Collins

ENGLISH

DICTIONARY

Published by Collins
An imprint of HarperCollins Publishers
Westerhill Road
Bishopbriggs
Glasgow G64 2QT

First Edition 2015

10 9 8 7 6 5 4 3 2 1

© HarperCollins Publishers 2015

ISBN 978-0-00-815048-8
ISBN 978-0-00-795137-6

Collins® is a registered trademark of
HarperCollins Publishers Limited

www.collinsdictionary.com

Typeset by Davidson Publishing
Solutions, Glasgow

Printed in Italy by GRAFICA VENETA S.p.A.

Entered words that we have reason to
believe constitute trademarks have been
designated as such. However, neither the
presence nor absence of such designation
should be regarded as affecting the legal
status of any trademark.

The contents of this publication are
believed correct at the time of printing.
Nevertheless the publisher can accept
no responsibility for errors or omissions,
changes in the detail given or for any
expense or loss thereby caused.

HarperCollins does not warrant that any
website mentioned in this title will be
provided uninterrupted, that any website
will be error-free, that defects will be
corrected, or that the website or the server
that makes it available are free of viruses
or bugs. For full terms and conditions
please refer to the site terms provided on
the website.

A catalogue record for this book is
available from the British Library.

If you would like to comment on any
aspect of this book, please contact us
at the given address or online.
E-mail: dictionaries@harpercollins.co.uk
 facebook.com/collinsdictionary
 @collinsdict

Acknowledgements
We would like to thank those authors and
publishers who kindly gave permission
for copyright material to be used in
the Collins Corpus. We would also like
to thank Times Newspapers Ltd for
providing valuable data.

MIX
Paper from
responsible sources
FSC® C007454

FSC™ is a non-profit international organisation established to promote
the responsible management of the world's forests. Products carrying the
FSC label are independently certified to assure consumers that they come
from forests that are managed to meet the social, economic and
ecological needs of present and future generations,
and other controlled sources.

Find out more about HarperCollins and the environment at
www.harpercollins.co.uk/green

Contents

Foreword

Collins English Dictionary provides clear and accessible information on contemporary vocabulary as well as Collins' famous and fascinating entries for people and places, all brought completely up to date especially for this edition of the dictionary.

All Collins Dictionaries are informed by an extensive reading, listening, and viewing programme, taking in broadcasts, websites, and publications from around the globe. These are fed into our monitoring system, an unparalleled 4.5 billion-word analytical database: the Collins Corpus. By analysing this data, Collins editors are able to build up a picture not just of the language being used today, but the people and places figuring large in history and in our times.

To help make this dictionary as useful as it can possibly be, the A-Z is complemented by a special supplement, *Improve your writing*, which offers quick tips and sound advice for the smartest use of language in all situations.

With more words, phrases, and definitions than any comparable dictionary, **Collins English Dictionary** provides support in all areas of the language, making it ideal for work, home, or study.

Using this dictionary

Main entry words	printed in large bold type, for example
	abbey
	All main entry words, including abbreviations and combining forms, in one alphabetical sequence, for example
	abbot **Abbott** **abbreviate** **ABC¹** **ABC²** **Abd Allah**
	Words with superscript numbers after the headwords are homographs – they have the same spelling but are derived from different sources, for example
	saw¹ *n* **1** a cutting tool … **saw²** *vb* the past tense of **see¹** **saw³** *n old-fashioned* a wise saying or proverb
	A word starting with a capital letter follows the lower-case form. For example, **Arras** follows **arras**.
Variant spellings	shown in full, for example
	adrenalin *or* **adrenaline**
	Note: where the spellings **-ize** and **-ization** are used at the end of a word, the alternative forms **-ise** and **-isation** are equally acceptable.
	Where different, US spellings are also recorded in the headword, for example
	centre *or* US **center**
Pronunciations	given in square brackets for words that are difficult or confusing; the word is respelt as it is pronounced, with the stressed syllable in bold type, for example
	antipodes (an-**tip**-pod-deez)

Parts of speech	shown in italics as an abbreviation, for example

ablaze *adj*

When a word can be used as more than one part of speech, the change of part of speech is shown after an arrow, for example

adept *adj* **1** proficient in something requiring skill ▷ *n* **2** a person skilled in something

Parts of speech may be combined for words, for example

awash *adv, adj* washed over by water

Irregular parts	or confusing forms of verbs, nouns, adjectives, and adverbs shown in bold type, for example

begin *vb* **-ginning, -gan, -gun**
regret *vb* **-gretting, -gretted**
anniversary *n, pl* **-ries**
angry *adj* **-grier, -griest**
well[1] *adv* **better, best**

Where inflections are not shown, it may be assumed that they are formed as follows:

nouns regular plurals are formed by adding **-s** (for example **pencils, monkeys**) or, in the case of nouns ending in **-s, -x, -z, -ch,** or **-sh,** by adding **-es** (for example **losses**).

verbs in regular inflected verbs: the third person singular of the present tense is formed by adding **-s** to the infinitive (for example **plays**) or, for verbs ending in **-s, -x, -z, -ch,** or **-sh,** by adding **-es** (for example **passes, reaches**); the past tense and past participle are formed by adding **-ed** to the infinitive (for example **played**); the present participle is formed by adding **-ing** to the infinitive (for example **playing**). Verbs that end in a consonant plus **-e** (for example **locate, snare**) regularly lose the final **-e** before adding **-ed** and **-ing**.

adjectives regular comparatives and superlatives of adjectives are formed by adding **-er** and **-est** to the base (for example **short**, **shorter**, **shortest**). Adjectives that end in a consonant plus **-e** regularly lose the **-e** before **-er** and **-est** (for example **fine**, **finer**, **finest**).

Meanings

separated by numbers, for example

> **absorb** *vb* **1** to soak up a liquid **2** to engage the interest of someone **3** to receive the force of an impact ...

Restrictive labels

immediately before a definition indicate that a particular meaning is restricted as to appropriateness, geographical area, subject field, etc., for example

> **bollard** *n* **1** *Brit and Austral* a small post marking a kerb or traffic island or barring cars from entering ...

If a label applies to all senses of a headword, it is placed immediately after the headword, or its pronunciation or inflections. If a label applies to a particular part of speech of a word, it is placed immediately after the part-of-speech label, for example

> **manifold** *adj formal* **1** numerous and varied: *her talents are manifold* ▷ *n* **2** a pipe with a number of inlets or outlets, esp. one in a car engine

Phrases and idioms

are included in the meanings of the main entry word, for example

> **hand** ... **22 keep one's hand in** to continue to practise something **23 (near) at hand** very close **24 on hand** close by; available

Derived words shown in the same paragraph as the main entry word, for example

> **absurd** *adj* obviously senseless or
> illogical; ridiculous [Latin *absurdus*]
> **> absurdity** *n* **> absurdly** *adv*

Note: where the meaning of a derived word is not given, it may be understood from the main entry word, or from another derived word.

Cross-references refer the reader to additional information elsewhere in the Dictionary. If the cross-reference is preceded by a solid arrow (▶), it applies to all senses of the headword that have gone before it, for example

> ▶ See also **back down, back off**, etc.

If there is no arrow, the cross-reference applies only to the sense immediately preceding it, for example

> **Babylon** *n* **1** the chief city of ancient
> Mesopotamia: first settled around
> 3000 BC. See also **Hanging Gardens**
> **of Babylon**

Variant spellings are generally entered as cross-references if their place in the alphabetical lists is considerably distant from the main entry, for example

> **foetus** *n*, *pl* **-tuses** same as **fetus**

Alternative names or terms are printed in bold type and introduced by the words 'Also' or 'Also called'. If the alternative name or term is preceded by a solid arrow (▶), it applies to all senses of the headword that have gone before it, for example

> **braaivleis** (brye-flayss) *S African n*
> **1** a grill on which food is cooked over
> hot charcoal, usually outdoors **2** an
> outdoor party at which food like this
> is served ▷ *vb* **3** to cook (food) in this
> way. ▶ Also: **braai**

Related adjectives   derived from Latin or French are shown in a
number of cases after the sense (or part-of speech
block) to which they are related, for example

> **wall** *n* **1** a vertical structure made of
> stone, brick, or wood, with a length
> and height much greater than its
> thickness, used to enclose, divide,
> or support. Related adjective: **mural**

Word histories   may appear at the end of an entry, inside square
brackets.

Words printed in SMALL CAPITALS refer to
other headwords where relevant or additional
information may be found, for example

> **bashful** *adj* shy or modest [*bash*, short for
> ABASH]

Language notes   appear in boxes to advise on the right words to
choose and words that are changing in meaning
or use, for example

> **USAGE** It was formerly considered correct
> to use *whether* after *doubtful* (*it is doubtful whether*
> *he will come*), but now *if* and *that* are also
> acceptable.

Abbreviations

AD	anno Domini
adj	adjective
adv	adverb
archit	architecture
astrol	astrology
Austral	Australia(n)
BC	before Christ
Brit	British
c	circa
cap	capital
chem	chemistry
conj	conjuction
crystallog	crystallography
E	East
eg	for example
esp.	especially
est	estimate
etc.	et cetera
fem	feminine
foll	followed
ft	feet
interj	interjection
km	kilometres
m	metres
masc	masculine
med	medicine
meteorol	meteorology
myth	mythology
n	noun
N	North
NE	Northeast(ern)
NW	Northwest(ern)
NZ	New Zealand
ornithol	ornithology
pathol	pathology

pharmacol	pharmacology
photog	photography
physiol	physiology
pl	plural
pop	population
prep	preposition
pron	pronoun
psychol	psychology
RC	Roman Catholic
S	South
Scot	Scottish
SE	Southeast(ern)
sing	singular
sociol	sociology
sq	square
SW	Southwest(ern)
theol	theology
US	United States
usu	usually
vb	verb
W	West

Az

Aa

a or **A** *n*, *pl* **a's, A's** or **As 1** the first letter of the English alphabet **2 from A to B** from one place to another: *I just want a car that takes me from A to B* **3 from A to Z** from start to finish

a *adj* (*indefinite article*) **1** used preceding a singular count noun that has not been mentioned before: *a book; a great shame* **2** used preceding a noun or adjective of quantity: *a litre of wine; a great amount has been written; I swim a lot and walk much more* **3** each or every; per: *I saw him once a week for six weeks*

A 1 *music* the sixth note of the scale of C major **2** ampere(s) **3** atomic: *an A-bomb*

Å angstrom unit

A. 1 acre(s) or acreage **2** America(n) **3** answer

a- or before a vowel **an-** prefix not or without: *atonal; asexual; anaemia* [Greek]

A1, A-1 or **A-one** *adj informal* first-class, excellent

A4 *n* a standard paper size, 297 × 210 mm

AA 1 Alcoholics Anonymous **2** (in Britain and South Africa) Automobile Association

AAA *Brit* (formerly) Amateur Athletic Association

Aachen *n* a city and spa in W Germany, in North Rhine-Westphalia: the northern capital of Charlemagne's empire. Pop: 256 605 (2003 est). French name: **Aix-la-Chapelle**

Aalborg or **Ålborg** *n* a city and port in Denmark, in N Jutland. Pop: 121 549 (2004 est)

Aalesund *n* a variant spelling of **Ålesund**

Aalst *n* the Flemish name for **Alost**

Aalto *n* Alvar. 1898–1976, Finnish architect and furniture designer, noted particularly for his public and industrial buildings, in which wood is much used. He invented bent plywood furniture (1932)

A & R artists and repertoire

Aarau *n* a town in N Switzerland, capital of Aargau canton: capital of the Helvetic Republic from 1798 to 1803. Pop: 15 470 (2000)

aardvark *n* a S African anteater with long ears and snout [obsolete Afrikaans: earth pig]

Aargau *n* a canton in N Switzerland. Capital: Aarau. Pop: 556 200 (2002 est). Area: 1404 sq km (542 sq miles). French name: **Argovie**

Aarhus *n* a variant spelling of **Århus**

A'asia Australasia

AB 1 able-bodied seaman **2** Alberta

ab- prefix away from or opposite to: *abnormal* [Latin]

aback *adv* **taken aback** startled or disconcerted

abacus (ab-a-cuss) *n* a counting device consisting of a frame holding beads on metal rods [Latin]

Abadan *n* a port in SW Iran, on an island in the Shatt-al-Arab delta. Pop: 307 000 (2005 est)

abaft *adv*, *adj nautical* closer to the stern of a ship [Old English *be* by + *æftan* behind]

Abakan *n* a city in S central Russia, capital of the Khakass Republic, at the confluence of the Yenisei and Abakan Rivers. Pop: 167 000 (2005 est)

abalone (ab-a-lone-ee) *n* an edible sea creature with a shell lined with mother-of-pearl [American Spanish *abulón*]

abandon *vb* **1** to desert or leave: *he had already abandoned his first wife* **2** to give up completely: *did you abandon all attempts at contact with the boy?* **3** to give oneself over completely to an emotion ▷ *n* **4 with abandon** uninhibitedly and without restraint [Old French *a bandon* under one's control] **> abandonment** *n*

abandoned *adj* **1** no longer used or occupied: *four people were found dead in an abandoned vehicle* **2** wild and uninhibited: *that fluffy abandoned laugh*

abase *vb* **abasing, abased abase oneself** to make oneself humble [Old French *abaissier*] **> abasement** *n*

abashed *adj* embarrassed and ashamed [Old French *esbair* to be astonished]

abate *vb* **abating, abated** to make or become less strong: *the tension has abated in recent months* [Old French *abatre* to beat down] **> abatement** *n*

abattoir (ab-a-twahr) *n* a slaughterhouse [French *abattre* to fell]

Abba *n* Swedish pop group (1972–82): comprised Benny Andersson (born 1946), Agnetha Faltskog (born 1950), Anni-Frid Lyngstad (born 1945), and Bjorn Ulvaeus (born 1945); numerous hit singles included "Waterloo" (1974), "Dancing Queen" (1977), and "The Winner Takes It All" (1980)

abbacy *n*, *pl* **-cies** the office or jurisdiction of an abbot or abbess [Church Latin *abbatia*]

Abbado *n* Claudio. 1933–2014, Italian conductor; principal conductor of the London Symphony Orchestra (1979–88); director of the Vienna State Opera (1986–91), and the Berlin Philharmonic (1989–2001)

Abbas *n* Ferhat. 1899–1985, Algerian nationalist leader: joined the National Liberation Front (1956); president of the provisional government of the Algerian republic (1958–61)

Abbas I *n* called *the Great*. 1557–1628, shah of Persia. He greatly extended Persian territory by defeating the Uzbeks and the Ottomans

Abbe *n* Ernst. 1840–1905, German physicist, noted for his work in optics and the microscope condenser known as the **Abbe condenser**

abbé (ab-bay) *n* a French abbot or other clergyman

abbess *n* the nun in charge of a convent [Church Latin *abbatissa*]

Abbeville *n* a town in N France: brewing, sugar-refining, and carpet industries. Pop: 24 567 (1999)

abbey *n* **1** a church associated with a community of monks or nuns **2** a community of monks or nuns **3** a building inhabited by monks or nuns [Church Latin *abbatia* ABBACY]

abbot *n* the head of an abbey of monks [Aramaic *abbā* father]

Abbott *n* Tony, full name *Anthony John Abbott*. born 1957, Australian Liberal politician; prime minister from 2013

a

abbreviate *vb* **-ating, -ated** **1** to shorten a word by leaving out some letters **2** to cut short [Latin *brevis* brief] **> abbreviation** *n*

ABC[1] *n* **1** the alphabet **2** an alphabetical guide **3** the basics of something

ABC[2] Australian Broadcasting Corporation

Abd Allah *n* 1846–99, Sudanese leader; he led the uprising against the Egyptian government of Sudan; defeated by Kitchener in 1898

Abd al-Malik ibn Marwan *n* ?646–705 AD, fifth caliph (685–705) of the Omayyad Arab dynasty. He pacified the Muslim empire and extended its territory in North Africa

Abdelkader *n* ?1807–83, Algerian nationalist, who resisted the French invasion of Algeria and established (1837) an independent state. He surrendered to the French in 1847

Abd-el-Krim *n* 1882–1963, Moroccan chief who led revolts against Spain and France, surrendered before their combined forces in 1926, but later formed the North African independence movement

abdicate *vb* **-cating, -cated** **1** to give up the throne formally **2** to give up one's responsibilities [Latin *abdicare* to disclaim] **> abdication** *n*

abdomen *n* the part of the body that contains the stomach and intestines [Latin] **> abdominal** *adj*

abdominoplasty *n* the surgical removal of excess skin and fat from the abdomen

abduct *vb* to remove (a person) by force; kidnap [Latin *abducere* to lead away] **> abduction** *n* **> abductor** *n*

Abdul-Hamid II *n* 1842–1918, sultan of Turkey (1876–1909), deposed by the Young Turks, noted for his brutal suppression of the Armenian revolt (1894–96)

Abdullah *n* 1882–1951, emir of Transjordan (1921–46) and first king of Jordan (1946–51). He joined the Arab revolt against Turkish rule in World War I; assassinated 1951

Abdullah II *n* born 1962, King of Jordan from 1999, son of King Hussein. See Hussein (1)

Abdul Rahman *n* Tunku. 1903–90, Malaysian statesman; prime minister of Malaya (1957–63) and of Malaysia (1963–70)

abeam *adv, adj* at right angles to the length of a ship or aircraft

Abelard *n* Peter. French name *Pierre Abélard*. 1079–1142, French scholastic philosopher and theologian whose works include *Historia Calamitatum* and *Sic et Non* (1121). His love for Héloïse is recorded in their correspondence

Abelson *n* Philip. 1913–2004, US physical chemist. He created (with Edwin McMillan) the first transuranic element, neptunium (1940)

Abeokuta *n* a town in W Nigeria, capital of Ogun state. Pop: 487 000 (2005 est)

Abercrombie *n* Sir (Leslie) Patrick. 1879–1957, British town planner and architect, best known for *The County of London Plan* (1943) and *The Greater London Plan* (1944)

Aberdare *n* a town in South Wales, in Rhondda Cynon Taff county borough. Pop: 31 705 (2001)

Aberdeen[1] *n* **1** a city in NE Scotland, on the North Sea: centre for processing North Sea oil and gas; university (1494). Pop: 184 788 (2001) **2 City of Aberdeen** a council area in NE Scotland, established in 1996. Pop: 206 600 (2003 est). Area: 186 sq km (72 sq miles)

Aberdeen[2] *n* George Hamilton-Gordon, 4th Earl of. 1784–1860, British statesman. He was foreign secretary under Wellington (1828) and Peel (1841–46); became prime minister of a coalition ministry in 1852 but was compelled to resign after mismanagement of the Crimean War (1855)

Aberdeen Angus *n* a black hornless breed of beef cattle originating in Scotland

Aberdeenshire *n* a council area and historical county of N Scotland, on the North Sea: became part of Grampian Region in 1975 but reinstated as an independent unitary authority (with adjusted borders) in 1996: rises to the Grampian and Cairngorm Mountains in the SW: chiefly agricultural (esp. sheep and stock raising). Administrative centre: Aberdeen. Pop: 229 330 (2003 est). Area 6319 sq km (2439 sq miles)

Aberdonian *n* **1** a native or inhabitant of Aberdeen ▷ *adj* **2** of or relating to Aberdeen or its inhabitants

Aberfan *n* a former coal-mining village in S Wales, in Merthyr Tydfil county borough: scene of a disaster in 1966 when a slag heap collapsed onto part of the village killing 144 people (including 116 children)

aberrant *adj* not normal, accurate, or correct: *aberrant behaviour*

aberration *n* **1** a sudden change from what is normal, accurate, or correct **2** a brief lapse in control of one's thoughts or feelings: *he suddenly had a mental aberration* [Latin *aberrare* to wander away]

Aberystwyth *n* a resort and university town in Wales, in Ceredigion on Cardigan Bay. Pop: 15 935 (2001)

abet *vb* **abetting, abetted** to help or encourage in wrongdoing [Old French *abeter* to lure on]

abeyance *n* **in abeyance** put aside temporarily [Old French *abeance*, literally: a gaping after]

abhor *vb* **-horring, -horred** to detest utterly [Latin *abhorrere* to shudder at]

abhorrent *adj* hateful or disgusting **> abhorrence** *n*

Abia *n* a state of SE Nigeria. Capital: Umuahia. Pop: 2 833 999 (2006 est). Area: 6320 sq km (2440 sq miles)

abide *vb* **1** to tolerate: *I can't abide stupid people* **2** to last or exist for a long time: *these instincts, while subdued in the individual, may abide in the race* **3 abide by** to act in accordance with: *he must abide by the findings of the report* **4** *archaic* to live [Old English *ābīdan*, from *a-* (intensive) + *bīdan* to wait]

abiding *adj* lasting for ever: *an abiding interest in history*

Abidjan *n* a port in Côte d'Ivoire, on the Gulf of Guinea: the legislative capital (Yamoussoukro became the administrative capital in 1983). Pop: 3 516 000 (2005 est)

Abilene *n* a city in central Texas. Pop: 114 889 (2003 est)

ability *n, pl* **-ties** **1** possession of the necessary skill or power to do something **2** great skill or competence: *his ability as a speaker was legendary* [Latin *habilitas*]

Abingdon *n* a market town in S England, in Oxfordshire. Pop: 36 010 (2001)

abject *adj* **1** utterly miserable: *one Mexican in five lives in abject poverty* **2** lacking all self-respect [Latin *abjectus* thrown away] **> abjectly** *adv*

abjure *vb* **-juring, -jured** to renounce or deny under oath [Latin *abjurare*] **> abjuration** *n*

Abkhazia *or* **Abkhaz Autonomous Republic** *n* a disputed region of NW Georgia, between the Black Sea and the Caucasus Mountains: a subtropical region, with mountains rising over 3900 m (13 000 ft); Abkhazian separatists seized control of the region in 1993; Russia formally recognized it as an independent republic following the Russian-Georgian war of 2008, although Georgia still claims the region as part of its territory. Capital: Sukhumi. Pop: 220 600 (2006 est). Area: 8600 sq km (3320 sq miles). Also called: **Abkhaz Autonomous Republic**

ablation *n* **1** the surgical removal of an organ or part **2** the wearing away of a rock or glacier **3** the melting of a part, such as the heat shield of a space re-entry vehicle [Latin *ablatus* carried away]

ablaze *adj* **1** on fire **2** brightly illuminated: *the sky was ablaze with the stars shining bright* **3** emotionally aroused: *his eyes were ablaze with anger*

able *adj* **1** having the necessary power, skill, or opportunity to do something **2** capable or talented [Latin *habilis* easy to hold]

-able *adj suffix* able to be acted upon as specified: *washable* [Latin *-abilis, -ibilis*] **> -ably** *suffix forming adverbs* **> -ability** *suffix forming nouns*

able-bodied *adj* strong and healthy

a

able-bodied seaman *or* **able seaman** *n* a seaman who is trained in certain skills

abled *adj* having a range of physical powers as specified: *less abled; differently abled*

ableism (ay-bel-iz-zum) *n* discrimination against disabled people

able rating *n* (in Britain) a seaman of the lowest rank in a navy

ablutions *pl n* the act of washing: *after the nightly ablutions, I settled down to read* [Latin *abluere* to wash away]

ably *adv* competently or skilfully

ABM antiballistic missile

abnegation *n* the act of giving something up [Latin *abnegare* to deny]

abnormal *adj* differing from the usual or typical > **abnormality** *n* > **abnormally** *adv*

Åbo *n* the Swedish name for **Turku**

aboard *adv, adj, prep* on, in, onto, or into (a ship, plane, or train)

abode *n* one's home [from ABIDE]

abolish *vb* to do away with (laws, regulations, or customs) [Latin *abolere* to destroy]

abolition *n* 1 the act of doing away with something: *the abolition of slavery* 2 **Abolition** the ending of slavery > **abolitionist** *n, adj*

A-bomb *n* short for **atomic bomb**

abominable *adj* very bad or unpleasant: *I think that what is being done here is utterly abominable* > **abominably** *adv*

abominable snowman *n* a large creature, like a man or an ape, that is said to live in the Himalayas [translation of Tibetan *metohkangmi* foul snowman]

abominate *vb* -**nating**, -**nated** to dislike intensely [Latin *abominari* to regard as an ill omen] > **abomination** *n*

aboriginal *adj* existing in a place from the earliest known period

Aboriginal *adj* 1 of or relating to (esp Australian) Aborigines ▷ *n* 2 an Aborigine

aborigine (ab-or-rij-in-ee) *n Brit, Austral and NZ* an original inhabitant of a country or region, esp. Australia [Latin *aborigines* the name of the inhabitants of Latium in pre-Roman times]

Aborigine *n* a member of a dark-skinned people who were already living in Australia when European settlers arrived

abort *vb* 1 (of a pregnancy) to end before the fetus is viable 2 to perform an abortion on a pregnant woman 3 to end a plan or process before completion [Latin *abortare*]

abortion *n* 1 an operation to end pregnancy 2 the premature ending of a pregnancy when a fetus is expelled from the womb before it can live independently 3 the failure of a mission or project 4 *informal* something that is grotesque > **abortionist** *n*

abortion pill *n* a drug used to terminate a pregnancy in its earliest stage

abortive *adj* failing to achieve its purpose

Aboukir Bay *or* **Abukir Bay** *n* a bay on the N coast of Egypt, where the Nile enters the Mediterranean: site of the Battle of the Nile (1798), in which Nelson defeated the French fleet. Arabic name: **Abu Qîr**

abound *vb* 1 to exist in large numbers 2 abound in to have a large number of [Latin *abundare* to overflow]

about *prep* 1 relating to or concerning 2 near to 3 carried on: *I haven't any money about me* 4 on every side of ▷ *adv* 5 near in number, time, or degree; approximately 6 nearby 7 here and there: *there were some fifteen other people scattered about on the first floor* 8 all around; on every side 9 in or to the opposite direction 10 in rotation: *turn and turn about* 11 used to indicate understatement: *it's about time somebody told the truth on that subject* 12 about to on the point of; intending to: *she was about to get in the car* 13 not about to determined not to: *we're not about to help her out* ▷ *adj* 14 active: *he was off the premises well before anyone was up and about* [Old English *abūtan, onbūtan* on the outside of]

about-turn *or US* **about-face** *n* 1 a complete change of opinion or direction 2 a reversal of the direction in which one is facing

above *prep* 1 higher than; over 2 greater than in quantity or degree: *above average* 3 superior to or higher than in quality, rank, or ability 4 too high-minded for: *he considered himself above the task of working* 5 too respected for; beyond: *his fleet was above suspicion* 6 too difficult to be understood by: *a discussion that was way above my head* 7 louder or higher than (other noise) 8 in preference to 9 above all most of all; especially ▷ *adv* 10 in or to a higher place: *the hills above* 11 in a previous place (in something written or printed) 12 higher in rank or position ▷ *n* 13 **the above** something previously mentioned ▷ *adj* 14 appearing in a previous place (in something written or printed): *for a copy of the free brochure write to the above address* [Old English *abufan*]

above board *adj* completely honest and open

abracadabra *n* a word used in magic spells, which is supposed to possess magic powers [Latin]

abrasion *n* 1 a scraped area on the skin; graze 2 *geography* the erosion of rock by rock fragments scratching and scraping it [Latin *abradere* to scrape away]

abrasive *adj* 1 rude and unpleasant in manner 2 tending to rub or scrape; rough ▷ *n* 3 a substance used for cleaning, smoothing, or polishing

abreast *adj* 1 alongside each other and facing in the same direction: *the two cars were abreast* 2 abreast of up to date with

abridge *vb* **abridging**, **abridged** to shorten a written work by taking out parts [Late Latin *abbreviare*] > **abridgment** *or* **abridgement** *n*

abroad *adv* 1 to or in a foreign country 2 generally known or felt: *there is a new spirit abroad*

abrogate *vb* -**gating**, -**gated** to cancel (a law or an agreement) formally [from Latin *ab-* away + *rogare* to propose a law] > **abrogation** *n*

abrupt *adj* 1 sudden or unexpected: *an abrupt departure* 2 rather rude in speech or manner [Latin *abruptus* broken off] > **abruptly** *adv* > **abruptness** *n*

Abruzzi *or* **Abruzzo** *n* a region of S central Italy, between the Apennines and the Adriatic. Capital: Aquila. Pop: 1 273 284 (2003 est). Area: 10 794 sq km (4210 sq miles)

abs *pl n* abdominal muscles

abscess (ab-sess) *n* 1 a swelling containing pus as a result of inflammation ▷ *vb* 2 to form a swelling containing pus [Latin *abscessus* literally: a throwing off] > **abscessed** *adj*

abscissa *n, pl* -**scissas** *or* -**scissae** *maths* (in a two-dimensional system of Cartesian coordinates) the distance from the vertical axis measured parallel to the horizontal axis [New Latin *linea abscissa* a cut-off line]

abscond *vb* to run away unexpectedly [Latin *abscondere* to conceal]

abseil (ab-sale) *vb* 1 to go down a steep drop by a rope fastened at the top and tied around one's body ▷ *n* 2 an instance of abseiling [German *abseilen*]

absence *n* 1 the state of being away 2 the time during which a person or thing is away 3 the fact of being without something

absent *adj* 1 not present in a place or situation 2 lacking 3 not paying attention ▷ *vb* 4 absent oneself to stay away [Latin *absens*] > **absently** *adv*

absentee *n* a person who should be present but is not

absenteeism *n* persistent absence from work or school

absent-minded *adj* inattentive or forgetful > **absent-mindedly** *adv*

absinthe *n* a strong, green, alcoholic drink, originally containing wormwood [Greek *apsinthion* wormwood]

absolute *adj* 1 total and complete: *he ordered an immediate and absolute ceasefire* 2 with unrestricted power and authority: *she has absolute control with fifty per cent of the shares* 3 undoubted or certain: *I was telling the absolute truth* 4 not dependent on or relative to anything else 5 pure;

a

unmixed: *absolute alcohol* ▷ *n* **6** a principle or rule believed to be unfailingly correct **7** the Absolute *philosophy* that which is totally unconditioned, perfect, or complete [Latin *absolutus*]

absolutely *adv* **1** completely or perfectly ▷ *interj* **2** yes indeed, certainly

absolute majority *n* a number of votes totalling over 50 per cent, such as the total number of votes that beats the combined opposition

absolute pitch *n* the ability to identify the pitch of a note, or to sing a given note, without reference to one previously sounded

absolute zero *n physics* the lowest temperature theoretically possible, at which the particles that make up matter would be at rest: equivalent to -273.15°C or -459.67°F

absolution *n Christianity* a formal forgiveness of sin pronounced by a priest

absolutism *n* a political system in which a monarch or dictator has unrestricted power

absolve *vb* **-solving, -solved** to declare to be free from blame or sin [Latin *absolvere*]

absorb *vb* **1** to soak up a liquid **2** to engage the interest of someone **3** to receive the force of an impact **4** *physics* to take in radiant energy and retain it **5** to take in or incorporate: *this country has absorbed almost one million refugees* [Latin *absorbere* to suck] **›** **absorbent** *adj* **›** **absorbing** *adj*

absorption *n* **1** the process of absorbing something or the state of being absorbed **2** *physiol* the process by which nutrients enter the tissues of an animal or a plant **›** **absorptive** *adj*

abstain *vb* **1** (usually foll. by *from*) to choose not to do or partake of something: *you will be asked to abstain from food prior to your general anaesthetic* **2** to choose not to vote [Latin *abstinere*] **›** **abstainer** *n*

abstemious (ab-**steem**-ee-uss) *adj* taking very little alcohol or food [Latin *abstemius*] **›** **abstemiously** *adv* **›** **abstemiousness** *n*

abstention *n* **1** the formal act of not voting **2** the act of abstaining from something, such as drinking alcohol

abstinence *n* the practice of choosing not to do something one would like **›** **abstinent** *adj*

abstract *adj* **1** referring to ideas or qualities rather than material objects: *an abstract noun* **2** not applied or practical; theoretical: *he was frustrated by the highly abstract mathematics being taught* **3** of art in which the subject is represented by shapes and patterns rather than by a realistic likeness ▷ *n* **4** a summary **5** an abstract painting or sculpture **6** an abstract word or idea **7** in the abstract without referring to specific circumstances ▷ *vb* **8** to summarize **9** to remove or extract [Latin *abstractus* drawn off]

abstracted *adj* lost in thought; preoccupied **›** **abstractedly** *adv*

abstraction *n* **1** a general idea rather than a specific example: *these absurd philosophical abstractions continued to bother him* **2** the quality of being abstract or abstracted

abstruse *adj* not easy to understand [Latin *abstrusus* concealed]

absurd *adj* obviously senseless or illogical; ridiculous [Latin *absurdus*] **›** **absurdity** *n* **›** **absurdly** *adv*

Abu-Bekr *or* **Abu-Bakr** *n* 573–634 AD, companion and father-in-law of Mohammed; the first caliph of Islam

Abu Dhabi *n* a sheikhdom (emirate) of SE Arabia, on the S coast of the Persian Gulf: the chief sheikhdom and capital of the United Arab Emirates, consisting principally of the port of Abu Dhabi and a desert hinterland; contains major oilfields. Pop: 476 000 (2005 est). Area: 67 350 sq km (25 998 sq miles)

Abu Hanifah *n* 700–67 AD, Muslim theologian and teacher of jurisprudence

Abuja *n* the federal capital of Nigeria, in the centre of the country. Pop: 467 000 (2005 est)

Abukir Bay *n* a variant spelling of **Aboukir Bay**

abundance *n* **1** a great amount **2** degree of plentifulness **3** in abundance in great amounts: *they had fish and fruit in abundance* [Latin *abundare* to abound] **›** **abundant** *adj*

abundantly *adv* **1** very: *he made his disagreement with the prime minister abundantly clear* **2** plentifully; in abundance

abuse *n* **1** prolonged ill-treatment of or violence towards someone: *child abuse* **2** insulting comments **3** improper use: *an abuse of power* ▷ *vb* **abusing, abused** **4** to take advantage of dishonestly: *these two ministers had abused their position for financial gain* **5** to ill-treat violently: *he had been sexually abused as a child* **6** to speak insultingly or cruelly to [Latin *abuti* to misuse] **›** **abuser** *n*

Abu Simbel *n* a former village in S Egypt: site of two temples of Rameses II, which were moved to higher ground (1966–67) before the area behind the Aswan High Dam was flooded. Also called: **Ipsambul**

abusive *adj* rude or insulting: *he was alleged to have used abusive language towards spectators* **›** **abusively** *adv*

abut *vb* **abutting, abutted** to be next to or touching [Old French *abouter*]

abutment *n* a construction that supports the end of a bridge

Abydos *n* **1** an ancient town in central Egypt: site of many temples and tombs **2** an ancient Greek colony on the Asiatic side of the Dardanelles (Hellespont): scene of the legend of Hero and Leander

abysmal *adj informal* extremely bad [Medieval Latin *abysmus* abyss] **›** **abysmally** *adv*

abyss *n* **1** a very deep hole in the ground **2** a frightening or threatening situation: *the abyss of revolution and war ahead* [Greek *abussos* bottomless]

Abyssinia *n* a former name for **Ethiopia**

Abyssinian *n* **1** a native or inhabitant of Abyssinia ▷ *adj* **2** of or relating to Abyssinia or its inhabitants

Ac *chem* actinium

AC **1** alternating current **2** athletic club

a/c **1** account **2** account current

acacia (a-**kay**-sha) *n* a shrub or tree with small yellow or white flowers [Greek *akakia*]

academic *adj* **1** relating to a college or university **2** (of pupils) having an aptitude for study **3** relating to studies such as languages and pure science rather than technical or professional studies **4** of theoretical interest only: *the argument is academic* ▷ *n* **5** a member of the teaching or research staff of a college or university **›** **academically** *adv*

academy *n, pl* **-mies** **1** a society for the advancement of literature, art, or science **2** a school for training in a particular skill: *sixteen hundred students would also spend their first year at the military academy* **3** (in Scotland) a secondary school [Greek *akadēmeia* the place where Plato taught]

Academy *n* the Academy **a** the grove or garden near Athens where Plato taught in the late 4th century BC **b** the school of philosophy founded by Plato **c** the members of this school and their successors

Acadia *n* **1 a** the Atlantic Provinces of Canada **b** the French-speaking areas of these provinces **2** (formerly) a French colony in the present-day Atlantic Provinces: ceded to Britain in 1713 ▶ French name: **Acadie**

Acadian *adj* **1** denoting or relating to Acadia or its inhabitants ▷ *n* **2** any of the early French settlers in Nova Scotia. See also **Cajun**

acanthus *n* **1** a plant with large spiny leaves and spikes of white or purplish flowers **2** a carved ornament based on the leaves of the acanthus plant [Greek *akantha* thorn]

Acapulco *n* a port and resort in SW Mexico, in Guerrero state. Pop: 761 000 (2005 est). Official name: **Acapulco de Juárez**

ACAS (in Britain) Advisory Conciliation and Arbitration Service

ACC (in New Zealand) Accident Compensation Corporation

acc. 1 *grammar* accusative 2 account

Accad *n* a variant spelling of **Akkad**

Accademia *n* an art gallery in Venice housing a collection of paintings by Venetian masters from the 13th to 18th centuries. Full name: **Galleria dell' Accademia**

Accardo *n* Salvatore. born 1941, Italian violinist and conductor

accede *vb* **-ceding, -ceded accede to 1** to agree to 2 to take up (an office or position): *he acceded to the throne after his Irish exile* [Latin *accedere*]

accelerando *adv music* with increasing speed [Italian]

accelerate *vb* **-ating, -ated 1** to move or cause to move more quickly 2 to cause to happen sooner than expected [Latin *accelerare*]

acceleration *n* 1 the act of increasing speed 2 the rate of increase of speed or the rate of change of velocity

accelerator *n* 1 a pedal in a motor vehicle that is pressed to increase speed 2 *physics* a machine for increasing the speed and energy of charged particles

accent *n* 1 the distinctive style of pronunciation of a person or group from a particular area, country, or social background 2 a mark used in writing to indicate the prominence of a syllable or the way a vowel is pronounced 3 particular emphasis: *there will be an accent on sport and many will enjoy rowing* 4 the stress on a syllable or musical note ▷ *vb* 5 to lay particular emphasis on [Latin *accentus*]

accentuate *vb* **-ating, -ated** to stress or emphasize > **accentuation** *n*

accept *vb* 1 to take or receive something offered 2 to agree to 3 to consider something as true 4 to tolerate or resign oneself to 5 to take on the responsibilities of: *he asked if I would become his assistant and I accepted that position* 6 to receive someone into a community or group 7 to receive something as adequate or valid [Latin *acceptare*]

acceptable *adj* 1 able to be endured; tolerable: *in war killing is acceptable* 2 good enough; adequate: *he found the article acceptable* > **acceptability** *n* > **acceptably** *adv*

acceptance *n* 1 the act of accepting something 2 favourable reception 3 belief or agreement

accepted *adj* commonly approved or recognized: *the accepted wisdom about old age*

access *n* 1 a means of approaching or entering a place 2 the condition of allowing entry, for example entry to a building by wheelchairs or prams 3 the right or opportunity to use something or enter a place: *the bourgeoisie gained access to political power* 4 the opportunity or right to see or approach someone: *my ex-wife sabotages my access to the children* ▷ *vb* 5 to obtain information from a computer [Latin *accedere* to accede]

accessible *adj* 1 easy to approach, enter, or use 2 easy to understand: *the most accessible opera by Wagner* > **accessibility** *n*

accession *n* the act of taking up an office or position: *the 40th anniversary of her accession to the throne*

accessory *n*, *pl* **-ries** 1 a supplementary part or object 2 a small item, such as a bag or belt, worn or carried by someone to complete his or her outfit 3 a person who is involved in a crime but who was not present when it took place [Late Latin *accessorius*]

access road *n* a road providing a way to a particular place or onto a motorway

access time *n* the time required to retrieve a piece of stored information from a computer

accident *n* 1 an unpleasant event that causes damage, injury, or death 2 an unforeseen event or one without apparent cause: *they had met in town by accident* [Latin *accidere* to happen]

accidental *adj* 1 occurring by chance or unintentionally ▷ *n* 2 *music* a symbol denoting a sharp, flat, or natural that is not a part of the key signature > **accidentally** *adv*

accident-prone *adj* (of a person) often involved in accidents

acclaim *vb* 1 to applaud or praise: *the highly acclaimed children's TV series* 2 to acknowledge publicly: *he was immediately acclaimed the new prime minister* ▷ *n* 3 an enthusiastic expression of approval [Latin *acclamare*]

acclamation *n* 1 an enthusiastic reception or display of approval 2 *Canad* an instance of being elected without opposition 3 **by acclamation** by a majority without a ballot

acclimatize or **-tise** *vb* **-tizing, -tized** or **-tising, -tised** to adapt to a new climate or environment > **acclimatization** or **-tisation** *n*

accolade *n* 1 an award, praise, or honour 2 a touch on the shoulder with a sword conferring knighthood [Latin *ad-* to + *collum* neck]

accommodate *vb* **-dating, -dated 1** to provide with lodgings 2 to have room for 3 to do a favour for 4 to adjust or become adjusted; to adapt [Latin *accommodare*]

accommodating *adj* willing to help; obliging

accommodation *n* a place in which to sleep, live, or work

accommodation address *n Brit* an address on letters to a person who cannot or does not wish to receive mail at a permanent address

accompaniment *n* 1 something that accompanies something else 2 *music* a supporting part for an instrument, a band, or an orchestra

accompanist *n* a person who plays a musical accompaniment

accompany *vb* **-nies, -nying, -nied 1** to go with (someone) 2 to happen or exist at the same time as 3 to provide a musical accompaniment for [Old French *accompaignier*]

accomplice *n* a person who helps someone else commit a crime [Late Latin *complex* partner]

accomplish *vb* 1 to manage to do; achieve: *most infants accomplish it immediately* 2 to complete [Latin *complere* to fill up]

accomplished *adj* 1 expert or proficient: *an accomplished liar* 2 successfully completed

accomplishment *n* 1 the successful completion of something 2 something successfully completed 3 (*often pl*) personal abilities or skills

accord *n* 1 agreement or harmony 2 a formal agreement between groups or nations: *the Paris peace accords* 3 **of one's own accord** voluntarily or willingly 4 **with one accord** unanimously ▷ *vb* 5 to grant: *she was at last accorded her true status* 6 **accord with** to fit in with or be consistent with [Latin *ad-* to + *cor* heart]

accordance *n* **in accordance with** conforming to or according to: *food is prepared in accordance with Jewish laws*

according *adv* 1 **according to a** as stated by: *according to her, they were once engaged* **b** in conformity with: *work hours varied according to the tides* 2 **according as** depending on whether

accordingly *adv* 1 in an appropriate manner 2 consequently

accordion *n* a box-shaped musical instrument played by moving the two sides apart and together, and pressing a keyboard or buttons to produce the notes [German *Akkordion*] > **accordionist** *n*

accost *vb* to approach, stop, and speak to [Latin *ad-* to + *costa* side, rib]

account *n* 1 a report or description 2 a person's money held in a bank 3 a statement of financial transactions with the resulting balance 4 part or behalf: *I am sorry that you suffered on my account* 5 **call someone to account** to demand an explanation from someone 6 **give a good** or **bad account of oneself** to perform well or fail to perform well 7 **of no account** of little importance or value 8 **on account of** because of 9 **take account of** or **take into account** to take into consideration; allow for ▷ *vb* 10 to consider as: *the evening was accounted a major step forward by all concerned* [Old French *aconit*]

accountable *adj* responsible to someone or for some action > **accountability** *n*

a

accountant *n* a person who maintains and audits business accounts **> accountancy** *n*

account for *vb* **1** to give reasons for **2** to explain or count up what has been spent

accounting *n* the skill or practice of maintaining and auditing business accounts

accoutrements (ak-koo-tra-ments) *or US*

accouterments (ak-koo-ter-ments) *pl n* clothing and equipment for a particular activity [Old French *accoustrer* to equip]

Accra *n* the capital of Ghana, a port on the Gulf of Guinea: built on the site of three 17th-century trading fortresses founded by the English, Dutch, and Danish. Pop: 1 970 000 (2005 est)

accredit *vb* **1** to give official recognition to **2** to send (a diplomat) with official credentials to a particular country **3** to certify as meeting required standards **4** to attribute (a quality or an action) to (a person) [French *accréditer*] **> accreditation** *n*

accretion (ak-kree-shun) *n* **1** a gradual increase in size, through growth or addition **2** something added, such as an extra layer [Latin *accretio*]

Accrington *n* a town in NW England, in SE Lancashire. Pop: 35 203 (2001)

accrue *vb* **-cruing, -crued 1** (of money or interest) to increase gradually over a period of time **2 accrue to** to fall naturally to: *some advantage must accrue to the weaker party* [Latin *accrescere*]

accumulate *vb* **-lating, -lated** to gather together in an increasing quantity; collect [Latin *accumulare* to heap up] **> accumulative** *adj*

accumulation *n* **1** something that has been collected **2** the collecting together of things

accumulator *n* **1** *Brit and Austral* a rechargeable device for storing electrical energy **2** *Brit horse racing* a collective bet on successive races, with both stake and winnings being carried forward to accumulate progressively

accuracy *n* faithful representation of the truth: *care is taken to ensure the accuracy of the content*

accurate *adj* faithfully representing the truth: *all the information was accurate* [Latin *accurare* to perform with care] **> accurately** *adv*

accursed (a-curse-id) *adj* **1** under a curse **2** hateful or detestable

accusation *n* **1** an allegation that a person is guilty of some wrongdoing **2** a formal charge brought against a person **> accusatory** *adj*

accusative *n grammar* a grammatical case in some languages that identifies the direct object of a verb

accuse *vb* **-cusing, -cused** to charge a person with wrongdoing [Latin *accūsāre*] **> accuser** *n* **> accusing** *adj* **> accusingly** *adv*

accused *n* **the accused** *law* the defendant appearing on a criminal charge

accustom *vb* **accustom oneself to** to become familiar with or used to from habit or experience [Old French *acostumer*]

accustomed *adj* **1** usual or customary: *he parked his motorcycle in its accustomed place* **2 accustomed to a** used to **b** in the habit of

ace *n* **1** a playing card with one symbol on it **2** *informal* an expert: *an American stock car ace* **3** *tennis* a winning serve that the opponent fails to reach **4** a fighter pilot who has destroyed several enemy aircraft ⊳ *adj* **5** *informal* superb or excellent: *an ace tennis player* [Latin *as* a unit]

Aceh *n* an autonomous region of N Indonesia, in N Sumatra; mountainous with rain forests; scene of separatist conflict since the late 1990s; coastal areas suffered badly in the Indian Ocean tsunami of December 2004. Capital: Banda Aceh. Pop: 3 930 905 (2000). Area: 55 392 sq km (21 381 sq miles)

acerbic (ass-sir-bik) *adj* harsh or bitter: *an acerbic critic* [Latin *acerbus* sharp, sour]

acerbity *n, pl* **-ties 1** bitter speech or temper **2** bitterness of taste

acetaldehyde (ass-it-tal-dee-hide) *n chem* a colourless volatile liquid, used as a solvent

acetate (ass-it-tate) *n* **1** *chem* any salt or ester of acetic acid **2** Also: **acetate rayon** a synthetic textile fibre made from cellulose acetate

acetic (ass-see-tik) *adj chem* of, containing, or producing acetic acid or vinegar [Latin *acetum* vinegar]

acetic acid *n chem* a strong-smelling colourless liquid used to make vinegar

acetone (ass-it-tone) *n chem* a strong-smelling colourless liquid used as a solvent for paints and lacquers

acetylene (ass-set-ill-een) *n chem* a colourless soluble flammable gas used in welding metals

Achaea *or* **Achaia** *n* **1** a department of Greece, in the N Peloponnese. Capital: Patras. Pop: 318 928 (2001). Area: 3209 sq km (1239 sq miles). Modern Greek name: Akhaïa **2** a province of ancient Greece, in the N Peloponnese on the Gulf of Corinth: enlarged as a Roman province in 27 BC

ache *vb* **aching, ached 1** to feel or be the source of a continuous dull pain **2** to suffer mental anguish ⊳ *n* **3** a continuous dull pain [Old English *ācan*]

Achebe *n* Chinua. 1930–2013, Nigerian novelist. His works include *Things Fall Apart* (1958), *A Man of the People* (1966), and *Anthills of the Savannah* (1987)

Acheson *n* Dean (**Gooderham**). 1893–1971, US lawyer and statesman: secretary of state (1949–53) under President Truman

achieve *vb* **achieving, achieved** to gain by hard work or effort [Old French *achever* to bring to an end] **> achiever** *n*

achievement *n* **1** something that has been accomplished by hard work, ability, or heroism **2** the successful completion of something

Achilles heel (ak-kill-eez) *n* a small but fatal weakness [*Achilles* in Greek mythology was killed by an arrow in his unprotected heel]

Achilles tendon *n* the fibrous cord that connects the muscles of the calf to the heel bone

Achill Island *n* an island in the Republic of Ireland, off the W coast of Co Mayo. Area: 148 sq km (57 sq miles). Pop: 2620 (2002)

achromatic *adj* **1** without colour **2** refracting light without breaking it up into its component colours **3** *music* involving no sharps or flats **> achromatically** *adv*

acid *n* **1** *chem* one of a class of compounds, corrosive and sour when dissolved in water, that combine with a base to form a salt **2** *slang* LSD **3** a sour-tasting substance ⊳ *adj* **4** *chem* of, from, or containing acid **5** sharp or sour in taste **6** sharp in speech or manner [Latin *acidus*] **> acidly** *adv*

Acid House *or* **Acid** *n* a type of funk-based, electronically edited disco music of the late 1980s, which has hypnotic sound effects and which is associated with hippy culture and the use of the drug ecstasy [*acid* (LSD) + *House* music]

acidic *adj* containing acid

acidify *vb* **-fies, -fying, -fied** to convert into acid **> acidification** *n*

acidity *n* **1** the quality of being acid **2** the amount of acid in a solution

acid rain *n* rain containing pollutants released into the atmosphere by burning coal or oil

acid reflux *n* the regurgitation of stomach acid into the oesophagus, causing heartburn

acid test *n* a rigorous and conclusive test of worth or value [from the testing of gold with nitric acid]

acknowledge *vb* **-edging, -edged 1** to recognize or admit the truth of a statement **2** to show recognition of a person by a greeting or glance **3** to make known that a letter or message has been received **4** to express gratitude for (a favour or compliment) [Old English *oncnāwan* to recognize]

a

acknowledgment *or* **acknowledgement** *n* **1** the act of acknowledging something or someone **2** something done or given as an expression of gratitude

acme (ak-mee) *n* the highest point of achievement or excellence [Greek *akmē*]

acne (ak-nee) *n* a skin disease in which pus-filled spots form on the face [New Latin]

acolyte *n* **1** a follower or attendant **2** *Christianity* a person who assists a priest [Greek *akolouthos*]

Aconcagua *n* a mountain in W Argentina: the highest peak in the Andes and in the W Hemisphere. Height: 6960 m (22 835 ft)

aconite *n* **1** a poisonous plant with hoodlike flowers **2** dried aconite root, used as a narcotic [Greek *akoniton*]

Açôres *n* the Portuguese name for (the) **Azores**

acorn *n* the fruit of the oak tree, consisting of a smooth nut in a cuplike base [Old English *æcern*]

A Coruña *n* the Galician name for **La Coruña**

acoustic *adj* **1** of sound, hearing, or acoustics **2** (of a musical instrument) without electronic amplification **3** designed to absorb sound: *acoustic tiles* [Greek *akouein* to hear] ⟩ **acoustically** *adv*

acoustics *n* **1** the scientific study of sound ▷ *pl n* **2** the characteristics of a room or auditorium determining how well sound can be heard within it

acquaint *vb* **acquaint with** to make (someone) familiar with [Latin *accognoscere* to know well]

acquaintance *n* **1** a person whom one knows slightly **2** slight knowledge of a person or subject **3 make the acquaintance of** to come into social contact with **4** the people one knows: *an actress of my acquaintance*

acquainted *adj* **1** on terms of familiarity but not intimacy **2 acquainted with** familiar with: *she became acquainted with the classics of Chinese literature*

acquiesce (ak-wee-ess) *vb* **-escing, -esced** to agree to what someone wants [Latin *acquiescere*] ⟩ **acquiescence** *n* ⟩ **acquiescent** *adj*

USAGE The use of *to* after *acquiesce* was formerly regarded as incorrect, but is now acceptable.

---

acquire *vb* **-quiring, -quired** to get or develop (something such as an object, trait, or ability) [Latin *acquirere*] ⟩ **acquirement** *n*

acquired taste *n* **1** a liking for something at first considered unpleasant **2** the thing liked

acquisition *n* **1** something acquired, often to add to a collection **2** the act of acquiring something

acquisitive *adj* eager to gain material possessions ⟩ **acquisitively** *adv* ⟩ **acquisitiveness** *n*

acquit *vb* **-quitting, -quitted 1** to pronounce someone not guilty: *he's been acquitted of negligence* **2** to behave in a particular way: *she acquitted herself well in the meeting* [Old French *aquiter*] ⟩ **acquittal** *n*

acre *n* **1** a unit of area equal to 4840 square yards (4046.86 square metres) **2 acres** *informal* a large amount: *acres of skin* [Old English *æcer*]

Acre *n* **1** a state of W Brazil: mostly unexplored tropical forests; acquired from Bolivia in 1903. Capital: Rio Branco. Pop: 586 942 (2002). Area: 152 589 sq km (58 899 sq miles) **2** a city and port in N Israel, strategically situated on the **Bay of Acre** in the E Mediterranean: taken and retaken during the Crusades (1104, 1187, 1191, 1291), taken by the Turks (1517), by Egypt (1832), and by the Turks again (1839). Pop: 45 600 (2001). Old Testament name: **Accho**. Arabic name: **'Akka**. Hebrew name: **'Akko**

acreage (ake-er-rij) *n* land area in acres

acrid (ak-rid) *adj* **1** unpleasantly strong-smelling **2** sharp in speech or manner [Latin *acer* sharp, sour] ⟩ **acridity** *n* ⟩ **acridly** *adv*

acrimony *n* bitterness and resentment felt about something [Latin *acrimonia*] ⟩ **acrimonious** *adj*

acrobat *n* an entertainer who performs gymnastic feats requiring skill, agility, and balance [Greek *akrobatēs* one who walks on tiptoe] ⟩ **acrobatic** *adj* ⟩ **acrobatically** *adv*

acrobatics *pl n* the skills or feats of an acrobat

acronym *n* a word made from the initial letters of other words, for example UNESCO for the *United Nations Educational, Scientific, and Cultural Organization* [Greek *akros* outermost + *onoma* name]

acrophobia *n* abnormal fear of being at a great height [Greek *akron* summit + *phobos* fear]

acropolis (a-**crop**-pol-liss) *n* the citadel of an ancient Greek city [Greek *akros* highest + *polis* city]

Acropolis *n* the citadel of Athens on which the Parthenon and the Erechtheum stand

across *prep* **1** from one side to the other side of **2** on or at the other side of ▷ *adv* **3** from one side to the other **4** on or to the other side [Old French *a croix* crosswise]

across-the-board *adj* affecting everyone in a particular group or place equally: *across-the-board tax cuts*

acrostic *n* a number of lines of writing, such as a poem, in which the first or last letters form a word or proverb [Greek *akros* outermost + *stikhos* line of verse]

acrylic *adj* **1** made of acrylic ▷ *n* **2** a man-made fibre used for clothes and blankets **3** a kind of paint made from acrylic acid [Latin *acer* sharp + *olere* to smell]

acrylic acid *n chem* a strong-smelling colourless corrosive liquid

acrylic resin *n chem* any of a group of polymers of acrylic acid, used as synthetic rubbers, in paints, and as plastics

act *n* **1** something done **2** a formal decision reached or law passed by a law-making body: *an act of parliament* **3** a major division of a play or opera **4** a short performance, such as a sketch or dance **5** a pretended attitude: *he appeared calm but it was just an act* **6 get in on the act** *informal* to become involved in something in order to share the benefit **7 get one's act together** *informal* to organize oneself ▷ *vb* **8** to do something **9** to perform (a part or role) in a play, film, or broadcast **10** to present (a play) on stage **11 act for** to be a substitute for: *Mr Lewis was acting for the head of the department* **12 act as** to serve the function of: *she is acting as my bodyguard* **13** to behave: *she acts as though she really hates you* **14** to behave in an unnatural way ▶ See also **act up** [Latin *actum* a thing done]

ACT Australian Capital Territory

acting *n* **1** the art of an actor ▷ *adj* **2** temporarily performing the duties of: *the acting president has declared a state of emergency*

actinide series *n chem* a series of 15 radioactive elements with increasing atomic numbers from actinium to lawrencium

actinium *n chem* a radioactive element of the actinide series, occurring as a decay product of uranium. Symbol: Ac [Greek *aktis* ray]

action *n* **1** doing something for a particular purpose **2** something done on a particular occasion **3** a lawsuit **4** movement during some physical activity **5** the operating mechanism in a gun or machine **6** the way in which something operates or works **7** *slang* the main activity in a place **8** the events that form the plot of a story or play **9** activity, force, or energy **10** a minor battle **11 actions** behaviour **12 out of action** not functioning

actionable *adj law* giving grounds for legal action

action painting *n* an art form in which paint is thrown, smeared, dripped, or spattered on the canvas

action replay *n* the rerunning of a small section of a television tape, for example of a sporting event

action stations *pl n* the positions taken up by individuals in preparation for battle or for some other activity

Actium *n* a town of ancient Greece that overlooked the naval battle in 31 BC at which Octavian's fleet under Agrippa defeated that of Mark Antony and Cleopatra

activate *vb* **-vating, -vated 1** to make something active **2** *physics* to make something radioactive **3** *chem* to increase the rate of a reaction ⟩ **activation** *n*

a

active *adj* **1** busy and energetic **2** energetically involved in or working hard for: *active in the peace movement* **3** happening now and energetically: *the plan is under active discussion* **4** functioning or causing a reaction: *the active ingredient is held within the capsule* **5** (of a volcano) erupting periodically **6** *grammar* denoting a form of a verb used to indicate that the subject is performing the action, for example *kicked* in *The boy kicked the football* ▷ *n* **7** *grammar* the active form of a verb **> actively** *adv*

active list *n military* a list of officers available for full duty

active service *n* military duty in an operational area

activist *n* a person who works energetically to achieve political or social goals **> activism** *n*

activity *n* **1** the state of being active **2** lively movement **3** (*pl* **-ties**) any specific action or pursuit: *he was engaged in political activities abroad*

act of God *n law* a sudden occurrence caused by natural forces, such as a flood

Acton¹ *n* a district of the London borough of Ealing

Acton² *n* **1** John Emerich Edward Dalberg, 1st Baron. 1834–1902, English historian: a proponent of Christian liberal ethics and adviser of Gladstone **2** his grandfather, Sir **John Francis Edward**. 1736–1811, European naval commander and statesman: admiral of Tuscany (1774–79) and Naples (1779 onwards) and chief minister of Naples (1779–1806)

actor *or fem* **actress** *n* a person who acts in a play, film, or broadcast

actual *adj* existing in reality or as a matter of fact [Latin *actus* act]

USAGE The excessive use of *actual* and *actually* should be avoided. They are unnecessary in sentences such as in *actual fact, he is forty-two*, and *he did actually go to the play but did not enjoy it*.

actuality *n, pl* **-ties** reality

actually *adv* as an actual fact; really

actuary *n, pl* **-aries** a person qualified to calculate commercial risks and probabilities involving uncertain future events, esp. in such contexts as life assurance [Latin *actuarius* one who keeps accounts] **> actuarial** *adj*

actuate *vb* **-ating, -ated** **1** to start up a mechanical device **2** to motivate someone [Medieval Latin *actuare*]

act up *vb informal* to behave in a troublesome way

acuity (ak-kew-it-ee) *n* keenness of vision or thought [Latin *acutus* acute]

acumen (ak-yew-men) *n* the ability to make good decisions [Latin: sharpness]

acupuncture *n* a medical treatment involving the insertion of needles at various parts of the body to stimulate the nerve impulses [Latin *acus* needle + PUNCTURE] **> acupuncturist** *n*

acute *adj* **1** severe or intense: *acute staff shortages* **2** penetrating in perception or insight **3** sensitive or keen: *it was amazing how acute your hearing got in the bush* **4** (of a disease) sudden and severe **5** *maths* (of an angle) of less than 90° **6** (of a hospital or bed) intended to accommodate short-term patients ▷ *n* **7** an acute accent [Latin *acutus*] **> acutely** *adv* **> acuteness** *n*

acute accent *n* the mark (´), used in some languages to indicate that the vowel over which it is placed is pronounced in a certain way

ad *n informal* an advertisement

AD (indicating years numbered from the supposed year of the birth of Christ) in the year of the Lord [Latin *anno Domini*]

ad- *prefix* **1** to or towards: *adverb* **2** near or next to: *adrenal* [Latin]

Ada *n* a high-level computer programming language, used esp. for military systems [after *Ada*, Countess of LOVELACE, pioneer in computer programming]

adage (ad-ij) *n* a traditional saying that is generally

accepted as being true [Latin *adagium*]

adagietto *music adv* **1** slowly, but more quickly than adagio ▷ *n, pl* **-tos** **2** a movement or piece to be performed fairly slowly

adagio (ad-dahj-yo) *music adv* **1** slowly ▷ *n, pl* **-gios** **2** a movement or piece to be performed slowly [Italian]

Adam¹ *n* **1** *Bible* the first man created by God **2 not know someone from Adam** to not know someone at all

Adam² *n* **1 Adolphe**. 1803–56, French composer, best known for his romantic ballet *Giselle* (1841) **2 Robert**. 1728–92, Scottish architect and furniture designer. Assisted by his brother, **James**, 1730–94, he emulated the harmony of classical and Italian Renaissance architecture

adamant *adj* unshakable in determination or purpose [Greek *adamas* unconquerable] **> adamantly** *adv*

Adamawa *n* **1** a state of Nigeria, in the E on the border with Cameroon. Capital: Yola. Pop: 3 168 101 (2006). Area: 36 917 sq km (14 254 sq miles) **2** a small group of languages of W Africa, spoken chiefly in E Nigeria, N Cameroon, the Central African Republic, and N Democratic Republic of Congo, forming a branch of the Niger-Congo family

Adami *n* Edward Fenech. born 1934, Maltese politician, president of Malta (2004–2009)

Adamkus *n* Valdas. born 1926, Lithuanian politician, president of Lithuania (1998–2003, 2004–2009)

Adamov *n* Arthur. 1908–70, French dramatist, born in Russia: one of the foremost exponents of the Theatre of the Absurd. His plays include *Le Professeur Taranne* (1953), *Le Ping-Pong* (1955), and *Le Printemps '71* (1960)

Adams¹ *n* a mountain in SW Washington, in the Cascade Range. Height: 3751 m (12 307 ft)

Adams² *n* **1 Gerry**, full name *Gerrard Adams*. born 1948, Northern Ireland politician; president of Sinn Féin from 1983: negotiated the Irish Republican Army ceasefires in 1994–96 and 1997; member of the parliament of the Irish Republic from 2011 **2 Henry** (Brooks). 1838–1918, US historian and writer. His works include *Mont Saint Michel et Chartres* (1913) and his autobiography *The Education of Henry Adams* (1918) **3 John**. 1735–1826, second president of the US (1797–1801); US ambassador to Great Britain (1785–88); helped draft the Declaration of Independence (1776) **4 John Coolidge**. born 1947, US composer; works include the operas *Nixon in China* (1987) and *The Death of Klinghoffer* (1991) **5 John Couch**. 1819–92, British astronomer who deduced the existence and position of the planet Neptune **6 John Quincey**. son of John Adams. 1767–1848, sixth president of the US (1825–29); secretary of state (1817–25) **7 Richard**. born 1920, British author; his novels include *Watership Down* (1972), *The Plague Dogs* (1977), and *Traveller* (1988) **8 Samuel**. 1722–1803, US revolutionary leader; one of the organizers of the Boston Tea Party; a signatory of the Declaration of Independence

Adam's apple *n* the projecting lump of thyroid cartilage at the front of a person's neck

Adana *n* a city in S Turkey, capital of Adana province. Pop: 1 248 000 (2005 est). Also called: **Seyhan**

adapt *vb* **1** to adjust (something or oneself) to different conditions **2** to change something to suit a new purpose [Latin *adaptare*] **> adaptable** *adj* **> adaptability** *n*

adaptation *n* **1** something that is produced by adapting something else: *a TV adaptation of a Victorian novel* **2** the act of adapting

adaptor *or* **adapter** *n* **1** a device used to connect several electrical appliances to a single socket **2** any device for connecting two parts of different sizes or types

ADC aide-de-camp

add *vb* **1** to combine (numbers or quantities) so as to make a larger number or quantity **2** to join something to something else so as to increase its size, effect, or scope: *these new rules will add an extra burden on already overworked officials* **3** to say or write something further **4 add in** to include ▶ See also **add up** [Latin *addere*]

a

Addams *n* Jane. 1860–1935, US social reformer, feminist, and pacifist, who founded Hull House, a social settlement in Chicago: Nobel peace prize 1931

addendum *n*, *pl* **-da** something added on, esp. an appendix to a book or magazine

adder *n* a small poisonous snake with a black zigzag pattern along the back [Old English *nædre*]

addict *n* **1** a person who is unable to stop taking narcotic drugs **2** *informal* a person who is devoted to something: *he's a telly addict* [Latin *addictus* given over] **> addictive** *adj*

addicted *adj* **1** dependent on a narcotic drug **2** *informal* devoted to something: *I'm a news freak and addicted to BBC Breakfast News* **> addiction** *n*

Addington *n* Henry, 1st Viscount Sidmouth. 1757–1844, British statesman; prime minister (1801–04) and Home Secretary (1812–21)

Addis Ababa *n* the capital of Ethiopia, on a central plateau 2400 m (8000 ft) above sea level: founded in 1887; became capital in 1896. Pop: 2 899 000 (2005 est)

Addison *n* Joseph. 1672–1719, English essayist and poet who, with Richard Steele, founded *The Spectator* (1711–14) and contributed most of its essays, including the *de Coverley Papers*

addition *n* **1** the act of adding **2** a person or thing that is added **3** a mathematical operation in which the total of two or more numbers or quantities is calculated **4 in addition (to)** besides; as well (as) **> additional** *adj* **> additionally** *adv*

additive *n* any substance added to something, such as food, to improve it or prevent deterioration

addled *adj* **1** confused or unable to think clearly **2** (of eggs) rotten [Old English *adela* filth]

add-on *n* a feature that can be added to a standard model to give increased benefits

address *n* **1** the place at which someone lives **2** the conventional form by which the location of a building is described **3** a formal speech **4** *computers* a number giving the location of a piece of stored information **> vb 5** to mark (a letter or parcel) with an address **6** to speak to **7** to direct one's attention to (a problem or an issue) **8 address oneself to a** to speak or write to **b** to apply oneself to: *we have got to address ourselves properly to this problem* [Latin *ad-* to + *directus* direct]

addressee *n* a person to whom a letter or parcel is addressed

adduce *vb* **-ducing, -duced** to mention something as evidence [Latin *adducere* to lead to]

add up *vb* **1** to calculate the total of (two or more numbers or quantities) **2** *informal* to make sense: *there's something about it that doesn't add up* **3 add up to** to amount to

Adelaide *n* the capital of South Australia: **Port Adelaide**, 11 km (7 miles) away on St Vincent Gulf, handles the bulk of exports. Pop: 1 225 235 (2011)

Adélie Land *n* a part of Antarctica, between Wilkes Land and George V Land: the mainland section of the French Southern and Antarctic Territories (claim suspended under the Antarctic Treaty). Also called: **Adélie Coast**. French name: **Terre Adélie**

Aden *n* **1** the main port and commercial capital of Yemen, on the N coast of the **Gulf of Aden**, an arm of the Indian Ocean at the entrance to the Red Sea: capital of South Yemen until 1990: formerly an important port of call on shipping routes to the East. Pop: 584 000 (2005 est) **2** a former British colony and protectorate on the S coast of the Arabian Peninsula: became part of South Yemen in 1967, now part of Yemen. Area: 195 sq km (75 sq miles)

Adenauer *n* Konrad. 1876–1967, German statesman; chancellor of West Germany (1949–63)

adenoidal *adj* having a nasal voice or impaired breathing because of enlarged adenoids

adenoids (ad-in-oidz) *pl n* a mass of tissue at the back of the throat [Greek *adenoeidēs* glandular]

adept *adj* **1** proficient in something requiring skill **> n 2** a person skilled in something [Latin *adipisci* to attain] **> adeptness** *n*

adequate *adj* just enough in amount or just good enough in quality [Latin *ad-* to + *aequus* equal] **> adequacy** *n* **> adequately** *adv*

à deux (ah duh) *adj*, *adv* of or for two people [French]

ADHD *med* attention deficit hyperactivity disorder

adhere *vb* **-hering, -hered 1** to stick to **2** to act according to (a rule or agreement) **3** to be a loyal supporter of (something) [Latin *adhaerere*]

> USAGE See at adhesion.

adherent *n* **1** a supporter or follower **> adj 2** sticking or attached **> adherence** *n*

adhesion *n* **1** the quality or condition of sticking together **2** *pathol* the joining together of two structures or parts of the body that are normally separate, for example after surgery

> USAGE *Adhesion* is preferred when talking about sticking or holding fast in a physical sense. *Adherence* is preferred when talking about attachment to a political party, cause, etc.

adhesive *n* **1** a substance used for sticking things together **> adj 2** able or designed to stick to things

ad hoc *adj*, *adv* for a particular purpose only [Latin: to this]

Adichie *n* Chimamanda Ngozi, born 1977, Nigerian novelist; her novels include *Purple Hibiscus* (2003) and *Half of a Yellow Sun* (2006), which won the 2007 Orange Prize for Fiction

Adie *n* Kathryn, known as Kate. born 1945, British television journalist, noted esp. for her frontline reporting of revolutions, wars, etc.

adieu (a-dew) *interj*, *n*, *pl* **adieux** or **adieus** (a-dewz) goodbye [French]

Adige *n* a river in N Italy, flowing southeast to the Adriatic. Length: 354 km (220 miles)

ad infinitum *adv* endlessly: *we would not be able to sustain the currency ad infinitum* [Latin]

adipose *adj* of or containing fat; fatty: *adipose tissue* [Latin *adeps* fat]

Adirondack Mountains or **Adirondacks** *pl n* a mountain range in NE New York State. Highest peak: Mount Marcy, 1629 m (5344 ft)

adj. adjective

adjacent *adj* **1** near or next: *the schools were adjacent but there were separate doors* **2** *geometry* (of a side of a right-angled triangle) lying between a specified angle and the right angle [Latin *ad-* near + *jacere* to lie]

adjective *n* a word that adds information about a noun or pronoun [Latin *nomen adjectivum* attributive noun] **> adjectival** *adj*

adjoin *vb* to be next to and joined onto **> adjoining** *adj*

adjourn *vb* **1** to close a court at the end of a session **2** to postpone or be postponed temporarily **3** *informal* to go elsewhere: *can we adjourn to the dining room?* [Old French *ajourner* to defer to an arranged day] **> adjournment** *n*

adjudge *vb* **-judging, -judged** to declare someone to be something specified: *my wife was adjudged to be the guilty party*

adjudicate *vb* **-cating, -cated 1** to give a formal decision on a dispute **2** to serve as a judge, for example in a competition [Latin *adjudicare*] **> adjudication** *n* **> adjudicator** *n*

adjunct *n* **1** something added that is not essential **2** a person who is subordinate to another [Latin *adjunctus* adjoined]

adjure *vb* **-juring, -jured 1** to command someone to do something **2** to appeal earnestly to someone [Latin *adjurare*] **> adjuration** *n*

a

adjust vb **1** to adapt to a new environment **2** to alter slightly, so as to be accurate or suitable **3** insurance to determine the amount payable in settlement of a claim [Old French adjuster] **>** **adjustable** adj **>** **adjuster** n

adjustment n **1** a slight alteration **2** the act of adjusting

adjutant (aj-oo-tant) n an officer in an army who acts as administrative assistant to a superior [Latin adjutare to aid]

Adler n **1** Alfred. 1870–1937, Austrian psychiatrist, noted for his descriptions of overcompensation and inferiority feelings **2** Larry, full name Lawrence Cecil Adler. 1914–2001, US harmonica player

ad-lib vb **-libbing, -libbed** **1** to improvise a speech or piece of music without preparation ▷ adj **2** improvised: ad-lib studio chat ▷ n **3** an improvised remark ▷ adv ad lib **4** spontaneously or freely [short for Latin ad libitum, literally: according to pleasure]

Adm. Brit Admiral

adman n, pl **-men** informal a man who works in advertising

admin n informal administration

administer vb **1** to manage (an organization or estate) **2** to organize and put into practice: anyone can learn to administer the test procedure **3** to give medicine to someone **4** to supervise the taking of (an oath) [Latin administrare]

administrate vb **-trating, -trated** to manage an organization

administration n **1** management of the affairs of an organization **2** the people who administer an organization **3** a government: the first non-communist administration in the country's history **4** the act of administering something, such as medicine or an oath **>** **administrative** adj

administrator n a person who administers an organization or estate

admirable (ad-mer-a-bl) adj deserving or inspiring admiration: the boldness of the undertaking is admirable **>** **admirably** adv

admiral n **1** Also called: **admiral of the fleet** a naval officer of the highest rank **2** any of various brightly coloured butterflies [Arabic amīr-al commander of]

Admiralty n Brit the former government department in charge of the Royal Navy

Admiralty House n the official residence of the Governor General of Australia, in Sydney

Admiralty Islands pl n a group of about 40 volcanic and coral islands in the SW Pacific, part of Papua New Guinea, in the Bismarck Archipelago: main island: Manus. Pop (whole province): 43 589 (2000). Area: about 2000 sq km (800 sq miles). Also called: **Admiralties**

Admiralty Range n a mountain range in Antarctica, on the coast of Victoria Land, northwest of the Ross Sea

admire vb **-miring, -mired** to respect and approve of (a person or thing) [Latin admirari to wonder at] **>** **admiration** n **>** **admirer** n **>** **admiring** adj **>** **admiringly** adv

admissible adj law allowed to be brought as evidence in court

admission n **1** permission or the right to enter **2** permission to join an organization **3** the price charged for entrance **4** a confession: she was, by her own admission, not educated

admit vb **-mitting, -mitted** **1** to confess or acknowledge (a crime or mistake) **2** to concede (the truth of something) **3** to allow (someone) to enter **4** to take (someone) in to a hospital for treatment: he was admitted for tests **5 admit to** to allow someone to participate in something **6 admit of** to allow for: these rules admit of no violation [Latin admittere]

admittance n **1** the right to enter **2** the act of entering a place

admittedly adv it must be agreed: my research is admittedly incomplete

admixture n **1** a mixture **2** an ingredient

admonish vb to reprimand sternly [Latin admonere] **>** **admonition** n **>** **admonitory** adj

ad nauseam (ad naw-zee-am) adv to a boring or sickening extent: she went on and on ad nauseam about her divorce [Latin: to (the point of) nausea]

ado n fuss: without further ado [Middle English at do a to-do]

adobe (ad-oh-bee) n **1** a sun-dried brick **2** the claylike material from which such bricks are made **3** a building made of such bricks [Spanish]

adolescence n the period between puberty and adulthood [Latin adolescere to grow up]

adolescent adj **1** of or relating to adolescence **2** informal (of behaviour) immature ▷ n **3** an adolescent person

Adonis n a handsome young man [name of a handsome youth in Greek myth]

adopt vb **1** law to take someone else's child as one's own **2** to choose (a plan or method) **3** to choose (a country or name) to be one's own [Latin adoptare] **>** **adoptee** n **>** **adoption** n

adoptive adj **1** acquired or related by adoption: an adoptive father **2** of or relating to adoption

adorable adj very attractive; lovable

adore vb **adoring, adored** **1** to love intensely or deeply **2** informal to like very much: I adore being in the country **3** to worship a god with religious rites [Latin adorare] **>** **adoration** n **>** **adoring** adj **>** **adoringly** adv

adorn vb to decorate; increase the beauty of [Latin adornare] **>** **adornment** n

Adorno n Theodor Wiesengrund. 1903–69, German philosopher, sociologist, and music critic. His writings include The Philosophy of the New Music (1949) and Negative Dialectics (1966)

Adowa n a variant spelling of **Aduwa**

ADP automatic data processing

adrenal (ad-reen-al) adj anatomy **1** on or near the kidneys **2** of or relating to the adrenal glands [Latin ad- near + renes kidneys]

adrenal glands pl n anatomy two endocrine glands covering the upper surface of the kidneys

adrenalin or **adrenaline** n biochem a hormone secreted by the adrenal gland in response to stress. It increases heart rate, pulse rate, and blood pressure

Adrian n Edgar Douglas, Baron Adrian. 1889–1977, English physiologist, noted particularly for his research into the function of neurons: shared with Sherrington the Nobel prize for physiology and medicine 1932

Adrian IV n original name Nicholas Breakspear. ?1100–59, the only English pope (1154–59)

Adrianople or **Adrianopolis** n former names of **Edirne**

Adriatic adj **1** of or relating to the Adriatic Sea, or to the inhabitants of its coast or islands ▷ n **2** the Adriatic short for the **Adriatic Sea**

Adriatic Sea n an arm of the Mediterranean between Italy and the Balkan Peninsula

adrift adj, adv **1** drifting **2** without a clear purpose **3** informal off course, wrong: it was obvious that something had gone adrift

adroit adj quick and skilful in how one behaves or thinks [French à droit rightly] **>** **adroitly** adv **>** **adroitness** n

adsorb vb (of a gas or vapour) to condense and form a thin film on a surface [Latin ad- to + sorbere to drink in] **>** **adsorbent** adj **>** **adsorption** n

ADT Atlantic Daylight Time

adulation n uncritical admiration [Latin adulari to flatter]

adult n **1** a mature fully grown person, animal, or plant ▷ adj **2** having reached maturity; fully developed **3** suitable for or typical of adult people: she had very adult features **4** sexually explicit: adult films [Latin adultus grown up] **>** **adulthood** n

adulterate vb **-ating, -ated** to spoil something by adding inferior material [Latin adulterare] **>** **adulteration** n

adulterer or fem **adulteress** n a person who has committed adultery

a

adultery n, pl **-teries** sexual unfaithfulness of a husband or wife [Latin *adulterium*] **> adulterous** adj

Aduwa or **Adowa** n a town in N Ethiopia: Emperor Menelik II defeated the Italians here in 1896. Pop: 46 272 (2005 est). Italian name: **Adua**

adv. adverb

advance vb **-vancing, -vanced 1** to go or bring forward **2** to make progress: *this student has advanced in reading and writing* **3** to further a cause: *an association founded to advance the interests of ex-soldiers* **4** advance on to move towards someone in a threatening manner **5** to present an idea for consideration **6** to lend a sum of money ▷ n **7** a forward movement **8** improvement or progress: *the greatest advance in modern medicine* **9** a loan of money **10** a payment made before it is legally due **11** an increase in price: *any advance on fifty pounds?* **12** in advance beforehand: *you have to pay in advance* **13** in advance of ahead of in time or development ▷ adj **14** done or happening before an event: *advance warning* ▶ See also **advances** [Latin *abante* from before]

advanced adj **1** at a late stage in development **2** not elementary: *he was taking the advanced class in economics*

Advanced level n Brit a formal name for **A level**

advancement n promotion in rank or status

advances pl n approaches made to a person with the hope of starting a romantic or sexual relationship

advantage n **1** a more favourable position or state **2** benefit or profit: *they could make this work to their advantage* **3** *tennis* the point scored after deuce **4** take advantage of **a** to use a person unfairly **b** to use an opportunity **5** to advantage to good effect: *her hair was shaped to display to advantage her superb neck* [Latin *abante* from before]

advantaged adj in a superior social or financial position

advantageous adj likely to bring benefits **> advantageously** adv

advection n physics the transferring of heat in a horizontal stream of gas [Latin *ad-* to + *vehere* to carry]

advent n an arrival: *the advent of the personal computer* [Latin *ad-* to + *venire* to come]

Advent n the season that includes the four Sundays before Christmas

Adventist n a member of a Christian group that believes in the imminent return of Christ

adventitious adj added or appearing accidentally [Latin *adventicius* coming from outside]

adventure n **1** a risky undertaking, the ending of which is uncertain: *our African adventure* **2** exciting or unexpected events [Latin *advenire* to happen to (someone), arrive]

adventure playground n Brit, Austral and NZ a playground for children that contains building materials and other equipment to build with or climb on

adventurer or fem **adventuress** n **1** a person who seeks money or power by unscrupulous means **2** a person who seeks adventure

adventurism n recklessness in politics or finance

adventurous adj daring or enterprising

adverb n a word that modifies a sentence, verb, adverb, or adjective, for example *easily, very,* and *happily* in *They could easily envy the very happily married couple* [Latin *adverbium,* literally: added word] **> adverbial** adj

adversary (ad-verse-er-ree) n, pl **-saries** an opponent in a fight, disagreement, or sporting contest [Latin *adversus* against]

adverse adj **1** unfavourable to one's interests: *adverse effects* **2** antagonistic or hostile [Latin *ad-* towards + *vertere* to turn] **> adversely** adv

adversity n, pl **-ties** very difficult or hard circumstances

advert n informal an advertisement

advertise vb **-tising, -tised 1** to present or praise (goods or a service) to the public, in order to encourage sales **2** to make (a vacancy, an event, or an article for sale) publicly known [Latin *advertere* to turn one's attention to] **> advertiser** n **> advertising** n

advertisement n any public announcement designed to sell goods or publicize an event

advertorial n advertising material presented under the guise of editorial material [from *advert* + *(edit)orial*]

advice n **1** recommendation as to an appropriate choice of action **2** formal notification of facts [Latin *ad* to + *visum* view]

advisable adj sensible and likely to achieve the desired result **> advisability** n

advise vb **-vising, -vised 1** to offer advice to **2** to inform or notify [Latin *ad-* to + *videre* to see] **> adviser** or **advisor** n

advised adj thought-out: *ill-advised*

advisedly (ad-vize-id-lee) adv deliberately; after careful consideration: *I use the word advisedly*

advisory adj **1** able to offer advice ▷ n, pl **-ries 2** a statement giving advice or a warning **3** a person or organization that gives advice: *the Prime Minister's media advisory*

advocaat n a liqueur with a raw egg base [Dutch]

advocacy n active support of a cause or course of action

advocate vb **-cating, -cated 1** to recommend a course of action publicly ▷ n **2** a person who upholds or defends a cause or course of action **3** a person who speaks on behalf of another in a court of law **4** *Scots Law* a barrister [Latin *advocare* to call, summon]

adware n *computers* **1** software that collects information about a user's browsing patterns in order to display relevant advertisements **2** software that is produced with advertisements embedded within it

Adygei Republic or **Adygea** n a constituent republic of SW Russia, bordering on the Caucasus Mountains: chiefly agricultural but with some mineral resources. Capital: Maikop. Pop: 447 000 (2002). Area: 7600 sq km (2934 sq miles)

adze or US **adz** n a tool with a blade at right angles to the handle, used for shaping timber [Old English *adesa*]

Adzhar Autonomous Republic or **Adzharia** n an administrative division of SW Georgia, on the Black Sea: part of Turkey from the 17th century until 1878; mostly mountainous, reaching 2805 m (9350 ft), with a subtropical coastal strip. Capital: Batumi. Pop: 376 016 (2002). Area: 3000 sq km (1160 sq miles)

AEA Atomic Energy Authority

AEC US Atomic Energy Commission

AEEU (in Britain) Amalgamated Engineering and Electrical Union

Aegean adj **1** of or relating to the Aegean Sea or Islands **2** of or relating to the Bronze Age civilization of Greece, Asia Minor, and the Aegean Islands

Aegean Islands pl n the islands of the Aegean Sea, including the Cyclades, Dodecanese, Euboea, and Sporades. The majority are under Greek administration

Aegean Sea n an arm of the Mediterranean between Greece and Turkey

Aegina n **1** an island in the Aegean Sea, in the Saronic Gulf. Area: 85 sq km (33 sq miles) **2** a town on the coast of this island: a city-state of ancient Greece **3** Gulf of Aegina another name for **Saronic Gulf** ▶ Greek name: **Aiyina**

aegis (ee-jiss) n under the aegis of with the sponsorship or protection of [Greek *aigis* shield of Zeus]

Aegospotami n a river of ancient Thrace that flowed into the Hellespont. At its mouth the Spartan fleet under Lysander defeated the Athenians in 405 BC, ending the Peloponnesian War

Ælfric n called *Grammaticus.* ?955–?1020, English abbot, writer, and grammarian

aeolian harp (ee-oh-lee-an) n a musical instrument that produces sounds when the wind passes over its strings [after *Aeolus,* god of winds in Greek myth]

Aeolian Islands pl n another name for the **Lipari Islands**

Aeolis or **Aeolia** n the ancient name for the coastal region of NW Asia Minor, including the island of Lesbos, settled by the Aeolian Greeks (about 1000 BC)

a

aeon *or US* **eon** (ee-on) *n* **1** an immeasurably long period of time **2** the longest division of geological time [Greek *aiōn*]

aerate *vb* **-ating, -ated** to put gas into a liquid, for example when making a fizzy drink **> aeration** *n*

aerial *n* **1** the metal pole or wire on a television or radio which transmits or receives signals ▷ *adj* **2** in, from, or operating in the air **3** extending high into the air **4** of or relating to aircraft [Greek *aēr* air]

aerial top dressing *n* NZ spreading of fertilizer from an aeroplane onto remote areas

aero-, aeri- *or* **aer-** *combining form* **1** relating to aircraft **2** relating to air, atmosphere, or gas [Greek *aēr* air]

aerobatics *n* spectacular manoeuvres, such as loops or rolls, performed by aircraft [AERO- + (ACRO)BATICS]

aerobe *n* biology an organism that requires oxygen to survive [Greek *aēr* air + *bios* life]

aerobic *adj* **1** (of an organism or process) depending on oxygen **2** of or relating to aerobes **3** designed for or relating to aerobics: *aerobic exercise*

aerobics *n* exercises to increase the amount of oxygen in the blood and strengthen the heart and lungs

aerodrome *n* a small airport

aerodynamics *n* the study of how air flows around moving objects **> aerodynamic** *adj* **> aerodynamicist** *n*

aero engine *n* an engine for an aircraft

aerofoil *n* a part of an aircraft, such as the wing, designed to give lift in flight

aerogram *n* an airmail letter on a single sheet of light paper that seals to form an envelope

aeronautics *n* the study or practice of flight through the air **> aeronautical** *adj*

aeroplane *or US and Canad* **airplane** *n* a heavier-than-air powered flying vehicle with fixed wings [AERO- + Greek *planos* wandering]

aerosol *n* a small metal pressurized can from which a substance can be dispensed in a fine spray [AERO- + SOL(UTION)]

aerospace *n* **1** the earth's atmosphere and space beyond ▷ *adj* **2** of rockets or space vehicles: *the aerospace industry*

Aeschines *n* ?389–?314 BC, Athenian orator; the main political opponent of Demosthenes

Aeschylus *n* ?525–?456 BC, Greek dramatist, regarded as the father of Greek tragedy. Seven of his plays are extant, including *Seven Against Thebes*, *The Persians*, *Prometheus Bound*, and the trilogy of the *Oresteia* **> Aeschylean** *adj*

Aesop *n* ?620–564 BC, Greek author of fables in which animals are given human characters and used to satirize human failings **> Aesopian** *or* **Aesopic** *adj*

aesthete *or US* **esthete** (eess-theet) *n* a person who has or who pretends to have a highly developed appreciation of beauty

aesthetic *or US* **esthetic** (iss-thet-ik) *adj* **1** relating to the appreciation of art and beauty ▷ *n* **2** a principle or set of principles relating to the appreciation of art and beauty [Greek *aisthanomai* to perceive, feel] **> aesthetically** *or US* **esthetically** *adv* **> aestheticism** *or US* **estheticism** *n*

aesthetics *or US* **esthetics** *n* **1** the branch of philosophy concerned with the study of the concepts of beauty and taste **2** the study of the rules and principles of art

aether *n* same as ether (2, 3)

aetiology (ee-tee-ol-a-jee) *n* same as etiology

Aetna *n* the Latin name for Mount Etna

Aetolia *n* a mountainous region forming (with the region of Acarnania) a department of W central Greece, north of the Gulf of Patras: a powerful federal state in the 3rd century BC. Chief city: Missolonghi. Pop (with Acarnania): 219 092 (2001). Area: 5461 sq km (2108 sq miles)

a.f. audio frequency

afar *n* from afar from or at a great distance

Afars and the Issas *n* Territory of the Afars and the Issas a former name (1967–77) of Djibouti

affable *adj* showing warmth and friendliness [Latin *affabilis*] **> affability** *n* **> affably** *adv*

affair *n* **1** an event or happening: *the Irangate affair* **2** a sexual relationship outside marriage **3** a thing to be done or attended to: *my wife's career is her own affair* **4** something previously specified: *lunch was a subdued affair* [Old French *à faire* to do]

affairs *pl n* **1** personal or business interests **2** matters of public interest: *foreign affairs*

affect¹ *vb* **1** to influence (someone or something): *the very difficult conditions continued to affect our performance* **2** (of pain or disease) to attack: *the virus can spread to affect the heart muscle* **3** to move someone emotionally: *the experience has affected him deeply* [Latin *afficere*]

affect² *vb* **1** to put on a show of: *he affects a certain disinterest* **2** to wear or use by preference: *he likes to be called Captain John and affects a nautical cap* [Latin *affectare* to strive after]

affectation *n* an attitude or manner put on to impress others

affected *adj* **1** behaving or speaking in a manner put on to impress others **2** pretended: *an affected indifference*

affecting *adj* arousing feelings of pity; moving

affection *n* **1** fondness or tenderness for a person or thing **2 affections** feelings of love; emotions: *I was angry with her for playing with their affections*

affectionate *adj* having or displaying tenderness, affection, or warmth **> affectionately** *adv*

affectless *adj* **1** showing no emotion or concern for others **2** not causing any emotion: *an affectless novel*

affianced (af-fie-anst) *adj* old-fashioned engaged to be married [Medieval Latin *affidare* to trust (oneself) to]

affidavit (af-fid-dave-it) *n* law a written statement made under oath [Medieval Latin, literally: he declares on oath]

affiliate *vb* **-ating, -ated** **1** (of a group) to link up with a larger group ▷ *n* **2** a person or organization that is affiliated with another [Medieval Latin *affiliatus* adopted as a son] **> affiliation** *n*

affinity *n, pl* **-ties** **1** a feeling of closeness to and understanding of a person **2** a close similarity in appearance, structure, or quality **3** a chemical attraction [Latin *affinis* bordering on, related]

affirm *vb* **1** to declare to be true **2** to state clearly one's support for (an idea or belief) [Latin *ad-* to + *firmare* to make firm] **> affirmation** *n*

affirmative *adj* **1** indicating agreement: *an affirmative answer* ▷ *n* **2** a word or phrase indicating agreement, such as *yes*

affix *vb* **1** to attach or fasten ▷ *n* **2** a word or syllable added to a word to produce a derived or inflected form, such as *-ment* in *establishment* [Medieval Latin *affixare*]

afflict *vb* to cause someone suffering or unhappiness [Latin *affligere* to knock against]

affliction *n* **1** something that causes physical or mental suffering **2** a condition of great distress or suffering

affluent *adj* having plenty of money [Latin *ad-* to + *fluere* to flow] **> affluence** *n*

affluent society *n* a society in which the material benefits of prosperity are widely available

afford *vb* **1 can afford** to be able to do or spare something without risking financial difficulties or undesirable consequences: *she can't afford to be choosy* **2** to give or supply: *afford me an opportunity to judge for myself* [Old English *geforthian* to further, promote] **> affordable** *adj* **> affordability** *n*

afforest *vb* to plant trees on [Medieval Latin *afforestare*] **> afforestation** *n*

affray *n* Brit, Austral and NZ a noisy fight in a public place [Vulgar Latin *exfridare* (unattested) to break the peace]

affront *n* **1** a deliberate insult ▷ *vb* **2** to hurt someone's pride or dignity [Old French *afronter* to strike in the face]

Afg. *or* **Afgh.** Afghanistan

afghan *n* NZ a type of biscuit

Afghan *adj* **1** of or relating to Afghanistan, its people, or their language ▷ *n* **2** a native or inhabitant of

Afghanistan **3** the language of Afghanistan

Afghan hound *n* a large slim dog with long silky hair

Afghani *n* Jamal ad-Din al-. 1839–97, Iranian Muslim religious and political reformer; a proponent of Muslim unity, he resisted European interference in Muslim countries

Afghanistan *n* a republic in central Asia: became independent in 1919; occupied by Soviet troops, 1979–89; controlled by mujaheddin forces from 1992 until 1996 when Taliban forces seized power; in the US-led 'war on terror' (2001) the Taliban were overthrown although their insurgency continues; generally arid and mountainous, with the Hindu Kush range rising over 7500 m (25 000 ft) and fertile valleys of the Amu Darya, Helmand, and Kabul Rivers. Official languages: Pashto and Dari (Persian), Tajik also widely spoken. Religion: Muslim. Currency: afghani. Capital: Kabul. Pop: 31 108 077 (2013 est). Area: 657 500 sq km (250 000 sq miles)

aficionado (af-fish-yo-nah-do) *n, pl* -dos an enthusiastic fan of a sport or interest [Spanish]

afield *adv* far afield far away: *they used to travel as far afield as Hungary*

aflame *adv, adj* **1** in flames **2** deeply aroused: *his face was aflame with self-contempt and embarrassment*

afloat *adj* **1** floating **2** free of debt: *his goal is to keep the company afloat* **3** aboard ship ▷ *adv* **4** floating **5** free of debt **6** aboard ship; at sea

afoot *adj, adv* happening; in operation: *I had no suspicion of what was afoot*

afore *adv, prep, conj* old-fashioned or dialect before

aforementioned *adj* mentioned before

aforesaid *adj* referred to previously

aforethought *adj* premeditated: *malice aforethought*

a fortiori (eh for-tee-**or**-rye) *adv* for similar but more convincing reasons [Latin]

afraid *adj* **1** feeling fear or apprehension **2** regretful: *I'm afraid I lost my temper* [Middle English *affraied*]

afresh *adv* once more

Africa *n* the second largest of the continents, on the Mediterranean in the north, the Atlantic in the west, and the Red Sea, Gulf of Aden, and Indian Ocean in the east. The Sahara desert divides the continent unequally into North Africa (an early centre of civilization, in close contact with Europe and W Asia, now inhabited chiefly by Arabs) and Africa south of the Sahara (relatively isolated from the rest of the world until the 19th century and inhabited chiefly by Black people). It was colonized mainly in the 18th and 19th centuries by Europeans and now comprises independent nations. The largest lake is Lake Victoria and the chief rivers are the Nile, Niger, Congo, and Zambezi. Pop: 1 100 000 000 (2013 est). Area: about 30 300 000 sq km (11 700 000 sq miles)

African *adj* **1** of or relating to Africa or its inhabitants ▷ *n* **2** a native or inhabitant of Africa

Africana *pl n* objects of cultural or historical interest from Africa

African-American *n* **1** an American of African descent ▷ *adj* **2** of African-Americans, their history, or their culture

Africander *n* a breed of humpbacked cattle originally from southern Africa [Afrikaans *Afrikander*]

African time *n* S African slang unpunctuality

African violet *n* a flowering house plant with pink or purple flowers and hairy leaves

Afrikaans *n* one of the official languages of South Africa, descended from Dutch [Dutch]

Afrikaner *n* a White South African whose native language is Afrikaans

Afro *n, pl* -ros a frizzy bushy hairstyle

Afro- *combining form* indicating Africa or African: *Afro-Caribbean*

Afro-American *n, adj* same as **African-American**

aft *adv, adj* at or towards the rear of a ship or aircraft [shortened from ABAFT]

after *prep* **1** following in time or place **2** in pursuit of: *he was after my mother's jewellery* **3** concerning: *he asked after Laura* **4** considering: *you seem all right after what happened last night* **5** next in excellence or importance to **6** in imitation of; in the manner of **7** in accordance with: *a man after his own heart* **8** with the same name as: *the street is named after the designer of the church* **9** US past (the hour of): *fifteen after twelve* **10 after all a** in spite of everything: *I was, after all, a suspect* **b** in spite of expectations or efforts **11 after you** please go before me ▷ *adv* **12** at a later time; afterwards ▷ *conj* **13** at a time later than the time when: *she arrived after the reading had begun* ▷ *adj* **14** nautical further aft: *the after cabin* [Old English *æfter*]

afterbirth *n* the placenta and fetal membranes expelled from the mother's womb after childbirth

aftercare *n* **1** the help and support given to a person discharged from a hospital or prison **2** the regular care required to keep something in good condition

afterdamp *n* a poisonous gas formed after the explosion of firedamp in a coal mine

aftereffect *n* any result occurring some time after its cause

afterglow *n* **1** the glow left after the source of a light has disappeared, for example after sunset **2** a pleasant feeling remaining after an enjoyable experience

afterlife *n* life after death

aftermath *n* effects or results of an event considered collectively: *the aftermath of the weekend violence* [after + Old English *mæth* a mowing]

afternoon *n* the period between noon and evening

afterpains *pl n* pains caused by contraction of a woman's womb after childbirth

afters *n* informal the sweet course of a meal

aftersales *n* any customer service that follows the sale of a product ▷ **after-sales** *adj*

aftershave *n* a scented lotion applied to a man's face after shaving

aftershock *n* one of a series of minor tremors occurring after the main shock of an earthquake

aftertaste *n* a taste that lingers on after eating or drinking

afterthought *n* **1** something thought of after the opportunity to use it has passed **2** an addition to something already completed

afterwards *or* **afterward** *adv* later [Old English *æfterweard*]

Ag *chem* silver [Latin *argentum*]

Agadir *n* a port in SW Morocco, which became the centre of an international crisis (1911), when a gunboat arrived to protect German interests. Britain issued a strong warning to Germany but the French negotiated and war was averted. In 1960 the town was virtually destroyed by an earthquake, about 10 000 people being killed. Pop: 385 000 (2003)

again *adv* **1** another or a second time: *I want to look at that atlas again* **2** once more in a previously experienced state or condition: *he pictured her again as she used to be* **3** in addition to the original amount: *twice as much again* **4** on the other hand **5** moreover or furthermore: *she is beautiful and, again, intelligent* **6** again and again continually or repeatedly [Old English *ongegn* opposite to]

against *prep* **1** standing or leaning beside: *he leaned against a tree* **2** opposed to or in disagreement with **3** in contrast to: *his complexion was a sickly white against the black stubble of his beard* **4** coming in contact with: *rain rattled against the window* **5** having an unfavourable effect on: *the system works against you when you don't have money* **6** as a protection from: *a safeguard against bacteria* **7** in exchange for or in return for: *the dollar has gained very slightly against the yen* **8 as against** as opposed to; as compared with [Middle English *ageines*]

Aga Khan IV *n* Prince Karim. born 1936, spiritual leader of the Ismaili sect of Muslims from 1957

Agaña *n* the former name for **Hagåtña**

agape *adj* **1** (of the mouth) wide open **2** (of a person) very surprised

agar (ayg-ar) *or* **agar-agar** *n* a jelly-like substance obtained from seaweed and used as a thickener in food [Malay]

agaric *n* any fungus with gills on the underside of the cap, such as a mushroom [Greek *agarikon*]

Agartala *n* a city in NE India, capital of the state of Tripura. Pop: 189 327 (2001)

Agassi *n* Andre. born 1970, US tennis player: winner of eight Grand Slam singles titles (1992–2003), including four Australian Opens (1995, 2000, 2001, 2003)

Agassiz *n* Jean Louis Rodolphe. 1807–73, Swiss natural historian and geologist, settled in the US after 1846

agate (ag-git) *n* a hard semiprecious form of quartz with striped colouring [Greek *akhatēs*]

Agate *n* James (Evershed). 1877–1947, British theatre critic; drama critic for *The Sunday Times* (1923–47) and author of a nine-volume diary *Ego* (1935–49)

agave (a-**gave**-vee) *n* a tropical American plant with tall flower stalks and thick leaves [Greek *agauos* illustrious]

age *n* **1** the length of time that a person or thing has existed **2** a period or state of human life **3** the latter part of human life **4** a period of history marked by some feature **5** **ages** *informal* a long time **6 come of age** to become legally responsible for one's actions (usually at 18 years) ▷ *vb* **ageing** *or* **aging, aged 7** to become old: *skin type changes as one ages* **8** to appear or cause to appear older: *the years had not aged her in any way* [Latin *aetas*]

aged *adj* **1** (ay-jid) advanced in years; old **2** (rhymes with raged) being at the age of: *a girl aged thirteen is missing*

Agee *n* James. 1909–55, US novelist, poet, and film critic. His works include the autobiographical novel *A Death in the Family* (1957)

ageing *or* **aging** *n* **1** the fact or process of growing old ▷ *adj* **2** becoming or appearing older

ageism *or* **agism** *n* discrimination against people on the grounds of age ▷ **ageist** *or* **agist** *n, adj*

ageless *adj* **1** apparently never growing old **2** seeming to have existed for ever; eternal: *an ageless profession*

Agen *n* a market town in SW France, on the Garonne river. Pop: 30 170 (1999)

agency *n, pl* **-cies 1** an organization providing a specific service: *an advertising agency* **2** the business or functions of an agent **3** action or power by which something happens: *the intervention of a human agency in the sequence of events* [Latin *agere* to do]

agenda *n* **1** a schedule or list of items to be attended to, for example at a meeting **2** *US and Canad* an appointment diary with room for storing addresses, telephone numbers, etc. [Latin: things to be done]

agent *n* **1** a person who arranges business for other people, esp. for actors or singers **2** a spy **3** a substance which causes change in other substances: *an emulsifying agent* **4** someone or something which causes an effect: *the agent of change*

agent noun *n grammar* a noun representing a person or thing performing the action of a verb, for example *performer* or *suspender*

agent provocateur (azh-on prov-vok-at-**tur**) *n, pl* **agents provocateurs** (azh-on prov-vok-at-**tur**) a person employed by the authorities to tempt people to commit illegal acts and so be discredited or punished [French]

age-old *adj* very old; ancient

agglomerate *vb* **-ating, -ated 1** to form or be formed into a mass ▷ *n* **2** a volcanic rock consisting of fused angular fragments of rock [Latin *agglomerare*]

agglomeration *n* a confused mass or cluster

agglutinate *vb* **-nating, -nated** to stick as if with glue [Latin *agglutinare*] ▷ **agglutination** *n*

aggrandize *or* **-dise** *vb* **-dizing, -dized** *or* **-dising, -dised** to make greater in size, power, or rank [Old French *aggrandir*] ▷ **aggrandizement** *or* **-disement** *n*

aggravate *vb* **-vating, -vated 1** to make (a disease,

situation, or problem) worse **2** *informal* to annoy [Latin *aggravare* to make heavier] ▷ **aggravating** *adj* ▷ **aggravation** *n*

aggravated *adj law* (of a criminal offence) made more serious by its circumstances

aggregate *n* **1** an amount or total formed from separate units **2** *geology* a rock, such as granite, consisting of a mixture of minerals **3** the sand and stone mixed with cement and water to make concrete ▷ *adj* **4** formed of separate units collected into a whole ▷ *vb* **-gating, -gated 5** to combine or be combined into a whole **6** to amount to (a particular number) [Latin *aggregare* to add to a flock or herd] ▷ **aggregation** *n*

aggression *n* **1** violent and hostile behaviour **2** an unprovoked attack [Latin *aggredi* to attack] ▷ **aggressor** *n*

aggressive *adj* **1** full of anger or hostility **2** forceful or determined: *an aggressive salesman* ▷ **aggressively** *adv* ▷ **aggressiveness** *n*

aggrieved *adj* upset and angry [Latin *aggravare* to aggravate]

aggro *slang n Brit, Austral and NZ* **1** aggressive behaviour ▷ *adj Austral and NZ* **2** aggressive [from *aggravation*]

aghast *adj* overcome with amazement or horror [Old English *gæstan* to frighten]

agile *adj* **1** quick in movement; nimble **2** mentally quick or acute [Latin *agilis*] ▷ **agility** *n*

agin *prep dialect* against or opposed to: *he gave the usual line of talk agin the government* [obsolete *again* against]

agitate *vb* **-tating, -tated 1** to excite, disturb, or trouble **2** to shake or stir (a liquid) **3** to attempt to stir up public opinion for or against something [Latin *agitare*] ▷ **agitated** *adj* ▷ **agitatedly** *adv* ▷ **agitation** *n* ▷ **agitator** *n*

agitprop *n* political agitation and propaganda [Russian *Agitpropbyuro*]

aglitter *adj* sparkling or glittering

aglow *adj* glowing

aglu *or* **agloo** *n Canad* a breathing hole made in ice by a seal [Inuit]

AGM annual general meeting

Agnes *n* Saint. ?292–?304 AD, Christian child martyr under Diocletian. Feast day: Jan 21

Agnesi *n* Maria Gaetana. 1718–99, Italian mathematician and philosopher, noted for her work on differential calculus

Agnew *n* Spiro Theodore. 1918–96, US Republican politician; vice president (1969–73)

Agnon *n* Shmuel Yosef, real name Samuel Josef Czaczkes. 1888–1970, Israeli novelist, born in Austria-Hungary. His works, which treat contemporary Jewish themes, include *The Day Before Yesterday* (1945). Nobel prize for literature 1966

agnostic *n* **1** a person who believes that it is impossible to know whether God exists **2** a person who claims that the answer to some specific question cannot be known with certainty ▷ *adj* **3** of or relating to agnostics [A- + *gnostic* having knowledge] ▷ **agnosticism** *n*

ago *adv* in the past: *fifty years ago* [Old English *āgān* to pass away]

USAGE The use of *ago* with *since* (*it's ten years ago since he wrote the novel*) is redundant and should be avoided: *it's ten years since he wrote the novel*.

---

agog *adj* eager or curious: *Marcia would be agog to hear his news* [Old French *en gogues* in merriments]

agonize *or* **-nise** *vb* **-nizing, -nized** *or* **-nising, -nised 1** to worry greatly **2** to suffer agony ▷ **agonizing** *or* **-nising** *adj* ▷ **agonizingly** *or* **-nisingly** *adv*

agony *n, pl* **-nies** acute physical or mental pain [Greek *agōnia* struggle]

agony aunt *n* a person who replies to readers' letters in an agony column

agony column *n* a newspaper or magazine feature offering advice on readers' personal problems

a

agoraphobia n a pathological fear of being in public places [Greek *agora* marketplace + *phobos* fear] ⟩ **agoraphobic** *adj, n*

Agostini n Giacomo. born 1942, Italian racing motorcyclist: world champion (500 cc. class) 1966–72, 1975; (350 cc. class) 1968–74

Agostino di Duccio n 1415–81, Italian sculptor, noted for his carved marble panels in the interior of the Tempio Malatestiano at Rimini

AGR advanced gas-cooled reactor

Agra n a city in N India, in W Uttar Pradesh on the Jumna River: a capital of the Mogul empire until 1658; famous for its Mogul architecture, esp. the Taj Mahal. Pop: 1 259 979 (2001)

Agram n the German name for **Zagreb**

agrarian *adj* of or relating to land or agriculture [Latin *ager* field] ⟩ **agrarianism** *n*

agree *vb* **agreeing, agreed** **1** to be of the same opinion **2** to give assent; consent **3** to be consistent **4** agree on to reach a joint decision about: *the ministers agreed on a strategy* **5** agree with to be agreeable or suitable to (one's health or appearance): *marriage and motherhood must agree with you* **6** to concede: *the unions have agreed that the results of appraisal are relevant* **7** *grammar* to be the same in number, gender, and case as a connected word [Old French *a gre* at will]

agreeable *adj* **1** pleasant and enjoyable **2** prepared to consent: *I cannot say that she was agreeable to the project but she was resigned* ⟩ **agreeably** *adv*

agreement n **1** the act or state of agreeing **2** a legally enforceable contract

agribusiness n **1** the use of intensive methods to increase profits in agriculture **2** all of the businesses that process, distribute, and support farm products [*agri*(*culture*) + *business*]

Agricola n Gnaeus Julius 40–93 AD, Roman general; governor of Britain who advanced Roman rule north to the Firth of Forth

agriculture n the rearing of crops and livestock; farming [Latin *ager* field + *cultura* cultivation] ⟩ **agricultural** *adj* ⟩ **agriculturalist** *n*

Agrigento n a town in Italy, in SW Sicily: site of six Greek temples. Pop: 54 619 (2001). Former name (until 1927): **Girgenti**

agrimony n a plant with small yellow flowers and bitter-tasting bristly fruits [Greek *argemōnē* poppy]

Agrippa n Marcus Vipsanius. 63–12 BC, Roman general: chief adviser and later son-in-law of Augustus

Agrippina n **1** called *the Elder. c.* 14 BC–33 AD, Roman matron: granddaughter of Augustus, wife of Germanicus, mother of Caligula and Agrippina the Younger **2** called *the Younger.* 15–59 AD, mother of Nero, who put her to death after he became emperor

agrochemical n a chemical used in agriculture

agrodolce (ag-gro-**dole**-chay) n an Italian sweet-and-sour sauce [Italian]

agronomy (ag-ron-om-mee) n the science of land cultivation, soil management, and crop production [Greek *agros* field + *nemein* to manage] ⟩ **agronomist** *n*

ground *adv* onto the bottom of shallow water: *they felt a jolt as the ship ran aground*

Aguascalientes n **1** a state in central Mexico. Pop: 943 506 (2000). Area: 5471 sq km (2112 sq miles) **2** a city in central Mexico, capital of Aguascalientes state, about 1900 m (6200 ft) above sea level, with hot springs. Pop: 830 000 (2005 est)

gue (aig-yew) n **1** *old-fashioned* malarial fever with shivering **2** a fit of shivering [Old French (*fievre*) *ague* acute fever]

gulhas n Cape Agulhas a headland in South Africa, the southernmost point of the African continent

h *interj* an exclamation expressing pleasure, pain, sympathy, etc.

ha *interj* an exclamation expressing triumph, surprise, etc.

ahead *adv* **1** at or in the front; before **2** forwards: *go straight ahead* **3** get ahead to achieve success: *I was young and hungry to get ahead* ⟩ *adj* **4** in a leading position: *he is ahead in the polls*

ahem *interj* a clearing of the throat, used to attract attention or express doubt

Ahern n Bertie. born 1951, Irish politician; leader of the Fianna Fáil party (1994–2008); prime minister of the Republic of Ireland (1997–2008)

ahi n another name for **yellowfin tuna** [Hawaiian]

Ahmadinejad n Mahmoud. born 1956, Iranian politician; president of Iran (2005–13)

Ahmedabad or **Ahmadabad** n a city in W India, in Gujarat: famous for its mosque. Pop: 3 515 361 (2001)

Ahmednagar or **Ahmadnagar** n a city in W India, in Maharashtra: formerly one of the kingdoms of Deccan. Pop: 307 455 (2001)

ahoy *interj nautical* a shout made to call a ship or to attract attention

Ahvenanmaa n the Finnish name for the **Åland Islands**

Ahwaz or **Ahvaz** n a town in SW Iran, on the Karun River. Pop: 967 000 (2005 est)

AI **1** artificial insemination **2** artificial intelligence

aid n **1** money, equipment, or services provided for people in need; assistance **2** a person or device that helps or assists ⟩ *vb* **3** to help financially or in other ways [Latin *adjutare* to help]

Aid or **-aid** *combining form* denoting a charitable organization that raises money for a particular cause: *Band Aid*

AID (formerly) artificial insemination by donor

Aidan n Saint. died 651 AD, Irish missionary in Northumbria, who founded the monastery at Lindisfarne (635). Feast day: Aug 31

aide n an assistant: *a senior aide to the Prime Minister*

aide-de-camp (aid-de-kom) *n, pl* **aides-de-camp** (aid-de-kom) a military officer serving as personal assistant to a senior [French: camp assistant]

Aidin n a variant spelling of **Aydin**

AIDS acquired immunodeficiency syndrome: a viral disease that destroys the body's ability to fight infection

AIH artificial insemination by husband

Aiken n **1** Conrad (Potter). 1889–1973, US poet, short-story writer, and critic. His works include *Collected Poems* (1953) and the novel *Blue Voyage* (1927) **2** Howard Hathaway. 1900–73, US mathematician; pioneered the construction of electronic computers

ail *vb literary* **1** to trouble or afflict **2** to feel unwell [Old English *eglan*]

aileron (ale-er-on) n a hinged flap on the back of an aircraft wing which controls rolling [French *aile* wing]

ailing *adj* unwell or unsuccessful over a long period: *an ailing company*

ailment n a slight illness

aim *vb* **1** to point (a weapon or missile) or direct (a blow or remark) at a particular person or object **2** to propose or intend: *they aim to provide full and equal rights to all groups* ⟩ *n* **3** the action of directing something at an object **4** intention or purpose **5** take aim to point a weapon or missile at a person or object [Latin *aestimare* to estimate]

aimless *adj* having no purpose or direction ⟩ **aimlessly** *adv*

Ain n **1** a department in E central France, in Rhône-Alpes region. Capital: Bourg. Pop: 539 006 (2003 est). Area: 5785 sq km (2256 sq miles) **2** a river in E France, rising in the Jura Mountains and flowing south to the Rhône. Length: 190 km (118 miles)

Ainsley n Sir Ben, full name *Charles Benedict Ainsley*. born 1977, English competitive sailor: won gold medals for Britain at four consecutive Olympics (2000–2012)

ain't *not standard* am not, is not, are not, have not, or has not: *it ain't fair*

Aintab n the former name (until 1921) of **Gaziantep**

Aintree n a suburb of Liverpool, in Merseyside: site of

the racecourse over which the Grand National steeplechase has been run since 1839

air *n* **1** the mixture of gases that forms the earth's atmosphere. It consists chiefly of nitrogen, oxygen, argon, and carbon dioxide **2** the space above and around the earth; sky. Related adjective: **aerial 3** a distinctive quality, appearance, or manner: *I thought he had an air of elegance and celebrity about him* **4** a simple tune **5** transportation in aircraft: *I went off to Italy by air and train* **6 in the air** in circulation; current: *a sense of expectation is in the air* **7 into thin air** leaving no trace behind **8 on the air** in the act of broadcasting on radio or television **9 up in the air** uncertain ▷ *vb* **10** to make known publicly: *these issues will be aired at a ministerial meeting* **11** to expose to air to dry or ventilate **12** (of a television or radio programme) to be broadcast ▶ See also **airs** [Greek *aēr*]

Aïr *n* a mountainous region of N central Niger, in the Sahara, rising to 1500 m (5000 ft): a former native kingdom. Area: about 77 700 sq km (30 000 sq miles). Also called: **Azbine, Asben**

airbag *n* a safety device in a car, consisting of a bag that inflates automatically in an accident to protect the driver or passenger

air base *n* a centre from which military aircraft operate

airborne *adj* **1** carried by air **2** (of aircraft) flying; in the air

air brake *n* a brake in heavy vehicles that is operated by compressed air

airbrush *n* **1** an atomizer which sprays paint by means of compressed air ▷ *vb* **2** to paint using an airbrush **3** to improve the image of (a person or thing) by hiding defects beneath a bland exterior

air chief marshal *n* a very senior officer in an air force

air commodore *n* a senior officer in an air force

air conditioning *n* a system for controlling the temperature and humidity of the air in a building ▷ **air-conditioned** *adj* ▷ **air conditioner** *n*

aircraft *n*, *pl* **-craft** any machine capable of flying, such as a glider or aeroplane

aircraft carrier *n* a warship with a long flat deck for the launching and landing of aircraft

aircraftman *n*, *pl* **-men** a serviceman of the most junior rank in an air force ▷ **aircraftwoman** *fem n*

air cushion *n* **1** an inflatable cushion **2** the pocket of air that supports a hovercraft

Airdrie *n* a town in W central Scotland, in North Lanarkshire, E of Glasgow: manufacturing and pharmaceutical industries. Pop: 36 326 (2001)

Aire *n* a river in N England rising in the Pennines and flowing southeast to the Ouse. Length: 112 km (70 miles)

Airedale *n* a large terrier with rough tan-coloured hair and a black patch covering most of the back

airfield *n* a place where aircraft can land and take off

air force *n* the branch of a nation's armed services that is responsible for air warfare

air gun *n* a gun fired by means of compressed air

airhead *n* *slang* a person who is stupid or incapable of serious thought

air hostess *n* *chiefly Brit* a female flight attendant on an airline

airily *adv* in a light-hearted and casual manner

airing *n* **1** exposure to air or warmth for drying or ventilation **2** exposure to public debate: *both these notions got an airing during the campaign*

airing cupboard *n* a heated cupboard in which laundry is aired and kept dry

airless *adj* lacking fresh air; stuffy

air letter *n* same as **aerogram**

airlift *n* **1** the transportation by air of troops or cargo when other routes are blocked ▷ *vb* **2** to transport by an airlift

airline *n* an organization that provides scheduled flights for passengers or cargo

airliner *n* a large passenger aircraft

airlock *n* **1** a bubble of air blocking the flow of liquid in a pipe **2** an airtight chamber between places that do not have the same air pressure, such as in a spacecraft or submarine

airmail *n* **1** the system of sending mail by aircraft **2** mail sent by aircraft

airman *or fem* **airwoman** *n*, *pl* **-men** *or* **-women** a person serving in an air force

air marshal *n* **1** a senior Royal Air Force officer of equivalent rank to a vice admiral in the Royal Navy **2** the rank of a Royal New Zealand Air Force officer when Chief of the Defence Force

Air Miles *pl n* *Brit* points awarded on buying flight tickets and certain other products which can be used to pay for other flights

airplane *n* *US and Canad* an aeroplane

airplay *n* the broadcast performances of a record on radio

air pocket *n* a small descending air current that causes an aircraft to lose height suddenly

airport *n* a landing and taking-off area for civil aircraft, with facilities for aircraft maintenance and passenger arrival and departure

air pump *n* a device for pumping air into or out of something

air rage *n* aggressive behaviour by an airline passenger that endangers the safety of the crew and other passengers

air raid *n* an attack by enemy aircraft in which bombs are dropped

air rifle *n* a rifle fired by means of compressed air

airs *pl n* manners put on to impress people: *we're poor and we never put on airs*

airship *n* a lighter-than-air self-propelled aircraft

airsick *adj* nauseated from travelling in an aircraft

airside *n* the part of an airport nearest the aircraft

airspace *n* the atmosphere above a particular country, regarded as its territory

airspeed *n* the speed of an aircraft relative to the air in which it moves

airstrip *n* a cleared area for the landing and taking-off of aircraft

air terminal *n* a building in a city from which air passengers are transported to an airport

airtight *adj* **1** sealed so that air cannot enter **2** having no weak points: *your reasoning is airtight and your evidence sound*

airtime *n* the time allocated to a particular programme, topic, or type of material on radio or television

air vice-marshal *n* a senior officer in an air force

airwaves *pl n* *informal* radio waves used in radio and television broadcasting

airway *n* an air route used regularly by aircraft

airworthy *adj* (of an aircraft) safe to fly ▷ **airworthiness** *n*

airy *adj* **airier, airiest 1** spacious and well ventilated **2** light-hearted and casual **3** having little basis in reality; fanciful: *airy assurances*

Airy *n* Sir George Biddell. 1801–92, British astronomer, noted for his estimate of the earth's density from gravity measurements in mines; astronomer royal (1835–81)

Aisha *or* **Ayesha** *n* ?613–678 AD, the favourite wife of Mohammed; daughter of Abu Bekr

aisle (rhymes with **mile**) *n* a passageway separating seating areas in a church, theatre, or cinema, or separating rows of shelves in a supermarket [Latin *ala* wing]

Aisne *n* **1** a department of NE France, in Picardy region. Capital: Laon. Pop: 535 326 (2003 est). Area: 7428 sq km (2897 sq miles) **2** a river in N France, rising in the Argonne Forest and flowing northwest and west to the River Oise: scene of a major Allied offensive in 1918 which turned the tide finally against Germany in World War I. Length: 282 km (175 miles)

a

aitchbone *n* a cut of beef from the rump bone [Middle English *nache-bone*]

Aitken *n* **1** Robert Grant. 1864–1951, US astronomer who discovered over three thousand double stars **2** William Maxwell. See Beaverbrook

Ai Weiwei *n* born 1957, Chinese multimedia artist and political activist. His works include *Sunflower Seeds* (2010), in which the floor of Tate Modern's Turbine Hall was covered with millions of tiny porcelain replicas of sunflower seeds

Aix-en-Provence *n* a city and spa in SE France: the medieval capital of Provence. Pop: 145 721 (2006). Also called: Aix

Aix-la-Chapelle *n* the French name for Aachen

Aix-les-Bains *n* a town in E France: a resort with sulphurous springs. Pop: 25 732 (1999)

Aíyina *n* transliteration of the Modern Greek name for Aegina

Ajaccio *n* the capital of Corsica, a port on the W coast. Pop: 64 432 (2007)

ajar *adj, adv* (of a door) slightly open [Old English *cierran* to turn]

Ajmer *n* a city in NW India, in Rajasthan: textile centre. Pop: 485 197 (2001)

AK Alaska

AK-47 *n trademark* same as Kalashnikov

Akbar *n* called *Akbar the Great*. 1542–1605, Mogul emperor of India (1556–1605), who extended the Mogul empire to include N India

Akhaïa *n* transliteration of the Modern Greek name for Achaea

Akhenaten *or* **Akhenaton** *n* original name *Amenhotep IV*. died ?1358 BC, king of Egypt, of the 18th dynasty; he moved his capital from Thebes to Tell El Amarna and introduced the cult of Aten

Akhmatova *n* Anna. pseudonym of *Anna Gorenko*. 1889–1966, Russian poet: noted for her concise and intensely personal lyrics

Akihito *n* born 1933, Emperor of Japan from 1989

akimbo *adv* (with) arms akimbo with hands on hips and elbows turned outwards [Middle English *in kenebowe* in keen (ie sharp) bow]

akin *adj* akin to similar or very close to: *the technique is akin to impressionist painting*

Akka *n* a city and port in N Israel, strategically situated on the Bay of Acre in the E Mediterranean: taken and retaken during the Crusades (1104, 1187, 1191, 1291), taken by the Turks (1517), by Egypt (1832), and by the Turks again (1839). Pop: 45 600 (2001). another name for Acre

Akkad *or* **Accad** *n* **1** a city on the Euphrates in N Babylonia, the centre of a major empire and civilization (2360–2180 BC). Ancient name: Agade **2** an ancient region lying north of Babylon, from which the Akkadian language and culture is named

Akkerman *n* the former name (until 1946) of Belgorod-Dnestrovski

Akko *n* a city and port in N Israel, strategically situated on the Bay of Acre in the E Mediterranean: taken and retaken during the Crusades (1104, 1187, 1191, 1291), taken by the Turks (1517), by Egypt (1832), and by the Turks again (1839). Pop: 45 600 (2001). another name for Acre

Akmola *or* **Aqmola** *n* a former name (1994–98) of Astana

Akmolinsk *n* a former name (until 1961) of Astana

Akron *n* a city in NE Ohio. Pop: 212 215 (2003 est)

Aksum *or* **Axum** *n* an ancient town in N Ethiopia, in the Tigre region: capital of the Aksumite Empire (1st to 6th centuries AD). According to tradition, the Ark of the Covenant was brought here from Jerusalem

Aktobe *n* an industrial city in W Kazakhstan. Pop: 291 000 (2005 est). Kazakh name: Aqtöbe. Former name (until 1991): Aktyubinsk

Aktyubinsk *n* the former name (until 1991) of Aktobe

Akure *n* a city in SW Nigeria, capital of Ondo state: agricultural trade centre. Pop: 434 000 (2005 est)

Akwa Ibom *n* a state of Nigeria, on the Gulf of Guinea. Capital: Uyo. Pop: 3 920 208 (2006). Area: 7081 sq km (2734 sq miles)

Al *chem* aluminium

AL Alabama

à la *prep* in the manner or style of: *laced with Gothic allusion à la David Lynch* [French]

Ala. Alabama

Alabama *n* **1** a state of the southeastern US, on the Gulf of Mexico: consists of coastal and W lowlands crossed by the Tombigbee, Black Warrior, and Alabama Rivers, with parts of the Tennessee Valley and Cumberland Plateau in the north; noted for producing cotton and white marble. Capital: Montgomery. Pop: 4 500 752 (2003 est). Area: 131 333 sq km (50 708 sq miles). Abbreviation: Ala., (with zip code) AL **2** a river in Alabama, flowing southwest to the Mobile and Tensaw Rivers. Length: 507 km (315 miles)

Alabamian *adj* **1** of or relating to Alabama or its inhabitants ▷ *n* **2** a native or inhabitant of Alabama

alabaster *n* a kind of white stone used for making statues and vases [Greek *alabastros*]

Alacant *n* the Catalan name for Alicante

à la carte *adj, adv* (of a menu) having dishes individually priced [French]

alacrity *n* speed or eagerness: *I accepted the invitation with alacrity* [Latin *alacer* lively]

Ala Dağ *or* **Ala Dagh** *n* **1** the E part of the Taurus Mountains, in SE Turkey, rising over 3600 m (12 000 ft) **2** a mountain range in E Turkey, rising over 3300 m (11 000 ft) **3** a mountain range in NE Turkey, rising over 3000 m (10 000 ft)

Alagez *or* **Alagöz** *n* the Turkish name for (Mount) Aragats

Alagna *n* Roberto. born 1963, Italian opera singer, born in France; a lyric tenor

Alagoas *n* a state in NE Brazil, on the Atlantic coast. Capital: Maceió. Pop: 2 887 535 (2002). Area: 30 776 sq km (11 031 sq miles)

Alai *n* a mountain range in central Asia, in SW Kyrgyzstan, running from the Tian Shan range in China into Tajikistan. Average height: 4800 m (16 000 ft), rising over 5850 m (19 500 ft)

Alain-Fournier *n* real name *Henri-Alban Fournier*. 1886–1914, French novelist; author of *Le Grand Meaulnes* (1913): translated as *The Lost Domain*, 1959)

Alamein *n* See El Alamein

Alamo *n* the Alamo a mission in San Antonio, Texas, the site of a siege and massacre in 1836 by Mexican forces under Santa Anna of a handful of American rebels fighting for Texan independence from Mexico

à la mode *adj* fashionable [French]

Alanbrooke *n* Alan Francis Brooke, 1st Viscount. 1883–1963, British field marshal; chief of Imperial General Staff (1941–46)

Åland Islands *pl n* a group of over 6000 islands under Finnish administration, in the Gulf of Bothnia. Capital: Mariehamn. Pop: 26 347 (2003 est). Finnish name: Ahvenanmaa

Alania *n* another name for North Ossetian Republic

al-Aqsa *n* See Dome of the Rock

Alarcón *n* Pedro Antonio de. 1833–91, Spanish novelist and short-story writer, noted for his humorous sketches of rural life, esp. in *The Three-Cornered Hat* (1874)

Alaric *n* ?370–410 AD, king of the Visigoths, who served under the Roman emperor Theodosius I but later invaded Greece and Italy, capturing Rome in 410

alarm *n* **1** fear aroused by awareness of danger **2** a noise warning of danger: *there had been no time to put on life jackets or to sound the alarm* **3** a device that transmits a warning **4** short for alarm clock ▷ *vb* **5** to fill with fear or activate a burglar alarm on (a house, car, etc.) [Old Italian *all'arme* to arms] **> alarming** *adj*

alarm clock *n* a clock that sounds at a set time to wake a person up

a

alarmist n 1 a person who alarms others needlessly ▷ adj 2 causing needless alarm

alas adv 1 unfortunately or regrettably: *the answer, alas, is that they cannot get any for the moment* ▷ interj 2 old-fashioned an exclamation of grief or alarm [Old French *ha las!*]

Alas. Alaska

Alaska n 1 the largest state of the US, in the extreme northwest of North America: the aboriginal inhabitants are Inuit and Yupik; the earliest White settlements were made by the Russians; it was purchased by the US from Russia in 1867. It is mostly mountainous and volcanic, rising over 6000 m (20 000 ft), with the Yukon basin in the central region; large areas are covered by tundra; it has important mineral resources (chiefly coal, oil, and natural gas). Capital: Juneau. Pop: 648 818 (2003 est). Area: 1 530 694 sq km (591 004 sq miles). Abbreviation: Alas., (with zip code) AK 2 Gulf of Alaska the N part of the Pacific, between the Alaska Peninsula and the Alexander Archipelago

Alaska Highway n a road extending from Dawson Creek, British Columbia, to Fairbanks, Alaska: built by the US Army (1942). Length: 2452 km (1523 miles). Originally called: Alcan Highway

Alaskan adj 1 of or relating to Alaska or its inhabitants ▷ n 2 a native or inhabitant of Alaska

Alaska Peninsula n an extension of the mainland of SW Alaska between the Pacific and the Bering Sea, ending in the Aleutian Islands. Length: about 644 km (400 miles)

Alaska Range n a mountain range in S central Alaska. Highest peak: Mount McKinley, 6194 m (20 320 ft)

alb n a long white linen robe worn by a Christian priest [Latin *albus* white]

Alb. Albania(n)

Albacete n a city in SE Spain: metal goods manufacturing. Pop: 155 142 (2003 est)

albacore n a tuna found in warm seas which is valued as a food fish [Arabic *al-bakrah*]

Alba Longa n a city of ancient Latium, southeast of modern Rome: the legendary birthplace of Romulus and Remus

Alban n Saint. 3rd century AD, the first English martyr. He was beheaded by the Romans on the site on which St Alban's Abbey now stands, for admitting his conversion to Christianity. Feast day: June 17

Albania n a republic in SE Europe, on the Balkan Peninsula: became independent in 1912 after more than four centuries of Turkish rule; established as a republic (1946) under Communist rule; multiparty constitution adopted in 1991. It is generally mountainous, rising over 2700 m (9000 ft), with extensive forests. Language: Albanian. Religion: Muslim majority. Currency: lek. Capital: Tirana. Pop: 3 011 405 (2013 est). Area: 28 749 sq km (11 100 sq miles)

Albanian adj 1 of or relating to Albania or its inhabitants ▷ n 2 a native or inhabitant of Albania 3 the language of Albania

Albany n 1 a city in E New York State, on the Hudson River: the state capital. Pop: 93 919 (2003 est) 2 a river in central Canada, flowing east and northeast to James Bay. Length: 982 km (610 miles) 3 a port in southwest Western Australia: founded as a penal colony. Pop: 22 415 (2001)

albatross n 1 a large sea bird with very long wings 2 golf a score of three strokes under par for a hole [Portuguese *alcatraz* pelican]

Albee n Edward. born 1928, US dramatist. His plays include *Who's Afraid of Virginia Woolf?* (1962), *Seascape* (1975), *Marriage Play* (1986), *Three Tall Women* (1990), and *Goat* (2004)

albeit conj even though: *these effects occur, albeit to a lesser degree* [Middle English *al be it* although it be (that)]

Albemarle Sound n an inlet of the Atlantic in NE North Carolina. Length: about 96 km (60 miles)

Albéniz n Isaac. 1860–1909, Spanish composer; noted for piano pieces inspired by folk music, such as the suite *Iberia*

Albers n Josef. 1888–1976, US painter, designer, and poet, born in Germany. His works include a series of abstract paintings entitled *Homage to the Square*

Albert¹ n Lake Albert a lake in E Africa, between the Democratic Republic of Congo and Uganda in the great Rift Valley, 660 m (2200 ft) above sea level: a source of the Nile, fed by the Victoria Nile, which leaves as the Albert Nile. Area: 5345 sq km (2064 sq miles). Former name: Lake Mobutu

Albert² n Prince. full name *Albert Francis Charles Augustus Emmanuel of Saxe-Coburg-Gotha*. 1819–61, Prince Consort of Queen Victoria of Great Britain and Ireland

Albert I n 1 c. 1255–1308, king of Germany (1298–1308) 2 1875–1934, king of the Belgians (1909–34) 3 called *Albert the Bear. c.* 1100–70. German military leader: first margrave of Brandenburg

Albert II n full name *Albert Felix Humbert Theodore Christian Eugene Marie*. born 1934, king of Belgium (1993–2013); abdicated in favour of his son Philippe

Alberta n a province of W Canada: mostly prairie, with the Rocky Mountains in the southwest Capital: Edmonton. Pop: 3 645 257 (2011 est). Area: 661 188 sq km (255 285 sq miles). Abbreviation: Alta, AB

Albertan adj 1 of or relating to Alberta or its inhabitants ▷ n 2 a native or inhabitant of Alberta

Albert Edward n a mountain in SE New Guinea, in the Owen Stanley Range. Height: 3993 m (13 100 ft)

Alberti n Leon Battista. 1404–72, Italian Renaissance architect, painter, writer, and musician; among his architectural designs are the façades of Sta. Maria Novella at Florence and S. Francesco at Rimini

Albertus Magnus n Saint. original name *Albert, Count von Böllstadt*. ?1193–1280, German scholastic philosopher; teacher of Thomas Aquinas and commentator on Aristotle. Feast day: Nov 15

Albi n a town in S France: connected with the Albigensian heresy and the crusade against it. Pop: 46 274 (1999)

albino n, pl -nos a person or animal with white or almost white hair and skin and pinkish eyes [Latin *albus* white] ▷ albinism n

Albinoni n Tomaso. 1671–1750, Italian composer and violinist. He wrote concertos and over 50 operas

Albion n poetic Britain or England [Latin]

Alboin n died 573 AD, king of the Lombards (565–73); conqueror of N Italy

Ålborg n a variant spelling of Aalborg

album n 1 a book with blank pages, for keeping photographs or stamps in 2 a long-playing record [Latin: blank tablet]

albumen n 1 egg white 2 biochem same as albumin [Latin *albus* white]

albumin or **albumen** n biochem a water-soluble protein found in blood plasma, egg white, milk, and muscle

Albuquerque¹ n a city in central New Mexico, on the Rio Grande. Pop: 471 856 (2003 est)

Albuquerque² n Afonso de. 1453–1515, Portuguese navigator who established Portuguese colonies in the East by conquering Goa, Ceylon (Sri Lanka), Malacca, and Ormuz

Albury-Wodonga n a town in SE Australia, in S central New South Wales, on the Murray River: commercial centre of an agricultural region. Pop: 69 880 (2001)

Alcaeus n 7th century BC, Greek lyric poet who wrote hymns, love songs, and political odes

Alcan Highway n original name of the Alaska Highway

Alcántara n a town in W Spain: a Roman bridge spans the River Tagus. Pop: 1739 (2003 est)

Alcatraz n an island in W California, in San Francisco Bay: a federal prison until 1963

Alcázar de San Juan n a town in S central Spain:

associated with Cervantes and Don Quixote. Pop: 27 229 (2003 est)

alchemy *n* a medieval form of chemistry concerned with trying to change base metals into gold and to find an elixir to prolong life indefinitely [Arabic *al* the + *kīmiyā'* transmutation] **> alchemist** *n*

Alchevsk *n* a city in E Ukraine. Pop: 117 000 (2005 est). Former name (until 1992): **Kommunarsk**

Alcibiades *n* 450–404 BC, Athenian statesman and general in the Peloponnesian War: brilliant, courageous, and unstable; he defected to the Spartans in 415, but returned and led the Athenian victories at Abydos (411) and Cyzicus (410) **> Alcibiadean** *adj*

Alcman *n* 7th century BC, Greek lyric poet

Alcock *n* Sir John William. 1892–1919, English aviator who with A.W. Brown made the first nonstop flight across the Atlantic (1919)

alcohol *n* **1** a colourless flammable liquid present in intoxicating drinks **2** intoxicating drinks generally [Arabic *al-kuhl* powdered antimony]

alcohol-free *adj* **1** (of beer or wine) containing only a trace of alcohol **2** (of a period of time) during which no alcohol is taken: *an alcohol-free evening*

alcoholic *n* **1** a person who is addicted to alcohol ▷ *adj* **2** of or relating to alcohol

alcoholism *n* a condition in which dependence on alcohol harms a person's health and everyday life

alcopop *n informal* an alcoholic drink that tastes like a soft drink [ALCO(HOL) + POP¹ (sense 9)]

Alcott *n* Louisa May. 1832–88, US novelist, noted for her children's books, esp. *Little Women* (1869)

alcove *n* a recess in the wall of a room [Arabic *al-qubbah* the vault]

Alcuin *or* **Albinus** *n* 735–804 AD, English scholar and theologian; friend and adviser of Charlemagne

Aldabra *n* an island group in the Indian Ocean: part of the British Indian Ocean Territory (1965–76); now administratively part of the Seychelles

Aldan *n* a river in E Russia in the SE Sakha Republic, rising in the **Aldan Mountains** and flowing north and west to the Lena River. Length: about 2700 km (1700 miles)

Aldeburgh *n* a small resort in SE England, in Suffolk: site of an annual music festival established in 1948 by Benjamin Britten. Pop: 2654 (2001)

aldehyde *n chem* any organic compound containing the group –CHO, derived from alcohol by oxidation [New Latin *al(cohol) dehyd(rogenatum)* dehydrogenated alcohol]

alder *n* a tree with toothed leaves and conelike fruits, often found in damp places [Old English *alor*]

alderman *n, pl* **-men 1** (formerly, in England and Wales) a senior member of a local council, elected by other councillors **2** (in the US, Canada and Australia) a member of the governing body of a city [Old English *ealdor* chief + *mann* man]

Aldermaston *n* a village in S England, in West Berkshire unitary authority, Berkshire, SW of Reading: site of the Atomic Weapons Research Establishment and starting point of the Aldermaston marches (1958–63), organized by the Campaign for Nuclear Disarmament. Pop: 927 (2001)

Alderney *n* **1** one of the Channel Islands, in the English Channel: separated from the French coast by a dangerous tidal channel (the **Race of Alderney**). Pop: 2294 (2001). Area: 8 sq km (3 sq miles). French name: **Aurigny 2** an early, but now extinct, breed of dairy cattle originating from the island of Alderney

Aldershot *n* a town in S England, in Hampshire: site of a large military camp. Pop: 58 170 (2001)

Aldington *n* Richard. 1892–1962, English poet, novelist, and biographer. His novels include *Death of a Hero* (1929) and *The Colonel's Daughter* (1931), which reflect postwar disillusion following World War I

Aldiss *n* Brian W(ilson). born 1925, British novelist, best known for his science fiction. His works include *Non-Stop* (1958), *Enemies of the System* (1978), *The Helliconia Trilogy* (1983–86), *Forgotten Life* (1988), and *The Detached Retina* (1995)

Aldridge-Brownhills *n* a town in central England, in Walsall unitary authority, West Midlands: formed by the amalgamation of neighbouring towns in 1966. Pop: 35 525 (2001)

Aldrin *n* Edwin Eugene Jr., known as *Buzz*. born 1930, US astronaut; the second man to set foot on the moon on July 20, 1969, during the Apollo 11 flight

Aldus Manutius *n* 1450–1515, Italian printer, noted for his fine editions of the classics. He introduced italic type

ale *n* **1** a beer fermented in an open vessel using yeasts that rise to the top of the brew **2** (formerly) an alcoholic drink that is unflavoured by hops **3** *Brit* another word for **beer** [Old English *alu, ealu*]

alehouse *n* old-fashioned a public house

Aleichem *n* Sholom, real name *Solomon Rabinowitz*. 1859–1916, US Jewish writer, born in Russia. His works include *Tevye the Milkman*, which was adapted for the stage musical *Fiddler on the Roof*

Aleixandre *n* Vicente. 1898–1984, Spanish poet, whose collections include *La destrucción o el amor* (1935; Destruction or Love): Nobel prize for literature 1977

Alekhine *n* Alexander. 1892–1946, Russian-born chess player who lived in France; world champion (1927–35, 1937–46)

Aleksandropol *n* the former name (from 1837 until after the Revolution) of **Kumayri**

Aleksandrovsk *n* the former name (until 1921) of **Zaporozhye**

Alemán *n* Mateo. 1547–?1614, Spanish novelist, author of the picaresque novel *Guzmán de Alfarache* (1599)

alembic *n* **1** an obsolete type of container used for distillation **2** anything that distils or purifies things [Arabic *al-anbīq* the still]

Alençon *n* a town in NW France: early lace-manufacturing centre. Pop: 28 935 (1999)

Aleppo *n* an ancient city in NW Syria: industrial and commercial centre; scene of heavy fighting from 2012 between various rebel forces and army units loyal to President Bashar al-Assad. Pop: 2 505 000 (2005 est). French name: **Alep**. Arabic name: **Haleb**

alert *adj* **1** watchful and attentive **2 alert to** aware of ▷ *n* **3** a warning or the period during which a warning remains in effect **4 on the alert** watchful ▷ *vb* **5** to warn of danger **6** to make aware of a fact [Italian *all'erta* on the watch] **> alertness** *n*

Alessandria *n* a town in NW Italy, in Piedmont. Pop: 85 438 (2001)

Ålesund *or* **Aalesund** *n* a port and market town in W Norway, on an island between Bergen and Trondheim: fishing and sealing fleets. Pop: 40 001 (2004 est)

Aleut *n* **1** a member of a people inhabiting the Aleutian Islands and SW Alaska, related to the Inuit **2** the language of this people, related to Inuktitut [from Russian *aleút*, probably of Chukchi origin]

Aleutian *adj* **1** of, denoting, or relating to the Aleutian Islands, the Aleuts, or their language ▷ *n* **2** another word for **Aleut**

Aleutian Islands *pl n* a chain of over 150 volcanic islands, extending southwestwards from the Alaska Peninsula between the N Pacific and the Bering Sea

A level *n* **1** *Brit* the advanced level of a subject taken for the General Certificate of Education **2** a pass in a subject at A level

Alexander *n* Harold (**Rupert Leofric George**), Earl Alexander of Tunis. 1891–1969, British field marshal in World War II, who organized the retreat from Dunkirk and commanded in North Africa (1943) and Sicily and Italy (1944–45); governor general of Canada (1946–52); British minister of defence (1952–54)

a

Allentown *n* a city in E Pennsylvania, on the Lehigh River. Pop: 105 958 (2003 est)

Alleppey *n* a port in S India, in Kerala on the Malabar Coast. Pop: 177 079 (2001)

allergen (al-ler-jen) *n* a substance capable of causing an allergic reaction ⟩ **allergenic** *adj*

allergic *adj* **1** having or caused by an allergy **2 allergic to** *informal* having a strong dislike of: *father and son seemed to have been allergic to each other from the start*

allergy *n, pl* **-gies** **1** extreme sensitivity to a substance such as a food or pollen, which causes the body to react to any contact with it **2** *informal* a strong dislike for something [Greek *allos* other + *ergon* activity]

alleviate *vb* **-ating, -ated** to lessen (pain or suffering) [Latin *levis* light] ⟩ **alleviation** *n*

> **USAGE** See at **ameliorate**.

alley *n* **1** a narrow passage within or behind buildings **2 a** a building containing lanes for tenpin bowling **b** a long narrow wooden lane down which the ball is rolled in tenpin bowling **3** a path in a garden, often lined with trees [Old French *alee*]

alleyway *n* a narrow passage with buildings or walls on both sides

all found *adv* (of charges for accommodation) including meals, heating, and other living expenses

Allhallows *n* same as **All Saints' Day**

alliance *n* **1** the state of being allied **2** a formal relationship between two or more countries or political parties to work together **3** the countries or parties involved [Old French *alier* to ally]

allied *adj* **1** united by a common aim or common characteristics: *the allied areas of telepathy and clairvoyance* **2 Allied** relating to the countries that fought against Germany and Japan in the Second World War: *the Allied bombing of German cities*

Allier *n* **1** a department of central France, in Auvergne region. Capital: Moulins. Pop: 342 307 (2003 est). Area: 7382 sq km (2879 sq miles) **2** a river in S central France, rising in the Cévennes and flowing north to the Loire. Length: over 403 km (250 miles)

alligator *n* a large reptile of the southern US, similar to the crocodile but with a shorter broader snout [Spanish *el lagarto* the lizard]

all in *adj* **1** *informal* exhausted **2** (of wrestling) with no style forbidden ▷ *adv* **3** with all expenses included

Allingham *n* Margery. 1904–66, British author of detective stories, featuring Albert Campion. Her works include *Tiger in the Smoke* (1952) and *The Mind Readers* (1965)

alliteration *n* the use of the same sound at the start of words occurring together, as in *round the rugged rock the ragged rascal ran* [Latin *litera* letter] ⟩ **alliterative** *adj*

Alloa *n* a town in E central Scotland, the administrative centre of Clackmannanshire. Pop: 18 989 (2001)

allocate *vb* **-cating, -cated** to assign to someone or for a particular purpose [Latin *locus* a place] ⟩ **allocation** *n*

allopathy (al-lop-ath-ee) *n med* an orthodox method of treating disease, by using drugs that produce an effect opposite to the effect of the disease being treated, as contrasted with homeopathy [Greek *allos* other + *pathos* suffering] ⟩ **allopathic** *adj*

allot *vb* **-lotting, -lotted** to assign as a share or for a particular purpose [Old French *lot* portion]

allotment *n* **1** *Brit* a small piece of land rented by a person to grow vegetables on **2** a portion allotted **3** distribution

allotrope *n chem* any of two or more physical forms in which an element can exist

allotropy *n chem* the existence of an element in two or more physical forms [Greek *allos* other + *tropos* manner] ⟩ **allotropic** *adj*

all-out *adj* *informal* using one's maximum powers: *an all-out attack on inflation*

allow *vb* **1** to permit someone to do something **2** to set aside: *I allowed plenty of time* **3** to acknowledge (a point or claim) **4 allow for** to take into account [Late Latin *allaudare* to extol] ⟩ **allowable** *adj*

allowance *n* **1** an amount of money given at regular intervals **2** (in Britain) an amount of a person's income that is not subject to income tax **3 make allowances for a** to treat or judge someone less severely because he or she has special problems **b** to take into account in one's plans

Alloway *n* a village in Scotland, in South Ayrshire, S of Ayr: birthplace of Robert Burns

alloy *n* **1** a mixture of two or more metals ▷ *vb* **2** to mix metals in order to obtain a substance with a desired property [Latin *alligare* to bind]

all-purpose *adj* useful for many purposes

all right *adj* **1** acceptable or satisfactory: *is everything all right?* **2** unharmed; safe: *I'm going to check if he's all right* ▷ *interj* **3** an expression of approval or agreement ▷ *adv* **4** satisfactorily **5** safely **6** without doubt: *it was him all right*

> **USAGE** See at **alright**.

all-round *adj* **1** having many skills; versatile: *an all-round player* **2** of broad scope; comprehensive: *we cannot do without up-to-date and all-round training*

all-rounder *n* a person with many skills and abilities

All Saints' Day *n* a Christian festival celebrated on November 1 to honour all the saints

All Souls' Day *n RC Church* a day of prayer (November 2) for the dead in purgatory

allspice *n* a spice used in cooking, which comes from the berries of a tropical American tree

Allston *n* Washington. 1779–1843, US painter and author, regarded as the earliest US Romantic painter. His paintings include *Elijah in the Desert* (1818) and *Moonlit Landscape* (1819)

all-time *adj informal* unsurpassed at a particular time: *one of boxing's all-time greats*

allude *vb* **-luding, -luded allude to** to refer indirectly to [Latin *alludere*]

> **USAGE** Avoid confusion with **elude**.

allure *n* attractiveness or appeal [Old French *alurer* to lure]

alluring *adj* extremely attractive

allusion *n* an indirect reference

alluvial *adj* **1** of or relating to alluvium ▷ *n* **2** same as **alluvium**

alluvium *n, pl* **-via** a fertile soil consisting of mud, silt, and sand deposited by flowing water [Latin]

ally *n, pl* **-lies** **1** a country, person, or group with an agreement to support another ▷ *vb* **-lies, -lying, -lied** **2** ally oneself with to agree to support another country, person, or group [Latin *ligare* to bind]

Alma-Ata *n* the former name of **Almaty**

Almada *n* a town in S central Portugal, on the S bank of the Tagus estuary opposite Lisbon: statue of Christ 110 m (360 ft) high, erected 1959. Pop: 160 826 (2001)

Almadén *n* a town in S Spain: rich cinnabar mines, worked since Roman times. Pop: 6659 (2003 est)

Al Madinah *n* the Arabic name for **Medina**

al-Maliki *n* Nouri. born 1950, Iraqi politician, prime minister of Iraq from 2006

alma mater *n* the school, college, or university that one attended [Latin: bountiful mother]

almanac *n* a yearly calendar with detailed information on matters like anniversaries and phases of the moon [Late Greek *almenikhiaka*]

Al Mansûrah *n* a variant of **El Mansûra**

Al Marj *n* an ancient town in N Libya: founded in about 550 BC Pop: 121 000 (2005 est). Italian name: **Barce**

Alma-Tadema n Sir Lawrence. 1836–1912, Dutch-English painter of studies of Greek and Roman life

Almaty n a city in SE Kazakhstan; capital of Kazakhstan (1991–97): an important trading centre. Pop: 1 103 000 (2005 est). Former name (until 1927): **Verny**. Also called: **Alma-Ata**

Almelo n a city in the E Netherlands, in Overijssel province. Pop: 72 000 (2003 est)

Almería n a port in S Spain. Pop: 176 727 (2003 est)

almighty adj 1 having power over everything 2 informal very great: there was an almighty bang ▷ n 3 **the Almighty** God

Almodóvar n Pedro. born 1949, Spanish film director. His provocative black comedies include Women on the Verge of a Nervous Breakdown (1988), The Flower of My Secret (1995), Talk to Her (2002), Volver (2006), and The Skin I Live In (2011)

almond n an edible oval nut with a yellowish-brown shell, which grows on a small tree [Greek amugdalē]

almoner n Brit a former name for a hospital social worker [Old French almosne alms]

almost adv very nearly

alms (ahmz) pl n old-fashioned donations of money or goods to poor people [Greek eleēmosunē pity]

almshouse n Brit (formerly) a house, financed by charity, which offered accommodation to poor people

aloe n 1 a plant with fleshy spiny leaves 2 **aloes** a bitter drug made from aloe leaves [Greek]

aloe vera n a plant producing a juice which is used to treat skin and hair

aloft adv 1 in the air 2 nautical in the rigging of a ship [Old Norse ā lopt]

alone adj 1 without anyone or anything else ▷ adv 2 without anyone or anything else 3 **leave someone** or **something alone** to refrain from annoying someone or interfering with something 4 **let alone** not to mention: it looked inconceivable that he could run again, let alone be elected [Old English al one all (entirely) one]

along prep 1 over part or all of the length of: we were going along the railway tracks ▷ adv 2 moving forward: they were roaring along at 40 mph 3 in company with another or others: let them go along for the ride 4 **along with** together with: I'm including the good days along with the bad [Old English andlang]

USAGE See at plus.

alongside prep 1 close beside ▷ adv 2 near the side of something

aloof adj distant or haughty in manner [obsolete a loof to windward]

alopecia (al-loh-pee-sha) n loss of hair, usually due to illness [Greek alōpekia mange in foxes]

Alost n a town in central Belgium, in East Flanders province. Pop: 76 852 (2004 est). Flemish name: **Aalst**

aloud adv in an audible voice

Aloysius n Saint. full name Aloysius Luigi Gonzaga. 1568–91, Italian Jesuit who died nursing plague victims; the patron saint of youth. Feast day: June 21

alp n 1 a high mountain 2 **the Alps** a high mountain range in S central Europe [Latin Alpes]

alpaca n 1 a South American mammal related to the llama, with dark shaggy hair 2 wool or cloth made from this hair [South American Indian allpaca]

alpenstock n a strong stick with an iron tip used by hikers and mountain climbers [German]

Alpes-de-Haute-Provence n a department of SE France in Provence-Alpes-Côte-d'Azur region. Capital: Digne. Pop: 144 508 (2003 est). Area: 6988 sq km (2725 sq miles). Former name: **Basses-Alpes**

Alpes-Maritimes n a department of the SE corner of France in Provence-Alpes-Côte-d'Azur region. Capital: Nice. Pop: 1 045 973 (2003 est). Area: 4298 sq km (1676 sq miles)

alpha n 1 the first letter in the Greek alphabet (A, α) 2 Brit the highest grade in an examination or for a piece of academic work 3 **alpha and omega** the first and last

alphabet n a set of letters in fixed conventional order, used in a writing system [alpha + beta, the first two letters of the Greek alphabet]

alphabetical adj in the conventional order of the letters of an alphabet ▷ **alphabetically** adv

alphabetize or **-ise** vb **-izing, -ized** or **-ising, -ised** to put in alphabetical order ▷ **alphabetization** or **-isation** n

alphanumeric adj consisting of alphabetical and numerical symbols

alpha particle n physics a positively charged particle, emitted during some radioactive transformations

alpha ray n physics a stream of alpha particles

alpine adj 1 of high mountains ▷ n 2 a plant grown on or native to mountains

Alpine adj 1 of or relating to the Alps or their inhabitants 2 geology a of or relating to an episode of mountain building in the Tertiary period during which the Alps were formed b of or relating to a high mountainous environment heavily modified by glacial erosion

alpinist n a mountain climber

Alps pl n 1 a mountain range in S central Europe, extending over 1000 km (650 miles) from the Mediterranean coast of France and NW Italy through Switzerland, N Italy, and Austria to Slovenia. Highest peak: Mont Blanc, 4807 m (15 771 ft) 2 a range of mountains in the NW quadrant of the moon, which is cut in two by a straight fracture, the **Alpine Valley**

already adv 1 before the present time 2 before an implied or expected time

alright adj, interj, adv not standard same as **all right**

USAGE The form alright, though very common, is still considered by many people to be wrong or less acceptable than all right.

Alsace n a region and former province of NE France, between the Vosges mountains and the Rhine: famous for its wines. Area: 8280 sq km (3196 sq miles). Ancient name: **Alsatia**. German name: **Elsass**

Alsace-Lorraine n an area of NE France, comprising the modern regions of Alsace and Lorraine: under German rule 1871–1919 and 1940–44. Area: 14 522 sq km (5607 sq miles). German name: **Elsass-Lothringen**

Alsatia n 1 the ancient name for **Alsace** 2 an area around Whitefriars, London, in the 17th century, which was a sanctuary for criminals and debtors

Alsatian n 1 Officially called: **German shepherd, German shepherd dog** a large wolflike breed of dog often used as a guard or guide dog and by the police 2 a native or inhabitant of Alsace 3 (in the 17th century) a criminal or debtor who took refuge in the Whitefriars area of London ▷ adj 4 of or relating to Alsace or its inhabitants

also adv in addition; too [Old English alswā]

also-ran n a loser in a race, competition, or election

Alta. Alberta

Altai Mountains pl n a mountain system of central Asia, in W Mongolia, W China, and S Russia. Highest peak: Belukha, 4506 m (14 783 ft)

Altai Republic n another name for **Gorno-Altai Republic**

Altamira n a cave in N Spain, SW of Santander, noted for Old Stone Age wall drawings

altar n 1 the table used for Communion in Christian churches 2 a raised structure on which sacrifices are offered and religious rites performed [Latin altus high]

altarpiece n a painting or a decorated screen set above and behind the altar in a Christian church

Altdorf n a town in central Switzerland, capital of Uri canton: setting of the William Tell legend. Pop: 8541 (2000)

Altdorfer n Albrecht. ?1480–?1538, German painter and

engraver: one of the earliest landscape painters

Alte Pinakothek *n* a museum in Munich housing a collection of paintings dating from the Middle Ages to the late 18th century

alter *vb* to make or become different; change [Latin *alter* other]

alteration *n* a change or modification

altercation *n* a noisy argument [Latin *altercari* to quarrel]

alter ego *n* **1** a hidden side to one's personality **2** a very close friend [Latin: other self]

alternate *vb* **-nating, -nated 1** to occur by turns **2** to interchange regularly or in succession ▷ *adj* **3** occurring by turns **4** every second (one) of a series: *alternate days* **5** being a second choice [Latin *alternare*] **>** **alternately** *adv* **>** **alternation** *n*

alternate angles *pl n geometry* two angles at opposite ends and on opposite sides of a line intersecting two other lines

alternating current *n* an electric current that reverses direction at frequent regular intervals

alternative *n* **1** a possibility of choice between two or more things **2** either or any of such choices ▷ *adj* **3** presenting a choice between two or more possibilities **4** of a lifestyle etc. that is less conventional or materialistic than is usual **>** **alternatively** *adv*

alternative energy *n* a form of energy obtained from natural resources like waves and wind

alternative medicine *n* the treatment of disease by unconventional methods like homeopathy, and involving attention to the patient's emotional wellbeing

alternator *n* an electrical machine that generates an alternating current

Althorp House *n* a mansion in Northamptonshire: seat of the Earls Spencer since 1508; originally a medieval house; altered (1787) to its present neoclassical style by Henry Holland. Diana, Princess of Wales is buried on Round Oval Island in the centre of the ornamental lake in Althorp Park

although *conj* in spite of the fact that

Althusser *n* Louis. 1918–90, French Marxist philosopher, author of *For Marx* (1965) and *Reading Capital* (1965): committed to a mental hospital (1981) after killing his wife

altimeter (al-tim-it-er) *n* an instrument that measures altitude [Latin *altus* high + -METER]

Altiplano *n* a plateau of the Andes, covering two thirds of Bolivia and extending into S Peru: contains Lake Titicaca. Height: 3000 m (10 000 ft) to 3900 m (13 000 ft)

altitude *n* height, esp. above sea level [Latin *altus* high, deep]

Altman *n* Robert. US film director, 1925–2006; his films include *M*A*S*H* (1970), *Nashville* (1975), *Short Cuts* (1994), and *Gosford Park* (2001)

alto *n, pl* **-tos 1** short for **contralto 2** the highest adult male voice **3** a singer with an alto voice **4** a musical instrument, for instance a saxophone, that is the second or third highest in its family ▷ *adj* **5** denoting such an instrument, singer, or voice: *an alto flute* [Italian: high]

altogether *adv* **1** completely: *an altogether different message* **2** on the whole: *this is not altogether a bad thing* **3** in total: *altogether, 25 aircraft took part* ▷ *n* **4** **in the altogether** *informal* naked

Alton Towers *n* a 19th-century Gothic Revival mansion with extensive gardens in NW central England, in Staffordshire: site of a large amusement park

Altrincham *n* a residential town in NW England, in Trafford unitary authority, Greater Manchester. Pop: 40 695 (2001)

alt.rock *n* a genre of rock music regarded by fans as being outside the mainstream

altruism *n* unselfish concern for the welfare of others [Italian *altrui* others] **>** **altruist** *n* **>** **altruistic** *adj*

alum *n chem* a double sulphate of aluminium and potassium, used in manufacturing and in medicine [Latin *alumen*]

aluminium *or US and Canad* **aluminum** *n chem* a light malleable silvery-white metallic element that does not rust. Symbol: Al

aluminize *or* **-ise** *vb* **-nizing, -nized** *or* **-nising, -nised** to cover with aluminium

alumnus (al-lumm-nuss) *or fem* **alumna** (al-lumm-na) *n pl* **-ni** (-nie) *or* **-nae** (-nee) *chiefly US and Canad* a graduate of a school or college [Latin: nursling, pupil]

Alva *or* **Alba** *n* Duke of, title of *Fernando Alvarez de Toledo.* 1508–82, Spanish general and statesman who suppressed the Protestant revolt in the Netherlands (1567–72) and conquered Portugal (1580)

Alvarez *n* Luis Walter. 1911–88, US physicist. He made (with Felix Bloch) the first measurement of the neutron's magnetic moment (1939). Nobel prize for physics 1968

alveolus (al-vee-ol-luss) *n, pl* **-li** (-lie) any small pit, cavity, or saclike dilation, such as a honeycomb cell, a tooth socket, or the tiny air sacs in the lungs [Latin: a little hollow]

always *adv* **1** without exception: *she was always at the top o her form in school work* **2** continually: *you're always shouting or whining* **3** in any case: *they're all adults, they can always say no* [Old English *ealne weg* all the way]

Alwyn *n* William. 1905–85, British composer. His works include the oratorio *The Marriage of Heaven and Hell* (1936) and the *Suite of Scottish Dances* (1946)

alyssum *n* a garden plant with clusters of small white flowers [Greek *alussos* curing rabies]

Alzheimer's disease (alts-hime-erz) *n* a disorder of the brain resulting in a progressive decline in intellectual and physical abilities and eventual dementia [after A. *Alzheimer*, German physician]

am *vb* (with "I" *as subject*) a form of the present tense of **be** [Old English *eam*]

Am *chem* americium

AM 1 amplitude modulation **2** (in Britain) Member of the National Assembly for Wales

Am. America(n)

a.m. before noon [Latin *ante meridiem*]

Amagasaki *n* an industrial city in Japan, in W Honshu on Osaka Bay. Pop: 463 256 (2002 est)

amah *n* (in the East, formerly) a nurse or maidservant [Portuguese *ama*]

amakhosi *n* the plural of inkhosi

amakwerekwere *n S African informal, disparaging* a term used by Black people to refer to foreign Africans [from Xhosa *ama*, a plural prefix, + *kwerekwere* imitative of unintelligible sound]

Amalfi *n* a town in Italy: a major Mediterranean port from the 10th to the 18th century, now a resort

amalgam *n* **1** a blend or combination **2** an alloy of mercury with another metal: *dental amalgam* [Medieval Latin *amalgama*]

amalgamate *vb* **-mating, -mated 1** to combine or unite **2** to alloy (a metal) with mercury **>** **amalgamation** *n*

amandla (a-mand-la) *n S African* a political slogan callin for power to the Black population [Nguni (language group of southern Africa): power]

amanuensis (am-man-yew-en-siss) *n, pl* **-ses** (-seez) a person who copies manuscripts or takes dictation [Lati *servus a manu* slave at hand]

Amanullah Khan *n* 1892–1960, emir (1919–26) and king (1926–29) of Afghanistan; he obtained Afghan independence from Britain (1919)

Amapá *n* a state of N Brazil, on the Amazon delta. Capital: Macapá. Pop: 516 511 (2002). Area: 143 716 sq km (55 489 sq miles)

amaranth *n* **1** *poetic* an imaginary flower that never fades **2** a lily-like plant with small green, red, or purple flowers [Greek *a*- not + *marainein* to fade]

a

amaretti *pl n* Italian almond biscuits [Italian *amaro* bitter]

Amarillo *n* an industrial city in NW Texas. Pop: 178 612 (2003 est)

amaryllis *n* a lily-like plant with large red or white flowers and a long stalk [*Amaryllis*, Greek name for a shepherdess]

amass *vb* to accumulate or collect: *the desire to amass wealth* [Latin *ad-* to + *massa* mass]

amateur *n* **1** a person who engages in a sport or other activity as a pastime rather than as a profession **2** a person unskilled in a subject or activity ▷ *adj* **3** doing something out of interest, not for money **4** amateurish [Latin *amator* lover] **>** **amateurism** *n*

amateurish *adj* lacking skill

Amati *n* **1** a family of Italian violin makers, active in Cremona in the 16th and 17th centuries, esp. **Nicolò**, 1596–1684, who taught Guarneri and Stradivari **2** (*pl* **Amatis**) a violin or other stringed instrument made by any member of this family

amatory *adj* of or relating to romantic or sexual love [Latin *amare* to love]

amaut *or* **amowt** *n Canad* a hood on an Inuit woman's parka for carrying a child

amaze *vb* **amazing, amazed** to fill with surprise; astonish [Old English *āmasian*] **>** **amazement** *n* **>** **amazing** *adj* **>** **amazingly** *adv*

Amazon¹ *n* **1** a strong and powerful woman **2** *Greek myth* one of a race of women warriors of Scythia [Greek] **>** **Amazonian** *adj*

Amazon² *n* a river in South America, rising in the Peruvian Andes and flowing east through N Brazil to the Atlantic: in volume, the largest river in the world; navigable for 3700 km (2300 miles). Length: over 6440 km (4000 miles). Area of basin: over 5 827 500 sq km (2 250 000 sq miles)

Amazonas *n* a state of W Brazil, consisting of the central Amazon basin: vast areas of unexplored tropical rainforest. Capital: Manaus. Pop: 2 961 801 (2002). Area: 1 542 512 sq km (595 474 sq miles)

Amazonia *n* the land around the Amazon river

Amazonian *adj* of or relating to the Amazon river, the land around it, or the inhabitants of this land

Ambala *n* a city in N India, in Haryana: site of archaeological remains of a prehistoric Indian civilization: grain, cotton, food processing. Pop: 139 222 (2001)

Ambartsumian *n* Viktor A(mazaspovich). 1908–96, Armenian astrophysicist, renowned for his description of radio sources as explosions in the core of galaxies

ambassador *n* **1** a diplomat of the highest rank, sent to another country as permanent representative of his or her own country **2** a representative or messenger: *he saw himself as an ambassador for the game* [Old Provençal *ambaisador*] **>** **ambassadorial** *adj*

amber *n* **1** a yellow translucent fossilized resin, used in jewellery ▷ *adj* **2** brownish-yellow [Arabic *'anbar* ambergris]

ambergris (am-ber-greece) *n* a waxy substance secreted by the sperm whale, which is used in making perfumes [Old French *ambre gris* grey amber]

ambidextrous *adj* able to use both hands with equal ease [Latin *ambi-* both + *dexter* right hand]

ambience *or* **ambiance** *n* the atmosphere of a place

ambient *adj* **1** surrounding: *low ambient temperatures* **2** creating a relaxing atmosphere: *ambient music* [Latin *ambi-* round + *ire* to go]

ambiguity *n*, *pl* **-ties** **1** the possibility of interpreting an expression in more than one way **2** an ambiguous situation or expression: *the ambiguities of feminine identity*

ambiguous *adj* having more than one possible interpretation [Latin *ambigere* to go around] **>** **ambiguously** *adv*

ambit *n* limits or boundary [Latin *ambire* to go round]

ambition *n* **1** strong desire for success **2** something so desired; a goal [Latin *ambitio* a going round (of candidates)]

ambitious *adj* **1** having a strong desire for success **2** requiring great effort or ability: *ambitious plans*

ambivalence (am-biv-a-lenss) *n* the state of feeling two conflicting emotions at the same time **>** **ambivalent** *adj*

amble *vb* **-bling, -bled** **1** to walk at a leisurely pace ▷ *n* **2** a leisurely walk or pace [Latin *ambulare* to walk]

Ambler *n* Eric. 1909–1998, English novelist. His thrillers include *The Mask of Dimitrios* (1939), *Journey into Fear* (1940), *A Kind of Anger* (1964), and *Doctor Frigo* (1974)

Ambleside *n* a town in NW England, in Cumbria: a tourist centre for the Lake District. Pop: 3064 (2001)

Amboise *n* a town in NW central France, on the River Loire: famous castle, a former royal residence. Pop: 11 457 (1999)

Ambon *n* **1** Also: **Amboina** an island in Indonesia, in the Moluccas. Capital: Amboina. Area: 1000 sq km (386 sq miles) **2** Also: **Amboina** a port in the Moluccas, the capital of Ambon (Amboina) island

Ambrose *n* **1** Saint. ?340–397 AD, bishop of Milan; built up the secular power of the early Christian Church; also wrote music and Latin hymns. Feast day: Dec 7 or April 4 **2** Sir Curtly. born 1963, Antiguan cricketer; a fast bowler, he took 405 wickets in 98 test matches for the West Indies (1988–2000) **>** **Ambrosian** *adj*

ambrosia *n* **1** something delightful to taste or smell **2** *Classical myth* the food of the gods [Greek: immortality]

ambulance *n* a motor vehicle designed to carry sick or injured people [Latin *ambulare* to walk]

ambulatory *adj* **1** of or relating to walking **2** able to walk ▷ *n*, *pl* **-ries** **3** a place for walking in, such as a cloister

ambush *n* **1** the act of waiting in a concealed position to make a surprise attack **2** an attack from such a position ▷ *vb* **3** to attack suddenly from a concealed position [Old French *embuschier* to position in ambush]

ameliorate (am-meal-yor-rate) *vb* **-rating, -rated** to make (something) better [Latin *melior* better] **>** **amelioration** *n*

> **USAGE** *Ameliorate* is often wrongly used where *alleviate* is meant. *Ameliorate* should be used to mean 'improve', not 'make easier to bear', so one should talk about *alleviating* pain or hardship, not *ameliorating* it.

amen *interj* so be it: used at the end of a prayer [Hebrew: certainly]

amenable (a-mean-a-bl) *adj* likely or willing to cooperate [Latin *minare* to drive (cattle)]

amend *vb* to make small changes to something such as a piece of writing or a contract, in order to improve it: *he has amended the basic design* [Old French *amender*]

amendment *n* an improvement or correction

amends *pl n* **make amends for** to compensate for some injury or insult

Amenhotep III *or* **Amenhotpe III** *n* Greek name *Amenophis*. ?1411–?1375 BC, Egyptian pharaoh who expanded Egypt's influence by peaceful diplomacy and erected many famous buildings

amenity *n*, *pl* **-ties** a useful or enjoyable feature: *all kinds of amenities including horse riding and golf* [Latin *amoenus* agreeable]

amenorrhoea *or especially US* **amenorrhea** (aim-men-or-ree-a) *n* abnormal absence of menstruation [Greek *a-* not + *mēn* month + *rhein* to flow]

Amen-Ra *n* an Egyptian god with a ram's head

Amer. America(n)

America *n* **1** short for the **United States of America** **2** Also called: **the Americas** the American continent, including North, South, and Central America [C16: from *Americus*, Latin form of *Amerigo*; after Amerigo VESPUCCI]

American *adj* **1** of or relating to the United States of America or the American continent ▷ *n* **2** a native or inhabitant of the United States of America or the American continent

American football *n* a game similar to rugby, played by two teams of eleven players

American Indian *n* **1** a member of any of the original peoples of America ▷ *adj* **2** of any of these peoples

Americanism *n* an expression or custom that is characteristic of the people of the United States

Americanize *or* **-ise** *vb* **-izing, -ized** *or* **-ising, -ised** to make American in outlook or form

Americano *n, pl* **-nos** a drink consisting of espresso coffee diluted with hot water [Italian (*caffè*) *Americano* American (coffee)]

American Samoa *n* the part of Samoa administered by the US. Capital: Pago Pago. Pop: 54 719 (2013 est). Area: 197 sq km (76 sq miles)

americium *n chem* a white metallic element artificially produced from plutonium. Symbol: **Am** [from *America* (where it was first produced)]

Amersfoort *n* a town in the central Netherlands, in E Utrecht province. Pop: 131 000 (2003 est)

amethyst (am-myth-ist) *n* **1** a purple or violet variety of quartz used as a gemstone ▷ *adj* **2** purple or violet [Greek *amethustos* not drunken]

Amex (aah-mex) **1** *trademark* American Express **2** American Stock Exchange

Amhara *n* **1** a region of NW Ethiopia: formerly a kingdom **2** an inhabitant of the former kingdom of Amhara

Amharic *n* the official language of Ethiopia

Amherst *n* Jeffrey, 1st Baron Amherst. 1717–97, British general who defeated the French in Canada (1758–60): governor general of British North America (1761–63)

amiable *adj* having a pleasant nature; friendly [Latin *amicus* friend] **> amiability** *n* **> amiably** *adv*

amicable *adj* characterized by friendliness: *ideally the parting should be amicable* [Latin *amicus* friend] **> amicability** *n* **> amicably** *adv*

amid *or* **amidst** *prep* in the middle of; among [Old English *on middan* in the middle]

amide *n chem* **1** any organic compound containing the group –CONH₂ **2** an inorganic compound having the general formula M(NH₂)ₓ, where M is a metal atom [from *ammonia*]

amidships *adv nautical* at, near, or towards the centre of a ship

Amiens *n* a city in N France: its Gothic cathedral is the largest church in France. Pop: 139 271 (2006)

Amin¹ *n* Lake Amin *or* Lake Idi Amin a former official name for (Lake) **Edward**

Amin² *n* Idi. 1925–2003, Ugandan soldier; dictator and head of state (1971–79). Notorious for his brutality, he was overthrown and exiled

amine (am-mean) *n chem* an organic base formed by replacing one or more of the hydrogen atoms of ammonia by organic groups [from *ammonium*]

amino acid (am-mean-oh) *n chem* any of a group of organic compounds containing the **amino** group, -NH₂, and one or more carboxyl groups, -COOH, esp. one that is a component of protein

amir (am-meer) *n* same as **emir** [Arabic]

Amis *n* **1** Sir Kingsley. 1922–95, British novelist and poet, noted for his novels *Lucky Jim* (1954), *Jake's Thing* (1978), *Stanley and the Women* (1984), *The Old Devils* (1986), and *The Folks that Live on the Hill* (1990) **2** his son, **Martin.** born 1949, British novelist. His works include *The Rachel Papers* (1974), *Money* (1984), *London Fields* (1989), *The Information* (1994), *Yellow Dog* (2003), and *Lionel Asbo: State of England* (2012)

amiss *adv* **1** wrongly or badly: *anxious not to tread amiss* **2** take something amiss to be offended by something ▷ *adj* **3** wrong or faulty [Middle English *a mis*, from *mis* wrong]

amity *n formal* friendship [from Latin *amicus* friend]

Amla *n* Hashim. born 1983, South African cricketer; first South African (2012) to score a triple century in a test match

Amman *n* the capital of Jordan, northeast of the Dead Sea: ancient capital of the Ammonites, rebuilt by Ptolemy in the 3rd century BC. Pop: 1 292 000 (2005 est). Ancient names: **Rabbath Ammon, Philadelphia**

ammeter *n* an instrument for measuring an electric current in amperes [am(pere) + -METER]

ammo *n informal* ammunition

ammonia *n* **1** a colourless strong-smelling gas containing hydrogen and nitrogen **2** a solution of this in water [ultimately from a substance found near the shrine of the Roman-Egyptian god Jupiter *Ammon*]

ammonite *n* the fossilized spiral shell of an extinct sea creature [Medieval Latin *cornu Ammonis* horn of Ammon]

ammonium *adj chem* of or containing the chemical group NH₄- or the ion NH₄⁺

ammunition *n* **1** bullets, bombs, and shells that can be fired from or as a weapon **2** facts that can be used in an argument [Latin *munitio* fortification]

amnesia *n* a partial or total loss of memory [Greek: forgetfulness] **> amnesiac** *adj, n*

amnesty *n, pl* **-ties 1** a general pardon for offences against a government **2** a period during which a law is suspended, to allow people to confess to crime or give up weapons without fear of prosecution [Greek *a-* not + *mnasthai* to remember]

amniocentesis *n, pl* **-ses** removal of amniotic fluid from the womb of a pregnant woman in order to detect possible abnormalities in the fetus [*amnion* + Greek *kentēsis* a pricking]

amnion *n, pl* **-nia** the innermost of two membranes enclosing an embryo [Greek: a little lamb] **> amniotic** *adj*

amniotic fluid *n* the fluid surrounding the fetus in the womb

amoeba *or US* **ameba** (am-mee-ba) *n, pl* **-bae** (-bee) *or* **-bas** a microscopic single-cell creature that is able to change its shape [Greek *ameibein* to change]

amok *or* **amuck** *adv* run amok to run about in a violent frenzy [Malay *amoq* furious assault]

among *or* **amongst** *prep* **1** in the midst of: *she decided to dwell among the Greeks* **2** in the group, class, or number of: *he is among the top trainers* **3** to each of: *the stakes should be divided among the players* **4** with one another within a group: *sort it out among yourselves* [Old English *amang*]

> **USAGE** See at **between**.

amoral (aim-mor-ral) *adj* without moral standards or principles **> amorality** *n*

> **USAGE** *Amoral* is often wrongly used where *immoral* is meant. *Immoral* should be used to talk about the breaking of moral rules, *amoral* about people who have no moral code or about places or situations where moral considerations do not apply.

amorous *adj* feeling, displaying, or relating to sexual love or desire [Latin *amor* love]

amorphous *adj* **1** lacking a definite shape **2** of no recognizable character or type [Greek *a-* not + *morphē* shape]

amortize *or* **-tise** *vb* **-tizing, -tized** *or* **-tising, -tised** *finance* to pay off (a debt) gradually by periodic transfers to a sinking fund [Latin *ad* to + *mors* death]

amount *n* **1** extent or quantity ▷ *vb* **2** amount to to be equal to or add up to [Old French *amonter* to go up]

> **USAGE** The use of a plural noun after *amount of* (*an amount of bananas; the amount of refugees*) should be avoided: *a quantity of bananas; the number of refugees*.

amour *n* a secret love affair [Latin *amor* love]

a

amour-propre (am-moor-**prop**-ra) *n* self-esteem

Amoy *n* **1** a port in SE China, in Fujian province on **Amoy Island**, at the mouth of the Jiulong River opposite Taiwan: one of the first treaty ports opened to European trade (1842). Pop: 746 000 (2005 est). Modern Chinese name: **Xiamen 2** the dialect of Chinese spoken in Amoy, Taiwan, and elsewhere: a Min dialect

amp *n* **1** an ampere **2** *informal* an amplifier

amperage *n* the strength of an electric current measured in amperes

ampere (am-**pair**) *n* the basic unit of electric current [after A. M. AMPÈRE]

Ampère *n* André Marie. 1775–1836, French physicist and mathematician, who made major discoveries in the fields of magnetism and electricity

ampersand *n* the character &, meaning *and* [shortened from *and per se and,* that is, the symbol & by itself (represents) *and*]

amphetamine (am-**fet**-am-mean) *n* a drug used as a stimulant [shortened from chemical name]

amphibian *n* **1** an animal, such as a newt, frog, or toad, that lives on land but breeds in water **2** a vehicle that can travel on both water and land

amphibious *adj* **1** living or operating both on land and in or on water **2** relating to a military attack launched from the sea against a shore [Greek *amphibios* having a double life]

amphitheatre *or US* **amphitheater** *n* a circular or oval building without a roof, in which tiers of seats rise from a central open arena [Greek *amphitheatron*]

amphora (am-for-ra) *n*, *pl* **-phorae** (-for-ree) an ancient Greek or Roman jar with two handles and a narrow neck [Greek *amphi-* on both sides + *phoreus* bearer]

ample *adj* **1** more than sufficient: *there is already ample evidence* **2** large: *ample helpings of stewed pomegranates and pears* [Latin *amplus*]

amplifier *n* an electronic device used to increase the strength of a current or sound signal

amplify *vb* **-fies, -fying, -fied 1** *electronics* to increase the strength of (a current or sound signal) **2** to explain in more detail **3** to increase the size, extent, or effect of [Latin *amplificare*] **> amplification** *n*

amplitude *n* **1** greatness of extent **2** *physics* the maximum displacement from the zero or mean position of a wave or oscillation [Latin *amplus* spacious]

amplitude modulation *n electronics* a method of transmitting information using radio waves in which the amplitude of the carrier wave is varied in accordance with the amplitude of the input signal

amply *adv* fully or generously: *she was amply rewarded for it*

ampoule *or US* **ampule** *n med* a small glass container in which liquids for injection are sealed [French]

ampulla *n, pl* **-pullae 1** *anatomy* the dilated end part of certain tubes in the body **2** *Christianity* a container for the wine and water, or the oil, used in church [Latin]

amputate *vb* **-tating, -tated** to cut off (a limb or part of a limb) for medical reasons [Latin *am-* around + *putare* to prune] **> amputation** *n*

amputee *n* a person who has had a limb amputated

Amravati *n* a town in central India, in NE Maharashtra: cotton centre. Pop: 549 370 (2001). Former name: **Amraoti**

Amritsar *n* a city in India, in NW Punjab: centre of the Sikh religion; site of a massacre in 1919 of unarmed supporters of Indian self-government by British troops; in 1984 the Golden Temple, fortified by Sikhs, was attacked by Indian troops with the loss of many Sikh lives. Pop: 975 695 (2001)

Amsterdam *n* the commercial capital of the Netherlands, a major industrial centre and port on the IJsselmeer, connected with the North Sea by canal: built on about 100 islands within a network of canals. Pop: 737 000 (2003 est)

amuck *adv* same as amok

Amu Darya *n* a river in central Asia, rising in the Pamirs and flowing northwest through the Hindu Kush and across Turkmenistan and Uzbekistan to its delta in the Aral Sea: forms much of the N border of Afghanistan and is important for irrigation. Length: 2400 km (1500 miles). Ancient name: **Oxus**

amulet *n* a trinket or jewel worn as a protection against evil [Latin *amuletum*]

Amundsen *n* Roald. 1872–1928, Norwegian explorer and navigator, who was the first man to reach the South Pole (1911)

Amundsen Sea *n* a part of the South Pacific Ocean, in Antarctica off Byrd Land

Amur *n* a river in NE Asia, rising in N Mongolia as the Argun and flowing southeast, then northeast to the Sea of Okhotsk: forms the boundary between Manchuria and Russia. Length: about 4350 km (2700 miles). Modern Chinese name: **Heilong Jiang**

amuse *vb* amusing, amused **1** to cause to laugh or smile **2** to entertain or keep interested [Old French *amuser* to cause to be idle] **> amusing** *adj* **> amusingly** *adv*

amusement *n* **1** the state of being amused **2** something that amuses or entertains someone

amusement arcade *n* a large room with coin-operated electronic games and fruit machines

amusement park *n* a large open-air entertainment area with rides and stalls

amylase *n* an enzyme present in saliva that helps to change starch into sugar

an *adj* (*indefinite article*) same as **a** used before an initial vowel sound: *an old man; an hour* [Old English *ān* one]

> USAGE *An* was formerly often used before words that begin with *h* and are unstressed on the first syllable: *an hotel; an historic meeting*: sometimes the initial *h* was not pronounced. This usage is now becoming obsolete.

an- *prefix* See a-

Anabaptist *n* **1** a member of a 16th-century Protestant movement that believed in adult baptism ▷ *adj* **2** of this movement [Late Greek *anabaptizein* to baptize again]

anabolic steroid *n* a synthetic steroid hormone used to stimulate muscle and bone growth

anabolism *n biology* a metabolic process in which body tissues are synthesized from food [Greek *anabolē* a rising up]

anachronism (an-nak-kron-iz-zum) *n* **1** the representation of something in a historical context in which it could not have occurred or existed **2** a person or thing that seems to belong to another time [Greek *ana* against + *khronos* time] **> anachronistic** *adj*

anaconda *n* a large S American snake which squeezes its prey to death [probably from Sinhalese *henakandayā* whip snake]

Anacreon *n* ?572–?488 BC, Greek lyric poet, noted for his short songs celebrating love and wine

Anadyr *n* **1** a town in Russia, in NE Siberia at the mouth of the Anadyr River; the capital of Chukot Autonomous Okrug. Pop: 11 038 (2002) **2** a mountain range in Russia, in NE Siberia, rising over 1500 m (5000 ft) **3** a river in Russia, rising in mountains on the Arctic Circle, south of the Anadyr Range, and flowing east to the Gulf of Anadyr. Length: 725 km (450 miles) **4 Gulf of Anadyr** an inlet of the Bering Sea, off the coast of NE Russia

anaemia *or US* **anemia** (an-**neem**-ee-a) *n* a deficiency of red blood cells or their haemoglobin content, resulting in paleness and lack of energy [Greek *an* without + *haima* blood]

anaemic *or US* **anemic** *adj* **1** having anaemia **2** pale and sickly-looking **3** lacking vitality

anaerobe *n biology* an organism that does not require oxygen [Greek *an* not + *aēr* air + *bios* life] **> anaerobic** *adj*

anaesthesia *or US* **anesthesia** (an-niss-**theez**-ee-a) *n* loss of bodily feeling caused by disease or accident or by

a

drugs such as ether: called **general anaesthesia** when consciousness is lost and **local anaesthesia** when only a specific area of the body is involved [Greek]

anaesthetic *or US* **anesthetic** (an-niss-**thet**-ik) *n* **1** a substance that causes anaesthesia ▷ *adj* **2** causing anaesthesia

anaesthetist (an-**neess**-thet-ist) *n Brit* a doctor who administers anaesthetics

anaesthetize, anaesthetise *or US* **anesthetize** *vb* **-tizing, -tized** *or* **-tising, -tised** to cause to feel no pain by administering an anaesthetic

Anaglypta *n trademark* a thick embossed wallpaper, designed to be painted

anagram *n* a word or phrase made by rearranging the letters of another word or phrase [Greek *anagrammatizein* to transpose letters]

Anaheim *n* a city in SW California: site of Disneyland. Pop: 332 361 (2003 est)

anal (**ain**-al) *adj* of or relating to the anus [New Latin *analis*]

analgesia *n* the absence of pain [Greek]

analgesic (an-nal-**jeez**-ik) *n* **1** a drug that relieves pain ▷ *adj* **2** pain-relieving: *an analgesic balm*

analog *n* same as **analogue**

> **USAGE** The spelling *analog* is a US variant of *analogue* in all its senses, and is also the generally preferred spelling in the computer industry.

analogize *or* **-gise** *vb* **-gizing, -gized** *or* **-gising, -gised** **1** to use analogy in argument **2** to reveal analogy between (one thing and another)

analogous *adj* similar in some respects [Greek *analogos* proportionate]

> **USAGE** The use of *with* after *analogous* should be avoided: *swimming has no event that is analogous to* (not *with*) *the 100 metres in athletics.*

analogue *or US* **analog** *n* **1** a physical object or quantity used to measure or represent another quantity **2** something that is analogous to something else ▷ *adj* **3** displaying information by means of a dial: *analogue speedometers*

> **USAGE** See at **analog.**

analogy *n, pl* **-gies** **1** a similarity, usually in a limited number of features **2** a comparison made to show such a similarity [Greek *analogia*] ▷ **analogical** *adj*

anal-retentive *adj* (of a person) excessively fussy and concerned with order and minute details

analyse *or US* **-lyze** (an-nal-lize) *vb* **-lysing, -lysed** *or* **-lyzing, -lyzed** **1** to examine (something) in detail in order to discover its meaning or essential features **2** to break (something) down into its components **3** to psychoanalyse (someone)

analysis (an-nal-liss-iss) *n, pl* **-ses** (-seez) **1** the separation of a whole into its parts for study or interpretation **2** a statement of the results of this **3** short for **psychoanalysis** [Greek *analusis* a dissolving]

analyst *n* **1** a person who is skilled in analysis **2** a psychoanalyst

analytical *or* **analytic** *adj* relating to or using analysis ▷ **analytically** *adv*

Anam *n* a variant spelling of **Annam**

Anambra *n* a state of S Nigeria. Capital: Awka. Pop: 4 182 031 (2006). Area: 4844 sq km (1870 sq miles)

Ananda *n* 5th century BC, the first cousin, favourite disciple, and personal attendant of the Buddha

anaphylactic shock *n* a severe, sometimes fatal, reaction to a substance to which a person has an extreme sensitivity, often involving respiratory difficulty and circulation failure [Greek *ana* again + *phulaxis* guarding]

Anapurna *n* a variant spelling of **Annapurna**

anarchism *n* a doctrine advocating the abolition of government and its replacement by a social system based on voluntary cooperation

anarchist *n* **1** a person who advocates anarchism **2** a person who causes disorder or upheaval ▷ **anarchistic** *adj*

anarchy (an-ark-ee) *n* **1** general lawlessness and disorder **2** the absence of government [Greek *an* without + *arkh-* leader] ▷ **anarchic** *adj*

Anastasia *n* Grand Duchess. 1901–?18, daughter of Tsar Nicholas II, believed to have been executed by the Bolsheviks in 1918, although several women subsequently claimed to be her

anastigmat *n* a lens corrected for astigmatism ▷ **anastigmatic** *adj*

anathema (an-**nath**-im-a) *n* a detested person or thing: *the very colour was anathema to him* [Greek: something accursed]

anathematize *or* **-tise** *vb* **-tizing, -tized** *or* **-tising, -tised** to curse: *he anathematized the world in general*

Anatolia *n* the Asian part of Turkey, occupying the peninsula between the Black Sea, the Mediterranean, and the Aegean: consists of a plateau, largely mountainous, with salt lakes in the interior. Historical name: **Asia Minor**

Anatolian *adj* **1** of or relating to Anatolia or its inhabitants **2** denoting, belonging to, or relating to an ancient family of languages related to the Indo-European family and including Hittite ▷ *n* **3** this family of languages, sometimes regarded as a branch of Indo-European **4** a native or inhabitant of Anatolia

anatomist *n* an expert in anatomy

anatomy *n, pl* **-mies** **1** the science of the physical structure of animals and plants **2** the structure of an animal or plant **3** *informal* a person's body: *the male anatomy* **4** a detailed analysis: *an anatomy of the massacre* [Greek *ana* up + *temnein* to cut] ▷ **anatomical** *adj*

Anaxagoras *n* ?500–428 BC, Greek philosopher who maintained that all things were composed of minute particles arranged by an eternal intelligence

Anaximander *n* 611–547 BC, Greek philosopher, astronomer, and mathematician who believed the first principle of the world to be the Infinite

Anaximenes *n* 6th century BC, Greek philosopher who believed air to be the primary substance

ANC African National Congress: South African political movement instrumental in bringing an end to apartheid

ancestor *n* **1** a person in former times from whom one is descended **2** a forerunner: *the immediate ancestor of rock and roll is rhythm and blues* [Latin *antecedere* to go before]

ancestral *adj* of or inherited from ancestors

ancestry *n, pl* **-tries** **1** family descent: *of Japanese ancestry* **2** origin or roots: *a vehicle whose ancestry dated back to the 1950s*

anchor *n* **1** a hooked device attached to a boat by a cable and dropped overboard to fasten the boat to the sea bottom **2** a source of stability or security: *a spiritual anchor* **3** *anchors slang* the brakes of a motor vehicle: *he rammed on the anchors* ▷ *vb* **4** to use an anchor to hold (a boat) in one place **5** to fasten securely: *we anchored his wheelchair to a rock* [Greek *ankura*]

anchorage *n* a place where boats can be anchored

Anchorage *n* the largest city in Alaska, a port in the south, at the head of Cook Inlet. Pop: 270 951 (2003 est)

anchor ice *n Canad* ice that forms at the bottom of a lake or river

anchorite *n* a person who chooses to live in isolation for religious reasons [Greek *anakhōrein* to retire]

anchorman *or* **anchorwoman** *n* **1** a broadcaster in a central studio, who links up and presents items from outside camera units and reporters in other studios **2** the last person to compete in a relay team

anchovy (an-chov-ee) *n, pl* **-vies** a small marine food fish with a salty taste [Spanish *anchova*]

ancien régime (on-syan ray-zheem) *n* **1** the political and social system of France before the 1789 Revolution **2** a former system [French: old regime]

ancient *adj* **1** dating from very long ago **2** very old **3** of the far past, esp. before the collapse of the Western Roman Empire (476 AD) ▷ *n* **4** ancients people who lived very long ago, such as the Romans and Greeks [Latin *ante* before]

ancillary *adj* **1** supporting the main work of an organization: *hospital ancillary workers* **2** used as an extra or supplement: *I had a small ancillary sleeping tent* [Latin *ancilla* female servant]

Ancohuma *n* one of the two peaks of Mount Sorata

Ancona *n* a port in central Italy, on the Adriatic, capital of the Marches: founded by Greeks from Syracuse in about 390 BC. Pop: 100 507 (2001)

and *conj* **1** in addition to: *plants and birds* **2** as a consequence: *she fell downstairs and broke her neck* **3** afterwards: *she excused herself and left* **4** used for emphasis or to indicate repetition or continuity: *they called again and again* **5** used to express a contrast between instances of something: *there are jobs and jobs* **6** *informal* used in place of *to* in infinitives after verbs such as *try, go,* and *come*: *come and see us again* [Old English]

> **USAGE** See at **try**.

Andalusia *n* a region of S Spain, on the Mediterranean and the Atlantic, with the Sierra Morena in the north, the Sierra Nevada in the southeast, and the Guadalquivir River flowing over fertile lands between them; a centre of Moorish civilization; it became an autonomous region in 1981. Area: about 87 280 sq km (33 700 sq miles). Spanish name: **Andalucía**

Andaman and Nicobar Islands *pl n* a territory of India, in the E Bay of Bengal, consisting of two groups of over 200 islands; suffered badly in the Indian Ocean tsunami of December 2004. Capital: Port Blair. Pop: 356 265 (2001). Area: 8140 sq km (3143 sq miles)

Andaman Islands *pl n* a group of islands in the E Bay of Bengal, part of the Indian territory of the Andaman and Nicobar Islands. Area: 6408 sq km (2474 sq miles). Pop: 314 804 (2001)

Andaman Sea *n* part of the Bay of Bengal, between the Andaman and Nicobar Islands and the Malay Peninsula

andante (an-dan-tay) *music adv* **1** moderately slowly ▷ *n* **2** a passage or piece to be performed moderately slowly [Italian *andare* to walk]

andantino (an-dan-tee-no) *music adv* **1** slightly faster than andante ▷ *n, pl* **-nos** **2** a passage or piece to be performed in this way

Andean *adj* of, relating to, or resembling the Andes

Anderlecht *n* a town in central Belgium, a suburb of Brussels. Pop: 92 755 (2004 est)

Andersen *n* Hans Christian. 1805–75, Danish author of fairy tales, including *The Ugly Duckling, The Tin Soldier,* and *The Snow Queen*

Anderson[1] *n* a river in N Canada, in the Northwest Territories, rising in lakes north of Great Bear Lake and flowing west and north to the Beaufort Sea. Length: about 580 km (360 miles)

Anderson[2] *n* **1** Carl David. 1905–91, US physicist, who discovered the positron in cosmic rays (1932): Nobel prize for physics 1936 **2** Elizabeth Garrett. 1836–1917, English physician and feminist: a campaigner for the admission of women to the professions **3** James (**Michael**). born 1982, English cricketer; first English bowler to take 400 test match wickets **4** John. 1893–1962, Australian philosopher, born in Scotland, whose theories are expounded in *Studies in Empirical Philosophy* (1962) **5** Dame Judith, real name *Frances Margaret Anderson*. 1898–1992, Australian stage and film actress **6** Lindsay (**Gordon**) 1923–94, British film and theatre director: his films include *This Sporting Life* (1963), *If* (1968), *O Lucky Man!*

(1973), and *The Whales of August* (1987) **7 Marian.** 1902–93, US contralto, the first Black permanent member of the Metropolitan Opera Company, New York **8** Philip Warren. born 1923, US physicist, noted for his work on solid-state physics. Nobel prize for physics 1977 **9** Sherwood. 1874–1941, US novelist and short-story writer, best known for *Winesburg Ohio* (1919), a collection of short stories illustrating small-town life

Anderssen *n* Adolf. 1818–79, German chess player: noted for the incisiveness of his combination play

Andes *pl n* a major mountain system of South America, extending for about 7250 km (4500 miles) along the entire W coast, with several parallel ranges or cordilleras and many volcanic peaks: rich in minerals, including gold, silver, copper, iron ore, and nitrates. Average height: 3900 m (13 000 ft). Highest peak: Aconcagua, 6960 m (22 835 ft)

Andhra Pradesh *n* a state of SE India, on the Bay of Bengal: formed in 1953 from parts of Tamil Nadu (then called Madras) and Hyderabad states. Capital: Hyderabad. Pop: 75 727 541 (2001). Area: about 275 068 sq km (106 204 sq miles)

andiron *n* either of a pair of metal stands for supporting logs in a fireplace [Old French *andier*]

Andizhan *n* a city in E Uzbekistan. Pop: 413 000 (2005 est)

Andong *n* another name for **Dandong**. Former spelling **Tan-tung**

and/or *conj not standard* either one or the other or both

> **USAGE** Many people think that *and/or* is only acceptable in legal and commercial contexts. In other contexts, it is better to use *or both*: *many drinkers lose their jobs or their driving licences or both* (not *their jobs and/or their driving licences*).

Andorra *n* a mountainous principality in SW Europe, between France and Spain: according to tradition, given independence by Charlemagne in the 9th century for helping to fight the Moors; placed under the joint sovereignty of the Comte de Foix and the Spanish bishop of Urgel in 1278; under the joint overlordship of the French head of state and the bishop of Urgel from the 16th century; adopted a constitution reducing the powers of the overlords in 1993. Languages: Catalan (official), French, and Spanish. Religion: Roman Catholic. Currency: euro. Capital: Andorra la Vella. Pop: 85 293 (2013 est). Area: 464 sq km (179 sq miles). Official name: **Principat d'Andorra**

Andorra la Vella *or* **Andorre la Vieille** *n* the capital of Andorra, situated in the west of the principality. Pop: 22 035 (2003 est). Spanish name: **Andorra la Vieja**. French name: **Andorre la Vieille**

Andorran *adj* **1** of or relating to Andorra or its inhabitants ▷ *n* **2** a native or inhabitant of Andorra

Andrássy *n* Count Gyula. 1823–90, Hungarian statesman; the first prime minister of Hungary under the Dual Monarchy of Austria-Hungary (1867)

André *n* John. 1751–80, British major who was hanged as a spy for conspiring with Benedict Arnold during the War of American Independence

Andreanof Islands *pl n* a group of islands in the central Aleutian Islands, Alaska. Area: 3710 sq km (1432 sq miles)

Andretti *n* Mario. born 1940, US racing driver: Formula One world champion (1978)

Andrewes *n* Lancelot. 1555–1626, English bishop and theologian

Andrews *n* Thomas. 1813–85, Irish physical chemist, noted for his work on the liquefaction of gases

Andrić *n* Ivo. 1892–1975, Serbian novelist: author of *The Bridge on the Drina* (1945): Nobel prize for literature 1961

androgen *n* any of the steroids that promote the development of male sexual organs and certain male sexual characteristics [Greek *anēr* man + *-gen* (suffix) producing]

a

androgynous *adj* having both male and female characteristics [Greek *anēr* man + *gunē* woman]

android *n* a robot resembling a human being [Late Greek *androeidēs* manlike]

andrology (an-drol-la-jee) *n* the branch of medicine concerned with diseases and conditions specific to men [Greek *anēr* man + -LOGY] **> andrologist** *n*

Andropov¹ *n* a former name (1984–91) for **Rybinsk**

Andropov² *n* Yuri Vladimirovich. 1914–84, Soviet statesman; president of the Soviet Union (1983–84)

Andros *n* **1** an island in the Aegean Sea, the northernmost of the Cyclades: long famous for wine. Capital: Andros. Pop: 10 009 (2001). Area: about 311 sq km (120 sq miles) **2** an island in the N Caribbean, the largest of the Bahamas. Pop: 7686 (2000). Area: 4144 sq km (1600 sq miles)

anecdote *n* a short amusing account of an incident [Greek *anekdotos* not published] **> anecdotal** *adj*

Aneirin *n* 6th century AD, Welsh poet. His Y *Gododdin*, preserved in *The Book of Aneirin*(?1250), is one of the earliest surviving Welsh poems

anemia *n US* anaemia

anemometer *n* an instrument for recording wind speed

anemone (an-nem-on-ee) *n* a flowering plant with white, purple, or red flowers [Greek: windflower]

aneroid barometer *n* a device for measuring air pressure, consisting of a partially evacuated chamber, in which variations in pressure cause a pointer on the lid to move [Greek *a* not + *nēros* wet]

anesthesia *n US* anaesthesia

Aneto *n* Pico de Aneto a mountain in N Spain, near the French border: the highest in the Pyrenees. Height: 3404 m (11 168 ft)

aneurysm *or* **aneurism** (an-new-riz-zum) *n med* a permanent swelling of a blood vessel [Greek *aneurunein* to dilate]

anew *adv* **1** once more **2** in a different way

Anfinsen *n* Christian Boehmer. 1916–95, US biochemist, noted for his research on the structure of enzymes. Nobel prize for chemistry 1972

Angara *n* a river in S Russia, in Siberia, flowing from Lake Baikal north and west to the Yenisei River: important for hydroelectric power. Length: 1840 km (1150 miles)

Angarsk *n* an industrial city in SE central Russia, northwest of Irkutsk. Pop: 244 000 (2005 est)

angel *n* **1** a spiritual being believed to be an attendant or messenger of God **2** a conventional representation of an angel as a human being with wings **3** *informal* a person who is kind, pure, or beautiful **4** *informal* an investor in a theatrical production [Greek *angelos* messenger]

angel cake *or especially US* **angel food cake** *n* a very light sponge cake

Angeleno *n, pl* **-nos** a native or inhabitant of Los Angeles

Angel Falls *n* a waterfall in SE Venezuela, on the Caroní River; regarded as the highest in the world. Height: 979 m (3212 ft)

angelfish *n, pl* **-fish** *or* **-fishes** a South American aquarium fish with large fins

angelic *adj* **1** very kind, pure, or beautiful **2** of or relating to angels **> angelically** *adv*

angelica (an-jell-ik-a) *n* a plant whose candied stalks are used in cookery [Medieval Latin (*herba*) *angelica* angelic herb]

Angelico *n* Fra, original name *Guido di Pietro;* monastic name Fra *Giovanni da Fiesole*. ?1400–55, Italian fresco painter and Dominican friar

Angell *n* Sir Norman, real name *Ralph Norman Angell Lane*. 1874–1967, English writer, pacifist, and economist, noted for his work on the economic futility of war, *The Great Illusion* (1910): Nobel peace prize 1933

Angel of the North *n* a steel sculpture of an angel with outstretched wings, created in 1998 by British sculptor Antony Gormley, which stands on a hilltop outside Gateshead, NE England. It stands 20 m (85 ft) high and has a wingspan of 54 m (175 ft)

Angelou *n* Maya, real name *Marguerite Johnson*. 1928–2014, US Black novelist, poet, and dramatist. Her works include the autobiographical novel I *Know Why the Caged Bird Sings* (1970) and its sequels

Angelus (an-jell-uss) *n RC Church* **1** prayers recited in the morning, at midday, and in the evening **2** the bell signalling the times of these prayers [Latin *Angelus domini nuntiavit Mariae* the angel of the Lord brought tidings to Mary]

anger *n* **1** a feeling of extreme annoyance or displeasure ▷ *vb* **2** to make (someone) angry [Old Norse *angr* grief]

Angers *n* a city in W France, on the River Maine. Pop: 156 965 (2006)

Angevin *n* **1** a native or inhabitant of Anjou **2** *history* a member of the Plantagenet royal line descended from Geoffrey, Count of Anjou, esp. one of the kings of England from Henry II to John (1154–1216) ▷ *adj* **3** of or relating to Anjou or its inhabitants **4** of or relating to the Plantagenet kings of England between 1154 and 1216 [from French, from medieval Latin *Andegavinus*, from *Andegavum*, ANGERS capital of ANJOU]

angina (an-jine-a) *or* **angina pectoris** (peck-tor-riss) *n* a sudden intense pain in the chest caused by a momentary lack of adequate blood supply to the heart muscle [Greek *ankhonē* a strangling]

Angkor *n* a large area of ruins in NW Cambodia, containing Angkor Thom, the capital of the former Khmer Empire, and Angkor Wat, a three-storey temple, which were overgrown with dense jungle from the 14th to 19th centuries

angle¹ *n* **1** the space between or shape formed by two straight lines or surfaces that meet **2** the divergence between two such lines or surfaces, measured in degrees **3** a recess or corner **4** point of view ▷ *vb* **-gling, -gled 5** to move in or place at an angle **6** to write (an article) from a particular point of view [Latin *angulus* corner]

angle² *vb* **-gling, -gled 1** to fish with a hook and line **2** angle for to try to get by hinting: *he's just angling for sympathy* [Old English *angul* fish-hook]

angler *n* a person who fishes with a hook and line

Angles *pl n* a race from N Germany who settled in E and N England in the 5th and 6th centuries AD [Latin *Anglus* a person from Angul, Germany]

Anglesey *n* an island and county of N Wales, formerly part of Gwynedd (1974–96), separated from the mainland by the Menai Strait. Administrative centre: Llangefni. Pop: 59 500 (2003 est). Area: 720 sq km (278 sq miles). Welsh name: Ynys Môn

Anglia *n* a Latin name for England

Anglican *adj* **1** of or relating to the Church of England ▷ *n* **2** a member of the Anglican Church [Latin *Anglicus* English, of the Angles] **> Anglicanism** *n*

Anglicism *n* an expression or custom that is peculiar to the English

anglicize *or* **-cise** *vb* **-cizing, -cized** *or* **-cising, -cised** to make or become English in outlook or form

angling *n* the art or sport of fishing with a hook and line

Anglo *n, pl* **-glos 1** *US* a White inhabitant of the US who is not of Latin extraction **2** *Canad* an English-speaking Canadian

Anglo- *combining form* English or British: *the history of Anglo-German relations* [Medieval Latin *Anglii* the English]

Anglo-Egyptian Sudan *n* the former name (1899–1956) of Sudan

Anglo-French *adj* **1** of England and France **2** of the Anglo-French language ▷ *n* **3** the Norman-French language of medieval England

Anglo-Indian *adj* **1** of England and India **2** denoting or relating to Anglo-Indians ▷ *n* **3** a person of mixed British and Indian descent **4** an English person who has lived for a long time in India

Anglo-Norman *adj* **1** of or relating to the Norman conquerors of England or their language ▷ *n* **2** a Norman inhabitant of England after 1066 **3** the Anglo-French language

Anglophile *n* a person who admires England or the English

Anglo-Saxon *n* **1** a member of any of the West Germanic tribes that settled in Britain from the 5th century AD **2** any White person whose native language is English **3** same as **Old English 4** *informal* plain, blunt, and often rude English ▷ *adj* **5** of the Anglo-Saxons or the Old English language **6** of the White Protestant culture of Britain and the US

Angola *n* a republic in SW Africa, on the Atlantic: includes the enclave of Cabinda, north of the River Congo; a Portuguese possession from 1575 until its independence in 1975; multiparty constitution adopted in 1991; factional violence. It consists of a narrow coastal plain with a large fertile plateau in the east. Currency: kwanza. Religion: Christian majority. Capital: Luanda. Pop: 18 565 269 (2013 est). Area: 1 246 693 sq km (481 351 sq miles)

Angolan *adj* **1** of or relating to Angola or its inhabitants ▷ *n* **2** a native or inhabitant of Angola

angora *n* **1** a variety of goat, cat, or rabbit with long silky hair **2** the hair of the angora goat or rabbit **3** cloth made from this hair [ANGORA]

Angora *n* the former name (until 1930) of **Ankara**

Angostura *n* the former name (1764–1846) for **Ciudad Bolívar**

Angostura Bitters *pl n trademark* a bitter tonic, used as a flavouring in alcoholic drinks [from ANGOSTURA]

Angra do Heroísmo *n* a port in the Azores, on Terceira Island. Pop: 35 581 (2001)

angry *adj* **-grier, -griest 1** feeling or expressing annoyance or rage **2** severely inflamed: *he had angry welts on his forehead* **3** dark and stormy: *angry waves* ❭ **angrily** *adv*

> **USAGE** It was formerly considered incorrect to talk about being *angry* at a person, but this use is now acceptable.

angst *n* a feeling of anxiety [German]

angstrom *n* a unit of length equal to 10^{-10} metre, used to measure wavelengths [after Anders J. ÅNGSTRÖM]

Ångström *n* **Anders Jonas**. 1814–74, Swedish physicist, noted for his work on spectroscopy and solar physics

Anguilla *n* an island in the Caribbean, in the Leeward Islands: part of the British associated state of St Kitts-Nevis-Anguilla from 1967 until 1980, when it reverted to the status of a British dependency and is now a UK Overseas Territory. Pop: 15 754 (2013 est). Area: 90 sq km (35 sq miles)

anguish *n* great mental pain [Latin *angustus* narrow]

anguished *adj* feeling or showing great mental pain: *anguished cries*

angular *adj* **1** lean and bony: *his angular face* **2** having an angle or angles **3** measured by an angle: *angular momentum* ❭ **angularity** *n*

Angus *n* a council area of E Scotland on the North Sea: the historical county of Angus became part of Tayside region in 1975; reinstated as a unitary authority (excluding City of Dundee) in 1996. Administrative centre: Forfar. Pop: 107 520 (2003 est). Area: 2181 sq km (842 sq miles)

Anhalt *n* a former duchy and state of central E Germany, now part of the state of Saxony-Anhalt: part of East Germany until 1990

Anhui *or* **Anhwei** *n* a province of E China, crossed by the Yangtze River. Capital: Hefei. Pop: 64 100 000 (2003 est). Area: 139 860 sq km (54 000 sq miles)

anhydride *n chem* a substance that combines with water to form an acid

anhydrous *adj chem* containing no water [Greek *an* without + *hudōr* water]

Aniakchak *n* an active volcanic crater in SW Alaska, on the Alaska Peninsula: the largest explosion crater in the world. Height: 1347 m (4420 ft). Diameter: 9 km (6 miles)

anil *n* a West Indian shrub which is a source of indigo [Arabic *an-nīl*, the indigo]

aniline *n chem* a colourless oily poisonous liquid, obtained from coal tar and used for making dyes, plastics, and explosives

animal *n* **1** *zoology* any living being that is capable of voluntary movement and possesses specialized sense organs **2** any living being other than a human being **3** any living being with four legs **4** a cruel or coarse person **5** *facetious* a person or thing: *there's no such animal* ▷ *adj* **6** of or from animals **7** of or relating to physical needs or desires [Latin *animalis* (adjective) living, breathing]

animalcule *n* a microscopic animal

animal husbandry *n* the science of breeding, rearing, and caring for farm animals

animalism *n* **1** preoccupation with physical matters; sensuality **2** the doctrine that human beings lack a spiritual nature

animality *n* **1** the animal instincts of human beings **2** the state of being an animal

animalize *or* **-ise** *vb* **-izing, -ized** *or* **-ising, -ised** to make (a person) brutal or sensual

animal magnetism *n* the quality of being sexually attractive

animal rights *pl n* the rights of animals to be protected from human abuse

animal spirits *pl n* outgoing and boisterous enthusiasm [from a vital force once supposed to be dispatched by the brain to all points of the body]

animate *vb* **-mating, -mated 1** to give life to **2** to make lively **3** to produce (a story) as an animated cartoon ▷ *adj* **4** having life [Latin *anima* breath, spirit]

animated *adj* **1** interesting and lively **2** (of a cartoon) made by using animation ❭ **animatedly** *adv*

animated cartoon *n* a film produced by photographing a series of gradually changing drawings, which give the illusion of movement when the series is projected rapidly

animation *n* **1** the techniques used in the production of animated cartoons **2** liveliness and enthusiasm: *there's an animation in her that is new*

animator *n* a person who makes animated cartoons

animism *n* the belief that natural objects possess souls [Latin *anima* breath, spirit] ❭ **animist** *n, adj* ❭ **animistic** *adj*

animosity *n, pl* **-ties** a powerful dislike or hostility [see ANIMUS]

animus *n* intense dislike; hatred [Latin: mind, spirit]

anion (an-eye-on) *n* an ion with negative charge [Greek *ana-* up + *ienai* to go] ❭ **anionic** *adj*

anise (an-niss) *n* a Mediterranean plant with liquorice-flavoured seeds [Greek *anison*]

aniseed *n* the liquorice-flavoured seeds of the anise plant, used for flavouring

Anjou *n* a former province of W France, in the Loire valley: a medieval countship from the 10th century, belonging to the English crown from 1154 until 1204; annexed by France in 1480. Related adjective: **Angevin**

Ankara *n* the capital of Turkey: an ancient city in the Anatolian highlands: first a capital in the 3rd century BC, in the Celtic kingdom of Galatia. Pop: 3 593 000 (2005 est). Ancient name: **Ancyra**. Former name (until 1930): **Angora**

ankh *n* a T-shaped cross with a loop on the top, which symbolized eternal life in ancient Egypt [Egyptian *'nh* life, soul]

Anking *n* a variant transliteration of the Chinese name for Anqing

ankle *n* **1** the joint connecting the leg and the foot **2** the

a

part of the leg just above the foot [Old Norse]

anklet n an ornamental chain worn round the ankle

ankylosis (ang-kill-**loh**-siss) n abnormal immobility of a joint, caused by a fibrous growth within the joint [Greek *ankuloun* to crook]

An Lu Shan n 703–57 AD, Chinese military governor. He declared himself emperor (756) and seized the capital Chang An; murdered by a eunuch slave

anna n a former Indian coin worth one sixteenth of a rupee [Hindi *ānā*]

Annaba n a port in NE Algeria: site of the Roman city of Hippo Regius. Pop: 382 000 (2005 est). Former name: **Bône**

annals pl n **1** yearly records of events **2** regular reports of the work of a society or other organization [Latin (*libri*) *annales* yearly (books)] **> annalist** n

Annam or **Anam** n a former kingdom (3rd century–1428), empire (1428–1884), and French protectorate (1884–1945) of E Indochina: now part of Vietnam

Annamese adj **1** of or relating to Annam ▷ adj, n **2** a former word for **Vietnamese**

Annan n Kofi. born 1938, Ghanaian international civil servant; secretary-general of the United Nations (1997–2007): Nobel peace prize 2001 with the UN

Annapolis n the capital of Maryland, near the mouth of the Severn River on Chesapeake Bay: site of the US Naval Academy. Pop: 36 178 (2003 est)

Annapolis Royal n a town in SE Canada in W Nova Scotia on an arm of the Bay of Fundy: the first settlement in Canada (1605). Pop: 550 (2001). Former name (until 1710): **Port Royal**

Annapurna or **Anapurna** n a massif of the Himalayas, in Nepal. Highest peak: 8078 m (26 502 ft)

Ann Arbor n a city in SE Michigan: seat of the University of Michigan. Pop: 114 498 (2003 est)

Anne n **1** Princess, the Princess Royal. born 1950, daughter of Elizabeth II of Great Britain and Northern Ireland; a noted horsewoman and president of the Save the Children Fund **2** Queen. 1665–1714, queen of Great Britain and Ireland (1702–14), daughter of James II, and the last of the Stuart monarchs **3** Saint. (in Christian tradition) the mother of the Virgin Mary. Feast day: July 26 or 25

anneal vb to toughen (glass or metal) by heat treatment [Old English *onǣlan*]

Annecy n **1** a city and resort in E France, on Lake Annecy. Pop: 52 890 (2006) **2** Lake Annecy a lake in E France, in the Alps

annelid n a worm with a segmented body, such as the earthworm [Latin *anulus* ring]

Anne of Austria n 1601–66, wife of Louis XIII of France and daughter of Philip III of Spain: regent of France (1643–61) for her son Louis XIV

Anne of Bohemia n 1366–94, queen consort of Richard II of England

Anne of Cleves n 1515–57, the fourth wife of Henry VIII of England: their marriage (1540) was annulled after six months

Anne of Denmark n 1574–1619, wife (from 1589) of James I of England and VI of Scotland

annex vb **1** to seize (territory) by conquest or occupation **2** to take without permission **3** to join or add (something) to something larger [Latin *annectere* to attach to] **> annexation** n

annexe or especially US **annex** n **1** an extension to a main building **2** a building used as an addition to a main one nearby

Annigoni n Pietro. 1910–88, Italian painter; noted esp. for his portraits of President Kennedy (1961) and Queen Elizabeth II (1955 and 1970)

annihilate vb **-lating, -lated 1** to destroy (a place or a group of people) completely **2** informal to defeat totally in an argument or a contest [Latin *nihil* nothing] **> annihilation** n

anniversary n, pl **-ries 1** the date on which an event,

such as a wedding, occurred in some previous year **2** the celebration of this [Latin *annus* year + *vertere* to turn]

anno Domini adv in the year of our Lord

annotate vb **-tating, -tated** to add critical or explanatory notes to a written work [Latin *nota* mark] **> annotation** n

announce vb **-nouncing, -nounced 1** to make known publicly **2** to proclaim **3** to declare the arrival of (a person) **4** to be a sign of: *snowdrops announced the arrival of spring* [Latin *annuntiare*] **> announcement** n

announcer n a person who introduces programmes on radio or television

annoy vb **1** to irritate or displease **2** to harass sexually [Latin *in odio (esse)* (to be) hated] **> annoyance** n **> annoying** adj

annual adj **1** occurring or done once a year: *the union's annual conference* **2** lasting for a year: *the annual subscription* ▷ n **3** a plant that completes its life cycle in one year **4** a book published once every year [Latin *annus* year] **> annually** adv

annualize or **-ise** vb **-izing, -ized** or **-ising, -ised** to calculate (a rate) for or as if for a year

annuity n, pl **-ties** a fixed sum payable at specified intervals over a period [Latin *annuus* annual]

annul vb **-nulling, -nulled** to declare (a contract or marriage) invalid [Latin *nullus* not any]

annular (an-new-lar) adj ring-shaped [Latin *anulus* ring]

annular eclipse n an eclipse of the sun in which a ring of sunlight can be seen surrounding the shadow of the moon

annulate (an-new-lit) adj having, composed of, or marked with rings [Latin *anulus* ring]

annulment n the formal declaration that a contract or marriage is invalid

Annunciation n **1** the Annunciation the announcement by the angel Gabriel to the Virgin Mary of her conception of Christ **2** the festival commemorating this, on March 25 (Lady Day) [Latin *annuntiare* to announce]

anode n electronics the positive electrode in an electrolytic cell or in an electronic valve [Greek *anodos* a way up]

anodize or **-dise** vb **-dizing, -dized** or **-dising, -dised** chem to coat (a metal) with a protective oxide film by electrolysis

anodyne n **1** something that relieves pain or distress ▷ adj **2** neutral **3** capable of relieving pain or distress [Greek *an-* without + *odunē* pain]

anoint vb to smear with oil as a sign of consecration [Latin *inunguere*]

anointing of the sick n RC Church a sacrament in which a person who is dying is anointed by a priest

anomalous adj different from the normal or usual order or type [Greek *an-* not + *homalos* even]

anomaly (an-nom-a-lee) n, pl **-lies** something that deviates from the normal; an irregularity

anomie or **anomy** (an-oh-mee) n sociol lack of social or moral standards [Greek *a-* without + *nomos* law]

anon adv old-fashioned or informal soon: *you shall see him anon* [Old English *on āne* in one, that is, immediately]

anon. anonymous

anonymize or **-ise** vb **-izing, -ized** or **-ising, -ised** to organize in a way that preserves anonymity: *anonymized AIDS screening*

anonymous adj **1** by someone whose name is unknown or withheld: *an anonymous letter* **2** having no known name: *an anonymous writer* **3** lacking distinguishing characteristics: *an anonymous little town* **4** Anonymous of an organization that helps applicants who remain anonymous: *Alcoholics Anonymous* [Greek *an-* without + *onoma* name] **> anonymity** n

anorak n **1** a waterproof hip-length jacket with a hood **2** Brit informal a socially inept person with a hobby considered to be boring [Greenland Inuktitut *ánorâq*]

anorexia or **anorexia nervosa** n a psychological

disorder characterized by fear of becoming fat and refusal to eat [Greek *an-* without + *orexis* appetite] **> anorexic** *adj, n*

another *adj* **1** one more: *they don't have the right to demand another chance* **2** different: *you'll have to find another excuse* ▷ *pron* **3** one more: *help yourself to another* **4** a different one: *one way or another* [originally *an other*]

Anouilh *n* Jean. 1910–87, French dramatist, noted for his reinterpretations of Greek myths: his works include *Eurydice* (1942), *Antigone* (1944), and *Becket* (1959)

Anqing *or* **Anking** *n* a city in E China, in SW Anhui province on the Yangtze River: famous seven-storeyed pagoda. Pop: 686 000 (2005 est)

Anselm *n* Saint. 1033–1109, Italian Benedictine monk; archbishop of Canterbury (1093–1109): one of the founders of scholasticism; author of *Cur Deus Homo?* (*Why did God become Man?*). Feast day: Aug 21

Ansermet *n* Ernest. 1883–1969, Swiss orchestral conductor; principal conductor of Diaghilev's Ballets Russes

Anshan *n* **1** a city in NE China, in Liaoning province. Pop: 1 459 000 (2005 est) **2** an ancient city and region in Persia, associated with Elam

answer *vb* **1** to reply or respond (to) by word or act **2** to be responsible (to a person) **3** to reply correctly to (a question) **4** to respond or react: *a dog that answers to the name of Pugg* **5** to meet the requirements of **6** to give a defence of (a charge) ▷ *n* **7** a reply to a question, request, letter, or article **8** a solution to a problem **9** a reaction or response [Old English *andswaru*]

answerable *adj* answerable for *or* to responsible for or accountable to

answer back *vb* to reply rudely (to)

answering machine *n* a device for answering a telephone automatically and recording messages

ant *n* a small often wingless insect, living in highly organized colonies [Old English *ǣmette*]

antacid *chem n* **1** a substance used to treat acidity in the stomach ▷ *adj* **2** having the properties of this substance

antagonism *n* openly expressed hostility

antagonist *n* an opponent or adversary **> antagonistic** *adj*

antagonize *or* **-nise** *vb* **-nizing, -nized** *or* **-nising, -nised** to arouse hostility in: *it was not prudent to antagonize a hired killer* [Greek *anti-* against + *agōn* contest]

Antakiya *n* the Arabic name for **Antioch**

Antakya *n* the Turkish name for **Antioch**

antalkali (ant-**alk**-a-lie) *n chem* a substance that neutralizes alkalis

Antalya *n* a port in SW Turkey, on the Gulf of Antalya. Pop: 751 000 (2005 est)

Antananarivo *n* the capital of Madagascar, on the central plateau: founded in the 17th century by a Hova chief; university (1961). Pop: 1 808 000 (2005 est). Former name: **Tananarive**

Antarctic *n* **1** the Antarctic the area around the South Pole ▷ *adj* **2** of this region [Greek *antarktikos*]

Antarctica *n* a continent around the South Pole: consists of an ice-covered plateau, 1800–3000 m (6000 ft to 10 000 ft) above sea level, and mountain ranges rising to 4500 m (15 000 ft) with some volcanic peaks; average temperatures all below freezing and human settlement is confined to research stations. All political claims to the mainland are suspended under the Antarctic Treaty of 1959

Antarctic Archipelago *n* the former name of the **Palmer Archipelago**

Antarctic Circle *n* the imaginary circle around the earth at latitude 66° 32´ S

Antarctic Ocean *n* the sea surrounding Antarctica, consisting of the most southerly parts of the Pacific, Atlantic, and Indian Oceans. Also called: **Southern Ocean**

Antarctic Peninsula *n* the largest peninsula of Antarctica, between the Weddell Sea and the Pacific: consists of Graham Land in the north and the Palmer Peninsula in the south. Former name (until 1964): **Palmer Peninsula**

ante *n* **1** the stake put up before the deal in poker by the players **2** *informal* a sum of money representing a person's share **3** up the ante *informal* to increase the costs or risks involved in an action ▷ *vb* **-teing, -ted** *or* **-teed 4** to place (one's stake) in poker **5** ante up *informal* to pay [Latin: before]

ante- *prefix* before in time or position: *antediluvian*; *antechamber* [Latin]

anteater *n* a mammal with a long snout used for eating termites

antecedent *n* **1** an event or circumstance that happens or exists before another **2** *grammar* a word or phrase to which a relative pronoun, such as *who*, refers **3** antecedents a person's ancestors and past history ▷ *adj* **4** preceding in time or order [Latin *antecedere* to go before]

antechamber *n* an anteroom

antedate *vb* **-dating, -dated 1** to be or occur at an earlier date than **2** to give (something) a date that is earlier than the actual date

antediluvian *adj* **1** belonging to the ages before the biblical Flood **2** old-fashioned [Latin *ante-* before + *diluvium* flood]

antelope *n, pl* **-lopes** *or* **-lope** any of a group of graceful deerlike mammals of Africa and Asia, which have long legs and horns [Late Greek *antholops* a legendary beast]

antenatal *adj* before birth; during pregnancy: *an antenatal clinic*

antenna *n* **1** (*pl* **-nae**) one of a pair of mobile feelers on the heads of insects, lobsters, and certain other creatures **2** (*pl* **-nas**) an aerial: *TV antennas* [Latin: sail yard]

antepenultimate *adj* **1** third from last ▷ *n* **2** anything that is third from last

ante-post *adj Brit* (of a bet) placed before the runners in a race are confirmed

anterior *adj* **1** at or towards the front **2** earlier [Latin]

anteroom *n* a small room leading into a larger room, often used as a waiting room

Antheil *n* George. 1900–59, US composer. His best known work is the controversial *Le Ballet Méchanique* (1924) for motor horns, bells, and aeroplane propellers

anthem *n* **1** a song of loyalty or devotion: *a national anthem* **2** a piece of music for a choir, usually set to words from the Bible [Late Latin *antiphona* antiphon]

anther *n botany* the part of the stamen of a flower which contains the pollen [Greek *anthos* flower]

ant hill *n* a mound of soil built by ants around the entrance to their nest

anthology *n, pl* **-gies** a collection of poems or other literary pieces by various authors [Greek *anthos* flower + *legein* to collect] **> anthologist** *n*

Anthony *n* Saint. ?251–?356 AD, Egyptian hermit, commonly regarded as the founder of Christian monasticism. Feast day: Jan 17

Anthony of Padua *n* Saint. 1195–1231, Franciscan friar, who preached in France and Italy. Feast day: June 13

anthracite *n* a hard coal that burns slowly with little smoke or flame but intense heat [Greek *anthrax* coal]

anthrax *n* a dangerous infectious disease of cattle and sheep, which can be passed to humans [Greek: carbuncle]

anthropocentric *adj* regarding the human being as the most important factor in the universe [Greek *anthrōpos* human being + Latin *centrum* centre]

anthropoid *adj* **1** resembling a human being ▷ *n* **2** an ape, such as the chimpanzee, that resembles a human being

anthropology *n* the study of human origins, institutions, and beliefs [Greek *anthrōpos* human being + *logos* word] **> anthropological** *adj* **> anthropologist** *n*

a

anthropomorphism *n* the attribution of human form or personality to a god, animal, or object
> **anthropomorphic** *adj*

anthropomorphous *adj* shaped like a human being [Greek *anthrōpos* human being + *morphē* form]

anti *informal adj* **1** opposed to a party, policy, or attitude ▷ *n* **2** an opponent of a party, policy, or attitude

anti- *prefix* **1** against or opposed to: *antiwar* **2** opposite to: *anticlimax* **3** counteracting or neutralizing: *antifreeze* [Greek]

anti-aircraft *adj* for defence against aircraft attack

antiballistic missile *n* a missile designed to destroy a ballistic missile in flight

Antibes *n* a port and resort in SE France, on the Mediterranean: an important Roman town. Pop: 76 925 (2006)

antibiotic *n* **1** a chemical substance capable of destroying bacteria ▷ *adj* **2** of or relating to antibiotics

antibody *n, pl* **-bodies** a protein produced in the blood which destroys bacteria

Antichrist *n* **1** *New Testament* the chief enemy of Christ **2** an enemy of Christ or Christianity

anticipate *vb* **-pating, -pated** **1** to foresee and act in advance of: *he anticipated some probing questions* **2** to look forward to **3** to make use of (something, such as one's salary) before receiving it **4** to mention (part of a story) before its proper time [Latin *ante-* before + *capere* to take]
> **anticipatory** *adj*

USAGE The use of *anticipate* to mean *expect* should be avoided.

anticipation *n* the act of anticipating; expectation, premonition, or foresight: *smiling in happy anticipation*

anticlerical *adj* opposed to the power and influence of the clergy in politics

anticlimax *n* a disappointing conclusion to a series of events > **anticlimactic** *adj*

anticline *n* *geology* a fold of rock raised up into a broad arch so that the strata slope down on both sides

anticlockwise *adv, adj* in the opposite direction to the rotation of the hands of a clock

anticoagulant (an-tee-koh-**ag**-yew-lant) *n* a substance that prevents the clotting of blood

Anticosti *n* an island of E Canada, in the Gulf of St Lawrence; part of Quebec. Area: 7881 sq km (3043 sq miles)

antics *pl n* absurd acts or postures [Italian *antico* something grotesque (from fantastic carvings found in ruins of ancient Rome)]

anticyclone *n* *meteorol* an area of moving air of high pressure in which the winds rotate outwards

antidepressant *n* **1** a drug used to treat depression ▷ *adj* **2** of or relating to such a drug

antidote *n* **1** *med* a substance that counteracts a poison **2** anything that counteracts a harmful condition: *exercise may be a good antidote to insomnia* [Greek *anti-* against + *didonai* to give]

Antietam *n* a creek in NW Maryland, flowing into the Potomac: scene of a Civil War battle (1862), in which the Confederate forces of General Robert E. Lee were defeated

antifreeze *n* a liquid added to water to lower its freezing point, used in the radiator of a motor vehicle to prevent freezing

antigen (an-tee-jen) *n* a substance, usually a toxin, that causes the body to produce antibodies [*anti(body)* + *-gen* (suffix) producing]

Antigonus I *n* known as *Cyclops*. 382–301 BC, Macedonian general under Alexander the Great; king of Macedon (306–301)

Antigua *n* an island in the Caribbean, one of the Leeward Islands: a British colony, with its dependency Barbuda, until 1967, when it became a British associated state; it became independent in 1981 as part of the state of Antigua and Barbuda. Area: 279 sq km (108 sq miles)

Antigua and Barbuda *n* a state in the Caribbean, comprising the islands of Antigua, Barbuda, and Redonda: gained independence in 1981: a member of the Commonwealth. Official language: English. Religion: Christian majority. Currency: East Caribbean dollar. Capital: St John's. Pop: 90 156 (2013 est). Area: 442 sq km (171 sq miles)

Antiguan *adj* **1** of or relating to Antigua or its inhabitants ▷ *n* **2** a native or inhabitant of Antigua

antihero *n, pl* **-roes** a central character in a novel, play, or film, who lacks the traditional heroic virtues

antihistamine *n* a drug that neutralizes the effects of histamine, used in the treatment of allergies

antiknock *n* a substance added to motor fuel to reduce knocking in the engine caused by too rapid combustion

Anti-Lebanon *n* a mountain range running north and south between Syria and Lebanon, east of the Lebanon Mountains. Highest peak: Mount Hermon, 2814 m (9232 ft)

Antilles *pl n* the Antilles a group of islands in the Caribbean. See also **Greater Antilles, Lesser Antilles**

antilogarithm *n* *maths* a number corresponding to a given logarithm

antimacassar *n* a cloth put over the back of a chair to prevent it getting dirty [*anti-* + *Macassar (oil)*]

antimatter *n* *physics* a hypothetical form of matter composed of antiparticles

antimony (an-tim-mon-ee) *n* *chem* a silvery-white metallic element that is added to alloys to increase their strength. Symbol: **Sb** [Medieval Latin *antimonium*]

antinomy (an-tin-nom-ee) *n, pl* **-mies** contradiction between two laws or principles that are reasonable in themselves [Greek *anti-* against + *nomos* law]

antinovel *n* a type of prose fiction in which conventional elements of the novel are rejected

antinuclear *adj* opposed to nuclear weapons or nuclear power

Antioch *n* a city in S Turkey, on the Orantes River: ancient commercial centre and capital of Syria (300–64 BC); early centre of Christianity. Pop: 155 000 (2005 est). Turkish name: **Antakya**

Antiochus III *n* known as *Antiochus the Great*. 242–187 BC, king of Syria (223–187), who greatly extended the Seleucid empire but was forced (190) to surrender most of Asia Minor to the Romans

Antiochus IV *n* ?215–164 BC, Seleucid king of Syria (175–164), who attacked the Jews and provoked the revolt of the Maccabees

antioxidant *n* *chem* a substance that slows down the process of oxidation

antiparticle *n* *nuclear physics* an elementary particle that has the same mass as its corresponding particle, but opposite charge and opposite magnetism

antipasto *n, pl* **-tos** an appetizer in an Italian meal [Italian: before food]

Antipater *n* ?398–319 BC, Macedonian general under Alexander the Great: regent of Macedon (334–323)

antipathy (an-tip-a-thee) *n* a feeling of strong dislike or hostility [Greek *anti-* against + *patheia* feeling]
> **antipathetic** *adj*

antipersonnel *adj* (of weapons or bombs) designed to be used against people rather than equipment

antiperspirant *n* a substance applied to the skin to reduce or prevent perspiration

antiphon *n* a hymn sung in alternate parts by two groups of singers [Greek *anti-* against + *phōnē* sound]

antipodes (an-tip-pod-deez) *pl n* **1** any two places that are situated diametrically opposite one another on the earth's surface **2** the Antipodes Australia and New Zealand [Greek plural of *antipous* having the feet opposite] > **antipodean** *adj*

Antipodes Islands *pl n* the Antipodes Islands a group of small uninhabited islands in the South Pacific, southeast of and belonging to New Zealand. Area: 62 sq km (24 sq miles)

antipope n a pope set up in opposition to the one chosen by church laws

antipyretic adj **1** reducing fever ▷ n **2** a drug that reduces fever

antiquarian adj **1** collecting or dealing with antiquities or rare books ▷ n **2** an antiquary

antiquary n, pl **-quaries** a person who collects, deals in, or studies antiques or ancient works of art

antiquated adj obsolete or old-fashioned [Latin antiquus ancient]

antique n **1** a decorative object or piece of furniture, of an earlier period, that is valued for its beauty, workmanship, and age ▷ adj **2** made in an earlier period **3** informal old-fashioned [Latin antiquus ancient]

antiquity n, pl **-ties 1** great age **2** the far distant past **3** antiquities objects dating from ancient times

antiracism n the policy of challenging racism or promoting racial tolerance ⟩ **antiracist** n, adj

antirrhinum n a two-lipped flower of various colours, such as the snapdragon [Greek anti- like, imitating + rhis nose]

Antisana n a volcano in N central Ecuador, in the Andes. Height: 5756 m (18 885 ft)

antiscorbutic adj preventing or curing scurvy

anti-Semitic adj discriminating against Jews ⟩ **anti-Semite** n ⟩ **anti-Semitism** n

antiseptic adj **1** preventing infection by killing germs ▷ n **2** an antiseptic substance

antiserum n blood serum containing antibodies used to treat or provide immunity to a disease

antishake adj (of photographic equipment) reducing the blurring caused by movement of the person taking a photograph

antisocial adj **1** avoiding the company of other people **2** (of behaviour) annoying or harmful to other people

antisocial behaviour order n a civil order made against a troublesome individual which restricts his or her activities or movements

antistatic adj reducing the effects of static electricity

Antisthenes n ?445–365 BC, Greek philosopher, founder of the Cynic school, who taught that the only good was virtue, won by self-control and independence from worldly needs

antitank adj (of weapons) designed to destroy military tanks

antithesis (an-tith-iss-iss) n, pl **-ses** (-seez) **1** the exact opposite **2** rhetoric the placing together of contrasting ideas or words to produce an effect of balance, such as where apes command, mere mortals must obey [Greek anti- against + tithenai to place] ⟩ **antithetical** adj

antitoxin n an antibody that acts against a toxin ⟩ **antitoxic** adj

antitrades pl n winds blowing in the opposite direction from and above the trade winds

antitrust adj US, Austral and S African (of laws) opposing business monopolies

antivirus adj **1** relating to software designed to protect computer files from viruses ▷ n **2** such a piece of software

antler n one of a pair of branched horns on the heads of male deer [Old French antoillier]

Antofagasta n a port in N Chile. Pop: 323 000 (2005 est)

Antonello da Messina n ?1430–?79, Italian painter, born in Sicily. His paintings include St Jerome in His Study and Portrait of a Man

Antonescu n Ion. 1882–1946, Romanian general and statesman; appointed prime minister (1940) by King Carol II. He was executed for war crimes

Antonine Wall n a Roman frontier defence work across S Scotland, extending between the River Clyde and the Firth of Forth. It was built in 142 AD on the orders of Antoninus Pius

Antoninus Pius n 86–161 AD, emperor of Rome (138–161); adopted son and successor of Hadrian

Antonioni n Michelangelo. 1912–2007, Italian film director; his films include L'Avventura (1959), La Notte (1961), Blow-Up (1966), Zabriskie Point (1970), Beyond the Clouds (1995), and Just To Be Together (2002)

Antonius n Marcus. Latin name of (Mark) **Antony**

Antony n Mark. Latin name Marcus Antonius. ?83–30 BC, Roman general who served under Julius Caesar in the Gallic wars and became a member of the second triumvirate (43). He defeated Brutus and Cassius at Philippi (42) but having repudiated his wife for Cleopatra, queen of Egypt, he was defeated by his brother-in-law Octavian (Augustus) at Actium (31)

antonym n a word that means the opposite of another [Greek anti- opposite + onoma name]

Antrim n **1** a historical county of NE Northern Ireland, famous for the Giant's Causeway on the N coast: in 1973 it was replaced for administrative purposes by the districts of Antrim, Ballymena, Ballymoney, Carrickfergus, Larne, Moyle, Newtownabbey, and parts of Belfast and Lisburn. Area: 3100 sq km (1200 sq miles) **2** a district of Northern Ireland, in Co Antrim. Pop: 49 260 (2003 est). Area: 415 sq km (160 sq miles)

antrum n, pl **-tra** anatomy a natural cavity, esp. in a bone [Latin: cave]

Antseranana or **Antsiranana** n a port in N Madagascar: former French naval base. Pop: 73 491 (2001). Former name: **Diégo-Suarez**

Antung n a variant transliteration of the Chinese name for **Andong**

Antwerp n **1** a province of N Belgium. Pop: 1 668 812 (2004 est). Area: 2859 sq km (1104 sq miles) **2** a port in N Belgium, capital of Antwerp province, on the River Scheldt: a major European port. Pop: 455 148 (2004 est) ▶ Flemish name: **Antwerpen**. French name: **Anvers**

Anubis n an Egyptian god with a jackal's head

Anuradhapura n a town in Sri Lanka: ancient capital of Ceylon; site of the sacred bo tree and place of pilgrimage for Buddhists. Pop: 53 151 (2001)

anus (ain-uss) n the opening at the end of the alimentary canal, through which faeces are discharged [Latin]

Anvers n the French name for **Antwerp**

anvil n a heavy iron block on which metals are hammered into particular shapes [Old English anfealt]

anxiety n, pl **-ties 1** a state of uneasiness about what may happen **2** eagerness: she was uneasy with his mixture of diffidence and anxiety to please

anxious adj **1** worried and tense **2** causing anxiety: he was anxious about the enormity of the task ahead **3** intensely desiring: both sides were anxious for a deal [Latin anxius] ⟩ **anxiously** adv

any determiner **1** one, some, or several, no matter how much or what kind: the jar opener fits over the top of any bottle or jar; have you left me any? **2** even the smallest amount or even one: we can't answer any questions; don't give her any **3** whatever or whichever: police may board any bus or train **4** an indefinite or unlimited amount or number: he would sign cheques for any amount of money ▷ adv **5** to even the smallest extent: the outcome wouldn't have been any different [Old English ǣnig]

Anyang n a town in E China, in Henan province: archaeological site and capital of the Shang dynasty. Pop: 808 000 (2005 est)

anybody pron same as **anyone**

anyhow adv same as **anyway**

anyone pron **1** any person: is anyone there? **2** a person of any importance: is he anyone?

anything pron **1** any object, event, or action whatever: they'll do anything to please you ▷ adv **2** in any way: it is not a computer nor anything like a computer **3** anything but not at all: the result is anything but simple

anyway adv **1** at any rate; nevertheless **2** in any manner **3** carelessly

a

anywhere adv 1 in, at, or to any place 2 get anywhere to be successful: *we will not get anywhere by being negative*

Anzac n (in the First World War) a soldier serving with the Australian and New Zealand Army Corps

Anzac biscuit n Austral and NZ a sweet biscuit containing oats, coconut and syrup

Anzac Day April 25, a public holiday in Australia and New Zealand commemorating the Anzac landing at Gallipoli in 1915

Anzio n a port and resort on the W coast of Italy: site of Allied landings in World War II. Pop: 36 952 (2001)

AOB (on the agenda for a meeting) any other business

Aoraki-Mount Cook or **Aorangi-Mount Cook** n official names for Mount **Cook**

aorta (eh-or-ta) n the main artery of the body, which carries oxygen-rich blood from the heart [Greek *aortē* something lifted]

Aosta n a town in NW Italy, capital of Valle d'Aosta region: Roman remains. Pop: 34 062 (2001)

Aotearoa n the Māori name for New Zealand [from Māori *ao tea roa* Land of the Long White Cloud]

Aouita n Saïd, born 1959, Moroccan middle-distance runner: set new world records for the 1500 metres (1987–93), 2000 metres (1987–95), and 5000 metres (1987–94)

apace adv literary quickly: *repairs to the grid continued apace*

Apache n, pl **Apaches** or **Apache** a member of a Native American people of the southwestern US and N Mexico [Mexican Spanish]

apart adj, adv 1 to or in pieces: *he took a couple of cars apart and rebuilt them* 2 separate in time, place, or position: *my father and myself stood slightly apart from them* 3 individual or distinct: *a nation apart* 4 not being taken into account: *early timing difficulties apart, they encountered few problems* 5 apart from other than: *apart from searching the house there is little more we can do* [Old French *a part* at (the) side]

apartheid n (formerly) the official government policy of racial segregation in South Africa [Afrikaans *apart* + *-heid* -hood]

apartment n 1 any room in a building, usually one of several forming a suite, used as living accommodation 2 chiefly US and Canad Also called (Brit): **flat** a set of rooms forming a home within a building usually incorporating other similar homes [French *appartement*]

apathy n lack of interest or enthusiasm [Greek *a-* without + *pathos* feeling] > **apathetic** adj

ape n 1 an animal, such as a chimpanzee or gorilla, which is closely related to human beings and the monkeys, and which has no tail 2 a stupid, clumsy, or ugly man ▷ vb **aping, aped** 3 to imitate [Old English *apa*] > **apelike** adj

Apeldoorn n a town in the Netherlands, in central Gelderland province: nearby is the summer residence of the Dutch royal family. Pop: 156 000 (2003 est)

Apelles n 4th century BC, Greek painter of mythological subjects, none of whose work survives, his fame resting on the testimony of Pliny and other writers

apeman n, pl **-men** an extinct primate thought to have been the forerunner of true humans

Apennines pl n 1 a mountain range in Italy, extending over 1250 km (800 miles) from the northwest to the southernmost tip of the peninsula. Highest peak: Monte Corno, 2912 m (9554 ft) 2 a mountain range lying in the N quadrants of the moon, extending over 950 km along the SE border of the Mare Imbrium and rising to 6200 m

aperient (ap-peer-ee-ent) med adj 1 having a mild laxative effect ▷ n 2 a mild laxative [Latin *aperire* to open]

aperitif (ap-per-rit-teef) n an alcoholic drink taken before a meal [French]

aperture n 1 a hole or opening 2 an opening in a camera or telescope that controls the amount of light entering it [Latin *aperire* to open]

apex n the highest point [Latin: point]

APEX Advance Purchase Excursion: a reduced fare for journeys booked a specified period in advance

aphasia n a disorder of the central nervous system that affects the ability to use and understand words [Greek *a-* not + *phanai* to speak]

aphelion (ap-heel-lee-on) n, pl **-lia** (-lee-a) astronomy the point in the orbit of a planet or comet when it is farthest from the sun [Greek *apo-* from + *hēlios* sun]

aphid (eh-fid) or **aphis** (eh-fiss) n, pl **aphids** or **aphides** (eh-fid-deez) a small insect which feeds by sucking the juices from plants [New Latin]

aphorism n a short clever saying expressing a general truth [Greek *aphorizein* to define]

aphrodisiac (af-roh-diz-zee-ak) n 1 a substance that arouses sexual desire ▷ adj 2 arousing sexual desire [Greek *aphrodisios* belonging to APHRODITE]

Aphrodite n Greek myth the goddess of love

Apia n the capital of (Western) Samoa: a port on the N coast of Upolu. Pop: 41 000 (2005 est)

apiary (ape-yar-ee) n, pl **-aries** a place where bees are kept [Latin *apis* bee] > **apiarist** n

apical (ape-ik-kl) adj of, at, or being an apex

apiculture n the breeding and care of bees [Latin *apis* bee + CULTURE] > **apiculturist** n

apiece adv each: *they had another cocktail apiece and then went down to dinner*

apish (ape-ish) adj 1 stupid or foolish 2 resembling an ape

aplomb (ap-plom) n calm self-possession [French: uprightness]

Apo n the highest mountain in the Philippines, on SE Mindanao: active volcano with three peaks. Height: 2954 m (9690 ft)

apocalypse n 1 the end of the world 2 an event of great destructive violence [Greek *apo-* away + *kaluptein* to hide] > **apocalyptic** adj

Apocalypse n the Apocalypse Bible the Book of Revelation, the last book of the New Testament

Apocrypha (ap-pok-rif-fa) pl n the Apocrypha the 14 books included as an appendix to the Old Testament, which are not accepted as part of the Hebrew scriptures [Late Latin *apocrypha (scripta)* hidden (writings), from Greek *apokruptein* to hide away]

apocryphal adj of questionable authenticity: *the paranoic and clearly apocryphal story*

apogee (ap-oh-jee) n 1 astronomy the point in its orbit around the earth when the moon or a satellite is farthest from the earth 2 the highest point: *the concept found its apogee in Renaissance Italy* [Greek *apogaios* away from the earth]

apolitical adj not concerned with political matters

Apollinaire n Guillaume, real name *Wilhelm Apollinaris de Kostrowitzki*. 1880–1918, French poet, novelist, and dramatist, regarded as a precursor of surrealism; author of *Alcoöls* (1913) and *Calligrammes* (1918)

Apollo n Classical myth the god of the sun, music, and medicine

Apollonius of Perga n ?261–?190 BC, Greek mathematician, remembered for his treatise on conic sections

Apollonius of Rhodes n 3rd century BC, Greek epic poet and head of the Library of Alexandria. His principal work is the four-volume *Argonautica*

apologetic adj showing or expressing regret > **apologetically** adv

apologetics n the branch of theology concerned with the reasoned defence of Christianity

apologia n a formal written defence of a cause

apologist n a person who offers a formal defence of a cause

apologize or **-gise** vb **-gizing, -gized** or **-gising, -gised** to say that one is sorry for some wrongdoing

apology n, pl **-gies** 1 an expression of regret for some wrongdoing **2** same as **apologia 3 an apology for** a poor example of: *an apology for a man* [Greek *apologia* a verbal defence, speech]

apophthegm (ap-poth-em) *n* a short clever saying expressing a general truth [Greek *apophthengesthai* to speak frankly]

apoplectic *adj* **1** of apoplexy **2** *informal* furious

apoplexy *n med* a stroke [Greek *apoplēssein* to cripple by a stroke]

apostasy (ap-poss-stass-ee) *n, pl* **-sies** abandonment of one's religious faith, political party, or cause [Greek *apostasis* desertion]

apostate *n* **1** a person who has abandoned his or her religion, political party, or cause ▷ *adj* **2** guilty of apostasy

a posteriori (eh poss-steer-ee-or-rye) *adj logic* involving reasoning from effect to cause [Latin: from the latter]

apostle *n* **1** one of the twelve disciples chosen by Christ to preach his gospel **2** an ardent supporter of a cause or movement [Greek *apostolos* a messenger]

apostolic (ap-poss-stoll-ik) *adj* **1** of or relating to the Apostles or their teachings **2** of or relating to the pope

Apostolic See *n* the see of the pope, at Rome

apostrophe¹ (ap-poss-trof-fee) *n* the punctuation mark (') used to indicate the omission of a letter or letters, such as *he's* for *he has* or *he is*, and to form the possessive, as in *John's father* [Greek *apostrephein* to turn away]

apostrophe² *n rhetoric* a digression from a speech to address an imaginary or absent person or thing [Greek: a turning away]

apostrophize *or* **-phise** *vb* **-phizing, -phized** *or* **-phising, -phised** *rhetoric* to address an apostrophe to

apothecary *n, pl* **-caries** *old-fashioned* a chemist [Late Latin *apothecarius* warehouseman]

apotheosis (ap-poth-ee-oh-siss) *n, pl* **-ses** (-seez) **1** a perfect example: *it was the apotheosis of elitism* **2** elevation to the rank of a god [Greek]

app *n* a computer program designed for a particular purpose, esp. one for a mobile phone

appal *or US* **appall** *vb* **-palling, -palled** to fill with horror; terrify [Old French *apalir* to turn pale]

Appalachia *n* a highland region of the eastern US, containing the Appalachian Mountains, extending from Pennsylvania to Alabama

Appalachian *adj* **1** of, from, or relating to the Appalachian Mountains **2** *geology* of or relating to an episode of mountain building in the late Palaeozoic era during which the Appalachian Mountains were formed

Appalachian Mountains *or* **Appalachians** *pl n* a mountain system of E North America, extending from Quebec province in Canada to central Alabama in the US: contains rich deposits of anthracite, bitumen, and iron ore. Highest peak: Mount Mitchell, 2038 m (6684 ft)

appalling *adj* **1** causing dismay, horror, or revulsion **2** very bad ▷ **appallingly** *adv*

apparatus *n* **1** a collection of equipment used for a particular purpose **2** any complicated device, system, or organization: *the whole apparatus of law enforcement* [Latin]

apparel (ap-par-rel) *n old-fashioned* clothing [Latin *parare* to prepare]

apparent *adj* **1** readily seen or understood; obvious **2** seeming as opposed to real: *he frowned in apparent bewilderment* [Latin *apparere* to appear] ▷ **apparently** *adv*

apparition *n* a ghost or ghostlike figure [Latin *apparere* to appear]

appeal *vb* **1** to make an earnest request **2 appeal to** to attract, please, or interest **3** *law* to apply to a higher court to review (a case or issue decided by a lower court) **4** to resort to a higher authority to change a decision **5** to call on in support of an earnest request: *he appealed for volunteers to help in relief work* **6** *cricket* to request the umpire to declare a batsman out ▷ *n* **7** an earnest request for money or help **8** the power to attract, please, or interest people **9** *law* a request for a review of a lower court's

decision by a higher court **10** an application to a higher authority to change a decision that has been made **11** *cricket* a request to the umpire to declare the batsman out [Latin *appellare* to entreat]

appealing *adj* attractive or pleasing

appear *vb* **1** to come into sight **2** to seem: *it appears that no one survived the crash* **3** to come into existence: *a rash and small sores appeared around the shoulder and neck* **4** to perform: *she hadn't appeared in a film for almost fifty years* **5** to be present in court before a magistrate or judge: *two men have appeared in court in London charged with conspiracy* **6** to be published or become available: *both books appeared in 1934* [Latin *apparere*]

appearance *n* **1** a sudden or unexpected arrival of someone or something at a place **2** the introduction or invention of something: *the appearance of credit cards* **3** an act or instance of appearing: *it will be his fiftieth appearance for his country* **4** the way a person or thing looks: *I spotted a man of extraordinary appearance* **5 keep up appearances** to maintain the public impression of wellbeing or normality **6 put in an appearance** to attend an event briefly **7 to all appearances** apparently: *to all appearances they seemed enthralled by what he was saying*

appease *vb* **-peasing, -peased** **1** to pacify (someone) by yielding to his or her demands **2** to satisfy or relieve (a feeling) [Old French *apaisier*] ▷ **appeasement** *n*

Appel *n* Karel. 1921–2006, Dutch abstract expressionist painter

appellant *law n* **1** a person who appeals to a higher court to review the decision of a lower court ▷ *adj* **2** same as **appellate**

appellate (ap-pell-it) *adj law* **1** of appeals **2** (of a tribunal) having the power to review appeals

appellation *n formal* a name or title

append *vb formal* to add as a supplement: *a series of notes appended to his translation of the poems* [Latin *pendere* to hang]

appendage *n* a secondary part attached to a main part

appendicectomy *or especially US, Canad and Austral* **appendectomy** *n, pl* **-mies** surgical removal of the appendix [*appendix* + Greek *tomē* a cutting]

appendicitis *n* inflammation of the appendix, causing abdominal pain

appendix (ap-pen-dix) *n, pl* **-dices** (-diss-seez) *or* **-dixes** **1** separate additional material at the end of a book **2** *anatomy* a short thin tube, closed at one end and attached to the large intestine at the other end [Latin]

Appenzell *n* **1** a canton of NE Switzerland, divided in 1597 into the Protestant demicanton of **Appenzell Outer Rhodes** and the Catholic demicanton of **Appenzell Inner Rhodes**. Capitals: Herisau and Appenzell, respectively. Pop: 53 200 and Pop: 15 000 (2002 est) respectively. Areas: 243 sq km (94 sq miles) and 171 sq km (66 sq miles) respectively **2** a town in NE Switzerland, capital of Appenzell Inner Rhodes demicanton. Pop: 5447 (2000)

appertain *vb* **appertain to** to belong to, relate to, or be connected with [Latin *ad-* to + *pertinere* to pertain]

appetence *or* **appetency** *n, pl* **-tences** *or* **-tencies** a craving or desire [Latin *appetentia*]

appetite *n* **1** a desire for food or drink **2** a liking or willingness: *he had an insatiable appetite for publicity* [Latin *appetere* to desire ardently]

appetizer *or* **-iser** *n* a small amount of food or drink taken at the start of a meal to stimulate the appetite

appetizing *or* **-ising** *adj* stimulating the appetite; looking or smelling deliciously delicious

Appian Way *n* a Roman road in Italy, extending from Rome to Brindisi: begun in 312 BC by Appius Claudius Caecus. Length: about 560 km (350 miles)

applaud *vb* **1** to show approval of by clapping one's hands **2** to express approval of: *we applaud her determination and ambition* [Latin *applaudere*]

applause *n* appreciation shown by clapping one's hands

apple *n* **1** a round firm fruit with red, yellow, or green skin and crisp whitish flesh, that grows on trees **2 apple**

a

of one's eye a person that one loves very much [Old English *æppel*]

Appleby *n* a town in NW England, in Cumbria: famous for its annual horse fair. Pop: 2862 (2001)

Apple Islander *n Austral informal* a native or inhabitant of Tasmania

Apple Isle *n* the Apple Isle *Austral informal* Tasmania

apple-pie bed *n* a bed made with the sheets folded so as to prevent the person from entering it

apple-pie order *n* in apple-pie order *informal* very tidy

applet *n computers* a computing program that runs within a page on the World Wide Web [*app(lication program)* + *-let* small or lesser]

Appleton *n* Sir Edward (Victor). 1892–1965, English physicist, noted particularly for his research on the ionosphere: Nobel prize for physics 1947

appliance *n* a machine or device that has a specific function

applicable *adj* appropriate or relevant

applicant *n* a person who applies for something, such as a job or grant

application *n* **1** a formal request, for example for a job **2** the act of applying something to a particular use: *you can make practical application of this knowledge to everyday living* **3** concentrated effort: *success would depend on their talent and application* **4** the act of putting something, such as a lotion or paint, onto a surface

applicator *n* a device for applying cosmetics, medication, or some other substance

applied *adj* put to practical use: *applied mathematics*

appliqué (ap-plee-kay) *n* a kind of decoration in which one material is cut out and sewn or fixed onto another [French: applied]

apply *vb* **-plies, -plying, -plied 1** to make a formal request for something, such as a job or a loan **2** to put to practical use: *he applied his calligrapher's skill* **3** to put onto a surface: *the hand lotion should be applied whenever possible throughout the day* **4** to be relevant or appropriate: *he had been involved in research applied to flying wing aircraft* **5** apply oneself to concentrate one's efforts or faculties [Latin *applicare* to attach to]

appoint *vb* **1** to assign officially to a job or position **2** to fix or decide (a time or place for an event) **3** to equip or furnish: *it was a beautifully appointed room with rows and rows of books* [Old French *apointer* to put into a good state] ⊳ **appointee** *n*

appointment *n* **1** an arrangement to meet a person **2** the act of placing someone in a job or position **3** the person appointed **4** the job or position to which a person is appointed **5 appointments** fixtures or fittings

Appomattox *n* a village in central Virginia where the Confederate army under Robert E. Lee surrendered to Ulysses S. Grant's Union forces on April 9, 1865, effectively ending the American Civil War

apportion *vb* to divide out in shares

apposite *adj* suitable or appropriate: *an apposite saying* [Latin *ad-* near + *ponere* to put]

apposition *n* a grammatical construction in which a noun or group of words is placed after another to modify its meaning, for example *my friend the mayor*

appraisal *n* an assessment of the worth or quality of a person or thing

appraise *vb* **-praising, -praised** to assess the worth, value, or quality of [Old French *aprisier*]

USAGE *Appraise* is sometimes wrongly used where *apprise* is meant: *they had been apprised* (not *appraised*) *of my arrival*.

appreciable *adj* enough to be noticed; significant ⊳ **appreciably** *adv*

appreciate *vb* **-ating, -ated 1** to value highly: *we appreciate his music but can't afford £400 a seat* **2** to be aware of and understand: *I can fully appreciate how desperate you must*

feel **3** to feel grateful for: *we do appreciate all you do for us* **4** to increase in value [Latin *pretium* price]

appreciation *n* **1** gratitude **2** awareness and understanding of a problem or difficulty **3** sensitive recognition of good qualities, as in art **4** an increase in value

appreciative *adj* feeling or expressing appreciation ⊳ **appreciatively** *adv*

apprehend *vb* **1** to arrest and take into custody **2** to grasp (something) mentally; understand [Latin *apprehendere* to lay hold of]

apprehension *n* **1** anxiety or dread **2** the act of arresting **3** understanding

apprehensive *adj* fearful or anxious about the future

apprentice *n* **1** someone who works for a skilled person for a fixed period in order to learn his or her trade ⊳ *vb* **-ticing, -ticed 2** to take or place as an apprentice [Old French *aprendre* to learn] ⊳ **apprenticeship** *n*

apprise *or* **-prize** *vb* **-prising, -prised** *or* **-prizing, -prized** to make aware: *I needed to apprise the students of the dangers that may be involved* [French *apprendre* to teach; learn]

USAGE See at appraise.

appro *n* on appro *informal* on approval

approach *vb* **1** to come close or closer to **2** to make a proposal or suggestion to **3** to begin to deal with (a matter) ⊳ *n* **4** the act of coming close or closer **5** a proposal or suggestion made to a person **6** the way or means of reaching a place; access **7** a way of dealing with a matter **8** an approximation **9** the course followed by an aircraft preparing for landing [Latin *ad-* to + *prope* near] ⊳ **approachable** *adj*

approach road *n NZ and S African* a smaller road leading into a major road

approbation *n* approval

appropriate *adj* **1** right or suitable ⊳ *vb* **-ating, -ated 2** to take for one's own use without permission **3** to put (money) aside for a particular purpose [Latin *ad-* to + *proprius* one's own] ⊳ **appropriately** *adv*

appropriation *n* **1** the act of putting money aside for a particular purpose **2** money put aside for a particular purpose

approval *n* **1** consent **2** a favourable opinion **3** on approval (of articles for sale) with an option to be returned without payment if unsatisfactory: *each volume in the collection will be sent to you on approval*

approve *vb* **-proving, -proved 1** approve of to consider fair, good, or right **2** to authorize or agree to [Latin *approbare*]

approx. approximate or approximately

approximate *adj* **1** almost but not quite exact ⊳ *vb* **-mating, -mated 2** approximate to **a** to come close to **b** to be almost the same as [Latin *ad-* to + *proximus* nearest] ⊳ **approximately** *adv* ⊳ **approximation** *n*

appurtenances *pl n* minor or additional features or possessions [Old French *apartenance* secondary thing]

APR annual percentage rate

Apr. April

après-ski (ap-ray-skee) *n* social activities after a day's skiing

apricot *n* **1** a yellowish-orange juicy fruit which resembles a small peach ⊳ *adj* **2** yellowish-orange [Latin *praecox* early-ripening]

April *n* the fourth month of the year [Latin *Aprilis*]

April fool *n* a victim of a practical joke played on April 1 (April Fools' Day *or* All Fools' Day)

a priori (eh pry-or-rye) *adj logic* involving reasoning from cause to effect [Latin: from the previous]

apron *n* **1** a garment worn over the front of the body to protect one's clothes **2** a hard-surfaced area at an airport or hangar for manoeuvring and loading aircraft **3** the part of a stage extending in front of the curtain **4 tied to someone's apron strings** dependent on or dominated by someone [Old French *naperon* little cloth]

apropos (ap-prop-poh) *adj* **1** appropriate ▷ *adv* **2** by the way; incidentally **3 apropos of** with regard to [French *à propos* to the purpose]

apse *n* an arched or domed recess at the east end of a church [Greek *apsis* a fitting together]

apsis (ap-siss) *n*, *pl* **apsides** (ap-sid-deez) *astronomy* either of two points lying at the extremities of the elliptical orbit of a planet or satellite [see **APSE**]

apt *adj* **1** having a specified tendency: *they are apt to bend the rules* **2** suitable or appropriate **3** quick to learn: *she was turning out to be a more apt pupil than he had expected* [Latin *aptus* fitting] ﹥ **aptly** *adv* ﹥ **aptness** *n*

APT *Brit* Advanced Passenger Train

apteryx *n* same as **kiwi** (1) [Greek *a-* without + *pteron* wing]

aptitude *n* natural tendency or ability

Apuleius *n* Lucius. 2nd century AD, Roman writer, noted for his romance *The Golden Ass*

Apulia *n* a region of SE Italy, on the Adriatic. Capital: Bari. Pop: 4 023 957 (2003 est). Area: 19 223 sq km (7422 sq miles). Italian name: **Puglia**

Apure *n* a river in W Venezuela, rising in the Andes and flowing east to the Orinoco. Length: about 676 km (420 miles)

Apurimac *n* a river in S Peru, rising in the Andes and flowing northwest into the Urubamba River. Length: about 885 km (550 miles)

Aqaba *or* **Akaba** *n* the only port in Jordan, in the southwest, on the **Gulf of Aqaba**. Pop: 80 790 (2004)

Aqmola *n* a variant spelling of **Akmola**

aqua *adj* short for **aquamarine** [Latin: water]

aqua fortis *n* obsolete nitric acid [Latin: strong water]

aqualung *n* an apparatus for breathing underwater, consisting of a mouthpiece attached to air cylinders

aquamarine *n* **1** a clear greenish-blue gemstone ▷ *adj* **2** greenish-blue [Latin *aqua marina* sea water]

aquaplane *n* **1** a board on which a person stands to be towed by a motorboat for sport ▷ *vb* **-planing, -planed** **2** to ride on an aquaplane **3** (of a motor vehicle) to skim uncontrollably on a thin film of water

aqua regia (ak-wa reej-ya) *n* a mixture of nitric acid and hydrochloric acid [New Latin: royal water; referring to its use in dissolving gold, the royal metal]

aquarium *n*, *pl* **aquariums** *or* **aquaria 1** a tank in which fish and other underwater creatures are kept **2** a building containing such tanks [Latin *aquarius* relating to water]

Aquarius *n* astrol the eleventh sign of the zodiac: the Water Carrier [Latin]

aquatic *adj* **1** growing or living in water **2** *sport* performed in or on water ▷ *n* **3** an aquatic animal or plant **4 aquatics** water sports [Latin *aqua* water]

aquatint *n* a print like a watercolour, produced by etching copper with acid [Italian *acqua tinta* dyed water]

aqua vitae (ak-wa vee-tie) *n* old-fashioned brandy [Medieval Latin: water of life]

aqueduct *n* a structure, often a bridge, that carries water across a valley or river [Latin *aqua* water + *ducere* to convey]

aqueous *adj* **1** of, like, or containing water **2** produced by the action of water [Latin *aqua* water]

aqueous humour *n* physiol the watery fluid in the eyeball, between the cornea and the lens

aquifer *n* a deposit of rock, such as sandstone, containing water that can be used to supply wells [Latin *aqua* water + *ferre* to carry]

Aquila *or* **L'Aquila** *n* a city in central Italy, capital of Abruzzi region; an earthquake in 2009 killed over 300 people and made over 60,000 homeless. Pop: 72 988 (2008). Official name: **Aquila degli Abruzzi**

Aquileia *n* a town in NE Italy, at the head of the Adriatic: important Roman centre, founded in 181 BC. Pop: 3329 (2001)

aquiline *adj* **1** (of a nose) curved like an eagle's beak **2** of or like an eagle [Latin *aquila* eagle]

Aquinas *n* Saint Thomas. 1225–74, Italian theologian, scholastic philosopher, and Dominican friar, whose works include *Summa contra Gentiles* (1259–64) and *Summa Theologiae* (1267–73), the first attempt at a comprehensive theological system. Feast day: Jan 28

Aquino *n* Corazón, known as *Cory*. 1933–2009, Philippine stateswoman: president (1986–92)

Aquitaine *n* a region of SW France, on the Bay of Biscay: a former Roman province and medieval duchy. It is generally flat in the west, rising to the slopes of the Massif Central in the northeast and the Pyrenees in the south; mainly agricultural. Ancient name: **Aquitania**

Ar *chem* argon

AR Arkansas

Ar. 1 Arabia(n) **2** Also: **Ar** Arabic

Arab *n* **1** a member of a Semitic people originally from Arabia ▷ *adj* **2** of the Arabs [Arabic *'Arab*]

arabesque (ar-ab-**besk**) *n* **1** a ballet position in which one leg is raised behind and the arms are extended **2** *arts* an elaborate design of intertwined leaves, flowers, and scrolls **3** an ornate piece of music [Italian *arabesco* in the Arabic style]

Arabia *n* a great peninsula of SW Asia, between the Red Sea and the Persian Gulf: consists chiefly of a desert plateau, with mountains rising over 3000 m (10 000 ft) in the west and scattered oases; includes the present-day countries of Saudi Arabia, Yemen, Oman, Bahrain, Qatar, Kuwait, and the United Arab Emirates. Area: about 2 600 000 sq km (1 000 000 sq miles)

Arabian *adj* **1** of Arabia or the Arabs ▷ *n* **2** same as **Arab**

Arabian Desert *n* **1** a desert in E Egypt, between the Nile, the Gulf of Suez, and the Red Sea: mountainous parts rise over 1800 m (6000 ft). Area: about 220 000 sq km (85 000 sq miles) **2** a desert, mainly in Saudi Arabia, forming the desert area of the Arabian Peninsula, esp. in the north. Area: about 2 330 000 sq km (900 000 sq miles)

Arabian Sea *n* the NW part of the Indian Ocean, between Arabia and India

Arabic *n* **1** the language of the Arabs ▷ *adj* **2** of this language, the Arabs, or Arabia

Arabic numerals *pl n* the symbols 1, 2, 3, 4, 5, 6, 7, 8, 9, 0, used to represent numbers

arable *adj* (of land) suitable for growing crops on [Latin *arare* to plough]

Araby *n* an archaic or poetic name for **Arabia**

Aracajú *n* a port in E Brazil, capital of Sergipe state. Pop: 701 000 (2005 est)

arachnid (ar-**rak**-nid) *n* an eight-legged insect-like creature, such as a spider, scorpion, or tick [Greek *arakhnē* spider]

Arad *n* a city in W Romania, on the Mureş River: became part of Romania after World War I, after belonging successively to Turkey, Austria, and Hungary. Pop: 155 000 (2005 est)

Arafat[1] *n* a hill in W Saudi Arabia, near Mecca: a sacred site of Islam, visited by pilgrims performing the **hajj**. Also called: **Jabal ar Rahm**

Arafat[2] *n* Yasser. 1929–2004, Palestinian leader; cofounder of Al Fatah (1956), leader from 1968 of the Palestine Liberation Organization, president of the Palestinian National Authority from 1996: signed a peace agreement with Israel (1993); Nobel peace prize 1994 with Shimon Peres and Yitzhak Rabin

Arafura Sea *n* a part of the W Pacific Ocean, between N Australia and SW New Guinea

Aragats *n* Mount Aragats a volcanic mountain in NW Armenia. Height: 4090 m (13 419 ft). Turkish name: **Alagez**

Aragon[1] *n* an autonomous region of NE Spain: independent kingdom from the 11th century until 1479, when it was united with Castile to form modern Spain.

Pop: 1 059 600 (2003 est). Area: 47 609 sq km (18 382 sq miles)

Aragon² *n* Louis. 1897–1982, French poet, essayist, and novelist; an early surrealist, later a committed Communist. His works include the verse collections *Le Crève-Cœur* (1941) and *Les Yeux d'Elsa* (1942) and the series of novels *Le Monde réel* (1933–51)

Aragonese *n, pl* **-nese** **1** a native or inhabitant of Aragon ▷ *adj* **2** of or relating to Aragon or its inhabitants

Araguaia *or* **Araguaya** *n* a river in central Brazil, rising in S central Mato Grosso state and flowing north to the Tocantins River. Length: over 1771 km (1100 miles)

arak *n* same as **arrack**

Arakan Yoma *n* a mountain range in Myanmar, between the Irrawaddy River and the W coast: forms a barrier between Myanmar and India; teak forests

Araks *n* the Russian name for the **Aras**

Aral Sea *n* a lake in Kazakhstan and Uzbekistan, east of the Caspian Sea, formerly the fourth largest lake in the world: shallow and saline, now badly polluted; use of its source waters for irrigation led to a loss of over 50% of its area between 1967 and 1997, after which the reduction began to be slowed. Area originally (to 1960) about 68 000 sq km (26 400 sq miles); water area reduced by 2004 to about 17 158 sq km (6625 sq miles) and the lake divided into sections. Also called: **Lake Aral**

Aram *n* the biblical name for ancient Syria

Aramaean *or* **Aramean** *adj* **1** of or relating to Aram (the biblical name for ancient Syria) ▷ *n* **2** a native or inhabitant of Aram

Aramaic *n* an ancient Semitic language spoken in parts of Syria and the Lebanon

Aran *adj* (of knitwear) knitted in a complicated pattern traditional to the Aran Islands

Aran Islands *pl n* a group of three islands in the Atlantic, off the W coast of the Republic of Ireland: Aranmore or Inishmore (the largest), Inishmaan, and Inisheer. Pop: 1280 (2002). Area: 46 sq km (18 sq miles)

Arany *n* János. 1817–82, Hungarian epic poet, ballad writer, and scholar

Ararat *n* an extinct volcanic mountain massif in E Turkey: two main peaks; **Great Ararat** 5155 m (16 916 ft), said to be the resting place of Noah's Ark after the Flood (Genesis 8:4), and **Little Ararat** 3914 m (12 843 ft)

Aras *n* a river rising in mountains in E Turkey and flowing east to the Caspian Sea: forms part of the E border of Turkey and the N border of Iran. Length: about 1100 km (660 miles). Ancient name: **Araxes**. Russian name: **Araks**

Araucania *n* a region of central Chile, inhabited by Araucanian Indians

Araxes *n* the ancient name for the **Aras**

Arbela *n* an ancient city in Assyria, near which the Battle of Arbela took place (331 BC), in which Alexander the Great defeated the Persians. Modern name: **Erbil**

Arber *n* Werner. born 1929, Swiss microbiologist, noted for his work on restriction enzymes. Nobel prize for physiology or medicine 1978

Arbil *n* a variant spelling of **Erbil**

arbiter *n* **1** a person empowered to judge in a dispute **2** a person with influential opinions about something: *the customer must be the ultimate arbiter of quality*

arbitrary *adj* **1** not done according to any plan or for any particular reason **2** without consideration for the wishes of others: *the arbitrary power of the king* ▷ **arbitrarily** *adv*

arbitrate *vb* **-trating, -trated** to settle (a dispute) by arbitration [Latin *arbitrari* to give judgment] ▷ **arbitrator** *n*

arbitration *n* the hearing and settlement of a dispute by an impartial referee chosen by both sides

arbor¹ *n* US same as **arbour**

arbor² *n* a revolving shaft or axle in a machine [Latin: tree]

arboreal (ahr-**bore**-ee-al) *adj* **1** of or resembling a tree **2** living in or among trees

arboretum (ahr-bore-**ee**-tum) *n, pl* **-ta** (-ta) a botanical garden where rare trees or shrubs are cultivated [Latin *arbor* tree]

arboriculture *n* the cultivation of trees or shrubs [Latin *arbor* tree + CULTURE]

arbor vitae (ahr-bore **vee**-tie) *n* an evergreen tree [New Latin: tree of life]

arbour *or* US **arbor** *n* a shelter in a garden shaded by trees or climbing plants [Latin *herba* grass]

Arbroath *n* a port and resort in E Scotland, in Angus: scene of the barons of Scotland's declaration of independence to Pope John XXII in 1320. Pop: 22 785 (2001)

Arbus *n* Diane, original name *Diane Nemerov*. 1923–71, US photographer, noted esp. for her portraits of vagrants, dwarfs, transvestites, etc.

Arbuthnot *n* John. 1667–1735, Scottish physician and satirist: author of *The History of John Bull* (1712) and, with others, of the *Memoirs of Martinus Scriblerus* (1741)

arbutus (ar-**byew**-tuss) *n* an evergreen shrub with berries like strawberries [Latin]

arc *n* **1** something curved in shape **2** *maths* a section of a circle or other curve **3** *electronics* a stream of very bright light that forms when an electric current flows across a small gap between two electrodes ▷ *vb* **4** to form an arc [Latin *arcus* bow, arch]

ARC AIDS-related complex: relatively mild symptoms suffered in the early stages of infection with the AIDS virus

arcade *n* **1** a covered passageway lined with shops **2** a set of arches and their supporting columns [Latin *arcus* bow, arch]

Arcadia *n* **1** a department of Greece, in the central Peloponnese. Capital: Tripolis. Pop: 91 326 (2001). Area: 4367 sq km (1686 sq miles) **2** Also called (poetic): **Arcady** the traditional idealized rural setting of Greek and Roman bucolic poetry and later in the literature of the Renaissance

Arcadian *literary adj* **1** rural, in an idealized way ▷ *n* **2** a person who leads a quiet simple country life [ARCADIA (2)]

arcane *adj* very mysterious [Latin *arcanus* secret]

Arc de Triomphe *n* the triumphal arch in Paris begun by Napoleon I to commemorate his victories of 1805–6 and completed in 1836

arch¹ *n* **1** a curved structure that spans an opening or supports a bridge or roof **2** something curved **3** the curved lower part of the foot ▷ *vb* **4** to form an arch [Latin *arcus* bow, arch]

arch² *adj* **1** knowing or superior **2** coyly playful: *he gave an arch smile to indicate his pride* [independent use of ARCH-] ▷ **archly** *adv*

arch- *or* **archi-** *combining form* chief or principal: *archbishop; archenemy* [Greek *arkhein* to rule]

archaeobotany *n* the study of plant remains found at archaeological sites ▷ **archaeobotanist** *n*

archaeology *or* **archeology** *n* the study of ancient cultures by the scientific analysis of physical remains [Greek *arkhaiologia* study of what is ancient] ▷ **archaeological** *or* **archeological** *adj* ▷ **archaeologist** *or* **archeologist** *n*

archaeopteryx *n* an extinct primitive bird with teeth, a long tail, and well-developed wings [Greek *arkhaios* ancient + *pterux* winged creature]

archaeozoology *n* the study of animal remains found at archaeological sites ▷ **archaeozoologist** *n*

archaic (ark-**kay**-ik) *adj* **1** of a much earlier period **2** out of date or old-fashioned **3** (of a word or phrase) no longer in everyday use [Greek *arkhē* beginning] ▷ **archaically** *adv*

archaism (ark-**kay**-iz-zum) *n* an archaic word or style ▷ **archaistic** *adj*

archangel (ark-ain-jell) *n* an angel of the highest rank

Archangel *n* a port in NW Russia, on the Dvina River: major centre for the timber trade and White Sea fisheries. Pop: 345 000 (2005 est). Russian name: Arkhangelsk

archbishop *n* a bishop of the highest rank

archbishopric *n* the rank, office, or diocese of an archbishop

archdeacon *n* a church official ranking just below a bishop **>** **archdeaconry** *n*

archdiocese *n* the diocese of an archbishop

archduchess *n* **1** a woman who holds the rank of archduke **2** the wife or widow of an archduke

archduchy *n*, *pl* -**duchies** the territory ruled by an archduke or archduchess

archduke *n* a duke of high rank, esp. one from Austria

archenemy *n*, *pl* -**mies** a chief enemy

archeology *n* same as **archaeology**

archer *n* a person who shoots with a bow and arrow [Latin *arcus* bow]

Archer *n* **1** Frederick Scott. 1813–57, British inventor and sculptor. He developed (1851) the wet collodion photographic process, enabling multiple copies of pictures to be made **2** Jeffrey (**Howard**), Baron Archer of Weston-Super-Mare. born 1940, British novelist and Conservative politician. He was an MP from 1969 until 1974. His novels include *Kane and Abel* (1979), *Honour Among Thieves* (1993), and *The Fourth Estate* (1996): from 2001 to 2003 he was imprisoned for perjury and attempting to pervert the course of justice **3** William. 1856–1924, Scottish critic and dramatist: made the first English translations of Ibsen

archery *n* the art or sport of shooting with a bow and arrow

archetype (ark-ee-type) *n* **1** a perfect or typical specimen **2** an original model; prototype [Greek *arkhetupos* first-moulded] **>** **archetypal** *adj*

archidiaconal (ark-ee-die-**ak**-on-al) *adj* of an archdeacon or his office

archiepiscopal (ark-ee-ip-**piss**-kop-al) *adj* of an archbishop or his office

Archilochus *n* 7th century BC, Greek poet of Paros, notable for using his own experience as subject matter

Archimedes *n* ?287–212 BC, Greek mathematician and physicist of Syracuse, noted for his work in geometry, hydrostatics, and mechanics **>** **Archimedean** *adj*

Archimedes' principle (ark-ee-**mee**-deez) *n physics* the principle that the apparent loss in weight of an object immersed in a fluid is equal to the weight of the displaced fluid [after ARCHIMEDES]

archipelago (ark-ee-**pel**-a-go) *n*, *pl* -**gos** **1** a group of islands **2** a sea full of small islands [Greek *arkhi-* chief + *pelagos* sea]

Archipenko *n* Aleksandr Porfiryevich. 1887–1964, Russian sculptor and painter, in the US after 1923, whose work is characterized by economy of form

architect *n* **1** a person qualified to design and supervise the construction of buildings **2** any planner or creator: *you will be the architect of your own future* [Greek *arkhi-* chief + *tektōn* workman]

architecture *n* **1** the style in which a building is designed and built: *Gothic architecture* **2** the science of designing and constructing buildings **3** the structure or design of anything: *computer architecture* **>** **architectural** *adj*

architrave (ark-ee-trave) *n archit* **1** a beam that rests on top of columns **2** a moulding around a doorway or window opening [Italian, from *arch-* + *trave* beam]

archive (ark-ive) *n* **1** a place where records or documents are kept **2** archives a collection of records or documents **3** *computers* data put on tape or disk for long-term storage **>** *vb* **4** to store in an archive

archivist (ark-iv-ist) *n* a person in charge of archives

archway *n* a passageway under an arch

Arcimboldo *n* Giuseppe. 1527–93, Italian painter, best remembered for painting grotesque figures composed of fruit, vegetables, and meat

arctic *adj* **1** of or relating to the Arctic: *arctic temperatures* **2** *informal* cold; freezing: *the weather at Christmas was arctic* **3** designed or suitable for conditions of extreme cold: *arctic clothing* **>** *n* **4** US a high waterproof overshoe with buckles [from Latin *arcticus,* from Greek *arktikos* northern, literally: pertaining to (the constellation of) the Bear, from *arktos* bear]

Arctic *n* **1** the Arctic the area around the North Pole **>** *adj* **2** of this region [Greek *arktikos* northern, literally: pertaining to (the constellation of) the Bear]

Arctic Circle *n* the imaginary circle around the earth at latitude 66° 32′ N

arctic hare *n* a large hare of the Canadian Arctic whose fur turns white in winter

Arctic Monkeys *pl n* British rock group (formed 2002): comprising Alex Turner (born 1986; vocals, guitar), Jamie Cook (born 1985, guitar), Matt Helders (born 1986, drums, vocals) and Nick O'Malley (born 1985, bass guitar); their albums include *Whatever People Say I Am, That's What I'm Not* (2006), *Favourite Worst Nightmare* (2007), and *AM* (2013)

Arctic Ocean *n* the ocean surrounding the North Pole, north of the Arctic Circle. Area: about 14 100 000 sq km (5 440 000 sq miles)

arctic willow *n* a low-growing shrub of the Canadian Arctic

Arctogaea *n* a zoogeographical area comprising the Palaearctic, Nearctic, Oriental, and Ethiopian regions. Compare **Neogaea**, **Notogaea**

Arctogaean *adj* of or relating to Arctogaea

arc welding *n* a technique in which metal is welded by heat generated by an electric arc

Ardèche *n* a department of S France, in Rhône-Alpes region. Capital: Privas. Pop: 294 933 (2003 est). Area: 5556 sq km (2167 sq miles)

Arden[1] *n* Forest of Arden a region of N Warwickshire, part of a former forest: scene of Shakespeare's *As You Like It*

Arden[2] *n* John. (1930–2012) British dramatist and novelist. His plays include *Serjeant Musgrave's Dance* (1959) and *The Workhouse Donkey* (1963); novels include *Silence Among the Weapons* (1982): he often worked in collaboration with his wife Margaretta D'Arcy

Ardennes *n* **1** a department of NE France, in Champagne-Ardenne region. Capital: Mézières. Pop: 288 806 (2003 est). Area: 5253 sq km (2049 sq miles) **2** the Ardennes a wooded plateau in SE Belgium, Luxembourg, and NE France: scene of heavy fighting in both World Wars

ardent *adj* **1** passionate **2** intensely enthusiastic [Latin *ardere* to burn] **>** **ardently** *adv*

ardour *or US* **ardor** *n* **1** emotional warmth; passion **2** intense enthusiasm [Latin *ardere* to burn]

Ards *n* a district of Northern Ireland, in Co Down. Pop: 74 369 (2003 est). Area: 368 sq km (142 sq miles)

arduous *adj* difficult to accomplish; strenuous [Latin *arduus* steep, difficult]

are[1] *vb* the plural form of the present tense of **be** used as the singular form with *you* [Old English *aron*]

are[2] *n* a unit of measure equal to one hundred square metres [Latin *area* piece of ground]

area *n* **1** a section, part, or region **2** a part having a specified function: *reception area* **3** the size of a two-dimensional surface **4** a subject field: *the area of literature* **5** a sunken area giving access to a basement **6** any flat, curved, or irregular expanse of a surface **7** range or scope [Latin: level ground, threshing floor]

area school *n* NZ a school in a rural area that includes primary and post-primary classes

Arecibo Observatory *n* an observatory in Puerto Rico at which the world's largest dish radio telescope

a

(diameter 305 m) is situated. It is operated by the National Astronomy and Ionosphere Center

arena *n* **1** a seated enclosure where sports events take place **2** the area of an ancient Roman amphitheatre where gladiators fought **3** a sphere of intense activity: *the political arena* [Latin *harena* sand]

Arendt *n* Hannah. 1906–75, US political philosopher, born in Germany. Her publications include *The Origins of Totalitarianism* (1951) and *Eichmann in Jerusalem* (1961)

aren't are not

areola *n, pl* **-lae** *or* **-las** a small circular area, such as the coloured ring around the human nipple [Latin]

Areopagus *n* **1 a** the hill to the northwest of the Acropolis in Athens **b** (in ancient Athens) the judicial council whose members (Areopagites) met on this hill **2** *literary* any high court [via Latin from Greek *Areiopagus*, contracted from *Areios pagos*, hill of Ares]

Arequipa *n* a city in S Peru, at an altitude of 2250 m (7500 ft): founded in 1540 on the site of an Inca city. Pop: 791 000 (2005 est)

Ares *n Greek myth* the god of war

arête *n* a sharp ridge separating valleys [French: fishbone]

Aretino *n* Pietro. 1492–1556, Italian satirist, poet, and dramatist, noted for his satirical attacks on leading political figures

Arezzo *n* a city in central Italy, in E Tuscany. Pop: 91 589 (2001). Ancient Latin name: **Arretium**

Arg. Argentina

Argenteuil *n* a suburb of Paris, France, with a convent (656) that became famous when Héloïse was abbess (12th century). Pop: 103 250 (2008)

Argentina *n* a republic in southern South America: colonized by the Spanish from 1516 onwards; gained independence in 1816 and became a republic in 1852; ruled by military dictatorships for much of the 20th century; civilian rule restored in 1983; consists chiefly of subtropical plains and forests (the Chaco) in the north, temperate plains (the pampas) in the central parts, the Andes in the west, and an infertile plain extending to Tierra del Fuego in the south (Patagonia); an important meat producer. Language: Spanish. Religion: Roman Catholic. Currency: peso. Capital: Buenos Aires. Pop: 42 610 981 (2013 est). Area: 2 776 653 sq km (1 072 067 sq miles). Also called: **the Argentine**

Argentine *or* **Argentinian** *adj* **1** of or relating to Argentina or its inhabitants ▷ *n* **2** a native or inhabitant of Argentina

Argerich *n* Martha. born 1941, Argentinian concert pianist

Argive *adj* **1** of or relating to Argos or Argolis ▷ *n* **2** an ancient Greek, esp. one from Argos or Argolis

Argolis *n* **1** a department and ancient region of Greece, in the NE Peloponnese. Capital: Nauplion. Pop: 102 392 (2001). Area: 2261 sq km (873 sq miles) **2 Gulf of Argolis** an inlet of the Aegean Sea, in the E Peloponnese

argon *n chem* an unreactive odourless element of the rare gas series, forming almost 1 per cent of the atmosphere. Symbol: **Ar** [Greek *argos* inactive]

Argonne *n* the Argonne a wooded region of NE France: scene of major battles in both World Wars

Argos *n* an ancient city in SE Greece, in the NE Peloponnese: one of the oldest Greek cities, it dominated the Peloponnese in the 7th century BC. Pop (municipality): 29 505 (2001)

argosy *n, pl* **-sies** *old-fashioned or poetic* a large merchant ship, or a fleet of such ships [Italian *Ragusea (nave)* (ship) of Ragusa, a former name for Dubrovnik]

argot (ahr-go) *n* slang or jargon peculiar to a particular group [French]

Argovie *n* the French name for Aargau

argue *vb* **-guing, -gued 1** to try to prove by presenting reasons **2** to debate **3** to quarrel **4** to persuade: *we argued her out of going* **5** to suggest: *her looks argue despair* [Latin

arguere to make clear, accuse] **> arguable** *adj* **> arguably** *adv*

argument *n* **1** a quarrel **2** a discussion **3** a point presented to support or oppose a proposition

argumentation *n* the process of reasoning methodically

argumentative *adj* likely to argue

argy-bargy *or* **argie-bargie** *n, pl* **-bargies** *Brit informal* a squabbling argument [Scots]

Argyll and Bute *n* a council area in W Scotland on the Atlantic Ocean: in 1975 the historical counties of Argyllshire and Bute became part of Strathclyde region; in 1996 they were reinstated as a single unitary authority. Argyll and Bute is mountainous and includes the islands of Bute, Mull, Islay, and Jura. Administrative centre: Lochgilphead. Pop: 91 300 (2003 est). Area: 6930 sq km (2676 sq miles)

Argyllshire *n* (until 1975) a county of W Scotland, part of Strathclyde region (1975–96), now part of Argyll and Bute

Århus *or* **Aarhus** *n* a city and port in Denmark, in E Jutland. Pop: 228 547 (2004 est)

aria (ah-ree-a) *n* an elaborate song for solo voice in an opera or choral work [Italian]

Arias Sánchez *n* Oscar. born 1940, Costa Rican statesman; president (1986–90, 2006–2010); Nobel peace prize 1987

Arica *n* a port in extreme N Chile: awarded to Chile in 1929 after the lengthy Tacna-Arica dispute with Peru; outlet for Bolivian and Peruvian trade. Pop: 180 000 (2005 est). See also **Tacna-Arica**

arid *adj* **1** having little or no rain **2** uninteresting [Latin *aridus*] **> aridity** *n*

Ariège *n* a department of SW France, in Midi-Pyrénées region. Capital: Foix. Pop: 139 612 (2003 est). Area: 4903 sq km (1912 sq miles)

Aries *n astrol* the first sign of the zodiac: the Ram [Latin]

aright *adv* correctly or properly

Arimathea *or* **Arimathaea** *n* a town in ancient Palestine: location unknown

Ariminum *n* the ancient name of **Rimini**

Ariosto *n* Ludovico. 1474–1533, Italian poet, famous for his romantic epic *Orlando Furioso* (1516)

arise *vb* **arising, arose, arisen 1** to come into being: *the opportunity for action did not arise* **2** to come into notice: *people can seek answers to their problems as and when they arise* **3** arise from to happen as a result of **4** *old-fashioned* to get or stand up [Old English *ārīsan*]

Aristarchus of Samos *n* 3rd century BC, Greek astronomer who anticipated Copernicus in advancing the theory that the earth revolves around the sun

Aristarchus of Samothrace *n* ?220–?150 BC, Greek scholar: librarian at Alexandria, noted for his edition of Homer

Aristides *n* known as *Aristides the Just*. ?530–?468 BC, Athenian general and statesman, who played a prominent part in the Greek victories over the Persians at Marathon (490), Salamis (480), and Plataea (479)

Aristippus *n* ?435–?356 BC, Greek philosopher, who believed pleasure to be the highest good and founded the Cyrenaic school

aristocracy *n, pl* **-cies 1** a class of people of high social rank **2** government by this class **3** a group of people considered to be outstanding in a particular sphere of activity [Greek *aristos* best + *kratein* to rule]

aristocrat *n* a member of the aristocracy

aristocratic *adj* **1** of the aristocracy **2** grand or elegant

Aristophanes *n* ?448–?380 BC, Greek comic dramatist, who satirized leading contemporary figures such as Socrates and Euripides. Eleven of his plays are extant, including *The Clouds, The Frogs, The Birds*, and *Lysistrata*

Aristotelian (ar-riss-tot-eel-ee-an) *adj* of Aristotle, 4th-century BC Greek philosopher, or his philosophy

Aristotle *n* 384–322 BC, Greek philosopher; pupil of Plato, tutor of Alexander the Great, and founder of the

Peripatetic school at Athens; author of works on logic, ethics, politics, poetics, rhetoric, biology, zoology, and metaphysics. His works influenced Muslim philosophy and science and medieval scholastic philosophy

arithmetic *n* **1** the branch of mathematics concerned with numerical calculations, such as addition, subtraction, multiplication, and division **2** calculations involving numerical operations **3** knowledge of or skill in arithmetic: *even simple arithmetic was beyond him* ▷ *adj* also: **arithmetical 4** of or using arithmetic [Greek *arithmos* number] **> arithmetically** *adv* **> arithmetician** *n*

arithmetic mean *n* the average value of a set of terms, expressed as their sum divided by their number: *the arithmetic mean of 3, 4, and 8 is 5*

arithmetic progression *n* a sequence, each term of which differs from the preceding term by a constant amount, such as 3, 6, 9, 12

Arius *n* ?250–336 AD, Greek Christian theologian, originator of the doctrine of Arianism

Ariz. Arizona

Arizona *n* a state of the southwestern US: consists of the Colorado plateau in the northeast, including the Grand Canyon, divided from desert in the southwest by mountains rising over 3750 m (12 500 ft). Capital: Phoenix. Pop: 5 580 811 (2003 est). Area: 293 750 sq km (113 417 sq miles). Abbreviation: **Ariz.**, (with zip code) **AZ**

ark *n Bible* the boat built by Noah, which survived the Flood [Latin *arca* box, chest]

Ark *n Judaism* **1** Also called: **Holy Ark** the cupboard in a synagogue in which the Torah scrolls are kept **2** Also called: **Ark of the Covenant** a chest containing the laws of the Jewish religion, regarded as the most sacred symbol of God's presence among the Hebrew people

Ark. Arkansas

Arkansan *n* **1** a native or inhabitant of Arkansas ▷ *adj* **2** of or relating to Arkansas

Arkansas *n* **1** a state of the southern US: mountainous in the north and west, with the alluvial plain of the Mississippi in the east; has the only diamond mine in the US; the chief US producer of bauxite. Capital: Little Rock. Pop: 2 725 714 (2003 est). Area: 134 537 sq km (51 945 sq miles). Abbreviation: **Ark.**, (with zip code) **AR** **2** a river in the S central US, rising in central Colorado and flowing east and southeast to join the Mississippi in Arkansas. Length: 2335 km (1450 miles)

Arkhangelsk *n* the Russian name for **Archangel**

Arkwright *n* Sir Richard. 1732–92, English cotton manufacturer: inventor of the spinning frame (1769) which produced cotton thread strong enough to be used as a warp

Arlberg *n* a mountain pass in W Austria: a winter sports region. Height: 1802 m (5910 ft)

Arles *n* **1** a city in SE France, on the Rhône: Roman amphitheatre. Pop: 53 058 (2006) **2** **Kingdom of Arles** a kingdom in SE France which had dissolved by 1378: known as the Kingdom of Burgundy until about 1200

Arlington *n* a county of N Virginia: site of **Arlington National Cemetery**

Arlon *n* a town in SE Belgium, capital of Luxembourg province. Pop: 25 766 (2004 est)

arm¹ *n* **1** (in humans, apes, and monkeys) either of the upper limbs from the shoulder to the wrist **2** the sleeve of a garment **3** the side of a chair on which one's arm can rest **4** a subdivision or section of an organization: *the London-based arm of a Swiss bank* **5** something resembling an arm in appearance or function: *the arm of a record player* **6** power or authority: *the long arm of the law* **7** **arm in arm** with arms linked **8** **at arm's length** at a distance **9** **with open arms** with warmth and hospitality [Old English]

arm² *vb* **1** to supply with weapons **2** to prepare (an explosive device) for use **3** to provide (a person or thing) with something that strengthens, or protects: *you will be armed with all the information you will ever need* ▶ See also **arms**

[Latin *arma* arms, equipment] **> armed** *adj*

armada *n* **1** a large number of ships **2** **the Armada** the great fleet sent by Spain against England in 1588 [Medieval Latin *armata* fleet, armed forces]

armadillo *n, pl* -**los** a small S American burrowing mammal covered in strong bony plates [Spanish *armado* armed (man)]

Armageddon *n* **1** *New Testament* the final battle between good and evil at the end of the world **2** a catastrophic and extremely destructive conflict [Hebrew *har megiddōn*, mountain district of *Megiddo* (in N Palestine)]

Armagh *n* **1** a historical county of S Northern Ireland: in 1973 it was replaced for administrative purposes by the districts of Armagh and Craigavon. Area: 1326 sq km (512 sq miles) **2** a district in Northern Ireland, in Co Armagh. Pop: 55 449 (2003 est). Area: 667 sq km (258 sq miles) **3** a town in S Northern Ireland, in Armagh district, Co Armagh: seat of Roman Catholic and Protestant archbishops. Pop: 14 590 (2001)

armament *n* **1** armaments the weapon equipment of a military vehicle, ship, or aircraft **2** preparation for war [Latin *armamenta* equipment]

Armani *n* Giorgio. born 1936, Italian fashion designer, noted for his restrained classical style

armature *n* **1** a revolving structure in an electric motor or generator, wound with the coils that carry the current **2** *sculpture* a framework to support the clay or other material used in modelling [Latin *armatura* armour, equipment]

armchair *n* **1** an upholstered chair with side supports for the arms ▷ *adj* **2** taking no active part: *we are, on the whole, a nation of armchair athletes*

armed forces *pl n* all the military forces of a nation or nations

Armenia *n* **1** a republic in NW Asia: originally part of the historic Armenian kingdom; acquired by Russia in 1828; became the Armenian Soviet Socialist Republic in 1936; gained independence in 1991. It is mountainous, rising over 4000 m (13 000 ft). Language: Armenian. Religion: Christian (Armenian Apostolic) majority. Currency: dram. Capital: Yerevan. Pop: 2 974 184 (2013 est). Area: 29 800 sq km (11 490 sq miles) **2** a former kingdom in W Asia, between the Black Sea and the Caspian Sea, south of Georgia **3** a town in central Colombia: centre of a coffee-growing district. Pop: 349 000 (2005 est)

Armenian *n* **1** a native or inhabitant of Armenia or an Armenian-speaking person elsewhere **2** the language of the Armenians: an Indo-European language probably belonging to the Thraco-Phrygian branch, but containing many non-Indo-European elements **3** an adherent of the Armenian Church or its doctrines ▷ *adj* **4** of or relating to Armenia, its inhabitants, their language, or the Armenian Church

Armentières *n* a town in N France: site of battles in both World Wars. Pop: 25 273 (1999)

armful *n* as much as can be held in the arms: *armfuls of lovely flowers*

armhole *n* the opening in a piece of clothing through which the arm passes

Armidale *n* a town in Australia, in NE New South Wales: a centre for tourism. Pop: 20 271 (2001)

Arminius *n* **1** Also: **Hermann** ?17 BC–?21 AD, Germanic chieftain: organized a revolt against the Romans in 9 AD **2** Jacobus, real name *Jacob Harmensen*. 1560–1609, Dutch Protestant theologian

armistice (arm-miss-stiss) *n* an agreement between opposing armies to stop fighting [Latin *arma* arms + *sistere* to stop]

Armistice Day *n* the anniversary of the signing of the armistice that ended the First World War, on November 11, 1918

Armitage *n* Simon (Robert). born 1963, British poet and writer, whose collections include *Zoom!* (1989), *Killing Time*

a

(1999), and *Universal Home Doctor* (2002)

armlet *n* a band or bracelet worn around the arm

armorial *adj* of or relating to heraldry or heraldic arms

Armorica *n* an ancient name for Brittany

Armorican *n* **1** a native or inhabitant of Armorica ▷ *adj* **2** of or relating to Armorica

armour *or US* **armor** *n* **1** metal clothing worn by medieval warriors for protection in battle **2** *military* armoured fighting vehicles in general **3** the protective metal plates on a tank or warship **4** protective covering, such as the shell of certain animals **5** a quality or attitude that gives protection ▷ *vb* **6** to equip or cover with armour [Latin *armātūra* armour, equipment]

armoured *or US* **armored** *adj* **1** having a protective covering **2** consisting of armoured vehicles: *an armoured brigade*

armourer *or US* **armorer** *n* **1** a person who makes or mends arms and armour **2** a person in charge of small arms in a military unit

armour plate *n* a tough heavy steel for protecting warships and vehicles ❭ **armour-plated** *adj*

armoury *or US* **armory** *n, pl* **-mouries** *or* **-mories** **1** a secure storage place for weapons **2** military supplies **3** resources on which to draw: *modern medicine has a large armoury of drugs for the treatment of mental illness*

armpit *n* **1** the hollow beneath the arm where it joins the shoulder **2** *slang* an extremely unpleasant place: *the armpit of the Mediterranean*

armrest *n* the part of a chair or sofa that supports the arm

arms *pl n* **1** weapons collectively **2** military exploits: *prowess in arms* **3** the heraldic symbols of a family or state **4 take up arms** to prepare to fight **5 under arms** armed and prepared for war **6 up in arms** prepared to protest strongly

Armstrong *n* **1 Edwin Howard**. 1890–1954, US electrical engineer; invented the superheterodyne radio receiver and the FM radio **2 (Daniel) Louis**, known as *Satchmo*. 1900–71, US jazz trumpeter, bandleader, and singer **3 Gillian**. born 1950, Australian film director; her films include *My Brilliant Career* (1978), *Little Women* (1994), and *Charlotte Gray* (2001) **4 Neil (Alden)**. 1930–2012, US astronaut; commanded Apollo 11 on the first manned lunar landing during which he became the first man to set foot on the moon on July 20, 1969 **5 Lance**. born 1971, US cyclist, winner of 7 Tour de France titles, 1999–2005; stripped of the titles in 2012 and banned for life, having been found to have used banned substances

army *n, pl* **-mies** **1** the military land forces of a nation **2** a large number of people or animals [Medieval Latin *armata* armed forces]

Arnaud *n* Yvonne. 1892–1958, French actress, who was well-known on the London stage and in British films. A theatre in Guildford is named after her

Arne *n* Thomas (Augustine). 1710–78, English composer, noted for his setting of Shakespearean songs and for his song *Rule Britannia*

Arnhem *n* a city in the E Netherlands, capital of Gelderland province, on the Rhine: site of a World War II battle. Pop: 142 000 (2003 est)

Arnhem Land *n* a region of N Australia in the N Northern Territory, large areas of which are reserved for native Australians

Arnim *n* Achim von. 1781–1831, German romantic poet. He published, with Clemens Brentano, the collection of folk songs, *Des Knaben Wunderhorn* (1805–08)

Arno *n* a river in central Italy, rising in the Apennines and flowing through Florence to the Ligurian Sea. Length: about 240 km (150 miles)

Arnold¹ *n* a town in N central England, in S Nottinghamshire. Pop: 37 402 (2001)

Arnold² *n* **1** Sir Malcolm. 1921–2006, English composer, esp. of orchestral works in a traditional idiom **2** Matthew. 1822–88, English poet, essayist, and literary

critic, noted particularly for his poems *Sohrab and Rustum* (1853) and *Dover Beach* (1867), and for his *Essays in Criticism* (1865) and *Culture and Anarchy* (1869) **3** his father, **Thomas**. 1795–1842, English historian and educationalist, headmaster of Rugby School, noted for his reforms in public-school education

aroha *n* NZ love, compassion, or affection [Māori]

aroma *n* **1** a distinctive pleasant smell **2** a subtle pervasive quality or atmosphere [Greek: spice]

aromatherapy *n* the use of fragrant essential oils as a treatment in alternative medicine, often to relieve tension

aromatic *adj* **1** having a distinctive pleasant smell **2** *chem* (of an organic compound) having an unsaturated ring of atoms, usually six carbon atoms ▷ *n* **3** something, such as a plant or drug, that gives off a fragrant smell

arose *vb* the past tense of **arise**

around *prep* **1** situated at various points in: *cameramen were positioned around the auditorium* **2** from place to place in: *he had spent twenty-five minutes driving around Amsterdam* **3** somewhere in or near **4** approximately in: *around 1980* ▷ *adv* **5** in all directions from a point of reference: *there wasn't a house for miles around* **6** in the vicinity, esp. restlessly but idly: *I couldn't hang around too long* **7** in no particular place or direction: *a few tropical fish tanks dotted around* **8** *informal* present in some unknown or unspecified place **9** *informal* available: *cancer drugs have been around for years* **10 have been around** *informal* to have gained considerable experience of a worldly or social nature

> **USAGE** In American English, *around* is usually used instead of *round* in adverbial and prepositional senses, except in a few fixed phrases such as *all year round*. The use of *around* in adverbial senses is less common in British English.

arouse *vb* **arousing, aroused** **1** to produce (a reaction, emotion, or response) **2** to awaken from sleep ❭ **arousal** *n*

Arp *n* Jean *or* Hans (hans). 1887–1966, Alsatian sculptor, painter, and poet, cofounder of the Dada movement in Zürich, noted particularly for his abstract organic sculptures based on natural forms

Árpád *n* died 907 AD, Magyar chieftain who conquered Hungary in the late 9th century

arpeggio (arp-pej-ee-oh) *n, pl* **-gios** a chord whose notes are played or sung in rapid succession [Italian]

arquebus (ark-wee-bus) *n* a portable long-barrelled gun dating from the 15th century [Middle Dutch *hakebusse* hook gun]

arrack *or* **arak** *n* a coarse alcoholic drink distilled in Eastern countries from grain or rice [Arabic *'araq* sweat, sweet juice]

arraign (ar-rain) *vb* **1** to bring (a prisoner) before a court to answer a charge **2** to accuse [Old French *araisnier* to accuse] ❭ **arraignment** *n*

Arran *n* an island off the SW coast of Scotland, in the Firth of Clyde. Pop: 5045 (2001). Area: 427 sq km (165 sq miles)

arrange *vb* **-ranging, -ranged** **1** to plan in advance: *my parents had arranged a surprise party* **2** to arrive at an agreement: *they had arranged to go to the cinema* **3** to put into a proper or systematic order **4** to adapt (a musical composition) for performance in a certain way [Old French *a-* to + *rangier* to put in a row, range]

arrangement *n* **1** a preparation or plan made for an event: *travel arrangements* **2** an agreement or a plan to do something **3** a thing composed of various ordered parts: *a flower arrangement* **4** the form in which things are arranged **5** an adaptation of a piece of music for performance in a different way

arrant *adj* utter or downright: *that's the most arrant nonsense*

I've ever heard [Middle English variant of *errant* (wandering, vagabond)]

arras *n* a tapestry wall-hanging [ARRAS]

Arras *n* a town in N France: formerly famous for tapestry; severely damaged in both World Wars. Pop: 43 663 (2006)

Arrau *n* Claudio. 1903–91, Chilean pianist

array *n* **1** an impressive display or collection **2** an orderly arrangement, such as of troops in battle order **3** *computers* a data structure in which elements may be located by index numbers **4** *poetic* rich clothing ▷ *vb* **5** to arrange in order **6** to dress in rich clothing [Old French *arayer* to arrange]

arrears *pl n* **1** money owed **2 in arrears** late in paying a debt [Latin *ad* to + *retro* backwards]

arrest *vb* **1** to take (a person) into custody **2** to slow or stop the development of **3** to catch and hold (one's attention) ▷ *n* **4** the act of taking a person into custody **5 under arrest** being held in custody by the police **6** the slowing or stopping of something: *a cardiac arrest* [Latin *ad* at, to + *restare* to stand firm, stop]

arresting *adj* attracting attention; striking

Arretium *n* the ancient Latin name of **Arezzo** ▷ **Arretine** *adj*

Arrhenius *n* Svante August. 1859–1927, Swedish chemist and physicist, noted for his work on the theory of electrolytic dissociation: Nobel prize for chemistry 1903

Ar Rimal *n* another name for **Rub' al Khali**

arrival *n* **1** the act of arriving **2** a person or thing that has just arrived **3** *informal* a recently born baby

arrive *vb* **-riving, -rived 1** to reach a place or destination **2 arrive at** to come to (a conclusion, idea, or decision) **3** to occur: *the crisis he predicted then has now arrived* **4** *informal* to be born **5** *informal* to attain success [Latin *ad* to + *ripa* river bank]

arrivederci (ar-reeve-a-der-chee) *interj* goodbye [Italian]

arrogant *adj* having an exaggerated opinion of one's own importance or ability [Latin *arrogare* to claim as one's own] ▷ **arrogance** *n* ▷ **arrogantly** *adv*

arrogate *vb* **-gating, -gated** to claim or seize without justification [Latin *arrogare*] ▷ **arrogation** *n*

arrow *n* **1** a long slender pointed weapon, with feathers at one end, that is shot from a bow **2** an arrow-shaped sign or symbol used to show the direction to a place [Old English *arwe*]

arrowhead *n* the pointed tip of an arrow

arrowroot *n* an easily digestible starch obtained from the root of a West Indian plant

Arroyo *n* Gloria Macapagal. born 1947, Filipino stateswoman; vice-president of the Philippines (1998–2001); president (2001–10)

Arru Islands *pl n* a variant spelling of **Aru Islands**

arse *or US and Canad* **ass** *n taboo* the buttocks or anus [Old English *ærs*]

arsehole *or US and Canad* **asshole** *n taboo* **1** the anus **2** a stupid or annoying person

arsenal *n* **1** a building in which arms and ammunition are made or stored **2** a store of anything regarded as weapons: *this new weapon in the medical arsenal* [Arabic *dār* house + *si_n'ah* manufacture]

arsenic *n* **1** a toxic metalloid element. Symbol: As **2** a nontechnical name for **arsenic trioxide**, a highly poisonous compound used as a rat poison and insecticide ▷ *adj* also: **arsenical 3** of or containing arsenic [Syriac *zarnīg*]

arson *n* the crime of intentionally setting fire to property [Latin *ardere* to burn] ▷ **arsonist** *n*

art *n* **1** the creation of works of beauty or other special significance **2** works of art collectively **3** human creativity as distinguished from nature **4** skill: *she was still new to the art of bargaining* **5** any branch of the visual arts, esp. painting **6 get something down to a fine art** to become proficient at something through practice ▸ See also **arts** [Latin *ars* craftsmanship]

Artaud *n* Antonin. 1896–1948, French stage director and dramatist, whose concept of the theatre of cruelty is expounded in *Manifeste du théâtre de la cruauté* (1932) and *Le Théâtre et son double* (1938)

Artaxerxes I *n* died 425 BC, king of Persia (465–425): son of Xerxes I

Artaxerxes II *n* died ?358 BC, king of Persia (?404–?358). He defeated his brother Cyrus the Younger at Cunaxa (401)

Art Deco (art deck-oh) *n* a style of design, at its height in the 1930s, characterized by geometrical shapes [French *art décoratif*]

artefact *or* **artifact** *n* something made by human beings, such as a tool or a work of art [Latin *ars* skill + *facere* to make]

Artemis *n* Greek myth the goddess of hunting

arterial *adj* **1** of or affecting an artery **2** being a major route: *an arterial road*

arteriosclerosis (art-ear-ee-oh-skler-**oh**-siss) *n* thickening and loss of elasticity of the walls of the arteries. Nontechnical name: **hardening of the arteries**

artery *n, pl* **-teries 1** any of the tubes that carry oxygenated blood from the heart to various parts of the body **2** a major road or means of communication [Latin *arteria*]

artesian well (art-**teez**-yan) *n* a well receiving water from a higher altitude, so the water is forced to flow upwards [from Old French *Arteis* Artois (in N France) where such wells were common]

Artex *n trademark Brit* a type of coating for walls and ceilings that gives a textured finish

art form *n* a recognized mode or medium of artistic expression

artful *adj* **1** cunning **2** skilful in achieving a desired end ▷ **artfully** *adv*

arthritis *n* inflammation of a joint or joints, causing pain and stiffness [Greek *arthron* joint] ▷ **arthritic** *adj, n*

arthropod *n* a creature, such as an insect or a spider, which has jointed legs and a hard case on its body [Greek *arthron* joint + *pous* foot]

Arthur *n* **1** a legendary king of the Britons in the sixth century AD, who led Celtic resistance against the Saxons: possibly based on a historical figure; represented as leader of the Knights of the Round Table at Camelot **2 Chester Alan.** 1830–86, 21st president of the US (1881–85) **3 not know whether one is Arthur or Martha** *Austral and NZ informal* to be in a state of confusion

artic *n Brit informal* an articulated lorry

artichoke *n* **1** Also called: **globe artichoke** the flower head of a thistle-like plant, cooked as a vegetable **2** same as **Jerusalem artichoke** [Arabic *al-kharshūf*]

article *n* **1** a written composition in a magazine or newspaper **2** an item or object **3** a clause in a written document **4** *grammar* any of the words *a, an,* or *the* [Latin *articulus* small joint]

articled *adj* bound by a written contract, such as one that governs a period of training: *an articled clerk*

articular *adj* of or relating to joints [Latin *articulus* small joint]

articulate *adj* **1** able to express oneself fluently and coherently **2** distinct, clear, or definite: *his amiable and articulate campaign attracted support* **3** *zoology* possessing joints ▷ *vb* **-lating, -lated 4** to speak clearly and distinctly **5** to express coherently in words [Latin *articulare* to divide into joints] ▷ **articulately** *adv*

articulated lorry *n* a large lorry in two separate sections connected by a pivoted bar

articulation *n* **1** the expressing of an idea in words **2** the process of articulating a speech sound or the sound so produced **3** a being jointed together **4** *zoology* a joint between bones or arthropod segments

artifact *n* same as **artefact**

artifice *n* **1** a clever trick **2** skill or cleverness [Latin *ars* skill + *facere* to make]

a

artificer (art-tiff-iss-er) *n* a skilled craftsman
artificial *adj* **1** man-made; not occurring naturally **2** made in imitation of a natural product: *artificial flavourings* **3** not sincere [Latin *artificialis* belonging to art] **> artificiality** *n* **> artificially** *adv*
artificial insemination *n* introduction of semen into the womb by means other than sexual intercourse
artificial intelligence *n* the branch of computer science aiming to produce machines which can imitate intelligent human behaviour
artificial respiration *n* any method of restarting a person's breathing after it has stopped
Artigas *n* José Gervasio. 1764–1850, the national hero of Uruguay. He fought for Uruguayan independence from Argentina, but was driven into exile in 1820
artillery *n* **1** large-calibre guns **2** military units specializing in the use of such guns [Old French *artillier* to equip with weapons]
artisan *n* a skilled workman; craftsman [French] **> artisanal** *adj*
artist *n* **1** a person who produces works of art such as paintings or sculpture **2** a person who is skilled at something **3** same as **artiste > artistic** *adj* **> artistically** *adv*
artiste *n* a professional entertainer such as a singer or dancer
artistry *n* **1** artistic ability **2** great skill
artless *adj* **1** free from deceit or cunning: *artless generosity* **2** natural or unpretentious **> artlessly** *adv*
Art Nouveau (ahr noo-voh) *n* a style of art and architecture of the 1890s, characterized by sinuous outlines and stylized natural forms [French: new art]
Artois *n* a former province of N France
arts *pl n* **1** the arts the nonscientific branches of knowledge **2** See fine art **3** cunning schemes
artwork *n* all the photographs and illustrations in a publication
arty *adj* **artier, artiest** *informal* having an affected interest in art **> artiness** *n*
Aruba *n* an island in the Caribbean, off the NW coast of Venezuela, a dependency of the Netherlands with special status; part of the Netherlands Antilles until 1986. Chief town: Oranjestad. Pop: 109 153 (2013 est). Area: about 181 sq km (70 sq miles)
Aru Islands *or* **Arru Islands** *pl n* a group of islands in Indonesia, in the SW Moluccas. Area: about 8500 sq km (3300 sq miles)
arum lily *n* a plant with a white funnel-shaped leaf surrounding a yellow spike of flowers
Arunachal Pradesh *n* a state in NE India, formed in 1986 from the former Union Territory. Capital: Itanagar. Pop: 1 091 117 (2001). Area: 83 743 sq km (32 648 sq miles). Former name (until 1972): North East Frontier Agency
Arundel *n* a town in S England, in West Sussex: 11th-century castle. Pop: 3297 (2001)
Aruwimi *n* a river in NE Democratic Republic of Congo, rising near Lake Albert as the Ituri and flowing west into the River Congo. Length: about 1288 km (800 miles)
Aryan (air-ree-an) *n* **1** (in Nazi ideology) a non-Jewish person of the Nordic type **2** a person supposedly descended from the Indo-Europeans ▷ *adj* **3** of Aryans [Sanskrit *ārya* of noble birth]
as *conj* **1** while or when: *he arrived just as the band finished the song* **2** in the way that: *they had talked and laughed as only the best of friends can* **3** that which; what: *George did as he was asked* **4** (of) which fact or event (referring to the previous statement): *to become wise, as we all know, is not easy* **5** as it were in a way; in a manner of speaking: *he was, as it were, on probation* **6** since; seeing that **7** for instance ▷ *adv, conj* **8** used to indicate amount or extent in comparisons: *he was as fat as his mum and dad* ▷ *prep* **9** in the role of; being: *my task, as his physician, is to do the best that I can* **10** as for *or* to with reference to **11** as if *or* though as it would be if: *she*

felt as if she had been run over by a bulldozer **12 as (it) is** in the existing state of affairs [Old English *alswā* likewise]

USAGE See at like¹.

As *chem* arsenic
ASA **1** (in Britain) Amateur Swimming Association **2** (in Britain) Advertising Standards Authority
asafoetida *n* a strong-smelling plant resin used as a spice in Eastern cookery [Medieval Latin *asa* gum + Latin *foetidus* evil-smelling]
a.s.a.p. as soon as possible
Asben *n* another name for Aïr
asbestos *n* a fibrous mineral which does not burn, formerly widely used as a heat-resistant material [Greek: inextinguishable]
asbestosis *n* inflammation of the lungs resulting from inhalation of asbestos fibre
ASBO Brit antisocial behaviour order
ascend *vb* **1** to go or move up **2** to slope upwards **3 ascend the throne** to become king or queen [Latin *ascendere*]
ascendancy *or* **ascendance** *n* the condition of being dominant: *when hardliners were in the ascendancy last winter*
ascendant *or* **ascendent** *adj* **1** dominant or influential ▷ *n* **2** *astrol* the sign of the zodiac that is rising on the eastern horizon at a particular moment **3 in the ascendant** increasing in power or influence
ascension *n* the act of ascending
Ascension *n* an island in the S Atlantic, northwest of St Helena: uninhabited until claimed by Britain in 1815. Pop: 884 (2010 est). Area: 88 sq km (34 sq miles)
Ascension Day *n Christianity* the 40th day after Easter, when the Ascension of Christ into Heaven is celebrated
ascent *n* **1** the act of ascending **2** an upward slope
ascertain *vb* to find out definitely [Old French *acertener* to make certain] **> ascertainment** *n*
ascetic (ass-set-tik) *n* **1** a person who abstains from worldly comforts and pleasures ▷ *adj* **2** rigidly abstinent and self-denying [Greek *askētikos*]
Asch *n* Sholem. 1880–1957, US writer, born in Poland, who wrote in Yiddish. His works include biblical novels
Aschaffenburg *n* a city in Germany, on the River Main in Bavaria: seat of the Imperial Diet (1447); ceded to Bavaria in 1814. Pop: 68 607 (2003 est)
Ascham *n* Roger. ?1515–68, English humanist writer and classical scholar: tutor to Queen Elizabeth I
ASCII (ass-kee) *n* a code for transmitting data between computers [A(merican) S(tandard) C(ode for) I(nformation) I(nterchange)]
Ascoli Piceno *n* a town in E central Italy, in the Marches: capital of the Roman province of Picenum; site of the massacre of all its Roman citizens in the Social War in 90 BC. Pop: 51 375 (2001). Latin name: Asculum Picenum
ascorbic acid (ass-core-bik) *n* a vitamin that occurs in citrus fruits, tomatoes, and green vegetables, and which prevents and cures scurvy. Also called: vitamin C [A- + SCORBUTIC]
Ascot *n* a town in S England, in Bracknell Forest unitary authority, Berkshire: noted for its horse-race meetings, esp. Royal Ascot, a four-day meeting held in June. Pop: 8755 (2001)
ascribe *vb* **-cribing, -cribed** **1** to attribute, as to a particular origin: *headaches which may be ascribed to stress* **2** to consider that (a particular quality) is possessed by something or someone: *specific human qualities are ascribed to each of the four elements* [Latin *ad* in addition + *scribere* to write] **> ascription** *n*

USAGE *Ascribe* is sometimes used where *subscribe* is meant: *I do not subscribe* (not *ascribe*) *to this view.*

aseptic (eh-sep-tik) *adj* free from harmful bacteria
asexual (eh-sex-yew-al) *adj* **1** having no apparent sex or

sex organs **2** (of reproduction) not involving sexual activity ▷ **asexually** *adv*

ash¹ *n* **1** the powdery substance formed when something is burnt **2** fine particles of lava thrown out by an erupting volcano [Old English *æsce*]

ash² *n* a tree with grey bark and winged seeds [Old English *æsc*]

ashamed *adj* **1** overcome with shame or remorse **2** unwilling through fear of humiliation or shame: *she'd be ashamed to admit to jealousy* [Old English *āscamod*]

Ashanti *n* **1** an administrative region of central Ghana: former native kingdom, suppressed by the British in 1900 after four wars. Capital: Kumasi. Pop: 3 187 607 (2000). Area: 24 390 sq km (9417 sq miles) **2** (*pl* **-ti** *or* **-tis**) a native or inhabitant of Ashanti

Ashby-de-la-Zouch *n* a town in central England, in Leicestershire: Mary, Queen of Scots, was imprisoned (1569) in the castle. Pop: 11 409 (2001)

ash can *n* US a dustbin

Ashcroft *n* Dame **Peggy**. 1907–91, English stage and film actress

Ashdod *n* a town in central Israel, on the Mediterranean coast: an important city in the Philistine Empire, with its artificial harbour (1961) it is now a major port. Pop: 192 000 (2003 est)

Ashdown *n* **Paddy**, Baron. real name *Jeremy John Durham Ashdown*. born 1941, British politician; leader of the Liberal Democrats (formerly the Social and Liberal Democrats) (1988–99); UN high representative in Bosnia-Herzegovina from 2002

Ashe *n* Arthur (**Robert**). 1943–93, US tennis player: US champion 1968; Wimbledon champion 1975

ashen *adj* pale with shock

ashes *pl n* **1** remains after burning **2** the remains of a human body after cremation

Ashes *pl n* **the Ashes** a cricket trophy competed for by England and Australia since 1882 [from a mock obituary of English cricket after a great Australian victory]

Ashford *n* a market town in SE England, in central Kent. Pop: 58 936 (2001)

Ashkenazy *n* **Vladimir**. born 1937, Soviet-born Icelandic pianist and conductor

Ashkhabad *or* **Ashgabat** *n* the capital of Turkmenistan. Pop: 598 000 (2005 est)

ashlar *or* **ashler** *n* **1** a square block of cut stone for use in building **2** a thin dressed stone used to face a wall [Old French *aisselier* crossbeam]

Ashley *n* **1** Jack, Baron. 1922–2012, British Labour politician and campaigner for deaf and disabled people **2** Laura. 1925–85, British designer, who built up a successful chain of retail stores selling dresses and fabrics based on traditional English patterns

Ashmolean Museum *n* a museum, attached to Oxford University and founded in 1683, noted for its paintings and archaeological collections [C19: named after Elias *Ashmole* (1617–92), English antiquary who donated the first collection]

ashore *adv* towards or on land

ashram *n* a religious retreat where a Hindu holy man lives [Sanskrit *āśrama*]

Ashton *n* **1** Catherine. Baroness. born 1956, British Labour politician; High Representative of the Union for Foreign Affairs and Security Policy for the European Union (2009–2014) **2** Sir **Frederick**. 1906–88, British ballet dancer and choreographer. His ballets include *Façade* (1931), to music by Walton, *La Fille mal gardée* (1960), *The Dream* (1964), and *A Month in the Country* (1976)

Ashton-under-Lyne *n* a town in NW England, in Tameside unitary authority, Greater Manchester. Pop: 43 236 (2001)

ashtray *n* a dish for tobacco ash and cigarette ends

Ashurbanipal *or* **Assurbanipal** *n* died ?626 BC, king of Assyria (?668–?626): son of Esarhaddon. He built the magnificent palace and library at Nineveh.

Greek name: **Sardanapalus**

Ash Wednesday *n* the first day of Lent, named from the Christian custom of sprinkling ashes on penitents' heads

ashy *adj* **ashier, ashiest** **1** pale greyish **2** covered with ash

'Asi *n* the Arabic name for the **Orontes**

Asia *n* the largest of the continents, bordering on the Arctic Ocean, the Pacific Ocean, the Indian Ocean, and the Mediterranean and Red Seas in the west. It includes the large peninsulas of Asia Minor, India, Arabia, and Indochina and the island groups of Japan, Indonesia, the Philippines, and Sri Lanka; contains the mountain ranges of the Hindu Kush, Himalayas, Pamirs, Tian Shan, Urals, and Caucasus, the great plateaus of India, Iran, and Tibet, vast plains and deserts, and the valleys of many large rivers including the Mekong, Irrawaddy, Indus, Ganges, Tigris, and Euphrates. Pop: 4 164 252 000 (2011 est). Area: 44 391 162 sq km (17 139 445 sq miles)

Asia Minor *n* the historical name for **Anatolia**

Asian *adj* **1** of or relating to Asia or its inhabitants **2** *Brit* of or relating to the Indian subcontinent or its inhabitants ▷ *n* **3** a native or inhabitant of Asia **4** *Brit* a native or inhabitant of the Indian subcontinent or a descendant of one

> **USAGE** The use of *Asian* or *Asiatic* as a noun can be offensive and should be avoided.

Asian pear *n* an apple-shaped pear with crisp juicy flesh

Asiatic *adj* Asian

> **USAGE** See at **Asian**.

aside *adv* **1** to one side **2** out of other people's hearing: *her mother took her aside for a serious talk* **3** out of mind: *she pushed aside her fears of being beaten or killed* **4** into reserve: *a certain amount must also be put aside for defence and government* ▷ *n* **5** a remark not meant to be heard by everyone present **6** a remark that is not connected with the subject being discussed

Asimov *n* **Isaac**. 1920–92, US writer and biochemist, born in Russia. His science-fiction works include *Foundation Trilogy* (1951–53; sequel 1982) and the collection of stories *I, Robot* (1950)

asinine (**ass-in-nine**) *adj* **1** obstinate or stupid **2** of or like an ass [Latin *asinus* ass]

Asir *n* a region of SW Saudi Arabia, in the Southern Province on the Red Sea: under Turkish rule until 1933. Area: 81 000 sq km (31 000 sq miles)

ask *vb* **1** to say or write (something) in a form that requires an answer: *I asked him his name; 'do you think we'll have trouble landing?' he asked* **2** to make a request or demand: *the chairman asked for a show of hands* **3** to invite **4** to inquire about: *I pretended to be lost and asked for directions* **5** to expect: *is that too much to ask?* [Old English *āscian*]

ask after *vb* to make polite inquiries about the health of: *he asked after you*

askance (**ass-kanss**) *adv* **look askance at a** to look at with an oblique glance **b** to regard with suspicion [origin unknown]

askari *n* S *African history* a former resistance fighter who collaborated with the authorities during the Apartheid regime [Arabic: soldier]

askew *adv*, *adj* towards one side; crooked

Askey *n* **Arthur**. 1900–82, British comedian

ask for *vb* **1** to seek to speak to **2** to request **3** *informal* to behave in a manner that is regarded as inviting (something): *you were asking for trouble there*

asking price *n* the price suggested by a seller

Askja *n* a volcano in E central Iceland: active in 1961; largest crater in Iceland. Height: 1510 m (4954 ft). Area of crater: 88 sq km (34 sq miles)

aslant *adv* **1** at a slant ▷ *prep* **2** slanting across

a

asleep *adj* **1** in or into a state of sleep **2** (of limbs) numb **3** *informal* not listening or paying attention

ASLEF (in Britain) Associated Society of Locomotive Engineers and Firemen

Asmara *n* the capital of Eritrea; cathedral (1922); Grand Mosque (1937); university (1958). Pop: 615 000 (2005 est)

Asnières *n* a suburb of Paris, France, on the Seine. Pop: 82 720 (2006)

Aso *n* a group of five volcanic cones in Japan on central Kyushu, one of which, Naka-dake, has the largest crater in the world, between 16 km (10 miles) and 24 km (15 miles) in diameter. Highest cone: 1592 m (5223 ft). Also called: **Asosan**

Asoka *n* died 232 BC, Indian emperor (?273–232 BC), who elevated Buddhism to the official state religion

asp *n* a small viper of S Europe [Greek *aspis*]

asparagus *n* the young shoots of a plant of the lily family, which can be cooked and eaten [Greek *asparagos*]

aspartame *n* an artificial sweetener

Aspasia *n* 5th century BC, Greek courtesan; mistress of Pericles

aspect *n* **1** a distinct feature or element in a problem or situation **2** a position facing a particular direction: *the room's east-facing aspect* **3** appearance or look: *a room with a somewhat gloomy aspect* [Latin *ad-* to, at + *specere* to look]

aspen *n* a poplar tree whose leaves quiver in the wind [Old English *æspe*]

asperity (ass-per-rit-ee) *n, pl* **-ties** roughness or sharpness of temper [Latin *asper* rough]

aspersion *n* **cast aspersions on** to make disparaging or malicious remarks about [Latin *aspergere* to sprinkle]

asphalt *n* **1** a black tarlike substance used in road-surfacing and roofing materials ▷ *vb* **2** to cover with asphalt [Greek *asphaltos*, probably from *a-* not + *sphallein* to cause to fall; referring to its use as a binding agent]

asphodel *n* a plant with clusters of yellow or white flowers

asphyxia (ass-fix-ee-a) *n* unconsciousness or death caused by lack of oxygen [Greek *a-* without + *sphuxis* pulse]

asphyxiate *vb* **-ating, -ated** to smother or suffocate ▷ **asphyxiation** *n*

aspic *n* a savoury jelly based on meat or fish stock, used as a mould for meat or vegetables [French]

aspidistra *n* a house plant with long tapered evergreen leaves [Greek *aspis* shield]

Aspinwall *n* the former name of **Colón**

aspirant *n* a person who aspires, such as to a powerful position

aspirate *phonetics vb* **-rating, -rated** **1** to pronounce (a word or syllable) with an initial h ▷ *n* **2** the sound represented in English and several other languages as h

aspiration *n* **1** a strong desire or aim **2** *phonetics* the pronunciation of an aspirated consonant ▷ **aspirational** *adj*

aspirator *n* a device for removing fluids from a body cavity by suction

aspire *vb* **-piring, -pired** to yearn for something or hope to do or be something: *it struck him as bizarre that somebody could aspire to be a dental technician* [Latin *aspirare* to breathe upon] ▷ **aspiring** *adj*

aspirin *n, pl* **-rin** or **-rins** **1** a drug used to relieve pain and fever **2** a tablet of aspirin [German]

Asquith *n* Herbert Henry, 1st Earl of Oxford and Asquith. 1852–1928, British statesman; prime minister (1908–16); leader of the Liberal Party (1908–26)

ass¹ *n* **1** a mammal resembling the horse but with longer ears **2** a foolish person [Old English *assa*]

ass² *n* US and Canad taboo same as **arse** [Old English *ærs*]

Assad *n* **1** Hafiz al. 1928–2000, Syrian statesman and general; president of Syria (1971–2000) **2** his son, Bashar al. born 1965, Syrian statesman; president of Syria from 2000

assagai *n* same as **assegai**

assail *vb* **1** to attack violently **2** to criticize strongly **3** to disturb: *he was assailed by a dizzy sensation* [Latin *assilire* to leap on] ▷ **assailant** *n*

Assam *n* **1** a state of NE India, situated in the central Brahmaputra valley: tropical forest, with the heaviest rainfall in the world; produces large quantities of tea. Capital: Dispur. Pop: 26 638 407 (2001 est). Area: 78 438 sq km (30 673 sq miles) **2** a high-quality black tea grown in the state of Assam

Assamese *n* **1** the state language of Assam, belonging to the Indic branch of the Indo-European family and closely related to Bengali **2** (*pl* **-mese**) a native or inhabitant of Assam ▷ *adj* **3** of or relating to Assam, its people, or their language

Assange *n* Julian (Paul). born 1971, Australian editor of WikiLeaks, a website that published (2010) thousands of leaked US diplomatic and military documents

assassin *n* a murderer of a prominent person [Arabic *hashshāshīn*, plural of *hashshāsh* one who eats hashish]

assassinate *vb* **-nating, -nated** to murder (a prominent person) ▷ **assassination** *n*

assault *n* **1** a violent attack, either physical or verbal ▷ *vb* **2** to attack violently [Old French *asaut*]

assault and battery *n criminal law* a threat of attack to another person followed by actual attack

assault course *n* an obstacle course designed to give soldiers practice in negotiating hazards

assay *vb* **1** to analyse (a substance, such as gold) to find out how pure it is ▷ *n* **2** an analysis of the purity of an ore or precious metal [Old French *assai*]

assegai or **assagai** *n, pl* **-gais** a sharp light spear used in southern Africa [Arabic *az zaghayah*]

assemblage *n* **1** a collection or group of things **2** the act of assembling

assemble *vb* **-bling, -bled** **1** to collect or gather together **2** to put together the parts of (a machine) [Old French *assembler*]

assembler *n* **1** a person or thing that assembles **2** a computer program that converts a set of low-level symbolic data into machine language

assembly *n, pl* **-blies** **1** a number of people gathered together for a meeting **2** the act of assembling

assembly line *n* a sequence of machines and workers in a factory assembling a product

assemblyman *n, pl* **-men** a member of a legislative assembly

Assen *n* a city in the N Netherlands, capital of Drenthe province. Pop: 62 000 (2003 est)

assent *n* **1** agreement, consent ▷ *vb* **2** to agree [Latin *assentiri*]

assert *vb* **1** to state or declare **2** to insist upon (one's rights, etc.) **3 assert oneself** to speak and act forcefully [Latin *asserere* to join to oneself]

assertion *n* **1** a positive statement, usually made without evidence **2** the act of asserting

assertive *adj* confident and direct in dealing with others ▷ **assertively** *adv* ▷ **assertiveness** *n*

assess *vb* **1** to judge the worth or importance of **2** to estimate the value of (income or property) for taxation purposes [Latin *assidere* to sit beside] ▷ **assessment** *n*

assessor *n* **1** a person who values property for taxation or insurance purposes **2** a person with technical expertise called in to advise a court **3** a person who evaluates the merits of something

asset *n* **1** a thing or person that is valuable or useful **2** any property owned by a person or company [Latin *ad-* to + *satis* enough]

asset-stripping *n commerce* the practice of taking over a failing company at a low price and then selling the assets piecemeal ▷ **asset-stripper** *n*

asseverate *vb* **-ating, -ated** *formal* to declare solemnly [Latin *asseverare* to do (something) earnestly] ▷ **asseveration** *n*

assiduous *adj* **1** hard-working **2** done with care [Latin *assidere* to sit beside] **> assiduity** *n* **> assiduously** *adv*

assign *vb* **1** to select (someone) for a post or task **2** to give a task or duty (to someone) **3** to attribute to a specified cause **4** to set apart (a place or time) for a particular function or event: *to assign a day for the meeting* **5** *law* to transfer (one's right, interest, or title to property) to someone else [Latin *assignare*]

assignation (ass-sig-**nay**-shun) *n* a secret arrangement to meet, esp. one between lovers [Latin *assignatio* a marking out]

assignment *n* **1** something that has been assigned, such as a task **2** the act of assigning **3** *law* the transfer to another person of a right, interest, or title to property

assimilate *vb* **-lating, -lated 1** to learn and understand (information) thoroughly **2** to adjust or become adjusted: *they became assimilated to German culture* **3** to absorb (food) [Latin *ad-* to + *similis* like] **> assimilable** *adj* **> assimilation** *n*

Assiniboine *n* a river in W Canada, rising in E Saskatchewan and flowing southeast and east to the Red River at Winnipeg. Length: over 860 km (500 miles)

Assisi *n* a town in central Italy, in Umbria: birthplace of St Francis, who founded the Franciscan religious order here in 1208. Pop: 25 304 (2001)

assist *vb* **1** to give help or support ▷ *n* **2** *sport* a pass by a player which enables another player to score a goal [Latin *assistere* to stand by]

assistance *n* help or support

assistant *n* **1** a helper or subordinate **2** same as **shop assistant** ▷ *adj* **3** junior or deputy: *assistant manager*

assistant referee *n soccer* the official name for linesman (1)

Assiut *n* a variant spelling of **Asyut**

assizes *pl n Brit* (formerly in England and Wales) the sessions of the principal court in each county [Latin *assidere* to sit beside]

assoc. association

associate *vb* **-ating, -ated 1** to connect in the mind **2** to mix socially: *addicts are driven to associate with criminals* **3 be associated** *or* **associate oneself with** to be involved with (a group) because of shared views: *she had long been associated with the far right* ▷ *n* **4** a partner in business **5** a companion or friend ▷ *adj* **6** having partial rights or subordinate status: *an associate member* **7** joined with in business: *an associate director* [Latin *ad-* to + *sociare* to join]

association *n* **1** a group of people with a common interest **2** the act of associating or the state of being associated **3** friendship: *their association still had to remain a secret* **4** a mental connection of ideas or feelings: *the place contained associations for her*

association football *n* same as **soccer**

associative *adj maths* (of an operation such as multiplication or addition) producing the same answer regardless of the way the elements are grouped, for example $(2 \times 3) \times 4 = 2 \times (3 \times 4)$

assonance *n* the rhyming of vowel sounds but not consonants, as in *time* and *light* [Latin *assonare* to sound]

assorted *adj* **1** consisting of various kinds mixed together **2** matched: *an ill-assorted childless couple* [Old French *assorter*]

assortment *n* a collection of various things or sorts

ASSR (formerly) Autonomous Soviet Socialist Republic

asst assistant

assuage (ass-**wage**) *vb* **-suaging, -suaged** to relieve (grief, pain, or thirst) [Latin *suavis* pleasant]

Assuan *or* **Assouan** *n* variant spellings of **Aswan**

assume *vb* **-suming, -sumed 1** to take to be true without proof **2** to undertake or take on: *every general staff officer was able to assume control of the army* **3** to make a pretence of: *the man had assumed a debonair attitude* **4** to take on: *her eyes assumed a scared haunted look* [Latin *ad-* to + *sumere* to take up]

assumed name *n* a false name used by someone to disguise his or her identity

assuming *conj* if it is assumed or taken for granted: *assuming the first two phases were successful, the third phase would follow*

assumption *n* **1** something that is taken for granted **2** the act of assuming power or possession [Latin *assumptio* a taking up]

Assumption *n Christianity* the taking up of the Virgin Mary into heaven when her earthly life was ended

Assur, Asur *or* **Asshur, Ashur** *n* **1** the supreme national god of the ancient Assyrians, chiefly a war god, whose symbol was an archer within a winged disc **2** one of the chief cities of ancient Assyria, on the River Tigris about 100 km (60 miles) downstream from the present-day city of Mosul

assurance *n* **1** a statement or assertion intended to inspire confidence **2** feeling of confidence; certainty **3** insurance that provides for events that are certain to happen, such as death

assure *vb* **-suring, -sured 1** to promise or guarantee **2** to convince: *they assured me that they had not seen the document* **3** to make (something) certain **4** *chiefly Brit* to insure against loss of life [Latin *ad-* to + *securus* secure]

assured *adj* **1** confident or self-assured **2** certain to happen **3** *chiefly Brit* insured **> assuredly** (a-**sure**-id-lee) *adv*

Assyria *n* an ancient kingdom of N Mesopotamia: it established an empire that stretched from Egypt to the Persian Gulf, reaching its greatest extent between 721 and 633 BC. Its chief cities were Assur and Nineveh

Assyrian *n* an inhabitant of ancient Assyria, a kingdom of Mesopotamia

AST Atlantic Standard Time

Astaire *n* Fred, real name *Frederick Austerlitz*. 1899–1987, US dancer, singer, and actor, whose films include *Top Hat* (1935), *Swing Time* (1936), and *The Band Wagon* (1953)

Astana *n* the capital of Kazakhstan, in the N of the country; replaced Almaty as capital in 1997; an important railway junction. Pop: 335 000 (2005 est). Former names: (until 1961) Akmolinsk, (1961–94) Tselinograd, (1994–98) Akmola

astatine *n chem* a radioactive element occurring naturally in minute amounts or artificially produced by bombarding bismuth with alpha particles. Symbol: At [Greek *astatos* unstable]

Astbury *n* John. 1688–1743, English potter; earliest of the great Staffordshire potters

aster *n* a plant with white, blue, purple, or pink daisy-like flowers [Greek: star]

asterisk *n* **1** a star-shaped character (*) used in printing or writing to indicate a footnote etc. ▷ *vb* **2** to mark with an asterisk [Greek *asteriskos* a small star]

astern *adv, adj nautical* **1** at or towards the stern of a ship **2** backwards **3** behind a vessel

asteroid *n* any of the small planets that orbit the sun between Mars and Jupiter [Greek *asteroeidēs* starlike]

asthma (ass-ma) *n* an illness causing difficulty in breathing [Greek] **> asthmatic** *adj, n*

Asti *n* a town in NW Italy: famous for its sparkling wine (Asti spumante). Pop: 71 276 (2001)

astigmatic *adj* relating to or affected with astigmatism [Greek *a-* without + *stigma* spot, focus]

astigmatism (eh-**stig**-mat-tiz-zum) *n* a defect of a lens, esp. of the eye, causing it not to focus properly

astir *adj* **1** out of bed **2** in motion

Aston *n* Francis William. 1877–1945, English physicist and chemist, who developed the first mass spectrograph, using it to investigate the isotopic structures of elements: Nobel prize for chemistry 1922

astonish *vb* to surprise greatly [Latin *ex-* out + *tonare* to thunder] **> astonishing** *adj* **> astonishment** *n*

Astor *n* **1** John Jacob, 1st Baron Astor of Hever. 1886–1971, British proprietor of *The Times* (1922–66) **2 Nancy (Witcher)**, Viscountess, original name *Nancy Langhorne*.

a

1879–1964, British Conservative politician, born in the US; the first woman to sit in the British House of Commons

Astoria *n* a port in NW Oregon, near the mouth of the Columbia River: founded as a fur-trading post in 1811 by John Jacob Astor. Pop: 9660 (2003 est)

astound *vb* to overwhelm with amazement [Old French *estoner*] **> astounding** *adj*

astraddle *prep* astride

astrakhan *n* **1** a fur made of the dark curly fleece of lambs from Astrakhan in Russia **2** a cloth resembling this

Astrakhan *n* a city in SE Russia, on the delta of the Volga River, 21 m (70 ft) below sea level. Pop: 507 000 (2005 est)

astral *adj* **1** relating to or resembling the stars **2** of the spirit world [Greek *astron* star]

astray *adj, adv* out of the right or expected way [Old French *estraier* to stray]

astride *adj* **1** with a leg on either side **2** with legs far apart ▷ *prep* **3** with a leg on either side of

astringent *adj* **1** causing contraction of body tissue **2** checking the flow of blood from a cut **3** severe or harsh ▷ *n* **4** an astringent drug or lotion [Latin *astringens* drawing together] **> astringency** *n*

astro- *combining form* indicating a star or stars: *astrology* [Greek]

astrolabe *n* an instrument formerly used to measure the altitude of stars and planets [Greek *astron* star + *lambanein* to take]

astrology *n* the study of the alleged influence of the stars, planets, sun, and moon on human affairs [Greek *astron* star + *logos* word, account] **> astrologer** or **astrologist** *n* **> astrological** *adj*

astronaut *n* a person trained for travelling in space [Greek *astron* star + *nautēs* sailor]

astronautics *n* the science and technology of space flight **> astronautical** *adj*

astronomical or **astronomic** *adj* **1** enormously large **2** of astronomy **> astronomically** *adv*

astronomical unit *n* a unit of distance equal to the average distance between the earth and the sun $(1.495 \times 10^{11}\text{m})$

astronomy *n* the scientific study of heavenly bodies [Greek *astron* star + *nomos* law] **> astronomer** *n*

astrophysics *n* the study of the physical and chemical properties of celestial bodies **> astrophysical** *adj* **> astrophysicist** *n*

Astroturf *n* *trademark* a brand of artificial grass [from the *Astro*(dome), sports stadium where it was first used + *turf*]

Asturian *adj* of or relating to Asturias

Asturias[1] *n* a region and former kingdom of NW Spain, consisting of a coastal plain and the Cantabrian Mountains: a Christian stronghold against the Moors (8th to 13th centuries); rich mineral resources

Asturias[2] *n* Miguel Ángel. 1899–1974, Guatemalan novelist and poet. His novels include *El Señor Presidente* (1946). Nobel prize for literature 1967

astute *adj* quick to notice or understand [Latin *astutus*] **> astutely** *adv* **> astuteness** *n*

Asunción *n* the capital and chief port of Paraguay, on the Paraguay River, 1530 km (950 miles) from the Atlantic. Pop: 1 750 000 (2005 est)

asunder *adv, adj* literary into parts or pieces; apart

Aswan, Assuan or **Assouan** *n* an ancient town in SE Egypt, on the Nile, just below the First Cataract. Pop: 249 000 (2005 est). Ancient name: **Syene**

Aswan High Dam *n* a dam on the Nile forming a reservoir (Lake Nasser) extending 480 km (300 miles) from the First to the Third Cataracts: opened in 1971, it was built 6 km (4 miles) upstream from the old **Aswan Dam** (built in 1902 and twice raised). Height of dam: 109 m (365 ft)

asylum *n* **1** refuge granted to a political refugee from a foreign country **2** (formerly) a mental hospital [Greek *asulon*]

asymmetric bars (ass-sim-**met**-rik, ay-sim-**met**-rik) *pl n* gymnastics a pair of bars parallel to each other but at different heights, used for various exercises

asymmetry *n* lack of symmetry **> asymmetric** or **asymmetrical** *adj*

asymptote (ass-im-tote) *n* a straight line that is closely approached but never met by a curve [Greek *asumptōtos* not falling together] **> asymptotic** *adj*

Asyut or **Assiut** *n* an ancient city in central Egypt, on the Nile. Pop: 417 000 (2005 est). Ancient Greek name: **Lycopolis**

at *prep* **1** indicating location or position: *she had planted a vegetable garden at the back* **2** towards; in the direction of: *she was staring at the wall behind him* **3** indicating position in time: *we arrived at 12.30* **4** engaged in: *the innocent laughter of children at play* **5** during the passing of: *she works at night as a nurse's aide* **6** for; in exchange for: *crude oil is selling at its lowest price since September* **7** indicating the object of an emotion: *I'm angry at you because you were rude to me* [Old English *æt*]

At *chem* astatine

at. **1** atmosphere **2** atomic

Atacama Desert *n* a desert region along the W coast of South America, mainly in N Chile: a major source of nitrates. Area: about 80 000 sq km (31 000 sq miles)

Atahualpa or **Atabalipa** *n* ?1500–33, the last Inca emperor of Peru (1525–33), who was put to death by the Spanish under Pizarro

Atatürk *n* Kemal, real name *Mustafa Kemal*. 1881–1938, Turkish general and statesman; founder of the Turkish republic and president of Turkey (1923–38), who westernized and secularized the country

atavism (at-a-viz-zum) *n* **1** the recurrence of primitive characteristics that were present in distant ancestors but not in more recent ones **2** reversion to a former type [Latin *atavus* great-grandfather's grandfather, ancestor] **> atavistic** *adj*

ataxia *n* pathol lack of muscular coordination [Greek] **> ataxic** *adj*

Atbara *n* **1** a town in NE Sudan. Pop: 110 000 (2005 est) **2** a river in NE Africa, rising in N Ethiopia and flowing through E Sudan to the Nile at Atbara. Length: over 800 km (500 miles)

ate *vb* the past tense of **eat**

atelier (at-tell-yay) *n* an artist's studio

Atget *n* (Jean) Eugène Auguste. 1856–1927, French photographer, noted for his pictures of Parisian life

Athabaska or **Athabasca** *n* **1** Lake Athabaska a lake in W Canada, in NW Saskatchewan and NE Alberta. Area: about 7770 sq km (3000 sq miles) **2** a river in W Canada, rising in the Rocky Mountains and flowing northeast to Lake Athabaska. Length: 1230 km (765 miles)

Athanasius *n* Saint. ?296–373 AD, patriarch of Alexandria who championed Christian orthodoxy against Arianism. Feast day: May 2 **> Athanasian** *adj*

atheism (aith-ee-iz-zum) *n* the belief that there is no God [Greek *a-* without + *theos* god] **> atheist** *n*

Athelstan *n* ?895–939 AD, king of Wessex and Mercia (924–939 AD), who extended his kingdom to include most of England

Athena or **Athene** *n* Greek myth the goddess of wisdom

Athenaeum or sometimes US **Atheneum** *n* **1** (in ancient Greece) a building sacred to the goddess Athena, esp. the Athenian temple that served as a gathering place for the learned **2** (in imperial Rome) the academy of learning established near the Forum in about 135 AD by Hadrian

Athenian *n* **1** a native or inhabitant of Athens ▷ *adj* **2** of or relating to Athens

Athens *n* the capital of Greece, in the southeast near the Saronic Gulf: became capital after independence in 1834; ancient city-state, most powerful in the 5th century BC;

a

contains the hill citadel of the Acropolis. Pop: 3 238 000 (2005 est). Greek name: **Athinai, Athina**

atherosclerosis *n, pl* **-ses** a disease in which deposits of fat cause the walls of the arteries to thicken [Greek *athērōma* tumour + SCLEROSIS] ⟩ **atherosclerotic** *adj*

Atherton *n* Mike, full name *Michael Andrew Atherton*. born 1968, English cricketer: played for Lancashire (1987–2001) and England (1989–2001); captain of England (1993–1998)

athlete *n* **1** a person trained to compete in sports or exercises **2** *chiefly Brit* a competitor in track-and-field events [Greek *athlos* a contest]

athlete's foot *n* a fungal infection of the skin of the foot

athletic *adj* **1** physically fit or strong **2** of or for an athlete or athletics ⟩ **athletically** *adv* ⟩ **athleticism** *n*

athletics *pl n Brit and Austral* track-and-field events

at-home *n Brit and Austral* a social gathering in a person's home

Athos *n* Mount Athos a mountainous peninsula in NE Greece: location of the Monastic Republic of Mount Athos, an autonomous administrative division of Greece since 1927; inhabited by Eastern Orthodox monks in about 20 monasteries, some founded in the 10th century; prohibited to women and children. Pop: 1942 (2001)

athwart *prep* **1** across ▷ *adv* **2** transversely; from one side to another

atigi *n* a type of parka worn by the Inuit in Canada

Atkins *n* Robert C. 1930–2003, US physician, cardiologist, and nutritionist. An advocate of complementary medicine, he devised a widely-used diet (the **Atkins diet**) based on controlled intake of carbohydrates for weight management and disease prevention

Atkinson *n* Sir Harry Albert. 1831–92, New Zealand statesman, born in England: prime minister of New Zealand (1876–77; 1883–84; 1887–91)

Atlanta *n* a city in N Georgia: the state capital. Pop: 423 019 (2003 est)

Atlantic *adj* of the Atlantic Ocean, the world's second largest ocean, bounded by the Arctic, the Antarctic, America, and Europe and Africa [Greek *(pelagos) Atlantikos* (the sea) of Atlas (so called because it lay beyond the Atlas Mountains)]

Atlantic City *n* a resort in SE New Jersey on Absecon Beach, an island on the Atlantic coast. Pop: 40 385 (2003 est)

Atlantic Intracoastal Waterway *n* a system of inland and coastal waterways along the Atlantic coast of the US from Cape Cod to Florida Bay. Length: 2495 km (1550 miles)

Atlanticism *n* belief in close economic and military cooperation between Europe and the United States ⟩ **Atlanticist** *n*

Atlantic Ocean *n* the world's second largest ocean, bounded in the north by the Arctic, in the south by the Antarctic, in the west by North and South America, and in the east by Europe and Africa. Greatest depth: 9220 m (30 246 ft). Area: about 81 585 000 sq km (31 500 000 sq miles)

Atlantic Provinces *pl n* the Atlantic Provinces certain of the Canadian provinces with coasts facing the Gulf of St Lawrence or the Atlantic: New Brunswick, Nova Scotia, Prince Edward Island, and Newfoundland and Labrador

Atlantis *n* (in ancient legend) a continent said to have sunk beneath the Atlantic west of Gibraltar

atlas *n* a book of maps [because *Atlas*, a Titan in Greek mythology, was shown supporting the heavens in 16th-century books of maps]

Atlas Mountains *pl n* a mountain system of N Africa, between the Mediterranean and the Sahara. Highest peak: Mount Toubkal, 4165 m (13 664 ft)

ATM automated teller machine

atmosphere *n* **1** the mass of gases surrounding the earth or any other heavenly body **2** the air in a particular place **3** a pervasive feeling or mood: *the atmosphere was tense* **4** a unit of pressure equal to the normal pressure of the air at sea level [Greek *atmos* vapour + *sphaira* sphere] ⟩ **atmospheric** *adj* ⟩ **atmospherically** *adv*

atmospherics *pl n* radio interference caused by electrical disturbance in the atmosphere

atoll *n* a circular coral reef surrounding a lagoon [*atollon*, native name in the Maldive Islands]

atom *n* **1 a** the smallest unit of matter which can take part in a chemical reaction **b** this entity as a source of nuclear energy **2** a very small amount [Greek *atomos* that cannot be divided]

atom bomb *n* same as **atomic bomb**

atomic *adj* **1** of or using atomic bombs or atomic energy **2** of atoms ⟩ **atomically** *adv*

atomic bomb *or* **atom bomb** *n* a type of bomb in which the energy is provided by nuclear fission

atomic energy *n* same as **nuclear energy**

atomic mass unit *n* a unit of mass that is equal to one twelfth of the mass of an atom of carbon-12

atomic number *n* the number of protons in the nucleus of an atom of an element

atomic theory *n* any theory in which matter is regarded as consisting of atoms

atomic weight *n* the ratio of the average mass per atom of an element to one twelfth of the mass of an atom of carbon-12

atomize *or* **-ise** *vb* **-izing, -ized** *or* **-ising, -ised** **1** to separate into free atoms **2** to reduce to fine particles or spray **3** to destroy by nuclear weapons

atomizer *or* **-iser** *n* a device for reducing a liquid to a fine spray

atonal (eh-tone-al) *adj* (of music) not written in an established key ⟩ **atonality** *n*

atone *vb* **atoning, atoned** to make amends (for a sin, crime, or wrongdoing)

atonement *n* **1** something done to make amends for wrongdoing **2** *Christian theol* the reconciliation of humankind with God through the sacrificial death of Christ [Middle English *at onement* in harmony]

atop *prep* on top of

atrium *n, pl* **atria** **1** *anatomy* the upper chamber of each half of the heart **2** a central hall that extends through several storeys in a modern building **3** the open main court of an ancient Roman house [Latin] ⟩ **atrial** *adj*

atrocious *adj* **1** extremely cruel or wicked **2** horrifying or shocking **3** *informal* very bad [Latin *atrox* dreadful] ⟩ **atrociously** *adv*

atrocity *n* **1** behaviour that is wicked or cruel **2** (*pl* **-ties**) an act of extreme cruelty

atrophy (at-trof-fee) *n, pl* **-phies** **1** a wasting away of a physical organ or part **2** a failure to grow ▷ *vb* **-phies, -phying, -phied** **3** to waste away [Greek *atrophos* ill-fed]

atropine *n* a poisonous alkaloid obtained from deadly nightshade [New Latin *atropa* deadly nightshade]

attach *vb* **1** to join, fasten, or connect **2** to attribute or ascribe: *he attaches particular importance to the proposed sale* **3** attach oneself *or* be attached to to become associated with or join [Old French *atachier*]

attaché (at-tash-shay) *n* a specialist attached to a diplomatic mission [French]

attaché case *n* a flat rectangular briefcase for carrying papers

attached *adj* **1** married, engaged, or in an exclusive sexual relationship **2** attached to fond of

attachment *n* **1** affection or regard for (someone or something) **2** an accessory that can be fitted to a device to change what it can do **3** a computer file sent with an e-mail

attack *vb* **1** to launch a physical assault (against) **2** to criticize vehemently **3** to set about (a job or problem) with vigour **4** to affect adversely: *BSE attacks the animal's*

a

brain **5** to take the initiative in a game or sport ▷ *n* **6** the act of attacking **7** any sudden appearance of a disease or symptoms: *a bad attack of mumps* [Old Italian *attaccare*]
> attacker *n*

attain *vb* **1** to manage to do or get (something): *the country attained economic growth* **2** to reach [Latin *attingere*]
> attainable *adj*

attainment *n* an achievement or the act of achieving something

attar *n* a perfume made from damask roses [Persian *'atir* perfumed]

attempt *vb* **1** to make an effort (to do or achieve something); try ▷ *n* **2** an endeavour to achieve something; effort **3 attempt on someone's life** an attack on someone with the intention to kill [Latin *attemptare*]

> **USAGE** *Attempt* should not be used in the passive when followed by an infinitive: *attempts were made to find a solution* (not *a solution was attempted to be found*).

Attenborough *n* **1** Sir David. born 1926, British naturalist and broadcaster; noted esp. for his TV series *Life on Earth* (1978), *The Living Planet* (1983), *The Life of Birds* (1998), *The Life of Mammals* (2002), and *First Life* (2010) **2** his brother, **Richard**, Baron Attenborough. 1923–2014, British film actor, director, and producer; his films include *Gandhi* (1982), *Cry Freedom* (1987), and *Shadowlands* (1993)

attend *vb* **1** to be present at (an event) **2** to go regularly to a school, college, etc. **3** to look after: *the actors lounged in their canvas chairs, attended by sycophants* **4** to pay attention **5 attend to** to apply oneself to: *I've a few things I must attend to* [Latin *attendere* to stretch towards]

attendance *n* **1** the act of attending **2** the number of people present **3** regularity in attending

attendant *n* **1** a person who assists, guides, or provides a service ▷ *adj* **2** associated: *nuclear power and its attendant dangers* **3** being in attendance

attendee *n* a person who is present at a specified event

attention *n* **1** concentrated direction of the mind **2** consideration, notice, or observation **3** detailed care or treatment **4** the alert position in military drill **5 attentions** acts of courtesy: *the attentions of men seemed to embarrass her*

attentive *adj* **1** paying close attention **2** considerately helpful: *at society parties he is attentive to his wife*
> attentively *adv* **> attentiveness** *n*

attenuated *adj* **1** weakened **2** thin and extended [Latin *attenuare* to weaken] **> attenuation** *n*

attest *vb* **1** to affirm or prove the truth of **2** to bear witness to (an act or event) [Latin *testari* to bear witness]
> attestation *n*

attested *adj* Brit (of cattle) certified to be free from a disease, such as tuberculosis

attic *n* a space or room within the roof of a house [from the ATTIC style of architecture]

Attic *adj* **1** of or relating to Attica, its inhabitants, or the dialect of Greek spoken there, esp. in classical times **2** (*often not cap*) classically elegant, simple, or pure: *an Attic style* ▷ *n* **3** the dialect of Ancient Greek spoken and written in Athens: the chief literary dialect of classical Greek

Attica *n* a region and department of E central Greece: in ancient times the territory of Athens. Capital: Athens. Pop: 3 336 700 (2001). Area: 14 157 sq km (5466 sq miles)

Attila *n* ?406–453 AD, king of the Huns, who devastated much of the Roman Empire, invaded Gaul in 451 AD, but was defeated by the Romans and Visigoths at Châlons-sur-Marne

attire *n* clothes, esp. fine or formal ones [Old French *atirier* to put in order]

attired *adj* dressed in a specified way

attitude *n* **1** the way a person thinks and behaves **2** a position of the body **3** *informal* a hostile manner **4** the

orientation of an aircraft or spacecraft in relation to some plane or direction [Latin *aptus* apt]

attitudinize *or* **-nise** *vb* **-nizing, -nized** *or* **-nising, -nised** to adopt a pose or opinion for effect

Attlee *n* Clement Richard, 1st Earl Attlee. 1883–1967, British statesman; prime minister (1945–51); leader of the Labour party (1935–55). His government instituted the welfare state, with extensive nationalization

attorney *n* **1** a person legally appointed to act for another **2** US a lawyer [Old French *atourner* to direct to]

attorney general *n*, *pl* **attorneys general** *or* **attorney generals** a chief law officer of some governments

attract *vb* **1** to arouse the interest or admiration of **2** (of a magnet) to draw (something) closer by exerting a force on it [Latin *attrahere* to draw towards]

attraction *n* **1** the act or quality of attracting **2** an interesting or desirable feature: *the Scottishness of Scott is an attraction, but by no means his only merit* **3** an object or place that people visit for interest: *this carefully preserved tourist attraction* **4** (of a magnet) a force by which one object attracts another

attractive *adj* appealing to the senses or mind
> attractively *adv* **> attractiveness** *n*

attribute *vb* **-uting, -uted** **1 attribute to** to regard as belonging to or produced by: *a play attributed to William Shakespeare* ▷ *n* **2** a quality or feature representative of a person or thing [Latin *attribuere* to associate with]
> attributable *adj* **> attribution** *n*

attributive *adj grammar* (of an adjective) coming before the noun modified

attrition *n* constant wearing down to weaken or destroy: *a war of attrition* [Latin *atterere* to weaken]

Attu *n* the westernmost of the Aleutian Islands, off the coast of SW Alaska: largest of the Near Islands

attune *vb* **-tuning, -tuned** to adjust or accustom (a person or thing)

ATV all-terrain vehicle: a vehicle with wheels designed to travel on rough ground

Atwood *n* Margaret (Eleanor) born 1939, Canadian poet and novelist. Her novels include *Lady Oracle* (1976), *The Handmaid's Tale* (1986), *Alias Grace* (1996), the Booker Prize-winning *The Blind Assassin* (2000), and *Oryx and Crake* (2003)

atypical (eh-**tip**-ik-kl) *adj* not typical **> atypically** *adv*

Au *chem* gold [Latin *aurum*]

AU **1** African Union **2** Also: **a.u.** angstrom unit **3** Also: **a.u.** astronomical unit

Aube *n* **1** a department of N central France, in Champagne-Ardenne region. Capital: Troyes. Pop: 293 925 (2003 est). Area: 6026 sq km (2350 sq miles) **2** a river in N central France, flowing northwest to the Seine. Length: about 225 km (140 miles)

Auber *n* Daniel François Esprit. 1782–1871, French composer, who was prominent in development of opéra comique. His works include 48 operas

aubergine (oh-bur-zheen) *n* Brit the dark purple fruit of a tropical plant, cooked and eaten as a vegetable [French, from Arabic *al-bādindjān*]

Aubervilliers *n* an industrial suburb of Paris, on the Seine. Pop: 63 136 (1999). Former name: *French* **Notre-Dame-des-Vertus**

Aubrey *n* John. 1626–97, English antiquary and author, noted for his vivid biographies of his contemporaries, *Brief Lives* (edited 1898)

aubrietia (aw-**bree**-sha) *n* a trailing purple-flowered rock plant [after Claude *Aubriet*, painter of flowers and animals]

auburn *adj* (of hair) reddish-brown [(originally meaning: blond) Latin *albus* white]

Aubusson *n* **1** a town in central France, in the Creuse department: a centre for flat-woven carpets and for tapestries since the 16th century. Pop: 4662 (1999) ▷ *adj* **2** denoting or relating to these carpets or tapestries

Auckland *n* the chief port of New Zealand, in the

northern part of North Island: former capital of New Zealand (1840–65). Pop: 450 300 (2010 est)

Auckland Islands *pl n* a group of six uninhabited islands, south of New Zealand. Area: 611 sq km (234 sq miles)

auction *n* **1** a public sale at which articles are sold to the highest bidder ▷ *vb* **2** to sell by auction [Latin *auctio* an increasing]

auctioneer *n* a person who conducts an auction

audacious *adj* **1** recklessly bold or daring **2** impudent or presumptuous [Latin *audax* bold] **> audacity** *n*

Aude *n* a department of S France on the Gulf of Lions, in Languedoc-Roussillon region. Capital: Carcassonne. Pop: 321 734 (2003 est). Area: 6342 sq km (2473 sq miles)

Auden *n* W(ystan) H(ugh). 1907–73, US poet, dramatist, critic, and librettist, born in Britain; noted for his lyric and satirical poems and for plays written in collaboration with Christopher Isherwood

audible *adj* loud enough to be heard [Latin *audire* to hear] **> audibility** *n* **> audibly** *adv*

audience *n* **1** a group of spectators or listeners at a concert or play **2** the people reached by a book, film, or radio or television programme **3** a formal interview [Latin *audire* to hear]

audio *adj* **1** of or relating to sound or hearing **2** of or for the transmission or reproduction of sound [Latin *audire* to hear]

audio book *n* a reading of a book recorded on tape

audio frequency *n* a frequency in the range 20 hertz to 20 000 hertz, audible to the human ear

audiometer (aw-dee-om-it-er) *n* an instrument for testing hearing

audiotypist *n* a typist trained to type from a dictating machine **> audiotyping** *n*

audiovisual *adj* involving both hearing and sight: *audiovisual teaching aids*

audit *n* **1** an official inspection of business accounts, conducted by an independent qualified accountant **2** any thoroughgoing assessment or review: *an audit of their lifestyle* ▷ *vb* **auditing, audited 3** to examine (business accounts) officially [Latin *audire* to hear]

audition *n* **1** a test of a performer's or musician's ability for a particular role or job ▷ *vb* **2** to test or be tested in an audition [Latin *audire* to hear]

auditor *n* a person qualified to audit accounts [Latin *auditor* a hearer]

auditorium *n, pl* **-toriums** *or* **-toria 1** the area of a concert hall or theatre in which the audience sits **2** *US and Canad* a building for public meetings [Latin]

auditory *adj* of or relating to hearing [Latin *audire* to hear]

Audubon *n* John James. 1785–1851, US naturalist and artist, noted particularly for his paintings of birds in *Birds of America* (1827–38)

Auer *n* Karl, Baron von Welsbach. 1858–1929, Austrian chemist who discovered the alloy of cerium and iron used for flints in cigarette lighters and invented the incandescent gas mantle

Auerbach *n* Frank (Helmuth). born 1931, British painter, born in Germany, noted esp. for his use of impasto

au fait (oh fay) *adj* **1** (usually foll. by *with*) fully informed (about) **2** expert [French: to the point]

auf Wiedersehen (owf vee-der-zay-en) *interj* goodbye [German]

Aug. August

Augean (aw-jee-an) *adj* extremely dirty or corrupt [from *Augeas*, in Greek mythology, king whose filthy stables Hercules cleaned in one day]

auger *n* a pointed tool for boring holes [Old English *nafugār* nave (ie hub of a wheel) spear]

aught *pron old-fashioned or literary* anything whatever: *for aught I know* [Old English *āwiht*]

augment *vb* to make or become greater in number or strength [Latin *augere* to increase] **> augmentation** *n*

augmented reality *n* an artificial environment created through the combination of real-world and computer-generated data

au gratin (oh grat-tan) *adj* cooked with a topping of breadcrumbs and sometimes cheese [French]

Augsburg *n* a city in S Germany, in Bavaria: founded by the Romans in 14 BC; site of the diet that produced the **Peace of Augsburg** (1555), which ended the struggles between Lutherans and Catholics in the Holy Roman Empire and established the principle that each ruler should determine the form of worship in his lands. Pop: 259 217 (2003 est). Roman name: **Augusta Vindelicorum**

augur *vb* to be a good or bad sign of future events: *a double fault on the opening point did not augur well* [Latin: diviner of omens]

augury *n* **1** the foretelling of the future **2** (*pl* **-ries**) an omen

august *adj* dignified and imposing [Latin *augustus*]

August *n* the eighth month of the year [Latin, after the emperor *Augustus*]

Augusta *n* **1** a city in the US, in Georgia. Pop: 193 316 (2003 est) (including Richmond) **2** a port in S Italy, in E Sicily. Pop: 33 820 (2001) **3** a town in the US, in Maine: the state capital; founded (1628) as a trading post; timber industry. Pop: 18 618 (2003 est)

Augustan *adj* **1** of the Roman emperor Augustus Caesar or the poets writing during his reign **2** of any literary period noted for refinement and classicism

Augustine *n* **1** Saint. 354–430 AD, one of the Fathers of the Christian Church; bishop of Hippo in North Africa (396–430), who profoundly influenced both Catholic and Protestant theology. His most famous works are *Confessions*, a spiritual autobiography, and *De Civitate Dei*, a vindication of the Christian Church. Feast day: Aug 28 **2** Saint. died 604 AD, Roman monk, sent to Britain (597 AD) to convert the Anglo-Saxons to Christianity and to establish the authority of the Roman See over the native Celtic Church; became the first archbishop of Canterbury (601–604). Feast day: May 26 or 27 **3** a member of an Augustinian order

Augustus *n* original name *Gaius Octavianus*; after his adoption by Julius Caesar (44 BC) known as *Gaius Julius Caesar Octavianus*. 63 BC–14 AD, Roman statesman, a member of the second triumvirate (43 BC–27 BC). After defeating Mark Antony at Actium (31 BC), he became first emperor of Rome, adopting the title Augustus (27 BC)

auk *n* a northern sea bird with a heavy body, short wings, and black-and-white plumage [Old Norse *ālka*]

auld lang syne *n* times past [Scots, literally: old long since]

Auld Reekie *n Scot* a nickname for **Edinburgh** [literally: Old Smoky]

Aulis *n* an ancient town in E central Greece, in Boeotia: traditionally the harbour from which the Greeks sailed at the beginning of the Trojan war

Auliye-Ata *n* a former name of **Taraz**

Aung San Suu Kyi *n* born 1945, Burmese politician; cofounder (1988) and general secretary (1988–91; 1995–) of the National League for Democracy; Nobel peace prize 1991; released (2010) from a lengthy house arrest; elected to the Burmese House of Representatives in 2012

aunt *n* **1** a sister of one's father or mother **2** the wife of one's uncle **3** a child's term of address for a female friend of the parents [Latin *amita* a father's sister]

auntie *or* **aunty** *n, pl* **-ies** *informal* an aunt

Aunt Sally *n, pl* **-lies 1** a figure used in fairgrounds as a target **2** any target for insults or criticism

au pair *n* a young foreign woman who does housework in return for board and lodging [French]

aura *n, pl* **auras** *or* **aurae 1** a distinctive air or quality associated with a person or thing **2** any invisible emanation [Greek: breeze]

aural *adj* of or using the ears or hearing [Latin *auris* ear] **> aurally** *adv*

Aurangzeb or **Aurungzeb** n 1618–1707, Mogul emperor of Hindustan (1658–1707), whose reign marked both the height of Mogul prosperity and the decline of its power through the revolts of the Marathas

aureate adj literary **1** covered with gold **2** (of a style of writing or speaking) excessively elaborate [Latin aurum gold]

Aurelian n Latin name Lucius Domitius Aurelianus. ?212–275 AD, Roman emperor (270–275), who conquered Palmyra (273) and restored political unity to the Roman Empire

aureole or **aureola** n **1** a ring of light surrounding the head of a figure represented as holy; halo **2** the sun's corona, visible as a faint halo during eclipses [Latin aurum gold]

au revoir (oh riv-vwahr) interj goodbye [French]

auric adj of or containing gold in the trivalent state [Latin aurum gold]

Auric n Georges. 1899–1983, French composer; one of Les Six. His works include ballet and film music

auricle n **1** the upper chamber of the heart **2** the outer part of the ear [Latin auris ear] **>** **auricular** adj

auricula n, pl **-lae** or **-las** an alpine primrose with leaves shaped like a bear's ear [Latin auris ear]

auriferous adj containing gold [Latin aurum gold + ferre to bear]

Aurigny n the French name for **Alderney** (1)

Auriol n Vincent. 1884–1966, French statesman; president of the Fourth Republic (1947–54)

aurochs n, pl **-rochs** a recently extinct European wild ox [German]

aurora n, pl **-ras** or **-rae 1** an atmospheric phenomenon of bands of light sometimes seen in the polar regions **2** poetic the dawn [Latin: dawn]

Aurora n another name for **Maewo**

aurora australis n the aurora seen around the South Pole [New Latin: southern aurora]

aurora borealis n the aurora seen around the North Pole [New Latin: northern aurora]

Aus. 1 Australia(n) **2** Austria(n)

Auschwitz n an industrial town in S Poland; site of a Nazi concentration camp during World War II. Pop: 40 686 (2007 est). Polish name: **Oświęcim**

auscultation n the listening to of the internal sounds of the body, usually with a stethoscope, to help with medical diagnosis [Latin auscultare to listen attentively]

Ausonius n Decimus Magnus. ?310–?395 AD, Latin poet, born in Gaul

auspices (aw-spiss-siz) pl n under the auspices of with the support and approval of [Latin auspicium augury from birds]

auspicious adj showing the signs of future success

> **USAGE** The use of auspicious to mean 'very special' (as in this auspicious occasion) should be avoided.

Aussie n, adj informal Australian

Aust. 1 Australia(n) **2** Austria(n)

Austen n Jane. 1775–1817, English novelist, noted particularly for the insight and delicate irony of her portrayal of middle-class families. Her completed novels are Sense and Sensibility (1811), Pride and Prejudice (1813), Mansfield Park (1814), Emma (1816), Northanger Abbey (1818), and Persuasion (1818)

austere adj **1** stern or severe: his austere and serious attitude to events **2** self-disciplined or ascetic: an extraordinarily austere and puritanical organization **3** severely simple or plain: the austere backdrop of grey [Greek austēros astringent]

austerity n, pl **-ties 1** the state of being austere **2** reduced availability of luxuries and consumer goods

Austerlitz n a town in the Czech Republic, in Moravia: site of Napoleon's victory over the Russian and Austrian armies in 1805. Pop: 1795 (2007 est). Czech name: **Slavkov**

Austin[1] n a city in central Texas, on the Colorado River: state capital since 1845. Pop: 672 011 (2003 est)

Austin[2] n **1** Herbert, 1st Baron. 1866–1941, British automobile engineer, who founded the Austin Motor Company **2** John. 1790–1859, British jurist, whose book The Province of Jurisprudence Determined (1832) greatly influenced legal theory and the English legal system **3** J(ohn) L(angshaw). 1911–60, English philosopher, whose lectures Sense and Sensibilia and How to do Things with Words were published posthumously in 1962

austral adj of or from the south [Latin auster the south wind]

Austral. 1 Australasia **2** Australia(n)

Australasia n **1** Australia, New Zealand, and neighbouring islands in the S Pacific Ocean **2** (loosely) the whole of Oceania

Australasian adj of Australia, New Zealand, and neighbouring islands

Australia n a country and the smallest continent, situated between the Indian Ocean and the Pacific: a former British colony, now an independent member of the Commonwealth, constitutional links with Britain formally abolished in 1986; consists chiefly of a low plateau, mostly arid in the west, with the basin of the Murray River and the Great Dividing Range in the east and the Great Barrier Reef off the NE coast. Official language: English. Religion: Christian majority. Currency: dollar. Capital: Canberra. Pop: 23 029 674 (2013 est). Area: 7 682 300 sq km (2 966 150 sq miles)

Australia Day n a public holiday in Australia on January 26

Australian adj **1** of or relating to Australia or its inhabitants **▷** n **2** a native or inhabitant of Australia

Australian Alps pl n a mountain range in SE Australia, in E Victoria and SE New South Wales. Highest peak: Mount Kosciuszko, 2195 m (7316 ft)

Australian Antarctic Territory n the area of Antarctica, other than Adélie Land, that is claimed by Australia (claims are suspended under the Antarctic Treaty), lying south of latitude 60°S and between longitudes 45°E and 160°E

Australian Capital Territory n a territory of SE Australia, within New South Wales: consists of two exclaves, one containing Canberra, the capital of Australia, and one at Jervis Bay (the latter sometimes regarded as a separate entity). Pop: 373 100 (2012 est). Former name: **Federal Capital Territory**

Austral Islands pl n another name for the **Tubuai Islands**

Austrasia n the eastern region of the kingdom of the Merovingian Franks that had its capital at Metz and lasted from 511 AD until 814 AD. It covered the area now comprising NE France, Belgium, and western Germany

Austria n a republic in central Europe: ruled by the Hapsburgs from 1282 to 1918; formed a dual monarchy with Hungary in 1867 and became a republic in 1919; a member of the European Union; contains part of the Alps, the Danube basin in the east, and extensive forests. Official language: German. Religion: Roman Catholic majority. Currency: euro. Capital: Vienna. Pop: 8 221 646 (2013 est). Area: 83 849 sq km (32 374 sq miles). German name: **Österreich**

Austria-Hungary n the Dual Monarchy established in 1867, consisting of what are now Austria, Hungary, the Czech Republic, Slovakia, Slovenia, Croatia, and Bosnia-Herzegovina, and parts of Poland, Romania, Ukraine, and Italy. The empire was broken up after World War I

Austrian adj **1** of or relating to Austria or its inhabitants **▷** n **2** a native or inhabitant of Austria

Austro-Hungarian adj of or relating to the Dual Monarchy of Austria-Hungary (1867–1918)

Austronesia n the islands of the central and S Pacific, including Indonesia, Melanesia, Micronesia, and Polynesia

Austronesian adj **1** of or relating to Austronesia, its peoples, or their languages ▷ *n* **2** another name for **Malayo-Polynesian**

autarchy (aw-tar-kee) *n, pl* **-chies** absolute power or autocracy [Greek *autarkhia*]

autarky (aw-tar-kee) *n, pl* **-kies** a policy of economic self-sufficiency [Greek *autarkeia*]

authentic *adj* **1** of undisputed origin or authorship; genuine **2** reliable or accurate **3** *music* using period instruments, scores, and playing techniques [Greek *authentikos*] ▷ **authentically** *adv* ▷ **authenticity** *n*

authenticate *vb* **-cating, -cated** to establish as genuine ▷ **authentication** *n*

author *n* **1** a person who writes a book, article, or other written work **2** an originator or creator [Latin *auctor*]

authoritarian *adj* **1** insisting on strict obedience to authority ▷ *n* **2** a person who insists on strict obedience to authority ▷ **authoritarianism** *n*

authoritative *adj* **1** recognized as being reliable: *the authoritative book on Shakespeare* **2** possessing authority; official ▷ **authoritatively** *adv*

authority *n, pl* **-ties** **1** the power to command, control, or judge others **2** a person or group with this power: *a third escapee turned himself in to the authorities* **3** a decision-making organization or government department: *the local authority* **4** an expert in a particular field **5** official permission: *he had no authority to negotiate* **6** a position that has the power to command, control, or judge others: *people in authority* **7** **on good authority** from reliable evidence **8** confidence resulting from expertise [Latin *auctor* author]

authorize *or* **-ise** *vb* **-izing, -ized** *or* **-ising, -ised** **1** to give authority to **2** to give official permission for ▷ **authorization** *or* **-isation** *n*

Authorized Version *n* the Authorized Version an English translation of the Bible published in 1611

authorship *n* **1** the origin or originator of a written work or plan **2** the profession of writing

autism *n* *psychiatry* abnormal self-absorption, usually affecting children, characterized by lack of response to people and limited ability to communicate [Greek *autos* self] ▷ **autistic** *adj*

auto *n, pl* **-tos** *US and Canad informal* short for **automobile**

auto- *or sometimes before a vowel* **aut-** *combining form* **1** self; of or by the same one: *autobiography* **2** self-propelling: *automobile* [Greek *autos* self]

autobahn *n* a motorway in German-speaking countries [German, from *Auto* car + *Bahn* road]

autobiography *n, pl* **-phies** an account of a person's life written by that person ▷ **autobiographer** *n* ▷ **autobiographical** *adj*

autoclave *n* an apparatus for sterilizing objects by steam under pressure [AUTO- + Latin *clavis* key]

autocracy *n, pl* **-cies** government by an individual with unrestricted authority

autocrat *n* **1** a ruler with absolute authority **2** a dictatorial person [AUTO- + Greek *kratos* power] ▷ **autocratic** *adj* ▷ **autocratically** *adv*

autocross *n* a sport in which cars race over a circuit of rough grass

Autocue *n* *trademark* an electronic television prompting device displaying a speaker's script, unseen by the audience

auto-da-fé (aw-toe-da-fay) *n, pl* **autos-da-fé** **1** *history* the ceremonial passing of sentence on heretics by the Spanish Inquisition **2** the burning to death of heretics [Portuguese, literally: act of the faith]

autofocus *n* a camera system in which the lens is focused automatically

autogiro *or* **autogyro** *n, pl* **-ros** a self-propelled aircraft resembling a helicopter but with an unpowered rotor

autograph *n* **1** a handwritten signature of a famous person ▷ *vb* **2** to write one's signature on or in [AUTO- + Greek *graphein* to write]

automat *n* *US* a vending machine

automate *vb* **-mating, -mated** to make (a manufacturing process) automatic

automated teller machine *n* *chiefly US* another name for **cash dispenser**

automatic *adj* **1** (of a device or mechanism) able to activate or regulate itself **2** (of a process) performed by automatic equipment **3** done without conscious thought **4** (of a firearm) utilizing some of the force of each explosion to reload and fire continuously **5** occurring as a necessary consequence: *the certificate itself carries no automatic legal benefits* ▷ *n* **6** an automatic firearm **7** a motor vehicle with automatic transmission [Greek *automatos* acting independently] ▷ **automatically** *adv*

automatic pilot *n* **1** a device that automatically maintains an aircraft on a preset course **2** **on automatic pilot** repeating an action or process without thought

automatic transmission *n* a transmission system in a motor vehicle in which the gears change automatically

automation *n* the use of automatic, often electronic, methods to control industrial processes

automaton *n, pl* **-tons** *or* **-ta** **1** a mechanical device operating under its own power **2** a person who acts mechanically [Greek *automatos* spontaneous]

automobile *n* *US and Canad* a motorcar

automotive *adj* **1** relating to motor vehicles **2** self-propelling

autonomous *adj* **1** having self-government **2** independent of others [AUTO- + Greek *nomos* law]

autonomy *n, pl* **-mies** **1** the right or state of self-government **2** freedom to determine one's own actions and behaviour [Greek *autonomia*]

autopilot *n* an automatic pilot

autopsy *n, pl* **-sies** examination of a corpse to determine the cause of death [Greek *autopsia* seeing with one's own eyes]

autoroute *n* a motorway in French-speaking countries [French, from *auto* car + *route* road]

autostrada *n* a motorway in Italian-speaking countries [Italian, from *auto* car + *strada* road]

autosuggestion *n* a process in which a person unconsciously supplies the means of influencing his or her own behaviour or beliefs

autumn *n* **1** the season of the year between summer and winter **2** a period of late maturity followed by a decline [Latin *autumnus*] ▷ **autumnal** *adj*

Auvergne *n* a region of S central France: largely mountainous, rising over 1800 m (6000 ft)

aux. auxiliary

Aux Cayes *n* the former name of **Les Cayes**

Auxerre *n* a town in central France, capital of Yonne department; Gothic cathedral. Pop: 38 800 (2006)

auxiliaries *pl n* foreign troops serving another nation

auxiliary *adj* **1** secondary or supplementary **2** supporting ▷ *n, pl* **-ries** **3** a person or thing that supports or supplements [Latin *auxilium* help]

auxiliary verb *n* a verb used to indicate the tense, voice, or mood of another verb, such as *will* in *I will go*

AV (of the Bible) Authorized Version

av. **1** average **2** avoirdupois

avail *vb* **1** to be of use, advantage, or assistance (to) **2** **avail oneself of** to make use of ▷ *n* **3** use or advantage: *to no avail* [Latin *valere* to be strong]

available *adj* **1** obtainable or accessible **2** able to be contacted and willing to talk: *a spokesman insisted she was not available for comment* ▷ **availability** *n* ▷ **availably** *adv*

avalanche *n* **1** a fall of large masses of snow and ice down a mountain **2** a sudden or overwhelming quantity of anything [French]

Avalon Peninsula *n* a large peninsula of Newfoundland, between Trinity and Placentia Bays. Area: about 10 000 sq km (4000 sq miles)

avant- (av-ong) *prefix* belonging to the avant-garde of a field: *avant-jazz*

a

avant-garde (av-ong-**gard**) *n* **1** those artists, writers, or musicians whose techniques and ideas are in advance of those generally accepted ▷ *adj* **2** using ideas or techniques in advance of those generally accepted [French: vanguard]

avarice (av-a-riss) *n* extreme greed for wealth [Latin *avere* to crave] **> avaricious** *adj*

avast *interj nautical* stop! cease! [probably Dutch *hou'vast* hold fast]

avatar *n* **1** *Hinduism* the appearance of a god in human or animal form **2** *computers* graphical representation of a person in a virtual environment, such as an online role-playing game [Sanskrit *avatāra* a going down]

Ave (ah-vay) *or* **Ave Maria** (ma-**ree**-a) *n* same as **Hail Mary** [Latin: hail, Mary!]

Ave. avenue

Avebury *n* a village in Wiltshire, site of an extensive Neolithic stone circle

Aveiro *n* a port in N central Portugal, on the **Aveiro lagoon**: ancient Roman town; linked by canal with the Atlantic Ocean. Pop: 73 335 (2001). Ancient name: **Talabriga**

Avellaneda *n* a city in E Argentina, an industrial suburb of Buenos Aires. Pop: 328 980 (2001)

avenge *vb* **avenging, avenged** to inflict a punishment in retaliation for (harm done) or on behalf of (the person harmed) [Latin *vindicare*] **> avenger** *n*

> **USAGE** The use of *avenge* with a reflexive pronoun was formerly considered incorrect, but is now acceptable: *she avenged herself on the man who killed her daughter.*

Aventine *n* one of the seven hills on which Rome was built

avenue *n* **1** a wide street **2** a road bordered by two rows of trees **3** a line of approach: *the United States was exhausting every avenue to achieve a diplomatic solution* [French, from *avenir* to come to]

aver (av-**vur**) *vb* **averring, averred** to state to be true [Latin *verus* true] **> averment** *n*

average *n* **1** the typical or normal amount or quality **2** the result obtained by adding the numbers or quantities in a set and dividing the total by the number of members in the set **3 on average** usually or typically ▷ *adj* **4** usual or typical **5** calculated as an average **6** mediocre or inferior ▷ *vb* **-aging, -aged 7** to calculate or estimate the average of **8** to amount to or be on average [Middle English *averay* loss arising from damage to ships, ultimately from Arabic *awār* damage]

Averno *n* a crater lake in Italy, near Naples: in ancient times regarded as an entrance to hell. Latin name: **Avernus** [from Latin, from Greek *aornos* without birds, from A⁻¹ + *ornis* bird; referring to the legend that the lake's sulphurous exhalations killed birds]

Averroës *n* Arabic name *ibn-Rushd*. 1126–88, Arab philosopher and physician in Spain, noted particularly for his attempts to reconcile Aristotelian philosophy with Islamic religion, which profoundly influenced Christian scholasticism

averse *adj* opposed: *he's not averse to publicity, of the right kind* [Latin *avertere* to turn from]

aversion *n* **1** extreme dislike or disinclination **2** a person or thing that arouses this

avert *vb* **1** to turn away: *he had to avert his eyes* **2** to ward off: *a final attempt to avert war* [Latin *avertere* to turn from]

Avesta *n* a collection of sacred writings of Zoroastrianism

Aveyron *n* a department of S France in Midi-Pyrénées region. Capital: Rodez. Pop: 266 940 (2003 est). Area: 8771 sq km (3421 sq miles)

avian (aiv-ee-an) *adj* of or like a bird: *the treatment of avian diseases* [Latin *avis* bird]

avian flu *n* another name for **bird flu** [Latin *avis* bird]

aviary *n, pl* **aviaries** a large enclosure in which birds are kept [Latin *avis* bird]

aviation *n* the art or science of flying aircraft [Latin *avis* bird]

aviator *n old-fashioned* the pilot of an aircraft **> aviatrix** *fem n*

Avicenna *n* Arabic name *ibn-Sina*. 980–1037, Arab philosopher and physician whose philosophical writings, which combined Aristotelianism with neo-Platonist ideas, greatly influenced scholasticism, and whose medical work *Qanun* was the greatest single influence on medieval medicine

avid *adj* **1** very keen or enthusiastic: *he is an avid football fan* **2** eager: *avid for economic development* [Latin *avere* to long for] **> avidity** *n* **> avidly** *adv*

Aviemore *n* a winter sports resort in Scotland, in Moray between the Monadhliath and Cairngorm Mountains. Pop: 2397 (2001)

Avignon *n* a city in SE France, on the Rhône: seat of the papacy (1309–77); famous 12th-century bridge, now partly destroyed. Pop: 94 787 (2006)

Ávila *n* a city in central Spain: 11th-century granite walls and Romanesque cathedral. Pop: 52 078 (2003 est)

Avlona *n* the ancient name for **Vlorë**

avocado *n, pl* **-dos** a pear-shaped tropical fruit with a leathery green skin and greenish-yellow flesh [Spanish *aguacate*]

avocation *n* **1** *Brit, Austral and NZ old-fashioned* a person's regular job **2** *formal* a hobby [Latin *avocare* to distract]

avocet *n* a long-legged shore bird with a long slender upward-curving bill [Italian *avocetta*]

Avogadro *n* Amedeo, *Conte di Quaregna*. 1776–1856, Italian physicist, noted for his work on gases

avoid *vb* **1** to refrain from doing **2** to prevent from happening **3** to keep out of the way of [Old French *esvuidier*] **> avoidable** *adj* **> avoidably** *adv* **> avoidance** *n*

avoirdupois *or* **avoirdupois weight** (av-er-de-**poise**) *n* a system of weights based on the pound, which contains 16 ounces [Old French *aver de peis* goods of weight]

Avon¹ *n* **1** a former county of SW England, created in 1974 from areas of N Somerset and S Gloucestershire: replaced in 1996 by the unitary authorities of Bath and North East Somerset (Somerset), North Somerset (Somerset), South Gloucestershire (Gloucestershire), and Bristol **2** a river in central England, rising in Northamptonshire and flowing southwest through Stratford-on-Avon to the River Severn at Tewkesbury. Length: 154 km (96 miles) **3** a river in SW England, rising in Gloucestershire and flowing south and west through Bristol to the Severn estuary at **Avonmouth**. Length: 120 km (75 miles) **4** a river in S England, rising in Wiltshire and flowing south to the English Channel. Length: about 96 km (60 miles)

Avon² *n* **Earl of**. title of (Anthony) **Eden**

avow *vb* **1** to state or affirm **2** to admit openly [Latin *advocare* to call upon] **> avowal** *n* **> avowed** *adj* **> avowedly** (a-**vow**-id-lee) *adv*

avuncular *adj* (of a man) friendly, helpful, and caring towards someone younger [Latin *avunculus* (maternal) uncle]

await *vb* **1** to wait for **2** to be in store for

awake *adj* **1** not sleeping **2** alert or aware: *awake to the danger* ▷ *vb* **awaking, awoke** *or* **awaked, awoken** *or* **awaked 3** to emerge or rouse from sleep **4** to become or cause to become alert [Old English *awacan*]

> **USAGE** See at wake¹.

awaken *vb* **1** to awake **2** to cause to be aware of: *anxieties awakened by reunification*

awakening *n* the start of a feeling or awareness in someone: *a picture of an emotional awakening*

award *vb* **1** to give (something) for merit **2** *law* to declare to be entitled, such as by decision of a court

▷ n **3** something awarded, such as a prize **4** *law* the decision of an arbitrator or court [Old French *eswarder* to decide after investigation]

aware *adj* **1 aware of** knowing about: *he's at least aware of the problem* **2** informed: *they are becoming more politically aware every day* [Old English *gewær*] **> awareness** *n*

awash *adv, adj* washed over by water

away *adv* **1** from a particular place: *I saw them walk away and felt absolutely desolated* **2** in or to another, a usual, or a proper place: *he decided to put the car away in the garage* **3** at a distance: *keep away from the windows* **4** out of existence: *the pillars rotted away* **5** indicating motion or distance from a normal or proper place: *the child shook her head and looked away* **6** continuously: *he continued to scribble away* ▷ *adj* **7** not present: *he had been away from home for years* **8** distant: *the castle was farther away than he had thought* **9** *sport* played on an opponent's ground [Old English *on weg* on way]

awayday *n* a day trip taken for pleasure [from *awayday ticket* a special-rate day return by train]

awe *n* **1** wonder and respect mixed with dread ▷ *vb*
awing, awed 2 to inspire with reverence or dread [Old Norse *agi*]

aweigh *adj nautical* (of an anchor) no longer hooked into the bottom

awesome *adj* **1** inspiring or displaying awe **2** *slang* excellent or outstanding

awestruck *adj* overcome or filled with awe

awful *adj* **1** very bad or unpleasant **2** *informal* considerable or great: *that's an awful lot of money, isn't it?* **3** *obsolete* inspiring reverence or dread ▷ *adv* **4** *not standard* very: *I'm working awful hard on my lines*

awfully *adv* **1** in an unpleasant way **2** *informal* very: *we were both awfully busy*

awhile *adv* for a brief period

awkward *adj* **1** clumsy or ungainly **2** embarrassed: *he was awkward and nervous around girls* **3** difficult to deal with: *the lawyer was in an awkward situation* **4** difficult to use or handle: *it was small but heavy enough to make it awkward to carry* **5** embarrassing: *there were several moments of awkward silence* [Old Norse *öfugr* turned the wrong way round] **> awkwardly** *adv* **> awkwardness** *n*

awl *n* a pointed hand tool for piercing wood, leather, etc. [Old English *æl*]

awn *n* any of the bristles growing from the flowering parts of certain grasses and cereals [Old English *agen* ear of grain]

awning *n* a canvas roof supported by a frame to give protection against the weather [origin unknown]

awoke *vb* a past tense and (now rare or dialectal) past participle of **awake**

awoken *vb* a past participle of **awake**

AWOL (eh-woll) *adj military* absent without leave but without intending to desert

awry (a-rye) *adv, adj* **1** with a twist to one side; askew: *my neck was really awry after the journey* **2** amiss or faulty: *if a gear gets stuck, the whole system goes awry* [Middle English *on wry*]

axe *or US* **ax** *n, pl* **axes 1** a hand tool with one side of its head sharpened to a cutting edge, used for felling trees and splitting timber **2 an axe to grind** a favourite topic one wishes to promote **3** *informal* a severe cut in spending or in the number of staff employed ▷ *vb* **axing, axed 4** *informal* to dismiss (employees), restrict (expenditure), or terminate (a project) [Old English *æx*]

Axelrod *n* Julius. 1912–2004, US neuropharmacologist, renowned for his work on catecholamines. Nobel prize for physiology or medicine (with von Euler and Bernard Katz) 1970

axes¹ *n* the plural of **axis**

axes² *n* the plural of **axe**

axial *adj* **1** forming or of an axis **2** in, on, or along an axis **> axially** *adv*

axil *n* the angle where the stalk of a leaf joins a stem [Latin *axilla* armpit]

axiom *n* **1** a generally accepted principle **2** a self-evident statement [Greek *axios* worthy]

axiomatic *adj* **1** containing axioms **2** self-evident or obvious **> axiomatically** *adv*

axis (ax-iss) *n, pl* **axes** (ax-eez) **1** a real or imaginary line about which a body can rotate or about which an object or geometrical construction is symmetrical **2** one of two or three reference lines used in coordinate geometry to locate a point in a plane or in space [Latin]

axle *n* a shaft on which a wheel or pair of wheels revolves [Old Norse *öxull*]

axolotl *n* an aquatic salamander of N America [Mexican Indian: water doll]

Axum *n* a variant spelling of **Aksum**

Ayacucho *n* a city in SE Peru: nearby is the site of the battle (1824) that won independence for Peru. Pop: 150 000 (2005 est)

ayah *n* (in parts of the former British Empire) a native maidservant or nursemaid [Hindi *āyā*]

ayatollah *n* one of a class of Islamic religious leaders in Iran [Arabic *aya* sign + *allah* God]

Ayckbourn *n* Sir Alan. born 1939, English dramatist. His plays include *Absurd Person Singular* (1973), the trilogy *The Norman Conquests* (1974), *A Chorus of Disapproval* (1985), *House and Garden* (2000), and *Private Fears in Public Places* (2004)

Aycliffe *n* a town in Co Durham: founded as a new town in 1947. Pop (including Newton Aycliffe): 25 655 (2001)

Aydin *or* **Aidin** *n* a town in SW Turkey: an ancient city of Lydia. Pop: 160 000 (2005 est). Ancient name: **Tralles**

aye *or* **ay** *interj* **1** *Brit, Austral and NZ* yes ▷ *n* **2** an affirmative vote or voter [probably from *I*, expressing assent]

Ayer *n* Sir Alfred Jules. 1910–89, English positivist philosopher, noted particularly for his antimetaphysical work *Language, Truth, and Logic* (1936)

Ayers Rock *n* another name for **Uluru**

Ayia Napa *n* a coastal resort in SE Cyprus. Pop: 9500 (2004 est)

Aykroyd *n* Dan. born 1952, Canadian film actor and screenwriter, best known for the television show *Saturday Night Live* (1975–80) and the films *The Blues Brothers* (1980), *Ghostbusters* (1984), and *Driving Miss Daisy* (1989)

Aylesbury *n* a town in SE central England, administrative centre of Buckinghamshire. Pop: 69 021 (2001)

Aylward *n* Gladys. 1903–70, English missionary in China

Aymé *n* Marcel. 1902–67, French writer: noted for his light and witty narratives

Ayodhya *n* an ancient town in N India, in Uttar Pradesh state: as the birthplace of Rama it is sacred to Hindus; also a Buddhist centre. Also called: **Ayodha, Awadh, Oudh**

Ayr *n* a port in SW Scotland, in South Ayrshire. Pop: 46 431 (2001)

Ayrshire *n* **1** a historical county of SW Scotland, formerly part of Strathclyde region (1975–96), now divided into the council areas of North Ayrshire, South Ayrshire, and East Ayrshire **2** any one of a hardy breed of brown-and-white dairy cattle

Ayub Khan *n* Mohammed. 1907–74, Pakistani field marshal; president of Pakistan (1958–69)

Ayutthaya *n* a city in S Thailand, on the Chao Phraya River: capital of the country until 1767; noted for its canals and ruins. Pop (province): 727 300 (2000). Also called: **Ayudhya, Ayuthia**

AZ Arizona

azalea (az-zale-ya) *n* a garden shrub grown for its showy flowers [Greek *azaleos* dry]

Azaña *n* Manuel. 1880–1940, Spanish statesman; president of the Spanish Republic (1936–39) until overthrown by Franco

Azania *n* another name for **South Africa** [perhaps from Arabic *Adzan* East Africa]

Azanian *n* **1** a native or inhabitant of Azania (another

a

name used esp. by many Black political activists for South Africa) ▷ *adj* **2** of or relating to Azania

Azbine *n* another name for Aïr

Azerbaijan *n* **1** a republic in NW Asia: the region was acquired by Russia from Persia in the early 19th century; became the Azerbaijan Soviet Socialist Republic in 1936 and gained independence in 1991; consists of dry subtropical steppes around the Aras and Kura rivers, surrounded by the Caucasus; contains the extensive Baku oilfields. Language: Azerbaijani (or Azeri). Religion: Shiite Muslim. Currency: manat. Capital: Baku. Pop: 9 590 159 (2013 est). Area: 86 600 sq km (33 430 sq miles) **2** a mountainous region of NW Iran, separated from the republic of Azerbaijan by the Aras River: divided administratively into **Eastern Azerbaijan** and **Western Azerbaijan**. Capitals: Tabriz and Orumiyeh. Pop: 2 119 524 (2002 est)

Azikiwe *n* Nnamdi 1904–96, Nigerian statesman; first president of Nigeria (1963–66)

azimuth *n* **1** the arc of the sky between the zenith and the horizon **2** *surveying* the horizontal angle of a bearing measured clockwise from the north [Arabic *as-samt* the path]

Azores *pl n* **the Azores** three groups of volcanic islands in the N Atlantic, since 1976 an autonomous region of Portugal. Capital: Ponta Delgada (on São Miguel). Pop: 241 762 (2001). Area: 2335 sq km (901 sq miles). Portuguese name: **Açores**

Azorín *n* real name *José Martínez Ruiz*. 1874–1967, Spanish writer: noted for his stories of the Spanish countryside

Azov *n* **Sea of Azov** a shallow arm of the Black Sea, to which it is connected by the Kerch Strait: almost entirely landlocked; fed chiefly by the River Don. Area: about 37 500 sq km (14 500 sq miles)

Aztec *n* **1** a member of a Mexican Indian race who established a great empire, overthrown by the Spanish in the early 16th century **2** the language of the Aztecs ▷ *adj* **3** of the Aztecs or their language [*Aztlan*, their traditional place of origin, literally: near the cranes]

azure *n* **1** the deep blue colour of a clear blue sky **2** *poetic* a clear blue sky ▷ *adj* **3** deep blue [Arabic *lāzaward* lapis lazuli]

Bb

b or **B** *n, pl* **b's, B's** or **Bs 1** the second letter of the English alphabet **2 from A to B** See **a** (2)

b *cricket* **1** bowled **2** bye

B 1 *music* the seventh note of the scale of C major **2** the second in a series, class, or rank **3** *chem* boron **4** *chess* bishop

b. born

B2B business-to-business; denoting trade between commercial organizations rather than between businesses and private customers

Ba *chem* barium

BA 1 Bachelor of Arts **2** British Airways

baa *vb* **baaing, baaed 1** (of a sheep) to make a characteristic bleating sound ▷ *n* **2** the cry made by a sheep

Baalbek *n* a town in E Lebanon: an important city in Phoenician and Roman times; extensive ruins. Pop: 150 000 (1998 est). Ancient name: **Heliopolis**

Baal Shem Tov or **Baal Shem Tob** *n* original name *Israel ben Eliezer* ?1700–60, Jewish religious leader, teacher, and healer in Poland: founder of modern Hasidism

baas *n S African* a boss [Afrikaans]

baaskap *n* (in South Africa) control by Whites of non-Whites [Afrikaans]

Bab *n* **the Bab** title of *Mirza Ali Mohammed*. 1819–50, Persian religious leader: founded Babism; executed as a heretic of Islam [from Persian *bāb* gate, from Arabic]

babaco *n* a greenish-yellow egg-shaped fruit

Babbage *n* **Charles** 1792–1871, English mathematician and inventor, who built a calculating machine that anticipated the modern electronic computer

babble *vb* **-bling, -bled 1** to talk in a quick, foolish, or muddled way **2** to make meaningless sounds: *children first gurgle and babble at random* **3** to disclose secrets carelessly **4** *literary* (of streams) to make a low murmuring sound ▷ *n* **5** muddled or foolish speech **6** a murmuring sound [probably imitative] ▸ **babbler** *n* ▸ **babbling** *n*

babe *n* **1** a baby **2 babe in arms** *informal* a naive or inexperienced person **3** *slang* a girl, esp. an attractive one

babel (babe-el) *n* **1** a confusion of noises or voices **2** a scene of noise and confusion [from the confusion of languages on the tower of *Babel* (Genesis 11:1–10)]

Babel *n* Issak Emmanuilovich 1894–1941, Russian short-story writer, whose works include *Stories from Odessa* (1924) and *Red Cavalry* (1926)

Bab el Mandeb *n* a strait between SW Arabia and E Africa, connecting the Red Sea with the Gulf of Aden

Baber, Babar or **Babur** *n* original name *Zahir ud-Din Mohammed* 1483–1530, founder of the Mogul Empire: conquered India in 1526

Babeuf *n* François Noël 1760–97, French political agitator: plotted unsuccessfully to destroy the Directory and establish a communistic system

babiche *n Canad* thongs or lacings of rawhide

Babinet *n* Jacques 1794–1872, French physicist, noted for his work on the diffraction of light

Babington *n* Anthony 1561–86, English conspirator, executed for organizing an unsuccessful plot (1586) to assassinate Elizabeth I and place Mary, Queen of Scots, on the English throne

baboon *n* a medium-sized monkey with a long face, large teeth, and a fairly long tail [Middle English *babewyn* gargoyle]

baby *n, pl* **-bies 1** a newborn child **2** the youngest or smallest of a family or group **3** a recently born animal **4** an immature person **5** *slang* a sweetheart **6** a project of personal concern **7 be left holding the baby** to be left with a responsibility ▷ *adj* **8** comparatively small of its type: *baby carrots* ▷ *vb* **-bies, -bying, -bied 9** to treat like a baby [probably childish reduplication] ▸ **babyhood** *n* ▸ **babyish** *adj*

baby bonus *n Canad informal* Family Allowance

Babylon *n* **1** the chief city of ancient Mesopotamia: first settled around 3000 BC. See also **Hanging Gardens of Babylon 2** *offensive* (in Protestant polemic) the Roman Catholic Church, regarded as the seat of luxury and corruption **3** *disparaging* any society or group in a society considered as corrupt or as a place of exile by another society or group, esp. White Britain as viewed by some West Indians [via Latin and Greek from Hebrew *Bābhēl*; see BABEL]

Babylonia *n* the southern kingdom of ancient Mesopotamia: a great empire from about 2200–538 BC, when it was conquered by the Persians

baby-sit *vb* **-sitting, -sat** to act or work as a baby-sitter ▸ **baby-sitting** *n, adj*

baby-sitter *n* a person who takes care of a child while the parents are out

Bacău *n* a city in E Romania on the River Bistrila: oil refining, textiles, paper. Pop: 128 000 (2005 est)

baccalaureate (back-a-law-ree-it) *n* the university degree of Bachelor of Arts [Medieval Latin *baccalarius* bachelor]

baccarat (back-a-rah) *n* a card game in which two or more punters gamble against the banker [French *baccara*]

bacchanalian (back-a-nail-ee-an) *adj literary* (of a party) unrestrained and involving a great deal of drinking and sometimes sexual activity [from BACCHUS]

Bacchus *n Classical myth* the god of wine; Dionysus

baccy *n Brit informal* tobacco

bach (batch) *NZ n* **1** a small holiday cottage ▷ *vb* **2** to look after oneself when one's spouse is away

Bach *n* **1** Johann Christian, 11th son of J. S. Bach. 1735–82, German composer, called *the English Bach*, resident in London from 1762 **2** Johann Christoph. 1642–1703, German composer: wrote oratorios, cantatas, and motets, some of which were falsely attributed to J. S. Bach, of whom he was a distant relative **3** Johann Sebastian. 1685–1750, German composer: church organist at Arnstadt (1703–07) and Mühlhausen (1707–08); court organist at Weimar (1708–17); musical

b

director for Prince Leopold of Köthen (1717–28); musical director for the city of Leipzig (1728–50). His output was enormous and displays great vigour and invention within the northern European polyphonic tradition. His works include nearly 200 cantatas and oratorios, settings of the *Passion according to St John* (1723) and *St Matthew* (1729), the six *Brandenburg Concertos* (1720–21), the 48 preludes and fugues of the *Well-tempered Clavier* (completed 1744), and the *Mass in B Minor* (1733–38) **4 Karl** (*or* **Carl**) **Philipp Emanuel**, 3rd son of J. S. Bach. 1714–88, German composer, chiefly of symphonies, keyboard sonatas, and church music **5 Wilhelm Friedemann**, eldest son of J. S. Bach. 1710–84, German composer: wrote nine symphonies and much keyboard and religious music

Bacharach *n* Burt. born 1928, US composer of popular songs, usually with lyricist Hal David

bachelor *n* **1** an unmarried man **2** a person who holds a first degree from a university or college [Old French *bacheler* youth, squire] **> bachelorhood** *n*

Bachelor of Arts *n* a person with a first degree from a university or college, usually in the arts

bacillary *adj* of or caused by bacilli

bacillus (bass-ill-luss) *n*, *pl* **-li** (-lie) a rod-shaped bacterium, esp. one causing disease [Latin *baculum* walking stick]

back *n* **1** the rear part of the human body, from the neck to the pelvis **2** the spinal column **3** the part or side of an object opposite the front **4** the part of anything less often seen or used **5** *ball games* a defensive player or position **6 at the back of one's mind** not in one's conscious thoughts **7 behind someone's back** secretly or deceitfully **8 put** *or* **get someone's back up** to annoy someone **9 turn one's back on someone** to refuse to help someone ▷ *vb* **10** to move or cause to move backwards **11** to provide money for (a person or enterprise) **12** to bet on the success of: *to back a horse* **13** to provide (a pop singer) with a musical accompaniment **14** (foll. by *on* or *onto*) to have the back facing (towards): *his garden backs onto a school* **15** (of the wind) to change direction anticlockwise ▷ *adj* **16** situated behind: *back garden* **17** owing from an earlier date: *back rent* **18** remote: *a back road* ▷ *adv* **19** at, to, or towards the rear **20** to or towards the original starting point or condition: *I went back home* **21** in reply or retaliation: *to hit someone back* **22** in concealment or reserve: *to keep something back* **23 back and forth** to and fro **24 back to front a** in reverse **b** in disorder ▶ See also **back down, back off**, etc. [Old English *bæc*]

backbencher *n* a Member of Parliament who does not hold office in the government or opposition

backbite *vb* **-biting, -bit, -bitten** *or* **-bit** to talk spitefully about an absent person **> backbiter** *n*

back boiler *n* Brit a tank at the back of a fireplace for heating water

backbone *n* **1** the spinal column **2** strength of character **3** *computers* a central section that connects segments of a network

back-breaking *adj* (of work) exhausting

backburn *Austral and NZ* *vb* **1** to clear (an area of bush) by creating a fire that burns in the opposite direction from the wind **2** to prevent a bush fire from spreading by clearing an area of land in front of it ▷ *n* **3** the act or result of backburning

back catalogue *n* a musician's previous recordings, as opposed to their current recordings

backchat *n informal* impudent replies

backcloth *n* a painted curtain at the back of a stage set. Also called: **backdrop**

backcomb *vb* to comb (the hair) towards the roots to give more bulk to a hairstyle

back country *n Austral and NZ* land far away from settled areas

backdate *vb* **-dating, -dated** to make (a document)

effective from a date earlier than its completion

back door *n* a means of entry to a job, position, etc. that is secret or obtained through influence: *the leaders may sneak a new treaty in through the back door*

back down *vb* to withdraw an earlier claim

backer *n* a person who gives financial or other support

backfire *vb* **-firing, -fired 1** (of a plan or scheme) to fail to have the desired effect **2** (of an internal-combustion engine) to make a loud noise as a result of an explosion of unburnt gases in the exhaust system

backgammon *n* a game for two people played on a board with pieces moved according to throws of the dice [*back* + obsolete *gammon* game]

background *n* **1** the events or circumstances that help to explain something **2** a person's social class, education, or experience **3** the part of a scene furthest from the viewer **4** an inconspicuous position: *in the background* **5** the space behind the chief figures or objects in a picture

backhand *n* **1** *tennis etc.* a stroke made from across the body with the back of the hand facing the direction of the stroke **2** the side on which backhand strokes are made

backhanded *adj* **1** (of a blow or shot) performed with the arm moving from across the body **2** ambiguous or implying criticism: *a backhanded compliment*

backhander *n* **1** *slang* a bribe **2** a backhanded stroke or blow

backing *n* **1** support **2** something that forms or strengthens the back of something **3** musical accompaniment for a pop singer

backing dog *n* NZ a dog that moves a flock of sheep by jumping on their backs

backlash *n* **1** a sudden and adverse reaction **2** a recoil between interacting badly fitting parts in machinery

backlog *n* an accumulation of things to be dealt with

backlot *n* an area outside a film or television studio used for outdoor filming

back number *n* **1** an old issue of a newspaper or magazine **2** *informal* a person or thing considered to be old-fashioned

back off *vb* **1** to retreat **2** to abandon an intention or objective

back office *n* **1** the administrative staff of a financial institution or other business ▷ *adj* **back-office 2** of or relating to such staff: *back-office operations*

back out *vb* (often foll. by *of*) to withdraw from (an agreement)

backpack *n* **1** a rucksack ▷ *vb* **2** to go hiking or travelling with a backpack **> backpacker** *n*

back passage *n* the rectum

back-pedal *vb* **-pedalling, -pedalled** *or US* **-pedaling, -pedaled** to retract or modify a previous opinion or statement

Back River *n* a river in N Canada, flowing northeast through Nunavut to the Arctic Ocean. Length: about 966 km (600 miles)

back room *n* **1** a place where secret research or planning is done ▷ *adj* **back-room 2** of or relating to secret research or planning: *back-room boys*

Backs *pl n* **the Backs** the grounds between the River Cam and certain Cambridge colleges

back seat *n informal* a less important or responsible position: *lyricism took a back seat to drama*

back-seat driver *n informal* a person who offers unwanted advice

backside *n informal* the buttocks

backslide *vb* **-sliding, -slid** to relapse into former bad habits or vices **> backslider** *n*

backspace *vb* **-spacing, -spaced** to move a typewriter carriage or computer cursor backwards

backspin *n sport* a backward spin given to a ball to reduce its speed at impact

backstabbing *n* treacherous actions or remarks that

are likely to cause harm to a person ⟩ **backstabber** *n* ⟩ **backstab** *vb*

backstage *adv* **1** behind the stage in a theatre ▷ *adj* **2** situated backstage

backstairs *or* **backstair** *adj* underhand: *backstairs gossip*

backstreet *n* **1** a street in a town far from the main roads ▷ *adj* **2** denoting secret or illegal activities: *a backstreet abortion*

backstroke *n swimming* a stroke performed on the back, using backward circular strokes of each arm

backtrack *vb* **1** to go back along the same route one has just travelled **2** to retract or reverse one's opinion or policy

back up *vb* **1** to support **2** *computers* to make a copy of (a data file), esp. as a security copy **3** (of traffic) to become jammed behind an obstruction ▷ *n* **backup 4** support or reinforcement **5** a reserve or substitute ▷ *adj* **backup 6** able to be substituted: *a backup copy*

backward *adj* **1** directed towards the rear **2** retarded in physical, material, or intellectual development **3** reluctant or bashful ▷ *adv* **4** same as **backwards** ⟩ **backwardness** *n*

backwards *or* **backward** *adv* **1** towards the rear **2** with the back foremost **3** in the reverse of the usual direction **4** into a worse state: *the Gothic novel's been going backwards since Radcliffe* **5** bend over backwards *informal* to make a special effort to please someone

backwash *n* **1** water washed backwards by the motion of oars or a ship **2** an unpleasant aftereffect of an event or situation

backwater *n* **1** an isolated or backward place or condition **2** a body of stagnant water connected to a river

backwoods *pl n* **1** any remote sparsely populated place **2** partially cleared, sparsely populated forests ⟩ **backwoodsman** *n*

back yard *n* **1** a yard at the back of a house, etc. **2** in one's own back yard **a** close at hand **b** involving or implicating one

Bacolod *n* a town in the Philippines, on the NW coast of Negros Island. Pop: 468 000 (2005 est)

bacon *n* **1** meat from the back and sides of a pig, dried, salted, and often smoked **2** bring home the bacon *informal* **a** to achieve success **b** to provide material support [Old French]

Bacon *n* **1** Francis, Baron Verulam, Viscount St Albans. 1561–1626, English philosopher, statesman, and essayist; described the inductive method of reasoning: his works include *Essays* (1625), *The Advancement of Learning* (1605), and *Novum Organum* (1620) **2** Francis. 1909–92, British painter, born in Dublin, noted for his distorted, richly coloured human figures, dogs, and carcasses **3** Roger. ?1214–92, English Franciscan monk, scholar, and scientist: stressed the importance of experiment, demonstrated that air is required for combustion, and first used lenses to correct vision. His *Opus Majus* (1266) is a compendium of all the sciences of his age

bacteria *pl n, sing* **-rium** a large group of microorganisms, many of which cause disease [Greek *baktron* rod] ⟩ **bacterial** *adj*

bacteriology *n* the study of bacteria ⟩ **bacteriologist** *n*

Bactria *n* an ancient country of SW Asia, between the Hindu Kush mountains and the Oxus River: forms the present Balkh region in N Afghanistan

Bactrian *adj* **1** of or relating to Bactria ▷ *n* **2** a native or inhabitant of Bactria

Bactrian camel *n* a two-humped camel [*Bactria*, ancient country of Asia]

bad *adj* **worse, worst 1** not good; of poor quality **2** lacking skill or talent: *I'm so bad at that sort of thing* **3** harmful: *smoking is bad for you* **4** evil or immoral **5** naughty or mischievous **6** rotten or decayed: *a bad egg* **7** severe: *a bad headache* **8** incorrect or faulty: *bad grammar* **9** sorry or upset: *I feel bad about saying no* **10** unfavourable or

distressing: *bad news* **11** offensive or unpleasant: *bad language* **12** not valid: *a bad cheque* **13** not recoverable: *a bad debt* **14** (**badder, baddest**) *slang* good; excellent **15** not bad *or* not so bad *informal* fairly good **16** too bad *informal* (often used dismissively) regrettable ▷ *n* **17** unfortunate or unpleasant events: *you've got to take the good with the bad* ▷ *adv* **18** *not standard* badly: *to want something bad* [Middle English] ⟩ **badness** *n*

Badajoz *n* a city in SW Spain: strategically positioned near the frontier with Portugal. Pop: 138 415 (2003 est)

Badalona *n* a port in NE Spain: an industrial suburb of Barcelona. Pop: 214 440 (2003 est)

bad blood *n* a feeling of intense hatred or hostility between people

bade *or* **bad** *vb* a past tense of **bid**

Baden *n* a former state of West Germany, now part of Baden-Württemberg

Baden-Baden *n* a spa in SW Germany, in Baden-Württemberg. Pop: 53 938 (2003 est)

Baden-Powell *n* Robert Stephenson Smyth, 1st Baron Baden-Powell. 1857–1941, British general, noted for his defence of Mafeking (1899–1900) in the Boer War; founder of the Boy Scouts (1908) and (with his sister Agnes) the Girl Guides (1910)

Baden-Württemberg *n* a state of SW Germany. Capital: Stuttgart. Pop: 53 938 (2003 est). Area: 35 742 sq km (13 800 sq miles)

Bader *n* Sir Douglas. 1910–82, British fighter pilot. Despite losing both legs after a flying accident (1931), he became a national hero as a pilot in World War II

badge *n* **1** a distinguishing emblem or mark worn to show membership or achievement **2** any revealing feature or mark [Old French *bage*]

badger *n* **1** a stocky burrowing mammal with a black and white striped head ▷ *vb* **2** to pester or harass [probably from *badge*]

Bad Godesberg *n* the official name for **Godesberg**

badinage (**bad-in-nahzh**) *n* playful and witty conversation [French]

Bad Lands *pl n* a deeply eroded barren region of SW South Dakota and NW Nebraska

badly *adv* **worse, worst 1** poorly; inadequately **2** unfavourably: *our plan worked out badly* **3** severely: *badly damaged* **4** very much: *he badly needed to improve his image* **5** badly off poor

badminton *n* a game played with rackets and a shuttlecock which is hit back and forth across a high net [*Badminton House*, Glos]

Badminton *n* a village in SW England, in South Gloucestershire unitary authority, Gloucestershire: site of Badminton House, seat of the Duke of Beaufort; annual horse trials

Badoglio *n* Pietro. 1871–1956, Italian marshal; premier (1943–44) following Mussolini's downfall: arranged an armistice with the Allies (1943)

Baeck *n* Leo. 1873–1956, German Jewish theologian: a leader of the German Jews during the Nazi period; major work *The Essence of Judaism* (1905)

Baeyer *n* Johann Friedrich Wilhelm Adolf von. 1835–1917, German chemist, noted for the synthesis of indigo: Nobel prize for chemistry 1905

Baez *n* Joan. born 1941, US rock and folk singer and songwriter, noted for the pure quality of her voice and for her committed pacifist and protest songs

BAF British Athletics Federation

Bafana bafana (bah-fan-na) *pl n S African* the South African national soccer team [from Nguni (language group of southern Africa) *bafana* the boys]

Baffin *n* William. c.1584–1622, English navigator and explorer who led several expeditions to find the North West Passage

Baffin Bay *n* part of the Northwest Passage, situated between Baffin Island and Greenland [named after William Baffin]

Baffin Island n the largest island of the Canadian Arctic, between Greenland and Hudson Bay. Area: 476 560 sq km (184 000 sq miles)

baffle vb **-fling, -fled 1** to perplex ▷ n **2** a mechanical device to limit or regulate the flow of fluid, light, or sound [origin unknown] **>** **bafflement** n **> baffling** adj

bag n **1** a flexible container with an opening at one end **2** the contents of such a container **3** a piece of luggage **4** a handbag **5** a loose fold of skin under the eyes **6** any sac in the body of an animal **7** offensive, slang an ugly or bad-tempered woman: an old bag **8** the amount of game taken by a hunter **9** in the bag slang assured of succeeding ▷ vb **bagging, bagged 10** to put into a bag **11** to bulge or cause to bulge **12** to capture or kill, as in hunting **13** informal to succeed in securing: he bagged the best chair ▶ See also **bags** [probably Old Norse baggi]

bagatelle n **1** something of little value **2** a board game in which balls are struck into holes **3** a short piece of music [French]

Bagdad n a variant spelling of **Baghdad**

Bagehot n Walter. 1826–77, English economist and journalist: editor of The Economist; author of The English Constitution (1867), Physics and Politics (1872), and Lombard Street (1873)

bagel (bay-gl) n a hard ring-shaped bread roll [Yiddish beygl]

baggage n **1** suitcases packed for a journey **2** an army's portable equipment **3** informal previous knowledge or experience that may have an influence in new circumstances: cultural baggage [Old French bagage]

baggy adj **-gier, -giest** (of clothes) hanging loosely **> bagginess** n

Baghdad or **Bagdad** n the capital of Iraq, on the River Tigris: capital of the Abbasid Caliphate (762–1258). Pop: 5 910 000 (2005 est)

bag lady n a homeless woman who carries around all her possessions in shopping bags

Bagnold n Enid (Algerine). 1889–1981, British novelist and playwright; her works include the novel National Velvet (1935) and the play The Chalk Garden (1955)

bagpipes pl n a musical wind instrument in which sounds are produced in reed pipes by air from an inflated bag

Bagram n an air base in NE Afghanistan, near Kabul; now under the control of US forces

bags pl n **1** informal a lot ▷ interj **2** Also: **bags I** children's slang, Brit and NZ an indication of the desire to do, be, or have something

Baguio n a city in the N Philippines, on N Luzon: summer capital of the Republic. Pop: 287 000 (2005 est)

bah interj an expression of contempt or disgust

Bahamas or **Bahama Islands** pl n the Bahamas a group of over 700 coral islands (about 20 of which are inhabited) in the Caribbean: a British colony from 1783 until 1964; an independent nation within the Commonwealth from 1973. Language: English. Currency: Bahamian dollar. Capital: Nassau. Pop: 319 031 (2013 est). Area: 13 939 sq km (5381 sq miles)

Bahamian adj **1** of or relating to the Bahamas ▷ n **2** a native or inhabitant of the Bahamas

Baha'ullah n title of Mirza Hosein Ali. 1817–92, Persian religious leader: originally a Shiite Muslim, later a disciple of the Bab; founder of the Baha'í Faith

Bahawalpur n an industrial city in Pakistan: cotton, soap. Pop: 563 000 (2005 est)

Bahia n **1** a state of E Brazil, on the Atlantic coast. Capital: Salvador. Pop: 13 323 212 (2002). Area: about 562 000 sq km (217 000 sq miles) **2** the former name of San Salvador

Bahía Blanca n a port in E Argentina. Pop: 276 000 (2005 est)

Bahia de los Cochinos n the Spanish name for the **Bay of Pigs**

Bahrain or **Bahrein** n an independent sheikhdom on the Persian Gulf, consisting of several islands: under British protection until the declaration of independence in 1971. It has large oil reserves. Language: Arabic. Religion: Muslim. Currency: dinar. Capital: Manama. Pop: 1 281 332 (2013 est). Area: 678 sq km (262 sq miles)

Bahraini or **Bahreini** adj **1** of or relating to Bahrain ▷ n **2** a native or inhabitant of Bahrain

Baikal n Lake Baikal a lake in Russia, in SE Siberia: the largest freshwater lake in Eurasia and the deepest in the world. Greatest depth: over 1500 m (5000 ft). Area: about 33 670 sq km (13 000 sq miles). Russian name: **Ozero Baykal**

Baikonur n a launching site for spacecraft in central Kazakhstan; formerly the centre for the Soviet space programme, now leased from Kazakhstan by Russia

bail[1] law n **1** a sum of money deposited with the court as security for a person's reappearance in court **2** the person giving such security **3** jump bail to fail to reappear in court after bail has been paid **4** stand or go bail to act as surety for someone ▷ vb **5** (foll. by out) to obtain the release of (a person) from custody by depositing money with the court [Old French: custody]

bail[2] or **bale** vb bail out to remove water from (a boat). See also **bail out** [Old French baille bucket]

bail[3] n **1** cricket either of two small wooden bars across the tops of the stumps **2** a partition between stalls in a stable or barn **3** Austral and NZ a framework in a cow shed used to secure the head of a cow during milking **4** a movable bar on a typewriter that holds the paper against the roller [Old French baile stake]

Baile Átha Cliath n the Irish Gaelic name for **Dublin**

bailey n the outermost wall or court of a castle [Old French baille enclosed court]

Bailey n **1** David. born 1938, English photographer **2** Nathan or Nathaniel. died 1742, English lexicographer: compiler of An Universal Etymological English Dictionary (1721–27)

Bailey bridge n a temporary bridge that can be rapidly assembled [after Sir Donald Coleman Bailey, its designer]

bailiff n **1** Brit a sheriff's officer who serves writs and summonses **2** the agent of a landlord or landowner [Old French baillif]

bailiwick n **1** law the area over which a bailiff has power **2** a person's special field of interest [bailie magistrate + obsolete wick district]

Baillie n Dame Isobel. 1895–1983, British soprano

bail out or **bale out** vb **1** to help (a person or organization) out of a predicament **2** to make an emergency parachute jump from an aircraft

bail up vb **1** Austral and NZ informal to confine (a cow) or (of a cow) to be confined by the head in a bail. See bail[3] **2** Austral history (of a bushranger) to hold under guard in order to rob **3** Austral to submit to robbery without offering resistance **4** Austral informal to accost or detain, esp. in conversation; buttonhole

Bainbridge n Beryl.1934–2010, British novelist and playwright. Novels include The Dressmaker (1973), Injury Time (1977), Master Georgie (1998), and According to Queeney (2001)

bain-marie (ban-mar-ee) n, pl bains-marie a container for holding hot water, in which sauces and other dishes are gently cooked or kept warm [French: bath of Mary]

Baird n John Logie. 1888–1946, Scottish engineer: inventor of a 240-line mechanically scanned system of television, replaced in 1935 by a 405-line electrically scanned system

bairn n Scot and N English a child [Old English bearn]

Bairnsfather n Bruce. 1888–1959, British cartoonist, born in India: best known for his cartoons of the war in the trenches during World War I

bait n **1** something edible fixed to a hook or in a trap to attract fish or animals **2** an enticement ▷ vb **3** to put a piece of food on or in (a hook or trap) **4** to persecute or tease **5** to set dogs upon (a bear or badger) [Old Norse *beita* to hunt]

> **USAGE** The phrase *with bated breath* is sometimes wrongly spelled *with baited breath*.

baize *n* a feltlike woollen fabric, usually green, which is used for the tops of billiard and card tables [Old French *bai* reddish-brown]

Baja California *n* **1** the Spanish name for **Lower California 2** short for **Baja California Norte**

Baja California Norte *n* a state of NW Mexico, in the N part of the Lower California peninsula. Capital: Mexicali. Pop: 2 487 700 (2000). Area: about 71 500 sq km (27 600 sq miles)

Baja California Sur *n* a state of NW Mexico, in the S part of the Lower California peninsula. Capital: La Paz. Pop: 423 516 (2000). Area: 73 475 sq km (28 363 sq miles)

Bajan *informal ▷ n* **1** a native of Barbados ▷ *adj* **2** of or relating to Barbados or its inhabitants [C20: variant of *Badian*, a shortened form of *Barbadian*]

bake *vb* **baking, baked 1** to cook by dry heat in an oven **2** to cook bread, pastry, or cakes **3** to make or become hardened by heat **4** *informal* to be extremely hot [Old English *bacan*]

bakeapple *n* cloudberry

baked beans *pl n* haricot beans, baked and tinned in tomato sauce

Bakelite (bake-a-lite) *n trademark* any of a class of resins used as electric insulators and for making plastics [after L. H. *Baekeland*, inventor]

bakeoff *n* a baking competition

baker *n* a person who makes or sells bread, cakes, etc.

Baker *n* **1** Sir **Benjamin**. 1840–1907, British engineer who, with Sir John Fowler, designed and constructed much of the London underground railway, the Forth Railway Bridge, and the first Aswan Dam **2** **Chet**, full name *Chesney H. Baker*. 1929–88, US jazz trumpeter and singer **3** Dame **Janet**. born 1933, British mezzo-soprano **4** Sir **Samuel White**. 1821–93, British explorer: discovered Lake Albert (1864)

baker's dozen *n* thirteen

bakery *n, pl* **-eries** a place where bread, cakes, etc. are made or sold

Bakewell *n* **Robert**. 1725–95, English agriculturist; radically improved livestock breeding, esp. of cattle and sheep

Bakhtaran *n* the former name (1987–1995) of **Kermanshah**

baking powder *n* a powdered mixture that contains sodium bicarbonate and cream of tartar: used in baking as a raising agent

bakkie (buck-ee) *n S African* a small truck with an enclosed cab and an open goods area at the back [Afrikaans *bak* container]

baksheesh *n* (in some Eastern countries) money given as a tip or present [Persian *bakhshīsh*]

Bakst *n* **Leon Nikolayevich**. 1866–1924, Russian painter and stage designer, noted particularly for his richly coloured sets for Diaghilev's Ballets Russes (1909–21)

Baku *n* the capital of Azerbaijan, a port on the Caspian Sea: important for its extensive oilfields. Pop: 1 830 000 (2005 est). Azerbaijani name: **Bakı**

Bakunin *n* **Mikhail**. 1814–76, Russian anarchist and writer: a prominent member of the First International, expelled from it after conflicts with Marx

Bala *n* **Lake Bala** a narrow lake in Gwynedd: the largest natural lake in Wales. Length: 6 km (4 miles)

Balaclava *or* **Balaclava helmet** *n* a close-fitting woollen hood that covers the ears and neck [after BALAKLAVA]

Balaguer *n* **Joaquin**. 1907–2002, Dominican statesman; president of the Dominican Republic (1960–62, 1966–78, 1986–96)

Balakirev *n* **Mily Alexeyevich**. 1837–1910, Russian composer, whose works include two symphonic poems, two symphonies, and many arrangements of Russian folk songs

Balaklava *or* **Balaclava** *n* a small port in S Crimea: scene of an inconclusive battle (1854), which included the charge of the Light Brigade, during the Crimean War

balalaika *n* a Russian musical instrument with a triangular body and three strings [Russian]

balance *n* **1** stability of mind or body: *lose one's balance* **2** a state of being in balance **3** harmony in the parts of a whole **4** the power to influence or control: *the balance of power* **5** something that remains: *the balance of what you owe* **6** *accounting* **a** the matching of debit and credit totals in an account **b** a difference between such totals **7** a weighing device **8 in the balance** in an undecided condition **9 on balance** after weighing up all the factors ▷ *vb* **-ancing, -anced 10** to weigh in or as if in a balance **11** to be or come into equilibrium **12** to bring into or hold in equilibrium **13** to compare the relative weight or importance of **14** to arrange so as to create a state of harmony **15** *accounting* to compare or equalize the credit and debit totals of (an account) [Latin *bilanx* having two scales]

balance of payments *n* the difference in value between a nation's total payments to foreign countries and its total receipts from foreign countries

balance of power *n* the equal distribution of military and economic power among countries

balance of trade *n* the difference in value between exports and imports of goods

balance sheet *n* a statement that shows the financial position of a business

Balanchine *n* **George**. 1904–83, US choreographer, born in Russia

Balaton *n* **Lake Balaton** a large shallow lake in W Hungary. Area: 689 sq km (266 sq miles)

Balbo *n* **Italo**. 1896–1940, Italian Fascist politician and airman: minister of aviation (1929–33)

Balboa¹ *n* **Vasco Núñez de**. ?1475–1519, Spanish explorer, who discovered the Pacific Ocean in 1513

Balboa² *n* a port in Panama at the Pacific end of the Panama Canal: the administrative centre of the former Canal Zone. Pop: 2750 (1990)

Balcon *n* Sir **Michael**. 1896–1977, British film producer; his films made at Ealing Studios include the comedies *Kind Hearts and Coronets* (1949) and *The Lavender Hill Mob* (1951)

balcony *n, pl* **-nies 1** a platform projecting from a building with a balustrade along its outer edge, often with access from a door **2** an upper tier of seats in a theatre or cinema [Italian *balcone*]

bald *adj* **1** having no hair or fur, esp. of a man having no hair on the scalp **2** lacking natural covering **3** plain or blunt: *the bald facts* **4** (of a tyre) having a worn tread [Middle English *ballede*] ▷ **baldly** *adv* ▷ **baldness** *n*

balderdash *n* stupid or illogical talk [origin unknown]

balding *adj* becoming bald

Baldwin *n* **1 James Arthur**. 1924–87, US Black writer, whose works include the novel *Go Tell it on the Mountain* (1954) **2 Stanley**, 1st Earl Baldwin of Bewdley. 1867–1947, British Conservative statesman: prime minister (1923–24, 1924–29, 1935–37)

Baldwin I *n* 1058–1118, crusader and first king of Jerusalem (1100–18), who captured Acre (1104), Beirut (1109), and Sidon (1110)

bale¹ *n* **1** a large bundle of hay or goods bound by ropes or wires for storage or transportation ▷ *vb* **baling, baled 2** to make (hay) or put (goods) into a bale or bales [Old High German *balla* ball]

bale² *vb* **baling, baled** same as **bail²**

Bâle *n* the French name for **Basle**

Balearic Islands *or* **Balearics** *pl n* a group of islands in

b

the W Mediterranean, consisting of Majorca, Minorca, Ibiza, Formentera, Cabrera, and 11 islets: a province of Spain. Capital: Palma, on Majorca. Pop: 1 071 500 (2003 est). Area: 5012 sq km (1935 sq miles). Spanish name: **(Islas) Baleares**

baleen *n* whalebone [Latin *balaena* whale]

baleen whale *n* same as **whalebone whale**

baleful *adj* harmful, menacing, or vindictive > **balefully** *adv*

Balenciaga *n* Cristobal. 1895–1972, Spanish couturier

bale out *vb* same as **bail out**

Balfour *n* Arthur James, 1st Earl of Balfour. 1848–1930, British Conservative statesman: prime minister (1902–05); foreign secretary (1916–19)

Bali *n* an island in Indonesia, east of Java: mountainous, rising over 3000 m (10 000 ft). Capital: Denpasar. Pop: 3 151 162 (2000). Area: 5558 sq km (2146 sq miles)

Balikpapan *n* a city in Indonesia, on the SE coast of Borneo. Pop: 409 023 (2000)

Balinese *adj* **1** of or relating to Bali, its people, or their language > *n* **2** (*pl* **-nese**) a native or inhabitant of Bali **3** the language of the people of Bali, belonging to the Malayo-Polynesian family

Baliol *or* **Balliol** *n* **1** Edward. ?1283–1364, king of Scotland (1332, 1333–56) **2** his father, John. 1249–1315, king of Scotland (1292–96): defeated and imprisoned by Edward I of England (1296)

balk *or* **baulk** *vb* **1** to stop short: *the horse balked at the jump* **2** to recoil: *France balked at the parliament having a veto* **3** to thwart, check, or foil: *he was balked in his plans* [Old English *balca* ridge]

Balkan *adj* of any of the countries of the Balkan Peninsula in SE Europe, between the Adriatic and Aegean Seas

Balkan Mountains *pl n* a mountain range extending across Bulgaria from the Black Sea to the eastern border. Highest peak: Mount Botev, 2376 m (7793 ft)

Balkan Peninsula *n* a large peninsula in SE Europe, between the Adriatic and Aegean Seas

Balkan States *pl n* the countries of the Balkan Peninsula: the former Yugoslavian Republics, Romania, Bulgaria, Albania, Greece, and the European part of Turkey. Also called: **the Balkans**

Balkh *n* a region of N Afghanistan, corresponding to ancient Bactria. Chief town: Mazar-i-Sharif

Balkhash *n* Lake Balkhash a salt lake in SE Kazakhstan: fed by the Ili River. Area: about 18 000 sq km (7000 sq miles)

ball¹ *n* **1** a spherical or nearly spherical mass: *a ball of wool* **2** a round or roundish object used in various games **3** a single delivery of the ball in a game **4** any more or less rounded part of the body: *the ball of the foot* **5** have the ball at one's feet to have the chance of doing something **6** on the ball *informal* alert; informed **7** play ball *informal* to cooperate **8** set *or* keep the ball rolling to initiate or maintain the progress of an action, discussion, or project > *vb* **9** to form into a ball ► See also **balls, balls-up** [Old Norse *böllr*]

ball² *n* **1** a lavish or formal social function for dancing **2** have a ball *informal* to have a very enjoyable time [Late Latin *ballare* to dance]

Ball *n* John. died 1381, English priest: executed as one of the leaders of the Peasants' Revolt (1381)

ballad *n* **1** a narrative song or poem often with a chorus that is repeated **2** a slow sentimental song [Old Provençal *balada* song accompanying a dance]

ballade *n* **1** *prosody* a verse form consisting of three stanzas and an envoy, all ending with the same line **2** *music* a romantic instrumental composition

Ballance *n* John. 1839–93, New Zealand statesman, born in Northern Ireland: prime minister of New Zealand (1891–93)

ball-and-socket joint *n* anatomy a joint in which a rounded head fits into a rounded cavity, allowing

a wide range of movement

Ballantyne *n* R(obert) M(ichael). 1825–94, British author, noted for such adventure stories as *The Coral Island* (1857)

Ballarat *n* a town in SE Australia, in S central Victoria: originally the centre of a gold-mining region. Pop: 72 999 (2001)

Ballard *n* J(ames) G(raham). 1930–2009, British novelist, born in China; his books include *Crash* (1973), *The Unlimited Dream Company* (1979), *Empire of the Sun* (1984), *Cocaine Nights* (1996), and *Super-Cannes* (2000)

ballast *n* **1** a substance, such as sand, used to stabilize a ship when it is not carrying cargo **2** crushed rock used for the foundation of a road or railway track > *vb* **3** to give stability or weight to [probably Low German]

ball bearing *n* **1** an arrangement of steel balls placed between moving parts of a machine in order to reduce friction **2** a metal ball used in such an arrangement

ball boy *or fem* **ball girl** *n* (in tennis) a person who retrieves balls that go out of play

ball cock *n* a device consisting of a floating ball and valve for regulating the flow of liquid into a tank or cistern

ballerina *n* a female ballet dancer [Italian]

Ballesteros *n* Severiano. 1957–2011, Spanish professional golfer: won the British Open Championship (1979; 1984; 1988) and the US Masters (1980; 1983)

ballet *n* **1** a classical style of expressive dancing based on precise conventional steps **2** a theatrical representation of a story performed by ballet dancers [Italian *balletto* a little dance] > **balletic** *adj*

ball game *n* **1** a game played with a ball **2** US and Canad a game of baseball **3** *informal* a state of affairs: *a whole new ball game*

ballistic missile *n* a launched weapon which is guided automatically in flight but falls freely at its target

ballistics *n* the study of the flight of projectiles, often in relation to firearms [Greek *ballein* to throw] > **ballistic** *adj*

ballocks *pl n, interj* same as **bollocks**

balloon *n* **1** an inflatable rubber bag used as a plaything or party decoration **2** a large bag inflated with a lighter-than-air gas, designed to rise and float in the atmosphere with a basket for carrying passengers **3** an outline containing the words or thoughts of a character in a cartoon > *vb* **4** to fly in a balloon **5** to swell or increase rapidly in size: *the cost of health care has ballooned* [Italian dialect *ballone* ball] > **balloonist** *n*

ballot *n* **1** the practice of selecting a representative or course of action by voting **2** the number of votes cast in an election **3** the actual vote or paper indicating a person's choice > *vb* **-loting, -loted** **4** to vote or ask for a vote from: *we balloted the members on this issue* **5** to vote for or decide on something by ballot [Italian *ballotta* a little ball]

ballot box *n* a box into which voting papers are dropped on completion

ballot paper *n* a paper used for voting

ballpark *n* **1** US and Canad a stadium used for baseball games **2** *informal* approximate range: *in the right ballpark*

ballpoint *or* **ballpoint pen** *n* a pen which has a small ball bearing as a writing point

ballroom *n* a large hall for dancing

ballroom dancing *n* social dancing in couples to music in conventional rhythms, such as the waltz

balls *pl n taboo, slang* **1** the testicles **2** nonsense **3** courage and determination > **ballsy** *adj*

balls-up *taboo, slang n* **1** something botched or muddled > *vb* balls up **2** to muddle or botch

bally *adj, adv* Brit old-fashioned, slang extreme or extremely: *a bally nuisance; he's too bally charming for his own good*

ballyhoo *n informal* unnecessary or exaggerated fuss [origin unknown]

Ballymena *n* a district in central Northern Ireland, in

b

Co Antrim. Pop: 59 516 (2003 est). Area: 634 sq km (247 sq miles)

Ballymoney *n* a district in N Northern Ireland, in Co Antrim. Pop: 27 809 (2003 est). Area: 417 sq km (161 sq miles)

balm *n* **1** an aromatic substance obtained from certain tropical trees and used for healing and soothing **2** something comforting or soothing: *her calmness was like a balm to my troubled mind* **3** an aromatic herb; lemon balm [Latin *balsamum* balsam]

Balmain *n* Pierre Alexandre. 1914–82, French couturier

Balmer *n* Johann Jakob. 1825–98, Swiss mathematician; discovered a formula giving the wavelengths of a series of lines in the hydrogen spectrum (the **Balmer series**)

Balmoral *n* a castle in NE Scotland, in SW Aberdeenshire: a private residence of the British sovereign

balmy *adj* **balmier, balmiest 1** (of weather) mild and pleasant **2** same as **barmy**

baloney *or* **boloney** *n informal* nonsense [*Bologna* (sausage)]

balsa (bawl-sa) *n* **1** a tree of tropical America which yields light wood **2** Also: **balsawood** the light wood of this tree, used for making rafts, models, etc. [Spanish: raft]

balsam *n* **1** an aromatic resin obtained from various trees and shrubs and used in medicines and perfumes **2** any plant yielding balsam **3** a flowering plant, such as busy lizzie [Greek *balsamon*]

Balthus *n* real name *Balthasar Klossowski de Rola*. 1908–2001, French painter of Polish descent, noted esp. for his paintings of adolescent girls

balti (boll-ti, bahl-ti) *n* a spicy Indian dish served in a metal dish [probably from the *Baltistan* region of Pakistan]

Baltic (bawl-tik) *adj* of the Baltic Sea in N Europe or the states bordering it

Baltic Centre for Contemporary Art *n* an arts centre in Gateshead, NE England: formerly a 1950s grain warehouse: used for its present purpose since 2002. It has no permanent collection, but rather hosts a programme of temporary exhibitions and events

Baltics *pl n* the Baltics another name for the **Baltic States**

Baltic Sea *n* a sea in N Europe, connected with the North Sea by the Skagerrak, Kattegat, and Öresund; shallow, with low salinity and small tidal ranges

Baltic States *pl n* the republics of Estonia, Latvia, and Lithuania, which became constituent republics of the former Soviet Union in 1940, regaining their independence in 1991. Sometimes shortened to: **the Baltics**

Baltimore[1] *n* a port in N Maryland, on Chesapeake Bay. Pop: 628 670 (2003 est)

Baltimore[2] *n* **1** David. born 1938, US molecular biologist: shared the Nobel prize for physiology or medicine (1975) for his discovery of reverse transcriptase **2** Lord. See **Calvert** (1)

Baluchi *or* **Balochi** *n* **1** (*pl* **-chis** *or* **-chi**) a member of a Muslim people living chiefly in coastal Pakistan and Iran **2** the language of this people, belonging to the West Iranian branch of the Indo-European family ▷ *adj* **3** of or relating to Baluchistan, its inhabitants, or their language

Baluchistan *or* **Balochistan** *n* **1** a mountainous region of SW Asia, in SW Pakistan and SE Iran **2** a province of SW Pakistan: a former territory of British India (until 1947). Capital: Quetta. Pop: 7 450 000 (2003 est)

baluster *n* a set of posts supporting a rail [French *balustre*]

balustrade *n* an ornamental rail supported by a set of posts [French]

Balzac *n* Honoré de. 1799–1850, French novelist: author of a collection of novels under the general title *La Comédie humaine*, including *Eugénie Grandet* (1833), *Le Père Goriot* (1834), and *La Cousine Bette* (1846)

Bamako *n* the capital of Mali, in the south, on the River Niger. Pop: 1 379 000 (2005 est)

Bamberg *n* a town in S Germany, in N Bavaria: seat of independent prince-bishops of the Holy Roman Empire (1007–1802). Pop: 69 899 (2003 est)

bamboo *n* a tall treelike tropical grass with hollow stems which are used to make canes, furniture, etc. [probably from Malay *bambu*]

bamboozle *vb* **-zling, -zled** *informal* **1** to cheat; mislead **2** to confuse [origin unknown] ▷ **bamboozlement** *n*

ban *vb* **banning, banned 1** to prohibit or forbid officially ▷ *n* **2** an official prohibition [Old English *bannan* to proclaim]

Banaba *n* an island in the SW Pacific, in the Republic of Kiribati. Phosphates were mined by Britain (1900–79). Area: about 5 sq km (2 sq miles). Pop: 301 (2005). Also called: **Ocean Island**

Banaban *adj* **1** of or relating to the SW Pacific island of Banaba ▷ *n* **2** a native or inhabitant of Banaba

banal (ban-nahl) *adj* lacking originality [Old French: common to all] ▷ **banality** *n*

banana *n* a crescent-shaped fruit that grows on a tropical or subtropical treelike plant [Spanish or Portuguese, of African origin]

banana republic *n informal, disparaging* a small politically unstable country whose economy is dominated by foreign interests

Banaras *n* a variant spelling of **Benares**

Banat *n* a fertile plain extending through Hungary, Romania, and Serbia

Banbridge *n* a district in S Northern Ireland, in Co Down. Pop: 43 083 (2003 est). Area: 442 sq km (170 sq miles)

Banbury *n* a town in central England, in N Oxfordshire: telecommunications, financial services. Pop: 43 867 (2001)

band[1] *n* **1** a group of musicians playing together, esp. on brass or percussion instruments **2** a group of people having a common purpose: *a band of revolutionaries* ▷ *vb* **3** (foll. by *together*) to unite [French *bande*]

band[2] *n* **1** a strip of some material, used to hold objects together: *a rubber band* **2** a strip of fabric used as an ornament or to reinforce clothing **3** a stripe of contrasting colour or texture **4** a driving belt in machinery **5** *physics* a range of frequencies or wavelengths between two limits ▷ *vb* **6** to fasten or mark with a band [Old French *bende*]

Banda *n* Hastings Kamuzu. 1906–97, Malawi statesman. As first prime minister of Nyasaland (from 1963), he led his country to independence (1964) as Malawi: president (1966–94)

Banda Aceh *n* a city in N Indonesia, in N Sumatra; the capital of Aceh region; suffered badly in the Indian Ocean tsunami of December 2004. Pop: 154 767 (2000)

bandage *n* **1** a piece of material used to dress a wound or wrap an injured limb ▷ *vb* **-daging, -daged 2** to cover or wrap with a bandage [French *bande* strip]

bandanna *or* **bandana** *n* a large brightly-coloured handkerchief or neckerchief [Hindi *bāndhnū* tie-dyeing]

Bandaranaike *n* **1** Chandrika. See **Kumaratunga 2** Sirimavo. 1916–2000, prime minister of Sri Lanka, formerly Ceylon (1960–65; 1970–77; 1994–2000); the world's first woman prime minister **3** her husband, **Solomon**. 1899–1959, prime minister of Ceylon (1956–59); assassinated

Bandar Lampung *n* a port in Indonesia, in S Sumatra on the Sunda Strait; formed by merging the cities of Tanjungkarang and Telukbetung, and sometimes still referred to as Tanjungkarang-Telukbetung. Pop: 742 749 (2000)

Bandar Seri Begawan *n* the capital of Brunei. Pop: 64 000 (2005 est). Former name: **Brunei**

Banda Sea *n* a part of the Pacific in Indonesia, between Sulawesi and New Guinea

B & B bed and breakfast

bandbox *n* a lightweight usually cylindrical box for hats

bandeau (ban-doe) *n, pl* **-deaux** (-doze) a narrow ribbon worn round the head [French]

banderole *n* **1** a narrow flag usually with forked ends **2** a ribbon-like scroll bearing an inscription [Old French]

bandicoot *n* **1** an Australian marsupial with a long pointed muzzle and a long tail **2** bandicoot rat any of three burrowing rats of S and SE Asia [Telugu (language of SE India) *pandikokku*]

bandit *n* a robber, esp. a member of an armed gang [Italian *bandito*] **> banditry** *n*

Bandjarmasin *or* **Bandjermasin** *n* former spellings of Banjarmasin

bandmaster *n* the conductor of a band

bandolier *n* a shoulder belt with small pockets for cartridges [Old French *bandouliere*]

band saw *n* a power-operated saw consisting of an endless toothed metal band running over two wheels

bandsman *n, pl* **-men** a player in a musical band

bandstand *n* a roofed outdoor platform for a band

Bandung *n* a city in Indonesia, in SW Java. Pop: 2 136 260 (2000)

bandwagon *n* jump *or* climb on the bandwagon to join a popular party or movement that seems assured of success

bandwidth *n* the range of frequencies used for transmitting electronic information

bandy *adj* **-dier, -diest 1** Also: **bandy-legged** having legs curved outwards at the knees **2** (of legs) curved outwards at the knees ▷ *vb* **-dies, -dying, -died 3** to exchange (words), sometimes in a heated manner **4 bandy about** to use (a name, term, etc.) frequently [probably from Old French *bander* to hit back and forth]

bane *n* a person or thing that causes misery or distress: *the bane of my life* [Old English *bana*] **> baneful** *adj*

Banff *n* **1** a town in NE Scotland, in Aberdeenshire. Pop: 3991 (2001) **2** a town in Canada, in SW Alberta, in the Rocky Mountains: surrounded by **Banff National Park**. Pop: 7135 (2001)

Banffshire *n* (until 1975) a county of NE Scotland: formerly (1975–96) part of Grampian region, now part of Aberdeenshire

bang *n* **1** a short loud explosive noise, such as the report of a gun **2** a hard blow or loud knock **3** *taboo, slang* an act of sexual intercourse **4 with a bang** successfully: *the party went with a bang* ▷ *vb* **5** to hit or knock, esp. with a loud noise **6** to close (a door) noisily **7** to make or cause to make a loud noise, as of an explosion **8** *taboo, slang* to have sexual intercourse with ▷ *adv* **9** with a sudden impact: *the car drove bang into a lamppost* **10** precisely: *bang in the middle* [Old Norse *bang, banga* hammer]

Bangalore *n* a city in S India, capital of Karnataka state: printing, textiles, pharmaceuticals. Pop: 4 292 223 (2001). Alternative official name: **Bengaluru**

banger *n* **1** *Brit and Austral informal* an old decrepit car **2** *slang* a sausage **3** *slang* a firework that explodes loudly

Bangka *or* **Banka** *n* an island in Indonesia, separated from Sumatra by the **Bangka Strait**. Chief town: Pangkalpinang. Area: about 11 914 sq km (4600 sq miles)

Bangkok *n* the capital and chief port of Thailand, on the Chao Phraya River: became a royal city and the capital in 1782. Pop: 6 604 000 (2005 est). Thai name: **Krung Thep**

Bangladesh *n* a republic in S Asia: formerly the Eastern Province of Pakistan; became independent in 1971 after civil war and the defeat of Pakistan by India; consists of the plains and vast deltas of the Ganges and Brahmaputra Rivers; prone to flooding: economy based on jute and jute products (over 70 per cent of world production); a member of the Commonwealth. Language: Bengali. Religion: Muslim. Currency: taka. Capital: Dhaka. Pop: 163 654 860 (2013 est). Area: 142 797 sq km (55 126 sq miles)

Bangladeshi *adj* **1** of or relating to Bangladesh or its

inhabitants ▷ *n* **2** a native or inhabitant of Bangladesh

bangle *n* a bracelet worn round the arm or sometimes round the ankle [Hindi *bangrī*]

Bangor *n* **1** a university town in NW Wales, in Gwynedd, on the Menai Strait. Pop: 15 280 (2001) **2** a town in SE Northern Ireland, in North Down district, Co Down, on Belfast Lough. Pop: 58 388 (2001)

Bangui *n* the capital of the Central African Republic, in the south part, on the Ubangi River. Pop: 732 000 (2005 est)

Bangweulu *n* Lake Bangweulu a shallow lake in NE Zambia, discovered by David Livingstone, who died there in 1873. Area: about 9850 sq km (3800 sq miles), including swamps

banian *n* same as **banyan**

banish *vb* **1** to send into exile **2** to drive away: *it's the only way to banish weeds from the garden* [Old French *banir*] **> banishment** *n*

banisters *or* **bannisters** *pl n* the railing and supporting balusters on a staircase [altered from BALUSTER]

Banja Luka *n* a city in NW Bosnia-Herzegovina, on the Vrbas River: scene of battles between the Austrians and Turks in 1527, 1688, and 1737; besieged by Serb forces (1992–95). Pop: 182 000 (2006 est)

Banjarmasin *or* **Banjermasin** *n* a port in Indonesia, in SW Borneo. Pop: 527 415 (2000). Former spelling: Bandjarmasin, Bandjermasin

banjo *n, pl* **-jos** *or* **-joes** a stringed musical instrument with a long neck and a circular drumlike body [US pronunciation of earlier *bandore*] **> banjoist** *n*

Banjul *n* the capital of The Gambia, a port at the mouth of the Gambia River. Pop: 392 000 (2005 est). Former name (until 1973): **Bathurst**

bank¹ *n* **1** an institution offering services, such as the safekeeping and lending of money at interest **2** the building used by such an institution **3** the funds held by a banker or dealer in some gambling games **4** any supply, store, or reserve: *a data bank* ▷ *vb* **5** to deposit (cash or a cheque) in a bank **6** to transact business with a bank ▶ See also **bank on** [probably from Italian *banca* bench, moneychanger's table]

bank² *n* **1** a long raised mass, esp. of earth **2** a slope, as of a hill **3** the sloping side and ground on either side of a river ▷ *vb* **4** to form into a bank or mound **5** to cover (a fire) with ashes and fuel so that it will burn slowly **6** (of an aircraft) to tip to one side in turning [Scandinavian]

bank³ *n* **1** an arrangement of similar objects in a row or in tiers ▷ *vb* **2** to arrange in a bank [Old French *banc* bench]

Banka *n* a variant spelling of **Bangka**

bankable *adj* likely to ensure financial success: *a bankable star* **> bankability** *n*

bank account *n* an arrangement whereby a customer deposits money at a bank and may withdraw it when it is needed

bank card *n* any plastic card issued by a bank, such as a cash card or a cheque card

banker¹ *n* **1** a person who owns or manages a bank **2** the keeper of the bank in various gambling games

banker² *n* *Austral and NZ informal* a stream almost overflowing its banks: *the creek was running a banker*

banker's order *n* same as **standing order** (1)

Bankhead *n* Tallulah (Brockman). 1902–68, US stage and film actress; her successes included the plays *The Little Foxes* (1939) and *The Skin of Our Teeth* (1942)

bank holiday *n* (in Britain) a public holiday when banks are traditionally closed

Ban Ki-moon *n* born 1944, South Korean international civil servant; secretary-general of the United Nations from 2007

banking *n* the business engaged in by a bank

bank machine *n* *chiefly Canad* another name for **cash dispenser**

banknote *n* a piece of paper money issued by a central bank

bank on vb to rely on

bankrupt n **1** a person, declared by a court to be unable to pay his or her debts, whose property is sold and the proceeds distributed among the creditors **2** a person no longer having a particular quality: *a spiritual bankrupt* ▷ adj **3** declared insolvent **4** financially ruined **5** no longer having a particular quality: *morally bankrupt* ▷ vb **6** to make bankrupt [Old Italian *banca* BANK¹ + *rotta* broken] ❯ **bankruptcy** n

Banks n **1** Iain (Menzies). 1954–2013, Scottish novelist and science fiction writer. His novels include *The Wasp Factory* (1984), *The Crow Road* (1992), and *The Steep Approach to Garbadale* (2007); science-fiction (under the name Iain M. Banks) includes *Look to Windward* (2000) **2** Sir Joseph. 1743–1820, British botanist and explorer: circumnavigated the world with James Cook (1768–71)

banksia n an Australian evergreen tree or shrub

Banks Island n **1** an island of N Canada, in the Northwest Territories: the westernmost island of the Arctic Archipelago. Area: about 67 340 sq km (26 000 sq miles) **2** an island of W Canada, off British Columbia. Length: about 72 km (45 miles)

banner n **1** a long strip of material displaying a slogan, advertisement, etc. **2** a placard carried in a demonstration **3** Also called: **banner headline** a large headline in a newspaper extending across the page **4** an advertisement, often animated, that extends across the width of a web page [Old French *baniere*]

Bannister n Sir Roger (Gilbert). born 1929, British athlete and doctor: first man to run a mile in under four minutes (1954)

bannock n Scot a round flat cake made from oatmeal or barley [Old English *bannuc*]

Bannockburn n a village in central Scotland, south of Stirling: nearby is the site of a victory (1314) of the Scots, led by Robert the Bruce, over the English. Pop: 7396 (2001)

banns pl n the public announcement of an intended marriage [plural of obsolete *bann* proclamation]

banquet n **1** an elaborate formal dinner often followed by speeches ▷ vb **-queting, -queted 2** to hold or take part in a banquet [Italian *banco* a table]

banshee n (in Irish folklore) a female spirit whose wailing warns of a coming death [Irish Gaelic *bean sídhe* woman of the fairy mound]

Banstead n a town in S England, in NE Surrey. Pop: 19 332 (2001)

bantam n **1** a small breed of domestic fowl **2** a small but aggressive person [after *Bantam*, village in Java, said to be the original home of this fowl]

bantamweight n a professional boxer weighing up to 118 lb (53.5 kg) or an amateur weighing up to 119 lb (54 kg)

banter vb **1** to tease jokingly ▷ n **2** teasing or joking conversation [origin unknown]

Banting n Sir Frederick Grant. 1891–1941, Canadian physiologist: discovered the insulin treatment for diabetes with Best and Macleod (1922) and shared the Nobel prize for physiology or medicine with Macleod (1923)

Bantock n Sir Granville. 1868–1946, British composer. His works include the *Hebridean Symphony* (1915), five ballets, and three operas

Bantu n **1** a group of languages of Africa **2** (pl **-tu** or **-tus**) offensive a Black speaker of a Bantu language ▷ adj **3** of the Bantu languages or the peoples who speak them [Bantu *Ba-ntu* people]

Bantustan n offensive formerly, an area reserved for occupation by a Black African people. Official name: **homeland** [Bantu + Hindi *-stan* country of]

Banville n Théodore de. 1823–91, French poet, who anticipated the Parnassian school in his perfection of form and command of rhythm

banyan or **banian** n an Indian tree whose branches grow down into the soil forming additional trunks [Hindi *baniyā*]

baobab (**bay-oh-bab**) n an African tree with a massive grey trunk, short angular branches, and large pulpy fruit [probably from a native African word]

Baoding, Paoting or **Pao-ting** n a city in NE China, in N Hebei province. Pop: 810 000 (2005 est). Former name: Ch'ing-yüan, Tsingyuan

Baotou or **Paotow** n an industrial city in N China, in the central Inner Mongolia AR on the Yellow River. Pop: 1 367 000 (2005 est)

bap n Brit a large soft bread roll [origin unknown]

baptism n a Christian religious rite in which a person is immersed in or sprinkled with water as a sign of being cleansed from sin and accepted as a member of the Church ❯ **baptismal** adj

baptism of fire n **1** any introductory ordeal **2** a soldier's first experience of battle

Baptist n **1** a member of a Protestant denomination that believes in the necessity of adult baptism by immersion **2 the Baptist** John the Baptist ▷ adj **3** of the Baptist Church

baptize or **-tise** vb **-tizing, -tized** or **-tising, -tised 1** Christianity to immerse (a person) in water or sprinkle water on (him or her) as part of the rite of baptism **2** to give a name to [Greek *baptein* to bathe, dip]

bar¹ n **1** a rigid usually straight length of metal, wood, etc. used as a barrier or structural part **2** a solid usually rectangular block of any material: *a bar of soap* **3** anything that obstructs or prevents: *a bar to women's mobility* **4** a counter or room where alcoholic drinks are served **5** a narrow band or stripe, as of colour or light **6** a heating element in an electric fire **7** See **Bar 8** the place in a court of law where the accused stands during trial **9** music a group of beats that is repeated with a consistent rhythm throughout a piece of music **10** football etc. same as **crossbar 11** heraldry a narrow horizontal line across a shield **12 behind bars** in prison ▷ vb **barring, barred 13** to secure with a bar: *to bar the door* **14** to obstruct: *the fallen tree barred the road* **15** to exclude: *he was barred from membership of the club* **16** to mark with a bar or bars ▷ prep **17** except for [Old French *barre*]

bar² n a unit of pressure equal to 10⁵ newtons per square metre [Greek *baros* weight]

Bar n **1 the Bar** barristers collectively **2 be called to the Bar** Brit to become a barrister

barachois n (in the Atlantic Provinces of Canada) a shallow lagoon formed by a sand bar

Barak n Ehud. born 1942, Israeli politician, prime minister (1999–2001); left the Labour Party (2011) to form the breakaway party Independence

Baranof Island n an island off SE Alaska, in the western part of the Alexander Archipelago. Area: 4162 sq km (1607 sq miles)

Bárány n Robert. 1876–1936, Austrian physician; devised the Bárány test, which detects diseases of the semicircular canals of the inner ear: Nobel prize for physiology or medicine 1914

barb n **1** a cutting remark **2** a point facing in the opposite direction to the main point of a fish-hook, harpoon, etc. **3** a beardlike growth, hair, or projection ▷ vb **4** to provide with a barb or barbs [Latin *barba* beard] ❯ **barbed** adj

Barbadian adj **1** of or relating to Barbados or its inhabitants ▷ n **2** a native or inhabitant of Barbados

Barbados n an island in the Caribbean, in the E Lesser Antilles: a British colony from 1628 to 1966, now an independent state within the Commonwealth. Language: English. Currency: Barbados dollar. Capital: Bridgetown. Pop: 288 725 (2013 est). Area: 430 sq km (166 sq miles)

barbarian n **1** a member of a primitive or uncivilized people **2** a coarse or vicious person ▷ adj **3** uncivilized or brutal

b

barbaric *adj* primitive or brutal

barbarism *n* **1** a brutal, coarse, or ignorant act **2** the condition of being backward, coarse, or ignorant **3** a substandard word or expression

barbarity *n, pl* **-ties 1** the state of being barbaric or barbarous **2** a vicious act

Barbarossa *n* **1** the nickname of the Holy Roman Emperor Frederick I. See Frederick Barbarossa **2** real name Khair ed-Din. c. 1465–1546, Turkish pirate and admiral: conquered Tunis for the Ottomans (1534)

barbarous *adj* **1** uncivilized: *a barbarous and uninhabitable jungle* **2** brutal or cruel: *the barbarous tortures inflicted on them* [Greek *barbaros* barbarian, non-Greek]

Barbary *n* a historic name for a region of N Africa extending from W Egypt to the Atlantic and including the former Barbary States of Tripolitania, Tunisia, Algeria, and Morocco

Barbary Coast *n* the Barbary Coast a historic name for the Mediterranean coast of North Africa: a centre of piracy against European shipping from the 16th to the 19th centuries

barbecue *n* **1** a grill on which food is cooked over hot charcoal, usually out of doors **2** food cooked over hot charcoal, usually out of doors **3** a party or picnic at which barbecued food is served ▷ *vb* **-cuing, -cued 4** to cook on a grill, usually over charcoal [American Spanish *barbacoa* frame made of sticks]

barbed wire *n* strong wire with sharp points protruding at close intervals

barbel *n* **1** a long thin growth that hangs from the jaws of certain fishes, such as the carp **2** a freshwater fish with such a growth [Latin *barba* beard]

barbell *n* a long metal rod to which heavy discs are attached at each end for weightlifting

barber *n* a person whose business is cutting men's hair and shaving beards [Latin *barba* beard]

Barber *n* Samuel. 1910–81, US composer: his works include an *Adagio for Strings*, adapted from the second movement of his string quartet No. 1 (1936) and the opera *Vanessa* (1958)

barberry *n, pl* **-ries** a shrub with orange or red berries [Arabic *barbāris*]

barbican *n* a walled defence to protect a gate or drawbridge of a fortification [Old French *barbacane*]

Barbican *n* the Barbican a building complex in the City of London: includes residential developments and the Barbican Arts Centre (completed 1982) housing concert and exhibition halls, theatres, cinemas, etc.

Barbirolli *n* Sir John. 1899–1970, English conductor of the Hallé Orchestra (1943–68)

barbiturate *n* a derivative of barbituric acid used in medicine as a sedative

barbituric acid *n* a crystalline solid used in the preparation of barbiturate drugs [German *Barbitursäure*]

Barbour[1] *n* trademark Brit a waterproof waxed jacket

Barbour[2] *n* John. c. 1320–95, Scottish poet: author of The Bruce (1376), a patriotic epic poem

Barbuda *n* a coral island in the E Caribbean, in the Leeward Islands: part of the independent state of Antigua and Barbuda. Area: 160 sq km (62 sq miles)

Barbusse *n* Henri. 1873–1935, French novelist and poet. His novels include L'Enfer (1908) and Le Feu (1916), reflecting the horror of World War I

barcarole *or* **barcarolle** *n* **1** a Venetian boat song **2** an instrumental composition resembling this [French]

Barce *or* **Barca** *n* the Italian name for Al Marj

Barcelona *n* the chief port of Spain, on the NE Mediterranean coast: seat of the Republican government during the Civil War (1936–39): the commercial capital of Spain. Pop: 1 582 738 (2003 est). Ancient name: Barcino

bar chart *or* **bar graph** *n* a diagram consisting of vertical or horizontal bars whose lengths are proportional to amounts or quantities

Barclay *n* Alexander. c. 1475–1552, English poet. His works include The Ship of Fools (1509) and Eclogues (c. 1513–14)

Barclay de Tolly *n* Prince Mikhail. 1761–1818, Russian field marshal: commander in chief against Napoleon in 1812

bar code *n* an arrangement of numbers and parallel lines on a package, which can be electronically scanned at a checkout to give the price of the goods

Barcoo River *n* a river in E central Australia, in SW Queensland: joins with the Thomson River to form Cooper Creek

bard *n* **1** archaic or literary a poet **2 a** (formerly) an ancient Celtic poet **b** a poet who wins a verse competition at a Welsh eisteddfod **3** the Bard William Shakespeare, English playwright and poet [Scottish Gaelic]

Bardeen *n* John. 1908–91, US physicist and electrical engineer, noted for his research on electrical conduction in solids; shared Nobel prize for physics 1956 for research on semiconductors leading to the invention of the transistor; shared Nobel prize for physics 1972 for contributions to the theory of superconductivity

Bardot *n* Brigitte. born 1934, French film actress and animal rights activist

bare *adj* **1** unclothed: used esp. of a part of the body **2** without the natural, conventional, or usual covering: *bare trees* **3** lacking appropriate furnishings, etc.: *a bare room* **4** simple: *the bare facts* **5** just sufficient: *the bare minimum* ▷ *vb* **baring, bared 6** to uncover [Old English *bær*] ➤ **bareness** *n*

bareback *adj, adv* (of horse-riding) without a saddle

bare-faced *or* **barefaced** *adj* obvious or shameless: *a bare-faced lie*

barefoot *or* **barefooted** *adj, adv* with the feet uncovered

bareheaded *adj, adv* with the head uncovered

Bareilly *n* a city in N India, in N central Uttar Pradesh. Pop: 699 839 (2001)

bare-knuckle *adj* **1** without boxing gloves **2** aggressive and without reservations

barely *adv* **1** only just: *barely enough* **2** scantily: *barely furnished*

USAGE See at hardly.

Barenboim *n* Daniel. born 1942, Israeli concert pianist and conductor, born in Argentina

Barents Sea *n* a part of the Arctic Ocean, bounded by Norway, Russia, and the islands of Novaya Zemlya, Spitsbergen, and Franz Josef Land [named after Willem Barents (1550–97), Dutch navigator and explorer]

bargain *n* **1** an agreement establishing what each party will give, receive, or perform in a transaction **2** something acquired or received in such an agreement **3** something bought or offered at a low price **4** drive a hard bargain to forcefully pursue one's own profit in a transaction **5** into the bargain besides ▷ *vb* **6** to negotiate the terms of an agreement or transaction [Old French *bargaigne*]

bargain for *vb* to anticipate

bargain on *vb* to rely or depend on

barge *n* **1** a flat-bottomed boat, used for transporting freight, esp. on canals **2** a boat, often decorated, used in pageants, etc. ▷ *vb* **barging, barged** informal **3** (foll. by into) to bump into **4** to push one's way violently **5** (foll. by into or in) to interrupt rudely: *he barged into our conversation* [Medieval Latin *barga*]

bargee *n* Brit a person in charge of a barge

bargepole *n* **1** a long pole used to propel a barge **2 not touch with a bargepole** informal to refuse to have anything to do with

Bari *n* a port in SE Italy, capital of Apulia, on the Adriatic coast. Pop: 316 532 (2001)

bariatric *adj* of or relating to the treatment of obesity: *bariatric surgery* [Greek *baros* weight + *iatrikos* of healing]

b

Baring n Evelyn, 1st Earl of Cromer. 1841–1917, English administrator. As consul general in Egypt with plenipotentiary powers, he controlled the Egyptian government from 1883 to 1907

barista (bar-ee-sta) n a person who makes and sells coffee in a coffee bar

baritone n **1** the second lowest adult male voice **2** a singer with such a voice [Greek *barus* low + *tonos* tone]

barium (bare-ee-um) n chem a soft silvery-white metallic chemical element. Symbol: **Ba** [Greek *barus* heavy]

barium meal n a preparation of barium sulphate, which is opaque to X-rays, used in X-ray examination of the alimentary canal

bark[1] n **1** the loud harsh cry of a dog or certain other animals ▷ vb **2** (of a dog or other animal) to make its typical cry **3** to shout in an angry tone: *he barked an order* **4 bark up the wrong tree** *informal* to misdirect one's attention or efforts [Old English *beorcan*]

bark[2] n **1** an outer protective layer of dead corklike cells on the trunks of trees ▷ vb **2** to scrape or rub off (skin), as in an injury **3** to remove the bark from (a tree) [Old Norse *börkr*]

barker n a person at a fairground who loudly addresses passers-by to attract customers

Barker n **1** Billy, full name *William George Barker*. 1894–1930, Canadian fighter pilot during World War I; the most decorated military serviceman in British Empire history **2 George** (Granville). 1913–91, British poet: author of *Calamiterror* (1937) and *The True Confession of George Barker* (1950) **3 Howard**. born 1946, British playwright: his plays include *Claw* (1975), *The Castle* (1985), *A Hard Heart* (1992), and *13 Objects* (2003) **4 Ronnie**, full name *Ronald William George Barker*. 1929–2005, British comedian: known esp. for his partnership with Ronnie Corbett (born 1930) in the TV series *The Two Ronnies* (1971–85)

Barkhausen n Heinrich Georg. 1881–1956, German physicist; discovered that ferromagnetic material in an increasing magnetic field becomes magnetized in discrete jumps (the **Barkhausen effect**)

barking *slang, chiefly Brit* adj **1** mad or crazy ▷ adv **2** extremely: *barking mad*

Barking and Dagenham n a borough of E Greater London. Pop: 165 900 (2003 est). Area: 34 sq km (13 sq miles)

Barkla n Charles Glover. 1877–1944, British physicist, noted for his work on X-rays: Nobel prize for physics 1917

Bar Kochba, Bar Kokhba or **Bar Kosba** n Simeon. died 135 AD, Jewish leader who led an unsuccessful revolt against the Romans in Palestine

Barletta n a port in SE Italy, in Apulia. Pop: 92 094 (2001)

barley n **1** a tall grasslike plant with dense bristly flower spikes, widely cultivated for grain **2** the grain of this grass used in making beer and whisky and for soups [Old English *bere*]

barleycorn n a grain of barley, or barley itself

barley sugar n a brittle clear amber-coloured sweet

barley water n a drink made from an infusion of barley

barm n the yeasty froth on fermenting malt liquors [Old English *bearm*]

barmaid n a woman who serves in a pub

barman n, pl **-men** a man who serves in a pub

bar mitzvah *Judaism* n **1** a ceremony marking the 13th birthday of a boy and his assumption of religious obligations ▷ adj **2** (of a Jewish boy) having undergone this ceremony [Hebrew: son of the law]

barmy adj **-mier, -miest** *slang* insane [originally, full of BARM, frothing, excited]

barn n a large farm outbuilding, chiefly for storing grain, but also for livestock [Old English *bere* barley + *ærn* room]

barnacle n a marine shellfish that lives attached to rocks, ship bottoms, etc. [Old French *bernac*] ▷ **barnacled** adj

barnacle goose n a goose with a black-and-white head

and body [it was formerly believed that the goose developed from a shellfish]

Barnard n **1** Christiaan (Neethling). 1923–2001, South African surgeon, who performed the first human heart transplant (1967) **2** Edward Emerson. 1857–1923, US astronomer: noted for his discovery of the fifth satellite of Jupiter and his discovery of comets, nebulae, and a red dwarf (1916)

Barnardo n Dr Thomas John. 1845–1905, British philanthropist, who founded homes for destitute children

Barnaul n a city in S Russia, on the River Ob. Pop: 605 000 (2005 est)

Barnave n Antoine Pierre. 1761–93, French revolutionary. A prominent member of the National Assembly, he was executed for his royalist sympathies

barn dance n **1** US and Canad a party with square-dancing **2** Brit a progressive round country dance

Barnes n **1** Djuna. 1892–1982, US novelist, noted for *Nightwood* (1936) **2** William. 1801–86, British poet, best known for *Poems of Rural Life in the Dorset Dialect* (1879)

Barnet n a borough of N Greater London: scene of a Yorkist victory (1471) in the Wars of the Roses. Pop: 324 400 (2003 est). Area: 89 sq km (34 sq miles)

barney n *informal* a noisy fight or argument [origin unknown]

barn owl n an owl with a pale brown-and-white plumage and a heart-shaped face

Barnsley n **1** an industrial town in N England, in Barnsley unitary authority, South Yorkshire. Pop: 71 599 (2001) **2** a unitary authority in N England, in South Yorkshire. Pop: 220 200 (2003 est). Area: 329 sq km (127 sq miles)

Barnstaple n a town in SW England, in Devon, on the estuary of the River Taw: tourism, agriculture. Pop: 30 765 (2001)

barnstorm vb **1** chiefly US and Canad to tour rural districts making speeches in a political campaign **2** to tour rural districts putting on shows ▷ **barnstorming** n, adj

Barnum n P(hineas) T(aylor). 1810–91, US showman, who created The Greatest Show on Earth (1871) and, with J. A. Bailey, founded the Barnum and Bailey Circus (1881)

barnyard n a yard adjoining a barn

Barocchio n Giacomo. See Vignola

Baroda n **1** a former state of W India, part of Gujarat since 1960 **2** the former name (until 1976) of **Vadodara**

barograph n *meteorol* a barometer that automatically keeps a record of changes in atmospheric pressure [Greek *baros* weight + *graphein* to write]

Baroja n Pio. 1872–1956, Spanish Basque novelist, who wrote nearly 100 novels, including a series of twenty-two under the general title *Memorias de un Hombre de Acción* (1944–9)

barometer n an instrument for measuring atmospheric pressure, used to determine weather or altitude changes [Greek *baros* weight + *metron* measure] ▷ **barometric** adj

baron n **1** a member of the lowest rank of nobility in the British Isles **2** a powerful businessman or financier: *a press baron* [Old French] ▷ **baronial** adj

Baron-Cohen n Sacha. born 1970, British television and film comedian, best known for his creation of the characters Ali G and Borat

baroness n **1** a woman holding the rank of baron **2** the wife or widow of a baron

baronet n a commoner who holds the lowest hereditary British title ▷ **baronetcy** n

barony n, pl **-nies** the domain or rank of a baron

baroque (bar-**rock**) n **1** a highly ornate style of architecture and art, popular in Europe from the late 16th to the early 18th century **2** a highly ornamented 17th-century style of music ▷ adj **3** ornate in style [French from Portuguese *barroco* imperfectly shaped pearl]

barque (bark) n **1** a sailing ship, esp. one with three masts **2** *poetic* any boat [Old Provençal *barca*]

Barquisimeto n a city in NW Venezuela. Pop: 1 009 000 (2005 est)

Barra n an island in NW Scotland, in the Outer Hebrides: fishing, crofting, tourism. Pop: 1078 (2001)

barrack¹ vb to house (soldiers) in barracks

barrack² vb 1 Brit, Austral and NZ informal to criticize loudly or shout against (a team or speaker) 2 Austral and NZ (foll. by for) to shout encouragement for (a team) [Irish: to boast]

barracks pl n 1 a building or group of buildings used to accommodate military personnel 2 a large and bleak building [French baraque]

barracuda (bar-rack-kew-da) n, pl -da or -das a tropical fish which feeds on other fishes [American Spanish]

barrage (bar-rahzh) n 1 a continuous delivery of questions, complaints, etc. 2 military the continuous firing of artillery over a wide area 3 a construction built across a river to control the water level [French barrer to obstruct]

barrage balloon n a balloon tethered by cables, often with net suspended from it, used to deter low-flying air attack

barramundi n an edible Australian fish

Barranquilla n a port in N Colombia, on the Magdalena River. Pop: 1 918 000 (2005 est)

Barras n Paul François Jean Nicolas, Vicomte de Barras. 1755–1829, French revolutionary: member of the Directory (1795–99)

Barrault n Jean-Louis. 1910–94, French actor and director, noted particularly as a mime

barre (bar) n a rail at hip height used for ballet practice [French]

barrel n 1 a cylindrical container, usually with rounded sides and flat ends, and held together by metal hoops 2 a unit of capacity of varying amount in different industries 3 the tube through which the bullet of a firearm is fired 4 over a barrel informal powerless ▷ vb -relling, -relled or US -reling, -reled 5 to put into a barrel or barrels [Old French baril]

barrel organ n a musical instrument played by turning a handle

barren adj 1 incapable of producing offspring 2 unable to support the growth of crops, fruit, etc.: barren land 3 unprofitable or unsuccessful: Real Madrid have had a barren two seasons 4 dull [Old French brahain]
> **barrenness** n

Barren Lands pl n the Barren Lands a region of tundra in N Canada, extending westwards from Hudson Bay: sparsely inhabited, chiefly by Inuit. Also known as: **the Barren Grounds**

Barrès n Maurice. 1862–1923, French novelist, essayist, and politician: a fervent nationalist and individualist

barricade n 1 a barrier, esp. one erected hastily for defence ▷ vb -**cading, -caded** 2 to erect a barricade across (an entrance) [Old French barrique a barrel]

Barrie n Sir James Matthew. 1860–1937, Scottish dramatist and novelist, noted particularly for his popular children's play Peter Pan (1904)

barrier n 1 anything that blocks a way or separates, such as a gate 2 anything that prevents progress: a barrier of distrust 3 anything that separates or hinders union: a language barrier [Old French barre bar]

barrier cream n a cream used to protect the skin

barrier reef n a long narrow ridge of coral, separated from the shore by deep water

barring prep unless something occurs; except for

Barrington n Jonah. born 1940, British squash player; winner of the Open Championship 1966–67, 1969–72

barrister n a lawyer who is qualified to plead in the higher courts [from BAR¹]

Barros n João de. 1496–1570, Portuguese historian: noted for his history of the Portuguese in the East Indies, Décadas da Ásia (1552–1615)

Barroso n José Manuel born 1956, Portuguese politician; prime minister of Portugal (2002–04); president of the European Commission (2004–2014)

barrow¹ n 1 same as wheelbarrow 2 a handcart used by street traders [Old English bearwe]

barrow² n a heap of earth placed over a prehistoric tomb [Old English beorg]

Barrow n 1 a river in SE Ireland, rising in the Slieve Bloom Mountains and flowing south to Waterford Harbour. Length: about 193 km (120 miles) 2 See Barrow-in-Furness, Barrow Point

barrow boy n Brit a man who sells goods from a barrow

Barrow-in-Furness n an industrial town in NW England, in S Cumbria. Pop: 47 194 (2001)

Barrow Point n the northernmost tip of Alaska, on the Arctic Ocean

Barry¹ n a port in SE Wales, in Vale of Glamorgan county borough on the Bristol Channel. Pop: 50 661 (2001)

Barry² n 1 Sir Charles. 1795–1860, English architect: designer of the Houses of Parliament in London 2 Comtesse du. See du Barry 3 John, real name John Barry Prendergast. 1933–2011, British composer of film scores, including several for films in the James Bond series

Barrymore n a US family of actors, esp. Ethel (1879–1959), John (1882–1942), Lionel (1878–1954), and Drew (born 1975)

Barry Mountains pl n a mountain range in SE Australia, in E Victoria: part of the Australian Alps

Bart n Lionel. 1930–99, British composer and playwright. His musicals include Oliver! (1960)

Bart. Baronet

barter vb 1 to trade goods or services in exchange for other goods or services, rather than for money ▷ n 2 trade by the exchange of goods [Old French barater to cheat]

Barth n 1 Heinrich. 1821–65, German explorer: author of Travels and Discoveries in North and Central Africa (1857–58) 2 John (Simmons). born 1930, US novelist; his novels include The Sot-Weed Factor (1960), Giles Goat-Boy (1966), and Once Upon a Time (1994) 3 Karl. 1886–1968, Swiss Protestant theologian. He stressed man's dependence on divine grace in such works as Commentary on Romans (1919)

Barthes n Roland. 1915–80, French writer and critic, who applied structuralist theory to literature and popular culture: his books include Mythologies (1957) and Elements of Semiology (1964)

Bartholdi n Frédéric August. 1834–1904, French sculptor and architect, who designed (1884) the Statue of Liberty

Bartók n Béla. 1881–1945, Hungarian composer, pianist, and collector of folk songs, by which his music was deeply influenced. His works include six string quartets, three piano concertos, several piano pieces including Mikrokosmos (1926–37), ballets (including The Miraculous Mandarin, 1919), and the opera Bluebeard's Castle (produced 1918)

Bartoli n Cecilia. born 1966, Italian mezzo-soprano, noted for her performances in Mozart and Rossini operas

Bartolommeo n Fra. original name Baccio della Porta. 1472–1517, Italian painter of the Florentine school, noted for his austere religious works

Barton n 1 Sir Derek (Harold Richard). 1918–98, British organic chemist: shared the Nobel prize for chemistry (1969) for his work on conformational analysis 2 Sir Edmund. 1849–1920, Australian statesman; first prime minister of Australia (1901–03) 3 Elizabeth, known as the Maid of Kent. ?1506–34, English nun, who claimed the gift of prophecy. Her criticism of Henry VIII's attempt to annul his first marriage led to her execution 4 John (Bernard Adie). born 1928, British theatre director, noted esp. for his productions of Shakespeare

baryon (bar-ree-on) n an elementary particle that has a mass greater than or equal to that of the proton [Greek barus heavy]

b

Baryshnikov n Mikhail. born 1948, Soviet-born ballet dancer, who defected (1974) to the West while on tour with the Kirov Ballet: director (1980–90) of the American Ballet Theatre

baryta (bar-rite-a) n a compound of barium, such as barium oxide [Greek *barus* heavy]

barytes (bar-rite-eez) n a colourless or white mineral: a source of barium [Greek *barus* heavy]

basal adj 1 at, of, or constituting a base 2 fundamental

basal metabolic rate n the amount of energy consumed by an animal's body at rest

basalt (bass-awlt) n a dark volcanic rock [Greek *basanitēs* touchstone] **> basaltic** adj

bascule n a drawbridge that operates by a counterbalanced weight [French: seesaw]

base¹ n 1 the bottom or supporting part of anything 2 the fundamental principle or part: *agriculture was the economic base of the city's growth* 3 a centre of operations, organization, or supply 4 a starting point: *the new discovery became the base for further research* 5 the main ingredient of a mixture: *to use rice as a base in cookery* 6 chem a compound that combines with an acid to form a salt 7 the lower side or face of a geometric construction 8 maths the number of units in a counting system that is equivalent to one in the next higher counting place: *10 is the base of the decimal system* 9 a starting or finishing point in any of various games ▷ vb **basing, based** 10 (foll. by *on* or *upon*) to use as a basis for 11 (foll. by *at* or *in*) to station, post, or place [Latin *basis* pedestal]

base² adj 1 dishonourable or immoral: *base motives* 2 of inferior quality or value: *a base coin* 3 debased; counterfeit: *base currency* [Late Latin *bassus* of low height]

baseball n 1 a team game in which the object is to score runs by batting the ball and running round all four bases 2 the ball used in this game

Basel n a variant spelling of **Basle**

baseless adj not based on fact

baseline n 1 a value or starting point on an imaginary scale with which other things are compared 2 a line at each end of a tennis court that marks the limit of play

baseliner n tennis a player who plays most of his or her shots from the back of the court

basement n a partly or wholly underground storey of a building

base metal n a common metal such as copper or lead, that is not a precious metal

base rate n 1 the rate of interest used by a bank as a basis for its lending rates 2 the rate at which the Bank of England lends to other financial organizations, which effectively controls interest rates throughout the UK

bases¹ n the plural of **basis**

bases² n the plural of **base¹**

Basescu n Traian. born 1951, Romanian politician, president of Romania from 2004

bash informal vb 1 to strike violently or crushingly 2 (foll. by *into*) to crash into ▷ n 3 a heavy blow 4 have a bash informal to make an attempt [origin unknown]

bashful adj shy or modest [*bash*, short for ABASH] **> bashfully** adv

-bashing combining form informal, slang a indicating a malicious attack on members of a group: *union-bashing* b indicating an activity undertaken energetically: *Bible-bashing* **> -basher** combining form

Bashir n Dame Marie (Roslyn). born 1930, Australian health administrator and campaigner: governor of New South Wales (2001–14)

Bashkir Republic n a constituent republic of E central Russia, in the S Urals: established as the first Soviet autonomous republic in 1919; rich mineral resources. Capital: Ufa. Pop: 4 012 900 (2002). Area: 143 600 sq km (55 430 sq miles). Also called: **Bashkiria**, *Russian* **Bashkortostan**

Bashkirtseff or **Bashkirtsev** n Marie, original name *Marya Konstantinovna Bashkirtseva*. 1858–84, Russian

painter and diarist who wrote in French, noted esp. for her *Journal* (1887)

Basho n full name **Matsuo Basho**, originally *Matsuo Munefusa*. 1644–94, Japanese poet and travel writer, noted esp. for his haiku

basic adj 1 of or forming a base or basis 2 elementary or simple: *a few basic facts* 3 excluding additions or extras: *basic pay* 4 chem of or containing a base ▷ n 5 **basics** fundamental principles, facts, etc. **> basically** adv

BASIC n a computer programming language that uses common English terms [b(*eginner's*) a(*ll-purpose*) s(*ymbolic*) i(*nstruction*) c(*ode*)]

basic slag n a slag produced in steel-making, containing calcium phosphate

Basie n William, known as *Count Basie*. 1904–84, US jazz pianist, bandleader, and composer: associated particularly with the polished phrasing and style of big-band jazz

basil n an aromatic herb used for seasoning food [Greek *basilikos* royal]

Basil n Saint, called *the Great*. ?329–379 AD, Greek patriarch: an opponent of Arianism and one of the founders of monasticism. Feast day: Jan 2, June 14, or Jan 1

Basil I n known as *the Macedonian*. died 886 AD, Byzantine emperor (876–86): founder of the Macedonian dynasty

Basilan n 1 a group of islands in the Philippines, SW of Mindanao 2 the main island of this group, separated from Mindanao by the **Basilan Strait**. Area: 1282 sq km (495 sq miles) 3 a city on Basilan Island. Pop: 381 000 (2005 est)

Basildon n a town in SE England, in S Essex: designated a new town in 1955. Pop: 99 876 (2001)

basilica n 1 a Roman building, used for public administration, which is rectangular with two aisles and a rounded end 2 a Christian church of similar design [Greek *basilikē oikia* the king's house]

Basilicata n a region of S Italy, between the Tyrrhenian Sea and the Gulf of Taranto. Capital: Potenza. Pop: 596 821 (2003 est). Area: 9985 sq km (3855 sq miles)

basilisk n (in classical legend) a serpent that could kill by its breath or glance [Greek *basiliskos* royal child]

basin n 1 a round wide container open at the top 2 the amount a basin will hold 3 a washbasin or sink 4 any partially enclosed area of water where ships or boats may be moored 5 the catchment area of a particular river 6 a depression in the earth's surface [Old French *bacin*]

Basingstoke n a town in S England, in N Hampshire. Pop: 90 171 (2001)

basis n, pl **bases** 1 something that underlies, supports, or is essential to an idea, belief, etc. 2 a principle on which something depends [Greek: step]

bask vb (foll. by *in*) 1 to lie in or be exposed (to pleasant warmth or sunshine) 2 to enjoy (approval or favourable conditions) [Old Norse *bathask* to bathe]

basket n 1 a container made of interwoven strips of wood or cane 2 the amount a basket will hold 3 *basketball* a the high horizontal hoop through which a player must throw the ball to score points b a point scored in this way [Middle English]

basketball n a team game in which points are scored by throwing the ball through a high horizontal hoop

basket weave n a weave of yarns, resembling that of a basket

basketwork n same as **wickerwork**

basking shark n a very large plankton-eating shark, which often floats at the sea surface

Basle or **Basel** n 1 a canton of NW Switzerland, divided into the demicantons of **Basle-Landschaft** and **Basle-Stadt**. Pops.: 263 200 and 186 900 (2002 est). Areas: 427 sq km (165 sq miles) and 36 sq km (14 sq miles) respectively 2 a city in NW Switzerland, capital of Basle canton, on the Rhine: oldest university in Switzerland.

Pop: 165 000 (2002 est) ▸ French name: **Bâle**

basmati rice *n* a variety of long-grain rice with slender aromatic grains, used for savoury dishes [Hindi: aromatic]

Basov *n* Nikolai Gennediyevich. 1922–2001, Russian physicist: shared the Nobel prize for physics (1964) for his pioneering work on the maser

basque *n* a tight-fitting bodice for women [origin unknown]

Basque *n* **1** a member of a people living in the W Pyrenees in France and Spain **2** the language of the Basques ▷ *adj* **3** of the Basques [Latin *Vasco*]

Basque Provinces *or* **Basque Country** *n* an autonomous region of N Spain, comprising the provinces of Álava, Guipúzcoa, and Vizcaya: inhabited mainly by Basques, who retained virtual autonomy from the 9th to the 19th century. Pop: 1 840 700 (2003 est). Area: about 7250 sq km (2800 sq miles)

Basra, Basrah *or* **Busra, Busrah** *n* a port in SE Iraq, on the Shatt-al-Arab. Pop: 1 187 000 (2005 est)

bas-relief *n* sculpture in which the figures project slightly from the background [Italian *basso rilievo*]

Bas-Rhin *n* a department of NE France in Alsace region. Capital: Strasbourg. Pop: 1 052 698 (2003 est). Area: 4793 sq km (1869 sq miles)

bass¹ (base) *n* **1** the lowest adult male voice **2** a singer with such a voice **3** *informal* same as **bass guitar, double bass** ▷ *adj* **4** of the lowest range of musical notes: *the system is engineered to give good bass sound from very small speakers* **5** denoting a musical instrument that is lowest or second lowest in pitch in its family: *bass trombone* **6** of or relating to a bass guitar or double bass: *the band is unusual in that it has two bass players* **7** of or written for a singer with the lowest adult male voice: *the bass soloist in next week's performance of Handel's 'Messiah'* [Middle English *bas*]

bass² (rhymes with **gas**) *n* **1** various Australian freshwater and sea fish **2** a European spiny-finned freshwater fish [Middle English]

bass clef (base) *n* the clef that establishes F a fifth below middle C on the fourth line of the staff

bass drum (base) *n* a large drum of low pitch

Bassein *n* a city in Myanmar, on the Irrawaddy delta: a port on the **Bassein River** (the westernmost distributary of the Irrawaddy). Pop: 231 000 (2005 est)

Basse-Normandie *n* a region of NW France, on the English Channel: consists of the Cherbourg peninsula in the west rising to the Normandy hills in the east; mainly agricultural

Bassenthwaite *n* a lake in NW England, in Cumbria near Keswick. Length: 6 km (4 miles)

Basses-Alpes *n* the former name for **Alpes-de-Haute-Provence**

Basses-Pyrénées *pl n* the former name for **Pyrénées-Atlantiques**

Basseterre *n* a port in the Caribbean, on St Kitts in the Leeward Islands: the capital of St Kitts-Nevis. Pop: 13 220 (2001)

Basse-Terre *n* **1** a mountainous island in the Caribbean, in the Leeward Islands, comprising part of Guadeloupe. Area: 848 sq km (327 sq miles) **2** a port in W Guadeloupe, on Basse-Terre Island: the capital of the French Overseas Department of Guadeloupe. Pop: 11 894 (2009)

basset hound *n* a smooth-haired dog with short legs and long ears [French *bas* low]

bass guitar (base) *n* an electric guitar with the same pitch and tuning as a double bass

bassinet *n* a wickerwork or wooden cradle or pram, usually hooded [French: little basin]

basso *n, pl* **-sos** *or* **-si** a singer with a bass voice [Late Latin *bassus* low]

bassoon *n* a woodwind instrument that produces a range of low sounds [Italian *basso* deep] ▸ **bassoonist** *n*

Bass Strait *n* a channel between mainland Australia and Tasmania, linking the Indian Ocean and the Tasman Sea

bastard *n* **1** *informal, offensive* an obnoxious or despicable person **2** *archaic or offensive* a person born of parents not married to each other **3** *informal* something extremely difficult or unpleasant ▷ *adj* **4** *archaic or offensive* illegitimate by birth **5** counterfeit; spurious [Old French *bastart*] ▸ **bastardy** *n*

bastardize *or* **-ise** *or* **-izing, -ized** *or* **-ising, -ised 1** to debase **2** to declare illegitimate

baste¹ *vb* **basting, basted** to sew with loose temporary stitches [Old French *bastir* to build]

baste² *vb* **basting, basted** to moisten (meat) during cooking with hot fat [origin unknown]

baste³ *vb* **basting, basted** to thrash [origin unknown]

Bastia *n* a port in NE Corsica: the main commercial and industrial town of the island: capital of Haute-Corse department. Pop: 43 315 (2007)

Bastille *n* a fortress in Paris, built in the 14th century: a prison until its destruction in 1789, at the beginning of the French Revolution [C14: from Old French *bastile* fortress, from Old Provençal *bastida*, from *bastir* to build, of Germanic origin; see BASTE¹]

bastinado *n, pl* **-does 1** a punishment or torture by beating on the soles of the feet with a stick ▷ *vb* **-doing, -doed 2** to beat (a person) in this way [Spanish *baston* stick]

bastion *n* **1** a projecting part of a fortification **2** a thing or person regarded as defending a principle or way of life: *a bastion of anti-communism* [French *bastille* fortress]

Bastogne *n* a town in SE Belgium: of strategic importance to Allied defences during the Battle of the Bulge; besieged by the Germans during the winter of 1944–45. Pop: 14 070 (2004 est)

Basutoland *n* the former name (until 1966) of **Lesotho**

bat¹ *n* **1** any of various types of club used to hit the ball in certain sports **2** *cricket* a batsman **3 off one's own bat a** of one's own accord **b** by one's own unaided efforts ▷ *vb* **batting, batted 4** to strike with or as if with a bat **5** *cricket etc.* to take a turn at batting [Old English *batt* club]

bat² *n* **1** a nocturnal mouselike flying animal with leathery wings **2 blind as a bat** having extremely poor eyesight [Scandinavian]

bat³ *vb* **batting, batted 1** to flutter (one's eyelids) **2 not bat an eyelid** *informal* to show no surprise [probably from obsolete *bate* flutter, beat]

Bataan *n* a peninsula in the Philippines, in W Luzon: scene of the surrender of US and Philippine forces to the Japanese during World War II, later retaken by American forces

Batangas *n* a port in the Philippines, in SW Luzon. Pop: 293 000 (2005 est)

Batan Islands *pl n* a group of islands in the Philippines, north of Luzon. Capital: Basco. Pop: 16 467 (2000). Area: 197 sq km (76 sq miles)

Batavia *n* **1** an ancient district of the Netherlands, on an island at the mouth of the Rhine **2** an archaic or literary name for **Holland 3** a former name for **Jakarta**

Batavian *adj* **1** of or relating to Batavia (a former name for Holland or Jakarta) or its inhabitants ▷ *n* **2** a native or inhabitant of Batavia

batch *n* **1** a group of similar objects or people dispatched or dealt with at the same time **2** the bread, cakes, etc. produced at one baking ▷ *vb* **3** to group (items) for efficient processing [Middle English *bache*]

batch processing *n* a system by which the computer programs of several users are submitted as a single batch

bated *adj* **with bated breath** in suspense or fear

Bates *n* **1** Sir Alan (Arthur). 1934–2003, British film and stage actor. His films include *A Kind of Loving* (1962), *Women in Love* (1969), *The Go-Between* (1971), and *The Cherry Orchard* (1999) **2** H(erbert) E(rnest). 1905–74, English

b

writer of short stories and novels, which include *The Darling Buds of May* (1958), *A Moment in Time* (1964), and *The Triple Echo* (1970)

bath *n* **1** a large container in which to wash the body **2** the act of washing in such a container **3** the amount of water in a bath **4 baths** a public swimming pool **5 a** a liquid in which something is immersed as part of a chemical process, such as developing photographs **b** the vessel containing such a liquid ▷ *vb* **6** *Brit* to wash in a bath [Old English *bæth*]

Bath *n* a city in SW England, in Bath and North East Somerset unitary authority, Somerset, on the River Avon: famous for its hot springs; a fashionable spa in the 18th century; Roman remains, notably the baths; university (1966). Pop: 90 144 (2001). Latin name: **Aquae Sulis**

Bath and North East Somerset *n* a unitary authority in SW England, in Somerset; formerly (1974–96) part of the county of Avon. Pop: 170 900 (2003 est). Area: 351 sq km (136 sq miles)

Bath chair *n* a wheelchair for invalids

bath cube *n* a cube of soluble scented material for use in a bath

bathe *vb* **bathing, bathed** **1** to swim in open water for pleasure **2** to apply liquid to (the skin or a wound) in order to cleanse or soothe **3** *chiefly US and Canad* to wash in a bath **4** to spread over: *bathed in moonlight* ▷ *n* **5** *Brit* a swim in open water [Old English *bathian*] **> bather** *n*

bathos (**bay**-thoss) *n* a sudden ludicrous descent from exalted to ordinary matters in speech or writing [Greek: depth] **> bathetic** *adj*

bathrobe *n* **1** a loose-fitting garment for wear before or after a bath or swimming **2** *US and Canad* a dressing gown

bathroom *n* **1** a room with a bath or shower, washbasin, and toilet **2** *US and Canad* a toilet

Bathurst *n* **1** a town in SE Australia, in E New South Wales: scene of a gold rush in 1851. Pop: 27 036 (2001) **2** a port in E Canada, in NE New Brunswick: rich mineral resources. Pop: 16 427 (2001) **3** the former name (until 1973) of **Banjul**

bathyscaph *or* **bathyscaphe** *n* a deep-sea diving vessel for observation [Greek *bathus* deep + *skaphē* light boat]

bathysphere *n* a strong steel deep-sea diving sphere, lowered by cable [Greek *bathus* deep + *sphere*]

batik (**bat-teek**) *n* **1** a process of printing fabric in which areas not to be dyed are covered by wax **2** fabric printed in this way [Javanese: painted]

Batista *n* Fulgencio, full name *Batista y Zaldívar*. 1901–73, Cuban military leader and dictator: president of Cuba (1940–44, 1952–59); overthrown by Fidel Castro

Batley *n* a town in N England, in Kirklees unitary authority, West Yorkshire. Pop: 49 448 (2001)

batman *n, pl* **-men** an officer's servant in the armed forces [Old French *bat* packsaddle]

Batman *n* John. 1801–39, a pioneer who selected the site of the city of Melbourne

baton *n* **1** a thin stick used by the conductor of an orchestra or choir **2** *athletics* a short bar transferred from one runner to another in a relay race **3** a police officer's truncheon **4** a short stick or something shaped like one [French]

Baton Rouge *n* the capital of Louisiana, in the SE part on the Mississippi River. Pop: 225 090 (2003 est)

baton round *n* same as **plastic bullet**

bats *adj informal* mad or eccentric

batsman *n, pl* **-men** *cricket etc.* a person who bats or specializes in batting

battalion *n* a military unit comprised of three or more companies [French *bataillon*]

batten¹ *n* **1** a strip of wood used to strengthen something or make it secure **2** a strip of wood used for holding a tarpaulin in place over a hatch on a ship ▷ *vb* **3** to strengthen or fasten with battens [French *bâton* stick]

batten² *vb* (foll. by *on*) to thrive at the expense of (someone else) [probably from Old Norse *batna* to improve]

Batten *n* Jean. 1909–82, New Zealand aviator: the first woman to fly single-handed from Australia to Britain (1935)

batter¹ *vb* **1** to hit repeatedly **2** to damage or injure, as by blows, heavy wear, etc. **3** to subject (someone, usually a close relative) to repeated physical violence [Middle English *bateren*] **> battered** *adj* **> batterer** *n* **> battering** *n*

batter² *n* a mixture of flour, eggs, and milk, used in cooking [Middle English *bater*]

batter³ *n* *baseball etc.* a player who bats

battering ram *n* (esp. formerly) a large beam used to break down fortifications

Battersea *n* a district in London, in Wandsworth: noted for its dogs' home, power station (now a leisure centre), and park

battery *n, pl* **-teries** **1** two or more primary cells connected to provide a source of electric current **2** a number of similar things occurring together: *a battery of questions* **3** *criminal law* unlawful beating or wounding of a person **4** *chiefly Brit* a series of cages for intensive rearing of poultry **5** a fortified structure on which artillery is mounted ▷ *adj* **6** kept in a series of cages for intensive rearing: *battery hens* [Latin *battuere* to beat]

battle *n* **1** a fight between large armed forces **2** conflict or struggle ▷ *vb* **-tling, -tled** **3** to fight in or as if in military combat: *shop stewards battling to improve conditions at work* **4** to struggle: *she battled through the crowd* [Latin *battuere* to beat]

Battle¹ *n* a town in SE England, in East Sussex: site of the Battle of Hastings (1066); medieval abbey. Pop: 5190 (2001)

Battle² *n* Kathleen. born 1948, US opera singer: a coloratura soprano, she made her professional debut in 1972 and sang with New York City's Metropolitan Opera (1977–94)

battle-axe *n* **1** a domineering woman **2** (formerly) a large broad-headed axe

battle cruiser *n* a high-speed warship with lighter armour than a battleship, but of the same size

battle cry *n* **1** a slogan used to rally the supporters of a campaign, movement, etc. **2** a shout uttered by soldiers going into battle

battledore *n* **1** Also called: **battledore and shuttlecock** an ancient racket game **2** a light racket used in this game [Middle English *batyldoure*]

battledress *n* the ordinary uniform of a soldier

battlefield *or* **battleground** *n* the place where a battle is fought

battlement *n* a wall with gaps, originally for firing through [Old French *bataille* battle]

battle royal *n* **1** a fight involving many combatants **2** a long violent argument

battleship *n* a large heavily armoured warship

batty *adj* **-tier, -tiest** *slang* **1** crazy **2** eccentric: *a batty OAP* [from BAT²]

Batum *or* **Batumi** *n* a city in Georgia: capital of the Adzhar Autonomous Republic; a major Black Sea port. Pop: 118 000 (2005 est)

bauble *n* **1** a trinket of little value **2** a small round ornament hung from a branch of a Christmas tree [Old French *baubel* plaything]

Bauchi *n* **1** a state of N Nigeria; tin mining. Capital: Bauchi. Pop: 4 676 465 (2006). Area: 45 837 sq km (17 698 sq miles) **2** a town in N central Nigeria, capital of Bauchi state. Pop: 76 070 (1991 est)

baud *n computers* a unit used to measure the speed of transmission of electronic data [after J. M. E. *Baudot*, inventor]

Baudelaire *n* Charles Pierre. 1821–67, French poet, noted

b

for his macabre imagery; author of *Les fleurs du mal* (1857)

Baudouin I *n* 1930–93, king of Belgium (1951–93)

Baudrillard *n* Jean. 1929–2007, French sociologist and theorist of postmodernism; his books include *Seduction* (1979), *America* (1986), and *The Spirit of Terrorism* (2002)

bauera *n* small evergreen Australian shrub

Bauhaus (bow-house) *adj* of a school of architecture and applied arts in Germany in the 1920s and 30s characterized by a functionalist approach to design [German: building house]

baulk *vb, n* same as **balk**

Baum *n* L(yman) Frank. 1856–1919, US novelist, author of *The Wonderful Wizard of Oz* (1900) and its sequels

Baumgarten *n* Alexander Gottlieb. 1714–62, German philosopher, noted for his pioneering work on aesthetics, a term that he originated

Bautzen *n* a town in E Germany, in Saxony: site of an indecisive battle in 1813 between Napoleon's army and an allied army of Russians and Prussians. Pop: 42 160 (2003 est)

bauxite *n* a claylike substance that is the chief source of aluminium [(Les) Baux in southern France, where originally found]

Bavaria *n* a state of S Germany: a former duchy and kingdom; mainly wooded highland, with the Alps in the south. Capital: Munich. Pop: 12 155 000 (2000 est). Area: 70 531 sq km (27 232 sq miles). German name: Bayern

Bavarian *adj* **1** of or relating to Bavaria or its inhabitants ▷ *n* **2** a native or inhabitant of Bavaria

bawdy *adj* **bawdier, bawdiest** (of language, writing, etc.) containing humorous references to sex [Old French *baud* merry] ▷ **bawdily** *adv* ▷ **bawdiness** *n*

bawdyhouse *n archaic* a brothel

bawl *vb* **1** to cry noisily **2** to shout loudly ▷ *n* **3** a loud shout or cry [imitative] ▷ **bawling** *n*

Bax *n* Sir Arnold (Edward Trevor). 1883–1953, English composer of romantic works, often based on Celtic legends, including the tone poem *Tintagel* (1917)

Baxter *n* **1** James (Keir). 1926–72, New Zealand lyric poet. His works include *The Fallen House* (1953) and *In Fires of No Return* (1958) **2** Richard. 1615–91, English Puritan divine and devotional writer: prominent in church affairs during the Restoration

bay¹ *n* a stretch of shoreline that curves inwards [Old French *baie*]

bay² *n* **1** a recess in a wall **2** an area set aside for a particular purpose: *a sick bay; a loading bay* **3** same as **bay window 4** an area off a road in which vehicles may park or unload **5** a compartment in an aircraft: *the bomb bay* [Old French *baee* gap]

bay³ *n* **1** a deep howl of a hound or wolf **2 at bay a** forced to turn and face attackers: *the stag at bay* **b** at a safe distance: *to keep his mind blank and his despair at bay* ▷ *vb* **3** to howl in deep prolonged tones [Old French *abaiier* to bark]

bay⁴ *n* **1** a Mediterranean laurel tree with glossy aromatic leaves **2 bays** a wreath of bay leaves [Latin *baca* berry]

bay⁵ *adj* **1** reddish-brown ▷ *n* **2** a reddish-brown horse [Latin *badius*]

Bayamón *n* a city in NE central Puerto Rico, south of San Juan. Pop: 224 915 (2003 est)

Bayard *n* Chevalier de, original name Pierre de Terrail. ?1473–1524, French soldier, known as *le chevalier sans peur et sans reproche* (the fearless and irreproachable knight)

Baybars I *n* 1223–77, sultan of Egypt and Syria (1260–77), of the Mameluke dynasty

bayberry *n, pl* **-ries** a tropical American tree that yields an oil used in making bay rum. Also: **bay**

Bayelsa *n* a state of Nigeria, on the Niger river delta on the Gulf of Guinea. Capital: Yenagoa. Pop: 1 703 358 (2006). Area: 10 773 sq km (4159 sq miles)

Bayern *n* the German name for **Bavaria**

Bayeux *n* a town in NW France, on the River Aure: its museum houses the Bayeux tapestry and there is a 13th-century cathedral: dairy foods, plastic. Pop: 13 478 (2008)

Bayezid II *n* ?1447–1512, sultan of Turkey; he greatly extended Turkish dominions in Greece and the Balkans

Bayle *n* Pierre. 1647–1706, French philosopher and critic, noted for his *Dictionnaire historique et critique* (1697), which profoundly influenced Voltaire and the French Encyclopedists

bay leaf *n* the dried leaf of a laurel, used for flavouring in cooking

Baylis *n* **1** Lillian Mary. 1874–1937, British theatre manager: founded the Old Vic (1912) and the Sadler's Wells company for opera and ballet (1931) **2** Trevor (Graham). born 1937, British inventor of the clockwork radio (1992)

Bay of Pigs *n* a bay on the SW coast of Cuba: scene of an unsuccessful invasion of Cuba by US-backed troops (April 17, 1961). Spanish name: Bahía de los Cochinos

bayonet *n* **1** a blade that can be attached to the end of a rifle and used as a weapon ▷ *vb* **-neting, -neted** or **-netting, -netted 2** to stab or kill with a bayonet [*Bayonne*, a port in France, where it originated]

Bayonne *n* a port in SW France: a commercial centre for the Basque region. Pop: 45 636 (2006)

Bayreuth *n* a city in E Germany, in NE Bavaria: home and burial place of Richard Wagner; annual festivals of his music. Pop: 74 818 (2003 est)

bay rum *n* an aromatic liquid, used in medicines and cosmetics, which was originally obtained by distilling bayberry leaves with rum

Bay Street *n* (in Canada) **1** the financial centre of Toronto, in which Canada's largest stock exchange is situated **2** the financial interests and powers of Toronto

bay window *n* a window projecting from a wall

bazaar *n* **1** a sale, esp. one in aid of charity **2** (esp. in the Orient) a market area, esp. a street of small stalls [Persian *bāzār*]

bazooka *n* a portable rocket launcher that fires a projectile capable of piercing armour [after a pipe instrument devised by an American comedian]

BB *Brit* Boys' Brigade

BBC British Broadcasting Corporation

BBQ barbecue

BC 1 (indicating years numbered back from the supposed year of the birth of Christ) before Christ **2** British Columbia

BCE (used, esp. by non-Christians, in numbering years BC) before Common Era

BCG *trademark* Bacillus Calmette-Guérin (antituberculosis vaccine)

BD Bachelor of Divinity

BDS Bachelor of Dental Surgery

be *vb, pres. sing 1st pers* **am** *or 2nd pers* **are** *or 3rd pers* **is** *or pres. pl* **are** *or past sing 1st pers* **was** *or 2nd pers* **were** *or 3rd pers* **was** *or past pl* **were** *or pres. part* **being** *or past part* **been 1** to exist; live: *I think, therefore I am* **2** to pay a visit; go: *have you been to Spain?* **3** to take place: *my birthday was last Thursday* **4** used as a linking verb between the subject of a sentence and its complement: *John is a musician; honey is sweet; the dance is on Saturday* **5** forms the progressive present tense: *the man is running* **6** forms the passive voice of all transitive verbs: *a good film is being shown on television tomorrow* **7** expresses intention, expectation, or obligation: *the president is to arrive at 9.30* [Old English *bēon*]

Be *chem* beryllium

BE Bachelor of Engineering

be- *prefix* **1** to surround or cover: *befog* **2** to affect completely: *bedazzle* **3** to consider as or cause to be: *befriend* **4** to provide or cover with: *bejewel* **5** (*from verbs*) at, for, against, on, or over: *bewail* [Old English *be-, bi-* by]

beach *n* **1** an area of sand or pebbles sloping down to the sea or a lake ▷ *vb* **2** to run or haul (a boat) onto a beach [origin unknown]

beachcomber *n* a person who searches shore debris for anything of worth

beachhead *n military* an area of shore captured by an attacking army, on which troops and equipment are landed

Beachy Head *n* a headland in East Sussex, on the English Channel, consisting of chalk cliffs 171 m (570 ft) high

beacon *n* 1 a signal fire or light on a hill or tower, used formerly as a warning of invasion 2 a lighthouse 3 a radio or other signal marking a flight course in air navigation 4 same as **Belisha beacon** [Old English *beacen* sign]

Beaconsfield¹ *n* a town in SE England, in Buckinghamshire. Pop: 12 292 (2001)

Beaconsfield² *n* 1st Earl of. title of (Benjamin) **Disraeli**

bead *n* 1 a small pierced piece of glass, wood, or plastic that may be strung with others to form a necklace, rosary, etc. 2 a small drop of moisture 3 a small metal knob acting as the sight of a firearm ▷ *vb* 4 to decorate with beads [Old English *bed* prayer] ❭ **beaded** *adj*

beading *n* a narrow rounded strip of moulding used for edging furniture

beadle *n* 1 *Brit* (formerly) a minor parish official who acted as an usher 2 *Scot* a church official who attends the minister [Old English *bydel*]

Beadle *n* George Wells. 1903–89, US biologist, who shared the Nobel prize for physiology or medicine in 1958 for his work in genetics

beady *adj* **beadier, beadiest** small, round, and glittering: *beady eyes*

beagle *n* a small hound with a smooth coat, short legs, and drooping ears [origin unknown]

Beaglehole *n* John. 1901–71, New Zealand historian and author. His works include *Exploration of the Pacific* (1934) and *The Journals of James Cook* (1955)

beak¹ *n* 1 the projecting horny jaws of a bird 2 *slang* a person's nose [Latin *beccus*] ❭ **beaky** *adj*

beak² *n Brit, Austral and NZ slang* a judge, magistrate, or headmaster [originally thieves' jargon]

beaker *n* 1 a tall drinking cup 2 a lipped glass container used in laboratories [Old Norse *bikarr*]

Beale *n* 1 Dorothea. 1831–1906, British schoolmistress, a champion of women's education and suffrage. As principal of Cheltenham Ladies' College (1858–1906) she introduced important reforms 2 Simon Russell. born 1961, English actor born in Malaya, noted for his work for the Royal Shakespeare Company

beam *n* 1 a broad smile 2 a ray of light 3 a narrow flow of electromagnetic radiation or particles: *an electron beam* 4 a long thick piece of wood, metal, etc. used in building 5 the central shaft of a plough to which all the main parts are attached 6 the breadth of a ship at its widest part 7 off (the) beam *informal* mistaken or irrelevant ▷ *vb* 8 to smile broadly 9 to send out or radiate 10 to divert or aim (a radio signal, light, etc.) in a certain direction: *the concert was beamed live from Geneva* [Old English]

beam-ends *pl n* on one's beam-ends out of money

bean *n* 1 the seed or pod of various climbing plants, eaten as a vegetable 2 any of various beanlike seeds, such as coffee 3 full of beans *informal* full of energy and vitality 4 not have a bean *slang* to be without money [Old English *bēan*]

beanbag *n* 1 a small cloth bag filled with dried beans and thrown in games 2 a very large cushion filled with polystyrene granules and used as a seat

bean curd *n* same as **tofu**

beanfeast *n Brit informal* any festive or merry occasion

beanie *n Brit, Austral and NZ* a close-fitting woollen hat

beano *n, pl* **beanos** *Brit old-fashioned, slang* a celebration or party

beanpole *n slang* a tall thin person

beansprout *n* a small edible shoot grown from a bean seed, often used in Chinese dishes

bear¹ *vb* **bearing, bore, borne** 1 to support or hold up 2 to bring: *to bear gifts* 3 to accept the responsibility of: *to bear a heavier burden of taxation* 4 to give birth to 5 to produce by natural growth: *to bear fruit* 6 to tolerate or endure 7 to stand up to; sustain: *his story does not bear scrutiny* 8 to hold in the mind: *to bear a grudge* 9 to show or be marked with: *he still bears the scars* 10 to have, be, or stand in (relation or comparison): *her account bears no relation to the facts* 11 to move in a specified direction: *bear left* 12 bring to bear to bring into effect ▸ See also **bear down on, bear on**, etc. [Old English *beran*]

> **USAGE** When *bear* means 'give birth to', the past participle used to form the passive voice can be either *born* or *borne*. When it is followed by the preposition *by*, *borne* should be used: *babies borne by American surrogates*. In all other cases the past participle should be *born*: *I was born in Glasgow; the baby born to hairdresser Maxine*.

bear² *n, pl* **bears** *or* **bear** 1 a large heavily-built mammal with a long shaggy coat 2 a bearlike animal, such as the koala 3 an ill-mannered person 4 *Stock Exchange* a person who sells shares in anticipation of falling prices to make a profit on repurchase 5 like a bear with a sore head *informal* bad-tempered, irritable [Old English *bera*]

bearable *adj* endurable; tolerable

bear-baiting *n history* an entertainment in which dogs attacked a chained bear

beard *n* 1 the hair growing on the lower parts of a man's face 2 any similar growth in animals ▷ *vb* 3 to oppose boldly: *I bearded my formidable employer in her den* [Old English] ❭ **bearded** *adj*

bear down on *vb* 1 to press down on 2 to approach (someone) in a determined manner

Beardsley *n* Aubrey (Vincent). 1872–98, English illustrator: noted for his stylized black-and-white illustrations, esp. those for Oscar Wilde's *Salome* and Pope's *Rape of the Lock*

bearer *n* 1 a person or thing that carries, presents, or upholds something 2 a person who presents a note or bill for payment

bear hug *n* a rough tight embrace

bearing *n* 1 (foll. by *on* or *upon*) relevance to: *it has no bearing on this problem* 2 a part of a machine supporting another part, and usually reducing friction 3 the act of producing fruit or young 4 a person's general social conduct 5 the angular direction of a point measured from a known position 6 the position, as of a ship, fixed with reference to two or more known points 7 bearings a sense of one's relative position: *I lost my bearings in the dark* 8 *heraldry* a device on a heraldic shield

bear on *vb* to be relevant to

bear out *vb* to show to be truthful: *the witness will bear me out*

bearskin *n* 1 the pelt of a bear 2 a tall fur helmet worn by certain British Army regiments

bear up *vb* to cope with hardships: *they are bearing up well under the pressure*

bear with *vb* to be patient with

beast *n* 1 a large wild animal 2 a brutal or uncivilized person 3 savage nature or characteristics: *the beast in man* [Latin *bestia*]

beastly *adj* **-lier, -liest** *informal* unpleasant; disagreeable

beat *vb* **beating, beat, beaten** *or* **beat** 1 to strike with a series of violent blows 2 to move (wings) up and down 3 to throb rhythmically 4 *cookery* to stir or whisk vigorously 5 to shape (metal) by repeated blows 6 *music* to indicate (time) by one's hand or a baton 7 to produce (a sound) by striking a drum 8 to overcome or defeat: *he was determined to beat his illness* 9 to form (a path or track) by repeated use 10 to arrive, achieve, or finish before (someone or something): *she beat her team mate fair and square* 11 (foll. by *back, down, off,* etc.) to drive, push, or thrust **12** to scour (woodlands or undergrowth) to rouse game for shooting **13** *slang* to puzzle or baffle: *it beats me* ▷ *n* **14** a stroke or blow **15** the sound made by a stroke or blow **16** a regular throb **17** an assigned route, as of a policeman **18** the basic rhythmic unit in a piece of music **19** pop or rock music characterized by a heavy rhythmic beat ▷ *adj* **20** *slang* totally exhausted ▶ See also **beat down**, **beat up** [Old English *bēatan*] ❭ **beating** *n*

beatbox *n* **1** a drum machine ▷ *vb* **2** to simulate percussion instruments with the voice, esp. in hip-hop music ❭ **beatboxing** *n*

beat down *vb* **1** (of the sun) to shine intensely **2** *informal* to force or persuade (a seller) to accept a lower price

beater *n* **1** a device used for beating: *a carpet beater* **2** a person who rouses wild game

beatific *adj literary* **1** displaying great happiness **2** having a divine aura [Latin *beatus*]

beatify (bee-at-if-fie) *vb* **-fies, -fying, -fied** **1** RC *Church* to declare (a deceased person) to be among the blessed in heaven: the first step towards canonization **2** to make extremely happy ❭ **beatification** *n*

beatitude *n* supreme blessedness or happiness [Latin *beatitudo*]

Beatitude *n Christianity* any of the blessings on the poor, meek, etc., in the Sermon on the Mount

Beat movement *n* a group of US writers who emerged in the 1950s, noted for their rejection of the social and political systems of the West and their espousal of alternative lifestyles

beatnik *n* a young person in the late 1950s who rebelled against conventional attitudes and styles of dress [BEAT (noun) + -NIK]

Beaton *n* Sir Cecil (**Walter Hardy**). 1904–80, British photographer, noted esp. for his society portraits

Beatrix *n* full name *Beatrix Wilhelmina Armgard*. born 1938, queen of the Netherlands (1980–2013); abdicated in favour of her eldest son Willem-Alexander

Beatty *n* **1** David, 1st Earl Beatty. 1871–1936, British admiral of the fleet in World War I **2** Warren, full name *Henry Warren Beatty*. born 1937, US film actor and director: his films include *Bonnie and Clyde* (1967), *Heaven Can Wait* (1978), *Reds* (1981, also directed), *Bugsy* (1991), and *Bulworth* (1998, also wrote and directed)

beat up *informal vb* **1** to inflict severe physical damage on (someone) by striking or kicking repeatedly ▷ *n* **2** *Austral and NZ* a small matter deliberately exaggerated ▷ *adj* **beat-up 3** dilapidated

beau (boh) *n, pl* **beaux** *or* **beaus** (bohz) **1** *chiefly US* a boyfriend **2** a man who is greatly concerned with his appearance [French]

Beaufort *n* **1** Henry. ?1374–1447, English cardinal, half-brother of Henry IV; chancellor (1403–04, 1413–17, 1424–26) **2** Lady Margaret, Countess of Richmond and Derby. ?1443–1509, mother of Henry VII. She helped to found two Cambridge colleges and was a patron of Caxton

Beaufort scale *n meteorol* a scale for measuring wind speeds, ranging from 0 (calm) to 12 (hurricane) [after Sir Francis Beaufort, who devised it]

Beaufort Sea *n* part of the Arctic Ocean off the N coast of North America

Beauharnais *n* **1** Alexandre, Vicomte de. 1760–94, French general, who served in the War of American Independence and the French Revolutionary wars; first husband of Empress Joséphine: guillotined **2** his son, Eugène de. 1781–1824, viceroy of Italy (1805–14) for his stepfather Napoleon I **3** (Eugénie) Hortense de. 1783–1837, queen of Holland (1806–10) as wife of Louis Bonaparte; daughter of Alexandre Beauharnais and sister of Eugène: mother of Napoleon III **4** Joséphine de, previous name of the Empress Josephine. See Josephine

Beaujolais *n* a red or white wine from southern Burgundy in France

Beaulieu *n* a village in S England, in Hampshire: site of Palace House, seat of Lord Montagu and once the gatehouse of the ruined 13th-century abbey; the National Motor Museum is in its grounds. Pop: 809 (2001)

Beaumarchais *n* Pierre Augustin Caron de. 1732–99, French dramatist, noted for his comedies *The Barber of Seville* (1775) and *The Marriage of Figaro* (1784)

Beaumaris *n* a resort in N Wales, on the island of Anglesey: 13th-century castle. Pop: 1513 (2001)

Beaumont[1] *n* a city in SE Texas. Pop: 112 434 (2003 est)

Beaumont[2] *n* Francis. 1584–1616, English dramatist, who collaborated with John Fletcher on plays including *The Knight of the Burning Pestle* (1607) and *The Maid's Tragedy* (1611)

Beaune *n* **1** a town in E France, near Dijon: an important trading centre for Burgundy wines. Pop: 22 218 (2008) **2** a wine produced in this district

beauteous *adj poetic* beautiful

beautician *n* a person who works in a beauty salon

beautiful *adj* **1** being very attractive to look at **2** highly enjoyable; very pleasant ❭ **beautifully** *adv*

beautify *vb* **-fies, -fying, -fied** to make beautiful ❭ **beautification** *n*

beauty *n, pl* **-ties** **1** the combination of all the qualities of a person or thing that delight the senses and mind **2** a very attractive woman **3** *informal* an outstanding example of its kind **4** *informal* an advantageous feature: *the beauty of this job is the short hours* [Latin *bellus* handsome]

beauty queen *n* a woman who has been judged the most beautiful in a contest

beauty salon *or* **beauty parlour** *n* an establishment that provides services such as hairdressing, facial treatment, and massage

beauty spot *n* **1** a place of outstanding beauty **2** a small dark-coloured spot formerly worn on a lady's face as decoration

Beauvais *n* a market town in N France, 64 km (40 miles) northwest of Paris. Pop: 55 392 (1999)

beaver *n* **1** a large amphibious rodent with soft brown fur, a broad flat tail, and webbed hind feet **2** its fur **3** a tall hat made of this fur ▷ *vb* **4** **beaver away** to work very hard and steadily [Old English *beofor*]

Beaverbrook *n* 1st Baron, title of *William Maxwell Aitken*. 1879–1964, British newspaper proprietor and Conservative politician, born in Canada, whose newspapers included the *Daily Express*; minister of information (1918); minister of aircraft production (1940–41)

Bebel *n* August. 1840–1913, German socialist leader: one of the founders of the Social Democratic Party (1869)

Bebington *n* a town in NW England, in Wirral unitary authority, Merseyside: docks and chemical works. Pop: 57 066 (2001)

bebop *n* same as **bop** [imitative of the rhythm]

becalmed *adj* (of a sailing ship) motionless through lack of wind

became *vb* the past tense of **become**

because *conj* **1** on account of the fact that: *because it's so cold we'll go home* **2** **because of** on account of: *I lost my job because of her* [Middle English *bi cause*]

> **USAGE** See at **reason**.

Beccaria *n* Cesare Bonesana, Marchese de. 1738–94, Italian legal theorist and political economist; author of the influential treatise *Crimes and Punishments* (1764), which attacked corruption, torture, and capital punishment

bechamel sauce (bay-sham-ell) *n* a thick white sauce flavoured with onion and seasonings [after the Marquis of *Béchamel*, its inventor]

Béchar *n* a city in NW Algeria: an oasis. Pop: 149 000 (2005 est). Former name: **Colomb-Béchar**

Bechet *n* Sidney (**Joseph**). 1897–1959, US jazz soprano saxophonist and clarinettist

Bechstein *n* Karl. 1826–1900, German piano maker; founder (1853) of the Bechstein company of piano manufacturers in Berlin

Bechuanaland *n* the former name (until 1966) of Botswana

beck¹ *n* at someone's beck and call having to be constantly available to do as someone asks [Middle English *becnen* to beckon]

beck² *n* (in N England) a stream [Old English *becc*]

Beckenbauer *n* Franz. born 1945, German footballer: team captain when West Germany won the World Cup (1974); manager of West Germany (1984–90), coaching the team to success in the 1990 World Cup

Becker *n* Boris. born 1967, German tennis player: Wimbledon champion 1985, 1986, and 1989: the youngest man ever to win Wimbledon

Becket *n* Saint Thomas à. 1118–70, English prelate; chancellor (1155–62) to Henry II; archbishop of Canterbury (1162–70): murdered following his opposition to Henry's attempts to control the clergy. Feast day: Dec 29 or July 7

Beckett *n* 1 Dame Margaret Mary. born 1943, British Labour politician; leader of the House of Commons (1998–2001); secretary of state for environment, food, and rural affairs (2001–2006); foreign secretary (2006– 07) 2 Samuel (Barclay). 1906–89, Irish dramatist and novelist writing in French and English, whose works portray the human condition as insignificant or absurd in a bleak universe. They include the plays *En attendant Godot* (*Waiting for Godot*, 1952), *Fin de partie* (*Endgame*, 1957), and *Not I* (1973) and the novel *Malone meurt* (*Malone Dies*, 1951): Nobel prize for literature 1969

Beckford *n* William. 1759–1844, English writer and dilettante; author of the oriental romance *Vathek* (1787)

Beckham *n* 1 David. born 1975, English footballer; played for Manchester United (1993–2003), Real Madrid (2003–07), Los Angeles Galaxy (2007–12), and England (1996–2009) for whom he won 115 caps 2 his wife, Victoria Caroline, née *Adams*, known as *Posh Spice*. born 1974, English pop singer and fashion designer, member of the Spice Girls

Beckmann *n* 1 Ernst Otto. 1853–1923, German chemist: devised the Beckmann thermometer, used for measuring small temperature changes in liquids 2 Max. 1884–1950, German expressionist painter

beckon *vb* 1 to summon with a gesture 2 to lure: *fame beckoned* [Old English *bīecnan*]

become *vb* -coming, -came, -come 1 to come to be: *he became Prime Minister last year* 2 (foll. by of) to happen to: *what became of him?* 3 to suit: *that dress becomes you* [Old English *becuman* happen]

becoming *adj* suitable or appropriate: *his conduct was not becoming to the rank of officer*

becquerel (beck-a-rell) *n* the SI unit of activity of a radioactive source [after A. H. BECQUEREL]

Becquerel *n* Antoine Henri. 1852–1908, French physicist, who discovered the photographic action of the rays emitted by uranium salts and so instigated the study of radioactivity: Nobel prize for physics 1903

bed *n* 1 a piece of furniture on which to sleep 2 a plot of ground in which plants are grown 3 the bottom of a river, lake, or sea 4 any underlying structure or part 5 a layer of rock 6 get out of bed on the wrong side *informal* to begin the day in a bad mood 7 go to bed with to have sexual intercourse with ▷ *vb* bedding, bedded 8 (foll. by down) to go to or put into a place to sleep or rest 9 to have sexual intercourse with 10 to place firmly into position: *the poles were bedded in concrete* 11 *geology* to form or be arranged in a distinct layer 12 to plant in a bed of soil [Old English *bedd*]

BEd Bachelor of Education

bed and breakfast *n chiefly Brit* overnight accommodation and breakfast

bedaub *vb* to smear over with something sticky or dirty

bedbug *n* a small blood-sucking wingless insect that infests dirty houses

bedclothes *pl n* coverings for a bed

bedding *n* 1 bedclothes, sometimes with a mattress 2 litter, such as straw, for animals 3 the distinct layered deposits of rocks

Beddoes *n* Thomas Lovell. 1803–49, British poet, noted for his macabre imagery, esp. in *Death's Jest-Book* (1850)

Bede *n* Saint, known as *the Venerable Bede*. ?673–735 AD, English monk, scholar, historian, and theologian, noted for his Latin *Ecclesiastical History of the English People* (731). Feast day: May 27 or 25. Latin name: **Baeda**

bedeck *vb* to cover with decorations

bedevil (bid-dev-ill) *vb* -illing, -illed *or US* -iling, -iled 1 to harass or torment 2 to throw into confusion ▷ **bedevilment** *n*

bedfellow *n* 1 a temporary associate 2 a person with whom one shares a bed

Bedford¹ *n* 1 a town in SE central England, in Bedfordshire, on the River Ouse; administrative centre of Bedford unitary authority. Pop: 82 488 (2001) 2 a unitary authority of SE central England. Pop: 154 900 (2007 est.). Area: 480 sq km (185 sq miles) 3 short for Bedfordshire

Bedford² *n* 1 David. 1937–2011, British composer, influenced by rock music 2 Duke of, title of *John of Lancaster*. 1389–1435, son of Henry IV of England: protector of England and regent of France (1422–35)

Bedfordshire *n* a county of S central England, administered since 2009 by the unitary authorities of Bedford and Central Bedfordshire: mainly low-lying, with the Chiltern Hills in the south: the geographical county includes Luton, which became a separate unitary authority in 1997. Area (excluding Luton): 1192 sq km (460 sq miles). Abbreviation: **Beds**

bedlam *n* a noisy confused situation [from Hospital of St Mary of *Bethlehem*, a former mental hospital in London]

bed linen *n* sheets and pillowcases for a bed

Bedloe's Island *or* **Bedloe Island** *n* the former name (until 1956) of Liberty Island

Bedouin *n* 1 (*pl* -ins *or* -in) a nomadic Arab tribesman of the deserts of Arabia, Jordan, and Syria 2 a wanderer [Arabic *badw* desert]

bedpan *n* a shallow container used as a toilet by people who are not well enough to leave bed

bedraggled *adj* with hair or clothing that is untidy, wet, or dirty

bedridden *adj* unable to leave bed because of illness

bedrock *n* 1 the solid rock beneath the surface soil 2 basic principles or facts

bedroom *n* 1 a room used for sleeping ▷ *adj* 2 containing references to sex: *a bedroom comedy*

Beds Bedfordshire

bedside *n* 1 the area beside a bed ▷ *adj* 2 placed at or near the side of the bed: *the bedside table*

bedsit *or* **bedsitter** *n* a furnished sitting room with a bed

bedsore *n* an ulcer on the skin, caused by a lengthy period of lying in bed due to illness

bedspread *n* a top cover on a bed

bedstead *n* the framework of a bed

bedstraw *n* a plant with small white or yellow flowers

bed-wetting *n* involuntarily urinating in bed

Bedworth *n* a town in central England, in N Warwickshire. Pop: 30 001 (2001)

bee¹ *n* 1 a four-winged insect that collects nectar and pollen to make honey and wax 2 have a bee in one's bonnet to be obsessed with an idea [Old English *bīo*]

bee² *n* a social gathering to carry out a communal task: *quilting bee* [probably from Old English *bēn* boon]

Beeb *n* the Beeb *Brit informal* the BBC

beech *n* 1 a tree with smooth greyish bark 2 the hard wood of this tree 3 See **copper beech** [Old English *bēce*]

b

Beecham n Sir Thomas. 1879–1961, English conductor who did much to promote the works of Delius, Sibelius, and Richard Strauss

Beecher n Henry Ward. 1813–87, US clergyman: a leader in the movement for the abolition of slavery

beechnut n the small brown triangular edible nut of the beech tree

beef n **1** the flesh of a cow, bull, or ox **2** slang a complaint ▷ vb **3** slang to complain ▶ See also **beef up** [Old French boef, from Latin bos ox]

beefburger n a flat fried or grilled cake of minced beef; hamburger

beefcake n slang musclemen as displayed in photographs

beefeater n a yeoman warder of the Tower of London

beef tea n a drink made by boiling pieces of lean beef

beef tomato or **beefsteak tomato** n a type of large fleshy tomato

beef up vb informal to strengthen

beefy adj **beefier, beefiest 1** informal muscular **2** like beef ▷ **beefiness** n

beehive n a structure in which bees are housed

Beehive n the Beehive informal **1** the dome-shaped building that houses sections of Parliament in Wellington, New Zealand **2** the New Zealand government

beekeeper n a person who keeps bees for their honey ▷ **beekeeping** n

beeline n **make a beeline for** to speedily take the most direct route to

Beelzebub (bee-ell-zib-bub) n Satan or any devil [Hebrew bá'al zebūb, literally: lord of flies]

been vb the past participle of **be**

beep n **1** a high-pitched sound, like that of a car horn ▷ vb **2** to make or cause to make such a noise [imitative]

beer n **1** an alcoholic drink brewed from malt, sugar, hops, and water **2** a glass, can, or bottle containing this drink [Old English beor]

beer and skittles n informal enjoyment or pleasure

Beerbohm n Sir (Henry) Max(imilian). 1872–1956, English critic, wit, and caricaturist, whose works include Zuleika Dobson (1911), a satire on Oxford undergraduates

beer parlour n Canad a licensed place in which beer is sold and drunk

Beersheba n a town in S Israel: commercial centre of the Negev. In biblical times it marked the southern limit of Palestine. Pop: 183 000 (2003 est)

beery adj **beerier, beeriest** smelling or tasting of beer

beeswax n **1** a wax produced by honeybees for making honeycombs **2** this wax after refining, used in polishes, etc.

beet n a plant with an edible root and leaves, such as the sugar beet and beetroot [Old English bēte]

Beethoven n Ludwig van. 1770–1827, German composer, who greatly extended the form and scope of symphonic and chamber music, bridging the classical and romantic traditions. His works include nine symphonies, 32 piano sonatas, 16 string quartets, five piano concertos, a violin concerto, two masses, the opera Fidelio (1805), and choral music

beetle¹ n **1** an insect with a hard wing-case closed over its back for protection ▷ vb **-tling, -tled 2** (foll. by along, off, etc.) informal to scuttle or scurry [Old English bitela]

beetle² vb **-tling, -tled** to overhang; jut: the eaves of the roof beetled out over the windows [origin unknown] ▷ **beetling** adj

beetle-browed adj having bushy or overhanging eyebrows

Beeton n Isabella Mary, known as Mrs Beeton. 1836–65, British cookery writer, author of The Book of Household Management (1861)

beetroot n a variety of the beet plant with a dark red root that may be eaten as a vegetable, in salads, or pickled

beet sugar n the sucrose obtained from sugar beet

befall vb **-falling, -fell, -fallen** archaic or literary to happen to [Old English befeallan]

befit vb **-fitting, -fitted** to be appropriate to or suitable for ▷ **befitting** adj

before conj **1** earlier than the time when **2** rather than: she'll resign before she agrees to it ▷ prep **3** preceding in space or time; in front of; ahead of: they stood before the altar **4** in the presence of: to be brought before a judge **5** in preference to: to put friendship before money ▷ adv **6** previously **7** in front [Old English beforan]

beforehand adj, adv early; in advance

befriend vb to become a friend to

befuddled adj stupefied or confused, as through alcoholic drink

beg vb **begging, begged 1** to ask for money or food in the street **2** to ask formally, humbly, or earnestly: I beg forgiveness; I beg to differ **3 beg the question** to put forward an argument that assumes the very point it is supposed to establish, or that depends on some other questionable assumption **4 go begging** to be unwanted or unused [probably from Old English bedecian]

began vb the past tense of **begin**

beget vb **-getting, -got** or **-gat, -gotten** or **-got** old-fashioned **1** to cause or create: repetition begets boredom **2** to father [Old English begietan]

beggar n **1** a person who lives by begging **2** chiefly Brit a fellow: lucky beggar! ▷ vb **3 beggar description** to be impossible to describe ▷ **beggarly** adj

begin vb **-ginning, -gan, -gun 1** to start (something) **2** to bring or come into being **3** to start to say or speak **4** to have the least capacity to do something: it doesn't even begin to address the problem [Old English beginnan] ▷ **beginner** n

Begin n Menachem. 1913–92, Israeli statesman, born in Poland. In Palestine after 1942, he became a leader of the militant Zionists; prime minister of Israel (1977–83); Nobel peace prize jointly with Sadat 1978. In 1979 he concluded the Camp David treaty with Anwar Sadat of Egypt

beginner's luck n exceptional luck supposed to attend a beginner

beginning n **1** a start **2 beginnings** an early part or stage **3** the place where or time when something starts **4** an origin; source

begone interj go away!

begonia n a tropical plant with ornamental leaves and waxy flowers [after Michel Bégon, patron of science]

begot vb a past tense and past participle of **beget**

begotten vb a past participle of **beget**

begrudge vb **-grudging, -grudged 1** to envy (someone) the possession of something **2** to give or allow unwillingly: he begrudged her an apology

beguile (big-gile) vb **-guiling, -guiled** to charm (someone) into doing something he or she would not normally do

beguiling adj charming, often in a deceptive way

beguine (big-geen) n **1** a dance of South American origin **2** music for this dance [French béguin flirtation]

begum (bay-gum) n (in certain Muslim countries) a woman of high rank [Turkish begim]

begun vb the past participle of **begin**

behalf n **on** or US and Canad **in behalf of** in the interest of or for the benefit of [Old English be by + halfe side]

Behan n Brendan. 1923–64, Irish writer, noted esp. for his plays The Quare Fellow (1954) and The Hostage (1958) and for an account of his detention as a member of the Irish Republican Army, Borstal Boy (1958)

behave vb **-having, -haved 1** to act or function in a particular way **2** to conduct oneself in a particular way: the baby behaved very well **3** to conduct oneself properly [Middle English]

behaviour or US **behavior** n **1** manner of behaving **2** psychol the response of an organism to a stimulus ▷ **behavioural** or US **behavioral** adj

behavioural science *n* the scientific study of the behaviour of organisms

behaviourism *or US* **behaviorism** *n* a school of psychology that regards objective observation of the behaviour of organisms as the only valid subject for study **> behaviourist** *or US* **behaviorist** *adj, n*

behead *vb* to remove the head from [Old English *behēafdian*]

beheld *vb* the past of **behold**

behemoth (bee-hee-moth) *n* a huge person or thing [Hebrew *běhēmāh* beast, name given to a huge beast in the Bible (Job 40:15)]

behest *n* an order or earnest request: *I came at her behest* [Old English *behǣs*]

behind *prep* **1** in or to a position further back than **2** in the past in relation to: *I want to leave the past behind me* **3** late according to: *running behind schedule* **4** concerning the circumstances surrounding: *the reasons behind his departure* **5** supporting: *I'm right behind you in your application* ▷ *adv* **6** in or to a position further back **7** remaining after someone's departure: *she left her books behind* **8** in arrears: *to fall behind with payments* ▷ *adj* **9** in a position further back ▷ *n* **10** *informal* the buttocks [Old English *behindan*]

behindhand *adj, adv* **1** in arrears **2** backward **3** late

Behistun, Bisitun *or* **Bisutun** *n* a village in W Iran by the ancient road from Ecbatana to Babylon. On a nearby cliff is an inscription by Darius in Old Persian, Elamite, and Babylonian describing his enthronement

Behn *n* Aphra. 1640–89, English dramatist and novelist, best known for her play *The Rover* (1678) and her novel *Oroonoko* (1688)

behold *vb* **-holding, -held** *archaic or literary* to look (at); observe [Old English *bihealdan*] **> beholder** *n*

beholden *adj* indebted; obliged: *I am beholden to you*

behove *vb* **-hoving, -hoved** *archaic* to be necessary or fitting for: *it behoves me to warn you* [Old English *behōfian*]

Behrens *n* Peter. 1868–1940, German architect

Behring *n* **1** Emil (Adolf) von. 1854–1917, German bacteriologist, who discovered diphtheria and tetanus antitoxins: Nobel prize for physiology or medicine 1901 **2** a variant spelling of **Bering**

Beiderbecke *n* Leon Bismarcke, known as Bix. 1903–31, US jazz cornettist, composer, and pianist

beige *adj* pale creamy-brown [Old French]

Beijing *n* the capital of the People's Republic of China, in the northeast in Beijing municipality (traditionally in Hebei province); the country's second largest city: dates back to the 12th century BC; consists of two central walled cities, the Outer City (containing the commercial quarter) and the Inner City, which contains the Imperial City, within which is the Purple or Forbidden City; many universities. Pop: 10 849 000 (2005 est). Former English name: **Peking**

being *n* **1** the state or fact of existing **2** essential nature; self **3** something that exists or is thought to exist: *a being from outer space* **4** a human being

Beira *n* a port in E Mozambique: terminus of a transcontinental railway from Lobito, Angola, through the Democratic Republic of Congo, Zambia, and Zimbabwe. Pop: 566 000 (2005 est)

Beirut *or* **Beyrouth** *n* the capital of Lebanon, a port on the Mediterranean: part of the Ottoman Empire from the 16th century until 1918; many universities (including Lebanese, American, French, and Arab). Pop: 1 875 000 (2005 est)

Béjart *n* Maurice. 1927–2007 French dancer and choreographer. His choreography is characterized by a combination of classic and modern dance and acrobatics

bejewelled *or US* **bejeweled** *adj* decorated with jewels

Bekaa *or* **Beqaa** *n* a broad valley in central Lebanon, between the Lebanon and Anti-Lebanon Mountains. Ancient name: **Coelesyria**

Békésy *n* Georg von. 1899–1972, US physicist, born in Hungary; noted for his work on the mechanism of hearing: Nobel prize for physiology or medicine 1961

bel *n* a unit for comparing two power levels or measuring the intensity of a sound, equal to 10 decibels [after A. G. BELL, scientist]

belabour *or US* **belabor** *vb* to attack verbally or physically

Belarus, Byelorussia *or* **Belorussia** *n* a republic in E Europe; part of the medieval Lithuanian and Polish empires before being occupied by Russia; a Soviet republic (1919–91); in 1997 formed a close political and economic union with Russia: mainly low-lying and forested. Languages: Belarussian; Russian. Religion: believers are mostly Christian. Currency: rouble. Capital: Minsk. Pop: 9 625 888 (2013 est). Area: 207 600 sq km (80 134 sq miles). Also called: **Byelorussian Republic, Bielorussia, White Russia**

Belarussian, Belarusian, Byelorussian *or* **Belorussian** *adj* **1** of, relating to, or characteristic of Belarus, its people, or their language ▷ *n* **2** the official language of Belarus: an East Slavonic language closely related to Russian **3** a native or inhabitant of Belarus ▶ Also called: **White Russian**

belated *adj* late or too late: *belated greetings* **> belatedly** *adv*

Belau *n* an alternative name for the (Republic of) **Palau**

belay *vb* **-laying, -layed** **1** *nautical* to secure (a line) to a pin or cleat **2** *nautical* to stop **3** *mountaineering* to secure (a climber) by fixing a rope round a rock or piton [Old English *belecgan*]

belch *vb* **1** to expel wind from the stomach noisily through the mouth **2** to expel or be expelled forcefully: *smoke belching from factory chimneys* ▷ *n* **3** an act of belching [Old English *bialcan*]

beleaguered *adj* **1** struggling against difficulties or criticism: *the country's beleaguered health system* **2** besieged by an enemy: *a ship bringing food to the beleaguered capital of Monrovia* [BE- + obsolete *leaguer* a siege]

Belém *n* a port in N Brazil, the capital of Pará state, on the Pará River: major trading centre for the Amazon basin. Pop: 2 097 000 (2005 est)

Belfast *n* **1** the capital of Northern Ireland, a port on Belfast Lough in Belfast district, Co Antrim and Co Down: became the centre of Irish Protestantism and of the linen industry in the 17th century; seat of the Northern Ireland assembly and executive. Pop: 281 000 (2011 est) **2** a district of W Northern Ireland, in Co Antrim and Co Down. Pop: 268 700 (2010 est). Area: 115 sq km (44 sq miles)

Belfort *n* **1** Territoire de Belfort a department of E France, now in Franche-Comté region: the only part of Alsace remaining to France after 1871. Capital: Belfort. Pop: 139 383 (2003 est). Area: 608 sq km (237 sq miles) **2** a fortress town in E France: strategically situated in the **Belfort Gap** between the Vosges and the Jura mountains. Pop: 50 417 (1999)

belfry *n, pl* **-fries** **1** the part of a tower or steeple in which bells are hung **2** a tower or steeple [Germanic]

Belg. *or* **Bel.** **1** Belgian **2** Belgium

Belgaum *n* a city in India, in Karnataka: cotton, furniture, leather. Pop: 399 600 (2001)

Belgian *adj* **1** of or relating to Belgium or its inhabitants ▷ *n* **2** a native or inhabitant of Belgium

Belgian Congo *n* a former name (1908–60) of **Congo** (1)

Belgium *n* a federal kingdom in NW Europe: at various times under the rulers of Burgundy, Spain, Austria, France, and the Netherlands before becoming an independent kingdom in 1830. It formed the Benelux customs union with the Netherlands and Luxembourg in 1948 and was a founder member of the Common Market, now the European Union. It consists chiefly of a low-lying region of sand, woods, and heath (the Campine) in the north and west, and a fertile undulating central plain rising to the Ardennes

b

Mountains in the southeast. Languages: French, Flemish (Dutch), German. Religion: Roman Catholic majority. Currency: euro. Capital: Brussels. Pop: 10 444 268 (2013 est). Area: 30 513 sq km (11 778 sq miles)

belgium sausage *n* NZ large smooth bland sausage

Belgorod-Dnestrovski *or* **Byelgorod-Dnestrovski** *n* a port in SW Ukraine, on the Dniester estuary: belonged to Romania from 1918 until 1940; under Soviet rule (1944–91). Pop: 48 100 (2004 est). Romanian name: **Cetatea Albă**. Former name (until 1946): **Akkerman**

Belgrade *n* the capital of Serbia, in the E part at the confluence of the Danube and Sava Rivers: became the capital of Serbia in 1878, of Yugoslavia in 1929, and later of the State Union of Serbia and Montenegro (2003–2006). Pop: 1 280 639 (2002). Serbian name: **Beograd**

Belgravia *n* a fashionable residential district of W central London, around Belgrave Square

Belial (bee-lee-al) *n* the devil or Satan [Hebrew *bəlīyya'al* worthless]

belie *vb* **-lying, -lied** 1 to show to be untrue: *the facts belied the theory* 2 to misrepresent: *the score belied the closeness of the match* 3 to fail to justify: *the promises were soon belied* [Old English *beléogan*]

belief *n* 1 trust or confidence: *belief in the free market* 2 opinion; conviction: *it's my firm belief* 3 a principle, etc., accepted as true, often without proof 4 religious faith

believe *vb* **-lieving, -lieved** 1 to accept as true or real: *I believe God exists* 2 to think, assume, or suppose: *I believe you know my father* 3 to accept the statement or opinion of (a person) as true 4 to have religious faith 5 **believe in** to be convinced of the truth or existence of: *I don't believe in ghosts* [Old English *beliefan*] ⟩ **believable** *adj* ⟩ **believer** *n*

Belisarius *n* ?505–565 AD, Byzantine general under Justinian I. He recovered North Africa from the Vandals and Italy from the Ostrogoths and led forces against the Persians

Belisha beacon (bill-lee-sha) *n* Brit a flashing orange globe mounted on a striped post, indicating a pedestrian crossing [after L. Hore-*Belisha*, politician]

belittle *vb* **-tling, -tled** to treat (something or someone) as having little value or importance

Belitung *n* another name for **Billiton**

Belize *n* a state in Central America, on the Caribbean Sea: site of a Mayan civilization until the 9th century AD; colonized by the British from 1638; granted internal self-government in 1964; became an independent state within the Commonwealth in 1981. Official language: English; Carib and Spanish are also spoken. Currency: Belize dollar. Capital: Belmopan. Pop: 334 297 (2013 est). Area: 22 965 sq km (8867 sq miles). Former name (until 1973): **British Honduras**

Belizean *adj* 1 of or relating to Belize or its inhabitants ▷ *n* 2 a native or inhabitant of Belize

Belize City *n* a port and the largest city in Belize, on the Caribbean coast: capital until 1973, when that function was transferred inland to Belmopan owing to hurricane risk. Pop: 53 000 (2005 est)

bell *n* 1 a hollow, usually metal, cup-shaped instrument that emits a ringing sound when struck 2 the sound made by such an instrument 3 an electrical device that rings or buzzes as a signal 4 something shaped like a bell 5 Brit slang a telephone call 6 **ring a bell** to sound familiar; recall something previously experienced [Old English *belle*]

Bell *n* 1 **Acton, Currer,** and **Ellis.** pen names of the sisters Anne, Charlotte, and Emily Brontë. See **Brontë** 2 **Alexander Graham.** 1847–1922, US scientist, born in Scotland, who invented the telephone (1876) 3 **Sir Francis Henry Dillon.** 1851–1936, New Zealand statesman; prime minister of New Zealand (1925) 4 **Gertrude** (**Margaret Lowthian**). 1868–1926, British traveller, writer, and diplomat; secretary to the British High Commissioner in Baghdad (1917–26) 5 **Joshua.** born 1967, US violinist 6 **Dame** (**Susan**) **Jocelyn**, married name

Jocelyn Burnell, born 1943, British radio astronomer, who discovered the first pulsar 7 **Vanessa**, original name *Vanessa Stephen*. 1879–1961, British painter; a member of the Bloomsbury group, sister of Virginia Woolf and wife of the art critic Clive Bell (1881–1964)

belladonna *n* 1 a drug obtained from deadly nightshade 2 same as **deadly nightshade** [Italian, literally: beautiful lady; supposed to refer to its use as a cosmetic]

Bellamy *n* David (James). born 1933, British botanist, writer, and broadcaster

Bellarmine *n* Saint Robert. 1542–1621, Italian Jesuit theologian and cardinal; an important influence during the Counter-Reformation

Bellay *n* Joachim du. 1522–60, French poet, a member of the Pléiade

bell-bottoms *pl n* trousers that flare from the knee ⟩ **bell-bottomed** *adj*

belle *n* a beautiful woman, esp. the most attractive woman at a function: *the belle of the ball* [French]

Belleau Wood *n* a forest in N France: site of a battle (1918) in which the US Marines halted a German advance on Paris

Belle Isle *n* an island in the Atlantic, at the N entrance to the **Strait of Belle Isle**, between Labrador and Newfoundland. Area: about 39 sq km (15 sq miles)

belles-lettres (bell-let-tra) *n* literary works, particularly essays and poetry [French]

bellicose *adj* warlike; aggressive [Latin *bellum* war]

belligerence *n* the act or quality of being belligerent or warlike

belligerent *adj* 1 marked by readiness to fight 2 relating to or engaged in a war ▷ *n* 3 a person or country engaged in war [Latin *bellum* war + *gerere* to wage]

Bellingshausen Sea *n* an area of the S Pacific Ocean off the coast of Antarctica [named after Fabian Gottlieb *Bellingshausen* (1778–1852), Russian explorer]

Bellini *n* 1 **Giovanni.** ?1430–1516, Italian painter of the Venetian school, noted for his altarpieces, landscapes, and Madonnas. His father **Jacopo** (?1400–70) and his brother **Gentile** (?1429–1507) were also painters 2 **Vincenzo.** 1801–35, Italian composer of operas, esp. *La Sonnambula* (1831) and *Norma* (1831)

Bellinzona *n* a town in SE central Switzerland, capital of Ticino canton. Pop: 16 463 (2000)

bell jar *n* a bell-shaped glass cover used to protect flower arrangements or cover apparatus to confine gases in experiments

Belloc *n* Hilaire. 1870–1953, British poet, essayist, and historian, born in France, noted particularly for his verse for children in *The Bad Child's Book of Beasts* (1896) and *Cautionary Tales* (1907)

bellow *vb* 1 to make a loud deep cry like that of a bull 2 to shout in anger ▷ *n* 3 the characteristic noise of a bull 4 a loud deep roar [probably from Old English *bylgan*]

Bellow *n* Saul. 1915–2005, US novelist, born in Canada. His works include *Dangling Man* (1944), *The Adventures of Angie March* (1954), *Herzog* (1964), *Humboldt's Gift* (1975), *The Dean's December* (1981), and *Ravelstein* (2000): Nobel prize for literature 1976

bellows *n* 1 a device consisting of an air chamber with flexible sides that is used to create and direct a stream of air 2 a flexible corrugated part, such as that connecting the lens system of some cameras to the body [plural of Old English *belig* belly]

bell pull *n* a handle or cord pulled to operate a bell

bell push *n* a button pressed to operate an electric bell

bell-ringer *n* a person who rings church bells or musical handbells ⟩ **bell-ringing** *n*

bells and whistles *pl n* attractive but nonessential additional features [from the bells and whistles which used to decorate fairground organs]

belly *n, pl* **-lies** 1 the part of the body of a vertebrate containing the intestines and other organs 2 the stomach 3 the front, lower, or inner part of something

4 go belly up *informal* to die, fail, or end ▷ *vb* **-lies, -lying, -lied 5** to swell out; bulge [Old English *belig*]

bellyache *n* **1** *informal* a pain in the abdomen ▷ *vb* **-aching, -ached 2** *slang* to complain repeatedly

bellybutton *n informal* the navel

belly dance *n* **1** a sensuous dance performed by women, with undulating movements of the abdomen ▷ *vb* **belly-dance (-dancing, -danced) 2** to dance thus **> belly dancer** *n*

belly flop *n* **1** a dive into water in which the body lands horizontally ▷ *vb* **belly-flop (-flopping, -flopped) 2** to perform a belly flop

bellyful *n* **1** *slang* more than one can tolerate **2** as much as one wants or can eat

belly laugh *n* a loud deep hearty laugh

Belmondo *n* Jean-Paul. born 1933, French film actor

Belmopan *n* (since 1973) the capital of Belize, about 50 miles inland: founded in 1970. Pop: 10 000 (2005 est)

Belo Horizonte *n* a city in SE Brazil, the capital of Minas Gerais state. Pop: 5 304 000 (2005 est)

belong *vb* **1** (foll. by *to*) to be the property of **2** (foll. by *to*) to be bound to (a person, organization, etc.) by ties of affection, association, membership, etc.: *the nations concerned belonged to NATO* **3** (foll. by *to, under, with,* etc.) to be classified with: *it belongs to a different class of comets* **4** (foll. by *to*) to be a part of: *this lid belongs to that tin* **5** to have a proper or usual place **6** *informal* to be acceptable, esp. socially [Middle English *belongen*]

belonging *n* a secure relationship: *they have a strong sense of belonging*

belongings *pl n* the things that a person owns or has with him or her

Belorussia *n* a variant spelling of **Belarus**

Belorussian *n, adj* a variant spelling of **Belarussian**

Belostok *n* transliteration of the Russian name for **Białystok**

beloved *adj* **1** dearly loved ▷ *n* **2** a person who is dearly loved

Belovo *n* a variant spelling of **Byelovo**

below *prep* **1** at or to a position lower than; under **2** less than **3** unworthy of; beneath ▷ *adv* **4** at or to a lower position **5** at a later place in something written **6** *archaic* on earth or in hell [Middle English *bilooghe*]

Belsen *n* a village in NE Germany: with Bergen, the site of a Nazi concentration camp (1943–45)

belt *n* **1** a band of leather or cloth worn around the waist **2** an area where a specific thing is found; zone: *a belt of high pressure* **3** same as **seat belt 4** a band of flexible material between rotating shafts or pulleys to transfer motion or transmit goods: *a fan belt; a conveyer belt* **5** *informal* a sharp blow **6 below the belt** *informal* unscrupulous or cowardly **7 tighten one's belt** to reduce expenditure **8 under one's belt** as part of one's experience: *he had a string of successes under his belt* ▷ *vb* **9** to fasten with or as if with a belt **10** to hit with a belt **11** *slang* to give (someone) a sharp blow **12** (foll. by *along*) *slang* to move very fast [Old English]

belter *n slang* an outstanding person or event: *a belter of a match*

belt out *vb informal* to sing (a song) loudly

belt up *vb* **1** *slang* to stop talking **2** to fasten with a belt

beluga (bill-loo-ga) *n* a large white sturgeon of the Black and Caspian Seas, from which caviar and isinglass are obtained [Russian *byeluga*]

belvedere *n* a building designed and situated to look out on pleasant scenery [Italian: beautiful sight]

Belvoir Castle *n* a castle in Leicestershire, near Grantham (in Lincolnshire): seat of the Dukes of Rutland; rebuilt by James Wyatt in 1816

Belyi or **Bely** *n* Andrei, real name *Boris Nikolayevich Bugaev*. 1880–1934, Russian poet, novelist, and critic: a leading exponent of symbolism. His novels include *Petersburg* (1913)

BEM British Empire Medal

Bembo *n* Pietro. 1470–1547, Italian scholar, poet, and cardinal (1539). His treatise *Prose della volgar lingua* (1525) helped to establish a standard form of literary Italian

bemoan *vb* to lament: *he's always bemoaning his fate*

bemused *adj* puzzled or confused

ben *n Scot and Irish* a mountain peak: *Ben Lomond* [Gaelic *beinn*]

Benacerraf *n* Baruj. 1920–2011, Venezuelan-born US immunologist: shared the Nobel prize for physiology or medicine (1980) for his work on histocompatibility antigens

Benares or **Banaras** *n* the former name of **Varanasi**

Benaud *n* Richard, known as *Richie*. 1930–2015, Australian cricketer; played in 63 test matches, 28 as captain; an all-rounder, he was the first to score 2000 runs and take 200 wickets in tests; TV commentator on the sport for many decades

Benavente y Martínez *n* Jacinto. 1866–1954, Spanish dramatist and critic, who wrote over 150 plays. Nobel prize for literature 1922

Ben Bella *n* Mohammed Ahmed. 1916–2012, Algerian statesman: first prime minister (1962–65) and president (1963–65) of independent Algeria: overthrown and imprisoned (1965–80)

Benbow *n* John. 1653–1702, English admiral, noted esp. for his heroic death during the War of the Spanish Succession

bench *n* **1** a long seat for more than one person **2 the bench a** a judge or magistrate sitting in court **b** judges or magistrates collectively **3** a long and strong worktable [Old English *benc*]

benchmark *n* **1** a mark on a fixed object, used as a reference point in surveying **2** a criterion by which to measure something: *the speech was a benchmark of his commitment*

bench press *n* an exercise in which a person pushes a barbell upwards while lying flat on a bench

bend[1] *vb* **bending, bent 1** to form a curve **2** to turn from a particular direction: *the road bends right* **3** (often foll. by *down* etc.) to incline the body **4** to submit: *to bend before public opinion* **5** to turn or direct (one's eyes, steps, or attention) **6 bend someone's ear** *informal* to complain to someone for a long time **7 bend the rules** *informal* to ignore or change rules to suit oneself ▷ *n* **8** a curved part **9** the act of bending **10 round the bend** *Brit slang* mad [Old English *bendan*] **> bendy** *adj*

bend[2] *n heraldry* a diagonal line across a shield [Old English: a band, strip]

Benda *n* Julien. 1867–1956, French philosopher and novelist, who defended reason and intellect and attacked the influence of Bergson: author of *La Trahison des clercs* (1927)

bender *n informal* **1** a drinking bout **2** a shelter made from plastic sheeting and woven branches

Bendigo *n* a city in SE Australia, in central Victoria: founded in 1851 after the discovery of gold. Pop: 68 715 (2001)

bends *pl n* **the bends** *informal* decompression sickness

bend sinister *n heraldry* a diagonal line across a shield, indicating a bastard line

beneath *prep* **1** below; under **2** too trivial for: *beneath his dignity* ▷ *adv* **3** below; underneath [Old English *beneothan*]

Benedict *n* Saint. ?480–?547 AD, Italian monk: founded the Benedictine order at Monte Cassino in Italy in about 540 AD. His *Regula Monachorum* became the basis of the rule of all Western Christian monastic orders. Feast day: July 11 or March 14

Benedict XV *n* original name *Giacomo della Chiesa*. 1854–1922, pope (1914–22); noted for his repeated attempts to end World War I and for his organization of war relief

Benedict XVI *n* original name *Joseph Alois Ratzinger*. born 1927 in Germany, pope (2005–2013): the first pope to resign since Gregory XII in 1415: on retirement he was accorded the title pope emeritus

b

b

Benedictine n 1 a monk or nun of the Christian order of Saint Benedict 2 a liqueur first made by Benedictine monks ▷ adj 3 of Saint Benedict or his order

benediction n 1 a prayer for divine blessing 2 a Roman Catholic service in which the congregation is blessed with the sacrament [Latin *benedictio*] ▷ **benedictory** adj

benefaction n 1 the act of doing good, particularly donating to charity 2 the donation or help given [Latin *bene* well + *facere* to do]

benefactor n a person who supports a person or institution by giving money ▷ **benefactress** fem n

benefice n Christianity a Church office that provides its holder with an income [Latin *beneficium* benefit]

beneficent (bin-eff-iss-ent) adj charitable; generous [Latin *beneficus*] ▷ **beneficence** n

beneficial adj helpful or advantageous [Latin *beneficium* kindness]

beneficiary n, pl -ciaries 1 a person who gains or benefits 2 law a person entitled to receive funds or property under a trust, will, etc.

benefit n 1 something that improves or promotes 2 advantage or sake: *I'm doing this for your benefit* 3 a payment made by an institution or government to a person who is ill, unemployed, etc. 4 a theatrical performance or sports event to raise money for a charity ▷ vb -fiting, -fited or US -fitting, -fitted 5 to do or receive good; profit [Latin *bene facere* to do well]

benefit society n US same as **friendly society**

Benelux n 1 the customs union formed by Belgium, the Netherlands, and Luxembourg in 1948; became an economic union in 1960 2 these countries collectively

Beneš n Eduard. 1884–1948, Czech statesman; president of Czechoslovakia (1935–38; 1946–48) and of its government in exile (1939–45)

Benét n Stephen Vincent. 1898–1943, US poet and novelist, best known for his poem on the American Civil War *John Brown's Body* (1928)

Benevento n a city in S Italy, in N Campania: at various times under Samnite, Roman, Lombard, Saracen, Norman, and papal rule. Pop: 61 791 (2001). Ancient name: **Beneventum**

benevolence n 1 inclination to do good 2 an act of kindness ▷ **benevolent** adj

Benfleet n a town in SE England, in S Essex on an inlet of the Thames estuary. Pop: 48 539 (2001)

Bengal n 1 a former province of NE India, in the great deltas of the Ganges and Brahmaputra Rivers: in 1947 divided into West Bengal (belonging to India) and East Bengal (Bangladesh) 2 **Bay of Bengal** a wide arm of the Indian Ocean, between India and Myanmar 3 a breed of medium-large cat with a spotted or marbled coat

Bengali n 1 a member of a people living chiefly in Bangladesh and West Bengal 2 the language of this people ▷ adj 3 of Bengal or the Bengalis

Bengaluru n the alternative official name for **Bangalore**

Bengbu, Pengpu or **Pang-fou** n a city in E China, in Anhui province. Pop: 779 000 (2005 est)

Benghazi or **Bengasi** n a port in N Libya, on the Gulf of Sidra: centre of Italian colonization (1911–42); scene of much fighting in World War II. Pop: 1 080 500 (2002 est). Ancient names: **Hesperides, Berenice**

Benguela n a port in W Angola: founded in 1617; a terminus (with Lobito) of the railway that runs from Beira in Mozambique through the Copper Belt of Zambia and Zimbabwe. Pop: about 200 000 (1990 est)

Ben-Gurion n David, original name *David Gruen*. 1886–1973, Israeli socialist statesman, born in Poland; first prime minister of Israel (1948–53, 1955–63)

Beni n a river in N Bolivia, rising in the E Cordillera of the Andes and flowing north to the Marmoré River. Length: over 1600 km (1000 miles)

Benidorm n a coastal resort town in W Spain, on the Costa Blanca

benighted adj lacking cultural, moral, or intellectual enlightenment

benign (bin-nine) adj 1 showing kindliness 2 favourable *a stroke of benign fate* 3 pathol (of a tumour, etc.) able to be controlled [Latin *benignus*] ▷ **benignly** adv

benignant adj 1 kind or gracious 2 same as **benign** (2, 3) ▷ **benignancy** n

benignity (bin-nig-nit-tee) n, pl -ties kindliness

Beni Hasan n a village in central Egypt, on the Nile, with cliff-cut tombs dating from 2000 BC

Benin n 1 a republic in W Africa, on the **Bight of Benin**, a section of the Gulf of Guinea: in the early 19th century a powerful kingdom, famed for its women warriors; became a French colony in 1893, gaining independence in 1960. It consists chiefly of coastal lagoons and swamps in the south, a fertile plain and marshes in the centre, and the Atakora Mountains in the northwest. Official language: French. Religion: animist majority. Currency: franc. Capital: Porto Novo (the government is based in Cotonou). Pop: 9 877 292 (2013 est). Area: 112 622 sq km (43 474 sq miles). Former name (until 1975): **Dahomey** 2 a former kingdom of W Africa, powerful from the 14th to the 17th centuries: now a province of S Nigeria: noted for its bronzes

Benin City n a city in S Nigeria, capital of Edo state: former capital of the kingdom of Benin. Pop: 1 022 000 (2005 est)

Beninese adj 1 of or relating to Benin or its people ▷ n 2 Also: **Beninois** a native or inhabitant of Benin

Benjamin n 1 Arthur. 1893–1960, Australian composer. In addition to *Jamaican Rumba* (1938), he wrote five operas and a harmonica concerto (1953) 2 Walter. 1892–1940, German critic and cultural theorist

Ben Lomond n 1 a mountain in W central Scotland, on the E side of Loch Lomond. Height: 973 m (3192 ft) 2 a mountain in NE Tasmania. Height: 1527 m (5010 ft) 3 a mountain in SE Australia, in NE New South Wales. Height: 1520 m (4986 ft)

Benn n Antony (Neil) Wedgwood, known as *Tony Benn*. 1925–2014, British Labour politician, a leading figure on the party's left wing. He renounced (1963) the title of Viscount Stansgate

Bennett n 1 Alan. born 1934, British actor and playwright. His plays include *Forty Years On* (1968), *The Old Country* (1977), *The Madness of George III* (1991), *The History Boys* (2004), and the monologues for television *Talking Heads* (1987, 1998) 2 (Enoch) Arnold. 1867–1931, British novelist, noted for *The Old Wives' Tale* (1908), *Clayhanger* (1910), and other works set in the Staffordshire Potteries 3 James Gordon. 1837–1931, US newspaper editor, born in Scotland. He founded (1835) the *New York Herald* and introduced techniques of modern news reporting 4 Jill. 1931–90, British actress 5 Richard Bedford, 1st Viscount. 1870–1947, Canadian Conservative statesman; prime minister (1930–35) 6 Sir Richard Rodney. born 1936, British composer, noted for film music and his operas *The Mines of Sulphur* (1965) and *Victory* (1970)

Ben Nevis n a mountain in W Scotland, in the Grampian mountains: highest peak in Great Britain. Height: 1344 m (4408 ft)

Bennington n a town in SW Vermont: the site of a British defeat (1777) in the War of American Independence. Pop: 15 637 (2003 est)

Benny n Jack, real name *Benjamin Kubelsky*. 1894–1974, US comedian

Benoît de Sainte-Maure n 12th-century French trouvère: author of the *Roman de Troie*, which contains the episode of Troilus and Cressida

Benoni n a city in NE South Africa: gold mines. Pop: 94 341 (2001)

Benson n E(dward) F(rederic). 1867–1940, British writer, noted esp. for a series of comic novels featuring the characters. Mapp and Lucia

bent adj 1 not straight; curved 2 slang a dishonest;

corrupt: *bent officials* **b** *Brit and Austral offensive, slang* homosexual **3 bent on** determined to pursue (a course of action) ▷ *n* **4** personal inclination or aptitude: *he had a strong practical bent in his nature*

Bentham *n* Jeremy. 1748–1832, British philosopher and jurist: a founder of utilitarianism. His works include *A Fragment on Government* (1776) and *Introduction to the Principles of Morals and Legislation* (1789)

Benthamism *n* the utilitarian philosophy of Jeremy Bentham, which holds that the ultimate goal of society should be to promote the greatest happiness of the greatest number ▷ **Benthamite** *n, adj*

Bentinck *n* Lord William Cavendish. 1774–1839, British statesman, governor general of Bengal (1828–35)

Bentley *n* Edmund Clerihew. 1875–1956, English journalist, noted for his invention of the clerihew

bento *or* **bento box** *n* a thin box, made of plastic or lacquered wood, divided into compartments, which contain small separate dishes comprising a Japanese meal, esp. lunch [Japanese *bento* box lunch]

Benton *n* Thomas Hart. 1889–1975, US painter of rural life; a leader of the American Regionalist painters in the 1930s

bentwood *n* **1** wood bent in moulds, used mainly for furniture ▷ *adj* **2** made from such wood: *a bentwood chair*

Benue *n* **1** a state of SE Nigeria. Capital: Makurdi. Pop: 4 219 244 (2006). Area: 34 059 sq km (13 150 sq miles) **2** a river in W Africa, rising in N Cameroon and flowing west across Nigeria: chief tributary of the River Niger. Length: 1400 km (870 miles)

benumb *vb* **1** to make numb or powerless **2** to stupefy (the mind, senses, will, etc.): *the work benumbed their minds and crushed their spirits*

Benxi, Penchi *or* **Penki** *n* an industrial city in SE China, in S Liaoning province. Pop: 967 000 (2005 est)

Benz *n* Karl (Friedrich). 1844–1929, German engineer; designed and built the first car to be driven by an internal-combustion engine (1885)

benzene *n* a flammable poisonous liquid used as a solvent, insecticide, etc. [from *benzoin*, a fragrant resin from certain Asiatic trees]

benzine *n* a volatile liquid obtained from coal tar and used as a solvent

Ben-Zvi *n* Itzhak. 1884–1963, Israeli statesman; president (1952–63)

Beograd *n* the Serbian name for **Belgrade**

bequeath *vb* **1** *law* to dispose of (property) as in a will **2** to hand down: *the author bequeaths no solutions* [Old English *becwethan*]

bequest *n* **1** the act of gifting money or property in a will **2** money or property that has been gifted in a will

Béranger *n* Pierre Jean de. 1780–1857, French lyric and satirical poet

Berar *n* a region of W central India: part of Maharashtra state since 1956; important for cotton growing

berate *vb* **-rating, -rated** to scold harshly

Berber *n* **1** a member of a Muslim people of N Africa **2** the language of this people ▷ *adj* **3** of the Berbers

Berbera *n* a port in N Somalia, (in the separatist area called Somaliland), on the Gulf of Aden. Pop: about 200 000 (2000 est)

berberis *n* a shrub with red berries [Medieval Latin]

berceuse (bare-suhz) *n* **1** a lullaby **2** an instrumental piece suggestive of this [French]

Berchtesgaden *n* a town in Germany, in SE Bavaria: site of the fortified mountain retreat of Adolf Hitler. Pop: 7667 (2003 est)

Bercow *n* John (Simon). born 1963, British Conservative politician; speaker of the House of Commons from 2009

Berdyayev *n* Nikolai Aleksandrovich. 1874–1948, Russian philosopher. Although he was a Marxist, his Christian views led him to criticize Soviet communism and he was forced into exile (1922)

bereaved *adj* having recently lost a close relative or

friend through death [Old English *bereafian* to deprive] ▷ **bereavement** *n*

bereft *adj* (foll. by *of*) deprived: *a government bereft of ideas*

Berenson *n* Bernard. 1865–1959, US art historian, born in Lithuania: an authority on art of the Italian Renaissance

Beresford *n* Bruce. born 1940, Australian film director. His films include *The Adventures of Barry McKenzie* (1972), *Breaker Morant* (1980), *Driving Miss Daisy* (1989) and *Evelyn* (2002)

beret (ber-ray) *n* a round flat close-fitting brimless cap [French]

Berezina *n* a river in Belarus, rising in the north and flowing south to the River Dnieper: linked with the River Dvina and the Baltic Sea by the **Berezina Canal**. Length: 563 km (350 miles)

Berezniki *n* a city in E Russia: chemical industries. Pop: 169 000 (2005 est)

berg[1] *n* short for **iceberg**

berg[2] *n S African* a mountain

Berg *n* **1** Alban (Maria Johannes). 1885–1935, Austrian composer: a pupil of Schoenberg. His works include the operas *Wozzeck* (1921) and *Lulu* (1935), a violin concerto (1935), chamber works, and songs **2** Paul. born 1926, US molecular biologist, the first to identify transfer RNA (1956). Nobel prize for chemistry 1980

Bergamo *n* a walled city in N Italy, in Lombardy. Pop: 113 143 (2001)

bergamot *n* **1** a small Asian tree with sour pear-shaped fruit **2 essence of bergamot** a fragrant essential oil from the fruit rind of this plant, used in perfumery [French *bergamote*]

Bergen *n* **1** a port in SW Norway: chief city in medieval times. Pop: 237 430 (2004 est) **2** the Flemish name for **Mons**

Bergius *n* Friedrich (Karl Rudolph). 1884–1949, German chemist, who invented a process for producing oil by high-pressure hydrogenation of coal: Nobel prize for chemistry 1931

Bergman *n* **1** (Ernst) Ingmar. 1918–2007, Swedish film and stage director, whose films include *The Seventh Seal* (1956), *Wild Strawberries* (1957), *Persona* (1966), *Scenes from a Marriage* (1974), *Autumn Sonata* (1978), and *Fanny and Alexander* (1982) **2** Ingrid. 1915–82, Swedish film and stage actress, working in Hollywood 1938–48; noted for her leading roles in many films, including *Casablanca* (1942), *For Whom the Bell Tolls* (1943), *Anastasia* (1956), and *The Inn of the Sixth Happiness* (1958)

Bergson *n* Henri Louis. 1859–1941, French philosopher, who sought to bridge the gap between metaphysics and science. His main works are *Memory and Matter* (1896, trans. 1911) and *Creative Evolution* (1907, trans. 1911): Nobel prize for literature 1927 ▷ **Bergsonian** *adj, n*

Bergström *n* Sune. 1916–2004, Swedish biochemist; shared the Nobel prize for medicine and physiology (1982) for work on prostaglandin

Beria *n* Lavrenti Pavlovich. 1899–1953, Soviet chief of secret police; killed by his associates shortly after Stalin's death

beri-beri *n* a disease caused by a dietary deficiency of thiamine (vitamin B_1) [Sinhalese]

Bering *or* **Behring** *n* Vitus. 1681–1741, Danish navigator, who explored the N Pacific for the Russians and discovered Bering Island and the Bering Strait

Bering Sea *n* a part of the N Pacific Ocean, between NE Siberia and Alaska. Area: about 2 275 000 sq km (878 000 sq miles)

Bering Strait *n* a strait between Alaska and Russia, connecting the Bering Sea and the Arctic Ocean

Berio *n* Luciano. 1925–2003, Italian composer, living in the US, noted esp. for works that exploit instrumental and vocal timbre and technique

Beriosova *n* Svetlana. 1932–98, British ballet dancer, born in Lithuania

b

berk or **burk** n Brit, Austral and NZ slang a stupid person; fool [Berkshire Hunt, rhyming slang for cunt]

Berkeley[1] n a city in W California, on San Francisco Bay: seat of the University of California. Pop: 102 049 (2003 est)

Berkeley[2] n **1** Busby. real name William Berkeley Enos. 1895–1976, US dance director, noted esp. for his elaborate choreography in film musicals **2** George. 1685–1753, Irish philosopher and Anglican bishop, whose system of subjective idealism was expounded in his works A Treatise concerning the Principles of Human Knowledge (1710) and Three Dialogues between Hylas and Philonous (1713). He also wrote Essay towards a New Theory of Vision (1709) **3** Sir Lennox (Randal Francis). 1903–89, British composer; his works include four symphonies, four operas, and the Serenade for Strings (1939)

Berkeley Castle n a castle in Gloucestershire: scene of the murder of Edward II in 1327

berkelium n chem an artificial radioactive element. Symbol: Bk [after BERKELEY[1], where it was discovered]

Berks Berkshire

Berkshire n **1** a historic county of S England: since reorganization in 1974 the River Thames has marked the N boundary while the **Berkshire Downs** occupy central parts; the county council was replaced by six unitary authorities in 1998. Area: 1259 sq km (486 sq miles). Abbreviation: **Berks 2** a rare breed of pork and bacon pig having a black body and white points

Berlichingen n Götz von, called the Iron Hand. 1480–1562, German warrior knight, who robbed merchants and kidnapped nobles for ransom

Berlin[1] n the capital of Germany (1871–1945 and from 1990), formerly divided (1945–90) into the eastern sector, capital of East Germany, and the western sectors, which formed an exclave in East German territory closely affiliated with West Germany: a wall dividing the sectors was built in 1961 by the East German authorities to stop the flow of refugees from east to west; demolition of the wall began in 1989 and the city was formally reunited in 1990: formerly (1618–1871) the capital of Brandenburg and Prussia. Pop: 3 388 477 (2003 est)

Berlin[2] n **1** Irving. original name Israel Baline, 1888–1989, US composer and writer of lyrics, born in Russia. His musical comedies include Annie Get Your Gun (1946); his most popular song is White Christmas **2** Sir Isaiah. 1909–97, British philosopher, born in Latvia, historian, and diplomat. His books include Historical Inevitability (1954) and The Magus of the North (1993)

Berliner n **1** a native or inhabitant of Berlin **2** a newspaper having a format between that of a broadsheet and a tabloid, approximately 18.5 inches by 12.4 inches (47 x 31.5 centimetres) [C20: (for sense 2) this format was first adopted by Berlin newspapers]

Berlioz n Hector (Louis). 1803–69, French composer, regarded as a pioneer of modern orchestration. His works include the cantata La Damnation de Faust (1846), the operas Les Troyens (1856–59) and Béatrice et Bénédict (1860–62), the Symphonie fantastique (1830), and the oratorio L'Enfance du Christ (1854)

Berlusconi n Silvio. born 1936, Italian politician and media tycoon: prime minister of Italy (1994–95, 2001–06, 2008–11); convicted of tax fraud and expelled from the Italian Senate in 2013

berm n NZ narrow grass strip between the road and the footpath in a residential area

Bermejo n a river in Argentina, rising in the northwest and flowing southeast to the Paraguay River. Length: about 1000 km (1000 miles)

Bermuda n a UK Overseas Territory consisting of a group of over 150 coral islands (**the Bermudas**) in the NW Atlantic: discovered in about 1503, colonized by the British by 1612, although not acquired by the British

crown until 1684. Capital: Hamilton. Pop: 69 467 (2013 est). Area: 53 sq km (20 sq miles)

Bermuda shorts pl n shorts that come down to the knees [after Bermudas, islands in NW Atlantic]

Bermuda Triangle n an area in the Atlantic Ocean bounded by Bermuda, Puerto Rico, and Florida where ships and aeroplanes are alleged to have disappeared mysteriously

Bermudian n **1** a native or inhabitant of Bermuda ▷ adj **2** of or relating to Bermuda or its inhabitants

Bern n **1** the capital of Switzerland, in the W part, on the Aar River: entered the Swiss confederation in 1353 and became the capital in 1848. Pop: 122 700 (2002 est) **2** a canton of Switzerland, between the French frontier and the Bernese Alps. Capital: Bern. Pop: 950 200 (2002 est). Area: 6884 sq km (2658 sq miles) ▶ French name: **Berne**

Bernadette of Lourdes n Saint. original name Marie Bernarde Soubirous. 1844–79, French peasant girl born in Lourdes, whose visions of the Virgin Mary led to the establishment of Lourdes as a centre of pilgrimage, esp for the sick or crippled. Feast day: Feb 18

Bernadotte n **1** Folke, Count. 1895–1948, Swedish diplomat, noted for his work with the Red Cross during World War II and as United Nations mediator in Palestine (1948). He was assassinated by Jewish terrorists **2** Jean Baptiste Jules. 1764–1844, French marshal under Napoleon; king of Norway and Sweden (1818–44) as Charles XIV

Bernanos n Georges. 1888–1948, French novelist and Roman Catholic pamphleteer, best known for The Diary of a Country Priest (1936)

Bernard n **1** Claude. 1813–78, French physiologist, noted for his research on the action of secretions of the alimentary canal and the glycogenic function of the liver **2** Saint, known as Bernard of Menthon and the Apostle of the Alps. 923–1008, French monk who founded hospices in the Alpine passes. Feast day: Aug 20

Bernard of Clairvaux n Saint. ?1090–1153, French abbot and theologian, who founded the stricter branch of the Cistercians in 1115

Berners-Lee n Sir Tim. born 1955, British computer scientist who in 1990 created the World Wide Web

Bernese Alps or **Bernese Oberland** n a mountain range in SW Switzerland, the N central part of the Alps. Highest peak: Finsteraarhorn, 4274 m (14 022 ft)

Bernhardt n Sarah. original name Rosine Bernard. 1844–1923, French actress, regarded as one of the greatest tragic actresses of all time

Bernina n Piz Bernina a mountain in SE Switzerland, the highest peak of the **Bernina Alps** in the S Rhaetian Alps. Height: 4049 m (13 284 ft)

Bernina Pass n a pass in the Alps between SE Switzerland and N Italy, east of Piz Bernina. Height: 2323 m (7622 ft)

Bernini n Gian Lorenzo. 1598–1680, Italian painter, architect, and sculptor: the greatest exponent of the Italian baroque

Bernoulli or **Bernouilli** n **1** Daniel, son of Jean Bernoulli 1700–82, Swiss mathematician and physicist, who developed an early form of the kinetic theory of gases and stated the principle of conservation of energy in fluid dynamics **2** Jacques or Jakob. 1654–1705, Swiss mathematician, noted for his work on calculus and the theory of probability **3** his brother, Jean or Johann. 1667–1748, Swiss mathematician who developed the calculus of variations

Bernoulli principle n physics the principle that the pressure in a moving fluid becomes less as the speed rises [after Daniel BERNOULLI]

Bernstein n Leonard. 1918–90, US conductor and composer, whose works include The Age of Anxiety (1949), the score of the musical West Side Story (1957), and Mass (1971)

berry n, pl **-ries** a small round fruit that grows on bushes or trees and is often edible [Old English *berie*]

Berry *n* **1 Chuck**, full name *Charles Edward Berry*. born 1926, US rock-and-roll guitarist, singer, and songwriter. His frequently covered songs include "Maybellene" (1955), "Roll Over Beethoven" (1956), "Johnny B. Goode" (1958), "Memphis, Tennessee" (1959), and "Promised Land" (1964) **2 Jean de France**, Duc de. 1340–1416, French prince, son of King John II; coregent (1380–88) for Charles VI and a famous patron of the arts

Berryman *n* **John**. 1914–72, US poet and critic, author of *Homage to Mistress Bradstreet* (1956) and *Dream Songs* (1964–68)

berserk *adj* **go berserk** to become violent or destructive [Icelandic *björn* bear + *serkr* shirt]

berth *n* **1** a bunk in a ship or train **2** *nautical* a place assigned to a ship at a mooring **3** *nautical* sufficient room for a ship to manoeuvre **4 give a wide berth to** to keep clear of ▷ *vb* **5** *nautical* to dock (a ship) **6** to provide with a sleeping place **7** *nautical* to pick up a mooring in an anchorage [probably from BEAR¹]

Bertolucci *n* **Bernardo**. born 1940, Italian film director: his films include *The Spider's Stratagem* (1970), *The Conformist* (1970), *1900* (1976), *The Last Emperor* (1987), *The Sheltering Sky* (1990), and *The Dreamers* (2003)

Berwick *n* **James Fitzjames**, Duke of Berwick. 1670–1734, marshal of France and illegitimate son of James II of England. He led French forces during the War of the Spanish Succession (1701–14)

Berwickshire *n* (until 1975) a county of SE Scotland: part of the Borders region from 1975 to 1996, now part of Scottish Borders council area

Berwick-upon-Tweed *n* a town in N England, in N Northumberland at the mouth of the Tweed: much involved in border disputes between England and Scotland between the 12th and 16th centuries; neutral territory 1551–1885. Pop: 12 870 (2001). Also called: **Berwick**

beryl *n* a transparent hard mineral, used as a source of beryllium and as a gemstone [Greek *bērullos*]

beryllium *n* a toxic silvery-white metallic element. Symbol: Be [Greek *bērullos*]

Berzelius *n* **Baron Jöns Jakob**. 1779–1848, Swedish chemist, who invented the present system of chemical symbols and formulas, discovered several elements, and determined the atomic and molecular weight of many substances

Besançon *n* a city in E France, on the Doubs River: university (1422). Pop: 121 012 (2006)

Besant *n* **Annie**, *née* Wood. 1847–1933, British theosophist, writer, and political reformer in England and India

beseech *vb* **-seeching, -sought** or **-seeched** to ask earnestly; beg [Middle English; see BE-, SEEK]

beset *vb* **-setting, -set 1** to trouble or harass constantly **2** to surround or attack from all sides

beside *prep* **1** next to; at, by, or to the side of **2** as compared with **3** away from: *beside the point* **4 beside oneself** overwhelmed; overwrought: *beside oneself with grief* ▷ *adv* **5** at, by, to, or along the side of something or someone [Old English *be sīdan*]

besides *adv* **1** in addition ▷ *prep* **2** apart from; even considering ▷ *conj* **3** anyway; moreover

besiege *vb* **-sieging, -sieged 1** to surround with military forces to bring about surrender **2** to hem in **3** to overwhelm, as with requests

Beslan *n* a town in the North Ossetian Republic in Russia: scene of a massacre in 2004 when Chechen extremists held a school hostage, leading to a siege in which 344 people were killed. Pop: 35 550 (2002)

besmirch *vb* to tarnish (someone's name or reputation)

besom *n* a broom made of a bundle of twigs tied to a handle [Old English *besma*]

besotted *adj* **1** having an irrational passion for a person or thing **2** stupefied with alcohol

besought *vb* a past of beseech

bespatter *vb* **1** to splash with dirty water **2** to dishonour or slander

bespeak *vb* **-speaking, -spoke, -spoken** or **-spoke 1** to indicate or suggest: *imitation bespeaks admiration* **2** to engage or ask for in advance: *she was bespoke to a family in the town*

bespectacled *adj* wearing spectacles

bespoke *adj chiefly Brit* **1** (esp. of a suit) made to the customer's specifications **2** making or selling such suits: *a bespoke tailor*

Bessarabia *n* a region in E Europe, mostly in Moldova and Ukraine: long disputed by the Turks and Russians; a province of Romania from 1918 until 1940. Area: about 44 300 sq km (17 100 sq miles)

Bessel *n* **Friedrich Wilhelm**. 1784–1846, German astronomer and mathematician. He made the first authenticated measurement of a star's distance (1841) and systematized a series of mathematical functions used in physics

best *adj* **1** the superlative of **good 2** most excellent of a particular group, category, etc. **3** most suitable, desirable, etc. ▷ *adv* **4** the superlative of **well¹ 5** in a manner surpassing all others; most attractively, etc. ▷ *n* **6 the best** the most outstanding or excellent person, thing, or group in a category **7** the utmost effort: *I did my best* **8** a person's finest clothes **9 at best a** in the most favourable interpretation **b** under the most favourable conditions **10 for the best a** for an ultimately good outcome **b** with good intentions **11 get the best of** to defeat or outwit **12 make the best of** to cope as well as possible with ▷ *vb* **13** to defeat [Old English *betst*]

Best *n* **1 Charles Herbert**. 1899–1978, Canadian physiologist: associated with Banting and Macleod in their discovery of insulin in 1922 **2 George**. 1946–2005, Northern Ireland footballer

bestial *adj* **1** brutal or savage **2** of or relating to a beast [Latin *bestia* beast]

bestiality *n, pl* **-ties 1** brutal behaviour, character, or action **2** sexual activity between a person and an animal

bestiary *n, pl* **-aries** a medieval collection of descriptions of animals

bestie *n slang* one's best friend

bestir *vb* **-stirring, -stirred** to cause (oneself) to become active

best man *n* the male attendant of the bridegroom at a wedding

bestow *vb* to present (a gift) or confer (an honour) ▷ **bestowal** *n*

bestrew *vb* **-strewing, -strewed, -strewn** or **-strewed** to scatter or lie scattered over (a surface)

bestride *vb* **-striding, -strode** to have or put a leg on either side of

bestseller *n* a book or other product that has sold in great numbers ▷ **bestselling** *adj*

bet *n* **1** the act of staking a sum of money or other stake on the outcome of an event **2** the stake risked **3** a course of action: *your best bet is to go by train* **4** *informal* an opinion: *my bet is that you've been up to no good* ▷ *vb* **betting, bet** or **betted 5** to make or place a bet with (someone) **6** to stake (money, etc.) in a bet **7** *informal* to predict (a certain outcome): *I bet she doesn't turn up* **8 you bet** *informal* of course [probably short for *abet*]

beta *n* **1** the second letter in the Greek alphabet (Β, β) **2** the second in a group or series

beta-blocker *n* a drug that decreases the activity of the heart: used in the treatment of high blood pressure and angina pectoris

beta-carotene *n biochem* the most important form of the plant pigment carotene, which occurs in milk, vegetables, and other foods and, when eaten by man and animals, is converted in the body to vitamin A

betake *vb* **-taking, -took, -taken betake oneself** *formal* to go or move: *he betook himself to the public house*

b

beta particle *n* a high-speed electron or positron emitted by a nucleus during radioactive decay or nuclear fission

betatron *n* a type of particle accelerator for producing high-energy beams of electrons

betel (bee-tl) *n* an Asian climbing plant, the leaves and nuts of which can be chewed [Malayalam (language of SW India) *vettila*]

bête noire (bet nwahr) *n*, *pl* **bêtes noires** a person or thing that one particularly dislikes or dreads [French, literally: black beast]

Bethany *n* a village in the West Bank, near Jerusalem at the foot of the Mount of Olives: in the New Testament, the home of Lazarus and the lodging place of Jesus during Holy Week

Bethe *n* Hans Albrecht. 1906–2005, US physicist, born in Germany; noted for his research on astrophysics and nuclear physics: Nobel prize for physics 1967

Bethel *n* **1** an ancient town in the West Bank, near Jerusalem: in the Old Testament, the place where the dream of Jacob occurred (Genesis 28:19) **2** a chapel of any of certain Nonconformist Christian sects **3** a seamen's chapel [C17: from Hebrew *bêth 'Ēl* house of God]

Bethlehem *n* a town in the West Bank, near Jerusalem: birthplace of Jesus and early home of King David

Bethmann Hollweg *n* Theobald von. 1856–1921, chancellor of Germany (1909–17)

Bethsaida *n* a ruined town in N Israel, near the N shore of the Sea of Galilee

Bethune *n* Norman. 1890–1939, Canadian physician and campaigner for socialized medicine; pioneered the use of mobile medical units during the Spanish Civil War and in China during the second Sino-Japanese War

betide *vb* **-tiding, -tided** to happen or happen to: *woe betide us if we're not ready on time* [BE- + obsolete *tide* to happen]

Betjeman *n* Sir John. 1906–84, English poet, noted for his nostalgic and humorous verse and essays and for his concern for the preservation of historic buildings, esp. of the Victorian era: Poet laureate (1972–84)

betoken *vb* to indicate; signify

betray *vb* **1** to hand over or expose (one's nation, friend, etc.) treacherously to an enemy **2** to disclose (a secret or confidence) treacherously **3** to reveal unintentionally: *his singing voice betrays his origins* [Latin *tradere* to hand over] **> betrayal** *n* **> betrayer** *n*

betroth *vb* archaic to promise to marry or to give in marriage [Middle English *betreuthen*] **> betrothal** *n*

betrothed old-fashioned *adj* **1** engaged to be married ▷ *n* **2** the person to whom one is engaged

better *adj* **1** the comparative of **good 2** more excellent than others **3** more suitable, attractive, etc. **4** improved or fully recovered in health **5 the better part of** a large part of ▷ *adv* **6** the comparative of **well¹ 7** in a more excellent manner **8** in or to a greater degree **9 better off** in more favourable circumstances, esp. financially **10 had better** would be sensible, etc. to: *I had better be off* ▷ *n* **11 the better** something that is the more excellent, useful, etc. of two such things **12 betters** people who are one's superiors, esp. in social standing **13 get the better of** to defeat or outwit ▷ *vb* **14** to improve upon [Old English *betera*]

better half *n* humorous one's spouse

betterment *n* improvement

better-off *adj* reasonably wealthy: *Catalonia aims to attract better-off tourists*

Betti *n* Ugo. 1892–1953, Italian writer, noted esp. for his plays, including *La Padrona* (1927), *Corruzione al palazzo di giustizia* (1949), and *La Regina e gli insorte* (1951)

betting shop *n* (in Britain) a licensed bookmaker's premises not on a racecourse

between *prep* **1** at a point intermediate to two other points in space, time, etc. **2** in combination; together: *between them, they saved enough money to buy a car* **3** confined

to: *between you and me* **4** indicating a linking relation or comparison **5** indicating alternatives, strictly only two alternatives ▷ *adv* also: **in between 6** between one specified thing and another [Old English *betwēonum*]

> **USAGE** After *distribute* and words with a similar meaning, *among* should be used rather than *between*: *this enterprise issued shares which were distributed among its workers.*

betwixt *prep*, *adv* **1** archaic between **2 betwixt and between** in an intermediate or indecisive position

Betws-y-Coed *n* a village in N Wales, in Conwy county borough, on the River Conwy: noted for its scenery. Pop: 534 (2001)

Beuthen *n* the German name for **Bytom**

Beuys *n* Joseph. 1921–86, German artist, a celebrated figure of the avant-garde, noted esp. for his sculptures made of felt and animal fat

Bevan *n* Aneurin, known as Nye. (1897–1960), British Labour statesman, born in Wales: noted for his oratory. As minister of health (1945–51) he introduced the National Health Service (1948) **> Bevanite** *n*, *adj*

bevel *n* **1** a slanting edge ▷ *vb* **-elling, -elled** or US **-eling, -eled 2** to be inclined; slope **3** to cut a bevel on (a piece of timber, etc.) [Old French *baer* to gape]

bevel gear *n* a toothed gear meshed with another at an angle to it

beverage *n* any drink other than water [Old French *bevrage*]

beverage room *n* Canad same as **beer parlour**

Beveridge *n* William Henry, 1st Baron Beveridge. 1879–1963, British economist, whose *Report on Social Insurance and Allied Services* (1942) formed the basis of social-security legislation in Britain

Beverley *n* a market town in NE England, the administrative centre of the East Riding of Yorkshire. Pop: 29 110 (2001)

Beverly Hills *n* a town in SW California, near Los Angeles: famous as the home of film stars. Pop: 34 941 (2003 est)

Bevin *n* Ernest. 1881–1951, British Labour statesman and trade unionist, who was largely responsible for the creation of the Transport and General Workers' Union (1922): minister of labour (1940–45); foreign secretary (1945–51)

bevvy *n*, *pl* **-vies** dialect **1** an alcoholic drink **2** a session of drinking [probably from Old French *bevee*, *buvee* drinking]

bevy *n*, *pl* **bevies** a flock; group [origin unknown]

bewail *vb* to express great sorrow over; lament

beware *vb* **-waring, -wared** (often foll. by *of*) to be wary (of); be on one's guard (against) [*be* (imperative) + obsolete *war* wary]

Bewick *n* Thomas. 1753–1828, English wood engraver; his best-known works are *Chillingham Bull* (1789), a large woodcut, *Aesop's Fables* (1818), and his *History of British Birds* (1797–1804)

bewilder *vb* to confuse utterly; puzzle [BE- + obsolete *wilder* to lose one's way] **> bewildering** *adj* **> bewilderment** *n*

bewitch *vb* **1** to attract and fascinate **2** to cast a spell over [Middle English *bewicchen*] **> bewitching** *adj*

Bexhill or **Bexhill-on-Sea** *n* a resort in S England, in East Sussex on the English Channel. Pop: 39 451 (2001)

Bexley *n* a borough of SE Greater London. Pop: 219 100 (2003 est). Area: 61 sq km (23 sq miles)

bey *n* **1** (in modern Turkey) a title of address, corresponding to *Mr* **2** (in the Ottoman Empire) a title given to provincial governors [Turkish: lord]

Beyoğlu *n* a district of Istanbul, north of the Golden Horn: the European quarter. Former name: **Pera**

beyond *prep* **1** at or to a point on the other side of: *beyond those hills* **2** outside the limits or scope of ▷ *adv* **3** at or to

b

the other or far side of something **4** outside the limits of something ▷ *n* **5 the beyond** the unknown, esp. life after death [Old English *begeondan*]

Beyrouth *n* a variant spelling of **Beirut**

bezel *n* **1** the sloping edge of a cutting tool **2** the slanting face of a cut gem **3** a groove holding a gem, watch crystal, etc. [French *biseau*]

Béziers *n* a city in S France: scene of a massacre (1209) during the Albigensian Crusade. It is a centre of the wine trade. Pop: 71 672 (2008)

bezique *n* a card game for two or more players [French *bésigue*]

Bezos *n* Jeff. real name *Jeffrey Preston Jorgensen*. born 1964, US entrepreneur: founder (1994) and CEO of the online retailer Amazon

Bezwada *n* the former name of **Vijayawada**

B/F or **b/f** *accounting* brought forward

BFPO British Forces Post Office

Bh *chem* bohrium

Bhagalpur *n* a city in India, in Bihar: agriculture, textiles, university (1960). Pop: 340 349 (2001)

Bhagavad-Gita (bug-a-vad-**geet**-a) *n* a sacred Hindu text composed about 200 BC [Sanskrit: song of the Blessed One]

bhaji *n*, *pl* **bhaji** or **bhajis** an Indian savoury made of chopped vegetables mixed in a spiced batter and deep-fried [Hindi]

bhang *n* a preparation of Indian hemp used as a narcotic and intoxicant [Hindi]

bhangra *n* a type of traditional Punjabi folk music combined with elements of Western pop music [Hindi]

Bharat *n* transliteration of the Hindi name for **India**

Bhaskar *n* Sanjeev. born 1964, British actor and writer of Indian origin, known for the TV comedy series *Goodness Gracious Me* (1998–2001) and *The Kumars at No. 42* (2001–06)

Bhatpara *n* a city in NE India, in West Bengal on the Hooghly River: jute and cotton mills. Pop: 441 956 (2001)

Bhavnagar *n* a port in W India, in S Gujarat. Pop: 510 958 (2001)

Bhisho *n* a town in S South Africa, on the Buffalo River adjacent to King Williams Town; the capital of Eastern Cape, it was formerly the capital of the Ciskei Bantu homeland: it is the centre of a sheep and cattle ranching area with various industries

Bhopal *n* a city in central India, the capital of Madhya Pradesh state and of the former state of Bhopal: site of a poisonous gas leak from a US-owned factory, which killed over 7000 people in 1984 and was implicated in a further 15 000 deaths afterwards. Pop: 1 433 875 (2001)

bhp brake horsepower

Bhubaneswar *n* an ancient city in E India, the capital of Odisha (formerly Orissa) state: many temples built between the 7th and 16th centuries. Pop: 647 302 (2001)

Bhutan *n* a kingdom in central Asia: disputed by Tibet, China, India, and Britain since the 18th century but most closely connected with India; contains inaccessible stretches of the E Himalayas in the north. Official language: Dzongka; Nepali is also spoken. Official religion: Mahayana Buddhist. Currencies: ngultrum and Indian rupee. Capital: Thimbu. Pop: 725 296 (2013 est). Area: about 46 600 sq km (18 000 sq miles)

Bhutanese *n* **1** a native or inhabitant of Bhutan ▷ *adj* **2** of or relating to Bhutan or its inhabitants

Bhutto *n* **1** Benazir. (1953–2007), Pakistani stateswoman; prime minister of Pakistan (1988–90; 1993–96); deposed and subsequently defeated in elections in 1997; assassinated during the 2007 election campaign **2** her father, Zulfikar Ali. 1928–79, Pakistani statesman; president (1971–73) and prime minister (1973–77) of Pakistan: executed for the murder of a political rival

Bi *chem* bismuth

bi- *combining form* **1** having two: *bifocal* **2** occurring or lasting for two: *biennial* **3** on both sides, directions, etc.: *bilateral* **4** occurring twice during: *biweekly* **5** *chem*

a denoting a compound containing two identical cyclical hydrocarbon systems: *biphenyl* **b** indicating an acid salt of a dibasic acid: *sodium bicarbonate* [Latin *bis* twice]

Biafra *n* **1** a region of E Nigeria, formerly a local government region: seceded as an independent republic (1967–70) during the Civil War, but defeated by Nigerian government forces **2 Bight of Biafra** former name (until 1975) of (the Bight of) **Bonny**

Biafran *adj* **1** of or relating to Biafra or its inhabitants ▷ *n* **2** a native or inhabitant of Biafra

Biak *n* an island in Indonesia, north of New Guinea: the largest of the Schouten Islands. Area: 2455 sq km (948 sq miles)

Bialik *n* Hayyim Nahman or Chaim Nachman. 1873–1934, Russian Jewish poet and writer. His long poems *The Talmud Student* (1894) and *In the City of Slaughter* (1903) established him as the major Hebrew poet of modern times

Białystok *n* a city in E Poland: belonged to Prussia (1795–1807) and to Russia (1807–1919). Pop: 315 000 (2005 est). Russian name: **Belostok**

biannual *adj* occurring twice a year **›biannually** *adv*

Biarritz *n* a town in SW France, on the Bay of Biscay: famous resort, patronized by Napoleon III and by Queen Victoria and Edward VII of Great Britain and Ireland. Pop: 27 398 (2006)

bias *n* **1** mental tendency, esp. prejudice **2** a diagonal cut across the weave of a fabric **3** *bowls* a bulge or weight inside one side of a bowl that causes it to roll in a curve ▷ *vb* **-asing, -ased** or **-assing, -assed 4** to cause to have a bias; prejudice [Old French *biais*] **›biased** or **biassed** *adj*

bias binding *n* a strip of material used for binding hems

biaxial *adj* (esp. of a crystal) having two axes

bib *n* **1** a piece of cloth or plastic worn to protect a very young child's clothes while eating **2** the upper front part of some aprons, dungarees, etc. [Middle English *bibben* to drink]

bibcock *n* a tap with a nozzle bent downwards

bibelot (bib-loh) *n* an attractive or curious trinket [Old French *beubelet*]

bibl. **1** bibliographical **2** bibliography

Bible *n* **1 the Bible** the sacred writings of the Christian religion, comprising the Old and New Testaments **2** *bible* a book regarded as authoritative: *this guide has long been regarded as the hill walkers' bible* [Greek *biblion* book] **›biblical** *adj*

Bible Belt *n* those states of the S US where Protestant fundamentalism is dominant

bibliography *n*, *pl* **-phies 1** a list of books on a subject or by a particular author **2** a list of sources used in a book, etc. **3** the study of the history, etc., of literary material [Greek *biblion* book + *graphein* to write] **›bibliographer** *n*

bibliophile *n* a person who collects or is fond of books [Greek *biblion* book + *philos* loving]

bibulous *adj* *literary* addicted to alcohol [Latin *bibere* to drink]

bicameral *adj* (of a legislature) consisting of two chambers [BI- + Latin *camera* chamber]

bicarb *n* short for **bicarbonate of soda**

bicarbonate *n* a salt of carbonic acid

bicarbonate of soda *n* sodium bicarbonate used as medicine or a raising agent in baking

bicentenary or US **bicentennial** *adj* **1** marking a 200th anniversary ▷ *n*, *pl* **-naries 2** a 200th anniversary

biceps *n*, *pl* **-ceps** *anatomy* a muscle with two origins, esp. the muscle that flexes the forearm [BI- + Latin *caput* head]

bicker *vb* to argue over petty matters; squabble [origin unknown]

bickie or **bikkie** *n* *informal* short for **biscuit** (1)

bicolour, bicoloured or US **bicolor, bicolored** *adj* two-coloured

bicuspid *adj* **1** having two points ▷ *n* **2** a bicuspid tooth

b

bicycle *n* **1** a vehicle with a metal frame and two wheels, one behind the other, pedalled by the rider ▷ *vb* **-cling, -cled 2** to ride a bicycle [BI- + Greek *kuklos* wheel]

bid *vb* **bidding, bad, bade** *or* **bid, bidden** *or* **bid 1** to offer (an amount) in an attempt to buy something **2** to say (a greeting): *to bid farewell* **3** to order: *do as you are bid!* **4** *bridge etc.* to declare how many tricks one expects to make ▷ *n* **5 a** an offer of a specified amount **b** the price offered **6 a** the quoting by a seller of a price **b** the price quoted **7** an attempt, esp. to attain power **8** *bridge etc.* the number of tricks a player undertakes to make [Old English *biddan*] **> bidder** *n*

Bida *or* **El Beda** *n* the former name of **Doha**

Bidault *n* Georges. 1899–1983, French statesman; prime minister (1946, 1949–50). His opposition to Algerian independence led him to support the OAS: he was charged with treason (1963) and fled abroad

biddable *adj* obedient

bidding *n* **1** an order or command: *she had done his bidding* **2** an invitation; summons: *he knew to knock and wait for bidding before he entered* **3** the bids in an auction, card game, etc.

Biddle *n* John. 1615–62, English theologian; founder of Unitarianism in England

biddy *n*, *pl* **-dies** *informal* a woman, esp. an old gossipy one [pet form of *Bridget*]

biddy-bid *or* **biddy-biddy** *n*, *pl* **-bids, -biddies** NZ a low-growing plant with hooked burrs

bide *vb* **biding, bided** *or* **bode, bided 1** *archaic or dialect* to remain **2** *bide one's time* to wait patiently for an opportunity [Old English *bīdan*]

bidet (bee-day) *n* a small low basin for washing the genital area [French: small horse]

Biel *n* **1 a** town in NW Switzerland, on Lake Biel. Pop: 48 655 (2000). French name: **Bienne 2 Lake Biel** a lake in NW Switzerland: remains of lake dwellings were discovered here in the 19th century. Area: 39 sq km (15 sq miles). German name: **Bielersee**

Bielefeld *n* a city in Germany, in NE North Rhine-Westphalia: food, textiles. Pop: 328 452 (2003 est)

Bielorussia *n* another name for **Belarus**

Bielsko-Biała *n* a town in S Poland: created in 1951 by the union of Bielsko and Biała Krakowska; a leading textile centre since the 16th century. Pop: 356 000 (2005 est)

Bien Hoa *n* a town in S Vietnam: a former capital of Cambodia. Pop: 520 000 (2005 est)

Bienne *n* the French name for **Biel**

biennial *adj* **1** occurring every two years ▷ *n* **2** a plant that completes its life cycle in two years

bier *n* a stand on which a corpse or a coffin rests before burial [Old English *bǣr*]

Bierce *n* Ambrose (Gwinett). 1842–?1914, US journalist and author of humorous sketches, horror stories, and tales of the supernatural: he disappeared during a mission in Mexico (1913)

biff *slang n* **1** a blow with the fist ▷ *vb* **2** to give (someone) such a blow [probably imitative]

bifid *adj* divided into two by a cleft in the middle [BI- + Latin *findere* to split]

bifocal *adj* having two different focuses, esp. (of a lens) permitting near and distant vision

bifocals *pl n* a pair of spectacles with bifocal lenses

bifurcate *vb* **-cating, -cated 1** to fork into two branches ▷ *adj* **2** forked into two branches [BI- + Latin *furca* fork] **> bifurcation** *n*

big *adj* **bigger, biggest 1** of great or considerable size, weight, number, or capacity **2** having great significance; important **3** important through having power, wealth, etc. **4 a** elder: *my big brother* **b** grown-up **5** generous: *that's very big of you* **6** extravagant; boastful: *big talk* **7** *too big for one's boots* conceited; unduly self-confident **8** in an advanced stage of pregnancy: *big with child* **9** *in a big way* in a very grand or enthusiastic

way ▷ *adv informal* **10** boastfully; pretentiously: *he talks big* **11** on a grand scale: *think big* [origin unknown]

bigamy *n* the crime of marrying a person while still legally married to someone else [BI- + Greek *gamos* marriage] **> bigamist** *n* **> bigamous** *adj*

Big Apple *n* the Big Apple *informal* New York City [C20: probably from US jazzmen's earlier use to mean any big, esp. northern, city; of obscure origin]

big-bang theory *n* a cosmological theory that suggests that the universe was created as the result of a massive explosion

Big Ben *n* **1** the bell in the clock tower of the Houses of Parliament, London **2** the clock in this tower **3** the tower [C19: named after Sir *Benjamin* Hall, Chief Commissioner of Works in 1856 when it was cast]

Big Brother *n* a person or organization that exercises total dictatorial control [from the novel *1984* by George Orwell]

big business *n* large commercial organizations collectively

big end *n* the larger end of a connecting rod in an internal-combustion engine

big game *n* large animals that are hunted or fished for sport

bighead *n informal* a conceited person **> big-headed** *adj*

bight *n* **1** a long curved shoreline **2** the slack part or a loop in a rope [Old English *byht*]

Bight *n* the Bight *Austral informal* the major indentation of the S coast of Australia, from Cape Pasley in W Australia to the Eyre Peninsula in S Australia. In full: **the Great Australian Bight**

big name *informal n* **1** a famous person ▷ *adj* **big-name 2** famous

bigot *n* a person who is intolerant, esp. regarding religion, politics, or race [Old French] **> bigoted** *adj* **> bigotry** *n*

big shot *n informal* an important person

Big Smoke *n* the Big Smoke *informal* a big city, esp. London

big stick *n informal* force or the threat of force

big time *n* the big time *informal* the highest level of a profession, esp. entertainment **> big-timer** *n*

big top *n informal* the main tent of a circus

bigwig *n informal* an important person

Bihar *n* a state of NE India: consists of part of the Ganges plain; important for rice: lost the S to the new state of Jharkhand in 2000. Capital: Patna. Pop: 82 878 796 (2001). Area: 99 225 sq km (38 301 sq miles)

Bihari *n* **1** (*pl* **Bihari** *or* **Biharis**) a member of an Indian people living chiefly in Bihar but also in other parts of NW India and Bangladesh **2** the language of this people comprising a number of highly differentiated dialects, belonging to the Indic branch of the Indo-European family ▷ *adj* **3** of or relating to this people, their language, or Bihar

Biisk *n* a variant spelling of **Biysk**

Bijapur *n* an ancient city in W India, in N Mysore: capital of a former kingdom, which fell at the end of the 17th century: cotton. Pop: 245 946 (2001)

bijou (bee-zhoo) *n*, *pl* **-joux** (-zhooz) **1** something small and delicately worked ▷ *adj* **2** small but tasteful: *a bijou residence* [French: a jewel]

Bikaner *n* a walled city in NW India, in Rajasthan: capital of the former state of Bikaner, on the edge of the Thar Desert. Pop: 529 007 (2001)

bike *n informal* a bicycle or motorcycle

biker *n* a person who rides a motorcycle

biker jacket *n* a short, close-fitting leather jacket often worn by motorcyclists

Bikila *n* Abebe. 1932–73, Ethiopian long-distance runner: winner of the Marathon at the Olympic Games in Rome (1960) and Tokyo (1964)

bikini *n* a woman's brief two-piece swimming costume [after BIKINI atoll, from a comparison between the devastating effect of the atomic-bomb test there and the effect caused by women wearing bikinis}

Bikini *n* an atoll in the N Pacific; one of the Marshall Islands: site of a US atomic-bomb test in 1946

Biko *n* Steven Bantu, known as *Steve*. 1946–77, Black South African civil rights leader; founder of the South African Students Organization. His death in police custody caused worldwide concern

bilateral *adj* affecting or undertaken by two parties; mutual

Bilbao *n* a port in N Spain, on the Bay of Biscay: the largest city in the Basque Provinces: famous since medieval times for the production of iron and steel goods: modern buildings include the Guggenheim Art Museum (1997). Pop: 353 567 (2003 est). Basque name: Bilbo

bilberry *n, pl* **-ries** a blue or blackish edible berry that grows on a shrub [probably Scandinavian]

bilby *n, pl* **-bies** an Australian marsupial with long pointed ears and grey fur

bile *n* **1** a greenish fluid secreted by the liver to aid digestion of fats **2** irritability or peevishness [Latin *bilis*]

bilge *n* **1** informal nonsense **2** nautical the bottom of a ship's hull **3** the dirty water that collects in a ship's bilge [probably variant of *bulge*]

bilharzia (bill-hart-see-a) *n* a disease caused by infestation of the body with blood flukes [after T. *Bilharz*, who discovered the blood fluke]

biliary *adj* of bile, the ducts that convey bile, or the gall bladder

bilingual *adj* **1** able to speak two languages **2** expressed in two languages **> bilingualism** *n*

bilious *adj* **1** nauseous; sick: *a bilious attack* **2** informal bad-tempered; irritable: *the regime's most persistent and bilious critic* **3** (of a colour) harsh and offensive [Latin *biliosus* full of bile]

bilk *vb* to cheat or deceive, esp. to avoid making payment to [perhaps variant of *balk*] **> bilker** *n*

bill¹ *n* **1** a statement of money owed for goods or services supplied **2** a draft of a proposed new law presented to a law-making body **3** a printed notice or advertisement **4** US and Canad a piece of paper money; note **5** any list of items, events, etc. such as a theatre programme ▷ *vb* **6** to send or present an account for payment to (a person) **7** to advertise by posters **8** to schedule as a future programme: *next week they will discuss what are billed as new ideas for economic reform* **9** fit or fill the bill informal to be suitable or adequate [Late Latin *bulla* document]

bill² *n* **1** the projecting jaws of a bird; beak ▷ *vb* **2** bill and coo (of lovers) to kiss and whisper amorously [Old English *bile*]

billabong *n* Austral a pool in the bed of a stream with an interrupted water flow [Aboriginal]

billboard *n* a hoarding

billet¹ *vb* **-leting, -leted 1** to assign a lodging to (a soldier) ▷ *n* **2** accommodation, esp. for a soldier, in civilian lodgings **3** Austral and NZ a person who is billeted [Old French *billette*, from *bulle* a document]

billet² *n* **1** a chunk of wood, esp. for fuel **2** a small bar of iron or steel [Old French *billette* a little log]

billet-doux (bill-ee-doo) *n, pl* **billets-doux** (bill-ee-dooz) old-fashioned or humorous a love letter [French: a sweet letter]

billhook *n* a tool with a hooked blade, used for chopping, etc.

billiards *n* a game in which a long cue is used to propel balls on a table [Old French *billard* curved stick]

Billingsgate *n* the largest fish market in London, on the N bank of the River Thames; moved to new site at Canary Wharf in 1982 and the former building converted into offices

billion *n, pl* **-lions** or **-lion 1** one thousand million: 1 000 000 000 or 10⁹ **2** (in Britain, originally) a million million: 1 000 000 000 000 or 10¹² **3** (often pl)

informal an extremely large but unspecified number: *billions of dollars* [French] **> billionth** *adj, n*

billionaire *n* a person who has money or property worth at least a billion pounds, dollars, etc.

Billiton *n* an island of Indonesia, in the Java Sea between Borneo and Sumatra. Chief town: Tanjungpandan. Area: 4833 sq km (1866 sq miles). Also called: **Belitung**

bill of exchange *n* a document instructing a third party to pay a stated sum at a designated date or on demand

bill of fare *n* a menu

bill of health *n* **1** a certificate that confirms the health of a ship's company **2** clean bill of health informal **a** a good report of one's physical condition **b** a favourable account of a person's or a company's financial position

bill of lading *n* a document containing full particulars of goods shipped

billow *n* **1** a large sea wave **2** a swelling or surging mass, as of smoke or sound ▷ *vb* **3** to rise up or swell out [Old Norse *bylgja*] **> billowing** *adj, n* **> billowy** *adj*

billy or **billycan** *n, pl* **-lies** or **-lycans** a metal can or pot for boiling water, etc. over a campfire [Scots *billypot*]

billy goat *n* a male goat

Billy the Kid *n* nickname of *William H. Bonney*. 1859–81, US outlaw

biltong *n* S African strips of meat dried and cured in the sun [Afrikaans]

bimbo *n, pl* **-bos** slang an attractive but empty-headed young woman [Italian: little child]

bimetallic *adj* consisting of two metals

bimetallism *n* the use of two metals, esp. gold and silver, in fixed relative values as the standard of value and currency **> bimetallist** *n*

bin *n* **1** a container for rubbish, etc. **2** a large container for storing something in bulk, such as coal, grain, or bottled wine ▷ *vb* **binning, binned 3** to put in a rubbish bin: *I bin my junk mail without reading it* [Old English *binne* basket]

binary (bine-a-ree) *adj* **1** composed of two parts **2** maths, computers of or expressed in a system with two as its base **3** chem containing atoms of two different elements ▷ *n, pl* **-ries 4** something composed of two parts [Late Latin *binarius*]

binary star *n* a system of two stars revolving around a common centre of gravity

Binchy *n* Maeve. 1940–2012, Irish novelist and journalist; her bestselling novels include *Circle of Friends* (1990) and *Quentins* (2002)

bind *vb* **binding, bound 1** to make secure, such as with a rope **2** to unite with emotional ties or commitment **3** to place (someone) under legal or moral obligation **4** to place under certain constraints: *bound by the rules* **5** to stick together or cause to stick: *egg binds fat and flour* **6** to enclose and fasten (the pages of a book) between covers **7** to provide (a garment) with an edging **8** (foll. by *up*) to bandage ▷ *n* **9** informal a difficult or annoying situation [Old English *bindan*]

binder *n* **1** a firm cover for holding loose sheets of paper together **2** a person who binds books **3** something used to fasten or tie, such as rope or twine **4** obsolete a machine for cutting and binding grain into sheaves

bindery *n, pl* **-eries** a place in which books are bound

binding *n* **1** anything that binds or fastens **2** the covering of a book ▷ *adj* **3** imposing an obligation or duty

bind over *vb* to place (a person) under a legal obligation, esp. to keep the peace

bindweed *n* a plant that twines around a support

binge *n* informal **1** a bout of excessive eating or drinking **2** excessive indulgence in anything [probably dialect: to soak]

binge drinking *n* the practice of drinking excessive amounts of alcohol regularly

Bingen *n* a town in W Germany on the Rhine: wine trade and tourist centre. Pop: 24 716 (2003 est)

bingo *n* a gambling game in which numbers called out

are covered by players on their individual cards. The first to cover a given arrangement is the winner [origin unknown]

bin Laden *n* Osama. 1957–2011, Saudi-born leader of the al-Qaida terrorist network: presumed architect of the terrorist attacks on New York and Washington of September 11 2001. Killed by US Special Forces in Abbottabad, Pakistan

binnacle *n* a housing for a ship's compass [Late Latin *habitaculum* dwelling-place]

Binnig *n* Gerd (**Karl**). born 1947, German physicist: shared the Nobel prize for physics (1986) for work on the superconductivity of semiconductors and development of the scanning tunnelling microscope

binocular *adj* involving or intended for both eyes: *binocular vision* [BI- + Latin *oculus* eye]

binoculars *pl n* an optical instrument for use with both eyes, consisting of two small telescopes joined together

binomial *n* **1** a mathematical expression consisting of two terms, such as $3x + 2y$ ▷ *adj* **2** referring to two names or terms [BI- + Latin *nomen* name]

binomial theorem *n* a general mathematical formula that expresses any power of a binomial without multiplying out, as in $(a+b)^2=a^2+2ab+b^2$

Binyon *n* (**Robert**) **Laurence**. 1869–1943, British poet and art historian, best known for his elegiac war poems "For the Fallen" (1914) and "The Burning of the Leaves" (1944)

bio- *combining form* **1** indicating life or living organisms: *biogenesis* **2** indicating a human life or career: *biography* [Greek *bios* life]

bioastronautics *n* the study of the effects of space flight on living organisms

Bío-Bío *n* a river in central Chile, rising in the Andes and flowing northwest to the Pacific. Length: about 390 km (240 miles)

biochemistry *n* the study of the chemical compounds, reactions, etc., occurring in living organisms ❯ **biochemical** *adj* ❯ **biochemist** *n*

biocide *n* a substance used to destroy living things [BIO- + Latin *caedere* to kill]

biocoenosis *or US* **biocenosis** (bye-oh-see-**no**-siss) *n* the relationships between animals and plants subsisting together [BIO- + Greek *koinōsis* sharing]

biodegradable *adj* (of sewage and packaging) capable of being decomposed by natural means ❯ **biodegradability** *n*

biodiesel *n* a biofuel intended for use in diesel engines

biodiversity *n* the existence of a wide variety of plant and animal species in their natural environments

bioengineering *n* the design and manufacture of aids, such as artificial limbs, to help people with disabilities

biofuel *n* fuel derived from renewable biological resources

biogas *n* gaseous fuel produced by the fermentation of organic waste

biogenesis *n* the principle that a living organism must originate from a similar parent organism

biogenic (bye-oh-**jen**-ik) *adj* originating from a living organism

biography *n*, *pl* **-phies** **1** an account of a person's life by another person **2** such accounts collectively [BIO- + Greek *graphein* to write] ❯ **biographer** *n* ❯ **biographical** *adj*

Bioko *n* an island in the Gulf of Guinea, off the coast of Cameroon: part of Equatorial Guinea. Capital: Malabo. Area: 2017 sq km (786 sq miles). Former names: (until 1973) **Fernando Po**, (1973–79) **Macías Nguema**

biol. **1** biological **2** biology

biological *adj* **1** of or relating to biology **2** (of a detergent) containing enzymes that remove natural stains, such as blood or grass ❯ **biologically** *adv*

biological clock *n* an inherent timing mechanism that controls the rhythmic repetition of processes in living organisms, such as sleeping

biological control *n* the control of destructive organisms, esp. insects, by nonchemical means, such a introducing a natural predator of the pest

biological warfare *n* the use of living organisms or their toxic products to induce death or incapacity in humans

biology *n* the study of living organisms ❯ **biologist** *n*

biomass *n* the total number of living organisms in a given area

biomechanics *n* the study of the mechanics of the movement of living organisms

biomedicine *n* **1** the medical and biological study of th effects of unusual environmental stress **2** the study of herbal remedies

biometric *adj* relating to the analysis of biological data using mathematical and statistical methods, esp. for purposes of identification: *biometric passport*

biometry *or* **biometrics** *n* the analysis of biological data using mathematical and statistical methods, esp. for purposes of identification

bionic *adj* **1** of or relating to bionics **2** (in science fiction) having physical functions augmented by electronic equipment [BIO- + (*electro*)*nic*]

bionics *n* **1** the study of biological functions in order to develop electronic equipment that operates similarly **2** the replacement of limbs or body parts by artificial electronically powered parts

biophysics *n* the physics of biological processes and the application of methods used in physics to biology ❯ **biophysical** *adj* ❯ **biophysicist** *n*

biopic (bye-oh-pick) *n informal* a film based on the life of famous person [*bio*(*graphical*) + *pic*(*ture*)]

biopsy *n*, *pl* **-sies** examination of tissue from a living body to determine the cause or extent of a disease [BIO- Greek *opsis* sight]

biorhythm *n* a complex recurring pattern of physiological states, believed to affect physical, emotional, and mental states

BIOS Basic Input Output System: built-in software which controls the primary functions of a PC

bioscope *n* **1** a kind of early film projector **2** *S African* a cinema

biosphere *n* the part of the earth's surface and atmosphere inhabited by living things

biosynthesis *n* the formation of complex compounds by living organisms ❯ **biosynthetic** *adj*

biotech *n* short for **biotechnology**

biotechnology *n* the use of microorganisms, such as cells or bacteria, in industry and technology

bioterrorism *n* the use of viruses, bacteria, etc. by terrorists ❯ **bioterrorist** *n*

biotin *n* a vitamin of the B complex, abundant in egg yolk and liver [Greek *biotē* life]

bipartisan *adj* consisting of or supported by two political parties

bipartite *adj* **1** consisting of or having two parts **2** affecting or made by two parties: *a bipartite agreement*

biped (bye-ped) *n* **1** any animal with two feet ▷ *adj* also: **bipedal** **2** having two feet [BI- + Latin *pes* foot]

biplane *n* an aeroplane with two sets of wings, one above the other

bipolar *adj* **1** having two poles **2** having two extremes ❯ **bipolarity** *n*

birch *n* **1** a tree with thin peeling bark and hard close-grained wood **2** **the birch** a bundle of birch twigs or a birch rod used, esp. formerly, for flogging offenders ▷ *vb* **3** to flog with the birch [Old English *bierce*]

bird *n* **1** a two-legged creature with feathers and wings, which lays eggs and can usually fly. Related adjective: **avian** **2** *slang, chiefly Brit* a girl or young woman **3** *informal* person: *he's a rare bird* **4 a bird in the hand** something definite or certain **5 birds of a feather** people with the same ideas or interests **6 kill two birds with one stone** t accomplish two things with one action [Old English *bridd*

ird flu *n* a form of influenza occurring in poultry caused by a virus capable of spreading to humans

irdie *n* **1** *informal* a bird **2** *golf* a score of one stroke under par for a hole

irdlime *n* a sticky substance smeared on twigs to catch small birds

ird of paradise *n* a songbird of New Guinea, the male of which has brilliantly coloured plumage

ird of prey *n* a bird, such as a hawk or owl, that hunts other animals for food

irdseed *n* a mixture of various kinds of seeds for feeding cage birds

ird's-eye view *n* **1** a view seen from above **2** a general or overall impression of something

ird-watcher *n* a person who studies wild birds in their natural surroundings

irendra Bir Bikram Shah Dev *n* 1945–2001, king of Nepal (1972–2001): he, his queen, and six other members of the royal family were shot dead by his son, Crown Prince Dipendra, who then committed suicide

iretta *n* RC *Church* a stiff square clerical cap [Italian *berretta*]

irgitta *n* Saint Birgitta See **Bridget** (2)

irkbeck *n* George. 1776–1841, British educationalist, who helped to establish vocational training for working men: founder and first president of the London Mechanics Institute (1824), which later became Birkbeck College

irkenhead¹ *n* a port in NW England, in Wirral unitary authority, Merseyside: former shipbuilding centre. Pop: 83 729 (2001)

irkenhead² *n* Frederick Edwin Smith, 1st Earl of, known as *F. E. Smith*. 1872–1930, British Conservative statesman, lawyer, and orator

irmingham *n* **1** an industrial city in central England, in Birmingham unitary authority, in the West Midlands: the second largest city in Great Britain; two cathedrals; three universities (1900, 1966, 1992). Pop: 970 892 (2001). Informal name: **Brum 2** a unitary authority in central England, in the West Midlands. Pop: 992 100 (2003 est). Area: 283 sq km (109 sq miles) **3** an industrial city in N central Alabama: rich local deposits of coal, iron ore, and other minerals. Pop: 236 620 (2003 est)

iro *n*, *pl* **-ros** *trademark* a kind of ballpoint pen

irobidzhan *or* **Birobijan** *n* **1** a city in SE Russia: capital of the Jewish Autonomous Region. Pop: 77 250 (2002) **2** another name for the **Jewish Autonomous Region**

irth *n* **1** the process of bearing young; childbirth **2** the act of being born **3** the beginning of something; origin **4** ancestry: *of noble birth* **5** give birth to **a** to bear (offspring) **b** to produce or originate (an idea, plan, etc.) [Old Norse *byrth*]

irth certificate *n* an official form stating the time and place of a person's birth

irth control *n* limitation of child-bearing by means of contraception

irthday *n* **1** an anniversary of the day of one's birth **2** the day on which a person was born

irthmark *n* a blemish on the skin formed before birth

irth mother *n* the woman who gives birth to a child, regardless of whether she is the genetic mother or subsequently brings up the child

irthplace *n* the place where someone was born or where something originated

irth rate *n* the ratio of live births to population, usually expressed per 1000 population per year

irthright *n* privileges or possessions that a person has or is believed to be entitled to as soon as he or she is born

irtwistle *n* Sir Harrison. born 1934, English composer, whose works include the operas *Punch and Judy* (1967), *The Mask of Orpheus* (1984), *Gawain* (1991), *Exody* (1998), and *The Minotaur* (2008)

isayas *pl n* the Spanish name for the **Visayan Islands**

iscay *n* Bay of Biscay a large bay of the Atlantic Ocean

between W France and N Spain: notorious for storms

biscuit *n* **1** a small flat dry sweet or plain cake **2** porcelain that has been fired but not glazed ▷ *adj* **3** pale brown or yellowish-grey [Old French *(pain) bescuit* twice-cooked (bread)]

bisect *vb* **1** *maths* to divide into two equal parts **2** to cut or split into two [BI- + Latin *secare* to cut] **> bisection** *n*

bisexual *adj* **1** sexually attracted to both men and women **2** showing characteristics of both sexes ▷ *n* **3** a bisexual person **> bisexuality** *n*

Bishkek *n* the capital of Kyrgyzstan. Pop: 828 000 (2005 est). Also called: **Pishpek**. Former name (1926–91): **Frunze**

bishop *n* **1** a clergyman having spiritual and administrative powers over a diocese **2** a chessman capable of moving diagonally [Greek *episkopos* overseer]

Bishop *n* **1** Billy, full name *William Avery Bishop*. 1894–1956, Canadian fighter pilot during World War I; played an important role in the training of Commonwealth pilots during World War II **2** Elizabeth. 1911–79, US poet, who lived in Brazil. Her poetry reflects her travelling experience, esp. in the tropics

Bishop Auckland *n* a town in N England, in central Durham: seat of the bishops of Durham since the 12th century: light industries. Pop: 24 764 (2001)

bishopric *n* the see, diocese, or office of a bishop

Bisitun *n* another name for **Behistun**

Bisk *n* a variant spelling of **Biysk**

Biskra *n* a town and oasis in NE Algeria, in the Sahara. Pop: 204 000 (2005 est)

Bisley *n* a village in SE England, in Surrey: annual meetings of the National Rifle Association

Bismarck¹ *n* a city in North Dakota, on the Missouri River: the state capital. Pop: 56 344 (2003 est)

Bismarck² *n* Prince Otto (**Eduard Leopold**) von, called *the Iron Chancellor*. 1815–98, German statesman; prime minister of Prussia (1862–90). Under his leadership Prussia defeated Austria and France, and Germany was united. In 1871 he became the first chancellor of the German Reich

Bismarck Archipelago *n* a group of over 200 islands in the SW Pacific, northeast of New Guinea: part of Papua New Guinea. Main islands: New Britain, New Ireland, Lavongai, and the Admiralty Islands. Chief town: Rabaul, on New Britain. Pop: 566 610 (2000). Area: 49 658 sq km (19 173 sq miles)

bismuth *n* *chem* a brittle pinkish-white metallic element. Some compounds are used in alloys and in medicine. Symbol: Bi [German *Wismut*]

bison *n*, *pl* **-son** an animal of the cattle family with a massive head, shaggy forequarters, and a humped back [Germanic]

bisque¹ *n* a thick rich soup made from shellfish [French]

bisque² *adj* **1** pink-to-yellowish-tan ▷ *n* **2** *ceramics* same as **biscuit** (2) [shortened from *biscuit*]

Bissau *or* **Bissão** *n* a port on the Atlantic, the capital of Guinea-Bissau (until 1974 Portuguese Guinea). Pop: 369 000 (2005 est)

bistable *adj* (of an electronic system) having two stable states

bistro *n*, *pl* **-tros** a small restaurant [French]

Bisutun *n* another name for **Behistun**

bit¹ *n* **1** a small piece, portion, or quantity **2** a short time or distance **3** a bit rather; somewhat: *a bit stupid* **4** a bit of rather: *a bit of a fool* **5** bit by bit gradually **6** do one's bit to make one's expected contribution [Old English *bite* action of biting]

bit² *n* **1** a metal mouthpiece on a bridle for controlling a horse **2** a cutting or drilling tool, part, or head in a brace, drill, etc. [Old English *bita*]

bit³ *vb* the past tense of **bite**

bit⁴ *n* *maths, computers* **1** a single digit of binary notation, represented either by 0 or by 1 **2** the smallest unit of information, indicating the presence or absence of a single feature [b(inary) + dig)it]

b

bitch *n* **1** a female dog, fox, or wolf **2** *slang, offensive* a malicious or spiteful woman **3** *informal* a difficult situation or problem ▷ *vb* **4** *informal* to complain; grumble [Old English *bicce*]

bitchy *adj* **bitchier, bitchiest** *informal* spiteful or malicious ▷ **bitchiness** *n*

bitcoin *n* a form of digital currency that is created, held, and exchanged electronically

bite *vb* **biting, bit, bitten 1** to grip, cut off, or tear with the teeth or jaws **2** (of animals or insects) to injure by puncturing (the skin) with the teeth or fangs **3** (of corrosive material) to eat away or into **4** to smart or cause to smart; sting **5** *angling* (of a fish) to take the bait or lure **6** to take firm hold of or act effectively upon: *turn the screw till it bites the wood* **7** *slang* to annoy or worry: *what's biting her?* ▷ *n* **8** the act of biting **9** a thing or amount bitten off **10** a wound or sting inflicted by biting **11** *angling* an attempt by a fish to take the bait or lure **12** a snack **13** a stinging or smarting sensation [Old English *bītan*] ▷ **biter** *n*

Bithynia *n* an ancient country on the Black Sea in NW Asia Minor

biting *adj* **1** piercing; keen: *a biting wind* **2** sarcastic; incisive

bitmap *n computers* a picture created by colour or shading on a visual display unit

Bitolj *or* **Bitola** *n* a city in SW Macedonia: under Turkish rule from 1382 until 1913 when it was taken by the Serbs. Pop: 77 000 (2005 est)

bit part *n* a very small acting role with few lines to speak

bitstream *n computers* a sequence of digital data transmitted electronically

bitten *vb* the past participle of **bite**

bitter *adj* **1** having an unpalatable harsh taste, as the peel of an orange **2** showing or caused by hostility or resentment **3** difficult to accept: *a bitter blow* **4** sarcastic: *bitter words* **5** bitingly cold: *a bitter night* ▷ *n* **6** *Brit* beer with a slightly bitter taste [Old English *biter*] ▷ **bitterly** *adv* ▷ **bitterness** *n*

Bitter Lakes *pl n* two lakes, the **Great Bitter Lake** and **Little Bitter Lake** in NE Egypt: part of the Suez Canal

bittern *n* a large wading marsh bird with a booming call [Old French *butor*]

bitters *pl n* bitter-tasting spirits flavoured with plant extracts

bittersweet *adj* **1** tasting of or being a mixture of bitterness and sweetness **2** pleasant but tinged with sadness

bitty *adj* **-tier, -tiest** lacking unity; disjointed ▷ **bittiness** *n*

bitumen *n* a sticky or solid substance that occurs naturally in asphalt and tar and is used in road surfacing [Latin] ▷ **bituminous** *adj*

bituminous coal *n* a soft black coal that burns with a smoky yellow flame

bivalve *n* **1** a sea creature, such as an oyster or mussel, that has a shell consisting of two hinged valves and breathes through gills ▷ *adj* **2** of these molluscs

bivouac *n* **1** a temporary camp, as used by soldiers or mountaineers ▷ *vb* **-acking, -acked 2** to make a temporary camp [French]

Biysk, Biisk *or* **Bisk** *n* a city in SW Russia, at the foot of the Altai Mountains. Pop: 216 000 (2005 est)

biz *n informal* business

bizarre *adj* odd or unusual, esp. in an interesting or amusing way [Italian *bizzarro* capricious]

Bizerte *or* **Bizerta** *n* a port in N Tunisia, on the Mediterranean at the canalized outlet of **Lake Bizerte**. Pop: 118 000 (2005 est)

Bizet *n* Georges. 1838–75, French composer, whose works include the opera *Carmen* (1875) and incidental music to Daudet's *L'Arlésienne* (1872)

Björneborg *n* the Swedish name for **Pori**

Bjørnson *n* Bjørnstjerne. 1832–1910, Norwegian poet,

dramatist, novelist, theatre director, and newspaper editor; mainly remembered for social dramas, such as *The Bankrupt* (1875): Nobel prize for literature 1903

Bk *chem* berkelium

BL 1 *chiefly Brit* Bachelor of Law **2** Bachelor of Letters **3** Barrister-at-Law

blab *vb* **blabbing, blabbed** to divulge (secrets) indiscreetly [Germanic]

blabber *n* **1** a person who blabs ▷ *vb* **2** to talk without thinking [Middle English *blabberen*]

black *adj* **1** having no hue, owing to the absorption of a[l] or almost all light; of the colour of coal **2** without light **3** without hope; gloomy: *the future looked black* **4** dirty or soiled **5** angry or resentful: *black looks* **6** unpleasant in a[ ] cynical or macabre manner: *black comedy* **7** (of coffee or tea) without milk or cream **8** wicked or harmful: *a blac[ ] lie* ▷ *n* **9** the darkest colour; the colour of coal **10** a dye o[ ] pigment producing this colour **11** black clothing, worn[ ] esp. in mourning: *she was in black, as though in mourning* **12** complete darkness: *the black of the night* **13** in the black in credit or without debt ▷ *vb* **14** same as **blacken 15** to polish (shoes or boots) with blacking **16** *Brit, Austral, and NZ* (of trade unionists) to organize a boycott of (specifi[ ] goods, work, etc.) ▶ See also **blackout** [Old English *blæc*] ▷ **blackness** *n* ▷ **blackish** *adj*

Black¹ *n* **1** a member of a dark-skinned race ▷ *adj* **2** of or[ ] relating to a Black person or Black people

Black² *n* **1** Sir James (Whyte). 1924–2010, British biochemist. He discovered beta-blockers and drugs for[ ] peptic ulcers: Nobel prize for physiology or medicine 1988 **2** Joseph. 1728–99, Scottish physician and chemist[ ] noted for his pioneering work on carbon dioxide and heat

black-and-blue *adj* (of the skin) bruised, as from a[ ] beating

black-and-white *n* **1** a photograph, film, etc., in black[ ] white, and shades of grey, rather than in colour **2** in **black and white a** in print or writing **b** in extremes: *he always sees things in black and white*

black-backed gull *n* a large common black-and-whit[ ] European gull

blackball¹ *vb* **1** to vote against **2** to exclude (someone) from a group, etc. [from *black ball*, used formerly to veto[ ]

blackball² *n NZ* a hard boiled sweet with black-and-white stripes

black bear *n* **1** a bear inhabiting forests of North America **2** a bear of central and E Asia

black belt *n judo, karate etc.* **1** a black belt that signifies that the wearer has reached a high standard in martia[ ] art **2** a person entitled to wear this

blackberry *n, pl* **-ries** a small blackish edible fruit that grows on a woody bush with thorny stems. Also called[ ] bramble

BlackBerry *n trademark* a hand-held device for sending and receiving e-mail

blackbird *n* a common European thrush, the male of which has black plumage and a yellow bill

blackboard *n* a hard or rigid surface made of a smooth[ ] usually dark substance, used for writing or drawing or[ ] with chalk, esp. in teaching

black box *n informal* a flight recorder

Blackburn¹ *n* **1** a city in NW England, in Blackburn wi[ ] Darwen unitary authority, Lancashire: formerly important for textiles, now has mixed industries. Pop:[ ] 105 085 (2001) **2** Mount Blackburn a mountain in SE Alaska, the highest peak in the Wrangell Mountains. Height: 5037 m (16 523 ft)

Blackburn² *n* Elizabeth (Helen). born 1948, Australian[ ] biologist who, with Carol W Greider and Jack W Szosta[ ] discovered the enzyme telomerase, for which they wo[ ] the Nobel Prize in Physiology or Medicine (2009)

Blackburn with Darwen *n* a unitary authority in NW[ ] England, in Lancashire. Pop: 139 800 (2003 est). Area: 137 sq km (53 sq miles)

blackcap n a brownish-grey warbler, the male of which has a black crown

blackcock n the male of the black grouse

Black Country n the Black Country the formerly heavily industrialized region of central England, northwest of Birmingham

blackcurrant n a very small blackish edible fruit that grows in bunches on a bush

blackdamp n air that is low in oxygen content and high in carbon dioxide as a result of an explosion in a mine

Black Death n the Black Death a form of bubonic plague in Europe and Asia during the 14th century

black economy n Brit, Austral and NZ that portion of the income of a nation that remains illegally undeclared

blacken vb 1 to make or become black or dirty 2 to damage (someone's reputation); discredit: they planned to blacken my father's name

Blackett n Patrick Maynard Stuart, Baron. 1897–1974, English physicist, noted for his work on cosmic radiation and his discovery of the positron. Nobel prize for physics 1948

black eye n bruising round the eye

Black Forest n the Black Forest a hilly wooded region of SW Germany, in Baden-Württemberg: a popular resort area. German name: der Schwarzwald

Black Friar n a Dominican friar

blackguard (blag-gard) n an unprincipled contemptible person [originally, lowest group at court]

blackhead n 1 a black-tipped plug of fatty matter clogging a pore of the skin 2 a bird with black plumage on the head

Blackheath n a residential district in SE London, mainly in the boroughs of Lewisham and Greenwich: a large heath formerly notorious for highwaymen

Black Hills pl n a group of mountains in W South Dakota and NE Wyoming: famous for the gigantic sculptures of US presidents on the side of Mount Rushmore. Highest peak: Harney Peak, 2207 m (7242 ft)

black hole n astronomy a hypothetical region of space resulting from the collapse of a star and surrounded by a gravitational field from which neither matter nor radiation can escape

black ice n a thin transparent layer of new ice on a road

blacking n any preparation for giving a black finish to shoes, metals, etc.

Black Isle n the Black Isle a peninsula in NE Scotland, in Highland council area, between the Cromarty and Moray Firths [so called because until the late 18th century much of it was uncultivated black moor]

blackjack¹ n pontoon or a similar card game [black + jack (the knave)]

blackjack² n chiefly US and Canad a truncheon of leather-covered lead with a flexible shaft [black + jack (implement)]

black lead n same as graphite

blackleg n Brit 1 a person who continues to work or does another's job during a strike ▷ vb **-legging, -legged 2** to refuse to join a strike

blacklist n 1 a list of people or organizations considered untrustworthy or disloyal ▷ vb 2 to put (someone) on a blacklist

black magic n magic used for evil purposes

blackmail n 1 the act of attempting to obtain money by threatening to reveal shameful information 2 the use of unfair pressure in an attempt to influence someone ▷ vb 3 to obtain or attempt to obtain money by intimidation 4 to attempt to influence (a person) by unfair pressure [black + Old English māl terms] **> blackmailer** n

Black Maria (mar-rye-a) n a police van for transporting prisoners

black mark n a discredit noted against someone

black market n a place or a system for buying or selling goods or currencies illegally, esp. in violation of controls or rationing **> black marketeer** n

black mass n a blasphemous travesty of the Christian Mass, used in black magic

Blackmore n R(ichard) D(oddridge). 1825–1900, English novelist; author of Lorna Doone (1869)

Black Mountain n the Black Mountain a mountain range in S Wales, in E Carmarthenshire and W Powys. Highest peak: Carmarthen Van, 802 m (2632 ft)

Black Mountains pl n a mountain range running from N Monmouthshire and SE Powys (Wales) to SW Herefordshire (England). Highest peak: Waun Fach, 811 m (2660 ft)

blackout n 1 (in wartime) the putting out or hiding of all lights as a precaution against a night air attack 2 a momentary loss of consciousness, vision, or memory 3 a temporary electrical power failure 4 the prevention of information broadcasts: a news blackout ▷ vb black out 5 to put out (lights) 6 to lose vision, consciousness, or memory temporarily 7 to stop (news, a television programme, etc.) from being broadcast

black pepper n a dark-coloured hot seasoning made from the dried berries and husks of the pepper plant

Blackpool n 1 a town and resort in NW England, in Blackpool unitary authority, Lancashire on the Irish Sea: famous for its tower, 158 m (518 ft) high, and its illuminations. Pop: 142 283 (2001) 2 a unitary authority in NW England, in Lancashire. Pop: 142 400 (2003 est). Area: 35 sq km (13 sq miles)

Black Power n a movement of Black people to obtain equality with Whites

Black Prince n the Black Prince See Edward (1)

black pudding n Brit a black sausage made from pig's blood, suet, etc.

Black Rod n (in Britain) the chief usher of the House of Lords and of the Order of the Garter

Black Sea n an inland sea between SE Europe and Asia: connected to the Aegean Sea by the Bosporus, the Sea of Marmara, and the Dardanelles, and to the Sea of Azov by the Kerch Strait. Area: about 415 000 sq km (160 000 sq miles). Ancient names: **Pontus Euxinus, Euxine Sea**

black sheep n a person who is regarded as a disgrace or failure by his or her family or peer group

Blackshirt n a member of the Italian Fascist party before and during the Second World War

blacksmith n a person who works iron with a furnace, anvil, and hammer

black spot n 1 a place on a road where accidents frequently occur 2 an area where a particular situation is exceptionally bad: an unemployment black spot

Blackstone n Sir William. 1723–80, English jurist noted particularly for his Commentaries on the Laws of England (1765–69), which had a profound influence on jurisprudence in the US

blackthorn n a thorny shrub with black twigs, white flowers, and small sour plumlike fruits

black tie n a black bow tie worn with a dinner jacket ▷ adj black-tie 2 denoting an occasion when a dinner jacket should be worn

Black Volta n a river in W Africa, rising in SW Burkina Faso and flowing northeast, then south into Lake Volta: forms part of the border of Ghana with Burkina-Faso and with Côte d'Ivoire. Length: about 800 km (500 miles)

Black Watch n the Black Watch the Royal Highland Regiment in the British Army

black widow n an American spider, the female of which is highly venomous and commonly eats its mate

Blackwood n Algernon (Henry). 1869–1951, British novelist and short-story writer; noted for his supernatural tales

bladder n 1 anatomy a membranous sac, usually containing liquid, esp. the urinary bladder 2 a hollow bag made of leather, etc. which becomes round when

b

filled with air or liquid **3** a hollow saclike part in certain plants, such as seaweed [Old English *blǣdre*] **> bladdery** *adj*

blade *n* **1** the part of a sharp weapon, tool, or knife, that forms the cutting edge **2** the thin flattish part of a propeller, oar, or fan **3** the flattened part of a leaf, sepal, or petal **4** the long narrow leaf of a grass or related plant [Old English *blæd*]

Blaenau Gwent *n* a county borough of SE Wales, created in 1996 from NW Gwent. Administrative centre: Ebbw Vale. Pop: 68 900 (2003 est). Area: 109 sq km (42 sq miles)

blag *vb* **blagging, blagged** *Brit slang* **1** to obtain by wheedling or cadging **2** to steal or rob [origin unknown]

Blagoveshchensk *n* a city and port in E Russia, in Siberia on the Amur River. Pop: 222 000 (2005 est)

blain *n* a blister, blotch, or sore on the skin [Old English *blegen*]

Blair *n* Tony, full name *Anthony Charles Lynton Blair*. born 1953, British politician; leader of the Labour Party (1994–2007); prime minister (1997–2007); Middle East peace envoy (2007–2015)

Blake *n* **1** Sir Peter. born 1932, British painter, a leading exponent of pop art in the 1960s: co-founder of the Brotherhood of Ruralists (1969) **2** Sir Quentin (Saxby). born 1932, British artist, illustrator, and children's writer; noted esp. for his illustrations to books by Roald Dahl **3** Robert. 1599–1657, English admiral, who commanded Cromwell's fleet against the Royalists, the Dutch, and the Spanish **4** William. 1757–1827, English poet, painter, engraver, and mystic. His literary works include *Songs of Innocence* (1789) and *Songs of Experience* (1794), *The Marriage of Heaven and Hell* (1793), and *Jerusalem* (1820). His chief works in the visual arts include engravings of a visionary nature, such as the illustrations for *The Book of Job* (1826), for Dante's poems, and for his own *Prophetic Books* (1783–1804)

Blakey *n* Art, full name *Arthur Blakey*. (1919–90), US Black jazz drummer and leader of the Jazz Messengers band

blame *vb* **blaming, blamed** **1** to consider (someone) responsible for: *I blame her for the failure* **2** (foll. by *on*) to put responsibility for (something) on (someone): *she blames the failure on me* **3** **be to blame** to be at fault ▷ *n* **4** responsibility for something that is wrong: *they must take the blame for the failure* **5** an expression of condemnation: *analysts lay the blame on party activists* [Late Latin *blasphemare* to blaspheme] **> blamable** *or* **blameable** *adj* **> blameless** *adj*

blameworthy *adj* deserving blame **> blameworthiness** *n*

Blanc¹ *n* **1** Mont Blanc See Mont Blanc **2** Cape Blanc a headland in N Tunisia: the northernmost point of Africa **3** Cape Blanc *or* Cape Blanco a peninsula in Mauritania, on the Atlantic coast

Blanc² *n* (Jean Joseph Charles) Louis (lwi). 1811–82, French socialist and historian: author of *L'Organisation du travail* (1840), in which he advocated the establishment of cooperative workshops subsidized by the state

blanch *vb* **1** to whiten **2** to become pale, as with sickness or fear **3** to prepare (meat or vegetables) by plunging them in boiling water **4** to cause (celery, chicory, etc.) to grow white from lack of light [Old French *blanc* white]

Blanche of Castile *n* ?1188–1252, queen consort (1223–26) of Louis VIII of France, born in Spain. The mother of Louis IX, she acted as regent during his minority (1226–36) and his absence on a crusade (1248–52)

Blanchett *n* Cate, full name *Catherine Elise Blanchett*. born 1969, Australian actress; her films include *Elizabeth* (1998), the *Lord of the Rings* trilogy (2001–03), *Notes on a Scandal* (2006), and *Blue Jasmine* (2013) for which she won an Academy Award

blancmange (blam-**monzh**) *n* a jelly-like dessert of milk, stiffened usually with cornflour [Old French *blanc manger* white food]

Blanco *n* Serge. born 1958, French Rugby Union footballer; won 93 caps (1980–91) and scored 38 tries in internationals (a French record)

bland *adj* **1** dull and uninteresting: *the bland predictability of the film* **2** (of food, drink, etc.) flavourless **3** smooth in manner: *he looked at his visitor with a bland smile* [Latin *blandus* flattering] **> blandly** *adv*

blandish *vb* to persuade by mild flattery; coax [Latin *blandiri*]

blandishments *pl n* flattery intended to coax or cajole

blank *adj* **1** (of a writing surface) not written on **2** (of a form, etc.) with spaces left for details to be filled in **3** without ornament or break: *a blank wall* **4** empty or void: *a blank space* **5** showing no interest or expression: *a blank look* **6** lacking ideas or inspiration: *his mind went blank* ▷ *n* **7** an empty space **8** an empty space for writing in **9** the condition of not understanding: *my mind went a complete blank* **10** a mark, often a dash, in place of a word **11** same as **blank cartridge** **12** draw a blank to get no results from something ▷ *vb* **13** (foll. by *out*) to cross out, blot, or obscure **14** blank something out to refuse to think about something; to clear something from one's mind **15** *slang* to ignore: *the crowd blanked her for the first four numbers* [Old French *blanc* white] **> blankly** *adv*

blank cartridge *n* a cartridge containing powder but no bullet

blank cheque *n* **1** a signed cheque on which the amount payable has not been specified **2** complete freedom of action

blanket *n* **1** a large piece of thick cloth for use as a bed covering **2** a concealing cover, as of smoke, leaves, or snow ▷ *adj* **3** applying to or covering a wide group or variety of people, conditions, situations, etc.: *a blanket ban on all supporters travelling to away matches* ▷ *vb* **-keting, -keted** **4** to cover as if with a blanket **5** to cover a wide area of; give blanket coverage to [Old French *blancquete*]

blanket stitch *n* a strong reinforcing stitch for the edges of blankets

blank verse *n* unrhymed verse

Blanqui *n* Louis Auguste. 1805–81, French revolutionary, who organized secret socialist societies and preached violent insurrection; he spent over 30 years in prison

Blantyre-Limbe *n* a city in S Malawi: largest city in the country; formed in 1956 from the adjoining towns of Blantyre and Limbe. Pop: 647 000 (2005 est)

blare *vb* **blaring, blared** **1** to sound loudly and harshly **2** to proclaim loudly: *the newspaper headlines blared the news* ▷ *n* **3** a loud harsh noise [Middle Dutch *bleren*]

blarney *n* flattering talk [after the BLARNEY STONE]

Blarney Stone *n* a stone in Blarney Castle, in the SW Republic of Ireland, said to endow whoever kisses it with the gift of the gab and skill in flattery

Blasco Ibáñez *n* Vicente. 1867–1928, Spanish novelist, whose books include *Blood and Sand* (1909) and *The Four Horsemen of the Apocalypse* (1916)

blasé (blah-**zay**) *adj* indifferent or bored, esp. through familiarity [French]

blaspheme *vb* **-pheming, -phemed** **1** to speak disrespectfully of (God or sacred things) **2** to utter curses [Greek *blasphēmos* evil-speaking] **> blasphemer** *n*

blasphemy *n, pl* **-mies** behaviour or language that shows disrespect for God or sacred things **> blasphemous** *adj*

blast *n* **1** an explosion, such as that caused by dynamite **2** the charge used in a single explosion **3** a sudden strong gust of wind or air **4** a sudden loud sound, such as that made by a trumpet **5** a violent verbal outburst, esp. critical **6** *slang* a very enjoyable or thrilling experience: *the party was a blast* **7** at full blast at maximum speed, volume, etc. ▷ *interj* **8** *slang* an exclamation of annoyance ▷ *vb* **9** to blow up (a rock, tunnel, etc.) with explosives **10** to make or cause to make a loud harsh noise **11** to criticize severely [Old English *blǣst*]

blasted *adj, adv slang* extreme or extremely: *a blasted idiot*

blast furnace *n* a furnace for smelting using a blast of preheated air

blastoff *n* **1** the launching of a rocket under its own power ▷ *vb* **blast off 2** (of a rocket) to be launched

blatant (blay-tant) *adj* **1** glaringly obvious: *a blatant lie* **2** offensively noticeable: *their blatant disregard for my feelings* [coined by Edmund Spenser, poet] **> blatantly** *adv*

blather *vb, n* same as blether

Blatter *n* Joseph, known as *Sepp.* born 1936, Swiss football administrator; President of FIFA 1998–2015

Blavatsky *n* Elena Petrovna, called *Madame Blavatsky.* 1831–91, Russian theosophist; author of *Isis Unveiled* (1877)

Blaydon *n* an industrial town in NE England, in Gateshead unitary authority, Tyne and Wear. Pop: 14 648 (2001)

blaze¹ *n* **1** a strong fire or flame **2** a very bright light or glare **3** an outburst (of passion, patriotism, etc.) ▷ *vb* **blazing, blazed 4** to burn fiercely **5** to shine brightly **6** to become stirred, as with anger or excitement **7 blaze away** to shoot continuously ▶ See also blazes [Old English *blǣse*]

blaze² *n* **1** a mark, usually indicating a path, made on a tree **2** a light-coloured marking on the face of an animal ▷ *vb* **blazing, blazed 3** to mark (a tree, path, etc.) with a blaze **4 blaze a trail** to explore new territories, areas of knowledge, etc. [probably from Middle Low German *bles* white marking]

blaze³ *vb* **blazing, blazed** blaze something abroad to make something widely known [Middle Dutch *blāsen*]

blazer *n* a fairly lightweight jacket, often in the colours of a sports club, school, etc.

blazes *pl n slang, euphemistic* hell

blazon *vb* **1** to proclaim publicly: *the newspaper photographs were blazoned on the front pages* **2** *heraldry* to describe or colour (heraldic arms) conventionally ▷ *n* **3** *heraldry* a coat of arms [Old French *blason* coat of arms]

bleach *vb* **1** to make or become white or colourless by exposure to sunlight, or by the action of chemical agents ▷ *n* **2** a bleaching agent [Old English *blǣcan*]

bleaching powder *n* a white powder consisting of chlorinated calcium hydroxide

bleak *adj* **1** exposed and barren **2** cold and raw **3** offering little hope; dismal: *a bleak future* [Old English *blāc* pale] **> bleakly** *adv* **> bleakness** *n*

bleary *adj* **blearier, bleariest 1** with eyes dimmed, by tears or tiredness: *a few bleary hacks* **2** indistinct or unclear **> blearily** *adv*

bleary-eyed *or* **blear-eyed** *adj* with eyes blurred, such as with old age or after waking

Bleasdale *n* Alan. born 1946, British playwright, best known for his television series *The Boys From the Blackstuff* (1983) and *GBH* (1991)

bleat *vb* **1** (of a sheep, goat, or calf) to utter its plaintive cry **2** to whine ▷ *n* **3** the characteristic cry of sheep, goats, and calves **4** a weak complaint or whine [Old English *blǣtan*]

bleed *vb* **bleeding, bled 1** to lose or emit blood **2** to remove or draw blood from (a person or animal) **3** (of plants) to exude (sap or resin), esp. from a cut **4** *informal* to obtain money, etc., from (someone), esp. by extortion **5** to draw liquid or gas from (a container or enclosed system) **6 my heart bleeds for you** I am sorry for you: often used ironically [Old English *blēdan*]

bleeding *adj, adv Brit slang* extreme or extremely: *a bleeding fool*

bleep *n* **1** a short high-pitched signal made by an electrical device **2** same as bleeper ▷ *vb* **3** to make a bleeping signal **4** to call (someone) by means of a bleeper [imitative]

bleeper *n* a small portable radio receiver that makes a bleeping signal

blemish *n* **1** a defect; flaw; stain ▷ *vb* **2** to spoil or tarnish

[Old French *blemir* to make pale]

blench *vb* to shy away, as in fear [Old English *blencan* to deceive]

blend *vb* **1** to mix or mingle (components) **2** to mix (different varieties of tea, whisky, etc.) **3** to look good together; harmonize **4** (esp. of colours) to shade gradually into each other ▷ *n* **5** a mixture produced by blending [Old English *blandan*]

blende *n* a mineral consisting mainly of zinc sulphide: the chief source of zinc

blender *n* an electrical kitchen appliance for pureeing vegetables, etc.

Blenheim *n* a village in SW Germany, site of a victory of Anglo-Austrian forces under the Duke of Marlborough and Prince Eugène of Savoy that saved Vienna from the French and Bavarians (1704) during the War of the Spanish Succession. Modern name: **Blindheim**

Blenheim Palace *n* a palace in Woodstock in Oxfordshire: built (1705–22) by Sir John Vanbrugh for the 1st Duke of Marlborough as a reward from the nation for his victory at Blenheim; gardens laid out by Henry Wise and Capability Brown; birthplace of Sir Winston Churchill (1874)

blenny *n, pl* **-nies** a small fish of coastal waters with a tapering scaleless body and long fins [Greek *blennos* slime]

Blériot *n* Louis. 1872–1936, French aviator and aeronautical engineer: made the first flight across the English Channel (1909)

bless *vb* **blessing, blessed** *or* **blest 1** to make holy by means of a religious rite **2** to give honour or glory to (a person or thing) as holy **3** to call upon God to protect **4** to worship or adore (God) **5 be blessed with** to be endowed with: *she is blessed with immense energy* **6 bless me!** an exclamation of surprise **7 bless you!** said to a person who has just sneezed [Old English *blǣdsian* to sprinkle with sacrificial blood]

blessed *adj* **1** made holy **2** *RC Church* (of a person) beatified by the pope **3** bringing great happiness or good fortune: *he was blessed with good looks* **4** *euphemistic* damned: *I'm blessed if I know*

blessing *n* **1** the act of invoking divine protection or aid **2** approval; good wishes **3** a happy event

blest *vb* a past of bless

Bletchley Park *n* the Buckinghamshire estate which was the centre of British code-breaking operations during World War II

blether *Scot vb* **1** to speak foolishly at length ▷ *n* **2** foolish talk **3** a person who blethers [Old Norse *blathr* nonsense]

blew *vb* the past tense of blow¹

Blida *n* a city in N Algeria, on the edge of the Mitidja Plain. Pop: 269 000 (2005 est)

Bligh *n* William. 1754–1817, British admiral; Governor of New South Wales (1806–9), deposed by the New South Wales Corps: as a captain, commander of *H.M.S. Bounty* when the crew mutinied in 1789

blight *n* **1** a person or thing that spoils or prevents growth **2** any plant disease characterized by withering and shrivelling without rotting **3** a fungus or insect that causes blight in plants **4** an ugly urban district ▷ *vb* **5** to cause to suffer a blight **6** to frustrate or disappoint: *blighted love* **7** to destroy: *the event blighted her life* [origin unknown]

blighter *n Brit, Austral and NZ informal* a despicable or irritating person or thing

Blighty *n Brit, Austral and NZ slang* **1** (used esp. by troops serving abroad) Britain; home **2** (*pl* **Blighties**) (esp. in the First World War) a wound that causes the recipient to be sent home to Britain [Hindi *bilāyatī* foreign land]

blimey *interj Brit and NZ slang* an exclamation of surprise or annoyance [short for *gorblimey* God blind me]

blimp¹ *n* **1** a small nonrigid airship **2** *films* a soundproof cover fixed over a camera during shooting [probably from (*type*) B-*limp*]

b

blimp² *n chiefly Brit* a person who is stupidly complacent and reactionary. Also called: **Colonel Blimp** [a cartoon character]

blind *adj* **1** unable to see **2** unable or unwilling to understand: *she is blind to his faults* **3** not determined by reason: *blind hatred* **4** acting or performed without control or preparation **5** done without being able to see, relying on instruments for information **6** hidden from sight: *a blind corner* **7** closed at one end: *a blind alley* **8** completely lacking awareness or consciousness: *a blind stupor* **9** having no openings: *a blind wall* ▷ *adv* **10** without being able to see ahead or using only instruments: *flying blind* **11** without adequate information: *we bought the house blind* **12 blind drunk** *informal* very drunk ▷ *vb* **13** to deprive of sight permanently or temporarily **14** to deprive of good sense, reason, or judgment **15** to darken; conceal **16** to overwhelm by showing detailed knowledge: *he tried to blind us with science* ▷ *n* **17** a shade for a window **18** any obstruction or hindrance to sight, light, or air **19** a person, action, or thing that serves to deceive or conceal the truth [Old English] **> blinding** *adj* **> blindly** *adv* **> blindness** *n*

> **USAGE** See at **disabled**.

blind alley *n* **1** an alley open at one end only **2** *informal* a situation in which no further progress can be made

blind date *n informal* a prearranged social meeting between two people who have not met before

blindfold *vb* **1** to prevent (a person or animal) from seeing by covering the eyes ▷ *n* **2** a piece of cloth used to cover the eyes ▷ *adj, adv* **3** having the eyes covered with a cloth [Old English *blindfellian* to strike blind]

Blindheim *n* the German name for **Blenheim**

blind man's buff *n* a game in which a blindfolded person tries to catch and identify the other players [obsolete *buff* a blow]

blind spot *n* **1** a small oval-shaped area of the retina which is unable to see **2** a place where vision is obscured **3** a subject about which a person is ignorant or prejudiced

blindworm *n* same as **slowworm**

bling *adj slang* **1** flashy, ostentatious, glitzy, etc. ▷ *n* **2** ostentatious jewellery

blink *vb* **1** to close and immediately reopen (the eyes), usually involuntarily **2** to shine intermittently or unsteadily ▷ *n* **3** the act or an instance of blinking **4** a glance; glimpse **5 on the blink** *slang* not working properly [variant of BLENCH]

blinker *vb* **1** to provide (a horse) with blinkers **2** to obscure or be obscured with or as with blinkers

blinkered *adj* **1** considering only a narrow point of view **2** (of a horse) wearing blinkers

blinkers *pl n Brit and Austral* leather side pieces attached to a horse's bridle to prevent sideways vision

blinking *adj, adv informal* extreme or extremely: *a blinking idiot*

blip *n* **1** a repetitive sound, such as the kind produced by an electronic device **2** the spot of light on a radar screen indicating the position of an object **3** a temporary irregularity in the performance of something [imitative]

bliss *n* **1** perfect happiness; serene joy **2** the joy of heaven [Old English *blīths*] **> blissful** *adj* **> blissfully** *adv*

Bliss *n* Sir Arthur. 1891–1975, British composer; Master of the Queen's Musick (1953–75). His works include the *Colour Symphony* (1922), film and ballet music, and a cello concerto (1970)

B list *n* **1** a category slightly below the most socially desirable ▷ *adj* **B-list 2** of the category slightly below the most socially desirable: *B-list celebrities*

blister *n* **1** a small bubble on the skin filled with a watery fluid **2** a swelling containing air or liquid, such as on a painted surface ▷ *vb* **3** to have or cause to have blisters

4 to attack verbally with great scorn [Old French *blestre*] **> blistering** *adj*

blithe *adj* **1** heedless; casual and indifferent **2** very happy or cheerful [Old English *blīthe*] **> blithely** *adv*

blithering *adj informal* stupid; foolish: *you blithering idiot* [variant of *blethering*]

BLitt Bachelor of Letters [Latin *Baccalaureus Litterarum*]

blitz *n* **1** a violent and sustained attack by enemy aircraft **2** any intensive attack or concerted effort ▷ *vb* **3** to attack suddenly and intensively [see BLITZKRIEG]

Blitz *n* **the Blitz** the systematic bombing of Britain in 1940–41 by the German Air Force

blitzkrieg *n* a swift intensive military attack designed to defeat the opposition quickly [German: lightning war]

Blixen *n* Karen. See Dinesen

blizzard *n* a blinding storm of wind and snow [origin unknown]

bloat *vb* **1** to cause to swell, as with a liquid or air **2** to cause to be puffed up, as with conceit **3** to cure (fish, esp herring) by half drying in smoke [Old Norse *blautr* soaked] **> bloated** *adj*

bloater *n Brit* a herring that has been salted in brine, smoked, and cured

blob *n* **1** a soft mass or drop **2** a spot of colour, ink, etc. **3** an indistinct or shapeless form or object [imitative]

bloc *n* a group of people or countries combined by a common interest [French]

Bloch *n* **1** Ernest. 1880–1959, US composer, born in Switzerland, who found inspiration in Jewish liturgical and folk music: his works include the symphonies *Israel* (1916) and *America* (1926) **2** Felix. 1905–83, US physicist, born in Switzerland: Nobel prize for physics (1952) for his work on the magnetic moments of atomic particles **3** Konrad Emil. 1912–2000, US biochemist, born in Germany: shared the Nobel prize for physiology or medicine in 1964 for his work on fatty-acid metabolism **4** Marc. 1886–1944, French historian and Resistance fighter; author of *Feudal Society* (1935) and *Strange Defeat* (1940), an essay on the fall of France: killed by the Nazis

block *n* **1** a large solid piece of wood, stone, etc. **2** such a piece on which particular tasks may be done, as chopping, cutting, etc. **3** a large building of offices, flats, etc. **4** a group of buildings in a city bounded by intersecting streets on each side **5** an obstruction or hindrance: *a writer with a block* **6** one of a set of wooden or plastic cubes as a child's toy **7** *slang* a person's head **8** a piece of wood, metal, etc., engraved for printing **9** a casing housing one or more freely rotating pulleys. See also **block and tackle 10** a quantity considered as a single unit ▷ *vb* **11** to obstruct or impede by introducing an obstacle: *lorry drivers had blocked the routes to Paris* **12** to impede, retard, or prevent (an action or procedure) **13** to stamp (a title or design) on (a book cover, etc.) **14** *cricket* to play (a ball) defensively ▶ See also **block out** [Dutch *blok*] **> blockage** *n*

blockade *n* **1** *military* the closing off of a port or region to prevent the passage of goods ▷ *vb* **-ading, -aded 2** to impose a blockade

block and tackle *n* a hoisting device in which a rope or chain is passed around a pair of blocks containing one or more pulleys

blockboard *n* a type of plywood consisting of strips of wood sandwiched between layers of veneer

blockbuster *n informal* **1** a film, novel, etc. that has been or is expected to be highly successful **2** a large bomb used to demolish extensive areas

blockhead *n* a stupid person **> blockheaded** *adj*

blockie *n Austral* an owner of a small property, esp. a farm

block letter *n* a plain capital letter. Also called: **block capital**

block out *vb* **1** to plan or describe (something) in a general fashion **2** to prevent the entry or consideration of (something)

Bloemfontein n a city in central South Africa: capital of Free State province and judicial capital of the country. Pop: 111 698 (2001)

blog n 1 a journal written online and accessible to users of the internet. Full name: weblog ▷ vb **blogging, blogged** 2 to write a blog 〉 **blogger** n 〉 **blogging** n

logosphere n informal a collective term for the weblogs on the internet

lois n a town in N central France, on the Loire: 13th-century castle. Pop: 46 013 (2009)

lok n Aleksandr Aleksandrovich. 1880–1921, Russian poet whose poems, which include *Verses about the Beautiful Lady* (1901–2) and *Rasput'ya* (1902–4), contain a mixture of symbolism, romanticism, tragedy, and irony

loke n Brit, Austral and NZ informal a man [Shelta] 〉 **blokeish** or **blokey** adj

londe or masc **blond** adj 1 (of hair) fair 2 (of a person) having fair hair and a light complexion ▷ n 3 a person having light-coloured hair and skin [Old French] 〉 **blondeness** or masc **blondness** n

londin n Charles, real name *Jean-François Gravelet*. 1824–97, French acrobat and tightrope walker; best known for walking a tightrope across Niagara Falls (1859)

lood n 1 a reddish fluid in vertebrates that is pumped by the heart through the arteries and veins. Related adjective: **haemal** 2 bloodshed, esp. when resulting in murder: *they were responsible for the spilling of blood throughout the country* 3 lifeblood 4 relationship through being of the same family, race, or kind; kinship 5 **the blood** royal or noble descent: *a prince of the blood* 6 **flesh and blood** a near kindred or kinship, esp. that between a parent and child **b** human nature: *it's more than flesh and blood can stand* 7 **in one's blood** as a natural or inherited characteristic or talent 8 newcomers viewed as an invigorating force: *new blood* 9 **in cold blood** showing no passion; ruthlessly 10 **make one's blood boil** to cause one to be angry or indignant 11 **make one's blood run cold** to fill one with horror ▷ vb 12 hunting to cause (young hounds) to taste the blood of a freshly killed quarry 13 to initiate (a person) to war or hunting [Old English *blōd*]

lood n Thomas, known as *Colonel Blood*. ?1618–80, Irish adventurer, who tried to steal the crown jewels (1671)

lood-and-thunder adj denoting melodramatic behaviour

lood bank n a place where blood is stored until required for transfusion

lood bath n a massacre

lood brother n a man or boy who has sworn to treat another as his brother, often in a ceremony in which their blood is mingled

lood count n determination of the number of red and white blood corpuscles in a specific sample of blood

lood-curdling or **bloodcurdling** adj terrifying

lood donor n a person who gives blood to be used for transfusion

lood group n any one of the various groups into which human blood is classified

lood heat n the normal temperature of the human body, 98.4°F or 37°C

loodhound n a large hound, formerly used in tracking and police work

loodless adj 1 without blood: *bloodless surgery* 2 conducted without violence: *a bloodless coup* 3 anaemic-looking; pale 4 lacking vitality; lifeless: *the bloodless ambience of supermarkets*

lood-letting n 1 bloodshed, esp. in a feud 2 the former medical practice of removing blood

loodlust n a desire for violence and carnage

lood money n 1 money obtained by ruthlessly sacrificing others 2 money paid to a hired murderer 3 compensation paid to the relatives of a murdered person

lood orange n a variety of orange, the pulp of which is dark red when ripe

blood poisoning n same as **septicaemia**

blood pressure n the pressure exerted by the blood on the inner walls of the blood vessels

blood relation or **blood relative** n a person related by birth

bloodshed n slaughter; killing

bloodshot adj (of an eye) inflamed

blood sport n any sport involving the killing of an animal

bloodstained adj discoloured with blood

bloodstock n thoroughbred horses

bloodstream n the flow of blood through the vessels of a living body

bloodsucker n 1 an animal that sucks blood, esp. a leech 2 informal a person who preys upon another person, esp. by extorting money

bloodthirsty adj -thirstier, -thirstiest taking pleasure in bloodshed or violence

blood vessel n a tube through which blood travels in the body

bloody adj **bloodier, bloodiest** 1 covered with blood 2 marked by much killing and bloodshed: *a bloody war* 3 cruel or murderous: *a bloody tyrant* ▷ adj, adv 4 slang extreme or extremely: *a bloody fool; a bloody good idea* ▷ vb **bloodies, bloodying, bloodied** 5 to stain with blood

Bloody Caesar n a drink consisting of vodka, juice made from clams and tomatoes, Worcester sauce and Tabasco

Bloody Mary n a drink consisting of tomato juice and vodka

bloody-minded adj Brit and NZ informal deliberately obstructive and unhelpful

bloom n 1 a blossom on a flowering plant 2 the state or period when flowers open 3 a healthy or flourishing condition; prime 4 a youthful or healthy glow 5 a fine whitish coating on the surface of fruits or leaves ▷ vb 6 (of flowers) to open 7 to bear flowers 8 to flourish or grow 9 to be in a healthy, glowing condition [Germanic]

bloomer n Brit informal a stupid mistake; blunder [from BLOOMING]

bloomers pl n 1 informal women's baggy knickers 2 (formerly) loose trousers gathered at the knee, worn by women [after Mrs A. *Bloomer*, social reformer]

Bloomfield n Leonard. 1887–1949, US linguist, influential for his strictly scientific and descriptive approach to comparative linguistics; author of *Language* (1933)

blooming adv, adj Brit informal extreme or extremely: *blooming painful* [euphemistic for *bloody*]

Bloomington n a city in central Indiana: seat of the University of Indiana (1820). Pop: 70 642 (2003 est)

Bloomsbury n 1 a district of central London in the borough of Camden: contains the British Museum, part of the University of London, and many publishers' offices ▷ adj 2 relating to or characteristic of the Bloomsbury Group

blossom n 1 the flower or flowers of a plant, esp. producing edible fruit 2 the period of flowering ▷ vb 3 (of plants) to flower 4 to come to a promising stage [Old English *blōstm*]

blot n 1 a stain or spot, esp. of ink 2 something that spoils 3 a stain on one's character ▷ vb **blotting, blotted** 4 to stain or spot 5 to cause a blemish in or on: *he blotted his copybook by missing a penalty* 6 to soak up (excess ink, etc.) by using blotting paper 7 **blot out a** to darken or hide completely: *the mist blotted out the sea* **b** to block from one's mind: *to blot out the memories* [Germanic]

blotch n 1 an irregular spot or discoloration ▷ vb 2 to become or cause to become marked by such discoloration [probably from *botch*, influenced by *blot*] 〉 **blotchy** adj

blotter n a sheet of blotting paper

blotting paper n a soft absorbent paper, used for soaking up surplus ink

b

blotto adj Brit, Austral and NZ slang extremely drunk [from blot (verb)]

blouse n 1 a woman's shirtlike garment 2 a waist-length belted jacket worn by soldiers ▷ vb **blousing**, **bloused** 3 to hang or cause to hang in full loose folds [French]

blouson (blew-zon) n a short loose jacket with a tight-fitting waist [French]

blow[1] vb **blowing, blew, blown** 1 (of a current of air, the wind, etc.) to be or cause to be in motion 2 to move or be carried by or as if by wind 3 to expel (air, etc.) through the mouth or nose 4 to breathe hard; pant 5 to inflate with air or the breath 6 (of wind, etc.) to make a roaring sound 7 to cause (a musical instrument) to sound by forcing air into it 8 (often foll. by up, down, in, etc.) to explode, break, or disintegrate completely 9 electronics (of a fuse or valve) to burn out because of excessive current 10 to shape (glass, etc.) by forcing air or gas through the material when molten 11 slang to spend (money) freely 12 slang to use (an opportunity) ineffectively 13 slang to expose or betray (a secret) 14 (past part **blowed**) informal same as **damn** 15 **blow hot and cold** informal to keep changing one's attitude towards someone or something 16 **blow one's top** informal to lose one's temper ▷ n 17 the act or an instance of blowing 18 the sound produced by blowing 19 a blast of air or wind 20 Brit slang cannabis ▶ See also **blow away**, **blow out**, etc. [Old English blāwan]

blow[2] n 1 a powerful or heavy stroke with the fist, a weapon, etc. 2 a sudden setback: the scheme was dealt a blow by the introduction of martial law 3 an attacking action: a blow for freedom 4 **come to blows a** to fight **b** to result in a fight [probably Germanic]

blow away vb slang 1 to kill by shooting 2 to defeat utterly

blow-by-blow adj explained in great detail: a blow-by-blow account

blow-dry vb **-dries, -drying, -dried** 1 to style (the hair) while drying it with a hand-held hair dryer ▷ n 2 this method of styling hair

blower n 1 a mechanical device, such as a fan, that blows 2 informal a telephone

blowfly n, pl **-flies** a fly that lays its eggs in meat

blowhole n 1 the nostril of a whale 2 a hole in ice through which seals, etc. breathe 3 a vent for air or gas 4 geology a hole in a cliff top leading to a sea cave

blowie n Austral informal a bluebottle

blown vb a past participle of **blow**[1]

blow out vb 1 (of a flame) to extinguish or be extinguished 2 (of a tyre) to puncture suddenly 3 (of an oil or gas well) to lose oil or gas in an uncontrolled manner ▷ n **blowout** 4 a sudden burst in a tyre 5 the uncontrolled escape of oil or gas from a well 6 slang a large filling meal 7 Austral informal an unexpectedly large financial deficit

blow over vb 1 to be forgotten 2 to cease or be finished: the crisis blew over

blowpipe n 1 a long tube from which poisoned darts, etc., are shot by blowing 2 a tube for blowing air into a flame to intensify its heat 3 an iron pipe used to blow glass into shape

blowsy adj **blowsier, blowsiest** 1 (of a woman) slovenly or sluttish 2 (of a woman) ruddy in complexion [dialect blowze beggar girl]

blowtorch or **blowlamp** n a small burner that produces a very hot flame, used to remove old paint, soften metal, etc.

blow up vb 1 to explode or cause to explode 2 to inflate with air 3 to increase the importance of (something): an affair blown up out of all proportion 4 informal to lose one's temper 5 informal to reprimand (someone) 6 informal to enlarge (a photograph) 7 to come into existence with sudden force: a crisis had blown up ▷ n **blow-up** 8 informal an enlarged photograph

blowy adj **blowier, blowiest** windy

blubber n 1 the fatty tissue of aquatic mammals such a the whale 2 informal flabby body fat ▷ vb 3 to sob witho restraint [probably imitative]

Blücher n Gebhard Leberecht von. 1742–1819, Prussian field marshal, who commanded the Prussian army against Napoleon at Waterloo (1815)

bludge Austral and NZ informal vb **bludging, bludged** 1 (fo by on) to scrounge from 2 to evade work ▷ n 3 a very eas task

bludgeon n 1 a stout heavy club, typically thicker at on end ▷ vb 2 to hit as if with a bludgeon 3 to force; bully; coerce [origin unknown]

blue n 1 the colour of a clear unclouded sky 2 anything blue, such as blue clothing or blue paint: she is clothed in blue 3 a sportsman who represents or has represented Oxford or Cambridge University 4 Brit informal a Tory 5 Austral and NZ slang an argument or fight 6 Also: **bluey** Austral and NZ slang a court summons 7 Austral and NZ informal a mistake 8 **out of the blue** unexpectedly ▷ adj **bluer, bluest** 9 of the colour blue; of the colour of a clea unclouded sky 10 (of the flesh) having a purple tinge from cold 11 depressed or unhappy 12 pornographic: bl movies ▷ vb **blueing, blued** 13 to make or becom blue or bluer 14 old-fashioned, informal to spend extravagantly or wastefully: I consoled myself by blueing my royalty cheque ▶ See also **blues** [Old French bleu] ▷ **blueness** n

blue baby n a baby born with a bluish tinge to the skin because of lack of oxygen in the blood

bluebell n a woodland plant with blue bell-shaped flowers

blueberry n, pl **-ries** a very small blackish edible fruit that grows on a North American shrub

bluebird n a North American songbird with a blue plumage

blue blood n royal or aristocratic descent

bluebook n 1 (in Britain) a government publication, usually the report of a commission 2 (in Canada) an annual statement of government accounts

bluebottle n 1 a large fly with a dark-blue body; blowfl 2 Austral and NZ informal a Portuguese man-of-war

blue cheese n cheese containing a blue mould, such a Stilton or Danish blue

blue chip n 1 finance a stock considered reliable ▷ adj **blue-chip** 2 denoting something considered to be a valuable asset

blue-collar adj denoting manual industrial workers

blue-eyed boy n informal a favourite

blue funk n slang a state of great terror

blue heeler n Austral and NZ informal a dog that controls cattle by biting their heels

Blue Mountains pl n 1 a mountain range in the US, in NE Oregon and SE Washington. Highest peak: Rock Creek Butte, 2773 m (9097 ft) 2 a mountain range in the Caribbean, in E Jamaica: Blue Mountain coffee is grow on its slopes. Highest peak: Blue Mountain Peak, 2256 m (7402 ft) 3 a plateau in SE Australia, in E New South Wales: part of the Great Dividing Range. Highes part: about 1134 m (3871 ft)

Blue Nile n a river in E Africa, rising in central Ethiopi as the Abbai and flowing southeast, then northwest to join the White Nile. Length: about 1530 km (950 miles)

bluenose n 1 US slang a puritanical or prudish person 2 Also: **bluenoser** (sometimes cap) Canad informal a native o inhabitant of Nova Scotia

blue pencil n 1 deletion or alteration of the contents of book or other work ▷ vb **blue-pencil (-cilling, -cilled)** or U **-ciling, -ciled** 2 to alter or delete parts of (a book, film, etc.)

blue peter n a signal flag of blue with a white square a the centre, displayed by a vessel about to leave port

blueprint n 1 an original description of a plan or idea that explains how it is expected to work 2 a photographic print of plans, technical drawings, etc.

consisting of white lines on a blue background

lue ribbon *n* **1** a badge awarded as the first prize in a competition **2** (in Britain) a badge of blue silk worn by members of the Order of the Garter

lue Ridge Mountains *pl n* a mountain range in the eastern US, extending from West Virginia into Georgia: part of the Appalachian mountains. Highest peak: Mount Mitchell, 2038 m (6684 ft)

lues *pl n* **the blues 1** a feeling of depression or deep unhappiness **2** a type of folk song originating among Black Americans

lue-screen *adj* relating to a film technique in which actors are filmed against a blue screen so that special effects can be added later

lue-sky *adj* of research done for theoretical reasons rather than for practical application

luestocking *n usually disparaging* a scholarly or intellectual woman [from the blue worsted stockings worn by members of an 18th-century literary society]

luetit *n* a small European bird with a blue crown, wings, and tail and yellow underparts

luetongue *n* an Australian lizard with a blue tongue

luetooth *n trademark* a short-range radio technology that allows wireless communication between computers, mobile phones, etc.

lue whale *n* a very large bluish-grey whale: the largest mammal

luff¹ *vb* **1** to pretend to be confident in order to influence someone) ▷ *n* **2** deliberate deception to create the impression of a strong position **3 call someone's bluff** to challenge someone to give proof of his or her claims [Dutch *bluffen* to boast]

luff² *n* **1** a steep promontory, bank, or cliff **2** *Canad* a clump of trees on the prairie; copse ▷ *adj* **3** good-naturedly frank and hearty [probably from Middle Dutch *blaf* broad]

luish *or* **blueish** *adj* slightly blue

lum *n* Léon. 1872–1950, French socialist statesman; premier of France (1936–37; 1938; 1946–47)

lumberg *n* Baruch Samuel.1925–2011, US physician, noted for work on antigens; shared the Nobel prize for physiology or medicine 1976

lunden *n* Edmund (Charles). 1896–1974, British poet and scholar, noted esp. for *Undertones of War* (1928), a memoir of World War I in verse and prose

lunder *n* **1** a stupid or clumsy mistake ▷ *vb* **2** to make stupid or clumsy mistakes **3** to act clumsily; stumble [Scandinavian] **> blundering** *n, adj*

lunderbuss *n* an obsolete gun with wide barrel and flared muzzle [Dutch *donderbus* thunder gun]

lunkett *n* David. born 1947, British Labour politician; secretary of state for education and employment (1997–2001); home secretary (2001–04); secretary of state for work and pensions (2005)

lunt *adj* **1** (esp. of a knife) lacking sharpness **2** not having a sharp edge or point: *a blunt knife* **3** (of people, manner of speaking, etc.) straightforward and uncomplicated ▷ *vb* **4** to make less sharp **5** to diminish the sensitivity or perception of: *prison life has blunted his mind* [Scandinavian] **> bluntly** *adv*

lunt *n* **1** Anthony. 1907–83, British art historian and Soviet spy **2** Wilfred Scawen. 1840–1922, British poet, traveller, and anti-imperialist

lur *vb* **blurring, blurred 1** to make or become vague or less distinct **2** to smear or smudge **3** to make (the judgment, memory, or perception) less clear; dim ▷ *n* **4** something vague, hazy, or indistinct **5** a smear or smudge [perhaps variant of *blear*] **> blurred** *adj* **> blurry** *adj*

lurb *n* a promotional description, such as on the jackets of books [coined by G. Burgess, humorist & illustrator]

lurt *vb* (foll. by *out*) to utter suddenly and involuntarily [probably imitative]

lush *vb* **1** to become suddenly red in the face, esp. from

embarrassment or shame ▷ *n* **2** a sudden reddening of the face, esp. from embarrassment or shame **3** a rosy glow **4** same as rosé [Old English *blȳscan*]

blusher *n* a cosmetic applied to the cheeks to give a rosy colour

bluster *vb* **1** to speak loudly or in a bullying way **2** (of the wind) to be gusty ▷ *n* **3** empty threats or protests [probably from Middle Low German *blüsteren* to blow violently] **> blustery** *adj*

Blyth¹ *n* a port in N England, in SE Northumberland, on the North Sea. Pop: 35 691 (2001)

Blyth² *n* Sir Chay. born 1940, British yachtsman. He sailed round the world alone (1970–71) and won many races

Blyton *n* Enid (Mary). 1897–1968, British writer of children's books; creator of Noddy and the *Famous Five* series of adventure stories

BM 1 Bachelor of Medicine **2** British Museum

BMA British Medical Association

BMI *n* body mass index: an index used to indicate whether or not a person is a healthy weight for his or her height

B-movie *n* a film originally made as a supporting film, now considered a genre in its own right

BMR basal metabolic rate

BMus Bachelor of Music

BMX *n* **1** bicycle motocross: stunt riding over an obstacle course on a bicycle **2** a bicycle designed for bicycle motocross

BO 1 *informal* body odour **2** box office

boa *n* **1** a large nonvenomous snake of Central and South America that kills its prey by constriction **2** a woman's long thin scarf of feathers or fur [Latin]

boab (boh-ab) *n Austral informal* short for **baobab**

Boabdil *n* original name *Abu-Abdullah*, called *El Chico*, ruled as *Mohammed XI*. died ?1538, last Moorish king of Granada (1482–83; 1486–92)

boa constrictor *n* a very large snake of tropical America and the West Indies that kills its prey by constriction

boar *n* **1** an uncastrated male pig **2** a wild pig [Old English *bār*]

board *n* **1** a long wide flat piece of sawn timber **2** a smaller flat piece of rigid material for a specific purpose: *ironing board* **3 a** a group of people who officially administer a company, trust, etc. **b** any other official group, such as examiners or interviewers **4** a person's meals, provided regularly for money **5** stiff cardboard or similar material, used for the outside covers of a book **6** a flat thin rectangular sheet of composite material, such as chipboard **7** *nautical* the side of a ship **8** a portable surface for indoor games such as chess or backgammon **9 go by the board** *informal* to be in disuse, neglected, or lost **10 on board** on or in a ship, aeroplane, etc. ▷ *vb* **11** to go aboard (a train or other vehicle) **12** to attack (a ship) by forcing one's way aboard **13** (foll. by *up, in*, etc.) to cover with boards **14** to receive meals and lodging in return for money **15 board out** to arrange for (someone, esp. a child) to receive food and lodging away from home **16** (in ice hockey and box lacrosse) to bodycheck an opponent against the boards ▶ See also **boards** [Old English *bord*]

boarder *n Brit* a pupil who lives at school during term time

boarding *n* **1** the act of embarking on an aircraft, train, ship, etc. **2** a structure of boards **3** timber boards collectively **4** (in ice hockey and box lacrosse) an act of bodychecking an opponent against the boards

boarding house *n* a private house that provides accommodation and meals for paying guests

boarding school *n* a school providing living accommodation for pupils

boardroom *n* a room where the board of directors of a company meets

boards *pl n* **1** a wooden wall forming the enclosure in

b

which ice hockey or box lacrosse is played **2 the boards** the stage

Boas n Franz. 1858–1942, US anthropologist, born in Germany. He made major contributions to cultural and linguistic anthropology in studies of North American Indians, including *The Mind of Primitive Man* (1911; 1938)

boast vb **1** to speak in excessively proud terms of one's possessions, talents, etc. **2** to possess (something to be proud of): *a team which boasts five current world record holders* ▷ n **3** a bragging statement **4** something that is bragged about: *this proved to be a false boast* [origin unknown]

boastful adj tending to boast

boat n **1** a small vessel propelled by oars, paddle, sails, or motor **2** informal a ship **3** See gravy boat, sauce boat **4 in the same boat** sharing the same problems **5 miss the boat** to lose an opportunity **6 rock the boat** informal to cause a disturbance in the existing situation ▷ vb **7** to travel or go in a boat, esp. as recreation [Old English *bāt*]

boater n a stiff straw hat with a straight brim and flat crown

boathouse n a shelter by the edge of a river, lake, etc., for housing boats

boating n rowing, sailing, or cruising in boats as a form of recreation

boatman n, pl **-men** a man who works on, hires out, or repairs boats

boatswain (boh-sn) n nautical same as **bosun**

boat train n a train scheduled to take passengers to or from a particular ship

Boa Vista n a town in N Brazil, capital of the state of Roraima, on the Rio Branco. Pop: 275 000 (2005 est)

bob¹ vb **bobbing, bobbed 1** to move or cause to move up and down repeatedly, such as while floating in water **2** to move or cause to move with a short abrupt movement, esp. of the head **3 bob up** to appear or emerge suddenly ▷ n **4** a short abrupt movement, as of the head [origin unknown]

bob² n **1** a hairstyle in which the hair is cut short evenly all round the head **2** a dangling weight on a pendulum or plumb line ▷ vb **bobbing, bobbed 3** to cut (the hair) in a bob [Middle English *bobbe* bunch of flowers]

bob³ n, pl **bob** Brit, Austral and NZ informal (formerly) a shilling: *two bob* [origin unknown]

bobbejaan n S African **1** a baboon **2** a large black spider **3** a monkey wrench [Afrikaans]

bobbin n a reel on which thread or yarn is wound [Old French *bobine*]

bobble n **1** a tufted ball, usually woollen, that is used for decoration ▷ vb **-bling, -bled 2** (of a ball) to bounce erratically because of an uneven playing surface [from BOB¹]

bobby n, pl **-bies** Brit informal a British policeman [after *Robert Peel*, who set up the Metropolitan Police Force]

bobby pin n US, Canad, Austral and NZ a metal hairpin

Bobo-Dioulasso n a city in W Burkina Faso. Pop: 396 000 (2005 est)

bobotie (ba-**boot**-ee) n S African a traditional Cape dish of curried minced meat [probably from Malay]

Bobruisk or **Bobruysk** n a port in Belarus, on the River Berezina: engineering, timber, tyre manufacturing. Pop: 219 000 (2005 est)

bobsleigh n **1** a sledge for racing down a steeply banked ice-covered run ▷ vb **2** to ride on a bobsleigh

bobtail n **1** a docked tail **2** an animal with such a tail ▷ adj also: **bobtailed 3** having the tail cut short

Boccaccio n Giovanni. 1313–75, Italian poet and writer, noted particularly for his *Decameron* (1353), a collection of 100 short stories. His other works include *Filostrato* (?1338) and *Teseida* (1341)

Boccherini n Luigi. 1743–1805, Italian composer and cellist

Boccioni n Umberto. 1882–1916, Italian painter and sculptor: principal theorist of the futurist movement

bocconcini (bok-on-**chee**-nee) pl n small bite-sized pieces of mozzarella cheese [Italian]

Boche (bosh) n offensive, slang a German, esp. a German soldier [French]

Bochum n an industrial city in NW Germany, in W North Rhine-Westphalia: university (1965). Pop: 387 28 (2003 est)

bod n informal **1** a person: *he's a queer bod* **2** short for **body** [short for *body*]

bode¹ vb **boding, boded** to be an omen of (good or ill); portend [Old English *bodian*]

bode² vb a past tense of **bide**

bodega n a shop in a Spanish-speaking country that sells wine [Spanish]

Bodensee n the German name for (Lake) **Constance**

bodge vb **bodging, bodged** Brit, Austral and NZ informal to make a mess of; botch

Bodh Gaya n a variant spelling of **Buddh Gaya**

Bodhidharma n 6th century AD, Indian Buddhist monk, who taught in China (from 520): considered to the founder of Zen Buddhism

bodice n **1** the upper part of a woman's dress, from the shoulder to the waist **2** a tight-fitting corset worn lac over a blouse, or (formerly) as a woman's undergarme [originally Scots *bodies*, plural of *body*]

bodily adj **1** relating to the human body ▷ adv **2** by tak hold of the body: *he threw him bodily from the platform* **3** in person; in the flesh

bodkin n a blunt large-eyed needle [origin unknown]

Bodmin n a market town in SW England, in Cornwall, near **Bodmin Moor**, a granite upland rising to 420 m (1375 ft). Pop: 12 778 (2001)

body n, pl **bodies 1** the entire physical structure of an animal or human. Related adjective: **corporal 2** the trunk or torso **3** a corpse **4** a group regarded as a single entity: *a local voluntary body* **5** the main part of anything *the body of a car* **6** a separate mass of water or land **7** the flesh as opposed to the spirit **8** fullness in the appearance of the hair **9** the characteristic full qualit of certain wines **10** informal a person: *all the important bod from the council were present* **11** a woman's one-piece undergarment **12 keep body and soul together** to manage to survive [Old English *bodig*]

bodyboard n a small polystyrene surfboard ▷ **bodyboarder** n

body building n regular exercising designed to enlarg the muscles

bodycheck sport n **1** obstruction of another player ▷ vb **2** to deliver a bodycheck to (an opponent)

bodyguard n a person or group of people employed to protect someone

body language n the communication of one's thoughts or feelings by the position or movements of one's body rather than by words

body politic n **the body politic** the people of a nation o the nation itself considered as a political entity

body search n **1** a search by police, customs officials, etc., that involves examination of a prisoner's or suspect's bodily orifices ▷ vb **body-search 2** to search (prisoner or suspect) in this manner

body shop n a repair yard for vehicle bodywork

body snatcher n (formerly) a person who robbed grav and sold the corpses for dissection

body stocking n **1** a one-piece undergarment for women, covering the torso **2** a tightly-fitting garmen covering the whole of the body, worn esp. for dancing exercising

body warmer n a sleeveless quilted jerkin, worn as ar outer garment

bodywork n the external shell of a motor vehicle

Boeotia n a region of ancient Greece, northwest of Athens. It consisted of ten city-states, which formed t Boeotian League, led by Thebes: at its height in the 4tł century BC. Modern Greek name: **Voiotia**

Boeotian n **1** a native or inhabitant of Boeotia ▷ adj **2** ◂

or relating to Boeotia or its inhabitants

Boer n a descendant of any of the Dutch or Huguenot colonists who settled in South Africa [Dutch]

boere- combining form S African rustic or country-style [from Afrikaans boer a farmer]

boeremeisie (boor-a-may-see) n S African a country girl of Afrikaans stock

boereseun (boor-a-see-oon) n S African a country boy of Afrikaans stock

boerewors (boor-a-vorss) n S African a traditional home-made farmer's sausage

Boethius n Anicius Manlius Severinus. ?480–?524 AD, Roman philosopher and statesman, noted particularly for his work De Consolatione Philosophiae. He was accused of treason and executed by Theodoric

boffin n informal, old-fashioned a scientist or expert [origin unknown]

bog n 1 a wet spongy area of land 2 slang a toilet [Gaelic bogach swamp] > **boggy** adj > **bogginess** n

Bogarde n Sir Dirk, real name Derek Jules Gaspard Ulric Niven van den Bogaerde. 1920–99, British film actor and writer: his films include The Servant (1963) and Death in Venice (1970). His writings include the autobiographical A Postillion Struck by Lightning (1977) and the novel A Period of Adjustment (1994)

Bogart n Humphrey (DeForest). nicknamed Bogie. 1899–1957, US film actor: his films include High Sierra (1941), Casablanca (1942), The Big Sleep (1946), The African Queen (1951), and The Caine Mutiny (1954)

Boğazköy n a village in central Asia Minor: site of the ancient Hittite capital

bog down vb **bogging, bogged** to impede physically or mentally

bogey or **bogy** n 1 an evil or mischievous spirit 2 something that worries or annoys 3 golf a score of one stroke over par on a hole 4 slang a piece of dried mucus from the nose [probably obsolete bug an evil spirit]

bogeyman n, pl **-men** a frightening person, real or imaginary, used as a threat, esp. to children

boggle vb **-gling, -gled** 1 to be surprised, confused, or alarmed: the mind boggles at the idea 2 to hesitate or be evasive when confronted with a problem [probably Scots]

bogie or **bogy** n an assembly of wheels forming a pivoted support at either end of a railway coach [origin unknown]

bogle (boh-gul) n a rhythmic dance performed to ragga music [origin unknown]

Bognor Regis n a resort in S England, in West Sussex on the English Channel: electronics industries. Regis was added to the name after King George V's convalescence there in 1929. Pop: 62 141 (2001)

Bogor n a city in Indonesia, in W Java: botanical gardens and research institutions. Pop: 750 819 (2000). Former name: **Buitenzorg**

Bogotá n the capital of Colombia, on a central plateau of the E Andes: originally the centre of Chibcha civilization; founded as a city in 1538 by the Spaniards. Pop: 7 594 000 (2005 est)

bog-standard adj Brit and Irish slang completely ordinary; run-of-the-mill

bogus (boh-guss) adj not genuine [origin unknown]

bogy n, pl **-gies** same as bogey, bogie

Bohai or **Pohai** n a large inlet of the Yellow Sea on the coast of NE China. Also called: **Gulf of Chihli**

Bohemia n 1 a former kingdom of central Europe, surrounded by mountains: independent from the 9th to the 13th century; belonged to the Hapsburgs from 1526 until 1918 2 an area of the W Czech Republic, formerly a province of Czechoslovakia (1918–1949). From 1939 until 1945 it formed part of the German protectorate of Bohemia-Moravia. Czech name: **Čechy**. German name: **Böhmen** 3 a district frequented by unconventional people, esp. artists or writers

bohemian n 1 a person, esp. an artist or writer, who lives an unconventional life ▷ adj 2 unconventional in appearance, behaviour, etc. > **bohemianism** n

Bohemian Forest n a mountain range between the SW Czech Republic and SE Germany. Highest peak: Arber, 1457 m (4780 ft). Czech name: **Český Les**. German name: **Böhmerwald**

Bohemond I n ?1056–?1111, prince of Antioch (1099–1111); a leader of the first crusade, he helped to capture Antioch (1098)

Böhm n Karl. 1894–1981, Austrian orchestral conductor

Böhme, Boehme or **Böhm** n Jakob. 1575–1624, German mystic

Bohol n an island of the central Philippines. Chief town: Tagbilaran. Pop: 1 139 130 (2000). Area: about 3900 sq km (1500 sq miles)

Bohr n 1 Aage Niels. 1922–2009, Danish physicist, noted for his work on nuclear structure. He shared the Nobel prize for physics 1975 2 his father, **Niels (Henrik David)**. 1885–1962, Danish physicist, who applied the quantum theory to Rutherford's model of the atom to explain spectral lines: Nobel prize for physics 1922

bohrium n chem an element artificially produced in minute quantities. Symbol: **Bh** [after N. BOHR]

Boiardo n Matteo Maria, conte de Scandiano. 1434–94, Italian poet; author of the historical epic Orlando Innamorato (1487)

boil¹ vb 1 to change or cause to change from a liquid to a vapour so rapidly that bubbles of vapour are formed in the liquid 2 to reach or cause to reach boiling point 3 to cook or be cooked by the process of boiling 4 to bubble and be agitated like something boiling: the sea was boiling 5 to be extremely angry ▷ n 6 the state or action of boiling ▶ See also boil away, boil down, boil over [Latin bullire to bubble]

boil² n a red painful swelling with a hard pus-filled core caused by infection of the skin [Old English bȳle]

boil away vb to cause (liquid) to evaporate completely by boiling or (of liquid) to evaporate completely

boil down vb 1 to reduce or be reduced in quantity by boiling 2 boil down to to be the essential element in

Boileau n Nicolas. full name Nicolas Boileau-Despréaux. 1636–1711, French poet and critic; author of satires, epistles, and L'Art poétique (1674), in which he laid down the basic principles of French classical literature

boiler n 1 a closed vessel in which water is heated to provide steam to drive machinery 2 a domestic device to provide hot water, esp. for central heating

boilermaker n a person who works with metal in heavy industry

boiler suit n Brit a one-piece overall

boiling point n 1 the temperature at which a liquid boils 2 informal the condition of being angered or highly excited

boil over vb 1 to overflow or cause to overflow while boiling 2 to burst out in anger or excitement

Bois de Boulogne n a large park in W Paris, formerly a forest: includes the racecourses of Auteuil and Longchamp

Boise or **Boise City** n a city in SW Idaho: the state capital. Pop: 190 117 (2003 est)

Bois-le-Duc n the French name for 's Hertogenbosch

boisterous adj 1 noisy and lively; unruly 2 (of the sea, etc.) turbulent or stormy [Middle English boistuous]

Boito n Arrigo. 1842–1918, Italian operatic composer and librettist, whose works include the opera Mefistofele (1868) and the librettos for Verdi's Otello and Falstaff

Bokassa I n original name Jean Bedel Bokassa. 1921–96, president of the Central African Republic (1972–76); emperor of the renamed Central African Empire from 1976 until overthrown in 1979

Bokhara n a variant spelling of Bukhara

Bol. Bolivia(n)

Boland n an area of high altitude in S South Africa

b

Bolan Pass *n* a mountain pass in W central Pakistan through the Brahui Range, between Sibi and Quetta, rising to 1800 m (5900 ft)

bold *adj* **1** courageous, confident, and fearless **2** immodest or impudent: *she gave him a bold look* **3** *Irish* (of a child) naughty; badly behaved **4** standing out distinctly; conspicuous: *a figure carved in bold relief* [Old English *beald*] **> boldly** *adv* **> boldness** *n*

Bolden *n* Buddy, real name *Charles Bolden*. 1868–1931, US Black jazz cornet player; a pioneer of the New Orleans style

Boldrewood *n* Rolf, real name *Thomas Alexander Browne*. 1826–1915, Australian writer, born in the UK, noted for his novels of the Australian outback, esp. *Robbery Under Arms* (1882–3)

bole *n* the trunk of a tree [Old Norse *bolr*]

bolero *n*, *pl* **-ros** **1** a Spanish dance, usually in triple time **2** music for this dance **3** a short open jacket not reaching the waist [Spanish]

Boleyn *n* Anne. 1507–36, second wife of Henry VIII of England; mother of Elizabeth I. She was executed on a charge of adultery

Bolger *n* James. born 1935, New Zealand politician; prime minister (1990–97)

Bolingbroke *n* **1** the surname of Henry IV of England. See Henry IV **2** Henry St John, 1st Viscount Bolingbroke. 1678–1751, English politician; fled to France in 1714 and acted as secretary of state to the Old Pretender; returned to England in 1723. His writings include *A Dissertation on Parties* (1733–34) and *Idea of a Patriot King* (1738)

Bolívar *n* Simon. 1783–1830, South American soldier and liberator. He drove the Spaniards from Venezuela, Colombia, Ecuador, and Peru and hoped to set up a republican confederation, but was prevented by separatist movements in Venezuela and Colombia (1829–30). Upper Peru became a separate state and was called Bolivia in his honour

Bolivia *n* an inland republic in central S America: original Aymara Indian population conquered by the Incas in the 13th century; colonized by Spain from 1538; became a republic in 1825; consists of low plains in the east, with ranges of the Andes rising to over 6400 m (21 000 ft) and the Altiplano, a plateau averaging 3900 m (13 000 ft) in the west; contains some of the world's highest inhabited regions; important producer of tin and other minerals. Official languages: Spanish, Quechua, and Aymara. Religion: Roman Catholic. Currency: boliviano. Capital: La Paz (administrative); Sucre (judicial). Pop: 10 461 053 (2013 est). Area: 1 098 580 sq km (424 260 sq miles)

Bolivian *adj* **1** of or relating to Bolivia or its inhabitants ⊳ *n* **2** a native or inhabitant of Bolivia

boll *n* the rounded seed capsule of flax, cotton, etc. [Dutch *bolle*]

Böll *n* Heinrich (Theodor). 1917–85, German novelist and short-story writer; his novels include *Group Portrait with Lady* (1971): Nobel prize for literature 1972

bollard *n* **1** *Brit and Austral* a small post marking a kerb or traffic island or barring cars from entering **2** a strong wooden or metal post on a wharf, quay, etc., used for securing mooring lines [perhaps from *bole*]

bollocks or **ballocks** *taboo, slang pl n* **1** the testicles ⊳ *n* **2** nonsense; rubbish ⊳ *interj* **3** an exclamation of annoyance, disbelief, etc. [Old English *beallucas*]

Bologna¹ *n* a city in N Italy, at the foot of the Apennines: became a free city in the Middle Ages; university (1088). Pop: 371 217 (2001). Ancient name: Bononia

Bologna² *n* Giovanni da Bologna See Giambologna

Bolognese *adj* **1** of or relating to Bologna or its inhabitants ⊳ *n* **2** a native or inhabitant of Bologna

Bolshevik *n* **1** (formerly) a Russian Communist **2** any Communist **3** *informal, offensive* any political radical, esp. a revolutionary [Russian *Bol'shevik* majority; from the fact that this group formed a majority of the Russian Social Democratic Party in 1903] **> Bolshevism** *n* **> Bolshevist** *adj, n*

bolshie or **bolshy** *Brit and NZ informal adj* **1** difficult to manage; rebellious **2** politically radical or left-wing ⊳ *pl* **-shies** **3** any political radical [from BOLSHEVIK]

bolster *vb* **1** to support or strengthen: *the government were unwilling to bolster sterling* ⊳ *n* **2** a long narrow pillow **3** an pad or support [Old English]

bolt¹ *n* **1** a bar that can be slid into a socket to lock a door, gate, etc. **2** a metal rod or pin that has a head and a screw thread to take a nut **3** a flash (of lightning) **4** a sudden movement, esp. in order to escape **5** an arrow, esp. for a crossbow **6 a bolt from the blue** a sudden, unexpected, and usually unwelcome event **7 shoot one** **bolt** to exhaust one's efforts ⊳ *vb* **8** to run away sudden **9** to secure or lock with or as if with a bolt **10** to attach firmly (one thing to another) by means of a nut and bol **11** to eat hurriedly: *bolting your food may lead to indigestion* **12** (of a horse) to run away without control **13** (of vegetables) to produce flowers and seeds too soon ⊳ *adv* **14 bolt upright** stiff and rigid [Old English: arrow]

bolt² or **boult** *vb* **1** to pass (flour, a powder, etc.) through a sieve **2** to examine and separate [Old French *bulter*]

Bolt *n* **1** Robert (Oxton). 1924–95, British playwright. Hi plays include *A Man for All Seasons* (1960) and he also wrot a number of screenplays **2** Usain (St Leo). born 1986, Jamaican athlete: winner of the 100 metres and the 200 metres in the 2008 Olympic Games, setting world records at both distances; successfully defended both titles at the 2012 Olympics

bolt hole *n* a place of escape

Bolton *n* **1** a town in NW England, in Bolton unitary authority, Greater Manchester: centre of the woollen trade since the 14th century; later important for cotton. Pop: 139 403 (2001) **2** a unitary authority in NW England in Greater Manchester. Pop: 263 800 (2003 est). Area: 140 sq km (54 sq miles)

Boltzmann *n* Ludwig. 1844–1906, Austrian physicist. H established the principle of the equipartition of energy and developed the kinetic theory of gases with J. C. Maxwell

Bolzano *n* a city in NE Italy, in Trentino-Alto Adige: belonged to Austria until 1919. Pop: 94 989 (2001). German name: Bozen

Boma *n* a port in the Democratic Republic of Congo, on the Congo River, capital of the Belgian Congo until 1926 forest decrease. Pop: 607 000 (2005 est)

bomb *n* **1** a hollow projectile containing explosive, incendiary, or other destructive substance **2** an object i which an explosive device has been planted: *a car bomb* **3** *chiefly Brit slang* a large sum of money: *it cost a bomb* **4** *slang* a disastrous failure: *the new play was a total bomb* **5 like a bomb** *informal* with great speed or success **6 the bomb** a hydrogen or an atom bomb considered as the ultimate destructive weapon ⊳ *vb* **7** to attack with a bomb or bombs; drop bombs (on) **8** (foll. by *along*) informal to move or drive very quickly **9** *slang* to fail disastrously ▸ See also **bomb out** [Greek *bombos* booming noise] **> bombing** *n*

bombard *vb* **1** to attack with concentrated artillery fire or bombs **2** to attack persistently **3** to attack verbally, esp with questions **4** *physics* to direct high-energy particles of photons against (atoms, nuclei, etc.) [Old French *bombarde* stone-throwing cannon] **> bombardment** *n*

bombardier *n* **1** *Brit* a noncommissioned rank in the Royal Artillery **2** *US* the member of a bomber aircrew responsible for releasing the bombs

Bombardier *n Canad trademark* a snow tractor, usually having caterpillar tracks at the rear and skis at the fron

bombast *n* pompous and flowery language [Medieval Latin *bombax* cotton] **> bombastic** *adj*

Bombay *n* **1** the former English name of **Mumbai 2** a breed of black short-haired medium-sized cat

Bombay duck *n* a fish that is eaten dried with curry

dishes as a savoury [through association with *Bombay* (now Mumbai), port in India]

ombay Hills *pl n* a row of hills marking the southern boundary of greater Auckland on the North Island, New Zealand

ombazine *n* a twill fabric, usually of silk and worsted, formerly worn dyed black for mourning [Latin *bombyx* silk]

omber *n* **1** a military aircraft designed to carry out bombing missions **2** a person who plants bombs

omberg *n* David. 1890–1957, British painter, noted esp. for his landscapes

omb out *vb informal* to fail disastrously

ombshell *n* a shocking or unwelcome surprise

omu *or* **Mbomu** *n* a river in central Africa, rising in the SE Central African Republic and flowing west into the Uele River, forming the Ubangi River. Length: about 800 km (500 miles)

on *n* **Cape Bon** a peninsula of NE Tunisia

ona *n* **Mount Bona** a mountain in S Alaska, in the Wrangell Mountains. Height: 5005 m (16 420 ft)

ona fide (bone-a **fide**-ee) *adj* **1** genuine: *a bona fide manuscript* **2** undertaken in good faith: *a bona fide agreement* [Latin]

onaire *n* an island in the S Caribbean, part of the Netherlands Antilles until its dissolution in 2010, now a special municipality of the Netherlands: one of the Leeward Islands. Chief town: Kralendijk. Pop: 11 537 (2007 est). Area: about 288 sq km (111 sq miles)

onanza *n* **1** sudden and unexpected luck or wealth **2** *US and Canad* a mine or vein rich in ore [Spanish: calm sea, hence, good luck]

onaparte *n* **1** See **Napoleon I 2 Jérôme**, brother of Napoleon I. 1784–1860, king of Westphalia (1807–13) **3 Joseph**, brother of Napoleon I. 1768–1844, king of Naples (1806–08) and of Spain (1808–13) **4 Louis**, brother of Napoleon I. 1778–1846, king of Holland (1806–10) **5 Lucien**, brother of Napoleon I. 1775–1840, prince of Canino

onar Law *n* See **Law (1)**

onaventura *or* **Bonaventure** *n* **Saint**, called *the Seraphic Doctor*. 1221–74, Italian Franciscan monk, mystic, theologian, and philosopher; author of a *Life of St Francis* and *Journey of the Soul to God*. Feast day: July 14

onbon *n* a sweet [French]

ond *n* **1** something that binds, fastens, or holds together **2** something that brings or holds people together; tie: *a bond of friendship* **3 bonds** something that restrains or imprisons **4** a written or spoken agreement, esp. a promise: *a marriage bond* **5** *chem* a means by which atoms are combined in a molecule **6** *finance* a certificate of debt issued in order to raise funds **7** *S African* the conditional pledging of property, esp. a house, as security for the repayment of a loan **8** *law* a written acknowledgment of an obligation to pay a sum or to perform a contract **9 in bond** *commerce* securely stored until duty is paid ▷ *vb* **10** to hold or be held together; bind **11** to form a friendship **12** to put or hold (goods) in bond [Old Norse *band*]

ond *n* Edward. born 1934, British dramatist: his plays, including *Saved* (1965), *Lear* (1971), *Restoration* (1981), and *In the Company of Men* (1990), are noted for their violent imagery and socialist commitment

ondage *n* **1** a sexual practice in which one partner is tied or chained up **2** slavery **3** subjection to some influence or duty

onded *adj* **1** *finance* consisting of, secured by, or operating under a bond or bonds **2** *commerce* in bond

ondi *n* Sir Hermann. 1919–2005, British mathematician and cosmologist, born in Austria; joint originator (with Sir Fred Hoyle and Thomas Gold) of the steady-state theory of the universe

ondi Beach *n* a beach in Sydney, Australia, popular with surfers

bond paper *n* superior quality writing paper

Bonds *n* Barry (**Lamar**). born 1964, US baseball player: holder of records for most home runs in a season (73) and a career (762)

bondservant *n* a serf or slave

bone *n* **1** any of the various structures that make up the skeleton in most vertebrates **2** the porous rigid tissue of which these parts are made **3** something consisting of bone or a bonelike substance **4 bones** the human skeleton **5** a thin strip of plastic, etc. used to stiffen corsets and brassieres **6 close to** *or* **near the bone** risqué or indecent **7 have a bone to pick** to have grounds for a quarrel **8 make no bones about a** to be direct and candid about **b** to have no scruples about **9 the bare bones** the essentials ▷ *vb* **boning, boned 10** to remove the bones from (meat for cooking, etc.) **11** to stiffen (a corset, etc.) by inserting bones ▸ See also **bone up on** [Old English *bān*] **> boneless** *adj*

Bône *n* a former name of **Annaba**

bone china *n* a type of fine porcelain containing powdered bone

bone-dry *adj informal* completely dry

bone-idle *adj* extremely lazy

bone meal *n* dried and ground animal bones, used as a fertilizer or in stock feeds

boneshaker *n slang* a decrepit or rickety vehicle

bone up on *vb informal* to study intensively

bonfire *n* a large outdoor fire [Middle English *bone-fire*, from the use of bones as fuel]

bongo *n, pl* **-gos** *or* **-goes** a small bucket-shaped drum, usually one of a pair, played by beating with the fingers [American Spanish]

Bongo *n* Omar. original name *Albert Bernard Bongo*. 1935–2009, Gabonese statesman; president of Gabon (1967–2009)

Bonheur *n* Rosa. 1822–99, French painter of animals

Bonhoeffer *n* Dietrich. 1906–45, German Lutheran theologian: executed by the Nazis

bonhomie (bon-om-**mee**) *n* exuberant friendliness [French]

Boniface *n* **Saint**, original name *Wynfrith*. ?680–?755 AD, Anglo-Saxon missionary: archbishop of Mainz (746–755). Feast day: June 5

Boniface VIII *n* original name *Benedict Caetano*. ?1234–1303, pope (1294–1303)

Bonington *n* **1** Sir Chris(**tian John Storey**). born 1934, British mountaineer and writer; led 1970 Annapurna I and 1975 Everest expeditions; reached Everest summit in 1985 **2 Richard Parkes**. 1801–28, British painter of landscapes and historical scenes

Bonin Islands *pl n* a group of 27 volcanic islands in the W Pacific: occupied by the US after World War II; returned to Japan in 1968. Largest island: Chichijima. Area: 103 sq km (40 sq miles). Japanese name: **Ogasawara Gunto**

bonito (ba-nee-toh) *n, pl* **-os 1** a small tunny-like marine food fish **2** a related fish, whose flesh is dried and flaked and used in Japanese cookery

bonk *vb informal* **1** to have sexual intercourse **2** to hit [probably imitative] **> bonking** *n*

bonkers *adj Brit, Austral and NZ slang* mad; crazy [origin unknown]

bon mot (bon moh) *n, pl* **bons mots** a clever and fitting remark [French, literally: good word]

Bonn *n* a city in W Germany, in North Rhine-Westphalia on the Rhine: the former capital (1949–90) of West Germany; university (1786). Pop: 311 052 (2003 est)

Bonnard *n* Pierre. 1867–1947, French painter and lithographer, noted for the effects of light and colour in his landscapes and sunlit interiors

bonnet *n* **1** *Brit* the hinged metal cover over a motor vehicle's engine **2** any of various hats tied with ribbons under the chin **3** (in Scotland) a soft cloth cap [Old French *bonet*]

bonny *adj* **-nier, -niest 1** *Scot and N English dialect* beautiful: *a bonny lass* **2** good or fine [Latin *bonus*]

Bonny *n* Bight of Bonny a wide bay at the E end of the Gulf of Guinea off the coasts of Nigeria and Cameroon. Former name (until 1975): **Bight of Biafra**

Bonporti *n* Francesco Antonio. 1672–1749, Italian composer and violinist, noted esp. for his *Invenzioni* (1712), a series of short instrumental suites

bonsai *n*, *pl* **-sai** an ornamental tree or shrub grown in a small shallow pot in order to stunt its growth [Japanese *bon* bowl + *sai* to plant]

bonsela (bon-**sell**-a) *n S African informal* a small gift of money [Zulu *ibanselo* gift]

Bontempelli *n* Massimo. 1878–1960, Italian dramatist, poet, novelist, and critic. His works include the play *Nostra Dea* (1925) and the novel *The Faithful Lover* (1953)

bonus *n* something given, paid, or received above what is due or expected [Latin: good]

bon voyage *interj* a phrase used to wish a traveller a pleasant journey [French]

bony *adj* **bonier, boniest 1** resembling or consisting of bone **2** thin **3** having many bones

Bonynge *n* Richard. born 1930, Australian conductor, esp. of opera

boo *interj* **1** a shout uttered to express dissatisfaction or contempt **2** an exclamation uttered to startle someone ▷ *vb* **booing, booed 3** to shout 'boo' at (someone or something) as an expression of disapproval

boob *slang n* **1** *Brit, Austral and NZ* an embarrassing mistake; blunder **2** a female breast **3** *Austral* a prison ▷ *vb* **4** *Brit, Austral and NZ* to make a blunder [from *booby*]

boobook (**boo**-book) *n* a small spotted Australian brown owl

booby *n*, *pl* **-bies 1** *old-fashioned* an ignorant or foolish person **2** a tropical marine bird related to the gannet [Latin *balbus* stammering]

booby prize *n* a mock prize given to the person with the lowest score in a competition

booby trap *n* **1** a hidden explosive device primed so as to be set off by an unsuspecting victim **2** a trap for an unsuspecting person, esp. one intended as a practical joke

boodle *n slang* money or valuables, esp. when stolen, counterfeit, or used as a bribe [Dutch *boedel* possessions]

boogie *vb* **-gieing, -gied** *slang* to dance to fast pop music [origin unknown]

boogie board *n* another name for **bodyboard**

boogie-woogie *n* a style of piano jazz using blues harmonies [perhaps imitative]

boohai *n NZ informal* **1** a very remote area **2 up the boohai** very mistaken or astray [from the remote township of *Puhoi*]

boohoo *vb* **-hooing, -hooed 1** to sob or pretend to sob noisily ▷ *n*, *pl* **-hoos 2** distressed or pretended sobbing

book *n* **1** a number of printed pages bound together along one edge and protected by covers **2** a written work or composition, such as a novel **3** a number of sheets of paper bound together: *an account book* **4 books** a record of the transactions of a business or society **5** the libretto of an opera or musical **6** a major division of a written composition, such as of a long novel or of the Bible **7** a number of tickets, stamps, etc. fastened together along one edge **8** a record of betting transactions **9 a closed book** a subject that is beyond comprehension: *art remains a closed book to him* **10 bring to book** to reprimand or require (someone) to give an explanation of his or her conduct **11 by the book** according to the rules **12 in someone's good or bad books** regarded by someone with favour or disfavour **13 throw the book at someone a** to charge someone with every relevant offence **b** to inflict the most severe punishment on someone ▷ *vb* **14** to reserve (a place, passage, etc.) or engage the services of (someone) in advance **15** (of a police officer) to take the name and address of (a person) for an alleged offence

with a view to prosecution **16** (of a football referee) to take the name of (a player) who has broken the rules seriously ▶ See also **book in** [Old English *bōc*]

bookcase *n* a piece of furniture containing shelves for books

book club *n* a club that sells books at low prices to members, usually by mail order

book end *n* one of a pair of supports for holding a row of books upright

bookie *n informal* short for **bookmaker**

book in *vb* chiefly *Brit and NZ* to register one's arrival at a hotel

booking *n* **1** *Brit, Austral and NZ* a reservation, as of a table or seat **2** *theatre* an engagement of a performer

bookish *adj* **1** fond of reading; studious **2** forming opinions through reading rather than experience

book-keeping *n* the skill or occupation of systematically recording business transactions ▷ **book-keeper** *n*

booklet *n* a thin book with paper covers

bookmaker *n* a person who as an occupation accepts bets, esp. on horse racing ▷ **bookmaking** *n*

bookmark *n* **1** a strip of some material put between the pages of a book to mark a place **2** *computers* an identifier put on a website that enables the user to return to it quickly and easily ▷ *vb* **3** *computers* to identify and store (a website) so that one can return to it quickly and easily

bookstall *n* a stall or stand where periodicals, newspapers, or books are sold

bookworm *n* **1** a person devoted to reading **2** a small insect that feeds on the binding paste of books

Boole *n* George. 1815–64, English mathematician. In *Mathematical Analysis of Logic* (1847) and *An Investigation of the Laws of Thought* (1854), he applied mathematical formulae to logic, creating Boolean algebra

Boolean algebra (**boo**-lee-an) *n* a system of symbolic logic devised to codify nonmathematical logical operations: used in computers [after George **Boole**]

boom[1] *vb* **1** to make a loud deep echoing sound **2** to prosper vigorously and rapidly: *business boomed* ▷ *n* **3** a loud deep echoing sound **4** a period of high economic growth [imitative]

boom[2] *n* **1** *nautical* a spar to which the foot of a sail is fastened to control its position **2** a pole carrying an overhead microphone and projected over a film or television set **3** a barrier across a waterway [Dutch: tree]

boomer *n Austral* a large male kangaroo

boomerang *n* **1** a curved wooden missile of Australian Aborigines which can be made to return to the thrower **2** an action or statement that recoils on its originator ▷ *vb* **3** (of a plan) to recoil unexpectedly, harming its originator [Aboriginal]

boomslang *n* a large greenish venomous tree-living snake of southern Africa [Afrikaans]

boon[1] *n* something extremely useful, helpful, or beneficial [Old Norse *bōn* request]

boon[2] *adj* close or intimate: *boon companion* [Latin *bonus* good]

Boone *n* Daniel. 1734–1820, American pioneer, explorer, and guide, esp. in Kentucky

boongary (boong-**gar**-ree) *n* a tree kangaroo of NE Queensland, Australia

boor *n* an ill-mannered, clumsy, or insensitive person [Old English *gebūr* dweller, farmer] ▷ **boorish** *adj*

boost *n* **1** encouragement or help: *a boost to morale* **2** an upward thrust or push **3** an increase or rise ▷ *vb* **4** to encourage or improve: *to boost morale* **5** to cause to rise; increase: *we significantly boosted our market share* **6** to advertise on a big scale [origin unknown]

booster *n* **1** a supplementary injection of a vaccine given to ensure that the first injection will remain effective **2** a radio-frequency amplifier to strengthen signals **3** the first stage of a multistage rocket

boot¹ n **1** an outer covering for the foot that extends above the ankle **2** Brit an enclosed compartment of a car for holding luggage **3** informal a kick: *he gave the door a boot* **4 lick someone's boots** to behave flatteringly towards someone **5 put the boot in** slang **a** to kick a person when already down **b** to finish something off with unnecessary brutality **6 the boot** slang dismissal from employment ▷ vb **7** to kick **8** to start up (a computer) **9 boot out** informal **a** to eject forcibly **b** to dismiss from employment [Middle English *bote*]

boot² n **to boot** as well; in addition [Old English *bōt* compensation]

boot camp n a centre for juvenile offenders, with strict discipline and hard physical exercise

bootee n a soft boot for a baby, esp. a knitted one

booth n, pl **booths 1** a small partially enclosed cubicle **2** a stall, esp. a temporary one at a fair or market [Scandinavian]

Booth n **1 Edwin Thomas**, son of Junius Brutus Booth. 1833–93, US actor **2 John Wilkes**, son of Junius Brutus Booth. 1838–65, US actor; assassin of Abraham Lincoln **3 Junius Brutus**. 1796–1852, US actor, born in England **4 William**. 1829–1912, British religious leader; founder and first general of the Salvation Army (1878)

Boothia Peninsula n a peninsula of N Canada: the northernmost part of the mainland of North America, lying west of the **Gulf of Boothia**, an arm of the Arctic Ocean

Boothroyd n **Betty**. Baroness. born 1929, British politician; speaker of the House of Commons (1992–2000)

Bootle n a port in NW England, in Sefton unitary authority, Merseyside; on the River Mersey adjoining Liverpool. Pop: 59 123 (2001)

bootleg vb **-legging**, **-legged 1** to make, carry, or sell (illicit goods, esp. alcohol) ▷ adj **2** produced, distributed, or sold illicitly [smugglers carried bottles of liquor concealed in their boots] **> bootlegger** n

bootless adj of little or no use; vain; fruitless [Old English *bōtlēas*]

bootlicker n informal one who seeks favour by grovelling to someone in authority

booty¹ n, pl **-ties** any valuable article or articles obtained as plunder [Old French *butin*]

booty² n slang the buttocks, esp. those of an attractive female [from **butt** the buttocks]

booze informal n **1** alcoholic drink ▷ vb **boozing**, **boozed 2** to drink alcohol, esp. in excess [Middle Dutch *būsen*] **> boozy** adj

booze bus n Austral and NZ informal a mobile police unit used to conduct drug and alcohol tests on drivers

boozer n informal **1** a person who is fond of drinking **2** Brit, Austral and NZ a bar or pub

booze-up n Brit, Austral and NZ slang a drinking spree

bop n **1** a form of jazz with complex rhythms and harmonies ▷ vb **bopping**, **bopped 2** informal to dance to pop music [from BEBOP] **> bopper** n

Bophuthatswana n (formerly) a Bantu homeland in N South Africa: consisted of six separate areas; declared independent by South Africa in 1977 although this was not internationally recognized; abolished in 1993. Capital: Mmabatho

bora n Austral an Aboriginal ceremony [from a native Australian language]

Bora Bora n an island in the S Pacific, in French Polynesia, in the Society Islands: one of the Leeward Islands. Area: 39 sq km (15 sq miles)

boracic adj same as **boric**

borage n a Mediterranean plant with star-shaped blue flowers [Arabic *abū 'āraq* literally: father of sweat]

Borås n a city in SW Sweden, chiefly producing textiles. Pop: 98 831 (2004 est)

borax n a white mineral in crystalline form used in making glass, soap, etc. [Persian *būrah*]

Bordeaux n **1** a port in SW France, on the River Garonne: a major centre of the wine trade. Pop: 235 878 (2006) **2** any of several red, white, or rosé wines produced around Bordeaux ▶ Related adjective: **Bordelais**

border n **1** the dividing line between political or geographic regions **2** a band or margin around or along the edge of something **3** a design around the edge of something **4** a narrow strip of ground planted with flowers or shrubs: *a herbaceous border* ▷ vb **5** to provide with a border **6 a** to be adjacent to; lie along the boundary of **b** to be nearly the same as; verge on: *a story that borders on the unbelievable* [Old French *bort* side of a ship]

Border¹ n **the Border 1** (often pl) the area straddling the border between England and Scotland **2** the area straddling the border between Northern Ireland and the Republic of Ireland **3** the region in S South Africa around East London

Border² n **Allan (Robert)**. born 1955, Australian cricketer; played in 156 test matches (1978–1994), 93 as captain; first Australian batsman to score 10,000 test runs

borderland n **1** land located on or near a boundary **2** an indeterminate state or condition

borderline n **1** a dividing line **2** an indeterminate position between two conditions: *the borderline between love and friendship* ▷ adj **3** on the edge of one category and verging on another: *a borderline failure*

Borders Region n a former local government region in S Scotland, formed in 1975 from Berwick, Peebles, Roxburgh, Selkirk, and part of Midlothian; replaced in 1996 by Scottish Borders council area

Bordet n **Jules (Jean Baptiste Vincent)**. 1870–1961, Belgian bacteriologist and immunologist, who discovered complement. Nobel prize for physiology or medicine 1919

bore¹ vb **boring**, **bored 1** to produce (a hole) with a drill, etc. **2** to produce (a tunnel, mine shaft, etc.) by drilling ▷ n **3** a hole or tunnel in the ground drilled in search of minerals, oil, etc. **4 a** the hollow of a gun barrel **b** the diameter of this hollow; calibre [Old English *borian*]

bore² vb **boring**, **bored 1** to tire or make weary by being dull, repetitious, or uninteresting ▷ n **2** a dull or repetitious person, activity, or state [origin unknown] **> bored** adj **> boring** adj

bore³ n a high wave moving up a narrow estuary, caused by the tide [Old Norse *bāra*]

bore⁴ vb the past tense of **bear¹**

boreal forest (bore-ee-al) n the forest of northern latitudes, esp. in Scandinavia, Canada, and Siberia, consisting mainly of spruce and pine [Latin *boreas* the north wind]

boredom n the state of being bored

boree (baw-ree) n Austral same as **myall**

Borg n **Björn**. born 1956, Swedish tennis player: Wimbledon champion 1976–80; French Open champion 1974–75, 1978–81

Borgerhout n a town in N Belgium, near Antwerp. Pop: 40 142 (2002 est)

Borges n **Jorge Luis**. 1899–1986, Argentinian poet, short-story writer, and literary scholar. The short stories collected in *Ficciones* (1944) he described as "games with infinity"

Borgia n **1 Cesare**, son of Rodrigo Borgia (Pope Alexander VI). 1475–1507, Italian cardinal, politician, and military leader; model for Machiavelli's *The Prince* **2** his sister, **Lucrezia**, daughter of Rodrigo Borgia. 1480–1519, Italian noblewoman. After her third marriage (1501), to the Duke of Ferrara, she became a patron of the arts and science **3 Rodrigo**. See **Alexander VI**

Borglum n **(John) Gutzon**. 1867–1941, US sculptor, noted for his monumental busts of US presidents carved in the mountainside of Mount Rushmore

b

boric *adj* of or containing boron

boric acid *n* a white soluble crystalline solid used as a mild antiseptic

Boris I *n* known as *Boris of Bulgaria*. died 907 AD, khan of Bulgaria. His reign saw the conversion of Bulgaria to Christianity and the birth of a national literature

Borlaug *n* Norman (**Ernest**). 1914–2009, US agronomist, who bred new strains of high-yielding cereal crops for use in developing countries. Nobel peace prize 1970

Bormann *n* Martin. 1900–45, German Nazi politician; Hitler's adviser and private secretary (1942–45): committed suicide

born *vb* 1 a past participle of **bear¹** 2 **not have been born yesterday** not to be gullible or foolish ▷ *adj* 3 possessing certain qualities from birth: *a born musician* 4 being in a particular social status at birth: *ignobly born*

> **USAGE** Care should be taken not to use *born* where *borne* is intended: *he had borne* (not *born*) *his ordeal with great courage: the following points should be borne in mind.*

Born *n* Max. 1882–1970, British nuclear physicist, born in Germany, noted for his fundamental contribution to quantum mechanics: Nobel prize for physics 1954

born-again *adj* 1 having experienced conversion, esp. to evangelical Christianity 2 showing the enthusiasm of someone newly converted to any cause: *a born-again romantic* ▷ *n* 3 a person with fervent enthusiasm for a newfound cause

borne *vb* a past participle of **bear¹**

> **USAGE** See at **born**.

Bornean *adj* 1 of or relating to Borneo or its inhabitants ▷ *n* 2 a native or inhabitant of Borneo

Borneo *n* an island in the W Pacific, between the Sulu and Java Seas, part of the Malay Archipelago: divided into Kalimantan (**Indonesian Borneo**), the Malaysian states of Sarawak and Sabah, and the sultanate of Brunei; mountainous and densely forested. Area: about 750 000 sq km (290 000 sq miles)

Bornholm *n* an island in the Baltic Sea, south of Sweden: administratively part of Denmark. Chief town: Rønne. Pop: 43 956 (2003 est). Area: 588 sq km (227 sq miles)

Borno *n* a state of NE Nigeria, on Lake Chad. Capital: Maiduguri. Pop: 4 151 193 (2006). Area: 70 898 sq km (27 374 sq miles)

Borodin *n* Aleksandr Porfirevich. 1834–87, Russian composer, whose works include the unfinished opera *Prince Igor*, symphonies, songs, and chamber music

Borodino *n* a village in E central Russia, about 110 km (70 miles) west of Moscow: scene of a battle (1812) in which Napoleon defeated the Russians but irreparably weakened his army

boron *n chem* a hard almost colourless crystalline metalloid element that is used in hardening steel. Symbol: **B** [*bor(ax)* + *(carb)on*]

boronia *n* an Australian aromatic flowering shrub

Borotra *n* Jean (**Robert**). 1898–1994, French tennis player: secretary general of physical education under the Vichy government (1940)

borough *n* 1 a town, esp. (in Britain) one that forms the constituency of an MP or that was originally incorporated by royal charter 2 any of the constituent divisions of Greater London or New York City [Old English *burg*]

Borromini *n* Francesco, original name *Francesco Castelli*. 1599–1667, Italian baroque architect, working in Rome: his buildings include the churches of San Carlo (1641) and Sant' Ivo (1660)

borrow *vb* 1 to obtain (something, such as money) on the understanding that it will be returned to the lender 2 to adopt (ideas, words, etc.) from another

source [Old English *borgian*] ▷ **borrower** *n* ▷ **borrowing** *n*

> **USAGE** The use of *off* after *borrow* was formerly considered incorrect, but is now acceptable in informal contexts.

Borrow *n* George (**Henry**). 1803–81, English traveller and writer. His best-known works are the semiautobiographica[l] novels of Gypsy life and language, *Lavengro* (1851) and its sequel *The Romany Rye* (1857)

borscht or **borsch** *n* a Russian soup based on beetroot [Russian *borshch*]

borstal *n* (formerly, in Britain) a prison for offenders aged 15 to 21 [after *Borstal*, village in Kent where the firs[t] institution was founded]

borzoi *n* a tall dog with a narrow head and a long coat [Russian: swift]

Bosch *n* 1 Carl. 1874–1940, German chemist, who adapte[d] the Haber process to produce ammonia for industrial use. He shared the Nobel prize for chemistry 1931
2 **Hieronymus**, original name probably *Jerome van Aken* (o[r] *Aeken*). ?1450–1516, Dutch painter, noted for his macabre allegorical representations of biblical subjects in brilliant transparent colours, esp. the triptych *The Garde[n] of Earthly Delights*

Bose *n* 1 Sir Jagadis Chandra. 1858–1937, Indian physicis[t] and plant physiologist 2 Satyendra Nath. 1894–1974, Indian physicist, who collaborated with Einstein in devising Bose-Einstein statistics 3 Subhas Chandra, known as *Netaji*. 1897–1945, Indian nationalist leader; president of the Indian National Congress (1938–39); organized the Indian National Army, with Japanese support, in Singapore to free India from British Rule

bosh *n Brit, Austral and NZ informal* meaningless talk or opinions; nonsense [Turkish *boş* empty]

Bosman *n* Herman Charles. (1905–1951), South African short-story writer and journalist; his experiences in prison are recounted in the semi-autobiographical *Col[d] Stone Jug* (1949)

Bosnia *n* a region of central Bosnia-Herzegovina: belonged to Turkey (1463–1878), to Austria-Hungary (1879–1918), then to Yugoslavia (1918–91)

Bosnia-Herzegovina *or especially US* **Bosnia and Herzegovina** *n* a country in SW Europe; a constituer[t] republic of Yugoslavia until 1991; in a state of civil war (1992–95); Serbian and Croatian forces were also involved: mostly barren and mountainous, with forest[s] in the east. Languages: Bosnian, Croatian, and Serbia[n] (formerly all regarded together as Serbo-Croat). Religion: Muslim, Serbian Orthodox, and Roman Catholic. Currency: marka (pegged to the euro). Capita[l] Sarajevo. Pop: 3 875 723 (2013 est). Area: 51 129 sq km (19 737 sq miles)

Bosnian *adj* 1 of or relating to Bosnia or its inhabitant[s] ▷ *n* 2 a native or inhabitant of Bosnia

bosom *n* 1 the chest or breast of a person, esp. the fema[le] breasts 2 a protective centre or part: *the bosom of the fam[ily]* 3 the breast considered as the seat of emotions ▷ *adj* 4 very dear: *a bosom friend* [Old English *bōsm*]

Bosporus or **Bosphorus** *n* the Bosporus a strait between European and Asian Turkey, linking the Blac[k] Sea and the Sea of Marmara

boss¹ *informal n* 1 a person in charge of or employing others ▷ *vb* 2 to employ, supervise, or be in charge of 3 **boss around** or **about** to be domineering or overbeari[ng] towards [Dutch *baas* master]

boss² *n* a raised knob or stud, esp. an ornamental one [on] a vault, shield, etc. [Old French *boce*]

bossa nova *n* 1 a dance similar to the samba, originating in Brazil 2 music for this dance [Portugue[se]

Bossuet *n* Jacques Bénigne. 1627–1704, French bishop: noted for his funeral orations

bossy *adj* **bossier, bossiest** *informal* domineering, overbearing, or authoritarian ▷ **bossiness** *n*

b

Boston n **1** a port in E Massachusetts, the state capital. Pop: 581 616 (2003 est) **2** a port in E England, in SE Lincolnshire. Pop: 35 124 (2001)

bosun or **boatswain** (boh-sn) n an officer who is responsible for the maintenance of a ship and its equipment

Boswell n James. 1740–95, Scottish author and lawyer, noted particularly for his *Life of Samuel Johnson* (1791) **> Boswellian** adj

Bosworth Field n English history the site, two miles south of Market Bosworth in Leicestershire, of the battle that ended the Wars of the Roses (August 1485). Richard III was killed and Henry Tudor was crowned king as Henry VII

bot. **1** botanical **2** botany

botany n, pl **-nies** the study of plants, including their classification, structure, etc. [Greek *botanē* plant] **> botanical** or **botanic** adj **> botanist** n

Botany Bay n **1** an inlet of the Tasman Sea, on the SE coast of Australia: surrounded by the suburbs of Sydney **2** (in the 19th century) a British penal settlement that was in fact at Port Jackson, New South Wales

botch vb **1** to spoil through clumsiness or ineptitude **2** to repair badly or clumsily ▷ also: **botch-up 3** a badly done piece of work or repair [origin unknown]

both adj **1** two considered together: *both parents were killed during the war* ▷ pron **2** two considered together: *both are to blame* ▷ conj **3** not just one but also the other of two (people or things): *both Darren and Keith enjoyed the match* [Old Norse *bāthir*]

Botha n **1** Louis. 1862–1919, South African statesman and general; first prime minister of the Union of South Africa (1910–19) **2** P(ieter) W(illem). 1916–2006, South African politician; defence minister (1965–78); prime minister (1978–84); state president (1984–89)

Botham n Sir Ian (Terence). born 1955, English cricketer: an all-rounder, he played in 102 test matches (1977–1992) taking 383 wickets

Bothe n Walther (Wilhelm Georg Franz). 1891–1957, German physicist, who developed new methods of detecting subatomic particles. He shared the Nobel prize for physics 1954

bother vb **1** to take the time or trouble: *don't bother to come with me* **2** to give annoyance, pain, or trouble to **3** to trouble (a person) by repeatedly disturbing; pester ▷ n **4** a state of worry, trouble, or confusion **5** a person or thing that causes fuss, trouble, or annoyance **6** informal a disturbance or fight: *a spot of bother* ▷ interj **7** Brit, Austral and NZ an exclamation of slight annoyance [origin unknown]

bothersome adj causing bother

Bothnia n Gulf of Bothnia an arm of the Baltic Sea, extending north between Sweden and Finland

Bothwell n Earl of, title of James Hepburn. 1535–78, Scottish nobleman; third husband of Mary Queen of Scots. He is generally considered to have instigated the murder of Darnley (1567)

bothy n, pl **bothies** chiefly Scot **1** a hut used for temporary shelter **2** (formerly) a farm worker's quarters [perhaps from *booth*]

Botox n trademark **1** a preparation of botulinum toxin used to treat muscle spasm and to remove wrinkles ▷ vb **2** to apply Botox to (a person or a part of the body) [from *BOT(ULINUM) (T)OX(IN)*]

Botswana n a republic in southern Africa: established as the British protectorate of Bechuanaland in 1885 as a defence against the Boers; became an independent state within the Commonwealth in 1966; consists mostly of a plateau averaging 1000 m (3300 ft), with the extensive Okavango swamps in the northwest and the Kalahari Desert in the southwest. Languages: English and Tswana. Religion: animist majority. Currency: pula. Capital: Gaborone. Pop: 2 127 825 (2013 est). Area: about 570 000 sq km (220 000 sq miles)

Botticelli n Sandro, original name *Alessandro di Mariano Filipepi*. 1444–1510, Italian (Florentine) painter, illustrator, and engraver, noted for the graceful outlines and delicate details of his mythological and religious paintings

bottle n **1** a container, often of glass and usually cylindrical with a narrow neck, for holding liquids **2** the amount such a container will hold **3** Brit slang courage; nerve: *you don't have the bottle* **4** the bottle informal drinking of alcohol, esp. to excess ▷ vb **-tling, -tled 5** to put or place in a bottle or bottles ▶ See also **bottle up** [Late Latin *buttis* cask]

bottle bank n a large container into which members of the public can throw glass bottles and jars for recycling

bottle-feed vb **-feeding, -fed** to feed (a baby) with milk from a bottle

bottle-green adj dark green

bottleneck n **1** a narrow stretch of road or a junction at which traffic is or may be held up **2** something that holds up progress

bottlenose dolphin n a grey or greenish dolphin with a bottle-shaped snout

bottle party n a party to which guests bring drink

bottler n Austral and NZ old-fashioned, informal an exceptional person or thing

bottle shop n Austral and NZ a shop licensed to sell alcohol for drinking elsewhere. Also called: **bottle-o**

bottle store n S African a shop licensed to sell alcohol for drinking elsewhere

bottle tree n an Australian tree with a bottle-shaped swollen trunk

bottle up vb to restrain (powerful emotion)

bottom n **1** the lowest, deepest, or farthest removed part of a thing: *the bottom of a hill* **2** the least important or successful position: *the bottom of a class* **3** the ground underneath a sea, lake, or river **4** the underneath part of a thing **5** the buttocks **6** at bottom in reality; basically **7** be at the bottom of to be the ultimate cause of **8** get to the bottom of to discover the real truth about ▷ adj **9** lowest or last [Old English *botm*]

bottomless adj **1** unlimited; inexhaustible: *bottomless resources* **2** very deep: *bottomless valleys*

bottom line n **1** the conclusion or main point of a process, discussion, etc. **2** the last line of a financial statement that shows the net profit or loss of a company or organization

bottom out vb to reach the lowest point and level out: *consumer spending has bottomed out*

Bottrop n an industrial city in W Germany, in North Rhine-Westphalia in the Ruhr. Pop: 120 324 (2003 est)

botulism n severe food poisoning resulting from the toxin botulin, produced in imperfectly preserved food [Latin *botulus* sausage]

Botvinnik n Mikhail Moiseivich. 1911–95, Soviet chess player; world champion (1948–57, 1958–60, 1961–63)

Bouaké n a market town in S central Côte d'Ivoire. Pop: 521 000 (2005 est)

Boucher n François. 1703–70, French rococo artist, noted for his delicate ornamental paintings of pastoral scenes and mythological subjects

Bouches-du-Rhône n a department of S central France, in Provence-Alpes-Côte d'Azur region. Capital: Marseille. Pop: 1 883 645 (2003 est). Area: 5284 sq km (2047 sq miles)

Boucicault n Dion, real name *Dionysius Lardner Boursiquot*. 1822–90, Irish dramatist and actor. His plays include *London Assurance* (1841), *The Octoroon* (1859), and *The Shaughran* (1874)

bouclé n a curled or looped yarn or fabric giving a thick knobbly effect [French: curly]

Boudicca n died 62 AD, a queen of the Iceni, who led a revolt against Roman rule in Britain; after being defeated she poisoned herself. Also called: **Boadicea**

Boudin n Eugène. 1824–98, French painter: one of the

b

first French landscape painters to paint in the open air; a forerunner of impressionism

boudoir (boo-dwahr) *n* a woman's bedroom or private sitting room [French, literally: room for sulking in]

bouffant (boof-fong) *adj* (of a hairstyle) having extra height and width through backcombing [French *bouffer* to puff up]

Bougainville¹ *n* an island in the W Pacific, in Papua New Guinea: the largest of the Solomon Islands: unilaterally declared independence in 1990; occupied by government troops in 1992, and granted autonomy in 2001. Chief town: Kieta. Area: 10 049 sq km (3880 sq miles)

Bougainville² *n* Louis Antoine de. 1729–1811, French navigator

bougainvillea *n* a tropical climbing plant with flowers surrounded by showy red or purple bracts [after L. A. de BOUGAINVILLE]

bough *n* any of the main branches of a tree [Old English *bōg* arm, twig]

bought *vb* the past of **buy**

bouillon (boo-yon) *n* a thin clear broth or stock [French *bouillir* to boil]

Boulanger *n* **1** Georges. 1837–91, French general and minister of war (1886–87). Accused of attempting a coup d'état, he fled to Belgium, where he committed suicide **2** Nadia (Juliette) (nadja). 1887–1979, French teacher of musical composition: her pupils included Elliott Carter, Aaron Copland, Darius Milhaud, and Virgil Thomson. She is noted also for her work in reviving the works of Monteverdi

boulder *n* a smooth rounded mass of rock shaped by erosion [Scandinavian]

boulder clay *n* an unstratified glacial deposit of fine clay, boulders, and pebbles

Boulder Dam *n* the former name (1933–47) of **Hoover Dam**

boules (bool) *n* a game, popular in France, in which metal bowls are thrown to land as close as possible to a target ball [French: balls]

boulevard *n* a wide usually tree-lined road in a city [Middle Dutch *bolwerc* bulwark; because originally often built on the ruins of an old rampart]

Boulez *n* Pierre. born 1925, French composer and conductor, whose works employ total serialism

Boulogne *n* a port in N France, on the English Channel. Pop: 45 036 (2006). Official name: *French* **Boulogne-sur-Mer**

Boulogne-Billancourt *n* an industrial suburb of SW Paris. Pop: 106 367 (1999). Also called: *French* **Boulogne-sur-Seine**

boult *vb* same as **bolt²**

Boult *n* Sir Adrian (Cedric). 1889–1983, English conductor

Boulton *n* Matthew. 1728–1809, British engineer and manufacturer, who financed Watt's steam engine and applied it to various industrial purposes

Boumédienne *n* Houari. 1927–78, Algerian statesman and soldier: president of Algeria (1965–78) after overthrowing Ben Bella in a coup

bounce *vb* **bouncing, bounced 1** (of a ball, etc.) to rebound from an impact **2** to cause (a ball, etc.) to hit a solid surface and spring back **3** to move or cause to move suddenly; spring: *I bounced down the stairs* **4** *slang* (of a bank) to send (a cheque) back or (of a cheque) to be sent back unredeemed because of lack of funds in the account ▷ *n* **5** the action of rebounding from an impact **6** a leap or jump **7** springiness **8** *informal* vitality; vigour **9** *informal* a temporary increase or rise: *a sales bounce* [probably imitative] > **bouncy** *adj*

bounce back *vb* to recover one's health, good spirits, confidence, etc., easily

bouncer *n* **1** *slang* a person employed at a club, disco, etc. to prevent unwanted people from entering and to eject

drunks or troublemakers **2** *cricket* a ball bowled so that i bounces high on pitching

bouncing *adj* vigorous and robust: *a bouncing baby*

Bouncy Castle *n trademark* a very large inflatable mode usually of a castle, on which children may bounce at fairs, etc.

bound¹ *vb* **1** the past of **bind** ▷ *adj* **2** tied as if with a rope **3** restricted or confined: *housebound* **4** certain: *it's bound to happen* **5** compelled or obliged: *they agreed to be bound by the board's recommendations* **6** (of a book) secured within a cover or binding **7** **bound up with** closely or inextricably linked with

bound² *vb* **1** to move forwards by leaps or jumps **2** to bounce; spring away from an impact ▷ *n* **3** a jump upwards or forwards **4** a bounce, as of a ball [Old Frencl *bondir*]

bound³ *vb* **1** to place restrictions on; limit: *bounded by tradition* **2** to form a boundary of ▷ *n* **3** See **bounds** [Old French *bonde*] > **boundless** *adj*

bound⁴ *adj* going or intending to go towards: *homeward bound* [Old Norse *buinn*, past participle of *būa* prepare]

boundary *n, pl* **-ries 1** something that indicates the farthest limit, such as of an area **2** *cricket* **a** the marked limit of the playing area **b** a stroke that hits the ball beyond this limit, scoring four or six runs

bounden *adj old-fashioned* morally obligatory: *bounden du*

bounder *n old-fashioned, Brit slang* a morally reprehensib person; cad

bounds *pl n* **1** a limit; boundary: *their jealousy knows no bounds* **2** something that restricts or controls, esp. the standards of a society: *within the bounds of good taste*

bountiful *or* **bounteous** *adj literary* **1** plentiful; ample: *bountiful harvest* **2** giving freely; generous

bounty *n, pl* **-ties 1** *literary* generosity; liberality **2** something provided in generous amounts: *nature's bounty* **3** a reward or premium by a government [Latin *bonus* good]

bouquet *n* **1** a bunch of flowers, esp. a large carefully arranged one **2** the aroma of wine [French: thicket]

bouquet garni *n, pl* **bouquets garnis** a bunch of herbs tied together and used for flavouring soups, stews, or stocks [French]

bourbon (bur-bn) *n* a whiskey distilled, chiefly in the US, from maize [after *Bourbon* county, Kentucky, where was first made]

bourgeois (boor-zhwah) *often disparaging adj* **1** characteristic of or comprising the middle class **2** conservative or materialistic in outlook **3** (in Marxis thought) dominated by capitalism ▷ *n, pl* **-geois 4** a member of the middle class, esp. one regarded as bein conservative and materialistic [Old French *borjois* citizen]

Bourgeois *n* Léon Victor Auguste. 1851–1925, French statesman; first chairman of the League of Nations: Nobel peace prize 1920

bourgeoisie (boor-zhwah-zee) *n* the bourgeoisie **1** the middle classes **2** (in Marxist thought) the capitalist ruling class

Bourges *n* a city in central France. Pop: 72 480 (1999)

Bourgogne *n* the French name for **Burgundy**

Bourguiba *n* Habib ben Ali. 1903–2000, Tunisian statesman: president of Tunisia (1957–87); a moderate and an advocate of gradual social change. He was deposed in a coup and kept under house arrest for the rest of his life

Bourke-White *n* Margaret. 1906–71, US photographer pioneer of modern photojournalism: noted esp. for he coverage of World War II

bourn *n chiefly S Brit* a stream [Old French *bodne* limit]

Bournemouth *n* **1** a resort in S England, in Bournemouth unitary authority, Dorset, on the English Channel. Pop: 167 527 (2001) **2** a unitary authority in SE Dorset. Pop: 163 700 (2003 est). Area: 46 sq km (17 sq miles)

b

bourrée (boor-ray) *n* **1** a traditional French dance in fast duple time **2** music for this dance [French]

Bourse (boorss) *n* a stock exchange, esp. of Paris [French: purse]

bout *n* **1 a** a period of time spent doing something, such as drinking **b** a period of illness: *a bad bout of flu* **2** a boxing, wrestling, or fencing match [obsolete *bought* turn]

boutique *n* a small shop, esp. one that sells fashionable clothes [French]

bouzouki *n* a Greek long-necked stringed musical instrument related to the mandolin [Modern Greek]

Bovet *n* Daniel. 1907–92, Italian pharmacologist, born in Switzerland, noted for his pioneering work on antihistamine drugs. Nobel prize for physiology or medicine 1957

bovine *adj* **1** of or relating to cattle **2** dull, sluggish, or ugly [Latin *bos* ox]

bow¹ (rhymes with **cow**) *vb* **1** to lower (one's head) or bend (one's knee or body) as a sign of respect, greeting, agreement, or shame **2** to comply or accept: *bow to the inevitable* **3 bow and scrape** to behave in a slavish manner ▷ *n* **4** a lowering or bending of the head or body as a mark of respect, etc. **5 take a bow** to acknowledge applause ▶ See also **bow out** [Old English *būgan*]

bow² (rhymes with **know**) *n* **1** a decorative knot usually having two loops and two loose ends **2** a long stick across which are stretched strands of horsehair, used for playing a violin, viola, cello, etc. **3** a weapon for shooting arrows, consisting of an arch of flexible wood, plastic, etc. bent by a string fastened at each end **4** something that is curved, bent, or arched ▷ *vb* **5** to form or cause to form a curve or curves [Old English *boga* arch, bow]

bow³ (rhymes with **cow**) *n* **1** chiefly *nautical* the front end or part of a vessel **2** *rowing* the oarsman at the bow [probably Low German *boog*]

Bow *n* Clara, known as the *It Girl*. 1905–65, US film actress, noted for her vivacity and sex appeal

bowdlerize or **-ise** *vb* **-izing, -ized** or **-ising, -ised** to remove passages or words regarded as indecent from (a play, novel, etc.) [after Thomas *Bowdler*, editor who expurgated Shakespeare] ❯ **bowdlerization** or **-isation** *n*

bowel *n* **1** an intestine, esp. the large intestine in humans **2 bowels** entrails **3 bowels** the innermost part: *the bowels of the earth* [Latin *botellus* a little sausage]

Bowen *n* Elizabeth (Dorothea Cole). 1899–1973, British novelist and short-story writer, born in Ireland. Her novels include *The Death of the Heart* (1938) and *The Heat of the Day* (1949)

bower *n* a shady leafy shelter in a wood or garden [Old English *būr* dwelling]

bowerbird *n* a brightly coloured songbird of Australia and New Guinea

Bowery *n* the Bowery a street in New York City noted for its cheap hotels and bars, frequented by vagrants and drunks [C17: from Dutch *bouwerij*, from *bouwen* to farm + *erij* -ERY; see BOOR, BOER]

Bowie *n* **1** David, real name *David Jones*. born 1947, British rock singer, songwriter, and film actor. His recordings include "Space Oddity" (1969), *The Rise and Fall of Ziggy Stardust and the Spiders from Mars* (1972), *Heroes* (1977), *Let's Dance* (1983), and *Heathen* (2002) **2** James, known as *Jim Bowie*. 1796–1836, US frontiersman. A hero of the Texas Revolution against Mexico (1835–36), he died at the Battle of the Alamo

bowie knife *n* a stout hunting knife [after Jim BOWIE]

bowl¹ *n* **1** a round container open at the top, used for holding liquid or serving food **2** the amount a bowl will hold **3** the hollow part of an object, esp. of a spoon or tobacco pipe [Old English *bolla*]

bowl² *n* **1 a** a wooden ball used in the game of bowls **b** a large heavy ball with holes for gripping used in the game of bowling ▷ *vb* **2** to roll smoothly or cause to roll smoothly along the ground **3** *cricket* **a** to send (a ball) from one's hand towards the batsman **b** Also: **bowl out** to dismiss (a batsman) by delivering a ball that breaks his wicket **4** to play bowls **5 bowl along** to move easily and rapidly, as in a car ▶ See also **bowl over, bowls** [French *boule*]

bow-legged *adj* having legs that curve outwards at the knees

bowler¹ *n* **1** a person who bowls in cricket **2** a player at the game of bowls

bowler² *n* a stiff felt hat with a rounded crown and narrow curved brim [after John *Bowler*, hatter]

Bowles *n* Paul. 1910–99, US novelist, short-story writer, and composer, living in Tangiers. His novels include *The Sheltering Sky* (1949) and *The Spider's House* (1955)

bowline *n* *nautical* **1** a line used to keep the sail taut against the wind **2** a knot used for securing a loop that will not slip at the end of a piece of rope [probably from Middle Low German *bōlīne*]

bowling *n* **1** a game in which a heavy ball is rolled down a long narrow alley at a group of wooden pins **2** *cricket* the act of delivering the ball to the batsman

bowl over *vb* **1** *informal* to surprise (a person) greatly, in a pleasant way **2** to knock down

bowls *n* a game played on a very smooth area of grass in which opponents roll biased wooden bowls as near a small bowl (the jack) as possible

bow out *vb* to retire or withdraw gracefully

bowsprit *n* *nautical* a spar projecting from the bow of a sailing ship [Middle Low German *bōch* BOW³ + *sprēt* pole]

bowstring *n* the string of an archer's bow

bow tie *n* a man's tie in the form of a bow

bow window *n* a curved bay window

bow-wow *n* **1** a child's word for **dog** **2** an imitation of the bark of a dog

box¹ *n* **1** a container with a firm base and sides and sometimes a removable or hinged lid **2** the contents of such a container **3** a separate compartment for a small group of people, as in a theatre **4** a compartment for a horse in a stable or a vehicle **5** a section of printed matter on a page, enclosed by lines or a border **6** a central agency to which mail is addressed and from which it is collected or redistributed: *a post-office box* **7** same as **penalty box 8 the box** *Brit informal* television ▷ *vb* **9** to put into a box ▶ See also **box in** [Greek *puxos* BOX³] ❯ **boxlike** *adj*

box² *vb* **1** to fight (an opponent) in a boxing match **2** to engage in boxing **3** to hit (esp. a person's ears) with the fist ▷ *n* **4** a punch with the fist, esp. on the ear [origin unknown]

box³ *n* a slow-growing evergreen tree or shrub with small shiny leaves [Greek *puxos*]

boxer *n* **1** a person who boxes **2** a medium-sized dog with smooth hair and a short nose

boxer shorts or **boxers** *pl n* men's underpants shaped like shorts but with a front opening

box girder *n* a girder that is hollow and square or rectangular in shape

box in *vb* to prevent from moving freely; confine

boxing *n* the act, art, or profession of fighting with the fists

Boxing Day *n* the first day after Christmas (in Britain, traditionally and strictly, the first weekday), observed as a holiday [from the former custom of giving Christmas boxes to tradesmen on this day]

box jellyfish *n* a highly venomous jellyfish with a cuboid body that lives in Australian tropical waters

box junction *n* (in Britain) a road junction marked with yellow crisscross lines which vehicles may only enter when their exit is clear

box lacrosse *n* *Canad* lacrosse played indoors

box number *n* a number used as an address for mail, esp. one used by a newspaper for replies to an advertisement

b

box office n 1 an office at a theatre, cinema, etc. where tickets are sold 2 the public appeal of an actor or production ▷ adj **box-office** 3 relating to the sales at the box office: *a box-office success*

box pleat n a flat double pleat made by folding under the fabric on either side of it

boxroom n a small room in which boxes, cases, etc. may be stored

box spring n a coiled spring contained in a boxlike frame, used for mattresses, chairs, etc.

boxwood n the hard yellow wood of the box tree, used to make tool handles, etc. See box³

boy n 1 a male child 2 a man regarded as immature or inexperienced 3 *S African offensive* a Black male servant [origin unknown] ▷ **boyhood** n ▷ **boyish** adj

Boyce n William. ?1710–79, English composer, noted esp. for his church music and symphonies

boycott vb 1 to refuse to deal with (an organization or country) as a protest against its actions or policy ▷ n 2 an instance of the use of boycotting [after Captain *Boycott*, Irish land agent, a victim of such practices for refusing to reduce rents]

Boycott n Geoff(rey). born 1940, English cricketer: played for Yorkshire (1962–86); played in 108 test matches (1964–82); first England batsman to score 8000 test runs

Boyd n 1 Arthur. 1920–99, Australian painter and sculptor, noted for his large ceramic sculptures and his series of engravings 2 Martin (A'Beckett). 1893–1972, Australian novelist, author of *Lucinda Brayford* (1946) and of the Langton tetralogy *The Cardboard Crown* (1952), *A Difficult Young Man* (1955), *Outbreak of Love* (1957), and *When Blackbirds Sing* (1962) 3 Sir Michael. born 1955, British theatre director; artistic director of the Royal Shakespeare Company from 2003

Boyd Orr n John, 1st Baron Boyd Orr of Brechin Mearns. 1880–1971, Scottish biologist; director general of the United Nations Food and Agriculture Organization: Nobel peace prize 1949

Boyer n Charles, known as *the Great Lover*. 1899–1978, French film actor

boyfriend n a male friend with whom a person is romantically or sexually involved

Boyle n 1 Robert. 1627–91, Irish scientist who helped to dissociate chemistry from alchemy. He established that air has weight and studied the behaviour of gases; author of *The Sceptical Chymist* (1661) 2 Danny. born 1956, English film director whose work includes *Trainspotting* (1996) and *Slumdog Millionaire* (2008); artistic director of the opening ceremony of the London 2012 Olympics

Boyle's law n the principle that the pressure of a gas varies inversely with its volume at constant temperature [after Robert Boyle]

Boyne n a river in the E Republic of Ireland, rising in the Bog of Allen and flowing northeast to the Irish Sea: William III of England defeated the deposed James II in a battle (**Battle of the Boyne**) on its banks in 1690, completing the overthrow of the Stuart cause in Ireland. Length: about 112 km (70 miles)

Boyoma Falls pl n a series of seven cataracts in the NE Democratic Republic of Congo, on the upper River Congo: forms an unnavigable stretch of 90 km (56 miles), which falls 60 m (200 ft). Former name: **Stanley Falls**

boy scout n See Queen's Guide

Bozcaada n the Turkish name for Tenedos

Bozen n the German name for Bolzano

BP 1 blood pressure 2 British Pharmacopoeia

bpi bits per inch (used of a computer tape)

Bq *physics* becquerel

Br *chem* bromine

Br. 1 Breton 2 Britain 3 British

bra n a woman's undergarment for covering and supporting the breasts [from *brassiere*]

braaivleis (brye-flayss) *S African*. n 1 a grill on which food is cooked over hot charcoal, usually outdoors 2 an outdoor party at which food like this is served ▷ vb 3 to cook (food) in this way ▶ Also: **braai** [Afrikaans]

Brabant n 1 a former duchy of W Europe: divided when Belgium became independent (1830), the south forming the Belgian provinces of Antwerp and Brabant and the north forming the province of North Brabant in the Netherlands 2 a former province of central Belgium; replaced in 1995 by the provinces of **Flemish Brabant** and **Walloon Brabant**

Brabham n Sir John Arthur, known as *Jack*. 1926–2014, Australian motor-racing driver: Formula One world champion 1959, 1960, and 1966

brace n 1 something that steadies, binds, or holds up another thing 2 a beam or prop, used to stiffen a framework 3 a hand tool for drilling holes 4 a pair, esp. of game birds 5 either of a pair of characters, {}, used for connecting lines of printing or writing 6 See **braces** ▷ vb **bracing, braced** 7 to steady or prepare (oneself) before an impact 8 to provide, strengthen, or fit with a brace [Latin *bracchia* arms]

brace and bit n a hand tool for boring holes, consisting of a cranked handle into which a drilling bit is inserted

bracelet n an ornamental chain or band worn around the arm or wrist [Latin *bracchium* arm]

bracelets pl n *slang* handcuffs

braces pl n 1 *Brit and NZ* a pair of straps worn over the shoulders for holding up the trousers 2 an appliance of metal bands and wires for correcting unevenness of teeth

brachiopod (brake-ee-oh-pod) n an invertebrate sea animal with a shell consisting of two valves [Greek *brakhiōn* arm + *pous* foot]

brachium (brake-ee-um) n, pl **brachia** (brake-ee-a) *anatomy* the arm, esp. the upper part [Latin *bracchium* arm]

bracing adj refreshing: *the bracing climate*

bracken n 1 a fern with large fronds 2 a clump of these ferns [Scandinavian]

bracket n 1 a pair of characters, [], (), or {}, used to enclose a section of writing or printing 2 a group or category falling within certain defined limits: *the lower income bracket* 3 an L-shaped or other support fixed to a wall to hold a shelf, etc. ▷ vb **-eting, -eted** 4 to put (written or printed matter) in brackets 5 to group or class together [Latin *braca* breeches]

brackish adj (of water) slightly salty [Middle Dutch *brac*]

Bracknell n a town in SE England, in Bracknell Forest unitary authority, Berkshire, designated a new town in 1949. Pop: 70 795 (2001)

Bracknell Forest n a unitary authority in SE England, in E Berkshire. Pop: 110 100 (2003 est). Area: 109 sq km (42 sq miles)

bract n a leaf, usually small and scaly, growing at the base of a flower [Latin *bractea* thin metal plate]

brad n a small tapered nail with a small head [Old English *brord* point]

Bradbury n 1 Sir Malcolm (Stanley). 1932–2000, British novelist and critic. His novels include *The History Man* (1975), *Rates of Exchange* (1983), *Cuts* (1988), and *Doctor Criminale* (1992) 2 Ray. 1920–2012, US science-fiction writer. His novels include *Fahrenheit 451* (1953), *Death is a Lonely Business* (1986), and *A Graveyard for Lunatics* (1990)

Bradford n 1 an industrial city in N England, in Bradford unitary authority, West Yorkshire: a centre of the woollen industry from the 14th century and of the worsted trade from the 18th century; university (1966). Pop: 293 717 (2001) 2 a unitary authority in West Yorkshire. Pop: 477 800 (2003 est). Area: 370 sq km (143 sq miles)

Bradlaugh n Charles. 1833–91, British radical and freethinker: barred from taking his seat in parliament (1880–86) for refusing to take the parliamentary oath

b

Bradley n 1 A(ndrew) C(ecil). 1851–1935, English critic; author of *Shakespearian Tragedy* (1904) 2 F(rancis) H(erbert). 1846–1924, English idealist philosopher and metaphysical thinker; author of *Ethical Studies* (1876), *Principles of Logic* (1883), and *Appearance and Reality* (1893) 3 Henry. 1845–1923, English lexicographer; one of the editors of the *Oxford English Dictionary* 4 James. 1693–1762, English astronomer, who discovered the aberration of light and the nutation of the earth's axis

Bradman n Sir Don(ald George). 1908–2001, Australian cricketer; in 52 test matches (1928–48) he scored 6,996 runs at an average of 99.94, by far the game's highest

Bradstreet n Anne (Dudley). ?1612–72, US poet, born in England: regarded as the first significant US poet

brae n Scot a hill or slope [Middle English bra]

Braemar n a village in NE Scotland, in Aberdeenshire; Balmoral Castle is nearby: site of the Royal Braemar Gathering, an annual Highland Games meeting

brag vb bragging, bragged 1 to speak arrogantly and boastfully ▷ n 2 boastful talk or behaviour 3 a card game similar to poker [origin unknown]

Braga n a city in N Portugal: capital of the Roman province of Lusitania; 12th-century cathedral, seat of the Primate of Portugal. Pop: 164 193 (2001). Ancient name: Bracara Augusta

Bragg n 1 Billy. born 1957, British rock singer and songwriter, noted for his political protest songs; recordings include *Between the Wars* (1985), *Workers' Playtime* (1988), *Mermaid Avenue* (1998), and *England, Half English* (2002) 2 Melvyn, Baron. born 1939, British novelist, broadcaster, and television executive; presenter of *The South Bank Show* since 1978 3 Sir William Henry. 1862–1942, British physicist, who shared a Nobel prize for physics (1915) with his son, for their study of crystal structures by means of X-rays 4 his son, Sir (William) Lawrence, 1890–1971, British physicist

braggart n a person who boasts loudly or exaggeratedly

Brahe n Tycho. 1546–1601, Danish astronomer, who designed and constructed instruments that he used to plot accurately the positions of the planets, sun, moon, and stars

Brahma n 1 a Hindu god, the Creator 2 same as Brahman (2)

Brahman n, pl -mans 1 Also: Brahmin a member of the highest or priestly caste in the Hindu caste system 2 Hinduism the ultimate and impersonal divine reality of the universe [Sanskrit: prayer] ▷ **Brahmanic** adj

Brahmaputra n a river in S Asia, rising in SW Tibet as the Tsangpo and flowing through the Himalayas and NE India to join the Ganges at its delta in Bangladesh. Length: about 2900 km (1800 miles)

Brahms n Johannes. 1833–97, German composer, whose music, though idealist in form, exhibits a strong lyrical romanticism. His works include four symphonies, four concertos, chamber music, and *A German Requiem* (1868)

braid vb 1 to interweave (hair, thread, etc.) 2 to decorate with an ornamental trim or border ▷ n 3 a length of hair that has been braided 4 narrow ornamental tape of woven silk, wool, etc. [Old English bregdan] ▷ **braiding** n

Brăila n a port in E Romania: belonged to Turkey (1544–1828). Pop: 192 000 (2005 est)

braille¹ n a system of writing for blind people consisting of raised dots interpreted by touch

braille² n Louis. 1809–52, French inventor, musician, and teacher of the blind, who himself was blind from the age of three and who devised the Braille system of raised writing

brain n 1 the soft mass of nervous tissue within the skull of vertebrates that controls and coordinates the nervous system 2 (often pl) informal intellectual ability: he's got brains 3 informal an intelligent person 4 on the brain informal constantly in mind: I had that song on the brain 5 the brains informal a person who plans and organizes something: the brains behind the bid ▷ vb 6 slang to hit

(someone) hard on the head [Old English brægen]

brainchild n informal an idea or plan produced by creative thought

braindead adj 1 having suffered brain death 2 informal stupid

brain death n complete stoppage of breathing due to irreparable brain damage

brain drain n informal the emigration of scientists, technologists, academics, etc.

Braine n John (Gerard). 1922–86, English novelist, whose works include *Room at the Top* (1957) and *Life at the Top* (1962)

brainfood n any foodstuff containing nutrients thought to promote brain function

brainless adj stupid or foolish

brainstorm n 1 informal a sudden mental aberration 2 a sudden and violent attack of insanity 3 informal same as brainwave

brainstorming n a thorough discussion to solve problems or create ideas

brains trust n a group of knowledgeable people who discuss topics in public or on radio or television

brain-teaser n informal a difficult problem

brainwash vb to cause (a person) to alter his or her beliefs, by methods based on isolation, sleeplessness, etc. ▷ **brainwashing** n

brainwave n Brit informal a sudden idea or inspiration

brain wave n a fluctuation of electrical potential in the brain

brainy adj brainier, brainiest informal clever; intelligent

braise vb braising, braised to cook (food) slowly in a closed pan with a small amount of liquid [Old French brese live coals]

brak¹ (bruck) n S African a crossbred dog; mongrel [Dutch]

brak² (bruck) adj S African (of water) slightly salty; brackish [Afrikaans]

brake¹ n 1 a device for slowing or stopping a vehicle 2 something that slows down or stops progress: he put a brake on my enthusiasm ▷ vb braking, braked 3 to slow down or cause to slow down, by or as if by using a brake [Middle Dutch braeke]

brake² n Brit an area of dense undergrowth; thicket [Old English bracu]

brake horsepower n the rate at which an engine does work, measured by the resistance of an applied brake

brake light n a red light at the rear of a motor vehicle that lights up when the brakes are applied

brake shoe n a curved metal casting that acts as a brake on a wheel

Brakpan n a city in E South Africa: gold-mining centre. Pop: 62 116 (2001)

Bramante n Donato. ?1444–1514, Italian architect and artist of the High Renaissance. He modelled his designs for domed centrally planned churches on classical Roman architecture

bramble n 1 a prickly plant or shrub such as the blackberry 2 Scot, N English and NZ a blackberry [Old English brǣmbel] ▷ **brambly** adj

bran n husks of cereal grain separated from the flour [Old French]

Branagh n Sir Kenneth. born 1961, British actor and director, born in Northern Ireland. He founded the Renaissance Theatre Company in 1986. His films include *Henry V* (1989), *Mary Shelley's Frankenstein* (1994), *Hamlet* (1997), and *Harry Potter and the Chamber of Secrets* (2002)

branch n 1 a secondary woody stem extending from the trunk or main branch of a tree 2 one of a number of shops, offices, or groups that belongs to a central organization: he was transferred to their Japanese branch 3 a subdivision or subsidiary section of something larger or more complex: branches of learning ▷ vb 4 to divide, then develop in different directions [Late Latin branca paw] ▷ **branchlike** adj

branch off vb to diverge from the main way, road, topic, etc.

branch out *vb* to expand or extend one's interests

Brancusi *n* Constantin. 1876–1957, Romanian sculptor, noted for his streamlined abstractions of animal forms

brand *n* **1** a particular product or a characteristic that identifies a particular producer **2** a trade name or trademark **3** a particular kind or variety **4** an identifying mark made, usually by burning, on the skin of animals as a proof of ownership **5** an iron used for branding animals **6** a mark of disgrace **7** *archaic or poetic* a flaming torch ▷ *vb* **8** to label, burn, or mark with or as if with a brand **9** to label (someone): *he was branded a war criminal* [Old English: fire]

Brandenburg *n* **1** a state in NE Germany, part of East Germany until 1990. A former electorate, it expanded under the Hohenzollerns to become the kingdom of Prussia (1701). The district east of the Oder River became Polish in 1945. Capital: Potsdam. Pop: 2 575 000 (2003 est). Area: 29 481 sq km (11 219 sq miles) **2** a city in NE Germany: former capital of the Prussian province of Brandenburg. Pop: 75 485 (2003 est)

Brandenburg Gate *n* the only remaining city gate in Berlin, built by Friedrich Wilhelm II of Prussia in 1788–1791 as a symbol of peace and now one of the city's landmarks

brandish *vb* to wave (a weapon, etc.) in a triumphant or threatening way [Old French *brandir*]

brand-new *adj* absolutely new

Brando *n* Marlon. 1924–2004, US actor; his films include *On the Waterfront* (1954) and *The Godfather* (1972), for both of which he won Oscars, *Last Tango in Paris* (1972), *Apocalypse Now* (1979), *A Dry White Season* (1989), and *Don Juan de Marco* (1995)

Brandt *n* **1** Bill, full name *William Brandt*. 1905–83, British photographer. His photographic books include *The English at Home* (1936) and *Perspectives of Nudes* (1961) **2** Georg. 1694–1768, Swedish chemist, who isolated cobalt (1742) and exposed fraudulent alchemists **3** Willy. 1913–92, German statesman; socialist chancellor of West Germany (1969–74); chairman of the Social Democratic party (1964–87). His policy of détente and reconciliation with E Europe brought him international acclaim. Nobel peace prize 1971

brandy *n*, *pl* **-dies** an alcoholic spirit distilled from wine [Dutch *brandewijn*]

brandy snap *n* a crisp sweet biscuit, rolled into a cylinder

Branson *n* Sir Richard. born 1950, British entrepreneur. In 1969 he founded the Virgin record company, adding other interests later, including Virgin Atlantic Airways (1984), Virgin Radio (1993), and the Virgin Rail Group (1996): made the fastest crossing of the Atlantic by boat (1986) and the first of the Pacific by hot-air balloon (1991)

Brantford *n* a city in central Canada, in SW Ontario. Pop: 86 417 (2001)

Branting *n* Karl Hjalmar. 1860–1925, Swedish politician; prime minister (1920; 1921–23; 1924–25). He founded Sweden's welfare state and shared the Nobel peace prize 1921

Braque *n* Georges. 1882–1963, French painter who developed cubism (1908–14) with Picasso

brash *adj* **1** tastelessly or offensively loud, or showy: *brash modernization* **2** impudent or bold: *I thought it was very brash of her to ask me* [origin unknown] ▶ **brashness** *n*

Brasil *n* the Portuguese spelling of **Brazil**

Brasília *n* the capital of Brazil (since 1960), on the central plateau: the former capital was Rio de Janeiro. Pop: 3 341 000 (2005 est)

Braşov *n* an industrial city in central Romania: formerly a centre for expatriate Germans; ceded by Hungary to Romania in 1920. Pop: 249 000 (2005 est). Former name (1950–61): Stalin. German name: Kronstadt. Hungarian name: Brassó

brass *n* **1** an alloy of copper and zinc **2** an object, ornament, or utensil made of brass **3 a** the large family of wind instruments including the trumpet, trombone, etc. made of brass **b** instruments of this family forming a section in an orchestra **4** same as **top brass 5** N English dialect money **6** Brit an engraved brass memorial tablet in a church **7** informal bold self-confidence; nerve [Old English *bræs*]

Brassaï *n* real name *Gyula Halész*. 1899–1984, French photographer, artist, and writer, born in Hungary: noted for his photographs of Paris by night

brass band *n* a group of musicians playing brass and percussion instruments

brasserie *n* a bar or restaurant serving drinks and cheap meals [French *brasser* to stir]

brass hat *n* Brit informal a top-ranking official, esp. a military officer

brassica *n* any plant of the cabbage and turnip family [Latin: cabbage]

brassiere *n* same as **bra** [French]

Brassó *n* the Hungarian name for **Braşov**

brass rubbing *n* an impression of an engraved brass tablet made by rubbing a paper placed over it with heelball or chalk

brass tacks *pl n* **get down to brass tacks** *informal* to discuss the realities of a situation

brassy *adj* **brassier, brassiest 1** brazen or flashy **2** like brass, esp. in colour **3** (of sound) harsh and strident

brat *n* a child, esp. one who is unruly [origin unknown]

Bratislava *n* the capital of Slovakia since 1918, a port on the River Danube; capital of Hungary (1541–1784) and seat of the Hungarian parliament until 1848. Pop: 428 672 (2001). German name: **Pressburg**. Hungarian name: **Pozsony**

Brattain *n* Walter Houser. 1902–87, US physicist, who shared the Nobel prize for physics (1956) with W. B. Shockley and John Bardeen for their invention of the transistor

Braun *n* **1** Eva. 1910–45, Adolf Hitler's mistress, whom he married shortly before their suicides in 1945 **2** Karl Ferdinand. 1850–1918, German physicist, who invented crystal diodes (leading to the development of crystal radio) and the oscilloscope. He shared the Nobel prize for physics (1909) with Marconi **3** See (Wernher) **von Braun**

Braunschweig *n* the German name for **Brunswick**

bravado *n* an outward display of self-confidence [Spanish *bravada*]

brave *adj* **1** having or displaying courage, resolution, or daring **2** fine; splendid: *a brave sight* ▷ *n* **3** a warrior of a Native American tribe of N America ▷ *vb* **braving, braved 4** to confront with resolution or courage: *she braved the 21 miles of Lake Tahoe* [Italian *bravo*] ▶ **bravery** *n*

bravo *interj* **1** well done! ▷ *n* **2** (*pl* **-vos**) a cry of 'bravo' **3** (*pl* **-voes** *or* **-vos**) a hired killer or assassin [Italian]

bravura *n* **1** a display of boldness or daring **2** *music* brilliance of execution [Italian]

brawl *n* **1** a loud disagreement or fight ▷ *vb* **2** to quarrel or fight noisily [probably from Dutch *brallen* to boast]

brawn *n* **1** strong well-developed muscles **2** physical strength **3** Brit and NZ a seasoned jellied loaf made from the head of a pig [Old French *braon* meat] ▶ **brawny** *adj*

bray *vb* **1** (of a donkey) to utter its characteristic loud harsh sound **2** to utter something with a loud harsh sound ▷ *n* **3** the loud harsh sound uttered by a donkey **4** a similar loud sound [Old French *braire*]

Braz. Brazil(ian)

braze *vb* **brazing, brazed** to join (two metal surfaces) by fusing brass between them [Old French: to burn]

brazen *adj* **1** shameless and bold **2** made of or resembling brass **3** having a ringing metallic sound ▷ **4 brazen it out** to face and overcome a difficult or embarrassing situation boldly or shamelessly ▶ **brazenly** *adv*

brazier¹ (bray-zee-er) *n* a portable metal container for burning charcoal or coal [French *braise* live coals]

brazier² *n* a worker in brass

brazil *n* **1** the red wood of various tropical trees of America **2** same as **brazil nut** [Old Spanish *brasa* glowing coals; referring to the redness of the wood]

Brazil *n* a republic in South America, comprising about half the area and half the population of South America: colonized by the Portuguese from 1500 onwards; became independent in 1822 and a republic in 1889; consists chiefly of the tropical Amazon basin in the north, semiarid scrub in the northeast, and a vast central tableland; an important producer of coffee and minerals, esp. iron ore. Official language: Portuguese. Religion: Roman Catholic majority. Currency: real. Capital: Brasília. Pop: 201 009 622 (2013 est). Area: 8 511 957 sq km (3 286 470 sq miles)

Brazilian *adj* **1** of or relating to Brazil or its inhabitants ▷ *n* **2** a native or inhabitant of Brazil

brazil nut *n* a large three-sided nut of a tropical American tree

Brazzaville *n* the capital of Congo-Brazzaville, in the south on the River Congo. Pop: 1 153 000 (2005 est) [C19: named after Pierre de *Brazza* (1852–1905), French explorer]

breach *n* **1** a breaking of a promise, obligation, etc. **2** any serious disagreement or separation **3** a crack, break, or gap ▷ *vb* **4** to break (a promise, law, etc.) **5** to break through or make an opening or hole in [Old English *bræc*]

USAGE See at breech.

breach of promise *n law* (formerly) failure to carry out one's promise to marry

breach of the peace *n law* an offence against public order causing an unnecessary disturbance of the peace

bread *n* **1** a food made from a dough of flour or meal mixed with water or milk, usually raised with yeast and then baked **2** necessary food **3** *slang* money ▷ *vb* **4** to cover (food) with breadcrumbs before cooking [Old English *brēad*]

bread and butter *n informal* a means of support; livelihood

breadboard *n* **1** a wooden board on which bread is sliced **2** an experimental arrangement of electronic circuits

breadfruit *n*, *pl* **-fruits** or **-fruit** a tree of the Pacific Islands, whose edible round fruit has a texture like bread when baked

breadline *n* **on the breadline** impoverished; living at subsistence level

breadth *n* **1** the extent or measurement of something from side to side **2** openness and lack of restriction, esp. of viewpoint or interest; liberality [Old English *brād* broad]

breadwinner *n* a person supporting a family with his or her earnings

break *vb* **breaking, broke, broken 1** to separate or become separated into two or more pieces **2** to damage or become damaged so as not to work **3** to burst or cut the surface of (skin) **4** to fracture (a bone) in (a limb, etc.) **5** to fail to observe (an agreement, promise, or law): *they broke their promise* **6** to reveal or be revealed: *she broke the news gently* **7** (foll. by *with*) to separate oneself from **8** to discontinue or become discontinued: *to break a journey* **9** to bring or come to an end: *the winter weather broke at last* **10** to weaken or overwhelm or be weakened or overwhelmed, as in spirit: *he felt his life was broken by his illness* **11** to cut through or penetrate: *silence broken by shouts* **12** to improve on or surpass: *she broke three world records* **13** (often foll. by *in*) to accustom (a horse) to the bridle and saddle, to being ridden, etc. **14** (foll. by *of*) to cause (a person) to give up (a habit): *this cure will break you of smoking* **15** to weaken the impact or force of: *this net will break his fall* **16** to decipher: *to break a code* **17** to lose the order of: *to break ranks* **18** to reduce to poverty or the state of bankruptcy **19** to come into being: *light broke over the mountains* **20** (foll. by *into*) **a** to burst into (song, laughter, etc.) **b** to change to (a faster pace) **21** to open with explosives: *to break a safe* **22 a** (often foll. by *against*) (of waves) to strike violently **b** (of waves) to collapse into foam or surf **23** *snooker* to scatter the balls at the start of a game **24** *boxing, wrestling* (of two fighters) to separate from a clinch **25** (of the male voice) to undergo a change in register, quality, and range at puberty **26** to interrupt the flow of current in (an electrical circuit) **27 break camp** to pack up and leave a camp **28 break even** to make neither a profit nor a loss **29 break the mould** to make a change that breaks an established habit or pattern ▷ *n* **30** the act or result of breaking; fracture **31** a brief rest **32** a sudden rush, esp. to escape: *they made a sudden break for freedom* **33** any sudden interruption in a continuous action **34** *Brit and NZ* a short period between classes at school **35 a** (short) holiday **36** *informal* a fortunate opportunity, esp. to prove oneself **37** *informal* a piece of good or bad luck **38** *billiards, snooker* a series of successful shots during one turn **39** *snooker* the opening shot that scatters the placed balls **40** a discontinuity in an electrical circuit **41 break of day** the dawn ▶ See also **breakaway, break down**, etc. [Old English *brecan*] ❭ **breakable** *adj*

breakage *n* **1** the act or result of breaking **2** compensation or allowance for goods damaged while in use, transit, etc.

breakaway *n* **1** loss or withdrawal of members from an association, club, etc. **2** *Austral* a stampede of cattle, esp. at the smell of water ▷ *adj* **3** dissenting: *a breakaway faction* ▷ *vb* **break away 4** to leave hastily or escape **5** to withdraw or quit

break dance *n* **1** an acrobatic dance style associated with hip-hop music, originating in the 1980s ▷ *vb* **break-dance (-dancing, -danced) 2** to perform a break dance ❭ **break dancing** *n*

break down *vb* **1** to cease to function; become ineffective **2** to give way to strong emotion or tears **3** to crush or destroy **4** to have a nervous breakdown **5** to separate into component parts: *with exercise the body breaks down fat to use as fuel* **6** to separate or cause to separate into simpler chemical elements; decompose **7** to analyse or be subjected to analysis ▷ *n* **breakdown 8** an act or instance of breaking down; collapse **9** same as **nervous breakdown 10** an analysis of something into its parts

breaker *n* **1** a large sea wave with a white crest or one that breaks into foam on the shore **2** a citizens' band radio operator

breakfast *n* **1** the first meal of the day ▷ *vb* **2** to eat breakfast [BREAK + FAST²]

break in *vb* **1** to enter a building, illegally, esp. by force **2** to interrupt **3** to accustom (a person or animal) to normal duties or practice **4** to use or wear (new shoes or new equipment) until comfortable or running smoothly ▷ *n* **break-in 5** the act of illegally entering a building, esp. by thieves

breaking point *n* the point at which something or someone gives way under strain

breakneck *adj* (of speed or pace) excessively fast and dangerous

break off *vb* **1** to sever or detach **2** to end (a relationship or association) **3** to stop abruptly

break out *vb* **1** to begin or arise suddenly: *fighting broke out between the two factions* **2** to make an escape, esp. from prison **3 break out in** to erupt in (a rash or spots) ▷ *n* **break-out 4** an escape, esp. from prison

break through *vb* **1** to penetrate **2** to achieve success after lengthy efforts ▷ *n* **breakthrough 3** a significant development or discovery

break up *vb* **1** to separate or cause to separate **2** to put an end to (a relationship) or (of a relationship) to come to an end **3** to dissolve or cause to dissolve: *the meeting broke up at noon* **4** *Brit* (of a school) to close for the holidays ▷ *n* **break-up 5** a separation or disintegration

breakwater *n* a massive wall built out into the sea to protect a shore or harbour from the force of waves

bream *n, pl* **bream 1** a freshwater fish covered with silvery scales **2** a food fish of European seas **3** a food fish of Australasian seas [Old French *bresme*]

Bream *n* Julian (Alexander). born 1933, English guitarist and lutenist

breast *n* **1** either of the two soft fleshy milk-secreting glands on a woman's chest **2** the front part of the body from the neck to the abdomen; chest **3** the corresponding part in certain other mammals **4** the source of human emotions **5** the part of a garment that covers the breast **6 make a clean breast of something** to divulge truths about oneself ▷ *vb literary* **7** to reach the summit of: *breasting the mountain top* **8** to confront boldly; face: *breast the storm* [Old English *brēost*]

breastbone *n* same as **sternum**

breast-feed *vb* **-feeding, -fed** to feed (a baby) with milk from the breast; suckle

breastplate *n* a piece of armour covering the chest

breaststroke *n* a swimming stroke in which the arms are extended in front of the head and swept back on either side

breastwork *n fortifications* a temporary defensive work, usually breast-high

breath *n* **1** the taking in and letting out of air during breathing **2** a single instance of this **3** the air taken in or let out during breathing **4** the vapour, heat, or odour of air breathed out **5** a slight gust of air **6** a short pause or rest **7** a suggestion or slight evidence; suspicion: *trembling at the least breath of scandal* **8** a whisper or soft sound **9 catch one's breath a** to rest until breathing is normal **b** to stop breathing momentarily from excitement, fear, etc. **10 out of breath** gasping for air after exertion **11 save one's breath** to avoid useless talk **12 take someone's breath away** to overwhelm someone with surprise, etc. **13 under one's breath** in a quiet voice or whisper [Old English *brǣth*]

breathable *adj* **1** (of air) fit to be breathed **2** (of material) allowing air to pass through so that perspiration can evaporate

Breathalyser *or* **-lyzer** *n Brit trademark* a device for estimating the amount of alcohol in the breath [*breath* + (*an*)*alyser*] ▷ **breathalyse** *or* **-lyze** *vb*

breathe *vb* **breathing, breathed 1** to take in oxygen and give out carbon dioxide; respire **2** to exist; be alive **3** to rest to regain breath or composure **4** (esp. of air) to blow lightly **5** to exhale or emit: *the dragon breathed fire* **6** to impart; instil: *a change that breathed new life into Polish industry* **7** to speak softly; whisper **8 breathe again** *or* **freely** *or* **easily** to feel relief **9 breathe one's last** to die

breather *n informal* a short pause for rest

breathing *n* **1** the passage of air into and out of the lungs to supply the body with oxygen **2** the sound this makes

breathing space *n* a short period during which a difficult situation temporarily becomes less severe: *the cut in interest rates creates a breathing space for struggling businesses*

breathless *adj* **1** out of breath; gasping, etc. **2** holding one's breath or having it taken away by excitement, etc. **3** (esp. of the atmosphere) motionless and stifling ▷ **breathlessness** *n*

breathtaking *adj* causing awe or excitement

breath test *n* a chemical test of a driver's breath to determine the amount of alcohol consumed

Brecht *n* Bertolt. 1898–1956, German dramatist, theatrical producer, and poet, who developed a new style of "epic" theatre and a new theory of theatrical alienation, notable also for his wit and compassion. His early works include *The Threepenny Opera* (1928) and *Rise and Fall of the City of Mahagonny* (1930) (both with music by Kurt Weill). His later plays are concerned with moral and political dilemmas and include *Mother Courage and her Children* (1941), *The Good Woman of Setzuan* (1943), and *The Caucasian Chalk Circle* (1955) ▷ **Brechtian** *adj, n*

Brecon *or* **Brecknock** *n* **1** a town in SE Wales, in Powys: textile and leather industries. Pop: 7901 (2001) **2** short for **Breconshire**

Breconshire *or* **Brecknockshire** *n* (until 1974) a count of SE Wales, now mainly in Powys: over half its area forms the **Brecon Beacons National Park**

bred *vb* the past of **breed**

Breda *n* a city in the S Netherlands, in North Brabant province: residence of Charles II of England during his exile. Pop: 164 000 (2003 est)

bredie (breed-ee) *n S African* a meat and vegetable stew [Portuguese *bredo* ragout]

breech *n* **1** the buttocks **2** the part of a firearm behind the barrel [Old English *brēc*, plural of *brōc* leg covering]

> **USAGE** *Breech* is sometimes wrongly used as a verb where *breach* is meant: *the barrier/agreement was breached* (not *breeched*).

breech delivery *n* birth of a baby with the feet or buttocks appearing first

breeches *pl n* trousers extending to the knee or just below, worn for riding, etc.

breeches buoy *n* a pulley device with a life buoy and pair of breeches attached, which is used as a means of transference between ships or rescue from the sea

breed *vb* **breeding, bred 1** to produce new or improved strains of (domestic animals and plants) **2** to produce c cause to produce by mating **3** to bear (offspring) **4** to bring up; raise: *she was city bred* **5** to produce or be produced: *the agreement bred confidence between the two* ▷ *n* **6** a group of animals, esp. domestic animals, of a species, that have certain clearly defined characteristi **7** a kind, sort, or group: *he was a gentleman, a breed not great admired* **8** a lineage or race [Old English *brēdan*] ▷ **breeder** *n*

breeder reactor *n* a nuclear reactor that produces mo fissionable material than it uses

breeding *n* **1** the process of producing plants or animal by controlled methods of reproduction **2** the process of bearing offspring **3** the result of good upbringing or training

Breed's Hill *n* a hill in E Massachusetts, adjoining Bunker Hill: the true site of the Battle of Bunker Hill (1775)

breeze¹ *n* **1** a gentle or light wind **2** *informal* an easy tas ▷ *vb* **breezing, breezed 3** to move quickly or casually: *he breezed into the room* [probably from Old Spanish *briza*]

breeze² *n* ashes of coal, coke, or charcoal [French *braise* live coals]

breeze block *n* a light building brick made from the ashes of coal, coke, etc. bonded together by cement

breezy *adj* **breezier, breeziest 1** fresh; windy **2** casual o carefree

Bregenz *n* a resort in W Austria, the capital of Vorarlbe province. Pop: 26 752 (2001)

brekky *n, pl* **-kies** *slang, chiefly Austral* short for **breakfast**

Brel *n* Jacques. 1929–78, Belgian-born composer and singer, based in Paris. His songs include "Ne me quitte pas" ("Don't Leave Me")

Bremen *n* **1** a state of NW Germany, centred on the city of Bremen and its outport Bremerhaven. Pop: 663 000 (2003 est). Area: 404 sq km (156 sq miles) **2** an industri city and port in NW Germany, on the Weser estuary. P 544 853 (2003 est)

Bremerhaven *n* a port in NW Germany: an outport fo Bremen. Pop: 118 276 (2003 est). Former name (until 1947): **Wesermünde**

Brendel *n* Alfred. born 1931, Austrian pianist and poet

Bren gun *n* an air-cooled gas-operated light machine gun [after Br(no), Czech Republic, and En(field), Englan where it was made]

b

Brennan n Christopher John. 1870–1932, Australian poet and classical scholar, disciple of Mallarmé and exponent of French symbolism in Australian verse

Brenner Pass n a pass over the E Alps, between Austria and Italy. Highest point: 1372 m (4501 ft)

brent or especially US **brant** n a small goose with dark grey plumage and a short neck

Brent n a borough of NW Greater London. Pop: 267 800 (2003 est). Area: 44 sq km (17 sq miles)

Brentano n Clemens (Maria). 1778–1842, German romantic poet and compiler of fairy stories and folk songs esp. (with Achim von Arnim) the collection Des Knaben Wunderhorn (1805–08)

Brenton n Howard. born 1942, British dramatist, author of such controversial plays as The Churchill Play (1974), The Romans in Britain (1980), (with David Hare) Pravda (1985), and several topical satires with Tariq Ali

Brentwood n a residential town in SE England, in SW Essex near London. Pop: 47 593 (2001)

Brescia n a city in N Italy, in Lombardy: at its height in the 16th century. Pop: 187 567 (2001). Ancient name: Brixia

Breslau n the German name for Wrocław

Bresson n Robert. 1901–99, French film director: his films include Le Journal d'un curé de campagne (1950), Une Femme douce (1969), and L'Argent (1983)

Brest n 1 a port in NW France, in Brittany: chief naval station of the country, planned by Richelieu in 1631 and fortified by Vauban. Pop: 148 316 (2006) 2 a city in SW Belarus: Polish until 1795 and from 1921 to 1945. Pop: 299 000 (2005 est). Former name (until 1921): **Brest Litovsk**. Polish name: **Brześć nad Bugiem**

Bretagne n the French name for **Brittany**

brethren pl n archaic a plural of **brother**

USAGE This plural of brother, which has existed since at least 1200 AD, is now archaic in English. It is, however, used between fellow members of a religious group or order, or sometimes between fellow members of a group, political party, or community with shared interests: Iranian Shia brethren across the border; Baker's Republican brethren; his sporting brethren
---

Breton¹ adj 1 of or relating to Brittany or its inhabitants ▷ n 2 a native or inhabitant of Brittany 3 the Celtic language of Brittany

Breton² n André. 1896–1966, French poet and art critic: founder and chief theorist of surrealism, publishing the first surrealist manifesto in 1924

Breuer n 1 Josef. 1842–1925, Austrian physician: treated the mentally ill by hypnosis 2 Marcel Lajos. 1902–81, US architect and furniture designer, born in Hungary. He developed bent plywood and tubular metal furniture and designed the UNESCO building in Paris (1953–58)

breve n an accent (˘) placed over a vowel to indicate that it is short or is pronounced in a specified way [Latin brevis short]

breviary n, pl **-ries** RC Church a book of psalms, hymns, prayers, etc., to be recited daily [Latin brevis short]

brevity n 1 a short duration; brief time 2 lack of verbosity [Latin brevitas]

brew vb 1 to make (beer, ale, etc.) from malt and other ingredients by steeping, boiling, and fermentation 2 to prepare (a drink, such as tea) by infusing 3 to devise or plan: to brew a plot 4 to be in the process of being brewed 5 to be about to happen or forming: a rebellion was brewing ▷ n 6 a beverage produced by brewing, esp. tea or beer ▷ an instance of brewing: last year's brew [Old English brēowan] ▷ **brewer** n

brewery n, pl **-eries** a place where beer, ale, etc., is brewed

Brewster n Sir David. 1781–1868, Scottish physicist, noted for his studies of the polarization of light

Brezhnev n Leonid Ilyich. 1906–82, Soviet statesman; president of the Soviet Union (1977–82); general secretary of the Soviet Communist Party (1964–82)

Brian n Havergal. 1876–1972, English composer, who wrote 32 symphonies, including the large-scale Gothic Symphony (1919–27)

Brian Boru n ?941–1014, king of Ireland (1002–14): killed during the defeat of the Danes at the battle of Clontarf

Briand n Aristide. 1862–1932, French socialist statesman: prime minister of France 11 times. He was responsible for the separation of Church and State (1905) and he advocated a United States of Europe. Nobel peace prize 1926

briar¹ or **brier** n 1 a shrub of S Europe, with a hard woody root (briarroot) 2 a tobacco pipe made from this root [French bruyère]

briar² n same as **brier¹**

bribe vb **bribing, bribed** 1 to promise, offer, or give something, often illegally, to (a person) to receive services or gain influence ▷ n 2 a reward, such as money or favour, given or offered for this purpose [Old French briber to beg] ▷ **bribery** n

bric-a-brac n miscellaneous small ornamental objects [French]

Brice n Fanny, real name Fannie Borach. 1891–1951, US actress and singer. The film Funny Girl was based on her life

brick n 1 a rectangular block of baked or dried clay, used in building construction 2 the material used to make such blocks 3 any rectangular block: a brick of ice cream 4 bricks collectively 5 informal a reliable, trustworthy, or helpful person 6 drop a brick Brit and NZ informal to make a tactless or indiscreet remark ▷ vb 7 (foll. by in or up or over) to construct, line, pave, fill, or wall up with bricks: they bricked up access to the historic pillar [Middle Dutch bricke]

brickbat n 1 blunt criticism 2 a piece of brick used as a weapon [BRICK + BAT¹]

bricklayer n a person who builds with bricks

brick-red adj reddish-brown

bridal adj of a bride or a wedding [Old English brȳdealu bride ale]

bride n a woman who has just been or is about to be married [Old English brȳd]

bridegroom n a man who has just been or is about to be married [Old English brȳdguma]

bridesmaid n a girl or young woman who attends a bride at her wedding

bridge¹ n 1 a structure that provides a way over a railway, river, etc. 2 a platform from which a ship is piloted and navigated 3 the hard ridge at the upper part of the nose 4 a dental plate containing artificial teeth that is secured to natural teeth 5 a piece of wood supporting the strings of a violin, guitar, etc. ▷ vb **bridging, bridged** 6 to build or provide a bridge over (something) 7 to connect or reduce the distance between: talks aimed at bridging the gap between the two sides [Old English brycg]

bridge² n a card game for four players, based on whist, in which the trump suit is decided by bidding between the players [origin unknown]

Bridge n Frank. 1879–1941, English composer, esp. of chamber music. He taught Benjamin Britten

bridgehead n military a fortified or defensive position at the end of a bridge nearest to the enemy

Bridgend n a county borough in S Wales, created in 1996 from S Mid Glamorgan. Administrative centre: Bridgend Pop: 129 900 (2003 est). Area: 264 sq km (102 sq miles)

Bridge of Sighs n a covered 16th-century bridge in Venice, between the Doges' Palace and the prisons, through which prisoners were formerly led to trial or execution

Bridgeport n a port in SW Connecticut, on Long Island Sound. Pop: 139 664 (2003 est)

Bridges n Robert (Seymour). 1844–1930, English poet: poet laureate (1913–30)

b

Bridget n Saint Bridget **1** Also: **Bride, Brigid** 453–523 AD, Irish abbess; a patron saint of Ireland. Feast day: Feb 1 **2** Also: **Birgitta** ?1303-73, Swedish nun and visionary; patron saint of Sweden. Feast day: July 23

Bridgetown n the capital of Barbados, a port on the SW coast. Pop: 144 000 (2005 est)

bridgework n a partial denture attached to the surrounding teeth

bridging loan n a loan made to cover the period between two transactions, such as the buying of another house before the sale of the first is completed

Bridgman n Percy Williams. 1882–1961, US physicist: Nobel prize for physics (1946) for his work on high-pressure physics and thermodynamics

Bridgwater n a town in SW England, in central Somerset. Pop: 36 563 (2001)

Bridie n James, real name *Osborne Henry Mavor*. 1888–1951, Scottish physician and dramatist, who founded the Glasgow Citizens' Theatre. His plays include *The Anatomist* (1930)

bridle n **1** headgear for controlling a horse, consisting of straps and a bit and reins **2** something that curbs or restrains ▷ vb **-dling, -dled 3** to show anger or indignation: *he bridled at the shortness of her tone* **4** to put a bridle on (a horse) **5** to restrain; curb [Old English *brigdels*]

bridle path n a path suitable for riding or leading horses

Brie n **1** a soft creamy white cheese, similar to Camembert but milder **2** a mainly agricultural area in N France, between the Rivers Marne and Seine: noted esp. for its cheese

brief adj **1** short in duration **2** short in length or extent; scanty: *a brief bikini* **3** terse or concise ▷ n **4** a condensed statement or written synopsis **5** law a document containing all the facts and points of law of a case by which a solicitor instructs a barrister to represent a client **6** RC Church a papal letter that is less formal than a bull **7** Also called: **briefing** instructions **8** hold a brief for to argue for; champion **9** in brief in short; to sum up ▷ vb **10** to prepare or instruct (someone) by giving a summary of relevant facts **11** English law **a** to instruct (a barrister) by brief **b** to retain (a barrister) as counsel [Latin *brevis*] **> briefly** adv

briefcase n a flat portable case for carrying papers, books, etc.

briefs pl n men's or women's underpants without legs

brier¹ or **briar** n any of various thorny shrubs or other plants, such as the sweetbrier [Old English *brēr, brǣr*]

brier² n same as **briar¹**

brig¹ n nautical a two-masted square-rigged ship [from BRIGANTINE]

brig² n Scot and N English a bridge

Brig. Brigadier

brigade n **1** a military formation smaller than a division and usually commanded by a brigadier **2** a group of people organized for a certain task: *a rescue brigade* [Old French]

brigadier n a senior officer in an army, usually commanding a brigade

brigalow n Austral a type of acacia tree [from a native Australian language]

brigand n a bandit, esp. a member of a gang operating in mountainous areas [Old French]

brigantine n a two-masted sailing ship [Old Italian *brigantino* pirate ship]

Briggs n Henry. 1561-1631, English mathematician: introduced common logarithms

Brighouse¹ n a town in N England, in Calderdale unitary authority, West Yorkshire: machine tools, textiles, engineering. Pop: 32 360 (2001)

Brighouse² n Harold. 1882–1958, British novelist and dramatist, best known for his play *Hobson's Choice* (1915)

bright adj **1** emitting or reflecting much light; shining **2** (of colours) intense or vivid **3** full of promise: *a bright future* **4** lively or cheerful **5** quick-witted or clever ▷ adv **6** brightly: *the light burned bright in his office* [Old English *beorht*] **> brightly** adv **> brightness** n

Bright n John. 1811–89, British liberal statesman, economist, and advocate of free trade: with Richard Cobden he led the Anti-Corn-Law League (1838–46)

brighten vb **1** to make or become bright or brighter **2** to make or become cheerful

Brighton n a coastal resort in S England, in Brighton and Hove unitary authority, East Sussex: patronized by the Prince Regent, who had the Royal Pavilion built (1782); seat of the University of Sussex (1966) and the University of Brighton (1992). Pop: 134 293 (2001)

Brighton and Hove n a city and unitary authority in S England, in East Sussex. Pop: 251 500 (2003 est). Area: 72 sq km (28 sq miles)

brill n, pl **brill** or **brills** a European flatfish similar to the turbot [probably Cornish *brȳthel* mackerel]

Brillat-Savarin n Anthelme. 1755–1826, French lawyer and gourmet; author of *Physiologie du Goût* (1825)

brilliance or **brilliancy** n **1** great brightness **2** excellence in physical or mental ability **3** splendour

brilliant adj **1** shining with light; sparkling **2** (of a colour) vivid **3** splendid; magnificent: *a brilliant show* **4** of outstanding intelligence or intellect ▷ n **5** a diamond cut with many facets to increase its sparkle [French *brillant* shining]

brilliantine n a perfumed oil used to make the hair smooth and shiny [French]

brim n **1** the upper rim of a cup, bowl, etc. **2** a projecting edge of a hat ▷ vb **brimming, brimmed 3** to be full to the brim: *he saw the tears that brimmed in her eyes* [Middle High German *brem*] **> brimless** adj

brimful adj (foll. by of) completely filled with

brimstone n obsolete sulphur [Old English *brynstān*]

Brindisi n a port in SE Italy, in SE Apulia: important naval base in Roman times and a centre of the Crusades in the Middle Ages. Pop: 89 081 (2001). Ancient name: **Brundisium**

brindled adj brown or grey streaked with a darker colour: *a brindled dog* [Middle English *brended*]

Brindley n James. 1716–72, British canal builder, who constructed (1759–61) the Bridgewater Canal, the first i England

brine n **1** a strong solution of salt and water, used for pickling **2** literary the sea or its water [Old English *brīne*]

bring vb **bringing, brought 1** to carry, convey, or take (something or someone) to a designated place or perso **2** to cause to happen: *responsibility brings maturity* **3** to cau to come to mind: *it brought back memories* **4** to cause to be a certain state, position, etc.: *the punch brought him to his knees* **5** to make (oneself): *she couldn't bring herself to do it* **6** sell for: *the painting brought a large sum* **7** law **a** to institute (proceedings, charges, etc.) **b** to put (evidence, etc.) before a tribunal ▶ See also **bring about, bring down, e** [Old English *bringan*]

bring about vb to cause to happen: *a late harvest brought about by bad weather*

bring-and-buy sale n Brit and NZ an informal sale, often for charity, to which people bring items for sale and buy those that others have brought

bring down vb to cause to fall

bring forth vb to give birth to

bring forward vb **1** to move (a meeting or event) to an earlier date or time **2** to present or introduce (a subjec for discussion **3** accounting to transfer (a sum) to the to of the next page or column

bring in vb **1** to yield (income, profit, or cash) **2** to introduce (a legislative bill, etc.) **3** to return (a verdict)

bring off vb to succeed in achieving (something difficult)

bring out vb **1** to produce, publish, or have (a book) published **2** to expose, reveal, or cause to be seen: *he brought out the best in me* **3** (foll. by in) to cause (a person) t

become covered with (a rash, spots, etc.)

bring over *vb* to cause (a person) to change allegiances

bring round *vb* **1** to restore (a person) to consciousness after a faint **2** to convince (another person) of an opinion or point of view

bring to *vb* to restore (a person) to consciousness: *the smelling salts brought her to*

bring up *vb* **1** to care for and train (a child); rear **2** to raise (a subject) for discussion; mention **3** to vomit (food)

brinjal *n S African and Indian* dark purple tropical fruit, cooked and eaten as a vegetable [Portuguese *berinjela*]

brink *n* **1** the edge or border of a steep place **2** the land at the edge of a body of water **3 on the brink of** very near; on the point of: *on the brink of disaster* [Middle Dutch *brinc*]

brinkmanship *n* the practice of pressing a dangerous situation to the limit of safety in order to win an advantage

briny *adj* **brinier, briniest 1** of or like brine; salty ▷ *n* **2 the briny** *informal* the sea

brio *n* liveliness; vigour [Italian]

briquette *n* a small brick made of compressed coal dust, used for fuel [French]

Brisbane *n* a port in E Australia, the capital of Queensland: founded in 1824 as a penal settlement; vast agricultural hinterland. Pop: 2 189 878 (2013)

brisk *adj* **1** lively and quick; vigorous: *brisk trade* **2** invigorating or sharp: *brisk weather* **3** practical and businesslike: *his manner was brisk* [probably variant of BRUSQUE] ❭ **briskly** *adv*

brisket *n* beef from the breast of a cow [probably Scandinavian]

brisling *n* same as **sprat** [Norwegian]

Brissot *n* Jacques-Pierre. 1754–93, French journalist and revolutionary; leader of the Girondists: executed by the Jacobins

bristle *n* **1** any short stiff hair, such as on a pig's back **2** something resembling these hairs: *toothbrush bristle* ▷ *vb* **-tling, -tled 3** to stand up or cause to stand up like bristles **4** to show anger or indignation: *she bristled at the suggestion* **5** to be thickly covered or set: *the hedges bristled with blossom* [Old English *byrst*] ❭ **bristly** *adj*

Bristol *n* **1 City of Bristol** a port and industrial city in SW England, mainly in Bristol unitary authority, on the River Avon seven miles from its mouth on the Bristol Channel: a major port, trading with America, in the 17th and 18th centuries; the modern port consists chiefly of docks at Avonmouth and Portishead; noted for the **Clifton Suspension Bridge** (designed by I. K. Brunel, 1834) over the Avon gorge; Bristol university (1909) and University of the West of England (1992). Pop: 420 556 (2001) **2 City of Bristol** a unitary authority in SW England, created in 1996 from part of Avon county. Pop: 391 500 (2003 est). Area: 110 sq km (42 sq miles)

Bristol Channel *n* an inlet of the Atlantic, between S Wales and SW England, merging into the Severn estuary. Length: about 137 km (85 miles)

Bristow *n* Eric. born 1957, British darts player: world champion five times (1980–81, 1984–86)

Brit *n informal* a British person

Brit. **1** Britain **2** British

Britain *n* another name for **Great Britain, United Kingdom**

Britannia *n* a female warrior carrying a trident and wearing a helmet, personifying Great Britain

Britannia metal *n* an alloy of tin with antimony and copper

Britannic *adj* of Britain; British: *Her Britannic Majesty*

britches *pl n* same as **breeches**

British *adj* **1** of Britain or the British Commonwealth **2** denoting the English language as spoken and written in Britain ▷ *pl n* **3 the British** the people of Britain

British Antarctic Territory *n* a UK Overseas Territory in the S Atlantic (claims are suspended under the Antarctic Treaty): created in 1962 and consisting of the South Shetland Islands, the South Orkney Islands, and Graham Land; formerly part of the Falkland Islands Dependencies

British Cameroons *pl n* a former British trust territory of West Africa. See **Cameroon**

British Columbia *n* a province of W Canada, on the Pacific coast: largely mountainous with extensive forests, rich mineral resources, and important fisheries. Capital: Victoria. Pop: 4 400 057 (2011 est). Area: 930 532 sq km (359 279 sq miles). Abbreviation: **BC**

British Columbian *adj* **1** of or relating to British Columbia or its inhabitants ▷ *n* **2** a native or inhabitant of British Columbia

British East Africa *n* the former British possessions of Uganda, Kenya, Tanganyika, and Zanzibar, before their independence in the 1960s

British Guiana *n* the former name (until 1966) of Guyana

British Honduras *n* the former name of **Belize**

British India *n* the 17 provinces of India formerly governed by the British under the British sovereign: ceased to exist in 1947 when the independent states of India and Pakistan were created

British Indian Ocean Territory *n* a UK Overseas Territory in the Indian Ocean: consists of the Chagos Archipelago (formerly a dependency of Mauritius) and formerly included (until 1976) Aldabra, Farquhar, and Des Roches, now administratively part of the Seychelles. Diego Garcia is an important US naval base

British Isles *pl n* a group of islands in W Europe, consisting of Great Britain, Ireland, the Isle of Man, Orkney, Shetland, the Channel Islands belonging to Great Britain, and the islands adjacent to these

British Museum *n* a museum in London, founded in 1753: contains one of the world's richest collections of antiquities and (until 1997) most of the British Library

British North America *n* (formerly) Canada or its constituent regions or provinces that formed part of the British Empire

British Somaliland *n* a former British protectorate (1884–1960) in E Africa, on the Gulf of Aden: united with Italian Somaliland in 1960 to form Somalia (or the Somali Republic); in 1991 the self-styled republic of Somaliland, covering the same area as the former British Somaliland, declared itself independent and continues to function largely as a separate entity, though without international recognition

British Summer Time *n* a time set one hour ahead of Greenwich Mean Time: used in Britain from the end of March to the end of October, providing an extra hour of daylight in the evening. Abbreviation: **BST**

British Virgin Islands *pl n* a UK Overseas Territory in the Caribbean, consisting of 36 islands in the E Virgin Islands: formerly part of the Federation of the Leeward Islands (1871–1956). Capital: Road Town, on Tortola. Pop: 31 912 (2013 est). Area: 153 sq km (59 sq miles)

British West Africa *n* the former British possessions of Nigeria, The Gambia, Sierra Leone, and the Gold Coast, and the former trust territories of Togoland and Cameroons

British West Indies *pl n* a former name for the states in the Caribbean that are members of the Commonwealth: the Bahamas, Barbados, Jamaica, Trinidad and Tobago, Antigua and Barbuda, Saint Kitts-Nevis, Dominica, Grenada, Saint Lucia, and Saint Vincent and the Grenadines; along with the islands which remain as United Kingdom dependencies: Anguilla, the Cayman Islands, Montserrat, the Turks and Caicos Islands and the British Virgin Islands

Briton *n* **1 a** a native or inhabitant of Britain **2** *history* any of the early Celtic inhabitants of S Britain [of Celtic origin]

Brittany *n* a region of NW France, the peninsula between the English Channel and the Bay of Biscay:

b

settled by Celtic refugees from Wales and Cornwall during the Anglo-Saxon invasions; disputed between England and France until 1364. Breton name: **Breiz**. French name: **Bretagne**. Related adjective: **Breton**

Britten *n* (Edward) Benjamin, Baron Britten. 1913–76, English composer, pianist, and conductor. His works include the operas *Peter Grimes* (1945) and *Billy Budd* (1951), the choral works *Hymn to St Cecilia* (1942) and *A War Requiem* (1962), and numerous orchestral pieces

brittle *adj* 1 easily cracked or broken; fragile 2 curt or irritable: *a brittle reply* 3 hard or sharp in quality: *a brittle laugh* [Old English *brēotan* to break] **> brittly** *adv*

Brno *n* a city in the Czech Republic; formerly the capital of Moravia: the country's second largest city. Pop: 375 000 (2005 est). German name: **Brünn**

broach *vb* 1 to initiate or introduce (a topic) for discussion 2 to tap or pierce (a container) to draw off (a liquid) 3 to open in order to begin to use ▷ *n* 4 a spit for roasting meat [Latin *brochus* projecting]

broad *adj* 1 having great breadth or width 2 of vast extent: *broad plains* 3 not detailed; general 4 clear and open: *broad daylight* 5 obvious: *broad hints* 6 tolerant: *a broad view* 7 extensive: *broad support* 8 vulgar or coarse 9 strongly marked: *he spoke broad Australian English* ▷ *n* 10 *slang, chiefly US and Canad* a woman [Old English *brād*] **> broadly** *adv*

Broad *n* Stuart (Christopher John). born 1986, English cricketer; he has taken over 300 test match wickets

B-road *n* a secondary road in Britain

broadband *n* a telecommunications technique that uses a wide range of frequencies to allow messages to be sent simultaneously

broad bean *n* the large edible flattened seed of a Eurasian bean plant

broadcast *n* 1 a transmission or programme on radio or television ▷ *vb* **-casting, -cast** *or* **-casted** 2 to transmit (announcements or programmes) on radio or television 3 to take part in a radio or television programme 4 to make widely known throughout an area: *to broadcast news* 5 to scatter (seed, etc.) **> broadcaster** *n* **> broadcasting** *n*

broaden *vb* to make or become broad or broader; widen

broad gauge *n* a railway track with a greater distance between the lines than the standard gauge of 56½ inches

Broadlands *n* a Palladian mansion near Romsey in Hampshire: formerly the home of Lord Palmerston and Lord Mountbatten

broad-leaved *adj* denoting trees other than conifers; having broad rather than needle-shaped leaves

broadloom *adj* of or designating carpets woven on a wide loom

broad-minded *adj* 1 tolerant of opposing viewpoints; liberal 2 not easily shocked

Broadmoor *n* an institution in Berkshire, England, for housing and treating mentally ill criminals

Broads *pl n* the Broads 1 a group of shallow navigable lakes, connected by a network of rivers, in E England, in Norfolk and Suffolk 2 the region around these lakes: a tourist centre; several bird sanctuaries

broadsheet *n* a newspaper in a large format

broadside *n* 1 a strong or abusive verbal or written attack 2 *naval* the simultaneous firing of all the guns on one side of a ship 3 *nautical* the entire side of a ship ▷ *adv* 4 with a broader side facing an object

broadsword *n* a broad-bladed sword used for cutting rather than stabbing

Broadway *n* 1 a thoroughfare in New York City, famous for its theatres: the centre of the commercial theatre in the US ▷ *adj* 2 of or relating to or suitable for the commercial theatre, esp. on Broadway

Broca *n* Paul. 1824–80, French surgeon and anthropologist who discovered the motor speech centre of the brain and did pioneering work in brain surgery

brocade *n* 1 a rich fabric woven with a raised design ▷ *vb* **-cading, -caded** 2 to weave with such a design [Spanish *brocado*]

broccoli *n* a variety of cabbage with greenish flower heads [Italian]

brochette (brosh-ett) *n* a skewer used for holding pieces of meat or vegetables while grilling [Old French *brochete*]

brochure *n* a pamphlet or booklet, esp. one containing introductory information or advertising [French]

Brocken *n* a mountain in central Germany: the highest peak of the Harz Mountains; important in German folklore. Height: 1142 m (3747 ft). The **Brocken Bow** or **Brocken Spectre** is an atmospheric phenomenon in which an observer, when the sun is low, may see his enlarged shadow against the clouds, often surrounded by coloured lights

broderie anglaise *n* open embroidery on white cotton, fine linen, etc. [French: English embroidery]

Brodsky *n* Joseph, original name *Iosif Aleksandrovich Brodsky*. 1940–96, US poet, born in the Soviet Union. His collections include *The End of a Beautiful Era* (1977). Nobel prize for literature 1987

broekies (brook-eez) *pl n* S African informal underpants [Afrikaans]

brogue¹ *n* a sturdy walking shoe, often with ornamental perforations [Irish Gaelic *bróg*]

brogue² *n* a broad gentle-sounding dialectal accent, esp that used by the Irish in speaking English [origin unknown]

broil *vb* same as **grill** (1) [Old French *bruillir*]

broiler *n* a young tender chicken suitable for roasting

broke *vb* 1 the past tense of **break** ▷ *adj* 2 *informal* having no money

broken *vb* 1 the past participle of **break** ▷ *adj* 2 fractured, smashed, or splintered 3 interrupted; disturbed: *broken sleep* 4 not functioning 5 (of a promise or contract) violated; infringed 6 (of the speech of a foreigner) imperfectly spoken: *broken English* 7 Also: **broken-in** made tame by training 8 exhausted or weakened, as through ill-health or misfortune

broken chord *n* same as **arpeggio**

broken-down *adj* 1 worn out, as by age or long use; dilapidated 2 not in working order

brokenhearted *adj* overwhelmed by grief or disappointment

Broken Hill *n* a town in SE Australia, in W New South Wales: mining centre for lead, silver, and zinc. Pop: 19 834 (2001)

broken home *n* a family which does not live together because the parents are separated or divorced

broker *n* 1 an agent who buys or sells goods, securities, etc.: *insurance broker* 2 a person who deals in second-hand goods [Anglo-French *brocour* broacher]

brokerage *n* commission charged by a broker

broker-dealer *n* same as **stockbroker**

brolga *n* a large grey Australian crane with a trumpeting call. Also called: **native companion**

brolly *n, pl* **-lies** *Brit, Austral and NZ informal* an umbrella

bromance *n informal* a close, non-sexual friendship between two men

Bromberg *n* the German name for **Bydgoszcz**

bromide *n* 1 *chem* any compound of bromine with another element or radical 2 a dose of sodium or potassium bromide given as a sedative 3 a boring, meaningless, or obvious remark

bromide paper *n* a type of photographic paper coated with an emulsion of silver bromide

bromine *n chem* a dark red liquid chemical element that gives off a pungent vapour. Symbol: **Br** [Greek *brōmos* bad smell]

Bromley *n* a borough of SE Greater London. Pop: 298 300 (2003 est). Area: 153 sq km (59 sq miles)

Bromsgrove *n* a town in W central England, in N Worcestershire. Pop: 29 237 (2001)

bronchial *adj* of or relating to both of the bronchi or the smaller tubes into which they divide

bronchiole *n* any of the smallest bronchial tubes

b

bronchitis *n* inflammation of the bronchial tubes, causing coughing and difficulty in breathing

bronchus (bronk-uss) *n, pl* **bronchi** (bronk-eye) either of the two main branches of the windpipe [Greek *bronkhos*]

bronco *n, pl* **-cos** (in the US and Canada) a wild or partially tamed horse [Mexican Spanish]

Brontë *n* **1** Anne, pen name *Acton Bell*. 1820–49, English novelist; author of *The Tenant of Wildfell Hall* (1847) **2** her sister, **Charlotte**, pen name *Currer Bell*. 1816–55, English novelist; author of *Jane Eyre* (1847), *Villette* (1853), and *The Professor* (1857) **3** her sister, **Emily** (**Jane**), pen name *Ellis Bell*. 1818–48, English novelist and poet; author of *Wuthering Heights* (1847)

brontosaurus *n* a very large plant-eating four-footed dinosaur that had a long neck and long tail [Greek *brontē* thunder + *sauros* lizard]

Bronx *n* **the Bronx** a borough of New York City, on the mainland, separated from Manhattan by the Harlem River. Pop: 1 363 198 (2003 est)

bronze *n* **1** an alloy of copper and smaller proportions of tin **2** a statue, medal, or other object made of bronze ▷ *adj* **3** made of or resembling bronze **4** yellowish-brown ▷ *vb* **bronzing, bronzed 5** (esp. of the skin) to make or become brown; tan [Italian *bronzo*]

Bronze Age *n* a phase of human culture, lasting in Britain from about 2000 to 500 BC during which weapons and tools were made of bronze

bronze medal *n* a medal awarded as third prize

Bronzino *n* Il, real name *Agnolo di Cosimo*. 1503–72, Florentine mannerist painter

brooch *n* an ornament with a hinged pin and catch, worn fastened to clothing [Old French *broche*]

brood *n* **1** a number of young animals, esp. birds, produced at one hatching **2** all the children in a family: often used jokingly ▷ *vb* **3** (of a bird) to sit on or hatch eggs **4** to think long and unhappily about something: *he brooded on his failure to avert the confrontation* [Old English *brōd*] ❯ **brooding** *n, adj*

broody *adj* **broodier, broodiest 1** moody; introspective **2** (of poultry) wishing to sit on or hatch eggs **3** *informal* (of a woman) wishing to have a baby

brook¹ *n* a natural freshwater stream [Old English *brōc*]

brook² *vb* to bear; tolerate: *she would brook no opposition* [Old English *brūcan*]

Brook *n* Peter (**Paul Stephen**). born 1925, British stage and film director, noted esp. for his experimental work in the theatre

Brooke *n* **1** Alan Francis. See Alanbrooke **2** Sir James. 1803–68, British soldier; first rajah of Sarawak (1841–63) **3** Rupert (**Chawner**). 1887–1915, British lyric poet, noted for his idealistic war poetry, which made him a national hero

Brooklyn *n* a borough of New York City, on the SW end of Long Island. Pop: 2 465 326 (2000)

Brookner *n* Anita. born 1928, British writer and art historian. Her novels include *Hotel du Lac* (1984), which won the Booker Prize, *Brief Lives* (1990), and *The Next Big Thing* (2002)

Brooks *n* **1** Geraldine. born 1955, Australian writer. Her novels include *March* (2005), which won the Pulitzer prize **2** Mel, real name *Melvyn Kaminsky*. born 1926, US comedy writer, actor, and film director. His films include *The Producers* (1968), *Blazing Saddles* (1974), *High Anxiety* (1977), and *Dracula: Dead and Loving It* (1996) **3** (**Troyal**) **Garth**. born 1962, US country singer and songwriter; his bestselling records include *Ropin' the Wind* (1991) and *Scarecrow* (2001)

Brooks Range *n* a mountain range in N Alaska. Highest peak: Mount Isto, 2761 m (9058 ft)

broom *n* **1** a type of long-handled sweeping brush **2** a yellow-flowered shrub **3 a new broom** a newly appointed official, etc., eager to make radical changes [Old English *brōm*]

broomstick *n* the long handle of a broom

Broonzy *n* William Lee Conley, called *Big Bill*. 1893–1958, US blues singer and guitarist

bros. *or* **Bros.** brothers

broth *n* a soup made by boiling meat, vegetables, etc. in water [Old English]

brothel *n* a house where men pay to have sexual intercourse with prostitutes [short for *brothel-house*, from Middle English *brothel* useless person]

brother *n* **1** a man or boy with the same parents as another person. Related adjective: **fraternal 2** a man belonging to the same group, trade union, etc. as another or others; fellow member **3** comrade; friend **4** *Christianity* a member of a male religious order [Old English *brōthor*]

brotherhood *n* **1** fellowship **2** an association, such as a trade union **3** the state of being a brother

brother-in-law *n, pl* **brothers-in-law 1** the brother of one's wife or husband **2** the husband of one's sibling

brotherly *adj* of or like a brother, esp. in showing loyalty and affection

brougham (brew-am) *n* a horse-drawn closed carriage with a raised open driver's seat in front [after Lord *Brougham*]

brought *vb* the past of **bring**

brouhaha *n* loud confused noise [French]

brow *n* **1** the part of the face from the eyes to the hairline; forehead **2** same as **eyebrow 3** the jutting top of a hill [Old English *brū*]

browbeat *vb* **-beating, -beat, -beaten** to frighten (someone) with threats

brown *adj* **1** of the colour of wood or the earth **2** (of bread) made from wheatmeal or wholemeal flour **3** deeply tanned ▷ *n* **4** the colour of wood or the earth **5** anything brown, such as brown paint or brown clothing: *clad in brown* ▷ *vb* **6** to make or become brown or browner, for example as a result of cooking [Old English *brūn*] ❯ **brownish** *adj*

Brown *n* **1** Sir Arthur Whitten. 1886–1948, British aviator who with J.W. Alcock made the first flight across the Atlantic (1919) **2** Ford Madox. 1821–93, British painter, associated with the Pre-Raphaelite Brotherhood. His paintings include *The Last of England* (1865) and *Work* (1865) **3** George (**Alfred**), Lord George-Brown. 1914–85, British Labour politician; vice-chairman and deputy leader of the Labour party (1960–70); foreign secretary 1966–68 **4** George Mackay. 1921–96, Scottish poet, novelist, and short-story writer. His works, which include the novels *Greenvoe* (1972) and *Magnus* (1973), reflect the history and culture of Orkney **5** (**James**) **Gordon**. born 1951, British Labour politician; Chancellor of the Exchequer (1997–2007); prime minister (2007–10) **6** Herbert Charles. 1912–2004, US chemist, who worked on the compounds of boron. Nobel prize for chemistry 1979 **7** James. 1933–2006, US soul singer and songwriter, noted for his dynamic stage performances and for his commitment to Black rights **8** John. 1800–59, US abolitionist leader, hanged after leading an unsuccessful rebellion of slaves at Harper's Ferry, Virginia **9** Lancelot, called *Capability Brown*. 1716–83, British landscape gardener **10** Michael (**Stuart**). born 1941, US physician: shared the Nobel prize for physiology or medicine (1985) for work on cholesterol **11** Robert. 1773–1858, Scottish botanist who was the first to observe the Brownian movement in fluids

brown bear *n* a large ferocious brownish bear of N America, Europe, and Asia

brown coal *n* same as **lignite**

Browne *n* **1** Coral (**Edith**). 1913–91, Australian actress: married to Vincent Price **2** Hablot Knight. See Phiz **3** Sir Thomas. 1605–82, English physician and author, noted for his magniloquent prose style. His works include *Religio Medici* (1642) and *Hydriotaphia or Urn Burial* (1658)

browned-off *adj informal, chiefly Brit* thoroughly bored and depressed

b

brownfield *adj* relating to an urban area which has previously been built on: *brownfield sites*

Brownian motion *n physics* the random movement of particles in a fluid, caused by continuous bombardment from molecules of the fluid [after Robert BROWN]

brownie *n* **1** (in folklore) an elf said to do helpful work, esp. household chores, at night **2** a small square nutty chocolate cake

Brownie Guide *or* **Brownie** *n* a member of the junior branch of the Guides

Brownie point *n* a notional mark to one's credit for being seen to do the right thing

browning *n Brit* a substance used to darken gravies

Browning *n* **1** Elizabeth Barrett. 1806–61, English poet and critic; author of the *Sonnets from the Portuguese* (1850) **2** her husband, **Robert**. 1812–89, English poet, noted for his dramatic monologues and *The Ring and the Book* (1868–69)

brown paper *n* a kind of coarse unbleached paper used for wrapping

brown rice *n* unpolished rice, in which the grains retain the outer yellowish-brown layer (bran)

Brown Shirt *n* **1** (in Nazi Germany) a storm trooper **2** a member of any fascist party or group

brown trout *n* a common brownish trout

browse *vb* **browsing, browsed** **1** to look through (a book or articles for sale) in a casual leisurely manner **2** *computers* to read hypertext, esp. on the World Wide Web **3** (of deer, goats, etc.) to feed upon vegetation by continual nibbling ▷ *n* **4** an instance of browsing [French *broust* bud]

browser *n computers* a software package that enables a user to read hypertext, esp. on the World Wide Web

Broz *n* Josip. original name of Marshal Tito. See **Tito**

Brubeck *n* Dave. 1920–2012, US modern jazz pianist and composer; formed his own quartet in 1951

Bruce *n* **1** James. 1730–94, British explorer, who discovered the source of the Blue Nile (1770) **2** Lenny. 1925–66, US comedian, whose satirical sketches, esp. of the sexual attitudes of his contemporaries, brought him prosecutions for obscenity, but are now regarded as full of insight as well as wit **3** Robert the Bruce. See **Robert I 4** Stanley Melbourne, 1st Viscount Bruce of Melbourne. 1883–1967, Australian statesman; prime minister, in coalition with Sir Earle Page's Country Party, of Australia (1923–29)

brucellosis *n* an infectious disease of cattle, goats, and pigs, caused by bacteria and transmittable to humans [after Sir David *Bruce*, bacteriologist]

Bruch *n* Max. 1838–1920, German composer, noted chiefly for his three violin concertos

Bruckner *n* Anton. 1824–96, Austrian composer and organist in the Romantic tradition. His works include nine symphonies, four masses, and a Te Deum

Brudenell *n* James Thomas, the 7th Earl of Cardigan. See **Cardigan**

Brueghel, Bruegel *or* **Breughel** *n* **1** Jan. 1568–1625, Flemish painter, noted for his detailed still lifes and landscapes **2** his father, **Pieter**, called *the Elder*. ?1525–69, Flemish painter, noted for his landscapes, his satirical paintings of peasant life, and his allegorical biblical scenes **3** his son, **Pieter**, called *the Younger*. ?1564–1637, Flemish painter, noted for his gruesome pictures of hell

Bruges *n* a city in NW Belgium, capital of West Flanders province: centre of the medieval European wool and cloth trade. Pop: 117 025 (2004 est). Flemish name: **Brugge**

bruise *vb* **bruising, bruised** **1** to injure (body tissue) without breaking the skin, usually with discoloration, or (of body tissue) to be injured in this way **2** to hurt (someone's feelings) **3** to damage (fruit) ▷ *n* **4** a bodily injury without a break in the skin, usually with discoloration [Old English *brȳsan*]

bruiser *n informal* a strong tough person, esp. a boxer or a bully

brumby *n, pl* **-bies** *Austral* **1** a wild horse **2** an unruly person [origin unknown]

Brummagem *n* **1** an informal name for **Birmingham**. Often shortened to: **Brum 2** (*sometimes not cap*) something that is cheap and flashy, esp. imitation jewellery ▷ *adj* **3** (*sometimes not cap*) cheap and gaudy; tawdry [C17: from earlier *Bromecham*, local variant of BIRMINGHAM]

Brummell *n* George Bryan, called *Beau Brummell*. 1778–1840, English dandy: leader of fashion in the Regency period

brunch *n* a meal eaten late in the morning, combining breakfast with lunch [BR(EAKFAST) + (L)UNCH]

Brundisium *n* the ancient name for **Brindisi**

Brunei *n* **1** a sultanate in NW Borneo, consisting of two separate areas on the South China Sea, otherwise bounded by Sarawak: controlled all of Borneo and parts of the Philippines and the Sulu Islands in the 16th century; under British protection since 1888; internally self-governing since 1971; became fully independent in 1984 as a member of the Commonwealth. The economy depends chiefly on oil and natural gas. Official language: Malay; English is also widely spoken. Religion: Muslim. Currency: Brunei dollar. Capital: Bandar Seri Begawan. Pop: 415 717 (2013 est). Area: 5765 sq km (2226 sq miles) **2** the former name of **Bandar Seri Begawan**

Brunel *n* **1** Isambard Kingdom. 1806–59, English engineer: designer of the Clifton Suspension Bridge (1828), many railway lines, tunnels, bridges, etc., and the steamships *Great Western* (1838), *Great Britain* (1845), and *Great Eastern* (1858) **2** his father, Sir **Marc Isambard**. 1769–1849, French engineer in England

Brunelleschi *n* Filippo. 1377–1446, Italian architect, whose works in Florence include the dome of the cathedral, the Pazzi chapel of Santa Croce, and the church of San Lorenzo

brunette *n* a girl or woman with dark brown hair [French]

Brüning *n* Heinrich. 1885–1970, German statesman; chancellor (1930–32). He was forced to resign in 1932, making way for the Nazis

Brünn *n* the German name for **Brno**

Bruno *n* **1** Franklin Roy, known as *Frank*. born 1961, British heavyweight boxer **2** Giordano. 1548–1600, Italian philosopher, who developed a pantheistic monistic philosophy: he was burnt at the stake for heresy

Brunswick *n* **1** a former duchy (1635–1918) and state (1918–46) of central Germany, now part of the state of Lower Saxony; formerly (1949–90) part of West German **2** a city in central Germany: formerly capital of the duchy and state of Brunswick. Pop: 245 076 (2003 est) ▶ German name: **Braunschweig**

brunt *n* the main force or shock of a blow, attack, etc.: *the town bore the brunt of the earthquake*

Brusa *n* the former name of **Bursa**

bruschetta (broo-**sket**-ta) *n* an Italian open sandwich toasted bread topped with olive oil and tomatoes, olive etc. [Italian]

brush[1] *n* **1** a device made of bristles, hairs, wires, etc. se into a firm back or handle: used to apply paint, groom the hair, etc. **2** the act of brushing **3** a brief encounter, esp. an unfriendly one **4** the bushy tail of a fox **5** an electric conductor, esp. one made of carbon, that conve current between stationary and rotating parts of a generator, motor, etc. ▷ *vb* **6** to clean, scrub, or paint with a brush **7** to apply or remove with a brush or brushing movement **8** to touch lightly and briefly ▶ Se also **brush aside, brush off, brush up** [Old French *broisse*]

brush[2] *n* a thick growth of shrubs and small trees; scru [Old French *broce*]

brush aside *or* **brush away** *vb* to dismiss (a suggestio or an idea) without consideration; disregard

brushed *adj textiles* treated with a brushing process to raise the nap and give a softer and warmer finish: *brushed nylon*

brush off *slang vb* **1** to dismiss and ignore (a person), esp. curtly ▷ *n* **brushoff 2 give someone the brushoff** to reject someone

brush turkey *n* a bird of New Guinea and Australia resembling the domestic fowl, with black plumage

brush up *vb* **1** (often foll. by *on*) to refresh one's knowledge or memory of (a subject) ▷ *n* **brush-up 2** *Brit* the act of tidying one's appearance: *have a wash and brush-up*

brushwood *n* **1** cut or broken-off tree branches, twigs, etc. **2** same as **brush²**

brushwork *n* a characteristic manner of applying paint with a brush: *Rembrandt's brushwork*

brusque *adj* blunt or curt in manner or speech [Italian *brusco* sour] ❭ **brusquely** *adv* ❭ **brusqueness** *n*

Brussels *n* the capital of Belgium, in the central part: became capital of Belgium in 1830; seat of the European Commission. Pop: 999 899 (2004 est). Flemish name: **Brussel.** French name: **Bruxelles**

Brussels sprout *n* a vegetable like a tiny cabbage

brut (broot) *adj* (of champagne or sparkling wine) very dry

brutal *adj* **1** cruel; vicious; savage **2** harsh or severe **3** extremely honest or frank in speech or manner ❭ **brutality** *n* ❭ **brutally** *adv*

brutalism *n* an austere architectural style of the 1950s on, characterized by the use of exposed concrete and angular shapes

brutalize *or* **-ise** *vb* **-izing, -ized** *or* **-ising, -ised 1** to make or become brutal **2** to treat (someone) brutally ❭ **brutalization** *or* **-isation** *n*

brute *n* **1** a brutal person **2** any animal except man; beast ▷ *adj* **3** wholly instinctive or physical, like that of an animal: *cricket is not a game of brute force* **4** without reason or intelligence **5** coarse and grossly sensual [Latin *brutus* irrational]

brutish *adj* **1** of or resembling a brute; animal **2** coarse; cruel; stupid

Bruton *n* John Gerard. born 1947, Irish politician: leader of the Fine Gael party (1990–2001); prime minister of the Republic of Ireland (1994–97)

Brutus *n* **1** Lucius Junius. late 6th century BC, Roman statesman who ousted the tyrant Tarquin (509) and helped found the Roman republic **2** Marcus Junius ?85–42 BC, Roman statesman who, with Cassius, led the conspiracy to assassinate Caesar (44): committed suicide after being defeated by Antony and Octavian (Augustus) at Philippi (42)

Bruxelles *n* the French name for **Brussels**

Bryansk *n* a city in W Russia. Pop: 428 000 (2005 est)

Bryant *n* David. born 1931, British bowler; many times world champion

bryony *n, pl* **-nies** a herbaceous climbing plant with greenish flowers and red or black berries [Greek *bruōnia*]

Brythonic (brith-on-ik) *n* **1** the S group of Celtic languages, consisting of Welsh, Cornish, and Breton ▷ *adj* **2** of this group of languages [Welsh *Brython* Celt]

Brześć nad Bugiem *n* the Polish name for **Brest** (2)

BS 1 Bachelor of Surgery **2** British Standard(s)

BSc Bachelor of Science

BSE bovine spongiform encephalopathy: a fatal virus disease of cattle

BSI British Standards Institution

-side *n* the less important side of a gramophone record

BSL British Sign Language

BST British Summer Time

Bt Baronet

BT British Telecom

Btu *or* **BThU** British thermal unit

bubble *n* **1** a small globule of air or a gas in a liquid or a solid **2** a thin film of liquid forming a ball around air or a gas: *a soap bubble* **3** a dome, esp. a transparent glass or plastic one **4** an unreliable scheme or enterprise ▷ *vb* **-bling, -bled 5** to form bubbles **6** to move or flow with a gurgling sound **7 bubble over** to express an emotion freely: *she was bubbling over with excitement* [probably Scandinavian]

bubble and squeak *n Brit, Austral and NZ* a dish of boiled cabbage and potatoes fried together

bubble bath *n* **1** a substance used to scent, soften, and foam in bath water **2** a bath with such a substance

bubble car *n Brit* a small car of the 1950s with a transparent bubble-shaped top

bubble gum *n* a type of chewing gum that can be blown into large bubbles

bubble wrap *n* a type of polythene wrapping containing many small air pockets, used to protect breakable goods

bubbly *adj* **-blier, -bliest 1** lively; animated; excited **2** full of or resembling bubbles ▷ *n* **3** *informal* champagne

Buber *n* Martin. 1878–1965, Jewish theologian, existentialist philosopher, and scholar of Hasidism, born in Austria, whose works include *I and Thou* (1923), *Between Man and Man* (1946), and *Eclipse of God* (1952)

bubo (byew-boh) *n, pl* **-boes** *pathol* inflammation and swelling of a lymph node, esp. in the armpit or groin [Greek *boubōn* groin] ❭ **bubonic** (bew-bonn-ik) *adj*

bubonic plague *n* an acute infectious disease characterized by the formation of buboes

Bucaramanga *n* a city in N central Colombia, in the Cordillera Oriental: centre of a district growing coffee, tobacco, and cotton. Pop: 1 069 000 (2005 est)

buccaneer *n* a pirate, esp. in the Caribbean in the 17th and 18th centuries [French *boucanier*]

Buchan *n* John, 1st Baron Tweedsmuir. 1875–1940, Scottish statesman, historian, and writer of adventure stories, esp. *The Thirty-Nine Steps* (1915) and *Greenmantle* (1916); governor general of Canada (1935–40)

Buchanan *n* **1** George. 1506–82, Scottish historian, who was tutor to Mary, Queen of Scots and James VI; author of *History of Scotland* (1582) **2** James. 1791–1868, 15th president of the US (1857–61)

Bucharest *n* the capital of Romania, in the southeast. Pop: 1 764 000 (2005 est). Romanian name: **Bucureşti**

Buchenwald *n* a village in E central Germany, near Weimar; site of a Nazi concentration camp (1937–45)

Buchner *n* Eduard. 1860–1917, German chemist who demonstrated that alcoholic fermentation is due to enzymes in the yeast: Nobel prize for chemistry 1907

Büchner *n* Georg. 1813–37, German dramatist; regarded as a forerunner of the Expressionists: author of *Danton's Death* (1835) and *Woyzeck* (1837)

buck¹ *n* **1** the male of the goat, hare, kangaroo, rabbit, and reindeer **2** *archaic* a spirited young man **3** the act of bucking ▷ *vb* **4** (of a horse or other animal) to jump vertically, with legs stiff and back arched **5** (of a horse, etc.) to throw (its rider) by bucking **6** *informal* to resist or oppose obstinately: *bucking the system* ▶ See also **buck up** [Old English *bucca* he-goat]

buck² *n US, Canad, Austral and NZ informal* a dollar [origin unknown]

buck³ *n* **pass the buck** *informal* to shift blame or responsibility onto another [probably from *buckhorn knife*, placed before a player in poker to indicate that he was the next dealer]

Buck *n* Pearl S(ydenstricker). 1892–1973, US novelist, noted particularly for her novel of Chinese life *The Good Earth* (1931): Nobel prize for literature 1938

bucket *n* **1** an open-topped cylindrical container with a handle **2** the amount a bucket will hold **3** a bucket-like part of a machine, such as the scoop on a mechanical shovel **4 kick the bucket** *slang* to die ▷ *vb* **-eting, -eted 5** (often foll. by *down*) (of rain) to fall very heavily [Old English *būc*]

b

bucket list *n informal* a list of experiences one wants to have before one dies

bucket shop *n* **1** *chiefly Brit* a travel agency specializing in cheap airline tickets **2** an unregistered firm of stockbrokers that engages in fraudulent speculation

Buckingham¹ *n* a town in S central England, in Buckinghamshire; university (1975). Pop: 12 512 (2001)

Buckingham² *n* **1** George Villiers, 1st Duke of. 1592–1628, English courtier and statesman; favourite of James I and Charles I: his arrogance, military incompetence, and greed increased the tensions between the King and Parliament that eventually led to the Civil War **2** his son, George Villiers, 2nd Duke of. 1628–87, English courtier and writer; chief minister of Charles II and member of the Cabal (1667–73)

Buckingham Palace *n* the London residence of the British sovereign: built in 1703, rebuilt by John Nash in 1821–36 and partially redesigned in the early 20th century

Buckinghamshire *n* a county in SE central England, containing the Vale of Aylesbury and parts of the Chiltern Hills: the geographic and ceremonial county includes Milton Keynes, which became an independent unitary authority in 1997. Administrative centre: Aylesbury. Pop (excluding Milton Keynes): 478 000 (2003 est). Area (excluding Milton Keynes): 1568 sq km (605 sq miles). Abbreviation: **Bucks**

Buckland *n* William. 1784–1856, English geologist; he became a proponent of the idea of catastrophic ice ages

buckle *n* **1** a clasp for fastening together two loose ends, esp. of a belt or strap ▷ *vb* **-ling, -led 2** to fasten or be fastened with a buckle **3** to bend or cause to bend out of shape, esp. as a result of pressure or heat [Latin *buccula* cheek strap]

buckle down *vb* to apply oneself with determination

buckler *n* a small round shield worn on the forearm [Old French *bocler*]

Bucks Buckinghamshire

buckshee *adj Brit slang* without charge; free [from BAKSHEESH]

buckshot *n* large lead pellets used for hunting game

buckskin *n* **1** a strong greyish-yellow suede leather, originally made from deerskin **2** buckskins trousers made of buckskin

buckteeth *pl n* projecting upper front teeth ▷ **buck-toothed** *adj*

buckthorn *n* a thorny shrub whose berries were formerly used as a purgative

buck up *vb informal* **1** to make or become more cheerful or confident **2** to make haste

buckwheat *n* **1** a type of small black seed used as animal fodder and in making flour **2** the flour obtained from such seeds [Middle Dutch *boecweite*]

bucolic (byew-koll-ik) *adj* **1** of the countryside or country life; rustic **2** of or relating to shepherds; pastoral ▷ *n* **3** a pastoral poem [Greek *boukolos* cowherd]

Bucovina *n* a variant spelling of **Bukovina**

București *n* the Romanian name for **Bucharest**

bud *n* **1** a swelling on the stem of a plant that develops into a flower or leaf **2** a partially opened flower: *rosebud* **3** any small budlike outgrowth: *taste buds* **4** nip something in the bud to put an end to something in its initial stages ▷ *vb* **budding, budded 5** (of plants and some animals) to produce buds **6** *horticulture* to graft (a bud) from one plant onto another [Middle English *budde*]

Budapest *n* the capital of Hungary, on the River Danube: formed in 1873 from the towns of Buda and Pest. Traditionally Buda, the old Magyar capital, was the administrative and Pest the trade centre: suffered severely in the Russian siege of 1945 and in the unsuccessful revolt against the Communist regime (1956). Pop: 1 719 342 (2003 est)

Buddh Gaya, Buddha Gaya *or* **Bodh Gaya** *n* a town in NE India, in Bihar: site of the sacred bo tree under which Gautama Siddhartha attained enlightenment and became the Buddha; pilgrimage centre. Pop: 30 883 (2001)

Buddhism *n* a religion founded by the Buddha that teaches that all suffering can be brought to an end by overcoming greed, hatred, and delusion ▷ **Buddhist** *n*, *adj*

budding *adj* beginning to develop or grow: *a budding acto*

buddleia *n* a shrub which has long spikes of purple flowers [after A. *Buddle*, botanist]

buddy *n, pl* **-dies 1** *chiefly US and Canad informal* a friend **2** a volunteer who helps and supports a person suffering from AIDS ▷ *vb* **-dies, -dying, -died 3** to act as a buddy to (a person suffering from AIDS) [probably variant of BROTHER]

budge *vb* **budging, budged 1** to move slightly: *he refuses t budge off that chair* **2** to change or cause to change opinions: *nothing would budge him from this idea* [Old French *bouger*]

Budge *n* Don(ald). 1915–2000, US tennis player, the first man to win the Grand Slam of singles championships (Australia, France, Wimbledon, and the US) in one year (1938)

budgerigar *n* a small cage bird bred in many different-coloured varieties [Aboriginal]

budget *n* **1** a plan of expected income and expenditure over a specified period **2** the total amount of money allocated for a specific purpose during a specified perio ▷ *adj* **3** inexpensive: *a budget hotel* ▷ *vb* **-eting, -eted 4** to enter or provide for in a budget **5** to plan the expenditure of (money or time) [Latin *bulga* leather pouch] ▷ **budgetary** *adj*

Budget *n* the Budget an annual estimate of British government expenditures and revenues and the financial plans for the following financial year

budget deficit *n* the amount by which government spending exceeds income from taxation, etc.

budgie *n informal* same as **budgerigar**

Budweis *n* the German name for **České Budějovice**

Buenaventura *n* a major port in W Colombia, on the Pacific coast. Pop: 250 000 (2005 est)

Buena Vista *n* a village in NE Mexico, near Saltillo: site of the defeat of the Mexicans by US forces (1847)

Buenos Aires *n* the capital of Argentina, a major port and industrial city on the Río de la Plata estuary: became capital in 1880; university (1821). Pop: 13 349 00 (2005 est)

buff¹ *n* **1** a soft thick flexible undyed leather **2** a cloth or pad of material used for polishing **3** in the buff *informal* completely naked ▷ *adj* **4** dull yellowish-brown **5** *informal* physically fit and attractive ▷ *vb* **6** to clean or polish (a metal, floor, shoes, etc.) with a buff [Late Lati *bufalus* buffalo]

buff² *n informal* an expert on or devotee of a given subjec *an opera buff* [from the buff-coloured uniforms worn by volunteer firemen in New York City]

buffalo *n, pl* **-loes** *or* **-lo 1** a type of cattle with upward-curving horns **2** same as **water buffalo 3** *US and Canad* a bison [Greek *bous* ox]

Buffalo *n* a port in W New York State, at the E end of La Erie. Pop: 285 018 (2003 est)

Buffalo Bill *n* nickname of William Frederick Cody. 1846–1917, US showman who toured Europe and the US with his famous *Wild West Show*

buffer¹ *n* **1** one of a pair of spring-loaded steel pads at th ends of railway vehicles and railway tracks that reduc shock on impact **2** a person or thing that lessens shocl or protects from damaging impact, circumstances, etc **3** *chem* **a** a substance added to a solution to resist changes in its acidity or alkalinity **b** Also called: **buffe solution** a solution containing such a substance **4** *computers* a device for temporarily storing data ▷ *vb* **5** to cushion; provide a buffer for [from BUFFET²]

buffer² n Brit informal a stupid or bumbling person, esp. a man: an old buffer [origin unknown]

buffer state n a small and usually neutral state between two rival powers

buffer zone n an area lying between two states, providing each with protection from the other

buffet¹ (boof-fay, buff-ay) n 1 a counter where light refreshments are served 2 a meal at which guests help themselves from a number of dishes [French]

buffet² (buff-it) vb -feting, -feted 1 to knock against or about; batter: the ship was buffeted by strong winds 2 to hit, esp. with the fist ▷ n 3 a blow, esp. with a hand [Old French buffeter]

buffet car (boof-fay) n Brit a railway coach where light refreshments are served

Buffett n Warren (Edward). born 1930, US financier, investor, and philanthropist

Buffon n Georges Louis Leclerc, Comte de. 1707–88, French encyclopedist of natural history; principal author of Histoire naturelle (36 vols., 1749–89), containing the Époques de la nature (1777), which foreshadowed later theories of evolution

buffoon n a person who amuses others by silly behaviour [Latin bufo toad] ▷ **buffoonery** n

bug n 1 any of various insects having piercing and sucking mouthparts 2 chiefly US and Canad any insect 3 informal a minor illness caused by a germ or virus 4 informal a small error, esp. in a computer or computer program 5 informal an obsessive idea or hobby 6 informal a concealed microphone used for recording conversations in spying 7 Austral a flattish edible shellfish ▷ vb **bugging, bugged** informal 8 to irritate or upset (someone) 9 to conceal a microphone in (a room or telephone) [origin unknown]

Bug n 1 Also called: **Southern Bug** a river in E Europe, rising in W Ukraine and flowing southeast to the Dnieper estuary and the Black Sea. Length: 853 km (530 miles) 2 Also called: **Western Bug** a river in E Europe, rising in SW Ukraine and flowing northwest to the River Vistula in Poland, forming part of the border between Poland and Ukraine. Length: 724 km (450 miles)

Buganda n a region of Uganda: a powerful Bantu kingdom from the 17th century

Bugatti n Ettore (Arco Isidoro). 1881–1947, Italian car manufacturer; founder of the Bugatti car factory at Molsheim (1909)

bugbear n a thing that causes obsessive anxiety [obsolete bug an evil spirit + BEAR²]

bugger n 1 taboo, slang a person or thing considered to be unpleasant or difficult 2 slang a humorous or affectionate term for someone: a friendly little bugger 3 a person who practises buggery ▷ vb 4 slang to tire; weary 5 to practise buggery with ▷ interj 6 taboo, slang an exclamation of annoyance or disappointment [Medieval Latin Bulgarus Bulgarian heretic]

bugger about or **bugger around** vb slang 1 to fool about and waste time 2 to create difficulties for: they really buggered me about when I tried to get my money back

bugger off vb taboo, slang to go away; depart

bugger up vb slang to spoil or ruin (something)

buggery n Brit, Austral and NZ anal intercourse

buggy n, pl -gies 1 a light horse-drawn carriage having two or four wheels 2 a lightweight folding pram for babies or young children [origin unknown]

bugle music n 1 a brass instrument used chiefly for military calls ▷ vb -gling, -gled 2 to play or sound (on) a bugle [short for bugle horn ox horn, from Latin buculus bullock] ▷ **bugler** n

build vb building, built 1 to make or construct by joining parts or materials: more than 100 bypasses have been built in the past decade 2 to establish and develop: it took ten years to build the business 3 to make in a particular way or for a particular purpose: she's built for speed, not stamina 4 (often foll. by up) to increase in intensity ▷ n 5 physical form,

figure, or proportions: he has an athletic build [Old English byldan]

builder n a person who constructs houses and other buildings

building n 1 a structure, such as a house, with a roof and walls 2 the business of building houses, etc.

building society n a cooperative banking enterprise where money can be invested and mortgage loans made available

build up vb 1 to construct (something) gradually, systematically, and in stages 2 to increase by degrees: he steadily built up a power base 3 to prepare for or gradually approach a climax ▷ n **build-up** 4 a progressive increase in number or size: the build-up of industry 5 a gradual approach to a climax 6 extravagant publicity or praise, esp. as a campaign

built vb the past of **build**

built-in adj 1 included as an essential part: a built-in cupboard 2 essential: a built-in instinct

built-up adj 1 having many buildings: a built-up area 2 increased by the addition of parts: built-up heels

Buitenzorg n the former name of **Bogor**

Bujumbura n the capital of Burundi, a port at the NE end of Lake Tanganyika. Pop: 419 000 (2005 est). Former name: **Usumbura**

Bukavu n a port in E Democratic Republic of Congo, on Lake Kivu: commercial and industrial centre. Pop: 294 000 (2005 est). Former name (until 1966): **Costermansville**

Bukhara or **Bokhara** n 1 a city in S Uzbekistan. Pop: 299 000 (2005 est) 2 a former emirate of central Asia: a powerful kingdom and centre of Islam; became a territory of the Soviet Union (1920) and was divided between the former Uzbek, Tajik, and Turkmen Soviet Socialist Republics

Bukharin n Nikolai Ivanovich. 1888–1938, Soviet Bolshevik leader: executed in one of Stalin's purges

Bukovina or **Bucovina** n a region of E central Europe, part of the NE Carpathians: the north was seized by the Soviet Union (1940) and later became part of Ukraine; the south remained Romanian

Bulawayo n a city in SW Zimbabwe founded (1893) on the site of the kraal of Lobengula, the last Matabele king; the country's main industrial centre. Pop: 693 000 (2005 est)

bulb n 1 same as **light bulb** 2 the onion-shaped base of the stem of some plants, which sends down roots 3 a plant, such as a daffodil, which grows from a bulb 4 any bulb-shaped thing [Greek bolbos onion] ▷ **bulbous** adj

Bulg. Bulgaria(n)

Bulgakov n Mikhail Afanaseyev. 1891–1940, Soviet novelist, dramatist, and short-story writer; his novels include The Master and Margerita (1966–67)

Bulganin n Nikolai Aleksandrovich. 1895–1975, Soviet statesman and military leader; chairman of the council of ministers (1955–58)

Bulgaria n a republic in SE Europe, on the Balkan Peninsula on the Black Sea: under Turkish rule from 1395 until 1878; became an independent kingdom in 1908 and a republic in 1946; joined the EU in 2007; consists chiefly of the Danube valley in the north and the Balkan Mountains in the central part, separated from the Rhodope Mountains of the south by the valley of the Maritsa River. Language: Bulgarian. Religion: Christian (Bulgarian Orthodox) majority. Currency: lev. Capital: Sofia. Pop: 6 981 642 (2013 est). Area: 110 911 sq km (42 823 sq miles)

Bulgarian adj 1 of or relating to Bulgaria or its inhabitants ▷ n 2 a native or inhabitant of Bulgaria 3 the language of Bulgaria

bulge n 1 a swelling or an outward curve on a normally flat surface 2 a sudden increase in number, esp. of population ▷ vb **bulging, bulged** 3 to swell outwards [Latin bulga bag] ▷ **bulging** adj

bulimia n a disorder characterized by compulsive overeating followed by vomiting [Greek *bous* ox + *limos* hunger] ⟩ **bulimic** adj, n

bulk n 1 volume or size, esp. when great 2 the main part: *he spends the bulk of his time abroad* 3 a large body, esp. of a person 4 the part of food which passes unabsorbed through the digestive system 5 in bulk in large quantities: *how frequently do you buy food in bulk for your family?* ⟩ vb 6 bulk large to be or seem important or prominent [Old Norse *bulki* cargo]

> **USAGE** The use of a plural noun after *bulk* was formerly considered incorrect, but is now acceptable.

bulk buying n the purchase of goods in large amounts, often at reduced prices

bulkhead n any upright partition in a ship or aeroplane [probably from Old Norse *bálkr* partition + HEAD]

bulky adj bulkier, bulkiest very large and massive, esp. so as to be unwieldy ⟩ **bulkiness** n

bull[1] n 1 a male of domestic cattle, esp. one that is sexually mature 2 the male of various other animals including the elephant and whale 3 a very large, strong, or aggressive person 4 Stock Exchange a speculator who buys in anticipation of rising prices in order to make a profit on resale 5 chiefly Brit same as **bull's-eye** (1, 2) 6 like a bull in a china shop clumsy 7 take the bull by the horns to face and tackle a difficulty without shirking [Old English *bula*]

bull[2] n a ludicrously self-contradictory or nonsensical statement [origin unknown]

bull[3] n a formal document issued by the pope [Latin *bulla* round object]

Bull n John. 1563–1628, English composer and organist

bull bars pl n a large protective metal grille on the front of some vehicles, esp. four-wheel-drive vehicles

bulldog n a thickset dog with a broad head and a muscular body

bulldog clip n a clip for holding papers together, consisting of two metal clamps and a spring

bulldoze vb -dozing, -dozed 1 to move, demolish, or flatten with a bulldozer 2 informal to coerce (someone) into doing something by intimidation [origin unknown]

bulldozer n a powerful tractor fitted with caterpillar tracks and a blade at the front, used for moving earth

bullet n a small metallic missile used as the projectile of a gun or rifle [French *boulette* little ball]

bulletin n 1 a broadcast summary of the news 2 an official statement on a matter of public interest 3 a periodical published by an organization for its members [Italian *bulla* papal edict]

bulletin board n 1 US same as **notice board** 2 computers a type of data-exchange system by which messages can be sent and read

bullfight n a public show, popular in Spain, in which a matador baits and usually kills a bull in an arena ⟩ **bullfighter** n ⟩ **bullfighting** n

bullfinch n a common European songbird with a black head and, in the male, a pinkish breast

bullfrog n any of various large frogs having a loud deep croak

bullion n gold or silver in the form of bars and ingots [Anglo-French: mint]

bull-necked adj having a short thick neck

bullock n a gelded bull; steer [Old English *bulluc*]

bullring n an arena for staging bullfights

bull's-eye n 1 the small central disc of a target or a dartboard 2 a shot hitting this 3 informal something that exactly achieves its aim 4 a peppermint-flavoured boiled sweet 5 a small circular window 6 a thick disc of glass set into a ship's deck, etc. to admit light 7 the glass boss at the centre of a sheet of blown glass 8 a a convex lens used as a condenser b a lamp or lantern containing such a lens

bullshit taboo, slang n 1 exaggerated or foolish talk; nonsense ⟩ vb -shitting, -shitted 2 to talk bullshit to: *don't bullshit me*

bull terrier n a terrier with a muscular body and a short smooth coat

bully n, pl -lies 1 a person who hurts, persecutes, or intimidates weaker people ⟩ vb -lies, -lying, -lied 2 to hurt, intimidate, or persecute (a weaker or smaller person) ⟩ interj 3 bully for you or him, etc informal well done! bravo!: now usually used sarcastically [originally sweetheart, fine fellow, swaggering coward, probably from Middle Dutch *boele* lover]

bully beef n canned corned beef [French *bœuf bouilli* boiled beef]

bully-off hockey n 1 the method of restarting play in which two opposing players stand with the ball between them and strike their sticks together three times before trying to hit the ball ⟩ vb bully off 2 to restart play with a bully-off [origin unknown]

Bülow n Prince **Bernhard von**. 1849–1929, chancellor of Germany (1900–09)

bulrush n 1 a tall reedlike marsh plant with brown spike flowers 2 Bible same as **papyrus** (1) [Middle English *bulrish*]

Bultmann n **Rudolf Karl**. 1884–1976, German theologian noted for his demythologizing approach to the New Testament

bulwark n 1 a wall or similar structure used as a fortification; rampart 2 a person or thing acting as a defence [Middle High German *bolwerk*]

bum[1] n Brit, Austral and NZ slang the buttocks or anus [origin unknown]

bum[2] informal n 1 a disreputable loafer or idler 2 a tramp; hobo ⟩ vb bumming, bummed 3 to get by begging; cadge: *to bum a lift* 4 bum around to spend time to no good purpose; loaf ⟩ adj 5 of poor quality; useless: *he hit a bum note* [probably from German *bummeln* to loaf]

bumbag n a small bag worn on a belt around the waist

bumble vb -bling, -bled 1 to speak or do in a clumsy, muddled, or inefficient way 2 to move in a clumsy or unsteady way [origin unknown] ⟩ **bumbling** adj, n

bumblebee n a large hairy bee [obsolete *bumble* to buzz]

Bumbry n **Grace**. born 1937, US soprano and mezzo-soprano

bumf or **bumph** n Brit, Austral and NZ 1 informal official documents or forms 2 slang toilet paper [short for *bumfodder*]

bump vb 1 to knock or strike (someone or something) with a jolt 2 to travel or proceed in jerks and jolts 3 to hurt by knocking ⟩ n 4 an impact; knock; jolt; collision 5 a dull thud from an impact or collision 6 a lump on the body caused by a blow 7 a raised uneven part, such as on a road surface ▸ See also **bump into, bump off, bump up** [probably imitative] ⟩ **bumpy** adj

bumper[1] n a horizontal bar attached to the front and rear of a vehicle to protect against damage from impact

bumper[2] n 1 a glass or tankard, filled to the brim, esp. a toast 2 an unusually large or fine example of something ⟩ adj 3 unusually large, fine, or abundant: *bumper crop* [probably obsolete *bump* to bulge]

bumph n same as **bumf**

bump into vb informal to meet (someone) by chance

bumpkin n an awkward simple rustic person: *a country bumpkin* [probably from Dutch]

bump off vb slang to murder (someone)

bumptious adj offensively self-assertive or conceited [probably *bump* + *fractious*]

bump up vb informal to increase (prices) by a large amount

bun n 1 a small sweetened bread roll, often containing currants or spices 2 a small round cake 3 a hairstyle in which long hair is gathered into a bun shape at the back of the head [origin unknown]

bunch *n* **1** a number of things growing, fastened, or grouped together: *a bunch of grapes; a bunch of keys* **2** a collection; group: *a bunch of queries* **3** a group or company: *a bunch of cowards* ▷ *vb* **4** to group or be grouped into a bunch [origin unknown]

Bunche *n* Ralph Johnson. 1904–71, US diplomat and United Nations official: awarded the Nobel peace prize in 1950 for his work as UN mediator in Palestine (1948–49); UN undersecretary (1954–71)

Bundaberg *n* a town in E Australia, near the E coast of Queensland: centre of a sugar-growing area, with a nearby deep-water port. Pop: 44 556 (2001)

Bundelkhand *n* a region of central India: formerly native states, now mainly part of Madhya Pradesh

bundle *n* **1** a number of things or a quantity of material gathered or loosely bound together: *a bundle of sticks* **2** something wrapped or tied for carrying; package **3** *biology* a collection of strands of specialized tissue such as nerve fibres **4** *botany* a strand of conducting tissue within plants ▷ *vb* **-dling, -dled** **5** (foll. by *out, off, into,* etc.) to cause (someone) to go, esp. roughly or unceremoniously: *she bundled them unceremoniously out into the garden* **6** to push or throw (something), esp. in a quick untidy way: *the soiled items were bundled into a black plastic bag* [probably from Middle Dutch *bundel*]

bundle up *vb* to make (something) into a bundle or bundles

bundu *n S African and Zimbabwean slang* a largely uninhabited wild region far from towns [from a Bantu language]

bun fight *n Brit, Austral and NZ slang* a tea party

bung *n* **1** a stopper, esp. of cork or rubber, used to close something such as a cask or flask **2** same as **bunghole** ▷ *vb* **3** (foll. by *up*) *informal* to close or seal (something) with or as if with a bung **4** *Brit, Austral and NZ slang* to throw (something) somewhere in a careless manner; sling [Middle Dutch *bonghe*]

bungalow *n* a one-storey house [Hindi *banglā* (house) of Bengali type]

bungee jumping *or* **bungy jumping** *n* a sport in which a person jumps from a high bridge, tower, etc., to which he or she is connected by a rubber rope [from *bungie,* slang word for India rubber]

bunghole *n* a hole in a cask or barrel through which liquid can be drained

bungle *vb* **-gling, -gled** **1** to spoil (an operation) through clumsiness or incompetence; botch ▷ *n* **2** a clumsy or unsuccessful performance; blunder [origin unknown] **> bungler** *n* **> bungling** *adj, n*

Bunin *n* Ivan Alekseyevich. 1870–1953, Russian novelist and poet; author of *The Gentleman from San Francisco* (1922)

bunion *n* an inflamed swelling of the first joint of the big toe [origin unknown]

bunk¹ *n* **1** a narrow shelflike bed fixed along a wall, esp. in a caravan or ship **2** same as **bunk bed** [probably from *bunker*]

bunk² *n informal* same as **bunkum**

bunk³ *n* **do a bunk** *Brit, Austral and NZ slang* to make a hurried and secret departure **2** *Brit, NZ and S African* be absent without permission [origin unknown]

bunk bed *n* one of a pair of beds constructed one above the other to save space

bunker *n* **1** an obstacle on a golf course, usually a sand-filled hollow bordered by a ridge **2** an underground shelter **3** a large storage container for coal etc. [Scots *bonkar*]

bunkum *n* empty talk; nonsense [after *Buncombe,* North Carolina, alluded to in an inane speech by its Congressional representative]

bunny *n, pl* **-nies** a child's word for **rabbit** [Scottish Gaelic *bun* rabbit's tail]

bunny girl *n* a night-club hostess whose costume includes a rabbit-like tail and ears

Bunsen *n* Robert Wilhelm. 1811–99, German chemist who with Kirchhoff developed spectrum analysis and discovered the elements caesium and rubidium. He invented the Bunsen burner and the ice calorimeter

Bunsen burner *n* a gas burner consisting of a metal tube with an adjustable air valve at the base [after R. W. BUNSEN]

bunting¹ *n* decorative flags, pennants, and streamers [origin unknown]

bunting² *n* a songbird with a short stout bill [origin unknown]

Bunting *n* Basil. 1900–85, British poet, author of *Briggflatts* (1966)

Buñuel *n* Luis. 1900–83, Spanish film director. He collaborated with Salvador Dali on the first surrealist films, *Un Chien andalou* (1929) and *L'Age d'or* (1930). His later films include *Viridiana* (1961), *Belle de jour* (1966), and *The Discreet Charm of the Bourgeoisie* (1972)

bunya *n* a tall dome-shaped Australian coniferous tree

Bunyan *n* John. 1628–88, English preacher and writer, noted particularly for his allegory *The Pilgrim's Progress* (1678)

bunyip *n Austral* a legendary monster said to live in swamps and lakes [from a native Australian language]

buoy *n* **1** a brightly coloured floating object anchored to the sea bed for marking moorings, navigable channels, or obstructions in the water ▷ *vb* **2** (foll. by *up*) to prevent from sinking: *the life belt buoyed him up* **3** to raise the spirits of; hearten: *exports are on the increase, buoyed by a weak dollar* **4** *nautical* to mark (a channel or obstruction) with a buoy or buoys [probably Germanic]

buoyant *adj* **1** able to float in or rise to the surface of a liquid **2** (of a liquid or gas) able to keep a body afloat **3** thriving: *a buoyant economy* **4** cheerful or resilient **> buoyancy** *n*

bur *or* **burr** *n* **1** a seed case or flower head with hooks or prickles **2** any plant that produces burs [probably from Old Norse]

Bur. Myanmar (Burma)

Buraydah *or* **Buraida** *n* a town and oasis in central Saudi Arabia. Pop: 462 000 (2005 est)

Burbage *n* **1** James. ?1530–97, English actor and theatre manager, who built (1576) the first theatre in England **2** his son, Richard. ?1567–1619, English actor, associated with Shakespeare

burble *vb* **-bling, -bled** **1** to make or utter with a bubbling sound; gurgle **2** to talk quickly and excitedly [probably imitative]

burbot *n, pl* **-bots** *or* **-bot** a freshwater fish of the cod family that has barbels around its mouth [Old French *bourbotte*]

Burckhardt *n* Jacob Christoph. 1818–97, Swiss art and cultural historian; author of *The Civilisation of the Renaissance in Italy* (1860)

burden¹ *n* **1** something that is carried; load **2** something that is difficult to bear. Related adjective: **onerous** ▷ *vb* **3** to put or impose a burden on; load **4** to weigh down; oppress [Old English *byrthen*] **> burdensome** *adj*

burden² *n* **1** a line of words recurring at the end of each verse of a song **2** the theme of a speech, book, etc. [Old French *bourdon* droning sound]

burdock *n* a weed with large heart-shaped leaves, and burlike fruits [BUR + DOCK⁴]

bureau (byew-roe) *n, pl* **-reaus** *or* **-reaux** (-rose) **1** an office or agency, esp. one providing services for the public **2** *US* a government department **3** *chiefly Brit* a writing desk with pigeonholes and drawers against which the writing surface can be closed when not in use **4** *US* a chest of drawers [French]

bureaucracy *n, pl* **-cies** **1** a rigid system of administration based upon organization into bureaus, division of labour, a hierarchy of authority, etc. **2** government by such a system **3** government officials collectively **4** any administration in which action is impeded by unnecessary official procedures

b

bureaucrat *n* **1** an official in a bureaucracy **2** an official who adheres rigidly to bureaucracy **> bureaucratic** *adj*

bureau de change *n* a place where foreign currencies can be exchanged [French]

burette *or US* **buret** *n* a graduated glass tube with a stopcock on one end for dispensing known volumes of fluids [Old French *buire* ewer]

Burgas *n* a port in SE Bulgaria on an inlet of the Black Sea. Pop: 177 000 (2005 est)

Burgenland *n* a state of E Austria. Capital: Eisenstadt. Pop: 276 419 (2003 est). Area: 3965 sq km (1531 sq miles)

burgeon *vb* to develop or grow rapidly; flourish [Old French *burjon*]

burger *n informal* same as **hamburger**

Bürger *n* Gottfried August. 1747–94, German lyric poet, noted particularly for his ballad *Lenore* (1773)

Burgess *n* **1** Anthony, real name *John Burgess Wilson*. 1917–93, English novelist and critic: his novels include *A Clockwork Orange* (1962), *Tremor of Intent* (1966), *Earthly Powers* (1980), and *Any Old Iron* (1989) **2** Guy. 1911–63, British spy, who fled to the Soviet Union (with Donald Maclean) in 1951

Burgess Shale *n* a bed of Cambrian sedimentary rock in the Rocky Mountains in British Columbia containing many unique invertebrate fossils [named after the *Burgess* Pass, where the bed is exposed]

burgh *n* (in Scotland until 1975) a town with a degree of self-government [Scots form of *borough*]

burgher *n archaic* a citizen, esp. one from the Continent [German *Bürger* or Dutch *burger*]

Burghley *or* **Burleigh** *n* William Cecil, 1st Baron Burghley. 1520–98, English statesman: chief adviser to Elizabeth I; secretary of state (1558–72) and Lord High Treasurer (1572–98)

Burghley House *n* an Elizabethan mansion near Stamford in Lincolnshire: seat of the Cecil family; site of the annual Burghley Horse Trials

burglar *n* a person who illegally enters a property to commit a crime [Medieval Latin *burglator*]

burglary *n*, *pl* **-ries** the crime of entering a building as a trespasser to commit theft or another offence

burgle *vb* **-gling, -gled** to break into (a house, shop, etc.)

burgomaster *n* the chief magistrate of a town in Austria, Belgium, Germany, or the Netherlands [Dutch *burgemeester*]

Burgos *n* a city in N Spain, in Old Castile: cathedral. Pop: 169 317 (2003 est)

Burgoyne *n* John. 1722–92, British general in the War of American Independence who was forced to surrender at Saratoga (1777)

Burgundian *adj* **1** of or relating to Burgundy or its inhabitants ▷ *n* **2** a native or inhabitant of Burgundy

Burgundy *n*, *pl* **-dies** **1** a region of E France famous for its wines, lying west of the Saône: formerly a semi-independent duchy; annexed to France in 1482. French name: **Bourgogne 2 Free County of Burgundy** another name for **Franche-Comté 3** a monarchy (1384–1477) of medieval Europe, at its height including the Low Countries, the duchy of Burgundy, and Franche-Comté **4 Kingdom of Burgundy** a kingdom in E France, established in the early 6th century AD, eventually including the later duchy of Burgundy, Franche-Comté, and the Kingdom of Provence: known as the Kingdom of Arles from the 13th century **5 a** any red or white wine produced in the region of Burgundy, around Dijon **b** any heavy red table wine **6** (*often not cap*) a blackish-purple to purplish-red colour

burial *n* the burying of a dead body

burin (byoor-in) *n* a steel chisel used for engraving metal, wood, or marble [French]

burk *n Brit slang* same as **berk**

burka *n* another spelling of **burqa**

Burke *n* **1** Edmund. 1729–97, British Whig statesman, conservative political theorist, and orator, born in Ireland: defended parliamentary government and campaigned for a more liberal treatment of the American colonies; denounced the French Revolution **2** Robert O'Hara. 1820–61, Irish explorer, who led the first expedition (1860–61) across Australia from south to north. He was accompanied by W. J. Wills, George Grey, and John King; King alone survived the return journey **3** William. 1792–1829, Irish murderer and body snatcher; associate of William Hare

Burkinabé *adj* **1** of or relating to Burkina Faso or its inhabitants ▷ *n* **2** a native or inhabitant of Burkina Faso

Burkina Faso *or* **Burkina** *n* an inland republic in W Africa: dominated by Mossi kingdoms (10th–19th centuries); French protectorate established in 1896; became an independent republic in 1960; consists mainly of a flat savanna plateau. Official language: French; Mossi and other African languages also widely spoken. Religion: mostly animist, with a large Muslim minority. Currency: franc. Capital: Ouagadougou. Pop: 17 812 961 (2013 est). Area: 273 200 sq km (105 900 sq miles). Former name (until 1984): **Upper Volta**

burl *or* **birl** *n informal* **1** *Scot, Austral and NZ* an attempt; try: *give it a burl* **2** *Austral and NZ* a ride in a car [from Scots *birl* to spin or turn]

burlesque *n* **1** an artistic work, esp. literary or dramatic, satirizing a subject by caricaturing it **2** *US and Canad theatre* a bawdy comedy show of the late 19th and early 20th centuries ▷ *adj* **3** of or characteristic of a burlesque [Italian *burla* a jest]

Burlington *n* **1** a city in S Canada on Lake Ontario, northeast of Hamilton. Pop: 150 836 (2001) **2** a town in NW Vermont on Lake Champlain: largest in the state; University of Vermont (1791). Pop: 39 148 (2003 est)

burly *adj* **-lier, -liest** large and thick of build; sturdy [Germanic]

Burma *n* the former official name (until 1989, though still widely used) of **Myanmar**

Burmese *adj also* **Burman 1** of, relating to, or characteristic of Burma (Myanmar), its people, or their language ▷ *n*, *pl* **-mese 2** a native or inhabitant of Burma (Myanmar) **3** the official language of Burma (Myanmar), belonging to the Sino-Tibetan family

burn[1] *vb* **burning, burnt** *or* **burned 1** to be or set on fire **2** to destroy or be destroyed by fire **3** to damage, injure, or mark by heat: *he burnt his hand* **4** to die or put to death by fire **5** to be or feel hot: *my forehead is burning* **6** to smart or cause to smart: *brandy burns your throat* **7** to feel strong emotion, esp. anger or passion **8** to use for the purposes of light, heat, or power: *to burn coal* **9** to form by or as if by fire: *to burn a hole* **10** to char or become charred: *the toast is burning* **11** to record data on (a compact disc) **12 burn one's bridges** *or* **boats** to commit oneself to a particular course of action with no possibility of turning back **13 burn one's fingers** to suffer from having meddled or interfered ▷ *n* **14** an injury caused by exposure to heat, electrical, chemical, or radioactive agents **15** a mark caused by burning ▶ See also **burn out** [Old English *beornan*]

burn[2] *n Scot and N English* a small stream [Old English *burna*]

Burne-Jones *n* Sir Edward. 1833–98, English Pre-Raphaelite painter and designer of stained-glass windows and tapestries

burner *n* the part of a stove or lamp that produces flame or heat

Burnet *n* **1** Gilbert. 1643–1715, Scottish bishop and historian, who played a prominent role in the Glorious Revolution (1688–89); author of *The History of My Own Time* (2 vols: 1724 and 1734) **2** Sir (Frank) Macfarlane. 1899–1985, Australian physician and virologist, who shared a Nobel prize for physiology or medicine in 1960 with P. B. Medawar for their work in immunology **3** Thomas. 1635–1715, English theologian who tried to reconcile science and religion in his *Sacred theory of the Earth* (1680–89)

Burnett n Frances Hodgson. 1849–1924, US novelist, born in England; author of *Little Lord Fauntleroy* (1886) and *The Secret Garden* (1911)

Burney n **1** Charles. 1726–1814, English composer and music historian, whose books include *A General History of Music* (1776–89) **2** his daughter, **Frances**. known as **Fanny**; married name *Madame D'Arblay*. 1752–1840, English novelist and diarist: author of *Evelina* (1778). Her *Diaries and Letters* (1768–1840) are of historical interest

burning adj **1** intense; passionate **2** urgent; crucial: *a burning problem*

burning glass n a convex lens for concentrating the sun's rays to produce fire

burnish vb to make or become shiny or smooth by friction; polish [Old French *brunir* to make brown]

Burnley n an industrial town in NW England, in E Lancashire. Pop: 73 021 (2001)

burnous n a long circular cloak with a hood, worn esp. by Arabs [Arabic *burnus*]

burn out vb **1** to become or cause to become inoperative as a result of heat or friction: *the clutch burnt out* ▷ n **burnout 2** total exhaustion and inability to work effectively as a result of excessive demands or overwork

Burns n Robert. 1759–96, Scottish lyric poet. His verse, written mostly in dialect, includes love songs, nature poetry, and satires. *Auld Lang Syne* and *Tam o' Shanter* are among his best known poems

burnt vb **1** a past of **burn**[1] ▷ adj **2** affected by or as if by burning; charred

burp n **1** informal a belch ▷ vb **2** informal to belch **3** to cause (a baby) to belch [imitative]

burqa or **burka** n a long enveloping garment worn by Muslim women in public, covering all but the wearer's eyes [from Arabic]

burr n **1** the soft trilling sound given to the letter (r) in some English dialects **2** a whirring or humming sound **3** a rough edge left on metal or paper after cutting **4** a small hand-operated drill [origin unknown]

Burr n Aaron. 1756–1836, US vice-president (1800–04), who fled after killing a political rival in a duel and plotted to create an independent empire in the western US; acquitted (1807) of treason

Burra n Edward (John). 1905–76, British painter, noted esp. for his depiction of squalid and grotesque subjects

burrawang n an Australian plant with fern-like flowers and an edible nut

Burrell Collection n a gallery in Glasgow, noted for its collection of paintings, textiles, furniture, ceramics, etc. [C20: named after Sir William *Burrell* (1861–1958), Scottish shipping magnate, and his wife Constance, who founded the collection]

Burren n the Burren a limestone area on the North Clare coast in the Irish Republic, famous for its wild flowers, caves, and dolmens

Burroughs n **1** Edgar Rice. 1875–1950, US novelist, author of the *Tarzan* stories **2** William S(eward). 1914–97, US novelist, noted for his experimental works exploring themes of drug addiction, violence, and homosexuality. His novels include *Junkie* (1953), *The Naked Lunch* (1959), and *Interzone* (1989)

burrow n **1** a hole dug in the ground by a rabbit or other small animal ▷ vb **2** to dig (a tunnel or hole) in, through, or under ground **3** to move through a place by or as if by digging **4** to delve deeply: *he burrowed into his coat pocket* **5** to live in or as if in a burrow [probably variant of *borough*]

Bursa n a city in NW Turkey: founded in the 2nd century BC; seat of Bithynian kings. Pop: 1 413 000 (2005 est). Former name: **Brusa**

bursar n a treasurer of a school, college, or university [Medieval Latin *bursarius* keeper of the purse]

bursary n, pl **-ries 1** a scholarship or grant awarded esp. in Scottish and New Zealand schools and universities **2** NZ a state examination for senior pupils at secondary school

burst vb **bursting, burst 1** to break or cause to break open or apart suddenly and noisily; explode **2** to come or go suddenly and forcibly: *he burst into the room* **3** to be full to the point of breaking open: *bursting at the seams* **4** (foll. by *into*) to give vent to (something) suddenly or loudly: *she burst into song* ▷ n **5** an instance of breaking open suddenly; explosion **6** a break; breach: *there was a burst in the pipe* **7** a sudden increase of effort; spurt: *a burst of speed* **8** a sudden and violent occurrence or outbreak: *a burst of applause* [Old English *berstan*]

burton n go for a burton Brit and NZ slang **a** to be broken, useless, or lost **b** to die [origin unknown]

Burton n **1** Sir Richard Francis. 1821–90, English explorer, Orientalist, and writer who discovered Lake Tanganyika with John Speke (1858); produced the first unabridged translation of *The Thousand Nights and a Night* (1885–88) **2** Richard, real name *Richard Jenkins*. 1925–84, Welsh stage and film actor: films include *Becket* (1964), *Who's Afraid of Virginia Woolf?* (1966), and *Equus* (1977) **3** Robert, pen name *Democritus Junior*. 1577–1640, English clergyman, scholar, and writer, noted for his *Anatomy of Melancholy* (1621) **4** Tim. born 1958, US film director whose work includes *Beetlejuice* (1988), *Batman* (1989), *Edward Scissorhands* (1990), *Ed Wood* (1994), *Corpse Bride* (2005), and *Alice in Wonderland* (2010)

Burton-upon-Trent n a town in W central England, in E Staffordshire: famous for brewing. Pop: 43 784 (2001)

Burundi n a republic in E central Africa: inhabited chiefly by the Hutu, Tutsi, and Twa (Pygmy); made part of German East Africa in 1899; part of the Belgian territory of Ruanda-Urundi from 1923 until it became independent in 1962; ethnic violence has erupted at times between Hutu and Tutsi, as in Rwanda; consists mainly of high plateaus along the main Nile-Congo dividing range, dropping rapidly to the Great Rift Valley in the west. Official languages: Kirundi and French. Religion: Christian majority. Currency: Burundi franc. Capital: Bujumbura. Pop: 10 888 321 (2013 est). Area: 27 731 sq km (10 707 sq miles). Former name (until 1962): Urundi

Burundian adj **1** of or relating to Burundi or its inhabitants ▷ n **2** a native or inhabitant of Burundi

bury vb **buries, burying, buried 1** to place (a corpse) in a grave **2** to place (something) in the earth and cover it with soil **3** to cover (something) from sight; hide **4** to occupy (oneself) with deep concentration: *he buried himself in his work* **5** to dismiss (a feeling) from the mind: *they decided to bury any hard feelings* [Old English *byrgan*]

Bury n **1** a town in NW England, in Bury unitary authority, Greater Manchester: an early textile centre. Pop: 60 178 (2001) **2** a unitary authority in NW England, in Greater Manchester. Pop: 181 900 (2003 est). Area: 99 sq km (38 sq miles)

Buryat Republic or **Buryatia** n a constituent republic of SE central Russia, on Lake Baikal: mountainous, with forests covering over half the total area. Capital: Ulan-Ude. Pop: 981 000 (2002). Area: 351 300 sq km (135 608 sq miles)

Bury St Edmunds n a market town in E England, in Suffolk. Pop: 36 218 (2001)

bus n **1** a large motor vehicle designed to carry passengers between stopping places along a regular route **2** informal a car or aircraft that is old and shaky **3** electronics, computers an electrical conductor used to make a common connection between several circuits ▷ vb **bussing, bussed** or **busing, bused 4** to travel or transport by bus **5** chiefly US and Canad to transport (children) by bus from one area to another in order to create racially integrated schools [short for OMNIBUS]

Busan n a port in SE South Korea, on the Korea Strait: the second largest city and chief port of the country; industrial centre; two universities. Pop: 3 527 000 (2005 est). Former name (until 2000): **Pusan**

busby *n*, *pl* **-bies** a tall fur helmet worn by certain British soldiers [origin unknown]

Busby *n* Sir Matthew, known as *Matt*. 1909–94, British footballer. He managed Manchester United (1946–69)

bush¹ *n* **1** a dense woody plant, smaller than a tree, with many branches; shrub **2** a dense cluster of such shrubs; thicket **3** something resembling a bush, esp. in density: *a bush of hair* **4** **the bush** an uncultivated area covered with trees or shrubs in Australia, Africa, New Zealand, and Canada **5** *Canad* an area on a farm on which timber is grown and cut **6** **beat about the bush** to avoid the point at issue [Germanic]

bush² *n* **1** a thin metal sleeve or tubular lining serving as a bearing ▷ *vb* **2** to fit a bush to (a casing or bearing) [Middle Dutch *busse* box]

Bush *n* **1** George. born 1924, US politician; vice president of the US (1981–89): 41st president of the US (1989–93) **2** his son, George W(alker). born 1946, US Republican politician; 43rd president of the US (2001–09) **3** Kate. born 1958, English singer and songwriter: her recordings include "Wuthering Heights" (1978), *Hounds of Love* (1985), and *Aerial* (2005)

bushbaby *n*, *pl* **-babies** a small agile tree-living mammal with large eyes and a long tail

bushed *adj informal* extremely tired; exhausted

bushel *n Brit* an obsolete unit of dry or liquid measure equal to 8 gallons (36.4 litres) [Old French *boissel*]

bushfire *n* an uncontrolled fire in the bush

Bushire *n* a port in SW Iran, on the Persian Gulf; nuclear power station. Pop: 166 000 (2005 est). Persian name: Bushehr

bush jacket *n* a casual jacket with four patch pockets and a belt

bush line *n Canad* an airline operating in the bush country of Canada's northern regions

bush lot *n Canad* same as **bush¹** (5)

bushman *n*, *pl* **-men** *Austral and NZ* a person who lives or travels in the bush

Bushman *n*, *pl* **-men** a member of a hunting and gathering people of southern Africa [Afrikaans *boschjesman*]

bush pilot *n Canad* a pilot who operates a plane in the bush country

bush sickness *n NZ* a disease of animals caused by mineral deficiency in old bush country ▷ **bush-sick** *adj*

bush telegraph *n* a means of spreading rumour or gossip

bush tucker *n Austral* **1** any wild animal, insect, plant, etc., traditionally used as food by Australian Aborigines **2** a style of cooking using these ingredients

bushveld *n S African* bushy countryside [Afrikaans]

bushwalking *n Austral* the leisure activity of walking in the bush ▷ **bushwalker** *n*

bushy *adj* **bushier**, **bushiest** **1** (of hair) thick and shaggy **2** covered or overgrown with bushes

business *n* **1** the purchase and sale of goods and services **2** a commercial or industrial establishment **3** a trade or profession **4** commercial activity: *the two countries should do business with each other* **5** proper or rightful concern or responsibility: *mind your own business* **6** an affair; matter: *it's a dreadful business* **7** serious work or activity: *get down to business* **8** a difficult or complicated matter: *it's a business trying to see him* **9** **mean business** to be in earnest [Old English *bisignis* care, attentiveness]

businesslike *adj* efficient and methodical

businessman *or fem* **businesswoman** *n*, *pl* **-men** *or* **-women** a person engaged in commercial or industrial business, usually an owner or executive

business park *n* an area specially designated to accommodate business offices, light industry, etc.

business rate *n* a tax levied on businesses, based on the value of their premises

business school *n* an institution that offers courses to managers in aspects of business, such as marketing, finance, and law

busker *n* a person who entertains for money in streets or stations [perhaps from Spanish *buscar* to look for] ▷ **busk** *vb*

busman's holiday *n informal* a holiday spent doing the same as one does at work

Busra *or* **Busrah** *n* variant spellings of **Basra**

Buss *n* Frances Mary. 1827–94, British educationalist; a pioneer of secondary education for girls, who campaigned for women's admission to university

Bussell *n* Darcey (Andrea). born 1969, British ballet dancer, principal ballerina with the Royal Ballet (1989–2006)

bust¹ *n* **1** a woman's bosom **2** a sculpture of the head, shoulders, and upper chest of a person [Italian *busto* a sculpture]

bust² *informal vb* **busting**, **busted** *or* **bust 1** to burst or break **2** (of the police) to raid or search (a place) or arrest (someone) **3** *US and Canad* to demote in military rank ▷ *adj* **4** broken **5** **go bust** to become bankrupt [from *burst*]

bustard *n* a bird with a long strong legs, a heavy body, a long neck, and speckled plumage

bustle¹ *vb* **-tling**, **-tled 1** (often foll. by *about*) to hurry with a great show of energy or activity ▷ *n* **2** energetic and noisy activity [probably obsolete *buskle* to prepare] ▷ **bustling** *adj*

bustle² *n* a cushion or framework worn by women in the late 19th century at the back in order to expand the skirt [origin unknown]

bust-up *informal n* **1** a serious quarrel, esp. one ending a relationship **2** *Brit, Austral and NZ* a disturbance or brawl ▷ *vb* **bust up 3** to quarrel and part **4** to disrupt (a meeting), esp. violently

busy *adj* **busier**, **busiest 1** actively or fully engaged; occupied **2** crowded with or characterized by activity **3** (of a telephone line) in use; engaged ▷ *vb* **busies**, **busying**, **busied 4** to make or keep (someone, esp. oneself) busy; occupy [Old English *bisig*] ▷ **busily** *adv*

busybody *n*, *pl* **-bodies** a meddlesome, prying, or officious person

but *conj* **1** contrary to expectation: *he cut his hand but didn't cry* **2** in contrast; on the contrary: *I like seafood but my husband doesn't* **3** other than: *we can't do anything but wait* **4** without it happening: *we never go out but it rains* ▷ *prep* **5** except: *they saved all but one* **6** **but for** were it not for: *but for you, we couldn't have managed* ▷ *adv* **7** only: *I can but try; he was but a child* ▷ *n* **8** an objection: *ifs and buts* [Old English *būtan* without, except]

but and ben *n Scot* a two-roomed cottage consisting of an outer room (**but**) and an inner room (**ben**) [Old English *būtan* outside + *binnan* inside]

butane (**byew**-tane) *n* a colourless gas used in the manufacture of rubber and fuels [from *butyl*]

butch *adj slang* (of a woman or man) markedly or aggressively masculine [from *butcher*]

butcher *n* **1** a person who sells meat **2** a person who kills animals for meat **3** a brutal murderer ▷ *vb* **4** to kill and prepare (animals) for meat **5** to kill (people) at random or brutally **6** to make a mess of; botch [Old French *bouchier*]

butcherbird *n* an Australian magpie that impales its prey on thorns

butchery *n*, *pl* **-eries 1** senseless slaughter **2** the business of a butcher

Bute¹ *n* an island off the coast of SW Scotland, in Argyll and Bute council area: situated in the Firth of Clyde, separated from the Cowal peninsula by the **Kyles of Bute**. Chief town: Rothesay. Pop: 7228 (2001). Area: 121 sq km (47 sq miles)

Bute² *n* John Stuart, 3rd Earl of Bute. 1713–92, British Tory statesman; prime minister (1762–63)

Butenandt *n* Adolf Frederick Johann. 1903–95, German organic chemist. He shared the Nobel prize for chemistry (1939) for his pioneering work on sex hormones

b

Buteshire *n* (until 1975) a county of SW Scotland, consisting of islands in the Firth of Clyde and Kilbrannan Sound: formerly part of Strathclyde region (1975–96), now part of Argyll and Bute council area

Buthelezi *n* Mangosouthu Gatsha, known as *Chief Buthelezi*. born 1928, Zulu leader, chief minister of the KwaZulu territory of South Africa from 1970 until its abolition in 1994; founder of the Inkatha movement and advocate of Zulu autonomy; minister of home affairs (1994–2004)

butler *n* the head manservant of a household, in charge of the wines, table, etc. [Old French *bouteille* bottle]

Butler *n* **1** Joseph. 1692–1752, English bishop and theologian, author of *Analogy of Religion* (1736) **2** Josephine (**Elizabeth**). 1828–1906, British social reformer, noted esp. for her campaigns against state regulation of prostitution **3** Reg, full name *Reginald Cotterell Butler*. 1913–81, British metal sculptor; his works include *The Unknown Political Prisoner* (1953) **4** R(**ichard**) A(**usten**), Baron Butler of Saffron Walden, known as *Rab Butler*. 1902–82, British Conservative politician: Chancellor of the Exchequer (1951–55); Home Secretary (1957–62); Foreign Secretary (1963–64) **5** Samuel. 1612–80, English poet and satirist; author of *Hudibras* (1663–78) **6** Samuel. 1835–1902, British novelist, noted for his satirical work *Erewhon* (1872) and his autobiographical novel *The Way of All Flesh* (1903)

butt¹ *n* **1** the thicker or blunt end of something, such as the stock of a rifle **2** the unused end of a cigarette or cigar; stub **3** *chiefly US and Canad slang* the buttocks [Middle English]

butt² *n* **1 a** a person or thing that is the target of ridicule or teasing **2** *shooting, archery* **a** a mound of earth behind the target **b** butts the target range [Old French *but*]

butt³ *n* **1** to strike (something or someone) with the head or horns **2** (foll. by in or into) to intrude, esp. into a conversation; interfere ▷ *n* **3** a blow with the head or horns [Old French *boter*]

butt⁴ *n* a large cask for collecting or storing liquids [Late Latin *buttis* cask]

Butt *n* Dame Clara. 1872–1936, English contralto

butte (byewt) *n US and Canad* an isolated steep flat-topped hill [Old French *bute* mound behind a target]

butter *n* **1** an edible fatty yellow solid made from cream by churning **2** any substance with a butter-like consistency, such as peanut butter ▷ *vb* **3** to put butter on or in (something) ▶ See also **butter up** [Greek *bous* cow + *turos* cheese] > **buttery** *adj*

butter bean *n* a large pale flat edible bean

buttercup *n* a small bright yellow flower

Butterfield *n* William. 1814–1900, British architect of the Gothic Revival; his buildings include Keble College, Oxford (1870) and All Saints, Margaret Street, London (1849–59)

butterfingers *n informal* a person who drops things by mistake or fails to catch things

butterflies *pl n informal* a nervous feeling in the stomach

butterfly *n, pl* **-flies 1** an insect with a slender body and brightly coloured wings **2** a swimming stroke in which the arms are plunged forward together in large circular movements **3** a person who never settles with one interest or occupation for long [Old English *buttorflēoge*]

butterfly nut *n* same as **wing nut**

Buttermere *n* a lake in NW England, in Cumbria, in the Lake District, southwest of Keswick. Length: 2 km (1.25 miles)

buttermilk *n* the sourish liquid remaining after the butter has been separated from milk

butterscotch *n* a hard brittle toffee made with butter, brown sugar, etc.

butter up *vb* to flatter

Butterworth *n* **1** George. 1885–1916, British composer, noted for his interest in folk song and his settings of Housman's poems **2** Nick. born 1946, English writer and illustrator of children's books, many of which feature Percy, the animal-loving park keeper

buttery *n, pl* **-teries** *Brit* (in some universities) a room in which food and drink are sold to students [Latin *butta* cask]

buttock *n* **1** either of the two large fleshy masses that form the human rump **2** the corresponding part in some mammals [perhaps from Old English *buttuc* round slope]

button *n* **1** a disc or knob of plastic, wood, etc., attached to a garment, which fastens two surfaces together by passing through a buttonhole **2** a small disc that operates a door bell or machine when pressed **3** a small round object, such as a sweet or badge **4** not worth a **button** *Brit* of no value; useless ▷ *vb* **5** to fasten (a garment) with a button or buttons [Old French *boton*]

buttonhole *n* **1** a slit in a garment through which a button is passed to fasten two surfaces together **2** a flower worn pinned to the lapel or in the buttonhole ▷ *vb* **-holing, -holed 3** to detain (a person) in conversation

button mushroom *n* an unripe mushroom

button up *vb* **1** to fasten (a garment) with a button or buttons **2** *informal* to conclude (business) satisfactorily: *we've got it all buttoned up*

buttress *n* **1** a construction, usually of brick or stone, built to support a wall **2** any support or prop ▷ *vb* **3** to support (a wall) with a buttress **4** to support or sustain: *his observations are buttressed by the most recent scholarly research* [Old French *bouter* to thrust]

butty *n, pl* **-ties** *chiefly N English dialect* a sandwich: *a jam butty* [from *buttered* (bread)]

Butung *n* an island of Indonesia, southeast of Sulawesi: hilly and forested. Chief town: Baubau. Area: 4555 sq km (1759 sq miles)

butyl (byew-tile) *adj* of or containing any of four isomeric forms of the group C_4H_9-: *butyl rubber* [Latin *butyrum* butter]

buxom *adj* (of a woman) healthily plump, attractive, and full-bosomed [Middle English *buhsum* compliant]

Buxtehude *n* Dietrich. 1637–1707, Danish composer and organist, resident in Germany from 1668, who influenced Bach and Handel

Buxton *n* a town in N England, in NW Derbyshire in the Peak District: thermal springs. Pop: 20 836 (2001)

buy *vb* **buying, bought 1** to acquire (something) by paying a sum of money for it; purchase **2** to be capable of purchasing: *money can't buy love* **3** to acquire by any exchange or sacrifice: *the rise in interest rates was just to buy time until the weekend* **4** to bribe (someone) **5** *slang* to accept (something) as true **6** (foll. by into) to purchase shares of (a company) ▷ *n* **7** a purchase: *a good buy* ▶ See also **buy in**, **buy into**, etc. [Old English *bycgan*]

> **USAGE** The use of *off* after buy as in *I bought this off my neighbour* was formerly considered incorrect, but is now acceptable in informal contexts.

buyer *n* **1** a person who buys; customer **2** a person employed to buy merchandise for a shop or factory

buy in *vb* to purchase (goods) in large quantities

buy into *vb* to agree with (an argument or theory)

buy off *vb* to pay (someone) to drop a charge or end opposition

buy-out *n* **1** the purchase of a company, often by its former employees ▷ *vb* **buy out 2** to purchase the ownership of a company or property from (someone)

buy up *vb* **1** to purchase all that is available of (something) **2** to purchase a controlling interest in (a company)

buzz *n* **1** a rapidly vibrating humming sound, such as of a bee **2** a low sound, such as of many voices in conversation **3** *informal* a telephone call **4** *informal* a sense of excitement ▷ *vb* **5** to make a vibrating sound like that of a prolonged *z* **6** (of a place) to be filled with an air of excitement: *the city buzzed with the news* **7** to summon (someone) with a buzzer **8** *informal* to fly an aircraft very low over (people, buildings, or another aircraft) **9 buzz about** *or* **around** to move around quickly and busily [imitative]

buzzard *n* a bird of prey with broad wings and tail and a soaring flight [Latin *buteo* hawk]

buzzer *n* an electronic device that produces a buzzing sound as a signal

buzzkill *or* **buzzkiller** *n informal* someone or something that stops people from enjoying themselves

buzz off *vb Brit and Austral informal* to go away; depart

buzz word *n informal* a word, originally from a particular jargon, which becomes a popular vogue word

by *prep* **1** used to indicate the performer of the action of a passive verb: *seeds eaten by the birds* **2** used to indicate the person responsible for a creative work: *three songs by Britten* **3** via; through: *enter by the back door* **4** used to indicate a means used: *he frightened her by hiding behind the door* **5** beside; next to; near: *a tree by the stream* **6** passing the position of; past: *I drove by the place she works* **7** not later than; before: *return the books by Tuesday* **8** used to indicate extent: *it is hotter by five degrees* **9** multiplied by: *four by three equals twelve* **10** during the passing of: *by night* **11** placed between measurements of the various dimensions of something: *a plank fourteen inches by seven* ▷ *adv* **12** near: *the house is close by* **13** away; aside: *he put some money by each week* **14** passing a point near something; past: *he drove by* ▷ *n, pl* **byes 15** same as **bye**[1] [Old English *bī*]

Byam Shaw *n* Glen Alexander. 1904–81, British actor and theatre director; director of the Shakespeare Memorial Theatre (1953–59)

by and by *adv* presently or eventually

by and large *adv* in general; on the whole

Byatt *n* Dame A(ntonia) S(usan). born 1936, British novelist; her books include *The Virgin in the Garden* (1978), *Possession* (1990), and *A Whistling Woman* (2002)

Bydgoszcz *n* an industrial city and port in N Poland: under Prussian rule from 1772 to 1919. Pop: 579 000 (2005 est). German name: **Bromberg**

bye[1] *n* **1** *sport* status of a player or team who wins a preliminary round by virtue of having no opponent **2** *cricket* a run scored off a ball not struck by the batsman **3 by the bye** incidentally; by the way [variant of *by*]

bye[2] *or* **bye-bye** *interj informal* goodbye

by-election *or* **bye-election** *n* an election held during the life of a parliament to fill a vacant seat

Byelgorod-Dnestrovski *n* a variant spelling of Belgorod-Dnestrovski

Byelorussia *or* **Byelorussian Republic** *n* a variant spelling of Belarus

Byelorussian *adj, n* a variant spelling of Belarussian

Byelostok *n* a Russian name for Białystok

Byelovo *or* **Belovo** *n* a city in W central Russia. Pop: 65 000 (2005 est)

bygone *adj* past; former: *a bygone age*

bygones *pl n* **let bygones be bygones** to agree to forget past quarrels

bylaw *or* **bye-law** *n* a rule made by a local authority [probably Scandinavian]

by-line *n* **1** a line under the title of an article in a newspaper or magazine, giving the author's name **2** same as **touchline**

Byng *n* **1** George, Viscount Torrington. 1663–1733, British admiral: defeated fleet of James Edward Stuart, the Old Pretender, off Scotland (1708); defeated Spanish fleet off Messina (1717) **2** his son John. 1704–57, English admiral: executed after failing to relieve Minorca **3** Julian Hedworth George, 1st Viscount Byng of Vimy. 1862–1935, British general in World War I; governor general of Canada (1921–26)

BYO *or* **BYOG** *n Austral and NZ* an unlicensed restaurant at which diners may bring their own alcoholic drink [*bring your own (grog)*]

bypass *n* **1** a main road built to avoid a city **2** a secondary pipe, channel, or appliance through which the flow of a substance, such as gas or electricity, is redirected **3** a surgical operation in which the blood flow is redirected away from a diseased or blocked part of the heart ▷ *vb* **4** to go around or avoid (a city, obstruction, problem, etc) **5** to proceed without reference to (regulations or a superior); get round; avoid

by-play *n* secondary action in a play, carried on apart while the main action proceeds

by-product *n* **1** a secondary or incidental product of a manufacturing process **2** a side effect

Byrd *n* **1** Richard Evelyn. 1888–1957, US rear admiral, aviator, and polar explorer **2** William. 1543–1623, English composer and organist, noted for his madrigals, masses, and music for virginals

Byrd Land *n* a part of Antarctica, east of the Ross Ice Shelf and the Ross Sea: claimed for the US by Admiral Richard E. Byrd in 1929, though all claims are suspended under the Antarctic Treaty of 1959. Former name: **Marie Byrd Land**

Byrds *pl n* **the**. US folk-rock and country-rock group (1964–73), noted for their vocal harmonies and 12-string guitar sound. Their albums include *Mr. Tambourine Man* (1965), *Younger Than Yesterday* (1967), and *Sweetheart of the Rodeo* (1968)

byre *n Brit* a shelter for cows [Old English *bȳre*]

byroad *n* a secondary or side road

Byron *n* George Gordon, 6th Baron. 1788–1824, British Romantic poet, noted also for his passionate and disastrous love affairs. His major works include *Childe Harold's Pilgrimage* (1812–18), and *Don Juan* (1819–24). He spent much of his life abroad and died while fighting for Greek independence ❯ **Byronic** *adj* ❯ **Byronically** *adv* ❯ **Byronism** *n*

bystander *n* a person present but not involved; onlooker; spectator

byte *n computers* a group of bits processed as one unit of data [origin unknown]

Bytom *n* an industrial city in SW Poland, in Upper Silesia: under Prussian and German rule from 1742 to 1945. Pop: 185 793 (2007 est). German name: **Beuthen**

byway *n* a secondary or side road, esp. in the country

byword *n* **1** a person or thing regarded as a perfect example of something: *their name is a byword for quality* **2** a common saying; proverb

Byzantine *adj* **1** of Byzantium, an ancient Greek city on the Bosporus **2** of the Byzantine Empire, the continuation of the Roman Empire in the East **3** of the style of architecture developed in the Byzantine Empire, with massive domes, rounded arches, and mosaics **4** (of attitudes, methods, etc.) inflexible or complicated ▷ *n* **5** an inhabitant of Byzantium

Byzantium *n* an ancient Greek city on the Bosporus: founded about 660 BC; rebuilt by Constantine I in 330 AD and called Constantinople; present-day Istanbul

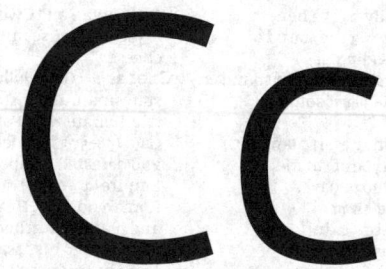

C 1 centi- 2 *cricket* caught 3 cubic 4 the speed of light in free space

C 1 *music* the first note of a major scale containing no sharps or flats (**C major**) 2 *chem* carbon 3 Celsius 4 centigrade 5 century: *C20* 6 coulomb 7 the Roman numeral for 100 8 a high-level computer programming language

c. (used preceding a date) about: *c. 1800* [Latin *circa*]

C. 1 (on maps as part of name) Cape 2 Catholic 3 Celtic 4 Conservative 5 Corps

Ca *chem* calcium

CA 1 California 2 Central America 3 Chartered Accountant

ca. (used preceding a date) about: *ca. 1930* [Latin *circa*]

cab *n* 1 a taxi 2 the enclosed driver's compartment of a lorry, bus, or train [from *cabriolet*]

cabal (kab-**bal**) *n* 1 a small group of political plotters 2 a secret plot or conspiracy [French *cabale*]

Caballé *n* **Montserrat**. born 1933, Spanish operatic soprano

cabaret (kab-a-ray) *n* 1 a floor show of dancing and singing at a nightclub or restaurant 2 a place providing such entertainment [French: tavern]

cabbage *n* 1 a vegetable with a large head of green or reddish-purple leaves 2 *informal, offensive* a person who is unable to move or think, as a result of brain damage [Norman French *caboche* head]

Cabbagetown *n* a former slum area of Toronto, now known for its Victorian architecture and thriving arts community

cabbage tree *n* NZ a palm-like tree with a bare trunk and spiky leaves

cabbage white *n* a large white butterfly whose larvae feed on cabbage leaves

cabbie *or* **cabby** *n, pl* **-bies** *informal* a taxi driver

caber *n* *Scot* a heavy section of trimmed tree trunk tossed in competition at Highland games [Gaelic *cabar* pole]

Cabernet Sauvignon (kab-er-nay so-veen-yon) *n* a dry red wine produced in the Bordeaux region of France and elsewhere [French]

Cabimas *n* a town in NW Venezuela, on the NE shore of Lake Maracaibo. Pop: 284 000 (2005 est)

cabin *n* 1 a room used as living quarters in a ship or boat 2 a small simple dwelling: *a log cabin* 3 the enclosed part of an aircraft in which the passengers or crew sit [Late Latin *capanna* hut]

cabin boy *n* a boy who waits on the officers and passengers of a ship

cabin cruiser *n* a motorboat with a cabin

Cabinda *n* an exclave of Angola, separated from the rest of the country by part of the Democratic Republic of Congo. Pop: about 300 000 (2002 est). Area: 7270 sq km (2807 sq miles)

cabinet *n* a piece of furniture containing shelves, cupboards, or drawers for storage or display: *a filing cabinet; a cocktail cabinet* [Old French *cabine* cabin]

Cabinet *n* a committee of senior government ministers or advisers to a president

cabinet-maker *n* a person who makes fine furniture ⟩ **cabinet-making** *n*

cabin fever *n* Canad acute depression resulting from being isolated or sharing cramped quarters

cable *n* 1 a strong thick rope of twisted hemp or wire 2 a bundle of wires covered with plastic or rubber that conducts electricity 3 a telegram sent abroad by submarine cable or telephone line 4 Also called: **cable stitch** a knitted design which resembles a twisted rope ▷ *vb* **-bling, -bled** 5 to send (someone) a message by cable [Late Latin *capulum* halter]

cable car *n* a vehicle that is pulled up a steep slope by a moving cable

cablegram *n* a more formal name for **cable** (3)

cable television *n* a television service in which the subscriber's television is connected to a central receiver by cable

caboodle *n* **the whole caboodle** *informal* the whole lot [origin unknown]

caboose *n* 1 US and Canad a railway car at the rear of a train, used as quarters for the crew 2 Canad a mobile building used as a cookhouse or bunkhouse for a work crew [Dutch *cabūse*]

Cabora Bassa *n* the site on the Zambezi River in N Mozambique of the largest dam in southern Africa

Cabot *n* 1 **John** Italian name *Giovanni Caboto*. 1450–98, Italian explorer, who landed in North America in 1497, under patent from Henry VII of England, and explored the coast from Nova Scotia to Newfoundland 2 his son, **Sebastian**. ?1476–1557, Italian navigator and cartographer, who served the English and Spanish crowns: explored the La Plata region of Brazil (1526–30)

Cabral *n* **Pedro Álvares**. ?1460–?1526, Portuguese navigator: discovered and took possession of Brazil for Portugal in 1500

cabriolet (kab-ree-oh-lay) *n* a small two-wheeled horse-drawn carriage with a folding hood [French: a little skip; referring to the lightness of movement]

cab sav *n* Austral informal short for **Cabernet Sauvignon**

cacao (kak-kah-oh) *n* a tropical American tree with seed pods (**cacao beans**) from which cocoa and chocolate are prepared [Mexican Indian *cacauatl* cacao beans]

Cáceres *n* a city in W Spain: held by the Moors (1142–1229). Pop: 87 088 (2003 est)

cachalot *n* the sperm whale [Portuguese *cachalote*]

cache (kash) *n* a hidden store of weapons, provisions, or treasure [French *cacher* to hide]

cachet (kash-shay) *n* prestige or distinction: *a Mercedes carries a certain cachet* [French]

cachou *n* a lozenge eaten to sweeten the breath [Malay *kāchu*]

cack-handed *adj informal* clumsy: *I open cans in a very cack-handed way* [dialect *cack* excrement]

cackle *vb* **-ling, -led 1** to laugh shrilly **2** (of a hen) to squawk with shrill broken notes ▷ *n* **3** the sound of cackling [probably imitative] ▷ **cackling** *adj*

cacophony (kak-**koff**-on-ee) *n* harsh discordant sound: *a cacophony of barking* [Greek *kakos* bad + *phōnē* sound] ▷ **cacophonous** *adj*

cactus *n, pl* **-tuses** *or* **-ti** a thick fleshy desert plant with spines but no leaves [Greek *kaktos* type of thistle]

cad *n old-fashioned, informal* a man who behaves dishonourably [from *caddie*] ▷ **caddish** *adj*

cadaver (kad-**dav**-ver) *n med* a corpse [Latin]

cadaverous *adj* pale, thin, and haggard

Cadbury *n* George. 1839–1922, British Quaker industrialist and philanthropist. He established, with his brother **Richard Cadbury** (1835–99), the chocolate-making company Cadbury Brothers and the garden village Bournville, near Birmingham, for their workers

caddie *n* **1** a person who carries a golfer's clubs ▷ *vb* **-dying, -died 2** to act as a caddie [from *cadet*]

caddis fly *n* an insect whose larva (the **caddis worm**) lives underwater in a protective case of silk, sand, and stones

caddy[1] *n, pl* **-dies** *chiefly Brit* a small container for tea [Malay *kati*]

caddy[2] *n, pl* **-dies,** *vb* **-dies, -dying, -died** same as **caddie**

Cade *n* Jack. died 1450, English leader of the Kentish rebellion against the misgovernment of Henry VI (1450)

cadence (**kade**-enss) *n* **1** the rise and fall in the pitch of the voice **2** the close of a musical phrase [Latin *cadere* to fall]

cadenza *n* a complex solo passage in a piece of music [Italian]

cadet *n* a young person training for the armed forces or the police [French]

cadge *vb* **cadging, cadged** *informal* to get (something) from someone by taking advantage of his or her generosity [origin unknown] ▷ **cadger** *n*

cadi *n* a judge in a Muslim community [Arabic *qāḍī* judge]

Cádiz *n* a port in SW Spain, on a narrow peninsula that forms the **Bay of Cádiz** at the E end of the **Gulf of Cádiz**, founded about 1100 BC as a Phoenician trading colony; centre of trade with America from the 16th to 18th centuries. Pop: 134 989 (2003 est)

cadmium *n chem* a bluish-white metallic element found in zinc ores and used in electroplating and alloys. Symbol: **Cd** [Latin *cadmia* zinc ore]

cadre (**kah**-der) *n* a small group of people selected and trained to form the core of a political organization or military unit [Latin *quadrum* square]

Cadwalader *n* 7th century AD, legendary king of the Britons, probably a confusion of several historical figures

caecum *or US* **cecum** (**seek**-um) *n, pl* **-ca** (-ka) the pouch at the beginning of the large intestine [short for Latin *intestinum caecum* blind intestine]

Cædmon *n* 7th century AD, Anglo-Saxon poet and monk, the earliest English poet whose name survives

Caelian *n* the southeasternmost of the Seven Hills of Rome

Caen *n* an industrial city in NW France. Pop: 112 790 (2008)

Caenozoic *adj* same as **Cenozoic**

Caerleon *n* a town in SE Wales, in Newport county borough on the River Usk: traditionally the seat of King Arthur's court. Pop: 9392 (2001)

Caernarfon, Caernarvon *or* **Carnarvon** *n* a port and resort in NW Wales, in Gwynedd on the Menai Strait: 13th-century castle. Pop: 9726 (2001)

Caernarvonshire *n* (until 1974) a county of NW Wales, now part of Gwynedd

Caerphilly *n* **1** a market town in SE Wales, in Caerphilly county borough: site of the largest castle in Wales (13th–14th centuries). Pop: 31 060 (2001) **2** a county borough in SE Wales, created in 1996 from parts of Mid

Glamorgan and Gwent. Pop: 170 200 (2003 est). Area: 275 sq km (106 sq miles) **3** a creamy white mild-flavoured cheese

Caesar *n* **1** Gaius Julius. 100–44 BC, Roman general, statesman, and historian. He formed the first triumvirate with Pompey and Crassus (60), conquered Gaul (58–50), invaded Britain (55–54), mastered Italy (49) and defeated Pompey (46). As dictator of the Roman Empire (49–44) he destroyed the power of the corrupt Roman nobility. He also introduced the Julian calendar and planned further reforms, but fear of his sovereign power led to his assassination (44) by conspirators led by Marcus Brutus and Cassius Longinus **2** any Roman emperor **3** (*sometimes not cap*) any emperor, autocrat, dictator, or other powerful ruler **4** a title of the Roman emperors from Augustus to Hadrian **5** (in the Roman Empire) **a** a title borne by the imperial heir from the reign of Hadrian **b** the heir, deputy, and subordinate ruler to either of the two emperors under Diocletian's system of government **6** short for **Caesar salad**

Caesaraugusta *n* the Latin name for **Zaragoza**

Caesarea *n* an ancient port in NW Israel, capital of Roman Palestine: founded by Herod the Great

Caesarea Mazaca *n* the ancient name of **Kayseri**

Caesarean, Caesarian *or US* **Cesarean** (siz-**zair**-ee-an) *n* short for **Caesarean section**

Caesarean section *n* surgical incision into the womb in order to deliver a baby [from the belief that Julius Caesar was delivered in this way]

Caesar salad *n* a salad of lettuce, cheese, and croutons with a dressing of olive oil, garlic, and lemon juice [after *Caesar Cardini*, its inventor]

caesium *or US* **cesium** *n chem* a silvery-white metallic element used in photocells. Symbol: **Cs** [Latin *caesius* bluish-grey]

caesura (siz-**your**-ra) *n, pl* **-ras** *or* **-rae** (-ree) a pause in a line of verse [Latin: a cutting]

Caetano *n* Marcello. 1906–80, prime minister of Portugal from 1968 until he was replaced by an army coup in 1974

café *n* **1** a small or inexpensive restaurant that serves drinks and snacks or light meals **2** *S African* a corner shop [French]

cafeteria *n* a self-service restaurant [American Spanish: coffee shop]

caff *n slang* a café

caffeine *n* a stimulant found in tea, coffee, and cocoa [German *Kaffee* coffee]

caftan *n* same as **kaftan**

cage *n* **1** an enclosure made of bars or wires, for keeping birds or animals in **2** the enclosed platform of a lift in a mine ▷ *vb* **caging, caged 3** to confine in a cage [Latin *cavea* enclosure] ▷ **caged** *adj*

Cage *n* John. 1912–92, US composer of experimental music for a variety of conventional, modified, or invented instruments. He evolved a type of music apparently undetermined by the composer, such as in *Imaginary Landscape* (1951) for 12 radio sets. Other works include *Reunion* (1968), *Apartment Building 1776* (1976), and *Europeras 3 and 4* (1990)

cagey *adj* **cagier, cagiest** *informal* reluctant to go into details; wary: *he is cagey about what he paid for the business* [origin unknown] ▷ **cagily** *adv*

Cagliari[1] *n* a port in Italy, the capital of Sardinia, on the coast. Pop: 164 249 (2001)

Cagliari[2] *n* Paolo. original name of (Paolo) **Veronese**

Cagliostro *n* Count Alessandro di, original name *Giuseppe Balsamo*. 1743–95, Italian adventurer and magician, who was imprisoned for life by the Inquisition for his association with freemasonry

Cagney *n* James. 1899–1986, US film actor, esp. in gangster roles; his films include *The Public Enemy* (1931), *Angels with Dirty Faces* (1938), *The Roaring Twenties* (1939), and *Yankee Doodle Dandy* (1942) for which he won an Oscar

cagoule (kag-**gool**) *n Brit* a lightweight hooded waterproof jacket [French]

Cahokia Mounds *pl n* the largest group of prehistoric Indian earthworks in the US, located northeast of East St Louis

cahoots *pl n* **in cahoots** *informal* conspiring together: *the loan sharks were in cahoots with the home-improvement companies* [origin unknown]

Caicos Islands *pl n* a group of islands in the Caribbean: part of the British dependency of the **Turks and Caicos Islands**

caiman *n, pl* **-mans** same as **cayman**

Caine *n* Sir Michael. real name *Maurice Micklewhite*. born 1933, British film actor. His films include *The Ipcress File* (1965), *Get Carter* (1971), *Educating Rita* (1983), *Hannah and Her Sisters* (1986), and *The Cider House Rules* (1999)

Caird Coast *n* a region of Antarctica: a part of Coats Land on the SE coast of the Weddell Sea; now included in the British Antarctic Territory (claim suspended under the Antarctic Treaty of 1959)

cairn *n* a mound of stones erected as a memorial or marker [Gaelic *carn*]

cairngorm *n* a smoky yellow or brown quartz gemstone [*Cairn Gorm* (blue cairn), mountain in Scotland]

Cairngorm Mountains *pl n* a mountain range of NE Scotland: part of the Grampians. Highest peak: Ben Macdui, 1309 m (4296 ft); designated a national park in 2003. Also called: **the Cairngorms**

Cairns *n* a port in NE Australia, in Queensland. Pop: 98 981 (2001)

Cairo *n* the capital of Egypt, on the Nile: the largest city in Africa and in the Middle East; industrial centre; site of the university and mosque of Al Azhar (founded in 972). Pop: 11 146 000 (2005 est). Arabic name: **El Qahira** > **Cairene** *n, adj*

caisson (kayss-on) *n* a watertight chamber used to carry out construction work under water [French]

Caithness *n* (until 1975) a county of NE Scotland, now part of Highland

Cajal *n* Santiago Ramon y. 1852–1934, Spanish histologist, a pioneer of modern neurophysiology: shared the Nobel prize for medicine 1906

cajole *vb* **-joling, -joled** to persuade by flattery; coax: *he allowed himself to be cajoled into staying on* [French *cajoler*] > **cajolery** *n*

Cajun *n* **1** a native of Louisiana descended from 18th-century Acadian immigrants **2** the dialect of French spoken by such people **3** the music of this ethnic group ▷ *adj* **4** denoting or relating to such people, their language, or their music [from ACADIAN]

cake *n* **1** a sweet food baked from a mixture of flour, sugar, eggs, etc. **2** a flat compact mass of something: *a cake of soap* **3** **have one's cake and eat it** to enjoy both of two incompatible alternatives **4** **piece of cake** *informal* something that is easy to do **5** **sell like hot cakes** *informal* to be sold very quickly: *commercial novels sell like hot cakes* ▷ *vb* **caking, caked 6** to form into a hardened mass or crust: *her hair was caked with grease and dust* [Old Norse *kaka*]

cal. calorie (small)

Cal. 1 Calorie (large) **2** California

Calabar *n* a port in SE Nigeria, capital of Cross River state. Pop: 418 000 (2005 est)

calabash *n* **1** a large round gourd that grows on a tropical American tree **2** a bowl made from the dried hollow shell of a calabash [obsolete French *calabasse*]

calabrese (kal-lab-**bray**-zee) *n* a kind of green sprouting broccoli [Italian: from *Calabria* (region of SW Italy)]

Calabria *n* **1** a region of SW Italy: mostly mountainous and subject to earthquakes. Chief town: Reggio di Calabria. Pop: 2 007 392 (2003 est). Area: 15 080 sq km (5822 sq miles) **2** an ancient region of extreme SE Italy (3rd century BC to about 668 AD); now part of Apulia

Calabrian *adj* **1** of or relating to Calabria or its inhabitants ▷ *n* **2** a native or inhabitant of Calabria

Calais *n* a port in N France, on the Strait of Dover: the nearest French port to England; belonged to England 1347–1558. Pop: 75 790 (2006)

calamari *n* squid cooked for eating, esp. cut into rings and fried in batter [from Italian, plural of *calamaro* squid]

calamine *n* a pink powder consisting chiefly of zinc oxide, used to make soothing skin lotions and ointments [Medieval Latin *calamina*]

calamitous *adj* resulting in or from disaster: *the country's calamitous economic decline*

calamity *n, pl* **-ties** a disaster or misfortune [Latin *calamitas*]

Calamity Jane *n* real name *Martha Canary*. ?1852–1903, US frontierswoman, noted for her skill at shooting and riding

calcareous (kal-**care**-ee-uss) *adj* of or containing calcium carbonate [Latin *calx* lime]

calciferol *n* a substance found in fish oils and used in the treatment of rickets. Also called: **vitamin D₂** [*calcif(erous* + *ergost)erol*, a substance in plants that is a source of vitamin D]

calciferous *adj* producing salts of calcium, esp. calcium carbonate

calcify *vb* **-fies, -fying, -fied** to harden by the depositing of calcium salts [Latin *calx* lime] > **calcification** *n*

calcine *vb* **-cining, -cined** to oxidize (a substance) by heating [Medieval Latin *calcinare* to heat] > **calcination** *n*

calcite *n* a colourless or white form of calcium carbonate

calcium *n chem* a soft silvery-white metallic element found in bones, teeth, limestone, and chalk. Symbol: **Ca** [Latin *calx* lime]

calcium carbonate *n* a white crystalline salt found in limestone, chalk, and pearl, used to make cement

calcium hydroxide *n* a white crystalline alkali used to make mortar and soften water

calcium oxide *n* same as **quicklime**

calculable *adj* able to be computed or estimated

calculate *vb* **-lating, -lated 1** to solve or find out by a mathematical procedure or by reasoning **2** to aim to have a particular effect: *this ad campaign is calculated to offend* [Latin *calculare*, from *calculus* pebble used as a counter]

calculated *adj* **1** undertaken after considering the likelihood of success: *a calculated gamble* **2** carefully planned: *a calculated and callous murder*

calculating *adj* selfishly scheming

calculation *n* **1** the act or result of calculating **2** selfish scheming: *there was an element of calculation in her insistence on arriving after dark*

calculator *n* a small electronic device for doing mathematical calculations

calculus *n* **1** the branch of mathematics dealing with infinitesimal changes to a variable number or quantity **2** (*pl* **-li**) *pathol* same as **stone** (7) [Latin: pebble]

Calcutta *n* the former official name (still widely used) of **Kolkata**

Calder *n* Alexander. 1898–1976, US sculptor, who originated mobiles and stabiles (moving or static abstract sculptures, generally suspended from wire)

Calderdale *n* a unitary authority in N England, in West Yorkshire. Pop: 193 200 (2003 est). Area: 364 sq km (140 sq miles)

Calderón de la Barca *n* Pedro. 1600–81, Spanish dramatist, whose best-known work is *La Vida es Sueño*. He also wrote *autos sacramentales*, outdoor plays for the feast of Corpus Christi, 76 of which survive

Caldwell *n* Erskine. 1903–87, US novelist whose works include *Tobacco Road* (1933)

Caledonia *n* the Roman name for **Scotland**

> **USAGE** *Caledonia* is now used poetically and, sometimes, humorously

Caledonian *adj* Scottish [from CALEDONIA]

Caledonian Canal n a canal in N Scotland, linking the Atlantic with the North Sea through the Great Glen: built 1803–47; now used mostly for leisure boating

calendar n **1** a chart showing a year divided up into months, weeks, and days **2** a system for determining the beginning, length, and divisions of years: *the Jewish calendar* **3** a schedule of events or appointments: *concerts were an important part of the social calendar of the Venetian nobility* [Latin *kalendae* the calends]

calender n **1** a machine in which paper or cloth is smoothed by passing it between rollers ▷ vb **2** to smooth in such a machine [French *calandre*]

calends or **kalends** pl n (in the ancient Roman calendar) the first day of each month [Latin *kalendae*]

calendula n a plant with orange-and-yellow rayed flowers [Medieval Latin]

calf¹ n, pl **calves 1** a young cow, bull, elephant, whale, or seal **2** same as **calfskin** [Old English *cealf*]

calf² n, pl **calves** the back of the leg between the ankle and the knee [Old Norse *kālfi*]

calf love n adolescent infatuation

calfskin n fine leather made from the skin of a calf

Calgary n a city in Canada, in S Alberta: centre of a large agricultural region; oilfields. Pop: 879 277 (2001)

Cali n a city in SW Colombia: commercial centre in a rich agricultural region. Pop: 2 583 000 (2005 est)

calibrate vb **-brating, -brated** to mark the scale or check the accuracy of (a measuring instrument) ▷ **calibration** n

calibre or US **caliber** (kal-lib-ber) n **1** a person's ability or worth: *a poet of Wordsworth's calibre* **2** the diameter of the bore of a gun or of a shell or bullet [Arabic *qālib* shoemaker's last, mould]

calico n a white or unbleached cotton fabric [*Calicut*, town in India]

Calicut n the former name for **Kozhikode**

Calif. California

California n **1** a state on the W coast of the US: the third largest state in area and the largest in population; consists of a narrow, warm coastal plain rising to the Coast Range, deserts in the south, the fertile central valleys of the Sacramento and San Joaquin Rivers, and the mountains of the Sierra Nevada in the east; major industries include the growing of citrus fruits and grapes, fishing, oil production, electronics, information technology, and films. Capital: Sacramento. Pop: 35 484 453 (2003 est). Area: 411 015 sq km (158 693 sq miles). Abbreviation: **Cal., Calif.**, (with zip code) **CA 2 Gulf of California** an arm of the Pacific Ocean, between Sonora and Lower California

Californian adj **1** of or relating to California or its inhabitants ▷ n **2** a native or inhabitant of California

californium n chem a radioactive metallic element produced artificially. Symbol: **Cf** [after the University of *California*, where it was discovered]

Caligula n original name *Gaius Caesar*, son of Germanicus. 12–41 AD, Roman emperor (37–41), noted for his cruelty and tyranny; assassinated

Calimere n **Point Calimere** a cape on the SE coast of India, on the Palk Strait

caliper n US same as **calliper**

caliph n Islam the title of the successors of Mohammed as rulers of the Islamic world [Arabic *khalifa* successor]

caliphate n the office, jurisdiction, or reign of a caliph

calisthenics n same as **callisthenics**

call vb **1** to name: *a town called Eyemouth* **2** to describe (someone or something) as being: *they called him a Hitler* **3** to speak loudly so as to attract attention **4** to telephone: *he left a message for Lynch to call him* **5** to summon: *a doctor must be called immediately* **6** to pay someone a visit: *the social worker called and she didn't answer the door* **7** to arrange: *the meeting was called for the lunch hour* **8 call someone's bluff** See **bluff¹** (3) ▷ n **9** a cry or shout **10** the cry made by a bird or animal **11** a communication

by telephone **12** a short visit: *I paid a call on an old friend* **13** a summons or invitation: *the police and fire brigade continued to respond to calls* **14** need, demand, or desire: *a call for economic sanctions* **15** allure or fascination: *the call of the open road* **16 on call** available when summoned: *there's a doctor on call in town* ▶ See also **call for**, **call in**, etc. [Old English *ceallian*] ▷ **caller** n

Callaghan n **1 (Leonard) James**, Baron Callaghan of Cardiff. 1912–2005, British Labour statesman; prime minister (1976–79) **2 Sir Paul (Terrence)**, 1947–2012, New Zealand physicist, noted for his work on magnetic resonance

Callao n a port in W Peru, near Lima, on **Callao Bay**: chief import centre of Peru. Pop: 813 264 (2005 est)

Callas n **Maria**, real name *Maria Anna Cecilia Kalageropoulos*. 1923–77, Greek operatic soprano, born in the US

call box n a soundproof enclosure for a public telephone

call centre n Brit, Austral and NZ an office where staff carry out an organization's telephone transactions

call for vb **1** to require: *appendicitis calls for removal of the appendix* **2** to come and fetch

call girl n a prostitute with whom appointments are made by telephone

Callicrates n 5th century BC, Greek architect: with Ictinus, designed the Parthenon

calligraphy n beautiful handwriting [Greek *kallos* beauty + **-GRAPHY**] ▷ **calligrapher** n ▷ **calligraphic** adj

Callimachus n **1** late 5th century BC, Greek sculptor, reputed to have invented the Corinthian capital **2** ?305–?240 BC, Greek poet of the Alexandrian School; author of hymns and epigrams

call in vb **1** to summon to one's assistance: *she called in a contractor to make the necessary repairs* **2** to pay a brief visit **3** to demand payment of (a loan): *if the share price continues to drop, some banks may call in their loans*

calling n **1** a strong urge to follow a particular profession or occupation, esp. a caring one **2** a profession or occupation, esp. a caring one

Calliope n Greek myth the Muse of epic poetry

calliper or US **caliper** n **1** a metal splint for supporting the leg **2** a measuring instrument consisting of two steel legs hinged together [variant of *calibre*]

callisthenics or **calisthenics** n light exercises designed to promote general fitness [Greek *kalli-* beautiful + *sthenos* strength] ▷ **callisthenic** or **calisthenic** adj

call off vb **1** to cancel or abandon: *the strike has now been called off* **2** to order (a dog or a person) to stop attacking someone

call on or **call upon** vb to make an appeal or request to: *church leaders called on political leaders to resume the discussions*

callous adj showing no concern for other people's feelings [Latin *callosus*] ▷ **callously** adv ▷ **callousness** n

calloused adj covered in calluses

call out vb **1** to shout loudly **2** to summon to one's assistance: *the army and air force have been called out to help drop food packets* **3** to order (workers) to strike

callow adj young and inexperienced: *a callow youth* [Old English *calu*]

Callow n Simon. born 1949, British actor and theatre director

call up vb **1** to summon for active military service **2** to cause one to remember ▷ n **call-up 3** a general order to report for military service

callus n, pl **-luses** an area of hard or thickened skin on the hand or foot [Latin *callum* hardened skin]

calm adj **1** not showing or not feeling agitation or excitement **2** not ruffled by the wind: *a flat calm sea* **3** (of weather) windless ▷ n **4** a peaceful state ▷ vb **5** (often foll. by *down*) to make or become calm [Late Latin *cauma* heat, hence a rest during the heat of the day] ▷ **calmly** adv ▷ **calmness** n

Calor Gas n trademark Brit butane gas liquefied under pressure in portable containers for domestic use

caloric (kal-or-ik) *adj* of heat or calories

calorie *n* **1** a unit of measure for the energy value of food **2** Also: **small calorie** the quantity of heat required to raise the temperature of 1 gram of water by 1°C [Latin *calor* heat]

Calorie *n* **1** Also: **large calorie** a unit of heat, equal to one thousand calories **2** the amount of a food capable of producing one calorie of energy

calorific *adj* of calories or heat

Calpe *n* the ancient name for (the Rock of) **Gibraltar**

Caltanissetta *n* a city in central Sicily: sulphur mines. Pop: 61 438 (2001)

calumniate *vb* **-ating, -ated** to make false or malicious statements about (someone)

calumny *n, pl* **-nies** a false or malicious statement; slander [Latin *calumnia* slander]

Calvados *n* **1** a department of N France in the Basse-Normandie region. Capital: Caen. Pop: 659 893 (2003 est). Area: 5693 sq km (2198 sq miles) **2** an apple brandy distilled from cider in this region

Calvary *n Christianity* the place just outside the walls of Jerusalem where Jesus Christ was crucified [Latin *calvaria* skull]

calve *vb* **calving, calved** to give birth to a calf

Calvert *n* **1** Sir George, 1st Baron Baltimore. ?1580–1632, English statesman; founder of the colony of Maryland **2** his son, **Leonard.** 1606–47, English statesman; first colonial governor of Maryland (1634–47)

calves *n* the plural of **calf**[1]

Calvin *n* **1** John, original name *Jean Cauvin, Caulvin,* or *Chauvin.* 1509–64, French theologian: a leader of the Protestant Reformation in France and Switzerland, establishing the first presbyterian government in Geneva. His theological system is described in his *Institutes of the Christian Religion* (1536) **2** Melvin. 1911–97, US chemist, noted particularly for his research on photosynthesis: Nobel prize for chemistry 1961

Calvinism *n* the theological system of Calvin, the 16th-century French theologian, stressing predestination and salvation solely by God's grace **> Calvinist** *n, adj* **> Calvinistic** *adj*

Calvino *n* Italo. 1923–85, Italian novelist and short-story writer. His works include *Our Ancestors* (1960) and *Invisible Cities* (1972)

calypso *n, pl* **-sos** a West Indian song with improvised topical lyrics [probably from *Calypso*, sea nymph in Greek mythology]

calyx (kale-ix) *n, pl* **calyxes** or **calyces** (kal-iss-seez) the outer leaves that protect the developing bud of a flower [Latin: shell, husk]

Calzaghe *n* Joe. born 1972, Welsh boxer: won all 46 of his professional fights (1993–2008); world champion in the super middleweight and light heavyweight divisions

calzone (kal-**zone**-ee) *n* a folded pizza filled with cheese, tomatoes, etc.

cam *n* a part of an engine that converts a circular motion into a to-and-fro motion [Dutch *kam* comb]

Cam *n* a river in E England, in Cambridgeshire, flowing through Cambridge to the River Ouse. Length: about 64 km (40 miles)

Camagüey *n* a city in E central Cuba. Pop: 320 000 (2005 est)

camaraderie *n* familiarity and trust between friends [French]

Camargue *n* la Camargue a delta region in S France, between the channels of the Grand and Petit Rhône, where cattle, esp. bulls for the Spanish bullrings, and horses are reared

Camb. Cambridge

Cambay *n* Gulf of Cambay an inlet of the Arabian Sea on the W coast of India, southeast of the Kathiawar Peninsula

camber *n* a slight upward curve to the centre of a road surface [Latin *camurus* curved]

Cambodia *n* a country in SE Asia: became part of French Indochina in 1887; achieved self-government in 1949 and independence in 1953; civil war (1970–74) ended in victory for the Khmer Rouge, who renamed the country Kampuchea (1975) and carried out extreme-radical political and economic reforms resulting in a considerable reduction of the population; Vietnamese forces ousted the Khmer Rouge in 1979 and set up a pro-Vietnamese government who reverted (1981) to the name Cambodia; after Vietnamese withdrawal in 1989 a peace settlement with exiled factions was followed in 1993 by the adoption of a democratic monarchist constitution restoring Prince Sihanouk to the throne. The country contains the central plains of the Mekong River and the Cardamom Mountains in the SW. Official language: Khmer; French is also widely spoken. Currency: riel. Capital: Phnom Penh. Pop: 15 205 539 (2013 est). Area: 181 000 sq km (69 895 sq miles)

Cambodian *adj* **1** of or relating to Cambodia or its inhabitants ▷ *n* **2** a native or inhabitant of Cambodia

Camborne-Redruth *n* a former (until 1974) urban district in SW England, in Cornwall: formed in 1934 by the amalgamation of the neighbouring towns of Camborne and Redruth. Pop: 39 936 (2001)

Cambrai *n* a town in NE France: textile industry: scene of a battle in which massed tanks were first used and broke through the German line (November, 1917). Pop: 33 738 (1999)

Cambria *n* the Medieval Latin name for **Wales**

Cambrian *adj geology* of the period of geological time about 600 million years ago

Cambrian Mountains *pl n* a mountain range in Wales, extending from Carmarthenshire in the S to Denbighshire in the N. Highest peak: Aran Fawddwy, 891 m (2970 ft)

cambric *n* a fine white linen fabric [Flemish *Kamerijk* Cambrai]

Cambridge *n* **1** a city in E England, administrative centre of Cambridgeshire, on the River Cam: centred around the university, founded in the 12th century: electronics, biotechnology. Pop: 117 717 (2001). Medieval Latin name: **Cantabrigia** **2** short for **Cambridgeshire** **3** a city in the US, in E Massachusetts: educational centre, with Harvard University (1636) and the Massachusetts Institute of Technology. Pop: 101 587 (2003 est) ▶ Related adjective: **Cantabrigian**

Cambridgeshire *n* a county of E England, in East Anglia: includes the former counties of the Isle of Ely and Huntingdon and lies largely in the Fens: Peterborough became an independent unitary authority in 1998. Administrative centre: Cambridge. Pop (excluding Peterborough): 571 000 (2003 est). Area (excluding Peterborough): 3068 sq km (184 sq miles). Abbreviation: **Cambs**

Cambs Cambridgeshire

Cambyses *n* died ?522 BC, king of Persia (529–?522 BC), who conquered Egypt (525); son of Cyrus the Great

camcorder *n* a combined portable video camera and recorder

Camden[1] *n* a borough of N Greater London. Pop: 210 700 (2003 est). Area: 21 sq km (8 sq miles)

Camden[2] *n* William. 1551–1623, English antiquary and historian; author of *Britannia* (1586)

came *vb* the past tense of **come**

camel *n* either of two humped mammals, the dromedary and Bactrian camel, that can survive long periods without food or water in desert regions [Greek *kamēlos*]

camellia (kam-**meal**-ya) *n* an ornamental shrub with glossy leaves and white, pink, or red flowers [after G. J. *Kamel*, Jesuit missionary]

camel's hair or **camelhair** *n* soft cloth, usually tan in colour, which is made from camel's hair and is used to make coats

Camembert (kam-mem-bare) *n* a soft creamy cheese [*Camembert*, village in Normandy]

cameo, *pl* **cameos** **1** a brooch or ring with a profile head carved in relief **2** a small but important part in a film or play played by a well-known actor or actress [Italian *cammeo*]

camera *n* **1** a piece of equipment used for taking photographs, video, or film **2** **in camera** in private [Greek *kamara* vault]

cameraman *n*, *pl* **-men** a man who operates a camera for television or cinema

camera obscura *n* a darkened room with an opening through which images of outside objects are projected onto a flat surface [New Latin]

camera phone *n* a mobile phone incorporating a camera

Cameron *n* **1** David (William Donald). born 1966, British politician; leader of the Conservative party from 2005; prime minister from 2010 **2** (Mark) James (Walter). 1911–85, British journalist, author, and broadcaster. His books include *Witness in Vietnam* (1966) and *Point of Departure* (1967) **3** James. born 1954, Canadian film director and screenwriter; his films include *The Terminator* (1984), *Aliens* (1986), *Titanic* (1997), and *Avatar* (2009) **4** Julia Margaret. 1815–79, British photographer, born in India, renowned for her portrait photographs

Cameroon *n* **1** a republic in West Africa, on the Gulf of Guinea: became a German colony in 1884; divided in 1919 into the Cameroons (administered by Britain) and Cameroun (administered by France); Cameroun and the S part of the Cameroons formed a republic in 1961 (the N part joined Nigeria); became a member of the Commonwealth in 1995. Official languages: French and English. Religions: Christian, Muslim, and animist. Currency: franc. Capital: Yaoundé. Pop: 20 549 221 (2013 est). Area: 475 500 sq km (183 591 sq miles). French name: Cameroun. German name: Kamerun **2** an active volcano in W Cameroon: the highest peak on the West African coast. Height: 4070 m (13 352 ft)

Cameroun *n* the French name for **Cameroon**

camiknickers *pl n* *Brit* a woman's undergarment consisting of knickers attached to a camisole top

camisole *n* a woman's bodice-like garment with shoulder straps [French]

Camoëns *or* **Camões** *n* Luis Vaz de. 1524–80, Portuguese epic poet; author of *The Lusiads* (1572)

camomile *or* **chamomile** (kam-mo-mile) *n* a sweet-smelling plant used to make herbal tea [Greek *khamaimēlon* earth-apple (referring to the scent of the flowers)]

camouflage (kam-moo-flahzh) *n* **1** the use of natural surroundings or artificial aids to conceal or disguise something ▷ *vb* **-flaging**, **-flaged** **2** to conceal by camouflage [French]

camp¹ *n* **1** a place where people stay in tents **2** a collection of huts and other buildings used as temporary lodgings for military troops or for prisoners of war **3** a group that supports a particular doctrine: *the socialist camp* ▷ *vb* **4** to stay in a camp [Latin *campus* field] ▷ **camper** *n* ▷ **camping** *n*

camp² *informal adj* **1** effeminate or homosexual **2** consciously artificial, vulgar, or affected ▷ *vb* **3** **camp it up** to behave in a camp manner [origin unknown]

Camp *n* Walter (Chauncey). 1859–1925, US sportsman and administrator; he introduced new rules to American football, which distinguished it from rugby

Campagna *n* a low-lying plain surrounding Rome, Italy: once fertile, it deteriorated to malarial marshes; but has since been reclaimed. Area: about 2000 sq km (800 sq miles). Also called: **Campagna di Roma**

campaign *n* **1** a series of coordinated activities designed to achieve a goal **2** *military* a number of operations aimed at achieving a single objective ▷ *vb* **3** to take part in a campaign: *he paid tribute to all those who'd campaigned for his release* [Latin *campus* field] ▷ **campaigner** *n*

Campanella *n* Tommaso. 1568–1639, Italian philosopher and Dominican friar. During his imprisonment by the Spaniards (1599–1626) he wrote his celebrated utopian fantasy, *La città del sole*

Campania *n* a region of SW Italy: includes the islands of Capri and Ischia. Chief town: Naples. Pop: 5 725 098 (2003 est). Area: 13 595 sq km (5248 sq miles)

campanile (camp-an-neel-lee) *n* a bell tower, usually one not attached to another building [Italian]

campanology *n* the art of ringing bells [Late Latin *campana* bell] ▷ **campanologist** *n*

campanula *n* a plant with blue or white bell-shaped flowers [New Latin: a little bell]

camp bed *n* a lightweight folding bed

Campbell *n* **1** Sir Colin, Baron Clyde. 1792–1863, British field marshal who relieved Lucknow for the second time (1857) and commanded in Oudh, suppressing the Indian Mutiny **2** Donald. 1921–67, English water speed record-holder **3** Kim, full name *Avril Phaedra Douglas Campbell*. born 1947, Canadian politician; prime minister of Canada (1993) **4** Sir Malcolm, father of Donald Campbell. 1885–1948, English racing driver and land speed record-holder **5** Mrs Patrick, original name *Beatrice Stella Tanner*. 1865–1940, English actress **6** Roy. 1901–57, South African poet. His poetry is often satirical and includes *The Flaming Terrapin* (1924) **7** Thomas. 1777–1844, Scottish poet and critic, noted particularly for his war poems *Hohenlinden* and *Ye Mariners of England*

Campbell-Bannerman *n* Sir Henry. 1836–1908, British statesman and leader of the Liberal Party (1899–1908); prime minister (1905–08), who granted self-government to the Transvaal and the Orange River Colony

Camp David *n* the US president's retreat in the Appalachian Mountains, Maryland: scene of the **Camp David Agreement** (Sept, 1978) between Anwar Sadat of Egypt and Menachem Begin of Israel, mediated by Jimmy Carter, which outlined a framework for establishing peace in the Middle East. This agreement was the basis of the peace treaty between Israel and Egypt signed in Washington (March, 1979)

Campeche *n* **1** a state of SE Mexico, on the SW of the Yucatán peninsula: forestry and fishing. Capital: Campeche. Pop: 205 000 (2005 est). Area: 56 114 sq km (21 666 sq miles) **2** a port in SE Mexico, capital of Campeche state. Pop: 195 000 (2000 est) **3** Bay of Campeche *or* Gulf of Campeche the SW part of the Gulf of Mexico

Campese *n* David. born 1962, Australian rugby union player: won 101 international caps (1982–1996), scoring 64 tries

camp follower *n* **1** a person who supports a particular group or organization without being a member of it **2** a civilian who unofficially provides services to military personnel

camphor *n* a sweet-smelling crystalline substance obtained from the wood of the **camphor tree**, which is used medicinally and in mothballs [Arabic *kāfūr*]

camphorated *adj* impregnated with camphor

Campin *n* Robert. 1379–1444, Flemish painter, noted esp for his altarpieces: usually identified with the so-called Master of Flémalle

Campina Grande *n* a city in NE Brazil, in E Paraíba state. Pop: 366 000 (2005 est)

Campinas *n* a city in SE Brazil, in São Paulo state: centre of a rich agricultural region, producing esp. coffee. Pop: 2 640 000 (2005 est)

campion *n* a red, pink, or white European wild flower [origin unknown]

Campion *n* **1** Saint Edmund. 1540–81, English Jesuit martyr. He joined the Jesuits in 1573 and returned to England (1580) as a missionary. He was charged with treason and hanged **2** Jane. born 1954, New Zealand film director and screenwriter: her films include *An Angel at My Table* (1990), *The Piano* (1993), *Holy Smoke* (1999), *In the Cu*

C

(2003), and *Bright Star* (2009) **3 Thomas**. 1567–1620, English poet and musician, noted particularly for his songs for the lute

Campobello *n* an island in the Bay of Fundy, off the coast of SE Canada: part of New Brunswick province. Pop: 1195 (2001). Area: about 52 sq km (20 sq miles)

Campo Formio *n* a village in NE Italy, in Friuli-Venezia Giulia: scene of the signing of a treaty in 1797 that ended the war between revolutionary France and Austria. Modern name: **Campoformido**

Campo Grande *n* a city in SW Brazil, capital of Mato Grosso do Sul state on the São Paulo–Corumbá railway: market centre. Pop: 746 000 (2005 est)

Campos *n* a city in E Brazil, in E Rio de Janeiro state on the Paraíba River. Pop: 388 000 (2005 est)

camp oven *n Austral and NZ* a heavy metal pot or box with a lid, used for baking over an open fire

camp site *n* a place where people can stay in tents

campus *n, pl* -**puses** the grounds and buildings of a university or college [Latin: field]

Cam Ranh *n* a port in SE Vietnam: large natural harbour, used at times as a naval base by French, Japanese, US, and Russian forces successively. Pop: 147 000 (2006 est)

camshaft *n* a part of an engine consisting of a rod to which cams are attached

Camus *n* **Albert**. 1913–60, French novelist, dramatist, and essayist, noted for his pessimistic portrayal of man's condition of isolation in an absurd world: author of the novels *L'Étranger* (1942) and *La Peste* (1947), the plays *Le Malentendu* (1945) and *Caligula* (1946), and the essays *Le Mythe de Sisyphe* (1942) and *L'Homme révolté* (1951): Nobel prize for literature 1957

can¹ *vb, past* **could** **1** be able to: *make sure he can breathe easily* **2** be allowed to: *you can swim in the large pool* [Old English *cunnan*]

USAGE See at **may¹**.

---

can² *n* **1** a metal container, usually sealed, for food or liquids ▷ *vb* **canning, canned** **2** to put (something) into a can [Old English *canne*]

Can. **1** Canada **2** Canadian

Canada *n* a country in North America: the second largest country in the world; first permanent settlements by Europeans were made by the French from 1605; ceded to Britain in 1763 after a series of colonial wars; established as the Dominion of Canada in 1867; a member of the Commonwealth. It consists generally of sparsely inhabited tundra regions, rich in natural resources, in the north, the Rocky Mountains in the west, the Canadian Shield in the east, and vast central prairies; the bulk of the population is concentrated along the US border and the Great Lakes in the south. Languages: English and French. Religion: Christian majority. Currency: Canadian dollar. Capital: Ottawa. Pop: 34 568 211 (2013 est). Area: 9 976 185 sq km (3 851 809 sq miles)

Canada Day *n* (in Canada) July 1, a public holiday marking the anniversary of the day in 1867 when Canada became a dominion

Canada goose *n* a greyish-brown North American goose with a black neck and head

Canada jay *n* a grey jay of northern N America, notorious for stealing

Canadian *adj* **1** of or relating to Canada or its inhabitants ▷ *n* **2** a native or inhabitant of Canada

Canadiana *pl n* objects relating to Canadian history and culture

Canadian football *n* a game like American football played on a grass field between teams of 12 players

Canadianism *n* **1** the Canadian national character or spirit **2** a linguistic feature peculiar to Canada or Canadians

Canadianize *or* -**ise** *vb* -**izing, -ized** *or* -**ising, -ised** to make Canadian

Canadian River *n* a river in the southern US, rising in NE New Mexico and flowing east to the Arkansas River in E Oklahoma. Length: 1458 km (906 miles)

Canadian Shield *n* (in Canada) the wide area of Precambrian rock extending west from the Labrador coast to the basin of the Mackenzie and north from the Great Lakes to Hudson Bay and the Arctic: rich in minerals

Canadien *or fem* **Canadienne** (kan-ad-ee-en) *n* a French Canadian [French: Canadian]

canaille (kan-nye) *n* the masses or rabble [French, from Italian *canaglia* pack of dogs]

canal *n* **1** an artificial waterway constructed for navigation or irrigation **2** a passage or duct in a person's body: *the alimentary canal* [Latin *canna* reed]

Canaletto *n* original name *Giovanni Antonio Canale*. 1697–1768, Italian painter and etcher, noted particularly for his highly detailed paintings of cities, esp. Venice, which are marked by strong contrasts of light and shade

canalize *or* -**lise** *vb* -**lizing, -lized** *or* -**lising, -lised** **1** to give direction to (a feeling or activity) **2** to convert into a canal ▷ **canalization** *or* -**lisation** *n*

Canal Zone *n* a former administrative region of the US, on the Isthmus of Panama around the Panama Canal: bordered on each side by the Republic of Panama, into which it was incorporated in 1979. Also called: **Panama Canal Zone**

canapé (kan-nap-pay) *n* a small piece of bread or toast spread with a savoury topping [French: sofa]

Canara *n* a variant spelling of **Kanara**

canard *n* a false report [French: a duck]

canary *n, pl* -**naries** a small yellow songbird often kept as a pet

Canary Islands *or* **Canaries** *pl n* a group of mountainous islands in the Atlantic off the NW coast of Africa, forming an Autonomous Community of Spain. Capital: Las Palmas. Pop: 1 944 700 (2003 est)

canasta *n* a card game like rummy, played with two packs of cards [Spanish: basket (because two packs, or a basketful, of cards are required)]

Canaveral *n* **Cape Canaveral** a cape on the E coast of Florida: site of the US Air Force Missile Test Centre, from which the majority of US space missions have been launched. Former name (1963–73): **Cape Kennedy**

Canberra *n* the capital of Australia, in Australian Capital Territory: founded in 1913 as a planned capital. Pop: 345 257 (2008)

cancan *n* a lively high-kicking dance performed by a female group [French]

cancel *vb* -**celling, -celled** *or US* -**celing, -celed** **1** to stop (something that has been arranged) from taking place **2** to mark (a cheque or stamp) with an official stamp to prevent further use **3 cancel out** to make ineffective by having the opposite effect: *economic vulnerability cancels out any possible political gain* [Late Latin *cancellare* to strike out, make like a lattice] ▷ **cancellation** *n*

cancer *n* **1** a serious disease resulting from a malignant growth or tumour, caused by abnormal and uncontrolled cell division **2** a malignant growth or tumour **3** an evil influence that spreads dangerously: *their country would remain a cancer of instability* [Latin: crab, creeping tumour] ▷ **cancerous** *adj*

Cancer *n* **1** *astrol* the fourth sign of the zodiac; the Crab **2 tropic of Cancer** See **tropic** (1) [Latin]

Cancún *n* a coastal resort in SE Mexico on the Yucatán Peninsula. Pop: 457 000 (2004 est)

candela (kan-dee-la) *n* the SI unit of luminous intensity (the amount of light a source gives off in a given direction) [Latin: candle]

Candela *n* **Felix**. 1910–97, Mexican architect, noted for his naturalistic modern style and thin prestressed concrete roofs

candelabrum or **candelabra** n, pl **-bra, -brums** or **-bras** a large branched holder for candles or overhead lights [Latin *candela* candle]

Candia n the Italian name for **Iráklion**

candid adj honest and straightforward in speech or behaviour [Latin *candere* to be white] **› candidly** adv

candidate n 1 a person seeking a job or position 2 a person taking an examination 3 a person or thing regarded as suitable or likely for a particular fate or position: *someone who smokes, drinks, or eats too much is a candidate for heart disease* [Latin *candidatus* clothed in white] **› candidacy** or **candidature** n

candied adj coated with or cooked in sugar: *candied peel*

Candiot or **Candiote** adj 1 of or relating to Candia (Iráklion) or Crete; Cretan ▷ n 2 a native or inhabitant of Crete; a Cretan

candle n 1 a stick or block of wax or tallow surrounding a wick, which is burned to produce light 2 **burn the candle at both ends** to exhaust oneself by doing too much [Latin *candela*]

candlelight n the light from a candle or candles **› candlelit** adj

Candlemas n *Christianity* February 2, the Feast of the Purification of the Virgin Mary

candlepower n the luminous intensity of a source of light: now expressed in candelas

candlestick or **candleholder** n a holder for a candle

candlewick n cotton with a tufted pattern, used to make bedspreads and dressing gowns

Candolle n Augustin Pyrame de. 1778–1841, Swiss botanist; his *Théorie élémentaire de la botanique* (1813) introduced a new system of plant classification

candour or US **candor** n honesty and straightforwardness of speech or behaviour [Latin *candor*]

candy n, pl **-dies** *chiefly US and Canad* a sweet or sweets [Arabic *qand* cane sugar]

candyfloss n *Brit* a light fluffy mass of spun sugar, held on a stick

candy-striped adj having narrow coloured stripes on a white background

candytuft n a garden plant with clusters of white, pink, or purple flowers

cane n 1 the long flexible stems of the bamboo or any similar plant 2 strips of such stems, woven to make wickerwork 3 a bamboo stem tied to a garden plant to support it 4 a flexible rod used to beat someone 5 a slender walking stick ▷ vb **caning, caned** 6 to beat with a cane [Greek *kanna*]

Canea or **Chania** n the chief port of Crete, on the NW coast. Pop: 55 838 (2001). Greek name: **Khaniá**

cane sugar n the sugar that is obtained from sugar cane

cane toad n a large toad used to control insects and other pests of sugar cane plantations

Canetti n Elias. 1905–94, British novelist and writer, born in Bulgaria, who usually wrote in German. His works include the novel *Auto da Fé* (1935). Nobel prize for literature 1981

canine (kay-nine) adj 1 of or like a dog ▷ n 2 a sharp-pointed tooth between the incisors and the molars [Latin *canis* dog]

canister n a metal container for dry food [Latin *canistrum* basket woven from reeds]

canker n 1 an ulceration or ulcerous disease 2 something evil that spreads and corrupts [Latin *cancer* crab, creeping tumour]

cannabis n a drug obtained from the dried leaves and flowers of the hemp plant [Greek *kannabis*]

Cannae n an ancient city in SE Italy: scene of a victory by Hannibal over the Romans (216 BC)

canned adj 1 preserved in a can 2 *informal* recorded in advance: *canned carols*

cannelloni or **canneloni** pl n tubular pieces of pasta filled with meat or cheese [Italian]

cannery n, pl **-neries** a place where foods are canned

Cannes n a port and resort in SE France: developed in the 19th century from a fishing village; annual film festival Pop: 72 939 (2008)

cannibal n 1 a person who eats human flesh 2 an animal that eats the flesh of other animals of its kind [Spanish *Canibales* natives of Cuba and Haiti] **› cannibalism** n

cannibalize or **-ise** vb **-izing, -ized** or **-ising, -ised** to use parts from (one machine or vehicle) to repair another

canning n the process of sealing food in cans to preserve it

Canning n 1 Charles John, 1st Earl Canning. 1812–62, British statesman; governor general of India (1856–58) and first viceroy (1858–62) 2 his father, **George**. 1770–1827, British Tory statesman; foreign secretary (1822–27) and prime minister (1827)

Canning Basin n an arid basin in NW Western Australia, largely unexplored. Area: 400 000 sq km (150 000 sq miles)

Cannock n a town in W central England, in S Staffordshire: **Cannock Chase** (a public area of heathland, once a royal preserve) is just to the east. Pop: 65 022 (2001)

cannon n, pl **-nons** or **-non** 1 a large gun consisting of a metal tube mounted on a carriage, formerly used in battles 2 an automatic aircraft gun 3 *billiards* a shot in which the cue ball strikes two balls successively ▷ vb 4 **cannon into** to collide with [Italian *canna* tube]

cannonade n continuous heavy gunfire

cannonball n a heavy metal ball fired from a cannon

cannon fodder n men regarded as expendable in war

cannot vb can not

canny adj **-nier, -niest** shrewd or cautious [from *can* (in the sense: to know how)] **› cannily** adv

canoe n a light narrow open boat, propelled by one or more paddles [Carib] **› canoeist** n

canoeing n the sport of rowing or racing in a canoe

canon[1] n a priest serving in a cathedral [Late Latin *canonicus* person living under a rule]

canon[2] n 1 *Christianity* a Church decree regulating moral or religious practices 2 a general rule or standard: *the Marx-Engels canon* 3 a list of the works of an author that are accepted as authentic: *the Yeats canon* 4 a piece of music in which a melody in one part is taken up in one or more other parts successively [Greek *kanōn* rule]

canonical adj 1 conforming with canon law 2 included in a canon of writings

canonical hour n RC Church one of the seven prayer times appointed for each day

canonicals pl n the official clothes worn by clergy when taking services

canonize or **-ise** vb **-izing, -ized** or **-ising, -ised** RC Church to declare (a dead person) to be a saint **› canonization** or **-isation** n

canon law n the body of laws of a Christian Church

canoodle vb **-dling, -dled** *slang* to kiss and cuddle [origin unknown]

canopied adj covered with a canopy: *canopied niches*

Canopus n a port in ancient Egypt east of Alexandria where granite monuments have been found inscribed with the name of Rameses II and written in languages similar to those of the Rosetta stone **› Canopic** adj

canopy n, pl **-pies** 1 an ornamental awning above a bed or throne 2 a rooflike covering over an altar, niche, or door 3 any large or wide covering: *the thick forest canopy* 4 the part of a parachute that opens out 5 the transparent hood of an aircraft cockpit [Greek *kōnōpeion* bed with a mosquito net]

Canossa n a ruined castle in N Italy, in Emilia near Reggio nell'Emilia: scene of the penance done by the Holy Roman Emperor Henry IV before Pope Gregory VII

Canova n Antonio. 1757–1822, Italian neoclassical sculptor

Canso *n* **1** a cape in Canada, at the NE tip of Nova Scotia **2 Strait of Canso** *or* **Gut of Canso** a channel in Canada, between the Nova Scotia mainland and S Cape Breton Island

cant[1] *n* **1** insincere talk concerning religion or morals **2** specialized vocabulary of a particular group, such as thieves or lawyers ▷ *vb* **3** to use cant: *canting hypocrites* [probably from Latin *cantare* to sing]

cant[2] *n* **1** a tilted position ▷ *vb* **2** to tilt or overturn: *the engine was canted to one side* [perhaps from Latin *canthus* iron hoop round a wheel]

Cant. 1 Canterbury **2** Bible Canticles

can't *vb* can not

Cantab. Cantabrigiensis [Latin: of Cambridge]

cantabile (kan-tah-bill-lay) *adv music* in a singing style, flowingly and melodiously [Italian]

Cantabria *n* a province and autonomous community in N Spain

Cantabrian Mountains *pl n* a mountain chain along the N coast of Spain, consisting of a series of high ridges that rise over 2400 m (8000 ft): rich in minerals (esp. coal and iron). Also called: **the Cantabrians**

Cantabrigia *n* the Medieval Latin name for **Cambridge** (1)

Cantabrigian *adj* **1** of, relating to, or characteristic of Cambridge or Cambridge University, or of Cambridge, Massachusetts, or Harvard University ▷ *n* **2** a member or graduate of Cambridge University or Harvard University **3** an inhabitant or native of Cambridge [C17: from Medieval Latin *Cantabrigia*]

Cantal *n* **1** a department of S central France, in the Auvergne region. Capital: Aurillac. Pop: 148 359 (2003 est). Area: 5779 sq km (2254 sq miles) **2** a hard strong cheese made in this area

cantaloupe *or* **cantaloup** *n Brit* a kind of melon with sweet-tasting orange flesh [*Cantaluppi*, near Rome, where first cultivated in Europe]

cantankerous *adj* quarrelsome or bad-tempered [origin unknown]

cantata (kan-tah-ta) *n* a musical setting of a text, consisting of arias, duets, and choruses [Italian]

canteen *n* **1** a restaurant attached to a workplace or school **2** a box containing a set of cutlery [Italian *cantina* wine cellar]

Canteloube *n* (Marie) Joseph. 1879–1957, French composer, best known for his *Chants d'Auvergne* (1923–30)

canter *n* **1** a gait of horses that is faster than a trot but slower than a gallop ▷ *vb* **2** (of a horse) to move at a canter [short for *Canterbury trot*, the pace at which pilgrims rode to Canterbury]

Canterbury *n* **1** a city in SE England, in E Kent: starting point for St Augustine's mission to England (597 AD); cathedral where St Thomas à Becket was martyred (1170); seat of the archbishop and primate of England; seat of the University of Kent (1965). Pop: 43 552 (2001). Latin name: **Durovernum 2** a regional council area of New Zealand, on E central South Island on **Canterbury Bight**: mountainous with coastal lowlands; agricultural. Chief town: Christchurch. Pop: 520 500 (2004 est). Area: 43 371 sq km (16 742 sq miles)

Can Tho *n* a town in S Vietnam, on the River Mekong. Pop: 368 000 (2005 est)

canticle *n* a short hymn with words from the Bible [Latin *canticulum*]

cantilever *n* a beam or girder fixed at one end only [origin unknown]

cantilever bridge *n* a bridge made of two cantilevers which meet in the middle

canto (kan-toe) *n*, *pl* **-tos** a main division of a long poem [Italian: song]

canton *n* a political division of a country, such as Switzerland [Old French: corner]

Canton *n* **1** a port in SE China, capital of Guangdong province, on the Zhu Jiang (Pearl River): the first Chinese port open to European trade. Pop: 3 881 000 (2005 est). Chinese names: **Guangzhou, Kwangchow 2** a city in the US, in NE Ohio. Pop: 80 806 (2000)

Cantonese *adj* **1** of or relating to Canton or its inhabitants ▷ *n* **2** (*pl* **-nese**) a native or inhabitant of Canton **3** the Chinese dialect of Canton

cantonment (kan-toon-ment) *n* a permanent military camp in British India [Old French *canton* corner]

Canton River *n* another name for the **Zhu Jiang**

cantor *n Judaism* a man employed to lead synagogue services [Latin: singer]

Canuck *n*, *adj US and Canad informal* Canadian [origin unknown]

Canute, Cnut *or* **Knut** *n* died 1035, Danish king of England (1016–35), Denmark (1018–35), and Norway (1028–35). He defeated Edmund II of England (1016), but divided the kingdom with him until Edmund's death. An able ruler, he invaded Scotland (1027) and drove Olaf II from Norway (1028)

canvas *n* **1** a heavy cloth of cotton, hemp, or jute, used to make tents and sails and for painting on in oils **2** an oil painting done on canvas **3 under canvas** in a tent: *sleeping under canvas* [Latin *cannabis* hemp]

canvass *vb* **1** to try to persuade (people) to vote for a particular candidate or party in an election **2** to find out the opinions of (people) by conducting a survey ▷ *n* **3** the activity of canvassing [probably from obsolete sense of *canvas* (to toss someone in a canvas sheet, hence, to criticize)] **› canvasser** *n* **› canvassing** *n*

canyon *n* a deep narrow steep-sided valley [Spanish *cañon*]

canyoning *n* the sport of travelling down a river situated in a canyon by a variety of means including scrambling, swimming, and abseiling

caoutchouc (cow-chook) *n* same as **rubber**[1] (1) [from S American Indian]

cap *n* **1** a soft close-fitting covering for the head **2** *sport* a cap given to someone selected for a national team **3** a small flat lid: *petrol cap* **4** a small amount of explosive enclosed in paper and used in a toy gun **5** a contraceptive device placed over the mouth of the womb **6** an upper financial limit **7 cap in hand** humbly ▷ *vb* **capping, capped 8** to cover or top with something: *a thick cover of snow capped the cars* **9** *sport* to select (a player) for a national team: *Australia's most capped player* **10** to impose an upper level on (a tax): *charge capping* **11** *informal* to outdo or excel: *capping anecdote with anecdote* [Late Latin *cappa* hood]

CAP (in the EU) Common Agricultural Policy

cap. capital

Capa *n* Robert, real name *André Friedmann*. 1913–54, Hungarian photographer, who established his reputation as a photojournalist during the Spanish Civil War

capability *n*, *pl* **-ties** the ability or skill to do something

Capablanca *n* José Raúl, called *Capa* or *the Chess Machine* 1888–1942, Cuban chess player; world champion 1921–27

capable *adj* **1** having the ability or skill to do something: *a side capable of winning the championship* **2** competent and efficient: *capable high achievers* [Latin *capere* to take] **› capably** *adv*

capacious *adj* having a large capacity or area [Latin *capere* to take]

capacitance *n physics* **1** the ability of a capacitor to store electrical charge **2** a measure of this

capacitor *n physics* a device for storing a charge of electricity

capacity *n*, *pl* **-ties 1** the ability to contain, absorb, or hold something **2** the maximum amount something can contain or absorb: *filled to capacity* **3** the ability to do something: *his capacity to elicit great loyalty* **4** a position or function: *acting in an official capacity* **5** the maximum output of which an industry or factory is capable: *the refinery had a capacity of three hundred thousand barrels a day*

6 *physics* same as **capacitance** ▷ *adj* **7** of the maximum amount or number possible: *a capacity crowd* [Latin *capere* to take]

caparisoned (kap-**par**-riss-sond) *adj* (esp. of a horse) magnificently decorated or dressed [Old Spanish *caparazón* saddlecloth]

cape¹ *n* a short sleeveless cloak [Late Latin *cappa*]

cape² *n* a large piece of land that juts out into the sea [Latin *caput* head]

Cape *n* the Cape **1** the SW region of South Africa, in Western Cape province **2** See **Cape of Good Hope**

Cape Breton Island *n* an island off SE Canada, in NE Nova Scotia, separated from the mainland by the Strait of Canso: its easternmost point is **Cape Breton**. Pop: 132 298 (2006). Area: 10 280 sq km (3970 sq miles)

Cape Cod *n* **1** a long sandy peninsula in SE Massachusetts, between **Cape Cod Bay** and the Atlantic **2** Also called: **Cape Cod cottage** a one-storey cottage of timber construction with a simple gable roof and a large central chimney: originated on Cape Cod in the 18th century

Cape Colony *n* the name from 1652 until 1910 of the former **Cape Province** of South Africa

Cape Flats *pl n* the strip of low-lying land in South Africa joining the Cape Peninsula proper to the African mainland

Cape Horn *n* a rocky headland on an island at the extreme S tip of South America, belonging to Chile. It is notorious for gales and heavy seas; until the building of the Panama Canal it lay on the only sea route between the Atlantic and the Pacific. Also called: **the Horn**

Čapek *n* Karel. 1890–1938, Czech dramatist and novelist; author of *R.U.R.* (1921), which introduced the word "robot", and (with his brother **Josef**) *The Insect Play* (1921)

Capello *n* Fabio. born 1946. Italian football player and coach; he won four Italian league titles with Milan and two Spanish league titles with Real Madrid; managed England (2008–12)

Cape of Good Hope *n* a cape in SW South Africa south of Cape Town

Cape Peninsula *n* (in South Africa) the peninsula and the part of the mainland on which Cape Town and most of its suburbs are located

Cape Province *n* a former province of S South Africa; replaced in 1994 by the new provinces of Northern Cape, Western Cape, Eastern Cape and part of North-West. Capital: Cape Town. Official name: **Cape of Good Hope Province**. Former name (1652–1910): **Cape Colony**

caper *n* **1** a high-spirited escapade ▷ *vb* **2** to skip about light-heartedly [probably from CAPRIOLE]

capercaillie *or* **capercailzie** (kap-per-**kale**-yee) *n* a large black European woodland grouse [Scottish Gaelic *capull coille* horse of the woods]

Capernaum *n* a ruined town in N Israel, on the NW shore of the Sea of Galilee: closely associated with Jesus Christ during his ministry

capers *pl n* the pickled flower buds of a Mediterranean shrub, used in making sauces [Greek *kapparis* caper plant]

Capet *n* Hugh *or* Hugues (yg). ?938–996 AD, king of France (987–96); founder of the Capetian dynasty

Cape Town *n* the legislative capital of South Africa and capital of Western Cape province, situated in the southwest on Table Bay: founded in 1652, the first White settlement in southern Africa; important port. Pop: 3 740 026 (2011)

Cape Verde *n* a republic in the Atlantic off the coast of West Africa, consisting of a group of ten islands and five islets: an overseas territory of Portugal until 1975, when the islands became independent. Official language: Portuguese. Religion: Christian (Roman Catholic) majority; animist minority. Currency: Cape Verdean escudo. Capital: Praia. Pop: 531 046 (2013 est). Area: 4033 sq km (1557 sq miles)

Cape Verdean *adj* **1** of or relating to Cape Verde or its inhabitants ▷ *n* **2** a native or inhabitant of Cape Verde

Cape York *n* the northernmost point of the Australian mainland, in N Queensland on the Torres Strait at the tip of **Cape York Peninsula** (a peninsula between the Coral Sea and the Gulf of Carpentaria)

Cap-Haitien *n* a port in N Haiti: capital during the French colonial period. Pop: 134 000 (2005 est). Also called: **le Cap**

capillarity *n physics* a phenomenon caused by surface tension that results in the surface of a liquid rising or falling in contact with a solid

capillary (kap-**pill**-a-ree) *n, pl* **-laries** **1** *anatomy* one of the very fine blood vessels linking the arteries and the veins ▷ *adj* **2** (of a tube) having a fine bore **3** *anatomy* of the capillaries [Latin *capillus* hair]

capital¹ *n* **1** the chief city of a country, where the government meets **2** the total wealth owned or used in business by an individual or group **3** wealth used to produce more wealth by investment **4** **make capital out of** to gain advantage from: *to make political capital out of the hostage situation* **5** a capital letter ▷ *adj* **6** *law* involving or punishable by death: *a capital offence* **7** denoting the large letter used as the initial letter in a sentence, personal name, or place name **8** *Brit, Austral and NZ old-fashioned* excellent or first-rate: *a capital dinner* [Latin *caput* head]

capital² *n* the top part of a column or pillar [Old French *capitel*, from Latin *caput* head]

capital gain *n* profit from the sale of an asset

capital goods *pl n econ* goods that are themselves utilized in the production of other goods

capitalism *n* an economic system based on the private ownership of industry

capitalist *adj* **1** based on or supporting capitalism: *capitalist countries* ▷ *n* **2** a supporter of capitalism **3** a person who owns a business ⟩ **capitalistic** *adj*

capitalize *or* **-ise** *vb* **-izing, -ized** *or* **-ising, -ised** **1** **capitalize on** to take advantage of: *to capitalize on the available opportunities* **2** to write or print (words) in capital letters **3** to convert (debt or earnings) into capital stock ⟩ **capitalization** *or* **-isation** *n*

capital levy *n* a tax on capital or property as contrasted with a tax on income

capitally *adv old-fashioned* in an excellent manner; admirably

capital punishment *n* the punishment of death for committing a serious crime

capital stock *n* **1** the value of the total shares that a company can issue **2** the total capital existing in an economy at a particular time

capitation *n* a tax of a fixed amount per person [Latin *caput* head]

Capitol *n* **1 a** another name for the **Capitoline b** the temple on the Capitoline **2** **the Capitol** the main building of the US Congress **3** Also called: **statehouse** (*sometimes not cap*) (in the US) the building housing any state legislature [C14: from Latin *Capitōlium*, from *caput* head]

Capitol Hill *n* **1** *US* the area around the Capitol in Washington, DC **2** the US Congress

Capitoline *n* **1** the **Capitoline** the most important of the Seven Hills of Rome. The temple of Jupiter was on the southern summit and the ancient citadel on the northern summit ▷ *adj* **2** of or relating to the Capitoline or the temple of Jupiter

capitulate *vb* **-lating, -lated** to surrender under agreed conditions [Medieval Latin *capitulare* to draw up under headings] ⟩ **capitulation** *n*

capo *n, pl* **-pos** a device fitted across the strings of a guitar or similar instrument so as to raise the pitch [Italian *capo tasto* head stop]

capoeira (kap-poo-**eer**-uh) *n* a combination of martial art and dance, which originated among African slaves in 19th-century Brazil [from Portuguese]

capon (kay-pon) *n* a castrated cock fowl fattened for eating [Latin *capo*]

caponata (kap-uh-**nah**-tuh) *n* a dish of fried seasoned aubergine and other vegetables, served as an appetizer [Italian]

Capone *n* Alphonse, called *Al*. 1899–1947, US gangster in Chicago during Prohibition

Caporetto *n* the Italian name for **Kobarid**

Capote *n* Truman. 1924–84, US writer; his novels include *Other Voices, Other Rooms* (1948) and *In Cold Blood* (1964), based on an actual multiple murder

Capp *n* Al, full name *Alfred Caplin*. 1909–79, US cartoonist, famous for his comic strip *Li'l Abner*

Cappadocia *n* an ancient region of E Asia Minor famous for its horses

Cappadocian *adj* **1** of or relating to Cappadocia or its inhabitants ▷ *n* **2** a native or inhabitant of Cappadocia

cappuccino (kap-poo-**cheen**-oh) *n*, *pl* **-nos** coffee with steamed milk, usually sprinkled with powdered chocolate [Italian]

Capra *n* Frank. 1896–1992, US film director born in Italy. His films include *It Happened One Night* (1934), *It's a Wonderful Life* (1946), and several propaganda films during World War II

Capri *n* an island off W Italy, in the Bay of Naples: resort since Roman times. Pop: 12 200 (2002 est). Area: about 13 sq km (5 sq miles)

caprice (kap-**reess**) *n* **1** a sudden change of attitude or behaviour **2** a tendency to have such changes [Italian *capriccio* a shiver, caprice]

capricious *adj* having a tendency to sudden unpredictable changes of attitude or behaviour ⟩ **capriciously** *adv*

Capricorn *n* **1** *astrol* the tenth sign of the zodiac; the Goat **2** tropic of Capricorn See **tropic** (1) [Latin *caper* goat + *cornu* horn]

Capricornia *n* the regions of Australia in the tropic of Capricorn

capriole *n* **1** an upward but not forward leap made by a horse ▷ *vb* **-oling, -oled 2** to perform a capriole [Latin *capreolus*, *caper* goat]

caps. capital letters

capsicum *n* a kind of pepper used as a vegetable or ground to produce a spice [Latin *capsa* box]

capsize *vb* **-sizing, -sized** (of a boat) to overturn accidentally [origin unknown]

capstan *n* a vertical rotating cylinder round which a ship's rope or cable is wound [Old Provençal *cabestan*]

capstone *n* same as **copestone** (2)

capsule *n* **1** a soluble gelatine case containing a dose of medicine **2** *botany* a plant's seed case that opens when ripe **3** *anatomy* a membrane or sac surrounding an organ or part **4** See **space capsule** ▷ *adj* **5** very concise: *capsule courses* [Latin *capsa* box]

capsulize *or* **-ise** *vb* **-izing, -ized** *or* **-ising, -ised 1** to state (information) in a highly condensed form **2** to enclose in a capsule

Capt. Captain

captain *n* **1** the person in charge of a ship, boat, or civil aircraft **2** a middle-ranking naval officer **3** a junior officer in the army **4** the leader of a team or group ▷ *vb* **5** to be captain of [Latin *caput* head] ⟩ **captaincy** *n*

caption *n* **1** a title, brief explanation, or comment accompanying a picture ▷ *vb* **2** to provide with a caption [Latin *captio* a seizing]

captious *adj* tending to make trivial criticisms [Latin *captio* a seizing]

captivate *vb* **-vating, -vated** to attract and hold the attention of; enchant [Latin *captivus* captive] ⟩ **captivating** *adj*

captive *n* **1** a person who is kept in confinement ▷ *adj* **2** kept in confinement **3** (of an audience) unable to leave [Latin *captivus*]

captivity *n* the state of being kept in confinement

captor *n* a person who captures a person or animal

capture *vb* **-turing, -tured 1** to take by force **2** to succeed in representing (something elusive) in words, pictures, or music: *today's newspapers capture the mood of the nation* **3** *physics* (of an atomic nucleus) to acquire (an additional particle) ▷ *n* **4** the act of capturing or the state of being captured [Latin *capere* to take]

Capua *n* a town in S Italy, in NW Campania: strategically important in ancient times, situated on the Appian Way. Pop: 19 041 (2001)

Capuana *n* Luigi. 1839–1915, Italian realist novelist, dramatist, and critic. His works include the novel *Giacinta* (1879) and the play *Malia* (1895)

capuchin (kap-yew-chin) *n* a S American monkey with a cowl of thick hair on the top of its head [Italian *cappuccio* hood]

Capuchin *n* **1** a friar belonging to a branch of the Franciscan Order founded in 1525 ▷ *adj* **2** of this order [Italian *cappuccio* hood]

capybara *n* the largest living rodent, found in S America

Caquetá *n* the Japurá River from its source in Colombia to the border with Brazil

car *n* **1** a motorized road vehicle designed to carry a small number of people **2** the passenger compartment of a cable car, airship, lift, or balloon **3** *US and Canad* a railway carriage [Latin *carra*, *carrum* two-wheeled wagon]

caracal *n* a lynx with reddish fur, which inhabits deserts of N Africa and S Asia [Turkish *kara kŭlăk* black ear]

Caracalla *n* real name *Marcus Aurelius Antoninus*, original name *Bassianus*. 188–217 AD, Roman emperor (211–17): ruled with cruelty and extravagance; assassinated

Caracas *n* the capital of Venezuela, in the north: founded in 1567; major industrial and commercial centre, notably for oil companies. Pop: 3 276 000 (2005 est)

carafe (kar-**raff**) *n* a wide-mouthed bottle for water or wine [Arabic *gharrāfah* vessel]

carambola *n* a yellow edible star-shaped fruit that grows on a Brazilian tree [Spanish]

caramel *n* **1** a chewy sweet made from sugar and milk **2** burnt sugar, used for colouring and flavouring food [French]

caramelize *or* **-ise** *vb* **-izing, -ized** *or* **-ising, -ised** to turn into caramel

carapace *n* the thick hard upper shell of tortoises and crustaceans [Spanish *carapacho*]

carat *n* **1** a unit of weight of precious stones, equal to 0.20 grams **2** a measure of the purity of gold in an alloy, expressed as the number of parts of gold in 24 parts of the alloy [Arabic *qīrāt* weight of four grains]

Caratacus, Caractacus *or* **Caradoc** *n* died ?54 AD, British chieftain: led an unsuccessful resistance against the Romans (43–50)

Caravaggio *n* Michelangelo Merisi da. 1571–1610, Italian painter, noted for his realistic depiction of religious subjects and for his dramatic use of chiaroscuro

caravan *n* **1** a large enclosed vehicle designed to be pulled by a car or horse and equipped to be lived in **2** (in some Eastern countries) a company of traders or other travellers journeying together [Persian *kārwān*]

caravanning *n* travelling or holidaying in a caravan

caravanserai *n* (in some Eastern countries, esp. formerly) a large inn enclosing a courtyard, providing accommodation for caravans [Persian *kārwānsarāī* caravan inn]

caraway *n* a Eurasian plant with seeds that are used as a spice in cooking [Arabic *karawyā*]

carb *n* *informal* short for **carbohydrate**

carbide *n* *chem* a compound of carbon with a metal

carbine *n* a type of light rifle [French *carabine*]

carbohydrate *n* any of a large group of energy-producing compounds, including sugars and starches, that contain carbon, hydrogen, and oxygen

C

carbolic acid n a disinfectant derived from coal tar
carbon n **1** a nonmetallic element occurring in three forms, charcoal, graphite, and diamond, and present in all organic compounds. Symbol: C **2** short for **carbon paper, carbon copy** [Latin *carbo* charcoal]
carbonaceous adj of, resembling, or containing carbon
carbonate n a salt or ester of carbonic acid
carbonated adj (of a drink) containing carbon dioxide; fizzy
carbon black n powdered carbon produced by partial burning of natural gas or petroleum, used in pigments and ink
carbon capture n the capture of carbon dioxide in the atmosphere, intended to prevent climate change
carbon copy n **1** a duplicate obtained by using carbon paper **2** informal a person or thing that is identical or very similar to another
carbon dating n a technique for finding the age of organic materials, such as wood, based on their content of radioactive carbon
carbon dioxide n a colourless odourless incombustible gas formed during breathing, and used in fire extinguishers and in making fizzy drinks
carbon footprint n a measure of the amount of carbon dioxide released into the atmosphere through a single endeavour or through the activities of a person, company, etc. over a given period
carbonic adj containing carbon
carbonic acid n a weak acid formed when carbon dioxide combines with water
carboniferous adj yielding coal or carbon
Carboniferous adj geology of the period of geological time about 330 million years ago, during which coal seams were formed
carbonize or **-ise** vb **-izing, -ized** or **-ising, -ised 1** to turn into carbon as a result of partial burning **2** to coat (a substance) with carbon ⟩ **carbonization** or **-isation** n
carbon monoxide n a colourless odourless poisonous gas formed by the incomplete burning of carbon compounds; part of the gases that come from a vehicle's exhaust
carbon-neutral adj not affecting the overall volume of carbon dioxide in the atmosphere
carbon offset n a compensatory measure made by an individual or company for carbon emissions, such as tree planting
carbon paper n a thin sheet of paper coated on one side with a dark waxy pigment, containing carbon, used to make a duplicate of something as it is typed or written
carbon tax n a tax on the emissions caused by the burning of coal, gas, and oil, aimed at reducing the production of greenhouse gases
carbon tetrachloride n a colourless nonflammable liquid used as a solvent, cleaning fluid, and insecticide
car boot sale n a sale of goods from car boots in a site hired for the occasion
Carborundum n trademark an abrasive material consisting of silicon carbide
carboxyl group or **carboxyl radical** n chem the chemical group –COOH: the functional group in organic acids
carboy n a large bottle protected by a basket or box [Persian *qarāba*]
carbuncle n a large painful swelling under the skin like a boil [Latin *carbo* coal]
carburettor or US and Canad **carburetor** n a device in an internal-combustion engine that mixes petrol with air and regulates the intake of the mixture into the engine
carcass or **carcase** n **1** the dead body of an animal **2** informal a person's body: *ask that person to move his carcass* [Old French *carcasse*]
Carcassonne n a city in SW France: extensive remains of medieval fortifications. Pop: 48 212 (2006)
Carchemish n an ancient city in Syria on the Euphrates,

lying on major trade routes; site of a victory of the Babylonians over the Egyptians (605 BC)
carcinogen n a substance that produces cancer [Greek *karkinos* cancer] ⟩ **carcinogenic** adj
carcinoma n, pl **-mas** or **-mata** a malignant tumour [Greek *karkinos* cancer]
card[1] n **1** a piece of stiff paper or thin cardboard used for identification, reference, proof of membership, or sending greetings or messages: *a Christmas card* **2** one of a set of small pieces of cardboard, marked with figures or symbols, used for playing games or for fortune-telling **3** a small rectangle of stiff plastic with identifying numbers for use as a credit card, cheque card, or charge card **4** old-fashioned, informal a witty or eccentric person ▷ See also **cards** [Greek *khartēs* leaf of papyrus]
card[2] n **1** a machine or tool for combing fibres of cotton or wool to disentangle them before spinning ▷ vb **2** to process with such a machine or tool [Latin *carduus* thistle]
cardamom n a spice that is obtained from the seeds of a tropical plant [Greek *kardamon* cress + *amōmon* an Indian spice]
cardboard n a thin stiff board made from paper pulp
card-carrying adj being an official member of an organization: *a card-carrying Conservative*
Cardenal n Ernesto. born 1925, Nicaraguan poet, revolutionary, and Roman Catholic priest; an influential figure in the Sandinista movement
Cárdenas n Lázaro. 1895–1970, Mexican statesman and general; president of Mexico (1934–40)
cardholder n a person who owns a credit or debit card
cardiac adj of or relating to the heart [Greek *kardia* heart]
Cardiff n **1** the capital of Wales, situated in the southeast, in Cardiff county borough: formerly an important port; seat of the Welsh assembly (1999); university (1883). Pop: 346 100 (2011) **2** a county borough in SE Wales, created in 1996 from part of South Glamorgan. Pop: 345 400 (2011 est). Area: 139 sq km (54 sq miles) ▷ Welsh name: **Caerdydd**
cardigan n a knitted jacket [after 7th Earl of *Cardigan*]
Cardigan n 7th Earl of, title of *James Thomas Brudenell*. 1797–1868, British cavalry officer. He led the charge of the Light Brigade at Balaklava (1854) during the Crimean War
Cardigan Bay n an inlet of St George's Channel, on the W coast of Wales
Cardiganshire n a former county of W Wales: became part of Dyfed in 1974; reinstated as **Ceredigion** in 1996
Cardin n Pierre. born 1922, French couturier, noted esp. for his collections for men
cardinal n **1** any of the high-ranking clergymen of the Roman Catholic Church who elect the pope and act as his chief counsellors ▷ adj **2** fundamentally important; principal [Latin *cardo* hinge]
cardinal number n a number denoting quantity but not order in a group, for example one, two, or three
cardinal points pl n the four main points of the compass: north, south, east, and west
cardinal virtues pl n the most important moral qualities, traditionally justice, prudence, temperance, and fortitude
card index n an index in which each item is separately listed on systematically arranged cards
cardiogram n an electrocardiogram. See **electrocardiograph**
cardiograph n an electrocardiograph ⟩ **cardiographer** n ⟩ **cardiography** n
cardiology n the branch of medicine dealing with the heart and its diseases ⟩ **cardiologist** n
cardiothoracic adj of or relating to the heart or the chest
cardiovascular adj of or relating to the heart and the blood vessels
Cardoso n Fernando Henrique. born 1931, Brazilian statesman; president (1995–2002)

cards *n* **1** any game played with cards, or card games generally **2** lay one's cards on the table to declare one's intentions openly **3** on the cards likely to take place: *a military coup was on the cards* **4** play one's cards right to handle a situation cleverly

cardsharp *or* **cardsharper** *n* a professional card player who cheats

Carducci *n* Giosuè. 1835–1907, Italian poet: Nobel prize for literature 1906

Cardus *n* Sir Neville. 1889–1975, British music critic and cricket writer

card vote *n* *Brit* and *NZ* a vote by delegates in which each delegate's vote counts as a vote by all his or her constituents

care *vb* **caring, cared** **1** to be worried or concerned: *he does not care what people think about him* **2** to like (to do something): *anybody care to go out?* **3 care for a** to look after or provide for: *it is still largely women who care for dependent family members* **b** to like or be fond of: *he did not care for his concentration to be disturbed; I don't suppose you could ever care for me seriously* **4** I couldn't care less I am completely indifferent ▷ *n* **5** careful or serious attention; caution: *treat all raw meat with extreme care to avoid food poisoning* **6** protection or charge: *the children are now in the care of a state orphanage* **7** trouble or worry: *his mind turned towards money cares* **8** care of (written on envelopes) at the address of **9** in *or* into care *Brit* and *NZ* (of a child) made the legal responsibility of a local authority or the state by order of a court **10** take care to be careful **11** take care of to look after: *women have to take greater care of themselves during pregnancy* [Old English *cearian*]

careen *vb* to tilt over to one side [Latin *carina* keel]

career *n* **1** the series of jobs in a profession or occupation that a person has through his or her life: *a career in child psychology* **2** the part of a person's life spent in a particular occupation or type of work: *a school career punctuated with exams* ▷ *vb* **3** to rush in an uncontrolled way ▷ *adj* **4** having chosen to dedicate his or her life to a particular occupation: *a career soldier* [Latin *carrus* two-wheeled wagon]

careerist *n* a person who seeks to advance his or her career by any means possible ➤ **careerism** *n*

carefree *adj* without worry or responsibility

careful *adj* **1** cautious in attitude or action **2** very exact and thorough ➤ **carefully** *adv* ➤ **carefulness** *n*

careless *adj* **1** done or acting with insufficient attention **2** unconcerned in attitude or action ➤ **carelessly** *adv* ➤ **carelessness** *n*

Carême *n* Marie Antonin. 1784–1833, French chef, regarded as the founder of *haute cuisine*

carer *n* a person who looks after someone who is ill or old, often a relative: *the group offers support for the carers of those with dementia*

caress *n* **1** a gentle affectionate touch or embrace ▷ *vb* **2** to touch gently and affectionately [Latin *carus* dear]

caret (kar-ret) *n* a symbol (⁁) indicating a place in written or printed matter where something is to be inserted [Latin: there is missing]

caretaker *n* **1** a person employed to look after a place or thing ▷ *adj* **2** performing the duties of an office temporarily: *a caretaker administration*

Carew *n* Thomas. ?1595–?1639, English Cavalier poet

careworn *adj* showing signs of stress or worry

Carey *n* **1** George (Leonard). born 1935, Archbishop of Canterbury (1991–2002) **2** Peter. born 1943, Australian novelist and writer; his novels include *Illywhacker* (1985), *Oscar and Lucinda* (1988), and *True History of the Kelly Gang* (2001) **3** William. 1761–1834, British orientalist and pioneer Baptist missionary in India

Carey Street *n* **1** (formerly) the street in which the London bankruptcy court was situated **2** the state of bankruptcy

cargo *n*, *pl* **-goes** *or especially US* **-gos** goods carried by a ship, aircraft, or other vehicle [Spanish *cargar* to load]

cargo pants *or* **cargo trousers** *pl n* loose trousers with a large external pocket on the side of each leg

Caria *n* an ancient region of SW Asia Minor, on the Aegean Sea: chief cities were Halicarnassus and Cnidus: corresponds to the present-day Turkish districts of S Aydin and W Muğla

Carib *n* **1** (*pl* **-ibs** *or* **-ib**) a member of a group of Native American peoples of NE South America and the S West Indies **2** any of the languages of these peoples [Spanish *Caribe*]

Caribbean *adj* **1** of or relating to the Caribbean Sea and its islands **2** of or relating to the Carib or any of their languages ▷ *n* **3** the Caribbean the states and islands of the Caribbean Sea, including the West Indies, when considered as a geopolitical region **4** short for the Caribbean Sea **5** a member of any of the peoples inhabiting the islands of the Caribbean Sea, such as a West Indian or a Carib

Caribbean Sea *n* an almost landlocked sea, part of the Atlantic Ocean, bounded by the Caribbean islands, Central America, and the N coast of South America. Area: 2 718 200 sq km (1 049 500 sq miles)

Caribbees *pl n* the Caribbees a former name for the Lesser Antilles

Cariboo *n* the Cariboo *Canad* a region in the W foothills of the Cariboo Mountains, scene of a gold rush beginning in 1860

Cariboo Mountains *pl n* a mountain range in SW Canada, in SE British Columbia. Highest peak: Mount Sir Wilfrid Laurier, 3520 m (11 549 ft)

caribou *n*, *pl* **-bou** *or* **-bous** a large North American reindeer [from a Native American language]

caricature *n* **1** a drawing or description of a person which exaggerates characteristic features for comic effect **2** a description or explanation of something that is so exaggerated or over-simplified that it is difficult to take seriously: *the classic caricature of the henpecked husband* ▷ *vb* **-turing, -tured** **3** to make a caricature of [Italian *caricatura* a distortion]

caries (care-reez) *n* tooth decay [Latin: decay]

carillon (kar-rill-yon) *n* **1** a set of bells hung in a tower and played either from a keyboard or mechanically **2** a tune played on such bells [French]

caring *adj* **1** feeling or showing care and compassion for other people **2** of or relating to professional social or medical care: *the caring professions*

Carinthia *n* a state of S Austria: an independent duchy from 976 to 1276; mainly mountainous, with many lakes and resorts. Capital: Klagenfurt. Pop: 559 440 (2003 est). Area: 9533 sq km (3681 sq miles). German name: **Kärnten**

Carisbrooke Castle *n* a castle near Newport on the Isle of Wight: Charles I was held prisoner here from 1647 until his execution in 1649

carjack *vb* to attack (a driver in a car) in order to rob the driver or to steal the car for another crime [CAR + (HI)JACK]

cark *vb* cark it *Austral* and *NZ slang* to die

Carling *n* Will(iam). born 1965, English Rugby Union player; won 72 caps (1988–97); captained England to three Grand Slams (1991, 1992, 1995)

Carlisle *n* a city in NW England, administrative centre of Cumbria: railway and industrial centre. Pop: 71 773 (2001). Latin name: **Luguvallum**

Carlos *n* Don. full name *Carlos María Isidro de Borbón*. 1788–1855, second son of Charles IV: pretender to the Spanish throne and leader of the Carlists

Carlota *n* original name *Marie Charlotte Amélie Augustine Victoire Clémentine Léopoldine*. 1840–1927, wife of Maximilian; empress of Mexico (1864–67)

Carlow *n* **1** a county of SE Republic of Ireland, in Leinster: mostly flat, with barren mountains in the southeast. County town: Carlow. Pop: 46 014 (2002). Area: 896 sq km (346 sq miles) **2** a town in SE Republic of Ireland, county town of Co Carlow. Pop: 18 487 (2002)

Carlsbad _n_ a variant spelling of the German name for Karlovy Vary

Carlton _n_ a town in N central England, in S Nottinghamshire. Pop: 48 493 (2001)

Carl XVI Gustaf _n_ born 1946, king of Sweden from 1973

Carlyle _n_ **1 Robert.** born 1961, Scottish actor; his work includes the television series _Cracker_ and _Hamish Macbeth_ and the films _Trainspotting_ (1996), _The Full Monty_ (1997), _The Beach_ (2000), and _28 Weeks Later_ (2007) **2 Thomas.** 1795–1881, Scottish essayist and historian. His works include _Sartor Resartus_ (1833–34), _The French Revolution_ (1837), lectures _On Heroes, Hero-Worship, and the Heroic in History_ (1841), and the _History of Frederick the Great_ (1858–65)

Carmarthen _n_ a market town in S Wales, the administrative centre of Carmarthenshire: Norman castle. Pop: 14 648 (2001)

Carmarthenshire _n_ a county of S Wales, formerly part of Dyfed (1974–96): on Carmarthen Bay, with the Cambrian Mountains in the N: generally agricultural (esp. dairying). Administrative centre: Carmarthen. Pop: 176 000 (2003 est). Area: 2398 sq km (926 sq miles)

Carmel _n_ **Mount Carmel** a mountain ridge in NW Israel, extending from the Samarian Hills to the Mediterranean. Highest point: about 540 m (1800 ft)

Carmelite _n_ **1** a Christian friar or nun belonging to the order of Our Lady of Carmel ▷ _adj_ **2** of this order [after Mount CARMEL, where the order was founded]

Carmichael _n_ **Hoaglund Howard**, known as _Hoagy_. 1899–1981, US pianist, singer, and composer of such standards as "Star Dust" (1929)

carminative _adj_ **1** able to relieve flatulence ▷ _n_ **2** a carminative drug [Latin _carminare_ to card wool, comb out]

carmine _adj_ vivid red [Arabic _qirmiz_ kermes]

Carnac _n_ a village in NW France: noted for its many megalithic monuments, including alignments of stone menhirs

carnage _n_ extensive slaughter of people [Latin _caro_ flesh]

carnal _adj_ of a sexual or sensual nature: _carnal knowledge_ [Latin _caro_ flesh] **› carnality** _n_

Carnap _n_ **Rudolf.** 1891–1970, US logical positivist philosopher, born in Germany: attempted to construct a formal language for the empirical sciences that would eliminate ambiguity

Carnarvon _n_ a variant spelling of **Caernarfon**

Carnatic _n_ a region of S India, between the Eastern Ghats and the Coromandel Coast: originally the country of the Kanarese; historically important as a rich and powerful trading centre; now part of Tamil Nadu state

carnation _n_ a cultivated plant with clove-scented white, pink, or red flowers [Latin _caro_ flesh]

Carné _n_ **Marcel.** 1906–96, French film director. His films include _Le Jour se lève_ (1939), _Les Portes de la nuit_ (1946), and _La Bible_ (1976)

Carnegie _n_ **Andrew.** 1835–1919, US steel manufacturer and philanthropist, born in Scotland: endowed public libraries, education, and research trusts

Carnegie Hall _n_ a famous concert hall in New York (opened 1891); endowed by Andrew Carnegie

carnelian _n_ a reddish-yellow variety of chalcedony, used as a gemstone [Old French _corneline_]

carnet (kar-nay) _n_ a customs licence permitting motorists to take their cars across certain frontiers [French: notebook]

Carney _n_ **Mark (Joseph).** born 1965, Canadian banker; governor of the Bank of Canada (2008–2013); governor of the Bank of England from 2013

Carniola _n_ a region of N Slovenia: a former duchy and crownland of Austria (1335–1919); divided between Yugoslavia and Italy in 1919; part of Yugoslavia (1947–92). German name: **Krain**. Slovene name: **Kranj**

carnival _n_ **1** a festive period with processions, music, and dancing in the street **2** a travelling funfair [Old Italian _carnelevare_ a removing of meat (referring to the Lenten fast)]

carnivore (car-niv-vore) _n_ **1** a meat-eating animal **2** _informal_ an aggressively ambitious person [Latin _caro_ flesh + _vorare_ to consume] **› carnivorous** (car-niv-or-uss) _adj_

Carnot _n_ **1 Lazare (Nicolas Marguerite)**, known as _the Organizer of Victory_. 1753–1823, French military engineer and administrator: organized the French Revolutionary army (1793–95) **2 Nicolas Léonard Sadi.** 1796–1832, French physicist, whose work formed the basis for the second law of thermodynamics, enunciated in 1850; author of _Réflexions sur la puissance motrice du feu_ (1824)

Caro _n_ **1 Sir Antony.** 1924–2013, British sculptor, best known for his abstract steel sculptures **2 Joseph (ben Ephraim)** 1488–1575, Jewish legal scholar and mystic, born in Spain; compiler of the _Shulhan Arukh_ (1564–65), the most authoritative Jewish legal code

carob _n_ the pod of a Mediterranean tree, used as a chocolate substitute [Arabic _al kharrūbah_]

carol _n_ **1** a joyful religious song sung at Christmas ▷ _vb_ **-olling, -olled** _or US_ **-oling, -oled 2** to sing carols **3** to sing joyfully [Old French]

Carol II _n_ 1893–1953, king of Romania (1930–40), who was deposed by the Iron Guard

Carolina _n_ a former English colony on the E coast of North America, first established in 1663: divided in 1729 into North and South Carolina, which are often referred to as the **Carolinas**

Caroline Islands _pl n_ an archipelago of over 500 islands and islets in the W Pacific Ocean east of the Philippines, all of which are now part of the Federated States of Micronesia, except for the Palau group: formerly part of the US Trust Territory of the Pacific Islands; centre of a typhoon zone. Area: (land) 1183 sq km (457 sq miles)

Caroline of Ansbach _n_ 1683–1737, wife of George II of Great Britain

Caroline of Brunswick _n_ 1768–1821, wife of George IV of the United Kingdom: tried for adultery (1820)

Carolinian _adj_ **1** of or relating to North or South Carolina ▷ _n_ **2** a native or inhabitant of North or South Carolina

carotene _n_ _biochem_ any of four orange-red hydrocarbons found in many plants, converted to vitamin A in the liver [from Latin _carota_ carrot]

carotid (kar-rot-id) _n_ **1** either of the two arteries that supply blood to the head and neck ▷ _adj_ **2** of either of these arteries [Greek _karoun_ to stupefy; so named because pressure on them produced unconsciousness]

carousal _n_ a merry drinking party

carouse _vb_ **-rousing, -roused** to have a merry drinking party: _carousing with friends_ [German (_trinken_) _gar aus_ (to drink) right out]

carousel (kar-roo-sell) _n_ **1** a revolving conveyor for luggage at an airport or for slides for a projector **2** _US and Canad_ a merry-go-round [Italian _carosello_]

carp¹ _n, pl_ **carp** _or_ **carps** a large freshwater food fish [Old French _carpe_]

carp² _vb_ to complain or find fault [Old Norse _karpa_ to boast] **› carping** _adj, n_

carpaccio (kar-patch-ee-oh) _n_ an Italian dish of thin slices of raw meat or fish [Italian]

Carpaccio _n_ **Vittore.** ?1460–?1525, Italian painter of the Venetian school

carpal _n_ a wrist bone [Greek _karpos_ wrist]

car park _n_ an area or building reserved for parking cars

Carpathian Mountains _or_ **Carpathians** _pl n_ a mountain system of central and E Europe, extending from Slovakia to central Romania: mainly forested, with rich iron ore resources. Highest peak: Gerlachovka 2663 m (8788 ft)

Carpatho-Ukraine _n_ another name for **Ruthenia**

carpel _n_ the female reproductive organ of a flowering plant [Greek _karpos_ fruit]

Carpentaria _n_ **Gulf of Carpentaria** a shallow inlet of the

Arafura Sea, in N Australia between Arnhem Land and Cape York Peninsula

carpenter *n* a person who makes or repairs wooden structures [Latin *carpentarius* wagon-maker]

Carpenter *n* **John Alden**. 1876–1951, US composer, who used jazz rhythms in orchestral music: his works include the ballet *Skyscrapers* (1926) and the orchestral suite *Adventures in a Perambulator* (1915)

Carpentier *n* **Georges**, known as *Gorgeous Georges*. 1894–1975, French boxer: world light-heavyweight champion (1920–22)

carpentry *n* the skill or work of a carpenter

carpet *n* **1** a heavy fabric for covering floors **2** a covering like a carpet: *a carpet of leaves* **3 on the carpet** *informal* being or about to be reprimanded **4 sweep something under the carpet** to conceal or keep silent about something that one does not want to be discovered ▷ *vb* **-peting, -peted 5** to cover with a carpet or a covering like a carpet [Latin *carpere* to pluck, card]

carpetbag *n* a travelling bag made of carpeting

carpetbagger *n* **1** a politician who seeks office in a place where he or she has no connections **2** *Brit* a person who makes a short-term investment in a mutual savings or life-assurance organization in order to benefit from free shares issued following the organization's conversion to a public limited company

carpeting *n* carpet material or carpets in general

carpet snake *n* a large nonvenomous Australian snake with a carpet-like pattern on its back

car phone *n* a telephone that operates by cellular radio for use in a car

carport *n* a shelter for a car, consisting of a roof supported by posts

carpus *n*, *pl* **-pi** the set of eight bones of the human wrist [Greek *karpos*]

Carracci *n* a family of Italian painters, born in Bologna: **Agostino** (1557–1602); his brother, **Annibale** (1560–1609), noted for his frescoes, esp. in the Palazzo Farnese, Rome; and their cousin, **Ludovico** (1555–1619). They were influential in reviving the classical tradition of the Renaissance and founded a teaching academy (1582) in Bologna

carrageen *n* an edible red seaweed of North America and N Europe [*Carragheen*, near Waterford, Ireland]

Carrantuohill or **Carrauntoohill** *n* a mountain in SW Republic of Ireland, in Macgillicuddy's Reeks in Kerry: the highest peak in Ireland. Height: 1041 m (3414 ft)

Carrara *n* a town in NW Italy, in NW Tuscany: famous for its marble. Pop: 65 034 (2001)

Carrel *n* **Alexis**. 1873–1944, French surgeon and biologist, active in the US (1905–39): developed a method of suturing blood vessels, making the transplantation of arteries and organs possible: Nobel prize for physiology or medicine 1912

Carreras *n* **José**. born 1947, Spanish tenor

Carrey *n* **Jim**. born 1962, Canadian-born Hollywood actor noted for his comedy roles; films include *Ace Ventura, Pet Detective* (1994), *Liar Liar* (1997), *The Truman Show* (1998), *The Majestic* (2001), and *Eternal Sunshine of the Spotless Mind* (2004)

carriage *n* **1** *Brit, Austral and NZ* one of the sections of a train for passengers **2** the way a person holds and moves his or her head and body **3** a four-wheeled horse-drawn passenger vehicle **4** the moving part of a machine, such as a typewriter, that supports and shifts another part **5** the charge made for conveying goods [Old French *cariage*]

carriage clock *n* a style of portable clock, originally used by travellers

carriageway *n* **1** *Brit* the part of a road along which traffic passes in one direction: *the westbound carriageway of the M4* **2** *NZ* the part of a road used by vehicles

Carrickfergus *n* **1** a town in E Northern Ireland, in Carrickfergus district, Co Antrim; historic settlement of Scottish Protestants on Belfast Lough; Norman castle. Pop: 27 201 (2001) **2** a district of E Northern Ireland, in Co Antrim. Pop: 37 659 (2001). Area: 83 sq km (32 sq miles)

carrier *n* **1** a person, vehicle, or organization that carries something: *armoured personnel carriers* **2** a person or animal that, without suffering from a disease, is capable of transmitting it to others **3** short for **aircraft carrier**

carrier bag *n* *Brit* a large plastic or paper bag for carrying shopping

carrier pigeon *n* a homing pigeon used for carrying messages

Carrington *n* **1 Dora**, known as *Carrington*. 1893–1932, British painter, engraver, and letter writer; a member of the Bloomsbury Group **2 Peter (Alexander Rupert)**, 6th Baron. born 1919, British Conservative politician: secretary of state for defence (1970–74); foreign secretary (1979–82); secretary general of NATO (1984–88)

carrion *n* dead and rotting flesh [Latin *caro* flesh]

carrion crow *n* a scavenging European crow with a completely black plumage and bill

Carroll *n* **Lewis**. real name *the Reverend Charles Lutwidge Dodgson*. 1832–98, English writer; an Oxford mathematics don who wrote *Alice's Adventures in Wonderland* (1865) and *Through the Looking-Glass* (1872) and the nonsense poem *The Hunting of the Snark* (1876)

carrot *n* **1** a long tapering orange root vegetable **2** something offered as an incentive [Greek *karōton*]

carroty *adj* (of hair) reddish-orange

carry *vb* **-ries, -rying, -ried 1** to take from one place to another **2** to have with one habitually, for example in one's pocket or handbag: *to carry a donor card* **3** to transmit or be transmitted: *to carry disease* **4** to have as a factor or result: *the charge of desertion carries a maximum penalty of twenty years* **5** to be pregnant with: *women carrying Down's Syndrome babies* **6** to hold (one's head or body) in a specified manner: *she always wears a sari and carries herself like an Indian* **7** to secure the adoption of (a bill or motion): *the resolution was carried by fewer than twenty votes* **8** (of a newspaper or television or radio station) to include in the contents: *several papers carried front-page pictures of the Russian president* **9** *maths* to transfer (a number) from one column of figures to the next **10** to travel a certain distance or reach a specified point: *his faint voice carried no farther than the front few rows* **11 carry the can** *informal* to take all the blame for something ▶ See also **carry away, carry forward**, etc. [Latin *carrum* transport wagon]

carry away *vb* **be** or **get carried away** to be engrossed in or fascinated by something to the point of losing self-control: *he could be carried away by his own rhetoric*

carrycot *n* a light portable bed for a baby, with handles and a hood, which usually also serves as the body of a pram

carry forward *vb* to transfer (an amount) to the next column, page, or accounting period

carry off *vb* **1** to lift and take (someone or something) away: *the German striker was carried off after snapping an Achilles tendon* **2** to win: *who will carry off this year's honours is unclear* **3** to handle (a situation) successfully: *he had the presence and social ability to carry off the job* **4** to cause to die: *the circulatory disorder which carried off other members of his family*

carry on *vb* **1** to continue: *we'll carry on exactly where we left off* **2** to do, run, or take part in: *the vast trade carried on in the city* **3** *informal* to cause a fuss: *I don't want to carry on and make a big scene* ▷ *n* **carry-on 4** *informal, chiefly Brit* a fuss

carry out *vb* **1** to follow (an order or instruction) **2** to accomplish (a task): *to carry out repairs*

carry over *vb* to extend from one period or situation into another: *major debts carried over from last year*

carry through *vb* to bring to completion: *these are difficult policies to carry through*

carsick *adj* nauseated from riding in a car

Carson *n* **1 Christopher**, known as *Kit Carson*. 1809–68, US frontiersman, trapper, scout, and Indian agent **2 Edward Henry**, Baron. 1854–1935, Anglo-Irish politician and lawyer; led northern Irish resistance to the British government's plan for home rule for Ireland **3 Rachel** (**Louise**). 1907–64, US marine biologist and science writer; author of *Silent Spring* (1962) **4 Willie**, full name *William Hunter Fisher Carson*. born 1942, Scottish jockey: rode four winners in the Derby (1979, 1980, 1989, 1994)

Carson City *n* a city in W Nevada, capital of the state. Pop: 55 311 (2003 est)

Carstensz *n* **Mount Carstensz** a former name of (Mount) Jaya

cart *n* **1** an open horse-drawn vehicle, usually with two wheels, used to carry goods or passengers **2** any small vehicle that is pulled or pushed by hand ▷ *vb* **3** to carry, usually with some effort: *men carted bricks and tiles and wooden boards* ▶ See also **cart off** [Old Norse *kartr*]

Cartagena *n* **1** a port in NW Colombia, on the Caribbean: centre for the Inquisition and the slave trade in the 16th century; chief oil port of Colombia. Pop: 1 002 000 (2005 est) **2** a port in SE Spain, on the Mediterranean: important since Carthaginian and Roman times for its minerals. Pop: 194 203 (2003 est)

carte blanche *n* complete authority: *she's got carte blanche to redecorate* [French: blank paper]

cartel *n* an association of competing firms formed in order to fix prices [German *Kartell*]

Carter *n* **1 Angela**. 1940–92, British novelist and writer; her novels include *The Magic Toyshop* (1967) and *Nights at the Circus* (1984) **2 Dan**(**iel William**). born 1982, New Zealand Rugby Union player; record points scorer in test match rugby **3 Elliot** (**Cook**). 1908–2012, US composer. His works include the *Piano Sonata* (1945–46), four string quartets, and other orchestral pieces: Pulitzer Prize 1960, 1973 **4 Howard**. 1873–1939, English Egyptologist: excavated the tomb of the Pharaoh Tutankhamen **5 James Earl**, known as *Jimmy*. born 1924, US Democratic statesman; 39th president of the US (1977–81); Nobel peace prize 2002

Carteret *n* **John**, 1st Earl Granville. 1690–1763, British statesman, diplomat, and orator who led the opposition to Walpole (1730–42), after whose fall he became a leading minister as secretary of state (1742–44)

Cartesian *adj* of René Descartes, 17th-century French philosopher and mathematician, or his works [*Cartesius*, Latin form of Descartes]

Cartesian coordinates *pl n* a set of numbers that determine the location of a point in a plane or in space by its distance from two fixed intersecting lines

Carthage *n* an ancient city state, on the N African coast near present-day Tunis. Founded about 800 BC by Phoenician traders, it grew into an empire dominating N Africa and the Mediterranean. Destroyed and then rebuilt by Rome, it was finally razed by the Arabs in 697 AD

Carthaginian *adj* **1** of or relating to Carthage or its inhabitants ▷ *n* **2** a native or inhabitant of Carthage

carthorse *n* a large heavily built horse kept for pulling carts or for farm work

Carthusian *n* **1** a Christian monk or nun belonging to a strict monastic order founded in 1084 ▷ *adj* **2** of this order [Latin *Carthusia* Chartreuse, near Grenoble]

Cartier *n* **Jacques**. 1491–1557, French navigator and explorer in Canada, who discovered the St Lawrence River (1535)

Cartier-Bresson *n* **Henri**. 1908–2004, French photographer

cartilage (**kar-till-ij**) *n* a strong flexible tissue forming part of the skeleton [Latin *cartilago*] **▷ cartilaginous** *adj*

Cartland *n* Dame **Barbara** (**Hamilton**). 1901–2000, British novelist, noted for her prolific output of popular romantic fiction

cart off *vb* to take (someone) somewhere forcefully: *we had been carted off to the security police building*

cartography *n* the art of making maps or charts [French *carte* map, chart] **▷ cartographer** *n* **▷ cartographic** *adj*

carton *n* **1** a cardboard box or container **2** a container of waxed paper in which drinks are sold [Italian *carta* card]

cartoon *n* **1** a humorous or satirical drawing in a newspaper or magazine **2** same as **comic strip 3** same as **animated cartoon** [Italian *cartone* pasteboard] **▷ cartoonist** *n*

cartouche *n* **1** an ornamental tablet or panel in the form of a scroll **2** (in ancient Egypt) an oblong or oval figure containing royal or divine names [French: scroll, cartridge]

cartridge *n* **1** a metal casing containing an explosive charge and bullet for a gun **2** the part of the pick-up of a record player that converts the movements of the stylus into electrical signals **3** a sealed container of film or tape, or ink for a special kind of pen [from French *cartouche*]

cartridge belt *n* a belt with loops or pockets for holding cartridges

cartridge clip *n* a metallic container holding cartridges for an automatic gun

cartridge paper *n* a type of heavy rough drawing paper

cartwheel *n* **1** a sideways somersault supported by the hands with legs outstretched **2** the large spoked wheel of a cart

Cartwright *n* **1 Edmund**. 1743–1823, British clergyman, who invented the power loom **2** Dame **Silvia** (née Poulter). born 1943, New Zealand lawyer. She became a High Court judge in 1993; governor general of New Zealand (2001–06)

Caruso *n* **Enrico**. 1873–1921, an outstanding Italian operatic tenor; one of the first to make gramophone records

carve *vb* **carving, carved 1** to cut in order to form something: *carving wood* **2** to form (something) by cutting: *the statue which was carved by Michelangelo* **3** to slice (cooked meat) ▶ See also **carve out, carve up** [Old English *ceorfan*] **▷ carver** *n*

carve out *vb informal* to make or create: *to carve out a political career*

Carver *n* **George Washington**. ?1864–1943, US agricultural chemist and botanist

carvery *n, pl* **-veries** a restaurant where customers pay a set price for unrestricted helpings of carved meat and other food

carve up *vb* **1** to divide or share out: *in 1795, Poland was carved up between three empires* ▷ *n* **carve-up 2** the division or sharing out of something: *a territorial carve-up*

carving *n* a figure or design produced by carving stone or wood

carving knife *n* a long-bladed knife for carving cooked meat

carwash *n* a place fitted with equipment for automatically washing cars

Cary *n* (**Arthur**) **Joyce** (**Lunel**). 1888–1957, British novelist; author of *Mister Johnson* (1939), *A House of Children* (1941), and *The Horse's Mouth* (1944)

caryatid (**kar-ree-at-id**) *n* a supporting column in the shape of a female figure [Greek *Karuatides* priestesses of Artemis at *Karuai* (Caryae), in Laconia]

Casablanca *n* a port in NW Morocco, on the Atlantic: largest city in the country; industrial centre. Pop: 3 523 000 (2003)

Casals *n* **Pablo**. 1876–1973, Spanish cellist and composer, noted for his interpretation of J. S. Bach's cello suites

Casanova *n* **1 Giovanni Jacopo**. 1725–98, Italian adventurer noted for his *Mémoires*, a vivid account of his sexual adventures and of contemporary society; rake **2** any man noted for his amorous adventures; rake

Casaubon *n* **Isaac**. 1559–1614, French Protestant theologian and classical scholar

casbah *n* the citadel of a North African city [Arabic *kasba* citadel]

cascade *n* **1** a waterfall or series of waterfalls over rocks **2** something flowing or falling like a waterfall: *a cascade* *of luxuriant hair* ▷ *vb* **-cading, -caded 3** to flow or fall in a cascade: *rays of sunshine cascaded down* [Italian *cascare* to fall]

Cascade Range *n* a chain of mountains in the US and Canada: a continuation of the Sierra Nevada range from N California through Oregon and Washington to British Columbia. Highest peak: Mount Rainier, 4392 m (14 408 ft)

cascading style sheet *n computers* a file recording style details, such as fonts, colours, etc., that ensures style is consistent over all the pages of a website

cascara *n* the bark of a N American shrub, used as a laxative [Spanish: bark]

case¹ *n* **1** a single instance or example of something: *cases of teenage pregnancies* **2** a matter for discussion: *the case before the Ethics Committee* **3** a specific condition or state of affairs: *a sudden-death play-off in the case of a draw* **4** a set of arguments supporting an action or cause: *I put my case before them* **5** a person or problem dealt with by a doctor, social worker, or solicitor **6 a** an action or lawsuit: *a rape case* **b** the evidence offered in court to support a claim: *he will try to show that the case against his client is largely circumstantial* **7** *grammar* a form of a noun, pronoun, or adjective showing its relation to other words in the sentence: *the accusative case* **8** *informal* an amusingly eccentric person **9 in any case** no matter what **10 in case** so as to allow for the possibility that: *the President has ordered a medical team to stand by in case hostages are released* **11 in case of** in the event of: *in case of a future conflict* [Old English *casus* (grammatical) case, associated with Old French *cas* a happening; both from Latin *cadere* to fall]

case² *n* **1** a container, such as a box or chest **2** a suitcase **3** a protective outer covering ▷ *vb* **casing, cased 4** *slang* to inspect carefully (a place one plans to rob) [Latin *capsa* box]

case-hardened *adj* having been made callous by experience: *a case-hardened senior policewoman*

case history *n* a record of a person's background or medical history

casein *n* a protein found in milk, which forms the basis of cheese [Latin *caseus* cheese]

case law *n* law established by following judicial decisions made in earlier cases

caseload *n* the number of cases that someone like a doctor or social worker deals with at any one time

casement *n* a window that is hinged on one side [probably from Old French *encassement* frame]

Casement *n* Sir **Roger** (**David**). 1864–1916, British diplomat and Irish nationalist: hanged by the British for treason in attempting to gain German support for Irish independence

Caserta *n* a town in S Italy, in Campania: centre of Garibaldi's campaigns for the unification of Italy (1860); Allied headquarters in World War II. Pop: 75 208 (2001)

case study *n* an analysis of a group or person in order to make generalizations about a larger group or society as a whole

casework *n* social work based on close study of the personal histories and circumstances of individuals and families **>** **caseworker** *n*

cash *n* **1** banknotes and coins, rather than cheques **2** *informal* money: *strapped for cash* ▷ *adj* **3** of, for, or paid in cash: *cash hand-outs* ▷ *vb* **4** to obtain or pay banknotes or coins for (a cheque or postal order) ▶ See also **cash in on** [Old Italian *cassa* money box]

Cash *n* **Johnny**. 1932–2003, US country-and-western singer, guitarist, and songwriter. His recordings include the hits "I Walk the Line" (1956), "Ring of Fire" (1963), "A Boy named Sue" (1969), and the *American Recordings* series of albums (1994–2003)

cash-and-carry *adj* operating on a basis of cash payment for goods that are taken away by the purchaser: *the cash-and-carry wholesalers*

cashback *n* **1** a discount offered in return for immediate payment **2** a service by which a customer in a shop can draw out cash on a debit card

cash-book *n accounting* a journal in which all money transactions are recorded

cash card *n* a card issued by a bank or building society which can be inserted into a cash dispenser in order to obtain money

cash crop *n* a crop produced for sale rather than for subsistence

cash desk *n* a counter or till in a shop where purchases are paid for

cash discount *n* a discount granted to a purchaser who pays within a specified period

cash dispenser *n* a computerized device outside a bank which supplies cash when a special card is inserted and the user's code number keyed in

cashew *n* an edible kidney-shaped nut [S American Indian *acajú*]

cash flow *n* the movement of money into and out of a business

cashier¹ *n* a person responsible for handling cash in a bank, shop, or other business [French *casse* money chest]

cashier² *vb* to dismiss with dishonour from the armed forces [Latin *quassare* to QUASH]

cash in on *vb informal* to gain profit or advantage from: *trying to cash in on the dispute*

cashmere *n* a very fine soft wool obtained from goats [from *Kashmir*, in SW central Asia]

Cashmere *n* a variant spelling of **Kashmir**

cash on delivery *n* a system involving cash payment to the carrier on delivery of merchandise. Abbreviation: COD

cash register *n* a till that has a mechanism for displaying and adding the prices of the goods sold

Casimir III *n* known as *the Great*. 1310–70, king of Poland (1333–70)

Casimir IV *n* 1427–92, grand duke of Lithuania (1440–92) and king of Poland (1447–92)

casing *n* a protective case or covering

casino *n*, *pl* **-nos** a public building or room where gambling games are played [Italian]

cask *n* **1** a strong barrel used to hold alcoholic drink **2** *Austral* a cubic carton containing wine, with a tap for dispensing [Spanish *casco* helmet]

casket *n* **1** a small box for valuables **2** *US* a coffin [probably from Old French *cassette* little box]

Caspian Sea *or* **Caspian** *n* a salt lake between SE Europe and Asia: the largest inland sea in the world; fed mainly by the River Volga. Area: 394 299 sq km (152 239 sq miles)

Cassandra *n* someone whose prophecies of doom are unheeded [Trojan prophetess in Greek mythology]

Cassatt *n* **Mary**. 1845–1926, US impressionist painter, who lived in France

cassava *n* a starch obtained from the root of a tropical American plant, used to make tapioca [West Indian *caçábi*]

Cassel *n* a variant spelling of **Kassel**

casserole *n* **1** a covered dish in which food is cooked slowly, usually in an oven, and served **2** a dish cooked and served in this way: *beef casserole* ▷ *vb* **-roling, -roled 3** to cook in a casserole [French]

cassette *n* a plastic case containing a reel of film or magnetic tape [French: little box]

cassia *n* **1** a tropical plant whose pods yield a mild laxative **2 cassia bark** a cinnamon-like spice obtained from the bark of a tropical Asian tree [Greek *kasia*]

Cassini *n* **Giovanni Domenico**. 1625–1712, French astronomer, born in Italy. He discovered (1675) **Cassini's division**, the gap that divides Saturn's rings into two parts, and four of Saturn's moons

Cassino *n* a town in central Italy, in Latium at the foot of Monte Cassino: an ancient Volscian (and later Roman) town and citadel. Pop: 32 762 (2001). Latin name: **Casinum**

C

Cassiodorus n Flavius Magnus Aurelius. ?490–?585 AD, Roman statesman, writer, and monk; author of *Variae*, a collection of official documents written for the Ostrogoths

Cassirer n Ernst. 1874–1945, German neo-Kantian philosopher. *The Philosophy of Symbolic Forms* (1923–29) analyses the symbols that underlie all manifestations, including myths and language, of human culture

Cassius Longinus n Gaius. died 42 BC, Roman general: led the conspiracy against Julius Caesar (44); defeated at Philippi by Antony (42)

Cassivelaunus n 1st century BC, British chieftain, king of the Catuvellauni tribe, who organized resistance to Caesar's invasion of Britain (54 BC)

cassock n an ankle-length garment, usually black, worn by some Christian priests [Italian *casacca* a long coat]

Casson n Sir Hugh (Maxwell). 1910–99, British architect; president of the Royal Academy of Arts (1976–84)

cassowary n, pl **-waries** a large flightless bird of Australia and New Guinea [Malay *kěsuari*]

cast n 1 the actors in a play collectively 2 a an object made of material that has been shaped, while molten, by a mould b the mould used to shape such an object 3 *surgery* a rigid casing made of plaster of Paris for immobilizing broken bones while they heal 4 a sort, kind, or style: *people of an academic cast of mind* 5 a slight squint in the eye ▷ vb **casting, cast** 6 to select (an actor) to play a part in a play or film 7 to give or deposit (a vote) 8 to express (doubts or aspersions) 9 to cause to appear: *a shadow cast by the grandstand; the gloom cast by the recession* 10 a to shape (molten material) by pouring it into a mould b to make (an object) by such a process 11 to throw (a fishing line) into the water 12 to throw with force: *cast into a bonfire* 13 to direct (a glance): *he cast his eye over the horse-chestnut trees* 14 to roll or throw (a dice) 15 **cast aside** to abandon or reject: *cast aside by her lover* 16 **cast a spell** a to perform magic b to have an irresistible influence ▶ See also **cast around, cast back**, etc. [Old Norse *kasta*]

Castalia n a spring on Mount Parnassus: in ancient Greece sacred to Apollo and the Muses and believed to be a source of inspiration ❯ **Cas'talian** adj

castanets pl n a musical instrument, used by Spanish dancers, consisting of curved pieces of hollow wood, held between the fingers and thumb and clicked together [Spanish *castañeta*, from *castaña* chestnut]

cast around or **cast about** vb to make a mental or visual search: *he cast around for a job*

castaway n a person who has been shipwrecked

cast back vb to turn (the mind) to the past

cast down vb to make (a person) feel discouraged or dejected

caste n 1 any of the four major hereditary classes into which Hindu society is divided 2 social rank [Latin *castus* pure, not polluted]

Castellammare di Stabia n a port and resort in SW Italy, in Campania on the Bay of Naples: site of the Roman resort of Stabiae, which was destroyed by the eruption of Vesuvius in 79 AD. Pop: 66 929 (2001)

castellated adj having turrets and battlements, like a castle [Medieval Latin *castellare* to fortify as a castle]

Castellón de la Plana n a port in E Spain. Pop: 160 714 (2003 est)

caster n same as **castor**

caster sugar n finely ground white sugar

castigate vb **-gating, -gated** to find fault with or reprimand (a person) harshly [Latin *castigare* to correct] ❯ **castigation** n

Castiglione n Count Baldassare. 1478–1529, Italian diplomat and writer, noted particularly for his dialogue on ideal courtly life, *Il Libro del Cortegiano* (The Courtier) (1528)

Castile or **Castilla** n a former kingdom comprising most of modern Spain: originally part of León, it became an independent kingdom in the 10th century and united with Aragon (1469), the first step in the formation of the Spanish state

Castilian n 1 the Spanish dialect of Castile; the standard form of European Spanish 2 a native or inhabitant of Castile ▷ adj 3 denoting, relating to, or characteristic of Castile, its inhabitants, or the standard form of European Spanish

Castilla la Vieja n the Spanish name for **Old Castile**

casting n an object that has been cast in metal from a mould

casting vote n the deciding vote used by the chairperson of a meeting when an equal number of votes are cast on each side

cast iron n 1 iron containing so much carbon that it is brittle and must be cast into shape rather than wrought ▷ adj **cast-iron** 2 made of cast iron 3 definite or unchallengeable: *cast-iron guarantees*

castle n 1 a a large fortified building or set of buildings, often built as a residence for a ruler or nobleman in medieval Europe 2 same as **rook²** [Latin: *castellum*]

Castlebar n the county town of Co Mayo, Republic of Ireland; site of the battle (1798) between the French and British known as Castlebar Races. Pop: 11 371 (2002)

Castleford n a town in N England, in Wakefield unitary authority, West Yorkshire on the River Aire. Pop: 37 525 (2001)

Castle Howard n a mansion near York in Yorkshire: designed in 1700 by Sir John Vanbrugh and Nicholas Hawksmoor; the grounds include the Temple of the Four Winds and a mausoleum

castle in the air or **in Spain** n a hope or desire unlikely to be realized

Castlereagh¹ n a district of E Northern Ireland, in Co Down. Pop: 66 076 (2003 est). Area: 85 sq km (33 sq miles)

Castlereagh² n Viscount. title of Robert Stewart, Marquis of Londonderry. 1769–1822, British statesman: as foreign secretary (1812–22) led the Grand Alliance against Napoleon and attended the Congress of Vienna (1815)

Castner n Hamilton Young. 1858–98, US chemist, who devised the **Castner process** for extracting sodium from sodium hydroxide

cast-off adj 1 discarded because no longer wanted or needed: *cast-off clothing* ▷ n 2 a person or thing that has been discarded because no longer wanted or needed ▷ vb **cast off 3** to discard (something no longer wanted or needed) 4 to untie a ship from a dock 5 to knot and remove (a row of stitches, esp. the final row) from the needle in knitting

cast on vb to make (a row of stitches) on the needle in knitting

castor n a small swivelling wheel fixed to a piece of furniture to enable it to be moved easily in any direction

castor oil n an oil obtained from the seeds of an Indian plant, used as a lubricant and purgative

castrate vb **-trating, -trated** 1 to remove the testicles of 2 to deprive of vigour or masculinity [Latin *castrare*] ❯ **castration** n

castrato n, pl **-ti** or **-tos** (in 17th- and 18th-century opera) a male singer whose testicles were removed before puberty, allowing the retention of a soprano or alto voice [Italian]

Castries n the capital and chief port of St Lucia. Pop: 14 000 (2005 est)

Castro n 1 Fidel. full name Fidel Castro Ruz. born 1927, Cuban revolutionary and statesman: led the communist overthrow of the Batista dictatorship in 1959; prime minister (1959–76), president (1976–2008) 2 his brother Raúl. full name Raúl Modesto Castro Ruz, born 1931, Cuban revolutionary and statesman; president from 2008

Castrop-Rauxel or **Kastrop-Rauxel** n an industrial city in W Germany, in North Rhine-Westphalia. Pop: 78 208 (2003 est)

casual adj 1 being or seeming careless or nonchalant: *he* was casual about security **2** occasional or irregular: *casual workers* **3** shallow or superficial: *casual relationships* **4** for informal wear: *a casual jacket* **5** happening by chance or without planning: *a casual comment* ▷ n **6** an occasional worker [Latin *casus* event, chance] ❭ **casually** *adv*

casuals *pl n* **1** informal clothing **2** Brit young men wearing expensive casual clothes who go to football matches in order to start fights

casualty *n, pl* **-ties** **1** a person who is killed or injured in an accident or war **2** the hospital department where victims of accidents are given emergency treatment **3** a person or thing that has suffered as the result of a particular event or circumstance: *583 job losses with significant casualties among public-sector employees*

casuarina (kass-yew-a-**reen**-a) *n* an Australian tree with jointed green branches [from Malay *kĕsuari*, referring to the resemblance of the branches to the feathers of the cassowary]

casuistry *n* reasoning that is misleading or oversubtle [Latin *casus* case] ❭ **casuist** *n*

cat *n* **1** a small domesticated mammal with thick soft fur and whiskers **2** a wild animal related to the cat, such as the lynx, lion, or tiger. Related adjective: **feline** **3** **let the cat out of the bag** to disclose a secret **4** **raining cats and dogs** raining very heavily **5** **set the cat among the pigeons** to stir up trouble [Latin *cattus*] ❭ **catlike** *adj*

catabolism *n* biology a metabolic process in which complex molecules are broken down into simple ones with the release of energy [Greek *kata-* down + *ballein* to throw] ❭ **catabolic** *adj*

cataclysm (kat-a-kliz-zum) *n* **1** a violent upheaval of a social, political, or military nature: *the cataclysm of the Second World War* **2** a disaster such as an earthquake or a flood [Greek *katakluzein* to flood] ❭ **cataclysmic** *adj*

catacombs (kat-a-koomz) *pl n* an underground burial place consisting of tunnels with side recesses for tombs [Late Latin *catacumbas* cemetery near Rome]

catafalque (kat-a-falk) *n* a raised platform on which a body lies in state before or during a funeral [Italian *catafalco*]

Catalan *adj* **1** of or relating to Catalonia or its inhabitants ▷ n **2** a language of Catalonia in NE Spain **3** a native or inhabitant of Catalonia

catalepsy *n* a trancelike state in which the body is rigid [Greek *katalēpsis* a seizing] ❭ **cataleptic** *adj*

Catalina Island *n* another name for **Santa Catalina**

catalogue *or US* **catalog** *n* **1** a book containing details of items for sale **2** a list of all the books of a library **3** a list of events, qualities, or things considered as a group: *a catalogue of killings* ▷ vb **-loguing, -logued** *or* **-loging, -loged** **4** to enter (an item) in a catalogue **5** to list a series of (events, qualities, or things): *the report catalogues two decades of human-rights violations* [Greek *katalegein* to list] ❭ **cataloguer** *n*

Catalonia *n* a region of NE Spain, with a strong separatist tradition: became an autonomous region with its own parliament in 1979; an important agricultural and industrial region, with many resorts. Pop: 7 012 600 (2003 est). Area: 31 929 sq km (12 328 sq miles). Catalan name: **Catalunya**. Spanish name: **Cataluña**

catalpa *n* a tree of N America and Asia with bell-shaped whitish flowers [Carolina Creek (a Native American language) *kutuhlpa* winged head]

catalyse *or US* **-lyze** *vb* **-lysing, -lysed** *or* **-lyzing, -lyzed** to influence (a chemical reaction) by catalysis

catalysis *n* acceleration of a chemical reaction by the action of a catalyst [Greek *kataluein* to dissolve] ❭ **catalytic** *adj*

catalyst *n* **1** a substance that speeds up a chemical reaction without itself undergoing any permanent chemical change **2** a person or thing that causes an important change to take place: *a catalyst for peace*

catalytic converter *n* a device which uses catalysts to reduce the quantity of poisonous substances emitted by the exhaust of a motor vehicle

catalytic cracker *n* a unit in an oil refinery in which mineral oils are converted into fuels by a catalytic process

catamaran *n* a boat with twin parallel hulls [Tamil *kattumaram* tied timber]

catamite *n* a boy kept as a homosexual partner [Latin *Catamitus*, variant of *Ganymedes* Ganymede, cupbearer to the gods in Greek mythology]

Catania *n* a port in E Sicily, near Mount Etna. Pop: 313 110 (2001)

Catanzaro *n* a city in S Italy, in Calabria. Pop: 95 251 (2001)

catapult *n* **1** a Y-shaped device with a loop of elastic fastened to the ends of the prongs, used by children for firing stones **2** a device used to launch aircraft from a warship ▷ vb **3** to shoot forwards or upwards violently: *traffic catapulted forward with a roar* **4** to cause (someone) suddenly to be in a particular situation: *catapulted to stardom* [Greek *kata-* down + *pallein* to hurl]

cataract *n* **1** pathol **a** a condition in which the lens of the eye becomes partially or totally opaque **b** the opaque area **2** a large waterfall [Greek *katarassein* to dash down]

catarrh (kat-**tar**) *n* excessive mucus in the nose and throat, often experienced during or following a cold [Greek *katarrhein* to flow down] ❭ **catarrhal** *adj*

catastrophe (kat-**ass**-trof-fee) *n* a great and sudden disaster or misfortune [Greek *katastrephein* to overturn] ❭ **catastrophic** *adj*

catatonia *n* a form of schizophrenia in which the sufferer experiences stupor, with outbreaks of excitement [Greek *kata-* down + *tonos* tension] ❭ **catatonic** *adj*

cat burglar *n* a burglar who enters buildings by climbing through upper windows

catcall *n* a shrill whistle or cry of disapproval or derision

catch *vb* **catching, caught** **1** to seize and hold **2** to capture (a person or a fish or animal) **3** to surprise in an act: *two boys were caught stealing* **4** to reach (a bus, train, or plane) in time to board it **5** to see or hear: *you'll have to be quick if you want to catch her DJ-ing* **6** to be infected with (an illness) **7** to entangle or become entangled **8** to attract (someone's attention, imagination, or interest) **9** to comprehend or make out: *you have to work hard to catch his tone and meaning* **10** to reproduce (a quality) accurately in a work of art **11** (of a fire) to start burning **12** cricket to dismiss (a batsman) by catching a ball struck by him before it touches the ground **13** **catch at a** to attempt to grasp **b** to take advantage of (an opportunity) **14** **catch it** *informal* to be punished ▷ n **15** a device such as a hook, for fastening a door, window, or box **16** the total number of fish caught **17** *informal* a concealed or unforeseen drawback **18** an emotional break in the voice **19** *informal* a person considered worth having as a husband or wife **20** *cricket* the act of catching a ball struck by a batsman before it touches the ground, resulting in him being out ▶ See also **catch on, catch out, catch up** [Latin *capere* to seize]

catch-22 *n* a situation in which a person is frustrated by a set of circumstances that prevent any attempt to escape from them [from the title of a novel by J Heller]

catchcry *n, pl* **-cries** *Austral* a well-known, frequently used phrase, esp. one associated with a particular group

catching *adj* infectious

catchment *n* **1** a structure in which water is collected **2** all the people served by a school or hospital in a particular catchment area

catchment area *n* **1** the area of land draining into a river, basin, or reservoir **2** the area served by a particular school or hospital

catch on *vb informal* **1** to become popular or fashionable **2** to understand: *I was slow to catch on to what she was trying to tell me*

catch out vb informal, chiefly Brit to trap (someone) in an error or a lie

catchpenny adj Brit designed to have instant appeal without regard for quality

catch phrase n a well-known phrase or slogan associated with a particular entertainer or other celebrity

catch up vb 1 be caught up in to be unwillingly or accidentally involved in: hundreds of civilians have been caught up in the clashes 2 catch up on or with to bring (something) up to date: he had a lot of paperwork to catch up on 3 catch up with to reach or pass (someone or something): she ran to catch up with him

catchword n a well-known and frequently used phrase or slogan

catchy adj catchier, catchiest (of a tune) pleasant and easily remembered

catechism (kat-tik-kiz-zum) n instruction in the doctrine of a Christian Church by a series of questions and answers [Greek katēkhizein to catechize]

catechize or **-echise** vb **-echizing, -echized** or **-echising, -echised** 1 to instruct in Christianity using a catechism 2 to question (someone) thoroughly [Greek katēkhizein] ⟩ **catechist** n

categorical or **categoric** adj absolutely clear and certain: he was categorical in his denial ⟩ **categorically** adv

categorize or **-rise** vb **-rizing, -rized** or **-rising, -rised** to put in a category ⟩ **categorization** or **-risation** n

category n, pl **-ries** a class or group of things or people with some quality or qualities in common [Greek katēgoria assertion]

cater vb 1 to provide what is needed or wanted: operating theatres that can cater for open-heart surgery 2 to provide food or services: chef is pleased to cater for vegetarians and vegans [Anglo-Norman acater to buy]

caterer n a person whose job is to provide food for social events such as parties and weddings

catering n the supplying of food for a social event

caterpillar n 1 the wormlike larva of a butterfly or moth 2 trademark Also: **caterpillar track** an endless track, driven by cogged wheels, used to propel a heavy vehicle such as a bulldozer [probably from Old French catepelose hairy cat]

caterwaul vb 1 to make a yowling noise like a cat ⟩ n 2 such a noise [imitative]

Catesby n Robert. 1573–1605, English conspirator, leader of the Gunpowder Plot (1605): killed while resisting arrest

catfish n, pl **-fish** or **-fishes** a freshwater fish with whisker-like barbels around the mouth

catgut n a strong cord made from dried animals' intestines, used to string musical instruments and sports rackets

catharsis (kath-thar-siss) n 1 the relief of strong suppressed emotions, for example through drama or psychoanalysis 2 evacuation of the bowels, esp. with the use of a laxative [Greek kathairein to purge, purify]

cathartic adj 1 causing catharsis ⟩ n 2 a drug that causes catharsis

Cathay n a literary or archaic name for China [C14: from Medieval Latin Cataya of Turkic origin]

cathedral n the principal church of a diocese [Greek kathedra seat]

Cather n Willa (Sibert). 1873–1947, US novelist, whose works include O Pioneers! (1913) and My Ántonia (1918)

Catherine n Saint. died 307 AD, Italian early Christian martyr of Alexandria, who was tortured on a spiked wheel and beheaded

Catherine I n ?1684–1727, second wife of Peter the Great, whom she succeeded as empress of Russia (1725–27)

Catherine II n known as Catherine the Great. 1729–96, empress of Russia (1762–96), during whose reign Russia extended her boundaries at the expense of Turkey, Sweden, and Poland: she was a patron of literature and the arts

Catherine de' Medici or **Catherine de Médicis** n 1519–89, queen of Henry II of France; mother of Francis II, Charles IX, and Henry III of France; regent of France (1560–74). She was largely responsible for the massacre of Protestants on Saint Bartholomew's Day (1572)

Catherine of Aragon n 1485–1536, first wife of Henry VIII of England and mother of Mary I. The annulment of Henry's marriage to her (1533) against papal authority marked an initial stage in the English Reformation

Catherine of Braganza n 1638–1705, wife of Charles II of England, daughter of John IV of Portugal

Catherine of Siena n Saint. 1347–80, Italian mystic and ascetic; patron saint of the Dominican order. Feast day: April 29

Catherine wheel n a firework that rotates, producing sparks and coloured flame [after St CATHERINE of Alexandria]

catheter (kath-it-er) n a slender flexible tube inserted into a body cavity to drain fluid [Greek kathienai to insert]

cathode n electronics the negative electrode in an electrolytic cell or in an electronic valve or tube [Greek kathodos a descent]

cathode rays pl n a stream of electrons emitted from the surface of a cathode in a valve

cathode-ray tube n a valve in which a beam of electrons is focused onto a fluorescent screen to produce a visible image, used in television receivers and visual display units

catholic adj (of tastes or interests) covering a wide range [Greek katholikos universal]

Catholic Christianity adj 1 of the Roman Catholic Church ⊳ n 2 a member of the Roman Catholic Church ⟩ **Catholicism** n

Catiline n Latin name Lucius Sergius Catilina. ?108–62 BC, Roman politician: organized an unsuccessful conspiracy against Cicero (63–62) ⟩ **Catilinarian** adj

cation (kat-eye-on) n a positively charged ion [Greek kata- down + ienai to go]

catkin n a drooping flower spike found on trees such as the birch, hazel, and willow [obsolete Dutch katteken kitten]

catmint n a Eurasian plant with scented leaves that attract cats. Also: **catnip**

catnap n 1 a short sleep or doze ⊳ vb **-napping, -napped** 2 to sleep or doze for a short time or intermittently

Cato n 1 Marcus Porcius, known as Cato the Elder or the Censor. 234–149 BC, Roman statesman and writer, noted for his relentless opposition to Carthage 2 his great-grandson, Marcus Porcius, known as Cato the Younger or Uticensis. 95–46 BC, Roman statesman, general, and Stoic philosopher; opponent of Catiline and Caesar

cat-o'-nine-tails n, pl **-tails** a rope whip with nine knotted thongs, formerly used to inflict floggings as a punishment

cat's cradle n a game played by making patterns with a loop of string between the fingers

catseyes pl n trademark Brit, Austral and NZ glass reflectors set into the road at intervals to indicate traffic lanes by reflecting light from vehicles' headlights

Catskill Mountains pl n a mountain range in SE New York State: resort. Highest peak: Slide Mountain, 1261 m (4204 ft). Also called: **Catskills**

cat's paw n a person used by someone else to do unpleasant things for him or her [from the tale of a monkey who used a cat's paw to draw chestnuts out of a fire]

Cattegat n a former spelling of **Kattegat**

Catterick n a village in N England, in North Yorkshire on the River Swale: site of an important army garrison and a racecourse

cattle pl n domesticated cows and bulls. Related adjective: **bovine** [Old French chatel chattel]

cattle-cake n concentrated food for cattle in the form of cakelike blocks

cattle-grid or NZ **cattle-stop** n a grid covering a hole dug in a road to prevent livestock crossing while allowing vehicles to pass unhindered

Catton n Eleanor. born 1985, Canadian-born New Zealand writer; her books include The Rehearsal (2008) and the Booker-prizewinning The Luminaries (2013)

catty adj **-tier, -tiest** informal spiteful: her remarks were amusing and only slightly catty > **cattiness** n

Catullus n Gaius Valerius. ?84–?54 BC, Roman lyric poet, noted particularly for his love poems > **Catullan** adj

catwalk n 1 a narrow pathway over the stage of a theatre or along a bridge 2 a narrow platform where models display clothes in a fashion show

Cauca n a river in W Colombia, rising in the northwest and flowing north to the Magdalena River. Length: about 1350 km (840 miles)

Caucasia n a region in SW Russia, Georgia, Armenia, and Azerbaijan, between the Caspian Sea and the Black Sea: contains the Caucasus Mountains, dividing it into Ciscaucasia in the north and Transcaucasia in the south; one of the most complex ethnic areas in the world, with over 50 different peoples. Also called: the Caucasus

Caucasian or **Caucasoid** adj 1 of the predominantly light-skinned racial group of humankind > n 2 a member of this group

Caucasus n the Caucasus 1 Also called: Caucasus Mountains a mountain range in SW Russia, running along the N borders of Georgia and Azerbaijan, between the Black Sea and the Caspian Sea: mostly over 2700 m (9000 ft). Highest peak: Mount Elbrus, 5642 m (18 510 ft) 2 another name for Caucasia

Cauchy n Augustin Louis, Baron Cauchy. 1789–1857, French mathematician, noted for his work on the theory of functions and the wave theory of light

caucus n, pl **-cuses** 1 a local committee or faction of a political party 2 a political meeting to decide future plans 3 NZ a formal meeting of all MPs of one party [probably of Native American origin]

caudal adj zoology at or near the tail or back part of an animal's body [Latin cauda tail]

Caudine Forks pl n a narrow pass in the Apennines, in S Italy, between Capua and Benevento: scene of the defeat of the Romans by the Samnites (321 BC)

caught vb the past of **catch**

caul n anatomy a membrane sometimes covering a child's head at birth [Old French calotte close-fitting cap]

cauldron or **caldron** n a large pot used for boiling [Latin caldarium hot bath]

Caulfield n Patrick (Joseph). 1936–2005, British painter and printmaker

cauliflower n a vegetable with a large head of white flower buds surrounded by green leaves [Italian caoli fiori cabbage flowers]

cauliflower ear n permanent swelling and distortion of the ear, caused by repeated blows usually received in boxing

caulk vb to fill in (cracks) with paste or some other material [Latin calcare to trample]

causal adj of or being a cause: a causal connection > **causally** adv

causation or **causality** n 1 the production of an effect by a cause 2 the relationship of cause and effect

causative adj producing an effect: bright lights seem to be a causative factor in some migraines

cause n 1 something that produces a particular effect 2 grounds for action; justification: there is cause for concern 3 an aim or principle which an individual or group is interested in and supports: the Socialist cause > vb **causing, caused** 4 to be the cause of [Latin causa] > **causeless** adj

cause célèbre (kawz sill-**leb**-ra) n, pl **causes célèbres** (kawz sill-**leb**-ra) a controversial legal case, issue, or person [French]

causeway n a raised path or road across water or marshland [Middle English cauciwey paved way]

caustic adj 1 capable of burning or corroding by chemical action: caustic soda 2 bitter and sarcastic: caustic critics > n 3 chem a caustic substance [Greek kaiein to burn] > **caustically** adv

caustic soda n same as **sodium hydroxide**

cauterize or **-ise** vb **-izing, -ized** or **-ising, -ised** to burn (a wound) with heat or a caustic agent to prevent infection [Greek kaiein to burn] > **cauterization** or **-isation** n

caution n 1 care or prudence, esp. in the face of danger 2 warning: a word of caution 3 law, chiefly Brit a formal warning given to a person suspected of an offence > vb 4 to warn or advise: he cautioned against an abrupt turnaround [Latin cautio] > **cautionary** adj

cautious adj showing or having caution > **cautiously** adv

Cauvery or **Kaveri** n a river in S India, rising in the Western Ghats and flowing southeast to the Bay of Bengal. Length: 765 km (475 miles)

Cavaco Silva n Aníbal. born 1939, Portuguese statesman; prime minister (1985–95); president from 2006

Cavafy n Constantine. Greek name Kavafis. 1863–1933, Greek poet of Alexandria in Egypt

cavalcade n a procession of people on horseback or in cars [Italian cavalcare to ride on horseback]

Cavalcanti n Guido. ?1255–1300, Italian poet, noted for his love poems

cavalier adj 1 showing haughty disregard; offhand > n 2 old-fashioned a gallant or courtly gentleman [Late Latin caballarius rider]

Cavalier n a supporter of Charles I during the English Civil War

Cavallini n Pietro. ?1250–?1330, Italian fresco painter and mosaicist. His works include the mosaics of the Life of the Virgin in Santa Maria, Trastevere, Rome

cavalry n the part of an army originally mounted on horseback, but now often using fast armoured vehicles [Italian cavaliere horseman] > **cavalryman** n

Cavan n 1 a county of N Republic of Ireland: hilly, with many small lakes and bogs. County town: Cavan. Pop: 56 546 (2002). Area: 1890 sq km (730 sq miles) 2 a market town in N Republic of Ireland, county town of Co Cavan. Pop: 6098 (2002)

cave n a hollow in the side of a hill or cliff, or underground [Latin cavus hollow]

caveat (kav-vee-at) n 1 law a formal notice requesting the court not to take a certain action without warning the person lodging the caveat 2 a caution [Latin: let him beware]

cave in vb 1 to collapse inwards 2 informal to yield completely under pressure: the government caved in to the revolutionaries' demands > n **cave-in** 3 the sudden collapse of a roof or piece of ground

Cavell n Edith Louisa. 1865–1915, English nurse: executed by the Germans in World War I for helping Allied prisoners to escape

caveman n, pl **-men** 1 a prehistoric cave dweller 2 informal a man who is primitive or brutal in behaviour

Cavendish n Henry. 1731–1810, British physicist and chemist: recognized hydrogen, determined the composition of water, and calculated the density of the earth by an experiment named after him

cavern n a large cave [Latin cavus hollow]

cavernous adj like a cavern in vastness, depth, or hollowness: the cavernous building

caviar or **caviare** n the salted roe of the sturgeon, regarded as a delicacy and usually served as an appetizer [Turkish havyār]

cavil vb **-illing, -illed** or US **-iling, -iled** 1 to raise annoying petty objections > n 2 a petty objection [Latin cavillari to jeer]

caving n the sport of climbing in and exploring caves > **caver** n

Cavite n a port in the N Philippines, in S Luzon on Manila Bay: a former US naval base. Pop: 109 000 (2005 est)

cavity n, pl **-ties** 1 a hollow space 2 dentistry a decayed area on a tooth [Latin cavus hollow]

cavort vb to skip about; caper

Cavour n Conte Camillo Benso di. 1810–61, Italian statesman and premier of Piedmont-Sardinia (1852–59; 1860–61): a leader of the movement for the unification of Italy

caw n 1 the cry of a crow, rook, or raven ▷ vb 2 to make this cry [imitative]

Cawdrey n Robert. 16th–17th-century English schoolmaster and lexicographer: compiled the first English dictionary (A Table Alphabeticall) in 1604

Cawley n Evonne (née Goolagong). born 1951, Australian tennis player: winner of seven Grand Slam singles titles including Wimbledon (1971,1980) and the Australian Open (1974–76, 1977 (December))

Cawnpore or **Cawnpur** n the former name of Kanpur

Caxton n William. ?1422–91, English printer and translator: published, in Bruges, the first book printed in English (1475) and established the first printing press in England (1477)

cay n a small low island or bank of sand and coral fragments [Spanish cayo]

Cayenne n the capital of French Guiana, on an island at the mouth of the Cayenne River: French penal settlement from 1854 to 1938. Pop: 57 229 (2011)

cayenne pepper or **cayenne** n a very hot red spice made from the dried seeds of capsicums [S American Indian quiynha]

Cayes n short for Les Cayes

Cayley n 1 Arthur. 1821–93, British mathematician, who invented matrices 2 Sir George. 1773–1857, British engineer and pioneer of aerial navigation. He constructed the first man-carrying glider (1853) and invented the caterpillar tractor

cayman or **caiman** n, pl **-mans** a tropical American reptile similar to an alligator [Carib]

Cayman Islands pl n three coral islands in the Caribbean Sea northwest of Jamaica: a dependency of Jamaica until 1962, now a UK Overseas Territory. Capital: George Town. Pop: 53 737 (2013 est). Area: about 260 sq km (100 sq miles)

caz adj slang short for casual

CB 1 Citizens' Band 2 Commander of the Order of the Bath

CBC Canadian Broadcasting Corporation

CBE Commander of the Order of the British Empire (a Brit. title)

CBI Confederation of British Industry

cc or **c.c.** 1 carbon copy 2 (in South Africa) closed corporation 3 cubic centimetre

CC 1 County Council 2 Cricket Club

CCS cascading style sheet

CCTV closed-circuit television

cd candela

Cd chem cadmium

CD compact disc

CDI compact disc interactive: a system for storing a mix of software, data, audio, and compressed video for interactive use under processor control

C.diff or **C.difficile** Clostridium difficile

Cdn. Canadian

CD player n a device for playing compact discs

Cdr Commander

CD-R compact disk recordable

CD-ROM compact disc read-only memory: a compact disc used with a computer system as a read-only optical disc

CD-RW compact disk read-write

CDT Central Daylight Time

CD-video n a compact-disc player that, when connected to a television and a hi-fi, produces high-quality stereo sound and synchronized pictures from a compact disc

Ce chem cerium

CE 1 chief engineer 2 Church of England 3 civil engineer 4 Common Entrance 5 Common Era 6 Communauté Européenne (European Union)

Ceará n 1 a state of NE Brazil: sandy coastal plain, rising to a high plateau. Capital: Fortaleza. Pop: 7 654 535 (2002). Area: 150 630 sq km (58 746 sq miles) 2 another name for Fortaleza

cease vb ceasing, ceased 1 to bring or come to an end ▷ n 2 without cease without stopping [Latin cessare]

ceasefire n a temporary period of truce

ceaseless adj without stopping › **ceaselessly** adv

Ceauşescu n Nicolae. 1918–89, Romanian statesman; chairman of the state council (1967–89) and president of Romania (1974–89): deposed and executed

Cebu n 1 an island in the central Philippines. Pop: 2 091 602 (latest est). Area: 4422 sq km (1707 sq miles) 2 a port in the Philippines, on E Cebu island. Pop: 796 000 (2005 est)

Čechy n the Czech name for Bohemia

Cecil n 1 Lord David. 1902–86, English literary critic and biographer 2 Robert. See (3rd Marquess of) Salisbury 3 William. See (William Cecil) Burghley

Cecilia n Saint. died ?230 AD, Roman martyr; patron saint of music. Feast day: Nov 22

cedar n 1 a coniferous tree with needle-like evergreen leaves and barrel-shaped cones 2 the sweet-smelling wood of this tree [Greek kedros]

Cedar Rapids n a city in the US, in E Iowa. Pop: 122 542 (2003 est)

cede vb ceding, ceded to transfer or surrender (territory or legal rights) [Latin cedere to yield]

cedilla n a character (¸) placed underneath a c, esp. in French or Portuguese, indicating that it is to be pronounced (s), not (k) [Spanish: little z]

ceilidh (kay-lee) n an informal social gathering in Scotland or Ireland with folk music and country dancing [Gaelic]

ceiling n 1 the inner upper surface of a room 2 an upper limit set on something such as a payment or salary 3 the upper altitude to which an aircraft can climb [origin unknown]

Cela n Camilo José. 1916–2002, Spanish novelist and essayist. His works include The Family of Pascual Duarte (1942), La Colmena (1951), and La Cruz de San Andrés (1994). Nobel prize for literature 1989

Celan n Paul, real name Paul Antschel. 1920–70, Romanian Jewish poet, writing in German, whose work reflects the experience of Nazi persecution

celandine n a wild plant with yellow flowers [Greek khelidōn swallow; the plant's season was believed to parallel the migration of swallows]

Celaya n a city in central Mexico, in Guanajuato state: market town, famous for its sweetmeats; textile-manufacturing. Pop: 727 000 (2005 est)

Celebes n the English name for Sulawesi

Celebes Sea n the part of the Pacific Ocean between Sulawesi, Borneo, and Mindanao

celebrant n a person who performs or takes part in a religious ceremony

celebrate vb **-brating, -brated** 1 to hold festivities: let's celebrate! 2 to hold festivities to mark (a happy event, birthday, or anniversary) 3 to perform (a solemn or religious ceremony) 4 to praise publicly: the novel is justly celebrated as a masterpiece [Latin celeber numerous, renowned] › **celebration** n › **celebratory** adj

celebrated adj well known: the celebrated musician

celebrity n, pl **-ties** 1 a famous person 2 the state of being famous

celeriac (sill-ler-ree-ak) n a variety of celery with a large turnip-like root

celerity (sill-ler-rit-tee) n formal swiftness [Latin celeritas]

celery n a vegetable with long green crisp edible stalks [Greek selinon parsley]

celesta *n* an instrument like a small piano in which key-operated hammers strike metal plates [French *céleste* heavenly]

celestial *adj* **1** heavenly or divine: *celestial music* **2** of or relating to the sky or space: *celestial objects such as pulsars and quasars* [Latin *caelum* heaven]

celestial equator *n* an imaginary circle lying on the celestial sphere in a plane perpendicular to the earth's axis

celestial sphere *n* an imaginary sphere of infinitely large radius enclosing the universe

celibate *adj* **1** unmarried or abstaining from sex, esp. because of a religious vow of chastity ▷ *n* **2** a celibate person [Latin *caelebs* unmarried] > **celibacy** *n*

Céline *n* Louis-Ferdinand, real name *Louis-Ferdinand Destouches*. 1894–1961, French novelist and physician; became famous with his controversial first novel *Journey to the End of the Night* (1932)

cell *n* **1** *biology* the smallest unit of an organism that is able to function independently **2** a small simple room in a prison, convent, or monastery **3** any small compartment, such as a cell of a honeycomb **4** a small group operating as the core of a larger organization: *Communist cells* **5** a device that produces electrical energy by chemical action **6** US and Canad a cellular telephone [Latin *cella* room, storeroom]

cellar *n* **1** an underground room, usually used for storage **2** a place where wine is stored **3** a stock of bottled wines [Latin *cellarium* food store]

cellarage *n* **1** the area of a cellar **2** a charge for storing goods in a cellar

Celle *n* a city in N Germany, on the Aller River in Lower Saxony: from 1378 to 1705 the residence of the Dukes of Brunswick-Lüneburg. Pop: 71 319 (2003 est)

Cellini *n* Benvenuto. 1500–71, Italian sculptor, goldsmith, and engraver, noted also for his autobiography

cello (**chell-oh**) *n, pl* **-los** a large low-pitched musical instrument of the violin family, held between the knees and played with a bow [short for *violoncello*] > **cellist** *n*

Cellophane *n trademark* a thin transparent material made from cellulose that is used as a protective wrapping, esp. for food [*cellulose* + Greek *phainein* to shine, appear]

cellular *adj* **1** of, consisting of, or resembling a cell or cells: *cellular changes* **2** woven with an open texture: *cellular blankets* **3** designed for or using cellular radio: *cellular phones*

cellular radio *n* radio communication, used esp. in car phones, based on a network of transmitters each serving a small area known as a cell

cellulite *n* fat deposits under the skin alleged to resist dieting

celluloid *n* **1** a kind of plastic made from cellulose nitrate and camphor, used to make toys and, formerly, photographic film **2** the cinema or films generally: *a Shakespeare play committed to celluloid*

cellulose *n* the main constituent of plant cell walls, used in making paper, rayon, and plastics

cellulose acetate *n* a nonflammable material used to make film, lacquers, and artificial fibres

cellulose nitrate *n* a compound used in plastics, lacquers, and explosives

Celsius *adj* denoting a measurement on the Celsius scale [after Anders *Celsius*, astronomer who invented it]

Celsius scale *n* a scale of temperature in which 0° represents the melting point of ice and 100° represents the boiling point of water

Celt (**kelt**) *n* **1** a person from Scotland, Ireland, Wales, Cornwall, or Brittany **2** a member of a people who inhabited Britain, Gaul, and Spain in pre-Roman times [Latin *Celtae* the Celts]

Celtic (**kel-tik, sel-tik**) *n* **1** a group of languages that includes Gaelic, Welsh, and Breton ▷ *adj* **2** of the Celts or the Celtic languages

Celtic Sea *n* the relatively shallow part of the Atlantic Ocean lying between S Ireland, SW Wales, Cornwall, and W Brittany

cement *n* **1 a** a fine grey powder made of limestone and clay, mixed with water and sand to make mortar or concrete **b** mortar or concrete **2** something that unites, binds, or joins things or people: *bone cement; the cement of fear and hatred of the Left* **3** *dentistry* a material used for filling teeth ▷ *vb* **4** to join, bind, or cover with cement **5** to make (a relationship) stronger: *this would cement a firm alliance between the army and rebels* [Latin *caementum* stone from the quarry]

cemetery *n, pl* **-teries** a place where dead people are buried: *a military cemetery* [Greek *koimētērion* room for sleeping]

Cenis *n* Mont Cenis a pass over the Graian Alps in SE France, between Lanslebourg (France) and Susa (Italy): nearby tunnel, opened in 1871. Highest point: 2082 m (6831 ft). Italian name: **Monte Cenisio**

cenotaph *n* a monument honouring soldiers who died in a war [Greek *kenos* empty + *taphos* tomb]

Cenotaph *n* the Cenotaph the monument in Whitehall, London, honouring the dead of both World Wars: designed by Sir Edwin Lutyens: erected in 1920

Cenozoic or **Caenozoic** (see-no-zoh-ik) *adj geology* of the most recent geological era, beginning 65 million years ago, characterized by the development and increase of the mammals [Greek *kainos* recent + *zōion* animal]

censer *n* a container for burning incense

censor *n* **1** a person authorized to examine films, letters, or publications, in order to ban or cut anything considered obscene or objectionable ▷ *vb* **2** to ban or cut portions of (a film, letter, or publication) [Latin *censere* to consider]

censorious *adj* harshly critical

censorship *n* the practice or policy of censoring films, letters, or publications

censure *n* **1** severe disapproval ▷ *vb* **-suring, -sured** **2** to criticize (someone or something) severely [Latin *censere* to assess]

census *n, pl* **-suses** an official periodic count of a population including such information as sex, age, and occupation [Latin *censere* to assess]

cent *n* a monetary unit worth one hundredth of the main unit of currency in many countries [Latin *centum* hundred]

cent. **1** central **2** century

centaur *n Greek myth* a creature with the head, arms, and torso of a man, and the lower body and legs of a horse [Greek *kentauros*]

centavo *n, pl* **-vos** a monetary unit worth one hundredth of the main unit of currency in Portugal and many Latin American countries [Spanish: one hundredth part]

centenarian *n* a person who is at least 100 years old

centenary (sen-teen-a-ree) *n, pl* **-naries** *chiefly Brit* a 100th anniversary or the celebration of one. US equivalent: **centennial** [Latin *centum* hundred]

center *n, vb* US same as **centre**

centesimal *n* **1** one hundredth ▷ *adj* **2** of or divided into hundredths [Latin *centum* hundred]

centi- *prefix* **1** denoting one hundredth: *centimetre* **2** a hundred: *centipede* [Latin *centum* hundred]

centigrade *adj* same as **Celsius**

> **USAGE** Although still used in meteorology, *centigrade*, when indicating the Celsius scale of temperature, is now usually avoided in other scientific contexts because of its possible confusion with the hundredth part of a grade.

centigram or **centigramme** *n* one hundredth of a gram
centilitre or US **centiliter** *n* a measure of volume equivalent to one hundredth of a litre

centime (son-teem) *n* a monetary unit worth one hundredth of the main unit of currency in a number of countries [Latin *centum* hundred]

centimetre *or US* **centimeter** *n* a unit of length equal to one hundredth of a metre

centipede *n* a small wormlike creature with many legs

central *adj* **1** of, at, or forming the centre of something: *eastern and central parts of the country* **2** main or principal: *a central issue* ⟩ **centrally** *adv* ⟩ **centrality** *n*

Central African Republic *n* a landlocked country of central Africa: joined with Chad as a territory of French Equatorial Africa in 1910; became an independent republic in 1960; a parliamentary monarchy (1976–79); consists of a huge plateau, mostly savanna, with dense forests in the south; drained chiefly by the Shari and Ubangi Rivers. Official language: French; Sango is the national language. Religion: Christian and animist. Currency: franc. Capital: Bangui. Pop: 5 166 510 (2013 est.). Area: 622 577 sq km (240 376 sq miles). Former names: (until 1958) **Ubangi-Shari**, (1976–79) **Central African Empire**. French name: **République Centrafricaine**

Central America *n* an isthmus joining the continents of North and South America, extending from the S border of Mexico to the NW border of Colombia and consisting of Belize, Guatemala, Honduras, El Salvador, Nicaragua, Costa Rica, and Panama. Area: about 518 000 sq km (200 000 sq miles)

Central American *adj* **1** of or relating to Central America or its inhabitants ⟩ *n* **2** a native or inhabitant of Central America

central bank *n* a national bank that acts as the government's banker, controls credit, and issues currency

Central Bedfordshire *n* a unitary authority of S central England. Pop: 252 100 (2007 est.). Area: 712 sq km (275 sq miles)

Central European Time *n* the standard time adopted by Western European countries one hour ahead of Greenwich Mean Time, corresponding to British Summer Time. Abbreviation: **CET**

central government *n* the government of a whole country, as opposed to the smaller organizations that govern counties, towns, and districts

central heating *n* a system for heating a building by means of radiators or air vents connected to a central source of heat ⟩ **centrally heated** *adj*

centralism *n* the principle of bringing a country or an organization under central control ⟩ **centralist** *adj*

centralize *or* **-ise** *vb* **-izing, -ized** *or* **-ising, -ised** to bring (a country or an organization) under central control ⟩ **centralization** *or* **-isation** *n*

Central Karoo *or* **Central Karroo** *n* an arid plateau of S central South Africa, in Cape Province, separated from the Little Karoo to the southwest by the Swartberg range. Average height: 750 m (2500 ft)

central locking *n* a system by which all the doors of a motor vehicle are locked automatically when the driver's door is locked manually

central nervous system *n* the part of the nervous system of vertebrates that consists of the brain and spinal cord

central processing unit *n* the part of a computer that performs logical and arithmetical operations on the data

Central Provinces *pl n* the Central Provinces the Canadian provinces of Ontario and Quebec

Central Provinces and Berar *n* a former province of central India: renamed Madhya Pradesh in 1950, Berar being transferred to Maharashtra in 1956

Central Region *n* a former local government region in central Scotland, formed in 1975 from Clackmannanshire, most of Stirlingshire, and parts of Perthshire, West Lothian, Fife, and Kinross-shire; in 1996 it was replaced by the council areas of Stirling, Clackmannanshire, and Falkirk

central reservation *n Brit and NZ* the strip that separates the two sides of a motorway or dual carriageway

centre *or US* **center** *n* **1** the middle point or part of something **2** a place where a specified activity takes place: *a shopping centre* **3** a person or thing that is a focus of interest: *the centre of a long-running dispute* **4** a place of activity or influence: *the parliament building was the centre of resistance* **5** a political party or group that favours moderation **6** *sport* a player who plays in the middle of the field rather than on a wing ▷ *vb* **-tring, -tred** *or US* **-tering, -tered 7** to put in the centre of something **8 centre on** to have as a centre or main theme: *the summit is expected to centre on expanding the role of the UN* [Greek *kentron* needle, sharp point]

Centre *n* **1 the Centre** the sparsely inhabited central region of Australia **2** a region of central France: generally low-lying; drained chiefly by the Rivers Loire, Loir, and Cher

centreboard *or US* **centerboard** *n* a supplementary keel for a sailing boat or dinghy

centrefold *or US* **centerfold** *n* a large coloured illustration, often a photograph of a naked or scantily dressed young woman, folded to form the centre pages of a magazine

centre forward *n sport* the middle player in the forward line of a team

centre half *or* **centre back** *n soccer* a defender who plays in the middle of the defence

centre of gravity *n* the point in an object around which its mass is evenly distributed

centre pass *n hockey* a push or hit made in any direction to start the game

centrepiece *or US* **centerpiece** *n* **1** the most important item of a group of things: *she was the centrepiece of this conference* **2** an ornament for the centre of a table

centrifugal (sent-riff-few-gl) *adj* **1** moving or tending to move away from a centre **2** of or operated by centrifugal force: *centrifugal extractors* [Greek *kentron* centre + Latin *fugere* to flee]

centrifugal force *n* a force that acts outwards on any body that rotates or moves along a curved path

centrifuge *n* a machine that separates substances by the action of centrifugal force

centripetal (sent-rip-it-al) *adj* moving or tending to move towards a centre [Greek *kentron* centre + Latin *petere* to seek]

centripetal force *n* a force that acts inwards on any body that rotates or moves along a curved path

centrist *n* a person who holds moderate political views

centurion *n* (in ancient Rome) the officer in command of a century [Latin *centurio*]

century *n, pl* **-ries 1** a period of 100 years **2** a score of 100 runs in cricket **3** (in ancient Rome) a unit of foot soldiers, originally consisting of 100 men [Latin *centuria*]

CEO chief executive officer

Cephalonia *or* **Kefallonia** *n* a mountainous island in the Ionian Sea, the largest of the Ionian Islands, off the W coast of Greece. Pop: 36 404 (2001). Area: 935 sq km (365 sq miles). Modern Greek name: **Kephallinía**

cephalopod (seff-a-loh-pod) *n* a sea mollusc with a head and tentacles, such as the octopus [Greek *kephalē* head + *pous* foot]

Ceram *n* a variant spelling of **Seram**

ceramic *n* **1** a hard brittle material made by heating clay to a very high temperature **2** an object made of this material ▷ *adj* **3** made of ceramic: *ceramic tiles* [Greek *keramos* potter's clay]

ceramics *n* the art of producing ceramic objects ⟩ **ceramicist** *or* **ceramist** *n*

Cerberus (sir-ber-uss) *n Greek myth* a three-headed dog who guarded the entrance to Hades

cere *n* a soft waxy swelling, containing the nostrils, at the base of the upper beak of a parrot [Latin *cera* wax]

cereal *n* **1** any grass that produces an edible grain, such as oat, wheat, or rice **2** the grain produced by such a plant **3** a breakfast food made from this grain, usually eaten mixed with milk [Latin *cerealis* concerning agriculture]

cerebellum (serr-rib-**bell**-lum) *n, pl* -**lums** *or* -**la** (-la) the back part of the brain, which controls balance and muscular coordination [Latin]

cerebral (serr-rib-ral) *adj* **1** of the brain: *a cerebral haemorrhage* **2** involving intelligence rather than emotions or instinct: *the cerebral joys of the literary world*

cerebral palsy *n* a condition in which the limbs and muscles are permanently weak, caused by damage to the brain

cerebrate (serr-rib-rate) *vb* -**brating, -brated** *usually facetious* to use the mind; think ▷ **cerebration** *n*

cerebrospinal *adj* of the brain and spinal cord: *a sample of cerebrospinal fluid*

cerebrovascular (serr-rib-roh-**vass**-kew-lar) *adj* of the blood vessels and blood supply of the brain

cerebrum (serr-rib-rum) *n, pl* -**brums** *or* -**bra** (-bra) the main part of the human brain, associated with thought, emotion, and personality [Latin: the brain]

Ceredigion *n* a county of W Wales, on Cardigan Bay: created in 1996 from part of Dyfed; corresponds to the former Cardiganshire (abolished 1974): mainly agricultural, with the Cambrian Mountains in the E and N. Administrative centre: Aberaeron. Pop: 77 200 (2003 est). Area: 1793 sq km (692 sq miles)

ceremonial *adj* **1** of ceremony or ritual ▷ *n* **2** a system of formal rites; ritual ▷ **ceremonially** *adv*

ceremonious *adj* excessively polite or formal ▷ **ceremoniously** *adv*

ceremony *n, pl* -**nies** **1** a formal act or ritual performed for a special occasion: *a wedding ceremony* **2** formally polite behaviour **3** **stand on ceremony** to insist on or act with excessive formality [Latin *caerimonia* what is sacred]

Ceres *n* the Roman goddess of agriculture

cerise (ser-reess) *adj* cherry-red [French: cherry]

cerium *n chem* a steel-grey metallic element found only in combination with other elements. Symbol: **Ce** [from *Ceres* (an asteroid)]

CERN Conseil Européen pour la Recherche Nucléaire: a European organization for research in high-energy particle physics

Cernăuţi *n* the Romanian name for Chernovtsy

Cernuda *n* Luis. 1902–63, Spanish poet. His major work is the autobiographical *Reality and Desire* (1936–64)

Cerro de Pasco *n* a town in central Peru, in the Andes: one of the highest towns in the world, 4400 m (14 436 ft) above sea level; mining centre. Pop: 70 000 (latest est)

Cerro Gordo *n* a mountain pass in E Mexico, between Veracruz and Jalapa: site of a battle in the Mexican War (1847) in which American forces under General Scott decisively defeated the Mexicans

cert *n* **a dead cert** *informal* something that is certain to happen or to be successful

cert. certificate

certain *adj* **1** positive and confident about something: *he was certain they would agree* **2** definitely known: *it is by no means certain the tomb still exists* **3** sure or bound: *the cuts are certain to go ahead* **4** some but not much: *a certain amount* **5** particular: *certain aspects* **6** named but not known: *a running commentary by a certain Mr Fox* **7 for certain** without doubt [Latin *certus* sure]

certainly *adv* without doubt: *he will certainly be back*

certainty *n* **1** the condition of being certain **2** (*pl* -**ties**) something established as inevitable

certifiable *adj* considered to be legally insane

certificate *n* an official document stating the details of something such as birth, death, or completion of an academic course [Old French *certifier* to certify]

certified *adj* **1** holding or guaranteed by a certificate: *a*

certified acupuncturist **2** declared legally insane

certify *vb* -**fies, -fying, -fied** **1** to confirm or attest to **2** to guarantee (that certain required standards have been met) **3** to declare legally insane [Latin *certus* certain + *facere* to make] ▷ **certification** *n*

certitude *n formal* confidence or certainty

Cervantes *n* Miguel de, full surname *Cervantes Saavedra*. 1547–1616, Spanish dramatist, poet, and prose writer, most famous for *Don Quixote* (1605), which satirizes the chivalric romances and greatly influenced the development of the novel

cervical smear *n med* a smear taken from the neck (cervix) of the womb for detection of cancer

Cervin *n* Mont Cervin the French name for **Matterhorn**

cervix *n, pl* **cervixes** *or* **cervices** **1** the lower part of the womb that extends into the vagina **2** *anatomy* the neck [Latin] ▷ **cervical** *adj*

Cesena *n* a city in N Italy, in Emilia-Romagna. Pop: 90 948 (2001)

cesium *n US* same as **caesium**

České Budějovice *n* a city in the S Czech Republic, on the Vltava (Moldau) River. Pop: 94 747 (2007 est). German name: **Budweis**

Československo *n* the Czech name for **Czechoslovakia**

cessation *n* an ending or pause: *a cessation of hostilities* [Latin *cessare* to be idle]

cession *n* the act of ceding territory or legal rights [Latin *cedere* to yield]

cesspool *or* **cesspit** *n* a covered tank or pit for collecting and storing sewage or waste water [Old French *souspirail* air vent]

CET Central European Time

cetacean (sit-**tay**-shun) *n* a sea creature such as a whale or dolphin, which belongs to a family of fish-shaped mammals and breathes through a blowhole [Greek *kētos* whale]

cetane (**see**-tane) *n* a colourless liquid hydrocarbon, used as a solvent [Latin *cetus* whale]

cetane number *n* a measure of the quality of a diesel fuel expressed as the percentage of cetane in it

Cetatea Albă *n* the Romanian name for Belgorod-Dnestrovski

Cetinje *n* a town in Montenegro, in the SW: former capital of Montenegro (until 1945); palace and fortified monastery, residences of Montenegrin prince-bishops. Pop: 15 137 (2003 est)

Cetshwayo *or* **Cetewayo** *n* ?1826–84, king of the Zulus (1873–79): defeated the British at Isandhlwana (1879) but was overwhelmed by them at Ulundi (1879); captured, he stated his case in London, and was reinstated as ruler of part of Zululand (1883)

Ceuta *n* an enclave in Morocco on the Strait of Gibraltar, consisting of a port and military station: held by Spain since 1580. Pop: 74 931 (2003 est)

Cévennes *n* a mountain range in S central France, on the SE edge of the Massif Central. Highest peak: 1754 m (5755 ft)

Ceylon *n* **1** the former name (until 1972) of **Sri Lanka** **2** an island in the Indian Ocean, off the SE coast of India: consists politically of the republic of Sri Lanka. Area: 64 644 sq km (24 959 sq miles)

Ceylonese *adj* of or relating to Ceylon or its inhabitants

Cézanne *n* Paul. 1839–1906, French postimpressionist painter, who was a major influence on modern art, esp. cubism, in stressing the structural elements latent in nature, such as the sphere and the cone

cf compare [Latin *confer*]

Cf *chem* californium

CF Canadian Forces

CFB Canadian Forces Base

CFC chlorofluorocarbon

CFL Canadian Football League

CFS chronic fatigue syndrome

cg centigram

C

CGI computer-generated image(s)

cgs units _pl n_ a metric system of units based on the centimetre, gram, and second: for scientific and technical purposes, replaced by SI units

CH Companion of Honour (a Brit. title)

ch. 1 chapter **2** church

Chablis (shab-lee) _n_ a dry white wine made around Chablis, France

Chabrier _n_ (Alexis) Emmanuel. 1841–94, French composer; noted esp. for the orchestral rhapsody _España_ (1883)

Chabrol _n_ Claude. 1930–2010, French film director, whose films, such as _Le Beau Serge_ (1958), _Les Biches_ (1968), _Le Boucher_ (1969), _Au coeur du mensonge_ (1999), and _La Fleur du mal_ (2003) explore themes of jealousy, guilt, and murder

cha-cha _or_ **cha-cha-cha** _n_ **1** a modern ballroom dance from Latin America **2** music for this dance [American (Cuban) Spanish]

Chaco _n_ See Gran Chaco

chaconne _n_ a musical form consisting of a set of variations on a repeated melodic bass line

chad _n_ the small pieces removed during the punching of holes in punch cards, printer paper, etc.

Chad _n_ **1** a republic in N central Africa: made a territory of French Equatorial Africa in 1910; became independent in 1960; contains much desert and the Tibesti Mountains, with Lake Chad in the west; produces chiefly cotton and livestock; suffered intermittent civil war from 1963 and prolonged drought. Official languages: Arabic; French. Religion: Muslim majority, also Christian and animist. Currency: franc. Capital: Ndjamena. Pop: 11 193 452 (2013 est). Area: 1 284 000 sq km (495 750 sq miles). French name: **Tchad 2** Lake Chad a lake in N central Africa: fed chiefly by the Shari River, it has no apparent outlet. Area: at fullest extent 10 000 to 26 000 sq km (4000 to 10 000 sq miles), varying seasonally; it has shrunk considerably in recent years

Chadderton _n_ a town in NW England, in Oldham unitary authority, in Greater Manchester. Pop: 33 001 (2001)

Chadwick _n_ **1** Sir Edwin. 1800–90, British social reformer, known for his _Report on the Sanitary Condition of the Labouring Population of Great Britain_ (1842) **2** Sir James. 1891–1974, British physicist: discovered the neutron (1932): Nobel prize for physics 1935 **3** Lynn (Russell). 1914–2003, British sculptor in metal

Chaeronea _n_ an ancient Greek town in W Boeotia: site of the victory of Philip of Macedon over the Athenians and Thebans (338 BC) and of Sulla over Mithridates (86 BC)

chafe _vb_ **chafing, chafed 1** to make sore or worn by rubbing **2** to be annoyed or impatient: _the lower castes are chafing against 20 years of servitude_ [Old French _chaufer_ to warm]

chafer _n_ a large slow-moving beetle [Old English _ceafor_]

chaff[1] _n_ **1** grain husks separated from the seeds during threshing **2** something of little worth; rubbish: _you had to be a very perceptive listener to sort the wheat from the chaff of his discourse_ [Old English _ceaf_]

chaff[2] _vb_ to tease good-naturedly [probably slang variant of _chafe_]

chaffinch _n_ a small European songbird with black-and-white wings and, in the male, a reddish body and blue-grey head [Old English _ceaf_ CHAFF[1] + _finc_ finch]

chafing dish _n_ a dish with a heating apparatus beneath it, for cooking or keeping food warm at the table

Chagall _n_ Marc. 1887–1985, French painter and illustrator, born in Russia, noted for his richly coloured pictures of men, animals, and objects in fantastic combinations and often suspended in space: his work includes 12 stained glass windows for a synagogue in Jerusalem (1961) and the decorations for the ceiling of the Paris Opera House (1964)

Chagres _n_ a river in Panama, flowing southwest through Gatún Lake, then northwest to the Caribbean Sea

chagrin (shag-grin) _n_ a feeling of annoyance and disappointment [French]

chagrined _adj_ annoyed and disappointed

chain _n_ **1** a flexible length of metal links, used for fastening, binding, or connecting, or in jewellery **2** chains anything that restricts or restrains someone: _bound by the chains of duty_ **3** a series of connected facts or events **4** a number of establishments, such as hotels or shops, that have the same owner or management **5** _chem_ a number of atoms or groups bonded together so that the resulting molecule, ion, or radical resembles a chain **6** a row of mountains or islands ▷ _vb_ **7** to restrict, fasten, or bind with or as if with a chain: _the demonstrators chained themselves to railings_ [Latin _catena_]

Chain _n_ Sir Ernst Boris. 1906–79, British biochemist, born in Germany: purified and adapted penicillin for clinical use; with Fleming and Florey shared the Nobel prize for physiology or medicine 1945

chain gang _n_ US a group of convicted prisoners chained together

chain letter _n_ a letter, often with a request for or promise of money, that is sent to many people who are asked to send copies to other people

chain mail _n_ same as mail[2]

chain reaction _n_ **1** a series of events, each of which causes the next **2** a chemical or nuclear reaction in which the product of one step triggers the following step

chain saw _n_ a motor-driven saw in which the cutting teeth form links in a continuous chain

chain-smoke _vb_ **-smoking, -smoked** to smoke continuously, lighting one cigarette from the preceding one **> chain smoker** _n_

chair _n_ **1** a seat with a back and four legs, for one person to sit on **2** an official position of authority or the person holding it: _the chair of the Security Council_ **3** a professorship **4** in the chair presiding over a meeting **5** the chair _informal_ the electric chair ▷ _vb_ **6** to preside over (a meeting) [Greek _kathedra_]

chairlift _n_ a series of chairs suspended from a moving cable for carrying people up a slope

chairman _n_, _pl_ **-men** a person who is in charge of a company's board of directors or a meeting **> chairwoman** _fem n_ **> chairmanship** _n_

> USAGE _Chairman_ can seem inappropriate when applied to a woman, while _chairwoman_ can be offensive. _Chair_ and _chairperson_ can be applied to either a man or a woman; _chair_ is generally preferred to _chairperson_.

chaise (shaze) _n_ a light horse-drawn carriage with two wheels [French]

chaise longue (long) _n_, _pl_ **chaise longues** _or_ **chaises longues** a couch with a back and a single armrest [French]

chalcedony (kal-sed-don-ee) _n_, _pl_ **-nies** a form of quartz composed of very fine crystals, often greyish or blue in colour [Greek _khalkēdōn_ a precious stone]

Chalcidice _n_ a peninsula of N central Greece, in Macedonia Central, ending in the three promontories of Kassandra, Sithonia, and Akti. Area: 2945 sq km (1149 sq miles). Modern Greek name: **Khalkidíki**

Chalcis _n_ a city on the island of Euboea in SE Greece, at the narrowest point of the Euripus strait: important since the 7th century BC, founding many colonies in ancient times. Pop (municipality): 55 264 (2001). Modern Greek name: **Khalkís**. Medieval English name: **Negropont**

Chaldea _or_ **Chaldaea** _n_ **1** an ancient region of Babylonia; the land lying between the Euphrates delta, the Persian Gulf, and the Arabian desert **2** another name for **Babylonia**

chalet _n_ **1** a type of Swiss wooden house with a steeply sloping roof **2** a similar house used as a ski lodge or holiday home [French]

Chaliapin *n* Fyodor Ivanovich. 1873–1938, Russian operatic bass singer

chalice (**chal**-liss) *n* **1** *poetic* a drinking cup or goblet **2** *Christianity* a gold or silver goblet containing the wine at communion [Latin *calix* cup]

chalk *n* **1** a soft white rock consisting of calcium carbonate **2** a piece of chalk, either white or coloured, used for writing and drawing on blackboards **3 as different as chalk and cheese** *informal* totally different **4 not by a long chalk** *informal* by no means: *you haven't finished by a long chalk* ▷ *vb* **5** to draw or mark with chalk [Latin *calx* limestone] **> chalky** *adj*

chalk up *vb informal* **1** to score or register: *the home side chalked up a 9-1 victory* **2** to charge or credit (money) to an account

challenge *n* **1** a demanding or stimulating situation **2** a call to engage in a contest, fight, or argument **3** a questioning of a statement or fact **4** a demand by a sentry for identification or a password **5** *law* a formal objection to a juror ▷ *vb* **-lenging, -lenged 6** to invite or call (someone) to take part in a contest, fight, or argument **7** to call (a decision or action) into question **8** to order (a person) to stop and be identified **9** *law* to make formal objection to (a juror) [Latin *calumnia* calumny] **> challenger** *n* **> challenging** *adj*

challenged *adj* disabled as specified: *physically challenged; mentally challenged*

Châlons-en-Champagne *n* a town in NE France, on the River Marne: scene of Attila's defeat by the Romans (451 AD). Pop: 47 339 (1999). Former name: **Châlons-sur-Marne**. Shortened form: **Châlons**

Chalon-sur-Saône *n* an industrial city in E central France, on the Saône River. Pop: 50 124 (1999). Shortened form: **Chalon**

chalybeate (kal-**lib**-bee-it) *adj* containing or impregnated with iron salts: *a natural chalybeate spring rises at the edge of the lake* [Greek *khalups* iron]

chamber *n* **1** a meeting hall, usually one used for a legislative or judicial assembly **2** a room equipped for a particular purpose: *a decompression chamber* **3** a legislative or judicial assembly: *the Senate, the upper chamber of Canada's parliament* **4** old-fashioned or poetic a room in a house, esp. a bedroom **5** a compartment or cavity: *the heart chambers* **6** a compartment for a cartridge or shell in a gun ▶ See also **chambers** [Greek *kamara* vault]

chamberlain *n history* an officer who managed the household of a king or nobleman [Old French *chamberlayn*]

Chamberlain *n* **1** Sir (**Joseph**) **Austen**. 1863–1937, British Conservative statesman; foreign secretary (1924–29); awarded a Nobel peace prize for his negotiation of the Locarno Pact (1925) **2** his father, **Joseph**. 1836–1914, British statesman; originally a Liberal, he resigned in 1886 over Home Rule for Ireland and became leader of the Liberal Unionists; a leading advocate of preferential trading agreements with members of the British Empire **3** his son, (**Arthur**) **Neville**. 1869–1940, British Conservative statesman; prime minister (1937–40): pursued a policy of appeasement towards Germany; following the German invasion of Poland, he declared war on Germany on Sept 3, 1939 **4 Owen**. 1920–2006, US physicist, who discovered the antiproton. Nobel prize for physics jointly with Emilio Segré 1959

chambermaid *n* a woman employed to clean bedrooms in a hotel

chamber music *n* classical music to be performed by a small group of musicians

Chamber of Commerce *n* an organization of local business people to promote, regulate, and protect their interests

chamber pot *n* a bowl for urine, formerly used in bedrooms

chambers *pl n* **1** a judge's room for hearing private cases not taken in open court **2** (in England) the set of rooms used as offices by a barrister

Chambéry *n* a city in SE France, in the Alps: skiing centre; former capital of the duchy of Savoy. Pop: 59 188 (2006)

Chambord *n* a village in N central France: site of a famous Renaissance chateau

chameleon (kam-**meal**-yon) *n* a small lizard with long legs that is able to change colour to blend in with its surroundings [Greek *khamai* on the ground + *leōn* lion]

chamfer (**cham**-fer) *n* **1** a bevelled surface at an edge or corner ▷ *vb* **2** to cut a chamfer on or in [Old French *chant* edge + *fraindre* to break]

chamois *n*, *pl* **-ois 1** (**sham**-wah) a small mountain antelope of Europe and SW Asia **2** (**sham**-ee) a soft suede leather made from the skin of this animal or from sheep or goats **3** (**sham**-ee) *Also:* **chamois leather, shammy, chammy** a piece of such leather or similar material, used for cleaning and polishing [Old French]

chamomile (**kam**-mo-mile) *n* same as **camomile**

Chamonix *n* a town in SE France, in the Alps at the foot of Mont Blanc: skiing and tourist centre. Pop: 9514 (2006)

champ¹ *vb* **1** to chew noisily **2 champ at the bit** *informal* to be restless or impatient to do something [probably imitative]

champ² *n informal* short for **champion** (1)

champagne *n* **1** a white sparkling wine produced around Reims and Épernay, France ▷ *adj* **2** denoting a luxurious lifestyle: *a champagne capitalist* [*Champagne*, region of France]

Champagne-Ardenne *n* a region of NE France: a countship and commercial centre in medieval times; it consists of a great plain, with sheep and dairy farms and many vineyards

Champaigne *n* Philippe de. 1602–74, French painter, born in Brussels: noted particularly for his portraits and historical and religious scenes

champers (**sham**-perz) *n slang* champagne

Champigny-sur-Marne *n* a suburb of Paris, on the River Marne. Pop: 75 556 (2006)

champion *n* **1** a person, plant, or animal that has defeated all others in a competition: *the Olympic 100 metres champion* **2** someone who defends a person or cause: *a champion of the downtrodden* ▷ *vb* **3** to support: *he unceasingly championed equal rights and opportunities* ▷ *adj* **4** N English dialect excellent [Latin *campus* field] **> championship** *n*

Champlain¹ *n* Lake Champlain a lake in the northeastern US, between the Green Mountains and the Adirondack Mountains: linked by the **Champlain Canal** to the Hudson River and by the Richelieu River to the St Lawrence; a major communications route in colonial times

Champlain² *n* Samuel de. ?1567–1635, French explorer; founder of Quebec (1608) and governor of New France (1633–35)

Champollion *n* Jean François. 1790–1832, French Egyptologist, who deciphered the hieroglyphics on the Rosetta stone

Champs-Elysées *n* a major boulevard in Paris, leading from the Arc de Triomphe: site of the Elysée Palace and government offices

chance *n* **1** the extent to which something is likely to happen; probability **2** an opportunity or occasion to do something: *a chance to escape rural poverty* **3** a risk or gamble: *the government is not in the mood to take any more chances* **4** the unknown and unpredictable element that causes something to happen in one way rather than another: *in Buddhism there is no such thing as chance or coincidence* **5 by chance** without planning: *by chance she met an old school friend* **6 on the off chance** acting on the slight possibility: *he had called on the agents on the off chance that he might learn something of value* ▷ *vb* **chancing, chanced 7** to risk or hazard: *a few picnickers chanced the perilous footpath* **8** to do something without planning to: *I chanced to look down* **9 chance on** or **upon** to discover by accident: *I chanced upon a copy of this book* [Latin *cadere* to occur]

chancel *n* the part of a church containing the altar and choir [Latin *cancelli* lattice]

chancellery or **chancellory** *n, pl* **-leries** or **-lories** **1** *Brit and Austral* the residence or office of a chancellor **2** *US* the office of an embassy or consulate [Anglo-French *chancellerie*]

chancellor *n* **1** the head of government in several European countries **2** *US* the president of a university **3** *Brit, Austral and Canad* the honorary head of a university [Late Latin *cancellarius* porter] **> chancellorship** *n*

Chancellor of the Exchequer *n Brit* the cabinet minister responsible for finance

Chancery *n* (in England) the Lord Chancellor's court, a division of the High Court of Justice [shortened from CHANCELLERY]

chancre (shang-ker) *n pathol* a painless ulcer that develops as a primary symptom of syphilis [French]

chancy *adj* **chancier, chanciest** *informal* uncertain or risky

chandelier (shan-dill-**eer**) *n* an ornamental hanging light with branches and holders for several candles or bulbs [French]

Chandernagore *n* a port in E India, in S West Bengal on the Hooghly River: a former French settlement (1686–1950). Pop: 162 166 (2001)

Chandigarh *n* a city and Union Territory of N India, joint capital of the Punjab and Haryana: modern city planned in the 1950s by Le Corbusier. Pop: 808 796 (2001), of city; 900 414 (2001), of union territory. Area (of union territory): 114 sq km (44 sq miles)

chandler *n* a dealer in a specified trade or merchandise: *a ship's chandler* [Old French *chandelier* dealer in candles] **> chandlery** *n*

Chandler *n* **Raymond** (**Thornton**). 1888–1959, US thriller writer: created Philip Marlowe, one of the first detective heroes in fiction

Chandragupta *n* Greek name *Sandracottos*. died ?297 BC, ruler of N India, who founded the Maurya dynasty (325) and defeated Seleucus (?305)

Chandrasekhar *n* **Subrahmanyan**. 1910–95, US astronomer born in Lahore, India (now Pakistan). His work on stellar evolution led to an understanding of white dwarfs: shared the Nobel prize for physics 1983

Chanel *n* **Gabrielle**, known as *Coco Chanel*. 1883–1971, French couturière and perfumer, who created "the little black dress" and the perfume Chanel No. 5

Chang *n* another name for the **Yangtze**

Changan *n* a former name for **Xi'an**

Changchiakow or **Changchiak'ou** *n* a variant transliteration of the Chinese name for **Zhangjiakou**

Changchow or **Ch'ang-chou** *n* **1** a variant transliteration of the Chinese name for **Zhangzhou** **2** former spellings of **Changzhou**

Changchun or **Ch'ang Ch'un** *n* a city in NE China, capital of Jilin province: as Hsinking, capital of the Japanese state of Manchukuo (1932–45). Pop: 3 092 000 (2005 est)

Changde, Changteh or **Ch'ang-te** *n* a port in SE central China, in N Hunan province, near the mouth of the Yuan River: severely damaged by the Japanese in World War II. Pop: 1 483 000 (2005 est)

change *n* **1** the fact of becoming different **2** variety or novelty: *they wanted to print some good news for a change* **3** a different set, esp. of clothes **4** money exchanged for its equivalent in a larger denomination or in a different currency **5** the balance of money when the amount paid is larger than the amount due **6** coins of a small denomination ▷ *vb* **changing, changed** **7** to make or become different **8** to replace with or exchange for another: *the Swedish Communist Party changed its name to the*

Left Party **9** to give and receive (something) in return: *slaves and masters changed places* **10** to give or receive (money) in exchange for its equivalent sum in a smaller denomination or different currency **11** to put on other clothes **12** to get off one bus, train or airliner, and on to another: *there's no direct train, so you'll need to change at York* ▶ See also **change down, changeover, change up** [Latin *cambire* to exchange, barter] **> changeless** *adj*

changeable *adj* changing often **> changeability** *n*

change down *vb* to select a lower gear when driving

changeling *n* a child believed to have been exchanged by fairies for the parents' real child

change of life *n* the menopause

changeover *n* **1** a complete change from one system, attitude, or product to another ▷ *vb* **change over** **2** to swap places or activities: *the train crews changed over at the frontier*

change up *vb* to select a higher gear when driving

Changsha or **Ch'ang-sha** *n* a port in SE China, capital of Hunan province, on the Xiang River. Pop: 2 051 000 (2005 est)

Changteh or **Ch'ang-te** *n* a variant transliteration of the Chinese name for **Changde**

Changzhou *n* a city in E China, in S Jiangsu province, on the Grand Canal: also known as Wutsin until 1949, when the 7th-century name was officially readopted. Pop: 2 085 500 (2004 est)

Chania or **Hania** *n* the chief port of Crete, on the NW coast. Pop: 82 000 (2005 est). Greek name: **Khaniá**

channel *n* **1** a band of radio frequencies assigned for the broadcasting of a radio or television signal **2** a path for an electrical signal or computer data **3** a means of access or communication: *reports coming through diplomatic channels* **4** a broad strait connecting two areas of sea **5** the bed or course of a river, stream, or canal **6** a navigable course through an area of water **7** a groove ▷ *vb* **-nelling, -nelled** or *US* **-neling, -neled** **8** to direct or convey through a channel or channels: *tunnels that channel the pilgrims into the area; to channel funds abroad* [Latin *canalis* pipe, conduit]

Channel *n* the Channel short for **English Channel**

Channel Country *n* the Channel Country an area of E central Australia, in SW Queensland: crossed by intermittent rivers and subject to both flooding and long periods of drought

channel-hop *vb* **-hopping, -hopped** to change television channels repeatedly using a remote control device

Channel Islands *pl n* a group of islands in the English Channel, off the NW coast of France, consisting of Jersey, Guernsey, Alderney, Brechou or Brecqhou, Sark, Herm, Jethou, and Lihou (all between them representing the United Kingdom Crown Dependencies of the Bailiwick of Jersey and the Bailiwick of Guernsey) – the only part of the duchy of Normandy remaining to Britain – and the Roches Douvres and the Îles Chausey (which belong to France). Pop: 149 878 (2001). Area: 194 sq km (75 sq miles)

chant *vb* **1** to repeat (a slogan) over and over **2** to sing or recite (a psalm) ▷ *n* **3** a rhythmic or repetitious slogan repeated over and over, usually by more than one person **4** a religious song with a short simple melody in which several words or syllables are sung on one note [Latin *canere* to sing]

chanter *n* the pipe on a set of bagpipes on which the melody is played

chanticleer *n* a name for a cock, used in fables [Old French *chanter cler* to sing clearly]

Chantilly *n* **1** a town in N France, near the **Forest of Chantilly** formerly famous for lace and porcelain. Pop: 10 902 (1999) **2** Also called: **Tiffany** a breed of medium-sized cat with silky semi-long hair ▷ *adj* **3** (of cream) lightly sweetened and whipped

chanty *n, pl* **-ties** same as **shanty²**

Chanukah or **Hanukkah** (hah-na-ka) *n* an eight-day Jewish festival, held in December, commemorating the rededication of the temple by Judas Maccabaeus [Hebrew]

Chaoan n the former name of **Chaozhou**

Chaochow n a former spelling of **Chaozhou**

Chao Phraya n a river in N Thailand, rising in the N highlands and flowing south to the Gulf of Thailand. Length: (including the headstreams Nan and Ping) 1200 km (750 miles). Also called: **Menam**

chaos n complete disorder or confusion [Greek *khaos*] ⟩ **chaotic** adj ⟩ **chaotically** adv

Chaozhou n a city in SE China, in E Guangdong province, on the Han River: river port. Pop: 480 000 (2005 est). Also called: **Chaochow**. Former name: **Chaoan**

chap n informal a man or boy [from Old English *cēapman* pedlar]

chapati or **chapatti** n (in Indian cookery) a kind of flat thin unleavened bread [Hindi]

chapel n 1 a place of worship with its own altar, in a church or cathedral 2 a similar place of worship in a large house or institution 3 (in England and Wales) a Nonconformist place of worship 4 (in Scotland) a Roman Catholic church 5 the members of a trade union in a newspaper office, printing house, or publishing firm [Latin *cappa* cloak: originally the sanctuary where the cloak of St Martin was kept]

chaperone (shap-per-rone) n 1 an older person who accompanies and supervises a young person or young people on social occasions ▷ vb **-oning, -oned** 2 to act as a chaperone to [Old French *chape* hood]

chaplain n a clergyman attached to a chapel, military body, or institution [Late Latin *cappella* chapel] ⟩ **chaplaincy** n

chaplet n a garland worn on the head [Old French *chapelet*]

Chaplin n Sir **Charles Spencer**, known as *Charlie Chaplin*. 1889–1977, English comedian, film actor, and director. He is renowned for his portrayal of a downtrodden little man with baggy trousers, bowler hat, and cane. His films, most of which were made in Hollywood, include *The Gold Rush* (1924), *Modern Times* (1936), and *The Great Dictator* (1940) ⟩ **Chaplin'esque** adj

chapman n, pl **-men** old-fashioned a travelling pedlar [Old English *cēapman*]

Chapman n George 1559–1634, English dramatist and poet, noted for his translation of Homer

chapped adj (of the skin) raw and cracked, through exposure to cold [probably Germanic]

Chappell n Greg(ory Stephen). born 1948, Australian cricketer: played in 87 test matches (1970–84); first Australian to score over 7000 test runs

chappie n informal a man or boy

chaps pl n leather leggings without a seat, worn by cowboys [shortened from Spanish *chaparejos*]

chapter n 1 a division of a book 2 a period in a life or history: *the latest chapter in the long and complex tale of British brewing* 3 a sequence of events: *a chapter of accidents* 4 a branch of some societies or clubs 5 a group of the canons of a cathedral 6 **chapter and verse** exact authority for an action or statement [Latin *caput* head]

char¹ vb **charring, charred** to blacken by partial burning [short for *charcoal*]

char² Brit informal n 1 short for **charwoman** ▷ vb **charring, charred** 2 to clean other people's houses as a job [Old English *cerr* turn of work]

char³ n Brit old-fashioned, slang tea [Chinese *ch'a*]

char⁴ n, pl **char** or **chars** a troutlike fish of cold lakes and northern seas [origin unknown]

charabanc (shar-rab-bang) n Brit old-fashioned a coach for sightseeing [French: wagon with seats]

character n 1 the combination of qualities distinguishing an individual person, group of people, or place: *the unique charm and character of this historic town* 2 a distinguishing quality or characteristic: *bodily movements of a deliberate character* 3 reputation, esp. good reputation:

a man of my Dad's character and standing in the community 4 an attractively unusual or interesting quality: *the little town was full of life and character* 5 a person represented in a play, film, or story 6 an unusual or amusing person: *quite a character* 7 informal a person: *a flamboyant character* 8 a single letter, numeral, or symbol used in writing or printing 9 **in** or **out of character** typical or not typical of the apparent character of a person [Greek *kharaktēr* engraver's tool] ⟩ **characterless** adj

character assassination n an attempt to destroy someone's good reputation by slander or deliberate misrepresentation of his or her views: *he described the accusation as 'an appalling piece of character assassination'*

characteristic n 1 a distinguishing feature or quality 2 maths the integral part of a logarithm: *the characteristic of 2.4771 is 2* ▷ adj 3 typical or representative of someone or something: *the prime minister fought with characteristic passion* ⟩ **characteristically** adv

characterization or **-isation** n 1 the description or portrayal of a person by an actor or writer: *a novel full of rich characterization and complex plotting* 2 the act or an instance of characterizing

characterize or **-ise** vb **-izing, -ized** or **-ising, -ised** 1 to be a characteristic of: *the violence that characterized the demonstrations* 2 to describe: *we have made what I would characterize as outstanding progress*

charade (shar-rahd) n an absurd pretence [French]

charades n a game in which one team acts out each syllable of a word or phrase, which the other team has to guess

charcoal n 1 a black form of carbon made by partially burning wood or other organic matter 2 a stick of this used for drawing 3 a drawing done in charcoal ▷ adj 4 Also: **charcoal-grey** very dark grey [origin unknown]

Charcot n Jean Martin. 1825–93, French neurologist, noted for his attempt using hypnotism to find an organic cause for hysteria, which influenced Freud

Chardin n Jean-Baptiste Siméon. 1699–1779, French still-life and genre painter, noted for his subtle use of scumbled colour

Chardonnay (shar-don-nay) n a white wine produced in the Burgundy region of France and elsewhere [French]

Chardonnet n (Louis Marie) Hilaire Bernigaud, Comte de. 1839–1924, French chemist and industrialist who produced rayon, the first artificial fibre

Charente n 1 a department of W central France, in Poitou-Charentes region. Capital: Angoulême. Pop: 341 275 (2003 est). Area: 5972 sq km (2329 sq miles) 2 a river in W France, rising in the Massif Central and flowing west to the Bay of Biscay. Length: 362 km (225 miles)

Charente-Maritime n a department of W France, in Poitou-Charentes region. Capital: La Rochelle. Pop: 576 855 (2003 est). Area: 7232 sq km (2820 sq miles)

Chargaff n Erwin. 1905–2002, US biochemist, born in Austria, noted esp. for his work on DNA

charge vb **charging, charged** 1 to ask (an amount of money) as a price 2 to enter a debit against a person's account for (a purchase) 3 to accuse (someone) formally of a crime in a court of law 4 to make a rush at or sudden attack upon 5 to fill (a glass) 6 to cause (an accumulator or capacitor) to take and store electricity 7 to fill or saturate with liquid or gas: *old mine workings charged with foul gas* 8 to fill with a feeling or mood: *the emotionally charged atmosphere* 9 formal to command or assign: *the president has charged his foreign minister with trying to open talks* ▷ n 10 a price charged for something; cost 11 a formal accusation of a crime in a court of law 12 an onrush or attack 13 custody or guardianship: *in the charge of the police* 14 a person or thing committed to someone's care: *a nanny reported the cruel father of one of her charges to social workers* 15 **a** a cartridge or shell **b** the explosive required to fire a gun 16 physics **a** the attribute of matter responsible for all electrical phenomena, existing in two forms, positive and negative **b** the total amount of electricity stored in a capacitor or an accumulator **17 in charge of** in control of and responsible for: *in charge of defence and foreign affairs* [Old French *chargier* to load]

chargeable *adj* **1** liable to be taxed or charged **2** liable to result in a legal charge

charge card *n* a card issued by a chain store, shop, or organization, that enables customers to obtain goods and services for which they pay later

chargé d'affaires (shar-zhay daf-**fair**) *n, pl* **chargés d'affaires** (shar-zhay daf-**fair**) **1** the temporary head of a diplomatic mission in the absence of the ambassador or minister **2** the head of a small or unimportant diplomatic mission [French]

charge hand *n* a workman ranked just below a foreman

charge nurse *n* a nurse in charge of a hospital ward

charger *n* **1** a device for charging a battery **2** (in the Middle Ages) a warhorse

char-grilled *adj* (of food) grilled over charcoal

Chari *or* **Shari** *n* a river in N central Africa, rising in the N Central African Republic and flowing north to Lake Chad. Length: about 2250 km (1400 miles)

Charing Cross *n* a district of London, in the city of Westminster: the modern cross (1863) in front of Charing Cross railway station replaces the one erected by Edward I (1290), the last of twelve marking the route of the funeral procession of his queen, Eleanor

chariot *n* a two-wheeled horse-drawn vehicle used in ancient times for wars and races [Old French *char* car]

charioteer *n* a chariot driver

charisma (kar-**rizz**-ma) *n* the quality or power of an individual to attract, influence, or inspire people [Greek *kharis* grace, favour] **> charismatic** (kar-rizz-**mat**-ik) *adj*

charismatic movement *n* Christianity a group that believes in divine gifts such as instantaneous healing and uttering unintelligible sounds while in a religious ecstasy

charitable *adj* **1** kind or lenient in one's attitude towards others **2** of or for charity: *a charitable organization* **> charitably** *adv*

charity *n* **1** (*pl* **-ties**) an organization set up to provide help to those in need **2** the giving of help, such as money or food, to those in need **3** help given to those in need; alms **4** a kindly attitude towards people [Latin *caritas* affection]

charlady *n, pl* **-ladies** *Brit* same as **charwoman**

charlatan (shar-lat-tan) *n* a person who claims expertise that he or she does not have [Italian *ciarlare* to chatter]

Charlemagne *n* ?742–814 AD, king of the Franks (768–814) and, as Charles I, Holy Roman Emperor (800–814). He conquered the Lombards (774), the Saxons (772–804), and the Avars (791–799). He instituted many judicial and ecclesiastical reforms, and promoted commerce and agriculture throughout his empire, which extended from the Ebro to the Elbe. Under Alcuin his court at Aachen became the centre of a revival of learning

Charleroi *n* a town in SW Belgium, in Hainaut province: centre of an industrial region. Pop: 200 608 (2004 est)

Charles *n* **1** *Prince of Wales.* born 1948, son of Elizabeth II; heir apparent to the throne of Great Britain and Northern Ireland. He married (1981) Lady Diana Spencer; they separated in 1992 and were divorced in 1996; their son, Prince William of Wales, was born in 1982 and their second son, Prince Henry, in 1984; married (2005) Camilla Parker Bowles **2 Ray** real name *Ray Charles Robinson.* 1930–2004, US singer, pianist, and songwriter, whose work spans jazz, blues, gospel, pop, and country music

Charles I *n* **1** title as Holy Roman Emperor of Charlemagne. See **Charlemagne 2** title as king of France of Charles II (Holy Roman Emperor). See **Charles II** (1) **3** title as king of Spain of Charles V (Holy Roman Emperor). See **Charles V** (2) **4** title of **Charles Stuart**

1600–49, king of England, Scotland, and Ireland (1625–49); son of James I. He ruled for 11 years (1629–40) without parliament, advised by his minister Strafford, until rebellion broke out in Scotland. Conflict with the Long Parliament led to the Civil War and after his defeat at Naseby (1645) he sought refuge with the Scots (1646). He was handed over to the English army under Cromwell (1647) and executed **5** 1887–1922, emperor of Austria, and, as Charles IV, king of Hungary (1916–18). The last ruler of the Austro-Hungarian monarchy, he was forced to abdicate at the end of World War I

Charles II *n* **1** known as *Charles the Bald.* 823–877 AD, Holy Roman Emperor (875–877) and, as Charles I, king of France (843–877) **2** the title as king of France of Charles III (Holy Roman Emperor). See **Charles III** (1) **3** 1630–85, king of England, Scotland, and Ireland (1660–85) following the Restoration (1660); son of Charles I. He did much to promote commerce, science, and the Navy, but his Roman Catholic sympathies caused widespread distrust **4** 1661–1700, the last Hapsburg king of Spain: his reign saw the end of Spanish power in Europe

Charles III *n* **1** known as *Charles the Fat.* 839–888 AD, Holy Roman Emperor (881–887) and, as Charles II, king of France (884–887). He briefly reunited the empire of Charlemagne **2** 1716–88, king of Spain (1759–88), who curbed the power of the Church and tried to modernize his country

Charles IV *n* **1** known as *Charles the Fair.* 1294–1328, king of France (1322–28): brother of Isabella of France, with whom he intrigued against her husband, Edward II of England **2** 1316–78, king of Bohemia (1346–78) and Holy Roman Emperor (1355–78) **3** 1748–1819, king of Spain (1788–1808), whose reign saw the domination of Spain by Napoleonic France: abdicated **4** title as king of Hungary of Charles I. See **Charles I** (5)

Charles V *n* **1** known as *Charles the Wise.* 1337–80, king of France (1364–80) during the Hundred Years' War **2** 1500–58, Holy Roman Emperor (1519–56), king of Burgundy and the Netherlands (1506–55), and, as Charles I, king of Spain (1516–56): his reign saw the empire threatened by Francis I of France, the Turks, and the spread of Protestantism; abdicated

Charles VI *n* **1** known as *Charles the Mad* or *Charles the Well-Beloved.* 1368–1422, king of France (1380–1422): defeated by Henry V of England at Agincourt (1415), he was forced by the Treaty of Troyes (1420) to recognize Henry as his successor **2** 1685–1740, Holy Roman Emperor (1711–40). His claim to the Spanish throne (1700) led to the War of the Spanish Succession

Charles VII *n* **1** 1403–61, king of France (1422–61), son of Charles VI. He was excluded from the French throne by the Treaty of Troyes, but following Joan of Arc's victory over the English at Orléans (1429), was crowned **2** 1697–1745, Holy Roman Emperor (1742–45) during the War of the Austrian Succession

Charles IX *n* 1550–74, king of France (1560–74), son of Catherine de' Medici and Henry II: his reign was marked by war between Huguenots and Catholics

Charles X *n* **1** title of *Charles Gustavus.* 1622–60, king of Sweden, who warred with Poland and Denmark in an attempt to create a unified Baltic state **2** 1757–1836, king of France (1824–30): his attempt to restore absolutism led to his enforced exile

Charles XI *n* 1655–97, king of Sweden (1660–97), established an absolute monarchy and defeated Denmark (1678)

Charles XII *n* 1682–1718, king of Sweden (1697–1718), who inflicted defeats on Denmark, Russia, and Poland during the Great Northern War (1700–21)

Charles Albert *n* 1798–1849, king of Sardinia-Piedmont (1831–49) during the Risorgimento: abdicated after the failure of his revolt against Austria

Charles' law *n* physics the principle that the volume of a gas varies in proportion to its temperature at constant pressure [after Jacques *Charles*, physicist]

Charles Martel *n* grandfather of Charlemagne. ?688–741 AD, Frankish ruler of Austrasia (715–41), who checked the Muslim invasion of Europe by defeating the Moors at Poitiers (732)

Charleston *n* a lively dance of the 1920s [after CHARLESTON, South Carolina]

Charleston *n* **1** a city in central West Virginia: the state capital. Pop: 51 394 (2003 est) **2** a port in SE South Carolina, on the Atlantic: scene of the first action in the Civil War. Pop: 101 024 (2003 est)

Charleville-Mézières *n* twin towns on opposite sides of the River Meuse in NE France. Pop: 55 490 (1999). See Mézières

charlie *n* Brit old-fashioned, informal a fool

charlock *n* a weed with hairy leaves and yellow flowers [Old English *cerlic*]

charlotte *n* a dessert made with fruit and bread or cake crumbs: *apple charlotte* [French]

Charlotte *n* a city in S North Carolina: the largest city in the state. Pop: 584 658 (2003 est)

Charlotte Amalie *n* the capital of the Virgin Islands of the United States, a port on St Thomas Island. Pop: 18 914 (2000). Former name (1921–37): **Saint Thomas**

Charlottenburg *n* a district of Berlin (of West Berlin until 1990), formerly an independent city. Pop: 315 473 (2005 est)

Charlottetown *n* a port in SE Canada, capital of the province of Prince Edward Island. Pop: 34 562 (2011)

Charlton *n* **1 Bobby**, full name *Sir Robert Charlton*. born 1937, English footballer; played for Manchester United (1956–73) and England (1958–70) for whom he played 106 times, scoring 49 goals (an England record) **2** his brother, **Jack**, full name *John Charlton*. born 1935, English footballer: played for Leeds United (1952–73) and England for whom he won 35 caps; manager of the Republic of Ireland (1986–95)

charm *n* **1** the quality of attracting, fascinating, or delighting people **2** a trinket worn on a bracelet **3** a small object worn for supposed magical powers **4** a magic spell ▷ *vb* **5** to attract, fascinate, or delight **6** to influence or obtain by personal charm: *you can easily be charmed into changing your mind* **7** to protect as if by magic: *a charmed life* [Latin *carmen* song] ⟩ **charmer** *n* ⟩ **charmless** *adj*

harminar *n* a 16th-century monument with four minarets at Hyderabad, India

charming *adj* delightful or attractive ⟩ **charmingly** *adv*

charm offensive *n* a concentrated attempt to gain favour by being helpful and obliging

charnel house *n* (formerly) a building or vault for the bones of the dead [Latin *carnalis* fleshly]

Charnley *n* Sir John. 1911–82, British surgeon noted for his invention of an artificial hip joint and his development of hip-replacement surgery

Charolais (sharr-ol-lay) *n* a breed of large white beef cattle [Monts du *Charollais*, E France]

Charpentier *n* **1 Gustave**. 1860–1956, French composer, whose best-known work is the opera *Louise* (1900) **2 Marc-Antoine**. ?1645–1704, French composer, best known for his sacred music, particularly the *Te Deum*

chart *n* **1** a graph, table, or sheet of information in the form of a diagram **2** a map of the sea or the stars **3 the charts** informal the weekly lists of the bestselling pop records or the most popular videos ▷ *vb* **4** to plot the course of **5** to make a chart of **6** to appear in the pop charts [Greek *khartēs* papyrus]

charter *n* **1** a formal document granting or demanding certain rights or liberties: *a children's charter* **2** the fundamental principles of an organization: *the UN Charter* **3** the hire or lease of transportation for private use ▷ *vb* **4** to lease or hire by charter **5** to grant a charter to [Latin *charta* leaf of papyrus]

chartered accountant *n* an accountant who has passed the examinations of the Institute of Chartered Accountants

Charteris *n* **Leslie**, original name *Leslie Charles Bowyer Yin*. 1907–93, British novelist, born in Singapore: created the character Simon Templar, known as The Saint, the central character in many adventure novels

Chartism *n* English history a movement (1838–48) for social and political reforms, demand for which was presented to Parliament in charters ⟩ **Chartist** *n*, *adj*

Chartres *n* a city in NW France: Gothic cathedral; market town. Pop: 41 588 (2006)

chartreuse (shar-truhz) *n* a green or yellow liqueur made from herbs [after *La Grande Chartreuse*, monastery near Grenoble, where the liqueur is produced]

Chartwell *n* a house near Westerham in Kent: home for 40 years of Sir Winston Churchill

charwoman *n*, *pl* **-women** Brit a woman whose job is to clean other people's houses

chary (chair-ee) *adj* **charier, chariest** wary or careful: *chary of interfering* [Old English *cearig*]

Charybdis (kar-rib-diss) *n* **1** a ship-devouring monster in classical mythology, identified with a whirlpool off the coast of Sicily **2 between Scylla and Charybdis** See Scylla

chase¹ *vb* **chasing, chased 1** to pursue (a person or animal) persistently or quickly **2** to force (a person or animal) to leave a place **3** informal to court (someone) in an unsubtle manner **4** informal to rush or run: *chasing around the world* **5** informal to pursue (something or someone) energetically in order to obtain results or information ▷ *n* **6** the act or an instance of chasing a person or animal [Latin *capere* to take]

chase² *vb* **chasing, chased** to engrave or emboss (metal) [Old French *enchasser*]

chaser *n* a drink drunk after another of a different kind, for example beer after whisky

chasm (kaz-zum) *n* **1** a very deep crack in the ground **2** a wide difference in interests or feelings: *a deep chasm separating science from politics* [Greek *khasma*]

chassis (shass-ee) *n*, *pl* **chassis** (shass-eez) the steel frame, wheels, and mechanical parts of a vehicle [French]

chaste *adj* **1** abstaining from sex outside marriage or from all sexual intercourse **2** (of conduct or speech) pure, decent, or modest: *a chaste kiss on the forehead* **3** simple in style: *chaste furniture* [Latin *castus* pure] ⟩ **chastely** *adv* ⟩ **chastity** *n*

chasten (chase-en) *vb* to subdue (someone) by criticism [Latin *castigare*]

chastise *vb* **-tising, -tised 1** to scold severely **2** old-fashioned to punish by beating [Middle English *chastisen*] ⟩ **chastisement** *n*

chasuble (chazz-yew-bl) *n* Christianity a long sleeveless robe worn by a priest when celebrating Mass [Late Latin *casubla* garment with a hood]

chat *n* **1** an informal conversation ▷ *vb* **chatting, chatted 2** to have an informal conversation ▶ See also chat up [short for *chatter*]

chateau (shat-toe) *n*, *pl* **-teaux** (-toe) or **-teaus** a French country house or castle [French]

Chateaubriand *n* **1 François René**, Vicomte de Chateaubriand. 1768–1848, French writer and statesman: a precursor of the romantic movement in France; his works include *Le Génie du Christianisme* (1802) and *Mémoires d'outre-tombe* (1849–50) **2** a thick steak cut from the fillet of beef

Châteauroux *n* a town in central France: 10th-century castle (**Château-Raoul**). Pop: 46 386 (2009)

Château-Thierry *n* a town in N central France, on the River Marne: scene of the second battle of the Marne (1918) during World War I. Pop: 14 967 (1999)

chatelaine (shat-tell-lane) *n* (formerly) the mistress of a large house or castle [French]

Chatham¹ *n* **1** a town in SE England, in N Kent on the River Medway: formerly royal naval dockyard. Pop:

73 468 (2001) **2** a town in SE Canada, in SE Ontario on the Thames River. Pop: 44 156 (2001)

Chatham² *n* 1st Earl of title of the elder (William) Pitt. See **Pitt** (1)

Chatham Island *n* a former name for **San Cristóbal** (1)

Chatham Islands *pl n* a group of islands in the S Pacific Ocean, forming a county of South Island, New Zealand: consists of the main islands of Chatham, Pitt, and several rocky islets. Chief settlement: Waitangi. Pop: 609 (2006 est). Area: 963 sq km (372 sq miles)

chatline *n* a telephone service enabling callers to join in general conversation with each other

chatroom *n* a site on the internet where users have group discussions by electronic mail

chat show *n* a television or radio show in which guests are interviewed informally

Chatsworth House *n* a mansion near Bakewell in Derbyshire: seat of the Dukes of Devonshire; built (1687–1707) in the classical style

Chattagam *n* the official name for **Chittagong**

Chattanooga *n* a city in SE Tennessee, on the Tennessee River: scene of two battles during the Civil War, in which the North defeated the Confederates, cleared Tennessee, and opened the way to Georgia (1863). Pop: 154 887 (2003 est)

chattels *pl n old-fashioned* possessions [Old French *chatel* personal property]

chatter *vb* **1** to speak quickly and continuously about unimportant things **2** (of birds or monkeys) to make rapid repetitive high-pitched noises **3** (of the teeth) to click together rapidly through cold or fear ▷ *n* **4** idle talk or gossip **5** the high-pitched repetitive noise made by a bird or monkey [imitative]

chatterbox *n informal* a person who talks a great deal, usually about unimportant things

chattering classes *pl n* **the chattering classes** *informal, often disparaging* the members of the educated sections of society who enjoy discussion of political, social, and cultural issues

Chatterton *n* Thomas. 1752–70, British poet; author of spurious medieval verse and prose: he committed suicide at the age of 17

chatty *adj* **-tier, -tiest** **1** (of a person) fond of friendly, informal conversation; talkative **2** (of a letter) informal and friendly; gossipy

chat up *vb Brit and Austral informal* to talk flirtatiously to (someone) with a view to starting a romantic or sexual relationship

Chaucer *n* Geoffrey. ?1340–1400, English poet, noted for his narrative skill, humour, and insight, particularly in his most famous work, *The Canterbury Tales*. He was influenced by the continental tradition of rhyming verse. His other works include *Troilus and Criseyde, The Legende of Good Women*, and *The Parlement of Foules*

chauffeur *n* **1** a person employed to drive a car for someone ▷ *vb* **2** to act as driver for (someone) [French: stoker] ▶ **chauffeuse** *fem n*

chauvinism (show-vin-iz-zum) *n* an irrational belief that one's own country, race, group, or sex is superior: *male chauvinism* [after Nicolas Chauvin, French soldier under Napoleon] ▶ **chauvinist** *n, adj* ▶ **chauvinistic** *adj*

chav *n Brit slang, disparaging* a young working-class person who dresses in casual sports clothes

Chavannes *n* See **Puvis de Chavannes**

Chavez *n* Hugo. 1954–2013, Venezuelan socialist politician; president of Venezuela (1999–2013)

cheap *adj* **1** costing relatively little; inexpensive **2** of poor quality; shoddy: *planks of cheap, splintery pine* **3** not valued highly; not worth much: *promises are cheap* **4** *informal* mean or despicable: *a cheap jibe* ▷ *n* **5 on the cheap** *Brit informal* at a low cost ▷ *adv* **6** at a low cost [Old English *ceap* barter, price] ▶ **cheaply** *adv* ▶ **cheapness** *n*

cheapen *vb* **1** to lower the reputation of; degrade **2** to reduce the price of

cheap-jack *n informal* a person who sells cheap and shoddy goods

cheapskate *n informal* a miserly person

cheat *vb* **1** to defraud: *he cheated her out of millions* **2** to act dishonestly in order to gain some advantage or profit **3 cheat on** *informal* to be unfaithful to (one's spouse or lover) ▷ *n* **4** a person who cheats **5** a fraud or deception [short for *escheat*]

Cheb *n* a town in the W Czech Republic, in W Bohemia on the Ohře River: 12th-century castle where Wallenstein was murdered (1634); a centre of the Sudeten-German movement after World War I. Pop: 34 036 (2007 est). German name: **Eger**

Cheboksary *n* a port in W central Russia on the River Volga: capital of the Chuvash Republic. Pop: 446 000 (2005 est)

Chechen Republic *n* a constituent republic of S Russia on the N slopes of the Caucasus Mountains: major oil and natural gas resources; formed an Autonomous Republic with Ingushetia from 1936 until 1944 and from 1957 until 1991; declared independence from Ingushetia in 1992; fighting between Chechen separatists and Russian forces (1994–96) led to de facto independence: reoccupied by Russia in 1999–2000. Capital: Grozny. Pop: 1 100 300 (2002). Area: 15 700 sq km (6010 sq miles). Also called: **Chechenia, Chechnya**

check *vb* **1** to examine, investigate, or make an inquiry into **2** to slow the growth or progress of **3** to stop abruptly **4** to correspond or agree: *that all checks with our data here* ▷ *n* **5** a test to ensure accuracy or progress **6** a means to ensure against fraud or error **7** a break in progress; stoppage **8** *US* same as **cheque** **9** *chiefly US and Canad* the bill in a restaurant **10** a pattern of squares or crossed lines **11** a single square in such a pattern **12** *chess* the state or position of a king under direct attack **13** in check under control or restraint ▷ *interj* **14** *chiefly US and Canad* an expression of agreement ▶ See also **check in, check out, check up on** [Old French *eschec* a check at chess]

checked *adj* having a pattern of squares

checker *n US and Canad* **1** same as **chequer** **2** same as **draughtsman** (3)

checkered *adj US and Canad* same as **chequered**

checkers *n US and Canad* same as **draughts**

check in *vb* **1 a** to register one's arrival at a hotel or airport **b** to register the arrival of (guests or passengers at a hotel or airport ▷ *n* **check-in** **2 a** the formal registration of arrival at a hotel or airport **b** the place where one registers one's arrival at a hotel or airport

check list *n* a list to be referred to for identification or verification

checkmate *n* **1** *chess* the winning position in which an opponent's king is under attack and unable to escape **2** utter defeat ▷ *vb* **-mating, -mated** **3** *chess* to place the king of (one's opponent) in checkmate **4** to thwart or defeat [Arabic *shāh māt* the king is dead]

check out *vb* **1** to pay the bill and leave a hotel **2** to investigate, examine, or look at: *he asked if he could check on the old man's theory; start the evening off by checking out one of the bars in the city* ▷ *n* **checkout** **3** a counter in a supermarket where customers pay

checkpoint *n* a place where vehicles or travellers are stopped for identification or inspection

checkup *n* a thorough examination to see if a person or thing is in good condition

check up on *vb* to investigate the background of

Cheddar *n* **1** (*sometimes not cap*) any of several types of smooth hard yellow or whitish cheese **2** a village in SW England, in N Somerset: situated near **Cheddar Gorge**, a pass through the Mendip Hills renowned for its stalactitic caverns and rare limestone flora. Pop: 4796 (2001)

cheek *n* **1** either side of the face below the eye **2** *informal* impudence, boldness, or lack of respect **3** *informal* a buttock **4 cheek by jowl** close together **5 turn the other cheek** to refuse to retaliate ▷ *vb* **6** *Brit, Austral and NZ informal* to speak or behave disrespectfully to someone [Old English *ceace*]

cheekbone *n* the bone at the top of the cheek, just below the eye

cheeky *adj* **cheekier, cheekiest** disrespectful; impudent **> cheekily** *adv* **> cheekiness** *n*

cheep *n* **1** the short weak high-pitched cry of a young bird ▷ *vb* **2** to utter a cheep [imitative]

cheer *vb* **1** to applaud or encourage with shouts **2 cheer up** to make or become happy or hopeful; comfort or be comforted ▷ *n* **3** a shout of applause or encouragement **4** a feeling of cheerfulness: *the news brought little cheer* [Middle English (in the sense: face, welcoming aspect), from Greek *kara* head]

cheerful *adj* **1** having a happy disposition **2** pleasantly bright: *a cheerful colour* **3** ungrudging: *a cheerful giver* **> cheerfully** *adv* **> cheerfulness** *n*

cheerio *interj* **1** *informal* a farewell greeting ▷ *n* **2** *Austral and NZ* a small red cocktail sausage

cheerleader *n* a person who leads a crowd in cheers, usually at sports events

cheerless *adj* dreary or gloomy

cheers *interj informal, chiefly Brit* **1** a drinking toast **2** a farewell greeting **3** an expression of gratitude

cheery *adj* **cheerier, cheeriest** cheerful **> cheerily** *adv*

cheese[1] *n* **1** a food made from coagulated milk curd **2** a block of this [Latin *caseus*]

cheese[2] *n* **big cheese** *slang* an important person [perhaps from Hindi *chiz* thing]

cheeseburger *n* a hamburger with a slice of cheese melted on top of it

cheesecake *n* **1** a dessert with a biscuit-crumb base covered with a sweet cream-cheese mixture and sometimes with a fruit topping **2** *slang* magazine photographs of naked or scantily dressed women

cheesecloth *n* a light, loosely woven cotton cloth

cheesed off *adj Brit, Austral and NZ slang* bored, disgusted, or angry [origin unknown]

cheeseparing *adj* **1** mean or miserly ▷ *n* **2** meanness or miserliness

cheesy *adj* **cheesier, cheesiest** **1** like cheese **2** *informal* (of a smile) broad but possibly insincere **3** *informal* in poor taste: *a cheesy game show*

cheetah *n* a large fast-running wild cat of Africa and SW Asia, which has a light brown coat with black spots [Hindi *cītā*]

Cheever *n* John. 1912–82, US novelist and short-story writer. His novels include *The Wapshot Chronicle* (1957) and *Bullet Park* (1969)

chef *n* a cook, usually the head cook, in a restaurant or hotel [French]

chef-d'oeuvre (shay-durv) *n, pl* **chefs-d'oeuvre** (shay-durv) a masterpiece [French]

Chefoo *n* another name for **Yantai**

Cheju *n* a volcanic island in the N East China Sea, southwest of Korea: constitutes a province (Cheju-do) of South Korea. Capital: Cheju. Pop: 302 000 (2005 est). Area: 1792 sq km (692 sq miles). Formerly called: **Quelpart**

Chekhov *or* **Chekov** *n* Anton Pavlovich. 1860–1904, Russian dramatist and short-story writer. His plays include *The Seagull* (1896), *Uncle Vanya* (1900), *The Three Sisters* (1901), and *The Cherry Orchard* (1904) **> Chekhovian** *or* **Chekovian** *adj*

Chekiang *n* a variant transliteration of the Chinese name for **Zhejiang**

Chelmsford *n* a city in SE England, administrative centre of Essex: electronics, retail; university (1992). Pop: 99 962 (2001)

Chelsea *n* a residential district of SW London, in the Royal Borough of Kensington and Chelsea: site of the Chelsea Royal Hospital for old and infirm soldiers (**Chelsea Pensioners**)

Cheltenham *n* **1** a town in W England, in central Gloucestershire: famous for its schools, racecourse, and saline springs (discovered in 1716). Pop: 98 875 (2001) **2** a style of type

Chelyabinsk *n* an industrial city in SW Russia; in 2013 a large meteor exploded in an airburst over the city's surrounding district. Pop: 1 067 000 (2005 est)

Chelyuskin *n* Cape Chelyuskin a cape in N central Russia, in N Siberia at the end of the Taimyr Peninsula: the northernmost point of Asia

chem. **1** chemical **2** chemist **3** chemistry

chemical *n* **1** any substance used in or resulting from a reaction involving changes to atoms or molecules ▷ *adj* **2** of or used in chemistry **3** of, made from, or using chemicals: *a chemical additive found in many foods* **> chemically** *adv*

chemical engineering *n* the applications of chemistry in industrial processes **> chemical engineer** *n*

chemical warfare *n* warfare using weapons such as gases and poisons

chemin de fer (shem-man de fair) *n* a gambling game, a variation of baccarat [French: railway, referring to the fast tempo of the game]

chemise (shem-meez) *n* a woman's old-fashioned loose-fitting slip or dress [Late Latin *camisa*]

chemist *n* **1** *Brit, Austral and NZ* a shop selling medicines and cosmetics **2** *Brit, Austral and NZ* a qualified dispenser of prescribed medicines **3** a specialist in chemistry [Medieval Latin *alchimista* alchemist]

chemistry *n* the branch of science concerned with the composition, properties, and reactions of substances

Chemnitz *n* a city in E Germany, in Saxony, at the foot of the Erzgebirge: textiles, engineering. Pop: 249 922 (2003 est). Also called (1953–90): **Karl-Marx-Stadt**

chemotherapy *n* the treatment of disease, often cancer, by means of chemicals

Chemulpo *n* a former name of **Inchon**

Chenab *n* a river rising in the Himalayas and flowing southwest to the Sutlej River in Pakistan. Length: 1087 km (675 miles)

Chen-chiang *or* **Cheng-chiang** *n* a variant transliteration of the Chinese name for **Zhenjiang**

Cheney *n* Richard B(ruce), known as *Dick*. born 1941, US Republican politician; vice-president from 2001 to 2009

Chengchow *or* **Cheng-chou** *n* a variant transliteration of the Chinese name for **Zhengzhou**

Chengde, Chengteh *or* **Ch'eng-te** *n* a city in NE China, in Hebei on the Luan River: summer residence of the Manchu emperors. Pop: 470 000 (2005 est)

Chengdu, Chengtu *or* **Ch'eng-tu** *n* a city in S central China, capital of Sichuan province. Pop: 3 478 000 (2005 est)

Chénier *n* **1** André (Marie de). 1762–94, French poet; his work was influenced by the ancient Greek elegiac poets. He was guillotined during the French Revolution **2** his brother, **Marie-Joseph** (**Blaise de**). 1764–1811, French dramatist and politician. He wrote patriotic songs and historical plays, such as *Charles IX* (1789)

chenille (shen-neel) *n* **1** a thick soft tufty yarn **2** a fabric made of this [French]

Chennai *n* a port in SE India, capital of Tamil Nadu, on the Bay of Bengal: founded in 1639 by the English East India Company as **Fort St George**; traditional burial place of St Thomas; university (1857). Pop: 4 216 268 (2001). Former name: **Madras**

Cheops *n* original name *Khufu*. Egyptian king of the fourth dynasty (?2613–?2494 BC), who built the largest pyramid at El Gîza

Chepstow *n* a town in S Wales, in Monmouthshire on the River Wye: tourism, light industry. Pop: 10 821 (2001)

cheque *or US* **check** *n* a written order to someone's bank to pay money from his or her account to the person to whom the cheque is made out [from *check* (in the sense: means of verification)]

C

cheque book n Brit a book of detachable blank cheques issued by a bank

cheque card n Brit a plastic card issued by a bank guaranteeing payment of a customer's cheques

chequer or US **checker** n a piece used in Chinese chequers. See also **chequers** [Middle English: chessboard]

chequered or US **checkered** adj **1** marked by varied fortunes: a chequered career **2** marked with alternating squares of colour

chequered flag n the black-and-white checked flag traditionally shown to the winner and all finishers at the end of a motor race by a senior race official

chequers or US **checkers** n the game of draughts

Chequers n an estate and country house in S England, in central Buckinghamshire: the official country residence of the British prime minister

Cher n **1** a department of central France, in E Centre region. Capital: Bourges. Pop: 312 277 (2003 est). Area: 7304 sq km (2849 sq miles) **2** a river in central France, rising in the Massif Central and flowing northwest to the Loire. Length: 354 km (220 miles)

Cherbourg n a port in NW France, on the English Channel. Pop: 25 370 (1999)

Cherenkov or **Cerenkov** n Pavel Alekseyevich. 1904–90, Soviet physicist: noted for work on the effects produced by high-energy particles: shared Nobel prize for physics 1958

Cheribon n a former spelling of **Cirebon**

cherish vb **1** to cling to (an idea or feeling): cherished notions **2** to care for [Latin carus dear]

Chernenko n Konstantin (Ustinovich). 1911–85, Soviet statesman; general secretary of the Soviet Communist Party (1984–85)

Chernigov n a city in N central Ukraine, on the River Desna: tyres, pianos, consumer goods. Pop: 308 000 (2005 est)

Chernobyl n a town in N Ukraine; site of a nuclear power station accident in 1986

Chernovtsy n a city in Ukraine on the Prut River: formerly under Polish, Austro-Hungarian, and Romanian rule; part of the Soviet Union (1947–91). Pop: 237 000 (2005 est). German name: **Czernowitz**. Romanian name: **Cernăuţi**

Cherokee n **1** a member of a Native American people, formerly of the Appalachian mountains, now living chiefly in Oklahoma **2** the language of this people

cheroot (sher-root) n a cigar with both ends cut off squarely [Tamil curuttu curl, roll]

cherry n, pl **-ries 1** a small round soft fruit with red or blackish skin and a hard stone **2** the tree on which this fruit grows ▷ adj **3** deep red: cherry lips [Greek kerasios]

cherry tomato n a miniature tomato, slightly bigger than a cherry

Chertsey n a town in S England, in N Surrey on the River Thames. Pop: 10 323 (2001)

cherub n **1** (pl **cherubim**) Christianity an angel, often represented as a winged child **2** (pl **cherubs**) an innocent or sweet child [Hebrew kĕrūbh] ❯ **cherubic** (chair-roo-bik) adj

Cherubini n (Maria) Luigi (Carlo Zenobio Salvatore). 1760–1842, Italian composer, noted particularly for his church music and his operas.

chervil n an aniseed-flavoured herb [Old English cerfelle]

Cherwell n 1st Viscount title of Frederick Alexander Lindemann. 1886–1957, British physicist, born in Germany, noted for his research on heat capacity, aeronautics, and atomic physics. He was scientific adviser to Winston Churchill during World War II

Ches Cheshire

Chesapeake Bay n the largest inlet of the Atlantic in the coast of the US: bordered by Maryland and Virginia

Cheshire[1] n a former administrative county of NW England; administered since 2009 by the unitary

authorities of Cheshire West and Chester, and Cheshire East: low-lying and undulating, bordering on the Pennines in the east; mainly agricultural: the geographic and ceremonial county includes Warrington and Halton, which became independent unitary authorities in 1998. Area 2077 sq km (802 sq miles). Abbreviation: **Ches**

Cheshire[2] n Group Captain (**Geoffrey**) **Leonard**. 1917–92, British philanthropist: awarded the Victoria Cross in World War II; founded the Leonard Cheshire Foundation Homes for the Disabled: married Sue, Baroness Ryder

Cheshire cheese n a mild white or pale orange cheese with a crumbly texture

Cheshire East n a unitary authority in NW England. Administrative centre: Sandbach. Pop: 358 900 (2008 est). Area: 1160 sq km (448 sq miles)

Cheshire West and Chester n a unitary authority in NW England. Administrative centre: Chester. Pop: 328 100 (2008 est). Area: 917 sq km (354 sq miles)

Cheshunt n a town in SE England, in SE Hertfordshire: dormitory town of London. Pop: 55 275 (2001)

chess n a game of skill for two players using a chessboard on which chessmen are moved, with the object of checkmating the opponent's king [Old French esches, plural of eschec check]

chessboard n a square board divided into 64 squares of two alternating colours, for playing chess

chessman n, pl **-men** a piece used in chess [Middle English chessemeyne chess company]

chest n **1** the front of the body, from the neck to the waist **2 get something off one's chest** informal to unburden oneself of worries or secrets by talking about them **3** a heavy box for storage or shipping: a tea chest [Greek kistē box]

Chester n a city in NW England, administrative centre of the unitary authority of Cheshire West and Chester, on the River Dee: intact surrounding walls; 16th- and 17th-century double-tier shops. Pop: 80 121 (2001). Latin name: **Deva**

chesterfield n **1** a large couch with high padded sides and back **2** Canad any sofa or couch [after a 19th-century Earl of Chesterfield]

Chesterfield[1] n an industrial town in N central England, in Derbyshire: famous 14th-century church with twisted spire. Pop: 70 260 (2001)

Chesterfield[2] n Philip Dormer Stanhope, 4th Earl of Chesterfield. 1694–1773, English statesman and writer, noted for his elegance, suavity, and wit; author of Letters to His Son (1774)

Chesterton n G(ilbert) K(eith). 1874–1936, English essayist, novelist, poet, and critic

chestnut n **1** a reddish-brown edible nut **2** the tree that this nut grows on **3** a horse of a reddish-brown colour **4** informal an old or stale joke ▷ adj **5** dark reddish-brown: chestnut hair [Greek kastanea]

chest of drawers n a piece of furniture consisting of a set of drawers in a frame

chesty adj **chestier, chestiest** Brit informal suffering from or symptomatic of chest disease: chesty colds ❯ **chestiness** n

cheval glass (shev-val) n a full-length mirror mounted so as to swivel within a frame [French cheval support (literally: horse)]

chevalier (shev-a-leer) n **1** a member of the French Legion of Honour **2** a chivalrous man [Medieval Latin caballarius horseman]

Chevalier n **1** Albert. 1861–1923, British music hall entertainer, remembered for his cockney songs **2** Maurice. 1888–1972, French singer and film actor

Cheviot n a large British sheep with a heavy medium-length fleece [CHEVIOT HILLS]

Cheviot Hills pl n a range of hills on the border between England and Scotland, mainly in Northumberland

chevron (shev-ron) n a V-shaped pattern, such as those

worn on the sleeve of a military uniform to indicate rank [Old French]

hew *vb* **1** to work the jaws and teeth in order to grind (food) ▷ *n* **2** the act of chewing **3** something that is chewed, such as a sweet or a piece of tobacco [Old English *ceowan*]

hewing gum *n* a flavoured gum which is chewed but not swallowed

hew over *vb* to consider carefully

hewy *adj* **chewier, chewiest** of a consistency requiring a lot of chewing

heyenne *n* a city in SE Wyoming, capital of the state. Pop: 54 374 (2003 est)

hez (**shay**) *prep* at the home of [French]

hhattisgarh *n* a state of E central India, created from the SE part of Madhya Pradesh in 2000: consists of a hilly plateau, with extensive forests; agricultural. Capital: Raipur. Pop: 20 795 956 (2001). Area: 135 194 sq km (52 199 sq miles)

hian *adj* **1** of or relating to Chios ▷ *n* **2** a native or inhabitant of Chios

hiang Ching-kuo or **Jiang Jing Guo** *n* 1910–88, Chinese statesman; the son of Chiang Kai-shek. He was prime minister of Taiwan (1971–78); president (1978–88)

hiang Kai-shek or **Jiang Jie Shi** *n* original name *Chiang Chung-cheng*, 1887–1975, Chinese general: president of China (1928–31; 1943–49) and of the Republic of China (Taiwan) (1950–75). As chairman of the Kuomintang, he allied with the Communists against the Japanese (1937–45), but in the Civil War that followed was forced to withdraw to Taiwan after his defeat by the Communists (1949)

hianti (**kee-ant-ee**) *n* a dry red wine produced in Tuscany, Italy

hianti *pl n* a mountain range in central Italy, in Tuscany, rising over 870 m (2900 ft): part of the Apennines

hiantishire *n* Brit informal a nickname for Tuscany [C20: from CHIANTI + SHIRE¹, alluding to the large numbers of British people living or holidaying in Tuscany]

hiapas *n* a state of S Mexico: mountainous and forested; Maya ruins in the northeast; rich mineral resources. Capital: Tuxtla Gutiérrez. Pop: 3 920 515 (2000). Area: 73 887 sq km (28 816 sq miles)

hiaroscuro (**kee-ah-roh-skew-roh**) *n*, *pl* -**ros** the distribution of light and shade in a picture [Italian *chiaro* clear + *oscuro* obscure]

hiba *n* an industrial city in central Japan, in SE Honshu on Tokyo Bay. Pop: 880 164 (2002 est)

hic (**sheek**) *adj* **1** stylish or elegant ▷ *n* **2** stylishness or elegance [French]

hicago *n* a port in NE Illinois, on Lake Michigan: the third largest city in the US; it is a major railway and air traffic centre. Pop: 2 869 121 (2003 est)

hicane (**shik-kane**) *n* an obstacle placed on a motor-racing circuit to slow the cars down [French *chicaner* to quibble]

hicanery *n* trickery or deception

hichagof Island *n* an island of Alaska, in the Alexander Archipelago. Area: 5439 sq km (2100 sq miles)

hichen Itzá *n* a village in Yucatán state in Mexico: site of important Mayan ruins

hichester¹ *n* a city in S England, administrative centre of West Sussex: Roman ruins; 11th-century cathedral; Festival Theatre. Pop: 27 477 (2001)

hichester² *n* Sir Francis. 1901–72, British yachtsman, who sailed alone round the world in *Gipsy Moth IV* (1966–67)

hichihaerh or **Ch'i-ch'i-haerh** *n* a variant transliteration of the Chinese name for Qiqihar

hick *n* **1** a baby bird, esp. a domestic fowl **2** slang a young woman [short for *chicken*]

hicken *n* **1** a domestic fowl bred for its flesh or eggs **2** the flesh of this bird used for food **3** slang a coward ▷ *adj*

4 slang cowardly [Old English *ciecen*]

chicken feed *n* slang a trifling amount of money

chicken-hearted *adj* easily frightened; cowardly

chicken out *vb informal* to fail to do something through cowardice

chickenpox *n* an infectious viral disease, usually affecting children, which produces an itchy rash

chicken wire *n* wire netting

chickpea *n* an edible hard yellow pealike seed [Latin *cicer*]

chickweed *n* a common garden weed with small white flowers

Chiclayo *n* a city in NW Peru. Pop: 434 000 (2005 est)

chicory *n* **1** a plant grown for its leaves, which are used in salads, and for its roots **2** the root of this plant, roasted, dried, and used as a coffee substitute [Greek *kikhōrion*]

chide *vb* **chiding, chided** or **chid** old-fashioned to rebuke or scold [Old English *cīdan*]

chief *n* **1** the head of a group or body of people **2** the head of a tribe ▷ *adj* **3** most important: *the chief suspects* **4** highest in rank: *the Chief Constable* [Latin *caput* head]

chiefly *adv* **1** especially or essentially **2** mainly or mostly

chief petty officer *n* a senior noncommissioned officer in a navy

chieftain *n* the leader of a tribe or clan [Late Latin *capitaneus* commander]

chief technician *n* a noncommissioned officer in the Royal Air Force

Chiengmai or **Chiang Mai** *n* a town in NW Thailand: teak, silver, silk industries: university (1964). Pop: 182 000 (2005 est)

chiffchaff *n* a European warbler with a yellowish-brown plumage [imitative]

chiffon (**shif-fon**) *n* a fine see-through fabric of silk or nylon [French *chiffe* rag]

chiffonier or **chiffonnier** (**shiff-on-near**) *n* **1** a tall elegant chest of drawers **2** a wide low open-fronted cabinet [French]

Chifley *n* Joseph Benedict. 1885–1951, Australian statesman; prime minister of Australia (1945–49)

chignon (**sheen-yon**) *n* a roll or knot of long hair pinned up at the back of the head [French]

chigoe (**chig-go**) *n* a tropical flea that burrows into the skin. Also: **chigger** [Carib *chigo*]

Chigwell *n* a town in S England, in W Essex. Pop: 10 128 (2001)

Chihli *n* Gulf of Chihli another name for Bohai

Chihuahua *n* **1** a state of N Mexico: mostly high plateau; important mineral resources, with many silver mines. Capital: Chihuahua. Pop: 728 000 (2005 est). Area: 247 087 sq km (153 194 sq miles) **2** a city in N Mexico, capital of Chihuahua state. Pop: 650 000 (2000 est) **3** a breed of tiny dog originally from Mexico, having short smooth hair, large erect ears, and protruding eyes

chilblain *n* an inflammation of the fingers or toes, caused by exposure to cold [CHILL (noun) + BLAIN]

child *n*, *pl* **children** **1** a young human being; boy or girl **2** a son or daughter. Related adjective: **filial** **3** a childish or immature person **4** the product of an influence or environment: *a child of the Army* **5** with child old-fashioned pregnant [Old English *cild*] ▷ **childless** *adj* ▷ **childlessness** *n*

childbearing *n* **1** the process of giving birth to a child ▷ *adj* **2** of childbearing age of an age when women are able to give birth to children

child benefit *n* Brit a regular government payment to parents of children up to a certain age

childbirth *n* the act of giving birth to a child. Related adjective: **natal**

Childers *n* (Robert) Erskine. 1870–1922, Irish politician, executed by the Irish Free State for his IRA activities: author of the spy story *The Riddle of the Sands* (1903)

childhood *n* the time or condition of being a child

childish *adj* **1** immature or silly: *childish fighting over who did what* **2** of or like a child: *childish illnesses*

childlike *adj* like a child, for example in being innocent or trustful

child minder *n* a person who looks after children whose parents are working

children *n* the plural of **child**

child's play *n informal* something that is easy to do

Chile *n* a republic in South America, on the Pacific, with a total length of about 4090 km (2650 miles) and an average width of only 177 km (110 miles): gained independence from Spain in 1818; the government of President Allende (elected 1970) attempted the implementation of Marxist policies within a democratic system until overthrown by a military coup (1973); democracy restored 1988. Chile consists chiefly of the Andes in the east, the Atacama Desert in the north, a central fertile region, and a huge S region of almost uninhabitable mountains, glaciers, fjords, and islands; an important producer of copper, iron ore, nitrates, etc. Language: Spanish. Religion: Roman Catholic majority. Currency: peso. Capital: Santiago. Pop: 17 216 945 (2013 est). Area: 756 945 sq km (292 256 sq miles)

Chilean *adj* **1** of or relating to Chile or its inhabitants ▷ *n* **2** a native or inhabitant of Chile

Chilkoot Pass *n* a mountain pass in North America between SE Alaska and NW British Columbia, over the Coast Range

chill *n* **1** a feverish cold **2** a moderate coldness **3** a feeling of coldness resulting from a cold or damp environment or from sudden fear ▷ *vb* **4** to make (something) cool or cold: *chilled white wine* **5** to cause (someone) to feel cold or frightened **6** *informal* to calm oneself ▷ *adj* **7** unpleasantly cold: *chill winds* [Old English *ciele*] > **chilling** *adj* > **chillingly** *adv*

Chillán *n* a city in central Chile. Pop: 149 000 (2005 est)

chilled *or* **chilled-out** *adj informal* relaxed or easy-going in character or behaviour

chiller *n* **1** short for **spine-chiller** **2** a cooling or refrigerating device

chilli *or* **chili** *n* **1** (*pl* **chillies** *or* **chilies**) the small red or green hot-tasting pod of a type of capsicum, used in cookery, often in powdered form **2** short for **chilli con carne** [Mexican Indian]

chilli con carne *n* a highly seasoned Mexican dish of meat, onions, beans, and chilli powder [Spanish: chilli with meat]

Chillon *n* a castle in W Switzerland, in Vaud at the E end of Lake Geneva

chill out *informal vb* **1** to relax, esp. after energetic dancing at a rave ▷ *adj* **chill-out** **2** suitable for relaxation after energetic dancing: *a chill-out area*

chilly *adj* **-lier, -liest** **1** causing or feeling moderately cold **2** without warmth; unfriendly: *a chilly reception*

chilly bin *n* NZ *informal* a portable insulated container for packing food and drink in ice

Chiloé Island *n* an island administered by Chile, off the W coast of South America in the Pacific Ocean: timber. Pop: 154 775 (2002, Chiloé province). Area: 8394 sq km (3240 sq miles)

Chilpancingo *n* a town in S Mexico, capital of Guerrero state, in the Sierra Madre del Sur. Pop: 166 000 (2005 est)

Chiltern Hills *pl n* a range of low chalk hills in SE England extending northwards from the Thames valley. Highest point: 260 m (852 ft)

Chiltern Hundreds *pl n* (in Britain) a nominal office that an MP applies for in order to resign his seat

Chilung *or* **Chi-lung** *n* a port in N Taiwan: fishing and industrial centre. Pop: 406 000 (2005 est). Also called: Keelung, Kilung

Chimborazo *n* an extinct volcano in central Ecuador, in the Andes: the highest peak in Ecuador. Height: 6267 m (20 561 ft)

Chimbote *n* a port in N central Peru: contains Peru's first steelworks (1958), using hydroelectric power from the Santa River. Pop: 328 000 (2005 est)

chime *n* **1** the musical ringing sound made by a bell or clock ▷ *vb* **chiming, chimed** **2** (of a bell) to make a clear musical ringing sound **3** (of a clock) to indicate (the time) by chiming [Latin *cymbalum* cymbal]

chime in *vb* to say something just after someone else has spoken

chimera (kime-meer-a) *n* **1** a wild and unrealistic dream or idea **2** *Greek myth* a fire-breathing monster with the head of a lion, body of a goat, and tail of a serpent [Greek *khimaira* she-goat]

chimerical *adj* wildly fanciful or imaginary

chime with *vb* to agree or be consistent with

Chimkent *n* the Russian name for **Shymkent**

chimney *n* a hollow vertical structure that carries smoke or steam away from a fire or engine [Greek *kaminos* oven]

chimney breast *n* the walls surrounding the base of a chimney or fireplace

chimneypot *n* a short pipe on the top of a chimney

chimney stack *n* the part of a chimney sticking up above a roof

chimney sweep *n* a person who cleans soot from chimneys

chimp *n informal* short for **chimpanzee**

chimpanzee *n* an intelligent small black ape of central W Africa [African dialect]

chin *n* the front part of the face below the mouth [Old English *cinn*]

Chin. **1** China **2** Chinese

china[1] *n* **1** ceramic ware of a type originally from China **2** dishes or ornamental objects made of china [Persian *chīnī*]

china[2] *n* *Brit and S African informal* a friend or companion [from cockney rhyming slang *china plate* mate]

China *n* **1** People's Republic of China, Communist China *or* Red China a republic in E Asia: the third largest and the most populous country in the world; the oldest continuing civilization (beginning over 2000 years BC); republic established in 1911 after the overthrow of the Manchu dynasty by Sun Yat-sen; People's Republic formed in 1949; the 1980s and 1990s saw economic liberalization but a rejection of political reform; contains vast deserts, steppes, great mountain ranges (Himalayas, Kunlun, Tian Shan, and Nan Shan), a central rugged plateau, and intensively cultivated E plains. Language: Chinese in various dialects, the chief of which is Mandarin. Religion: nonreligious majority; Buddhist and Taoist minorities. Currency: yuan. Capital: Beijing. Pop: 1 349 586 000 (2013 est). Area: 9 560 990 sq km (3 691 502 sq miles) **2 Republic of China, Nationalist China** *or* **Taiwan** a republic (recognized as independent by only 24 nations) in E Asia occupying the island of Taiwan, 13 nearby islands, and 64 islands of the Penghu (Pescadores) group: established in 1949 by the Nationalist government of China under Chiang Kai-shek after its expulsion by the Communists from the mainland; its territory claimed by the People's Republic of China since the political separation from the mainland; under US protection 1954–79; lost its seat at the UN to the People's Republic of China in 1971; state of war with the People's Republic of China formally ended in 1991, though tensions continue owing to the unresolved territorial claim. Language: Mandarin Chinese. Religion: nonreligious majority, Buddhist and Taoist minorities. Currency: New Taiwan dollar. Capital: Taipei. Pop: 22 610 000 (2003 est). Area: 35 981 sq km (13 892 sq miles). Former name: **Formosa** ▶ Related adjective: **Sinitic**

china clay *n* same as **kaolin**

Chinaman *n, pl* **-men** *old-fashioned, offensive* a man from China

Chinan or **Chi-nan** n a variant transliteration of the Chinese name for **Jinan**

China Sea n a part of the Pacific Ocean off the coast of China: divided by Taiwan into the East China Sea in the north and the South China Sea in the south

Chinatown n a section of a town or city outside China with a mainly Chinese population

chinchilla n **1** a small S American rodent bred in captivity for its soft silvery-grey fur **2** the fur of this animal [Spanish]

Chin-Chou or **Chin-chow** n a variant transliteration of the Chinese name for **Jinzhou**

Chindia n China and India considered together in economic and strategic terms

Chindwin n a river in N Myanmar, rising in the Kumôn Range and flowing northwest then south to the Irrawaddy, of which it is the main tributary. Length: about 966 km (600 miles)

chine n **1** a cut of meat including part of the backbone ▷ vb **chining, chined 2** to cut (meat) along the backbone [Old French *eschine*]

Chinese adj **1** of or relating to China or its inhabitants ▷ n **2** (pl **-nese**) a native or inhabitant of China or a descendant of one **3** any of the languages of China

Chinese chequers n a game played with marbles or pegs on a six-pointed star-shaped board

Chinese lantern n a collapsible lantern made of thin paper

Chinese leaves pl n the edible leaves of a Chinese cabbage

Chinese puzzle n a complicated puzzle or problem

Chinese Turkestan n the E part of the central Asian region of Turkestan: corresponds generally to the present-day Xinjiang Uygur Autonomous Region of China

Chinghai or **Ch'ing-hai** n a variant transliteration of the Chinese name for **Qinghai**

Chingtao or **Ch'ing-tao** n a variant transliteration of the Chinese name for **Qingdao**

Ch'ing-yüan n a former name of **Baoding**

Chin Hills pl n a mountainous region of W Myanmar; part of the Arakan Yoma system. Highest peak: Mount Victoria, 3053 m (10 075 ft)

Chin-Hsien n the former name (1913–47) of **Jinzhou**

chink¹ n a small narrow opening: *a chink of light* [Old English *cine* crack]

chink² vb **1** to make a light ringing sound ▷ n **2** a light ringing sound [imitative]

chinless wonder n Brit informal a person, usually upper-class, lacking strength of character

chinoiserie (sheen-**wahz**-a-ree) n **1** a style of decorative art based on imitations of Chinese motifs **2** objects in this style [French *chinois* Chinese]

Chinook n **1** (pl **-nook** or **-nooks**) a member of a Native American people of the Pacific coast of N America **2** the language of this people

Chinook salmon n a Pacific salmon valued as a food fish

chinos (chee-**nohz**) pl n trousers made of a kind of hard-wearing cotton [*chino*, the cloth; origin unknown]

chintz n a printed patterned cotton fabric with a glazed finish, used for curtains and chair coverings [Hindi *chīnt*]

chintzy adj **chintzier, chintziest 1** of or covered with chintz **2** (of a room or house) decorated in an excessively fussy or twee way

chinwag n Brit, Austral and NZ informal a chat

Chios n **1** an island in the Aegean Sea, off the coast of Turkey: belongs to Greece. Capital: Chios. Pop: 51 936 (2001). Area: 904 sq km (353 sq miles) **2** a port on the island of Chios: in ancient times, one of the 12 Ionian city-states. Pop (municipality): 25 671 (2001). ▶ Modern Greek name: **Khíos**

chip n **1** a thin strip of potato fried in deep fat **2** US, Canad,

Austral and NZ a potato crisp **3** electronics a tiny wafer of semiconductor material, such as silicon, processed to form an integrated circuit **4** a counter used to represent money in gambling games **5** a small piece removed by chopping, cutting, or breaking **6** a mark left where a small piece has been broken off something **7 chip off the old block** informal a person who resembles one of his or her parents in personality **8 have a chip on one's shoulder** informal to be resentful or bear a grudge **9 when the chips are down** informal at a time of crisis ▷ vb **chipping, chipped 10** to break small pieces from [Old English *cipp*]

chip and PIN n a system for authorizing credit- or debit-card payment requiring the purchaser to enter a personal identification number

chipboard n thin rigid board made of compressed wood particles

chip in vb informal **1** to contribute to a common fund **2** to interrupt with a remark

chipmunk n a squirrel-like striped burrowing rodent of North America and Asia [from a Native American language]

chipolata n chiefly Brit a small sausage [Italian *cipolla* onion]

Chippendale n **1** Thomas. ?1718–79, English cabinet-maker and furniture designer ▷ adj **2** (of furniture) designed by, made by, or in the style of Thomas Chippendale, characterized by the use of Chinese and Gothic motifs, cabriole legs, and massive carving

chipset n a highly integrated circuit on the motherboard of a computer that controls many of its data transfer functions

Chirac n Jacques (René). born 1932, French Gaullist politician: president of France (1995–2007); prime minister (1974–76 and 1986–88); mayor of Paris (1977–95)

Chirico n Giorgio de. 1888–1978, Italian artist born in Greece: profoundly influenced the surrealist movement

chiropody (kir-**rop**-pod-ee) n the treatment of minor foot complaints like corns **>** **chiropodist** n

chiropractic (kire-oh-**prak**-tik) n a system of treating bodily disorders by manipulation of the spine [Greek *kheir* hand + *praktikos* practical] **>** **chiropractor** n

chirp vb **1** (of some birds and insects) to make a short high-pitched sound **2** Brit, Austral and NZ to speak in a lively fashion ▷ n **3** a chirping sound [imitative]

chirpy adj **chirpier, chirpiest** informal lively and cheerful **>** **chirpiness** n

chirrup vb **1** (of some birds) to chirp repeatedly ▷ n **2** a chirruping sound [variant of *chirp*]

chisel n **1** a metal tool with a sharp end for shaping wood or stone ▷ vb **-elling, -elled** or US **-eling, -eled 2** to carve or form with a chisel [Latin *caesus* cut]

chiselled or US **chiseled** adj finely or sharply formed: *chiselled angular features*

Chishima n the Japanese name for the **Kuril Islands**

Chisimaio n a port in S Somalia, on the Indian Ocean. Pop: reliable recent estimates are not available. Also called: **Kismayu**

Chişinău n the capital of Moldova on the Bîk River: manufacturing centre of a rich agricultural region; university (1945). Pop: 662 000 (2005 est). Russian name: **Kishinev**

chit¹ n a short official note, such as a memorandum, requisition, or receipt. Also: **chitty** [Hindi *cittha* note]

chit² n Brit, Austral and NZ old-fashioned a pert or impudent girl [Middle English: young animal, kitten]

Chita n an industrial city in SE Russia, on the Trans-Siberian railway. Pop: 309 000 (2005 est)

chitchat n chat or gossip

chitin (**kite**-in) n the tough substance forming the outer layer of the bodies of arthropods [Greek *khitōn* tunic]

Chittagong n a port in E Bangladesh, on the Bay of Bengal: industrial centre. Pop: 4 171 000 (2005 est). Official name: **Chattagam**

C

C

chitterlings *pl n* the intestines of a pig or other animal prepared as food [origin unknown]

chivalrous *adj* gallant or courteous **>** **chivalrously** *adv*

chivalry *n* **1** courteous behaviour, esp. by men towards women **2** the medieval system and principles of knighthood [Old French *chevalier* knight] **>** **chivalric** *adj*

chives *pl n* the long slender hollow leaves of a small Eurasian plant, used in cooking for their onion-like flavour [Latin *caepa* onion]

chivvy *vb* **-vies, -vying, -vied** *Brit* to harass or nag [probably from *Chevy Chase*, a Scottish ballad]

Chkalov *n* the former name (1938–57) of **Orenburg**

chloral hydrate *n* a colourless crystalline solid used as a sedative

chlorate *n chem* any salt containing the ion ClO₃⁻

chloride *n chem* **1** any compound of chlorine and another element and radical **2** any salt or ester of hydrochloric acid

chlorinate *vb* **-ating, -ated** **1** to disinfect (water) with chlorine **2** *chem* to combine or treat (a substance) with chlorine: *chlorinated hydrocarbons* **>** **chlorination** *n*

chlorine *n* a poisonous strong-smelling greenish-yellow gaseous element, used in water purification and as a disinfectant, and, combined with sodium, to make common salt. Symbol: **Cl**

chloro- *combining form* green [Greek *khlōros*]

chlorofluorocarbon *n chem* any of various gaseous compounds of carbon, hydrogen, chlorine, and fluorine, used as refrigerants and aerosol propellants, some of which break down the ozone in the atmosphere

chloroform *n* a sweet-smelling liquid, used as a solvent and cleansing agent, and formerly as an anaesthetic [CHLORO- + *formyl:* see FORMIC ACID]

chlorophyll *or US* **chlorophyl** *n* the green colouring matter of plants, which enables them to convert sunlight into energy [CHLORO- + Greek *phullon* leaf]

chloroplast *n biology* one of the parts of a plant cell that contains chlorophyll [CHLORO- + Greek *plastos* formed]

chock *n* **1** a block or wedge of wood used to prevent the sliding or rolling of a heavy object ▷ *vb* **2** to fit with or secure by a chock [origin unknown]

chock-a-block *adj* filled to capacity

chockers *or* **chocker** *adj slang, chiefly Austral* completely full

chock-full *adj* completely full

chocolate *n* **1** a food made from roasted ground cacao seeds, usually sweetened and flavoured **2** a sweet or drink made from this ▷ *adj* **3** deep brown [Aztec *xocolatl*] **>** **chocolaty** *adj*

choice *n* **1** the act of choosing or selecting **2** the opportunity or power of choosing: *parental choice* **3** a person or thing chosen or that may be chosen: *the president's choice as the new head of the CIA* **4** an alternative action or possibility: *they had no choice but to accept* **5** a range from which to select: *a choice of weapons* ▷ *adj* **6** of high quality: *choice government jobs* **7** carefully chosen: *a few choice words* **8** vulgar: *choice language* [Old French *choisir* to choose]

choir *n* **1** an organized group of singers, usually for singing in church **2** the part of a church, in front of the altar, occupied by the choir [Latin *chorus*]

choirboy *n* a boy who sings in a church choir

Choiseul¹ *n* an island in the SW Pacific Ocean, in the Solomon Islands: hilly and densely forested. Area: 3885 sq km (1500 sq miles)

Choiseul² *n* Étienne François, Duc de. 1719–85, French statesman; foreign minister (1758–70)

choke *vb* **choking, choked** **1** to hinder or stop the breathing of (a person or animal) by strangling or smothering **2** to have trouble in breathing, swallowing, or speaking **3** to block or clog up: *the old narrow streets become choked to a standstill* **4** to hinder the growth of: *weeds would outgrow and choke the rice crop* ▷ *n* **5** a device in a vehicle's engine that enriches the petrol-air mixture by

reducing the air supply [Old English *ācēocian*]

choke back *vb* to suppress (tears or anger)

choked *adj informal* disappointed or angry: *I still feel choked about him leaving*

choker *n* a tight-fitting necklace

choke up *vb* **1** to block completely **2** **choked up** *informal* overcome with emotion

choko *n, pl* **-kos** *Austral and NZ* the pear-shaped fruit of a tropical American vine, eaten as a vegetable [Brazilian Indian]

choler (kol-ler) *n archaic* anger or bad temper [Greek *kholē* bile]

cholera (kol-ler-a) *n* a serious infectious disease causing severe diarrhoea and stomach cramps, caught from contaminated water or food [Greek *kholē* bile]

choleric *adj* bad-tempered

cholesterol (kol-**lest**-er-oll) *n* a fatty alcohol found in all animal fats, tissues, and fluids, an excess of which is thought to contribute to heart and artery disease [Greek *kholē* bile + *stereos* solid]

Cholon *n* a city in S Vietnam: a suburb of Ho Chi Minh City

Cholula *n* a town in S Mexico, in Puebla state: ancient ruins, notably a pyramid, 53 m (177 ft) high. Pop: 82 964 (2005)

Chomolungma *or* **Chomolangma** *n* a Chinese name for (Mount) **Everest**

chomp *vb* to chew (food) noisily

Chomsky *n* (Avram) Noam. born 1928, US linguist and political critic. His theory of language structure, transformational generative grammar, superseded the behaviourist view of Leonard Bloomfield **>** **Chomskyan** *or* **Chomskyite** *n, adj*

Chǒngjin *or* **Chungjin** *n* a port in E North Korea, on the Sea of Japan (East Sea). Pop: 603 000 (2005 est)

Chongqing, Chungking *or* **Ch'ung-ch'ing** *n* a river port in SW China, capital of Chongqing municipality (traditionally in Sichuan province) at the confluence of the Yangtze and Jialing rivers: site of a city since the 3rd millennium BC; wartime capital of China (1938–45); major trade centre for W China. Pop: 4 975 000 (2005 est) Former name: **Pahsien**

Chǒnju *n* a city in SW South Korea: centre of large rice-growing region. Pop: 643 000 (2005 est)

chook *n informal, chiefly Austral and NZ* a hen or chicken

choose *vb* **choosing, chose, chosen** **1** to select (a person, thing, or course of action) from a number of alternatives **2** to like or please: *when she did choose to reveal her secret, the group were initially hushed* **3** to consider it desirable or proper: *I don't choose to read that sort of book* [Old English *ceosan*]

choosy *adj* **choosier, choosiest** *informal* fussy; hard to please

chop¹ *vb* **chopping, chopped** **1** (often foll. by *down* or *off*) to cut (something) with a blow from an axe or other sharp tool **2** to cut into pieces **3** *boxing, karate* to hit (an opponent) with a short sharp blow **4** *Brit, Austral and NZ informal* to dispense with or reduce **5** *sport* to hit (a ball) sharply downwards ▷ *n* **6** a cutting blow **7** a slice of mutton, lamb, or pork, usually including a rib **8** *sport* a sharp downward blow or stroke **9** **the chop** *slang* dismissal from employment [variant of *chap:* see CHAPPED]

chop² *vb* **chopping, chopped** **1** **chop and change** to change one's mind repeatedly **2** **chop logic** to use excessively subtle or involved argument [Old English *ceapian* to barter]

chop chop *adv slang* quickly

Chopin *n* Frédéric (François) (frederik). 1810–49, Polish composer and pianist active in France, who wrote chiefly for the piano: noted for his harmonic imagination and his lyrical and melancholy qualities

chopper *n* **1** *informal* a helicopter **2** *chiefly Brit* a small hand axe **3** a butcher's cleaver **4** a type of bicycle or motorcycle with very high handlebars **5** NZ a child's bicycle

hoppy *adj* **-pier, -piest** (of the sea) fairly rough ▷ **choppiness** *n*

hops *pl n Brit, Austral and NZ informal* **1** the jaws or cheeks **2 lick one's chops** to anticipate something with pleasure [origin unknown]

hopsticks *pl n* a pair of thin sticks of ivory, wood, or plastic, used for eating Chinese or other East Asian food [pidgin English, from Chinese]

hop suey *n* a Chinese-style dish of chopped meat, bean sprouts, and other vegetables in a sauce [Chinese *tsap sui* odds and ends]

horal *adj* of or for a choir

horale (kor-rahl) *n* **1** a slow stately hymn tune **2** *chiefly US* a choir or chorus [German *Choralgesang* choral song]

hord[1] *n* **1** *maths* a straight line connecting two points on a curve **2** *anatomy* same as **cord 3 strike** *or* **touch a chord** to bring about an emotional response, usually of sympathy [Greek *khordē* string]

hord[2] *n* the simultaneous sounding of three or more musical notes [short for *accord*]

hordate *n* any animal that has a long fibrous rod just above the gut to support the body, such as the vertebrates

hore *n* **1** a small routine task **2** an unpleasant task [Old English *cerr* a turn of work]

horea (kor-ree-a) *n* a disorder of the nervous system characterized by uncontrollable brief jerky movements [Greek *khoreia* dance]

horeograph *vb* to compose the steps and dances for (a piece of music or ballet)

horeography *n* **1** the composition of steps and movements for ballet and other dancing **2** the steps and movements of a ballet or dance [Greek *khoreia* dance + -GRAPHY] ▷ **choreographer** *n* ▷ **choreographic** *adj*

horister *n* a singer in a church choir

horley *n* a town in NW England, in S Lancashire: cotton textiles. Pop: 33 424 (2001)

hortle *vb* **-tling, -tled 1** to chuckle with amusement ▷ *n* **2** an amused chuckle [coined by Lewis Carroll]

horus *n, pl* **-ruses 1** a large choir **2** a piece of music to be sung by a large choir **3** a part of a song repeated after each verse **4** something expressed by many people at once: *a chorus of boos* **5** the noise made by a group of birds or small animals: *the dawn chorus* **6** a group of singers or dancers who perform together in a show **7** (in ancient Greece) a group of actors who commented on the action of a play **8** (in Elizabethan drama) the actor who spoke the prologue and epilogue **9 in chorus** in unison ▷ *vb* **10** to sing or say together [Greek *khoros*]

horus girl *n* a young woman who dances or sings in the chorus of a show or film

horzów *n* an industrial city in SW Poland: under German administration from 1794 to 1921. Pop: 113 739 (2007 est). German name: **Königshütte**

hose *vb* the past tense of **choose**

hosen *vb* **1** the past participle of **choose** ▷ *adj* **2** selected for some special quality: *the chosen one*

hosen *n* the official name for Korea when it was a Japanese province (1910–45)

hosŏn *n* the Korean name for **North Korea**

hota Nagpur *n* a plateau in E India, mainly in Jharkhand state since 2000: forested, with rich mineral resources and much heavy industry; produces chiefly lac (world's leading supplier), coal (half India's total output), and mica

hou En-lai *or* **Zhou En Lai** *n* 1898–1976, Chinese Communist statesman; foreign minister of the People's Republic of China (1949–58) and premier (1949–76)

hough (chuff) *n* a large black bird of the crow family [origin unknown]

houx pastry (shoo) *n* a very light pastry made with eggs [French *pâte choux* cabbage dough]

chow *n* **1** a thick-coated dog with a curled tail, originally from China **2** *informal* food [pidgin English]

chowder *n* a thick soup containing clams or fish [French *chaudière* kettle]

chow mein *n* a Chinese-American dish consisting of chopped meat or vegetables fried with noodles [from Chinese]

Chrétien *n* (**Joseph Jacques**) **Jean**. born 1934, Canadian Liberal politician; prime minister of Canada (1993–2003)

Chrétien de Troyes *n* 12th century, French poet, who wrote the five Arthurian romances *Erec; Cligès; Lancelot, le chevalier de la charette; Yvain, le chevalier au lion*; and *Perceval, le conte del Graal* (?1155–?1190), the first courtly romances

chrism *n* consecrated oil used for anointing in some churches [Greek *khriein* to anoint]

Christ *n* **1** Jesus of Nazareth (Jesus Christ), regarded by Christians as the Messiah of Old Testament prophecies **2** the Messiah of Old Testament prophecies **3** an image or picture of Christ ▷ *interj* **4** *taboo, slang* an oath expressing annoyance or surprise [Greek *khristos* anointed one]

Christchurch *n* **1** a city in New Zealand, on E South Island: manufacturing centre of a rich agricultural region; suffered major damage and loss of life in a series of earthquakes in 2010–11. Pop: 366 000 (2013 est) **2** a town and resort in S England, in SE Dorset. Pop: 47 900 (2011)

christen *vb* **1** same as **baptize 2** to give a name to (a person or thing) **3** *informal* to use for the first time [Old English *cristnian*] ▷ **christening** *n*

Christendom *n* all Christian people or countries

Christian[1] *n* **1** a person who believes in and follows Jesus Christ **2** *informal* a person who displays the virtues of kindness and mercy encouraged in the teachings of Jesus Christ ▷ *adj* **3** of Jesus Christ, Christians, or Christianity **4** kind or good

Christian[2] *n* **Charlie**. 1919–42, US jazz guitarist

Christian IV *n* 1577–1648, king of Denmark and Norway (1588–1648): defeated in the Thirty Years' War (1629) and by Sweden (1645)

Christian X *n* 1890–1947, king of Denmark (1912–47) and Iceland (1918–44)

Christian Era *n* the period beginning with the year of Christ's birth

Christiania *n* a former name (1624–1877) of **Oslo**

Christianity *n* **1** the religion based on the life and teachings of Christ **2** Christian beliefs or practices **3** same as **Christendom**

Christianize *or* **-ise** *vb* **-izing, -ized** *or* **-ising, -ised 1** to convert to Christianity **2** to fill with Christian principles, spirit, or outlook ▷ **Christianization** *or* **-isation** *n*

Christian name *n* a personal name formally given to Christians at baptism: loosely used to mean a person's first name

Christiansand *n* a variant spelling of **Kristiansand**

Christian Science *n* the religious system founded by Mary Baker Eddy (1866), which emphasizes spiritual regeneration and healing through prayer ▷ **Christian Scientist** *n*

Christie *n* **1** Dame **Agatha** (**Mary Clarissa**). 1890–1976, British author of detective stories, many featuring Hercule Poirot, and several plays, including *The Mousetrap* (1952) **2** **John** (**Reginald Halliday**). 1898–1953, British murderer. His trial influenced legislation regarding the death penalty after he was found guilty of a murder for which Timothy Evans had been hanged **3** **Linford**. born 1960, British athlete: Commonwealth (1990), Olympic (1992), World (1993), and European (1994) 100 metres gold medallist **4** **William** (**Lincoln**). born 1944, French harpsichord player, organist, and conductor, born in the US; founder (1979) and director of the early-music group Les Arts Florissants

Christina *n* 1626–89, queen of Sweden (1632–54),

daughter of Gustavus Adolphus, noted particularly for her patronage of literature

Christine de Pisan *n* ?1364–?1430, French poet and prose writer, born in Venice. Her works include ballads, rondeaux, lays, and a biography of Charles V of France

Christmas *n* **1 a** *Christianity* a festival commemorating the birth of Christ, held by most Churches to have occurred on December 25 **b** Also: **Christmas Day** December 25, as a day of secular celebrations when gifts and greetings are exchanged ▷ *adj* **2** connected with or taking place at the time of year when this festival is celebrated: *the Christmas holidays* [Old English *Cristes mæsse* Mass of Christ] ➤ **Christmassy** *adj*

Christmas box *n* a tip or present given at Christmas, esp. to postmen or tradesmen

Christmas Eve *n* the evening or the whole day before Christmas Day

Christmas Island *n* **1** the former name (until 1981) of **Kiritimati 2** an island in the Indian Ocean, south of Java: administered by Singapore (1900–58), now by Australia; phosphate mining. Pop: 1496 (2013 est). Area: 135 sq km (52 sq miles)

Christmas pudding *n* *Brit and Austral* a rich steamed pudding containing suet, dried fruit, and spices

Christmas rose *n* an evergreen plant with white or pink winter-blooming flowers

Christmas tree *n* an evergreen tree or an imitation of one, decorated as part of Christmas celebrations

Christo *n* full name **Christo Javacheff**. born 1935, US artist, born in Bulgaria; best known for works in which he wraps buildings, monuments, or natural features in canvas or plastic

Christoff *n* Boris. 1919–93, Bulgarian bass-baritone, noted esp. for his performance in the title role of Mussorgsky's *Boris Godunov*

Christophe *n* Henri. 1767–1820, Haitian revolutionary leader; king of Haiti (1811–20)

Christopher *n* Saint. 3rd century AD, Christian martyr; patron saint of travellers

chromate *n* *chem* any salt or ester of chromic acid

chromatic *adj* **1** of or in colour or colours **2** *music* **a** involving the sharpening or flattening of notes or the use of such notes **b** of the chromatic scale [Greek *khrōma* colour] ➤ **chromatically** *adv*

chromatics *n* the science of colour

chromatic scale *n* a twelve-note scale including all the semitones of the octave

chromatin *n* *biochem* the part of the nucleus of a cell that forms the chromosomes and can easily be dyed [from *chrome*]

chromatography *n* the technique of separating and analysing the components of a mixture of liquids or gases by slowly passing it through an adsorbing material [Greek *khrōma* colour + -GRAPHY]

chrome *n* **1** same as **chromium 2** anything plated with chromium ▷ *vb* **chroming, chromed 3** to plate with chromium [Greek *khrōma* colour]

chromite *n* a brownish-black mineral which is the only commercial source of chromium

chromium *n* *chem* a hard grey metallic element, used in steel alloys and electroplating to increase hardness and corrosion resistance. Symbol: **Cr** [from *chrome*]

chromosome *n* any of the microscopic rod-shaped structures that appear in a cell nucleus during cell division, consisting of units (genes) that are responsible for the transmission of hereditary characteristics [Greek *khrōma* colour + *sōma* body]

chromosphere *n* a gaseous layer of the sun's atmosphere extending from the photosphere to the corona

chronic *adj* **1** (of a disease) developing slowly or lasting for a long time **2** (of a bad habit or bad behaviour) having continued for a long time; habitual: *chronic drug addiction* **3** very serious or severe: *chronic food shortages*

4 *Brit, Austral and NZ informal* very bad: *the play was chronic* [Greek *khronos* time] ➤ **chronically** *adv*

chronic fatigue syndrome *n* a condition characterized by painful muscles and general weakness sometimes persisting long after a viral illness

chronicle *n* **1** a record of events in chronological order ▷ *vb* **-cling, -cled 2** to record in or as if in a chronicle [Greek *khronika* annals] ➤ **chronicler** *n*

chronological *adj* **1** (of a sequence of events) arranged in order of occurrence **2** relating to chronology ➤ **chronologically** *adv*

chronology *n, pl* **-gies 1** the arrangement of dates or events in order of occurrence **2** the determining of the proper sequence of past events **3** a table of events arranged in order of occurrence [Greek *khronos* time + -LOGY] ➤ **chronologist** *n*

chronometer *n* a timepiece designed to be accurate in all conditions [Greek *khronos* time + -METER]

chrysalis (kriss-a-liss) *n* an insect in the stage between larva and adult, when it is in a cocoon [Greek *khrusos* gold]

chrysanthemum *n* a garden plant with large round flowers made up of many petals [Greek *khrusos* gold + *anthemon* flower]

Chrysostom *n* Saint John. ?345–407 AD, Greek patriarch: archbishop of Constantinople (398–404). Feast day: Sep 13 or Nov 13

chub *n, pl* **chub** or **chubs** a common freshwater game fish of the carp family with a dark greenish body [origin unknown]

chubby *adj* **-bier, -biest** plump and round [perhaps from *chub*] ➤ **chubbiness** *n*

Chu Chiang *n* a variant transliteration of the Chinese name for the **Zhu Jiang**

chuck¹ *vb* **1** *informal* to throw carelessly **2** *informal* (sometimes foll. by *in* or *up*) to give up; reject: *he chucked in his job* **3** to pat (someone) affectionately under the chin **4** *Austral and NZ informal* to vomit ▷ *n* **5** a throw or toss **6** a pat under the chin ▶ See also **chuck off, chuck out** [origin unknown]

chuck² *n* **1** Also: **chuck steak** a cut of beef from the neck to the shoulder blade **2** a device that holds a workpiece in a lathe or a tool in a drill [variant of *chock*]

chuck³ *n* *W Canad* **1** a large body of water **2** Also: **saltchuck** the sea [Chinook]

chuckle *vb* **-ling, -led 1** to laugh softly or to oneself ▷ *n* **2** a partly suppressed laugh [probably from *chuck* cluck]

chuck off *vb* (often foll. by *at*) *Austral and NZ informal* to abuse or make fun of

chuck out *vb* *informal* to throw out

chuddies *pl n* *Indian informal* underpants

Chudskoye Ozero *n* the Russian name for Lake **Peipus**

chuff *vb* to move while making a puffing sound, as a steam engine [imitative]

chuffed *adj* *informal* pleased or delighted: *I suppose you're feeling pretty chuffed* [origin unknown]

chug *n* **1** a short dull sound like the noise of an engine ▷ *vb* **chugging, chugged 2** (esp. of an engine) to operate or move with this sound: *lorries chug past* [imitative]

Chukchi Peninsula *n* a peninsula in the extreme NE of Russia, in NE Siberia: mainly tundra. Also called: **Chukot Peninsula**

Chukchi Sea *n* part of the Arctic Ocean, north of the Bering Strait between Asia and North America. Russian name: **Chukotskoye More**. Also called: **Chukot Sea**

Chu Kiang *n* a variant transliteration of the Chinese name for the **Zhu Jiang**

chukka or **chukker** *n* *polo* a period of continuous play, usually 7½ minutes [Hindi *cakkar*]

chum *n* **1** *informal* a close friend ▷ *vb* **chumming, chummed 2 chum up with** to form a close friendship with [probably from *chamber fellow*]

chummy *adj* **-mier, -miest** *informal* friendly ➤ **chummily** *adv* ➤ **chumminess** *n*

chump n 1 informal a stupid person 2 a thick piece of meat 3 a thick block of wood 4 off one's chump Brit slang crazy [origin unknown]

chunder slang, chiefly Austral vb 1 to vomit ▷ n 2 vomit [origin unknown]

chungjin n a variant spelling of **Chŏngjin**

chungking or **Ch'ung-ch'ing** n a variant transliteration of the Chinese name for **Chongqing**

chunk n 1 a thick solid piece of something 2 a considerable amount [variant of CHUCK²]

chunky adj chunkier, chunkiest 1 thick and short 2 containing thick pieces 3 chiefly Brit (of clothes, esp. knitwear) made of thick bulky material ➤ **chunkiness** n

chuquisaca n the former name (until 1839) of **Sucre**

chur n a city in E Switzerland, capital of Graubünden canton. Pop: 32 989 (2000). Ancient name: **Curia Rhaetorum**. French name: **Coire**

church n 1 a building for public Christian worship 2 religious services held in a church 3 a particular Christian denomination 4 Christians collectively 5 the clergy as distinguished from the laity 6 Church institutional religion as a political or social force: conflict between Church and State [Greek kuriakon (dōma) the Lord's (house)]

churchgoer n a person who attends church regularly

churchill¹ n 1 a river in E Canada, rising in SE Labrador and flowing north and southeast over Churchill Falls, then east to the Atlantic. Length: about 1000 km (600 miles). Former name: **Hamilton River** 2 a river in central Canada, rising in NW Saskatchewan and flowing east through several lakes to Hudson Bay. Length: about 1600 km (1000 miles)

churchill² n 1 **Caryl**. born 1938, British playwright; her plays include Cloud Nine (1978), Top Girls (1982), Serious Money (1987), and Far Away (2000) 2 **Charles**. 1731–64, British poet, noted for his polemical satires. His works include The Rosciad (1761) and The Prophecy of Famine (1763) 3 **John**. See (1st Duke of) **Marlborough** 4 **Lord Randolph**. 1849–95, British Conservative politician: secretary of state for India (1885–86) and chancellor of the Exchequer and leader of the House of Commons (1886) 5 his son, **Sir Winston (Leonard Spencer)**. 1874–1965, British Conservative statesman, orator, and writer, noted for his leadership during World War II. He held various posts under both Conservative and Liberal governments, including 1st Lord of the Admiralty (1911–15), before becoming prime minister (1940–45; 1951–55). His writings include The World Crisis (1923–29), Marlborough (1933–38), The Second World War (1948–54), and History of the English-Speaking Peoples (1956–58): Nobel prize for literature 1953

churchill Falls pl n a waterfall in E Canada, in SW Labrador on the Churchill River: site of one of the largest hydroelectric power projects in the world. Height: 75 m (245 ft). Former name (until 1965): **Grand Falls**

churchman n, pl -men a clergyman

church of England n the reformed established state Church in England, with the sovereign as its temporal head

church of Scotland n the established Presbyterian church in Scotland

churchwarden n 1 Church of England, Episcopal Church a lay assistant of a parish priest 2 an old-fashioned long-stemmed tobacco pipe made of clay

churchyard n the grounds round a church, used as a graveyard

churl n 1 a surly ill-bred person 2 archaic a farm labourer [Old English ceorl]

churlish adj surly and rude

churn n 1 a machine in which cream is shaken to make butter 2 a large container for milk ▷ vb 3 to stir (milk or cream) vigorously in order to make butter 4 to move about violently: a hot tub of churning water [Old English ciern]

churn out vb informal to produce (something) rapidly and in large numbers

chute¹ (shoot) n a steep sloping channel or passage down which things may be dropped [Old French cheoite fallen]

chute² n informal short for **parachute**

Chu Teh or **Zhu De** n 1886–1976, Chinese military leader and politician; he became commander in chief of the Red Army (1931) and was chairman of the Standing Committee of the National People's Congress of the People's Republic of China (1959–76)

chutney n a pickle of Indian origin, made from fruit, vinegar, spices, and sugar: mango chutney [Hindi catni]

chutzpah (hoots-pa) n informal unashamed self-confidence; impudence [Yiddish]

Chuvash Republic n a constituent republic of W central Russia, in the middle Volga valley: generally low-lying with undulating plains and large areas of forest. Capital: Cheboksary. Pop: 1 313 900 (2002). Area: 18 300 sq km (7064 sq miles). Also called: **Chuvashia**

Chu Xi or **Chu Hsi** n 1130–1200, Chinese philosopher, known for his neo-Confucian commentaries, the Ssu shu or Four Books

chyle n a milky fluid formed in the small intestine during digestion [Greek khulos juice]

chyme n the thick fluid mass of partially digested food that leaves the stomach [Greek khumos juice]

chypre (sheep-ra) n a perfume made from sandalwood [French: Cyprus]

Ci curie

CI Channel Islands

CIA Central Intelligence Agency; a US bureau responsible for espionage and intelligence activities

ciabatta (cha-bat-ta) n a type of bread made with olive oil [Italian: slipper]

Ciano n **Galeazzo**, full name Conte Galeazzo Ciano di Cortellazzo. 1903–44, Italian fascist politician; minister of foreign affairs (1936–43) and son-in-law of Mussolini, whose supporters shot him

Cibber n **Colley**. 1671–1757, English actor and dramatist; poet laureate (1730–57)

cicada (sik-kah-da) n a large broad insect, found in hot countries, that makes a high-pitched drone [Latin]

cicatrix (sik-a-trix) n, pl **cicatrices** (sik-a-trice-eez) the tissue that forms in a wound during healing; scar [Latin: scar]

Cicero n **Marcus Tullius**. 106–43 BC, Roman consul, orator, and writer. He foiled Catiline's conspiracy (63) and was killed by Mark Antony's agents after he denounced Antony in the Philippics. His writings are regarded as a model of Latin prose. Formerly known in English as: **Tully**

cicerone (siss-a-rone-ee) n, pl -nes or -ni literary a person who guides and informs sightseers [after CICERO]

Cid n **El** or **the**. original name Rodrigo Díaz de Vivar. ?1043–99, Spanish soldier and hero of the wars against the Moors

CID (in Britain) Criminal Investigation Department; the detective division of a police force

cider n an alcoholic drink made from fermented apple juice [Hebrew shēkhār strong drink]

Cienfuegos n a port in S Cuba, on Cienfuegos Bay. Pop: 147 000 (2005 est)

cigar n a tube-like roll of cured tobacco leaves for smoking [Spanish cigarro]

cigarette n a thin roll of shredded tobacco in thin paper, for smoking [French: a little cigar]

ciggie n informal short for **cigarette**

cilantro (sil-lan-tro) n chiefly US and Canad a European plant, cultivated for its aromatic seeds and leaves, used in flavouring foods. Also called: **coriander** [Spanish]

Cilicia n an ancient region and former kingdom of SE Asia Minor, between the Taurus Mountains and the Mediterranean: corresponds to the region around present-day Adana

C

Cilician *adj* **1** of or relating to Cilicia or its inhabitants ▷ *n* **2** a native or inhabitant of Cilicia

Cilician Gates *pl n* a pass in S Turkey, over the Taurus Mountains. Turkish name: **Gülek Bogaz**

cilium *n, pl* **cilia** *biology* **1** any of the short threads projecting from a cell or organism, whose rhythmic beating causes movement **2** an eyelash [Latin] **> ciliary** *adj*

Çiller *n* Tansu. born 1945, Turkish politician; first female prime minister (1993–96)

Cimabue *n* Giovanni. ?1240–?1302, Italian painter of the Florentine school, who anticipated the movement, led by Giotto, away from the Byzantine tradition in art towards a greater naturalism

Cimarosa *n* Domenico. 1749–1801, Italian composer, chiefly remembered for his opera buffa *The Secret Marriage* (1792)

Cimon *n* died 449 BC, Athenian military and naval commander: defeated the Persians at Eurymedon (?466)

C in C *military* Commander in Chief

cinch (**sinch**) *n* **1** *informal* an easy task **2** *slang* a certainty [Spanish *cincha* saddle girth]

cinchona (sing-**kone**-a) *n* **1** a South American tree or shrub with medicinal bark **2** its dried bark which yields quinine **3** a drug made from cinchona bark [after the Countess of *Chinchón*]

Cincinnati *n* a city in SW Ohio, on the Ohio River. Pop: 317 361 (2003 est)

Cincinnatus *n* Lucius Quinctius. ?519–438 BC, Roman general and statesman, regarded as a model of simple virtue; dictator of Rome during two crises (458; 439), retiring to his farm after each one

cincture *n* *literary* something, such as a belt or girdle, that goes around another thing [Latin *cingere* to gird]

cinder *n* **1** a piece of material that will not burn, left after burning coal or wood **2** cinders ashes [Old English *sinder*]

Cinderella *n* a poor, neglected, or unsuccessful person or thing [after *Cinderella*, the heroine of a fairy tale]

cine camera *n* a camera for taking moving pictures

cinema *n* **1** a place designed for showing films **2** the cinema **a** the art or business of making films **b** films collectively [shortened from *cinematograph*] **> cinematic** *adj*

cinematograph *n* *chiefly Brit* a combined camera, printer, and projector [Greek *kinēma* motion + -GRAPH] **> cinematographer** *n* **> cinematographic** *adj*

cinematography *n* the technique of making films: *he won an Oscar for his stunning cinematography*

cineraria *n* a garden plant with daisy-like flowers [Latin *cinis* ashes]

cinerarium *n, pl* **-raria** a place for keeping the ashes of the dead after cremation [Latin *cinerarius* relating to ashes] **> cinerary** *adj*

Cinna *n* Lucius Cornelius. died 84 BC, Roman patrician; an opponent of Sulla

cinnabar *n* **1** a heavy red mineral containing mercury **2** a large red-and-black European moth [Greek *kinnabari*]

cinnamon *n* the spice obtained from the aromatic bark of a tropical Asian tree [Hebrew *qinnamown*]

cinquefoil *n* **1** a plant with five-lobed compound leaves **2** an ornamental carving in the form of five arcs arranged in a circle [Latin *quinquefolium* plant with five leaves]

Cinque Ports *pl n* an association of ports on the SE coast of England, with certain ancient duties and privileges

Cintra *n* the former name for **Sintra**

cipher *or* **cypher** (**sife**-er) *n* **1** a method of secret writing using substitution of letters according to a key **2** a secret message **3** the key to a secret message **4** a person or thing of no importance **5** *obsolete* the numeral zero ▷ *vb* **6** to put (a message) into secret writing [Arabic *sifr* zero]

circa (**sir**-ka) *prep* (used with a date) approximately; about: *circa 1788* [Latin]

circadian *adj* of biological processes that occur regularly at 24-hour intervals [Latin *circa* about + *dies* day]

Circassia *n* a region of S Russia, on the Black Sea north of the Caucasus Mountains

Circassian *n* **1** a native of Circassia **2** a language or languages spoken in Circassia, belonging to the North-West Caucasian family ▷ *adj also* **Circassic** **3** relating to Circassia, its people, or language

circle *n* **1** a curved line surrounding a central point, every point of the line being the same distance from the centre **2** the figure enclosed by such a curve **3** something formed or arranged in the shape of a circle: *they ran round in little circles* **4** a group of people sharing an interest, activity, or upbringing: *his judgment is well respected in diplomatic circles* **5** *theatre* the section of seats above the main level of the auditorium **6** a process or chain of events or parts that forms a connected whole; cycle **7 come full circle** to arrive back at one's starting point ▷ *vb* **-cling, -cled 8** to move in a circle (around) **9** to enclose in a circle [Latin *circus*]

circlet *n* a small circle or ring, esp. a circular ornament worn on the head [Old French *cerclet* little circle]

circuit *n* **1** a complete route or course, esp. one that is circular or that lies around an object **2** a complete path through which an electric current can flow **3 a** a periodical journey around an area, as made by judges or salesmen **b** the places visited on such a journey **4** a motor-racing track **5** *sport* a series of tournaments in which the same players regularly take part: *the professional golf circuit* **6** a number of theatres or cinemas under one management [Latin *circum* around + *ire* to go]

circuit breaker *n* a device that stops the flow of current in an electrical circuit if there is a fault

circuitous (sir-**kew**-it-uss) *adj* indirect and lengthy: *a circuitous route*

circuitry (**sir**-kit-tree) *n* **1** the design of an electrical circuit **2** the system of circuits used in an electronic device

circular *adj* **1** of or in the shape of a circle **2** travelling in a circle **3** (of an argument) not valid because a statement is used to prove the conclusion and the conclusion to prove the statement **4** (of letters or announcements) intended for general distribution ▷ *n* **5** a letter or advertisement sent to a large number of people at the same time **> circularity** *n*

circularize *or* **-ise** *vb* **-izing, -ized** *or* **-ising, -ised** to distribute circulars to

circular saw *n* a power-driven saw in which a circular disc with a toothed edge is rotated at high speed

circulate *vb* **-lating, -lated 1** to send, go, or pass from place to place or person to person: *rumours were circulating that he was about to resign* **2** to move through a circuit or system, returning to the starting point: *regular exercise keeps the blood circulating around the body* **3** to move around the guests at a party, talking to different people: *it wasn't like her not to circulate among all the guests* [Latin *circulari*] **> circulatory** *adj*

circulation *n* **1** the flow of blood from the heart through the arteries, and then back through the veins to the heart, where the cycle is renewed **2** the number of copies of a newspaper or magazine that are sold **3** the distribution of newspapers or magazines **4** sending or moving around: *the circulation of air* **5 in circulation a** (of currency) being used by the public **b** (of people) active in a social or business context

circum- *prefix* around; on all sides: *circumlocution* [Latin]

circumcise *vb* **-cising, -cised 1** to remove the foreskin of (a male) **2** to cut or remove the clitoris of (a female) **3** to perform such an operation as a religious rite on (someone) [Latin CIRCUM- + *caedere* to cut] **> circumcision** *n*

circumference *n* **1** the boundary of a specific area or figure, esp. of a circle **2** the distance round this [Latin CIRCUM- + *ferre* to bear] **> circumferential** *adj*

circumflex *n* a mark (^) placed over a vowel to show tha it is pronounced in a particular way, for instance as a long vowel in French [Latin CIRCUM- + *flectere* to bend]

circumlocution *n* **1** an indirect way of saying something **2** an indirect expression **>** **circumlocutory** *adj*

circumnavigate *vb* **-gating, -gated** to sail, fly, or walk right around **>** **circumnavigation** *n*

circumscribe *vb* **-scribing, -scribed 1** *formal* to limit or restrict within certain boundaries: *the President's powers are circumscribed by the Constitution* **2** *geometry* to draw a geometric figure around (another figure) so that the two are in contact but do not intersect [Latin CIRCUM- + *scribere* to write] **>** **circumscription** *n*

circumspect *adj* cautious and careful not to take risks [Latin CIRCUM- + *specere* to look] **>** **circumspection** *n* **>** **circumspectly** *adv*

circumstance *n* **1** an occurrence or condition that accompanies or influences a person or event **2** unplanned events and situations which cannot be controlled: *a victim of circumstance* **3** pomp and circumstance formal display or ceremony **4** under *or* in no circumstances in no case; never **5** under the circumstances because of conditions [Latin CIRCUM- + *stare* to stand]

circumstantial *adj* **1** (of evidence) strongly suggesting something but not proving it **2** fully detailed

circumstantiate *vb* **-ating, -ated** to prove by giving details

circumvent *vb formal* **1** to avoid or get round (a rule, restriction, etc.) **2** to outwit (a person) [Latin CIRCUM- + *venire* to come] **>** **circumvention** *n*

circus *n, pl* **-cuses 1** a travelling company of entertainers such as acrobats, clowns, trapeze artists, and trained animals **2** a public performance given by such a company **3** *Brit* an open place in a town where several streets meet **4** *informal* a hectic or well-published situation: *her second marriage turned into a media circus* **5** (in ancient Rome) an open-air stadium for chariot races or public games **6** a travelling group of professional sportsmen: *the Formula One circus* [Greek *kirkos* ring]

Cirebon *n* a port in S central Indonesia, on N Java on the Java Sea: scene of the signing of the **Tjirebon Agreement** of Indonesian independence (1946) by the Netherlands. Pop: 272 263 (2000). Former spelling: **Tjirebon, Cheribon**

Cirenaica *n* a variant spelling of **Cyrenaica**

Cirencester *n* a market town in S England, in Gloucestershire: Roman amphitheatre. Pop: 15 861 (2001). Latin name: **Corinium**

cirque (**sirk**) *n* a steep-sided semicircular hollow found in mountainous areas

cirrhosis (sir-roh-siss) *n* a chronic progressive disease of the liver, often caused by drinking too much alcohol [Greek *kirrhos* orange-coloured]

cirrocumulus (sirr-oh-kew-myew-luss) *n, pl* **-li** (-lie) a high cloud of ice crystals grouped into small separate globular masses

cirrostratus (sirr-oh-strah-tuss) *n, pl* **-ti** (-tie) a uniform layer of cloud above about 6000 metres

cirrus *n, pl* **-ri 1** a thin wispy cloud found at high altitudes **2** a plant tendril **3** a slender tentacle in certain sea creatures [Latin: curl]

CIS Commonwealth of Independent States

cisalpine *adj* on this (the southern) side of the Alps, as viewed from Rome

Ciscaucasia *n* the part of Caucasia north of the Caucasus Mountains

cisco *n, pl* **-coes** *or* **-cos** a whitefish, esp. the lake herring of cold deep lakes of North America [from a Native American language]

Ciskei *n* (formerly) a Bantu homeland in SE South Africa; declared independent in 1981 but this was not recognized outside South Africa; abolished in 1993. Capital: Bisho (now Bhisho)

cissy *n, pl* **-sies**, *adj* same as **sissy**

Cistercian *n* **1** a Christian monk or nun belonging to an especially strict Benedictine order **▷** *adj* **2** of or relating to this order [*Cîteaux*, original home of the order]

cistern *n* **1** a water tank, esp. one which holds water for flushing a toilet **2** an underground reservoir [Latin *cista* box]

citadel *n* a fortress in a city [Latin *civitas*]

citation *n* **1** an official commendation or award, esp. for bravery **2** the quoting of a book or author **3** a quotation

cite *vb* **citing, cited 1** to quote or refer to (a passage, book, or author) **2** to bring forward as proof **3** to summon to appear before a court of law **4** to mention or commend (someone) for outstanding bravery **5** to enumerate: *the president cited the wonders of the American family* [Old French *citer* to summon]

citified *adj* *often disparaging* having the customs, manners, or dress of city people

citizen *n* **1** a native or naturalized member of a state or nation **2** an inhabitant of a city or town

citizenry *n* citizens collectively

Citizens' Band *n* a range of radio frequencies for use by the public for private communication

citizenship *n* the condition or status of a citizen, with its rights and duties

Citlaltépetl *n* a volcano in SE Mexico, in central Veracruz state: the highest peak in the country. Height: 5636 m (18 492 ft), though this is disputed between different sources. Spanish name: **Pico de Orizaba**

citrate *n* any salt or ester of citric acid

citric *adj* of or derived from citrus fruits or citric acid

citric acid *n* a weak acid found especially in citrus fruits and used as a flavouring (**E330**)

citron *n* **1** a lemon-like fruit of a small Asian tree **2** the candied rind of this fruit, for decorating foods [Latin *citrus* citrus tree]

citronella *n* **1** a tropical Asian grass with lemon-scented leaves **2** the aromatic oil obtained from this grass

citrus fruit *n* juicy, sharp-tasting fruit such as oranges, lemons, or limes [Latin *citrus* citrus tree]

Città del Vaticano *n* the Italian name for **Vatican City**

city *n, pl* **cities 1** any large town **2** (in Britain) a town that has received this title from the Crown **3** the people of a city collectively **4** (in the US and Canada) a large town with its own government established by charter from the state or provincial government [Latin *civis* citizen]

City *n* the City **1** short for **City of London**: the original settlement of London on the N bank of the Thames; a municipality governed by the Lord Mayor and Corporation. Resident pop: 7186 (2001) **2** the area in central London in which the United Kingdom's major financial business is transacted **3** the various financial institutions located in this area

city editor *n* **1** *Brit* (on a newspaper) the editor in charge of business news **2** *US and Canad* (on a newspaper) the editor in charge of local news

city-state *n history* a state consisting of a sovereign city and its dependencies

Ciudad Bolívar *n* a port in E Venezuela, on the Orinoco River: accessible to ocean-going vessels. Pop: 344 000 (2005 est). Former name (1764–1846): **Angostura**

Ciudad Guayana *n* an industrial conurbation in E Venezuela, on the River Orinoco: iron and steel processing, gold mining. Pop: 807 000 (2005 est). Former name: **Santo Tomé de Guayana**

Ciudad Juárez *n* a city in N Mexico, in Chihuahua state on the Río Grande, opposite El Paso, Texas. Pop: 1 469 000 (2005 est). Former name (until 1888): **El Paso del Norte**

Ciudad Real *n* a market town in S central Spain. Pop: 65 703 (2003 est)

Ciudad Trujillo *n* the former name (1936–61) of **Santo Domingo**

Ciudad Victoria *n* a city in E central Mexico, capital of Tamaulipas state. Pop: 285 000 (2005 est)

civet (siv-vit) *n* **1** a spotted catlike mammal of Africa and

S Asia **2** the musky fluid produced by this animal, used in perfumes [Arabic *zabād* civet perfume]

civic *adj* of a city or citizens > **civically** *adv*

civic centre *n Brit and NZ* a complex of public buildings, including recreational facilities and offices of local government

civics *n* the study of the rights and responsibilities of citizenship

civil *adj* **1** of or occurring within the state or between citizens: *civil unrest* **2** of or relating to the citizen as an individual: *civil rights* **3** not part of the military, legal, or religious structures of a country: *civil aviation* **4** polite or courteous: *he seemed very civil and listened politely* [Latin *civis* citizen] > **civilly** *adv*

civil defence *n* the organizing of civilians to deal with enemy attacks and natural disasters

civil disobedience *n* nonviolent protest, such as a refusal to obey laws or pay taxes

civil engineer *n* a person qualified to design and construct public works, such as roads or bridges > **civil engineering** *n*

civilian *n* **1** a person who is not a member of the armed forces or police ▷ *adj* **2** not relating to the armed forces or police: *civilian clothes*

civility *n*, *pl* **-ties 1** polite or courteous behaviour **2** civilities polite words or actions

civilization *or* **-lisation** *n* **1** the total culture and way of life of a particular people, nation, region, or period **2** a human society that has a complex cultural, political, and legal organization **3** the races collectively who have achieved such a state **4** cities or populated areas, as contrasted with sparsely inhabited areas **5** intellectual, cultural, and moral refinement

civilize *or* **-lise** *vb* **-lizing**, **-lized** *or* **-lising**, **-lised 1** to bring out of barbarism into a state of civilization **2** to refine, educate, or enlighten > **civilized** *or* **-lised** *adj*

civil law *n* **1** the law of a state, relating to private and civilian affairs **2** a system of law based on that of ancient Rome

civil liberties *pl n* a person's rights to freedom of speech and action

civil list *n* (in Britain) the annual amount given by Parliament to the royal household and the royal family

civil marriage *n law* a marriage performed by an official other than a clergyman

civil partnership *n* a legal union, similar to a marriage, between two people of the same sex

civil rights *pl n* the personal rights of the individual citizen to have equal treatment and equal opportunities

civil servant *n* a member of the civil service

civil service *n* the service responsible for the public administration of the government of a country

civil war *n* war between people of the same country

civvies *pl n Brit, Austral and NZ slang* civilian clothes as opposed to uniform

civvy street *n slang* civilian life

CJD Creutzfeldt-Jakob disease: a fatal virus disease that affects the central nervous system

cl centilitre

Cl *chem* chlorine

clack *n* **1** the sound made by two hard objects striking each other ▷ *vb* **2** to make this sound [imitative]

Clackmannan *n* a town in E central Scotland, in Clackmannanshire. Pop: 3450 (2001)

Clackmannanshire *n* a council area and historical county of central Scotland; became part of the Central region in 1975 but reinstated as an independent unitary authority in 1996; mainly agricultural. Administrative centre: Alloa. Pop: 47 680 (2003 est). Area: 142 sq km (55 sq miles)

Clacton *or* **Clacton-on-Sea** *n* a town and resort in SE England, in E Essex. Pop: 51 284 (2001)

clad *vb* a past participle of **clothe**

cladding *n* **1** the material used to cover the outside of a building **2** a protective metal coating attached to another metal [special use of CLAD]

cladistics *n* a method of grouping animals by measurable likenesses [Greek *klados* branch]

claim *vb* **1** to assert as a fact: *he had claimed to be too ill to return* **2** to demand as a right or as one's property: *you can claim housing benefit to help pay your rent* **3** to call for or need: *this problem claims our attention* **4** to cause the death of: *violence which has claimed at least fifty lives* **5** to succeed in obtaining; win: *she claimed her fifth European tour victory with a closing round of 64* ▷ *n* **6** an assertion of something as true or real **7** an assertion of a right; a demand for something as due **8** a right or just title to something: *a claim to fame* **9** anything that is claimed, such as a piece of land staked out by a miner **10 a** a demand for payment in connection with an insurance policy **b** the sum of money demanded [Latin *clamare* to shout] > **claimant** *n*

Clair *n* René, real name *René Chomette*. 1898–1981, French film director; noted for his comedies including *An Italian Straw Hat* (1928) and pioneering sound films such as *Sous les toits de Paris* (1930); later films include *Les Belles de nuit* (1952)

clairvoyance *n* the alleged power of perceiving things beyond the natural range of the senses [French: clear-seeing]

clairvoyant *n* **1** a person claiming to have the power to foretell future events ▷ *adj* **2** of or possessing clairvoyance

clam *n* an edible shellfish with a hinged shell. See also **clam up** [earlier *clamshell* shell that clamps]

clamber *vb* **1** to climb awkwardly, using hands and feet ▷ *n* **2** a climb performed in this manner [probably variant of *climb*]

clammy *adj* **-mier**, **-miest** unpleasantly moist and sticky [Old English *clǣman* to smear] > **clammily** *adv* > **clamminess** *n*

clamour *or US* **clamor** *n* **1** a loud protest **2** a loud and persistent noise or outcry ▷ *vb* **3** clamour for to demand noisily **4** to make a loud noise or outcry [Latin *clamare* to cry out] > **clamorous** *adj*

clamp¹ *n* **1** a mechanical device with movable jaws for holding things together tightly **2** See wheel clamp ▷ *vb* **3** to fix or fasten with a clamp **4** to immobilize (a car) by means of a wheel clamp [Dutch or Low German *klamp*]

clamp² *n* a mound of a harvested root crop, covered with straw and earth to protect it from winter weather [Middle Dutch *klamp* heap]

clamp down *vb* **1** clamp down on **a** to become stricter about **b** to suppress (something regarded as undesirable) ▷ *n* **clampdown 2** a sudden restriction placed on an activity

clam up *vb* **clamming**, **clammed** *informal* to keep or become silent

clan *n* **1** a group of families with a common surname and a common ancestor, esp. among Scottish Highlanders **2** an extended family related by ancestry or marriage: *America's leading political clan, the Kennedys* **3** a group of people with common characteristics, aims, or interests [Scottish Gaelic *clann*] > **clansman** *n*

Clancy *n* Tom. 1947–2013, US novelist; his thrillers, many of which have been filmed, include *The Hunt for Red October* (1984), *Clear and Present Danger* (1989), *Debt of Honour* (1994) and *Red Rabbit* (2002)

clandestine *adj formal* secret and concealed: *a base for clandestine activities* [Latin *clam* secretly] > **clandestinely** *adv*

clang *vb* **1** to make a loud ringing noise, as metal does when it is struck ▷ *n* **2** a ringing metallic noise [Latin *clangere*]

clanger *n* drop a clanger *informal* to make a very noticeable mistake

clangour *or US* **clangor** *n* a loud continuous clanging sound [Latin *clangor*] > **clangorous** *adj*

lank *n* **1** an abrupt harsh metallic sound ▷ *vb* **2** to make such a sound [imitative]

lannish *adj* (of a group) tending to exclude outsiders: *the villagers can be very clannish*

lap[1] *vb* **clapping, clapped 1** to applaud by striking the palms of one's hands sharply together **2** to place or put quickly or forcibly: *in former times he would have been clapped in irons or shot* **3** to strike (a person) lightly with an open hand as in greeting **4** to make a sharp abrupt sound like two objects being struck together **5 clap eyes on** *informal* to catch sight of ▷ *n* **6** the act or sound of clapping **7** a sharp abrupt sound, esp. of thunder **8** a light blow [Old English *clæppan*]

lap[2] *n slang* gonorrhoea [Old French *clapier* brothel]

apped out *adj informal* worn out; dilapidated

apper *n* **1** a small piece of metal hanging inside a bell, which causes it to sound when struck against the side **2 like the clappers** *Brit informal* extremely quickly: *he left, pedalling like the clappers*

apperboard *n* a pair of hinged boards clapped together during film shooting to help in synchronizing sound and picture

lapton *n* Eric. born 1945, British rock guitarist, noted for his virtuoso style, his work with the Yardbirds (1963–65), Cream (1966–68), and, with Derek and the Dominos, the album *Layla* (1970); later solo work includes *Unplugged* (1992)

aptrap *n informal* foolish or pretentious talk: *pseudo-intellectual claptrap*

aque *n formal* **1 a** a group of people hired to applaud **2** a group of fawning admirers [French *claquer* to clap]

lare[1] *n* a county of W Republic of Ireland, in Munster between Galway Bay and the Shannon estuary. County town: Ennis. Pop: 103 277 (2002). Area: 3188 sq km (1231 sq miles)

lare[2] *n* **1** Anthony (Ward). 1942–2007, Irish psychiatrist and broadcaster; presenter of the radio series *In the Psychiatrist's Chair* from 1982 **2** John. 1793–1864, English poet, noted for his descriptions of country life, particularly in *The Shepherd's Calendar* (1827) and *The Rural Muse* (1835). He was confined in a lunatic asylum from 1837

larendon[1] *n* a village near Salisbury in S England: site of a council held by Henry II in 1164 that produced a code of laws (the **Constitutions of Clarendon**) defining relations between church and state

larendon[2] *n* 1st Earl of, title of *Edward Hyde*. 1609–74, English statesman and historian; chief adviser to Charles II (1660–67); author of *History of the Rebellion and Civil Wars in England* (1704–07)

lare of Assisi *n* Saint. 1194–1253, Italian nun; founder of the Franciscan Order of Poor Clares. Feast day: Aug 11

aret (klar-rit) *n* **1 a** a dry red wine, esp. one from Bordeaux ▷ *adj* **2** purplish-red [Latin *clarus* clear]

arify *vb* **-fies, -fying, -fied 1** to make or become clear or easy to understand **2** to make or become free of impurities, esp. by heating: *clarified butter* [Latin *clarus* clear + *facere* to make] **> clarification** *n*

arinet *n* a keyed woodwind instrument with a single reed [French *clarinette*] **> clarinettist** *n*

arion *n* **1** an obsolete high-pitched trumpet **2** its sound [Latin *clarus* clear]

arion call *n* strong encouragement to do something

arity *n* clearness [Latin *claritas*]

ark *n* **1** Helen. born 1950, New Zealand Labour politician; prime minister (1999–2008); administrator of the United Nations Development Programme from 2009 **2** James, known as *Jim*. 1936–68, Scottish racing driver; Formula One World Champion (1963, 1965) **3** Kenneth, Baron Clark of Saltwood. 1903–83, English art historian: his books include *Civilization* (1969), which he first presented as a television series **4** William. 1770–1838, US explorer and frontiersman: best known for his expedition to the Pacific Northwest (1804–06) with Meriwether Lewis

Clarke *n* **1** Sir Arthur C(harles). 1917–2008, British science-fiction writer, who helped to develop the first communications satellites. He scripted the film *2001, A Space Odyssey* (1968) **2** Austin. 1896–1974, Irish poet and verse dramatist. His volumes include *The Vengeance of Fionn* (1917), *Night and Morning* (1938), and *Ancient Lights* (1955) **3** Jeremiah. ?1673-1707, English composer and organist, best known for his *Trumpet Voluntary*, formerly attributed to Purcell **4** Kenneth Harry. born 1940, British Conservative politician: secretary of state for health (1988-1990); secretary of state for education (1990–1992); home secretary (1992-93); chancellor of the exchequer (1993-97); secretary of state for justice and Lord Chancellor (2010–2012) **5** Marcus (Andrew Hislop). 1846–81, Australian novelist born in England, noted for his novel *For the Term of His Natural Life*, published in serial form (1870–72); other works include *Twixt Shadow and Shine* (1875) **6** Michael (John). born 1981, Australian cricketer; a batsman, he has played in over 100 test matches (from 2004), scored over 8000 test runs, and captained Australia to a World Cup win (2015)

Clarkson *n* Thomas. 1760–1846, British campaigner for the abolition of slavery

clash *vb* **1** to come into conflict **2** to be incompatible **3** (of dates or events) to coincide **4** (of colours or styles) to look ugly or incompatible together: *patterned fabrics which combine seemingly clashing shades to great effect* **5** to make a loud harsh sound, esp. by striking together ▷ *n* **6** a collision or conflict **7** a loud harsh noise [imitative]

clasp *n* **1** a fastening, such as a catch or hook, for holding things together **2** a firm grasp or embrace ▷ *vb* **3** to grasp or embrace tightly **4** to fasten together with a clasp [origin unknown]

clasp knife *n* a large knife with blades which fold into the handle

class *n* **1** a group of people sharing a similar social and economic position **2** the system of dividing society into such groups **3** a group of people or things sharing a common characteristic **4 a** a group of pupils or students who are taught together **b** a meeting of a group of students for tuition **5** a standard of quality or attainment: *second class* **6** *informal* excellence or elegance, esp. in dress, design, or behaviour: *a full-bodied red wine with real class* **7** *biology* one of the groups into which a phylum is divided, containing one or more orders **8 in a class of its own** *or* **in a class by oneself** without an equal for ability, talent, etc. ▷ *adj* **9** *informal* excellent, skilful, or stylish: *a class act* ▷ *vb* **10** to place in a class [Latin *classis* class, rank]

class-conscious *adj* aware of belonging to a particular social rank

classic *adj* **1** serving as a standard or model of its kind; typical: *it is a classic symptom of iron deficiency* **2** of lasting interest or significance because of excellence: *the classic work on Central America* **3** characterized by simplicity and purity of form: *a classic suit* ▷ *n* **4** an author, artist, or work of art of the highest excellence **5** a creation or work considered as definitive [Latin *classicus* of the first rank]

classical *adj* **1** of or in a restrained conservative style: *it had been built in the 18th century in a severely classical style* **2** *music* **a** in a style or from a period marked by stability of form, intellectualism, and restraint **b** denoting serious art or music in general **3** of or influenced by ancient Greek and Roman culture **4** of the form of a language historically used for formal and literary purposes: *classical Chinese* **5** (of an education) based on the humanities and the study of Latin and Greek **> classically** *adv*

classic car *n chiefly Brit* a car that is more than 25 years old

classicism *n* **1** an artistic style based on Greek and Roman models, showing emotional restraint and regularity of form **2** knowledge of the culture of ancient Greece and Rome **> classicist** *n*

C

C

classics *pl n* **1** the study of ancient Greek and Roman literature and culture **2 the classics a** those works of literature regarded as great or lasting **b** the ancient Greek and Latin languages

classification *n* **1** placing things systematically in categories **2** a division or category in a classifying system [French] **>** **classificatory** *adj*

classified *adj* **1** arranged according to some system of classification **2** *government* (of information) not available to people outside a restricted group, esp. for reasons of national security

classify *vb* **-fies, -fying, -fied** **1** to arrange or order by classes **2** *government* to declare (information) to be officially secret **>** **classifiable** *adj*

classless *adj* **1** not belonging to a class **2** distinguished by the absence of economic or social distinctions: *a classless society*

classmate *n* a friend or contemporary in the same class of a school

classroom *n* a room in a school where lessons take place

classy *adj* **classier, classiest** *informal* stylish and sophisticated **>** **classiness** *n*

clatter *vb* **1** to make a rattling noise, as when hard objects hit each other ▷ *n* **2** a rattling sound or noise [Old English *clatrung* clattering]

Claude *n* Albert. 1898–1983, US cell biologist, born in Belgium: shared the Nobel prize for physiology or medicine (1974) for work on microsomes and mitochondria

Claudel *n* Paul (**Louis Charles Marie**). 1868–1955, French dramatist, poet, and diplomat, whose works testify to his commitment to the Roman Catholic faith. His plays include *L'Annonce faite à Marie* (1912) and *Le Soulier de satin* (1919–24)

Claude Lorrain *n* real name *Claude Gelée*. 1600–82, French painter, esp. of idealized landscapes, noted for his subtle depiction of light

Claudius *n* full name *Tiberius Claudius Drusus Nero Germanicus*. 10 BC–54 AD, Roman emperor (41–54); invaded Britain (43); poisoned by his fourth wife, Agrippina

Claudius II *n* full name *Marcus Aurelius Claudius*, called *Gothicus*. 214–270 AD, Roman emperor (268–270)

clause *n* **1** a section of a legal document such as a will or contract **2** *grammar* a group of words, consisting of a subject and a predicate including a finite verb, that does not necessarily constitute a sentence [Latin *clausula* conclusion] **>** **clausal** *adj*

Clausewitz *n* Karl von. 1780–1831, Prussian general, noted for his works on military strategy, esp. *Vom Kriege* (1833)

Clausius *n* Rudolf Julius. 1822–88, German physicist and mathematician. He enunciated the second law of thermodynamics (1850) and developed the kinetic theory of gases

claustrophobia *n* an abnormal fear of being in a confined space [Latin *claustrum* cloister + -PHOBIA] **>** **claustrophobic** *adj*

clavichord *n* an early keyboard instrument with a very soft tone [Latin *clavis* key + *chorda* string]

clavicle *n* either of the two bones connecting the shoulder blades with the upper part of the breastbone; the collarbone [Latin *clavis* key]

claw *n* **1** a curved pointed nail on the foot of birds, some reptiles, and certain mammals **2** a similar part in some invertebrates, such as a crab's pincer ▷ *vb* **3** to scrape, tear, or dig with claws or nails: *she clawed his face with her fingernails* **4** to achieve (something) only after overcoming great difficulties: *he clawed his way to power and wealth*; *settlers attempting to claw a living from the desert* [Old English *clawu*]

claw back *vb* **1** to get back (something) with difficulty **2** to recover (a part of a grant or allowance) in the form of a tax or financial penalty

clay *n* **1** a very fine-grained earth, soft when moist and

hardening when baked, used to make bricks and potter▪ **2** earth or mud **3** *poetic* the material of the human body [Old English *clæg*] **>** **clayey, clayish** or **claylike** *adj*

Clay *n* **1** Cassius. See Muhammad Ali **2** Henry. 1777–1852, US statesman and orator; secretary of state (1825–29)

claymore *n* a large two-edged broadsword used formerly by Scottish Highlanders [Gaelic *claidheamh mōr* great sword]

clay pigeon *n* a disc of baked clay hurled into the air from a machine as a target for shooting

Clayton's *adj* *Austral* and *NZ informal* acting as an imitation or substitute: *this latest ploy is simply a Clayton's resignation* [from the trademark of a non-alcoholic drink marketed as 'the drink you have when you're not havir▪ a drink']

CLC Canadian Labour Congress

clean *adj* **1** free from dirt or impurities: *clean water* **2** habitually hygienic and neat **3** morally sound: *clean living* **4** without objectionable language or obscenity: *good clean fun* **5** without anything in it or on it: *a clean she* *of paper* **6** causing little contamination or pollution: *rape▪ seed oil may provide a clean alternative to petrol* **7** recently washed; fresh **8** thorough or complete: *a clean break with the past* **9** skilful and done without fumbling; dexterous: *a clean catch* **10** *sport* played fairly and without fouls **11** free from dishonesty or corruption: *clean government* **12** simple and streamlined in design: *the clean lines and colourful simplicity of these ceramics* **13** (esp. of a driving licence) showing or having no record of offences **14** *slan* **a** innocent **b** not carrying illegal drugs, weapons, etc. ▷ *vb* **15** to make or become free of dirt: *he wanted to help me clean the room* ▷ *adv* **16** in a clean way **17** *not standard* completely: *she clean forgot to face the camera* **18 come clean** *informal* to make a revelation or confession ▷ *n* **19** the ac or an instance of cleaning: *the fridge could do with a clean* **>** See also **clean up** [Old English *clǣne*]

clean-cut *adj* **1** clearly outlined **2** wholesome in appearance

cleaner *n* **1** a person, device, or substance that removes dirt **2** a shop or firm that provides a dry-cleaning servic▪ **3 take someone to the cleaners** *informal* to rob or defrau▪ someone

cleanly (kleen-lee) *adv* **1** easily or smoothly **2** in a fair manner ▷ *adj* (klen-lee) **-lier, -liest** **3** habitually clean or neat **>** **cleanliness** *n*

cleanse *vb* **cleansing, cleansed** **1** to remove dirt from **2** to remove evil or guilt from **>** **cleanser** *n*

clean-shaven *adj* (of men) having the facial hair shave▪ off

clean sheet *n* *sport* an instance of conceding no goals o▪ points in a match

cleanskin *n* *informal, chiefly Austral* and *NZ* **1** a person without a criminal record **2** a bottle of wine without a▪ official label

clean-tech *informal* *adj* **1** using clean technology ▷ *n* **2** same as **clean technology**

clean technology *n* techniques that minimize the damage caused to the environment as a result of manufacturing processes

Cleanthes *n* ?300–?232 BC, Greek philosopher: succeede▪ Zeno as head of the Stoic school

clean up *vb* **1** to make (something) free from dirt **2** to make tidy or presentable **3** to rid (a place) of undesirabl▪ people or conditions **4** *informal* to make a great profit ▷ **cleanup** **5** the process of cleaning up

clear *adj* **1** free from doubt or confusion: *clear evidence of police thuggery* **2** certain in the mind; sure: *I am still not clec about what they can and cannot do* **3** easy to see or hear; distinct **4** perceptive; alert: *clear thinking* **5** evident or obvious: *it is not clear how he died* **6** transparent: *clear glass doors* **7** free from darkness or obscurity; bright **8** (of sounds or the voice) not harsh or hoarse **9** even and pu▪ in tone or colour **10** free of obstruction; open: *a clear path runs under the trees* **11** (of weather) free from dullness or

c

clouds 12 without blemish or defect: *a clear skin* **13** free of suspicion, guilt, or blame: *a clear conscience* **14** (of money) without deduction; net **15** free from debt or obligation **16** without qualification or limitation; complete: *a clear road* ▷ *adv* **17** in a clear or distinct manner **18** completely **19 clear of** out of the way of: *once we were clear of the harbour we headed east* ▷ *n* **20 in the clear** free of suspicion, guilt, or blame ▷ *vb* **21** to free from doubt or confusion **22** to rid of objects or obstructions **23** to make or form (a path) by removing obstructions **24** to move or pass by or over without contact: *he cleared the fence easily* **25** to make or become free from darkness or obscurity **26** to rid (one's throat) of phlegm **27 a** (of the weather) to become free from dullness, fog, or rain **b** (of mist or fog) to disappear **28** (of a cheque) to pass through one's bank and be charged against one's account **29** to free from impurity or blemish **30** to obtain or give (clearance) **31** to prove (someone) innocent of a crime or mistake **32** to permit (someone) to see or handle classified information **33** to make or gain (money) as profit **34** to discharge or settle (a debt) **35 clear the air** to sort out a misunderstanding ▷ See also **clear away**, **clear off**, etc. [Latin *clarus*] **clearly** *adv*

clearance *n* **1** the act of clearing: *slum clearance* **2** permission for a vehicle or passengers to proceed **3** official permission to have access to secret information or areas **4** space between two parts in motion

clearance sale *n* a sale in which a shop sells off unwanted goods at reduced prices

clear away *vb* to remove (dishes, etc.) from the table after a meal

clear-cut *adj* **1** easy to distinguish or understand: *there is no clear-cut distinction between safe and unsafe areas of the city* **2** clearly outlined

clearing *n* an area with few or no trees or shrubs in wooded or overgrown land

clearing bank *n* (in Britain) any bank that makes use of the central clearing house in London

clearing house *n* **1** *banking* an institution where cheques and other commercial papers drawn on member banks are cancelled against each other so that only net balances are payable **2** a central agency for the collection and distribution of information or materials

clear off *vb informal* to go away: often used as a command

clear out *vb* **1** to remove and sort the contents of (a room or container) **2** *informal* to go away: often used as a command ▷ *n* **clear-out 3** an act of clearing someone or something out

clear up *vb* **1** to put (a place or thing that is disordered) in order **2** to explain or solve (a mystery or misunderstanding) **3** (of an illness) to become better **4** (of the weather) to become brighter

clearway *n* *Brit and Austral* a stretch of road on which motorists may stop only in an emergency

cleat *n* **1** a wedge-shaped block attached to a structure to act as a support **2** a piece of wood or iron with two projecting ends round which ropes are fastened [Germanic]

cleavage *n* **1** the space between a woman's breasts, as revealed by a low-cut dress **2** a division or split **3** (of crystals) the act of splitting or the tendency to split along definite planes so as to make smooth surfaces

cleave¹ *vb* **cleaving, cleft, cleaved** or **clove, cleft, cleaved** or **cloven 1** to split apart: *cleave the stone along the fissures* **2** to make by or as if by cutting: *a two-lane highway that eats its way through the northern extremities of the Everglades* [Old English *clēofan*]

cleave² *vb* **cleaving, cleaved** to cling or stick: *a farmhouse cleaved to the hill* [Old English *cleofian*]

cleaver *n* a heavy knife with a square blade, used for chopping meat

cleavers *n* a plant with small white flowers and sticky fruits [Old English *clīfe*]

Cleese *n* John (Marwood). born 1939, British comedy writer and actor, noted for the TV series *Monty Python's Flying Circus* (1969–74) and *Fawlty Towers* (1975, 1978). His films include *A Fish Called Wanda* (1988) and *Fierce Creatures* (1997)

Cleethorpes *n* a resort in E England, in North East Lincolnshire unitary authority, Lincolnshire. Pop: 31 853 (2001)

clef *n* *music* a symbol placed at the beginning of each stave indicating the pitch of the music written after it [French]

cleft *n* **1** a narrow opening in a rock **2** an indentation or split ▷ *adj* **3 in a cleft stick** in a very difficult position ▷ *vb* **4** a past of **cleave¹**

cleft palate *n* a congenital crack in the mid line of the hard palate

Clegg *n* Nick, full name *Nicholas William Peter Clegg*. born 1967, British politician; leader of the Liberal Democrats (2007–2015); deputy prime minister of a Conservative and Liberal Democrat coalition (2010–2015)

Cleisthenes *n* 6th century BC, Athenian statesman: democratized the political structure of Athens

Cleland *n* John. 1709–89, British writer, best known for his bawdy novel *Fanny Hill* (1748–49)

clematis *n* a climbing plant grown for its large colourful flowers [Greek *klēma* vine twig]

Clemenceau *n* Georges Eugène Benjamin. 1841–1929, French statesman; prime minister of France (1906–09; 1917–20); negotiated the Treaty of Versailles (1919)

clemency *n* mercy

Clemens *n* Samuel Langhorne. See **Twain**

clement *adj* **1** (of the weather) mild **2** merciful [Latin *clemens* mild]

Clement *n* Jemaine. born 1974, New Zealand comic actor, noted for his partnership with Bret McKenzie as the musical comedy duo Flight of the Conchords

Clement I *n* Saint, called *Clement of Rome*. pope (?88–?97 AD). Feast day: Nov 23

Clement V *n* original name *Bertrand de Got*. ?1264–1314, pope (1305–14): removed the papal seat from Rome to Avignon in France (1309)

Clement VII *n* original name *Giulio de' Medici*. 1478–1534, pope (1523–34): refused to authorize the annulment of the marriage of Henry VIII of England to Catherine of Aragon (1533)

clementine *n* a citrus fruit resembling a tangerine [French]

Clement of Alexandria *n* Saint. original name *Titus Flavius Clemens*. ?150–?215 AD, Greek Christian theologian: head of the catechetical school at Alexandria; teacher of Origen. Feast day: Dec 5

clench *vb* **1** to close or squeeze together (the teeth or a fist) tightly **2** to grasp or grip firmly ▷ *n* **3** a firm grasp or grip [Old English *beclencan*]

Clendinnen *n* Inga. born 1934, Australian historian and writer. Her books include *Reading the Holocaust* (1998) and *Tiger's Eye – a Memoir* (2000)

Cleon *n* died 422 BC, Athenian demagogue and military leader

Cleopatra *n* ?69–30 BC, queen of Egypt (51–30), renowned for her beauty: the mistress of Julius Caesar and later of Mark Antony. She killed herself with an asp to avoid capture by Octavian (Augustus)

clerestory (clear-store-ee) *n*, *pl* **-ries** a row of windows in the upper part of the wall of the nave of a church above the roof of the aisle [*clear* + *storey*] ▷ **clerestoried** *adj*

clergy *n*, *pl* **-gies** priests and ministers as a group [see **CLERK**]

clergyman *n*, *pl* **-men** a member of the clergy

cleric *n* a member of the clergy

clerical *adj* **1** of clerks or office work: *a clerical job* **2** of or associated with the clergy: *a Lebanese clerical leader*

clerical collar *n* a stiff white collar with no opening at the front, worn by the clergy in certain Churches

clerihew *n* a form of comic or satiric verse, consisting of two couplets and containing the name of a well-known person [after E. *Clerihew* BENTLEY, who invented it]

clerk *n* **1** an employee in an office, bank, or court who keeps records, files, and accounts **2** *US and Canad* a hotel receptionist **3** *archaic* a scholar ▷ *vb* **4** to work as a clerk [Greek *klērikos* cleric, from *klēros* heritage] **> clerkship** *n*

clerk of works *n* an employee who oversees building work

Clermont-Ferrand *n* a city in S central France: capital of Puy-de-Dôme department; industrial centre. Pop: 140 957 (2011)

Cleveland¹ *n* **1** a former county of NE England formed in 1974 from parts of E Durham and N Yorkshire; replaced in 1996 by the unitary authorities of Hartlepool (Durham), Stockton-on-Tees (Durham), Middlesbrough (North Yorkshire) and Redcar and Cleveland (North Yorkshire) **2** a port in NE Ohio, on Lake Erie: major heavy industries. Pop: 461 324 (2003 est) **3** a hilly region of NE England, extending from the **Cleveland Hills** to the River Tees

Cleveland² *n* Stephen Grover. 1837–1908, US Democratic politician; the 22nd and 24th president of the US (1885–89; 1893–97)

clever *adj* **1** displaying sharp intelligence or mental alertness **2** skilful with one's hands **3** smart in a superficial way **4** *Brit informal* sly or cunning [Middle English *cliver*] **> cleverly** *adv* **> cleverness** *n*

clianthus *n* a plant of Australia and New Zealand with clusters of ornamental scarlet flowers [probably from Greek *kleos* glory + *anthos* flower]

cliché (klee-shay) *n* an expression or idea that is no longer effective because of overuse [French] **> clichéd** or **cliché'd** *adj*

Clichy *n* an industrial suburb of NW Paris: residence of the Merovingian kings (7th century). Pop: 58 646 (2007). Official name: *French* **Clichy-la-Garenne**

click *n* **1** a short light often metallic sound ▷ *vb* **2** to make a clicking sound: *cameras clicked and whirred* **3** Also: **click on** *computers* to press and release (a button on a mouse) or select (a particular function) by pressing and releasing a button on a mouse **4** *informal* to become suddenly clear: *it wasn't until I saw the photograph that everything clicked into place* **5** *slang* (of two people) to get on well together: *I met him at a dinner party and we clicked straight away* **6** *slang* to be a great success: *the film cost so much that if it hadn't clicked at the box office we'd have been totally wiped out* [imitative]

click bait *n informal* a link on a website that is intended to lure the user to another website

client *n* **1** someone who uses the services of a professional person or organization **2** a customer **3** *computers* a program or work station that requests data from a server [Latin *cliens* retainer]

clientele (klee-on-tell) *n* customers or clients collectively

cliff *n* a steep rock face, esp. along the seashore [Old English *clif*]

cliffhanger *n* a film, game, etc. which is exciting and full of suspense because its outcome is uncertain **> cliffhanging** *adj*

climacteric *n* **1** same as **menopause** **2** the period in the life of a man corresponding to the menopause, during which sexual drive and fertility diminish [Greek *klimakter* rung of a ladder]

climate *n* **1** the typical weather conditions of an area **2** an area with a particular kind of climate **3** a prevailing trend: *the current economic climate* [Greek *klima* inclination, region] **> climatic** *adj* **> climatically** *adv*

> USAGE Climatic is sometimes wrongly used where *climactic* is meant. *Climatic* should be used to talk about things relating to climate; *climactic* is used to describe something which forms a climax.

climate change *n* the long-term shift in the world's weather patterns and temperatures

climax *n* **1** the most intense or highest point of an experience or of a series of events: *a striking climax to the year's efforts to promote tourism* **2** a decisive moment in a dramatic or other work: *the film has a climax set atop a gale-swept lighthouse* **3** an orgasm ▷ *vb* **4** *not standard* to reach or bring to a climax [Greek *klimax* ladder] **> climactic** *adj*

climb *vb* **1** to go up or ascend (stairs, a mountain, etc.) **2** to move or go with difficulty: *she climbed through a wind▮* **3** to rise to a higher point or intensity: *I grew increasingly delirious as my temperature climbed* **4** to increase in value or amount: *the number could eventually climb to half a million* **5** ▮ ascend in social position: *he climbed the ranks of the organization* **6** (of plants) to grow upwards by twining, using tendrils or suckers **7** to incline or slope upwards: *the road climbed up through the foothills* **8** **climb into** *informal* put on or get into: *I climbed into the van* ▷ *n* **9** the act or an▮ instance of climbing **10** a place or thing to be climbed, esp. a route in mountaineering [Old English *climban*] **> climbable** *adj* **> climber** *n* **> climbing** *n, adj*

climb down *vb* **1** to retreat (from an opinion or positio▮ ▷ *n* **climb-down 2** a retreat from an opinion or position▮

clime *n poetic* a region or its climate

clinch *vb* **1** to settle (an argument or agreement) decisively **2** to secure (a nail) by bending the protrudir▮ point over **3** to engage in a clinch, as in boxing or wrestling ▷ *n* **4** the act of clinching **5** *boxing, wrestling* a movement in which one or both competitors hold on t▮ the other to avoid punches or regain wind **6** *slang* a lovers' embrace [variant of *clench*]

clincher *n informal* something decisive, such as a fact, argument, or point scored

Cline *n* Patsy, original name *Virginia Patterson Hensley*. 1932–63, US country singer; her bestselling records include "Walking After Midnight", "I Fall to Pieces", an▮ "Leavin' On Your Mind"

cling *vb* **clinging, clung 1** (often foll. by *to*) to hold fast o▮ stick closely (to something) **2** to be emotionally overdependent on **3** to continue to do or believe in: *he clings to the belief that people are capable of change* [Old Englis▮ *clingan*] **> clinging** or **clingy** *adj*

clingfilm *n Brit* a thin polythene material used for wrapping food

clinic *n* **1** a place in which outpatients are given medic▮ treatment or advice **2** a similar place staffed by specialist physicians or surgeons: *I have an antenatal clin▮ on Friday afternoon* **3** *Brit and NZ* a private hospital or nursing home **4** the teaching of medicine to students ▮ the bedside [Greek *klinē* bed]

clinical *adj* **1** of or relating to the observation and treatment of patients directly: *clinical trials of a new drug* **2** of or relating to a clinic **3** logical and unemotional: *th▮ have a somewhat clinical attitude to their children's upbringing* **4** (of a room or buildings) plain, simple, and usually unattractive **> clinically** *adv*

clinical thermometer *n* a thermometer for measurin▮ the temperature of the body

clink¹ *vb* **1** to make a light sharp metallic sound ▷ *n* **2** such a sound [perhaps from Middle Dutch *klinken*]

clink² *n slang* prison [after *Clink*, a former prison in London]

clinker *n* the fused coal left over in a fire or furnace [Dutch *klinker* a type of brick]

clinker-built *adj* (of a boat or ship) with a hull made from overlapping planks [obsolete *clinker* a nailing together, probably from *clinch*]

Clinton *n* **1** Bill, full name *William Jefferson Clinton*. born 1946, US Democrat politician; 42nd president of the US (1993–2001) **2** his wife, **Hillary Rodham**. born 1947, US Democrat politician and lawyer: first lady (1993–2001), senator (2001–09); secretary of state (2009–13)

Clio *n Greek myth* the Muse of history

clip¹ *vb* **clipping, clipped 1** to cut or trim with scissors o▮ shears **2** to remove a short section from (a film or newspaper) **3** *Brit and Austral* to punch a hole in something, esp. a ticket) **4** *informal* to strike with a sharp, often slanting, blow **5** to shorten (a word) **6** *slang* to obtain (money) by cheating ▷ *n* **7** the act of clipping **8** a short extract from a film **9** something that has been clipped **10** *informal* a sharp, often slanting, blow: *a clip on the ear* **11** *informal* speed: *proceeding at a smart clip* **12** *Austral and NZ* the total quantity of wool shorn, as in one place or season [Old Norse *klippa* to cut]

clip² *n* **1** a device for attaching or holding things together **2** an article of jewellery that can be clipped onto a dress or hat **3** short for **paperclip, cartridge clip** ▷ *vb* **clipping, clipped** **4** to attach or hold together with a clip [Old English *clyppan* to embrace]

clipboard *n* a portable writing board with a clip at the top for holding paper

clip joint *n slang* a nightclub in which customers are overcharged

clipped *adj* (of speech) abrupt, clearly pronounced, and using as few words as possible

clipper *n* a fast commercial sailing ship

clippers *pl n* a tool used for clipping and cutting

Clipperton Island *n* an uninhabited atoll in the E Pacific SW of Mexico, under French administration. Area: 6 sq km (2.3 sq miles). French name: **Île Clipperton**

clippie *n Brit old-fashioned, informal* a bus conductress

clipping *n* something cut out, esp. an article from a newspaper

clique (kleek) *n* a small exclusive group of friends or associates [French] ❭ **cliquey, cliquy** or **cliquish** *adj*

clit *n taboo, slang* short for **clitoris**

clitoris (klit-or-riss) *n* a small sexually sensitive organ at the front of the vulva [Greek *kleitoris*] ❭ **clitoral** *adj*

Clive *n* Robert, Baron Clive of Plassey. 1725–74, British general and statesman, whose victory at Plassey (1757) strengthened British control in India

Cliveden *n* a mansion in Buckinghamshire, on the N bank of the Thames near Maidenhead: formerly the home of Nancy Astor and the scene of gatherings of politicians and others (known as the **Cliveden Set**); now a hotel

clr councillor

cloaca (kloh-ake-a) *n, pl* **-cae** a cavity in most animals, except higher mammals, into which the alimentary canal and the genital and urinary ducts open [Latin: sewer]

cloak *n* **1** a loose sleeveless outer garment, fastened at the throat and falling straight from the shoulders **2** something that covers or conceals ▷ *vb* **3** to hide or disguise **4** to cover with or as if with a cloak [Medieval Latin *clocca* cloak, bell]

cloak-and-dagger *adj* of or involving mystery and secrecy

cloakroom *n* **1** a room in which coats may be left temporarily **2** *Brit euphemistic* a toilet

clobber¹ *vb informal* **1** to batter **2** to defeat utterly **3** to criticize severely [origin unknown]

clobber² *n Brit, Austral and NZ informal* personal belongings, such as clothes [origin unknown]

cloche (klosh) *n* **1** *Brit, Austral and NZ* a small glass or plastic cover for protecting young plants **2** a woman's close-fitting hat [French: bell]

clock¹ *n* **1** a device for showing the time, either through pointers that revolve over a numbered dial, or through a display of figures **2** a device with a dial for recording or measuring **3** the downy head of a dandelion that has gone to seed **4** short for **time clock** **5** *informal* same as **speedometer, mileometer** **6** *Brit slang* the face **7** round the clock all day and all night ▷ *vb* **8** to record (time) with a stopwatch, esp. in the calculation of speed **9** *Brit, Austral and NZ slang* to strike, esp. on the face or head **10** *informal* to turn back the mileometer on (a car) illegally so that its mileage appears less **11** *Brit slang* to see or notice [Medieval Latin *clocca* bell]

clock² *n* an ornamental design on the side of a sock [origin unknown]

clock in or **clock on** *vb* to register one's arrival at work on an automatic time recorder

clock out or **clock off** *vb* to register one's departure from work on an automatic time recorder

clock up *vb* to record or reach (a total): *he has now clocked up over 500 games for the club*

clockwise *adv, adj* in the direction in which the hands of a clock rotate

clockwork *n* **1** a mechanism similar to that of a spring-driven clock, as in a wind-up toy **2** like clockwork with complete regularity and precision

clod *n* **1** a lump of earth or clay **2** *Brit, Austral and NZ* a dull or stupid person [Old English] ❭ **cloddish** *adj*

clodhopper *n informal* **1** a clumsy person **2** clodhoppers large heavy shoes

clog *vb* **clogging, clogged** **1** to obstruct or become obstructed with thick or sticky matter **2** to encumber **3** to stick in a mass ▷ *n* **4** a wooden or wooden-soled shoe [origin unknown]

cloisonné (klwah-**zon**-nay) *n* a design made by filling in a wire outline with coloured enamel [French]

cloister *n* **1** a covered pillared walkway within a religious building **2** a place of religious seclusion, such as a monastery ▷ *vb* **3** to confine or seclude in or as if in a monastery [Medieval Latin *claustrum* monastic cell, from Latin *claudere* to close]

cloistered *adj* sheltered or protected

clomp *n, vb* same as **clump** (2, 3)

clone *n* **1** a group of organisms or cells of the same genetic constitution that have been reproduced asexually from a single plant or animal **2** *informal* a person who closely resembles another **3** *slang* a mobile phone that has been given the electronic identity of an existing mobile phone, so that calls made on it are charged to that owner ▷ *vb* **cloning, cloned** **4** to produce as a clone **5** *informal* to produce near copies of (a person) **6** *slang* to give (a mobile phone) the electronic identity of an existing mobile phone so that calls made on it are charged to that owner [Greek *klōn* twig, shoot] ❭ **cloning** *n*

clonk *vb* **1** to make a loud dull thud **2** *informal* to hit ▷ *n* **3** a loud thud [imitative]

Clonmel *n* the county town of Co Tipperary, Republic of Ireland; birthplace of Laurence Sterne; meat processing and enamelware. Pop: 16 910 (2002)

Clooney *n* George. born 1961, US film actor; starred in the television series ER (1994–99) and the films *The Perfect Storm* (2000), *Ocean's Eleven* (2001), *Confessions of a Dangerous Mind* (2002, also directed), *Syriana* (2005, also directed), and *The American* (2010)

close¹ *vb* **closing, closed** **1** to shut: *he lay back and closed his eyes* **2** to bar, obstruct, or fill up (an entrance, a hole, etc.): *the blockades had closed major roads, railways, and border crossings* **3** to cease or cause to cease giving service: *both stores closed at 9 p.m.; the Shipping Company closed its offices in Bangkok* **4** to end; terminate: *'Never,' she said, so firmly that it closed the subject* **5** (of agreements or deals) to complete or be completed successfully **6** to come closer (to): *he was still in second place but closing fast on the leader* **7** to take hold: *his small fingers closed around the coin* **8** *Stock Exchange* to have a value at the end of a day's trading, as specified: *the pound closed four-and-a-half cents higher* **9** to join the ends or edges of something: *to close a circuit* ▷ *n* **10** the act of closing **11** the end or conclusion: *the close of play* **12** (rhymes with dose) *Brit* a courtyard or quadrangle enclosed by buildings **13** *Scot* the entry from the street to a tenement building ▶ See also **close down, close in**, etc. [Latin *claudere*]

close² *adj* **1** near in space or time **2** intimate: *we were such close friends in those days* **3** near in relationship: *the dead man seems to have had no close relatives* **4** careful, strict, or searching: *their research will not stand up to close scrutiny*

5 having the parts near together: *a close formation* **6** near to the surface; short: *an NCO's haircut, cropped close on top, shaved clean at sides and back* **7** almost equal: *a close game* **8** not deviating or varying greatly from something: *a close resemblance* **9** confined or enclosed **10** oppressive, heavy, or airless: *damp, close weather* **11** strictly guarded: *he had been placed in close arrest* **12** secretive or reticent **13** miserly; not generous **14** restricted as to public admission or membership ▷ *adv* **15** closely; tightly **16** near or in proximity [Old French *clos*] **> closely** *adv* **> closeness** *n*

closed *adj* **1** blocked against entry **2** only admitting a selected group of people; exclusive: *he had a fairly closed circle of friends* **3** not open to question or debate **4** *maths* **a** (of a curve or surface) completely enclosing an area or volume **b** (of a set) made up of members on which a specific operation, such as addition, gives as its result another existing member of the set

closed circuit *n* a complete electrical circuit through which current can flow

closed-circuit television *n* a television system used within a limited area such as a building

close down *vb* **1** to stop operating or working: *the factory closed down many years ago* ▷ *n* **close-down** **2** *Brit and NZ radio, television* the end of a period of broadcasting

closed shop *n Brit, Austral and NZ* (formerly) a place of work in which all workers had to belong to a particular trade union

close harmony *n* a type of singing in which all parts except the bass lie close together

close in *vb* **1** (of days) to become shorter with the approach of winter **2 close in on** to advance on so as to encircle or surround

close quarters *pl n* **at close quarters a** engaged in hand-to-hand combat **b** very near together

close season *n* **1** the period of the year when it is illegal to kill certain game or fish **2** *sport* the period of the year when there is no domestic competition

close shave *n informal* a narrow escape

closet *n* **1** *US and Austral* a small cupboard **2** a small private room **3** short for **water closet** ▷ *adj* **4** private or secret: *a closet homosexual* ▷ *vb* **-eting, -eted** **5** to shut away in private, esp. in order to talk: *he was closeted with the President* [Old French *clos* enclosure]

close-up *n* **1** a photograph or film or television shot taken at close range **2** a detailed or intimate view or examination ▷ *vb* **close up** **3** to shut entirely: *every other shop front seemed to be closed up* **4** to draw together: *the ranks closed up and marched on* **5** (of wounds) to heal completely

close with *vb* to engage in battle with (an enemy)

Clostridium difficile *n* a bacterium of the human intestine which is a common cause of colitis in hospital patients. Often shortened to: **C.diff, C.difficile**

closure *n* **1** the act of closing or the state of being closed **2** something that closes or shuts **3** a procedure by which a debate may be stopped and an immediate vote taken **4** *chiefly US* **a** a resolution of a significant event or relationship in a person's life **b** the sense of contentment experienced after such a resolution

clot *n* **1** a soft thick lump formed from liquid **2** *informal* a stupid person ▷ *vb* **clotting, clotted** **3** to form soft thick lumps [Old English *clott*]

cloth *n, pl* **cloths** **1** a fabric formed by weaving, felting, or knitting fibres **2** a piece of such fabric used for a particular purpose **3 the cloth** the clergy [Old English *clāth*]

clothe *vb* **clothing, clothed** or **clad** **1** to put clothes on **2** to provide with clothes **3** to cover or envelop (something) so as to change its appearance: *a small valley clothed in thick woodland* [Old English *clāthian*]

clothes *pl n* **1** articles of dress **2** *chiefly Brit* short for **bedclothes** [Old English *clāthas*, plural of *clāth* cloth]

clotheshorse *n* **1** a frame on which to hang laundry for drying or airing **2** a person who is extremely concerned with his or her appearance

clothesline *n* a piece of rope from which clean washing is hung to dry

clothes peg *n* a small wooden or plastic clip for attaching washing to a clothesline

clothier *n* a person who makes or sells clothes or cloth

clothing *n* **1** garments collectively **2** something that covers or clothes

Clotilda *n* ?475–?545 AD, wife of Clovis I of the Franks, whom she converted (496) to Christianity

clotted cream *n Brit* a thick cream made from scalded milk

cloud *n* **1** a mass of water or ice particles visible in the sky **2** a floating mass of smoke, dust, etc. **3** a large number of insects or other small animals in flight **4** something that darkens, threatens, or carries gloom **5 in the clouds** not in contact with reality **6 on cloud nine** *informal* elated; very happy **7 under a cloud a** under reproach or suspicion **b** in a state of gloom or bad temper ▷ *vb* **8** to make or become more difficult to see through: *my glasses kept clouding up; mud clouded the water* **9** to confuse or impair: *his judgment was no longer clouded by alcohol* **10** to make or become gloomy or depressed: *insanity clouded the last years of his life* ▶ See also **cloud over** [Old English *clūd* rock, hill] **> cloudless** *adj*

cloudburst *n* a heavy fall of rain

cloud chamber *n physics* an apparatus for detecting high-energy particles by observing their tracks through a chamber containing a supersaturated vapour

cloud computing *n* a system in which services stored on the internet are accessible to users on a temporary basis

cloud-cuckoo-land *n* a place of fantasy or impractical ideas

cloud over *vb* **1** (of the sky or weather) to become cloud: *it was clouding over and we thought it would rain* **2** (of a person's face or eyes) to suddenly look gloomy or depressed: *Grace's face clouded over and she turned away*

cloudy *adj* **cloudier, cloudiest** **1** covered with cloud or clouds **2** (of liquids) opaque or muddy **3** confused or unclear **> cloudily** *adv* **> cloudiness** *n*

Clouet *n* François, ?1515–72, and his father, Jean, ?1485–?1540, French portrait painters

Clough *n* **1** Arthur Hugh. 1819–61, British poet, author of *Amours de Voyage* (1858) and *Dipsychus* (1865) **2** Brian. 1935–2004, English footballer and manager

clout *n* **1** *informal* a fairly hard blow **2** power or influence ▷ *vb* **3** *informal* to hit hard [Old English *clūt* piece of cloth]

clove¹ *n* a dried closed flower bud of a tropical tree, used as a spice [Latin *clavus* nail]

clove² *n* a segment of a bulb of garlic [Old English *clufu* bulb]

clove³ *vb* a past tense of **cleave¹**

clove hitch *n* a knot used to fasten a rope to a spar or a larger rope

Clovelly *n* a village in SW England, in Devon on the Bristol Channel: famous for its steep cobbled streets: tourism, fishing. Pop: 472 (2001)

cloven *vb* **1** a past participle of **cleave¹** ▷ *adj* **2** split or divided

cloven hoof or **cloven foot** *n* the divided hoof of a pig, goat, cow, or deer

clover *n* **1** a plant with three-lobed leaves and dense flower heads **2 in clover** *informal* in ease or luxury [Old English *clāfre*]

Clovis I *n* German name Chlodwig. ?466–511 AD, king of the Franks (481–511), who extended the Merovingian kingdom to include most of Gaul and SW Germany

clown *n* **1** a comic entertainer, usually bizarrely dressed and made up, appearing in the circus **2** an amusing person **3** a clumsy rude person ▷ *vb* **4** to behave foolishly **5** to perform as a clown [origin unknown] **> clownish** *adj*

clownfish *n, pl* **-fish** or **-fishes** a brightly coloured striped fish of the Pacific and Indian Oceans

cloying *adj* so sweet or pleasurable that it ultimately becomes sickly: *cloying sentimentality* [Middle English *cloy* riginally to nail, hence, to obstruct] **> cloyingly** *adv*

club *n* **1** a group or association of people with common aims or interests **2** the building used by such a group **3** a stout stick used as a weapon **4** a stick or bat used to strike the ball in various sports, esp. golf **5** an establishment or regular event at which people dance to records; disco: *a new weekly club with resident DJ* **6** a building in which members go to meet, dine, read, etc. **7** chiefly *Brit* an organization, esp. in a shop, set up as a means of saving **8** a playing card marked with one or more black trefoil symbols **9** short for **Indian club** **>** *vb* **clubbing, clubbed 10** to beat with a club **11 club together** to combine resources or efforts for a common purpose [Old Norse *klubba*]

club class *n* **1** a class of air travel which is less luxurious than first class but more luxurious than economy class **>** *adj* **club-class 2** of this class of air travel

club foot *n* a congenital deformity of the foot

clubhouse *n* the premises of a sports or other club, esp. a golf club

club root *n* a fungal disease of cabbages and related plants, in which the roots become thickened and distorted

cluck *n* **1** the low clicking noise made by a hen **>** *vb* **2** (of a hen) to make a clicking sound **3** to express (a feeling) by making a similar sound: *the landlady was clucking feverishly behind them* [imitative]

clue *n* **1** something that helps to solve a problem or unravel a mystery **2 not have a clue a** to be completely baffled **b** to be ignorant or incompetent **>** *adj* **3 clued-up** shrewd and well-informed [variant of *clew* ball of thread]

clueless *adj slang* helpless or stupid

Cluj *n* an industrial city in NW Romania, on the Someşul-Mic River: former capital of Transylvania. Pop: 297 000 (2005 est). German name: **Klausenburg**. Hungarian name: **Kolozsvár**

clump *n* **1** a small group of things or people together **2** a dull heavy tread **>** *vb* **3** to walk or tread heavily **4** to form into clumps [Old English *clympe*] **> clumpy** *adj*

clumsy *adj* **-sier, -siest 1** lacking in skill or physical coordination: *an extraordinarily clumsy player* **2** badly made or done **3** said or done without thought or tact: *I took the clumsy hint and left* [Middle English *clumse* to benumb] **> clumsily** *adv* **> clumsiness** *n*

clung *vb* the past of **cling**

Cluniac *adj* of or relating to a reformed Benedictine order founded at the French town of Cluny in 910

clunk *n* **1** a dull metallic sound **>** *vb* **2** to make such a sound [imitative]

Cluny *n* a town in E central France: reformed Benedictine order founded here in 910; important religious and cultural centre in the Middle Ages. Pop: 4835 (2006)

cluster *n* **1** a number of things growing, fastened, or occurring close together **2** a number of people or things grouped together **>** *vb* **3** to gather or be gathered in clusters [Old English *clyster*]

clutch¹ *vb* **1** to seize with or as if with hands or claws **2** to grasp or hold firmly **3 clutch at** to attempt to get hold or possession of **>** *n* **4** a device that enables two revolving shafts to be joined or disconnected, esp. one that transmits the drive from the engine to the gearbox in a vehicle **5** the pedal which operates the clutch in a car **6** a firm grasp **7 clutches a** hands or claws in the act of clutching: *his free kick escaped the clutches of the rival goalkeeper* **b** power or control: *rescued from the clutches of the Gestapo* [Old English *clyccan*]

clutch² *n* **1** a set of eggs laid at the same time **2** a group, bunch, or cluster: *a clutch of gloomy economic reports* [Old Norse *klekja* to hatch]

clutch bag *n* a handbag without handles

Clutha *n* a river in New Zealand, the longest river in South Island; rising in the Southern Alps it flows southeast to the Pacific. Length: 338 km (210 miles)

clutter *vb* **1** to scatter objects about (a place) in an untidy manner **>** *n* **2** an untidy heap or mass of objects **3** a state of untidiness [Middle English *clotter*]

Clwyd *n* a former county in NE Wales, formed in 1974 from Flintshire, most of Denbighshire, and part of Merionethshire; replaced in 1996 by Flintshire, Denbighshire, Wrexham county borough, and part of Conwy county borough

Clyde *n* **1 Firth of Clyde** an inlet of the Atlantic in SW Scotland. Length: 103 km (64 miles) **2** a river in S Scotland, rising in South Lanarkshire and flowing northwest to the Firth of Clyde: formerly extensive shipyards. Length: 170 km (106 miles)

Clydebank *n* a town in W Scotland, in West Dunbartonshire on the north bank of the River Clyde. Pop: 29 858 (2001)

Clydesdale *n* a heavy powerful carthorse, originally from Scotland

cm centimetre

Cm *chem* curium

Cmdr Commander

Cn *chem* copernicium

CND Campaign for Nuclear Disarmament

Cnidus *n* an ancient Greek city in SW Asia Minor: famous for its school of medicine

Cnossus *n* a variant spelling of **Knossos**

CNS *biology* central nervous system

Co *chem* cobalt

CO 1 Colorado **2** Commanding Officer

Co.¹ *or* **co. 1** Company **2 and co.** *informal* and the rest of them: *Harold and co.*

Co.² County

co- *prefix* **1** together; joint or jointly: *coproduction* **2** indicating partnership or equality: *co-star*; *copilot* **3** to the same or a similar degree: *coextend* **4** (*maths, astronomy*) of the complement of an angle: *cosecant* [Latin; see COM-]

c/o 1 care of **2** *accounting* carried over

coach *n* **1** a large comfortable single-decker bus used for sightseeing or long-distance travel **2** a railway carriage **3** a large four-wheeled enclosed carriage, usually horse-drawn **4** a trainer or instructor: *the coach of the Mexican national team* **5** a tutor who prepares students for examinations **>** *vb* **6** to train or teach [from *Kocs*, village in Hungary where horse-drawn coaches were first made] **> coaching** *n*

coachman *n, pl* **-men** the driver of a horse-drawn coach or carriage

coachwork *n* the body of a car

coagulate (koh-ag-yew-late) *vb* **-lating, -lated** to change from a liquid into a soft semisolid mass; clot [Latin *coagulare*] **> coagulant** *n* **> coagulation** *n*

Coahuila *n* a state of N Mexico: mainly plateau, crossed by several mountain ranges that contain rich mineral resources. Capital: Saltillo. Pop: 2 295 808 (2000). Area: 151 571 sq km (59 112 sq miles)

coal *n* **1** a compact black or dark brown rock consisting largely of carbon formed from partially decomposed vegetation: a fuel and a source of coke, coal gas, and coal tar **2** one or more lumps of coal **3 coals to Newcastle** something supplied to a place where it is already plentiful [Old English *col*]

coalesce (koh-a-less) *vb* **-lescing, -lesced** to unite or come together in one body or mass [Latin *co-* together + *alescere* to increase] **> coalescence** *n* **> coalescent** *adj*

coalface *n* the exposed seam of coal in a mine

coalfield *n* an area rich in deposits of coal

coal gas *n* a mixture of gases produced by the distillation of bituminous coal and used for heating and lighting

coalition (koh-a-lish-un) *n* a temporary alliance, esp.

C

between political parties [Latin *coalescere* to coalesce]

coal scuttle *n* a container for holding coal for a domestic fire

coal tar *n* a black tar, produced by the distillation of bituminous coal, used for making drugs and chemical products

coal tit *n* a small songbird with a black head with a white patch on the nape

coaming *n* a raised frame round a ship's hatchway for keeping out water [origin unknown]

coarse *adj* **1** rough in texture or structure **2** unrefined or indecent: *coarse humour* **3** of inferior quality [origin unknown] **>** **coarsely** *adv* **> coarseness** *n*

coarse fish *n Brit* a freshwater fish that is not of the salmon family **> coarse fishing** *n*

coarsen *vb* to make or become coarse

coast *n* **1** the place where the land meets the sea **2 the coast is clear** *informal* the obstacles or dangers are gone ▷ *vb* **3** to move by momentum or force of gravity, without the use of power **4** to proceed without great effort: *they coasted to a 31-9 win in the pairs* [Latin *costa* side, rib] **> coastal** *adj*

coaster *n* **1** a small mat placed under a bottle or glass to protect a table **2** *Brit* a small ship used for coastal trade

coastguard *n* **1** an organization which aids shipping, saves lives at sea, and prevents smuggling **2** a member of such an organization

coastline *n* the outline of a coast

Coast Mountains *pl n* a mountain range in Canada, on the Pacific coast of British Columbia. Highest peak: Mount Waddington, 4043 m (13 266 ft)

coat *n* **1** an outer garment with sleeves, covering the body from the shoulders to below the waist **2** the hair, wool, or fur of an animal **3** any layer that covers a surface ▷ *vb* **4** to cover with a layer [Old French *cote*]

Coatbridge *n* an industrial town in central Scotland, in North Lanarkshire. Pop: 41 170 (2001)

Coates *n* Joseph Gordon. 1878–1943, New Zealand statesman; prime minister of New Zealand (1925–28)

coat hanger *n* a curved piece of wood, wire, or plastic, fitted with a hook and used to hang up clothes

coating *n* a layer or film spread over a surface: *a thick coating of breadcrumbs*

coat of arms *n* the heraldic emblem of a family or organization

coat of mail *n history* a protective garment made of linked metal rings or plates

coax *vb* **1** to persuade (someone) gently **2** to obtain (something) by persistent coaxing **3** to work on (something) carefully and patiently so as to make it function as desired: *I watched him coax the last few drops of beer out of his glass* [obsolete *cokes* a fool]

coaxial (koh-**ax**-ee-al) *adj* **1** *electronics* (of a cable) transmitting by means of two concentric conductors separated by an insulator **2** having a common axis

cob *n* **1** a male swan **2** a thickset type of horse **3** the stalk of an ear of maize **4** *Brit and Austral* a round loaf of bread **5** *Brit* a hazel tree or hazelnut [origin unknown]

cobalt *n chem* a brittle hard silvery-white metallic element used in alloys. Symbol: **Co** [Middle High German *kobolt* goblin; from the miners' belief that goblins placed it in the silver ore]

cobber *n Austral or old-fashioned, NZ informal* a friend [dialect *cob* to take a liking to someone]

Cobbett *n* William. 1763–1835, English journalist and social reformer; founded *The Political Register* (1802); author of *Rural Rides* (1830)

cobble *n* a cobblestone

cobbled *adj* (of a street or road) paved with cobblestones

cobbler *n* a person who makes or mends shoes [origin unknown]

cobblers *pl n Brit, Austral and NZ slang* nonsense [rhyming slang *cobblers' awls* balls]

cobblestone *n* a rounded stone used for paving [from *cob*]

cobble together *vb* **-bling, -bled** to put together clumsily: *a coalition cobbled together from parties with widely differing aims*

Cobden *n* Richard. 1804–65, British economist and statesman: with John Bright a leader of the successful campaign to abolish the Corn Laws (1846)

Cóbh *n* a port in S Republic of Ireland, in SE Co Cork: po of call for Atlantic liners. Pop: 9811 (2002). Former nam (1849–1922): **Queenstown**

Cobham *n* Lord Cobham title of Sir John Oldcastle. See **Oldcastle**

cobia (koh-bee-a) *n* a large dark-striped game fish of tropical and subtropical seas

Coblenz *n* a variant spelling of **Koblenz**

COBOL *n* a high-level computer programming langua designed for general commercial use [*co(mmon) b(usines o(riented) l(anguage)*]

cobra *n* a highly venomous hooded snake of tropical Africa and Asia [Latin *colubra* snake]

Coburg *n* a city in E Germany, in N Bavaria. Pop: 42 257 (2003 est)

cobweb *n* **1** a web spun by certain spiders **2** a single thread of such a web [Old English *(ātor)coppe* spider] **> cobwebbed** *adj* **> cobwebby** *adj*

cobwebs *pl n* mustiness, confusion, or obscurity: *her election dusted away the cobwebs that normally surround the presidency*

coca *n* the dried leaves of a S American shrub which contain cocaine [S American Indian *kúka*]

Coca-Cola *n trademark* a carbonated soft drink

cocaine *n* an addictive drug derived from coca leaves, used as a narcotic and local anaesthetic

coccyx (kok-**six**) *n, pl* **coccyges** (kok-**sije**-eez) *anatomy* a small triangular bone at the base of the spine in huma beings and some apes [Greek *kokkux* cuckoo, from its likeness to a cuckoo's beak] **> coccygeal** *adj*

Cochabamba *n* a city in central Bolivia. Pop: 561 000 (2005 est)

Cochin *n* **1** a region and former state of SW India: part Kerala state since 1956 **2** a port in SW India, on the Malabar Coast: the first European settlement in India founded by Vasco da Gama in 1502: shipbuilding, engineering. Pop: 596 473 (2001). Local official name: **Kochi 3** a large breed of domestic fowl, with dense plumage and feathered legs, that originated in Cochir China

Cochin China *n* a former French colony of Indochina (1862–1948): now the part of Vietnam that lies south of Phan Thiet

cochineal *n* a scarlet dye obtained from a Mexican insect, used for colouring food [Greek *kokkos* kermes berry]

Cochise *n* died 1874, Apache Indian chief

cochlea (kok-lee-a) *n, pl* **-leae** (-lee-ee) *anatomy* the spira tube in the internal ear, which converts sound vibrations into nerve impulses [Greek *kokhlias* snail] **> cochlear** *adj*

cock *n* **1** a male bird, esp. of domestic fowl **2** a stopcock **3** *taboo, slang* a penis **4** the hammer of a gun **5** *Brit inforn* friend: used as a term of address ▷ *vb* **6** to draw back th hammer of (a gun) so that it is ready to fire **7** to lift anc turn (part of the body) in a particular direction ▶ See also **cockup** [Old English *cocc*]

cockabully *n* a small freshwater fish of New Zealand [Māori *kokopu*]

cockade *n* a feather or rosette worn on the hat as a bad [French *coq* cock]

cock-a-hoop *adj Brit, Austral and NZ* in very high spirits [origin unknown]

cock-a-leekie *n* a Scottish soup of chicken boiled with leeks

cock-and-bull story *n informal* an obviously improbal story, esp. one used as an excuse

cockatiel *n* a crested Australian parrot with a

eyish-brown and yellow plumage

ckatoo *n*, *pl* **-toos** a light-coloured crested parrot of ustralia and the East Indies [Malay *kakatua*]

ckatrice *n* a legendary monster that could kill with a ance [Late Latin *calcatrix* trampler]

ckchafer *n* a large flying beetle [COCK + *chafer* beetle]

ckcroft *n* Sir John Douglas. 1897–1967, English nuclear nysicist. With E. T. S. Walton, he produced the first rtificial transmutation of an atomic nucleus (1932) and nared the Nobel prize for physics 1951

cked hat *n* **1** a hat with three corners and a turned-up rim **2 knock into a cocked hat** *slang* to outdo or defeat

ckerel *n* a young domestic cock, less than a year old

ckerell *n* Sir Christopher Sydney. 1910–99, British ngineer, who invented the hovercraft

cker spaniel *n* a small spaniel [from *cocking* hunting oodcocks]

ckeyed *adj informal* **1** crooked or askew **2** foolish or bsurd **3** cross-eyed

ckfight *n* a fight between two gamecocks fitted with narp metal spurs

ckie *or* **cocky** *n*, *pl* **-kies** *Austral and NZ informal* a ockatoo

ckle *n* **1** an edible bivalve shellfish **2** its shell **3 warm ne cockles of one's heart** to make one feel happy [Greek *nkhule* mussel]

ckleshell *n* **1** the rounded shell of the cockle **2** a small ght boat

ckney *n* **1** a native of London, esp. of its East End **2** the rban dialect of London or its East End ▷ *adj* characteristic of cockneys or their dialect [Middle nglish *cokeney* cock's egg, later applied contemptuously o townsmen]

ckpit *n* **1** the compartment in an aircraft for the pilot nd crew **2** the driver's compartment in a racing car nautical a space in a small vessel containing the wheel nd tiller **4** the site of many battles or conflicts: *the south the country is a cockpit of conflicting interests* **5** an enclosure sed for cockfights

ckroach *n* a beetle-like insect which is a household est [Spanish *cucaracha*]

ckscomb *n* same as **coxcomb**

cksure *adj* overconfident or arrogant [origin nknown]

cktail *n* **1** a mixed alcoholic drink **2** an appetizer of eafood or mixed fruits **3** any combination of diverse ements: *Central America was a cocktail of death, poverty, and struction* [origin unknown]

ckup *Brit and Austral slang n* **1** something done badly vb **cock up 2** to ruin or spoil

cky *adj* **cockier**, **cockiest** excessively proud of oneself **cockily** *adv* ▷ **cockiness** *n*

co *n*, *pl* **-cos** the coconut palm [Portuguese: grimace; om the likeness of the three holes of the coconut to a ce]

coa *or* **cacao** *n* **1** a powder made by roasting and rinding cocoa beans **2** a hot or cold drink made from ocoa powder [from CACAO]

coa bean *n* a cacao seed

coa butter *n* a fatty solid obtained from cocoa beans nd used for confectionery and toiletries

conut *n* **1** the fruit of a type of palm tree (**coconut alm**), which has a thick fibrous oval husk and a thin ard shell enclosing edible white flesh. The hollow entre is filled with a milky fluid (**coconut milk**) **2** the esh of the coconut

conut matting *n* coarse matting made from the usk of the coconut

coon *n* **1** a silky protective covering produced by a lkworm or other insect larva, in which the pupa evelops **2** a protective covering ▷ *vb* **3** to wrap in or rotect as if in a cocoon [Provençal *coucoun* eggshell]

cos Islands *pl n* a group of 27 coral islands in the ndian Ocean, southwest of Java: a Territory of Australia since 1955. Pop: 596 (2010). Area: 13 sq km (5 sq miles). Also called: **Keeling Islands**

cocotte *n* a small fireproof dish in which individual portions of food are cooked and served [French]

Cocteau *n* Jean. 1889–1963, French dramatist, novelist, poet, critic, designer, and film director. His works include the novel *Les Enfants terribles* (1929) and the play *La Machine infernale* (1934)

cod[1] *n*, *pl* **cod** *or* **cods** a large food fish [probably Germanic]

cod[2] *adj Brit slang* having the character of an imitation or parody: *the chorus were dressed in exuberant cod-medieval costumes* [origin unknown]

Cod *n* See **Cape Cod**

COD cash (in the US, collect) on delivery

coda (kode-a) *n music* the final part of a musical movement or work [Italian: tail]

coddle *vb* **-dling**, **-dled 1** to pamper or overprotect **2** to cook (eggs) in water just below boiling point [origin unknown]

code *n* **1** a system of letters, symbols, or prearranged signals, by which information can be communicated secretly or briefly: *binary code*; *Morse code* **2** a set of principles or rules: *a code of practice* **3** a system of letters or digits used for identification purposes: *area code*; *tax code* ▷ *vb* **coding, coded 4** to translate or arrange into a code **5** to write computer programs [Latin *codex* book, wooden block]

codeine (kode-een) *n* a drug made mainly from morphine, used as a painkiller and sedative [Greek *kōdeia* head of a poppy]

codex (koh-dex) *n*, *pl* **-dices** (-diss-seez) a volume of manuscripts of an ancient text [Latin: wooden block, book]

codfish *n*, *pl* **-fish** *or* **-fishes** a cod

codger *n Brit, Austral and NZ informal* an old man [probably variant of *cadger*]

codicil (cod-iss-ill) *n law* an addition to a will [from CODEX]

codify (kode-if-fie) *vb* **-fies, -fying, -fied** to organize or collect together (rules or procedures) systematically ▷ **codification** *n*

codling *n* a young cod

cod-liver oil *n* an oil extracted from fish, rich in vitamins A and D

codpiece *n history* a bag covering the male genitals, attached to breeches [obsolete *cod* scrotum]

codswallop *n Brit, Austral and NZ slang* nonsense [origin unknown]

Coe *n* Sebastian, Baron. born 1956, English middle-distance runner, Conservative politician, and sports administrator: winner of the 1500 metres in the 1980 and 1984 Olympic Games; held records at 800m, 1000m, 1500m, and a mile: member of parliament (1992–97), chairman of the London Organising Committee for the Olympic Games of 2012

coeducation *n* the education of boys and girls together ▷ **coeducational** *adj*

coefficient *n* **1** *maths* a number or constant placed before and multiplying another quantity: *the coefficient of the term 3xyz is 3* **2** *physics* a number or constant used to calculate the behaviour of a given substance under specified conditions

coelacanth (seel-a-kanth) *n* a primitive marine fish, thought to be extinct until a living specimen was discovered in 1938 [Greek *koilos* hollow + *akanthos* spine]

coelenterate (seel-lent-a-rate) *n* any invertebrate that has a saclike body with a single opening, such as a jellyfish or coral [Greek *koilos* hollow + *enteron* intestine]

coeliac *or US* **celiac** *n* **1** a person who suffers from coeliac disease ▷ *adj* **2** of or related to the abdomen [Greek *koilia* belly]

coeliac disease (seel-ee-ak) *n* a disease which makes the digestion of food difficult [Greek *koilia* belly]

C

Coen _n_ Jan Pieterszoon. 1587–1629, Dutch colonial administrator; governor general of the Dutch East Indies (1618–23, 1627–29)

coenobite (**seen**-oh-bite) _n_ a member of a religious order in a monastic community [Greek _koinos_ common + _bios_ life]

coequal _adj, n_ equal

coerce (koh-**urss**) _vb_ **-ercing, -erced** to compel or force [Latin _co-_ together + _arcere_ to enclose] **> coercion** _n_

coercive _adj_ using force or authority to make a person do something against his or her will

Coetzee _n_ J(ohn) M(ichael). born 1940, South African novelist: his works include _Life and Times of Michael K_ (1983), which won the Booker Prize, _Age of Iron_ (1990), _Disgrace_ (1999), which won his second Booker Prize, and _Elizabeth Costello_ (2003); Nobel prize for literature (2003)

Coeur _n_ Jacques. ?1395–1456, French merchant; councillor and court banker to Charles VII of France

coeval (koh-**eev**-al) _adj_ 1 contemporary 2 ▷ _n_ 3 a contemporary [Latin _co-_ together + _aevum_ age] **> coevally** _adv_

coexist _vb_ 1 to exist together at the same time or in the same place 2 to exist together in peace despite differences **> coexistence** _n_ **> coexistent** _adj_

coextensive _adj_ covering the same area, either literally or figuratively: _the concepts of 'the nation' and 'the people' are not coextensive_

C of E Church of England

coffee _n_ 1 a drink made from the roasted and ground seeds of a tall tropical shrub 2 Also called: **coffee beans** the beanlike seeds of this shrub 3 the shrub yielding these seeds 4 medium-brown [Turkish _kahve_, from Arabic _qahwah_ coffee, wine]

coffee bar _n_ a café; snack bar

coffee house _n_ a place where coffee is served, esp. one that was a fashionable meeting place in 18th-century London

coffee mill _n_ a machine for grinding roasted coffee beans

coffee table _n_ a small low table

coffee-table book _n_ a large expensive illustrated book

coffer _n_ 1 a chest for storing valuables 2 **coffers** a store of money 3 an ornamental sunken panel in a ceiling or dome [Greek _kophinos_ basket]

cofferdam _n_ a watertight enclosure pumped dry to enable construction work or ship repairs to be done

coffered _adj_ (of a ceiling or dome) decorated with ornamental sunken panels

coffin _n_ a box in which a corpse is buried or cremated [Latin _cophinus_ basket]

cog _n_ 1 one of the teeth on the rim of a gearwheel 2 a gearwheel, esp. a small one 3 an unimportant person in a large organization or process [Scandinavian]

cogent (koh-**jent**) _adj_ forcefully convincing [Latin _co-_ together + _agere_ to drive] **> cogency** _n_

cogitate (koj-it-tate) _vb_ **-tating, -tated** to think deeply about (something) [Latin _cogitare_] **> cogitation** _n_ **> cogitative** _adj_

Cognac _n_ 1 a town in SW France: centre of the district famed for its brandy. Pop: 19 066 (2008) 2 (_sometimes not cap_) a high-quality grape brandy

cognate _adj_ 1 derived from a common original form: _cognate languages_ 2 related to or descended from a common ancestor ▷ _n_ 3 a cognate word or language 4 a relative [Latin _co-_ same + _gnatus_ born] **> cognation** _n_

cognition _n_ formal 1 the processes of getting knowledge, including perception, intuition, and reasoning 2 the results of such a process [Latin _cognoscere_ to learn] **> cognitive** _adj_

cognizance or **cognisance** _n_ formal 1 knowledge or understanding 2 **take cognizance of** to take notice of 3 the range or scope of knowledge or understanding [Latin _cognoscere_ to learn] **> cognizant** or **cognisant** _adj_

cognomen (kog-noh-men) _n, pl_ **-nomens** or **-nomina** (-nom-min-a) _formal_ 1 a nickname 2 a surname 3 an ancient Roman's third name or nickname [Latin: additional name]

cognoscenti (kon-yo-shen-tee) _pl n, sing_ **-te** (-tee) connoisseurs [obsolete Italian]

cogwheel _n_ same as **gearwheel**

cohabit _vb_ to live together as a couple without being married [Latin _co-_ together + _habitare_ to live] **> cohabitation** _n_

cohabitee _n_ a person who lives with, and has a sexual and romantic relationship with, someone to whom he or she is not married

Cohen _n_ 1 Leonard. born 1934, Canadian singer, songwriter, and poet; recordings include _Songs of Leona Cohen_ (1968), _Songs of Love and Hate_ (1971), _I'm Your Man_ (1988), and _Ten New Songs_ (2001) 2 Stanley. born 1922, US biochemist: shared the Nobel prize for physiology or medicine 1986

cohere _vb_ **-hering, -hered** 1 to hold or stick firmly together 2 to be logically connected or consistent [Latin _co-_ together + _haerere_ to cling]

coherent _adj_ 1 logical and consistent 2 capable of intelligible speech 3 cohering or sticking together 4 _physics_ (of two or more waves) having the same frequency and a constant fixed phase difference **> coherence** _n_

cohesion _n_ 1 sticking together 2 _physics_ the force that holds together the atoms or molecules in a solid or liquid **> cohesive** _adj_

cohort _n_ 1 a band of associates 2 a tenth part of an ancient Roman Legion [Latin _cohors_ yard, company of soldiers]

coif _n_ 1 a close-fitting cap worn in the Middle Ages 2 a hairstyle ▷ _vb_ **coiffing, coiffed** 3 to arrange (the hair) [Late Latin _cofea_ helmet, cap]

coiffeur _n_ a hairdresser [French] **> coiffeuse** _fem n_

coiffure _n_ a hairstyle [French]

coil¹ _vb_ 1 to wind or be wound into loops 2 to move in a winding course ▷ _n_ 3 something wound in a connecte[d] series of loops 4 a single loop of such a series 5 a contraceptive device in the shape of a coil, inserted in the womb 6 an electrical conductor wound into a spir[al] to provide inductance [Old French _coillir_ to collect together]

coil² _n_ **mortal coil** the troubles of the world [coined by William Shakespeare]

Coimbatore _n_ an industrial city in SW India, in W Tamil Nadu. Pop: 923 085 (2001)

Coimbra _n_ a city in central Portugal: capital of Portug[al] from 1190 to 1260; seat of the country's oldest universi[ty]. Pop: 148 474 (2001)

coin _n_ 1 a metal disc used as money 2 metal currency collectively ▷ _vb_ 3 to invent (a new word or phrase) 4 t[o] make or stamp (coins) 5 **coin it in** or **coin money** informa[l] to make money rapidly [Latin _cuneus_ wedge]

coinage _n_ 1 coins collectively 2 the currency of a count[ry] 3 a newly invented word or phrase 4 the act of coining

coincide _vb_ **-ciding, -cided** 1 to happen at the same tim[e] 2 to agree or correspond exactly: _what she had said coincid[ed] exactly with his own thinking_ 3 to occupy the same place i[n] space [Latin _co-_ together + _incidere_ to occur]

coincidence _n_ 1 a chance occurrence of simultaneous apparently connected events 2 a coinciding

coincident _adj_ 1 having the same position in space or time 2 **coincident with** in exact agreement with

coincidental _adj_ resulting from coincidence; not intentional **> coincidentally** _adv_

coir _n_ coconut fibre, used in making rope and matting [Malayalam (a language of SW India) _kāyar_ rope]

Coire _n_ the French name for Chur

coitus (koh-it-uss) or **coition** (koh-ish-un) _n_ sexual intercourse [Latin _coire_ to meet] **> coital** _adj_

coke¹ _n_ 1 a solid fuel left after gas has been distilled fro[m] coal ▷ _vb_ **coking, coked** 2 to become or convert into co[ke] [probably dialect _colk_ core]

C

oke² n slang cocaine

Coke¹ n trademark short for **Coca-Cola**

Coke² n 1 **Sir Edward.** 1552–1634, English jurist, noted for his defence of the common law against encroachment from the Crown: the Petition of Right (1628) was largely his work 2 **Thomas William,** 1st Earl of Leicester, known as *Coke of Holkham.* 1752–1842, English agriculturist: pioneered agricultural improvement and considerably improved productivity at his Holkham estate in Norfolk

ol n the lowest point of a ridge connecting two mountain peaks [French: neck]

Col. Colonel

ola n 1 a soft drink flavoured with an extract from the nuts of a tropical tree 2 the W African tree whose nuts contain this extract [probably variant of W African *kolo* nut]

olander n a bowl with a perforated bottom for straining or rinsing foods [Latin *colum* sieve]

olbert n 1 **Claudette,** real name **Claudette Lily Chauchoin.** 1905–96, French-born Hollywood actress, noted for her sophisticated comedy roles; her films include *It Happened One Night* (1934) and *The Palm Beach Story* (1942) 2 **Jean Baptiste.** 1619–83, French statesman; chief minister to Louis XIV: reformed the taille and pursued a mercantilist policy, creating a powerful navy and merchant fleet and building roads and canals

olchester n a town in E England, in NE Essex; university (1964). Pop: 104 390 (2001). Latin name: **Camulodunum**

olchis n an ancient country on the Black Sea south of the Caucasus; the land of Medea and the Golden Fleece in Greek mythology

old adj 1 low in temperature: *the cold March wind*; *cans of cold beer* 2 not hot enough: *eat your food before it gets cold!* 3 lacking in affection or enthusiasm 4 not affected by emotion: *the cold truth* 5 dead 6 (of a trail or scent in hunting) faint 7 (of a colour) giving the impression of coldness 8 slang unconscious 9 informal (of a seeker) far from the object of a search 10 denoting the contacting of potential customers without previously approaching them to establish their interest: *cold mailing* 11 **cold comfort** little or no comfort 12 **have** or **get cold feet** to be or become fearful or reluctant 13 **in cold blood** deliberately and without mercy 14 **leave someone cold** informal to fail to excite or impress someone 15 **throw cold water on** informal to discourage ▷ n 16 the absence of heat 17 a viral infection of the nose and throat characterized by catarrh and sneezing 18 the sensation caused by loss or lack of heat 19 **(out) in the cold** informal neglected or ignored ▷ adv 20 informal unrehearsed or unprepared: *he played his part cold* [Old English *ceald*] ▷ **coldly** adv ▷ **coldness** n

old-blooded adj 1 callous or cruel 2 zoology (of all animals except birds and mammals) having a body temperature that varies according to the temperature of the surroundings

old chisel n a toughened steel chisel

old cream n a creamy preparation used for softening and cleansing the skin

old frame n an unheated wooden frame with a glass top, used to protect young plants

old front n meteorol the boundary line between a warm air mass and the cold air pushing it from beneath and behind

old-hearted adj lacking in feeling or warmth ▷ **cold-heartedness** n

olditz n a town in E Germany, on the River Mulde: during World War II its castle was used as a top-security camp for Allied prisoners of war; many daring escape attempts, some successful, were made

old shoulder informal n 1 **give someone the cold shoulder** to snub someone ▷ vb **cold-shoulder** 2 to treat with indifference

old snap n a short period of cold and frosty weather

cold sore n a cluster of blisters near the lips, caused by a virus

cold storage n 1 the storage of things in a refrigerated place 2 informal a state of temporary disuse: *the idea has been in cold storage ever since*

Coldstream n a town in SE Scotland, in Scottish Borders on the English border: the Coldstream Guards were formed here (1660). Pop: 1813 (2001)

cold sweat n informal coldness and sweating as a bodily reaction to fear or nervousness

cold turkey n slang a method of curing drug addiction by the sudden withdrawal of all doses

cold war n a state of political hostility between two countries without actual warfare

cole n any of various plants such as the cabbage and rape [Latin *caulis* cabbage]

Cole n **Nat 'King',** real name *Nathaniel Adams Cole.* 1917–65, US popular singer and jazz pianist

Coleman n **Ornette.** 1930–2015, US avant-garde jazz alto saxophonist and multi-instrumentalist

Colenso n **John William.** 1814–83, British churchman; Anglican bishop of Natal from 1853: charged with heresy for questioning the accuracy of the Pentateuch

Coleraine n 1 a town in N Northern Ireland, in Coleraine district, Co Antrim, on the River Bann; light industries; university (1965). Pop: 24 089 (2001) 2 a district in N Northern Ireland, in Co Antrim and Co Londonderry. Pop: 56 024 (2003 est). Area: 485 sq km (187 sq miles)

Coleridge n **Samuel Taylor.** 1772–1834, English Romantic poet and critic, noted for poems such as *The Rime of the Ancient Mariner* (1798), *Kubla Khan* (1816), and *Christabel* (1816), and for his critical work *Biographia Literaria* (1817)

Coleridge-Taylor n **Samuel.** 1875–1912, British composer, best known for his trilogy of oratorios *Song of Hiawatha* (1898–1900)

coleslaw n a salad dish of shredded raw cabbage in a dressing [Dutch *koolsalade* cabbage salad]

Colet n **John.** ?1467–1519, English humanist and theologian; founder of St Paul's School, London (1509)

Colette n full name *Sidonie Gabrielle Claudine Colette.* 1873–1954, French novelist; her works include *Chéri* (1920), *Gigi* (1944), and the series of *Claudine* books

coley n Brit an edible fish with white or grey flesh [perhaps from *coalfish*]

colic n severe pains in the stomach and bowels [Greek *kolon* COLON²] ▷ **colicky** adj

Coligny or **Coligni** n **Gaspard de,** Seigneur de Châtillon. 1519–72, French Huguenot leader

Colima n 1 a state of SW Mexico, on the Pacific coast: mainly a coastal plain, rising to the foothills of the Sierra Madre, with important mineral resources. Capital: Colima. Pop: 238 000 (2005 est). Area: 5455 sq km (2106 sq miles) 2 a city in SW Mexico, capital of Colima state, on the Colima River. Pop: 106 967 (1990) 3 **Nevado de Colima** a volcano in SW Mexico, in Jalisco state. Height: 4339 m (14 235 ft)

colitis (koh-lie-tiss) n inflammation of the colon, usually causing diarrhoea and lower abdominal pain

collaborate vb **-rating, -rated** 1 to work with another or others on a joint project 2 to cooperate with an enemy invader [Latin *com-* together + *laborare* to work] ▷ **collaboration** n ▷ **collaborative** adj ▷ **collaborator** n

collage (kol-lahzh) n 1 an art form in which various materials or objects are glued onto a surface to make a picture 2 a picture made in this way 3 a work, such as a piece of music, created by combining unrelated styles [French] ▷ **collagist** n

collagen n a protein found in cartilage and bone that yields gelatine when boiled [Greek *kolla* glue]

collapse vb **-lapsing, -lapsed** 1 to fall down or cave in suddenly 2 to fail completely: *a package holiday company which collapsed last year* 3 to fall down from lack of strength, exhaustion, or illness: *he collapsed with an asthma attack* 4 to sit down and rest because of tiredness or lack of energy: *she collapsed in front of the telly when she got home* **5** to fold compactly, esp. for storage ▷ *n* **6** the act of falling down or falling to pieces **7** a sudden failure or breakdown [Latin *collabi* to fall in ruins]

collapsible *adj* able to be folded up for storage

collar *n* **1** the part of a garment round the neck **2** a band of leather, rope, or metal placed around an animal's neck **3** *biology* a ringlike marking around the neck of a bird or animal **4** a cut of meat, esp. bacon, from the neck of an animal **5** a ring or band around a pipe, rod, or shaft ▷ *vb Brit, Austral and NZ informal* **6** to seize; arrest **7** to catch in order to speak to **8** to take for oneself [Latin *collum* neck]

collarbone *n* same as **clavicle**

collate *vb* **-lating, -lated** **1** to examine and compare carefully **2** to gather together and put in order [Latin *com-* together + *latus* brought] ▷ **collator** *n*

collateral *n* **1** security pledged for the repayment of a loan **2** a person, animal, or plant descended from the same ancestor as another but through a different line ▷ *adj* **3** descended from a common ancestor but through different lines **4** additional but subordinate: *a spokeswoman said that there was no collateral information to dispute the assurances the government had been given* **5** situated or running side by side: *collateral ridges of mountains* [Latin *com-* together + *lateralis* of the side]

collateral damage *n military* unintentional civilian casualties or damage to civilian property caused by military action: *to minimize collateral damage maximum precision in bombing is required*

collation *n* **1** the act or result of collating **2** *formal* a light meal

colleague *n* a fellow worker, esp. in a profession [Latin *collega*]

collect[1] *vb* **1** to gather together or be gathered together **2** to gather (objects, such as stamps) as a hobby or for study **3** to go to a place to fetch (a person or thing) **4** to receive payments of (taxes, dues, or contributions) **5** to regain control of (oneself or one's emotions) [Latin *com-* together + *legere* to gather]

collect[2] *n Christianity* a short prayer said during certain church services [Medieval Latin *oratio ad collectam* prayer at the assembly]

collected *adj* **1** calm and self-controlled **2** brought together into one book or set of books: *the collected works of Dickens*

collection *n* **1** things collected or accumulated **2** a group of people **3** the act or process of collecting **4** a selection of clothes usually presented by a particular designer **5** a sum of money collected, as in church **6** a regular removal of letters from a postbox

collective *adj* **1** done by or characteristic of individuals acting as a group: *the army's collective wisdom regarding peacekeeping* ▷ *n* **2** a group of people working together on an enterprise and sharing the benefits from it ▷ **collectively** *adv*

collective bargaining *n* negotiation between a trade union and an employer on the wages and working conditions of the employees

collective noun *n* a noun that is singular in form but that refers to a group of people or things, as *crowd* or *army*

USAGE Collective nouns are usually used with singular verbs: *the family is on holiday; General Motors is mounting a big sales campaign*. In British usage, however, plural verbs are sometimes employed in this context, esp. where reference is being made to a collection of individual objects or people rather than to the group as a unit: *the family are all on holiday*. Care should be taken that the same collective noun is not treated as both singular and plural in the same sentence: *the family is well and sends its best wishes* or *the family are all well and send their best wishes*, but not *the family is well and send their best wishes*.

collectivism *n* the theory that the state should own all means of production ▷ **collectivist** *adj*

collectivize *or* **-vise** *vb* **-vizing, -vized** *or* **-vising, -vised** to organize according to the theory of collectivism ▷ **collectivization** *or* **-visation** *n*

collector *n* **1** a person who collects objects as a hobby **2** a person employed to collect debts, rents, or tickets

collector's item *n* an object highly valued by collectors for its beauty or rarity

colleen *n Irish* a girl [Irish Gaelic *cailín*]

college *n* **1** an institution of higher or further education that is not a university **2** a self-governing section of certain universities **3** *Brit and NZ* a name given to some secondary schools **4** an organized body of people with specific rights and duties: *the president is elected by an electoral college* **5** a body organized within a particular profession, concerned with regulating standards **6** the staff and students of a college [Latin *collega* colleague]

collegian *n* a member of a college

collegiate *adj* **1** of a college or college students **2** (of a university) composed of various colleges

Collette *n* Toni, full name *Antonia Collette*. born 1972, Australian film actress. Her films include *Muriel's Wedding* (1994), *The Sixth Sense* (1999) and *Little Miss Sunshine* (2006)

collide *vb* **-liding, -lided** **1** to crash together violently **2** to conflict or disagree [Latin *com-* together + *laedere* to strike]

collie *n* a silky-haired dog used for herding sheep and cattle [Scots, probably from earlier *colie* black]

collier *n chiefly Brit* **1** a coal miner **2** a ship designed to carry coal

colliery *n, pl* **-lieries** *chiefly Brit* a coal mine and its buildings

Collins *n* **1** Michael. 1890–1922, Irish republican revolutionary: a leader of Sinn Féin; member of the Irish delegation that negotiated the treaty with Great Britain (1921) that established the Irish Free State **2** (William) Wilkie. 1824–89, British author, noted particularly for his suspense novel *The Moonstone* (1868) **3** William. 1721–59, British poet, noted for his odes; regarded as a precursor of romanticism

collision *n* **1** a violent crash between moving objects **2** the conflict of opposed ideas or wishes [Latin *collidere* to collide]

collision course *n* **1** a trajectory of movement likely to result in a collision **2** a course of action likely to result in a serious disagreement or confrontation: *the union is on a inevitable collision course with the government*

collocate *vb* **-cating, -cated** (of words) to occur together regularly ▷ **collocation** *n*

colloid *n* a mixture of particles of one substance suspended in a different substance [Greek *kolla* glue] ▷ **colloidal** *adj*

collop *n* a small slice of meat [Scandinavian]

colloquial *adj* suitable for informal speech or writing ▷ **colloquially** *adv*

colloquialism *n* **1** a colloquial word or phrase **2** the use of colloquial words and phrases

colloquium *n, pl* **-quiums** *or* **-quia** an academic conference or seminar [Latin; see COLLOQUY]

colloquy *n, pl* **-quies** *formal* a conversation or conference [Latin *com-* together + *loqui* to speak] ▷ **colloquist** *n*

collude *vb* **-luding, -luded** to cooperate secretly or dishonestly with someone [Latin *colludere* to conspire]

collusion *n* secret or illegal agreement or cooperation ▷ **collusive** *adj*

collywobbles *pl n slang* **1** an intense feeling of nervousness **2** an upset stomach [probably from *colic* + *wobble*]

Colmar *n* a city in NE France: annexed to Germany 1871–1919 and 1940–45; textile industry. Pop: 65 136 (1999) German name: **Kolmar**

Colo. Colorado

cologne n a perfumed toilet water [*Cologne*, Germany, where it was first manufactured]

Cologne n an industrial city and river port in W Germany, in North Rhine-Westphalia on the Rhine: important commercially since ancient times; university (1388). Pop: 965 954 (2003 est). German name: **Köln**

Colomb-Béchar n the former name of **Béchar**

Colombes n an industrial and residential suburb of NW Paris. Pop: 83 220 (2006)

Colombia n a republic in NW South America: inhabited by Chibchas and other Indians before Spanish colonization in the 16th century; independence won by Bolívar in 1819; became the Republic of Colombia in 1886; violence and unrest have been endemic since the 1970s. It consists chiefly of a hot swampy coastal plain, separated by ranges of the Andes from the pampas and the equatorial forests of the Amazon basin in the east. Language: Spanish. Religion: Roman Catholic majority. Currency: peso. Capital: Bogotá. Pop: 45 745 783 (2013 est). Area: 1 138 908 sq km (439 735 sq miles)

Colombian adj **1** of or relating to Colombia or its inhabitants ▷ n **2** a native or inhabitant of Colombia

Colombo n the capital and chief port of Sri Lanka, on the W coast, with one of the largest artificial harbours in the world. Pop: 653 000 (2005 est)

colon[1] n, pl **-lons** the punctuation mark (:) used before an explanation or an example, a list, or an extended quotation [Greek *kōlon* limb, clause]

colon[2] n, pl **-lons** or **-la** the part of the large intestine connected to the rectum [Greek *kolon* large intestine] ▷ **colonic** adj

Colón n **1** a port in Panama, at the Caribbean entrance to the Panama Canal. Chief Caribbean port. Pop: 157 000 (2005 est). Former name: **Aspinwall 2 Archipiélago de Colón** the official name of the **Galápagos Islands**

colonel n a senior commissioned officer in the army or air force [Old Italian *colonnello* column of soldiers] ▷ **colonelcy** n

colonial adj **1** of or inhabiting a colony or colonies **2** of a style of architecture popular in North America in the 17th and 18th centuries: *a colonial mansion* **3** *Austral* of a style of architecture popular during Australia's colonial period ▷ n **4** an inhabitant of a colony

colonial goose n NZ old-fashioned stuffed roast mutton

colonialism n the policy of acquiring and maintaining colonies, esp. for exploitation ▷ **colonialist** n, adj

colonist n a settler in or inhabitant of a colony

colonize or **-nise** vb **-nizing, -nized** or **-nising, -nised 1** to establish a colony in (an area) **2** to settle in (an area) as colonists ▷ **colonization** or **-nisation** n

colonnade n a row of evenly spaced columns, usually supporting a roof [French *colonne* column] ▷ **colonnaded** adj

Colonsay n an island in W Scotland, in the Inner Hebrides. Area: about 41 sq km (16 sq miles)

colony n, pl **-nies 1** a group of people who settle in a new country but remain under the rule of their homeland **2** the territory occupied by such a settlement **3** a group of people with the same nationality or interests, forming a community in a particular place: *an artists' colony* **4** zoology a group of the same type of animal or plant living or growing together **5** bacteriol a group of microorganisms when grown on a culture medium [Latin *colere* to cultivate, inhabit]

colophon n a publisher's symbol on a book [Greek *kolophōn* a finishing stroke]

color n, vb US same as **colour**

Colorado n **1** a state of the central US: consists of the Great Plains in the east and the Rockies in the west; drained chiefly by the Colorado, Arkansas, South Platte, and Rio Grande Rivers. Capital: Denver. Pop: 4 550 688 (2003 est). Area: 269 998 sq km (104 247 sq miles). Abbreviation: **Colo.**, (with zip code) **CO 2** a river in SW North America, rising in the Rocky Mountains and

flowing southwest to the Gulf of California: famous for the 1600 km (1000 miles) of canyons along its course. Length: about 2320 km (1440 miles) **3** a river in central Texas, flowing southeast to the Gulf of Mexico. Length: about 1450 km (900 miles) **4** a river in central Argentina, flowing southeast to the Atlantic. Length: about 850 km (530 miles) [Spanish, literally: red, from Latin *colōrātus* coloured, tinted red; see COLOUR]

Colorado beetle n a black-and-yellow beetle that is a serious pest of potatoes [*Colorado*, state of central US]

Colorado Desert n an arid region of SE California and NW Mexico, west of the Colorado River. Area: over 5000 sq km (2000 sq miles)

Colorado Springs n a city and resort in central Colorado. Pop: 370 448 (2003 est)

coloration or **colouration** n arrangement of colours: *a red coloration of the eyes*

coloratura n music **1** a part for a solo singer which has much complicated ornamentation of the basic melody **2** a soprano who specializes in such music [obsolete Italian, literally: colouring]

Colossae n an ancient city in SW Phrygia in Asia Minor: seat of an early Christian Church

colossal adj **1** very large in size: *the turbulent rivers and colossal mountains of New Zealand* **2** very serious or significant: *a colossal legal blunder*

Colosseum n an amphitheatre in Rome built about 75–80 AD

colossus n, pl **-si** or **-suses 1** a very large statue **2** a huge or important person or thing [Greek *kolossos*]

colostomy n, pl **-mies** an operation to form an opening from the colon onto the surface of the body, for emptying the bowel [COLON[2] + Greek *stoma* mouth]

colour or US **color** n **1** a property of things that results from the particular wavelengths of light which they reflect or give out, producing a sensation in the eye **2** a colour, such as a red or green, that possesses hue, as opposed to black, white, or grey **3** a substance, such as a dye, that gives colour **4** the skin complexion of a person **5** the use of all the colours in painting, drawing, or photography **6** the distinctive tone of a musical sound **7** details which give vividness or authenticity: *I walked the streets and absorbed the local colour* **8** semblance or pretext: *under colour of* ▷ vb **9** to apply colour to (something) **10** to influence or distort: *anger coloured her judgment* **11** to become red in the face, esp. when embarrassed or annoyed **12** to give a convincing appearance to: *he coloured his account of what had happened* ▷ See also **colours** [Latin *color*]

colour bar n racial discrimination by whites against non-whites

colour-blind adj **1** unable to distinguish between certain colours, esp. red and green **2** not discriminating on grounds of skin colour: *colour-blind policies* ▷ **colour blindness** n

coloured or US **colored** adj **1** having a colour or colours other than black or white: *coloured glass bottles; a peach-coloured outfit with matching hat* **2** offensive (of a person) not White ▷ n **3** offensive a person who is not White

Coloured or US **Colored** S African n **1** a person of racially mixed parentage or descent ▷ adj **2** of mixed White and non-White parentage

colourful or US **colorful** adj **1** with bright or richly varied colours **2** vivid or distinctive in character

colouring or US **coloring** n **1** the application of colour **2** something added to give colour **3** appearance with regard to shade and colour **4** the colour of a person's complexion

colourless or US **colorless** adj **1** without colour: *a colourless gas* **2** dull and uninteresting: *a colourless personality* **3** grey or pallid in tone or hue: *a watery sun hung low in the colourless sky*

colours or US **colors** pl n **1** the flag of a country, regiment, or ship **2** Brit sport a badge or other symbol showing membership of a team, esp. at a school or college **3 nail one's colours to the mast** to commit oneself publicly to a course of action **4 show one's true colours** to display one's true nature or character

colour sergeant *n* a sergeant who carries the regimental, battalion, or national colours

colour supplement *n Brit* an illustrated magazine accompanying a newspaper

colt *n* **1** a young male horse or pony **2** *sport* a young and inexperienced player [Old English: young ass]

Coltrane *n* John (William). 1926–67, US jazz tenor and soprano saxophonist and composer

coltsfoot *n, pl* **-foots** a weed with yellow flowers and heart-shaped leaves

Colum *n* Padraic. 1881–1972, Irish lyric poet, resident in the US (1914–72)

Columba *n* Saint. ?521–597 AD, Irish missionary: founded the monastery at Iona (563) from which the Picts were converted to Christianity. Feast day: June 9

Columbia *n* **1** a river in NW North America, rising in the Rocky Mountains and flowing through British Columbia, then west to the Pacific. Length: about 1930 km (1200 miles) **2** a city in central South Carolina, on the Congaree River: the state capital. Pop: 117 357 (2003 est)

Columbian *adj* **1** of or relating to the United States **2** relating to Christopher Columbus ▷ *n* **3** a size of printer's type, approximately equal to 16 point; two-line Brevier

columbine *n* a plant that has brightly coloured flowers with five spurred petals [Medieval Latin *columbina herba* dovelike plant]

Columbus¹ *n* **1** a city in central Ohio: the state capital. Pop: 728 432 (2003 est) **2** a city in W Georgia, on the Chattahoochee River. Pop: 185 702 (2003 est)

Columbus² *n* Christopher. Spanish name *Cristóbal Colón*, Italian name *Cristoforo Colombo*. 1451–1506, Italian navigator and explorer in the service of Spain, who discovered the New World (1492)

column *n* **1** an upright pillar usually having a cylindrical shaft, a base, and a capital **2** a form or structure in the shape of a column: *a column of smoke* **3** a vertical division of a newspaper page **4** a regular feature in a paper: *a cookery column* **5** a vertical arrangement of numbers **6** *military* a narrow formation in which individuals or units follow one behind the other [Latin *columna*] ❯ **columnar** *adj*

columnist *n* a journalist who writes a regular feature in a newspaper

Colwyn Bay *n* a town and resort in N Wales, in Conwy county borough. Pop: 30 269 (2001)

com- *or* **con-** *prefix* used with a main word to mean together; with; jointly: *commingle* [Latin, from *cum* with]

coma *n* a state of unconsciousness from which a person cannot be aroused, caused by injury, disease, or drugs [Greek *kōma* heavy sleep]

Comanche (kom-man-chee) *n, pl* **-ches** *or* **-che** a member of a N American Indian people, formerly living in the plains to the east of the Rockies, now chiefly in Oklahoma

Comaneci *n* Nadia. born 1961, Romanian gymnast: gold medal winner in the 1976 Olympic Games where she became the first female gymnast to be awarded a perfect score of 10; defected to the US in 1989

comatose *adj* **1** in a coma **2** sound asleep

comb *n* **1** a toothed instrument for disentangling or arranging hair **2** a tool or machine that cleans and straightens wool or cotton **3** a fleshy serrated crest on the head of a domestic fowl **4** a honeycomb ▷ *vb* **5** to use a comb on **6** to search with great care: *police combed the streets for the missing cat* [Old English *camb*]

combat *n* **1** a fight or struggle ▷ *vb* **-bating, -bated** **2** to fight: *a coordinated approach to combating the growing drugs problem* [Latin *com-* with + *battuere* to beat] ❯ **combative** *adj*

combatant *n* **1** a person taking part in a combat ▷ *adj* **2** engaged in or ready for combat

combat trousers *or* **combats** *pl n* loose casual trouser with large pockets on the sides of the legs

combe *n* same as **coomb**

comber *n* a long curling wave

combination *n* **1** the act of combining or state of being combined **2** people or things combined **3** the set of numbers or letters that opens a combination lock **4** a motorcycle with a sidecar **5** *maths* an arrangement of the members of a set into specified groups without regard to order in the group

combination lock *n* a lock that can only be opened when a set of dials is turned to show a specific sequence of numbers or letters

combinations *pl n Brit* a one-piece undergarment with long sleeves and legs

combine *vb* **-bining, -bined** **1** to join together **2** to form a chemical compound ▷ *n* **3** an association of people or firms for a common purpose **4** short for **combine harvester** [Latin *com-* together + *bini* two by two]

combine harvester *n* a machine used to reap and thresh grain in one process

combings *pl n* the loose hair or fibres removed by combing, esp. from animals

combining form *n* a part of a word that occurs only as part of a compound word, such as *anthropo-* in *anthropolog*

combo *n, pl* **-bos** a small group of jazz musicians

combustible *adj* capable of igniting and burning easily

combustion *n* **1** the process of burning **2** a chemical reaction in which a substance combines with oxygen t produce heat and light [Latin *comburere* to burn up]

come *vb* **coming, came, come** **1** to move towards a place considered near to the speaker or hearer: *come and see me as soon as you can* **2** to arrive or reach: *turn left and continue until you come to a cattle-grid; he came to Britain in the 1920s* **3** to occur: *Christmas comes but once a year* **4** to happen as a result: *no good will come of this* **5** to occur to the mind: *the truth suddenly came to me* **6** to reach a specified point, state or situation: *a dull brown dress that came down to my ankles; he'd come to a decision* **7** to be produced: *it also comes in other colours* **8 come from** to be or have been a resident or native (of): *my mother comes from Greenock* **9** to become: *it was like a dream come true* **10** *slang* to have an orgasm **11** *Brit and NZ informal* to play the part of: *don't come the innocent with me* **12** (subjunctive use) when a specified time arrives: *come next August* **13 as … as they come** the most characteristic example of a type: *he's an arrogant swine and as devious as they come* **14 come again?** *informal* what did yo say? **15 come to light** to be revealed ▷ *interj* **16** an exclamation expressing annoyance or impatience: *com now!* ▶ See also **come about, come across**, etc. [Old English *cuman*]

come about *vb* to happen

come across *vb* **1** to meet or find by accident **2** to communicate the intended meaning or impression **3 come across as** to give a certain impression

come at *vb* to attack: *he came at me with an axe*

comeback *n informal* **1** a return to a former position or status **2** a response or retaliation ▷ *vb* **come back** **3** to return, esp. to the memory **4** to become fashionable again

come between *vb* to cause the estrangement or separation of (two people)

come by *vb* to find or obtain, esp. accidentally: *Graham filled him in on how he came by the envelope*

Comecon (kom-meek-on) *n* (formerly) an economic league of Soviet-oriented Communist nations [*Co(uncil for)* M(utual) Econ(omic Aid)]

comedian *or fem* **comedienne** *n* **1** an entertainer who tells jokes **2** a person who performs in comedy

comedown *n* **1** a decline in status or prosperity **2** *informal* a disappointment ▷ *vb* **come down** **3** (of prices to become lower **4** to reach a decision: *a 1989 court ruling* came down in favour of three councils who wanted Sunday trading banned **5** to be handed down by tradition or inheritance **6 come down with** to begin to suffer from (illness) **7 come down on** to reprimand sharply **8 come down to** to amount to: *at the end the case came down to the one simple issue* **9 come down in the world** to lose status or prosperity

comedy *n, pl* **-dies 1** a humorous film, play, or broadcast **2** such works as a genre **3** the humorous aspect of life or of events **4** (in classical literature) a play which ends happily [Greek *kōmos* village festival + *aeidein* to sing]

come forward *vb* **1** to offer one's services **2** to present oneself

come-hither *adj informal* flirtatious and seductive: *a come-hither look*

come in *vb* **1** to prove to be: *it came in useful* **2** to become fashionable or seasonable **3** to finish a race (in a certain position) **4** to be received: *reports of more deaths came in today* **5** (of money) to be received as income **6** to be involved in a situation: *where do I come in?* **7 come in for** to be the object of: *she came in for a lot of criticism*

come into *vb* **1** to enter **2** to inherit

comely *adj* **-lier, -liest** *old-fashioned* good-looking [Old English *cȳmlic* beautiful] **> comeliness** *n*

Comenius *n* John Amos, Czech name *Jan Amos Komensky*. 1592–1670, Czech educational reformer

come of *vb* to result from: *nothing came of it*

come off *vb* **1** to emerge from a situation in a certain position: *the people who have come off worst are the poorest in society* **2** *informal* to take place **3** to have the intended effect: *it was a gamble that didn't come off*

come-on *n* **1** *informal* a lure or enticement ▷ *vb* **come on 2** (of power or water) to start running or functioning **3** to make progress: *my plants are coming on nicely* **4** to begin: *I think I've got a cold coming on* **5** to make an entrance on stage **6** to make a certain impression: *he comes on like a hard man* **7 come on to** *informal* to make sexual advances to

come out *vb* **1** to be made public or revealed: *it was only then that the truth came out* **2** to be published or put on sale: *their latest album which came out last month* **3** Also: **come out of the closet** to reveal something formerly concealed, esp. that one is a homosexual **4** *chiefly Brit* to go on strike **5** to declare oneself: *the report has come out in favour of maintaining child benefit* **6** to end up or turn out: *this wine consistently came out top in our tastings*; *the figures came out exactly right* **7 come out in** to become covered with (a rash or spots) **8 come out with** to say or disclose: *she came out with a remark that left me speechless* **9** to enter society formally

come over *vb* **1** to influence or affect: *I don't know what's come over me* **2** to communicate the intended meaning or impression **3** to give a certain impression **4** to change sides or opinions **5** *informal* to feel a particular sensation: *it makes him come over slightly queasy*

come round *vb* **1** to recover consciousness **2** to change one's opinion

comestibles *pl n* food [Latin *comedere* to eat up]

comet *n* a heavenly body that travels round the sun, leaving a long bright trail behind it [Greek *komētēs* long-haired]

come through *vb* to survive or endure (an illness or difficult situation) successfully

come to *vb* **1** to regain consciousness **2** to amount to (a total figure)

come up *vb* **1** to be mentioned or arise: *we hope that the difficulties that have arisen in the past will not keep coming up* **2** to be about to happen: *the club has important games coming up* **3 come up against** to come into conflict with **4 come up in the world** to rise in status **5 come up to** to meet a standard **6 come up with** to produce or propose: *he has a knack for coming up with great ideas*

come upon *vb* to meet or encounter unexpectedly

comeuppance *n informal* deserved punishment [from *come up* (in the sense: to appear before a court)]

comfit *n* a sugar-coated sweet [Latin *confectum* something prepared]

comfort *n* **1** a state of physical ease or well-being **2** relief from suffering or grief **3** a person or thing that brings ease **4 comforts** things that make life easier or more pleasant: *the comforts of home* ▷ *vb* **5** to soothe or console **6** to bring physical ease to [Latin *con-* (intensive) + *fortis* strong] **> comforting** *adj*

comfortable *adj* **1** giving comfort; relaxing **2** free from trouble or pain **3** *informal* well-off financially **4** not afraid or embarrassed: *he was not comfortable expressing sympathy* **> comfortably** *adv*

comforter *n* **1** a person or thing that comforts **2** *Brit* a baby's dummy **3** *Brit* a woollen scarf

comfrey *n* a tall plant with bell-shaped blue, purple, or white flowers [Latin *conferva* water plant]

comfy *adj* **-fier, -fiest** *informal* comfortable

comic *adj* **1** humorous; funny **2** of or relating to comedy ▷ *n* **3** a comedian **4** a magazine containing comic strips [Greek *kōmikos*]

comical *adj* causing amusement, often because of being ludicrous or ridiculous: *an enthusiasm comical to behold* **> comically** *adv*

comic opera *n* an opera with speech and singing that tells an amusing story

comic strip *n* a sequence of drawings in a newspaper or magazine, telling a humorous story or an adventure

Comines or **Commines** *n* Philippe de. ?1447–?1511, French diplomat and historian, noted for his *Mémoires* (1489–98)

coming *adj* **1** (of time or events) approaching or next: *in the coming weeks* **2** likely to be important in the future: *he was regarded as a coming man at the Foreign Office* **3 have it coming to one** *informal* to deserve what one is about to suffer ▷ *n* **4** arrival or approach

comity *n, pl* **-ties** *formal* friendly politeness, esp. between different countries [Latin *comis* affable]

comma *n* the punctuation mark indicating a slight pause and used where there is a list of items or to separate the parts of a sentence [Greek *komma* clause]

command *vb* **1** to order or compel **2** to have authority over **3** to deserve and get: *a public figure who commands almost universal respect* **4** to look down over: *the house commands a magnificent view of the sea and the islands* ▷ *n* **5** an authoritative instruction that something must be done **6** the authority to command **7** knowledge; control: *a fluent command of French* **8** a military or naval unit with a specific function **9** *computers* a part of a program consisting of a coded instruction to the computer to perform a specified function [Latin *com-* (intensive) + *mandare* to order]

commandant *n* an officer in charge of a place or group of people

commandeer *vb* **1** to seize for military use **2** to take as if by right: *he commandeered the one waiting taxi outside the station* [Afrikaans *kommandeer*]

commander *n* **1** an officer in command of a military group or operation **2** a middle-ranking naval officer **3** a high-ranking member of some orders of knights

commander-in-chief *n, pl* **commanders-in-chief** the supreme commander of a nation's armed forces

commanding *adj* **1** being in charge: *the commanding officer* **2** in a position or situation where success looks certain: *a commanding lead* **3** having the air of authority: *a commanding voice* **4** having a wide view

commandment *n* a divine command, esp. one of the Ten Commandments in the Old Testament

commando *n, pl* **-dos** or **-does 1** a military unit trained to make swift raids in enemy territory **2** a member of such a unit [Dutch *commando* command]

commedia dell'arte (kom-**made**-ee-a dell-**art**-tay) *n* a form of improvised comedy popular in Italy in the 16th century, with stock characters and a stereotyped plot [Italian]

commemorate *vb* **-rating, -rated** to honour or keep alive the memory of: *a series of events to commemorate the end of the Second World War* [Latin *com-* (intensive) + *memorare* to remind] **> commemoration** *n* **> commemorative** *adj*

commence *vb* **-mencing, -menced** to begin [Latin *com-* (intensive) + *initiare* to begin]

commencement *n* **1** the beginning; start **2** US and Canad a graduation ceremony

commend *vb* **1** to praise in a formal manner: *the judge commended her bravery* **2** to recommend: *he commended the scheme warmly* **3** to entrust: *I commend my child to your care* [Latin *com-* (intensive) + *mandare* to entrust] **> commendable** *adj* **> commendation** *n*

commensurable *adj* **1** measurable by the same standards **2** *maths* **a** having a common factor **b** having units of the same dimensions and being related by whole numbers **> commensurability** *n*

commensurate *adj* **1** corresponding in degree, size, or value **2** commensurable [Latin *com-* same + *mensurare* to measure]

comment *n* **1** a remark, criticism, or observation **2** a situation or event that expresses some feeling: *a sad comment on the nature of many relationships* **3** talk or gossip **4** a note explaining or criticizing a passage in a text **5** no comment I decline to say anything about the matter ▷ *vb* **6** to remark or express an opinion [Latin *commentum* invention]

commentariat *n* the journalists and broadcasters who analyse and comment on current affairs [from COMMENTATOR + PROLETARIAT]

commentary *n*, *pl* **-taries 1** a spoken accompaniment to an event, broadcast, or film **2** a series of explanatory notes on a subject

commentate *vb* **-tating, -tated** to act as a commentator

USAGE The verb *commentate*, derived from *commentator*, is sometimes used as a synonym for *comment on* or *provide a commentary for*. It is not yet fully accepted as standard, though widespread in sports reporting and journalism.

---

commentator *n* **1** a person who provides a spoken commentary for a broadcast, esp. of a sporting event **2** an expert who reports on and analyses a particular subject

commerce *n* **1** the buying and selling of goods and services **2** *literary* social relations [Latin *commercium*]

commercial *adj* **1** of or engaged in commerce: *commercial exploitation of sport* **2** sponsored or paid for by an advertiser: *commercial radio* **3** having profit as the main aim: *this is a more commercial, accessible album than its predecessor* ▷ *n* **4** a radio or television advertisement

commercialism *n* **1** the principles and practices of commerce **2** exclusive or inappropriate emphasis on profit

commercialize *or* **-ise** *vb* **-izing, -ized** *or* **-ising, -ised 1** to make commercial **2** to exploit for profit, esp. at the expense of quality **> commercialization** *or* **-isation** *n*

commercial traveller *n* a travelling salesman

commie *n*, *pl* **-mies**, *adj informal, offensive* Communist

commingle *vb* **-gling, -gled** to mix or be mixed

commis (kom-iss, kom-ee) *adj Brit* (of a waiter or chef) apprentice: *the commis chef* [French]

commiserate *vb* **-ating, -ated** (usually foll. by *with*) to express sympathy or pity (for) [Latin *com-* together + *miserari* to bewail] **> commiseration** *n*

commissar *n* (formerly) an official responsible for political education in Communist countries

commissariat *n* a military department in charge of food supplies [Medieval Latin *commissarius* commissary]

commissary *n*, *pl* **-saries 1** US a shop supplying food or equipment, as in a military camp **2** a representative or deputy [Medieval Latin *commissarius* official in charge]

commission *n* **1** an order for a piece of work, esp. a work of art or a piece of writing **2** a duty given to a person or group to perform **3** the fee or percentage paid to a salesperson for each sale made **4** a group of people appointed to perform certain duties: *a new parliamentary commission on defence* **5** the act of committing a sin or crime **6** *military* the rank or authority officially given to an officer **7** authority to perform certain duties **8** in or out of commission in or not in working order ▷ *vb* **9** to place an order for: *a report commissioned by the United Nation. a new work commissioned by the BBC Symphony Orchestra* **10** *military* to give a commission to **11** to prepare (a ship) for active service **12** to grant authority to [Latin *committere* to commit]

commissionaire *n chiefly Brit* a uniformed doorman at a hotel, theatre, or cinema [French]

commissioned officer *n* a military officer holding a rank by a commission

commissioner *n* **1** an appointed official in a government department or other organization **2** a member of a commission

commit *vb* **-mitting, -mitted 1** to perform (a crime or error) **2** to hand over or allocate: *a marked reluctance to commit new money to business* **3** to pledge to a cause or a course of action **4** to send (someone) to prison or hospital **5** commit to memory to memorize **6** commit to paper to write down [Latin *committere* to join]

commitment *n* **1** dedication to a cause or principle **2** an obligation, responsibility, or promise that restricts freedom of action **3** the act of committing or state of being committed

committal *n* the official consignment of a person to a prison or mental hospital

committed *adj* having pledged oneself to a particular belief or course of action: *a committed pacifist*

committee *n* a group of people appointed to perform a specified service or function [Middle English *committen* to entrust]

commode *n* **1** a chair with a hinged flap concealing a chamber pot **2** a chest of drawers [French]

commodious *adj* with plenty of space [Latin *commodus* convenient]

commodity *n*, *pl* **-ties** something that can be bought or sold [Latin *commoditas* suitability]

commodore *n* **1** *Brit* a senior commissioned officer in the navy **2** the president of a yacht club [probably from Dutch *commandeur*]

Commodus *n* **Lucius Aelius Aurelius**, son of Marcus Aurelius. 161–192 AD, Roman emperor (180–192), noted for his tyrannical reign

common *adj* **1** frequently encountered: *a fairly common plant*; *this disease is most common in kittens and young cats* **2** widespread among people in general: *common practice* **3** belonging to two or more people: *we share common interests* **4** belonging to the whole community: *common property* **5** low-class, vulgar, or coarse **6** *maths* belonging to two or more: *the lowest common denominator* **7** not belonging to the upper classes: *the common people* **8** common or garden *informal* ordinary ▷ *n* **9** a piece of open land belonging to all the members of a communit **10** in common shared, in joint use ▶ See also **Commons** [Latin *communis* general] **> commonly** *adv*

commonality *n*, *pl* **-ties 1** the sharing of common attributes **2** the ordinary people

commonalty *n*, *pl* **-ties 1** the ordinary people **2** the members of an incorporated society

common cold *n* same as **cold** (17)

commoner *n* a person who does not belong to the nobility

common fraction *n* same as **simple fraction**

common law *n* **1** law based on judges' decisions and custom, as distinct from written laws ▷ *adj* **common-law 2** (of a relationship) regarded as a marriage throug being long-standing

Common Market *n* a former name for **European Union**

commonplace *adj* **1** so common or frequent as not to be worth commenting on: *foreign holidays have now become commonplace* **2** dull or unoriginal: *a commonplace observation* ▷ *n* **3** a cliché **4** an ordinary thing [translation of Latin *locus communis* argument of wide application]

common room *n chiefly Brit and Austral* a sitting room for students or staff in schools or colleges

commons *pl n* **1** *Brit* shared food or rations **2** short commons reduced rations

Commons *n* the Commons same as **House of Commons**

common sense *n* **1** good practical understanding ▷ *adj* common-sense **2** inspired by or displaying this

common time *n music* a time signature with four crotchet beats to the bar; four-four time: *a dance in common time*

commonwealth *n* the people of a state or nation viewed politically

Commonwealth *n* the Commonwealth **a** Official name: the Commonwealth of Nations an association of sovereign states that are or at some time have been ruled by Britain **b** the official title of the federated states of Australia

commotion *n* noisy disturbance [Latin *com-* (intensive) + *movere* to move]

communal *adj* **1** belonging to or used by a community as a whole **2** of a commune ▷ **communally** *adv*

communautaire (kom-myune-aw-ter) *adj* supporting the principles of the European Union [French: community]

commune¹ *n* **1** a group of people living together and sharing possessions and responsibilities **2** the smallest district of local government in Belgium, France, Italy, and Switzerland [Latin *communia* things held in common]

commune² *vb* **-muning, -muned** commune with **a** to experience strong emotion for: *communing with nature* **b** to talk intimately with [Old French *comuner* to hold in common]

communicable *adj* **1** capable of being communicated **2** (of a disease) capable of being passed on easily

communicant *n Christianity* a person who receives Communion

communicate *vb* **-cating, -cated** **1** to exchange (thoughts) or make known (information or feelings) by speech, writing, or other means **2** (usually foll. by *to*) to transmit (to): *the reaction of the rapturous audience communicated itself to the performers* **3** to have a sympathetic mutual understanding **4** *Christianity* to receive Communion [Latin *communicare* to share] ▷ **communicator** *n* ▷ **communicative** *adj*

communicating *adj* making or having a direct connection from one room to another: *the suite is made up of three communicating rooms*; *the communicating door*

communication *n* **1** the exchange of information, ideas, or feelings **2** something communicated, such as a message **3** communications means of travelling or sending messages

communication cord *n Brit* a chain in a train which may be pulled by a passenger to stop the train in an emergency

communion *n* **1** a sharing of thoughts, emotions, or beliefs **2** communion with strong feelings for: *private communion with nature* **3** a religious group with shared beliefs and practices: *the Anglican communion* [Latin *communis* common]

Communion *n Christianity* **1** a ritual commemorating Christ's Last Supper by the consecration of bread and wine **2** the consecrated bread and wine. ▶ Also called: Holy Communion

communiqué (kom-mune-ik-kay) *n* an official announcement [French]

communism *n* the belief that private ownership should be abolished and all work and property should be shared by the community [French *communisme*] ▷ **communist** *n, adj*

Communism *n* **1** a political movement based upon the writings of Karl Marx that advocates communism **2** the political and social system established in countries with a ruling Communist Party ▷ **Communist** *n, adj*

Communism Peak *n* a former name for **Ismoil Somoni**

Communist China *n* another name for (the People's Republic of) China

community *n, pl* **-ties** **1** all the people living in one district **2** a group of people with shared origins or interests: *the local Jewish community* **3** a group of countries with certain interests in common **4** the public; society **5** a group of interdependent plants and animals inhabiting the same region [Latin *communis* common]

community centre *n* a building used by a community for social gatherings or activities

community charge *n* in Britain, the formal name for poll tax

community college *n US and Canad* a nonresidential college offering two-year courses of study

community service *n* organized unpaid work intended for the good of the community: often used as a punishment for minor criminals

commutative *adj maths* giving the same result irrespective of the order of the numbers or symbols

commutator *n* a device used to change alternating electric current into direct current

commute *vb* **-muting, -muted** **1** to travel some distance regularly between one's home and one's place of work **2** *law* to reduce (a sentence) to one less severe **3** to substitute **4** to pay (an annuity or pension) at one time, instead of in instalments ▷ *n* **5** a journey made by commuting [Latin *com-* mutually + *mutare* to change] ▷ **commutable** *adj* ▷ **commutation** *n*

commuter *n* a person who regularly travels a considerable distance to work

Como *n* a city in N Italy, in Lombardy at the SW end of Lake Como: tourist centre. Pop: 78 680 (2001). Latin name: Comum

Comorin *n* Cape Comorin a headland at the southernmost point of India, in Tamil Nadu state

Comoros *pl n* a republic consisting of three volcanic islands in the Indian Ocean, off the NW coast of Madagascar; a French territory from 1947; became independent in 1976 except for Mayotte, the fourth island in the group, which chose to remain French. Official languages: Comorian, French, and Arabic; Swahili is used commercially. Religion: Muslim. Currency: franc. Capital: Moroni. Pop: 752 288 (2013 est). Area: 1862 sq km (719 sq miles). Official name: Union of the Comoros

compact¹ *adj* **1** closely packed together **2** neatly fitted into a restricted space **3** concise; brief ▷ *vb* **4** to pack closely together ▷ *n* **5** a small flat case containing a mirror and face powder [Latin *com-* together + *pangere* to fasten] ▷ **compactly** *adv* ▷ **compactness** *n*

compact² *n* a contract or agreement [Latin *com-* together + *pacisci* to contract]

compact disc *n* a small digital audio disc on which the sound is read by an optical laser system

companion *n* **1** a person who associates with or accompanies someone: *a travelling companion* **2** a woman paid to live or travel with another woman **3** a guidebook or handbook **4** one of a pair [Late Latin *companio* one who eats bread with another] ▷ **companionship** *n*

companionable *adj* friendly and pleasant to be with ▷ **companionably** *adv*

companionway *n* a ladder from one deck to another in a ship

company *n, pl* **-nies** **1** a business organization **2** a group of actors **3** a small unit of troops **4** the officers and crew of a ship **5** the fact of being with someone: *I enjoy her company* **6** a number of people gathered together **7** a guest or guests **8** a person's associates **9** keep someone company to accompany someone **10** part company to disagree or separate [see COMPANION]

company sergeant-major *n military* the senior noncommissioned officer in a company

comparable *adj* **1** worthy of comparison **2** able to be compared (with) **> comparability** *n*

comparative *adj* **1** relative: *despite the importance of his discoveries, he died in comparative poverty* **2** involving comparison: *comparative religion* **3** *grammar* the form of an adjective or adverb that indicates that the quality denoted is possessed to a greater extent. In English the comparative is marked by the suffix *-er* or the word *more* ▷ *n* **4** the comparative form of an adjective or adverb **> comparatively** *adv*

compare *vb* **-paring, -pared** **1** to examine in order to observe resemblances or differences: *the survey compared the health of three groups of children* **2 compare to** to declare to be like: *one ambulance driver compared the carnage to an air crash* **3** (usually foll. by *with*) to resemble: *his storytelling compares with the likes of Le Carré* **4** to bear a specified relation when examined: *this full-flavoured white wine compares favourably with more expensive French wines* **5 compare notes** to exchange opinions ▷ *n* **6 beyond compare** without equal [Latin *com-* together + *par* equal]

comparison *n* **1** a comparing or being compared **2** likeness or similarity: *there is no comparison at all between her and Catherine* **3** *grammar* the positive, comparative, and superlative forms of an adjective or adverb **4 in comparison to** or *with* compared to **5 bear** or *stand* **comparison with** to be able to be compared with (something else), esp. favourably: *his half-dozen best novels can stand comparison with anyone's*

compartment *n* **1** one of the sections into which a railway carriage is sometimes divided **2** a separate section: *filing the information away in some compartment of his mind* **3** a small storage space: *the ice-making compartment of the fridge* [French *compartiment*]

compartmentalize or **-ise** *vb* **-izing, -ized** or **-ising, -ised** to put into categories or sections

compass *n* **1** an instrument for finding direction, with a magnetized needle which points to magnetic north **2** limits or range: *within the compass of a normal sized book such a comprehensive survey is not possible* **3 compasses** an instrument used for drawing circles or measuring distances, that consists of two arms, joined at one end [Latin *com-* together + *passus* step]

compassion *n* a feeling of distress and pity for the suffering or misfortune of another [Latin *com-* with + *pati* to suffer]

compassionate *adj* showing or having compassion **> compassionately** *adv*

compassionate leave *n* leave from work granted on the grounds of family illness or bereavement

compatible *adj* **1** able to exist together harmoniously **2** consistent: *his evidence is fully compatible with the other data* **3** (of pieces of equipment) capable of being used together [Late Latin *compati* to suffer with] **> compatibility** *n*

compatriot *n* a fellow countryman or countrywoman [French *compatriote*]

compel *vb* **-pelling, -pelled** **1** to force (to be or do something) **2** to obtain by force: *his performance compelled attention* [Latin *com-* together + *pellere* to drive]

compelling *adj* **1** arousing strong interest: *a compelling new novel* **2** convincing: *compelling evidence*

compendious *adj* brief but comprehensive

compendium *n, pl* **-diums** or **-dia** **1** *Brit* a selection of different table games in one container **2** a concise but comprehensive summary [Latin: a saving, literally: something weighed]

compensate *vb* **-sating, -sated** **1** to make amends to (someone), esp. for loss or injury **2** to cancel out the effects of (something): *the car's nifty handling fails to compensate for its many flaws* **3** to serve as compensation for (injury or loss) [Latin *compensare*] **> compensatory** *adj*

compensation *n* **1** payment made as reparation for loss or injury **2** the act of making amends for something

compere *Brit, Austral and NZ n* **1** a person who introduces a stage, radio, or television show ▷ *vb* **-pering, -pered** **2** to be the compere of [French: godfather]

compete *vb* **-peting, -peted** **1** to take part (in a contest o competition) **2** to strive (to achieve something or to be successful): *able to compete on the international market* [Latin *com-* together + *petere* to seek]

competence or **competency** *n* **1** the ability to do something well or effectively **2** a sufficient income to live on **3** the state of being legally competent or qualified

competent *adj* **1** having sufficient skill or knowledge: *he was a very competent engineer* **2** suitable or sufficient for the purpose: *it was a competent performance, but hardly a remarkable one* **3** having valid legal authority: *lawful detention after conviction by a competent court* [Latin *competens*]

competition *n* **1** the act of competing; rivalry: *competition for places was keen* **2** an event in which people compete **3** the opposition offered by competitors **4** people against whom one competes

competitive *adj* **1** involving rivalry: *the increasingly competitive computer industry* **2** characterized by an urge to compete: *her naturally competitive spirit* **3** of good enough value to be successful against commercial rivals: *we offer worldwide flights at competitive prices* **> competitiveness** *n*

competitor *n* a person, team, or firm that competes

Compiègne *n* a city in N France, on the Oise River: scen of the armistice at the end of World War I (1918) and of the Franco-German armistice of 1940. Pop: 41 714 (2007)

compile *vb* **-piling, -piled** **1** to collect and arrange (information) from various sources **2** *computers* to convert (commands for a computer) from the language used by the person using it into machine code suitable for the computer, using a compiler [Latin *com-* together + *pilare* to thrust down, pack] **> compilation** *n*

compiler *n* **1** a person who compiles information **2** a computer program that converts a high-level programming language into the machine language used by a computer

complacency *n* extreme self-satisfaction **> complacen** *adj* **> complacently** *adv*

complain *vb* **1** to express resentment or displeasure **2 complain of** to state that one is suffering from a pain c illness: *he complained of breathing trouble and chest pains* **3** to make a formal protest: *he complained to the police about his rowdy neighbours* [Latin *com-* (intensive) + *plangere* to bewail]

complainant *n law* a plaintiff

complaint *n* **1** the act of complaining **2** a reason for complaining **3** a mild illness **4** a formal protest

complaisant (kom-**play**-zant) *adj* willing to please or oblige [Latin *complacere* to please greatly] **> complaisance** *n*

complement *n* **1** a person or thing that completes something **2** a complete amount or number: *a full complement of staff nurses and care assistants* **3** the officers an crew needed to man a ship **4** *grammar* a word or words added to the verb to complete the meaning of the predicate in a sentence, as *a fool* in He is a fool or *that he would come* in I hoped that he would come **5** *maths* the angle that when added to a specified angle produces a right angle ▷ *vb* **6** to complete or form a complement to [Lati *com-* (intensive) + *plere* to fill]

USAGE Avoid confusion with **compliment**.

complementary *adj* **1** forming a complete or balanced whole **2** forming a complement

complementary medicine *n* same as **alternative medicine**

complete *adj* **1** thorough; absolute: *it was a complete shambles* **2** perfect in quality or kind: *he is the complete modern footballer* **3** finished **4** having all the necessary parts **5 complete with** having as an extra feature or part: *a mansion complete with swimming pool* ▷ *vb* **-pleting, -pleted 6** to finish **7** to make whole or perfect [Latin *complere* to fill up] ❭ **completely** *adv* ❭ **completion** *n*

complex *adj* **1** made up of interconnected parts **2** intricate or complicated **3** *maths* of or involving complex numbers ▷ *n* **4** a whole made up of related parts: *a leisure complex including a gymnasium, squash courts, and a 20-metre swimming pool* **5** *psychoanalysis* a group of unconscious feelings that influences a person's behaviour **6** *informal* an obsession or phobia: *I have never had a complex about my height* [Latin *com-* together + *plectere* to braid]

> **USAGE** *Complex* is sometimes used where *complicated* is meant. *Complex* should be used to say only that something consists of several parts rather than that, because something consists of many parts, it is difficult to understand or analyse.

complex fraction *n maths* a fraction in which the numerator or denominator or both contain fractions
complexion *n* **1** the colour and general appearance of the skin of a person's face **2** character or nature: *the political complexion of the government* [Latin *complexio* a combination]
complexity *n, pl* **-ties 1** the state or quality of being intricate or complex **2** something complicated
complex number *n* any number of the form $a + bi$, where a and b are real numbers and $i = \sqrt{-1}$
compliance *n* **1** complying **2** a tendency to do what others want ❭ **compliant** *adj*
complicate *vb* **-cating, -cated** to make or become complex or difficult to deal with [Latin *complicare* to fold together]
complicated *adj* difficult to understand or deal with

> **USAGE** See at **complex.**

complication *n* **1** something which makes a situation more difficult to deal with: *an added complication is the growing concern for the environment* **2** a medical condition arising as a consequence of another
complicity *n, pl* **-ties** the fact of being an accomplice in a crime
compliment *n* **1** an expression of praise **2 compliments** formal greetings ▷ *vb* **3** to express admiration for [Italian *complimento*]

> **USAGE** Avoid confusion with **complement.**

complimentary *adj* **1** expressing praise **2** free of charge: *a complimentary drink*
comply *vb* **-plies, -plying, -plied** to act in accordance with a rule, order, or request) [Spanish *cumplir* to complete]
component *n* **1** a constituent part or feature of a whole **2** *maths* one of a set of two or more vectors whose resultant is a given vector ▷ *adj* **3** forming or functioning as a part or feature: *over 60 component parts* [Latin *componere* to put together]
comport *vb formal* **1 comport oneself** to behave in a specified way **2 comport with** to suit or be appropriate to [Latin *comportare* to collect] ❭ **comportment** *n*
compose *vb* **-posing, -posed 1** to put together or make up **2** to be the component elements of **3** to create (a musical or literary work) **4** to calm (oneself) **5** to arrange artistically **6** *printing* to set up (type) [Latin *componere* to put in place]
composed *adj* (of people) in control of their feelings
composer *n* a person who writes music
composite *adj* **1** made up of separate parts **2** (of a plant) with flower heads made up of many small flowers, such as the dandelion **3** *maths* capable of being factorized: *a*

composite function ▷ *n* **4** something composed of separate parts **5** a composite plant [Latin *compositus* well arranged]
Composite *adj* of a style of classical architecture which combines elements of the Ionic and Corinthian styles
composite school *n Canad* a secondary school which offers both academic courses and vocational training
composition *n* **1** the act of putting together or composing **2** something composed **3** the things or parts which make up a whole **4** a work of music, art, or literature **5** the harmonious arrangement of the parts of a work of art **6** a written exercise; an essay **7** *printing* the act or technique of setting up type
compositor *n* a person who arranges type for printing
compos mentis *adj* sane [Latin]
compost *n* **1** a mixture of decaying plants and manure, used as a fertilizer **2** soil mixed with fertilizer, used for growing plants ▷ *vb* **3** to make (vegetable matter) into compost [Latin *compositus* put together]
Compostela *n* See **Santiago de Compostela**
composure *n* the state of being calm or unworried
compote *n* fruit stewed with sugar or in a syrup [French]
compound¹ *n* **1** *chem* a substance that contains atoms of two or more chemical elements held together by chemical bonds **2** any combination of two or more parts, features, or qualities **3** a word formed from two existing words or combining forms ▷ *vb* **4** to combine so as to create a compound **5** to make by combining parts or features: *the film's score is compounded from surging strings, a heavenly chorus and jazzy saxophones* **6** to intensify by an added element: *the problems of undertaking relief work are compounded by continuing civil war* **7** *law* to agree not to prosecute in return for payment: *to compound a crime* ▷ *adj* **8** composed of two or more parts or elements **9** *music* with a time in which the number of beats per bar is a multiple of three: *such tunes are usually in a form of compound time, for example six-four* [Latin *componere* to put in order] ❭ **compoundable** *adj*
compound² *n* a fenced enclosure containing buildings, such as a camp for prisoners of war [Malay *kampong* village]
compound fracture *n* a fracture in which the broken bone pierces the skin
compound interest *n* interest paid on a sum and its accumulated interest
comprehend *vb* **1** to understand **2** to include [Latin *comprehendere*] ❭ **comprehensible** *adj*
comprehension *n* **1** understanding **2** inclusion
comprehensive *adj* **1** of broad scope or content **2** (of car insurance) providing protection against most risks, including third-party liability, fire, theft, and damage **3** *Brit* of the comprehensive school system ▷ *n* **4** *Brit* a comprehensive school
comprehensive school *n Brit* a secondary school for children of all abilities
compress *vb* **1** to squeeze together **2** to condense ▷ *n* **3** a cloth or pad applied firmly to some part of the body to cool inflammation or relieve pain [Latin *comprimere*]
compression *n* **1** the act of compressing **2** the reduction in volume and increase in pressure of the fuel mixture in an internal-combustion engine before ignition
compressor *n* a device that compresses a gas
comprise *vb* **-prising, -prised 1** to be made up of: *the group comprised six French diplomats, five Italians, and three Bulgarians* **2** to form or make up: *women comprised 57 per cent of all employees, but less than 10 per cent of managers* [French *compris* included]

> **USAGE** The use of *of* after *comprise* should be avoided: *the library comprises* (not *comprises of*) *500 000 books and manuscripts.*

compromise (kom-prom-mize) *n* **1** settlement of a dispute by concessions on each side: *everyone pleaded for* compromise; the compromise was only reached after hours of hard bargaining **2** the terms of such a settlement **3** something midway between different things ▷ vb **-mising, -mised 4** to settle (a dispute) by making concessions **5** to put (oneself or another person) in a dishonourable position ▷ adj **6** being, or having the nature of, a compromise: a compromise solution [Latin compromittere to promise at the same time] **> compromising** adj

Compton n **1** Arthur Holly. 1892–1962, US physicist, noted for his research on X-rays, gamma rays, and nuclear energy: Nobel prize for physics 1927 **2 Denis.** 1918–97, English cricketer, who played for Middlesex and England (1937–57); broke two records in 1947 scoring 3816 runs and 18 centuries in one season

Compton-Burnett n Dame **Ivy.** 1884–1969, English novelist. Her novels include Men and Wives (1931) and Mother and Son (1955)

comptroller n a financial controller

compulsion n **1** an irresistible urge to perform some action **2** compelling or being compelled [Latin compellere to compel]

compulsive adj **1** resulting from or acting from a compulsion **2** irresistible or absorbing **> compulsively** adv

compulsory adj required by regulations or laws

compulsory purchase n the enforced purchase of a property by a local authority or government department

compunction n a feeling of guilt or regret [Latin compungere to sting]

computation n a calculation involving numbers or quantities **> computational** adj

compute vb **-puting, -puted** to calculate (an answer or result), often by using a computer [Latin computare]

computer n an electronic device that processes data according to a set of instructions

computer game n a game played on a home computer by manipulating a joystick or keys in response to the graphics on the screen

computerize or **-ise** vb **-izing, -ized** or **-ising, -ised 1** to equip with a computer **2** to control or perform (operations) by means of a computer **> computerization** or **-isation** n

computing n **1** the activity of using computers and writing programs for them **2** the study of computers and their application

comrade n **1** a fellow member of a union or a socialist political party **2** a companion [French camarade] **> comradely** adj **> comradeship** n

Comte n (Isidore) Auguste (Marie François). 1798–1857, French mathematician and philosopher; the founder of positivism **> Comtism** n **> Comtist** or **Comtian** adj, n

con¹ informal n **1** same as confidence trick ▷ vb **conning, conned 2** to swindle or defraud

con² n See pros and cons

con³ n slang a convict

Con politics Conservative

con- prefix See com-

Conakry or **Konakri** n the capital of Guinea, a port on the island of Tombo. Pop: 1 465 000 (2005 est)

Conan Doyle n Sir Arthur. 1859–1930, British author of detective stories and historical romances and the creator of Sherlock Holmes

concatenation n formal a series of linked events [Latin com- together + catena chain]

concave adj curving inwards like the inside surface of a ball [Latin concavus arched] **> concavity** n

conceal vb **1** to cover and hide **2** to keep secret [Latin com- (intensive) + celare to hide] **> concealment** n

concede vb **-ceding, -ceded 1** to admit (something) as true or correct **2** to give up or grant (something, such as a right) **3** to acknowledge defeat in (a contest or argument) [Latin concedere]

conceit n **1** an excessively high opinion of oneself **2** literary a far-fetched or clever comparison [see CONCEIVE]

conceited adj having an excessively high opinion of oneself **> conceitedness** n

conceivable adj capable of being understood, believed, or imagined **> conceivably** adv

conceive vb **-ceiving, -ceived 1** to imagine or think **2** to consider in a certain way: we must do what we conceive to be right **3** to form in the mind **4** to become pregnant [Latin concipere to take in]

concentrate vb **-trating, -trated 1** to focus all one's attention, thoughts, or efforts on something: she tried hard to concentrate, but her mind kept flashing back to the previous night **2** to bring or come together in large numbers or amounts in one place: a flawed system that concentrates power in the hands of the few **3** to make (a liquid) stronger by removing water from it ▷ n **4** a concentrated substance [Latin com- same + centrum centre] **> concentrated** adj

concentration n **1** intense mental application **2** the act of concentrating **3** something that is concentrated **4** the amount or proportion of a substance in a mixture or solution

concentration camp n a prison camp for civilian prisoners, as in Nazi Germany

concentric adj having the same centre: concentric circles [Latin com- same + centrum centre]

Concepción n an industrial city in S central Chile. Pop: 378 000 (2005 est)

concept n an abstract or general idea: one of the basic concepts of quantum theory [Latin concipere to conceive]

conception n **1** a notion, idea, or plan **2** the fertilizatio of an egg by a sperm in the Fallopian tube followed by implantation in the womb **3** origin or beginning: the ga between the conception of an invention and its production [Latin concipere to conceive]

conceptual adj of or based on concepts

conceptualize or **-ise** vb **-izing, -ized** or **-ising, -ised** to form a concept or idea of **> conceptualization** or **-isation** n

concern n **1** anxiety or worry: the current concern over teena pregnancies **2** something that is of interest or importanc to a person **3** regard or interest: a scrupulous concern for clie confidentiality **4** a business or firm ▷ vb **5** to worry or mal anxious **6** to involve or interest: he had converted the buildi into flats without concerning himself with the niceties of planning permission **7** to be relevant or important to [Latin com- together + cernere to sift]

concerned adj **1** interested or involved: I have spoken to th person concerned and he has no recollection of saying such a thing **2** worried or anxious: we are increasingly concerned for her safety

concerning prep about; regarding

concert n **1** a performance of music by players or singer in front of an audience **2 in concert a** working togethe **b** (of musicians or singers) performing live [Latin com- together + certare strive]

concerted adj decided or planned by mutual agreement: a concerted effort

Concertgebouw n a concert hall in Amsterdam, inaugurated in 1888: the **Concertgebouw Orchestra** established in 1888, has been independent of the hall since World War II

concertina n **1** a small musical instrument similar to an accordion ▷ vb **-naing, -naed 2** to collapse or fold up like a concertina [from concert]

concerto (kon-**chair**-toe) n, pl **-tos** or **-ti** (-tee) a large-scale composition for an orchestra and one or more soloists [Italian]

concert pitch n the internationally agreed pitch to which concert instruments are tuned for performance

concession n **1** any grant of rights, land, or property by a government, local authority, or company **2** a reductio in price for a certain category of person: fare concessions fo senior citizens **3** the act of yielding or conceding **4** something conceded **5** Canad **a** a land subdivision in township survey **b** same as **concession road** [Latin

C

concedere to concede] **> concessionary** *adj*

concessionaire *n* someone who holds a concession

concession road *n Canad* one of a series of roads separating concessions in a township

conch *n, pl* **conchs** *or* **conches** **1** a marine mollusc with a large brightly coloured spiral shell **2** its shell [Greek *konkhē* shellfish]

concierge (kon-see-airzh) *n* (esp. in France) a caretaker in a block of flats [French]

conciliate *vb* **-ating, -ated** to try to end a disagreement with or pacify (someone) [Latin *conciliare* to bring together] **> conciliator** *n*

conciliation *n* **1** the act of conciliating **2** a method of helping the parties in a dispute to reach agreement, esp. divorcing or separating couples to part amicably

conciliatory *adj* intended to end a disagreement

concise *adj* brief and to the point [Latin *concidere* to cut short] **> concisely** *adv* **> conciseness** *or* **concision** *n*

conclave *n* **1** a secret meeting **2** *RC Church* a private meeting of cardinals to elect a new pope [Latin *clavis* key]

conclude *vb* **-cluding, -cluded** **1** to decide by reasoning: *the investigation concluded that key data from the paper were faked* **2** to come or bring to an end: *the festival concludes on December 19th* **3** to arrange or settle finally: *officials have refused to comment on the failure to conclude an agreement* [Latin *concludere*]

conclusion *n* **1** a final decision, opinion, or judgment based on reasoning: *the obvious conclusion is that something is being covered up* **2** end or ending **3** outcome or result: *if you take that strategy to its logical conclusion you end up with communism* **4** in conclusion finally **5** jump to conclusions to come to a conclusion too quickly, without sufficient thought or evidence

conclusive *adj* putting an end to doubt: *there is no conclusive proof of this* **> conclusively** *adv*

concoct *vb* **1** to make by combining different ingredients **2** to invent or make up (a story or plan) [Latin *coquere* to cook] **> concoction** *n*

concomitant *adj* **1** existing or along with (something else): *the concomitant health gains* ▷ *n* **2** something that is concomitant [Latin *com-* with + *comes* companion]

concord *n* **1** agreement or harmony **2** peaceful relations between nations **3** *music* a harmonious combination of musical notes [Latin *com-* same + *cor* heart] **> concordant** *adj*

Concord *n* **1** a town in NE Massachusetts: scene of one of the opening military actions (1775) of the War of American Independence. Pop: 16 937 (2003 est) **2** a city in New Hampshire, the state capital: printing, publishing. Pop: 41 823 (2003 est)

concordance *n* **1** a state of harmony or agreement **2** an alphabetical list of words in a literary work, with the context and often the meaning

concordat *n formal* a treaty or agreement, such as one between the Vatican and another state [Latin *concordatum* something agreed]

concourse *n* **1** a large open space in a public place, where people can meet: *a crowded concourse at Heathrow Airport* **2** a crowd [Latin *concurrere* to run together]

concrete *n* **1** a building material made of cement, sand, stone, and water that hardens to a stonelike mass ▷ *vb* **-creting, -creted** **2** to cover with concrete ▷ *adj* **3** made of concrete **4** specific as opposed to general **5** relating to things that can be perceived by the senses, as opposed to abstractions [Latin *concrescere* to grow together]

concretion *n* **1** a solidified mass **2** the act of solidifying

concubine (kon-kew-bine) *n* **1** *old-fashioned* a woman living with a man as his wife, but not married to him **2** a secondary wife in polygamous societies [Latin *concumbere* to lie together] **> concubinage** *n*

concupiscence (kon-kew-piss-enss) *n formal* strong sexual desire [Latin *concupiscere* to covet] **> concupiscent** *adj*

concur *vb* **-curring, -curred** to agree; be in accord [Latin *concurrere* to run together]

concurrence *n* **1** agreement **2** simultaneous occurrence

concurrent *adj* **1** taking place at the same time or place **2** meeting at, approaching, or having a common point: *concurrent lines* **3** in agreement **> concurrently** *adv*

concuss *vb* to injure (the brain) by a fall or blow [Latin *concutere* to disturb greatly]

concussion *n* **1** a brain injury caused by a blow or fall, usually resulting in loss of consciousness **2** violent shaking

Condé *n* **Prince de,** title of *Louis II de Bourbon, Duc d'Enghien,* called *the Great Condé.* 1621–86, French general, who led Louis XIV's armies against the Fronde (1649) but joined the Fronde in a new revolt (1650–52). He later fought for both France and Spain

condemn *vb* **1** to express strong disapproval of **2** to pronounce sentence on in a court of law **3** to force into a particular state: *a system that condemns most of our youngsters to failure* **4** to judge or declare (something) unfit for use **5** to indicate the guilt of: *everything the man had said condemned him, morally if not technically* [Latin *condemnare*] **> condemnation** *n* **> condemnatory** *adj*

condensation *n* **1** anything that has condensed from a vapour, esp. on a window **2** the act of condensing, or the state of being condensed

condense *vb* **-densing, -densed** **1** to express in fewer words **2** to increase the density of; concentrate **3** to change from a gas to a liquid or solid [Latin *condensare*]

condensed milk *n* milk thickened by evaporation, with sugar added

condenser *n* **1** an apparatus for reducing gases to their liquid or solid form by the removal of heat **2** same as **capacitor** **3** a lens that concentrates light

condescend *vb* **1** to behave patronizingly towards (one's supposed inferiors) **2** to do something as if it were beneath one's dignity [Church Latin *condescendere*] **> condescending** *adj* **> condescension** *n*

Condillac *n* **Étienne Bonnot de.** 1715–80, French philosopher. He developed Locke's view that all knowledge derives from the senses in his *Traité des sensations* (1754)

condiment *n* any seasoning for food, such as salt, pepper, or sauces [Latin *condire* to pickle]

condition *n* **1** a particular state of being: *the human condition; the van is in very poor condition* **2** conditions circumstances: *worsening weather conditions; the government pledged to improve living and working conditions* **3** a necessary requirement for something else to happen: *food is a necessary condition for survival* **4** a restriction or a qualification **5** a term of an agreement: *the conditions of the lease are set out* **6** state of physical fitness, esp. good health: *she is in a serious condition in hospital; out of condition* **7** an ailment **8** on condition that provided that ▷ *vb* **9** to accustom to or alter the reaction of (a person or animal) to a particular stimulus or situation **10** to treat with a conditioner **11** to make fit or healthy **12** to influence or determine the form that something takes: *he argued that the failure of Latin American industry was conditioned by international economic structures* [Latin *con-* together + *dicere* to say] **> conditioning** *n, adj*

conditional *adj* **1** depending on other factors **2** *grammar* expressing a condition on which something else depends, for example 'If he comes' is a conditional clause in the sentence 'If he comes I shall go'

conditioner *n* a thick liquid used when washing to make hair or clothes feel softer

condo *n, pl* **-dos** *US and Canad informal* a condominium building or apartment

condolence *n* sympathy expressed for someone in grief or pain [Latin *com-* together + *dolere* to grieve] **> condole** *vb*

condom *n* a rubber sheath worn on the penis or in the vagina during sexual intercourse to prevent conception or infection [origin unknown]

condominium *n, pl* **-ums** **1** *Austral, US and Canad* **a** an apartment building in which each apartment is individually owned **b** an apartment in such a building **2** joint rule of a state by two or more other states [Latin *com-* together + *dominium* ownership]

condone *vb* **-doning, -doned** to overlook or forgive (an offence or wrongdoing) [Latin *com-* (intensive) + *donare* to donate]

condor *n* a very large rare S American vulture [S American Indian *kuntur*]

Condorcet *n* Marie Jean Antoine Nicolas de Caritat, Marquis de. 1743–94, French philosopher and politician. His works include *Sketch for a Historical Picture of the Progress of the Human Mind* (1795)

conducive *adj* (often foll. by *to*) likely to lead to or produce (a result) [Latin *com-* together + *ducere* to lead]

conduct *n* **1** behaviour **2** the management or handling of an activity or business ▷ *vb* **3** to carry out: *the police are conducting an investigation into the affair* **4 conduct oneself** to behave (oneself) **5** to control (an orchestra or choir) by the movements of the hands or a baton **6** to accompany and guide (people or a party): *a conducted tour* **7** to transmit (heat or electricity) [Latin *com-* together + *ducere* to lead]

conductance *n* the ability of a specified body to conduct electricity

conduction *n* the transmission of heat or electricity

conductivity *n* the property of transmitting heat, electricity, or sound

conductor *n* **1** a person who conducts an orchestra or choir **2** an official on a bus who collects fares **3** *US, Canad and NZ* a railway official in charge of a train **4** something that conducts electricity or heat ▷ **conductress** *fem n*

conduit (kon-dew-it) *n* **1** a route or system for transferring things from one place to another: *a conduit for smuggling cocaine into the United States* **2** a channel or tube for carrying a fluid or electrical cables **3** a means of access or communication [Latin *conducere* to lead]

cone *n* **1** a geometric solid consisting of a circular or oval base, tapering to a point **2** a cone-shaped wafer shell used to contain ice cream **3** the scaly fruit of a conifer tree **4** *Brit, Austral and NZ* a plastic cone used as a temporary traffic marker on roads **5** a type of cell in the retina, sensitive to colour and bright light [Greek *kōnus* pine cone, geometrical cone]

coney *n* same as cony

Coney Island *n* an island off the S shore of Long Island, New York: site of a large amusement park

confab *n informal* a conversation

confabulation *n formal* a conversation [Latin *confabulari* to talk together]

confection *n* **1** any sweet food, such as a cake or a sweet **2** *old-fashioned* an elaborate piece of clothing [Latin *confectio* a preparing]

confectioner *n* a person who makes or sells confectionery

confectionery *n, pl* **-eries** **1** sweets and chocolates collectively: *a drop in confectionery sales* **2** the art or business of a confectioner

confederacy *n, pl* **-cies** a union of states or people joined for a common purpose [Late Latin *confoederatio* agreement] ▷ **confederal** *adj*

Confederacy *n* the Confederacy another name for Confederate States of America

confederate *n* **1** a state or individual that is part of a confederacy **2** an accomplice or conspirator ▷ *adj* **3** united; allied ▷ *vb* **-ating, -ated** **4** to unite in a confederacy [Late Latin *confoederare* to unite by a league]

Confederate *adj* of or supporting those American states which withdrew from the USA in 1860–61, leading to the American Civil War

Confederate States of America *pl n US history* the 11 Southern states (Alabama, Arkansas, Florida, Georgia, North Carolina, South Carolina, Texas, Virginia, Tennessee, Louisiana, and Mississippi) that seceded from the Union in 1861, precipitating a civil war with

the North. The Confederacy was defeated in 1865 and th South reincorporated into the US

confederation *n* **1** a union or alliance of states or groups **2** confederating or being confederated **3** a federation

confer *vb* **-ferring, -ferred** **1** to discuss together **2** to grant or give: *the power conferred by wealth* [Latin *com-* together + *ferre* to bring] ▷ **conferment** *n* ▷ **conferrable** *adj*

conference *n* a meeting for formal consultation or discussion [Medieval Latin *conferentia*]

confess *vb* **1** to admit (a fault or crime) **2** to admit to be true, esp. reluctantly **3** *Christianity* to declare (one's sins) to God or to a priest, so as to obtain forgiveness [Latin *confiteri* to admit]

confession *n* **1** something confessed **2** an admission of one's faults, sins, or crimes **3 confession of faith** a formal public statement of religious beliefs

confessional *n* **1** *Christianity* a small room or enclosed stall in a church where a priest hears confessions ▷ *adj* **2** of or suited to a confession

confessor *n* **1** *Christianity* a priest who hears confessions and gives spiritual advice **2** *history* a person who demonstrates his or her Christian religious faith by the holiness of his or her life: *Edward the Confessor*

confetti *n* small pieces of coloured paper thrown at weddings [Italian]

confidant *or fem* **confidante** *n* a person to whom private matters are confided [French *confident*]

confide *vb* **-fiding, -fided** **1** confide in to tell (something to someone) in confidence to **2** *formal* to entrust into another's keeping [Latin *confidere*]

confidence *n* **1** trust in a person or thing **2** belief in one's own abilities **3** trust or a trustful relationship: *she won first the confidence, then the admiration, of her bosses* **4** something confided, such as a secret **5 in confidence** as a secret

confidence trick *n* a swindle in which the swindler gains the victim's trust in order to cheat him or her

confident *adj* **1** having or showing certainty: *we are now confident that this technique works* **2** sure of oneself [Latin *confidere* to have complete trust in] ▷ **confidently** *adv*

confidential *adj* **1** spoken or given in confidence **2** entrusted with another's secret affairs: *a confidential secretary* **3** suggestive of intimacy: *a halting, confidential manner* ▷ **confidentiality** *n* ▷ **confidentially** *adv*

confiding *adj* trusting: *a close and confiding relationship* ▷ **confidingly** *adv*

configuration *n* **1** the arrangement of the parts of something **2** the form or outline of such an arrangement [Late Latin *configurare* to model on something]

confine *vb* **-fining, -fined** **1** to keep within bounds **2** to restrict the free movement of: *a nasty dose of flu which confined her to bed for days* ▷ *n* **3 confines** boundaries or limits [Latin *finis* boundary]

confinement *n* **1** being confined **2** the period of childbirth

confirm *vb* **1** to prove to be true or valid **2** to reaffirm (something), so as to make (it) more definite: *confirmed that she is about to resign as leader of the council* **3** to strengthen: *this cruise confirmed my first impressions of the boat's performance* **4** to formally make valid **5** to administer the rite of confirmation to [Latin *confirmare*]

confirmation *n* **1** the act of confirming **2** something that confirms **3** a rite in several Christian churches tha admits a baptized person to full church membership

confirmed *adj* long-established in a habit or condition *a confirmed bachelor*

confiscate *vb* **-cating, -cated** to seize (property) by authority [Latin *confiscare* to seize for the public treasur ▷ **confiscation** *n*

conflagration *n* a large destructive fire [Latin *com-* (intensive) + *flagrare* to burn]

conflate vb **-flating, -flated** to combine or blend into a whole [Latin conflare to blow together] **> conflation** n

conflict n **1** opposition between ideas or interests **2** a struggle or battle ▷ vb **3** to be incompatible [Latin confligere to combat] **> conflicting** adj

confluence n **1** a place where rivers flow into one another **2** a gathering [Latin confluere to flow together] **> confluent** adj

conform vb **1** to comply with accepted standards, rules, or customs **2** (usually foll. by with) to be like or in accordance with: people tend to absorb ideas that conform with their existing beliefs, and reject those that do not [Latin confirmare to strengthen]

conformation n **1** the general shape of an object **2** the arrangement of the parts of an object

conformist adj **1 a** (of a person) behaving or thinking like most other people rather than in an original or unconventional way: a shy and conformist type of boy **b** (of an organization or society) expecting everyone to behave in the same way: the school was a dull, conformist place for staff and students alike ▷ n **2** a person who behaves or thinks like most other people rather than in an original or unconventional way

conformity n, pl **-ities 1** compliance in actions or behaviour with certain accepted rules, customs, or standards **2** likeness

confound vb **1** to astound or bewilder **2** to fail to distinguish between **3 confound it!** damn it! [Latin confundere to mingle, pour together]

confounded adj **1** informal damned: what a confounded nuisance! **2** bewildered; confused: her silent, utterly confounded daughter

confrere (kon-frair) n a colleague: their Gallic confreres [Medieval Latin confrater]

confront vb **1** (of a problem or task) to present itself to **2** to meet face to face in hostility or defiance **3** to present (someone) with something, esp. in order to accuse or criticize: she finally confronted him with her suspicions [Latin com- together + frons forehead]

confrontation n a serious argument or fight

Confucianism n the teachings of Confucius (551–479 BC), the ancient Chinese philosopher, which emphasize moral order **> Confucian** n, adj **> Confucianist** n

Confucius n Chinese name Kong Zi or K'ung Fu-tse. 551–479 BC, Chinese philosopher and teacher of ethics (see **Confucianism**). His doctrines were compiled after his death under the title The Analects of Confucius

confuse vb **-fusing, -fused 1** to fail to distinguish (between one thing and another) **2** to perplex or disconcert **3** to make unclear: he confused his talk with irrelevant detail **4** to throw into disorder [Latin confundere to pour together] **> confusing** adj **> confusingly** adv

confused adj **1** lacking a clear understanding of something **2** disordered and difficult to understand or make sense of: a confused dream

confusion n **1** mistaking one person or thing for another **2** bewilderment **3** lack of clarity **4** disorder

confute vb **-futing, -futed** to prove to be wrong [Latin confutare to check, silence] **> confutation** n

conga n **1** a Latin American dance performed by a number of people in single file **2** a large single-headed drum played with the hands ▷ vb **-gaing, -gaed 3** to dance the conga [from American Spanish]

congeal vb to change from a liquid to a semisolid state [Latin com- together + gelare to freeze]

congenial adj **1** friendly, pleasant, or agreeable: he found the Botanic Gardens a most congenial place for strolling **2** having a similar disposition or tastes [con- (same) + genial] **> congeniality** n

congenital adj (of an abnormal condition) existing at birth but not inherited: congenital heart disease [Latin con- together + genitus born] **> congenitally** adv

conger n a large sea eel [Greek gongros]

congested adj **1** crowded to excess **2** clogged or blocked [Latin congerere to pile up] **> congestion** n

conglomerate n **1** a large corporation made up of many different companies **2** a thing composed of several different elements **3** a type of rock consisting of rounded pebbles or fragments held together by silica or clay ▷ vb **-ating, -ated 4** to form into a mass ▷ adj **5** made up of several different elements **6** (of rock) consisting of rounded pebbles or fragments held together by silica or clay [Latin conglomerare to roll up] **> conglomeration** n

Congo n **1 Democratic Republic of Congo** a republic in S central Africa, with a narrow strip of land along the Congo estuary leading to the Atlantic in the west: Congo Free State established in 1885, with Leopold II of Belgium as absolute monarch; became the Belgian Congo colony in 1908; gained independence in 1960, followed by civil war and the secession of Katanga (until 1963); President Mobutu Sese Seko seized power in 1965; declared a one-party state in 1978, and was overthrown by rebels in 1997. The country consists chiefly of the Congo basin, with large areas of dense tropical forest and marshes, and the Mitumba highlands reaching over 5000 m (16 000 ft) in the east. Official language: French. Religion: Christian majority, animist minority. Currency: Congolese franc. Capital: Kinshasa. Pop: 75 507 308 (2013 est). Area: 2 344 116 sq km (905 063 sq miles). Former names: (1885–1908) **Congo Free State**, (1908–60) **Belgian Congo**, (1960–71) **Congo-Kinshasa**, (1971–97) **Zaïre 2 Republic of Congo** another name for **Congo-Brazzaville 3** the second longest river in Africa, rising as the Lualaba on the Katanga plateau in the Democratic Republic of Congo and flowing in a wide northerly curve to the Atlantic: forms the border between Congo-Brazzaville and the Democratic Republic of Congo. Length: about 4800 km (3000 miles). Area of basin: about 3 000 000 sq km (1 425 000 sq miles). Former Zaïrese name (1971–97): **Zaïre**

Congo-Brazzaville, Congo or **Republic of Congo** n a republic in W Central Africa: formerly the French colony of Middle Congo, part of French Equatorial Africa; it became independent in 1960; consists mostly of equatorial forest, with savanna and extensive swamps; drained chiefly by the Rivers Congo and Ubangi. Official language: French. Religion: Christian majority. Currency: franc. Capital: Brazzaville. Pop: 4 492 689 (2013 est). Area: 342 000 sq km (132 018 sq miles). Former names: (until 1958) **Middle Congo**

Congo Free State n a former name (1885–1908) of (**Democratic Republic of**) **Congo** (1)

Congolese adj **1** of or relating to the Republic of Congo or the Democratic Republic of Congo or their inhabitants ▷ n **2** a native or inhabitant of the Republic of Congo or the Democratic Republic of Congo

congratulate vb **-lating, -lated 1** to express one's pleasure to (a person) at his or her success or good fortune **2 congratulate oneself** to consider oneself clever or fortunate (as a result of): she congratulated herself on her own business acumen [Latin congratulari] **> congratulatory** adj

congratulations pl n, interj expressions of pleasure or joy on another's success or good fortune

congregate vb **-gating, -gated** to collect together in or as a crowd [Latin congregare to collect into a flock]

congregation n a group of worshippers **> congregational** adj

Congregationalism n a system of Protestant church government in which each church is self-governing **> Congregationalist** adj, n

congress n a formal meeting of representatives for discussion [Latin com- together + gradi to walk] **> congressional** adj

Congress n the federal legislature of the US, consisting of the House of Representatives and the Senate **> Congressional** adj **> Congressman** n **> Congresswoman** fem n

C

Congreve n William. 1670–1729, English dramatist, a major exponent of Restoration comedy; author of *Love for Love* (1695) and *The Way of the World* (1700)

congruent adj **1** agreeing or corresponding **2** geometry identical in shape and size: *congruent triangles* [Latin *congruere* to agree] **> congruence** n

congruous adj formal **1** appropriate or in keeping: *an elegant, though not altogether congruous, wing was added to the house in 1735* **2** corresponding or agreeing: *this finding is congruous with Adam's 1982 study* [Latin *congruere* to agree] **> congruity** n

conical adj in the shape of a cone

conic section n a figure, either a circle, ellipse, parabola, or hyperbola, formed by the intersection of a plane and a cone

conifer n a tree or shrub bearing cones and evergreen leaves, such as the fir or larch [Latin *conus* cone + *ferre* to bear] **> coniferous** adj

Coniston Water n a lake in NW England, in Cumbria: scene of the establishment of world water speed records by Sir Malcolm Campbell (1939) and his son Donald Campbell (1959). Length: 8 km (5 miles)

conjecture n **1** the formation of conclusions from incomplete evidence **2** a guess ▷ vb **-turing, -tured 3** to form (an opinion or conclusion) from incomplete evidence [Latin *conjicere* to throw together] **> conjectural** adj

conjoin vb to join or become joined

conjoined twins pl n the technical name for **Siamese twins**

conjugal (kon-jew-gal) adj of marriage: *conjugal rights* [Latin *conjunx* wife or husband]

conjugate vb (kon-jew-gate) **-gating, -gated 1** grammar to give the inflections of (a verb) **2** (of a verb) to undergo inflection according to a specific set of rules **3** formal to combine: *a country in which conjugating Marxism with Christianity has actually been tried* ▷ n (kon-jew-git) **4** formal something formed by conjugation: *haemoglobin is a conjugate of a protein with an iron-containing pigment* [Latin *com-* together + *jugare* to connect]

conjugation n **1** grammar **a** inflection of a verb for person, number, tense, voice, and mood **b** the complete set of the inflections of a given verb **2** a joining

conjunction n **1** joining together **2** simultaneous occurrence of events **3** a word or group of words that connects words, phrases, or clauses; for example *and*, *if*, and *but* **4** astronomy the apparent nearness of two heavenly bodies to each other **> conjunctional** adj

conjunctiva n, pl **-vas** or **-vae** the delicate mucous membrane that covers the eyeball and inner eyelid [New Latin *membrana conjunctiva* the conjunctive membrane] **> conjunctival** adj

conjunctive adj **1** joining or joined **2** used as a conjunction: *a conjunctive adverb* ▷ n **3** a word or words used as a conjunction [Latin *conjungere* to join]

conjunctivitis n inflammation of the conjunctiva

conjuncture n a combination of events, esp. one that leads to a crisis

conjure vb **-juring, -jured 1** to make (something) appear, as if by magic **2** to perform tricks that appear to be magic **3** to summon (a spirit or demon) by magic **4** formal or literary to appeal earnestly to: *I conjure you by all which you profess: answer me!* [Latin *conjurare* to swear together] **> conjuring** n

conjure up vb **1** to create an image in the mind: *the name Versailles conjures up a past of sumptuous grandeur* **2** to produce as if from nowhere: *he conjured up a fabulous opening goal*

conjuror or **conjurer** n a person who performs magic tricks for people's entertainment

conk Brit, Austral and NZ slang n **1** the head or nose ▷ vb **2** to strike (someone) on the head or nose [probably changed from *conch*]

conker n same as **horse chestnut** (2)

conkers n Brit a game in which a player swings a horse chestnut (conker), threaded onto a string, against that of another player to try to break it [dialect *conker* snail shell, originally used in the game]

conk out vb informal **1** (of a machine or car) to break down **2** to become tired or fall asleep suddenly [origin unknown]

con man n informal a person who swindles someone by means of a confidence trick

Conn n 2nd century AD, king of Leinster and high king of Ireland

Conn. Connecticut

Connacht or **Connaught** n a province and ancient kingdom of NW Republic of Ireland: consists of the counties of Galway, Leitrim, Mayo, Roscommon, and Sligo. Pop: 464 296 (2002). Area: 17 122 sq km (6611 sq miles)

Connaught n another name for **Connacht**

connect vb **1** to link or be linked: *high blood pressure is closely connected to heart disease* **2** to put into telephone communication with **3** (of two public vehicles) to have the arrival of one timed to occur just before the departure of the other, for the convenience of passengers **4** to associate in the mind: *he had always connected sex with violence and attacks rather than loving and concern* **5** to relate by birth or marriage: *she was distantly connected with the Wedgwood family* [Latin *connectere* to bind together] **> connective** adj

Connecticut n **1** a state of the northeastern US, in New England. Capital: Hartford. Pop: 3 483 372 (2003 est). Area: 12 973 sq km (5009 sq miles). Abbreviation: **Conn.**, (with zip code) **CT 2** a river in the northeastern US, rising in N New Hampshire and flowing south to Long Island Sound. Length: 651 km (407 miles)

connection or **connexion** n **1** a relationship or association **2** a link or bond **3** a link between two components in an electric circuit **4 a** an opportunity to transfer from one public vehicle to another **b** vehicle scheduled to provide such an opportunity **5** an influential acquaintance **6** a relative **7** logical sequence in thought or expression **8** a telephone link **9** slang a supplier of illegal drugs, such as heroin **10 in connection with** with reference to: *a number of people have been arrested in connection with the explosion*

connective tissue n body tissue that supports organs, fills the spaces between them, and forms tendons and ligaments

Connell n Desmond. born 1926, Irish cardinal; Archbishop of Dublin and primate of Ireland (1988–2004)

Connemara n a barren coastal region of W Republic of Ireland, in Co Galway: consists of quartzite mountains, peat bogs, and many lakes; noted for its breed of pony originating from the hilly regions

Connery n Sir Sean, real name *Thomas Connery*. born 1929, Scottish film actor, who played James Bond in such films as *Goldfinger* (1964). His later films include *The Name of the Rose* (1986), *Indiana Jones and the Last Crusade* (1989), and *Finding Forrester* (2000)

conning tower n the raised observation tower containing the periscope on a submarine [*con* to steer a ship]

connivance n encouragement or permission of wrongdoing

connive vb **-niving, -nived 1 connive at** to allow or encourage (wrongdoing) by ignoring it **2** to conspire [Latin *connivere* to blink, hence, leave uncensured]

connoisseur (kon-noss-**sir**) n a person with special knowledge of the arts, food, or drink [French]

Connolly n **1** Billy. born 1942, Scottish comedian, musician, and actor: his films include *Mrs Brown* (1997) **2** Cyril (**Vernon**). 1903–74, British critic and writer, founder and editor of *Horizon* (1939–50): his books include *Enemies of Promise* (1938) **3** James. 1868–1916, Irish labour leader: executed by the British for his part in the Easter Rising (1916)

Connors n Jimmy. born 1952, US tennis player: Wimbledon champion 1974 and 1982; US champion 1974, 1976, 1978, 1982, and 1983

connotation n an additional meaning or association implied by a word: *the German term carries a connotation of elitism* [Latin *con-* + together *notare* to mark, note] **> connote** vb

connubial (kon-**new**-bee-al) adj formal of marriage: *connubial bliss* [Latin *conubium* marriage]

conquer vb **1** to defeat (an opponent or opponents) **2** to overcome (a difficulty or feeling) **3** to gain possession of (a place) by force or war [Latin *conquirere* to search for] **> conquering** adj **> conqueror** n

conquest n **1** the act of conquering **2** a person or thing that has been conquered **3** a person whose affections have been won

conquistador n, pl **-dors** or **-dores** one of the Spanish conquerors of Mexico and Peru in the 16th century [Spanish: conqueror]

Conrad n Joseph. real name *Teodor Josef Konrad Korzeniowski*. 1857–1924, British novelist born in Poland, noted for sea stories such as *The Nigger of the Narcissus* (1897) and *Lord Jim* (1900) and novels of politics and revolution such as *Nostromo* (1904) and *Under Western Eyes* (1911)

Cons. Conservative

consanguineous adj formal related by birth [Latin *con-* with + *sanguis* blood] **> consanguinity** n

conscience n **1** the sense of right and wrong that governs a person's thoughts and actions **2** a feeling of guilt: *he showed no hint of conscience over the suffering he had inflicted* **3** in (all) conscience in fairness **4** on one's conscience causing feelings of guilt [Latin *conscire* to know]

conscience-stricken adj feeling guilty because of having done something wrong

conscientious adj **1** painstaking or thorough in one's work **2** governed by conscience **> conscientiously** adv **> conscientiousness** n

conscientious objector n a person who refuses to serve in the armed forces on moral or religious grounds

conscious adj **1** alert and awake **2** aware of one's surroundings and of oneself **3** aware (of something): *he was conscious of a need to urinate* **4** deliberate or intentional: *a conscious attempt* **5** of the part of the mind that is aware of a person's self, surroundings, and thoughts, and that to a certain extent determines choices of action ▷ n **6** the conscious part of the mind [Latin *com-* with + *scire* to know] **> consciously** adv **> consciousness** n

conscript n **1** a person who is enrolled for compulsory military service ▷ vb **2** to enrol (someone) for compulsory military service [Latin *conscriptus* enrolled]

conscription n compulsory military service

consecrate vb **-crating, -crated 1** to make or declare sacred or for religious use **2** to devote or dedicate (something) to a specific purpose **3** Christianity to sanctify (bread and wine) to be received as the body and blood of Christ [Latin *consecrare*] **> consecration** n

consecutive adj following in order without interruption: *three consecutive nights of rioting* [Latin *consequi* to pursue] **> consecutively** adv

consensus n general or widespread agreement [Latin *consentire* to agree]

USAGE Since *consensus* refers to a collective opinion, the words *of opinion* in the phrase *consensus of opinion* are redundant and should therefore be avoided.

consent n **1** agreement, permission, or approval **2** age of consent the age at which sexual intercourse is permitted by law ▷ vb **3** to permit or agree (to) [Latin *consentire* to agree] **> consenting** adj

consequence n **1** a logical result or effect **2** significance or importance: *we said little of consequence to each other; a*

woman of little consequence **3** in consequence as a result **4** take the consequences to accept whatever results from one's action

consequent adj **1** following as an effect **2** following as a logical conclusion [Latin *consequens* following closely]

USAGE See at consequential.

consequential adj **1** important or significant **2** following as a result

USAGE Although both *consequential* and *consequent* can refer to something which happens as the result of something else, *consequent* is more common in this sense in modern English: *the new measures were put into effect, and the consequent protest led to the dismissal of those responsible.*

consequently adv as a result; therefore

conservancy n environmental conservation

conservation n **1** protection and careful management of the environment and natural resources **2** protection from change, loss, or injury **3** physics the principle that the quantity of a specified aspect of a system, such as momentum or charge, remains constant **> conservationist** n

conservative adj **1** favouring the preservation of established customs and values, and opposing change **2** moderate or cautious: *a conservative estimate* **3** conventional in style: *people in this area are conservative in their tastes* ▷ n **4** a conservative person **> conservatism** n

Conservative adj **1** of or supporting the Conservative Party, the major right-wing political party in Britain, which believes in private enterprise and capitalism **2** of or supporting a similar right-wing party in other countries ▷ n **3** a supporter or member of the Conservative Party

conservatoire (kon-**serv**-a-twahr) n a school of music [French]

conservatory n, pl **-tories 1** a greenhouse attached to a house **2** a conservatoire

conserve vb **-serving, -served 1** to protect from harm, decay, or loss **2** to preserve (fruit or other food) with sugar ▷ n **3** fruit preserved by cooking in sugar [Latin *conservare* to keep safe]

Consett n a town in N England, in N Durham. Pop: 20 659 (2001)

consider vb **1** to be of the opinion that **2** to think carefully about (a problem or decision) **3** to bear in mind: *Corsica is well worth considering for those seeking a peaceful holiday in beautiful surroundings* **4** to have regard for or care about: *you must try to consider other people's feelings more* **5** to discuss (something) in order to make a decision **6** to look at: *he considered her and she forced herself to sit calmly under his gaze* [Latin *considerare* to inspect closely]

considerable adj **1** large enough to reckon with: *a considerable number of people* **2** a lot of: *he was in considerable pain* **> considerably** adv

considerate adj thoughtful towards other people

consideration n **1** careful thought **2** a fact to be taken into account when making a decision **3** thoughtfulness for other people **4** payment for a service **5** take into consideration to bear in mind **6** under consideration being currently discussed

considered adj **1** presented or thought out with care: *a considered opinion* **2** thought of in a specified way: *highly considered*

considering conj, prep **1** taking (a specified fact) into account: *considering the mileage the car had done, it was lasting well* ▷ adv **2** informal taking into account the circumstances: *it's not bad considering*

consign vb **1** to give into the care or charge of **2** to put irrevocably: *those events have been consigned to history* **3** to put (in a specified place or situation): *only a few months ago such*

C

demands would have consigned the student leaders to prisons and labour camps **4** to address or deliver (goods): *a cargo of oil drilling equipment consigned to Saudi Arabia* [Latin *consignare* to put one's seal to, sign] **> consignee** *n* **> consignor** *n*

consignment *n* **1** a shipment of goods **2** the act or an instance of consigning: *the goods are sent to Hong Kong for onward consignment to customers in the area*

consist *vb* **1 consist of** to be made up of: *a match consists of seven games* **2 consist in** to have as its main or only part: *his madness, if he is mad, consists in believing that he is a sundial* [Latin *consistere* to stand firm]

consistency *n, pl* **-encies 1** degree of thickness or smoothness **2** being consistent

consistent *adj* **1** holding to the same principles **2** in agreement **> consistently** *adv*

consolation *n* **1** a person or thing that is a comfort in a time of sadness or distress **2** a consoling or being consoled

consolation prize *n* something given to console the loser of a game

console¹ *vb* **-soling, -soled** to comfort (someone) in sadness or distress [Latin *consolari*] **> consolable** *adj*

console² *n* **1** a panel of controls for electronic equipment **2** a cabinet for a television or audio equipment **3** an ornamental bracket used to support a wall fixture **4** the desklike case of an organ, containing the pedals, stops, and keys [Old French *consolateur* one that provides support]

consolidate *vb* **-dating, -dated 1** to make or become stronger or more stable **2** to combine into a whole [Latin *consolidare* to make firm] **> consolidation** *n* **> consolidator** *n*

consommé (kon-som-may) *n* a thin clear meat soup [French]

consonance *n formal* agreement or harmony

consonant *n* **1 a** a speech sound made by partially or completely blocking the breath streams, for example *b* or *f* **b** a letter representing this ▷ *adj* **2 consonant with** in keeping or agreement with: *an individualistic style of religion, more consonant with liberal society* **3** harmonious: *this highly-dissonant chord is followed by a more consonant one* [Latin *consonare* to sound at the same time]

consort *vb* **1 consort with** to keep company with ▷ *n* **2** a husband or wife of a reigning monarch **3** a small group of voices or instruments [Latin *consors* partner]

consortium *n, pl* **-tia** an association of business firms [Latin: partnership]

conspectus *n formal* a survey or summary [Latin: a viewing]

conspicuous *adj* **1** clearly visible **2** noteworthy or striking: *conspicuous bravery* [Latin *conspicuus*] **> conspicuously** *adv*

conspiracy *n, pl* **-cies 1** a secret plan to carry out an illegal or harmful act **2** the act of making such plans

conspire *vb* **-spiring, -spired 1** to plan a crime together in secret **2** to act together as if by design: *the weather and the recession conspired to hit wine production and sales* [Latin *conspirare* to plot together] **> conspirator** *n* **> conspiratorial** *adj*

constable *n* a police officer of the lowest rank [Late Latin *comes stabuli* officer in charge of the stable]

Constable *n* John. 1776–1837, English landscape painter, noted particularly for his skill in rendering atmospheric effects of changing light

constabulary *n, pl* **-laries** *chiefly Brit* the police force of an area

Constance *n* **1** a city in S Germany, in Baden-Württemberg on Lake Constance: tourist centre. Pop: 80 716 (2003 est). German name: **Konstanz 2 Lake Constance** a lake in W Europe, bounded by S Germany, W Austria, and N Switzerland, through which the Rhine flows. Area: 536 sq km. (207 sq miles). German name: **Bodensee**

constant *adj* **1** continuous: *she has endured constant criticism, mockery, and humiliation* **2** unchanging: *the average speed of the winds remained constant over this period* **3** faithful ▷ *n* **4** *maths, physics* a quantity or number which remains invariable: *the velocity of light is a constant* **5** something that is unchanging [Latin *constare* to be steadfast] **> constancy** *n* **> constantly** *adv*

Constant *n* Benjamin. real name Henri Benjamin Constant de Rebecque. 1767–1830, French writer and politician: author of the psychological novel *Adolphe* (1816)

Constanţa *n* a port and resort in SE Romania, on the Black Sea: founded by the Greeks in the 6th century BC and rebuilt by Constantine the Great (4th century); exports petroleum. Pop: 265 000 (2005 est)

Constantia *n S African* **1** a region of the Cape Peninsula **2** any of several red or white wines produced around Constantia

Constantine *n* a walled city in NE Algeria: built on an isolated rock; military and trading centre. Pop: 482 000 (2005 est)

Constantine I *n* **1** known as *Constantine the Great*. Latin name *Flavius Valerius Aurelius Constantinus*. ?280–337 AD, first Christian Roman emperor (306–337): moved his capital to Byzantium, which he renamed Constantinople (330) **2** 1868–1923, king of Greece (1913–17; 1920–22): deposed (1917), recalled by a plebiscite (1920), but forced to abdicate again (1922) after defeat by the Turks

Constantine II *n* official title *Constantine XIII*. born 1940, king of Greece (1964–73): went into exile when the army seized power in 1967. He was officially deposed in 1973 and Greece became a republic

Constantine VII *n* known as *Porphyrogenitus*. 905–59 AD, Byzantine emperor (913–59) and scholar: his writings are an important source for Byzantine history

Constantine XI *n* 1404–53, last Byzantine emperor (1448–53): killed when Constantinople was captured by the Turks

Constantinople *n* the former name (330–1926) of Istanbul

constellation *n* **1** a group of stars which form a pattern and are given a name **2** a group of people or things: *the constellation of favourable circumstances* [Latin *com-* together + *stella* star]

consternation *n* a feeling of anxiety or dismay

constipated *adj* unable to empty one's bowels [Latin *constipare* to press closely together]

constipation *n* a condition in which emptying one's bowels is difficult

constituency *n, pl* **-cies 1** the area represented by a Member of Parliament **2** the voters in such an area

constituent *n* **1** a person living in an MP's constituency **2** a component part ▷ *adj* **3** forming part of a whole: *the constituent parts of the universe* **4** having the power to make or change a constitution of a state: *a constituent assembly* [Latin *constituere* to constitute]

constitute *vb* **-tuting, -tuted 1** to form or make up: *the amazing range of crags that constitute the Eglwyseg Mountains* **2** to set up (an institution) formally [Latin *com-* (intensive) + *statuere* to place]

constitution *n* **1** the principles on which a state is governed **2 the Constitution** (in certain countries) the statute embodying such principles **3** a person's state of health **4** the make-up or structure of something: *change in the very constitution of society*

constitutional *adj* **1** of a constitution **2** authorized by or in accordance with the Constitution of a nation: *constitutional monarchy* **3** inherent in the nature of a person or thing: *a constitutional sensitivity to cold* ▷ *n* **4** a regular walk taken for the good of one's health **> constitutionally** *adv*

constitutive *adj* **1** forming a part of something **2** with the power to appoint or establish

constrain *vb* **1** to compel or force: *he felt constrained to apologize* **2** to limit, restrict, or inhibit: *the mobility of workers is constrained by the serious housing shortage* [Latin *constringere* to bind together]

constrained *adj* embarrassed or unnatural: *his constrained expression*

constraint *n* **1** something that limits a person's freedom of action **2** repression of natural feelings **3** a forced unnatural manner

constrict *vb* **1** to make smaller or narrower by squeezing **2** to limit or restrict [Latin *constringere* to tie up together] > **constrictive** *adj*

constriction *n* **1** a feeling of tightness in some part of the body, such as the chest **2** a narrowing **3** something that constricts

constrictor *n* **1** a snake that coils around and squeezes its prey to kill it **2** a muscle that contracts an opening

construct *vb* **1** to build or put together **2** *geometry* to draw (a figure) to specified requirements **3** to compose (an argument or sentence) > *n* **4** a complex idea resulting from the combination of simpler ideas **5** something formulated or built systematically [Latin *construere* to build] > **constructor** *n*

construction *n* **1** the act of constructing or manner in which a thing is constructed **2** something that has been constructed **3** the business or work of building houses or other structures **4** formal an interpretation: *the financial markets will put the worst possible construction on any piece of news which might affect them* **5** *grammar* the way in which words are arranged in a sentence, clause, or phrase > **constructional** *adj*

constructive *adj* **1** useful and helpful: *constructive criticism* **2** *law* deduced by inference; not openly expressed > **constructively** *adv*

construe *vb* **-struing, -strued 1** to interpret the meaning of (something): *her indifference was construed as rudeness* **2** to analyse the grammatical structure of (a sentence) **3** to combine (words) grammatically **4** old-fashioned to translate literally [Latin *construere* to build]

consul *n* **1** an official representing a state in a foreign country **2** one of the two chief magistrates in ancient Rome [Latin] > **consular** *adj* > **consulship** *n*

consulate *n* **1** the workplace and official home of a consul **2** the position or period of office of a consul

consult *vb* **1** to ask advice from or discuss matters with (someone): *he never consults his wife about what he's about to do* **2** to refer to for information: *he consulted his watch* [Latin *consultare*]

consultant *n* **1** a specialist doctor with a senior position in a hospital **2** a specialist who gives expert professional advice > **consultancy** *n*

consultation *n* **1** the act of consulting **2** a meeting for discussion or the seeking of advice > **consultative** *adj*

consulting *adj* acting as an adviser on professional matters: *consulting engineers*

consulting room *n* a room in which a doctor sees patients

consume *vb* **-suming, -sumed 1** to eat or drink **2** to use up **3** to destroy: *the ship blew up and was consumed by flames* **4** to obsess: *he was consumed with jealousy over the ending of their affair* [Latin *com-* (intensive) + *sumere* to take up] > **consumable** *adj* > **consuming** *adj*

consumer *n* a person who buys goods or uses services

consumer durables *pl n* manufactured products that have a relatively long life, such as cars or televisions

consumer goods *pl n* goods bought for personal needs rather than those required for the production of other goods or services

consumerism *n* **1** the belief that a high level of consumer spending is desirable and beneficial to the economy: *the obsessive consumerism of the 80s* **2** protection of the rights of consumers

consummate *vb* (kon-sum-mate) **-mating, -mated 1** to make (a marriage) legal by sexual intercourse **2** to complete or fulfil > *adj* (kon-**sum**-mit) **3** supremely skilled: *a consummate craftsman* **4** complete or extreme: *consummate skill; consummate ignorance* [Latin *consummare* to complete] > **consummation** *n*

consumption *n* **1** the quantity of something consumed or used: *for such a powerful car, fuel consumption is modest* **2** the act of eating or drinking something: *this meat is unfit for human consumption* **3** *econ* purchase of goods and services for personal use **4** old-fashioned tuberculosis of the lungs

consumptive *adj* **1** wasteful or destructive **2** of tuberculosis of the lungs > *n* **3** a person with tuberculosis of the lungs

cont. continued

contact *n* **1** the state or act of communication: *the airport lost contact with the plane shortly before the crash* **2** the state or act of touching: *rugby is a game of hard physical contact* **3** an acquaintance who might be useful in business **4** a connection between two electrical conductors in a circuit **5** a person who has been exposed to a contagious disease > *vb* **6** to come or be in communication or touch with [Latin *contingere* to touch on all sides]

contact lens *n* a small lens placed on the eyeball to correct defective vision

contagion *n* **1** the passing on of disease by contact **2** a contagious disease **3** a corrupting influence that tends to spread [Latin *contagio* infection]

contagious *adj* **1** (of a disease) capable of being passed on by contact **2** (of a person) capable of passing on a transmissible disease **3** spreading from person to person: *contagious enthusiasm*

contain *vb* **1** to hold or be capable of holding: *the bag contained a selection of men's clothing* **2** to have as one of its ingredients or constituents: *tea and coffee both contain appreciable amounts of caffeine* **3** to consist of: *the book contains 13 very different and largely separate chapters* **4** to check or restrain (feelings or behaviour) **5** to prevent from spreading or going beyond fixed limits: *the blockade was too weak to contain the French fleet* [Latin *continere*] > **containable** *adj*

container *n* **1** an object used to hold or store things in **2** a large standard-sized box for transporting cargo by lorry or ship

containerize or **-ise** *vb* **-izing, -ized** or **-ising, -ised 1** to pack (cargo) in large standard-sized containers **2** to fit (a port, ship, or lorry) to carry goods in standard-sized containers > **containerization** or **-isation** *n*

containment *n* the prevention of the spread of something harmful

contaminate *vb* **-nating, -nated 1** to make impure; pollute **2** to make radioactive [Latin *contaminare* to defile] > **contaminant** *n* > **contamination** *n*

contemn *vb* formal to regard with contempt [Latin *contemnere*]

contemplate *vb* **-plating, -plated 1** to think deeply about **2** to consider as a possibility **3** to look at thoughtfully **4** to meditate [Latin *contemplare*] > **contemplation** *n*

contemplative *adj* **1** of or given to contemplation > *n* **2** a person dedicated to religious contemplation

contemporaneous *adj* happening at the same time > **contemporaneity** *n*

contemporary *adj* **1** existing or occurring at the present time **2** living or occurring in the same period **3** modern in style or fashion **4** of approximately the same age > *n, pl* **-raries 5** a person or thing living at the same time or of approximately the same age as another [Latin *com-* together + *temporarius* relating to time]

> **USAGE** Since *contemporary* can mean either of the same period or of the present period, it is best to avoid this word where ambiguity might arise as in *a production of Othello in contemporary dress. Modern dress* or *Elizabethan dress* should be used in such contexts to avoid ambiguity.

contempt *n* **1** scorn **2** hold in contempt to scorn or despise **3** deliberate disrespect for the authority of a court of law: *contempt of court* [Latin *contemnere* to scorn]

contemptible *adj* deserving to be despised or hated: *a contemptible lack of courage*

contemptuous *adj* showing or feeling strong dislike or disrespect > **contemptuously** *adv*

contend *vb* **1** contend with to deal with **2** to assert **3** to compete or fight **4** to argue earnestly [Latin *contendere* to strive] > **contender** *n*

content¹ *n* **1** contents everything inside a container **2** contents a list of chapters at the front of a book **3** the meaning or substance of a piece of writing, often as distinguished from its style or form **4** the amount of a substance contained in a mixture: *the water vapour content of the atmosphere* [Latin *contentus* contained]

content² *adj* **1** satisfied with things as they are **2** willing to accept a situation or a proposed course of action ▷ *vb* **3** to satisfy (oneself or another person) ▷ *n* **4** peace of mind [Latin *contentus* contented, having restrained desires] > **contentment** *n*

contented *adj* satisfied with one's situation or life > **contentedly** *adv* > **contentedness** *n*

contention *n* **1** disagreement or dispute **2** a point asserted in argument **3** bone of contention a point of dispute [Latin *contentio*]

contentious *adj* **1** causing disagreement **2** tending to quarrel > **contentiousness** *n*

contest *n* **1** a game or match in which people or teams compete **2** a struggle for power or control ▷ *vb* **3** to dispute: *he has said he will not contest the verdict* **4** to take part in (a contest or struggle for power): *all parties which meet the legal requirements will be allowed to contest the election* [Latin *contestari* to introduce a lawsuit] > **contestable** *adj*

contestant *n* a person who takes part in a contest

context *n* **1** the circumstances relevant to an event or fact **2** the words before and after a word or passage in a piece of writing that contribute to its meaning: *taken out of context, lines like these sound ridiculous, but, as part of a scrupulously written play, they are just right* [Latin *com-* together + *texere* to weave] > **contextual** *adj*

contiguous *adj* formal very near or touching [Latin *contiguus*]

continent¹ *n* one of the earth's large landmasses (Asia, Australia, Africa, Europe, North and South America, and Antarctica) [Latin *terra continens* continuous land] > **continental** *adj*

continent² *adj* **1** able to control one's bladder and bowels **2** sexually restrained [Latin *continere* to contain, retain] > **continence** *n*

Continent *n* the Continent the mainland of Europe as distinct from the British Isles > **Continental** *adj*

continental breakfast *n* a light breakfast of coffee and rolls

continental climate *n* a climate with hot summers, cold winters, and little rainfall, typical of the interior of a continent

continental drift *n* geology the theory that the earth's continents drift gradually over the surface of the planet, due to currents in its mantle

continental quilt *n* Brit a large quilt used as a bed cover in place of the top sheet and blankets

continental shelf *n* the gently sloping shallow sea bed surrounding a continent

contingency *n*, *pl* **-cies 1** an unknown or unforeseen future event or condition **2** something dependent on a possible future event

contingent *n* **1** a group of people with a common interest, that represents a larger group: *a contingent of European scientists* **2** a military group that is part of a larger force: *the force includes a contingent of the Foreign Legion* ▷ *adj* **3** (foll. by on or upon) dependent (on something uncertain) **4** happening by chance [Latin *contingere* to touch, befall]

continual *adj* **1** occurring without interruption **2** recurring frequently [Latin *continuus* uninterrupted] > **continually** *adv*

USAGE See at **continuous**.

continuance *n* **1** the act of continuing **2** duration

continuation *n* **1** the act of continuing **2** a part or thing added, such as a sequel **3** a renewal of an interrupted action or process

continue *vb* **-tinuing, -tinued 1** to remain or cause to remain in a particular condition or place **2** to carry on (doing something): *we continued kissing; heavy fighting continued until Thursday afternoon* **3** to resume after an interruption: *we'll continue after lunch* **4** to go on to a further place: *the road continues on up the hill* [Latin *continuar* to join together]

continuity *n*, *pl* **-ties 1** a smooth development or sequence **2** the arrangement of scenes in a film so that they follow each other logically and without breaks

continuo *n*, *pl* **-tinuos** music a continuous bass accompaniment played usually on a keyboard instrument [Italian]

continuous *adj* **1** without end: *a continuous process* **2** not having any breaks or gaps in it: *a continuous line of boats; continuous rain* [Latin *continuus*] > **continuously** *adv*

USAGE Both *continual* and *continuous* can be used to say that something continues without interruption, but only *continual* can correctly be used to say that something keeps happening repeatedly.

continuum *n*, *pl* **-tinua** or **-tinuums** a continuous series or whole, no part of which is noticeably different from the parts immediately next to it, although the ends or extremes of it are very different from each other: *the continuum from minor misbehaviour to major crime* [Latin]

contort *vb* to twist or bend out of shape [Latin *contortus* intricate] > **contortion** *n*

contortionist *n* a performer who contorts his or her body to entertain others

contour *n* **1** an outline **2** same as **contour line** ▷ *vb* **3** to shape so as to form or follow the contour of something [Italian *contornare* to sketch]

contour line *n* a line on a map or chart joining points o equal height or depth

contra- prefix **1** against or contrasting: *contraceptive* **2** (in music) lower in pitch: *contrabass* [Latin *contra* against]

contraband *n* **1** smuggled goods ▷ *adj* **2** (of goods) smuggled [Spanish *contrabando*]

contraception *n* the deliberate use of artificial or natural means to prevent pregnancy [CONTRA- + CONCEPTION]

contraceptive *n* **1** a device, such as a condom, that is used to prevent pregnancy ▷ *adj* **2** providing or relating to contraception: *the contraceptive pill*

contract *n* **1** a formal agreement between two or more parties **2** a document setting out a formal agreement ▷ *vb* **3** to make a formal agreement with (a person or company) to do or deliver (something) **4** to enter into (a relationship or marriage) formally: *she had contracted an alliance with a wealthy man* **5** to make or become smaller, narrower, or shorter **6** to become affected by (an illness **7** to draw (muscles) together or (of muscles) to be drawn together **8** to shorten (a word or phrase) by omitting letters or syllables, usually indicated in writing by an apostrophe [Latin *contractus* agreement] > **contractible** *adj*

contract bridge *n* the most common variety of bridge, in which only tricks bid and won count towards the game

contraction *n* **1** a contracting or being contracted **2** a shortening of a word or group of words, often marked b an apostrophe, for example *I've come* for *I have come* **3** contractions med temporary shortening and tensing o the uterus during pregnancy and labour

contractor *n* a person or firm that supplies materials o labour for other companies

contract out vb Brit to agree not to take part in a scheme
contractual adj of or in the nature of a contract
contradict vb 1 to declare the opposite of (a statement) to be true 2 (of a fact or statement) to suggest that (another fact or statement) is wrong [Latin contra- against + dicere to speak] › **contradiction** n
contradictory adj (of facts or statements) inconsistent
contradistinction n a distinction made by contrasting different qualities › **contradistinctive** adj
contraflow n a flow of road traffic going alongside but in an opposite direction to the usual flow
contralto n, pl -tos or -ti 1 the lowest female voice 2 a singer with such a voice [Italian]
contraption n informal a strange-looking device or gadget [origin unknown]
contrapuntal adj music of or in counterpoint [Italian contrappunto counterpoint]
contrariwise adv 1 from a contrasting point of view 2 in the opposite way
contrary n, pl -ries 1 on or to the contrary in opposition to what has just been said or implied ▷ adj 2 opposed; completely different: a contrary view, based on equally good information 3 perverse; obstinate 4 (of the wind) unfavourable ▷ adv contrary to 5 in opposition or contrast to: contrary to popular belief 6 in conflict with: contrary to nature [Latin contrarius opposite] › **contrariness** n
contrast n 1 a difference which is clearly seen when two things are compared 2 a person or thing showing differences when compared with another 3 the degree of difference between the colours in a photograph or television picture ▷ vb 4 to compare or be compared in order to show the differences between (things): he contrasts that society with contemporary America 5 contrast with to be very different from: her speed of reaction contrasted with her husband's vagueness [Latin contra- against + stare to stand] › **contrasting** adj
contravene vb -vening, -vened formal to break (a rule or law) [Latin contra- against + venire to come] › **contravention** n
contretemps (kon-tra-tahn) n, pl -temps an embarrassing minor disagreement [French]
contribute vb -buting, -buted (often foll. by to) 1 to give (support or money) for a common purpose or fund 2 to supply (ideas or opinions) 3 contribute to to be partly responsible for: his own unconvincing play contributed to his defeat 4 to write (an article) for a publication [Latin contribuere to collect] › **contribution** n › **contributory** adj › **contributor** n
contrite adj full of guilt or regret [Latin contritus worn out] › **contritely** adv › **contrition** n
contrivance n 1 an ingenious device 2 an elaborate or deceitful plan 3 the act or power of contriving
contrive vb -triving, -trived 1 to make happen: he had already contrived the murder of King Alexander 2 to devise or construct ingeniously: he contrived a plausible reason to fly back to London; he contrived a hook from a bent nail [Old French controver]
control n 1 power to direct something: the province is mostly under guerrilla control 2 a curb or check: import controls 3 controls instruments used to operate a machine 4 a standard of comparison used in an experiment 5 an experiment used to verify another by having all aspects identical except for the one that is being tested ▷ vb -trolling, -trolled 6 to have power over: the gland which controls the body's metabolic rate 7 to limit or restrain: he could not control his jealousy 8 to regulate or operate (a machine) 9 to restrict the authorized supply of (certain drugs) [Old French conteroller to regulate] › **controllable** adj
controller n 1 a person who is in charge 2 a person in charge of the financial aspects of a business
control tower n a tall building at an airport from which air traffic is controlled
controversy n, pl -sies argument or debate concerning a

matter about which there is strong disagreement [Latin contra- against + vertere to turn] › **controversial** adj
contumacy (kon-tume-mass-ee) n, pl -cies literary obstinate disobedience [Latin contumax obstinate] › **contumacious** (kon-tume-may-shuss) adj
contumely (kon-tume-mill-ee) n, pl -lies literary 1 scornful or insulting treatment 2 a humiliating insult [Latin contumelia]
contusion n formal a bruise [Latin contusus bruised] › **contuse** vb
conundrum n 1 a puzzling question or problem 2 a riddle whose answer contains a pun [origin unknown]
conurbation n a large heavily populated urban area formed by the growth and merging of towns [Latin con- together + urbs city]
convalesce vb -lescing, -lesced to recover health after an illness or operation [Latin com- (intensive) + valescere to grow strong]
convalescence n 1 gradual return to health after illness or an operation 2 the period during which such recovery occurs › **convalescent** n, adj
convection n the transmission of heat caused by movement of molecules from cool regions to warmer regions of lower density [Latin convehere to bring together]
convector n a heating device which gives out hot air
convene vb -vening, -vened to gather or summon for a formal meeting [Latin convenire to assemble]
convener or **convenor** n a person who calls or chairs a meeting: the shop stewards' convener at the factory › **convenership** or **convenorship** n
convenience n 1 the quality of being suitable or convenient 2 at your convenience at a time suitable to you 3 an object that is useful: a house with every modern convenience 4 euphemistic, chiefly Brit a public toilet
convenience food n food that needs little preparation and can be used at any time
convenient adj 1 suitable or opportune 2 easy to use 3 nearby [Latin convenire to be in accord with]
convent n 1 a building where nuns live 2 a school in which the teachers are nuns 3 a community of nuns [Latin conventus meeting]
conventicle n Brit history, US history a secret or unauthorized religious meeting [Latin conventiculum]
convention n 1 the established view of what is thought to be proper behaviour 2 an accepted rule or method: a convention used by printers 3 a formal agreement or contract between people and nations 4 a large formal assembly of a group with common interests [Latin conventio an assembling]
conventional adj 1 following the accepted customs and lacking originality 2 established by accepted usage or general agreement 3 (of weapons or warfare) not nuclear › **conventionally** adv
conventionality n, pl -ties 1 the quality of being conventional 2 something conventional
conventionalize or -ise vb -izing, -ized or -ising, -ised to make conventional
converge vb -verging, -verged 1 to move towards or meet at the same point 2 (of opinions or effects) to move towards a shared conclusion or result [Latin com- together + vergere to incline] › **convergence** n › **convergent** adj
conversant adj conversant with having knowledge or experience of [Latin conversari to keep company with]
conversation n informal talk between two or more people
conversational adj 1 of or used in conversation: conversational French 2 resembling informal spoken language: the author's easy, conversational style
conversationalist n a person with a specified ability at conversation: a brilliant conversationalist
conversation piece n something, such as an unusual object, that provokes conversation

converse¹ *vb* **-versing, -versed** to have a conversation [Latin *conversari* to keep company with]

converse² *adj* **1** reversed or opposite ▷ *n* **2** a statement or idea that is the opposite of another [Latin *conversus* turned around] > **conversely** *adv*

conversion *n* **1** a change or adaptation **2** *maths* a calculation in which a weight, volume, or distance is worked out in a different system of measurement: *the conversion from Fahrenheit to Celsius* **3** a change to another belief or religion **4** *rugby* a score made after a try by kicking the ball over the crossbar from a place kick [Latin *conversio* a turning around]

convert *vb* **1** to change or adapt **2** to cause (someone) to change in opinion or belief **3** to change (a measurement) from one system of units to another **4** to change (money) into a different currency **5** *rugby* to make a conversion after (a try) ▷ *n* **6** a person who has been converted to another belief or religion [Latin *convertere* to turn around, alter] > **converter** *or* **convertor** *n*

convertible *adj* **1** capable of being converted **2** *finance* (of a currency) freely exchangeable into other currencies ▷ *n* **3** a car with a folding or removable roof

convex *adj* curving outwards like the outside surface of a ball [Latin *convexus* vaulted, rounded] > **convexity** *n*

convey *vb* **1** to communicate (information) **2** to carry or transport from one place to another **3** (of a channel or path) to transfer or transmit **4** *law* to transfer (the title to property) [Old French *conveier*] > **conveyable** *adj* > **conveyor** *n*

conveyance *n* **1** *old-fashioned* a vehicle **2** *law* **a** a transfer of the legal title to property **b** the document effecting such a transfer **3** the act of conveying: *the conveyance of cycles on peak hour trains* > **conveyancer** *n*

conveyancing *n* the branch of law dealing with the transfer of ownership of property

conveyor belt *n* an endless moving belt driven by rollers and used to transport objects, esp. in a factory

convict *vb* **1** to declare (someone) guilty of an offence ▷ *n* **2** a person serving a prison sentence [Latin *convictus* convicted]

conviction *n* **1** a firmly held belief or opinion **2** an instance of being found guilty of a crime: *he had several convictions for petty theft* **3** a convincing or being convinced **4** **carry conviction** to be convincing

convince *vb* **-vincing, -vinced** to persuade by argument or evidence [Latin *convincere* to demonstrate incontrovertibly] > **convinced** *adj* > **convincible** *adj* > **convincing** *adj*

convivial *adj* sociable or lively: *a convivial atmosphere; convivial company* [Late Latin *convivialis*] > **conviviality** *n*

convocation *n* *formal* a large formal meeting

convoke *vb* **-voking, -voked** *formal* to call together [Latin *convocare*]

convoluted *adj* **1** coiled or twisted **2** (of an argument or sentence) complex and difficult to understand

convolution *n* **1** a coil or twist **2** an intricate or confused matter or condition **3** a convex fold in the surface of the brain

convolvulus *n, pl* **-luses** *or* **-li** a twining plant with funnel-shaped flowers and triangular leaves [Latin: bindweed]

convoy *n* a group of vehicles or ships travelling together [Old French *convoier* to convey]

convulse *vb* **-vulsing, -vulsed** **1** to shake or agitate violently **2** (of muscles) to undergo violent spasms **3** *informal* to be overcome (with laughter or rage) **4** to disrupt the normal running of: *student riots have convulsed India* [Latin *con-* together + *vellere* to pluck, pull] > **convulsive** *adj*

convulsion *n* **1** a violent muscular spasm **2** a violent upheaval **3 convulsions** *informal* uncontrollable laughter: *I was in convulsions*

Conwy *n* **1** a market town and resort in N Wales, in Conwy county borough on the estuary of the River Conwy: medieval town walls, 13th-century castle. Pop: 3847 (2001). Former name: **Conway 2** a county borough in N Wales, created in 1996 from parts of Gwynedd and Clwyd. Pop: 110 900 (2003 est). Area: 1130 sq km (436 sq miles)

cony *or* **coney** *n, pl* **-nies** *or* **-neys** *Brit* **1** a rabbit **2** rabbit fur [Latin *cuniculus* rabbit]

Conybeare *n* **William Daniel**. 1787–1857, British geologist. He summarized all that was known about rocks at the time in *Outlines of the Geology of England and Wales* (1822)

coo *vb* **cooing, cooed 1** (of a dove or pigeon) to make a soft murmuring sound **2 bill and coo** to murmur softly or lovingly ▷ *n* **3** a cooing sound ▷ *interj* **4** *Brit slang* an exclamation of surprise or amazement [imitative] > **cooing** *adj, n*

Cooch Behar *or* **Kuch Bihar** *n* **1** a former state of NE India: part of West Bengal since 1950 **2** a city in India, in NE West Bengal: capital of the former state of Cooch Behar. Pop: 76 812 (2001)

cooee *interj* **1** *Brit, Austral and NZ* a call used to attract attention **2** *Austral and NZ* **within cooee** within calling distance: *the school was within cooee of our house* [Aboriginal]

cook *vb* **1** to prepare (food) by heating or (of food) to be prepared in this way **2** *slang* to alter or falsify (figures or accounts): *she had cooked the books* ▷ *n* **3** a person who prepares food for eating ▶ See also **cook up** [Latin *coquere*]

Cook¹ *n* **Mount Cook 1** a mountain in New Zealand, in the South Island, in the Southern Alps: the highest peak in New Zealand. Height: reduced in 1991 by a rockfall from 3764 m (12 349 ft) to 3754 m (12 316 ft); further erosion has reduced the height to 3724 m (12 217 ft). Official name: **Aoraki-Mount Cook 2** a mountain in SE Alaska, in the St Elias Mountains. Height: 4194 m (13 760 ft)

Cook² *n* **1 Captain James**. 1728–79, British navigator and explorer: claimed the E coast of Australia for Britain, circumnavigated New Zealand, and discovered several Pacific and Atlantic islands (1768–79) **2 Sir Joseph**. 1860–1947, Australian statesman, born in England: prime minister of Australia (1913–14) **3 Peter (Edward)**. 1937–95, British comedy actor and writer, noted esp. for his partnership (1960–73) with Dudley Moore **4 Robin**, full name *Robert Finlayson Cook*. 1946–2005, British Labour politician; foreign secretary (1997–2001), Leader of the House (2001-2003) **5 Thomas**. 1808–92, British travel agent; innovator of conducted excursions and founder of the travel agents Thomas Cook and Son

cook-chill *n* a method of food preparation used by caterers, in which cooked dishes are chilled rapidly and reheated as required

cooker *n* **1** *chiefly Brit* an apparatus for cooking heated by gas or electricity **2** *Brit* an apple suitable for cooking but not for eating raw

cookery *n* the art or practice of cooking. Related adjective: **culinary**

cookery book *or* **cookbook** *n* a book containing recipes for cooking

cookie *n, pl* **cookies 1** *US and Canad* a biscuit **2 that's the way the cookie crumbles** *informal* that is how things inevitably are **3** *informal* a person: *a real tough cookie* **4** *computers* a piece of data downloaded from a website to a user's computer, allowing the user to be identified on future visits to the website [Dutch *koekje* little cake]

Cook Inlet *n* an inlet of the Pacific on the coast of S Alaska: part of the Gulf of Alaska

Cook Islands *pl n* a group of islands in the SW Pacific, an overseas territory of New Zealand: consists of the Lower Cooks and the Northern Cooks Capital: Avarua, on Rarotonga. Pop: 10 447 (2013 est). Area: 234 sq km (90 sq miles)

Cookson *n* **Dame Catherine**. 1906-98, British novelist, known for her popular novels set in northeast England

Cookstown n a district of central Northern Ireland, in Co Tyrone. Pop: 33 387 (2003 est). Area: 622 sq km (240 sq miles)

Cook Strait n the strait between North and South Islands, New Zealand. Width: 26 km (16 miles)

cook up vb to invent (a story or scheme)

cool adj **1** moderately cold: it should be served cool, even chilled **2** comfortably free of heat: it was one of the few cool days that summer **3** calm and unemotional: a cool head **4** indifferent or unfriendly: the idea met with a cool response **5** calmly impudent **6** informal (of a large sum of money) without exaggeration: a cool million **7** informal sophisticated or elegant **8** (of a colour) having violet, blue, or green predominating **9** informal marvellous ▷ vb **10** to make or become cooler **11** to calm down ▷ n **12** coolness: in the cool of the evening **13** slang calmness; composure: he lost his cool and wantonly kicked the ball away [Old English cōl] ⟩ **coolly** adv ⟩ **coolness** n

coolant n a fluid used to cool machinery while it is working

cool drink n S African a soft drink

cooler n a container for making or keeping things cool

coolibah n an Australian eucalypt that grows beside rivers [Aboriginal]

Coolidge n (John) **Calvin**. 1872–1933, 30th president of the US (1923–29)

coolie n old-fashioned, offensive an unskilled Oriental labourer [Hindi kulī]

cooling tower n a tall hollow structure in a factory or power station, inside which hot water cools as it trickles down

Coomaraswamy n Ananda (Kentish). 1877–1947, Ceylonese art historian and interpreter of Indian culture to the West

coomb or **coombe** n a short valley or deep hollow [Old English cumb]

coon n **1** informal short for **raccoon 2** offensive, slang a Black person of African origin or an Australian Aborigine **3** S African offensive a person of mixed race

coop¹ n **1** a cage or pen for poultry or small animals ▷ vb **2** **coop up** to confine in a restricted space [Latin cupa basket, cask]

coop² or **co-op** (koh-op) n Brit, Austral and NZ a cooperative society or a shop run by a cooperative society

cooper n a person who makes or repairs barrels or casks [see COOP¹]

Cooper n **1** Anthony Ashley. See (Earl of) **Shaftesbury 2** Cary (Lynn). born 1940, British psychologist, noted for his studies of behaviour at work and the causes and treatment of stress **3** Gary, real name Frank James Cooper. 1901–61, US film actor; his many films include Sergeant York (1941) and High Noon (1952), for both of which he won Oscars **4** Sir Henry. 1934–2011, British boxer; European heavyweight champion (1964; 1968–71) **5** James Fenimore 1789–1851, US novelist, noted for his stories of Native Americans, esp. The Last of the Mohicans (1826) **6** Leon Neil. born 1930, US physicist, noted for his work on the theory of superconductivity. He shared the Nobel prize for physics 1972 **7** Samuel 1609–72, English miniaturist

cooperate or **co-operate** vb **1** to work or act together **2** to assist or be willing to assist [Latin co- with + operari to work] ⟩ **cooperation** or **co-operation** n

cooperative or **co-operative** adj **1** willing to cooperate **2** (of an enterprise or farm) owned and managed collectively ▷ n **3** a cooperative organization

cooperative society n a commercial enterprise owned and run by customers or workers, in which the profits are shared among the members

Cooper Creek n an intermittent river in E central Australia, in the Channel Country: rises in central Queensland and flows generally southwest, reaching Lake Eyre only during wet-year floods; scene of the death of the explorers Burke and Wills in 1861; the surrounding basin provides cattle pastures after the floods subside. Total length: 1420 km (880 miles)

coopt or **co-opt** (koh-opt) vb to add (someone) to a group by the agreement of the existing members [Latin cooptare to choose, elect]

coordinate or **co-ordinate** vb **-nating, -nated 1** to bring together and cause to work together efficiently ▷ n **2** maths any of a set of numbers defining the location of a point with reference to a system of axes ▷ adj **3** of or involving coordination **4** of or involving the use of coordinates: coordinate geometry [Latin co- together + ordinatio arranging] ⟩ **coordination** or **co-ordination** n ⟩ **coordinator** or **co-ordinator** n

coordinates or **co-ordinates** pl n clothes designed to be worn together

Coorg n a former province of SW India: since 1956 part of Karnataka state

coot n **1** a small black water bird **2** Brit, Austral and NZ a foolish person [probably Low German]

cop slang n **1** a policeman **2** not much cop of little value or worth ▷ vb **copping, copped 3** to take or seize **4** cop it to get into trouble or be punished: he copped it after he was spotted driving a car without a seat belt ▶ See also **cop out** [perhaps from Old French caper to seize]

copal n a resin used in varnishes

Copán n a village in W Honduras: site of a ruined Mayan city

copartner n a partner or associate ⟩ **copartnership** n

cope¹ vb **coping, coped 1** to deal successfully (with): well-nourished people cope better with stress **2** to tolerate or endure: the ability to cope with his pain [Old French coper to strike, cut]

cope² n a large ceremonial cloak worn by some Christian priests [Late Latin cappa hooded cloak]

cope³ vb **coping, coped** to provide (a wall) with a coping [probably from French couper to cut]

copeck n same as kopeck

Copenhagen n the capital of Denmark, a port on Zealand and the Amager Islands on a site inhabited for some 6000 years: exports chiefly agricultural products; iron and steel works; university (1479). Pop: 501 664 (2004 est). Danish name: København

Copernican (kop-per-nik-an) adj of the theory that the earth and the planets rotate round the sun [after COPERNICUS]

copernicium n a highly radioactive element that is produced synthetically. Symbol: **Cn** [after COPERNICUS]

Copernicus n Nicolaus. Polish name Mikolaj Kopernik. 1473–1543, Polish astronomer, whose theory of the solar system (the **Copernican system**) was published in 1543 ⟩ **Copernican** adj

copestone n **1** Also called: **coping stone** a stone used to form a coping **2** the stone at the top of a building or wall

copier n a person or machine that copies

copilot n the second pilot of an aircraft

coping n a layer of rounded or sloping bricks on the top of a wall

coping saw n a handsaw with a U-shaped frame, used for cutting curves in wood

copious (kope-ee-uss) adj existing or produced in large quantities [Latin copiosus] ⟩ **copiously** adv

Copland n Aaron. 1900–90, US composer of orchestral and chamber music, ballets, and film music

Copley n John Singleton. 1738–1815, US painter

cop out slang vb **1** to avoid taking responsibility or committing oneself ▷ n **cop-out 2** a way or an instance of avoiding responsibility or commitment [probably from COP]

copper¹ n **1** a soft reddish metallic element, used in such alloys as brass and bronze. Symbol: **Cu 2** informal any copper or bronze coin **3** chiefly Brit a large metal container used to boil water ▷ adj **4** reddish-brown [Latin Cyprium aes Cyprian metal, from Greek Kupris Cyprus]

copper² *n Brit slang* a policeman [from COP (verb)]

copper beech *n* a European beech with reddish leaves

Copper Belt *n* a region of Central Africa, along the border between Zambia and the Democratic Republic of Congo: rich deposits of copper

copper-bottomed *adj* financially reliable [from the practice of coating the bottom of ships with copper to prevent the timbers rotting]

copperhead *n* a poisonous snake with a reddish-brown head

copperplate *n* **1** an elegant handwriting style **2** a polished copper plate engraved for printing **3** a print taken from such a plate

copper sulphate *n* a blue crystalline copper salt used in electroplating and in plant sprays

coppice *n* a small group of trees or bushes growing close together [Old French *copeiz*]

Coppola *n* Francis Ford. born 1939, US film director. His films include *The Godfather* (1972), *The Godfather Part II* (1974), *Apocalypse Now* (1979), *Tucker* (1988), and *The Rainmaker* (1997)

copra *n* the dried oil-yielding kernel of the coconut [Malayalam (a language of SW India) *koppara* coconut]

copse *n* same as **coppice**

Copt *n* **1** a member of the Coptic Church, a part of the Christian Church which was founded in Egypt **2** an Egyptian descended from the ancient Egyptians [Coptic *kyptios* Egyptian]

Coptic *n* **1** the language of the Copts, descended from Ancient Egyptian and surviving only in the Coptic Church ▷ *adj* **2** of the Copts or the Coptic Church

copula *n*, *pl* **-las** *or* **-lae** a verb, such as *be*, that is used to link the subject with the complement of a sentence, as in *he became king* [Latin: bond]

copulate *vb* **-lating, -lated** to have sexual intercourse [Latin *copulare* to join together] ▷ **copulation** *n*

copy *n*, *pl* **copies** **1** a thing made to look exactly like another **2** a single specimen of a book, magazine, or record of which there are many others exactly the same: *my copy of 'Death on the Nile'* **3** written material for printing **4** the text of an advertisement **5** *journalism informal* suitable material for an article: *disasters are always good copy* ▷ *vb* **copies, copying, copied** **6** to make a copy (of) **7** to act or try to be like another [Latin *copia* abundance]

copybook *n* **1** a book of specimens of handwriting for imitation **2 blot one's copybook** *informal* to spoil one's reputation by a mistake or indiscretion ▷ *adj* **3** done exactly according to the rules **4** trite or unoriginal

copycat *n informal* a person who imitates or copies someone

copyist *n* **1** a person who makes written copies **2** an imitator: *although the songs are derivative, it is unfair to dismiss the band as mere copyists*

copyright *n* **1** the exclusive legal right to reproduce and control an original literary, musical, or artistic work ▷ *vb* **2** to take out a copyright on ▷ *adj* **3** protected by copyright

copy typist *n* a typist who types from written or typed drafts rather than dictation

copywriter *n* a person employed to write advertising copy

coquette *n* a woman who flirts [French] ▷ **coquetry** *n* ▷ **coquettish** *adj*

coracle *n* a small round boat made of wicker covered with skins [Welsh *corwgl*]

coral *n* **1** the stony substance formed by the skeletons of marine animals called polyps, often forming an island or reef **2** any of the polyps whose skeletons form coral ▷ *adj* **3** orange-pink [Greek *korallion*]

Coral Sea *n* the SW arm of the Pacific, between Australia, New Guinea, and Vanuatu

cor anglais *n*, *pl* **cors anglais** *music* an alto woodwind instrument of the oboe family [French: English horn]

Corantijn *n* the Dutch name of **Courantyne**

corbel *n archit* a stone or timber support sticking out of a wall [Old French: a little raven]

corbie *n Scot* a raven or crow [Latin *corvus*]

Corby *n* a town in central England, in N Northamptonshire: designated a new town in 1950. Pop 49 222 (2001)

Corcovado *n* **1** a volcano in S Chile, in the Andes. Height: 2300 m (7546 ft) **2** a mountain in SE Brazil, in SW Rio de Janeiro city, famous for a massive statue of Christ the Redeemer. Height of mountain: 704 m (2310 ft)

Corcyra *n* the ancient name for **Corfu**

cord *n* **1** string or thin rope made of twisted strands **2** *anatomy* a structure in the body resembling a rope: *the vocal cords* **3** a ribbed fabric like corduroy **4** *US, Canad, Austral and NZ* an electrical flex **5** a unit for measuring cut wood, equal to 128 cubic feet ▷ *adj* **6** (of fabric) ribbed ▷ **See also cords** [Greek *khordē*]

cordate *adj* heart-shaped

Corday *n* Charlotte, full name Marie Anne Charlotte Corday d'Armont. 1768–93, French Girondist revolutionary, who assassinated Marat

corded *adj* **1** tied or fastened with cord **2** (of a fabric) ribbed: *white corded silk* **3** (of muscles) standing out like cords

cordial *adj* **1** warm and friendly: *a cordial atmosphere* **2** heartfelt or sincere: *I developed a cordial dislike for the place* ▷ *n* **3** a drink with a fruit base: *lime cordial* [Latin *cor* heart] ▷ **cordially** *adv*

cordiality *n* warmth of feeling

Cordilleras *pl n* **the Cordilleras** the complex of mountain ranges on the W side of the Americas, extending from Alaska to Cape Horn and including the Andes and the Rocky Mountains

cordite *n* a smokeless explosive used in guns and bombs [from *cord*, because of its stringy appearance]

cordless *adj* (of an electrical appliance such as a kettle or telephone) powered by an internal battery or kept in a holder which is connected to the mains, so that there is no cable connecting the appliance itself to the electrical mains

Córdoba¹ *n* **1** a city in central Argentina: university (1613). Pop: 1 592 000 (2005 est) **2** a city in S Spain, on the Guadalquivir River: centre of Moorish Spain (711–1236). Pop: 318 628 (2003 est). English name: **Cordova**

Córdoba² *or* **Córdova** *n* Francisco Fernández de. died 1518, Spanish soldier and explorer, who discovered Yucatán

cordon *n* **1** a chain of police, soldiers, or vehicles guarding an area **2** an ornamental braid or ribbon **3** *horticulture* a fruit tree trained to grow as a single stem bearing fruit ▷ *vb* **4 cordon off** to put or form a cordon round [Old French: a little cord]

cordon bleu (bluh) *adj* (of cookery or cooks) of the highest standard: *a cordon bleu chef* [French: blue ribbon]

cordon sanitaire *n* **1** a line of buffer states shielding a country **2** a guarded line isolating an infected area [French, literally: sanitary line]

Cordova *n* the English name for **Córdoba** (2)

Cordovan *n* **1** a native or inhabitant of Córdoba, Spain ▷ *adj* **2** of or relating to Córdoba, Spain

cords *pl n* trousers made of corduroy

corduroy *n* a heavy cotton fabric with a velvety ribbed surface [origin unknown]

corduroys *pl n* trousers made of corduroy

core *n* **1** the central part of certain fleshy fruits, containing the seeds **2** the central or essential part of something: *the historic core of the city* **3** a piece of magnetic soft iron inside an electromagnet or transformer **4** *geology* the central part of the earth **5** a cylindrical sample of rock or soil, obtained by the use of a hollow drill **6** *physics* the region of a nuclear reactor containing the fissionable material **7** *computers* the main internal memory of a computer ▷ *vb* **coring, cored** **8** to remove the core from (fruit) [origin unknown]

corella *n* a white Australian cockatoo

Corelli *n* **1** Arcangelo. 1653–1713, Italian violinist and composer of sonatas and concerti grossi **2** Marie, real name *Mary Mackay*. 1854–1924, British novelist. Her melodramatic works include *The Sorrows of Satan* (1895) and *The Murder of Delicia* (1896)

co-respondent *n* a person with whom someone being sued for divorce is claimed to have committed adultery

Corfu *n* **1** an island in the Ionian Sea, in the Ionian Islands: forms, with neighbouring islands, a department of Greece. Pop: 107 879 (2001). Area: 641 sq km (247 sq miles) **2** a port on E Corfu island. Pop (municipality): 41 532 (2001) ▶ Modern Greek name: **Kérkyra**. Ancient name: **Corcyra**

corgi *n* a short-legged sturdy dog [Welsh *cor* dwarf + *ci* dog]

Cori *n* Carl Ferdinand. 1896–1984, US biochemist, born in Bohemia; shared a Nobel prize for physiology or medicine (1947) with his wife **Gerty Theresa Radnitz Cori** (1896–1957) and Bernardo Houssay, for elucidating the stages of glycolysis

coriander *n* a European plant, cultivated for its aromatic seeds and leaves, used in flavouring foods [Greek *koriannon*]

Corinth *n* **1** a port in S Greece, in the NE Peloponnese: the modern town is near the site of the ancient city, the largest and richest of the city-states after Athens. Pop (municipality): 36 991 (2001). Modern Greek name: **Kórinthos 2** a region of ancient Greece, occupying most of the Isthmus of Corinth and part of the NE Peloponnese **3** Gulf of Corinth *or* Gulf of Lepanto an inlet of the Ionian Sea between the Peloponnese and central Greece **4** Isthmus of Corinth a narrow strip of land between the Gulf of Corinth and the Saronic Gulf: crossed by the **Corinth Canal** making navigation possible between the gulfs

Corinthian *adj* **1** of or relating to Corinth or its inhabitants **2** of a style of classical architecture characterized by a bell-shaped capital with carved leaf-shaped ornaments ▷ *n* **3** a native or inhabitant of Corinth

Coriolanus *n* Gaius Marcius. 5th century BC, a legendary Roman general, who allegedly led an army against Rome but was dissuaded from conquering it by his mother and wife

cork *n* **1** the thick light porous outer bark of a Mediterranean oak **2** a piece of cork used as a stopper **3** *botany* the outer bark of a woody plant ▷ *vb* **4** to stop up (a bottle) with a cork [probably from Arabic *qurq*]

Cork *n* **1** a county of SW Republic of Ireland, in Munster province: crossed by ridges of low mountains; scenic coastline. County town: Cork. Pop: 447 829 (2002). Area: 7459 sq km (2880 sq miles) **2** a city and port in S Republic of Ireland, county town of Co Cork, at the mouth of the River Lee: seat of the University College of Cork (1849). Pop: 186 239 (2002) ▶ Gaelic name: **Corcaigh**

corkage *n* a charge made at a restaurant for serving wine bought elsewhere

corked *adj* (of wine) spoiled through being stored in a bottle with a decayed cork

corker *n* *old-fashioned, slang* a splendid or outstanding person or thing

corkscrew *n* **1** a device for pulling corks from bottles, usually consisting of a pointed metal spiral attached to a handle ▷ *adj* **2** like a corkscrew in shape ▷ *vb* **3** to move in a spiral or zigzag course

corm *n* the scaly bulblike underground stem of certain plants [Greek *kormos* tree trunk]

cormorant *n* a large dark-coloured long-necked sea bird [Old French *corp* raven + *-mareng* of the sea]

corn¹ *n* **1** a cereal plant such as wheat, oats, or barley **2** the grain of such plants **3** US, Canad, Austral and NZ maize **4** *slang* something unoriginal or oversentimental [Old English]

corn² *n* a painful hardening of the skin around a central point in the foot, caused by pressure [Latin *cornu* horn]

corn circle *n* same as **crop circle**

corncob *n* the core of an ear of maize, to which the kernels are attached

corncrake *n* a brown bird with a harsh grating cry

cornea (korn-ee-a) *n* the transparent membrane covering the eyeball [Latin *cornu* horn] ▷ **corneal** *adj*

corned beef *n* cooked beef preserved in salt

Corneille *n* Pierre. 1606–84, French tragic dramatist often regarded as the founder of French classical drama. His plays include *Médée* (1635), *Le Cid* (1636), *Horace* (1640), and *Polyeucte* (1642)

cornelian *n* same as **carnelian**

corner *n* **1** the place or angle formed by the meeting of two converging lines or surfaces **2** the space within the angle formed, as in a room **3** the place where two streets meet **4** a sharp bend in a road **5** a remote place: *far-flung corners of the world* **6** any secluded or private place **7** *sport* a free kick or shot taken from the corner of the field **8** cut corners to take the shortest or easiest way at the expense of high standards **9** turn the corner to pass the critical point of an illness or a difficult time ▷ *adj* **10** on or in a corner: *a corner seat* ▷ *vb* **11** to force (a person or animal) into a difficult or inescapable position **12** (of a vehicle or its driver) to turn a corner **13** to obtain a monopoly of [Latin *cornu* point, horn]

Corner *n* the Corner *informal* an area in central Australia, at the junction of the borders of Queensland and South Australia

corner shop *n* a small general shop serving a neighbourhood

cornerstone *n* **1** an indispensable part or basis: *the food we eat is one of the cornerstones of good health* **2** a stone at the corner of a wall

cornet *n* **1** a brass instrument of the trumpet family **2** *Brit* a cone-shaped ice-cream wafer [Latin *cornu* horn] ▷ **cornetist** *n*

corn exchange *n* a building where corn is bought and sold

cornflakes *pl n* a breakfast cereal made from toasted maize

cornflour *n* **1** a fine maize flour, used for thickening sauces **2** NZ fine wheat flour

cornflower *n* a small plant with blue flowers

Cornforth *n* Sir John Warcup. 1917–2014, Australian chemist, who shared the 1975 Nobel prize for chemistry with Vladimir Prelog for their work on stereochemistry

cornice (korn-iss) *n* **1** a decorative moulding round the top of a wall or building **2** *archit* the projecting mouldings at the top of a column [Old French]

Cornish *adj* **1** of Cornwall ▷ *n* **2** a Celtic language of Cornwall, extinct by 1800 ▷ *pl n* **3** the Cornish the people of Cornwall

Cornishman *n, pl* -men a man who is a native or inhabitant of Cornwall

Cornish pasty *n* a pastry case with a filling of meat and vegetables

Corno *n* Monte Corno a mountain in central Italy: the highest peak in the Apennines. Height: 2912 m (9554 ft)

cornucopia (korn-yew-kope-ee-a) *n* **1** a great abundance: *a cornucopia of rewards* **2** a symbol of plenty, consisting of a horn overflowing with fruit and flowers [Latin *cornu copiae* horn of plenty]

Cornwall *n* a former administrative county of SW England; became a unitary authority in 2009: hilly, with a deeply indented coastline. Administrative centre: Truro. Pop: 513 500 (2003 est). Area: 3564 sq km (1376 sq miles). Cornish name: **Kernow**

Cornwallis *n* Charles, 1st Marquis Cornwallis. 1738–1805, British general in the War of American Independence: commanded forces defeated at Yorktown (1781): defeated Tipu Sahib (1791): governor general of Bengal (1786–93, 1805): negotiated the Treaty of Amiens (1801)

Cornwell *n* Patricia D (aniels). born 1956, US crime novelist; her novels, many of which feature the pathologist Dr Kay Scarpetta, include *Postmortem* (1990), *The Last Precinct* (2000), and *Isle of Dogs* (2002)

corny *adj* **cornier, corniest** *slang* unoriginal or oversentimental

corolla *n* the petals of a flower collectively [Latin: garland]

corollary (kor-oll-a-ree) *n, pl* **-laries 1** a proposition that follows directly from another that has been proved **2** a natural consequence [Latin *corollarium* money paid for a garland]

Coromandel Coast *n* the SE coast of India, along the Bay of Bengal, extending from Point Calimere to the mouth of the Krishna River

corona (kor-rone-a) *n, pl* **-nas** or **-nae** (-nee) **1** a circle of light around a luminous body, usually the moon **2** the outermost part of the sun's atmosphere, visible as a faint halo during a total eclipse **3** a long cigar with blunt ends **4** *botany* a crownlike part of some flowers on top of the seed or on the inner side of the corolla **5** *physics* an electrical glow appearing around the surface of a charged conductor [Latin: crown]

coronary (kor-ron-a-ree) *adj* **1** *anatomy* of the arteries that supply blood to the heart ▷ *n, pl* **-naries 2** a coronary thrombosis [Latin *coronarius* belonging to a wreath or crown]

coronary thrombosis *n* a condition where the blood flow to the heart is blocked by a clot in a coronary artery

coronation *n* the ceremony of crowning a monarch [Latin *coronare* to crown]

coronavirus *n* a type of airborne virus accounting for 10–30% of all colds [from its corona-like appearance under an electron microscope]

coroner *n* a public official responsible for the investigation of violent, sudden, or suspicious deaths [Anglo-French *corouner*]

coronet *n* **1** a small crown worn by princes or peers **2** a band of jewels worn as a headdress [Old French *coronete*]

Corot *n* Jean Baptiste Camille. 1796–1875, French landscape and portrait painter

corpora *pl n* the plural of **corpus**

corporal[1] *n* a noncommissioned officer in an army [Old French *caporal*, from Latin *caput* head]

corporal[2] *adj* of the body [Latin *corpus* body]

corporal punishment *n* physical punishment, such as caning

corporate *adj* **1** relating to business corporations: *corporate finance* **2** shared by a group **3** forming a corporation; incorporated [Latin *corpus* body]

corporation *n* **1** a large business or company **2** a city or town council **3** *informal* a large paunch ▷ **corporative** *adj*

corporatism *n* organization of a state on the lines of a business enterprise, with substantial government management of the economy

corporeal (kore-pore-ee-al) *adj* of the physical world rather than the spiritual [Latin *corpus* body]

corps (kore) *n, pl* **corps 1** a military unit with a specific function: *medical corps* **2** an organized body of people: *the diplomatic corps* [French]

corps de ballet *n* the members of a ballet company [French]

corpse *n* a dead body, esp. of a human being [Latin *corpus*]

corpulent *adj* fat or plump [Latin *corpulentus*] ▷ **corpulence** *n*

corpus *n, pl* **-pora** a collection of writings, such as one by a single author or on a specific topic: *the corpus of Marxist theory* [Latin: body]

Corpus Christi *n* a port in S Texas, on **Corpus Christi Bay**, an inlet of the Gulf of Mexico. Pop: 279 208 (2003 est)

corpuscle *n* a red blood cell (see **erythrocyte**) or white blood cell (see **leucocyte**) [Latin *corpusculum* a little body] ▷ **corpuscular** *adj*

corral *US and Canad n* **1** an enclosure for cattle or horses ▷ *vb* **-ralling, -ralled 2** to put in a corral [Spanish]

corrasion *n geology* erosion of rocks caused by fragments transported over them by water, wind, or ice [Latin *corradere* to scrape together]

correct *adj* **1** free from error; true: *the correct answer* **2** in conformity with accepted standards: *in most cultures there is a strong sense of correct sexual conduct* ▷ *vb* **3** to make free from or put right errors **4** to indicate the errors in (something) **5** to rebuke or punish in order to improve: *I stand corrected* **6** to make conform to a standard [Latin *corrigere* to make straight] ▷ **correctly** *adv* ▷ **correctness** *n*

correction *n* **1** an act or instance of correcting **2** an alteration correcting something: *corrections to the second proofs* **3** a reproof or punishment ▷ **correctional** *adj*

corrective *adj* intended to put right something that is wrong: *corrective action*

Correggio *n* Antonio Allegri da. 1494–1534, Italian painter, noted for his striking use of perspective and foreshortening

Corregidor *n* an island at the entrance to Manila Bay, in the Philippines: site of the defeat of American forces by the Japanese (1942) in World War II

correlate *vb* **-lating, -lated 1** to place or be placed in a mutual relationship: *water consumption is closely correlated to the number of people living in a house* ▷ *n* **2** either of two things mutually related ▷ **correlation** *n*

correlative *adj* **1** having a mutual relationship **2** *grammar* (of words, usually conjunctions) corresponding to each other and occurring regularly together, for example *neither* and *nor*

correspond *vb* **1** to be consistent or compatible (with) **2** to be similar (to) **3** to communicate (with) by letter [Latin *com-* together + *respondere* to respond] ▷ **corresponding** *adj* ▷ **correspondingly** *adv*

correspondence *n* **1** communication by letters **2** the letters exchanged in this way **3** relationship or similarity

correspondence course *n* a course of study conducted by post

correspondent *n* **1** a person who communicates by letter **2** a person employed by a newspaper or news service to report on a special subject or from a foreign country

Corrèze *n* a department of central France, in Limousin region. Capital: Tulle. Pop: 234 144 (2003 est). Area: 5888 sq km (2296 sq miles)

corridor *n* **1** a passage in a building or a train **2** a strip of land or airspace that provides access through the territory of a foreign country **3 corridors of power** the higher levels of government or the Civil Service [Old Italian *corridore*, literally: place for running]

corrie *n* (in Scotland) a circular hollow on the side of a hill [Gaelic *coire* cauldron]

Corrientes *n* a port in NE Argentina, on the Paraná River. Pop: 340 000 (2005 est)

corrigendum (kor-rij-end-um) *n, pl* **-da** (-da) **1** an error to be corrected **2** a slip of paper inserted into a book after printing, listing corrections [Latin: that which is to be corrected]

corroborate *vb* **-rating, -rated** to support (a fact or opinion) by giving proof [Latin *com-* (intensive) + *roborare* to make strong] ▷ **corroboration** *n* ▷ **corroborative** *adj*

corroboree *n Austral* **1** an Aboriginal gathering or dance of festive or warlike character **2** *informal* any noisy gathering [Aboriginal]

corrode *vb* **-roding, -roded 1** to eat away or be eaten away by chemical action or rusting **2** to destroy gradually: *rumours corroding the public's affection for the royal family* [Latin *corrodere* to gnaw to pieces]

corrosion *n* **1** the process by which something, esp. a metal, is corroded **2** the result of corrosion ▷ **corrosive** *adj*

corrugate *vb* **-gating, -gated** to fold into alternate grooves and ridges [Latin *corrugare*] ▷ **corrugation** *n*

corrugated iron n a thin sheet of iron or steel, formed with alternating ridges and troughs

corrupt adj 1 open to or involving bribery or other dishonest practices: corrupt practices 2 morally depraved 3 (of a text or data) made unreliable by errors or alterations ▷ vb 4 to make corrupt [Latin corruptus spoiled] > **corruptive** adj

corruptible adj capable of being corrupted

corruption n 1 dishonesty and illegal behaviour 2 the act of corrupting morally or sexually 3 the process of rotting or decaying 4 an unintentional or unauthorized alteration in a text or data 5 an altered form of a word

corsage (kore-sahzh) n a small bouquet worn on the bodice of a dress [Old French cors body]

corsair n 1 a pirate 2 a pirate ship 3 a privateer [Old French corsaire]

corse n archaic a corpse

Corse n the French name for Corsica

corselet n 1 a woman's one-piece undergarment, combining corset and bra 2 a piece of armour to cover the trunk [Old French cors bodice]

corset n 1 a close-fitting undergarment worn by women to shape the torso 2 a similar garment worn by either sex to support and protect the back [Old French: a little bodice] > **corsetry** n

Corsica n an island in the Mediterranean, west of N Italy: forms, with 43 islets, a region of France; mountainous; settled by Greeks in about 560 BC; sold by Genoa to France in 1768. Capital: Ajaccio. Pop: 265 999 (2003 est). Area: 8682 sq km (3367 sq miles). French name: Corse

Corsican adj 1 of or relating to Corsica or its inhabitants ▷ n 2 a native or inhabitant of Corsica

cortege (kore-**tayzh**) n a funeral procession [Italian corteggio]

Cortés or **Cortez** n Hernando or Hernán. 1485–1547, Spanish conquistador: defeated the Aztecs and conquered Mexico (1523)

cortex (kore-tex) n, pl **-tices** (-tiss-seez) anatomy the outer layer of the brain or some other internal organ [Latin: bark, outer layer] > **cortical** adj

cortisone n a steroid hormone used in treating rheumatoid arthritis, allergies, and skin diseases [corticosterone, a hormone]

Cortona n a town in central Italy, in Tuscany: Roman and Etruscan remains, 15th-century cathedral. Pop: 22 048 (2001)

Cortot n Alfred. 1877–1962, French pianist, born in Switzerland

corundum n a hard mineral used as an abrasive, and of which the ruby and white sapphire are precious forms [Tamil kuruntam]

Corunna n the English name for **La Coruña**

coruscate vb **-cating, -cated** formal to emit flashes of light; sparkle [Latin coruscare to flash] > **coruscating** adj > **coruscation** n

corvette n a lightly armed escort warship [perhaps from Middle Dutch corf]

corymb n botany a flat-topped flower cluster with the stems growing progressively shorter towards the centre [Greek korumbos cluster]

cos¹ or **cos lettuce** n a lettuce with a long slender head and crisp leaves [after Kos, where it originated]

cos² cosine

Cos n a variant spelling of **Kos**

cosec (koh-sek) cosecant

cosecant (koh-seek-ant) n (in trigonometry) the ratio of the length of the hypotenuse to that of the opposite side in a right-angled triangle

Cosenza n a city in S Italy, in Calabria. Pop: 72 998 (2001)

Cosgrave n 1 Liam. born 1920, Irish statesman; prime minister of the Republic of Ireland (1973–77) 2 his father, **W**(illiam) **T**(homas). 1880–1965, Irish statesman; first prime minister (president of the executive council) of the Irish Free State (1922–32)

cosh chiefly Brit n 1 a heavy blunt weapon, often made of hard rubber ▷ vb 2 to hit on the head with a cosh [Romany kosh]

cosignatory n, pl **-ries** a person or country that signs a document jointly with others

cosine (koh-sine) n (in trigonometry) the ratio of the length of the adjacent side to that of the hypotenuse in a right-angled triangle [see CO-, SINE]

cosmetic n 1 anything applied to the face or body in order to improve the appearance ▷ adj 2 done or used to improve the appearance of the face or body 3 improving in appearance only: glossy brochures are part of a cosmetic exercise [Greek kosmētikos, from kosmein to arrange]

cosmetic surgery n surgery performed to improve the appearance, rather than for medical reasons

cosmic adj 1 of or relating to the whole universe: the cosmic order 2 occurring in or coming from outer space: cosmic dust

cosmogony n, pl **-nies** the study of the origin of the universe [Greek kosmos world + gonos creation]

cosmology n the study of the origin and nature of the universe [Greek kosmos world + -LOGY] > **cosmological** adj > **cosmologist** n

cosmonaut n the Russian name for an astronaut [Russian kosmonavt, from Greek kosmos universe + nautēs sailor]

cosmopolitan adj 1 composed of people or elements from many different countries or cultures 2 having lived and travelled in many countries 3 sophisticated and cultured ▷ n 4 a cosmopolitan person [Greek kosmos world + politēs citizen] > **cosmopolitanism** n

cosmos n the universe considered as an ordered system [Greek kosmos order]

Cossack n 1 a member of a S Russian people, famous as horsemen and dancers ▷ adj 2 of the Cossacks: a Cossack dance [Russian kazak vagabond]

cosset vb **-seting, -seted** to pamper or pet [origin unknown]

cossie (coz-zee) n informal a swimming costume

cost n 1 the amount of money, time, or energy required to obtain or produce something 2 suffering or sacrifice: these were crucial truths which rugby never grasped, to its cost 3 the amount paid for a commodity by its seller: to sell at cost 4 costs law the expenses of a lawsuit 5 at all costs regardless of any cost or effort involved 6 at the cost of at the expense of losing: they eventually triumphed, but at the cost of many lives ▷ vb costing, cost 7 to be obtained or obtainable in exchange for: calls cost 36p a minute cheap rate, 48p at other times 8 to involve the loss or sacrifice of: a fall which almost cost him his life 9 (costing, costed) to estimate the cost of producing something [Latin constare to stand at, cost]

Costa Brava n a coastal region of NE Spain along the Mediterranean, extending from Barcelona to the French border: many resorts

cost accounting n the recording and controlling of all the costs involved in running a business > **cost accountant** n

costal adj of the ribs

Costa Rica n a republic in Central America: gained independence from Spain in 1821; mostly mountainous and volcanic, with extensive forests. Official language: Spanish. Official religion: Roman Catholic. Currency: colón. Capital: San José. Pop: 4 695 942 (2013 est). Area: 50 900 sq km (19 652 sq miles)

Costa Rican adj 1 of or relating to Costa Rica or its inhabitants ▷ n 2 a native or inhabitant of Costa Rica

cost-effective adj providing adequate financial return in relation to outlay

Costello n Elvis, real name Declan McManus. born 1954, British rock singer and songwriter. His recordings include This Year's Model (1978), "Oliver's Army" (1979),

Spike (1989), *Brutal Youth* (1994), and *When I Was Cruel* (2003)

Costermansville *n* the former name (until 1966) of Bukavu

costermonger *n Brit* a person who sells fruit and vegetables from a barrow in the street [*costard* a kind of apple + *monger* trader]

costive *adj old-fashioned* having or causing constipation [Old French *costivé*]

costly *adj* **-lier, -liest 1** expensive **2** involving great loss or sacrifice: *a bitter and costly war* **> costliness** *n*

Costner *n* Kevin. born 1955, US film actor: his films include *Robin Hood: Prince of Thieves* (1990), *Dances with Wolves* (1990; also directed), *JFK* (1991), *Waterworld* (1995), *Open Range* (2003), and the TV mini-series *Hatfields & McCoys* (2012)

cost of living *n* the average cost of the basic necessities of life, such as food, housing, and clothing

costume *n* **1** a style of dressing, including all the clothes and accessories, typical of a particular country or period **2** the clothes worn by an actor or performer: *a jester's costume* **3** short for **swimming costume** ▷ *vb* **-tuming, -tumed 4** to provide with a costume: *she was costumed by many of the great Hollywood designers* [Italian: dress, custom] **> costumed** *adj*

costume jewellery *n* inexpensive but attractive jewellery

costumier *n* a maker or supplier of theatrical or fancy dress costumes

cosy *or US* **cozy** *adj* **-sier, -siest** *or US* **-zier, -ziest 1** warm and snug **2** intimate and friendly: *a cosy chat* ▷ *n, pl* **-sies** *or US* **-zies 3** a cover for keeping things warm: *a tea cosy* [Scots] **> cosiness** *or US* **coziness** *n*

cot¹ *n* **1** a bed with high sides for a baby or very young child **2** a small portable bed [Hindi *khāt* bedstead]

cot² *n* **1** *literary or archaic* a small cottage **2** a cote [Old English]

cot³ cotangent

cotangent *n* (in trigonometry) the ratio of the length of the adjacent side to that of the opposite side in a right-angled triangle

cot death *n* the unexplained sudden death of a baby while asleep

cote *or* **cot** *n* a small shelter for birds or animals [Old English]

Côte d'Azur *n* the Mediterranean coast of France, including the French Riviera: forms an administrative region with Provence

Côte d'Ivoire *n* a republic in West Africa, on the Gulf of Guinea: Portuguese trading for ivory and slaves began in the 16th century; made a French protectorate in 1842 and became independent in 1960; major producer of coffee and cocoa. Official language: French. Religion: Muslim majority, with animist, atheist, and Roman Catholic minorities. Currency: franc. Capital: Yamoussoukro (administrative); Abidjan (legislative). Pop: 22 400 835 (2013 est). Area: 319 820 sq km (123 483 sq miles). Former name (until 1986): the Ivory Coast

Côte-d'Or *n* a department of E central France, in NE Burgundy. Capital: Dijon. Pop: 510 334 (2003 est). Area: 8787 sq km (3427 sq miles)

coterie (kote-er-ee) *n* a small exclusive group of friends or people with common interests [French]

Côtes-d'Armor *n* a department of W France, on the N coast of Brittany. Capital: St Brieuc. Pop: 553 969 (2003 est). Area: 6878 sq km (2656 sq miles). Former name: Côtes-du-Nord

Côtes-du-Nord *n* the former name of Côtes-d'Armor

Cotman *n* John Sell. 1782–1842, English landscape watercolourist and etcher

cotoneaster (kot-tone-ee-ass-ter) *n* a garden shrub with red berries

Cotonou *n* the chief port and official capital of Benin, on the Bight of Benin. Pop: 891 000 (2005 est)

Cotopaxi *n* a volcano in central Ecuador, in the Andes: the world's highest active volcano Height: 5896 m (19 344 ft)

Cotswolds *pl n* a range of low hills in SW England, mainly in Gloucestershire: formerly a centre of the wool industry

cottage *n* a small simple house, usually in the country [from COT²] **> cottager** *n*

cottage cheese *n* a mild soft white cheese made from skimmed milk curds

cottage industry *n* a craft industry in which employees work at home

cottage pie *n* a dish of minced meat topped with mashed potato

cottaging *n Brit, Austral and NZ slang* homosexual activity between men in a public lavatory [from *cottage* (in the sense: a public lavatory)]

Cottbus *n* an industrial city in E Germany, in Brandenburg on the Spree River. Pop: 107 549 (2003 est)

cotter¹ *n machinery* a bolt or wedge that is used to secure parts of machinery [Middle English *cotterel*]

cotter² *n Scot history* a farm labourer occupying a cottage and land rent-free [see COT²]

cotter pin *n machinery* a split pin used to hold parts together and fastened by having the ends spread apart after it is inserted

Cottian Alps *pl n* a mountain range in SW Europe, between NW Italy and SE France: part of the Alps. Highest peak: Monte Viso, 3841 m (12 600 ft)

cotton *n* **1** the soft white downy fibre surrounding the seeds of a plant grown in warm climates, used to make cloth and thread **2** cloth or thread made from cotton fibres [Arabic *qutn*] **> cottony** *adj*

Cotton *n* Sir Henry. 1907–87, English golfer: three times winner of the British Open (1934, 1937, 1948)

cotton bud *n* a small stick with cotton wool tips used for cleaning the ears, applying make-up, etc.

cotton on *vb informal* to understand or realize the meaning (of): *it has taken the world 20 years to cotton on to this idea*

cotton wool *n Brit* absorbent fluffy cotton, used for surgical dressings and to apply creams to the skin

cotyledon (kot-ill-ee-don) *n* the first leaf produced by a plant embryo [Greek *kotulē* cup]

couch *n* **1** a piece of upholstered furniture for seating more than one person **2** a bed on which patients of a doctor or a psychoanalyst lie during examination or treatment ▷ *vb* **3** to express in a particular style of language: *a proclamation couched in splendidly archaic phraseology* **4** *archaic* (of an animal) to crouch, as when preparing to leap [Old French *coucher* to lay down]

couchette (koo-shett) *n* a bed converted from seats on a train or ship [French]

couch grass *n* a grassy weed which spreads quickly

couch potato *n slang* a physically lazy person, esp. one who spends most of the day in front of the television

Coué *n* Émile. 1857–1926, French psychologist and pharmacist: advocated psychotherapy by autosuggestion **> Couéism** *n*

cougan *n Austral slang* a drunk and rowdy person

cougar (koo-gar) *n* same as **puma** [from S American Indian]

cough *vb* **1** to expel air abruptly and noisily from the lungs **2** (of an engine or other machine) to make a sound similar to this ▷ *n* **3** an act or sound of coughing **4** an illness which causes frequent coughing [Old English *cohhetten*]

cough up *vb* **1** to give up (money or information) **2** to bring up into the mouth by coughing: *to cough up blood*

could *vb* **1** used to make the past tense of **can¹ 2** used to make the subjunctive mood of **can¹**, esp. in polite requests or conditional sentences: *could I have a word with you, please?* **3** used to indicate the suggestion of a course of action: *we could make a fortune from selling players, but that would not be in the long-term interests of the club* **4** used to indicate a possibility: *it could simply be a spelling mistake* [Old English *cūthe*]

couldn't could not

coulis (koo-lee) *n* a thin purée of vegetables or fruit, usually served as a sauce surrounding a dish: *rum truffle cake with raspberry coulis* [French: purée]

coulomb (koo-lom) *n* the SI unit of electric charge [after C. A. de COULOMB]

Coulomb *n* Charles Augustin de. 1736–1806, French physicist: made many discoveries in the field of electricity and magnetism

coulter (kole-ter) *n* a vertical blade on a plough in front of the ploughshare [Latin *culter* ploughshare, knife]

council *n* **1** a group meeting for discussion or consultation **2** a legislative or advisory body: *the United Nations Security Council* **3** *Brit* the local governing authority of a town or county **4** *Austral* the local governing authority of a district or shire ▷ *adj* **5** of or provided by a local council: *a council house* [Latin *concilium* assembly]

> USAGE Avoid confusion with **counsel**.

councillor *or US* **councilor** *n* a member of a council

> USAGE Avoid confusion with **counsellor**.

council tax *n* (in Britain) a tax based on the relative value of property, levied to fund local council services

counsel *n* **1** advice or guidance **2** discussion or consultation: *when it was over they took counsel of their consciences* **3** a barrister or group of barristers who conduct cases in court and advise on legal matters ▷ *vb* **-selling, -selled** *or US* **-seling, -seled** **4** to give advice or guidance to **5** to recommend or urge [Latin *consilium* deliberating body] **> counselling** *or US* **counseling** *n*

> USAGE Avoid confusion with **council**.

counsellor *or US* **counselor** *n* **1** an adviser **2** *US* a lawyer who conducts cases in court

> USAGE Avoid confusion with **councillor**.

count¹ *vb* **1** to say numbers in ascending order up to and including: *count from one to ten* **2** to add up or check (each thing in a group) in order to find the total: *he counted the money he had left* **3** to be important: *it's the thought that counts* **4** to consider: *he can count himself lucky* **5** to take into account or include: *the time he'd spent in prison on remand counted towards his sentence* **6** **not counting** excluding **7** *music* to keep time by counting beats ▷ *n* **8** the act of counting **9** the number reached by counting: *a high pollen count* **10** *law* one of a number of charges **11** **keep** *or* **lose count** to keep or fail to keep an accurate record of items or events **12** **out for the count** unconscious ▶ See also **count against, countdown**, etc. [Latin *computare* to calculate] **> countable** *adj*

count² *n* a middle-ranking European nobleman [Latin *comes* associate]

count against *vb* to have an effect or influence that makes something more unlikely: *his age counts against him getting promotion*

countdown *n* the act of counting backwards to zero to time exactly an operation such as the launching of a rocket

countenance *n* **1** *literary* the face or facial expression ▷ *vb* **-nancing, -nanced** **2** to support or tolerate [Latin *continentia* restraint, control]

counter¹ *n* **1** a long flat surface in a bank or shop, on which business is transacted **2** a small flat disc used in board games **3** a disc or token used as an imitation coin **4** **under the counter** (of the sale of goods) illegal [Latin *computare* to compute]

counter² *n* an apparatus for counting things

counter³ *vb* **1** to say or do (something) in retaliation or response **2** to oppose or act against **3** to return the attack of (an opponent) ▷ *adv* **4** in an opposite or opposing direction or manner **5** **run counter to** to be in direct contrast with ▷ *adj* **6** opposing or opposite ▷ *n* **7** something that is contrary or opposite to something else **8** an opposing action **9** a return attack, such as a blow in boxing [Latin *contra* against]

counter- *prefix* **1** against or opposite: *counterattack* **2** complementary or corresponding: *counterpart* [Latin *contra*]

counteract *vb* to act against or neutralize **> counteraction** *n* **> counteractive** *adj*

counterattack *n* **1** an attack in response to an attack ▷ *vb* **2** to make a counterattack (against)

counterbalance *n* **1** a weight or influence that balances or neutralizes another ▷ *vb* **-ancing, -anced** **2** to act as a counterbalance to

counterbid *n* a bid made in response to a bid from another party, offering more favourable terms to the seller

counterblast *n* an aggressive response to a verbal attack

counterclockwise *adv, adj US and Canad* same as **anticlockwise**

counterespionage *n* activities to counteract enemy espionage

counterfeit *adj* **1** made in imitation of something genuine with the intent to deceive or defraud: *counterfeit currency* **2** pretended: *counterfeit friendship* ▷ *n* **3** an imitation designed to deceive or defraud ▷ *vb* **4** to make a fraudulent imitation of **5** to feign: *surprise is an easy emotion to counterfeit* [Old French *contrefait*]

counterfoil *n Brit* the part of a cheque or receipt kept as a record

counterintelligence *n* activities designed to frustrate enemy espionage

countermand *vb* to cancel (a previous order) [Old French *contremander*]

countermeasure *n* an action taken to counteract some other action

counterpane *n* a bed covering [Medieval Latin *culcita puncta* quilted mattress]

counterpart *n* **1** a person or thing complementary to or corresponding to another **2** a duplicate of a legal document

counterpoint *n* **1** the harmonious combining of two or more parts or melodies **2** a melody or part combined in this way ▷ *vb* **3** to set in contrast [Old French *contrepoint* an accompaniment set against the notes of a melody]

counterpoise *vb* **-poising, -poised** to oppose with something of equal weight or effect: *counterpoising humour and horror*

counterproductive *adj* having an effect opposite to the one intended

countersign *vb* **1** to sign (a document already signed by another) as confirmation ▷ *n* **2** the signature so written

countersink *vb* **-sinking, -sank, -sunk** to drive (a screw) into a shaped hole so that its head is below the surface

countertenor *n* **1** an adult male voice with an alto range **2** a singer with such a voice

counterterrorism *n* activities intended to prevent terrorist acts or to eradicate terrorist groups **> counterterrorist** *adj*

countess *n* **1** a woman holding the rank of count or earl **2** the wife or widow of a count or earl

countless *adj* too many to count

count noun *n* a noun that may be preceded by an indefinite article and can be used in the plural, such as *telephone* or *thing*

count on *vb* to rely or depend on

count out *vb* **1** to exclude **2** to declare (a boxer) defeated when he has not risen from the floor within ten seconds

countrified *adj* having an appearance or manner

C

associated with the countryside rather than a town

country *n, pl* **-tries 1** an area distinguished by its people, culture, language, or government **2** the territory of a nation or state **3** the people of a nation or state **4** the part of the land that is away from cities or industrial areas **5** a person's native land **6** same as **country and western 7** across country not keeping to roads **8 go to the country** *Brit and NZ* to dissolve Parliament and hold a general election [Medieval Latin *contrata (terra)* (land) lying opposite]

country and western *or* **country music** *n* popular music based on American White folk music

country club *n* a club in the country, which has sporting and social facilities

country dance *n* a type of British folk dance performed in rows or circles

countryman *n, pl* **-men 1** a person from one's own country **2** *Brit, Austral and NZ* a person who lives in the country ▷ **countrywoman** *fem n*

countryside *n* land away from the cities

county *n, pl* **-ties 1** (in some countries) a division of a country ▷ *adj* **2** *Brit informal* upper-class [Old French *conté* land belonging to a count]

coup (koo) *n* **1** a brilliant and successful action **2** a coup d'état [French]

coup de grâce (koo de grahss) *n, pl* **coups de grâce** (koo de grahss) a final or decisive action [French]

coup d'état (koo day-**tah**) *n, pl* **coups d'état** (kooz day-**tah**) a sudden violent or illegal overthrow of a government [French]

coupé (koo-**pay**) *n* a sports car with two doors and a sloping fixed roof [French *carrosse coupé* cut-off carriage]

Couperin *n* François. 1668–1733, French composer, noted for his harpsichord suites and organ music

Coupland *n* Douglas. born 1961, Canadian novelist and journalist; novels include *Generation X* (1991), *Girlfriend in a Coma* (1998), and *City of Glass* (2000)

couple *n* **1** two people who are married or romantically involved **2** two partners in a dance or game **3 a couple of a** a pair of: *a couple of guys* **b** *informal* a few: *a couple of weeks* ▷ *pron* **4 a couple a** two **b** *informal* a few: *give him a couple* ▷ *vb* **-pling, -pled 5** to connect or link: *an ingrained sense of shame, coupled with a fear of ridicule* **6** *literary* to have sexual intercourse [Latin *copula* a bond]

couplet *n* two successive lines of verse, usually rhyming and of the same metre

coupling *n* a device for connecting things, such as railway cars or trucks

coupon *n* **1** a piece of paper entitling the holder to a discount or free gift **2** a detachable slip that can be used as a commercial order form **3** *Brit* a football pools entry form [Old French *colpon* piece cut off]

courage *n* **1** the ability to face danger or pain without fear **2 the courage of one's convictions** the confidence to act according to one's beliefs [Latin *cor* heart]

courageous *adj* showing courage ▷ **courageously** *adv*

Courantyne *n* a river in S South America, rising in S Guyana and flowing north to the Atlantic, forming the boundary between Guyana and Surinam. Length: 765 km (475 miles). Dutch name: **Corantijn**

Courbet *n* Gustave. 1819–77, French painter, a leader of the realist movement; noted for his depiction of contemporary life

Courbevoie *n* an industrial suburb of Paris, on the Seine. Pop: 85 716 (2006)

courgette *n* a type of small vegetable marrow [French]

courier *n* **1** a person who looks after and guides travellers **2** a person paid to deliver urgent messages [Latin *currere* to run]

Courland *or* **Kurland** *n* a region of Latvia, between the Gulf of Riga and the Lithuanian border. Latvian name: **Kurzeme**

Cournand *n* André (Frederic). 1895–1988, US physician, born in France: shared the 1956 Nobel prize for

physiology or medicine for his work on heart catheterization

Courrèges *n* André. born 1923, French couturier: helped to launch unisex fashion in the mid-1960s

course *n* **1** a complete series of lessons or lectures: *a training course* **2** a sequence of medical treatment prescribed for a period of time: *a course of antibiotics* **3** an onward movement in time or space: *during the course of his career he worked with many leading actors* **4** a route or direction taken: *the ships were blown off course by a gale* **5** the path or channel along which a river moves **6** an area on which a sport is played or a race is held: *a golf course* **7** any of the successive parts of a meal **8** a continuous, usually horizontal layer of building material, such as bricks or tiles, at one level in a building **9** a mode of conduct or action: *the safest course of action was to do nothing* **10** the natural development of a sequence of events: *allow the fever to run its course* **11** a period of time: *over the course of the last two years* **12 as a matter of course** as a natural or normal consequence or event **13 in the course of** in the process of **14 in due course** at the natural or appropriate time **15 of course a** (*adv*) as expected; naturally **b** (*interj*) certainly; definitely ▷ *vb* **coursing, coursed 16** (of a liquid) to run swiftly **17** to hunt with hounds that follow the quarry by sight and not scent [Latin *cursus* a running

coursebook *n* a book that is used as part of an educational course

courser¹ *n* **1** a person who courses hounds **2** a hound trained for coursing

courser² *n literary* a swift horse; steed [Old French *coursier*

coursework *n* work done by a student and assessed as part of an educational course

coursing *n* hunting with hounds trained to hunt game by sight

court *n* **1** *law* **a** a judicial body which hears and makes decisions on legal cases **b** the room or building in which such a body meets **2** a marked area used for playing a racket game **3** an area of ground wholly or partly surrounded by walls or buildings **4** a name given to some short streets, blocks of flats, or large country houses as a part of their address: *Carlton Court* **5** the residence or retinue of a sovereign **6** any formal assembly held by a sovereign **7 go to court** to take legal action **8 hold court** to preside over a group of admirers **9 out of court** without a trial or legal case **10 pay court to** to give flattering attention to ▷ *vb* **11** to attempt to gain the love of **12** to pay attention to (someone) in order to gain favour **13** to try to obtain (something): *he has not courted controversy, but he has certainly attracted it* **14** to make oneself open or vulnerable to: *courting disaster* [Latin *cohor, cohort*]

Court *n* Margaret (née *Smith*). born 1942, Australian tennis player, winner of a record 24 Grand Slam singles titles: Australian Open champion 1960–66, 1969–71, and 1973; US Open champion 1962, 1965, 1969–70, and 1973; Wimbledon champion 1963, 1965, and 1970; French Open champion 1962, 1965, 1969–70, and 1973

court card *n* (in a pack of playing cards) a king, queen, or jack [earlier *coat-card*, from the decorative coats worn by the figures depicted]

courteous *adj* polite and considerate in manner [Middle English *corteis* with courtly manners] ▷ **courteously** *adv* ▷ **courteousness** *n*

courtesan (kore-tiz-**zan**) *n history* a mistress or high-class prostitute [Old French *courtisane*]

courtesy *n, pl* **-sies 1** politeness; good manners **2** a courteous act or remark **3 by courtesy of** with the consent of [Old French *corteis* courteous]

courthouse *n* a public building in which courts of law are held

courtier *n* an attendant at a royal court

courtly *adj* **-lier, -liest 1** ceremoniously polite **2** of or suitable for a royal court ▷ **courtliness** *n*

court martial *n, pl* **court martials** *or* **courts martial**

1 the trial of a member of the armed forces charged with breaking military law ▷ *vb* **court-martial** (**-tialling, -tialled**) *or US* **-tialing, -tialed 2** to try by court martial

Courtrai *n* a town in W Belgium, in West Flanders on the Lys River; the largest producer of linen in W Europe. Pop: 73 984 (2004 est). Flemish name: **Kortrijk**

courtship *n* the courting of an intended spouse or mate

court shoe *n* a low-cut shoe for women, without laces or straps

courtyard *n* an open area of ground surrounded by walls or buildings

couscous (kooss-kooss) *n* **1** a type of semolina used in North African cookery **2** a spicy North African dish, consisting of steamed semolina served with a stew [Arabic *kouskous*]

cousin *n* the child of one's aunt or uncle. Also called: **first cousin** [Latin *consobrinus*]

Cousin *n* Victor. 1792–1867, French philosopher and educational reformer

Cousteau *n* Jacques Yves. 1910–97, French underwater explorer

couture (koo-toor) *n* **1** high-fashion designing and dressmaking ▷ *adj* **2** relating to high fashion design and dress-making: *couture clothes* [French: sewing]

couturier *n* a person who designs fashion clothes for women [French]

covalency *or US* **covalence** *n chem* **1** the ability to form a bond in which two atoms share a pair of electrons **2** the number of covalent bonds which a particular atom can make with others ❭ **covalent** *adj*

cove¹ *n* a small bay or inlet [Old English *cofa*]

cove² *n old-fashioned, slang* a fellow; chap [probably from Romany *kova*]

coven (kuv-ven) *n* a meeting of witches [Latin *convenire* to come together]

covenant (kuv-ven-ant) *n* **1** *chiefly Brit* a formal agreement to make an annual payment to charity **2** *law* a formal sealed agreement **3** *Bible* God's promise to the Israelites and their commitment to worship him alone ▷ *vb* **4** to agree by a legal covenant [Latin *convenire* to come together, agree] ❭ **covenanter** *n*

Covenanter *n Scot history* a person upholding either of two 17th-century covenants to establish and defend Presbyterianism

Covent Garden *n* **1** a district of central London: famous for its former fruit, vegetable, and flower market, now a shopping precinct **2** the Royal Opera House (built 1858) in Covent Garden

Coventry *n* **1** a city in central England, in Coventry unitary authority, West Midlands: devastated in World War II; modern cathedral (1954–62); industrial centre, esp. for motor vehicles; two universities (1965, 1992). Pop: 303 475 (2001) **2** a unitary authority in central England, in West Midlands. Pop: 305 000 (2003 est). Area: 97 sq km (37 sq miles) **3 send to Coventry** to ostracize or ignore

cover *vb* **1** to place something over so as to protect or conceal **2** to put a garment on; clothe **3** to extend over or lie thickly on the surface of: *the ground was covered with dry leaves* **4** (sometimes foll. by *up*) to screen or conceal; hide from view **5** to travel over **6** to protect (an individual or group) by taking up a position from which fire may be returned if those being protected are fired upon **7** to keep a gun aimed at **8 a** to insure against loss or risk **b** to provide for (loss or risk) by insurance **9** to include or deal with: *the course covers accounting, economics, statistics, law, and computer applications* **10** to act as reporter or photographer on (a news event) for a newspaper or magazine **11** (of a sum of money) to be enough to pay for (something) **12** *music* to record a cover version of **13** *sport* to guard or obstruct (an opponent, team-mate, or area) **14 cover for** to deputize for (a person) **15** (foll. by *for* or *up for*) to provide an alibi (for): *can my men count on your friends at City Hall to cover for us?* ▷ *n* **16** anything which covers **17** a blanket or bedspread **18** the outside of a book or

magazine **19** a pretext or disguise: *he claimed UN resolutions were being used as a cover for planned American aggression* **20** an envelope or other postal wrapping: *under plain cover* **21** an individual table setting **22** insurance **23** a cover version **24 the covers** *cricket* the area roughly at right angles to the pitch on the off side and about halfway to the boundary **25 break cover** to come out from a shelter or hiding place **26 take cover** to make for a place of safety or shelter **27 under cover** protected or in secret ▶ See also **cover-up** [Latin *cooperire* to cover completely] ❭ **covering** *adj*, *n*

coverage *n journalism* the amount of reporting given to a subject or event

cover charge *n* a fixed service charge added to the bill in a restaurant

Coverdale *n* Miles. 1488–1568, the first translator of the complete Bible into English (1535)

cover girl *n* an attractive woman whose picture appears on the cover of a magazine

covering letter *n* an accompanying letter sent as an explanation

coverlet *n* same as **bedspread**

cover note *n Brit and Austral* a temporary certificate from an insurance company giving proof of a current policy

covert *adj* **1** concealed or secret ▷ *n* **2** a thicket or woodland providing shelter for game **3** *ornithol* any of the small feathers on the wings and tail of a bird that surround the bases of the larger feathers [Old French: covered] ❭ **covertly** *adv*

cover-up *n* **1** concealment or attempted concealment of a mistake or crime ▷ *vb* **cover up 2** to cover completely **3** to attempt to conceal (a mistake or crime)

cover version *n* a version by a different artist of a previously recorded musical item

covet *vb* **-eting, -eted** to long to possess (something, esp. something belonging to another person) [Latin *cupiditas* cupidity]

covetous *adj* jealously longing to possess something ❭ **covetously** *adv* ❭ **covetousness** *n*

covey (kuv-vee) *n* **1** a small flock of grouse or partridge **2** a small group of people [Old French *cover* to sit on, hatch]

Covilhã *n* Pero da. ?1460–?1526, Portuguese explorer, who established relations between Portugal and Ethiopia

cow¹ *n* **1** the mature female of cattle **2** the mature female of various other mammals, such as the elephant or whale **3** *no longer in technical use* any domestic species of cattle **4** *informal, offensive* a disagreeable woman [Old English *cū*]

cow² *vb* to frighten or subdue with threats [Old Norse *kūga* to oppress]

coward *n* a person who is easily frightened and avoids dangerous or difficult situations [Latin *cauda* tail] ❭ **cowardly** *adj*

Coward *n* Sir Noël (Pierce). 1899–1973, English dramatist, actor, and composer, noted for his sophisticated comedies, which include *Private Lives* (1930) and *Blithe Spirit* (1941)

cowardice *n* lack of courage

cowbell *n* a bell hung around a cow's neck

cowboy *n* **1** (in the US and Canada) a ranch worker who herds and tends cattle, usually on horseback **2** a conventional character of Wild West folklore or films **3** *Brit, Austral and NZ informal* an irresponsible or unscrupulous worker or businessman ❭ **cowgirl** *fem n*

cowcatcher *n US and Canad* a fender on the front of a locomotive to clear the track of animals or other obstructions

cow cocky *n Austral and NZ* a one-man dairy farmer

Cowdrey *n* (Michael) Colin, Baron. 1932–2000, English cricketer. He played for Kent and in 114 Test matches (captaining England 27 times)

Cowell *n* Simon. born 1959, British manager of pop groups and TV personality, best known as an outspoken judge on the TV talent contests *Pop Idol* (2001–04), *The X Factor* (from 2004), and *Britain's Got Talent* (from 2007)

cower *vb* to cringe or shrink in fear [Middle Low German *kūren* to lie in wait]

Cowes *n* a town in S England, on the Isle of Wight: famous for its annual regatta. Pop: 19 110 (2001)

cowl *n* **1** a loose hood **2** a monk's hooded robe **3** a cover fitted to a chimney to increase ventilation and prevent draughts [Latin *cucullus* hood] ⟩ **cowled** *adj*

Cowley *n* Abraham. 1618–67, English poet and essayist, who introduced the Pindaric ode to English literature

cowlick *n* a tuft of hair over the forehead

cowling *n* a streamlined detachable metal covering around an engine

co-worker *n* a fellow worker: *these habits can drive your boss and co-workers crazy*

cow parsley *n* a hedgerow plant with umbrella-shaped clusters of white flowers

cowpat *n* a pool of cow dung

Cowper *n* William. 1731–1800, English poet, noted for his nature poetry, such as in *The Task* (1785), and his hymns

cowpox *n* a contagious disease of cows, the virus of which is used to make smallpox vaccine

cowrie *n*, *pl* **-ries** the glossy brightly-marked shell of a marine mollusc [Hindi *kaurī*]

cowslip *n* a European wild plant with yellow flowers [Old English *cūslyppe*, from *cū* cow + *slyppe* slime, dung]

cox *n* **1** a coxswain ⟩ *vb* **2** to act as coxswain of (a boat)

Cox *n* **1** Brian (Edward). born 1968, English physicist, educator, and broadcaster; noted esp. for his TV programmes on physics and astronomy. **2** David. 1783–1859, English landscape painter

coxcomb *or* **cockscomb** *n* **1** the comb of a domestic cock **2** *informal* a conceited dandy

coxswain (kok-sn) *n* the person who steers a lifeboat or rowing boat [*cock* a ship's boat + SWAIN]

coy *adj* **1** affectedly shy and modest **2** unwilling to give information [Latin *quietus* quiet] ⟩ **coyly** *adv* ⟩ **coyness** *n*

coyote (koy-ote-ee) *n*, *pl* **-otes** *or* **-ote** a small wolf of the deserts and prairies of North America [Mexican Indian *coyotl*]

Coypel *n* Antoine. 1661–1722, French baroque painter, noted esp. for his large biblical compositions

coypu *n*, *pl* **-pus** *or* **-pu** a beaver-like amphibious rodent, bred for its fur [From a Native American language, *kóypu*]

cozen *vb literary* to cheat or trick [originally a cant term] ⟩ **cozenage** *n*

Cpl Corporal

CPU *computers* central processing unit

Cr *chem* chromium

CR **1** Community of the Resurrection **2** Costa Rica

crab *n* **1** an edible shellfish with five pairs of legs, the first pair modified into pincers **2** short for **crab louse** **3** catch a crab *rowing* to make a stroke in which the oar misses the water or digs too deeply, causing the rower to fall backwards [Old English *crabba*]

crab apple *n* a kind of small sour apple

Crabbe *n* George. 1754–1832, English narrative poet, noted for his depiction of impoverished rural life in *The Village* (1783) and *The Borough* (1810)

crabbed *adj* **1** (of handwriting) cramped and hard to read **2** bad-tempered [probably from *crab*, because of its sideways movement and *crab apple*, because of its sourness]

crabby *adj* **-bier, -biest** bad-tempered

crab louse *n* a parasitic louse living in the pubic area of humans

crack *vb* **1** to break or split without complete separation of the parts **2** to break with a sudden sharp sound **3** to make or cause to make a sudden sharp sound: *the coachman cracked his whip* **4** (of the voice) to become harsh or change pitch suddenly **5** *informal* to fail or break down: *he had cracked under the strain of losing his job* **6** to yield or cease to resist: *he had cracked under torture* **7** to hit with a forceful or resounding blow **8** to break into or force open: *it'll take me longer if I have to crack the safe myself* **9** to solve or decipher (a code or problem) **10** *informal* to tell (a joke) **11** to break (a molecule) into smaller molecules or radicals by heat or catalysis as in the distillation of petroleum **12** to open (a bottle) for drinking **13** **crack it** *informal* to achieve something ⟩ *n* **14** a sudden sharp noise **15** a break or fracture without complete separation of the two parts **16** a narrow opening or fissure **17** *informal* a sharp blow **18** **crack of dawn** daybreak **19** a broken or cracked tone of voice **20** *informal* an attempt **21** *informal* a gibe or joke **22** *slang* a highly addictive form of cocaine **23** *chiefly Irish informal* fun; informal entertainment **24** **a fair crack of the whip** *informal* a fair chance or opportunity ⟩ *adj* **25** *slang* first-class or excellent: *crack troops* ▸ See also **crack down**, **crack up** [Old English *cracian*]

crackbrained *adj* idiotic or crazy: *a crackbrained scheme*

crack down *vb* **1 crack down on** to take severe measures against ⟩ *n* **crackdown** **2** severe or repressive measures

cracked *adj* **1** damaged by cracking **2** harsh-sounding **3** *informal* crazy

cracked wheat *n* whole wheat cracked between rollers so that it will cook more quickly

cracker *n* **1** a thin crisp unsweetened biscuit **2** a decorated cardboard tube, pulled apart with a bang, containing a paper hat and a joke or a toy **3** a small explosive firework **4** *slang* an excellent or notable thing or person

crackers *adj* *Brit and NZ slang* insane

cracking *adj* **1 get cracking** *informal* to start doing something immediately **2 a cracking pace** *informal* a high speed ⟩ *adv*, *adj* **3** *Brit informal* first-class: *five cracking good saves* ⟩ *n* **4** the oil-refining process in which heavy oils are broken down into smaller molecules by heat or catalysis

crackle *vb* **-ling, -led 1** to make small sharp popping noises ⟩ *n* **2** a crackling sound ⟩ **crackly** *adj*

crackling *n* **1** a series of small sharp popping noises **2** the crisp browned skin of roast pork

crackpot *informal* ⟩ *n* **1** an eccentric person ⟩ *adj* **2** eccentric: *crackpot philosophies*

crack up *vb* **1** to have a physical or mental breakdown **2** to begin to break into pieces: *there are worrying reports of buildings cracking up as the earth dries out and foundations move* **3 not all it is cracked up to be** *informal* not as good as people have claimed it to be ⟩ *n* **crackup 4** *informal* a physical or mental breakdown

Cracow *n* an industrial city in S Poland, on the River Vistula: former capital of the country (1320–1609); university (1364). Pop: 822 000 (2005 est). Polish name: Kraków. German name: Krakau

-cracy *combining form* indicating a type of government or rule: *plutocracy*; *mobocracy*. See also **-crat** [Greek *kratos* power]

cradle *n* **1** a baby's bed on rockers **2** a place where something originates: *the cradle of civilization* **3** a supporting framework or structure **4** a platform or trolley in which workmen are suspended on the side of a building or ship ⟩ *vb* **-dling, -dled 5** to hold gently as if in a cradle [Old English *cradol*]

cradle-snatcher *n informal* a person who marries or has a sexual relationship with someone much younger than himself or herself

craft *n* **1** an occupation requiring skill or manual dexterity **2** skill or ability **3** cunning or guile **4** (*pl* **craft**) a boat, ship, aircraft, or spacecraft ⟩ *vb* **5** to make skilfully [Old English *cræft* skill, strength]

craftsman *or fem* **craftswoman** *n*, *pl* **-men** *or* **-women 1** a skilled worker **2** a skilled artist ⟩ **craftsmanship** *n*

crafty *adj* **-tier, -tiest** skilled in deception ⟩ **craftily** *adv* ⟩ **craftiness** *n*

crag *n* a steep rugged rock or peak [Celtic] ⟩ **craggy** *adj*

craic *n* an Irish spelling of **crack** (23)

Craig *n* Edward Gordon. 1872–1966, English theatrical designer, actor, and director. His nonrealistic scenic design greatly influenced theatre in Europe and the US

Craigavon *n* a district in central Northern Ireland, in Co Armagh. Pop: 57 685 (2001). Area: 279 sq km (108 sq miles)

Craigie *n* Sir William A(lexander). 1867–1957, Scottish lexicographer; joint editor of the *Oxford English Dictionary* (1901–33), and of *A Dictionary of American English on Historical Principles* (1938–44)

Craiova *n* a city in SW Romania, on the Jiul River. Pop: 285 000 (2005 est)

crake *n zoology* a bird of the rail family, such as the corncrake [Old Norse *krāka* crow or *krākr* raven]

cram *vb* **cramming, crammed** **1** to force (more people or things) into (a place) than it can hold **2** to eat or feed to excess **3** *chiefly Brit* to study hard just before an examination [Old English *crammian*]

Cram *n* Steve. born 1960, English middle-distance runner: European 1500 m champion (1981, 1986); world 1500 m champion (1983)

crammer *n* a person or school that prepares pupils for an examination

cramp¹ *n* **1** a sudden painful contraction of a muscle **2** temporary stiffness of a muscle group from overexertion: *writer's cramp* **3** severe stomach pain **4** a clamp for holding masonry or timber together ▷ *vb* **5** to affect with a cramp [Old French *crampe*]

cramp² *vb* **1** to confine or restrict **2** **cramp someone's style** *informal* to prevent someone from impressing another person or from behaving naturally: *shyness will cramp their style* [Middle Dutch *crampe* hook]

cramped *adj* **1** closed in **2** (of handwriting) small and irregular

crampon *n* a spiked iron plate strapped to a boot for climbing on ice [French]

Cranach *n* Lucas, known as *the Elder*, real name *Lucas Müller*. 1472–1553, German painter, etcher, and designer of woodcuts

cranberry *n, pl* **-ries** a sour edible red berry [Low German *kraanbere* crane berry]

crane *n* **1** a machine for lifting and moving heavy objects, usually by suspending them from a movable projecting arm **2** a large wading bird with a long neck and legs ▷ *vb* **3** **craning, craned** to stretch out (the neck) in order to see something [Old English *cran*]

Crane *n* **1** (Harold) Hart. 1899–1932, US poet; author of *The Bridge* (1930) **2** Stephen. 1871–1900, US novelist and short-story writer, noted particularly for his novel *The Red Badge of Courage* (1895) **3** Walter. 1845–1915, British painter, illustrator of children's books, and designer of textiles and wallpaper

crane fly *n* a fly with long legs, slender wings, and a narrow body

cranesbill *n* a plant with pink or purple flowers

cranial *adj* of or relating to the skull

craniology *n* the scientific study of the human skull [Greek *kranion* skull + -LOGY]

cranium *n, pl* **-niums** *or* **-nia** *anatomy* **1** the skull **2** the part of the skull that encloses the brain [Greek *kranion*]

crank *n* **1** a device for transmitting or converting motion, consisting of an arm projecting at right angles from a shaft **2** a handle incorporating a crank, used to start an engine or motor **3** *informal* an eccentric or odd person ▷ *vb* **4** to turn with a crank **5** to start (an engine) with a crank [Old English *cranc*]

crankcase *n* the metal case that encloses the crankshaft in an internal-combustion engine

Cranko *n* John. 1927–73, British choreographer, born in South Africa: director of the Stuttgart Ballet (1961–73)

crankpin *n* a short cylindrical pin in a crankshaft, to which the connecting rod is attached

crankshaft *n* a shaft with one or more cranks, to which the connecting rods are attached

cranky *adj* **-kier, -kiest** *informal* **1** eccentric **2** bad-tempered ▷ **crankiness** *n*

Cranmer *n* Thomas. 1489–1556, the first Protestant archbishop of Canterbury (1533–56) and principal author of the Book of Common Prayer. He was burnt as a heretic by Mary I

cranny *n, pl* **-nies** a narrow opening [Old French *cran*]

Cranwell *n* a village in E England, in Lincolnshire: Royal Air Force College (1920)

crap¹ *slang n* **1** nonsense **2** junk **3** *taboo* faeces ▷ *vb* **crapping, crapped** *taboo* to defecate [Middle English *crappe* chaff] ▷ **crappy** *adj*

crap² *n* same as **craps**

crape *n* same as **crepe**

craps *n* **1** a gambling game played with two dice **2** **shoot craps** to play this game [probably from *crabs* lowest throw at dice]

crapulent *or* **crapulous** *adj literary* given to or resulting from excessive eating or drinking [Latin *crapula* drunkenness] ▷ **crapulence** *n*

crash *n* **1** a collision involving a vehicle or vehicles **2** a sudden descent of an aircraft as a result of which it crashes **3** a sudden loud noise **4** a breaking and falling to pieces **5** the sudden collapse of a business or stock exchange ▷ *vb* **6** to cause (a vehicle or aircraft) to collide with another vehicle, the ground, or some other object or (of vehicles or aircraft) to be involved in a collision **7** to make or cause to make a loud smashing noise **8** to drop with force and break into pieces with a loud noise **9** to break or smash into pieces with a loud noise **10** (of a business or stock exchange) to collapse or fail suddenly **11** to move violently or noisily **12** (of a computer system or program) to fail suddenly because of a malfunction **13** *Brit and Austral informal* to gate-crash ▷ *adj* **14** requiring or using great effort in order to achieve results quickly: *a crash course* [probably Middle English *crasen* to smash + *dasshen* to strike]

Crashaw *n* Richard. 1613–49, English religious poet, noted esp. for the *Steps to the Temple* (1646)

crash barrier *n* a safety barrier along the centre of a motorway, around a racetrack, or at the side of a dangerous road

crash dive *n* **1** a sudden steep emergency dive by a submarine ▷ *vb* **crash-dive (-diving, -dived)** **2** to perform a crash dive

crash helmet *n* a helmet worn by motorcyclists to protect the head in case of a crash

crashing *adj informal* extreme: *a crashing bore*

crash-land *vb* (of an aircraft) to land in an emergency, causing damage ▷ **crash-landing** *n*

crash out *vb informal* **1** to go to sleep or become unconscious **2** to be eliminated from a competition in a way that brings disgrace or embarrassment

crash team *n* a medical team with special equipment who can arrive quickly to treat a patient having a heart attack

crass *adj* stupid and insensitive: *the enquiry is crass and naive* [Latin *crassus* thick] ▷ **crassly** *adv* ▷ **crassness** *n*

Crassus *n* Marcus Licinius. ?115–53 BC, Roman general; member of the first triumvirate with Caesar and Pompey

-crat *combining form* indicating a supporter or member of a particular form of government: *autocrat; democrat* [Greek *-kratēs*] ▷ **-cratic** *or* **-cratical** *combining form*

crate *n* **1** a large container made of wooden slats, used for packing goods **2** *slang* an old car or aeroplane ▷ *vb* **crating, crated** **3** to put in a crate [Latin *cratis* wickerwork] ▷ **crateful** *n*

crater *n* **1** the bowl-shaped opening in a volcano or a geyser **2** a cavity made by the impact of a meteorite or an explosion **3** a roughly circular cavity on the surface of the moon and some planets ▷ *vb* **4** to make or form craters in (a surface, such as the ground) [Greek *kratēr* mixing bowl] ▷ **cratered** *adj*

cravat *n* a scarf worn round the neck instead of a tie [French *cravate*]

crave *vb* **craving, craved 1** to desire intensely: *a vulnerable, unhappy girl who craved affection* **2** *formal* to beg or plead for: *may I crave your lordship's indulgence?* [Old English *crafian*] **> craving** *n*

craven *adj* **1** cowardly ▷ *n* **2** a coward [Middle English *cravant*]

craw *n* **1** the crop of a bird **2** the stomach of an animal **3 stick in one's craw** *informal* to be difficult for one to agree with or accept [Middle English]

crawfish *n, pl* **-fish** or **-fishes** same as crayfish

Crawford *n* **1 Joan**, real name *Lucille le Sueur*. 1908–77, US film actress, who portrayed ambitious women in such films as *Mildred Pierce* (1945) **2 Michael**, real name *Michael Dumbell Smith*. born 1942, British actor and singer, noted for his role in the sitcom *Some Mothers Do 'Ave 'Em* (1973–78) and performances in West End musicals esp. *Barnum* (1981) and *The Phantom of the Opera* (1986)

crawl *vb* **1** to move on one's hands and knees **2** (of insects, worms, or snakes) to creep slowly **3** to move very slowly **4** to act in a servile manner **5** to be or feel as if covered with crawling creatures: *the kind of smile that made your hair stand on end and your flesh crawl* ▷ *n* **6** a slow creeping pace or motion **7** *swimming* a stroke in which the feet are kicked like paddles while each arm in turn reaches forward and pulls back through the water [probably from Old Norse *krafla*]

Crawley *n* a town in S England, in NE West Sussex: designated a new town in 1956. Pop: 100 547 (2001)

Craxi *n* Bettino. 1934–2000, Italian socialist statesman; prime minister (1983–87)

crayfish or especially US **crawfish** *n, pl* **-fish** or **-fishes** an edible shellfish like a lobster [Old French *crevice* crab]

crayon *n* **1** a small stick or pencil of coloured wax or clay ▷ *vb* **2** to draw or colour with a crayon [Latin *creta* chalk]

craze *n* **1** a short-lived fashion or enthusiasm ▷ *vb* **crazing, crazed 2** to make mad **3** *ceramics, metallurgy* to develop or cause to develop fine cracks: *you must prevent the drill crazing the glazed surface of the tile* [probably from Old Norse]

crazed *adj* **1** wild and uncontrolled in behaviour **2** (of porcelain) having fine cracks

crazy *adj* **-zier, -ziest** *informal* **1** ridiculous **2 crazy about** extremely fond of: *he was crazy about me* **3** extremely annoyed or upset **4** insane **> crazily** *adv* **> craziness** *n*

Crazy Horse *n* Native American name *Ta-Sunko-Witko*. ?1849–77, Sioux chief, remembered for his attempts to resist White settlement in Sioux territory

crazy paving *n* Brit, Austral and NZ a form of paving on a path, made of irregular slabs of stone

creak *vb* **1** to make or move with a harsh squeaking sound ▷ *n* **2** a harsh squeaking sound [imitative] **> creaky** *adj* **> creakiness** *n*

cream *n* **1** the fatty part of milk, which rises to the top **2** a cosmetic or medication that resembles cream in consistency **3** any of various foods resembling or containing cream **4** the best part of something **5 cream sherry** a full-bodied sweet sherry ▷ *adj* **6** yellowish-white ▷ *vb* **7** to beat (foodstuffs) to a light creamy consistency **8** to remove the cream from (milk) **9** to prepare or cook (foodstuffs) with cream or milk **10 cream off** to take away the best part of [Late Latin *cramum*] **> creamy** *adj*

cream cheese *n* a type of very rich soft white cheese

creamer *n* chiefly Brit a powdered milk substitute for coffee

creamery *n, pl* **-eries** a place where dairy products are made or sold

cream of tartar *n* a purified form of the tartar produced in wine-making, an ingredient in baking powder

crease *n* **1** a line made by folding or pressing **2** a wrinkle or furrow, esp. on the face **3** *cricket* any of four lines near each wicket marking positions for the bowler or batsman ▷ *vb* **creasing, creased 4** to make or become wrinkled or furrowed [Middle English *crēst*] **> creasy** *adj*

create *vb* **-ating, -ated 1** to cause to come into existence **2** to be the cause of **3** to appoint to a new rank or position **4** Brit slang to make an angry fuss [Latin *creare*]

creation *n* **1** a creating or being created **2** something brought into existence or created

Creation *n* Christianity **1** God's act of bringing the universe into being **2** the universe as thus brought into being by God

creationism *n* the doctrine that ascribes the origins of all things to God's acts of creation rather than to evolution **> creationist** *n, adj*

creative *adj* **1** having the ability to create **2** imaginative or inventive ▷ *n* **3** a creative person, esp. one who devises advertising campaigns **> creativity** *n*

creator *n* a person who creates

Creator *n* the Creator God

creature *n* **1** an animal, bird, or fish **2** a person **3** a person or thing controlled by another

crèche *n* **1** a day nursery for very young children **2** a supervised play area provided for young children for short periods [French]

Crécy *n* a village in N France: scene of the first decisive battle of the Hundred Years' War when the English defeated the French (1346). Official name: **Crécy-en-Ponthieu**. Former English name: **Cressy**

cred *n* slang short for street cred

credence (kreed-enss) *n* belief in the truth or accuracy of a statement: *the question is, how much credence to give to their accounts?* [Latin *credere* to believe]

credentials *pl n* **1** something that entitles a person to credit or confidence **2** a document giving evidence of the bearer's identity or qualifications

credibility gap *n* the difference between claims or statements made and the true facts

credible *adj* **1** capable of being believed; convincing: *there is no credible evidence* **2** trustworthy or reliable: *the latest claim is the only one to involve a credible witness* [Latin *credere* to believe] **> credibility** *n*

credit *n* **1 a** the system of allowing customers to receive goods or services before payment **b** the time allowed for paying for such goods or services **2** a reputation for trustworthiness in paying debts **3 a** the positive balance in a person's bank account **b** the sum of money that a bank makes available to a client in excess of any deposit **4** a sum of money or equivalent purchasing power, available for a person's use **5** *accounting* **a** acknowledgment of a sum of money by entry on the right-hand side of an account **b** an entry or total of entries on this side **6** praise or approval, as for an achievement or quality: *you must give him credit for his perseverance* **7** a person or thing who is a source of praise or approval: *he is a credit to his family* **8** influence or reputation based on the good opinion of others: *he acquired credit within the community* **9** belief or confidence in someone or something: *this theory is now gaining credit among the scientific community* **10** *education* **a** a distinction awarded to an examination candidate obtaining good marks **b** certification that a section of an examination syllabus has been satisfactorily completed **11 on credit** with payment to be made at a future date ▷ *vb* **-iting, -ited 12** *accounting* **a** to enter (an item) as a credit in an account **b** to acknowledge (a payer) by making such an entry **13 credit with** to give credit for: *credit us with some intelligence* **14** to believe ▶ See also **credits** [Latin *credere* to believe]

creditable *adj* deserving praise or honour **> creditably** *adv*

credit account *n* Brit a credit system in which shops allow customers to obtain goods and services before payment

credit card *n* a card issued by banks or shops, allowing the holder to buy on credit

credit crunch *n* a period during which there is a sudden reduction in the availability of credit from banks, mortgage lenders, etc.

creditor *n* a person or company to whom money is owed

credit rating *n* an evaluation of the ability of a person or business to repay money lent

credits *pl n* a list of people responsible for the production of a film, programme, or record

creditworthy *adj* (of a person or a business) regarded as deserving credit on the basis of earning power and previous record of debt repayment **> creditworthiness** *n*

credo *n*, *pl* **-dos** a creed

credulity *n* willingness to believe something on little evidence

credulous *adj* **1** too willing to believe: *he has convinced only a few credulous American intellectuals* **2** arising from or showing credulity: *credulous optimism* [Latin *credere* to believe]

creed *n* **1** a system of beliefs or principles **2** a formal statement of the essential parts of Christian belief [Latin *credo* I believe]

Creed *n* Frederick. 1871–1957, Canadian inventor, resident in Scotland from 1897, noted for his invention of the teleprinter, first used in 1912

creek *n* **1** a narrow inlet or bay **2** *US, Canad, Austral and NZ* a small stream or tributary **3 up the creek** *slang* in a difficult position [Old Norse *kriki* nook]

creel *n* a wickerwork basket used by fishermen [Scots]

creep *vb* **creeping, crept 1** to move quietly and cautiously **2** to crawl with the body near to or touching the ground **3** to have the sensation of something crawling over the skin, from fear or disgust: *she makes my flesh creep* **4** (of plants) to grow along the ground or over rocks ▷ *n* **5** a creeping movement **6** *slang* an obnoxious or servile person [Old English *crēopan*]

creeper *n* **1** a plant, such as ivy, that grows by creeping **2** *US and Canad* same as **tree creeper**

creeps *pl n* **give someone the creeps** to give someone a feeling of fear or disgust

creepy *adj* **creepier, creepiest** *informal* causing a feeling of fear or disgust **> creepiness** *n*

creepy-crawly *n*, *pl* **-crawlies** *Brit informal* a small crawling creature

cremate *vb* **-mating, -mated** to burn (a corpse) to ash [Latin *cremare*] **> cremation** *n*

crematorium *n*, *pl* **-riums** *or* **-ria** a building where corpses are cremated

crème de la crème *n* the very best: *the crème de la crème of cities* [French]

crème de menthe *n* a liqueur flavoured with peppermint [French]

Cremona *n* a city in N Italy, in Lombardy on the River Po: noted for the manufacture of fine violins in the 16th–18th centuries. Pop: 70 887 (2001)

crenellated *or US* **crenelated** *adj* having battlements [Late Latin *crena* a notch] **> crenellation** *or US* **crenelation** *n*

creole *n* **1** a language developed from a mixture of different languages which has become the main language of a place ▷ *adj* **2** of or relating to a creole [Spanish]

Creole *n* **1** (in the West Indies and Latin America) a native-born person of mixed European and African descent **2** (in the Gulf States of the US) a native-born person of French descent **3** the French creole spoken in the Gulf States ▷ *adj* **4** of or relating to any of these peoples: *Creole cooking*

creosote *n* **1** a thick dark liquid made from coal tar and used for preserving wood **2** a colourless liquid made from wood tar and used as an antiseptic ▷ *vb* **-soting, -soted 3** to treat with creosote [Greek *kreas* flesh + *sōtēr* preserver]

crepe (**krayp**) *n* **1** a thin light fabric with a crinkled

texture **2** a very thin pancake, often folded around a filling **3** a type of rubber with a wrinkled surface, used for the soles of shoes [French]

crepe paper *n* paper with a crinkled texture, used for decorations

crept *vb* the past of **creep**

crepuscular *adj* **1** of or like twilight **2** (of animals) active at twilight [Latin *crepusculum* dusk]

Cres. Crescent

crescendo (krish-**end**-oh) *n*, *pl* **-dos 1** a gradual increase in loudness **2** a musical passage that gradually gets louder ▷ *adv* **3** gradually getting louder [Italian]

crescent *n* **1** the curved shape of the moon when in its first or last quarter **2** *chiefly Brit and NZ* a crescent-shaped street ▷ *adj* **3** crescent-shaped [Latin *crescere* to grow]

cress *n* a plant with strong-tasting leaves, used in salads and as a garnish [Old English *cressa*]

Cressent *n* Charles. 1685–1768, French cabinetmaker, noted esp. for his marquetry using coloured woods

Cressy *n rare* the former English name for **Crécy**

crest *n* **1** the top of a mountain, hill, or wave **2** a tuft or growth of feathers or skin on the top of a bird's or animal's head **3** a heraldic design or figure used on a coat of arms and elsewhere **4** an ornamental plume or emblem on top of a helmet ▷ *vb* **5** to come or rise to a high point **6** to lie at the top of **7** to reach the top of (a hill or wave) [Latin *crista*] **> crested** *adj*

crestfallen *adj* disappointed or disheartened

Cretaceous *adj geology* of the period of geological time about 135 million years ago, at the end of which the dinosaurs died out [Latin *creta* chalk]

Cretan *adj* **1** of or relating to Crete or its inhabitants ▷ *n* **2** a native or inhabitant of Crete

Crete *n* a mountainous island in the E Mediterranean, the largest island of Greece: of archaeological importance for the ruins of Minoan civilization. Pop: 601 131 (2001). Area: 8331 sq km (3216 sq miles). Modern Greek name: **Krîti**

cretin *n* **1** *informal* a very stupid person **2** *no longer in technical use, offensive* a person with learning difficulties and physical disabilities because of a thyroid deficiency [French from Latin *Christianus* Christian, alluding to the humanity of such people despite their handicaps] **> cretinism** *n* **> cretinous** *adj*

cretonne *n* a heavy printed cotton or linen fabric, used in furnishings [French]

Creuse *n* a department of central France, in Limousin region. Capital: Guéret. Pop: 122 713 (2003 est). Area: 5606 sq km (2186 sq miles)

crevasse *n* a deep open crack in a glacier [French]

crevice *n* a narrow crack or gap in rock [Latin *crepare* to crack]

crew[1] *n* **1** the people who man a ship or aircraft **2** a group of people working together: *a film crew* **3** *informal* any group of people ▷ *vb* **4** to serve as a crew member on a ship or boat [Middle English *crue* reinforcement, from Latin *crescere* to increase]

crew[2] *vb archaic* a past tense of **crow**[2]

crew cut *n* a closely cut haircut for men

Crewe *n* a town in NW England, in Cheshire: major railway junction. Pop: 67 683 (2001)

crewel *n* a loosely twisted worsted yarn, used in embroidery [origin unknown] **> crewelwork** *n*

crew neck *n* a plain round neckline **> crew-neck** *or* **crew-necked** *adj*

crib *n* **1** a piece of writing stolen from elsewhere **2** a translation or list of answers used by students, often dishonestly **3** a baby's cradle **4** a rack or manger for fodder **5** a model of the manger scene at Bethlehem **6** short for **cribbage 7** *NZ* a small holiday house ▷ *vb* **cribbing, cribbed 8** to copy (someone's work) dishonestly **9** to confine in a small space [Old English *cribb*]

cribbage *n* a card game for two to four players, who each try to win a set number of points before the others [origin unknown]

crib sheet *n* **1** a sheet containing notes on a subject, used as a study aid **2** a sheet with information on a complicated topic, used in a debate

crib-wall *n* NZ a retaining wall built against an earth bank

Crichton *n* **1** James. 1560–82, Scottish scholar and writer, called the *Admirable Crichton* because of his talents **2** (John) Michael. 1942–2008, US novelist, screenwriter, and film director; his thrillers, many of which have been filmed, include *The Andromeda Strain* (1969), *Jurassic Park* (1990), and *Disclosure* (1994)

crick *informal n* **1** a painful muscle spasm or cramp in the neck or back ▷ *vb* **2** to cause a crick in [origin unknown]

Crick *n* Francis Harry Compton. 1916–2004, English molecular biologist: helped to discover the helical structure of DNA; Nobel prize for physiology or medicine shared with James Watson and Maurice Wilkins 1962

cricket¹ *n* **1** a game played by two teams of eleven players using a ball, bats, and wickets **2 not cricket** *informal* not fair play [Old French *criquet* wicket] ❯ **cricketer** *n*

cricket² *n* a jumping insect like a grasshopper, which produces a chirping sound by rubbing together its forewings [Old French *criquer* to creak, imitative]

cried *vb* the past of **cry**

crier *n* an official who makes public announcements

crime *n* **1** an act prohibited and punished by law **2** unlawful acts collectively **3** *informal* a disgraceful act: *to be a woman writing music is neither a crime against nature nor a freakish rarity* [Latin *crimen*]

Crimea *n* a peninsula between the Black Sea and the Sea of Azov, disputed between Ukraine and Russia: a former autonomous republic of the Soviet Union (1921–54); part of the Ukrainian SSR from (1954–1991); an autonomous republic of independent Ukraine (1991–2014); annexation by Russia in 2014 not recognized internationally. Capital: Simferopol. Pop: 1 966 801 (2014 est). Russian name: **Krym**

Crimean *adj* **1** of or relating to the Crimea or its inhabitants ▷ *n* **2** a native or inhabitant of the Crimea

criminal *n* **1** a person guilty of a crime ▷ *adj* **2** of or relating to crime or its punishment **3** *informal* senseless or disgraceful ❯ **criminally** *adv* ❯ **criminality** *n*

criminalize *or* **-ise** *vb* **-izing, -ized** *or* **-ising, -ised 1** to make (an action or activity) criminal **2** to treat (a person) as a criminal

criminology *n* the scientific study of crime [Latin *crimen* crime + -LOGY] ❯ **criminologist** *n*

crimp *vb* **1** to fold or press into ridges **2** to curl (hair) tightly with curling tongs **3** *chiefly US informal* to restrict or hinder: *a slowdown in the US economy could crimp some big Swedish concerns' profits* ▷ *n* **4** the act or result of crimping [Old English *crympan*]

Crimplene *n trademark* a crease-resistant synthetic fabric

crimson *adj* deep purplish-red [Arabic *qirmizi* kermes (dried bodies of insects used to make a red dye)]

cringe *vb* **cringing, cringed 1** to shrink or flinch in fear: *he cringed and shrank against the wall* **2** to behave in a submissive or timid way: *women who cringe before abusive husbands* **3** *informal* to be very embarrassed: *I cringe every time I see that old photo of me* ▷ *n* **4** the act of cringing [Old English *cringan* to yield in battle]

crinkle *vb* **-kling, -kled 1** to become slightly creased or folded ▷ *n* **2** a crease or fold [Old English *crincan* to bend] ❯ **crinkly** *adj*

crinoline *n* a petticoat stiffened with hoops to make the skirt stand out [Latin *crinis* hair + *lino* flax]

Crippen *n* Hawley Harvey, known as *Doctor Crippen*. 1862–1910, US doctor living in England: executed for poisoning his wife; the first criminal to be apprehended by the use of radiotelegraphy

cripple *n offensive* **1** a person who is lame or disabled **2** a

person with a mental or social problem: *an emotional cripple* ▷ *vb* **-pling, -pled 3** to make a cripple of **4** to damage (something) [Old English *crypel*] ❯ **crippled** *adj* ❯ **crippling** *adj*

Cripple Creek *n* a village in central Colorado: gold-mining centre since 1891, once the richest in the world

Cripps *n* Sir (Richard) Stafford. 1889–1952, British Labour statesman; Chancellor of the Exchequer (1947–50)

crisis *n, pl* **-ses 1** a crucial stage or turning point in the course of anything **2** a time of extreme trouble or danger [Greek *krisis* decision]

crisp *adj* **1** fresh and firm: *a crisp green salad* **2** dry and brittle: *bake until crisp and golden brown* **3** clean and neat: *crisp white cotton* **4** (of weather) cold but invigorating: *a crisp autumn day* **5** clear and sharp: *the telescope is designed to provide the first crisp images of distant galaxies* **6** lively or brisk: *the service is crisp and efficient* ▷ *n* **7** Brit a very thin slice of potato fried till crunchy ▷ *vb* **8** to make or become crisp [Latin *crispus* curled] ❯ **crisply** *adv* ❯ **crispness** *n*

crispbread *n* a thin dry biscuit made of wheat or rye

Crispi *n* Francesco. 1819–1901, Italian statesman; premier (1887–91; 1893–96)

Crispin *n* Saint, 3rd century AD, legendary Roman Christian martyr, with his brother **Crispinian**: they are the patron saints of shoemakers. Feast day: Oct 25

crispy *adj* **crispier, crispiest** hard and crunchy ❯ **crispiness** *n*

crisscross *vb* **1** to move in or mark with a crosswise pattern ▷ *adj* **2** (of lines) crossing one another in different directions

criterion *n, pl* **-ria** *or* **-rions** a standard by which something can be judged or decided [Greek *kritērion*]

USAGE *Criteria*, the plural of *criterion*, is not acceptable as a singular noun: *this criterion is not valid; these criteria are not valid.*

---

critic *n* **1** a professional judge of art, music, or literature **2** a person who finds fault and criticizes [Greek *kritēs* judge]

critical *adj* **1** very important or dangerous: *this was a critical moment in her career* **2** so seriously ill or injured as to be in danger of dying: *he is in a critical condition in hospital* **3** fault-finding or disparaging: *the article is highly critical of the government* **4** examining and judging analytically and without bias: *he submitted the plans to critical examination* **5** of a critic or criticism **6** *physics* denoting a constant value at which the properties of a system undergo an abrupt change: *the critical temperature above which the material loses its superconductivity* **7** (of a nuclear power station or reactor) having reached a state in which a nuclear chain reaction becomes self-sustaining ❯ **critically** *adv*

criticism *n* **1** fault-finding or censure **2** an analysis of a work of art or literature **3** the occupation of a critic **4** a work that sets out to analyse

criticize *or* **-cise** *vb* **-cizing, -cized** *or* **-cising, -cised 1** to find fault with **2** to analyse (something)

critique *n* **1** a critical essay or commentary **2** the act or art of criticizing [French]

Croagh Patrick *n* a mountain in NW Republic of Ireland, in Mayo: a place of pilgrimage as Saint Patrick is said to have prayed and fasted there. Height: 765 m (2510 ft)

croak *vb* **1** (of a frog or crow) to make a low hoarse cry **2** to utter or speak with a croak **3** *slang* to die ▷ *n* **4** a low hoarse sound [Old English *crācettan*] ❯ **croaky** *adj*

Croat (kroh-at) *adj, n* same as **Croatian**

Croatia *n* a republic in SE Europe: settled by Croats in the 7th century; belonged successively to Hungary, Turkey, and Austria; formed part of Yugoslavia (1918–91); became independent in 1991 but was invaded by Serbia and fighting continued until 1995; involved in the civil war in Bosnia-Herzegovina (1991–95); joined the European Union in 2013. Language: Croatian. Religion:

Roman Catholic majority. Currency: kuna. Capital: Zagreb. Pop: 4 475 611 (2013 est). Area: 55 322 sq km (21 359 sq miles). Croatian name: **Hrvatska**

Croatian (kroh-ay-shun) *adj* **1** of or relating to Croatia or its inhabitants ▷ *n* **2** a native or inhabitant of Croatia **3** the dialect of Serbo-Croat spoken in Croatia

Croce *n* Benedetto. 1866–1952, Italian philosopher, critic, and statesman: an opponent of Fascism, he helped re-establish liberalism in postwar Italy

crochet (kroh-shay) *vb* **-cheting, -cheted 1** to make (a piece of needlework) by looping and intertwining thread with a hooked needle ▷ *n* **2** work made by crocheting [French: small hook]

crock[1] *n* an earthenware pot or jar [Old English *crocc* pot]

crock[2] *n* old crock *Brit, Austral and NZ slang* a person or thing that is old or broken-down [Scots]

crockery *n* china dishes or earthenware vessels collectively

Crockett *n* David, known as *Davy Crockett*. 1786–1836, US frontiersman, politician, and soldier

crocodile *n* **1** a large amphibious tropical reptile with a tapering snout **2** *Brit, Austral and NZ informal* a line of schoolchildren walking two by two [Greek *krokodeilos* lizard]

Crocodile River *n* **1** a river in N South Africa, rising north of Johannesburg and flowing north-westerly into the Marico River on the Botswanan border; a tributary of the Limpopo **2** a river that rises in NE South Africa, in the Kruger National Park, and flows south-easterly into Mozambique

crocodile tears *pl n* an insincere show of grief [from the belief that crocodiles wept over their prey to lure further victims]

crocus *n, pl* **-cuses** a plant with white, yellow, or purple flowers in spring [Greek *krokos* saffron]

Croesus *n* **1** died ?546 BC, the last king of Lydia (560–546), noted for his great wealth **2** any very rich man

croft *n* a small farm worked by one family in Scotland [Old English] ▷ **crofter** *n* ▷ **crofting** *adj, n*

croissant (krwah-son) *n* a flaky crescent-shaped bread roll [French]

Crome *n* John, known as *Old Crome*. 1768–1821, English landscape painter and etcher

Cromer *n* a resort in E England, on the Norfolk coast: fishing. Pop: 8836 (2001)

cromlech *n Brit* **1** a circle of prehistoric standing stones **2** *no longer in technical use* a dolmen [Welsh]

Crompton *n* **1** Richmal, full name *Richmal Crompton Lamburn*. 1890–1969, British children's author, best known for her *Just William* stories **2** Samuel. 1753–1827, British inventor of the spinning mule (1779)

Cromwell *n* **1** Oliver. 1599–1658, English general and statesman. A convinced Puritan, he was an effective leader of the parliamentary army in the Civil War. After the execution of Charles I he quelled the Royalists in Scotland and Ireland, and became Lord Protector of the Commonwealth (1653–58) **2** his son, Richard. 1626–1712, Lord Protector of the Commonwealth (1658–59) **3** Thomas, Earl of Essex. ?1485–1540, English statesman. He was secretary to Cardinal Wolsey (1514), after whose fall he became chief adviser to Henry VIII. He drafted most of the Reformation legislation, securing its passage through parliament, the power of which he thereby greatly enhanced. He was executed after losing Henry's favour ▷ **Cromwellian** *adj, n*

crone *n* a witchlike old woman [Old French *carogne* carrion]

Cronin *n* **1** A(rchibald) J(oseph). 1896–1981, British novelist and physician. His works include *Hatter's Castle* (1931), *The Judas Tree* (1961), and *Dr Finlay's Casebook*, a TV series based on his medical experiences **2** James Watson. born 1931, US physicist; shared the Nobel prize for physics (1980) for his work on parity conservation in weak interactions

Cronje *n* Hansie, full name *Wessel Johannes Cronje* (1969–2002); South African cricketer. He captained South Africa (1994–2000); banned for life from cricket for match-fixing in 2001

crony *n, pl* **-nies** a close friend [Greek *khronios* long-lasting]

crook *n* **1** *informal* a dishonest person **2** a bent or curved place or thing: *she held the puppy in the crook of her arm* **3** a bishop's or shepherd's staff with a hooked end ▷ *adj* **4** *Austral and NZ informal* **a** ill **b** of poor quality **c** unpleasant; bad **5** go (off) crook *Austral and NZ informal* to lose one's temper **6** go crook at or on *Austral and NZ informal* to rebuke or upbraid ▷ *vb* **7** to bend or curve [Old Norse *krokr* hook]

crooked *adj* **1** bent or twisted **2** set at an angle **3** *informal* dishonest or illegal ▷ **crookedly** *adv* ▷ **crookedness** *n*

Crookes *n* Sir William. 1832–1919, English chemist and physicist: he investigated the properties of cathode rays and invented a type of radiometer and the lens named after him

croon *vb* to sing, hum, or speak in a soft low tone [Middle Dutch *crōnen* to groan] ▷ **crooner** *n*

crop *n* **1** a cultivated plant, such as a cereal, vegetable, or fruit plant **2** the season's total yield of farm produce **3** any group of things appearing at one time: *a remarkable crop of new Scottish plays* **4** the handle of a whip **5** short for **riding crop 6** a pouchlike part of the gullet of a bird, in which food is stored or prepared for digestion **7** a short cropped hairstyle ▷ *vb* **cropping, cropped 8** to cut (something) very short **9** to produce or harvest as a crop **10** (of animals) to feed on (grass) **11** to clip part of (the ear or ears) of (an animal), esp. for identification ▶ See also **crop up** [Old English *cropp*]

crop circle *n* a pattern made up of ring shapes formed by the unexplained flattening of cereals growing in a field

cropper *n* **come a cropper** *informal* **a** to fail completely **b** to fall heavily

crop top *n* a short T-shirt or vest that reveals the wearer's midriff

crop up *vb informal* to occur or appear unexpectedly

croquet (kroh-kay) *n* a game played on a lawn in which balls are hit through hoops [French]

croquette (kroh-kett) *n* a fried cake of mashed potato, meat, or fish [French]

Crosby[1] *n* a town in NW England, in Sefton unitary authority, Merseyside. Pop: 51 789 (2001)

Crosby[2] *n* Bing, real name *Harry Lillis Crosby*. 1904–77, US singer and film actor; famous for his style of crooning: best known for the song "White Christmas" from the film *Holiday Inn* (1942)

crosier *n* same as **crozier**

Crosland *n* Anthony. 1918–77, British Labour politician and socialist theorist, author of *The Future of Socialism* (1957)

cross *vb* **1** to move or go across (something): *she crossed the street to the gallery* **2** to meet and pass: *further south, the way is crossed by Brewer Street* **3** *Brit and NZ* to draw two parallel lines across (a cheque) and so make it payable only into a bank account **4** to mark with a cross or crosses **5** to cancel or delete with a cross or with lines: *she crossed out the first three words* **6** to place across or crosswise: *he sat down and crossed his legs* **7** to make the sign of the cross upon as a blessing **8** to annoy or anger (someone) by challenging or opposing their wishes and plans **9** to interbreed or cross-fertilize **10** *football* to pass (the ball) from a wing to the middle of the field **11** (of each of two letters in the post) to be sent before the other is received **12** (of telephone lines) to interfere with each other so that several callers are connected together at one time **13 cross one's fingers** to fold one finger across another in the hope of bringing good luck **14 cross one's heart** to promise by making the sign of a cross over one's heart **15 cross one's mind** to occur to one briefly or suddenly ▷ *n* **16** a structure, symbol, or mark consisting of two

C

intersecting lines **17** an upright post with a bar across it, used in ancient times as a means of execution **18** a representation of the Cross on which Jesus Christ was executed as an emblem of Christianity **19** a symbol (×) used as a signature or error mark **20 the sign of the cross** a sign made with the hand by some Christians to represent the Cross **21** a medal or monument in the shape of a cross **22** the place in a town or village where a cross has been set up **23** *biology* **a** the process of crossing; hybridization **b** a hybrid **24** a mixture of two things **25** a hindrance or misfortune: *we've all got our own cross to bear* **26** *football* a pass of the ball from a wing to the middle of the field ▷ *adj* **27** angry **28** lying or placed across: *a cross beam* [Latin *crux*] **> crossly** *adv* **> crossness** *n*

Cross[1] *n* **the Cross a** the cross on which Jesus Christ was crucified **b** Christianity

Cross[2] *n* Richard Assheton, 1st Viscount. 1823–1914, British Conservative statesman, home secretary (1874–80); noted for reforms affecting housing, public health, and the employment of women and children in factories

cross- *combining form* **1** indicating action from one individual or group to another: *cross-cultural*; *cross-refer* **2** indicating movement or position across something: *crosscurrent*; *crosstalk* **3** indicating a crosslike figure or intersection: *crossbones*

crossbar *n* **1** a horizontal bar across a pair of goalposts **2** the horizontal bar on a man's bicycle

cross-bench *n* *Brit* a seat in Parliament for a member belonging to neither the government nor the opposition **> cross-bencher** *n*

crossbill *n* a finch that has a bill with crossed tips

crossbow *n* a weapon consisting of a bow fixed across a wooden stock, which releases an arrow when the trigger is pulled

crossbreed *vb* **-breeding, -bred 1** to produce (a hybrid animal or plant) by crossing two different species ▷ *n* **2** a hybrid animal or plant

crosscheck *vb* **1** to check the accuracy of (something) by using a different method ▷ *n* **2** a crosschecking

cross-country *adj, adv* **1** by way of open country or fields ▷ *n* **2** a long race held over open ground

crosscut *vb* **-cutting, -cut 1** to cut across ▷ *adj* **2** cut across ▷ *n* **3** a transverse cut or course

cross-examine *vb* **-examining, -examined 1** *law* to question (a witness for the opposing side) in order to check his or her testimony **2** to question closely or relentlessly **> cross-examination** *n* **> cross-examiner** *n*

cross-eyed *adj* with one or both eyes turning inwards towards the nose

cross-fertilize *or* **-lise** *vb* **-lizing, -lized** *or* **-lising, -lised** to fertilize (an animal or plant) by fusion of male and female reproductive cells from different individuals of the same species **> cross-fertilization** *or* **-lisation** *n*

crossfire *n* **1** *military* gunfire crossing another line of fire **2** a lively exchange of ideas or opinions

crosshatch *vb* *drawing* to shade with two or more sets of parallel lines that cross one another

crossing *n* **1** a place where a street, railway, or river may be crossed **2** the place where one thing crosses another **3** a journey across water

cross-legged *adj* sitting with the legs bent and the knees pointing outwards

Crossman *n* Richard (Howard Stafford). 1907–74, British Labour politician. His diaries, published posthumously as the *Crossman Papers* (1975), revealed details of cabinet discussions

crosspatch *n* *informal* a bad-tempered person [*cross* + obsolete *patch* fool]

cross-ply *adj* (of a tyre) having the fabric cords in the outer casing running diagonally to stiffen the sidewalls

cross-purposes *pl n* **at cross-purposes** misunderstanding each other in a discussion

cross-question *vb* to cross-examine

cross-refer *vb* **-referring, -referred** to refer from one part of something to another

cross-reference *n* **1** a reference within a text to another part of the text ▷ *vb* **-referencing, -referenced 2** to cross-refer

Cross River *n* a state of SE Nigeria, on the Gulf of Guinea. Capital: Calabar. Pop: 2 888 966 (2006). Area: 20 156 sq km (7782 sq miles). Former name (until 1976): South-Eastern State

crossroad *n* *US and Canad* **1** a road that crosses another road **2** a road that connects one main road to another

crossroads *n* **1** the point at which roads cross one another **2 at the crossroads** at the point at which an important choice has to be made

cross section *n* **1** *maths* a surface formed by cutting across a solid, usually at right angles to its longest axis **2** a random sample regarded as representative: *a cross section of society* **> cross-sectional** *adj*

cross-stitch *n* an embroidery stitch made from two crossing stitches

crosstalk *n* **1** *Brit* rapid or witty talk **2** unwanted signals transferred between communication channels

crosswalk *n* *US and Canad* a place marked where pedestrians may cross a road

crosswise *or* **crossways** *adj* **1** across **2** in the shape of a cross ▷ *adv* **3** across: *slice the celery crosswise* **4** in the shape of a cross

crossword puzzle *or* **crossword** *n* a puzzle in which vertically and horizontally crossing words suggested by clues are written into a grid of squares

crotch *n* **1** the forked part of the human body between the legs **2** the corresponding part of a pair of trousers or pants **3** any forked part formed by the joining of two things: *the crotch of the tree* [probably variant of CRUTCH] **> crotched** *adj*

crotchet *n* *Brit music* a note having the time value of a quarter of a semibreve [Old French *crochet* little hook]

crotchety *adj* *informal* bad-tempered

Crotone *n* a town in S Italy, on the coast of Calabria: founded in about 700 BC by the Achaeans; chemical works and zinc-smelting. Pop: 60 010 (2001)

crouch *vb* **1** to bend low with the legs and body pulled close together ▷ *n* **2** this position [Old French *crochir* to become bent like a hook]

croup[1] (kroop) *n* a throat disease of children, with a hoarse cough and laboured breathing [Middle English: to cry hoarsely, probably imitative]

croup[2] (kroop) *n* the hindquarters of a horse [Old French *croupe*]

croupier (kroop-ee-ay) *n* a person who collects bets and pays out winnings at a gambling table [French]

crouton *n* a small piece of fried or toasted bread served in soup [French]

crow[1] *n* **1** a large black bird with a harsh call **2 as the crow flies** in a straight line [Old English *crāwa*]

crow[2] *vb* **1** (*past* **crowed** *or* **crew**) (of a cock) to utter a shrill squawking sound **2** to boast about one's superiority **3** (of a baby) to utter cries of pleasure ▷ *n* **4** a crowing sound [Old English *crāwan*]

crowbar *n* a heavy iron bar used as a lever

crowd *n* **1** a large number of things or people gathered together **2** a particular group of people: *we got to know a French crowd from Lyons* **3 the crowd** the masses ▷ *vb* **4** to gather together in large numbers **5** to press together into a confined space **6** to fill or occupy fully **7** *informal* to make (someone) uncomfortable by coming too close [Old English *crūdan*] **> crowded** *adj*

crowdfunding *n* the practice of funding a project by getting small donations from many supporters, often via the internet

crowd-pleaser *n* a person or thing that appeals to a large proportion of an audience **> crowd-pleasing** *adj*

Crowe *n* Russell. born 1964, Australian film actor, born in New Zealand. His films include *LA Confidential* (1997),

Gladiator (2000), for which he won an Oscar, *A Beautiful Mind* (2001), *Master and Commander* (2003), and *American Gangster* (2007)

crown *n* **1** a monarch's ornamental headdress, usually made of gold and jewels **2** a wreath for the head, given as an honour **3** the highest or central point of something arched or curved: *the crown of the head* **4 a** the enamel-covered part of a tooth projecting beyond the gum **b** a substitute crown, usually of gold or porcelain, fitted over a decayed or broken tooth **5** a former British coin worth 25 pence **6** the outstanding quality or achievement: *the last piece is the crown of the evening* ▷ *vb* **7** to put a crown on the head of (someone) to proclaim him or her monarch **8** to put on the top of **9** to reward **10** to form the topmost part of **11** to put the finishing touch to (a series of events): *he crowned a superb display with three goals* **12** to attach a crown to (a tooth) **13** *Brit, Austral and NZ slang* to hit over the head **14** *draughts* to promote (a draught) to a king by placing another draught on top of it [Greek *korōnē*]

Crown *n* **the Crown** the power or institution of the monarchy

crown colony *n* a British colony controlled by the Crown

crown court *n* a local criminal court in England and Wales

Crown Derby *n* a type of fine porcelain made at Derby

crown jewels *pl n* the jewellery used by a sovereign on ceremonial occasions

crown-of-thorns *n* a starfish with a spiny outer covering that feeds on living coral

crown prince *n* the male heir to a sovereign throne **> crown princess** *n*

crow's feet *pl n* wrinkles at the outer corners of the eye

crow's nest *n* a lookout platform fixed at the top of a ship's mast

Croydon *n* a borough in S Greater London (since 1965): formerly important for its airport (1915–59). Pop: 336 700 (2003 est). Area: 87 sq km (33 sq miles)

crozier *or* **crosier** *n* a hooked staff carried by bishops as a symbol of office [Old French *crossier* staff-bearer]

crucial *adj* **1** of exceptional importance **2** *Brit slang* very good [Latin *crux* cross] **> crucially** *adv*

cruciate *adj* shaped or arranged like a cross [Latin *crux* cross] **> cruciately** *adv*

cruciate ligament *n anatomy* either of a pair of ligaments that cross each other in the knee

crucible *n* a pot in which metals or other substances are melted [Medieval Latin *crucibulum* night lamp]

Crucible *n* **the Crucible** a Sheffield theatre, venue of the annual world professional snooker championship

crucifix *n* a model cross with a figure of Christ upon it [Church Latin *crucifixus* the crucified Christ]

crucifixion *n* a method of execution by fastening to a cross, normally by the hands and feet

Crucifixion *n* **1** the Crucifixion the crucifying of Christ **2** a representation of this

cruciform *adj* shaped like a cross

crucify *vb* **-fies, -fying, -fied 1** to put to death by crucifixion **2** to treat cruelly **3** *slang* to defeat or ridicule totally [Latin *crux* cross + *figere* to fasten]

crud *n slang* a sticky or encrusted substance [earlier form of CURD] **> cruddy** *adj*

crude *adj* **1** rough and simple: *crude farm implements* **2** tasteless or vulgar **3** in a natural or unrefined state ▷ *n* **4** short for **crude oil** [Latin *crudus* bloody, raw] **> crudely** *adv* **> crudity** *or* **crudeness** *n*

Cruden *n* Alexander. 1701–70, Scottish bookseller and compiler of a well-known biblical concordance (1737)

crude oil *n* unrefined petroleum

crudités (crew-dit-tay) *pl n* a selection of raw vegetables often served with a variety of dips before a meal [French *crudité* rawness]

cruel *adj* **1** deliberately causing pain without pity

2 causing pain or suffering [Latin *crudelis*] **> cruelly** *adv* **> cruelty** *n*

cruet *n* **1** a small container for pepper, salt, etc., at table **2** a set of such containers on a stand [Old French *crue* flask]

Cruft *n* Charles. 1852–1938, British dog breeder, who organized the first (1886) of the annual dog shows known as Cruft's

Cruikshank *n* George. 1792–1878, English illustrator and caricaturist

cruise *n* **1** a sail taken for pleasure, stopping at various places ▷ *vb* **cruising, cruised 2** to sail about from place to place for pleasure **3** (of a vehicle, aircraft, or ship) to travel at a moderate and efficient speed **4** to proceed steadily or easily: *they cruised into the final of the qualifying competition* [Dutch *kruisen* to cross]

Cruise *n* Tom, original name *Thomas Cruise Mapother*. born 1962, US film actor; his films include *Risky Business* (1983), *Top Gun* (1986), *Jerry Maguire* (1989), *Eyes Wide Shut* (1999), *War of the Worlds* (2005), and *Valkyrie* (2008)

cruise missile *n* a low-flying subsonic missile that is guided throughout its flight

cruiser *n* **1** a large fast warship armed with medium-calibre weapons **2** Also called: **cabin cruiser** a motorboat with a cabin

cruiserweight *n* a professional boxer weighing up to 195 pounds (88.5 kg)

crumb *n* **1** a small fragment of bread or other dry food **2** a small bit or scrap: *a crumb of comfort* [Old English *cruma*]

crumble *vb* **-bling, -bled 1** to break into crumbs or fragments **2** to fall apart or decay ▷ *n* **3** a baked pudding consisting of stewed fruit with a crumbly topping: *rhubarb crumble* **> crumbly** *adj* **> crumbliness** *n*

crumby *adj* **crumbier, crumbiest 1** full of crumbs **2** same as **crummy**

Crummock Water *n* a lake in NW England, in Cumbria in the Lake District. Length: 4 km (2.5 miles)

crummy *adj* **-mier, -miest** *slang* **1** of very bad quality: *a crummy hotel* **2** unwell: *I felt really crummy* [variant spelling of *crumby*]

crumpet *n* **1** a light soft yeast cake, eaten buttered **2** *chiefly Brit slang* sexually attractive women collectively [origin unknown]

crumple *vb* **-pling, -pled 1** to crush or become crushed into untidy wrinkles or creases **2** to collapse in an untidy heap: *her father lay crumpled on the floor* ▷ *n* **3** an untidy crease or wrinkle [obsolete *crump* to bend] **> crumply** *adj*

crunch *vb* **1** to bite or chew with a noisy crushing sound **2** to make a crisp or brittle sound ▷ *n* **3** a crunching sound **4** **the crunch** *informal* the critical moment or situation [imitative] **> crunchy** *adj* **> crunchiness** *n*

crupper *n* **1** a strap that passes from the back of a saddle under a horse's tail **2** the horse's rump [Old French *crupiere*]

crusade *n* **1** any of the medieval military expeditions undertaken by European Christians to recapture the Holy Land from the Muslims **2** a vigorous campaign in favour of a cause ▷ *vb* **-sading, -saded 3** to take part in a crusade [Latin *crux* cross] **> crusader** *n*

cruse *n* a small earthenware container for liquids [Old English *crūse*]

crush *vb* **1** to press or squeeze so as to injure, break, or put out of shape **2** to break or grind into small pieces **3** to control or subdue by force **4** to extract (liquid) by pressing: *crush a clove of garlic* **5** to defeat or humiliate utterly **6** to crowd together ▷ *n* **7** a dense crowd **8** the act of crushing **9** *informal* an infatuation: *I had a teenage crush on my French teacher* **10** a drink made by crushing fruit: *orange crush* [Old French *croissir*]

crush barrier *n* a barrier put up to separate sections of large crowds and prevent crushing

crust *n* **1** the hard outer part of bread **2** the baked shell of a pie or tart **3** any hard outer layer: *a thin crust of snow*

c

4 the solid outer shell of the earth ▷ *vb* **5** to cover with or form a crust [Latin *crusta* hard surface, rind]

crustacean *n* **1** an animal with a hard outer shell and several pairs of legs, which usually lives in water, such as a crab or lobster ▷ *adj* **2** of crustaceans [Latin *crusta* shell]

crusty *adj* **crustier, crustiest** **1** having a crust **2** rude or irritable ▶ **crustiness** *n*

crutch *n* **1** a long staff with a rest for the armpit, used by a lame person to support the weight of the body **2** something that supports **3** *Brit* same as **crotch** (1) [Old English *crycc*]

crutchings *pl n Austral and NZ* the wool clipped from a sheep's hindquarters

crux *n, pl* **cruxes** *or* **cruces** a crucial or decisive point [Latin: cross]

Cruyff *n* Johan, born 1947, Dutch footballer and manager: played for Ajax and Barcelona; European Footballer of the Year (1971, 1973, 1974); capped 48 times for the Netherlands, scoring 33 goals; as a manager he won the European Cup with Barcelona (1992)

cry *vb* **cries, crying, cried** **1** to shed tears **2** to make a loud vocal sound, usually to express pain or fear or to appeal for help **3** to utter loudly or shout **4** (of an animal or bird) to utter loud characteristic sounds **5 cry for** to appeal urgently for ▷ *n, pl* **cries** **6** a fit of weeping **7** the act or sound of crying **8** the characteristic utterance of an animal or bird **9** an urgent appeal: *a cry for help* **10** a public demand: *a cry for more law and order on the streets* **11 a far cry** from something very different from **12 in full cry** **a** in eager pursuit **b** in the middle of talking or doing something ▶ See also **cry off** [Old French *crier*]

crying *adj* **a crying shame** something that demands immediate attention

cry off *vb informal* to withdraw from an arrangement

cryogenics *n* the branch of physics concerned with very low temperatures and their effects [Greek *kruos* cold + *-genēs* born] ▶ **cryogenic** *adj*

crypt *n* a vault or underground chamber, such as one beneath a church, used as a burial place [Greek *kruptē*]

cryptic *adj* having a hidden or secret meaning; puzzling: *no-one knew what he meant by that cryptic remark* [Greek *kruptos* concealed] ▶ **cryptically** *adv*

cryptogam *n botany* a plant that reproduces by spores not seeds [Greek *kruptos* hidden + *gamos* marriage]

cryptography *n* the art of writing in and deciphering codes [Greek *kruptos* hidden + -GRAPHY] ▶ **cryptographer** *n* ▶ **cryptographic** *adj*

crystal *n* **1** a solid with a regular internal structure and symmetrical arrangement of faces **2** a single grain of a crystalline substance **3** a very clear and brilliant glass **4** something made of crystal **5** crystal glass articles collectively **6** *electronics* a crystalline element used in certain electronic devices, such as a detector or oscillator ▷ *adj* **7** bright and clear: *the crystal waters of the pool* [Greek *krustallos* ice, crystal]

crystal ball *n* the glass globe used in crystal gazing

crystal gazing *n* **1** the act of staring into a crystal ball, supposedly in order to see future events **2** the act of trying to foresee or predict ▶ **crystal gazer** *n*

crystalline *adj* **1** of or like crystal or crystals **2** clear

crystallize, crystalize *or* **-ise** *vb* **-izing, -ized** *or* **-ising, -ised** **1** to make or become definite **2** to form into crystals **3** to preserve (fruit) in sugar ▶ **crystallization, crystalization** *or* **-isation** *n*

crystallography *n* the science of crystal structure

crystalloid *n* a substance that in solution can pass through a membrane

crystal meth *n informal* crystal methamphetamine, a concentrated and highly potent form of methamphetamine with dangerous side effects

Crystal Palace *n* a building of glass and iron designed by Joseph Paxton to house the Great Exhibition of 1851. Erected in Hyde Park, London, it was moved to Sydenham (1852–53): destroyed by fire in 1936

Cs *chem* caesium

CSA (in Britain) Child Support Agency

CSE (formerly, in Britain) Certificate of Secondary Education: an examination the first grade pass of which was an equivalent to a GCE O level

CS gas *n* a gas causing tears and painful breathing, used to control civil disturbances [initials of its US inventors, Ben Carson and Roger Staughton]

CST Central Standard Time

CT Connecticut

Ctesiphon *n* an ancient city on the River Tigris about 100 km (60 miles) above Babylon. First mentioned in 221 BC, it was destroyed in the 7th and 8th centuries AD

CT scanner *n* an X-ray machine that can produce cross-sectional images of the soft tissues [*c*(omputerized) *t*(omography) *scanner*]

CTV Canadian Television (Network Limited)

Cu *chem* copper [Late Latin *cuprum*]

cu. cubic

cub *n* **1** the young of certain mammals, such as the lion or bear **2** a young or inexperienced person ▷ *vb* **cubbing, cubbed** **3** to give birth to (cubs) [origin unknown]

Cub *n* short for **Cub Scout**

Cuba *n* a republic and the largest island in the Caribbean, at the entrance to the Gulf of Mexico: became a Spanish colony after its discovery by Columbus in 1492; gained independence after the Spanish-American War of 1898 but remained subject to US influence until declared a people's republic under Castro in 1960; subject of an international crisis in 1962, when the US blockaded the island in order to compel the Soviet Union to dismantle its nuclear missile base. Sugar comprises about 80 per cent of total exports; the economy was badly affected by loss of trade following the collapse of the Soviet Union and by the continuing US trade embargo. Diplomatic ties with the US restored in 2014. Language: Spanish. Religion: nonreligious majority. Currency: peso. Capital: Havana. Pop: 11 061 886 (2013 est). Area: 110 922 sq km (42 827 sq miles)

Cuban *adj* **1** of or relating to Cuba or its inhabitants ▷ *n* **2** a native or inhabitant of Cuba

cubbyhole *n* a small enclosed space or room [dialect *cub* cattle pen]

cube *n* **1** an object with six equal square faces **2** the product obtained by multiplying a number by itself twice: *the cube of 2 is 8* ▷ *vb* **cubing, cubed** **3** to find the cube of (a number) **4** to cut into cubes [Greek *kubos*]

cube root *n* the number or quantity whose cube is a given number or quantity: *2 is the cube root of 8*

cubic *adj* **1 a** having three dimensions **b** having the same volume as a cube with length, width, and depth each measuring the given unit: *a cubic metre* **2** having the shape of a cube **3** *maths* involving the cubes of numbers

cubicle *n* an enclosed part of a large room, screened for privacy [Latin *cubiculum*]

cubic measure *n* a system of units for the measurement of volumes

cubism *n* a style of art, begun in the early 20th century, in which objects are represented by geometrical shapes ▶ **cubist** *adj, n*

cubit *n* an ancient measure of length based on the length of the forearm [Latin *cubitum* elbow, cubit]

cuboid *adj* **1** shaped like a cube ▷ *n* **2** *maths* a geometric solid whose six faces are rectangles

Cub Scout *or* **Cub** *n* a member of a junior branch of the Scout Association

cuckold *literary or old-fashioned* *n* **1** a man whose wife has been unfaithful to him ▷ *vb* **2** to make a cuckold of [Middle English *cukeweld*]

cuckoo *n, pl* **cuckoos** **1** a migratory bird with a characteristic two-note call, noted for laying its eggs in the nests of other birds ▷ *adj* **2** *informal* insane or foolish [Old French *cucu*, imitative]

cuckoopint n a plant with arrow-shaped leaves, purple flowers, and red berries

cuckoo spit n a white frothy mass produced on plants by the larvae of some insects

cucumber n 1 a long fruit with thin green rind and crisp white flesh, used in salads 2 **as cool as a cucumber** calm and self-possessed [Latin *cucumis*]

Cúcuta n a city in E Colombia: commercial centre of a coffee-producing region. Pop: 883 000 (2005 est). Official name: **San José de Cúcuta**

cud n 1 partially digested food which a ruminant brings back into its mouth to chew again 2 **chew the cud** to think deeply [Old English *cudu*]

cuddle vb **-dling, -dled** 1 to hug or embrace fondly 2 **cuddle up** to lie close and snug ▷ n 3 a fond hug [origin unknown] ▷ **cuddly** adj

cudgel n a short thick stick used as a weapon [Old English *cycgel*]

Cudlipp n Hugh, Baron. 1913–98, British newspaper editor, a pioneer of tabloid journalism: editorial director of the *Daily Mirror* (1952–63)

Cudworth n Ralph. 1617–88, English philosopher and theologian. His works include *True Intellectual System of the Universe* (1678) and *A Treatise concerning Eternal and Immutable Morality* (1731)

cue¹ n 1 a signal to an actor or musician to begin speaking or playing 2 a signal or reminder 3 **on cue** at the right moment ▷ vb **cueing, cued** 4 to give a cue to [perhaps from the letter *q*, used in an actor's script to represent Latin *quando* when]

cue² n 1 a long tapering stick used to hit the balls in billiards, snooker, or pool ▷ vb **cueing, cued** 2 to hit (a ball) with a cue [variant of QUEUE]

cue ball n snooker the ball struck by the cue, as distinguished from the object balls

Cuenca n 1 a city in SW Ecuador: university (1868). Pop: 311 000 (2005 est) 2 a town in central Spain: prosperous in the Middle Ages for its silver and textile industries. Pop: 47 201 (2003 est)

Cuernavaca n a city in S central Mexico, capital of Morelos state: resort with nearby Cacahuamilpa Caverns. Pop: 723 000 (2005 est)

cuff¹ n 1 the end of a sleeve 2 US, Canad, Austral and NZ a turn-up on trousers 3 **off the cuff** informal impromptu: *he delivers many speeches off the cuff* [Middle English *cuffe* glove]

cuff² Brit, Austral and NZ vb 1 to strike with an open hand ▷ n 2 a blow with an open hand [origin unknown]

cuff link n one of a pair of decorative fastenings for shirt cuffs

Cuiabá or **Cuyabá** n 1 a port in W Brazil, capital of Mato Grosso state, on the Cuiabá River. Pop: 777 000 (2005 est) 2 a river in SW Brazil, rising on the Mato Grosso plateau and flowing southwest into the São Lourenço River. Length: 483 km (300 miles)

cuisine (quiz-**zeen**) n 1 a style of cooking: *Italian cuisine* 2 the range of food served in a restaurant [French]

Culbertson n Ely. 1891–1955, US authority on contract bridge

cul-de-sac n, pl **culs-de-sac** or **cul-de-sacs** a road with one end blocked off [French: bottom of the bag]

Culebra Cut n the former name of **Gaillard Cut**

Culham n a village in S central England, in Oxfordshire: site of the UK centre for thermonuclear reactor research and of the Joint European Torus (JET) programme

Culiacán n a city in NW Mexico, capital of Sinaloa state. Pop: 799 000 (2005 est)

culinary adj of the kitchen or cookery [Latin *culina* kitchen]

cull vb 1 to choose or gather 2 to remove or kill (the inferior or surplus) animals from a herd ▷ n 3 the act of culling [Latin *colligere* to gather together]

Cullen n William Douglas, Baron. born 1935, Scottish judge who conducted public inquiries into the Piper Alpha disaster (1990), the Dunblane school shootings

(1996), and the Ladbroke Grove rail disaster (1999); led the tribunal which turned down the appeal (2002) of Abdelbaset al-Megrahi against his conviction for the 1988 Lockerbie bombing

Culloden n a moor near Inverness in N Scotland: site of a battle in 1746 in which government troops under the Duke of Cumberland defeated the Jacobites under Prince Charles Edward Stuart

culminate vb **-nating, -nated** to reach the highest point or climax: *the parade culminated in a memorial service* [Latin *culmen* top] ▷ **culmination** n

culottes pl n women's flared trousers cut to look like a skirt [French]

culpable adj deserving blame [Latin *culpa* fault] ▷ **culpability** n

Culpeper n Nicholas. 1616–54, English herbalist and astrologer; his unauthorized translation (1649) of the College of Physicians' *Pharmacopoeia* and his *Herbal* (1653) popularized herbalism

culprit n the person guilty of an offence or misdeed [Anglo-French *culpable* guilty + *prit* ready]

cult n 1 a specific system of religious worship 2 a sect devoted to the beliefs of a cult 3 devoted attachment to a person, idea, or activity 4 a popular fashion: *the bungee-jumping cult* ▷ adj 5 very popular among a limited group of people: *a cult TV series* [Latin *cultus* cultivation, refinement]

cultish adj intended to appeal to a small group of fashionable people

cultivate vb **-vating, -vated** 1 to prepare (land) to grow crops 2 to grow (plants) 3 to develop or improve (something) by giving special attention to it: *he tried to cultivate a reputation for fairness* 4 to try to develop a friendship with (a person) [Latin *colere* to till]

cultivated adj well-educated: *a civilized and cultivated man*

cultivation n 1 the act of cultivating 2 culture or refinement

cultivator n a farm implement used to break up soil and remove weeds

culture n 1 the ideas, customs, and art of a particular society 2 a particular civilization at a particular period 3 a developed understanding of the arts 4 development or improvement by special attention or training: *physical culture* 5 the cultivation and rearing of plants or animals 6 a growth of bacteria for study ▷ vb **-turing, -tured** 7 to grow (bacteria) in a special medium [Latin *colere* to till] ▷ **cultural** adj

cultured adj 1 showing good taste or manners 2 artificially grown or synthesized

cultured pearl n a pearl artificially grown in an oyster shell

culture shock n sociol the feelings of isolation and anxiety experienced by a person on first coming into contact with a culture very different from his or her own

culvert n a drain or pipe that crosses under a road or railway [origin unknown]

Culzean Castle n a Gothic Revival castle near Ayr in South Ayrshire, in SW Scotland: designed by Robert Adam (1772–92); includes a room dedicated to General Eisenhower

cum prep with: *a small living-cum-dining room* [Latin]

Cumaná n a city in NE Venezuela: founded in 1523; the oldest European settlement in South America. Pop: 271 000 (2005 est)

Cumberland¹ n (until 1974) a county of NW England, now part of Cumbria

Cumberland² n 1 Richard. 1631–1718, English theologian and moral philosopher; bishop of Peterborough (1691–1718) 2 William Augustus, Duke of Cumberland, known as *Butcher Cumberland*. 1721–65, English soldier, younger son of George II, noted for his defeat of Charles Edward Stuart at Culloden (1746) and his subsequent ruthless destruction of Jacobite rebels

Cumbernauld *n* a town in central Scotland, in North Lanarkshire, northeast of Glasgow: developed as a new town since 1956. Pop: 49 664 (2001)

cumbersome *or* **cumbrous** *adj* **1** awkward because of size or shape **2** difficult because of complexity: *the cumbersome appeals procedure*

Cumbria *n* (since 1974) a county of NW England comprising the former counties of Westmorland and Cumberland together with N Lancashire: includes the Lake District mountain area and surrounding coastal lowlands with the Pennine uplands in the extreme east. Administrative centre: Carlisle. Pop: 489 800 (2003 est). Area: 6810 sq km (2629 sq miles)

Cumbrian *adj* **1** of or relating to Cumbria or its inhabitants ▷ *n* **2** a native or inhabitant of Cumbria

Cumbrian Mountains *pl n* a mountain range in NW England, in Cumbria. Highest peak: Scafell Pike, 977 m (3206 ft)

cumin *or* **cummin** *n* **1** the spicy-smelling seeds of a Mediterranean herb, used in cooking **2** the plant from which these seeds are obtained [Greek *kuminon*]

cummerbund *n* a wide sash worn round the waist, esp. with a dinner jacket [Hindi *kamarband*, from Persian *kamar* loins + *band* band]

Cummings *n* Edward Estlin, (preferred typographical representation of name **e. e. cummings**). 1894–1962, US poet

cumquat *n* same as kumquat

cumulative (kew-myew-la-tiv) *adj* growing in amount, strength, or effect by small steps: *the cumulative effect of twelve years of war*

cumulus (kew-myew-luss) *n, pl* **-li** (-lie) a thick or billowing white or dark grey cloud [Latin: mass]

Cunard *n* Sir Samuel (1787–1865). Canadian shipping magnate, founder of the Cunard line

Cunaxa *n* the site near the lower Euphrates where Artaxerxes II defeated Cyrus the Younger in 401 BC

cuneiform (kew-nif-form) *n* **1** an ancient system of writing using wedge-shaped characters ▷ *adj* **2** written in cuneiform [Latin *cuneus* wedge]

Cuneo *n* a city in NW Italy, in Piedmont. Pop: 52 334 (2001)

cunjevoi *n Austral* **1** a plant of tropical Asia and Australia with small flowers, cultivated for its edible rhizome **2** a sea squirt

cunnilingus *n* the kissing and licking of a woman's genitals by her sexual partner [Latin *cunnus* vulva + *lingere* to lick]

cunning *adj* **1** clever at deceiving **2** made with skill ▷ *n* **3** cleverness at deceiving **4** skill or ingenuity [Old English *cunnende*]

Cunningham *n* Merce. 1919–2009 US dancer and choreographer. His experimental ballets include *Suite for Five* (1956) and *Travelogue* (1977)

Cunninghame Graham *n* R(obert) B(ontine). 1852–1936, Scottish traveller, writer, and politician, noted for his essays and short stories: first president (1928) of the Scottish Nationalist Party

Cunobelinus *n* also called *Cymbeline*. died ?42 AD, British ruler of the Catuvellauni tribe (?10–?42); founder of Colchester (?10)

cunt *n taboo* **1** the female genitals **2** *offensive, slang* a stupid or obnoxious person [Middle English]

cup *n* **1** a small bowl-shaped drinking container with a handle **2** the contents of a cup **3** something shaped like a cup: *a bra with padded cups* **4** a cup-shaped trophy awarded as a prize **5** a sporting contest in which a cup is awarded to the winner **6** a mixed drink with fruit juice or wine as a base: *claret cup* **7** one's lot in life: *his cup of bitterness was full to overflowing* **8** someone's cup of tea *informal* someone's chosen or preferred thing ▷ *vb* **cupping, cupped** **9** to form (the hands) into the shape of a cup **10** to hold in cupped hands [Old English *cuppe*]

cupboard *n* a piece of furniture or a recess with a door, for storage

cupboard love *n* a show of love put on in order to gain something

Cup Final *n* **1** the annual final of the FA or Scottish Cup soccer competition **2** the final of any cup competition

Cupid *n* **1** the Roman god of love, represented as a winged boy with a bow and arrow **2** a picture or statue of Cupid [Latin *cupido* desire]

cupidity (kew-pid-it-ee) *n formal* strong desire for wealth or possessions [Latin *cupere* to long for]

cupola (kew-pol-la) *n* **1** a domed roof or ceiling **2** a small dome on the top of a roof **3** an armoured revolving gun turret on a warship [Latin *cupa* tub]

cupreous (kew-pree-uss) *adj* of or containing copper [Latin *cuprum* copper]

cupric (kew-prick) *adj* of or containing copper in the divalent state

cupronickel (kew-proh-nik-el) *n* a copper alloy containing up to 40 per cent nickel

cup tie *n Brit sport* an eliminating match between two teams in a cup competition

cur *n* **1** a vicious mongrel dog **2** a contemptible person [Middle English *kurdogge*]

curable *adj* capable of being cured ▷ **curability** *n*

curaçao (kew-rah-so) *n* an orange-flavoured liqueur

Curaçao *n* **1** an island in the Caribbean, formerly a part of the Netherlands Antilles until their dissolution in 2010, now a constituent country of the Netherlands. Capital: Willemstad. Pop: 146 836 (2013 est). Area: 444 sq km (171 sq miles) **2** (*also without cap*) an orange-flavoured liqueur originally made there

curacy (kew-rah-see) *n, pl* **-cies** the work or position of a curate

curare (kew-rah-ree) *n* a poisonous resin obtained from a South American tree, used as a muscle relaxant in medicine [Carib *kurari*]

curate *n* a clergyman who assists a vicar or parish priest [Medieval Latin *cura* spiritual oversight]

curative *adj* **1** able to cure ▷ *n* **2** something able to cure

curator *n* the person in charge of a museum or art gallery [Latin: one who cares] ▷ **curatorial** *adj* ▷ **curatorship** *n*

curb *n* **1** something that restrains or holds back **2** a horse's bit with an attached chain or strap, used to check the horse **3** a raised edge that strengthens or encloses ▷ *vb* **4** to control or restrain ▶ See also **kerb** [Latin *curvus* curved]

curcumin *n* a yellow pigment, present in turmeric, that is an antioxidant and has anti-inflammatory properties

curd *n* **1** coagulated milk, used in making cheese or as a food **2** any similar substance: *bean curd* [origin unknown]

curd cheese *n* a mild smooth white cheese made from skimmed milk curds

curdle *vb* **-dling, -dled** **1** to turn into curd; coagulate **2** make someone's blood curdle to fill someone with horror

cure *vb* **curing, cured** **1** to get rid of (an ailment or problem) **2** to restore (someone) to health **3** to preserve (meat or fish) by salting or smoking **4** to preserve (leather or tobacco) by drying **5** to vulcanize (rubber) ▷ *n* **6** a restoration to health **7** medical treatment that restores health **8** a means of restoring health or improving a situation **9** a curacy [Latin *cura* care]

cure-all *n* something supposed to cure all ailments or problems

curette *or* **curet** *n* **1** a surgical instrument for scraping tissue from body cavities ▷ *vb* **-retting, -retted** **2** to scrape with a curette [French] ▷ **curettage** *n*

curfew *n* **1** a law which states that people must stay inside their houses after a specific time at night **2** the time set as a deadline by such a law **3** *history* the ringing of a bell at a fixed time, as a signal for putting out fires and lights [Old French *cuevrefeu* cover the fire]

Curia *n, pl* **-riae** the court and government of the Roman Catholic Church [Latin] ▷ **curial** *adj*

curie n the standard unit of radioactivity [after Pierre CURIE]

Curie n **1** Marie. 1867–1934, French physicist and chemist, born in Poland: discovered with her husband Pierre the radioactivity of thorium, and discovered and isolated radium and polonium. She shared a Nobel prize for physics (1903) with her husband and Henri Becquerel, and was awarded a Nobel prize for chemistry (1911) **2** her husband, Pierre. 1859–1906, French physicist and chemist

curio (kew-ree-oh) n, pl **-rios** a rare or unusual thing valued as a collector's item [from curiosity]

curiosity n, pl **-ties 1** eagerness to know or find out **2** a rare or unusual thing

curious adj **1** eager to learn or know **2** eager to find out private details **3** unusual or peculiar [Latin curiosus taking pains over something] **> curiously** adv

Curitiba n a city in SE Brazil, capital of Paraná state: seat of the University of Paraná (1946). Pop: 2 871 000 (2005 est)

curium (kew-ree-um) n chem a silvery-white metallic radioactive element artificially produced from plutonium. Symbol: **Cm** [after Pierre & Marie CURIE]

curl vb **1** to twist (hair) or (of hair) to grow in coils or ringlets **2** to twist into a spiral or curve **3** to play the game of curling **4 curl one's lip** to show contempt by raising a corner of the lip ▷ n **5** a coil of hair **6** a curved or spiral shape ▶ See also **curl up** [probably from Middle Dutch crullen] **> curly** adj

curler n **1** a pin or small tube for curling hair **2** a person who plays curling

curlew n a large wading bird with a long downward-curving bill [Old French corlieu]

curlicue n an intricate ornamental curl or twist [curly + CUE²]

curling n a game played on ice, in which heavy stones with handles are slid towards a target circle

curl up vb **1** to lie or sit with legs drawn up **2** to be embarrassed or horrified

curmudgeon n a bad-tempered or mean person [origin unknown] **> curmudgeonly** adj

Curnow n (Thomas) Allen (Monro). 1911–2001, New Zealand poet and anthologist

currajong n same as kurrajong

currant n **1** a small dried seedless raisin **2** a small round acid berry, such as the redcurrant [earlier rayson of Corannte raisin of Corinth]

currawong n an Australian songbird [Aboriginal]

currency n, pl **-cies 1** the system of money or the actual coins and banknotes in use in a particular country **2** general acceptance or use: ideas that had gained currency during the early 1960s [Latin currere to run, flow]

current adj **1** of the immediate present: current affairs; the current economic climate **2** most recent or up-to-date: the current edition **3** commonly accepted: current thinking on this issue **4** circulating and valid at present: current coins ▷ n **5** a flow of water or air in a particular direction **6** physics a flow or rate of flow of electric charge through a conductor **7** a general trend or drift: two opposing currents of thought [Latin currere to run, flow] **> currently** adv

current account n a bank account from which money may be drawn at any time using a chequebook or computerized card

curriculum n, pl **-la** or **-lums 1** all the courses of study offered by a school or college **2** a course of study in one subject at a school or college: the history curriculum [Latin: course] **> curricular** adj

curriculum vitae (vee-tie) n, pl **curricula vitae** an outline of someone's educational and professional history, prepared for job applications [Latin: the course of one's life]

curry¹ n, pl **-ries 1** a dish of Indian origin consisting of meat or vegetables in a hot spicy sauce **2** curry seasoning or sauce **3 curry powder** a mixture of spices for making curry ▷ vb **-ries, -rying, -ried 4** to prepare (food) with curry powder [Tamil kari sauce, relish]

curry² vb **-ries, -rying, -ried 1** to groom (a horse) **2** to dress (leather) after it has been tanned **3 curry favour** to ingratiate oneself with an important person [Old French correer to make ready]

Curry n John (Anthony). 1949–94, British ice skater: won the figure-skating gold medal in the 1976 Olympic Games

currycomb n a ridged comb used for grooming horses

curse vb **cursing, cursed 1** to swear or swear at (someone) **2** to call on supernatural powers to bring harm to (someone or something) ▷ n **3** a profane or obscene expression, usually of anger **4** an appeal to a supernatural power for harm to come to a person **5** harm resulting from a curse **6** something that causes great trouble or harm **7 the curse** informal menstruation or a menstrual period [Old English cursian]

cursed adj **1** under a curse **2** deserving to be cursed; hateful

cursive adj **1** of handwriting or print in which letters are joined in a flowing style ▷ n **2** a cursive letter or printing type [Medieval Latin cursivus running]

cursor n **1** a movable point of light that shows a specific position on a visual display unit **2** the sliding part of a slide rule or other measuring instrument

cursory adj hasty and usually superficial [Late Latin cursorius of running] **> cursorily** adv

curt adj so blunt and brief as to be rude [Latin curtus cut short] **> curtly** adv **> curtness** n

curtail vb **1** to cut short: the opening round was curtailed by heavy rain **2** to restrict: a plan to curtail drinks advertising [obsolete curtal to dock] **> curtailment** n

curtain n **1** a piece of material hung at an opening or window to shut out light or to provide privacy **2** a hanging cloth that conceals all or part of a theatre stage from the audience **3** the end of a scene or a performance in the theatre, marked by the fall or closing of the curtain **4** the rise or opening of the curtain at the start of a performance **5** something forming a barrier or screen: a curtain of rain ▷ vb **6** to shut off or conceal with a curtain **7** to provide with curtains [Late Latin cortina]

curtain call n theatre a return to the stage by performers to receive applause

curtain-raiser n **1** theatre a short play performed before the main play **2** a minor event happening before a major one

curtains pl n informal death or ruin; the end

Curtin n John Joseph. 1885–1945, Australian statesman; prime minister of Australia (1941–45)

curtsy or **curtsey** n, pl **-sies** or **-seys 1** a woman's formal gesture of respect made by bending the knees and bowing the head ▷ vb **-sies, -sying, -sied** or **-seys, -seying, -seyed 2** to make a curtsy [variant of courtesy]

curvaceous adj informal having a curved shapely body

curvature n the state or degree of being curved

curve n **1** a continuously bending line with no straight parts **2** something that curves or is curved **3** curvature **4** maths a system of points whose coordinates satisfy a given equation **5** a line representing data on a graph ▷ vb **curving, curved 6** to form into or move in a curve [Latin curvare to bend] **> curvy** adj

curvet n **1** a horse's low leap with all four feet off the ground ▷ vb **-vetting, -vetted** or **-veting, -veted 2** to make such a leap [Latin curvare to bend]

curvilinear adj consisting of or bounded by a curved line

Curzon n **1** Sir Clifford. 1907–82, English pianist **2** George Nathaniel, 1st Marquis Curzon of Kedleston. 1859–1925, British Conservative statesman; viceroy of India (1898–1905)

Cusack n Cyril (James). 1910–93, Irish actor

Cusco n a variant of Cuzco

cuscus n, pl **-cuses** a large nocturnal possum of N

Australia and New Guinea [probably from a native word in New Guinea]

Cushing *n* Harvey Williams. 1869–1939, US neurosurgeon: identified a pituitary tumour as a cause of the disease named after him

cushion *n* **1** a bag filled with a soft material, used to make a seat more comfortable **2** something that provides comfort or absorbs shock **3** the resilient felt-covered rim of a billiard table ▷ *vb* **4** to protect from injury or shock **5** to lessen the effects of **6** to provide with cushions [Latin *culcita* mattress] ➤ **cushiony** *adj*

cushy *adj* **cushier, cushiest** *informal* easy: *a cushy job* [Hindi *khush* pleasant]

cusp *n* **1** a small point on the grinding or chewing surface of a tooth **2** a point where two curves meet **3** *astrol* any division between houses or signs of the zodiac **4** *astronomy* either of the points of a crescent moon [Latin *cuspis* pointed end]

cuss *informal n* **1** a curse or oath **2** an annoying person ▷ *vb* **3** to swear or swear at

cussed (kuss-id) *adj informal* **1** obstinate: *the older she got the more cussed she became* **2** same as **cursed** ➤ **cussedness** *n*

custard *n* **1** a sauce made of milk and sugar thickened with cornflour **2** a baked sweetened mixture of eggs and milk [Middle English *crustade* kind of pie]

Custer *n* George Armstrong. 1839–76, US cavalry general: Civil War hero, killed fighting the Sioux at Little Bighorn, Montana

custodian *n* the person in charge of a public building ➤ **custodianship** *n*

custody *n, pl* **-dies** **1** the act of keeping safe **2** imprisonment prior to being tried [Latin *custos* guard, defender] ➤ **custodial** *adj*

custom *n* **1** a long-established activity, action, or festivity: *the custom of serving port after dinner* **2** the long-established habits or traditions of a society **3** a usual practice or habit: *she held his hand more tightly than was her custom in public* **4** regular use of a shop or business ▷ *adj* **5** made to the specifications of an individual customer: *a custom car; custom-tailored suits* ▶ See also **customs** [Latin *consuetudo*]

customary *adj* **1** usual **2** established by custom ➤ **customarily** *adv* ➤ **customariness** *n*

custom-built *or* **-made** *adj* made according to the specifications of an individual customer

customer *n* **1** a person who buys goods or services **2** *informal* a person with whom one has to deal: *a tricky customer*

custom house *n* a government office where customs are collected

customize *or* **-ise** *vb* **-izing, -ized** *or* **-ising, -ised** to make (something) according to a customer's individual requirements

customs *n* **1** duty charged on imports or exports **2** the government department responsible for collecting this **3** the area at a port, airport, or border where baggage and freight are examined for dutiable goods

cut *vb* **cutting, cut** **1** to open up or penetrate (a person or thing) with a sharp instrument **2** (of a sharp instrument) to penetrate or open up (a person or thing) **3** to divide or be divided with or as if with a sharp instrument **4** to trim **5** to abridge or shorten **6** to reduce or restrict: *cut your intake of fried foods* **7** to form or shape by cutting **8** to reap or mow **9** *sport* to hit (the ball) so that it spins and swerves **10** to hurt the feelings of (a person): *her rudeness cut me to the core* **11** *informal* to pretend not to recognize **12** *informal* to absent oneself from without permission: *he found the course boring, and was soon cutting classes* **13** to stop (doing something): *cut the nonsense* **14** to dilute or adulterate: *heroin cut with talcum powder* **15** to make a sharp or sudden change in direction: *the path cuts to the right just after you pass the quarry* **16** to grow (teeth) through the gums **17** *films* **a** to call a halt to a shooting sequence **b** *cut to* to move quickly to (another scene) **18** *films* to edit (film) **19** to switch off (a light or engine) **20** to make (a commercial recording): *he cut his first solo album in 1971* **21** *cards* **a** to divide (the pack) at random into two parts after shuffling **b** to pick cards from a spread pack to decide the dealer or who plays first **22** *cut a dash* to make a stylish impression **23** *cut a person dead informal* to ignore a person completely **24** *cut and run informal* to escape quickly from a difficult situation **25** *cut both ways* **a** to have both good and bad effects **b** to serve both sides of an argument **26** *cut it fine informal* to allow little margin of time or space **27** *cut no ice informal* to fail to make an impression **28** *cut one's teeth on informal* to get experience from ▷ *n* **29** the act of cutting **30** a stroke or incision made by cutting **31** a piece cut off **32** a channel or path cut or hollowed out **33** a reduction: *a pay cut* **34** a deletion in a text, film, or play **35** *informal* a portion or share **36** the style in which hair or a garment is cut **37** a direct route; short cut **38** *sport* a stroke which makes the ball spin and swerve **39** *films* an immediate transition from one shot to the next **40** *Brit* a canal **41** *a cut above informal* superior to; better than ▷ *adj* **42** made or shaped by cutting **43** reduced by cutting: *the shop has hundreds of suits, all at cut prices* **44** adulterated or diluted **45** *cut and dried informal* settled in advance ▶ See also **cut across**, **cutback**, etc. [probably from Old Norse]

cut across *vb* **1** to go against (ordinary restrictions or expectations): *this dilemma has cut across class divisions* **2** to cross or traverse

cutaneous (kew-tane-ee-uss) *adj* of the skin [Latin *cutis* skin]

cutaway *adj* (of a drawing or model) having part of the outside omitted to reveal the inside

cutback *n* **1** a decrease or reduction ▷ *vb* **cut back 2** to shorten by cutting **3** (often foll. by *on*) to make a reduction: *we may cut back on other expenditure*

Cutch *n* a variant spelling of **Kutch**

cut down *vb* **1** to fell **2** (often foll. by *on*) to make a reduction: *cut down on the amount of salt you eat* **3** to kill **4** *cut someone down to size* to cause someone to feel less important or to be less conceited

cute *adj* **1** appealing or attractive **2** *informal* clever or shrewd [from ACUTE] ➤ **cuteness** *n*

cut glass *n* **1** glass with patterns cut into the surface ▷ *adj* **cut-glass 2** upper-class; refined: *Victoria with her cut-glass accent*

Cuthbert *n* Saint. ?635–87 AD, English monk; bishop of Lindisfarne. Feast day: March 20

cuticle (kew-tik-kl) *n* **1** hardened skin round the base of a fingernail or toenail **2** same as **epidermis** [Latin *cuticula* skin]

cut in *vb* **1** to interrupt **2** to move in front of another vehicle, leaving too little space

cutlass *n* a curved one-edged sword formerly used by sailors [French *coutelas*]

cutler *n* a person who makes or sells cutlery [Latin *culter* knife]

cutlery *n* knives, forks, and spoons, used for eating

cutlet *n* **1** a small piece of meat taken from the neck or ribs **2** a flat croquette of chopped meat or fish [Old French *costelette* a little rib]

cut off *vb* **1** to remove or separate by cutting **2** to stop the supply of **3** to interrupt (a person who is speaking), esp. during a telephone conversation **4** to bring to an end **5** to disinherit: *cut off without a penny* **6** to intercept so as to prevent retreat or escape ▷ *n* **cutoff 7** the point at which something is cut off; limit **8** *chiefly US* a short cut **9** a device to stop the flow of a fluid in a pipe

cut out *vb* **1** to shape by cutting **2** to delete or remove **3** *informal* to stop doing (something) **4** (of an engine) to cease to operate suddenly **5** (of an electrical device) to switch off, usually automatically **6** *be cut out for* to be suited or equipped for: *you're not cut out for this job* **7** *have one's work cut out* to have as much work as one can manage ▷ *n* **cutout 8** a device that automatically switches off a circuit or engine as a safety device **9** something that has been cut out from something else

cut-price *or especially US* **cut-rate** *adj* **1** at a reduced price **2** offering goods or services at prices below the standard price

Cuttack *n* a city in NE India, in E Odisha (formerly Orissa) near the mouth of the Mahanadi River: former state capital until 1948. Pop: 535 139 (2001)

cutter *n* **1** a person or tool that cuts **2** a small fast boat

cut-throat *adj* **1** fierce or ruthless in competition: *the cut-throat world of international finance* **2** (of a card game) played by three people: *cut-throat poker* ▷ *n* **3** a murderer **4** *Brit and NZ* a razor with a long blade that folds into its handle

cutting *n* **1** an article cut from a newspaper or magazine **2** a piece cut from a plant for rooting or grafting **3** a passage cut through high ground for a road or railway **4** the editing process of a film ▷ *adj* **5** (of a remark) likely to hurt the feelings **6** keen; piercing: *a cutting wind* **7** designed for cutting: *the hatchet's blade is largely stone, but its cutting edge is made of copper*

cutting edge *n* the leading position in any field; forefront: *the cutting edge of space technology*

cuttlefish *n*, *pl* **-fish** *or* **-fishes** a flat squidlike mollusc which squirts an inky fluid when in danger [Old English *cudele*]

cut up *vb* **1** to cut into pieces **2** *informal* (of a driver) to overtake or pull in front of (another driver) in a dangerous manner **3 be cut up** *informal* to be very upset **4 cut up rough** *Brit informal* to become angry or violent

Cuvier *n* Georges (Jean-Leopold-Nicolas-Frédéric), Baron. 1769–1832, French zoologist and statesman; founder of the sciences of comparative anatomy and palaeontology

Cuxhaven *n* a port in NW Germany, at the mouth of the River Elbe. Pop: 52 876 (2003 est)

Cuyabá *n* a variant spelling of **Cuiabá**

Cuyp *or* **Kuyp** *n* Aelbert. 1620–91, Dutch painter of landscapes and animals

Cuzco *or* **Cusco** *n* a city in S central Peru: former capital of the Inca Empire, with extensive Inca remains; university (1692). Pop: 307 000 (2005 est)

CV curriculum vitae

cwm (koom) *n* (in Wales) a valley [Welsh]

Cwmbran *n* a new town in SE Wales, in Torfaen county borough, developed in the 1950s. Pop: 47 254 (2001)

cwt hundredweight

cyanic acid *n* a colourless poisonous volatile liquid acid

cyanide *n* any of a number of highly poisonous substances containing a carbon-nitrogen group of atoms

cyanogen *n* a poisonous colourless flammable gas [Greek *kuanos* dark blue]

cyanosis *n pathol* a blue discoloration of the skin, caused by a deficiency of oxygen in the blood [Greek *kuanos* dark blue]

cyber- *combining form* indicating computers: *cyberspace* [from CYBERNETICS]

cyberbully *n* a person who bullies another person via electronic technology such as mobile phones and social media

cybercafé *n* a café equipped with computer terminals which customers can use to access the internet [CYBER- + CAFÉ]

cybernetics *n* the branch of science in which electronic and mechanical systems are studied and compared to biological systems [Greek *kubernētēs* steersman] ▷ **cybernetic** *adj*

cyberspace *n* the hypothetical environment which contains all the data stored in computers [CYBER- + SPACE]

cybersquatting *n* the practice of registering an internet domain name that is likely to be wanted by

another person or organization in the hope that it can be sold to them for a profit ▷ **cybersquatter** *n*

cyberterrorism *n* the illegal use of computers and the internet to achieve some goal ▷ **cyberterrorist** *n*

Cyclades *pl n* a group of over 200 islands in the S Aegean Sea, forming a department of Greece. Capital: Hermoupolis (Ermoupoli, on Syros). Pop: 112 615 (2001). Area: 2572 sq km (993 sq miles). Modern Greek name: Kikládhes

Cycladic *adj* of or relating to the Cyclades or their inhabitants

cyclamen (sik-la-men) *n* a plant with white, pink, or red flowers, with turned-back petals [Greek *kuklaminos*]

cycle *vb* **-cling, -cled 1** to ride a bicycle **2** to occur in cycles ▷ *n* **3** *Brit, Austral and NZ* a bicycle **4** *US* a motorcycle **5** a complete series of recurring events **6** the time taken or needed for one such series **7** a single complete movement in an electrical, electronic, or mechanical process **8** a set of plays, songs, or poems about a figure or event [Greek *kuklos*] ▷ **cycling** *n*

cyclical *or* **cyclic** *adj* **1** occurring in cycles **2** *chem* (of an organic compound) containing a closed ring of atoms

cyclist *n* a person who rides a bicycle

cyclo- *or before a vowel* **cycl-** *combining form* **1** indicating a circle or ring: *cyclotron* **2** *chem* denoting a cyclical compound: *cyclopropane* [Greek *kuklos* cycle]

cyclometer (sike-lom-it-er) *n* a device that records the number of revolutions made by a wheel and the distance travelled

cyclone *n* **1** a body of moving air below normal atmospheric pressure, which often brings rain **2** a violent tropical storm [Greek *kuklōn* a turning around] ▷ **cyclonic** *adj*

cyclopedia *or* **cyclopaedia** *n* same as **encyclopedia**

Cyclops *n*, *pl* **Cyclopes** *or* **Cyclopses** *Classical myth* one of a race of giants having a single eye in the middle of the forehead [Greek *Kuklōps* round eye]

cyclotron *n* an apparatus, used in atomic research, which accelerates charged particles by means of a strong vertical magnetic field

cyder *n* same as **cider**

Cydnus *n* the ancient name for the (River) **Tarsus**

cygnet *n* a young swan [Latin *cygnus* swan]

cylinder *n* **1** a solid or hollow body with circular equal ends and straight parallel sides **2** a container or other object shaped like a cylinder **3** the chamber in an internal-combustion engine within which the piston moves **4** the rotating mechanism of a revolver, containing cartridge chambers [Greek *kulindein* to roll] ▷ **cylindrical** *adj*

cymbal *n* a percussion instrument consisting of a round brass plate which is struck against another or hit with a stick [Greek *kumbē* something hollow] ▷ **cymbalist** *n*

cyme *n botany* a flower cluster which has a single flower on the end of each stem and of which the central flower blooms first [Greek *kuma* anything swollen] ▷ **cymose** *adj*

Cymric (kim-rik) *adj* **1** of Wales ▷ *n* **2** the Celtic language of Wales

Cymru *n* the Welsh name for **Wales**

Cynewulf, Kynewulf *or* **Cynwulf** *n* ?8th century AD, Anglo-Saxon poet; author of *Juliana*, *The Ascension*, *Elene*, and *The Fates of the Apostles*

cynic (sin-ik) *n* a person who believes that people always act selfishly [Greek *kuōn* dog]

Cynic *n* a member of an ancient Greek philosophical school that had contempt for worldly things ▷ **Cynicism** *n*

cynical *adj* **1** believing that people always act selfishly **2** sarcastic or sneering ▷ **cynically** *adv*

cynicism *n* the attitude or beliefs of a cynic

cynosure (sin-oh-zyure) *n literary* a centre of interest or attention [Greek *Kunosoura* dog's tail (name of the constellation of Ursa Minor)]

cypher (sife-er) *n, vb* same as **cipher**

cypress *n* **1** an evergreen tree with dark green leaves **2** the wood of this tree [Greek *kuparissos*]

Cyprian[1] *n, adj* same as **Cypriot**

Cyprian[2] *n* Saint. ?200–258 AD, bishop of Carthage and martyr. Feast day: Sept 26 or 16

Cypriot *adj* **1** of or relating to Cyprus or its inhabitants ▷ *n* **2** a native or inhabitant of Cyprus **3** the dialect of Greek spoken in Cyprus

Cyprus *n* an island in the E Mediterranean: ceded to Britain by Turkey in 1878 and made a colony in 1925; became an independent republic in 1960 as a member of the Commonwealth; invaded by Turkey in 1974 following a Greek-supported military coup, leading to the partition of the island. In 1983 the Turkish-controlled northern sector declared itself to be an independent state as the Turkish Republic of Northern Cyprus but failed to receive international recognition. Attempts by the UN to broker a reunification agreement have failed. Cyprus joined the EU in 2004. The UK maintains two enclaves as military bases (Akrotiri and Dhekelia Sovereign Base Areas), which are not included in Cyprus politically. Languages: Greek and Turkish. Religions: Greek Orthodox and Muslim. Currency: euro and Turkish lira. Capital: Nicosia. Pop (Greek): 838 897 (2011 est); (Turkish): 265 100 (2006 est). Area: 9251 sq km (3571 sq miles)

Cyrano de Bergerac *n* Savinien. 1619–55, French writer and soldier, famous as a duellist and for his large nose. He became widely known through the verse drama *Cyrano de Bergerac* (1897) by Edmond Rostand

Cyrenaica *or* **Cirenaica** *n* a region and former province (1951–63) of E Libya: largely desert; settled by the Greeks in about 630 BC; ruled successively by the Egyptians, Romans, Arabs, Turks, and Italians. Area: 855 370 sq km (330 258 sq miles)

Cyrene *n* an ancient Greek city of N Africa, near the coast of Cyrenaica: famous for its medical school

Cyril *n* Saint. ?827–869 AD, Greek Christian theologian, missionary to the Moravians and inventor of the Cyrillic alphabet; he and his brother Saint Methodius were called *the Apostles of the Slavs*. Feast day: Feb 14 or May 11

Cyrillic *adj* of the Slavic alphabet devised supposedly by Saint Cyril, now used primarily for Russian and Bulgarian

Cyril of Alexandria *n* Saint. ?375–444 AD, Christian theologian and patriarch of Alexandria. Feast day: June 27 or June 9

Cyrus *n* **1** known as *Cyrus the Great* or *Cyrus the Elder*. died ?529 BC, king of Persia and founder of the Persian empire **2** called *the Younger*. died 401 BC, Persian satrap of Lydia: revolted against his brother Artaxerxes II, but was killed at the battle of Cunaxa

cyst (sist) *n* **1** *pathol* an abnormal membranous sac containing fluid or diseased matter **2** *anatomy* any normal sac in the body [Greek *kustis* pouch, bag]

cystic fibrosis *n* a congenital disease, usually affecting

young children, which causes breathing disorders and malfunctioning of the pancreas

cystitis (siss-tite-iss) *n* inflammation of the bladder, causing a desire to urinate frequently, accompanied by a burning sensation

-cyte *combining form* indicating a cell: *leucocyte* [Greek *kutos* vessel]

Cythera *n* **1** a Greek island off the SE coast of the Peloponnese: in ancient times a centre of the worship of Aphrodite. Pop: 3354 (2001). Area: about 285 sq km (110 sq miles) **2** the chief town of this island, on the S coast. Pop: 297 (2001) ▶ Modern Greek name: **Kíthira**

cytology (site-ol-a-jee) *n* the study of plant and animal cells ❯ **cytological** *adj* ❯ **cytologically** *adv* ❯ **cytologist** *n*

cytoplasm *n* the protoplasm of a cell excluding the nucleus ❯ **cytoplasmic** *adj*

Cyzicus *n* an ancient Greek colony in NW Asia Minor on the S shore of the Sea of Marmara: site of Alcibiades' naval victory over the Peloponnesians (410 BC)

czar (zahr) *n* same as **tsar**

Czech *adj* **1** of or relating to the Czech Republic or its inhabitants ▷ *n* **2** a native or inhabitant of the Czech Republic **3** the language of the Czech Republic

Czechoslovak *adj* **1** of, relating to, or characteristic of the former Czechoslovakia, its peoples, or their languages ▷ *n* **2** (loosely) either of the two mutually intelligible languages of the former Czechoslovakia; Czech or Slovak

Czechoslovakia *n* a former republic in central Europe: formed after the defeat of Austria-Hungary (1918) as a nation of Czechs in Bohemia and Moravia and Slovaks in Slovakia; occupied by Germany from 1939 until its liberation by the Soviet Union in 1945; became a people's republic under the Communists in 1948; invaded by Warsaw Pact troops in 1968, ending Dubček's attempt to liberalize communism; in 1989 popular unrest led to the resignation of the politburo and the formation of a non-Communist government. It consisted of two federal republics, the Czech Republic and Slovakia, which separated in 1993. Czech name: **Československo**. See also **Czech Republic**, **Slovakia**

Czechoslovakian *adj* **1** of, relating to, or characteristic of the former republic of Czechoslovakia, its peoples, or their languages ▷ *n* **2** a native or inhabitant of the former republic of Czechoslovakia

Czech Republic *n* a country in central Europe: formed part of Czechoslovakia until 1993; mostly wooded, with lowlands surrounding the River Morava, rising to the Bohemian plateau in the W and to highlands in the N; joined the EU in 2004. Language: Czech. Religion: Christian majority. Currency: koruna. Capital Prague. Pop: 10 162 921 (2013 est). Area: 78 864 sq km (30 450 sq miles)

Czernowitz *n* the German name for **Chernovtsy**

Czerny *n* Karl. 1791–1857, Austrian pianist, composer, and teacher, noted for his studies

Częstochowa *n* an industrial city in S Poland, on the River Warta: pilgrimage centre. Pop: 293 000 (2005 est)

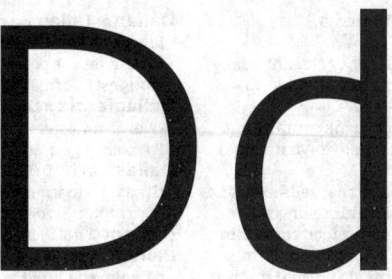

d **1** *physics* density **2** deci-

D **1** *music* the second note of the scale of C major **2** *chem* deuterium **3** the Roman numeral for 500

d. **1** *Brit and NZ* (before decimalization) penny *or* pennies **2** died **3** daughter

dab¹ *vb* **dabbing, dabbed** **1** to pat lightly and quickly **2** to apply with short tapping strokes: *dabbing antiseptic on cuts* ▷ *n* **3** a small amount of something soft or moist **4** a light stroke or tap **5 dabs** *slang, chiefly Brit* fingerprints [imitative]

dab² *n* a small European flatfish covered with rough toothed scales [Anglo-French *dabbe*]

dabble *vb* **-bling, -bled** **1** to be involved in an activity in a superficial way: *she dabbles in right-wing politics* **2** to splash (one's toes or fingers) in water [probably from Dutch *dabbelen*] ▷ **dabbler** *n*

dab hand *n informal* a person who is particularly skilled at something: *a dab hand with a needle and thread* [origin unknown]

Dacca *n* the former name (until 1982) of **Dhaka**

dace *n, pl* **dace** *or* **daces** a European freshwater fish of the carp family [Old French *dars* dart]

Dachau *n* a town in S Germany, in Bavaria: site of a Nazi concentration camp. Pop: 39 474 (2003 est)

dachshund *n* a small dog with short legs and a long body [German *Dachs* badger + *Hund* dog]

Dacia *n* an ancient region bounded by the Carpathians, the Tisza, and the Danube, roughly corresponding to modern Romania. United under kings from about 60 BC, it later contained the Roman province of the same name (about 105 to 270 AD) ▷ **Dacian** *adj, n*

dactyl *n prosody* a metrical foot of three syllables, one long followed by two short [Greek *daktulos* finger, comparing the finger's three joints to the three syllables] ▷ **dactylic** *adj*

dad *or* **daddy** *n informal* father [from child's *da da*]

Dada *or* **Dadaism** *n* an art movement of the early 20th century that systematically used arbitrary and absurd concepts [French: hobbyhorse] ▷ **Dadaist** *n, adj*

Dadd *n* Richard. 1817–86, British painter of mythological and fairy scenes. He was committed to an asylum for patricide

daddy-longlegs *n informal* **1** *Brit* crane fly **2** a small web-spinning spider with long legs

dado (day-doe) *n, pl* **-does** *or* **-dos** **1** the lower part of an interior wall, often separated by a rail, that is decorated differently from the upper part **2** *archit* the part of a pedestal between the base and the cornice [Italian: die, die-shaped pedestal]

Dadra and Nagar Haveli *n* a union territory of W India, on the Gulf of Cambay: until 1961 administratively part of Portuguese Damão. Capital: Silvassa. Pop: 220 451 (2001). Area: 489 sq km (191 sq miles)

daemon (deem-on) *n* same as **demon**

daffodil *n* **1** a spring plant with yellow trumpet-shaped flowers ▷ *adj* **2** brilliant yellow [variant of Latin *asphodelus* asphodel]

daft *adj informal, chiefly Brit* **1** foolish or crazy **2 daft about** very enthusiastic about: *he's daft about football* [Old English *gedæfte* gentle, foolish]

Dafydd ap Gruffudd *n* died 1283, Welsh leader. Claiming the title Prince of Wales (1282), he led an unsuccessful revolt against Edward I: executed

Dafydd ap Gwilym *n* ?1320–?1380, Welsh poet

dag *Austral and NZ n* **1** the dried dung on a sheep's rear **2** *informal* an amusing person **3 rattle one's dags** *informal* hurry up ▷ *vb* **4** to remove the dags from a sheep [origin unknown]

Dagenham *n* part of the Greater London borough of Barking and Dagenham: engineering and chemicals

Dagestan Republic *n* a constituent republic of S Russia, on the Caspian Sea: annexed from Persia in 1813; rich mineral resources. Capital: Makhachkala. Pop: 2 584 200 (2002). Area: 50 278 sq km (19 416 sq miles). Also called: **Dagestan, Daghestan**

dagga (duhh-a) *n S African* a local name for marijuana [probably from Khoi (language of southern Africa) *daxa*]

dagger *n* **1** a short knifelike weapon with a double-edged pointed blade **2** a character (†) used to indicate a cross-reference **3 at daggers drawn** in a state of open hostility **4 look daggers** to glare with hostility [origin unknown]

daggy *adj Austral and NZ informal* **1** untidy; dishevelled **2** eccentric

Daguerre *n* Louis Jacques Mandé. 1789–1851, French inventor, who devised one of the first practical photographic processes (1838)

daguerreotype (dag-**gair**-oh-type) *n* a type of early photograph produced on chemically treated silver [after L. DAGUERRE]

Dahl *n* Roald. 1916–90, British writer with Norwegian parents, noted for his short stories and such children's books as *Charlie and the Chocolate Factory* (1964)

dahlia (day-lya) *n* a garden plant with showy flowers [after Anders Dahl, botanist]

Dahna *n* a desert area in central Saudi Arabia, to the N of the Rub' al Khali (Empty Quarter)

Dahomey *n* the former name (until 1975) of **Benin**

Dáil Éireann (doil air-in) *or* **Dáil** *n* (in the Republic of Ireland) the lower chamber of parliament [Irish *dáil* assembly + *Éireann* of Eire]

daily *adj* **1** occurring every day or every weekday: *there have been daily airdrops of food, blankets, and water* **2** of or relating to a single day or to one day at a time: *her home help comes in on a daily basis; exercise has become part of our daily lives* ▷ *adv* **3** every day ▷ *n, pl* **-lies** **4** *Brit and Austral* a daily newspaper **5** *Brit informal* a woman employed to clean someone's house [Old English *dæglīc*]

Daimler *n* Gottlieb (Wilhelm). 1834–1900, German engineer and car manufacturer, who collaborated with

Nikolaus Otto in inventing the first internal-combustion engine (1876)

dainty *adj* **-tier, -tiest** **1** delicate, pretty, or elegant: *dainty little pink shoes* ▷ *n, pl* **-ties** **2** Brit a small choice cake or sweet [Old French *deintié*] ▷ **daintily** *adv*

daiquiri (dak-eer-ee) *n, pl* **-ris** an iced drink containing rum, lime juice, and sugar [after *Daiquiri*, town in Cuba]

Dairen *n* a former name of Dalian

dairy *n, pl* **dairies** **1** a company or shop that sells milk and milk products **2** a place where milk and cream are stored or made into butter and cheese **3** food containing milk or milk products: *I can't eat dairy* **4** NZ a small shop selling groceries and milk often outside normal trading hours ▷ *adj* **5** of milk or milk products: *dairy produce* [Old English *dæge* servant girl]

dairy cattle *n* cows reared mainly for their milk

dairy farm *n* a farm where cows are kept mainly for their milk

dairymaid *n* Brit, Austral and NZ archaic a woman employed to milk cows

dairyman *n* Brit, Austral and S African a man employed to look after cows

dais (day-iss) *n* a raised platform in a hall or meeting place used by a speaker [Old French *deis*]

daisy *n, pl* **-sies** a small low-growing flower with a yellow centre and pinkish-white petals [Old English *dægesēge* day's eye]

daisy chain *n* a string of daisies joined together by their stems to make a necklace

daisywheel *n* a flat disc in a word processor with radiating spokes for printing characters

Dak. Dakota

Dakar *n* the capital and chief port of Senegal, on the SE side of Cape Verde peninsula. Pop: 2 313 000 (2005 est)

Dakota *n* a former territory of the US: divided into the states of North Dakota and South Dakota in 1889

Dakotan *adj* **1** of or relating to Dakota or its inhabitants ▷ *n* **2** a native or inhabitant of Dakota

dal¹ *n* same as **dhal**

dal² decalitre(s)

Daladier *n* Édouard. 1884–1970, French radical socialist statesman; premier of France (1933; 1934; 1938–40) and signatory of the Munich Pact (1938)

Dalai Lama *n* **1** (until 1959) the chief lama and ruler of Tibet **2** born 1935, the 14th holder of this office (1940), who fled to India (1959): Nobel peace prize 1989 [from Mongolian *dalai* ocean; see LAMA]

dale *n* an open valley [Old English *dæl*]

Dale *n* Sir Henry Hallet. 1875–1968, English physiologist: shared a Nobel prize for physiology or medicine in 1936 with Otto Loewi for their work on the chemical transmission of nerve impulses

d'Alembert *n* Jean Le Rond. 1717–83, French mathematician, physicist, and rationalist philosopher, noted for his contribution to Newtonian physics in *Traité de dynamique* (1743) and for his collaboration with Diderot in editing the *Encyclopédie*

Dalén *n* Nils Gustaf. 1869–1937, Swedish engineer, inventor of an automatic light-controlled valve known as 'Solventil'. Nobel prize for physics 1912

Dales *pl n* **the Dales** (*sometimes not cap*) short for the **Yorkshire Dales**

Dalglish *n* Kenny, born 1951, Scottish footballer: a striker, he played for Celtic (1968–77) and for Liverpool (1977–89): manager of Liverpool (1985–91; 2011–12), of Blackburn Rovers (1991–95), Newcastle United (1997–98), and Celtic (2000): Scotland's most-capped footballer (102 appearances, 1971–86)

Dalhousie *n* **1** 9th Earl of, title of *George Ramsay*. 1770–1838, British general; governor of the British colonies in Canada (1819–28) **2** his son, 1st Marquis and 10th Earl of, title of *James Andrew Broun Ramsay*. 1812–60, British statesman: governor general of India (1848–56)

Dali *n* Salvador. 1904–89, Spanish surrealist painter

Dalian *or* **Talien** *n* a city in NE China, at the end of the Liaodong Peninsula: with the adjoining city of Lüshun comprises the port complex of Lüda. Pop: 2 709 000 (2005 est). Former name: Dairen

Dallapiccola *n* Luigi. 1904–75, Italian composer of twelve-tone music. His works include the opera *Il Prigioniero* (1944–48) and the ballet *Marsia* (1948)

Dallas *n* a city in NE Texas, on the Trinity River: scene of the assassination of President John F. Kennedy (1963). Pop: 1 208 318 (2003 est)

dalliance *n* old-fashioned flirtation

dally *vb* **-lies, -lying, -lied** **1** old-fashioned to waste time or dawdle **2** **dally with** to deal frivolously with: *to dally with someone's affections* [Anglo-French *dalier* to gossip]

Dalmatia *n* a region of W Croatia along the Adriatic: mountainous, with many offshore islands

Dalmatian *n* **1** a large dog with a smooth white coat and black spots **2** a native or inhabitant of Dalmatia ▷ *adj* **3** of or relating to Dalmatia or its inhabitants

Dalton *n* John. 1766–1844, English chemist and physicist who formulated the modern form of the atomic theory and the law of partial pressures for gases. He also gave the first accurate description of colour blindness, from which he suffered

dam¹ *n* **1** a barrier built across a river to create a lake **2** a lake created by such a barrier ▷ *vb* **damming, dammed** **3** to block up (a river) by a dam [probably from Middle Low German]

dam² *n* the female parent of an animal such as a sheep or horse [variant of *dame*]

dam³ decametre(s)

Dam *n* (Carl Peter) Henrik. 1895–1976, Danish biochemist who discovered vitamin K (1934): Nobel prize for physiology or medicine 1943

damage *vb* **-aging, -aged** **1** to harm or injure ▷ *n* **2** injury or harm caused to a person or thing **3** informal cost: *what's the damage?* [Latin *damnum* injury, loss] ▷ **damaging** *adj*

damages *pl n* law money awarded as compensation for injury or loss

Daman *n* a coastal town in W India, the chief town of Daman and Diu. Pop: 35 743 (2001). Portuguese name: Damão

Daman and Diu *n* a union territory in W India: formerly a district of Portuguese India (1559–1961) then part of the union territory of Goa, Daman, and Diu (1961–87). Area: 112 sq km (43 sq miles). Pop: 158 059 (2001)

Damanhûr *n* a city in NE Egypt, in the Nile delta. Pop: 229 000 (2005 est)

Damão *n* the Portuguese name for Daman

Damaraland *n* a plateau region of central Namibia, the traditional homeland of the Damara people

Damascene *adj* **1** of or relating to Damascus ▷ *n* **2** a native or inhabitant of Damascus **3** a variety of domestic fancy pigeon with silvery plumage

Damascus *n* the capital of Syria, in the southwest: reputedly the oldest city in the world, having been inhabited continuously since before 2000 BC. Pop: 2 317 000 (2005 est). Arabic names: Dimashq, Esh Sham

damask *n* a heavy fabric with a pattern woven into it, used for tablecloths, curtains, etc. [*Damascus*, where fabric originally made]

dame *n* slang a woman [Latin *domina* lady]

Dame *n* (in Britain) the title of a woman who has been awarded the Order of the British Empire or another order of chivalry

Damien *n* Joseph, known as *Father Damien*. 1840–89, Belgian Roman Catholic missionary to the leper colony at Molokai, Hawaii

Damietta *n* a town in NE Egypt, in the Nile delta: important medieval commercial centre. Arabic name: Dumyat

damn *interj* **1** slang an exclamation of annoyance ▷ *adv* **2** slang Also: **damned** extremely ▷ *adj* **3** slang Also:

damned extreme: *a damn good idea* ▷ *vb* **4** to condemn as bad or worthless **5** to curse **6** (of God) to condemn to hell or eternal punishment **7** to prove (someone) guilty **8** damn with faint praise to praise so unenthusiastically that the effect is condemnation ▷ *n* **9** not give a damn *informal* not care [Latin *damnum* loss, injury] **> damning** *adj*

damnable *adj* very unpleasant or annoying **> damnably** *adv*

damnation *interj* **1** an exclamation of anger ▷ *n* **2** *theol* eternal punishment

damned *adj* **1** condemned to hell ▷ *adv, adj slang* **2** extreme or extremely: *a damned good try* **3** used to indicate amazement or refusal: *I'm damned if I'll do it!*

damnedest *n* do one's damnedest *informal* to do one's best: *I'm doing my damnedest to make myself clear*

Damodar *n* a river in NE India, rising in Jharkhand and flowing east through West Bengal to the Hooghly River: the **Damodar Valley** is an important centre of heavy industry

Damon *n* Matt. born 1970, US film actor and screenwriter. His films include *Good Will Hunting* (1997, which he co-wrote), *Saving Private Ryan* (1998), *The Talented Mr Ripley* (1999) and, from 2002, the *Bourne* series

damp *adj* **1** slightly wet ▷ *n* **2** slight wetness; moisture ▷ *vb* **3** to make slightly wet **4 damp down a** to reduce the intensity of (someone's emotions or reactions): *they attempted to damp down protests* **b** to reduce the flow of air to (a fire) to make it burn more slowly [Middle Low German: steam] **> damply** *adv* **> dampness** *n*

dampcourse or **damp-proof course** *n* a layer of waterproof material built into the base of a wall to prevent moisture rising

dampen *vb* **1** to reduce the intensity of **2** to make damp

damper *n* **1** put a damper on to produce a depressing or inhibiting effect on **2** a movable plate to regulate the draught in a stove or furnace **3** the pad in a piano or harpsichord that deadens the vibration of each string as its key is released **4** *chiefly Austral and NZ* any of various unleavened loaves and scones, typically cooked on an open fire

Dampier *n* William. 1652–1715, English navigator, pirate, and writer: sailed around the world twice

damsel *n* *archaic or poetic* a young woman [Old French *damoisele*]

damson *n* a small blue-black edible plumlike fruit that grows on a tree [Latin *prunum damascenum* Damascus plum]

dan *n* **1** *judo, karate* **2** any of the 10 black-belt grades of proficiency **3** a competitor entitled to dan grading [Japanese]

Dan. **1** *Bible* Daniel **2** Danish

Dana *n* James Dwight. 1813–95, American geologist; noted for his work *The System of Mineralogy* (1837)

Da Nang *n* a port in central Vietnam, on the South China Sea. Pop: 448 000 (2005 est). Former name: **Tourane**

Danby *n* **1** 1st Earl of, title of *Thomas Osborne*. 1631–1712, English politician; Lord Treasurer (1673–78): regarded as the founder of the Tory party. Also called (from 1694): **1st Duke of Leeds 2** Francis. 1793–1861, Irish painter of romantic landscapes and historical subjects

dance *vb* **dancing, danced 1** to move the feet and body rhythmically in time to music **2** to perform (a particular dance): *to dance a tango* **3** to skip or leap **4** to move in a rhythmic way: *their reflection danced in the black waters* **5 dance attendance on someone** to carry out someone's slightest wish in an overeager manner ▷ *n* **6** a social meeting arranged for dancing **7** a series of rhythmic steps and movements in time to music **8** a piece of music in the rhythm of a particular dance [Old French *dancier*] **> dancer** *n* **> dancing** *n, adj*

dancehall *n* a style of dance-oriented reggae

D and C *n med* dilatation of the cervix and curettage of the uterus: a minor operation to clear the womb or remove tissue for diagnosis

dandelion *n* a wild plant with yellow rayed flowers and deeply notched leaves [Old French *dent de lion* tooth of a lion, referring to its leaves]

dander *n* get one's dander up *Brit, Austral and NZ slang* to become angry [from *dandruff*]

dandified *adj* dressed like or resembling a dandy

dandle *vb* **-dling, -dled** to move (a young child) up and down on one's knee [origin unknown]

Dandolo *n* Enrico. *c*. 1108–1205, Venetian statesman; doge (1192–1205). During the fourth Crusade he won Greek colonies for Venice

Dandong *n* a port in E China, in Liaoning province at the mouth of the Yalu River. Pop: 730 000 (2005 est). Also called: **Andong**. Former spelling: **Tan-tung**

dandruff *n* loose scales of dry dead skin shed from the scalp [origin unknown]

dandy *n, pl* **-dies 1** a man who is greatly concerned with the elegance of his appearance ▷ *adj* **-dier, -diest 2** *informal* very good or fine [origin unknown]

dandy-brush *n* a stiff brush used for grooming a horse

Dane *n* a native or inhabitant of Denmark

Danelaw or **Danelagh** *n* the northern, central and eastern parts of Anglo-Saxon England in which Danish law and custom were observed [Old English *Dena lagu* Danes' law; term revived in the 19th century]

danger *n* **1** the possibility that someone may be injured or killed **2** someone or something that may cause injury or harm **3** a likelihood that something unpleasant will happen: *the danger of flooding* [Middle English *daunger* power, hence power to inflict injury]

danger money *n* extra money paid to compensate for the risks involved in dangerous work

dangerous *adj* likely or able to cause injury or harm **> dangerously** *adv*

dangle *vb* **-gling, -gled 1** to hang loosely **2** to display (something attractive) as an enticement [probably imitative]

Daniel *n* **1** Paul (Wilson). born 1958, English conductor; musical director of the English National Opera (1997–2005) **2** Samuel. ?1562–1619, English poet and writer: author of the sonnet sequence *Delia* (1592)

Danish *adj* **1** of or relating to Denmark or its inhabitants ▷ *n* **2** the language of Denmark

Danish blue *n* a white cheese with blue veins and a strong flavour

Danish pastry *n* a rich puff pastry filled with apple, almond paste, etc. and topped with icing

Danish West Indies *pl n* the former possession of Denmark in the W Lesser Antilles, sold to the US in 1917. Name since 1917: **Virgin Islands of the United States**

dank *adj* (esp. of cellars or caves) unpleasantly damp and chilly [probably from Old Norse]

Dankworth *n* Sir John (Philip William). 1927–2010, British jazz composer, bandleader, and saxophonist: married to Cleo Laine

Danmark *n* the Danish name for **Denmark**

D'Annunzio *n* Gabriele. 1863–1938, Italian poet, dramatist, novelist, national hero, and Fascist. His works include the poems in *Alcione* (1904) and the drama *La Figlia di Iorio* (1904)

Dante *n* full name **Dante Alighieri**. 1265–1321, Italian poet famous for *La Divina Commedia* (?1309–?1320), an allegorical account of his journey through Hell, Purgatory, and Paradise, guided by Virgil and his idealized love Beatrice. His other works include *La Vita Nuova* (?1292), in which he celebrates his love for Beatrice **> Dantean** or **Dantesque** *adj*

Danton *n* Georges Jacques. 1759–94, French revolutionary leader: a founder member of the Committee of Public Safety (1793) and minister of justice (1792–94). He was overthrown by Robespierre and guillotined

d

Danube n a river in central and SE Europe, rising in the Black Forest in Germany and flowing to the Black Sea. Length: 2859 km (1776 miles). German name: **Donau**. Czech name: **Dunaj**. Hungarian name: **Duna**. Croatian and Serbian name: **Dunav**. Romanian name: **Dunărea**

Danubian adj of or relating to the river Danube

Danzig n **1** the German name for **Gdańsk 2** a rare variety of domestic fancy pigeon originating in this area

Da Ponte n **Lorenzo**, real name *Emmanuele Conegliano* 1749–1838, Italian writer; Mozart's librettist for *The Marriage of Figaro* (1786), *Don Giovanni* (1787), and *Così fan tutte* (1790)

dapper adj (of a man) neat in appearance and slight in build [Middle Dutch]

dappled adj **1** marked with spots of a different colour; mottled **2** covered in patches of light and shadow [origin unknown]

dapple-grey n a horse with a grey coat and darker coloured spots

Dapsang n another name for **K2**

Darby n **Abraham**. 1677–1717, British iron manufacturer: built the first coke-fired blast furnace (1709)

Darby and Joan n *chiefly Brit* a happily married elderly couple [couple in 18th-century ballad]

Darcy n **(James) Les**(lie). 1895–1917, Australian boxer and folk hero, who lost only five professional fights and was never knocked out, considered a martyr after his death from septicaemia during a tour of the United States

Dardanelles n the strait between the Aegean and the Sea of Marmara, separating European from Asian Turkey. Ancient name: **Hellespont**

dare vb **daring, dared 1** to be courageous enough to try (to do something) **2** to challenge (someone) to do something risky **3** I dare say **a** it is quite possible **b** probably ▷ n **4** a challenge to do something risky [Old English *durran*]

USAGE When used negatively or interrogatively, *dare* does not usually add *-s: he dare not come; dare she come?* When used negatively in the past tense, however, *dare* usually adds *-d: he dared not come.*
---

daredevil n **1** a recklessly bold person ▷ adj **2** recklessly bold or daring

Dar es Salaam n the chief port of Tanzania, on the Indian Ocean: capital of German East Africa (1891–1916); capital of Tanzania until 1983 when it was officially replaced by Dodoma, though still retaining some functions; university (1963). Pop: 2 683 000 (2005 est)

Darfur n a region of the W Sudan; an independent kingdom until conquered by Egypt in 1874; since 2003 conflict between the Janjaweed and rebel groups has left thousands dead and homeless

Darien n **1** the E part of the Isthmus of Panama, between the **Gulf of Darien** on the Caribbean coast and the Gulf of San Miguel on the Pacific coast; chiefly within the republic of Panama but extending also into Colombia: site of a disastrous attempt to establish a Scottish colony in 1698 **2 Isthmus of Darien** the former name of the Isthmus of **Panama** ▶ Spanish name: **Darién**

daring adj **1** willing to do things that may be dangerous ▷ n **2** the courage to do things that may be dangerous ▷ **daringly** adv

Dario n **Rubén**, real name *Félix Rubén García Sarmiento*. 1867–1916, Nicaraguan poet whose poetry includes *Prosas Profanas* (1896)

Darius I n known as *Darius the Great*, surname *Hystaspis*. ?550–486 BC, king of Persia (521–486), who extended the Persian empire and crushed the revolt of the Ionian city states (500). He led two expeditions against Greece but was defeated at Marathon (490)

Darius III n died 330 BC, last Achaemenid king of Persia (336–330), who was defeated by Alexander the Great

Darjeeling n **1** a town in NE India, in West Bengal in the Himalayas, at an altitude of about 2250 m (7500 ft). Pop: 107 530 (2001). Official name: **Darjiling 2** a high-quality black tea grown in the mountains around Darjeeling

dark adj **1** having little or no light **2** (of a colour) reflecting little light: *dark brown* **3** (of hair or skin) brown or black **4** (of thoughts or ideas) gloomy or sad **5** sinister or evil: *a dark deed* **6** sullen or angry: *a dark scowl* **7** secret or mysterious: *keep it dark* ▷ n **8** absence of light; darkness **9** night or nightfall **10 in the dark** in ignorance [Old English *deorc*] ▷ **darkly** adv ▷ **darkness** n

dark age n a period of ignorance or barbarism

Dark Ages pl n the period of European history between 500 and 1000 AD

Dark Continent n **the Dark Continent** a term for Africa when it was relatively unexplored

darken vb **1** to make or become dark or darker **2** to make gloomy, angry, or sad

dark horse n a person who reveals little about himself or herself, esp. someone who has unexpected talents

darkroom n a darkened room in which photographs are developed

Darlan n **Jean Louis Xavier François**. 1881–1942, French admiral and member of the Vichy government. He cooperated with the Allies after their invasion of North Africa; assassinated

darling n **1** a person very much loved: used as a term of address **2** a favourite: *the darling of the gossip columns* ▷ adj **3** beloved **4** pleasing: *a darling film* [Old English *dēorling*]

Darling n **1 Alistair (Maclean)**. born 1953, British Labour politician: Chancellor of the Exchequer (2007–10) **2 Grace**. 1815–42, English national heroine, famous for her rescue (1838) of some shipwrecked sailors with her father, a lighthouse keeper

Darling Downs pl n a plateau in NE Australia, in SE Queensland: a vast agricultural and stock-raising area

Darling Range n a ridge in SW Western Australia, parallel to the coast. Highest point: about 582 m (1669 ft

Darling River n a river in SE Australia, rising in the Eastern Highlands and flowing southwest to the Murray River. Length: 2740 km (1702 miles)

Darlington n **1** an industrial town in NE England in Darlington unitary authority, S Durham: developed mainly with the opening of the Stockton-Darlington railway (1825). Pop: 86 082 (2001) **2** a unitary authority in NE England, in Durham. Pop: 98 200 (2003 est). Area: 198 sq km (77 sq miles)

Darmstadt n an industrial city in central Germany, in Hesse: former capital of the grand duchy of Hesse-Darmstadt (1567–1945). Pop: 139 698 (2003 est)

darmstadtium n a radioactive element produced synthetically in small quantities. Symbol: Ds [after DARMSTADT]

darn¹ vb **1** to mend a hole in (a knitted garment) with a series of interwoven stitches ▷ n **2** a patch of darned work on a garment [origin unknown]

darn² interj, adj, adv, vb, n euphemistic same as **damn**

darnel n a weed that grows in grain fields [origin unknown]

Darnley n **Lord**. title of *Henry Stuart* (or *Stewart*). 1545–67, Scottish nobleman; second husband of Mary, Queen of Scots and father of James I of England. After murdering his wife's secretary, Rizzio (1566), he was himself assassinated (1567)

dart n **1** a small narrow pointed missile that is thrown or shot, as in the game of darts **2** a sudden quick movement **3** a tapered tuck made in dressmaking ▷ vb **4** to move or throw swiftly and suddenly [Germanic] ▷ **darting** adj

dartboard n a circular board used as the target in the game of darts

Dartford n a town in SE England, in NW Kent. Pop: 56 818 (2001)

Dartmoor n **1** a moorland plateau in SW England, in SW Devon: a national park since 1951. Area: 945 sq km

(365 sq miles) **2** a prison in SW England, on Dartmoor: England's main prison for long-term convicts **3** a small strong breed of pony, originally from Dartmoor **4** a hardy coarse-woolled breed of sheep originally from Dartmoor

Dartmouth *n* **1** a port in SW England, in S Devon: Royal Naval College (1905). Pop: 5512 (2001) **2** a city in SE Canada, in S Nova Scotia, on Halifax Harbour: oil refineries and shipyards. Pop: 65 741 (2001)

darts *n* a game in which darts are thrown at a dartboard

Darwin¹ *n* a port in N Australia, capital of the Northern Territory: destroyed by a cyclone in 1974 but rebuilt on the same site. Pop: 129 062 (2011). Former name (1869–1911): Palmerston

Darwin² *n* **1** Charles (**Robert**). 1809–82, English naturalist who formulated the theory of evolution by natural selection, expounded in *On the Origin of Species* (1859) and applied to man in *The Descent of Man* (1871) **2** his grandfather, **Erasmus**. 1731–1802, English physician and poet; author of *Zoonomia, or the Laws of Organic Life* (1794–96), anticipating Lamarck's views on evolution **3** Sir **George Howard**, son of Charles Darwin. 1845–1912, English astronomer and mathematician noted for his work on tidal friction **›** **Darwinian** *adj, n*

Darwinism *or* **Darwinian theory** *n* the theory of the origin of animal and plant species by evolution [after Charles DARWIN] **›** **Darwinist** *n, adj*

dash *vb* **1** to move hastily; rush **2** to hurl; crash: *deep-sea rollers dashing spray over jagged rocks* **3** to frustrate: *prospects for peace have been dashed* **▷** *n* **4** a sudden quick movement **5** a small amount: *a dash of milk* **6** a mixture of style and courage: *the commander's dash did not impress him* **7** the punctuation mark (—), used to indicate a change of subject **8** the symbol (–), used in combination with the symbol *dot* (.) in Morse code **▶** See also **dash off** [Middle English *daschen, dassen*]

dashboard *n* the instrument panel in a car, boat, or aircraft

dasher *n Canad* one of the boards surrounding an ice-hockey rink

dashing *adj* stylish and attractive: *a splendidly dashing character*

dash off *vb* to write down or finish off hastily

Dasht-i-Kavir *or* **Dasht-e-Kavir** *n* a salt waste on the central plateau of Iran: a treacherous marsh beneath a salt crust. Also called: **Kavir Desert**

Dasht-i-Lut *or* **Dasht-e-Lut** *n* a desert plateau in central and E central Iran

dassie *n S African* a hyrax, esp. a rock hyrax [Afrikaans]

dastardly *adj old-fashioned* mean and cowardly [Middle English *dastard* dullard]

dasyure (dass-ee-your) *n* a small marsupial of Australia, New Guinea, and adjacent islands

DAT digital audio tape

dat. dative

data *n* **1** a series of observations, measurements, or facts; information **2** *computers* the numbers, digits, characters, and symbols operated on by a computer [Latin: (things) given]

> **USAGE** Although now often used as a singular noun, *data* is in fact a plural.

database *n* **1** a store of information in a form that can be easily handled by a computer **2** a large store of information: *a database of knowledge*

data capture *n* a process for converting information into a form that can be handled by a computer

data processing *n* a sequence of operations performed on data, esp. by a computer, in order to extract or interpret information

date¹ *n* **1** a specified day of the month **2** the particular day or year when an event happened **3 a** an appointment, esp. with a person to whom one is

romantically or sexually attached **b** the person with whom the appointment is made **4 to date** up to now **▷** *vb* **dating, dated 5** to mark (a letter or cheque) with the date **6** to assign a date of occurrence or creation to **7** to reveal the age of: *that dress dates her* **8** to make or become old-fashioned: *it's the freshest look this year but may date quickly* **9** *informal, chiefly US and Canad* to be a boyfriend or girlfriend of **10 date from** *or* **date back to** to have originated at (a specified time) [Latin *dare* to give, as in *epistula data Romae* letter handed over at Rome]

> **USAGE** See at **year**.

date² *n* the dark-brown, sweet-tasting fruit of the date palm [Greek *daktulos* finger]

dated *adj* unfashionable; outmoded

dateless *adj* likely to remain fashionable or interesting regardless of age

dateline *n journalism* information placed at the top of an article stating the time and place the article was written

Date Line *n* short for **International Date Line**

date palm *n* a tall palm grown in tropical regions for its fruit

date rape *n* the act of a man raping a woman or pressuring her into having sex while they are on a date together

dative *n grammar* the grammatical case in certain languages that expresses the indirect object [Latin *dativus*]

datum *n, pl* **-ta** a single piece of information usually in the form of a fact or statistic [Latin: something given]

daub *vb* **1** to smear (paint or mud) quickly or carelessly over a surface **2** to paint (a picture) clumsily or badly **▷** *n* **3** a crude or badly done painting: *a typical child's daub* [Old French *dauber* to paint]

Daubigny *n* Charles François. 1817–78, French landscape painter associated with the Barbizon School

Daudet *n* Alphonse. 1840–97, French novelist, short-story writer, and dramatist: noted particularly for his humorous sketches of Provençal life, as in *Lettres de mon moulin* (1866)

Daugava *n* the Latvian name for the Western **Dvina**

Daugavpils *n* a city in SE Latvia on the Western Dvina River: founded in 1274 by Teutonic Knights; ruled by Poland (1559–1772) and Russia (1772–1915); retaken by the Russians in 1940. Pop: 112 609 (2002 est). German name (until 1893): **Dünaburg**. Former Russian name (1893–1920): **Dvinsk**

daughter *n* **1** a female child **2** a girl or woman who comes from a certain place or is connected with a certain thing: *a daughter of the church* **▷** *adj* **3** *biology* denoting a cell, chromosome, etc. produced by the division of one of its own kind **4** *physics* (of a nuclide) formed from another nuclide by radioactive decay [Old English *dohtor*] **›** **daughterly** *adj*

daughter-in-law *n, pl* **daughters-in-law** the wife of one's son or daughter

Daumier *n* Honoré. 1808–79, French painter and lithographer, noted particularly for his political and social caricatures

daunting *adj* intimidating or worrying: *this project grows more daunting every day* [Latin *domitare* to tame]

dauntless *adj* fearless; not discouraged

dauphin (daw-fin) *n* formerly, the eldest son of the king of France [Old French: originally a family name]

Dauphiné *n* a former province of SE France: its rulers, the Counts of Vienne, assumed the title of *dauphin*; annexed to France in 1457

Davao *n* a port in the S Philippines, in SE Mindanao. Pop: 1 326 000 (2005 est)

Davenant *n* Sir William. 1606–68, English dramatist and poet: poet laureate (1638–68). His plays include *Love and Honour* (1634)

davenport *n* **1** *chiefly Brit* a writing desk with drawers at the side **2** _Austral, US and Canad_ a large sofa [sense 1 supposedly after Captain _Davenport,_ who commissioned the first ones]

Daventry _n_ a town in central England, in Northamptonshire: light industries, site of an important international radio transmitter. Pop: 21 731 (2001)

David _n_ **1** the second king of the Hebrews (about 1000–962 BC), who united Israel as a kingdom with Jerusalem as its capital **2 Elizabeth**. 1914–92, British cookery writer. Her books include _Mediterranean Food_ (1950) and _An Omelette and a Glass of Wine_ (1984) **3 Jacques Louis**. 1748–1825, French neoclassical painter of such works as the _Oath of the Horatii_ (1784), _Death of Socrates_ (1787), and _The Intervention of the Sabine Women_ (1799). He actively supported the French Revolution and became court painter to Napoleon Bonaparte in 1804; banished at the Bourbon restoration **4 Saint**. 6th century AD, Welsh bishop; patron saint of Wales. Feast day: March 1

David I _n_ 1084–1153, king of Scotland (1124–53) who supported his niece Matilda's claim to the English throne and unsuccessfully invaded England on her behalf

David II _n_ 1324–71, king of Scotland (1329–71): he was forced into exile in France (1334–41) by Edward de Baliol; captured following the battle of Neville's Cross (1346), and imprisoned by the English (1346–57)

Davies _n_ **1** Sir **John**. 1569–1626, English poet, author of _Orchestra or a Poem of Dancing_ (1596) and the philosophical poem _Nosce Teipsum_ (1599) **2** Sir **Peter Maxwell**. born 1934, British composer whose works include the operas _Taverner_ (1967), _The Martyrdom of St Magnus_ (1977), and _Resurrection_ (1988), nine symphonies, and the ten Strathclyde Concertos; Master of the Queen's Music (2004–2014) **3 (William) Robertson**. 1913–95, Canadian novelist and dramatist. His novels include _Leaven of Malice_ (1954), _Fifth Business_ (1970), _The Rebel Angels_ (1981), _What's Bred in the Bone_ (1985), and _The Cunning Man_ (1994) **4** W(illiam) H(enry). 1871–1940, Welsh poet, noted also for his _Autobiography of a Super-tramp_ (1908)

Davis _n_ **1** Sir **Andrew (Frank)**. born 1944, British conductor; chief conductor of the BBC Symphony Orchestra (1989–2000) and of the Chicago Lyric Opera from 2000 **2 Bette**, real name _Ruth Elizabeth Davis._ 1908–89, US film actress, whose films include _Of Human Bondage_ (1934), _Jezebel_ (1938) for which she won an Oscar, _All About Eve_ (1950), _Whatever Happened to Baby Jane?_ (1962), _The Nanny_ (1965), and _The Whales of August_ (1987) **3** Sir **Colin (Rex)**. 1927–2013, English conductor, noted for his interpretation of the music of Berlioz **4** Jefferson. 1808–89, president of the Confederate States of America during the Civil War (1861–65) **5** Joe. 1901–78, English billiards and snooker player: world champion from 1927 to 1946 **6** John. Also called: **John Davys**. ?1550–1605, English navigator: discovered the Falkland Islands (1592); searched for a Northwest Passage **7** Miles (Dewey). 1926–91, US jazz trumpeter and composer **8** Steve. born 1957, English snooker player: world champion 1981, 1983–84, 1987–89

Davisson _n_ Clinton Joseph. 1881–1958, US physicist, noted for his discovery of electron diffraction; shared the Nobel prize for physics in 1937

Davis Strait _n_ a strait between Baffin Island, in Canada, and Greenland [named after John DAVIS]

davit (dav-vit) _n_ a crane, usually one of a pair, on the side of a ship for lowering or hoisting a lifeboat [Anglo-French _daviot,_ from _Davi_ David]

Davos _n_ a mountain resort in Switzerland: winter sports, site of the Parsenn ski run. Pop: 11 417 (2000). Height: about 1560 m (5118 ft). Romansch name: **Tarau**

Davy _n_ Sir Humphry. 1778–1829, English chemist who isolated sodium, magnesium, chlorine, and other elements and suggested the electrical nature of chemical combination. He invented the **Davy lamp**

Davy Jones's locker _n_ the ocean's bottom, regarded as the grave of those lost or buried at sea [origin unknown]

Davy lamp _n_ same as **safety lamp** [after Sir Humphrey DAVY]

dawdle _vb_ **-dling, -dled** to walk slowly or lag behind [origin unknown]

Dawes _n_ Charles Gates. 1865–1951, US financier, diplomat, and statesman, who devised the Dawes Plan for German reparations payments after World War I; vice president of the US (1925–29); Nobel peace prize 1925

Dawkins _n_ Richard. born 1941, British zoologist, noted for such works as _The Selfish Gene_ (1976), _The Blind Watchmaker_ (1986), _The God Delusion_ (2006), and _The Greatest Show on Earth_ (2009)

dawn _n_ **1** daybreak **2** the beginning of something ▷ _vb_ **3** to begin to grow light after the night **4** to begin to develop or appear **5 dawn on** or **upon** to become apparent (to someone) [Old English _dagian_ to dawn]

dawn chorus _n_ the singing of birds at dawn

Dawson _n_ a town in NW Canada, in the Yukon on the Yukon River: a boom town during the Klondike gold rush (at its height in 1899). Pop: 1251 (2001)

Dawson Creek _n_ a town in W Canada, in NE British Columbia: SE terminus of the Alaska Highway. Pop: 10 754 (2001)

day _n_ **1** the period of 24 hours from one midnight to the next **2** the period of light between sunrise and sunset **3** the part of a day occupied with regular activity, esp. work **4** a period or point in time: _in days gone by; in Shakespeare's day_ **5** a day of special observance: _Christmas Day_ **6** a time of success or recognition: _his day will come_ **7 all in a day's work** part of one's normal activity **8 at the end of the day** in the final reckoning **9 call it a day** to stop work or other activity **10 day in, day out** every day without changing **11 that'll be the day a** that is most unlikely to happen **b** I look forward to that. Related adjective: **diurnal** [Old English _dæg_]

Day _n_ Sir Robin. 1923–2000, British radio and television journalist, noted esp. for his political interviews

Dayan _n_ Moshe. 1915–81, Israeli soldier and statesman; minister of defence (1967; 1969–74) and foreign minister (1977–79)

daybreak _n_ the time in the morning when light first appears

day centre _n_ a place that provides care where elderly or disabled people can spend the day

daydream _n_ **1** a pleasant fantasy indulged in while awake ▷ _vb_ **2** to indulge in idle fantasy ❭ **daydreamer** _n_

Day-Glo _adj_ (of a colour) luminous in daylight: _Day-Glo pink_ [from a trade name for a brand of fluorescent paint]

Day-Lewis or **Day Lewis** _n_ **1** C(ecil). 1904–72, British poet, critic, and (under the pen name _Nicholas Blake_) author of detective stories; poet laureate (1968–72) **2** his son, Sir **Daniel**, born 1957, English actor; winner of three Academy Awards for best actor: _My Left Foot_ (1989), _There Will Be Blood_ (2007), and _Lincoln_ (2012)

daylight _n_ **1** light from the sun **2** daytime **3** daybreak **4 see daylight** to realize that the end of a difficult task is approaching ▶ See also **daylights**

daylight robbery _n_ _informal_ blatant overcharging

daylights _pl n_ _informal_ **1** beat the living daylights out of someone to beat someone soundly **2 scare the living daylights out of someone** to frighten someone greatly

daylight-saving time _n_ time set one hour ahead of the local standard time, to provide extra daylight in the evening in summer

Day of Atonement _n_ same as **Yom Kippur**

day release _n_ _Brit_ a system whereby workers go to college one day a week for vocational training

day return _n_ a reduced fare for a train or bus journey travelling both ways in one day

day room _n_ a communal living room in a hospital or similar institution

daytime _n_ the time from sunrise to sunset

day-to-day *adj* routine; everyday

Dayton *n* an industrial city in SW Ohio: aviation research centre. Pop: 161 696 (2003 est)

Daytona Beach *n* a city in NE Florida, on the Atlantic: a resort with a beach of hard white sand, used since 1903 for motor speed trials. Pop: 64 581 (2003 est)

Da Yunhe *n* the Pinyin transliteration of the Chinese name for the **Grand Canal** (1)

daze *vb* **dazing, dazed 1** to cause to be in a state of confusion or shock ▷ *n* **2** a state of confusion or shock: *in a daze* [Old Norse *dasa*] **> dazed** *adj*

dazzle *vb* **-zling, -zled 1** to impress greatly: *she was dazzled by his wit* **2** to blind for a short time by sudden excessive light: *he passed two cars and they dazzled him with their headlights* ▷ *n* **3** bright light that dazzles [from *daze*] **> dazzling** *adj* **> dazzlingly** *adv*

dB *or* **db** decibel(s)

Db *chem* dubnium

DBE Dame (Commander of the Order) of the British Empire

DC 1 direct current **2** District of Columbia

DCC digital compact cassette: a magnetic tape cassette on which sound can be recorded digitally

DD Doctor of Divinity

D-day *n* the day selected for the start of some operation [after D(*ay*)*-day*, the day of the Allied invasion of Europe on June 6, 1944]

DDR Deutsche Demokratische Republik (the former East Germany; GDR)

DDS *or* **DDSc** Doctor of Dental Surgery or Science

DDT *n* dichlorodiphenyltrichloroethane; an insecticide, now banned in many countries

DE Delaware

de- *prefix* **1** indicating removal: *dethrone* **2** indicating reversal: *declassify* **3** indicating departure from: *decamp* [Latin]

deacon *n Christianity* **1** (in episcopal churches) an ordained minister ranking immediately below a priest **2** (in some Protestant churches) a lay official who assists the minister [Greek *diakonos* servant]

deactivate *vb* **-vating, -vated** to make (a bomb or other explosive device) harmless

dead *adj* **1** no longer alive **2** no longer in use or finished: *a dead language*; *a dead match* **3** unresponsive **4** (of a limb) numb **5** complete or absolute: *there was dead silence* **6** *informal* very tired **7** (of a place) lacking activity **8** *electronics* **a** drained of electric charge **b** not connected to a source of electric charge **9** *sport* (of a ball) out of play **10** **dead from the neck up** *informal* stupid **11** **dead to the world** *informal* fast asleep ▷ *n* **12** a period during which coldness or darkness is most intense: *the dead of winter* ▷ *adv* **13** *informal* extremely: *dead easy* **14** suddenly and abruptly: *stop dead* **15** **dead on** exactly right [Old English *dēad*]

deadbeat *n informal* a lazy or socially undesirable person

dead beat *adj informal* exhausted

dead duck *n slang* something that is doomed to failure

deaden *vb* to make (something) less intense: *drugs deaden the pain*; *heavy curtains deadened the echo* **> deadening** *adj*

dead end *n* **1** a cul-de-sac **2** a situation in which further progress is impossible: *efforts to free the hostages had reached a dead end*

deadhead *n* **1** *US and Canad informal* a person who does not pay on a bus, at a game, etc. **2** *US and Canad informal* a commercial vehicle travelling empty **3** *slang* a dull person **4** *US and Canad* a totally or partially submerged log floating in a lake

Dead Heart *n* **the Dead Heart** *Austral* the remote interior of Australia [C20: from the title *The Dead Heart of Australia* (1906) by J. W. Gregory (1864–1932), British geologist]

dead heat *n* a tie for first place between two or more participants in a race or contest

dead letter *n* **1** a letter that cannot be delivered or returned due to lack of information **2** a law or rule that is no longer enforced

deadline *n* a time or date by which a job or task must be completed

deadlock *n* a point in a dispute at which no agreement can be reached

deadlocked *adj* having reached a deadlock

dead loss *n informal* a useless person or thing

deadly *adj* **-lier, -liest 1** likely to cause death: *deadly poison* **2** *informal* extremely boring ▷ *adv, adj* **3** like or suggestive of death: *deadly pale* ▷ *adv* **4** extremely: *she was being deadly serious*

deadly nightshade *n* a poisonous plant with purple bell-shaped flowers and black berries

dead man's handle *or* **dead man's pedal** *n* a safety device which only allows equipment to operate when a handle or pedal is being pressed

dead march *n* solemn funeral music played to accompany a procession

dead-nettle *n* a plant with leaves like nettles but without stinging hairs

deadpan *adj* **1** deliberately emotionless ▷ *adv* **2** in a deliberately emotionless manner

dead reckoning *n* a method of establishing one's position using the distance and direction travelled

Dead Sea *n* a lake between Israel, Jordan, and the West Bank, now 420 m (1378 ft) below sea level; originally 390 m (1285 ft): the lowest lake in the world, with no outlet and very high salinity; outline, esp. at the southern end, reduced considerably in recent years. Area: originally about 950 sq km (365 sq miles); by 2003 about 625 sq km (240 sq miles)

dead set *adv* firmly decided: *he is dead set on leaving*

dead soldier *or* **dead marine** *n informal* an empty beer or spirit bottle

dead weight *n* **1** a heavy weight or load **2** the difference between the loaded and the unloaded weights of a ship

dead wood *n informal* people or things that are no longer useful

deaf *adj* **1** unable to hear **2** **deaf to** refusing to listen or take notice of [Old English *dēaf*] **> deafness** *n*

> **USAGE** See at **disabled**.

deaf-and-dumb *adj offensive* unable to hear or speak

deafblind *adj* unable to hear or see

deafen *vb* to make deaf, esp. momentarily by a loud noise **> deafening** *adj*

deaf-mute *n old-fashioned, offensive* a person who is unable to hear or speak

Deak *n* Ferenc. 1803–76, Hungarian statesman: minister of justice following the 1848 Hungarian uprising. The Austro-Hungarian dual monarchy was largely his creation

Deakin *n* Alfred. 1856–1919, Australian statesman. He was a leader of the movement for Australian federation; prime minister of Australia (1903–04; 1905–08; 1909–10)

deal¹ *n* **1** an agreement or transaction **2** a particular type of treatment received: *a fair deal* **3** a large amount: *the land alone is worth a good deal* **4** *cards* a player's turn to distribute the cards **5** **big deal** *slang* an important matter: often used sarcastically ▷ *vb* **dealing, dealt** (delt) **6** to inflict (a blow) on **7** *slang* to sell any illegal drug **8** **deal in** to engage in commercially **9** **deal out** to apportion or distribute ▶ See also **deal with** [Old English *dǣlan*]

deal² *n* **1** a plank of softwood timber **2** the sawn wood of various coniferous trees [Middle Low German *dele* plank]

Deal *n* a town in SE England, in Kent, on the English Channel: two 16th-century castles: tourism, light industries. Pop: 96 670 (2003 est)

dealbreaker *n informal* an issue that prevents an agreement from being reached or that nullifies an existing agreement

dealer *n* **1** a person or organization whose business involves buying and selling things **2** *slang* a person who

d

sells illegal drugs **3** *cards* the person who distributes the cards

dealings *pl n* business relations with a person or organization

dealt *vb* the past of **deal**¹

deal with *vb* **1** to take action on: *he was not competent to deal with the legal aspects* **2** to be concerned with: *I do not wish to deal with specifics* **3** to do business with

dean *n* **1** the chief administrative official of a college or university faculty **2** *chiefly Church of England* the chief administrator of a cathedral or collegiate church [Late Latin *decanus* one set over ten people]

Dean¹ *n* **Forest of Dean** a forest in W England, in Gloucestershire, between the Rivers Severn and Wye: formerly a royal hunting ground

Dean² *n* **1** Christopher. See **Torvill and Dean 2** James (Byron). 1931–55, US film actor, who became a cult figure; his films include *East of Eden* and *Rebel Without a Cause* (both 1955). He died in a car crash

Deane *n* Sir William Patrick. born 1931, Australian lawyer. He became a High Court judge in 1982 and governor-general of Australia (1996–2001)

deanery *n, pl* **-eries 1** a place where a dean lives **2** the parishes presided over by a rural dean

dear *n* **1** (often used in direct address) someone regarded with affection ▷ *adj* **2** beloved; precious **3 a** highly priced **b** charging high prices **4** a form of address used at the beginning of a letter before the name of the recipient: *Dear Mr Anderson* **5 dear to** important or close to ▷ *interj* **6** an exclamation of surprise or dismay: *oh dear, I've broken it* ▷ *adv* **7** dearly: *her errors have cost her dear* [Old English *dēore*] ▷ **dearly** *adv*

Dearborn *n* a city in SE Michigan, near Detroit: automobile industry. Pop: 96 670 (2003 est)

dearth (dirth) *n* an inadequate amount; scarcity [Middle English *derthe*]

death *n* **1** the permanent end of life in a person or animal **2** an instance of this: *his sudden death* **3** ending or destruction **4 at death's door** likely to die soon **5 catch one's death (of cold)** *informal* to contract a severe cold **6 like death warmed up** *informal* looking or feeling very ill or very tired **7 put to death** to execute **8 to death a** until dead **b** very much: *I had probably scared him to death* [Old English *dēath*]

deathbed *n* the bed in which a person dies or is about to die

deathblow *n* a thing or event that destroys hope

death certificate *n* a document signed by a doctor certifying the death of a person and stating the cause of death if known

death duty *n* (in Britain) the former name for **inheritance tax**

death knell *n* something that heralds death or destruction

deathless *adj* everlasting because of fine qualities: *highbrow, deathless, and often endless prose*

deathly *adj* **1** resembling death: *a deathly pallor* **2** deadly

death mask *n* a cast taken from the face of a person who has recently died

death rate *n* the ratio of deaths in an area or group to the population of that area or group

death row *n* US part of a prison where convicts awaiting execution are imprisoned

death's-head *n* a human skull or a picture of one used to represent death or danger

death trap *n* a place or vehicle considered very unsafe

Death Valley *n* a desert valley in E California and W Nevada: the lowest, hottest, and driest area of the US. Lowest point: 86 m (282 ft) below sea level. Area: about 3885 sq km (1500 sq miles)

death warrant *n* **1** the official authorization for carrying out a sentence of death **2 sign one's (own) death warrant** to cause one's own destruction

deathwatch beetle *n* a beetle that bores into wood

and produces a tapping sound

Deauville *n* a town and resort in NW France: casino. Pop: 3968 (2008)

deb *n informal* a debutante

debacle (day-bah-kl) *n* something that ends in a disastrous failure, esp. because it has not been properly planned [French]

debar *vb* **-barring, -barred** to prevent (someone) from doing something

> **USAGE** See at **disbar**.

debase *vb* **-basing, -based** to lower in quality, character, or value [see DE-, BASE²] ▷ **debasement** *n*

debatable *adj* not absolutely certain: *her motives are highly debatable*

debate *n* **1** a discussion **2** a formal discussion, as in a parliament, in which opposing arguments are put forward ▷ *vb* **-bating, -bated 3** to discuss (something) formally **4** to consider (possible courses of action) [Old French *debatre*]

debauch (dib-bawch) *vb* to make someone bad or corrupt, esp. sexually [Old French *desbaucher* to corrupt]

debauched *adj* immoral; sexually corrupt

debauchery *n* excessive drunkenness or sexual activity

de Beauvoir *n* Simone. 1908–86, French existentialist novelist and feminist, whose works include *Le Sang des autres* (1944), *Le Deuxième Sexe* (1949), and *Les Mandarins* (1954)

debenture *n* a long-term bond, bearing fixed interest and usually unsecured, issued by a company or governmental agency [Latin *debentur mihi* there are owed to me] ▷ **debentured** *adj*

debenture stock *n* shares issued by a company, guaranteeing a fixed return at regular intervals

de Bèze *n* Théodore.1519–1605, French Calvinist theologian and scholar, who lived in Switzerland. He succeeded Calvin as leader of the Swiss Protestants

debilitate *vb* **-tating, -tated** to make gradually weaker [Latin *debilis* weak] ▷ **debilitating** *adj* ▷ **debilitation** *n*

debility *n, pl* **-ties** a state of weakness, esp. caused by illness

debit *n* **1** the money, or a record of the money, withdrawn from a person's bank account **2** *accounting* **a** acknowledgment of a sum owing by entry on the left side of an account **b** an entry or the total of entries on this side ▷ *vb* **-iting, -ited 3** to charge (an account) with a debt: *they had debited our account* **4** *accounting* to record (an item) as a debit in an account [Latin *debitum* debt]

debit card *n* a card issued by a bank or building society enabling customers to pay for goods by inserting it into a computer-controlled device at the place of sale, which is connected through the telephone network to the bank or building society

debonair *or* **debonnaire** *adj* (of a man) confident, charming, and well-dressed [Old French]

debouch *vb* **1** (esp. of troops) to move into a more open space **2** (of a river, glacier, etc.) to flow into a larger area or body [Old French *dé-* from + *bouche* mouth] ▷ **debouchment** *n*

Debrecen *n* a city in E Hungary: seat of the revolutionary government of 1849. Pop: 205 881 (2003 est)

debrief *vb* to interrogate (a soldier, diplomat, astronaut, etc.) on the completion of a mission ▷ **debriefing** *n*

debris (deb-ree) *n* **1** fragments of something destroyed; rubble **2** a mass of loose stones and earth [French]

de Broglie *n* **1** Prince Louis Victor. 1892–1987, French physicist, noted for his research in quantum mechanics and his development of wave mechanics: Nobel prize for physics 1929 **2** his brother, **Maurice**, Duc de Broglie. 1875–1960, French physicist, noted for his research into X-ray spectra

Debs *n* Eugene Victor. 1855–1926, US labour leader; five times Socialist presidential candidate (1900–20)

debt n **1** a sum of money owed **2 bad debt** a debt that is unlikely to be paid **3 in debt** owing money **4 in someone's debt** grateful to someone for his or her help: *I couldn't have managed without you – I'm in your debt* [Latin *debitum*]

debt of honour n a debt that is morally but not legally binding

debtor n a person who owes money

debug vb **-bugging, -bugged** *informal* **1** to locate and remove defects in (a computer program) **2** to remove concealed microphones from (a room or telephone)

debunk vb *informal* to expose the falseness of: *many commonly held myths are debunked by the book* [DE- + BUNK²] **> debunker** n

Debussy n (**Achille**) **Claude.** 1862–1918, French composer and critic, the creator of impressionism in music and a profound influence on contemporary composition. His works include *Prélude à l'après-midi d'un faune* (1894) and *La Mer* (1905) for orchestra, the opera *Pelléas et Mélisande* (1902), and many piano pieces and song settings

debut (**day**-byoo) n the first public appearance of a performer [French]

debutante (**day**-byoo-tont) n a young upper-class woman who is formally presented to society [French]

Debye n Peter Joseph Wilhelm. 1884–1966, Dutch chemist and physicist, working in the US: Nobel prize for chemistry (1936) for his work on dipole moments

Dec. December

decade n a period of ten years [Greek *deka* ten]

decadence (**deck**-a-denss) n a decline in morality or culture [Medieval Latin *decadentia* a falling away] **> decadent** adj

decaf (**dee**-kaf) *informal* n **1** decaffeinated coffee ▷ adj **2** decaffeinated

decaffeinated (dee-kaf-fin-ate-id) adj with the caffeine removed: *decaffeinated tea*

decagon n *geometry* a figure with ten sides [Greek *deka* ten + *gōnia* angle] **> decagonal** adj

decahedron (deck-a-heed-ron) n a solid figure with ten plane faces [Greek *deka* ten + *hedra* base] **> decahedral** adj

decalitre or US **decaliter** n a measure of volume equivalent to 10 litres

Decalogue n same as **Ten Commandments** [Greek *deka* ten + *logos* word]

decametre or US **decameter** n a unit of length equal to ten metres

decamp vb to leave secretly or suddenly

decant vb **1** to pour (a liquid, esp. wine) from one container to another **2** *chiefly Brit* to rehouse (people) while their homes are being renovated [Medieval Latin *de-* from + *canthus* spout, rim]

decanter n a stoppered bottle into which a drink is poured for serving

decapitate vb **-tating, -tated** to behead [Latin *de-* from + *caput* head] **> decapitation** n

decapod n **1** a creature, such as a crab, with five pairs of walking limbs **2** a creature, such as a squid, with eight short tentacles and two longer ones [Greek *deka* ten + *pous* foot]

decarbonize or **-ise** vb **-izing, -ized** or **-ising, -ised** to remove carbon from (an internal-combustion engine) **> decarbonization** or **-isation** n

decathlon n an athletic contest in which each athlete competes in ten different events [Greek *deka* ten + *athlon* contest] **> decathlete** n

Decatur n Stephen. 1779–1820, US naval officer, noted for his raid on Tripoli harbour (1804) and his role in the War of 1812

decay vb **1** to decline gradually in health, prosperity, or quality **2** to rot or cause to rot **3** *physics* (of an atomic nucleus) to undergo radioactive disintegration ▷ n **4** the process of something rotting: *too much sugar can cause tooth*

decay **5** the state brought about by this process **6** *physics* disintegration of a nucleus, occurring spontaneously or as a result of electron capture [Latin *de-* from + *cadere* to fall]

Deccan n the Deccan **1** a plateau in S India, between the Eastern Ghats, the Western Ghats, and the Narmada River **2** the whole Indian peninsula south of the Narmada River

decease n *formal* death [Latin *decedere* to depart]

deceased adj *formal* **1** dead ▷ n **2** a dead person: *the deceased*

deceit n behaviour intended to deceive

deceitful adj full of deceit

deceive vb **-ceiving, -ceived** **1** to mislead by lying **2 deceive oneself** to refuse to acknowledge something one knows to be true **3** to be unfaithful to (one's sexual partner) [Latin *decipere* to ensnare, cheat]

decelerate vb **-ating, -ated** to slow down [DE- + (AC)CELERATE] **> deceleration** n

December n the twelfth month of the year [Latin: the tenth month (the Roman year originally began with March)]

decencies pl n generally accepted standards of good behaviour

decency n conformity to the prevailing standards of what is right

decennial adj **1** lasting for ten years **2** occurring every ten years

decent adj **1** conforming to an acceptable standard or quality: *a decent living wage*; *he's made a few decent films* **2** polite or respectable: *he's a decent man* **3** fitting or proper: *that's the decent thing to do* **4** conforming to conventions of sexual behaviour **5** *informal* kind; generous: *she was pretty decent to me* [Latin *decens* suitable] **> decently** adv

decentralize or **-ise** vb **-izing, -ized** or **-ising, -ised** to reorganize into smaller local units **> decentralization** or **-isation** n

deception n **1** the act of deceiving someone or the state of being deceived **2** something that deceives; trick

deceptive adj likely or designed to deceive **> deceptively** adv **> deceptiveness** n

deci- *combining form* denoting one tenth: *decimetre* [Latin *decimus* tenth]

decibel n a unit for comparing two power levels or measuring the intensity of a sound [DECI- + BEL]

decide vb **-ciding, -cided** **1** to reach a decision: *we must decide on suitable action*; *he decided to stay on* **2** to cause to reach a decision **3** to settle (a question): *possible profits decided the issue* **4** to influence the outcome of (a contest) decisively: *the goal that decided the match came just before half-time* [Latin *decidere* to cut off]

decided adj **1** definite or noticeable: *a decided improvement* **2** strong and definite: *he has decided views on the matter* **> decidedly** adv

deciduous adj **1** (of a tree) shedding all leaves annually **2** (of antlers or teeth) being shed at the end of a period of growth [Latin *deciduus* falling off]

decilitre or US **deciliter** n a measure of volume equivalent to one tenth of a litre

decimal n **1** a fraction written in the form of a dot followed by one or more numbers, for example $.2 = \frac{2}{10}$ ▷ adj **2** relating to or using powers of ten **3** expressed as a decimal [Latin *decima* a tenth]

decimal currency n a system of currency in which the units are parts or powers of ten

decimalize or **-ise** vb **-izing, -ized** or **-ising, -ised** to change (a system or number) to the decimal system **> decimalization** or **-isation** n

decimal point n the dot between the unit and the fraction of a number in the decimal system

decimal system n a number system with a base of ten, in which numbers are expressed by combinations of the digits 0 to 9

d

decimate vb -mating, -mated to destroy or kill a large proportion of [Latin decimare] **> decimation** n

> USAGE You would talk about the whole of something being *decimated*, not a part: *disease decimated the population*, not *disease decimated most of the population*.

decimetre or US **decimeter** n a unit of length equal to one tenth of a metre

decipher vb 1 to make out the meaning of (something obscure or illegible) 2 to convert from code into plain text **> decipherable** adj

decision n 1 a choice or judgment made about something 2 the act of making up one's mind 3 the ability to make quick and definite decisions [Latin decisio a cutting off]

decisive adj 1 having great influence on the result of something: *the decisive goal was scored in the closing minutes* 2 having the ability to make quick decisions **> decisively** adv **> decisiveness** n

deck n 1 an area of a ship that forms a floor, at any level 2 a similar area in a bus 3 same as **tape deck** 4 US and Austral a pack of playing cards 5 **clear the decks** informal to prepare for action, as by removing obstacles ▷ vb 6 slang to knock (a person) to the ground [Middle Dutch dec a covering]

deck chair n a folding chair with a wooden frame and a canvas seat

decking n a wooden deck or platform, esp. one in a garden for deck chairs, etc.

deckle edge n a rough edge on paper, often left as ornamentation [the *deckle* is the frame that holds the pulp in paper making] **> deckle-edged** adj

deck out vb to make more attractive by decorating: *the village was decked out in the blue-and-white flags*

declaim vb 1 to speak loudly and dramatically 2 **declaim against** to protest against loudly and publicly [Latin declamare] **> declamation** n **> declamatory** adj

declaration n 1 a firm, emphatic statement 2 an official announcement or statement **> declaratory** adj

declare vb -claring, -clared 1 to state firmly and forcefully 2 to announce publicly or officially: *a state of emergency has been declared* 3 to state officially that (someone or something) is as specified: *he was declared fit to play* 4 to acknowledge (dutiable goods or income) for tax purposes 5 cards to decide (the trump suit) by making the winning bid 6 cricket to bring an innings to an end before the last batsman is out 7 **declare for** or **against** to state one's support or opposition for something [Latin declarare to make clear]

declassify vb -fies, -fying, -fied to state officially that (information or a document) is no longer secret **> declassification** n

declension n grammar changes in the form of nouns, pronouns, or adjectives to show case, number, and gender [Latin declinatio a bending aside, hence variation]

declination n 1 astronomy the angular distance of a star or planet north or south from the celestial equator 2 the angle made by a compass needle with the direction of the geographical north pole

decline vb -clining, -clined 1 to become smaller, weaker, or less important 2 to politely refuse to accept or do (something) 3 grammar to list the inflections of (a noun, pronoun, or adjective) ▷ n 4 a gradual weakening or loss [Latin declinare to bend away]

declivity n, pl -ties a downward slope [Latin declivitas] **> declivitous** adj

declutch vb to disengage the clutch of a motor vehicle

decoct vb to extract the essence from (a substance) by boiling [Latin decoquere to boil down] **> decoction** n

decode vb -coding, -coded to convert from code into ordinary language **> decoder** n

decoke vb -coking, -coked same as **decarbonize**

décolletage (day-kol-**tahzh**) n a low-cut dress or neckline [French]

décolleté (day-kol-tay) adj 1 (of a woman's garment) low-cut ▷ n 2 a low-cut neckline [French]

decommission vb to dismantle or remove from service (a nuclear reactor, weapon, ship, etc. which is no longer required)

decompose vb -posing, -posed 1 to rot 2 to break up or separate into constituent parts **> decomposition** n

decompress vb 1 to free from pressure 2 to return (a diver) to normal atmospheric pressure **> decompression** n

decompression sickness n a disorder characterized by severe pain and difficulty in breathing caused by a sudden and sustained change in atmospheric pressure

decongestant n a drug that relieves nasal congestion

decontaminate vb -nating, -nated to make (a place or object) safe by removing poisons, radioactivity, etc. **> decontamination** n

decor (day-core) n a style or scheme of interior decoration and furnishings in a room or house [French]

decorate vb -rating, -rated 1 to make more attractive by adding some ornament or colour 2 to paint or wallpaper 3 to confer a mark of distinction, esp. a medal, upon [Latin decorare] **> decorative** adj **> decorator** n

Decorated style or **Decorated architecture** n a 14th-century style of English architecture characterized by the ogee arch, geometrical tracery, and floral decoration

decoration n 1 an addition that makes something more attractive or ornate 2 the way in which a room or building is decorated 3 something, esp. a medal, conferred as a mark of honour

decorous (deck-or-uss) adj polite, calm, and sensible in behaviour [Latin decorus] **> decorously** adv **> decorousness** n

decorum (dik-**core**-um) n polite and socially correct behaviour

decoy n 1 a person or thing used to lure someone into danger 2 an image of a bird or animal, used to lure game into a trap or within shooting range ▷ vb 3 to lure into danger by means of a decoy [probably from Dutch de kooi the cage]

decrease vb -creasing, -creased 1 to make or become less in size, strength, or quantity ▷ n 2 a lessening; reduction 3 the amount by which something has been diminished [Latin decrescere to grow less] **> decreasing** adj **> decreasingly** adv

decree n 1 a law made by someone in authority 2 a judgment of a court ▷ vb **decreeing, decreed** 3 to order by decree [Latin decretum ordinance]

decree absolute n the final decree in divorce proceedings, which leaves the parties free to remarry

decree nisi n a provisional decree in divorce proceedings, which will later be made absolute unless cause is shown why it should not [Latin nisi unless]

decrepit adj weakened or worn out by age or long use [Latin crepare to creak] **> decrepitude** n

decretal n RC Church a papal decree [Late Latin decretalis]

decry vb -cries, -crying, -cried to express open disapproval of [Old French descrier]

decrypt vb 1 to decode (a message) with or without previous knowledge of its key 2 to make intelligible (a television or other signal) that has been deliberately distorted for transmission ▶ See also **encrypt** [DE- + (EN) CRYPT] **> decryption** n

Dedéagach, Dedeagatch or **Dedeağac** n a former name (until the end of World War I) of **Alexandroúpolis**

Dedekind n (Julius Wilhelm) Richard. 1831–1916, German mathematician, who devised a way (the **Dedekind cut**) of according irrational and rational numbers the same status

dedicate vb -cating, -cated 1 to devote (oneself or one's time) wholly to a special purpose or cause 2 to inscribe or address (a book, piece of music, etc.) to someone as a token of affection or respect **3** to play (a record) on radio for someone as a greeting **4** to set apart for sacred uses [Latin *dedicare* to announce]

edicated *adj* **1** devoted to a particular purpose or cause **2** *computers* designed to fulfil one function

edication *n* **1** wholehearted devotion **2** an inscription in a book dedicating it to a person

educe *vb* **-ducing, -duced** to reach (a conclusion) by reasoning from evidence; work out [Latin *de-* away + *ducere* to lead] > **deducible** *adj*

educt *vb* to subtract (a number, quantity, or part) [Latin *deducere* to deduce]

eductible *adj* **1** capable of being deducted **2** US tax-deductible

eduction *n* **1** the act or process of subtracting **2** something that is deducted **3** *logic* **a** a process of reasoning by which a conclusion necessarily follows from a set of general premises **b** a conclusion reached by this process > **deductive** *adj*

e Duve *n* Christian. 1917–2013, Belgian biochemist, who discovered lysosomes: shared the Nobel prize (1974) for his work in cell biology

ee[1] *n* **1** a river in N Wales and NW England, rising in S Gwynedd and flowing east and north to the Irish Sea. Length: about 112 km (70 miles) **2** a river in NE Scotland, rising in the Cairngorms and flowing east to the North Sea. Length: about 140 km (87 miles) **3** a river in S Scotland, flowing south to the Solway Firth. Length: about 80 km (50 miles)

ee[2] *n* John. 1527–1608, English mathematician, astrologer, and magician: best known for his preface (1570) to the first edition of Euclid in English

eed *n* **1** something that is done **2** a notable achievement **3** action as opposed to words **4** *law* a legal document, esp. one concerning the ownership of property [Old English *dēd*]

eed box *n* a strong box in which deeds and other documents are kept

eed poll *n law* a deed made by one party only, esp. to change one's name

eejay *n informal* a disc jockey [from the initials DJ]

eem *vb* to judge or consider: *common sense is deemed to be a virtue* [Old English *dēman*]

eep *adj* **1** extending or situated far down from a surface: *a deep ditch* **2** extending or situated far inwards, backwards, or sideways **3** of a specified dimension downwards, inwards, or backwards: *six metres deep* **4** coming from or penetrating to a great depth **5** difficult to understand **6** of great intensity: *deep doubts* **7** deep in totally absorbed in: *deep in conversation* **8** (of a colour) intense or dark **9** low in pitch: *a deep laugh* **10** go off the deep end *informal* to lose one's temper **11** in deep water *informal* in a tricky position or in trouble ▷ *n* **12** any deep place on land or under water **13** the deep a *poetic* the ocean b *cricket* the area of the field relatively far from the pitch **14** the most profound, intense, or central part: *the deep of winter* ▷ *adv* **15** late: *deep into the night* **16** profoundly or intensely: *deep down I was afraid it was all my fault* [Old English *dēop*] > **deeply** *adv*

eepen *vb* to make or become deeper or more intense

eep-freeze *n* **1** same as freezer ▷ *vb* **-freezing, -froze, -frozen** **2** to freeze or keep in a deep-freeze

eep-fry *vb* **-fries, -frying, -fried** to cook in hot oil deep enough to completely cover the food

eep-laid *adj* (of a plan) carefully worked out and kept secret

eep-rooted or **deep-seated** *adj* (of ideas, beliefs, etc.) firmly fixed or held

eep South *n* the SE part of the US, esp. South Carolina, Georgia, Alabama, Mississippi, and Louisiana

eep-vein thrombosis *n* a blood clot in one of the major veins, usually in the legs or pelvis

eer *n*, *pl* **deer** or **deers** a large hoofed mammal [Old English *dēor* beast]

deerstalker *n* a cloth hat with peaks at the front and back and earflaps

de-escalate *vb* to reduce the intensity of (a problem or situation) > **de-escalation** *n*

def *adj* **deffer, deffest** *slang* very good [perhaps from definitive]

deface *vb* **-facing, -faced** to deliberately spoil the surface or appearance of > **defacement** *n*

de facto *adv* **1** in fact ▷ *adj* **2** existing in fact, whether legally recognized or not [Latin]

defalcate *vb* **-cating, -cated** *law* to make wrong use of funds entrusted to one [Medieval Latin *defalcare* to cut off] > **defalcation** *n*

defame *vb* **-faming, -famed** to attack the good reputation of [Latin *diffamare* to spread by unfavourable report] > **defamation** *n* > **defamatory** (dif-**fam**-a-tree) *adj*

default *n* **1** a failure to do something, esp. to meet a financial obligation or to appear in court **2** *computers* an instruction to a computer to select a particular option unless the user specifies otherwise **3** by default happening because something else has not happened: *they gained a colony by default because no other European power wanted it* **4** in default of in the absence of ▷ *vb* **5** to fail to fulfil an obligation, esp. to make payment when due [Old French *defaillir* to fail] > **defaulter** *n*

defeat *vb* **1** to win a victory over **2** to thwart or frustrate: *this accident has defeated all his hopes of winning* ▷ *n* **3** the act of defeating or state of being defeated [Old French *desfaire* to undo, ruin]

defeatism *n* a ready acceptance or expectation of defeat > **defeatist** *n*, *adj*

defecate *vb* **-cating, -cated** to discharge waste from the body through the anus [Latin *defaecare*] > **defecation** *n*

defect *n* **1** an imperfection or blemish ▷ *vb* **2** to desert one's country or cause to join the opposing forces [Latin *deficere* to forsake, fail] > **defection** *n* > **defector** *n*

defective *adj* imperfect or faulty: *defective hearing*

defence or US **defense** *n* **1** resistance against attack **2** something that provides such resistance **3** an argument or piece of writing in support of something that has been criticized or questioned **4** a country's military resources **5** *law* a defendant's denial of the truth of a charge **6** *law* the defendant and his or her legal advisers collectively **7** *sport* the players in a team whose function is to prevent the opposing team from scoring **8** defences fortifications [Latin *defendere* to defend] > **defenceless** or US **defenseless** *adj*

defend *vb* **1** to protect from harm or danger **2** to support in the face of criticism: *I spoke up to defend her* **3** to represent (a defendant) in court **4** to protect (a title or championship) against a challenge [Latin *defendere* to ward off] > **defender** *n*

defendant *n* a person accused of a crime

defensible *adj* capable of being defended because believed to be right > **defensibility** *n*

defensive *adj* **1** intended for defence **2** guarding against criticism or exposure of one's failings: *he can be highly defensive and wary* ▷ *n* **3** on the defensive in a position of defence, as in being ready to reject criticism > **defensively** *adv*

defer[1] *vb* **-ferring, -ferred** to delay until a future time; postpone: *payment was deferred indefinitely* [Old French *differer* to be different, postpone] > **deferment** or **deferral** *n*

defer[2] *vb* **-ferring, -ferred** defer to to comply with the wishes (of) [Latin *deferre* to bear down]

deference *n* polite and respectful behaviour

deferential *adj* showing respect > **deferentially** *adv*

defiance *n* open resistance to authority or opposition > **defiant** *adj*

defibrillator *n med* an apparatus for stopping fibrillation of the heart by application of an electric current

deficiency *n, pl* **-cies 1** the state of being deficient **2** a lack or shortage

deficiency disease *n* any condition, such as scurvy, caused by a lack of vitamins or other essential substances

deficient *adj* **1** lacking something essential **2** inadequate in quantity or quality [Latin *deficere* to fall short]

deficit *n* the amount by which a sum is lower than that expected or required [Latin: there is lacking]

defile¹ *vb* **-filing, -filed 1** to make foul or dirty **2** to make unfit for ceremonial use [Old French *defouler* to trample underfoot, abuse] › **defilement** *n*

defile² *n* a narrow pass or gorge: *the sandy defile of Wadi Rum* [French *défiler* to file off]

define *vb* **-fining, -fined 1** to describe the nature of **2** to state precisely the meaning of **3** to show clearly the outline of: *the picture was sharp and cleanly defined* **4** to fix with precision; specify: *define one's duties* [Latin *definire* to set bounds to] › **definable** *adj*

definite *adj* **1** firm, clear, and precise: *I have very definite views on this subject* **2** having precise limits or boundaries **3** known for certain: *it's definite that they have won* [Latin *definitus* limited, distinct] › **definitely** *adv*

definite article *n grammar* the word 'the'

definition *n* **1** a statement of the meaning of a word or phrase **2** a description of the essential qualities of something **3** the quality of being clear and distinct **4** sharpness of outline

definitive *adj* **1** final and unable to be questioned or altered: *a definitive verdict* **2** most complete, or the best of its kind: *the book was hailed as the definitive Dickens biography* › **definitively** *adv*

deflate *vb* **-flating, -flated 1** to collapse or cause to collapse through the release of gas **2** to take away the self-esteem or conceit from **3** to cause deflation of (an economy) [DE- + (IN)FLATE]

deflation *n* **1** *econ* a reduction in economic activity resulting in lower levels of output and investment **2** a feeling of sadness following excitement › **deflationary** *adj*

deflect *vb* to turn or cause to turn aside from a course [Latin *deflectere*] › **deflection** *n* › **deflector** *n*

deflower *vb literary* to deprive (a woman) of her virginity

Defoe *n* Daniel. ?1660–1731, English novelist, journalist, spymaster, and pamphleteer, noted particularly for his novel *Robinson Crusoe* (1719). His other novels include *Moll Flanders* (1722) and *A Journal of the Plague Year* (1722)

defoliate *vb* **-ating, -ated** to deprive (a plant) of its leaves [Latin *de-* from + *folium* leaf] › **defoliant** *n* › **defoliation** *n*

De Forest *n* Lee. 1873–1961, US inventor of telegraphic, telephonic, and radio equipment: patented the first triode valve (1907)

deforestation *n* the cutting down or destruction of forests

deform *vb* to put (something) out of shape or spoil its appearance [Latin *de-* from + *forma* shape beauty]

deformed *adj* disfigured or misshapen

deformity *n, pl* **-ties 1** *pathol* a distortion of an organ or part **2** the state of being deformed

defraud *vb* to cheat out of money, property, or a right to do something

defray *vb* to provide money to cover costs or expenses [Old French *deffroier* to pay expenses] › **defrayal** *n*

defrock *vb* to deprive (a priest) of ecclesiastical status

defrost *vb* **1** to make or become free of frost or ice **2** to thaw (frozen food) by removing from a deep-freeze

deft *adj* quick and skilful in movement; dexterous [Middle English variant of *daft* (in the sense: gentle)] › **deftly** *adv* › **deftness** *n*

defunct *adj* no longer existing or working properly [Latin *defungi* to discharge (one's obligations), die]

defuse *or US sometimes* **defuze** *vb* **-fusing, -fused** *or* **-fuzing, -fuzed 1** to remove the fuse of (an explosive

device) **2** to reduce the tension in (a difficult situation): *I said it in a bid to defuse the situation*

> USAGE Avoid confusion with **diffuse**.

defy *vb* **-fies, -fying, -fied 1** to resist openly and boldly **2** to elude in a baffling way: *his actions defy explanation* **3** *formal* to challenge (someone to do something) [Old French *desfier*]

Degas *n* (Hilaire Germain) Edgar. 1834–1917, French impressionist painter and sculptor, noted for his brilliant draughtsmanship and ability to convey movement, esp in his studies of horse racing and ballet dancers

De Gasperi *n* Alcide. 1881–1954, Italian statesman; prime minister (1945–53). An antifascist, he led the Christian Democratic party during World War II from the Vatican City

de Gaulle *n* Charles (André Joseph Marie). 1890–1970, French general and statesman. During World War II, he refused to accept Pétain's armistice with Germany and founded the Free French movement in England (1940). He was head of the provisional governments (1944–46) and, as first president of the Fifth Republic (1959–69), he restored political and economic stability to France

degenerate *adj* **1** having deteriorated to a lower mental, moral, or physical level ▷ *n* **2** a degenerate person ▷ *vb* **-ating, -ated 3** to become degenerate [Latin *degener* departing from its kind, ignoble] › **degeneracy** *n*

degeneration *n* **1** the process of degenerating **2** *biology* the loss of specialization or function by organisms

degenerative *adj* (of a disease or condition) getting steadily worse

degrade *vb* **-grading, -graded 1** to reduce to dishonour or disgrace **2** to reduce in status or quality **3** *chem* to decompose into atoms or smaller molecules [Latin *de-* from + *gradus* rank, degree] › **degradation** *n* › **degrading** *adj*

degree *n* **1** a stage in a scale of relative amount or intensity: *this task involved a greater degree of responsibility* **2** an academic award given by a university or college on successful completion of a course **3** *grammar* any of the forms of an adjective used to indicate relative amount or intensity **4** a unit of temperature. Symbol: ° **5** a measure of angle equal to one three-hundred-and-sixtieth of the circumference of a circle. Symbol: ° **6** a unit of latitude or longitude. Symbol: ° **7 by degrees** little by little; gradually [Latin *de-* down + *gradus* step]

de Havilland *n* Sir Geoffrey. 1882–1965, British aircraft designer. He produced many military aircraft and the first jet airliners

dehisce *vb* **-hiscing, -hisced** (of the seed capsules of some plants) to burst open spontaneously [Latin *dehiscere* to split open] › **dehiscence** *n* › **dehiscent** *adj*

Dehra Dun *n* a city in N India, the capital of Uttarakhand (formerly Uttaranchal): Indian military academy (1932). Pop: 447 808 (2001)

dehumanize *or* **-ise** *vb* **-izing, -ized** *or* **-ising, -ised 1** to deprive of the qualities thought of as being best in human beings, such as kindness **2** to make (an activity) mechanical or routine › **dehumanization** *or* **-isation** *n*

dehydrate *vb* **-drating, -drated 1** to remove water from (food) in order to preserve it **2 be dehydrated** (of a person) to be weak or ill through losing too much water from the body › **dehydration** *n*

de-ice *vb* **de-icing, de-iced** to free of ice › **de-icer** *n*

deify (day-if-fie) *vb* **-fies, -fying, -fied** to treat or worship (someone or something) as a god [Latin *deus* god + *facere* to make] › **deification** *n*

Deighton *n* Len. born 1929, British thriller writer. His books include *The Ipcress File* (1962), *Bomber* (1970), and the trilogy *Berlin Game, Mexico Set,* and *London Match* (1983–85)

deign (dane) *vb* to do something that one considers beneath one's dignity: *she did not deign to reply* [Latin *dignari* to consider worthy]

deindustrialization *or* **-sation** *n* a decline in the importance of a country's manufacturing industry

deism (dee-iz-zum) *n* belief in the existence of God based only on natural reason, without reference to revelation › **deist** *n, adj* › **deistic** *adj*

deity (dee-it-ee) *n, pl* **-ties** 1 a god or goddess 2 the state of being divine [Latin *deus* god]

Deity *n* the Deity God

déjà vu (day-zhah **voo**) *n* a feeling of having experienced before something that is happening at the present moment [French: already seen]

ejected *adj* in low spirits; downhearted [Latin *deicere* to cast down] › **dejectedly** *adv* › **dejection** *n*

e jure *adv* according to law [Latin]

eke *Canad slang* *vb* **deking, deked** 1 (in ice hockey or box lacrosse) to draw (a defending player) out of position by faking a shot or movement ▷ *n* 2 such a shot or movement [from *decoy*]

ekker *or* **Decker** *n* Thomas. ?1572–?1632, English dramatist and pamphleteer, noted particularly for his comedy *The Shoemaker's Holiday* (1600) and his satirical pamphlet *The Gull's Hornbook* (1609)

ekko *n* have a dekko *Brit, Austral and NZ slang* have a look [Hindi *dekhnā* to see]

e Klerk *n* F(rederik) W(illem). born 1936, South African statesman; president (1989–94), second executive deputy president (1994–97). In 1990 he legalized the ANC and released Nelson Mandela from prison, and initiated the abolition of apartheid: Nobel peace prize 1993 jointly with Mandela

e Kooning *n* Willem. 1904–97, US abstract expressionist painter, born in Holland

el. Delaware

e la Beche *n* Henry. 1796–1855, English geologist. His work led to the founding of the Geological Survey (1835)

elacroix *n* (Ferdinand Victor) Eugène. 1798–1863, French romantic painter whose use of colour and free composition influenced impressionism. His paintings of historical and contemporary scenes include *The Massacre at Chios* (1824)

elagoa Bay *n* an inlet of the Indian Ocean, in S Mozambique. Official name: **Baía de Lourenço Marques**

e la Mare *n* Walter (John). 1873–1956, English poet and novelist, noted esp. for his evocative verse for children. His works include the volumes of poetry *The Listeners and Other Poems* (1912) and *Peacock Pie* (1913) and the novel *Memoirs of a Midget* (1921)

elaroche *n* (Hippolyte) Paul. 1797–1859, French painter of portraits and sentimental historical scenes, such as *The Children of Edward IV in the Tower* (1830)

elaunay *n* Robert. 1885–1941, French painter, whose abstract use of colour characterized Orphism, an attempt to introduce more colour into austere forms of Cubism

elaware *n* 1 a state of the northeastern US, on the Delmarva Peninsula: mostly flat and low-lying, with hills in the extreme north and cypress swamps in the extreme south. Capital: Dover. Pop: 817 491 (2003 est). Area: 5004 sq km (1932 sq miles). Abbreviation: **Del.**, (with zip code) **DE** 2 a river in the northeastern US, rising in the Catskill Mountains and flowing south into **Delaware Bay**, an inlet of the Atlantic. Length 660 km (410 miles)

elawarean *adj* 1 of or relating to the state of Delaware or its inhabitants 2 of or relating to the Delaware river

e La Warr *n* Baron, title of *Thomas West*, known as *Lord Delaware*. 1577–1618, English administrator in America; first governor of Virginia (1610)

elay *vb* 1 to put (something) off to a later time 2 to slow up or cause to be late 3 a to hesitate in doing something b to deliberately take longer than necessary to do something ▷ *n* 4 the act of delaying 5 a period of inactivity or waiting before something happens or continues [Old French *des-* off + *laier* to leave]

Delbrück *n* Max. 1906–81, US molecular biologist, born in Germany. Noted for his work on bacteriophages, he shared the Nobel prize for physiology or medicine in 1969

delectable *adj* delightful or very attractive [Latin *delectare* to delight]

delectation *n formal* great pleasure and enjoyment

Deledda *n* Grazia. 1875–1936, Italian novelist, noted for works, such as *La Madre* (1920), on peasant life in Sardinia: Nobel prize for literature 1926

delegate *n* 1 a person chosen to represent others at a conference or meeting ▷ *vb* **-gating, -gated** 2 to entrust (duties or powers) to another person 3 to appoint as a representative [Latin *delegare* to send on a mission]

delegation *n* 1 a group chosen to represent others 2 the act of delegating

de Lesseps *n* Vicomte Ferdinand Marie. 1805–94, French diplomat: directed the construction of the Suez Canal (1859–69) and the unsuccessful first attempt to build the Panama Canal (1881–89)

delete *vb* **-leting, -leted** to remove or cross out (something printed or written) [Latin *delere*] › **deletion** *n*

deleterious (del-lit-eer-ee-uss) *adj formal* harmful or injurious [Greek *dēlētērios*]

Delft *n* 1 a town in the SW Netherlands, in South Holland province. Pop: 97 000 (2003 est) 2 Also called: **delftware** tin-glazed earthenware made in Delft since the 17th century, typically having blue decoration on a white ground 3 a similar earthenware made in England

Delgado *n* Cape Delgado a headland on the NE coast of Mozambique

Delhi *n* 1 the capital of India, in the N central part, on the Jumna river: consists of **Old Delhi** (a walled city reconstructed in 1639 on the site of former cities of Delhi, which date from the 15th century BC) and **New Delhi** to the south, chosen as the capital in 1912, replacing Kolkata (then called Calcutta); university (1922). Pop: 9 817 439 (2001) 2 an administrative division (National Capital Territory) of N India, formerly a Union Territory. Capital: Delhi. Area: 1483 sq km (572 sq miles). Pop: 13 782 976 (2001)

Delian *n* 1 a native or inhabitant of Delos ▷ *adj* 2 of or relating to Delos 3 of or relating to Delius

deliberate *adj* 1 carefully thought out in advance; intentional 2 careful and unhurried: *a deliberate gait* ▷ *vb* **-ating, -ated** 3 to consider (something) deeply; think over [Latin *deliberare* to consider well] › **deliberately** *adv* › **deliberative** *adj*

deliberation *n* 1 careful consideration 2 calmness and absence of hurry 3 deliberations formal discussions

Delibes *n* (Clément Philibert) Léo (leo). 1836–91, French composer, noted particularly for his ballets *Coppélia* (1870) and *Sylvia* (1876), and the opera *Lakmé* (1883)

delicacy *n, pl* **-cies** 1 fine or subtle quality, construction, etc.: *delicacy of craftsmanship* 2 fragile or graceful beauty 3 something that is considered particularly nice to eat 4 frail health 5 refinement of feeling, manner, or appreciation: *the delicacy of the orchestra's playing* 6 need for careful or tactful treatment

delicate *adj* 1 fine or subtle in quality or workmanship 2 having a fragile beauty 3 (of colour, smell, or taste) pleasantly subtle 4 easily damaged; fragile 5 precise or sensitive in action: *the delicate digestive system* 6 requiring tact: *a delicate matter* 7 showing consideration for the feelings of other people [Latin *delicatus* affording pleasure] › **delicately** *adv*

delicatessen *n* a shop selling unusual or imported foods, often already cooked or prepared [German *Delikatessen* delicacies]

delicious *adj* 1 very appealing to taste or smell 2 extremely enjoyable [Latin *deliciae* delights] › **deliciously** *adv*

delight *n* 1 extreme pleasure 2 something or someone that causes this ▷ *vb* 3 to please greatly 4 delight in to take great pleasure in [Latin *delectare* to please] › **delightful** *adj* › **delightfully** *adv*

delighted *adj* greatly pleased

delimit *vb* **-iting, -ited** to mark or lay down the limits of ⟩ **delimitation** *n*

delineate (dill-lin-ee-ate) *vb* **-ating, -ated** **1** to show by drawing **2** to describe in words [Latin *delineare* to sketch out] ⟩ **delineation** *n*

delinquent *n* **1** someone, esp. a young person, who breaks the law ▷ *adj* **2** repeatedly breaking the law [Latin *delinquens* offending] ⟩ **delinquency** *n*

deliquesce *vb* **-quescing, -quesced** (esp. of certain salts) to dissolve in water absorbed from the air [Latin *deliquescere* to melt away] ⟩ **deliquescence** *n* ⟩ **deliquescent** *adj*

delirious *adj* **1** suffering from delirium **2** wildly excited and happy ⟩ **deliriously** *adv*

delirium *n* **1** a state of excitement and mental confusion, often with hallucinations **2** violent excitement [Latin: madness]

delirium tremens (trem-enz) *n* a severe condition characterized by delirium and trembling, caused by chronic alcoholism [New Latin: trembling delirium]

Delius *n* Frederick. 1862–1934, English composer, who drew inspiration from folk tunes and the sounds of nature. His works include the opera *A Village Romeo and Juliet* (1901), *A Mass of Life* (1905), and the orchestral variations *Brigg Fair* (1907)

deliver *vb* **1** to carry (goods or mail) to a destination **2** to hand over: *the tenants were asked to deliver up their keys* **3** to aid in the birth of (offspring) **4** to present (a lecture or speech) **5** to release or rescue (from captivity or danger) **6** to strike (a blow) suddenly **7** *informal* Also: **deliver the goods** to produce something promised [Latin *de-* from + *liberare* to free] ⟩ **deliverance** *n*

delivery *n, pl* **-eries 1 a** the act of delivering goods or mail **b** something that is delivered **2** the act of giving birth to a baby **3** manner or style in public speaking: *her delivery was clear and humorous* **4** *cricket* the act or manner of bowling a ball **5** *S African* a semi-official slogan for the provision of services to previously disadvantaged communities

dell *n chiefly Brit* a small wooded hollow [Old English]

Deller *n* Alfred (George). 1912–79, British countertenor

Del Mar *n* Norman. 1919–94, British conductor, associated esp. with 20th-century British music

Delmarva Peninsula *n* a peninsula of the northeast US, between Chesapeake Bay and the Atlantic

Delorme or **de l'Orme** *n* Philibert. ?1510–70, French Renaissance architect of the Tuileries, Paris

Delors *n* Jacques (Lucien Jean). born 1925, French politician and economist, President of the European Commission (1985–94): originator of the **Delors plan** for closer European union

Delos *n* a Greek island in the SW Aegean Sea, in the Cyclades: a commercial centre in ancient times; the legendary birthplace of Apollo and Artemis. Area: about 5 sq km (2 sq miles). Modern Greek name: **Dhílos**

de los Angeles *n* Victoria. 1923–2005, Spanish soprano

delouse *vb* **-lousing, -loused** to rid (a person or animal) of lice

Delphi *n* an ancient Greek city on the S slopes of Mount Parnassus: site of the most famous oracle of Apollo

Delphic or **Delphian** *adj* **1** of or relating to Delphi or its oracle or temple **2** obscure or ambiguous

delphinium *n, pl* **-iums** or **-ia** a large garden plant with spikes of blue flowers [Greek *delphis* dolphin]

delta *n* **1** the fourth letter in the Greek alphabet (Δ, δ) **2** the flat area at the mouth of some rivers where the main stream splits up into several branches

Delta *n* a state of Nigeria, on the Niger river delta on the Gulf of Guinea. Capital: Asaba. Pop: 4 098 391 (2006). Area: 17 698 sq km (6833 sq miles)

delude *vb* **-luding, -luded** to make someone believe something that is not true [Latin *deludere*]

deluge (del-lyooj) *n* **1** a great flood of water **2** torrential rain **3** an overwhelming number ▷ *vb* **-uging, -uged 4** to flood **5** to overwhelm [Latin *diluere* to wash away]

Deluge *n* the Deluge same as the **Flood¹**

delusion *n* **1** a mistaken idea or belief **2** the state of being deluded ⟩ **delusive** *adj* ⟩ **delusory** *adj*

de luxe *adj* rich or sumptuous; superior in quality: *a de luxe hotel* [French]

Delvaux *n* Paul. 1897–1994, Belgian surrealist painter: his works portray dreamlike figures in mysterious settings

delve *vb* **delving, delved 1** to research deeply or intensively (for information) **2** *old-fashioned* to dig [Old English *delfan*]

demagnetize or **-ise** *vb* **-izing, -ized** or **-ising, -ised** to remove magnetic properties ⟩ **demagnetization** or **-isation** *n*

demagogue or *US sometimes* **demagog** *n* a political agitator who attempts to win support by appealing to the prejudice and passions of the mob [Greek *dēmagōgos* people's leader] ⟩ **demagogic** *adj* ⟩ **demagogy** *n*

demand *vb* **1** to request forcefully **2** to require as just, urgent, etc.: *the situation demands intervention* **3** to claim as a right ▷ *n* **4** a forceful request **5** something that requires special effort or sacrifice: *demands upon one's time* **6** *econ* willingness and ability to purchase goods and services **7 in demand** sought after; popular **8 on demand** as soon as requested: *the funds will be available on demand* [Latin *demandare* to commit to]

demanding *adj* requiring a lot of skill, time, or effort: *a demanding relationship*

demarcation *n* the act of establishing limits or boundaries, esp. between the work performed by members of different trade unions [Spanish *demarcar* to appoint the boundaries of]

Demavend or **Damavand** *n* Mount Demavend a volcanic peak in N Iran, in the Elburz Mountains. Height: 5671 m (18 606 ft)

demean *vb* **1** to undermine the status or dignity of (someone or something) **2 demean oneself** to do something unworthy of one's status or character: *there is no doubt that he will lose face with the boss by having to demean himself in this way* [DE- + MEAN²]

demeanour or *US* **demeanor** *n* the way a person behaves [Old French *de-* (intensive) + *mener* to lead]

demented *adj* mad; insane [Late Latin *dementare* to drive mad] ⟩ **dementedly** *adv*

dementia (dim-men-sha) *n* a state of serious mental deterioration [Latin: madness]

Demerara *n* **1 the Demerara** a river in Guyana, rising in the central forest area and flowing north to the Atlantic at Georgetown. Length: 346 km (215 miles) **2** a former region of what is now Guyana, on the Demerara river

Demeraran *adj* originating from or native to Demerara

demerara sugar *n* brown crystallized cane sugar from the West Indies [after DEMERARA (2)]

demerit *n* **1** a fault or disadvantage **2** *US and Canad* a mark given against a student for failure or misconduct

demesne (dim-mane) *n* **1** land surrounding a house or manor **2** *property law* the possession of one's own property or land **3** a region or district; domain [Old French *demeine*]

Demeter *n* *Greek myth* the goddess of agriculture

demi- *combining form* **1** half: *demirelief* **2** of less than full size, status, or rank: *demigod* [Latin *dimidius* half]

demigod *n* **1 a** a being who is part mortal, part god **b** a lesser deity **2** a godlike person

demijohn *n* a large bottle with a short narrow neck, often encased in wickerwork [probably from French *dame-jeanne*]

demilitarize or **-rise** *vb* **-rizing, -rized** or **-rising, -rised** to remove all military forces from (an area): *demilitarized zone* ⟩ **demilitarization** or **-risation** *n*

De Mille *n* Cecil B(lount). 1881–1959, US film producer and director

demimonde n 1 (esp. in the 19th century) a class of women considered to be outside respectable society because of promiscuity 2 any group considered not wholly respectable [French: half-world]

Demirel n Süleyman. born 1924, Turkish statesman; prime minister (1965–71; 1975–77; 1977–78; 1979–80; 1991–93) and president (1993–2000)

demise n 1 the eventual failure of something originally successful 2 *euphemistic, formal* death 3 *property law* a transfer of an estate by lease ▷ vb **-mising, -mised** 4 *property law* to transfer for a limited period; lease [Old French *demis* dismissed]

demi-sec adj (of wines) medium-sweet

demisemiquaver n *music* a note with the time value of one thirty-second of a semibreve

demist vb to make or become free of condensation › **demister** n

demo n, pl **-os** *informal* 1 short for **demonstration** (1) 2 a demonstration record or tape

demob vb **-mobbing, -mobbed** *Brit, Austral and NZ informal* to demobilize

demobilize or **-lise** vb **-lizing, -lized** or **-lising, -lised** to release from the armed forces › **demobilization** or **-lisation** n

democracy n, pl **-cies** 1 a system of government or organization in which the citizens or members choose leaders or make other important decisions by voting 2 a country in which the citizens choose their government by voting [Greek *dēmokratia*]

democrat n a person who believes in democracy

Democrat n *US politics* a member or supporter of the Democratic Party, the more liberal of the two main political parties in the US › **Democratic** adj

democratic adj of or relating to a country, organization, or system in which leaders are chosen or decisions are made by voting › **democratically** adv

Democratic Republic of Congo n the Democratic Republic of Congo See Congo (1)

Democritus n ?460–?370 BC, Greek philosopher who developed the atomist theory of matter of his teacher, Leucippus

demodulation n *electronics* the process by which an output wave or signal is obtained having the characteristics of the original modulating wave or signal

demography n the study of population statistics, such as births and deaths [Greek *dēmos* the populace + **-GRAPHY**] › **demographic** adj

de Molina n Tirso. Pen name of *Gabriel Téllez*. ?1571–1648, Spanish dramatist; author of the first dramatic treatment of the Don Juan legend *El Burlador de Sevilla* (1630)

demolish vb 1 to tear down or break up (buildings) 2 to put an end to; destroy: *I demolished her argument in seconds* 3 *facetious* to eat up: *he demolished the whole cake* [Latin *demoliri* to throw down] › **demolisher** n › **demolition** n

demon n 1 an evil spirit 2 a person, obsession, etc., thought of as evil or persistently tormenting 3 a person extremely skilful in or devoted to a given activity: *a demon at cricket* [Greek *daimōn* spirit, fate] › **demonic** adj

demonetize or **-tise** vb **-tizing, -tized** or **-tising, -tised** to withdraw from use as currency › **demonetization** or **-tisation** n

demoniac or **demoniacal** adj 1 appearing to be possessed by a devil 2 suggesting inner possession or inspiration: *the demoniac fire of genius* 3 frantic or frenzied: *demoniac activity* › **demoniacally** adv

demonize or **-ise** vb **-izing, -ized** or **-ising, -ised** 1 to make into a demon 2 to describe as evil or guilty: *America is demonized by many in France*

demonolatry n the worship of demons [*demon* + Greek *latreia* worship]

demonology n the study of demons or demonic beliefs [*demon* + **-LOGY**]

demonstrable adj able to be proved › **demonstrably** adv

demonstrate vb **-strating, -strated** 1 to show or prove by reasoning or evidence 2 to display and explain the workings of (a machine, product, etc.) 3 to reveal the existence of: *the adult literacy campaign demonstrated the scale of educational deprivation* 4 to show support or opposition by public parades or rallies [Latin *demonstrare* to point out]

demonstration n 1 a march or public meeting to demonstrate opposition to something or support for something 2 an explanation, display, or experiment showing how something works 3 proof or evidence leading to proof

demonstrative adj 1 tending to show one's feelings freely and openly 2 *grammar* denoting a word used to point out the person or thing referred to, such as *this* and *those* 3 **demonstrative of** giving proof of › **demonstratively** adv

demonstrator n 1 a person who demonstrates how a device or machine works 2 a person who takes part in a public demonstration

demoralize or **-ise** vb **-izing, -ized** or **-ising, -ised** to deprive (someone) of confidence or enthusiasm: *she had been demoralized and had just given up* › **demoralization** or **-isation** n

Demosthenes n 384–322 BC, Athenian statesman, orator, and lifelong opponent of the power of Macedonia over Greece

demote vb **-moting, -moted** to lower in rank or position [DE- + (PRO)MOTE] › **demotion** n

demotic adj of or relating to the common people [Greek *dēmotikos*]

Dempsey n Jack. real name *William Harrison Dempsey*. 1895–1983, US boxer; world heavyweight champion (1919–26)

demur vb **-murring, -murred** 1 to show reluctance; object ▷ n 2 without demur without objecting [Latin *demorari* to linger]

demure adj quiet, reserved, and rather shy [perhaps from Old French *demorer* to delay, linger] › **demurely** adv › **demureness** n

demutualize or **-ise** vb **-izing, -ized** or **-ising, -ised** (of a mutual savings or life-assurance organization) to convert to a public limited company › **demutualization** or **-isation** n

demystify vb **-fies, -fying, -fied** to remove the mystery from: *he attempted to demystify the contemporary jargon of psychology* › **demystification** n

den n 1 the home of a wild animal; lair 2 *chiefly US* a small secluded room in a home, often used for a hobby 3 a place where people indulge in criminal or immoral activities: *a den of iniquity* [Old English *denn*]

Den. Denmark

Denali n another name for Mount **McKinley**

Denali National Park and Preserve n a national park in S central Alaska: contains part of the Alaska Range Area: 7847 sq km (3030 sq miles). Former name: **Mount McKinley National Park**

denarius (din-air-ee-uss) n, pl **-narii** (-nair-ee-eye) a silver coin of ancient Rome, often called a penny in translation [Latin]

denary (dean-a-ree) adj calculated by tens; decimal [Latin *denarius*]

denationalize or **-ise** vb **-izing, -ized** or **-ising, -ised** to transfer (an industry or a service) from public to private ownership › **denationalization** or **-isation** n

denature vb **-turing, -tured** 1 to change the nature of 2 to make (alcohol) unfit to drink by adding another substance

Denbighshire n a county of N Wales: split between Clwyd and Gwynedd in 1974; reinstated with different boundaries in 1996: borders the Irish Sea, with the Cambrian Mountains in the south: chiefly agricultural. Administrative centre: Ruthin. Pop: 94 900 (2003 est). Area: 844 sq km (327 sq miles)

Den Bosch *n* another name for **'s Hertogenbosch**

Dench *n* Dame Judi (Olivia). born 1934, British actress and theatre director: her film roles include *Mrs Brown* (1997), *Notes on a Scandal* (2006), and, since 1995, 'M' in the James Bond series of films

dendrology *n* the study of trees [Greek *dendron* tree + -LOGY]

dene *or* **dean** *n* chiefly Brit a narrow wooded valley

Deneuve *n* Catherine, original name *Catherine Dorléac*. born 1943, French film actress: her films include *Les Parapluies de Cherbourg* (1964), *Belle de jour* (1967), *Indochine* (1992), and *Dancer in the Dark* (2000)

dengue (deng-gee) *n* a viral disease transmitted by mosquitoes, characterized by headache, fever, pains in the joints, and a rash [probably of African origin]

Deng Xiaoping *or* **Teng Hsiao-ping** *n* 1904–97, Chinese Communist statesman; deputy prime minister (1973–76; 1977–80) and the dominant figure in the Chinese government from 1977 until his death. He was twice removed from office (1967–73, 1976–77) and rehabilitated. He introduced economic liberalization, but suppressed demands for political reform, most notably in 1989 when over 2500 demonstrators were killed by the military in Tiananmen Square in Beijing

Den Haag *n* a Dutch name for (The) **Hague**

Den Helder *n* a port in the W Netherlands, in North Holland province: fortified by Napoleon in 1811; naval station. Pop: 60 000 (2003 est)

denial *n* **1** a statement that something is not true **2** a rejection of a request **3** *psychol* a process by which painful thoughts are not permitted into the consciousness

denier (den-yer) *n* a unit of weight used to measure the fineness of silk and man-made fibres [Old French: coin]

denigrate *vb* -grating, -grated to criticize (someone or something) unfairly [Latin *denigrare* to make very black] **> denigration** *n* **> denigrator** *n*

denim *n* **1** a hard-wearing cotton fabric used for jeans, skirts, etc. **2** denims jeans made of denim [French (*serge*) *de Nîmes* (serge) of Nîmes, in S France]

De Niro *n* Robert. born 1943, US film actor. His films include *Taxi Driver* (1976), *Raging Bull* (1980), *GoodFellas* (1990), *Casino* (1995), and *Meet the Parents* (2000)

Denis *n* **1** Maurice. 1870–1943, French painter and writer on art. One of the leading Nabis, he defined a picture as "essentially a flat surface covered with colours assembled in a certain order" **2** Saint Denis *or* Saint Denys 3rd century AD, first bishop of Paris; patron saint of France. Feast day: Oct 9

denizen *n* **1** a person, animal, or plant that lives or grows in a particular place **2** an animal or plant established in a place to which it is not native [Old French *denzein*]

Denmark *n* a kingdom in N Europe, between the Baltic and the North Sea: consists of the mainland of Jutland and about 100 inhabited islands (chiefly Zealand, Lolland, Funen, Falster, Langeland, and Bornholm); extended its territory throughout the Middle Ages, ruling Sweden until 1523 and Norway until 1814, and incorporating Greenland as a province from 1953 to 1979; joined the Common Market (now the EU) in 1973; an important exporter of dairy produce. Language: Danish. Religion: Christian, Lutheran majority. Currency: krone. Capital: Copenhagen. Pop: 5 556 452 (2013 est). Area: 43 031 sq km (16 614 sq miles). Danish name: Danmark. Related adjective: Danish

Denmark Strait *n* a channel between SE Greenland and Iceland, linking the Arctic Ocean with the Atlantic

Denning *n* Baron Alfred Thompson. 1899–1999, English judge; Master of the Rolls 1962-82

Dennis *n* C(larence) J(ames). 1876–1938, Australian poet best known for his humorous poems, esp. in *The Songs of a Sentimental Bloke* (1915) and *The Moods of Ginger Mick* (1916)

denominate *vb* -nating, -nated to give a specific name to; designate [Latin *denominare*]

denomination *n* **1** a group which has slightly different beliefs from other groups within the same faith **2** a unit in a system of weights, values, or measures: *coins of small denomination have been withdrawn* **3** a name given to a class or group; classification **> denominational** *adj*

denominator *n* the number below the line in a fraction, as 8 in $\frac{7}{8}$

denote *vb* -noting, -noted **1** to be a sign or indication of: *these contracts denote movement on the widest possible scale* **2** (of a word or phrase) to have as a literal or obvious meaning [Latin *denotare* to mark] **> denotation** *n*

denouement (day-noo-mon) *n* the final outcome or solution in a play or other work [French]

denounce *vb* -nouncing, -nounced **1** to condemn openly or vehemently **2** to give information against [Latin *denuntiare* to make an official proclamation, threaten]

dense *adj* **1** thickly crowded or closely packed **2** difficult to see through: *dense clouds of smoke* **3** *informal* stupid or dull **4** (of a film, book, etc.) difficult to follow or understand: *the content should be neither too dense nor too abstract* [Latin *densus* thick] **> densely** *adv*

density *n*, *pl* -ties **1** the degree to which something is filled or occupied: *an average population density* **2** *physics* a measure of the compactness of a substance, expressed as its mass per unit volume **3** a measure of a physical quantity per unit length, area, or volume

dent *n* **1** a hollow in the surface of something ▷ *vb* **2** to make a dent in [variant of *dint*]

dental *adj* of or relating to the teeth or dentistry [Latin *dens* tooth]

dental floss *n* a waxed thread used to remove particles of food from between the teeth

dental surgeon *n* same as **dentist**

dentate *adj* having teeth or toothlike notches [Latin *dentatus*]

dentifrice (den-tif-riss) *n* paste or powder for cleaning the teeth [Latin *dens* tooth + *fricare* to rub]

dentine (den-teen) *n* the hard dense tissue that forms the bulk of a tooth [Latin *dens* tooth]

dentist *n* a person qualified to practise dentistry [French *dentiste*]

dentistry *n* the branch of medicine concerned with the teeth and gums

dentition *n* the typical arrangement, type, and number of teeth in a species [Latin *dentitio* a teething]

Denton *n* a town in NW England, in Tameside unitary authority, Greater Manchester. Pop: 26 866 (2001)

D'Entrecasteaux Islands *pl n* a group of volcanic islands in the Pacific, off the SE coast of New Guinea: part of Papua New Guinea. Pop: 49 167 (1990 est). Area: 3141 sq km (1213 sq miles)

denture *n* (*often pl*) a partial or full set of artificial teeth [French *dent* tooth]

denude *vb* -nuding, -nuded **1** to make bare; strip: *the atrocious weather denuded the trees* **2** *geology* to expose (rock) by the erosion of the layers above **> denudation** *n*

denumerable *adj* maths countable

denunciation *n* open condemnation; denouncing [Latin *denuntiare* to proclaim]

Denver *n* a city in central Colorado: the state capital. Pop: 557 478 (2003 est)

deny *vb* -nies, -nying, -nied **1** to declare (a statement) to be untrue **2** to refuse to give or allow: *we have been denied permission* **3** to refuse to acknowledge: *the baron denied his wicked son* [Latin *denegare*]

deodar *n* a Himalayan cedar with drooping branches [Hindi]

deodorant *n* a substance applied to the body to prevent or disguise the odour of perspiration

deodorize *or* -ise *vb* -izing, -ized *or* -ising, -ised to remove or disguise the odour of **> deodorization** *or* -isation *n*

deoxyribonucleic acid *n* same as DNA

Depardieu *n* Gérard. born 1948, French film actor, granted Russian citizenship in 2013. His films include *Jean de Florette* (1986), *Cyrano de Bergerac* (1990), *Green Card*

1991), *The Man in the Iron Mask* (1997), and *Tais-toi* (2003)

depart *vb* **1** to leave **2** to differ or deviate: *to depart from the original concept* [Old French *departir*]

departed *euphemistic adj* **1** dead ▷ *n* **the departed 2 a** a dead person **b** dead people collectively

department *n* **1** a specialized division of a large business organization, hospital, university, etc. **2** a major subdivision of the administration of a government **3** an administrative division in several countries, such as France **4** *informal* a specialized sphere of activity: *wine-making is my wife's department* [French *département*] **> departmental** *adj*

department store *n* a large shop divided into departments selling many kinds of goods

departure *n* **1** the act of departing **2** a divergence from previous custom, rule, etc. **3** a course of action or venture: *the album represents a new departure for them*

depend *vb* **depend on a** to put trust (in); rely (on) **b** to be influenced or determined (by): *the answer depends on four main issues* **c** to rely (on) for income or support [Latin *dependere* to hang from]

dependable *adj* reliable and trustworthy **> dependability** *n* **> dependably** *adv*

dependant *n* a person who depends on another for financial support

USAGE Avoid confusion with **dependent**.

dependence *n* **1** the state of relying on something in order to be able to survive or operate properly **2** reliance or trust: *they had a bond between them of mutual dependence and trust*

dependency *n, pl* **-cies 1** a territory subject to a state on which it does not border **2** *psychol* overreliance on another person or on a drug

dependent *adj* **1** depending on a person or thing for aid or support **2 dependent on** *or* **upon** influenced or conditioned by

USAGE Avoid confusion with **dependant**.

depict *vb* **1** to represent by drawing, painting, etc. **2** to describe in words [Latin *depingere*] **> depiction** *n*

depilatory (dip-pill-a-tree) *adj* **1** able or serving to remove hair ▷ *n, pl* **-ries 2** a chemical used to remove hair [Latin *depilare* to pull out the hair]

deplete *vb* **-pleting, -pleted 1** to use up (supplies or money) **2** to reduce in number [Latin *deplere* to empty out] **> depletion** *n*

deplorable *adj* very bad or unpleasant **> deplorably** *adv*

deplore *vb* **-ploring, -plored** to express or feel strong disapproval of [Latin *deplorare* to weep bitterly]

deploy *vb* to organize (troops or resources) into a position ready for immediate and effective action [Latin *displicare* to scatter] **> deployment** *n*

deponent *n law* a person who makes a statement on oath [Latin *deponens* putting down]

depopulate *vb* **-lating, -lated** to cause to be reduced in population **> depopulation** *n*

deport *vb* **1** to remove forcibly from a country **2 deport oneself** to behave in a specified manner [Latin *deportare* to carry away, banish]

deportation *n* the act of expelling someone from a country

deportee *n* a person deported or awaiting deportation

deportment *n* the way in which a person moves and stands: *she had the manners and deportment of a great lady* [Old French *deporter* to conduct (oneself)]

depose *vb* **-posing, -posed 1** to remove from an office or position of power **2** *law* to testify on oath [Latin *deponere* to put aside]

deposit *vb* **-iting, -ited 1** to put down **2** to entrust (money or valuables) for safekeeping **3** to place (money) in a bank account or other savings account **4** to lay

down naturally: *the river deposits silt* ▷ *n* **5** a sum of money placed in a bank account or other savings account **6** money given in part payment for goods or services **7** an amount of a substance left on a surface as a result of a chemical or geological process [Latin *depositus* put down]

deposit account *n Brit* a bank account that earns interest

depositary *n, pl* **-taries** a person or group to whom something is entrusted for safety

deposition *n* **1** *law* the sworn statement of a witness used in court in his or her absence **2** the act of deposing **3** the act of depositing **4** something deposited [Late Latin *depositio* a laying down, testimony]

depositor *n* a person who places or has money on deposit in a bank or similar organization: *panic-stricken depositors*

depository *n, pl* **-ries 1** a store where furniture, valuables, etc. can be kept for safety **2** same as **depositary**

depot (dep-oh) *n* **1** a place where goods and vehicles are kept when not in use **2** *US, Canad and NZ* a bus or railway station [French]

Depp *n* Johnny, full name *John Christopher*, born 1963, US actor; his films include *Edward Scissorhands* (1990), *Sleepy Hollow* (1999), and the *Pirates of the Caribbean* series (from 2003)

depraved *adj* morally bad; corrupt [Latin *depravare* to distort, corrupt]

depravity *n, pl* **-ties** moral corruption

deprecate *vb* **-cating, -cated** to express disapproval of [Latin *deprecari* to avert, ward off] **> deprecation** *n* **> deprecatory** *adj*

USAGE Avoid confusion with **depreciate**.

depreciate *vb* **-ating, -ated 1** to decline in value or price **2** to deride or criticize [Latin *de-* down + *pretium* price] **> depreciatory** *adj*

USAGE Avoid confusion with **deprecate**.

depreciation *n* **1** *accounting* the reduction in value of a fixed asset through use, obsolescence, etc. **2** a decrease in the exchange value of a currency **3** the act or an instance of belittling

depredation *n* plundering; pillage [Latin *depraedare* to pillage]

depress *vb* **1** to make sad and gloomy **2** to lower (prices) **3** to push down [Old French *depresser*] **> depressing** *adj* **> depressingly** *adv*

depressant *adj* **1** *med* able to reduce nervous or functional activity; sedative ▷ *n* **2** a depressant drug

depressed *adj* **1** low in spirits; downcast **2** suffering from economic hardship, such as unemployment: *the current depressed conditions* **3** pressed down or flattened

depression *n* **1** a mental state in which a person has feelings of gloom and inadequacy **2** an economic condition in which there is substantial unemployment, low output and low investment; slump **3** *meteorol* a mass of air below normal atmospheric pressure, which often causes rain **4** a sunken place

Depression *n* **the Depression** the worldwide economic depression of the early 1930s

depressive *adj* causing sadness and lack of energy

Depretis *n* Agostino. 1813–87, Italian statesman; prime minister (1876–78; 1878–79; 1881–87). His policy led to the Triple Alliance (1882) between Italy, Austria-Hungary, and Germany

deprive *vb* **-priving, -prived** **deprive of** to prevent from having or enjoying [Latin *de-* from + *privare* to deprive of] **> deprivation** *n*

deprived *adj* lacking adequate living conditions, education, etc.: *deprived ghettos*

dept department

d

Deptford n a district in the Greater London borough of Lewisham, on the S bank of the River Thames: formerly the site of the Royal Naval dockyard

depth n 1 the distance downwards, backwards, or inwards 2 intensity of emotion or feeling 3 the quality of having a high degree of knowledge, insight, and understanding 4 intensity of colour 5 lowness of pitch 6 depths a a remote inaccessible region: *the depths of the forest* b the most severe part: *the depths of depression* c a low moral state 7 out of one's depth a in water deeper than one is tall b beyond the range of one's competence or understanding [Middle English *dep* deep]

depth charge n a bomb used to attack submarines that explodes at a preset depth of water

deputation n a body of people appointed to represent others

depute vb -puting, -puted to appoint (someone) to act on one's behalf [Late Latin *deputare* to assign, allot]

deputize or -**tise** vb -tizing, -tized or -tising, -tised (usually foll. by for) to act as deputy

deputy n, pl -ties a person appointed to act on behalf of another [Old French *deputer* to appoint]

De Quincey n Thomas. 1785–1859, English critic and essayist, noted particularly for his *Confessions of an English Opium Eater* (1821)

derail vb to cause (a train or tram) to go off the rails ➤ **derailment** n

derailleur (dee-rail-yer) n a type of gear-change mechanism for bicycles

Derain n André. 1880–1954, French painter, noted for his Fauvist pictures (1905–08)

deranged adj 1 mad, or behaving in a wild and uncontrolled way 2 in a state of disorder [from Old French *desrengier* to disorder, disturb] ➤ **derangement** n

Derbent n a port in S Russia, in the Dagestan Republic on the Caspian Sea: founded by the Persians in the 6th century. Pop: 106 000 (2005 est)

derby n, pl -bies US and Canad a bowler hat

Derby[1] n, pl -bies 1 the Derby an annual horse race for three-year-olds, run at Epsom Downs, Surrey 2 local derby a sporting event between teams from the same area [after the Earl of *Derby*, who founded the race in 1780]

Derby[2] n 1 a city in central England, in Derby unitary authority, Derbyshire: engineering industries (esp. aircraft engines and railway rolling stock); university (1991). Pop: 229 407 (2001) 2 a unitary authority in central England, in Derbyshire. Pop: 233 200 (2003 est). Area: 78 sq km (30 sq miles) 3 a firm-textured pale-coloured type of cheese 4 sage Derby a green-and-white Derby cheese flavoured with sage

Derby[3] n Earl of. title of *Edward George Geoffrey Smith Stanley*. 1799–1869, British statesman; Conservative prime minister (1852; 1858–59; 1866–68)

Derbyshire n a county of N central England: contains the Peak District and several resorts with mineral springs: the geographical and ceremonial county includes the city of Derby, which became an independent unitary authority in 1997. Administrative centre: Matlock. Pop (excluding Derby city): 743 000 (2003 est). Area (excluding Derby city): 2551 sq km (985 sq miles)

deregulate vb -lating, -lated to remove regulations or controls from ➤ **deregulation** n

derelict adj 1 abandoned or unused and falling into ruins ➤ n 2 a social outcast or vagrant [Latin *derelinquere* to abandon]

dereliction n 1 the state of being abandoned 2 dereliction of duty wilful neglect of one's duty

derestrict vb Brit, Austral and NZ to make (a road) free from speed limits ➤ **derestriction** n

deride vb -riding, -rided to speak of or treat with contempt or ridicule [Latin *deridere* to laugh at, scorn] ➤ **derision** n

de rigueur (de rig-gur) adj required by fashion [French, literally: of strictness]

derisive adj mocking or scornful ➤ **derisively** adv

derisory adj too small or inadequate to be considered seriously: *the shareholders have dismissed the offer as derisory*

derivation n the origin or descent of something, such a a word

derivative adj 1 based on other sources; not original ➤ ▪ 2 a word, idea, etc., that is derived from another 3 maths the rate of change of one quantity with respect to another

derive vb -riving, -rived to draw or be drawn (from) in source or origin [Old French *deriver* to spring from]

dermatitis n inflammation of the skin [Greek *derma* skin]

dermatology n the branch of medicine concerned with the skin [Greek *derma* skin + -LOGY] ➤ **dermatologist** n

Dermot MacMurrough n ?1110–71, king of Leinster, who, by enlisting the support of the English to win bac his kingdom, was responsible for the English conquest of Ireland

derogate vb -gating, -gated derogate from to cause to seem inferior; detract from [Latin *derogare* to diminish] ➤ **derogation** n

derogatory (dir-rog-a-tree) adj expressing or showing a low opinion of someone or something

derrick n 1 a simple crane that has lifting tackle slung from a boom 2 the framework erected over an oil well to enable drill tubes to be raised and lowered [after *Derrick,* famous hangman]

Derrida n Jacques. 1930–2004, French philosopher and literary critic, regarded as the founder of deconstruction: author of *L'Ecriture et la différence* (1967)

derring-do n archaic or literary a daring spirit or deed [Middle English *durring don* daring to do]

Derry n 1 a district in NW Northern Ireland, in Co Londonderry. Pop: 106 456 (2003 est). Area: 387 sq km (149 sq miles) 2 another name for **Londonderry**

derv n Brit diesel oil, when used for road transport [*d(iese e(ngine) r(oad) v(ehicle)*]

dervish n a member of a Muslim religious order noted for a frenzied, ecstatic, whirling dance [Persian *darvīsh* mendicant monk]

Derwent n 1 a river in S Australia, in S Tasmania, flowing southeast to the Tasman Sea. Length: 172 km (107 miles) 2 a river in N central England, in N Derbyshire, flowing southeast to the River Trent. Length: 96 km (60 miles) 3 a river in N England, in Yorkshire, rising on the North York Moors and flowing south to the River Ouse. Length: 92 km (57 miles) 4 a river in NW England, in Cumbria, rising on the Borrowdale Fells and flowing north and west to the Iris Sea. Length: 54 km (34 miles)

Derwentwater n a lake in NW England, in Cumbria in the Lake District. Area: about 8 sq km (3 sq miles)

Desai n 1 Morarji (Ranchhodji). 1896–1995, Indian statesman, noted for his asceticism. He founded the Janata party in opposition to Indira Gandhi, whom he defeated in the 1977 election; prime minister of India (1977–79) 2 Kiran, born 1971, Indian writer; her novel The *Inheritance of Loss* (2006) won the Man Booker Prize

desalination n the process of removing salt, esp. from sea water

descale vb to remove the hard coating which sometime forms inside kettles, pipes, etc.

descant n 1 a tune played or sung above a basic melody ➤ adj 2 of the highest member in a family of musical instruments: *a descant clarinet* [Latin *dis-* apart + *cantus* song]

Descartes n René. 1596–1650, French philosopher and mathematician. He provided a mechanistic basis for the philosophical theory of dualism and is regarded as the founder of modern philosophy. He also founded analytical geometry and contributed greatly to the science of optics. His works include *Discours de la méthode* (1637), *Meditationes de Prima Philosophia* (1641), and *Principia Philosophiae* (1644) ▶ Related adjective: **Cartesian**

descend *vb* **1** to move down (a slope, staircase, etc.) **2** to move or fall to a lower level, pitch, etc. **3 be descended from** to be connected by a blood relationship to **4 descend on** to visit unexpectedly **5 descend to** to stoop to (unworthy behaviour) [Latin *descendere*]

descendant *n* a person or animal descended from an individual, race, or species

descendent *adj* descending

descent *n* **1** the act of descending **2** a downward slope **3** a path or way leading downwards **4** derivation from an ancestor; family origin **5** a decline or degeneration

eschamps *n* **1** Émile (*French* emil), full name Émile Deschamps de Saint-Armand. 1791–1871, French poet, dramatist, and librettist: a leading figure in the French romantic movement **2** Eustache. ?1346–?1406, French poet, noted for his *Miroir de mariage*, a satirical attack on women

describe *vb* **-scribing, -scribed 1** to give an account of something (or someone) in words **2** to trace the outline of (a circle, etc.) [Latin *describere* to copy off, write out]

description *n* **1** a statement or account that describes someone or something **2** the act of describing **3** sort, kind, or variety: *antiques of every description*

descriptive *adj* describing something: *it was a very descriptive account of the play* ▶ **descriptively** *adv*

descry *vb* **-scries, -scrying, -scried 1** to catch sight of **2** to discover by looking carefully [Old French *descrier* to proclaim]

desecrate *vb* **-crating, -crated** to violate the sacred character of (an object or place) [DE- + (CON)SECRATE] ▶ **desecration** *n*

desegregate *vb* **-gating, -gated** to end racial segregation in (a school or other public institution) ▶ **desegregation** *n*

deselect *vb* **1** *computers* to cancel (a highlighted selection of data) on a computer screen **2** *Brit politics* (of a constituency organization) to refuse to select (an MP) for re-election ▶ **deselection** *n*

desensitize *or* **-tise** *vb* **-tizing, -tized** *or* **-tising, -tised** to make insensitive or less sensitive: *the patient was desensitized to the allergen*; *to desensitize photographic film*

desert¹ *n* a region that has little or no vegetation because of low rainfall [Church Latin *desertum*]

desert² *vb* **1** to abandon (a person or place) without intending to return **2** *chiefly military* to leave (a post or duty) with no intention of returning [Latin *deserere*] ▶ **deserted** *adj* ▶ **deserter** *n* ▶ **desertion** *n*

desertification *n* a process by which fertile land turns into desert

desert island *n* a small uninhabited island in the tropics

deserts *pl n* **get one's just deserts** get the punishment one deserves [Old French *deserte* something deserved]

deserve *vb* **-serving, -served** to be entitled to or worthy of [Latin *deservire* to serve devotedly]

deserved *adj* rightfully earned ▶ **deservedly** (diz-zerv-d-lee) *adv*

deserving *adj* worthy of a reward, help, or praise

deshabille (day-zab-beel) *or* **dishabille** *n* the state of being partly dressed [French *déshabillé*]

desi *Indian adj* **1** indigenous or local ▶ *n* **2** *informal* a person considered to be of South Asian origin [Hindi]

De Sica *n* Vittorio. 1902–74, Italian film actor and director. His films, in the neorealist tradition, include *Shoeshine* (1946) and *Bicycle Thieves* (1948)

desiccate *vb* **-cating, -cated** to remove most of the water from; dry [Latin *desiccare* to dry up] ▶ **desiccated** *adj* ▶ **desiccation** *n*

design *vb* **1** to work out the structure or form of (something), by making a sketch or plans **2** to plan and make (something) artistically **3** to intend (something)

for a specific purpose: *the move is designed to reduce travelling costs* ▶ *n* **4** a sketch, plan, or preliminary drawing **5** the arrangement or features of an artistic or decorative work: *he built it to his own design* **6** a finished artistic or decorative creation **7** the art of designing **8** an intention; purpose **9 have designs on** to plot to gain possession of [Latin *designare* to mark out, describe]

designate (dez-zig-nate) *vb* **-nating, -nated 1** to give a name to or describe as: *vessels sunk during battle are designated as war graves* **2** to select (someone) for an office or duty; appoint ▶ *adj* **3** appointed, but not yet in office: *a Prime Minister designate* [Latin *designatus* marked out]

designated driver *n* a person who volunteers not to drink alcohol at a social event, in order to drive people who have been drinking

designation *n* **1** something that designates, such as a name **2** the act of designating

designedly (dee-zine-id-lee) *adv* by intention

designer *n* **1** a person who draws up original sketches or plans from which things are made ▶ *adj* **2** designed by a well-known fashion designer: *a wardrobe full of designer clothes* **3** having an appearance of fashionable trendiness: *designer stubble*

designing *adj* cunning and scheming

desirable *adj* **1** worth having or doing: *a desirable lifestyle* **2** arousing sexual desire ▶ **desirability** *n* ▶ **desirably** *adv*

desire *vb* **-siring, -sired 1** to want very much **2** *formal* to request: *we desire your company at the wedding of our daughter* ▶ *n* **3** a wish or longing **4** sexual appetite **5** a person or thing that is desired [Latin *desiderare*]

desirous *adj* (usually foll. by *of*) having a desire for: *deeply desirous of regaining the leadership*

desist *vb* to stop doing: *please desist from talking* [Latin *desistere*]

desk *n* **1** a piece of furniture with a writing surface and usually drawers **2** a service counter in a public building, such as a hotel **3** the section of a newspaper or television station responsible for a particular subject: *the picture desk* [Medieval Latin *desca* table]

deskill *vb* **1** to mechanize or computerize (a job) thereby reducing the skill required to do it **2** to deprive (employees) of the opportunity to use their skills ▶ **deskilling** *n*

desktop *n* **1** the main screen display on a personal computer **2** a personal computer that is small enough to use at a desk ▶ *adj* **3** (esp. of a computer system) for use at a desk

desktop publishing *n* a computer system which combines text and graphics and presents them in a professional-looking printed format

Des Moines *n* **1** a city in S central Iowa: state capital. Pop: 196 093 (2003 est) **2** a river in the N central US, rising in SW Minnesota and flowing southeast to join the Mississippi. Length: 861 km (535 miles)

Desmond *n* 15th Earl of, title of *Gerald Fitzgerald*. died 1583, Anglo-Irish nobleman, who led a Catholic rebellion (1579) against English domination of Ireland

Desmoulins *n* (Lucie Simplice) Camille (Benoît) (kamij). 1760–94, French revolutionary leader, pamphleteer, and orator

desolate *adj* **1** uninhabited and bleak **2** made uninhabitable; devastated **3** without friends, hope, or encouragement **4** gloomy or dismal; depressing ▶ *vb* **-lating, -lated 5** to deprive of inhabitants **6** to make barren; devastate **7** to make wretched or forlorn [Latin *desolare* to leave alone] ▶ **desolately** *adv* ▶ **desolateness** *n*

desolation *n* **1** ruin or devastation **2** solitary misery; wretchedness

De Soto *n* Hernando. ?1500–42, Spanish explorer, who discovered the Mississippi River (1541). Also: **Fernando De Soto**

despair *n* **1** total loss of hope ▶ *vb* **2** to lose or give up hope: *we must not despair of finding a peaceful solution* [Old French *despoir*] ▶ **hopelessness**]

despatch *vb, n* same as **dispatch**

Despenser *n* Hugh le, Earl of Winchester. 1262–1326, English statesman, a favourite of Edward II. Together with his son **Hugh**, *the Younger* (?1290–1326), he was executed by the king's enemies

desperado *n, pl* **-does** or **-dos** a reckless person ready to commit any violent illegal act [probably pseudo-Spanish]

desperate *adj* **1** willing to do anything to improve one's situation **2** (of an action) undertaken as a last resort **3** very grave: *in desperate agony* **4** having a great need or desire: *I was desperate for a child* [Latin *desperare* to have no hope] **› desperately** *adv*

desperation *n* **1** desperate recklessness **2** the state of being desperate

despicable *adj* deserving contempt **› despicably** *adv*

despise *vb* **-pising, -pised** to look down on with contempt [Latin *despicere* to look down]

despite *prep* in spite of [Old French *despit*]

despoil *vb formal* to plunder [Latin *despoliare*]
› despoliation *n*

despondent *adj* dejected or depressed [Latin *despondere* to lose heart] **› despondency** *n* **› despondently** *adv*

despot *n* any person in power who acts tyrannically [Greek *despotēs* lord, master] **› despotic** *adj*
› despotically *adv*

despotism *n* **1** absolute or tyrannical government **2** tyrannical behaviour

des Prés *or* **Desprez** *n* Josquin. ?1450–1521, Flemish Renaissance composer of masses, motets, and chansons

Dessalines *n* Jean-Jacques. ?1758–1806, emperor of Haiti (1804–06) after driving out the French; assassinated

Dessau *n* an industrial city in E Germany, in Saxony-Anhalt: capital of Anhalt state from 1340 to 1918. Pop: 78 380 (2003 est)

dessert *n* the sweet course served at the end of a meal [French]

dessertspoon *n* a spoon between a tablespoon and a teaspoon in size

destination *n* the place to which someone or something is going

destined (dess-tinnd) *adj* **1** certain to be or do something: *the school is destined to close this summer* **2** heading towards a specific destination: *some of the oil was destined for Eastern Europe* [Latin *destinare* to appoint]

destiny *n, pl* **-nies 1** the future destined for a person or thing **2** the predetermined course of events **3** the power that predetermines the course of events [Old French *destinee*]

destitute *adj* lacking the means to live; totally impoverished [Latin *destituere* to leave alone]
› destitution *n*

de-stress *vb* to become or cause to become less stressed or anxious

destroy *vb* **1** to ruin; demolish **2** to put an end to **3** to kill (an animal) **4** to crush or defeat [Latin *destruere* to pull down]

destroyer *n* **1** a small heavily armed warship **2** a person or thing that destroys

destructible *adj* capable of being destroyed

destruction *n* **1** the act of destroying something or state of being destroyed **2** a cause of ruin [Latin *destructio* a pulling down]

destructive *adj* **1** causing or capable of causing harm, damage, or injury **2** intended to discredit, esp. without positive suggestions or help: *destructive speeches against the platform* **› destructively** *adv*

desuetude (diss-syoo-it-tude) *n formal* the condition of not being in use [Latin *desuescere* to lay aside a habit]

desultory (dez-zl-tree) *adj* **1** passing or jumping from one thing to another; disconnected: *desultory conversation* **2** occurring in a random way: *a desultory thought* [Latin *de-* from + *salire* to jump] **› desultorily** *adv*

detach *vb* **1** to disengage and separate **2** *military* to send (a regiment, officer, etc.) on a special assignment [Old French *destachier*] **› detachable** *adj*

detached *adj* **1** *Brit, Austral and S African* separate or standing apart: *a detached farmhouse* **2** showing no emotional involvement: *she continued to watch him in her grave and detached manner*

detachment *n* **1** the state of not being personally involved in something **2** *military* a small group of soldiers separated from the main group

detail *n* **1** an item that is considered separately **2** an item considered to be unimportant: *a mere detail* **3** treatment of individual parts: *the census provides a considerable amount of detail* **4** a small section of a work of art often enlarged to make the smaller features more distinct **5** *chiefly military* **a** personnel assigned a specific duty **b** the duty **6** in detail including all the important particulars ▷ *vb* **7** to list fully **8** *chiefly military* to select (personnel) for a specific duty [Old French *detailler* to cut in pieces]

detailed *adj* having many details

detain *vb* **1** to delay (someone) **2** to force (someone) to stay: *the police detained him for questioning* [Latin *detinere*] **› detainee** *n* **› detainment** *n*

detect *vb* **1** to perceive or notice: *to detect a note of sarcasm* **2** to discover the existence or presence of: *to detect alcohol in the blood* [Latin *detegere* to uncover] **› detectable** *adj* **› detector** *n*

detection *n* **1** the act of noticing, discovering, or sensing something **2** the act or process of extracting information

detective *n* **a** a police officer who investigates crimes **b** same as **private detective**

detente (day-tont) *n* the easing of tension between nations [French]

detention *n* **1** imprisonment, esp. of a suspect awaiting trial **2** a form of punishment in which a pupil is detained after school

detention centre *n* a place where young people may be detained for short periods of time by order of a court

deter *vb* **-terring, -terred** to discourage or prevent someone from doing something by instilling fear or doubt in them [Latin *deterrere*]

detergent *n* **1** a chemical substance used for washing clothes, dishes, etc. ▷ *adj* **2** having cleansing power [Latin *detergens* wiping off]

deteriorate *vb* **-rating, -rated** to become worse [Latin *deterior* worse] **› deterioration** *n*

determinant *adj* **1** serving to determine or affect ▷ *n* **2** a factor that controls or influences what will happen **3** *maths* a square array of elements that represents the sum of certain products of these elements

determinate *adj* definitely limited or fixed

determination *n* **1** the condition of being determined resoluteness **2** the act of making a decision

determine *vb* **-mining, -mined 1** to settle (an argument or a question) conclusively **2** to find out the facts about (something): *the tests determined it was in fact cancer* **3** to fix in scope, extent, etc.: *to determine the degree of the problem* **4** to make a decision [Latin *determinare* to set boundaries to]

determined *adj* firmly decided **› determinedly** *adv*

determiner *n grammar* a word, such as a number, article or personal pronoun, that determines the meaning of a noun phrase

determinism *n* the theory that human choice is not free, but is decided by past events **› determinist** *n, adj*

deterrent *n* **1** something that deters **2** a weapon or set of weapons held by one country to deter another country attacking ▷ *adj* **3** tending to deter [Latin *deterrens* hindering] **› deterrence** *n*

detest *vb* to dislike intensely [Latin *detestari*]
› detestable *adj*

detestation *n* intense hatred

dethrone *vb* **-throning, -throned** to remove from a throne or deprive of any high position **› dethronement** *n*

Detmold n a city in NW Germany, in North Rhine-Westphalia. Pop: 73 880 (2003 est)

detonate vb **-nating, -nated** to make (an explosive device) explode or (of an explosive device) to explode [Latin *detonare* to thunder down] **> detonation** n

detonator n a small amount of explosive or a device used to set off an explosion

detour n a deviation from a direct route or course of action [French]

detoxify vb **-fies, -fying, -fied** to remove poison from **> detoxification** n

detract vb detract from to make (something) seem less good, valuable, or impressive: *I wouldn't want to detract from your triumph* [Latin *detrahere* to pull away, disparage] **> detraction** n **> detractor** n

> **USAGE** *Detract* is sometimes wrongly used where *distract* is meant: *a noise distracted* (not *detracted*) *my attention.*

detriment n disadvantage or damage [Latin *detrimentum* a rubbing off] **> detrimental** adj **> detrimentally** adv

detritus (dit-**trite**-uss) n **1** a loose mass of stones and silt worn away from rocks **2** debris [Latin: a rubbing away] **> detrital** adj

Detroit n **1** a city in SE Michigan, on the Detroit River: a major Great Lakes port; once the largest car-manufacturing centre in the world. Pop: 911 402 (2003 est) **2** a river in central North America, flowing along the US-Canadian border from Lake St Clair to Lake Erie

de trop (de **troh**) adj unwanted or unwelcome: *I know when I'm de trop, so I'll leave you two together* [French]

detumescence n the subsidence of a swelling [Latin *detumescere* to cease swelling]

deuce (dyooss) n **1** *tennis* a tied score that requires one player to gain two successive points to win the game **2** a playing card or dice with two spots [Latin *duo* two]

Deurne n a town in N Belgium, a suburb of E Antwerp: site of Antwerp airport. Pop: 68 308 (2002 est)

deus ex machina n an unlikely development introduced into a play or film to resolve the plot

deuterium n a stable isotope of hydrogen. Symbol: D, ^{2}H [Greek *deuteros* second]

deuterium oxide n same as **heavy water**

Deutsch n Otto Erich. 1883–1967, Austrian music historian and art critic, noted for his catalogue of Schubert's works (1951)

Deutschland n the German name for **Germany**

Deutschmark (**doytch**-mark) or **Deutsche Mark** (doytch-a) n a former monetary unit of Germany [German: German mark]

Deutzia (dyewt-see-a) n a shrub with clusters of pink or white flowers

Deux-Sèvres n a department of W France, in Poitou-Charentes region. Capital: Niort. Pop: 347 652 (2003 est). Area: 6054 sq km (2337 sq miles)

de Valera n Eamon. 1882–1975, Irish statesman; president of Sinn Féin (1917–26) and of the Dáil (1918–22); formed the Fianna Fáil party (1927); prime minister (1937–48; 1951–54; 1957–59) and president (1959–73) of the Irish Republic

de Valois n Dame Ninette. original name *Edris Stannus*. 1898–2001, British ballet dancer and choreographer, born in Ireland: a founder of the Vic-Wells Ballet Company (1931), which under her direction became the Royal Ballet (1956)

devalue vb **-valuing, -valued 1** to reduce the exchange value of (a currency) **2** to reduce the value of (something or someone) **> devaluation** n

devastate vb **-tating, -tated** to damage (a place) severely or destroy it [Latin *devastare*] **> devastation** n

devastated adj shocked and extremely upset **> devastating** adj **> devastatingly** adv

develop vb **1** to grow or bring to a later, more elaborate,

or more advanced stage **2** to come or bring into existence: *the country has developed a consumer society* **3** to make or become gradually clearer or more widely known **4** to follow as a result of something: *Cubism developed from attempts to give painting a more intellectual concept of form* **5** to contract (an illness) **6** to improve the value or change the use of (land) **7** to exploit the natural resources of (a country or region) **8** *photog* to treat (a photographic plate or film) to produce a visible image [Old French *desveloper* to unwrap]

developer n **1** a person who develops property **2** *photog* a chemical used to develop photographs or films

developing country n a poor or nonindustrial country that is seeking to develop its resources by industrialization

development n **1** the process of growing or developing **2** the product of developing **3** an event or incident that changes a situation **4** an area of land that has been developed **> developmental** adj

development area n (in Britain) an area which has experienced economic depression and which is given government assistance to establish new industry

Deventer n an industrial city in the E Netherlands, in Overijssel province, on the River IJssel: medieval intellectual centre; early centre of Dutch printing. Pop: 88 000 (2003 est)

deviant adj **1** deviating from what is considered acceptable behaviour ▷ n **2** a person whose behaviour deviates from what is considered to be acceptable **> deviance** n

deviate vb **-ating, -ated 1** to differ from others in belief or thought **2** to depart from one's usual or previous behaviour [Late Latin *deviare* to turn aside from the direct road] **> deviation** n

device n **1** a machine or tool used for a particular purpose **2** *euphemistic* a bomb **3** a scheme or plan **4** a design or emblem **5** leave someone to his *or* her own devices to leave someone alone to do as he or she wishes [Old French *devis* contrivance + *devise* intention]

devil n **1** *theol* the Devil the chief spirit of evil and enemy of God **2** any evil spirit **3** a person regarded as wicked **4** a person: *lucky devil* **5** a person regarded as daring: *be a devil!* **6** *informal* something difficult or annoying **7** between the devil and the deep blue sea between equally undesirable alternatives **8** give the devil his due to acknowledge the talent or success of an unpleasant person **9** talk of the devil! used when an absent person who has been the subject of conversation arrives unexpectedly **10** the devil used as an exclamation to show surprise or annoyance: *what the devil is she doing here?* ▷ vb **-villing, -villed** *or US* **-viling, -viled 11** to prepare (food) by coating with a highly flavoured spiced mixture **12** *chiefly Brit* to do routine literary work for a lawyer or author [Greek *diabolos* enemy, accuser]

devilish adj **1** of or like a devil; fiendish ▷ adv, adj **2** *old-fashioned, informal* extreme or extremely: *devilish good food* **> devilishly** adv

de Villiers n A(braham) B(enjamin), born 1984, South African cricketer; a prolific run-scorer in all forms of international cricket

devil-may-care adj happy-go-lucky; reckless

devilment n mischievous conduct

devilry n **1** reckless fun or mischief **2** wickedness

devil's advocate n a person who takes an opposing or unpopular point of view for the sake of argument

Devil's Island n one of the three Safety Islands, off the coast of French Guiana: formerly a leper colony, then a French penal colony from 1895 until 1938. Area: less than 2 sq km (1 sq mile). French name: **Île du Diable**

Devine n George (*Alexander Cassady*). 1910–65, British stage director and actor: founded (1956) the English Stage Company in London's Royal Court Theatre

devious adj **1** insincere and dishonest **2** (of a route or course of action) indirect [Latin *devius* lying to one side of the road] **> deviously** adv

devise *vb* **-vising, -vised** to work out (something) in one's mind [Old French *deviser* to divide]

Devizes *n* a market town in S England, in Wiltshire: agricultural and dairy products. Pop: 14 379 (2001)

devoid *adj* **devoid of** completely lacking in a particular quality: *she was a woman totally devoid of humour* [Old French *devoider* to remove]

devolution *n* a transfer of authority from a central government to regional governments [Medieval Latin *devolutio* a rolling down] **› devolutionist** *n, adj*

devolve *vb* **-volving, -volved** to pass or cause to pass to a successor or substitute, as duties or power [Latin *devolvere* to roll down]

Devon *n* **1** Also called: **Devonshire** a county of SW England, between the Bristol Channel and the English Channel, including the island of Lundy: the geographic and ceremonial county includes Plymouth and Torbay, which became independent unitary authorities in 1998; hilly, rising to the uplands of Exmoor and Dartmoor, with wooded river valleys and a rugged coastline. Administrative centre: Exeter. Pop (excluding unitary authorities): 714 900 (2003 est). Area (excluding unitary authorities): 6569 sq km (2536 sq miles) **2** a breed of large red beef cattle originally from Devon

Devonian *adj* **1** *geology* of the period of geological time about 405 million years ago **2** of or relating to Devonshire

Devonshire *n* **8th Duke of,** title of *Spencer Compton Cavendish.* 1833–1908, British politician, also known (1858–91) as Lord Hartington. He led the Liberal Party (1874–80) and left it to found the Liberal Unionist Party (1886)

devote *vb* **-voting, -voted** to apply or dedicate (one's time, money, or effort) to a particular purpose [Latin *devovere* to vow]

devoted *adj* feeling or demonstrating loyalty or devotion: *he was clearly devoted to his family* **› devotedly** *adv*

devotee (dev-vote-**tee**) *n* **1** a person fanatically enthusiastic about a subject or activity **2** a zealous follower of a religion

devotion *n* **1** strong attachment to or affection for someone or something **2** religious zeal; piety **3 devotions** religious observance or prayers **› devotional** *adj*

devour *vb* **1** to eat up greedily **2** to engulf and destroy **3** to read avidly [Latin *devorare* to gulp down] **› devouring** *adj*

devout *adj* **1** deeply religious **2** sincere; heartfelt: *a devout confession* [Latin *devotus* faithful] **› devoutly** *adv*

Devoy *n* Dame Susan (**Elizabeth Anne**). born 1964, New Zealand squash player; winner of the World Open Championship 1985, 1987, 1990, and 1992

De Vries *n* Hugo. 1848–1935, Dutch botanist, who rediscovered Mendel's laws and developed the mutation theory of evolution

dew *n* drops of water that form on the ground or on a cool surface at night from vapour in the air [Old English *dēaw*] **› dewy** *adj*

Dewar *n* **1** Donald. 1937–2000, Scottish Labour politician; secretary of state for Scotland (1997–99); first minister of Scotland (1999–2000) **2** Sir James. 1842–1923, Scottish chemist and physicist. He worked on the liquefaction of gases and the properties of matter at low temperature, invented the vacuum flask, and (with Sir Frederick Abel) was the first to prepare cordite

dewberry *n, pl* **-berries** a type of bramble with blue-black fruits

dewclaw *n* a nonfunctional claw on a dog's leg

de Wet *n* Christian Rudolf. 1854–1922, Afrikaner military commander and politician, who led the Orange Free State army in the second Boer War (1899–1902). He was imprisoned for treason (1914) after organizing an Afrikaner nationalist rebellion

Dewey *n* John. 1859–1952, US pragmatist philosopher and educator: an exponent of progressivism in education, he formulated an instrumentalist theory of learning through experience. His works include *The School and Society* (1899), *Democracy and Education* (1916), and *Logic: the Theory of Inquiry* (1938)

Dewey Decimal System *n* a system of library book classification with ten main subject classes [after Melv Dewey, educator]

de Wint *n* Peter. 1784–1849, English landscape painter

de Witt *n* Johan. 1625–72, Dutch statesman; chief minister of the United Provinces of the Netherlands (1653–72)

dewlap *n* a loose fold of skin hanging under the throat in cattle, dogs, etc. [Middle English *dew* + *lap* hanging flap]

Dewsbury *n* a town in N England, in Kirklees unitary authority, West Yorkshire: formerly a centre of the woollen industry. Pop: 54 341 (2001)

dew-worm *n* US and Canad a large earthworm used as fishing bait

dewy-eyed *adj* innocent and inexperienced

dexter *adj* of or on the right side of a shield, etc., from the bearer's point of view [Latin]

Dexter *n* John. 1925–90, British actor and theatre director

dexterity *n* **1** skill in using one's hands **2** mental quickness [Latin *dexteritas* aptness, readiness]

dexterous *adj* possessing or done with dexterity **› dexterously** *adv*

dextrin or **dextrine** *n* a sticky substance obtained from starch: used as a thickening agent in food [French *dextrine*]

dextrose *n* a glucose occurring in fruit, honey, and in the blood of animals

Dezhnev *n* Cape Dezhnev a cape in NE Russia at the E end of Chukchi Peninsula: the northeasternmost point of Asia. Former name: **East Cape**

DFC (in Britain) Distinguished Flying Cross

dg decigram

DH Brit Department of Health

Dhahran *n* a town in E Saudi Arabia: site of the original discovery of oil in the country (1938)

Dhaka or **Dacca** *n* the capital of Bangladesh, in the E central part: capital of Bengal (1608–39; 1660–1704) and of East Pakistan (1949–71); jute and cotton mills; university (1921). Pop: 12 560 000 (2005 est)

dhal or **dal** *n* **1** the nutritious pealike seed of a tropical shrub **2** a curry made from lentils or other pulses [Hind *dāl*]

dharma *n* **1** Hinduism moral law or behaviour **2** Buddhism ideal truth [Sanskrit]

Dhaulagiri *n* a mountain in W central Nepal, in the Himalayas. Height: 8172 m (26 810 ft)

Dhílos *n* a transliteration of the Modern Greek name for Delos

Dhodhekánisos *n* a transliteration of the Modern Greek name for the Dodecanese

dhoti *n, pl* **-tis** a long loincloth worn by men in India [Hindi]

DI Brit **1** Detective Inspector **2** Donor Insemination: a method of making a woman pregnant by transferring sperm from a man other than her husband or regular partner using artificial means

di- *prefix* **1** twice; two; double: *dicotyledon* **2** containing tw specified atoms or groups of atoms: *carbon dioxide* [Greek]

diabetes (die-a-**beet**-eez) *n* a medical condition in whic the body is unable to control the level of sugar in the blood [Greek: a passing through]

diabetic *n* **1** a person who has diabetes ▷ *adj* **2** of or having diabetes **3** suitable for people suffering from diabetes: *diabetic chocolate*

diabolic *adj* of the Devil; satanic [Greek *diabolos* devil]

diabolical *adj* informal **1** unpleasant or annoying: *the weather was diabolical* **2** extreme: *diabolical cheek* **3** same as **diabolic** **› diabolically** *adv*

diabolism n 1 witchcraft or sorcery 2 worship of devils > **diabolist** n

diaconate n the position or period of office of a deacon [Late Latin diaconatus] > **diaconal** adj

diacritic n a sign placed above or below a character or letter to indicate phonetic value or stress [Greek diakritikos serving to distinguish]

diadem n old-fashioned a small jewelled crown or headband, usually worn by royalty: a gold diadem [Greek: royal headdress]

diaeresis or especially US **dieresis** (die-air-iss-iss) n, pl **-ses** (-seez) the mark (¨) placed over the second of two adjacent vowels to indicate that it is to be pronounced separately, as in naïve [Greek: a division]

Diaghilev n Sergei (**Pavlovich**). 1872–1929, Russian ballet impresario. He founded (1909) and directed (1909–29) the Ballets Russes in Paris, introducing Russian ballet to the West

diagnose vb **-nosing, -nosed** to determine by diagnosis

diagnosis (die-ag-no-siss) n, pl **-ses** (-seez) the discovery and identification of diseases from the examination of symptoms [Greek: a distinguishing] > **diagnostic** adj

diagonal adj 1 maths connecting any two vertices in a polygon that are not adjacent 2 slanting ▷ n 3 a diagonal line, plane, or pattern [Greek dia- through + gōnia angle] > **diagonally** adv

diagram n a sketch or plan showing the form or workings of something [Greek diagraphein to mark out] > **diagrammatic** adj

dial n 1 the face of a clock or watch, marked with divisions representing units of time 2 the graduated disc on a measuring instrument 3 the control on a radio or television set used to change the station 4 a numbered disc on the front of some telephones ▷ vb **dialling, dialled** or US **dialing, dialed** 5 to try to establish a telephone connection with (someone) by operating the dial or buttons on a telephone [Latin dies day]

dialect n a form of a language spoken in a particular geographical area [Greek dialektos speech, dialect] > **dialectal** adj

dialectic n 1 logical debate by question and answer to resolve differences between two views 2 the art of logical argument [Greek dialektikē (tekhnē) (the art) of argument] > **dialectical** adj

dialling tone or US, Canad, Austral and NZ **dial tone** n a continuous sound heard on picking up a telephone receiver, indicating that a number can be dialled

dialogue or US sometimes **dialog** n 1 conversation between two people 2 a conversation in a literary or dramatic work 3 a discussion between representatives of two nations or groups [Greek dia- between + legein to speak]

dialysis (die-al-iss-iss) n, pl **-ses** (-seez) 1 med the filtering of blood through a semipermeable membrane to remove waste products 2 the separation of the particles in a solution by filtering through a semipermeable membrane [Greek dialuein to tear apart, dissolve] > **dialyser** or US **-lyzer** n > **dialytic** adj

diamagnetism n the phenomenon exhibited by substances that are repelled by both poles of a magnet

diamanté (die-a-man-tee) adj decorated with glittering bits of material, such as sequins [French]

diameter n 1 a straight line through the centre of a circle or sphere 2 the length of such a line [Greek dia- through + metron measure]

diametric or **diametrical** adj 1 of or relating to a diameter 2 completely opposed: the diametric opposition of the two camps > **diametrically** adv

diamond n 1 a usually colourless exceptionally hard precious stone of crystallized carbon 2 geometry a figure with four sides of equal length forming two acute and two obtuse angles 3 a playing card marked with one or more red diamond-shaped symbols 4 baseball the playing field ▷ adj 5 (of an anniversary) the sixtieth: diamond wedding [Latin adamas the hardest iron or steel, diamond]

Diana n 1 the virginal Roman goddess of the hunt and the moon. Greek counterpart: **Artemis** 2 title Diana, Princess of Wales, original name Lady Diana Frances Spencer. 1961–97, she married Charles, Prince of Wales, in 1981; they were divorced in 1996: died in a car crash

Diaoyu Islands n the Chinese name for **Senkaku Islands**

diapason (die-a-pay-zon) n music 1 either of two stops found throughout the range of a pipe organ 2 the range of an instrument or voice [Greek dia pasōn through all (the notes)]

diaper n US and Canad a nappy [Medieval Greek diaspros pure white]

diaphanous (die-af-fan-uss) adj (of fabrics) fine and translucent [Greek diaphanēs transparent]

diaphoretic n 1 a drug that causes perspiration or sweat ▷ adj 2 relating to or causing perspiration or sweat

diaphragm (die-a-fram) n 1 anatomy the muscular partition that separates the abdominal cavity and chest cavity 2 same as **cap** (5) 3 a device to control the amount of light entering an optical instrument 4 a thin vibrating disc which converts sound to electricity or vice versa, as in a microphone or loudspeaker [Greek dia- across + phragma fence]

diapositive n a positive transparency; slide

diarist n a person who writes a diary that is subsequently published

diarrhoea or especially US **diarrhea** (die-a-ree-a) n frequent discharge of abnormally liquid faeces [Greek dia- through + rhein to flow]

diary n, pl **-ries** 1 a book containing a record of daily events, appointments, or observations 2 a written record of daily events, appointments, or observations [Latin dies day]

Dias or **Diaz** n Bartholomeu. ?1450–1500, Portuguese navigator who discovered the sea route from Europe to the East via the Cape of Good Hope (1488)

Diaspora (die-ass-spore-a) n 1 the dispersion of the Jews after the Babylonian conquest of Palestine 2 a dispersion of people originally belonging to one nation [Greek: a scattering]

diastase (die-ass-stayss) n an enzyme that converts starch into sugar [Greek diastasis a separation] > **diastasic** adj

diastole (die-ass-stoh-lee) n dilation of the chambers of the heart > **diastolic** adj

diatom n a microscopic unicellular alga [Greek diatomos cut in two]

diatomic adj containing two atoms

diatonic adj of or relating to any scale of five tones and two semitones produced by playing the white keys of a keyboard instrument [Greek diatonos extending]

diatribe n a bitter critical attack [Greek dia- through + tribein to rub]

Diaz n 1 a variant spelling of **Dias** 2 **Cameron**. born 1972, US film actress; films include The Mask (1994), There's Something About Mary (1998), and Gangs of New York (2003) 3 (José de la Cruz) **Porfirio**. 1830–1915, Mexican general and statesman; president of Mexico (1877–80; 1884–1911)

Díaz de Vivar n Rodrigo. the original name of El Cid. See **Cid**

dibble n a small hand tool used to make holes in the ground for bulbs, seeds, or roots [origin unknown]

DiCaprio n **Leonardo**. born 1974, US film actor; his films include Romeo and Juliet (1996), Titanic (1997), Gangs of New York (2002), The Departed (2006), and Django Unchained (2012)

dice n, pl **dice** 1 a small cube, each of whose sides has a different number of spots (1 to 6), used in games of chance ▷ vb **dicing, diced** 2 to cut (food) into small cubes 3 **dice with death** to take a risk [originally plural of DIE²]

dicey adj **dicier, diciest** informal dangerous or tricky

d

dichotomy (die-kot-a-mee) *n, pl* **-mies** division into two opposed groups or parts [Greek *dicha* in two + *temnein* to cut] ➤ **dichotomous** *adj*

> **USAGE** *Dichotomy* should always refer to a division of some kind into two groups. It is sometimes used to refer to a puzzling situation which seems to involve a contradiction, but this use is generally thought to be incorrect.

dichromatic *adj* having two colours [Greek *di-* double + *khrōma* colour]

dick *n slang* **1** *taboo* a penis **2** clever dick an opinionated person [*Dick* familiar form of *Richard*]

dickens *n* the dickens *informal* used as an exclamation to show surprise, confusion, or annoyance: *what the dickens do you think you're doing?* [from the name *Dickens*]

Dickens *n* Charles (John Huffam), pen name Boz. 1812–70, English novelist, famous for the humour and sympathy of his characterization and his criticism of social injustice. His major works include *The Pickwick Papers* (1837), *Oliver Twist* (1839), *Nicholas Nickleby* (1839), *Old Curiosity Shop* (1840–41), *Martin Chuzzlewit* (1844), *David Copperfield* (1850), *Bleak House* (1853), *Little Dorrit* (1857), and *Great Expectations* (1861)

Dickensian *adj* **1** of Charles Dickens **2** denoting poverty, distress, and exploitation, as depicted in the novels of Dickens

Dickinson *n* Emily. 1830–86, US poet, noted for her short, mostly unrhymed, mystical lyrics

dicky¹ *n, pl* **dickies** *informal* a false shirt front [from *Dick*, name]

dicky² *adj* **dickier, dickiest** *Brit and NZ informal* shaky or weak: *a dicky heart* [origin unknown]

dicky-bird *n* a child's word for a bird

dicky-bow *n Brit informal* a bow tie

dicotyledon (die-kot-ill-**leed**-on) *n* a flowering plant with two seed leaves

dictate *vb* **-tating, -tated** **1** to say (words) aloud for another person to transcribe **2** to seek to impose one's will on others ▷ *n* **3** an authoritative command **4** a guiding principle: *the dictates of reason* [Latin *dictare* to say repeatedly]

dictation *n* **1** the act of dictating words to be taken down in writing **2** the words dictated

dictator *n* **1** a ruler who has complete power **2** a person who behaves in a tyrannical manner ➤ **dictatorship** *n*

dictatorial *adj* **1** of or pertaining to a dictator **2** tyrannical; overbearing ➤ **dictatorially** *adv*

diction *n* the manner of pronouncing words and sounds [Latin *dicere* to speak]

dictionary *n, pl* **-aries** **1 a** a book that consists of an alphabetical list of words with their meanings **b** a similar book giving equivalent words in two languages **2** a reference book listing terms and giving information about a particular subject [Late Latin *dictio* word]

dictum *n, pl* **-tums** *or* **-ta 1** a formal statement; pronouncement **2** a popular saying or maxim [Latin]

did *vb* the past tense of **do¹**

didactic *adj* intended to teach or instruct people: *an Impressionist work can be as didactic in its way as a sermon* [Greek *didaktikos* skilled in teaching] ➤ **didactically** *adv* ➤ **didacticism** *n*

diddle *vb* **-dling, -dled** *informal* to swindle [Jeremy *Diddler*, a scrounger in a 19th-century play] ➤ **diddler** *n*

Diderot *n* Denis. 1713–84, French philosopher, noted particularly for his direction (1745–72) of the great French *Encyclopédie*

didgeridoo *n* an Australian Aboriginal deep-toned wind instrument [imitative]

didn't did not

die¹ *vb* **dying, died 1** (of a person, animal, or plant) to cease all biological activity permanently **2** (of something inanimate) to cease to exist **3** to lose

strength, power, or energy by degrees **4** to stop working *the engine died* **5 be dying** to be eager (for something or to do something) **6 be dying of** *informal* to be nearly overcome with (laughter, boredom, etc.) **7 die hard** to change or disappear only slowly: *old loyalties die hard* **8 to die for** *informal* highly desirable: *a salary to die for* ▶ See also **die down, die out** [Old English *dīegan*]

> **USAGE** It was formerly considered incorrect to use the preposition *from* after *die*, but *of* and *from* are now both acceptable: *he died of/from his injuries.*

die² *n* **1** a shaped block used to cut or form metal **2** a casting mould **3** same as **dice** (1) **4 the die is cast** an irrevocable decision has been taken [Latin *dare* to give, play

die down *vb* **1** to lose strength or power by degrees **2** to become calm: *the storm has died down now*

Diefenbaker *n* John George. 1895–1979, Canadian Conservative statesman; prime minister of Canada (1957–63)

Diégo-Suarez *n* the former name of **Antseranana**

die-hard *or* **diehard** *n* a person who resists change

dieldrin *n* a highly toxic crystalline insecticide

dielectric *n* **1** a substance of very low electrical conductivity; insulator ▷ *adj* **2** having the properties of dielectric [Greek *dia-* through + ELECTRIC]

Dien Bien Phu *n* a village in NW Vietnam: French military post during the Indochina War; scene of a major defeat of French forces by the Vietminh (1954)

die out *or* **die off** *vb* to become extinct or disappear after a gradual decline

Dieppe *n* a port and resort in N France, on the English Channel. Pop: 34 670 (2006)

dieresis (die-**air**-iss-iss) *n, pl* **-ses** (-seez) *especially US* same as diaeresis

diesel *n* **1** same as **diesel engine 2** a vehicle driven by a diesel engine **3** *informal* diesel oil [after R. DIESEL]

Diesel *n* Rudolf. 1858–1913, German engineer, who invented the diesel engine (1892)

diesel-electric *n* a locomotive with a diesel engine driving an electric generator

diesel engine *n* an internal-combustion engine in which oil is ignited by compression

diesel oil *or* **diesel fuel** *n* a fuel obtained from petroleum distillation, used in diesel engines

diet¹ *n* **1** the food that a person or animal regularly eats **2** a specific allowance or selection of food, to control weight or for health reasons: *a high-fibre diet* ▷ *vb* **3** to follow a special diet so as to lose weight ▷ *adj* **4** suitable for eating with a weight-reduction diet: *diet soft drinks* [Greek *diaita* mode of living] ➤ **dietary** *adj* ➤ **dieter** *n*

diet² *n* a legislative assembly in some countries [Medieval Latin *dieta* public meeting]

dietary fibre *n* the roughage in fruits and vegetables that aids digestion

dietetic *adj* prepared for special dietary requirements

dietetics *n* the study of diet, nutrition, and the preparation of food

dietician *n* a person qualified to advise people about healthy eating

Dietrich *n* Marlene, real name *Maria Magdalene von Losch*. 1901–92, US film actress and cabaret singer, born in Germany

differ *vb* **1** to be dissimilar in quality, nature, or degree **2** to disagree [Latin *differre* to scatter, be different]

difference *n* **1** the state or quality of being unlike **2** a disagreement or argument **3** the result of the subtraction of one number or quantity from another **4 make a difference** to have an effect **5 split the difference a** to compromise **b** to divide a remainder equally

different *adj* **1** partly or completely unlike **2** new or unusual **3** not identical or the same; other: *he wears a different tie every day* ➤ **differently** *adv*

ferential *adj* 1 of, relating to, or using a difference *maths* involving differentials ▷ *n* 3 a factor that ifferentiates between two comparable things 4 *maths* a minute difference between two values in a scale 5 *chiefly Brit* the difference between rates of pay for different types of abour, esp. within a company or industry

ferential calculus *n* the branch of mathematics oncerned with derivatives and differentials

ferential gear *n* the gear in the driving axle of a road ehicle that permits one driving wheel to rotate faster han the other when cornering

ferentiate *vb* **-ating, -ated** 1 to perceive or show the ifference (between) 2 to make (one thing) distinct rom other such things 3 *maths* to determine the erivative of a function or variable ❯ **differentiation** *n*

ficult *adj* 1 not easy to do, understand, or solve 2 not asily pleased or satisfied: *a difficult patient* 3 full of ardships or trials: *he had recently had a difficult time with his* ob *as a self-employed builder*

ficulty *n, pl* **-ties** 1 the state or quality of being ifficult 2 a task or problem that is hard to deal with 3 a roublesome or embarrassing situation: *in financial ifficulties* 4 an objection or obstacle: *you're just making ifficulties* 5 lack of ease; awkwardness: *he could run only* ith difficulty [Latin *difficultas*]

fident *adj* lacking self-confidence; shy [Latin *dis-* not + *dere* to trust] ❯ **diffidence** *n* ❯ **diffidently** *adv*

fract *vb* to cause to undergo diffraction ❯ **diffractive** *adj*

fraction *n* 1 *physics* a deviation in the direction of a vave at the edge of an obstacle in its path 2 the ormation of light and dark fringes by the passage of ight through a small aperture [Latin *diffringere* to shatter]

ffuse *vb* **-fusing, -fused** 1 to spread over a wide area *physics* to cause to undergo diffusion ▷ *adj* 3 spread out ver a wide area 4 lacking conciseness [Latin *diffusus* pread abroad] ❯ **diffuser** *n* ❯ **diffusible** *adj*

ffusion *n* 1 the act of diffusing or the fact of being iffused; dispersion 2 *physics* the random thermal motion of atoms and molecules in gases, liquids, and ome solids 3 *physics* the transmission or reflection of ight, in which the radiation is scattered in many irections

g *vb* **digging, dug** 1 to cut into, break up, and turn over r remove (earth), esp. with a spade 2 to excavate (a hole r tunnel) by digging, usually with an implement or (of nimals) with claws 3 to obtain by digging: *dig out potatoes* to find by effort or searching: *he dug out a mini cassette om his pocket* 5 *informal* to like or understand 6 (foll. by *in* r *into*) to thrust or jab ▷ *n* 7 the act of digging 8 an rchaeological excavation 9 a thrust or poke 10 a utting remark ▶ See also **dig in** [Middle English *diggen*]

gest *vb* 1 to subject (food) to a process of digestion 2 to bsorb mentally ▷ *n* 3 a shortened version of a book, eport, or article [Latin *digerere* to divide] ❯ **digestible** *adj*

gestion *n* 1 the process of breaking down food into asily absorbed substances 2 the body's system for oing this

digestive *adj* relating to digestion

digger *n* a machine used for excavation

dig in *vb* 1 to mix (compost or fertilizer) into the soil by digging 2 to begin to eat vigorously 3 *informal* (of soldiers) to dig a trench and prepare for an enemy attack 4 **dig one's heels in** *informal* to refuse to move or be persuaded

digit (dij-it) *n* 1 a finger or toe 2 any numeral from 0 to 9 [Latin *digitus* toe, finger]

digital *adj* 1 displaying information as numbers rather than with a dial 2 representing data as a series of numerical values 3 of or possessing digits ❯ **digitally** *adv*

digital audio tape *n* magnetic tape on which sound is recorded digitally, giving high-fidelity reproduction

digital clock *or* **digital watch** *n* a clock or watch in which the time is indicated by digits rather than by hands on a dial

digital computer *n* a computer in which the input consists of numbers, letters, and other characters that are represented internally in binary notation

digitalis *n* a drug made from foxglove leaves: used as a heart stimulant [Latin: relating to a finger (from the shape of the foxglove flowers)]

digital recording *n* a sound recording process that converts audio or analogue signals into a series of pulses

digital switchover *n* the process of changing the method of transmitting television from analogue to digital format

digital television *n* television in which the picture information is transmitted in digital form and decoded at the television receiver

digitate *adj* 1 (of leaves) having leaflets in the form of a spread hand 2 (of animals) having digits

digitize *or* **-ise** *vb* **-izing, -ized** *or* **-ising, -ised** to transcribe (data) into a digital form for processing by a computer ❯ **digitizer** *or* **-iser** *n*

dignified *adj* calm, impressive, and worthy of respect

dignify *vb* **-fies, -fying, -fied** 1 to add distinction to: *the meeting was dignified by the minister* 2 to add a semblance of dignity to by the use of a pretentious name or title: *she dignifies every plant with its Latin name* [Latin *dignus* worthy + *facere* to make]

dignitary *n, pl* **-taries** a person of high official position or rank

dignity *n, pl* **-ties** 1 serious, calm, and controlled behaviour or manner 2 the quality of being worthy of honour 3 sense of self-importance: *he considered the job beneath his dignity* [Latin *dignus* worthy]

digraph *n* two letters used to represent a single sound, such as *gh* in *tough*

digress *vb* to depart from the main subject in speech or writing [Latin *digressus* turned aside] ❯ **digression** *n*

digs *pl n Brit, Austral and S African informal* lodgings [from *diggings*, perhaps referring to where one digs or works]

dihedral *adj* having or formed by two intersecting planes

Dijon *n* a city in E France: capital of the former duchy of Burgundy. Pop: 151 576 (2008)

dilapidated *adj* (of a building) having fallen into ruin [Latin *dilapidare* to waste] ❯ **dilapidation** *n*

dilate *vb* **-lating, -lated** to make or become wider or larger: *her eyes dilated in the dark* [Latin *dilatare* to spread out] ❯ **dilation** *or* **dilatation** *n*

dilatory (dill-a-tree) *adj* tending or intended to waste time [Late Latin *dilatorius*] ❯ **dilatorily** *adv* ❯ **dilatoriness** *n*

dildo *n, pl* **-dos** an object used as a substitute for an erect penis [origin unknown]

dilemma *n* a situation offering a choice between two equally undesirable alternatives [Greek *di-* double + *lēmma* proposition]

dilettante (dill-it-tan-tee) *n, pl* **-tantes** *or* **-tanti** a person whose interest in a subject is superficial rather than serious [Italian] > **dilettantism** *n*

Dili *or* **Dilli** *n* the capital (from 2002) of independent East Timor: the former capital (until 1976) of Portuguese Timor. Pop: 50 000 (2005 est)

diligent *adj* **1** careful and persevering in carrying out tasks or duties **2** carried out with care and perseverance: *a diligent approach to work* [Latin *diligere* to value] > **diligence** *n* > **diligently** *adv*

dill *n* a sweet-smelling herb used for flavouring [Old English *dile*]

dilly-dally *vb* **-lies, -lying, -lied** *Brit, Austral and NZ informal* to dawdle or waste time [reduplication of *dally*]

dilute *vb* **-luting, -luted** **1** to make (a liquid) less concentrated by adding water or another liquid **2** to make (someone's power, idea, or role) weaker or less effective: *socialists used their majority in parliament to dilute legislation crucial to developing a market economy* > *adj* **3** *chem* (of a solution) having a low concentration [Latin *diluere*] > **dilution** *n*

diluvian *or* **diluvial** *adj* of a flood, esp. the great Flood described in the Old Testament [Latin *diluere* to wash away]

dim *adj* **dimmer, dimmest** **1** badly lit **2** not clearly seen; faint: *a dim figure in the doorway* **3** not seeing clearly: *eyes dim with tears* **4** *informal* mentally dull **5** not clear in the mind; obscure: *a dim awareness* **6** lacking in brightness or lustre: *a dim colour* **7** **take a dim view of** to disapprove of > *vb* **dimming, dimmed** **8** to become or cause to become dim **9** to cause to seem less bright **10** *US and Canad* same as **dip** (4) [Old English *dimm*] > **dimly** *adv* > **dimness** *n*

DiMaggio *n* Joe. 1914–99, US baseball player

Dimashq *n* an Arabic name for **Damascus**

Dimbleby *n* Richard. 1913–65, British broadcaster

dime *n* a coin of the US and Canada worth ten cents [Latin *decem* ten]

dimension *n* **1** an aspect or factor: *the attack brought a whole new dimension to the bombing campaign* **2 dimensions** scope or extent **3** (*often pl*) a measurement of the size of something in a particular direction [Latin *dimensio* an extent] > **dimensional** *adj*

dimer *n chem* a molecule made up of two identical molecules bonded together

diminish *vb* **1** to make or become smaller, fewer, or less **2** *music* to decrease (a minor interval) by a semitone **3** to reduce in authority or status [Latin *deminuere* to make smaller + archaic *minish* to lessen]

diminuendo *music* *n, pl* **-dos** **1 a** a gradual decrease in loudness **b** a passage which gradually decreases in loudness > *adv* **2** gradually decreasing in loudness [Italian]

diminution *n* reduction in size, volume, intensity, or importance [Latin *deminutio*]

diminutive *adj* **1** very small; tiny **2** *grammar* **a** denoting an affix added to a word to convey the meaning *small* or *unimportant* or to express affection, as for example, the suffix *-ette* in French **b** denoting a word formed by the addition of a diminutive affix > *n* **3** *grammar* a diminutive word or affix > **diminutiveness** *n*

Dimitrovo *n* the former name (1949–62) of **Pernik**

dimmer *n* **1** a device for dimming an electric light **2** *US* **a** a dipped headlight on a road vehicle **b** a parking light on a car

dimple *n* **1** a small natural dent on the cheeks or chin > *vb* **-pling, -pled** **2** to produce dimples by smiling [Middle English *dympull*]

dimwit *n informal* a stupid person > **dim-witted** *adj*

din *n* **1** a loud unpleasant confused noise > *vb* **dinning, dinned** **2** **din something into someone** to instil something into someone by constant repetition [Old English *dynn*]

Dinan *n* a town in NW France, in Brittany, on the estuary of the River Rance: medieval buildings, including town walls and castle: tourism, hosiery, cider: Pop: 10 953 (2008)

Dinant *n* a town in S Belgium, on the River Meuse below steep limestone cliffs: 11th-century citadel: famous in the Middle Ages for fine brassware, known as *dinanderie*: tourism, metalwork, biscuits. Pop: 12 719 (2004 est)

dinar (dee-nahr) *n* a monetary unit of various Balkan, Middle Eastern, and North African countries [Latin *denarius* a Roman coin]

Dinaric Alps *pl n* a mountain range in W Croatia, Bosnia-Herzegovina, and Serbia: connected with the main Alpine system by the Julian Alps. Highest peak: Troglav, 1913 m (6277 ft)

d'Indy *n* (Paul Marie Theodore) Vincent. 1851–1931, French composer. His works include operas, chamber music, and the *Symphony on a French Mountaineer's Song* (1866)

dine *vb* **dining, dined** **1** to eat dinner **2 dine on** *or* **off** to make one's meal of: *the guests dined on roast beef* [Old French *disner*]

diner *n* **1** a person eating a meal in a restaurant **2** *chiefly US and Canad* a small cheap restaurant **3** short for **dining car**

Dinesen *n* Isak, pen name of *Baroness Karen Blixen*. 1885–1962, Danish author of short stories in Danish and English, including *Seven Gothic Tales* (1934) and *Winter's Tales* (1942). Her life story was told in the film *Out of Africa* (1986)

dinette *n* an alcove or small area for use as a dining room

ding *n chiefly US, Canad, Austral and NZ informal* a small dent in a vehicle

Dingaan *n* died 1840, Zulu chief (1828–40), who fought the Boer colonists in Natal

ding-dong *n* **1** the sound of a bell **2** *Brit informal* a violent exchange of blows or words [imitative]

dinges (ding-uss) *n S African informal* a jocular word for something whose name is unknown or forgotten; thingumabob [Dutch *ding* thing]

dinghy (ding-ee, ding-gee) *n, pl* **-ghies** a small boat, powered by sail, oars, or outboard motor [Hindi or Bengali *dingi*]

dingle *n* a small wooded hollow or valley [origin unknown]

dingo *n, pl* **-goes** an Australian native wild dog [Aboriginal]

dingy (din-jee) *adj* **-gier, -giest** **1** *Brit, Austral and NZ* dull, neglected, and drab: *he waited in this dingy little outer office* **2** shabby and discoloured: *she was wearing dingy white overalls* [origin unknown] > **dinginess** *n*

dining car *n* a railway coach in which meals are served

dining room *n* a room where meals are eaten

dinkum *adj Austral and NZ informal* genuine or right: *a fair dinkum offer* [English dialect: work]

dinky *adj* **dinkier, dinkiest** *chiefly Brit informal* small and neat; dainty [dialect *dink* neat]

dinky-di *adj Austral informal* typical [variant of DINKUM]

dinner *n* **1** the main meal of the day, eaten either in the evening or at midday **2** a formal social occasion at which an evening meal is served [Old French *disner* to dine]

dinner jacket *n* a man's semiformal black evening jacket without tails

dinner service *n* a set of matching dishes suitable for serving a meal

dinosaur *n* any of a large order of extinct prehistoric reptiles many of which were gigantic [Greek *deinos* fearful + *sauros* lizard]

dint *n* **by dint of** by means of: *by dint of their own efforts* [Old English *dynt* a blow]

D'Inzeo *n* Piero, born 1923, and his brother Raimondo, 1925–2013, Italian showjumping riders

Dio Cassius *n* ?155–?230 AD, Roman historian. His *History of Rome* covers the period of Rome's transition from Republic to Empire

d

...ocesan adj of or relating to a diocese

...ocese (die-a-siss) n the district over which a bishop ...as control [Greek dioikēsis administration]

...o Chrysostom n 2nd century AD, Greek orator and ...hilosopher

...ocletian n full name Gaius Aurelius Valerius Diocletianus. ...45–313 AD, Roman emperor (284–305), who divided the ...mpire into four administrative units (293) and ...nstigated the last severe persecution of the Christians ...303)

...ode n **1** a semiconductor device for converting ...lternating current to direct current **2** an electronic ...alve with two electrodes between which a current can ...low only in one direction [Greek di- double + hodos a way, ...oad]

...odorus Siculus n 1st century BC, Greek historian, ...oted for his history of the world in 40 books, of which ...5 are extant

...oecious (die-eesh-uss) adj (of plants) having the male ...nd female reproductive organs on separate plants ...Greek di- twice + oikia house]

...ogenes n ?412–?323 BC, Greek Cynic philosopher, who ...ejected social conventions and advocated self- ...ufficiency and simplicity of life

...omede Islands pl n two small islands in the Bering ...trait, separated by the international date line and by ...he boundary line between the US and Russia

...on n Céline. born 1968, Canadian singer. Her ...vorldwide hit singles include 'My Heart Will Go On' ...1998)

...onysian (die-on-niz-zee-an) adj wild or orgiastic [from ...DIONYSUS]

...onysius n called the Elder. ?430–367 BC, tyrant of ...yracuse (405–367), noted for his successful campaigns ...gainst Carthage and S Italy

...onysius Exiguus n died ?556 AD, Scythian monk and ...cholar, who is believed to have introduced the current ...nethod of reckoning dates on the basis of the Christian ...ra

...onysius of Halicarnassus n died ?7 BC, Greek ...istorian and rhetorician; author of a history of Rome

...onysius the Areopagite n 1st century AD, Greek ...hristian, thought to have been the first Bishop of ...\thens: long considered the author of influential ...heological works actually written c. 500

...onysus n Greek myth the god of wine

...ophantus n 3rd century AD, Greek mathematician, ...oted for his treatise on the theory of numbers, ...rithmetica

...optre or US **diopter** (die-op-ter) n a unit for measuring ...he refractive power of a lens [Greek dia- through + ...vsesthai to see]

...or n Christian. 1905–57, French couturier, noted for his ...Jew Look of narrow waist with a long full skirt (1947); ...e also created the waistless sack dress

...orama n **1** a miniature three-dimensional scene, in ...vhich models of figures are seen against a background ...a picture made up of illuminated translucent curtains, ...iewed through an aperture [Greek dia- through + horama ...iew]

...oxide n an oxide containing two oxygen atoms per ...nolecule

...p vb **dipping, dipped 1** to plunge or be plunged quickly ...r briefly into a liquid **2** to put one's hands into ...omething, esp. to obtain an object: she dipped into her ...andbag looking for change **3** to slope downwards **4** to ...witch (car headlights) from the main to the lower ...eam **5** to undergo a slight decline, esp. temporarily: ...ales dipped in November **6** to immerse (farm animals) ...riefly in a chemical to rid them of insects **7** to lower or ...e lowered briefly: she dipped her knee in a curtsy ▷ n **8** the ...ct of dipping **9** a brief swim **10** a liquid chemical in ...vhich farm animals are dipped **11** a depression, esp. in a ...andscape **12** a momentary sinking down **13** a creamy

mixture into which pieces of food are dipped before being eaten ▶ See also **dip into** [Old English dyppan]

Dip Ed (in Britain) Diploma in Education

diphtheria (dif-theer-ree-a) n a contagious disease producing fever and difficulty in breathing and swallowing [Greek diphthera leather; from the membrane that forms in the throat]

diphthong n a vowel sound, occupying a single syllable, in which the speaker's tongue moves continuously from one position to another, as in the pronunciation of a in late [Greek di- double + phthongos sound]

dip into vb **1** to draw upon: he dipped into his savings **2** to read passages at random from (a book or journal)

diploid adj biology denoting a cell or organism with pairs of homologous chromosomes [Greek di- double + -ploos -fold]

diploma n a document conferring a qualification or recording successful completion of a course of study [Latin: official document, literally: letter folded double]

diplomacy n **1** the conduct of the relations between nations by peaceful means **2** skill in the management of international relations **3** tact or skill in dealing with people

diplomat n an official, such as an ambassador, engaged in diplomacy

diplomatic adj **1** of or relating to diplomacy **2** skilled in negotiating between nations **3** tactful in dealing with people [French diplomatique concerning the documents of diplomacy; see DIPLOMA] **> diplomatically** adv

diplomatic immunity n the freedom from legal action and exemption from taxation which diplomats have in the country where they are working

dipole n **1** two equal but opposite electric charges or magnetic poles separated by a small distance **2** a molecule that has two such charges or poles **> dipolar** adj

dipper n **1** a ladle used for dipping **2** a songbird that inhabits fast-flowing streams

diprotodont (die-pro-toe-dont) n a marsupial with fewer than three upper incisor teeth on each side of the jaw

dipsomania n a compulsive desire to drink alcoholic beverages [Greek dipsa thirst + mania madness] **> dipsomaniac** n, adj

dipstick n a rod with notches on it dipped into a container to indicate the fluid level

dip switch n a device for dipping headlights on a vehicle

dipterous adj having two wings or winglike parts [Greek dipteros two-winged]

diptych (dip-tik) n a painting on two hinged panels [Greek di- double + ptuchē a panel]

Dirac n Paul (Adrien Maurice). 1902–84, English physicist, noted for his work on the application of relativity to quantum mechanics and his prediction of electron spin and the positron: shared the Nobel prize for physics 1933

dire adj disastrous, urgent, or terrible: he was now in dire financial straits [Latin dirus ominous]

direct adj **1** shortest; straight: a direct route **2** without intervening people: they secretly arranged direct links to their commanders **3** honest; frank: he was polite but very direct **4** diametric: the direct opposite **5** in an unbroken line of descent: a direct descendant ▷ adv **6** directly; straight ▷ vb **7** to conduct or control the affairs of **8** to give orders with authority to (a person or group) **9** to tell (someone) the way to a place **10** to address (a letter, parcel, etc.) **11** to address (a look or remark) at someone: the look she directed at him was one of unconcealed hatred **12 a** to provide guidance to (actors, cameramen, etc.) in (a play or film) **b** to supervise the making or staging of (a film or play) [Latin dirigere to guide] **> directness** n

direct access n a method of reading data from a computer file without reading through the file from the beginning

direct current *n* an electric current that flows in one direction only

direct debit *n* an order given to a bank or other financial institution by an account holder to pay an amount of money from the account to a specified person or company at regular intervals

direction *n* 1 the course or line along which a person or thing moves, points, or lies 2 management or guidance: *the campaign was successful under his direction* 3 the work of a stage or film director

directional *adj* 1 of or showing direction 2 *electronics* (of an aerial) transmitting or receiving radio waves more effectively in some directions than in others

directions *pl n* instructions for doing something or for reaching a place

directive *n* an instruction; order

directly *adv* 1 in a direct manner 2 at once; without delay 3 immediately or very soon: *I'll do that directly* ▷ *conj* 4 as soon as: *we left directly the money arrived*

direct object *n grammar* a noun, pronoun, or noun phrase denoting the person or thing receiving the direct action of a verb. For example, *a book* in *They bought Anne a book*

director *n* 1 a person or thing that directs or controls 2 a member of the governing board of a business, trust, etc. 3 the person responsible for the artistic and technical aspects of the making of a film or television programme ▷ **directorial** *adj* ▷ **directorship** *n*

directorate *n* 1 a board of directors 2 the position of director

director-general *n, pl* **directors-general** a person in overall charge of certain large organizations

directory *n, pl* **-ries** 1 a book listing names, addresses, and telephone numbers of individuals or business companies 2 *computers* an area of a disk containing the names and locations of the files it currently holds

direct speech *n* the reporting of what someone has said by quoting the exact words

direct tax *n* a tax paid by the person or organization on which it is levied

dirge *n* 1 a chant of lamentation for the dead 2 any mournful song [Latin *dirige* direct (imperative), opening word of antiphon used in the office of the dead]

Dirichlet *n* Peter Gustav Lejeune. 1805–59, German mathematician, noted for his work on number theory and calculus

dirigible (dir-rij-jib-bl) *adj* 1 able to be steered ▷ *n* 2 same as **airship** [Latin *dirigere* to direct]

dirk *n* a dagger, formerly worn by Scottish Highlanders [Scots *durk*]

dirndl *n* 1 a woman's dress with a full gathered skirt and fitted bodice 2 a gathered skirt of this kind [from German]

dirt *n* 1 any unclean substance, such as mud; filth 2 loose earth; soil 3 packed earth, cinders, etc., used to make a racetrack 4 obscene speech or writing 5 *informal* harmful gossip [Old Norse *drit* excrement]

dirt-cheap *adj, adv* at an extremely low price

dirt-poor *adj chiefly US* extremely poor

dirt track *n* a racetrack made of packed earth or cinders

dirty *adj* **dirtier, dirtiest** 1 covered or marked with dirt; filthy 2 causing one to become grimy: *a dirty job* 3 (of a colour) not clear and bright 4 unfair, dishonest, or unkind: *dirty tricks* 5 a obscene: *dirty jokes* b sexually clandestine: *a dirty weekend* 6 revealing dislike or anger: *a dirty look* 7 (of weather) rainy or stormy 8 **dirty work** unpleasant or illicit activity ▷ *n* 9 **do the dirty on** *informal* to behave meanly towards ▷ *vb* **dirties, dirtying, dirtied** 10 to make dirty; soil ▷ **dirtiness** *n*

dirty bomb *n informal* a bomb made from nuclear waste combined with conventional explosives that is capable of spreading radioactive material over a wide area

dis *vb* **disses, dissing, dissed** *slang, chiefly US* same as **diss**

dis- *prefix* 1 indicating reversal: *disconnect* 2 indicating negation or lack: *dissimilar; disgrace* 3 indicating removal or release: *disembowel*

disability *n, pl* **-ties** 1 a severe physical or mental illness that restricts the way a person lives his or her life 2 something that disables someone

disable *vb* **-abling, -abled** to make ineffective, unfit, or incapable ▷ **disablement** *n*

disabled ▷ *adj* lacking one or more physical powers, such as the ability to walk or to coordinate one's movements

> **USAGE** The use of *the disabled, the blind*, etc. can be offensive and should be avoided. Instead you should talk about *disabled people, blind people*, etc.

disabuse *vb* **-abusing, -abused** to rid (someone) of a mistaken idea: *Arnold felt unable to disabuse her of her prejudices*

disaccharide (die-sack-a-ride) *n* a sugar, such as sucrose, whose molecules consist of two linked monosaccharides

disadvantage *n* 1 an unfavourable or harmful circumstance 2 **at a disadvantage** in a less favourable position than other people: *he continued to insist that he was at a disadvantage at the hearings* ▷ **disadvantageous** *adj*

disadvantaged *adj* socially or economically deprived

disaffected *adj* having lost loyalty to or affection for someone or something; alienated: *three million disaffected voters* ▷ **disaffection** *n*

disagree *vb* **-greeing, -greed** 1 to have differing opinions or argue about (something) 2 to fail to correspond; conflict 3 to cause physical discomfort to: *curry disagrees with me*

disagreeable *adj* 1 (of an incident or situation) unpleasant 2 (of a person) bad-tempered or disobliging ▷ **disagreeably** *adv*

disagreement *n* 1 refusal or failure to agree 2 a difference between results, totals, etc., which shows that they cannot all be true 3 an argument

disallow *vb* to reject as untrue or invalid; cancel

disappear *vb* 1 to cease to be visible; vanish 2 to go away or become lost, esp. without explanation 3 to cease to exist: *the pain has disappeared* ▷ **disappearance** *n*

disappoint *vb* 1 to fail to meet the expectations or hopes of; let down 2 to prevent the fulfilment of (a plan, etc.) frustrate [Old French *desapointier*] ▷ **disappointed** *adj* ▷ **disappointing** *adj*

disappointment *n* 1 the feeling of being disappointed 2 a person or thing that disappoints

disapprobation *n* disapproval

disapprove *vb* **-proving, -proved** to consider wrong or bad ▷ **disapproval** *n* ▷ **disapproving** *adj*

disarm *vb* 1 to deprive of weapons 2 to win the confidence or affection of 3 (of a country) to decrease the size and capability of one's armed forces

disarmament *n* the reduction of fighting capability by a country

disarming *adj* removing hostility or suspicion ▷ **disarmingly** *adv*

disarrange *vb* **-ranging, -ranged** to throw into disorder ▷ **disarrangement** *n*

disarray *n* 1 confusion and lack of discipline 2 extreme untidiness ▷ *vb* 3 to throw into confusion

disassociate *vb* **-ating, -ated** same as **dissociate** ▷ **disassociation** *n*

disaster *n* 1 an accident that causes great distress or destruction 2 something, such as a project, that fails or has been ruined [Italian *disastro*] ▷ **disastrous** *adj* ▷ **disastrously** *adv*

disavow *vb* to deny connection with or responsibility for (something) ▷ **disavowal** *n*

sband *vb* to stop or cause to stop functioning as a unit or group > **disbandment** *n*

sbar *vb* **-barring, -barred** to deprive (a barrister) of the ight to practise

> **USAGE** *Disbar* is sometimes wrongly used where *debar* is meant: *he was debarred* (not *disbarred*) *from attending meetings.*

sbelieve *vb* **-lieving, -lieved 1** to reject (a person or tatement) as being untruthful **2 disbelieve in** to have o faith or belief in: *to disbelieve in the supernatural* > **disbelief** *n*

sburse *vb* **-bursing, -bursed** to pay out [Old French *esborser*] > **disbursement** *n*

> **USAGE** *Disburse* is sometimes wrongly used where *disperse* is meant: *the police used water cannon to disperse* (not *disburse*) *the crowd.*

sc *n* **1** a flat circular object **2** a gramophone record **3** *anatomy* a circular flat structure in the body, esp. etween the vertebrae **4** *computers* same as **disk** [Latin *iscus* discus]

scard *vb* to get rid of (something or someone) as seless or undesirable [DIS- + *card* (the playing card)]

sc brake *n* a brake in which two pads rub against a *d*at disc

scern *vb* to see or be aware of (something) clearly [Latin *discernere* to divide] > **discernible** *adj*

scerning *adj* having or showing good judgment > **discernment** *n*

scharge *vb* **-charging, -charged 1** to release or allow to o **2** to dismiss (someone) from duty or employment , to fire (a gun) **4** to cause to pour forth: *the scar was red and* wollen *and began to discharge pus* **5** to remove (the cargo) rom a boat, etc.; unload **6** to meet the demands of (a uty or responsibility) **7** to relieve oneself of (a debt) *physics* to take or supply electrical current from (a cell or attery) ⊳ *n* **9** something that is discharged o dismissal or release from an office, job, etc. **11** a ouring out of a fluid; emission **12** *physics* a conduction f electricity through a gas

sciple (diss-*sipe*-pl) *n* **1** a follower of the doctrines of a eacher **2** one of the personal followers of Christ during is earthly life [Latin *discipulus* pupil]

sciplinarian *n* a person who practises strict discipline

sciplinary *adj* of or imposing discipline; corrective

scipline *n* **1** the practice of imposing strict rules of ehaviour on other people **2** the ability to behave and vork in a controlled manner **3** a particular area of cademic study ⊳ *vb* **-plining, -plined 4** to improve or ttempt to improve the behaviour of (oneself or omeone else) by training or rules **5** to punish [Latin isciplina teaching]

sciplined *adj* able to behave and work in a controlled vay

sc jockey *n* a person who announces and plays ecorded pop records on a radio programme or at a lisco

sclaim *vb* **1** to deny (responsibility for or knowledge f something) **2** to give up (any claim to)

sclaimer *n* a statement denying responsibility for or nowledge of something

sclose *vb* **-closing, -closed 1** to make (information) nown **2** to allow to be seen: *she agreed to disclose the* ontents *of the box* > **disclosure** *n*

sco *n, pl* **-cos 1** a nightclub for dancing to amplified op records **2** an occasion at which people dance to mplified pop records **3** mobile equipment for roviding music for a disco [from DISCOTHEQUE]

scography *n, pl* **-phies** a classified list of gramophone ecords

---

discolour *or US* **discolor** *vb* to change in colour; to fade or stain > **discoloration** *n*

discomfit *vb* **-fiting, -fited** to make uneasy or confused [Old French *desconfire* to destroy] > **discomfiture** *n*

discomfort *n* **1** a mild pain **2** a feeling of worry or embarrassment **3 discomforts** conditions that cause physical uncomfortableness: *the physical discomforts of pregnancy*

discommode *vb* **-moding, -moded** to cause inconvenience [DIS- + obsolete *commode* to suit] > **discommodious** *adj*

discompose *vb* **-posing, -posed** to disturb or upset someone > **discomposure** *n*

disconcert *vb* to disturb the confidence or self-possession of; upset, embarrass, or take aback > **disconcerting** *adj*

disconnect *vb* **1** to undo or break the connection between (two things) **2** to stop the supply of (gas or electricity to a building) ⊳ *n* **3** a lack of connection: disconnection: *a disconnect between political discourse and the public* > **disconnection** *n*

disconnected *adj* (of speech or ideas) not logically connected

disconsolate *adj* sad beyond comfort [Medieval Latin *disconsolatus*] > **disconsolately** *adv*

discontent *n* lack of contentment, as with one's condition or lot in life > **discontented** *adj* > **discontentedly** *adv*

discontinue *vb* **-nuing, -nued** to come or bring to an end; stop

discontinuous *adj* characterized by interruptions; intermittent > **discontinuity** *n*

discord *n* **1** lack of agreement or harmony between people **2** harsh confused sounds **3** a combination of musical notes that lacks harmony [Latin *discors* at variance]

discordant *adj* **1** at variance; disagreeing **2** harsh in sound; inharmonious > **discordance** *n*

discotheque *n* same as **disco** [French]

discount *vb* **1** to leave (something) out of account as being unreliable, prejudiced, or irrelevant **2** to deduct (an amount or percentage) from the price of something ⊳ *n* **3** a deduction from the full amount of a price **4 at a discount** below the regular price

discountenance *vb* **-nancing, -nanced** to make (someone) ashamed or confused

discourage *vb* **-raging, -raged 1** to deprive of the will or enthusiasm to persist in something **2** to oppose by expressing disapproval > **discouragement** *n* > **discouraging** *adj*

discourse *n* **1** conversation **2** a formal treatment of a subject in speech or writing ⊳ *vb* **-coursing, -coursed 3** to speak or write (about) at length [Medieval Latin *discursus* argument]

discourteous *adj* showing bad manners; rude > **discourteously** *adv* > **discourtesy** *n*

discover *vb* **1** to be the first to find or find out about **2** to learn about for the first time **3** to find after study or search > **discoverer** *n*

discovery *n, pl* **-veries 1** the act of discovering **2** a person, place, or thing that has been discovered

Discovery Bay *n* an inlet of the Indian Ocean in SE Australia

discredit *vb* **-diting, -dited 1** to damage the reputation of (someone) **2** to cause (an idea) to be disbelieved or distrusted ⊳ *n* **3** something that causes disgrace > **discreditable** *adj*

discreet *adj* **1** careful to avoid embarrassment when dealing with secret or private matters **2** unobtrusive: *there was a discreet entrance down a side alley* [Old French *discret*] > **discreetly** *adv*

> **USAGE** Avoid confusion with **discrete**.

discrepancy *n*, *pl* **-cies** a conflict or variation between facts, figures, or claims [Latin *discrepare* to differ in sound] **> discrepant** *adj*

> **USAGE** Discrepancy is sometimes wrongly used where *disparity* is meant. A *discrepancy* exists between things which ought to be the same; it can be small but is usually significant. A *disparity* is a large difference between measurable things such as age, rank, or wages.

discrete *adj* separate or distinct [Latin *discretus* separated] **> discreteness** *n*

> **USAGE** Avoid confusion with **discreet**.

discretion (diss-kresh-on) *n* 1 the quality of behaving so as to avoid social embarrassment or distress 2 freedom or authority to make judgments and to act as one sees fit: *at his discretion* **> discretionary** *adj*

discriminate *vb* **-nating, -nated** 1 to make a distinction against or in favour of a particular person or group 2 to recognize or understand a difference: *to discriminate between right and wrong* [Latin *discriminare* to divide] **> discriminating** *adj*

discrimination *n* 1 unfair treatment of a person, racial group, or minority 2 subtle appreciation in matters of taste 3 the ability to see fine distinctions

discriminatory *adj* based on prejudice

discursive *adj* passing from one topic to another [Latin *discursus* a running to and fro]

discus *n* athletics a disc-shaped object with a heavy middle, thrown by athletes [Greek *diskos*]

discuss *vb* 1 to consider (something) by talking it over 2 to treat (a subject) in speech or writing [Latin *discutere* to dash to pieces] **> discussion** *n*

disdain *n* 1 a feeling of superiority and dislike; contempt ▷ *vb* 2 to refuse or reject with disdain: *he disdained domestic conventions* [Old French *desdeign*] **> disdainful** *adj* **> disdainfully** *adv*

disease *n* an unhealthy condition in a person, animal, or plant which is caused by bacteria or infection [Old French *desaise*] **> diseased** *adj*

diseconomy *n* econ a disadvantage, such as higher costs, resulting from the scale on which a business operates

disembark *vb* to land or cause to land from a ship, aircraft, or other vehicle **> disembarkation** *n*

disembodied *adj* 1 lacking a body 2 seeming not to be attached to or come from anyone **> disembodiment** *n*

disembowel *vb* **-welling, -welled** or US **-weling, -weled** to remove the entrails of **> disembowelment** *n*

disempower *vb* to deprive (a person) of power or authority **> disempowerment** *n*

disenchanted *adj* disappointed and disillusioned (with something) **> disenchantment** *n*

disenfranchise *vb* **-chising, -chised** to deprive (someone) of the right to vote or of other rights of citizenship

disengage *vb* **-gaging, -gaged** 1 to release from a connection 2 military to withdraw from close action **> disengagement** *n*

disentangle *vb* **-gling, -gled** 1 to release from entanglement or confusion 2 to unravel or work out **> disentanglement** *n*

disequilibrium *n* a loss or absence of stability or balance

disestablish *vb* to deprive (a church or religion) of established status **> disestablishment** *n*

disfavour or US **disfavor** *n* 1 disapproval or dislike 2 the state of being disapproved of or disliked

disfigure *vb* **-guring, -gured** to spoil the appearance or shape of **> disfigurement** *n*

disfranchise *vb* **-chising, -chised** same as **disenfranchise**

disgorge *vb* **-gorging, -gorged** 1 to vomit 2 to discharge (contents)

disgrace *n* 1 a condition of shame, loss of reputation, o dishonour 2 a shameful person or thing 3 exclusion from confidence or trust: *he was sent home in disgrace* ▷ *vb* **-gracing, -graced** 4 to bring shame upon (oneself or others) **> disgraceful** *adj* **> disgracefully** *adv*

disgruntled *adj* sulky or discontented: *the disgruntled home supporters* [DIS- + obsolete *gruntle* to complain] **> disgruntlement** *n*

disguise *vb* **-guising, -guised** 1 to change the appearan or manner in order to conceal the identity of (someone or something) 2 to misrepresent (something) in order obscure its actual nature or meaning ▷ *n* 3 a mask, costume, or manner that disguises 4 the state of being disguised [Old French *desguisier*] **> disguised** *adj*

disgust *n* 1 a great loathing or distaste ▷ *vb* 2 to sicken fill with loathing [Old French *desgouster* to sicken] **> disgusted** *adj* **> disgusting** *adj*

dish *n* 1 a container used for holding or serving food, es an open shallow container 2 the food in a dish 3 a particular kind of food 4 short for **dish aerial** 5 informal an attractive person ▶ See also **dish out**, **dish up** [Old English *disc*]

dishabille (diss-a-beel) *n* same as **deshabille**

dish aerial *n* a large disc-shaped aerial with a concave reflector, used to receive signals in radar, radio telescopes, and satellite broadcasting

disharmony *n* lack of agreement or harmony **> disharmonious** *adj*

dishcloth *n* a cloth for washing dishes

dishearten *vb* to weaken or destroy the hope, courage, enthusiasm of **> disheartened** *adj* **> disheartening** *adj*

dishevelled or US **disheveled** *adj* (of a person's hair, clothes, or general appearance) disordered and untidy [Old French *deschevelé*]

dishonest *adj* not honest or fair **> dishonestly** *adv* **> dishonesty** *n*

dishonour or US **dishonor** *vb* 1 to treat with disrespect 2 to refuse to pay (a cheque) ▷ *n* 3 a lack of honour or respect 4 a state of shame or disgrace 5 something tha causes a loss of honour **> dishonourable** or US **dishonorable** *adj* **> dishonourably** or US **dishonorably** *adv*

dish out *vb* 1 to distribute 2 **dish it out** to inflict punishment

dish up *vb* to serve (food)

dishwasher *n* a machine for washing and drying dishes, cutlery, etc.

dishwater *n* 1 water in which dishes have been washe 2 like dishwater (of tea) very weak

dishy *adj* **dishier, dishiest** informal good-looking

disillusion *vb* 1 to destroy the illusions or false ideas of (someone) ▷ *n* also: **disillusionment** 2 the state of being disillusioned

disillusioned *adj* disappointed at finding out reality does not match one's ideals

disincentive *n* something that discourages someone from behaving or acting in a particular way

disinclined *adj* unwilling or reluctant **> disinclination** *n*

disinfect *vb* to rid of harmful germs by cleaning with a chemical substance **> disinfection** *n*

disinfectant *n* a substance that destroys harmful germ

disinformation *n* false information intended to mislead

disingenuous *adj* dishonest and insincere **> disingenuously** *adv*

disinherit *vb* **-iting, -ited** law to deprive (an heir) of inheritance **> disinheritance** *n*

disintegrate *vb* **-grating, -grated** 1 to lose cohesion; break up: *the business disintegrated* 2 (of an object) to brea into fragments; shatter 3 physics **a** to undergo nuclear fission or include nuclear fission in **b** same as **decay** (3 **> disintegration** *n*

disinter *vb* **-terring, -terred** 1 to dig up 2 to bring to light; expose

disinterested *adj* **1** free from bias; objective **2** *not standard* feeling or showing a lack of interest; uninterested **> disinterest** *n*

> **USAGE** Many people consider that the use of *disinterested* to mean not interested is incorrect and that *uninterested* should be used.

disjointed *adj* having no coherence; disconnected: *a disjointed conversation*

disjunctive *adj* serving to disconnect or separate

disk *n* **1** *chiefly US and Canad* same as **disc 2** *computers* a storage device, consisting of a stack of plates coated with a magnetic layer, which rotates rapidly as a single unit [see DISC]

disk drive *n computers* the controller and mechanism for reading and writing data on computer disks

Disko *n* an island in Davis Strait, off the W coast of Greenland: extensive coal deposits

dislike *vb* **-liking, -liked 1** to consider unpleasant or disagreeable ▷ *n* **2** a feeling of not liking something or someone

dislocate *vb* **-cating, -cated 1** to displace (a bone or joint) from its normal position **2** to disrupt or shift out of place **> dislocation** *n*

dislodge *vb* **-lodging, -lodged** to remove (something) from a previously fixed position

disloyal *adj* not loyal; deserting one's allegiance or duty **> disloyalty** *n*

dismal *adj* **1** gloomy and depressing **2** *informal* of poor quality [Medieval Latin *dies mali* unlucky days] **> dismally** *adv*

Dismal Swamp *or* **Great Dismal Swamp** *n* a coastal marshland in SE Virginia and NE North Carolina: partly reclaimed. Area: about 1940 sq km (750 sq miles). Area before reclamation: 5200 sq km (2000 sq miles)

dismantle *vb* **-tling, -tled 1** to take apart piece by piece **2** to cause (an organization or political system) to stop functioning by gradually reducing its power or purpose [Old French *desmanteler*]

dismay *vb* **1** to fill with alarm or depression ▷ *n* **2** a feeling of alarm or depression [Old French *des-* intensive) + *esmayer* to frighten]

dismember *vb* **1** to remove the limbs of **2** to cut to pieces **> dismemberment** *n*

dismiss *vb* **1** to remove (an employee) from a job **2** to allow (someone) to leave **3** to put out of one's mind; no longer think about **4** (of a judge) to state that (a case) will not be brought to trial **5** *cricket* to bowl out (a side) for a particular number of runs [Latin *dis-* from + *mittere* to send] **> dismissal** *n* **> dismissive** *adj*

dismount *vb* to get off a horse or bicycle

Disney *n* Walt(er Elias). 1901–66, US film producer, who pioneered animated cartoons: noted esp. for his creations *Mickey Mouse* and *Donald Duck* and films such as *Fantasia* (1940) **> Disneyesque** *adj*

Disneyland *n* an amusement park in Anaheim, California, founded by Walt Disney and opened in 1955. **Walt Disney World**, a second amusement park, opened in 1971 near Orlando, Florida. Further parks operate in Paris, Tokyo, and Hong Kong

disobedient *adj* refusing to obey **> disobedience** *n*

disobey *vb* to neglect or refuse to obey (a person or an order)

disobliging *adj* unwilling to help

disorder *n* **1** a state of untidiness and disorganization **2** public violence or rioting **3** an illness **> disordered** *adj*

disorderly *adj* **1** untidy and disorganized **2** uncontrolled; unruly **3** *law* violating public peace

disorganize *or* **-ise** *vb* **-izing, -ized** *or* **-ising, -ised** to disrupt the arrangement or system of **> disorganization** *or* **-isation** *n*

disorientate *or* **disorient** *vb* **-tating, -tated** *or* **-enting, -ented** to cause (someone) to lose his or her bearings **> disorientation** *n*

disown *vb* to deny any connection with (someone)

disparage *vb* **-aging, -aged** to speak contemptuously of [Old French *desparagier*] **> disparagement** *n* **> disparaging** *adj*

disparate *adj* utterly different in kind [Latin *disparare* to divide]

disparity *n* inequality or difference

> **USAGE** See at **discrepancy**.

dispassionate *adj* not influenced by emotion; objective **> dispassionately** *adv*

dispatch *or* **despatch** *vb* **1** to send off to a destination or to perform a task **2** to carry out (a duty or task) promptly **3** to murder ▷ *n* **4** an official communication or report, sent in haste **5** a report sent to a newspaper by a correspondent **6** murder **7 with dispatch** quickly [Italian *dispacciare*]

dispatch rider *n Brit, Austral and NZ* a motorcyclist who carries dispatches

dispel *vb* **-pelling, -pelled** to disperse or drive away [Latin *dispellere*]

dispensable *adj* not essential; expendable

dispensary *n, pl* **-ries** a place where medicine is prepared and given out

dispensation *n* **1** the act of distributing or dispensing **2** *chiefly RC Church* permission to dispense with an obligation of church law **3** any exemption from an obligation **4** the ordering of life and events by God

dispense *vb* **-pensing, -pensed 1** to distribute in portions **2** to prepare and distribute (medicine) **3** to administer (the law, etc.) **4 dispense with** to do away with or manage without [Latin *dispendere* to weigh out] **> dispenser** *n*

> **USAGE** *Dispense with* is sometimes wrongly used where *dispose of* is meant: *this task can be disposed of* (not *dispensed with*) *quickly and easily.*

dispensing optician *n* See **optician** (2)

disperse *vb* **-persing, -persed 1** to scatter over a wide area **2** to leave or cause to leave a gathering: *police dispersed rioters* **3** to separate (light) into its different wavelengths **4** to separate (particles) throughout a solid, liquid, or gas [Latin *dispergere* to scatter widely] **> dispersal** *or* **dispersion** *n*

> **USAGE** See at **disburse**.

dispirit *vb* to make downhearted **> dispirited** *adj* **> dispiriting** *adj*

displace *vb* **-placing, -placed 1** to move (something) from its usual place **2** to remove (someone) from a post or position of authority

displaced person *n* a person forced from his or her home or country, esp. by war or revolution

displacement *n* **1** the act of displacing **2** *physics* the weight or volume of liquid displaced by an object submerged or floating in it **3** *maths* the distance measured in a particular direction from a reference point. Symbol: *s*

display *vb* **1** to show **2** to reveal or make evident: *to display anger* ▷ *n* **3** the act of exhibiting or displaying **4** something displayed **5** an exhibition **6** *electronics* a device capable of representing information visually, as on a screen **7** *zoology* a pattern of behaviour by which an animal attracts attention while courting, defending its territory, etc. [Anglo-French *despleier* to unfold]

displease *vb* **-pleasing, -pleased** to annoy or offend (someone) **> displeasure** *n*

disport *vb* **disport oneself** to indulge oneself in pleasure [Anglo-French *desporter*]

disposable *adj* **1** designed for disposal after use: *disposable cigarette lighters* **2** available for use if needed: *disposable capital*

disposal n 1 the act or means of getting rid of something 2 **at one's disposal** available for use
dispose vb **-posing, -posed** 1 **dispose of** a to throw away b to give, sell, or transfer to another c to deal with or settle: *I disposed of that problem right away* d to kill 2 to arrange or place in a particular way: *around them are disposed the moulded masks of witch doctors* [Latin *disponere* to set in different places]

> **USAGE** See at **dispense.**

disposed adj 1 willing or eager (to do something): *few would feel disposed to fault his judgment* 2 having an inclination as specified (towards someone or something): *my people aren't too well disposed towards defectors*
disposition n 1 a person's usual temperament 2 a tendency or habit 3 arrangement; layout
dispossess vb to deprive (someone) of (a possession) > **dispossessed** adj > **dispossession** n
disproportion n lack of proportion or equality
disproportionate adj out of proportion > **disproportionately** adv
disprove vb **-proving, -proved** to show (an assertion or claim) to be incorrect
dispute n 1 a disagreement between workers and their employer 2 an argument between two or more people 3 **beyond dispute** unable to be questioned or denied: *it's beyond dispute that tensions already existed between them* ▷ vb **-puting, -puted** 4 to argue or quarrel about (something) 5 to doubt the validity of 6 to fight over possession of [Latin *disputare* to discuss] > **disputation** n > **disputatious** adj
disqualify vb **-fies, -fying, -fied** 1 to officially ban (someone) from doing something: *he was disqualified from driving for ten years* 2 to make ineligible, as for entry to an examination > **disqualification** n
disquiet n 1 a feeling of anxiety or uneasiness ▷ vb 2 to make (someone) anxious > **disquieting** adj > **disquietude** n
disquisition n a formal written or oral examination of a subject
Disraeli n Benjamin, 1st Earl of Beaconsfield. 1804–81, British Tory statesman and novelist; prime minister (1868; 1874–80). He gave coherence to the Tory principles of protectionism and imperialism, was responsible for the Reform Bill (1867) and, as prime minister, bought a controlling interest in the Suez Canal. His novels include *Coningsby* (1844) and *Sybil* (1845)
disregard vb 1 to give little or no attention to; ignore ▷ n 2 lack of attention or respect
disrepair n the condition of being worn out or in poor working order
disreputable adj having or causing a bad reputation > **disreputably** adv
disrepute n a loss or lack of good reputation
disrespect n contempt or lack of respect > **disrespectful** adj
disrobe vb **-robing, -robed** literary to undress
disrupt vb to interrupt the progress of [Latin *disruptus* burst asunder] > **disruption** n > **disruptive** adj
diss vb slang, chiefly US to treat (a person) with contempt [from DISRESPECT]
dissatisfied adj displeased or discontented > **dissatisfaction** n
dissect vb 1 to cut open (a corpse) to examine it 2 to examine critically and minutely: *the above conclusion causes one to dissect that policy more closely* [Latin *dissecare*] > **dissection** n
dissemble vb **-bling, -bled** to conceal one's real motives or emotions by pretence [Latin *dissimulare*] > **dissembler** n
disseminate vb **-nating, -nated** to spread (information, ideas, etc.) widely [Latin *disseminare*] > **dissemination** n
dissension n disagreement and argument [Latin *dissentire* to dissent]

dissent vb 1 to disagree 2 Christianity to reject the doctrines of an established church ▷ n 3 a disagreemen 4 Christianity separation from an established church [Latin *dissentire* to disagree] > **dissenter** n > **dissenting** ad
Dissenter n Christianity, chiefly Brit a Protestant who refuses to conform to the established church
dissentient adj dissenting from the opinion of the majority
dissertation n 1 a written thesis, usually required for a higher degree 2 a long formal speech [Latin *dissertare* to debate]
disservice n a harmful action
dissident n 1 a person who disagrees with a governmen or a powerful organization ▷ adj 2 disagreeing or dissenting [Latin *dissidere* to be remote from] > **dissidence** n
dissimilar adj not alike; different > **dissimilarity** n
dissimulate vb **-lating, -lated** to conceal one's real feelings by pretence > **dissimulation** n
dissipate vb **-pating, -pated** 1 to waste or squander 2 to scatter or break up [Latin *dissipare* to disperse]
dissipated adj showing signs of overindulgence in alcohol or other physical pleasures
dissipation n 1 the process of dissipating 2 unrestrained indulgence in physical pleasures
dissociate vb **-ciating, -ciated** 1 **dissociate oneself from** to deny or break an association with (a person or organization) 2 to regard or treat as separate > **dissociation** n
dissoluble adj same as **soluble** [Latin *dissolubilis*] > **dissolubility** n
dissolute adj leading an immoral life [Latin *dissolutus* loose]
dissolution n 1 the act of officially breaking up an organization or institution 2 the act of officially endin a formal agreement, such as a marriage 3 the formal ending of a meeting or assembly, such as a Parliament
dissolve vb **-solving, -solved** 1 to become or cause to become liquid; melt 2 to officially break up (an organization or institution) 3 to formally end: *the campaign started as soon as Parliament was dissolved last month* 4 to collapse emotionally: *she dissolved in loud tears* 5 films, television to fade out one scene and replace with another to make two scenes merge imperceptibly [Latin *dissolver* to make loose]
dissonance n a lack of agreement or harmony between things: *this dissonance of colours* > **dissonant** adj
dissuade vb **-suading, -suaded** to deter (someone) by persuasion from doing something or believing in something [Latin *dissuadere*] > **dissuasion** n
dissyllable or **disyllable** n a word of two syllables > **dissyllabic** or **disyllabic** adj
distaff n the rod on which flax is wound for spinning [Old English *distæf*]
distaff side n the female side of a family
distance n 1 the space between two points or places 2 the state of being apart 3 a distant place 4 remotenes in manner 5 **the distance** the most distant part of the visible scene 6 **go the distance** a boxing to complete a bout without being knocked out b to complete an assigned task or responsibility 7 **keep one's distance** to maintain a reserved attitude to another person ▷ vb **-tancing, -tanced** 8 **distance oneself from** or **be distance from** to separate oneself or be separated mentally from
distance learning n a teaching system involving vide and written material for studying at home
distant adj 1 far-off; remote 2 far apart 3 separated by a specified distance: *five kilometres distant* 4 apart in relationship: *a distant cousin* 5 going to a faraway place 6 remote in manner; aloof 7 abstracted: *a distant look entere her eyes* [Latin *dis-* apart + *stare* to stand] > **distantly** adv
distaste n a dislike of something offensive
distasteful adj unpleasant or offensive > **distastefulness** n

Di Stéfano *n* Alfredo. 1926–2014, Argentinian-born football player, who played for Argentina, Colombia, Spain, and Real Madrid

distemper¹ *n* a highly contagious viral disease that can affect young dogs [Latin *dis-* apart + *temperare* to regulate]

distemper² *n* 1 paint mixed with water, glue, etc. which is used for painting walls ▷ *vb* 2 to paint with distemper [Latin *dis-* (intensive) + *temperare* to mingle]

distend *vb* to expand by pressure from within; swell [Latin *distendere*] > **distensible** *adj* > **distension** *n*

distich (diss-stick) *n prosody* a unit of two verse lines [Greek *di-* two + *stikhos* row, line]

distil *or US* **distill** *vb* **-tilling, -tilled** 1 to subject to or obtain by distillation 2 to give off (a substance) in drops 3 to extract the essence of [Latin *de-* down + *stillare* to drip]

distillation *n* 1 the process of evaporating a liquid and condensing its vapour 2 Also: **distillate** a concentrated essence

distiller *n* a person or company that makes spirits

distillery *n, pl* **-eries** a place where alcoholic drinks are made by distillation

distinct *adj* 1 not the same; different: *these two areas produce wines with distinct characteristics* 2 clearly seen, heard, or recognized: *it is not possible to draw a distinct line between the two categories; there's a distinct smell of burning* 3 clear and definite: *there is a distinct possibility of rain* 4 obvious: *a distinct improvement* [Latin *distinctus*] > **distinctly** *adv*

distinction *n* 1 the act of distinguishing or differentiating 2 a distinguishing feature 3 the state of being different or distinguishable 4 special honour, recognition, or fame 5 excellence of character 6 a symbol of honour or rank

distinctive *adj* easily recognizable; characteristic > **distinctively** *adv* > **distinctiveness** *n*

distingué (diss-tang-gay) *adj* distinguished or noble [French]

distinguish *vb* 1 to make, show, or recognize a difference: *I have tried to distinguish between fact and theory* 2 to be a distinctive feature of: *what distinguishes the good teenage reader from the less competent one?* 3 to make out by hearing, seeing, or tasting: *she listened but could distinguish nothing except the urgency of their discussion* 4 **distinguish oneself** to make oneself noteworthy [Latin *distinguere* to separate] > **distinguishable** *adj* > **distinguishing** *adj*

distinguished *adj* 1 dignified in appearance or behaviour 2 highly respected: *a distinguished historian*

distort *vb* 1 to alter or misrepresent (facts) 2 to twist out of shape; deform 3 *electronics* to reproduce or amplify (a signal) inaccurately [Latin *distorquere* to turn different ways] > **distorted** *adj* > **distortion** *n*

distract *vb* 1 to draw (a person or his or her attention) away from something 2 to amuse or entertain [Latin *strahere* to pull in different directions]

> **USAGE** See at **detract**.

distracted *adj* unable to concentrate because one's mind is on other things

distraction *n* 1 something that diverts the attention 2 something that serves as an entertainment 3 mental turmoil

distrain *vb law* to seize (personal property) to enforce payment of a debt [Latin *di-* apart + *stringere* to draw tight] > **distraint** *n*

distrait (diss-tray) *adj* absent-minded or abstracted [French]

distraught (diss-trawt) *adj* upset or agitated [obsolete *stract*]

distress *n* 1 extreme unhappiness or worry 2 great physical pain 3 financial trouble 4 **in distress** in dire need of help ▷ *vb* 5 to upset badly [Latin *districtus* divided in mind] > **distressing** *adj* > **distressingly** *adv*

distressed *adj* 1 much troubled; upset 2 in great physical pain 3 in financial difficulties 4 (of furniture or fabric) having signs of ageing artificially applied

distributary *n, pl* **-taries** one of several outlet streams draining a river, esp. on a delta

distribute *vb* **-uting, -uted** 1 to hand out or deliver (leaflets, mail, etc.) 2 to share (something) among the members of a particular group [Latin *distribuere*]

distribution *n* 1 the delivering of leaflets, mail, etc., to individual people or organizations 2 the sharing out of something among a particular group 3 the arrangement or spread of anything over an area, space, or period of time: *the unequal distribution of wealth* 4 *commerce* the process of satisfying the demand for goods and services

distributive *adj* 1 of or relating to distribution 2 *maths* of the rule that the same result is produced when multiplication is performed on a set of numbers as when performed on the members of the set individually

distributor *n* 1 a wholesaler who distributes goods to retailers in a specific area 2 the device in a petrol engine that sends the electric current to the sparking plugs

district *n* 1 an area of land regarded as an administrative or geographical unit 2 an area which has recognizable or special features: *an upper-class residential district* [Medieval Latin *districtus* area of jurisdiction]

district court judge *n Austral and NZ* a judge presiding over a lower court

district nurse *n* (in Britain) a nurse who attends to patients in their homes within a particular district

District of Columbia *n* a federal district of the eastern US, coextensive with the federal capital, Washington. Pop: 564 326 (2003 est). Area: 178 sq km (69 sq miles). Abbreviation: **D.C.**, (with zip code) **DC**

District Six *n* an area of Cape Town that was inhabited by a racially mixed community until it was forcibly removed in 1966

Distrito Federal *n* a district in S central Brazil, containing Brasília: detached from Goiás state in 1960. Pop: 2 145 839 (2002). Area: 5815 sq km (2245 sq miles)

distrust *vb* 1 to regard as untrustworthy ▷ *n* 2 a feeling of suspicion or doubt > **distrustful** *adj*

disturb *vb* 1 to intrude on; interrupt 2 to upset or worry 3 to disarrange; muddle 4 to inconvenience [Latin *disturbare*] > **disturbing** *adj* > **disturbingly** *adv*

disturbance *n* 1 an interruption or intrusion 2 an unruly outburst in public

disturbed *adj psychiatry* emotionally upset, troubled, or maladjusted

disunite *vb* **-niting, -nited** to cause disagreement among > **disunion** *n* > **disunity** *n*

disuse *n* the state of being neglected or no longer used; neglect

disused *adj* no longer used

disyllable *n* same as **dissyllable**

ditch *n* 1 a narrow channel dug in the earth for drainage or irrigation ▷ *vb* 2 *slang* to abandon or discard: *she ditched her boyfriend last month* [Old English *dīc*]

Ditch *n Austral and NZ* **the Ditch** an informal name for the Tasman Sea

dither *vb* 1 *chiefly Brit and NZ* to be uncertain or indecisive ▷ *n* 2 *chiefly Brit* a state of indecision or agitation [Middle English *didder*] > **ditherer** *n* > **dithery** *adj*

dithyramb *n* (in ancient Greece) a passionate choral hymn in honour of Dionysus [Greek *dithurambos*] > **dithyrambic** *adj*

ditto *n, pl* **-tos** 1 the above; the same: used in lists to avoid repetition, and represented by the mark (Ð) placed under the thing repeated ▷ *adv* 2 in the same way [Italian (dialect) *detto* said]

ditty *n, pl* **-ties** a short simple song or poem [Latin *dictare* to say repeatedly]

ditzy *or* **ditsy** *adj* **ditzier, ditziest** *or* **ditsier, ditsiest** *slang* silly and scatterbrained [perhaps from DOTTY + DIZZY]

Diu *n* a small island off the NW coast of India: together with a mainland area, it formed a district of Portuguese India (1535–1961); formerly part of the Indian Union Territory of Goa, Daman, and Diu (1962–87)

diuretic (die-yoor-et-ik) *n* a drug that increases the flow of urine [Greek *dia*- through + *ourein* to urinate]

diurnal (die-urn-al) *adj* 1 happening during the day or daily 2 (of animals) active during the day [Latin *diurnus*]

diva *n*, *pl* **-vas** *or* **-ve** a distinguished female singer; prima donna [Latin: a goddess]

divalent *adj chem* having two valencies or a valency of two **> divalency** *n*

divan *n* 1 a low bed with a thick base under the mattress 2 a couch with no back or arms [Turkish *dīvān*]

dive *vb* **diving, dived** *or US* **dove, dived** 1 to plunge headfirst into water 2 (of a submarine or diver) to submerge under water 3 (of a bird or aircraft) to fly in a steep nose-down descending path 4 to move quickly in a specified direction: *he dived for the door* 5 **dive in** *or* **into** a to put (one's hand) quickly or forcefully into b to start doing (something) enthusiastically ▷ *n* 6 a headlong plunge into water 7 the act of diving 8 a steep nose-down descent of a bird or aircraft 9 *slang* a disreputable bar or club [Old English *dȳfan*]

dive bomber *n* a military aircraft designed to release bombs on a target during a dive **> dive-bomb** *vb*

diver *n* 1 a person who works or explores underwater 2 a person who dives for sport 3 a large diving bird of northern oceans with a straight pointed bill and webbed feet

diverge *vb* **-verging, -verged** 1 to separate and go in different directions 2 to be at variance; differ: *the two books diverge in setting and in style* 3 to deviate (from a prescribed course) [Latin *dis*- apart + *vergere* to turn] **> divergence** *n* **> divergent** *adj*

diverse *adj* 1 having variety; assorted 2 different in kind [Latin *diversus* turned in different directions]

diversify *vb* **-fies, -fying, -fied** 1 to create different forms of; vary 2 (of an enterprise) to vary (products or operations) in order to expand or reduce the risk of loss [Latin *diversus* different + *facere* to make] **> diversification** *n*

diversion *n* 1 *chiefly Brit* an official detour used by traffic when a main route is closed 2 something that distracts someone's attention or concentration 3 the act of diverting from a specified course 4 a pleasant or amusing pastime or activity **> diversionary** *adj*

diversity *n* 1 the quality of being different or varied 2 a point of difference

divert *vb* 1 to change the course or direction of (traffic) 2 to distract the attention of 3 to entertain or amuse [Latin *divertere* to turn aside]

diverticulitis *n* inflammation of pouches in the wall of the colon, causing lower abdominal pain [Latin *deverticulum* path, track]

divertimento *n*, *pl* **-ti** a piece of entertaining music in several movements [Italian]

divest *vb* 1 to strip (of clothes) 2 to deprive of a role, function, or quality: *the chairman felt duty-bound to stay with the company after it was divested of all its aviation interests* [earlier *devest*]

divide *vb* **-viding, -vided** 1 to separate into parts 2 to share or be shared out in parts 3 to disagree or cause to disagree: *experts are divided over the plan* 4 to keep apart or be a boundary between 5 to categorize or classify 6 to calculate how many times one number can be contained in another ▷ *n* 7 a division or split 8 *chiefly US and Canad* an area of high ground separating drainage basins [Latin *dividere* to force apart]

dividend *n* 1 a portion of a company's profits paid to its shareholders 2 an extra benefit: *Saudi progressives saw a dividend to the crisis* 3 *maths* a number to be divided by another number [Latin *dividendum* what is to be divided]

divider *n* a screen placed so as to divide a room into separate areas

dividers *pl n* compasses with two pointed arms, used fo measuring or dividing lines

divination *n* the art of discovering future events as though by supernatural powers

divine *adj* 1 of God or a god 2 godlike 3 *informal* splendid or perfect ▷ *n* 4 a priest who is learned in theology ▷ *vb* **-vining, -vined** 5 to discover (something) by intuition guessing [Latin *divus* a god] **> divinely** *adv* **> diviner** *n*

diving bell *n* a diving apparatus with an open bottom, supplied with compressed air from above

diving board *n* a platform from which swimmers may dive

diving suit *n* a waterproof suit used for diving with a detachable helmet and an air supply

divining rod *n* a forked twig said to move when held over ground in which water or metal is to be found

divinity *n*, *pl* **-ties** 1 the study of religion 2 a god or goddess 3 the state of being divine

divisible *adj* capable of being divided **> divisibility** *n*

division *n* 1 the separation of something into two or more distinct parts 2 the act of dividing or sharing ou 3 one of the parts into which something is divided 4 th mathematical operation of dividing 5 a difference of opinion 6 a part of an organization that has been mad into a unit for administrative or other reasons 7 a formal vote in Parliament 8 one of the groups of team that make up a football or other sports league 9 *army* a major formation containing the necessary arms to sustain independent combat 10 *biology* one of the majo groups into which the plant kingdom is divided, corresponding to a phylum [Latin *dividere* to divide] **> divisional** *adj*

division sign *n* the symbol ÷, placed between two numbers to indicate that the first number should be divided by the second, as in $12 \div 6 = 2$

divisive (div-vice-iv) *adj* tending to cause disagreemen *he played an important role in defusing potentially divisive issues*

divisor *n* a number to be divided into another number

divorce *n* 1 the legal ending of a marriage 2 a separation, esp. one that is permanent ▷ *vb* **-vorcing, -vorced** 3 to separate or be separated by divorce 4 to remove or separate [Latin *divertere* to separate]

divorcee *or masc* **divorcé** *n* a person who is divorced

divot *n* a small piece of turf

divulge *vb* **-vulging, -vulged** to make known: *I am not permitted to divulge his name* [Latin *divulgare*] **> divulgence** *n*

divvy¹ *vb* **-vies, -vying, -vied** **divvy up** *informal* to divide and share

divvy² *n*, *pl* **-vies** *Brit dialect* a stupid person

Diwali (duh-wah-lee) *n* an annual Hindu festival honouring Lakshmi, the goddess of wealth

Dixie *n* 1 Also called: **Dixieland** the southern states of th US; the states that joined the Confederacy during the Civil War 2 a song adopted as a marching tune by the Confederate states during the American Civil War ▷ *ad* 3 of, relating to, or characteristic of the southern states of the US [C19: perhaps from the nickname of New Orleans, from *dixie* a ten-dollar bill printed there, from French *dix* ten]

Dixieland *n* 1 a form of jazz that originated in New Orleans, becoming popular esp. with White musicians in the second decade of the 20th century 2 a revival of this style in the 1950s 3 See **Dixie** (1)

Dixon *n* Willie, full name *William James Dixon*. 1915–92, US blues musician, songwriter, and record producer, who songs have been recorded by many other artists

DIY *or* **d.i.y.** *Brit, Austral and NZ* do-it-yourself

Diyarbakir *or* **Diyarbekir** *n* a city in SE Turkey, on the River Tigris: ancient black basalt walls. Pop: 607 000 (2005 est). Ancient name: **Amida**

dizzy *adj* **-zier, -ziest** 1 feeling giddy 2 unable to think clearly; confused 3 tending to cause giddiness or confusion ▷ *vb* **-zies, -zying, -zied** 4 to cause to feel

...ddy or confused [Old English *dysig* silly] **> dizzily** *adv*

...**dizziness** *n*

...or **dj 1** disc jockey **2** *Brit* dinner jacket

...**ailolo** or **Jilolo** *n* the Dutch name for **Halmahera**

...**aja** *n* the former spelling of (Mount) **Jaya**

...**ajapura** *n* the former spelling of **Jayapura**

...**akarta** *n* the former spelling of **Jakarta**

...**ambi** *n* the former spelling of **Jambi**

...**awa** *n* the former spelling of **Java**

...**erba** or **Jerba** *n* an island off the SE coast of Tunisia, in ...he Gulf of Gabès: traditionally Homer's land of the ...tus-eaters. Pop: about 100 000 (latest est). Area: ...0 sq km (197 sq miles). Ancient name: **Meninx**

...**ibouti** or **Jibouti** *n* **1** a republic in E Africa, on the Gulf ...f Aden: a French overseas territory (1946–77); became ...dependent in 1977; mainly desert. Official languages: ...rabic and French. Religion: Muslim majority. ...urrency: Djibouti franc. Capital: Djibouti. Pop: 792 198 ...013 est). Area: 23 200 sq km (8950 sq miles). Former ...ame (until 1977): **(Territory of the) Afars and the Issas** ...the capital of Djibouti, a port on the Gulf of Aden: an ...utlet for Ethiopian goods. Pop: 523 000 (2005 est)

...**ilas** *n* Milovan. 1911–95, Yugoslav politician and writer; ...ice president (1953–54): imprisoned (1956–61, 1962–66) ...or his criticism of the communist system

...**nni** or **djinny** *n*, *pl* **djinn** same as **jinni**

...**decilitre(s)**

...**itt** or **DLit 1** Doctor of Letters **2** Doctor of Literature ...atin *Doctor Litterarum*]

...**L** *computers* dynamic link library: a set of programs ...hat can be activated and then discarded by other ...rograms

...**1** decimetre(s)

...**M** Deutschmark

...**Mus** Doctor of Music

...**NA** deoxyribonucleic acid, the main constituent of the ...hromosomes of all organisms

...**NA fingerprinting** or **DNA profiling** *n* same as ...enetic fingerprinting

...**neprodzerzhinsk** *n* an industrial city in E Ukraine on ...he Dnieper River. Pop: 250 000 (2005 est)

...**nepropetrovsk** *n* a city in E central Ukraine on the ...nieper River: a major centre of the metallurgical ...ndustry. Pop: 1 036 000 (2005 est). Former name ...787–1796, 1802–1926): **Yekaterinoslav**

...**nieper** *n* a river in NE Europe, rising in Russia, in the ...aldai Hills NE of Smolensk and flowing south to the ...lack Sea: the third longest river in Europe; a major ...avigable waterway. Length: 2200 km (1370 miles). ...ussian name: **Dnepr**

...**niester** *n* a river in E Europe, rising in Ukraine, in the ...arpathian Mountains and flowing generally southeast ...the Black Sea. Length: 1411 km (877 miles). Russian ...ame: **Dnestr**. Romanian name: **Nistru**

...**notice** *n* *Brit* and *Austral* an official notice sent to ...ewspapers prohibiting the publication of certain ...ecurity information [from this administrative ...lassification letter]

...**1** *vb* **does, doing, did, done 1** to perform or complete (a ...eed or action): *we do a fair amount of entertaining* **2** to be ...dequate: *it's not what I wanted but it will have to do* **3** to ...rovide: *this hotel only does bed and breakfast* **4** to make tidy ...: elegant: *he watched her do her hair* **5** to improve: *that style* ...*oes nothing for you* **6** to find an answer to (a problem or ...uzzle) **7** to conduct oneself: *do as you want* **8** to cause or ...roduce: *herbal teas have active ingredients that can do good* **9** to ...ive or grant: *do me a favour* **10** to work at as a course of ...tudy or a job **11** to mimic **12** to achieve a particular ...peed, amount, or rate: *this computer system can do 40 ...fferent cross checks; this car can do sixty miles to the gallon* ...**a** used to form questions: *do you like it?* **b** used to ...ntensify positive statements and commands: *tensions do ...xist* **c** used to form negative statements or commands: ...*o not talk while I'm talking!* **d** used to replace an earlier

verb: *he drinks much more than I do* **14** *informal* to visit (a place) as a tourist: *we plan to do the States this year* **15** *slang* to serve (a period of time) as a prison sentence **16** *informal* to cheat or rob: *I was done out of ten pounds* **17** *slang* **a** to arrest **b** to convict of a crime: *he was done for 3 years for housebreaking* **18** *slang, chiefly Brit* to assault **19** *slang* to take or use (drugs) **20 make do** to manage with whatever is available ▷ *n, pl* **dos** or **do's 21** *informal, chiefly Brit and NZ* a party or other social event **22 do's and don'ts** *informal* rules ▶ See also **do away with, do by,** etc. [Old English *dōn*]

do² *n, pl* **dos** *music* same as **doh**

do away with *vb* to get rid of (someone or something)

Dobbyn *n* Dave. born 1957, New Zealand singer and songwriter; member of Th'Dudes (1976–80) with whom he had the hit singles "Be Mine Tonight" (1979) and "Bliss" (1979); founder of DD Smash (1981–85) with whom he released the album *Cool Bananas* (1982); solo albums include: *Loyal* (1986) and *Footrot Flats: The Dog's Tale* (1986)

Dobell *n* Sir William. 1899–1970, Australian portrait and landscape painter. Awarded the Archibald prize (1943) for his famous painting of *Joshua Smith* which resulted in a heated clash between the conservatives and the moderns and led to a lawsuit. His other works include *The Cypriot* (1940), *The Billy Boy* (1943), and *Portrait of a strapper* (1941)

Doberman pinscher or **Doberman** *n* a large dog with a glossy black-and-tan coat [after L. *Dobermann*, dog breeder]

dob in *vb* **dobbing, dobbed** *Austral* and *NZ informal* **1** to inform against **2** to contribute to a fund

Dobruja *n* a region of E Europe, between the River Danube and the Black Sea: the north passed to Romania and the south to Bulgaria after the Berlin Congress (1878). Romanian name: **Dobrogea**

do by *vb* to treat in the manner specified: *he felt badly done by*

Dobzhansky *n* Theodosius. 1900–75, US biologist, born in Russia, noted for work on evolution and genetic variation

doc *n informal* same as **doctor**

DOC (in New Zealand) Department of Conservation

docile *adj* (of a person or animal) easily controlled [Latin *docilis* easily taught] **> docilely** *adv* **> docility** *n*

dock¹ *n* **1** an enclosed area of water where ships are loaded, unloaded, or repaired **2** a wharf or pier ▷ *vb* **3** to moor or be moored at a dock **4** to link (two spacecraft) or (of two spacecraft) to be linked together in space [Middle Dutch *docke*]

dock² *vb* **1** to deduct (an amount) from (a person's wages) **2** to remove part of (an animal's tail) by cutting through the bone [Middle English *dok*]

dock³ *n* an enclosed space in a court of law where the accused person sits or stands [Flemish *dok sty*]

dock⁴ *n* a weed with broad leaves [Old English *docce*]

docker *n Brit* a person employed to load and unload ships

docket *chiefly Brit n* **1** a label on a package or other delivery, stating contents, delivery instructions, etc. ▷ *vb* **-eting, -eted 2** to fix a docket to (a package or other delivery) [origin unknown]

dockyard *n* a place where ships are built or repaired

Doc Martens *pl n trademark* a brand of lace-up boots with thick lightweight resistant soles

doctor *n* **1** a person licensed to practise medicine **2** a person who has been awarded a doctorate **3** *chiefly US and Canad* a person licensed to practise dentistry or veterinary medicine ▷ *vb* **4** to change in order to deceive: *she confessed to having doctored the figures* **5** to poison or drug (food or drink) **6** to castrate (an animal) [Latin: teacher] **> doctoral** *adj*

doctorate *n* the highest academic degree in any field of knowledge

doctrinaire *adj* stubbornly insistent on the application of a theory without regard to practicality

d

doctrine (dock-trin) *n* **1** a body of teachings of a religious, political, or philosophical group **2** a principle or body of principles that is taught or advocated [Latin *doctrina* teaching] > **doctrinal** *adj*

docudrama *n* a film or television programme based on true events, presented in a dramatized form

document *n* **1** a piece of paper that provides an official record of something ▷ *vb* **2** to record or report (something) in detail **3** to support (a claim) with evidence [Latin *documentum* a lesson]

documentary *n, pl* **-ries 1** a film or television programme presenting the facts about a particular subject ▷ *adj* **2** of or based on documents: *vital documentary evidence has been found*

documentation *n* documents supplied as proof or evidence of something

docu-soap *n* a television documentary series presenting the lives of the people filmed as entertainment

Dodd *n* C(harles) H(arold). 1884–1973, British New Testament scholar. His works include *The Parables of the Kingdom* (1935)

dodder *vb* to move unsteadily [variant of earlier *dadder*] > **dodderer** *n* > **doddery** *adj*

doddle *n* Brit, Austral and NZ informal something easily accomplished: *the test turned out to be a doddle* [origin unknown]

dodecagon (doe-**deck**-a-gon) *n* a polygon with twelve sides [Greek *dōdeka* twelve + *gōnia* angle]

dodecahedron (doe-deck-a-**heed**-ron) *n* a solid figure with twelve plane faces

Dodecanese *pl n* a group of islands in the SE Aegean Sea, forming a department of Greece: part of the Southern Sporades. Capital: Rhodes. Pop: 190 071 (2001). Area: 2663 sq km (1028 sq miles). Modern Greek name: Dhodhekánisos

dodge *vb* **dodging, dodged 1** to avoid being hit, caught, or seen by moving suddenly **2** to evade by cleverness or trickery: *the Government will not be able to dodge the issue* ▷ *n* **3** a cunning and deceitful trick [origin unknown]

Dodge City *n* a city in SW Kansas, on the Arkansas River: famous as a frontier town on the Santa Fe Trail. Pop: 25 568 (2003 est)

Dodgem *n* trademark a small electric car driven and bumped against similar cars in a rink at a funfair

dodger *n* a person who evades a duty or obligation

Dodgson *n* Charles Lutwidge. the real name of Lewis Carroll. See Carroll

dodgy *adj* **dodgier, dodgiest** Brit, Austral and NZ informal **1** dangerous, risky, or unreliable: *he's in a very dodgy political position* **2** untrustworthy: *they considered him a very dodgy character*

dodo *n, pl* **dodos** or **dodoes 1** a large extinct bird that could not fly **2 as dead as a dodo** no longer existing [Portuguese *duodo* stupid]

Dodoma *n* a city in central Tanzania, the official capital of the country. Pop: 169 000 (2005 est)

Dodona *n* an ancient Greek town in Epirus: seat of an ancient sanctuary and oracle of Zeus and later the religious centre of Pyrrhus' kingdom > **Dodonaean** or **Dodonean** *adj*

do down *vb* to belittle or humiliate: *the moderate constructionist does not wish to do science down*

doe *n, pl* **does** or **doe** the female of the deer, hare, or rabbit [Old English *dā*]

DOE (in Britain) Department of the Environment

doek (rhymes with **book**) *n* S African informal a square of cloth worn on the head by women [Afrikaans]

doer *n* an active or energetic person

does *vb* third person singular of the present tense of **do**[1]

doff *vb* to take off or lift (one's hat) in salutation [Old English *dōn of*]

do for *vb informal* **1** to cause the ruin, death, or defeat of: *I'm done for if this error comes to light* **2** to do housework for

3 do well for oneself to thrive or succeed

dog *n* **1** a domesticated canine mammal occurring in many different breeds **2** any other member of the dog family, such as the dingo or coyote. Related adjective: **canine 3** the male of animals of the dog family **4** inform a person: *you lucky dog!* **5** US and Canad informal something unsatisfactory or inferior **6 a dog's life** a wretched existence **7 dog eat dog** ruthless competition **8 like a dog's dinner** dressed smartly and ostentatiously ▷ *vb* **dogging, dogged 9** to follow (someone) closely **10** to trouble: *dogged by ill health* ▶ See also **dogs** [Old English *docga*]

dog box *n* Austral and NZ informal same as **doghouse**

dogcart *n* a light horse-drawn two-wheeled cart

dog collar *n* **1** a collar for a dog **2** informal a clerical colla

dog days *pl n* Brit, Austral and NZ the hottest period of th summer [in ancient times reckoned from the heliacal rising of the Dog Star]

doge (doje) *n* (formerly) the chief magistrate of Venice Genoa [Latin *dux* leader]

dog-eared *adj* **1** (of a book) having pages folded down the corner **2** shabby or worn

dog-end *n* Brit, Austral and NZ informal a cigarette end

dogfight *n* **1** close-quarters combat between fighter aircraft **2** any rough fight

dogfish *n, pl* **-fish** or **-fishes** a small shark

dogged (dog-gid) *adj* obstinately determined > **doggec** *adv* > **doggedness** *n*

Dogger Bank *n* an extensive submerged sandbank in the North Sea between N England and Denmark: fishing ground

doggerel *n* poorly written, usually comic, verse [Midd English *dogerel* worthless]

doggo *adv* **lie doggo** informal to hide and keep quiet [probably from *dog*]

doggy or **doggie** *n, pl* **-gies 1** a child's word for a dog ▷ *adj* **-gier, -giest 2** of or like a dog **3** fond of dogs: *I suppc dogs are all right but doggy folk can be real bores*

doggy bag *n* a bag in which leftovers from a meal may be taken away, supposedly for the diner's dog

doghouse *n* **1** US and Canad a kennel **2 in the doghouse** informal in disfavour

dogie, dogy or **dogey** (dohg-ee) *n, pl* **-gies** or **-geys** US a Canad a motherless calf [from *dough-guts*, because they were fed on flour-and-water paste]

dog in the manger *n* a person who prevents others from using something he has no use for

dogleg *n* a sharp bend

dogma *n* a doctrine or system of doctrines proclaimed authority as true [Greek: opinion]

dogmatic *adj* habitually stating one's opinions in a forceful or arrogant manner > **dogmatically** *adv* > **dogmatism** *n*

do-gooder *n informal* a well-intentioned but naive or impractical person

dog paddle *n* a swimming stroke in which the hands are paddled in imitation of a swimming dog. Also calle **doggy paddle**

dogs *pl n* **1 the dogs** Brit and Austral informal greyhound racing **2 go to the dogs** informal to go to ruin physically morally **3 let sleeping dogs lie** to leave things undisturbed

Dogs *n* **Isle of Dogs** a district in the East End of London, bounded on three sides by the River Thames, and a foc of major office development (Canary Wharf) in recent years

dogsbody *n, pl* **-bodies** informal a person who carries ou boring or unimportant tasks for others

dog-tired *adj informal* exhausted

dogwatch *n* either of two watches aboard ship, from four to six pm or from six to eight pm

doh or **do** *n music* (in tonic sol-fa) the first note of any ascending major scale

Doha *n* the capital and chief port of Qatar, on the E coa of the peninsula. Pop: 370 000 (2002 est). Former name: Bida, El Beda

Dohnányi n Ernö or Ernst von. 1877–1960, Hungarian pianist and composer whose works include *Variations on a Nursery Theme* (1913) for piano and orchestra

doily or **doyley** n, pl **-lies** or **-leys** a decorative lacelike paper mat laid on a plate [after *Doily*, a London draper]

do in vb slang **1** to kill **2** to exhaust

doings pl n **1** deeds or actions: *her brother's doings upset her terribly* ▷ n **2** informal anything of which the name is not known or is left unsaid: *do you have the doings to open this?*

Doisy n Edward Adelbert. 1893–1986, US biochemist. He discovered (1939) the nature of vitamin K and shared a Nobel prize for medicine with Carl Dam (1943)

do-it-yourself n the practice of constructing and repairing things oneself

Dolby n trademark **1** a system used in tape recorders which reduces noise level on recorded or broadcast sound **2** a system used in cinemas and television sets which provides surround sound

doldrums n the doldrums **1 a** a feeling of depression **b** a state of inactivity **2** a belt of sea along the equator noted for absence of winds [probably from Old English *dol* dull]

dole n **1 the dole** Brit, Austral and NZ informal money received from the state while unemployed **2 on the dole** Brit, Austral and NZ informal receiving benefit while unemployed ▷ vb **doling, doled 3 dole out** to distribute in small quantities [Old English *dāl* share]

dole bludger n Austral and NZ informal a person who chooses to live off unemployment benefit

doleful adj dreary or mournful [from Latin *dolere* to lament] ▷ **dolefully** adv ▷ **dolefulness** n

Dolgellau n a market town and tourist centre in NW Wales, in Gwynedd. Pop: 2407 (2001). Former spelling: Dolgelley

Dolin n Sir Anton, real name *Sydney Healey-Kay*. 1904–83, British ballet dancer and choreographer: with Alicia Markova he founded (1949) the London Festival Ballet

D'Oliviera n Basil (Lewis). 1931–2011, South African-born cricketer who played for England. The South African government's refusal to admit him to the country as part of the England touring party in 1968 led to South Africa being banned from international cricket

doll n **1** a small model of a human being, used as a toy **2** slang a pretty girl or young woman [probably from *Doll*, pet name for *Dorothy*]

dollar n the standard monetary unit of various countries [Low German *daler*]

Dollfuss n Engelbert. 1892–1934, Austrian statesman, chancellor (1932–34), who was assassinated by Austrian Nazis

dollop n informal an amount of food served in a lump: *he shook the bottle and added a large dollop of ketchup* [origin unknown]

doll up vb get dolled up slang to dress (oneself) in a stylish or showy manner

dolly n, pl **-lies 1** a child's word for a **doll** (1) **2** films, television a wheeled support on which a camera may be mounted **3** Also called: **dolly bird** old-fashioned, slang, chiefly Brit an attractive and fashionable girl

dolman sleeve n a sleeve that is very wide at the armhole and tapers to a tight wrist [Turkish *dolaman* a winding round]

dolmen n a prehistoric monument consisting of a horizontal stone supported by vertical stones, thought to be a tomb [French]

Dolmetsch n Arnold. 1858–1940, British musician, born in France. He contributed greatly to the revival of interest in early music and instruments

dolomite n a mineral consisting of calcium magnesium carbonate [after Déodat de *Dolomieu*, mineralogist]

Dolomites pl n a mountain range in NE Italy: part of the Alps; formed of dolomitic limestone. Highest peak: Marmolada, 3342 m (10 965 ft)

dolphin n a sea mammal of the whale family, with a long pointed snout [Greek *delphis*]

dolphinarium n an aquarium for dolphins, esp. one in which they give public displays

dolt n a stupid person [probably related to Old English *dol* stupid] ▷ **doltish** adj

Domagk n Gerhard. 1895–1964, German biochemist: Nobel prize for medicine (1939) for isolating sulphanilamide for treating bacterial infections

domain n **1** a particular area of activity or interest **2** land under one ruler or government **3** computers a group of computers that have the same suffix in their names on the internet, specifying the country, type of institution, etc. where they are located **4** NZ a public park [French *domaine*]

dome n **1** a rounded roof built on a circular base **2** something shaped like this [Latin *domus* house]

domed adj shaped like a dome

Domenichino n full name Domenico Zampieri. 1581–1641, Italian Baroque painter, noted for his frescoes and the altarpiece *Last Communion of St Jerome* (1614)

Domenico Veneziano n died 1461, Italian painter, noted for the St Lucy Altarpiece

Dome of the Rock n the mosque in Jerusalem, Israel, built in 691 AD by caliph Abd al-Malik: the third most holy place of Islam; stands on the Temple Mount alongside the **al-Aqsa** mosque. Also called (not in Muslim usage): **Mosque of Omar**

domestic adj **1** of one's own country or a specific country: *the domestic economy was generally better* **2** of the home or family **3** enjoying home or family life: *she was never a very domestic sort of person* **4** intended for use in the home: *the kitchen was equipped with all the latest domestic appliances* **5** (of an animal) bred or kept as a pet or for the supply of food ▷ n **6** a household servant [Latin *domesticus* belonging to the house] ▷ **domestically** adv

domesticate vb **-cating, -cated 1** to bring or keep (wild animals or plants) under control or cultivation **2** to accustom (someone) to home life ▷ **domestication** n

domesticity n, pl **-ties 1** home life **2** devotion to home life

domestic science n the study of cooking, needlework, and other household skills

Domett n Alfred. 1811–87, New Zealand poet, colonial administrator, and statesman, born in England: prime minister of New Zealand (1862–63)

domicile (**dom-miss-ile**) n **1** formal a person's regular dwelling place **2** law the country in which a person has his or her permanent legal residence [Latin *domus* house] ▷ **domiciliary** adj

domiciled adj living or established in a particular place: *the holding company was domiciled in Bermuda*

dominant adj **1** having control, authority, or influence: *a dominant leader* **2** main or chief: *coal is still, worldwide, the dominant fuel* **3** genetics (in a pair of genes) designating the gene that produces a particular character in an organism ▷ **dominance** n

dominate vb **-nating, -nated 1** to control or govern **2** to tower above (surroundings): *the building had been designed to dominate the city skyscape* **3** to predominate in [Latin *dominari* to be lord over] ▷ **dominating** adj ▷ **domination** n

dominee (**doom-in-nee**) n S African a minister of the Dutch Reformed Church [Dutch, from Latin *dominus* master]

domineering adj acting arrogantly or tyrannically [Dutch *domineren*]

Domingo n Placido. born 1941, Spanish operatic tenor

Dominic n Saint. original name *Domingo de Guzman*. ?1170–1221, Spanish priest; founder of the Dominican order. Feast day: Aug 7

Dominica n a republic in the E Caribbean, comprising a volcanic island in the Windward Islands group; a former British colony; became independent as a member of the Commonwealth in 1978. Official language: English.

Religion: Roman Catholic majority. Currency: East Caribbean dollar. Capital: Roseau. Pop: 73 286 (2013 est). Area: 751 sq km (290 sq miles). Official name: **Commonwealth of Dominica**

Dominican[1] *n* **1** a friar or nun of the Christian order founded by Saint Dominic ▷ *adj* **2** of the Dominican order

Dominican[2] *adj* **1** of or relating to the Dominican Republic or Dominica ▷ *n* **2** a native or inhabitant of the Dominican Republic or Dominica

Dominican Republic *n* a republic in the Caribbean, occupying the eastern half of the island of Hispaniola: colonized by the Spanish after its discovery by Columbus in 1492; gained independence from Spain in 1821. It is generally mountainous, dominated by the Cordillera Central, which rises over 3000 m (10 000 ft), with fertile lowlands. Language: Spanish. Religion: Roman Catholic majority. Currency: peso. Capital: Santo Domingo. Pop: 10 219 630 (2013 est). Area: 48 441 sq km (18 703 sq miles). Former name (until 1844): **Santo Domingo**

dominion *n* **1** control or authority **2** the land governed by one ruler or government **3** (formerly) a self-governing division of the British Empire [Latin *dominium* ownership]

domino[1] *n*, *pl* **-noes** a small rectangular block marked with dots, used in dominoes [Italian, perhaps from *domino!* master!, said by the winner]

domino[2] *n*, *pl* **-noes** or **-nos** a large hooded cloak worn with an eye mask at a masquerade [Latin *dominus* lord, master]

Domino *n* Fats. real name *Antoine Domino* born 1928, US rhythm-and-blues and rock-and-roll pianist, singer, and songwriter. His singles include "Ain't that a Shame" (1955) and "Blueberry Hill" (1956)

dominoes *n* a game in which dominoes with matching halves are laid together

Domitian *n* Latin name *Titus Flavius Domitianus*. 51–96 AD, Roman emperor (81–96): instigated a reign of terror (93); assassinated

Domrémy-la-Pucelle or **Domrémy** *n* a village in NE France, in the Vosges: birthplace of Joan of Arc

don[1] *vb* **donning, donned** to put on (clothing) [Middle English]

don[2] *n* **1** Brit a member of the teaching staff at a university or college **2** a Spanish gentleman or nobleman **3** (in the Mafia) the head of a family [Latin *dominus* lord]

Don *n* **1** a river rising in W Russia, southeast of Tula and flowing generally south, to the Sea of Azov: linked by canal to the River Volga. Length: 1870 km (1162 miles) **2** a river in NE Scotland, rising in the Cairngorm Mountains and flowing east to the North Sea. Length: 100 km (62 miles) **3** a river in N central England, rising in S Yorkshire and flowing northeast to the Humber. Length: about 96 km (60 miles)

Donald *n* ?1031–1100, king of Scotland (1093–94; 1094–97)

donate *vb* **-nating, -nated** to give (something) to a charity or other organization

Donatello *n* real name *Donato di Betto Bardi*. 1386–1466, Florentine sculptor, regarded as the greatest sculptor of the quattrocento, who was greatly influenced by classical sculpture and contemporary humanist theories. His marble relief of *St George Killing the Dragon* (1416–17) shows his innovative use of perspective. Other outstanding works are the classic bronze *David*, and the bronze equestrian monument to Gattamelatta, which became the model of subsequent equestrian sculpture

donation *n* **1** the act of donating **2** a contribution to a charity or other organization [Latin *donum* gift]

Donatus *n* **1** Aelius. 4th century AD, Latin grammarian, who taught Saint Jerome; his textbook *Ars Grammatica* was used throughout the Middle Ages **2** 4th century AD, bishop of Carthage; leader of the Donatists, a heretical

Christian sect originating in N Africa in 311 AD

Donau *n* the German name for the **Danube**

Donbass or **Donbas** *n* an industrial region in E Ukraine in the plain of the Rivers Donets and lower Dnieper: the site of a major coalfield. Also called: **Donets Basin**

Doncaster *n* **1** an industrial town in N England, in Doncaster unitary authority, South Yorkshire, on the River Don. Pop: 67 977 (2001) **2** a unitary authority in N England, in South Yorkshire. Pop: 288 400 (2003 est). Area: 582 sq km (225 sq miles)

donder *S African slang vb* **1** to beat (someone) up ▷ *n* **2** a wretch; swine [Dutch *donderen* to swear, bully]

done *vb* **1** the past participle of **do**[1] ▷ *interj* **2** an expression of agreement: *£60 seems reasonable, done!* ▷ *adj* **3** (of a task) completed **4** (of food) cooked enough **5** used up: *the milk is done* **6** Brit, Austral and NZ socially acceptable *the done thing* **7** *informal* cheated or tricked **8** done in or up *informal* exhausted

Donegal *n* a county in NW Republic of Ireland, on the Atlantic: mountainous, with a rugged coastline and many offshore islands. County town: Lifford. Pop: 137 57 (2002). Area: 4830 sq km (1865 sq miles)

doner kebab *n* a dish of grilled minced lamb, served in a split slice of unleavened bread [Turkish *döner* rotating]

Donets *n* a river rising in SW Russia, in the Kursk stepp and flowing southeast, through Ukraine, to the Don River. Length: about 1078 km (670 miles)

Donets Basin *n* another name for the **Donbass**

Donetsk *n* a city in E Ukraine: the chief industrial centre of the Donbass; first ironworks founded by a Welshman, John Hughes (1872), after whom the town wa named **Yuzovka** (Hughesovka). Pop: 992 000 (2005 est). Former names (from 1924 until 1961): **Stalin, Stalino**

dongle *n computers* **1** a plug-in device that allows a computer user to access the internet via mobile broadband **2** an electronic device that accompanies software to prevent the unauthorized copying of programs

Dongola *n* a small town in the N Sudan, on the Nile: built on the site of Old Dongola, the capital of the Christian Kingdom of Nubia (6th to 14th centuries). Po 16 900 (2001 est)

Dongting, Tungting or **Tung-t'ing** *n* a lake in S China in NE Hunan province: main outlet flows to the Yangtze rice-growing in winter. Area: (in winter) 3900 sq km (1500 sq miles)

Dönitz or **Doenitz** *n* Karl. 1891–1980, German admiral; commander in chief of the German navy (1943–45); as head of state after Hitler's death he surrendered to the Allies (May 7, 1945)

Donizetti *n* Gaetano. 1797–1848, Italian operatic composer: his works include *Lucia di Lammermoor* (1835), L *Fille du régiment* (1840), and *Don Pasquale* (1843)

donjon *n* the heavily fortified central tower of a castle [archaic variant of *dungeon*]

Don Juan *n* a successful seducer of women [after the legendary Spanish philanderer]

donkey *n* **1** a long-eared member of the horse family **2** a person who is considered to be stupid or stubborn [origin unknown]

donkey jacket *n* Brit, Austral and NZ a man's thick hip-length jacket with a waterproof panel across the shoulders

donkey's years *pl n informal* a long time

donkey-work *n* uninteresting groundwork

Donleavy *n* J(ames) P(atrick). born 1926, Irish-American novelist. His books include *The Ginger Man* (1956), *The Onion Eaters* (1971), *Are You Listening Rabbi Löw?* (1987), and *The Lady Who Liked Clean Rest Rooms* (1995)

Donne *n* John. 1573–1631, English metaphysical poet and preacher. He wrote love and religious poems, sermons, epigrams, and elegies

donnish *adj* resembling a university don; pedantic or fussy

onor *n* **1** *med* a person who gives blood or organs for use in the treatment of another person **2** a person who makes a donation [Latin *donare* to give]

onor card *n* a card carried by someone to show that the body parts specified may be used for transplants after the person's death

onostia-San Sebastián *n* the official name (including the Basque name Donostia) for **San Sebastián**

on Quixote (don kee-hoe-tee) *n* an impractical idealist [after the hero of Miguel de Cervantes' novel *Don Quixote de la Mancha*]

on't do not

oodle *vb* **-dling, -dled 1** to scribble or draw aimlessly ▷ *n* **2** a shape or picture drawn aimlessly [originally, a foolish person]

oohan *n* Michael K (**Mick**). born 1965, Australian racing motorcyclist; 500 cc world champion 1994–98

oolittle *n* Hilda. known as H.D. 1886–1961, US imagist poet and novelist, living in Europe

oom *n* **1** death or a terrible fate ▷ *vb* **2** to destine or condemn to death or a terrible fate [Old English *dōm*]

oomsday *or* **domesday** *n* **1** the day on which the Last Judgment will occur **2** any dreaded day [Old English *dōmes dæg* Judgment Day]

oona *n Austral* a large quilt used as a bed cover in place of the top sheet and blankets

oor *n* **1** a hinged or sliding panel for closing the entrance to a building, room, or cupboard **2** a doorway or entrance **3** a means of access or escape: *the door to happiness* **4 lay something at someone's door** to blame someone for something **5 out of doors** in the open air [Old English *duru*]

oorjamb *n* one of the two vertical posts that form the sides of a door frame. Also called: **doorpost**

oorman *n, pl* **-men** a man employed to be on duty at the main entrance of a large building

oormat *n* **1** a mat, placed at an entrance, for wiping dirt from shoes **2** *informal* a person who offers little resistance to being treated badly

oorn *n* a town in the central Netherlands, in Utrecht province: residence of Kaiser Wilhelm II of Germany from his abdication (1919) until his death (1941)

oornik *n* the Flemish name for **Tournai**

oors *pl n* **the**. US rock group (1965–73), originally comprising Jim Morrison (1943–71), Ray Manzarek (1935–2013), Robby Krieger (born 1946), and John Densmore (born 1945). See also **Morrison** (2)

oorstep *n* **1** a step in front of a door **2** *informal* a thick slice of bread

oorstop *n* a heavy object or one fixed to the floor, which prevents a door from closing or from striking a wall

oor-to-door *adj* **1** (of selling) from one house to the next **2** (of a journey) direct

oorway *n* an opening into a building or room

oosra (dooz-ruh) *n cricket* a delivery bowled by an off-spinner that turns the opposite way from an off-break [Urdu, Hindi]

op *n S African informal* a tot or small drink, usually alcoholic [Afrikaans]

ope *n* **1** *slang* an illegal drug, such as cannabis **2** a drug administered to a person or animal to affect performance in a race or other sporting competition **3** *informal* a slow-witted person **4** *informal* confidential information **5** a thick liquid, such as a lubricant ▷ *vb* **doping, doped 6** to administer a drug to [Dutch *doop* sauce]

opey *or* **dopy** *adj* **dopier, dopiest 1** *informal* half-asleep, as when under the influence of a drug **2** *slang* silly

oppelgänger (dop-pl-geng-er) *n legend* a ghostly duplicate of a living person [German *Doppelgänger* double-goer]

oppler effect *n* a change in the apparent frequency of a sound or light wave as a result of relative motion between the observer and the source [after C. J. Doppler, physicist]

Doráti *n* Antal. 1906–88, US conductor and composer, born in Hungary

dorba *n Austral informal* a stupid, inept, or clumsy person

Dorchester *n* a town in S England, administrative centre of Dorset: associated with Thomas Hardy, esp. as the Casterbridge of his novels. Pop: 16 171 (2001). Latin name: Durnovaria

Dordogne *n* **1** a river in SW France, rising in the Auvergne Mountains and flowing southwest and west to join the Garonne river and form the Gironde estuary. Length: 472 km (293 miles) **2** a department of SW France, in Aquitaine region. Capital: Périgueux. Pop: 392 291 (2003 est). Area: 9224 sq km (3597 sq miles)

Dordrecht *n* a port in the SW Netherlands, in South Holland province: chief port of the Netherlands until the 17th century. Pop: 120 000 (2003 est). Also called: **Dort**

Doré *n* (Paul) Gustave. 1832–83, French illustrator, whose style tended towards the grotesque. He illustrated the Bible, Dante's *Inferno,* Cervantes' *Don Quixote,* and works by Rabelais

Dorgon *n* 1612–50, Manchurian prince, who ruled China as regent (1643–50) and helped to establish the Ching dynasty

Dorian *n* a member of a Hellenic people who invaded Greece around 1100 BC, overthrew the Mycenaean civilization, and settled chiefly in the Peloponnese

Doric *adj* **1** of a style of classical architecture characterized by a heavy fluted column and a simple capital ▷ *n* **2** a rustic dialect, esp. a Scots one [*Doris,* in ancient Greece]

Doris *n* (in ancient Greece) **1** a small landlocked area north of the Gulf of Corinth. Traditionally regarded as the home of the Dorians, it was perhaps settled by some of them during their southward migration **2** the coastal area of Caria in SW Asia Minor, settled by Dorians

Dorkland *n NZ informal* an offensive name for Auckland ▷ **'Dorklander** *n*

dormant *adj* **1** temporarily quiet, inactive, or not being used **2** *biology* alive but in a resting condition [Latin *dormire* to sleep] ▷ **dormancy** *n*

dormer *or* **dormer window** *n* a window that is built upright in a sloping roof [Latin *dormitorium* dormitory]

dormitory *n, pl* **-ries 1** a large room, esp. at a school, containing several beds **2** a building, esp. at a college, providing living accommodation ▷ *adj* **3** *Brit and Austral* denoting an area from which most of the residents commute to work: *the swelling suburban dormitory areas* [Latin *dormitorium,* from *dormire* to sleep]

Dormobile *n trademark* a vanlike vehicle specially equipped for living in while travelling

dormouse *n, pl* **-mice** a small rodent resembling a mouse with a furry tail [origin unknown]

Dornbirn *n* a city in W Austria, in Vorarlberg. Pop: 42 301 (2001)

dorp *n S African* a small town or village [Dutch]

Dorpat *n* the German name for **Tartu**

dorsal *adj anatomy, zoology* of or on the back [Latin *dorsum* back]

Dorset *n* a county in SW England, on the English Channel: mainly hilly but low-lying in the east: the geographical and ceremonial county includes Bournemouth and Poole, which became independent unitary authorities in 1997. Administrative centre: Dorchester. Pop (excluding unitary authorities): 398 200 (2003 est). Area (excluding unitary authorities): 2544 sq km (982 sq miles). Abbreviation: **Dors**

Dort *n* another name for **Dordrecht**

Dortmund *n* an industrial city in W Germany, in North Rhine-Westphalia at the head of the **Dortmund–Ems Canal**: university (1966). Pop: 589 661 (2003 est)

dory *n, pl* **-ries** a spiny-finned food fish. Also called: **John Dory** [French *dorée* gilded]

DOS *computers* disk operating system

d

dose n **1** a specific quantity of a medicine taken at one time **2** informal something unpleasant to experience: a dose of the cold **3** the total energy of radiation absorbed **4** slang a sexually transmitted infection ▷ vb **dosing, dosed 5** to administer a quantity of medicine to (someone) [Greek dosis a giving] **> dosage** n

dosh n slang money

dosing strip n (in New Zealand) an area for treating dogs suspected of having hydatid disease

Dos Passos n John (Roderigo). 1896–1970, US novelist of the Lost Generation; author of Three Soldiers (1921), Manhattan Transfer (1925), and the trilogy USA (1930–36)

doss slang vb **1 doss down** to sleep on a makeshift bed **2** to pass time aimlessly: I doss around a lot ▷ n **3** a task requiring little effort [origin unknown]

dosshouse n slang a cheap lodging house for homeless people

dossier (doss-ee-ay) n a collection of papers about a subject or person [French]

Dostoevsky, Dostoyevsky, Dostoevski or **Dostoyevski** n Fyodor Mikhailovich. 1821–81, Russian novelist, the psychological perception of whose works has greatly influenced the subsequent development of the novel. His best-known works are Crime and Punishment (1866), The Idiot (1868), The Possessed (1871), and The Brothers Karamazov (1879–80)

dot n **1** a small round mark **2** the small round mark used to represent the short sound in Morse code **3 on the dot** at exactly the arranged time ▷ vb **dotting, dotted 4** to mark with a dot **5** to scatter or intersperse: there are numerous churches dotted around Rome **6 dot one's i's and cross one's t's** informal to pay meticulous attention to detail [Old English dott head of a boil]

dotage n feebleness of mind as a result of old age [Middle English doten to dote]

dotard n a person who is feeble-minded through old age

dotcom or **dot.com** n a company that conducts most of its business on the internet [from .com, the domain name suffix of businesses trading on the internet]

dote vb **doting, doted dote on** or **upon** to love (someone or something) to an excessive degree [Middle English doten] **> doting** adj

dotterel n a shore bird with reddish-brown underparts and white bands around the head and neck [Middle English dotrelle]

dottle n the tobacco left in a pipe after smoking [obsolete dot lump]

dotty adj **-tier, -tiest** slang slightly crazy [from dot] **> dottiness** n

Dou, Dow or **Douw** n Gerard. 1613–75, Dutch portrait and genre painter

Douai n an industrial city in N France: the political and religious centre of exiled English Roman Catholics in the 16th and 17th centuries. Pop: 42 796 (1999)

Douala or **Duala** n the chief port and largest city in W Cameroon, on the Bight of Bonny: capital of the German colony of Kamerun (1901–16). Pop: 1 980 000 (2005 est)

double adj **1** as much again in size, strength, number, etc.: a double scotch **2** composed of two equal or similar parts **3** designed for two users: a double bed **4** folded in half: the blanket had been folded double **5** stooping: she was bent double over the flower bed **6** ambiguous: a double meaning **7** false, deceitful, or hypocritical: double standards **8** music (of an instrument) sounding an octave lower: a double bass ▷ adv **9** twice over: that's double the amount requested ▷ n **10** twice the size, strength, number, etc. **11** a double measure of spirits **12** a person who closely resembles another person **13** a bet on two horses in different races in which any winnings from the first race are placed on the horse in the later race **14** at or on the double quickly or immediately ▷ vb **-bling, -bled 15** to make or become twice as much **16** to bend or fold so that one part covers another **17** to play two parts or serve two roles **18** to turn sharply **19** bridge to make a call that will double certain

scoring points if the preceding bid becomes the contrac **20 double for** to act as substitute for ▶ See also **double back, doubles, double up** [Latin duplus twofold] **> doubler** n

double agent n a spy employed by two enemy countrie at the same time

double back vb to go back in the opposite direction: I doubled back searching for the track

double-barrelled or US **-barreled** adj **1** (of a gun) having two barrels **2** Brit (of a surname) having hyphenated parts

double bass n a stringed instrument, the largest and lowest member of the violin family

double-breasted adj (of a garment) having overlapping fronts

double-check vb to make certain by checking again

double chin n a fold of fat under the chin

double cream n Brit and Austral thick cream with a high fat content

double-cross vb **1** to cheat or betray ▷ n **2** an instance o double-crossing

double-dealing n treacherous or deceitful behaviour

double-decker n **1** chiefly Brit a bus with two passenger decks one on top of the other ▷ adj **2** informal having two layers: a double-decker sandwich

double-double n **1** chiefly US and Canad basketball the feat of scoring 10 or more in each of two classes of quantifiable positive action (such as points, assists, rebounds, etc.) **2** Canad a cup of coffee served with two helpings of cream and sugar

double Dutch n informal speech or writing that is difficult to understand: it was double Dutch to me

double-edged adj **1** (of a remark) malicious in intent though apparently complimentary **2** (of a knife) having a cutting edge on either side of the blade

double entendre (doob-bl on-tond-ra) n a word or phrase with two interpretations, esp. with one meanin that is rude [obsolete French]

double entry n a book-keeping system in which a transaction is entered as a debit in one account and as a credit in another

double glazing n a window consisting of two layers of glass separated by a space, fitted to reduce heat loss

double Gloucester (glost-er) n a smooth orange-red cheese with a mild flavour

double-jointed adj (of a person) having unusually flexible joints

double knitting n a medium thickness of knitting woo

double negative n a grammatical construction, considered incorrect, in which two negatives are used where one is needed, for example I wouldn't never have believed it

double-park vb to park (a vehicle) alongside another vehicle, causing an obstruction

double pneumonia n pneumonia affecting both lung

double-quick adj **1** very quick ▷ adv **2** in a very quick manner

doubles n a game between two pairs of players

double standard n a set of principles that allows greater freedom to one person or group than to another

doublet (dub-lit) n history a man's close-fitting jacket, with or without sleeves [Old French]

double take n a delayed reaction by a person to a remark or situation: she did a double take when he said he was leaving

double talk n deceptive or ambiguous talk

doublethink n the acceptance of conflicting facts or principles at the same time

double time n **1** Brit, Austral and NZ a doubled wage rate sometimes paid for overtime work **2** music two beats per bar

double up vb **1** to bend or cause to bend in two: she was doubled up with stomach cramps **2** to share with other people we only took two cars, so we had to double up

d

double whammy *n informal* a devastating setback made up of two elements

doubloon *n* a former Spanish gold coin [Spanish *doblón*]

doubly *adv* **1** to or in a greater degree, quantity, or measure: *I have to be doubly careful* **2** in two ways: *the defence debate was doubly complicated*

Doubs *n* **1** a department of E France, in Franche-Comté region. Capital: Besançon. Pop: 505 557 (2003 est). Area: 5258 sq km (2030 sq miles) **2** a river in E France, rising in the Jura Mountains, becoming part of the border between France and Switzerland and flowing generally southwest to the Saône River. Length: 430 km (267 miles)

doubt *n* **1** uncertainty about the truth, facts, or existence of something **2** an unresolved difficulty or point **3** give someone the benefit of the doubt accept that someone is speaking the truth **4** no doubt almost certainly ▷ *vb* **5** to be inclined to disbelieve: *I doubt that we are late* **6** to distrust or be suspicious of: *he doubted their motives* [Latin *dubitare* to hesitate] **> doubter** *n*

USAGE Where a clause follows *doubt* in a positive sentence, it was formerly considered correct to use *whether*: (*I doubt whether he will come*), but now *if* and *that* are also acceptable. In negative statements, *doubt* is followed by *that*: *I do not doubt that he is telling the truth.* In such sentences, *but* (*I do not doubt but that he is telling the truth*) is redundant.

doubtful *adj* **1** unlikely or improbable: *it's doubtful that I will marry again* **2** unsure or uncertain: *I was doubtful about some of his ideas* **> doubtfully** *adv* **> doubtfulness** *n*

USAGE It was formerly considered correct to use *whether* after *doubtful* (*it is doubtful whether he will come*), but now *if* and *that* are also acceptable.

doubtless *adv* probably or almost certainly: *somebody will now and doubtless somebody will ring us*

douche (doosh) *n* **1** a stream of water directed onto or into the body for cleansing or medical purposes **2** an instrument for applying a douche ▷ *vb* **douching, douched** **3** to cleanse or treat by means of a douche [French]

dough *n* **1** a thick mixture of flour and water or milk, used for making bread, pastry, or biscuits **2** *slang* money [Old English *dāg*]

doughnut *n* a small cake of sweetened dough cooked in hot fat

doughty (dowt-ee) *adj* **-tier, -tiest** *old-fashioned* brave and determined [Old English *dohtig*]

Doughty *n* Charles Montagu. 1843–1926, English writer and traveller; author of *Travels in Arabia Deserta* (1888)

Douglas[1] *n* a town and resort on the Isle of Man, capital of the island, on the E coast. Pop: 25 347 (2001)

Douglas[2] *n* **1** C(lifford) H(ugh). 1879–1952, British economist, who originated the theory of social credit **2** Gavin. ?1474–1522, Scottish poet, the first British translator of the *Aeneid* **3** Keith (Castellain). 1920–44, British poet, noted for his poems of World War II: killed in action **4** Michael (Kirk). born 1944, US film actor; his films include *Romancing the Stone* (1984), *Wall Street* (1987), *Basic Instinct* (1992), and *Wonder Boys* (2000) **5** (George) Norman. 1868–1952, British writer, esp. of books on southern Italy such as *South Wind* (1917) **6** Tommy, full name *Thomas Clement Douglas* (1904–86). Canadian statesman: premier of Saskatchewan 1944–61

Dounreay *n* the site in N Scotland of a nuclear power station, which contained the world's first fast-breeder reactor (1962–77). A prototype fast-breeder operated from 1974 until 1994: a nuclear fuel reprocessing plant has also operated at the site

do up *vb* **1** to wrap and make into a bundle: *he did up the parcel* **2** to fasten: *to do up one's blouse* **3** to renovate or redecorate

dour (doo-er, dow-er) *adj* sullen and unfriendly [probably from Latin *durus* hard] **> dourness** *n*

Douro *n* a river in SW Europe, rising in N central Spain and flowing west to NE Portugal, then south as part of the border between the two countries and finally west to the Atlantic. Length: 895 km (556 miles). Spanish name: Duero

douse *or* **dowse** (rhymes with **mouse**) *vb* **dousing, doused** *or* **dowsing, dowsed** **1** to drench with water or other liquid **2** to put out (a light) [origin unknown]

dove *n* **1** a bird with a heavy body, small head, and short legs **2** *politics* a person opposed to war [Old English *dūfe*]

dovecote *or* **dovecot** *n* a box, shelter, or part of a house built for doves or pigeons to live in

dove-grey *adj* greyish-brown

Dover *n* **1** a port in SE England, in E Kent on the Strait of Dover: the only one of the Cinque Ports that is still important; a stronghold since ancient times and Caesar's first point of attack in the invasion of Britain (55 BC). Pop: 34 087 (2001) **2** Strait of Dover a strait between SE England and N France, linking the English Channel with the North Sea. Width: about 32 km (20 miles). French name: Pas de Calais **3** a city in the US, the capital of Delaware, founded in 1683: 18th-century buildings. Pop: 32 808 (2003 est)

dovetail *n* **1** Also called: **dovetail joint** a wedge-shaped joint used to fit two pieces of wood tightly together ▷ *vb* **2** to fit together closely or neatly: *her resignation dovetails well with the new structure*

Dovzhenko *n* Aleksandr Petrovitch. 1894–1956, Soviet film director. His films include *Zemlya* (1930) and *Ivan* (1932)

dowager *n* a woman possessing property or a title obtained from her dead husband [Old French *douagiere*]

Dowding *n* Baron Hugh Caswall Tremenheere, nicknamed *Stuffy*. 1882–1970, British air chief marshal. As commander in chief of Fighter Command (1936–40), he contributed greatly to the British victory in the Battle of Britain (1940)

dowdy *adj* **-dier, -diest** wearing dull and unfashionable clothes [Middle English *dowd* slut] **> dowdily** *adv* **> dowdiness** *n*

dowel *n* a wooden or metal peg that fits into two corresponding holes to join larger pieces of wood or metal together [Middle Low German *dövel* plug]

Dowell *n* Sir Anthony. born 1943, British ballet dancer. He became director of the Royal Ballet in 1986

dower *n* **1** the life interest in a part of her husband's estate allotted to a widow by law **2** *archaic* a dowry [Latin *dos* gift]

dower house *n* a house for the use of a widow, often on her deceased husband's estate

do with *vb* **1** could do with need or would benefit from: *I could do with some royal treatment* **2** have to do with to be associated with: *his illness has a lot to do with his failing the exam* **3** to do with concerning; related to: *this book has to do with the occult*

do without *vb* to manage without

Dowland *n* John. ?1563–1626, English lutenist and composer of songs and lute music

down[1] *prep* **1** from a higher to a lower position in or on **2** at a lower or further level or position on, in, or along: *I wandered down the corridor* ▷ *adv* **3** at or to a lower level or position: *he bent down* **4** indicating lowering or destruction: *to bring down an aircraft* **5** indicating intensity or completion: *calm down and mind your manners* **6** immediately: *cash down* **7** on paper: *she copied it down* **8** away from a more important place: *he came down from head office* **9** reduced to a state of lack: *he was down to his last pound* **10** lacking a specified amount: *down several pounds* **11** lower in price **12** from an earlier to a later time: *the ring was handed down from my grandmother* **13** to a finer state: *to grind down* **14** *sport* being a specified number of points or goals behind an opponent **15** (of a person) being

inactive, owing to illness: *down with the cold* ▷ *adj*
16 depressed or unhappy: *he seems very down today* ▷ *vb*
17 *informal* to eat or drink quickly **18** to fell (someone or
something) ▷ *n* **19 have a down on** *informal* to feel hostile
towards: *you seem to have a down on the family tonight* [Old
English *dūne* from the hill]

down² *n* soft fine feathers [Old Norse *dūnn*] ❯ **downy** *adj*

Down *n* **1 a** district of SE Northern Ireland, in Co Down.
Pop: 65 195 (2003 est). Area: 649 sq km (250 sq miles) **2 a**
historical county of SE Northern Ireland, on the Irish
Sea: generally hilly, rising to the Mountains of Mourne:
in 1973 it was replaced for administrative purposes by
the districts of Ards, Banbridge, Castlereagh, Down,
Newry and Mourne, North Down, and part of Lisburn.
Area: 2466 sq km (952 sq miles)

down-and-out *n* **1** a person who is homeless and
destitute ▷ *adj* **2** without any means of support;
destitute

downbeat *adj informal* **1** depressed or gloomy: *she was in
one of her downbeat moods* **2** casual and restrained: *the
chairman's statement was decidedly downbeat* ▷ *n* **3** *music* the
first beat of a bar

downcast *adj* **1** sad and dejected **2** (of the eyes) directed
downwards

downer *n slang* **1 a** barbiturate, tranquillizer, or narcotic
2 on a downer in a state of depression

downfall *n* **1 a** sudden loss of position or reputation
2 the cause of this

downgrade *vb* **-grading, -graded** to reduce in
importance or value

downhearted *adj* sad and discouraged

downhill *adj* **1** going or sloping down ▷ *adv* **2** towards
the bottom of a hill **3 go downhill** *informal* to deteriorate

Downing Street *n* **1** a street in W central London, in
Westminster: official residences of the British prime
minister and the chancellor of the exchequer **2** the
prime minister or the British Government [named after
Sir George *Downing* (1623–84), English statesman]

download *vb* **1** to transfer (data) from the memory of
one computer to that of another ▷ *n* **2 a** file transferred
in this way

down-market *adj* cheap, popular, and of poor quality

Downpatrick *n* a market town in Northern Ireland:
reputedly the burial place of Saint Patrick. Pop: 10 316
(2001)

down payment *n* the deposit paid on an item
purchased on hire-purchase, mortgage, etc.: *an initial
down payment is usually required*

downpour *n* a heavy continuous fall of rain

downright *adv* **1** extremely: *it's just downright cruel* ▷ *adj*
2 absolute; utter: *Crozier is a downright thief*

down-river *adj, adv* nearer the mouth of a river

downs *pl n* an area of low grassy hills, esp. in S England

Downs *n* the Downs **1** any of various ranges of low chalk
hills in S England, esp. the South Downs in Sussex **2 a**
roadstead off the SE coast of Kent, protected by the
Goodwin Sands

downshifting *n* the practice of simplifying one's
lifestyle and becoming less materialistic

downside *n* the disadvantageous aspect of a situation:
the downside of capitalism

downsize *vb* **1** to reduce the number of people employed
by (a company) **2** to reduce the size of or produce a
smaller version of (something)

Down's syndrome *or especially US, Canad and Austral*
Down syndrome *n pathol* a genetic disorder
characterized by mental impairment and physical
abnormalities, including a flattish face and a vertical
fold of skin at the inner edge of the eye [after John
Langdon-Down, physician]

downstairs *adv* **1** down the stairs; to or on a lower floor
▷ *n* **2 a** lower or ground floor

downstream *adv, adj* in or towards the lower part of a
stream; with the current

downtime *n commerce* time during which a computer o
other machine is not working

down-to-earth *adj* sensible or practical

downtown *chiefly US, Canad and NZ n* **1** the central or
lower part of a city, esp. the main commercial area ▷ *ad*
2 towards, to, or into this area

downtrodden *adj* oppressed and lacking the will to
resist

downturn *n* a drop in the success of an economy or a
business

down under *informal n* **1** Australia or New Zealand ▷ *ad*
2 in or to Australia or New Zealand

downward *adj* **1** descending from a higher to a lower
level, condition, or position ▷ *adv* **2** same as **downward**
❯ **downwardly** *adv*

downwards *or* **downward** *adv* **1** from a higher to a
lower level, condition, or position **2** from an earlier tim
or source to a later one

downwind *adv, adj* in the same direction towards whic
the wind is blowing; with the wind from behind

dowry *n, pl* **-ries** the property brought by a woman to he
husband at marriage [Latin *dos*]

dowse (rhymes with **cows**) *vb* **dowsing, dowsed 1** to
search for underground water or minerals using a
divining rod **2** same as **douse** [origin unknown]
❯ **dowser** *n*

Dowson *n* Ernest (Christopher). 1867–1900, English
Decadent poet noted for his lyric *Cynara*

doxology *n, pl* **-gies** a hymn or verse of praise to God
[Greek *doxologos* uttering praise]

doyen (doy-en) *n* the senior member of a group,
profession, or society [French] ❯ **doyenne** (doy-en) *fem n*

D'Oyly Carte *n* Richard. 1844–1901, British impresario
noted for his productions of the operettas of Gilbert an
Sullivan

doze *vb* **dozing, dozed 1** to sleep lightly or for a short
period **2 doze off** to fall into a light sleep ▷ *n* **3 a** short
sleep [probably from Old Norse *dūs* lull]

dozen *adj, n* twelve [Latin *duodecim*] ❯ **dozenth** *adj*

dozy *adj* **dozier, doziest 1** feeling sleepy **2** *Brit informal*
stupid and slow-witted

DP displaced person

DPB (in New Zealand) Domestic Purposes Benefit

dpi *computers* dots per inch

DPP (in Britain) Director of Public Prosecutions

Dr 1 Doctor **2** Drive

drab *adj* **drabber, drabbest 1** dull and dreary **2** light
olive-brown [Old French *drap* cloth] ❯ **drabness** *n*

Drabble *n* Dame Margaret. born 1939, British novelist
and editor. Her novels include *The Needle's Eye* (1972), *The
Radiant Way* (1987), and *The Seven Sisters* (2002). She edited
the 1985 and 2000 editions of the *Oxford Companion to
English Literature*

drachm (dram) *n Brit* a unit of liquid measure equal to
one eighth of a fluid ounce (3.55 ml) [variant of DRAM]

drachma *n, pl* **-mas** *or* **-mae** a former monetary unit of
Greece [Greek *drakhmē* a handful]

Draco *n* 7th century BC, Athenian statesman and
lawmaker, whose code of laws (621) prescribed death fc
almost every offence

draconian *adj* severe or harsh: *draconian measures were
taken by the government* [after DRACO]

draft *n* **1 a** preliminary outline of a letter, book, or speec
2 a written order for payment of money by a bank **3** *US
and Austral* selection for compulsory military service ▷ *v*
4 to write a preliminary outline of a letter, book, or
speech **5** to send (personnel) from one place to another
to carry out a specific job **6** *chiefly US* to select for
compulsory military service ▷ *n, vb* **7** *US* same as
draught [variant of DRAUGHT]

drag *vb* **dragging, dragged 1** to pull with force along th
ground **2** to trail on the ground **3** to persuade (someon
to go somewhere): *he didn't want to come so I had to drag him
along* **4** to move (oneself) slowly and with difficulty: *I h*

d

to drag myself out of bed this morning **5** to linger behind: *she dragged along behind her mother* **6** to search (a river) with a dragnet or hook **7** to draw (on a cigarette) **8** *computers* to move (a graphics image) from one place to another on the screen by manipulating a mouse with its button held down **9 drag away** *or* **from** to force (oneself) to come away from something interesting: *I was completely spellbound and couldn't drag myself away from the film* **10 drag on** *or* **out** to last or be prolonged tediously: *winter dragged on* **11 drag one's feet** *informal* to act with deliberate slowness ▷ *n* **12** a person or thing that slows up progress **13** *informal* a tedious or boring thing: *it was a drag having to walk two miles to the station every day* **14** *informal* a draw on a cigarette **15** an implement, such as a dragnet, used for dragging **16** *aeronautics* the resistance to the motion of a body passing through air **17** in **drag** (of a man) wearing women's clothes, usually as a form of entertainment ▶ See also **drag up** [Old English *dragan* to draw]

draggle *vb* **-gling, -gled** to make or become wet or dirty by trailing on the ground [Middle English]

dragnet *n* a net used to scour the bottom of a pond or river when searching for something

dragoman *n, pl* **-mans** *or* **-men** (in some Middle Eastern countries) a professional interpreter or guide [Arabic *targumān*]

dragon *n* **1** a mythical monster that resembles a large fire-breathing lizard **2** *informal* a fierce woman **3 chase the dragon** *slang* to smoke opium or heroin [Greek *drakōn*]

dragonfly *n, pl* **-flies** a brightly coloured insect with a long slender body and two pairs of wings

dragoon *n* **1** a heavily armed cavalryman ▷ *vb* **2** to coerce or force: *we were dragooned into participating* [French *dragon*]

drag race *n* a race in which specially built or modified cars or motorcycles are timed over a measured course ▷ **drag racing** *n*

drag up *vb informal* to revive (an unpleasant fact or story)

drain *n* **1** a pipe that carries off water or sewage **2** a cause of a continuous reduction in energy or resources: *the expansion will be a drain on resources* **3** a metal grid on a road or pavement through which rainwater flows **4 down the drain** wasted ▷ *vb* **5** to draw off or remove (liquid) from **6** to flow (away) or filter (off) **7** to dry or be emptied as a result of liquid running off or flowing away **8** to drink the entire contents of (a glass or cup) **9** to make constant demands on (energy or resources); exhaust **10** (of a river) to carry off the surface water from (an area) [Old English *drēahnian*]

drainage *n* **1** a system of pipes, drains, or ditches used to drain water or other liquids **2** the process or a method of draining

draining board *n* a grooved surface at the side of a sink, used for draining washed dishes

drainpipe *n* a pipe for carrying off rainwater or sewage

drake *n* the male of a duck [origin unknown]

Drake *n* Sir Francis. ?1540–96, English navigator and buccaneer, the first Englishman to sail around the world (1577–80). He commanded a fleet against the Spanish Armada (1588) and contributed greatly to its defeat

Drakensberg *n* a mountain range in southern Africa, extending through Lesotho, E South Africa, and Swaziland. Highest peak: Thabana Ntlenyana, 3482 m (11 425 ft). Sotho name: **Quathlamba**

Drake Passage *n* a strait between S South America and the South Shetland Islands, connecting the Atlantic and Pacific Oceans

dram *n* **1** a small amount of spirits, such as whisky **2** a unit of weight equal to one sixteenth of an ounce (avoirdupois) [Greek *drakhmē*; see DRACHMA]

drama *n* **1** a serious play for theatre, television, or radio **2** plays in general, as a form of literature **3** the art of writing, producing, or acting in a play **4** a situation that is exciting or highly emotional [Greek: something performed]

dramatic *adj* **1** of or relating to drama **2** like a drama in suddenness or effectiveness: *the government's plan has had a dramatic effect on employment in television* **3** acting or performed in a flamboyant way: *he spread his hands in a dramatic gesture of helplessness* ▷ **dramatically** *adv*

dramatics *n* **1** the art of acting or producing plays ▷ *pl n* **2** exaggerated, theatrical behaviour

dramatis personae (drah-mat-tiss per-**soh**-nigh) *pl n* the characters in a play [New Latin]

dramatist *n* a playwright: *Austria's greatest living dramatist*

dramatize *or* **-tise** *vb* **-tizing, -tized** *or* **-tising, -tised** **1** to rewrite (a book or story) in a form suitable for performing on stage **2** to express (something) in a dramatic or exaggerated way: *he dramatizes his illness* ▷ **dramatization** *or* **-tisation** *n*

Drammen *n* a port in S Norway. Pop: 56 688 (2004 est)

Drancy *n* a residential suburb of NE Paris. Pop: 66 454 (2006)

drank *vb* the past tense of **drink**

drape *vb* **draping, draped** **1** to cover with material or fabric **2** to hang or arrange in folds **3** to place casually: *he draped his arm across the back of the seat* ▶ See also **drapes** [Old French *draper*]

draper *n Brit* a person who sells fabrics and sewing materials

Draper *n* **1** Henry. 1837–82, US astronomer, who contributed to stellar classification and spectroscopy **2** his father, **John William**. 1811–82, US chemist and historian, born in England, made the first photograph of the moon

drapery *n, pl* **-peries 1** fabric or clothing arranged and draped **2** fabrics and cloth collectively

drapes *pl n Austral, NZ, US and Canad* material hung at an opening or window to shut out light or to provide privacy

drastic *adj* strong and severe: *the police are taking drastic measures against car thieves* [Greek *drastikos*] ▷ **drastically** *adv*

drat *interj slang* an exclamation of annoyance [probably alteration of *God rot*]

draught *or US* **draft** *n* **1** a current of cold air, usually one coming into a room or vehicle **2** a portion of liquid to be drunk, esp. a dose of medicine **3** a gulp or swallow: *she took a deep draught then a sip* **4** one of the flat discs used in the game of draughts. US and Canad equivalent: **checker 5 feel the draught** to be short of money **6 on draught** (of beer) drawn from a cask ▷ *adj* **7** (of an animal) used for pulling heavy loads: *horses are specialized draught animals* [probably Old Norse *drahtr*]

draught beer *n* beer stored in a cask

draughtboard *n* a square board divided into 64 squares, used for playing draughts

draughts *n* a game for two players using a draughtboard and 12 draughtsmen each [plural of *draught* (in obsolete sense: a chess move)]

draughtsman *or US* **draftsman** *n, pl* **-men 1** a person employed to prepare detailed scale drawings of equipment, machinery, or buildings **2** a person skilled in drawing **3** US and Canad equivalent: **checker** *Brit* a flat disc used in the game of draughts ▷ **draughtsmanship** *n*

draughty *or US* **drafty** *adj* **draughtier, draughtiest** *or US* **draftier, draftiest** exposed to draughts of air ▷ **draughtily** *adv* ▷ **draughtiness** *n*

Drava *or* **Drave** *n* a river in S central Europe, rising in N Italy and flowing east through Austria, then southeast along the southern Hungarian border to join the River Danube. Length: 725 km (450 miles). German name: **Drau**

draw *vb* **drawing, drew, drawn 1** to sketch (a picture, pattern, or diagram) with a pen or pencil **2** to cause (a person or thing) to move closer or further away from a place by pulling **3** to bring, take, or pull (something) out of a container: *he drew a gun and laid it on the table* **4** to take (something) from a particular source: *the inhabitants drew water from the well two miles away* **5** to move in a specified

d

direction: *he drew alongside me* **6** to attract: *she drew enthusiastic audiences from all over the country* **7** to formulate or decide: *he drew similar conclusions* **8** to cause to flow: *the barman nodded and drew two pints* **9** to choose or be given by lottery: *Brazil have drawn Spain in the semi-final of the Cup* **10** (of two teams or contestants) to finish a game with an equal number of points **11** *archery* to bend (a bow) by pulling the string **12** to cause (pus) to discharge from an abscess or wound ▷ *n* **13** a raffle or lottery **14** *informal* a person, place, show, or event that attracts a large audience **15** a contest or game ending in a tie ▶ See also **drawback, draw in**, etc. [Old English *dragan*]

drawback *n* **1** a disadvantage or hindrance ▷ *vb* **draw back 2** to move backwards: *the girl drew back as though in pain* **3** to turn aside from an undertaking: *the prime minister drew back from his original intention*

drawbridge *n* a bridge that may be raised to prevent access or to enable vessels to pass

drawer *n* **1** a sliding box-shaped part of a piece of furniture used for storage **2** a person or thing that draws

drawers *pl n old-fashioned* an undergarment worn on the lower part of the body

draw in *vb* **1** (of a train) to arrive at a station **2 the nights are drawing in** the hours of daylight are becoming shorter

drawing *n* **1** a picture or plan made by means of lines on a surface **2** the art of making drawings

drawing pin *n Brit and NZ* a short tack with a broad smooth head used for fastening papers to a drawing board or other surface

drawing room *n* a room where visitors are received and entertained

drawl *vb* **1** to speak slowly with long vowel sounds ▷ *n* **2** the way of speech of someone who drawls [probably frequentative of *draw*] ❯ **drawling** *adj*

drawn *vb* **1** the past participle of **draw** ▷ *adj* **2** haggard, tired, or tense in appearance

draw off *vb* to cause (a liquid) to flow from something

draw on *vb* **1** to make use of from a source or fund: *they are able to draw on a repertoire of around 400 songs* **2** (of a period of time) to come near or pass by: *summer draws on; time draws on*

draw out *vb* **1** (of a train) to leave a station **2** to encourage (someone) to talk freely: *therapy groups will continue to draw her out* **3 draw out of** to find out (information) from

drawstring *n* a cord run through a hem around an opening, so that when it is pulled tighter, the opening closes

draw up *vb* **1** to prepare and write out: *the signatories drew up a draft agreement* **2** (of a vehicle) to come to a halt

dray *n* a low cart used for carrying heavy loads [Old English *drǣge* dragnet]

Drayton *n* Michael. 1563–1631, English poet. His work includes odes and pastorals, and *Poly-Olbion* (1613–22), on the topography of England

dread *vb* **1** to anticipate with apprehension or terror ▷ *n* **2** great fear [Old English *ondrǣdan*]

dreadful *adj* **1** extremely disagreeable or shocking **2** extreme: *there were dreadful delays* ❯ **dreadfully** *adv*

dreadlocks *pl n* hair worn in the Rastafarian style of tightly curled strands

dreadnought *n* **1** a type of battleship with heavy guns **2** a heavy overcoat

dream *n* **1** an imagined series of events experienced in the mind while asleep **2** a daydream: *the dream of success turning into a nightmare* **3** a goal or aim: *Unity has been their constant dream* **4** a wonderful person or thing: *her house is a dream* ▷ *vb* **dreaming, dreamed** or **dreamt 5** to experience (a dream) **6** to indulge in daydreams **7** to be unrealistic: *you're dreaming if you think we can win* **8 dream of** to consider the possibility of: *she would not dream of taking his advice* **9 dream of** or **about** to have an image of or fantasy about: *they often dream about what life will be like for them on*

the outside ▷ *adj* **10** beautiful or pleasing: *a dream kitchen* [Old English *drēam* song] ❯ **dreamer** *n*

dream team *n informal* a group of people regarded as having the perfect combination of talents

dream ticket *n* a combination of two people, esp. candidates in an election, that is considered to be ideal

dream up *vb* to formulate in the imagination: *a character dreamed up by a scriptwriter*

dreamy *adj* **dreamier, dreamiest 1** vague or impractical: *she was wild-eyed and dreamy* **2** relaxing or gentle: *I felt this dreamy contentment* **3** *informal* wonderful or impressive: *he drives a dreamy Jaguar* ❯ **dreamily** *adv* ❯ **dreaminess** *n*

dreary *adj* **drearier, dreariest** dull or uninteresting: *there are long streets of dreary red houses spreading everywhere* [Old English *drēorig* gory] ❯ **drearily** *adv* ❯ **dreariness** *n*

dredge¹ *n* **1** a machine used to scoop or suck up silt or mud from a river bed or harbour ▷ *vb* **dredging, dredged 2** to remove silt or mud from (a river bed or harbour) by means of a dredge **3** to search for (a submerged object) with or as if with a dredge [origin unknown] ❯ **dredger** *n*

dredge² *vb* **dredging, dredged** to sprinkle (food) with a substance, such as flour [Old French *dragie*] ❯ **dredger** *n*

dredge up *vb informal* to remember (something obscure or half-forgotten): *I didn't retain you to dredge up unfortunate incidents from my past*

dregs *pl n* **1** solid particles that settle at the bottom of some liquids **2 the dregs** the worst or most despised elements: *the dregs of colonial society* [Old Norse *dregg*]

Dreiser *n* Theodore (Herman Albert). 1871–1945, US novelist; his works include *Sister Carrie* (1900) and *An American Tragedy* (1925)

drench *vb* **1** to make completely wet **2** to give medicine to (an animal) [Old English *drencan* to cause to drink] ❯ **drenching** *n, adj*

Drenthe *n* a province of the NE Netherlands: a low plateau, with many raised bogs, partially reclaimed; agricultural, with oil deposits. Capital: Assen. Pop: 481 000 (2003 est). Area: 2647 sq km (1032 sq miles)

Dresden *n* **1** an industrial city in SE Germany, the capital of Saxony on the River Elbe: it was severely damaged in the Seven Years' War (1760); the baroque city was almost totally destroyed in World War II by Allied bombing (1945). Pop: 483 632 (2003 est) **2** Also: **Dresden china** delicate and decorative porcelain made near Dresden ▷ *adj* **3** relating to, designating, or made of Dresden china

dress *n* **1** a one-piece garment worn by a woman or girl, with a skirt and bodice and sometimes sleeves **2** complete style of clothing: *contemporary dress* ▷ *adj* **3** suitable for a formal occasion: *he was wearing a dress shirt* ▷ *vb* **4** to put clothes on **5** to put on formal clothes **6** to apply protective covering to (a wound) **7** to cover (a salad) with dressing **8** to prepare (meat, poultry, or fish for selling or cooking by cleaning or gutting **9** to put a finish on (the surface of stone, metal, or other building material) ▶ See also **dress up** [Old French *drecier* to arrange]

dressage (dress-ahzh) *n* **a** the method of training horses to perform manoeuvres as a display of obedience **b** the manoeuvres performed [French]

dress circle *n* the first gallery in a theatre

dress code *n* a set of rules regarding the style of dress acceptable in an office, restaurant, etc.

dresser¹ *n* **1** a piece of furniture with shelves and cupboards, used for storing or displaying dishes **2** *US* a chest of drawers [Old French *drecier* to arrange]

dresser² *n* **1** a person who dresses in a specified way: *Lara was a meticulous, elegant dresser* **2** *theatre* a person employed to assist performers with their costumes

dressing *n* **1** a sauce for food: *salad dressing* **2** *US and Canad* same as **stuffing** (1) **3** a covering for a wound **4** manure or fertilizer spread on land **5** a gluey material used for stiffening paper, textiles, etc.

dressing-down n informal a severe reprimand

dressing gown n a loose-fitting garment worn over one's pyjamas or nightdress

dressing room n a room used for changing clothes and applying make-up, esp. a backstage room in a theatre

dressing table n a piece of bedroom furniture with a mirror and a set of drawers

dressmaker n a person who makes clothes for women **> dressmaking** n

dress rehearsal n 1 the last rehearsal of a play, opera, or show using costumes, lighting, and other effects 2 any full-scale practice: astronauts are in the midst of a two day dress rehearsal of their launch countdown

dress shirt n a man's evening shirt, worn as part of formal evening dress

dress suit n a man's evening suit

dress up vb 1 to put on glamorous or stylish clothes 2 to put fancy dress on: the guests dressed up like cowboys 3 to disguise (something) to make it more attractive or acceptable: the offer was simply an old one dressed up in new terms

dressy adj **dressier, dressiest** 1 (of clothes or occasions) elegant 2 (of people) dressing stylishly **> dressiness** n

drew vb the past tense of **draw**

drey or **dray** n Brit and Austral a squirrel's nest [origin unknown]

Dreyfus n Alfred. 1859–1935, French army officer, a Jew whose false imprisonment for treason (1894) raised issues of anti-semitism and militarism that dominated French politics until his release (1906)

dribble vb **-bling, -bled** 1 to flow or allow to flow in a thin stream or drops 2 to allow saliva to trickle from the mouth 3 (in football, hockey, etc.) to propel (the ball) by kicking or tapping in quick succession ▷ n 4 a small quantity of liquid falling in drops or flowing in a thin stream 5 a small supply: there's only a dribble of milk left 6 an act or instance of dribbling [obsolete drib, variant of drip] **> dribbler** n

ribs and drabs pl n informal small occasional amounts

dried vb the past of **dry**

drier¹ adj a comparative of **dry**

drier² n same as **dryer¹**

Driesch n Hans Adolf Eduard. 1867–1941, German zoologist and embryologist

driest adj a superlative of **dry**

drift vb 1 to be carried along by currents of air or water 2 to move aimlessly from one place or activity to another 3 to wander away from a fixed course or point 4 (of snow) to pile up in heaps ▷ n 5 something piled up by the wind or current, as a snowdrift 6 a general movement or development: there has been a drift away from family control 7 the main point of an argument or speech: I was beginning to get his drift 8 the extent to which a vessel or aircraft is driven off course by winds, etc. 9 a current of water created by the wind [Old Norse]

drifter n 1 a person who moves aimlessly from place to place 2 a boat used for drift-net fishing

drift net n a fishing net that is allowed to drift with the tide

driftwood n wood floating on or washed ashore by the sea

drill¹ n 1 a machine or tool for boring holes 2 military training in procedures or movements, as for parades 3 strict and often repetitive training 4 informal correct procedure: he knows the drill as well as anybody ▷ vb 5 to bore a hole in (something) with or as if with a drill 6 to instruct or be instructed in military procedures or movements 7 to teach by rigorous exercises or training [Middle Dutch drillen]

drill² n 1 a machine for planting seeds in rows 2 a furrow in which seeds are sown 3 a row of seeds planted by means of a drill ▷ vb 4 to plant (seeds) by means of a drill [origin unknown]

drill³ n a hard-wearing cotton cloth, used for uniforms [German Drillich]

drill⁴ n a W African monkey, related to the mandrill [from a West African word]

drilling platform n an offshore structure that supports a drilling rig

drilling rig n the complete machinery, equipment, and structures needed to drill an offshore oil well

drily or **dryly** adv in a dry manner

Drin n a river in S Europe, rising in SW Macedonia and flowing north and west, through Albania, into the Adriatic Sea. Length: about 270 km (170 miles)

drink vb **drinking, drank, drunk** 1 to swallow (a liquid) 2 to consume alcohol, esp. to excess 3 to bring (oneself) into a specified condition by consuming alcohol: he drank himself senseless every night 4 drink someone's health to wish someone health or happiness with a toast 5 drink in to pay close attention to: I drank in what the speaker said 6 drink to to drink a toast to: I drank to their engagement ▷ n 7 liquid suitable for drinking 8 a portion of liquid for drinking 9 alcohol, or the habit of drinking too much of it [Old English drincan] **> drinkable** adj **> drinker** n

drink-driving adj of or relating to driving a car after drinking alcohol: a drink-driving offence

Drinkwater n John. 1882–1937, English dramatist, poet, and critic; author of chronicle plays such as Abraham Lincoln (1918) and Mary Stuart (1921)

drip vb **dripping, dripped** 1 to fall or let fall in drops ▷ n 2 a drop of liquid 3 the falling of drops of liquid 4 the sound made by falling drops 5 informal a weak or foolish person 6 med a device that administers a liquid drop by drop into a vein [Old English dryppan]

drip-dry adj 1 (of clothes or fabrics) designed to dry without creases if hung up when wet ▷ vb **-dries, -drying, -dried** 2 to dry or become dry thus

drip-feed vb **-feeding, -fed** 1 to feed (someone) a liquid drop by drop, usually through a vein ▷ n **drip feed** 2 same as **drip** (6)

dripping n the fat that comes from meat while it is being roasted

drive vb **driving, drove, driven** 1 to guide the movement of (a vehicle) 2 to transport or be transported in a vehicle 3 to goad into a specified state: the black despair that finally drove her to suicide 4 to push or propel: he drove the nail into the wall with a hammer 5 sport to hit (a ball) very hard and straight 6 golf to strike (the ball) with a driver 7 to chase (game) from cover 8 drive home to make (a point) clearly understood by emphasis ▷ n 9 a journey in a driven vehicle 10 a road for vehicles, esp. a private road leading to a house 11 a special effort made by a group of people for a particular purpose: a charity drive 12 energy, ambition, or initiative 13 psychol a motive or interest: sex drive 14 a sustained and powerful military offensive 15 the means by which power is transmitted in a machine 16 sport a hard straight shot or stroke [Old English drīfan]

drive at vb to intend or mean: he had no idea what she was driving at

drive-by n informal an incident in which a person is shot at by a person in a moving vehicle

drive-in n 1 a cinema, restaurant, etc. offering a service where people remain in their cars while using the service provided ▷ adj 2 denoting a cinema, etc. of this kind

drivel n 1 foolish talk ▷ vb **-velling, -velled** or US **-veling, -veled** 2 to speak foolishly 3 to allow (saliva) to flow from the mouth [Old English dreflian to slaver]

driven vb the past participle of **drive**

driver n 1 a person who drives a vehicle 2 golf a long-shafted club with a large head and steep face, used for tee shots

drive-thru n 1 a takeaway restaurant, bank, etc., designed so that customers can use it without leaving their cars ▷ adj 2 denoting a restaurant, etc. of this kind

drive-time n 1 the time of day when many people are driving to or from work, considered as a broadcasting slot ▷ *adj* **2** of this time of day: *the daily drive-time show*

driveway *n* a path for vehicles connecting a building to a public road

driving licence *n* an official document authorizing a person to drive a motor vehicle. Also called: (Canada and Australia) **driver's licence**, (US) **driver's license**, (New Zealand) **driver license**

drizzle *n* **1** very light rain ▷ *vb* **-zling, -zled 2** to rain lightly [Old English *drēosan* to fall] **> drizzly** *adj*

Drnovsek *n* Janez. 1950–2008, Slovenian politician, president of Slovenia from 2002

Drobny *n* Jaroslav (; *Czech*). 1921–2001, British tennis and ice-hockey player, born in Czechoslovakia: Wimbledon champion 1954: a member of the Czech ice-hockey team in the 1948 Olympic Games

Drogheda *n* a port in NE Republic of Ireland, in Co Louth near the mouth of the River Boyne: captured by Cromwell in 1649 and its inhabitants massacred. Pop: 31 020 (2002)

droll *adj* quaintly amusing [French *drôle* scamp] **> drollery** *n* **> drolly** *adv*

Drôme *n* a department of SE France, in Rhône-Alpes region. Capital: Valence. Pop: 452 652 (2003 est. Area: 6561 sq km (2559 sq miles)

dromedary (drom-mid-er-ee) *n*, *pl* **-daries** a camel with a single hump [Greek *dromas* running]

drone¹ *n* **1** a male honeybee **2** a person who lives off the work of others [Old English *drān*]

drone² *vb* **droning, droned 1** to make a monotonous low dull sound **2 drone on** to talk in a monotonous tone without stopping ▷ *n* **3** a monotonous low dull sound **4** a single-reed pipe in a set of bagpipes [related to DRONE¹]

drongo *n* a tropical songbird with a glossy black plumage, a forked tail, and a stout bill

drool *vb* **1 drool over** to show excessive enthusiasm for or pleasure in **2** same as **drivel** (2, 3) [probably alteration of DRIVEL]

droop *vb* **1** to sag, as from weakness or lack of support **2** to be overcome by weariness: *her eyelids drooped as if she were falling asleep* [Old Norse *drūpa*] **> drooping** *adj*

droopy *adj* hanging or sagging downwards: *a droopy moustache*

drop *vb* **dropping, dropped 1** to fall or allow (something) to fall vertically **2** to decrease in amount, strength, or value **3** to fall to the ground, as from exhaustion **4** to sink to a lower position, as on a scale **5** to mention casually: *he dropped a hint* **6** to set down (passengers or goods): *can you drop me at the hotel?* **7** *informal* to send: *drop me a letter* **8** to discontinue: *can we drop the subject?* **9** *informal* to be no longer friendly with: *I dropped him when I discovered his political views* **10** to leave out in speaking: *he has a tendency to drop his h's* **11** (of animals) to give birth to (offspring) **12** *sport* to omit (a player) from a team **13** to lose (a game or point) **14 drop back** to progress more slowly than other people going in the same direction **15 drop in** or *by informal* to pay someone a casual visit ▷ *n* **16** a small quantity of liquid forming a round shape **17** a small quantity of liquid **18** a small round sweet: *a lemon drop* **19** a decrease in amount, strength, or value **20** the vertical distance that anything may fall **21** the act of unloading troops or supplies by parachute ▶ See also **drop off, dropout, drops** [Old English *dropian*]

drop curtain *n theatre* a curtain that can be raised and lowered onto the stage

drop kick *n* a kick in certain sports such as rugby, in which the ball is dropped and kicked as it bounces from the ground

droplet *n* a very small drop of liquid

drop off *vb* **1** to set down (passengers or goods) **2** to fall asleep **3** to decrease or decline: *sales dropped off during our period of transition*

dropout *n* **1** a person who rejects conventional society **2** a student who does not complete a course of study ▷ *vb*

drop out 3 to abandon or withdraw (from an institution or group)

dropper *n* a small tube with a rubber part at one end for drawing up and dispensing drops of liquid

droppings *pl n* the dung of certain animals, such as rabbits or birds

drops *pl n* any liquid medication applied by means of a dropper

drop scone *n* a flat spongy cake made by dropping a spoonful of batter on a hot griddle

dropsy *n* an illness in which watery fluid collects in the body [Middle English *ydropesie*, from Greek *hudōr* water] **> dropsical** *adj*

drosky or **droshky** *n*, *pl* **-kies** an open four-wheeled carriage, formerly used in Russia [Russian *drozhki*]

dross *n* **1** the scum formed on the surfaces of molten metals **2** anything of inferior quality: *we can't publish this dross* [Old English *drōs* dregs]

drought (rhymes with **out**) *n* a prolonged period of time during which no rain falls [Old English *drūgoth*]

drove¹ *vb* the past tense of **drive**

drove² *n* **1** a herd of livestock being driven together **2** a moving crowd of people [Old English *drāf* herd]

drover *n* a person who drives sheep or cattle

drown *vb* **1** to die or kill by immersion in liquid **2** to drench thoroughly **3** to make (a sound) impossible to hear by making a loud noise [probably from Old English *druncnian*]

drowse *vb* **drowsing, drowsed** to be sleepy, dull, or sluggish [probably from Old English *drūsian* to sink]

drowsy *adj* **drowsier, drowsiest 1** feeling sleepy **2** peaceful and quiet: *row upon row of windows looked out over drowsy parkland* **> drowsily** *adv* **> drowsiness** *n*

drubbing *n* an utter defeat, as in a contest: *the Communist received a drubbing* [probably from Arabic *dáraba* to beat]

drudge *n* **1** a person who works hard at an uninteresting task ▷ *vb* **drudging, drudged 2** to work at such tasks [origin unknown]

drudgery *n* uninteresting work that must be done

drug *n* **1** any substance used in the treatment, prevention, or diagnosis of disease **2** a chemical substance, such as a narcotic, taken for the effects it produces ▷ *vb* **drugging, drugged 3** to administer a drug to (a person or animal) in order to induce sleepiness or unconsciousness **4** to mix a drug with (food or drink): *who drugged my wine?* [Old French *drogue*]

drug addict *n* a person who is dependent on narcotic drugs

druggist *n* US and Canad a pharmacist

drugstore *n* US and Canad a pharmacy where a wide variety of goods are available

Druid *n* a member of an ancient order of Celtic priests [Latin *druides*] **> Druidic** or **Druidical** *adj*

drum *n* **1** a percussion instrument sounded by striking a skin stretched across the opening of a hollow cylinder **2** the sound produced by a drum **3** an object shaped like a drum: *an oil drum* **4** same as **eardrum** ▷ *vb* **drumming, drummed 5** to play (music) on a drum **6** to tap rhythmically or regularly: *he drummed his fingers on the desk* **7** to fix in someone's mind by constant repetition: *my father always drummed into us how privileged we were* ▶ See also **drum up** [Middle Dutch *tromme*] **> drummer** *n*

drumbeat *n* the sound made by beating a drum

drumhead *n* the part of a drum that is struck

drum machine *n* a synthesizer programmed to reproduce the sound of percussion instruments

drum major *n* the noncommissioned officer in the army who is in command of the drums and the band when paraded together

drum majorette *n* a girl who marches at the head of a procession, twirling a baton

Drummond of Hawthornden *n* William. 1585–1649, Scottish poet, historian, and royalist pamphleteer

drumstick *n* **1** a stick used for playing a drum **2** the lower joint of the leg of a cooked fowl

drum up *vb* to obtain (support or business) by making requests or canvassing

drunk *vb* **1** the past participle of **drink** ▷ *adj* **2** intoxicated with alcohol to the extent of losing control over normal functions **3** overwhelmed by strong influence or emotion: *he was half drunk with satisfaction at his victory over the intruder* ▷ *n* **4** a person who is drunk or drinks habitually to excess [Old English *druncen*, past participle of *drincan* to drink]

drunkard *n* a person who is frequently or habitually drunk

drunken *adj* **1** intoxicated with alcohol **2** habitually drunk **3** caused by or relating to alcoholic intoxication: *a drunken argument* **> drunkenly** *adv* **> drunkenness** *n*

drupe *n* a fleshy fruit with a stone, such as the peach or cherry [Greek *druppa* olive]

Drury Lane *n* a street in the West End of London, formerly famous for its theatres

dry *adj* **drier, driest** *or* **dryer, dryest 1** lacking moisture **2** having little or no rainfall **3** having the water drained away or evaporated: *a dry gully for the most part of the year* **4** not providing milk: *a dry cow* **5** (of the eyes) free from tears **6** *Brit, Austral and NZ informal* thirsty **7** eaten without butter or jam: *a dry cracker* **8** (of wine) not sweet **9** dull and uninteresting: *a dry subject* **10** (of humour) subtle and sarcastic **11** prohibiting the sale of alcoholic liquor: *a dry district* ▷ *vb* **dries, drying, dried 12** to make or become dry **13** to preserve (food) by removing the moisture ▶ See also **dry out, dry up** [Old English *drȳge*] **> dryness** *n*

dryad *n, pl* **dryads** *or* **dryades** (dry-ad-deez) *Greek myth* a wood nymph [Greek *druas*]

dry battery *n* an electric battery composed of dry cells

dry cell *n* an electric cell in which the electrolyte is in the form of a paste to prevent it from spilling

dry-clean *vb* to clean (clothes, etc.) with a solvent other than water **> dry-cleaner** *n* **> dry-cleaning** *n*

Dryden *n* John. 1631–1700, English poet, dramatist, and critic of the Augustan period, commonly regarded as the chief exponent of heroic tragedy. His major works include the tragedy *All for Love* (1677), the verse satire *Absalom and Achitophel* (1681), and the *Essay of Dramatick Poesie* (1668)

dry dock *n* a dock that can be pumped dry to permit work on a ship's bottom

dryer¹ *n* any device that removes moisture by heating or by hot air

dryer² *adj* same as **drier¹**

dry ice *n* solid carbon dioxide used as a refrigerant

dryly *adv* same as **drily**

dry out *vb* **1** to make or become dry **2** to undergo or cause to undergo treatment for alcoholism or drug addiction

dry rot *n* **1** crumbling and drying of timber, caused by certain fungi **2** a fungus causing this decay

dry run *n informal* a rehearsal

Drysdale *n* Sir George Russell. 1912–81, Australian painter, esp. of landscapes

dry stock *n NZ* cattle raised for meat

dry-stone *adj* (of a wall) made without mortar

Dry Tortugas *n* a group of eight coral islands at the entrance to the Gulf of Mexico: part of Florida

dry up *vb* **1** to make or become dry **2** to dry (dishes, cutlery, etc.) with a tea towel after they have been washed **3** (of a resource) to come to an end **4** *informal* to stop speaking: *she suddenly dried up in the middle of her speech*

Ds *chem* darmstadtium

DSC *Brit military* Distinguished Service Cross

DSO *Brit military* Distinguished Service Order

DSS *Brit* Department of Social Security

DSW (in New Zealand) Department of Social Welfare

DTP *computers* desktop publishing

DT's *informal* delirium tremens

dual *adj* having two parts, functions, or aspects: *dual controls; dual nationality* [Latin *duo* two] **> duality** *n*

dual carriageway *n Brit, Austral and NZ* a road with a central strip of grass or concrete to separate traffic travelling in opposite directions

dub¹ *vb* **dubbing, dubbed** to give (a person or place) a name or nickname: *he is dubbed a racist despite his strong denials* [Old English *dubbian*]

dub² *vb* **dubbing, dubbed 1** to provide (a film) with a new soundtrack in a different language **2** to provide (a film or tape) with a soundtrack ▷ *n* **3** *music* a style of reggae record production involving exaggeration of instrumental parts, echo, etc. [shortened from DOUBLE]

Dubai *n* a sheikhdom in the NE United Arab Emirates, consisting principally of the port of Dubai, on the Persian Gulf: oilfields. Pop: 1 026 000 (2005 est)

du Barry *n* Comtesse, original name *Marie Jeanne Bécu*. ?1743–93, mistress of Louis XV, guillotined in the French Revolution

dubbin *n* a kind of thick grease applied to leather to soften it and make it waterproof [*dub* to dress leather]

Dubček *n* Alexander. 1921–92, Czechoslovak statesman. His reforms as first secretary of the Czechoslovak Communist Party prompted the Russian invasion of 1968

dubious (dew-bee-uss) *adj* **1** not entirely honest, safe, or reliable: *this allegation was at best dubious and at worst an outright fabrication* **2** unsure or undecided: *she felt dubious about the entire proposition* **3** of doubtful quality or worth: *she had the dubious honour of being taken for his mother* [Latin *dubius* wavering] **> dubiety** (dew-by-it-ee) *n* **> dubiously** *adv*

Dublin *n* **1** the capital of the Republic of Ireland, on Dublin Bay: under English rule from 1171 until 1922; commercial and cultural centre; contains one of the world's largest breweries and exports whiskey, stout, and agricultural produce. Pop: 1 004 614 (2002). Gaelic name: **Baile Átha Cliath 2** a county in E Republic of Ireland, in Leinster on the Irish Sea: mountainous in the south but low-lying in the north and centre. County seat: Dublin. Pop: 1 122 821 (2002). Area: 922 sq km (356 sq miles)

Dubliner *n* a native or inhabitant of Dublin

Dubna *n* a new town in W Russia, founded in 1956: site of the United Institute of Nuclear Research. Pop: 60 951 (2002)

dubnium *n chem* an element produced in minute quantities by bombarding plutonium with high-energy neon ions. Symbol: **Db** [after DUBNA, where it was first reported]

Dubois *n* W(illiam) E(dward) B(urghardt). 1868–1963, US Black sociologist, writer, and political activist; a founder of the National Association for the Advancement of Colored People (NAACP)

Dubrovnik *n* a port in W Croatia, on the Dalmatian coast: an important commercial centre in the Middle Ages; damaged in 1991 when it was shelled by Serbian artillery. Pop: 43 770 (2001). Former Italian name (until 1918): **Ragusa**

Dubuffet *n* Jean. 1901–85, French painter, inspired by graffiti and the untrained art of children and psychotics

ducal (duke-al) *adj* of a duke

ducat (duck-it) *n* a former European gold or silver coin [Old Italian *ducato*]

Duccio di Buoninsegna *n* ?1255–?1318, Italian painter; founder of the Sienese school

Duchamp *n* Marcel. 1887–1968, US painter and sculptor, born in France; noted as a leading exponent of Dada. His best-known work is *Nude Descending a Staircase* (1912)

duchess *n* **1** a woman who holds the rank of duke **2** the wife or widow of a duke [Old French *duchesse*]

duchy *n, pl* **duchies** the area of land owned or ruled by a duke or duchess [Old French *duché*]

duck¹ *n, pl* **ducks** *or* **duck 1** a water bird with short legs, webbed feet, and a broad blunt bill **2** the flesh of this bird used for food **3** the female of such a bird **4** *cricket* a score of nothing **5** like water off a duck's back without effect: *I reprimanded him but it was like water off a duck's back* [Old English *dūce*]

duck² *vb* **1** to move (the head or body) quickly downwards, to escape being seen or avoid a blow **2** to plunge suddenly under water **3** *informal* to dodge (a duty or responsibility) [Middle English]

duck-billed platypus *n* See platypus

duckling *n* a young duck

ducks and drakes *n* **1** a game in which a flat stone is bounced across the surface of water **2** play ducks and drakes with *informal* to use recklessly: *he has played ducks and drakes with his life*

duct *n* **1** a tube, pipe, or channel through which liquid or gas is sent **2** a tube in the body through which liquid such as tears or bile can pass [Latin *ducere* to lead]

ductile *adj* (of a metal) able to be shaped into sheets or drawn out into threads [Latin *ductilis*] **> ductility** *n*

dud *informal* *n* **1** an ineffectual person or thing: *they had the foresight to pick on someone who was not a total dud* ▷ *adj* **2** bad or useless: *a dud cheque* [origin unknown]

dude *n informal* **1** *US and Canad* a man: *he was a black dude in his late twenties* **2** *chiefly US and Canad old-fashioned* a dandy **3** *Western US and Canad* a city dweller who spends his or her holiday on a ranch [origin unknown]

dudgeon *n* in high dudgeon angry or resentful: *the scientist departed in high dudgeon* [origin unknown]

Dudley *n* **1** a town in W central England, in Dudley unitary authority, West Midlands: wrought-iron industry. Pop: 194 919 (2001) **2** a unitary authority in W central England, in West Midlands. Pop: 304 800 (2003 est). Area: 98 sq km (38 sq miles)

due *adj* **1** expected to happen, be done, or arrive at a particular time: *he is due to return on Thursday* **2** immediately payable: *the balance is now due* **3** owed as a debt: *they finally agreed to pay her the money she was due* **4** fitting or proper: *he was found guilty of driving without due care and attention* **5** due to happening or existing as a direct result of someone or something else: *the cause of death was chronic kidney failure due to diabetes* ▷ *n* **6** something that is owed or required **7** give someone his or her due to acknowledge someone's good points: *I'll give him his due, he's resourceful* ▷ *adv* **8** directly or exactly: *due west* [Latin *debere* to owe]

USAGE The use of *due to* as a compound preposition (*the performance has been cancelled due to bad weather*) was formerly considered incorrect, but is now acceptable.

duel *n* **1** a formal fight between two people using guns, swords, or other weapons to settle a quarrel ▷ *vb* **duelling, duelled** *or US* **dueling, dueled 2** to fight in a duel [Latin *duellum*, poetical variant of *bellum* war] **> duellist** *or US* **duelist** *n*

duenna *n* (esp. in Spain) an elderly woman acting as chaperone to girls [Spanish *dueña*]

Duero *n* the Spanish name for the Douro

dues *pl n* membership fees paid to a club or organization: *union dues*

duet *n* a piece of music sung or played by two people [Latin *duo* two] **> duettist** *n*

duff *adj* **1** *chiefly Brit informal* broken or useless: *my car had a duff clutch* ▷ *vb* **2** *golf informal* to bungle (a shot) **3** duff up *Brit slang* to beat (someone) severely [probably from *duffer*]

duffel *or* **duffle** *n* same as duffel coat [after *Duffel*, Belgian town]

duffel bag *n* a cylinder-shaped canvas bag fastened with a drawstring

duffel coat *n* a wool coat usually with a hood and fastened with toggles

duffer *n informal* a dull or incompetent person [origin unknown]

Duffy *n* Dame **Carol Ann**. born 1955, British poet and writer; poet laureate from 2009, her collections include *Standing Female Nude* (1985), *The World's Wife* (1999), and *Rapture* (2005)

Du Fu *or* **Tu Fu** *n* 712–770 AD, Chinese poet of the Tang dynasty

Dufy *n* **Raoul**. 1877–1953, French painter and designer whose style is characterized by swift calligraphic draughtsmanship and bright colouring

dug¹ *vb* the past of dig

dug² *n* a teat or udder of a female animal [Scandinavian]

dugite (doo-gyte) *n* a medium-sized Australian venomous snake

dugong *n* a whalelike mammal found in tropical waters [Malay *duyong*]

dugout *n* **1** a canoe made by hollowing out a log **2** *Brit* (at a sports ground) the covered bench where managers and substitutes sit **3** *military* a covered shelter dug in the ground to provide protection

Du Guesclin *n* **Bertrand**. ?1320–80, French military leader; as constable of France (1370–80), he helped to drive the English from France

Duhamel *n* **Georges**. 1884–1966, French novelist, poet, and dramatist; author of *La Chronique des Pasquier* (1933–45)

duiker *or* **duyker** (dike-er) *n*, *pl* **-kers** *or* **-ker** a small African antelope [Dutch: diver]

Duisburg *n* an industrial city in NW Germany, in North Rhine-Westphalia at the confluence of the Rivers Rhine and Ruhr: one of the world's largest and busiest inland ports; university (1972). Pop: 506 496 (2003 est)

Duisenberg *n* **Willem Frederik**, known as *Wim*. 1935–2005, Dutch economist; president of the European Central Bank (1998–2003)

du jour (doo zhoor) *adj informal* currently fashionable [French, literally: of the day]

Dukas *n* **Paul**. 1865–1935, French composer best known for the orchestral scherzo *The Sorcerer's Apprentice* (1897)

duke *n* **1** a nobleman of the highest rank **2** the prince or ruler of a small principality or duchy [Latin *dux* leader] **> dukedom** *n*

Dulbecco *n* **Renato**. 1914–2012, US physician and molecular biologist, born in Italy: shared the Nobel prize for physiology or medicine (1975) for cancer research

dulcet (dull-sit) *adj* (of a sound) soothing or pleasant: *she smiled and, in dulcet tones, told me I would be next* [Latin *dulcis* sweet]

dulcimer *n* a tuned percussion instrument consisting of a set of strings stretched over a sounding board and struck with hammers [Old French *doulcemer*]

dull *adj* **1** not interesting: *the finished article would make dull reading* **2** slow to learn or understand **3** (of an ache) not intense: *I have a dull ache in the middle of my back* **4** (of weather) not bright or clear **5** not lively or energetic: *she appeared, looking dull and apathetic* **6** (of colour) lacking brilliance **7** (of the blade of a knife) not sharp **8** (of a sound) not loud or clear: *his head fell back to the carpet with a dull thud* ▷ *vb* **9** to make or become dull [Old English *dol*] **> dullness** *n* **> dully** *adv*

dullard *n* old-fashioned a dull or stupid person

Dulles *n* **John Foster**. 1888–1959, US statesman and lawyer; secretary of state (1953–59)

dulse *n* a seaweed with large red edible fronds [Irish *duilesc* seaweed]

Duluth *n* a port in E Minnesota, at the W end of Lake Superior. Pop: 85 734 (2003 est)

Dulwich *n* a residential district in the Greater London borough of Southwark: site of an art gallery and the public school, Dulwich College

duly *adv* **1** in a proper manner: *my permit was duly stamped* **2** at the proper time: *the photographer duly arrived*

Dumas *n* **1** **Alexandre**, known as *Dumas père*. 1802–70, French novelist and dramatist, noted for his historical romances *The Count of Monte Cristo* (1844) and *The Three Musketeers* (1844) **2** his son, **Alexandre**, known as *Dumas*

d

fils. 1824–95, French novelist and dramatist, noted esp. for the play he adapted from an earlier novel, *La Dame aux camélias* (1852) **3 Jean-Baptiste André.** 1800–84, French chemist, noted for his research on vapour density and atomic weight **4 Marlene.** born 1953, South African-born painter resident in the Netherlands; noted for her expressionist portraits and nudes

Du Maurier *n* **1** Dame **Daphne.** 1907–89, English novelist; author of *Rebecca* (1938) and *My Cousin Rachel* (1951) **2** her grandfather, **George Louis Palmella Busson.** 1834–96, British novelist and illustrator; author *Trilby* (1894) **3** his son, Sir **Gerald (Hubert Edward).** 1873–1934, British actor-manager: father of Daphne Du Maurier

dumb *adj* **1** old-fashioned, offensive lacking the power to speak **2** lacking the power of human speech: *the event was denounced as cruelty to dumb animals* **3** temporarily unable to speak: *I was struck dumb when I heard the news* **4** done or performed without speech: *I looked at her in dumb puzzlement* **5** *informal* stupid or slow to understand ► See also **dumb down** [Old English] ⟩ **dumbly** *adv*

Dumbarton *n* a town in W Scotland, in West Dunbartonshire near the confluence of the Rivers Leven and Clyde: centred around the **Rock of Dumbarton,** an important stronghold since ancient times; engineering and distilling. Pop: 20 527 (2001)

Dumbarton Oaks *n* an estate in the District of Columbia in the US: scene of conferences in 1944 concerned with creating the United Nations

dumbbell *n* **1** a short bar with a heavy ball or disc at either end, used for physical exercise **2** slang, chiefly US and Canad a stupid person

dumb down *vb* to make (something) less intellectually demanding or sophisticated: *a move to dumb down its news coverage*

dumbfounded *adj* speechless with amazement: *she sat open-mouthed and dumbfounded* [dumb + (con)found]

dumb show *n* meaningful gestures without speech

dumbstruck *adj* temporarily speechless through shock or surprise

dumbwaiter *n* **1** a lift for carrying food, etc. from one floor of a building to another **2** Brit **a** a stand placed near a dining table to hold food **b** a revolving circular tray placed on a table to hold food

dumdum or **dumdum bullet** *n* a soft-nosed bullet that expands on impact and causes large and serious wounds [after Dum-Dum, town near Calcutta where originally made]

Dumfries *n* a town in S Scotland on the River Nith, administrative centre of Dumfries and Galloway. Pop: 31 146 (2001)

Dumfries and Galloway *n* a council area in SW Scotland: created in 1975 from the counties of Dumfries, Kirkcudbright, and Wigtown; became a unitary authority in 1996; chiefly agricultural. Administrative centre: Dumfries. Pop: 147 210 (2003 est). Area: 6439 sq km (2486 sq miles)

Dumfriesshire *n* (until 1975) a county in S Scotland, on the Solway Firth, now part of Dumfries and Galloway

dummy *n*, *pl* **-mies 1** a large model that looks like a human being, used for displaying clothes in a shop, as a target, etc. **2** a copy of an object, often lacking some essential feature of the original **3** slang a stupid person **4** bridge **a** the hand exposed on the table by the declarer's partner and played by the declarer **b** the declarer's partner **5** a rubber teat for babies to suck ▷ adj **6** imitation or substitute: *you can train them with dummy bombs and live ammunition* [from dumb]

dummy run *n* a practice or test carried out to test if any problems remain: *we'll do a dummy run on the file to see if the program works*

Du Mont *n* Allen Balcom. 1901–65, US inventor and electronics manufacturer. He developed the cathode-ray tube used in television sets and oscilloscopes

dump *vb* **1** to drop or let fall in a careless manner: *he dumped the books on the bed* **2** informal to abandon (someone or something) without proper care: *the unwanted babies were dumped in orphanages* **3** to dispose of (nuclear waste) **4** commerce to sell (goods) in bulk and at low prices, usually in another country, in order to keep prices high in the home market **5** computers to record (the contents of the memory) on a storage device at a series of points during a computer run ▷ *n* **6** a place where rubbish is left **7** informal a dirty, unattractive place: *you're hardly in this dump out of choice* **8** military a place where weapons or supplies are stored [probably from Old Norse]

dumpling *n* **1** a small ball of dough cooked and served with stew **2** a round pastry case filled with fruit: *an apple dumpling* [obsolete *dump* lump]

dumps *pl n* **down in the dumps** informal feeling depressed and miserable [probably from Middle Dutch *domp* haze]

dumpy *adj* **dumpier, dumpiest** short and plump [perhaps related to DUMPLING]

Dumyat *n* the Arabic name for **Damietta**

dun¹ *vb* **dunning, dunned 1** to press (a debtor) for payment ▷ *n* **2** a demand for payment [origin unknown]

dun² *adj* brownish-grey [Old English *dunn*]

Duna *n* the Hungarian name for the **Danube**

Dünaburg *n* the German name (until 1893) for **Daugavpils**

Dunaj *n* the Czech name for the **Danube**

Dunant *n* **(Jean) Henri.** 1828–1910, Swiss humanitarian, founder of the International Red Cross (1864): shared the Nobel peace prize 1901

Dunărea *n* the Romanian name for the **Danube**

Dunbar¹ *n* a port and resort in SE Scotland, in East Lothian: scene of Cromwell's defeat of the Scots (1650). Pop: 6354 (2001)

Dunbar² *n* **William.** ?1460–?1520, Scottish poet, noted for his satirical, allegorical, and elegiac works

Dunbartonshire *n* a historical county of W Scotland: became part of Strathclyde region in 1975; administered since 1996 by the council areas of East Dunbartonshire and West Dunbartonshire

Duncan *n* **Isadora.** 1878–1927, US dancer and choreographer, who influenced modern ballet by introducing greater freedom of movement

Duncan I *n* died 1040, king of Scotland (1034–40); killed by Macbeth

Duncan Smith *n* **(George) Iain.** born 1954, British politician; leader of the Conservative Party (2001–03); secretary of state for work and pensions (from 2010)

dunce *n* Brit, Austral and NZ a person who is stupid or slow to learn [*Dunses*, term of ridicule applied to the followers of John *Duns Scotus*, scholastic theologian]

Dundalk *n* a town in NE Republic of Ireland, on **Dundalk Bay:** county town of Co Louth. Pop: 32 505 (2002)

Dundee¹ *n* **1** a port in E Scotland, in City of Dundee council area, on the Firth of Tay: centre of the former British jute industry; university (1967). Pop: 154 674 (2001) **2 City of Dundee** a council area in E Scotland. Pop: 143 090 (2003 est). Area: 65 sq km (25 sq miles)

Dundee² *n* **1st Viscount,** title of *John Graham of Claverhouse.* ?1649–89, Scottish Jacobite leader, who died from his wounds after winning the battle of Killiecrankie

dunderhead *n* Brit, Austral and NZ a slow-witted person [probably from Dutch *donder* thunder + HEAD]

Dundonian *n* **1** a native or inhabitant of Dundee ▷ adj **2** of or relating to Dundee or its inhabitants

dune *n* a mound or ridge of drifted sand [Middle Dutch]

Dunedin *n* a port in New Zealand, on SE South Island: founded (1848) by Scottish settlers. Pop: 119 100 (2013 est)

Dunfermline *n* a city in E Scotland, in SW Fife: ruined palace, a former residence of Scottish kings. Pop: 39 229 (2001)

dung *n* the faeces from large animals [Old English: prison]

Dungannon *n* a district of S Northern Ireland, in Co Tyrone. Pop: 48 695 (2003 est). Area: 783 sq km (302 sq miles)

dungarees *pl n* trousers with a bib attached [*Dungrī*, district of Bombay, where the fabric used originated]

Dungeness *n* a low shingle headland on the S coast of England, in Kent: two nuclear power stations: automatic lighthouse

dungeon *n* a prison cell, often underground [Old French *donjon*]

dunghill *n* a heap of dung

dunk *vb* **1** to dip (a biscuit or piece of bread) in a drink or soup before eating it **2** to put (something) in liquid: *dunk the garment in the dye for 15 minutes* **3** *basketball* to drop (the ball) through the hoop after having leapt high enough to have the hands above the rim ▷ *n* **4** *basketball* a scoring shot in which one player drops the ball through the hoop after having leapt high enough to have the hands above the rim [Old High German *dunkōn*]

Dunkerque *n* a port in N France, on the Strait of Dover: scene of the evacuation of British and other Allied troops after the fall of France in 1940; industrial centre with an oil refinery and naval shipbuilding yards. Pop: 70 654 (2006). English name: **Dunkirk**

Dún Laoghaire *n* a port in E Republic of Ireland, on Dublin Bay. Pop: 24 447 (2002). Former names: (until 1821) **Dunleary**, (1821–1921) **Kingstown**

dunlin *n* a small sandpiper, of northern and arctic regions, with a brown back and a black breast [from *DUN²*]

Dunlop *n* John Boyd. 1840–1921, Scottish veterinary surgeon, who devised the first successful pneumatic tyre, which was manufactured by the company named after him

dunnock *n* same as **hedge sparrow** [from *DUN²*]

dunny *n, pl* **-nies** *Austral and NZ informal* a toilet [of obscure origin]

Dunois *n* Jean, Comte de Dunois, known as *the Bastard of Orléans*. ?1403–68, French military commander, who defended Orléans against the English until the siege was raised by Joan of Arc (1429)

Dunoon *n* a town and resort in W Scotland, in Argyll and Bute, on the Firth of Clyde. Pop: 8251 (2001)

Dunsany *n* 18th Baron, title of *Edward John Moreton Drax Plunkett*. 1878–1957, Irish dramatist and short-story writer

Dunsinane *n* a hill in central Scotland, in the Sidlaw Hills: the ruined fort at its summit is regarded as Macbeth's castle. Height: 308 m (1012 ft)

Duns Scotus *n* John. ?1265–1308, Scottish scholastic theologian and Franciscan priest: opposed the theology of St Thomas Aquinas

Dunstable¹ *n* an industrial town in SE central England, in Bedfordshire. Pop: 50 775 (2001)

Dunstable² *n* John. died 1453, English composer, esp. of motets and mass settings, noted for his innovations in harmony and rhythm

Dunstan *n* Saint. ?909–988 AD, English prelate and statesman; archbishop of Canterbury (959–988). He revived monasticism in England on Benedictine lines and promoted education. Feast day: May 19

Duntroon *n* a suburb of Canberra: seat of the Royal Military College of Australia

duo *n, pl* **duos 1** two singers or musicians who sing or play music together as a pair **2** *informal* two people who have something in common or do something together: *when they're together they make an impressive duo* [Latin: two]

duodecimal *adj* relating to twelve or twelfths [Latin *duodecim* twelve]

duodenum (dew-oh-deen-um) *n* the first part of the small intestine, just below the stomach [Medieval Latin *intestinum duodenum digitorum* intestine of twelve fingers' length] ▷ **duodenal** *adj*

duologue *or US sometimes* **duolog** *n* a part or all of a play in which the speaking roles are limited to two actors [DUO + (MONO)LOGUE]

DUP (in Northern Ireland) Democratic Unionist Party

Duparc *n* Henri, full name *Marie Eugène Henri Fouques Duparc*. 1848–1933, French composer of songs noted for their sad brooding quality

dupe *vb* **duping, duped 1** to deceive or cheat: *you duped me into doing exactly what you wanted* ▷ *n* **2** a person who is easily deceived [French]

duple *adj* **1** same as **double 2** *music* having two beats in a bar [Latin *duplus* double]

Dupleix *n* Marquis Joseph François. 1697–1763, French governor general in India (1742–54). His plan to establish a French empire in India was frustrated by Clive

duplex *n* **1** *US and Canad* **a** an apartment on two floors **b** *US and Austral* a semidetached house ▷ *adj* **2** having two parts [Latin: twofold]

duplicate *adj* **1** copied exactly from an original: *he had a duplicate key to the front door* ▷ *n* **2** an exact copy **3** in duplicate in two exact copies: *submit the draft in duplicate, please* ▷ *vb* **-cating, -cated 4** to make an exact copy of **5** to do again (something that has already been done) [Latin *duplicare* to double] ▷ **duplication** *n* ▷ **duplicator** *n*

duplicity *n* deceitful behaviour: *he is a man of duplicity, who turns things to his advantage* [Old French *duplicite*]

Dupré *n* Marcel. 1886–1971, French organist and composer, noted as an improviser

du Pré *n* Jacqueline. 1945–87, English cellist. Multiple sclerosis ended her performing career (1973) after which she became a cello teacher

Duque de Caxias *n* a city in SE Brazil, near Rio de Janeiro. Pop: 116 000 (2005 est)

Dur Durham

durable *adj* strong and long-lasting: *the car's body was made of a light but durable plastic* [Latin *durare* to last] ▷ **durability** *n*

durable goods *pl n* goods that do not require frequent replacement. Also called: **durables**

Durán *n* Roberto. born 1951, Panamanian boxer: held world titles at four different weights, most notably lightweight (1972–79)

Durance *n* a river in S France, rising in the Alps and flowing generally southwest into the Rhône. Length: 304 km (189 miles)

Durango *n* **1** a state in N central Mexico: high plateau, with the Sierra Madre Occidental in the west; irrigated agriculture (esp. cotton) and rich mineral resources. Capital: Durango. Pop: 1 448 661 (2000). Area: 119 648 sq km (46 662 sq miles) **2** a city in NW central Mexico, capital of Durango state: mining centre. Pop: 520 000 (2005 est). Official name: **Victoria de Durango**

Durante *n* Jimmy, known as *Schnozzle*. 1893–1980, US comedian

Duras *n* Marguerite, real name *Marguerite Donnadieu*. 1914–96, French novelist born in Giadinh, Indochina (now in Vietnam). Her works include *The Sea Wall* (1950) *Practicalities* (1990), *Écrire* (1993), and the script for the film *Hiroshima mon amour* (1960)

duration *n* the length of time that something lasts [Latin *durare* to last]

Durazzo *n* the Italian name for **Durrës**

Durban *n* a port in E South Africa, in E KwaZulu/Natal province on the Indian Ocean: University of Natal (1909); resort and industrial centre, with oil refineries, shipbuilding yards, etc. Pop: 595 061 (2011)

durbar *n* **a** (formerly) the court of a native ruler or a governor in India **b** a reception at such a court [Hindi *darbār*]

Düren *n* a city in W Germany, in North Rhine-Westphalia. Pop: 92 966 (2003 est)

Dürer *n* Albrecht. 1471–1528, German painter and engraver, regarded as the greatest artist of the German Renaissance and noted particularly as a draughtsman and for his copper engravings and woodcuts

duress *n* physical or moral pressure used to force someone to do something: *confessions obtained under duress* [Latin *durus* hard]

Durgapur *n* a city in NE India, in West Bengal: heavy industry, including steelworks. Pop: 492 996 (2001)

Durham *n* 1 a former administrative county of NE England; became a unitary authority in 2009; on the North Sea: rises to the N Pennines in the west: the geographical and ceremonial county includes the unitary authorities of Hartlepool and Stockton-on-Tees (both part of Cleveland until 1996) and Darlington (created in 1997). Administrative centre: Durham. Pop (of Durham unitary authority): 494 200 (2003 est). Area (of Durham unitary authority): 2434 sq km (940 sq miles). Abbreviation: **Dur** 2 a city in NE England, administrative centre of Co Durham, on the River Wear: Norman cathedral; 11th-century castle (founded by William the Conqueror), now occupied by the University of Durham (1832). Pop: 42 939 (2001) 3 a rare variety of shorthorn cattle

during *prep* throughout or within the limit of (a period of time) [Latin *durare* to last]

Durkan *n* (John) **Mark.** born 1960, Northern Irish politician; leader of the Social Democratic and Labour Party (SDLP) from 2001 to 2010

Durkheim *n* Émile. 1858–1917, French sociologist, whose pioneering works include *De la Division du travail social* (1893)

Durrell *n* 1 Gerald (**Malcolm**). 1925–95, British zoologist and writer: his books include *The Bafut Beagles* (1954), *My Family and Other Animals* (1956), and *The Aye-aye and I* (1992) 2 his brother, **Lawrence (George**). 1912–90, British poet and novelist; author of *The Alexandria Quartet* of novels, consisting of *Justine* (1957), *Balthazar* (1958), *Mountolive* (1958), and *Clea* (1960). Later works include *The Avignon Quintet* of novels (1974–85)

Dürrenmatt *n* Friedrich. 1921–90, Swiss dramatist and writer of detective stories, noted for his grotesque and paradoxical treatment of the modern world: author of *The Visit* (1956) and *The Physicists* (1962)

Durrës *n* a port in W Albania, on the Adriatic. Pop: 114 000 (2003 est). Italian name: **Duraz**. Ancient names: **Epidamnus, Dyrrachium**

Duruflé *n* Maurice. 1902–86, French composer and organist, best known for his *Requiem* (1947)

Duse *n* Eleonora. 1858–1924, Italian actress, noted as a tragedienne

Dushanbe *n* the capital of Tajikistan; a cultural centre. Pop: 551 000 (2005 est). Former name (1929–61): **Stalinabad**

dusk *n* the time just before nightfall when it is almost dark [Old English *dox*]

dusky *adj* **duskier, duskiest** 1 dark in colour: *her gold earrings gleamed against her dusky cheeks* 2 dim or shadowy: *the dusky room was crowded with absurd objects* **> duskily** *adv* **> duskiness** *n*

Düsseldorf *n* an industrial city in W Germany, capital of North Rhine-Westphalia, on the Rhine: commercial centre of the Rhine-Ruhr industrial area. Pop: 572 511 (2003 est)

dust *n* 1 small dry particles of earth, sand, or dirt 2 **bite the dust a** to stop functioning: *my television has finally bitten the dust* **b** to fall down dead 3 **shake the dust off one's feet** to depart angrily 4 **throw dust in someone's eyes** to confuse or mislead someone **> vb** 5 to remove dust from (furniture) by wiping 6 to sprinkle (something) with a powdery substance: *serve dusted with brown sugar and cinnamon* [Old English *dūst*]

dustbin *n* a large, usually cylindrical, container for household rubbish

dust bowl *n* a dry area in which the surface soil is exposed to wind erosion

Dust Bowl *n* **the Dust Bowl** the area of the south central US that became denuded of topsoil by wind erosion during the droughts of the mid-1930s

dustcart *n* chiefly Brit and NZ a lorry for collecting household rubbish

dust cover *n* 1 same as **dustsheet** 2 same as **dust jacket**

duster *n* a cloth used for dusting

dust jacket or **dust cover** *n* a removable paper cover used to protect a book

dustman *n*, *pl* **-men** Brit a man whose job is to collect household rubbish

dust mite *n* one of two varieties of mites that feed on shed human skin cells and whose excrement is a household allergen

dustpan *n* a short-handled shovel into which dust is swept from floors

dustsheet or **dust cover** *n* a large cloth cover used to protect furniture from dust

dust-up *n* informal a fight or argument

dusty *adj* **dustier, dustiest** 1 covered with dust 2 (of a colour) tinged with grey

Dutch *adj* 1 of or relating to the Netherlands or its inhabitants **> n** 2 the language of the Netherlands **> pl n** 3 **the Dutch** the people of the Netherlands **> adv** 4 **go Dutch** informal to go on an outing where each person pays his or her own expenses

Dutch auction *n* an auction in which the price is lowered by stages until a buyer is found

Dutch barn *n* Brit a farm building with a steel frame and a curved roof

Dutch courage *n* false courage gained from drinking alcohol

Dutch East Indies *n* **the Dutch East Indies** a former name (1798–1945) of **Indonesia**. Also called: **the Netherlands East Indies**

Dutch elm disease *n* a fungal disease of elm trees

Dutch Guiana or **Netherlands Guiana** *n* the former name of **Surinam**

Dutchman or fem **Dutchwoman** *n*, *pl* **-men** or **-women** a native or inhabitant of the Netherlands

Dutch New Guinea *n* a former name (until 1963) of Papua

Dutch oven *n* 1 an iron or earthenware container with a lid, used for stews, etc. 2 a metal box, open in front, for cooking in front of an open fire

Dutch treat *n* informal an outing where each person pays his or her own expenses

Dutch uncle *n* informal a person who criticizes or scolds frankly and severely

Dutch West Indies *pl n* **the Dutch West Indies** a former name of the **Netherlands Antilles**

duteous *adj* formal, archaic dutiful or obedient

dutiable *adj* (of goods) requiring payment of duty

dutiful *adj* doing what is expected: *she is a responsible and dutiful mother* **> dutifully** *adv*

Dutton *n* Clarence Edward. 1841–1912, American geologist who first developed the theory of isostasy

duty *n*, *pl* **-ties** 1 the work performed as part of one's job: *it is his duty to supervise the memorial services* 2 an obligation to fulfil one's responsibilities: *it's my duty as a doctor to keep it confidential* 3 a government tax on imports 4 **on** or **off duty** at (or not at) work [Anglo-French *dueté*]

duty-bound *adj* morally obliged to do something: *we are duty-bound to take whatever measures are necessary*

duty-free *adj*, *adv* with exemption from customs or excise duties

duty-free shop *n* a shop, esp. at an airport, that sells duty-free goods

Duvalier *n* 1 François, known as *Papa Doc*. 1907–71, president of Haiti (1957–71) 2 his son, **Jean-Claude**, known as *Baby Doc*. 1951–2014, Haitian statesman; president of Haiti 1971–86; deposed; lived in exile in France before returning to Haiti in 2011

duvet (doo-vay) *n* same as **continental quilt** [French]

Du Vigneaud *n* Vincent. 1901–78, US biochemist: Nobel prize for chemistry (1955) for his synthesis of the hormones oxytocin and vasopressin

DVD Digital Versatile or Video Disk: a type of compact disc that can store large amounts of video and audio information

Dvina n **1 Northern Dvina** a river in NW Russia, formed by the confluence of the Sukhona and Yug Rivers and flowing northwest to *Dvina Bay* in the White Sea. Length: 750 km (466 miles). Russian name: **Severnaya Dvina 2 Western Dvina** a river rising in W Russia, in the Valdai Hills and flowing south and southwest then northwest to the Gulf of Riga. Length: 1021 km (634 miles). Russian name: **Zapadnaya Dvina**. Latvian name: **Daugava**

Dvina Bay or **Dvina Gulf** n an inlet of the White Sea, off the coast of NW Russia

Dvinsk n transliteration of the former Russian name for **Daugavpils**

DVLA Brit Driver and Vehicle Licensing Agency

Dvořák n Antonín, sometimes known as *Anton*. 1841–1904, Czech composer, much of whose work reflects the influence of folk music. His best-known work is the *Symphony No. 9 From the New World* (1893)

DVT deep-vein thrombosis

dwaal n S African a state of absent-mindedness; a daze [Afrikaans]

dwang n NZ and S African a short piece of wood inserted in a timber-framed wall

dwarf vb **1** to cause (someone or something) to seem small by being much larger ▷ adj **2** (of an animal or plant) much below the average size for the species: *a dwarf evergreen shrub* ▷ n, pl **dwarfs** or **dwarves 3** a person who is smaller than average size as a result of a medical condition **4** (in folklore) a small ugly manlike creature, often possessing magical powers [Old English *dweorg*]

dwarf planet n any celestial body orbiting the sun within the solar system, larger than a satellite but smaller than a planet

dwell vb **dwelling, dwelt** or **dwelled** formal, literary to live as a permanent resident [Old English *dwellan* to seduce, get lost] **> dweller** n

dwelling n formal, literary a place of residence

dwell on or **dwell upon** vb to think, speak, or write at length about (something)

dwindle vb **-dling, -dled** to grow less in size, strength, or number [Old English *dwīnan*]

Dy chem dysprosium

dye n **1** a colouring substance **2** the colour produced by dyeing ▷ vb **dyeing, dyed 3** to colour (hair or fabric) by applying a dye [Old English *dēag*] **> dyer** n

dyed-in-the-wool adj having strong and unchanging attitudes or opinions: *he's a dyed-in-the-wool communist*

Dyfed n a former county in SW Wales: created in 1974 from Cardiganshire, Pembrokeshire, and Carmarthenshire; in 1996 it was replaced by Pembrokeshire, Carmarthenshire, and Ceredigion

dying vb **1** the present participle of **die¹** ▷ adj **2** occurring at the moment of death: *in accordance with his dying wish* **3** (of a person or animal) very ill and likely to die soon **4** becoming less important or less current: *coal mining is a dying industry*

dyke¹ or especially US **dike** n **1** a wall built to prevent flooding **2** a ditch **3** Scot a dry-stone wall [Old English *dic* ditch]

dyke² or **dike** n offensive, slang a lesbian [origin unknown]

Dyke n Greg(ory). born 1947, British television executive; director-general of the BBC (2000–04)

Dylan n Bob. real name *Robert Allen Zimmerman*. born 1941, US rock singer and songwriter, also noted for his acoustic protest songs in the early 1960s. His albums include *The Freewheelin' Bob Dylan* (1963), *Highway 61 Revisited* (1965), *Blonde on Blonde* (1966), *John Wesley Harding* (1968), *Blood on the Tracks* (1974), *Oh Mercy* (1989), *Time Out of Mind* (1997), and *Love and Theft* (2001) **> Dylanesque** adj

dynamic adj **1** (of a person) full of energy, ambition, and new ideas **2** relating to a force of society, history, or the mind that produces a change: *the government needs a more dynamic policy towards the environment* **3** physics relating to energy or forces that produce motion [Greek *dunamis* power] **> dynamically** adv

dynamics n **1** the branch of mechanics concerned with the forces that change or produce the motions of bodies ▷ pl n **2** those forces that produce change in any field or system **3** music the various degrees of loudness called for in a performance

dynamism n great energy or enthusiasm

dynamite n **1** an explosive made of nitroglycerine **2** informal a dangerous or exciting person or thing: *she's still dynamite* ▷ vb **-miting, -mited 3** to mine or blow (something) up with dynamite [Greek *dunamis* power]

dynamo n, pl **-mos** a device for converting mechanical energy into electricity [short for *dynamoelectric machine*]

dynamoelectric adj of the conversion of mechanical energy into electricity or vice versa

dynamometer (dine-a-mom-it-er) n an instrument for measuring mechanical power or force

dynast n a hereditary ruler [Greek *dunasthai* to be powerful]

dynasty n, pl **-ties 1** a series of rulers of a country from the same family **2** a period of time during which a country is ruled by the same family [Greek *dunastēs* dynast] **> dynastic** adj

dysentery n infection of the intestine which causes severe diarrhoea [Greek *dusentera* bad bowels]

dysfunction n **1** med any disturbance or abnormality in the function of an organ or part **2** (esp. of a family) failure to show the characteristics or fulfil the purposes accepted as normal or beneficial **> dysfunctional** adj

dyslexia n a developmental disorder that causes learning difficulty with reading, writing, and numeracy [Greek *dus-* not + *lexis* word] **> dyslexic** adj, n

dysmenorrhoea or especially US **dysmenorrhea** n painful or difficult menstruation [Greek *dus-* bad + *mēn* month + *rhoia* a flowing]

Dyson n Sir James. born 1947, British businessman and industrial designer; inventor of the bagless vacuum cleaner (1979–93)

dyspepsia n indigestion [Greek *dus-* bad + *pepsis* digestion] **> dyspeptic** adj, n

dysprosium n chem a metallic element of the lanthanide series. Symbol: **Dy** [Greek *dusprositos* difficult to get near]

dystrophy (diss-trof-fee) n See **muscular dystrophy** [Greek *dus-* not + *trophē* food]

Dzaudzhikau n the former name (1944–54) of Vladikavkaz

Dzerzhinsk n an industrial city and port in central Russia. Pop: 257 000 (2005 est)

Dzhambul n a former name of **Taraz**

Dzungaria n another name for **Junggar Pendi**

e *maths* a number used as the base of natural logarithms. Approximate value: 2.718 282...

E **1** *music* the third note of the scale of C major **2** East(ern) **3** English **4** *physics* **a** energy **b** electromotive force **5** *slang* the drug ecstasy or an ecstasy tablet

e- *prefix* electronic: *e-mail; e-tailer*

E- *prefix* used with a number following it to indicate that something, such as a food additive, conforms to an EU standard

each *adj* **1** every one of two or more people or things considered individually: *each year* ▷ *pron* **2** every one of two or more people or things: *each had been given one room to design* ▷ *adv* **3** for, to, or from each person or thing: *twenty pounds each* **4 each other** (of two or more people) each one to or at the other or others; one another: *they stared at each other* [Old English *ǣlc*]

> USAGE *Each* is a singular pronoun and should be used with a singular form of a verb: *each of the candidates was* (not *were*) *interviewed separately*. See also at **either**.

Eadred *n* died 955 AD, king of England (946–55): regained Northumbria (954) from the Norwegian king Eric Bloodaxe

Eadwig or **Edwy** *n* died 959 AD, king of England (955–57)

eager *adj* very keen to have or do something [Latin *acer* sharp, keen] **▷ eagerly** *adv* **▷ eagerness** *n*

eagle *n* **1** a large bird of prey with broad wings and strong soaring flight **2** *golf* a score of two strokes under par for a hole [Latin *aquila*]

eagle-eyed *adj* having very sharp eyesight

eaglet *n* a young eagle

Eakins *n* Thomas. 1844–1916, US painter of portraits and sporting life: a noted realist

Ealing *n* a borough of W Greater London, formed in 1965 from Acton, Ealing, and Southall. Pop: 3 050 000 (2003 est). Area: 55 sq km (21 sq miles)

ear¹ *n* **1** the part of the body with which a person or animal hears **2** the external visible part of the ear **3** the ability to hear musical and other sounds and interpret them accurately: *a good ear for languages* **4** willingness to listen: *they are always willing to lend an ear* **5 be all ears** to be prepared to listen attentively to something **6 fall on deaf ears** to be ignored: *his words fell on deaf ears* **7 in one ear and out the other** heard but quickly forgotten or ignored **8 out on one's ear** *informal* dismissed suddenly and unpleasantly **9 play by ear** to play without written music **10 play it by ear** *informal* to make up one's plan of action as one goes along **11 turn a deaf ear to** to be deliberately unresponsive to: *many countries have turned a deaf ear to their cries for help* **12 up to one's ears in** *informal* deeply involved in [Old English *ēare*]

ear² *n* the part of a cereal plant, such as wheat or barley, that contains the seeds [Old English *ēar*]

earache *n* pain in the ear

earbash *vb* *Brit, Austral and NZ informal* to talk incessantly **▷ earbashing** *n*

eardrum *n* the thin membrane separating the external ear from the middle ear

earful *n* *informal* a scolding or telling-off

Earhart *n* Amelia. 1898–1937, US aviator: the first woman to fly the Atlantic (1928). She disappeared on a Pacific flight (1937)

earl *n* (in Britain) a nobleman ranking below a marquess and above a viscount [Old English *eorl*] **▷ earldom** *n*

Earl Grey *n* a variety of China tea flavoured with oil of bergamot

ear lobe *n* the soft hanging lowest part of the human ear

early *adj* **-lier, -liest** **1** before the correct or expected time **2** in the first part of a period of time: *early April* **3** near the beginning of the development or history of something: *early Britain was very primitive; early models of this car rust easily* ▷ *adv* **4** occurring or arriving before the correct or expected time **5** in the first part of a period of time **6** near the beginning of the development or history of something: *early in the war* [Old English *ǣrlīce*]

Early English *n* a style of architecture used in England in the 12th and 13th centuries, characterized by narrow pointed arches and ornamental intersecting stonework in windows

earmark *vb* **1** to set (something) aside for a specific purpose ▷ *n* **2** a feature that enables the nature of something to be identified: *it had all the earmarks of a disaster*

earn *vb* **1** to gain or be paid (money) in return for work **2** to acquire or deserve through one's behaviour or action: *you've earned a good night's sleep* **3** to make (money) as interest or profit: *her savings earned 8% interest* [Old English *earnian*] **▷ earner** *n*

earnest¹ *adj* **1** serious and sincere, often excessively so ▷ *n* **2 in earnest** with serious or sincere intentions [Old English *eornost*] **▷ earnestly** *adv* **▷ earnestness** *n*

earnest² *n* *Brit, Austral and NZ old-fashioned* a part payment given in advance as a guarantee of the remainder, esp. to confirm a contract [Old French *erres* pledges]

earnings *pl n* money earned

earphone *n* a small device connected to a radio or tape recorder and worn over the ear, so that a person can listen to a broadcast or tape without anyone else hearing it

ear-piercing *adj* extremely loud or shrill

earplug *n* a piece of soft material placed in the ear to keep out noise or water

earring *n* a piece of jewellery worn in or hanging from the ear lobe

earshot *n* the range within which a sound can be heard: *out of earshot*

ear-splitting *adj* extremely loud or shrill

earth *n* **1** (*sometimes cap*) the planet that we live on, the third planet from the sun, the only one on which life is known to exist. Related adjective: **terrestrial 2** the part of the surface of this planet that is not water **3** the soil in which plants grow **4** the hole in which a fox lives **5** a wire in a piece of electrical equipment through which electricity can escape into the ground if a fault develops **6 come down to earth** to return to reality from a daydream or fantasy **7 on earth** used for emphasis: *what on earth happened?* ▷ *vb* **8** to fit (a piece of electrical equipment) with an earth [Old English *eorthe*]

earthbound *adj* **1** unable to leave the surface of the earth **2** lacking in imagination

earthen *adj* made of earth or baked clay: *an earthen floor*

earthenware *n* dishes and other objects made of baked clay: *an earthenware flowerpot*

earthly *adj* **-lier, -liest 1** of life on earth as opposed to any heavenly or spiritual state **2** *informal* conceivable or possible: *what earthly reason would they have for lying?*

earthquake *n* a series of vibrations at the earth's surface caused by movement of the earth's crust

earth science *n* any science, such as geology, concerned with the structure, age, etc., of the earth

earth-shattering *adj* very surprising or shocking: *an earth-shattering event*

earthwards *adv* towards the earth

earthwork *n* **1** excavation of earth, as in engineering construction **2** a fortification made of earth

earthworm *n* a common worm that burrows in the soil

earthy *adj* **earthier, earthiest 1** open and direct in the treatment of sex, excretion, etc. **2** of or like earth: *earthy colours* ➤ **earthiness** *n*

earwig *n* a thin brown insect with pincers at the tip of its abdomen [Old English *ēarwicga*, from *ēare* ear + *wicga* beetle]

ease *n* **1** lack of difficulty **2** freedom from discomfort or worry **3** rest, leisure, or relaxation **4** freedom from poverty: *a life of leisure and ease* **5 at ease a** *military* (of a soldier) standing in a relaxed position with the feet apart **b** in a relaxed attitude or frame of mind ▷ *vb* **easing, eased 6** to make or become less difficult or severe: *the pain gradually eased* **7** to move into or out of a place or situation slowly and carefully **8 ease off** *or* **up** to lessen or cause to lessen in severity, pressure, tension, or strain: *the rain eased off* [Old French *aise*]

easel *n* a frame on legs, used for supporting an artist's canvas, a display, or a blackboard [Dutch *ezel* ass]

easily *adv* **1** without difficulty **2** without doubt; by far: *easily the most senior Chinese leader to visit the West*

USAGE See at **easy.**

---

east *n* **1** one of the four cardinal points of the compass, at 90° clockwise from north **2** the direction along a line of latitude towards the sunrise **3 the east** any area lying in or towards the east ▷ *adj* **4** situated in, moving towards, or facing the east **5** (esp. of the wind) from the east ▷ *adv* **6** in, to, or towards the east [Old English *ēast*]

East *n* **1 the East a** the southern and eastern parts of Asia **b** (esp. formerly) the countries in Eastern Europe and Asia which are or have been under Communist rule ▷ *adj* **2** of or denoting the eastern part of a country or region

East Africa *n* a region of Africa comprising Kenya, Uganda, and Tanzania

East African *adj* **1** of or relating to East Africa or its inhabitants ▷ *n* **2** a native or inhabitant of East Africa

East Anglia *n* **1** a region of E England south of the Wash: consists of Norfolk and Suffolk, and parts of Essex and Cambridgeshire **2** an Anglo-Saxon kingdom that consisted of Norfolk and Suffolk in the 6th century AD; became a dependency of Mercia in the 8th century

East Anglian *adj* **1** of or relating to East Anglia or its inhabitants ▷ *n* **2** a native or inhabitant of East Anglia

East Ayrshire *n* a council area of SW Scotland, comprising the E part of the historical county of

Ayrshire: part of Strathclyde region from 1975 to 1996: chiefly agricultural. Administrative centre: Kilmarnock. Pop: 119 530 (2003 est). Area: 1252 sq km (483 sq miles)

East Bengal *n* the part of the former Indian province of Bengal assigned to Pakistan in 1947 (now Bangladesh)

East Bengali *adj* **1** of or relating to East Bengal (now Bangladesh) or its inhabitants ▷ *n* **2** a native or inhabitant of East Bengal

East Berlin *n* (formerly) the part of Berlin under East German control

East Berliner *n* a native or inhabitant of the former East Berlin

eastbound *adj* going towards the east

Eastbourne *n* a resort in SE England, in East Sussex on the English Channel. Pop: 106 592 (2001)

East Cape *n* **1** the easternmost point of New Guinea, on Milne Bay **2** the easternmost point of New Zealand, on North Island **3** the former name for Cape **Dezhnev**

East China Sea *n* part of the N Pacific, between the E coast of China and the Ryukyu Islands

East Dunbartonshire *n* a council area of central Scotland to the N of Glasgow: part of Strathclyde region from 1975 until 1996: mainly agricultural and residential. Administrative centre: Kirkintilloch. Pop: 106 970 (2003 est). Area: 172 sq km (66 sq miles)

East End *n* **the East End** a densely populated part of E London containing former industrial and dock areas, now extensively redeveloped for offices

East Ender *n* a native or inhabitant of the East End of London

Easter *n* **1** *Christianity* a festival commemorating the Resurrection of Christ ▷ *adj* **2** taking place at the time of the year when this festival is celebrated: *the Easter holidays* [Old English *ēastre*]

Easter egg *n* a chocolate egg given at Easter

Easter Island *n* an isolated volcanic island in the Pacific, 3700 km (2300 miles) west of Chile, of which it is a dependency: discovered on Easter Sunday, 1722; annexed by Chile in 1888; noted for the remains of an aboriginal culture, which includes gigantic stone figures. Pop: 3791 (2002). Area: 166 sq km (64 sq miles). Polynesian name: **Rapa Nui**. Spanish name: **Isla de Pascua**

Easter Islander *n* a native or inhabitant of Easter Island

easterly *adj* **1** of or in the east ▷ *adv, adj* **2** towards the east **3** from the east: *an easterly breeze*

eastern *adj* **1** situated in or towards the east **2** facing or moving towards the east **3** (*sometimes cap*) of or characteristic of the east or East ➤ **easternmost** *adj*

Eastern Cape *n* a province of S South Africa; formed in 1994 from the E part of the former Cape Province: service industries, agriculture, and mining. Capital: Bhisho (formerly Bisho). Pop: 6 562 053 (2011 est). Area: 169 600 sq km (65 483 sq miles). Also called: **Eastern Province**

Easterner *n* a person from the east of a country or region

Eastern Ghats *pl n* a mountain range in S India, parallel to the Bay of Bengal: united with the Western Ghats by the Nilgiri Hills; forms the E margin of the Deccan plateau

eastern hemisphere *n* the half of the globe that contains Europe, Asia, Africa, and Australia

Eastern Townships *n* an area of central Canada, in S Quebec: consists of 11 townships south of the St Lawrence

East Flanders *n* a province of W Belgium: low-lying, with reclaimed land in the northeast: textile industries Capital: Ghent. Pop: 1 373 720 (2004 est). Area: 2979 sq km (1150 sq miles)

East German *adj* **1** of or relating to the former republic of East Germany or its inhabitants ▷ *n* **2** a native or inhabitant of the former East Germany

East Germany *n* a former republic in N central Europe:

established in 1949 and declared a sovereign state by the Soviet Union in 1954; Communist regime replaced by a multiparty democracy in 1989; reunited with West Germany in 1990. Official name: **German Democratic Republic**, (Abbreviation) **DDR**, (Abbreviation) **GDR**. See also **Germany**

East Indies *pl n* **the East Indies 1** the Malay Archipelago, including or excluding the Philippines **2** SE Asia in general

eastings *pl n* a series of numbers in a grid reference indicating the distance eastwards from a given meridian

East Kilbride *n* a town in W Scotland, in South Lanarkshire near Glasgow: designated a new town in 1947. Pop: 73 796 (2001)

Eastleigh *n* a town in S England, in S Hampshire: railway engineering industry. Pop: 52 894 (2001)

East London *n* a port in S South Africa, in S Eastern Cape province. Pop: 135 560 (2001)

East Lothian *n* a council area and historical county of E central Scotland, on the Firth of Forth and the North Sea: part of Lothian region from 1975 to 1996: chiefly agricultural. Administrative centre: Haddington. Pop: 91 090 (2003 est). Area: 678 sq km (262 sq miles)

Eastman *n* George. 1854–1932, US manufacturer of photographic equipment: noted for the introduction of roll film and developments in colour photography

East Pakistan *n* the former name (until 1971) of **Bangladesh**

East Pakistani *adj* **1** of or relating to East Pakistan (now Bangladesh) or its inhabitants ▷ *n* **2** a native or inhabitant of the former East Pakistan

East Prussia *n* a former province of NE Germany on the Baltic Sea: separated in 1919 from the rest of Germany by the Polish Corridor and Danzig: in 1945 Poland received the south part, the Soviet Union the north. German name: **Ostpreussen**

East Prussian *adj* **1** of or relating to the former German province of East Prussia or its inhabitants ▷ *n* **2** a native or inhabitant of the former East Prussia

East Renfrewshire *n* a council area of W central Scotland, comprising part of the historical county of Renfrewshire; part of Strathclyde region from 1975 to 1996: chiefly agricultural and residential. Administrative centre: Giffnock. Pop: 89 680 (2003 est). Area: 173 sq km (67 sq miles)

East Riding of Yorkshire *n* a county of NE England, a historical division of Yorkshire on the North Sea and the Humber estuary: became part of Humberside in 1974; reinstated as an independent unitary authority in 1996, with a separate authority for Kingston upon Hull: chiefly agricultural and low-lying, with various industries in Hull. Administrative centre: Beverley. Pop (excluding Hull): 321 300 (2003 est). Area (excluding Hull): 748 sq km (675 sq miles)

East Sea *n* the Korean name for **Sea of Japan**

East Sussex *n* a county of SE England comprising part of the former county of Sussex: mainly undulating agricultural land, with the South Downs and seaside resorts in the south: Brighton and Hove became an independent unitary authority in 1997 but is part of the geographical and ceremonial county. Administrative centre: Lewes. Pop (excluding Brighton and Hove): 496 100 (2003 est). Area (excluding Brighton and Hove): 1795 sq km (693 sq miles)

East Timor *n* a small country in SE Asia, comprising part of the island of Timor: colonized by Portugal in the 19th century; declared independence in 1975 but immediately invaded by Indonesia; under UN administration from 1999 and an independent state from 2002. It is mountainous with a monsoon climate; subsistence agriculture is the main occupation. Languages: Portuguese, Tetun (a lingua franca), and Bahasa Indonesia. Religion: Roman Catholic majority.

Currency: US dollar. Capital: Dili. Pop: 1 172 390 (2013 est). Area: 14 874 sq km (5743 sq miles). Official name: **Timor-Leste**

East Timorese *adj* **1** of or relating to East Timor or its inhabitants ▷ *n* **2** a native or inhabitant of East Timor

eastward *adj, adv also:* **eastwards 1** towards the east ▷ *n* **2** the eastward part or direction

Eastwood *n* Clint. born 1930, US film actor and director. His films include *The Good The Bad and The Ugly* (1966), *Dirty Harry* (1971), and as actor and director *Play Misty for Me* (1971), *Unforgiven* (1993), *Mystic River* (2003), *Million Dollar Baby* (2004), and *Gran Torino* (2008)

easy *adj* **easier, easiest 1** not difficult; simple: *the house is easy to keep clean* **2** free from pain, care, or anxiety: *an easy life* **3** tolerant and undemanding; easy-going **4** defenceless or readily fooled: *easy prey* **5** moderate and not involving any great effort: *an easy ride* **6** *informal* ready to fall in with any suggestion made: *he wanted to do something and I was easy about it* **7** *informal* pleasant and not involving any great effort to enjoy: *easy on the eye* ▷ *adv* **8 go easy on a** to avoid using too much of: *he'd tried to go easy on the engines* **b** to treat less severely than is deserved: *go easy on him, he's just a kid* **9 take it easy** to relax and avoid stress or undue hurry [Old French *aisié*] ⟩ **easiness** *n*

> **USAGE** *Easy* should only be used as an adverb in certain set phrases: *to take it easy; easy does it.* Where a fixed expression is not involved, the usual adverbial form of *easy* is preferred: *this polish goes on more easily* (not *easier*) *than the other.*

easy chair *n* a comfortable upholstered armchair

easy-going *adj* relaxed in manner or attitude; very tolerant

eat *vb* **eating, ate, eaten 1** to take (food) into the mouth and swallow it **2** to have a meal: *sometimes we eat out of doors* **3** *informal* to make anxious or worried: *what's eating you?* **4 eat away** *or* **into** *or* **up** to destroy or use up partly or wholly: *inflation ate into the firm's profits* ▶ See also **eat out, eat up** [Old English *etan*] ⟩ **eater** *n*

eatable *adj* fit or suitable for eating

eating *n* **1** food in relation to its quality or taste: *these add up to lots of vitamins and minerals, and good eating* ▷ *adj* **2** suitable for eating uncooked: *eating apples*

eat out *vb* to eat at a restaurant

eat up *vb* **1** to eat or consume entirely: *eat up these potatoes* **2** *informal* to affect severely: *I was eaten up by jealousy*

eau de Cologne (oh de kol-**lone**) *n* full form of **cologne** [French: water of Cologne]

eau de vie (oh de **vee**) *n* brandy or a similar alcoholic drink [French: water of life]

eaves *pl n* the edge of a sloping roof that overhangs the walls [Old English *efes*]

eavesdrop *vb* **-dropping, -dropped** to listen secretly to a private conversation [Old English *yfesdrype* water dripping from the eaves] ⟩ **eavesdropper** *n*

eavestrough *n* Canad a gutter at the eaves of a building

e-banking *n* the use of the internet for banking transactions

ebb *vb* **1** (of the sea or the tide) to flow back from its highest point **2** to fall away or decline: *her anger ebbed away* ▷ *n* **3** the flowing back of the tide from high to low water **4 at a low ebb** in a weak state: *her creativity was at a low ebb* [Old English *ebba* ebb-tide]

Ebbinghaus *n* Hermann. 1850–1909, German experimental psychologist who undertook the first systematic and large-scale studies of memory and devised tests using nonsense syllables

Ebbw Vale *n* a town in S Wales, in Blaenau Gwent county borough: a former coal mining centre. Pop: 18 558 (2001)

Eberhard *n* Johann August. 1739–1809, German philosopher and lexicographer, best known for his German dictionary (1795–1802)

Ebert n Friedrich. 1871–1925, German Social Democratic statesman; first president of the German Republic (1919–25)

Ebola virus disease n a severe infectious disease characterized by fever, vomiting, and internal bleeding [after the Ebola River in Democratic Republic of Congo, where an outbreak occurred in 1976]

Ebonji n a state of Nigeria, in the SE. Capital: Abakiliki. Pop: 2 173 501(2006). Area: 5670 sq km (2189 sq miles)

ebony n 1 a very hard dark-coloured wood used to make furniture, etc. ▷ adj 2 very deep black [Greek ebenos]

e-book n 1 a book in electronic form ▷ vb 2 to book (tickets, appointments, etc.) through the internet

Eboracum n the Roman name for York (1)

Ebro n the second largest river in Spain, rising in the Cantabrian Mountains and flowing southeast to the Mediterranean. Length: 910 km (565 miles)

ebullient adj full of enthusiasm or excitement [Latin ebullire to bubble forth, be boisterous] > **ebullience** n

EC 1 European Commission 2 European Community: a former name for the European Union

Ecbatana n an ancient city in Iran, on the site of modern Hamadān; capital of Media and royal residence of the Persians and Parthians

eccentric adj 1 unconventional or odd 2 (of circles) not having the same centre ▷ n 3 a person who behaves unconventionally or oddly [Greek ek- away from + kentron centre] > **eccentrically** adv

eccentricity n 1 unconventional or odd behaviour 2 (pl -ties) an unconventional or odd habit or act

Eccles¹ n a town in NW England, in Salford unitary authority, Greater Manchester. Pop: 36 610 (2001)

Eccles² n Sir John Carew. 1903–97, Australian physiologist: shared the Nobel prize for physiology (1963) with A. L. Hodgkin and A. F. Huxley for their work on conduction of nervous impulses

ecclesiastic n 1 a member of the clergy ▷ adj 2 of or relating to the Christian Church or its clergy [Greek ekklēsia assembly]

ecclesiastical adj of or relating to the Christian Church or its clergy

Ecclestone n Bernard, known as Bernie. born 1930, British businessman and sports administrator; head of Formula One motor racing from 1995

Ecevit n Bülent. 1925–2006, Turkish politician and journalist: prime minister of Turkey (1974, 1977, 1978–79, 1998–2002)

ECG electrocardiogram

Echegaray y Eizaguirre n José. 1832–1916, Spanish dramatist, statesman, and mathematician. His plays include Madman or Saint (1877); Nobel prize for literature 1904

echelon (esh-a-lon) n 1 a level of power or responsibility: the upper echelons of society 2 military a formation in which units follow one another but are spaced out sideways to allow each a line of fire ahead [French échelon rung of a ladder]

echidna (ik-kid-na) n, pl -nas, -nae (-nee) an Australian spiny egg-laying mammal. Also called: **spiny anteater**

echinoderm (ik-kine-oh-durm) n a sea creature with a five-part symmetrical body, such as a starfish or sea urchin [Greek ekhinos sea urchin + derma skin]

echo n, pl -oes 1 a the reflection of sound by a solid object b a sound reflected by a solid object 2 a repetition or imitation of someone else's opinions 3 something that brings back memories: an echo of the past 4 the signal reflected back to a radar transmitter by an object ▷ vb -oing, -oed 5 (of a sound) to be reflected off an object in such a way that it can be heard again 6 (of a place) to be filled with a sound and its echoes: the church echoed with singing 7 (of people) to repeat or imitate (what someone else has said): his conclusion echoed that of Jung [Greek ēkhō] > **echoing** adj

echo chamber n a room with walls that reflect sound,

used to create an echo effect

echolocation n the discovery of an object's position by measuring the time taken for an echo to return from it

echo sounder n a navigation device that determines depth by measuring the time taken for a pulse of sound to reach the sea bed and for the echo to return

e-cigarette n an electronic vaporizer which dispenses inhalable nicotine, for simulating the effect of smoking. In full: **electronic cigarette**. Short form (informal): **e-cig**

Eck n Johann, original name Johann Mayer. 1486–1543, German Roman Catholic theologian; opponent of Luther and the Reformation

Eckert n John Presper. 1919–95, US electronics engineer: built the first electronic computer with John W. Mauchly in 1946

Eckhart n Johannes, called Meister Eckhart. ?1260–?1327, German Dominican theologian, mystic, and preacher

éclair n a finger-shaped cake of choux pastry, filled with cream and coated with chocolate [French: lightning (probably because it does not last long)]

eclampsia n pathol a serious condition that can develop towards the end of a pregnancy, causing high blood pressure, swelling, and convulsions

eclectic adj 1 composed of elements selected from a wide range of styles, ideas, or sources: the eclectic wine list includes bottles from all round the world 2 selecting elements from a wide range of styles, ideas, or sources: an eclectic approach that takes the best from all schools of psychology ▷ n 3 a person who takes an eclectic approach [Greek eklegein to select] > **eclecticism** n

eclipse n 1 the obscuring of reflected light from a celestial body as it passes through the shadow of another; a **lunar eclipse** occurs when the moon passes through the shadow of the earth 2 a loss of importance, power, or fame: communism eventually went into eclipse ▷ vb eclipsing, eclipsed 3 to overshadow or surpass 4 (of a star or planet) to hide (another planet or star) from view [Greek ekleipsis a forsaking]

ecliptic n astronomy the great circle on the celestial sphere representing the apparent annual path of the sun relative to the stars

Eco n Umberto. born 1932, Italian semiologist and writer. His novels include The Name of the Rose (1981) and Foucault's Pendulum (1988)

eco- combining form denoting ecology or ecological: ecotourism

E.coli (ee-koal-eye) n a common bacterium often found in the intestines [shortened from Escherichia coli, after Theodor Escherich, paediatrician]

ecological adj 1 of or relating to ecology 2 tending or intended to benefit or protect the environment: an ecological approach to agriculture > **ecologically** adv

ecology n the study of the relationships between people, animals, and plants, and their environment [Greek oikos house] > **ecologist** n

e-commerce or **ecommerce** n business transactions conducted on the internet

econ. economy

economic adj 1 of or relating to an economy or economics 2 Brit and Austral capable of being produced or operated for profit 3 informal inexpensive or cheap

economical adj 1 not requiring a lot of money to use: low fuel consumption makes this car very economical 2 (of a person) spending money carefully and sensibly 3 using no more time, effort, or resources than is necessary 4 **economical with the truth** euphemistic deliberately withholding information > **economically** adv

economics n 1 the study of the production and consumption of goods and services and the commercial activities of a society ▷ pl n 2 financial aspects: the economics of health care

economist n a person who specializes in economics

economize or **-mise** vb -mizing, -mized or -mising,

-mised to reduce expense or waste: *people are being advised to economize on fuel use*

conomy *n*, *pl* **-mies** 1 the system by which the production, distribution, and consumption of goods and services is organized in a country or community: *the rural economy* 2 the ability of a country to generate wealth through business and industry: *unless the economy improves, more jobs will be lost* 3 careful use of money or resources to save expense, time, or energy 4 an instance of this: *we can make economies by reusing envelopes* ▷ *adj* 5 denoting a class of air travel that is cheaper than first-class 6 offering a larger quantity for a lower price: *an economy pack* [Greek *oikos* house + *nemein* to manage]

conomy-class syndrome *n* a deep-vein thrombosis that has developed in the legs or pelvis of a person travelling for a long time in cramped conditions [reference to the restricted legroom of cheaper seats on passenger aircraft]

conomy of scale *n econ* a fall in average costs resulting from an increase in the scale of production

cosystem *n ecology* the system of relationships between animals and plants and their environment

coterrorism *n* the use of violence in order to achieve environmentalist aims [from *eco* + *terrorism*]

coterrorist *n* a person who uses violence in order to achieve environmentalist aims [from *eco* + *terrorist*]

cotourism *n* tourism designed to contribute to the protection of the environment or at least minimize damage to it ▷ **ecotourist** *n*

COWAS *n acronym for* Economic Community of West African States; an economic association established in 1975 whose members are Benin, Burkina Faso, Cape Verde, Côte d'Ivoire, The Gambia, Ghana, Guinea, Guinea-Bissau, Liberia, Mali, Niger, Nigeria, Senegal, Sierra Leone, and Togo. Mauritania joined but withdrew in 2002

cru *adj* pale creamy-brown [French]

cstasy *n*, *pl* **-sies** 1 a state of extreme delight or joy 2 *slang* a strong drug that acts as a stimulant and can cause hallucinations [Greek *ekstasis* displacement, trance] ▷ **ecstatic** *adj* ▷ **ecstatically** *adv*

CT electroconvulsive therapy: the treatment of depression and some other mental disorders by passing a current of electricity through the brain, producing a convulsion

ctomorph *n physiol* a person with a thin body build. See also **endomorph**, **mesomorph** [Greek *ektos* outside + *morphē* shape] ▷ **ectomorphic** *adj*

ctopic *adj med* (of an organ or other body part) congenitally displaced or abnormally positioned [Greek *ektopos* out of position]

ctoplasm *n* (in spiritualism) the substance that supposedly is emitted from the body of a medium during a trance [Greek *ektos* outside + *plasma* something moulded]

cua. Ecuador

cuador *n* a republic in South America, on the Pacific: under the Incas when Spanish colonization began in 1532; gained independence in 1822; declared a republic in 1830. It consists chiefly of a coastal plain in the west, separated from the densely forested upper Amazon basin (Oriente) by ranges and plateaus of the Andes. Official language: Spanish; Quechua is also widely spoken. Religion: Roman Catholic majority. Currency: US dollar. Capital: Quito. Pop: 15 439 429 (2013 est). Area: 283 560 sq km (109 483 sq miles)

cuadorean *adj* 1 of or relating to Ecuador or its inhabitants ▷ *n* 2 a native or inhabitant of Ecuador

cumenical *adj* 1 of or relating to the Christian Church throughout the world 2 tending to promote unity among Christian churches [Greek *oikoumenikos* of the inhabited world]

cumenism *or* **ecumenicism** *n* the aim of unity among Christian churches throughout the world

eczema (ek-sim-a, ig-**zeem**-a) *n pathol* a condition in which the skin becomes inflamed and itchy [Greek *ek-* out + *zein* to boil]

ed. 1 edition 2 editor

Edam *n* 1 a town in the NW Netherlands, in North Holland province, on the IJsselmeer: cheese, light manufacturing. Pop: 28 000 (2003 est; includes Volendam) 2 a hard round mild-tasting Dutch cheese, yellow in colour with a red outside covering

Edberg *n* Stefan. born 1966, Swedish tennis player; winner of six Grand Slam singles titles: Wimbledon (1988, 1990), the US Open (1991–2), and the Australian Open (1985, 1987)

Eddery *n* Patrick, known as *Pat*. born 1952, Irish jockey: Champion Jockey eleven times; rode three winners in the Derby (1975, 1982, 1990)

Eddington *n* Sir Arthur Stanley. 1882–1944, English astronomer and physicist, noted for his research on the motion, internal constitution, and luminosity of stars and for his elucidation of the theory of relativity

eddo (ed-doh) *n*, *pl* **eddoes** same as **taro**

eddy *n*, *pl* **-dies** 1 a circular movement of air, water, or smoke ▷ *vb* **-dies**, **-dying**, **-died** 2 to move with a gentle circular motion; swirl gently [probably from Old Norse]

Eddy *n* Mary Baker. 1821–1910, US religious leader; founder of the Christian Science movement (1866)

Eddystone Rocks *n* a dangerous group of rocks at the W end of the English Channel, southwest of Plymouth: lighthouse

Ede *n* a city in the central Netherlands, in Gelderland province. Pop: 105 000 (2003 est)

Edelman *n* Gerald Maurice. born 1929, US biochemist: he shared the Nobel prize for physiology or medicine (1972) with Rodney Porter for determining the structure of antibodies

edelweiss (ade-el-vice) *n* a small white alpine flower [German: noble white]

edema (id-**deem**-a) *n*, *pl* **-mata** same as **oedema**

Eden¹ *n* 1 Also called: **Garden of Eden** *Bible* the garden in which Adam and Eve were placed at the Creation 2 a place of great delight or contentment [Hebrew *'ēdhen* place of pleasure]

Eden² *n* Sir (Robert) Anthony, Earl of Avon. 1897–1977, British Conservative statesman; foreign secretary (1935–38; 1940–45; 1951–55) and prime minister (1955–57). He resigned after the controversy caused by the occupation of the Suez Canal zone by British and French forces (1956)

Eden Project *n* an environmental complex containing the world's largest greenhouse, built in a disused clay pit near St Austell, Cornwall, to study plant populations in a variety of environments

edentate *n* 1 a mammal with few or no teeth, such as an armadillo or a sloth ▷ *adj* 2 denoting such a mammal [Latin *edentatus* lacking teeth]

Edessa *n* 1 an ancient city on the N edge of the Syrian plateau, founded as a Macedonian colony by Seleucus I: a centre of early Christianity. Modern name: **Urfa** 2 a market town in Greece: ancient capital of Macedonia. Pop (municipality): 25 729 (2001). Ancient name: **Aegae**. Modern Greek name: **Édhessa**

Edgar *n* 1 944–975 AD, king of Mercia and Northumbria (957–975) and of England (959–975) 2 ?1074–1107, king of Scotland (1097–1107), fourth son of Malcolm III. He overthrew his uncle Donald to gain the throne 3 **David**. born 1948, British dramatist, noted for political plays such as *Destiny* (1976), *Maydays* (1983), and *Albert Speer* (1999): he adapted (1980) *Nicholas Nickleby* and (1991) *Dr Jekyll and Mr Hyde* for the RSC

Edgar Atheling *n* ?1050–?1125, grandson of Edmund II; Anglo-Saxon pretender to the English throne in 1066

edge *n* 1 a border or line where something ends or begins: *the edge of the city* 2 a line along which two faces or surfaces of a solid meet 3 the sharp cutting side of a blade **4** keenness, sharpness, or urgency: *there was a nervous edge to his voice* **5 have the edge on** to have a slight advantage over **6 on edge** nervous and irritable **7 set someone's teeth on edge** to make someone acutely irritated ▷ *vb* **edging, edged 8** to make, form, or be an edge or border for: *a pillow edged with lace* **9** to move very gradually in a particular direction: *I edged through to the front of the crowd* [Old English *ecg*]

Edgehill *n* a ridge in S Warwickshire: site of the indecisive first battle between Charles I and the Parliamentarians (1642) in the Civil War

edgeways *or especially US and Canad* **edgewise** *adv* **1** with the edge forwards or uppermost **2 get a word in edgeways** to interrupt a conversation in which someone else is talking continuously

Edgeworth *n* Maria. 1767–1849, Anglo-Irish novelist: her works include *Castle Rackrent* (1800) and *The Absentee* (1812)

edging *n* anything placed along an edge for decoration

edgy *adj* **edgier, edgiest** nervous, irritable, or anxious ▷ **edginess** *n*

Édhessa *n* transliteration of the Modern Greek name for Edessa

edible *adj* fit to be eaten; eatable [Latin *edere* to eat] ▷ **edibility** *n*

edict (ee-dikt) *n* a decree or order given by any authority [Latin *edicere* to declare]

edifice (ed-if-iss) *n* **1** a large or impressive building **2** an elaborate system of beliefs and institutions: *the crumbling edifice of Communist rule* [Latin *aedificare* to build]

edify (ed-if-fie) *vb* **-fies, -fying, -fied** to inform or instruct (someone) with a view to improving his or her morals or understanding [Latin *aedificare* to build] ▷ **edification** *n* ▷ **edifying** *adj*

Edinburgh[1] *n* **1** the capital of Scotland and seat of the Scottish Parliament (from 1999), in City of Edinburgh council area on the S side of the Firth of Forth: became the capital in the 15th century; castle; three universities (including University of Edinburgh, 1583); commercial and cultural centre, noted for its annual festival. Pop: 482 640 (2012) **2 City of** a council area in central Scotland, created from part of Lothian region in 1996. Pop: 448 370 (2003 est). Area: 262 sq km (101 sq miles)

Edinburgh[2] *n* **Duke of**, title of Prince *Philip Mountbatten*. born 1921, husband of Elizabeth II of Great Britain and Northern Ireland

Edirne *n* a city in NW Turkey: a Thracian town, rebuilt and renamed by the Roman emperor Hadrian. Pop: 126 000 (2005 est). Former name: **Adrianople**

Edison *n* Thomas Alva. 1847–1931, US inventor. He patented more than a thousand inventions, including the phonograph, the incandescent electric lamp, the microphone, and the kinetoscope

edit *vb* **editing, edited 1** to prepare (text) for publication by checking and improving its accuracy or clarity **2** to be in charge of (a newspaper or magazine) **3** to prepare (a film, tape, etc.) by rearranging or selecting material **4 edit out** to remove (a section) from a text, film, etc.

edition *n* **1** a particular version of a book, newspaper, or magazine produced at one time: *the revised paperback edition* **2** a single television or radio programme which forms part of a series: *the first edition goes on the air in 30 minutes*

editor *n* **1** a person who edits **2** a person in overall charge of a newspaper or magazine **3** a person in charge of one section of a newspaper or magazine: *the Political Editor* **4** a person in overall control of a television or radio programme [Latin *edere* to publish] ▷ **editorship** *n*

editorial *n* **1** an article in a newspaper expressing the opinion of the editor or publishers ▷ *adj* **2** of editing or editors: *an editorial meeting* **3** relating to the contents and opinions of a magazine or newspaper: *the paper's editorial policy* ▷ **editorially** *adv*

Edmonton *n* a city in W Canada, capital of Alberta: oil industry. Pop: 812 201 (2011)

Edmund *n* **Saint**, also called *Saint Edmund Rich*. 1175–1240, English churchman: archbishop of Canterbury (1234–40). Feast day: Nov 16.

Edmund I *n* ?922–946 AD, king of England (940–946)

Edmund II *n* called *Edmund Ironside*. ?980–1016, king of England in 1016. His succession was contested by Canute and they divided the kingdom between them

Edo *n* **1** (*pl* **Edo** *or* **Edos**) a member of a people of SW Nigeria around Benin, noted for their 16th-century bronze sculptures **2** Also called: **Bini** the language of this people, belonging to the Kwa branch of the Niger-Congo family **3** a state of Nigeria, in the S. Capital: Benin City. Pop: 3 218 332 (2006). Area: 17 802 sq km (6873 sq miles)

EDP electronic data processing

EDT Eastern Daylight Time

educate *vb* **-cating, -cated 1** to teach (someone) over a long period of time so that he or she acquires knowledge and understanding of a range of subjects **2** to send (someone) to a particular educational establishment: *he was educated at mission schools* **3** to teach (someone) about a particular matter: *a campaign to educate people to the dangers of smoking* [Latin *educare* to rear, educate] ▷ **educative** *adj*

educated *adj* **1** having an education, esp. a good one **2** displaying culture, taste, and knowledge **3 educated guess** a guess that is based on experience

education *n* **1** the process of acquiring knowledge and understanding **2** knowledge and understanding acquired through study and training: *education is the key to a good job* **3** the process of teaching, esp. at a school, college, or university **4** the theory of teaching and learning ▷ **educational** *adj* ▷ **educationally** *adv* ▷ **educationalist** *or* **educationist** *n*

Edward[1] *n* **Lake Edward** a lake in central Africa, between Uganda and the Democratic Republic of Congo in the Great Rift Valley: empties through the Semliki River into Lake Albert. Area: about 2150 sq km (830 sq miles). Former official name: **Lake Amin**

Edward[2] *n* **1** known as *the Black Prince*. 1330–76, Prince of Wales, the son of Edward III of England. He won victories over the French at Crécy (1346) and Poitiers (1356) in the Hundred Years' War **2 Prince**. born 1964, Earl of Wessex, third son of Elizabeth II of Great Britain and Northern Ireland. In 1999 he married Sophie Rhys-Jones (born 1965); their daughter Louise was born in 2003 and their son James in 2007

Edward I *n* 1239–1307, king of England (1272–1307); son of Henry III. He conquered Wales (1284) but failed to subdue Scotland

Edward II *n* 1284–1327, king of England (1307–27); son of Edward I. He invaded Scotland but was defeated by Robert Bruce at Bannockburn (1314). He was deposed by his wife Isabella and Roger Mortimer; died in prison

Edward III *n* 1312–77, king of England (1327–77); son of Edward II. His claim to the French throne in right of his mother Isabella provoked the Hundred Years' War (1337)

Edward IV *n* 1442–83, king of England (1461–70; 1471–83); son of Richard, duke of York. He defeated Henry VI in the Wars of the Roses and became king (1461). In 1470 Henry was restored to the throne, but Edward recovered the crown by his victory at Tewkesbury

Edward V *n* 1470–?83, king of England in 1483; son of Edward IV. He was deposed by his uncle, Richard, Duke of Gloucester (Richard III), and is thought to have been murdered with his brother in the Tower of London

Edward VI *n* 1537–53, king of England (1547–53), son of Henry VIII and Jane Seymour. His uncle the Duke of Somerset was regent until 1552, when he was executed. Edward then came under the control of Dudley, Duke of Northumberland

Edward VII *n* 1841–1910, king of Great Britain and Ireland (1901–10); son of Queen Victoria

Edward VIII *n* 1894–1972, king of Great Britain and Ireland in 1936; son of George V and brother of George VI. He abdicated in order to marry an American divorcée,

Mrs Wallis Simpson (1896–1986); created Duke of Windsor (1937)

Edwardian *adj* of or in the reign of King Edward VII of Great Britain and Ireland (1901–10)

Edwards *n* **1** Gareth (**Owen**). born 1947, Welsh Rugby Union footballer: halfback for Wales (1967–78) and the British Lions (1968–74) **2** Jonathan. 1703–58, American Calvinist theologian and metaphysician; author of *The Freedom of the Will* (1754) **3** Jonathan. born 1966, British athlete: gold medallist in the triple jump at the Olympics (2000) and the World Championships (1995, 2001)

Edward the Confessor *n* Saint. ?1002–66, king of England (1042–66); son of Ethelred II; founder of Westminster Abbey. Feast day: Oct 13

Edward the Elder *n* died 924 AD, king of England (899–924), son of Alfred the Great

Edward the Martyr *n* Saint. ?963–978 AD, king of England (975–78), son of Edgar: murdered. Feast day: March 18

Edwin *n* ?585–633 AD, king of Northumbria (617–633) and overlord of all England except Kent

EEC European Economic Community: a former name for the European Union

EEG electroencephalogram

eel *n* a slimy snakelike fish [Old English *ǣl*]

e'er *adv poetic* short for **ever**

eerie *adj* **eerier, eeriest** strange and frightening [probably from Old English *earg* cowardly] **> eerily** *adv*

efface *vb* **-facing, -faced 1** to obliterate or make dim: *nothing effaced the memory* **2** to rub out or erase **3** efface oneself to make oneself inconspicuous [French *effacer* to obliterate the face] **> effacement** *n*

effect *n* **1** a change or state of affairs caused by something or someone: *the gales have had a serious effect on the crops* **2** power to influence or produce a result: *the wine had little effect on him* **3** the condition of being operative: *a new law has come into effect* **4** the overall impression: *the whole effect is one of luxury* **5** basic meaning or purpose: *words to that effect* **6** an impression, usually a contrived one: *he paused for effect* **7** a physical phenomenon: *the greenhouse effect* **8** in effect for all practical purposes: *in effect he has no choice* **9** take effect to begin to produce results **▷** *vb* **10** to cause (something) to take place: *a peace treaty was effected* [Latin *efficere* to accomplish]

effective *adj* **1** producing a desired result: *an effective vaccine against HIV* **2** officially coming into operation: *the new rates become effective at the end of May* **3** impressive: *a highly effective speech* **4** in reality, although not officially or in theory: *he is in effective control of the company* **> effectively** *adv* **> effectiveness** *n*

effects *pl n* **1** personal belongings **2** lighting, sounds, etc., to accompany a stage, film, or broadcast production

effectual *adj* **1** producing the intended result **2** (of a document etc.) having legal force **> effectually** *adv*

effeminate *adj* (of a man) displaying characteristics regarded as typical of a woman [Latin *femina* woman] **> effeminacy** *n*

effervescent *adj* **1** (of a liquid) giving off bubbles of gas **2** (of a person) lively and enthusiastic [Latin *effervescere* to foam up] **> effervescence** *n*

effete (if-feet) *adj* weak, powerless, and decadent [Latin *effetus* exhausted by bearing young]

efficacious *adj* producing the intended result [Latin *efficere* to achieve] **> efficacy** *n*

efficient *adj* working or producing effectively without wasting effort, energy, or money [Latin *efficiens* effecting] **> efficiency** *n* **> efficiently** *adv*

effigy (ef-fij-ee) *n, pl* **-gies 1** a statue or carving of someone, often as a memorial: *a 14th-century wooden effigy of a knight* **2** a crude representation of someone, used as a focus for contempt: *an effigy of the president was set on fire* [Latin *effingere* to portray]

efflorescence *n* **1** the blooming of flowers on a plant **2** a

brief period of high-quality artistic activity [Latin *efflorescere* to blossom]

effluent *n* liquid discharged as waste, for instance from a factory or sewage works [Latin *effluere* to flow out]

effluvium *n, pl* **-via** an unpleasant smell, such as the smell of decaying matter [Latin: a flowing out]

efflux *n* **1** the process of flowing out **2** something that flows out

effort *n* **1** physical or mental energy needed to do something **2** a determined attempt to do something **3** an achievement or creation: *his earliest literary efforts* [Latin *fortis* strong] **> effortless** *adj* **> effortlessly** *adv*

effrontery *n* insolence or boldness [Late Latin *effrons* putting forth one's forehead]

effusion *n* **1** an unrestrained verbal expression of emotions or ideas **2** a sudden pouring out: *small effusions of blood* [Latin *effundere* to shed]

effusive *adj* enthusiastically showing pleasure, gratitude, or approval **> effusively** *adv* **> effusiveness** *n*

EFL English as a Foreign Language

EFTA European Free Trade Association

EFTPOS electronic funds transfer at point of sale

eg *or* **e.g.** for example [Latin *exempli gratia*]

Eg. 1 Egypt(ian) **2** Egyptology

egalitarian *adj* **1** expressing or supporting the idea that all people should be equal **▷** *n* **2** a person who believes that all people should be equal [French *égal* equal] **> egalitarianism** *n*

Egas Moniz *n* Antonio Caetanio de Abreu Freire. 1874–1955, Portuguese neurologist: shared the Nobel prize for physiology or medicine (1949) with Walter Hess for their development of prefrontal leucotomy

Egbert *n* ?775–839 AD, king of Wessex (802–839); first overlord of all England (829–830)

Eger *n* **1** a city in N central Hungary. Pop: 56 696 (2003 est) **2** the German name for **Cheb**

egg *n* **1** the oval or round object laid by the females of birds, reptiles, and other creatures, containing a developing embryo **2** a hen's egg used for food **3** a type of cell produced in the body of a female animal which can develop into a baby if fertilized by a male reproductive cell **4** have egg on one's face *informal* to have been made to look ridiculous **5** put all one's eggs in one basket to rely entirely on one action or decision, with no alternative in case of failure [Old Norse]

egg cup *n* a small cup for holding a boiled egg

egghead *n informal* an intellectual person

eggnog *n* a drink made of raw eggs, milk, sugar, spice, and brandy or rum [*egg* + *nog* strong ale]

egg on *vb* to encourage (someone) to do something foolish or daring [Old English *eggian*]

eggplant *n* US, Canad, Austral and NZ a dark purple tropical fruit, cooked and eaten as a vegetable

eggshell *n* **1** the hard porous outer layer of a bird's egg **▷** *adj* **2** (of paint) having a very slight sheen

Egham *n* a town in S England, in N Surrey on the River Thames. Pop: 27 666 (2001)

Egmont¹ *n* Mount Egmont an extinct volcano in New Zealand, in W central North Island in the **Egmont National Park**: an almost perfect cone. Height: 2518 m (8261 ft). Official name: **Mount Taranaki**

Egmont² *n* Lamoral, Count of Egmont, Prince of Gavre. 1522–68, Flemish statesman and soldier. He attempted to secure limited reforms and religious tolerance in the Spanish government of the Netherlands, refused to join William the Silent's rebellion, but was nevertheless executed for treason by the Duke of Alva

ego *n, pl* **egos 1** the part of a person's self that is able to recognize that person as being distinct from other people and things **2** a person's opinion of his or her own worth: *men with fragile egos* [Latin: I]

egocentric *adj* thinking only of one's own interests and feelings **> egocentricity** *n*

e

Egoli *n* a local name for **Johannesburg** [from Zulu *eGoli* place of gold]

egomania *n* an obsessive concern with fulfilling one's own needs and desires, regardless of the effect on other people **> egomaniac** *n*

egotism *or* **egoism** *n* concern only for one's own interests and feelings **> egotist** *or* **egoist** *n* **> egotistical, egoistical, egotistic** *or* **egoistic** *adj*

ego trip *n informal* something that a person does in order to boost his or her self-image

egregious (ig-**greej**-uss) *adj* shockingly bad: *egregious government waste* [Latin *egregius* outstanding (literally: standing out from the herd)]

egress (**ee**-gress) *n formal* **1** the act of going out **2** a way out or exit [Latin *egredi* to come out]

egret (**ee**-grit) *n* a wading bird like a heron, with long white feathery plumes [Old French *aigrette*]

Egypt *n* a republic in NE Africa, on the Mediterranean and Red Sea: its history dates back about 5000 years. Occupied by the British from 1882, it became an independent kingdom in 1922 and a republic in 1953. Over 96 per cent of the total area is desert, with the chief areas of habitation and cultivation in the Nile delta and valley. Cotton is the main export. Official language: Arabic. Official religion: Muslim; Sunni majority. Currency: pound. Capital: Cairo. Pop: 85 294 388 (2013 est). Area: 997 739 sq km (385 229 sq miles). Official name: **Arab Republic of Egypt**. Former official name (1958–71): **United Arab Republic**

Egyptian *adj* **1** of or relating to Egypt or its inhabitants **2** of the ancient Egyptians ▷ *n* **3** a native or inhabitant of Egypt **4** a member of an ancient people who established an advanced civilization in Egypt **5** the language of the ancient Egyptians

Egyptology *n* the study of the culture of ancient Egypt **> Egyptologist** *n*

eh *interj* **1** an exclamation used to ask for repetition or confirmation **2** *Canad and E Scot* a filler phrase used to make a pause in speaking, or add slight emphasis: *it's broken, eh, so I can't play for six weeks*

Ehrenburg *or* **Erenburg** *n* Ilya Grigorievich. 1891–1967, Soviet novelist and journalist. His novel *The Thaw* (1954) was the first published in the Soviet Union to deal with repression under Stalin

Ehrlich *n* Paul. 1854–1915, German bacteriologist, noted for his pioneering work in immunology and chemotherapy and for his discovery of a remedy for syphilis: Nobel prize for physiology or medicine 1908

EI 1 East Indian **2** East Indies **3** *social psychol* emotional intelligence **4** (in Canada) Employment Insurance: a regular payment to a person who is out of work, funded by contributions from workers and employers

Eichendorff *n* Joseph, Freiherr von. 1788–1857, German poet and novelist, regarded as one of the greatest German romantic lyricists

Eichler *n* August Wilhelm. 1839–87, German botanist: devised the system on which modern plant classification is based

Eichmann *n* Karl Adolf. 1902–62, Austrian Nazi official, who took a leading role in organizing the extermination of the European Jews. He escaped to Argentina after World War II, but was captured and executed in Israel as a war criminal

eider *or* **eider duck** *n* a large sea duck of the N hemisphere [Old Norse *æthr*]

eiderdown *n* a thick warm cover for a bed, filled with soft feathers, originally the breast feathers of the female eider duck

Eid-ul-Adha (eed-ool-**ah**-da) *n* an annual Muslim festival, marking the end of the pilgrimage to Mecca [from Arabic *id ul adha* festival of sacrifice]

Eid-ul-Fitr (eed-ool-**feet**-er) *n* an annual Muslim festival, marking the end of Ramadan [from Arabic *id ul fitr* festival of fast-breaking]

Eifel *n* a plateau region in W Germany, between the River Moselle and the Belgian frontier: quarrying

Eiffel *n* Alexandre Gustave. 1832–1923, French engineer

Eiffel Tower *n* a tower in Paris: designed by A. G. Eiffel; erected for the 1889 Paris Exposition. Height: 300 m (984 ft), raised in 1959 to 321 m (1052 ft)

Eigen *n* Manfred. born 1927, German physical chemist: shared the Nobel prize for chemistry (1967) for developing his relaxation technique for studying fast reactions

Eiger *n* a mountain in central Switzerland, in the Bernese Alps. Height: 3970 m (13 025 ft)

eight *n* **1** the cardinal number that is the sum of one and seven **2** a numeral, 8 or VIII, representing this number **3** something representing or consisting of eight units **4** *rowing* **a** a light narrow boat rowed by eight people **b** the crew of such a boat ▷ *adj* **5** amounting to eight: *eight apples* [Old English *eahta*] **> eighth** *adj, n*

eighteen *n* **1** the cardinal number that is the sum of ten and eight **2** a numeral, 18 or XVIII, representing this number **3** something representing or consisting of 18 units ▷ *adj* **4** amounting to eighteen: *eighteen months* **> eighteenth** *adj, n*

eightfold *adj* **1** having eight times as many or as much **2** composed of eight parts ▷ *adv* **3** by eight times as many or as much

eightsome reel *n* a lively Scottish country dance for eight people

eighty *n, pl* **eighties 1** the cardinal number that is the product of ten and eight **2** a numeral, 80 or LXXX, representing this number **3** something representing or consisting of 80 units ▷ *adj* **4** amounting to eighty: *eighty miles* **> eightieth** *adj, n*

Eijkman *n* Christiaan. 1858–1930, Dutch physician, who discovered that beriberi is caused by nutritional deficiency: Nobel prize for physiology or medicine 1929

Eilat, Elat *or* **Elath** *n* a port in S Israel, on the Gulf of Aqaba: Israel's only outlet to the Red Sea. Pop: 43 500 (2003 est)

Eilean Donan Castle *n* a castle near the Kyle of Lochalsh in Highland, Scotland: built in the 13th century; famous for its picturesque setting

Eilean Siar *n* the Scottish Gaelic name for **Western Isles**

eina (**ay**-na) *interj* S African an exclamation of pain [Khoi (language of southern Africa)]

Eindhoven *n* a city in the SE Netherlands, in North Brabant province: radio and electrical industry. Pop: 206 000 (2003 est)

Einstein *n* Albert. 1879–1955, US physicist and mathematician, born in Germany. He formulated the special theory of relativity (1905) and the general theory of relativity (1916), and made major contributions to the quantum theory, for which he was awarded the Nobel prize for physics in 1921. He was noted also for his work for world peace **> Ein'steinian** *adj*

einsteinium *n chem* a radioactive metallic element artificially produced from plutonium. Symbol: **Es** [after Albert EINSTEIN]

Einthoven *n* Willem. 1860–1927, Dutch physiologist. A pioneer of electrocardiography, he was awarded the Nobel prize for physiology or medicine in 1924

Eire *n* **1** the Irish Gaelic name for **Ireland 2** a former official name (1937–49) for **Republic of Ireland**

EIS Educational Institute of Scotland

Eisenach *n* a city in central Germany, in Thuringia: birthplace of Johann Sebastian Bach. Pop: 44 081 (2003 est)

Eisenhower *n* Dwight David, known as *Ike*. 1890–1969, US general and Republican statesman; Supreme Commander of the Allied Expeditionary Force (1943–45) and 34th president of the US (1953–61). He commanded Allied forces in Europe and North Africa (1942), directed the invasion of Italy (1943), and was Supreme Commander of the combined land forces of NATO (1950–52)

Eisenstadt *n* a town in E Austria, capital of Burgenland province: Hungarian until 1921. Pop: 11 334 (2001)

Eisenstaedt *n* Alfred. 1898–1995, US photographer, born in Germany; noted for his photograph of a sailor kissing a woman in Times Square, New York on V-J Day in 1945

Eisenstein *n* Sergei Mikhailovich. 1898–1948, Soviet film director. His films include *Battleship Potemkin* (1925), *Alexander Nevsky* (1938), and *Ivan the Terrible* (1944)

Eisk or **Eysk** *n* variant transliterations of the Russian name for Yeisk

eisteddfod (ice-**sted**-fod) *n* a Welsh festival with competitions in music, poetry, drama, and art [Welsh: session]

either *adj, pron* **1** one or the other (of two): *we were offered either fish or beef* **2** both one and the other: *we sat at either end of a long settee* ▷ *conj* **3** used preceding two or more possibilities joined by or: *it must be stored either in the fridge or in a cool place* ▷ *adv* **4** likewise: *I don't eat meat and my husband doesn't either* **5** used to qualify or modify a previous statement: *he wasn't exactly ugly, but he wasn't an oil painting either* [Old English *ægther*]

> **USAGE** Either should be followed by a singular verb: *either is good; either of these books is useful*. Care should be taken to avoid ambiguity when using *either* to mean *both* or *each*, as in the following sentence: *a ship could be moored on either side of the channel*. Agreement between the verb and its subject in *either...or...* constructions follows the pattern given for *neither...nor...* See at **neither**.

Eivissa *n* the Catalan name for Ibiza

ejaculate *vb* **-lating, -lated 1** to discharge semen from the penis while having an orgasm **2** *literary* to say or shout suddenly [Latin *ejaculari* to hurl out] **> ejaculation** *n* **> ejaculatory** *adj*

eject *vb* **1** to push or send out forcefully **2** to compel (someone) to leave a place or position **3** to leave an aircraft rapidly in mid-flight, using an ejector seat [Latin *ejicere*] **> ejection** *n* **> ejector** *n*

ejector seat or **ejection seat** *n* a seat in a military aircraft that throws the pilot out in an emergency

Ekaterinburg *n* a variant transliteration of the Russian name for Yekaterinburg

Ekaterinodar *n* the former name (until 1920) of Krasnodar

Ekaterinoslav *n* the former name (1787–96, 1802–1926) of Dnepropetrovsk

eke out *vb* **eking, eked 1** to make (a supply) last for a long time by using as little as possible **2** to manage to sustain (a living) despite having barely enough food or money [obsolete *eke* to enlarge]

Ekiti *n* a state of Nigeria, in the SW. Capital: Ado-Ekiti. Pop: 2 384 212(2006). Area: 6353 sq km (2453 sq miles)

Ekman *n* Vagn Walfrid. 1874–1954, Swedish oceanographer: discoverer of the **Ekman spiral** (a complex interaction on the surface of the sea between wind, rotation of the earth, and friction forces) and the **Ekman Layer** (the thin top layer of the sea that flows at 90° to the wind direction)

El Aaiún *n* a city in Western Sahara, controlled by Morocco: the capital of the former Spanish Sahara; port facilities for rich phosphate deposits nearby. Pop: 197 000 (2005 est). Moroccan (French) name: Laâyoune

elaborate *adj* **1** very complex because of having many different parts: *elaborate equipment* **2** having a very complicated design: *elaborate embroidery* ▷ *vb* **-rating, -rated 3** elaborate on to describe in more detail: *he did not elaborate on his plans* **4** to develop (a plan or theory) in detail [Latin *elaborare* to take pains] **> elaborately** *adv* **> elaboration** *n*

El Alamein or **Alamein** *n* a village on the N coast of Egypt, about 112 km (70 miles) west of Alexandria: scene of a decisive Allied victory over the Axis forces (1942)

Elam *n* an ancient kingdom east of the River Tigris: established before 4000 BC; probably inhabited by a non-Semitic people

élan (ale-**an**) *n* style and liveliness [French]

eland (**eel**-and) *n* a large spiral-horned antelope of southern Africa [Dutch: elk]

elapse *vb* **elapsing, elapsed** (of time) to pass by [Latin *elabi* to slip away]

elastane *n* a synthetic fibre that is able to return to its original shape after being stretched

elastic *adj* **1** capable of returning to its original shape after stretching, compression, or other distortion **2** capable of being adapted to meet the demands of a particular situation: *an elastic interpretation of the law* **3** made of elastic ▷ *n* **4** tape, cord, or fabric containing flexible rubber [Greek *elastikos* propellent] **> elastically** *adv* **> elasticated** *adj* **> elasticity** *n*

elastic band *n* a rubber band

Elat or **Elath** *n* variant spellings of Eilat

elated *adj* extremely happy and excited [Latin *elatus* carried away] **> elatedly** *adv*

elation *n* a feeling of great happiness and excitement

Elba *n* a mountainous island off the W coast of Italy, in the Mediterranean: Napoleon Bonaparte's first place of exile (1814–15). Pop: 30 000 (latest est). Area: 223 sq km (86 sq miles)

Elbe *n* a river in central Europe, rising in the N Czech Republic and flowing generally northwest through Germany to the North Sea at Hamburg. Length: 1165 km (724 miles). Czech name: Labe

Elbert *n* Mount Elbert a mountain in central Colorado, in the Sawatch range. Height: 4399 m (14 431 ft)

Elbląg *n* a port in N Poland: metallurgical industries. Pop: 129 000 (2005 est). German name: Elbing

elbow *n* **1** the joint between the upper arm and the forearm **2** the part of a garment that covers the elbow ▷ *vb* **3** to push with one's elbow or elbows: *she elbowed him aside; he elbowed his way to the bar* [Old English elnboga]

elbow grease *n facetious* vigorous physical labour, esp. hard rubbing

elbow room *n* sufficient scope to move or to function

Elbrus *n* a mountain in SW Russia, on the border with Georgia, in the Caucasus Mountains, with two extinct volcanic peaks: the highest mountain in Europe. Height: 5642 m (18 510 ft)

Elburz Mountains *pl n* a mountain range in N Iran, parallel to the SW and S shores of the Caspian Sea. Highest peak: Mount Demavend, 5671 m (18 606 ft)

El Capitan *n* a mountain in E central California, in the Sierra Nevada: a monolith with a precipice rising over 1100 m (3600 ft) above the floor of the Yosemite Valley. Height: 2306 m (7564 ft)

Elche *n* a town in S Spain, in Valencia: noted for Iberian and Roman archaeological finds and the medieval religious drama performed there annually: fruit growing, esp. dates, pomegranates, figs. Pop: 207 163 (2003 est). Catalan name: Elx

elder¹ *adj* **1** (of one of two people) born earlier ▷ *n* **2** an older person: *have some respect for your elders* **3** a senior member of a tribe, who has authority **4** (in certain Protestant Churches) a member of the church who has certain administrative, teaching, or preaching powers [Old English eldra]

elder² *n* a shrub or small tree with clusters of small white flowers and dark purple berries [Old English ellern]

Elder *n* Sir Mark Philip. born 1947, British conductor; musical director of the English National Opera (1979–93) and of the Hallé Orchestra from 2000

elderberry *n, pl* **-ries 1** the fruit of the elder **2** same as elder²

elderly *adj* **1** rather old ▷ *pl n* **2** the elderly old people

elder statesman *n* a respected influential older person, esp. a politician

eldest *adj* (of a person, esp. a child) oldest [Old English *eldesta*]

Eldon *n* Earl of, title of **John Scott**. 1751–1838, British statesman and jurist; Lord Chancellor (1801–06, 1807–27): an inflexible opponent of parliamentary reform, Catholic emancipation, and the abolition of slavery

El Dorado (el dor-**rah**-doe) *n* **1** a fabled city in South America, supposedly rich in treasure **2** Also: **eldorado** any place of great riches or fabulous opportunity [Spanish: the golden (place)]

eldritch *adj poetic, Scot* unearthly or weird [origin unknown]

Elea *n* (in ancient Italy) a Greek colony on the Tyrrhenian coast of Lucana

Eleanor of Aquitaine *n* ?1122–1204, queen of France (1137–52) by her marriage to Louis VII and queen of England (1154–89) by her marriage to Henry II; mother of the English kings Richard I and John

Eleanor of Castile *n* 1246–90, Spanish wife of Edward I of England. **Eleanor Crosses** were erected at each place at which her body rested between Nottingham, where she died, and London, where she is buried

elect *vb* **1** to choose (someone) to fill a position by voting for him or her: *she was elected President in 1990* **2** to choose or decide: *those who elected to stay* ▷ *adj* **3** voted into office but not yet having taken over from the current office-bearer: *the President elect* ▷ *pl n* **4 the elect** any group of people specially chosen for some privilege [Latin *eligere* to select] ▷ **electable** *adj*

election *n* **1 a** a process whereby people vote for a person or party to fill a position: *last month's presidential election* **b** short for **general election 2** the gaining of political power or taking up of a position in an organization as a result of being voted for: *he will be seeking election as the President of Romania*

electioneering *n* the act of taking an active part in a political campaign, for example by canvassing

elective *adj* **1** of or based on selection by vote: *an elective office* **2** not compulsory or necessary: *an elective hysterectomy*

elector *n* **1** someone who is eligible to vote in an election **2** (in the Holy Roman Empire) any of the German princes who were entitled to elect a new emperor: *the Elector of Hanover*

electoral *adj* of or relating to elections: *the electoral system* ▷ **electorally** *adv*

electoral register *n* the official list of all the people in an area who are eligible to vote in elections

electorate *n* **1** all the people in an area or country who have the right to vote in an election **2** the rank or territory of an elector of the Holy Roman Empire

electric *adj* **1** produced by, transmitting, or powered by electricity: *an electric fire* **2** very tense or exciting: *the atmosphere was electric* ▷ *n* **3 electrics** *Brit* an electric circuit or electric appliances [Greek *ēlektron* amber (because friction causes amber to become electrically charged)]

> USAGE See at **electronic**.

electrical *adj* of or relating to electricity ▷ **electrically** *adv*

> USAGE See at **electronic**.

electrical engineering *n* the branch of engineering concerned with practical applications of electricity and electronics ▷ **electrical engineer** *n*

electric blanket *n* a blanket fitted with an electric heating element, used to warm a bed

electric chair *n* (in the US) a chair for executing criminals by passing a strong electric current through them

electric eel *n* an eel-like South American freshwater fish, which can stun or kill its prey with a powerful electric shock

electric field *n physics* a region of space surrounding a charged particle within which another charged particle experiences a force

electric guitar *n* an electrically amplified guitar

electrician *n* a person trained to install and repair electrical equipment

electricity *n* **1** a form of energy associated with stationary or moving electrons, ions, or other charged particles **2** the supply of electricity to houses, factories, etc., for heating, lighting, etc.

electric shock *n* pain and muscular spasms caused by an electric current passing through the body

electrify *vb* **-fies, -fying, -fied 1** to adapt or equip (a system or device) to work by electricity: *the whole track has now been electrified* **2** to provide (an area) with electricity **3** to startle or excite intensely ▷ **electrification** *n*

electrifying *adj* very exciting and surprising

electro- *combining form* electric or electrically: *electroconvulsive* [Greek *ēlektron* amber; see ELECTRIC]

electrocardiograph *n* an instrument for making tracings (**electrocardiograms**) recording the electrical activity of the heart

electrocute *vb* **-cuting, -cuted** to kill or injure by an electric shock [ELECTRO- + (EXE)CUTE] ▷ **electrocution** *n*

electrode *n* a small piece of metal used to take an electric current to or from a power source, piece of equipment, or living body

electrodynamics *n* the branch of physics concerned with the interactions between electrical and mechanical forces

electroencephalograph (ill-lek-tro-en-sef-a-loh-graf) *n* an instrument for making tracings (**electroencephalograms**) recording the electrical activity of the brain

electrolysis (ill-lek-**troll**-iss-iss) *n* **1** the process of passing an electric current through a liquid in order to produce a chemical reaction in the liquid **2** the destruction of living tissue, such as hair roots, by an electric current

electrolyte *n* a solution or molten substance that conducts electricity ▷ **electrolytic** *adj*

electromagnet *n* a magnet consisting of a coil of wire wound round an iron core through which a current is passed

electromagnetic *adj* **1** of or operated by an electromagnet **2** of or relating to electromagnetism ▷ **electromagnetically** *adv*

electromagnetism *n* magnetism produced by an electric current

electromotive *adj physics* of or producing an electric current

electromotive force *n physics* **1** a source of energy that can cause current to flow in an electrical circuit **2** the rate at which energy is drawn from such a source when a unit of current flows through the circuit, measured in volts

electron *n physics* an elementary particle in all atoms that has a negative electrical charge

electronegative *adj physics* **1** having a negative electric charge **2** tending to gain or attract electrons

electronic *adj* **1** (of a device, circuit, or system) containing transistors, silicon chips, etc., which control the current passing through it **2** making use of electronic systems: *electronic surveillance devices* ▷ **electronically** *adv*

> USAGE *Electronic* refers to equipment, such as television sets, computers, etc., in which the current is controlled by transistors, valves, and similar components. *Electrical* is used in a more general sense to refer to the use of electricity as a whole as opposed to other forms of energy: *electrical engineering; an electrical appliance. Electric* can be used interchangeably with *electrical*, but is often restricted to the

description of particular devices or to concepts relating to the flow of current: *electric fire; electric charge.*

electronic paper *or* **electronic ink** *n* a material used in e-readers, consisting of black particles suspended in white fluid which become visible in response to an electronic charge

electronic publishing *n* the publication of information on discs, magnetic tape, etc., so that it can be accessed by computer

electronics *n* the technology concerned with the development, behaviour, and applications of devices and circuits, for example televisions and computers, which make use of electronic components such as transistors or silicon chips

electron microscope *n* a powerful microscope that uses electrons, rather than light, to produce a magnified image

electronvolt *n physics* a unit of energy equal to the work done on an electron accelerated through a potential difference of 1 volt

electroplate *vb* **-plating, -plated 1** to coat (an object) with metal by dipping it in a special liquid through which an electric current is passed ▷ *n* **2** electroplated articles collectively

electropositive *adj physics* **1** having a positive electric charge **2** tending to release electrons

electrostatics *n* the branch of physics concerned with static electricity ▷ **electrostatic** *adj*

elegant *adj* **1** attractive and graceful or stylish **2** cleverly simple and clear: *an elegant summary* [Latin *elegans* tasteful] ▷ **elegance** *n* ▷ **elegantly** *adv*

elegiac *adj literary* sad, mournful, or plaintive

elegy (el-lij-ee) *n, pl* **-gies** a mournful poem or song, esp. a lament for the dead [Greek *elegos* lament]

USAGE Avoid confusion with eulogy.

Eleia *n* a variant spelling of **Elia**

element *n* **1** one of the fundamental components making up a whole **2** *chem* any of the known substances that cannot be separated into simpler substances by chemical means **3** a distinguishable section of a social group: *liberal elements in Polish society* **4** a degree: *an element of truth* **5** a metal part in an electrical device, such as a kettle, that changes the electric current into heat **6** one of the four substances (earth, air, water, and fire) formerly believed to make up the universe **7** *maths* any of the members of a set **8 in one's element** in a situation in which one is happy and at ease: *she was in her element behind the wheel* **9 elements a** the basic principles of something **b** weather conditions, esp. wind, rain, and cold: *only 200 braved the elements* [Latin *elementum*]

elemental *adj* of or like basic and powerful natural forces or passions

elementary *adj* **1** simple, basic, and straightforward: *elementary precautions* **2** involving only the most basic principles of a subject: *elementary mathematics*

elementary particle *n physics* any of several entities, such as electrons, neutrons, or protons, that are less complex than atoms

elementary school *n* **1** *Brit* same as **primary school 2** *US and Canad* a state school for the first six to eight years of a child's education

elephant *n* **1** a very large four-legged animal that has a very long flexible nose called a trunk, large ears, and two ivory tusks, and lives in Africa or India **2 elephant in the room** an obvious truth deliberately ignored by all parties in a situation [Greek *elephas*]

elephantiasis (el-lee-fan-tie-a-siss) *n pathol* a skin disease, caused by parasitic worms, in which the affected parts of the body become extremely enlarged

elephantine *adj* like an elephant, esp. in being huge, clumsy, or ponderous

Eleusis *n* a town in Greece, in Attica about 23 km (14 miles) west of Athens, of which it is now an industrial suburb. Modern Greek name: Elevsís ▷ **Eleusinian** *n, adj*

elevate *vb* **-vating, -vated 1** to raise in rank or status: *she had elevated flirting to an art form* **2** to lift to a higher place: *this action elevates the upper back* [Latin *elevare*]

elevated *adj* **1** higher than normal: *elevated cholesterol levels* **2** (of ideas or pursuits) on a high intellectual or moral level: *elevated discussions about postmodernism* **3** (of land or part of a building) higher than the surrounding area

elevation *n* **1** the act of elevating someone or something: *his elevation to the peerage* **2** height above sea level **3** a raised area **4** a scale drawing of one side of a building

elevator *n* **1** *Austral, US and Canad* a lift for carrying people **2** a mechanical hoist

eleven *n* **1** the cardinal number that is the sum of ten and one **2** a numeral, 11 or XI, representing this number **3** something representing or consisting of 11 units **4** a team of 11 players in football, cricket, etc. ▷ *adj* **5** amounting to eleven: *eleven years* [Old English *endleofan*] ▷ **eleventh** *adj, n*

eleven-plus *n* (in Britain, esp. formerly) an examination taken by children aged 10 or 11 that determines the type of secondary education they will be given

elevenses *pl n Brit, Austral, S African and NZ informal* a mid-morning snack

eleventh hour *n* **1** the latest possible time ▷ *adj* **eleventh-hour 2** done at the latest possible time: *an eleventh-hour rescue*

Elevsís *n* a transliteration of the Modern Greek name for Eleusis

elf *n, pl* **elves** (in folklore) a small mischievous fairy [Old English *ælf*]

El Faiyûm *or* **Al Faiyûm** *n* a city in N Egypt: a site of towns going back at least to the 12th dynasty. Pop: 311 000 (2005 est)

El Ferrol *n* a port in NW Spain, on the Atlantic: fortified naval base, with a deep natural harbour. Pop: 78 764 (2003 est). Former name: El Ferrol del Caudillo

elfin *adj* **1** small and delicate: *her elfin features* **2** of or relating to elves

Elgar *n* Sir Edward (William). 1857–1934, English composer, whose works include the *Enigma Variations* (1899), the oratorio *The Dream of Gerontius* (1900), two symphonies, a cello concerto, and a violin concerto

Elgin *n* a market town in NE Scotland, the administrative centre of Moray, on the River Lossie: ruined 13th-century cathedral; distilling, engineering. Pop: 20 829 (2001)

El Gîza *or* **Giza** *n* a city in NE Egypt, on the W bank of the Nile opposite Cairo: nearby are the Great Pyramid of Cheops (Khufu) and the Sphinx. Pop: 2 221 868 (1996)

Elgon *n* Mount Elgon an extinct volcano in E Africa, on the Kenya-Uganda border. Height: 4321m (14 178 ft)

El Greco *n* real name *Domenikos Theotocopoulos*. 1541–1614, Spanish painter, born in Crete; noted for his elongated human forms and dramatic use of colour

Elia *or* **Eleia** *n* a department of SW Greece, in the W Peloponnese: in ancient times most of the region formed the state of Elis. Pop: 183 521 (2001). Area: 2681 sq km (1035 sq miles). Modern Greek name: Ilía

Eliade *n* Mircea. 1907–86, Romanian scholar and writer, noted for his study of religious symbolism. His works include *Patterns of Comparative Religion* (1949)

elicit *vb* **1** to bring about (a response or reaction): *her remarks elicited a sharp retort* **2** to draw out (information) from someone: *a phone call elicited the fact that she had just awakened* [Latin *elicere*]

elide *vb* **eliding, elided** to omit (a syllable or vowel) from a spoken word [Latin *elidere* to knock]

e

eligible *adj* **1** meeting the requirements or qualifications needed: *he may be eligible for free legal services* **2** old-fashioned desirable as a spouse [Latin *eligere* to elect] > **eligibility** *n*

Elikón *n* a transliteration of the Modern Greek name for Helicon

eliminate *vb* **-nating, -nated** **1** to get rid of (something or someone unwanted, unnecessary, or not meeting the requirements needed): *he can be eliminated from the list of suspects* **2** to remove (a competitor or team) from a contest, esp. following a defeat: *they were eliminated in the third round* **3** slang to murder in cold blood: *Stalin had thousands of his former comrades eliminated* [Latin *eliminare* to turn out of the house] > **elimination** *n*

> **USAGE** *Eliminate* is sometimes wrongly used to talk about avoiding the repetition of something undesirable: *we must prevent* (not *eliminate*) *further mistakes of this kind.*

Eliot *n* **1** George, real name *Mary Ann Evans*. 1819–80, English novelist, noted for her analysis of provincial Victorian society. Her best-known novels include *Adam Bede* (1859), *The Mill on the Floss* (1860), *Silas Marner* (1861), and *Middlemarch* (1872) **2** Sir **John**. 1592–1632, English statesman, a leader of parliamentary opposition to Charles I **3** **T(homas) S(tearns)**. 1888–1965, British poet, dramatist, and critic, born in the US. His poetry includes *Prufrock and Other Observations* (1917), *The Waste Land* (1922), *Ash Wednesday* (1930), and *Four Quartets* (1943). Among his verse plays are *Murder in the Cathedral* (1935), *The Family Reunion* (1939), *The Cocktail Party* (1950), and *The Confidential Clerk* (1954): Nobel prize for literature 1948

Elis *n* an ancient city-state of SW Greece, in the NW Peloponnese: site of the ancient Olympic games

Élisabethville *n* the former name (until 1966) of Lubumbashi

Elisavetgrad *n* a former name (until 1924) of Kirovograd

Elisavetpol *n* a former name (until 1920) of Kirovabad

elision *n* the omission of a syllable or vowel from a spoken word [Latin *elidere* to elide]

elite (ill-eet) *n* the most powerful, rich, or gifted members of a group or community

elitism *n* **1** the belief that society should be governed by a small group of people who are superior to everyone else **2** pride in being part of an elite > **elitist** *n, adj*

elixir (ill-ix-er) *n* **1** an imaginary substance that is supposed to be capable of prolonging life and changing base metals into gold **2** a liquid medicine mixed with syrup [Arabic *al iksīr*]

Elizabeth¹ *n* **1** a city in NE New Jersey, on Newark Bay. Pop: 123 215 (2003 est) **2** a town in SE South Australia, part of Adelaide. Pop: 26 428 (2006)

Elizabeth² *n* **1** Saint Elizabeth *or* Saint Elisabeth *New Testament* the wife of Zacharias, mother of John the Baptist, and kinswoman of the Virgin Mary. Feast day: Nov 5 or 8 **2** pen name *Carmen Sylva*. 1843–1916, queen of Romania (1881–1914) and author **3** Russian name *Yelizaveta Petrovna*. 1709–62, empress of Russia (1741–62); daughter of Peter the Great **4** title *the Queen Mother*; original name *Lady Elizabeth Bowes-Lyon*. 1900–2002, queen of Great Britain and Northern Ireland (1936–52) as the wife of George VI; mother of Elizabeth II

Elizabeth I *n* 1533–1603, queen of England (1558–1603); daughter of Henry VIII and Anne Boleyn. She established the Church of England (1559) and put an end to Catholic plots, notably by executing Mary Queen of Scots (1587) and defeating the Spanish Armada (1588). Her reign was notable for commercial growth, maritime expansion, and the flourishing of literature, music, and architecture

Elizabeth II *n* born 1926, queen of Great Britain and Northern Ireland from 1952; daughter of George VI

Elizabethan *adj* **1** of or in the reign of Queen Elizabeth I of England (1558–1603) ▷ *n* **2** a person who lived during the reign of Queen Elizabeth I

Elizabeth of Hungary *n* Saint. 1207–31, Hungarian princess who devoted herself to charity and asceticism. Feast day: Nov 17 and 19

elk *n* a very large deer of N Europe and Asia with broad flat antlers

El Khalil *n* transliteration of the Arabic name for **Hebron**

Ellás *n* transliteration of the Modern Greek name for Greece

Ellenborough *n* **Earl of**, title of Edward Law. 1780–1871, British colonial administrator: governor general of India (1742–44)

Ellesmere Island *n* a Canadian island in the Arctic Ocean: part of Nunavut; mountainous, with many glaciers. Area: 212 688 sq km (82 119 sq miles)

Ellesmere Port *n* a port in NW England, in NW Cheshire on the Mersey estuary and Manchester Ship Canal. Pop: 66 265 (2001)

Ellice Islands *pl n* the former name (until 1975) of **Tuvalu**

Ellington *n* **Duke**, nickname of *Edward Kennedy Ellington*. 1899–1974, US jazz composer, pianist, and conductor, famous for such works as "Mood Indigo" and "Creole Love Call"

ellipse *n* an oval shape resembling a flattened circle

ellipsis (ill-lip-siss) *n, pl* **-ses** (-seez) **1** the omission of a word or words from a sentence **2** printing three dots (...) indicating an omission [Greek *elleipein* to leave out]

ellipsoid *n* geometry a surface whose plane sections are ellipses or circles

elliptical *or* **elliptic** *adj* **1** oval-shaped **2** (of speech or writing) obscure or ambiguous

> **USAGE** The use of *elliptical* to mean *circumlocutory* should be avoided as it may be interpreted wrongly as meaning *condensed* or *concise.*

Ellis *n* **1** Alexander John. 1814–90, English philologist: made the first systematic survey of the phonology of British dialects **2** (Henry) Havelock. 1859–1939, English essayist: author of works on the psychology of sex

elm *n* **1** a tall tree with broad leaves **2** the hard heavy wood of this tree [Old English]

El Mansûra *or* **Al Mansûrah** *n* a city in NE Egypt: scene of a battle (1250) in which the Crusaders were defeated by the Mamelukes and Louis IX of France was captured; cotton-manufacturing centre. Pop: 423 000 (2005 est)

El Minya *n* a river port in central Egypt on the Nile. Pop: 225 000 (2005 est)

El Misti *n* a volcano in S Peru, in the Andes. Height: 5852 m (19 199 ft)

El Obeid *n* a city in the central Sudan, in Kordofan province: scene of the defeat of a British and Egyptian army by the Mahdi (1883). Pop: 423 000 (2005 est)

elocution *n* the art of speaking clearly in public [Latin *e-* out + *loqui* to speak] > **elocutionist** *n*

elongate (eel-long-gate) *vb* **-gating, -gated** to make or become longer [Latin *e-* away + *longe* (adverb) far] > **elongation** *n*

elope *vb* **eloping, eloped** (of two people) to run away secretly to get married [Anglo-French *aloper*] > **elopement** *n*

eloquence *n* the ability to speak or write in a skilful and convincing way

eloquent *adj* **1** (of speech or writing) fluent and persuasive **2** (of a person) able to speak in a fluent and persuasive manner **3** visibly or vividly expressive: *he raised an eloquent eyebrow* [Latin *e-* out + *loqui* to speak] > **eloquently** *adv*

El Paso *n* a city in W Texas, on the Rio Grande opposite Ciudad Juárez, Mexico. Pop: 584 113 (2003 est)

Els *n* Ernie, full name *Theodore Ernest Els*. born 1969; South African golfer: won the British Open Championship (2002, 2012) and the US Open Championship (1994, 1997)

El Salvador n a republic in Central America, on the Pacific: colonized by the Spanish from 1524; declared independence in 1841, becoming a republic in 1856. It consists of coastal lowlands rising to a central plateau. Coffee constitutes over a third of the total exports. Official language: Spanish. Religion: Roman Catholic majority. Currency: US dollar. Capital: San Salvador. Pop: 6 108 590 (2013 est). Area: 21 393 sq km (8236 sq miles)

Elsass n the German name for **Alsace**

Elsass-Lothringen n the German name for Alsace-Lorraine

else adv 1 in addition or more: *what else do you want to know?* 2 other or different: *it was unlike anything else that had happened* 3 **or else** a if not, then: *tell us soon or else we shall go mad* b informal or something terrible will result: used as a threat: *do it our way or else* [Old English *elles*]

elsewhere adv in or to another place

Elsinore n the English name for **Helsingør**

ELT English Language Teaching

Elton n 1 **Ben(jamin) (Charles)**. born 1959, British comedian, scriptwriter, playwright, and novelist; his work includes the *Blackadder* series for television (1987–89), the play *Gasping* (1990), the novel *High Society* (2002), and the lyrics to the musical *We Will Rock You* (2002) 2 **Charles Sutherland**. 1900–91, British zoologist: initiated the study of animal ecology

Éluard n **Paul**, real name *Eugène-Émile-Paul Grindel*. 1895–1952, French surrealist poet, noted for his political and love poems

elucidate vb -dating, -dated to make (something obscure or difficult) clear [Late Latin *elucidare* to enlighten] > **elucidation** n

elude vb eluding, eluded 1 to avoid or escape from (someone or something) 2 to fail to be understood or remembered by: *the mysteries of commerce elude me* [Latin *eludere* to deceive]

> **USAGE** Elude is sometimes wrongly used where *allude* is meant: *he was alluding (not eluding) to his previous visit to the city.*

elusive adj 1 difficult to find or catch 2 difficult to remember or describe > **elusiveness** n

> **USAGE** See at illusory.

elver n a young eel [variant of *eelfare* eel-journey]

elves n the plural of elf

Elx n the Catalan name for **Elche**

Ely n 1 a cathedral city in E England, in E Cambridgeshire on the River Ouse. Pop: 13 954 (2001) 2 a former county of E England, part of Cambridgeshire since 1965

Elyot n Sir **Thomas**. ?1490–1546, English scholar and diplomat; author of *The Boke named the Governour* (1531), a treatise in English on education

Élysée n a palace in Paris, in the Champs Elysées: official residence of the president of France

Elysium n 1 Greek myth the dwelling place of the blessed after death 2 a state or place of perfect bliss [Greek *ēlusion pedion* blessed fields] > **Elysian** adj

Elytis n **Odysseus**, real name *Odysseus Alepoudelis*. 1912–96, Greek poet, author of the long poems *To Axion Esti* (1959) and *Maria Nefeli* (1978): Nobel prize for literature 1979

emaciated (im-mace-ee-ate-id) adj extremely thin through illness or lack of food [Latin *macer* thin] > **emaciation** n

e-mail or **email** (ee-mail) n 1 the transmission of messages from one computer terminal to another ▷ vb 2 to contact (a person) by e-mail 3 to send (a message) by e-mail

emanate (em-a-nate) vb -nating, -nated to come or seem to come from someone or something: *an aura of power emanated from him* [Latin *emanare* to flow out] > **emanation** n

emancipate vb -pating, -pated to free from social, political, or legal restrictions [Latin *emancipare* to give independence (to a son)] > **emancipation** n

emasculate vb -lating, -lated to deprive of power or strength [Latin *emasculare* to remove the testicles of] > **emasculation** n

embalm vb to preserve (a corpse) by the use of chemicals and oils [Old French *embaumer*]

embankment n a man-made ridge of earth or stone that carries a road or railway or prevents a river or lake from overflowing

embargo n, pl -goes 1 an order by a government or international body prohibiting trade with a country: *the world trade embargo against Iraq* ▷ vb -going, -goed 2 to place an official prohibition on [Spanish]

embark vb 1 to go on board a ship or aircraft 2 **embark on** to begin (a new project or venture) [Old Provençal *embarcar*] > **embarkation** n

embarrass vb 1 to make (someone) feel shy, ashamed, or guilty about something 2 to cause political problems for (a government or party) 3 to cause to have financial difficulties [Italian *imbarrare* to confine within bars] > **embarrassed** adj > **embarrassing** adj > **embarrassingly** adv > **embarrassment** n

embassy n, pl -sies 1 the residence or place of business of an ambassador 2 an ambassador and his or her assistants and staff [Old Provençal *ambaisada*]

embattled adj 1 (of a country) involved in fighting a war, esp. when surrounded by enemies 2 facing many problems and difficulties: *the embattled Mayor*

embed vb -bedding, -bedded 1 to fix firmly in a surrounding solid mass: *the boy has shrapnel embedded in his spine* 2 to fix (an attitude or idea) in a society or in someone's mind: *corruption was deeply embedded in the ruling party*

embellish vb 1 to make (something) more attractive by adding decorations 2 to make (a story) more interesting by adding details which may not be true [Old French *embelir*] > **embellishment** n

ember n a smouldering piece of coal or wood remaining after a fire has died [Old English *ǣmyrge*]

embezzle vb -zling, -zled to steal (money that belongs to the company or organization that one works for) [Anglo-French *embeseiller* to destroy] > **embezzlement** n > **embezzler** n

embittered adj feeling anger and despair as a result of misfortune: *embittered by poverty* > **embitterment** n

emblazon (im-blaze-on) vb 1 to decorate with a coat of arms, slogan, etc.: *a jacket emblazoned with his band's name* 2 to proclaim or publicize: *I am not sure he would want his name emblazoned in my column*

emblem n an object or design chosen to symbolize an organization or idea [Greek *emblēma* insertion] > **emblematic** adj

embody vb -bodies, -bodying, -bodied 1 to be an example of or express (an idea or other abstract concept) 2 to include as part of a whole: *the proposal has been embodied in a draft resolution* > **embodiment** n

embolden vb to make bold

embolism n pathol the blocking of a blood vessel by a blood clot, air bubble, etc.

embolus n, pl -li pathol a blood clot, air bubble, or other stoppage that blocks a small blood vessel [Greek *embolos* stopper]

emboss vb to mould or carve a decoration on (a surface) so that it stands out from the surface [Old French *embocer*]

embrace vb -bracing, -braced 1 to clasp (someone) with one's arms as an expression of affection or a greeting 2 to accept eagerly: *he has embraced the Islamic faith* 3 to include or be made up of: *a church that embraces two cultures* ▷ n 4 an act of embracing [Latin *im-* in + *brachia* arms]

embrasure n 1 an opening for a door or window which is wider on the inside of the wall than on the outside

2 an opening in a battlement or wall, for shooting through [French]

embrocation *n* a lotion rubbed into the skin to ease sore muscles [Greek *brokhē* a moistening]

embroider *vb* **1** to do decorative needlework on (a piece of cloth or a garment) **2** to add imaginary details to (a story) [Old French *embroder*] **› embroiderer** *n*

embroidery *n* **1** decorative needlework, usually on cloth or canvas **2** the act of adding imaginary details to a story

embroil *vb* to involve (oneself or another person) in problems or difficulties [French *embrouiller*]
› embroilment *n*

embryo (em-bree-oh) *n, pl* **-bryos 1** an unborn animal or human being in the early stages of development, in humans up to approximately the end of the second month of pregnancy **2** something in an early stage of development: *the embryo of a serious comic novel* [Greek *embruon*]

embryology *n* the scientific study of embryos

embryonic *adj* **1** of or relating to an embryo **2** in an early stage

Emden *n* a port in NW Germany, in Lower Saxony at the mouth of the River Ems. Pop: 51 445 (2003 est)

emend *vb* to make corrections or improvements to (a text) [Latin *e-* out + *mendum* a mistake] **› emendation** *n*

emerald *n* **1** a green transparent variety of beryl highly valued as a gem ▷ *adj* **2** bright green [Greek *smaragdos*]

Emerald Isle *n* a poetic name for **Ireland**

emerge *vb* **emerging, emerged 1** to come into view out of something: *two men emerged from the pub* **2** to come out of a particular state of mind or way of existence: *she emerged from the trance* **3** to come to the end of a particular event or situation: *no party emerged from the election with a clear majority* **4** to become apparent, esp. as the result of a discussion or investigation: *it emerged that he had been drinking* **5** to come into existence over a long period of time: *a new style of dance music emerged in the late 1980s* [Latin *emergere* to rise up from] **› emergence** *n* **› emergent** *adj*

emergency *n, pl* **-cies 1** an unforeseen or sudden occurrence, esp. of danger demanding immediate action **2 state of emergency** a time of crisis, declared by a government, during which normal laws and civil rights can be suspended ▷ *adj* **3** for use in an emergency: *the emergency exit* **4** made necessary because of an emergency: *emergency surgery*

emeritus (im-mer-rit-uss) *adj* retired, but retaining one's title on an honorary basis: *a professor emeritus* [Latin *merere* to deserve]

Emerson *n* Ralph Waldo. 1803–82, US poet, essayist, and transcendentalist

emery *n* a hard greyish-black mineral used for smoothing and polishing [Greek *smuris* powder for rubbing]

emery board *n* a strip of cardboard coated with crushed emery, for filing one's fingernails

emetic (im-met-ik) *n* **1** a substance that causes vomiting ▷ *adj* **2** causing vomiting [Greek *emetikos*]

EMF electromotive force

emigrate *vb* **-grating, -grated** to leave one's native country to settle in another country [Latin *emigrare*] **› emigrant** *n, adj* **› emigration** *n*

émigré (em-mig-gray) *n* someone who has left his or her native country for political reasons [French]

Emilia-Romagna *n* a region of N central Italy, on the Adriatic: rises from the plains of the Po valley in the north to the Apennines in the south. Capital: Bologna. Pop: 4 030 220 (2003 est). Area: 22 123 sq km (8628 sq miles)

Emin *n* Tracey. born 1963, British artist, noted for provocative multimedia works such as *Everyone I Have Ever Slept With* (1995) and *My Bed* (1999)

Eminem *n* real name *Marshall Mathers III*. born 1972, US White rap performer noted for his controversial lyrics; recordings include *The Slim Shady LP* (1999) and *The Eminem*

Show (2002); he also starred in the film *8 Mile* (2002)

eminence *n* **1** the state of being well-known and well-respected **2** a piece of high ground

Eminence *n* Your or His Eminence a title used to address or refer to a cardinal

éminence grise (em-in-nonss greez) *n, pl* **éminences grises** a person who wields power and influence unofficially [French, literally: grey eminence, originally applied to Père Joseph, secretary of Cardinal Richelieu]

eminent *adj* well-known and well-respected [Latin *eminere* to stand out]

eminently *adv* extremely: *eminently sensible*

emir (em-meer) *n* an independent ruler in the Islamic world [Arabic *'amīr* commander] **› emirate** *n*

emissary *n, pl* **-saries** an agent sent on a mission by a government or head of state [Latin *emissarius*]

emission *n* **1** the act of giving out heat, light, a smell, etc. **2** energy or a substance given out by something: *exhaust emissions from motor vehicles*

emit *vb* **emitting, emitted 1** to give or send forth (heat, light, a smell, etc.) **2** to produce (a sound) [Latin *emittere* to send out]

Emmen *n* a city in the NE Netherlands, in Drenthe province: a new town developed since World War II. Pop: 108 000 (2003 est)

Emmental (em-men-tahl) *n* a hard Swiss cheese with holes in it [after *Emmenthal*, valley in Switzerland]

Emmet *n* Robert. 1778–1803, Irish nationalist, executed for leading an uprising for Irish independence

emoji (im-moh-jee) *n* an image used in electronic messages to convey an emotion [Japanese *e* letter + *moji* character]

emollient *adj* **1** (of skin cream or lotion) having a softening effect **2** helping to avoid confrontation; calming: *his emollient political style* ▷ *n* **3** a cream or lotion that softens the skin [Latin *emollire* to soften]

emolument *n* fees or wages from employment [Latin *emolumentum* benefit; originally, fee paid to a miller]

emote *vb* **emoting, emoted** to display exaggerated emotion, as if acting

emoticon (im-mote-ik-kon) *n computers* same as **smiley** (3) [EMOT(ION) + ICON]

emotion *n* **1** any strong feeling, such as joy or fear **2** the part of a person's character based on feelings rather than thought: *the conflict between emotion and logic* [Latin *emovere* to disturb]

emotional *adj* **1** of or relating to the emotions: *emotional abuse* **2** influenced by feelings rather than rational thinking: *he was too emotional to be a good doctor* **3** appealing to the emotions: *emotional appeals for public support* **4** showing one's feelings openly, esp. when upset: *he became very emotional and burst into tears* **› emotionalism** *n* **› emotionally** *adv*

emotive *adj* tending or designed to arouse emotion

USAGE *Emotional* is preferred to *emotive* when describing a display of emotion: *he was given an emotional (not emotive) welcome.*

empathize *or* **-thise** *vb* **-thizing, -thized** *or* **-thising, -thised** (often foll. by *with*) to sense and understand someone else's feelings as if they were one's own

empathy *n* the ability to sense and understand someone else's feelings as if they were one's own [Greek *empatheia* affection, passion] **› empathic** *adj*

Empedocles *n* ?490–430 BC, Greek philosopher and scientist, who held that the world is composed of four elements, air, fire, earth, and water, which are governed by the opposing forces of love and discord

emperor *n* a man who rules an empire [Latin *imperare* to command]

emperor penguin *n* a very large Antarctic penguin with orange-yellow patches on its neck

emphasis *n, pl* **-ses 1** special importance or significance given to something, such as an object or idea **2** stress on a particular syllable, word, or phrase in speaking [Greek]

emphasize or **-sise** vb **-sizing, -sized** or **-sising, -sised** to give emphasis or prominence to: *to emphasize her loyalty*

emphatic adj **1** expressed, spoken, or done forcefully: *an emphatic denial of the allegations* **2** forceful and positive: *he was emphatic about his desire for peace talks* [Greek *emphainein* to display] **> emphatically** adv

emphysema (em-fiss-see-ma) n pathol a condition in which the air sacs of the lungs are grossly enlarged, causing breathlessness [Greek *emphusēma* a swelling up]

empire n **1** a group of countries under the rule of a single person or sovereign state **2** a large industrial organization that is controlled by one person: *the heiress to a jewellery empire* [Latin *imperare* to command]

empire-builder n informal a person who seeks extra power by increasing the number of his or her staff **> empire-building** n, adj

Empire State n nickname of New York

empirical adj derived from experiment, experience, and observation rather than from theory or logic: *there is no empirical data to support this claim* [Greek *empeirikos* practised] **> empirically** adv

empiricism n philosophy the doctrine that all knowledge derives from experience **> empiricist** n

emplacement n a prepared position for an artillery gun

employ vb **1** to hire (someone) to do work in return for money **2** to keep busy or occupy: *she was busily employed cutting the grass* **3** to use as a means: *you can employ various methods to cut your heating bills* ▷ n **4 in the employ of** doing regular paid work for: *he is in the employ of The Sunday Times* [Old French *emploier*] **> employable** adj

employee or US **employe** n a person who is hired to work for someone in return for payment

employer n a person or company that employs workers

employment n **1** the act of employing or state of being employed **2** a person's work or occupation **3** the availability of jobs for the population of a town, country, etc.: *the party's commitment to full employment*

emporium n, pl **-riums** or **-ria** old-fashioned a large retail shop with a wide variety of merchandise [Latin, from Greek *emporos* merchant]

empower vb to give (someone) the power or authority to do something

empowerment n **1** the giving or delegation of power; authority **2** S African a semi-official slogan for the empowering of previously disadvantaged populations

empress n **1** a woman who rules an empire **2** the wife or widow of an emperor [Latin *imperatrix*]

Empson n Sir William. 1906–84, English poet and critic; author of *Seven Types of Ambiguity* (1930)

empty adj **-tier, -tiest 1** containing nothing **2** without inhabitants; unoccupied **3** without purpose, substance, or value: *he contemplated yet another empty weekend* **4** insincere or trivial: *empty words* **5** informal drained of energy or emotion **6** maths, logic (of a set or class) containing no members ▷ vb **-ties, -tying, -tied 7** to make or become empty **8** to remove from something: *they emptied out the remains of the tin of paint* ▷ n, pl **-ties 9** an empty container, esp. a bottle [Old English *ǣmtig*] **> emptiness** n

empty-handed adj having gained nothing: *the robbers ran off empty-handed*

empty-headed adj silly or incapable of serious thought

Empty Quarter n another name for **Rub' al Khali**

empyrean (em-pie-ree-an) n poetic the sky or the heavens [Greek *empuros* fiery]

Ems or **Bad Ems** n **1** a town in W Germany, in the Rhineland-Palatinate: famous for the **Ems Telegram** (1870), Bismarck's dispatch that led to the outbreak of the Franco-Prussian War. Pop: 9666 (2003 est) **2** a river in W Germany, rising in the Teutoburger Wald and flowing generally north to the North Sea. Length: about 370 km (230 miles)

EMS European Monetary System: the system enabling some EU members to coordinate their exchange rates

emu n a large Australian long-legged bird that cannot fly [Portuguese *ema* ostrich]

EMU 1 European Monetary Union **2** Economic and Monetary Union

emulate vb **-lating, -lated** to imitate (someone) in an attempt to do as well as or better than him or her [Latin *aemulus* competing with] **> emulation** n **> emulator** n

emulsifier n a substance that helps to combine two liquids, esp. a water-based liquid and an oil

emulsify vb **-fies, -fying, -fied** to make or form into an emulsion

emulsion n **1** a mixture of two liquids in which particles of one are suspended evenly throughout the other **2** photog a light-sensitive coating for paper or film **3** a type of water-based paint [Latin *emulgere* to milk out]

enable vb **-abling, -abled 1** to provide (someone) with the means or opportunity to do something **2** to make possible: *to enable the best possible chance of cure*

enabling act n a legislative act giving certain powers to a person or organization

enact vb **1** to establish by law: *plans to enact a bill of rights* **2** to perform (a story or play) by acting **> enactment** n

enamel n **1** a coloured glassy coating on the surface of articles made of metal, glass, or pottery **2** an enamel-like paint or varnish **3** the hard white substance that covers teeth ▷ vb **-elling, -elled** or US **-eling, -eled 4** to decorate or cover with enamel [Old French *esmail*]

enamoured or US **enamored** adj enamoured of **a** in love with **b** very fond of and impressed by: *he is not enamoured of Moscow* [Latin *amor* love]

en bloc adv as a whole; all together [French]

enc. 1 enclosed **2** enclosure

encamp vb formal to set up a camp **> encampment** n

encapsulate vb **-lating, -lated 1** to put in a concise form; summarize **2** to enclose in, or as if in, a capsule **> encapsulation** n

encase vb **-casing, -cased** to enclose or cover completely: *her arms were encased in plaster* **> encasement** n

encephalitis (en-sef-a-lite-iss) n inflammation of the brain [Greek *en-* in + *kephalē* head] **> encephalitic** adj

encephalogram n an electroencephalogram [Greek *en-* in + *kephalē* head + *gramma* drawing]

enchant vb **1** to delight and fascinate **2** to cast a spell on [Latin *incantare* to chant a spell] **> enchanted** adj **> enchanter** n **> enchantress** fem n

enchilada (en-chill-lah-da) n a Mexican dish consisting of a tortilla filled with meat, served with chilli sauce

encircle vb **-cling, -cled** to form a circle round **> encirclement** n

Encke n Johann Franz. 1791–1865, German astronomer, who discovered **Encke's Division** in the outer ring of Saturn

enclave n a part of a country entirely surrounded by foreign territory: *a Spanish enclave* [Latin *in-* in + *clavis* key]

enclose vb **-closing, -closed 1** to surround completely: *the house enclosed a courtyard* **2** to include along with something else: *he enclosed a letter with the parcel*

enclosed adj kept separate from the normal everyday activities of the outside world: *an enclosed community of nuns*

enclosure n **1** an area of land enclosed by a fence, wall, or hedge **2** something, such as a cheque, enclosed with a letter

encode vb **-coding, -coded** to convert (a message) into code

encomium n a formal expression of praise [Latin]

encompass vb **1** to enclose within a circle; surround **2** to include all of: *the programme encompasses the visual arts, music, literature, and drama*

encore interj **1** again: used by an audience to demand a short extra performance ▷ n **2** an extra song or piece performed at a concert in response to enthusiastic demand from the audience [French]

encounter *vb* **1** to meet (someone) unexpectedly **2** to be faced with: *he had rarely encountered such suffering* **3** to meet (an opponent or enemy) in a competition or battle ▷ *n* **4** a casual or unexpected meeting **5** a game or battle: *a fierce encounter between the army and armed rebels* [Latin *in-* in + *contra* against, opposite]

encourage *vb* **-raging, -raged 1** to give (someone) the confidence to do something **2** to stimulate (something or someone) by approval or help [French *encourager*] **›encouragement** *n* **›encouraging** *adj*

encroach *vb* to intrude gradually on someone's rights or on a piece of land [Old French *encrochier* to seize] **›encroachment** *n*

encrust *vb* to cover (a surface) with a layer of something, such as jewels or ice **›encrustation** *n*

encrypt *vb* **1** to put (a message or data) into a coded form **2** to distort (a television or other signal) so that it cannot be received without the use of specific equipment ▶ See also **decrypt** [Greek *en-* in + *kruptos* hidden] **›encryption** *n*

encumber *vb* **1** to hinder or impede: *neither was greatly encumbered with social engagements* **2** to burden with a load or with debts [Old French *en-* into + *combre* a barrier]

encumbrance *n* something that impedes or is burdensome

encyclical (en-sik-lik-kl) *n* a letter sent by the pope to all Roman Catholic bishops [Greek *kuklos* circle]

encyclopedia *or* **encyclopaedia** *n* a book or set of books, often in alphabetical order, containing facts about many different subjects or about one particular subject [Greek *enkuklios* general + *paideia* education]

encyclopedic *or* **encyclopaedic** *adj* (of knowledge or information) very full and thorough; comprehensive

end *n* **1** one of the two extreme points of something such as a road **2** the surface at one of the two extreme points of an object: *a pencil with a rubber at one end* **3** the extreme extent or limit of something: *the end of the runway* **4** the most distant place or time that can be imagined: *the ends of the earth* **5** the act or an instance of stopping doing something or stopping something from continuing: *I want to put an end to all the gossip* **6** the last part of something: *at the end of the story* **7** a remnant or fragment: *cigarette ends* **8** death or destruction **9** the purpose of an action: *he will only use you to achieve his own ends* **10** *sport* either of the two defended areas of a playing field **11** **in the end** finally **12** **make ends meet** to have just enough money to meet one's needs **13** **no end** used for emphasis: *these moments give me no end of trouble* **14** **on end** *informal* without pause or interruption: *for months on end* **15** **the end** *slang* the worst, esp. beyond the limits of endurance ▷ *vb* **16** to bring or come to a finish **17** **end it all** *informal* to commit suicide ▶ See also **end up** [Old English *ende*]

endanger *vb* to put in danger

endangered *adj* (of a species of animal) in danger of becoming extinct

endear *vb* to cause to be liked: *his wit endeared him to a great many people* **›endearing** *adj*

endearment *n* an affectionate word or phrase

endeavour *or US* **endeavor** *formal vb* **1** to try (to do something) ▷ *n* **2** an effort to do something [Middle English *endeveren*]

endemic *adj* present within a localized area or only found in a particular group of people: *he found 100 species of plant endemic to that ridge* [Greek *en-* in + *dēmos* the people]

Enderby Land *n* part of the coastal region of Antarctica, between Kemp Land and Queen Maud Land: the westernmost part of the Australian Antarctic Territory (claims are suspended under the Antarctic Treaty); discovered in 1831

Enders *n* John Franklin. 1897–1985, US microbiologist: shared the Nobel prize for physiology or medicine (1954) with Frederick Robbins and Thomas Weller for their work on viruses

ending *n* **1** the last part or conclusion of something: *the film has a happy ending* **2** the tip or end of something: *nerve endings*

endive *n* a plant with crisp curly leaves, used in salads [Old French]

endless *adj* **1** having no end; eternal or infinite **2** continuing too long or continually recurring: *an endless stream of visitors* **›endlessly** *adv*

endmost *adj* nearest the end

endocrine *adj* of or denoting a gland that secretes hormones directly into the blood stream, or a hormone secreted by such a gland [Greek *endon* within + *krinein* to separate]

endogenous (en-dodge-in-uss) *adj* biology developing or originating from within

endometrium (end-oh-meet-tree-um) *n* the mucous membrane lining the womb [Greek *endon* within + *mētra* womb] **›endometrial** *adj*

endomorph *n physiol* a person with a fat and heavy body build. See also **ectomorph, mesomorph** [Greek *endon* within + *morphē* shape] **›endomorphic** *adj*

endorphin *n* any of a group of chemicals found in the brain, which have an effect similar to morphine

endorsation *n Canad* approval or support

endorse *vb* **-dorsing, -dorsed 1** to give approval or support to **2** to sign the back of (a cheque) to specify the payee **3** *chiefly Brit* to record a conviction on (a driving licence) [Old French *endosser* to put on the back] **›endorsement** *n*

endoscope *n med* a long slender medical instrument used for examining the interior of hollow organs **›endoscopy** *n*

endoskeleton *n zoology* an internal skeleton, such as the bony skeleton of vertebrates

endothermic *adj* (of a chemical reaction) involving or requiring the absorption of heat

endow *vb* **1** to provide with a source of permanent income, esp. by leaving money in a will **2 endowed with** provided with or possessing (a quality or talent) [Old French *endouer*]

endowment *n* **1** the money given to an institution, such as a hospital **2** a natural talent or quality

endowment assurance *or* **endowment insurance** *n* a kind of life insurance that pays a specified sum directly to the policyholder at a designated date or to his or her beneficiary should he or she die before this date

endpaper *n* either of two leaves at the front and back of a book pasted to the inside of the cover

end product *n* the final result of a process

end up *vb* **1** to arrive at a place by a roundabout route or without intending to: *the van somehow ended up in Bordeaux* **2** to arrive at a particular condition or situation without expecting to: *I thought I was going to hate it, but I ended up enjoying myself*

endurance *n* the ability to withstand prolonged hardship

endure *vb* **-during, -dured 1** to bear (hardship) patiently **2** to tolerate or put up with: *I cannot endure your disloyalty any longer* **3** to last for a long time [Latin *indurare* to harden] **›endurable** *adj*

enduring *adj* long-lasting

endways *or especially US and Canad* **endwise** *adv* having the end forwards or upwards

enema (en-im-a) *n med* a quantity of fluid inserted into the rectum to empty the bowels, for example before an operation [Greek: injection]

enemy *n, pl* **-mies 1** a person who is hostile or opposed to a person, group, or idea **2** a hostile nation or people **3** something that harms or opposes something: *oil is an enemy of the environment.* Related adjective: **inimical** ▷ *adj* **4** of or belonging to an enemy: *enemy troops* [Latin *inimicus* hostile]

energetic *adj* **1** having or showing energy and enthusiasm: *an energetic campaigner for democracy*

2 involving a lot of movement and physical effort: *energetic exercise* **> energetically** *adv*

energize *or* **-gise** *vb* **-gizing, -gized** *or* **-gising, -gised** to stimulate or enliven

energy *n, pl* **-gies 1** capacity for intense activity; vigour **2** intensity or vitality of action or expression; forcefulness **3** *physics* the capacity to do work and overcome resistance **4** a source of power, such as electricity [Greek *energeia* activity]

energy drink *n* a soft drink designed to boost the drinker's energy levels

enervate *vb* **-vating, -vated** to deprive of strength or vitality [Latin *enervare* to remove the nerves from] **> enervating** *adj* **> enervation** *n*

Enesco *n* Georges, original name *George Enescu*. 1881–1955, Romanian violinist and composer

Enewetak *n* the official name for Eniwetok

enfant terrible (on-fon ter-reeb-la) *n, pl* **enfants terribles** a talented but unconventional or indiscreet person [French, literally: terrible child]

enfeeble *vb* **-bling, -bled** to make (someone or something) weak

Enfield *n* a borough of Greater London: a N residential suburb. Pop: 280 300 (2003 est). Area: 55 sq km (31 sq miles)

enfilade *military n* **1** a burst of gunfire sweeping from end to end along a line of troops ▷ *vb* **-lading, -laded 2** to attack with an enfilade [French *enfiler* to thread on string]

enfold *vb* **1** to cover (something) by, or as if by, wrapping something round it: *darkness enfolded the city* **2** to embrace or hug

enforce *vb* **-forcing, -forced 1** to ensure that (a law or decision) is obeyed **2** to impose (obedience) by, or as if by, force **> enforceable** *adj* **> enforcement** *n*

enfranchise *vb* **-chising, -chised** to grant (a person or group of people) the right to vote **> enfranchisement** *n*

Eng. 1 England **2** English

Engadine *n* the upper part of the valley of the River Inn in Switzerland, in Graubünden canton: tourist and winter sports centre

engage *vb* **-gaging, -gaged 1** Also: **be engaged** (usually foll. by *in*) to take part or participate: *he engaged in criminal and illegal acts; they were engaged in espionage* **2** to involve (a person or his or her attention) intensely: *there's nothing to engage the intellect in this film* **3** to employ (someone) to do something **4** to promise to do something **5** *military* to begin a battle with **6** to bring (part of a machine or other mechanism) into operation, esp. by causing components to interlock **7 engage in conversation** to start a conversation with [Old French *en-* in + *gage* a pledge]

engaged *adj* **1** having made a promise to get married **2** *Brit* (of a telephone line or a toilet) already being used

engagement *n* **1** a business or social appointment **2** the period when a couple has agreed to get married but the wedding has not yet taken place **3** a limited period of employment, esp. in the performing arts **4** a battle

engagement ring *n* a ring worn by a woman engaged to be married

engaging *adj* pleasant and charming **> engagingly** *adv*

Engels *n* Friedrich. 1820–95, German socialist leader and political philosopher, in England from 1849. He collaborated with Marx on *The Communist Manifesto* (1848) and his own works include *Condition of the Working Classes in England* (1844) and *The Origin of the Family, Private Property and the State* (1884)

engender *vb* to produce (a particular feeling, atmosphere, or situation) [Latin *ingenerare*]

engine *n* **1** any machine designed to convert energy into mechanical work, esp. one used to power a vehicle **2** a railway locomotive [Latin *ingenium* nature, talent]

engineer *n* **1** a person trained in any branch of engineering **2** a person who repairs and maintains mechanical or electrical devices **3** a soldier trained in

engineering and construction work **4** an officer responsible for a ship's engines **5** *US and Canad* a train driver ▷ *vb* **6** to cause or plan (an event or situation) in a clever or devious manner **7** to design or construct as a professional engineer

engineering *n* the profession of applying scientific principles to the design and construction of engines, cars, buildings, bridges, roads, and electrical machines

England *n* the largest division of Great Britain, bordering on Scotland and Wales: unified in the mid-tenth century and conquered by the Normans in 1066; united with Wales in 1536 and Scotland in 1707; monarchy overthrown in 1649 but restored in 1660. Capital: London. Pop: 53 012 456 (2011 est). Area: 130 439 sq km (50 352 sq miles). See **United Kingdom, Great Britain**

English *adj* **1** of or relating to England or the English language ▷ *n* **2** the principal language of Britain, Ireland, Australia, New Zealand, the US, Canada, and several other countries ▷ *pl n* **3 the English** the people of England

English breakfast *n* a breakfast including cooked food, such as bacon and eggs

English Channel *n* an arm of the Atlantic Ocean between S England and N France, linked with the North Sea by the Strait of Dover. Length: about 560 km (350 miles). Width: between 32 km (20 miles) and 161 km (100 miles). French name: **La Manche**

Englishman *or fem* **Englishwoman** *n, pl* **-men** *or* **-women** a native or inhabitant of England

engorge *vb* **-gorging, -gorged** *pathol* to clog or become clogged with blood **> engorgement** *n*

engrave *vb* **-graving, -graved 1** to carve or etch a design or inscription into (a surface) **2** to print (designs or characters) from a plate into which they have been cut or etched **3** to fix deeply or permanently in the mind [*en-* in + obsolete *grave* to carve] **> engraver** *n*

engraving *n* **1** a printing surface that has been engraved **2** a print made from this

engross (en-*groce*) *vb* to occupy the attention of (someone) completely [*en-* in + Latin *grossus* thick] **> engrossing** *adj*

engulf *vb* **1** to immerse, plunge, or swallow up: *engulfed by flames* **2** to overwhelm: *a terrible fear engulfed her*

enhance *vb* **-hancing, -hanced** to improve or increase in quality, value, or power: *grilling on the barbecue enhances the flavour* [Old French *enhaucier*] **> enhancement** *n* **> enhancer** *n*

enigma *n* something or someone that is mysterious or puzzling [Greek *ainissesthai* to speak in riddles] **> enigmatic** *adj* **> enigmatically** *adv*

Eniwetok *n* an atoll in the W Pacific Ocean, in the NW Marshall Islands: taken by the US from Japan in 1944; became a naval base and later a testing ground for atomic weapons. Pop: 820 (1999 est). Official name: **Enewetak**

enjoin *vb* **1** to order (someone) to do something **2** to impose (a particular kind of behaviour) on someone: *the sect enjoins poverty on its members* **3** *law* to prohibit (someone) from doing something by an injunction [Old French *enjoindre*]

enjoy *vb* **1** to receive pleasure from **2** to have or experience (something, esp. something good): *many fat people enjoy excellent health* **3 enjoy oneself** to have a good time [Old French *enjoir*] **> enjoyable** *adj* **> enjoyably** *adv* **> enjoyment** *n*

enlarge *vb* **-larging, -larged 1** to make or grow larger **2 enlarge on** to speak or write about in greater detail **> enlargement** *n* **> enlarger** *n*

enlighten *vb* to give information or understanding to **> enlightening** *adj*

enlightened *adj* **1** rational and having beneficial effects: *an enlightened approach to social welfare* **2** (of a person) tolerant and unprejudiced

enlightenment n the act of enlightening or the state of being enlightened

enlist vb 1 to enter the armed forces 2 to obtain (someone's help or support) **> enlistment** n

enlisted adj (of a man or woman in the US Army or Navy) being below the rank of an officer

enliven vb to make lively, cheerful, or bright **> enlivening** adj

en masse adv all together; as a group [French]

enmeshed adj deeply involved: enmeshed in turmoil

enmity n a feeling of hostility or ill will [Latin inimicus hostile]

EnnerdaleWater n a lake in NW England, in Cumbria in the Lake District. Length: 4 km (2.5 miles)

Ennis n a town in the W Republic of Ireland, county town of Co Clare. Pop: 22 051 (2002)

Ennis-Hill n Jessica (née Ennis). born 1986, English athlete: won gold for Britain in the heptathlon at the World Championships (2009) and the Olympics (2012)

Enniskillen or formerly **Inniskilling** n a town in SW Northern Ireland, in Fermanagh, on an island in the River Erne: scene of the defeat of James II's forces in 1689. Pop: 13 599 (2001)

Ennius n Quintus. 239–169 BC, Roman epic poet and dramatist

ennoble vb -bling, -bled 1 to make (someone) a member of the nobility 2 to make (someone or his or her life) noble or dignified: poverty does not ennoble people

ennui (on-nwee) n literary boredom and dissatisfaction resulting from lack of activity or excitement [French]

Eno n Brian (Peter George St Baptiste de la Salle). born 1948, English musician, noted esp. as a member (1971–73) of Roxy Music, a collaborator with David Bowie (1977–79), a pioneer of ambient music, and record producer of acts such as U2 and Coldplay

enormity n 1 extreme wickedness 2 (pl -ties) an act of great wickedness 3 the vastness or extent of a problem or difficulty

> **USAGE** In modern English, it is common to talk about the enormity of something such as a task or a problem, but one should not talk about the enormity of an object or area: distribution is a problem because of India's enormous size (not India's enormity).

enormous adj unusually large in size, extent, or degree [Latin e- out of, away from + norma rule, pattern] **> enormously** adv

enough adj 1 as much as or as many as necessary 2 that's enough! used to stop someone behaving in a particular way ▷ pron 3 an adequate amount or number: I don't know enough about the subject to be able to speak about it ▷ adv 4 as much as necessary 5 fairly or quite: that's a common enough experience 6 very: used to give emphasis to the preceding word: funnily enough, I wasn't alarmed 7 just adequately: he sang well enough [Old English genōh]

en passant (on pass-on) adv in passing: references made en passant [French]

enquire vb -quiring, -quired same as inquire **> enquiry** n

enrage vb -raging, -raged to make extremely angry

enraptured adj filled with delight and fascination

enrich vb 1 to improve or increase the quality or value of: his poetry has vastly enriched the English language 2 to improve in nutritional value, colour, or flavour: a sauce enriched with beer 3 to make wealthy or wealthier **> enriched** adj **> enrichment** n

Enright n D(ennis) J(oseph). 1920–2002, British poet, essayist, and editor

enrol or US **enroll** vb -rolling, -rolled to become or cause to become a member **> enrolment** or US **enrollment** n

en route adv on or along the way [French]

Enschede n a city in the E Netherlands, in Overijssel province: a major centre of the Dutch cotton industry. Pop: 152 000 (2003 est)

ensconce vb -sconcing, -sconced to settle firmly or comfortably [Middle English en- in + sconce fortification]

ensemble (on-som-bl) n 1 all the parts of something considered as a whole 2 the complete outfit of clothes a person is wearing 3 a group of musicians or actors performing together 4 music a passage in which all or most of the performers are playing or singing at once [French: together]

enshrine vb -shrining, -shrined to contain and protect (an idea or right) in a society, legal system, etc.: the university's independence is enshrined in its charter

enshroud vb to cover or hide (an object) completely, as if by draping something over it: fog enshrouded the forest

ensign n 1 a flag flown by a ship to indicate its nationality 2 any flag or banner 3 (in the US Navy) a commissioned officer of the lowest rank 4 (formerly, in the British infantry) a commissioned officer of the lowest rank [Latin insignia badges]

enslave vb -slaving, -slaved to make a slave of (someone) **> enslavement** n

ensnare vb -snaring, -snared 1 to trap or gain power over (someone) by dishonest or underhand means 2 to catch (an animal) in a snare

Ensor n James (Sydney). 1860–1949, Belgian expressionist painter, noted for his macabre subjects

ensue vb -suing, -sued 1 to happen next 2 to occur as a consequence: if glaucoma is not treated, blindness can ensue [Latin in- in + sequi to follow] **> ensuing** adj

en suite adj, adv (of a bathroom) connected to a bedroom and entered directly from it: an en-suite bathroom; a room with a bathroom en suite [French, literally: in sequence]

ensure or especially US **insure** vb -suring, -sured 1 to make certain: we must ensure that similar accidents do not happen again 2 to make safe or protect: female athletes should take extra iron to ensure against anaemia

ENT med ear, nose, and throat

entablature n archit the part of a classical building supported by the columns, consisting of an architrave, a frieze, and a cornice [Italian intavolatura something put on a table, hence, something laid flat]

entail vb 1 to bring about or impose inevitably: few women enter marriage knowing what it really entails 2 Brit, Austral and NZ property law to restrict the ability to inherit (a piece of property) to designated heirs [Middle English en- in + taille limitation]

entangle vb -gling, -gled 1 to catch very firmly in something, such as a net or wire: a fishing line had entangled his legs 2 to involve in a complicated series of problems or difficulties: he entangles himself in contradictions 3 to involve in a troublesome relationship: she kept getting entangled with unsuitable boyfriends **> entanglement** n

Entebbe n a town in S Uganda, on Lake Victoria: British administrative centre of Uganda (1893–1958); international airport. Pop: 57 518 (2002 est)

entente (on-tont) n short for **entente cordiale** [French: understanding]

entente cordiale (cord-ee-ahl) n a friendly understanding between two or more countries [French: cordial understanding]

enter vb 1 to come or go into (a particular place): he entered the room 2 to join (a party or organization) 3 to become involved in or take part in: 1500 schools entered the competition 4 to become suddenly present or noticeable in: a note of anxiety entered his voice 5 to record (an item) in a journal or list 6 theatre to come on stage: used as a stage direction: enter Joseph 7 to begin (a new process or period of time): the occupation of the square has entered its eleventh day [Latin intrare]

enteric (en-ter-ik) adj of the intestines [Greek enteron intestine]

enter into vb 1 to be an important factor in (a situation or plan): money doesn't enter into it: it's a matter of principle 2 to start to do or be involved in (a process or series of events): the government will not enter into negotiations with terrorists

enteritis (en-ter-rite-iss) *n* inflammation of the small intestine

enterprise *n* **1** a business firm **2** a project or undertaking, esp. one that requires boldness or effort **3** boldness and energy [Old French *entreprendre* to undertake]

enterprising *adj* full of boldness and initiative > **enterprisingly** *adv*

entertain *vb* **1** to provide amusement for (a person or audience) **2** to show hospitality to (guests) **3** to consider (an idea or suggestion) [Old French *entre-* mutually + *tenir* to hold]

entertainer *n* a person who entertains, esp. professionally

entertaining *adj* **1** interesting, amusing, and enjoyable ▷ *n* **2** the provision of hospitality to guests: *the smart kitchen is perfect for entertaining*

entertainment *n* **1** enjoyment and interest: *a match of top-quality entertainment and goals* **2** an act or show that entertains, or such acts and shows collectively

enthral *or US* **enthrall** (en-thrawl) *vb* **-thralling, -thralled** to hold the attention or interest of > **enthralling** *adj* > **enthralment** *or US* **enthrallment** *n*

enthrone *vb* **-throning, -throned** **1** to place (a person) on a throne in a ceremony to mark the beginning of his or her new role as a monarch or bishop **2** to give an important or prominent position to (something): *the religious fundamentalism now enthroned in American life* > **enthronement** *n*

enthuse *vb* **-thusing, -thused** to feel or cause to feel enthusiasm

enthusiasm *n* ardent and lively interest or eagerness: *your enthusiasm for literature* [Greek *enthousiazein* to be possessed by a god]

enthusiast *n* a person who is very interested in and keen on something > **enthusiastic** *adj* > **enthusiastically** *adv*

entice *vb* **-ticing, -ticed** to attract (someone) away from one place or activity to another [Old French *enticier*] > **enticement** *n* > **enticing** *adj*

entire *adj* made up of or involving all of something, including every detail, part, or aspect [Latin *integer* whole] > **entirely** *adv*

entirety *n, pl* **-ties** **1** all of a person or thing: *you must follow this diet for the entirety of your life* **2** in its entirety as a whole

entitle *vb* **-tling, -tled** **1** to give (someone) the right to do or have something **2** to give a name or title to (a book or film) > **entitlement** *n*

entity *n, pl* **-ties** something that exists in its own right and not merely as part of a bigger thing [Latin *esse* to be]

entomb *vb* **1** to place (a corpse) in a tomb **2** to bury or trap: *a circulatory system entombed in fat* > **entombment** *n*

entomology *n* the study of insects [Greek *entomon* insect] > **entomological** *adj* > **entomologist** *n*

entourage (on-toor-ahzh) *n* a group of people who assist or travel with an important or well-known person [French *entourer* to surround]

entozoon (en-toe-zoe-on) *n, pl* **-zoa** (-zoe-a) a parasite, such as a tapeworm, that lives inside another animal

entrails *pl n* **1** the internal organs of a person or animal; intestines **2** the innermost parts of anything [Latin *interanea* intestines]

entrance¹ *n* **1** something, such as a door or gate, through which it is possible to enter a place **2** the act of coming into a place, esp. with reference to the way in which it is done: *she made a sudden startling entrance* **3** theatre the act of appearing on stage **4** the right to enter a place: *he refused her entrance because she was carrying her Scottie dog* **5** ability or permission to join or become involved with a group or organization: *entrance to the profession should be open to men and women alike* ▷ *adj* **6** necessary in order to enter something: *they have paid entrance fees for English-language courses*

entrance² *vb* **-trancing, -tranced** to fill with delight

> **entrancement** *n* > **entrancing** *adj*

entrant *n* a person who enters a university, competition, etc.

entrap *vb* **-trapping, -trapped** **1** to trick (someone) into danger or difficulty **2** to catch in a trap > **entrapment** *n*

entreat *vb* to ask (someone) earnestly to do something [Old French *entraiter*]

entreaty *n, pl* **-treaties** an earnest request or plea

entrecote (on-tra-coat) *n* a steak of beef cut from between the ribs [French]

entrée (on-tray) *n* **1** the right to enter a place **2** a dish served before a main course **3** chiefly US the main course [French]

entrench *vb* **1** to fix or establish firmly: *the habit had become entrenched* **2** military to fortify (a position) by digging trenches around it > **entrenchment** *n*

entrepreneur *n* the owner of a business who attempts to make money by risk and initiative [French] > **entrepreneurial** *adj*

entropy (en-trop-ee) *n* **1** formal lack of pattern or organization **2** physics a thermodynamic quantity that represents the amount of energy present in a system that cannot be converted into work because it is tied up in the atomic structure of the system [Greek *entropē* a turning towards]

entrust *vb* **1** to give (someone) a duty or responsibility: *Miss Conway, who was entrusted with the child's education* **2** to put (something) into the care of someone: *he stole all the money we had entrusted to him*

USAGE It is usually considered incorrect to talk about *entrusting* someone *to do* something: *the army cannot be trusted* (not *entrusted*) *to carry out orders.*

---

entry *n, pl* **-tries** **1** something, such as a door or gate, through which it is possible to enter a place **2** the act of coming in to a place, esp. with reference to the way in which it is done **3** the right to enter a place: *he was refused entry to Britain* **4** the act of joining an organization or group: *Britain's entry into the EU* **5** a brief note, article, or group of figures in a diary, book, or computer file **6** a quiz form, painting, etc., submitted in an attempt to win a competition **7** a person, horse, car, etc., entering a competition ▷ *adj* **8** necessary in order to enter something: *entry fee*

entwine *vb* **-twining, -twined** to twist together or round something else

Enugu *n* **1** a state of S Nigeria. Capital: Enugu. Pop: 3 257 298 (2006). Area: 7161 sq km (2765 sq miles) **2** a city in S Nigeria, capital of Enugu state: capital of the former Eastern region and of the breakaway state of Biafra during the Civil War (1967–70): coal-mining. Pop: 549 000 (2005 est)

E number *n* any of a series of numbers with the prefix E- indicating a specific food additive recognized by the EU

enumerate *vb* **-ating, -ated** **1** to name or list one by one **2** to count **3** Canad to compile the voting list for an area [Latin *e-* out + *numerare* to count] > **enumeration** *n* > **enumerator** *n*

enunciate *vb* **-ating, -ated** **1** to pronounce (words) clearly **2** to state precisely or formally [Latin *enuntiare* to declare] > **enunciation** *n*

enuresis (en-yoo-reece-iss) *n* involuntary urination, esp. during sleep [Greek *en-* in + *ouron* urine]

envelop *vb* to cover, surround, or enclose [Old French *envoluper*] > **envelopment** *n*

envelope *n* **1** a flat covering of paper, that can be sealed, used to enclose a letter, etc. **2** any covering, wrapper, or enclosing structure: *an envelope of filo pastry* **3** geometry a curve that is tangential to each one of a group of curves [French *envelopper* to wrap round]

Enver Pasha *n* 1881–1922, Turkish soldier and leader of the Young Turks: minister of war (1914–18)

enviable *adj* so desirable or fortunate that it is likely to cause envy ❯ **enviably** *adv*

envious *adj* feeling, showing, or resulting from envy ❯ **enviously** *adv*

environment (en-vire-on-ment) *n* **1** the surroundings in which a person, animal, or plant lives **2** *ecology* the environment the natural world of land, sea, air, plants, and animals: *nuclear waste must be prevented from leaking into the environment* [French *environs* surroundings] ❯ **environmental** *adj*

environmentalist *n* a person concerned with the protection and preservation of the natural environment

environs *pl n* a surrounding area, esp. the outskirts of a city

envisage *or US* **envision** *vb* **-aging, -aged** *or* **-ioning, -ioned** to believe to be possible or likely in the future: *the commission envisages a mix of government and private funding* [French *en-* in + *visage* face]

> **USAGE** It was formerly considered incorrect to use a clause after *envisage* as in *it is envisaged that the new centre will cost £40 million*, but this use is now acceptable.

envoy *n* **1** a messenger or representative **2** a diplomat ranking next below an ambassador [French *envoyer* to send]

envy *n, pl* **-vies 1** a feeling of discontent aroused by someone else's possessions, achievements, or qualities **2** something that causes envy: *their standards are the envy of the world* ▷ *vb* **-vies, -vying, -vied 3** to wish that one had the possessions, achievements, or qualities of (someone else) [Latin *invidia*] ❯ **envyingly** *adv*

Enzed *n Austral and NZ informal* **1** New Zealand **2** Also called: **Enzedder** a New Zealander

enzyme *n* any of a group of complex proteins that act as catalysts in specific biochemical reactions [Greek *en-* in + *zumē* leaven] ❯ **enzymatic** *adj*

Eocene (ee-oh-seen) *adj* of the epoch of geological time about 55 million years ago [Greek *ēos* dawn + *kainos* new]

Eolithic *adj* of the early period of the Stone Age, when crude stone tools were used

Eötvös *n* Baron **Roland von.** 1848–1919, Hungarian physicist noted for his studies of gravity and surface tension

EP *n* an extended-play gramophone record, which is 7 inches in diameter and has a longer recording on each side than a single does

Epaminondas *n* ?418–362 BC, Greek Theban statesman and general: defeated the Spartans at Leuctra (371) and Mantinea (362) and restored power in Greece to Thebes

epaulette *n* a piece of ornamental material on the shoulder of a garment, esp. a military uniform [French]

épée (ep-pay) *n* a straight-bladed sword used in fencing

ephedrine (eff-fid-dreen) *n* an alkaloid used for the treatment of asthma and hay fever [*Ephedra,* genus of plants which produce it]

ephemera (if-fem-a-ra) *pl n* items designed to last only for a short time, such as programmes or posters

ephemeral *adj* lasting only for a short time [Greek *hēmera* day]

Ephesus *n* (in ancient Greece) a major trading city on the W coast of Asia Minor: famous for its temple of Artemis (Diana); sacked by the Goths (262 AD)

epic *n* **1** a long exciting book, poem, or film, usually telling of heroic deeds **2** a long narrative poem telling of the deeds of a legendary hero ▷ *adj* **3** very large or grand: *a professional feud of epic proportions* [Greek *epos* word, song]

epicene *adj* (esp. of a man) having characteristics or features that are not definitely male or female [Greek *epikoinos* common to many]

epicentre *or US* **epicenter** *n* the point on the earth's surface immediately above the origin of an earthquake [Greek *epi* above + *kentron* point]

Epictetus *n* ?50–?120 AD, Greek Stoic philosopher, who

stressed self-renunciation and the brotherhood of man

epicure *n* a person who enjoys good food and drink [after EPICURUS] ❯ **epicurism** *n*

epicurean *adj* **1** devoted to sensual pleasures, esp. food and drink ▷ *n* **2** same as **epicure** ❯ **epicureanism** *n*

Epicurus *n* 341–270 BC, Greek philosopher, who held that the highest good is pleasure and that the world is a series of fortuitous combinations of atoms

Epidaurus *n* an ancient port in Greece, in the NE Peloponnese, in Argolis on the Saronic Gulf

epidemic *n* **1** a widespread occurrence of a disease **2** a rapid development or spread of something: *an epidemic of rape* ▷ *adj* **3** (esp. of a disease) affecting many people in an area: *stress has now reached epidemic proportions* [Greek *epi* among + *dēmos* people]

epidemiology (ep-pid-deem-ee-ol-a-jee) *n* the branch of medical science concerned with the occurrence and control of diseases in populations ❯ **epidemiologist** *n*

epidermis *n* the thin protective outer layer of the skin [Greek *epi* upon + *derma* skin] ❯ **epidermal** *adj*

epidural (ep-pid-dure-al) *adj* **1** on or over the outermost membrane covering the brain and spinal cord (**dura mater**) ▷ *n* **2 a** an injection of anaesthetic into the space outside the outermost membrane enveloping the spinal cord **b** anaesthesia produced by this method [from *dura mater*]

epiglottis *n* a thin flap of cartilage at the back of the mouth that covers the entrance to the larynx during swallowing [Greek *epi* upon + *glōtta* tongue]

epigram *n* **1** a witty remark **2** a short poem with a witty ending [Greek *epi* upon + *graphein* to write] ❯ **epigrammatic** *adj*

epigraph *n* **1** a quotation at the beginning of a book **2** an inscription on a monument or building [Greek *epi* upon + *graphein* to write]

epilepsy *n* a disorder of the central nervous system which causes periodic loss of consciousness and sometimes convulsions [Greek *epi* upon + *lambanein* to take]

epileptic *adj* **1** of or having epilepsy ▷ *n* **2** a person who has epilepsy

> **USAGE** The use of *epileptic* as a noun can be offensive and should be avoided. Instead you should talk about *a person with epilepsy.*

epilogue *n* a short concluding passage or speech at the end of a book or play [Greek *epi* upon + *logos* word, speech]

epiphany (ip-piff-a-nee) *n, pl* **-nies** a moment of great or sudden revelation [Greek *epiphaneia* an appearing]

Epiphany *n, pl* **-nies** a Christian festival held on January 6 commemorating, in the Western church, the manifestation of Christ to the Magi and, in the Eastern church, the baptism of Christ

Epirus *n* **1** a region of NW Greece, part of ancient Epirus ceded to Greece after independence in 1830 **2** (in ancient Greece) a region between the Pindus mountains and the Ionian Sea, straddling the modern border with Albania

episcopacy (ip-piss-kop-a-see) *n* **1** government of a Church by bishops **2** (*pl* **-cies**) same as **episcopate**

episcopal (ip-piss-kop-al) *adj* of or relating to bishops [Greek *episkopos* overseer]

Episcopal Church *n* (in Scotland and the US) a self-governing branch of the Anglican Church

episcopalian *adj* also: **episcopal 1** practising or advocating Church government by bishops ▷ *n* **2** an advocate of such Church government

Episcopalian (ip-piss-kop-pale-ee-an) *adj* **1** of or relating to the Episcopal Church ▷ *n* **2** a member of this Church ❯ **Episcopalianism** *n*

episcopate (ip-piss-kop-it) *n* **1** the office, status, or term of office of a bishop **2** bishops collectively

episiotomy (ip-peez-ee-ot-tom-ee) *n, pl* **-tomies** an operation involving cutting into the area between the genitals and the anus sometimes performed during childbirth to make the birth easier

episode *n* **1** an event or series of events **2** any of the sections into which a novel or a television or radio serial is divided [Greek *epi* in addition + *eisodios* coming in]

episodic *adj* **1** resembling or relating to an episode **2** occurring at irregular and infrequent intervals

epistemology (ip-iss-stem-**ol**-a-jee) *n* the theory of knowledge, esp. the critical study of its validity, methods, and scope [Greek *epistēmē* knowledge] **>** **epistemological** *adj* **>** **epistemologist** *n*

epistle *n* **1** *formal or humorous* a letter **2** a literary work in letter form, esp. a poem [Greek *epistolē*]

Epistle *n New Testament* any of the letters written by the apostles

epistolary *adj* **1** of or relating to letters **2** (of a novel) presented in the form of a series of letters

epitaph *n* **1** a commemorative inscription on a tombstone **2** a commemorative speech or written passage [Greek *epi* upon + *taphos* tomb]

epithelium *n, pl* **-lia** *anatomy* a cellular tissue covering the external and internal surfaces of the body [Greek *epi* upon + *thēlē* nipple] **>** **epithelial** *adj*

epithet *n* a word or short phrase used to describe someone or something: *these tracks truly deserve that overworked epithet 'classic'* [Greek *epitithenai* to add]

epitome (ip-pit-a-mee) *n* **1** a person or thing that is a typical example of a characteristic or class: *the epitome of rural tranquillity* **2** a summary, esp. of a written work [Greek *epitemnein* to abridge]

epitomize *or* **-mise** *vb* **-mizing, -mized** *or* **-mising, -mised** to be or make a perfect or typical example of

EPNS electroplated nickel silver

epoch (ee-pok) *n* **1** a long period of time marked by some predominant characteristic: *the cold-war epoch* **2** the beginning of a new or distinctive period: *the invention of nuclear weapons marked an epoch in the history of warfare* **3** *geology* a unit of time within a period during which a series of rocks is formed [Greek *epokhē* cessation] **>** **epochal** *adj*

epoch-making *adj* very important or significant

eponymous (ip-pon-im-uss) *adj* **1** (of a person) being the person after whom a literary work, film, etc., is named: *the eponymous heroine in the film of Jane Eyre* **2** (of a literary work, film, etc.) named after its central character or creator: *The Stooges' eponymous debut album* [Greek *epōnumos* giving a significant name]

epoxy *chem adj* **1** of or containing an oxygen atom joined to two different groups that are themselves joined to other groups **2** of or consisting of an epoxy resin **>** *n, pl* **epoxies 3** an epoxy resin [Greek *epi* upon + OXY(GEN)]

epoxy resin *n* a tough resistant thermosetting synthetic resin, used in laminates and adhesives

Epping *n* a town in E England, in Essex, on the edge of Epping Forest: a residential centre for London. Pop: 9889 (2001)

Epping Forest *n* a forest in E England, northeast of London: formerly a royal hunting ground

EPROM *n computers* erasable programmable read-only memory: a storage device that can be reprogrammed to hold different data

Epsom *n* a town in SE England, in Surrey: famous for its mineral springs and for horse racing. Pop (with Ewell): 64 492 (2001)

Epsom salts *pl n* a medicinal preparation of hydrated magnesium sulphate, used to empty the bowels [after EPSOM]

Epstein *n* Sir Jacob. 1880–1959, British sculptor, born in the US of Russo-Polish parents

equable (ek-wab-bl) *adj* **1** even-tempered and reasonable **2** (of a climate) not varying much throughout the year, and neither very hot nor very cold [Latin *aequabilis*] **>** **equably** *adv*

equal *adj* **1** identical in size, quantity, degree, or intensity **2** having identical privileges, rights, or status **3** applying in the same way to all people or in all circumstances: *equal rights* **4 equal to** having the necessary strength, ability, or means for: *she was equal to any test the corporation put to her* **>** *n* **5** a person or thing equal to another **>** *vb* **equalling, equalled** *or US* **equaling, equaled 6** to be equal to; match **7** to make or do something equal to: *he has equalled his world record in the men's 100 metres* [Latin *aequalis*] **>** **equally** *adv*

> **USAGE** The use of *more equal* as in *from now on their relationship will be a more equal one* is acceptable in modern English usage. *Equally* is preferred to *equally as* in sentences such as *reassuring the victims is equally important*. *Just as* is preferred to *equally as* in sentences such as *their surprise was just as great as his*.

equality *n, pl* **-ties** the state of being equal

equalize *or* **-ise** *vb* **-izing, -ized** *or* **-ising, -ised 1** to make equal or uniform **2** (in a sport) to reach the same score as one's opponent or opponents **>** **equalization** *or* **-isation** *n* **>** **equalizer** *or* **-iser** *n*

equal opportunity *n* the offering of employment or promotion equally to all, without discrimination as to sex, race, colour, etc.

equanimity *n* calmness of mind or temper; composure [Latin *aequus* even + *animus* mind, spirit]

equate *vb* **equating, equated 1** to make or regard as equivalent **2** *maths* to form an equation from **>** **equatable** *adj*

equation *n* **1** a mathematical statement that two expressions are equal **2** a situation or problem in which a number of different factors need to be considered: *this plan leaves human nature out of the equation* **3** the act of equating **4** *chem* a representation of a chemical reaction using symbols of the elements

equator *n* an imaginary circle around the earth at an equal distance from the North Pole and the South Pole [Medieval Latin *(circulus) aequator (diei et noctis)* (circle) that equalizes (the day and night)]

equatorial *adj* of, like, or existing at or near the equator

Equatorial Guinea *n* a republic of W Africa, consisting of Río Muni on the mainland and the island of Bioko in the Gulf of Guinea, with four smaller islands: ceded by Portugal to Spain in 1778; gained independence in 1968. Official languages: Spanish and French. Religion: Roman Catholic majority. Currency: franc. Capital: Malabo. Pop: 704 000 (2013 est). Area: 28 049 sq km (10 830 sq miles). Former name (until 1964): **Spanish Guinea**

equerry (ek-kwer-ee) *n, pl* **-ries** *Brit* an officer of the royal household who acts as a personal attendant to a member of the royal family [Old French *escuirie* group of squires]

equestrian *adj* **1** of or relating to horses and riding **2** on horseback: *an equestrian statue of the Queen* [Latin *equus* horse] **>** **equestrianism** *n*

equidistant *adj* equally distant

equilateral *adj* **1** having all sides of equal length **>** *n* **2** a geometric figure having all sides of equal length

equilibrium *n, pl* **-ria** **1** a stable condition in which forces cancel one another **2** a state of mental and emotional balance; composure [Latin *aequi-* equal + *libra* balance]

equine *adj* of or like a horse [Latin *equus* horse]

equinoctial *adj* **1** relating to or occurring at an equinox **>** *n* **2** a storm at or near an equinox

equinox *n* either of the two occasions when day and night are of equal length, around March 21 and September 23 [Latin *aequi-* equal + *nox* night]

equip *vb* **equipping, equipped 1** to provide with supplies, components, etc.: *the car comes equipped with a catalytic converter* **2** to provide with abilities, understanding, etc.: *stress is something we are all equipped to cope with* [Old French *eschiper* to fit out (a ship)]

equipment n 1 a set of tools or devices used for a particular purpose: *communications equipment* 2 an act of equipping

equipoise n the state of being perfectly balanced; equilibrium

equitable adj fair and reasonable › **equitably** adv

equitation n the study of riding and horsemanship [Latin *equitare* to ride]

equities pl n same as **ordinary shares**

equity n, pl -ties 1 the quality of being impartial; fairness 2 *law* a system of using principles of natural justice and fair conduct to reach a judgment when common law is inadequate or inappropriate 3 the difference in value between a person's debts and the value of the property on which they are secured: *negative equity* [Latin *aequus* level, equal]

Equity n Brit, Austral and NZ the actors' trade union

equivalent n 1 something that has the same use or function as something else: *Denmark's equivalent to Silicon Valley* ▷ adj 2 equal in value, quantity, significance, etc. 3 having the same or a similar effect or meaning [Latin *aequi-* equal + *valere* to be worth] › **equivalence** n

equivocal adj 1 capable of varying interpretations; ambiguous 2 deliberately misleading or vague 3 of doubtful character or sincerity: *the party's commitment to genuine reform is equivocal* [Latin *aequi-* equal + *vox* voice] › **equivocally** adv

equivocate vb -cating, -cated to use vague or ambiguous language in order to deceive someone or to avoid telling the truth › **equivocation** n › **equivocator** n

er interj a sound made when hesitating in speech

Er chem erbium

ER Queen Elizabeth [Latin *Elizabeth Regina*]

era n 1 a period of time considered as distinctive; epoch 2 an extended period of time measured from a fixed point: *the Communist era* 3 *geology* a major division of time [Latin *aera* counters, pieces of brass money]

eradicate vb -cating, -cated to destroy or get rid of completely: *measures to eradicate racism* [Latin *e-* out + *radix* root] › **eradicable** adj › **eradication** n › **eradicator** n

erase vb erasing, erased 1 to destroy all traces of: *he could not erase the memory of his earlier defeat* 2 to rub or wipe out (something written) 3 to remove sound or information from (a magnetic tape or disk) [Latin *e-* out + *radere* to scrape] › **erasable** adj

eraser n an object, such as a piece of rubber, for erasing something written

Erasmus n Desiderius, real name *Gerhard Gerhards*. ?1466–1536, Dutch humanist, the leading scholar of the Renaissance in northern Europe. He published the first Greek edition of the New Testament in 1516; his other works include the satirical *Encomium Moriae* (1509); *Colloquia* (1519), a series of dialogues, and an attack on the theology of Luther, *De Libero Arbitrio* (1524)

erasure n 1 an erasing 2 the place or mark where something has been erased

Erato n Greek myth the Muse of love poetry

Eratosthenes n ?276–?194 BC, Greek mathematician and astronomer, who calculated the circumference of the earth by observing the angle of the sun's rays at different places

Erbil, Irbil or **Arbil** n a city in N Iraq: important in Assyrian times. Pop: 870 000 (2005 est). Ancient name: **Arbela**

erbium n chem a soft silvery-white element of the lanthanide series of metals. Symbol: **Er** [after *Ytterby*, Sweden, where it was first found]

Erciyas Daği n an extinct volcano in central Turkey. Height 3916 m (12 848 ft)

ere conj, prep poetic before [Old English *ǣr*]

e-reader n a portable device that allows users to download and read texts in electronic form

Erebus n Mount Erebus a volcano in Antarctica, on Ross Island: discovered by Sir James Ross in 1841 and named after his ship. Height: 3794 m (12 448 ft)

Erechtheum or **Erechtheion** n a temple on the Acropolis at Athens, which has a porch of caryatids

erect vb 1 to build 2 to raise to an upright position 3 to found or form: *the caricature of socialism erected by Lenin* ▷ adj 4 upright in posture or position 5 *physiol* (of the penis, clitoris, or nipples) firm or rigid after swelling with blood, esp. as a result of sexual excitement [Latin *erigere* to set up] › **erection** n

erectile adj physiol (of an organ, such as the penis) capable of becoming erect

eremite (air-rim-mite) n a Christian hermit [Greek *erēmos* lonely]

Eretria n an ancient city in Greece, on the S coast of Euboea: founded as an Ionian colony; destroyed by the Persians in 490 BC following which it never regained its former significance

Erevan n a variant spelling of **Yerevan**

Erfurt n an industrial city in central Germany, the capital of Thuringia: university (1392). Pop: 201 645 (2003 est)

ergo conj therefore [Latin]

ergonomic adj 1 designed to minimize effort and discomfort 2 of or relating to ergonomics

ergonomics n the study of the relationship between workers and their environment [Greek *ergon* work + (ECO)NOMICS]

ergot n 1 a disease of a cereal, such as rye, caused by a fungus 2 the dried fungus used in medicine [French spur (of a cock)]

Erhard n Ludwig. 1897–1977, German statesman: chief architect of the *Wirtschaftswunder* ("economic miracle") of West Germany's recovery after World War II; chancellor (1963–66)

Eric XIV n 1533–77, king of Sweden (1560–68). His attempts to dominate the Baltic led to war with Denmark (1563–70); deposed and imprisoned

Ericson or **Ericsson** or **Leif**. 10th–11th centuries AD, Norse navigator, who discovered Vinland (?1000), variously identified as the coast of New England, Labrador, or Newfoundland; son of Eric the Red

Eric the Red n ?940–?1010 AD, Norse navigator: discovered and colonized Greenland; father of Leif Ericson

Erie n 1 Lake Erie a lake between the US and Canada: the southernmost and the shallowest of the Great Lakes; empties by the Niagara River into Lake Ontario. Area: 25 718 sq km (9930 sq miles) 2 a port in NW Pennsylvania, on Lake Erie. Pop: 101 373 (2003 est)

Erie Canal n a canal in New York State between Albany and Buffalo, linking the Hudson River with Lake Erie. Length: 579 km (360 miles)

Erigena n John Scotus. ?800–?877 AD, Irish Neo-Platonist philosopher

Eriksson n Sven-Goran. born 1948, Swedish football manager; honours as a club manager include the UEFA Cup (1982) with Gothenburg, three Portuguese league titles with Benfica (1983, 1984, 1990), and the Italian league with Lazio (2000); head coach of the England national team (2001–06)

Erin n an archaic or poetic name for **Ireland** [from Irish Gaelic *Éirinn*, dative of *Ériu* Ireland]

Eritrea n a small country in NE Africa, on the Red Sea: became an Italian colony in 1890; federated with Ethiopia (1952–93); an independence movement was engaged in war with the Ethiopian government from 1961 until independence was gained in 1993; consists of hot and arid coastal lowlands, rising to the foothills of the Ethiopian highlands. Languages: Tigrinya, Arabic, English, Afar, and others. Religions: Muslim and Christian Currency: nakfa. Capital: Asmara. Pop: 6 233 682 (2013 est). Area: 117 400 sq km (45 300 sq miles)

Eritrean adj 1 of or relating to Eritrea or its inhabitants

▷ *n* **2** a native or inhabitant of Eritrea

Erivan *n* a variant spelling of **Yerevan**

Erlangen *n* a town in central Germany, in Bavaria: university (1743). Pop: 102 449 (2003 est)

Erlanger *n* Joseph. 1874–1965, US physiologist. He shared a Nobel prize for physiology or medicine (1944) with Gasser for their work on the electrical signs of nervous activity

Ermanaric *n* died ?375 AD, king of the Ostrogoths: ruled an extensive empire in eastern Europe, which was overrun by the Huns in the 370s

ermine *n, pl* **-mines** *or* **-mine** **1** the stoat in northern regions, where it has a white winter coat **2** the fur of this animal, used to trim state robes of judges, nobles, etc. [Medieval Latin *Armenius (mus)* Armenian (mouse)]

Ermoupoli *n* the modern Greek name for **Hermoupolis**

erne *or* **ern** *n* a fish-eating sea eagle [Old English *earn*]

Erne *n* a river in N central Republic of Ireland, rising in County Cavan and flowing north across the border, through **Upper Lough Erne** and **Lower Lough Erne** and then west to Donegal Bay. Length: about 96 km (60 miles)

Ernie *n* (in Britain) a machine that randomly selects winning numbers of Premium Bonds [acronym of Electronic Random Number Indicator Equipment]

Ernst *n* Max. 1891–1976, German painter, resident in France and the US, a prominent exponent of Dada and surrealism: developed the technique of collage

erode *vb* **eroding, eroded** **1** to wear down or away **2** to deteriorate or cause to deteriorate [Latin *e-* away + *rodere* to gnaw]

erogenous (ir-roj-in-uss) *adj* sensitive to sexual stimulation: *an erogenous zone* [Greek *erōs* love + *-genēs* born]

erosion *n* **1** the wearing away of rocks or soil by the action of water, ice, or wind **2** a gradual lessening or reduction: *an erosion of national sovereignty* ❭ **erosive** *or* **erosional** *adj*

erotic *adj* of, concerning, or arousing sexual desire or giving sexual pleasure [Greek *erōs* love] ❭ **erotically** *adv*

erotica *pl n* explicitly sexual literature or art

eroticism *n* **1** erotic quality or nature **2** the use of sexually arousing symbolism in literature or art **3** sexual excitement or desire

err *vb* **1** to make a mistake **2** to sin [Latin *errare*]

errand *n* **1** a short trip to get or do something for someone **2** **run an errand** to make such a trip [Old English *ǣrende*]

errant *adj* **1** behaving in a way considered to be unacceptable: *an errant schoolboy* **2** old-fashioned *or* literary wandering in search of adventure: *a knight errant* [Latin *iter* journey] ❭ **errantry** *n*

erratic *adj* **1** irregular or unpredictable: *his increasingly erratic behaviour* ▷ *n* **2** geology a rock that has been transported by glacial action [Latin *errare* to wander] ❭ **erratically** *adv*

erratum *n, pl* **-ta** an error in writing or printing [Latin]

Er Rif *n* a mountainous region of N Morocco, near the Mediterranean coast

erroneous *adj* based on or containing an error or errors; incorrect ❭ **erroneously** *adv*

error *n* **1** a mistake, inaccuracy, or misjudgment **2** the act or state of being wrong or making a misjudgment: *the plane was shot down in error* **3** the amount by which the actual value of a quantity might differ from an estimate: *a 3% margin of error* [Latin]

ersatz (air-zats) *adj* made in imitation of something more expensive: *ersatz coffee* [German *ersetzen* to substitute]

Erse *n, adj* Irish Gaelic [Lowland Scots *Erisch* Irish]

Ershad *n* Hussain Mohammed. born 1930, Bangladeshi soldier and statesman. He seized power in a coup in 1982, becoming president in 1983. He was deposed in 1990 and has served prison sentences for corruption

Erskine *n* Thomas, 1st Baron. 1750–1823, Scottish lawyer: noted as a defence advocate, esp. in cases involving civil liberties

erstwhile *adj* **1** former ▷ *adv* **2** archaic formerly

Erté *n* real name *Romain de Tirtoff*. 1892–1990, French fashion illustrator and designer, born in Russia, noted for his extravagant costumes and tableaux for the Folies-Bergère in Paris

eruct *or* **eructate** *vb* formal to belch [Latin *e-* out + *ructare* to belch] ❭ **eructation** *n*

erudite (air-rude-ite) *adj* having or showing great academic knowledge [Latin *erudire* to polish] ❭ **erudition** *n*

erupt *vb* **1** (of a volcano) to throw out molten lava, ash, and steam in a sudden and violent way **2** to burst forth suddenly and violently: *riots erupted across the country* **3** (of a group of people) to suddenly become angry and aggressive: *the meeting erupted in fury* **4** (of a blemish) to appear on the skin [Latin *e-* out + *rumpere* to burst] ❭ **eruptive** *adj* ❭ **eruption** *n*

Erymanthus *n* **Mount Erymanthus** a mountain in SW Greece, in the NW Peloponnese. Height: 2224 m (7297 ft). Modern Greek name: **Erímanthos**

erysipelas (air-riss-sip-ill-ass) *n* an acute disease of the skin, with fever and raised purplish patches [Greek *erusi-* red + *-pelas* skin]

erythrocyte (ir-rith-roe-site) *n* a red blood cell that transports oxygen through the body [Greek *eruthros* red + *kutos* hollow vessel]

Erzgebirge *pl n* a mountain range on the border between Germany and the Czech Republic: formerly rich in mineral resources. Highest peak: Mount Klínovec (Keilberg), 1244 m (4081 ft). Czech name: **Krušné Hory**. Also called: **Ore Mountains**

Erzurum *n* a city in E Turkey: a strategic centre; scene of two major battles against Russian forces (1877 and 1916); important military base. Pop: 436 000 (2005 est)

Es *chem* einsteinium

Esbjerg *n* a port in SW Denmark, in Jutland on the North Sea: Denmark's chief fishing port. Pop: 72 550 (2004 est)

escalate *vb* **-lating, -lated** to increase or be increased in size, seriousness, or intensity [from *escalator*] ❭ **escalation** *n*

escalator *n* a moving staircase consisting of stair treads fixed to a conveyor belt [Latin *scala* ladder]

escalope (ess-kal-lop) *n* a thin slice of meat, usually veal [Old French: shell]

escapade *n* a mischievous act or adventure [French]

escape *vb* **-caping, -caped** **1** to get away or break free from (confinement) **2** to manage to avoid (something dangerous, unpleasant, or difficult) **3** (of gases, liquids, etc.) to leak gradually **4** to elude; be forgotten by: *those little round cakes whose name escapes me* ▷ *n* **5** the act of escaping or state of having escaped **6** a way of avoiding something difficult, dangerous, or unpleasant: *his frequent illnesses provided an escape from intolerable stress* **7** a means of relaxation or relief: *he found temporary escape through the local cinema* **8** a leakage of gas or liquid [Late Latin *e-* out + *cappa* cloak]

escapee *n* a person who has escaped, esp. from prison

escapement *n* the mechanism in a clock or watch which connects the hands to the pendulum or balance

escape road *n* a small road leading off a steep hill, into which a car can be driven if the brakes fail

escape velocity *n* the minimum velocity necessary for a particle, space vehicle, etc. to escape from the gravitational field of the earth or other celestial body

escapism *n* an inclination to retreat from unpleasant reality, for example through fantasy ❭ **escapist** *n, adj*

escapologist *n* an entertainer who specializes in freeing himself or herself from chains, ropes, etc. ❭ **escapology** *n*

escarpment *n* the long continuous steep face of a ridge or mountain [French *escarpement*]

Escaut *n* the French name for the **Scheldt**

eschatology (ess-cat-**tol**-a-jee) *n* the branch of theology concerned with the end of the world [Greek *eskhatos* last] **> eschatological** *adj*

escheat (iss-**cheat**) *law n* **1** formerly, the return of property to the state in the absence of legal heirs **2** the property so reverting ▷ *vb* **3** to obtain (land) by escheat [Old French *escheoir* to fall to the lot of]

eschew (iss-**chew**) *vb* to avoid doing or being involved in (something disliked or harmful) [Old French *eschiver*] **> eschewal** *n*

Escoffier *n* (Georges) Auguste. 1846–1935, French chef at the Savoy Hotel, London (1890–99)

Escorial *or* **Escurial** *n* a village in central Spain, northwest of Madrid: site of an architectural complex containing a monastery, palace, and college, built by Philip II between 1563 and 1584

escort *n* **1** people or vehicles accompanying another to protect or guard them **2** a person who accompanies someone of the opposite sex on a social occasion ▷ *vb* **3** to act as an escort to [French *escorte*]

escritoire (ess-kree-**twahr**) *n* a writing desk with compartments and drawers [Medieval Latin *scriptorium* writing room in a monastery]

escudo (ess-**kew**-doe) *n*, *pl* **-dos** a former monetary unit of Portugal [Spanish: shield]

esculent *formal adj* **1** edible ▷ *n* **2** any edible substance [Latin *esculentus* good to eat]

Escurial *n* a variant of **Escorial**

escutcheon *n* **1** a shield displaying a coat of arms **2** blot on one's escutcheon a stain on one's honour [Latin *scutum* shield]

Esdraelon *n* a plain in N Israel, east of Mount Carmel. Also called: **Plain of Jezreel**

Esenin *or* **Yesenin** *n* Sergey Aleksandrovich. 1895–1925, Soviet poet, author of *Confessions of a Hooligan* (1924): married to Isadora Duncan

Eşfahān *n* a variant of **Isfahan**

Esher *n* a town in SE England, in NE Surrey near London: racecourse. Pop: 25 172 (2001)

Eskilstuna *n* an industrial city in SE Sweden. Pop: 91 137 (2004 est)

Eskimo *n* **1** (*pl* **-mos** *or* **-mo**) a member of a group of peoples who live in N Canada, Greenland, Alaska, and E Siberia **2** the language of these peoples ▷ *adj* **3** of the Eskimos [Algonquian *esquimawes*]

> **USAGE** The peoples native to the area from western Greenland to NW Canada prefer to be called *Inuit* rather than *Eskimo*.

Eskişehir *n* an industrial city in NW Turkey: founded around hot springs in Byzantine times. Pop: 519 000 (2005 est)

ESN *Brit* educationally subnormal; formerly used to designate a child who needs special schooling

esoteric (ee-so-**ter**-rik) *adj* understood by only a small number of people, esp. because they have special knowledge [Greek *esōterō* inner] **> esoterically** *adv*

ESP extrasensory perception

esp. especially

espadrille (ess-pad-drill) *n* a light canvas shoe with a braided cord sole [French]

espalier (ess-**pal**-yer) *n* **1** a shrub or fruit tree trained to grow flat **2** the trellis on which such plants are grown [French]

España *n* the Spanish name for **Spain**

esparto *or* **esparto grass** *n*, *pl* **-tos** any of various grasses of S Europe and N Africa, used to make ropes, mats, etc. [Greek *spartos* a kind of rush]

especial *adj formal* same as **special** [Latin *specialis* individual]

> **USAGE** *Especial* and *especially* have a more limited use than *special* and *specially*. *Special* is preferred to *especial* when the sense is one of being out of the ordinary: *a special lesson; he has been specially trained*. *Special* is also used when something is referred to as being for a particular purpose: *the word was specially underlined for you*. Where an idea of pre-eminence or individuality is involved, either *especial* or *special* may be used: *he is my especial* (or *special*) *friend; he is especially* (or *specially*) *good at his job*. In informal English, however, *special* is usually preferred in all contexts.

especially *adv* **1** particularly: *people are dying, especially children and babies* **2** more than usually: *an especially virulent disease*

Esperanto *n* an international artificial language [literally: the one who hopes, pseudonym of Dr L. L. Zamenhof, its Polish inventor] **> Esperantist** *n, adj*

espionage (ess-pyon-ahzh) *n* **1** the use of spies to obtain secret information, esp. by governments **2** the act of spying [French *espionnage*]

Espírito Santo *n* a state of E Brazil, on the Atlantic: swampy coastal plain with mountains in the west; heavily forested. Capital: Vitória. Pop: 3 201 722 (2002). Area: 45 597 sq km (17 601 sq miles)

Espíritu Santo *n* an island in the SW Pacific: the largest and westernmost of the Vanuatu islands. Area: 4856 sq km (1875 sq miles)

esplanade *n* a long open level stretch of ground, esp. beside the seashore or in front of a fortified place [French]

Espoo *n* a city in S Finland. Pop: 224 231 (2003 est)

espousal *n* **1** adoption or support: *his espousal of the free market* **2** *old-fashioned* a marriage or engagement ceremony

espouse *vb* **-pousing, -poused 1** to adopt or give support to (a cause, ideal, etc.) **2** *old-fashioned* (esp. of a man) to marry [Latin *sponsare*]

espresso *n, pl* **-sos** coffee made by forcing steam or boiling water through ground coffee [Italian: pressed]

esprit (ess-pree) *n* spirit, liveliness, or wit [French]

esprit de corps (de **kore**) *n* consciousness of and pride in belonging to a particular group [French]

espy *vb* **espies, espying, espied** to catch sight of [Old French *espier*]

Esq. esquire

Esquiline *n* one of the seven hills on which ancient Rome was built

esquire *n* **1** *chiefly Brit* a title of respect placed after a man's name and usually shortened to *Esq.*: *I Davies, Esquire* **2** (in medieval times) the attendant of a knight [Late Latin *scutarius* shield bearer]

Essaouira *n* a port in SW Morocco on the Atlantic. Pop: 84 000 (2003). Former name (until 1956): **Mogador**

essay *n* **1** a short literary composition on a single subject **2** a short piece of writing on a subject done as an exercise by a student **3** an attempt ▷ *vb* **4** *formal* to attempt: *he essayed a faint smile* [Old French *essai* an attempt]

essayist *n* a person who writes essays

Essen *n* a city in W Germany, in North Rhine-Westphalia: the leading administrative centre of the Ruhr; university. Pop: 589 499 (2003 est)

essence *n* **1** the most important and distinctive feature of something, which determines its identity **2** a concentrated liquid used to flavour food **3** in essence essentially **4** of the essence vitally important [Latin *esse* to be]

essential *adj* **1** vitally important; absolutely necessary: *it is essential to get this finished on time* **2** basic or fundamental: *she translated the essential points of the lecture into English* ▷ *n* **3** something fundamental or indispensable **> essentially** *adv*

essential oil *n* any of various volatile oils in plants, which have the odour or flavour of the plant from which they are extracted

Essequibo n a river in Guyana, rising near the Brazilian border and flowing north to the Atlantic: drains over half of Guyana. Length: 1014 km (630 miles)

Essex[1] n **1** a county of SE England, on the North Sea and the Thames estuary: the geographical and ceremonial county includes Thurrock and Southend-on-Sea, which became independent unitary authorities in 1998. Administrative centre: Chelmsford. Pop (excluding unitary authorities): 1 324 100 (2003 est). Area (excluding unitary authorities): 3446 sq km (1310 sq miles) **2** an Anglo-Saxon kingdom that in the early 7th century AD comprised the modern county of Essex and much of Hertfordshire and Surrey. By the late 8th century, Essex had become a dependency of the kingdom of Mercia

Essex[2] n **2nd Earl of**, title of *Robert Devereux*. ?1566–1601, English soldier and favourite of Queen Elizabeth I; executed for treason

Esslingen n a town in SW Germany, on the River Neckar: Gothic church, medieval buildings: wines, light industry. Pop: 91 980 (2003 est)

Essonne n a department of N France, south of Paris in Île-de-France region: formed in 1964. Capital: Évry. Pop: 1 153 434 (2003 est). Area: 1811 sq km (706 sq miles)

EST 1 Eastern Standard Time **2** electric-shock treatment

est. 1 established **2** estimate(d)

establish vb **1** to create or set up (an organization, link, etc.): *the regime wants to establish better relations with neighbouring countries* **2** to become firmly associated with a particular activity or reputation: *the play that established him as a major dramatist* **3** to prove: *a test to establish if your baby has any chromosomal disorder* **4** to cause (a principle) to be accepted: *our study establishes the case for further research* [Latin *stabilis* firm, stable]

Established Church n a church, such as the Church of England, that is recognized as the official church of a country

establishment n **1** the act of establishing or state of being established **2 a** a business organization or other institution **b** a place of business **3** the people employed by an organization

Establishment n **the Establishment** a group of people having authority within a society: usually seen as conservative

estate n **1** a large piece of landed property, esp. in the country **2** Brit and Austral a large area of land with houses or factories built on it: *an industrial estate* **3** law property or possessions, esp. of a deceased person **4** history any of the orders or classes making up a society [Latin *status* condition]

estate agent n Brit and Austral a person whose job is to help people buy and sell houses and other property

estate car n Brit a car which has a long body with a door at the back end and luggage space behind the rear seats

estate duty n a former name for **inheritance tax**

esteem n **1** admiration and respect ▷ vb **2** to have great respect or high regard for (someone) **3** formal to judge or consider: *I should esteem it a kindness* [Latin *aestimare* to assess the worth of] ▷ **esteemed** adj

ester n chem a compound produced by the reaction between an acid and an alcohol [German]

Esterházy n a noble Hungarian family that produced many soldiers, diplomats, and patrons of the arts. Prince **Miklós József Esterházy** (1714–90) rebuilt the family castle of Esterháza and employed Haydn as his musical director (1766–90)

Esthonia n a former spelling of **Estonia**

Estienne or **Étienne** n a family of French printers, scholars, and dealers in books, including **Henri**, ?1460–1520, who founded the printing business in Paris, his son **Robert**, 1503–59, and his grandson **Henri**, 1528–98

estimable adj worthy of respect

estimate vb **-mating, -mated 1** to form an approximate idea of (size, cost, etc.); calculate roughly **2** to form an opinion about; judge **3** to submit an approximate price

for a job to a prospective client ▷ n **4** an approximate calculation **5** a statement of the likely charge for certain work **6** an opinion [Latin *aestimare* to assess the worth of] ▷ **estimator** n

estimation n **1** a considered opinion; judgment: *overall, he went up in my estimation* **2** the act of estimating

Estonia or formerly **Esthonia** n a republic in NE Europe, on the Gulf of Finland and the Baltic: low-lying with many lakes and forests, it includes numerous islands in the Baltic Sea. It was under Scandinavian and Teutonic rule from the 13th century to 1721, when it passed to Russia: it was an independent republic from 1920 to 1940, when it was annexed by the Soviet Union; became independent in 1991 and joined the EU in 2004. Official language: Estonian. Religion: believers are mostly Christian. Currency: euro. Capital: Tallinn. Pop: 1 266 375 (2013 est). Area: 45 227 sq km (17 462 sq miles)

Estonian adj **1** of or relating to Estonia or its inhabitants ▷ n **2** a native or inhabitant of Estonia

Estoril n a resort in W Portugal, near Lisbon, on the Atlantic Ocean: noted esp. for a famous avenue of palm trees leading to the seafront. Pop: 23 769 (2001)

estranged adj **1** no longer living with one's husband or wife: *his estranged wife* **2** having quarrelled and lost touch with one's family or friends: *I am estranged from my son* [from Latin *extraneus* foreign] ▷ **estrangement** n

estuary n, pl **-aries** the widening channel of a river where it nears the sea [Latin *aestus* tide] ▷ **estuarine** adj

ET Brit Employment Training: a government scheme offering training in technology and business skills for unemployed people

ETA estimated time of arrival

e-tail (ee-tail) n retail conducted via the internet

et al. 1 and elsewhere **2** and others [Latin *et alii*]

etc. et cetera

et cetera or **etcetera** (et set-ra) adv **1** and the rest; and others; or the like **2** and so forth [Latin *et* and + *cetera* the other (things)]

> **USAGE** It is unnecessary to use and before etc. as etc. (et cetera) already means and other things. The repetition of etc., as in he brought paper, ink, notebooks, etc., etc., is avoided except in informal contexts.

etceteras pl n miscellaneous extra things or people

etch vb **1** to wear away the surface of (a metal, glass, etc.) by the action of an acid **2** to cut (a design or pattern) into a printing plate with acid **3** to imprint vividly: *the scene is etched on my mind* [Dutch *etsen*] ▷ **etcher** n

etching n **1** the art or process of preparing or printing etched designs **2** a print made from an etched plate

eternal adj **1** without beginning or end; lasting for ever **2** unchanged by time: *eternal truths* **3** seemingly unceasing: *his eternal whingeing* **4** of or like God or a god: *the Eternal Buddha* [Latin *aeternus*] ▷ **eternally** adv

Eternal City n the Eternal City Rome

eternal triangle n an emotional or sexual relationship in which there are conflicts between a man and two women or a woman and two men

eternity n, pl **-ties 1** endless or infinite time **2** a seemingly endless period of time: *it seemed an eternity before he could feel his heart beating again* **3** the timeless existence after death **4** the state of being eternal

eternity ring n a ring given as a token of lasting affection, esp. one set all around with stones to symbolize continuity

Eth. Ethiopia(n)

ethane n a flammable gaseous alkane obtained from natural gas and petroleum: used as a fuel [from *ethyl*]

ethanoic acid n same as **acetic acid**

ethanol n same as **alcohol** (1)

Ethelbert or **Æthelbert** n Saint. ?552–616 AD, king of Kent (560–616): converted to Christianity by St Augustine; issued the earliest known code of

English laws. Feast day: Feb 24 or 25

Ethelred I *or* **Æthelred I** *n* died 871, king of Wessex (866–71). He led resistance to the Danish invasion of England; died following his victory at Ashdown

Ethelred II *or* **Æthelred II** *n* known as *Ethelred the Unready*. ?968–1016 AD, king of England (978–1016). He was temporarily deposed by the Danish king Sweyn (1013) but was recalled on Sweyn's death (1014)

Ethelwulf *or* **Æthelwulf** *n* died 858 AD, king of Wessex (839–858)

ethene *n* same as ethylene

ether *n* **1** a colourless sweet-smelling liquid used as a solvent and anaesthetic **2** the substance formerly believed to fill all space and to transmit electromagnetic waves **3** the upper regions of the atmosphere; clear sky. ▶ Also (for senses 2 and 3): **aether** [Greek *aithein* to burn]

ethereal (eth-eer-ee-al) *adj* **1** extremely delicate or refined **2** heavenly or spiritual [Greek *aithēr* ether] **>** **ethereally** *adv*

Etherege *n* Sir George. ?1635–?92, English Restoration dramatist; author of the comedies *The Comical Revenge* (1664), *She would if she could* (1668), and *The Man of Mode* (1676)

ethic *n* a moral principle or set of moral values held by an individual or group [Greek *ēthos* custom]

ethical *adj* **1** of or based on a system of moral beliefs about right and wrong **2** in accordance with principles of professional conduct **3** of or relating to ethics **>** **ethically** *adv*

ethics *pl n* **1** a code of behaviour, esp. of a particular group, profession, or individual: *business ethics* **2** the moral fitness of a decision, course of action, etc. ▷ *n* **3** the study of the moral value of human conduct

Ethiopia *n* a state in NE Africa, on the Red Sea: consolidated as an empire under Menelik II (1889–1913); federated with Eritrea from 1952 until 1993; Emperor Haile Selassie was deposed by the military in 1974 and the monarchy was abolished in 1975; an independence movement in Eritrea was engaged in war with the government from 1961 until 1993. It lies along the Great Rift Valley and consists of deserts in the southeast and northeast and a high central plateau with many rivers (including the Blue Nile) and mountains rising over 4500 m (15 000 ft); the main export is coffee. Language: Amharic. Religion: Christian majority. Currency: birr. Capital: Addis Ababa. Pop: 93 877 025 (2013 est). Area: 1 128 215 sq km (435 614 sq miles). Former name: **Abyssinia**

Ethiopian *adj* **1** of or relating to Ethiopia or its inhabitants ▷ *n* **2** a native or inhabitant of Ethiopia

ethnic *or* **ethnical** *adj* **1** of or relating to a human group with racial, religious, and linguistic characteristics in common **2** characteristic of another culture, esp. a peasant one: *ethnic foodstuffs* [Greek *ethnos* race] **>** **ethnically** *adv*

ethnic cleansing *n* the practice, by the dominant ethnic group in an area, of removing other ethnic groups by expulsion or extermination

ethnocentric *adj* of or relating to the belief that one's own nation, culture, or group is intrinsically superior **>** **ethnocentricity** *n*

ethnology *n* the branch of anthropology that deals with races and peoples and their relations to one another **>** **ethnological** *adj* **>** **ethnologist** *n*

ethos (eeth-oss) *n* the distinctive spirit and attitudes of a people, culture, etc. [Greek]

ethyl (eth-ill) *adj* of, consisting of, or containing the monovalent group C_2H_5– [from *ether*]

ethyl alcohol *n* same as alcohol (1)

ethylene *or* **ethene** *n* a colourless flammable gaseous alkene used to make polythene and other chemicals

etiolate (ee-tee-oh-late) *vb* **-lating, -lated** **1** *formal* to become or cause to become weak **2** *botany* to make a green plant paler through lack of sunlight [French *étioler* to make pale] **>** **etiolation** *n*

etiology *n, pl* **-gies 1** the study of causation **2** the study of the cause of diseases [Greek *aitia* cause + -LOGY] **>** **etiological** *adj*

etiquette *n* **1** the customs or rules of behaviour regarded as correct in social life **2** a conventional code of practice in certain professions [French]

Etna *n* Mount Etna an active volcano in E Sicily: the highest volcano in Europe and the highest peak in Italy south of the Alps. Height: 3323 m (10 902 ft)

Eton *n* **1** a town in S England, in Windsor and Maidenhead unitary authority, Berkshire, near the River Thames: site of **Eton College**, a public school for boys founded in 1440. Pop: 3821 (2001 est) **2** this college

Etruria *n* **1** an ancient country of central Italy, between the Rivers Arno and Tiber, roughly corresponding to present-day Tuscany and part of Umbria **2** a factory established in Staffordshire by Josiah Wedgwood in 1769

étude (ay-tewd) *n music* a short composition for a solo instrument, esp. intended to be played as an exercise or to demonstrate virtuosity [French: study]

etymology *n, pl* **-gies 1** the study of the sources and development of words **2** an account of the source and development of a word [Greek *etumon* basic meaning + -LOGY] **>** **etymological** *adj* **>** **etymologist** *n*

Eu *chem* europium

EU European Union

Euboea *n* an island in the W Aegean Sea: the largest island after Crete of the Greek archipelago; linked with the mainland by a bridge across the Euripus channel. Capital: Chalcis. Pop: 198 130 (2001). Area: 3908 sq km (1509 sq miles). Modern Greek name: **Évvoia**. Former English name: **Negropont**

Euboean *adj* **1** of or relating to the Greek island of Euboea ▷ *n* **2** a native or inhabitant of Euboea

eucalyptus *or* **eucalypt** *n, pl* **-lyptuses, -lyptus** *or* **-lypts** any of a mostly Australian genus of trees, widely cultivated for timber and gum, and for the medicinal oil in their leaves (**eucalyptus oil**) [Greek *eu-* well + *kaluptos* covered]

Eucharist (yew-kar-ist) *n* **1** the Christian sacrament commemorating Christ's Last Supper by the consecration of bread and wine **2** the consecrated elements of bread and wine [Greek *eukharistos* thankful] **>** **Eucharistic** *adj*

Eucken *n* Rudolph Christoph. 1846–1926, German idealist philosopher: Nobel prize for literature 1908

Euclid *n* **1** 3rd century BC, Greek mathematician of Alexandria; author of *Elements*, which sets out the principles of geometry and remained a text until the 19th century at least **2** the works of Euclid, esp. his system of geometry **>** **Euclidean** *or* **Euclidian** *adj*

Eudoxus of Cnidus *n* ?406–?355 BC, Greek astronomer and mathematician; believed to have calculated the length of the solar year

Eugène *n* Prince, title of *François Eugène de Savoie-Carignan*. 1663–1736, Austrian general, born in France: with Marlborough defeated the French at Blenheim (1704), Oudenaarde (1708), and Malplaquet (1709)

eugenics (yew-jen-iks) *n* the study of methods of improving the human race, esp. by selective breeding [Greek *eugenēs* well-born] **>** **eugenic** *adj* **>** **eugenically** *adv* **>** **eugenicist** *n*

Eugénie *n* original name *Eugenia María de Montijo de Guzmán, Comtesse de Téba*. 1826–1920, Empress of France (1853–71) as wife of Napoleon III

Euler *n* **1** Leonhard. 1707–83, Swiss mathematician, noted esp. for his work on the calculus of variation: considered the founder of modern mathematical analysis **2** Ulf (Svante) von. 1905–83, Swedish physiologist: shared the Nobel prize (1970) for physiology or medicine with Julius Axelrod and Bernard Katz for their work on the catecholamines: son of Hans von Euler-Chelpin

Euler-Chelpin *n* Hans (Karl August) von. 1873–1964, Swedish biochemist, born in Germany: shared the Nobel prize for chemistry (1929) with Sir Arthur Harden for their work on enzymes: father of Ulf von Euler

eulogize or **-gise** *vb* **-gizing, -gized** or **-gising, -gised** to praise (a person or thing) highly in speech or writing ⊳ **eulogistic** *adj*

eulogy *n, pl* **-gies** **1** a speech or piece of writing praising a person or thing, esp. a person who has recently died **2** high praise [Greek *eulogia* praise]

> USAGE Avoid confusion with **elegy**.

eunuch *n* a man who has been castrated, esp. (formerly) a guard in a harem [Greek *eunoukhos* bedchamber attendant]

Eupen and Malmédy *n* a region of Belgium in Liège province: ceded by Germany in 1919. Pop: 29 372 (2004 est)

euphemism *n* an inoffensive word or phrase substituted for one considered offensive or upsetting, such as *departed* for *dead* [Greek *eu-* well + *phēmē* speech] ⊳ **euphemistic** *adj* ⊳ **euphemistically** *adv*

euphonious *adj* pleasing to the ear

euphonium *n* a brass musical instrument with four valves, resembling a small tuba [*euph(ony* + *harm)onium*]

euphony *n, pl* **-nies** a pleasing sound, esp. in speech [Greek *eu-* well + *phōnē* voice]

euphoria *n* a feeling of great but often unjustified or exaggerated happiness [Greek *eu-* well + *pherein* to bear] ⊳ **euphoric** *adj*

Euphrates *n* a river in SW Asia, rising in E Turkey and flowing south across Syria and Iraq to join the Tigris, forming the Shatt-al-Arab, which flows to the head of the Persian Gulf: important in ancient times for the extensive irrigation of its valley (in Mesopotamia). Length: 3598 km (2235 miles)

Eur. **1** Europe **2** European

Eurasia *n* the continents of Europe and Asia considered as a whole

Eurasian *adj* **1** of Europe and Asia **2** of mixed European and Asian descent ⊳ *n* **3** a person of mixed European and Asian descent

Eure *n* a department of N France, in Haute Normandie region. Capital: Évreux. Pop: 550 056 (2003 est). Area: 6037 sq km (2354 sq miles)

Eure-et-Loir *n* a department of N central France, in Centre region. Capital: Chartres. Pop: 412 094 (2003 est). Area: 5940 sq km (2317 sq miles)

eureka (yew-reek-a) *interj* an exclamation of triumph on discovering or solving something [Greek *heurēka* I have found (it)]

Euripides *n* ?480–406 BC, Greek tragic dramatist. His plays, 18 of which are extant, include *Alcestis, Medea, Hippolytus, Hecuba, Trojan Women, Electra, Iphigeneia in Tauris, Iphigeneia in Aulis,* and *Bacchae*

euro *n, pl* **euros** the unit of the European Union's single currency

Euro- *combining form* Europe or European

Eurocentric *adj* chiefly concerned with Europe and European culture: *a Eurocentric view of British history*

Euroland or **Eurozone** *n* the geographical area containing the countries that have joined the European single currency

Europe *n* **1** the second smallest continent, forming the W extension of Eurasia: the border with Asia runs from the Urals to the Caspian and the Black Sea. The coastline is generally extremely indented and there are several peninsulas (notably Scandinavia, Italy, and Iberia) and offshore islands (including the British Isles and Iceland). It contains a series of great mountain systems in the south (Pyrenees, Alps, Apennines, Carpathians, Caucasus), a large central plain, and a N region of lakes and mountains in Scandinavia. Pop: 739 165 030 (2011 est). Area: about 10 400 000 sq km (4 000 000 sq miles) **2** *Brit* the continent of Europe except for the British Isles: *we're going to Europe for our holiday* **3** *Brit* the European Union:

when did Britain go into Europe? **4** a type of dinghy, designed to be sailed by one person

European *adj* **1** of or relating to Europe or its inhabitants ⊳ *n* **2** a native or inhabitant of Europe **3** a person of European descent **4** an advocate of closer links between the countries of Europe, esp. those in the European Union ⊳ **Europeanism** *n*

European Community or **European Economic Community** *n* former names for **European Union**

European Union *n* an economic organization of W European states, which have some shared monetary, social, and political goals

Europhile (you-roh-file) *n* **1** a person who admires Europe or the European Union ⊳ *adj* **2** marked by admiration of Europe or the European Union

europium *n chem* a silvery-white element of the lanthanide series. Symbol: **Eu** [after EUROPE]

Europoort *n* a port in the Netherlands near Rotterdam: developed in the 1960s; handles chiefly oil

Euro-sceptic *n* **1** (in Britain) a person who is opposed to closer links with the European Union ⊳ *adj* **2** (in Britain) opposing closer links with the European Union: *three Euro-sceptic MPs*

Eurozone *n* same as **Euroland**

Eusebio *n* Silva Ferreira da. 1942–2014, Portuguese footballer; played for Benfica (1960-75) and Portugal, for whom he scored 41 goals in 64 games; European Footballer of the Year (1965)

Eusebius *n* ?265–?340 AD, bishop of Caesarea: author of a history of the Christian Church to 324 AD

Eustachian tube *n* a tube that connects the middle ear with the pharynx and equalizes the pressure between the two sides of the eardrum [after Bartolomeo *Eustachio,* anatomist]

Euterpe *n Greek myth* the Muse of lyric poetry

euthanasia *n* the act of killing someone painlessly, esp. to relieve suffering from an incurable illness [Greek: easy death]

Euxine Sea *n* an ancient name for the **Black Sea**

eV electronvolt

evacuate *vb* **-ating, -ated** **1** to send away from a dangerous place to a safe place: *200 people were evacuated from their homes because of the floods* **2** to empty (a place) of people because it has become dangerous: *the entire street was evacuated until the fire was put out* **3** *physiol* to discharge waste from the body [Latin *evacuare* to empty] ⊳ **evacuation** *n* ⊳ **evacuee** *n*

evade *vb* **evading, evaded** **1** to get away from or avoid (imprisonment, captors, etc.) **2** to get around, shirk, or dodge (the law, a duty, etc.) **3** to avoid answering (a question) [Latin *evadere* to go forth]

evaluate *vb* **-ating, -ated** to find or judge the quality or value of (something) [French *évaluer*] ⊳ **evaluation** *n*

evanesce *vb* **-nescing, -nesced** *formal* to fade gradually from sight [Latin *evanescere*]

evanescent *adj formal* quickly fading away; ephemeral or transitory ⊳ **evanescence** *n*

evangelical *Christianity adj* **1** of or following from the Gospels **2** of certain Protestant sects which emphasize salvation through faith alone and a belief in the absolute authority of the Bible **3** displaying missionary zeal in promoting something ⊳ *n* **4** a member of an evangelical sect [Greek *evangelion* good news] ⊳ **evangelicalism** *n* ⊳ **evangelically** *adv*

evangelism *n* the practice of spreading the Christian gospel

evangelist *n* a preacher, sometimes itinerant ⊳ **evangelistic** *adj*

Evangelist *n* any of the writers of the Gospels: Matthew, Mark, Luke, or John

evangelize or **-lise** *vb* **-lizing, -lized** or **-lising, -lised** to preach the Christian gospel (to) ⊳ **evangelization** or **-lisation** *n*

e

Evans n 1 Sir Arthur (John). 1851–1941, British archaeologist, whose excavations of the palace of Knossos in Crete provided evidence for the existence of the Minoan civilization 2 Dame **Edith** (**Mary Booth**). 1888–1976, British actress 3 Sir **Geraint** (**Llewellyn**). 1922–92, Welsh operatic baritone 4 **Herbert McLean**. 1882–1971, US anatomist and embryologist; discoverer of vitamin E (1922) 5 **Mary Ann**. real name of (George) **Eliot** (1) 6 **Oliver**. 1755–1819, US engineer: invented the continuous production line and a high-pressure steam engine 7 **Walker**. 1903–75, US photographer, noted esp. for his studies of rural poverty in the Great Depression

Evanston n a city in NE Illinois, on Lake Michigan north of Chicago: Northwestern University (1851). Pop: 74 360 (2003 est)

Evansville n a city in SW Indiana, on the Ohio River. Pop: 117 881 (2003 est)

evaporate vb **-rating, -rated** 1 to change from a liquid or solid to a vapour 2 to become less and less and finally disappear: *faith in the government evaporated rapidly after the election* [Latin e- out + vapor steam] ⟩ **evaporable** adj ⟩ **evaporation** n

evaporated milk n thick unsweetened tinned milk from which some of the water has been removed

evasion n 1 the act of evading something, esp. a duty or responsibility, by cunning or illegal means: *tax evasion* 2 cunning or deception used to dodge a question, duty, etc.

evasive adj 1 seeking to evade; not straightforward: *an evasive answer* 2 avoiding or seeking to avoid trouble or difficulties: *evasive action* ⟩ **evasively** adv

Evatt n Herbert Vere. 1894–1965, Australian jurist and Labor political leader, president of the General Assembly of the United Nations 1948–49

eve n 1 the evening or day before some special event 2 the period immediately before an event: *on the eve of the Second World War* 3 poetic or old-fashioned evening [variant of EVEN²]

Eve n Bible the first woman, created by God from Adam's rib

Evelyn n John. 1620–1706, English author, noted chiefly for his diary (1640–1706)

even¹ adj 1 level and regular; flat 2 on the same level: *make sure the surfaces are even with one another* 3 regular and unvarying: *an even pace* 4 equally balanced between two sides 5 equal in number, quantity, etc. 6 (of a number) divisible by two 7 denoting alternatives, events, etc., that have an equal probability: *they have a more than even chance of winning the next election* 8 having scored the same number of points 9 **even money** or **evens** a bet in which the winnings are exactly the same as the amount staked 10 **get even with** informal to exact revenge on; settle accounts with ▷ adv 11 used to suggest that the content of a statement is unexpected or paradoxical: *it's chilly in Nova Scotia, even in August* 12 used to intensify a comparative adjective or adverb: *an even greater demand* 13 used to introduce a word that is stronger and more accurate than one already used: *a normal, even inevitable aspect of ageing* 14 used preceding a hypothesis to emphasize that, whether or not the condition is fulfilled, the statement remains valid: *the remark didn't call for an answer even if he could have thought of one* 15 **even so** in spite of any assertion to the contrary; nevertheless 16 **even though** despite the fact that ▶ See also **even out**, **even up** [Old English efen] ⟩ **evenly** adv ⟩ **evenness** n

even² n poetic or old-fashioned 1 eve 2 evening [Old English æfen]

even-handed adj fair; impartial

evening n 1 the latter part of the day, esp. from late afternoon until nightfall ▷ adj 2 of or in the evening: *the evening meal* [Old English æfnung]

evening class n Brit, Austral and NZ an educational class for adults, held during the evening

evening dress n clothes for a formal occasion during the evening

evening primrose n a plant with yellow flowers that open in the evening

evening star n a planet, usually Venus, seen shining brightly just after sunset

even out vb to make or become even, by the removal of bumps, inequalities, etc.

evensong n Church of England the daily evening service. Also called: **Evening Prayer**

event n 1 anything that takes place, esp. something important 2 a planned and organized occasion: *the wedding was one of the social events of the year* 3 any one contest in a sporting programme 4 **in any event** or **at all events** whatever happens 5 **in the event** when it came to the actual or final outcome: *in the event, neither of them turned up* 6 **in the event of** if (such a thing) happens 7 **in the event that** if it should happen that [Latin evenire to happen]

even-tempered adj calm and not easily angered

eventful adj full of exciting or important incidents

eventide n archaic or poetic evening

eventing n Brit, Austral and NZ riding competitions (esp. three-day events), usually involving cross-country riding, jumping, and dressage

eventual adj happening or being achieved at the end of a situation or process: *the Fascists' eventual victory in the Spanish Civil War* ⟩ **eventually** adv

eventuality n, pl **-ties** a possible occurrence or result: *I was utterly unprepared for such an eventuality*

even up vb to make or become equal

ever adv 1 at any time: *it was the fourth fastest time ever* 2 always: *ever present* 3 used to give emphasis: *tell him to put to sea as soon as ever he can* 4 **ever so** or **ever such** informal, chiefly Brit used to give emphasis: *I'm ever so sorry* [Old English æfre]

Everest n 1 **Mount Everest** a mountain in S Asia on the border between Nepal and Tibet, in the Himalayas: the highest mountain in the world; first climbed by members of a British-led expedition (1953). Height: established as 8848 m (29 028 ft) for many years, but the latest of a series of more recent reassessments (in 1999), not currently accepted by all authorities or by either of the controlling governments, puts it at 8850 m (29 035 ft). Nepalese name: **Sagarmatha**. Chinese names: **Qomolangma, Chomolungma** 2 any high point of ambition or achievement [C19: named after Sir G. *Everest* (1790–1866), Surveyor-General of India]

Everglades pl n the Everglades a subtropical marshy region of Florida, south of Lake Okeechobee: contains the **Everglades National Park** established to preserve the flora and fauna of the swamps. Area: over 13 000 sq km (5000 sq miles)

evergreen adj 1 (of certain trees and shrubs) bearing foliage throughout the year ▷ n 2 an evergreen tree or shrub

everlasting adj 1 never coming to an end; eternal 2 lasting so long or occurring so often as to become tedious ⟩ **everlastingly** adv

Everly Brothers pl n the. US pop singing duo comprising Don Everly (born 1937) and Phil Everly 1939–2014, noted for their close harmonies

evermore adv all time to come

Evert n Chris(tine). born 1954, US tennis player: winner of eighteen Grand Slam singles titles (1974–86), including the French Open a record seven times, the US Open a record six times, and Wimbledon three times

every adj 1 each without exception: *they were winning every battle* 2 the greatest or best possible: *there is every reason to believe in the sincerity of their commitment* 3 each: *every 20 years* 4 **every bit as** informal just as: *she's every bit as clever as you* 5 **every other** each alternate: *every other month* [Old English æfre ever + ælc each]

everybody *pron* every person; everyone

USAGE See at **everyone**.

everyday *adj* **1** commonplace or usual **2** happening each day **3** suitable for or used on ordinary days
Everyman *n* the ordinary person; common man [after the central figure in a medieval morality play]
everyone *pron* every person; everybody

USAGE *Everyone* and *everybody* are interchangeable, as are *no one* and *nobody*, and *someone* and *somebody*. Care should be taken to distinguish between *everyone* and *someone* as single words and *every one* and *some one* as two words, the latter form correctly being used to refer to each individual person or thing in a particular group: *every one of them is wrong.*

everything *pron* **1** the whole; all things: *everything had been carefully packed* **2** the thing that is most important: *work was everything to her*
everywhere *adv* to or in all parts or places
Evesham *n* a town in W central England, in W Worcestershire, on the River Avon: scene of the Battle of Evesham in 1265 (Lord Edward's defeat of Simon de Montfort and the barons); centre of the **Vale of Evesham**, famous for market gardens and orchards. Pop: 22 179 (2001)
Évian-les-Bains or **Évian** *n* a resort and spa town in E France, on Lake Geneva opposite Lausanne; noted for its bottled mineral waters. Pop: 8064 (2006)
evict *vb* to expel (someone) legally from his or her home or land [Latin *evincere* to vanquish utterly] **> eviction** *n*
evidence *n* **1** something which provides ground for belief or disbelief: *there is no evidence that depression is inherited* **2** *law* matter produced before a court of law in an attempt to prove or disprove a point in issue **3** in evidence on display; apparent ▷ *vb* **-dencing, -denced** **4** to show clearly; demonstrate: *you evidenced no talent for music*
evident *adj* easy to see or understand [Latin *videre* to see] **> evidently** *adv*
evidential *adj* of, serving as, or based on evidence **> evidentially** *adv*
evil *n* **1** a force or power that brings about wickedness and harm: *the battle between good and evil* **2** a wicked or morally wrong act or thing: *the evil of racism* ▷ *adj* **3** (of a person) deliberately causing great harm and misery; wicked: *an evil dictator* **4** (of an act, idea, etc.) causing great harm and misery; morally wrong: *what you did was deeply evil* **5** very unpleasant: *it was fascinating to see people vanish as if we had some very evil smell* [Old English *yfel*] **> evilly** *adv*
evildoer *n* a person who does evil **> evildoing** *n*
evil eye *n* the evil eye a look superstitiously supposed to have the power of inflicting harm
evince *vb* **evincing, evinced** *formal* to show or display (a quality or feeling) clearly: *a humility which he had never evinced in earlier days* [Latin *evincere* to overcome]

USAGE *Evince* is sometimes wrongly used where *evoke* is meant: *the proposal evoked* (not *evinced*) *a storm of protest.*

eviscerate *vb* **-ating, -ated** to remove the internal organs of; disembowel [Latin *e-* out + *viscera* entrails] **> evisceration** *n*
evocation *n* the act of evoking **> evocative** *adj*
evoke *vb* **evoking, evoked** **1** to call or summon up (a memory or feeling) from the past **2** to provoke or bring about: *his sacking evoked a huge public protest* [Latin *evocare* to call forth]

USAGE See at **evince** and **invoke**.

evolution *n* **1** *biology* a gradual change in the characteristics of a population of animals or plants over successive generations **2** a gradual development, esp. to a more complex form [Latin *evolutio* an unrolling] **> evolutionary** *adj*
evolve *vb* **evolving, evolved** **1** to develop gradually **2** (of animal or plant species) to undergo evolution [Latin *evolvere* to unfold]
Évora *n* a city in S central Portugal: ancient Roman settlement; occupied by the Moors from 712 to 1166; residence of the Portuguese court in 15th and 16th centuries. Pop: 56 525 (2001). Ancient name: **Ebora**
e-voting *n* the application of electronic technology to cast and count votes in an election
Évreux *n* an industrial town in NW France: severely damaged in World War II; cathedral (12th–16th centuries). Pop: 50 772 (2008)
Évros *n* a transliteration of the Modern Greek name for the **Maritsa**
Évvoia *n* a transliteration of the Modern Greek name for **Euboea**
Ewart *n* Gavin (Buchanan). 1916–95, British poet, noted for his light satirical verse
ewe *n* a female sheep [Old English *ēowu*]
ewer *n* a large jug with a wide mouth [Latin *aqua* water]
ex¹ *prep finance* excluding or without: *ex dividend* [Latin: out of, from]
ex² *n, pl* **exes** *informal* one's former wife or husband
ex- *prefix* **1** out of, outside, or from: *exit* **2** former: *his glamorous ex-wife* [Latin]
exacerbate (ig-zass-er-bate) *vb* **-bating, -bated** to make (pain, emotion, or a situation) worse [Latin *acerbus* bitter] **> exacerbation** *n*
exact *adj* **1** correct in every detail; strictly accurate **2** precise, as opposed to approximate **3** based on measurement and the formulation of laws: *forecasting floods is not an exact science* ▷ *vb* **4** to obtain or demand as a right, esp. through force or strength: *the rebels called for revenge to be exacted for the killings* [Latin *exigere* to demand]
exacting *adj* making rigorous or excessive demands
exaction *n formal* **1** the act of obtaining or demanding money as a right **2** a sum or payment exacted
exactitude *n* the quality of being exact; precision
exactly *adv* **1** with complete accuracy and precision: *I don't know exactly where they live* **2** in every respect: *he looks exactly like his father* ▷ *interj* **3** just so! precisely!
exaggerate *vb* **-rating, -rated** **1** to regard or represent as greater than is true **2** to make greater or more noticeable [Latin *exaggerare* to heap up] **> exaggerated** *adj* **> exaggeratedly** *adv* **> exaggeration** *n*
exalt *vb* **1** to praise highly **2** to raise to a higher rank [Latin *exaltare* to raise] **> exalted** *adj* **> exaltation** *n*

USAGE *Exalt* is sometimes wrongly used where *exult* is meant: *he was exulting* (not *exalting*) *in his win earlier that day.*

exam *n* short for **examination**
examination *n* **1** the act of examining **2** *education* exercises, questions, or tasks set to test a person's knowledge and skill **3** *med* physical inspection of a patient **4** *law* the formal questioning of a person on oath
examine *vb* **-mining, -mined** **1** to inspect carefully or in detail; investigate **2** *education* to test the knowledge of (a candidate) in (a subject) by written or oral questions **3** *med* to investigate the state of health of (a patient) **4** *law* to formally question (someone) on oath [Latin *examinare* to weigh] **> examinee** *n* **> examiner** *n*
example *n* **1** a specimen that is typical of its group; sample: *a fine example of Georgian architecture* **2** a particular event, object, or person that demonstrates a point or supports an argument, theory, etc.: *Germany is a good example of how federalism works in practice* **3** a person, action, or thing that is worthy of imitation **4** a punishment or the person punished regarded as a warning to others

5 for example as an illustration [Latin *exemplum*]

exasperate *vb* **-rating, -rated** to cause great irritation to [Latin *exasperare* to make rough] **> exasperated** *adj* **> exasperating** *adj* **> exasperation** *n*

ex cathedra *adj, adv* **1** with the authority of one's official position **2** *RC Church* (of doctrines of faith or morals) defined by the pope as infallibly true [Latin: from the chair]

excavate *vb* **-vating, -vated** **1** to unearth (buried objects) methodically to discover information about the past **2** to make a hole in something by digging into it or hollowing it out: *one kind of shrimp excavates a hole for itself* [Latin *excavare* to make hollow] **> excavation** *n* **> excavator** *n*

exceed *vb* **1** to be greater in degree or quantity **2** to go beyond the limit of (a restriction) [Latin *excedere* to go beyond]

exceedingly *adv* very; extremely

excel *vb* **-celling, -celled** **1** to be better than; surpass **2 excel in** *or* **at** to be outstandingly good at [Latin *excellere* to rise up]

excellence *n* the quality of being exceptionally good

Excellency *or* **Excellence** *n, pl* **-lencies** *or* **-lences** **Your** *or* **His** *or* **Her Excellency** a title used to address a high-ranking official, such as an ambassador

excellent *adj* exceptionally good; outstanding

except *prep* **1** Also: **except for** not including; apart from: *everyone except Jill laughed* **2 except that** but for the fact that ▷ *vb* **3** to leave out or exclude [Latin *excipere* to take out]

excepting *prep* except

> **USAGE** The use of *excepting* is considered by many people to be acceptable only after *not*, *only*, *always*, or *without*. Elsewhere *except* is preferred: *every country agreed to the proposal except* (not *excepting*) *Spain; he was well again except for* (not *excepting*) *a slight pain in his chest*.

exception *n* **1** anything excluded from or not conforming to a general rule or classification **2 take exception to** to make objections to

exceptionable *adj* open to objection

exceptional *adj* **1** forming an exception **2** having much more than average intelligence, ability, or skill **> exceptionally** *adv*

excerpt *n* **1** a passage taken from a book, speech, etc.; extract ▷ *vb* **2** to take a passage from a book, speech, etc. [Latin *excerptum* (something) picked out]

excess *n* **1** the state or act of going beyond normal or permitted limits **2** an immoderate or abnormal amount **3** the amount, number, etc., by which one thing exceeds another **4** behaviour regarded as too extreme or immoral to be acceptable: *a life of sex, drugs, and drunken excess* **5 excesses** acts or actions that are unacceptably cruel or immoral: *one of the bloodiest excesses of a dictatorial regime* **6 in excess of** more than **7 to excess** to an extreme or unhealthy extent: *he had started to drink to excess* ▷ *adj* **8** more than normal, necessary, or permitted: *excess fat* [Latin *excedere* to go beyond] **> excessive** *adj* **> excessively** *adv*

excess luggage *or* **excess baggage** *n* luggage that is more in weight or number of pieces than an airline, etc., will carry free

exchange *vb* **-changing, -changed** **1** (of two or more people, governments, etc.) to give each other (something similar) at the same time: *they nervously exchanged smiles* **2** to replace (one thing) with another, esp. to replace unsatisfactory goods: *could I exchange this for a larger size, please?* ▷ *n* **3** the act of exchanging **4** anything given or received as an equivalent or substitute for something else **5** an argument **6** Also called: **telephone exchange** a centre in which telephone lines are interconnected **7** a place where securities or commodities are traded, esp. by brokers or merchants

8 a transfer of sums of money of equivalent value, as between different currencies **9** the system by which commercial debts are settled, esp. by bills of exchange, without direct payment of money [Latin *cambire* to barter] **> exchangeable** *adj*

exchange rate *n* the rate at which the currency unit of one country may be exchanged for that of another

Exchequer *n* *government* (in Britain and certain other countries) the accounting department of the Treasury [Old French *eschequier* counting table]

excise[1] *n* **1** a tax on goods, such as spirits, produced for the home market **2** *Brit* that section of the government service responsible for the collection of excise, now the Board of Customs and Excise [Latin *assidere* to sit beside, assist in judging]

excise[2] *vb* **-cising, -cised** **1** to delete a passage from a book **2** to remove an organ or part surgically [Latin *excidere* to cut down] **> excision** *n*

exciseman *n, pl* **-men** *Brit* (formerly) a government agent who collected excise and prevented smuggling

excitable *adj* nervous and easily excited **> excitability** *n*

excite *vb* **-citing, -cited** **1** to make (a person) feel so happy that he or she is unable to relax because he or she is looking forward eagerly to something: *he was excited at the long-awaited arrival of a son* **2** to cause or arouse (an emotion, response, etc.): *the idea strongly excited his interest* **3** to arouse sexually **4** *physiol* to cause a response in (an organ, tissue, or part) **5** *physics* to raise (an atom, molecule, etc.) to a higher energy level [Latin *exciere* to stimulate] **> excited** *adj* **> excitedly** *adv*

excitement *n* **1** the state of being excited **2** a person or thing that excites

exciting *adj* causing excitement; stirring; stimulating **> excitingly** *adv*

exclaim *vb* to cry out or speak suddenly or excitedly, as from surprise, delight, horror, etc. [Latin *exclamare*]

exclamation *n* **1** an abrupt or excited cry or utterance **2** the act of exclaiming **> exclamatory** *adj*

exclamation mark *or* US **exclamation point** *n* the punctuation mark (!) used after exclamations and forceful commands

exclude *vb* **-cluding, -cluded** **1** to keep out; prevent from entering **2** to leave out of consideration [Latin *excludere*] **> exclusion** *n*

excluding *prep* excepting

exclusive *adj* **1** excluding or incompatible with anything else: *these two theories are mutually exclusive* **2** not shared: *exclusive rights* **3** used or lived in by a privileged minority, esp. a fashionable clique: *an exclusive skiing resort* **4** not including the numbers, dates, etc., mentioned **5 exclusive of** except for; not taking account of **6 exclusive to** limited to; found only in ▷ *n* **7** a story reported in only one newspaper **> exclusively** *adv* **> exclusivity** *or* **exclusiveness** *n*

excommunicate *vb* **-cating, -cated** to expel (someone) from membership of a church and ban him or her from taking part in its services [Late Latin *excommunicare* to exclude from the community] **> excommunication** *n*

excoriate *vb* **-ating, -ated** **1** *literary* to censure severely **2** to strip skin from (a person or animal) [Late Latin *excoriare* to strip, flay] **> excoriation** *n*

excrement *n* waste matter discharged from the body; faeces [Latin *excernere* to sift, excrete] **> excremental** *adj*

excrescence *n* something that protrudes, esp. an outgrowth from a part of the body [Latin *excrescere* to grow out] **> excrescent** *adj*

excreta (ik-skree-ta) *pl n* urine and faeces discharged from the body

excrete *vb* **-creting, -creted** to discharge waste matter, such as urine, sweat, or faeces, from the body [Latin *excernere* to discharge] **> excretion** *n* **> excretory** *adj*

excruciating *adj* **1** unbearably painful; agonizing **2** hard to bear: *never had an afternoon passed with such excruciating slowness* [Latin *excruciare* to torture]

> excruciatingly *adv*

exculpate *vb* **-pating, -pated** to free from blame or guilt [Latin *ex* from + *culpa* fault]

excursion *n* a short outward and return journey, esp. for sightseeing, etc.; outing [Latin *excurrere* to run out]

excuse *n* **1** an explanation offered to justify an action which has been criticized or as a reason for not fulfilling an obligation, etc. ▷ *vb* **-cusing, -cused 2** to put forward a reason or justification for (an action, fault, or offending person) **3** to pardon (a person) or overlook (a fault) **4** to free (someone) from having to carry out a task, obligation, etc.: *a doctor's letter excusing him from games at school* **5** to allow to leave **6 be excused** *euphemistic* to go to the toilet **7 excuse me!** an expression used to catch someone's attention or to apologize for an interruption, disagreement, etc. [Latin *ex* out + *causa* cause, accusation] **> excusable** *adj*

ex-directory *adj Brit and NZ* not listed in a telephone directory by request

execrable (eks-sik-rab-bl) *adj* of very poor quality [see EXECRATE] **> execrably** *adv*

execrate *vb* **-crating, -crated 1** to feel and express loathing and hatred of (someone or something) **2** to curse (a person or thing) [Latin *exsecrari* to curse] **> execration** *n*

executable *adj computers* **1** (of a program) able to be run ▷ *n* **2** a file containing a program that will run as soon as it is opened

execute *vb* **-cuting, -cuted 1** to put (a condemned person) to death **2** to carry out or accomplish **3** to produce or create (a work of art) **4** *law* to render (a deed) effective, for example by signing it **5** to carry out the terms of (a contract, will, etc.) [Old French *executer*] **> executer** *n*

execution *n* **1** the act of executing **2** the carrying out or undergoing of a sentence of death **3** the manner in which something is performed; technique

executioner *n* a person whose job is to kill people who have been sentenced to death

executive *n* **1** a person or group responsible for the administration of a project or business **2** the branch of government responsible for carrying out laws, decrees, etc. ▷ *adj* **3** having the function of carrying out plans, orders, laws, etc., into effect: *the executive producer* **4** of or for executives: *the executive car park* **5** *informal* very expensive or exclusive: *executive cars*

executor *n law* a person appointed by someone to ensure that the conditions set out in his or her will are carried out **> executorial** *adj* **> executrix** *fem n*

exegesis (eks-sij-jee-siss) *n, pl* **-ses** (-seez) explanation of a text, esp. of the Bible [Greek *exēgeisthai* to interpret]

exemplar *n* **1** a person or thing to be copied; model **2** a typical specimen; example [Latin *exemplum* example]

exemplary *adj* **1** so good as to be an example worthy of imitation **2** (of a punishment) extremely harsh, so as to discourage others from committing a similar crime

exemplify *vb* **-fies, -fying, -fied 1** to show by example **2** to serve as an example of [Latin *exemplum* example + *facere* to make] **> exemplification** *n*

exempt *adj* **1** not subject to an obligation, tax, etc. ▷ *vb* **2** to release (someone) from an obligation, tax, etc. [Latin *exemptus* removed] **> exemption** *n*

exequies (eks-sik-weez) *pl n, sing* **-quy** funeral rites [Latin *exequiae*]

exercise *n* **1** physical exertion, esp. for training or keeping fit **2** an activity planned to achieve a particular purpose: *the group's meeting was mainly an exercise in mutual reassurance* **3** a set of movements, tasks, etc., designed to improve or test one's ability or fitness **4** the use or practice of (a right, power, or authority) **5** *military* a manoeuvre or simulated combat operation ▷ *vb* **-cising, -cised 6** to put into use; make use of: *we urge all governments involved to exercise restraint* **7** to take exercise or perform exercises **8** to practise using in order to develop

or train: *to exercise one's voice* **9** to worry or vex: *Western governments have been exercised by the need to combat international terrorism* **10** *military* to carry out simulated combat, manoeuvres, etc. [Latin *exercere* to drill] **> exerciser** *n*

exert *vb* **1** to use influence, authority, etc. forcefully or effectively **2 exert oneself** to make a special effort [Latin *exserere* to thrust out]

exertion *n* **1** effort or exercise, esp. physical effort: *the sudden exertion of running for a bus* **2** the act or an instance of using one's influence, powers, or authority: *the exertion of parental authority*

Exeter *n* a city in SW England, administrative centre of Devon; university (1955). Pop: 106 772 (2001)

exeunt (eks-see-unt) they go out: used as a stage direction [Latin]

exfoliate *vb* **-ating, -ated 1** to peel off in scales or layers **2** to remove dead cells from the skin by washing with a granular cosmetic preparation **> exfoliation** *n*

ex-gratia (eks-gray-sha) *adj* given as a favour where no legal obligation exists: *an ex-gratia payment* [New Latin: out of kindness]

exhale *vb* **-haling, -haled 1** to expel breath or smoke from the lungs; breathe out **2** to give off or be given off as gas, fumes, etc.: *the crater exhaled smoke* [Latin *exhalare*] **> exhalation** *n*

exhaust *vb* **1** to tire out **2** to use up totally **3** to discuss (a topic) so thoroughly that no more remains to be said ▷ *n* **4** gases ejected from an engine as waste products **5** the parts of an engine through which waste gases pass [Latin *exhaurire* to draw out] **> exhausted** *adj* **> exhaustible** *adj*

exhaustion *n* **1** extreme tiredness **2** the act of exhausting or state of being exhausted

exhaustive *adj* very thorough; comprehensive **> exhaustively** *adv*

exhibit *vb* **1** to display (a work of art) to the public **2** to show (a quality or feeling): *they exhibited extraordinary courage* ▷ *n* **3** an object exhibited to the public **4** *law* a document or object produced in court as evidence [Latin *exhibere* to hold forth] **> exhibitor** *n*

exhibition *n* **1** a public display of art, skills, etc. **2** the act of exhibiting or the state of being exhibited: *an exhibition of bad temper* **3 make an exhibition of oneself** to behave so foolishly that one attracts public attention

exhibitionism *n* **1** a compulsive desire to attract attention to oneself **2** a compulsive desire to expose one's genitals publicly **> exhibitionist** *n*

exhilarate *vb* **-rating, -rated** to make (someone) feel lively and cheerful [Latin *exhilarare*] **> exhilaration** *n*

exhilarating *adj* causing strong feelings of excitement and happiness

exhort *vb formal* to urge (someone) earnestly [Latin *exhortari*] **> exhortation** *n*

exhume (ig-zyume) *vb* **-huming, -humed** *formal* to dig up (something buried), esp. a corpse [Latin *ex* out + *humus* the ground] **> exhumation** *n*

exigency *n, pl* **-gencies** *formal* **1** an urgent demand or need **2** an emergency [Latin *exigere* to require] **> exigent** *adj*

exiguous *adj formal* scanty or meagre [Latin *exiguus*] **> exiguity** *n*

exile *n* **1** a prolonged, usually enforced absence from one's country **2** a person banished or living away from his or her country ▷ *vb* **-iling, -iled 3** to expel (someone) from his or her country; banish [Latin *exsilium*]

exist *vb* **1** to have being or reality: *does God exist?* **2** to only just be able to keep oneself alive, esp. because of poverty or hunger **3** to be living; live **4** to be present under specified conditions or in a specified place [Latin *exsistere* to step forth] **> existing** *adj*

existence *n* **1** the fact or state of being real, live, or actual **2** a way of life, esp. a poor or hungry one **3** everything that exists **> existent** *adj*

e

existential *adj* 1 of or relating to existence, esp. human existence 2 of or relating to existentialism

existentialism *n* a philosophical movement stressing personal experience and responsibility of the individual, who is seen as a free agent > **existentialist** *adj, n*

exit *n* 1 a way out 2 the act of going out 3 *theatre* the act of going offstage 4 *Brit and Austral* a point at which vehicles may leave or join a motorway ▷ *vb* **exiting, exited** 5 to go away or out; depart 6 *theatre* to go offstage: used as a stage direction: *exit bleeding from the room* [Latin *exire* to go out]

Exmoor *n* 1 a high moorland in SW England, in W Somerset and N Devon: chiefly grazing ground for Exmoor ponies, sheep, and red deer 2 a small stocky breed of pony with a fawn-coloured nose, originally from Exmoor

Exmouth *n* a town in SW England, in Devon, at the mouth of the River Exe: tourism, fishing. Pop: 32 972 (2001)

exocrine *adj* of or denoting a gland, such as the sweat gland, that discharges its product through a duct [Greek *exō* outside + *krinein* to separate]

exodus (eks-so-duss) *n* the departure of a large number of people [Greek *ex* out + *hodos* way]

Exodus *n Bible* the second book of the Old Testament, containing a description of the departure of the Israelites from Egypt

ex officio (eks off-fish-ee-oh) *adv, adj* by right of position or office [Latin]

exonerate *vb* **-ating, -ated** to clear (someone) of blame or a criminal charge [Latin *exonerare* to free from a burden] > **exoneration** *n*

exorbitant *adj* (of prices, demands, etc.) excessively great or high: *an exorbitant rent* [Latin *ex* out, away + *orbita* track] > **exorbitantly** *adv*

exorcize or **-cise** *vb* **-cizing, -cized** or **-cising, -cised** to expel (evil spirits) by prayers and religious rites [Greek *ex* out + *horkos* oath] > **exorcism** *n* > **exorcist** *n*

exoskeleton *n zoology* the protective or supporting structure covering the outside of the body of many animals, for example insects or crabs

exothermic *adj* (of a chemical reaction) involving or leading to the giving off of heat

exotic *adj* 1 having a strange allure or beauty 2 originating in a foreign country; not native ▷ *n* 3 a non-native plant [Greek *exō* outside] > **exotically** *adv*

exotica *pl n* exotic objects, esp. as a collection

expand *vb* 1 to make or become greater in extent, size, or scope 2 to spread out; unfold 3 **expand on** to go into more detail about (a story or subject) 4 to become increasingly relaxed, friendly, and talkative 5 *maths* to express a function or expression as the sum or product of terms [Latin *expandere* to spread out] > **expandable** *adj*

expanse *n* an uninterrupted wide area; stretch: *a large expanse of water*

expansible *adj* able to expand or be expanded

expansion *n* 1 the act of expanding 2 an increase or development, esp. in the activities of a company

expansionism *n* the practice of expanding the economy or territory of a country > **expansionist** *n, adj*

expansive *adj* 1 wide or extensive 2 friendly, open, and talkative > **expansiveness** *n*

expat *adj, n* short for **expatriate**

expatiate (iks-pay-shee-ate) *vb* **-ating, -ated expatiate on** *formal* to speak or write at length on (a subject) [Latin *exspatiari* to digress] > **expatiation** *n*

expatriate (eks-pat-ree-it) *adj* 1 living away from one's native country; *an expatriate American* 2 exiled ▷ *n* 3 a person living away from his or her native country 4 an exile [Latin *ex* out, away + *patria* native land] > **expatriation** *n*

expect *vb* 1 to regard as likely 2 to look forward to or be waiting for 3 to require (something) as an obligation: *he expects an answer by January* 4 **be expecting** *informal* to be pregnant [Latin *exspectare* to watch for]

expectancy *n* 1 something expected, esp. on the basis of a norm: *a life expectancy of 78* 2 anticipation or expectation

expectant *adj* 1 expecting or hopeful 2 a pregnant b married to or living with a woman who is pregnant: *an expectant father* > **expectantly** *adv*

expectation *n* 1 the state of expecting or of being expected 2 something looked forward to, whether feared or hoped for 3 belief that someone should behave in a particular way: *women with expectations of old-fashioned gallantry*

expectorant *med adj* 1 helping to bring up phlegm from the respiratory passages ▷ *n* 2 an expectorant medicine

expectorate *vb* **-rating, -rated** *formal* to cough up and spit out (phlegm from the respiratory passages) [Latin *expectorare* to drive from the breast, expel] > **expectoration** *n*

expediency or **expedience** *n, pl* **-encies** or **-ences** 1 the use of methods that are advantageous rather than fair or just 2 appropriateness or suitability

expedient (iks-pee-dee-ent) *n* 1 something that achieves a particular purpose: *income controls were used only as a short-term expedient* ▷ *adj* 2 useful or advantageous in a given situation: *they only talk about human rights when it is politically expedient* [Latin *expediens* setting free; see EXPEDITE]

expedite *vb* **-diting, -dited** *formal* 1 to hasten the progress of 2 to do quickly [Latin *expedire* to free the feet]

expedition *n* 1 an organized journey or voyage, esp. for exploration 2 the people and equipment comprising an expedition 3 a pleasure trip or excursion: *an expedition to the seaside* [Latin *expedire* to prepare, expedite] > **expeditionary** *adj*

expeditious *adj* done quickly and efficiently

expel *vb* **-pelling, -pelled** 1 to drive out with force 2 to dismiss from a school, club, etc., permanently [Latin *expellere*]

expend *vb* *formal* to spend or use up (time, energy, or money) [Latin *expendere* to weigh out, pay]

expendable *adj* 1 not worth preserving 2 able to be sacrificed to achieve an objective, esp. a military one

expenditure *n* 1 something expended, esp. money 2 the amount expended

expense *n* 1 a particular payment of money; expenditure 2 the amount of money needed to buy or do something; cost 3 **expenses** money spent in the performance of a job, etc. 4 something requiring money for its purchase or upkeep 5 **at the expense of** to the detriment of [Latin *expensus* weighed out]

expense account *n* 1 an arrangement by which an employee's expenses are refunded by his or her employer 2 a record of such expenses

expensive *adj* costing a great deal of money > **expensiveness** *n*

experience *n* 1 direct personal participation or observation of something: *his experience of prison life* 2 a particular incident, feeling, etc., that a person has undergone 3 accumulated knowledge, esp. of practical matters ▷ *vb* **-encing, -enced** 4 to participate in or undergo 5 to be moved by; feel [Latin *experiri* to prove]

experienced *adj* skilful or knowledgeable as a result of having done something many times before

experiential *adj philosophy* relating to or derived from experience

experiment *n* 1 a test or investigation to provide evidence for or against a theory: *a scientific experiment* 2 the trying out of a new idea or method ▷ *vb* 3 to carry out an experiment or experiments [Latin *experiri* to test] > **experimentation** *n* > **experimenter** *n*

experimental *adj* 1 relating to, based on, or having the nature of an experiment 2 trying out new ideas or methods > **experimentally** *adv*

expert n **1** a person who has extensive skill or knowledge in a particular field ▷ adj **2** skilful or knowledgeable **3** of, involving, or done by an expert [Latin *expertus* known by experience] ▶ **expertly** adv

expertise (eks-per-teez) n special skill, knowledge, or judgment [French]

expiate vb -ating, -ated formal to make amends for (a sin or wrongdoing) [Latin *expiare*] ▶ **expiation** n

expiration n **1** the finish of something; expiry **2** the act, process, or sound of breathing out ▶ **expiratory** adj

expire vb -piring, -pired **1** to finish or run out; come to an end **2** to breathe out air **3** to die [Latin *exspirare* to breathe out]

expiry n, pl -ries a coming to an end, esp. of the period of a contract

explain vb **1** to make something easily understandable, esp. by giving a clear and detailed account of it **2** explain oneself to justify or attempt to justify oneself by giving reasons for one's actions **3** explain away to offer excuses or reasons for (mistakes) [Latin *explanare* to flatten, make clear]

explanation n **1** the reason or reasons why a particular event or situation happened: *there is no reasonable explanation for her behaviour* **2** a detailed account or description: *a 90-minute explanation of his love of jazz*

explanatory adj serving or intended to serve as an explanation

expletive (iks-plee-tiv) n an exclamation or swearword expressing emotion rather than meaning [Latin *explere* to fill up]

explicable adj capable of being explained

explicate vb -cating, -cated formal to make clear; explain [Latin *explicare* to unfold] ▶ **explication** n

explicit adj **1** precisely and clearly expressed, leaving nothing to implication: *an explicit commitment to democracy* **2** leaving little to the imagination; graphically detailed: *the film contains some sexually explicit scenes* **3** (of a person) expressing something in a precise and clear way, so as to leave no doubt about what is meant [Latin *explicitus* unfolded] ▶ **explicitly** adv

explode vb -ploding, -ploded **1** to burst with great violence; blow up **2** (of a gas) to undergo a sudden violent expansion as a result of a fast chemical or nuclear reaction **3** to react suddenly or violently with emotion **4** (esp. of a population) to increase rapidly **5** to show (a theory, etc.) to be baseless [Latin *explodere* to drive off by clapping]

exploit vb **1** to take advantage of (a person or situation) for one's own ends **2** to make the best use of ▷ n **3** a notable deed or feat [Old French: accomplishment] ▶ **exploitation** n ▶ **exploiter** n

exploitative adj tending to take advantage of a person or situation for one's own ends

explore vb -ploring, -plored **1** to examine or investigate, esp. systematically **2** to travel into an unfamiliar region, esp. for scientific purposes [Latin *ex* out + *plorare* to cry aloud] ▶ **exploration** n ▶ **exploratory** or **explorative** adj ▶ **explorer** n

explosion n **1** an exploding **2** a violent release of energy resulting from a rapid chemical or nuclear reaction **3** a sudden or violent outburst of activity, noise, emotion, etc. **4** a rapid increase

explosive adj **1** able or likely to explode **2** potentially violent: *an explosive situation* ▷ n **3** a substance capable of exploding ▶ **explosiveness** n

expo n, pl -pos short for **exposition** (3)

exponent n **1** a person who advocates an idea, cause, etc.: *an exponent of free speech* **2** a person who is a skilful performer of some activity: *one of the greatest modern exponents of the blues* **3** maths a number placed as a superscript to another number indicating how many times the number is to be used as a factor [Latin *exponere* to expound]

exponential adj **1** maths of or involving numbers raised to an exponent **2** informal very rapid ▶ **exponentially** adv

export n **1** the sale of goods and services to a foreign country: *a ban on the export of arms* **2** exports goods or services sold to a foreign country ▷ vb **3** to sell (goods or services) or transport (goods) to a foreign country [Latin *exportare* to carry away] ▶ **exporter** n

expose vb -posing, -posed **1** to uncover (something previously covered) **2** to reveal the truth about (someone or something), esp. when it is shocking or scandalous: *an MP whose private life was recently exposed in the press* **3** to leave (a person or thing) unprotected in a potentially harmful situation: *workers were exposed to relatively low doses of radiation* **4** expose someone to to give someone an introduction to or experience of (something new) **5** photog to subject (a film) to light **6** expose oneself to display one's sexual organs in public [Latin *exponere* to set out]

exposé (iks-pose-ay) n the bringing of a scandal, crime, etc. to public notice [French]

exposed adj **1** not concealed; displayed for viewing: *the exposed soles of his shoes* **2** without shelter from the elements **3** vulnerable: *the enemy attacked our army's exposed flank*

exposition n **1** a systematic explanation of a subject **2** the act of expounding or setting out a viewpoint **3** a large public exhibition **4** music the first statement of the themes of a movement [Latin *exponere* to display]

expository adj explanatory

ex post facto adj having retrospective effect [Latin *ex* from + *post* afterwards + *factus* done]

expostulate vb -lating, -lated expostulate with to reason or argue with, esp. in order to dissuade or as a protest [Latin *expostulare* to require] ▶ **expostulation** n ▶ **expostulatory** adj

exposure n **1** the state of being exposed to, or lacking protection from, something: *the body cannot cope with sudden exposure to stress* **2** the revealing of the truth about someone or something, esp. when it is shocking or scandalous: *the exposure of a loophole in the tax laws* **3** the harmful effect on a person's body caused by lack of shelter from the weather, esp. the cold **4** appearance before the public, as on television **5** photog **a** the act of exposing a film to light **b** an area on a film that has been exposed **6** photog **a** the intensity of light falling on a film multiplied by the time for which it is exposed **b** a combination of lens aperture and shutter speed used in taking a photograph

exposure meter n photog an instrument for measuring the intensity of light so that suitable camera settings can be chosen

expound vb to explain (a theory, belief, etc.) in detail [Latin *exponere* to set forth]

express vb **1** to state (an idea or feeling) in words; utter: *two record labels have expressed an interest in signing the band* **2** to show (an idea or feeling): *his body and demeanour expressed distrust* **3** to indicate through a symbol or formula **4** to squeeze out (juice, etc.) **5** express oneself to communicate one's thoughts or ideas ▷ adj **6** explicitly stated **7** deliberate and specific: *she came with the express purpose of causing a row* **8** of or for rapid transportation of people, mail, etc. ▷ n **9** a fast train stopping at only a few stations **10** chiefly US and Canad a system for sending mail rapidly ▷ adv **11** using a system for rapid transportation of people, mail, etc.: *please send this letter express; it's very urgent!* [Latin *exprimere* to force out] ▶ **expressible** adj

expression n **1** the transforming of ideas into words **2** a showing of emotion without words **3** communication of emotion through music, painting, etc. **4** a look on the face that indicates mood or emotion **5** a particular phrase used conventionally to express something **6** maths a variable, function, or some combination of these ▶ **expressionless** adj

expressionism n an early 20th-century artistic and literary movement which sought to express emotions

rather than to represent the physical world
> **expressionist** n, adj

expression mark n music one of a set of symbols indicating how a piece or passage is to be performed

expressive adj 1 of or full of expression 2 expressive of showing or suggesting: *looks expressive of hatred and revenge*

expressly adv 1 definitely 2 deliberately and specifically

expressway n chiefly US a motorway

expropriate vb -ating, -ated formal (of a government or other official body) to take (money or property) away from its owners [Medieval Latin *expropriare* to deprive of possessions] > **expropriation** n > **expropriator** n

expulsion n the act of expelling or the fact of being expelled [Latin *expellere* to expel] > **expulsive** adj

expunge (iks-sponge) vb -punging, -punged formal to remove all traces of: *he had tried to expunge his failure from his mind* [Latin *expungere* to blot out]

expurgate (eks-per-gate) vb -gating, -gated to amend (a piece of writing) by removing sections thought to be offensive [Latin *expurgare* to clean out] > **expurgation** n > **expurgator** n

exquisite adj 1 extremely beautiful or attractive 2 showing unusual delicacy and craftsmanship 3 sensitive or discriminating: *exquisite manners* 4 intensely felt: *exquisite joy* [Latin *exquisitus* excellent] > **exquisitely** adv

ex-serviceman or fem **ex-servicewoman** n, pl -men or -women a person who has served in the armed forces

extant adj still in existence; surviving [Latin *exstans* standing out]

> **USAGE** *Extant* is sometimes wrongly used simply to say that something exists, without any connotation of survival: *plutonium is perhaps the deadliest element in existence* (not *the deadliest element extant*).

extemporaneous adj spoken or performed without preparation > **extemporaneously** adv

extempore (iks-temp-or-ee) adj, adv without planning or preparation [Latin *ex tempore* instantaneously]

extemporize or -**rise** vb -rizing, -rized or -rising, -rised to perform or speak without preparation
> **extemporization** or -**risation** n > **extemporizer** or -**riser** n

extend vb 1 to make bigger or longer than before: *they extended the house by building a conservatory* 2 to reach to a certain distance or in a certain direction: *the suburbs extend for many miles* 3 to last for a certain time: *in Norway maternity leave extends to 52 weeks* 4 to broaden the meaning or scope of: *the law was extended to ban all guns* 5 to make something exist or be valid for longer than before: *her visa was extended for three months* 6 to present or offer: *a tradition of extending asylum to refugees* 7 to straighten or stretch out (part of the body): *she extended a hand in welcome* 8 **extend oneself** to make use of all one's ability or strength, often because forced to: *she'll have to really extend herself if she wants to win* [Latin *extendere* to stretch out] > **extendable** adj

extended family n a social unit in which parents, children, grandparents, and other relatives live as a family unit

extensible adj capable of being extended

extension n 1 a room or rooms added to an existing building 2 a development that includes or affects more people or things than before: *an extension of democracy within the EU* 3 an additional telephone connected to the same line as another 4 an extra period of time in which something continues to exist or be valid: *an extension of the contract for another 2 years* ▷ adj 5 denoting something that can be extended or that extends another object: *an extension ladder* 6 of or relating to the provision of teaching and other facilities by a school or college to people who cannot attend full-time courses

extensive adj 1 covering a large area: *extensive moorland*

2 very great in effect: *the bomb caused extensive damage* 3 containing many details, ideas, or items on a particular subject: *an extensive collection of modern art* > **extensively** adv

extensor n any muscle that stretches or extends an arm leg, or other part of the body

extent n 1 the length, area, or size of something 2 the scale or seriousness of a situation or difficulty: *the extent of the damage* 3 the degree or amount to which something applies: *to a certain extent that's true*

extenuate vb -ating, -ated formal to make (an offence or fault) less blameworthy, by giving reasons that partly excuse it [Latin *extenuare* to make thin] > **extenuating** ad > **extenuation** n

exterior n 1 a part or surface that is on the outside 2 the outward appearance of a person: *Jim's grumpy exterior concealed a warm heart* 3 a film scene shot outside ▷ adj 4 of, situated on, or suitable for the outside 5 coming or acting from outside or abroad [Latin comparative of *exterus* on the outside]

exterior angle n an angle of a polygon contained between one side extended and the adjacent side

exterminate vb -nating, -nated to destroy (a group or type of people, animals, or plants) completely [Latin *exterminare* to drive away] > **extermination** n > **exterminator** n

external adj 1 of, situated on, or suitable for the outside: *there was damage to the house's external walls* 2 coming or acting from outside: *most ill health is caused by external influences* 3 of or involving foreign nations: *Hong Kong's external trade* 4 anatomy situated on or near the outside of the body: *the external ear* 5 brought into an organization to do a task which must be done impartially, esp. one involving testing or checking: *external examiners* 6 of or relating to someone taking a university course, but not attending a university: *an external degree* ▷ n 7 **externals** obvious circumstances or aspects, esp. superficial ones: *despite the war, the externals of life in the city remain normal* [Latin *externus*] > **externality** n > **externally** adv

externalize or -**ise** vb -izing, -ized or -ising, -ised to express (thoughts or feelings) in words or actions > **externalization** or -**isation** n

extinct adj 1 (of an animal or plant species) having died out 2 no longer in existence, because of social changes: *shipbuilding is virtually extinct in Scotland* 3 (of a volcano) no longer liable to erupt [Latin *exstinguere* to extinguish]

extinction n 1 the dying out of a plant or animal species 2 the end of a particular way of life or type of activity

extinguish vb 1 to put out (a fire or light) 2 to remove or destroy entirely [Latin *exstinguere*] > **extinguishable** adj > **extinguisher** n

extirpate (eks-ter-pate) vb -pating, -pated to remove or destroy completely: *the Romans attempted to extirpate the Celtic religion* [Latin *exstirpare* to root out] > **extirpation** n

extol or US **extoll** vb -tolling, -tolled to praise lavishly [Latin *extollere* to elevate]

extort vb to obtain (money or favours) by intimidation, violence, or the misuse of authority [Latin *extorquere* to wrest away] > **extortion** n

extortionate adj (of prices, profits, etc.) much higher than is fair > **extortionately** adv

extra adj 1 more than is usual, expected or needed; additional ▷ n 2 a person or thing that is additional 3 something for which an additional charge is made 4 films a person temporarily engaged, usually for crowd scenes 5 cricket a run not scored from the bat 6 an additional edition of a newspaper ▷ adv 7 unusually; exceptionally [probably from *extraordinary*]

extra- prefix outside or beyond an area or scope: *extracellular; extraterrestrial* [Latin]

extract vb 1 to pull out or uproot by force 2 to remove from a container 3 to derive (pleasure, information, etc. from some source 4 informal to obtain (money, information, etc.) from someone who is not willing to provide it: *a confession extracted by force* **5** to obtain (a substance) from a material or the ground by mining, distillation, digestion, etc.: *oil extracted from shale* **6** to copy out (an article, passage, etc.) from a publication ▷ *n* **7** something extracted, such as a passage from a book, etc. **8** a preparation containing the concentrated essence of a substance [Latin *extrahere* to draw out] **>extractive** *adj* **>extractor** *n*

> **USAGE** *Extract* is sometimes wrongly used where *extricate* would be better: *he will find it difficult extricating* (not *extracting*) *himself from this situation.*

extraction *n* **1** the act or an instance of extracting **2** the removal of a tooth by a dentist: *few patients need an extraction* **3** the origin or ancestry of a person: *he is of German extraction*

extractor fan *n* a fan used to remove stale air from a room

extracurricular *adj* not part of the normal courses taken by students: *her free time is devoted to extracurricular duties*

extradite *vb* **-diting, -dited** to hand over (an alleged offender) to the country where the crime took place for trial: *an agreement to extradite him to Hong Kong* [Latin *ex* away + *traditio* a handing over] **>extraditable** *adj* **>extradition** *n*

extrajudicial *adj* **1** outside the ordinary course of legal proceedings: *extrajudicial evidence* **2** beyond the jurisdiction or authority of the court: *an extrajudicial opinion*

extramarital *adj* occurring between a married person and a person other than his or her spouse: *an extramarital affair*

extramural *adj* connected with but outside the normal courses of a university or college [Latin *extra* beyond + *murus* wall]

extraneous (iks-**train**-ee-uss) *adj* not essential or relevant to the situation or subject being considered [Latin *extraneus* external]

extraordinary *adj* **1** very unusual or surprising: *the extraordinary sight of my grandfather wearing a dress* **2** having some special or extreme quality: *an extraordinary first novel* **3** (of a meeting, ambassador, etc.) specially called or appointed to deal with one particular topic [Latin *extraordinarius* beyond what is usual] **>extraordinarily** *adv*

extraordinary rendition *n* the process by which a country seizes a terrorist suspect and then transports him or her for interrogation to a country where due process of law is unlikely to be respected

extrapolate (iks-**trap**-a-late) *vb* **-lating, -lated 1** to infer (something not known) from the known facts, using logic and reason **2** *maths* to estimate (the value of a function or measurement) beyond the known values, by the extension of a curve [EXTRA- + -*polate*, as in *interpolate*] **>extrapolation** *n*

extrasensory *adj* of or relating to extrasensory perception

extrasensory perception *n* the supposed ability to obtain information without the use of normal senses of sight, hearing, etc.

extravagant *adj* **1** spending more than is reasonable or affordable **2** costing more than is reasonable or affordable: *an extravagant gift* **3** going beyond usual or reasonable limits: *extravagant expectations* **4** (of behaviour or gestures) extreme, esp. in order to make a particular impression: *an extravagant display of affection* **5** very elaborate and impressive: *extravagant costumes* [Latin *extra* beyond + *vagari* to wander] **>extravagance** *n*

extravaganza *n* **1** an elaborate and lavish entertainment **2** any fanciful display, literary composition, etc. [Italian: extravagance]

extravert *adj, n* same as **extrovert**

Extremadura *n* a region of W Spain: arid and sparsely populated except in the valleys of the Tagus and Guardiana rivers. Area: 41 593 sq km (16 059 sq miles)

extreme *adj* **1** of a high or the highest degree or intensity **2** exceptionally severe or unusual: *people can survive extreme conditions* **3** (of an opinion, political group, etc.) beyond the limits regarded as acceptable; fanatical **4** farthest or outermost ▷ *n* **5** either of the two limits of a scale or range **6 go to extremes** to be unreasonable in speech or action **7 in the extreme** to the highest or furthest degree: *the effect was dramatic in the extreme* [Latin *extremus* outermost] **>extremely** *adv*

extreme sport *n* any of various sports with a high risk of injury or death

extreme unction *n* RC Church a former name for anointing of the sick

extremist *n* **1** a person who favours or uses extreme or violent methods, esp. to bring about political change ▷ *adj* **2** holding extreme opinions or using extreme methods **>extremism** *n*

extremity *n, pl* **-ties 1** the farthest point **2** an unacceptable or extreme nature or degree: *the extremity of his views alienated other nationalists* **3** an extreme condition, such as misfortune **4 extremities** hands and feet

extricate *vb* **-cating, -cated** to free from a difficult or complicated situation or place [Latin *extricare*] **>extricable** *adj* **>extrication** *n*

> **USAGE** See at **extract**.

extrinsic *adj* **1** not an integral or essential part **2** originating or acting from outside [Latin *exter* outward + *secus* alongside] **>extrinsically** *adv*

extroversion *n psychol* the directing of one's interests outwards, esp. towards making social contacts

extrovert *adj* **1** lively and outgoing **2** *psychol* concerned more with external reality than inner feelings ▷ *n* **3** a person who has these characteristics [*extro-* (variant of EXTRA-, contrasting with *intro-*) + Latin *vertere* to turn] **>extroverted** *adj*

extrude *vb* **-truding, -truded 1** to squeeze or force out **2** to produce (moulded sections of plastic, metal, etc.) by forcing through a shaped die [Latin *extrudere* to thrust out] **>extruded** *adj* **>extrusion** *n*

exuberant *adj* **1** full of vigour and high spirits **2** (of vegetation) growing thickly; flourishing [Latin *exuberans* abounding] **>exuberance** *n*

exude *vb* **-uding, -uded 1** (of a liquid or smell) to seep or flow out slowly and steadily **2** to seem to have (a quality or feeling) to a great degree: *the Chancellor exuded confidence* [Latin *exsudare*] **>exudation** *n*

exult *vb* to be joyful or jubilant [Latin *exsultare* to jump for joy] **>exultation** *n* **>exultant** *adj*

> **USAGE** See at **exalt**.

Eyam *n* a village in N central England, in Derbyshire. When plague reached the village in 1665 the inhabitants, led by the Rev. Mompesson, isolated themselves to prevent it spreading further: as a result most of them died, including Mompesson's family

eye *n* **1** the organ of sight in humans and animals **2** the external part of an eye, often including the area around it **3** (*often pl*) the ability to see or record what is happening: *the eyes of an entire nation were upon us* **4** a look, glance, or gaze **5** attention or observation: *his new shirt caught my eye* **6** the ability to judge or appreciate something: *his shrewd eye for talent* **7** (*often pl*) opinion, judgment, or authority: *in the eyes of the law* **8** a dark spot on a potato from which new shoots can grow **9** a small hole, such as the one at the blunt end of a sewing needle **10** a small area of calm in the centre of a storm, hurricane, or tornado **11 all eyes** *informal* acutely vigilant

12 an eye for an eye justice consisting of an equivalent action to the original wrong or harm **13 have eyes for** to be interested in **14 in one's mind's eye** imagined or remembered vividly **15 in the public eye** exposed to public curiosity **16 keep an eye on** to take care of **17 keep an eye open** *or* **out for** to watch with special attention for **18 keep one's eyes peeled** *or* **skinned** to watch vigilantly **19 look someone in the eye** to look openly and without embarrassment at someone **20 make eyes at someone** to look at someone in an obviously attracted manner **21 more than meets the eye** hidden motives, meanings, or facts **22 my eye!** *old-fashioned, informal* nonsense! **23 see eye to eye with** to agree with **24 set** *or* **lay** *or* **clap eyes on** to see: *I never laid eyes on him again* **25 turn a blind eye to** *or* **close one's eyes to** to pretend not to notice **26 up to one's eyes in** extremely busy with **27 with an eye to** with the intention of **28 with one's eyes open** in full knowledge of all the facts ▷ *vb* **eyeing** *or* **eying, eyed 29** to look at carefully or warily ► See also **eye up** [Old English *ēage*] ⟩ **eyeless** *adj* ⟩ **eyelike** *adj*

eyeball *n* **1** the entire ball-shaped part of the eye **2 eyeball to eyeball** in close confrontation ▷ *vb* **3** *slang* to stare at

eyebrow *n* **1** the bony ridge over each eye **2** the arch of hair on this ridge **3 raise an eyebrow** to show doubt or disapproval

eye-catching *adj* very striking and tending to catch people's attention ⟩ **eye-catcher** *n*

eye dog *n* NZ a dog trained to control sheep by staring at them

eyeful *n* **1** *slang* a good look at or view of something **2** *slang* an attractive sight, esp. a woman **3** an amount of liquid, dust, etc., that has got into someone's eye

eyeglass *n* a lens for aiding defective vision

eyelash *n* any of the short hairs that grow from the edge of the eyelids

eyelet *n* **1** a small hole for a lace or cord to be passed through **2** a small metal ring reinforcing such a hole

eyelevel *adj* level with a person's eyes: *an eyelevel oven*

eyelid *n* either of the two folds of skin that cover an eye when it is closed

eyeliner *n* a cosmetic used to outline the eyes

eye-opener *n informal* something startling or revealing

eyepiece *n* the lens in a microscope, telescope, etc., into which the person using it looks

eye shadow *n* a coloured cosmetic worn on the upper eyelids

eyesight *n* the ability to see: *poor eyesight*

eyesore *n* something very ugly

eyestrain *n* fatigue or irritation of the eyes, caused by tiredness or a failure to wear glasses

eyetooth *n*, *pl* **-teeth 1** either of the two canine teeth in the upper jaw **2 give one's eyeteeth for** to go to any lengths to achieve or obtain (something)

eye up *vb informal* to look at (someone) in a way that indicates sexual interest

eyewash *n* **1** a lotion for the eyes **2** *informal* nonsense; rubbish

eyewitness *n* a person present at an event who can describe what happened

Eyjafjallajökull *n* a cone-shaped ice cap in south Iceland that covers an active volcano. The volcano's eruption in 2010 resulted in large high-altitude clouds of volcanic ash that caused major disruption to European passenger air traffic. Height: 1666 m (5466 ft)

Eyre[1] *n* **Lake Eyre** a shallow salt lake or salt flat in NE central South Australia, about 11 m (35 ft) below sea level, divided into two areas (North and South); it usually contains little or no water. Maximum area: 9600 sq km (3700 sq miles) [C19: named after Edward John EYRE]

Eyre[2] *n* **1 Edward John**. 1815–1901, British explorer and colonial administrator. He was governor of Jamaica (1864–66) until his authorization of 400 executions to suppress an uprising led to his recall **2 Sir Richard**. born 1943, British theatre director: director of the Royal National Theatre (1988–97)

Eyre Peninsula *n* a peninsula of South Australia, between the Great Australian Bight and Spencer Gulf [C19: named after Edward John EYRE]

eyrie *n* **1** the nest of an eagle, built in a high inaccessible place **2** any high isolated place [Latin *area* open field, hence, nest]

Eysenck *n* **Hans Jürgen**. 1916–97, British psychologist, born in Germany, who developed a dimensional theory of personality that stressed the influence of heredity

Ff

f¹ *physics* frequency

f², f/ *or* **f:** f-number

F **1** *music* the fourth note of the scale of C major **2** Fahrenheit **3** farad(s) **4** *chem* fluorine **5** *physics* force **6** franc(s)

f. *or* **F.** **1** fathom(s) **2** female **3** *grammar* feminine **4** (*pl* **ff.**) following (page)

fa *n music* same as **fah**

FA (in Britain) Football Association

F.A.B. *interj Brit informal* an expression of agreement to, or acknowledgement of, a command [from British television series, *Thunderbirds*]

Fabergé *n* Peter Carl. 1846–1920, Russian goldsmith and jeweller, known for the golden Easter eggs and other ornate and fanciful objects that he created for the Russian and other royal families

Fabian (fay-bee-an) *adj* **1** of the Fabian Society, which aims to establish socialism gradually and democratically ▷ *n* **2** a member of the Fabian Society [after FABIUS] **›** **Fabianism** *n*

Fabius Maximus *n* full name *Quintus Fabius Maximus Verrucosus*, called *Cunctator* (the delayer). died 203 BC, Roman general and statesman. As commander of the Roman army during the Second Punic War, he withstood Hannibal by his strategy of harassing the Carthaginians while avoiding a pitched battle

fable *n* **1 a** a short story, often one with animals as characters, that illustrates a moral **2** an unlikely story which is usually untrue **3** a story about mythical characters or events [Latin *fabula* story]

fabled *adj* well-known from anecdotes and stories rather than experience

Fablon *n trademark* a brand of adhesive-backed plastic used for covering surfaces

Fabre *n* JeanHenri. 1823–1915, French entomologist; author of many works on insect life, remarkable for their vivid and minute observation, esp. *Souvenirs Entomologiques* (1879–1907). Nobel prize for literature 1910

fabric *n* **1** any cloth made from yarn or fibres by weaving or knitting **2** the structure that holds a system together: *the fabric of society* **3** the walls, floor, and roof of a building [Latin *faber* craftsman]

fabricate *vb* **-cating, -cated** **1** to invent (a story or lie): *fabricated reports about the opposition* **2** to make or build [Latin *fabrica* workshop] **›** **fabrication** *n*

Fabry *n* Charles. 1867–1945, French physicist: discovered ozone in the upper atmosphere

fabulous *adj* **1** *informal* extremely good **2** almost unbelievable: *a city of fabulous wealth* **3** told of in fables and legends: *a fabulous horned creature* [Latin *fabulosus* celebrated in fable] **›** **fabulously** *adv*

facade (fass-sahd) *n* **1** the front of a building **2** a front or deceptive outer appearance

face *n* **1** the front of the head from the forehead to the lower jaw **2 a** one's expression: *as his eyes met hers his face sobered* **b** a distorted expression to show disgust or

defiance: *she was pulling a face at him* **3** the front or main side of an object, building, etc. **4** the surface of a clock or watch that has the numbers or hands on it **5** the functional side of an object, such as a tool or playing card **6** the exposed area of a mine from which coal or metal can be mined **7** *Brit slang* a well-known or important person **8** **in the face of** in spite of: *a determined character in the face of adversity* **9** **lose face** to lose one's credibility **10** **on the face of it** to all appearances **11** **put a good** *or* **brave face on something** to maintain a cheerful appearance despite misfortune **12** **save face** to keep one's good reputation **13** **set one's face against** to oppose with determination **14** **to someone's face** directly and openly ▷ *vb* **facing, faced** **15** to look towards **16** to be opposite **17** to be confronted by: *they were faced with the prospect of high inflation* **18** to provide with a surface of a different material ▸ See also **face up to** [Latin *facies* form]

Facebook *n* a popular social networking site

face card *n* a playing card showing a king, queen, or jack

faceless *adj* without individual identity or character: *faceless government officials*

face-lift *n* **1** cosmetic surgery for tightening sagging skin and smoothing wrinkles on the face **2** an outward improvement designed to give a more modern appearance: *the stadium was given a face-lift*

facer *n Brit old-fashioned, informal* a difficulty or problem

face-saving *adj* preventing damage to one's reputation **›** **face-saver** *n*

facet *n* **1** an aspect of something, such as a personality **2** any of the surfaces of a cut gemstone [French *facette* little face]

facetious (fass-see-shuss) *adj* joking, or trying to be amusing, esp. at inappropriate times [Old French *facetie* witticism] **›** **facetiously** *adv*

face up to *vb* to accept (an unpleasant fact or reality)

face value *n* apparent worth or meaning: *only a fool would take it at face value*

facia (fay-shee-a) *n, pl* **-ciae** (-shee-ee) same as **fascia**

facial *adj* **1** of the face ▷ *n* **2** a beauty treatment for the face **›** **facially** *adv*

facile (fass-ile) *adj* **1** (of a remark, argument, etc.) overly simple and showing lack of real thought **2** easily performed or achieved: *a facile winner of his only race this year* [Latin *facilis* easy]

facilitate *vb* **-tating, -tated** to make easier the progress of: *the agreement helped facilitate trade between the countries* **›** **facilitation** *n*

facility *n, pl* **-ties** **1** **facilities** the means or equipment needed for an activity: *leisure and shopping facilities* **2** the ability to do things easily and well **3** skill or ease: *grown human beings can forget with remarkable facility* [Latin *facilis* easy]

facing *n* **1** a piece of material used esp. to conceal the seam of a garment **2** **facings** contrasting collar and cuffs on a jacket **3** an outer layer of material applied to the surface of a wall

facsimile (fak-sim-ill-ee) *n* **1** an exact copy **2** same as **fax** (1, 2) [Latin *fac simile!* make something like it!]

fact *n* **1** an event or thing known to have happened or existed **2** a truth that can be proved from experience or observation **3** a piece of information **4 after** or **before the fact** *criminal law* after or before the commission of the offence **5 as a matter of fact** or **in fact** in reality or actuality **6 fact of life** an inescapable truth, esp. an unpleasant one ▶ See also **facts of life** [Latin *factum* something done]

faction[1] *n* **1** a small group of people within a larger body, but differing from it in certain aims and ideas **2** strife within a group [Latin *factio* a making] **> factional** *adj*

faction[2] *n* a dramatized presentation of actual events [blend of FACT + FICTION]

factious *adj* inclined to quarrel and cause divisions: *a factious political party is unelectable*

> **USAGE** See at **fractious**.

factitious *adj* artificial rather than natural [Latin *facticius*]

factor *n* **1** an element that contributes to a result: *reliability was an important factor in the success of the car* **2** *maths* any whole number that will divide exactly into a given number, for example 2 and 3 are factors of 6 **3** a quantity by which an amount is multiplied or divided to become that number of times bigger or smaller: *production increased by a factor of 3* **4** *med* any of several substances that participate in the clotting of blood: *factor VIII* **5** a level on a scale of measurement: *suntan oil with a factor of 5* **6** (in Scotland) the manager of an estate [Latin: one who acts]

> **USAGE** Factor (sense 1) should only be used to refer to something which contributes to a result. It should not be used to refer to a part of something such as a plan or arrangement; instead a word such as *component* or *element* should be used.

factorial *maths n* **1** the product of all the whole numbers from one to a given whole number ▷ *adj* **2** of factorials or factors

factorize or **-rise** *vb* **-rizing, -rized** or **-rising, -rised** *maths* to resolve (a whole number) into factors **> factorization** or **-risation** *n*

factory *n, pl* **-ries** a building where goods are manufactured in large quantities [Late Latin *factorium*, from *facere* to make]

factory farm *n Brit, Austral and NZ* a farm in which animals are given foods that increase the amount of meat, eggs, or milk they yield **> factory farming** *n*

factory ship *n* a vessel that processes fish supplied by a fleet

factotum *n* a person employed to do all kinds of work [Latin *fac!* do! + *totum* all]

facts of life *pl n* the details of sexual behaviour and reproduction

factual *adj* concerning facts rather than opinions or theories: *a factual report* **> factually** *adv*

faculty *n, pl* **-ties** **1** one of the powers of the mind or body, such as memory, sight, or hearing **2** any ability or power, either inborn or acquired: *his faculties of reasoning were considerable* **3 a** a department within a university or college **b** its staff **c** *chiefly US and Canad* all the teaching staff of a university, school, or college [Latin *facultas* capability]

fad *n informal* **1** an intense but short-lived fashion: *the skateboard fad* **2** a personal whim [origin unknown] **> faddish** *adj*

Fadden *n* Sir Arthur William. 1895–1973, Australian statesman; prime minister of Australia (1941)

faddy *adj* **-dier, -diest** unreasonably fussy, particularly about food

fade *vb* **fading, faded** **1** to lose brightness, colour, or strength **2 fade away** or **out** to vanish slowly [Middle English *fade* dull]

fade in or **fade out** *vb* (of vision or sound in a film or broadcast) to increase or decrease gradually

faeces or *especially US* **feces** (fee-seez) *pl n* bodily waste matter discharged through the anus [Latin: dregs] **> faecal** or *especially US* **fecal** (fee-kl) *adj*

Faenza *n* a city in N Italy, in Emilia-Romagna: famous in the 15th and 16th centuries for its majolica earthenware, esp. faïence. Pop: 53 641 (2001)

Faeroes or **Faroes** *pl n* a group of 21 basalt islands in the North Atlantic between Iceland and the Shetland Islands: a self-governing community within the kingdom of Denmark; fishing. Capital: Thorshavn. Pop: 49 709 (2013 est). Area: 1400 sq km (540 sq miles). Also called: **Faeroe Islands, Faroe Islands**

Faeroese or **Faroese** (fair-oh-eez) *adj* **1** of or relating to the Faeroes or their inhabitants ▷ *n* **2** (*pl* **-ese**) a native or inhabitant of the Faeroes **3** the language of the Faeroes

faff about *vb Brit and S African informal* to dither or fuss [origin unknown]

fag[1] *n* **1** *informal* a boring or tiring task: *weeding was a fag* **2** *Brit* (esp. formerly) a young public school boy who performs menial chores for an older boy ▷ *vb* **fagging, fagged** **3** *Brit* to do menial chores in a public school [origin unknown]

fag[2] *n slang* a cigarette [origin unknown]

fag[3] *n offensive, slang, chiefly US and Canad* short for **faggot**[2]

fag end *n* **1** the last and worst part: *another dull game at the fag end of the football season* **2** *Brit and NZ informal* the stub of a cigarette

fagged *adj informal* exhausted by hard work. Also: **fagged out**

faggot[1] or *especially US* **fagot** *n* **1** *Brit, Austral and NZ* a ball of chopped liver bound with herbs and bread **2** a bundle of sticks [from Old French]

faggot[2] *n offensive, slang* a male homosexual [special use of FAGGOT[1]]

fah *n music* (in tonic sol-fa) the fourth note of any ascending major scale

Fahd ibn Abdul Aziz *n* 1923–2005, king of Saudi Arabia (1982–2005)

Fahrenheit[1] (far-ren-hite) *adj* of or measured according to the scale of temperature in which 32° represents the melting point of ice and 212° the boiling point of water

Fahrenheit[2] *n* Gabriel Daniel. 1686–1736, German physicist, who invented the mercury thermometer and devised the temperature scale that bears his name

Faial or **Fayal** *n* an island in the central Azores archipelago. Chief town: Horta. Area: 171 sq km (66 sq miles)

Faidherbe *n* Louis Léon César. 1818–89, French soldier and governor of Senegal (1854–65); founder of Dakar

faïence (fie-ence) *n* tin-glazed earthenware [*Faenza*, N Italy, where made]

fail *vb* **1** to be unsuccessful in an attempt **2** to stop operating **3** to judge or be judged as being below the officially accepted standard required in a course or examination **4** to prove disappointing or useless to (someone): *the government has failed the homeless* **5** to neglect or be unable (to do something): *he failed to repair the car* **6** to go bankrupt ▷ *n* **7** a failure to attain the required standard **8 without fail a** regularly or without exception: *use this shampoo once a week without fail* **b** definitely: *they agreed to enforce the embargo without fail* [Latin *fallere* to disappoint]

failing *n* **1** a weak point ▷ *prep* **2 failing that** alternatively: *your doctor will normally be able to advise you or, failing that, one of the self-help agencies*

fail-safe *adj* **1** designed to return to a safe condition in the event of a failure or malfunction **2** safe from failure

failure n **1** the act or an instance of failing **2** someone or something that is unsuccessful: *he couldn't help but regard his own son as a failure* **3** the fact of something required or expected not being done or not happening: *his failure to appear at the meeting* **4** a halt in normal operation: *heart failure* **5** a decline or loss of something: *crop failure* **6** the fact of not reaching the required standard in an examination or test

fain *adv* old-fashioned gladly or willingly [Old English *fægen*]

faint *adj* **1** lacking clarity, brightness, or volume: *her voice was very faint* **2** feeling dizzy or weak **3** lacking conviction or force: *a faint attempt to smile* ▷ *vb* **4** to lose consciousness ▷ *n* **5** a sudden loss of consciousness [Old French *faindre* to be idle] > **faintly** *adv*

faint-hearted *adj* lacking courage and confidence

fair[1] *adj* **1** reasonable and just: *a move towards fair trade* **2** in agreement with rules **3** light in colour: *her fair skin* **4** old-fashioned young and beautiful: *a fair maiden* **5** quite good: *a fair attempt at making a soufflé* **6** quite large: *they made a fair amount of money* **7** (of the tide or wind) favourable to the passage of a ship or plane **8** fine or cloudless **9** fair and square in a correct or just way ▷ *adv* **10** in a fair way **11** absolutely or squarely: *he was caught fair off his guard* [Old English *fæger*] > **fairness** n

fair[2] n **1** a travelling entertainment with sideshows, rides, and amusements **2** an exhibition of goods produced by a particular industry to promote business: *the Frankfurt book fair* [Latin *feriae* holidays]

Fairbanks[1] n a city in central Alaska, at the terminus of the Alaska Highway. Pop: 30 970 (2003 est)

Fairbanks[2] n **1** Douglas (Elton), real name *Julius Ullman*. 1883–1939, US film actor and producer **2** his son, Douglas, Jnr. 1909–2000, US film actor

fair copy n a neat copy, without mistakes or alterations, of a piece of writing

Fairfax n Thomas, 3rd Baron Fairfax. 1612–71, English general and statesman: commanded the Parliamentary army (1645–50), defeating Charles I at Naseby (1645). He was instrumental in restoring Charles II to the throne (1660)

fair game n a person regarded as a justifiable target for criticism or ridicule

fairground n an open space used for a fair

fairing n a metal structure fitted around parts of an aircraft, car, etc., to reduce drag [*fair* to streamline]

Fair Isle n an intricate multicoloured knitted pattern [after one of the Shetland Islands where this type of pattern originated]

fairly *adv* **1** to a moderate degree or extent: *in the Philippines labour is fairly cheap* **2** to a great degree or extent: *the folder fairly bulged with documents* **3** as deserved: *the pound was fairly valued against the Deutschmark*

fair play n a conventional standard of honourable behaviour

fair sex n the fair sex old-fashioned women collectively

fair trade n the practice of buying goods from producers in the developing world at a guaranteed price

fairway n **1** (on a golf course) the mown areas between tees and greens **2** nautical a part of a river or sea on which ships may sail

Fairweather n Mount Fairweather a mountain in W North America, on the border between Alaska and British Columbia. Height: 4663 m (15 300 ft)

fair-weather *adj* not reliable in difficult situations: *a fair-weather friend*

fairy n, pl fairies **1** an imaginary supernatural being with magical powers **2** offensive, slang a male homosexual [Old French *faerie* fairyland, from *feie* fairy]

fairy bread n Austral and NZ slices of white bread covered with small beads of brightly coloured sugar, served as a children's snack

fairy floss n Austral a light fluffy mass of spun sugar, held on a stick. Also called: **candy floss**

fairy godmother n a generous friend who appears unexpectedly and offers help in time of trouble

fairyland n **1** an imaginary place where fairies live **2** an enchanted or wonderful place

fairy lights pl n small coloured electric bulbs used as decoration, esp. on a Christmas tree

fairy penguin n a small penguin with a bluish head and back, found on the Australian coast

fairy ring n a ring of dark grass caused by fungi

fairy tale or **fairy story** n **1** a story about fairies or magical events **2** a highly improbable account: *his report was little more than a fairy tale* ▷ *adj* **fairy-tale 3** of or like a fairy tale: *a fairy-tale wedding* **4** highly improbable: *a fairy-tale account of his achievements*

Faisal I or **Feisal I** n 1885–1933, king of Syria (1920) and first king of Iraq (1921–33): a leader of the Arab revolt against the Turks (1916–18)

Faisal II or **Feisal II** n 1935–58, last king of Iraq (1939–58)

Faisalabad n a city in NE Pakistan: commercial and manufacturing centre of a cotton- and wheat-growing region; university (1961). Pop: 2 533 000 (2005 est). Former name (until 1979): Lyallpur

Faisal Ibn Abdul Aziz n 1905–75, king of Saudi Arabia (1964–75)

fait accompli (fate ak-kom-plee) n something already done and beyond alteration: *they had to accept the invasion as a fait accompli* [French]

faith n **1** strong belief in something, esp. without proof **2** a specific system of religious beliefs **3** complete confidence or trust, such as in a person or remedy **4** allegiance to a person or cause **5** bad faith dishonesty **6** good faith honesty [Latin *fides* trust, confidence]

faithful *adj* **1** remaining true or loyal **2** maintaining sexual loyalty to one's lover or spouse **3** consistently reliable: *my old, but faithful, four-cylinder car* **4** accurate in detail: *a faithful translation of the book* ▷ *pl n* **the faithful 5 a** the believers in a religious faith **b** loyal followers > **faithfully** *adv* > **faithfulness** n

faith healing n treatment of a sick person through the power of religious faith > **faith healer** n

faithless *adj* treacherous or disloyal

Faiyûm or **Fayum** n See El Faiyûm

fajitas (fa-hee-taz) pl n a Mexican dish of soft tortillas wrapped around fried strips of meat or vegetables [Mexican Spanish]

fake *vb* faking, faked **1** to cause (something not genuine) to appear real or more valuable by fraud **2** to pretend to have (an illness, emotion, etc.) ▷ *n* **3** an object, person, or act that is not genuine ▷ *adj* **4** not genuine: *fake fur* [probably from Italian *facciare* to make or do]

fakir (fay-keer) n **1** a Muslim religious ascetic who spurns worldly possessions **2** a Hindu holy man [Arabic *faqīr* poor]

falcon n a type of bird of prey that can be trained to hunt other birds and small animals [Late Latin *falco* hawk]

falconry n **1** the art of training falcons to hunt **2** the sport of hunting with falcons > **falconer** n

Faldo n Sir Nick , full name *Nicholas Alexander Faldo*, born 1957, English golfer: winner of the British Open Championship (1987, 1990, 1992) and the US Masters (1989, 1990, 1996)

Falerii n an ancient city of S Italy, in Latium: important in pre-Roman times

Faliraki n a coastal resort in SE Greece, on Rhodes. Pop: 400 (2000 est)

Falkirk n **1** a town in Scotland, the administrative centre of Falkirk council area: scene of Edward I's defeat of Wallace (1298) and Prince Charles Edward's defeat of General Hawley (1746); formerly a major iron and steel centre; the Falkirk Wheel, an innovative rotating canal boat lift, is nearby. Pop: 32 379 (2001) **2** a council area in central Scotland, on the Firth of Forth: created in 1996 from part of Central Region: largely agricultural, with heavy industry in Falkirk and Grangemouth.

Administrative centre: Falkirk. Pop: 145 920 (2003 est). Area: 299 sq km (115 sq miles)

Falkland Islands *pl n* a group of over 100 islands in the S Atlantic: a UK Overseas Territory; invaded by Argentina, who had long laid claim to the islands, on 2 April 1982; recaptured by a British expeditionary force on 14 June 1982. Chief town: Stanley. Pop: 3140 (2008 est). Area: about 12 200 sq km (4700 sq miles). Spanish name: **Islas Malvinas**

Falkland Islands Dependencies *pl n* the former name (until 1985) for South Georgia and the South Sandwich Islands

fall *vb* **falling, fell, fallen 1** to descend by the force of gravity from a higher to a lower place **2** to drop suddenly from an upright position **3** to collapse to the ground **4** to become less or lower in number or quality: *inflation fell by one percentage point* **5** to slope downwards **6** to be badly wounded or killed **7** to give in to attack: *in 1939 Barcelona fell to the Nationalists* **8** to lose power or status **9** to pass into a specified condition: *I fell asleep* **10** to adopt a downhearted expression: *his face fell and he pouted like a child* **11** (of night or darkness) to begin **12** to occur at a specified time: *Christmas falls on a Sunday* **13** to give in to temptation or sin **14 fall apart a** to break owing to long use or poor construction: *the chassis is falling apart* **b** to become disorganized and ineffective: *since you resigned, the office has fallen apart* **15 fall short** to prove inadequate **16 fall short of** to fail to reach (a standard) ▷ *n* **17** an instance of falling **18** an amount of something, such as snow or soot, that has fallen **19** a decrease in value or number **20** a decline in status or importance: *the town's fall from prosperity* **21** a capture or overthrow: *the fall of Budapest in February 1945* **22** *wrestling* a scoring move, pinning both shoulders of one's opponent to the floor for a specified period **23** *chiefly US* autumn ▶ See also **fall about, fall away, falls,** etc. [Old English *feallan*]

Fall *n* **the Fall** *theol* the state of mankind's innate sinfulness following Adam's sin of disobeying God

Falla *n* Manuel de. 1876–1946, Spanish composer and pianist, composer of the opera *La Vida Breve* (1905), the ballet *The Three-Cornered Hat* (1919), guitar and piano music, and songs

fall about *vb* to laugh uncontrollably

fallacy *n, pl* **-cies 1** an incorrect or misleading notion based on inaccurate facts or faulty reasoning: *the fallacy underlying the government's industrial policy* **2** reasoning that is unsound [Latin *fallere* to deceive] ▷ **fallacious** *adj*

fall away *vb* **1** to slope down: *the ground fell away sharply to the south* **2** to decrease in size or intensity: *obstacles to all-party talks are falling away with amazing speed*

fall back *vb* **1** to retreat **2 fall back on** to have to choose (a less acceptable alternative): *they had to fall back on other lines of defence*

fall behind *vb* **1** to fail to keep up **2** to be in arrears, such as with a payment

fall down *vb* **1** to drop suddenly or collapse **2** to fail to meet requirements **3** (of an argument or idea) to fail at a specific point: *in one area only did the case fall down*

fallen *vb* **1** the past participle of **fall** ▷ *adj* **2** old-fashioned (of a woman) having had sex outside marriage **3** killed in battle

fall for *vb* **1** to become strongly attracted to (someone) **2** to be deceived by (a lie or trick)

fall guy *n informal* **1** the victim of a confidence trick **2** a person who is publicly blamed for something, though it may not be his or her fault

fallible *adj* **1** (of a person) liable to make mistakes **2** capable of error: *our all-too-fallible economic indicators* [Latin *fallere* to deceive] ▷ **fallibility** *n*

fall in *vb* **1** to collapse **2** to get into line or formation in a display, march, or procession **3 fall in with a** to meet and join **b** to agree with or support (a person or a suggestion)

falling star *n informal* a meteor

Fall Line *n* a natural junction, running parallel to the E coast of the US, between the hard rocks of the Appalachians and the softer coastal plain, along which rivers form falls and rapids

fall off *vb* **1** to drop unintentionally to the ground from (a bicycle, horse, etc.) **2** to decrease in size or intensity: *demand for beef began to fall off*

fall on *vb* **1** to attack (an enemy) **2** to meet with (something unpleasant): *his family had fallen on hard times* **3** to affect: *a horrified hush fell on the company* **4 fall on one's feet** to emerge unexpectedly well from a difficult situation

Fallopian tube *n* either of a pair of slender tubes through which eggs pass from the ovaries to the uterus in female mammals [after Gabriello *Fallopio*, anatomist]

fallout *n* **1** radioactive material in the atmosphere following a nuclear explosion **2** unpleasant circumstances following an event: *the political fallout of the riots* ▷ *vb* **fall out 3** *informal* to disagree and quarrel: *I hope we don't fall out over this issue* **4** to leave a military formation

fallow¹ *adj* (of land) left unseeded after being ploughed to regain fertility for a future crop [Old English *fealga*]

fallow² *adj* light yellowish-brown [Old English *fealu*]

fallow deer *n* a deer that has a reddish coat with white spots in summer

falls *pl n* a waterfall

fall through *vb* to fail before completion: *his transfer deal fell through*

fall to *vb* **1** to become the responsibility of: *it fell to the Prime Minister to announce the plans* **2** to begin (some activity, such as eating, working, or fighting)

Fallujah *n* a town in central Iraq, about 60 km W of Baghdad; a centre of resistance against the US-led invasion of Iraq, from 2003. Pop: 223 000 (2005 est)

Falmouth *n* a port and resort in SW England, in S Cornwall. Pop: 21 635 (2001)

false *adj* **1** not in accordance with the truth or facts: *false allegations* **2** not real or genuine but intended to seem so: *false teeth* **3** misleading or deceptive: *their false promises* **4** forced or insincere: *false cheer* **5** based on mistaken ideas [Latin *falsus*] ▷ **falsely** *adv* ▷ **falseness** *n*

false alarm *n* a situation that appears to be dangerous but turns out not to be: *air-raid sirens sounded once but it turned out to be a false alarm*

False Bay *n* a bay in SW South Africa, near the Cape of Good Hope

falsehood *n* **1** the quality of being untrue **2** a lie

false pretences *pl n* under false pretences so as to mislead people about one's true intentions

false start *n athletics, swimming* an occasion when one competitor starts a race before the starter's signal has been given, which means that all competitors have to be recalled and the race restarted

falsetto *n, pl* **-tos** a voice pitch higher than one's normal range [Italian]

falsies *pl n informal* pads worn to exaggerate the size of a woman's breasts

falsify *vb* **-fies, -fying, -fied** to make (a report or evidence) false by alteration in order to deceive [Latin *falsus* false + *facere* to make] ▷ **falsification** *n*

falsity *n, pl* **-ties 1** the state of being false **2** a lie

Falster *n* an island in the Baltic Sea, part of SE Denmark. Chief town: Nykøbing. Pop: 43 537 (2003 est). Area: 513 sq km (198 sq miles)

falter *vb* **1** to be hesitant, weak, or unsure **2** (of a machine) to lose power or strength in an uneven way: *the engine began to falter and the plane lost height* **3** to speak nervously and without confidence **4** to stop moving smoothly and start moving unsteadily: *as he neared the house his steps faltered* [origin unknown] ▷ **faltering** *adj*

Falun *n* a city in central Sweden: iron and pyrites mines. Pop: 55 009 (2004 est)

Famagusta *n* a port in E Cyprus, on Famagusta Bay: became one of the richest cities in Christendom in the 14th century. Pop: 35 453 (2006)

ame n the state of being widely known or recognized [Latin *fama* report]

amed adj extremely well-known: *a nation famed for its efficiency*

amilial adj formal of or relating to the family

amiliar adj 1 well-known 2 frequent or common: *it was a familiar argument* 3 familiar with well acquainted with 4 friendly and informal 5 more intimate than is acceptable ▷ n 6 an animal or bird believed to share with a witch her supernatural powers 7 a friend [Latin *familia* family] ⟩ **familiarly** adv ⟩ **familiarity** n

amiliarize or **-rise** vb -rizing, -rized or -rising, -rised to make (oneself or someone else) fully aware of a particular subject ⟩ **familiarization** or **-risation** n

amily n, pl **-lies** 1 a social group consisting of parents and their offspring. Related adjective: **familial** 2 one's wife or husband and one's children 3 one's children 4 a group descended from a common ancestor 5 all the people living together in one household 6 any group of related objects or beings: *a family of chemicals* 7 biology one of the groups into which an order is divided, containing one or more genera: *the cat family* ▷ adj 8 of or suitable for a family or any of its members: *films for a family audience* 9 in the family way informal pregnant [Latin *familia*]

amily Allowance n 1 in Britain, a former name for **child benefit** 2 (in Canada) an allowance formerly paid by the Federal Government to the parents of dependent children, replaced by Canada Child Tax Benefit

amily assistance n (in New Zealand) a tax credit formerly given to families on the basis of their income and family size, replaced by Working for Families Tax Credits

amily doctor n Brit, Austral and NZ informal same as **general practitioner**

amily man n 1 a man with a wife and children 2 a man who loves his family and spends a lot of time with them

amily name n a surname, esp. when regarded as representing a family's good reputation

amily planning n the control of the number of children in a family by the use of contraceptives

amily tree n a chart showing the relationships between individuals in a family over many generations

amine n a severe shortage of food [Latin *fames* hunger]

amish vb be famished or famishing to be very hungry [Latin *fames* hunger]

amous adj known to or recognized by many people [Latin *famosus*]

amously adv 1 well-known: *her famously relaxed manner* 2 very well: *the two got on famously*

an¹ n 1 any device for creating a current of air, esp. a rotating machine of blades attached to a central hub 2 a hand-held object, usually made of paper, which creates a draught of cool air when waved 3 something shaped like such a fan, such as the tail of certain birds ▷ vb **fanning, fanned** 4 to create a draught of air in the direction of (someone or something) 5 fan out to spread out in the shape of a fan: *the troops fanned out along the beach* [Latin *vannus*]

an² n a person who admires or is enthusiastic about a pop star, actor, sport, or hobby: *he was a big fan of Woody Allen* [from fanatic]

anatic n 1 a person whose enthusiasm for something, esp. a political or religious cause, is extreme 2 informal a person devoted to a particular hobby or pastime ▷ adj also: **fanatical** 3 excessively enthusiastic [Latin *fanaticus* belonging to a temple, hence, inspired by a god, frenzied] ⟩ **fanatically** adv ⟩ **fanaticism** n

anbase n a body of admirers of a particular pop singer, sports team, etc.

an belt n the belt that drives a cooling fan in a car engine

ancier n a person with a keen interest in the thing specified: *a pigeon fancier*

anciful adj 1 not based on fact 2 made in a curious or imaginative way: *fanciful architecture* 3 guided by unrestrained imagination: *fanciful tales of fairy folk* ⟩ **fancifully** adv

fan club n 1 an organized group of admirers of a particular pop singer or star 2 be a member of someone's fan club informal to approve of someone strongly

fancy adj -cier, -ciest 1 special, unusual, and elaborate 2 (often used ironically) superior in quality 3 (of a price) higher than expected ▷ n, pl -cies 4 a sudden spontaneous idea 5 a sudden or irrational liking for a person or thing 6 old-fashioned or literary a person's imagination ▷ vb -cies, -cying, -cied 7 Brit informal to be physically attracted to (another person) 8 informal to have a wish for 9 to picture in the imagination 10 to think or suppose: *I fancy I am redundant here* 11 fancy oneself to have a high opinion of oneself ▷ interj 12 Also: fancy that! an exclamation of surprise [Middle English *fantsy*] ⟩ **fancily** adv

fancy dress n clothing worn for a party at which people dress up to look like a particular animal or character

fancy-free adj free from commitments, esp. marriage

fancy goods pl n small decorative gifts

fancy man n old-fashioned, slang a woman's lover

fancy woman n old-fashioned, slang a man's lover

fancywork n ornamental needlework

fandango n, pl **-gos** 1 a lively Spanish dance 2 music for this dance [Spanish]

fanfare n a short rousing tune played on brass instruments [French]

fang n 1 the long pointed tooth of a poisonous snake through which poison is injected 2 the canine tooth of a meat-eating mammal [Old English: what is caught, prey]

Fangio n Juan Manuel. 1911–95, Argentinian racing driver who won the Formula One World Championship five times between 1951 and 1957

Fang Lizhi n 1936–2012, Chinese astrophysicist and human-rights campaigner, lived in the US from 1990

Fa Ngum n 1316–74, founder and first king of Lan Xang (1354–73), a kingdom that included the present-day republic of Laos; abdicated

fanjet n same as turbofan

fanlight n a semicircular window over a door or another window

fanny n, pl **-nies** slang 1 Brit and Austral taboo the female genitals 2 chiefly US and Canad the buttocks [origin unknown]

fantail n 1 a breed of domestic pigeon with a large tail like a fan 2 a fly-catching bird of Australia, New Zealand, and SE Asia with a broad fan-shaped tail

fantasia n 1 any musical work not composed in a strict form 2 a mixture of popular tunes arranged as a continuous whole [Italian: fancy]

fantasize or **-sise** vb -sizing, -sized or -sising, -sised to imagine pleasant but unlikely events

fantastic adj 1 informal excellent 2 informal very large in degree or amount: *a fantastic amount of money* 3 strange or exotic in appearance: *fantastic costumes* 4 difficult to believe or unlikely to happen ⟩ **fantastically** adv

fantasy n, pl **-sies** 1 a far-fetched idea 2 imagination unrestricted by reality 3 a daydream 4 fiction with a large fantasy content 5 music same as fantasia ▷ adj 6 of a competition in which a participant selects players for an imaginary, ideal team and points are awarded according to the actual performances of the chosen players: *fantasy football* [Greek *phantazein* to make visible]

Fantin-Latour n (Ignace) Henri (Joseph Théodore). 1836–1904, French painter, noted for his still lifes and portrait studies

fan vaulting n archit vaulting with ribs that radiate like those of a fan from the top part of a pillar

fanzine (fan-zeen) n a magazine produced by fans of a specific interest, football club, etc., for fellow fans

fanzone n an area set aside to provide organized

entertainment for travelling fans before a major event and often to relay the event itself on a large screen

FAQ *n computers* frequently asked question *or* questions: a text file containing basic information on a particular subject

far *adv* **farther, farthest** *or* **further, furthest 1** at, to, or from a great distance **2** at or to a remote time: *as far back as 1984* **3** by a considerable degree: *far greater* **4 as far as a** to the degree or extent that **b** to the distance or place of **c** *informal* with reference to **5 by far** by a considerable margin **6 far and away** by a very great margin: *far and away the ugliest building in the city* **7 far and wide** in a great many places over a large area **8 go far a** to be successful **b** to be sufficient or last long: *her wages didn't go far* **9 go too far** to go beyond reasonable limits: *the press have gone too far this time* **10 so far a** up to the present moment **b** up to a certain point, extent, or degree ▷ *adj* **11** distant in space or time: *the far south* **12** extending a great distance **13** more distant: *over in the far corner* **14 far from** by no means: *the battle is far from over* [Old English *feorr*]

farad *n physics* the SI unit of electric capacitance [after Michael FARADAY]

Faraday *n* **Michael.** 1791–1867, English physicist and chemist who discovered electromagnetic induction, leading to the invention of the dynamo. He also carried out research into the principles of electrolysis

Farage *n* **Nigel (Paul).** born 1964, British politician; leader of UKIP (2006–09 and from 2010); member of the European Parliament from 1999

Farah *n* **Mo(hamed).** born 1983, British long-distance runner, born in Somalia: winner of the 5000 metres and the 10,000 metres at the 2012 Olympics; winner of the 5000 metres at the World Championships (2011, 2013)

faraway *adj* **1** very distant **2** dreamy or absent-minded: *a faraway look in his eyes*

farce *n* **1** a humorous play involving characters in unlikely and ridiculous situations **2** the style of comedy of this kind **3** a ludicrous situation: *the game degenerated into farce* [Latin *farcire* to stuff, interpolate passages (in plays)] ▷ **farcical** *adj* ▷ **farcically** *adv*

fare *n* **1** the amount charged or paid for a journey in a bus, train, or plane **2** a paying passenger **3** a range of food and drink: *marvellous picnic fare* ▷ *vb* **faring, fared 4** to get on (in a specified way): *he fared well in the exam* [Old English *faran*]

Far East *n* **the Far East** the countries of E Asia, usually including China, Japan, North and South Korea, Indonesia, Malaysia, and the Philippines: sometimes extended to include all territories east of Afghanistan

Far Eastern *adj* of or relating to the Far East (E Asia) or its inhabitants

Fareham *n* a market town in S England, in S Hampshire. Pop: 37 440 (2001 est)

fare stage *n* **1** a section of a bus journey for which a set charge is made **2** the bus stop marking the end of such a section

farewell *interj* **1** *old-fashioned* goodbye ▷ *n* **2** the act of saying goodbye and leaving ▷ *vb* **3** NZ to say goodbye ▷ *adj* **4** parting or closing: *the President's farewell speech*

far-fetched *adj* unlikely to be true

far-flung *adj* **1** distributed over a wide area **2** far distant or remote

Fargo *n* **William.** 1818–81, US businessman: founded (1852) with Henry Wells the express mail service Wells, Fargo and Company

Farhi *n* **Nicole.** born 1946, French fashion designer based in Britain: married to Sir David Hare

Faridabad *n* a city in NE India, in Haryana: industrial centre. Pop: 1 054 981 (2001)

farinaceous *adj* containing starch or having a starchy texture [Latin *far* coarse meal]

farm *n* **1** a tract of land, usually with a house and buildings, cultivated as a unit or used to rear livestock **2** a unit of land or water devoted to the growing or rearing of some particular type of fruit, animal, or fish: *a salmon farm; an ostrich farm* ▷ *vb* **3 a** to cultivate (land) **b** t rear (animals or fish) on a farm **4** to do agricultural work as a way of life **5** to collect and keep the profits from a (tax district or business) ▶ See also **farm out** [Old French *ferme* rented land]

farmed *adj* (of fish or game) reared on a farm rather tha caught in the wild

farmer *n* a person who owns or manages a farm

Farmer *n* **John.** ?1565–1605, English madrigal composer and organist

farmers' market *n* a market at which farm produce is sold directly to the public by the producer

farm hand *n* a person who is hired to work on a farm

farmhouse *n* a house attached to a farm

farming *n* the business or skill of agriculture

farmland *n* land that is used for or suitable for farming

farm out *vb* **1** to send (work) to be done by another person or firm **2** (of the state) to put (a child) into the care of a private individual

farmstead *n* a farm and its main buildings

farmyard *n* the small area of land enclosed by or around the farm buildings

Farnborough *n* a town in S England, in NE Hampshire military base, with an aeronautical research centre. Pop: 57 147 (2001)

Farnese *n* **1 Alesandro.** original name of Pope Paul III. See also **Paul III 2 Alessandro,** duke of Parma and Piacenza. 1545–92, Italian general, statesman, and diplomat in the service of Philip II of Spain. As governor of the Netherlands (1578–92), he successfully suppressed revolts against Spanish rule

Farnham *n* a town in S England, in NW Surrey. Pop: 36 296 (2001)

Far North *n* **the Far North** the Arctic and sub-Arctic regions of the world

Faro *n* a port and resort in S Portugal: destroyed by earthquakes in 1722 and 1755. Pop: 58 051 (2001)

Faroes *n* a variant spelling of **Faeroes**

Faroese *adj, n* a variant spelling of **Faeroese**

far-off *adj* distant in space or time: *a far-off land*

Farouk I *or* **Faruk I** *n* 1920–65, last king of Egypt (1936–52). He was forced to abdicate (1952)

far-out *adj* **1** very unusual or strange: *the idea was so far-ou it was ludicrous* **2** *informal* wonderful

Farquhar *n* **George.** 1678–1707, Irish-born dramatist; author of comedies such as *The Recruiting Officer* (1706) and *The Beaux' Stratagem* (1707)

Farquhar Islands *pl n* an island group in the Indian Ocean: administratively part of the Seychelles

farrago (far-rah-go) *n, pl* **-gos** *or* **-goes** a hotchpotch or mixture, esp. a ridiculous or unbelievable one: *a farrago of patriotic nonsense*

far-reaching *adj* extensive in influence, effect, or range

Farrell *n* **1 Colin (James).** born 1976, Irish film actor; he appeared in the TV series *Ballykissangel* before starring in the films *Tigerland* (2000), *Minority Report* (2002), *Alexander* (2004), and *In Bruges* (2008) **2 J(ames) G(ordon)** 1935–79, British novelist: author of *Troubles* (1970), *The Siege of Krishnapur* (1973), and *The Singapore Grip* (1978) **3 James T(homas)** 1904–79, US writer. His works include the trilogy *Young* (1932), *The Young Manhood of Studs Lonigan* (1934), and *Judgment Day* (1935)

farrier *n chiefly Brit* a person who shoes horses [Latin *ferrarius* smith]

farrow *n* **1** a litter of piglets ▷ *vb* **2** (of a sow) to give birth to a litter [Old English *fearh*]

far-seeing *adj* having wise judgment

far-sighted *adj* **1** able to look forward and plan ahead **2** US long-sighted

fart *taboo n* **1** an emission of intestinal gas from the anus ▷ *vb* **2** to break wind [Middle English *farten*]

farther *adv* **1** to or at a greater distance in space or time

2 in addition ▷ *adj* **3** more distant or remote in space or time [Middle English]

> **USAGE** *Farther, farthest, further,* and *furthest* can all be used to refer to literal distance, but *further* and *furthest* are regarded as more correct for figurative senses denoting greater or additional amount, time, etc.: *further to my letter.* *Further* and *furthest* are also preferred for figurative distance.

farthermost *adj* most distant or remote

farthest *adv* **1** to or at the greatest distance in space or time ▷ *adj* **2** most distant or remote in space or time [Middle English *ferthest*]

farthing *n* a former British coin worth a quarter of an old penny [Old English *fēorthing*]

farthingale *n* a hoop worn under skirts in the Elizabethan period [Old Spanish *verdugo* rod]

fasces (fass-eez) *pl n, sing* **-cis** (-siss) (in ancient Rome) a bundle of rods containing an axe with its blade pointing out; a symbol of a magistrate's power [Latin]

fascia *or* **facia** (fay-shee-a) *n, pl* **-ciae** (-shee-ee) **1** the flat surface above a shop window **2** *archit* a flat band or surface **3** *Brit* the outer panel which surrounds the instruments and dials of a motor vehicle [Latin: band]

fascinate *vb* **-nating, -nated** to attract and delight by arousing interest [Latin *fascinum* a bewitching] ＞ **fascinating** *adj* ＞ **fascinatingly** *adv* ＞ **fascination** *n*

> **USAGE** A person can be fascinated *by* or *with* another person or thing. It is correct to speak of someone's fascination *with* a person or thing; you can also say a person or thing has a fascination *for* someone.

fascism (fash-iz-zum) *n* **1** the authoritarian and nationalistic political movement in Italy (1922–43) **2** any ideology or movement like this [Italian *fascio* political group] ＞ **Fascist** *n, adj*

fashion *n* **1** style in clothes, hairstyles, behaviour, etc., that is popular at a particular time **2** the way that something happens or is done: *conversing in a very animated fashion* **3 after a fashion** in some way, but not very well: *he apologized, after a fashion, for his haste* ▷ *vb* **4** to form, make, or shape: *he had fashioned a crude musical instrument* [Latin *facere* to make]

fashionable *adj* **1** popular with a lot of people at a particular time **2** popular among well-off or famous people: *the fashionable Côte d'Azur* ＞ **fashionably** *adv*

Fashoda *n* a small town in SE Sudan: scene of a diplomatic incident (1898) in which French occupation of the fort at Fashoda caused a crisis between France and Great Britain. Modern name: **Kodok**

Fassbinder *n* Rainer Werner. 1946–82, West German film director. His films include *The Bitter Tears of Petra von Kant* (1972), *Fear Eats the Soul* (1974), and *The Marriage of Maria Braun* (1978)

fast¹ *adj* **1** acting or moving quickly **2** accomplished in or lasting a short time **3** adapted to or allowing for rapid movement: *the fast lane* **4** (of a clock or watch) indicating a time in advance of the correct time **5** given to a life of expensive and exciting activities: *the desire for a fast life* **6** firmly fixed, fastened, or shut **7** (of colours and dyes) not likely to fade **8** *photog* very sensitive and able to be used in low-light conditions **9 fast friends** devoted and loyal friends **10 pull a fast one** *informal* to play an unscrupulous trick ▷ *adv* **11** quickly **12 fast asleep** in a deep sleep **13** firmly and tightly: *stuck fast* **14 play fast and loose** to behave in an insincere or unreliable manner [Old English *fæst* strong, tight]

fast² *vb* **1** to go without food for a period of time, esp. for religious reasons ▷ *n* **2** a period of fasting [Old English *fæstan*]

fast-breeder reactor *n* a nuclear reactor that produces more fissionable material (plutonium) than it

consumes for the purposes of generating electricity

fasten *vb* **1** to make or become secure or joined **2** to close by fixing firmly in place or locking **3 fasten on a** to direct one's attention in a concentrated way towards: *the mind needs such imagery to fasten on to* **b** to take a firm hold on [Old English *fæstnian*] ＞ **fastener** *n*

fastening *n* something that fastens something, such as a clasp or lock

fast food *n* food, such as hamburgers, that is prepared and served very quickly

fastidious *adj* **1** paying great attention to neatness, detail, and order: *a fastidious dresser* **2** excessively concerned with cleanliness [Latin *fastidiosus* scornful] ＞ **fastidiously** *adv* ＞ **fastidiousness** *n*

fast lane *n* **1** the outside lane on a motorway for overtaking or travelling fast **2** *informal* the quickest but most competitive route to success: *the hectic pace of life in the corporate fast lane*

fastness *n* *Brit and Austral literary* a stronghold or safe place that is hard to get to

fast-track *adj* **1** taking the quickest but most competitive route to success or personal advancement: *a fast-track marketer's dream* ▷ *vb* **2** to speed up the progress of (a project or person)

fat *adj* **fatter, fattest 1** having more flesh on the body than is thought necessary or desirable; overweight **2** (of meat) containing a lot of fat **3** thick or wide: *his obligatory fat cigar* **4** profitable or productive: *fat years for the farmers are few and far between* **5 a fat chance** *slang* unlikely to happen **6 a fat lot of good** *slang* not at all good or useful ▷ *n* **7** extra or unwanted flesh on the body **8** a greasy or oily substance obtained from animals or plants and used in cooking **9 the fat is in the fire** an action has been taken from which disastrous consequences are expected **10 the fat of the land** the best that is obtainable [Old English *fætt* crammed] ＞ **fatless** *adj* ＞ **fatness** *n*

fatal *adj* **1** resulting in death: *a fatal accident* **2** resulting in unfortunate consequences: *Gorbachov's second fatal mistake* [Latin *fatum* fate] ＞ **fatally** *adv*

fatalism *n* the belief that all events are decided in advance by God or Fate so that human beings are powerless to alter their destiny ＞ **fatalist** *n* ＞ **fatalistic** *adj* ＞ **fatalistically** *adv*

fatality *n, pl* **-ties** a death caused by an accident or disaster

fate *n* **1** the ultimate force that supposedly predetermines the course of events **2** the inevitable fortune that happens to a person or thing **3** death or downfall: *Custer met his fate at Little Bighorn* [Latin *fatum*]

fated *adj* **1** certain to be or do something: *he was always fated to be a musician* **2** doomed to death or destruction

fateful *adj* having important, and usually disastrous, consequences ＞ **fatefully** *adv*

Fates *pl n Classical myth* the goddesses who control human destiny

fathead *n informal* a stupid person ＞ **fatheaded** *adj*

father *n* **1** a male parent **2** a person who founds a line or family; forefather **3** a man who starts, creates, or invents something: *the father of democracy in Costa Rica* **4** a leader of an association or council: *the city fathers* ▷ *vb* **5** (of a man) to be the biological cause of the conception and birth of (a child) [Old English *fæder*] ＞ **fatherhood** *n*

Father *n* **1** God **2** a title used for Christian priests **3** any of the early writers on Christian doctrine

Father Christmas *n* same as **Santa Claus**

father-in-law *n, pl* **fathers-in-law** the father of one's wife or husband

fatherland *n* a person's native country

fatherly *adj* kind or protective, like a father

Father's Day *n* a day celebrated in honour of fathers

fathom *n* **1** a unit of length, used in navigation, equal to six feet (1.83 metres) ▷ *vb* **2** to understand by thinking carefully about: *I couldn't fathom his intentions* [Old English *fæthm*] ＞ **fathomable** *adj*

fathomless *adj* too deep or difficult to fathom

fatigue (fat-eeg) *n* **1** extreme physical or mental tiredness **2** the weakening of a material caused by repeated stress or movement **3** the duties of a soldier that are not military **4 fatigues** a soldier's clothing for nonmilitary or battlefield duties ▷ *vb* **-tiguing, -tigued 5** to make or become weary or exhausted [Latin *fatigare* to tire]

Fatima *n* ?606–632 AD daughter of Mohammed; wife of Ali

Fátima *n* a village in central Portugal: Roman Catholic shrine and pilgrimage centre

Fatshan *n* a variant transliteration of the Chinese name for Foshan

fat stock *n* livestock fattened and ready for market

fatten *vb* to grow or cause to grow fat or fatter ▷ **fattening** *adj*

fatty *adj* **-tier, -tiest 1** containing or derived from fat **2** greasy or oily ▷ *n, pl* **-ties 3** *informal* a fat person

fatty acid *n* any of a class of organic acids some of which, such as stearic acid, are found in animal or vegetable fats

fatuity *n, pl* **-ties 1** foolish thoughtlessness **2** a fatuous remark

fatuous *adj* foolish, inappropriate, and showing no thought [Latin *fatuus*] ▷ **fatuously** *adv*

faucet (faw-set) *n* **1** a tap fitted to a barrel **2** *US and Canad* a tap [Old French *fausset*]

Faulkner *or* **Falkner** *n* William. 1897–1962, US novelist and short-story writer. Most of his works portray the problems of the southern US, esp. the novels set in the imaginary county of Yoknapatawpha in Mississippi. Other novels include *The Sound and the Fury* (1929) and *Light in August* (1932): Nobel prize for literature 1949 ▷ **Faulknerian** *adj*

fault *n* **1** responsibility for something wrong **2** a defect or failing: *they shut the production line to remedy a fault* **3** a weakness in a person's character **4** *geology* a fracture in the earth's crust with displacement of the rocks on either side **5** *tennis, squash etc.* a serve that bounces outside the proper service court or fails to get over the net **6** (in showjumping) a penalty mark for failing to clear, or refusing, a fence **7 at fault** to be to blame for something wrong **8 find fault with** to seek out minor imperfections in **9 to a fault** more than is usual or necessary: *generous to a fault* ▷ *vb* **10** to criticize or blame **11** *geology* to undergo or cause to undergo a fault [Latin *fallere* to fail] ▷ **faultless** *adj* ▷ **faultlessly** *adv*

fault-finding *n* continual criticism

faulty *adj* **faultier, faultiest** badly designed or not working properly: *a faulty toaster*

faun *n* (in Roman legend) a creature with the head and torso of a man and the legs, ears, and horns of a goat [Latin *Faunus*, god of forests]

fauna *n, pl* **-nas** *or* **-nae** all the animal life of a given place or time: *the fauna of the Arctic* [Late Latin *Fauna*, a goddess of living things]

Fauré *n* Gabriel (Urbain). 1845–1924, French composer and teacher, noted particularly for his song settings of French poems, esp. those of Verlaine, his piano music, and his *Messe de Requiem* (1887)

faux pas (foe pah) *n, pl* **faux pas** (foe pahz) a socially embarrassing action or mistake [French]

favour *or US* **favor** *n* **1** an approving attitude: *the company looked with favour on his plan* **2** an act done out of goodwill or generosity **3** bias at the expense of others: *his fellow customs officers, showing no favour, demanded to see his luggage* **4** **in** *or* **out of favour** regarded with approval or disapproval **5 in favour of a** approving **b** to the benefit of ▷ *vb* **6** to prefer **7** to show bias towards (someone) at the expense of others: *parents sometimes favour the youngest child in the family* **8** to support or agree with (something): *he favours the abolition of capital punishment* [Latin *favere* to protect] ▷ **favoured** *or US* **favored** *adj*

favourable *or US* **favorable** *adj* **1** advantageous, encouraging, or promising: *a favourable climate for business expansion* **2** giving consent or approval ▷ **favourably** *or U* **favorably** *adv*

favourite *or US* **favorite** *adj* **1** most liked ▷ *n* **2** a person or thing regarded with especial preference or liking **3** *sport* a competitor thought likely to win [Latin *favere* to protect]

favouritism *or US* **favoritism** *n* the practice of giving special treatment to a person or group: *favouritism in the allocation of government posts*

Fawcett *n* Dame Millicent Garrett. 1847–1929, British suffragette

Fawkes *n* Guy. 1570–1606, English conspirator, executed for his part in the Gunpowder Plot to blow up King James I and VI and the Houses of Parliament (1605). Effigies of him (guys) are burnt in Britain on Guy Fawkes Day (Nov 5)

fawn[1] *n* **1** a young deer aged under one year ▷ *adj* **2** pale greyish-brown [Latin *fetus* offspring]

fawn[2] *vb* **fawn on 1** to seek attention from (someone) by insincere flattery: *it makes me sick to see the way you fawn on that awful woman* **2** (of a dog) to try to please (someone) b a show of extreme friendliness [Old English *fægnian* to b glad] ▷ **fawning** *adj*

fax *n* **1** an electronic system for transmitting an exact copy of a document **2** a document sent by this system **3** Also called: **fax machine, facsimile machine** a machine which transmits and receives exact copies of documen ▷ *vb* **4** to send (a document) by this system [short for *facsimile*]

Fa Xian *or* **Fa-hsien** *n* original name *Sehi*. 5th century AD, Chinese Buddhist monk: his pilgrimage to India (399–414) began relations between China and India

Fayal *n* a variant spelling of Faial

Fayum *n* See El Faiyûm

fazed *adj* worried or disconcerted [Old English *fēsian*]

FBI (in the US) Federal Bureau of Investigation

FC (in Britain) Football Club

FD Defender of the Faith: the title of the British sovereign as head of the Church of England [Latin *Fidei Defensor*]

Fe *chem* iron [Latin *ferrum*]

fealty *n, pl* **-ties** (in feudal society) the loyalty sworn to a lord by his tenant or servant [Latin *fidelitas* fidelity]

fear *n* **1** a feeling of distress or alarm caused by danger o pain that is about to happen **2** something that causes fear **3** possibility or likelihood: *there is no fear of her agreeing to that* **4 no fear** *informal* certainly not ▷ *vb* **5** to be afraid of (someone or something) **6** *formal* to be sorry: *I fear the children were not very good yesterday* **7 fear for** to feel anxiety about [Old English *fēr*] ▷ **fearless** *adj* ▷ **fearlessly** *adv*

fearful *adj* **1** afraid and full of fear **2** frightening or causing fear: *the ship hit a fearful storm* **3** *informal* very bad: *they were making a fearful noise* ▷ **fearfully** *adv*

fearsome *adj* terrible or frightening

feasible *adj* able to be done: *a manned journey to Mars is now feasible* [Anglo-French *faisable*] ▷ **feasibility** *n* ▷ **feasibly** *adv*

feast *n* **1** a large and special meal for many people **2** something extremely pleasing: *a feast of colour* **3** an annual religious celebration ▷ *vb* **4** to take part in a feas **5** to give a feast to **6 feast on** to eat a large amount of: *down come hundreds of vultures to feast on the remains* **7 feast one's eyes on** to look at (someone or something) with a great deal of attention and pleasure [Latin *festus* joyful]

Feast of Tabernacles *n* same as Sukkoth

feat *n* a remarkable, skilful, or daring action: *an extraordinary feat of engineering* [Anglo-French *fait*]

feather *n* **1** any of the flat light structures that form the plumage of birds, each consisting of a shaft with soft thin hairs on either side **2 feather in one's cap** a cause for pleasure at one's achievements ▷ *vb* **3** to fit, cover, o supply with feathers **4** *rowing* to turn an oar parallel to the water between strokes, in order to lessen wind resistance **5 feather one's nest** to collect possessions and money to make one's life comfortable, often dishonestly [Old English *fether*] **> feathered** *adj* **> feathery** *adj*

feather bed *n* **1** a mattress filled with feathers or down ▷ *vb* **featherbed** (**-bedding, -bedded**) **2** to pamper or spoil (someone)

featherbedding *n* the practice of working in a factory or office deliberately slowly and inefficiently so that more workers are employed than are necessary

featherbrain *n* an empty-headed or forgetful person **> featherbrained** *adj*

featherweight *n* **1** a professional or an amateur boxer weighing up to 126 pounds (57 kg) **2** something very light or of little importance

feature *n* **1 features** any one of the parts of the face, such as the nose, chin, or mouth **2** a prominent or distinctive part of something: *regular debates were a feature of our final year* **3** the main film in a cinema programme **4** an item appearing regularly in a newspaper or magazine **5** a prominent story in a newspaper ▷ *vb* **-turing, -tured 6** to have as a feature or make a feature of: *this cooker features a fan-assisted oven* **7** to give special prominence to: *the film features James Mason as Rommel* [Anglo-French *feture*] **> featureless** *adj*

Feb. February

febrile (fee-brile) *adj formal* **1** very active and nervous: *increasingly febrile activity at the Stock Exchange* **2** of or relating to fever [Latin *febris* fever]

February *n, pl* **-aries** the second month of the year [Latin *Februarius mensis* month of expiation]

Fechner *n* Gustav Theodor. 1801–87, German physicist, philosopher, and psychologist, noted particularly for his work on psychophysics, *Elemente der Psychophysik* (1860)

feckless *adj* irresponsible and lacking character and determination: *her feckless brother was always in debt* [obsolete *feck* value, effect]

fecund *adj literary* **1** fertile or capable of producing many offspring **2** intellectually productive or creative: *an extraordinarily fecund year even by Mozart's standards* [Latin *fecundus*] **> fecundity** *n*

fed *vb* the past of **feed**

federal *adj* **1** of a form of government in which power is divided between one central and several regional governments **2** of the central government of a federation **3** *Austral* of a style of house built around the time of Federation [Latin *foedus* league] **> federalism** *n* **> federalist** *n, adj*

Federal *adj* of or supporting the Union government during the American Civil War

Federal Capital Territory *n* **1** an administrative division of Nigeria, in the centre. Capital: Abuja (also national capital). Pop: 1 405 201 (2006). Area: 7315 sq km (2824 sq miles) **2** the former name of **Australian Capital Territory**

Federal Government *n* the national government of a federated state, such as that of Canada located in Ottawa or of Australia in Canberra

federalize *or* **-lise** *vb* **-lizing, -lized** *or* **-lising, -lised 1** to unite in a federal union **2** to subject to federal control **> federalization** *or* **-isation** *n*

Federal Republic of Germany *n* the official name of Germany, formerly used to refer to West Germany

federate *vb* **-rating, -rated** to unite in a federal union **> federative** *adj*

Federated Malay States *pl n* See Malay States

federation *n* **1** the union of several provinces, states, etc. **2** any alliance or association of organizations which have freely joined together for a common purpose: *a federation of twenty regional unions*

Federation of Rhodesia and Nyasaland *n* a federation (1953–63) of Northern Rhodesia, Southern Rhodesia, and Nyasaland

Federer *n* Roger. born 1981, Swiss tennis player: winner

of a record seventeen Grand Slam singles titles (2003–12), including seven at Wimbledon and five at the US Open

fed up *adj informal* annoyed or bored

fee *n* **1** a charge paid to be allowed to do something: *many people resent the licence fee* **2** a payment asked by professional people for their services **3** *property law* an interest in land that can be inherited. The interest can be with unrestricted rights (**fee simple**) or restricted (**fee tail**) [Old French *fie*]

feeble *adj* **1** lacking in physical or mental strength **2** not effective or convincing: *feeble excuses for Scotland's latest defeat* [Old French *feble*] **> feebly** *adv*

feeble-minded *adj* unable to think or understand effectively

feed *vb* **feeding, fed 1** to give food to (a person or an animal) **2** to give (something) as food: *people feeding bread to their cattle* **3** to eat food: *red squirrel feed in the pines* **4** to supply or prepare food for **5** to provide what is needed for the continued existence, operation, or growth of: *illustrations which will feed an older child's imagination; pools fed by waterfalls* ▷ *n* **6** the act of feeding **7** food, esp. that given to animals or babies **8** *Brit, Austral and NZ informal* a meal [Old English *fēdan*]

feedback *n* **1** information in response to an inquiry or experiment: *considerable feedback from the customers* **2** the return of part of the output of an electronic circuit to its input **3** the return of part of the sound output of a loudspeaker to the microphone, so that a high-pitched whine is produced

feeder *n* **1** a device used to feed an animal, child, or sick person **2** an animal or a person who feeds: *these larvae are voracious feeders* **3** a road, rail, or air service that links outlying areas to the main network **4** a tributary or channel of a river

feel *vb* **feeling, felt 1** to have a physical or emotional sensation of: *he felt a combination of shame and relief* **2** to become aware of or examine by touching **3** Also: **feel in one's bones** to sense by intuition **4** to believe or think: *I felt I got off pretty lightly* **5 feel for** to show compassion towards **6 feel like** to have an inclination for (something or doing something): *I feel like going to the cinema* **7 feel up to** to be fit enough for (something or doing something) ▷ *n* **8** the act of feeling **9** an impression: *all this mixing and matching has a French feel to it* **10** the sense of touch **11** an instinctive ability: *a feel for art* [Old English *fēlan*]

feeler *n* **1** an organ on an insect's head that is sensitive to touch **2 put out feelers** to make informal suggestions or remarks designed to probe the reactions of others

feeling *n* **1** an emotional reaction: *a feeling of discontent* **2 feelings** emotional sensitivity: *I don't want to hurt your feelings* **3** instinctive appreciation and understanding: *your feeling for language* **4** an intuitive understanding that cannot be explained: *I began to have a sinking feeling that I was not going to get rid of her* **5** opinion or view: *it was his feeling that the report was a misinterpretation of what had been said* **6** capacity for sympathy or affection: *moved by feeling for his fellow citizens* **7 a** the ability to experience physical sensations: *he has no feeling in his left arm* **b** the sensation so experienced **8** the impression or mood created by something: *a feeling of excitement in the air* **9 bad feeling** resentment or anger between people, for example after an argument or an injustice: *his refusal may have triggered bad feeling between the two men* **> feelingly** *adv*

feet *n* **1** the plural of **foot 2 be run** *or* **rushed off one's feet** to be very busy **3 feet of clay** a weakness that is not widely known **4 have** *or* **keep one's feet on the ground** to be practical and reliable **5 put one's feet up** to take a rest **6 stand on one's own feet** to be independent **7 sweep off one's feet** to fill with enthusiasm

feign (fane) *vb* to pretend to experience (a particular feeling): *he didn't have to feign surprise* [Old French *feindre*] **> feigned** *adj*

Feininger *n* Lyonel. 1871–1956, US artist, who worked at the Bauhaus, noted for his use of superimposed translucent planes of colour

feint¹ (faint) *n* **1** a misleading movement designed to distract an opponent, such as in boxing or fencing ▷ *vb* **2** to make a feint [Old French *feindre* to feign]

feint² (faint) *n printing* paper that has pale lines across it for writing on [variant of *faint*]

feisty (fie-stee) *adj* **feistier, feistiest** *informal* **1** showing courage or spirit **2** *US and Canad* frisky **3** *US and Canad* irritable [from dialect *feist* small dog]

feldspar *or* **felspar** *n* a hard mineral that is the main constituent of igneous rocks [German *feldspath*] **>feldspathic** *or* **felspathic** *adj*

felicitations *pl n, interj* expressions of pleasure at someone's success or good fortune; congratulations

felicitous *adj* appropriate and well-chosen: *a felicitous combination of architectural styles*

felicity *n* **1** great happiness and pleasure **2** the quality of being pleasant or desirable: *small moments of architectural felicity amidst acres of monotony* **3** (*pl* **-ties**) an appropriate and well-chosen remark: *Nietzsche's verbal felicities are not lost in translation* [Latin *felicitas* happiness]

feline *adj* **1** of or belonging to the cat family **2** like a cat, esp. in stealth or grace ▷ *n* **3** any member of the cat family [Latin *feles* cat] **>felinity** *n*

Felipe VI *n* born 1968, king of Spain from 2014; succeeded his father Juan Carlos, who abdicated

Felixstowe *n* a port and resort in E England, in Suffolk: ferry connections to Rotterdam and Zeebrugge. Pop: 29 349 (2001)

fell¹ *vb* the past tense of **fall**

fell² *vb* **1** to cut down (a tree) **2** to knock down (a person), esp. in a fight [Old English *fellan*]

fell³ *adj* **in one fell swoop** in one single action or on one single occasion: *they arrested all the hooligans in one fell swoop* [Middle English *fel*]

fell⁴ *n Scot and N English* a mountain, hill, or moor [Old Norse *fjall*]

fell⁵ *n* an animal's skin or hide with its hair [Old High German *fel* skin]

fellatio (fill-**lay**-shee-oh) *n* a sexual activity in which the penis is stimulated by the partner's mouth [Latin *fellare* to suck]

Felling *n* a town in NE England, in Gateshead unitary authority, Tyne and Wear; formerly noted for coal mining. Pop: 34 196 (2001)

Fellini *n* Federico. 1920–93, Italian film director. His films include *La Dolce Vita* (1959), *Satyricon* (1969), and *Intervista* (1987)

felloe *or* **felly** *n, pl* **-loes** *or* **-lies** a segment or the whole rim of a wooden wheel [Old English *felge*]

fellow *n* **1** a man or boy **2** a comrade or associate **3** a person in the same group or condition: *he earned the respect of his fellows at Dunkirk* **4** a member of the governing body at any of various universities or colleges **5** (in Britain) a postgraduate research student ▷ *adj* **6** in the same group or condition: *a conversation with a fellow passenger* [Old English *fēolaga*]

Fellow *n* a senior member of an academic institution

fellow feeling *n* sympathy existing between people who have shared similar experiences

fellowship *n* **1** the state of sharing mutual interests or activities **2** a society of people sharing mutual interests or activities **3** companionship or friendship **4** *education* a financed research post providing study facilities

fellow traveller *n history* a person who sympathized with the Communist Party but was not a member of it

felon *n criminal law* (formerly) a person who committed a serious crime [Old French: villain]

felony *n, pl* **-nies** *criminal law* (formerly) a serious crime, such as murder or arson **>felonious** *adj*

felspar *n* same as **feldspar**

felt¹ *vb* the past of **feel**

felt² *n* a matted fabric of wool, made by working the fibres together under pressure [Old English]

felt-tip pen *n* a pen with a writing point made from pressed fibres

fem. **1** female **2** feminine

female *adj* **1** of the sex producing offspring **2** of or characteristic of a woman **3** (of reproductive organs such as the ovary and carpel) capable of producing reproductive cells (**gametes**) that are female **4** (of flowers) not having parts in which pollen is produced (**stamens**) **5** (of a mechanical component) having an opening into which a projecting male component can be fitted ▷ *n* **6** a female person, animal, or plant [Latin *femina* a woman]

feminine *adj* **1** possessing qualities considered typical of or appropriate to a woman **2** of women **3** *grammar* denoting a gender of nouns that includes some female animate things [Latin *femina* a woman] **>femininity** *n*

feminism *n* a doctrine or movement that advocates equal rights for women **>feminist** *n, adj*

femme fatale (fam fat-**tahl**) *n, pl* **femmes fatales** (fam fat-**tahlz**) an alluring or seductive woman who leads men into dangerous or difficult situations by her charm [French]

femto- *combining form* denoting 10^{-15}: *femtometer* [Danish *femten* fifteen]

femur (**fee**-mer) *n, pl* **femurs** *or* **femora** (**fee**-mer-ra) the thighbone [Latin: thigh] **>femoral** *adj*

fen *n Brit* low-lying flat marshy land [Old English *fenn*]

fence *n* **1** a barrier that encloses an area such as a garden or field, usually made of posts connected by wire rails or boards **2** an obstacle for a horse to jump in steeplechasing or showjumping **3** *slang* a dealer in stolen property **4** *machinery* a guard or guide, esp. in a circular saw or plane **5** (**sit**) **on the fence** (to be) unwilling to commit oneself ▷ *vb* **fencing, fenced** **6** to construct a fence on or around (a piece of land) **7** fence in *or* off to close in *or* separate off with or as if with a fence **8** to fight using swords or foils **9** to argue cleverly but evasively: *they fenced for a while, weighing each other up* [Middle English *fens*, from *defens* defence]

fencing *n* **1** the sport of fighting with swords or foils **2** materials used for making fences

fend *vb* **1** fend for oneself to look after oneself; be independent **2** fend off to defend oneself against (verbal or physical attack) [Middle English *fenden*]

fender *n* **1** a low metal barrier that stops coals from falling out of a fireplace **2** a soft but solid object, such as a coil of rope, hung over the side of a vessel to prevent damage when docking **3** *US and Canad* the wing of a car

Fénelon *n* François de Salignac de La Mothe. 1651–1715, French theologian and writer; author of *Maximes des saints* (1697), a defence of quietism, and *Les aventures de Télémaque* (1699), which was construed as criticizing the government of Louis XIV

fenestration *n* the arrangement of windows in a building [Latin *fenestra* window]

feng shui (fung shway) *n* the Chinese art of deciding the best design or position of a grave, building, etc., in order to bring good luck [Chinese *feng* wind + *shui* water]

Fenian (**feen**-yan) *n* (formerly) a member of an Irish revolutionary organization founded to fight for an independent Ireland [after *Fianna*, legendary band of Irish warriors] **>Fenianism** *n*

fenland *n Brit* an area of low-lying flat marshy land

fennel *n* a fragrant plant whose seeds, leaves, and root are used in cookery [Old English *fenol*]

Fens *pl n* the Fens a flat low-lying area of E England, west and south of the Wash: consisted of marshes until reclaimed in the 17th to 19th centuries

Fenton *n* James (Martin). born 1949, British poet, journalist, and critic. His poetry includes the collection *A German Requiem* (1980) and *Out of Danger* (1993)

fenugreek *n* a Mediterranean plant grown for its heavily scented seeds [Old English *fēnogrēcum*]

feoff (feef) *n* same as **fief** [Anglo-French]

eral *adj* **1** (of animals and plants) existing in a wild state, esp. after being domestic or cultivated **2** savage [Latin *ferus* savage]

erdinand I *n* **1** known as *Ferdinand the Great*. ?1016–65, king of Castile (1035–65) and León (1037–65): achieved control of the Moorish kings of Saragossa, Seville, and Toledo **2** 1503–64, king of Hungary and Bohemia (1526–64); Holy Roman Emperor (1558–64), bringing years of religious warfare to an end **3** 1751–1825, king of the Two Sicilies (1816–25); king of Naples (1759–1806; 1815–25), as Ferdinand IV, being dispossessed by Napoleon (1806–15) **4** 1793–1875, king of Hungary (1830–48) and emperor of Austria (1835–48): abdicated after the Revolution of 1848 in favour of his nephew, Franz Josef I **5** 1861–1948, ruling prince of Bulgaria (1887–1908) and tsar from 1908 until his abdication in 1918 **6** 1865–1927, king of Romania (1914–27): sided with the Allies in World War I

erdinand II *n* **1** 1578–1637, Holy Roman Emperor (1619–37); king of Bohemia (1617–19; 1620–37) and of Hungary (1617–37). His anti-Protestant policies led to the Thirty Years' War **2** title as king of Aragon and Sicily of Ferdinand V

erdinand III *n* **1** 1608–57, Holy Roman Emperor (1637–57) and king of Hungary (1625–57); son of Ferdinand II **2** title as king of Naples of Ferdinand V

erdinand V *n* known as *Ferdinand the Catholic*. 1452–1516, king of Castile (1474–1504); as Ferdinand II, king of Aragon (1479–1516) and Sicily (1468–1516); as Ferdinand III, king of Naples (1504–16). His marriage to Isabella I of Castile (1469) led to the union of Aragon and Castile and his reconquest of Granada from the Moors (1492) completed the unification of Spain. He introduced the Inquisition (1478), expelled the Jews from Spain (1492), and financed Columbus' voyage to the New World

erdinand VII *n* 1784–1833, king of Spain (1808; 1814–33). He precipitated the Carlist Wars by excluding his brother Don Carlos as his successor

ergana *or* **Ferghana** *n* **1** a region of W central Asia, surrounded by high mountains and accessible only from the west; mainly in Uzbekistan and partly in Tajikistan and Kyrgyzstan **2** the chief city of this region, in E Uzbekistan. Pop: 230 000 (2005 est)

erguson *n* Sir Alex(ander) Chapman. born 1941, Scottish footballer and manager: manager of Aberdeen (1978–86) with whom he won the European Cup Winners' Cup (1983); manager of Manchester United (1986–2013) with whom he won thirteen English league titles, five FA Cups, and the Champions League twice (1999, 2008)

erlinghetti *n* Lawrence. born 1919, US poet of the Beat Generation. His poetry includes the collections *Pictures of the Gone World* (1955) and *When I Look at Pictures* (1990)

ermanagh *n* a district and historical county of SW Northern Ireland: contains the Upper and Lower Lough Erne. Pop: 58 705 (2003 est). Area (excluding water): 1700 sq km (656 sq miles)

ermat *n* Pierre de. 1601–65, French mathematician, regarded as the founder of the modern theory of numbers. He studied the properties of whole numbers and, with Pascal, investigated the theory of probability

erment *n* **1** excitement and unrest caused by change or uncertainty **2** any substance, such as yeast, that causes fermentation ▷ *vb* **3** to undergo or cause to undergo fermentation [Latin *fermentum* yeast]

> USAGE See at foment.

ermentation *n* a chemical reaction in which an organic molecule splits into simpler substances, esp. the conversion of sugar to ethyl alcohol by yeast

ermi *n* Enrico. 1901-54, Italian nuclear physicist, in the US from 1939. He was awarded a Nobel prize for physics in 1938 for his work on radioactive substances and nuclear bombardment and headed the group that produced the first controlled nuclear reaction (1942)

fermium *n chem* an element artificially produced by neutron bombardment of plutonium. Symbol: Fm [after Enrico FERMI]

Fermor *n* Sir Patrick (Michael) Leigh. 1915–2011, British traveller and author, noted esp. for the travel books *A Time of Gifts* (1977) and *Between the Woods and the Water* (1986)

fern *n* a flowerless plant with roots, stems, and long feathery leaves that reproduces by releasing spores [Old English *fearn*] > **ferny** *adj*

Fernandel *n* real name *Fernand Joseph Désiré Contandin*. 1903–71, French comic film actor

Fernando de Noronha *n* a volcanic island in the S Atlantic northeast of Cape São Roque: constitutes a federal territory of Brazil; a penal colony since the 18th century; inhabited by military personnel. Area: 26 sq km (10 sq miles)

Fernando Po *n* a former name (until 1973) of Bioko

ferocious *adj* savagely fierce or cruel [Latin *ferox*] > **ferocity** *n*

Ferrar *n* Nicholas. 1592–1637, English mystic. He founded (1625) an Anglican religious community at Little Gidding, Huntingdonshire

Ferrara *n* a city in N Italy, in Emilia–Romagna: a centre of the Renaissance under the House of Este; university (1391). Pop: 130 992 (2001)

Ferrari *n* Enzo. 1898–1988, Italian designer and manufacturer of racing cars

ferret *n* **1** a small yellowish-white animal related to the weasel and bred for hunting rats and rabbits ▷ *vb* **-reting, -reted** **2** to hunt rabbits or rats with ferrets **3** to search around **4 ferret out a** to drive from hiding **b** to find by determined investigation: *she could ferret out little knowledge of his background* [Latin *fur* thief]

ferric *adj* of or containing iron in the trivalent state [Latin *ferrum* iron]

Ferrier *n* Kathleen. 1912–53, British contralto; noted for her expressive voice

Ferris wheel *n* a large vertical fairground wheel with hanging seats for riding on [after G. W. G. Ferris, American engineer]

ferroconcrete *n* same as reinforced concrete

Ferrol *n* See El Ferrol

ferrous *adj* of or containing iron in the divalent state [Latin *ferrum* iron]

ferruginous (fur-rooj-in-uss) *adj* (of a mineral or rock) containing iron [Latin *ferrum* iron]

ferrule *n* a metal ring or cap placed over the end of a stick for added strength [Latin *viria* bracelet]

ferry *n, pl* **-ries** **1** a boat for transporting passengers and vehicles across a body of water, esp. as a regular service **2** such a service ▷ *vb* **-ries, -rying, -ried** **3** to transport or go by ferry **4** to transport (passengers or goods) on a regular basis [Old English *ferian* to carry] > **ferryman** *n*

fertile *adj* **1** capable of producing offspring, crops, or vegetation **2** *biology* capable of growth and development: *fertile seeds* **3** highly productive: *a fertile imagination* **4** *physics* (of a substance) able to be transformed into fissile or fissionable material [Latin *fertilis*] > **fertility** *n*

Fertile Crescent *n* an area of fertile land in the Middle East, extending around the Rivers Tigris and Euphrates in a semicircle from Israel to the Persian Gulf, where the Sumerian, Babylonian, Assyrian, Phoenician, and Hebrew civilizations flourished

fertilize *or* **-lise** *vb* **-lizing, -lized** *or* **-lising, -lised** **1** to provide (an animal or plant) with sperm or pollen to bring about fertilization **2** to supply (soil) with nutrients > **fertilization** *or* **-lisation** *n*

fertilizer *or* **-liser** *n* any substance, such as manure, added to soil to increase its productivity

fervent *or* **fervid** *adj* intensely sincere and passionate [Latin *fervere* to boil] > **fervently** *adv*

fervour *or* US **fervor** *n* great intensity of feeling or belief [Latin *fervere* to boil]

Fès or **Fez** n a city in N central Morocco, traditional capital of the north: became an independent kingdom in the 11th century, at its height in the 14th century; religious centre; university (850). Pop: 664 000 (2003)

fescue n a pasture and lawn grass with stiff narrow leaves [Old French *festu*]

Fessenden n Reginald (Aubrey). 1866–1932, Canadian physicist and radio engineer; a pioneer of radio transmission, he made the first sound broadcast in North America (1906)

fest n an event at which the emphasis is on a particular activity: *fashion fest* [German: festival]

fester vb **1** to grow worse and increasingly hostile: *the bitterness which had been festering beneath the surface* **2** (of a wound) to form pus **3** to rot and decay: *rubbish festered in the heat* [Old French *festre* suppurating sore]

festival n **1** an organized series of special events and performances: *the Edinburgh Festival* **2** a day or period set aside for celebration [Latin *festivus* joyful]

Festival Hall n a concert hall in London, on the South Bank of the Thames: constructed for the 1951 Festival of Britain; completed 1964–65. Official name: **Royal Festival Hall**

festive adj of or like a celebration [Latin *festivus* joyful]

festivity n, pl **-ties 1** happy celebration: *a spirit of joy and festivity* **2** festivities celebrations

festoon vb **1** to drape with decorations: *Christmas trees festooned with fairy lights* ▷ n **2** a decorative chain of flowers or ribbons suspended in loops [Italian *festone* ornament for a feast]

feta n a white Greek cheese made from sheep's or goat's milk [Modern Greek]

fetal alcohol syndrome n a condition in newborn babies caused by excessive alcohol intake by the mother during pregnancy: characterized by various defects including mental retardation

fetch[1] vb **1** to go after and bring back **2** to be sold for (a certain price): *Impressionist pictures fetch very high prices* **3** informal to give someone (a blow or slap) **4** fetch and carry to perform menial tasks [Old English *feccan*]

fetch[2] n the ghost or apparition of a living person [origin unknown]

fetching adj informal attractive: *a fetching dress*

fetch up vb **1** US and NZ informal to arrive or end up **2** slang to vomit food

fete (fate) n **1** an event, usually outdoors, with stalls, competitions, etc., held to raise money for charity ▷ vb **feting, feted 2** to honour and entertain (someone) publicly: *the President was feted with an evening of music and dancing* [French]

fetid or **foetid** adj having a stale and unpleasant smell [Latin *fetere* to stink]

fetish n **1 a** a form of behaviour in which a person derives sexual satisfaction from handling an object **b** any object that is involved in such behaviour **2** any object, activity, etc., to which one is excessively devoted: *cleanliness is almost a fetish with her* **3** an object that is believed to have magical powers [Portuguese *feitiço* sorcery] **> fetishism** n **> fetishist** n

fetlock n **1** the back part of a horse's leg, just behind the hoof **2** the tuft of hair growing from this part [Middle English *fetlak*]

fetter n **1** fetters checks or restraints: *free from the fetters of religion* **2** a chain fixed around a prisoner's ankle ▷ vb **3** to prevent from behaving freely and naturally: *fettered by bureaucracy* **4** to tie up in fetters [Old English *fetor*]

fettle n in fine fettle in good spirits or health [Old English *fetel* belt]

fetus or **foetus** (fee-tuss) n, pl **-tuses** the embryo of a mammal in the later stages of development [Latin: offspring] **> fetal** or **foetal** adj

feu n Scots Law a right to the use of land in return for a fixed annual payment (**feu duty**) [Old French]

Feuchtwanger n Lion. 1884–1958, German novelist and

dramatist, lived in the US (1940–58): noted for his historical novels, including *Die hässliche Herzogin* (1923) and *Jud Süss* (1925)

feud n **1** long and bitter hostility between two families, clans, or individuals ▷ vb **2** to carry on a feud [Old French *feide*]

feudal adj of or characteristic of feudalism [Medieval Latin *feudum* fief]

feudalism n the legal and social system in medieval Europe, in which people were given land and protection by a lord in return for which they worked and fought for him. Also called: **feudal system**

Feuerbach n Ludwig Andreas. 1804–72, German materialist philosopher: in *The Essence of Christianity* (1841), translated into English by George Eliot (1853), he maintained that God is merely an outward projection of man's inner self

fever n **1** an abnormally high body temperature, accompanied by a fast pulse rate, shivering, and nausea. Related adjective: **febrile 2** any disease characterized by a high temperature **3** intense nervous excitement: *she waited in a fever of anxiety* [Latin *febris*]

feverish or **fevered** adj **1** suffering from fever **2** in a state of nervous excitement: *a feverish scramble to buy shares* **> feverishly** adv

fever pitch n a state of intense excitement

few adj **1** hardly any: *few homes had telephones in Paris in the 1930s* **2** a few a small number of: *a few days ago* **3** a good few informal several **4** few and far between scarce **5** quite a few informal several [Old English *fēawa*]

> **USAGE** See at less.

fey adj **1** vague and whimsically strange **2** having the ability to look into the future [Old English *fæge* marked out for death]

Feydeau n Georges. 1862–1921, French dramatist, noted for his farces, esp. *La Dame de chez Maxim* (1899) and *Occupe-toi d'Amélie* (1908)

Feynman n Richard. 1918–88, US physicist, noted for his research on quantum electrodynamics; shared the Nobel prize for physics in 1965

fez n, pl **fezzes** a round red brimless hat with a flat top and a tassel hanging from it. Formerly worn by men in Turkey and some Arab countries [Turkish]

Fez n a variant of Fès

Fezzan n a region of SW Libya, in the Sahara: a former province (until 1963)

ff. and the following (pages, lines, etc.)

Ffestiniog n a town in N Wales, in Gwynedd: tourist attractions include former slate quarries and a narrow-gauge railway at nearby Blaenau Ffestiniog. Pop: 4830 (2001)

FI Falkland Islands

fiancé or fem **fiancée** (fee-on-say) n a person who is engaged to be married [Old French *fiancier* to promise, betroth]

fiasco n, pl **-cos** or **-coes** an action or attempt that fails completely in a ridiculous or disorganized way: *the invasion of Cuba ended in a fiasco* [Italian: flask; sense development obscure]

fiat (fie-at) n **1** an official order issued without the consultation of those expected to obey it: *the junta ruled by fiat* **2** official permission [Latin: let it be done]

fib n **1** a trivial and harmless lie ▷ vb **fibbing, fibbed 2** to tell such a lie [origin unknown] **> fibber** n

Fibiger n Johannes Andreas Grib. 1867–1928, Danish physician: Nobel prize for physiology or medicine (1926) for his work in cancer research

Fibonacci n Leonardo, also called *Leonardo of Pisa*. ?1170–?1250, Italian mathematician: popularized the decimal system in Europe

fibre or US **fiber** n **1** a natural or synthetic thread that may be spun into yarn **2** a threadlike animal or plant tissue: *a simple network of nerve fibres* **3** a fibrous substance that helps the body digest food: *fruits, vegetables, grains, lentils, and beans are high in fibre* **4** strength of character: *moral fibre* **5** essential substance or nature: *my every fibre sang out in sudden relief* [Latin *fibra* filament, entrails] **> fibrous** *adj*

breboard *n* a building material made of compressed wood

breglass *n* **1** material consisting of matted fine glass fibres, used as insulation **2** a light strong material made by bonding fibreglass with a synthetic resin, used for boats and car bodies

bre optics *n* the transmission of information by light along very thin flexible fibres of glass **> fibre optic** *adj*

bril (fibe-rill) *n* a small fibre

brillation *n* uncontrollable twitching of muscle fibres, esp. those of the heart

brin *n* a white insoluble elastic protein formed when blood clots

brinogen (fib-rin-no-jen) *n biology* a soluble plasma protein involved in blood clotting

bro *n Austral* a mixture of cement and asbestos fibre, used in sheets for building. Short for: fibrocement

broid (fibe-royd) *adj* **1** *anatomy* (of structures or tissues) containing or resembling fibres ▷ *n* **2** a harmless tumour composed of fibrous connective tissue

brosis (fibe-roh-siss) *n* the formation of an abnormal amount of fibrous tissue

brositis (fibe-roh-site-iss) *n* inflammation of fibrous tissue, esp. of the back muscles, causing pain and stiffness

bula (fib-yew-la) *n, pl* **-lae** (-lee) *or* **-las** the outer and thinner of the two bones between the knee and ankle of the human leg [Latin: a clasp] **> fibular** *adj*

che (feesh) *n* a sheet of film for storing publications in miniature form

ichte *n* Johann Gottlieb. 1762–1814, German philosopher: expounded ethical idealism

icino *n* Marsilio. 1433–99, Italian Neoplatonist philosopher: attempted to integrate Platonism with Christianity

ckle *adj* **1** changeable in purpose, affections, etc.: *notoriously fickle voters* **2** (of the weather) changing often and suddenly [Old English *ficol* deceitful] **> fickleness** *n*

ction *n* **1** literary works invented by the imagination, such as novels **2** an invented story or explanation: *the fiction that the Baltic states freely joined the USSR* **3** *law* something assumed to be true for the sake of convenience, though probably false [Latin *fictio* a fashioning] **> fictional** *adj*

ctionalize *or* **-lise** *vb* **-lizing, -lized** *or* **-lising, -lised** to make into fiction

ctitious *adj* **1** not genuine: *rumours of false accounting and fictitious loans had surrounded the bank for years* **2** of or in fiction

ddle *n* **1** *informal or disparaging* the violin **2** a violin played as a folk instrument **3** *Brit and NZ informal* a dishonest action or scheme **4 on the fiddle** *informal* engaged in an illegal or fraudulent undertaking **5 fit as a fiddle** *informal* in very good health **6 play second fiddle** *informal* to undertake a role that is less important or powerful than someone else's ▷ *vb* **-dling, -dled** **7** to play (a tune) on the fiddle **8** *informal* to do (something) by illegal or dishonest means **9** *informal* to falsify (accounts) **10 fiddle with** to move or touch (something) restlessly or nervously **11 fiddle about** *or* **around** *informal* to waste time [Old English *fithele*]

ddle-faddle *interj* old-fashioned nonsense [reduplication of *fiddle*]

ddler *n* **1** a person who plays the fiddle **2** a small burrowing crab **3** *informal* a person who dishonestly alters something or lies in order to get money

ddlesticks *interj* an expression of annoyance or disagreement

fiddling *adj* small or unimportant

fiddly *adj* **-dlier, -dliest** small and awkward to do or handle

fidelity *n, pl* **-ties** **1** faithfulness to one's spouse or lover **2** loyalty to a person, belief, or cause **3** accuracy in reporting detail: *an account of the invasion written with objectivity and fidelity* **4** *electronics* the degree to which an amplifier or radio accurately reproduces the input signal [Latin *fides* faith]

fidget *vb* **-dgeting, -dgeted** **1** to move about restlessly **2 fidget with** to make restless or uneasy movements with (something): *he broke off, fidgeting with the papers, unable to meet their gaze* ▷ *n* **3** a person who fidgets **4 the fidgets** a state of restlessness: *these youngsters are very highly strung and tend to get the fidgets* [earlier *fidge*] **> fidgety** *adj*

fiduciary (fid-yewsh-ya-ree) *law* *n* **1** a person bound to act for someone else's benefit, as a trustee ▷ *adj* **2** of or relating to a trust or trustee [Latin *fiducia* trust]

fie *interj obsolete or facetious* an exclamation of disapproval [Old French *fi*]

fief (feef) *n* (in feudal Europe) land granted by a lord in return for military service [Old French *fie*]

fiefdom *n* **1** (in Feudal Europe) the property owned by a lord **2** an area over which a person has influence or authority

field *n* **1** an area of uncultivated grassland; meadow **2** a piece of cleared land used for pasture or growing crops **3** a marked off area on which sports or athletic competitions are held **4** an area that is rich in minerals or other natural resources: *an oil field* **5 a** all the competitors in a competition **b** the competitors in a competition excluding the favourite **6** a battlefield **7** *cricket* the fielders collectively **8** a wide expanse of land covered by some substance such as snow or lava **9** an area of human activity or knowledge: *the most distinguished physicist in the field of quantum physics* **10** a place away from the laboratory or classroom where practical work is done **11** the surface or background of something, such as a flag **12** *physics* In full: **field of force** the region surrounding a body, such as a magnet, within which it can exert a force on another similar body not in contact with it **13 play the field** *informal* to have many romantic relationships ▷ *adj* **14** *military* of equipment or personnel for operations in the field: *field guns* ▷ *vb* **15** *sport* to catch or return (the ball) as a fielder **16** *sport* to send (a player or team) onto the field to play **17** *sport* (of a player or team) to act or take turn as a fielder or fielders **18** *informal* to deal successfully with (a question or remark) [Old English *feld*]

Field *n* John. 1782–1837, Irish composer and pianist, lived in Russia from 1803: invented the nocturne

field day *n* **1** *informal* an opportunity or occasion for unrestrained action, esp. if previously denied or restricted: *the revelations gave the press a field day* **2** *military* a day devoted to manoeuvres or exercises

fielder *n cricket etc.* a member of the fielding side

field event *n* a competition, such as the discus, that takes place on a field as opposed to the track

fieldfare *n* a type of large thrush [Old English *feldefare*]

field glasses *pl n* binoculars

field hockey *n US and Canad* hockey played on a field, as distinguished from ice hockey

Fielding *n* Henry. 1707–54, English novelist and dramatist, noted particularly for his picaresque novel *Tom Jones* (1749) and for *Joseph Andrews* (1742), which starts as a parody of Richardson's *Pamela*: also noted as an enlightened magistrate and a founder of the Bow Street runners (1749)

field marshal *n* an officer holding the highest rank in certain armies

fieldmouse *n, pl* **-mice** a nocturnal mouse that lives in woods and fields

field officer *n* an officer holding the rank of major, lieutenant colonel, or colonel

Fields n 1 Dame **Gracie**. real name *Grace Stansfield*. 1898–1979, English popular singer and entertainer 2 **W. C.** real name *William Claude Dukenfield*. 1880–1946, US film actor, noted for his portrayal of comic roles

fieldsman n, pl -**men** *cricket* a fielder

field sports pl n sports carried on in the countryside, such as hunting or fishing

field trip n an expedition, esp. by students, to study something at first hand

fieldwork n *military* a temporary structure used in defending a place or position

field work n an investigation made in the field as opposed to the classroom or laboratory > **field worker** n

fiend (feend) n 1 an evil spirit 2 a cruel or wicked person 3 *informal* a person who is extremely interested in or fond of something: *a fitness fiend* [Old English *fēond*] > **fiendish** adj > **fiendishly** adv

Fiend n the Fiend the devil

Fiennes n 1 Ralph (**Nathanial**). born 1962, British actor; his films include *Schindler's List* (1993), *The English Patient* (1997), *The End of the Affair* (2000), *Spider* (2002), and three films (2005–11) in the *Harry Potter* series 2 Sir **Ranulph** (**Twistleton-Wykeham-**). born 1944, British explorer; led the first surface journey around the earth's polar axis (1979–82); unsupported crossing of Antarctica (1992–93); in 2003 he raised money for a heart charity by running seven marathons in seven days on seven continents

fierce adj 1 very aggressive or angry: *a fierce dog* 2 intense or strong: *a fierce wind* [Latin *ferus*] > **fiercely** adv

fiery (fire-ee) adj **fierier, fieriest** 1 consisting of or like fire: *a fiery explosion* 2 displaying strong passion, esp. anger: *a fiery speech* 3 (of food) very spicy > **fierily** adv > **fieriness** n

Fiesole n a town in central Italy, in Tuscany near Florence: Etruscan and Roman remains. Pop: 14 085 (2001). Ancient name: **Faesulae**

fiesta n (esp. in Spain and Latin America) a religious festival or carnival [Spanish]

FIFA (fee-fa) International Association Football Federation [French *Fédération Internationale de Football Association*]

fife n a small high-pitched flute, often used in military bands [Old High German *pfifa*]

Fife n a council area and historical county of E central Scotland, bordering on the North Sea between the Firths of Tay and Forth: coastal lowlands in the north and east, with several ranges of hills; mainly agricultural. Administrative centre: Glenrothes. Pop: 352 040 (2003 est). Area: 1323 sq km (511 sq miles)

fifteen n 1 the cardinal number that is the sum of ten and five 2 a numeral, 15 or XV, representing this number 3 something representing or consisting of 15 units 4 a Rugby Union team ▷ adj 5 amounting to fifteen: *fifteen trees* > **fifteenth** adj, n

fifth adj 1 of or being number five in a series ▷ n 2 one of five equal parts of something 3 *music* the interval between one note and the note three-and-a-half tones higher or lower than it 4 an additional high gear fitted to some vehicles, esp. certain sports cars

fifth column n any group that secretly helps the enemies of its own country or organization > **fifth columnist** n

fifty n, pl -**ties** 1 the cardinal number that is the product of ten and five 2 a numeral, 50 or L, representing this number 3 something representing or consisting of 50 units ▷ adj 4 amounting to fifty: *fifty bodies* > **fiftieth** adj, n

fifty-fifty adj, adv *informal* 1 in equal parts 2 just as likely to happen as not to happen: *a fifty-fifty chance of survival*

fig n 1 a soft sweet fruit full of tiny seeds, which grows on a tree 2 **not care** *or* **give a fig** not to care at all: *he did not give a fig for his enemies* [Latin *ficus* fig tree]

fig. 1 figurative(ly) 2 figure

fight vb **fighting, fought** 1 to struggle against (an enemy) in battle or physical combat 2 to struggle to overcome o destroy: *to fight drug trafficking* 3 to carry on (a battle or contest) 4 to make (one's way) somewhere with difficulty: *they fought their way upstream* 5 **fight for** to uphold (a cause) by struggling: *fight for your rights* 6 **fight out** to struggle or compete until a decisive result is obtained 7 **fight shy of** to avoid: *they fought shy of direct involvement in the conflict* ▷ n 8 a battle 9 a quarrel or contest 10 a boxing match 11 **put up a fight** to offer resistance [Old English *feohtan*] > **fighting** n

fighter n 1 a professional boxer 2 a person who has determination 3 *military* an armed aircraft for destroyin other aircraft

fighting chance n a slight chance of success dependent on a struggle

fight off vb 1 to drive away (an attacker) 2 to struggle to avoid: *to fight off infection*

fig leaf n 1 a representation of a leaf of the fig tree used in sculpture to cover the genitals of nude figures 2 anything used to conceal something thought to be shameful: *the agreement was a fig leaf for Hitler's violation of th treaty*

figment n a figment of one's imagination something nonexistent and only imagined by someone [Latin *fingere* to shape]

figuration n ornamentation

figurative adj 1 (of language) abstract, imaginative, or symbolic; not literal 2 (of art) involving realistic representation of people and things > **figuratively** adv

figure n 1 a written symbol for a number 2 an amount expressed in numbers 3 figures calculations with numbers 4 visible shape or form; outline 5 a slim bodil shape: *it's not good for your figure* 6 a well-known person: *a public figure* 7 a representation in painting or sculpture, esp. of the human body 8 an illustration or diagram in text 9 a decorative pattern 10 a fixed set of movements in dancing or skating 11 *geometry* any combination of points, lines, curves, or planes 12 *music* a characteristic short pattern of notes 13 **figure of fun** a person who is often laughed at by other people ▷ vb -**uring, -ured** 14 t calculate (sums or amounts) 15 *US, Canad, Austral and NZ informal* to consider 16 to be included or play a part: *a house which figures in several of White's novels* 17 *informal* to be consistent with expectation: *he's a small-time crook, earns most of his cash as an informer. – That figures* [Latin *figura* a shape]

figured adj 1 decorated with a design: *a chair upholstered ir figured velvet* 2 *music* ornamental

figurehead n 1 a person who is formally the head of a movement or an organization, but has no real authorit 2 a carved bust on the bow of some sailing vessels

figure of speech n an expression, such as a simile, in which words do not have their literal meaning

figure out vb *informal* to work out, solve, or understand: *can't figure him out*

figure skating n ice skating in which the skater traces outlines of selected patterns > **figure skater** n

figurine n a small carved or moulded figure [French]

Fiji n 1 an independent republic, consisting of 844 island (chiefly Viti Levu and Vanua Levu) in the SW Pacific: a British colony (1874–1970); a member of the Commonwealth (1970–87 and from 1997); the large islands are of volcanic origin, surrounded by coral reefs smaller ones are of coral. Official language: English. Religion: Christian and Hindu. Currency: dollar. Capital: Suva. Pop: 896 758 (2013 est). Area: 18 272 sq km (7055 sq miles) ▷ n, adj 2 another word for **Fijian**

Fijian n 1 a member of the indigenous people of mixed Melanesian and Polynesian descent inhabiting Fiji 2 the language of this people, belonging to the Malayo-Polynesian family ▷ adj 3 of, relating to, or characteristic of Fiji or its inhabitants ▶ Also: **Fiji**

filament n 1 the thin wire inside a light bulb that emit light 2 *electronics* a high-resistance wire forming the cathode in some valves **3** a single strand of fibre **4** *botany* the stalk of a stamen [Latin *filum* thread] **>filamentary** *adj*

lbert *n* the brown edible nuts of the hazel [after St Philbert, because the nuts are ripe around his feast day, August 22]

lch *vb* to steal in small amounts [Middle English *filchen* to steal, attack]

le¹ *n* **1** a folder or box used to keep documents in order **2** the documents, etc., kept in this way **3** documents or information about a specific subject or person: *the doctor handed him his file* **4** a line of people in marching formation, one behind another **5** *computers* an organized collection of related records **6** **on file** recorded for reference, as in a file ▷ *vb* **filing, filed** **7** to place (a document) in a file **8** to place (a legal document) on public or official record **9** to bring a lawsuit, esp. for divorce **10** to submit (a report or story) to a newspaper **11** to march or walk in a line [Latin *filum* a thread]

le² *n* **1** a hand tool consisting of a steel blade with small cutting teeth on its faces, used for shaping or smoothing ▷ *vb* **filing, filed** **2** to shape or smooth (a surface) with a file [Old English *fīl*]

le sharing *n* the practice of sharing computer data on space on a network

lial *adj* of or suitable to a son or daughter: *filial duty* [Latin *filius* son]

libuster *n* **1** the process of obstructing legislation by means of long speeches so that time runs out and a vote cannot be taken **2** a legislator who engages in such obstruction ▷ *vb* **3** to obstruct (legislation) with such delaying tactics [probably from Dutch *vrijbuiter* pirate]

ligree *n* **1** delicate ornamental work of gold or silver wire ▷ *adj* **2** made of filigree [Latin *filum* thread + *granum* grain]

lings *pl n* shavings or particles removed by a file: *iron filings*

ilipino (fill-lip-pee-no) *adj* **1** of or relating to the Philippines or their inhabitants ▷ *n, pl* **-nos** **2** Also (fem): **Filipina** a native or inhabitant of the Philippines

ll *vb* (often foll. by *up*) **1** to make or become full **2** to occupy the whole of: *their supporters filled the entire stand* **3** to plug (a gap or crevice) **4** to meet (a requirement or need) satisfactorily: *this book fills a major gap* **5** to cover (a page or blank space) with writing or drawing **6** to hold and perform the duties of (an office or position) **7** to appoint or elect an occupant to (an office or position) ▷ *n* **8** **one's fill** sufficient for one's needs or wants ► See also **fill in, fill out, fill up** [Old English *fyllan*]

ller *n* **1** a paste used for filling in cracks or holes in a surface before painting **2** *journalism* an item to fill space between more important articles

llet *n* **1** a piece of boneless meat or fish **2** a thin strip of ribbon or lace worn in the hair or around the neck **3** *archit* a narrow flat moulding ▷ *vb* **-leting, -leted** **4** to cut or prepare (meat or fish) as a fillet [Latin *filum* thread]

ll in *vb* **1** to complete (a form) **2** to act as a substitute **3** to put material into (a hole) so as to make it level with a surface **4** *informal* to give (a person) fuller details

lling *n* **1** a substance or thing used to fill something: *a sandwich filling* **2** *dentistry* a substance that fills a gap or cavity of a tooth ▷ *adj* **3** (of food or a meal) substantial and satisfying

lling station *n chiefly Brit* a place where petrol and other supplies for motorists are sold

llip *n* **1** something that adds stimulation or enjoyment **2** the action of holding a finger towards the palm with the thumb and suddenly releasing it with a snapping sound [imitative]

illmore *n* Millard. 1800-74, 13th president of the US (1850-53); a leader of the Whig Party

ll out *vb* **1** to fill in (a form or application) **2** to make or become plumper, thicker, or rounder **3** to make more substantial: *he filled out his speech with a few jokes*

ll up *vb* **1** to complete (a form or application) **2** to make or become full

lly *n, pl* **-lies** a young female horse [Old Norse *fylja*]

film *n* **1 a** a sequence of images projected onto a screen, creating the illusion of movement **b** a form of entertainment in such a sequence of images. Related adjective: **cinematic** **2** a thin flexible strip of cellulose coated with a photographic emulsion, used to make negatives and slides **3** a thin coating, covering, or layer: *a fine film of dust covered the floor* **4** a thin sheet of any material, as of plastic for packaging ▷ *vb* **5 a** to photograph with a movie or video camera **b** to make a film of (a screenplay or event) **6 film over** to cover or become covered with a thin layer ▷ *adj* **7** of or relating to films or the cinema [Old English *filmen* membrane]

filmic *adj* of or suggestive of films or the cinema **>filmically** *adv*

film star *n* a popular film actor or actress

film strip *n* a strip of film composed of different images projected separately as slides

filmy *adj* **filmier, filmiest** very thin and almost transparent: *a shirt of filmy black chiffon* **>filmily** *adv* **>filminess** *n*

filo *or* **filo pastry** (feel-o) *n* a type of flaky Greek pastry in very thin sheets [Modern Greek *phullon* leaf]

Filofax *n trademark* a type of loose-leaf ring binder, used as a portable personal filing system

filter *n* **1** a substance, such as paper or sand, that allows fluid to pass but retains solid particles **2** any device containing such a substance, esp. a tip on the mouth end of a cigarette **3** any electronic or acoustic device that blocks signals of certain frequencies while allowing others to pass **4** any transparent disc of gelatine or glass used to reduce the intensity of given frequencies from the light leaving a lamp or entering a camera **5** *Brit* a traffic signal which permits vehicles to turn either left or right when the main signals are red ▷ *vb* **6** Also: **filter out** to remove or separate (particles) from (a liquid or gas) by a filter **7** Also: **filter through** to pass through a filter or something like a filter [Medieval Latin *filtrum* piece of felt used as a filter]

filter out *or* **filter through** *vb* to become known gradually: *the crowd broke up when the news filtered through*

filter paper *n* a porous paper used for filtering liquids

filter tip *n* **1** an attachment to the mouth end of a cigarette for trapping impurities **2** a cigarette with such an attachment **>filter-tipped** *adj*

filth *n* **1** disgusting dirt and muck **2** offensive material or language [Old English *fӯlth*] **>filthy** *adj* **>filthiness** *n*

filtrate *n* **1** a liquid or gas that has been filtered ▷ *vb* **-trating, -trated** **2** to filter [Medieval Latin *filtrare* to filter] **>filtration** *n*

fin *n* **1** any of the winglike projections from a fish's body enabling it to balance and swim **2** *Brit* a vertical surface to which the rudder is attached at the rear of an aeroplane **3** a swimmer's flipper [Old English *finn*] **>finned** *adj*

Fin 1 Finland **2** Finnish

fin. 1 finance **2** financial

finagle (fin-nay-gl) *vb* **-gling, -gled** *informal* to use or achieve by craftiness or trickery [origin unknown]

final *adj* **1** of or occurring at the end; last **2** having no possibility of further discussion, action, or change: *a final decision* ▷ *n* **3** a deciding contest between the winners of previous rounds in a competition ► See also **finals** [Latin *finis* limit, boundary] **>finality** *n* **>finally** *adv*

finale (fin-nah-lee) *n* the concluding part of a dramatic performance or musical composition [Italian]

finalist *n* a contestant who has reached the last stage of a competition

finalize *or* **-lise** *vb* **-lizing, -lized** *or* **-lising, -lised** to put into final form; settle: *plans have yet to be finalized* **>finalization** *or* **-lisation** *n*

USAGE Although *finalize* has been in widespread use for some time, many speakers and writers still prefer to use *complete*, *conclude*, or *make final*, esp. in formal contexts.

finals *pl n* **1** the deciding part of a competition **2** *education, Brit and S African* the last examinations in an academic course

finance *vb* **-nancing, -nanced 1** to provide or obtain funds for (a project or large purchase) ▷ *n* **2** the system of money, credit, and investment **3** management of money, loans, or credits: *the dangerous political arena of public-sector finance* **4** funds or the provision of funds **5 finances** money resources: *the company's crumbling finances* [Old French *finer* to end, settle by payment]

financial *adj* **1** of or relating to finance, finances, or people who manage money **2** *Austral and NZ informal* having ready money **> financially** *adv*

financial year *n* any annual accounting period

financier *n* a person who is engaged in large-scale financial operations

finch *n* a small songbird with a short strong beak [Old English *finc*]

Finchley *n* a residential district of N London, part of the Greater London borough of Barnet from 1965

find *vb* **finding, found 1** to discover by chance **2** to discover by search or effort **3** to realize or become aware: *I have found that if you make the effort then people will be more willing to help you* **4** to consider (someone or something) to have a particular quality: *his business partner had found that odd* **5** to experience (a particular feeling): *she found comfort in his words* **6** *law* to pronounce (the defendant) guilty or not guilty **7** to reach (a target) **8** to provide, esp. with difficulty: *we'll find room for you too* **9 find one's feet** to become capable or confident ▷ *n* **10** a person or thing that is found, esp. a valuable discovery: *the archaeological find of the century* [Old English *findan*]

finder *n* **1** a small telescope fitted to a larger one **2** a person or thing that finds **3** *photog* short for **viewfinder**

finding *n* the conclusion reached after an inquiry or investigation

find out *vb* **1** to learn something that one did not already know **2 find someone out** to discover that someone has been dishonest or deceitful

fine¹ *adj* **1** very good **2** superior in skill: *a fine doctor* **3** (of weather) clear and dry **4** *informal* quite well: *I felt fine* **5** satisfactory: *as far as we can tell, everything is fine* **6** of delicate or careful workmanship: *fine porcelain* **7** subtle: *too fine a distinction* **8** very thin or slender: *fine soft hair* **9** very small: *fine print* **10** (of edges or blades) sharp **11** fancy, showy, or smart **12** good-looking **13** *humorous* disappointing or terrible: *a fine mess!* ▷ *adv* **14** *informal* very well: *that's what we've always done, and it suits us just fine* ▷ *vb* **fining, fined 15** to make (something) finer or thinner **16 fine down** to make (a theory or criticism) more precise or exact [Latin *finis* end, boundary, as in *finis honorum* the highest degree of honour] **> finely** *adv*

fine² *n* **1** a payment imposed as a penalty ▷ *vb* **fining, fined 2** to impose a fine on [Old French *fin*]

fine art *n* **1** art produced chiefly to appeal to the sense of beauty **2** any of the fields in which such art is produced, such as painting, sculpture, and engraving

fine-drawn *adj* **1** (of arguments or distinctions) subtle **2** (of wire) drawn out until very fine

finery *n* elaborate or showy decoration, esp. clothing and jewellery: *the actress dressed up in her finery*

fines herbes (feenz airb) *pl n* finely chopped mixed herbs, used to flavour omelettes [French]

finespun *adj* **1** spun or drawn out to a fine thread **2** excessively subtle or concerned with minute detail: *a finespun theological debate*

finesse (fin-ness) *n* **1** elegant and delicate skill **2** subtlety and tact in handling difficult situations: *a lack of diplomatic finesse* **3** *bridge, whist* an attempt to win a trick when opponents hold a high card in the suit led by playing a lower card ▷ *vb* **-nessing, -nessed 4** to bring about with finesse **5** *bridge, whist* to play (a card) as a finesse [Old French]

fine-tooth comb *or* **fine-toothed comb** *n* **1** a comb with fine teeth set closely together **2 go over with a fine-tooth comb** to examine very thoroughly

fine-tune *vb* **-tuning, -tuned** to make fine adjustments to (something) so that it works really well

Fingal's Cave *n* a cave in W Scotland, on the Isle of Staffa in the Inner Hebrides: basaltic pillars. Length: 69 m (227 ft). Height: 36 m (117 ft)

finger *n* **1** one of the four long jointed parts of the hand **2** the part of a glove made to cover a finger **3** something that resembles a finger in shape or function **4** a quantity of liquid in a glass as deep as a finger is wide **5 get** *or* **pull one's finger out** *Brit and NZ informal* to begin or speed up activity, esp. after initial delay **6 put one's finger on** to identify precisely **7 put the finger on** *informal* to inform on or identify, esp. for the police **8 twist around one's little finger** to have easy and complete influence over ▷ *vb* **9** to touch or manipulate with the fingers; handle **10** to use one's fingers in playing (a musical instrument) **11** *informal, chiefly US* to identify as a criminal or suspect [Old English] **> fingerless** *adj*

fingerboard *n* the long strip of hard wood on a violin, guitar, etc., upon which the strings are stopped by the fingers

finger bowl *n* a small bowl of water for rinsing the fingers at table during a meal, esp. at a formal dinner

fingering *n* **1** the technique of using one's fingers in playing a musical instrument **2** the numerals in a musical part indicating this ▷ *vb*

fingernail *n* a thin hard clear plate covering part of the upper surface of the end of each finger

fingerprint *n* **1** an impression of the pattern of ridges on the inner surface of the end of each finger and thumb ▷ *vb* **2** to take an inked impression of the fingerprints of (a person) **3** to take a sample of the DNA of (a person)

fingerstall *n* a protective covering for a finger

fingertip *n* **1** the end of a finger **2 have at one's fingertips** to know thoroughly

finicky *or* **finicking** *adj* **1** extremely fussy **2** overelaborate or ornate: *finicky designer patterns* [earlier *finical*, from FINE¹]

finis *n* the end: used at the end of books [Latin]

finish *vb* **1** to bring to an end; conclude or stop **2** to be at or come to the end; use up **3** to bring to a desired or complete condition **4** to put a particular surface texture on (wood, cloth, or metal) **5 finish off a** to complete by doing the last part of: *he finished off his thesis last week* **b** to destroy or defeat completely: *he finished off Faldo at the 16th hole* **6 finish with** to end a relationship with (someone) ▷ *n* **7** the final stage or part; end **8** death or absolute defeat **9** the surface texture of wood, cloth, or metal **10** a thing or event that completes [Latin *finire*]

finishing school *n* a private school for girls that teaches social skills and polite behaviour

Finistère *n* a department of NW France, at the tip of the Breton peninsula. Capital: Quimper. Pop: 863 798 (2003 est). Area: 7029 sq km (2741 sq miles)

Finisterre *n* **1 Cape Finisterre** a headland in NW Spain: the westernmost point of the Spanish mainland **2** an English name for **Finistère**

finite (fine-ite) *adj* **1** having limits in size, space, or time: *finite supplies of fossil fuels* **2** *maths, logic* having a countable number of elements **3** *grammar* denoting any form of a verb inflected for person, number, and tense [Latin *finitus* limited]

Finland *n* **1** a republic in N Europe, on the Baltic Sea: ceded to Russia by Sweden in 1809; gained independence in 1917; Soviet invasion successfully withstood in 1939–40, with the loss of Karelia; a member of the European Union. It is generally low-lying, with about 50 000 lakes, extensive forests, and peat bogs.

Official languages: Finnish and Swedish. Religion: Christian, Lutheran majority. Currency: euro. Capital: Helsinki. Pop: 5 266 114 (2013 est). Area: 337 000 sq km (130 120 sq miles). Finnish name: **Suomi 2 Gulf of Finland** an arm of the Baltic Sea between Finland, Estonia, and Russia

inlay n Carlos Juan. 1833–1915, Cuban physician: discovered that the mosquito was the vector of yellow fever

inn¹ n a native or inhabitant of Finland

inn² n Neil (**Mullane**). born 1958, New Zealand singer and songwriter; lead singer with the group Crowded House (from 1985) with whom he recorded the albums *Crowded House* (1986), *Woodface* (1991), and *Time on Earth* (2007). Solo albums include *Try Whistling This* (1998)

nnan haddock or **finnan haddie** n a smoked haddock [*Findon*, town near Aberdeen]

inney n 1 Albert. born 1936, British stage and film actor: his films include *Saturday Night and Sunday Morning* (1960), *Murder on the Orient Express* (1974), and *The Gathering Storm* (2002) 2 Sir Tom. 1922–2014, English footballer: a winger, he played for Preston North End (1946–60) and won 76 caps for England, scoring 30 goals

innish adj 1 of or relating to Finland or its inhabitants ▷ n 2 the language of Finland

innmark n a county of N Norway: the largest, northernmost, and least populated county; mostly a barren plateau. Capital: Vadsø. Pop: 73 210 (2004 est). Area: 48 649 sq km (18 779 sq miles)

no (fee-no) n a very dry sherry [Spanish: fine]

insen n Niels Ryberg. 1860–1904, Danish physician; founder of phototherapy: Nobel prize for physiology or medicine 1903

insteraarhorn n a mountain in S central Switzerland: highest peak in the Bernese Alps. Height: 4274 m (14 022 ft)

inzi n Gerald. 1901–56, British composer. His works include the cantata *Dies Natalis* (1940)

ord (fee-ord) n same as **fjord**

pple flute n an end-blown flute with a plug (**fipple**) at the mouthpiece, such as the recorder or flageolet

r n a pyramid-shaped tree with needle-like leaves and erect cones [Old English *furh*]

irbank n (Arthur Annesley) Ronald. 1886–1926, English novelist, whose works include *Valmouth* (1919), *The Flower beneath the Foot* (1923), and *Concerning the Eccentricities of Cardinal Pirelli* (1926)

irdausi or **Firdusi** n pen name of *Abul Qasim Mansur* ?935–1020 AD, Persian epic poet; author of *Shah Nama* (*The Book of Kings*), a chronicle of the legends and history of Persia

re n 1 the state of combustion producing heat, flames, and often smoke 2 Brit burning coal or wood, esp. in a hearth to heat a room 3 a destructive uncontrolled burning that destroys buildings, crops, etc. 4 an electric or gas device for heating a room 5 the act of shooting weapons 6 passion and enthusiasm: *her questions brought new fire to the debate* 7 **catch fire** to start burning 8 **on fire** a burning b ardent or eager 9 **open fire** to start firing a gun, artillery, etc. 10 **play with fire** to be involved in something risky 11 **set fire to** or **set on fire** a to ignite b to arouse or excite 12 **under fire** being attacked, such as by weapons or by harsh criticism ▷ vb **firing, fired** 13 to discharge (a firearm) 14 to detonate (an explosive device) 15 *informal* to dismiss from employment 16 to ask (a lot of questions) quickly in succession 17 *ceramics* to bake in a kiln to harden the clay 18 to kindle or be kindled 19 (of an internal-combustion engine) to produce an electrical spark which causes the fuel to burn and the engine to start 20 to provide with fuel 21 to arouse to strong emotion: *he fired his team mates with enthusiasm* [Old English *fȳr*]

ire alarm n a device to give warning of fire

irearm n a weapon, such as a pistol, that fires bullets

fireball n 1 ball-shaped lightning 2 the hot ionized gas at the centre of a nuclear explosion 3 a large bright meteor 4 *slang* an energetic person

firebomb n a bomb that is designed to cause fires

firebrand n a person who arouses passionate political feelings, often causing trouble

firebreak n a strip of open land in a forest to stop the advance of a fire

firebrick n a heat-resistant brick, used for lining furnaces, flues, and fireplaces

fire brigade n Brit and Austral an organized body of firefighters

fire clay n a heat-resistant clay used in making firebricks and furnace linings

firecracker n a firework which produces a loud bang

firedamp n Brit, Austral and NZ an explosive mixture of hydrocarbons, chiefly methane, formed in coal mines

firedog n same as **andiron**

fire door n a door made of noncombustible material that prevents a fire spreading within a building

fire drill n a rehearsal of procedures for escape from a fire

fire-eater n 1 a performer who pretends to swallow flaming rods 2 a very quarrelsome person

fire engine n a vehicle that carries firefighters and firefighting equipment to a fire

fire escape n a metal staircase or ladder on the outside of a building for escape in the event of fire

fire-extinguisher n a portable device for spraying water, foam, or powder to extinguish a fire

firefighter n a person whose job is to put out fires and rescue people endangered by them ▷ **firefighting** adj, n

firefly n, pl **-flies** a beetle that glows in the dark

fireguard n a screen made of wire mesh put before an open fire to protect against sparks

fire hall n Canad a fire station

fire hydrant n an outlet from a water main in the street, from which firefighters can draw water in an emergency

fire irons pl n a shovel, poker, and tongs for tending a domestic fire

fireman n, pl **-men** 1 a man whose job is to put out fires and rescue people endangered by them 2 (on steam trains) the man who stokes the fire

Firenze n the Italian name for **Florence**

fireplace n an open recess at the base of a chimney for a fire; hearth

fireplug n chiefly US and NZ same as **fire hydrant**

fire power n *military* the amount of fire that can be delivered by a unit or weapon

fire raiser n Brit a person who deliberately sets fire to property ▷ **fire raising** n

fire ship n *history* a ship loaded with explosives, set on fire and left to drift among an enemy's warships

fireside n the hearth

fire station n a building where firefighting vehicles and equipment are stationed

firetrap n a building that would burn easily or one without fire escapes

firewall n *computers* software that prevents unauthorized access to a computer network from the internet

firewater n *informal* any alcoholic spirit

firework n a device containing chemicals that is ignited to produce coloured sparks and sometimes bangs

fireworks pl n 1 a show in which fireworks are let off 2 *informal* an outburst of temper 3 an exciting and impressive performance, speech, or piece of writing: *Dickens' verbal fireworks*

firie n Austral informal a firefighter

firing n 1 a discharge of a firearm 2 the process of baking ceramics in a kiln 3 something used as fuel

firing line n 1 *military* the positions from which fire is delivered 2 the leading or most vulnerable position in an activity: *the manager is in the firing line after a string of bad results*

firing squad n a group of soldiers appointed to shoot a condemned criminal dead

firkin n **1** a small wooden barrel or similar container **2** Brit a unit of capacity equal to nine gallons [Middle Dutch *vierde* fourth]

firm¹ adj **1** not soft or yielding to a touch or pressure **2** securely in position **3** definitely established: *a firm agreement* **4** having determination or strength: *if you are firm and consistent she will come to see things your way* ▷ adv **5** stand firm to refuse to give in ▷ vb **6** to make or become firm: *to firm up flabby thighs* [Latin *firmus*] **> firmly** adv **> firmness** n

firm² n **1** a business company **2** Brit slang a gang of criminals or football hooligans [Spanish *firma* signature]

firmament n literary the sky or the heavens [Late Latin *firmamentum*]

first adj **1** earliest in time or order **2** rated, graded, or ranked above all other levels: *the First Lord of the Admiralty* **3** denoting the lowest forward gear in a motor vehicle **4** music denoting the highest voice part in a chorus or one of the sections of an orchestra: *the first violin* ▷ n **5** the person or thing coming before all others **6** the beginning or outset **7** education, chiefly Brit an honours degree of the highest class **8** the lowest forward gear in a motor vehicle ▷ adv **9** before anything else: *I would advise you to try surgery first* **10** for the first time: *this story first came to public attention in January 1984* [Old English *fyrest*]

first aid n immediate medical assistance given in an emergency

first-born adj **1** eldest of the children in a family ▷ n **2** the eldest child in a family

first class n **1** the class or grade of the best or highest value, rank, or quality ▷ adj **first-class 2** of the best or highest class or grade **3** excellent **4** denoting the most comfortable class of accommodation in a hotel, aircraft, or train **5** denoting mail that is handled faster than second-class mail ▷ adv **first-class 6** by first-class mail, transport, etc.

first-day cover n philately an envelope postmarked on the first day of the issue of its stamps

first-degree burn n a burn in which the skin surface is red and painful

first floor n **1** the storey of a building immediately above the one at ground level **2** US the storey at ground level

first-foot Scot and NZ n **1** the first person to enter a household in the New Year ▷ vb **2** to visit (someone) as first-foot **> first-footing** n

first fruits pl n **1** the first results or profits of an undertaking **2** fruit that ripens first

first-hand adj **1** obtained directly from the original source ▷ adv **2** directly from the original source **3** at first hand directly

First Lady n (in the US) the wife of the president

firstly adv same as first (9)

first mate n an officer second in command to the captain of a merchant ship

First Minister n **1** the chief minister of the Scottish Parliament **2** the chief minister of the Northern Ireland Assembly

First Nation n one of the formally recognized Canadian aboriginal communities

first night n the first public performance of a play or other production

first offender n a person convicted of a criminal offence for the first time

first officer n same as first mate

First Peoples pl n Canad a collective term for the Native Canadian peoples, the Inuit, and the Métis

first person n the form of a pronoun or verb used by the speaker to refer to himself or herself, or a group including himself or herself

first-person shooter n a computer game in which the player aims and shoots at targets, and the graphics displayed are seen from the viewpoint of the shooter

first-rate adj of the best quality; excellent

First Secretary n the chief minister of the National Assembly for Wales

First World n the economically advanced countries of North America, Europe, Australia, E Asia, etc.

firth n a narrow inlet of the sea, esp. in Scotland [Old Norse *fjörthr* fjord]

fiscal adj **1** of or relating to government finances, esp. ta revenues ▷ n **2** (in Scotland) same as **procurator fiscal** [Latin *fiscalis* concerning the state treasury]

Fischer n **1** Emil Hermann. 1852–1919, German chemist, noted particularly for his work on synthetic sugars and the purine group: Nobel prize for chemistry 1902 **2** Erns Otto. 1918–94, German chemist: shared the Nobel prize for chemistry in 1973 with Geoffrey Wilkinson for his work on inorganic complexes **3** Hans. 1881–1945, Germa chemist, noted particularly for his work on chlorophyll haemin, and the porphyrins: Nobel prize for chemistry 1930 **4** Robert James, known as Bobby. 1943–2008, US chess player; world champion 1972–75

Fischer-Dieskau n Dietrich. 1925–2012, German baritone, noted particularly for his interpretation of Schubert's song cycles

Fischer von Erlach n Johann Bernhard. 1656–1723, Austrian architect: a leading exponent of the German baroque

fish n, pl fish or fishes **1** a cold-blooded animal with a backbone, gills, and usually fins and a skin covered in scales, that lives in water. Related adjective: **piscine 2** the flesh of fish used as food **3** cold fish a person who shows little emotion **4** drink like a fish to drink alcohol to excess **5** have other fish to fry to have other more important concerns **6** like a fish out of water ill at ease in an unfamiliar situation ▷ vb **7** to attempt to catch fish **8** to fish in (a particular area of water): *the first trawl to fish these waters* **9** to grope for and find with some difficulty: *he fished a cigarette from his pocket* **10** fish for to seek (something) indirectly: *he was fishing for compliments* [Old English *fisc*]

fishcake n a fried flattened ball of flaked fish mixed with mashed potatoes

Fisher n **1** Andrew. 1862–1928, Australian statesman, born in Scotland: prime minister of Australia (1908–09; 1910–13; 1914–15) **2** Saint John. ?1469–1535, English prela and scholar: executed for refusing to acknowledge Henry VIII as supreme head of the church. Feast day: June 22 **3** John Arbuthnot 1st Baron Fisher of Kilverstone 1841–1920, British admiral; First Sea Lord (1904–10; 1914–15); introduced the dreadnought

fisherman n, pl -men a person who fishes as a professio or for sport

fishery n, pl -eries **1 a** the industry of catching, processing, and selling fish **b** a place where this is carried on **2** a place where fish are reared

fish-eye lens n photog a lens with a highly curved front that covers almost 180°

fishfinger n an oblong piece of fish coated in breadcrumbs

Fishguard n a port and resort in SW Wales, in Pembrokeshire: ferry connections to Cork and Rosslare Pop: 3193 (2001)

fishing n the occupation of catching fish

fishing rod n a long tapered flexible pole for use with a fishing line and, usually, a reel

fishmeal n ground dried fish used as feed for farm animals or as a fertilizer

fishmonger n chiefly Brit a seller of fish

fishnet n an open mesh fabric resembling netting, sometimes used for tights or stockings

fishplate n a flat piece of metal joining one rail or beam to the next, esp. on railway tracks

fishtail n a nozzle having a long narrow slot at the top, placed over a Bunsen burner to produce a thin fanlike flame

shwife *n, pl* **-wives** a coarse or bad-tempered woman with a loud voice

shy *adj* **fishier, fishiest** **1** of or suggestive of fish **2** *informal* suspicious or questionable: *something a bit fishy about his explanation* **> fishily** *adv*

ssile *adj* **1** capable of undergoing nuclear fission **2** tending to split

ssion *n* **1** the act or process of splitting into parts **2** *biology* a form of asexual reproduction involving a division into two or more equal parts **3** the splitting of atomic nuclei with the release of a large amount of energy [Latin *fissio* a splitting] **> fissionable** *adj*

ssure (fish-er) *n* any long narrow cleft or crack, esp. in a rock [Latin *fissus* split]

st *n* a hand with the fingers clenched into the palm [Old English *fȳst*]

sticuffs *n* fighting with the fists [probably from obsolete *fisty* with the fist + CUFF²]

stula (fist-yew-la) *n pathol* a long narrow ulcer [Latin: tube, ulcer]

t¹ *vb* **fitting, fitted** **1** to be appropriate or suitable for **2** to be of the correct size or shape (for) **3** to adjust in order to make appropriate **4** to try clothes on (someone) and note any adjustments needed **5** to make competent or ready: *the experience helped to fit him for the task* **6** to correspond with the facts or circumstances: *this part doesn't fit in with the rest of his theory* **> adj fitter, fittest 7** appropriate **8** in good health **9** worthy or suitable: *houses fit for human habitation* **10** *slang* (of a person) sexually attractive **> n 11** the manner in which something fits: *the suit was an excellent fit* ► See also **fit in, fit out** [probably from Middle Dutch *vitten*] **> fitly** *adv* **> fitness** *n*

t² *n* **1 a** sudden attack or convulsion, such as an epileptic seizure **2 a** sudden short burst or spell: *fits of laughter; a fit of pique* **3** in fits and starts in spasmodic spells **4** have a fit *informal* to become very angry [Old English *fitt* conflict]

tful *adj* occurring in irregular spells **> fitfully** *adv*

t in *vb* **1** to give a place or time to (someone or something) **2** to belong or conform, esp. after adjustment

tment *n* **1** an accessory attached to a machine **2** *chiefly Brit* a detachable part of the furnishings of a room

t out *vb* to equip: *he started to fit out a ship in secret*

tted *adj* **1** designed for excellent fit: *a fitted suit* **2** (of a carpet) covering a floor completely **3 a** (of furniture) built to fit a particular space **b** (of a kitchen, bathroom, etc.) having equipment and furniture built or selected to suit the measurements of the room **4** (of sheets) having ends that are elasticated to fit tightly over a mattress

tter *n* **1** a person who is skilled in the installation and adjustment of machinery **2** a person who fits garments

tting *adj* **1** appropriate or proper **> n 2** an accessory or part **3** the trying-on of clothes so that they can be adjusted to fit **4** fittings furnishings or accessories in a building **> fittingly** *adv*

ittipaldi *n* Emerson. born 1946, Brazilian motor-racing driver: Formula One world champion (1972,1974)

itzgerald *n* **1** Edward. 1809–83, English poet, noted particularly for his free translation of the *Rubáiyát of Omar Khayyám* (1859) **2** Ella. 1918–96, US jazz singer, noted esp. for her vocal range and scat singing **3** F(rancis) Scott (Key). 1896–1940, US novelist and short-story writer, noted particularly for his portrayal of the 1920s in *The Great Gatsby* (1925) and *Tender is the Night* (1934) **4** Garret. 1926–2011, Irish politician; leader of Fine Gael Party (1977–87); prime minister of the Republic of Ireland (1981–82 and 1982–87)

itzpatrick *n* Sean. born 1963, New Zealand Rugby Union footballer; played in 92 test matches (1986–97), 51 as captain

itzrovia *n informal* the district north of Oxford Street, London, around Fitzroy Square and its pubs, noted in the 1930s and 40s as a haunt of poets

Fitzsimmons *n* Bob. 1862–1917, New Zealand boxer, born in England: world middleweight (1891–97), heavyweight (1897–99), and light-heavyweight (1903–05) champion

Fitzwilliam Museum *n* a museum, attached to Cambridge University and founded in 1816, noted esp. for its paintings and collections devoted to the applied arts [C19: named after the 7th Viscount *Fitzwilliam* of *Merrion*, who donated the first collection]

Fiume *n* the Italian name for **Rijeka**

five *n* **1** the cardinal number that is the sum of one and four **2** a numeral, 5 or V, representing this number **3** something representing or consisting of five units **⊳ adj 4** amounting to five: *five years* ► See also **fives** [Old English *fīf*]

five-eighth *n* **1** *Austral* (in rugby) a player positioned between the scrum-half and the inside-centre **2** *NZ* (in rugby) either of two players positioned between the halfback and the centre

fivefold *adj* **1** having five times as many or as much **2** composed of five parts **⊳ adv 3** by five times as many or as much

fivepins *n* a bowling game played esp. in Canada

fiver *n Brit, Austral and NZ informal* a five-pound or five-dollar note

fives *n* a ball game similar to squash but played with bats or the hands

Five Towns *n* the Five Towns the name given in his fiction by Arnold Bennett to the Potteries towns (actually six in number) of Burslem, Fenton, Hanley, Longton, Stoke-upon-Trent, and Tunstall, now part of the city of Stoke-on-Trent

fix *vb* **1** to make or become firm, stable, or secure **2** to repair **3** to attach or place permanently: *fix the mirror to the wall* **4** to settle definitely or decide upon: *the meeting is fixed for the 12th* **5** to direct (the eyes, etc.) steadily: *she fixed her eyes upon the jewels* **6** *informal* to unfairly influence the outcome of: *the fight was fixed by the promoter* **7** *informal* to put a stop to the activities of (someone): *the Party was determined to fix him* **8** *informal* to prepare: *let me fix you a drink* **9** *photog* to treat (a film, plate, or paper) with fixer to make the image permanent **10** to convert (atmospheric nitrogen) into nitrogen compounds **11** *slang* to inject a narcotic drug **⊳ n 12** *informal* a difficult situation **13** the reckoning of a navigational position of a ship by radar, etc. **14** *slang* an injection of a narcotic ► See also **fix up** [Latin *fixus* fixed]

fixation *n* **1** an obsessive interest in something **2** *psychol* a strong attachment of a person to another person or an object in early life **3** *chem* the conversion of nitrogen in the air into a compound, esp. a fertilizer **> fixated** *adj*

fixative *n* **1** a fluid sprayed over drawings to prevent smudging **2** a liquid used to hold objects, esp. dentures, in place **3** a substance added to a perfume to make it less volatile

fixed *adj* **1** attached or placed so as to be immovable **2** stable: *fixed rates* **3** unchanging and appearing artificial: *a fixed smile* **4** established as to relative position: *a fixed point* **5** always at the same time **6** (of ideas) firmly maintained **7** *informal* equipped or provided for, esp. with money or possessions **8** *informal* illegally arranged: *a fixed trial* **> fixedly** (fix-id-lee) *adv*

fixed star *n* an extremely distant star that appears to be almost stationary

fixer *n* **1** *photog* a solution used to make an image permanent **2** *slang* a person who makes arrangements, esp. illegally

fixity *n, pl* **-ties** the state or quality of a person's gaze, attitude, or concentration not changing or weakening: *a remarkable fixity of purpose*

fixture *n* **1** an object firmly fixed in place, esp. a household appliance **2** something or someone regarded as fixed in a particular place or position: *the diplomatic wife seems a fixture of international politics* **3 a** a sports match **b** the date of it

fix up vb 1 to arrange 2 **fix up with** to provide with: *can you fix me up with tickets?*

fizz vb 1 to make a hissing or bubbling sound 2 (of a drink) to produce bubbles of carbon dioxide ▷ n 3 a hissing or bubbling sound 4 releasing of small bubbles of gas by a liquid 5 any effervescent drink [imitative] **> fizzy** adj **> fizziness** n

fizzle vb **-zling, -zled** 1 to make a hissing or bubbling sound 2 **fizzle out** informal to fail or die out, esp. after a promising start [probably from obsolete *fist* to break wind]

fjord (fee-ord) n a long narrow inlet of the sea between high cliffs, esp. in Norway [Norwegian, from Old Norse *fjörthr*]

FL Florida

fl. fluid

Fla. Florida

flab n unsightly or unwanted fat on the body [from *flabby*]

flabbergasted adj informal completely astonished [origin unknown]

flabby adj **-bier, -biest** 1 having flabby flesh 2 loose or limp 3 weak and lacking purpose: *flabby hesitant leaders* [alteration of *flappy*, from *flap*] **> flabbiness** n

flaccid (flak-sid) adj soft and limp [Latin *flaccidus*] **> flaccidity** n

flag[1] n 1 a piece of cloth often attached to a pole, used as an emblem or for signalling 2 a code inserted into a computer file to distinguish certain information ▷ vb **flagging, flagged** 3 to mark with a tag or sticker 4 NZ to give up an activity 5 **flag down** to signal (a vehicle) to stop 6 **flag up** bring something to someone's attention [origin unknown]

flag[2] n same as **iris** (2) [origin unknown]

flag[3] vb **flagging, flagged** 1 to lose enthusiasm or energy 2 to become limp [origin unknown] **> flagging** adj

flag[4] n short for **flagstone**

flag day n Brit a day on which money is collected by a charity and small stickers are given to contributors

flagellate vb (flaj-a-late) **-lating, -lated** 1 to whip, esp. in religious penance or for sexual pleasure ▷ adj (flaj-a-lit) 2 possessing one or more flagella 3 like a whip [Latin *flagellare* to whip] **> flagellation** n

flagellum (flaj-jell-lum) n, pl **-la** (-la) or **-lums** 1 biology a long whiplike outgrowth that acts as an organ of movement 2 botany a long thin shoot or runner [Latin: a little whip]

flageolet (flaj-a-let) n a high-pitched musical instrument of the recorder family [French]

flag fall n Austral the minimum charge for hiring a taxi, to which the rate per kilometre is added

flagged adj paved with flagstones

flag of convenience n a foreign flag flown by a ship registered in that country to gain financial or legal advantage

flag of truce n a white flag indicating an invitation to an enemy to negotiate

flagon n 1 a large bottle of wine, cider, etc. 2 a narrow-necked jug for containing liquids [Late Latin *flasco* flask]

flagpole or **flagstaff** n a pole on which a flag is flown

flagrant (flayg-rant) adj openly outrageous: *flagrant violation of international law* [Latin *flagrare* to blaze, burn] **> flagrancy** n

flagship n 1 a ship aboard which the commander of a fleet is quartered 2 the most important ship belonging to a shipping company 3 the most modern or impressive product or asset of an organization: *the company has opened its own flagship store*

Flagstad n Kirsten. 1895–1962, Norwegian operatic soprano, noted particularly for her interpretations of Wagner

flagstone n a flat slab of hard stone for paving [Old Norse *flaga* slab]

flag-waving n informal an emotional appeal to patriotic feeling

Flaherty n Robert (Joseph). 1884–1951, US film director, pioneer of documentary film; his work includes *Nanook of the North* (1922) and *Elephant Boy* (1935)

flail n 1 a tool formerly used for threshing grain by hand ▷ vb 2 to wave about wildly: *arms flailing, they staggered abou* 3 to beat with or as if with a flail [Latin *flagellum* whip]

flair n 1 natural ability: *she has a flair for languages* 2 originality and stylishness: *to dress with flair* [French]

flak n 1 anti-aircraft fire 2 severe criticism: *most of the fla was directed at the umpire* [German Fl(ieger)a(bwehr)k(anone) aircraft defence gun]

flake[1] n 1 a small thin piece chipped off an object or substance 2 a small piece: *flakes of snow* 3 slang an eccentric or unreliable person ▷ vb **flaking, flaked** 4 to peel or cause to peel off in flakes 5 to break into small thin pieces: *bake for 30 minutes, or until the fish is firm and flake easily* [from Old Norse] **> flaky** adj

flake[2] n (in Australia) the commercial name for the mea of the gummy shark

flake out vb informal to collapse or fall asleep from exhaustion

flak jacket n a reinforced sleeveless jacket for protectio against gunfire or shrapnel

flambé (flahm-bay) vb **flambéeing, flambéed** to cook or serve (food) in flaming brandy [French]

Flamborough Head n a chalk promontory in NE England, on the coast of the East Riding of Yorkshire

flamboyant adj 1 behaving in a very noticeable, extravagant way: *a flamboyant jazz pianist* 2 very bright and showy [French: flaming] **> flamboyance** n

flame n 1 a hot luminous body of burning gas coming i flickering streams from burning material 2 **flames** the state of burning: *half the building was in flames* 3 intense passion: *the flame of love* 4 informal an abusive message sent by e-mail ▷ vb **flaming, flamed** 5 to burn brightly 6 to become red or fiery: *colour flamed in Sally's cheeks* 7 to become angry or excited 8 informal to send (someone) ar abusive message by e-mail [Latin *flamma*]

flamenco n, pl **-cos** 1 a rhythmic Spanish dance accompanied by a guitar and vocalist 2 music for this dance [Spanish]

flame-thrower n a weapon that ejects a stream or spra of burning fluid

flaming adj 1 burning with flames 2 glowing brightly 3 very angry and heated: *a flaming row* 4 informal extreme; damned: *what the flaming hell do you think you're doing?* ▷ adv 5 informal extremely; damned: *I was flaming mad about wha happened*

flamingo n, pl **-gos** or **-goes** a large pink wading bird with a long neck and legs [Portuguese *flamengo*]

Flaminian Way n an ancient road in Italy, extending north from Rome to Rimini: constructed in 220 BC by Gaius Flaminius. Length: over 322 km (200 miles). Latin name: **Via Flaminia**

Flamininus n Titus Quinctius. ?230–?174 BC, Roman general and statesman: defeated Macedonia (197) and proclaimed the independence of the Greek states (196)

Flaminius n Gaius. died 217 BC, Roman statesman and general: built the Flaminian Way; defeated by Hanniba at Trasimene (217)

flammable adj easily set on fire; inflammable **> flammability** n

---

USAGE *Flammable* and *inflammable* are interchangeable when used of the properties of materials. *Flammable* is, however, often preferred for warning labels as there is less likelihood of misunderstanding (*inflammable* being sometimes taken to mean *not flammable*). *Inflammable* is preferred in figurative contexts: *this could prove to be an inflammable situation.*

Flamsteed n John. 1646–1719, English astronomer: the first Astronomer Royal and first director of the Royal

bservatory, Greenwich (1675). He increased the
ccuracy of existing stellar catalogues, greatly aiding
avigation

an *n* an open sweet or savoury tart [French]

anagan *n* Richard (**Miller**). born 1961, Australian
writer. His novels include *Wanting* (2008) and the 2014
ooker prizewinner *The Narrow Road to the Deep North*

anders *n* a powerful medieval principality in the SW
art of the Low Countries, now in the Belgian provinces
f East and West Flanders, the Netherlands province of
eeland, and the French department of the Nord; scene
f battles in many wars

ange *n* a projecting collar or rim on an object for
trengthening it or for attaching it to another object
origin unknown]

ank *n* **1** the side of a man or animal between the ribs
nd the hip **2** a cut of beef from the flank **3** the side of a
aval or military formation ▷ *vb* **4** to be positioned at
he side of (a person or thing) [Old French *flanc*]

annel *n* **1** *Brit* a small piece of towelling cloth used to
wash the face **2** a soft light woollen fabric used for
lothing **3 flannels** trousers made of flannel **4** *Brit
nformal* evasive talk that avoids giving any commitment
r direct answer ▷ *vb* **-nelling, -nelled** or *US* **-neling,
neled 5** *Brit informal* to flatter or talk evasively [Welsh
wlân wool]

annelette *n* a cotton imitation of flannel, used to
make sheets and nightdresses

annery *n* Tim, full name *Timothy Fridtjof Flannery*. born
956, Australian zoologist, palaeontologist and
nvironmentalist. His books include *The Weather Makers*
2006)

ap *vb* **flapping, flapped 1** to move backwards and
orwards or up and down, like a bird's wings in flight
▷ *n* **2** the action of or noise made by flapping **3** a piece of
material attached at one edge and usually used to cover
n opening, such as on a pocket **4** a hinged section of an
ircraft wing that is raised or lowered to control the
ircraft's speed **5** *informal* a state of panic or agitation
probably imitative]

apjack *n* **1** *Brit* a chewy biscuit made with rolled oats
NZ a small thick pancake

apper *n* (in the 1920s) a lively young woman who
.ressed and behaved unconventionally

are *vb* **flaring, flared 1** to burn with an unsteady or
udden bright flame **2** (of temper, violence, or trouble)
o break out suddenly **3** to spread outwards from a
arrow to a wider shape ▷ *n* **4** an unsteady flame **5** a
udden burst of flame **6 a** a blaze of light used to
lluminate, signal distress, alert, etc. **b** the device
roducing such a blaze **7 flares** trousers with legs that
lare out at the bottom [origin unknown] ▷ **flared** *adj*

are up *vb* **1** to burst suddenly into fire **2** *informal* to burst
nto anger

ash *n* **1 a** a sudden short blaze of intense light or flame
a sudden occurrence of a particular emotion or
xperience: *a flash of anger* **3** a very brief time: *in a flash he
vas inside and locked the door behind him* **4** a short
nscheduled news announcement **5** *Brit and Austral* an
mblem on a uniform or vehicle to identify its military
ormation **6** *photog* short for **flashlight 7 flash in the pan**
project, person, etc., that enjoys only short-lived
uccess ▷ *adj* **8** *informal* ostentatious or vulgar **9** brief and
apid: *a flash fire* ▷ *vb* **10** to burst or cause to burst
uddenly into flame **11** to shine with a bright light
uddenly or repeatedly **12** to move very fast **13** to come
apidly (into the mind or vision) **14 a** to signal very fast:
warning was flashed onto a computer screen in the cockpit **b** to
ignal by use of a light, such as car headlights **15** *informal*
o display in a boastful and extravagant way: *flashing
ranknotes around* **16** *informal* to show briefly **17** *Brit slang* to
xpose oneself indecently [origin unknown] ▷ **flasher** *n*

ashback *n* a scene in a book, play, or film that shows
arlier events

flashbulb *n photog* a small light bulb that produces a
bright flash of light

flash drive *n* a portable computer hard drive and data
storage device

flash flood *n* a sudden short-lived flood

flashing *n* a weatherproof material used to cover the
joins in a roof

flashlight *n* **1** *photog* the brief bright light emitted by a
flashbulb **2** *chiefly US and Canad* a torch

flash point *n* **1** a critical time beyond which a situation
will inevitably erupt into violence **2** the lowest
temperature at which the vapour above a liquid can be
ignited

flashy *adj* **flashier, flashiest** showy in a vulgar way: *a loud
and flashy tie* ▷ **flashily** *adv* ▷ **flashiness** *n*

flask *n* **1** same as **vacuum flask 2** a small flat container
for alcoholic drink designed to be carried in a pocket **3** a
bottle with a narrow neck, esp. used in a laboratory
[Medieval Latin *flasca, flasco*]

flat¹ *adj* **flatter, flattest 1** horizontal or level: *roofs are now
flat instead of slanted* **2** even or smooth: *a flat surface* **3** lying
stretched out at full length **4** (of a tyre) deflated **5** (of
shoes) having an unraised heel **6** without qualification;
total: *a flat rejection* **7** fixed: *a flat rate* **8** unexciting: *a picture
curiously flat in tone* **9** without variation or emotion: *a flat
voice* **10** (of drinks) no longer fizzy **11** (of a battery) fully
discharged **12** (of paint) without gloss **13** *music*
a denoting a note that has been lowered in pitch by one
chromatic semitone: *B flat* **b** (of an instrument, voice,
etc.) out of tune by being too low in pitch ▷ *adv* **14** in or
into a level or flat position: *the boat was knocked almost flat*
15 completely: *flat broke* **16** exactly: *in three months flat*
17 *music* **a** lower than a standard pitch **b** too low in pitch:
singing flat **18 fall flat (on one's face)** to fail to achieve a
desired effect **19 flat out** *informal* with maximum speed
and effort ▷ *n* **20** a flat object or part **21** low-lying land,
esp. a marsh **22** a mud bank exposed at low tide **23** *music*
a an accidental that lowers the pitch of a note by one
semitone. Symbol: ♭ **b** a note affected by this accidental
24 *theatre* a wooden frame covered with painted canvas,
used to form part of a stage setting **25** a punctured car
tyre **26 the flat** *chiefly Brit* the season of flat racing [Old
Norse *flatr*] ▷ **flatly** *adv*

flat² *n* **1** a set of rooms forming a home entirely on one
floor of a building ▷ *vb* **flatting, flatted 2** *Austral and NZ*
to share a flat **3 go flatting** *Austral and NZ* to leave home to
share a flat [Old English *flett* floor, hall, house]

flatboat *n* a flat-bottomed boat for transporting goods
on a canal

flatfish *n, pl* **-fish** or **-fishes** a sea fish, such as the sole,
which has a flat body with both eyes on the uppermost
side

flat-footed *adj* **1** having less than the usual degree of
arching in the insteps of the feet **2** *informal* clumsy or
insensitive

flathead *n* a common Australian flatfish

flatiron *n* (formerly) an iron for pressing clothes that
was heated by being placed on a stove

flatlet *n Brit, Austral and S African* a small flat

flatmate *n* a person with whom one shares a flat

flat-pack *adj* (of furniture, etc.) supplied in pieces in a
flat box for assembly by the buyer

flat racing *n* the racing of horses on racecourses
without jumps

flatscreen *n* a slimline television set or computer
monitor with a flat screen

flat spin *n* **1** an aircraft spin in which the longitudinal
axis is more nearly horizontal than vertical **2** *informal* a
state of confusion

flatten *vb* **1** to make or become flat or flatter **2** *informal*
a to knock down or injure **b** to crush or subdue

flatter *vb* **1** to praise insincerely, esp. in order to win
favour **2** to show to advantage: *she wore a simple green cotton
dress which she knew flattered her* **3** to make (a person) appear

more attractive than in reality: *a portrait that flattered him* **4** to cater to the vanity of (a person): *I was flattered by her praise* **5 flatter oneself** to believe, perhaps mistakenly, something good about oneself [Old French *flater* to lick, fawn upon] ⟩ **flatterer** *n*

flattery *n, pl* **-teries** excessive or insincere praise

flattie *n NZ and S African informal* flat tyre

flatulent *adj* suffering from or caused by too much gas in the stomach or intestines [Latin *flatus* blowing] ⟩ **flatulence** *n*

flatworm *n* a worm, such as a tapeworm, with a flattened body

Flaubert *n* Gustave. 1821–80, French novelist and short-story writer, regarded as a leader of the 19th-century naturalist school. His most famous novel, *Madame Bovary* (1857), for which he was prosecuted (and acquitted) on charges of immorality, and *L'Éducation sentimentale* (1869) deal with the conflict of romantic attitudes and bourgeois society. His other major works include *Salammbô* (1862), *La Tentation de Saint Antoine* (1874), and *Trois contes* (1877)

flaunt *vb* to display (oneself or one's possessions) arrogantly: *flaunting his new car* [origin unknown]

> **USAGE** *Flaunt* is sometimes wrongly used where *flout* is meant: *they must be prevented from flouting* (not *flaunting*) *the law.*

flautist (flaw-tist) *n* a flute player [Italian *flautista*]

flavour *or US* **flavor** *n* **1** taste perceived in food or liquid in the mouth **2** a distinctive quality or atmosphere: *Rome has its own particular flavour* ▷ *vb* **3** to give flavour to: *salmon flavoured with dill* [Old French *flaour*] ⟩ **flavourless** *or US* **flavorless** *adj*

flavouring *or US* **flavoring** *n* a substance used to flavour food

flaw *n* **1** an imperfection or blemish **2** a mistake in something that makes it invalid: *a flaw in the system* [probably from Old Norse *flaga* stone slab] ⟩ **flawed** *adj* ⟩ **flawless** *adj*

flax *n* **1** a plant that has blue flowers and is cultivated for its seeds and the fibres of its stems **2** its fibres, made into linen fabrics **3** NZ a perennial plant producing a fibre that is used by Māoris for decorative work and weaving baskets [Old English *fleax*]

flaxen *adj* **1** of flax **2** (of hair) pale yellow

Flaxman *n* John. 1755–1826, English neoclassical sculptor and draughtsman, noted particularly for his monuments and his engraved illustrations for the *Iliad*, the *Odyssey*, and works by Dante and Aeschylus

flay *vb* **1** to strip off the skin of, esp. by whipping **2** to criticize severely [Old English *flēan*]

flea *n* **1** a small wingless jumping insect feeding on the blood of mammals and birds **2 flea in one's ear** *informal* a sharp rebuke [Old English *flēah*]

fleabite *n* **1** the bite of a flea **2** a slight annoyance or discomfort

flea-bitten *adj* **1** bitten by or infested with fleas **2** *informal* shabby or decrepit: *a flea-bitten hotel*

flea market *n* an open-air market selling cheap second-hand goods

fleapit *n informal* a shabby cinema or theatre

fleck *n* **1** a small marking or streak **2** a small or tiny piece of something: *a fleck of grit* ▷ *vb* **3** to speckle: *a grey suit flecked with white* [probably from Old Norse *flekkr* stain, spot]

Flecker *n* James Elroy. 1884–1915, English poet and dramatist; author of *Hassan* (1922)

fled *vb* the past of **flee**

fledged *adj* **1** (of young birds) able to fly **2** qualified and competent: *a fully fledged doctor* [Old English *-flycge*, as in *unflycge* unfledged]

fledgling *or* **fledgeling** *n* **1** a young bird that has grown feathers ▷ *adj* **2** new or inexperienced: *Poland's fledgling market economy*

flee *vb* **fleeing, fled** **1** to run away from (a place, danger, etc.) **2** to run or move quickly [Old English *flēon*]

fleece *n* **1** the coat of wool that covers a sheep **2** the wool removed from a sheep at one shearing **3** sheepskin or a fabric with soft pile, used as a lining for coats, etc. **4** a jacket or top made of this fabric **5** a warm outdoor jacket or top made from a polyester fabric with a brushed nap ▷ *vb* **fleecing, fleeced** **6** to defraud or overcharge **7** same as **shear** (1) [Old English *flēos*]

fleecy *adj* **1** of or resembling fleece ▷ *n, pl* **-ies** **2** NZ *informal* a person who collects fleeces after shearing and prepares them for baling

fleet¹ *n* **1** a number of warships organized as a tactical unit **2** all the ships of a nation or company: *the British merchant fleet* **3** a number of vehicles under the same ownership [Old English *flēot* ship, flowing water]

fleet² *adj* rapid in movement [probably from Old English *flēotan* to float]

Fleet *n* **the Fleet** **1** a stream that formerly ran into the Thames between Ludgate Hill and Fleet Street and is now a covered sewer **2** Also called: **Fleet Prison** (formerly) a London prison, esp. used for holding debtors

fleet chief petty officer *n* a noncommissioned officer in a navy

fleeting *adj* rapid and soon passing: *a fleeting moment* ⟩ **fleetingly** *adv*

Fleet Street *n* **1** the street in London where many newspaper offices were formerly situated **2** British national newspapers collectively: *Fleet Street's obsession with the Royal Family*

Fleetwood *n* a fishing port in NW England, in Lancashire. Pop: 26 841 (2001)

Flem. Flemish

Fleming¹ *n* a native or inhabitant of Flanders or Flemish-speaking Belgium

Fleming² *n* **1** Sir Alexander. 1881–1955, Scottish bacteriologist: discovered lysozyme (1922) and penicillin (1928): shared the Nobel prize for physiology or medicine in 1945 **2** Ian (Lancaster). 1908–64, English author of spy novels; creator of the secret agent James Bond **3** Sir John Ambrose. 1849–1945, English electrical engineer: invented the thermionic valve (1904) **4** Renée. born 1959, US operatic soprano and songwriter

Flemish *adj* **1** of Flanders, in Belgium ▷ *n* **2** one of the two official languages of Belgium ▷ *pl n* **3 the Flemish** people from Flanders or Flemish-speaking Belgium

Flemish Brabant *n* a province of central Belgium, formed in 1995 from the N part of Brabant province: densely populated and intensively farmed, with large industrial centres. Pop: 1 031 904 (2004 est). Area: 2106 sq km (813 sq miles)

Flensburg *n* a port in N Germany, in Schleswig-Holstein: taken from Denmark by Prussia in 1864; vote to remain German in 1920. Pop: 85 300 (2003 est)

flesh *n* **1** the soft part of the body of an animal or human, esp. muscular tissue. Related adjective: **carnal** **2** *informal* excess weight; fat **3** the meat of animals as opposed to that of fish or, sometimes, fowl **4** the thick soft part of fruit or vegetable **5 the flesh** sexuality or sensuality: *pleasures of the flesh* **6 flesh and blood** human beings or human nature: *it is almost more than flesh and blood can bear* **7 in the flesh** in person; actually present **8 one's own flesh and blood** one's own family **9 press the flesh** *informal* to shake hands with large numbers of people, esp. in political campaigning [Old English *flǣsc*]

flesh-coloured *adj* yellowish-pink

fleshly *adj* **-lier, -liest** **1** relating to sexuality or sensuality: *the fleshly implications of their love* **2** worldly as opposed to spiritual

flesh out *vb* to expand on or give more details to: *further meetings will be needed to flesh out the agreement*

fleshpots *pl n* places, such as brothels and strip clubs, where sexual desires are catered to [from the Biblical use as applied to Egypt (Exodus 16:3)]

esh wound n a wound affecting superficial tissues

eshy adj **fleshier, fleshiest 1** plump **2** resembling flesh **3** botany (of some fruits) thick and pulpy ⊳ **fleshiness** n

etcher n John. 1579–1625, English Jacobean dramatist, noted for his romantic tragicomedies written in collaboration with Francis Beaumont, esp. *Philaster* (1610) and *The Maid's Tragedy* (1611)

eur-de-lys or **fleur-de-lis** (flur-de-lee) n, pl **fleurs-de-lys** or **fleurs-de-lis** (flur-de-leez) a representation of a lily with three distinct petals [Old French *flor de lis* lily lower]

eury n André Hercule de. 1653–1743, French cardinal and statesman: Louis XV's chief adviser and virtual uler of France (1726–43)

evoland n a province of the central Netherlands, created in 1986 on land reclaimed from the IJsselmeer (formerly the Zuiderzee); entirely below sea level. Capital: Lelystad. Pop: 352 000 (2003 est). Area: 1420 sq km (548 sq miles)

ew vb the past tense of **fly**[1]

ews pl n the fleshy hanging upper lip of a bloodhound or similar dog [origin unknown]

ex n **1** Brit and Austral a flexible insulated electric cable: *a oiled kettle flex* ⊳ vb **2** to bend **3** to bend and stretch (a muscle) [Latin *flexus* bent, winding]

exible adj **1** able to be bent easily without breaking **2** adaptable to changing circumstances: *flexible working arrangements* ⊳ **flexibility** n ⊳ **flexibly** adv

exitime n a system permitting flexibility of working hours at the beginning or end of the day, provided an agreed total is worked

bbertigibbet n old-fashioned an irresponsible, silly, gossipy person [origin unknown]

ick vb **1** to touch or move with the finger or hand in a quick jerky movement **2** to move with a short sudden movement, often repeatedly: *the windscreen wipers flicked back and forth* **3 flick through** to look at (a book or magazine) quickly or idly ⊳ n **4** a tap or quick stroke **5 give someone the flick** slang, chiefly Austral to reject someone [imitative]

icker vb **1** to give out an unsteady or irregular light **2** to move quickly to and fro ⊳ n **3** an unsteady or brief light **4** a brief or faint indication of emotion: *a flicker of fear in his voice* [Old English *flicorian*]

ick knife n a knife with a retractable blade that springs out when a button is pressed

icks pl n slang, old-fashioned the cinema

ier n same as **flyer**

ight[1] n **1** a journey by aircraft **2** the act or manner of flying **3** a group of flying birds or aircraft **4** an aircraft flying on a scheduled journey **5** a set of stairs between one landing and the next **6 flight of fancy** an idea that is imaginative but not practical **7** small plastic or feather fins at the rear of an arrow or dart which make it stable in flight [Old English *flyht*]

ight[2] n **1** the act of running away, esp. from danger **2 put to flight** to cause to run away **3 take (to) flight** to run away [Old English *flyht* (unattested)]

ight attendant n a person who attends to the needs of passengers on a commercial flight

ight deck n **1** the crew compartment in an airliner **2** the upper deck of an aircraft carrier from which aircraft take off

ightless adj (of certain birds and insects) unable to fly

ight lieutenant n a junior commissioned officer in an air force

ight recorder n an electronic device in an aircraft for storing information concerning its performance in flight. It is often used to determine the cause of a crash. Also called: **black box**

ight sergeant n a noncommissioned officer in an air force

ighty adj **flightier, flightiest** frivolous and not very reliable or serious ⊳ **flightiness** n

flimsy adj **-sier, -siest 1** not strong or substantial **2** light and thin: *a flimsy gauze mask* **3** not very convincing: *flimsy evidence* [origin unknown] ⊳ **flimsily** adv ⊳ **flimsiness** n

flinch vb **1** to draw back suddenly from pain or something unpleasant **2 flinch from** to avoid: *I wouldn't flinch from saying that to his face* [Old French *flenchir*]

Flinders Island n an island off the coast of NE Tasmania: the largest of the Furneaux Islands. Pop: 850 (2004 est). Area: 2077 sq km (802 sq miles)

Flinders Range n a mountain range in E South Australia, between Lake Torrens and Lake Frome. Highest peak: 1188 m (3898 ft)

fling vb **flinging, flung 1** to throw with force **2** to move or go hurriedly or violently: *she flung her arms open wide* **3** to put or send without warning: *they used to fling me in jail* **4** to put (something) somewhere hurriedly or carelessly **5 fling oneself into** to apply oneself with enthusiasm to ⊳ n **6** a short spell of self-indulgent enjoyment **7** a brief romantic or sexual relationship **8** a vigorous Scottish country dance: *a Highland fling* [from Old Norse]

flint n **1** a very hard stone that produces sparks when struck with steel **2** any piece of flint, esp. one used as a primitive tool **3** a small piece of an iron alloy, used in cigarette lighters [Old English] ⊳ **flinty** adj

Flint n **1** a town in NE Wales, in Flintshire, on the Dee estuary. Pop: 11 936 (2001) **2** a city in SE Michigan: closure of the car production plants led to a high level of unemployment. Pop: 120 292 (2003 est)

flintlock n an obsolete gun in which the powder was lit by a spark produced by a flint

Flintoff n Andrew. born 1977, English cricketer; an all-rounder, he played 79 test matches for England (1998–2009)

Flintshire n a county of NE Wales, on the Irish Sea and the Dee estuary: became part of Clwyd in 1974, reinstated with reduced borders in 1996: includes the industrialized Deeside region in the E and the Clwydian Hills in the SW. Administrative centre: Mold. Pop: 149 400 (2003 est). Area: 437 sq km (169 sq miles)

flip vb **flipping, flipped 1** to throw (something light or small) carelessly **2** to turn (something) over: *flip the fish on its back* **3** to turn (a device or machine) on or off by quickly pressing a switch **4** to throw (an object such as a coin) so that it turns in the air **5** to buy and sell an asset (often property) quickly for profit **6** (in Britain) to change the designation of an MP's primary and secondary residences in order to maximize a claim from public funds **7 flip through** to look at (a book or magazine) idly **8** Also: **flip one's lid** slang to fly into an emotional outburst ⊳ n **9** a snap or tap, usually with the fingers ⊳ adj **10** informal flippant or pert [probably imitative]

flipchart n a large pad of paper mounted on a stand, used in giving lectures, etc.

flip-flop n **1** Brit and S African a rubber-soled sandal attached to the foot by a thong between the big toe and the next toe **2** informal a reversal of opinion, policy, etc. ⊳ vb informal **3** to reverse one's opinion, policy, etc. [reduplication of *flip*]

flippant adj treating serious matters with inappropriate light-heartedness or lack of respect [probably from *flip*] ⊳ **flippancy** n

flipper n **1** the flat broad limb of seals, whales, and other aquatic animals specialized for swimming **2** either of a pair of rubber paddle-like devices worn on the feet as an aid in swimming

flirt vb **1** to behave as if sexually attracted to someone **2** (foll. by with) to consider lightly: *he had often flirted with the idea of emigrating* ⊳ n **3** a person who flirts [origin unknown] ⊳ **flirtation** n ⊳ **flirtatious** adj

flit vb **flitting, flitted 1** to fly or move along rapidly and lightly **2** to pass quickly: *a shadow flitted across his face* **3** Scot and N English dialect to move house **4** Brit informal to leave hurriedly and stealthily in order to avoid debts ⊳ n **5** the act of flitting **6 do a flit** NZ informal to abandon rented accommodation [Old Norse flytja to carry]

flitch n a side of pork salted and cured [Old English flicce]

flitter vb rare same as **flutter**

float vb **1** to rest on the surface of a fluid without sinking **2** to move lightly or freely across a surface or through air or water **3** to move about aimlessly, esp. in the mind: a pleasant image floated into his mind **4 a** to launch (a commercial enterprise, etc.) **b** to offer for sale on the stock market **5** finance to allow (a currency) to fluctuate against other currencies ▷ n **6** an inflatable object that helps people learning to swim stay afloat **7** angling an indicator attached to a baited line that moves when a fish bites **8** a long rigid boatlike structure, of which there are usually two, attached to an aircraft instead of wheels so that it can land on and take off from water **9** a decorated lorry that is part of a procession **10** a small delivery vehicle: a milk float **11** Austral and NZ a vehicle for transporting horses **12** a sum of money used to cover small expenses or provide change **13** the hollow floating ball of a ball cock [Old English flotian]

floatation n same as **flotation**

floating adj **1** (of a population) moving about; not settled **2** (of an organ or part) displaced or abnormally movable: a floating kidney **3** (of a voter) not committed to one party **4** finance **a** (of capital) available for current use **b** (of a currency) free to fluctuate against other currencies

floating rib n a lower rib not attached to the breastbone

floats pl n theatre footlights

flocculent adj like tufts of wool [Latin floccus tuft of wool] ▷ **flocculence** n

flock¹ n **1** a group of animals of one kind, esp. sheep or birds **2** a large number of people **3** a congregation of Christians regarded as the responsibility of a member of the clergy ▷ vb **4** to gather together or move in large numbers [Old English flocc]

flock² n **1** waste from fabrics such as cotton or wool, used for stuffing mattresses ▷ adj **2** (of wallpaper) having a velvety raised pattern [Latin floccus tuft of wool]

Flodden n a hill in Northumberland where invading Scots were defeated by the English in 1513 and James IV of Scotland was killed. Also called: **Flodden Field**

floe n a sheet of floating ice [probably from Norwegian flo slab, layer]

flog vb **flogging, flogged 1** to beat harshly, esp. with a whip or stick **2** (sometimes foll. by off) informal to sell **3** Austral and NZ informal to steal **4 flog a dead horse** chiefly Brit to waste one's energy [probably from Latin flagellare] ▷ **flogging** n

flood n **1** an overflowing of water on an area that is normally dry **2** a large amount of water **3** the rising of the tide from low to high water. Related adjectives: **diluvial, diluvian 4** a large amount: a flood of letters **5** theatre short for **floodlight** ▷ vb **6** to cover or become covered with water **7** to fill to overflowing **8** to put a large number of goods on sale on (a market) at the same time, often at a cheap price: the US was flooded with cheap televisions **9** to flow or surge: the memories flooded back **10** to supply excess petrol to (a petrol engine) so that it cannot work properly **11** to bleed profusely from the womb [Old English flōd] ▷ **flooding** n

Flood¹ n the Flood Old Testament the flood from which Noah and his family and livestock were saved in the ark (Genesis 7–8)

Flood² n Henry. 1732–91, Anglo-Irish politician: leader of the parliamentary opposition to English rule

floodgate n **1** a gate used to control the flow of water **2** floodgates controls against an outpouring of emotion: it had opened the floodgates of her anxiety

floodlight n **1** a lamp that casts a broad intense light, used in the theatre or to illuminate sports grounds or the exterior of buildings ▷ vb **-lighting, -lit 2** to illuminate by floodlight

flood plain n geography a flat area bordering a river, made of sediment deposited during flooding

floor n **1** the lower surface of a room **2** a storey of a building **3** a flat bottom surface: the ocean floor **4** that pa of a legislative hall in which debate is conducted **5** a minimum limit: a wages floor for low-paid employees **6** have the floor to have the right to speak in a debate or discussion ▷ vb **7** to knock to the ground **8** informal to disconcert or defeat [Old English flōr]

floorboard n one of the boards forming a floor

floored adj covered with a floor: an attic floored with pine planks

flooring n **1** the material used in making a floor: pine flooring **2** a floor

floor plan n a scale drawing of the arrangement of rooms on one floor of a building

floor show n a series of entertainments, such as singi and dancing, in a nightclub

floozy, floozie or **floosie** n, pl **-zies** or **-sies** slang, old-fashioned a woman considered to be disreputable or immoral [origin unknown]

flop vb **flopping, flopped 1** to bend, fall, or collapse loosely or carelessly **2** informal to fail: his first big film flopp **3** to fall or move with a sudden noise ▷ n **4** informal a complete failure **5** the act of flopping [variant of flap] ▷ **floppy** adj

floppy disk n a flexible magnetic disk that stores data the memory of a digital computer

flora n all the plant life of a given place or time [Flora, Roman goddess of flowers]

floral adj decorated with or consisting of flowers or patterns of flowers

Florence n a city in central Italy, on the River Arno in Tuscany: became an independent republic in the 14th century; under Austrian and other rule intermittently from 1737 to 1859; capital of Italy 1865–70. It was the major cultural and artistic centre of the Renaissance and is still one of the world's chief art centres. Pop: 356 118 (2001). Ancient name: **Florentia**. Italian name: **Firenze**

Florentine adj **1** of or relating to Florence or its inhabitants ▷ n **2** a native or inhabitant of Florence

Flores n **1** an island in Indonesia, one of the Lesser Sunda Islands, between the Flores Sea and the Savu Sea: mountainous, with active volcanoes and unexplored forests. Chief town: Ende. Area: 17 150 sq kr (6622 sq miles) **2** an island in the Atlantic, the westernmost of the Azores. Chief town: Santa Cruz. Area: 142 sq km (55 sq miles)

Flores Sea n a part of the Pacific Ocean in Indonesia between Celebes and the Lesser Sunda Islands

floret (flaw-ret) n a small flower forming part of a composite flower head [Old French florete]

Florey n Howard Walter, Baron Florey. 1898–1968, Australian pathologist: shared the Nobel prize for physiology or medicine (1945) with E. B. Chain and Alexander Fleming for their work on penicillin

Florianópolis n a port in S Brazil, capital of Santa Catarina state, on the W coast of Santa Catarina Island Pop: 884 000 (2005 est)

floribunda n a type of rose whose flowers grow in large clusters [New Latin floribundus flowering freely]

florid adj **1** having a red or flushed complexion **2** very ornate and extravagant: florid prose [Latin floridus blooming]

Florida n **1** a state of the southeastern US, between the Atlantic and the Gulf of Mexico: consists mostly of a low-lying peninsula ending in the **Florida Keys** a chair of small islands off the coast of S Florida, extending southwest for over 160 km (100 miles). Capital: Tallahassee. Pop: 17 019 068 (2003 est). Area: 143 900 sq k (55 560 sq miles). Abbreviation: **Fla.**, (with zip code) **FL 2 Straits of Florida** a sea passage between the Florida Keys and Cuba, linking the Atlantic with the Gulf of Mexico

oridian n **1** a native or inhabitant of Florida ▷ adj **2** of or relating to Florida or its inhabitants

orin n a former British, Australian, and New Zealand oin, equivalent to ten pence or twenty cents [Old talian *fiorino* Florentine coin]

orio n John. ?1553–?1625, English lexicographer, noted or his translation of Montaigne's *Essays* (1603)

orist n a person or shop selling flowers

oss n **1** fine silky fibres, such as those obtained from ilkworm cocoons **2** See **dental floss** ▷ vb **3** to clean between the teeth) with dental floss [probably from Old French *flosche* down] **> flossy** adj

otation or **floatation** n the launching or financing of a commercial enterprise by bond or share issues

otilla n a small fleet or a fleet of small ships [Spanish *lota* fleet]

otow n Friedrich von. 1812–83, German composer of operas, esp. *Martha* (1847)

otsam n **1** floating wreckage from a ship **2** flotsam and etsam **a** odds and ends **b** Brit homeless or vagrant people [Anglo-French *floteson*]

ounce[1] vb **flouncing, flounced 1** to move or go with emphatic movements ▷ n **2** the act of flouncing Scandinavian]

ounce[2] n an ornamental frill on a garment or ablecloth [Old French *froncir* to wrinkle]

ounder[1] vb **1** to struggle to move or stay upright, esp. in water or mud **2** to behave or speak in an awkward, confused way [probably a blend of FOUNDER + BLUNDER]

> **USAGE** *Flounder* is sometimes wrongly used where *founder* is meant: *the project foundered* (not *floundered*) *because of a lack of funds.*

ounder[2] n, pl **-der** or **-ders** an edible flatfish Scandinavian]

our n **1** a powder prepared by grinding grain, esp. wheat ▷ vb **2** to sprinkle (food or utensils) with lour [Middle English *flur* 'flower', i.e. best part] **• floury** adj

ourish vb **1** to be active, successful, or widespread; prosper **2** to be at the peak of development **3** to wave something) dramatically ▷ n **4** a dramatic waving or sweeping movement: *he created a flourish with an imaginary wand* **5** an ornamental curly line in writing **6** a fancy or extravagant action or part of something: *he took his tie off with a flourish* [Latin *florere* to flower] **> flourishing** adj

out (rhymes with out) vb to deliberately disobey (a rule, aw, etc.) [probably from Middle English *flouten* to play the flute]

> **USAGE** See at **flaunt**.

ow vb **1** (of liquids) to move in a stream **2** (of blood, electricity, etc.) to circulate **3** to move steadily and smoothly: *a golf club with rich-looking cars flowing into it* **4** to be produced effortlessly: *words flowed from him in a steady stream* **5** to hang freely: *her hair loose and flowing down her back* **6** to be abundant: *at the buffet lunch, wine flowed like water* **7** (of tide water) to rise ▷ n **8** the act, rate, or manner of flowing: *the abundant flow of water through domestic sprinklers* **9** a continuous stream or discharge **10** the advancing of the tide [Old English *flōwan*]

ow chart or **flow sheet** n a diagram showing a sequence of operations in an industrial process, computer program, etc.

low Country n an area of moorland and peat bogs in northern Scotland known for its wildlife, now partly afforested

ower n **1** the part of a plant that is, usually, brightly coloured, and quickly fades, producing seeds **2** a plant grown for its colourful flowers. Related adjective: **floral 3** the best or finest part: *in the flower of her youth* **4 in flower** with flowers open ▷ vb **5** to produce flowers; bloom **6** to

reach full growth or maturity: *liberty only flowers in times of peace* [Latin *flos*]

flowered adj decorated with flowers or a floral design

flowerpot n a pot in which plants are grown

flowery adj **1** decorated with flowers or floral patterns **2** (of language or style) containing elaborate literary expressions **> floweriness** n

flown vb the past participle of **fly**[1]

fl. oz. fluid ounce(s)

Flt Lt Flight Lieutenant

Flt Sgt Flight Sergeant

flu n informal short for **influenza**

fluctuate vb **-ating, -ated** to change frequently and erratically: *share prices fluctuated wildly throughout the day* [Latin *fluctus* a wave] **> fluctuation** n

flue n a passage or pipe in a chimney, used to carry off smoke, gas, or hot air [origin unknown]

fluent adj **1** able to speak or write with ease: *they spoke fluent English; fluent in French* **2** spoken or written with ease [Latin *fluere* to flow] **> fluency** n **> fluently** adv

fluff n **1** soft light particles, such as the down of cotton or wool **2** informal a mistake, esp. in speaking or reading lines ▷ vb **3** to make or become soft and puffy **4** informal to make a mistake in performing [probably from earlier *flue* downy matter] **> fluffy** adj **> fluffiness** n

fluid n **1** a substance, such as a liquid or gas, that can flow and has no fixed shape ▷ adj **2** capable of flowing and easily changing shape **3** constantly changing or apt to change [Latin *fluere* to flow] **> fluidity** n

fluid ounce n **1** Brit a unit of liquid measure equal to one twentieth of an Imperial pint (28.4 ml) **2** US a unit of liquid measure equal to one sixteenth of a US pint (29.6 ml)

fluke[1] n an accidental stroke of luck [origin unknown] **> fluky** adj

fluke[2] n **1** the flat triangular point of an anchor **2** either of the two lobes of the tail of a whale [perhaps a special use of FLUKE[3] (in the sense: a flounder, flatfish)]

fluke[3] n any parasitic flatworm, such as the liver fluke [Old English *flōc*]

flume n **1** a narrow sloping channel for water **2** an enclosed water slide at a swimming pool

flummery n informal silly or trivial talk [Welsh *llymru*]

flummox vb to puzzle or confuse [origin unknown]

flung vb the past of **fling**

flunk vb US, Canad, Austral, NZ and S African informal to fail (an examination, course, etc.) [origin unknown]

flunky or **flunkey** n, pl **flunkies** or **flunkeys 1** a manservant who wears ceremonial dress **2** a person who performs small unimportant tasks for a powerful or important person in the hope of being rewarded [origin unknown]

fluor (flew-or) n same as **fluorspar** [Latin: a flowing; so called from its use as a metallurgical flux]

fluoresce vb **-rescing, -resced** to exhibit fluorescence [back formation from FLUORESCENCE]

fluorescence n **1** physics the emission of light from atoms or molecules that are bombarded by particles, such as electrons, or by radiation from a separate source **2** the radiation emitted as a result of fluorescence [from *fluor*] **> fluorescent** adj

fluorescent lamp n a lamp in which ultraviolet radiation from an electrical gas discharge causes a thin layer of phosphor on a tube's inside surface to fluoresce

fluoridate vb **-dating, -dated** to add fluoride to (water) as protection against tooth decay **> fluoridation** n

fluoride n chem any compound containing fluorine and another element or radical

fluorinate vb **-nating, -nated** to treat or combine with fluorine **> fluorination** n

fluorine n chem a poisonous strong-smelling pale yellow gas that is the most reactive of all the elements. Symbol: F

fluoroscopy (floor-**oss**-kop-ee) n same as **radioscopy**

fluorspar, fluor *or US and Canad* **fluorite** *n* a white or colourless mineral, consisting of calcium fluoride in crystalline form: the chief ore of fluorine

flurry *n, pl* **-ries** **1** a short rush of vigorous activity or movement **2** a light gust of wind or rain, or fall of snow ▷ *vb* **-ries, -rying, -ried** **3** to confuse or bewilder [obsolete *flurr* to scatter]

flush[1] *vb* **1** to blush or cause to blush **2** to send water quickly through (a pipe or a toilet) so as to clean it **3** to elate: *she was flushed with excitement* ▷ *n* **4** a rosy colour, esp. in the cheeks **5** a sudden flow, such as of water **6** a feeling of elation: *in the flush of victory* **7** freshness: *in the first flush of youth* [perhaps from FLUSH[3]] > **flushed** *adj*

flush[2] *adj* **1** level with another surface **2** *informal* having plenty of money ▷ *adv* **3** so as to be level [probably from FLUSH[1] (in the sense: spring out)]

flush[3] *vb* to drive out of a hiding place [Middle English *flusshen*]

flush[4] *n* (in poker and similar games) a hand containing only one suit [Latin *fluxus* flux]

Flushing *n* a port in the SW Netherlands, in Zeeland province, on Walcheren Island, at the mouth of the West Scheldt river: the first Dutch city to throw off Spanish rule (1572). Pop: 45 000 (2003 est). Dutch name: **Vlissingen**

fluster *vb* **1** to make or become nervous or upset ▷ *n* **2** a nervous or upset state [from Old Norse]

flute *n* **1** a wind instrument consisting of a tube of wood or metal with holes in the side stopped either by the fingers or keys. The breath is directed across a mouth hole in the side **2** a tall narrow wineglass, used esp. for champagne ▷ *vb* **fluting, fluted** **3** to utter in a high-pitched tone [Old French *flahute*] > **fluty** *adj*

fluted *adj* having decorated grooves

fluting *n* a design or decoration of flutes on a column

flutter *vb* **1** to wave rapidly **2** (of birds or butterflies) to flap the wings **3** to move with an irregular motion **4** *pathol* (of the heart) to beat abnormally rapidly **5** to move about restlessly ▷ *n* **6** a quick flapping or vibrating motion **7** a state of nervous excitement or confusion **8** excited interest **9** *Brit informal* a modest bet **10** *pathol* an abnormally rapid beating of the heart **11** *electronics* a slow variation in pitch in a sound-reproducing system [Old English *floterian* to float to and fro]

fluvial (flew-vee-al) *adj* of or relating to a river [Latin *fluvius* river]

flux *n* **1** continuous change or instability **2** a flow or discharge **3** a substance mixed with a metal oxide to assist in fusion **4** *physics* **a** the rate of flow of particles, energy, or a fluid **b** the strength of a field in a given area: *magnetic flux* [Latin *fluxus* a flow]

fly[1] *vb* **flies, flying, flew, flown** **1** to move through the air on wings or in an aircraft **2** to control the flight of (an aircraft) **3** to float, flutter, display, or be displayed in the air: *the Red Cross flag flew at each corner of the compound* **4** to transport or be transported through the air by aircraft, wind, etc. **5** to move very quickly or suddenly: *the front door flew open* **6** to pass quickly: *how time flies* **7** to escape from (an enemy or a place) **8 fly a kite** to release information or take a step in order to test public opinion **9 fly at** to attack (someone) **10 fly high** *informal* to have a high aim **11 let fly** *informal* to lose one's temper: *a young child letting fly at you in a sudden moment of temper* ▷ *n, pl* **flies** **12** Also: **flies** a closure that conceals a zip, buttons, or other fastening, as on trousers **13** a flap forming the entrance to a tent **14 flies** *theatre* the space above the stage, used for storing scenery [Old English *flēogan*]

fly[2] *n, pl* **flies** **1** a small insect with two pairs of wings **2** any of various similar but unrelated insects, such as the dragonfly **3** *angling* a lure made from a fish-hook attached with feathers to resemble a fly **4 fly in the ointment** *informal* a slight flaw that detracts from value or enjoyment **5 fly on the wall** a person who watches others, while not being noticed himself or herself

6 there are no flies on him *or* **her** *informal* he *or* she is no fool [Old English *flēoge*]

fly[3] *adj slang, chiefly Brit* sharp and cunning [origin unknown]

flyaway *adj* **1** (of hair) very fine and soft **2** frivolous or light-hearted: *a flyaway remark*

flyblown *adj* **1** covered with blowfly eggs **2** in a dirty or bad condition

fly-by-night *informal adj* **1** unreliable or untrustworthy, esp. in money matters ▷ *n* **2** an untrustworthy person

flycatcher *n* a small insect-eating songbird

flyer *or* **flier** *n* **1** a small advertising leaflet **2** a person or thing that flies or moves very fast **3** *old-fashioned* an aircraft pilot

fly-fishing *n angling* fishing using artificial flies as lure

flying *n* **1** the act of piloting, navigating, or travelling in an aircraft ▷ *adj* **2** hurried and brief: *a flying visit* **3** fast or built for speed: *Australia's flying fullback* **4** hanging, waving, or floating freely: *flags flying proudly*

flying boat *n* a seaplane in which the fuselage consists of a hull that provides buoyancy

flying buttress *n* an arch and vertical column that supports a wall from the outside

flying colours *pl n* conspicuous success; triumph: *they passed with flying colours*

flying fish *n* a fish of warm and tropical seas, with winglike fins used for gliding above the water

flying fox *n* **1** a large fruit bat of tropical Africa and Asia **2** *Austral and NZ* a platform suspended from an overhead cable, used for transporting people or materials

flying officer *n* a junior commissioned officer in an air force

flying saucer *n* an unidentified disc-shaped flying object alleged to come from outer space

flying squad *n* a small group of police or soldiers ready to move into action quickly

flying start *n* **1** any promising beginning: *a flying start to the new financial year* **2** a start to a race in which the competitor is already travelling at speed as he or she passes the starting line

flyleaf *n, pl* **-leaves** the inner leaf of the endpaper of a book

Flynn *n* **1** Errol. 1909–59, Australian-born Hollywood actor, who was noted for his swashbuckling roles; his films included *Captain Blood* (1935), *The Adventures of Robin Hood* (1938), and *Too Much Too Soon* (1958) **2** Rev. **John.** 1880–1951, founder of the Australian flying doctor service

flyover *n* an intersection of two roads at which one is carried over the other by a bridge

flypaper *n* paper with a sticky and poisonous coating, hung up to trap flies

fly-past *n* a ceremonial flight of aircraft over a given area

Fly River *n* a river in W Papua New Guinea, flowing southeast to the Gulf of Papua. Length: about 1300 km (800 miles)

fly sheet *n* a piece of canvas drawn over the ridgepole of a tent to form an outer roof

fly spray *n* a liquid used to destroy flies, sprayed from an aerosol

flyweight *n* a professional or an amateur boxer weighing up to 112 pounds (51 kg)

flywheel *n* a heavy wheel that regulates the speed of a machine

Fm *chem* fermium

FM **1** frequency modulation **2** (in Scotland) First Minister

f-number *n photog* the ratio of the effective diameter of a lens to its focal length

Fo *n* Dario. born 1926, Italian playwright and actor. His plays include *The Accidental Death of an Anarchist* (1970), *Trumpets and Raspberries* (1984), and *The Tricks of the Trade* (1991): Nobel prize for literature 1997

foal *n* **1** the young of a horse or related animal ▷ *vb* **2** to give birth to a foal [Old English *fola*]

...am *n* **1** a mass of small bubbles of gas formed on the surface of a liquid **2** frothy saliva **3** a light spongelike solid used for insulation, packing, etc. ▷ *vb* **4** to produce or cause to produce foam **5 foam at the mouth** to be very angry [Old English *fām*] **> foamy** *adj*

...b *n* **1** a chain by which a pocket watch is attached to a waistcoat **2** a small pocket in a man's waistcoat, for holding a watch [Germanic]

...o.b. or **FOB** *commerce* free on board

...b off *vb* **fobbing, fobbed 1** to pretend to satisfy (a person) with lies or excuses **2** to sell or pass off (inferior goods) as valuable [probably from German *foppen* to trick]

...cal *adj* **1** of or relating to a focus **2** situated at or measured from the focus

...cal length *n* the distance from the focal point of a lens or mirror to the surface of the mirror or the centre of the lens

...cal point *n* **1** the point where the rays of light from a lens or mirror meet **2** the centre of attention or interest: *focal point for the new high-technology industries*

...ch *n* Ferdinand. 1851–1929, marshal of France; commander in chief of Allied armies on the Western Front in World War I (1918)

...cus (foe-kuss) *vb* **-cusing, -cused** or **-cussing, -cussed 1** to adjust one's eyes or an instrument on an object so that its image is clear **2** to concentrate ▷ *n*, *pl* **-cuses** or **-ci** (-sigh, -kye, -kee) **3** a point of convergence of light or sound waves, or a point from which they appear to diverge **4 in focus** (of an object or image being viewed) clear and sharp **5 out of focus** (of an object or image being viewed) blurred and fuzzy **6** same as **focal point**, **focal length 7** *optics* the state of an optical image when it is distinct or the state of an instrument producing this image **8** a point upon which attention or activity is concentrated: *the focus was on health and education* **9** *geometry* a fixed reference point on the concave side of a conic section, used when defining its eccentricity [Latin: hearth, fireplace]

...cus group *n* a group of people gathered by a market research company to discuss and assess a product or service

...dder *n* bulk feed for livestock, esp. hay or straw [Old English *fōdor*]

...e *n* formal or literary an enemy [Old English *fāh* hostile]

...E or **FOE** Friends of the Earth

...etid *adj* same as **fetid**

...etus *n*, *pl* **-tuses** same as **fetus**

...g *n* **1** a mass of droplets of condensed water vapour suspended in the air, often greatly reducing visibility **2** *photog* a blurred area on a developed negative, print, or transparency ▷ *vb* **fogging, fogged 3** to envelop or become enveloped with or as if with fog [probably from Old Norse] **> foggy** *adj*

...ogarty *n* Carl (George). born 1965, British racing motorcyclist; Superbike world champion 1994, 1995, 1998, 1999

...g bank *n* a distinct mass of fog, esp. at sea

...gbound *adj* prevented from operating by fog

...gey or **fogy** *n*, *pl* **-geys** or **-gies** an extremely old-fashioned person: *a stick-in-the-mud old fogey* [origin unknown] **> fogeyish** or **fogyish** *adj*

...oggia *n* a city in SE Italy, in Apulia: seat of Emperor Frederick II; centre for Carbonari revolutionary societies in the revolts of 1820, 1848, and 1860. Pop: 155 203 (2001)

...ghorn *n* a large horn sounded at intervals as a warning to ships in fog

...ible *n* a slight peculiarity or minor weakness: *he was intolerant of other people's foibles* [obsolete French form of *faible* feeble]

...il¹ *vb* to baffle or frustrate (a person or an attempt) [Middle English *foilen* to trample]

...il² *n* **1** metal in the form of very thin sheets **2** a person

or thing setting off another thing to advantage: *mint sauce is an excellent foil to lamb* [Latin *folia* leaves]

foil³ *n* a light slender flexible sword tipped by a button, used in fencing [origin unknown]

foist *vb* **foist on** to force (someone) to have or experience (something): *the tough economic policies which have been foisted on the developing world* [probably from obsolete Dutch *vuisten* to enclose in one's hand]

Fokine *n* Michel. 1880–1942, US choreographer, born in Russia, regarded as the creator of modern ballet. He worked with Diaghilev as director of the Ballets Russes (1909–15), producing works such as *Les Sylphides* and *Petrushka*

Fokker *n* Anthony Herman Gerard. 1890–1939, Dutch designer and builder of aircraft, born in Java

fold¹ *vb* **1** to bend double so that one part covers another **2** to bring together and intertwine (the arms or legs) **3 fold up** to enclose in a surrounding material **4** *literary* to clasp (a person) in one's arms **5** Also: **fold in** to mix (ingredients) by gently turning one over the other with a spoon **6** *informal* (of a business, organization, or project) to fail or go bankrupt ▷ *n* **7** a piece or section that has been folded **8** a mark, crease, or hollow made by folding **9** a bend in stratified rocks that results from movements within the earth's crust [Old English *fealdan*]

fold² *n* **1** *Brit, Austral and S African* a small enclosure for sheep **2** a church or the members of it [Old English *falod*]

folder *n* a binder or file for holding loose papers

folding door *n* a door with two or more vertical hinged leaves that can be folded one against another

foliaceous *adj* **1** like a leaf **2** *geology* consisting of thin layers [Latin *foliaceus*]

foliage *n* **1** the green leaves of a plant **2** leaves together with the stems, twigs, and branches they are attached to, esp. when used for decoration [Old French *fuellage*]

foliation *n* **1** *botany* **a** the process of producing leaves **b** the state of being in leaf **2** a leaflike decoration

folio *n*, *pl* **-lios 1** a sheet of paper folded in half to make two leaves for a book **2** a book of the largest common size made up of such sheets **3 a** a leaf of paper numbered on the front side only **b** the page number of a book **4** NZ a collection of related material ▷ *adj* **5** of or made in the largest book size, common esp. in early centuries of European printing: *the entire series is being reissued, several in the original folio format* [Latin *in folio* in a leaf]

folk *pl n* **1** people in general, esp. those of a particular group or class: *ordinary folk* **2** Also: **folks** *informal* members of one's family; relatives ▷ *n* **3** *informal* short for **folk music 4** a people or tribe ▷ *adj* **5** originating from or traditional to the common people of a country: *folk art* [Old English *folc*]

folk dance *n* **1** a traditional country dance **2** music for such a dance

Folkestone *n* a port and resort in SE England, in E Kent. Pop: 45 273 (2001)

folk etymology *n* the gradual change in the form of a word through the influence of a more familiar word, as for example *crayfish* from its Middle English form *crevis*

folklore *n* the traditional beliefs of a people as expressed in stories and songs

folk music *n* **1** music that is passed on from generation to generation **2** a piece written in the style of this music

folk song *n* **1** a song handed down among the common people **2** a modern song like this **> folk singer** *n*

folksy *adj* **-sier, -siest** simple and unpretentious, sometimes in an artificial way

follicle *n* any small sac or cavity in the body, esp. one from which a hair grows [Latin *folliculus* small bag] **> follicular** *adj*

follow *vb* **1** to go or come after **2** to accompany: *he followed Isabel everywhere* **3** to be a logical or natural consequence of **4** to keep to the course or track of **5** to act in accordance with: *follow the rules below and it will help you a* great deal **6** to accept the ideas or beliefs of **7** to understand (an explanation) **8** to have a keen interest in: *he's followed the singer's career for more than 25 years* **9** to choose to receive messages or blogs posted online by (a particular person) ▶ See also **follow-on, follow through, follow up** [Old English *folgian*]

follower *n* **1** a person who accepts the teachings of another: *a follower of Nietzsche* **2** a supporter, such as of a sport or team

following *adj* **1** about to be mentioned **2** next in time **3** (of winds or currents) moving in the same direction as a vessel ▷ *prep* **4** as a result of: *uncertainty following the collapse of communism* ▷ *n* **5** a group of supporters or enthusiasts

USAGE The use of *following* to mean as a result of is very common in journalism, but should be avoided in other kinds of writing.

follow-on *cricket n* **1** an immediate second innings forced on a team scoring a prescribed number of runs fewer than its opponents in the first innings ▷ *vb* **follow on 2** to play a follow-on: *England had to follow on*

follow through *vb* **1** to continue an action or series of actions until finished **2** *sport* to continue a stroke, kick, etc., after striking the ball ▷ *n* **follow-through** *sport* continuation of a kick, stroke, etc., after striking the ball: *Faldo's controlled follow-through*

follow up *vb* **1** to investigate (a person, evidence, etc.) closely **2** to continue (action) after a beginning, esp. to increase its effect ▷ *n* **follow-up 3** something done to reinforce an initial action: *a routine follow-up to his operation*

folly *n, pl* **-lies 1** the quality of being foolish **2** a foolish action, idea, etc. **3** an imitation castle, temple, etc., built as a decoration in a large garden or park [Old French *folie* madness]

foment (foam-ent) *vb* to encourage or stir up (trouble) [Latin *fomentum* a poultice] ▶ **fomentation** *n*

USAGE Both *foment* and *ferment* can be used to talk about stirring up trouble: *he was accused of fomenting/fermenting unrest.* Only *ferment* can be used intransitively or as a noun: *his anger continued to ferment* (not *foment*); *rural areas were unaffected by the ferment in the cities.*

fond *adj* **1 fond of** having a liking for **2** loving and affectionate: *his fond parents* **3** (of hopes or wishes) cherished but unlikely to be realized [Middle English *fonnen* to be foolish] ▶ **fondly** *adv* ▶ **fondness** *n*

Fonda *n* **1** Henry. 1905–82, US film actor. His many films include *Young Mr Lincoln* (1939), *The Grapes of Wrath* (1940), *Twelve Angry Men* (1957), and *On Golden Pond* (1981) for which he won an Oscar **2** his daughter **Jane**. born 1937, US film actress. Her films include *Klute* (1971) for which she won an Oscar, *Julia* (1977), *The China Syndrome* (1979), *On Golden Pond* (1981), and *Old Gringo* (1989) **3** her brother, **Peter**. born 1939, US film actor, who made his name in *Easy Rider* (1969); later films include *Ulee's Gold* (1997) and *3:10 to Yuma* (2007)

fondant *n* (a sweet made from) a thick flavoured paste of sugar and water [French]

fondle *vb* **-dling, -dled** to touch or stroke tenderly [obsolete *fond* to fondle]

fondue *n* a Swiss dish, consisting of melted cheese into which small pieces of bread are dipped [French: melted]

Fonseca *n* Gulf of Fonseca an inlet of the Pacific Ocean in W Central America

font[1] *n* a large bowl in a church for baptismal water [Latin *fons* fountain]

font[2] *n* printing same as **fount**[2]

Fontainebleau *n* a town in N France, in the **Forest of Fontainebleau**: famous for its palace (now a museum), one of the largest royal residences in France, built

largely by Francis I (16th century). Pop: 16 236 (2006)

Fontane *n* Theodor. 1819–98, German novelist and journalist; his novels include *Vor dem Sturm* (1878) and *E[ffi] Briest* (1898)

fontanelle *or especially US* **fontanel** *n anatomy* a soft membranous gap between the bones of a baby's skull [Old French *fontanele* a little spring]

Fontenelle *n* Bernard le Bovier de. 1657–1757, French philosopher. His writings include *Digressions sur les ancie[ns] et les modernes* (1688) and *Éléments de la géométrie de l'infini* (1727)

Fonteyn *n* Dame Margot. real name *Margaret Hookham*. 1919–91, English classical ballerina

Fonthill Abbey *n* a ruined Gothic Revival mansion in Wiltshire: rebuilt (1790–1810) for William Beckford by James Wyatt; the main tower collapsed in 1800 and, after rebuilding, again in 1827

Foochow *n* a variant transliteration of the Chinese name for **Fuzhou**

food *n* any substance that can be taken into the body by a living organism and changed into energy and body tissue. Related adjective: **gastronomy** [Old English *fōda*]

foodbank *n* a charity that provides food to people in financial trouble

food chain *n ecology* a series of organisms in a community, each member of which feeds on another i[n] the chain and is in turn eaten

food group *n* any of the categories into which differen[t] foods may be placed according to the type of nourishment they supply

foodie *n informal* a person with a keen interest in food and cookery

food poisoning *n* an acute illness caused by food that [is] contaminated by bacteria

food processor *n* a machine for chopping, mixing, or liquidizing food

foodstuff *n* any substance that can be used as food

fool[1] *n* **1** a person who lacks sense or judgment **2** a person who is made to appear ridiculous **3** (formerly) a professional jester living in a royal or noble household **4 play** *or* **act the fool** to deliberately act foolishly ▷ *vb* **5** [to] deceive (someone), esp. in order to make them look ridiculous **6 fool around** *or* **about** with *informal* to act or play with irresponsibly or aimlessly **7** to speak or act in [a] playful or jesting manner [Latin *follis* bellows]

fool[2] *n chiefly Brit* a dessert made from a puree of fruit with cream [perhaps from FOOL[1]]

foolery *n* foolish behaviour

foolhardy *adj* **-hardier, -hardiest** recklessly adventurou[s] [Old French *fol* foolish + *hardi* bold] ▶ **foolhardily** *adv* ▶ **foolhardiness** *n*

foolish *adj* very silly, unwise, or absurd ▶ **foolishly** *adv* ▶ **foolishness** *n*

foolproof *adj informal* **1** incapable of going wrong; infallible: *a foolproof identification system* **2** (of machines etc.) guaranteed to function as intended despite huma[n] misuse or error

foolscap *n chiefly Brit* a standard paper size, 34.3 × 43.2 centimetres [from the watermark of a *fool's* (i.e. dunce's *cap*, formerly used on it]

fool's errand *n* a fruitless undertaking

fool's gold *n* a yellow-coloured mineral, such as pyrite that is sometimes mistaken for gold

fool's paradise *n* a state of happiness based on false hopes or beliefs

foosball *n US and Canad* a game in which opponents on either side of a purpose-built table attempt to strike a ball into the other side's goal by moving horizontal bar[s] with miniatures of footballers attached

foot *n, pl* **feet 1** the part of the leg below the ankle joint that is in contact with the ground during standing and walking **2** the part of a garment covering a foot **3** a uni[t] of length equal to 12 inches (0.3048 metre) **4** the bottom[,] base, or lower end of something: *at the foot of the hill; the* foot of the page **5** old-fashioned infantry **6** prosody a group of two or more syllables in which one syllable has the major stress, forming the basic unit of poetic rhythm **7 one foot in the grave** informal near to death **8 on foot** walking **9 put one's best foot forward** to try to do one's best **10 put one's foot down** informal to act firmly **11 put one's foot in it** informal to make an embarrassing and tactless mistake **12 under foot** on the ground ▷ vb **13 foot it** informal to travel on foot **14 foot the bill** to pay the entire cost of something ▸ See also **feet** [Old English fōt] ❭ **footless** adj

USAGE In front of another noun, the plural for the unit of length is foot: a 20-foot putt; his 70-foot ketch. Foot can also be used instead of feet when mentioning a quantity and in front of words like tall: four foot of snow; he is at least six foot tall.

Foot n Michael (Mackintosh). 1913–2010, British Labour politician and journalist; secretary of state for employment (1974–76); leader of the House of Commons (1976–79); leader of the Labour Party (1980–83)

footage n **1** a length of film **2** the sequences of filmed material: footage of refugees leaving the city

foot-and-mouth disease n a highly infectious viral disease of cattle, pigs, sheep, and goats, in which blisters form in the mouth and on the feet

football n **1** any of various games played with a ball in which two teams compete to kick, head, or propel the ball into each other's goal **2** the ball used in any of these games ❭ **footballer** n

football pools pl n same as **pools**

footbridge n a narrow bridge for the use of pedestrians

footfall n the sound of a footstep

foothills pl n relatively low hills at the foot of a mountain

foothold n **1** a secure position from which further progress may be made: a firm foothold in Europe's telecommunications market **2** a ledge or other place where a foot can be securely positioned, as during climbing

footing n **1** basis or foundation: on a sound financial footing **2** the relationship between two people or groups: on an equal footing **3** a secure grip by or for the feet

footle vb **-ling, -led** chiefly Brit informal to loiter aimlessly [probably from French foutre to copulate with] ❭ **footling** adj

footlights pl n theatre lights set in a row along the front of the stage floor

footloose adj free to go or do as one wishes

footman n, pl **-men** a male servant in uniform

footnote n a note printed at the bottom of a page

footpad n old-fashioned a highwayman, on foot rather than horseback

footpath n **1** a narrow path for walkers only **2** Austral a raised space alongside a road, for pedestrians

footplate n chiefly Brit a platform in the cab of a locomotive on which the crew stand to operate the controls

footprint n **1** an indentation or outline of the foot on a surface **2** the shape and size of the area something occupies: enlarging the footprint of the building

footsie n informal flirtation involving the touching together of feet

footsore adj having sore or tired feet, esp. from much walking

footstep n **1** a step in walking **2** the sound made by walking **3** a footmark **4 follow in someone's footsteps** to continue the example of another

footstool n a low stool used for supporting the feet of a seated person

footwear n anything worn to cover the feet

footwork n the way in which the feet are used, for example in sports or dancing: nimble footwork

fop n a man who is excessively concerned with fashion

[perhaps from Middle English foppe fool] ❭ **foppery** n ❭ **foppish** adj

for prep **1** directed or belonging to: a bottle of beer for himself **2** to the advantage of: he spelt it out for her **3** in the direction of: he headed for the door **4** over a span of (time or distance): she considered him coolly for a moment **5** in favour of: support for the war **6** in order to get: for a bit of company **7** designed to meet the needs of: the instructions are for right-handed players **8** at a cost of: two dishes for one **9** in place of: she had to substitute for her mother because they woke late **10** because of: dancing for joy **11** regarding the usual characteristics of: unusually warm for the time of year **12** concerning: our idea for the last scene **13** as being: do you take me for an idiot? **14** at (a specified time): multiparty elections are planned for next year **15** to do or take part in: two guests for dinner **16** in the duty or task of: that's for you to decide **17** in relation to; as it affects: it's too hard for me **18** in order to preserve or retain: fighting for survival **19** as a direct equivalent to: word for word **20** in order to become or enter: training for the priesthood **21** in exchange for: the cash was used to pay for food, shelter, and medical supplies **22 for all** See **all** (12) **23 for it** Brit and Austral informal liable for punishment or blame: you'll be for it if you get caught ▷ conj **24** formal because or seeing that: implausibility cries aloud, and this is a pity, for much of the narrative is entertaining [Old English]

forage (**for**-ridge) vb **-aging, -aged 1** to search for food **2** to obtain (something) by searching about: she foraged for her shoes ▷ n **3** food for horses or cattle, esp. hay or straw **4** the act of searching for food or provisions [Old French fourrage]

forage cap n a cap with a flat round crown and a visor, worn by soldiers when not in battle or on parade

foramen (for-**ray**-men) n, pl **-ramina** (-**ram**-in-a) or **-ramens** anatomy a natural hole, esp. one in a bone through which nerves pass [Latin]

forasmuch as conj old-fashioned or law seeing that or since

foray n **1** a short raid or incursion **2** a first attempt or new undertaking: his first foray into films [Middle English forrayen to pillage]

forbade or **forbad** vb the past tense of **forbid**

forbear¹ vb **-bearing, -bore, -borne** to cease or refrain (from doing something) [Old English forberan] ❭ **forbearance** n

forbear² n same as **forebear**

Forbes n George William. 1869–1947, New Zealand statesman; prime minister of New Zealand (1930–35)

forbid vb **-bidding, -bade** or **-bad**, **-bidden** or **-bid** to prohibit or refuse to allow [Old English forbēodan]

USAGE It was formerly considered incorrect to talk of forbidding someone from doing something, but in modern usage either from or to can be used: he was forbidden from entering/to enter the building.

Forbidden City n the Forbidden City **1** Lhasa, Tibet: once famed for its inaccessibility and hostility to strangers **2** a walled section of Beijing, China, enclosing the Imperial Palace and associated buildings of the former Chinese Empire

forbidding adj severe and threatening in appearance or manner: a very large and forbidding building

forbore vb the past tense of **forbear¹**

forborne vb the past participle of **forbear¹**

force¹ n **1** strength or power: the force of the impact had thrown him into the fireplace **2** exertion or the use of exertion against a person or thing that resists: they used force and repression against those who opposed their policies **3** physics an influence that changes a body from a state of rest to one of motion or changes its rate of motion. Symbol: F **4 a** intellectual or moral influence: the Superintendent acknowledged the force of the Chief Constable's argument **b** a person or thing with such influence: Hitler quickly became the decisive force behind German foreign policy **5** drive or intensity: he reacted with frightening speed and force **6** a group of people organized for particular duties or tasks: *a UN peacekeeping force* **7 in force a** (of a law) having legal validity **b** in great strength or numbers ▷ *vb* **forcing, forced 8** to compel (a person, group, etc.) to do something through effort, superior strength, etc.: *forced into an arranged marriage* **9** to acquire or produce through effort, superior strength, etc.: *he forced a smile* **10** to propel or drive despite resistance **11** to break down or open (a lock, door, etc.) **12** to impose or inflict: *a series of opposition strikes forced the appointment of a coalition government* **13** to cause (plants or farm animals) to grow at an increased rate [Latin *fortis* strong]

force² *n* (in N England) a waterfall [Old Norse *fors*]

forced *adj* **1** done because of force: *forced labour* **2** false or unnatural: *forced jollity* **3** due to an emergency: *a forced landing*

force-feed *vb* **-feeding, -fed** to force (a person or animal) to swallow food

forceful *adj* **1** strong, emphatic, and confident: *a forceful speech* **2** effective **> forcefully** *adv*

forcemeat *n* a mixture of chopped ingredients used for stuffing [from *force* (see FARCE) + *meat*]

forceps *n, pl* **-ceps** a surgical instrument in the form of a pair of pincers [Latin *formus* hot + *capere* to seize]

forcible *adj* **1** involving physical force **2** convincing or effective: *a strong shrewd mind and a steady forcible manner* **> forcibly** *adv*

ford *n* **1** a shallow area in a river that can be crossed by car, on horseback, etc. ▷ *vb* **2** to cross (a river) over a shallow area [Old English] **> fordable** *adj*

Ford *n* **1** Ford Maddox original name *Ford Madox Hueffer*. 1873–1939, English novelist, editor, and critic; works include *The Good Soldier* (1915) and the war tetralogy *Parade's End* (1924–28) **2** Gerald R(udolph). 1913–2006, US politician; 38th president of the US (1974–77) **3** Harrison. born 1942, US film actor. His films include *Star Wars* (1977) and its sequels, *Raiders of the Lost Ark* (1981) and its sequels, *Bladerunner* (1982), *Clear and Present Danger* (1994), and *What Lies Beneath* (2000) **4** Henry. 1863–1947, US car manufacturer, who pioneered mass production **5** John. 1586–?1639, English dramatist; author of revenge tragedies such as *'Tis Pity She's a Whore* (1633) **6** John, real name *Sean O'Feeney*. 1895–1973, US film director, esp. of Westerns such as *Stagecoach* (1939) and *She Wore a Yellow Ribbon* (1949)

Forde *n* Frank, full name *Francis Michael Forde*.1890–1983, Australian politician; prime minister of Australia for eight days (1945)

fore *adj* **1** at, in, or towards the front: *the fore foot* ▷ *n* **2** the front part **3** fore and aft located at both ends of a vessel: *two double cabins fore and aft* **4** to the fore to the front or prominent position ▷ *interj* **5** a golfer's shouted warning to a person in the path of a flying ball [Old English]

fore- *prefix* **1** before in time or rank: *foregoing* **2** at or near the front: *foreground* [Old English]

forearm¹ *n* the part of the arm from the elbow to the wrist

forearm² *vb* to prepare or arm beforehand

forebear *or* **forbear** *n* an ancestor

foreboding *n* a strong feeling that something bad is about to happen

forecast *vb* **-casting, -cast** *or* **-casted 1** to predict or calculate (weather, events, etc.), in advance ▷ *n* **2** a statement predicting the weather **3** a prediction **> forecaster** *n*

forecastle, fo'c's'le *or* **fo'c'sle** (foke-sl) *n* the raised front part of a ship

foreclose *vb* **-closing, -closed** *law* to take possession of property bought with borrowed money because repayment has not been made: *the banks have been reluctant to foreclose on troubled borrowers* [Old French *for-* out + *clore* to close] **> foreclosure** *n*

forecourt *n* a courtyard in front of a building, such as one in a filling station

forefather *n* an ancestor

forefinger *n* the finger next to the thumb. Also called: index finger

forefoot *n, pl* **-feet** either of the front feet of an animal

forefront *n* **1** the most active or prominent position: *at the forefront of medical research* **2** the very front

foregather *or* **forgather** *vb* to gather together or assemble

forego¹ *vb* **-going, -went, -gone** to precede in time, plac etc. [Old English *foregān*]

forego² *vb* **-going, -went, -gone** same as forgo

foregoing *adj* (esp. of writing or speech) going before; preceding

foregone conclusion *n* an inevitable result

foreground *n* **1** the part of a view, esp. in a picture, nearest the viewer **2** an important or prominent position

forehand 1 *tennis, squash etc.* ▷ *adj* **2** (of a stroke) made so that the racket is held with the wrist facing the direction of play ▷ *n* **3** a forehand stroke

forehead *n* the part of the face between the natural hairline and the eyes [Old English *forhēafod*]

foreign *adj* **1** of, located in, or coming from another country, area, or people **2** dealing or concerned with another country, area, or people: *the Foreign Minister* **3** no familiar; strange **4** in an abnormal place or position: *a foreign body in the food* [Latin *foris* outside]

foreigner *n* **1** a person from a foreign country **2** an outsider

foreign minister *or* **foreign secretary** *n* (in Britain) cabinet minister who is responsible for a country's dealings with other countries

foreign office *n* (in Britain) the ministry of a country that is concerned with dealings with other states

foreknowledge *n* knowledge of something before it actually happens

Foreland *n* either of two headlands (**North Foreland** an **South Foreland**) in SE England, on the coast of Kent

foreleg *n* either of the front legs of an animal

forelock *n* a lock of hair growing or falling over the forehead

foreman *n, pl* **-men 1** a person who supervises other workmen **2** *law* the leader of a jury

Foreman *n* George. born 1949, US boxer; world heavyweight champion (1973–74); retired in 1977 but re-entered the ring in 1987 and won the heavyweight championship in 1994 at age 45; also noted for the grilling appliance that bears his name

foremast *n* the mast nearest the bow of a ship

foremost *adj* **1** first in time, place, or importance: *Germany's foremost conductor* ▷ *adv* **2** first in time, place, o importance [Old English *formest*, from *forma* first]

forename *n* first name

forenoon *n* the daylight hours before noon

forensic (for-ren-sik) *adj* used in or connected with a court of law [Latin *forensis* public] **> forensically** *adv*

forensic medicine *n* the application of medical knowledge for the purposes of the law, such as in determining the cause of death

foreordain *vb* to determine (events, etc.) in the future

forepaw *n* either of the front feet of a land mammal that does not have hooves

foreplay *n* sexual stimulation before intercourse

forerunner *n* **1** a person or thing that existed or happened before another and is similar in some way: *a forerunner of the surrealist painters* **2** a person or thing that a sign of what will happen in the future

foresail *n* the main sail on the foremast of a ship

foresee *vb* **-seeing, -saw, -seen** to see or know beforehand **> foreseeable** *adj*

foreshadow *vb* to show, indicate, or suggest in advanc

foreshore *n* the part of the shore between high- and low-tide marks

foreshorten *vb* to see or draw (an object) from such an angle that it appears to be shorter than it really is

foresight n 1 the ability to anticipate and provide for future needs 2 the front sight on a firearm

foreskin n anatomy the fold of skin covering the tip of the penis

forest n 1 a large wooded area with a thick growth of trees and plants 2 a group of narrow or tall objects standing upright: a forest of waving arms 3 NZ an area planted with pines or other trees that are not native to the country [Medieval Latin forestis unfenced woodland, from Latin foris outside] **> forested** adj

forestall vb to delay, stop, or guard against beforehand: an action forestalling any further talks [Middle English forestallen to waylay]

forestation n the planting of trees over a wide area

forester n a person skilled in forestry or in charge of a forest

forester n C(ecil) S(cott) 1899–1966, English novelist; creator of Captain Horatio Hornblower in a series of novels on the Napoleonic Wars

forestry n the science or skill of growing and maintaining trees in a forest, esp. to obtain wood

foretaste n an early but limited experience of something to come

foretell vb -telling, -told literary to correctly predict (an event, a result, etc.) beforehand

forethought n thoughtful planning for future events: a little forethought can avoid a lot of problems later

foretoken n a sign of a future event

for ever or **forever** adv 1 without end 2 at all times 3 informal for a long time: I could go on for ever about similar incidents

forewarn vb to warn beforehand

foreword n an introductory statement to a book

Forfar n a market town in E Scotland, the administrative centre of Angus: site of a castle, residence of Scottish kings between the 11th and 14th centuries. Pop: 13 206 (2001)

forfeit (for-fit) n 1 something lost or given up as a penalty for a fault, mistake, etc. ▷ vb 2 to lose as a forfeit ▷ adj 3 lost as a forfeit [Old French forfet offence] **> forfeiture** n

forgather vb same as **foregather**

forgave vb the past tense of **forgive**

forge[1] n 1 a place in which metal is worked by heating and hammering; smithy 2 a furnace used for heating metal ▷ vb forging, forged 3 to shape (metal) by heating and hammering 4 to make a fraudulent imitation of (a signature, money, a painting, etc.) 5 to create (an alliance, relationship, etc.) [Old French forgier to construct] **> forger** n

forge[2] vb forging, forged 1 to move at a steady pace 2 forge ahead to increase speed or progress; take the lead [origin unknown]

forgery n, pl -geries 1 an illegal copy of a painting, banknote, antique, etc. 2 the crime of making a fraudulent imitation

forget vb -getting, -got, -gotten 1 to fail to remember someone or something once known) 2 to neglect, either by mistake or on purpose 3 to leave behind by mistake 4 forget oneself to act in an uncharacteristically unrestrained or unacceptable manner: behave yourself or I might forget myself and slap your wrists [Old English forgietan] **> forgettable** adj

forgetful adj 1 tending to forget 2 forgetful of inattentive to or neglectful of: Fiona, forgetful of the time, was still in bed **> forgetfully** adv

forget-me-not n a low-growing plant with clusters of small blue flowers

forgive vb -giving, -gave, -given 1 to stop feeling anger and resentment towards (a person) or at (an action that has caused upset or harm) 2 to pardon (a mistake) 3 to free from (a debt) [Old English forgiefan]

forgiveness n the act of forgiving or the state of being forgiven

forgiving adj willing to forgive

forgo or **forego** vb -going, -went, -gone to give up or do without [Old English forgān]

forgot vb 1 the past tense of **forget** 2 old-fashioned or dialect a past participle of **forget**

forgotten vb a past participle of **forget**

fork n 1 a small tool with long thin prongs on the end of a handle, used for lifting food to the mouth 2 a larger similar-shaped gardening tool, used for lifting or digging 3 forks the part of a bicycle that links the handlebars to the front wheel 4 a (of a road, river, etc.) a division into two or more branches b the point where the division begins c such a branch ▷ vb 5 to pick up, dig, etc., with a fork 6 to be divided into two or more branches 7 to take one or other branch at a fork in a road, etc. [Latin furca]

forked adj 1 having a fork or forklike parts 2 zigzag: forked lightning

fork-lift truck n a vehicle with two moveable arms at the front that can be raised and lowered for transporting and unloading goods

fork out vb slang to pay, esp. with reluctance

Forlì n a city in N Italy, in Emilia-Romagna. Pop: 108 335 (2001). Ancient name: **Forum Livii**

forlorn adj 1 lonely, unhappy, and uncared-for 2 (of a place) having a deserted appearance 3 desperate and without any expectation of success: a final, apparently forlorn attempt to save the war-torn country [Old English forloren lost] **> forlornly** adv

forlorn hope n 1 a hopeless enterprise 2 a faint hope [changed (by folk etymology) from Dutch verloren hoop lost troop]

form n 1 the shape or appearance of something 2 a visible person or animal 3 the particular mode in which a thing or person appears: wood in the form of paper 4 a type or kind: abortion was widely used as a form of birth control 5 physical or mental condition 6 a printed document, esp. one with spaces in which to fill details or answers 7 the previous record of a horse, athlete, etc. 8 Brit slang a criminal record 9 education, chiefly Brit and NZ a group of children who are taught together 10 manners and etiquette: it is considered bad form not to wear a tie 11 the structure and arrangement of a work of art or piece of writing as distinguished from its content 12 a bench 13 a hare's nest 14 any of the various ways in which a word may be spelt or inflected ▷ vb 15 to give shape to or take shape, esp. a particular shape 16 to come or bring into existence: glaciers dammed the valley bottoms with debris behind which lakes have formed 17 to make or construct or be made or constructed 18 to train or mould by instruction or example 19 to acquire or develop: they've formed this impression; we formed a bond 20 to be an element of: they had formed part of a special murder unit [Latin forma shape, model]

formal adj 1 of or following established conventions: formal talks; a formal announcement 2 characterized by conventional forms of ceremony and behaviour: a small formal dinner party 3 suitable for occasions organized according to conventional ceremony: formal cocktail frocks 4 methodical and organized: a formal approach 5 (of education and training) given officially at a school, college, etc.: he had no formal training in maths 6 symmetrical in form: a formal garden 7 relating to the form or structure of something as distinguished from its substance or content: they addressed the formal elements of the structure of police work 8 philosophy logically deductive rather than based on facts and observation [Latin formalis] **> formally** adv

formaldehyde (for-mal-de-hide) n a colourless poisonous strong-smelling gas, used as formalin and in synthetic resins. Also: **methanal** [form(ic) + aldehyde]

formalin n a solution of formaldehyde in water, used as a disinfectant and as a preservative for biological specimens

formalism n concerned with outward appearances and

structure at the expense of content **>formalist** *n*

formality *n, pl* **-ties** **1** something done as a requirement of custom or good manners: *he dealt with the formalities regarding the cremation* **2** a necessary procedure without real effect: *trials were often a mere formality with the verdict decided beforehand* **3** strict observance of ceremony

formalize *or* **-ise** *vb* **-izing, -ized** *or* **-ising, -ised** **1** to make official or valid **2** to give a definite form to **>formalization** *or* **-isation** *n*

Forman *n* Miloš. born 1932, Czech film director working in the USA since 1968. His films include *One Flew over the Cuckoo's Nest* (1976), *Amadeus* (1985), and *The People vs Larry Flynt* (1996)

format *n* **1** the shape, size, and general appearance of a publication **2** style or arrangement, such as of a television programme: *a chat-show format* **3** *computers* the arrangement of data on disk or magnetic tape to comply with a computer's input device ▷ *vb* **-matting, -matted** **4** to arrange in a specified format [Latin *formatus* formed]

formation *n* **1** the act of having or taking form or existence **2** something that is formed **3** the manner in which something is arranged **4** an arrangement of people or things acting as a unit, such as a troop of soldiers **5** a series of rocks or clouds of a particular structure or shape

formative *adj* **1** of or relating to formation, development, or growth: *formative years at school* **2** shaping or moulding: *the formative influence on his life*

Formby *n* George. Real name *George Booth*. 1904–61, British comedian. He made many musical films in the 1930s, accompanying his songs on the ukulele

former *adj* **1** belonging to or occurring in an earlier time: *a grotesque parody of a former greatness* **2** having been at a previous time: *the former prime minister* ▷ *n* **3 the former** the first or first mentioned of two

formerly *adv* in the past

Formica *n trademark* a hard laminated plastic used esp. for heat-resistant surfaces

formic acid *n* an acid derived from ants [Latin *formica* ant]

formidable *adj* **1** frightening because very difficult to deal with or overcome: *the Finnish winter presents formidable problems to drivers* **2** extremely impressive: *a formidable Juventus squad* [Latin *formido* fear] **>formidably** *adv*

formless *adj* without a definite shape or form

Formosa *n* the former name of **Taiwan**

Formosa Strait *n* an arm of the Pacific between Taiwan and mainland China, linking the East and South China Seas. Also called: **Taiwan Strait**

formula (form-yew-la) *n, pl* **-las** *or* **-lae** (-lee) **1** a group of letters, numbers, or other symbols which represents a mathematical or scientific rule **2** a plan or set of rules for doing or producing something: *a formula for peace in the Middle East* **3** an established form of words, as used in religious ceremonies, legal proceedings, etc. **4** a powder used to make a milky drink for babies **5** *motor racing* the category in which a car competes, judged according to engine size [Latin *forma* form] **>formulaic** *adj*

formulary *n, pl* **-laries** a book of prescribed formulas

formulate *vb* **-lating, -lated** **1** to express in a formula **2** to plan or describe precisely and clearly: *formulate a regional energy strategy* **>formulation** *n*

fornicate *vb* **-cating, -cated** to have sexual intercourse without being married [Latin *fornix* vault, brothel situated therein] **>fornicator** *n*

fornication *n* voluntary sexual intercourse outside marriage

Forrest *n* John, 1st Baron Forrest 1847–1918, Australian statesman and explorer; first premier of Western Australia (1890–1901)

forsake *vb* **-saking, -sook, -saken** **1** to withdraw support or friendship from **2** to give up (something valued or enjoyed) [Old English *forsacan*]

forsooth *adv old-fashioned* in truth or indeed [Old English *forsōth*]

Forster *n* E(dward) M(organ). 1879–1970, English novelist, short-story writer, and essayist. His best-known novels are *A Room with a View* (1908), *Howard's End* (1910), and *A Passage to India* (1924), in all of which he stresses the need for sincerity and sensitivity in human relationships and criticizes English middle-class value

forswear *vb* **-swearing, -swore, -sworn** **1** to reject or renounce with determination **2** to testify falsely in a court of law [Old English *forswearian*]

Forsyth *n* **1** Bill. born 1947, Scottish writer and director. His films include *Gregory's Girl* (1981), *Local Hero* (1983), an *Gregory's Two Girls* (1999) **2** Frederick born 1938, British thriller writer. His books include *The Day of the Jackal* (1970), *The Odessa File* (1972), and *The Fourth Protocol* (1984)

forsythia (for-syth-ee-a) *n* a shrub with yellow flowers which appear in spring before the leaves [after William Forsyth, botanist]

fort *n* **1** a fortified building or position **2 hold the fort** *informal* to keep things in operation during someone's absence [Latin *fortis* strong]

Fortaleza *n* a port in NE Brazil, capital of Ceará state. Pop: 3 261 000 (2005 est). Also called: **Ceará**

Fort-de-France *n* the capital of Martinique, a port on the W coast: commercial centre of the French Antilles. Pop: 91 249 (2007)

forte¹ (for-tay) *n* something at which a person excels: *cooking is his forte* [Latin *fortis* strong]

forte² *adv music* loudly [Italian]

forth *adv* **1** *formal or old-fashioned* forward, out, or away: *running back and forth across the street; Christopher Columbus set forth on his epic voyage of discovery* **2 and so forth** and so on [Old English]

Forth *n* **1 Firth of Forth** an inlet of the North Sea in SE Scotland: spanned by a cantilever railway bridge 1600 r (almost exactly 1 mile) long (1889), and by a road bridge (1964) **2** a river in S Scotland, flowing generally east to the Firth of Forth. Length: about 104 km (65 miles)

forthcoming *adj* **1** about to appear or happen: *the forthcoming elections* **2** given or made available **3** (of a person) willing to give information

forthright *adj* direct and outspoken

forthwith *adv* at once

fortification *n* **1** the act of fortifying **2 fortifications** walls, mounds, etc., used to strengthen the defences of place

fortified wine *n* wine mixed with a small amount of brandy or alcohol, such as port or sherry

fortify *vb* **-fies, -fying, -fied** **1** to make (a place) defensible, such as by building walls **2** to strengthen physically, mentally, or morally: *the news fortified their resolve to succeed* **3** to increase the nutritious value of (a food), such as by adding vitamins [Latin *fortis* strong + *facere* to make]

fortissimo *adv music* very loudly [Italian]

fortitude *n* calm and patient courage in trouble or pain [Latin *fortitudo* courage]

Fort Knox *n* a military reservation in N Kentucky: site of the US Gold Bullion Depository. Pop: 12 377 (2000)

Fort Lamy *n* the former name (until 1973) of **Ndjamena**

Fort Lauderdale *n* a city in SE Florida, on the Atlantic Pop: 162 917 (2003 est)

fortnight *n* a period of 14 consecutive days [Old English *fēowertīene niht* fourteen nights]

fortnightly *chiefly Brit adj* **1** occurring or appearing once each fortnight ▷ *adv* **2** once a fortnight

FORTRAN *n* a high-level computer programming language designed for mathematical and scientific purposes [*for(mula) tran(slation)*]

fortress *n* a large fort or fortified town [Latin *fortis* strong]

Fort Sumter *n* a fort in SE South Carolina, guarding Charleston Harbour. Its capture by Confederate forces (1861) was the first action of the Civil War

fortuitous (for-tyew-it-uss) *adj* happening by chance,

esp. by a lucky chance [Latin *fortuitus*] **> fortuitously** *adv*

ortunate *adj* **1** having good luck **2** occurring by good luck **> fortunately** *adv*

ortune *n* **1** a very large sum of money **2** luck, esp. when favourable **3** (*often pl*) a person's destiny **4** a power regarded as being responsible for human affairs **5** wealth or material prosperity [Latin *fors* chance]

ortune-teller *n* a person who claims to predict events in other people's lives

ort Wayne *n* a city in NE Indiana. Pop: 219 495 (2003 est)

ort William *n* a town in W Scotland, in Highland at the head of Loch Linnhe: tourist centre; the fort itself, built in 1655 and renamed after William III in 1690, was demolished in 1866. Pop: 9908 (2001)

ort Worth *n* a city in N Texas, at the junction of the Clear and West forks of the Trinity River: aircraft works, electronics. Pop: 585 122 (2003 est)

orty *n, pl* **-ties** **1** the cardinal number that is the product of ten and four **2** a numeral, 40 or XL, representing this number **3** something representing or consisting of 40 units ▷ *adj* **4** amounting to forty: *forty pages* **> fortieth** *adj, n*

orty-ninth parallel *n Canad informal* the border with the USA, which is in part delineated by the parallel line of latitude at 49°N

orty winks *n informal* a short light sleep

orum *n* **1** a meeting or medium for the open discussion of subjects of public interest **2** (in ancient Roman cities) an open space serving as a marketplace and centre of public business **3** (in South Africa) a pressure group of leaders and representatives [Latin]

orward *adj* **1** directed or moving ahead **2** at, in, or near the front **3** overfamiliar or disrespectful **4** well developed or advanced **5** of or relating to the future or favouring change ▷ *n* **6** an attacking player in any of various sports, such as soccer ▷ *adv* **7** same as **forwards** ▷ *vb* **8** to send (a letter, etc.) on to an ultimate destination **9** to advance or promote: *the veneer of street credibility he had used to forward his career* [Old English *foreweard*]

orwards *or* **forward** *adv* **1** towards or at a place ahead or in advance, esp. in space but also in time **2** towards the front

oscolo *n* Ugo, real name Niccolò Foscolo. 1778–1827, Italian poet and writer; his patriotic verse includes *Dei sepolcri* (1807)

oshan *or* **Fatshan** *n* a city in SE China, in W Guangdong province. Pop: 483 000 (2005 est). Also called: **Namhoi**

osse *or* **foss** *n* a ditch or moat, esp. one dug as a fortification [Latin *fossa*]

osse Way *n* a Roman road in Britain between Lincoln and Exeter, with a fosse on each side

ossick *vb Austral and NZ* **1** to search for gold or precious stones in abandoned workings, rivers, etc. **2** to search for, through, or in something; to forage [probably from English dialect *fussock* to bustle about]

ossil *n* **1** remains of a plant or animal that existed in a past geological age, occurring in the form of mineralized bones, shells, etc. ▷ *adj* **2** of, like, or being a fossil [Latin *fossilis* dug up]

ossil fuel *n* fuel, such as coal or oil, formed from the decayed remains of prehistoric animals and plants

ossilize *or* **-ise** *vb* **-izing, -ized** *or* **-ising, -ised** **1** to convert or be converted into a fossil **2** to become out-of-date or inflexible: *fossilized political attitudes*

oster *adj* **1** of or involved in the bringing up of a child not one's own: *foster care* ▷ *vb* **2** to bring up (a child not one's own) **3** to promote the growth or development of: *Catherine fostered knowledge and patronized the arts* [Old English *fōstrian* to feed] **> fostering** *n*

oster *n* **1** Jodie, born 1962, US film actress and director: her films include *Taxi Driver* (1976), *The Accused* (1988), *The*

Silence of the Lambs (1990), *Little Man Tate* (1991; also directed), *Nell* (1995), and *Panic Room* (2002) **2** Norman, Baron. born 1935, British architect. His works include the Willis Faber building (1978) in Ipswich, Stansted Airport, Essex (1991), Chek Lap Kok Airport, Hong Kong (1998), the renovation of the Reichstag, Berlin (1999), and City Hall, London (2002) **3** Stephen Collins. 1826–64, US composer of songs such as *The Old Folks at Home* and *Oh Susanna*

Fotheringhay *n* a village in E England, in NE Northamptonshire: ruined castle, scene of the imprisonment and execution of Mary Queen of Scots (1587)

Foucault *n* **1** Jean Bernard Léon. 1819–68, French physicist. He determined the velocity of light and proved that light travels more slowly in water than in air (1850). He demonstrated by means of the pendulum named after him the rotation of the earth on its axis (1851) and invented the gyroscope (1852) **2** Michel. 1926–84, French philosopher and historian of ideas. His publications include *Histoire de la folie* (1961) and *Les Mots et les choses* (1966)

fought *vb* the past of **fight**

foul *adj* **1** offensive or loathsome: *a foul deed* **2** stinking or dirty **3** full of dirt or offensive matter **4** (of language) obscene or vulgar **5** unfair: *by fair or foul means* **6** (of weather) unpleasant **7** very bad-tempered and irritable: *he was in a foul mood* **8** *informal* disgustingly bad ▷ *n* **9** *sport* a violation of the rules ▷ *vb* **10** to make dirty or polluted **11** to make or become entangled **12** to make or become clogged **13** *sport* to commit a foul against (an opponent) ▷ *adv* **14** **fall foul of** to come into conflict with [Old English *fūl*]

foul-mouthed *adj* habitually using swearwords and bad language

Foulness *n* a flat marshy island in SE England, in Essex north of the Thames estuary

foul play *n* **1** violent activity, esp. murder **2** a violation of the rules in a game

foul up *vb* **1** *informal* to mismanage or bungle **2** to contaminate **3** to block or choke ▷ *n* **foul-up 4** a state of disorder resulting from mistakes or carelessness: *a foul-up by their computers*

found¹ *vb* the past of **find**

found² *vb* **1** to bring into being or establish (something, such as an institution) **2** to lay the foundation of **3 founded on** to have a basis in: *a political system founded on fear* [Latin *fundus* bottom] **> founder** *n* **> founding** *adj*

found³ *vb* **1** to cast (metal or glass) by melting and pouring into a mould **2** to make (articles) in this way [Latin *fundere* to melt] **> founder** *n*

foundation *n* **1** the basic experience, idea, or attitude on which a way of life or belief is based: *respect for the law is the foundation of commercial society* **2** a construction below the ground that distributes the load of a building, wall, etc. **3** the base on which something stands **4** the act of founding **5** an endowment for the support of an institution, such as a college **6** an institution supported by an endowment **7** a cosmetic used as a base for make-up

foundation stone *n* a stone laid at a ceremony to mark the foundation of a new building

founder *vb* **1** to break down or fail: *his negotiations have foundered on economic grounds* **2** (of a ship) to sink **3** to sink into or become stuck in soft ground **4** (of a horse) to stumble or go lame [Old French *fondrer* to submerge]

USAGE *Founder* is sometimes wrongly used where *flounder* is meant: *this unexpected turn of events left him floundering* (not *foundering*).

foundling *n chiefly Brit* an abandoned baby whose parents are not known [Middle English *foundeling*]

foundry *n, pl* **-ries** a place where metal is melted and cast

fount[1] *n* **1** *poetic* a spring or fountain **2** a source or supply: *a fount of knowledge* [from *fountain*]

fount[2] *n* *printing, chiefly Brit* a complete set of type of one style and size [Old French *fonte* a founding, casting]

fountain *n* **1** an ornamental feature in a pool or lake consisting of a jet of water forced into the air by a pump **2** a jet or spray of water **3** a natural spring of water **4** a source or supply: *a fountain of many new ideas about the causes of cancer* **5** a cascade of sparks, lava, etc. [Latin *fons* spring]

fountainhead *n* a principal or original source

fountain pen *n* a pen supplied with ink from a container inside it

Fountains Abbey *n* a ruined Cistercian abbey near Ripon in Yorkshire: founded 1132, dissolved 1539; landscaped 1720

Fouqué *n* Friedrich Heinrich Karl, Baron de la Motte. 1777–1843, German romantic writer; author of *Undine* (1811)

Fouquet *n* **1** Jean. ?1420–?80, French painter and miniaturist **2** Also: **Foucquet Nicolas**, *Marquis de Belle-Isle*. 1615–80, French statesman; superintendent of finance (1653–61) under Louis XIV. He was imprisoned for embezzlement, having been denounced by Colbert

Fouquier-Tinville *n* Antoine Quentin. 1746–95, French revolutionary; as public prosecutor (1793–94) during the Reign of Terror, he sanctioned the guillotining of Desmoulins, Danton, and Robespierre

four *n* **1** the cardinal number that is the sum of one and three **2** a numeral, 4 or IV, representing this number **3** something representing or consisting of four units **4** *cricket* a score of four runs, obtained by hitting the ball so that it crosses the boundary after hitting the ground **5** *rowing* **a** a rowing boat propelled by four oarsmen **b** the crew of such a rowing boat ▷ *adj* **6** amounting to four: *four zones* [Old English *fēower*]

four-by-four *n* a vehicle with four-wheel drive

fourfold *adj* **1** having four times as many or as much **2** composed of four parts ▷ *adv* **3** by four times as many or as much

Fourier *n* **1** (François Marie) Charles. 1772–1837, French social reformer: propounded a system of cooperatives known as Fourierism, esp. in his work *Le Nouveau monde industriel* (1829–30) **2** Jean Baptiste Joseph. 1768–1830, French mathematician, Egyptologist, and administrator, noted particularly for his research on the theory of heat and the method of analysis named after him

four-in-hand *n* a carriage drawn by four horses and driven by one driver

four-letter word *n* any of several short English words referring to sex or excrement: regarded generally as offensive or obscene

four-poster *n* a bed with posts at each corner supporting a canopy and curtains

fourscore *adj* *old-fashioned* eighty

foursome *n* **1** a group of four people **2** *golf* a game between two pairs of players

foursquare *adv* **1** squarely or firmly ▷ *adj* **2** solid and strong **3** forthright and uncompromising

four-stroke *adj* designating an internal-combustion engine in which the piston makes four strokes for every explosion

fourteen *n* **1** the cardinal number that is the sum of ten and four **2** a numeral, 14 or XIV, representing this number **3** something representing or consisting of 14 units ▷ *adj* **4** amounting to fourteen: *fourteen points* ▷ **fourteenth** *adj, n*

fourth *adj* **1** of or being number four in a series **2** denoting the highest forward gear in a motor vehicle ▷ *n* **3** the highest forward gear in a motor vehicle

fourth dimension *n* **1** the dimension of time, which in addition to three spatial dimensions specifies the position of a point or particle **2** the concept in science fiction of an extra dimension ▷ **fourth-dimensional** *adj*

fourth estate *n* the press

four-wheel drive *n* a system in a vehicle in which all four wheels are connected to the source of power

Fowey *n* a resort and fishing village in SW England, in Cornwall, linked administratively with St Austell from 1968 to 1974. Pop: 2064 (2001)

fowl *n* **1** a domesticated bird such as a hen **2** any other bird that is used as food or hunted as game **3** the meat o fowl **4** *old-fashioned* a bird ▷ *vb* **5** to hunt or snare wild birds [Old English *fugol*]

Fowler *n* Henry Watson. 1858–1933, English lexicographer and grammarian; compiler of *Modern English Usage* (1926)

Fowles *n* John (Martin). 1926–2005, British novelist. His books include *The Collector* (1963), *The Magus* (1966), *The French Lieutenant's Woman* (1969), and *The Tree* (1991)

Fowliang or **Fou-liang** *n* a variant transliteration of th Chinese name for Jingdezhen

fox *n, pl* **foxes** or **fox** **1** a doglike wild animal with a pointed muzzle and a bushy tail **2** its reddish-brown or grey fur **3** a person who is cunning and sly ▷ *vb* **4** inform to confuse or puzzle [Old English]

Fox *n* **1** Charles James. 1749–1806, British Whig statesma and orator. He opposed North over taxation of the American colonies and Pitt over British intervention against the French Revolution. He advocated parliamentary reform and the abolition of the slave trade **2** George. 1624–91, English religious leader; founder (1647) of the Society of Friends (Quakers) **3** Terry, full name *Terrance Stanley Fox* (1958–81). Canadian athlete: he lost a leg to cancer and subsequently attempted a coast-to-coast run across Canada to raise funds for cancer research **4** Vicente. born 1942, Mexican politician; president of Mexico (2000–06) **5** Sir William. 1812–93, New Zealand statesman, born in England: prime minister of New Zealand (1856; 1861–62; 1869–72; 1873)

Foxe *n* John. 1516–87, English Protestant clergyman; author of *History of the Acts and Monuments of the Church* (1563), popularly known as the *Book of Martyrs*

Foxe Basin *n* an arm of the Atlantic in NE Canada, between Melville Peninsula and Baffin Island

foxglove *n* a tall plant with purple or white flowers

foxhole *n* *military* a small pit dug to provide shelter against enemy fire

foxhound *n* a breed of short-haired terrier, originally kept for hunting foxes

fox-hunting *n* the activity of hunting foxes with hounds

foxtrot *n* **1** a ballroom dance with slow and quick steps **2** music for this ▷ *vb* **-trotting, -trotted** **3** to perform th dance

foxy *adj* **foxier, foxiest** **1** of or resembling a fox, esp. in craftiness **2** reddish-brown ▷ **foxily** *adv* ▷ **foxiness** *n*

foyer (foy-ay) *n* an entrance hall in a hotel, theatre, or cinema [French: fireplace]

fp forte-piano

FP **1** fire plug **2** freezing point

Fr **1** *Christianity* **a** Father **b** Frater **2** *chem* francium

fr. **1** franc **2** from

fracas (frak-ah) *n* a noisy quarrel or fight [French]

fracking *n* a method of extracting oil or gas from rock b forcing liquid at high pressure into the rock [from *fracture*]

fraction *n* **1** *maths* a numerical quantity that is not a whole number **2** any part or subdivision **3** a very small proportion or amount of something **4** *chem* a compone of a mixture separated by distillation [Latin *fractus* broken] ▷ **fractional** *adj* ▷ **fractionally** *adv*

fractional distillation or **fractionation** *n* *chem* the process of separating the constituents of a liquid mixture by heating it and condensing the components separately according to their different boiling points

fractious *adj* (esp. of children) easily upset and angered often due to tiredness [obsolete *fraction* discord]

USAGE *Fractious* is sometimes wrongly used where *factious* is meant: *this factious* (not *fractious*) *dispute has split the party still further.*

---

fracture *n* **1** breaking, esp. the breaking or cracking of a bone ▷ *vb* **-turing, -tured 2** to break [Latin *frangere* to break] ▷ **fractural** *adj*

fragile *adj* **1** able to be broken or damaged easily **2** in a weakened physical state: *you're looking a bit fragile this morning* [Latin *fragilis*] ▷ **fragility** *n*

fragment *n* **1** a piece broken off **2** an incomplete piece: *fragments of information* ▷ *vb* **3** to break into small pieces or different parts [Latin *fragmentum*] ▷ **fragmentation** *n*

fragmentary *adj* made up of small or unconnected pieces: *fragmentary evidence to support his theory*

Fragonard *n* Jean-Honoré. 1732–1806, French artist, noted for richly coloured paintings typifying the frivolity of 18th-century French court life

fragrance *n* **1** a pleasant smell **2** a perfume or scent

fragrant *adj* having a pleasant smell [Latin *fragrare* to emit a smell]

frail *adj* **1** physically weak and delicate **2** easily damaged: *the frail aircraft* **3** easily tempted [Old French *frele*]

frailty *n* **1** physical or moral weakness **2** (*pl* **-ties**) an inadequacy or fault resulting from moral weakness

frame *n* **1** an open structure that gives shape and support to something, such as a building **2** an enclosing case or border into which something is fitted: *the window frame* **3** the system around which something is built up: *caught up in the frame of the revolution* **4** the structure of the human body **5** one of a series of exposures on film used in making motion pictures **6** a television picture scanned by electron beams at a particular frequency **7** *snooker* **a** a single game in a match **b** a wooden triangle used to arrange the red balls in formation before the start of a game **8** short for **cold frame 9** *slang* a frame-up **10 frame of mind** a state of mind: *in a complacent frame of mind* ▷ *vb* **framing, framed 11** to construct by fitting parts together **12** to create and develop (plans or a policy) **13** to construct (a statement) in a particular kind of language **14** to provide or enclose with a frame **15** *slang* to conspire to incriminate (someone) on a false charge [Old English *framian* to avail]

Frame *n* Janet. 1924–2004, New Zealand writer: author of the novels *Owls Do Cry* (1957) and *Faces in the Water* (1961), the collection of verse *The Pocket* (1967), and volumes of autobiography including *An Angel at My Table* (1984), which was made into a film in 1990

frame of reference *n* **1** a set of standards that determines behaviour **2** any set of planes or curves, such as the three coordinate axes, used to locate a point in space

frame-up *n* *slang* a conspiracy to incriminate someone on a false charge

framework *n* **1** a particular set of beliefs, ideas, or rules referred to in order to solve a problem: *a moral framework* **2** a structure supporting something

franc *n* the standard monetary unit of Switzerland, various African countries, and formerly of France and Belgium [Latin *Rex Francorum* King of the Franks, inscribed on 14th-century francs]

France¹ *n* a republic in W Europe, between the English Channel, the Mediterranean, and the Atlantic: the largest country wholly in Europe; became a republic in 1793 after the French Revolution and an empire in 1804 under Napoleon; reverted to a monarchy (1815–48), followed by the Second Republic (1848–52), the Second Empire (1852–70), the Third Republic (1870–1940), and the Fourth and Fifth Republics (1946 and 1958); a member of the European Union. It is generally flat or undulating in the north and west and mountainous in the south and east. Official language: French. Religion: Roman Catholic majority. Currency: euro. Capital: Paris. Pop: 62 814 233 (2013 est). Area: (including Corsica) 551 600 sq km (212 973 sq miles). Related adjectives: **French, Gallic**

France² *n* Anatole, real name *Anatole François Thibault.* 1844–1924, French novelist, short-story writer, and critic. His works include *Le Crime de Sylvestre Bonnard* (1881), *L'Île des Pingouins* (1908), and *La Révolte des anges* (1914): Nobel prize for literature 1921

Franche-Comté *n* a region of E France, covering the Jura and the low country east of the Saône: part of the Kingdom of Burgundy (6th century AD–1137); autonomous as the Free County of Burgundy (1137–1384); under Burgundian rule again (1384–1477) and Hapsburg rule (1493–1674); annexed by France (1678)

franchise *n* **1** the right to vote, esp. for a member of parliament **2** any exemption, privilege, or right granted by a public authority **3** *commerce* authorization granted to a distributor to sell a company's goods ▷ *vb* **-chising, -chised 4** *commerce, chiefly US and Canad* to grant (a person, firm, etc.) a franchise [Old French *franchir* to set free]

Francis *n* **1** original name *Jorge Mario Bergoglio.* born 1936 in Argentina, pope from 2013 **2** Dick, full name *Richard Stanley Francis.* 1920–2010, British thriller writer, formerly a champion jockey. His books include *Dead Cert* (1962), *The Edge* (1988), and *Come to Grief* (1995) **3** Sir Philip. 1740–1818, British politician; probable author of the *Letters of Junius* (1769–72). He played an important part in the impeachment of Warren Hastings (1788–95)

Francis I *n* **1** 1494–1547, king of France (1515–47). His reign was dominated by his rivalry with Emperor Charles V for the control of Italy. He was a noted patron of the arts and learning **2** 1708–65, duke of Lorraine (1729–37), grand duke of Tuscany (1737–65), and Holy Roman Emperor (1745–65). His marriage (1736) to Maria Theresa led to the War of the Austrian Succession (1740–48) **3** title as emperor of Austria of **Francis II**

Francis II *n* **1** 1544–60, king of France (1559–60); son of Henry II and Catherine de' Medici; first husband of Mary, Queen of Scots **2** 1768–1835, last Holy Roman Emperor (1792–1806) and, as Francis I, first emperor of Austria (1804–35). The Holy Roman Empire was dissolved (1806) following his defeat by Napoleon at Austerlitz

Franciscan *n* **1** a member of a Christian religious order of friars or nuns founded by Saint Francis of Assisi ▷ *adj* **2** of this order

Francis of Assisi *n* Saint original name *Giovanni di Bernardone.* ?1181–1226, Italian monk; founder of the Franciscan order of friars. He is remembered for his humility and love for all creation and was the first person to exhibit stigmata (1224). Feast day: Oct 4

Francis of Sales *n* Saint. 1567–1622, French ecclesiastic and theologian; bishop of Geneva (1602–22) and an opponent of Calvinism; author of *Introduction to a Devout Life* (1609) and founder of the Order of the Visitation (1610). Feast day: Jan 24

francium *n* *chem* an unstable radioactive element of the alkali-metal group. Symbol: **Fr** [from *France*, because first found there]

Franck *n* **1** César (Auguste) (sezar). 1822–90, French composer, organist, and teacher, born in Belgium. His works, some of which make use of cyclic form, include a violin sonata, a string quartet, the *Symphony in D Minor* (1888), and much organ music **2** James. 1882–1964, US physicist, born in Germany: shared a Nobel prize for physics with Gustav Hertz (1925) for work on the quantum theory, particularly the effects of bombarding atoms with electrons

Franco *n* Francisco, called *el Caudillo*. 1892–1975, Spanish general and statesman; head of state (1939–1975). He was commander-in-chief of the Falangists in the Spanish Civil War (1936–39), defeating the republican government and establishing a dictatorship (1939).

He kept Spain neutral in World War II

Franco- *combining form* indicating France or French: *the Franco-Prussian war* [Medieval Latin *Francus*]

Franconia *n* a medieval duchy of Germany, inhabited by the Franks from the 7th century, now chiefly in Bavaria, Hesse, and Baden-Württemberg

Franconian *adj* of or relating to Franconia, the Franks, or their languages

frangipani (fran-jee-**pah**-nee) *n* **1** an Australian evergreen tree with large yellow fragrant flowers **2** a tropical shrub with fragrant white or pink flowers

frank *adj* **1** honest and straightforward in speech or attitude ▷ *vb* **2** to put a mark on (a letter), ensuring free carriage ▷ *n* **3** an official mark stamped to a letter ensuring free delivery [Medieval Latin *francus* free] › **frankly** *adv* › **frankness** *n*

Frank¹ *n* a member of the West Germanic peoples who in the late 4th century AD gradually conquered most of Gaul [Old English *Franca*]

Frank² *n* **1** Anne. 1929–45, German Jewess, whose *Diary* (1947) recorded the experiences of her family while in hiding from the Nazis in Amsterdam (1942–44). They were betrayed and she died in a concentration camp **2** Robert. born 1924, US photographer and film maker, born in Switzerland; best known for his photographic book *The Americans* (1959)

Frankenstein *n* a creation or monster that brings disaster and is beyond the control of its creator. Also called: **Frankenstein's monster** [after Baron *Frankenstein*, who created a monster from parts of corpses in the novel by Mary Shelley]

Frankfort *n* **1** a city in N Kentucky: the state capital. Pop: 27 408 (2003 est) **2** *rare* an English spelling of **Frankfurt¹**

Frankfurt¹ *or* **Frankfurt am Main** *n* a city in central Germany, in Hesse on the Main River: a Roman settlement in the 1st century; a free imperial city (1372–1806); seat of the federal assembly (1815–66); university (1914); trade fairs since the 13th century. Pop: 643 432 (2003 est)

Frankfurt² *or* **Frankfurt an der Oder** *n* a city in E Germany on the Polish border: member of the Hanseatic League (1368–1450). Pop: 67 014 (2003 est)

frankfurter *n* a smoked sausage of pork or beef [short for German *Frankfurter Wurst* sausage from Frankfurt]

frankincense *n* an aromatic gum resin burnt as incense [Old French *franc* free, pure + *encens* incense]

Frankish *n* **1** the ancient West Germanic language of the Franks ▷ *adj* **2** of the Franks or their language

Franklin *n* **1** Aretha. born 1942, US soul, pop, and gospel singer; noted for her songs "Respect" (1967), "I Say a Little Prayer" (1968), and, with George Michael, "I Knew You Were Waiting (For Me)" (1987) **2** Benjamin. 1706–90, American statesman, scientist, and author. He helped draw up the Declaration of Independence (1776) and, as ambassador to France (1776–85), he negotiated an alliance with France and a peace settlement with Britain. As a scientist, he is noted particularly for his researches in electricity, esp. his invention of the lightning conductor **3** Sir John. 1786–1847, English explorer of the Arctic: lieutenant-governor of Van Diemen's Land (now Tasmania) (1836–43): died while on a voyage to discover the Northwest Passage **4** Rosalind. 1920–58, British x-ray crystallographer. She contributed to the discovery of the structure of DNA, before her death from cancer

frantic *adj* **1** distracted with fear, pain, joy, etc. **2** hurried and disorganized: *frantic activity* [Latin *phreneticus* mad] › **frantically** *adv*

Franz Ferdinand *n* English name *Francis Ferdinand*. 1863–1914, archduke of Austria; heir apparent of Franz Josef I. His assassination contributed to the outbreak of World War I

Franz Josef I *n* English name *Francis Joseph I*. 1830–1916,

emperor of Austria (1848–1916) and king of Hungary (1867–1916)

Franz Josef Land *n* an archipelago of over 100 islands in the Arctic Ocean, administratively part of Russia. Area: about 21 000 sq km (8000 sq miles). Russian name **Zemlya Frantsa Iosifa**

frappé *adj* (esp. of drinks) chilled [French]

Fraser¹ *n* a river in SW Canada, in S central British Columbia, flowing northwest, south, and west through spectacular canyons in the Coast Mountains to the Strait of Georgia. Length: 1370 km (850 miles)

Fraser² *n* **1** (John) Malcolm.1930–2015, Australian statesman; prime minister of Australia (1975–83) **2** Peter. 1884–1950, New Zealand statesman, born in Scotland; prime minister (1940–49) **3** Simon. (1776–1862), Canadian explorer: explored British Columbia and the river which was named after him

Fraser Island *n* an island off the south-east coast of Queensland and the largest sand island in the world: contains rainforests, heathlands, and freshwater lakes; a national park (since 1976) and a World Heritage site (since 1992). Area: 1840 sq km (710 sq miles). Pop: 194 (2011)

fraternal *adj* **1** of a brother; brotherly **2** designating twins that developed from two separate fertilized ova [Latin *frater* brother] › **fraternally** *adv*

fraternity *n, pl* **-ties 1** a body of people united in interests, aims, etc. **2** friendship between groups of people **3** *US and Canad* a society of male students

fraternize *or* **-nise** *vb* **-nizing, -nized** *or* **-nising, -nised** to associate on friendly terms: *fraternizing with the customers is off-limits* › **fraternization** *or* **-nisation** *n*

fratricide *n* **1** the act of killing one's brother **2** a person who kills his or her brother [Latin *frater* brother + *caedere* to kill] › **fratricidal** *adj*

Frau (rhymes with **how**) *n, pl* **Frauen** *or* **Fraus** a German form of address equivalent to *Mrs* or *Ms* [German]

fraud *n* **1** deliberate deception or cheating intended to gain an advantage **2** an act of such deception **3** *informal* a person who acts in a false or deceitful way [Latin *fraus*]

fraudster *n* a person who commits a fraud; swindler

fraudulent *adj* **1** acting with intent to deceive **2** proceeding from fraud [Latin *fraudulentus*] › **fraudulence** *n*

Frauenfeld *n* a town in NE Switzerland, capital of Thurgau canton. Pop: 21 954 (2000)

fraught (frawt) *adj* **1 fraught with** involving or filled with: *we expected the trip to be fraught with difficulties* **2** tense or anxious [Middle Dutch *vrachten*]

Fräulein (**froy**-line) *n, pl* **-lein** *or* **-leins** a German form of address equivalent to *Miss* [German]

Fraunhofer *n* Joseph von. 1787–1826, German physicist and optician, who investigated spectra of the sun, planets, and fixed stars, and improved telescopes and other optical instruments

fray¹ *n* **1** *Brit, Austral and NZ* a noisy quarrel or brawl **2** the fray any challenging conflict: *the game got more scrappy when the substitutes entered the fray* [short for *affray*]

fray² *vb* **1** to wear away into loose threads, esp. at an edg **2** to make or become strained or irritated [French *frayer* t rub]

Fray Bentos *n* a port in W Uruguay, on the River Uruguay: noted for meat-packing. Pop: 23 122 (2004 est)

Frayn *n* Michael. born 1933, British playwright, novelist and translator; his plays include *The Two of Us* (1970), *Noises Off* (1982), *Copenhagen* (1998), and *Democracy* (2004); novels include *A Landing on the Sun* (1991) and *Spies* (2002)

Frazer *n* Sir James George. 1854–1941, Scottish anthropologist; author of many works on primitive religion, and magic, esp. *The Golden Bough* (1890)

Frazier *n* Joe. 1944–2011, US boxer: won the world heavyweight title in 1970 and was the first to beat Muhammad Ali professionally (1971)

frazil (**fray**-zil) *n* small pieces of ice that form in water moving turbulently enough to prevent the formation of a sheet of ice [French *fraisil* cinders]

razzle *n informal* the state of being exhausted: *worn to a frazzle* [probably from Middle English *faselen* to fray]

reak *n* **1** a person, animal, or plant that is abnormal or deformed **2** an object, event, etc., that is abnormal: *a statistical freak* **3** *informal* a person whose appearance or behaviour is very unusual **4** *informal* a person who is very enthusiastic about something specified: *a health freak* ▷ *adj* **5** abnormal or unusual: *a freak accident* [origin unknown] ❭ **freakish** *adj* ❭ **freaky** *adj*

reak out *vb informal* to be or cause to be in a heightened emotional state

reckle *n* **1** a small brownish spot on the skin ▷ *vb* **-ling, -led** **2** to mark or become marked with freckles [Old Norse *freknur* freckles] ❭ **freckled** *adj*

redericia *n* a port in Denmark, in E Jutland at the N end of the Little Belt. Pop: 37 054 (2004 est)

rederick I *n* **1** See **Frederick Barbarossa 2** 1657–1713, first king of Prussia (1701–13); son of Frederick William

rederick II *n* **1** 1194–1250, Holy Roman Emperor (1220–50), king of Germany (1212–50), and king of Sicily (1198–1250) **2** See **Frederick the Great**

rederick III *n* **1** 1415–93, Holy Roman Emperor (1452–93) and, as Frederick IV, king of Germany (1440–93) **2** called *the Wise*. 1463–1525, elector of Saxony (1486–1525). He protected Martin Luther in Wartburg Castle after the Diet of Worms (1521)

rederick V *n* called *the Winter King*. 1596–1632, elector of the Palatinate (1610–23) and king of Bohemia (1619–20). He led the revolt of Bohemian Protestants at the beginning of the Thirty Years' War

rederick IX *n* 1899–1972, king of Denmark (1947–72)

rederick Barbarossa *n* official title *Frederick I*. ?1123–90, Holy Roman Emperor (1155–90), king of Germany (1152–90). His attempt to assert imperial rights in Italy ended in his defeat at Legnano (1176) and the independence of the Lombard cities (1183)

rederick Henry *n* 1584–1647, prince of Orange and count of Nassau; son of William (I) the Silent

rederick the Great *n* official title *Frederick II*. 1712–86, king of Prussia (1740–86); son of Frederick William I. He gained Silesia during the War of Austrian Succession (1740–48) and his military genius during the Seven Years' War (1756–63) established Prussia as a European power. He was also a noted patron of the arts

rederick William *n* called *the Great Elector*. 1620–88, elector of Brandenburg (1640–88)

rederick William I *n* 1688–1740, king of Prussia (1713–40); son of Frederick I: reformed the Prussian army

rederick William II *n* 1744–97, king of Prussia (1786–97)

rederick William III *n* 1770–1840, king of Prussia (1797–1840)

rederick William IV *n* 1795–1861, king of Prussia (1840–61). He submitted to the 1848 Revolution but refused the imperial crown offered by the Frankfurt Parliament (1849). In 1857 he became insane and his brother, William I, became regent (1858–61)

redericton *n* a city in SE Canada, capital of New Brunswick, on the St John River. Pop: 56 224 (2011)

rederiksberg *n* a city in E Denmark, within the area of greater Copenhagen: founded in 1651 by King Frederick III. Pop: 91 721 (2004 est)

redrikstad *n* a port in SE Norway at the entrance to Oslo Fjord. Pop: 69 867 (2004 est)

ee *adj* **freer, freest** **1** able to act at will; not under compulsion or restraint **2** not enslaved or confined **3** (of a country) independent **4** (of a translation) not exact or literal **5** provided without charge: *free school meals* **6** not occupied or in use; available: *is this seat free?* **7** (of a person) not busy **8** open or available to all **9** not fixed or joined; loose: *the free end* **10** without obstruction or blockage: *the free flow of capital* **11** *chem* chemically uncombined: *free nitrogen* **12** **free and easy** casual or tolerant **13** **free from**

not subject to: *free from surveillance* **14** **free with** using or giving (something) a lot: *he was free with his tongue* **15** **make free with** to behave too familiarly towards ▷ *adv* **16** in a free manner **17** without charge or cost ▷ *vb* **freeing, freed** **18** to release or liberate **19** to remove obstructions or impediments from **20** to make available or usable: *capital freed by the local authority* **21** **free of** *or* **from** to relieve or rid of (obstacles, pain, etc.) [Old English *frēo*] ❭ **freely** *adv*

-free *combining form* free from: *duty-free*; *nuclear-free zones*

freebie *n slang* something provided without charge

freeboard *n* the space or distance between the deck of a vessel and the water line

freebooter *n* a pirate [Dutch *vrijbuit* booty]

freeborn *adj history* not born in slavery

Free Church *n chiefly Brit* any Protestant Church other than the Established Church

Freecycle *n trademark* **1** an informal network of citizens who promote recycling online by offering one another unwanted items free of charge ▷ *vb* **freecycle 2** to recycle (an unwanted item) by offering it free of charge

freediving *n* the sport or activity of diving without the aid of breathing apparatus

freedman *n, pl* **-men** *history* a man freed from slavery

freedom *n* **1** the state of being free, esp. to enjoy political and civil liberties **2** exemption or immunity: *freedom from government control* **3** liberation, such as from slavery **4** the right or privilege of unrestricted access: *freedom of the skies* **5** self-government or independence **6** the power to order one's own actions **7** ease or frankness of manner

free enterprise *n* an economic system in which commercial organizations compete for profit with little state control

free fall *n* **1** the part of a parachute descent before the parachute opens **2** free descent of a body in which gravity is the only force acting on it

free-for-all *n informal* a disorganized brawl or argument involving all those present

free hand *n* **1** unrestricted freedom to act: *the president must be able to deal with foreign hostilities with a free hand* ▷ *adj, adv* **freehand 2** (done) by hand without the use of guiding instruments

freehold *property law* *n* **1** tenure of property for life without restrictions ▷ *adj* **2** of or held by freehold ❭ **freeholder** *n*

free house *n Brit* a public house not bound to sell only one brewer's products

free kick *n soccer* an unopposed kick of the ball awarded for a foul or infringement

freelance *n* **1** a self-employed person doing specific pieces of work for various employers ▷ *vb* **-lancing, -lanced 2** to work as a freelance ▷ *adj, adv* **3** of or as a freelance [originally applied to a mercenary soldier]

freeloader *n slang* a person who habitually depends on others for food, accommodation, etc.

free love *n old-fashioned* the practice of having sexual relationships outside marriage, often several relationships at the same time

freeman *n, pl* **-men** a person who has been given the freedom of a city as an honour in return for public service

Freeman *n* Cathy, full name *Catherine Astrid Salome Freeman*. born 1973, Australian sprinter; winner of the 200m and 400m in the 1994 Commonwealth Games and the 400m in the 2000 Olympic Games

free-market *adj* denoting an economic system which allows supply and demand to regulate prices and wages

Freemason *n* Also called: **Mason** a member of a widespread secret order whose members are pledged to help each other ❭ **Freemasonry** *n*

free-range *adj* kept or produced in natural conditions: *free-range eggs*

freesia *n* a plant with fragrant tubular flowers [after F. H. T. *Freese*, physician]

free space n a region that has no gravitational and electromagnetic fields

freestanding adj not attached to or supported by another object

Free State n 1 a province of central South Africa; replaced the former province of Orange Free State in 1994: gold and uranium mining. Capital: Bloemfontein. Pop: 2 745 590 (2011 est). Area: 129 480 sq km (49 992 sq miles) 2 US history (before the Civil War) any state prohibiting slavery 3 short for **Irish Free State**

freestyle n 1 a competition, such as in swimming, in which each participant may use a style of his or her choice 2 Also called: **all-in wrestling** a style of professional wrestling with no internationally agreed set of rules

freethinker n a person who forms his or her ideas independently of authority, esp. in matters of religion

Freetown n the capital and chief port of Sierra Leone: founded in 1787 for slaves freed and destitute in England. Pop: 1 007 000 (2005 est)

free trade n international trade that is free of such government interference as protective tariffs and import quotas

free verse n unrhymed verse without a fixed rhythm

Freeview n trademark (in Britain) a free service providing digital terrestrial television

freeway n US and Austral a motorway

freewheel vb 1 to travel downhill on a bicycle without pedalling ▷ n 2 a device in the rear hub of a bicycle wheel that permits it to rotate freely while the pedals are stationary

freewheeling adj behaving in a relaxed spontaneous manner, without any long-term plans or commitments: he had to change his freewheeling lifestyle after his son was born

free will n 1 the ability to make a choice without outside coercion or pressure: you walked in here of your own free will 2 philosophy the belief that human behaviour is an expression of personal choice and is not determined by physical forces, Fate, or God

Free World n the non-Communist countries collectively

freeze vb **freezing, froze, frozen** 1 to change from a liquid to a solid by the reduction of temperature, such as water to ice 2 to preserve (food) by subjection to extreme cold 3 to cover or become covered with ice 4 to fix fast or become fixed (to something) because of frost 5 to feel or cause to feel the effects of extreme cold 6 to die of extreme cold 7 to become motionless through fear, shock, etc. 8 to cause (moving film) to stop at a particular frame 9 to fix (prices, incomes, etc.) at a particular level 10 to forbid by law the exchange or collection of (loans, assets, etc.) ▷ n 11 the act of freezing or state of being frozen 12 meteorol a spell of temperatures below freezing point 13 the fixing of incomes, prices, etc. by legislation [Old English frēosan]

freeze-dry vb **-dries, -drying, -dried** to preserve (food) by rapid freezing and drying in a vacuum

freeze out vb to prevent (someone) from being involved in an activity, conversation, etc., by being unfriendly or reserved

freezer n an insulated cabinet for cold-storage of perishable foods

freezing adj informal very cold

freezing point n the temperature below which a liquid turns into a solid

freezing works n Austral and NZ a slaughterhouse at which animals are slaughtered and carcasses frozen, esp. for export

Frege n Gottlob. 1848–1925, German logician and philosopher, who laid the foundations of modern formal logic and semantics in his Begriffsschrift (1879)

Freiburg n 1 a city in SW Germany, in SW Baden-Württemberg: under Austrian rule (1368–1805); university (1457). Pop: 212 495 (2003 est). Official name: **Freiburg im Breisgau** 2 the German name for **Fribourg**

freight (frate) n 1 a commercial transport of goods **b** the cargo transported **c** the cost of this 2 chiefly Brit a ship's cargo or part of it ▷ vb 3 to transport (goods) by freight 4 to load with goods for transport [Middle Dutch vrecht]

freighter n a ship or aircraft designed for transporting cargo

Fremantle n a port in SW Western Australia, on the Indian Ocean. Pop: 25 197 (2001)

French[1] adj 1 of or relating to France or its inhabitants ▷ n 2 the official language of France and an official language of Switzerland, Belgium, Canada, and certain other countries ▷ pl n 3 **the French** the people of France [Old English Frencisc French, Frankish]

French[2] n Sir John Denton Pinkstone, 1st Earl of Ypres. 1852–1925, British field marshal in World War I: commanded the British Expeditionary Force in France and Belgium (1914–15); Lord Lieutenant of Ireland (1918–21)

French beans pl n green beans, the pods of which are eaten

French bread n white bread in a long thin crusty loaf

French Cameroons pl n the part of Cameroon formerly administered by France (1919–60)

French Canada n the areas of Canada, esp. in the province of Quebec, where French Canadians predominate

French Canadian n a Canadian citizen whose native language is French

French chalk n a variety of talc used to mark cloth or remove grease stains

French dressing n a salad dressing made from oil and vinegar with seasonings

French Equatorial Africa n the former French overseas territories of Chad, Gabon, Middle Congo, and Ubangi-Shari (1910–58)

French fries pl n chiefly US and Canad potato chips

French Guiana n a French overseas region in NE South America, on the Atlantic: colonized by the French in about 1637; tropical forests. Capital: Cayenne. Pop: 229 000 (2009 est). Area: about 91 000 sq km (23 000 sq miles)

French Guianese or **French Guianan** adj 1 of or relating to French Guiana or its inhabitants ▷ n 2 a native or inhabitant of French Guiana

French Guinea n a former French territory of French West Africa: became independent as Guinea in 1958

French horn n music a valved brass wind instrument with a coiled tube

Frenchify vb **-fies, -fying, -fied** informal to make or become French in appearance, etc.

French India n a former French overseas territory in India, including Chandernagore and Pondicherry (now Puducherry): restored to India between 1949 and 1954

French Indochina n the territories of SE Asia that were colonized by France and held mostly until 1954: include Cochin China, Annam, and Tonkin (now largely Vietnam), Cambodia, Laos, and Kuang-Chou Wan (returned to China in 1945, now Zhanjiang)

French letter n Brit and NZ slang a condom

Frenchman or fem **Frenchwoman** n, pl **-men** or **-women** a native or inhabitant of France

French Morocco n a former French protectorate in NW Africa, united in 1956 with Spanish Morocco and Tangier to form the kingdom of Morocco

French North Africa n the former French possessions of Algeria, French Morocco, and Tunisia

French Oceania n a former name (until 1958) of French Polynesia

French polish n a shellac varnish for wood, giving a high gloss

French Polynesia n a French Overseas Country (formerly Territory) in the S Pacific Ocean, including the Society Islands, the Tuamotu group, the Gambier group, the Tubuai Islands, and the Marquesas Islands. Capital

Papeete, on Tahiti. Pop: 277 293 (2013 est). Area: about 4000 sq km (1500 sq miles). Former name (until 1958): French Oceania

French seam *n* a seam in which the edges are enclosed

French Somaliland *n* a former name (until 1967) of Djibouti

French Southern and Antarctic Territories *pl n* a French overseas territory, comprising Adélie Land in Antarctica, the islands of Amsterdam and St Paul and the Kerguelen and Crozet archipelagos in the S Indian Ocean, and (from 2007), the Îles Éparses ("scattered islands") previously administered from Réunion, consisting of Bassas da India, Europa, the Glorioso Islands (Îles Glorieuses), Juan de Nova, and Tromelin Island; no permanent population: all claims to the mainland of Antarctica are suspended under the Antarctic Treaty of 1959

French Sudan *n* a former name (1898–1959) of Mali

French Togoland *n* a former United Nations Trust Territory in W Africa, administered by France (1946–60), now the independent republic of Togo

French West Africa *n* a former group (1895–1958) of French Overseas Territories: consisted of Senegal, Mauritania, French Sudan, (now Mali), Upper Volta (now Burkina Faso), Niger, French Guinea, Côte d'Ivoire, and Dahomey (now Benin)

French West Indies *pl n* the French West Indies various islands in the Lesser Antilles, administered by France; chiefly Guadeloupe, Martinique, Saint-Barthélemy and the French part of Saint Martin. Pop: 838 000 (2004 est). Area: 2792 sq km (1077 sq miles)

French windows *pl n* a window extending to floor level, used as a door

Freneau *n* Philip. 1752–1832, US poet, journalist, and patriot; editor of the *National Gazette* (1791–93)

frenetic (frin-net-ik) *adj* wild, excited, and uncontrolled [Greek *phrenitis* insanity] **> frenetically** *adv*

frenzy *n, pl* **-zies** **1** violent or wild and uncontrollable behaviour **2** excited or agitated activity: *a frenzy of speculation* [Late Latin *phrenesis* madness, from Greek *phren* mind] **> frenzied** *adj*

freon *n trademark* any of a group of gas or liquid chemical compounds of methane with chlorine and fluorine: used in propellants, aerosols, and solvents

frequency *n, pl* **-cies** **1** the number of times that an event occurs within a given period **2** the state of being frequent **3** *physics* the number of times a wave repeats itself in a given time

frequency distribution *n* statistical data arranged to show the frequency with which the possible values of a variable occur

frequency modulation *n* a method of transmitting information by varying the frequency of the carrier wave in accordance with the amplitude of the input signal

frequent *adj* **1** happening often **2** habitual ▷ *vb* **3** to visit often: *a spa town frequented by the Prussian nobility* [Latin *frequens* numerous] **> frequently** *adv*

frequentative *grammar adj* **1** denoting a verb or an affix meaning repeated action ▷ *n* **2** a frequentative verb or affix

fresco *n, pl* **-coes** *or* **-cos** **1** a method of wall-painting using watercolours on wet plaster **2** a painting done in this way [Italian: fresh plaster]

Frescobaldi *n* Girolamo. 1583–1643, Italian organist and composer, noted esp. for his organ and harpsichord music

fresh *adj* **1** newly made, acquired, etc. **2** not thought of before; novel: *fresh ideas* **3** most recent: *fresh allegations* **4** further or additional: *a fresh supply* **5** (of food) not canned or frozen **6** (of water) not salty **7** bright and clear: *a fresh morning* **8** (of a wind) cold and fairly strong **9** not tired; alert **10** not worn or faded: *the fresh colours of spring* **11** having a healthy or ruddy appearance **12** having

recently come (from somewhere): *cakes fresh from the oven* **13** youthful or inexperienced **14** *informal* overfamiliar or disrespectful ▷ *adv* **15** recently: *a delicious fresh-baked cake* [Old English *fersc*] **> freshly** *adv* **> freshness** *n*

freshen *vb* **1** to make or become fresh or fresher **2** (of the wind) to become stronger **3 freshen up** to wash and tidy up one's appearance: *I'll go and freshen up*

fresher *or* **freshman** *n, pl* **-ers** *or* **-men** *Brit and US* a first-year student at college or university

freshet *n* **1** the sudden overflowing of a river **2** a stream of fresh water emptying into the sea

freshwater *adj* of or living in fresh water

Fresnel *n* Augustin Jean. 1788–1827, French physicist: worked on the interference of light, contributing to the wave theory of light

Fresno *n* a city in central California, in the San Joaquin Valley. Pop: 451 455 (2003 est)

fret¹ *vb* **fretting, fretted** **1** to worry: *he would fret about the smallest of problems* **2** to rub or wear away **3** to feel or give annoyance ▷ *n* **4** a state of irritation or anxiety [Old English *fretan* to eat]

fret² *n* **1** a repetitive geometrical figure used for ornamentation ▷ *vb* **fretting, fretted** **2** to ornament with fret or fretwork [Old French *frete* interlaced design used on a shield]

fret³ *n* a small metal bar set across the fingerboard of a musical instrument, such as a guitar, as a guide to fingering [origin unknown]

fretful *adj* irritable or upset **> fretfully** *adv*

fret saw *n* a fine-toothed saw with a long thin narrow blade, used for cutting designs in thin wood or metal

fretwork *n* decorative geometrical carving in wood

Freud *n* **1** Anna. 1895–1982, Austrian psychiatrist: daughter of Sigmund Freud and pioneer of child psychoanalysis **2** Sir Clement. 1924–2009, British broadcaster, writer, politician, and chef; best known as a panellist on the radio game show *Just a Minute*; grandson of Sigmund Freud **3** Lucian. 1922–2011, British painter, esp. of nudes and portraits; grandson of Sigmund Freud **4** Sigmund. 1856–1939, Austrian psychiatrist; originator of psychoanalysis, based on free association of ideas and analysis of dreams. He stressed the importance of infantile sexuality in later development, evolving the concept of the Oedipus complex. His works include *The Interpretation of Dreams* (1900) and *The Ego and the Id* (1923)

Freudian (froy-dee-an) *adj* of or relating to Sigmund Freud (1856–1939), Austrian psychiatrist, or his ideas **> Freudianism** *n*

Freudian slip *n* a slip of the tongue that may reveal an unconscious wish

Freytag *n* Gustav. 1816–95, German novelist and dramatist; author of the comedy *Die Journalisten* (1853) and *Soll und Haben* (1855), a novel about German commercial life

FRG Federal Republic of Germany

Fri. Friday

friable (fry-a-bl) *adj* easily broken up [Latin *friare* to crumble] **> friability** *n*

friar *n* a member of a male Roman Catholic religious order [Latin *frater* brother]

friar's balsam *n* a compound with a camphor-like smell, used as an inhalant to relieve bronchitis

friary *n, pl* **-aries** a house of friars

Fribourg *n* **1** a canton in W Switzerland. Capital: Fribourg. Pop: 242 700 (2002 est). Area: 1676 sq km (645 sq miles) **2** a town in W Switzerland, capital of Fribourg canton: university (1889). Pop: 35 547 (2000) ▶ German name: **Freiburg**

fricassee *n* stewed meat, esp. chicken or veal, served in a thick white sauce [Old French]

fricative *n* **1** a consonant produced by friction of breath through a partly closed mouth, such as (f) or (z) ▷ *adj* **2** relating to or being a fricative [Latin *fricare* to rub]

friction *n* **1** a resistance encountered when one body moves relative to another body with which it is in contact **2** the act of rubbing one object against another **3** disagreement or conflict [Latin *fricare* to rub] > **frictional** *adj*

Friday *n* the sixth day of the week [Old English *Frīgedæg* day of Freya, Norse goddess]

fridge *n* a cabinet for keeping food and drink cool. In full: refrigerator

fried *vb* the past of fry¹

Friedan *n* Betty. 1921–2006, US feminist, founder and first president (1966–70) of the National Organization for Women. Her books include *The Feminine Mystique* (1963), *The Second Stage* (1982), and *The Fountain of Life* (1993)

Friedman *n* Milton. 1912–2006. US economist, particularly associated with monetarism; a forceful advocate of free-market capitalism; Nobel Prize for Economics (1976) > **Friedmanite** *n, adj*

Friedrich *n* Caspar David. 1774–1840, German romantic landscape painter, noted for his skill in rendering changing effects of light

friend *n* **1** a person known well to another and regarded with liking, affection, and loyalty **2** an ally in a fight or cause **3** a patron or supporter: *our cause has many influential friends throughout Europe* **4 make friends (with)** to become friendly (with) ▷ *vb* **5** to add (a person) as a contact on a social networking site [Old English *frēond*] > **friendless** *adj* > **friendship** *n*

Friend *n* a member of the Society of Friends; Quaker

friendly *adj* **-lier, -liest** **1** showing or expressing liking, goodwill, or trust **2** on the same side; not hostile **3** tending to help or support ▷ *n, pl* **-lies** **4** *sport* a match played for its own sake and not as part of a competition > **friendliness** *n*

-friendly *combining form* helpful, easy, or good for the person or thing specified: *a user-friendly computer system; the development of an environment-friendly weedkiller*

Friendly Islands *pl n* another name for **Tonga**

friendly society *n* Brit an association of people who pay regular dues in return for old-age pensions, sickness benefits, etc.

frier *n* a fryer

fries *pl n* short for **French fries**

Friese-Greene *n* William. 1855–1921, British photographer. He invented (with Mortimer Evans) the first practicable motion-picture camera

Friesian (free-zhan) *n* any of several breeds of black-and-white dairy cattle

Friesland *n* **1** a province of the N Netherlands, on the IJsselmeer and the North Sea: includes four of the West Frisian Islands; flat, with sand dunes and fens (under reclamation), canals, and lakes. Capital: Leeuwarden. Pop: 640 000 (2003 est). Area: 3319 sq km (1294 sq miles). Official and Frisian name: **Fryslân** **2** an area comprising the province of Friesland in the Netherlands along with the regions of **East Friesland** and **North Friesland** in Germany

frieze (freeze) *n* **1** a sculptured or decorated band on a wall **2** *archit* the horizontal band between the architrave and cornice of a classical temple [French *frise*]

frigate (frig-it) *n* **1** a fast warship, smaller than a destroyer **2** a medium-sized warship of the 18th and 19th centuries [French *frégate*]

fright *n* **1** sudden fear or alarm **2** a sudden alarming shock **3** *informal* a very strange or unattractive person or thing [Old English *fryhto*]

frighten *vb* **1** to terrify or scare **2** to force (someone) to do something from fear > **frightening** *adj*

frightful *adj* **1** very alarming or horrifying **2** annoying or disagreeable: *a frightful pair of socks* **3** *informal* extreme: *a frightful mess* > **frightfully** *adv*

frigid (frij-id) *adj* **1** (esp. of a woman) lacking sexual responsiveness **2** very cold: *the frigid air* **3** formal or stiff in behaviour or temperament [Latin *frigidus* cold] > **frigidity** *n*

frill *n* **1** a long narrow strip of fabric with many folds in i attached at one edge of something as a decoration **2** an unnecessary part of something added to make it more attractive or interesting: *no fuss, no frills, just a purity of soun, and clarity of vision* [origin unknown] > **frilly** or **frilled** *adj*

frilled lizard *n* a large tree-living Australian lizard with an erectile fold of skin around the neck

fringe *n* **1** *chiefly Brit* hair cut short and hanging over the forehead **2** an ornamental edge of hanging threads, tassels, etc. **3** an outer edge: *London's southern fringe* **4** the minor and less important parts of an activity or organization: *two agents on the fringes of espionage activity* **5** a small group of people within a larger body, but differing from it in certain aims and ideas: *the radical fringe of the Green Party* ▷ *adj* **6** (of theatre) unofficial or unconventional ▷ *vb* **fringing, fringed** **7** to form a border for: *sandy paths fringing the water's edge* **8** to decorate with a fringe: *tinsel fringed the desk* [Latin *fimbria* fringe, border]

fringe benefit *n* a benefit given in addition to a regular salary or wage

fringed *adj* **1** (of clothes, curtains, etc.) decorated with a fringe **2 fringed with** or **by** bordered with or by: *a field fringed with trees*

Frink *n* Dame Elisabeth. 1930–93, British sculptor

frippery *n, pl* **-peries** **1** showy but useless ornamentatio **2** unimportant or trivial matters [Old French *frepe* frill, rag]

Frisbee *n* trademark a light plastic disc thrown with a spinning motion for recreation

Frisch *n* **1** Karl von. 1886–1982, Austrian zoologist; studied animal behaviour, esp. of bees; shared the Nobe prize for physiology or medicine 1973 **2** Max. 1911–91, Swiss dramatist and novelist. His works are predominantly satirical and include the plays *Biedermann und die Brandstifter* (1953) and *Andorra* (1961), anc the novel *Stiller* (1954) **3** Otto. 1904–79, British nuclear physicist, born in Austria, who contributed to the development of the first atomic bomb **4** Ragnar (Anton Kittil). 1895–1973, Norwegian economist, who pioneerec the study of econometrics and greatly influenced the management of the Norwegian economy from 1945: shared the first Nobel prize for economics (1969) with Jan Tinbergen

Frisches Haff *n* the German name for **Vistula** (2)

Frisian (free-zhan) *n* **1** a language spoken in the NW Netherlands **2** a speaker of this language ▷ *adj* **3** of this language or its speakers [Latin *Frisii* people of northern Germany]

Frisian Islands *pl n* a chain of islands in the North Sea along the coasts of the Netherlands, Germany, and Denmark: separated from the mainland by shallows

frisk *vb* **1** to leap, move about, or act in a playful manner **2** *informal* to search (someone) by feeling for concealed weapons, etc. ▷ *n* **3** a playful movement **4** *informal* an instance of frisking a person [Old French *frisque*]

frisky *adj* **friskier, friskiest** lively, high-spirited, or playful > **friskily** *adv*

frisson (freess-on) *n* a short sudden feeling of fear or excitement [French]

fritter *n* a piece of food, such as apple, that is dipped in batter and fried in deep fat [Latin *frigere* to fry]

fritter away *vb* to waste: *he did not fritter away his energy on trivialities* [obsolete *fitter* to break into small pieces]

Friuli *n* a historic region of SW Europe, between the Carnic Alps and the Gulf of Venice: the W part (**Venetian Friuli**) was ceded by Austria to Italy in 1866 and **Eastern Friuli** in 1919; in 1947 Eastern Friuli (except Gorizia) was ceded to Yugoslavia

Friulian *n* **1** the Rhaetian dialect spoken in parts of Friuli **2** an inhabitant of Friuli or a speaker of Friulian ▷ *adj* **3** of or relating to Friuli, its inhabitants, or their language

Friuli-Venezia Giulia *n* a region of NE Italy, formed in

1947 from **Venetian Friuli** and part of **Eastern Friuli**. Capital: Trieste. Pop: 1 191 588 (2003 est). Area: 7851 sq km (3031 sq miles)

frivolous *adj* **1** not serious or sensible in content, attitude, or behaviour **2** unworthy of serious or sensible treatment: *frivolous distractions* [Latin *frivolus*] **> frivolity** *n*

frizz *vb* **1** (of hair) to form or cause (hair) to form tight curls ▷ *n* **2** hair that has been frizzed [French *friser* to curl] **> frizzy** *adj*

frizzle¹ *vb* **-zling, -zled 1** to form (hair) into tight crisp curls ▷ *n* **2** a tight curl [probably related to Old English *frīs* curly]

frizzle² *vb* **-zling, -zled** to cook or heat until crisp or shrivelled up [probably blend of *fry* + *sizzle*]

Frobisher *n* Sir **Martin**. ?1535–94, English navigator and explorer: made three unsuccessful voyages in search of the Northwest Passage (1576; 1577; 1578), visiting Labrador and Baffin Island

Frobisher Bay *n* **1** an inlet of the Atlantic in NE Canada, in the SE coast of Baffin Island **2** the former name of **Iqaluit**

frock *n* old-fashioned **1** a girl's or woman's dress **2** a loose garment, formerly worn by peasants [Old French *froc*]

frock coat *n* a man's skirted coat, as worn in the 19th century

Fröding *n* Gustaf. 1860–1911, Swedish poet. His popular lyric verse includes the collections *Guitar and Concertina* (1891), *New Poems* (1894), and *Splashes and Rags* (1896)

Froebel *or* **Fröbel** *n* **1** Friedrich (**Wilhelm August**). 1782–1852, German educator: founded the first kindergarten (1840) ▷ *adj* **2** of, denoting, or relating to a system of kindergarten education developed by him or to the training and qualification of teachers to use this system

frog¹ *n* **1** a smooth-skinned tailless amphibian with long back legs used for jumping **2 a frog in one's throat** phlegm on the vocal cords, hindering speech [Old English *frogga*]

frog² *n* a military-style fastening on a coat consisting of a button and a loop [origin unknown] **> frogging** *n*

frog³ *n* horny material in the centre of the sole of a horse's foot [origin unknown]

frogman *n, pl* **-men** a swimmer equipped with a rubber suit, flippers, and breathing equipment for working underwater

frogmarch *n* **1** a method of carrying a resisting person in which each limb is held and the victim is face downwards ▷ *vb* **2** to carry in a frogmarch or cause to move forward unwillingly

frogspawn *n* a jelly-like substance containing a frog's eggs

Froissart *n* Jean. ?1333–?1400, French chronicler and poet, noted for his *Chronique*, a vivid history of Europe from 1325 to 1400

frolic *vb* **-icking, -icked 1** to run and play in a lively way ▷ *n* **2** lively and merry behaviour **3** a light-hearted occasion [Dutch *vrolijk*]

frolicsome *adj* merry and playful

from *prep* **1** indicating the original location, situation, etc.: *from America* **2** in a period of time starting at: *from 1950 to the current year* **3** indicating the distance between two things or places: *60 miles from the Iraqi border* **4** indicating a lower amount: *from 5 to 6* **5** showing the model of: *drawn from life* **6** used with a verbal noun to denote prohibition, etc.: *she was banned from smoking at meetings* **7** because of: *five hundred horses collapsed from exhaustion* [Old English *fram*]

fromage frais (from-ahzh fray) *n* a low-fat soft cheese with a smooth light texture [French: fresh cheese]

Frome *n* Lake Frome a shallow salt lake in NE South Australia: intermittently filled with water. Length: 100 km (60 miles). Width: 48 km (30 miles)

Fromm *n* Erich. 1900–80, US psychologist and philosopher, born in Germany. His works include *The Art of Loving* (1956) and *To Have and To Be* (1976)

frond *n* **1** the compound leaf of a fern **2** the leaf of a palm [Latin *frons*]

front *n* **1** that part or side that is forward, or most often seen or used **2** a position or place directly before or ahead **3** the beginning, opening, or first part **4** the position of leadership **5** a promenade at a seaside resort **6** *military* **a** the total area in which opposing armies face each other **b** the space in which a military unit is operating **7** *meteorol* the dividing line between two different air masses **8** an outward appearance: *he put on a bold front* **9** *informal* a business or other activity serving as a respectable cover for another, usually criminal, organization **10** Also called: **front man** a nominal leader of an organization **11** a particular field of activity: *on the economic front* **12** a group of people with a common goal: *the National Liberation Front* ▷ *adj* **13** of, at, or in the front ▷ *vb* **14** to face (onto) **15** to be a front of or for **16** to appear as a presenter in (a television show) **17** to be the leader of (a band) on stage [Latin *frons* forehead, foremost part]

frontage *n* **1** the facade of a building or the front of a plot of ground **2** the extent of the front of a shop, plot of land, etc.

frontal *adj* **1** of, at, or in the front **2** of or relating to the forehead [Latin *frons* forehead]

front bench *n* (in Britain) the leadership of either the Government or Opposition in the House of Commons or in various other legislative assemblies **> front-bencher** *n*

Frontenac *or* **Frontenac et Palluau** *n* Comte de. title of *Louis de Buade*. 1620–98, governor of New France (1672–82; 1689–98)

frontier *n* **1** the region of a country bordering on another or a line marking such a boundary **2** the edge of the settled area of a country **3 frontiers** the limit of knowledge in a particular field: *twenty years ago, laser spectroscopy was on the frontiers of chemical research* [Old French *front* part which is opposite]

frontispiece *n* an illustration facing the title page of a book [Late Latin *frontispicium* facade]

frontrunner *n* *informal* the leader or a favoured contestant in a race or election

frosh *n* US and Canad informal a freshman

frost *n* **1** a white deposit of ice particles **2** an atmospheric temperature of below freezing point, producing this deposit ▷ *vb* **3** to cover with frost **4** to kill or damage (plants) with frost [Old English]

Frost *n* **1** Sir David (**Paradine**). 1939–2013, British television presenter and executive, noted esp. for political interviews **2** Robert (**Lee**). 1874–1963, US poet, noted for his lyrical verse on country life in New England. His books include *A Boy's Will* (1913), *North of Boston* (1914), and *New Hampshire* (1923)

frostbite *n* destruction of tissues, esp. of the fingers, ears, toes, and nose, by freezing **> frostbitten** *adj*

frosted *adj* (of glass) having the surface roughened so that it cannot be seen through clearly

frosting *n* chiefly US and Canad icing

frosty *adj* **frostier, frostiest 1** characterized by frost: *the frosty air* **2** covered by frost **3** unfriendly or disapproving: *a frosty reception from the bank manager* **> frostily** *adv* **> frostiness** *n*

froth *n* **1** a mass of small bubbles of air or a gas in a liquid **2** a mixture of saliva and air bubbles formed at the lips in certain diseases, such as rabies **3** trivial but superficially attractive ideas or entertainment ▷ *vb* **4** to produce or cause to produce froth [Old Norse *frotha*] **> frothy** *adj*

Froude *n* **1** James Anthony. 1818–94, English historian; author of a controversial biography (1882–84) of Carlyle. **2** his brother **William**. 1810–79, English civil engineer

frown *vb* **1** to wrinkle one's brows in worry, anger, or concentration **2 frown on** to disapprove of: *smoking at work is frowned on* ▷ *n* **3** the act of frowning **4** a look of disapproval or displeasure [Old French *froignier*]

f

frowsty *adj* **frowstier, frowstiest** *Brit* stale or musty [from *frowzy*]

frowzy *or* **frowsy** *adj* **frowzier, frowziest** *or* **frowsier, frowsiest 1** slovenly or unkempt in appearance **2** musty and stale [origin unknown]

froze *vb* the past tense of **freeze**

frozen *vb* **1** the past participle of **freeze** ▷ *adj* **2** turned into or covered with ice **3** killed or stiffened by extreme cold **4** (of food) preserved by a freezing process **5 a** (of prices or wages) officially fixed at a certain level **b** (of business assets) not convertible into cash **6** motionless: *she was frozen in horror*

FRS (in Britain) Fellow of the Royal Society

fructify *vb* **-fies, -fying, -fied** to bear or cause to bear fruit [Latin *fructus* fruit + *facere* to produce]

fructose *n* a crystalline sugar occurring in honey and many fruits [Latin *fructus* fruit]

frugal (froo-gl) *adj* **1** economical in the use of money or resources; thrifty **2** meagre and inexpensive: *a frugal meal* [Latin *frugi* useful, temperate] **> frugality** *n* **> frugally** *adv*

fruit *n* **1** any fleshy part of a plant that supports the seeds and is edible, such as the strawberry **2** *botany* the ripened ovary of a flowering plant, containing one or more seeds **3** any plant product useful to man, including grain and vegetables **4** fruits the results of an action or effort, esp. if pleasant: *they have enjoyed the fruits of a complete victory* ▷ *vb* **5** to bear fruit [Latin *fructus* enjoyment, fruit]

fruiterer *n chiefly Brit and Austral* a person who sells fruit

fruit fly *n* **1** a small fly that feeds on and lays its eggs in plant tissues **2** a similar fly that feeds on plant sap, decaying fruit, etc., and is widely used in genetic experiments

fruitful *adj* **1** producing good and useful results: *a fruitful relationship* **2** bearing much fruit **> fruitfully** *adv*

fruition (froo-ish-on) *n* **1** the fulfilment of something worked for or desired **2** the act or condition of bearing fruit [Latin *frui* to enjoy]

fruitless *adj* **1** producing nothing of value: *a fruitless debate* **2** without fruit **> fruitlessly** *adv*

fruit machine *n Brit and NZ* a coin-operated gambling machine that pays out money when a particular combination of symbols, usually representing fruit, appears on a screen

fruit salad *or* **fruit cocktail** *n* a dish consisting of pieces of different kinds of fruit

fruit sugar *n* same as **fructose**

fruity *adj* **fruitier, fruitiest 1** of or like fruit **2** (of a voice) mellow or rich **3** *informal, chiefly Brit* referring humorously to things relating to sex **> fruitiness** *n*

frump *n* a woman who dresses in a dull and old-fashioned way [Middle Dutch *verrompelen* to wrinkle] **> frumpy** *or* **frumpish** *adj*

Frunze *n* the former name (until 1991) of **Bishkek**

frustrate *vb* **-trating, -trated 1** to upset or anger (a person) by presenting difficulties that cannot be overcome: *his lack of ambition frustrated me* **2** to hinder or prevent (the efforts, plans, or desires of) [Latin *frustrare* to cheat] **> frustrating** *adj* **> frustration** *n*

frustrated *adj* dissatisfied or unfulfilled

frustum *n, pl* **-tums** *or* **-ta** *geometry* the part of a solid, such as a cone or pyramid, contained between the base and a plane parallel to the base that intersects the solid [Latin: piece]

fry¹ *vb* **fries, frying, fried 1** to cook or be cooked in fat or oil, usually over direct heat ▷ *n, pl* **fries 2** Also: **fry-up** *informal* a dish of mixed fried food ▶ See also **fries** [Latin *frigere*] **> fryer** *or* **frier** *n*

fry² *pl n* **1** the young of various species of fish **2** See **small fry** [Old French *freier* to spawn]

Fry *n* **1** Christopher. 1907–2005, English dramatist; author of the verse dramas *A Phoenix Too Frequent* (1946), *The Lady's Not For Burning* (1948), and *Venus Observed* (1950) **2** Elizabeth. 1780–1845, English prison reformer and Quaker **3** Roger Eliot. 1866–1934, English art critic and painter who helped to introduce the postimpressionists to Britain. His books include *Vision and Design* (1920) and *Cézanne* (1927) **4** Stephen (John). born 1957, British writer, actor, and comedian; his novels include *The Liar* (1991) and *The Stars' Tennis Balls* (2000)

frying pan *n* **1** a long-handled shallow pan used for frying **2** out of the frying pan into the fire from a bad situation to a worse one

FSH *biology* follicle-stimulating hormone: a hormone secreted by the pituitary gland

f-stop *n photog* any of the lens aperture settings of a camera

ft. foot or feet

ftp file transfer protocol: a standard protocol for transferring files across a network, esp. the internet

Fuad I *n* original name *Ahmed Fuad Pasha*. 1868–1936, sultan of Egypt (1917–22) and king (1922–36)

Fu-chou *n* a variant transliteration of the Chinese name for Fuzhou

Fuchs *n* **1** Klaus Emil. 1911–88, East German physicist. He was born in Germany, became a British citizen (1942), and was imprisoned (1950–59) for giving secret atomic research information to the Soviet Union **2** Sir Vivian Ernest. 1908–99, English explorer and geologist: led the Commonwealth Trans-Antarctic Expedition (1955–58)

fuchsia (fyew-sha) *n* an ornamental shrub with hanging purple, red, or white flowers [after Leonhard Fuchs, botanist]

fuck *taboo vb* **1** to have sexual intercourse with (someone) ▷ *n* **2** an act of sexual intercourse **3** *slang* a partner in sexual intercourse **4** not give a fuck not to care at all ▷ *interj* **5** *offensive* an expression of strong disgust or anger [Germanic] **> fucking** *n, adj, adv*

fuck off *vb offensive, taboo* to go away

fuck up *vb offensive, taboo* to make a mess of (something)

fuddle *vb* **-dling, -dled 1** to cause to be confused or intoxicated ▷ *n* **2** a confused state [origin unknown] **> fuddled** *adj*

fuddy-duddy *n, pl* **-dies** *informal* a person, esp. an elderly one, who is extremely conservative or dull [origin unknown]

fudge¹ *n* a soft sweet made from sugar, butter, and milk [origin unknown]

fudge² *vb* **fudging, fudged 1** to make (an issue or problem) less clear deliberately **2** to avoid making a firm statement or decision [origin unknown]

Fuegian *adj* **1** of or relating to Tierra del Fuego or its indigenous Indians ▷ *n* **2** an Indian of Tierra del Fuego

fuel *n* **1** any substance burned for heat or power, such as coal or petrol **2** the material that produces energy by fission in a nuclear reactor **3** add fuel to to make (a difficult situation) worse ▷ *vb* **fuelling, fuelled** *or US* **fueling, fueled 4** to supply with or receive fuel **5** to intensify or make worse (a feeling or situation): *the move is bound to fuel speculation* [Old French *feu* fire]

fuel cell *n* a cell in which chemical energy is converted directly into electrical energy

Fuentes *n* Carlos. 1928–2012, Mexican novelist and writer. His novels include *A Change of Skin* (1967), *Terra Nostra* (1975), and *Cristóbal Nonato* (1987)

Fuerteventura *n* the second largest of the Canary Islands; tourism, fishing. Pop: 74 983 (2003 est). Area: 1,660 sq km (640 sq miles)

fug *n chiefly Brit and NZ* a hot stale atmosphere [origin unknown] **> fuggy** *adj*

Fugard *n* Athol. born 1932, South African dramatist, theatre director, and novelist. His plays include *The Blood-Knot* (1961), *Sizwe Bansi is Dead* (1972), *Statements after an Arrest under the Immorality Act* (1974), and *The Captain's Tiger* (1999). The film of his novel *Tsotsi* won an Academy Award for best foreign language film (2006)

fugitive (fyew-jit-iv) *n* **1** a person who flees, esp. from arrest or pursuit ▷ *adj* **2** fleeing **3** not permanent;

fleeting [Latin *fugere* to take flight]

fugu *n* any of various marine pufferfish eaten in Japan once certain lethally poisonous parts have been removed [Japanese]

fugue (fyewg) *n* a musical form consisting of a theme repeated above or below the continuing first statement [French] **> fugal** *adj*

führer *n* a leader: the title used by Hitler as Nazi dictator [German]

Fuji *n* Mount Fuji an extinct volcano in central Japan, in S central Honshu: the highest mountain in Japan, famous for its symmetrical snow-capped cone. Height: 3776 m (12 388 ft). Also known as: **Fujiyama, Fuji-san**

Fujian or **Fukien** *n* **1** a province of SE China: mountainous and forested, drained chiefly by the Min River; noted for the production of flower-scented teas. Capital: Fuzhou. Pop: 34 880 000 (2003 est). Area: 123 000 sq km (47 970 sq miles) **2** any of the Chinese dialects of this province

Fukuoka *n* an industrial city and port in SW Japan, in N Kyushu: an important port in ancient times; site of Kyushu university. Pop: 1 302 454 (2002 est)

Fukushima *n* a city in Japan, in N Honshu: noted for production of silk; site of a serious nuclear power station accident following an earthquake and tsunami in 2011. Pop: 290 064 (2011 est)

Fukuyama *n* a city in Japan, in SW Honshu: industrial and commercial centre. Pop: 381 098 (2002 est)

ful *suffix* **1** full of or characterized by: *painful; restful* **2** able or tending to: *useful* **3** as much as will fill the thing specified: *mouthful*

fulcrum *n, pl* **-crums** or **-cra** the pivot about which a lever turns [Latin: foot of a couch]

fulfil or US **fulfill** *vb* **-filling, -filled 1** to bring about the achievement of (a desire or promise) **2** to carry out (a request or order) **3** to satisfy (demands or conditions) **4 fulfil oneself** to achieve one's potential [Old English *fulfyllan*] **> fulfilment** or US **fulfillment** *n*

Fulham *n* a district of the Greater London borough of Hammersmith and Fulham (since 1965): contains **Fulham Palace** (16th century), residence of the Bishop of London

full¹ *adj* **1** holding as much or as many as possible **2** abundant in supply: *full of enthusiasm* **3** having consumed enough food or drink **4** (of the face or figure) rounded or plump **5** complete: *the full amount* **6** with all privileges or rights: *full membership* **7** *music* powerful or rich in volume and sound **8** (of a garment) containing a large amount of fabric **9 full of** engrossed with: *she had been full of her own plans lately* **10 full of oneself** full of pride or conceit **11 full up** filled to capacity ▷ *adv* **12** completely or entirely **13** directly or right: *she hit him full in the face* **14 full well** very or extremely well: *we knew full well that she was watching every move we made* ▷ *n* **15 in full** without omitting or shortening **16 to the full** thoroughly or fully [Old English] **> fullness** or especially US **fulness** *n*

full² *vb* to make (cloth) more compact during manufacture through shrinking and beating [Old French *fouler*]

fullback *n* soccer, hockey, rugby a defensive player

full-blooded *adj* **1** vigorous or enthusiastic **2** (esp. of horses) having ancestors of a single race or breed

full-blown *adj* fully developed

full board *n* the daily provision by a hotel of bed, breakfast, and midday and evening meals

full-bodied *adj* having a full rich flavour or quality: *a full-bodied vintage port*

Fuller *n* **1** (Richard) Buckminster. 1895–1983, US architect and engineer: developed the geodesic dome **2** Roy (Broadbent). 1912–91, British poet and writer, whose collections include *The Middle of a War* (1942) and *A Lost Season* (1944), both of which are concerned with World War II, *Epitaphs and Occasions* (1949), and *Available for Dreams* (1989) **3** Thomas. 1608–61, English clergyman and

antiquarian; author of *The Worthies of England* (1662)

fuller's earth *n* a natural absorbent clay used for fulling cloth

full-frontal *adj* informal exposing the genitals to full view

full house *n* **1** a theatre filled to capacity **2** (in bingo) the set of numbers needed to win

full-length *adj* **1** (of a mirror, portrait, etc.) showing the complete human figure **2** not abridged

full moon *n* the phase of the moon when it is visible as a fully illuminated disc

full-on *adj* informal complete; unrestrained: *full-on military intervention*

full-scale *adj* **1** (of a plan) of actual size **2** using all resources; all-out

full stop *n* the punctuation mark (.) used at the end of a sentence and after abbreviations. Also called (esp. US and Canad): **period**

full-time *adj* **1** for all of the normal working week: *a full-time job* ▷ *adv* **full time 2** on a full-time basis: *she worked full time until she was 72* ▷ *n* **full time 3** soccer, rugby, hockey the end of the game

full toss or **full pitch** *n* cricket a bowled ball that reaches the batsman without bouncing

fully *adv* **1** to the greatest degree or extent **2** amply or adequately **3** at least: *fully a hundred people*

fully-fashioned *adj* (of stockings or knitwear) shaped and seamed so as to fit closely

fulmar *n* a heavily-built Arctic sea bird with a short tail [Scandinavian]

fulminate *vb* **-nating, -nated fulminate against** to criticize or denounce angrily [Latin *fulmen* lightning that strikes] **> fulmination** *n*

fulsome *adj* **1** exaggerated and elaborate, and often sounding insincere: *fulsome praise* **2** not standard extremely complimentary

Fulton *n* Robert. 1765–1815, US engineer: designed the first successful steamboat (1807) and steam warship (1814)

fumble *vb* **-bling, -bled 1** to use the hands clumsily or grope about blindly: *fumbling for a cigarette* **2** to say or do awkwardly ▷ *n* **3** the act of fumbling [probably Scandinavian]

fume *vb* **fuming, fumed 1** to be overcome with anger or fury **2** to give off (fumes) or (of fumes) to be given off, esp. during a chemical reaction **3** to treat with fumes ▷ *n* **4** (often pl) pungent or toxic vapour, gas, or smoke: *exhaust fumes* [Latin *fumus* smoke, vapour]

fumigate (fyew-mig-gate) *vb* **-gating, -gated** to treat (something contaminated) with fumes [Latin *fumus* smoke + *agere* to drive] **> fumigation** *n*

fun *n* **1** pleasant, enjoyable, and light-hearted activity or amusement **2 for** or **in fun** for amusement or as a joke **3 make fun of** or **poke fun at** to ridicule or tease ▷ *adj* **4** (of a person) amusing and likeable **5** (of a place or activity) amusing and enjoyable [obsolete *fon* to make a fool of]

Funchal *n* the capital and chief port of the Madeira Islands, on the S coast of Madeira. Pop: 103 962 (2001)

function *n* **1** the intended role or purpose of a person or thing **2** an official or formal social gathering **3** a factor, the precise nature of which depends upon another thing in some way: *muscle breakdown is a function of vitamin E deficiency* **4** maths a quantity, the value of which depends on the varying value of another quantity **5** a sequence of operations that a computer or calculator performs when a specified key is pressed ▷ *vb* **6** to operate or work **7 function as** to perform the action or role of (something or someone else) [Latin *functio*]

functional *adj* **1** of or performing a function **2** practical rather than decorative **3** in working order **4** med affecting a function of an organ without structural change **> functionally** *adv*

functional food *n* a food containing additives which provide extra nutritional value. Also called: **nutraceutical**

functionalism *n* the theory that the form of a thing should be determined by its use ➤ **functionalist** *n, adj*

functionary *n, pl* **-aries** a person acting in an official capacity, such as for a government; official

fund *n* **1** a reserve of money set aside for a certain purpose **2** a supply or store of something ▷ *vb* **3** to provide money to **4** *finance* to convert (short-term debt) into long-term debt bearing fixed interest ▶ See also **funds** [Latin *fundus* the bottom, piece of land] ➤ **funder** *n*

fundamental *adj* **1** essential or primary: *fundamental mathematical concepts* **2** basic: *a fundamental error* ▷ *n* **3** fundamentals the most important and basic parts of a subject or activity **4** the lowest note of a harmonic series ➤ **fundamentally** *adv*

fundamentalism *n* **1** *Christianity* the view that the Bible is literally true **2** *Islam* a movement favouring strict observance of Islamic law ➤ **fundamentalist** *n, adj*

fundamental particle *n physics* same as **elementary particle**

fundholding *n* the system in which general practitioners may choose to receive a fixed budget from which they pay for non-urgent hospital treatment and drug costs for patients

fundi (foon-dee) *n S African* an expert [Nguni (language group of southern Africa) *umfindisi*]

funding *n* **1** the provision of money for a project or organization **2** the amount of money provided

fundraiser *n* **1** a person involved in organizing fundraising activities **2** an event held to raise money for a cause

fundraising *n* **1** the activity involved in raising money for a cause ▷ *adj* **2** of, for, or relating to fundraising: *a fundraising disco*

funds *pl n* money that is readily available

Fundy *n* Bay of Fundy an inlet of the Atlantic in SE Canada, between S New Brunswick and W Nova Scotia: remarkable for its swift tides of up to 21 m (70 ft)

Funen *n* the second largest island of Denmark, between the Jutland peninsula and the island of Zealand. Pop: 441 795 (2003 est). Area: 3481 sq km (1344 sq miles). Danish name: **Fyn**. German name: **Fünen**.

funeral *n* **1** a ceremony at which a dead person is buried or cremated **2** it's your funeral *informal* a mistake has been made and you alone will be responsible for its consequences ▷ *adj* **3** of or for a funeral [Latin *funus*] ➤ **funerary** *adj*

funeral director *n* an undertaker

funeral parlour *n* a place where the dead are prepared for burial or cremation

funereal (fyew-neer-ee-al) *adj* suggestive of a funeral; gloomy or sombre ➤ **funereally** *adv*

funfair *n Brit* an amusement park with machines to ride on and stalls

fungicide *n* a substance used to destroy fungi [FUNGUS + Latin *caedere* to kill]

fungoid *adj* resembling a fungus

fungous *adj* appearing suddenly and spreading quickly like a fungus

fungus *n, pl* **fungi** *or* **funguses** a plant without leaves, flowers, or roots, that reproduces by spores, including moulds, yeasts, and mushrooms [Latin] ➤ **fungal** *adj*

funicular (fyew-nik-yew-lar) *n* a railway up the side of a mountain, consisting of two cars at either end of a cable passing round a driving wheel at the summit. Also called: **funicular railway** [Latin *funis* rope]

funk¹ *old-fashioned, Brit n* **1** a state of nervousness, fear, or depression **2** a coward ▷ *vb* **3** to avoid doing (something) through fear [origin unknown]

funk² *n* a type of Black dance music with a strong beat [from *funky*]

Funk *n* Casimir. 1884–1967, US biochemist, born in Poland: studied and named vitamins

funky *adj* **-kier, -kiest** (of jazz or pop) having a strong beat [from obsolete *funk* to smoke tobacco, perhaps referring to music that is smelly, i.e. earthy]

funnel *n* **1** a tube with a wide mouth tapering to a small hole, used for pouring liquids into narrow openings **2** a chimney of a ship or steam train ▷ *vb* **-nelling, -nelled** *or* US **-neling, -neled 3** to move or cause to move through, or as if through, a funnel [Old Provençal *fonilh*]

funnel-web *n Austral* a large poisonous black spider that builds funnel-shaped webs

funny *adj* **-nier, -niest 1** causing amusement or laughter; humorous **2** peculiar or odd **3** *informal* faint or ill: *this smell is making me feel a bit funny* **4** funny business *informal* suspicious or dubious behaviour ➤ **funnily** *adv* ➤ **funniness** *n*

funny bone *n* a sensitive area near the elbow where the nerve is close to the surface of the skin

fur *n* **1** the dense coat of fine silky hairs on many mammals **2** the skin of certain animals, with the hair left on **3** a garment made of fur **4** make the fur fly to cause a scene or disturbance **5** *informal* a whitish coating on the tongue, caused by illness **6** *Brit* a deposit on the insides of water pipes or kettles, caused by hard water ▷ *vb* **furring, furred 7** Also: **fur up** to cover or become covered with a furlike deposit [Old French *fuerre* sheath]

furbelow *n old-fashioned* **1** a pleated or gathered piece of material used as a decoration on a woman's garment; ruffle **2** furbelows showy ornamentation [French dialect *farbella* a frill]

furbish *vb formal* to brighten up or renovate [Old French *fourbir* to polish]

furcate *vb* **-cating, -cated 1** to divide into two parts ▷ *adj* **2** forked: *furcate branches* [Latin *furca* a fork] ➤ **furcation** *n*

Furies *pl n, sing* **Fury** *Classical myth* the goddesses of vengeance, who pursued unpunished criminals

furious *adj* **1** extremely angry or annoyed **2** violent or unrestrained, such as in speed or energy: *fast and furious dance routines* ➤ **furiously** *adv*

furl *vb* to roll up (an umbrella, flag, or sail) neatly and securely [Old French *ferm* tight + *lier* to bind]

furlong *n* a unit of length equal to 220 yards (201.168 metres) [Old English *furlang*, from *furh* furrow + *lang* long]

furlough (fur-loh) *n* leave of absence from military or other duty [Dutch *verlof*]

furnace *n* **1** an enclosed chamber in which heat is produced to destroy refuse or smelt ores **2** *informal* a very hot place [Latin *fornax*]

Furness *n* a region in NW England in Cumbria, forming a peninsula between the Irish Sea and Morecambe Bay

furnish *vb* **1** to provide (a house or room) with furniture, etc. **2** to supply or provide [Old French *fournir*] ➤ **furnished** *adj*

furnishings *pl n* furniture, carpets, and fittings with which a room or house is furnished

furniture *n* the large movable articles, such as chairs and tables, that equip a room or house [Old French *fourn* to equip]

Furnivall *n* Frederick James. 1825–1910, English philologist: founder of the Early English Text Society and one of the founders of the *Oxford English Dictionary*

furore (fyew-ror-ee) *n* a very angry or excited reaction by people to something: *the furore over 'The Satanic Verses'* [Latin *furor* frenzy]

Furphy *n* Joseph, pen name *Tom Collins*. 1843–1912, Australian author. His works include the classic Australian novel *Such is Life* (1903) and *The Buln-Buln and the Brolga* (1948)

furrier *n* a person who makes or sells fur garments [Middle English *furour*]

furrow *n* **1** a long narrow trench made in the ground by plough **2** any long deep groove, esp. a deep wrinkle on the forehead ▷ *vb* **3** to become wrinkled **4** to make furrows in (land) [Old English *furh*]

furry *adj* **-rier, -riest** like or covered with fur or something furlike

Fur Seal Islands *pl n* another name for **Pribilof Islands**

Fürth *n* a city in S central Germany, in Bavaria northwest of Nuremberg: Pop: 111 892 (2003 est)

further *adv* **1** in addition **2** to a greater degree or extent **3** to or at a more advanced point **4** to or at a greater distance in time or space ▷ *adj* **5** additional **6** more distant or remote in time or space ▷ *vb* **7** to assist the progress of (something) [Old English *furthor*]
❭ **furtherance** *n*

> **USAGE** See at **farther**.

further education *n* (in Britain, Australia, and South Africa) formal education beyond school other than at university

furthermore *adv* in addition

furthest *adv* **1** to the greatest degree or extent **2** to or at the greatest distance in time or space; farthest ▷ *adj* **3** most distant in time or space; farthest

furtive *adj* sly, cautious, and secretive [Latin *furtivus* stolen] ❭ **furtively** *adv*

Furtwängler *n* Wilhelm. 1886–1954, German conductor, noted for his interpretations of Wagner

fury *n, pl* **-ries 1** violent anger **2** uncontrolled violence: *the fury of the sea* **3** an outburst of violent anger **4** a person with a violent temper **5** *like fury old-fashioned* with great energy, strength, or power [Latin *furere* to be furious]

Fury *n, pl* **-ries** See **Furies**

furze *n* gorse [Old English *fyrs*] ❭ **furzy** *adj*

fuse¹ *or US* **fuze** *n* **1** a lead containing an explosive for detonating a bomb ▷ *vb* **fusing, fused** *or US* **fuzing, fuzed 2** to equip with such a fuse [Latin *fusus* spindle]

fuse² *n* **1** a protective device for safeguarding electric circuits, containing a wire that melts and breaks the circuit when the current exceeds a certain value ▷ *vb* **fusing, fused 2** *Brit* to fail or cause to fail as a result of a fuse blowing **3** to equip (a plug or circuit) with a fuse **4** to join or become combined: *the two ideas fused in his mind* **5** to unite or become united by melting **6** to become or cause to become liquid, esp. by the action of heat [Latin *fusus* melted, cast]

fuselage (**fyew**-zill-lahzh) *n* the main body of an aircraft [French]

Fuseli *n* Henry. original name *Johann Heinrich Füssli.* 1741–1825, British painter, born in Switzerland. His paintings include *Nightmare* (1782)

Fushih *or* **Fu-shih** *n* another name for **Yanan**

Fushun *n* a city in NE China, in central Liaoning province near Shenyang: situated on one of the richest coalfields in the world; site of the largest thermal power plant in NE Asia. Pop: 1 425 000 (2005 est)

fusible *adj* capable of being melted

fusilier (fyew-zill-**leer**) *n* (formerly) an infantryman armed with a light musket: a term still used in the names of certain British regiments [French]

fusillade (fyew-zill-**lade**) *n* **1** a rapid continual discharge of firearms **2** a sudden outburst of criticism, questions, etc. [French *fusiller* to shoot]

fusilli (foo-**zee**-li) *n* pasta in the form of short spirals [Italian]

fusion *n* **1** the act or process of melting together **2** something produced by fusing **3** a kind of popular music that is a blend of two or more styles, such as jazz and funk **4** something new created by a mixture of qualities, ideas, or things **5** See **nuclear fusion** ▷ *adj* **6** relating to a style of cooking that combines traditional Western techniques and ingredients with those used in Eastern cuisine [Latin *fusio* a melting]

fuss *n* **1** needless activity and worry **2** complaint or objection: *it was silly to make a fuss over seating arrangements* **3** an exhibition of affection or admiration: *when I arrived my nephews made a big fuss of me* ▷ *vb* **4** to worry unnecessarily **5** to be excessively concerned over trivial matters **6** to bother (a person) **7 fuss over** to show great or excessive concern or affection for [origin unknown]

fusspot *n informal* a person who is difficult to please and complains often

fussy *adj* **fussier, fussiest 1** inclined to fuss **2** very particular about detail **3** overelaborate: *a fussy, overdecorated palace* ❭ **fussily** *adv*

fustian *n* **1** (formerly) a hard-wearing fabric of cotton mixed with flax or wool **2** pompous talk or writing [Old French *fustaigne*]

fusty *adj* **-tier, -tiest 1** smelling of damp or mould **2** old-fashioned [Middle English *fust* wine cask]
❭ **fustiness** *n*

futile (**fyew**-tile) *adj* **1** useless or having no chance of success **2** foolish and of no value: *her futile remarks began to annoy me* [Latin *futtilis* pouring out easily] ❭ **futility** *n*

futon (**foo**-tonn) *n* a Japanese padded quilt, laid on the floor as a bed

future *n* **1** the time yet to come **2** undetermined events that will occur in that time **3** the condition of a person or thing at a later date **4** prospects: *he had faith in its future* **5** *grammar* a tense of verbs used when the action specified has not yet taken place **6 in future** from now on ▷ *adj* **7** that is yet to come or be **8** of or expressing time yet to come **9** destined to become **10** *grammar* in or denoting the future as a tense of verbs ▶ See also **futures** [Latin *futurus* about to be]

future perfect *grammar adj* **1** denoting a tense of verbs describing an action that will have been performed by a certain time ▷ *n* **2** the future perfect tense

futures *pl n* commodities bought or sold at an agreed price for delivery at a specified future date

futurism *n* an early 20th-century artistic movement making use of the characteristics of the machine age
❭ **futurist** *n, adj*

futuristic *adj* **1** of design or technology that appears to belong to some future time **2** of futurism

futurity *n, pl* **-ties 1** future **2** a future event

futurology *n* the study or prediction of the future of mankind

Fuzhou, Foochow *or* **Fuchou** *n* a port in SE China, capital of Fujian province on the Min Jiang: one of the original five treaty ports (1842). Pop: 1 398 000 (2005 est)

fuzz¹ *n* a mass or covering of fine or curly hairs, fibres, etc. [probably from Low German *fussig* loose]

fuzz² *n Brit, Austral and NZ slang* the police or a policeman [origin unknown]

fuzzy *adj* **fuzzier, fuzziest 1** of, like, or covered with fuzz **2** unclear, blurred, or distorted: *some fuzzy pictures from a Russian radar probe* **3** (of hair) tightly curled ❭ **fuzzily** *adv*
❭ **fuzziness** *n*

fwd forward

FX *films informal* special effects [a phonetic respelling of *effects*]

Fylde *n* a region in NW England in Lancashire between the Wyre and Ribble estuaries

Fyn *n* the Danish name for **Funen**

FYROM Former Yugoslav Republic of Macedonia

Gg

g 1 gallon(s) **2** gram(s) **3** acceleration due to gravity

G 1 *music* the fifth note of the scale of C major **2** gravity **3** good **4** giga- **5** *slang* grand (a thousand pounds or dollars)

G. *or* **g. 1** Gulf **2** guilder(s) **3** guinea(s)

G8 Group of Eight

G20 Group of Twenty: an international organization established to promote global economic stability

Ga *chem* gallium

Ga. *or* **GA** Georgia

gab *informal vb* **gabbing, gabbed 1** to talk a lot, esp. about unimportant things ▷ *n* **2** idle talk **3 gift of the gab** the ability to talk easily and persuasively [probably from Irish Gaelic *gob* mouth]

gabardine *or* **gaberdine** *n* **1** a strong twill cloth used esp. for raincoats **2** a coat made of this cloth [Old French *gauvardine* pilgrim's garment]

Gabba *n* **the Gabba** *Austral informal* the Queensland Cricket Association ground at Woolloongabba, Brisbane

gabble *vb* **-bling, -bled 1** to speak rapidly and indistinctly: *the interviewee started to gabble furiously* ▷ *n* **2** rapid and indistinct speech [Middle Dutch *gabbelen*]

Gaberones *n* the former name for **Gaborone**

Gabès *n* **1** a port in E Tunisia. Pop: 116 000 (2005 est) **2** **Gulf of Gabès** an inlet of the Mediterranean on the E coast of Tunisia ▶ Ancient name: **Syrtis Minor**. Arabic name: **Qabis**

gable *n* the triangular upper part of a wall between the sloping ends of a ridged roof [probably from Old Norse *gafl*] ▷ **gabled** *adj*

Gable *n* (**William**) **Clark**. 1901–60, US film actor. His films include *It Happened One Night* (1934), *San Francisco* (1936), *Gone with the Wind* (1939), *Mogambo* (1953), and *The Misfits* (1960)

Gabo *n* Naum, original name *Naum Neemia Pevsner*. 1890–1977, US sculptor, born in Russia: a leading constructivist

Gabon *n* a republic in W central Africa, on the Atlantic: settled by the French in 1839; made part of the French Congo in 1888; became independent in 1960; almost wholly forested. Official language: French. Religion: Christian majority; significant animist minority. Currency: franc. Capital: Libreville. Pop: 1 640 286 (2013 est). Area: 267 675 sq km (103 350 sq miles). Former English spelling: **Gaboon**

Gabonese *adj* **1** of or relating to Gabon or its inhabitants ▷ *n* **2** a native or inhabitant of Gabon

Gabor *n* Dennis. 1900–79, British electrical engineer, born in Hungary. He invented holography: Nobel prize for physics 1971

Gaborone *n* the capital of Botswana (since 1964), in the extreme southeast. Pop: 186 007 (2001). Former name: Gaberones

Gabriel *n* Jacques-Ange. 1698–1782, French architect: designed the Petit Trianon at Versailles

Gabrieli *or* **Gabrielli** *n* **1** Andrea. 1520–86, Italian organist and composer; chief organist of St Mark's, Venice **2** his nephew, **Giovanni**. 1558–1612, Italian organist and composer

gad *vb* **gadding, gadded** (foll. by *about* or *around*) to go about in search of pleasure [obsolete *gadling* companion]

gadabout *n informal* a person who restlessly seeks amusement

Gaddafi *or* **Qaddafi** *n* Mu'ammar Muhammad al-, 1942–2011, Libyan army officer and statesman; head of state 1969–2011; deposed and executed 2011

gadfly *n, pl* **-flies 1** a large fly that bites livestock **2** a constantly irritating person [obsolete *gad* sting]

gadget *n* a small mechanical device or appliance [perhaps from French *gâchette* trigger] ▷ **gadgetry** *n*

gado-gado *n* an Indonesian dish of cooked mixed vegetables and hard-boiled eggs served with a peanut sauce [Bahasa Indonesia]

gadoid (gay-doid) *adj* **1** of or belonging to the cod family of marine fishes ▷ *n* **2** any gadoid fish [New Latin *gadus* cod]

gadolinium *n chem* a silvery-white metallic element of the rare-earth group. Symbol: **Gd** [after Johan *Gadolin*, mineralogist]

Gadsden Purchase *n* an area of about 77 000 sq km (30 000 sq miles) in present-day Arizona and New Mexico, bought by the US from Mexico for 10 million dollars in 1853. The purchase was negotiated by James Gadsden (1788–1858), US diplomat

gadzooks *interj archaic* a mild oath [perhaps from *God's hooks* the nails of the cross, from *Gad*, archaic euphemism for God]

Gael (gayl) *n* a Gaelic-speaker of Scotland, Ireland, or the Isle of Man [Gaelic *Gaidheal*] ▷ **Gaeldom** *n*

Gaelic (gal-lik, gay-lik) *n* **1** any of the closely related Celtic languages of Scotland, Ireland, or the Isle of Man ▷ *adj* **2** of the Celtic people of Scotland, Ireland, or the Isle of Man, or their language

Gaeltacht *or* **Gaedhealtacht** *n* any of the regions in Ireland in which Irish Gaelic is the vernacular speech. The form *Gaeltacht* is sometimes also used to mean the region of Scotland in which Scottish Gaelic is spoken. See also **Gaidhealtachd** [C20: from Irish Gaelic]

gaff¹ *n* **1** *angling* a pole with a hook attached for landing large fish **2** *nautical* a spar hoisted to support a fore-and-aft sail [Provençal *gaf* boathook]

gaff² *n* **blow the gaff** *Brit slang* to give away a secret [origin unknown]

gaffe *n* something said or done that is socially upsetting or incorrect [French]

gaffer *n* **1** *informal, chiefly Brit* a boss or foreman **2** an old man: often used affectionately **3** *informal* the senior electrician on a television or film set [from *godfather*]

gag¹ *vb* **gagging, gagged 1** to choke as if about to vomit or as if struggling for breath **2** to stop up (a person's mouth), usually with a piece of cloth, to prevent them from speaking or crying out **3** to deprive of free speech

▷ *n* **4** something, usually a piece of cloth, stuffed into or tied across the mouth **5** any restraint on free speech **6** a device for keeping the jaws apart: *a dentist's gag* [Middle English *gaggen*]

gag² *informal n* **1** a joke, usually one told by a professional comedian ▷ *vb* **gagging, gagged 2** to tell jokes [origin unknown]

gaga (**gah**-gah) *adj informal* **1** confused and suffering some memory loss as a result of old age **2** foolishly doting: *she's gaga over him* [French]

Gagarin *n* Yuri. 1934–68, Soviet cosmonaut: made the first manned space flight (1961)

gage¹ *n* (formerly) a glove or other object thrown down to indicate a challenge to fight [Old French]

gage² *n, vb* **gaging, gaged** US same as **gauge**

Gage *n* Thomas. 1721–87, British general and governor in America; commander in chief of British forces at Bunker Hill (1775)

gaggle *n* **1** *informal* a group of people gathered together **2** a flock of geese [Germanic]

Gaidhealtachd *n* **1** the area of Scotland in which Scottish Gaelic is the vernacular speech. See also **Gaeltacht 2** the culture and traditions of the Scottish Gaels [Scottish Gaelic]

gaiety *n, pl* **-ties 1** a state of lively good spirits **2** festivity; merrymaking

> **USAGE** See at **gay.**

Gaillard Cut *n* the SE section of the Panama Canal, cut through Culebra Mountain. Length: about 13 km (8 miles). Former name: **Culebra Cut** [C19: named after David Du Bose *Gaillard* (1859–1913), US army engineer in charge of the work]

gaily *adv* **1** in a lively manner; cheerfully **2** with bright colours

gain *vb* **1** to acquire (something desirable) **2** to increase, improve, or advance: *wholesale prices gained 5.6 percent* **3** to get to; reach: *gaining the top of the hill* **4** (of a watch or clock) to become or be too fast **5 gain on** to get nearer to or catch up on ▷ *n* **6** something won or acquired; profit; advantage: *a clear gain would result* **7** an increase in size or amount **8** *electronics* the ratio of the output signal of an amplifier to the input signal, usually measured in decibels [Old French *gaignier*]

gainful *adj* useful or profitable **> gainfully** *adv*

gainsay *vb* **-saying, -said** *archaic or literary* to deny or contradict [Middle English *gainsaien*, from *gain-* against + *saien* to say]

Gainsborough *n* Thomas. 1727–88, English painter, noted particularly for his informal portraits and for his naturalistic landscapes

gait *n* **1** manner of walking **2** (of horses and dogs) the pattern of footsteps at a particular speed, such as a trot [variant of *gate*]

gaiters *pl n* cloth or leather coverings for the legs or ankles [French *guêtre*]

Gaitskell *n* Hugh (**Todd Naylor**). 1906–63, British politician; leader of the Labour Party (1955–63)

Gaius or **Caius** *n* **1** ?110–?180 AD, Roman jurist. His *Institutes* were later used as the basis for those of Justinian **2** Gaius Caesar. See **Caligula**

gal *n slang* a girl

gala (**gah**-la) *n* **1** a special social occasion, esp. a special performance **2** *chiefly Brit* a sporting occasion with competitions in several events: *next week's sports gala* [Old French *galer* to make merry]

galactic *adj* of the Galaxy or other galaxies

Galápagos Islands *pl n* a group of 15 islands in the Pacific west of Ecuador, of which they form a province: discovered (1535) by the Spanish; main settlement on San Cristóbal. Pop: 18 640 (2001). Area: 7844 sq km (3028 sq miles). Official Spanish name: **Archipiélago de Colón**

Galashiels *n* a town in SE Scotland, in central Scottish Borders. Pop: 14 361 (2001)

Galata *n* a port in NW Turkey, a suburb and the chief business section of Istanbul

Galaţi *n* an inland port in SE Romania, on the River Danube. Pop: 251 000 (2005 est)

Galatia *n* an ancient region in central Asia Minor, conquered by Gauls 278–277 BC: later a Roman province

Galatian *adj* **1** of or relating to Galatia or its inhabitants ▷ *n* **2** a native or inhabitant of Galatia

galaxy *n, pl* **-axies 1** a star system held together by gravitational attraction **2** a collection of brilliant people or things: *a galaxy of legal talent* [Middle English (in the sense: the Milky Way); from Greek *gala* milk]

Galaxy *n* the Galaxy the spiral galaxy that contains the solar system. Also called: **Milky Way**

Galba *n* Servius Sulpicius. ?3 BC–69 AD, Roman emperor (68–69) after the assassination of Nero

Galbraith *n* John Kenneth. 1908–2006, US economist and diplomat born in Canada; author of *The Affluent Society* (1958), *The New Industrial State* (1967), and *The Culture of Contentment* (1992) **> Galbraithian** *adj*

gale *n* **1** a strong wind, specifically one of force 8 on the Beaufort scale **2 gales** a loud outburst: *gales of laughter* [origin unknown]

Galen *n* Latin name *Claudius Galenus*. ?130–?200 AD, Greek physician, anatomist, and physiologist. He codified existing medical knowledge and his authority continued until the Renaissance

galena or **galenite** *n* a soft bluish-grey mineral consisting of lead sulphide: the chief source of lead [Latin: lead ore]

Galerius *n* full name *Gaius Galerius Valerius Maximianus*. ?250–311 AD, Eastern Roman Emperor (305–311): noted for his persecution of Christians

Galia melon *n* a kind of melon with a raised network texture on the skin and sweet flesh

Galicia *n* **1** a region of E central Europe on the N side of the Carpathians, now in SE Poland and Ukraine **2** an autonomous region and former kingdom of NW Spain, on the Bay of Biscay and the Atlantic. Pop: 1 969 000 (2003 est)

Galician *adj* **1** of or relating to Galicia in E central Europe **2** of or relating to Galicia in NW Spain ▷ *n* **3** a native or inhabitant of either Galicia **4** the Romance language or dialect of Spanish Galicia, sometimes regarded as a dialect of Spanish, although historically it is more closely related to Portuguese

Galilee *n* **1** Sea of Galilee, Lake Tiberias or Lake Kinneret a lake in NE Israel, 209 m (686 ft) below sea level, through which the River Jordan flows. Area: 165 sq km (64 sq miles) **2** a northern region of Israel: scene of Christ's early ministry

Galileo *n* full name *Galileo Galilei*. 1564–1642, Italian mathematician, astronomer, and physicist. He discovered the isochronism of the pendulum and demonstrated that falling bodies of different weights descend at the same rate. He perfected the refracting telescope, which led to his discovery of Jupiter's satellites, sunspots, and craters on the Earth's moon. He was forced by the Inquisition to recant his support of the Copernican system

gall¹ (**gawl**) *n* **1** *informal* bold impudence: *she was stunned I had the gall to ask* **2** a feeling of great bitterness **3** *physiol obsolete* same as **bile** [Old Norse]

gall² (**gawl**) *vb* **1** to annoy or irritate **2** to make the skin sore by rubbing ▷ *n* **3** something that causes annoyance **4** a sore on the skin caused by rubbing [Germanic]

gall³ (**gawl**) *n* an abnormal outgrowth on a tree or plant caused by parasites [Latin *galla*]

gallant *adj* **1** persistent and courageous in the face of overwhelming odds: *a gallant fight* **2** (of a man) making a show of polite attentiveness to women **3** having a reputation for bravery: *Police Medal for gallant and* *meritorious services* ▷ *n* **4** *history* a young man who tried to impress women with his fashionable clothes or daring acts [Old French *galer* to make merry] **>** **gallantly** *adv*

gallantry *n* **1** showy, attentive treatment of women **2** great bravery in war or danger

gall bladder *n* a muscular sac, attached to the liver, that stores bile

Galle *n* a port in SW Sri Lanka; along with other coastal settlements, it suffered badly in the Indian Ocean tsunami of December 2004. Pop: 90 270 (2001). Former name: **Point de Galle**

galleon *n* a large three-masted sailing ship used from the 15th to the 18th centuries [Spanish *galeón*]

gallery *n, pl* **-leries** **1** a room or building for displaying works of art **2** a balcony running along or around the inside wall of a church, hall, or other building **3** *theatre* **a** an upper floor that projects from the rear and contains the cheapest seats **b** the audience seated there **4** an underground passage in a mine or cave **5** a group of spectators, for instance at a golf match **6** **play to the gallery** to try to gain approval by appealing to popular taste [Old French *galerie*]

galley *n* **1** the kitchen of a ship, boat, or aircraft **2** a ship propelled by oars or sails, used in ancient or medieval times [Old French *galie*]

galley slave *n* **1** a criminal or slave forced to row in a galley **2** *informal* a drudge

Gallia *n* the Latin name of **Gaul**

Gallic *adj* **1** French **2** of ancient Gaul or the Gauls

Gallicism *n* a word or idiom borrowed from French

gallinaceous *adj* of an order of birds, including poultry, pheasants, and grouse, that have a heavy rounded body [Latin *gallina* hen]

Gallinas Point *n* a cape in NE Colombia: the northernmost point of South America. Spanish name: **Punta Gallinas**

galling (gawl-ing) *adj* annoying or bitterly humiliating

Gallipoli *n* **1** a peninsula in NW Turkey, between the Dardanelles and the Gulf of Saros: scene of a costly but unsuccessful Allied campaign in 1915 **2** a port in NW Turkey, at the entrance to the Sea of Marmara: historically important for its strategic position. Pop: 22 000 (latest est) ▶ Turkish name: **Gelibolu**

gallium *n chem* a silvery metallic element used in high-temperature thermometers and low-melting alloys. Symbol: **Ga** [Latin *gallus* cock, translation of French *coq* in the name of its discoverer, Lecoq de Boisbaudran]

gallivant *vb* to go about in search of pleasure [perhaps from *gallant*]

Gällivare *n* a town in N Sweden, within the Arctic Circle: iron mines. Pop: 19 191 (2004 est)

gallon *n* **1** *Brit* a unit of liquid measure equal to 4.55 litres **2** *US* a unit of liquid measure equal to 3.79 litres [Old Northern French *galon*]

gallop *vb* **1** (of a horse) to run fast with a two-beat stride in which all four legs are off the ground at once **2** to ride (a horse) at a gallop **3** to move or progress rapidly ▷ *n* **4** the fast two-beat gait of horses **5** an instance of galloping [Old French *galoper*]

Gallovidian *n* **1** a native or inhabitant of Galloway ▷ *adj* **2** of or relating to Galloway ▶ Also called: **Galwegian**

Galloway *n* **1** an area of SW Scotland, on the Solway Firth: consists of the former counties of Kirkcudbright and Wigtown, now part of Dumfries and Galloway; in the west is a large peninsula, the **Rhinns of Galloway**, with the **Mull of Galloway**, a promontory, at the south end of it (the southernmost point of Scotland) **2** a breed of hardy beef cattle, usually black, originally bred in Galloway

gallows *n, pl* **-lowses** or **-lows** **1** a wooden structure consisting of two upright posts with a crossbeam, used for hanging criminals **2** **the gallows** execution by hanging [Old Norse *galgi*]

gallstone *n* a small hard mass formed in the gall bladder or its ducts

Gallup *n* George Horace. 1901–84, US statistician: devised the Gallup Poll; founded the American Institute of Public Opinion (1935) and its British counterpart (1936)

Gallup Poll *n* a sampling of the views of a representative cross section of the population, usually used to forecast voting [after G. H. GALLUP]

galop *n* **1** a 19th-century dance in quick duple time **2** music for this dance [French]

galore *adj* in abundance: *there were bargains galore* [Irish Gaelic *go leór* to sufficiency]

galoshes *pl n Brit, Austral and NZ* a pair of waterproof overshoes [Old French *galoche* wooden shoe]

Galsworthy *n* John. 1867–1933, English novelist and dramatist, noted for *The Forsyte Saga* (1906–28): Nobel prize for literature 1932

Galt *n* John. 1779–1839, Scottish novelist, noted for his ironic humour, esp. in *Annals of the Parish* (1821), *The Provost* (1822), and *The Entail* (1823)

Galton *n* Sir Francis. 1822–1911, English explorer and scientist, a cousin of Charles Darwin, noted for his researches in heredity, meteorology, and statistics. He founded the study of eugenics and the theory of anticyclones

galumph *vb Brit, Austral and NZ informal* to leap or move about clumsily or joyfully [probably a blend of GALLOP + TRIUMPH]

Galvani *n* Luigi. 1737–98, Italian physiologist: observed that muscles contracted on contact with dissimilar metals. This led to the galvanic cell and the electrical theory of muscle control by nerves

galvanic *adj* **1** of or producing an electric current by chemical means, such as in a battery **2** *informal* stimulating, startling, or energetic

galvanize or **-nise** *vb* **-nizing, -nized** or **-nising, -nised** **1** to stimulate into action **2** to cover (metal) with a protective zinc coating **3** to stimulate by an electric current [after Luigi GALVANI] **>** **galvanization** or **-nisation** *n*

galvanometer *n* a sensitive instrument for detecting or measuring small electric currents

Galway *n* **1** a county of W Republic of Ireland, in S Connacht, on **Galway Bay** and the Atlantic: it has a deeply indented coastline and many offshore islands, including the Aran Islands. County town: Galway. Pop: 209 077 (2002). Area: 5939 sq km (2293 sq miles) **2** a port in W Republic of Ireland, county town of Co Galway, on Galway Bay: important fisheries (esp. for salmon). Pop: 66 163 (2002) **3** a breed of sheep with long wool, originally from W Ireland. Former name: **Roscommon**

Galwegian *n* **1** another word for **Gallovidian** (1) **2** a native or inhabitant of the town or county of Galway in W Republic of Ireland ▷ *adj* **3** another word for **Gallovidian** (2) **4** of or relating to the town or county of Galway in W Republic of Ireland [C18: influenced by *Norway, Norwegian*]

Gama *n* Vasco da. ?1469–1524, Portuguese navigator, who discovered the sea route from Portugal to India around the Cape of Good Hope (1498)

Gambetta *n* Léon. 1838–82, French statesman; prime minister (1881–82). He organized resistance during the Franco-Prussian War (1870–71) and was a founder of the Third Republic (1871)

Gambia *n* a republic in W Africa, entirely surrounded by Senegal except for an outlet to the Atlantic: sold to English merchants by the Portuguese in 1588; became a British colony in 1843; gained independence and was a member of the Commonwealth between 1965 and 2013; joined with Senegal to form the Confederation of Senegambia (1982–89); consists of a strip of land about 16 km (10 miles) wide, on both banks of the **Gambia River**, extending inland for about 480 km (300 miles). Official language: English. Religion: Muslim majority.

Currency: dalasi. Capital: Banjul. Pop: 1 883 051 (2013 est). Area: 11 295 sq km (4361 sq miles). Also: **The Gambia**

Gambian *adj* **1** of or relating to Gambia or its inhabitants ▷ *n* **2** a native or inhabitant of Gambia

Gambier Islands *pl n* a group of islands in the S Pacific Ocean, in French Polynesia. Chief settlement: Rikitéa. Pop: 1097 (2002). Area: 30 sq km (11 sq miles)

gambit *n* **1** an opening remark or action intended to gain an advantage **2** *chess* an opening move in which a piece, usually a pawn, is sacrificed to gain an advantageous position [Italian *gambetto* a tripping up]

gamble *vb* **-bling, -bled** **1** to play games of chance to win money or prizes **2** to risk or bet (something) on the outcome of an event or sport **3 gamble away** to lose by gambling **4 gamble on** to act with the expectation of: *she has gambled on proving everyone wrong* ▷ *n* **5** a risky act or venture **6** a bet or wager [probably variant of GAME[1]] ▷ **gambler** *n* ▷ **gambling** *n*

gamboge (gam-**boje**) *n* a gum resin obtained from a tropical Asian tree, used as a yellow pigment and as a purgative [from *Cambodia*, where first found]

gambol *vb* **-bolling, -bolled** *or US* **-boling, -boled** **1** to jump about playfully; frolic ▷ *n* **2** the act of playfully jumping about; the act of frolicking [French *gambade*]

game[1] *n* **1** an amusement for children **2** a competitive activity with rules **3** a single period of play in such an activity **4** (in some sports) the score needed to win **5** a single contest in a series; match **6** short for **computer game 7** style or ability in playing a game: *in the second set his overall game improved markedly* **8** an activity that seems to operate according to unwritten rules: *the political game of power* **9** an activity undertaken in a spirit of playfulness: *people who regard life as a game* **10** wild animals, birds, or fish, hunted for sport or food **11** the flesh of such animals, used as food **12** an object of pursuit: *fair game* **13** *informal* a trick or scheme: *what's his game?* **14 games** an event consisting of various sporting contests, usually in athletics: *Commonwealth Games* **15 give the game away** to reveal one's intentions or a secret **16 on the game** *slang* working as a prostitute **17 play the game** to behave fairly **18 the game is up** the scheme or trick has been found out and so cannot succeed ▷ *adj* **19** *informal* full of fighting spirit; plucky **20** *informal* prepared or willing: *I'm always game for a new sensation* ▷ *vb* **gaming, gamed 21** to play games of chance for money; gamble [Old English *gamen*] ▷ **gamely** *adv* ▷ **gameness** *n*

game[2] *adj Brit, Austral and NZ* lame: *he had a game leg* [probably from Irish *cam* crooked]

gamekeeper *n Brit* a person employed to take care of game on an estate

game plan *n* **1** *US and Canad* a strategy for playing a particular game **2** any plan or strategy

gamer *n* a person who plays computer games

games console *n* a small machine, linked to a television set, used for playing video games

gamesmanship *n informal* the art of winning by cunning practices without actually cheating

gamester *n* a gambler

gamete (gam-**eet**) *n* a cell that can fuse with another in reproduction [Greek *gametē* wife] ▷ **gametic** *or* **gametal** *adj*

gamey *or* **gamy** *adj* **gamier, gamiest** having the smell or flavour of game

gamin *n* a street urchin [French]

gamine (gam-**een**) *n* a slim and boyish girl or young woman [French]

gaming *n* gambling

gamma *n* the third letter in the Greek alphabet (Γ, γ)

gamma radiation *n* electromagnetic radiation of shorter wavelength and higher energy than X-rays

gamma rays *pl n* streams of gamma radiation

gammon *n* **1** cured or smoked ham **2** the hindquarter of a side of bacon [Old French *gambe* leg]

gammy *adj* **-mier, -miest** *Brit and NZ slang* (of the leg) lame [dialect variant of GAME[2]]

gamp *n Brit informal* an umbrella [after Mrs *Gamp* in Dickens' *Martin Chuzzlewit*]

gamut *n* **1** entire range or scale: *a rich gamut of facial expressions* **2** *music* **a** a scale **b** the whole range of notes [Medieval Latin, from *gamma*, the lowest note of the hexachord as established by Guido d'Arezzo + *ut* (now, *doh*), the first of the notes of the scale *ut, re, mi, fa, sol, la, si*]

gamy *adj* same as **gamey**

Gäncä *n* a variant transliteration of the Azerbaijani name for Gandzha

Gance *n* Abel. 1889–1981, French film director, whose works include *J'accuse* (1919, 1937) and *Napoléon* (1927), which introduced the split-screen technique

Gand *n* the French name for **Ghent**

gander *n* **1** a male goose **2** *informal* a quick look: *have a gander* [Old English *gandra, ganra*]

Gandhi *n* **1** Indira (Priyadarshini), daughter of Jawaharlal Nehru. 1917–84, Indian stateswoman; prime minister of India (1966–77; 1980–84); assassinated **2** Mohandas Karamchand, known as *Mahatma Gandhi*. 1869–1948, Indian political and spiritual leader and social reformer. He played a major part in India's struggle for home rule and was frequently imprisoned by the British for organizing acts of civil disobedience. He advocated passive resistance and hunger strikes as means of achieving reform, campaigned for the untouchables, and attempted to unite Muslims and Hindus. He was assassinated by a Hindu extremist **3** Rajiv, son of Indira Gandhi. 1944–91, Indian statesman; prime minister of India (1984–89); assassinated

Gandzha *or* **Gäncä** *n* a city in NW Azerbaijan: annexed by the Russians in 1804; centre of a cotton-growing region. Pop: 314 000 (2005 est). Former names: (1813–1920) Yelisavetpol, (1936–91) Kirovabad

gang[1] *n* **1** a group of people who go around together, often to commit crime **2** an organized group of workmen ▷ *vb* **3** to become or act as a gang ▶ See also **gang up on** [Old English: journey]

gang[2] *vb Scot* to go or walk [Old English *gangan*]

Ganga *n* the Hindi name for the **Ganges**

gangbang *n slang* sexual intercourse between one woman and several men one after the other, esp. against her will

Ganges *n* the great river of N India and central Bangladesh: rises in two headstreams in the Himalayas and flows southeast to Allahabad, where it is joined by the Jumna; continues southeast into Bangladesh, where it enters the Bay of Bengal in a great delta; the most sacred river to Hindus, with many places of pilgrimage, esp. Varanasi. Length: 2507 km (1557 miles). Hindi name: **Ganga**

Gangetic *adj* of or relating to the river Ganges

gangland *n* the criminal underworld

gangling *or* **gangly** *adj* lanky and awkward in movement [see GANG[2]]

ganglion *n, pl* **-glia** *or* **-glions** a collection of nerve cells outside the brain and spinal cord [Greek: cystic tumour] ▷ **ganglionic** *adj*

gangplank *n nautical* a portable bridge for boarding and leaving a ship

gangrene *n* decay of body tissue caused by the blood supply being interrupted by disease or injury [Greek *gangraina* an eating sore] ▷ **gangrenous** *adj*

gangsta rap *n* a style of rap music originating from US Black street culture [phonetic rendering of GANGSTER]

gangster *n* a member of an organized gang of criminals ▷ **gangsterism** *n*

Gangtok *n* a town in NE India: capital of Sikkim state. Pop: 29 162 (2001)

gangue *n* valueless material in an ore [German *Gang* vein of metal, course]

gang up on *or* **gang up against** *vb informal* to combine in a group against

gangway n **1** Brit an aisle between rows of seats **2** same as **gangplank** **3** an opening in a ship's side to take a gangplank

gannet n **1** a heavily built white seabird **2** Brit slang a greedy person [Old English *ganot*]

ganoid adj **1** (of the scales of certain fishes) consisting of an inner bony layer covered with an enamel-like substance **2** (of a fish) having such scales ▷ n **3** a ganoid fish [Greek *ganos* brightness]

Gansu or **Kansu** n a province of NW China, between Tibet and Inner Mongolia: mountainous, with desert regions; forms a corridor, the Old Silk Road, much used in early and medieval times for trade with Turkestan, India, and Persia. Capital: Lanzhou. Pop: 26 030 000 (2003 est). Area: 366 500 sq km (141 500 sq miles)

gantry n, pl **-tries** a large metal framework used to support something, such as a travelling crane, or to position a rocket on its launch pad [Latin *cantherius* supporting frame, pack ass]

Gao n a town in E Mali, on the River Niger: a small river port. Pop: 57 978 (2005 est)

gaol (jayl) n, vb Brit and Austral same as **jail** ▷ **gaoler** n

Gao Xingjian n born 1940, Chinese dramatist, novelist, and dissident, living in France from 1987; his works include the play *Chezhan* (*Bus Stop*, 1983) and the novel *Lingshan* (*Soul Mountain*, 1989): Nobel prize for literature 2000

Gaoxiong n a variant transliteration of the Chinese name for **Kaohsiung**

gap n **1** a break or opening in something **2** an interruption or interval **3** a difference in ideas or viewpoint: *the generation gap* [Old Norse: chasm] ▷ **gappy** adj

gape vb **gaping, gaped** **1** to stare in wonder with the mouth open **2** to open the mouth wide, as in yawning **3** to be or become wide open: *a hole gaped in the roof* [Old Norse *gapa*] ▷ **gaping** adj

gap year n a year's break between leaving school and starting further education

garage n **1** a building used to keep cars **2** a place where cars are repaired and petrol is sold ▷ vb **-aging, -aged** **3** to put or keep a car in a garage [French]

garage sale n a sale of household items held at a person's home, usually in the garage

garb n **1** clothes, usually the distinctive dress of an occupation or group: *modern military garb* ▷ vb **2** to clothe [Old French *garbe* graceful contour]

garbage n **1** US, Austral and NZ household waste **2** worthless rubbish or nonsense [probably from Anglo-French]

garbled adj (of a story, message, etc.) jumbled and confused [Old Italian *garbellare* to strain, sift]

garbo n, pl **-bos** Austral informal a person who collects garbage

Garbo n Greta, real name *Greta Lovisa Gustafson*. 1905–90, US film actress, born in Sweden. Her films include *Grand Hotel* (1932), *Queen Christina* (1933), *Anna Karenina* (1935), *Camille* (1936), and *Ninotchka* (1939)

García Márquez n Gabriel. 1927–2014, Colombian novelist and short-story writer. His novels include *One Hundred Years of Solitude* (1967), *The Autumn of the Patriarch* (1977), *Love in the Time of Cholera* (1985), and *News of a Kidnapping* (1996). Nobel prize for literature 1982

garçon (garss-on) n a waiter [French]

Gard n a department of S France, in Languedoc-Roussillon region. Capital: Nîmes. Pop: 648 522 (2003 est). Area: 5881 sq km (2294 sq miles)

garda n, pl **gardaí** a member of the police force of the Republic of Ireland [Irish Gaelic: guard]

Garda n Lake Garda a lake in N Italy: the largest lake in the country. Area: 370 sq km (143 sq miles)

garden n **1** an area of land usually next to a house, for growing flowers, fruit, or vegetables. Related adjective: **horticultural** **2** Also: **gardens** a cultivated area of land

open to the public: *Kensington Gardens* **3** lead someone up the garden path informal to mislead or deceive someone ▷ vb **4** to work in or take care of a garden [Old French *gardin*] ▷ **gardener** n ▷ **gardening** n

garden centre n a place where plants and gardening tools and equipment are sold

garden city n Brit a planned town of limited size surrounded by countryside

gardenia (gar-deen-ya) n **1** a large fragrant waxy white flower **2** the evergreen shrub on which it grows [after Dr Alexander *Garden*, botanist]

gardening leave n chiefly Brit informal a period during which an employee who is about to leave a company continues to receive a salary but does not work

Gardiner n **1** Sir John Eliot. born 1943, British conductor, noted for performances using period instruments; founded the Monteverdi Choir in 1965, the English Baroque Soloists in 1978, and the Orchestre Révolutionnaire et Romantique in 1990 **2** Stephen. ?1483–1555, English bishop and statesman; lord chancellor (1553–55). He opposed Protestantism, supporting the anti-Reformation policies of Mary I

Gardner n Ava. 1922–90, US film actress. Her films include *The Killers* (1946), *The Sun also Rises* (1957), and *The Night of the Iguana* (1964)

Garfield n James Abram. 1831–81, 20th president of the US (1881); assassinated in office

garfish n **1** a freshwater fish with a long body and very long toothed jaws **2** a sea fish with similar characteristics

gargantuan adj huge or enormous [after *Gargantua*, a giant in Rabelais' *Gargantua and Pantagruel*]

USAGE Some people think that *gargantuan* should only be used to describe things connected with food: *a gargantuan meal; his gargantuan appetite.*

---

gargle vb **-gling, -gled** **1** to rinse the mouth and throat with (a liquid) by slowly breathing out through the liquid ▷ n **2** the liquid used for gargling **3** the act or sound of gargling [Old French *gargouille* throat]

gargoyle n (on ancient buildings) a waterspout below the roof, carved in the form of a grotesque face or figure [Old French *gargouille* gargoyle, throat]

Garibaldi n Giuseppe. 1807–82, Italian patriot; a leader of the Risorgimento. He fought against the Austrians and French in Italy (1848–49; 1859) and, with 1000 volunteers, conquered Sicily and Naples for the emerging kingdom of Italy (1860)

garish adj crudely bright or colourful [obsolete *gaure* to stare] ▷ **garishly** adv ▷ **garishness** n

garland n **1** a wreath of flowers and leaves worn round the head or neck or hung up ▷ vb **2** to decorate with a garland or garlands [Old French *garlande*]

Garland n Judy, real name *Frances Gumm*. 1922–69, US singer and film star. Already a child star, she achieved international fame with *The Wizard of Oz* (1939). Later films included *Meet Me in St Louis* (1944) and *A Star is Born* (1954)

garlic n the bulb of a plant of the onion family, with a strong taste and smell, made up of small segments which are used in cooking [Old English *gārlēac*] ▷ **garlicky** adj

garment n an article of clothing [Old French *garniment*]

garner vb to collect or gather: *the financial rewards garnered by his book* [Latin *granum* grain]

Garner n **1** Erroll. 1921–77, US jazz pianist and composer, noted for the jazz standard 'Misty' (1954) **2** Helen. born 1942, Australian novelist and journalist. Her books include the novels *Monkey Grip* (1977), *The Idea of Perfection* (2002), *The Children's Bach* (1984), and *The Spare Room* (2008), and the nonfiction *The First Stone* (1995)

garnet n a red semiprecious gemstone [Old French *grenat* red, from *pome grenate* pomegranate]

Garnett *n* **1** Constance. 1862–1946, British translator of Russian novels **2** her son, **David**. 1892–1981, British novelist and editor. His novels include *Lady Into Fox* (1922) and *Aspects of Love* (1955)

garnish *vb* **1** to decorate (food) with something to add to its appearance or flavour ▷ *n* **2** a decoration for food [Old French *garnir* to adorn, equip]

Garonne *n* a river in SW France, rising in the central Pyrenees in Spain and flowing northeast then northwest into the Gironde estuary. Length: 580 km (360 miles)

garret *n* an attic in a house [Old French *garite* watchtower]

Garrett *n* Lesley. born 1955, British soprano; principal soprano with the English National Opera (1984–98)

Garrick *n* David. 1717–79, English actor and theatre manager

garrison *n* **1** soldiers who guard a base or fort **2** the place itself ▷ *vb* **3** to station (soldiers) in (a fort or base) [Old French *garir* to defend]

garrotte *or* **garotte** *n* **1** a Spanish method of execution by strangling **2** a cord, wire, or iron collar, used to strangle someone ▷ *vb* **-rotting, -rotted 3** to execute with a garrotte [Spanish *garrote*]

garrulous *adj* constantly chattering; talkative [Latin *garrire* to chatter] **> garrulousness** *n*

garter *n* **1** a band, usually of elastic, worn round the leg to hold up a sock or stocking **2** *US and Canad* a suspender [Old French *gartier*]

Garter *n* **the Order of the Garter** the highest order of British knighthood

garter stitch *n* knitting in which all the rows are knitted in plain stitch

Garvey *n* Marcus. 1887–1940, Jamaican Black nationalist leader, active in the US. He founded (1914) the Universal Negro Improvement Association and led the Back-to-Africa movement: gaoled for fraud (1925–27)

Gary *n* a port in NW Indiana, on Lake Michigan: a major world steel producer. Pop: 99 961 (2003 est)

gas *n*, *pl* **gases** *or* **gasses 1** an airlike substance that is neither liquid nor solid at room temperature and atmospheric pressure **2** a fossil fuel in the form of a gas, used as a source of heat **3** an anaesthetic in the form of a gas **4** *mining* firedamp or the explosive mixture of firedamp and air **5** *US, Canad, Austral and NZ* petrol **6** a poisonous gas used in war **7** *informal* idle talk or boasting **8** *slang* an entertaining person or thing: *Monterey was a gas for musicians and fans alike* **9** *US informal* gas generated in the alimentary canal ▷ *vb* **gases** *or* **gasses, gassing, gassed 10** to subject to gas fumes so as to make unconscious or to suffocate **11** *informal* to talk a lot; chatter [coined from Greek *khaos* atmosphere]

gasbag *n informal* a person who talks too much

gas chamber *n* an airtight room which is filled with poison gas to kill people

Gascoigne *n* Paul, known as *Gazza*. born 1967, English footballer: won 57 caps for England (1988–98); his clubs included Newcastle United, Tottenham Hotspur, Lazio, and Rangers

Gascony *n* a former province of SW France. French name: **Gascogne**

gaseous *adj* of or like a gas

gash *n* **1** a long deep cut ▷ *vb* **2** to make a long deep cut in [Old French *garser* to scratch, wound]

gasholder *n* a large tank for storing gas before distributing it to users

gasify *vb* **-fies, -fying, -fied** to change into a gas **> gasification** *n*

Gaskell *n* Mrs. married name of *Elizabeth Cleghorn Stevenson*. 1810–65, English novelist. Her novels include *Mary Barton* (1848), an account of industrial life in Manchester, and *Cranford* (1853), a social study of a country village

gasket *n* a piece of paper, rubber, or metal sandwiched

between the faces of a metal joint to provide a seal [probably from French *garcette* rope's end]

gaslight *n* **1** a lamp in which light is produced by burning gas **2** the light produced by such a lamp

gasman *n*, *pl* **-men** a man employed to read household gas meters and install or repair gas fittings, etc.

gas mask *n* a mask fitted with a chemical filter to protect the wearer from breathing in harmful gases

gas meter *n* a device for measuring and recording the amount of gas passed through it

gasoline *or* **gasolene** *n US and Canad* petrol

gasometer (gas-som-it-er) *n* same as **gasholder**

gasp *vb* **1** to draw in the breath sharply or with difficulty **2** to utter breathlessly ▷ *n* **3** a short sudden intake of breath [Old Norse *geispa* to yawn]

Gasparovic *n* Ivan. born 1941, Slovakian politician, president of Slovakia from 2004

Gaspé Peninsula *n* a peninsula in E Canada, in SE Quebec between the St Lawrence River and New Brunswick: mountainous and wooded with many lakes and rivers. Area: about 29 500 sq km (11 400 sq miles). Also called: **the Gaspé**

gas ring *n* a circular metal pipe with several holes in it fed with gas for cooking

Gassendi *n* Pierre. 1592–1655, French physicist and philosopher, who promoted an atomic theory of matter

Gasser *n* Herbert Spencer. 1888–1963, US physiologist: shared a Nobel prize for physiology or medicine (1944) with Erlanger for work on electrical signs of nervous activity

gassy *adj* **-sier, -siest** filled with, containing, or like gas **> gassiness** *n*

gastric *adj* of the stomach

gastric band *n* an adjustable band fitted inside the stomach to reduce its capacity as an aid to weight loss

gastric juice *n* a digestive fluid secreted by the stomach

gastric ulcer *n* an ulcer on the lining of the stomach

gastritis *n* inflammation of the lining of the stomach, causing vomiting or gastric ulcers

gastroenteritis *n* inflammation of the stomach and intestine, causing vomiting and diarrhoea

gastronomy *n* the art of good eating [Greek *gastēr* stomach + *nomos* law] **> gastronomic** *adj*

gastropod *n* a mollusc, such as a snail or whelk, that has a single flat muscular foot, eyes on stalks, and usually a spiral shell [Greek *gastēr* stomach + *-podos* -footed]

gasworks *n* a factory in which coal gas is made

gate *n* **1** a movable barrier, usually hinged, for closing an opening in a wall or fence **2 a** the number of people admitted to a sporting event or entertainment **b** the total entrance money received from them **3** an exit at an airport by which passengers get to an aircraft **4** *electronics* a circuit with one or more input terminals and one output terminal, the output being determined by the combination of input signals **5** a slotted metal frame that controls the positions of the gear lever in a motor vehicle [Old English *geat*]

gateau (gat-toe) *n*, *pl* **-teaux** (-toes) a large rich layered cake [French]

gate-crash *vb informal* to gain entry to (a party) without invitation **> gate-crasher** *n*

gatehouse *n* a building at or above a gateway

gate-leg table *or* **gate-legged table** *n* a table with leaves supported by hinged legs that can swing back to let the leaves hang from the frame

Gates *n* **1** Bill, full name *William Henry Gates*. born 1955, US computer-software executive and philanthropist; founder (1976) of Microsoft Corporation **2** Henry Louis. born 1950, US scholar and critic, who pioneered African-American studies in such works as *Figures in Black* (1987) **3** Horatio. ?1728–1806, American Revolutionary general: defeated the British at Saratoga (1777)

g

Gateshead *n* **1** a port in NE England, in Gateshead unitary authority, Tyne and Wear: engineering works, cultural centre. Pop: 78 403 (2001) **2** a unitary authority in NE England, in Tyne and Wear. Pop: 191 000 (2003 est). Area: 142 sq km (55 sq miles)

gateway *n* **1** an entrance that may be closed by a gate **2** a means of entry or access: *his only gateway to the outside world* **3** *computers* hardware and software that connect incompatible computer networks, allowing them to communicate

gather *vb* **1** to come or bring together **2** to increase gradually in (pace, speed, or momentum) **3** to prepare oneself for a task or challenge by collecting one's thoughts, strength, or courage **4** to learn from information given; conclude: *this is pretty important, I gather* **5** to draw (fabric) into small folds or tucks **6** to pick or harvest (crops) ▷ *n* **7** gathers small folds or tucks in fabric [Old English *gadrian*]

gathering *n* a group of people, usually meeting for some particular purpose: *the Braemar Highland Gathering*

GATT General Agreement on Tariffs and Trade: a former name for the World Trade Organization

Gatún Lake *n* a lake in Panama, part of the Panama Canal: formed in 1912 on the completion of the **Gatún Dam** across the Chagres River. Area: 424 sq km (164 sq miles)

gatvol (hut-fol) *adj S African slang* disenchanted; fed up [Afrikaans, literally: completely full]

gauche (gohsh) *adj* socially awkward [French]

gaucho (gow-choh) *n, pl* **-chos** a cowboy of the South American pampas [American Spanish]

Gaudí *n* Antonio. 1852–1926, Spanish architect, regarded as one of the most original exponents of Art Nouveau in Europe and noted esp. for the church of the Sagrada Familia, Barcelona

Gaudier-Brzeska *n* Henri, original name *Henri Gaudier*. 1891–1915, French vorticist sculptor

gaudy *adj* **gaudier, gaudiest** vulgarly bright or colourful [from *gaud* trinket] ▷ **gaudily** *adv* ▷ **gaudiness** *n*

gauge (gayj) *vb* **gauging, gauged 1** to estimate or judge (people's feelings or reactions) **2** to measure using a gauge ▷ *n* **3** an instrument for measuring quantities: *a petrol gauge* **4** a scale or standard of measurement **5** a standard for estimating people's feelings or reactions: *a gauge of public opinion* **6** the diameter of the barrel of a gun **7** the distance between the rails of a railway track [from Old French]

Gauguin *n* Paul. 1848–1903, French postimpressionist painter, who worked in the South Pacific from 1891. Inspired by primitive art, his work is characterized by flat contrasting areas of pure colours

Gauhati *n* a city in NE India, in Assam on the River Brahmaputra: centre of British administration in Assam (1826–74). Pop: 808 021 (2001)

Gaul *n* **1** an ancient region of W Europe corresponding to N Italy, France, Belgium, most of Germany, and the S Netherlands: divided into Cisalpine Gaul, which became a Roman province before 100 BC, and Transalpine Gaul, which was conquered by Julius Caesar (58–51 BC). Latin name: **Gallia 2** a native of ancient Gaul **3** a French person

Gaultier *n* Jean-Paul. born 1952, French fashion designer

gaunt *adj* **1** bony and emaciated in appearance **2** (of a place) bleak or desolate: *the gaunt disused flour mill* [origin unknown] ▷ **gauntness** *n*

gauntlet[1] *n* **1** a long heavy protective glove **2** a medieval armoured glove **3** take up the gauntlet to accept a challenge [Old French *gantelet*]

gauntlet[2] *n* run the gauntlet to be exposed to criticism or harsh treatment [Swedish *gatlopp* passageway]

gauss (rhymes with mouse) *n, pl* **gauss** the cgs unit of magnetic flux density [after K. F. GAUSS]

Gauss *n* Karl Friedrich. 1777–1855, German mathematician: developed the theory of numbers and applied mathematics to astronomy, electricity and magnetism, and geodesy ▷ **Gaussian** *adj*

Gauteng *n* a province of N South Africa; formed in 1994 from part of the former province of Transvaal: service industries, mining, and manufacturing. Capital: Johannesburg. Pop: 12 272 263 (2011 est). Area: 18 810 sq km (7262 sq miles)

Gautier *n* Théophile. 1811–72, French poet, novelist, and critic. His early extravagant romanticism gave way to a preoccupation with poetic form and expression that anticipated the Parnassians

gauze *n* a transparent, loosely woven cloth, often used for surgical dressings [French *gaze*] ▷ **gauzy** *adj*

Gavaskar *n* Sunil (Manohar). born 1949, Indian cricketer: played in 125 test matches (1971–87), 47 as captain; first batsman to score more than 10,000 test runs

gave *vb* the past tense of **give**

gavel (gav-vl) *n* a small hammer used by a judge, auctioneer, or chairman to call for order or attention [origin unknown]

Gävle *n* a port in E Sweden, on an inlet of the Gulf of Bothnia. Pop: 92 025 (2004 est)

gavotte *n* **1** an old formal dance in quadruple time **2** music for this dance [French]

gawk *vb* **1** to stare stupidly ▷ *n* **2** a clumsy stupid person [Old Danish *gaukr*]

gawky *adj* **gawkier, gawkiest** clumsy and awkward

gawp *vb slang* to stare stupidly [Middle English *galpen*] ▷ **gawper** *n*

gay *adj* **1** homosexual **2** carefree and merry: *with gay abandon* **3** bright and cheerful: *smartly dressed in gay colours* ▷ *n* **4** a homosexual, esp. a homosexual man: *solidarity amongst lesbians and gays* [Old French *gai*]

USAGE *Gayness* is the state of being homosexual. The noun which refers to the state of being carefree and merry is *gaiety*.

Gay *n* John. 1685–1732, English poet and dramatist; author of *The Beggar's Opera* (1728)

Gaya *n* a city in NE India, in Bihar: Hindu place of pilgrimage and one of the holiest sites of Buddhism. Pop: 383 197 (2001)

gaydar *n informal* the supposed ability of a homosexual person to determine whether or not another person is homosexual

Gaye *n* Marvin. 1939–84, US soul singer and songwriter; recordings include "I Heard It Through the Grapevine" (1969), *What's Going On* (1971), and "Sexual Healing" (1982): shot dead by his father

Gay-Lussac *n* Joseph Louis. 1778–1850, French physicist and chemist: discovered the law named after him (1808), investigated the effects of terrestrial magnetism, isolated boron and cyanogen, and discovered methods of manufacturing sulphuric and oxalic acids

Gay-Lussac's law *n* the principle that gases react together in volumes (measured at the same temperature and pressure) that bear a simple ratio to each other and to the gaseous products

gayness *n* homosexuality

Gaza *n* a city in the Gaza Strip: a Philistine city in biblical times. It was under Egyptian administration from 1949 until occupied by Israel (1967). Pop: 787 000 (2005 est). Arabic name: **Ghazzah**

Gazankulu *n* (formerly) a Bantu homeland in South Africa; abolished in 1993. Capital: Giyani

Gaza Strip *n* a coastal region on the SE corner of the Mediterranean: administered by Egypt from 1949; occupied by Israel from 1967; granted autonomy in 1993 and administered by the Palestinian National Authority from 1994. Pop: 1 763 387 (2013 est). Area: 363 sq km (140 sq miles)

gaze *vb* **gazing, gazed 1** to look long and steadily at someone or something ▷ *n* **2** a long steady look

[Swedish dialect *gasa* to gape at]

gazebo (gaz-zee-boh) *n, pl* **-bos** a summerhouse or pavilion with a good view [perhaps a pseudo-Latin coinage based on *gaze*]

gazelle *n* a small graceful fawn-coloured antelope of Africa and Asia [Arabic *ghazāl*]

gazette *n* an official newspaper that gives lists of announcements, for instance in legal or military affairs [French]

gazetteer *n* a book or section of a book that lists and describes places

Gaziantep *n* a city in S Turkey: base for Ibrahim Pasha's campaign against the Turks (1839) and centre of Turkish resistance to French forces (1921). Pop: 1 004 000 (2005 est). Former name (until 1921): **Aintab**

gazump *vb Brit and Austral informal* to raise the price of a house after agreeing a price verbally with an intending buyer [origin unknown]

gazunder *vb Brit informal* to reduce an offer on a house immediately before exchanging contracts, having earlier agreed a higher price with (the seller) **> gazunderer** *n*

GB 1 Great Britain **2** Also: **Gb** gigabyte

GBH (in Britain and South Africa) grievous bodily harm

GC George Cross (a British award for bravery)

GCE 1 (formerly in Britain) General Certificate of Education **2** *informal* a pass in a GCE examination

GCSE 1 (in Britain) General Certificate of Secondary Education; an examination in specified subjects which replaced the GCE O level and CSE **2** *informal* a pass in a GCSE examination

Gd *chem* gadolinium

Gdańsk *n* **1** the chief port of Poland, on the Baltic: a member of the Hanseatic league; under Prussian rule (1793–1807 and 1814–1919); a free city under the League of Nations from 1919 until annexed by Germany in 1939; returned to Poland in 1945. Pop: 851 000 (2005 est). German name: **Danzig 2 Bay of Gdańsk** a wide inlet of the Baltic Sea on the N coast of Poland

g'day *interj Austral and NZ informal* same as **good day**

GDP gross domestic product

GDR German Democratic Republic (East Germany; DDR)

Gdynia *n* a port in N Poland, near Gdańsk: developed 1924–39 as the outlet for trade through the Polish Corridor; naval base. Pop: 251 183 (2007 est)

Ge *chem* germanium

gear *n* **1** a set of toothed wheels that engages with another or with a rack in order to change the speed or direction of transmitted motion **2** a mechanism for transmitting motion by gears **3** the setting of a gear to suit engine speed or direction: *a higher gear; reverse gear* **4** clothing or personal belongings **5** equipment for a particular task: *police in riot gear* **6 in** or **out of gear** with the gear mechanism engaged or disengaged ▷ *vb* **7** to prepare or organize for something: *to gear for war* ▶ See also **gear up** [Old Norse *gervi*]

gearbox *n* the metal casing enclosing a set of gears in a motor vehicle

gearing *n* a system of gears designed to transmit motion

gear lever or *US and Canad* **gearshift** *n* a lever used to engage or change gears in a motor vehicle

gear up *vb* to prepare for an activity: *to gear up for a massive relief operation*

gearwheel *n* one of the toothed wheels in the gears of a motor vehicle

Geber *n* Latinized form of Jabir, assumed in honour of Jabir ibn Hayyan by a 14th-century alchemist, probably Spanish: he described the preparation of nitric and sulphuric acids

Gebrselassie *n* Haile. born 1973, Ethiopian athlete; won gold medals in the 10,000 metres at the Olympics (1996, 2000) and in four consecutive World Championships (1993–99)

gecko *n, pl* **geckos** a small tropical lizard [Malay *ge'kok*]

gee *interj US and Canad informal* a mild exclamation of surprise, admiration, etc. Also: **gee whizz** [euphemism for *Jesus*]

Gee *n* Maurice. born 1931, New Zealand writer, noted for his trilogy of novels *Plumb* (1978), *Meg* (1981), and *Sole Survivor* (1983)

geebung (gee-bung) *n* **1** an Australian tree or shrub with an edible but tasteless fruit **2** the fruit of this tree

geek *n informal* a boring and unattractive person [perhaps from Scottish *geck* fool] **> geeky** *adj*

geelbek (heel-bek) *n S African* an edible marine fish with yellow jaws [Afrikaans *geel* yellow + *bek* mouth]

Geelong *n* a port in SE Australia, in S Victoria on Port Phillip Bay. Pop: 130 194 (2001)

geese *n* the plural of **goose**[1]

geezer *n Brit, Austral and NZ informal* a man [probably dialect pronunciation of *guiser*, a mummer]

Gehry *n* Frank O(wen). born 1929, US architect and furniture designer, born in Canada; best known for the Guggenheim Museum in Bilbao, Spain (1997)

Geiger *n* Hans. 1882–1945, German physicist: developed the Geiger counter

Geiger counter (guy-ger) or **Geiger-Müller counter** *n* an instrument for detecting and measuring radiation [after Hans GEIGER]

Geikie *n* Sir Archibald. 1835–1924, Scottish geologist noted for his study of British volcanic rocks

geisha (gay-sha) *n* a professional female companion for men in Japan, trained in music, dancing, and conversation [Japanese]

gel (jell) *n* **1** a thick jelly-like substance, esp. one used to keep a hairstyle in shape ▷ *vb* **gelling, gelled 2** to become a gel **3** same as **jell** (1) **4** to apply gel to (one's hair) [from *gelatine*]

gelatine (jell-a-teen) or **gelatin** *n* a clear water-soluble protein made by boiling animal hides and bones, used in cooking, photography, etc. [Latin *gelare* to freeze]

gelatinous (jill-at-in-uss) *adj* with a thick, semiliquid consistency

geld *vb* **gelding, gelded** or **gelt** to castrate (a horse or other animal) [Old Norse *gelda*]

Gelderland or **Guelderland** *n* a province of the E Netherlands: formerly a duchy, belonging successively to several different European powers. Capital: Arnhem. Pop: 1 960 000 (2003 est). Area: 5014 sq km (1955 sq miles). Also called: **Guelders**

gelding *n* a castrated male horse [Old Norse *geldingr*]

Geldof *n* Bob. Full name *Robert Frederick Zenon Geldof.* born 1954, Irish rock singer and philanthropist: formerly lead vocalist with the Boomtown Rats (1977–86): organizer of the Band Aid charity (from 1984) for famine relief in Africa. He received an honorary knighthood in 1986

Gelibolu *n* the Turkish name for **Gallipoli**

gelignite *n* a type of dynamite used for blasting [GELATINE + Latin *ignis* fire]

Gelligaer *n* a town in S Wales, in Caerphilly county borough. Pop (including Ystrad Mynach): 17 185 (2001)

Gell-Mann *n* Murray. born 1929, US physicist, noted for his research on the interaction and classification of elementary particles: Nobel prize for physics in 1969

Gelsenkirchen *n* an industrial city in W Germany, in North Rhine-Westphalia. Pop: 272 445 (2003 est)

gem *n* **1** a precious stone used for decoration. Related adjective: **lapidary 2** a person or thing regarded as precious or special: *a perfect gem of a hotel* [Latin *gemma* bud, precious stone]

gemfish *n* an Australian food fish with a delicate flavour

Gemini *n astrol* the third sign of the zodiac; the Twins [Latin]

gemsbok (hemss-bok) *n S African* same as **oryx** [Afrikaans]

gemstone *n* a precious or semiprecious stone, esp. one which has been cut and polished

gen n Brit, Austral and NZ informal information: *I want to get as much gen as I can about the American market*. See also **gen up on** [from gen(eral information)]

Gen. General

Genck n a variant spelling of **Genk**

gendarme (zhahn-darm) n a member of the French police force [French]

gender n 1 the state of being male, female, or neuter 2 the classification of nouns in certain languages as masculine, feminine, or neuter [Latin *genus* kind]

gene (jean) n a unit composed of DNA forming part of a chromosome, by which inherited characteristics are transmitted from parent to offspring [German *Gen*]

genealogy (jean-ee-al-a-jee) n 1 the direct descent of an individual or group from an ancestor 2 (pl **-gies**) a chart showing the descent of an individual or group [Greek *genea* race] › **genealogical** adj › **genealogist** n

genera (jen-er-a) n a plural of **genus**

general adj 1 common or widespread: *general goodwill* 2 of, affecting, or including all or most of the members of a group 3 not specialized or specializing: *a general hospital* 4 including various or miscellaneous items: *general knowledge* 5 not definite; vague: *the examples used will give a general idea* 6 highest in authority or rank: *the club's general manager* ▷ n 7 a very senior military officer 8 **in general** generally; mostly or usually [Latin *generalis*]

general anaesthetic n a substance that causes general anaesthesia. See **anaesthesia**

general election n an election in which representatives are chosen in all constituencies of a state

generalissimo n, pl **-mos** a supreme commander of combined armed forces [Italian]

generality n 1 (pl **-ties**) a general principle or observation: *speaking in generalities* 2 old-fashioned the majority: *the generality of mankind*

generalization or **-lisation** n a principle or statement based on specific instances but applied generally: *the argument sinks to generalizations and name-calling*

generalize or **-lise** vb **-lizing, -lized** or **-lising, -lised** 1 to form general principles or conclusions from specific instances 2 to speak in generalities 3 to make widely used or known: *generalized violence*

generally adv 1 usually; as a rule: *these protests have generally been peaceful* 2 commonly or widely: *it's generally agreed he has performed well* 3 not specifically; broadly: *what are your thoughts generally about the war?*

general practitioner n a doctor who does not specialize but has a general medical practice in which he or she treats all illnesses

general-purpose adj having a variety of uses: *general-purpose cooking oil*

general staff n officers who assist commanders in the planning and execution of military operations

general strike n a strike by all or most of the workers of a country

generate vb **-rating, -rated** to produce or create [Latin *generare* to beget]

generation n 1 all the people of approximately the same age: *the younger generation* 2 a successive stage in descent of people or animals: *passed on from generation to generation* 3 the average time between two generations of a species, about 35 years for humans: *an alliance which has lasted a generation* 4 a specified stage of development: *the next generation of fighter aircraft* 5 production, esp. of electricity or heat

generation X n people born between the mid-1960s and mid-1970s who are highly educated and underemployed [from the novel *Generation X: Tales for an Accelerated Culture* by Douglas Coupland]

generation gap n the difference in outlook and the lack of understanding between people of different generations

generative adj capable of producing or originating something

generator n a device for converting mechanical energy into electrical energy

generic (jin-ner-ik) adj of a whole class, or group, or genus [Latin *genus* kind, race] › **generically** adv

generous adj 1 ready to give freely; unselfish 2 free from pettiness in character and mind 3 large or plentiful: *a generous donation* [Latin *generosus* nobly born] › **generosity** n › **generously** adv

genesis (jen-iss-iss) n, pl **-ses** (-seez) the beginning or origin of anything [Greek]

Genesis n Bible the first book of the Old Testament, containing a description of the creation of the world

Genet n Jean, 1910–86, French dramatist and novelist; his novels include *Notre-Dame des Fleurs* (1944) and his plays *Les Bonnes* (1947) and *Le Balcon* (1956)

gene therapy n genetics the replacement or alteration of defective genes in order to prevent the occurrence of inherited diseases

genetic (jin-net-tik) adj of genetics, genes, or the origin of something [from *genesis*] › **genetically** adv

genetically modified adj (of an organism) having DNA which has been altered for the purpose of improvement or correction of defects

genetic code n biochem the order in which the four nucleic acid bases of DNA are arranged in the molecule for transmitting genetic information to the cells

genetic engineering n alteration of the genetic structure of an organism in order to produce more desirable traits

genetic fingerprinting n the use of a person's unique pattern of DNA, which can be obtained from blood, saliva, or tissue, as a means of identification › **genetic fingerprint** n

genetics n the study of heredity and variation in organisms › **geneticist** n

Geneva n 1 a city in SW Switzerland, in the Rhône valley on Lake Geneva: centre of Calvinism; headquarters of the International Red Cross (1864), the International Labour Office (1925), the League of Nations (1929–46), the World Health Organization, and the European office of the United Nations; banking centre. Pop: 177 500 (2002 est) 2 a canton in SW Switzerland. Capital: Geneva. Pop: 419 300 (2002 est). Area: 282 sq km (109 sq miles). French name: **Genève**. German name: **Genf** 3 **Lake Geneva** a lake between SW Switzerland and E France: fed and drained by the River Rhône, it is the largest of the Alpine lakes; the surface is subject to considerable changes of level. Area: 580 sq km (224 sq miles). French name: **Lac Léman**. German name: **Genfersee**

Genevan or **Genevese** adj 1 of, relating to, or characteristic of Geneva 2 of, adhering to, or relating to the teachings of Calvin or the Calvinists ▷ n, pl **-vans** or **-vese** 3 a native or inhabitant of Geneva

Genève n the French name for **Geneva** (1, 2)

Geneviève n Saint. ?422–?512 AD, French nun; patron saint of Paris. Feast day: Jan 3

Genf n the German name for **Geneva** (1, 2)

Genfersee n the German name for (Lake) **Geneva**

Genghis Khan n original name *Temuchin* or *Temujin*. ?1162–1227, Mongol ruler, whose empire stretched from the Black Sea to the Pacific. Also: **Jinghis Khan, Jenghis Khan**

genial (jean-ee-al) adj cheerful, easy-going, and friendly [Latin *genius* guardian deity] › **geniality** n › **genially** adv

genie (jean-ee) n (in fairy tales) a servant who appears by magic and fulfils a person's wishes [Arabic *jinni* demon]

Genie n Canad an award given by the Academy of Canadian Cinema and Television in recognition of Canadian cinematic achievements

genital adj of the sexual organs or reproduction [Latin *genitalis* concerning birth]

genitals or **genitalia** (jen-it-ail-ya) pl n the external sexual organs

genitive n grammar a grammatical case in some

languages used to indicate a relation of ownership or association [Latin *genetivus* relating to birth]

genius (jean-yuss) *n, pl* **-uses** 1 a person with exceptional ability in a particular subject or activity 2 such ability 3 a person considered as exerting influence of a certain sort: *the evil genius behind the drug-smuggling empire* [Latin]

Genk *or* **Genck** *n* a town in NE Belgium, in Limburg province: coal-mining. Pop: 106 213 (2004 est)

Genoa *n* a port in NW Italy, capital of Liguria, on the **Gulf of Genoa**: Italy's main port; an independent commercial city with many colonies in the Middle Ages; university (1243); heavy industries. Pop: 610 307 (2001). Italian name: **Genova**

genocide (jen-no-side) *n* the deliberate killing of a people or nation [Greek *genos* race + Latin *caedere* to kill] > **genocidal** *adj*

Genoese *or* **Genovese** *n, pl* **-ese** *or* **-vese** 1 a native or inhabitant of Genoa ▷ *adj* 2 of or relating to Genoa or its inhabitants

genome *n* 1 the full complement of genetic material within an organism 2 all the genes comprising a haploid set of chromosomes [from GENE + CHROMOSOME]

genomics *n* the branch of molecular genetics concerned with the study of genomes

genotoxic *adj* harmful to genetic material

Genova *n* the Italian name for **Genoa**

genre (zhahn-ra) *n* 1 a kind or type of literary, musical, or artistic work: *the mystery and supernatural genres* 2 a kind of painting depicting incidents from everyday life [French]

Genseric *or* **Gaiseric** *n* ?390–477 AD, king of the Vandals (428–77). He seized Roman lands, esp. extensive parts of N Africa, and sacked Rome (455)

gent *n* Brit, Austral and NZ informal short for **gentleman**

Gent *n* the Flemish name for **Ghent**

genteel *adj* 1 overly concerned with being polite 2 respectable, polite, and well-bred [French *gentil* well-born] > **genteelly** *adv*

gentian (jen-shun) *n* a mountain plant with blue or purple flowers [Latin *gentiana*]

gentian violet *n* a violet-coloured solution used as an antiseptic and in the treatment of burns

Gentile[1] *n* 1 a person who is not a Jew ▷ *adj* 2 not Jewish [Latin *gentilis* belonging to the same tribe]

Gentile[2] *n* Giovanni. 1875–1944, Italian Idealist philosopher and Fascist politician: minister of education (1922–24)

Gentile da Fabriano *n* original name *Niccolo di Giovanni di Massio*. ?1370–1427, Italian painter. His works, in the International Gothic style, include the *Adoration of the Magi* (1423)

gentility *n, pl* **-ties** 1 noble birth or ancestry 2 respectability and good manners [Old French *gentilite*]

gentle *adj* 1 kind and calm in character 2 temperate or moderate: *gentle autumn rain* 3 soft; not sharp or harsh: *gentle curves* [Latin *gentilis* belonging to the same family] > **gentleness** *n* > **gently** *adv*

gentlefolk *pl n* old-fashioned people regarded as being of good breeding

gentleman *n, pl* **-men** 1 a cultured, courteous, and well-bred man 2 a man who comes from a family of high social position 3 a polite name for a man > **gentlemanly** *adj*

gentrification *n* a process by which the character of a traditionally working-class area is made fashionable by middle-class people > **gentrify** *vb*

gentry *n* Brit old-fashioned people just below the nobility in social rank [Old French *genterie*]

gents *n* Brit and Austral informal a men's public toilet

genuflect *vb* to bend the knee as a sign of reverence or deference, esp. in church [Latin *genu* knee + *flectere* to bend] > **genuflection** *n*

genuine *adj* 1 real and exactly what it appears to be: *a genuine antique* 2 sincerely felt: *genuine concern* 3 (of a

person) honest and without pretence [Latin *genuinus* inborn] > **genuinely** *adv* > **genuineness** *n*

gen up on *vb* **genning, genned** Brit and Austral informal to become, or make someone else, fully informed about

genus (jean-uss) *n, pl* **genera** *or* **genuses** 1 biology one of the groups into which a family is divided, containing one or more species 2 a class or group [Latin: race]

geocentric *adj* 1 having the earth as a centre 2 measured as from the centre of the earth

geodesic *adj* 1 relating to the geometry of curved surfaces ▷ *n* 2 the shortest line between two points on a curved surface

geodesy *n* the study of the shape and size of the earth [Greek *gē* earth + *daiein* to divide]

Geoffrey of Monmouth *n* ?1100–54, Welsh bishop and chronicler; author of *Historia Regum Britanniae*, the chief source of Arthurian legends

geography *n* 1 the study of the earth's surface, including physical features, climate, and population 2 the physical features of a region [Greek *gē* earth + -GRAPHY] > **geographer** *n* > **geographical** *or* **geographic** *adj* > **geographically** *adv*

geology *n* 1 the study of the origin, structure, and composition of the earth 2 the geological features of an area [Greek *gē* earth + -LOGY] > **geological** *adj* > **geologically** *adv* > **geologist** *n*

geometric *or* **geometrical** *adj* 1 of geometry 2 consisting of shapes used in geometry, such as circles, triangles, and straight lines: *geometric design* > **geometrically** *adv*

geometric progression *n* a sequence of numbers, each of which differs from the succeeding one by a constant ratio, for example 1, 2, 4, 8

geometry *n* the branch of mathematics concerned with points, lines, curves, and surfaces [Greek *geōmetrein* to measure the land] > **geometrician** *n*

geophysics *n* the study of the earth's physical properties and the physical forces which affect it > **geophysical** *adj* > **geophysicist** *n*

Geordie Brit *n* 1 a native or inhabitant of Tyneside 2 the Tyneside dialect ▷ *adj* 3 of or relating to Tyneside or its inhabitants: *a Geordie accent*

George *n* 1 David Lloyd. See **Lloyd George** 2 Sir **Edward** (**Alan John**), known as *Eddie*. 1938–2009, British economist, governor of the Bank of England (1993–2003) 3 **Henry**. 1839–97, US economist: advocated a single tax on land values, esp. in *Progress and Poverty* (1879) 4 **Saint**. died ?303 AD, Christian martyr, the patron saint of England; the hero of a legend in which he slew a dragon. Feast day: April 23 5 **Stefan** (**Anton**). 1868–1933, German poet and aesthete. Influenced by the French Symbolists, esp Mallarmé and later by Nietzsche, he aimed for an idealized purity of form in his verse. He refused Nazi honours and went into exile in 1933

George I 1660–1727, first Hanoverian king of Great Britain and Ireland (1714–27) and elector of Hanover (1698–1727). His dependence in domestic affairs on his ministers led to the emergence of Walpole as the first prime minister

George II *n* 1 1683–1760, king of Great Britain and Ireland and elector of Hanover (1727–60); son of George I. His victory over the French at Dettingen (1743) in the War of the Austrian Succession was the last appearance on a battlefield by a British king 2 1890–1947, king of Greece (1922–24; 1935–47). He was overthrown by the republicans (1924) and exiled during the German occupation of Greece (1941–45)

George III 1738–1820, king of Great Britain and Ireland (1760–1820) and of Hanover (1814–20). During his reign the American colonies were lost. He became insane in 1811, and his son acted as regent for the rest of the reign

George IV *n* 1762–1830, king of Great Britain and Ireland and also of Hanover (1820–30); regent (1811–20). His father (George III) disapproved of his profligate ways, which undermined the prestige of the crown, and of his association with the Whig opposition

George V *n* 1865–1936, king of Great Britain and Northern Ireland and emperor of India (1910–36)

George VI *n* 1895–1952, king of Great Britain and Northern Ireland (1936–52) and emperor of India (1936–47). The second son of George V, he succeeded to the throne after the abdication of his brother, Edward VIII

George Cross *n* a British award for bravery, usually awarded to civilians

Georgetown *n* the capital and chief port of Guyana, at the mouth of the Demerara River: became capital of the Dutch colonies of Essequibo and Demerara in 1784; seat of the University of Guyana. Pop: 237 000 (2005 est). Former name (until 1812): **Stabroek**

George Town *n* **1** Also called: **Penang** a port in NW Malaysia, capital of Penang state, in NE Penang Island: the first chartered city of the Malayan federation. Pop: 162 000 (2005 est) **2** the capital of the Cayman Islands: a port on Grand Cayman Island. Pop: 30 600 (2004 est)

georgette (jor-jet) *n* a thin crepe dress material [after Mme *Georgette*, a French dressmaker]

Georgia *n* **1** a republic in NW Asia, on the Black Sea: an independent kingdom during the Middle Ages, it was divided by Turkey and Persia in 1555; became part of Russia in 1918 and a separate Soviet republic in 1936; its independence was recognized internationally in 1992. It is rich in minerals and has hydroelectric resources. Official language: Georgian. Religion: believers are mainly Christian or Muslim. Currency: lari. Capital: Tbilisi. Pop: 4 555 911 (2013 est). Area: 69 493 sq km (26 831 sq miles) **2** a state of the southeastern US, on the Atlantic: consists of coastal plains with forests and swamps, rising to the Cumberland Plateau and the Appalachians in the northwest. Capital: Atlanta. Pop: 8 684 715 (2003 est). Area: 152 489 sq km (58 876 sq miles). Abbreviation: **Ga.**, (with zip code) **GA**

Georgian *adj* **1** of, characteristic of, or relating to any or all of the four kings who ruled Great Britain and Ireland from 1714 to 1830, or to their reigns **2** of or relating to George V of Great Britain and Northern Ireland or his reign (1910–36): *the Georgian poets* **3** of or relating to the republic of Georgia, its people, or their language **4** of or relating to the American State of Georgia or its inhabitants **5** in or imitative of the style prevalent in England during the 18th century (reigns of George I, II, and III), in architecture, dominated by the ideas of Palladio, and in furniture, represented typically by the designs of Sheraton ▷ *n* **6** the official language of Georgia, belonging to the South Caucasian family **7** a native or inhabitant of Georgia **8** an aboriginal inhabitant of the Caucasus **9** a native or inhabitant of the American State of Georgia **10** a person belonging to or imitating the styles of either of the Georgian periods in England

Georgian Bay *n* a bay in S central Canada, in Ontario, containing many small islands: the NE part of Lake Huron. Area: 15 000 sq km (5800 sq miles)

geospatial *adj* of or relating to the relative position of things on the earth's surface

geostationary *adj* (of a satellite) orbiting so as to remain over the same point on the earth's surface

geotechnical *adj* relating to the application of technology to engineering problems caused by geological factors

geothermal *adj* of or using the heat in the earth's interior

Ger. **1** German **2** Germany

Gera *n* an industrial city in E central Germany, in Thuringia. Pop: 106 365 (2003 est)

geranium *n* a cultivated plant with scarlet, pink, or white flowers [Latin: cranesbill]

Gérard *n* François (**Pascal Simon**), Baron. 1770–1837,

French painter, court painter to Napoleon I and Louis XVIII

gerbil (jur-bill) *n* a small rodent with long back legs, often kept as a pet [French *gerbille*]

Gergiev *n* Valery Abesalovich. born 1953, Russian conductor; musical director of the Kirov (now the Mariinsky) Opera from 1988; principal conductor of the London Symphony Orchestra from 2007

geriatric *adj* **1** of geriatrics or old people ▷ *n* **2** an old person, esp. as a patient

geriatrics *n* the branch of medicine concerned with illnesses affecting old people

Géricault *n* (Jean Louis André) Théodore. 1791–1824, French romantic painter, noted for his skill in capturing movement, esp. of horses

Gerlachovka *n* a mountain in N Slovakia, in the Tatra Mountains: the highest peak of the Carpathian Mountains. Height: 2663 m (8737 ft)

germ *n* **1** a tiny living thing, esp. one that causes disease: *a diphtheria germ* **2** the beginning from which something may develop: *the germ of a book* [Latin *germen* sprout, seed]

German *adj* **1** of or relating to Germany or its inhabitants ▷ *n* **2** a native or inhabitant of Germany **3** the official language of Germany, Austria, and parts of Switzerland

German Democratic Republic *n* (formerly) the official name of **East Germany**. Abbreviations: **GDR**, **DDR**

germane *adj* relevant: *the studies provided some evidence germane to these questions* [Latin *germanus* of the same race]

German East Africa *n* a former German territory in E Africa, consisting of Tanganyika and Ruanda-Urundi: divided in 1919 between Great Britain and Belgium; now in Tanzania, Rwanda, and Burundi

Germanic *n* **1** the ancient language from which English, German, and the Scandinavian languages developed ▷ *adj* **2** of this ancient language or the languages that developed from it **3** characteristic of German people or things: *Germanic-looking individuals*

Germanicus Caesar *n* 15 BC–19 AD, Roman general; nephew of the emperor Tiberius; waged decisive campaigns against the Germans (14–16)

germanium *n chem* a brittle grey metalloid element that is a semiconductor and is used in transistors. Symbol: **Ge** [after GERMANY]

German measles *n* same as **rubella**

German Ocean *n* a former name for the **North Sea**

German shepherd dog *n* same as **Alsatian** (1)

Germany *n* a country in central Europe: in the Middle Ages the centre of the Holy Roman Empire; dissolved into numerous principalities; united under the leadership of Prussia in 1871 after the Franco-Prussian War; became a republic with reduced size in 1919 after being defeated in World War I; under the dictatorship of Hitler from 1933 to 1945; defeated in World War II and divided by the Allied Powers into four zones, which became established as East and West Germany in the late 1940s; reunified in 1990: a member of the European Union. It is flat and low-lying in the north with plateau and uplands (including the Black Forest and the Bavarian Alps) in the centre and south. Official language: German. Religion: Christianity, Protestant majority. Currency: euro. Capital: Berlin. Pop: 81 147 265 (2013 est). Area: 357 041 sq km (137 825 sq miles). German name: **Deutschland**. Official name: **Federal Republic of Germany**. See also **East Germany**, **West Germany**. Related adjective: **Teutonic**

germ cell *n* a sexual reproductive cell

germicide *n* a substance used to destroy germs [germ + Latin *caedere* to kill]

germinal *adj* **1** of or in the earliest stage of development: *the germinal phases of the case* **2** of germ cells

germinate *vb* -nating, -nated to grow or cause to grow [Latin *germinare* to sprout] **> germination** *n*

Germiston *n* a city in South Africa, southeast of Johannesburg: industrial centre, with the world's largest gold refinery, serving the Witwatersrand mines. Pop: 139 721 (2001)

germ warfare *n* the military use of disease-spreading bacteria against an enemy

Gerona *n* a city in NE Spain: city walls and 14th-century cathedral; often besieged, in particular by the French (1809). Pop: 81 220 (2003 est). Catalan name: **Girona**. Ancient name: **Gerunda**

Geronimo *n* **1** 1829–1909, Apache Indian chieftain: led a campaign against the White settlers until his final capture in 1886 ▷ *interj* **2** *US* a shout given by paratroopers as they jump into battle **3** an exclamation expressing exhilaration, esp. when jumping from a great height

gerontology *n* the scientific study of ageing and the problems of old people [Greek *gerōn* old man + -LOGY] **> gerontologist** *n*

gerrymandering *n* the practice of dividing the constituencies of a voting area so as to give one party an unfair advantage [from Elbridge *Gerry*, US politician + (*sala*)*mander*, from the salamander-like outline of a reshaped electoral district]

Gers *n* a department of SW France, in Midi-Pyrénées region. Capital: Auch. Pop: 175 055 (2003 est). Area: 6291 sq km (2453 sq miles)

Gershwin *n* **1** **George**, original name *Jacob Gershvin*. 1898–1937, US composer: incorporated jazz into works such as *Rhapsody in Blue* (1924) for piano and jazz band and the opera *Porgy and Bess* (1935) **2** **Ira**, original name *Israel Gershvin*. 1896–1983, US song lyricist, noted esp. for his collaboration with his brother, George Gershwin

gerund (jer-rund) *n* a noun formed from a verb, ending in -*ing*, denoting an action or state, for example *running* [Latin *gerundum* something to be carried on]

Gervais *n* **Ricky**. born 1961, British comedian, writer, and actor; his TV series include *The Office* (2001–03), and *Extras* (2005–07)

gesso (jess-oh) *n* plaster used for painting or in sculpture [Italian: chalk]

Gestapo *n* the secret state police of Nazi Germany [German *Ge(heime) Sta(ats)po(lizei)* secret state police]

gestation *n* **1** the process of carrying and developing babies in the womb during pregnancy, or the time during which this process takes place **2** the process of developing a plan or idea in the mind [Latin *gestare* to bear]

gesticulate *vb* -**lating, -lated** to make expressive movements with the hands and arms, usually while talking [Latin *gesticulari*] **> gesticulation** *n*

gesture *n* **1** a movement of the hands, head, or body to express or emphasize an idea or emotion **2** something said or done to indicate intention, or as a formality: *a gesture of goodwill* ▷ *vb* -**turing, -tured 3** to make expressive movements with the hands and arms [Latin *gestus*]

Gesualdo *n* **Carlo**, Prince of Venosa. ?1560–1613, Italian composer, esp. of madrigals

get *vb* **getting, got 1** to come into possession of **2** to bring or fetch **3** to catch (an illness) **4** to become: *they get frustrated and angry* **5** to cause to be done or to happen: *he got a wart removed; to get steamed up* **6** to hear or understand: *did you get that joke?* **7** to reach (a place or point): *we could not get to the airport in time* **8** to catch (a bus or train) **9** to persuade: *she was trying to get him to give secrets away* **10** *informal* to annoy: *you know what really gets me?* **11** *informal* to baffle: *now you've got me* **12** *informal* to hit: *a bit of grenade got me on the left hip* **13** *informal* to be revenged on **14** *informal* to start: *we got talking about it; it got me thinking* ▷ *n* **15** Brit slang same as **git**. ▶ See also **get about, get across,** etc. [Old English *gietan*]

get about *or* **get around** *vb* **1** to be socially active **2** (of news or a rumour) to circulate

get across *vb* to make (something) understood

get at *vb* **1** to gain access to: *to get at the information on these disks* **2** to imply or mean: *it is hard to see what he is getting at* **3** to annoy or criticize persistently: *people who know they're being got at*

get away *vb* **1** to escape or leave **2 get away with** to do (something wrong) without being caught or punished ▷ *interj* **3** an exclamation of disbelief ▷ *n* **getaway 4** the act of escaping, usually by criminals ▷ *adj* **getaway 5** used to escape: *the getaway car was abandoned*

get back *vb* **1** to have (something) returned to one **2** to return to a former state or activity: *get back to normal* **3 get back at** to retaliate against **4 get one's own back** *informal* to get one's revenge

get by *vb informal* to manage in spite of difficulties: *he saw for himself what people did to get by*

get in *vb* **1** to arrive **2** to be elected **3 get in on** to join in (an activity)

get off *vb* **1** to leave (a bus, train, etc.) **2** to escape the consequences of or punishment for an action: *the real culprits have got off scot-free* **3 get off with** *Brit and Austral informal* to begin a romantic or sexual relationship with

get on *vb* **1** to enter (a bus, train, etc.) **2** to have a friendly relationship: *he had a flair for getting on with people* **3** to grow old: *he was getting on in years* **4** (of time) to elapse: *the time was getting on* **5** to make progress: *how are the children getting on?* **6 get on with** to continue to do: *you can get on with whatever you were doing before* **7 getting on for** approaching (a time, age, or amount): *getting on for half a century ago*

get out *vb* **1** to leave or escape **2** to become known **3** to gain something of significance or value: *that's all I got out of it* **4 get out of** to avoid: *to get out of doing the dishes*

get over *vb* **1** to recover from (an illness or unhappy experience) **2** to overcome (a problem) **3 get over with** to bring (something necessary but unpleasant) to an end: *better to get it over with*

get round *vb* **1** to overcome (a problem or difficulty) **2** (of news or a rumour) to circulate **3** *informal* to gain the indulgence of (someone) by praise or flattery: *a child who learned to get round everybody and have her own way* **4 get round to** to come to (a task) eventually: *I will get round to paying the bill*

get through *vb* **1** to complete (a task or process) **2** to use up (money or supplies) **3** to succeed in (an examination or test) **4 get through to a** to succeed in making (someone) understand **b** to contact (someone) by telephone

get-together *n* **1** *informal* a small informal social gathering ▷ *vb* **get together 2** to meet socially or in order to have a discussion

Getty *n* **J(ean) Paul**. 1892–1976, US oil executive, millionaire, and art collector

Gettysburg *n* a small town in S Pennsylvania, southwest of Harrisburg: scene of a crucial battle (1863) during the American Civil War, in which Meade's Union forces defeated Lee's Confederate army; site of the national cemetery dedicated by President Lincoln. Pop: 7825 (2003 est)

get up *vb* **1** to get out of bed **2 get up to** *informal* to be involved in: *I don't know what those guys got up to down there* ▷ *n* **get-up 3** a costume or outfit

get-up-and-go *n informal* energy or drive

Getz *n* **Stanley**, known as **Stan**. 1927–91, US jazz saxophonist: leader of his own group from 1949

geyser (geez-er) *n* **1** a spring that discharges steam and hot water **2** *Brit and S African* a domestic gas water heater [Icelandic *Geysir*]

Gezira *n* a region of the E central Sudan between the Blue and White Niles: site of a large-scale irrigation system

Ghana *n* a republic in W Africa, on the Gulf of Guinea: a powerful empire from the 4th to the 13th centuries; a major source of gold and slaves for Europeans after 1471; British colony of the Gold Coast established in 1874; united with British Togoland in 1957 and became a republic and a member of the Commonwealth in 1960. Official language: English. Religions: Christian, Muslim, and animist. Currency: cedi. Capital: Accra. Pop: 25 199 609 (2013 est). Area: 238 539 sq km (92 100 sq miles)

Ghanaian or **Ghanian** adj **1** of or relating to Ghana or its inhabitants ▷ n **2** a native or inhabitant of Ghana

ghastly adj **-lier, -liest 1** informal very unpleasant **2** deathly pale **3** horrible: a ghastly accident [Old English gāstlīc spiritual]

ghat n (in India) **1** stairs leading down to a river **2** a place of cremation **3** a mountain pass [Hindi]

Ghats pl n See **Eastern Ghats, Western Ghats**

Ghazali n al-. 1058–1111, Muslim theologian, philosopher, and mystic

Ghazzah n transliteration of the Arabic name for **Gaza**

GHB gamma hydroxybutyrate: a substance with anaesthetic properties, used medically as a sedative and also as a recreational drug

ghee (gee) n clarified butter, used in Indian cookery [Hindi ghī]

Ghent n an industrial city and port in NW Belgium, capital of East Flanders province, at the confluence of the Rivers Lys and Scheldt: formerly famous for its cloth industry; university (1816). Pop: 229 344 (2004 est). Flemish name: **Gent**. French name: **Gand**

Gheorghiu n Angela. born 1965, Romanian soprano: noted for her performances and recordings of Italian opera

gherkin n a small pickled cucumber [Dutch agurkkijn]

Gherkin n the Gherkin an informal name for **Swiss Re Tower**

ghetto n, pl **-tos** or **-toes** an area that is inhabited by people of a particular race, religion, nationality, or class [Italian]

ghetto blaster n informal a large portable CD player or cassette recorder with built-in speakers

ghettoize or **-ise** vb **-izing, -ized** or **-ising, -ised** to confine (someone or something) to a particular area or category: to ghettoize women as housewives ▷ **ghettoization** or **-isation** n

Ghiberti n Lorenzo. 1378–1455, Italian sculptor, painter, and goldsmith of the quattrocento: noted esp. for the bronze doors of the baptistry of Florence Cathedral

ghillie n same as gillie

Ghirlandaio or **Ghirlandajo** n Domenico. original name Domenico Bigordi. 1449–94, Italian painter of frescoes

ghost n **1** the disembodied spirit of a dead person, supposed to haunt the living **2** a faint trace: the ghost of a smile on his face **3** a faint secondary image in an optical instrument or on a television screen ▷ vb **4** short for ghostwrite [Old English gāst]

ghost gum n Austral a eucalyptus with a white trunk and branches

ghostly adj **-lier, -liest** frightening in appearance or effect: ghostly noises

ghost town n a town that used to be busy but is now deserted

ghostwrite vb **-writing, -wrote, -written** to write (an article or book) on behalf of a person who is then credited as author ▷ **ghostwriter** n

ghoul (gool) n **1** a person who is interested in morbid or disgusting things **2** a demon that eats corpses [Arabic ghūl] ▷ **ghoulish** adj ▷ **ghoulishly** adv

GHQ military General Headquarters

GI¹ n, pl **GIs** or **GI's** US informal a soldier in the US Army [abbreviation of government issue]

GI² See glycaemic index

Giacometti n Alberto. 1901–66, Swiss sculptor and painter, noted particularly for his long skeletal statues of isolated figures

Giambologna n original name Giovanni da Bologna or Jean de Boulogne. 1529–1608, Italian mannerist sculptor, born in Flanders: noted for his fountains and such

works as Samson Slaying a Philistine (1565)

giant n **1** a mythical figure of superhuman size and strength **2** a person or thing of exceptional size, ability, or importance: industrial giants ▷ adj **3** remarkably large **4** (of an atom or ion or its structure) having large numbers of particles present in a crystal lattice, with each particle exerting a strong force of attraction on those near to it [Greek gigas]

giant panda n See panda

Giant's Causeway n a promontory of columnar basalt on the N coast of Northern Ireland, in Antrim: consists of several thousand pillars, mostly hexagonal, that were formed by the rapid cooling of lava and the inward contraction of the lava flow

Gib an informal name for **Gibraltar**

gibber¹ (jib-ber) vb to talk in a fast and unintelligible manner [imitative]

gibber² (gib-ber) n Austral **1** a boulder **2** barren land covered with stones [Aboriginal]

Gibberd n Sir Frederick. 1908–84, British architect and town planner. His buildings include the Liverpool Roman Catholic cathedral (1960–67) and the Regent's Park Mosque in London (1977). Harlow in the UK and Santa Teresa in Venezuela were built to his plans

gibberish n rapid incomprehensible talk; nonsense

gibbet (jib-bit) n a gallows [Old French gibet]

gibbon (gib-bon) n a small agile ape of the forests of S Asia [French]

Gibbon n **1** Edward. 1737–94, English historian; author of The History of the Decline and Fall of the Roman Empire (1776–88), controversial in its historical criticism of Christianity **2** Lewis Grassic, real name James Leslie Mitchell. 1901–35, Scottish writer: best known for his trilogy of novels A Scots Quair (1932–34)

Gibbons n **1** Grinling. 1648–1721, English sculptor and woodcarver, noted for his delicate carvings of fruit, flowers, birds, etc. **2** Orlando. 1583–1625, English organist and composer, esp. of anthems, motets, and madrigals

gibbous (gib-bus) adj (of the moon) more than half but less than fully illuminated [Latin gibba hump]

Gibbs n **1** James. 1682–1754, British architect; his buildings include St Martin's-in-the-Fields, London (1722–26), and the Radcliffe Camera, Oxford (1737–49) **2** Josiah Willard. 1839–1903, US physicist and mathematician: founder of chemical thermodynamics

gibe (jibe) n, vb **gibing, gibed** same as jibe¹ [perhaps from Old French giber to treat roughly]

Gibeon n an ancient town of Palestine: the excavated site thought to be its remains lies about 9 kilometres (6 miles) northwest of Jerusalem

giblets (jib-lits) pl n the gizzard, liver, heart, and neck of a fowl [Old French gibelet stew of game birds]

Gibraltar n **1** City of Gibraltar a city on the Rock of Gibraltar, a limestone promontory at the tip of S Spain: settled by Moors in 711 and taken by Spain in 1462; ceded to Britain in 1713; a British crown colony (1830–1969), still politically associated with Britain; a naval and air base of strategic importance. Pop: 29 111 (2013 est). Area: 6.5 sq km (2.5 sq miles). Ancient name: Calpe **2** Strait of Gibraltar a narrow strait between the S tip of Spain and the NW tip of Africa, linking the Mediterranean with the Atlantic

Gibraltarian adj **1** of or relating to Gibraltar or its inhabitants ▷ n **2** a native or inhabitant of Gibraltar

Gibran n Kahlil. 1883–1931, Syro-Lebanese poet, mystic, and painter, resident in the US after 1910; author of The Prophet (1923)

Gibson n Mel. born 1956, Australian film actor and director: his films include Mad Max (1979), Hamlet (1990), Braveheart (1996; also directed), What Women Want (2000), The Passion of the Christ (2004; director only), and Apocalypto (2006; director and co-writer)

Gibson Desert n a desert in W central Australia,

between the Great Sandy Desert and the Victoria Desert: salt marshes, salt lakes, and scrub. Area: about 220 000 sq km (85 000 sq miles)

gidday *interj Austral and NZ* a variant of **g'day**

giddy *adj* **-dier, -diest 1** feeling weak and unsteady on one's feet, as if about to fall **2** happy and excited: *a state of giddy expectation* [Old English *gydig* mad, frenzied, possessed by God] **>** **giddiness** *n*

Gide *n* André. 1869–1951, French novelist, dramatist, critic, diarist, and translator, noted particularly for his exploration of the conflict between self-fulfilment and conventional morality. His novels include *L'Immoraliste* (1902), *La Porte étroite* (1909), and *Les Faux-Monnayeurs* (1926): Nobel prize for literature 1947

Gielgud *n* Sir John. 1904–2000, English stage, film, and television actor and director

Giessen *n* a city in central Germany, in Hesse: university (1607). Pop: 74 001 (2003 est)

GIF *computers* **a** graphic interchange format: a standard compressed file format used for pictures **b** a picture held in this format

gift *n* **1** something given to someone: *a birthday gift* **2** a special ability or power: *a gift for caricature* [Old English: payment for a wife, dowry]

gifted *adj* having natural talent or aptitude: *that era's most gifted director*

giftwrap *vb* **-wrapping, -wrapped** to wrap (a gift) in decorative wrapping paper

Gifu *n* a city in Japan, on central Honshu: hot springs, textile and paper lantern manufacturing. Pop: 401 269 (2002 est)

gig¹ *n* **1 a** a single performance by jazz or pop musicians ▷ *vb* **gigging, gigged 2** to play gigs [origin unknown]

gig² *n* a light open two-wheeled one-horse carriage [origin unknown]

gig³ *n computers informal* short for **gigabyte**

giga- *prefix* **1** denoting 10⁹: *gigavolt* **2** *computers* denoting 2³⁰: *gigabyte* [Greek *gigas* giant]

gigabyte *n computers* one thousand and twenty-four megabytes

gigantic *adj* extremely large: *the most gigantic gold paperweight ever* [Greek *gigantikos*]

giggle *vb* **-gling, -gled 1** to laugh nervously or foolishly ▷ *n* **2** a nervous or foolish laugh **3** *informal* an amusing person or thing [imitative] **>** **giggly** *adj*

Gigli *n* Beniamino. 1890–1957, Italian operatic tenor

gigolo *(jig-a-lo)* *n, pl* **-los** a man who is paid by an older woman to be her escort or lover [French]

gigot *n chiefly Brit* a leg of lamb or mutton [French]

Gijón *n* a port in NW Spain, on the Bay of Biscay: capital of the kingdom of Asturias until 791. Pop: 270 875 (2003 est). Asturian name: **Xixón**. Ancient name: **Gigia**

Gilbert *n* **1** Grove Karl. 1843–1918, US geologist who pioneered the study of river development and valley erosion **2** Sir Humphrey. ?1539–83, English navigator: founded the colony at St John's, Newfoundland (1583) **3** William. 1540–1603, English physician and physicist, noted for his study of terrestrial magnetism in *De Magnete* (1600) **4** Sir W(illiam) S(chwenck). 1836–1911, English dramatist, humorist, and librettist. He collaborated (1871–96) with Arthur Sullivan on the famous series of comic operettas, including *The Pirates of Penzance* (1879), *Iolanthe* (1882), and *The Mikado* (1885)

Gilbert and George *n* a team of artists, **Gilbert Proesch**, Italian, born 1942, and **George Passmore**, British, born 1943: noted esp. for their photomontages and performance works

Gilbert Islands *pl n* a group of islands in the W Pacific: with Banaba, the Phoenix Islands, and three of the Line Islands they constitute the independent state of Kiribati; until 1975 they formed part of the British colony of **Gilbert and Ellice Islands**; achieved full independence in 1979. Pop: 82 902 (2005). Area: 295 sq km (114 sq miles)

Gilchrist *n* Adam (Craig). born 1971, Australian cricketer; a wicketkeeper-batsman, he took an Australian-record 416 dismissals in tests (1999–2008) and a world-record 472 dismissals in ODIs (1996–2008); his 33 international centuries is a record for a wicketkeeper

gild *vb* **gilding, gilded** *or* **gilt 1** to cover with a thin layer of gold **2** to make (something) appear golden: *the morning sun gilded the hills* **3 gild the lily a** to adorn unnecessarily something already beautiful **b** to praise someone excessively [Old English *gyldan*]

Gilead *n* a historic mountainous region east of the River Jordan, rising over 1200 m (4000 ft)

Giles *n* **1** Saint. 7th century AD, Greek hermit in France; patron saint of cripples, beggars, and lepers. Feast day: Sept 1 **2** William Ernest Powell. 1835–97, Australian explorer, born in England. He was noted esp. for his exploration of the western desert (1875–76)

gill (jill) *n* a unit of liquid measure equal to one quarter of a pint (0.14 litres) [Old French *gille* vat, tub]

Gill *n* (Arthur) Eric (Rowton). 1882–1940, British sculptor, engraver, and typographer: his sculptures include the *Stations of the Cross* in Westminster Cathedral, London

Gillard *n* Julia (Eileen). born 1961, Australian Labor politician, born in Wales: Deputy Prime Minister (2007–10); Prime Minister (2010-13)

Gillespie *n* Dizzy, nickname of *John Birks Gillespie*. 1917–93, US jazz trumpeter

gillie *or* **ghillie** *n Scot* a sportsman's attendant or guide for hunting or fishing [Scottish Gaelic *gille* boy, servant]

Gillingham *n* a town in SE England, in Medway unitary authority, Kent, on the Medway estuary: former dockyards. Pop: 98 403 (2001)

Gillray *n* James. 1757–1815, English caricaturist

gills (gillz) *pl n* the breathing organs of fish and other water creatures [from Old Norse]

Gilolo *n* See Halmahera

gilt *vb* **1 a** past of **gild** ▷ *adj* **2** covered with a thin layer of gold ▷ *n* **3** a thin layer of gold, used as decoration

gilt-edged *adj* denoting government securities on which interest payments and final repayments are guaranteed

gilts *pl n* gilt-edged securities

gimcrack (jim-krak) *adj* showy but cheap; shoddy [origin unknown]

gimlet (gim-let) *n* **1** a small hand tool with a pointed spiral tip, used for boring holes in wood ▷ *adj* **2** penetrating or piercing: *gimlet eyes* [Old French *guimbelet*]

gimmick *n informal* something designed to attract attention or publicity [origin unknown] **>** **gimmickry** *n* **>** **gimmicky** *adj*

gin¹ *n* an alcoholic drink distilled from malted grain and flavoured with juniper berries [Dutch *genever* juniper]

gin² *n* a noose of thin strong wire for catching small mammals [Middle English *gyn*]

gin³ *n Austral offensive* an Aboriginal woman [Aboriginal]

ginger *n* **1** the root of a tropical plant, powdered and used as a spice or sugared and eaten as a sweet ▷ *adj* **2** light reddish-brown: *ginger hair* [Old French *gingivre*] **>** **gingery** *adj*

ginger ale *n* a nonalcoholic fizzy drink flavoured with ginger extract

ginger beer *n* a drink made by fermenting a mixture of syrup and root ginger

gingerbread *n* a moist brown cake flavoured with ginger

ginger group *n Brit, Austral and NZ* a group within a larger group that agitates for a more active policy

gingerly *adv* carefully or cautiously: *she sat gingerly on the edge of the chair* [perhaps from Old French *gensor* dainty]

ginger nut *or* **ginger snap** *n* a hard biscuit flavoured with ginger

gingham *n* a cotton fabric with a checked or striped design [Malay *ginggang* striped cloth]

gingivitis (jin-jiv-**vite**-iss) *n* inflammation of the gums [Latin *gingiva* gum]

ginormous *adj informal* very large [*gi(gantic)* + *(e)normous*]

gin rummy *n* a version of rummy in which a player may finish if the odd cards in his hand total less than ten points [GIN¹ + *rummy*]

Ginsberg *n* Allen. 1926–97, US poet of the Beat Generation. His poetry includes *Howl* (1956) and *Kaddish* (1961)

ginseng (jin-seng) *n* the root of a plant of China and N America, believed to have tonic and energy-giving properties [Mandarin Chinese *jen shen*]

Ginzburg *n* Natalia. 1916–91, Italian writer and dramatist. Her books include *The Road to the City* (1942), *Voices in the Evening* (1961), and *Family Sayings* (1963)

Giorgione *n* Il. original name *Giorgio Barbarelli*. ?1478–1511, Italian painter of the Venetian school, who introduced a new unity between figures and landscape

Giotto *n* also known as *Giotto di Bondone*. ?1267–1337, Florentine painter, who broke away from the stiff linear design of the Byzantine tradition and developed the more dramatic and naturalistic style characteristic of the Renaissance: his work includes cycles of frescoes in Assisi, the Arena Chapel in Padua, and the Church of Santa Croce, Florence

gip (jip) *n* same as **gyp**

Gippsland *n* a fertile region of SE Australia, in SE Victoria, extending east along the coast from Melbourne to the New South Wales border. Area: 35 200 sq km (13 600 sq miles)

Gipsy *n*, *pl* **-sies** same as **Gypsy**

giraffe *n* a cud-chewing African mammal with a very long neck and long legs and a spotted yellowy skin [Arabic *zarāfah*]

Giraldus Cambrensis *n* literary name of *Gerald de Barri*. ?1146–?1223, Welsh chronicler and churchman, noted for his accounts of his travels in Ireland and Wales

Giraud *n* Henri Honoré. 1879–1949, French general, who commanded French forces in North Africa (1942–43)

Giraudoux *n* (Hippolyte) Jean. 1882–1944, French dramatist. His works include the novel *Suzanne et le Pacifique* (1921) and the plays *Amphitryon 38* (1929) and *La Guerre de Troie n'aura pas lieu* (1935)

gird *vb* **girding, girded** *or* **girt 1** to put a belt or girdle around **2 gird (up) one's loins** to prepare oneself for action [Old English *gyrdan*]

girder *n* a large steel or iron beam used in the construction of bridges and buildings

girdle *n* **1** a woman's elastic corset that covers the stomach and hips **2** anything that surrounds something or someone: *his girdle of supporters* **3** *anatomy* an encircling arrangement of bones: *the shoulder girdle* ▷ *vb* **-dling, -dled 4** to surround: *a ring of volcanic ash girdling the earth* [Old English *gyrdel*]

Girgenti *n* a former name (until 1927) of **Agrigento**

girl *n* **1** a female child **2** a young woman [Middle English *girle*] ❯ **girlhood** *n* ❯ **girlish** *adj*

girlfriend *n* **1** a female friend with whom a person is romantically or sexually involved **2** any female friend

Girl Guide *n* a former name for **Guide**

girlie *adj informal* **1** featuring naked or scantily dressed women: *girlie magazines* **2** suited to or designed to appeal to young women: *a real girlie night out*

giro (jire-oh) *n*, *pl* **-ros 1** (in some countries) a system of transferring money within a bank or post office, directly from one account into another **2** *Brit informal* a social-security payment by giro cheque [Greek *guros* circuit]

Girona *n* the Catalan name for **Gerona**

Gironde *n* **1** a department of SW France, in Aquitaine region. Capital: Bordeaux. Pop: 1 330 683 (2003 est). Area: 10 726 sq km (4183 sq miles) **2** an estuary in SW France, formed by the confluence of the Rivers Garonne and Dordogne. Length: 72 km (45 miles)

girt *vb* a past of **gird**

girth *n* **1** the measurement around something **2** a band fastened round a horse's middle to keep the saddle in position [Old Norse *gjörth* belt]

Gisborne *n* a port in N New Zealand, on E North Island on Poverty Bay. Pop: 44 900 (2004 est)

Giscard d'Estaing *n* Valéry. born 1926, French politician; minister of finance and economic affairs (1962–66; 1969–74); president (1974–81)

Gish *n* **1** Dorothy. 1898–1968, US film actress, chiefly in silent films **2** her sister, Lillian. 1896–1993, US film and stage actress, noted esp. for her roles in such silent films as *The Birth of a Nation* (1915) and *Intolerance* (1916)

Gissing *n* George (Robert). 1857–1903, English novelist, noted for his depiction of middle-class poverty. His works include *Demos* (1886) and *New Grub Street* (1891)

gist (jist) *n* the main point or meaning of something: *the gist of the letter* [Anglo-French, as in *cest action gist en* this action consists in]

git *n* *Brit slang* a contemptible person [from *get* (in the sense: to beget, hence a bastard, fool)]

Gitmo *n* *informal, chiefly US* Guantánamo: referring more specifically to the detainment camp run there by the US military, in which suspected terrorists are detained and questioned

Giulini *n* Carlo Maria. 1914–2005, Italian orchestral conductor, esp. of opera

Giulio Romano *n* ?1499–1546, Italian architect and painter; a founder of mannerism

give *vb* **giving, gave, given 1** to present or hand (something) to someone **2** to pay (an amount of money) for a purchase **3** to grant or provide: *to give an answer* **4** to utter (a shout or cry) **5** to perform, make, or do: *the prime minister gave a speech* **6** to host (a party) **7** to sacrifice or devote: *comrades who gave their lives for their country* **8** to concede: *he was very efficient, I have to give him that* **9** to yield or break under pressure: *something has got to give* **10 give or take** plus or minus: *about one hundred metres, give or take five* ▷ *n* **11** a tendency to yield under pressure; elasticity ▶ See also **give away, give in,** etc. [Old English *giefan*] ❯ **giver** *n*

give-and-take *n* **1** mutual concessions and cooperation **2** a smoothly flowing exchange of ideas and talk: *a relaxed give-and-take about their past involvement*

give away *vb* **1** to donate as a gift **2** to reveal (a secret) **3** to present (a bride) formally to her spouse in a marriage ceremony **4 give something away** NZ to give something up ▷ *n* **giveaway 5** something that reveals hidden feelings or intentions ▷ *adj* **giveaway 6** very cheap or free: *a giveaway rent*

give in *vb* to admit defeat

given *vb* **1** the past participle of **give** ▷ *adj* **2** specific or previously stated: *priorities within the given department* **3** to be assumed: *any given place on the earth* **4 given to** inclined to: *a man not given to undue optimism*

give off *vb* to send out (heat, light, or a smell)

give out *vb* **1** to hand out: *the bloke that was giving out those tickets* **2** to send out (heat, light, or a smell) **3** to make known: *the man who gave out the news* **4** to fail: *the engine gave out*

give over *vb* **1** to set aside for a specific purpose: *the amount of space given over to advertisements* **2** *informal* to stop doing something annoying: *tell him to give over*

give up *vb* **1** to stop (doing something): *I did give up smoking* **2** to resign from (a job or position) **3** to admit defeat or failure **4** to abandon (hope) **5 give oneself up a** to surrender to the police or other authorities **b** to devote oneself completely: *she gave herself up to her work*

Giza *n* See **El Gîza**

gizzard *n* the part of a bird's stomach in which hard food is broken up [Old French *guisier* fowl's liver]

Gk Greek

glacé (**glass**-say) *adj* preserved in a thick sugary syrup: *glacé cherries* [French: iced]

glacial *adj* **1** of glaciers or ice **2** extremely cold

3 cold and unfriendly: *a glacial stare*

glacial period *n* same as **ice age**

glaciation *n* the process of covering part of the earth's surface with glaciers or masses of ice ▷ **glaciated** *adj*

glacier *n* a slowly moving mass of ice formed by an accumulation of snow [Latin *glacies* ice]

glad *adj* **gladder, gladdest 1** happy and pleased **2** very willing: *he was only too glad to help* **3** *archaic* causing happiness: *glad tidings* [Old English *glæd*] ▷ **gladden** *vb* ▷ **gladly** *adv* ▷ **gladness** *n*

Gladbeck *n* a city in NW Germany, in North Rhine-Westphalia. Pop: 77 166 (2003 est)

glade *n* an open space in a forest: *a peaceful and sheltered glade* [origin unknown]

gladiator *n* (in ancient Rome) a man trained to fight in arenas to provide entertainment [Latin: swordsman] ▷ **gladiatorial** *adj*

gladiolus (glad-ee-oh-luss) *n, pl* **-li** (-lie) a garden plant with brightly coloured funnel-shaped flowers [Latin: a small sword]

glad rags *pl n informal* one's best clothes

gladsome *adj old-fashioned* joyous or cheerful

Gladstone *n* **1** William Ewart. 1809–98, British statesman. He became leader of the Liberal Party in 1867 and was four times prime minister (1868–74; 1880–85; 1886; 1892–94). In his first ministry he disestablished the Irish Church (1869) and introduced educational reform (1870) and the secret ballot (1872). He succeeded in carrying the Reform Act of 1884 but failed to gain support for a Home Rule Bill for Ireland, to which he devoted much of the latter part of his career **2** a light four-wheeled horse-drawn vehicle

gladwrap *Austral, NZ and S African n* **1** *trademark* thin polythene material for wrapping ▷ *vb* **2** to wrap in gladwrap

Glamis Castle *n* a castle near Glamis in Angus, Scotland: ancestral seat of the Lyons family, forebears of Elizabeth, the Queen Mother; famous for its legend of a secret chamber

Glamorgan *or* **Glamorganshire** *n* a former county of SE Wales: divided into West Glamorgan, Mid Glamorgan, and South Glamorgan in 1974; since 1996 administered by the county of Swansea and the county boroughs of Neath Port Talbot, Bridgend, Rhondda Cynon Taff, Vale of Glamorgan, Merthyr Tydfil, and part of Caerphilly

glamorous *adj* attractive and fascinating

glamour *or US* **glamor** *n* exciting or alluring charm or beauty [Scots variant of *grammar* (hence a spell, because occult practices were popularly associated with learning)] ▷ **glamorize** *or* **-ise** *vb*

glance *n* **1** a quick look ▷ *vb* **glancing, glanced 2** to look quickly at something **3** to be deflected off an object at an oblique angle: *the ball glanced off a spectator* [Middle English *glacen* to strike obliquely] ▷ **glancing** *adj*

> **USAGE** Glance is sometimes wrongly used where *glimpse* is meant: *he caught a glimpse* (not *glance*) *of her making her way through the crowd.*

gland *n* **1** an organ that synthesizes and secretes chemical substances for the body to use or eliminate **2** a similar organ in plants [Latin *glans* acorn]

glandular *adj* of or affecting a gland or glands

glandular fever *n* an acute infectious viral disease that causes fever, sore throat, and painful swollen lymph nodes

glare *vb* **glaring, glared 1** to stare angrily **2** (of light or colour) to be too bright ▷ *n* **3** an angry stare **4** a dazzling light or brilliance **5 in the glare of publicity** receiving a lot of attention from the media or the public [Middle English]

glaring *adj* conspicuous or obvious: *glaring inconsistencies* ▷ **glaringly** *adv*

Glarus *n* **1** an Alpine canton of E central Switzerland. Capital: Glarus. Pop: 38 400 (2002 est). Area 684 sq km (264 sq miles) **2** a town in E central Switzerland, the capital of Glarus canton. Pop: 5556 (2000) ▶ French name: Glaris

Glaser *n* Donald Arthur. 1926–2013, US physicist: invented the bubble chamber; Nobel prize for physics 1960

Glasgow *n* **1** a city in W central Scotland, in City of Glasgow council area on the River Clyde: the largest city in Scotland; centre of a major industrial region, formerly an important port; universities (1451, 1964, 1992). Pop: 598 830 (2011). Related adjective: **Glaswegian 2** City of Glasgow a council area in W central Scotland. Pop: 593 000 (2010 est). Area: 175 sq km (68 sq miles)

glasnost *n* a policy of public frankness and accountability, developed in the USSR in the 1980s under Mikhail Gorbachev [Russian: publicity, openness]

glass *n* **1** a hard brittle transparent solid, consisting of metal silicates or similar compounds **2** a drinking vessel made of glass **3** the amount contained in a drinking glass: *a glass of wine* **4** objects made of glass, such as drinking glasses and bowls [Old English *glæs*]

Glass *n* Philip. born 1937, US composer noted for his minimalist style: his works include *Music in Fifths* (1970), *Akhnaten* (1984), *The Voyage* (1992), and *Monsters of Grace* (1998); his film music includes scores for *Kundun* (1998), *The Truman Show* (1999), and *The Hours* (2002)

glass-blowing *n* the process of shaping a mass of molten glass by blowing air into it through a tube ▷ **glass-blower** *n*

glass ceiling *n* a situation in which progress, esp. promotion, appears to be possible, but restrictions or discrimination create a barrier that prevents it

glasses *pl n* a pair of lenses for correcting faulty vision, in a frame that rests on the nose and hooks behind the ears

glasshouse *n* Brit and NZ same as **greenhouse**

glassy *adj* **glassier, glassiest 1** smooth, clear, and shiny, like glass: *the glassy sea* **2** expressionless: *that glassy look*

Glastonbury *n* a town in SW England, in Somerset: remains of prehistoric lake villages; the reputed burial place of King Arthur; site of a ruined Benedictine abbey, probably the oldest in England; the Glastonbury Festival of music and other arts is held most summers in nearby Pilton. Pop: 8429 (2001)

Glaswegian (glaz-weej-an) *adj* **1** of or relating to Glasgow or its inhabitants ▷ *n* **2** a native or inhabitant of Glasgow **3** the Glasgow dialect

glaucoma *n* an eye disease in which increased pressure in the eyeball causes gradual loss of sight [Greek *glaukos* silvery, bluish-green]

glaze *vb* **glazing, glazed 1** to fit or cover with glass **2** to cover (a piece of pottery) with a protective shiny coating **3** to cover (food) with beaten egg or milk before cooking, in order to produce a shiny coating ▷ *n* **4** a protective shiny coating applied to a piece of pottery **5** a shiny coating of beaten egg or milk applied to food ▶ See also **glaze over** [Middle English *glasen*] ▷ **glazed** *adj* ▷ **glazing** *n*

glaze over *vb* to become dull through boredom or inattention: *the listener's eyes glaze over*

glazier *n* a person who fits windows or doors with glass

Glazunov *n* Aleksandr Konstantinovich. 1865–1936, Russian composer, in France from 1928. A pupil of Rimsky-Korsakov, he wrote eight symphonies and concertos for piano and for violin among other works

gleam *n* **1** a small beam or glow of light **2** a brief or dim indication: *a gleam of anticipation in his eye* ▷ *vb* **3** to shine [Old English *glǣm*] ▷ **gleaming** *adj*

glean *vb* **1** to gather (information) bit by bit **2** to gather the useful remnants of (a crop) after harvesting [Old French *glener*] ▷ **gleaner** *n*

gleanings *pl n* pieces of information that have been gleaned

g

g

glebe *n Brit and Austral* land granted to a member of the clergy as part of his or her benefice [Latin *glaeba*]

glee *n* great merriment or joy, esp. caused by the misfortune of another person [Old English *glēo*]

gleeful *adj* merry or joyful, esp. over someone else's mistake or misfortune **> gleefully** *adv*

Gleiwitz *n* the German name for **Gliwice**

glen *n* a deep narrow mountain valley [Scottish Gaelic *gleann*]

Glen Albyn *n* another name for the **Great Glen**

Glencoe *n* a glen in W Scotland, in S Highland: site of a massacre of MacDonalds by Campbells and English troops (1692)

Glendower *n* Owen, Welsh name *Owain Glyndŵr*. ?1350–?1416, Welsh chieftain, who led a revolt against Henry IV's rule in Wales (1400–15)

glengarry *n, pl* -**ries** a brimless Scottish cap with a crease down the crown [after *Glengarry*, Scotland]

Glen More *n* another name for the **Great Glen**

Glenn *n* John. born 1921, US astronaut and politician. The first American to orbit the earth (Feb, 1962), he later became a senator (1975–99) and in 1998 returned to space at the age of 77

Glennie *n* Dame Evelyn (**Elizabeth Ann**). born 1965, Scottish percussionist and composer; profoundly deaf since the age of twelve

Glenrothes *n* a new town in E central Scotland, the administrative centre of Fife: founded in 1948. Pop: 38 679 (2001)

glib *adj* **glibber, glibbest** fluent and easy, often in an insincere or deceptive way: *there were no glib or easy answers* [probably from Middle Low German *glibberich* slippery] **> glibly** *adv* **> glibness** *n*

glide *vb* **gliding, glided** **1** to move easily and smoothly **2** (of an aircraft) to land without engine power **3** to fly a glider **4** to float on currents of air [Old English *glīdan*]

glider *n* **1** an aircraft that does not use an engine, but flies by floating on air currents **2** *Austral* a flying phalanger

glide time *n NZ* same as **flexitime**

gliding *n* the sport of flying in a glider

glimmer *vb* **1** (of a light) to glow faintly or flickeringly ▷ *n* **2** a faint indication: *a glimmer of hope* **3** a glow or twinkle [Middle English]

glimpse *n* **1** a brief view: *a glimpse of a rare snow leopard* **2** a vague indication: *glimpses of insecurity* ▷ *vb* **glimpsing, glimpsed 3** to catch sight of momentarily [Germanic]

USAGE *Glimpse* is sometimes wrongly used where *glance* is meant: *he gave a quick glance* (not *glimpse*) *at his watch.*

Glinka *n* Mikhail Ivanovich. 1804–57, Russian composer who pioneered the Russian national school of music. His works include the operas *A Life for the Tsar* (1836) and *Russlan and Ludmilla* (1842)

glint *vb* **1** to gleam brightly ▷ *n* **2** a bright gleam [probably from Old Norse]

glissade *n* **1** a gliding step in ballet **2** a controlled slide down a snow slope ▷ *vb* -**sading, -saded 3** to perform a glissade [French]

glissando *n, pl* -**dos** *music* a slide between two notes in which all intermediate notes are played [mock Italian, from French *glisser* to slide]

glisten *vb* (of a wet or glossy surface) to gleam by reflecting light: *sweat glistened above his eyes* [Old English *glisnian*]

glitch *n* a small problem that stops something from working properly [Yiddish *glitsh* a slip]

glitter *vb* **1** (of a surface) to reflect light in bright flashes **2** (of light) to be reflected in bright flashes **3** to be brilliant in a showy way: *she glitters socially* ▷ *n* **4** a sparkling light **5** superficial glamour: *the trappings and glitter of the European aristocracy* **6** tiny pieces of shiny

decorative material **7** *Canad* ice formed from freezing rain [Old Norse *glitra*] **> glittering** *adj* **> glittery** *adj*

glitzy *adj* **glitzier, glitziest** *slang* showily attractive [probably from German *glitzern* to glitter]

Gliwice *n* an industrial city in S Poland. Pop: 197 874 (2007 est). German name: **Gleiwitz**

gloaming *n Scot poetic* twilight; dusk [Old English *glōmung*]

gloat *vb* to regard one's own good fortune or the misfortune of others with smug or malicious pleasure [probably Scandinavian]

glob *n informal* a rounded mass of thick fluid [probably from *globe*, influenced by *blob*]

global *adj* **1** of or applying to the whole earth: *global environmental problems* **2** of or applying to the whole of something: *a global total for local-authority revenue* **> globally** *adv*

globalize *or* -**lise** *vb* -**izing, -ized** *or* -**ising, -ised** to put (something) into effect worldwide **> globalization** *or* -**lisation** *n*

global warming *n* an increase in the overall temperature worldwide believed to be caused by the greenhouse effect

globe *n* **1 a** a sphere on which a map of the world is drawn **2 the globe** the earth **3** a spherical object, such as a glass lamp shade or fishbowl **4** *S African* an electric light bulb [Latin *globus*]

globetrotter *n* a habitual worldwide traveller **> globetrotting** *n, adj*

globular *adj* shaped like a globe or globule

globule *n* a small round drop of liquid [Latin *globulus*]

globulin *n* a simple protein found in living tissue

glockenspiel *n* a percussion instrument consisting of tuned metal plates played with a pair of small hammers [German *Glocken* bells + *Spiel* play]

Glomma *n* a river in SE Norway, rising near the border with Sweden and flowing generally south to the Skagerrak: the largest river in Scandinavia; important for hydroelectric power and floating timber. Length: 588 km (365 miles)

gloom *n* **1** depression or melancholy: *all doom and gloom* **2** partial or total darkness [Middle English *gloumben* to look sullen]

gloomy *adj* **gloomier, gloomiest 1** despairing or sad **2** causing depression or gloom: *gloomy economic forecasts* **3** dark or dismal **> gloomily** *adv*

gloop *or US* **glop** *n informal* any messy sticky fluid or substance [origin unknown] **> gloopy** *or US* **gloppy** *adj*

glorify *vb* -**fies, -fying, -fied 1** to make (something) seem more important than it really is: *computers are just glorified adding machines* **2** to praise: *few countries have glorified success in business more than the United States* **3** to worship (God) **> glorification** *n*

glorious *adj* **1** brilliantly beautiful: *in glorious colour* **2** delightful or enjoyable: *the glorious summer weather* **3** having or full of glory: *glorious successes* **> gloriously** *adv*

glory *n, pl* -**ries 1** fame, praise, or honour: *tales of glory* **2** splendour: *the glory of the tropical day* **3** something worthy of praise: *the Lady Chapel is the great glory of Lichfield* **4** adoration or worship: *the greater glory of God* ▷ *vb* -**ries, -rying, -ried 5 glory in** to take great pleasure in: *the workers were glorying in their new-found freedom* [Latin *gloria*]

glory box *n Austral and NZ old-fashioned, informal* a box in which a young woman stores her trousseau

glory hole *n* an untidy cupboard or storeroom

Glos Gloucestershire

gloss[1] *n* **1 a** a bright shine on a surface **2** a superficially attractive appearance **3** a paint with a shiny finish **4 a** cosmetic used to give a shiny appearance: *lip gloss* ▷ *vb* **5** to paint with gloss **6 gloss over** to conceal (an error, failing, or awkward moment) by minimizing it: *don't try to gloss over bad news* [probably Scandinavian]

gloss[2] *n* **1** an explanatory comment added to the text of a book ▷ *vb* **2** to add a gloss or glosses to [Latin *glossa* unusual word requiring explanatory note]

glossary *n, pl* **-ries** an alphabetical list of technical or specialist words in a book, with explanations [Late Latin *glossarium*; see GLOSS²]

glossy *adj* **glossier, glossiest 1** smooth and shiny: *glossy black hair* **2** superficially attractive or sophisticated: *his glossy Manhattan flat* **3** (of a magazine) produced on expensive shiny paper

glottal stop *n phonetics* a speech sound produced by tightly closing and then opening the glottis

glottis *n* the opening at the top of the windpipe, between the vocal cords [Greek *glōtta* tongue]

Gloucester¹ *n* a city in SW England, administrative centre of Gloucestershire, on the River Severn; cathedral (founded 1100). Pop: 123 205 (2001). Latin name: **Glevum**

Gloucester² *n* **1** Humphrey, Duke of. 1391–1447, English soldier and statesman; son of Henry IV. He acted as protector during Henry VI's minority (1422–29) and was noted for his patronage of humanists **2** Duke of. See **Richard III 3** Duke of. See **Thomas of Woodstock**

Gloucestershire *n* a county of SW England, situated around the lower Severn valley: contains the Forest of Dean and the main part of the Cotswold Hills: the geographical and ceremonial county includes the unitary authority of South Gloucestershire (part of Avon county from 1974 to 1996). Administrative centre: Gloucester. Pop (excluding South Gloucestershire): 568 500 (2003 est). Area (excluding South Gloucestershire): 2643 sq km (1020 sq miles). Abbreviation: **Glos**

glove *n* **1** a shaped covering for the hand with individual sheaths for each finger and the thumb **2** a protective hand covering worn in sports such as boxing [Old English *glōfe*]

glove compartment *n* a small storage area in the dashboard of a car

gloved *adj* covered by a glove or gloves: *a gloved hand*

glow *n* **1** light produced as a result of great heat **2** a steady light without flames **3** brightness of complexion **4** a feeling of wellbeing or satisfaction ▷ *vb* **5** to produce a steady light without flames **6** to shine intensely **7** to experience a feeling of wellbeing or satisfaction: *she glowed with pleasure* **8** (of the complexion) to have a strong bright colour: *his pale face glowing at the recollection* [Old English *glōwan*]

glower (rhymes with **power**) *vb* **1** to stare angrily ▷ *n* **2** an angry stare [origin unknown]

glowing *adj* full of praise: *a glowing tribute*

glow-worm *n* a European beetle, the females and larvae of which have organs producing a soft greenish light

gloxinia *n* a plant with white, red, or purple bell-shaped flowers [after Benjamin P. *Gloxin*, botanist]

Gluck *n* Christoph Willibald von. 1714–87, German composer, esp. of operas, including *Orfeo ed Euridice* (1762) and *Alceste* (1767)

glucose *n* a white crystalline sugar found in plant and animal tissues [Greek *gleukos* sweet wine]

glue *n* **1** a substance used for sticking things together ▷ *vb* **gluing** or **glueing, glued 2** to join or stick together with glue **3 glued to** paying full attention to: *golf fans will be glued to their televisions today for the Open Championship* [Late Latin *glus*] ▷ **gluey** *adj*

glue ear *n* an accumulation of fluid in the middle ear of children, caused by infection and causing deafness

glue-sniffing *n* the practice of inhaling glue fumes to produce intoxicating or hallucinatory effects ▷ **glue-sniffer** *n*

glum *adj* **glummer, glummest** gloomy and quiet, usually because of a disappointment [variant of *gloom*] ▷ **glumly** *adv*

glut *n* **1** an excessive supply ▷ *vb* **glutting, glutted 2** to supply (a market) with a commodity in excess of the demand for it **3 glut oneself** to eat or drink more than one really needs [probably from Old French *gloutir* to swallow]

glute *n* short for **gluteus**

gluten (gloo-ten) *n* a sticky protein found in cereal grains, such as wheat [Latin: glue]

gluteus or **glutaeus** *n* any of the three muscles of the buttock [Greek *gloutos* rump]

glutinous (gloo-tin-uss) *adj* gluelike in texture

glutton *n* **1** someone who eats and drinks too much **2** a person who has a great capacity for something: *a glutton for work* [Latin *gluttire* to swallow] ▷ **gluttonous** *adj*

gluttony *n* the practice of eating too much

glycaemic index or US **glycemic index** *n* an index indicating the effects of various foods on blood sugar. Abbreviation: **GI**

glycerine (gliss-ser-reen) or **glycerin** *n* a nontechnical name for **glycerol** [Greek *glukeros* sweet]

glycerol (gliss-ser-ol) *n* a colourless odourless syrupy liquid obtained from animal and vegetable fats, used as a solvent, antifreeze, and sweetener, and in explosives

glycogen (glike-oh-jen) *n* a starchlike carbohydrate stored in the liver and muscles of humans and animals

glycolysis (glike-kol-iss-iss) *n biochem* the breakdown of glucose by enzymes, with the release of energy

Glyndebourne *n* an estate in SE England, in East Sussex: site of a famous annual festival of opera founded in 1934 by John Christie

gm gram

GM 1 genetically modified **2** *Brit* grant-maintained

G-man *n, pl* **G-men** *US slang* an FBI agent

GMB (in Britain) General, Municipal and Boilermakers (Trade Union)

GMO genetically modified organism

GMT Greenwich Mean Time

gnarled *adj* rough, twisted, and knobbly, usually through age

gnash *vb* to grind (the teeth) together in pain or anger [probably from Old Norse]

gnat *n* a small biting two-winged insect [Old English *gnætt*]

gnaw *vb* **1** to bite or chew constantly so as to wear away bit by bit **2 gnaw at** to cause constant distress or anxiety to: *uneasiness gnawed at his mind* [Old English *gnagan*] ▷ **gnawing** *adj*

gneiss *n* a coarse-grained layered metamorphic rock [German *Gneis*]

gnome *n* **1** an imaginary creature in fairy tales that looks like a little old man **2** a small statue of a gnome in a garden [French]

gnomic (no-mik) *adj literary* of or containing short clever sayings: *gnomic pronouncements*

Gnosticism (noss-tiss-siz-zum) *n* a religious movement involving belief in intuitive spiritual knowledge ▷ **Gnostic** *n, adj*

GNP gross national product

gnu (noo) *n, pl* **gnus** or **gnu** a sturdy African antelope with an oxlike head [Xhosa *nqu*]

go *vb* **goes, going, went, gone 1** to move or proceed to or from a place: *go forward* **2** to be in regular attendance at (work, church, or a place of learning) **3** to lead to a particular place: *the path that goes right along the bank* **4** to be kept in a particular place: *where does this go?* **5** to do or become as specified: *he went white; the gun went bang* **6** to be or continue to be in a specified state: *to go to sleep* **7** to operate or function: *the car wouldn't go* **8** to follow a specified course; fare: *I'd hate the meeting to go badly* **9** to be allotted to a particular purpose or recipient: *a third of the total budget goes on the army* **10** to be sold: *the portrait went for a fortune to a telephone bidder* **11** (of words or music) to be expressed or sung: *the song goes like this* **12** to fail or break down: *my eyesight is going; he was on lap 19 when the engine went* **13** to die: *he went quickly at the end* **14** to be spent or finished: *all tension and all hope had gone* **15** to proceed up to or beyond certain limits: *I think this is going too far* **16** to carry authority: *what Daddy says goes* **17** to endure or last out: *they go for eight or ten hours without resting* **18** not standard to say: *then she goes, 'shut up'* **19 anything goes** anything is acceptable **20 be going to** to intend or be about to: *she was afraid of what was going to happen next* **21 let go** to relax one's hold on; release **22 let oneself go a** to act in an uninhibited manner **b** to lose interest in one's appearance **23 to go** remaining: *two days to go till the holidays* ▷ *n, pl* **goes 24** an attempt: *he had a go at the furniture business* **25** a verbal or physical attack: *he couldn't resist having another go at me* **26** a turn to do something in a game: *'Your go now!' I shouted* **27** *informal* the quality of being active and energetic: *a grand old man, full of go and determination* **28 from the word go** *informal* from the very beginning **29 make a go of** *informal* to be successful in (a business venture or a relationship) **30 on the go** *informal* active and energetic ▶ See also **go about, go against**, etc. [Old English *gān*]

Goa *n* a state on the W coast of India: a Portuguese overseas territory from 1510 until annexed by India in 1961. Capital: Panjim (or Panaji). Pop: 1 343 998 (2001). Area: 3702 sq km (1430 sq miles)

go about *vb* **1** to tackle (a problem or task): *he went about it in the wrong way* **2** to busy oneself with: *people have been going about their business as usual*

goad *vb* **1** to provoke (someone) to take some kind of action, usually in anger ▷ *n* **2** something that provokes someone to take some kind of action **3** a sharp pointed stick for driving cattle [Old English *gād*]

Goa, Daman, and Diu *n* a former Union Territory of India consisting of the widely separated districts of Goa and Daman and the island of Diu. Capital: Panjim (or Panaji). Area: 3814 sq km (1472 sq miles)

go against *vb* **1** to conflict with (someone's wishes or beliefs) **2** to be unfavourable to (a person): *a referendum would almost certainly go against them*

go-ahead *n* **1 give the go-ahead** *informal* to give permission to proceed ▷ *adj* **2** enterprising or ambitious: *prosperous and go-ahead republics*

goal *n* **1** *sport* the space into which players try to propel the ball or puck to score **2** *sport* **a** a successful attempt at scoring **b** the score so made **3** an aim or purpose: *the goal is to get homeless people on their feet* [origin unknown] ❭ **goalless** *adj*

goalie *n* *informal* a goalkeeper

goalkeeper *n* *sport* a player whose duty is to prevent the ball or puck from entering the goal

goal line *n* *sport* the line marking each end of the pitch, on which the goals stand

goalpost *n* **1** either of two uprights supporting the crossbar of a goal **2 move the goalposts** to change the aims of an activity to ensure the desired results

goanna *n* a large Australian lizard [from IGUANA]

goat *n* **1** an agile cud-chewing mammal with hollow horns **2 act the goat** *informal* to behave in a silly manner **3 get someone's goat** *slang* to annoy someone [Old English *gāt*]

goatee *n* a small pointed beard that does not cover the cheeks

goatherd *n* a person who looks after a herd of goats

goatskin *n* leather made from the skin of a goat

goatsucker *n* *US and Canad* same as **nightjar**

go-away bird *n* *S African* a grey lourie [imitative]

gob¹ *n* a thick mass of a soft substance [Old French *gobe* lump]

gob² *n* *Brit, Austral and NZ slang* the mouth [origin unknown]

go back on *vb* to fail to fulfil (a promise): *he went back on his promise not to raise taxes*

gobbet *n* a chunk or lump [Old French *gobet*]

Gobbi *n* Tito. 1915–84, Italian operatic baritone

gobble¹ *vb* **-bling, -bled** to eat quickly and greedily [probably from GOB¹]

gobble² *n* **1** the loud rapid gurgling sound made by a turkey ▷ *vb* **-bling, -bled 2** to make this sound [probably imitative]

gobbledegook *or* **gobbledygook** *n* pretentious or unintelligible language [whimsical formation from GOBBLE²]

gobbler *n* *informal* a turkey

go-between *n* a person who acts as a messenger between two people or groups

Gobi *or* **Gobi Desert** *n* a desert in E Asia, mostly in Mongolia and the Inner Mongolian Autonomous Region of China: sometimes considered to include all the arid regions east of the Pamirs and north of the plateau of Tibet and the Great Wall of China: one of the largest deserts in the world. Length: about 1600 km (1000 miles). Width: about 1000 km (625 miles). Average height: 900 m (3000 ft). Chinese name: **Shamo**

Gobian *adj* of or relating to the Gobi desert

Gobind Singh *or* **Govind Singh** *n* 1666–1708, tenth and last guru of the Sikhs (1675–1708): assassinated

goblet *n* a drinking vessel with a base and stem but without handles [Old French *gobelet* a little cup]

goblin *n* a small grotesque creature in fairy tales that causes trouble for people [Old French]

gobshite *n* *Irish taboo, slang* a stupid person [GOB² + *shite* excrement]

gobsmacked *adj* *Brit, Austral and NZ slang* astonished; astounded

goby *n, pl* **-by** *or* **-bies** a small spiny-finned fish [Latin *gobius* gudgeon]

go by *vb* **1** to pass: *as time goes by* **2** to be guided by: *if my experience is anything to go by*

go-cart *n* same as **go-kart**

god *n* **1** a supernatural being, worshipped as the controller of the universe or some aspect of life, or as the personification of some force **2** an image of such a being **3** a person or thing to which excessive attention is given: *the All Blacks are gods in New Zealand* **4 the gods** the top balcony in a theatre [Old English] ❭ **goddess** *fem n*

God *n* **1** the sole Supreme Being, Creator and ruler of all, in religions such as Christianity, Judaism, and Islam ▷ *interj* **2** an oath or exclamation of surprise or annoyance

Godard *n* Jean-Luc. born 1930, French film director and writer associated with the New Wave of the 1960s. His works include *À bout de souffle* (1960), *Weekend* (1967), *Sauve qui peut* (1980), *Nouvelle Vague* (1990), and *Éloge de l'amour* (2003)

Godavari *n* a river in central India, rising in the Western Ghats and flowing southeast to the Bay of Bengal: extensive delta, linked by canal with the Krishna delta; a sacred river to Hindus. Length: about 1500 km (900 miles)

godchild *n, pl* **-children** a person who is sponsored by godparents at baptism

Goddard *n* Robert Hutchings. 1882–1945, US physicist. He made the first workable liquid-fuelled rocket

goddaughter *n* a female godchild

Godefroy de Bouillon *n* ?1060–1100, French leader of the First Crusade (1096–99), becoming first ruler of the Latin kingdom of Jerusalem

Gödel *n* Kurt. 1906–78, US logician and mathematician, born in Austria-Hungary. He showed (**Gödel's proof**) that in a formal axiomatic system, such as logic or mathematics, it is impossible to prove consistency without using methods from outside the system

Goderich *n* Viscount, title of *Frederick John Robinson*, 1st Earl of Ripon. 1782–1859, British statesman; prime minister (1827–28)

Godesberg *n* a town and spa in W Germany, in North Rhine-Westphalia on the Rhine: a SE suburb of Bonn. Official name: **Bad Godesberg**

godetia *n* a garden plant with showy flowers [after C. H. *Godet*, botanist]

godfather *n* **1** a male godparent **2** the head of a Mafia family or other criminal ring

God-fearing *adj* deeply religious

godforsaken *adj* desolate or dreary: *some godforsaken village in the Himalayas*

Godhead *n* the nature and condition of being God

Godiva *n* Lady. ?1040–1080, wife of Leofric, Earl of Mercia. According to legend, she rode naked through Coventry in order to obtain remission for the townspeople from the heavy taxes imposed by her husband

godless *adj* 1 wicked or unprincipled 2 not religious ➤ **godlessness** *n*

godly *adj* **-lier, -liest** deeply religious ➤ **godliness** *n*

godmother *n* a female godparent

Godolphin *n* Sidney. 1st Earl of Godolphin. 1645–1712, English statesman; as Lord Treasurer, he managed the financing of Marlborough's campaigns in the War of the Spanish Succession

Godoy *n* Manuel de. 1767–1851, Spanish statesman: Charles IV's unpopular chief minister (1792–97; 1801–08)

godparent *n* a person who promises at a person's baptism to look after his or her religious upbringing

godsend *n* a person or thing that comes unexpectedly but is very welcome

godson *n* a male godchild

Godspeed *interj* an expression of good wishes for a person's safe journey and success

Godthaab *or* **Godthåb** *n* the Danish and former official name for Nuuk

Godunov *n* Boris (Fyodorovich). ?1551–1605, Russian regent (1584–98) and tsar (1598–1605)

Godwin *n* 1 died 1053, Earl of Wessex. He was chief adviser to Canute and Edward the Confessor. His son succeeded Edward to the throne as Harold II 2 Mary. See (Mary) Wollstonecraft 3 William. 1756–1836, British political philosopher and novelist. In *An Enquiry concerning Political Justice* (1793), he rejected government and social institutions, including marriage. His views greatly influenced English romantic writers

Godwin-Austen *n* another name for K2

Goebbels *n* (Paul) Joseph. 1897–1945, German Nazi politician; minister of propaganda (1933–45)

goer *n* a person who attends something regularly: *a church goer*

Goes *n* Hugo van der. ?1440–82, Flemish painter: works include the *Pontinari Altarpiece* and *The Death of a Virgin*

Goethe *n* Johann Wolfgang von. 1749–1832, German poet, novelist, and dramatist, who settled in Weimar in 1775. His early works of the *Sturm und Drang* period include the play *Götz von Berlichingen* (1773) and the novel *The Sorrows of Young Werther* (1774). After a journey to Italy (1786–88) his writings, such as the epic play *Iphigenie auf Tauris* (1787) and the epic idyll *Hermann und Dorothea* (1797), showed the influence of classicism. Other works include the *Wilhelm Meister* novels (1796–1829) and his greatest masterpiece *Faust* (1808; 1832)

go for *vb* 1 to choose: *any politician will go for the soft option* 2 informal to like very much 3 to attack 4 to apply equally to: *the same might go for the other woman*

go-getter *n* informal an ambitious enterprising person ➤ **go-getting** *adj*

gogga (hohh-a) *n* S African informal an insect [Nama (language of southern Africa) *xo xo*]

goggle *vb* **-gling, -gled** to stare with wide-open eyes. See also **goggles** [Middle English *gogelen* to look aside] ➤ **goggle-eyed** *adj*

gogglebox *n* Brit slang a television set

goggles *pl n* close-fitting protective spectacles

go-go *adj* denoting a type of dancing performed to pop music by young women wearing few clothes

Gogol *n* Nikolai (Vasilievich). 1809–52, Russian novelist, dramatist, and short-story writer. His best-known works are *The Government Inspector* (1836), a comedy satirizing bureaucracy, and the novel *Dead Souls* (1842) ➤ **Go·golian** *adj*

Gogra *n* a river in N India, rising in Tibet, in the Himalayas, and flowing southeast through Nepal as the Karnali, then through Uttar Pradesh to join the Ganges. Length: about 1000 km (600 miles)

Goiânia *n* a city in central Brazil, capital of Goiás state: planned in 1933 to replace the old capital, Goiás; two universities. Pop: 1 878 000 (2005 est)

Goiás *n* a state of central Brazil, in the Brazilian Highlands: contains Brasília, the capital of Brazil. Capital: Goiânia. Pop: 5 210 335 (2002). Area: 341 289 sq km (131 772 sq miles)

Goidelic *n* 1 the group of Celtic languages, consisting of Irish Gaelic, Scottish Gaelic, and Manx ▷ *adj* 2 of this group of languages [Old Irish *Goidel* Celt]

go in for *vb* 1 to enter (a competition) 2 to take up or take part in (an activity)

going *n* 1 the condition of the ground with regard to walking or riding: *the going for the cross-country is perfect* 2 informal speed or progress: *not bad going for a lad of 58* ▷ *adj* 3 thriving: *the racecourse was a going concern* 4 current or accepted: *this is the going rate for graduates*

going-over *n, pl* **goings-over** informal 1 a thorough examination or investigation 2 a physical beating

goings-on *pl n* informal mysterious or shady activities

go into *vb* to describe or investigate in detail

goitre *or US* **goiter** (goy-ter) *n* pathol a swelling of the thyroid gland in the neck [French]

go-kart *n* a small four-wheeled motor vehicle, used for racing

Golan Heights *pl n* a range of hills in the Middle East, possession of which is disputed between Israel and Syria: under Syrian control until 1967 when they were stormed by Israeli forces; Jewish settlements have since been established. Highest peak: 2224 m (7297 ft)

Golconda *n* 1 a ruined town and fortress in S central India, in W Andhra Pradesh near Hyderabad city: capital of one of the five Muslim kingdoms of the Deccan from 1512 to 1687, then annexed to the Mogul empire; renowned for its diamonds 2 (*sometimes not cap*) a source of wealth or riches, esp. a mine

gold *n* 1 a bright yellow precious metal, used as a monetary standard and in jewellery and plating. Symbol: Au 2 jewellery or coins made of this metal 3 short for **gold medal** ▷ *adj* 4 deep yellow [Old English]

Gold *n* Thomas. 1920–2004, Austrian-born astronomer, working in England and the US: with Bondi and Hoyle he proposed the steady-state theory of the universe

Gold Coast *n* 1 the former name (until 1957) of **Ghana** 2 a city comprising a line of beach resorts in E Australia, extending for over 30 km (20 miles) along the SE coast of Queensland and the NE coast of New South Wales. Pop: 527 828 (2010)

goldcrest *n* a small bird with a bright yellow-and-black crown

gold-digger *n* informal a woman who marries or has a relationship with a man for his money

gold dust *n* 1 gold in the form of small particles or powder 2 like gold dust in great demand because difficult to obtain: *kidney machines were like gold dust*

golden *adj* 1 made of gold: *golden bangles* 2 of the colour of gold: *golden corn* 3 informal very successful or destined for success: *the golden girl of British athletics* 4 excellent or valuable: *a golden opportunity for peace* 5 (of an anniversary) the fiftieth: *golden wedding*; *Golden Jubilee*

golden age *n* the most flourishing and outstanding period in the history of an art or nation: *the golden age of Dixieland jazz*

golden eagle *n* a large mountain eagle of the N hemisphere with golden-brown feathers

Golden Gate *n* a strait between the Pacific and San Francisco Bay: crossed by the **Golden Gate Bridge**, with a central span of 1280 m (4200 ft)

golden goal *n* soccer (in certain matches) the first goal scored in extra time, which instantly wins the match for the side scoring it

g

golden handshake *n informal* money given to an employee either on retirement or to compensate for loss of employment

Golden Horn *n* an inlet of the Bosporus in NW Turkey, forming the harbour of Istanbul. Turkish name: **Haliç**

golden hour *n* the first hour after a serious accident, when medical treatment for the victim is crucial

golden mean *n* the middle course between extremes

golden retriever *n* a retriever with silky wavy gold-coloured hair

goldenrod *n* a tall plant with spikes of small yellow flowers

golden rule *n* an important principle: *the golden rule is to start with the least difficult problems*

golden syrup *n* a light golden-coloured treacle used for sweetening food

golden triangle *n* **1 the Golden Triangle** an opium-producing area of SE Asia, comprising parts of Myanmar, Laos, and Thailand **2** any more or less triangular area or region noted for its success, prosperity, influence, etc. **3** *maths* a triangle which has two 72-degree angles and one 36-degree angle

golden wattle *n* an Australian plant with yellow flowers that yields a useful gum and bark

goldfinch *n* a European finch, the adult of which has yellow-and-black wings

goldfish *n, pl* **-fish** *or* **-fishes** a gold or orange-red freshwater fish, often kept as a pet

gold foil *n* thin gold sheet that is thicker than gold leaf

Golding *n* Sir **William** (**Gerald**). 1911–93, English novelist noted for his allegories of man's proclivity for evil. His novels include *Lord of the Flies* (1954), *Darkness Visible* (1979), *Rites of Passage* (1980), *Close Quarters* (1987), and *Fire Down Below* (1989). Nobel prize for literature 1983

gold leaf *n* very thin gold sheet made by rolling or hammering gold and used for gilding

gold medal *n* a medal made of gold, awarded to the winner of a race or competition

Goldoni *n* **Carlo**. 1707–93, Italian dramatist; author of over 250 plays in Italian or French, including *La Locandiera* (1753). His work introduced realistic Italian comedy, superseding the commedia dell'arte

gold-plated *adj* covered with a very thin coating of gold

gold rush *n* a large-scale migration of people to a territory where gold has been found

Goldschmidt *n* **Richard Benedikt**. 1878–1958, US geneticist, born in Germany. He advanced the theory that heredity is determined by the chemical configuration of the chromosome molecule rather than by the qualities of the individual genes

goldsmith *n* a person who makes gold jewellery and other articles

Goldsmith *n* **Oliver**. ?1730–74, Irish poet, dramatist, and novelist. His works include the novel *The Vicar of Wakefield* (1766), the poem *The Deserted Village* (1770), and the comedy *She Stoops to Conquer* (1773)

gold standard *n* a monetary system in which the basic currency unit equals a specified weight of gold

golf *n* **1** a game in which a ball is struck with clubs into a series of eighteen holes in a grassy course ▷ *vb* **2** to play golf [origin unknown] **> golfer** *n*

golf club *n* **1** a long-shafted club used to strike a golf ball **2 a** an association of golf players **b** the premises of such an association

golf course *or* **golf links** *n* an area of ground laid out for golf

Golgi *n* **Camillo**. 1844–1926, Italian neurologist and histologist, noted for his work on the central nervous system and his discovery in animal cells of the bodies known by his name: shared the Nobel prize for physiology or medicine 1906

golliwog *n* a soft doll with a black face, usually made of cloth [from a doll in a series of American children's books]

golly *interj* an exclamation of mild surprise [originally a euphemism for *God*]

Gombe *n* a state of Nigeria, in the NE. Capital: Gombe. Pop: 2 353 879(2006). Area: 18 768 sq km (7246 sq miles)

Gomberg *n* **Moses**. 1866–1947, US chemist, born in Russia, noted for his work on free radicals

Gomel *n* an industrial city in SE Belarus, on the River Sozh; an industrial centre. Pop: 480 000 (2005 est)

Gompers *n* **Samuel**. 1850–1924, US labour leader, born in England; a founder of the American Federation of Labor and its president (1886–94; 1896–1924)

Gomulka *n* **Władysław**. 1905–82, Polish statesman; first secretary of the Polish Communist Party (1956–70)

gonad *n* an organ in which reproductive cells are produced, such as a testis or ovary [Greek *gonos* seed]

Gonaïves *n* a port in W Haiti, on the Gulf of Gonaïves; scene of the proclamation of Haiti's independence (1804). Pop: 104 825 (2003)

Goncharov *n* **Ivan** (**Aleksandrovich**). 1812–91, Russian novelist: his best-known work is *Oblomov* (1859)

Goncourt *n* **Edmond** (**Louis Antoine Huot**) **de**, 1822–96, and his brother, **Jules** (**Alfred Huot**) **de**, 1830–70, French writers, noted for their collaboration, esp. on their *Journal*, and for the Académie Goncourt founded by Edmond's will

Gondar *n* a city in NW Ethiopia: capital of Ethiopia from the 17th century until 1868. Pop: 191 000 (2005 est)

gondola *n* **1 a** long narrow flat-bottomed boat with a high ornamented stem, traditionally used on the canals of Venice **2** a moving cabin suspended from a cable, used as a ski lift [Italian]

gondolier *n* a person who propels a gondola

Gondwanaland *or* **Gondwana** *n* one of the two ancient supercontinents produced by the first split of the even larger supercontinent Pangaea about 200 million years ago, comprising chiefly what is now Africa, South America, Australia, Antarctica, and the Indian subcontinent [C19: from *Gondwana* region in central north India, where the rock series was originally found]

gone *vb* **1** the past participle of **go** ▷ *adj* **2** no longer present or no longer in existence

goner *n slang* a person who is about to die or who is beyond help

gong *n* **1** a flat circular metal disc that is hit with a hammer to give out a loud sound **2** *Brit slang* a medal [Malay]

Góngora y Argote *n* **Luis de**. 1561–1627, Spanish lyric poet, noted for the exaggerated pedantic style of works such as *Las Soledades*

gonorrhoea *or especially US* **gonorrhea** (gon-or-ree-a) *n* a sexually transmitted disease that causes inflammation and a discharge from the genital organs [Greek *gonos* semen + *rhoia* flux]

González *n* **Julio**. 1876–1942, Spanish sculptor: one of the first to create abstract geometric forms with soldered iron

González Márquez *n* **Felipe**. born 1942, Spanish statesman; prime minister of Spain (1982–96)

goo *n informal* a sticky substance [origin unknown]

Gooch *n* **Graham** (**Alan**). born 1953, English cricketer: played in 118 test matches (1975–95), 34 as captain; scored 8,900 test runs

good *adj* **better, best 1** having admirable, pleasing, or superior qualities: *a good listener* **2** morally excellent; virtuous: *a good person* **3** beneficial: *exercise is good for the heart* **4** kindly or generous: *he is so good to us* **5** competent or talented: *she's good at physics* **6** obedient or well-behaved: *a good boy* **7** reliable or recommended: *a good make* **8** complete or thorough: *she went to have a good look round* **9** appropriate or opportune: *a good time to clear the air* **10** satisfying or enjoyable: *a good holiday* **11** newest or of the best quality: *keep the good dishes for guests* **12** fairly large, extensive, or long: *they contain a good amount of protein* **13 as**

good as virtually or practically: *the war was as good as over* ▷ *n* **14** advantage or benefit: *what is the good of it all?* **15** positive moral qualities; virtue **16 for good** for ever; permanently: *his political career was over for good* ▶ See also **goods** [Old English *gōd*]

goodbye *interj* **1** an expression used on parting ▷ *n* **2** the act of saying goodbye: *he said his goodbyes* [from *God be with ye*]

good day *interj* an expression of greeting or farewell used during the day

good-for-nothing *n* **1** an irresponsible or worthless person ▷ *adj* **2** irresponsible or worthless

Good Friday *n* Christianity the Friday before Easter, observed as a commemoration of the Crucifixion of Jesus Christ

Good Hope *n* Cape of Good Hope See **Cape of Good Hope**

goodies *pl n* any things considered particularly desirable

goodly *adj* **-lier, -liest** fairly large: *a goodly number of children*

Goodman *n* Benny, full name *Benjamin David Goodman*. 1909–86, US jazz clarinetist and bandleader, whose treatment of popular songs created the jazz idiom known as swing

good morning *interj* an expression of greeting or farewell used in the morning

good-natured *adj* tolerant and kindly

goodness *n* **1** the quality of being good ▷ *interj* **2** an exclamation of surprise

good night *interj* an expression of farewell used in the evening or at night

goods *pl n* **1** articles produced to be sold: *consumer goods* **2** movable personal property: *houses and goods are insured from fire* **3 deliver the goods** *informal* to do what is expected or required **4 have the goods on someone** *US and Canad slang* to know something incriminating about someone

Good Samaritan *n* a person who helps someone in difficulty or distress [from a parable in Luke 10: 30–37]

good-tempered *adj* tolerant and kindly

good turn *n* a helpful and friendly act

goodwill *n* **1** kindly feelings towards other people **2** the popularity and good reputation of a well-established business, considered as a valuable asset

Goodwin *n* Fred(erick Anderson). born 1958, Scottish banker; CEO of Royal Bank of Scotland (2001–2009); losses in 2008 of £24 billion led to the bank's effective nationalization; his knighthood (2004) was annulled in 2012

Goodwin Sands *pl n* a dangerous stretch of shoals at the entrance to the Strait of Dover: separated from the E coast of Kent by the Downs roadstead

Goodwood *n* an area in SE England, in Sussex: site of a famous racecourse and of **Goodwood House**, built 1780–1800

goody *interj* **1** a child's exclamation of pleasure ▷ *n, pl* **goodies 2** *informal* the hero in a film or book ▶ See also **goodies**

Goodyear *n* Charles. 1800–60, US inventor of vulcanized rubber

goody-goody *informal n, pl* **-goodies 1** a person who behaves well in order to please people in authority ▷ *adj* **2** behaving well in order to please people in authority

gooey *adj* **gooier, gooiest** *informal* **1** sticky, soft, and often sweet **2** sentimental: *one knows the whole gooey performance is an act*

goof *vb informal* **1** to bungle or botch **2 goof off** *US and Canad* to spend time in a lazy or foolish way: *he's goofing off on the Costa del Sol* [probably from dialect *goff* simpleton]

go off *vb* **1** to stop functioning: *the heating went off* **2** to make a sudden loud noise: *a bomb went off* **3** to occur as specified: *the actual launch went off perfectly* **4** *informal* (of food) to become stale or rotten **5** *Brit informal* to stop liking

goofy *adj* **goofier, goofiest** *informal* silly or ridiculous

google *vb* **1** to search for (something) on the internet

using a search engine **2** to check (someone's credentials) by searching for websites containing his or her name [from *Google*, a popular search engine on the internet]

googly *n, pl* **-lies** *cricket* a ball bowled like a leg break but spinning from off to leg on pitching [Australian English]

Goole *n* an inland port in NE England, in the East Riding of Yorkshire at the confluence of the Ouse and Don Rivers, 75 km (47 miles) from the North Sea. Pop: 18 741 (2001)

goon *n* **1** a stupid person **2** *US informal* a hired thug [dialect *gooney* fool; influenced by US cartoon character Alice the *goon*]

go on *vb* **1** to continue or proceed **2** to take place: *there's a war going on* **3** to talk at length and annoyingly

goosander *n* a duck of Europe and North America with a dark head and white body [probably from GOOSE[1] + Old Norse *önd* (genitive *andar*) duck]

goose[1] *n, pl* **geese 1** a fairly large web-footed long-necked migratory bird **2** the female of such a bird **3** the flesh of the goose used for food **4** *informal* a silly person [Old English *gōs*]

goose[2] *vb* **goosing, goosed** *slang* to prod (someone) playfully in the bottom [from the jabbing of a goose's bill]

gooseberry *n, pl* **-ries 1** a small edible green berry with tiny hairs on the skin **2 play gooseberry** *Brit and NZ informal* to be an unwanted single person accompanying a couple

goose flesh *n* the bumpy condition of the skin due to cold or fear, in which the muscles at the base of the hair follicles contract, making the hair bristle. Also: **goose pimples**

Goosen *n* Retief. born 1969, South African golfer: winner of the US Open Championship (2001, 2004)

goose-step *vb* **-stepping, -stepped** to march raising the legs high alternately while keeping the legs straight

Goossens *n* **1** Sir Eugene. 1893–1962, British composer and conductor, born in Belgium **2** his brother, **Leon**. 1896–1988, British oboist

go out *vb* **1** to go to entertainments or social functions **2** to be extinguished or cease to function: *the lights went out* **3** (of information) to be released publicly **4** (of a broadcast) to be transmitted **5 go out with** to have a romantic relationship with

go over *vb* **1** to examine very carefully **2 go over to** to change to: *he went over to the Free Orthodox Church*

gopher (go-fer) *n* an American burrowing rodent with wide cheek pouches [origin unknown]

Gorakhpur *n* a city in N India, in SE Uttar Pradesh: formerly an important Muslim garrison. Pop: 624 570 (2001)

Gorbachev or **Gorbachov** *n* Mikhail (Sergeevich). born 1931, Soviet statesman; general secretary of the Soviet Communist Party (1985–91): president (1988–91). Nobel peace prize 1990. His reforms ended the Communist monopoly of power and led to the break-up of the Soviet Union

Gorbals *n* the Gorbals a district of Glasgow, formerly known for its slums

Gordian knot *n* cut the Gordian knot to solve a complicated problem by bold or forceful action [after *Gordius*, in Greek legend, who tied a knot that Alexander the Great cut with a sword]

Gordimer *n* Nadine. born 1923, South African novelist. Her books include *The Lying Days* (1952), *The Conservationist* (1974), which won the Booker prize, *None to Accompany Me* (1994), and *The House Gun* (1998). Her works were banned in South Africa for their condemnation of apartheid. Nobel prize for literature 1991

Gordon *n* **1** Adam Lindsay. 1833–70, Australian poet and horseman, born in the Azores, who developed the bush ballad as a literary form, esp. in *Bush Ballads and Galloping*

Rhymes (1870) **2 Charles George**, known as *Chinese Gordon*. 1833–85, British general and administrator. He helped to crush the Taiping rebellion (1863–64), and was governor of Sudan (1877–80), returning in 1884 to aid Egyptian forces against the Mahdi. He was killed in the siege of Khartoum **3 Dexter (Keith)**. 1923–90, US jazz tenor saxophonist **4 Sir Donald**. born 1930, South African businessman **5 Lord George**. 1751–93, English religious agitator. He led the Protestant opposition to legislation relieving Roman Catholics of certain disabilities, which culminated in the Gordon riots (1780) **6 George Hamilton**. See (4th Earl of) **Aberdeen**

gore¹ *n* blood shed from a wound [Old English *gor* dirt]

gore² *vb* **goring, gored** (of an animal) to pierce or stab (a person or another animal) with a horn or tusk [probably from Old English *gār* spear]

gore³ *n* a tapering piece of material in a garment, sail, or umbrella [Old English *gāra*]

Gore *n* Al(bert) Jr. born 1948, US Democrat politician; vice president of the US (1993–2001); defeated in the disputed presidential election of 2000; leading environmental campaigner; shared the 2007 Nobel Peace Prize with the Intergovernmental Panel For Climate Change

Górecki *n* Henryk (Mikołaj). 1933–2010, Polish composer, best known for his sombre third symphony (1979)

Gorey *n* Edward St John. 1925–2000, US illustrator and author, noted for his bizarre humour in such works as *The Unstrung Harp* (1953) and *The Wuggly Ump* (1963)

gorge *n* **1** a deep narrow steep-sided valley **2** one's gorge rises one feels disgusted or nauseated ▷ *vb* **gorging, gorged 3** Also: **gorge oneself** to eat greedily [Latin *gurges* whirlpool]

gorgeous *adj* **1** strikingly beautiful or attractive **2** *informal* warm, sunny, and very pleasant: *a gorgeous day* [Old French *gorgias* elegant] ▷ **gorgeously** *adv*

Gorgias *n* ?485–?380 BC, Greek sophist and rhetorician, subject of a dialogue by Plato

Gorgon *n* **1** *Greek myth* one of three monstrous sisters who had live snakes for hair, and were so horrifying that anyone who looked at them was turned to stone **2** *informal* a terrifying or repulsive woman [Greek *gorgos* terrible]

Gorgonzola *n* a sharp-flavoured blue-veined Italian cheese [after *Gorgonzola*, Italian town where it originated]

Gorica *n* the Bosnian, Croatian, and Serbian name for **Gorizia**

gorilla *n* a very large W African ape with coarse black hair [Greek *Gorillai*, an African tribe renowned for their hairy appearance]

Göring or **Goering** *n* Hermann Wilhelm. 1893–1946, German Nazi leader and field marshal. He commanded Hitler's storm troops (1923) and as Prussian prime minister and German commissioner for aviation (1933–45) he founded the Gestapo and mobilized Germany for war. Sentenced to death at Nuremberg, he committed suicide

Gorizia *n* a city in NE Italy, in Friuli-Venezia Giulia, on the Isonzo River: cultural centre under the Hapsburgs. Pop: 35 667 (2001). German name: **Görz**. Bosnian, Croatian, and Serbian name: **Gorica**

Gorki¹ or **Gorky** *n* the former name (until 1991) of **Nizhni Novgorod**

Gorki² or **Gorky** *n* Maxim, pen name of *Aleksey Maximovich Peshkov*. 1868–1936, Russian novelist, dramatist, and short-story writer, noted for his depiction of the outcasts of society. His works include the play *The Lower Depths* (1902), the novel *Mother* (1907), and an autobiographical trilogy (1913–23)

Gorky *n* Arshile. 1904–48, US abstract expressionist painter, born in Armenia. Influenced by Picasso and Miró, his style is characterized by fluid lines and resonant colours

Görlitz *n* a city in E Germany, in Saxony on the Neisse River: divided in 1945, the area on the E bank of the river becoming the Polish town of **Zgorzelec**. Pop: 58 518 (2003 est)

Gorlovka *n* a city in SE Ukraine in the centre of the Donets Basin: a major coal-mining centre. Pop: 280 000 (2005 est)

gormless *adj Brit and NZ informal* stupid or dull-witted [obsolete *gaumless*]

Gormley *n* Sir Antony. born 1950, British sculptor, noted for *Angel of the North* (1998) and *Another Place* (1997), an installation of cast-iron figures facing out to sea on Crosby beach, near Liverpool

Gorno-Altai Republic *n* a constituent republic of S Russia: mountainous, rising over 4350 m (14 500 ft) in the Altai Mountains of the south. Capital: Gorno-Altaisk. Pop: 202 900 (2002). Area: 92 600 sq km (35 740 sq miles). Also called: **Altai Republic**

Gorno-Badakhshan Autonomous Republic *n* an administrative division of Tajikistan: generally mountainous and inaccessible. Capital: Khorog. Pop: 206 000 (2000 est). Area: 63 700 sq km (24 590 sq miles). Also called: **Badakhshan**

go round *vb* to be sufficient: *there wasn't enough money to go round*

gorse *n* an evergreen shrub with small yellow flowers and prickles, which grows wild in the countryside [Old English *gors*]

Gorton *n* Sir John Grey. 1911–2002, Australian statesman; prime minister (1968–71)

gory *adj* **gorier, goriest 1** horrific or bloodthirsty: *the gory details* **2** bloody: *gory remains*

Görz *n* the German name for **Gorizia**

gosh *interj* an exclamation of mild surprise or wonder [euphemistic for *God*]

goshawk *n* a large swift short-winged hawk [Old English *gōshafoc*]

Goshen *n* **1** a region of ancient Egypt, east of the Nile delta: granted to Jacob and his descendants by the king of Egypt and inhabited by them until the Exodus (Genesis 45:10) **2** a place of comfort and plenty

Goslar *n* a city in N central Germany, in Lower Saxony: imperial palace and other medieval buildings, silver mines. Pop: 43 727 (2003 est)

gosling *n* a young goose [Old Norse *gæslingr*]

go-slow *n Brit and NZ* a deliberate slowing of the rate of production by workers as a tactic in industrial conflict

gospel *n* **1 a** the teachings of Jesus Christ **b** the story of Christ's life and teachings **2** a doctrine held to be of great importance: *the gospel of self-help* **3** Also called: **gospel truth** unquestionable truth: *gross inaccuracies which are sometimes taken as gospel* ▷ *adj* **4** denoting a kind of religious music originating in the churches of the Black people in the Southern US [Old English *gōdspell*, from *gōd* good + *spell* message]

Gospel *n Christianity* any of the first four books of the New Testament, namely Matthew, Mark, Luke, and John, which tell the story of Jesus Christ

Gosport *n* a town in S England, in Hampshire on Portsmouth harbour: naval base since the 16th century. Pop: 69 348 (2001)

gossamer *n* **1 a** very fine fabric **2 a** filmy cobweb often seen on foliage or floating in the air [probably Middle English *gos* goose + *somer* summer; referring to *St Martin's summer*, a period in November when goose was eaten and cobwebs abound]

Gosse *n* Sir Edmund William. 1849–1928, English critic and poet, noted particularly for his autobiographical work *Father and Son* (1907)

gossip *n* **1** idle talk, usually about other people's private lives, esp. of a disapproving or malicious nature: *office gossip* **2** an informal conversation, esp. about other people's private lives: *to have a gossip and a giggle* **3** a person who habitually talks about other people, usually maliciously ▷ *vb* **4** to talk idly or maliciously, esp. about other people's private lives [Old English *godsibb* godparent, applied to a woman's female friends at the birth of a child] **> gossipy** *adj*

got *vb* **1** the past of **get 2** have got to possess **3** have got to must: *you have got to be prepared to work hard*

Göta *n* a river in S Sweden, draining Lake Vänern and flowing south-southwest to the Kattegat: forms part of the **Göta Canal**, which links Göteborg in the west with Stockholm in the east. Length: 93 km (58 miles)

Göteborg *or* **Gothenburg** *n* a port in SW Sweden, at the mouth of the Göta River: the largest port and second largest city in the country; developed through the Swedish East India Company and grew through Napoleon's continental blockade and with the opening of the Göta Canal (1832); university (1891). Pop: 481 523 (2004 est)

Gotha *n* a town in central Germany, in Thuringia on the N edge of the Thuringian forest: capital of Saxe-Coburg-Gotha (1826–1918); noted for the *Almanach de Gotha*, a record of the royal and noble houses of Europe, first published in 1764). Pop: 47 158 (2003 est)

Gotham *n* US an informal name for **New York**

Gothenburg *n* the English name for **Göteborg**

Gothic *adj* **1** of a style of architecture used in W Europe from the 12th to the 16th centuries, characterized by pointed arches, ribbed vaults, and flying buttresses **2** of a literary style featuring stories of gloom, horror, and the supernatural, popular in the late 18th century **3** of or in a heavy ornate script typeface ▷ *n* **4** Gothic architecture or art [Greek *Gothoi*]

go through *vb* **1** to experience (a difficult time or process) **2** to name or describe: *the president went through a list of government ministers* **3** to qualify for the next stage of a competition: *Belgium, Spain and Uruguay all went through from Group E* **4** to be approved: *the bill went through parliament* **5** go through with to bring to a successful conclusion, often by persistence

Gotland, Gothland *or* **Gottland** *n* an island in the Baltic Sea, off the SE coast of Sweden: important trading centre since the Bronze Age; long disputed between Sweden and Denmark, finally becoming Swedish in 1645; tourism and agriculture now important. Capital: Visby. Pop: (including associated islands) 57 677 (2004 est). Area: 3140 sq km (1212 sq miles)

gotten *vb* chiefly US a past participle of **get**

Gottfried von Strassburg *n* early 13th-century German poet; author of the incomplete epic *Tristan and Isolde*, the version of the legend that served as the basis of Wagner's opera

Göttingen *n* a city in central Germany, in Lower Saxony: important member of the Hanseatic League (14th century); university, founded in 1734 by George II of England. Pop: 122 883 (2003 est)

Gottsched *n* Johann Christoph. 1700–66, German critic, dramatist, and translator

gouache *n* opaque watercolour paint bound with glue [French]

Gouda *n* **1** a town in the W Netherlands, in South Holland province: important medieval cloth trade; famous for its cheese. Pop: 72 000 (2003 est) **2** a large round Dutch cheese, mild and similar in taste to Edam

gouge (gowj) *vb* **gouging, gouged 1** to scoop or force (something) out of its position **2** to cut (a hole or groove) in something with a pointed object ▷ *n* **3** a mark or groove made by gouging [French]

goulash (goo-lash) *n* a rich stew seasoned with paprika, originating in Hungary [Hungarian *gulyás hus* herdsman's meat]

Gould *n* **1** Benjamin Apthorp. 1824–96, US astronomer: the first to use the telegraph to determine longitudes; founded the *Astronomical Journal* (1849) **2** Glenn. 1932–82, Canadian pianist

Gounod *n* Charles François. 1818–93, French composer of the operas *Faust* (1859) and *Romeo and Juliet* (1867)

gourd (goord) *n* **1** a large hard-shelled fruit similar to a cucumber or marrow **2** a container made from a dried gourd shell [Old French *gourde*]

gourmand (goor-mand) *n* a person devoted to eating and drinking, usually to excess [Old French *gourmant*]

gourmet (goor-may) *n* an expert on good food and drink [French]

Gourmont *n* Remy de. 1858–1915, French symbolist critic and novelist

gout (gowt) *n* a disease that causes painful inflammation of certain joints, for example of the big toe [Latin *gutta* a drop] **> gouty** *adj*

govern *vb* **1** to direct and control the policy and affairs of (a country or an organization) **2** to control or determine: *the international organizations governing athletics and rugby* [Latin *gubernare* to steer] **> governable** *adj*

governance *n* government, control, or authority

governess *n* a woman employed in a private household to teach the children

government *n* **1** the executive policy-making body of a country or state **2** the state and its administration: *the assembled heads of state and government* **3** the system by which a country or state is ruled: *the old hard-line government* **> governmental** *adj*

governor *n* **1** the chief political administrator of a region, such as a US state or a colony. Related adjective: **gubernatorial 2** Brit the senior administrator of a school, prison, or other institution **3** Brit informal one's employer or father **> governorship** *n*

governor general *n, pl* **governors general** *or* **governor generals** the chief representative of the British government in a Commonwealth country

Gower[1] *n* the Gower a peninsula in S Wales, in Swansea county on the Bristol Channel: mainly agricultural with several resorts

Gower[2] *n* **1** David (Ivon). born 1957, English cricketer: played in 117 test matches (1978–1992), 32 as captain; scored 8,231 test runs **2** John. ?1330–1408, English poet, noted particularly for his tales of love, the *Confessio Amantis*

go with *vb* **1** to blend or harmonize with: *the style goes well with modern art* **2** to be linked with: *respect goes with age*

go without *vb* to be denied or deprived of: *no-one should go without food*

gown *n* **1** a woman's long formal dress **2** a surgeon's overall **3** a loose wide official robe worn by clergymen, judges, lawyers, and academics [Late Latin *gunna* garment made of fur]

goy *n, pl* **goyim** *or* **goys** a Jewish word for a **Gentile[1]** [Yiddish]

Goya *n* Francisco de, full name *Francisco José de Goya y Lucientes*. 1746–1828, Spanish painter and etcher; well known for his portraits, he became court painter to Charles IV of Spain (1799). He recorded the French invasion of Spain in a series of etchings *The Disasters of War* (1810–14) and two paintings *2 May 1808* and *3 May 1808* (1814)

Goyen *n* Jan Josephszoon van. 1596–1656, Dutch landscape painter and etcher

GP general practitioner

GPMU (in Britain) Graphical, Paper and Media Union

GPO (in Britain and Australia) general post office

GPS Global Positioning System: a satellite-based navigation system

Gr. 1 Grecian **2** Greece **3** Greek

Graafian follicle *n* anatomy a cavity in the ovary that contains a developing egg cell [after R. de Graaf, anatomist]

grab *vb* **grabbing, grabbed 1** to seize hold of **2** to take (food, drink, or rest) hurriedly **3** to take (an opportunity) eagerly **4** to seize illegally or unscrupulously: *land grabbing* **5** informal to interest or impress ▷ *n* **6** the act of grabbing [probably from Middle Dutch *grabben*]

grab bag *n* **1** a collection of miscellaneous things **2** US,

Canad and *Austral* a bag from which gifts are drawn at random

Gracchus *n* Tiberius Sempronius. ?163–133 BC, and his younger brother, **Gaius Sempronius**, 153–121 BC, known as *the Gracchi*. Roman tribunes and reformers. Tiberius attempted to redistribute public land among the poor but was murdered in the ensuing riot. Violence again occurred when the reform was revived by Gaius, and he too was killed

grace *n* **1** elegance and beauty of movement, form, or expression **2** a pleasing or charming quality: *architecture with few redeeming graces* **3** courtesy or decency: *at least she had the grace to laugh* **4** a delay granted for the completion of a task or payment of a debt: *another year's grace* **5** *Christian theol* the free and unmerited favour of God shown towards humankind **6** a short prayer of thanks for a meal **7** airs and graces an affected manner **8** with bad grace unwillingly or grudgingly: *independence was granted with bad grace* **9** with good grace willingly or ungrudgingly: *to accept with good grace* ▷ *vb* **gracing**, **graced 10** to honour or favour: *graced by the presence of Henry Fonda* **11** to decorate or make more attractive: *bedsit walls graced by Che Guevara and James Dean* [Latin *gratia*]

Grace[1] *n* Your *or* His *or* Her Grace a title used to address or refer to a duke, duchess, or archbishop

Grace[2] *n* W(illiam) G(ilbert). 1848–1915, English cricketer

graceful *adj* having beauty of movement, style, or form ▷ **gracefully** *adv* ▷ **gracefulness** *n*

graceless *adj* **1** lacking elegance **2** lacking manners

grace note *n music* a note that ornaments a melody

Graces *pl n Greek myth* the three sister goddesses of charm and beauty

gracious *adj* **1** showing kindness and courtesy **2** characterized by elegance, ease, and indulgence: *gracious living* ▷ *interj* **3** an expression of mild surprise or wonder ▷ **graciously** *adv* ▷ **graciousness** *n*

gradation *n* **1** a series of systematic stages; gradual progression **2** a stage in such a series or progression

grade *n* **1** a place on a scale of quality, rank, or size **2** a mark or rating indicating a student's level of achievement **3** a rank or level of importance in a company or organization **4** *US, Canad, Austral and S African* a class or year in a school **5** make the grade *informal* to be successful by reaching a required standard ▷ *vb* **grading**, **graded 6** to arrange according to quality or rank: *passes are graded from A down to E* **7** to give a grade to: *senior secretaries will need shorthand and be graded accordingly* [Latin *gradus* step]

gradient *n* **1** Also (esp. US): **grade** a sloping part of a railway, road, or path **2** Also (esp. US): **grade** a measure of the steepness of such a slope **3** a measure of the change in something, such as the angle of a curve, over a specified distance [Latin *gradiens* stepping]

gradual *adj* occurring, developing, or moving in small stages: *a gradual handover of power* [Latin *gradus* a step] ▷ **gradually** *adv*

gradualism *n* the policy of changing something gradually ▷ **gradualist** *adj*

graduate *n* **1** a person who holds a university or college degree **2** *US and Canad* a student who has completed a course of studies at a high school and received a diploma **3** same as **postgraduate** ▷ *vb* **-ating, -ated 4** to receive a degree or diploma **5** to change by degrees: *the winds graduate from tropical storms to cyclones* **6** to mark (a measuring flask or instrument) with units of measurement [Latin *gradus* a step]

graduation *n* **1** the act of graduating from university or college **2** *US and Canad* the act of graduating from high school **3** the ceremony at which degrees and diplomas are given to graduating students **4** a mark indicating measure on an instrument or container

Graeco-Roman *or especially* US **Greco-Roman** (greek-oh-**rome**-an) *adj* of, or showing the influence of, both Greek and Roman cultures

Graf *n* Steffi. born 1969, German tennis player: won 22 Grand Slam singles titles (1987–99), including seven at Wimbledon; won (1988) a unique 'golden slam' of each Grand Slam singles title and a gold medal in the women's singles at the Olympics

graffiti (graf-**fee**-tee) *n* drawings or words scribbled or sprayed on walls or posters [Italian: little scratches]

graft[1] *n* **1** *surgery* a piece of tissue transplanted to an area of the body in need of the tissue **2** a small piece of tissue from one plant that is joined to another plant so that they grow together as one ▷ *vb* **3** to transplant (tissue) to an area of the body in need of the tissue **4** to join (part of one plant) onto another plant so that they grow together as one **5** to attach or incorporate: *to graft Japanese production methods onto the American talent for innovation* [Greek *graphein* to write]

graft[2] *n* **1** *Brit informal* hard work **2** the practice of obtaining money by taking advantage of one's position ▷ *vb* **3** *informal* to work hard [origin unknown]

Graham *n* **1** Martha. 1893–1991, US dancer and choreographer **2** Thomas. 1805–69, British physicist: proposed **Graham's law** (1831) of gaseous diffusion and coined the terms osmosis, crystalloids, and colloids **3** William Franklin, known as *Billy Graham*. born 1918, US evangelist

Grahame *n* Kenneth. 1859–1932, Scottish author, noted for the children's classic *The Wind in the Willows* (1908)

Graham Land *n* the N part of the Antarctic Peninsula: became part of the British Antarctic Territory in 1962 (formerly part of the Falkland Islands Dependencies; claims are suspended under the Antarctic Treaty)

Graian Alps *pl n* the N part of the Western Alps, in France and NW Piedmont, Italy. Highest peak: Gran Paradiso, 4061 m (13 323 ft)

Grail *n* See Holy Grail

grain *n* **1** the small hard seedlike fruit of a cereal plant **2** a mass of such fruits gathered for food **3** cereal plants in general **4** a small hard particle: *a grain of salt* **5** a very small amount: *a grain of compassion* **6 a** the arrangement of the fibres, layers, or particles in wood, leather, or stone **b** the pattern or texture resulting from this **7** go against the grain to be contrary to one's natural inclinations [Latin *granum*] ▷ **grainy** *adj*

Grainger *n* Percy Aldridge. 1882–1961, Australian pianist, composer, and collector of folk music on which many of his works are based

gram *or* **gramme** *n* a metric unit of weight equal to one thousandth of a kilogram [Greek *gramma* small weight]

graminivorous *adj* (of an animal) grass-eating [Latin *gramen* grass + *vorare* to swallow]

grammar *n* **1** the rules of a language, that show how sentences are formed, or how words are inflected **2** the way in which grammar is used: *the teacher found errors of spelling and grammar* **3** a book on the rules of grammar [Greek *gramma* letter]

grammarian *n* a person who studies or writes about grammar for a living

grammar school *n* **1** *Brit* (esp. formerly) a secondary school for children of high academic ability **2** *US* same as **elementary school 3** *Austral* a private school, usually one controlled by a church

grammatical *adj* **1** of grammar **2** (of a sentence) following the rules of grammar ▷ **grammatically** *adv*

gramme *n* same as **gram**

gramophone *n* an old-fashioned type of record player [inversion of *phonogram*]

Grampian *adj* **1** of or relating to the area of Scotland occupied by the Grampian Mountains ▷ *n* **2** another name for **Grampian Region**

Grampian Mountains *pl n* **1** a mountain system of central Scotland, extending from the southwest to the northeast and separating the Highlands from the Lowlands. Highest peak: Ben Nevis, 1344 m (4408 ft) **2** a mountain range in SE Australia, in W Victoria ▶ Also called: **the Grampians**

Grampian Region *n* a former local government region in NE Scotland, formed in 1975 from Aberdeenshire, Kincardineshire, and most of Banffshire and Morayshire; replaced in 1996 by the council areas of Aberdeenshire, City of Aberdeen, and Moray

grampus *n, pl* **-puses** a dolphin-like mammal with a blunt snout [Old French *gras* fat + *pois* fish]

Gramsci *n* Antonio. 1891–1937, Italian politician and Marxist theorist: founder (1921) of the Italian Communist party. His important works were written during his imprisonment (1926–37) by the Fascists

gran *n Brit, Austral and NZ informal* a grandmother

Granada *n* **1** a former kingdom of S Spain, in Andalusia: founded in the 13th century and divided in 1833 into the present-day provinces of Granada, Almería, and Málaga **2** a city in S Spain, in Andalusia: capital of the Moorish kingdom of Granada from 1238 to 1492 and a great commercial and cultural centre, containing the Alhambra palace (13th and 14th centuries); university (1531). Pop: 237 663 (2003 est) **3** a city in SW Nicaragua, on the NW shore of Lake Nicaragua: the oldest city in the country, founded in 1523 by Córdoba; attacked frequently by pirates in the 17th century. Pop: 95 000 (2005 est)

Granados *n* Enrique, full name *Enrique Granados y Campina.* 1867–1916, Spanish composer, noted for the *Goyescas* (1911) for piano, which formed the basis for an opera of the same name

granary *n, pl* **-ries 1** a building for storing threshed grain **2** a region that produces a large amount of grain [Latin *granarium*]

Granary *adj trademark* (of bread or flour) containing malted wheat grain

Gran Canaria *n* an island in the Atlantic, in the Canary Islands: part of the Spanish province of Las Palmas. Capital: Las Palmas. Pop: 771 333 (2002 est). Area: 1533 sq km (592 sq miles). English name: **Grand Canary**

Gran Chaco *n* a plain of S central South America, between the Andes and the Paraguay River in SE Bolivia, E Paraguay, and N Argentina: huge swamps and scrub forest Area: about 780 000 sq km (300 000 sq miles). Often shortened to: **Chaco**

grand *adj* **1** large or impressive in size or appearance; magnificent: *the grand hall* **2** ambitious or important: *grand themes* **3** dignified or haughty **4** *informal* excellent or wonderful **5** comprehensive or complete: *the grand total* ▷ *n* **6** (*pl* **grand**) *slang* a thousand pounds or dollars **7** short for **grand piano** [Latin *grandis*] ▶ **grandly** *adv*

grandad, granddad *or US* **granddaddy** *n, pl* **-dads** *or* **-daddies** *informal* a grandfather

Grand Bahama *n* an island in the Atlantic, in the W Bahamas. Pop: 46 994 (2000). Area: 1114 sq km (430 sq miles)

Grand Banks *pl n* a part of the continental shelf in the Atlantic, extending for about 560 km (350 miles) off the SE coast of Newfoundland: meeting place of the cold Labrador Current and the warm Gulf Stream, producing frequent fogs and formerly rich fishing grounds

Grand Canal *n* **1** a canal in E China, extending north from Hangzhou to Tianjin: the longest canal in China, now partly silted up; central section, linking the Yangtze and Yellow Rivers, finished in 486 BC; north section finished by Kublai Khan between 1282 and 1292. Length: about 1600 km (1000 miles). Chinese name: **Da Yunhe 2** a canal in Venice, forming the main water thoroughfare: noted for its bridges, the Rialto, and the fine palaces along its banks

Grand Canary *n* the English name for **Gran Canaria**

Grand Canyon *n* a gorge of the Colorado River in N Arizona, extending from its junction with the Little Colorado River to Lake Mead; cut by vertical river erosion through the multicoloured strata of a high plateau; partly contained in the **Grand Canyon National Park,**

covering 2610 sq km (1008 sq miles). Length: 451 km (280 miles). Width: 6 km (4 miles) to 29 km (18 miles). Greatest depth: over 1.5 km (1 mile)

grandchild *n, pl* **-children** a son or daughter of one's son or daughter

Grand Coulee *n* a canyon in central Washington State, over 120 m (400 ft) deep, at the N end of which is situated the **Grand Coulee Dam**, on the Columbia River. Height of dam: 168 m (550 ft). Length of dam: 1310 m (4300 ft)

granddad *or US* **granddaddy** *n informal* See **grandad**

granddaughter *n* a daughter of one's son or daughter

grand duke *n* a prince or nobleman who rules a territory, state, or principality ▶ **grand duchess** *fem n* ▶ **grand duchy** *n*

grande dame (grond **dam**) *n* a woman regarded as the most prominent or respected member of her profession or group: *the grande dame of international fashion* [French]

grandee *n* **1** a high-ranking Spanish nobleman **2** a person who has a high rank or position: *the Party's grandees* [Spanish *grande*]

Grande-Terre *n* a French island in the Caribbean, in the Lesser Antilles: one of the two main islands which constitute Guadeloupe. Chief town: Pointe-à-Pitre

grandeur *n* **1** personal greatness, dignity, or nobility: *delusions of grandeur* **2** magnificence or splendour: *cathedral-like grandeur*

Grand Falls *pl n* the former name (until 1965) of **Churchill Falls**

grandfather *n* the father of one's father or mother

grandfather clock *n* an old-fashioned clock in a tall wooden case that stands on the floor

grandiloquent *adj* using pompous or unnecessarily complicated language [Latin *grandiloquus*] ▶ **grandiloquence** *n*

grandiose *adj* impressive, or meant to impress: *grandiose plans for constructing a new stadium* [French]

grand jury *n law, chiefly US* a jury that investigates accusations of crime to decide whether the evidence is adequate to bring a prosecution

grandma *n informal* a grandmother. Also (old-fashioned): **grandmama**

grand mal *n* a form of epilepsy in which there is loss of consciousness and violent convulsions [French: great illness]

Grand Manan *n* a Canadian island, off the SW coast of New Brunswick: separated from the coast of Maine by the **Grand Manan Channel**. Area: 147 sq km (57 sq miles)

grandmaster *n* a person who is exceptionally good at a particular activity or skill, esp. chess

grandmother *n* the mother of one's father or mother

Grand National *n* an annual steeplechase for horses, run at Aintree, Liverpool

grandnephew *n* same as **great-nephew**

grandniece *n* same as **great-niece**

grand opera *n* an opera that has a serious plot and no spoken dialogue

grandpa *n informal* a grandfather. Also (old-fashioned): **grandpapa**

grandparent *n* the father or mother of one's father or mother

grand piano *n* a large piano in which the strings are arranged horizontally

Grand Pré *n* a village in SE Canada, in W Nova Scotia: setting of Longfellow's *Evangeline*

Grand Prix (gron **pree**) *n* **1** an international formula motor race **2** a very important international competitive event in other sports, such as athletics [French: great prize]

Grand Rapids *n* (*functioning as sing*) a city in SW Michigan: electronics, car parts. Pop: 195 601 (2003 est)

grandsire *n old-fashioned* a grandfather

grand slam *n* **1** the achievement of winning all the games or major tournaments in a sport in one season **2** See **slam²**

g

grandson *n* a son of one's son or daughter

grandstand *n* the main block of seats giving the best view at a sports ground

grand tour *n* **1** (formerly) an extended tour of continental Europe **2** *informal* a tour of inspection: *a grand tour of the house*

Grand Union Canal *n* a canal in S England linking London and the Midlands: opened in 1801

grange *n Brit* a farmhouse or country house with its farm buildings [Anglo-French *graunge*]

Grangemouth *n* a port in Scotland, in Falkirk council area: now Scotland's second port, with oil refineries, shipyards, and chemical industries. Pop: 17 771 (2001)

Granicus *n* an ancient river in NW Asia Minor where Alexander the Great won his first major battle against the Persians (334 BC)

granite (gran-nit) *n* a very hard rock consisting of quartz and feldspars that is widely used for building [Italian *granito* grained]

granivorous *adj* (of an animal) grain-eating [Latin *granum* grain + *vorare* to swallow]

granny *or* **grannie** *n*, *pl* -**nies** *informal* a grandmother

granny flat *n* a flat in or joined on to a house, suitable for an elderly relative to live in

granny knot *n* a reef knot with the ends crossed the wrong way, making it liable to slip or jam

Gran Paradiso *n* a mountain in NW Italy, in NW Piedmont: the highest peak of the Graian Alps. Height: 4061 m (13 323 ft)

grant *vb* **1** to give (a sum of money or a right) formally: *to grant a 38% pay rise*; *only the President can grant a pardon* **2** to consent to perform or fulfil: *granting the men's request for sanctuary* **3** to admit that (something) is true: *I grant that her claims must be true* **4 take for granted a** to accept that something is true without requiring proof **b** to take advantage of (someone or something) without showing appreciation ▷ *n* **5** a sum of money provided by a government or public fund to a person or organization for a specific purpose: *student grants* [Old French *graunter*]

Grant *n* **1** Cary, real name *Alexander Archibald Leach*. 1904–86, US film actor, born in England. His many films include *Bringing up Baby* (1938), *The Philadelphia Story* (1940), *Arsenic and Old Lace* (1944), and *Mr Blandings Builds his Dream House* (1948) **2** Duncan (James Corrowr). 1885–1978, British painter and designer **3** Ulysses S(impson), real name *Hiram Ulysses Grant*. 1822–85, 18th president of the US (1869–77); commander in chief of Union forces in the American Civil War (1864–65)

Granta *n* the original name, still in use locally, for the River Cam

Granth (grunt) *n* the sacred scripture of the Sikhs [Hindi]

Grantham *n* a town in E England, in Lincolnshire: birthplace of Sir Isaac Newton and Margaret Thatcher. Pop: 34 592 (2001)

grant-maintained school *n Brit* a school funded directly by central government

granular *adj* of, like, or containing granules: *granular materials such as powders*

granulated *adj* (of sugar) in the form of coarse grains

granule *n* a small grain of something: *gravy granules* [Late Latin *granulum* a small grain]

Granville *n* **1** 1st Earl, title of *John Carteret*. 1690–1763, British statesman: secretary of state (1742–44); a leading opponent of Walpole **2** 2nd Earl, title of *Granville George Leveson-Gower*. 1815–91, British Liberal politician: Gladstone's foreign secretary (1870–74; 1880–85) and a supporter of Irish Home Rule

Granville-Barker *n* Harley. 1877–1946, English dramatist, theatre director, and critic, noted particularly for his *Prefaces to Shakespeare* (1927–47)

grape *n* a small round sweet juicy fruit with a purple or green skin, which can be eaten raw, dried to make raisins, currants, or sultanas, or used to make wine [Old French *grape* bunch of grapes]

grapefruit *n*, *pl* -**fruit** *or* -**fruits** a large round yellow juicy citrus fruit with a slightly bitter taste

grapeshot *n* ammunition for cannons consisting of a cluster of iron balls that scatter after firing

grapevine *n* **1** a vine grown for its grapes **2** *informal* an unofficial means of passing on information from person to person: *he'd doubtless heard rumours on the grapevine*

graph *n* a diagram showing the relation between certain sets of numbers or quantities by means of a series of dots or lines plotted with reference to a set of axes [short for *graphic formula*]

-graph *combining form* **1** an instrument that writes or records: *tachograph* **2** a writing or record: *autograph* [Greek *graphein* to write] ▷ **-graphic** *or* **-graphical** *combining form* ▷ **-graphically** *combining form*

graphic *adj* **1** vividly described: *a graphic account of her three days in captivity* **2** of the graphic arts: *graphic design* **3** Also: **graphical** *maths* of or using a graph: *a graphic presentation* [Greek *graphikos*] ▷ **graphically** *adv*

graphic arts *pl n* the visual arts based on drawing or the use of line

graphics *n* ▷ *pl n* **1** (*functioning as sing*) the art of drawing in accordance with mathematical rules **2** the illustrations in a magazine or book, or in a television or film production **3** *computers* information displayed in the form of diagrams or graphs

graphite *n* a soft black form of carbon used in pencils, as a lubricant, and in some nuclear reactors [German *Graphit*]

graphology *n* the study of handwriting, usually to analyse the writer's character ▷ **graphologist** *n*

graph paper *n* paper printed with a design of small squares for drawing graphs or diagrams on

-graphy *combining form* **1** indicating a form of writing or representing things: *calligraphy*; *photography* **2** indicating an art or descriptive science: *choreography*; *topography* [Greek *graphein* to write]

grapnel *n* a device with several hooks at one end, which is used to grasp or secure an object, esp. in sailing [Old French *grapin* a little hook]

Grappelli *or* **Grappelly** *n* Stéphane 1908–97, French jazz violinist: with Django Reinhardt, he led the Quintet of the Hot Club of France between 1934 and 1939

grapple *vb* -**pling**, -**pled** **grapple with a** to try to cope with: *a difficult concept to grapple with* **b** to come to grips with (someone) in hand-to-hand combat [Old French *grappelle* a little hook]

grappling iron *n* same as **grapnel**

Grasmere *n* a village in NW England, in Cumbria at the head of **Lake Grasmere**: home of William Wordsworth and of Thomas de Quincey

grasp *vb* **1** to grip firmly **2** to understand: *his failure to grasp the gravity of the crisis* ▷ *n* **3** a very firm grip **4** understanding or comprehension: *a good grasp of detail* **5** within someone's grasp almost certain to be accomplished or won: *he now has this prize within his grasp* [Low German *grapsen*]

grasping *adj* greedy for money

grass *n* **1** a very common green plant with jointed stems and long narrow leaves, eaten by animals such as sheep and cows, and used for lawns and sports fields **2** a particular kind of grass, such as bamboo **3** a lawn **4** *slang* marijuana **5** *Brit and Austral slang* a person who informs, usually on criminals ▷ *vb* **6 grass on** *or* up *Brit slang* to inform on (someone) to the police or some other authority **7 grass over** to cover with grass [Old English *græs*] ▷ **grassy** *adj*

Grass *n* Günter (Wilhelm). 1927–2015, German novelist, dramatist, and poet. His novels include *The Tin Drum* (1959), *Dog Years* (1963), *The Rat* (1986), *Crabwalk* (2002), and *Peeling the Onion* (2007). Nobel prize for literature 1999

grass hockey *n* (in W Canada) field hockey, as contrasted with ice hockey

grasshopper _n_ an insect with long hind legs which it uses for leaping

grassland _n_ **1** land covered with grass **2** pasture land

grass roots _pl n_ **1** ordinary members of a group or organization, as distinct from its leaders ▷ _adj_ **grassroots 2** of the ordinary members of a group or organization: _the focus of a virulent grassroots campaign_

grass snake _n_ a harmless snake with a brownish-green body

grass tree _n_ an Australian plant with stiff grass-like leaves and small white flowers

grass widow _n_ a woman whose husband is regularly absent for a time [perhaps an allusion to a grass bed as representing an illicit relationship]

grate¹ _vb_ **grating, grated 1** to reduce to shreds by rubbing against a rough surface: _grated cheese_ **2** to produce a harsh rasping sound by scraping against an object or surface: _the clutch plates grated_ **3** grate on to annoy: _his manner always grated on me_ [Old French _grater_]

grate² _n_ **1** a framework of metal bars for holding coal or wood in a fireplace **2** same as **grating¹** [Latin _cratis_ hurdle]

grateful _adj_ feeling or showing thanks [Latin _gratus_] ▷ **gratefully** _adv_

grater _n_ a tool with a sharp surface for grating food

Gratian _n_ Latin name _Flavius Gratianus_. 359–383 AD, Roman emperor (367–383): ruled with his father Valentinian I (367–375); ruled the Western Roman Empire with his brother Valentinian II (375-83); appointed Theodosius I emperor of the Eastern Roman Empire (379)

gratify _vb_ **-fies, -fying, -fied 1** to satisfy or please (someone) **2** to yield to (a desire or whim): _all his wishes were to be gratified_ [Latin _gratus_ grateful + _facere_ to make] ▷ **gratification** _n_

grating¹ _n_ a framework of metal bars covering an opening in a wall or in the ground

grating² _adj_ **1** (of a sound) rough or unpleasant **2** annoying or irritating: _his cringing obsequiousness was grating_

gratis _adv, adj_ without payment; free: _the gifts are gratis_ [Latin]

gratitude _n_ a feeling of being grateful for gifts or favours [Latin _gratus_ grateful]

Grattan _n_ Henry. 1746–1820, Irish statesman and orator: led the movement that secured legislative independence for Ireland (1782), opposed union with England (1800), and campaigned for Catholic emancipation

gratuitous (grat-**tyoo**-it-uss) _adj_ **1** unjustified or unreasonable: _gratuitous violence_ **2** given or received without charge or obligation: _his gratuitous voluntary services_ [Latin _gratuitus_] ▷ **gratuitously** _adv_

gratuity (grat-**tyoo**-it-ee) _n, pl_ **-ties** money given for services rendered; tip

Graubünden _n_ an Alpine canton of E Switzerland: the largest of the cantons, but sparsely populated. Capital: Chur. Pop: 186 100 (2002 est). Area: 7109 sq km (2773 sq miles). Italian name: **Grigioni**. Romansch name: **Grischun**. French name: **Grisons**

grave¹ _adj_ (rhymes with **save**) **1** serious and worrying: _grave concern_ **2** serious and solemn in appearance or behaviour: _the man looked grave and respectful_ **3** (rhymes with **halve**) denoting an accent (ˋ) over a vowel in some languages, such as French, which indicates that the vowel is pronounced in a particular way ▷ _n_ (rhymes with **halve**) **4** a grave accent [Latin _gravis_] ▷ **gravely** _adv_

grave² (rhymes with **save**) _n_ **1** a place where a dead person is buried. Related adjective: **sepulchral 2** death: _people are smoking themselves to an early grave_ **3** make someone turn in his _or_ her grave to do something that would have shocked a person who is now dead [Old English _græf_]

gravel _n_ **1** a mixture of rock fragments and pebbles that

is coarser than sand **2** _pathol_ small rough stones in the kidneys or bladder ▷ _vb_ **-elling, -elled** _or US_ **-eling, -eled 3** to cover with gravel [Old French _gravele_]

gravelly _adj_ **1** covered with gravel **2** (of a voice or sound) harsh and grating

Gravenhage _n_ 's Gravenhage a Dutch name for (The) Hague

graven image _n_ _chiefly Bible_ a carved image used as an idol

Graves _n_ Robert (Ranke). 1895–1985, English poet, novelist, and critic, whose works include his World War I autobiography, _Goodbye to All That_ (1929), and the historical novels _I, Claudius_ (1934) and _Claudius the God_ (1934)

Gravesend _n_ a river port in SE England, in NW Kent on the Thames. Pop: 53 045 (2001)

gravestone _n_ a stone marking a grave

graveyard _n_ a place where dead people are buried, esp. one by a church

graveyard slot _n_ _television_ the hours from late night until early morning when relatively few people are watching television

gravid (grav-id) _adj med_ pregnant [Latin _gravis_ heavy]

gravimeter (grav-**vim**-it-er) _n_ **1** an instrument for measuring the force of gravity **2** an instrument for measuring relative density [French _gravimètre_]

gravitas (grav-vit-tass) _n_ seriousness or solemnity [Latin: weight]

gravitate _vb_ **-tating, -tated 1** gravitate towards to be attracted or influenced by: _the mathematically inclined often gravitate towards computers_ **2** _physics_ to move under the influence of gravity

gravitation _n_ _physics_ **1** the force of attraction that bodies exert on one another as a result of their mass **2** the process or result of this interaction ▷ **gravitational** _adj_

gravity _n, pl_ **-ties 1** _physics_ **a** the force that attracts bodies towards the centre of the earth, a moon, or any planet **b** same as **gravitation 2** seriousness or importance: _the gravity of the situation_ **3** seriousness or solemnity of appearance or behaviour: _his priestly gravity_ [Latin _gravitas_ weight]

gravy _n, pl_ **-vies a** the juices that come from meat during cooking **b** the sauce made by thickening and flavouring these juices [Old French _gravé_]

gravy boat _n_ a small boat-shaped dish with a spout, used for serving gravy or sauce

gravy train _n_ _slang_ a job or scheme that produces a lot of money for little effort

gray _adj, n, vb chiefly US_ grey

Gray _n_ **1** Simon (James Holiday). 1936–2008, British writer: his plays include _Butley_ (1971), _The Common Pursuit_ (1988), _Life Support_ (1997), and _Japes_ (2001) **2** Thomas. 1716–71, English poet, best known for his _Elegy written in a Country Churchyard_ (1751)

Graz _n_ an industrial city in SE Austria, capital of Styria province: the second largest city in the country. Pop: 226 244 (2001)

graze¹ _vb_ **grazing, grazed a** (of an animal) to eat (grass or other growing plants) **b** to feed (animals) on grass or other growing plants [Old English _grasian_]

graze² _vb_ **grazing, grazed 1** to break the skin of (a part of the body) by scraping **2** to brush against someone gently in passing ▷ _n_ **3** an injury on the skin caused by scraping [probably a special use of GRAZE¹]

grazier _n_ a rancher or farmer who keeps cattle or sheep on grazing land

grazing _n_ land where grass is grown for farm animals to feed upon

grease _n_ **1** soft melted animal fat **2** a thick oily substance, such as the kind put on machine parts to make them work smoothly ▷ _vb_ **greasing, greased 3** to apply grease to: _lightly grease a baking tin_ **4** grease someone's palm _slang_ to bribe someone [Latin _crassus_ thick]

g

greasepaint n theatrical make-up

greaseproof paper n any paper that is resistant to penetration by grease and oil, esp. one used for lining baking dishes or wrapping food

greasy adj **greasier, greasiest 1** covered with or containing grease **2** excessively pleasant or flattering in an insincere manner **> greasiness** n

great adj **1** large in size **2** large in number or amount: *the great majority* **3** larger than others of its kind: *the great white whale* **4** extreme or more than usual: *great difficulty* **5** of importance or consequence: *a great discovery* **6** of exceptional talents or achievements: *a great artist* **7** skilful: *he's a great storyteller; they are great at problem solving* **8** informal excellent ▷ n **9** the greats the most successful people in a particular field: *the all-time greats of golf* ▶ See also **Greats** [Old English *grēat*] **> greatly** adv **> greatness** n

great- prefix (in expressing relationship) one generation older or younger than: *great-grandmother*

great auk n an extinct large auk that could not fly

great-aunt n an aunt of one's father or mother

Great Australian Bight n a wide bay of the Indian Ocean, in S Australia, extending from Cape Pasley to the Eyre Peninsula: notorious for storms

Great Barrier Reef n a coral reef in the Coral Sea, off the NE coast of Australia, for about 2000 km (1250 miles) from the Torres Strait along the coast of Queensland; the largest coral reef in the world

Great Basin n a semiarid region of the western US, between the Wasatch and the Sierra Nevada Mountains, having no drainage to the ocean: includes Nevada, W Utah, and parts of E California, S Oregon, and Idaho. Area: about 490 000 sq km (189 000 sq miles)

Great Bear Lake n a lake in NW Canada, in the Northwest Territories: the largest freshwater lake entirely in Canada; drained by the **Great Bear River**, which flows to the Mackenzie River. Area: 31 792 sq km (12 275 sq miles)

Great Belt n a strait in Denmark, between Zealand and Funen islands, linking the Kattegat with the Baltic. Danish name: **Store Bælt**

Great Britain n England, Wales, and Scotland including those adjacent islands governed from the mainland (i.e. excluding the Isle of Man and the Channel Islands). The United Kingdom of Great Britain was formed by the Act of Union (1707), although the term Great Britain had been in use since 1603, when James VI of Scotland became James I of England (including Wales). Later unions created the United Kingdom of Great Britain and Ireland (1801) and the United Kingdom of Great Britain and Northern Ireland (1922). Pop: 57 851 100 (2003 est). Area: 229 523 sq km (88 619 sq miles). See also **United Kingdom**

great circle n maths a circular section of a sphere that has a radius equal to the sphere's radius

greatcoat n a heavy overcoat

Great Dane n a very large dog with short smooth hair

Great Dividing Range pl n a series of mountain ranges and plateaus roughly parallel to the E coast of Australia, in Queensland, New South Wales, and Victoria; the highest range is the Australian Alps, in the south

Greater adj (of a city) considered with the inclusion of the outer suburbs: *Greater London*

Greater Antilles pl n the Greater Antilles a group of islands in the Caribbean, including Cuba, Jamaica, Hispaniola, and Puerto Rico

Greater London n See London (2)

Greater Manchester n a metropolitan county of NW England, administered since 1986 by the unitary authorities of Wigan, Bolton, Bury, Rochdale, Salford, Manchester, Oldham, Trafford, Stockport, and Tameside. Area: 1286 sq km (496 sq miles)

Greater Sunda Islands pl n a group of islands in the W Malay Archipelago, forming the larger part of the Sunda Islands: consists of Borneo, Sumatra, Java, and Sulawesi

Great Glen n the Great Glen a fault valley across the whole of Scotland, extending southwest from the Moray Firth in the east to Loch Linnhe and containing Loch Ness and Loch Lochy. Also known as: **Glen More, Glen Albyn**

Great Indian Desert n another name for the **Thar Desert**

Great Lakes pl n a group of five lakes in central North America with connecting waterways: the largest group of lakes in the world: consists of Lakes Superior, Huron, Erie, and Ontario, which are divided by the border between the US and Canada and Lake Michigan, which is wholly in the US; constitutes the most important system of inland waterways in the world, discharging through the St Lawrence into the Atlantic. Total length: 3767 km (2340 miles). Area: 246 490 sq km (95 170 sq miles)

great-nephew n a son of one's nephew or niece

great-niece n a daughter of one's nephew or niece

Great Ouse n See Ouse (1)

Great Plains pl n a vast region of North America east of the Rocky Mountains, extending from the lowlands of the Mackenzie River (Canada), south to the Big Bend of the Rio Grande

Great Rift Valley n the most extensive rift in the earth's surface, extending from the Jordan valley in Syria to Mozambique; marked by a chain of steep-sided lakes, volcanoes, and escarpments

Greats pl n **1** the Honours course in classics, ancient history, and philosophy at Oxford University **2** the final examinations at the end of this course

Great Salt Lake n a shallow salt lake in NW Utah, in the Great Basin at an altitude of 1260 m (4200 ft): the area has fluctuated from less than 2500 sq km (1000 sq miles) to over 5000 sq km (2000 sq miles)

Great Sandy Desert n **1** a desert in NW Australia. Area: about 415 000 sq km (160 000 sq miles) **2** an English name for the **Rub' al Khali**

Great Slave Lake n a lake in NW Canada, in the Northwest Territories: drained by the Mackenzie River into the Arctic Ocean. Area: 28 440 sq km (10 980 sq miles)

Great Slave River n another name for the **Slave River**

Great Smoky Mountains or **Great Smokies** pl n the W part of the Appalachians, in W North Carolina and E Tennessee. Highest peak: Clingman's Dome, 2024 m (6642 ft)

Great St Bernard Pass n a pass over the W Alps, between SW central Switzerland and N Italy: noted for the hospice at the summit, founded in the 11th century. Height: 2469 m (8100 ft)

Great Stour n another name for Stour (1)

great-uncle n an uncle of one's father or mother

Great Victoria Desert n a desert in S Australia, in SE Western Australia and W South Australia. Area: 323 750 sq km (125 000 sq miles)

Great Wall of China n a defensive wall in N China, extending from W Gansu to the Gulf of Liaodong: constructed in the 3rd century BC as a defence against the Mongols; substantially rebuilt in the 15th century. Length: over 2400 km (1500 miles). Average height: 6 m (20 ft). Average width: 6 m (20 ft)

Great War n same as World War I

Great Yarmouth n a port and resort in E England, in E Norfolk. Pop: 58 032 (2001)

Great Zimbabwe n See Zimbabwe (2)

greave n a piece of armour for the shin [Old French *greve*]

Greaves n Jimmy. born 1940, English footballer and television commentator on the sport; played for a number of clubs including Tottenham Hotspur and Chelsea; scored 44 goals in 57 matches for England (1959–67)

grebe n a diving water bird [French]

Grecian (gree-shan) *adj* of ancient Greece

Greece *n* a republic in SE Europe, occupying the S part of the Balkan Peninsula and many islands in the Ionian and Aegean Seas; site of two of Europe's earliest civilizations (the Minoan and Mycenaean); in the classical era divided into many small independent city-states, the most important being Athens and Sparta; part of the Roman and Byzantine Empires; passed under Turkish rule in the late Middle Ages; became an independent kingdom in 1827; taken over by a military junta (1967–74); the monarchy was abolished in 1973; became a republic in 1975; a member of the European Union. Official language: Greek. Official religion: Eastern (Greek) Orthodox. Currency: euro. Capital: Athens. Pop: 10 772 967 (2013 est). Area: 131 944 sq km (50 944 sq miles). Modern Greek name: **Ellás**. Related adjective: **Hellenic**

greed *n* excessive desire for something, such as food or money

greedy *adj* **greedier**, **greediest** having an excessive desire for something, such as food or money: *greedy for personal possessions* [Old English *grǣdig*] ❯ **greedily** *adv*

Greek *adj* 1 of or relating to Greece or its inhabitants ▷ *n* 2 a person from Greece 3 the language of Greece

Greek cross *n* a cross with each of the four arms of the same length

Greeley *n* Horace. 1811–72, US journalist and political leader: founder (1841) and editor of the *New York Tribune*, which championed the abolition of slavery

green *adj* 1 of a colour between yellow and blue; of the colour of grass 2 covered with grass, plants, or trees: *green fields* 3 of or concerned with conservation and improvement of the environment: used in a political context: *green issues* 4 (of fruit) fresh, raw, or unripe 5 pale and sick-looking 6 inexperienced or gullible 7 **green with envy** very envious ▷ *n* 8 a colour between yellow and blue 9 anything green, such as green clothing or green ink: *printed in green* 10 a small area of grassy land: *the village green* 11 an area of smooth turf kept for a special purpose: *putting greens* 12 **greens** the leaves and stems of certain plants, eaten as a vegetable: *turnip greens* 13 **Green** a person who supports environmentalist issues [Old English *grēne*] ❯ **greenish** or **greeny** *adj* ❯ **greenness** *n*

Green *n* 1 Henry, real name *Henry Vincent Yorke*. 1905–73, British novelist: author of *Living* (1929), *Loving* (1945), and *Back* (1946) 2 John Richard. 1837–83, British historian; author of *A Short History of the English People* (1874) 3 T(homas) H(ill). 1836–82, British idealist philosopher. His chief work, *Prolegomena to Ethics*, was unfinished at his death

Greenaway *n* 1 Kate. 1846–1901, English painter, noted as an illustrator of children's books 2 Peter. born 1942, British film director; noted for such cerebral films as *The Draughtsman's Contract* (1982), *Prospero's Books* (1990), and *Eight and a Half Women* (1999)

green beans *pl n* long narrow green beans that are cooked and eaten as a vegetable

green belt *n* a protected zone of parkland or open country surrounding a town or city

green card *n* an official permit allowing the holder permanent residence and employment, issued to foreign nationals in the US

Green Cross Code *n* Brit a code for children giving rules on road safety

Greene *n* 1 Graham. 1904–91, English novelist and dramatist; his works include the novels *Brighton Rock* (1938), *The Power and the Glory* (1940), *The End of the Affair* (1951), and *Our Man in Havana* (1958), and the film script *The Third Man* (1949) 2 Robert. ?1558–92, English poet, dramatist, and prose writer, noted for his autobiographical tract *A Groatsworth of Wit bought with a Million of Repentance* (1592), which contains an attack on Shakespeare

greenery *n* green leaves or growing plants: *lush greenery*

green-eyed monster *n* jealousy

greenfield *adj* relating to a rural area which has not previously been built on: *greenfield factory sites*

greenfinch *n* a European finch, the male of which has olive-green feathers

green fingers *pl n* skill in growing plants

greenfly *n*, *pl* **-flies** a green aphid commonly occurring as a pest on plants

greengage *n* a green sweet variety of plum [after Sir W. Gage, botanist]

Greengrass *n* Paul. born 1955, English film director and writer; his films include *Bloody Sunday* (2002), *The Bourne Supremacy* (2004), *United 93* (2006), and *The Bourne Ultimatum* (2007)

greengrocer *n* Brit and Austral a shopkeeper who sells fruit and vegetables

Greenham Common *n* a village in West Berkshire unitary authority, Berkshire; site of a US cruise missile base, and, from 1981, a camp of women protesters against nuclear weapons; although the base had closed by 1991 a small number of women remained until 2000

greenhorn *n* an inexperienced person; novice [originally an animal with *green* (that is, young) horns]

greenhouse *n* 1 a building with glass walls and roof where plants are grown under controlled conditions ▷ *adj* 2 relating to or contributing to the greenhouse effect: *greenhouse gases such as carbon dioxide*

greenhouse effect *n* the gradual rise in temperature in the earth's atmosphere due to heat being absorbed from the sun and being trapped by gases such as carbon dioxide in the air around the earth

greenhouse gas *n* any gas that contributes to the greenhouse effect

greenkeeper *n* a person responsible for maintaining a golf course or bowling green

Greenland *n* a large island, lying mostly within the Arctic Circle off the NE coast of North America: first settled by Icelanders in 986; resettled by Danes from 1721 onwards; integral part of Denmark (1953–79); granted internal autonomy 1979; mostly covered by an icecap up to 3300 m (11 000 ft) thick, with ice-free coastal strips and coastal mountains; the population is largely Inuit, with a European minority; fishing, hunting, and mining. Capital: Nuuk (Godthåb). Pop: 57 714 (2013 est). Area: 175 600 sq km (840 000 sq miles). Danish name: **Grønland**. Greenlandic name: **Kalaallit Nunaat**

Greenlander *n* a native or inhabitant of Greenland

Greenlandic *adj* 1 of, relating to, or characteristic of Greenland, the Greenlanders, or the Inuit dialect spoken in Greenland ▷ *n* 2 the dialect of Inuktitut spoken in Greenland

Greenland Sea *n* the S part of the Arctic Ocean, off the NE coast of Greenland

green light *n* 1 a signal to go 2 permission to proceed with a project ▷ *vb* **greenlight** (**-lighting**, **-lighted**) 3 to permit (a project) to proceed

Green Mountains *pl n* a mountain range in E North America, extending from Canada through Vermont into W Massachusetts: part of the Appalachian system. Highest peak: Mount Mansfield, 1338 m (4393 ft)

Greenock *n* a port in SW Scotland, in Inverclyde on the Firth of Clyde: shipbuilding and other marine industries. Pop: 45 467 (2001)

Greenough *n* George Bellas. 1778–1855, English geologist, founder of the Geological Society of London

green paper *n* a government document containing policy proposals to be discussed

green pepper *n* the green unripe fruit of the sweet pepper, eaten as a vegetable

Green River *n* a river in the western US, rising in W central Wyoming and flowing south into Utah, east through NW Colorado, re-entering Utah before joining the Colorado River. Length: 1175 km (730 miles)

g

greenroom *n* (esp. formerly) a backstage room in a theatre where performers rest or receive visitors

Greensboro *n* a city in N central North Carolina. Pop: 229 110 (2003 est)

greenstick fracture *n* a fracture in which the bone is partly bent and splinters only on the outer side of the bend

greenstone *n* NZ a type of green jade used for Māori carvings and ornaments

greensward *n* archaic or literary an area of fresh green turf

green tea *n* tea made from leaves that have been dried quickly without fermenting

greenway *n* US a corridor of protected open space that is maintained for conservation, recreation, and non-motorized transportation

Greenwich *n* a Greater London borough on the Thames: site of a Royal Naval College (now used as the National Maritime Museum), including Inigo Jones' Queen's House (1617), and of the original Royal Observatory designed by Christopher Wren (1675), accepted internationally as the prime meridian of longitude since 1884, and the basis of Greenwich Mean Time. Pop: 223 700 (2003 est). Area: 46 sq km (18 sq miles)

Greenwich Mean Time (gren-itch) *n* the local time of the 0° meridian passing through Greenwich, England: a basis for calculating times throughout most of the world. Abbreviation: **GMT**

Greenwich Village *n* a part of New York City in the lower west side of Manhattan; traditionally the home of many artists and writers

Green Zone *n* (since the invasion of Iraq by US-led forces, and the fall of Saddam Hussein in 2003) the area of central Baghdad used by the coalition and civilian authorities, subject to high security

Greer *n* Germaine. born 1939, Australian writer, academic, and feminist. Her books include *The Female Eunuch* (1970), *Sex and Destiny* (1984), and *The Whole Woman* (1998)

greet[1] *vb* **1** to address or meet with expressions of friendliness or welcome **2** to receive in a specified manner: *a direct request would be greeted coolly* **3** to be immediately noticeable to: *the scene of devastation which greeted him* [Old English *grētan*]

greet[2] *vb* Scot to weep [Old English *grætan*]

greeting *n* the act or words of welcoming on meeting

greetings *interj* an expression of friendly salutation

gregarious *adj* **1** enjoying the company of others **2** (of animals) living together in herds or in flocks [Latin *grex* flock]

Gregorian calendar *n* the revision of the calendar introduced in 1582 by Pope Gregory XIII and still widely used

Gregorian chant *n* same as **plainsong**

Gregory *n* Lady (Isabella) Augusta (Persse). 1852–1932, Irish dramatist; a founder and director of the Abbey Theatre, Dublin

Gregory I *n* Saint, known as *Gregory the Great*. ?540–604 AD, pope (590–604), who greatly influenced the medieval Church. He strengthened papal authority by centralizing administration, tightened discipline, and revised the liturgy. He appointed Saint Augustine missionary to England. Feast day: March 12 or Sept 3

Gregory VII *n* Saint, monastic name *Hildebrand*. ?1020—85, pope (1073–85), who did much to reform abuses in the Church. His assertion of papal supremacy and his prohibition (1075) of lay investiture was opposed by the Holy Roman Emperor Henry IV, whom he excommunicated (1076). He was driven into exile when Henry captured Rome (1084). Feast day: May 25

Gregory IX *n* original name *Ugolino of Segni*. ?1148–1241, pope (1227–41). He excommunicated and waged war against Emperor Frederick II

Gregory XIII *n* 1502–85, pope (1572–85). He promoted the Counter-Reformation and founded seminaries. His reformed (Gregorian) calendar was issued in 1582

Gregory of Nazianzus *n* Saint. ?329–89 AD, Cappadocian theologian: bishop of Caesarea (370–79). Feast days: Jan 2, 25, and 30

Gregory of Nyssa *n* Saint. ?335–394 AD, Cappadocian theologian and brother of St Basil: bishop of Nyssa. Feast day: March 9

Gregory of Tours *n* Saint. ?538–?594 AD, Frankish bishop and historian. His *Historia Francorum* is the chief source of knowledge of 6th-century Gaul. Feast day: Nov 17

gremlin *n* an imaginary imp jokingly blamed for malfunctions in machinery [origin unknown]

Grenada *n* an island state in the Caribbean, in the Windward Islands: formerly a British colony (1783–1967); since 1974 an independent state within the Commonwealth; occupied by US troops (1983–85); mainly agricultural. Official language: English. Religion: Christian majority. Currency: East Caribbean dollar. Capital: St George's. Pop: 109 590 (2013 est). Area: 344 sq km (133 sq miles)

grenade *n* a small bomb filled with explosive or gas, thrown by hand or fired from a rifle [Spanish *granada* pomegranate]

Grenadian *adj* **1** of or relating to Grenada or its inhabitants ▷ *n* **2** a native or inhabitant of Grenada

grenadier *n* military **1** (in the British Army) a member of the senior regiment of infantry in the Household Brigade (the **Grenadier Guards**) **2** (formerly) a soldier trained to throw grenades [French]

grenadine (gren-a-**deen**) *n* a syrup made from pomegranate juice, often used as an ingredient in cocktails

Grenadines *pl n* **the Grenadines** a chain of about 600 islets in the Caribbean, part of the Windward Islands, extending for about 100 km (60 miles) between St Vincent and Grenada and divided administratively between the two states. Largest island: Carriacou

Grenfell *n* Joyce, real name Joyce Irene Phipps. 1910–79, British comedy actress and writer

Grenoble *n* a city in SE France, on the Isère River: university (1339). Pop: 156 659 (2008)

Grenville *n* **1** George. 1712–70, British statesman; prime minister (1763–65). His policy of taxing the American colonies precipitated the War of Independence **2** Kate. born 1950. Australian writer. Her novels include *Lilian's Story* (1985), *The Idea of Perfection* (2002), and *The Secret River* (2005) **3** Sir Richard. ?1541–91, English naval commander. He was fatally wounded aboard his ship, the *Revenge*, during a lone battle with a fleet of Spanish treasure ships **4** William Wyndham, Baron Grenville, son of George Grenville. 1759–1834, British statesman; prime minister (1806–07) of the coalition government known as the "ministry of all the talents"

Gresham *n* Sir Thomas. ?1519–79, English financier, who founded the Royal Exchange in London (1568)

Gretna Green *n* a village in S Scotland, in Dumfries and Galloway on the border with England: famous smithy where eloping couples were married by the blacksmith from 1754 until 1940, when such marriages became illegal. Pop: 2705 (2001)

Gretzky *n* Wayne. born 1961, Canadian ice-hockey player and coach; in his playing career (1979–99) he became the record point scorer in the National Hockey League

Greuze *n* Jean Baptiste. 1725–1805, French genre and portrait painter

Greville *n* Fulke, 1st Baron Brooke. 1554–1628, English poet, writer, politician, and diplomat; Chancellor of the Exchequer (1614–22); author of *The Life of the Renowned Sir Philip Sidney* (1652)

grevillea *n* any of various Australian evergreen trees and shrubs [after C. F. Greville, botanist]

grew *vb* the past tense of **grow**

grey *or US* **gray** *adj* **1** of a colour between black and white; of the colour of ashes **2 a** (of hair) having partly turned white **b** (of a person) having grey hair **3** dismal, dark, or gloomy: *a grey and misty morning* **4** dull or boring: *in 1948 life generally was grey* ▷ *n* **5** a colour between black and white **6** anything grey, such as grey paint or grey clothing: *available in grey or brown* **7** a grey or whitish horse [Old English *grǣg*] **> greyish** *adj* **> greyness** *n*

Grey *n* **1 Charles,** 2nd Earl Grey. 1764–1845, British statesman. As Whig prime minister (1830–34), he carried the Reform Bill of 1832 and the bill for the abolition of slavery throughout the British Empire (1833) **2 Sir Edward,** 1st Viscount Grey of Fallodon. 1862–1933, British statesman; foreign secretary (1905–16) **3 Sir George.** 1812–98, British statesman and colonial administrator; prime minister of New Zealand (1877–79) **4 Lady Jane.** 1537–54, queen of England (July 9–19, 1553); great-granddaughter of Henry VII. Her father-in-law, the Duke of Northumberland, persuaded Edward VI to alter the succession in her favour, but after ten days as queen she was imprisoned and later executed **5 Zane.** 1875–1939, US author of Westerns, including *Riders of the Purple Sage* (1912)

grey area *n* a situation or area that has no clearly defined characteristics or that falls somewhere between two categories

greyed out *adj* (of a navigation button, menu item, etc. on a computer screen) not highlighted, indicating that the function is not available

Grey Friar *n* a Franciscan friar

greyhound *n* a tall slender dog that can run very fast and is used for racing

greying *adj* becoming grey: *greying hair*

greylag *or* **greylag goose** *n* a large grey Eurasian goose [GREY + LAG, because it migrates later than other species]

grey matter *n informal* intellect or brains: *those who don't have lots of grey matter*

Grey Owl *n* Grey Owl, original name *Archibald Belaney* (1888–1938). Canadian writer and conservationist, born in England; adopted Native American identity

grey squirrel *n* a grey-furred squirrel, native to E North America but now common in Britain

Grey-Thompson *n* Tanni (Carys Davina) Baroness. born 1969, Welsh wheelchair athlete; won eleven gold medals for Britain in wheelchair racing in the Paralympic Games (1988–2004); a crossbench peer in the House of Lords since 2010

grid *n* **1** a network of crossing parallel lines on a map, plan, or graph paper for locating points **2 the grid** the national network of cables or pipes by which electricity, gas, or water is distributed **3** *electronics* an electrode that controls the flow of electrons between the cathode and anode of a valve [from *gridiron*]

griddle *n* a thick round iron plate placed on top of a cooker and used to cook food [Old French *gridil*]

gridiron *n* **1** a utensil of parallel metal bars, used to grill food **2 a** the field of play in American football **b** *informal* same as American football [Middle English *gredire*]

gridlock *n* **1** obstruction of traffic caused by queues of vehicles forming across junctions and so causing queues in intersecting streets **2** a point in a dispute at which no agreement can be reached: *political gridlock* ▷ *vb* **3** (of traffic) to obstruct (an area)

grid reference *n* a series of numbers indicating the location of a point on a map

grief *n* **1** deep or intense sorrow **2** *informal* trouble or annoyance: *people were giving me grief for leaving ten minutes early* **3 come to grief** to have an unfortunate or unsuccessful end or outcome

grief-stricken *adj* deeply affected by sorrow

Grieg *n* Edvard (Hagerup). 1843–1907, Norwegian composer. His works, often inspired by Norwegian folk music, include the incidental music for *Peer Gynt* (1876), a piano concerto, and many songs

Grierson *n* John. 1898–1972, Scottish film director. He coined the noun *documentary*, of which genre his *Industrial Britain* (1931) and *Song of Ceylon* (1934) are notable examples

grievance *n* **1** a real or imaginary cause for complaint **2** a feeling of resentment at having been unfairly treated

grieve *vb* **grieving, grieved** to feel or cause to feel great sorrow or distress [Old French *grever*] **> grieved** *adj* **> grieving** *adj*

grievous *adj* **1** very severe or painful: *grievous injuries* **2** very serious or worrying: *a grievous loss* **> grievously** *adv*

grievous bodily harm *n criminal law* serious injury caused by one person to another

griffin, griffon *or* **gryphon** *n* a mythical winged monster with an eagle's head and a lion's body [Old French *grifon*]

Griffith *n* **1 Arthur.** 1872–1922, Irish journalist and nationalist: founder of Sinn Féin (1905); president of the Free State assembly (1922) **2 D(avid Lewelyn) W(ark).** 1875–1948, US film director and producer. He introduced several cinematic techniques, including the flashback and the fade-out, in his masterpiece *The Birth of a Nation* (1915)

Griffith-Joyner *n* Florence, known as *Flojo*. 1959–98, US sprinter, winner of two gold medals at the 1988 Olympic Games

griffon *n* **1** a large vulture with pale feathers and black wings **2** a small wire-haired breed of dog [French]

Grigioni *n* the Italian name for **Graubünden**

grill *vb* **1** to cook by direct heat under a grill or over a hot fire **2** *informal* to subject to relentless questioning: *the jury pool was grilled for signs of prejudice* ▷ *n* **3** a device on a cooker that radiates heat downwards for grilling food **4** a gridiron for cooking food **5** a dish of grilled food **6** See **grillroom** [Latin *craticula* fine wickerwork] **> grilled** *adj* **> grilling** *n*

grille *or* **grill** *n* a metal or wooden grating, used as a screen or partition [Latin *craticula* fine hurdlework]

Grillparzer *n* Franz. 1791–1872, Austrian dramatist and poet, noted for his historical and classical tragedies, which include *Sappho* (1818), the trilogy *The Golden Fleece* (1819–22), and *The Jewess of Toledo* (1872)

grillroom *n* a restaurant specializing in grilled foods

grilse (grillss) *n, pl* **grilses** *or* **grilse** a salmon on its first return from the sea to fresh water [origin unknown]

grim *adj* **grimmer, grimmest** **1** unfavourable and worrying: *grim figures on unemployment* **2** harsh and unpleasant: *grim conditions in the detention centres* **3** stern or resolute: *a grim determination to fight on* **4** informal unpleasant or disagreeable [Old English *grimm*] **> grimly** *adv* **> grimness** *n*

grimace *n* **1** an ugly or distorted facial expression of disgust, pain, or displeasure ▷ *vb* **-macing, -maced** **2** to make a grimace [French]

Grimaldi *n* Joseph. 1779–1837, English actor, noted as a clown in pantomime

grime *n* **1** ingrained dirt ▷ *vb* **griming, grimed** **2** to make very dirty: *sweat-grimed faces* [Middle Dutch] **> grimy** *adj*

Grimm *n* Jakob Ludwig Karl, 1785–1863, and his brother, Wilhelm Karl, 1786–1859, German philologists and folklorists, who collaborated on *Grimm's Fairy Tales* (1812–22) and began a German dictionary. Jakob is noted also for his philological work *Deutsche Grammatik* (1819–37)

Grimsby *n* a port in E England, in North East Lincolnshire unitary authority, Lincolnshire, formerly important for fishing. Pop: 87 574 (2001)

grin *vb* **grinning, grinned** **1** to smile broadly, showing one's teeth **2 grin and bear it** *informal* to suffer hardship without complaint ▷ *n* **3** a broad smile [Old English *grennian*] **> grinning** *adj*

grind *vb* **grinding, ground** **1** to reduce to small particles by pounding or rubbing: *grinding coffee* **2** to smooth, sharpen, or polish by friction **3** (of two objects) to scrape together with a harsh rasping sound **4 an axe to grind**

See **axe** (2) **5 grind one's teeth** to rub one's upper and lower teeth against each other, as if chewing **6 grind to a halt** to come to an end or a standstill: *without enzymes life would grind to a halt* ▷ *n* **7** *informal* hard or tedious work: *the grind of everyday life* ▶ See also **grind down** [Old English *grindan*]

grind down *vb* to treat harshly so as to suppress resistance: *to grind down the opposition*

Grindelwald *n* a valley and resort in central Switzerland, in the Bernese Oberland: mountaineering centre, with the Wetterhorn and the Eiger nearby

grinder *n* a device for grinding substances: *an electric coffee grinder*

grindstone *n* **1** a revolving stone disc used for sharpening, grinding, or polishing things **2 keep one's nose to the grindstone** to work hard and steadily

grip *n* **1** a very tight hold: *he felt a grip at his throat* **2** the style or manner of holding something, such as a golf club or tennis racket **3** power or control over a situation, person, or activity: *rebel forces tighten their grip around the capital* **4** a travelling bag or holdall **5** a small bent clasp used to fasten the hair **6** a handle **7** a person who manoeuvres the cameras in a film or television studio **8 get** *or* **come to grips with** to face up to and deal with (a problem or subject) ▷ *vb* **gripping, gripped 9** to take a tight hold of **10** to affect strongly: *sudden panic gripped her* **11** to hold the interest or attention of: *gripped by the intensity of the film; the story gripped him* [Old English *gripe* grasp]

gripe *vb* **griping, griped 1** *informal* to complain persistently **2** to cause sudden intense pain in the bowels ▷ *n* **3** *informal* a complaint **4 the gripes** a sudden intense pain in the bowels [Old English *grīpan*]

grippe *n* a former name for **influenza** [French]

gripping *adj* very interesting and exciting: *a gripping story*

Griqualand East *n* an area of central South Africa: settled in 1861 by Griquas led by Adam Kok III; annexed to the Cape Colony in 1879; part of the Transkei, 1903–93. Chief town: Kokstad. Area: 17 100 sq km (6602 sq miles)

Griqualand West *n* an area of N South Africa, north of the Orange river: settled after 1803 by the Griquas; annexed by the British in 1871 following a dispute with the Orange Free State; became part of the Cape Colony in 1880. Chief town: Kimberley. Area: 39 360 sq km (15 197 sq miles)

Gris *n* Juan. 1887–1927, Spanish cubist painter, resident in France from 1906

Grisham *n* John. born 1955, US novelist and lawyer; his legal thrillers, many of which have been filmed, include *A Time to Kill* (1989), *The Pelican Brief* (1992), and *The Summons* (2002)

Grishun *n* the Romansch name for **Graubünden**

grisly *adj* **-lier, -liest** causing horror or dread: *grisly murders* [Old English *grislic*]

> **USAGE** See at **grizzly**.

Grisons *n* the French name for **Graubünden**

grist *n* **1** grain that is to be or that has been ground **2 grist to the mill** anything that can be turned to profit or advantage [Old English *grīst*]

gristle *n* tough stringy animal tissue found in meat [Old English] ▷ **gristly** *adj*

grit *n* **1** small hard particles of sand, earth, or stone **2** courage and determination ▷ *vb* **gritting, gritted 3** to cover (an icy road) with grit **4 grit one's teeth a** to rub one's upper and lower teeth against each other, as if chewing **b** to decide to carry on in a difficult situation: *he urged the Cabinet to grit its teeth and continue cutting public spending* [Old English *grēot*]

grits *pl n* coarsely ground grain, a popular dish in the Southern US [Old English *grytt*]

gritter *n* a vehicle that spreads grit on the roads in icy weather

gritty *adj* **-tier, -tiest 1** courageous and tough **2** covered with grit

grizzle *vb* **-zling, -zled** *Brit, Austral and NZ informal* to whine or complain [Germanic]

grizzled *adj* **1** (of hair) streaked or mixed with grey **2** (of a person) having grey hair

grizzly *n, pl* **-zlies** a large fierce greyish-brown bear of N America. In full: **grizzly bear**

> **USAGE** Grizzly is sometimes wrongly used where grisly is meant: *a grisly (not grizzly) murder.*

groan *n* **1** a long deep cry of pain, grief, or disapproval **2** *informal* a grumble or complaint ▷ *vb* **3** to give a long deep cry of pain, grief, or disapproval **4** *informal* to complain or grumble **5 groan under** to be weighed down by: *chemists' shelves groan under the weight of slimming aids* [Old English *grānian*] ▷ **groaning** *adj, n*

groat *n* a former British coin worth four old pennies [Middle Dutch *groot*]

groats *pl n* the crushed grain of various cereals [Old English *grot* particle]

grocer *n* a shopkeeper who sells food and other household supplies [Old French *grossier*]

groceries *pl n* food and other household supplies

grocery *n, pl* **-ceries** the business or premises of a grocer

Grodno *n* a city in W Belarus on the Neman River: part of Poland (1921–39); an industrial centre. Pop: 318 000 (2005 est)

Groening *n* Matt(hew). born 1954, US cartoonist and writer, creator and producer of *The Simpsons* television series from 1989

grog *n* **1** an alcoholic drink, usually rum, diluted with water **2** *Brit, Austral and NZ informal* any alcoholic drink [after Old *Grog*, nickname of Edward Vernon, British admiral, who in 1740 issued naval rum diluted with water]

groggy *adj* **-gier, -giest** *informal* faint, weak, or dizzy

groin *n* **1** the part of the body where the abdomen joins the legs **2** *archit* a curved edge formed where two intersecting vaults meet [origin unknown]

grommet *n* **1** a rubber, plastic, or metal ring or eyelet **2** *med* a small tube inserted into the eardrum to drain fluid from the middle ear [obsolete French *gourmer* bridle]

Gromyko *n* Andrei Andreyevich. 1909–89, Soviet statesman and diplomat; foreign minister (1957–85); president (1985–88)

Groningen *n* **1** a province in the NE Netherlands: mainly agricultural. Capital: Groningen. Pop: 573 000 (2003 est). Area: 2336 sq km (902 sq miles) **2** a city in the NE Netherlands, capital of Groningen province. Pop: 177 000 (2003 est)

Grønland *n* the Danish name for **Greenland**

groom *n* **1** a person employed to clean and look after horses **2** short for **bridegroom** ▷ *vb* **3** to clean and smarten (a horse or other animal) **4** to keep (oneself or one's appearance) clean and tidy: *carefully groomed hair* **5** to train (someone) for a particular task or occupation: *groomed for future leadership* [Middle English *grom* manservant] ▷ **grooming** *n*

groove *n* **1** a long narrow furrow cut into a surface **2** the spiral channel in a gramophone record [obsolete Dutch *groeve*] ▷ **grooved** *adj*

groovy *adj* **groovier, grooviest** *slang, often humorous* attractive, fashionable, or exciting

grope *vb* **groping, groped 1** to feel about uncertainly for something **2** to find (one's way) by groping **3** to search uncertainly for a solution or expression: *the new democracies are groping for stability* **4** *slang* to fondle (someone) in a rough sexual way ▷ *n* **5** an instance of groping [Old English *grāpian*]

Gropius *n* Walter. 1883–1969, US architect, designer, and teacher, born in Germany. He founded (1919) and directed (1919–28) the Bauhaus in Germany. His influence stemmed from his adaptation of architecture to modern social needs and his pioneering use of industrial materials, such as concrete and steel. His buildings include the Fagus factory at Alfeld (1911) and the Bauhaus at Dessau (1926)

Gros n Baron Antoine Jean. 1771–1835, French painter, noted for his battle scenes

gros point (groh point) n **1** a cross-stitch in embroidery **2** work done in this stitch [Old French: large point]

gross adj **1** outrageously wrong: *gross violations of human rights* **2** very coarse or vulgar: *gross bad taste* **3** slang disgusting or repulsive: *I think beards are gross* **4** repulsively fat **5** with no deductions for tax or the weight of the container; total: *gross income; a gross weight of 20 000 lbs* ▷ n **6** (pl **gross**) twelve dozen (144) **7** the entire amount or weight ▷ vb **8** to earn as total revenue, before deductions [Old French *gros* large] **> grossly** adv

gross domestic product n the total value of all goods and services produced domestically by a nation during a year

Grosseteste n Robert. ?1175–1253, English prelate and scholar; bishop of Lincoln (1235–53). He attacked ecclesiastical abuses and wrote commentaries on Aristotle and treatises on theology, philosophy, and science

gross national product n the total value of all final goods and services produced annually by a nation: equivalent to gross domestic product plus net investment income from abroad

gross profit n accounting the difference between total revenue from sales and the total cost of purchases or materials

Grosswardein n the German name for **Oradea**

Grosz n George. 1893–1959, German painter, in the US from 1932, whose works satirized German militarism and bourgeois society

Grote n George. 1794–1871, English historian, noted particularly for his *History of Greece* (1846–56)

grotesque (groh-tesk) adj **1** strangely distorted or bizarre: *a grotesque and pervasive personality cult* **2** ugly or repulsive ▷ n **3** a grotesque person or thing **4** an artistic style in which parts of human, animal, and plant forms are distorted and mixed, or a work of art in this style [Old Italian *(pittura) grottesca* cave (painting)] **> grotesquely** adv

Grotius n Hugo, original name *Huig de Groot*. 1583–1645, Dutch jurist and statesman, whose *De Jure Belli ac Pacis* (1625) is regarded as the foundation of modern international law **> 'Grotian** adj **> 'Grotianism** n

grotto n, pl **-toes** or **-tos** a small picturesque cave [Old Italian *grotta*]

grotty adj **-tier, -tiest** Brit and NZ slang **1** nasty or unattractive **2** in bad condition [from *grotesque*]

grouch informal vb **1** to complain or grumble ▷ n **2** a person who is always complaining **3** a persistent complaint [Old French *grouchier*]

grouchy adj **grouchier, grouchiest** bad-tempered

ground[1] n **1** the land surface **2** earth or soil **3** an area used for a particular purpose: *a cricket ground* **4** a matter for consideration or discussion: *there is no need to cover the same ground* **5** an advantage in an argument or competition: *neither side seems willing to give ground in this trial of strength* **6** the background colour of a painting **7** US and Canad an electrical earth **8** grounds **a** the land around a building **b** reason or justification: *the hostages should be freed on humanitarian grounds* **c** sediment or dregs: *coffee grounds* **9** break new ground to do something that has not been done before **10** common ground an agreed basis for identifying issues in an argument **11** get something off the ground to get something started: *to get the peace conference off the ground* **12** into the ground to exhaustion or excess: *he was running himself into the ground* **13** suit someone down to the ground Brit informal to be totally suitable or

appropriate for someone ▷ adj **14** on the ground: *ground troops* ▷ vb **15** to confine (an aircraft or pilot) to the ground **16** nautical to move (a ship) onto the bottom of shallow water, so that it cannot move **17** to instruct in the basics of a subject: *the student who is not grounded in the elements cannot understand the advanced teaching* **18** to provide a basis for; establish: *a scientifically grounded documentation* **19** to forbid (a child) to go out and enjoy himself or herself as a punishment **20** US and Canad to connect (a circuit or electrical device) to an earth [Old English *grund*]

ground[2] vb **1** the past of **grind** ▷ adj **2** reduced to fine particles by grinding: *ground glass*

ground bass n music a short melodic bass line that is repeated over and over again

ground beef n finely chopped beef, sometimes used to make hamburgers

ground-breaking adj innovative

ground control n the people and equipment on the ground that monitor the progress of aircraft or spacecraft

ground cover n dense low plants that spread over the surface of the ground

ground floor n the floor of a building that is level, or almost level, with the ground

grounding n a foundation, esp. the basic general knowledge of a subject

groundless adj without reason or justification: *the scare turned out to be groundless*

groundnut n Brit a peanut

groundsel (grounce-el) n a yellow-flowered weed [Old English *grundeswelge*]

groundsheet n a waterproof sheet placed on the ground in a tent to keep out damp

groundsman n, pl **-men** a person employed to maintain a sports ground or park

groundswell n a rapidly developing general feeling or opinion

ground water n water that has seeped through from the surface and is held underground

groundwork n preliminary work as a foundation or basis

ground zero n **1** a point on the surface of land or water at or directly above or below the centre of a nuclear explosion **2** a scene of great devastation **3** (sometimes caps) the name given to the devastated site of the collapsed World Trade Center towers in New York after September 11 2001

group n **1** a number of people or things considered as a unit **2** a small band of players or singers, esp. of popular music **3** an association of business firms that have the same owner **4** chem two or more atoms that are bound together in a molecule and behave as a single unit: *a methyl group* $-CH_3$ **5** chem a vertical column of elements in the periodic table that all have similar properties: *the halogen group* ▷ vb **6** to put into or form into a group [French *groupe*]

group captain n a middle-ranking officer in some air forces

groupie n slang an ardent fan of a celebrity or of a sport or activity: *a polo groupie*

grouping n a set of people or organizations who act or work together to achieve a shared aim: *a pro-democracy grouping within China*

group therapy n psychol the treatment of people by bringing them together to share their problems in group discussion

grouse[1] n, pl **grouse** **1** a game bird with a stocky body and feathered legs and feet **2** the flesh of this bird used for food [origin unknown]

grouse[2] vb **grousing, groused** **1** to complain or grumble ▷ n **2** a persistent complaint [origin unknown]

grouse[3] adj Austral and NZ slang fine or excellent [origin unknown]

grout _n_ **1** a thin mortar for filling joints between tiles or masonry ▷ _vb_ **2** to fill with grout [Old English _grūt_]

grove _n_ a small wood or group of trees: _orange groves_ [Old English _grāf_]

grovel (grov-el) _vb_ **-elling, -elled** _or US_ **-eling, -eled** **1** to behave excessively humbly towards someone, esp. a superior, in an attempt to win his or her favour **2** to crawl on the floor, often in search of something: _grovelling on the floor for missing cards_ [Middle English _on grufe_ on the face] **> grovelling** _or US_ **groveling** _adj, n_

Groves _n_ Sir Charles. 1915–92, English orchestral conductor

grow _vb_ **growing, grew, grown** **1** (of a person or animal) to increase in size and develop physically **2** (of a plant) to exist and increase in size: _an ancient meadow where wild flowers grow_ **3** to produce (a plant) by planting seeds, bulbs, or cuttings, and looking after it: _many farmers have expressed a wish to grow more cotton_ **4** to let (one's hair or nails) develop: _to grow a beard_ **5** to increase in size or degree: _the gulf between rich and poor is growing_ **6** to originate or develop: _Melbourne grew from a sheep-farming outstation and occasional port to a city_ **7** to become increasingly as specified: _as the night wore on the audience grew more intolerant_ ▶ See also **grow on, grow out of**, etc. [Old English _grōwan_] **> grower** _n_ **> growing** _adj_

growing pains _pl n_ **1** pains in muscles or joints sometimes experienced by growing children **2** difficulties experienced in the early stages of a new enterprise

growl _vb_ **1** (of a dog or other animal) to make a low rumbling sound, usually in anger **2** to say in a gruff or angry manner: _'You're late,' he growled_ **3** to make a deep rumbling sound: _his stomach growled_ ▷ _n_ **4** the act or sound of growling [Old French _grouller_ to grumble]

grown _adj_ developed or advanced: _fully grown; a grown man_

grown-up _adj_ **1** having reached maturity; adult **2** of or suitable for an adult ▷ _n_ **3** an adult

grow on _vb_ to become progressively more acceptable or pleasant to: _I didn't like that programme at first but it has grown on me_

grow-op _n Canad_ an illegal scheme to grow marijuana plants

grow out of _vb_ to become too big or mature for: _I used to be into the fifties scene but grew out of it_

growth _n_ **1** the process of growing **2** an increase in size, number, or significance: _the growth of drug trafficking_ **3** something grown or growing: _a thick growth of ivy_ **4** any abnormal tissue, such as a tumour ▷ _adj_ **5** of or relating to growth: _growth hormone_

grow up _vb_ to reach maturity; become adult

groyne _n_ a wall or breakwater built out from a shore to control erosion [Old French _groign_ snout]

Grozny _n_ a city in S Russia, capital of the Chechen Republic: a major oil centre: it was badly damaged during fighting between separatists and Russian troops (1994–95, 1999–2000). Pop: 199 000 (2005 est)

grub _n_ **1** _slang_ food **2** the thick legless larva of certain insects, such as beetles ▷ _vb_ **grubbing, grubbed** **3** to search carefully for something by digging or by moving things about **4 grub up** to dig (roots or plants) out of the ground [Germanic]

grubby _adj_ **-bier, -biest** **1** rather dirty **2** unsavoury or morally unacceptable: _grubby activities_ **> grubbiness** _n_

grudge _n_ **1** a persistent feeling of resentment against a person who has caused harm or upset ▷ _vb_ **grudging, grudged** **2** to give unwillingly: _the rich men who grudged pennies for the poor_ **3** to resent or envy the success or possessions of: _none of their guests grudged them this celebration_ ▷ _adj_ **4** planned or carried out in order to settle a grudge: _a grudge match_ [Old French _grouchier_ to grumble]

grudging _adj_ felt or done unwillingly: _grudging admiration for his opponent_ **> grudgingly** _adv_

gruel _n_ thin porridge made by boiling oatmeal in water or milk [Old French]

gruelling _or US_ **grueling** _adj_ extremely severe or tiring: _a gruelling journey_ [obsolete _gruel_ to punish]

gruesome _adj_ inspiring horror and disgust [Scandinavian]

gruff _adj_ **1** rough or surly in manner or speech **2** (of a voice) low and throaty [Germanic] **> gruffly** _adv_ **> gruffness** _n_

grumble _vb_ **-bling, -bled** **1** to complain in a nagging way: _his neighbour grumbled about the long wait_ **2** to make low rumbling sounds: _the storm grumbled in the distance_ ▷ _n_ **3** a complaint **4** a low rumbling sound: _a distant grumble of artillery fire_ [Middle Low German _grommelen_] **> grumbling** _adj, n_

grumpy _adj_ **grumpier, grumpiest** sulky and bad-tempered [imitative] **> grumpily** _adv_

Grünewald _n_ Matthias, original name _Mathis Gothardt._ ?1470–1528, German painter, the greatest exponent of late Gothic art in Germany. The _Isenheim Altarpiece_ is regarded as his masterpiece

grunge _n_ **1** a style of rock music with a fuzzy guitar sound **2** a deliberately untidy and uncoordinated fashion style [from US slang: dirt, rubbish]

grungy _adj_ **grungier, grungiest** _slang_ **1** _chiefly US and Canad_ squalid or seedy **2** (of pop music) characterized by a loud fuzzy guitar sound

grunt _vb_ **1** to make a low short gruff noise, such as the sound made by a pig, or by a person to express annoyance **2** to express (something) gruffly: _he grunted his thanks_ ▷ _n_ **3** a low short gruff noise, such as the sound made by a pig, or by a person to express annoyance [Old English _grunnettan_]

Gruyère (grew-yair) _n_ a hard flat pale yellow cheese with holes [after _Gruyère_, Switzerland, where it originated]

gryphon _n_ same as **griffin**

GST (in Australia, New Zealand, and Canada) Goods and Services Tax

G-string _n_ a strip of cloth worn between the legs and attached to a waistband

G-suit _n_ a close-fitting pressurized garment that is worn by the crew of high-speed aircraft [from _g_(ravity) suit]

GT gran turismo: a touring car, usually a fast sports car with a hard fixed roof

GTA Greater Toronto Area

Guadalajara _n_ **1** a city in W Mexico, capital of Jalisco state: the second largest city of Mexico: centre of the Indian slave trade until its abolition, declared here in 1810; two universities (1792 and 1935). Pop: 3 905 000 (2005 est) **2** a city in central Spain, in New Castile. Pop: 70 732 (2003 est)

Guadalcanal _n_ a mountainous island in the SW Pacific, the largest of the Solomon Islands: under British protection until 1978; occupied by the Japanese (1942–43) Pop: 109 382 (1999). Area: 6475 sq km (2500 sq miles)

Guadalquivir _n_ the chief river of S Spain, rising in the Sierra de Segura and flowing west and southwest to the Gulf of Cádiz: navigable by ocean-going vessels to Seville. Length: 560 km (348 miles)

Guadalupe Hidalgo _n_ the former name (until 1931) of Gustavo A. Madero

Guadeloupe _n_ an overseas region of France in the E Caribbean, in the Leeward Islands, formed by the islands of Basse-Terre and Grande-Terre and several offlying islands; in 2007 the island of Saint-Barthélemy and the part-island dependency of Saint-Martin were separated from Guadeloupe to become Overseas Collectivities directly subordinate to France. Capital: Basse-Terre. Pop: 405 500 (2007 est). Area: 1780 sq km (687 sq miles)

Guadiana _n_ a river in SW Europe, rising in S central Spain and flowing west, then south as part of the border between Spain and Portugal, to the Gulf of Cádiz. Length: 578 km (359 miles)

Guam _n_ an island in the N Pacific, the largest and southernmost of the Marianas: belonged to Spain from the 17th century until 1898, when it was ceded to the US; site of naval and air force bases. Capital: Agana (now officially spelt Hagåtña). Pop: 160 378 (2013 est). Area: 541 sq km (209 sq miles)

Guamanian *adj* **1** of or relating to Guam or its inhabitants ▷ *n* **2** a native or inhabitant of Guam

Guanabara *n* (until 1975) a state of SE Brazil, on the Atlantic and **Guanabara Bay**, now amalgamated with the state of Rio de Janeiro

Guanajuato *n* **1** a state of central Mexico, on the great central plateau: mountainous in the north, with fertile plains in the south; important mineral resources. Capital: Guanajuato. Pop: 4 656 761 (2000). Area: 30 588 sq km (11 810 sq miles) **2** a city in central Mexico, capital of Guanajuato state: founded in 1554, it became one of the world's richest silver-mining centres. Pop: 80 000 (2005 est)

Guangdong *or* **Kwangtung** *n* a province of SE China, on the South China Sea: includes the Leizhou Peninsula, with densely populated river valleys; traditionally also including Macao and Hong Kong; the only true tropical climate in China. Capital: Canton. Pop: 79 540 000 (2003 est). Area: 197 100 sq km (76 100 sq miles)

Guangxi Zhuang Autonomous Region *or* **Kwangsi-Chuang Autonomous Region** *n* an administrative division of S China. Capital: Nanning. Pop: 48 570 000 (2003 est). Area: 220 400 sq km (85 100 sq miles)

Guangzhou *n* the Pinyin transliteration of the Chinese name for **Canton**

guano (gwah-no) *n* the dried manure of sea birds, used as a fertilizer [S American Indian *huano* dung]

Guantánamo *n* a city in SE Cuba, on **Guantánamo Bay**. Pop: 214 000 (2005 est)

Guantánamo Bay Naval Base *n* a US naval base on Guantánamo Bay; since 2002, a detainment camp for suspected al-Qaeda and Taliban operatives

Guaporé *n* **1** a river in W central South America, rising in SW Brazil and flowing northwest as part of the border between Brazil and Bolivia, to join the Mamoré River. Length: 1750 km (1087 miles). Spanish name: **Iténez 2** the former name (until 1956) of **Rondônia**

guarantee *n* **1** a formal assurance in writing that a product or service will meet certain standards or specifications **2** something that makes a specified condition or outcome certain: *there was no guarantee that there would not be another military coup* **3** same as **guaranty** ▷ *vb* **-teeing**, **-teed 4** to promise or make certain: *to guarantee absolute loyalty* **5** (of a company) to provide a guarantee in writing for (a product or service) **6** to take responsibility for the debts or obligations of (another person) [Germanic]

guarantor *n* a person who gives or is bound by a guarantee or guaranty

guaranty *n*, *pl* **-ties 1** a pledge of responsibility for fulfilling another person's obligations in case of that person's default **2** a thing given or taken as security for a guaranty

guard *vb* **1** to watch over or shield from danger or harm; protect: *US marines who guard the American embassy* **2** to keep watch over (a prisoner) to prevent escape **3** to protect (a right or privilege) **4** to take precautions: *to guard against a possible coup attempt* ▷ *n* **5** a person or group of people who protect or watch over people or things **6** *Brit, Austral and NZ* the official in charge of a train **7** a device or part of a machine designed to protect the user against injury **8** anything that provides protection: *a guard against future shocks* **9 off guard** having one's defences down; unprepared: *England were caught off guard as the Dutch struck two telling blows* **10 on guard** on duty to protect or watch over people or things **11 on one's guard** prepared to face danger or difficulties: *parents have been warned to be on their guard against kidnappers* **12 stand guard** (of a sentry) to keep watch [Old French *garder* to protect]

Guardafui *n* **Cape Guardafui** a cape at the NE tip of Somalia, extending into the Indian Ocean

guarded *adj* cautious and avoiding any commitment: *a guarded welcome* ▷ **guardedly** *adv*

guardhouse *or* **guardroom** *n military* a military police office in which prisoners can be detained

Guardi *n* **Francesco**. 1712–93, Venetian landscape painter

guardian *n* **1** one who looks after, protects, or defends someone or something: *the nation's moral guardians* **2** someone legally appointed to manage the affairs of another person, such as a child or a person who is mentally ill ▷ **guardianship** *n*

guardsman *n*, *pl* **-men** *military* a member of a regiment responsible for ceremonial duties

guard's van *n Brit, Austral and NZ* a small railway carriage in which the guard travels

Guat. Guatemala

Guatemala *n* a republic in Central America: original Maya Indians conquered by the Spanish in 1523; became the centre of Spanish administration in Central America; gained independence and was annexed to Mexico in 1821, becoming an independent republic in 1839. Official language: Spanish. Religion: Roman Catholic majority. Currency: quetzal and US dollar. Capital: Guatemala City. Pop: 14 373 472 (2013 est). Area: 108 889 sq km (42 042 sq miles)

Guatemala City *n* the capital of Guatemala, in the southeast: founded in 1776 to replace the former capital, Antigua Guatemala, after an earthquake; university (1676). Pop: 982 000 (2005 est)

Guatemalan *adj* **1** of or relating to Guatemala or its inhabitants ▷ *n* **2** a native or inhabitant of Guatemala

guava (gwah-va) *n* a round tropical fruit with yellow skin and pink pulp [from S American Indian]

Guayaquil *n* a port in W Ecuador: the largest city in the country and its chief port; university (1867). Pop: 2 387 000 (2005 est)

gubernatorial *adj chiefly US* of or relating to a governor [Latin *gubernator* governor]

gudgeon¹ *n* a small slender European freshwater fish, used as bait by anglers [Old French *gougon*]

gudgeon² *n* the socket of a hinge, which fits round the pin [Old French *goujon*]

guelder rose (geld-er) *n* a Eurasian shrub with clusters of white flowers [from *Gelderland*, province of Holland]

Guelders *n* another name for **Gelderland**

Guelph *n* a city in Canada, in SE Ontario. Pop: 106 920 (2001)

Guericke *n* **Otto von**. 1602–86, German physicist: invented the air pump (1650) and demonstrated the power of a vacuum with the Magdeburg hemispheres

Guernica *n* a town in N Spain: formerly the seat of a Basque parliament; destroyed in 1937 by German bombers during the Spanish Civil War, an event depicted in one of Picasso's most famous paintings. Pop: 15 454 (2003 est). Basque name: **Gernika**

Guernsey *n* **1** an island in the English Channel: the second largest of the Channel Islands, which, with Alderney and Sark, Herm, Jethou, and some islets, forms the bailiwick of Guernsey; finance, market gardening, dairy farming, and tourism. Capital: St Peter Port. Pop: 65 605 (2013). Area: 63 sq km (24.5 sq miles) **2** a breed of dairy cattle producing rich creamy milk, originating from the island of Guernsey **3** (*sometimes not cap*) a seaman's knitted woollen sweater **4 guernsey** *Austral* a sleeveless woollen shirt or jumper worn by a football player **5 get a guernsey** *Austral* to be selected or gain recognition for something

Guerrero *n* a mountainous state of S Mexico, on the Pacific: rich mineral resources. Capital: Chilpancingo. Pop: 3 075 083 (2000 est). Area: 63 794 sq km (24 631 sq miles)

guerrilla *or* **guerilla** *n* a member of an irregular, politically motivated, armed force that fights regular forces [Spanish]

Guesclin *n* Bertrand du ?1320–80, French commander during the Hundred Years' War

guess *vb* **1** to form an estimate or conclusion about (something), without proper knowledge: *a competition to guess the weight of the cake* **2** to arrive at a correct estimate of (something) by guessing: *I had a notion that he guessed my thoughts* **3** *informal* to think or suppose: *I guess he must have been a great athlete* ▷ *n* **4** an estimate or conclusion arrived at by guessing: *we can hazard a guess at the answer* [probably from Old Norse]

guesswork *n* the process of arriving at conclusions or estimates by guessing

guest *n* **1** a person who receives hospitality at someone else's home **2** a person who is taken out socially by someone else who pays all the expenses **3** a performer or speaker taking part in an event, show, or film by special invitation **4** a person who is staying in a hotel ▷ *vb* **5** to be a guest in an event, show, or film: *he guested in concert with Eric Clapton* [Old English *giest* guest, stranger, enemy]

guesthouse *n* a private home or boarding house offering accommodation

guest of honour *n* a famous or important person who is the most important guest at a dinner or other social occasion

Guevara *n* Ernesto, known as *Che Guevara*. 1928–67, Latin American politician and soldier, born in Argentina. He developed guerrilla warfare as a tool for revolution and was instrumental in Castro's victory in Cuba (1959), where he held government posts until 1965. He was killed while training guerrillas in Bolivia

guff *n* Brit, Austral and NZ slang ridiculous talk; nonsense [imitative]

guffaw *vb* **1** to laugh loudly and raucously ▷ *n* **2** a loud raucous laugh [imitative]

Guggenheim Museum *n* an international chain of art museums, some of which are architecturally important buildings in their own right, most notably one in New York, designed by Frank Lloyd Wright (1956–59), and one in Bilbao, designed by Frank O Gehry (1997)

GUI (goo-ee) *computers* graphical user interface

Guiana *or* **The Guianas** *n* a region of NE South America, including Guyana, Surinam, French Guiana, and the **Guiana Highlands** (largely in SE Venezuela and partly in N Brazil). Area: about 1 787 000 sq km (690 000 sq miles)

Guianese *or* **Guianan** *adj* **1** of or relating to the South American region of Guiana or its inhabitants ▷ *n* **2** a native or inhabitant of Guiana

guidance *n* help, advice, or instruction, usually from someone more experienced or more qualified: *marriage guidance*

guide *n* **1** a person who conducts parties of tourists around places of interest, such as museums **2** a person who leads travellers to a place, usually in a dangerous area: *a mountain guide* **3** something that can be used to gauge something or to help in planning one's actions: *starting salary was not an accurate guide to future earnings* **4** same as **guidebook** **5** a book that explains the basics of a subject or skill: *a guide to higher education* ▷ *vb* **guiding, guided** **6** to lead the way for (tourists or travellers) **7** to control the movement or course of; steer **8** to direct the affairs of (a person, team, or country): *he will stay with the club he guided to promotion to the First Division* **9** to influence (a person) in his or her actions or opinions: *to be guided by the law* [Germanic] ▷ **guiding** *adj*

Guide *n* a member of an organization for girls that encourages discipline and practical skills

guidebook *n* a book which gives tourist information on a place

guided missile *n* a missile whose course is controlled electronically

guide dog *n* a dog that has been trained to lead a blind person

guideline *n* a principle put forward to set standards or determine a course of action: *guidelines for arms exporting*

Guido d'Arezzo *n* ?995–?1050 AD, Italian Benedictine monk and musical theorist: reputed inventor of solmization

Guienne *or* **Guyenne** *n* a former province of SW France: formed, with Gascony, the duchy of Aquitaine during the 12th century

guild *n* **1** an organization or club for people with shared interests **2** (in Medieval Europe) an association of men in the same trade or craft [Old Norse *gildi*]

guilder *n, pl* **-ders** *or* **-der** a former monetary unit of the Netherlands [Middle Dutch *gulden*]

Guildford *n* a city in S England, in Surrey: cathedral (1936–68); seat of the University of Surrey (1966). Pop: 69 400 (2001)

guildhall *n* Brit a hall where members of a guild meet

guile (gile) *n* craftiness or deviousness [Old French] ▷ **guileless** *adj*

Guilin, Kweilin *or* **Kuei-lin** *n* a city in S China, in Guangxi on the Li River: noted for the unusual caves and formations of the surrounding karst scenery; trade and manufacturing centre. Pop: 631 000 (2005 est)

Guillaume de Lorris *n* 13th-century French poet who wrote the first 4058 lines of the allegorical romance, the *Roman de la rose*, continued by Jean de Meung

Guillem *n* Sylvie. born 1965, French ballet dancer based in Britain; with the Royal Ballet (1989–2006)

guillemot (gil-lee-mot) *n* a northern oceanic black-and-white diving sea bird [French]

guillotine *n* **1** a device formerly used, esp. in France, for beheading people, consisting of a weighted blade between two upright posts, which was dropped on the neck **2** a device with a blade for cutting paper ▷ *vb* **-tining, -tined** **3** to behead with a guillotine [after J. I. Guillotin, who advocated its use]

guilt *n* **1** the fact or state of having done wrong: *the court was unable to establish guilt* **2** remorse or self-reproach caused by feeling that one has done something wrong: *he feels no guilt about the planned cutbacks* [Old English *gylt*]

guiltless *adj* free of all responsibility for wrongdoing or crime; innocent

guilty *adj* **guiltier, guiltiest** **1** *law* judged to have committed a crime: *she has been found guilty of drug trafficking* **2** responsible for doing something wrong: *students who are guilty of cheating* **3** showing, feeling, or indicating guilt: *guilty conscience* ▷ **guiltily** *adv*

Guin. Guinea

guinea *n* a former British unit of currency worth £1.05 (21 shillings), sometimes still used in quoting professional fees [the coin was originally made of gold from Guinea]

Guinea *n* **1** a republic in West Africa, on the Atlantic: established as the colony of French Guinea in 1890 and became an independent republic in 1958. Official language: French. Religion: Muslim majority and animist. Currency: franc. Capital: Conakry. Pop: 11 176 026 (2013 est). Area: 245 855 sq km (94 925 sq miles) **2** (formerly) the coastal region of West Africa, between Cape Verde and Namibe (formerly Moçâmedes; Angola): divided by a line of volcanic peaks into **Upper Guinea** (between The Gambia and Cameroon) and **Lower Guinea** (between Cameroon and S Angola) **3 Gulf of Guinea** a large inlet of the S Atlantic on the W coast of Africa, extending from Cape Palmas, Liberia, to Cape Lopez, Gabon: contains two large bays, the Bight of Bonny and the Bight of Benin, separated by the Niger delta

Guinea-Bissau *n* a republic in West Africa, on the Atlantic: first discovered by the Portuguese in 1446 and of subsequent importance in the slave trade; made a colony in 1879; became an independent republic in 1974. Official language: Portuguese; Cape Verde creole is widely spoken. Religion: animist majority and Muslim. Currency: franc. Capital: Bissau. Pop: 1 660 870 (2013 est). Area: 36 125 sq km (13 948 sq miles). Former name (until 1974): **Portuguese Guinea**

guinea fowl *n* a domestic bird with a heavy rounded body and speckled feathers

Guinean *adj* **1** of or relating to Guinea or its inhabitants ▷ *n* **2** a native or inhabitant of Guinea

guinea pig *n* **1** a tailless S American rodent, commonly kept as a pet or used in scientific experiments **2** a person used in an experiment [origin unknown]

Guinness *n* Sir Alec. 1914–2000, British stage and film actor. His films include *Kind Hearts and Coronets* (1949), *The Bridge on the River Kwai* (1957), for which he won an Oscar, and *Star Wars* (1977); TV roles include Le Carré's George Smiley

guipure (geep-**pure**) *n* heavy lace that has its pattern connected by threads, rather than supported on a net mesh [French]

Guiscard *n* Robert. ?1015–85, Norman conqueror in S Italy

guise (rhymes with **size**) *n* **1** a false appearance: *in the guise of a wood-cutter* **2** general appearance or form: *haricot beans are best known in Britain in their popular guise of baked beans* [Old French]

guitar *n* a stringed instrument with a flat back and a long neck with a fretted fingerboard, which is played by plucking or strumming [Spanish *guitarra*] ▷ **guitarist** *n*

Guitry *n* Sacha. 1885–1957, French actor, dramatist, and film director, born in Russia: plays include *Nono* (1905)

Guiyang, Kweiyang *or* **Kuei-yang** *n* a city in S China, capital of Guizhou province: reached by rail in 1959, with subsequent industrial growth. Pop: 2 467 000 (2005 est)

Guizhou, Kweichow *or* **Kueichou** *n* a province of SW China, between the Yangtze and Xi Rivers: a high plateau. Capital: Guiyang. Pop: 38 700 000 (2003 est). Area: 174 000 sq km (69 278 sq miles)

Guizot *n* François Pierre Guillaume. 1787–1874, French statesman and historian. As chief minister (1840–48), his reactionary policies contributed to the outbreak of the revolution of 1848

Gujarat *or* **Gujerat** *n* **1** a state of W India: formed in 1960 from the N and W parts of the former Bombay State; one of India's most industrialized states. Capital: Gandhinagar. Pop: 50 596 992 (2001). Area: 196 024 sq km (75 268 sq miles) **2** a region of W India, north of the Narmada River: generally includes the areas north of Mumbai city where Gujarati is spoken

Gujarati *or* **Gujerati** *n* **1** (*pl* **-ti**) a member of a people of India living chiefly in Gujarat **2** the state language of Gujarat, belonging to the Indic branch of the Indo-European family ▷ *adj* **3** of or relating to Gujarat, its people, or their language

Gujranwala *n* a city in NE Pakistan: textile manufacturing. Pop: 1 466 000 (2005 est)

Gulag *n* a system or department that silences dissidents, esp. in the former Soviet Union [Russian *G(lavnoye) U(pravleniye Ispravitelno-Trudovykh) Lag(erei)* Main Administration for Corrective Labour Camps]

Gulbenkian *n* **1** Calouste Sarkis. 1869–1955, British industrialist, born in Turkey. He endowed the international Gulbenkian Foundation for the advancement of the arts, science, and education **2** his son, Nubar Sarkis. 1896–1972, British industrialist, diplomat, and philanthropist

gulch *n* US and Canad a narrow ravine with a stream running through it [origin unknown]

Gülek Bogaz *n* the Turkish name for the Cilician Gates

gulf *n* **1** a large deep bay **2** something that divides or separates people, such as a lack of understanding: *gradually the gulf between father and son has lessened* [Greek *kolpos*]

Gulf *n* the Gulf **1** the Persian Gulf **2** *Austral* the Gulf of Carpentaria **3** *NZ* the Hauraki Gulf

Gulf States *pl n* the Gulf States **1** the oil-producing states around the Persian Gulf: Iran, Iraq, Kuwait, Saudi Arabia, Bahrain, Qatar, the United Arab Emirates, and Oman **2** the states of the US that border on the Gulf of Mexico: Alabama, Florida, Louisiana, Mississippi, and Texas

Gulf War syndrome *n* a group of various debilitating symptoms experienced by many soldiers who served in the Gulf War of 1991, claimed to be associated with damage to the central nervous system

gull *n* a large sea bird with white feathers tipped with black or grey [Celtic]

gullet *n* the muscular tube through which food passes from the throat to the stomach [Latin *gula* throat]

gullible *adj* easily tricked; too trusting ▷ **gullibility** *n*

gully *or* **gulley** *n, pl* **-lies** *or* **-leys 1** a channel or small valley originally worn away by running water **2** *cricket* a fielding position on the off side, between the slips and point [French *goulet* neck of a bottle]

gulp *vb* **1** to swallow (a drink or food) rapidly in large mouthfuls **2** to gasp or breathe in violently, for example when nervous or when swimming **3** **gulp back** to stifle or suppress: *he gulped back the tears as he said his goodbyes* ▷ *n* **4** the act of gulping **5** the quantity taken in a gulp [imitative]

gum¹ *n* **1** a sticky substance obtained from certain plants, which hardens on exposure to air and dissolves in water **2** a substance used for sticking things together **3** short for **chewing gum, bubble gum 4** *chiefly Brit* a gumdrop ▷ *vb* **gumming, gummed 5** to stick with gum ▶ See also **gum up** [Old French *gomme*]

gum² *n* the fleshy tissue that covers the bases of the teeth [Old English *gōma* jaw]

gum arabic *n* a gum obtained from certain acacia trees, used to make ink, food thickeners, and pills

gumboil *n* an abscess on the gum

gumboots *pl n* *Brit and NZ* long rubber boots, worn in wet or muddy conditions

gumdrop *n* a small hard fruit-flavoured jelly-like sweet

gummy¹ *adj* **-mier, -miest 1** sticky or tacky **2** producing gum

gummy² *adj* **-mier, -miest** toothless

gumption *n* *Brit and NZ informal* common sense or initiative [origin unknown]

gumtree *n* **1** any of various trees that yield gum, such as the eucalyptus **2** **up a gumtree** *Brit and NZ informal* in an awkward position; in difficulties

gum up *vb* **gum up the works** *informal* to spoil a plan or hinder progress

gun *n* **1** a weapon with a metallic tube or barrel from which a missile is fired, usually by force of an explosion **2** a device used to force out (a substance, such as grease or paint) under pressure: *a spray gun* **3** **jump the gun** *informal* to act prematurely **4** **stick to one's guns** *informal* to stand by one's opinions or intentions in spite of opposition ▷ *vb* **gunning, gunned 5** to press hard on the accelerator of (a vehicle's engine) **6** **gun down** to shoot (someone) with a gun ▷ *adj* **7** *NZ slang* expert: *a gun surfer* ▶ See also **gun for** [Middle English *gonne*]

gunboat *n* a small ship carrying mounted guns

gunboat diplomacy *n* diplomacy conducted by threats of military intervention

guncotton *n* a form of cellulose nitrate used as an explosive

gun dog *n* **1** a dog trained to locate or retrieve birds or animals that have been shot in a hunt **2** a dog belonging to any breed traditionally used for these activities

gunfire *n* the repeated firing of guns

gun for *vb informal* to search for (someone) in order to harm him or her in some way

gunge *n* *informal* a sticky or congealed substance [imitative] ▷ **gungy** *adj*

gunk *n* *informal* a slimy, oily, or dirty substance [perhaps imitative]

gunman *n, pl* **-men** a man who uses a gun to commit a crime

gunmetal *n* **1** a type of bronze containing copper, tin, and zinc ▷ *adj* **2** dark grey

g

Gunn *n* Thom(son William). 1929–2004, British poet who lived in the USA. His works include *Fighting Terms* (1954), *My Sad Captains* (1961), *Jack Straw's Castle* (1976), *The Man with the Night Sweats* (1992), and *Boss Cupid* (2000)

gunnel (gun-nel) *n* same as **gunwale**

Gunnell *n* Sally. born 1966, British athlete: Olympic 400-metre hurdles gold medallist (1992)

gunner *n* a member of the armed forces who works with, uses, or specializes in guns

gunnery *n* the art and science of the efficient design and use of large guns

gunny *n* chiefly US a coarse hard-wearing fabric, made from jute and used for sacks [Hindi *gōnī*]

gunpoint *n* at gunpoint being under or using the threat of being shot: *eight tourists have been kidnapped at gunpoint by unidentified men*

gunpowder *n* an explosive mixture of potassium nitrate, charcoal, and sulphur, used to make fireworks

gunrunning *n* the practice of smuggling guns and ammunition into a country **> gunrunner** *n*

gunshot *n* **1** bullets fired from a gun **2** the sound of a gun being fired **3** the firing range of a gun: *within gunshot*

gunslinger *n* slang a person who can shoot very accurately and has been involved in many fights using guns, esp. in the frontier days of the American West

gunstock *n* the wooden handle to which the barrel of a rifle is attached

Gunter *n* Edmund. 1581–1626, English mathematician and astronomer, who invented various measuring instruments

Guntur *n* a city in E India, in central Andhra Pradesh: founded by the French in the 18th century; ceded to Britain in 1788. Pop: 514 707 (2001)

gunwale (gun-nel) *n* nautical the top of the side of a ship [*wale*, ridge of planking originally supporting guns]

gunyah *n* Austral a hut or shelter in the bush [Aboriginal]

guppy *n, pl* **-pies** a small brightly coloured tropical fish, often kept in aquariums in people's homes [after R. J. L. *Guppy*, who gave specimens to the British Museum]

Gurdjieff *n* Georgei Ivanovitch. ?1877–1949, Russian mystic: founded a teaching centre in Paris (1922)

gurdwara *n* a Sikh place of worship [from Punjabi]

gurgle *vb* **-gling, -gled** **1** (of water) to make low bubbling noises when flowing **2** to make low throaty bubbling noises: *the baby gurgled in delight* ▷ *n* **3** the sound of gurgling [origin unknown]

Gurkha *n* **1** a member of a Hindu people living mainly in Nepal **2** a member of a Gurkha regiment in the Indian or British Army [Sanskrit]

gurnard *n, pl* **-nard** or **-nards** a sea fish with a spiny head and long finger-like pectoral fins [Old French *gornard* grunter]

Gurney *n* Ivor (Bertie). 1890–1937, British poet and composer, noted esp. for his songs and his poems of World War I

guru *n* **1** a Hindu or Sikh religious teacher or leader **2** a leader or adviser of a person or group of people: *inside a team of advertising gurus are at work* [Hindi]

Guru Granth Sahib *n* same as **Granth**

Guru Nanak *n* 1469–1539, Indian religious leader and founder of Sikhism. Born near Lahore in India, he spent many years as a missionary before returning to the Punjab, where he gained many followers

gush *vb* **1** to pour out suddenly and profusely **2** to speak or behave in an overenthusiastic manner: *I'm not about to start gushing about raspberry coulis* ▷ *n* **3** a sudden large flow of liquid **4** a sudden surge of strong feeling: *she felt a gush of pure affection for her mother* [probably imitative]

gusher *n* **1** a person who gushes **2** a spurting oil well

gushing *adj* behaving in an overenthusiastic manner: *gushing television commentators*

gusset *n* a piece of material sewn into a garment to strengthen it [Old French *gousset*]

gust *n* **1** a sudden blast of wind **2** a sudden surge of

strong feeling: *a gust of joviality* ▷ *vb* **3** to blow in gusts [Old Norse *gustr*] **> gusty** *adj*

Gustavo A. Madero *n* a city in central Mexico, northeast of Mexico City: became a pilgrimage centre after an Indian convert had a vision of the Virgin Mary here in 1531. Pop: 668 500 (2000 est). Former name (until 1931): Guadalupe Hidalgo

Gustavus I *n* called *Gustavus Vasa*. ?1496–1560, king of Sweden (1523–60). He was elected king after driving the Danes from Sweden (1520–23)

Gustavus VI *n* title of *Gustaf Adolf*. 1882–1973, king of Sweden (1950–73)

Gustavus Adolphus or **Gustavus II** *n* 1594–1632, king of Sweden (1611–32). A brilliant general, he waged successful wars with Denmark, Russia, and Poland and in the Thirty Years' War led a Protestant army against the Catholic League and the Holy Roman Empire (1630–32). He defeated Tilly at Leipzig (1631) and Lech (1632) but was killed at the battle of Lützen

gusto *n* vigorous enjoyment: *he downed a pint with gusto* [Spanish: taste]

gut *n* **1** same as **intestine 2** slang a stomach, esp. a fat one **3** short for **catgut 4** a silky fibrous substance extracted from silkworms and used in the manufacture of fishing tackle ▷ *vb* **gutting, gutted 5** to remove the internal organs from (a dead animal or fish) **6** (of a fire) to destroy the inside of (a building): *a local pub was gutted* ▷ *adj* **7** informal basic, essential, or natural: *I have a gut feeling she's after something* ▶ See also **guts** [Old English *gutt*]

Gutenberg *n* Johann, original name *Johannes Gensfleisch*. ?1398–1468, German printer; inventor of printing by movable type

Gütersloh *n* a town in NW Germany, in North Rhine-Westphalia. Pop: 95 928 (2003 est)

Guthrie *n* **1** Samuel. 1782–1848, US chemist: invented percussion priming powder and a punch lock for exploding it, and discovered chloroform (1831) **2** Sir (William) Tyrone. 1900–71, English theatrical director **3** Woody, full name *Woodrow Wilson Guthrie*. 1912–67, US folk singer and songwriter. His songs include "So Long, it's been Good to Know you" (1940) and "This Land is your Land" (1944)

gutless *adj* informal lacking courage or determination

guts *pl n* **1** the internal organs of a person or an animal **2** courage, willpower, or daring **3** informal the inner or essential part: *the new roads have torn apart the guts of the city*

gutsy *adj* **gutsier, gutsiest** slang **1** bold or courageous: *the gutsy kid who lost a leg to cancer* **2** robust or vigorous: *a gutsy rendering of 'Bobby Shaftoe'*

gutta-percha *n* a whitish rubber substance, obtained from a tropical Asian tree and used in electrical insulation and dentistry [Malay *getah* gum + *percha* gumtree]

gutted *adj* Brit, Austral and NZ informal disappointed and upset: *the supporters will be absolutely gutted if the manager leaves the club*

gutter *n* **1** a channel on the roof of a building or alongside a kerb, used to collect and carry away rainwater **2** tenpin bowling one of the channels on either side of an alley **3** the gutter a poverty-stricken, degraded, or criminal environment: *he dragged himself up from the gutter* ▷ *vb* **4** (of a candle) to flicker and be about to go out [Latin *gutta* a drop] **> guttering** *n*

gutter press *n* informal the section of the popular press that concentrates on the sensational aspects of the new

guttersnipe *n* Brit a child who spends most of his or her time in the streets, usually in a slum area

guttural (gut-ter-al) *adj* **1** phonetics pronounced at the back of the throat **2** harsh-sounding [Latin *guttur* gullet]

guy[1] *n* **1** informal a man or boy **2** informal a person of either sex: *it's been very nice talking to you guys again* **3** Brit a crude model of Guy Fawkes, that is burnt on top of a bonfire on Guy Fawkes Day (November 5) [short for *Guy Fawkes*, who plotted to blow up the Houses of Parliament]

guy² *n* a rope or chain for steadying or securing something such as a tent. Also: **guyrope** [probably Low German]

Guy *n* **Buddy**, real name *George Guy*. born 1936, US blues singer and guitarist

Guyana *n* a republic in NE South America, on the Atlantic: colonized chiefly by the Dutch in the 17th and 18th centuries; became a British colony in 1831 and an independent republic within the Commonwealth in 1966. Official language: English. Religions: Christian and Hindu. Currency: dollar. Capital: Georgetown. Pop: 739 903 (2013 est). Area: about 215 000 sq km (83 000 sq miles). Former name (until 1966): **British Guiana**

Guyanese *or* **Guyanan** *adj* **1** of or relating to Guyana or its inhabitants ▷ *adj* **2** a native or inhabitant of Guyana

Guyenne *n* a variant spelling of **Guienne**

Guzmán Blanco *n* Antonio. 1829–99, Venezuelan statesman; president (1873–77; 1879–84; 1886–87). He was virtual dictator of Venezuela from 1870 until his overthrow (1889)

guzzle *vb* **-zling, -zled** to eat or drink quickly or greedily: *the guests guzzled their way through squid with mushrooms* [origin unknown]

Gwalior *n* **1** a city in N central India, in Madhya Pradesh: built around the fort, which dates from before 525; industrial and commercial centre. Pop: 826 919 (2001) **2** a former princely state of central India, established in the 18th century: merged with Madhya Bharat in 1948, which in turn merged with Madhya Pradesh in 1956

Gwent *n* a former county of SE Wales: formed in 1974 from most of Monmouthshire and part of Breconshire; replaced in 1996 by Monmouthshire and the county boroughs of Newport, Torfaen, Blaenau Gwent, and part of Caerphilly

Gweru *n* a city in central Zimbabwe. Pop: 140 000 (2005 est). Former name (until 1982): **Gwelo**

Gwyn *n* Nell, original name *Eleanor Gwynne*. 1650–87, English actress; mistress of Charles II

Gwynedd *n* a county of NW Wales, formed in 1974 from Anglesey, Caernarvonshire, part of Denbighshire, and most of Merionethshire; lost Anglesey and part of the NE in 1996: generally mountainous with many lakes, much of it lying in Snowdonia National Park. Administrative centre: Caernarfon. Pop: 117 500 (2003 est). Area: 2550 sq km (869 sq miles)

gybe *or* **jibe** (jibe) *nautical vb* **gybing, gybed** *or* **jibing, jibed** **1** (of a fore-and-aft sail) to swing suddenly from one side

of a ship to the other **2** to change the course of (a ship) by letting the sail gybe ▷ *n* **3** an instance of gybing [obsolete Dutch *gijben*]

gym *n* short for **gymnasium**, **gymnastics**

gymkhana (jim-kah-na) *n Brit, Austral and NZ* an event in which horses and riders take part in various races and contests [Hindi *gend-khānā* ball house]

gymnasium *n* a large room containing equipment such as bars, weights, and ropes, for physical exercise [Greek *gumnazein* to exercise naked]

gymnast *n* a person who is skilled or trained in gymnastics

gymnastics *n* **1** practice or training in exercises that develop physical strength and agility ▷ *pl n* **2** such exercises **>** **gymnastic** *adj*

gym shoes *pl n* same as **plimsolls**

gymslip *n* a tunic formerly worn by schoolgirls as part of school uniform

gynaecology *or US* **gynecology** (guy-nee-kol-la-jee) *n* the branch of medicine concerned with diseases and conditions specific to women [Greek *gunē* woman + -LOGY] **>** **gynaecological** *or US* **gynecological** *adj* **>** **gynaecologist** *or US* **gynecologist** *n*

Győr *n* an industrial town in NW Hungary: medieval Benedictine abbey. Pop: 128 913 (2003 est)

gyp *or* **gip** *n* **give someone gyp** *Brit, Austral and NZ slang* to cause someone severe pain: *her back's still giving her gyp* [probably a contraction of *gee up*!]

gypsophila *n* a garden plant with small white flowers

gypsum *n* a mineral used in making plaster of Paris [Greek *gupsos*]

Gypsy *or* **Gipsy** *n, pl* **-sies** a member of a travelling people scattered throughout Europe and North America [from *Egyptian*, since they were thought to have come originally from Egypt]

gyrate (jire-rate) *vb* **-rating, -rated** to turn round and round in a circle [Greek *guros* circle] **>** **gyration** *n*

gyrfalcon (jur-fawl-kon) *n* a very large rare falcon of northern regions [Old French *gerfaucon*]

gyro *n, pl* **-ros** short for **gyroscope**

gyrocompass *n* a nonmagnetic compass that uses a motor-driven gyroscope to indicate true north [Greek *guros* circle + COMPASS]

gyroscope (jire-oh-skope) *n* a device containing a disc rotating on an axis that can turn freely in any direction, so that the disc maintains the same position regardless of the movement of the surrounding structure [Greek *guros* circle + *skopein* to watch] **>** **gyroscopic** *adj*

Hh

H 1 *chem* hydrogen **2** *physics* henry

h. *or* **H. 1** height **2** hour

ha¹ *or* **hah** *interj* an exclamation expressing triumph, surprise, or scorn

ha² hectare

Ha *chem* hahnium

Ha. Hawaii

Haakon IV *n* surnamed *Haakonsson*. 1204–63, king of Norway (1217–63). He strengthened the monarchy and extended Norwegian territory to include Iceland and Greenland

Haakon VII *n* 1872–1957, king of Norway (1905–57). During the Nazi occupation of Norway (1940–45) he led Norwegian resistance from England

Haarlem *n* a city in the W Netherlands, capital of North Holland province. Pop: 147 000 (2003 est)

Habana¹ *n* the Spanish name for **Havana**

Habana² *n* Bryan. born 1983; South African Rugby Union player: scored a record-equalling eight tries for the South Africa side that won the 2007 World Cup

habeas corpus (hay-bee-ass **kor**-puss) *n law* a writ ordering a person to be brought before a judge, so as to decide whether his or her detention is lawful [Latin: you may have the body]

haberdasher *n Brit, Austral and NZ* a dealer in small articles used for sewing [Anglo-French *hapertas* small items of merchandise] ▷ **haberdashery** *n*

Habermas *n* Jürgen. born 1929, German social theorist: his chief works are *Theory and Practice* (1963) and *Knowledge and Human Interests* (1968)

Haber process (hah-ber) *n chem* a method of making ammonia by reacting nitrogen with hydrogen at high pressure in the presence of a catalyst [after Fritz *Haber*, German chemist]

habiliments *pl n old-fashioned* clothes [Old French *habillement*]

habit *n* **1** a tendency to act in a particular way **2** established custom or use: *the English habit of taking tea in the afternoon* **3** an addiction to a drug **4** mental disposition or attitude: *deference was a deeply ingrained habit of mind* **5** the costume of a nun or monk **6** a woman's riding costume [Latin *habitus* custom]

habitable *adj* fit to be lived in ▷ **habitability** *n*

habitant *n* an early French settler in Canada or Louisiana or a descendant of one, esp. a farmer

habitat *n* the natural home of an animal or plant [Latin: it inhabits]

habitation *n* **1** occupation of a dwelling place: *unfit for human habitation* **2** *formal* a dwelling place

habitaunce *n* a place where a person or an animal lives or resides

habit-forming *adj* tending to become a habit or addiction

habitual *adj* **1** done regularly and repeatedly: *habitual behaviour patterns* **2** by habit: *a habitual criminal* ▷ **habitually** *adv*

habituate *vb* **-ating, -ated** to accustom; get used to: *habituated to failure* ▷ **habituation** *n*

habitué (hab-**it**-yew-ay) *n* a frequent visitor to a place [French]

hachure (hash-yoor) *n* shading of short lines drawn on a map to indicate the degree of steepness of a hill [French]

hacienda (hass-ee-**end**-a) *n* (in Spanish-speaking countries) a ranch or large estate with a house on it [Spanish]

hack¹ *vb* **1** to chop roughly or violently **2** to cut and clear (a way) through undergrowth **3** (in sport) to foul (an opposing player) by kicking his or her shins **4** *Brit and NZ informal* to tolerate **5** to manipulate a computer program skilfully, esp., to gain unauthorized access to another computer system ▷ *n* **6** a cut or gash **7** a tool, such as a pick **8** a chopping blow **9** a kick on the shins, such as in rugby [Old English *haccian*]

hack² *n* **1** a writer or journalist who produces work fast and on a regular basis **2** a horse kept for riding, often one for hire **3** *Brit* a country ride on horseback ▷ *vb* **4** *Brit* to ride (a horse) cross-country for pleasure ▷ *adj* **5** unoriginal or of a low standard: *clumsily contrived hack verse* [short for *hackney*]

hacker *n slang* a computer enthusiast, esp. one who through a personal computer breaks into the computer system of a company or government ▷ **hacking** *or* **hackery** *n*

hacking *adj* (of a cough) dry, painful, and harsh-sounding

hacking jacket *n* a jacket with vents at the side and sloping pockets, originally designed for wearing on horseback

hackles *pl n* **1** the hairs or feathers on the back of the neck of certain animals or birds, which rise when they are angry **2 raise someone's hackles** to make someone feel angry or hostile [Middle English *hakell*]

Hackman *n* Gene. born 1930, US film actor; his films include *The French Connection* (1971), *Mississippi Burning* (1988), *Absolute Power* (1997), and *The Royal Tenenbaums* (2001)

hackney *n* **1** *Brit* a taxi **2** same as **hack²** (2) [probably after HACKNEY, where horses were formerly raised]

Hackney *n* a borough of NE Greater London: formed in 1965 from the former boroughs of Shoreditch, Stoke Newington, and Hackney; nearby are **Hackney Marshes**, the largest recreation ground in London. Pop: 208 400 (2003 est). Area: 19 sq km (8 sq miles)

hackneyed (hak-need) *adj* (of a word or phrase) unoriginal and overused

hacksaw *n* a small saw for cutting metal

had *vb* the past of **have**

haddock *n, pl* **-dock** a North Atlantic food fish [origin unknown]

hadedah *or* **hadeda** (hah-dee-dah) *n* a large grey-green S African ibis [imitative]

Haden *n* Charles (**Edward**). born 1937, US jazz bassist, esp.

noted for his collaborations with Ornette Coleman and Keith Jarrett

Hades (hay-deez) *n Greek myth* **1** the underworld home of the souls of the dead **2** the god of the underworld

Hadfield *n* Chris (**Austin**). born 1959, Canadian astronaut: in 2013 he became the first Canadian to command the International Space Station

Hadhramaut *or* **Hadramaut** *n* a plateau region of the S Arabian Peninsula, in SE Yemen on the Indian Ocean; formerly in South Yemen: corresponds roughly to the former East Aden Protectorate. Area: about 151 500 sq km (58 500 sq miles)

Hadid *n* Dame Zaha (**Mohammad**). born 1950, Iraqi-British architect, born in Baghdad; her buildings include the MAXXI in Rome (Stirling Prize, 2010) and the Evelyn Grace Academy in London (Stirling Prize, 2011)

Hadith (had-dith, hah-deeth) *n Islam* the body of tradition and legend about Mohammed and his followers, used as a basis of Islamic law [Arabic]

hadj *n* same as **hajj**

hadji *n, pl* **hadjis** same as **hajji**

Hadlee *n* Sir Richard (**John**). born 1951, New Zealand cricketer: an all-rounder, he played in 86 test matches in which he took 431 wickets and scored 3124 runs

hadn't had not

Hadrian *or* **Adrian** *n* Latin name *Publius Aelius Hadrianus*. 76–138 AD, Roman emperor (117–138); adopted son and successor of Trajan. He travelled throughout the Roman Empire, strengthening its frontiers and encouraging learning and architecture, and in Rome he reorganized the army and codified Roman law

Hadrian's Wall *n* a fortified Roman wall, of which substantial parts remain, extending across N England from the Solway Firth in the west to the mouth of the River Tyne in the east. It was built in 120–123 AD on the orders of the emperor Hadrian as a defence against the N British tribes

Haeckel *n* Ernst Heinrich. 1834–1919, German biologist and philosopher. He formulated the recapitulation theory of evolution and was an exponent of the philosophy of materialistic monism ▷ **Haeckelian** *adj*

haemal *or US* **hemal** (heem-al) *adj* of the blood [Greek *haima* blood]

haematic *or US* **hematic** (hee-mat-ik) *adj* relating to or containing blood

haematite *or US* **hematite** *n* a type of iron ore which is reddish-brown when powdered

haematology *or US* **hematology** *n* the branch of medical science concerned with the blood [Greek *haima* blood + -LOGY] ▷ **haematologist** *or US* **hematologist** *n*

haemoglobin *or US* **hemoglobin** (hee-moh-globe-in) *n* a protein in red blood cells that carries oxygen from the lungs to the tissues [Greek *haima* blood + Latin *globus* ball]

haemophilia *or US* **hemophilia** (hee-moh-fill-lee-a) *n* a hereditary disorder, usually affecting males, in which the blood does not clot properly [Greek *haima* blood + *philos* loving] ▷ **haemophiliac** *n*

haemorrhage *or US* **hemorrhage** (hem-or-ij) *n* **1** heavy bleeding from ruptured blood vessels ▷ *vb* **-rhaging, -rhaged** **2** to bleed heavily [Greek *haima* blood + *rhēgnunai* to burst]

haemorrhoids *or US* **hemorrhoids** (hem-or-oydz) *pl n pathol* swollen veins in the wall of the anus [Greek *haimorrhoos* discharging blood]

haere mai (hire-a-my) *interj NZ* an expression of greeting or welcome [Māori]

Ha-erh-pin *n* a transliteration of the Chinese name for Harbin

Hafiz *n* Shams al-Din Muhammad. ?1326–90, Persian lyric poet, best known for his many short poems about love and wine, often treated as religious symbols

hafnium *n chem* a metallic element found in zirconium ores. Symbol: Hf [after *Hafnia*, Latin name of Copenhagen]

haft *n* the handle of an axe, knife, or dagger [Old English *hæft*]

hag *n* **1** an unpleasant or ugly old woman **2** a witch [Old English *hægtesse* witch] ▷ **haggish** *adj*

Hagåtña *n* the capital of the Pacific island of Guam, on its W coast. Pop: 1100 (2000). Former name: **Agana**

Hagen¹ *n* an industrial city in NW Germany, in North Rhine-Westphalia. Pop: 200 039 (2003 est)

Hagen² *n* Walter. 1892–1969, US golfer

haggard *adj* looking tired and ill [Old French *hagard* wild]

Haggard *n* Sir (Henry) Rider. 1856–1925, British author of romantic adventure stories, including *King Solomon's Mines* (1885)

haggis *n* a Scottish dish made from sheep's or calf's offal, oatmeal, suet, and seasonings boiled in a skin made from the animal's stomach [origin unknown]

haggle *vb* **-gling, -gled** to bargain or wrangle (over a price) [Scandinavian]

hagiography *n, pl* **-phies** the writing of lives of the saints [Greek *hagios* holy + *graphein* to write] ▷ **hagiographer** *n*

hagiology *n, pl* **-gies** literature about the lives and legends of saints [Greek *hagios* holy + -LOGY]

hag-ridden *adj* distressed or worried

Hague¹ *n* The Hague the seat of government of the Netherlands and capital of South Holland province, situated about 3 km (2 miles) from the North Sea. Pop: 464 000 (2003 est). Dutch names: **'s Gravenhage, Den Haag**

Hague² *n* William Jefferson. born 1961, British politician; leader of the Conservative party (1997–2001); foreign secretary (2010–2014); as a writer he is noted for his biography of William Pitt the Younger (2004)

hah *interj* same as **ha¹**

ha-ha¹ *or* **haw-haw** *interj* a written representation of the sound of laughter

ha-ha² *n* a wall set in a ditch so as not to interrupt a view of the landscape [French]

Hahn *n* **1** Kurt. 1886–1974, German educationalist. During the Nazi era he escaped to Britain, where he founded Gordonstoun School (1935) and helped to establish the Duke of Edinburgh's award scheme **2** Otto. 1879–1968, German physicist: discovered the radioactive element protactinium with Meitner (1917); with Strassmann, demonstrated the nuclear fission of uranium, when it is bombarded with neutrons: Nobel prize for chemistry 1944

Hahnemann *n* (Christian Friedrich) Samuel. 1755–1843, German physician; founder of homeopathy

hahnium *n chem* another name, not in technical use, for dubnium. Symbol: Ha

Haifa *n* a port in NW Israel, near Mount Carmel, on the Bay of Acre: Israel's chief port, with an oil refinery and other heavy industry. Pop: 269 400 (2003 est)

Haig *n* Douglas, 1st Earl Haig. 1861–1928, British field marshal; commander in chief of the British forces in France and Flanders (1915–18)

haiku (hie-koo) *n, pl* **-ku** a Japanese verse form in 17 syllables [Japanese]

hail¹ *n* **1** small pellets of ice falling from thunderclouds **2** words, ideas, missiles, etc., directed with force and in great quantity: *a hail of abuse* ▷ *vb* **3** to fall as hail: *it's hailing* **4** to fall like hail: *blows hailed down on him* [Old English *hægl*]

hail² *vb* **1** to call out to; greet: *a voice from behind hailed him* **2** to praise, acclaim, or acknowledge: *his crew had been hailed as heroes* **3** to stop (a taxi) by shouting or gesturing **4** hail from to come originally from: *she hails from Nova Scotia* ▷ *n* **5** within hailing distance within hearing range ▷ *interj* **6** *poetic* an exclamation of greeting [Old Norse *heill* healthy]

Haile Selassie *n* title of *Ras Tafari Makonnen*. 1892–1975, emperor of Ethiopia (1930–36; 1941–74). During the

Italian occupation of Ethiopia (1936–41), he lived in exile in England. He was a prominent figure in the Pan-African movement: deposed 1974

hail-fellow-well-met *adj* genial and familiar in an offensive way

Hail Mary *n RC Church* a prayer to the Virgin Mary

Hailsham of St Marylebone *n* Baron, title of Quintin (McGarel) Hogg. 1907–2001, British Conservative politician; Lord Chancellor (1970–74; 1979–87). He renounced his viscountcy in 1963 when he made an unsuccessful bid for the Conservative Party leadership; he became a life peer in 1970

hailstone *n* a pellet of hail

hailstorm *n* a storm during which hail falls

Hailwood *n* Mike, full name *Stanley Michael Bailey Hailwood*. 1940–81, English racing motorcyclist: world champion (250 cc.) 1961 and 1966–67; (350 cc.) 1966–67; and (500 cc.) 1962–65

Hainan *or* **Hainan Tao** *n* an island and province in the South China Sea, separated from the mainland of S China by the **Hainan Strait**: part of Guangdong province until 1988; mainland China's largest offshore island. Pop: 8 110 000 (2003 est). Area: 33 572 sq km (12 962 sq miles)

Hainaut *or* **Hainault** *n* a province of SW Belgium: stretches from the Flanders Plain in the north to the Ardennes in the south. Capital: Mons. Pop: 1 283 200 (2004 est). Area: 3797 sq km (1466 sq miles)

Haiphong *n* a port in N Vietnam, on the Red River delta: a major industrial centre. Pop: 1 817 000 (2005 est)

hair *n* **1** any of the threadlike outgrowths on the skin of mammals **2** a mass of such outgrowths, such as on a person's head or an animal's body **3** *botany* a threadlike growth from the outer layer of a plant **4** a very small distance or margin: *he missed death by a hair* **5 get in someone's hair** *informal* to annoy someone **6 hair of the dog** an alcoholic drink taken as a cure for a hangover **7 let one's hair down** to enjoy oneself without restraint **8 not turn a hair** to show no reaction **9 split hairs** to make petty and unnecessary distinctions [Old English *hær*] ⟩ **hairless** *adj*

hairclip *n NZ and S African* a small bent metal hairpin

hairdo *n, pl* **-dos** *informal* the style of a person's hair

hairdresser *n* **1** a person who cuts and styles hair. Related adjective: **tonsorial 2** a hairdresser's premises ⟩ **hairdressing** *n*

hairgrip *n chiefly Brit* a small bent clasp used to fasten the hair

hairline *n* **1** the edge of hair at the top of the forehead ▷ *adj* **2** very fine or narrow: *a hairline crack*

hairpiece *n* a section of false hair added to a person's real hair

hairpin *n* a thin U-shaped pin used to fasten the hair

hairpin bend *n* a bend in the road that curves very sharply

hair-raising *adj* very frightening or exciting

hair's-breadth *n* an extremely small margin or distance

hair shirt *n* a shirt made of horsehair cloth worn against the skin as a penance

hair slide *n* a decorative clasp used to fasten the hair

hairsplitting *n* **1** the act of making petty distinctions ▷ *adj* **2** characterized by petty distinctions

hairspring *n* a fine spring in some clocks and watches which regulates the timekeeping

hairstyle *n* the cut and arrangement of a person's hair ⟩ **hairstylist** *n*

hair trigger *n* a trigger that responds to the slightest pressure

hairy *adj* **hairier, hairiest 1** covered with hair **2** *slang* dangerous, exciting, and difficult ⟩ **hairiness** *n*

Haiti *n* **1** a republic occupying the W part of the island of Hispaniola in the Caribbean, the E part consisting of the Dominican Republic: ceded by Spain to France in 1697

and became one of the richest colonial possessions in the world, with numerous plantations; slaves rebelled under Toussaint L'Ouverture in 1793 and defeated the French; taken over by the US (1915–41) after long political and economic chaos; under the authoritarian regimes of François Duvalier ('Papa Doc') (1957–71) and his son Jean-Claude Duvalier ('Baby Doc') (1971–86); returned to civilian rule in 1990, but another coup in 1991 brought military rule, which was ended in 1994 with US intervention; in 2010 the area around Port-au-Prince was devastated by an earthquake that killed at least 100,000 people. Official languages: French and Haitian creole. Religions: Roman Catholic and voodoo. Currency: gourde. Capital: Port-au-Prince. Pop: 9 893 934 (2013 est). Area: 27 749 sq km (10 714 sq miles) **2** a former name for Hispaniola

Haitian *adj* **1** relating to or characteristic of Haiti, its inhabitants, or their language ▷ *n* **2** a native, citizen, or inhabitant of Haiti **3** the creolized French spoken in Haiti ▶ Former spelling: **Haytian**

Haitink *n* Bernard. born 1929, Dutch orchestral conductor; received an honorary knighthood in 1977

Haji-Ioannou *n* Sir Stelios. born 1967, British businessman; born in Greece; founder (1995) and chairman (until 2002) of the low-cost airline company Easyjet

hajj *or* **hadj** *n* the pilgrimage a Muslim makes to Mecca [Arabic]

hajji *or* **hadji** *n, pl* **hajjis** *or* **hadjis** a Muslim who has made a pilgrimage to Mecca

haka *n NZ* **1** a Māori war chant accompanied by actions **2** a similar chant by a sports team

hake *n, pl* **hake** *or* **hakes 1** an edible fish of the cod family **2** *Austral* same as **barracuda** [origin unknown]

hakea (hah-kee-a) *n* an Australian tree or shrub with hard woody fruit

Hakluyt *n* Richard. ?1552–1616, English geographer, who compiled *The Principal Navigations, Voyages, and Discoveries of the English Nation* (1589)

Hakodate *n* a port in N Japan, on S Hokkaido: fishing industry and shipbuilding. Pop: 284 690 (2002 est)

hakuna matata *interj African* no problem [from Swahili, there is no problem]

Halabja *n* a Kurdish town in NE Iraq; in March 1998 Iraqi forces used poison gas on the population, killing hundreds of civilians. Pop: estimates vary between 45 000 and 80 000

halal *or* **hallal** *n* meat from animals that have been slaughtered according to Muslim law [Arabic: lawful]

halberd *n history* a tall spear that includes an axe blade and a pick [Middle High German *helm* handle + *barde* axe]

Halberstadt *n* a town in central Germany, in Saxony-Anhalt: industrial centre noted for its historic buildings. Pop: 40 014 (2003 est)

halcyon (hal-see-on) *adj* **1** peaceful, gentle, and calm **2 halcyon days** a time, usually in the past, of greatest happiness or success [Greek *alkuōn* kingfisher]

Haldane *n* **1** J(ohn) B(urdon) S(anderson) 1892–1964, Scottish biochemist, geneticist, and writer on science **2** his father, **John Scott**. 1860–1936, Scottish physiologist noted particularly for his research into industrial diseases **3** his brother, **Richard Burdon**, 1st Viscount Haldane of Cloan. 1856–1928, British statesman and jurist. As secretary of state for war (1905–12) he reorganized the army and set up the territorial reserve

hale *adj* healthy and robust: *hale and hearty* [Old English *hæl* whole]

Hale *n* **1** George Ellery. 1868–1938, US astronomer: undertook research into sunspots and invented the spectroheliograph **2** Sir Matthew. 1609–76, English judge and scholar; Lord Chief Justice (1671–76)

Haleakala *n* a volcano in Hawaii, on E Maui island. Height: 3057 m (10 032 ft). Area of crater: 49 sq km (19 sq miles). Depth of crater: 829 m (2720 ft)

Halesowen *n* a town in W central England, in Dudley unitary authority, West Midlands. Pop: 55 273 (2001)

Halévy *n* 1 (Jacques François) Fromental, original name *Elias Levy*. 1799–1862, French composer, noted for his operas, which include *La Juive* (1835) 2 his nephew, Ludovic. 1834–1908, French dramatist and novelist, who collaborated with Meilhac on opera libretti

Haley *n* Bill, full name *William John Clifton Haley*. 1925–81, US rock and roll singer, best known for his recording of "Rock Around the Clock" (1955)

half *n, pl* **halves 1** either of two equal or corresponding parts that together make up a whole **2** the fraction equal to one divided by two **3** half a pint, esp. of beer **4** *sport* one of two equal periods of play in a game **5** a half-price ticket **6 by half** to an excessive degree: *too clever by half* **7 by halves** without being thorough: *in Italy they rarely do things by halves* **8 go halves** to share expenses ▷ *adj* **9** denoting one of two equal parts: *a half chicken* ▷ *adv* **10** half in degree or quantity: *half as much* **11** partially; to an extent: *half hidden in the trees* **12 not half** *informal* **a** *Brit* very; indeed: *it isn't half hard to look at these charts* **b** yes, indeed [Old English *healf*]

half-and-half *adj* half one thing and half another thing

halfback *n rugby* a player positioned immediately behind the forwards

half-baked *adj informal* poorly planned: *half-baked policies*

half board *n Brit* the daily provision by a hotel of bed, breakfast, and evening meal

half-bottle *n* a bottle of spirits or wine that contains half the quantity of a standard bottle

half-breed *n offensive* a person whose parents are of different races

half-brother *n* the son of either one's mother or father by another partner

half-caste *n offensive* a person whose parents are of different races

half-cock *n* **go off at half-cock** *or* **half-cocked** to fail because of lack of preparation

half-crown *or* **half-a-crown** *n* a former British coin worth two shillings and sixpence (12½p)

half-cut *adj Brit slang* rather drunk

half-day *n* a day when one works only in the morning or only in the afternoon

half-dozen *n* six

half-hearted *adj* without enthusiasm or determination ▷ **half-heartedly** *adv*

half-hitch *n* a knot made by passing the end of a piece of rope around itself and through the loop so made

half-hour *n* **1** a period of 30 minutes **2** the point of time 30 minutes after the beginning of an hour ▷ **half-hourly** *adv, adj*

half-life *n* the time taken for radioactive material to lose half its radioactivity

half-light *n* a dim light, such as at dawn or dusk

half-mast *n* the halfway position of a flag on a mast as a sign of mourning

half measures *pl n* inadequate actions or solutions: *the education system cannot be reformed by half measures*

half-moon *n* **1** the moon when half its face is illuminated **2** the time at which a half-moon occurs **3** something shaped like a half-moon

half-nelson *n* a wrestling hold in which a wrestler places an arm under his opponent's arm from behind and exerts pressure with his palm on the back of his opponent's neck

halfpenny *or* **ha'penny** (hayp-nee) *n, pl* **-pennies** a former British coin worth half a penny

half-pie *adj NZ informal* badly planned; not properly thought out: *a half-pie scheme* [Māori *pai* good]

half-pipe *n* a structure with a U-shaped cross section, used in skateboarding, snowboarding, Rollerblading, etc.

half-price *adj, adv* for half the normal price: *special half-price tickets; jeans bought half-price in a sale*

half-sister *n* the daughter of either one's mother or father by another partner

half term *n Brit education* a short holiday midway through a term

half-timbered *adj* (of a building) having an exposed timber framework filled with brick or plaster

half-time *n sport* an interval between the two halves of a game

half-title *n* the first right-hand page of a book, with only the title on it

halftone *n* a photographic illustration in which the image is composed of a large number of black and white dots

half-track *n* a vehicle with moving tracks on the rear wheels

half-truth *n* a partially true statement ▷ **half-true** *adj*

half volley *sport n* **1** a stroke or shot in which the ball is hit immediately after it bounces ▷ *vb* **half-volley 2** to hit or kick (a ball) immediately after it bounces

halfway *adv* **1** at or to half the distance **2** at or towards the middle of a period of time or of an event or process **3** rather: *halfway decent* **4 meet someone halfway** to compromise with someone ▷ *adj* **5** at the same distance from two points: *the halfway line*

halfway house *n* **1** a place to rest midway on a journey **2** the halfway stage in any process: *a halfway house between the theatre and cinema is possible*

halfwit *n* a foolish or feeble-minded person ▷ **halfwitted** *adj*

halibut *n* a large edible flatfish [Middle English *hali* holy (because it was eaten on holy days) + *butte* flatfish]

Haliç *n* the Turkish name for the **Golden Horn**

Halicarnassian *adj* of or relating to the ancient Greek city of Halicarnassus

Halicarnassus *n* a Greek colony on the SW coast of Asia Minor: one of the major Hellenistic cities

Halifax¹ *n* **1** a port in SE Canada, capital of Nova Scotia, on the Atlantic: founded in 1749 as a British stronghold. Pop: 390 096 (2011) **2** a town in N England, in Calderdale unitary authority, West Yorkshire: textiles. Pop: 83 570 (2001)

Halifax² *n* **1** Charles Montagu, Earl of Halifax. 1661–1715, British statesman; founder of the National Debt (1692) and the Bank of England (1694) **2** Edward Frederick Lindley Wood, Earl of Halifax. 1881–1959, British Conservative statesman. He was viceroy of India (1926–31), foreign secretary (1938–40), and ambassador to the US (1941–46) **3** George Savile, 1st Marquess of Halifax, known as *the Trimmer*. 1633–95, British politician, noted for his wavering opinions. He opposed the exclusion of the Catholic James II from the throne but later supported the Glorious Revolution

Haligonian *n* **1** a native or resident of Halifax, Canada ▷ *adj* **2** of or relating to Halifax, Canada

halitosis *n* bad-smelling breath [Latin *halitus* breath]

hall *n* **1** an entry area to other rooms in a house **2** a building or room for public meetings, dances, etc. **3** a residential building in a college or university **4** *Brit* a great house of an estate; manor **5** a large dining room in a college or university **6** the large room of a castle or stately home [Old English *heall*]

Hall *n* **1** Charles Martin. 1863–1914, US chemist: discovered the electrolytic process for producing aluminium **2** Sir John. 1824–1907, New Zealand statesman, born in England: prime minister of New Zealand (1879–82) **3** Sir Peter. born 1930, English stage director: director of the Royal Shakespeare Company (1960–73) and of the National Theatre (1973–88) **4** (Marguerite) Radclyffe. 1883–1943, British novelist and poet. Her frank treatment of a lesbian theme in the novel *The Well of Loneliness* (1928) led to an obscenity trial

Halle *n* a city in E central Germany, in Saxony-Anhalt, on the River Saale: early saltworks; a Hanseatic city in the late Middle Ages; university (1694). Pop: 240 119

(2003 est). Official name: **Halle an der Saale**

Hallé *n* Sir Charles, original name Karl Hallé. 1819–95, German conductor and pianist, in Britain from 1848. In 1857 he founded the Hallé Orchestra in Manchester

hallelujah, halleluiah (hal-ee-loo-ya) *or* **alleluia** *interj* an exclamation of praise to God [Hebrew *hellēl* to praise + *yāh* the Lord]

Haller *n* Albrecht von. 1708–77, Swiss biologist: founder of experimental physiology

Halley *n* Edmund. 1656–1742, English astronomer and mathematician. He predicted the return of the comet now known as **Halley's comet**, constructed charts of magnetic declination, and produced the first wind maps

Hall-Jones *n* Sir William. 1851–1936, New Zealand statesman, born in England: prime minister of New Zealand (1906)

hallmark *n* **1** a typical feature: *secrecy became the hallmark of government* **2** Brit an official stamped on gold, silver, or platinum articles to guarantee purity and date of manufacture **3** a mark of authenticity or excellence ▷ *vb* **4** to stamp with a hallmark [after Goldsmiths' *Hall* in London, where items were stamped]

hallo *interj, n* same as **hello**

halloo *interj* chiefly Brit a shout used to call hounds at a hunt [perhaps variant of *hallow* to encourage hounds by shouting]

halloumi *or* **haloumi** *n* a salty white sheep's cheese from Greece or Turkey, usually eaten grilled [from Arabic *haluma* be mild]

hallowed *adj* **1** regarded as holy: *hallowed ground* **2** respected and revered because of age, importance, or reputation: *the hallowed pitch at Lord's* [Old English *hālgian* to consecrate]

Halloween *or* **Hallowe'en** *n* October 31, celebrated by children by dressing up as ghosts, witches, etc. [*all hallow even* all saints' eve]

hallucinate *vb* **-nating, -nated** to seem to see something that is not really there [Latin *alucinari*]

hallucination *n* the experience of seeming to see something that is not really there ❯ **hallucinatory** *adj*

hallucinogen *n* any drug that causes hallucinations ❯ **hallucinogenic** *adj*

hallway *n* an entrance area

Halmahera *n* an island in NE Indonesia, the largest of the Moluccas: consists of four peninsulas enclosing three bays; mountainous and forested. Area: 17 780 sq km (6865 sq miles). Former names: **Djailolo**, **Gilolo**, **Jilolo**

Halmstad *n* a port in SW Sweden, on the Kattegat. Pop: 88 032 (2004 est)

halo (hay-loh) *n, pl* **-loes** *or* **-los** **1** a ring of light around the head of a sacred figure **2** a circle of refracted light around the sun or moon ▷ *vb* **-loes** *or* **-los, -loing, -loed** **3** to surround with a halo [Greek *halōs* circular threshing floor]

halogen (hal-oh-jen) *n* chem any of the nonmetallic chemical elements fluorine, chlorine, bromine, iodine, and astatine, which form salts when combined with metal [Greek *hals* salt + *-genēs* born]

Hals *n* Frans. ?1580–1666, Dutch portrait and genre painter: his works include *The Laughing Cavalier* (1624)

Hälsingborg *n* the former name (until 1971) of **Helsingborg**

halt *vb* **1** to come to a stop or bring (someone or something) to a stop ▷ *n* **2** a temporary standstill **3** a military command to stop **4** chiefly Brit a minor railway station without a building: *Deeside Halt* **5 call a halt to** to put an end to [German *halten* to stop]

halter *n* **1** a strap around a horse's head with a rope to lead it with ▷ *vb* **2** to put a halter on (a horse) [Old English *hælfter*]

halterneck *n* a woman's top or dress which fastens behind the neck, leaving the back and arms bare

halting *adj* hesitant or uncertain: *she spoke halting Italian*

Halton *n* a unitary authority in NW England, in N Cheshire. Pop: 118 400 (2003 est). Area: 75 sq km (29 sq miles)

halve *vb* **halving, halved** **1** to divide (something) into two equal parts **2** to reduce (the size or amount of something) by half **3** golf to draw with one's opponent on (a hole or round)

halyard *n* nautical a line for hoisting or lowering a ship's sail or flag [Middle English *halier*]

ham¹ *n* smoked or salted meat from a pig's thigh [Old English *hamm*]

ham² *n* **1** informal an amateur radio operator **2** theatre informal an actor who overacts and exaggerates the emotions and gestures of a part ▷ *adj* **3** (of actors or their performances) exaggerated and overstated ▷ *vb* **hamming, hammed** **4 ham it up** informal to overact [special use of HAM¹]

Hama *n* a city in W Syria, on the Orontes River: an early Hittite settlement; famous for its huge water wheels, used for irrigation since the Middle Ages. Pop: 439 000 (2005 est). Biblical name: **Hamath**

Hamadān *or* **Hamedān** *n* a city in W central Iran, at an altitude of over 1830 m (6000 ft): changed hands several times from the 17th century between Iraq, Persia, and Turkey; trading centre. Pop: 508 000 (2005 est)

Hamamatsu *n* a city in central Japan, in S central Honshu: cotton textiles and musical instruments. Pop: 573 504 (2002 est)

hamba *interj* S African usually offensive go away [Nguni (language group of southern Africa): to go]

Hamburg *n* a city-state and port in NW Germany, on the River Elbe: the largest port in Germany; a founder member of the Hanseatic League; became a free imperial city in 1510 and a state of the German empire in 1871; university (1919); extensive shipyards. Pop: 1 734 083 (2003 est)

hamburger *n* a flat round of minced beef, often served in a bread roll [*Hamburger steak*, steak in the fashion of *Hamburg*, Germany]

Hameln *n* an industrial town in N Germany, in Lower Saxony on the Weser River: famous for the legend of the Pied Piper (supposedly took place in 1284). Pop: 58 902 (2003 est). English name: **Hamelin**

Hamersley Range *n* a mountain range in N Western Australia: iron-ore deposits. Highest peak: 1236 m (4056 ft)

ham-fisted *or* **ham-handed** *adj* informal very clumsy or awkward

Hamhung *or* **Hamheung** *n* an industrial city in central North Korea: commercial and governmental centre of NE Korea during the Yi dynasty (1392–1910). Pop: 753 000 (2005 est)

Hamilcar Barca *n* died ?228 BC, Carthaginian general; father of Hannibal. He held command (247–41) during the first Punic War and established Carthaginian influence in Spain (237–?228)

Hamilton¹ *n* **1** a port in central Canada, in S Ontario on Lake Ontario: iron and steel industry. Pop: 618 820 (2001) **2** a city in New Zealand, on central North Island. Pop: 150 200 (2011 est) **3** a town in S Scotland, in South Lanarkshire near Glasgow. Pop: 48 546 (2001) **4** the capital and chief port of Bermuda. Pop: 3461 (2000) **5** the former name of **Churchill** (1)

Hamilton² *n* **1** Alexander. ?1757–1804, American statesman. He was a leader of the Federalists and as first secretary of the Treasury (1789–95) established a federal bank **2** Lady **Emma**. ?1765–1815, mistress of Nelson **3** James, 1st Duke of Hamilton. 1606–49, Scottish supporter of Charles I in the English Civil War: defeated by Cromwell at the Battle of Preston and executed **4** Lewis (**Carl**). born 1985, English racing driver; Formula One world champion (2008, 2014) **5** Richard. 1922–2011, British artist: a pioneer of the pop art style **6** Sir William Rowan. 1805–65, Irish mathematician: founded

Hamiltonian mechanics and formulated the theory of quaternions

hamlet *n* a small village [Old French *hamelet*]

Hamlisch *n* Marvin. 1944–2012, US composer, best known for the musical *A Chorus Line* (1975)

Hamlyn *n* Baron Paul. 1926–2001, British businessman and publisher

Hamm *n* an industrial city in NW Germany, in North Rhine-Westphalia: a Hanse town from 1417; severely damaged in World War II. Pop: 184 961 (2003 est)

Hammarskjöld *n* Dag (Hjalmar Agne Carl). 1905–61, Swedish statesman; secretary-general of the United Nations (1953–61): Nobel peace prize 1961

hammer *n* **1** a hand tool consisting of a heavy metal head on the end of a handle, used for driving in nails, beating metal, etc. **2** the part of a gun that causes the bullet to shoot when the trigger is pulled **3** *athletics* **a** a heavy metal ball attached to a flexible wire: thrown in competitions **b** the sport of throwing the hammer **4** an auctioneer's mallet **5** the part of a piano that hits a string when a key is pressed **6 come** *or* **go under the hammer** to be on sale at auction **7 hammer and tongs** with great effort or energy ▷ *vb* **8** to hit with or as if with a hammer **9** *Brit* to criticize severely **10** *informal* to defeat heavily **11** to feel or sound like hammering: *his heart was hammering* **12 hammer in** to force (facts or ideas) into someone through repetition **13 hammer away at** to work at (something) constantly: *the paper hammered away at the same theme all the way through the campaign* ▶ See also **hammer out** [Old English *hamor*]

hammer and sickle *n* the emblem on the flag of the former Soviet Union, representing the industrial workers and the peasants

Hammerfest *n* a port in N Norway, on the W coast of Kvalöy Island: the northernmost town in Europe, with uninterrupted daylight from May 17 to July 29 and no sun between Nov 21 and Jan 21; fishing and tourist centre. Pop: 9157 (2004 est)

hammerhead *n* a shark with a wide flattened head

hammer out *vb* to produce (an agreement) with great effort

Hammersmith and Fulham *n* a borough of Greater London on the River Thames: established in 1965 by the amalgamation of Fulham and Hammersmith. Pop: 174 200 (2003 est). Area: 16 sq km (6 sq miles)

Hammerstein II *n* Oscar. 1895–1960, US librettist and songwriter: collaborated with the composer Richard Rodgers in musicals such as *South Pacific* (1949) and *The Sound of Music* (1959)

hammertoe *n* a condition in which the toe is permanently bent at the joint

Hammett *n* Dashiell. 1894–1961, US writer of detective novels. His books include *The Maltese Falcon* (1930) and *The Thin Man* (1932)

hammock *n* a hanging bed made of canvas or net [Spanish *hamaca*]

Hammond¹ *n* a city in NW Indiana, adjacent to Chicago. Pop: 80 547 (2003 est)

Hammond² *n* **1** Dame Joan. 1912–96, Australian operatic singer, born in New Zealand **2** Walter Reginald, known as Wally. 1903–65, English cricketer. An all-rounder, he played for England 85 times between 1928 and 1946

Hammurabi *or* **Hammurapi** *n* ?18th century BC, king of Babylonia; promulgator of one of the earliest known codes of law

hammy *n*, *pl* **-mies** *informal* short for **hamstring** (1)

Hampden *n* John. 1594–1643, English statesman; one of the leaders of the Parliamentary opposition to Charles I

hamper¹ *vb* to make it difficult for (someone or something) to move or progress [origin unknown]

hamper² *n* **1** a large basket with a lid **2** *Brit* a selection of food and drink packed as a gift [Middle English *hanaper* a small basket]

Hampshire¹ *n* a county of S England, on the English Channel: crossed by the **Hampshire Downs** and the South Downs, with the New Forest in the southwest and many prehistoric and Roman remains: the geographical and ceremonial county includes Portsmouth and Southampton, which became independent unitary authorities in 1997. Administrative centre: Winchester. Pop (excluding unitary authorities): 1 251 000 (2003 est). Area (excluding unitary authorities): 3679 sq km (1420 sq miles). Abbreviation: **Hants**

Hampshire² *n* Sir Stuart. 1914–2004, British philosopher: his publications include *Thought and Action* (1959), *Two Theories of Morality* (1977), and *Innocence and Experience* (1989)

Hampstead *n* a residential district in N London: part of the Greater London borough of Camden since 1965; nearby is **Hampstead Heath**, a popular recreation area

Hampton¹ *n* **1** a city in SE Virginia, on the harbour of **Hampton Roads** on Chesapeake Bay. Pop: 146 878 (2003 est) **2** a district of the Greater London borough of Richmond-upon-Thames, on the River Thames: famous for **Hampton Court Palace** (built in 1515 by Cardinal Wolsey)

Hampton² *n* **1** Christopher (James). born 1946, British playwright: his works include *When Did You Last See My Mother?* (1964), the screenplay for the film *Dangerous Liaisons* (1988), the book for the musical *Sunset Boulevard* (1993), and the screenplay for the film *Atonement* (2007) **2** Lionel. 1913–2002, US jazz-band leader and vibraphone player

hamster *n* a small rodent with a stocky body, short tail, and cheek pouches [German]

hamstring *n* **1** one of the tendons at the back of the knee ▷ *vb* **-stringing, -strung 2** to make it difficult for someone to take any action [*ham* (in the sense: leg)]

Hamsun *n* Knut, pen name of *Knut Pedersen*. 1859–1952, Norwegian novelist, whose works include *The Growth of the Soil* (1917): Nobel prize for literature 1920

Han *n* a river in E central China, rising in S Shaanxi and flowing southeast through Hubei to the Yangtze River at Wuhan. Length: about 1450 km (900 miles)

Hanau *n* a city in central Germany, in Hesse east of Frankfurt am Main: a centre of the jewellery industry. Pop: 88 897 (2003 est)

Han Cities *pl n* a group of three cities in E central China (Hanyang, Hankow, and Wuchang), in SE Hubei at the confluence of the Han and Yangtze Rivers; united in 1950 to form the conurbation of Wuhan, the capital of Hubei province

Hancock *n* **1** Anthony John, known as *Tony*. 1924–68, British comedian, noted for his radio series *Hancock's Half Hour* **2** John. 1737–93, American statesman; first signatory of the Declaration of Independence

hand *n* **1** the part of the body at the end of the arm, consisting of a thumb, four fingers, and a palm. Related adjective: **manual 2** a person's style of writing: *scrolls written in her own hand* **3** the influence a person or thing has over a particular situation: *the hand of the military in shaping policy was obvious* **4** a part in some activity: *I remember with gratitude Fortune's hand in starting my collection* **5** assistance: *give me a hand with the rice* **6** a round of applause: *give a big hand to the most exciting duo in the game* **7** consent to marry someone: *he asked for her hand in marriage* **8** a manual worker **9** a member of a ship's crew **10** a pointer on a dial or gauge, esp. on a clock **11 a** the cards dealt in one round of a card game **b** one round of a card game **12** a position indicated by its location to the side of an object or the observer: *on the right hand* **13** a contrasting aspect or condition: *on the other hand* **14** source: *I had experienced at first hand many management styles* **15** a person who creates something: *a good hand at baking* **16** a unit of length equalling four inches, used for measuring the height of horses **17 by hand a** by manual rather than mechanical means **b** by messenger: *the letter was delivered by hand* **18 from hand to mouth** with no food or money in

h

reserve: *living from hand to mouth* **19 hand in glove** in close association **20 hand over fist** steadily and quickly: *losing money hand over fist* **21 in hand a** under control **b** receiving attention: *the business in hand* **c** available in reserve: *Pakistan have a game in hand* **22 keep one's hand in** to continue to practise something **23 (near) at hand** very close **24 on hand** close by; available **25 out of hand a** beyond control **b** decisively, without possible reconsideration: *he dismissed the competition out of hand* **26 show one's hand** to reveal one's plans **27 to hand** accessible ▷ *vb* **28** to pass or give by the hand or hands **29 hand it to someone** to give credit to someone ▶ See also **hand down, hand on, hands**, etc. [Old English] **> handless** *adj*

handbag *n* a woman's small bag carried to contain personal articles

handball *n* a game in which two teams of seven players try to throw a ball into their opponent's goal

handbill *n* a small printed notice for distribution by hand

handbook *n* a reference manual giving practical information on a subject

handbrake *n* a brake in a motor vehicle operated by a hand lever

h & c hot and cold (water)

handcart *n* a simple cart pushed or pulled by hand, used for transporting goods

handcrafted *adj* made by handicraft

handcuff *n* **1 handcuffs** a linked pair of locking metal rings used for securing prisoners ▷ *vb* **2** to put handcuffs on (a person)

hand down *vb* **1** to pass on (knowledge, possessions, or skills) to a younger generation **2** to pass (outgrown clothes) on from one member of a family to a younger one **3** *US and Canad law* to announce (a verdict)

Handel *n* George Frideric. German name *Georg Friedrich Händel*. 1685–1759, German composer, resident in England, noted particularly for his oratorios, including the *Messiah* (1741) and *Samson* (1743). Other works include over 40 operas, 12 concerti grossi, organ concertos, chamber and orchestral music, esp. *Water Music* (1717)

handful *n, pl* **-fuls 1** the amount that can be held in the hand **2** a small number: *a handful of parents* **3** *informal* a person or animal that is difficult to control: *as a child she was a real handful*

hand-held *adj* **1** held in position by the hand ▷ *n* **2** a device, such as a computer, that can be held in the hand

handicap *n* **1** a physical or mental disability **2** something that makes progress difficult **3 a** a contest in which competitors are given advantages or disadvantages in an attempt to equalize their chances **b** the advantage or disadvantage given **4** *golf* the number of strokes by which a player's averaged score exceeds par for the course ▷ *vb* **-capping, -capped 5** to make it difficult for (someone) to do something [probably *hand in cap*, a lottery game in which players drew forfeits from a cap]

handicapped *adj* physically or mentally disabled

> **USAGE** Many disabled people find the use of the word *handicapped* to describe them or their condition offensive. See **disabled**

handicraft *n* **1** a skill performed with the hands, such as weaving **2** the objects produced by people with such skills

handiwork *n* **1** the result of someone's work or activity **2** work produced by hand

handkerchief *n* a small square of fabric used to wipe the nose

handle *n* **1** the part of an object that is held or operated in order that it may be used **2** a small lever used to open and close a door or window **3** *slang* a person's name **4** a reason for doing something: *trying to get a handle on why*

companies borrow money **5 fly off the handle** *informal* to become suddenly extremely angry ▷ *vb* **-dling, -dled 6** to hold, move, operate, or touch with the hands **7** to have responsibility for: *she handles all their affairs personally* **8** to manage successfully: *I can handle this challenge* **9** to discuss (a subject) **10** to deal with in a specified way: *the affair was neatly handled* **11** to trade or deal in (specified merchandise): *we handle 1800 properties in Normandy* **12** to react or respond in a specified way to operation or control: *it's light and handles well* [Old English] **> handling** *n*

handlebars *pl n* a metal tube with handles at each end, used for steering a bicycle or motorcycle

handler *n* **1** a person who trains and controls an animal **2** a person who handles something: *a baggage handler*

Handler *n* Daniel. born 1970, US writer for older children best known for the macabre humour of his *A Series of Unfortunate Events*, a sequence of books written in the persona of Lemony Snicket

handmade *adj* made by hand, not by machine

handmaiden *or* **handmaid** *n* **1** *old-fashioned* a female servant **2** a person or thing that serves a useful but lesser purpose: *these policies resulted in agriculture becoming the poor handmaiden of industry*

hand-me-down *n* *informal* an item of clothing that someone has finished with and passed on to someone else

hand on *vb* to pass (something) to the next person in a succession

hand-out *n, pl* **hand-outs 1** clothing, food, or money given to a needy person **2** a leaflet, free sample, etc., given out to publicize something **3** a piece of written information given out to the audience at a talk, lecture, etc. ▷ *vb* **hand out 4** to distribute

hand over *vb* to give up possession of or transfer (something)

hand-pick *vb* to select (a person) with great care, such as for a special job **> hand-picked** *adj*

handrail *n* a rail alongside a stairway, to provide support

hands *pl n* **1 change hands** to pass from the possession of one person to another **2 have one's hands full** to be completely occupied **3 in someone's hands** in someone's control or power: *that's in the hands of the courts* **4 off one's hands** no longer one's responsibility **5 on one's hands** for which one is responsible: *what a problem case I've got on my hands* **6 wash one's hands of** to have nothing more to do with **7 win hands down** to win easily

Hands *n* Terence David, known as *Terry*. born 1941, British theatre director: chief executive and artistic director (1986–91) of the Royal Shakespeare Company

handset *n* a telephone mouthpiece and earpiece in a single unit

hands-free *adj, n* (of) a device allowing the user to make and receive phonecalls without holding the handset

handshake *n* the act of grasping and shaking a person's hand, such as in greeting or when agreeing on a deal

handsome *adj* **1** (esp. of a man) good-looking **2** (of a building, garden, etc.) large, well-made, and with an attractive appearance: *a handsome building* **3** (of an amount of money) generous or large: *a handsome dividend* [obsolete *handsom* easily handled] **> handsomely** *adv*

hands-on *adj* involving practical experience of equipment: *Navy personnel joined the 1986 expedition for hands-on operating experience*

handspring *n* a gymnastic exercise in which a person leaps forwards or backwards into a handstand and then onto his or her feet

handstand *n* the act of supporting the body on the hands in an upside-down position

hand-to-hand *adj, adv* at close quarters, with fists or knives: *hand-to-hand combat*; *they fought hand-to-hand*

hand-to-mouth *adj, adv* with barely enough money or food to live on: *a hand-to-mouth existence*; *they lived hand-to-mouth*

handwork *n* work done by hand rather than by machine

handwriting n **1** writing by hand rather than by typing or printing **2** a person's characteristic writing style ⟩ **handwritten** adj

handy adj **handier, handiest 1** conveniently within reach **2** easy to handle or use **3** good at manual work ⟩ **handily** adv

Handy n W(illiam) C(hristopher). 1873–1958, US blues musician and songwriter, esp. noted for the song "St Louis Blues"

handyman n, pl **-men** a man skilled at odd jobs

Han Fei Zu n died 233 BC, Chinese diplomat and philosopher of law

hang vb **hanging, hung 1** to fasten or be fastened from above **2** to place (something) in position, for instance by a hinge, so as to allow free movement: to hang a door **3** to be suspended so as to allow movement from the place where it is attached: her long hair hung over her face **4** to decorate with something suspended, such as pictures **5** (of cloth or clothing) to fall or flow in a particular way: the fine gauge knit hangs loosely with graceful femininity **6** (past, past part **hanged**) to suspend or be suspended by the neck until dead **7** to hover: clouds hung over the mountains **8** to fasten to a wall: to hang wallpaper **9** to exhibit or be exhibited in an art gallery **10** (past, past part **hanged**) slang to damn: used in mild curses or interjections **11** hang fire to put off doing something **12** hang over to threaten or overshadow: the threat of war hung over the Middle East ▷ n **13** the way in which something hangs **14 get the hang of** something informal to understand the technique of doing something ▶ See also **hang about, hang back,** etc. [Old English hangian]

hang about or **hang around** vb **1** to stand about idly somewhere **2** (foll. by with) to spend a lot of time in the company (of someone)

hangar n a large building for storing aircraft [French: shed]

hang back vb to be reluctant to do something

Hangchow n a variant transliteration of the Chinese name for **Hangzhou**

hangdog adj dejected, ashamed, or guilty in appearance or manner

hanger n same as **coat hanger**

hanger-on n, pl **hangers-on** an unwanted follower, esp. of a rich or famous person

hang-glider n an unpowered aircraft consisting of a large cloth wing stretched over a light framework from which the pilot hangs in a harness ⟩ **hang-gliding** n

hangi (hung-ee) n NZ **1** an open-air cooking pit **2** the food cooked in it **3** the social gathering at the resultant meal [Māori]

hanging n **1** the act or practice of putting a person to death by suspending the body by the neck **2** a large piece of cloth hung on a wall as a decoration

Hanging Gardens of Babylon n (in ancient Babylon) gardens, probably planted on terraces of a ziggurat: one of the Seven Wonders of the World

hanging valley n geography a tributary valley that enters a main valley high up because the main valley has been deepened through erosion by a glacier

hangman n, pl **-men** an official who carries out a sentence of hanging

hangnail n a piece of skin partly torn away from the base or side of a fingernail

hang on vb **1** informal to wait: hang on a minute, will you? **2** to continue or persist with effort or difficulty **3** to grasp or hold **4** to depend on: a lot hangs on its success **5** to listen attentively to: she hangs on every word our leader says

hang out vb **1** to suspend, be suspended, or lean **2** informal to live or spend a lot of time in a place: fishermen hang out in waterfront bars **3 let it all hang out** informal, chiefly US to relax completely; act or speak freely ▷ n **hang-out 4** a place where someone spends a lot of time

hangover n a feeling of sickness and headache after drinking too much alcohol

hang together vb **1** to be united **2** to be consistent: the story simply did not hang together

Hanguk n the Korean name for **South Korea**

hang up vb **1** to replace (a telephone receiver) at the end of a conversation **2** to put on a hook or hanger ▷ n **hang-up 3** an emotional or psychological problem

Hangzhou or **Hangchow** n a port in E China, capital of Zhejiang province, on **Hangzhou Bay** (an inlet of the East China Sea), at the foot of the Eye of Heaven Mountains: regarded by Marco Polo as the finest city in the world; seat of two universities (1927, 1959). Pop: 1 955 000 (2005 est)

Hania n a variant spelling of **Chania**

hank n a loop or coil, esp. of yarn [from Old Norse]

hanker vb (foll. by for or after) to have a great desire for [probably from Dutch dialect hankeren] ⟩ **hankering** n

Hankow or **Han-k'ou** n a former city in SE China, in SE Hubei at the confluence of the Han and Yangtze Rivers: one of the Han Cities; merged with Hanyang and Wuchang in 1950 to form the conurbation of Wuhan

Hanks n Tom. born 1956, US film actor: his films include Splash (1984), Philadelphia (1993), Forrest Gump (1994), Saving Private Ryan (1998), and The Terminal (2004)

hanky or **hankie** n, pl **hankies** informal short for **handkerchief**

hanky-panky n informal **1** casual sexual relations **2** mischievous behaviour [variant of hocus-pocus]

Hanna n William. 1910–2001, US animator and film producer who with Joseph Barbera (1911–2006) created the cartoon characters Tom and Jerry in the 1940s; the Hanna–Barbera company later produced numerous cartoon series for television.

Hannibal n 247–182 BC, Carthaginian general; son of Hamilcar Barca. He commanded the Carthaginian army in the Second Punic War (218–201). After capturing Saguntum in Spain, he invaded Italy (218), crossing the Alps with an army of about 40 000 men and defeating the Romans at Trasimene (217) and Cannae (216). In 203 he was recalled to defend Carthage and was defeated by Scipio at Zama (202). He was later forced into exile and committed suicide to avoid capture

Hannover n a city in N Germany, capital of Lower Saxony: capital of the kingdom of Hannover (1815–66); situated on the Mittelland canal. Pop: 516 160 (2003 est). English spelling: **Hanover**

Hanoi n the capital of Vietnam, on the Red River: became capital of Tonkin in 1802, of French Indochina in 1887, of Vietnam in 1945, and of North Vietnam (1954–75); university (1917); industrial centre. Pop: 4 147 000 (2005 est)

Hanover n the English spelling of **Hannover**

Hanoverian[1] (han-no-**veer**-ee-an) adj of or relating to the British royal house ruling from 1714 to 1901 [after Hanover, Germany]

Hanoverian[2] adj of, relating to, or situated in Hannover

Hanratty n James. 1936–62, Englishman executed, despite conflicting evidence, for a murder on the A6 road. Subsequent public concern played a major part in the abolition of capital punishment in Britain. New DNA evidence led to an appeal by Hanratty's supporters being dismissed in 2002

Hansard n the official report of the proceedings of the British or Canadian parliament [after L. Hansard, its original compiler]

Hanseatic League (han-see-**at**-ik) n history a commercial organization of towns in N Germany formed in the 14th century to protect and control trade

hansom n formerly, a two-wheeled one-horse carriage with a fixed hood. Also called: **hansom cab** [after its designer J. A. Hansom]

Hants Hampshire

Hanukkah n same as **Chanukah**

Hanyang or **Han-yang** n a former city in SE China, in SE Hubei at the confluence of the Han and Yangtze

Rivers: one of the Han Cities; merged with Hankow and Wuchang in 1950 to form the conurbation of Wuhan

haphazard *adj* not organized or planned [Old Norse *happ* chance, good luck + HAZARD] ▷ **haphazardly** *adv*

hapless *adj* unlucky: *the hapless victim of a misplaced murder attempt* [Old Norse *happ* chance, good luck]

haploid *adj* biology denoting a cell or organism with unpaired chromosomes [Greek *haplous* single]

haplotype *n* genetics a set of alleles inherited by an individual from a single parent

happen *vb* 1 to take place; occur 2 to chance (to be or do something): *I happen to know him* 3 to be the case, esp. by chance: *it happens that I know him* 4 **happen to** (of some unforeseen event, such as death) to be the experience or fate of: *if anything happens to me you will know* [obsolete *hap*]

> **USAGE** See at occur.

happening *n* an event that often occurs in a way that is unexpected or hard to explain: *some strange happenings in the village recently*

happy *adj* **-pier, -piest** 1 feeling or expressing joy 2 causing joy or gladness: *the happiest day of my life* 3 fortunate or lucky: *it was a happy coincidence* 4 satisfied or content: *he seems happy to let things go on as they are* 5 willing: *I'll be happy to arrange a loan for you* [Old Norse *happ* chance, good luck] ▷ **happily** *adv* ▷ **happiness** *n*

happy-go-lucky *adj* carefree or easy-going

hara-kiri *n* (formerly, in Japan) ritual suicide by disembowelment when disgraced or under sentence of death [Japanese *hara* belly + *kiri* cut]

Harald I *n* called *Harald Fairhair*. ?850–933, first king of Norway: his rule caused emigration to the British Isles

Harald III *n* surname *Hardraade*. 1015–66, king of Norway (1047–66); invaded England (1066) and died at the battle of Stamford Bridge

harangue *vb* **-ranguing, -rangued** 1 to address (a person or group) in an angry or forcefully persuasive way ▷ *n* 2 a forceful or angry speech [Old Italian *aringa* public speech]

Harappa *n* an ancient city in the Punjab in NW Pakistan: one of the centres of the Indus civilization that flourished from 2500 to 1700 BC; probably destroyed by Indo-European invaders

Harappan *adj* 1 of or relating to Harappa or its inhabitants ▷ *n* 2 a native or inhabitant of Harappa

Harar or **Harrer** *n* a city in E Ethiopia: former capital of the Muslim state of Adal. Pop: 96 000 (2005 est)

Harare *n* the capital of Zimbabwe, in the northeast: University of Zimbabwe (1957); industrial and commercial centre. Pop: 1 527 000 (2005 est). Former name (until 1982): **Salisbury**

harass *vb* to trouble or annoy (someone) by repeated attacks, questions, or problems [French *harasser*] ▷ **harassed** *adj* ▷ **harassment** *n*

Harbin *n* a city in NE China, capital of Heilongjiang province on the Songhua River: founded by the Russians in 1897; centre of tsarist activities after the October Revolution in Russia (1917). Pop: 2 989 000 (2005 est). Also called: **Ha-erh-pin**

harbinger (har-binge-er) *n* literary a person or thing that announces or indicates the approach of something: *a harbinger of death* [Old French *herbergere*]

harbour or US **harbor** *n* 1 a sheltered port 2 a place of refuge or safety ▷ *vb* 3 to maintain secretly in the mind: *he might be harbouring a death wish* 4 to give shelter or protection to: *the government accused her of harbouring criminals* [Old English *hereborg*, from *here* army + *beorg* shelter]

harbour master *n* an official in charge of a harbour

hard *adj* 1 firm, solid, or rigid 2 difficult to do or understand: *a hard sum* 3 showing or requiring a lot of effort or application: *hard work* 4 unkind or unfeeling: *she's very hard, no pity for anyone* 5 causing pain, sorrow, or

hardship: *the hard life of a northern settler* 6 tough or violent: *a hard man* 7 forceful: *a hard knock* 8 cool or uncompromising: *we took a long hard look at our profit factor* 9 indisputable and proven to be true: *hard facts* 10 (of water) containing calcium salts which stop soap lathering freely 11 practical, shrewd, or calculating: *he is a hard man in business* 12 harsh: *hard light* 13 (of currency) high and stable in exchange value 14 (of alcoholic drink) being a spirit rather than a wine or beer 15 (of a drug) highly addictive 16 hard-core 17 phonetics denoting the consonants *c* and *g* when they are pronounced as in *cat* and *got* 18 politically extreme: *the hard left* 19 **hard of hearing** slightly deaf 20 **hard up** informal in need of money ▷ *adv* 21 with great energy or force: *they fought so hard and well in Spain* 22 with great intensity: *thinking hard about the conversation* 23 **hard by** very close to: *Cleveland Place, hard by Bruntsfield Square* 24 **hard put (to it)** scarcely having the capacity (to do something) ▷ *n* 25 **have a hard on** taboo, slang to have an erection of the penis [Old English *heard*] ▷ **hardness** *n*

hard-and-fast *adj* (of rules) fixed and not able to be changed

hardback *n* 1 a book with stiff covers ▷ *adj* 2 of or denoting a hardback

hardball *n* US and Canad 1 baseball as distinct from softball 2 **play hardball** informal to act in a ruthless or uncompromising way

hard-bitten *adj* informal tough and determined

hardboard *n* stiff board made in thin sheets of compressed sawdust and wood pulp

hard-boiled *adj* 1 (of an egg) boiled until solid 2 informal tough, realistic, and unemotional

hard cash *n* money or payment in money, as opposed to payment by cheque, credit, etc.

hard copy *n* computer output printed on paper

hardcore *n* 1 a style of rock music with short fast songs and little melody 2 a type of dance music with a very fast beat

hard core *n* 1 the members of a group who most resist change 2 broken stones used to form a foundation for a road ▷ *adj* **hard-core** 3 (of pornography) showing sexual acts in explicit detail 4 extremely committed or fanatical: *a hard-core Communist*

hard disk *n* computers an inflexible disk in a sealed container

hard drive *n* computers the mechanism that handles the reading, writing, and storage of data on the hard disk

Hardecanute or **Hardicanute** *n* ?1019–42, king of Denmark (1035–42) and of England (1040–42); son of Canute

harden *vb* 1 to make or become hard; freeze, stiffen, or set 2 to make or become tough or unfeeling: *life in the camp had hardened her considerably* 3 to make or become stronger or firmer: *they hardened defences* 4 to make or become more determined or resolute: *the government has hardened its attitude to the crisis* 5 commerce (of prices or a market) to cease to fluctuate

Hardenberg *n* 1 Friedrich von. the original name of Novalis. See **Novalis** 2 **Fürst Karl (August) von** ( ). 1750–1822, Prussian statesman: foreign minister (1804–06): prime minister (1807; 1810–22). His reforms enabled Prussia to break away from Napoleonic control in 1813

hardened *adj* toughened by experience: *a hardened criminal*

hardfill *n* NZ and S African a stone waste material used for landscaping

hard-headed *adj* tough, realistic, or shrewd, esp. in business

hardhearted *adj* unsympathetic and uncaring

Hardie *n* (James) **Keir**. 1856–1915, British Labour leader and politician, born in Scotland; the first parliamentary leader of the Labour Party

hardihood *n* courage or daring

h

Harding n Warren G(amaliel). 1865–1923, 29th president of the US (1921–23)

Hardinge n Henry, 1st Viscount Hardinge of Lahore. 1785–1856, British politician, soldier, and colonial administrator; governor general of India (1844–48)

hard labour n difficult and tiring physical work: used as a punishment for a crime in some countries

hard line n **1** an uncompromising policy: *a hard line on drugs* ▷ adj **hard-line 2** tough and uncompromising: *a hard-line attitude to the refugee problem* **> hardliner** n

hardly adv **1** scarcely; barely: *he'd hardly sipped his whisky* **2** humorous not at all: *it was hardly in the Great Train Robbery league* **3** with difficulty: *their own families would hardly recognize them*

> USAGE Since *hardly*, *scarcely*, and *barely* already have negative force, it is redundant to use another negative in the same clause: *he had hardly had* (not *he hadn't hardly had*) *time to think*; *there was scarcely any* (not *scarcely no*) *bread left.*

hard pad n (in dogs) an abnormal increase in the thickness of the foot pads: a sign of distemper

hard palate n the bony front part of the roof of the mouth

hard-pressed adj **1** under a great deal of strain and worry: *hard-pressed companies having to cut costs* **2** closely pursued

hard science n one of the natural or physical sciences, such as physics, chemistry, or biology

hard sell n an aggressive insistent technique of selling

hardship n **1** conditions of life that are difficult to endure **2** something that causes suffering

hard shoulder n Brit and NZ a surfaced verge running along the edge of a motorway and other roads for emergency stops

hardtack n a kind of hard saltless biscuit, formerly eaten by sailors

hardware n **1** metal tools or implements, esp. cutlery or cooking utensils **2** computers the physical equipment used in a computer system **3** heavy military equipment, such as tanks and missiles

Hardwick Hall n an Elizabethan mansion near Chesterfield in Derbyshire: built 1591–97 for Elizabeth, Countess of Shrewsbury (Bess of Hardwick)

hard-wired adj (of a circuit or instruction) permanently wired into a computer

hardwood n the wood of a deciduous tree such as oak, beech, or ash

hardy adj **-dier, -diest 1** able to stand difficult conditions **2** (of plants) able to live out of doors throughout the winter [Old French *hardi* emboldened] **> hardiness** n

Hardy n **1** Oliver. See Laurel and Hardy **2** Thomas. 1840–1928, British novelist and poet. Most of his novels are set in his native Dorset (part of his fictional Wessex) and include *Far from the Madding Crowd* (1874), *The Return of the Native* (1878), *The Mayor of Casterbridge* (1886), *Tess of the d'Urbervilles* (1891), and *Jude the Obscure* (1895), after which his work consisted chiefly of verse **3** Sir Thomas Masterman. 1769–1839, British naval officer, flag captain under Nelson (1799–1805): 1st Sea Lord (1830)

are n, pl **hares** or **hare 1** a mammal like a large rabbit, with longer ears and legs ▷ vb **haring, hared 2** (foll. by *off* or *after*) Brit and Austral informal to run fast or wildly [Old English *hara*]

are n **1** Sir David. born 1947, British dramatist and theatre director: his plays include *Plenty* (1978), *Pravda* (with Howard Brenton, 1985), *The Secret Rapture* (1989), *Racing Demon* (1990), *The Permanent Way* (2003), and *Stuff Happens* (2004) **2** William. 19th century, Irish murderer and bodysnatcher: associate of William Burke

arebell n a blue bell-shaped flower

arebrained adj foolish or impractical: *harebrained schemes*

harelip n a slight split in the mid line of the upper lip

harem n **1** a Muslim man's wives and concubines collectively **2** the part of an Oriental house reserved for wives and concubines [Arabic *harīm* forbidden (place)]

Harewood House n a mansion near Harrogate in Yorkshire: built 1759–71 by John Carr for the Lascelles family; interior decoration by Robert Adam

Harfleur n a port in N France, in Seine-Maritime department: important centre in the Middle Ages. Pop: 8602 (2005)

Hargeisa n a city in NW Somalia: former capital of British Somaliland (1941–60) and functioning as the capital of the separatist republic of Somaliland; trading centre for nomadic herders. Pop: reliable recent estimates are not available

Hargreaves n James. died 1778, English inventor of the spinning jenny

haricot bean or **haricot** (har-rik-oh) n a white edible bean, which can be dried [French *haricot*]

Haringey n a borough of N Greater London. Pop: 224 700 (2003 est). Area: 30 sq km (12 sq miles)

Harishchandra n also known as *Bharatendu*. 1850–85, Indian poet, dramatist, and essayist, who established Hindi as a literary language

harissa n a hot paste or sauce made from chilli peppers, tomatoes, spices, and olive oil, used in North African cuisine

hark vb old-fashioned to listen; pay attention: *hark, the cocks are crowing* [Old English *heorcnian*]

hark back vb to return (to an earlier subject in speech or thought): *he keeps harking back to his music-hall days*

Harlech n a town in N Wales, in Gwynedd: noted for its ruined 13th-century castle overlooking Cardigan Bay: tourism. Pop: 1233 (2001)

Harlem n a district of New York City, in NE Manhattan: now largely a Black ghetto

harlequin n **1** theatre a stock comic character, usually wearing a diamond-patterned multicoloured costume and a black mask ▷ adj **2** in varied colours [Old French *Herlequin* leader of a band of demon horsemen]

harlequinade n theatre a play in which harlequin has a leading role

Harley n Robert, 1st Earl of Oxford. 1661–1724, British statesman; head of the government (1710–14), negotiated the treaty of Utrecht (1713)

Harley Street n a street in central London famous for its large number of medical specialists' consulting rooms

harlot n literary a prostitute [Old French *herlot* rascal] **> harlotry** n

Harlow[1] n a town in SE England, in W Essex: designated a new town in 1947. Pop: 78 389 (2001 est)

Harlow[2] n Jean, real name *Harlean Carpentier*. 1911–37, US film actress, whose films include *Hell's Angels* (1930), *Red Dust* (1932), and *Bombshell* (1933)

harm vb **1** to injure physically, morally, or mentally ▷ n **2** physical, moral, or mental injury [Old English *hearm*]

harmful adj causing or tending to cause harm, esp. to a person's health

harmless adj **1** safe to use, touch, or be near **2** unlikely to annoy or worry people: *a harmless habit*

harmonic adj **1** of, producing, or characterized by harmony; harmonious ▷ n **2** music an overtone of a musical note produced when that note is played, but not usually heard as a separate note ▶ See also **harmonics** [Latin *harmonicus* relating to harmony] **> harmonically** adv

harmonica n a small wind instrument in which reeds enclosed in a narrow oblong box are made to vibrate by blowing and sucking

harmonics n the science of musical sounds

harmonious adj **1** (esp. of colours or sounds) consisting of parts which blend together well **2** showing agreement, peacefulness, and friendship: *a harmonious* *relationship* **3** tuneful or melodious

harmonium *n* a musical keyboard instrument in which air from pedal-operated bellows causes the reeds to vibrate

harmonize *or* **-nise** *vb* **-nizing, -nized** *or* **-nising, -nised 1** to sing or play in harmony, such as with another singer or player **2** to make or become harmonious

harmony *n, pl* **-nies 1** a state of peaceful agreement and cooperation **2** *music* a pleasant combination of two or more notes sounded at the same time **3** the way parts combine well together or into a whole [Greek *harmonia*]

Harnack *n* Adolf von. 1851–1930, German Protestant theologian, author of the influential *History of Dogma* (1886–90)

harness *n* **1** an arrangement of straps for attaching a horse to a cart or plough **2** something resembling this, for attaching something to a person's body: *a parachute harness* **3 in harness** at one's routine work ▷ *vb* **4** to put a harness on (a horse or other animal) **5** to control something in order to make use of it: *learning to harness the power of your own mind* [Old French *harneis* baggage]

Harney Peak *n* a mountain in SW South Dakota: the highest peak in the Black Hills. Height: 2207 m (7242 ft)

Harnoncourt *n* Nikolaus. born 1929, Austrian conductor and cellist, noted for his performances using period instruments

Harold I *n* surname *Harefoot*. died 1040, king of England (1037–40); son of Canute

Harold II *n* ?1022–66, king of England (1066); son of Earl Godwin and successor of Edward the Confessor. His claim to the throne was disputed by William the Conqueror, who defeated him at the Battle of Hastings (1066)

harp *n* **1** a large upright triangular stringed instrument played by plucking the strings with the fingers ▷ *vb* **2 harp on** to speak in a persistent and tedious manner (about a subject) [Old English *hearpe*] ▷ **harpist** *n*

Harper *n* Stephen (Joseph). Born 1959. Canadian statesman; prime minister from 2006

Harper's Ferry *n* a village in NE West Virginia, at the confluence of the Potomac and Shenandoah Rivers: site of an arsenal seized by John Brown (1859). Pop: 302 (2003 est)

harpoon *n* **1** a barbed spear attached to a long rope and thrown or fired when hunting whales, etc. ▷ *vb* **2** to spear with a harpoon [probably from Dutch *harpoen*]

harpsichord *n* a keyboard instrument, resembling a small piano, with strings that are plucked mechanically [Late Latin *harpa* harp + Latin *chorda* string] ▷ **harpsichordist** *n*

harpy *n, pl* **-pies** a violent, unpleasant, or greedy woman [from Greek *Harpuiai* the Harpies, literally: snatchers (mythical birdlike female monsters)]

Harrer *n* a variant spelling of Harar

harridan *n* a scolding old woman; nag [origin unknown]

harrier¹ *n* a cross-country runner [from *hare*]

harrier² *n* a bird of prey with broad wings and long legs and tail

Harriman *n* W(illiam) Averell. 1891–1986, US diplomat: negotiated the Nuclear Test Ban Treaty with the Soviet Union (1963); governor of New York (1955–58)

Harrington *n* James. 1611–77, English republican and writer. He described his ideal form of government in *Oceana* (1656)

Harris¹ *n* the S part of the island of Lewis with Harris, in the Outer Hebrides. Pop: about 3000 (2001). Area: 500 sq km (190 sq miles)

Harris² *n* **1** Sir Arthur Travers, known as *Bomber Harris*. 1892–1984, British air marshal. He was commander-in-chief of Bomber Command of the RAF (1942–45) **2** Frank. 1856–1931, British writer and journalist; his books include his autobiography *My Life and Loves* (1923–27) and *Contemporary Portraits* (1915–30) **3** Joel Chandler. 1848–1908, US writer; creator of Uncle Remus **4** Roy. 1898–1979, US

composer, esp. of orchestral and choral music incorporating American folk tunes

Harrisburg *n* a city in S Pennsylvania, on the Susquehanna River: the state capital. Pop: 48 322 (2003 est)

Harrison *n* **1** Benjamin. 1833–1901, 23rd president of the US (1889–93) **2** George. 1943–2001, British rock singer, guitarist, and songwriter: a member of the Beatles (1962–70). His solo recordings include *All Things Must Pass* (1970) and *Cloud Nine* (1987) **3** Rex (Carey). 1908–90, British actor. His many films include *Major Barbara* (1940), *Blithe Spirit* (1945), and *My Fair Lady* (1964) **4** Tony. born 1937, British poet, dramatist, and translator: best known for his poems for television and his translations for the stage **5** grandfather of Benjamin, William Henry. 1773–1841, 9th president of the US (1841)

Harrogate *n* a town in N England, in North Yorkshire: a former spa, now a centre for tourism and conferences. Pop: 70 811 (2001 est)

harrow *n* **1** an implement used to break up clods of soil ▷ *vb* **2** to draw a harrow over (land) [from Old Norse]

Harrow *n* a borough of NW Greater London; site of an English boys' public school founded in 1571 at Harrow-on-the-Hill, a part of this borough. Pop: 210 700 (2003 est). Area: 51 sq km (20 sq miles)

harrowing *adj* very upsetting or disturbing

harry *vb* **-ries, -rying, -ried** to keep asking (someone) to do something; pester [Old English *hergian*]

harsh *adj* **1** severe and difficult to cope with: *harsh winters* **2** unkind and showing no understanding: *the judge was very harsh on the demonstrators* **3** excessively hard, bright, or rough: *harsh sunlight* **4** (of sounds) unpleasant and grating [probably Scandinavian] ▷ **harshly** *adv* ▷ **harshness** *n*

hart *n, pl* **harts** *or* **hart** the male of the deer, esp. the red deer [Old English *heorot*]

Hart *n* **1** Lorenz. 1895–1943, US lyricist: collaborated with Richard Rodgers in writing musicals **2** Moss. 1904–61, US dramatist: collaborated with George Kaufman on Broadway comedies and wrote libretti for musicals

Harte *n* (Francis) Bret. 1836–1902, US poet and short-story writer, noted for his sketches of Californian gold miners, such as *The Luck of Roaring Camp* (1870)

hartebeest *n* a large African antelope with curved horns and a fawn-coloured coat [Dutch]

Hartford *n* a port in central Connecticut, on the Connecticut River: the state capital. Pop: 124 387 (2003 est)

Harthacanute *n* same as Hardecanute

Hartlepool *n* **1** a port in NE England, in Hartlepool unitary authority, Co Durham, on the North Sea: greatl▯ enlarged in 1967 by its amalgamation with West Hartlepool; engineering, clothing, food processing. Pop: 86 075 (2001) **2** a unitary authority in NE England, in Co Durham: formerly (1974–96) part of the county of Cleveland. Pop: 90 200 (2003 est). Area: 93 sq km (36 sq miles)

Hartley *n* **1** David. 1705–57, English philosopher and physician. In *Observations of Man* (1749) he introduced the theory of psychological associationism **2** L(eslie) P(oles). 1895–1972, British novelist. His novels include the trilog▯ *The Shrimp and the Anemone* (1944), *The Sixth Heaven* (1946), and *Eustace and Hilda* (1947) as well as *The Go-Between* (1953▯

Hartnell *n* Sir Norman. 1901–79, English couturier

harum-scarum *adj* **1** reckless ▷ *adv* **2** recklessly ▷ *n* **3** an impetuous person [origin unknown]

Harun al-Rashid *n* ?763–809 AD, Abbasid caliph of Isla▯ (786–809), whose court at Baghdad was idealized in the *Arabian Nights*

harvest *n* **1** the gathering of a ripened crop **2** the crop itself **3** the season for gathering crops **4** the product of an effort or action ▷ *vb* **5** to gather (a ripened crop) **6** *chiefly US* to remove (an organ) from the body for transplantation [Old English *hærfest*]

harvester *n* **1** a harvesting machine, esp. a combine harvester **2** a person who harvests

harvest festival *n* **1** a Christian church service held every year to thank God for the harvest **2** any of various ceremonies celebrating the harvest in other religions

harvest moon *n* the full moon occurring nearest to the autumn equinox

harvest mouse *n* a very small reddish-brown mouse that lives in cornfields or hedgerows

Harvey *n* William. 1578–1657, English physician who discovered the mechanism of blood circulation, expounded in *On the motion of the heart* (1628)

Harwell *n* a village in S England, in Oxfordshire: atomic research station (1947)

Harwich *n* a port in SE England, in NE Essex on the North Sea. Pop: 20 130 (2001)

Haryana *n* a state of NE India, formed in 1966 from the Hindi-speaking parts of the state of Punjab. Capital: Chandigarh (shared with Punjab). Pop: 21 082 989 (2001 est). Area: 44 506 sq km (17 182 sq miles)

Harz *or* **Harz Mountains** *pl n* a range of wooded hills in central Germany, between the Rivers Weser and Elbe: source of many legends. Highest peak: Brocken, 1142 m (3746 ft)

has *vb* third person singular of the present tense of **have**

Hasan al-Basri *n* died 728 AD, Muslim religious thinker

has-been *n informal* a person who is no longer popular or successful

Hasdrubal *n* died 207 BC, Carthaginian general: commanded the Carthaginian army in Spain (218–211); joined his brother Hannibal in Italy and was killed at the Metaurus

Hašek *n* Jaroslav. 1883–1923, Czech novelist and short-story writer; author of *The Good Soldier Schweik* (1923)

hash¹ *n* **1** a dish of diced cooked meat, vegetables, etc., reheated: *corned-beef hash* **2** a reworking of old material **3** **make a hash of** *informal* to mess up or destroy [Old French *hacher* to chop up]

hash² *n slang* short for **hashish**

hash³ *or* **hashmark** *n* the character (#) used to precede a number

Hashemite Kingdom of Jordan *n* the official name of Jordan

hashish (hash-eesh) *n* a drug made from the hemp plant, smoked for its intoxicating effects [Arabic]

hashtag *n* (on the Twitter website) a word or phrase preceded by a hash, indicating the topic being discussed

hasn't has not

hasp *n* a clasp which fits over a staple and is secured by a pin, bolt, or padlock, used as a fastening [Old English *hæpse*]

Hassan II *n* 1929–1999, king of Morocco (1961–99)

Hasselt *n* a market town in E Belgium, capital of Limburg province. Pop: 69 127 (2004 est)

hassium *n chem* an element synthetically produced in small quantities by high-energy ion bombardment. Symbol: Hs [Latin, from *Hesse*, the German state where it was discovered]

hassle *informal n* **1** a great deal of trouble **2** a prolonged argument ▷ *vb* **-sling, -sled** **3** to cause annoyance or trouble to (someone): *stop hassling me!* [origin unknown]

hassock *n* a cushion for kneeling on in church [Old English *hassuc* matted grass]

haste *n* **1** speed, esp. in an action **2** the act of hurrying in a careless manner **3** **make haste** to hurry or rush ▷ *vb* **hasting, hasted** **4** *poetic* to hasten [Old French]

hasten *vb* **1** to hurry or cause to hurry **2** to be anxious (to say something)

Hastings¹ *n* **1** a port in SE England, in East Sussex on the English Channel: near the site of the **Battle of Hastings** (1066), in which William the Conqueror defeated King Harold; chief of the Cinque Ports. Pop: 85 828 (2001) **2** a town in New Zealand, on E North Island: centre of a rich agricultural and fruit-growing region. Pop: 71 100 (2004 est)

Hastings² *n* **1** Gavin. born 1962, Scottish Rugby Union footballer; played for Scotland (1986–95), scoring 667 points in 61 games **2** Warren. 1732–1818, British administrator in India; governor general of Bengal (1773–85). He implemented important reforms but was impeached by parliament (1788) on charges of corruption; acquitted in 1795

hasty *adj* **-tier, -tiest** **1** done or happening suddenly or quickly **2** done too quickly and without thought; rash ▷ **hastily** *adv*

hat *n* **1** a head covering, often with a brim, usually worn to give protection from the weather **2** *informal* a role or capacity: *I'm wearing my honorary consul's hat* **3** **keep something under one's hat** to keep something secret **4** **pass the hat round** to collect money for a cause **5** **take off one's hat to someone** to admire or congratulate someone [Old English *hætt*]

hatband *n* a band or ribbon around the base of the crown of a hat

hatch¹ *vb* **1** to cause (the young of various animals, esp. birds) to emerge from the egg or (of young birds, etc.) to emerge from the egg **2** (of eggs) to break and release the young animal within **3** to devise (a plot or plan) [Germanic]

hatch² *n* **1** a hinged door covering an opening in a floor or wall **2 a** short for **hatchway b** a door in an aircraft or spacecraft **3** Also called: **serving hatch** an opening in a wall between a kitchen and a dining area **4** *informal* short for **hatchback** [Old English *hæcc*]

hatch³ *vb drawing, engraving etc.* to mark (a figure, etc.) with fine parallel or crossed lines to indicate shading [Old French *hacher* to chop] ▷ **hatching** *n*

hatchback *n* a car with a single lifting door in the rear

hatchet *n* **1** a short axe used for chopping wood, etc. **2** **bury the hatchet** to make peace or resolve a disagreement ▷ *adj* **3** narrow and sharp: *a hatchet face* [Old French *hachette*]

hatchet job *n informal* a malicious verbal or written attack

hatchet man *n informal* a person who carries out unpleasant tasks on behalf of an employer

hatchling *n* a young animal that has newly hatched from an egg

hatchway *n* an opening in the deck of a vessel to provide access below

hate *vb* **hating, hated** **1** to dislike (someone or something) intensely **2** to be unwilling (to do something): *I hate to trouble you* ▷ *n* **3** intense dislike **4** *informal* a person or thing that is hated: *my own pet hate is restaurants* [Old English *hatian*] ▷ **hater** *n*

hateful *adj* causing or deserving hate

Hatfield *n* a market town in S central England, in Hertfordshire, with a new town of the same name built on the outskirts: university (1992); site of **Hatfield House** (1607–11), the seat of the Cecil family. Pop: 32 281 (2001)

Hathaway *n* Anne. ?1557–1623, wife of William Shakespeare

Hathor *n* an Egyptian goddess of creation

hatred *n* intense dislike

Hatshepsut *or* **Hatshepset** *n* queen of Egypt of the 18th dynasty (?1512–1482 BC). She built a great mortuary temple at Deir el Bahri near Thebes

hatter *n* **1** a person who makes and sells hats **2** **mad as a hatter** eccentric

Hatteras *n* **Cape Hatteras** a promontory off the E coast of North Carolina, on **Hatteras Island**, which is situated between Pamlico Sound and the Atlantic: known as the "Graveyard of the Atlantic" for its danger to shipping

Hattersley *n* Roy (**Sydney George**), Baron Hattersley of Sparkbrook. born 1932, British Labour politician; deputy leader of the Labour Party (1983–92); shadow home secretary (1980–83; 1987–92)

hat trick *n* **1** *cricket* the achievement of a bowler in taking three wickets with three successive balls **2** any

h

achievement of three successive goals, victories, etc.

hauberk *n history* a long sleeveless coat of mail [Old French *hauberc*]

Haughey *n* Charles James. 1925–2006, Irish politician; leader of the Fianna Fáil party; prime minister of the Republic of Ireland (1979–81; 1982; 1987–92)

haughty *adj* **-tier, -tiest** having or showing excessive pride or arrogance [Latin *altus* high] **› haughtily** *adv* **› haughtiness** *n*

haul *vb* **1** to drag or pull (something) with effort **2** to transport, such as in a lorry **3** *nautical* to alter the course of (a vessel) ▷ *n* **4** the act of dragging with effort **5** a quantity of something obtained: *a good haul of fish; a huge haul of stolen goods* **6 long haul a** a long journey **b** a long difficult process [Old French *haler*]

haulage *n* **1** the business of transporting goods **2** a charge for transporting goods

haulier *n* Brit and Austral a person or firm that transports goods by road

haulm (**hawm**) *n* the stalks of beans, peas, or potatoes collectively [Old English *healm*]

haunch *n* **1** the human hip or fleshy hindquarter of an animal **2** the leg and loin of an animal, used for food [Old French *hanche*]

haunt *vb* **1** to visit (a person or place) in the form of a ghost **2** to remain in the memory or thoughts of: *it was a belief which haunted her* **3** to visit (a place) frequently ▷ *n* **4** a place visited frequently [Old French *hanter*]

haunted *adj* **1** (of a place) frequented or visited by ghosts **2** (of a person) obsessed or worried

haunting *adj* having a quality of great beauty or sadness so as to be memorable: *a haunting melody*

Hauptmann *n* Gerhart. 1862–1946, German naturalist, dramatist, novelist, and poet. His works include the historical drama *The Weavers* (1892): Nobel prize for literature 1912

Hauraki Gulf *n* an inlet of the Pacific in New Zealand, on the N coast of North Island

Haussmann *n* Georges-Eugène, Baron. 1809–91, French town planner, noted for his major rebuilding of Paris in the reign of Napoleon III

hautboy (oh-boy) *n old-fashioned* an oboe [French *haut* high + *bois* wood]

haute couture (oat koo-ture) *n* high fashion [French]

Haute-Garonne *n* a department of SW France, in Midi-Pyrénées region. Capital: Toulouse. Pop: 1 102 919 (2003 est). Area: 6367 sq km (2483 sq miles)

Haute-Loire *n* a department of S central France, in Auvergne region. Capital: Le Puy. Pop: 213 993 (2003 est). Area: 5001 sq km (1950 sq miles)

Haute-Marne *n* a department of NE France, in Champagne-Ardenne region. Capital: Chaumont. Pop: 190 983 (2003 est). Area: 6257 sq km (2440 sq miles)

Haute-Normandie *n* a region of NW France, on the English Channel: generally fertile and flat

Hautes-Alpes *n* a department of SE France in Provence-Alpes-Côte d'Azur region. Capital: Gap. Pop: 126 810 (2003 est). Area: 5643 sq km (2201 sq miles)

Haute-Saône *n* a department of E France, in Franche-Comté region. Capital: Vesoul. Pop: 232 283 (2003 est). Area: 5375 sq km (2096 sq miles)

Haute-Savoie *n* a department of E France, in Rhône-Alpes region. Capital: Annecy. Pop: 663 810 (2003 est). Area: 4958 sq km (1934 sq miles)

Hautes-Pyrénées *n* a department of SW France, in Midi-Pyrénées region. Capital: Tarbes. Pop: 224 053 (2003 est). Area: 4534 sq km (1768 sq miles)

hauteur (oat-ur) *n* haughtiness [French *haut* high]

Haute-Vienne *n* a department of W central France, in Limousin region. Capital: Limoges. Pop: 353 788 (2003 est). Area: 5555 sq km (2166 sq miles)

Haut-Rhin *n* a department of E France in Alsace region. Capital: Colmar. Pop: 722 692 (2003 est). Area: 3566 sq km (1377 sq miles)

Hauts-de-Seine *n* a department of N central France, in Île-de-France region just west of Paris: formed in 1964. Capital: Nanterre. Pop: 1 470 706 (2003 est). Area: 175 sq km (68 sq miles)

Havana *n* **1** the capital of Cuba, a port in the northwest on the Gulf of Mexico: the largest city in the Caribbean; founded in 1514 as San Cristóbal de la Habana by Diego Velásquez. Pop: 2 192 000 (2005 est). Spanish name: Habana. Related adjective: **Habanero 2** a fine-quality hand-rolled cigar from Cuba

Havant *n* a market town in S England, in SE Hampshire. Pop: 45 435 (2001)

have *vb* **has, having, had 1** to possess: *he has a massive collection of old movies*; *I have an iron constitution* **2** to receive, take, or obtain: *I had a long letter* **3** to hold in the mind: *she always had a yearning to be a schoolteacher* **4** to possess a knowledge of: *I have no German* **5** to experience or be affected by: *a good way to have a change* **6** to suffer from: *to have a blood pressure problem* **7** to gain control of or advantage over: *you have me on that point* **8** *slang* to cheat or outwit: *I've been had* **9** to show: *have mercy on me* **10** to take part in; hold: *I had a telephone conversation* **11** to cause to be done: *have my shoes mended by Friday* **12** to eat or drink **13** *taboo, slang* to have sexual intercourse with **14** to tolerate or allow: *I won't have all this noise* **15** to receive as a guest: *we have visitors* **16** to be pregnant with or give birth to (offspring): *I have gone; I had gone* **18 have had it** *informal* **a** to be exhausted or killed **b** to have lost one's last chance **19 have it off** *taboo, Brit slang* to have sexual intercourse **20 have to** used to express compulsion or necessity: *you'd have to wait six months* ▷ *n* **21 haves** *informal* people who have wealth, security, etc.: *the haves and the have-nots* ▶ See also **have on**, **have out**, etc. [Old English *habban*]

have-a-go *adj informal* (of people attempting arduous or brave tasks) brave or spirited: *have-a-go pensioner*

Havel[1] *n* a river in E Germany, flowing south to Berlin, then west and north to join the River Elbe. Length: about 362 km (225 miles)

Havel[2] *n* Václav. 1936–2011, Czech dramatist and statesman: founder of the Civic Forum movement for political change: president of Czechoslovakia (1989–92) and of the Czech Republic (1993–2003). His plays include *The Garden Party* (1963) and *Redevelopment* (1989)

haven *n* **1** a place of safety **2** a harbour for shipping [Old English *hæfen*]

haven't have not

have on *vb* **1** to wear: *he'd got a long pair of trousers on* **2** to have a commitment: *what do you have on this afternoon?* **3** *informal* to trick or tease: *he's having you on* **4** to have (information, esp. when incriminating) about (a person): *she's got something on him*

have out *vb* to settle (a matter), esp. by fighting or by frank discussion: *I went to Carl's office to have it out with him*

haver *vb* **1** *Scot and N English dialect* to talk nonsense **2** to be unsure and hesitant; dither [origin unknown]

Havering *n* a borough of NE Greater London, formed in 1965 from Romford and Hornchurch (both previously in Essex). Pop: 224 600 (2003 est). Area: 120 sq km (46 sq miles)

haversack *n* a canvas bag carried on the back or shoulder [French *havresac*]

have up *vb* to bring to trial: *what, and get me had up for kidnapping?*

havoc *n* **1** *informal* chaos, disorder, and confusion **2 play havoc with** to cause a great deal of damage or confusion to [Old French *havot* pillage]

Havre *n* See Le Havre

haw[1] *n* the fruit of the hawthorn [Old English *haga*]

haw[2] *vb* hum (*or* hem) and haw to hesitate in speaking [imitative]

Hawaii *n* a state of the US in the central Pacific, consisting of over 20 volcanic islands and atolls, including Hawaii, Maui, Oahu, Kauai, and Molokai:

discovered by Captain Cook in 1778; annexed by the US in 1898; naval base at Pearl Harbor attacked by the Japanese in 1941, a major cause of US entry into World War II; became a state in 1959. Capital: Honolulu. Pop: 1 257 608 (2003 est). Area: 16 640 sq km (6425 sq miles). Former name: **Sandwich Islands**. Abbreviation: **Ha.**, (with zip code) **HI**

Hawaiian adj **1** of or relating to Hawaii, its people, or their language ▷ n **2** a native or inhabitant of Hawaii, esp. one descended from Melanesian or Tahitian immigrants **3** a language of Hawaii belonging to the Malayo-Polynesian family

Hawaiki n NZ a legendary Pacific island from which the Māoris migrated to New Zealand by canoe [Māori]

Hawes Water n a lake in NW England, in the Lake District: provides part of Manchester's water supply; extended by damming from 4 km (2.5 miles) to 6 km (4 miles)

Haw-Haw n Lord Haw-Haw See Joyce (2)

Hawick n a town in SE Scotland, in S central Scottish Borders: knitwear industry. Pop: 14 573 (2001)

hawk[1] n **1** a bird of prey with short rounded wings and a long tail **2** a supporter or advocate of warlike policies ▷ vb **3** to hunt with falcons or hawks [Old English hafoc] **> hawkish** adj **> hawklike** adj

hawk[2] vb to offer (goods) for sale in the street or door-to-door [from hawker pedlar]

hawk[3] vb **1** to clear the throat noisily **2** to force (phlegm) up from the throat [imitative]

Hawke n **1** Edward, 1st Baron. 1705–81, British admiral. He destroyed the French fleet in Quiberon Bay (1759), preventing a French invasion of England **2** Robert (James Lee), known as Bob. Born 1929, Australian statesman; prime minister of Australia (1983–91)

hawker n a person who travels from place to place selling goods [probably from Middle Low German hōken to peddle]

awk-eyed adj having extremely keen eyesight

Hawking n Stephen William. Born 1942, British physicist. Stricken with a progressive nervous disease since the 1960s, he has nevertheless been a leader in cosmological theory. His publications intended for a wide audience include A Brief History of Time (1987) and The Grand Design (2010)

Hawkins n **1** Coleman. 1904–69, US pioneer of the tenor saxophone for jazz **2** Sir John. 1532–95, English naval commander and slave trader, treasurer of the navy (1577–89); commander of a squadron in the fleet that defeated the Spanish Armada (1588)

Hawks n Howard (Winchester). 1896–1977, US film director. His films include Sergeant York (1941) and The Big Sleep (1946)

Hawksmoor n Nicholas. 1661–1736, English architect. His designs include All Souls', Oxford, and a number of London churches, notably St Anne's, Limehouse

Haworth[1] n a village in N England, in Bradford unitary authority, West Yorkshire: home of Charlotte, Emily, and Anne Brontë. Pop: 6078 (2001)

Haworth[2] n Sir Walter Norman. 1883–1950, British biochemist, who shared the Nobel prize for chemistry (1937) for being the first to synthesize ascorbic acid (vitamin C)

hawser n nautical a large heavy rope [Anglo-French hauceour]

hawthorn n a thorny tree or shrub with white or pink flowers and reddish fruits [Old English haguthorn]

Hawthorne n Nathaniel. 1804–64, US novelist and short-story writer: his works include the novels The Scarlet Letter (1850) and The House of the Seven Gables (1851) and the children's stories Tanglewood Tales (1853)

hay n **1** grass cut and dried as fodder **2 hit the hay** slang to go to bed **3 make hay while the sun shines** to take full advantage of an opportunity [Old English hieg]

Hay n Will. 1888–1949, British music-hall comedian, who

later starred in films, such as Oh, Mr Porter! (1937)

Haydn n **1** (Franz) Joseph. 1732–1809, Austrian composer, who played a major part in establishing the classical forms of the symphony and the string quartet. His other works include the oratorios The Creation (1796–98) and The Seasons (1798–1801) **2** his brother, (Johann) Michael. 1737–1806, Austrian composer, esp. of Church music

Haydon n Benjamin (Robert). 1786–1846, British historical painter and art critic, best known for his Autobiography and Journals (1853)

Hayek n Friedrich August von. 1899–1992, British economist and political philosopher, born in Austria: noted for his advocacy of free-market ideas; shared the Nobel prize for economics 1974

Hayes n Rutherford B(irchard). 1822–93, 19th president of the US (1877–81)

hay fever n an allergic reaction to pollen, which causes sneezing, runny nose, and watery eyes

haystack or **hayrick** n a large pile of hay built in the open and covered with thatch

haywire adj **go haywire** informal to stop functioning properly

hazard n **1** a thing likely to cause injury, loss, etc. **2** risk or likelihood of injury, loss, etc.: evaluate the level of hazard in a situation **3** golf an obstacle such as a bunker **4 at hazard** at risk ▷ vb **5** to risk: hazarding the health of his crew **6** hazard a guess to make a guess [Arabic az-zahr the die]

hazard lights or **hazard warning lights** pl n the indicator lights on a motor vehicle when flashing simultaneously to indicate that the vehicle is stationary

hazardous adj involving great risk

haze n **1** meteorol reduced visibility as a result of condensed water vapour, dust, etc., in the air **2** confused or unclear understanding or feeling [from hazy]

hazel n **1** a shrub with edible rounded nuts ▷ adj **2** greenish-brown: hazel eyes [Old English hæsel]

hazelnut n the nut of a hazel shrub, which has a smooth shiny hard shell

Hazlitt n William. 1778–1830, English critic and essayist: works include Characters of Shakespeare's Plays (1817), Table Talk (1821), and The Plain Speaker (1826)

hazy adj **-zier, -ziest 1** (of the sky or a view) unable to be seen clearly because of dust or heat **2** dim or vague: my memory is a little hazy on this [origin unknown] **> hazily** adv **> haziness** n

Hb haemoglobin

HB Brit and Austral (of pencil lead) hard-black: denoting a medium-hard lead

H-bomb n short for **hydrogen bomb**

HDD hard disk drive

HD-DVD High Definition DVD: a DVD capable of storing between two and four times as much data as a standard DVD

he pron **1** (refers to) a male person or animal **2** (refers to) a person or animal of unknown or unspecified sex: a member may vote as he sees fit ▷ n **3** (refers to) a male person or animal: a he-goat [Old English hē]

He chem helium

HE His or Her Excellency

head n **1** the upper or front part of the body that contains the brain, eyes, mouth, nose, and ears **2** a person's mind and mental abilities: I haven't any head for figures **3** the most forward part of a thing: the head of a queue **4** the highest part of a thing; upper end: the head of the pass **5** something resembling a head in form or function, such as the top of a tool **6** the position of leadership or command **7** the person commanding most authority within a group or an organization **8** botany the top part of a plant, where the leaves or flowers grow in a cluster **9** a culmination or crisis: the matter came to a head in December 1928 **10** the froth on the top of a glass of beer **11** the pus-filled tip of a pimple or boil **12** part of a computer or tape recorder that can read, write, or erase information **13** the source of a river or stream **14** the side of a coin that usually bears a portrait of the head of a monarch, etc. **15** a headland or promontory: *Beachy Head* **16** pressure of water or steam in an enclosed space **17** (*pl* **head**) a person or animal considered as a unit: *the cost per head of Paris's refuse collection*; *six hundred head of cattle* **18** a headline or heading **19** *informal* short for headmaster, headmistress, head teacher **20** *informal* short for headache **21** give someone his head to allow someone greater freedom or responsibility **22** go to one's head **a** (of an alcoholic drink) to make one slightly drunk **b** to make one conceited: *success has gone to his head* **23** head over heels (in love) very much (in love) **24** keep one's head to remain calm **25** not make head nor tail of not to understand (a problem, etc.) **26** off one's head *slang* very foolish or insane **27** on one's own head at one's own risk **28** over someone's head **a** to a higher authority: *the taboo of going over the head of their immediate boss* **b** beyond a person's understanding **29** put our *or* your *or* their heads together *informal* to consult together **30** turn someone's head to make someone conceited ▷ *vb* **31** to be at the front or top of: *Barnes headed the list* **32** to be in charge of **33** (often foll. by *for*) to go or cause to go (towards): *to head for the Channel ports* **34** *soccer* to propel (the ball) by striking it with the head **35** to provide with a heading ▸ See also **head off, heads** [Old English *hēafod*]

Head *n* Edith. 1907–81, US dress designer: won many Oscars for her Hollywood film costume designs

headache *n* **1** a continuous pain in the head **2** *informal* any cause of worry, difficulty, or annoyance: *financial headaches*

head-banger *n Brit, Austral and NZ slang* **1** a person who shakes his head violently to the beat of heavy-metal music **2** a crazy or stupid person

headboard *n* a vertical board at the head of a bed

headdress *n* any decorative head covering

headed *adj* **1** having a head or heads: *two-headed; bald-headed* **2** having a heading: *headed notepaper*

header *n* **1** *soccer* the action of striking a ball with the head **2** *informal* a headlong fall or dive

headfirst *adv* **1** with the head foremost **2** quickly and without thinking carefully: *she jumped into marriage headfirst*

headgear *n* hats collectively

head-hunting *n* **1** (of companies) the practice of actively searching for new high-level personnel, often from rival companies **2** the practice among certain peoples of removing the heads of enemies they have killed and preserving them as trophies ▸ **head-hunter** *n*

heading *n* **1** a title for a page, chapter, etc. **2** a main division, such as of a speech **3** *mining* a horizontal tunnel

headland *n* a narrow area of land jutting out into a sea

headlight *or* **headlamp** *n* a powerful light on the front of a vehicle

headline *n* **1** a phrase in heavy large type at the top of a newspaper or magazine article indicating the subject **2** headlines the main points of a television or radio news broadcast

headlong *adv* **1** with the head foremost; headfirst **2** with great haste and without much thought: *they rushed headlong into buying a house* ▷ *adj* **3** hasty or reckless

headmaster *or fem* **headmistress** *n* the principal of a school

head off *vb* **1** to intercept and force to change direction: *police head off New Age travellers* **2** to prevent or avert: *trying to head off the prospect of civil war* **3** to depart or set out: *to head off to school*

head-on *adv, adj* **1** front foremost: *a head-on collision* **2** with directness or without compromise: *a head-on confrontation with the unions*

headphones *pl n* two small loudspeakers held against the ears, worn to listen to the radio or recorded music without other people hearing it

headquarters *pl n* any centre from which operations are directed

headroom *or* **headway** *n* the space below a roof or bridge which allows an object to pass or stay underneath it without touching it

heads *adv* with the side of a coin uppermost which has a portrait of a head on it

headship *n* the position or state of being a leader, esp. the head teacher of a school

headshrinker *n slang* a psychiatrist

headstall *n* the part of a bridle that fits round a horse's head

head start *n* an initial advantage in a competitive situation

headstone *n* a memorial stone at the head of a grave

headstrong *adj* determined to do something in one's own way and ignoring the advice of others

head teacher *n* the principal of a school

head-to-head *adv, adj informal* in direct competition

headwaters *pl n* the tributary streams of a river in the area in which it rises

headway *n* **1** progress towards achieving something: *have the police made any headway?* **2** motion forward: *we felt our way out to the open sea, barely making headway* **3** same as headroom

headwind *n* a wind blowing directly against the course of an aircraft or ship

heady *adj* **headier, headiest** **1** (of an experience or period of time) extremely exciting **2** (of alcoholic drink, atmosphere, etc.) strongly affecting the physical senses: *a powerful, heady scent of cologne* **3** rash and impetuous

heal *vb* **1** (of a wound) to repair by natural processes, such as by scar formation **2** to restore (someone) to health **3** to repair (a rift in a personal relationship or an emotional wound) [Old English *hælan*] ▸ **healer** *n* ▸ **healing** *n, adj*

Healey *n* Denis (Winston), Baron. born 1917, British Labour politician; Chancellor of the Exchequer (1974–79) deputy leader of the Labour Party (1980–83)

health *n* **1** the general condition of body and mind: *better health* **2** the state of being bodily and mentally vigorous and free from disease **3** the condition of an organization, society, etc.: *the economic health of the republic* [Old English *hǣlth*]

health camp *n* NZ a camp for children with health or behavioural problems

health centre *n Brit* the surgery and offices of the doctors in a district

health farm *n* a residential establishment for people wishing to improve their health by losing weight, exercising, etc.

health food *n* natural food, organically grown and free from additives

healthful *adj* same as healthy (1, 2, 3)

health stamp *n* NZ a postage stamp with a small surcharge used to support health camps

health visitor *n* (in Britain) a nurse employed to visit mothers, their preschool children, and elderly people in their homes

healthy *adj* **healthier, healthiest** **1** having or showing good health **2** likely to produce good health: *healthy seaside air* **3** functioning well or being sound: *this is a very healthy business to be in* **4** *informal* considerable: *healthy profit* **5** sensible: *a healthy scepticism about his promises* ▸ **healthily** *adv* ▸ **healthiness** *n*

Healy *n* Ian. born 1964, Australian cricketer; a wicketkeeper, he took 395 dismissals in 119 test matches (1988–99)

Heaney *n* Seamus (Justin). 1939–2013, Irish poet and critic, born in Northern Ireland. His collections include *Death of a Naturalist* (1966), *North* (1975), *The Haw Lantern* (1987), *The Spirit Level* (1996), *District and Circle* (2006), and *Human Chain* (2010). Nobel prize for literature 1995

heap *n* **1** a pile of things lying one on top of another **2** (often *pl*) *informal* a large number or quantity ▷ *adv* **3** heaps *informal* much: *he was heaps better* ▷ *vb* **4** to collect into a pile **5** to give freely (to): *film roles were heaped on her* [Old English *hēap*]

hear *vb* **hearing, heard 1** to perceive (a sound) with the sense of hearing **2** to listen to: *I didn't want to hear what he had to say* **3** to be informed (of something); receive information (about something): *I hear you mean to join the crusade* **4** *law* to give a hearing to (a case) **5 hear from** to receive a letter or telephone call from **6 hear! hear!** an exclamation of approval **7 hear of** to allow: *she wouldn't hear of it* [Old English *hieran*] **> hearer** *n*

Heard and McDonald Islands *pl n* a group of islands in the S Indian Ocean: an external territory of Australia from 1947. Area: 412 sq km (159 sq miles)

hearing *n* **1** the sense by which sound is perceived **2** an opportunity for someone to be listened to **3** the range within which sound can be heard; earshot **4** the investigation of a matter by a court of law

hearing aid *n* a small amplifier worn by a partially deaf person in or behind the ear to improve his or her hearing

hearing dog *n* a dog that has been trained to help a deaf person by alerting him or her to various sounds

hearken *vb archaic* to listen [Old English *heorcnian*]

hearsay *n* gossip or rumour

hearse *n* a large car used to carry a coffin at a funeral [Latin *hirpex* harrow]

Hearst *n* William Randolph. 1863–1951, US newspaper publisher, whose newspapers were noted for their sensationalism

heart *n* **1 a** a hollow muscular organ whose contractions pump the blood throughout the body **2** this organ considered as the centre of emotions, esp. love **3** tenderness or pity: *my heart went out to her* **4** courage or spirit **5** the most central part or important part: *at the heart of Italian motor racing* **6** (of vegetables such as cabbage) the inner compact part **7** the breast: *she held him to her heart* **8** a shape representing the heart, with two rounded lobes at the top meeting in a point at the bottom **9 a** a red heart-shaped symbol on a playing card **b** a card with one or more of these symbols or (*when pl*) the suit of cards so marked **10 break someone's heart** to cause someone to grieve very deeply, esp. by ending a love affair **11 by heart** by memorizing **12 have a change of heart** to experience a profound change of outlook or attitude **13 have one's heart in one's mouth** to be full of apprehension, excitement, or fear **14 have the heart to** have the necessary will or callousness (to do something): *I didn't have the heart to tell him* **15 set one's heart on something** to have something as one's ambition **16 take heart** to become encouraged **17 take something to heart** to take something seriously or be upset about something **18 wear one's heart on one's sleeve** to show one's feelings openly **19 with all one's heart** deeply and sincerely [Old English *heorte*]

heartache *n* very great sadness and emotional suffering

heart attack *n* a sudden severe malfunction of the heart

heartbeat *n* one complete pulsation of the heart

heartbreak *n* intense and overwhelming grief, esp. after the end of a love affair **> heartbreaking** *adj* **> heartbroken** *adj*

heartburn *n* a burning sensation in the chest caused by indigestion

hearten *vb* to encourage or make cheerful **> heartening** *adj*

heart failure *n* **1** a condition in which the heart is unable to pump an adequate amount of blood to the tissues **2** sudden stopping of the heartbeat, resulting in death

heartfelt *adj* sincerely and strongly felt: *heartfelt thanks*

hearth *n* **1** the floor of a fireplace **2** this as a symbol of the home [Old English *heorth*]

heartland *n* **1** the central region of a country or continent: *we headed west towards the heartland of Tibet* **2** the area where the thing specified is most common or strongest: *Germany's industrial heartland*

heartless *adj* unkind or cruel **> heartlessly** *adv*

heart-rending *adj* causing great sadness and pity: *a heart-rending story*

hearts and minds *pl n* the collective trust or approval of a body of people such as a populace, esp. for a foreign military force: *we must win the hearts and minds of the people*

heart-searching *n* examination of one's feelings or conscience

heartstrings *pl n often facetious* deep emotions: *tugging our heartstrings with pictures of suffering* [originally referring to the tendons supposed to support the heart]

heart-throb *n* a man, esp. a film or pop star, who is attractive to a lot of women or girls

heart-to-heart *adj* **1** (of a talk) concerned with personal problems or intimate feelings ▷ *n* **2** an intimate conversation

heart-warming *adj* inspiring feelings of happiness: *the heart-warming spectacle of a family reunion*

heartwood *n* the central core of dark hard wood in tree trunks

hearty *adj* **heartier, heartiest 1** warm, friendly, and enthusiastic **2** strongly felt: *a hearty dislike* **3** (of a meal) substantial and nourishing **> heartily** *adv*

heat *vb* **1** to make or become hot or warm ▷ *n* **2** the state of being hot **3** the energy transferred as a result of a difference in temperature. Related adjectives: **thermal, calorific 4** hot weather: *he loves the heat of Africa* **5** intensity of feeling: *the heat of their argument* **6** the most intense part: *in the heat of an election campaign* **7** pressure: *political heat on the government* **8** *sport* a preliminary eliminating contest in a competition **9 on** or **in heat** (of some female mammals) ready for mating [Old English *hætu*] **> heating** *n*

heated *adj* impassioned or highly emotional: *a heated debate* **> heatedly** *adv*

heater *n* a device for supplying heat

heath *n* **1** *Brit* a large open area, usually with sandy soil, low shrubs, and heather **2** a low-growing evergreen shrub with small bell-shaped pink or purple flowers [Old English *hæth*]

Heath *n* Sir Edward (Richard George). 1916–2005, British statesman; leader of the Conservative Party (1965–75); prime minister (1970–74)

heathen *n, pl* **-thens** or **-then** *old-fashioned* **1** a person who does not believe in an established religion; pagan ▷ *adj* **2** of or relating to heathen peoples [Old English *hæthen*]

heather *n* a shrub with small bell-shaped flowers growing on heaths and mountains [origin unknown]

Heath Robinson *adj* (of a mechanical device) absurdly complicated in design for a simple function [after William *Heath Robinson*, cartoonist]

heatstroke *n* same as sunstroke

heat wave *n* a spell of unusually hot weather

heave *vb* **heaving, heaved 1** to lift or move (something) with a great effort **2** to throw (something heavy) with effort **3** to utter (a sigh) noisily or unhappily **4** to rise and fall heavily **5** (*past, past part* **hove**) *nautical* **a** to move in a specified direction: *heave her bows around and head north* **b** (of a vessel) to pitch or roll **6** to vomit or retch ▷ *n* **7** the act of heaving [Old English *hebban*]

heaven *n* **1** the place where God is believed to live and where those leading good lives are believed to go when they die **2** a place or state of happiness **3 heavens** the sky **4** Also: **heavens** God or the gods, used in exclamatory phrases: *for heaven's sake!* [Old English *heofon*]

heavenly *adj* **1** *informal* wonderful or very enjoyable: *a heavenly meal* **2** of or occurring in space: *a heavenly body* **3** of or relating to heaven

heave to *vb* to stop (a ship) or (of a ship) to stop

Heaviside *n* Oliver. 1850–1925, English physicist. Independently of Kennelly, he predicted (1902) the existence of an ionized gaseous layer in the upper atmosphere (the **Heaviside layer**); he also contributed to telegraphy

heavy *adj* **heavier, heaviest** **1** of comparatively great weight **2** with a relatively high density: *lead is a heavy metal* **3** great in degree or amount: *heavy traffic* **4** considerable: *heavy emphasis* **5** hard to fulfil: *an exceptionally heavy demand for this issue* **6** using or consuming a lot of something quickly: *a heavy drinker* **7** deep and loud: *heavy breathing* **8** clumsy and slow: *a heavy lumbering trot* **9** (of a movement or action) with great downward force or pressure: *a heavy blow with a club* **10** solid or fat: *mountain animals acquire a heavy layer of fat* **11** not easily digestible: *a heavy meal* **12** (of cakes or bread) insufficiently raised **13** (of soil) with a high clay content **14** sad or dejected: *you feel heavy or sad afterwards* **15** (of facial features) looking sad and tired **16** (of a situation) serious and causing anxiety or sadness **17** cloudy or overcast: *heavy clouds obscured the sun* **18** (of an industry) engaged in the large-scale manufacture of large objects or extraction of raw materials **19** *military* (of guns, etc.) large and powerful **20** dull and uninteresting: *Helen finds his friends very heavy going* **21** (of music, literature, etc.) difficult to understand or not immediately appealing **22** *slang* (of rock music) loud and having a powerful beat **23** *slang* using, or prepared to use, violence or brutality ▷ *n, pl* **heavies 24** *slang* a large strong man hired to threaten violence or deter others by his presence **25 a** a villainous role **b** an actor who plays such a part **26 the heavies** *informal* serious newspapers ▷ *adv* **27** heavily: *time hung heavy* [Old English *hefig*] ▷ **heavily** *adv* ▷ **heaviness** *n*

heavy-duty *adj* made to withstand hard wear, bad weather, etc.

heavy-handed *adj* acting forcefully and without care and thought

heavy-hearted *adj* sad and discouraged

heavy hydrogen *n* same as **deuterium**

heavy metal *n* a type of very loud rock music featuring guitar riffs

heavy water *n* water formed of oxygen and deuterium

heavyweight *n* **1** a professional boxer weighing over 195 pounds (88.5 kg) or an amateur weighing over 91 kg **2** a person who is heavier than average **3** *informal* an important or highly influential person

Heb. *or* **Hebr.** Hebrew (language)

Hebbel *n* Christian Friedrich. 1813–63, German dramatist and lyric poet, whose historical works were influenced by Hegel; his major plays are *Maria Magdalena* (1844), *Herodes und Marianne* (1850), and the trilogy *Die Nibelungen* (1862)

Hebei, Hopeh *or* **Hopei** *n* a province of NE China, on the Gulf of Chihli: important for the production of winter wheat, cotton, and coal. Capital: Shijiazhuang. Pop: 67 690 000 (2003 est). Area: 202 700 sq km (79 053 sq miles)

Hébert *n* Jacques René. 1755–94, French journalist and revolutionary: a leader of the sans-culottes during the French Revolution. He was guillotined under Robespierre

Hebraic (hib-ray-ik) *adj* of the Hebrews or their language or culture

Hebrew *n* **1** the ancient language of the Hebrews, revived as the official language of Israel **2** a member of an ancient Semitic people; an Israelite ▷ *adj* **3** of the Hebrews or their language [Hebrew *'ibhrī* one from beyond (the river)]

Hebridean *or* **Hebridian** *adj* **1** of or relating to the Hebrides or their inhabitants ▷ *n* **2** a native or inhabitant of the Hebrides

Hebrides *pl n* **the Hebrides** a group of over 500 islands off the W coast of Scotland: separated by the North Minch, Little Minch, and the Sea of the Hebrides: the chief islands are Skye, Raasay, Rum, Eigg, Coll, Tiree, Mull,

Jura, Colonsay, and Islay (**Inner Hebrides**), and Lewis with Harris, North Uist, Benbecula, South Uist, and Barra (**Outer Hebrides**). Also known as: **the Western Isles**

Hebron *n* a city in the West Bank: famous for the Haram, which includes the cenotaphs of Abraham and Sarah, Isaac and Rebecca, and Jacob and Leah. Pop: 168 000 (2005 est). Arabic name: **El Khalil**

heck *interj* a mild exclamation of surprise, irritation, etc. [euphemistic for *hell*]

heckle *vb* **-ling, -led** to interrupt (a public speaker) with comments, questions, or taunts [form of *hackle*] ▷ **heckler** *n*

hectare *n* a unit of measure equal to one hundred ares (10 000 square metres or 2.471 acres) [French]

hectic *adj* involving a lot of rushed activity [Greek *hektikos* hectic, consumptive]

hector *vb* **1** to bully or torment ▷ *n* **2** a blustering bully [after *Hector*, legendary Trojan warrior]

he'd he had *or* he would

hedge *n* **1** a row of shrubs or bushes forming a boundary **2** a barrier or protection against something, esp. against the risk of loss on an investment ▷ *vb* **hedging, hedged** **3** to avoid making a decision by making noncommittal statements **4 hedge against** to guard against the risk of loss in (a bet or disagreement), by supporting the opposition as well [Old English *hecg*]

hedgehog *n* a small mammal with a protective covering of spines

hedgerow *n* a hedge of shrubs or low trees bordering a field

hedge sparrow *n* a small brownish songbird

Hedjaz *n* a variant spelling of **Hejaz**

hedonism *n* the doctrine that the pursuit of pleasure is the most important thing in life [Greek *hēdonē* pleasure] ▷ **hedonist** *n* ▷ **hedonistic** *adj*

heebie-jeebies *pl n* **the heebie-jeebies** *slang* nervous apprehension [coined by W. De Beck, cartoonist]

heed *formal n* **1** careful attention: *he must have taken heed of her warning* ▷ *vb* **2** to pay close attention to (a warning or piece of advice) [Old English *hēdan*]

heedless *adj* taking no notice; careless or thoughtless ▷ **heedlessly** *adv*

heehaw *interj* a representation of the braying sound of a donkey

heel[1] *n* **1** the back part of the foot **2** the part of a stocking or sock designed to fit the heel **3** the part of a shoe supporting the heel **4** *slang* a contemptible person **5 at one's heels** following closely behind one **6 down at heel** untidy and in poor condition **7 kick** *or* **cool one's heels** to be kept waiting **8 take to one's heels** to run off **9 to heel** under control, such as a dog walking by a person's heel ▷ *vb* **10** to repair or replace the heel of (a shoe or boot) [Old English *hēla*]

heel[2] *vb* to lean to one side [Old English *hieldan*]

heelball *n* **a** a mixture of beeswax and lampblack used by shoemakers **b** a similar substance used to take brass rubbings

heeler *n Austral and NZ* a dog that herds cattle by biting at their heels

Heerlen *n* a city in the SE Netherlands, in Limburg province: industrial centre of a coal-mining region. Pop 94 000 (2003 est)

Hefei *or* **Hofei** *n* a city in SE China, capital of Anhui province: administrative and commercial centre in a rice- and cotton-growing region. Pop: 1 320 000 (2005 est)

hefty *adj* **heftier, heftiest** *informal* **1** large in size, weight, or amount **2** forceful and vigorous: *a hefty slap on the back* **3** involving a large amount of money: *a hefty fine*

Hegel *n* Georg Wilhelm Friedrich. 1770–1831, German philosopher, who created a fundamentally influential system of thought. His view of man's mind as the highest expression of the Absolute is expounded in *The Phenomenology of Mind* (1807). He developed his concept of dialectic, in which the contradiction between a proposition (thesis) and its antithesis is resolved at a higher level of truth (synthesis), in *Science of Logic* (1812–16) **> Hegelian** *adj* **> He'gelian,ism** *n*

hegemony (hig-em-on-ee) *n, pl* **-nies** domination of one state, country, or class within a group of others [Greek *hēgemonia*]

hegira *n* the flight of Mohammed from Mecca to Medina in 622 AD, regarded as being the starting point of the Muslim era [Arabic *hijrah* flight]

Heidegger *n* Martin. 1889–1976, German existentialist philosopher: he expounded his ontological system in *Being and Time* (1927)

Heidelberg *n* a city in SW Germany, in NW Baden-Württemberg on the River Neckar: capital of the Palatinate from the 13th century until 1719; famous castle (begun in the 12th century) and university (1386), the oldest in Germany. Pop: 142 959 (2003 est)

heifer (hef-fer) *n* a young cow [Old English *heahfore*]

Heifetz *n* Jascha. 1901–87, US violinist, born in Russia

height *n* **1** the vertical distance from the bottom of something to the top **2** the vertical distance of a place above sea level **3** relatively great distance from bottom to top **4** the topmost point; summit **5** the period of greatest intensity: *the height of the shelling* **6** an extreme example: *the height of luxury* **7 heights** extremes: *dizzy heights of success* [Old English *hīehthu*]

heighten *vb* to make or become higher or more intense **> heightened** *adj*

height of land *n* US and Canad a ridge of high ground dividing two river basins

Heilbronn *n* a city in SW Germany, in N Baden-Württemberg on the River Neckar. Pop: 120 705 (2003 est)

Heilongjiang *or* **Heilungkiang** *n* a province of NE China, in Manchuria: coal-mining, with placer gold in some rivers. Capital: Harbin. Pop: 38 150 000 (2003 est). Area: 464 000 sq km (179 000 sq miles)

Heilong Jiang *n* the Pinyin transliteration of the Chinese name for the **Amur**

Heine *n* Heinrich. 1797–1856, German poet and essayist, whose chief poetic work is *Das Buch der Lieder* (1827). Many of his poems have been set to music, notably by Schubert and Schumann

Heinkel *n* Ernst Heinrich. 1888–1958, German aircraft designer. His company provided many military aircraft in World Wars I and II, including the first jet-powered plane

heinous *adj* evil and shocking [Old French *haineus*]

heir *n* the person legally succeeding to the property of a deceased person [Latin *heres*] **> heiress** *fem n*

heir apparent *n, pl* **heirs apparent** **1** *law* a person whose right to succeed to certain property cannot be defeated **2** a person whose succession to a role or position is extremely likely: *heir apparent to the England captaincy*

heirloom *n* an object that has been in a family for generations [HEIR + *lome* tool]

heir presumptive *n property law* a person who expects to succeed to an estate but whose right may be defeated by the birth of an heir nearer in blood to the ancestor

Heisenberg *n* Werner Karl. 1901–76, German physicist. He contributed to quantum mechanics and formulated the uncertainty principle (1927): Nobel prize for physics 1932

heist *n slang* a robbery [from HOIST]

Heitler *n* Walter. 1904–81, German physicist, noted for his work on chemical bonds

hejab *n* another spelling of hijab

Hejaz, Hedjaz *or* **Hijaz** *n* a region of W Saudi Arabia, along the Red Sea and the Gulf of Aqaba: formerly an independent kingdom; united with Nejd in 1932 to form Saudi Arabia. Area: about 348 600 sq km 134 600 sq miles)

Hekla *n* a volcano in SW Iceland: several craters, subject to fairly frequent eruptions in recent times.

Height: 1491 m (4892 ft)

held *vb* the past of **hold**[1]

Helena[1] *n* a city in W Montana: the state capital. Pop: 26 718 (2003 est)

Helena[2] *n* Saint. ?248–?328 AD, Roman empress, mother of Constantine I. After converting to Christianity (313) she made a pilgrimage to the Holy Land (?326) where she supposedly discovered the cross on which Christ died. Feast day: May 21

Helengrad *n* NZ a satirical name for Wellington as the seat of Helen Clark's socialist government from 1999 to 2008 [C20: from *Helen* + *-grad* common suffix in Russian place names; likening the policies of Clark's government to the communism of the former Soviet Union]

Helgoland *n* the German name for **Heligoland**

helical *adj* of or like a helix

Helicon *n* a mountain in Greece, in Boeotia: location of the springs of Hippocrene and Aganippe, believed by the Ancient Greeks to be the source of poetic inspiration and the home of the Muses. Height: 1749 m (5738 ft). Modern Greek name: **Elikón**

helicopter *n* an aircraft, powered by rotating overhead blades, that is capable of hovering, vertical flight, and horizontal flight in any direction [Greek *helix* spiral + *pteron* wing]

helicopter parent *n* a parent who is excessively involved in all areas of his or her child's life [from the idea of a parent hovering over a child]

Heligoland *n* a small island in the North Sea, one of the North Frisian Islands, separated from the coast of NW Germany by the **Heligoland Bight**: administratively part of the German state of Schleswig-Holstein: a large island in early medieval times, now eroded to an area of about 150 hectares (380 acres); ceded by Britain to Germany in 1890 in exchange for Zanzibar. German name: **Helgoland**

Heliogabalus *or* **Elagabalus** *n* original name *Varius Avitus Bassianus*. ?204–222 AD, Roman emperor (218–222). His reign was notorious for debauchery and extravagance

heliograph *n* an instrument with mirrors and a shutter used for sending messages in Morse code by reflecting the sun's rays [Greek *hēlios* sun + -GRAPHY]

Heliopolis *n* **1** (in ancient Egypt) a city near the apex of the Nile delta: a centre of sun worship. Ancient Egyptian name: **On 2** the Ancient Greek name for **Baalbek**

heliotrope *n* a plant with small fragrant purple flowers [Greek *hēlios* sun + *trepein* to turn]

heliport *n* an airport for helicopters [*heli(copter)* + *port*]

helium (heel-ee-um) *n chem* a very light colourless odourless inert gas. Symbol: He [Greek *hēlios* sun, because first detected in the solar spectrum]

helix (heel-iks) *n, pl* **helices** (hell-iss-seez) *or* **helixes** a spiral [Greek: spiral]

hell *n* **1** (in Christianity and some other religions) the place or state of eternal punishment of the wicked after death **2** (in various religions and cultures) the abode of the spirits of the dead **3** *informal* a situation that causes suffering or extreme difficulty: *war is hell* **4 come hell or high water** *informal* whatever difficulties may arise **5 for the hell of it** *informal* for the fun of it **6 from hell** *informal* denoting a person or thing that is particularly bad or alarming: *the neighbour from hell* **7 give someone hell** *informal* **a** to give someone a severe reprimand or punishment **b** to be a torment to someone **8 hell for leather** at great speed **9 the hell** *informal* **a** used for emphasis: *what the hell* **b** an expression of strong disagreement: *the hell you do!* ▷ *interj* **10** *informal* an exclamation of anger or surprise [Old English]

he'll he will or he shall

Hellas *n* transliteration of the Ancient Greek name for **Greece**

hellbent *adj informal* rashly intent: *hellbent on revenge*

hellebore *n* a plant with white flowers that bloom in winter [Greek *helleboros*]

Hellene *n* a Greek

Hellenic *adj* **1** of the Greeks or their language **2** of or relating to ancient Greece during the classical period (776–323 BC)

Hellenism *n* **1** the principles and ideals of classical Greek civilization **2** the spirit or national character of the Greeks ▷ **Hellenist** *n*

Hellenistic *adj* of Greek civilization during the period 323–30 BC

Heller *n* Joseph. 1923–99, US novelist. His works include *Catch 22* (1961), *God Knows* (1984), *Picture This* (1988), and *Closing Time* (1994)

Helles *n* Cape Helles a cape in NW Turkey, at the S end of the Gallipoli Peninsula

Hellespont *n* the ancient name for the **Dardanelles**

hellfire *n* the torment of hell, imagined as eternal fire

hellish *adj informal* very unpleasant

Hellman *n* Lillian. 1905–84, US dramatist. Her works include the plays *The Little Foxes* (1939), *The Searching Wind* (1944), and the autobiographical *Scoundrel Time* (1976)

hello, hallo *or* **hullo** *interj* **1** an expression of greeting or surprise **2** a call used to attract attention ▷ *n, pl* **-los** **3** the act of saying 'hello' [French *holà*]

Hell's Angel *n* a member of a motorcycle gang noted for their lawless behaviour

helm *n* **1** *nautical* the tiller or wheel for steering a ship **2** at the helm in a position of leadership or control [Old English *helma*] ▷ **helmsman** *n*

Helmand *n* **1** a river in S Asia, rising in E Afghanistan and flowing generally southwest to a marshy lake, Hamun Helmand, on the border with Iran. Length: 1400 km (870 miles) **2** a province of SW Afghanistan; scene of strong Taliban insurgency since 2006. Capital: Lashkar Gah. Pop: 1 441 769 (2010 est). Area: 58 584 sq km (23 058 sq miles)

helmet *n* a piece of protective headgear worn by motorcyclists, soldiers, policemen, divers, etc. [Old French]

Helmholtz *n* Baron **Hermann Ludwig Ferdinand von**. 1821–94, German physiologist, physicist, and mathematician: helped to found the theory of the conservation of energy; invented the ophthalmoscope (1850); and investigated the mechanics of sight and sound

Helmont *n* Jean Baptiste van. 1577–1644, Flemish chemist and physician. He was the first to distinguish gases and claimed to have coined the word *gas*

Héloïse *n* ?1101–64, pupil, mistress, and wife of Abelard

helot *n* (in ancient Greece) a serf or slave [Greek *Heilōtes* serfs, literally: inhabitants of Helos]

help *vb* **1** to assist (someone to do something) **2** to contribute to: *to help Latin America's economies* **3** to improve a situation: *a felt or rubber underlay will help* **4 a** to refrain from: *I couldn't help feeling foolish* **b** to be responsible for: *you must not blame him, he simply can't help it* **5** to serve (a customer) **6 help oneself** to take something, esp. food or drink, for oneself, without being served ▷ *n* **7** the act of helping **8** a person or thing that helps, esp. a farm worker or domestic servant **9** a remedy: *there's no help for it* ▷ *interj* **10** used to call for assistance ▶ See also **help out** [Old English *helpan*] ▷ **helper** *n*

helpful *adj* giving help ▷ **helpfully** *adv* ▷ **helpfulness** *n*

helping *n* a single portion of food

helpless *adj* **1** unable to manage independently **2** made weak: *it reduced her to helpless laughter* ▷ **helplessly** *adv* ▷ **helplessness** *n*

helpline *n* a telephone line set aside for callers to contact an organization for help with a problem

Helpmann *n* Sir Robert. 1909–86, Australian ballet dancer and choreographer: his ballets include *Miracle in the Gorbals* (1944), *Display* (1965), and *Yugen* (1965)

helpmate *or* **helpmeet** *n* a companion and helper, esp.

a husband or wife

help out *vb* to assist (someone) by sharing the burden or cost of something

Helsingborg *n* a port in SW Sweden, on the Sound opposite Helsingør, Denmark: changed hands several times between Denmark and Sweden, finally becoming Swedish in 1710; shipbuilding. Pop: 121 097 (2004 est). Former name (until 1971): **Hälsingborg**

Helsingør *n* a port in NE Denmark, in NE Zealand: site of Kronborg Castle (16th century), famous as the scene of Shakespeare's *Hamlet*. Pop: 35 002 (2004 est). English name: **Elsinore**

Helsinki *n* the capital of Finland, a port in the south on the Gulf of Finland: founded by Gustavus I of Sweden in 1550; replaced Turku as capital in 1812, while under Russian rule; university. Pop: 559 330 (2003 est). Swedish name: **Helsingfors**

helter-skelter *adj* **1** hurried or disorganized ▷ *adv* **2** in a hurried or disorganized manner ▷ *n* **3** *Brit* a high spiral slide at a fairground [probably imitative]

Helvellyn *n* a mountain in NW England, in the Lake District. Height: 949 m (3114 ft)

Helvetia *n* **1** the Latin name for Switzerland **2** a Roman province in central Europe (1st century BC to the 5th century AD), corresponding to part of S Germany and parts of W and N Switzerland

Helvetian *adj* **1** another word for **Swiss** ▷ *n* **2** a native or citizen of Switzerland

Helvétius *n* Claude Adrien. 1715–71, French philosopher. In his chief work *De l'Esprit* (1758), he asserted that the mainspring of human action is self-interest and that differences in human intellects are due only to differences in education

hem¹ *n* **1** the bottom edge of a garment, folded under and stitched down ▷ *vb* **hemming, hemmed** **2** to provide (a garment) with a hem ▶ See also **hem in** [Old English *hemm*]

hem² *n* **1** a representation of the sound of clearing the throat, used to gain attention ▷ *vb* **hemming, hemmed** **2** to make this sound **3 hem and haw** See **haw²**

he-man *n, pl* **-men** *informal* a strong man, esp. one who shows off his strength

Hemel Hempstead *n* a town in SE England, in W Hertfordshire: designated a new town in 1947. Pop: 83 11? (2001)

hemi- *prefix* half: *hemisphere* [Greek]

hem in *vb* to surround and prevent from moving

Hemingway *n* Ernest. 1899–1961, US novelist and short-story writer. His novels include *The Sun Also Rises* (1926), *A Farewell to Arms* (1929), *For Whom the Bell Tolls* (1940), and *The Old Man and the Sea* (1952): Nobel prize for literature 1954

hemipterous *or* **hemipteran** *adj* of an order of insects with sucking or piercing mouthparts [Greek *hēmi* half + *pteron* wing]

hemisphere *n* one half of a sphere, esp. of the earth (**northern** and **southern hemisphere**) or of the brain ▷ **hemispherical** *adj*

hemline *n* the level to which the hem of a skirt or dress hangs: *the hemline debate*

hemlock *n* a poisonous drug derived from a plant with spotted stems and small white flowers [Old English *hymlic*]

hemp *n* **1** an Asian plant with tough fibres **2** the fibre of this plant, used to make canvas and rope **3** a narcotic drug obtained from this plant [Old English *hænep*] ▷ **hempen** *adj*

hen *n* the female of any bird, esp. the domestic fowl [Old English *henn*]

Henan *or* **Honan** *n* a province of N central China: the chief centre of early Chinese culture; mainly agricultural (the largest wheat-producing province in China). Capital: Zhengzhou. Pop: 96 670 000 (2003 est)

henbane *n* a poisonous plant with sticky hairy leaves

hence *adv* **1** for this reason; therefore **2** from this time: *two weeks hence* **3** *archaic* from here [Old English *hionane*]

henceforth *or* **henceforward** *adv* from now on

henchman *n, pl* **-men** a person employed by someone powerful to carry out orders [Middle English *hengestman*]

Henderson *n* Arthur. 1863–1935, British Labour politician. As foreign secretary (1929–31) he supported the League of Nations and international disarmament; Nobel peace prize 1934

Hendrix *n* Jimi, full name *James Marshall Hendrix*. 1942–70, US rock guitarist, singer, and songwriter, noted for his innovative guitar technique. His recordings include "Purple Haze" (1967) and *Are you Experienced?* (1967)

Hendry *n* Stephen. born 1969, Scottish snooker player: world champion 1990, 1992–96, and 1999

henge *n* a circular monument, often containing a circle of stones, dating from the Neolithic and Bronze Ages [from *Stonehenge*]

Hengelo *n* a city in the E Netherlands, in Overijssel province on the Twente Canal: industrial centre, esp. for textiles. Pop: 81 000 (2003 est)

Hengist *n* died ?488 AD, a leader, with his brother Horsa, of the first Jutish settlers in Britain; he is thought to have conquered Kent (?455). See also **Horsa**

Hengyang *n* a city in SE central China, in Hunan province on the Xiang River. Pop: 853 000 (2005 est)

Henie *n* Sonja. 1912–69, Norwegian figure-skater

Henley-on-Thames *n* a town in S England, in SE Oxfordshire on the River Thames: a riverside resort with an annual regatta. Pop: 10 513 (2001). Often shortened to: **Henley**

henna *n* **1** a reddish dye, obtained from a shrub or tree of Asia and N Africa which is used to colour hair ▷ *vb* **2** to dye (the hair) with henna [Arabic *hinnā'*]

hen night *n informal* a party for women only, esp. held for a woman shortly before she is married

hen party *n informal* a party at which only women are present

henpecked *adj* (of a man) harassed by the persistent nagging of his wife

Henri *n* born 1955, full name *Henri Albert Gabriel Félix Marie Guillaume*, grand duke of Luxembourg from 2000

Henrietta Maria *n* 1609–69, queen of England (1625–49), the wife of Charles I; daughter of Henry IV of France. Her Roman Catholicism contributed to the unpopularity of the crown in the period leading to the Civil War

henry *n, pl* **-ry, -ries** *or* **-rys** the SI unit of electric inductance [after Joseph HENRY]

Henry *n* **1** Joseph. 1797–1878, US physicist. He discovered the principle of electromagnetic induction independently of Faraday and constructed the first electromagnetic motor (1829). He also discovered self-induction and the oscillatory nature of electric discharges (1842) **2** Patrick. 1736–99, American statesman and orator, a leading opponent of British rule during the War of American Independence **3** Prince, known as **Harry**. born 1984, second son of Charles, Prince of Wales, and Diana, Princess of Wales

Henry I *n* **1** known as *Henry the Fowler*. ?876–936 AD, duke of Saxony (912–36) and king of Germany (919–36): founder of the Saxon dynasty (918–1024) **2** 1068–1135, king of England (1100–35) and duke of Normandy (1106–35); son of William the Conqueror: crowned in the absence of his elder brother, Robert II, duke of Normandy; conquered Normandy (1106)

Henry II *n* **1** known as *Henry the Saint*. 973–1024, king of Germany and Holy Roman Emperor (1014–24): canonized in 1145 **2** 1133–89, first Plantagenet king of England (1154–89): extended his Anglo-French domains and instituted judicial and financial reforms. His attempts to control the church were opposed by Becket **3** 1519–59, king of France (1547–59); husband of Catherine de' Medici. He recovered Calais from the English (1558) and

suppressed the Huguenots

Henry III *n* **1** 1017–56, king of Germany and Holy Roman Emperor (1046–56). He increased the power of the Empire but his religious policy led to rebellions **2** 1207–72, king of England (1216–72); son of John. His incompetent rule provoked the Barons' War (1264–67), during which he was captured by Simon de Montfort **3** 1551–89, king of France (1574–89). He plotted the massacre of Huguenots on St Bartholomew's Day (1572) with his mother Catherine de' Medici, thus exacerbating the religious wars in France

Henry IV *n* **1** 1050–1106, Holy Roman Emperor (1084–1105) and king of Germany (1056–1105). He was excommunicated by Pope Gregory VII, whom he deposed (1084) **2** surnamed *Bolingbroke*. 1367–1413, first Lancastrian king of England (1399–1413); son of John of Gaunt: deposed Richard II (1399) and suppressed rebellions led by Owen Glendower and the Earl of Northumberland **3** known as *Henry of Navarre*. 1553–1610, first Bourbon king of France (1589–1610). He obtained toleration for the Huguenots with the Edict of Nantes (1598) and restored prosperity to France following the religious wars (1562–98)

Henry V *n* **1** 1081–1125, king of Germany (1089–1125) and Holy Roman Emperor (1111–25) **2** 1387–1422, king of England (1413–22); son of Henry IV. He defeated the French at the Battle of Agincourt (1415), conquered Normandy (1419), and was recognized as heir to the French throne (1420)

Henry VI *n* **1** 1165–97, king of Germany (1169–97) and Holy Roman Emperor (1190–97): added Sicily to the Empire **2** 1421–71, last Lancastrian king of England (1422–61; 1470–71); son of Henry V. His weak rule was blamed for the loss by 1453 of all his possessions in France except Calais; from 1454 he suffered periods of insanity which contributed to the outbreak of the Wars of the Roses (1455–85). He was deposed by Edward IV (1461) but was briefly restored to the throne (1470)

Henry VII *n* **1** ?1275–1313, Holy Roman Emperor (1312–13) and, as Henry VI, count of Luxembourg (1288–1313). He became king of the Lombards in 1313 **2** 1457–1509, first Tudor king of England (1485–1509). He came to the throne (1485) after defeating Richard III at the Battle of Bosworth Field, ending the Wars of the Roses. Royal power and the prosperity of the country greatly increased during his reign

Henry VIII *n* 1491–1547, king of England (1509–47); second son of Henry VII. The declaration that his marriage to Catherine of Aragon was invalid and his marriage to Anne Boleyn (1533) precipitated the Act of Supremacy, making Henry supreme head of the Church in England. Anne Boleyn was executed (1536) and Henry subsequently married Jane Seymour, Anne of Cleves, Catherine Howard, and Catherine Parr. His reign is also noted for the fame of his succession of advisers, Cardinal Wolsey, Sir Thomas More, and Thomas Cromwell

Henryson *n* Robert. ?1430–?1506, Scottish poet. His works include *Testament of Cresseid* (1593), a sequel to Chaucer's *Troilus and Cressida*, the 13 *Moral Fables of Esope the Phrygian*, and the pastoral dialogue *Robene and Makyne*

Henry the Lion *n* ?1129–95, duke of Saxony (1142–81). His ambitions led to conflict with the Holy Roman Emperors, notably Frederick Barbarossa

Henry the Navigator *n* 1394–1460, prince of Portugal, noted for his patronage of Portuguese voyages of exploration of the W coast of Africa

Henslowe *n* Philip. died 1616, English theatre manager, noted also for his diary

Henze *n* Hans Werner. 1926–2012, German composer, whose works, in many styles, include the operas *The Stag King* (1956), *The Bassarids* (1965), *The English Cat* (1983), and *Das verratene Meer* (1990) and the oratorio *The Raft of the Medusa* (1968)

h

hepatic *adj* of the liver [Greek *hēpar* liver]

hepatitis *n* inflammation of the liver, causing fever, jaundice, and weakness

Hepburn *n* **1** Audrey. 1929–93, US actress, born in Belgium. Her films include *Roman Holiday* (1955), *Funny Face* (1957), and *My Fair Lady* (1964) **2** Katharine. 1907–2003, US film actress, whose films include *The Philadelphia Story* (1940), *Adam's Rib* (1949), *The African Queen* (1951), *The Lion in Winter* (1968) for which she won an Oscar, and *On Golden Pond* (1981)

Hephaestus *n* Greek myth the god of fire

hepta- *combining form* seven: *heptameter*

heptagon *n* geometry a figure with seven sides [Greek *heptagōnos* having seven angles] **> heptagonal** *adj*

heptathlon *n* an athletic contest for women in which athletes compete in seven different events

Hepworth *n* Dame Barbara. 1903–75, British sculptor of abstract works

her *pron* **1** (refers to) a female person or animal: *he loves her* **2** (refers to) things personified as feminine, such as ships and nations ▷ *adj* **3** of, belonging to, or associated with her: *her hair* [Old English *hire*]

> USAGE See at me¹.

Hera *or* **Here** *n* Greek myth the queen of the gods

Heraclea *n* any of several ancient Greek colonies. The most famous is the S Italian site where Pyrrhus of Epirus defeated the Romans (280 BC)

Heracleides *or* **Heraclides of Pontus** *n* ?390–?322 BC, Greek astronomer and philosopher: the first to state that the earth rotates on its axis

Heraclitus *n* ?535–?475 BC, Greek philosopher, who held that fire is the primordial substance of the universe and that all things are in perpetual flux

Heraclius *n* ?575–641 AD, Byzantine emperor, who restored the Holy Cross to Jerusalem (629)

Herakleion *or* **Heraklion** *n* variants of Iráklion

herald *n* **1** a person who announces important news **2** often literary a forerunner ▷ *vb* **3** to announce or signal the approach of: *his arrival was heralded by excited barking* [Germanic] **> heraldic** *adj*

heraldry *n, pl* -ries the study of coats of arms and family trees

Herat *n* a city in NW Afghanistan, on the Hari Rud River: on the site of several ancient cities; at its height as a cultural centre in the 15th century. Pop: 344 000 (2005 est)

Hérault *n* a department of S France, in Languedoc-Roussillon region. Capital: Montpellier. Pop: 945 901 (2003 est). Area: 6224 sq km (2427 sq miles)

herb *n* **1** an aromatic plant that is used for flavouring in cookery, and in medicine **2** botany a seed-bearing plant whose parts above ground die back at the end of the growing season [Latin *herba* grass, green plants] **> herbal** *adj* **> herby** *adj*

herbaceous *adj* designating plants that are soft-stemmed rather than woody

herbaceous border *n* a flower bed that contains perennials rather than annuals

herbage *n* herbaceous plants collectively, esp. those on which animals graze

herbalist *n* a person who grows or specializes in the use of medicinal herbs

Herbert *n* **1** Edward, 1st Baron Herbert of Cherbury. 1583–1648, English philosopher and poet, noted for his deistic views **2** his brother, George. 1593–1633, English Metaphysical poet. His chief work is *The Temple: Sacred Poems and Private Ejaculations* (1633) **3** Zbigniew, 1924–98, Polish poet and dramatist, noted esp. for his dramatic monologues

herbicide *n* a substance used to destroy plants, esp. weeds [Latin *herba* plant + *caedere* to kill]

herbivore (her-biv-vore) *n* **1** an animal that feeds only on plants **2** informal a liberal or idealistic person [Latin *herba* plant + *vorare* to swallow] **> herbivorous** (her-biv-or-uss) *adj*

Hercegovina *n* a variant of Herzegovina

Herculaneum *n* an ancient city in SW Italy, of marked Greek character, on the S slope of Vesuvius: buried along with Pompeii by an eruption of the volcano (79 AD). Excavation has uncovered well-preserved streets, houses, etc.

Herculean (her-kew-lee-an) *adj* **1** (often not cap) (of a task) requiring tremendous effort or strength **2** resembling Hercules, hero of classical myth, in strength or courage

herd *n* **1 a** large group of mammals, esp. cattle, living and feeding together **2** often disparaging a large group of people ▷ *vb* **3** to collect or be collected into, or as if into, a herd [Old English *heord*]

Herder *n* Johann Gottfried von. 1744–1803, German philosopher, critic, and poet, the leading figure in the *Sturm und Drang* movement in German literature. His chief work is *Outlines of a Philosophy of the History of Man* (1784–91)

herd instinct *n* psychol the inborn tendency to associate with others and follow the group's behaviour

herdsman *n, pl* -men chiefly Brit a man who looks after a herd of animals

here *adv* **1** in, at, or to this place, point, case, or respect: *I am pleased to be back here* **2** here and there at several places in or throughout an area **3** here's to a convention used in proposing a toast **4** neither here nor there of no relevance ▷ *n* **5** this place: *they leave here tonight* [Old English *hēr*]

hereabouts *or* **hereabout** *adv* in this region

hereafter *adv* **1** formal or law in a subsequent part of this document, matter, or case **2** at some time in the future ▷ *n* **3** the hereafter **a** life after death **b** the future

hereby *adv* (used in official statements and documents) by means of or as a result of this

hereditable *adj* same as heritable

hereditary *adj* **1** passed on genetically from one generation to another **2** law passed on to succeeding generations by inheritance

heredity (hir-red-it-ee) *n, pl* -ties the passing on from one generation to another of genetic factors that determine individual characteristics [Latin *hereditas* inheritance]

Hereford *n* **1** a city in W England, in Herefordshire on the River Wye: trading centre for agricultural produce; cathedral (begun 1079). Pop: 56 373 (2001) **2** a hardy breed of beef cattle characterized by a red body, red and white head, and white markings

Hereford and Worcester *n* a former county of the W Midlands of England, created in 1974 from the historic counties of Herefordshire and (most of) Worcestershire: abolished in 1998 when Herefordshire became an independent unitary authority

Herefordshire *n* a county of W England: from 1974 to 1998 part of Hereford and Worcester: drained chiefly by the River Wye; agricultural (esp. fruit and cattle). Administrative centre: Hereford. Pop: 176 900 (2003 est) Area: 2180 sq km (842 sq miles)

herein *adv* formal or law in this place, matter, or document

hereinafter *adv* formal or law from this point on in this document, matter, or case

hereof *adv* formal or law of or concerning this

heresy (herr-iss-ee) *n, pl* -sies **1** an opinion contrary to the principles of a religion **2** any belief thought to be contrary to official or established theory [Greek *hairein* to choose]

heretic (herr-it-ik) *n* **1** chiefly RC Church a person who maintains beliefs contrary to the established teachings of the Church **2** a person who holds unorthodox opinions in any field **> heretical** (hir-ret-ik-kl) *adj*

hereto *adv* formal or law to this place, matter, or document

heretofore *adv* formal or law until now

hereupon adv following immediately after this; at this stage

Hereward n called *Hereward the Wake*. 11th-century Anglo-Saxon rebel, who defended the Isle of Ely against William the Conqueror (1070–71): a subject of many legends

herewith adv formal together with this: *a schedule of the event is appended herewith*

Hering n Ewald. 1834–1918, German physiologist and experimental psychologist who studied vision and propounded the doctrine of nativism, the policy of favouring the natives of a country over the immigrants

Herisau n a town in NE Switzerland, capital of Appenzell Outer Rhodes demicanton. Pop: 15 882 (2000)

heritable adj capable of being inherited

heritage n 1 something inherited at birth 2 anything that has been carried over from the past or handed down by tradition 3 the evidence of the past, such as historical sites, considered as the inheritance of present-day society

Hermannstadt n the German name for **Sibiu**

hermaphrodite (her-maf-roe-dite) n an animal, flower, or person that has both male and female reproductive organs [after *Hermaphroditus*, son of Hermes and Aphrodite, who merged with the nymph Salmacis to form one body] ➤ **hermaphroditic** adj

Hermes n Greek myth the messenger of the gods

hermetic adj sealed so as to be airtight [after the god *Hermes* (*Trismegistus*), traditionally the inventor of a magic seal] ➤ **hermetically** adv

hermit n a person living in solitude, esp. for religious reasons [Greek *erēmos* lonely]

hermitage n 1 the home of a hermit 2 any retreat

hermitage n 1 the Hermitage an art museum in St Petersburg, originally a palace built by Catherine the Great 2 a full-bodied red or white wine from the Rhône valley at Tain-l'Ermitage, in SE France

hermit crab n a small crab that lives in the empty shells of other shellfish

Hermon n Mount a mountain on the border between Lebanon and SW Syria, in the Anti-Lebanon Range: represented the NE limits of Israelite conquests under Moses and Joshua. Height: 2814 m (9232 ft)

Hermosillo n a city in NW Mexico, capital of Sonora state, on the Sonora River: university (1938); winter resort and commercial centre for an agricultural and mining region. Pop: 668 000 (2005 est)

Hermoupolis n a port in Greece, capital of Cyclades department, on the E coast of Syros Island. Pop: (municipality): 13 496 (2001). Modern Greek name: Ermoupoli

Herne n an industrial city in W Germany, in North Rhine-Westphalia, in the Ruhr on the Rhine-Herne Canal. Pop: 172 870 (2003 est)

hernia n protrusion of an organ or part through the lining of the body cavity in which it is normally situated [Latin]

hero n, pl **-roes** 1 the principal male character in a novel, play, etc. 2 a man of exceptional courage, nobility, etc. 3 a man who is idealized for having superior qualities in any field [Greek *hērōs*]

Hero or **Heron** n 1st century AD, Greek mathematician and inventor

Herod n called *the Great*. ?73–4 BC, king of Judaea (37–4). The latter part of his reign was notable for his cruelty: according to the New Testament he ordered the Massacre of the Innocents

Herod Agrippa I n 10 BC–44 AD, king of Judaea (41–44), grandson of Herod (the Great). A friend of Caligula and Claudius, he imprisoned Saint Peter and executed Saint James

Herod Agrippa II n died ?93 AD, king of territories in N Palestine (50–?93 AD). He presided (60) at the trial of Saint Paul and sided with the Roman authorities in the Jewish rebellion of 66

Herod Antipas n died ?40 AD, tetrarch of Galilee and Peraea (4 BC–40 AD); son of Herod the Great. At the instigation of his wife Herodias, he ordered the execution of John the Baptist

Herodias n ?14 BC–?40 AD, niece and wife of Herod Antipas and mother of Salome, whom she persuaded to ask for the head of John the Baptist. Her ambition led to the banishment of her husband

Herodotus n called *the Father of History*. ?485–?425 BC, Greek historian, famous for his *History* dealing with the causes and events of the wars between the Greeks and the Persians (490–479)

heroic adj 1 brave and courageous: *heroic work by the army engineers* 2 of, like, or befitting a hero ➤ **heroically** adv

heroics pl n behaviour or language considered too melodramatic or extravagant for the particular situation in which they are used

heroin n a highly addictive drug derived from morphine [probably from *hero*, referring to its aggrandizing effect on the personality]

heroine n 1 the principal female character in a novel, play, etc. 2 a woman of exceptional courage, nobility, etc. 3 a woman who is idealized for having superior qualities in any field

heroism (herr-oh-izz-um) n great courage and bravery

heron n a wading bird with a long neck, long legs, and grey or white feathers [Old French *hairon*]

Heron n 1 same as Hero 2 Patrick. 1920–99, British abstract painter and art critic

heronry n, pl **-ries** a colony of breeding herons

Herophilus n died ?280 BC, Greek anatomist in Alexandria. He was the first to distinguish sensory from motor nerves

hero worship n admiration for heroes or idealized people

herpes (her-peez) n any of several inflammatory skin diseases, including shingles and cold sores [Greek *herpein* to creep]

herpes simplex n an acute viral disease causing clusters of watery blisters [New Latin: simple herpes]

herpes zoster n same as **shingles** [New Latin: girdle herpes]

Herr (hair) n, pl **Herren** a German form of address equivalent to *Mr* [German]

Herrick n Robert. 1591–1674, English poet. His chief work is the *Hesperides* (1648), a collection of short, delicate, sacred, and pastoral lyrics

herring n, pl **-rings** or **-ring** a food fish of northern seas, with a long silver-coloured body [Old English *hǣring*]

herringbone n a zigzag pattern consisting of short lines of V shapes

herring gull n a common gull that has white and grey feathers with black-tipped wings

herring-pond n the herring-pond informal the Atlantic Ocean

Herriot n 1 Édouard. 1872–1957, French Radical statesman and writer; premier (1924–25; 1932) 2 James. real name *James Alfred Wight*. 1916–95, British veterinary surgeon and writer. His books based on his experiences in Yorkshire have been adapted for television and films

hers pron 1 something belonging to her: *hers is the highest paid part-time job*; *the money which is rightfully hers* 2 of hers belonging to her

Herschel n 1 Caroline Lucretia. 1750–1848, British astronomer, born in Germany, noted for her catalogue of nebulae and star clusters: sister of Sir William Herschel 2 Sir John Frederick William. 1792–1871, British astronomer. He discovered and catalogued over 525 nebulae and star clusters 3 his father, Sir (**Frederick**) William, original name *Friedrich Wilhelm Herschel*. 1738–1822, British astronomer, born in Germany. He constructed a reflecting telescope, which led to his discovery of the planet Uranus (1781), two of its satellites, and two of the satellites of Saturn. He also discovered the motions of binary stars

herself *pron* **1 a** the reflexive form of *she* or *her*: *she busied herself at the stove* **b** used for emphasis: *none other than The Great Mother herself* **2** her normal self: *she hasn't been herself all week*

Herstmonceux *or* **Hurstmonceux** *n* a village in S England, in E Sussex north of Eastbourne: 15th-century castle, site of the Royal Observatory, which was transferred from Greenwich between 1948 and 1958, until 1990

Hertford *n* a town in SE England, administrative centre of Hertfordshire. Pop: 24 460 (2001)

Hertfordshire *n* a county of S England, bordering on Greater London in the south: mainly low-lying, with the Chiltern Hills in the northwest; largely agricultural; light industries, esp. in the new towns. Administrative centre: Hertford. Pop: 1 040 900 (2003 est). Area: 1634 sq km (631 sq miles). Abbreviation: **Herts**

Hertogenbosch *n* See 's Hertogenbosch

Herts Hertfordshire

hertz *n*, *pl* **hertz** the SI unit of frequency, equal to one cycle per second [after H. R. HERTZ]

Hertz *n* **1** Gustav. 1887–1975, German atomic physicist. He provided evidence for the quantum theory by his research with Franck on the effects produced by bombarding atoms with electrons: they shared the Nobel prize for physics (1925) **2** Heinrich Rudolph. 1857–94, German physicist. He was the first to produce electromagnetic waves artificially ▷ **'Hertzian** *adj*

Hertzog *n* James Barry Munnik. 1866–1942, South African politician; prime minister (1924–39): founded the Nationalist Party (1913), advocating complete South African independence from Britain; opposed South African participation in World Wars I and II

Hertzsprung *n* Ejnar. 1873–1967, Danish astronomer: he discovered the existence of giant and dwarf stars, originating one form of the Hertzsprung-Russell diagram

Herzegovina *or* **Hercegovina** *n* a region in Bosnia-Herzegovina: originally under Austro-Hungarian rule; became part of the province of Bosnia-Herzegovina (1878), which was a constituent republic of Yugoslavia (1946–92)

Herzen *n* Aleksandr (Ivanovich). 1812–70, Russian socialist political philosopher: best known for his autobiography *My Past and Thoughts* (1861–67)

Herzl *n* Theodor. 1860–1904, Austrian writer, born in Hungary; founder of the Zionist movement. In *The Jewish State* (1896), he advocated resettlement of the Jews in a state of their own

Herzog *n* **1** Roman. born 1934, German politician; president of Germany (1994–99) **2** Werner. born 1942, German film director. His films include *Signs of Life* (1967), *Fata Morgana* (1970), *Fitzcarraldo* (1982), *Little Dieter Needs to Fly* (1997), and *Grizzly Man* (2005)

he's he is *or* he has

hESC human embryonic stem cell

Heseltine *n* **1** Michael (Ray Dibden) Baron. born 1933, British Conservative politician; secretary of state for defence (1983–86); secretary of state for the environment (1990–92); secretary of state for trade and industry (1992–95); deputy prime minister (1995–97) **2** Philip Arnold. the real name of composer Peter Warlock. See Warlock

Hesiod *n* 8th century BC, Greek poet and the earliest author of didactic verse. His two complete extant works are the *Works and Days*, dealing with the agricultural seasons, and the *Theogony*, concerning the origin of the world and the genealogies of the gods ▷ **Hesi'odic** *adj*

hesitant *adj* doubtful and unsure in speech or action ▷ **hesitancy** *n* ▷ **hesitantly** *adv*

hesitate *vb* **-tating, -tated 1** to be slow and uncertain in acting **2** to be reluctant (to do something): *I hesitate to use the word 'squandered'* **3** to pause during speech because of uncertainty [Latin *haesitare*] ▷ **hesitation** *n*

Hesperia *n* a poetic name used by the ancient Greeks for Italy and by the Romans for Spain or beyond [Latin, from Greek: land of the west, from *hesperos* western]

Hesperian *adj* **1** poetic western ▷ *n* **2** a native or inhabitant of a western land

Hess *n* **1** Dame Myra. 1890–1965, English pianist **2** (Walther Richard) Rudolf. 1894–1987, German Nazi leader. He made a secret flight to Scotland (1941) to negotiate peace with Britain but was held as a prisoner of war; later sentenced to life imprisonment at the Nuremberg trials (1946); committed suicide **3** Victor Francis. 1883–1964, US physicist, born in Austria: pioneered the investigation of cosmic rays: shared the Nobel prize for physics (1936)

Hesse¹ *n* a state of central Germany, formed in 1945 from the former Prussian province of Hesse-Nassau and part of the former state of Hesse; part of West Germany until 1990. Capital: Wiesbaden. Pop: 6 089 000 (2003 est). Area: 21 111 sq km (8151 sq miles). German name: **Hessen**

Hesse² *n* Hermann. 1877–1962, German novelist, short-story writer, and poet. His novels include *Der Steppenwolf* (1927) and *Das Glasperlenspiel* (1943): Nobel prize for literature 1946

Hesse-Nassau *n* a former province of Prussia, now part of the state of Hesse, Germany

hessian *n* a coarse jute fabric similar to sacking [after HESSE, Germany]

Hessian *n* **1** a native or inhabitant of Hesse **2 a** a Hessian soldier in any of the mercenary units of the British Army in the War of American Independence or the Napoleonic Wars **b** US any German mercenary in the British Army during the War of American Independence **3** *chiefly US* a mercenary or ruffian ▷ *adj* **4** of or relating to Hesse or its inhabitants

hetero- *combining form* other, another, or different: *heterosexual* [Greek *heteros* other]

heterodox *adj* different from established or accepted doctrines or beliefs [HETERO- + Greek *doxa* opinion] ▷ **heterodoxy** *n*

heterodyne *electronics vb* **-dyning, -dyned 1** to combine (two alternating signals) so as to produce two signals with frequencies corresponding to the sum and the difference of the original frequencies ▷ *adj* **2** produced or operating by heterodyning two signals [HETERO- + Greek *dunamis* power]

heterogeneous (het-er-oh-jean-ee-uss) *adj* varied in content; composed of different parts: *a heterogeneous collection of art* [HETERO- + Greek *genos* sort] ▷ **heterogeneity** *n*

heteromorphic *adj* biology **1** differing from the normal form **2** (esp. of insects) having different forms at different stages of the life cycle [HETERO- + Greek *morphē* form] ▷ **heteromorphism** *n*

heterosexual *n* **1** a person who is sexually attracted to members of the opposite sex ▷ *adj* **2** (of a person) sexually attracted to members of the opposite sex **3** (of sexual relationship) between a man and a woman ▷ **heterosexuality** *n*

heterozygous *adj* biology having two different alleles of the same gene [HETERO- + Greek *zugōtos* yoked]

het up *adj informal* agitated or excited: *he was very het up about the traffic* [dialect for *heated*]

heuristic (hew-rist-ik) *adj* (of a method of teaching) allowing students to learn things for themselves by trial and error [Greek *heuriskein* to discover]

Hevelius *n* Johannes. 1611–87, German astronomer, who published one of the first detailed maps of the lunar surface

Hever Castle *n* a Tudor mansion near Edenbridge in Kent: home of Anne Boleyn before her marriage; Italian garden added in the 20th century by the Astor family

Hevesy *n* Georg von. 1885–1966, Hungarian chemist. H

worked on radioactive tracing and, with D. Coster, discovered the element hafnium (1923): Nobel prize for chemistry 1943

ew vb **hewing, hewed, hewed** or **hewn 1** to chop or cut with an axe **2** to carve (something) from a substance: *a tunnel hewn out of the living rock* [Old English *hēawan*]

ewish n Antony. born 1924, British radio astronomer, noted esp. for his role in the discovery of pulsars (1967): shared the Nobel prize for physics 1974

ewitt n Lleyton. born 1981, Australian tennis player; US Open champion 2001, Wimbledon singles champion 2002

ex n **1** short for **hexadecimal notation** ▷ adj **2** of or relating to hexadecimal notation: *hex code*

exa- combining form six: **hexameter** [Greek *hex* six]

exadecimal notation n a number system with a base of 16, the numbers 10–15 being represented by the letters A–F

exagon n geometry a figure with six sides ▷ **hexagonal** adj

exagram n geometry a star formed by extending the sides of a regular hexagon to meet at six points

examter (hek-**sam**-it-er) n prosody a verse line consisting of six metrical feet

ey interj **1** an expression of surprise or for catching attention **2 hey presto!** an exclamation used by conjurors at the climax of a trick [imitative]

eyday n the time of most power, popularity, or success: *the heyday of classical composition* [probably based on *hey*]

eyer n Georgette. 1902–74, British historical novelist and writer of detective stories, noted esp. for her romances of the Regency period

eyerdahl n Thor. 1914–2002, Norwegian anthropologist. In 1947 he demonstrated that the Polynesians could originally have been migrants from South America, by sailing from Peru to the Pacific islands of Tuamotu in the *Kon-Tiki*, a raft made of balsa wood. DNA testing in the late 1990s indicated that such a migration did not actually take place

eysham n a port in NW England, in NW Lancashire. Pop (with Morecambe): 16 136 (2001)

eywood[1] n a town in NW England, in Rochdale unitary authority, Greater Manchester, near Bury. Pop: 28 024 (2001)

eywood[2] n **1** John. ?1497–?1580, English dramatist, noted for his comic interludes **2** Thomas. ?1574–1641, English dramatist, noted esp. for his domestic drama *A Woman Killed with Kindness* (1607)

f chem hafnium

FEA Brit Human Fertilization and Embryology Authority

g chem mercury

GV (in Britain, formerly) heavy goods vehicle

H 1 His (or Her) Highness **2** His Holiness (title of the pope)

i interj informal hello [probably from *how are you?*]

I Hawaii

ialeah n a city in SE Florida, near Miami: racetrack. Pop: 226 401 (2003 est)

iatus (hie-**ay**-tuss) n, pl **-tuses** or **-tus** a pause or an interruption in continuity: *diplomatic relations restored after a four-year hiatus* [Latin: gap, cleft]

iatus hernia n protrusion of the stomach through the diaphragm at the hole for the gullet

iawatha n a 16th-century Onondaga Indian chief: credited with the organization of the Five Nations

ib n Haemophilus influenzae type b: a vaccine against a specific type of bacterial meningitis, administered to children under four years of age

ibernate vb **-nating, -nated** (of some animals) to pass the winter in a resting state in which heartbeat, temperature, and breathing rate are very low [Latin *hibernare* to spend the winter] ▷ **hibernation** n

ibernia n the Roman name for Ireland

USAGE This name is now used poetically

Hibernian adj **1** of or relating to Ireland or its inhabitants ▷ n **2** a native or inhabitant of Ireland

Hiberno- combining form denoting Irish or Ireland: *Hiberno-English*

hibiscus n, pl **-cuses** a tropical plant with large brightly coloured flowers [Greek *hibiskos* marsh mallow]

hiccup n **1** a spasm of the breathing organs with a sharp coughlike sound **2 hiccups** the state of having such spasms **3** informal a minor difficulty ▷ vb **-cuping, -cuped** or **-cupping, -cupped 4** to make a hiccup or hiccups. Also: **hiccough** [imitative]

hick n US, Austral and NZ informal an unsophisticated country person [after *Hick*, familiar form of *Richard*]

Hickok n James Butler, known as *Wild Bill Hickok*. 1837–76, US frontiersman and marshal

hickory n, pl **-ries 1** a North American tree with edible nuts **2** the hard wood of this tree [Native American *pawcohiccora*]

Hickox n Richard (Sidney). 1948–2008, British conductor; musical director of the City of London Sinfonia and Singers (1971–2008)

Hidalgo n a state of central Mexico: consists of a high plateau, with the Sierra Madre Oriental in the north and east; ancient remains of Teltec culture (at Tula); rich mineral resources. Capital: Pachuca. Pop: 2 231 392 (2000). Area: 20 987 sq km (8103 sq miles)

hidden vb **1** a past participle of **hide**[1] ▷ adj **2** not easily noticed or obscure: *hidden dangers* **3** difficult to find

hidden agenda n a set of motives or intentions concealed from others who might object to them

hide[1] vb **hiding, hid, hidden** or **hid 1** to conceal (oneself or an object) from view or discovery: *in an attempt to hide from his wife* **2** to keep (information or one's feelings) secret **3** to obscure or cover (something) from view: *the collar hid his face* ▷ n **4** Brit a place of concealment, disguised to appear as part of its surroundings, used by hunters, bird-watchers, etc. [Old English *hȳdan*]

hide[2] n the skin of an animal, either tanned or raw [Old English *hȳd*]

hide-and-seek n a game in which one player covers his or her eyes while the others hide, and that player then tries to find them

hideaway n a hiding place or secluded spot

hidebound adj restricted by petty rules and unwilling to accept new ideas

hideous (hide-ee-uss) adj extremely ugly or unpleasant [Old French *hisdos*]

hide-out n a hiding place

Hideyoshi Toyotomi n 1536–98, Japanese military dictator (1582–98). He unified all Japan (1590)

hiding[1] n **1** a state of concealment: *in hiding* **2 hiding place** a place of concealment

hiding[2] n informal a severe beating

hie vb **hieing** or **hying, hied** archaic or poetic to hurry [Old English *hīgian* to strive]

hierarchy (hire-ark-ee) n, pl **-chies 1** a system of people or things arranged in a graded order **2 the hierarchy** the people in power in any organization [Late Greek *hierarkhēs* high priest] ▷ **hierarchical** adj

hieroglyphic (hire-oh-gliff-ik) adj **1** of or relating to a form of writing using picture symbols, as used in ancient Egypt ▷ n also: **hieroglyph 2** a symbol that is difficult to decipher **3** a picture or symbol representing an object, idea, or sound [Greek *hieros* holy + *gluphein* to carve]

hieroglyphics n **1** a form of writing, as used in ancient Egypt, in which pictures or symbols are used to represent objects, ideas, or sounds **2** writing that is difficult to decipher

Hieronymus n Eusebius. the Latin name of Saint Jerome. See **Jerome** (1) ▷ **Hieronymic** or **Hieronymian** adj

hi-fi n informal **1** a set of high-quality sound-reproducing equipment **2** short for **high fidelity** ▷ *adj* **3** producing high-quality sound: *a hi-fi amplifier*

Higgins *n* **1 Alex,** known as *Hurricane Higgins.* 1949–2010, Northern Irish snooker player: world champion (1972, 1982) **2 Jack,** real name *Harry Patterson.* born 1929, British novelist; his thrillers include *The Eagle Has Landed* (1975), *Confessional* (1985), and *Midnight Runner* (2002) **3 Michael** (Daniel). born 1941, Irish politician: president of Ireland from 2011

higgledy-piggledy *informal adj, adv* in a muddle [origin unknown]

high *adj* **1** being a relatively great distance from top to bottom: *a high stone wall* **2** being at a relatively great distance above sea level: *a high village* **3** being a specified distance from top to bottom: *three feet high* **4** coming up to a specified level: *waist-high* **5** being at its peak: *high summer* **6** of greater than average height: *a high ceiling* **7** greater than usual in intensity or amount: *high blood pressure*; *high fees* **8** (of a sound) acute in pitch **9** (of food) slightly decomposed, regarded as enhancing the flavour of game **10** towards the top of a scale of importance or quality: *high fashion* **11** intensely emotional: *high drama* **12** very cheerful: *high spirits* **13** *informal* under the influence of alcohol or drugs **14** luxurious or extravagant: *high life* **15** advanced in complexity: *high finance* **16** formal and elaborate: *High Mass* **17 high and dry** abandoned in a difficult situation **18 high and mighty** *informal* too confident and full of self-importance **19 high opinion** a favourable opinion ▷ *adv* **20** at or to a height: *flying high* ▷ *n* **21** a high level **22** same as **anticyclone 23 on a high** *informal* **a** in a state of intoxication by alcohol or drugs **b** in a state of great excitement and happiness [Old English *hēah*]

High Arctic *n* the regions of Canada, esp. the northern islands, within the Arctic Circle

highball *n chiefly US* a long iced drink consisting of whisky with soda water or ginger ale

highbrow *often disparaging adj* **1** concerned with serious, intellectual subjects ▷ *n* **2** a person with such tastes

highchair *n* a long-legged chair with a table-like tray, used for a child at meal times

High Church *n* **1** the movement within the Church of England stressing the importance of ceremony and ritual ▷ *adj* **High-Church 2** of or relating to this movement

high commissioner *n* the senior diplomatic representative sent by one Commonwealth country to another

high country *n* **the high country** NZ sheep pastures in the foothills of the Southern Alps

High Court *n* (in England, Wales, Australia, and New Zealand) the supreme court dealing with civil and criminal law cases

high-energy *adj* providing or inspiring a lot of energy: *a high-energy drink*; *a high-energy workout*

Higher *n* **1** (in Scotland) the advanced level of the Scottish Certificate of Education **2** a pass in a subject at this level: *she has got four Highers*

higher education *n* education and training at colleges, universities, and polytechnics

higher-up *n informal* a person of higher rank

highest common factor *n* the largest number that divides equally into each member of a group of numbers

high explosive *n* an extremely powerful chemical explosive, such as TNT or gelignite

highfalutin (hie-fa-loot-in) *adj informal* (of behaviour) excessively grand or pompous [-*falutin* perhaps variant of *fluting*]

high fidelity *n* **1** the electronic reproduction of sound with little or no distortion ▷ *adj* **high-fidelity 2** able to produce sound with little or no distortion: *high-fidelity stereo earphones*

high-five *n slang* a gesture of greeting or congratulation in which two people slap raised palms together

high-flown *adj* extravagant or pretentious: *high-flown language*

high-flyer or **high-flier** *n* **1** a person who is extremely ambitious **2** a person of great ability in a career ▷ **high-flying** *adj, n*

high frequency *n* a radio frequency between 30 and 3 megahertz

High German *n* the standard German language

high-handed *adj* using authority in an unnecessarily forceful way ▷ **high-handedness** *n*

high jump *n* **the high jump a** an athletic event in which competitors have to jump over a high bar **b** *Brit and Austral informal* a severe reprimand or punishment: *I was for the high jump again*

Highland *n* **1** a council area in N Scotland, formed in 1975 (as Highland Region) from Caithness, Sutherland Nairnshire, most of Inverness-shire, and Ross and Cromarty except for the Outer Hebrides. Administrativ centre: Inverness. Pop: 209 080 (2003 est). Area: 25 149 sq k (9710 sq miles) ▷ *adj* **2** of, relating to, or denoting the Highlands of Scotland

Highland cattle *n* a breed of cattle with shaggy reddish-brown hair and long horns

Highland fling *n* an energetic Scottish solo dance

highlands *pl n* relatively high ground

Highlands *n* **the Highlands 1 a** the part of Scotland that lies to the northwest of the great fault that runs from Dumbarton to Stonehaven **b** a smaller area consisting of the mountainous north of Scotland: distinguished b Gaelic culture **2** (*often not cap*) the highland region of an country ▷ **Highlander** *n*

high-level language *n* a computer programming language that is close to human language

highlight *n* **1** Also called: **high spot** the most exciting or memorable part of something **2** an area of the lightest tone in a painting or photograph **3** a lightened streak i the hair produced by bleaching ▷ *vb* **4** to give emphasis to: *the prime minister repeatedly highlighted the need for lower pa*

highlighter *n* **1** a cosmetic cream or powder applied to the face to highlight the cheekbones or eyes **2** a fluorescent felt-tip pen used as a marker to emphasize section of text without obscuring it

highly *adv* **1** extremely: *highly desirable* **2** towards the top of a scale of importance, admiration, or respect: *highly paid doctors*

highly strung or *US and Canad* **high-strung** *adj* tense and easily upset

high-maintenance *adj* **1** (of a piece of equipment, motor vehicle, etc.) requiring regular maintenance to keep it in working order **2** *informal* (of a person) requirin a high level of care and attention; demanding

High Mass *n* a solemn and elaborate Mass

high-minded *adj* having high moral principles

Highness *n* (preceded by *Your* or *His* or *Her*) a title used to address or refer to a royal person

high-octane *adj* **1** (of petrol) having a high octane number **2** *informal* dynamic or intense: *a high-octane lifestyle*

high-pitched *adj* (of a sound, esp. a voice) pitched high in tone

high-powered *adj* **1** (of machinery or equipment) powerful, advanced, and sophisticated **2** important, successful, or influential: *a high-powered business contact*

high-pressure *adj informal* (of selling) persuasive in an aggressive and persistent manner

high priest *n* the head of a cult or movement ▷ **high priestess** *fem n*

high-rise *adj* **1** of or relating to a building that has many storeys: *a high-rise estate* ▷ *n* **2** a building that has many storeys

high-risk *adj* denoting a group or area that is particularly subject to a danger

highroad *n* a main road

high school *n* a secondary school

gh seas *pl n* the open seas, which are outside the authority of any one nation

gh season *n* the most popular time of year at a holiday resort, etc.

ghsmith *n* Patricia. 1921–95, US author of crime fiction. Her novels include *Strangers on a Train* (1950) and *Ripley's Game* (1974)

gh-spirited *adj* lively and wishing to have fun and excitement

gh Street *often not caps n* the **High Street 1** *Brit* the main street of a town, usually where the principal shops are situated **2** the market constituted by the general public ▷ *adj* **High-Street, high-street 3** *Brit* the main street of a town, usually where the principal shops are situated **4** the market constituted by the general public geared to meet the requirements of, and readily available for purchase by, the general public: *High-Street fashion*

gh Tatra *n* another name for the **Tatra Mountains**

gh tea *n* *Brit* an early evening meal consisting of a cooked dish, bread, cakes, and tea

gh-tech *adj* same as **hi-tech**

gh technology *n* any type of sophisticated industrial process, esp. one involving electronics

gh-tension *adj* (of electricity cable) carrying a powerful current

gh tide *n* the sea at its highest level on the coast

gh time *adv* *informal* the latest possible time: *it was high time she got married*

gh treason *n* a serious crime directly affecting a sovereign or state

gh-water mark *n* **1** the level reached by sea water at high tide or a river in flood **2** the highest or most successful stage: *the premature high-water mark of his career*

ghway *n* **1** a public road that everyone may use **2** *US, Canad, Austral and NZ* a main road, esp. one that connects towns

ghway Code *n* (in Britain) a booklet of regulations and recommendations for all road users

ghwayman *n, pl* **-men** (formerly) a robber, usually on horseback, who held up travellers on public roads

gh Wycombe *n* a town in S central England, in S Buckinghamshire: furniture industry. Pop: 77 178 (2001)

jab *or* **hejab** *n* a covering for the head and face, worn by some Muslim women [Arabic: curtain]

jack *vb* **1** to seize control of or divert (a vehicle or aircraft) while travelling ▷ *n* **2** an instance of hijacking: *Indonesian ferry hijack ends* [origin unknown] ▷ **hijacker** *n*

jaz *n* a variant spelling of **Hejaz**

ke *vb* **hiking, hiked 1** to walk a long way in the country, usually for pleasure **2** to raise (prices) **3** to pull up with a quick movement: *he hiked up his trouser legs* ▷ *n* **4** a long walk **5** a rise in price [origin unknown] ▷ **hiker** *n*

larious *adj* very funny [Greek *hilaros* cheerful]

hilariously *adv* ▷ **hilarity** *n*

lary of Poitiers *n* Saint. ?315–?367 AD, French bishop, an opponent of Arianism. Feast day: Jan 13 or 14

lbert *n* David. 1862–1943, German mathematician, who made outstanding contributions to the theories of number fields and invariants and to geometry

ildegard of Bingen *n* Saint. 1098–1179, German abbess, poet, composer, and mystic

ildesheim *n* a city in N central Germany, in Lower Saxony: a member of the Hanseatic League. Pop: 103 245 (2003 est)

ll *n* **1** a natural elevation of the earth's surface, less high than a mountain **2** a heap or mound **3** an incline or slope [Old English *hyll*] ▷ **hilly** *adj*

ill *n* **1** Archibald Vivian. 1886–1977, British biochemist, noted for his research into heat loss in muscle contraction: shared the Nobel prize for physiology or medicine (1922) **2** Damon Graham Devereux, son of Graham Hill. born 1960, British motor-racing driver; Formula One world champion (1996) **3** David Octavius

1802–70, Scottish painter and portrait photographer, noted esp. for his collaboration with the chemist Robert Adamson (1821–48) **4** Sir **Geoffrey (William)**. born 1932, British poet: his books include *King Log* (1968), *Mercian Hymns* (1971), *The Mystery of the Charity of Charles Péguy* (1983), and *The Orchards of Syon* (2002) **5** Graham. 1929–75, British motor-racing driver: Formula One world champion (1962, 1968) **6** Octavia. 1838–1912, British housing reformer; a founder of the National Trust **7** Sir **Rowland**. 1795–1879, British originator of the penny postage **8** Susan **(Elizabeth)**. born 1942, British novelist and writer of short stories: her books include *I'm the King of the Castle* (1970) *The Woman in Black* (1983), and *Felix Derby* (2002)

Hilla *n* a market town in central Iraq, on a branch of the Euphrates: built partly of bricks from the nearby site of Babylon. Pop: 364 000 (2005 est). Also called: **Al Hillah**

Hillary *n* Sir Edmund. 1919–2008, New Zealand explorer and mountaineer. He and his Sherpa guide, Tenzing Norgay, were the first to reach the summit of Mount Everest (1953); New Zealand ambassador to India (1984–89)

hillbilly *n, pl* **-lies 1** *usually disparaging* an unsophisticated person from the mountainous areas in the southeastern US **2** same as **country and western** [hill + Billy (the nickname)]

Hillel *n* ?60 BC–?9 AD, rabbi, born in Babylonia; president of the Sanhedrin. He was the first to formulate principles of biblical interpretation

Hiller *n* Dame Wendy. 1912–2003, British actress. Her many films include *Pygmalion* (1938), *Major Barbara* (1940), and *Separate Tables* (1958)

Hilliard *n* Nicholas. 1537–1619, English miniaturist, esp. of portraits

Hillingdon *n* a residential borough of W Greater London. Pop: 247 600 (2003 est). Area: 110 sq km (43 sq miles)

hillock *n* a small hill or mound

hilt *n* **1** the handle or shaft of a sword, dagger, or knife **2** to the hilt to the full: *he plays the role to the hilt* [Old English]

Hilton *n* Walter. died 1396, English mystical writer: author of *The Scale of Perfection*

hilum *n, pl* **-la** *botany* a scar on a seed marking its point of attachment to the seed vessel [Latin: trifle]

Hilversum *n* a city in the central Netherlands, in North Holland province: Dutch radio and television centre. Pop: 83 000 (2003 est))

him *pron* refers to a male person or animal: *I greeted him at the hotel*; *I must send him a note of congratulation* [Old English]

USAGE See at **me**[1].

Himachal Pradesh *n* a state of N India, in the W Himalayas: rises to about 6700 m (22 000 ft) and is densely forested. Capital: Simla. Pop: 6 077 248 (2001). Area: 55 658 sq km (21 707 sq miles)

Himalayan *adj* of or relating to the Himalayas or their inhabitants

Himalayas *or* **Himalaya** *pl n* the **Himalayas** a vast mountain system in S Asia, extending 2400 km (1500 miles) from Kashmir (west) to Assam (east), between the valleys of the Rivers Indus and Brahmaputra: covers most of Nepal, Sikkim, Bhutan, and the S edge of Tibet; the highest range in the world, with several peaks over 7500 m (25 000 ft). Highest peak: Mount Everest, 8848 m (29 028 ft)

Himeji *n* a city in central Japan, on W Honshu: cotton textile centre. Pop: 475 892 (2002 est)

Himmler *n* Heinrich. 1900–45, German Nazi leader, head of the SS and the Gestapo (1936–45); committed suicide

Hims *n* a former name of **Homs**

himself *pron* **1 a** the reflexive form of *he* or *him*: *he secretly asked himself* **b** used for emphasis: *approved of by the Creator himself* **2** his normal self: *he was almost himself again*

Himyarite n **1** a member of an ancient people of SW Arabia, sometimes regarded as including the Sabeans ▷ adj **2** of or relating to this people or their culture [C19: named after *Himyar* legendary king in ancient Yemen]

Hinckley n a town in central England, in Leicestershire. Pop: 43 246 (2001)

hind¹ adj **hinder, hindmost** situated at the back: *a hind leg* [Old English *hindan* at the back]

hind² n, pl **hinds** or **hind** the female of the deer, esp. the red deer [Old English]

Hind. 1 Hindi **2** Hindu **3** Hindustan **4** Hindustani

Hindemith n Paul. 1895–1963, German composer and musical theorist, who opposed the twelve-tone technique. His works include the song cycle *Das Marienleben* (1923) and the opera *Mathis der Maler* (1938)

Hindenburg¹ n the German name for **Zabrze**

Hindenburg² n Paul von Beneckendorff und von. 1847–1934, German field marshal and statesman; president (1925–34). During World War I he directed German strategy together with Ludendorff (1916–18)

hinder¹ vb to get in the way of (someone or something) [Old English *hindrian*]

hinder² adj situated at the back [Old English]

Hindi n **1** a language or group of dialects of N central India **2** a formal literary dialect of this language, the official language of India [Old Persian *Hindu* the river Indus]

hindmost adj furthest back; last

hindquarters pl n the rear of a four-legged animal

hindrance n **1** an obstruction or snag **2** the act of hindering

hindsight n the ability to understand, after something has happened, what should have been done or what caused the event

Hindu n, pl **-dus 1** a person who practises Hinduism ▷ adj **2** of Hinduism

Hinduism n the dominant religion of India, which involves the worship of many gods and belief in reincarnation

Hindu Kush pl n a mountain range in central Asia, extending about 800 km (500 miles) east from the Koh-i-Baba Mountains of central Afghanistan to the Pamirs. Highest peak: Tirich Mir, 7690 m (25 230 ft)

Hindustan n **1** the land of the Hindus, esp. India north of the Deccan and excluding Bengal **2** the general area around the Ganges where Hindi is the predominant language **3** the areas of India where Hinduism predominates, as contrasted with those areas where Islam predominates

Hindustani n a group of northern Indian languages that includes Hindi and Urdu

Hines n Earl, known as *Earl "Fatha" Hines*. 1905–83, US jazz pianist, conductor, and songwriter

hinge n **1** a device for holding together two parts, such as a door and its frame, so that one can swing freely ▷ vb **hinging, hinged 2** to join or open (something) by means of a hinge **3 hinge on** to depend on: *billions of dollars of western aid hinged on the outcome of the talks* [probably Germanic] ▷ **hinged** adj

Hinglish n a variety of English incorporating elements of Hindi [blend of HINDI + ENGLISH]

hinny n, pl **-nies** the offspring of a male horse and a female donkey [Greek *hinnos*]

Hinshelwood n Sir Cyril Norman. 1897–1967, English chemist, who shared the Nobel prize for chemistry (1956) for the study of reaction kinetics

hint n **1** a suggestion given in an indirect or subtle manner **2** a helpful piece of advice **3** a small amount: *a hint of irony* ▷ vb **4** (sometimes foll. by at) to suggest indirectly: *a solution has been hinted at by a few politicians* [origin unknown]

hinterland n **1** land lying behind a coast or the shore of a river **2** an area near and dependent on a large city, esp. a port [German *hinter* behind + LAND]

hip¹ n either side of the body below the waist and above the thigh [Old English *hype*]

hip² n the berry-like brightly coloured fruit of a rose bush. Also called: **rosehip** [Old English *hēope*]

hip³ interj an exclamation used to introduce cheers: *hip, hip, hurrah* [origin unknown]

hip⁴ adj **hipper, hippest** slang aware of or following the latest trends [variant of earlier *hep*]

hip bath n a portable bath in which the bather sits

hipbone n either of the two bones that form the sides of the pelvis

hip flask n a small metal flask for whisky, brandy, etc.

hip-hop n a US pop-culture movement originating in the 1980s, comprising rap music, graffiti, and break dancing

Hipparchus n **1** 2nd century BC, Greek astronomer. He discovered the precession of the equinoxes, calculated the length of the solar year, and developed trigonometry **2** died 514 BC, tyrant of Athens (527–514)

hippie n same as **hippy²**

hippo n, pl **-pos** informal short for **hippopotamus**

Hippocrates n ?460–?377 BC, Greek physician, commonly regarded as the father of medicine ▷ **Hippocratic** or **Hippocratical** adj

Hippocratic oath n an oath taken by a doctor to observe a code of medical ethics [from HIPPOCRATES]

hippodrome n **1** a music hall, variety theatre, or circus **2** (in ancient Greece or Rome) an open-air course for horse and chariot races [Greek *hippos* horse + *dromos* race]

hippopotamus n, pl **-muses** or **-mi** a very large mammal with thick wrinkled skin and short legs, which lives around the rivers of tropical Africa [Greek *hippopotamos* river horse]

Hippo Regius n an ancient Numidian city, adjoining present-day Annaba, Algeria. Often shortened to: **Hippo**

hippy¹ adj **-pier, -piest** informal having large hips

hippy² or **hippie** n, pl **-pies** (esp. during the 1960s) a person whose behaviour and dress imply a rejection of conventional values [from HIP⁴]

hipster n informal a person who believes he or she is following trends that are outside the mainstream

hipsters pl n Brit trousers cut so that the top encircles the hips

Hiram n 10th century BC, king of Tyre, who supplied Solomon with materials and craftsmen for the building of the Temple (II Samuel 5:11; I Kings 5:1–18)

hire vb **hiring, hired 1** to acquire the temporary use of (a thing) or the services of (a person) in exchange for payment **2** to employ (a person) for wages **3** to provide (something) or the services of (oneself or others) for payment **4 hire out** chiefly Brit to pay independent contractors for (work to be done) ▷ n **5** the act of hiring **6 for hire** available to be hired [Old English *hȳrian*]

hireling n disparaging a person who works only for money

hire-purchase n a system in which a buyer takes possession of merchandise on payment of a deposit and completes the purchase by paying a series of instalments while the seller retains ownership until the final instalment is paid

Hirohito n 1901–89, emperor of Japan 1926–89. In 1946 he became a constitutional monarch

Hiroshige n Ando. 1797–1858, Japanese artist, esp. of colour wood-block prints

Hiroshima n a port in SW Japan, on SW Honshu on the delta of the Ota River: largely destroyed on August 6, 1945, by the first atomic bomb to be used in warfare, dropped by the US, which killed over 75 000 of its inhabitants. Pop: 1 113 786 (2002 est)

Hirst n Damien. born 1965, British artist, noted esp. for his works featuring dead animals preserved. in tanks of formaldehyde, and for his 2007 sculpture, *For the Love of God*, a human skull encrusted with flawless diamonds

hirsute (her-suit) adj hairy [Latin *hirsutus* shaggy]

his adj **1** of, belonging to, or associated with him: *his*

irthday ▷ *pron* **2** something belonging to him: *his is on the eft; that book is his* **3** of his belonging to him [Old English]

ispania *n* the Iberian peninsula in the Roman world

ispanic *adj* **1** of or derived from Spain or the Spanish ▷ *n* **2** US a US citizen of Spanish or Latin-American lescent [Latin *Hispania* Spain]

ispaniola *n* the second largest island in the Caribbean, n the Greater Antilles: divided politically into Haiti and he Dominican Republic; discovered in 1492 by Christopher Columbus, who named it La Isla Española. Area: 18 703 sq km (29 418 sq miles). Former name: **Santo Domingo**

iss *n* **1** a sound like that of a prolonged s **2** such a sound as an expression of dislike or disapproval ▷ *vb* **3** to utter a hiss **4** to express with a hiss: *she hissed the name* **5** to show dislike or disapproval towards (a speaker or performer) by hissing [imitative]

iss *n* Alger. 1904–96, US government official: imprisoned (1950–54) for perjury in connection with alleged espionage activities

issy fit *n informal* a childish temper tantrum

istamine (hiss-ta-meen) *n* a chemical compound released by the body tissues in allergic reactions [Greek *histos* tissue + *amine*]

istogram *n* a statistical graph that represents the frequency of values of a quantity by vertical bars of varying heights and widths [probably *histo(ry)* + Greek *grammē* line]

istology *n* the study of the tissues of an animal or plant [Greek *histos* tissue + -LOGY]

istorian *n* a person who writes or studies history

istoric *adj* important in history, or likely to be seen as important in the future

USAGE A distinction is usually made between *historic* (important, significant) and *historical* (pertaining to history): *a historic decision; a historical perspective.*

istorical *adj* **1** occurring in the past **2** describing or representing situations or people that existed in the past: *a historical novel* **3** belonging to or typical of the study of history: *historical perspective* ▷ **historically** *adv*

USAGE See at **historic**.

istoricism *n* **1** the belief that natural laws govern historical events **2** excessive respect for historical institutions, such as traditions or laws

istoricity *n* historical authenticity

istoriographer *n* **1** a historian, esp. one concerned with historical method and the writings of other historians **2** a historian employed to write the history of a group or public institution ▷ **historiography** *n*

istory *n, pl* **-ries** **1** a record or account of past events and developments **2** all that is preserved of the past, esp. in written form **3** the study of interpreting past events **4** the past events or previous experiences of a place, thing, or person: *he knew the whole history of the place* **5** a play that depicts historical events [Greek *historia* inquiry]

istrionic *adj* **1** very dramatic and full of exaggerated emotion: *histrionic bursts of invective* ▷ *n* **2** histrionics behaviour of this kind [Latin *histrio* actor] ▷ **histrionically** *adv*

it *vb* **hitting, hit** **1** to strike or touch (a person or thing) forcefully **2** to come into violent contact with: *a helicopter hit a Volvo* **3** to propel (a ball) by striking **4** *cricket* to score (runs) **5** to affect (a person, place, or thing) badly: *the airline says that its revenue will be hit* **6** to reach (a point or place): *the city's crime level hit new heights* **7** hit the bottle *slang* to start drinking excessive amounts of alcohol **8** hit the road *informal* to set out on a journey ▷ *n* **9** an impact or collision **10** a shot or blow that reaches its target **11** *informal* a person or thing that gains wide appeal: *those*

early collections made her a hit with the club set **12** *computers slang* a single visit to a website: *over 500 000 hits a day to its site* ▷ See also **hit off, hit on, hit out at** [Old English *hittan*]

Hitachi *n* a city in Japan, in E Honshu: a centre of the electronics industry. Pop: 193 080 (2002 est)

hit-and-miss *adj informal* happening in an unplanned way: *farming can be very much a hit-and-miss affair*

hit-and-run *adj* denoting a motor-vehicle accident in which the driver does not stop to give assistance or inform the police

hitch *n* **1** a temporary or minor problem or difficulty **2** a knot that can be undone by pulling against the direction of the strain that holds it ▷ *vb* **3** *informal* **a** to obtain (a ride) by hitchhiking **b** to hitchhike **4** to fasten with a knot or tie **5** get hitched *slang* to get married **6** hitch up to pull up (one's trousers, etc.) with a quick jerk [origin unknown]

Hitchcock *n* Sir **Alfred** (**Joseph**). 1899–1980, English film director, noted for his mastery in creating suspense. His films include *The Thirty-Nine Steps* (1935), *Rebecca* (1940), *Psycho* (1960), and *The Birds* (1963)

hitchhike *vb* **-hiking, -hiked** to travel by getting free lifts in motor vehicles ▷ **hitchhiker** *n*

hi-tech *adj* using sophisticated, esp. electronic, technology

hither *adv old-fashioned* to or towards this place: *come hither* [Old English *hider*]

hitherto *adv formal* until this time: *fundamental questions which have hitherto been ignored*

Hitler *n* **1** Adolf. Grandmother's maiden name and father's original surname *Schicklgruber*. 1889–1945, German dictator, born in Austria. After becoming president of the National Socialist German Workers' Party (Nazi party), he attempted to overthrow the government of Bavaria (1923). While in prison he wrote *Mein Kampf*, expressing his philosophy of the superiority of the Aryan race and the inferiority of the Jews. He was appointed chancellor of Germany (1933), transforming it from a democratic republic into the totalitarian Third Reich, of which he became Führer in 1934. He established concentration camps to exterminate the Jews, rearmed the Rhineland (1936), annexed Austria (1938) and Czechoslovakia, and invaded Poland (1939), which precipitated World War II. He committed suicide **2** a person who displays dictatorial characteristics

hit list *n informal* **1** a list of people to be murdered **2** a list of targets to be eliminated: *the Treasury draws up a hit list for spending cuts*

hit man *n* a person hired by terrorists or gangsters to murder someone

hit off *vb* hit it off *informal* to have a good relationship with someone

hit on *or* hit upon *vb* to think of (an idea or a solution)

hit-or-miss *adj informal* unplanned or unpredictable: *hit-or-miss service*. Also: **hit-and-miss**

hit out at *vb* **1** to direct blows forcefully and vigorously at (someone) **2** to make a verbal attack upon (someone)

hit wicket *n cricket* a batsman breaking the wicket while playing a stroke and so being out

HIV human immunodeficiency virus, the cause of AIDS

hive *n* **1** a structure in which bees live **2** hive of activity a busy place with many people working hard [Old English *hȳf*]

hive off *vb* **hiving, hived** to transfer (part of a business, esp. the profitable part of a nationalized industry) to new ownership

hives *n pathol* an allergic reaction in which itchy red or whitish raised patches develop on the skin [origin unknown]

HM (in Britain) Her (*or* His) Majesty

H.M.A.S. *or* **HMAS** (in Australia) Her (*or* His) Majesty's Australian Ship

HMI (in Britain) Her (*or* His) Majesty's Inspector; a government official who examines and supervises schools

hmm *interj* a sound made when considering or puzzling over something

HMRC (in Britian) Her Majesty's Revenue and Customs: a government department responsible for collecting taxes

H.M.S. *or* **HMS** (in Britain) Her (*or* His) Majesty's Ship

HMSO (in Britain) Her (*or* His) Majesty's Stationery Office

HNC (in Britain) Higher National Certificate; a qualification recognized by many national technical and professional institutions

HND (in Britain) Higher National Diploma; a qualification in a technical subject equivalent to an ordinary degree

ho *n US Black* a derogatory term for a woman [from *Black* or *Southern US* pronunciation of WHORE]

Ho *chem* holmium

hoar *n* short for **hoarfrost** [Old English *hār*]

hoard *n* **1** a store of money, food, etc., hidden away for future use ▷ *vb* **2** to save or store (money, food, etc.) [Old English *hord*] **⟩ hoarder** *n*

> **USAGE** *Hoard* is sometimes wrongly written where *horde* is meant: *hordes* (not *hoards*) *of tourists*.

hoarding *n* a large board at the side of a road, used for displaying advertising posters [Old French *hourd* palisade]

hoarfrost *n* a white layer of ice crystals formed on the ground by condensation at temperatures below freezing point

hoarse *adj* **1** (of a voice) rough and unclear through illness or too much shouting **2** having a rough and unclear voice [from Old Norse] **⟩ hoarsely** *adv* **⟩ hoarseness** *n*

hoary *adj* **hoarier, hoariest 1** having grey or white hair **2** very old: *a hoary old problem*

hoax *n* **1** a deception, esp. a practical joke ▷ *vb* **2** to deceive or play a joke on (someone) [probably from *hocus* to trick]

hob *n Brit* the flat top part of a cooker, or a separate flat surface, containing hotplates or burners [perhaps from *hub*]

Hobart *n* a port in Australia, capital of the island state of Tasmania on the estuary of the Derwent: excellent natural harbour; University of Tasmania (1890). Pop: 216 656 (2011)

Hobbema *n* Meindert. 1638–1709, Dutch painter of peaceful landscapes, usually including a watermill

Hobbes *n* Thomas. 1588–1679, English political philosopher. His greatest work is the *Leviathan* (1651), which contains his defence of absolute sovereignty **⟩ 'Hobbesian** *n, adj*

hobble *vb* **-bling, -bled 1** to walk with a lame awkward movement **2** to tie the legs of (a horse) together in order to restrict its movement [probably from Low German]

Hobbs *n* Sir John Berry, known as *Jack Hobbs*. 1882–1963, English cricketer: scored 197 centuries

hobby *n, pl* **-bies** an activity pursued in one's spare time for pleasure or relaxation [probably variant of the name *Robin*]

hobbyhorse *n* **1** a favourite topic about which a person likes to talk at every opportunity: *public transport is his hobbyhorse* **2** a toy consisting of a stick with a figure of a horse's head at one end **3** a figure of a horse attached to a performer's waist in a morris dance

hobgoblin *n* a small, mischievous creature in fairy stories [*hob*, variant of the name *Rob* + GOBLIN]

hobnail boots *pl n* old-fashioned heavy boots with short nails in the soles to lessen wear and tear [*hob* (in archaic sense: peg)]

hobnob *vb* **-nobbing, -nobbed** to socialize or talk informally: *hobnobbing with the rich* [*hob or nob* to drink to one another in turns]

hobo *n, pl* **-bos** *or* **-boes** *US, Canad, Austral and NZ* a tramp o vagrant [origin unknown]

Hoboken *n* **1** a city in N Belgium, in Antwerp province, on the River Scheldt. Pop: 33 476 (2002 est) **2** a city in NE New Jersey, on the Hudson River. Pop: 50 005 (2010)

Hobson's choice *n* the choice of taking what is offered or nothing at all [after Thomas *Hobson*, liveryman who gave his customers no choice]

Hochhuth *n* Rolf. born 1933, Swiss dramatist. His best-known works are the controversial documentary drama *The Representative* (1963), on the papacy's attitude to the Jews in World War II, *Soldiers* (1967), *German Love Story* (1980), and *Wessis in Weimar* (1992)

Ho Chi Minh *n* original name *Nguyen That Tan*. 1890–196 Vietnamese statesman; president of North Vietnam (1954–69). He headed the Vietminh (1941), which won independence for Vietnam from the French (1954)

Ho Chi Minh City *n* a port in S Vietnam, 97 km (60 mile from the South China Sea, on the Saigon River: capture by the French in 1859; merged with adjoining Cholon in 1932; capital of the former Republic of Vietnam (South Vietnam) from 1954 to 1976; university (1917); US headquarters during the Vietnam War. Pop: 5 030 000 (2005 est). Former name (until 1976): **Saigon**

hock[1] *n* the joint in the leg of a horse or similar animal that corresponds to the human ankle [Old English *hōhsinu* heel sinew]

hock[2] *n* a white wine from the German Rhine [German *Hochheimer*]

hock[3] *informal vb* **1** to pawn or pledge ▷ *n* **2 in hock a** in debt **b** in pawn [Dutch *hok* prison, debt]

hockey *n* **1 a** game played on a field by two teams of 11 players who try to hit a ball into their opponents' goal using long sticks curved at the end **2** *US and Canad* ice hockey [origin unknown]

Hockney *n* David. born 1937, English painter, best known for his etchings, such as those to Cavafy's poem (1966), naturalistic portraits such as *Mr and Mrs Clark and Percy* (1971), and for paintings of water, swimmers, and swimming pools

hocus-pocus *n informal* something said or done in orde to confuse or trick someone [a dog Latin exclamation used by conjurors]

hod *n* an open metal or plastic box attached to a pole, for carrying bricks or mortar [Old French *hotte* pannier]

Hodeida *n* a port in N Yemen, on the Red Sea. Pop: 547 000 (2005 est)

hodgepodge *n chiefly US and Canad* same as **hotchpotch**

Hodgkin *n* **1** Sir Alan Lloyd. 1914–98, English physiologist. With A. F. Huxley, he explained the conduction of nervous impulses in terms of the physica and chemical changes involved: shared the Nobel prize for physiology or medicine (1963) **2** Dorothy Crowfoot. 1910–94, English chemist and crystallographer, who determined the three-dimensional structure of insulin Nobel prize for chemistry (1964) **3** Sir Howard. born 1932 British painter, noted for his brightly coloured semi-abstract works

Hodgkin's disease *n* a malignant disease that causes enlargement of the lymph nodes, spleen, and liver [afte Thomas *Hodgkin*, physician]

hoe *n* **1** a long-handled implement used to loosen the soil or to weed ▷ *vb* **hoeing, hoed 2** to scrape or weed with a hoe [Germanic]

Hoek van Holland *n* the Dutch name for the **Hook of Holland**

Hofei *n* a variant transliteration of the Chinese name fo **Hefei**

Hoffman *n* Dustin (Lee). born 1937, US stage and film actor. His films include *The Graduate* (1967), *Midnight Cowboy* (1969), *All the President's Men* (1976), *Kramer vs Kramer* (1979), *Rain Man* (1989), *Accidental Hero* (1992), and *Moonligh Mile* (2002)

Hofmann *n* Hans. 1880–1966, US painter, born in

ermany: a pioneer of the abstract expressionist style

fmannsthal *n* Hugo von. 1874–1929, Austrian lyric
oet and dramatist, noted as the librettist for Richard
trauss' operas, esp. *Der Rosenkavalier* (1911), *Elektra* (1909),
nd *Ariadne auf Naxos* (1912)

fuf *n* another name for **Al Hufuf**

g *n* **1** a castrated male pig **2** *US and Canad* any mammal
f the pig family **3** *informal* a greedy person **4 go the
hole hog** *slang* to do something in the most complete
ay possible ▷ *vb* **hogging, hogged 5** *slang* to take more
han one's share of (something) [Old English *hogg*]

ogan *n* Ben, full name *William Benjamin Hogan*. 1912–97,
S golfer: winner of nine major championships
946–53) including the US Open four times

ogarth *n* James. 1697–1764, English engraver and
ainter. He is noted particularly for his series of
ngravings satirizing the vices and affectations of his
ge, such as *A Rake's Progress* (1735) and *Marriage à la Mode*
745) ▷ **Hogarthian** *adj*

ogg *n* **1** James, known as *the Ettrick Shepherd*. 1770–1835,
cottish poet and writer. His works include the volume
f poems *The Queen's Wake* (1813) and the novel *The
onfessions of a Justified Sinner* (1824) **2** Quintin See **Hailsham
f St Marylebone**

ogmanay *n* New Year's Eve in Scotland [probably from
ld French *aguillanneuf* a New Year's Eve gift]

ogshead *n* a large cask for storing alcoholic drinks
origin unknown]

ogtown *n* *Canad* a slang name for **Toronto**

ogue *n* See La Hogue

ogwash *n* *informal* nonsense

ogwood *n* Christopher (Jarvis Haley). (1941–2014),
ritish harpsichordist, conductor, and musicologist;
ounder and director of the Academy of Ancient Music
1973–2006)

ohenlinden *n* a village in S Germany, in Bavaria east
f Munich: scene of the defeat of the Austrians by the
rench during the Napoleonic Wars (1800)

ohenlohe *n* Chlodwig, Prince of Hohenlohe-
chillingsfürst. 1819–1901, Prussian statesman;
hancellor of the German empire (1894–1900)

ohhot, Huhehot *or* **Hu-ho-hao-t'e** *n* a city in N
hina, capital of Inner Mongolia (since 1954); previously
apital of the former Suiyüan province; Inner Mongolia
University (1957). Pop: 998 000 (2005 est)

o-ho *interj* a written representation of the sound of a
eep laugh

o-hum *adj informal* uninteresting or mediocre: *a ho-hum
erformance*

oick *vb* **1** to raise abruptly and sharply **2** *NZ* to clear the
hroat and spit [origin unknown]

oi polloi *pl n* the ordinary people when compared to the
ich or well-educated [Greek: the many]

oisin *n* a sweet spicy sauce of soya beans, sugar, garlic,
nd vinegar, used in Chinese cookery [from Cantonese]

oist *vb* **1** to raise or lift up, esp. by mechanical means
▷ *n* **2** an apparatus or device for lifting things [probably
from Low German]

oity-toity *adj informal* arrogant or haughty [obsolete
noit to romp]

okey-pokey *n* *NZ* a brittle toffee sold in lumps

okkaido *n* the second largest and northernmost of the
our main islands of Japan, separated from Honshu by
the Tsugaru Strait and from the island of Sakhalin,
Russia, by La Pérouse Strait: constitutes an autonomous
administrative division. Capital: Sapporo. Pop: 5 670 000
(2002 est). Area: 78 508 sq km (30 312 sq miles)

okum *n* *slang, chiefly US and Canad* **1** nonsense; bunk
2 obvious sentimental material in a play or film
[probably a blend of *hocus-pocus* + *bunkum*]

okusai *n* Katsushika. 1760–1849, Japanese artist, noted
for the draughtsmanship of his colour wood-block
prints, which influenced the impressionists

olbein *n* **1** Hans, known as *Holbein the Elder*. 1465–1524,

German painter **2** his son, **Hans**, known as *Holbein the
Younger*. 1497–1543, German painter and engraver; court
painter to Henry VIII of England (1536–43). He is noted
particularly for his portraits, such as those of Erasmus
(1524; 1532) and Sir Thomas More (1526)

Holberg *n* Ludvig, Baron. 1684–1754, Danish playwright,
poet, and historian, born in Norway: considered the
founder of modern Danish literature

hold¹ *vb* **holding, held 1** to keep (an object or a person)
with or within the hands or arms **2** to support: *a rope
made from 1000 hairs would hold a large adult* **3** to maintain in a
specified state or position: *his reputation continued to hold
secure* **4** to have the capacity for: *trains designed to hold more
than 400* **5** to set aside or reserve: *they will hold our tickets until
tomorrow* **6** to restrain or keep back: *designed to hold
dangerous criminals* **7** to remain unbroken: *if the elastic holds*
8 (of the weather) to remain dry and bright **9** to keep
(the attention of): *a writer holds a reader by his temperament*
10 to arrange and cause to take place: *we must hold an
inquiry* **11** to have the ownership or possession of: *she holds
a degree in Egyptology* **12** to have responsibility for: *she
cannot hold an elective office* **13** to be able to control the
outward effects of drinking (alcohol): *he can't hold his liquor*
14 to (cause to) remain committed to (a promise, etc.)
15 to claim or believe: *some Sufis hold that all religious leaders
were prophets* **16** to remain valid or true: *the categories are not
the same and equivalency does not hold* **17** to consider in a
specified manner: *philosophies which we hold so dear* **18** to
defend successfully: *the Russians were holding the Volga front*
19 *music* to sustain the sound of (a note) ▷ *n* **20** a way of
holding something or the act of holding it **21** something
to hold onto for support **22** controlling influence: *drugs
will take a hold* **23 with no holds barred** with all
limitations removed ▶ See also **hold back, hold down,**
etc. [Old English *healdan*] ▷ **holder** *n*

hold² *n* the space in a ship or aircraft for storing cargo
[variant of *hole*]

holdall *n* *Brit* a large strong travelling bag

hold back *vb* **1** to restrain (someone) or refrain from
doing something: *managers declined to hold back the crowds*;
buyers held back in the expectation of further price decreases **2** to
withhold: *holding back the wages*

hold down *vb* **1** to restrain or control someone **2** *informal*
to manage to keep (a job) **3** to prevent (wages, prices,
etc.) from rising much

Hölderlin *n* Friedrich. 1770–1843, German lyric poet,
whose works include the poems *Menon's Lament for Diotima*
and *Bread and Wine* and the novel *Hyperion* (1797–99)

hold forth *vb* to speak for a long time

hold in *vb* to control or conceal (one's feelings)

holding *n* **1** land held under a lease **2** property to which
the holder has legal title, such as land, stocks, or shares

holding company *n* a company that holds the
controlling shares in one or more other companies

holding paddock *n* *Austral and NZ* a paddock in which
cattle or sheep are kept temporarily, such as when
awaiting sale

hold off *vb* **1** to keep (an attacker or attacking force) at a
distance **2** to put off (doing something): *he held off
distributing weapons*

hold on *vb* **1** to maintain a firm grasp (of something or
someone) **2** to wait, esp. on the telephone **3 hold on to** to
keep: *he held on to his world No. 1 ranking*

hold out *vb* **1** to offer (something) **2** to last: *I could hold out
until we return home* **3** to continue to stand firm and
manage to resist opposition **4 hold out for** to wait
patiently for (the fulfilment of one's wishes) **5 hold out
on someone** *informal* to keep from telling someone some
important information

hold over *vb* to postpone: *several cases had to be held over
pending further investigation*

hold-up *n* **1** an armed robbery **2** a delay: *a traffic hold-up*
▷ *vb* **hold up 3** to delay **4** to support (an object) **5** to stop
and rob (someone), using a weapon **6** to exhibit or

h

present (something) as an example: *he was held up as a model professional*

hold with *vb* to approve of: *I don't hold with divorce*

hole *n* **1** an area hollowed out in a solid **2** an opening in or through something **3** an animal's burrow **4** *informal* a fault or error: *this points to a very big hole in parliamentary security* **5** *informal* an unattractive town or other place **6** (on a golf course) any one of the divisions of a course (usually 18) represented by the distance between the tee and the sunken cup on the green into which the ball is to be played **7 in a hole** *slang* in a difficult and embarrassing situation **8 make a hole in** *informal* to use a great amount of (one's money or food supply) **9 pick holes in** to point out faults in ▷ *vb* **holing, holed 10** to make a hole or holes in (something) **11** to hit (a golf ball) into a hole ▶ See **hole up** [Old English *hol*] ▷ **holey** *adj*

hole-and-corner *adj informal* furtive or secretive

hole in one *n golf* a shot from the tee that finishes in the hole

hole in the heart *n* a congenital defect of the heart, in which there is an abnormal opening in the partition between the left and right halves

hole up *vb informal* to go into hiding

Holguín *n* a city in NE Cuba, in Holguín province: trading centre. Pop: 278 000 (2005 est)

Holi (holl-lee) *n* an annual Hindu spring festival, honouring Krishna

holiday *n* **1 a** a period of time spent away from home for enjoyment and relaxation **2** (*often pl*) *chiefly Brit and NZ* a period in which a break is taken from work or studies for rest or recreation **3** a day on which work is suspended by law or custom, such as a bank holiday ▷ *vb* **4** *chiefly Brit* to spend a holiday [Old English *hāligdæg* holy day]

Holiday *n* Billie. real name *Eleanora Fagan*; known as *Lady Day*. 1915–59, US jazz singer

holier-than-thou *adj* offensively self-righteous

Holiness *n* (preceded by *His* or *Your*) a title reserved for the pope

Holinshed *or* **Holingshed** *n* Raphael. died ?1580, English chronicler. His *Chronicles of England, Scotland, and Ireland* (1577) provided material for Shakespeare's historical and legendary plays

holism *n* **1** the view that a whole is greater than the sum of its parts **2** (in medicine) consideration of the complete person in the treatment of disease [Greek *holos* whole] ▷ **holistic** *adj*

Holkar State *n* a former state of central India, ruled by the Holkar dynasty of Maratha rulers of Indore (18th century until 1947)

Holkham Hall *n* a Palladian mansion near Wells in Norfolk: built 1734–59 by William Kent for Thomas Coke

Holland¹ *n* **1** another name for the **Netherlands 2** a county of the Holy Roman Empire, corresponding to the present-day North and South Holland provinces of the Netherlands **3 Parts of** an area in E England constituting a former administrative division of Lincolnshire

Holland² *n* **1** Henry. 1745–1806, British neoclassical architect. His work includes Brooks's Club (1776) and Carlton House (1783), both in London **2** Sir Sidney George. 1893–1961, New Zealand statesman; prime minister of New Zealand (1949–57)

hollandaise sauce *n* a rich sauce of egg yolks, butter, vinegar, and lemon juice [French *sauce hollandaise* Dutch sauce]

Hollande *n* François. born 1954, French socialist politician, president of France from 2012

Hollandia *n* a former name of **Jayapura**

holler *informal vb* **1** to shout or yell ▷ *n* **2** a shout or yell [French *holà* stop!]

Holliger *n* Heinz. born 1939, Swiss oboist and composer

hollow *adj* **1** having a hole or space within; not solid: *a hollow tree* **2** curving inwards: *hollow cheeks* **3** (of sounds)

as if echoing in a hollow place **4** without any real valu or worth: *a hollow enterprise, lacking purpose, and lacking soul* ▷ *adv* **5 beat someone hollow** *Brit and NZ informal* to defe someone thoroughly ▷ *n* **6** a cavity or space in something **7** a dip in the land ▷ *vb* **8** (often foll. by *out*) form a hole or cavity in [Old English *holh* cave] ▷ **hollowly** *adv*

holly *n* an evergreen tree with prickly leaves and brigh red berries, used for Christmas decorations [Old English *holegn*]

Holly *n* Buddy. real name *Charles Harden Holley*. 1936–59, U rock-and-roll singer, guitarist, and songwriter. His hit (all 1956–59) include "That'll be the Day", "Maybe Baby "Peggy Sue", "Oh, Boy", "Think It Over", and "It Doesn' Matter Anymore"

hollyhock *n* a tall garden plant with spikes of colourfu flowers [*holy* + obsolete *hock* mallow]

Hollywood *n* **1** a NW suburb of Los Angeles, Californi centre of the American film industry. Pop: 167 664 (200 **2** the American film industry

Holmes *n* **1** Oliver Wendell. 1809–94, US author, esp. of humorous essays, such as *The Autocrat of the Breakfast Tab* (1858) and its sequels **2** his son, **Oliver Wendell.** 1841–1935, US jurist, noted for his liberal judgments **3** S Paul. 1950–2013, New Zealand radio and television broadcaster; presenter of *The Paul Holmes Breakfast*, (1987–2008)

holmium *n chem* a silver-white metallic element, the compounds of which are highly magnetic. Symbol: Ho [after *Holmia*, Latin name of Stockholm]

holm oak *n* an evergreen oak tree with prickly leaves like holly

holocaust *n* **1** destruction or loss of life on a massive scale **2 the Holocaust** mass murder of the Jews in Euro by the Nazis (1940–45) [Greek *holos* whole + *kaiein* to bur

Holocene *adj* of the current geological epoch, which began about 10 000 years ago

hologram *n* a three-dimensional photographic image produced by means of a split laser beam [Greek *holos* whole + *grammē* line]

holograph *n* a book or document handwritten by its author [Greek *holos* whole + *graphein* to write]

holography *n* the science of using lasers to produce holograms [Greek *holos* whole + -GRAPHY] ▷ **holographi** *adj* ▷ **holographically** *adv*

hols *pl n Brit and S African school slang* holidays

Holst *n* **1** Dame Alison. born 1938, New Zealand chef. **2** Gustav (**Theodore**). 1874–1934, English composer. His works include operas, choral music, and orchestral music such as the suite *The Planets* (1917)

Holstein *n* a region of N Germany, in S Schleswig-Holstein: in early times a German duchy of Saxony; became a duchy of Denmark in 1474; finally incorporat into Prussia in 1866

holster *n* a sheathlike leather case for a pistol, worn attached to a belt [Germanic]

holt *n* the lair of an otter [from HOLD²]

Holt *n* Harold Edward. 1908–67, Australian statesman; prime minister (1966–67); believed drowned

holy *adj* **-lier, -liest 1** of or associated with God or a deity **2** (of a person) religious and leading a virtuous life [Old English *hālig, hǣlig*] ▷ **holiness** *n*

Holy Communion *n Christianity* a church service in which people take bread and wine in remembrance of Christ's Last Supper and His atonement for the sins of the world

Holy Ghost *n* the Holy Ghost same as **Holy Spirit**

Holy Grail *n* **1 the Holy Grail** (in medieval legend) the bowl used by Jesus at the Last Supper **2** *informal* any ambition or goal [*grail* from Medieval Latin *gradalis* bowl

Holyhead *n* a town in NW Wales, in Anglesey, the chie town of Holy Island: a port on the N coast. Pop: 11 237 (2001)

Holy Island *n* **1** Also called: **Lindisfarne** an island off the

NE coast of Northumberland, linked to the mainland by road but accessible only at low water: site of a monastery founded by St Aidan in 635 **2** an island off the NW coast of Anglesey. Area: about 62 sq km (24 sq miles)

oly Land *n* the Holy Land another name for **Palestine** (1)

olyoake *n* Sir Keith Jacka. 1904–83, New Zealand politician; prime minister (1957; 1960–72); governor general (1977–80)

oly of holies *n* **1** any sacred place or a place considered as if it were sacred: *the holy of holies they called the Captain's Cabin* **2** the innermost chamber of a Jewish temple

oly orders *pl n* the status of an ordained Christian minister

olyrood *n* **1** the Scottish Parliament building in Edinburgh, located beside Holyroodhouse **2** *informal* the Scottish Government

olyroodhouse *n* a royal palace in Edinburgh in Scotland: official residence of the Queen when in Scotland; begun in 1501 by James IV of Scotland; scene of the murder of David Rizzio in 1566

oly See *n* the Holy See *RC Church* the see of the pope as bishop of Rome

oly Spirit *n* the Holy Spirit *Christianity* one of the three aspects of God

oly Week *n Christianity* the week before Easter Sunday

omage *n* a public show of respect or honour towards someone or something: *the master's jazzy-classical homage to Gershwin* [Latin *homo* man]

omburg *n* a man's soft felt hat with a dented crown and a stiff upturned brim

ome *n* **1** the place where one lives **2** the country or area of one's birth **3** a building or organization set up to care for people in a certain category, such as orphans or elderly people **4** the place where something is invented or started: *the home of the first aircraft* **5** *sport* a team's own ground: *the match is at home* **6** *baseball, rounders etc.* the objective towards which a player runs after striking the ball **7** at home **a** in one's own home or country **b** at ease: *he felt more at home with the Russians* **c** receiving visitors ▷ *adj* **8** of one's home, birthplace, or native country **9** (of an activity) done in one's house: *home movies* **10** *sport* played on one's own ground: *a home game* **11** home and dry *Brit slang* definitely safe or successful ▷ *adv* **12** to or at home: *I came home* **13** to or on the point: *the message struck home* **14** to the fullest extent: *they drove their spears home* **15** bring something home to someone to make something clear to someone ▷ *vb* **homing, homed 16** (of birds) to return home accurately from a distance **17** home in on to be directed towards (a goal or target) [Old English *hām*]

USAGE See at hone.

---

lome *n* Baron See Home of the Hirsel

lomeboy *n slang* **1** a close friend **2** a member of a gang

lome-brew *n* beer or other alcoholic drink brewed at home

lomecoming *n* a return home, esp. after a long absence

lome Counties *pl n* the counties surrounding London

lome economics *n* the study of diet, budgeting, child care, and other subjects concerned with running a home

lome farm *n Brit* a farm that belonged to and provided food for a large country house

lome Guard *n* a part-time military force of volunteers recruited for the defence of the United Kingdom in the Second World War

lome help *n Brit, Austral and NZ* a person employed by a local authority to do housework in an elderly or disabled person's home

lomeland *n* **1** the country from which the ancestors of a person or group came: *defending their homeland* **2** the official name in S Africa for a **Bantustan**

lomeless *adj* **1** having nowhere to live ▷ *pl n* **2** (the homeless) people who have nowhere to live: *night shelters for the homeless* ▷ **homelessness** *n*

homely *adj* **-lier, -liest 1** simple, ordinary, and comfortable **2 a** *Brit* (of a person) warm and friendly **b** *chiefly US and Canad* (of a person) plain or unattractive ▷ **homeliness** *n*

home-made *adj* (esp. of foods) made at home or on the premises

Home Office *n Brit government* the department responsible for law and order, immigration, and other domestic affairs

Home of the Hirsel *n* Baron, title of *Sir Alec Douglas-Home*, formerly 14th Earl of Home. 1903–95, British Conservative statesman: he renounced his earldom to become prime minister of Great Britain and Northern Ireland (1963–64); foreign secretary (1970–74)

homeopathy or **homoeopathy** (home-ee-**op**-ath-ee) *n* a method of treating disease by the use of small amounts of a drug that produces symptoms of the disease in healthy people [Greek *homoios* similar + *patheia* suffering] ▷ **homeopath** or **homoeopath** (home-ee-oh-path) *n* ▷ **homeopathic** or **homoeopathic** *adj*

homeostasis or **homoeostasis** (hom-ee-oh-**stass**-iss) *n* the tendency of an organism to achieve a stable metabolic state by compensating automatically for violent changes in the environment and other disruptions [Greek *homoios* similar + *stasis* a standing]

homeowner *n* a person who owns the home in which he or she lives

home page *n internet* the introductory information about a website with links to the information or services provided

Homer *n* **1** c. 800 BC, Greek poet to whom are attributed the *Iliad* and the *Odyssey*. Almost nothing is known of him, but it is thought that he was born on the island of Chios and was blind **2 Winslow**. 1836–1910, US painter, noted for his seascapes and scenes of working life

Homeric (home-**mer**-rik) *adj* of or relating to Homer, Greek epic poet

home rule *n* self-government in domestic affairs

Home Secretary *n Brit government* the head of the Home Office

homesick *adj* depressed by being away from home and family ▷ **homesickness** *n*

homespun *adj* (of philosophies or opinions) plain and unsophisticated

homestead *n* **1** a farmhouse and the adjoining land **2** (in the western US & Canada) a house and adjoining tract of land (originally often 160 acres) that was granted by the government for development as a farm

homesteader *n* (in the western US & Canada) a person who lives on and farms a homestead

homestead law *n* (in the western US & Canada) any of various laws granting certain privileges to owners of homesteads

home truths *pl n* unpleasant facts told to a person about himself or herself

home unit *n Austral and NZ* a self-contained residence that is part of a block of such residences

homeward *adj* **1** going home ▷ *adv* also: **homewards 2** towards home

homework *n* **1** school work done at home **2** research or preparation

homicide *n* **1** the act of killing someone **2** a person who kills someone [Latin *homo* man + *caedere* to kill] ▷ **homicidal** *adj*

homie *n slang, chiefly US* short for **homeboy**

homily *n, pl* **-lies** a moralizing lecture or piece of writing [Greek *homilia* discourse] ▷ **homiletic** *adj*

homing *adj* **1** *zoology* denoting the ability to return home after travelling great distances **2** (of a missile) capable of guiding itself onto a target

homing pigeon *n* a pigeon developed for its homing instinct, used for racing

hominid n 1 any member of the family of primates that includes modern man and the extinct forerunners of man ▷ adj 2 of or belonging to this family [Latin *homo* man]

hominoid adj 1 of or like man; manlike ▷ n 2 a manlike animal [Latin *homo* man]

hominy n chiefly US coarsely ground maize prepared as a food by boiling in milk or water [probably from a Native American language]

homo¹ n informal, disparaging short for **homosexual**

homo² n Canad informal homogenized milk

homo- combining form same or like: *homologous* [Greek *homos* same]

homogeneous (home-oh-**jean**-ee-uss) adj having parts or members which are all the same or which consist of only one substance: *the Arabs are not a single, homogeneous nation* [Greek *homos* same + *genos* kind] **> homogeneity** n

homogenize or **-nise** vb **-nizing, -nized** or **-nising, -nised** 1 to break up the fat globules in (milk or cream) so that they are evenly distributed 2 to make different elements the same or similar: *homogenized products for a mass market*

homogenous (hom-oj-in-uss) adj having a similar structure because of common ancestry

homograph n a word spelt the same as another, but having a different meaning, such as *bear* (to carry) and *bear* (the animal) [Greek *homos* same + *graphein* to write]

homologous (hom-ol-log-uss) adj 1 having a related or similar position or structure 2 biology (of organs and parts) having the same origin but different functions: *the wing of a bat and the arm of a monkey are homologous* [Greek *homos* same + *logos* ratio]

homology (hom-ol-a-jee) n the condition of being homologous

homonym n a word pronounced and spelt the same as another, but having a different meaning, such as *novel* (a book) and *novel* (new)

homophobia n intense hatred or fear of homosexuals [*homo(sexual)* + *phobia*]

homophone n a word pronounced the same as another, but having a different meaning or spelling or both, such as *bear* and *bare* [Greek *homos* same + *phōnē* sound]

Homo sapiens (home-oh **sap**-ee-enz) n the name for modern man as a species [Latin *homo* man + *sapiens* wise]

homosexual n 1 a person who is sexually attracted to members of the same sex ▷ adj 2 (of a person) sexually attracted to members of the same sex 3 (of a sexual relationship) between members of the same sex [Greek *homos* same] **> homosexuality** n

homozygous adj biology having two identical alleles of the same gene [Greek *homos* same + *zugōtos* yoked]

Homs or **Hums** n a city in W Syria, near the Orontes River: important in Roman times as the capital of Phoenicia-Lebanesia. Pop: 915 000 (2005 est). Ancient name: **Emesa**. Former name: **Hims**

homy or especially US **homey** adj **homier, homiest** like a home; pleasant and cosy

Hon. Honourable (title)

Honan n a variant transliteration of the Chinese name for **Henan**

Hond. Honduras

Hondo n another name for **Honshu**

Honduran adj 1 of or relating to Honduras or its inhabitants ▷ n 2 a native or inhabitant of Honduras

Honduras n 1 a republic in Central America: an early centre of Mayan civilization; colonized by the Spanish from 1524 onwards; gained independence in 1821. Official language: Spanish; English is also widely spoken. Religion: Roman Catholic majority. Currency: lempira. Capital: Tegucigalpa. Pop: 8 448 465 (2013 est). Area: 112 088 sq km (43 277 sq miles) 2 Gulf of Honduras an inlet of the Caribbean, on the coasts of Honduras, Guatemala, and Belize

hone vb **honing, honed** 1 to develop and improve (a

quality or ability): *a workshop to hone interview techniques* 2 to sharpen (a tool) ▷ n 3 a fine whetstone used for sharpening edged tools and knives [Old English *hān* stone]

> **USAGE** Hone is sometimes wrongly used where home is meant: *this device makes it easier to home in on* (not *hone in on*) *the target.*

Honecker n Erich. 1912–94, German statesman; head of state of East Germany (1976–89)

Honegger n Arthur. 1892–1955, French composer, one of Les Six. His works include the oratorios *King David* (1921) and *Joan of Arc at the Stake* (1935), and *Pacific 231* (1924) for orchestra

honest adj 1 truthful and moral in behaviour; trustworthy 2 open and sincere in relationships and attitudes; without pretensions 3 gained or earned fairly: *an honest income* [Latin *honos* esteem]

honestly adv 1 in an honest manner 2 truly: *honestly, that's all I can recall*

honesty n, pl **-ties** 1 the quality of being truthful and trustworthy 2 a plant with flattened silvery pods which are used for indoor decoration

honey n 1 a sweet edible sticky substance made by bees from nectar 2 chiefly US and Canad a term of affection 3 informal, chiefly US and Canad something very good of its kind: *a honey of a picture about American family life* [Old English *huneg*]

honeybee n a bee widely domesticated as a source of honey and beeswax

honeycomb n a waxy structure, constructed by bees in a hive, that consists of many six-sided cells in which honey is stored

honeydew n a sugary substance excreted by aphids and similar insects

honeydew melon n a melon with yellow skin and sweet pale flesh

honeyed adj poetic flattering or soothing: *honeyed words*

honeymoon n 1 a holiday taken by a newly married couple 2 the early period of an undertaking or activity, such as the start of a new government's term of office, when an attitude of goodwill prevails ▷ vb 3 to take a honeymoon [traditionally, referring to the feelings of married couples as changing with the phases of the moon] **> honeymooner** n

honeysuckle n a climbing shrub with sweet-smelling white, yellow, or pink flowers [Old English *hunigsūce*]

honeytrap n Brit informal a scheme in which a victim is lured into a compromising sexual situation that provides the opportunity for blackmail

hongi (hong-jee) n NZ a Māori greeting in which people touch noses

Hong Kong n 1 a Special Administrative Region of China, in the south of the country, with some autonomy; formerly a British Crown Colony: consists of Hong Kong Island, leased by China to Britain from 1842 until 1997, Kowloon Peninsula, Stonecutters Island, the New Territories (mainland), leased by China in 1898 for a 99-year period, and over 230 small islands; important entrepôt trade and manufacturing centre, esp. for textiles and other consumer goods; university (1912). It retains its own currency, the Hong Kong dollar. Administrative centre: Victoria. Pop: 7 182 724 (2013 est). Area: 1046 sq km (404 sq miles) 2 an island in Hong Kong region, south of Kowloon Peninsula: contains the capital, Victoria. Pop: 1 337 800 (2001). Area: 75 sq km (29 sq miles)

Hong-wu or **Hung-wu** n title of *Chu Yuan-Zhang* (or *Chu Yüan-Chang*), 1328–98, first emperor (1368–98) of the Ming dynasty, uniting China under his rule by 1382

Hong Xiu Quan or **Hung Hsiu-Ch'uan** n 1814–64, Chinese religious leader and revolutionary. Claiming

1851) to be Christ's brother, he led the Taiping rebellion; committed suicide when it was defeated

oniara *n* the capital of the Solomon Islands, on NW Guadalcanal Island. Pop: 61 000 (2005 est)

onk *n* **1** the sound made by a motor horn **2** the sound made by a goose ▷ *vb* **3** to make or cause (something) to make a honking sound

onky-tonk *n* **1** *US and Canad slang* a cheap disreputable nightclub or dance hall **2** a style of ragtime piano-playing, esp. on a tinny-sounding piano [rhyming compound based on HONK]

onolulu *n* a port in Hawaii, on S Oahu island: the state capital. Pop: 380 149 (2003 est)

onorarium *n, pl* **-iums** *or* **-ia** a voluntary fee paid for a service which is usually free [Latin *honorarium (donum)* honorary gift]

onorary *adj* **a** held or given as a mark of respect, without the usual qualifications, payment, or work: *an honorary degree* **b** (of a secretary, treasurer, etc.) unpaid

onorific *adj* showing respect: *an honorific title*

onour *or US* **honor** *n* **1** allegiance to moral principles **2** a person's good reputation and the respect they are given by other people **3 a** fame or glory **b** a person who wins fame or glory for his or her country, school, etc.: *he was an honour to his nation* **4** great respect or esteem, or an outward sign of this **5** a privilege or pleasure: *it was an honour to meet him* **6** *old-fashioned* a woman's virginity **7** *bridge, whist* any of the top four or five cards in a suit **8** *golf* the right to tee off first **9 in honour of** out of respect for **10 on one's honour** under a moral obligation ▷ *vb* **11** to hold someone in respect **12** to give (someone) special praise, attention, or an award **13** to accept and then pay (a cheque or bill) **14** to keep (one's promise); fulfil (a previous agreement) [Latin *honor* esteem]

onour *n* (preceded by *Your* or *His* or *Her*) a title used to address or refer to certain judges

onourable *or US* **honorable** *adj* **1** principled **2** worthy of respect or esteem **> honourably** *adv*

onourable *adj* **the Honourable** a title of respect placed before a name: used of various officials, of the children of certain peers, and in Parliament by one member speaking of another

onours *or US* **honors** *pl n* **1** (in a university degree course) a rank or mark of the highest academic standard: *an honours degree* **2** observances of respect, esp. at a funeral **3 do the honours** to serve as host or hostess by serving food or pouring drinks

onshu *n* the largest of the four main islands of Japan, between the Pacific and the Sea of Japan; regarded as the Japanese mainland; includes a number of offshore islands and contains most of the main cities. Pop: 102 324 961 (2000). Area: 230 448 sq km (88 976 sq miles). Also called: **Hondo**

ooch (rhymes with **smooch**) *n informal* alcoholic drink, esp. illegally distilled spirits [from a Native American language]

ooch *or* **Hoogh** *n* Pieter de. 1629–?1684, Dutch genre painter, noted esp. for his light effects

ood[1] *n* **1** a loose head covering either attached to a coat or made as a separate garment **2** *US, Canad and Austral* the bonnet of a car **3** the folding roof of a convertible car or a pram ▷ *vb* **4** to cover with or as if with a hood [Old English *hōd*] **> hoodlike** *adj*

ood[2] *n slang* short for **hoodlum**

ood *n* **1** Samuel, 1st Viscount. 1724–1816, British admiral. He fought successfully against the French during the American Revolution and the French Revolutionary Wars **2** Thomas. 1799–1845, British poet and humorist: his work includes protest poetry, such as *The Song of the Shirt* (1843) and *The Bridge of Sighs* (1844)

ooded *adj* **1** (of a garment) having a hood **2** (of eyes) having heavy eyelids that appear to be half-closed

ooded crow *n* a crow that has a grey body and black head, wings, and tail

hoodie *n informal* **1** a hooded sweatshirt **2** a young person who wears a hooded sweatshirt, regarded by some as a potential hooligan

hoodlum *n* a violent criminal, esp. one who is a member of a gang [origin unknown]

hoodoo *n, pl* **-doos 1** *informal* bad luck **2** *informal* a person or thing that brings bad luck **3** *chiefly US* same as **voodoo**

hoodwink *vb* to trick or deceive [originally, to cover the eyes with a hood]

hooey *n slang* nonsense [origin unknown]

hoof *n, pl* **hooves** *or* **hoofs 1** the horny covering of the end of the foot in the horse, deer, and certain other mammals **2 on the hoof** (of livestock) alive **3** in an impromptu way: *thinking on the hoof* ▷ *vb* **3 hoof it** *slang* to walk [Old English *hōf*] **> hoofed** *adj*

hoofer *n slang* a professional dancer

Hooft *n* Pieter Corneliszoon. 1581–1647, Dutch poet, historian, and writer: noted esp. for his love poetry and his 27-volume *History of the Netherlands* (1626–47)

Hooghly *n* a river in NE India, in West Bengal: the westernmost and commercially most important channel by which the River Ganges enters the Bay of Bengal. Length: 232 km (144 miles)

hoo-ha *n* a noisy commotion or fuss [origin unknown]

hook *n* **1** a curved piece of metal or plastic used to hang, hold, or pull something **2** something resembling a hook, such as a sharp bend in a river or a sharply curved strip of land **3** *boxing* a short swinging blow with the elbow bent **4** *cricket, golf* a shot that causes the ball to go to the player's left **5 by hook or by crook** by any means: *get into the charts by hook or by crook* **6 hook, line, and sinker** *informal* completely: *we fell for it hook, line, and sinker* **7 let someone off the hook** *slang* to free someone from an obligation or a difficult situation **8 sling one's hook** *Brit and Austral slang* to leave ▷ *vb* **9** to fasten with, or as if with, a hook **10** to catch (a fish) on a hook **11** *cricket, golf* to play (a ball) with a hook **12** *rugby* to obtain and pass (the ball) backwards from a scrum, using the feet [Old English *hōc*]

hookah *n* an oriental pipe for smoking marijuana or tobacco, with a long flexible stem connected to a container of water through which smoke is drawn and cooled [Arabic *huqqah*]

Hooke *n* Robert. 1635–1703, English physicist, chemist, and inventor. He formulated Hooke's law (1678), built the first Gregorian telescope, and invented a balance spring for watches

hooked *adj* **1** bent like a hook **2** (often foll. by *on*) **a** *slang* addicted (to): *hooked on drugs* **b** obsessed with: *hooked on football*

hooker *n* **1** *slang* a prostitute **2** *rugby* a player who uses his feet to get the ball in a scrum

Hooker *n* **1** John Lee. 1917–2001, US blues singer and guitarist **2** Sir Joseph Dalton. 1817–1911, British botanist; director of Kew Gardens (1865–85) **3** Richard. 1554–1600, British theologian, who influenced Anglican theology with *The Laws of Ecclesiastical Polity* (1593–97) **4** Sir William Jackson. 1785–1865, British botanist; first director of Kew Gardens: father of Sir Joseph Dalton Hooker

Hooke's law *n physics* the principle that a solid stretches or contracts in proportion to the force placed on it, within the limits of its elasticity [after Robert HOOKE]

Hook of Holland *n* the Hook of Holland **1** a cape on the SW coast of the Netherlands, in South Holland province **2** a port on this cape ▶ Dutch name: **Hoek van Holland**

hook-up *n* **1** the linking of broadcasting equipment or stations to transmit a special programme **2 a** a person, esp. a stranger or recent acquaintance, with whom one has casual, unplanned sex **b** an instance of having casual, unplanned sex with a person, esp. a stranger or recent acquaintance

hookworm *n* a blood-sucking worm with hooked mouthparts

hooligan *n slang* a young person who behaves in a noisy

and violent way in public [origin unknown]
> **hooliganism** n

hoon Austral and NZ slang n **1** a loutish youth who drives irresponsibly ▷ vb **2** to drive irresponsibly

hoop n **1** a rigid circular band of metal, plastic, or wood **2** a child's toy shaped like a hoop and rolled on the ground or whirled around the body **3** croquet any of the iron arches through which the ball is driven **4** a large ring through which performers or animals jump **5 go** or **be put through the hoops** to go through an ordeal or test ▷ vb **6** to surround (something) with a hoop [Old English hōp] > **hooped** adj

hoopla n Brit and Austral a fairground game in which hoops are thrown over objects in an attempt to win them

hoopoe (hoop-oo) n a bird with pinkish-brown plumage with black-and-white wings and a fanlike crest [imitative]

hoop pine n an Australian tree or shrub with flowers in dense spikes

hooray interj, n same as **hurrah**

Hooray Henry (hoo-ray) n, pl **Hooray Henries** or **-rys** Brit informal a young upper-class man with an affectedly loud and cheerful manner

hoot n **1** the sound of a car horn **2** the cry of an owl **3** a high-pitched noise showing disapproval **4** informal an amusing person or thing ▷ vb **5** Brit to blow (a car horn) **6** to make a hoot **7** to jeer or yell contemptuously at someone **8** to drive (speakers or performers on stage) off by hooting [imitative]

hooter n chiefly Brit **1** a device that hoots, such as a car horn **2** slang a nose

Hoover[1] n **1** trademark a vacuum cleaner ▷ vb **hoover 2** to vacuum-clean (a carpet) **3** (often foll. by up) to devour (something) quickly and completely

Hoover[2] n **1** Herbert (Clark). 1874–1964, US statesman; 31st president of the US (1929–33). He organized relief for Europe during and after World War I, but as president he lost favour after his failure to alleviate the effects of the Depression **2** J(ohn) Edgar. 1895–1972, US lawyer: director of the FBI (1924–72). He used new scientific methods to combat crime, including the first fingerprint file

Hoover Dam n a dam in the western US, on the Colorado River on the border between Nevada and Arizona; forms Lake Mead. Height: 222 m (727 ft). Length: 354 m (1180 ft). Former name (1933–47): **Boulder Dam**

hooves n a plural of **hoof**

hop[1] vb **hopping, hopped 1** to jump forwards or upwards on one foot **2** (of frogs, birds, etc.) to move forwards in short jumps **3** to jump over something **4** informal to move quickly (in, on, out of, etc.): hop into bed **5 hop it** Brit and Austral slang to go away ▷ n **6** an instance of hopping **7** informal an informal dance **8** informal a short journey, usually in an aircraft **9 on the hop** informal **a** active or busy: he keeps me on the hop **b** unawares or unprepared: you caught me on the hop [Old English hoppian]

hop[2] n a climbing plant with green conelike flowers. See also **hops** [Middle Dutch hoppe]

hope vb **hoping, hoped 1** to desire (something), usually with some possibility of fulfilment: you would hope for their cooperation **2** to trust or believe: I hope I've arranged that ▷ n **3** a feeling of desire for something, usually with confidence in the possibility of its fulfilment: the news was greeted by some as hope for further interest rate cuts **4** a reasonable ground for this feeling: there is hope for you yet **5** the person, thing, situation, or event that gives cause for hope or is desired: the young are a symbol of hope for the future [Old English hopa]

Hope n **1** Anthony, real name Sir Anthony Hope Hawkins. 1863–1933, English novelist; author of The Prisoner of Zenda (1894) **2** Bob, real name Leslie Townes Hope. 1903–2003, US comedian and comic actor, born in England. His films include The Cat and the Canary (1939), Road to Morocco (1942),

and The Paleface (1947). He was awarded an honorary knighthood in 1998 **3** David (**Michael**). Baron. born 194[?] British churchman, Archbishop of York (1995–2005)

hopeful adj **1** having, inspiring, or expressing hope ▷ n[?] **2** a person considered to be on the brink of success: a young hopeful

hopefully adv **1** in a hopeful manner **2** informal it is hoped: hopefully I've got a long career ahead of me

> **USAGE** The use of hopefully to mean it is hoped used to be considered incorrect by some people but has now become acceptable in informal contexts.

Hopeh or **Hopei** n a variant transliteration of the Chinese name for **Hebei**

hopeless adj **1** having or offering no hope **2** impossible to solve **3** informal without skill or ability: I'm hopeless at maths > **hopelessly** adv > **hopelessness** n

Hopkins n **1** Sir Anthony. born 1937, Welsh actor: his films include Bounty (1984), The Silence of the Lambs (1991), Shadowlands (1994), Nixon (1995), and Hannibal (2001) **2** Si[?] Frederick Gowland. 1861–1947, British biochemist, who pioneered research into what came to be called vitamins: shared the Nobel prize for physiology or medicine (1929) **3** Gerard Manley. 1844–89, British poet and Jesuit priest, who experimented with sprung rhythm in his highly original poetry **4** Harry L(loyd). 1890–1946, US administrator. During World War II he was a personal aide to President Roosevelt and administered the lend-lease programme

hopper n a funnel-shaped device from which solid materials can be discharged into a receptacle below

Hopper n Edward. 1882–1967, US painter, noted for his realistic depiction of everyday scenes

hops pl n the dried flowers of the hop plant, used to give[?] bitter taste to beer

hopscotch n a children's game in which a player throws a stone to land in one of a pattern of squares marked on the ground and then hops over to it to pick i[?] up [hop + obsolete scotch a line, scratch]

Horace n Latin name Quintus Horatius Flaccus. 65–8 BC, Roman poet and satirist: his verse includes the lyrics in the Epodes and the Odes, the Epistles and Satires, and the A[?] Poetica

Horatius Cocles n a legendary Roman hero of the 6th century BC, who defended a bridge over the Tiber against Lars Porsena

horde n a very large crowd, often frightening or unpleasant [Turkish ordū camp]

> **USAGE** Horde is sometimes wrongly written where hoard is meant: a hoard (not horde) of gold coins.

Hordern n Sir Michael (Murray). 1911–95, British actor

horehound n a plant that produces a bitter juice formerly used as a cough medicine [Old English hārhūn[?]]

horizon n **1** the apparent line that divides the earth and the sky **2 horizons** the limits of a person's interests and activities: seeking to broaden his horizons at college **3 on the horizon** almost certainly going to happen or be done in the future: a new type of computer is on the horizon [Greek horizein to limit]

horizontal adj **1** flat and level with the ground or with a line considered as a base **2** affecting or happening at one level in a system or organization: a horizontal division labour ▷ n **3** a horizontal plane, position, or line > **horizontally** adv

Horkheimer n Max. 1895–1973, German social theorist o[?] the Frankfurt school. His books include Eclipse of Reason (1947) and Critical Theory (1968)

hormone n **1** a chemical substance produced in an endocrine gland and transported in the blood to a certain tissue, on which it has a specific effect **2** a similar substance produced by a plant that is essential for growth **3** a synthetic substance having the same effects [Greek *hormōn*] **> hormonal** *adj*

Hormuz *or* **Ormuz** *n* an island off the SE coast of Iran, in the **Strait of Hormuz**: ruins of the ancient city of Hormuz, a major trading centre in the Middle Ages. Area: about 41 sq km (16 sq miles)

horn *n* **1** either of a pair of permanent bony outgrowths on the heads of animals such as cattle and antelopes **2** any hornlike projection, such as the eyestalk of a snail **3** the antler of a deer **4** the hard substance of which horns are made **5** a musical wind instrument made from horn **6** any musical instrument consisting of a pipe or tube of brass fitted with a mouthpiece **7** a device, such as on a vehicle, for producing a warning or signalling noise [Old English] **> horned** *adj*

Horn *n* **Cape** See **Cape Horn**

hornbeam *n* a tree with smooth grey bark

hornbill *n* a tropical bird with a bony growth on its large beak

hornblende *n* a green-to-black mineral containing aluminium, calcium, sodium, magnesium, and iron

Hornby *n* Nick. born 1958, British writer; his books include the memoir *Fever Pitch* (1992; filmed 1997) and the bestselling novels *About a Boy* (1998; filmed 2002), *How To Be Good* (2001), and *Juliet, Naked* (2009)

hornet *n* **1** a large wasp that can inflict a severe sting **2 hornet's nest** a very unpleasant situation that is difficult to deal with: *you'll stir up a hornet's nest* [Old English *hyrnetu*]

Horn of Africa *n* a region of NE Africa, comprising Somalia and adjacent territories

horn of plenty *n* same as **cornucopia**

hornpipe *n* **1** a solo dance, traditionally performed by sailors **2** music for this dance

horny *adj* **hornier, horniest 1** of, like, or hard as horn **2** *slang* **a** sexually aroused **b** provoking sexual arousal **c** sexually eager

horology *n* the art of making clocks and watches or of measuring time [Greek *hōra* hour + -LOGY] **> horological** *adj*

horoscope *n* **1** the prediction of a person's future based on the positions of the planets, sun, and moon at the time of birth **2** a diagram showing the positions of the planets, sun, and moon at a particular time and place [Greek *hōra* hour + *skopos* observer]

Horowitz *n* Vladimir. 1904–89, Russian virtuoso pianist, in the US from 1928

horrendous *adj* very unpleasant or shocking [Latin *horrendus* fearful]

horrible *adj* **1** disagreeable and unpleasant: *a horrible hotel room* **2** causing fear, shock, or disgust: *he died a horrible death* [Latin *horribilis*] **> horribly** *adv*

horrid *adj* **1** disagreeable or unpleasant: *it had been a horrid day at school* **2** *informal* (of a person) unkind and nasty: *her horrid parents* [Latin *horridus* prickly]

horrific *adj* provoking horror: *horrific injuries* **> horrifically** *adv*

horrify *vb* **-fies, -fying, -fied** to cause feelings of horror in (someone); shock (someone) greatly

horror *n* **1** extreme fear or terror **2** intense hatred: *she had a horror of violence* **3** a thing or person causing fear, loathing, or distaste ▷ *adj* **4** having a frightening subject, usually concerned with the supernatural: *a horror film* [Latin: a trembling with fear]

horrors *pl n* **the horrors** *slang* a fit of nervousness or anxiety

Horsa *n* died ?455 AD, leader, with his brother Hengist, of the first Jutish settlers in Britain. See also **Hengist**

hors d'oeuvre (or durv) *n*, *pl* **hors d'oeuvre** *or* **hors d'oeuvres** (or durv) an appetizer, usually served before the main meal [French]

horse *n* **1** a four-footed mammal with hooves, a mane, and a tail, used for riding and pulling carts, etc. Related adjectives: **equestrian, equine 2** the adult male of this

species; stallion **3** *gymnastics* a padded apparatus on legs, used for vaulting **4 be** *or* **get on one's high horse** *informal* to act in a haughty manner **5 the horses** *informal* horse races on which bets may be placed: *an occasional flutter on the horses* **6 the horse's mouth** the most reliable source: *I'll tell you straight from the horse's mouth* ▶ See also **horse around** [Old English *hors*]

horse around *or* **horse about** *vb informal* to play roughly or boisterously

horseback *n* a horse's back: *on horseback*

horsebox *n Brit, S African, NZ and Austral* a van or trailer used for transporting horses

horse brass *n* a decorative brass ornament, originally attached to a horse's harness

horse chestnut *n* **1** a tree with broad leaves and brown shiny inedible nuts enclosed in a spiky case **2** the nut of this tree

horseflesh *n* **1** horses collectively: *Ascot's annual parade of fashion and horseflesh* **2** the flesh of a horse as food

horsefly *n*, *pl* **-flies** a large fly which sucks the blood of horses, cattle, and people

Horse Guards *pl n* **1** the mounted squadrons supplied by the Household Cavalry for ceremonial duties **2** their headquarters in Whitehall, London: also the headquarters of the British Army

horsehair *n* hair from the tail or mane of a horse, used in upholstery

horse laugh *n* a loud and coarse laugh

horseman *n*, *pl* **-men 1** a man who is skilled in riding **2** a man riding a horse **> horsemanship** *n* **> horsewoman** *fem n*

Horsens *n* a port in Denmark, in E Jutland at the head of Horsens Fjord. Pop: 49 652 (2004 est)

horseplay *n* rough or rowdy play

horsepower *n* a unit of power (equivalent to 745.7 watts), used to measure the power of an engine

horseradish *n* a plant with a white strong-tasting root, which is used to make a sauce

horse sense *n* same as **common sense**

horseshoe *n* **1** a piece of iron shaped like a U, nailed to the bottom of a horse's hoof to protect the foot **2** an object of similar shape: often regarded as a symbol of good luck

horsetail *n* a plant with small dark toothlike leaves

horsewhip *n* **1** a whip with a long thong, used for managing horses ▷ *vb* **-whipping, -whipped 2** to beat (a person or animal) with such a whip

horsey *or* **horsy** *adj* **horsier, horsiest 1** of or relating to horses: *a horsey smell* **2** devoted to horses: *the horsey set* **3** like a horse: *a horsey face*

Horta¹ *n* a port in the Azores, on the SE coast of Fayal Island

Horta² *n* Victor. 1861–1947, Belgian architect, best known for his early buildings in Art Nouveau style

hortatory *or* **hortative** *adj formal* encouraging [Latin *hortari* to encourage]

Horthy *n* Miklós, full name *Horthy de Nagybánya*. 1868–1957, Hungarian admiral: suppressed Kun's Communist republic (1919); regent of Hungary (1920–44)

horticulture *n* the art or science of cultivating gardens [Latin *hortus* garden + CULTURE] **> horticultural** *adj* **> horticulturalist** *or* **horticulturist** *n*

Horus *n* an Egyptian god with a falcon's head

hosanna *interj* an exclamation of praise to God [Hebrew *hōshi 'āh nnā* save now, we pray]

hose¹ *n* **1** a flexible pipe, for conveying a liquid or gas ▷ *vb* **hosing, hosed 2** to wash or water (a person or thing) with a hose [later use of HOSE²]

hose² *n* **1** old-fashioned stockings, socks, and tights collectively **2** *history* a man's garment covering the legs and reaching up to the waist [Old English *hosa*]

hoser *n* **1** *US slang* a person who swindles or deceives others **2** *Canad slang* an unsophisticated, esp. rural, person

h

hosiery *n* stockings, socks, and knitted underclothing collectively

hospice (hoss-piss) *n* **1** a nursing home that specializes in caring for the terminally ill **2** *archaic* a place of shelter for travellers, esp. one kept by a religious order [Latin *hospes* guest]

hospitable *adj* generous, friendly, and welcoming to guests or strangers: *charming and hospitable lodgings* [Medieval Latin *hospitare* to receive as a guest] **> hospitably** *adv*

hospital *n* an institution for the medical or psychiatric care and treatment of patients [Latin *hospes* guest]

Hospitalet *n* a city in NE Spain, a SW suburb of Barcelona. Pop: 246 415 (2003 est)

hospitality *n, pl* **-ties** kindness in welcoming strangers or guests

hospitalize *or* **-lise** *vb* **-lizing, -lized** *or* **-lising, -lised** to admit or send (a person) into a hospital **> hospitalization** *or* **-lisation** *n*

hospitaller *or US* **hospitaler** *n* a member of a religious order dedicated to hospital work, ambulance services, etc.

host¹ *n* **1** a person who receives or entertains guests, esp. in his own home **2** the organization or country providing the facilities for a function or event: *Barcelona, host of the 1992 Olympic Games* **3** the compere of a radio or television programme **4** *biology* an animal or plant in or on which a parasite lives **5** *computers* a computer connected to a network and providing facilities to other computers and their users **6** *old-fashioned* the owner or manager of an inn ▷ *vb* **7** to be the host of (a party, programme, or event): *he's hosting a radio show* [Latin *hospes* guest, host]

host² *n* a great number; multitude [Latin *hostis* stranger]

Host *n Christianity* the bread used in Holy Communion [Latin *hostia* victim]

hostage *n* a person who is illegally held prisoner until certain demands are met by other people [Old French *hoste* guest]

hostel *n* **1** a building providing overnight accommodation at a low cost for particular groups of people, such as the homeless **2** same as **youth hostel** **3** *Brit and NZ* a supervised lodging house for nurses, students, etc. [Medieval Latin *hospitale* hospice] **> hosteller** *or US* **hosteler** *n*

hostelry *n, pl* **-ries** *archaic or facetious* an inn

hostel school *n Canad* same as **residential school**

hostess *n* **1** a woman who receives and entertains guests, esp. in her own house **2** a woman who receives and entertains patrons of a club, restaurant, or dance hall

hostile *adj* **1** unfriendly and aggressive **2** opposed (to): *hostile to the referendum* **3** relating to or involving the enemies of a country [Latin *hostis* enemy]

hostility *n, pl* **-ties** **1** unfriendly and aggressive feelings or behaviour **2** hostilities acts of warfare

hot *adj* **hotter, hottest** **1** having a relatively high temperature **2** having a temperature higher than desirable **3** spicy or causing a burning sensation on the tongue: *hot chillies* **4** (of a temper) quick to flare up **5** (of a contest or conflict) intense **6** recent or new: *hot from the press* **7** much favoured: *a hot favourite* **8** *informal* having a dangerously high level of radioactivity **9** *slang* stolen or otherwise illegally obtained **10** (of a colour) intense; striking: *hot pink* **11** following closely: *this LP appeared hot on the heels of the debut smash* **12** *informal* dangerous or unpleasant: *they're making it hot for me here* **13** (in various games) very near the answer **14 hot on** *informal* **a** strict about: *they are extremely hot on sloppy language* **b** particularly knowledgeable about **15 hot under the collar** *informal* aroused with anger, annoyance, or resentment **16 in hot water** *informal* in trouble ▶ See also **hot up** [Old English *hāt*] **> hotly** *adv*

hot air *n informal* empty and usually boastful talk

Hotan, Hotien *or* **Ho-t'ien** *n* **1** an oasis in W China, in the Taklimakan Shamo desert of central Xinjiang, around the seasonal Hotan River **2** the chief town of this oasis, situated at the foot of the Kunlun Mountains. Pop: 114 000 (2006 est) ▶ Also called: **Khotan, Hetian**

hotbed *n* a place offering ideal conditions for the growth of an idea or activity: *a hotbed of resistance*

hot-blooded *adj* passionate or excitable

hot-button *adj informal* indicating a controversial subject that is likely to arouse strong emotions: *the hot-button issue of abortion*

hotchpotch *or especially US and Canad* **hodgepodge** *n* a jumbled mixture [Old French *hochepot* shake pot]

hot cross bun *n* a yeast bun marked with a cross and traditionally eaten on Good Friday

hot-desking *n* the practice of not assigning permanent desks in a workplace, so that employees may work at an available desk

hot dog *n* a long roll split lengthways with a hot sausage inside

hotel *n* a commercially run establishment providing lodging and meals for guests [French]

hotelier *n* an owner or manager of a hotel

Hotere *n* **Ralph.** 1931–2013, New Zealand artist of Māori origin, noted esp. for his minimalist *Black Paintings*

hotfoot *adv* with all possible speed: *hotfoot to the accident*

hot-gospeller *n informal* a revivalist preacher with a highly enthusiastic delivery

hot-headed *adj* impetuous, rash, or hot-tempered **> hot-headedness** *n*

hothouse *n* a greenhouse in which the temperature is maintained at a fixed level

Hotien *or* **Ho-t'ien** *n* a variant transliteration of the Chinese name for **Hotan**

hot key *n computers* a single key on a computer keyboard which provides a shortcut to a function in an application

hotline *n* a direct telephone link between heads of government for emergency use

hot money *n* capital that is transferred from one financial centre to another seeking the best opportunity for short-term gain

hotplate *n* **1** a heated metal surface on an electric cooker **2** a portable device on which food can be kept warm

hot pool *n NZ* a geothermally heated pool

hotpot *n* a casserole of meat and vegetables covered with a layer of potatoes

hot rod *n* a car with an engine that has been modified to produce increased power

hot seat *n* **1** *US slang* the electric chair **2 in the hot seat** *informal* in a difficult and responsible position

hotspot *n* **1** a place where there is a lot of exciting activity or entertainment: *Birmingham's fashionable hot spots* **2** an area where there is fighting or political unrest: *a political hot spot in the Caucasus* **3** a small area of abnormally high temperature or radioactivity **4** *computers* a place (esp. a public building or commercial premises) offering a wireless internet connection

Hotspur *n* **Harry Hotspur** the nickname of Sir Henry Percy. See **Percy (1)**

hot stuff *n informal* **1** a person, object, or activity considered attractive, exciting, or important: *they're still hot stuff* **2** pornographic or erotic books, plays, films, etc.

Hottentot *n offensive* same as **Khoikhoi**

hotting *n Brit informal* the performing of high-speed stunts in a stolen car **> hotter** *n*

hot up *vb* **hotting, hotted** *informal* to make or become more active and exciting

hot-water bottle *n* a rubber container, designed to be filled with hot water and used for warming a bed

Houdini *n* **Harry,** real name *Ehrich Weiss.* 1874–1926, US magician and escapologist

Houdon *n* **Jean Antoine.** 1741–1828, French neoclassical portrait sculptor

Houghton-le-Spring *n* a town in N England, in Sunderland unitary authority, Tyne and Wear: coal-mining. Pop: 36 746 (2001)

hound *n* **1** a dog used for hunting: *to ride with the hounds* **2** a despicable person ▷ *vb* **3** to pursue, disturb, or criticize relentlessly: *hounded by the press* [Old English *hund*]

Hounslow *n* a borough of Greater London, on the River Thames: site of London's first civil airport (1919). Pop: 212 900 (2003 est). Area: 59 sq km (23 sq miles)

Houphouet-Boigny *n* Félix. 1905–93, Côte d'Ivoire statesman; president of the Côte d'Ivoire (1960–93)

hour *n* **1** a period of time equal to 60 minutes; $\frac{1}{24}$ of a day **2** any of the points on the face of a clock or watch that indicate intervals of 60 minutes: *in my hurry I mistook the hour* **3** the time of day **4** the time allowed for, or used for, something: *a three-and-a-half-hour test* **5** the distance covered in an hour: *an hour from the heart of Tokyo* **6** a special moment: *the decisive hour*. See also **hours** [Latin *hora*]

hourglass *n* a device consisting of two transparent sections linked by a narrow channel, containing a quantity of sand that takes an hour to trickle from one section to the other

houri *n*, *pl* **-ris** (in Muslim belief) any of the nymphs of Paradise [Arabic *haurā'* woman with dark eyes]

hourly *adj* **1** of, occurring, or done once every hour **2** measured by the hour: *hourly charges* **3** frequent ▷ *adv* **4** once every hour **5** by the hour: *hourly paid* **6** frequently **7** at any moment: *the arrival of the men was hourly expected*

hours *pl n* **1** an indefinite time: *they play on their bikes for hours* **2** a period regularly appointed for work or business **3** one's times of rising and going to bed: *you keep very late hours* **4** RC Church prayers recited at seven specified times of the day

Hours *pl n* Classical myth the goddesses of the seasons

house *n* **1** a building used as a home; dwelling **2** the people in a house **3** a building for some specific purpose: *beach house* **4** a family or dynasty: *the House of Windsor* **5** a commercial company: *auction house* **6** a law-making body or the hall where it meets **7** a division of a large school: *he was captain of the house rugby team* **8** the audience in a theatre or cinema **9** *astrol* any of the 12 divisions of the zodiac **10** *informal* a brothel **11 get on like a house on fire** *informal* (of people) to get on very well together **12 on the house** (usually of drinks) paid for by the management **13 put one's house in order** to settle or organize one's affairs ▷ *adj* **14** (of wine) sold unnamed by a restaurant, at a lower price than wines specified on the wine list: *house red* ▷ *vb* **housing, housed** **15** to give accommodation to **16** to contain or cover (something) [Old English *hūs*]

house arrest *n* confinement to one's own home rather than in prison

houseboat *n* a stationary boat used as a home

housebound *adj* unable to leave one's house, usually because of illness

housebreaking *n* criminal law the act of entering a building as a trespasser for an unlawful purpose **▷ housebreaker** *n*

housecoat *n* a woman's loose robelike garment for casual wear

housefly *n*, *pl* **-flies** a common fly often found in houses

household *n* **1** all the people living together in one house ▷ *adj* **2** relating to the running of a household: *household budget*

householder *n* a person who owns or rents a house

household name or **household word** *n* a person or thing that is very well known

housekeeper *n* a person employed to run someone else's household

housekeeping *n* **1** the running of a household **2** money allotted for this

house lights *pl n* the lights in the auditorium of a theatre or cinema

housemaid *n* (esp. formerly) a female servant employed to do housework

housemaid's knee *n* a fluid-filled swelling of the kneecap

houseman *n*, *pl* **-men** med a junior doctor in a hospital

house martin *n* a swallow with a slightly forked tail

House music or **House** *n* a type of disco music of the late 1980s, based on funk, with fragments of other recordings edited in electronically

House of Commons *n* (in Britain and Canada) the lower chamber of Parliament

House of Keys *n* the lower chamber of the law-making body of the Isle of Man

House of Lords *n* (in Britain) the upper chamber of Parliament, composed of the peers of the realm

House of Representatives *n* **1** (in the US) the lower chamber of Congress, or of many state legislatures **2** (in Australia) the lower chamber of Parliament **3** the sole chamber of New Zealand's Parliament

house party *n* **1** a party, usually in a country house, at which guests are invited to stay for several days **2** the guests who are invited

house-proud *adj* excessively concerned with the appearance, cleanliness, and tidiness of one's house

houseroom *n* not give something houseroom not to want to have something in one's house

house-train *vb* to train (a pet) to urinate and defecate outside

housewares *pl n* US and Canad kitchenware and other utensils for use in the home

house-warming *n* a party given after moving into a new home

housewife *n*, *pl* **-wives** a woman who runs her own household and does not have a paid job **▷ housewifely** *adj*

housework *n* the work of running a home, such as cleaning, cooking, and shopping

housing *n* **1** houses collectively **2** the job of providing people with accommodation **3** a part designed to contain and support a component or mechanism: *the inspection panel set within the concrete housing*

Housman *n* A(lfred) E(dward). 1859–1936, English poet and classical scholar, author of *A Shropshire Lad* (1896) and *Last Poems* (1922)

Houston *n* an inland port in SE Texas, linked by the Houston Ship Canal to the Gulf of Mexico and the Gulf Intracoastal Waterway: capital of the Republic of Texas (1837–39; 1842–45); site of the Manned Spacecraft Center (1964). Pop: 2 009 690 (2003 est)

hove *vb* chiefly nautical a past of **heave**

Hove *n* a town and coastal resort in S England, in Brighton and Hove unitary authority, East Sussex. Pop: 72 335 (2001)

hovea *n* an Australian plant with purple flowers

hovel *n* a small house or hut that is dirty or badly in need of repair [origin unknown]

hover *vb* **1** (of a bird, insect, or helicopter) to remain suspended in one place in the air **2** to linger uncertainly in a place **3** to be in an unsettled or uncertain situation or frame of mind: *hovering between two options* [Middle English *hoveren*]

hovercraft *n* a vehicle that is able to travel across both land and water on a cushion of air

how *adv* **1** in what way, by what means: *how did you spend the evening?*; *observing how elderly people coped* **2** to what extent: *they don't know how tough I am* **3** used to inquire about the quality of something: *how good is your steak?* **4 how about?** used to suggest something: *how about some tea?* **5 how are you?** what is your state of health? **6 how's that? a** what is your opinion?: *we'll go out for a late-night supper – how's that?* **b** cricket Also written: **howzat** (an appeal to the umpire) is the batsman out? [Old English *hu*]

Howard *n* **1** Catherine. ?1521–42, fifth wife of Henry VIII of England; beheaded **2** Charles, Lord Howard of Effingham and 1st Earl of Nottingham. 1536–1624, Lord

High Admiral of England (1585–1618). He commanded the fleet that defeated the Spanish Armada (1588) **3** Sir **Ebenezer**. 1850–1928, English town planner, who introduced garden cities **4 Henry Howard** See **Surrey 5 John**. 1726–90, English prison reformer **6 John Winston**. born 1939, Australian politician; prime minister of Australia (1996–2007) **7 Leslie**. real name *Leslie Howard Stainer*. 1890–1943, British actor of Hungarian descent. His many films included *The Scarlet Pimpernel* (1938), *Pygmalion* (1938), and *Gone With the Wind* (1939) **8 Trevor**. 1916-88, British actor. His many films include *Brief Encounter* (1946), *The Third Man* (1949), *Ryan's Daughter* (1970), and *White Mischief* (1987)

howdah *n* a seat for riding on an elephant's back [Hindi *haudah*]

Howe *n* **1 Elias**. 1819–67, US inventor of the sewing machine (1846) **2 Gordon**, known as *Gordie*. born 1928, Canadian ice-hockey player, who scored1071 goals in a professional career lasting 32 years. **3 Howe of Aberavon, Baron**, title of (*Richard Edward*) *Geoffrey Howe*. born 1926, British Conservative politician; Chancellor of the Exchequer (1979–83); foreign secretary (1983–89); deputy prime minister (1989–90) **4 Richard**, 4th Viscount Howe. 1726–99, British admiral: served (1776–78) in the War of American Independence and commanded the Channel fleet against France, winning the Battle of the Glorious First of June (1794) **5** his brother, **William**, 5th Viscount Howe. 1729–1814, British general; commander in chief (1776–78) of British forces in the War of American Independence

however *adv* **1** still; nevertheless: *the book does, however, almost get funny* **2** by whatever means: *get there however you can* **3** (with an adjective or adverb) no matter how: *however low we plunge, there is always hope*

howitzer *n* a large gun that fires shells at a steep angle [Czech *houfnice* stone-sling]

howl *n* **1** the long, loud wailing noise made by a wolf or dog **2** a similar cry of pain or sorrow **3** a loud burst of laughter ▷ *vb* **4** to express (something) in a howl or utter such cries **5** (of the wind, etc.) to make a wailing noise [Middle English *houlen*]

Howland Island *n* a small island in the central Pacific, near the equator northwest of Phoenix Island: US airfield. Area: 2.6 sq km (1 sq mile)

howl down *vb* to prevent (a speaker) from being heard by shouting disapprovingly

howler *n informal* a glaring mistake

howling *adj informal* great: *a howling success*

Howlin' Wolf *n* real name *Chester Burnett*. 1910–76, US blues singer and songwriter

Howrah *n* an industrial city in E India, in West Bengal on the Hooghly River opposite Kolkata (Calcutta). Pop: 1 008 704 (2001)

howzit *sentence substitute S African* an informal word for hello [from the phrase *how is it?*]

Hoxha *n* **Enver**. 1908–85, Albanian statesman: founded the Albanian Communist Party in 1941 and was its first secretary (1954–85)

hoy *interj* a cry used to attract someone's attention [variant of *hey*]

Hoy *n* Sir **Chris**(*topher Andrew*). born 1976, Scottish cyclist: in his international career (1999–2012) he won eleven World Championship gold medals and six Olympic gold medals for Britain

hoyden *n old-fashioned* a wild boisterous girl; tomboy [perhaps from Middle Dutch *heidijn* heathen]
> hoydenish *adj*

Hoylake *n* a town and resort in NW England, in Wirral unitary authority, Merseyside, on the Irish Sea. Pop: 25 524 (2001)

Hoyle *n* Sir **Fred**. 1915–2001, English astronomer and writer: his books include *The Nature of the Universe* (1950) and *Frontiers of Astronomy* (1955), and science-fiction writings

HP *or* **h.p.** **1** *Brit* hire-purchase **2** horsepower
HQ *or* **h.q.** headquarters
hr hour
Hradec Králové *n* a town in the N Czech Republic, on the Elbe River. Pop: 97 000 (2005 est). German name: Königgrätz
HRH Her (*or* His) Royal Highness
HRT **1** hormone replacement therapy **2** *Austral and NZ* high rising terminal
Hrvatska *n* the Croatian name for **Croatia**
Hs *chem* hassium
Hsi *n* a variant spelling of **Xi**
Hsia-men *n* a transliteration of the modern Chinese name for **Amoy**
Hsian *n* a variant transliteration of the Chinese name for **Xi'an**
Hsiang *n* a variant transliteration of the Chinese name for **Xiang**
Hsin-hai-lien *n* a variant transliteration of the alternative name of **Lianyungang**
Hsining *n* a variant transliteration of the Chinese name for **Xining**
Hsinking *n* the former name (1932–45) of **Changchun**
Hsü-chou *n* a variant transliteration of the Chinese name for **Xuzhou**
HTML *n computers* a text description language that is use on the World Wide Web [hypertext markup language]
Hts (in place names) Heights
HTTP *n computers* hypertext transfer protocol: a system o rules for transferring files on the internet
Hua Guo Feng *or* **Hua Kuo-feng** *n* 1921–2008, Chinese Communist statesman; prime minister of China 1976–80
Huainan *n* a city in E China, in Anhui province north o Hefei. Pop: 1 422 000 (2005 est)
Huambo *n* a town in central Angola: designated at one time by the Portuguese as the future capital of the country. Pop: 756 000 (2005 est). Former name (1928–73) Nova Lisboa
Huang Hai *n* the Pinyin transliteration of the Chinese name for the **Yellow Sea**
Huang He *n* the modern transliteration of the Chinese name (formerly Huang Ho) for the **Yellow River**
Huang Hua *n* 1913–2010, Chinese Communist statesman; minister for foreign affairs (1976–83)
Huáscar *n* died 1533, Inca ruler (1525–33): murdered by his half brother Atahualpa
Huascarán *or* **Huascán** *n* an extinct volcano in W Peru in the Peruvian Andes: the highest peak in Peru; avalanche in 1962 killed over 3000 people. Height: 6768 1 (22 205 ft)
hub *n* **1** the central portion of a wheel, through which the axle passes **2** the central, most important, or active part of a place or organization [probably variant of *hob*]
Hubble *n* **Edwin Powell**. 1889–1953, US astronomer, note for his investigations of nebulae and the recession of the galaxies
hubble-bubble *n* **1** same as **hookah 2** *archaic* turmoil or confusion [imitative]
hubbub *n* **1** a confused noise of many voices **2** great confusion or excitement [probably from Irish *hooboobbe*]
hubby *n*, *pl* -**bies** *informal* a husband
hubcap *n* a metal disc that fits on to and protects the hub of a wheel, esp. on a car
Hubei *or* **Hupeh** *or* **Hupei** *n* a province of central China: largely low-lying with many lakes. Capital: Wuhan. Pop: 60 020 000 (2003 est). Area: 187 500 sq km (72 394 sq miles)
Hubli *n* a city in W India, in NW Mysore: incorporated with Dharwar in 1961; educational and trading centre. Pop (with Dharwar): 786 018 (2001)
hubris (hew-briss) *n formal* pride or arrogance [Greek]
> hubristic *adj*
huckster *n* **1** a person who uses aggressive methods of

selling **2** *rare* a person who sells small articles or fruit in the street [probably from Middle Dutch *hoekster*]

Huddersfield *n* a town in N England, in Kirklees unitary authority, West Yorkshire, on the River Colne: former textile centre, now with varied manufacturing and services; university 1992. Pop: 146 234 (2001)

huddle *n* **1** a small group of people or things standing or lying close together **2 go into a huddle** *informal* to have a private conference ▷ *vb* **-dling, -dled 3** (of a group of people) to crowd or nestle closely together **4** to curl up one's arms and legs close to one's body through cold or fear [origin unknown]

Huddleston *n* Trevor. 1913–98, British Anglican prelate; suffragan bishop of Stepney (1968–78) and bishop of Mauritius (1978–83); president of the Anti-Apartheid Movement (1981–94)

Hudson *n* **1** Henry. died 1611, English navigator: he explored the Hudson River (1609) and Hudson Bay (1610), where his crew mutinied and cast him adrift to die **2** W(illiam) H(enry). 1841–1922, British naturalist and novelist, born in Argentina, noted esp. for his romance *Green Mansions* (1904) and the autobiography *Far Away and Long Ago* (1918)

Hudson Bay *n* an inland sea in NE Canada: linked with the Atlantic by **Hudson Strait**; the S extension forms James Bay; discovered in 1610 by Henry Hudson. Area (excluding James Bay): 647 500 sq km (250 000 sq miles)

Hudson River *n* a river in E New York State, flowing generally south into Upper New York Bay: linked to the Great Lakes, the St Lawrence Seaway, and Lake Champlain by the New York State Barge Canal and the canalized Mohawk River. Length: 492 km (306 miles)

hue *n* **1** the feature of colour that enables an observer to classify it as red, blue, etc. **2** a shade of a colour [Old English *hīw* beauty]

Hué *n* a port in central Vietnam, on the delta of the **Hué River** near the South China Sea: former capital of the kingdom of Annam, of French Indochina (1883–1946), and of Central Vietnam (1946–54). Pop: 377 000 (2005 est)

hue and cry *n* a loud public outcry [Old French *hue* outcry]

Huelva *n* a port in SW Spain, between the estuaries of the Odiel and Tinto Rivers: exports copper and other ores. Pop: 144 831 (2003 est)

Huesca *n* a city in NE Spain: Roman town, site of Quintus Sertorius' school (76 BC); 15th-century cathedral and ancient palace of Aragonese kings. Pop: 47 609 (2003 est). Latin name: Osca

huff *n* **1** a passing mood of anger or resentment: *in a huff* ▷ *vb* **2** to blow or puff heavily **3** *draughts* to remove (an opponent's draught) from the board for failure to make a capture **4** huffing and puffing empty threats or objections [imitative] ❯ **huffily** *adv* ❯ **huffy** *adj*

Hufuf *n* See Al Hufuf

hug *vb* **hugging, hugged 1** to clasp (someone or something) tightly, usually with affection **2** to keep close to (a shore or the kerb) ▷ *n* **3** a tight or fond embrace [probably Scandinavian]

huge *adj* extremely large [Old French *ahuge*] ❯ **hugely** *adv*

huggermugger *archaic n* **1** confusion or secrecy ▷ *adj*, *adv* **2** in confusion [origin unknown]

Huggins *n* Sir William. 1824–1910, British astronomer. He pioneered the use of spectroscopy in astronomy and discovered the red shift in the line of a stellar spectrum

Hughes *n* **1** Howard. 1905–76, US industrialist, aviator, and film producer. He became a total recluse during the last years of his life **2** (James Mercer) Langston. 1902–67, US Black poet and writer. His collections include *The Weary Blues* (1926) and *The Panther and the Lash* (1967) **3** Richard (Arthur Warren). 1900–76, British novelist. He wrote *A High Wind in Jamaica* (1929), *In Hazard* (1938), and *The Fox in the Attic* (1961) **4** Robert (Studley Forrest). 1938–2012, Australian art critic, writer, and broadcaster; his work includes the television series *The Shock of the New* (1981)

and the book *The Culture of Complaint* (1993) **5** Ted, full name Edward James Hughes. 1930–98, British poet: his works include *The Hawk in the Rain* (1957), *Crow* (1970), and *Birthday Letters* (1998). Poet laureate (1984–98) **6** Thomas. 1822–96, British novelist; author of *Tom Brown's Schooldays* (1857) **7** William Morris. 1864–1952, Australian statesman, born in England: prime minister of Australia (1915–23)

Hugo *n* Victor (Marie). 1802–85, French poet, novelist, and dramatist; leader of the romantic movement in France. His works include the volumes of verse *Les Feuilles d'automne* (1831) and *Les Contemplations* (1856), the novels *Notre-Dame de Paris* (1831) and *Les Misérables* (1862), and the plays *Hernani* (1830) and *Ruy Blas* (1838)

Huguenot (hew-gan-oh) *n* a French Calvinist of the 16th or 17th centuries [French]

huh *interj* an exclamation of derision, bewilderment, or inquiry

Huhehot or **Hu-ho-hao-t'e** *n* a variant transliteration of the Chinese name for Hohhot

hui (hoo-ee) *n*, *pl* **huis** NZ **1** a Māori social gathering **2** a meeting to discuss Māori matters **3** any party [Māori]

Hu Jintao *n* born 1942, Chinese Communist statesman; president of China (2003–2013)

hula *n* a Hawaiian dance performed by a woman [Hawaiian]

Hula Hoop *n* *trademark* a plastic hoop swung round the body by wiggling the hips

hulk *n* **1** the body of an abandoned ship **2** *disparaging* a large ungainly person or thing [Old English *hulc*]

hulking *adj* big and ungainly

hull *n* **1** the main body of a boat **2** the outer covering of a fruit or seed such as a pea or bean **3** the leaves round the stem of a strawberry, raspberry, or similar fruit ▷ *vb* **4** to remove the hulls from (fruit or seeds) [Old English *hulu*]

Hull¹ *n* **1** a city and port in NE England, in Kingston upon Hull unitary authority, East Riding of Yorkshire: fishing, food processing; two universities. Pop: 301 416 (2001). Official name: **Kingston upon Hull 2** a city in SE Canada, in SW Quebec on the River Ottawa: a centre of the timber trade and associated industries. Pop: 66 246 (2001)

Hull² *n* Cordell. 1871–1955, US statesman; secretary of state (1933–44). He helped to found the U.N.: Nobel peace prize 1945

hullabaloo *n*, *pl* **-loos** a loud confused noise or commotion [*hallo* + Scots *baloo* lullaby]

hullo *interj*, *n* same as hello

Hulme *n* T(homas) E(rnest). 1883–1917, English literary critic and poet; a proponent of imagism

hum *vb* **humming, hummed 1** to make a low continuous vibrating sound **2** (of a person) to sing with the lips closed **3** to utter an indistinct sound when hesitating **4** *informal* to be in a state of feverish activity: *the town hums with activity and life* **5** *slang* to smell unpleasant **6 hum and haw** See haw² ▷ *n* **7** a low continuous murmuring sound **8** an unpleasant smell ▷ *interj*, *n* **9** an indistinct sound of hesitation [imitative]

human *adj* **1** of or relating to people: *human occupants* **2** having the qualities of people as opposed to animals, divine beings, or machines: *human nature* **3** kind or considerate ▷ *n* **4** a human being [Latin *humanus*]

human being *n* a man, woman, or child

humane *adj* **1** showing kindness and sympathy **2** inflicting as little pain as possible: *a humane method of killing minke whales* **3** considered to have a civilizing effect on people: *the humane tradition of a literary education* [variant of *human*]

humanism *n* the rejection of religion in favour of a belief in the advancement of humanity by its own efforts ❯ **humanist** *n*, *adj* ❯ **humanistic** *adj*

humanitarian *adj* **1** having the interests of mankind at heart ▷ *n* **2** a person who has the interests of mankind at heart ❯ **humanitarianism** *n*

humanity *n*, *pl* **-ties 1** the human race **2** the quality of being human **3** kindness or mercy **4** humanities the study of literature, philosophy, and the arts

humanize or **-ise** vb **-izing, -ized** or **-ising, -ised** to make human or humane ➤ **humanization** or **-isation** n

humankind n the human race; humanity

> **USAGE** See at mankind.

humanly adv by human powers or means: as fast as is humanly possible

humanoid adj **1** like a human being in appearance ▷ n **2** (in science fiction) a robot or creature resembling a human being

human race n all men, women, and children collectively

human resources pl n **1** the people employed in an organization or for a service **2** (functioning as sing) the department in an organization that appoints or keeps records of employees

human rights pl n the basic rights of individuals to liberty, justice, etc.

Humber n an estuary in NE England, into which flow the Rivers Ouse and Trent: flows east into the North Sea; navigable for large ocean-going ships as far as Hull; crossed by the **Humber Bridge** (1981), a single-span suspension bridge with a main span of 1410 m (4626 ft). Length: 64 km (40 miles)

Humberside n a former county of N England around the Humber estuary, formed in 1974 from parts of the East and West Ridings of Yorkshire and N Lincolnshire: replaced in 1996 by the unitary authorities of East Riding of Yorkshire, Kingston upon Hull, North Lincolnshire, and North East Lincolnshire

humble adj **1** conscious of one's failings **2** modest and unpretentious: humble domestic objects **3** ordinary or not very important: humble beginnings ▷ vb **-bling, -bled 4** to cause to become humble; humiliate [Latin humilis low] ➤ **humbly** adv

humble pie n eat humble pie to be forced to behave humbly; be humiliated [earlier an umble pie, from numbles offal of a deer]

Humboldt n **1** Baron (**Friedrich Heinrich**) **Alexander von**. 1769–1859, German scientist, who made important scientific explorations in Central and South America (1799–1804). In Kosmos (1845–62), he provided a comprehensive description of the physical universe **2** his brother, Baron (**Karl**) **Wilhelm von**. 1767–1835, German philologist and educational reformer

humbug n **1** Brit a hard peppermint sweet with a striped pattern **2** a speech or piece of writing that is obviously untrue, dishonest, or nonsense **3** a dishonest person [origin unknown]

humdinger n slang **1** something unusually large **2** an excellent person or thing [origin unknown]

humdrum adj ordinary, dull, and uninteresting [probably based on hum]

Hume n **1** (**George**) **Basil**. 1923–99, English Roman Catholic Benedictine monk and cardinal; archbishop of Westminster (1976–99) **2 David**. 1711–76, Scottish empiricist philosopher, economist, and historian, whose sceptic philosophy restricted human knowledge to that which can be perceived by the senses. His works include A Treatise of Human Nature (1740), An Enquiry concerning the Principles of Morals (1751), Political Discourses (1752), and History of England (1754–62) **3 John**. born 1937, Northern Ireland politician; leader of the Social Democratic and Labour Party (SDLP) (1979–2001). Nobel peace prize jointly with David Trimble in 1998 ➤ **Humism** n

humerus (hew-mer-uss) n, pl **-meri** (-mer-rye) the bone from the shoulder to the elbow [Latin umerus] ➤ **humeral** adj

humid adj (of the weather) damp and warm [Latin umidus]

humidex (hew-mid-ex) n Canad a system of measuring discomfort showing the combined effect of humidity and temperature

humidify vb **-fies, -fying, -fied** to make the air in (a room) more humid or damp ➤ **humidifier** n

humidity n **1** dampness **2** a measure of the amount of moisture in the air

humiliate vb **-ating, -ated** to hurt the dignity or pride o the English cricket team was humiliated by Australia [Latin humilis humble] ➤ **humiliating** adj ➤ **humiliation** n

humility n the quality of being humble and modest

Hummel n Johann Nepomuk. 1778–1837, German composer and pianist

hummingbird n a very small brightly-coloured American bird with a long slender bill, and powerful wings that hum as they vibrate

hummock n a very small hill or a mound [origin unknown]

hummus n a creamy dip originating in the Middle East made from puréed chickpeas [from Turkish humus]

humongous a variant of humungous

humorist n a person who speaks or writes in a humorous way

humorous adj amusing, esp. in a witty or clever way ➤ **humorously** adv

humour or US **humor** n **1** the quality of being funny **2** the ability to appreciate or express things that are humorous: a sense of humour **3** situations, speech, or writings that are humorous **4** a state of mind; mood: in astoundingly good humour **5** archaic any of various fluids in the body: aqueous humour ▷ vb **6** to be kind and indulgent to: he decided the patient needed to be humoured [Latin humor liquid] ➤ **humourless** adj

hump n **1** a rounded lump on the ground **2** a rounded deformity of the back **3** a rounded lump on the back of a camel or related animal **4 the hump** Brit informal a fit of sulking: you've got the hump today ▷ vb **5** slang to carry or heave: who would be responsible if they were injured humping heavy gear around? [probably from humpbacked]

humpback n **1** same as hunchback **2** Also called: **humpback whale** a large whalebone whale with a hump on its back **3** Also called: **humpback bridge** Brit a road bridge with a sharp slope on either side ➤ **humpbacked** adj

Humperdinck n Engelbert. 1854–1921, German composer, esp. of operas, including Hansel and Gretel (1893

humph interj an exclamation of annoyance or scepticism

Humphrey n **1** Duke Humphrey See Gloucester (1) **2** Hubert Horatio. 1911–78, US statesman; vice-president of the US under President Johnson (1965–69)

Humphreys Peak n a mountain in N central Arizona, in the San Francisco Peaks: the highest peak in the state. Height: 3862 m (12 670 ft)

Humphries n (John) Barry. born 1934, Australian comic actor and writer, best known for creating the character Dame Edna Everage

Hums n a variant of Homs

humungous or especially US **humongous** (hew-mung-gus) adj informal very large; enormous: it was not a humungous box office hit [probably from huge + enormous]

humus (hew-muss) n a dark brown or black mass of partially decomposed plant and animal matter in the soil [Latin: soil]

Humvee n a four-wheel drive military vehicle [h(igh-mobility) + m(ulti-purpose) v(ehicle) + -EE]

Hun n, pl **Huns** or **Hun 1** a member of any of several Asiatic peoples who invaded the Roman Empire in the 4th and 5th centuries AD **2** offensive, informal (esp. in World War I) a German [Old English Hūnas]

Hunan n a province of S China, between the Yangtze River and the Nan Ling Mountains: drained chiefly by the Xiang and Yüan Rivers; valuable mineral resources. Capital: Changsha. Pop: 66 630 000 (2003 est). Area: 210 500 sq km (82 095 sq miles)

unch n **1** a feeling or suspicion not based on facts: *she said that she had had a hunch that the coup would not succeed* **2** same as **hump** ▷ vb **3** to draw (oneself or one's shoulders) up or together [origin unknown]

unchback n *offensive* a person who has an abnormal curvature of the spine **> hunchbacked** adj

undred n, pl **-dreds** or **-dred 1** the cardinal number that is the product of ten and ten **2** a numeral, 100 or C, representing this number **3** (often pl) a large but unspecified number ▷ adj **4** amounting to a hundred: *a hundred yards* [Old English] **> hundredth** adj, n

undreds and thousands pl n tiny beads of coloured sugar, used in decorating cakes and sweets

undredweight n, pl **-weights** or **-weight 1** Brit a unit of weight equal to 112 pounds or 50.802kg **2** US and Canad a unit of weight equal to 100 pounds or 45.359kg **3** a metric unit of weight equal to 50 kilograms

ung vb **1** the past of **hang** ▷ adj **2** (of a parliament or jury) with no side having a clear majority **3 hung over** *informal* suffering the effects of a hangover

> **USAGE** When *hang* means 'execute', the past tense and past participle is *hanged* instead of *hung*

ung. 1 Hungarian **2** Hungary

ungarian adj **1** of or relating to Hungary or its inhabitants ▷ n **2** a native or inhabitant of Hungary **3** the language of Hungary

ungary n a republic in central Europe: Magyars first unified under Saint Stephen, the first Hungarian king (1001–38); taken by the Hapsburgs from the Turks at the end of the 17th century; gained autonomy with the establishment of the dual monarchy of Austria-Hungary (1867) and became a republic in 1918; passed under Communist control in 1949; a popular rising in 1956 was suppressed by Soviet troops; a multi-party democracy replaced Communism in 1989 after mass protests; joined the EU in 2004. It consists chiefly of the Middle Danube basin and plains. Official language: Hungarian. Religion: Christian majority. Currency: forint. Capital: Budapest Pop: 9 939 470 (2013 est). Area: 93 030 sq km (35 919 sq miles). Hungarian name: **Magyarország**

unger n **1** a feeling of emptiness or weakness caused by lack of food **2** a lack of food that causes suffering or death: *refugees dying of hunger and disease* **3** desire or craving: *Europe's hunger for bullion* ▷ vb **4 hunger for** to have a great desire for [Old English *hungor*]

unger strike n a refusal of all food, usually by a prisoner, as a means of protest

ungnam n a port in E North Korea, on the Sea of Japan (East Sea) southeast of Hamhung. Pop: about 200 000 (latest est), but the city was merged administratively with Hamhung in 2005 and figures are not normally published separately

ungry adj **-grier, -griest 1** desiring food **2** (foll. by *for*) having a craving, desire, or need for: *hungry for revenge* **3** expressing greed, craving, or desire: *the media's hungry search for impact* **> hungrily** adv

unk n **1** a large piece: *a hunk of bread* **2** slang a well-built, sexually attractive man [probably related to Flemish *hunke*]

unkers pl n informal haunches [origin unknown]

unt vb **1** to seek out and kill (animals) for food or sport **2 hunt down** to track in an attempt to capture (someone): *hunting down villains* **3 hunt for** to search for: *Western companies are hunting for opportunities to invest* ▷ n **4** the act or an instance of hunting **5** a party organized for the pursuit of wild animals for sport **6** the members of such a party [Old English *huntian*] **> hunting** n

unt n **1** Henry, known as *Orator Hunt*. 1773–1835, British radical, who led the mass meeting that ended in the Peterloo Massacre (1819) **2** (William) Holman. 1827–1910, British painter; a founder of the Pre-Raphaelite

Brotherhood (1848) **3** James. 1947–93, British motor-racing driver: world champion 1976 **4** (Henry Cecil) John, Baron. 1910–98, British army officer and mountaineer. He planned and led the expedition that first climbed Mount Everest (1953) **5** (James Henry) Leigh. 1784–1859, British poet and essayist: a founder of *The Examiner* (1808) in which he promoted the work of Keats and Shelley **6** Sam(uel Percival Maitland). born 1946, New Zealand poet, noted for his public performances

huntaway n NZ a sheepdog trained to drive sheep by barking

hunter n **1** a person or animal that seeks out and kills or captures game **2** a person who looks carefully for something: *a house hunter* **3** a horse or dog bred for hunting **4** a watch with a hinged metal lid or case to protect the glass

Hunter n **1** John. 1728–93, British physician, noted for his investigation of venereal and other diseases **2** his brother, William. 1718–83, British anatomist and obstetrician

hunter-gatherer n a member of a society that lives by hunting and gathering naturally occurring resources

Huntingdon[1] n a town in E central England, in Cambridgeshire: birthplace of Oliver Cromwell. Pop (with Godmanchester): 20 600 (2001)

Huntingdon[2] n Selina, Countess of Huntingdon. 1707–91, English religious leader, who founded a Calvinistic Methodist sect

Huntingdonshire n (until 1974) a former county of E England, now part of Cambridgeshire

huntsman n, pl **-men 1** a person who hunts **2** a person who trains hounds and manages them during a hunt

Huntsville n a city in NE Alabama: space-flight and guided-missile research centre. Pop: 164 237 (2003 est)

Hunyadi n János. ?1387–1456, Hungarian general, who led Hungarian resistance to the Turks, defeating them notably at Belgrade (1456)

Hupeh or **Hupei** n a variant transliteration of the Chinese name for Hubei

Hurd n Douglas (Richard), Baron Hurd of Westwell. born 1930, British Conservative politician; home secretary (1985–89); foreign secretary (1989–95)

hurdle n **1** athletics one of a number of light barriers over which runners leap in certain events **2** a difficulty or problem: *the main technical hurdle is the environment* **3 hurdles** a race involving hurdles ▷ vb **-dling, -dled 4** to jump over (a hurdle or other obstacle) [Old English *hyrdel*] **> hurdler** n

hurdy-gurdy n, pl **hurdy-gurdies** a mechanical musical instrument, such as a barrel organ [probably imitative]

hurl vb **1** to throw (something) with great force **2** to utter (something) with force; yell: *onlookers hurled abuse at them* [probably imitative]

hurling or **hurley** n a traditional Irish game resembling hockey

hurly-burly n great noise and activity; commotion [obsolete *hurling* uproar]

Huron n **1** Lake Huron a lake in North America, between the US and Canada: the second largest of the Great Lakes. Area: 59 570 sq km (23 000 sq miles) **2** (pl **-rons** or **-ron**) a member of a North American Indian people formerly living in the region east of Lake Huron **3** the Iroquoian language of this people

hurrah or **hooray** interj, n a cheer of joy or victory [probably from German *hurra*]

hurricane n a severe, often destructive storm, esp. a tropical cyclone [Spanish *huracán*]

hurricane lamp n a paraffin lamp with a glass covering

hurried adj done quickly or too quickly **> hurriedly** adv **> hurriedness** n

hurry vb **-ries, -rying, -ried 1** to move or act, or cause to move or act, in great haste: *the umpires hurried the players off the ground* **2** to speed up the completion or progress of: *eat a small snack rather than hurry a main meal* ▷ n **3** haste

h

h

4 urgency or eagerness **5 in a hurry** *informal* **a** easily: *a striking old guy, not the sort you'd forget in a hurry* **b** willingly: *he would not ease interest rates again in a hurry* [probably imitative]

Hurstmonceux *n* a variant spelling of **Herstmonceux**

hurt *vb* **hurting, hurt 1** to cause physical or mental injury to: *is she badly hurt?* **2** to cause someone to feel pain: *my head hurt* **3** *informal* to feel pain: *she was hurting* ▷ *n* **4** physical or mental pain or suffering ▷ *adj* **5** injured or pained: *his hurt head; a hurt expression* [Old French *hurter* to knock against] **> hurtful** *adj*

hurtle *vb* **-ling, -led** to move very quickly or violently [Middle English *hurtlen*]

Hus *n* Jan. the Czech name of John Huss. See **Huss**

Husain *n* **1** ?629–680 AD, Islamic caliph, the son of Ali and Fatima and the grandson of Mohammed **2** same as **Hussein**

husband *n* **1** the man to whom a person is married ▷ *vb* **2** to use (resources, finances, etc.) economically [Old English *hūsbonda*]

husbandry *n* **1** the art or skill of farming **2** management of resources

Husein ibn-Ali *n* 1856–1931, first king of Hejaz (1916–24): initiated the Arab revolt against the Turks (1916–18); forced to abdicate by ibn-Saud

hush *vb* **1** to make or be silent ▷ *n* **2** stillness or silence ▷ *interj* **3** a plea or demand for silence ▶ See also **hush up** [earlier *husht* quiet!] **> hushed** *adj*

hush-hush *adj informal* (esp. of official work) secret and confidential

hush money *n slang* money given to a person to ensure that something is kept secret

hush up *vb* to suppress information or rumours about (something)

husk *n* **1** the outer covering of certain fruits and seeds ▷ *vb* **2** to remove the husk from [probably from Middle Dutch *hūs* house]

husky¹ *adj* **huskier, huskiest 1** (of a voice) slightly hoarse **2** *informal* (of a man) big and strong [probably from *husk*, from the toughness of a corn husk] **> huskily** *adv*

husky² *n, pl* **huskies** an Arctic sledge dog with thick hair and a curled tail [probably based on *Eskimo*]

Huss *n* John, Czech name *Jan Hus*. ?1372–1415, Bohemian religious reformer. Influenced by Wycliffe, he anticipated the Reformation in denouncing doctrines and abuses of the Church. His death at the stake precipitated the Hussite wars in Bohemia and Moravia

Hussain *n* Nasser. born 1968, British cricketer born in India; played in 96 test matches for England (1990–2004), 56 as captain

hussar (hoo-**zar**) *n history* a member of a light cavalry regiment [Hungarian *huszár*]

Hussein *n* **1** Also: **Husain** 1935–99, king of Jordan (1952–99) **2 Saddam**. 1937–2006, Iraqi politician: president (1979–2003) and prime minister (1994–2003) of Iraq. He led Iraq into the Iran-Iraq War (1980–88) and the Gulf War (1991) but was deposed and captured in the US-led invasion of 2003; executed 2006

Husserl *n* Edmund. 1859–1938, German philosopher; founder of phenomenology

hussy *n, pl* **-sies** *old-fashioned* a woman considered sexually immoral or improper [from *hussif* housewife]

hustings *pl n* the campaigns and speeches at a parliamentary election [Old Norse *hūsthing*, from *hūs* house + *thing* assembly]

hustle *vb* **-tling, -tled 1** to make (someone) move by pushing or jostling them: *he hustled her away* **2** to deal with (something) hurriedly: *they did not heedlessly hustle the tempo* **3** *US and Canad slang* (of a prostitute) to solicit clients ▷ *n* **4** lively activity and excitement [Dutch *husselen* to shake]

hustler *n US informal* a person who tries to make money or gain an advantage from every situation, often by immoral or dishonest means

Huston *n* John. 1906–87, US film director. His films include *The Treasure of the Sierra Madre* (1947), for which he won an Oscar, *The African Queen* (1951), *The Man Who Would Be King* (1975), *Prizzi's Honour* (1985), and *The Dead* (1987)

hut *n* a small house or shelter [French *hutte*]

hutch *n* a cage for small animals [Old French *huche*]

Hutcheson *n* Francis. 1694–1746, Scottish philosopher: he published books on ethics and aesthetics, including *System of Moral Philosophy* (1755)

Hutton *n* **1** James. 1726–97, Scottish geologist, regarded as the founder of modern geology **2** Sir **Leonard**, known as Len Hutton. 1916–90, English cricketer; the first professional captain of England (1953)

Huxley *n* **1** Aldous (Leonard). 1894–1963, British novelist and essayist, noted particularly for his novel *Brave New World* (1932), depicting a scientifically controlled civilization of human robots **2** his half-brother, Sir **Andrew Fielding**, 1917–2012, English biologist: noted for his research into nerve cells and the mechanism by which nerve impulses are transmitted; Nobel prize for physiology or medicine shared with Alan Hodgkin and John Eccles 1963; president of the Royal Society (1980–85) **3** brother of Aldous, Sir **Julian (Sorrel)**. 1887–1975, English biologist; first director-general of UNESCO (1946–48). His works include *Essays of a Biologist* (1923) and *Evolution: the Modern Synthesis* (1942) **4** their grandfather, **Thomas Henry**. 1825–95, English biologist, the leading British exponent of Darwin's theory of evolution; his works include *Man's Place in Nature* (1863) and *Evolution and Ethics* (1893)

Hu Yaobang *n* 1915–89, Chinese statesman; leader of the Chinese Communist Party (1981–87)

Huygens *n* Christiaan. 1629–95, Dutch physicist: first formulated the wave theory of light

Huysmans *n* Joris Karl. 1848–1907, French novelist of the Decadent school, whose works include *À rebours* (1884)

Hwange *n* a town in W Zimbabwe: coal mines. Pop: 42 581 (1992). Former name (until 1982): **Wankie**

Hwang Hai *n* a former transliteration of the Chinese name for **Yellow Sea**

Hwang Ho *n* a former transliteration of the Chinese name for **Yellow River**

hyacinth *n* a plant with bell-shaped sweet-smelling flowers [Greek *huakinthos*]

hyaena *n* same as **hyena**

hybrid *n* **1** an animal or plant resulting from a cross between two different types of animal or plant **2** a vehicle that is powered by an internal-combustion engine and another source of power **3** anything that is a mixture of two different things ▷ *adj* **4** of mixed origin **5** (of a vehicle) powered by an internal-combustion engine and another source of power [Latin *hibrida*]

hybridize *or* **-dise** *vb* **-dizing, -dized** *or* **-dising, -dised** to produce or cause (species) to produce hybrids; crossbreed **> hybridization** *or* **-disation** *n*

hydatid disease (hide-at-id) *n* a condition caused by the presence of bladder-like cysts (**hydatids**) in the liver, lungs, or brain [Greek *hudatis* watery sac]

Hyde¹ *n* a town in NW England, in Tameside unitary authority, Greater Manchester: textiles, footwear, engineering. Pop: 31 253 (2001)

Hyde² *n* **1** Douglas. 1860–1949, Irish scholar and author; first president of Eire (1938–45) **2** Edward Hyde See **Clarendon**

Hyde Park *n* a park in W central London: popular for open-air meetings

Hyderabad *n* **1** a city in S central India, capital of Andhra Pradesh state and capital of former Hyderabad state; university (1918). Pop: 3 449 878 (2001) **2** a former state of S India: divided in 1956 between the states of Andhra Pradesh, Mysore, and Maharashtra **3** a city in SW Pakistan, on the River Indus: seat of the University of Sind (1947). Pop: 1 392 000 (2005 est)

Hyder Ali *or* **Haidar Ali** *n* 1722–82, Indian ruler of Mysore

(1766–82), who waged two wars against the British in India (1767–69; 1780–82)

hydra *n* **1** a mythical many-headed serpent **2** a persistent problem: *killing the hydra of drug production is impossible* **3** a microscopic freshwater creature with a slender tubular body and tentacles around the mouth [Greek *hudra* water serpent]

hydrangea *n* an ornamental shrub with large clusters of white, pink, or blue flowers [Greek *hudōr* water + *angeion* vessel]

hydrant *n* an outlet from a water main, from which water can be tapped for fighting fires

hydrate *chem n* **1** a compound containing water chemically combined with a substance: *chloral hydrate* ▷ *vb* **-drating, -drated** **2** to treat or impregnate (a substance) with water ▷ **hydration** *n*

hydraulic *adj* operated by pressure transmitted through a pipe by a liquid, such as water or oil [Greek *hudōr* water + *aulos* pipe] ▷ **hydraulically** *adv*

hydraulics *n* the study of the mechanical properties of fluids as they apply to practical engineering

hydride *n chem* a compound of hydrogen with another element

hydro¹ *n, pl* **-dros** *Brit* a hotel offering facilities for hydropathic treatment

hydro² *adj* **1** short for **hydroelectric** ▷ *n* **2** *Canad* electricity as supplied to a residence, business, etc.

hydro- *or before a vowel* **hydr-** *combining form* **1** indicating water or fluid: *hydrodynamics* **2** *chem* indicating hydrogen in a chemical compound: *hydrochloric acid* [Greek *hudōr* water]

hydrocarbon *n chem* a compound containing only carbon and hydrogen

hydrocephalus *n* accumulation of fluid in the cavities of the brain, causing enlargement of the head in children [Greek *hudōr* water + *kephalē* head] ▷ **hydrocephalic** *adj*

hydrochloric acid *n chem* a solution of hydrogen chloride in water: a strong acid used in many industrial and laboratory processes

hydrodynamics *n* the branch of science concerned with the mechanical properties of fluids

hydroelectric *adj* **1** generated by the pressure of falling water: *hydroelectric power* **2** of the generation of electricity by water pressure: *a hydroelectric scheme* ▷ **hydroelectricity** *n*

hydrofoil *n* **1** a fast light vessel the hull of which is raised out of the water on one or more pairs of fins **2** any of these fins

hydrogen *n chem* a colourless gas that burns easily and is the lightest element in the universe. It occurs in water and in most organic compounds. Symbol: H [HYDRO- + *-gen* producing; because its combustion produces water] ▷ **hydrogenous** *adj*

hydrogenate (hide-roj-in-nate) *vb* **-ating, -ated** *chem* to combine (a substance) with hydrogen: *hydrogenated vegetable oil* ▷ **hydrogenation** *n*

hydrogen bomb *n* an extremely powerful bomb in which energy is released by fusion of hydrogen nuclei to give helium nuclei

hydrogen peroxide *n* a colourless oily unstable liquid chemical used as a hair bleach and as an antiseptic

hydrogen sulphide *n* a colourless poisonous gas with an odour of rotten eggs

hydrography (hide-rog-ra-fee) *n* the study of the oceans, seas, and rivers ▷ **hydrographer** *n* ▷ **hydrographic** *adj*

hydrology *n* the study of the distribution, conservation, and use of the water of the earth and its atmosphere

hydrolysis (hide-rol-iss-iss) *n chem* a process of decomposition in which a compound reacts with water to produce other compounds [Greek *hudōr* water + *lusis* a loosening]

hydrometer (hide-rom-it-er) *n* an instrument for measuring the density of a liquid

hydropathy *n* a method of treating disease by the use of large quantities of water both internally and externally [Greek *hudōr* water + *patheia* suffering] ▷ **hydropathic** *adj*

hydrophilic *adj chem* tending to dissolve in or mix with water: *a hydrophilic layer*

hydrophobia *n* **1** same as **rabies** **2** (esp. of a person with rabies) a fear of drinking fluids ▷ **hydrophobic** *adj*

hydroplane *n* **1** a motorboat that raises its hull out of the water at high speeds **2** a fin on the hull of a submarine for controlling its vertical motion

hydroponics *n* a method of growing plants in gravel, etc., through which water containing the necessary nutrients is pumped [HYDRO- + (*geo*)*ponics* science of agriculture]

hydrosphere *n* the watery part of the earth's surface

hydrostatics *n* the branch of science concerned with the properties and behaviour of fluids that are not in motion ▷ **hydrostatic** *adj*

hydrotherapy *n med* the treatment of certain diseases by exercise in water

hydrous *adj* containing water

hydroxide *n chem* a compound containing a hydroxyl group or ion

hydroxyl *adj chem* of or containing the monovalent group –OH or the ion OH⁻: *forming a hydroxyl radical*

hyena *or* **hyaena** *n* a meat-eating doglike mammal of Africa and S Asia [Greek *hus* hog]

hygiene *n* **1** the principles and practices of health and cleanliness: *personal hygiene* **2** Also called: **hygienics** the science concerned with the maintenance of health [Greek *hugieinē*] ▷ **hygienic** *adj* ▷ **hygienically** *adv* ▷ **hygienist** *n*

hygrometer (hie-grom-it-er) *n* an instrument for measuring humidity [Greek *hugros* wet]

hygroscope *n* any device that indicates the humidity of the air without necessarily measuring it, such as an animal or vegetable fibre which contracts with moisture [Greek *hugros* wet + *skopein* to observe]

hygroscopic *adj* (of a substance) tending to absorb water from the air

hymen *n anatomy* a membrane that partly covers the entrance to the vagina and is usually ruptured when sexual intercourse takes place for the first time [Greek: membrane]

hymenopterous *adj* of or belonging to an order of insects with two pairs of membranous wings [Greek *humēn* membrane + *pteron* wing]

Hymettian *or* **Hymettic** *adj* of or relating to Hymettus

Hymettus *n* a mountain in SE Greece, in Attica east of Athens: famous for its marble and for honey. Height: 1032 m (3386 ft). Modern Greek name: **Imittós**

hymn *n* a Christian song of praise sung to God or a saint [Greek *humnos*]

hymnal *n* a book of hymns. Also: **hymn book**

hymnody *n* **1** the composition or singing of hymns **2** hymns collectively

hymnology *n* the study of hymn composition ▷ **hymnologist** *n*

Hypatia *n* died 415 AD, Neo-Platonist philosopher and politician, who lectured at Alexandria. She was murdered by a Christian mob

hype *slang n* **1** intensive or exaggerated publicity or sales promotion ▷ *vb* **hyping, hyped** **2** to market or promote (a commodity) using intensive or exaggerated publicity [origin unknown]

hyped up *adj old-fashioned, slang* stimulated or excited by, or as if by, drugs

hyper *adj informal* overactive or overexcited

hyper- *prefix* above, over, or in excess: *hypercritical* [Greek *huper* over]

hyperactive *adj* (of a person) unable to relax and always in a state of restless activity

hyperbola (hie-per-bol-a) *n geometry* a curve produced

when a cone is cut by a plane at a steeper angle to its base than its side [Greek *huperbolē*]

hyperbole (hie-per-bol-ee) *n* a deliberate exaggeration of speech or writing used for effect, such as *he embraced her a thousand times* [Greek *huper* over + *ballein* to throw]

hyperbolic *or* **hyperbolical** *adj* **1** exaggerated **2** of a hyperbola or a hyperbole

hypercritical *adj* excessively critical

hyperglycaemia *or US* **hyperglycemia** (hie-per-glice-seem-ea-a) *n pathol* an abnormally large amount of sugar in the blood [Greek *huper* over + *glukus* sweet]

hyperlink *computers n* **1** a word, picture, etc., in a computer document on which a user may click to move to another part of the document or to another document ▷ *vb* **2** to link (files) in this way

hypermarket *n* a huge self-service store [translation of French *hypermarché*]

hypersensitive *adj* **1** unduly emotionally vulnerable **2** abnormally sensitive to an allergen, a drug, or high or low temperatures

hypersexual *adj* **1** excessively interested in sexual activity **2** inappropriately sexualized: *hypersexual and explicit portrayals of women*

hypersonic *adj* having a speed of at least five times the speed of sound

hypertension *n pathol* abnormally high blood pressure

hypertext *n* computer software and hardware that allows users to store and view text and move between related items easily

hypertrophy (hie-per-trof-fee) *n, pl* **-phies** enlargement of an organ or part resulting from an increase in the size of the cells [Greek *huper* over + *trophē* nourishment]

hyperventilation *n* an increase in the rate of breathing at rest, sometimes resulting in cramp and dizziness ▷ **hyperventilate** *vb*

hyphen *n* the punctuation mark (-), used to separate parts of compound words and between syllables of a word split between two consecutive lines [Greek *huphen* together]

hyphenate *vb* **-ating, -ated** to separate (words) with a hyphen ▷ **hyphenation** *n*

hyphenated *adj* having two words or syllables connected by a hyphen

hypnosis *n* an artificially induced state of relaxation in which the mind is more than usually receptive to suggestion

hypnotherapy *n* the use of hypnosis in the treatment of emotional and mental problems ▷ **hypnotherapist** *n*

hypnotic *adj* **1** of or producing hypnosis or sleep **2** having an effect resembling hypnosis: *the film makes for hypnotic viewing* ▷ *n* **3** a drug that induces sleep [Greek *hupnos* sleep] ▷ **hypnotically** *adv*

hypnotism *n* the practice of or process of inducing hypnosis ▷ **hypnotist** *n*

hypnotize *or* **-tise** *vb* **-tizing, -tized** *or* **-tising, -tised** **1** to induce hypnosis in (a person) **2** to hold the attention of (someone) completely; fascinate; mesmerize: *hypnotized by her beauty*

hypo- *or before a vowel* **hyp-** *prefix* beneath; less than: *hypodermic* [Greek *hupo* under]

hypoallergenic *adj* not likely to cause an allergic reaction

hypocaust *n* an ancient Roman heating system in which hot air circulated under the floor and between double walls [Latin *hypocaustum*, from Greek *hupokauston* room heated from below]

hypochondria *n* abnormal anxiety concerning one's health [Late Latin: abdomen, supposedly the seat of melancholy]

hypochondriac *n* a person abnormally concerned about his or her health

hypocrisy (hip-ok-rass-ee) *n, pl* **-sies** **1** the practice of claiming to have standards or beliefs that are contrary to one's real character or actual behaviour **2** an act or instance of this

hypocrite (hip-oh-krit) *n* a person who pretends to be what he or she is not [Greek *hupokrinein* to pretend] ▷ **hypocritical** *adj*

hypodermic *adj* **1** used for injecting ▷ *n* **2** a hypodermic syringe or needle

hypodermic syringe *n med* a syringe consisting of a hollow cylinder, a piston, and a hollow needle, used for withdrawing blood samples or injecting drugs under the skin

hypotension *n pathol* abnormally low blood pressure

hypotenuse (hie-pot-a-news) *n* the side in a right-angled triangle that is opposite the right angle [Greek *hupoteinousa grammē* subtending line]

hypothalamus *n, pl* **-mi** an area at the base of the brain which controls hunger, thirst, and other functions

hypothermia *n pathol* an abnormally low body temperature, as a result of exposure to cold weather

hypothesis (hie-poth-iss-iss) *n, pl* **-ses** (-seez) a suggested explanation for a group of facts, accepted either as a basis for further verification or as likely to be true [Greek *hupotithenai* to propose, literally: put under] ▷ **hypothesize** *or* **-ise** *vb*

hypothetical *adj* based on assumption rather than fact or reality ▷ **hypothetically** *adv*

hyrax (hire-ax) *n, pl* **hyraxes** *or* **hyraces** (hire-a-seez) a genus of hoofed rodent-like animals

Hyrcania *n* an ancient district of Asia, southeast of the Caspian Sea

Hyrcanian *adj* of or relating to Hyrcania

hyssop *n* **1** an aromatic plant used in herbal medicine **2** a Biblical plant, used for sprinkling in the ritual practices of the Hebrews [Greek *hussōpos*]

hysterectomy *n, pl* **-mies** surgical removal of the womb [Greek *hustera* womb + *tomē* a cutting]

hysteria *n* **1 a** mental disorder marked by emotional outbursts and, often, symptoms such as paralysis **2** any uncontrolled emotional state, such as of panic, anger, or excitement [Greek *hustera* womb, from the belief that hysteria in women originated in disorders of the womb]

hysteric *n* a hysterical person

hysterical *adj* **1** in a state of uncontrolled panic, anger, or excitement: *a crazy hysterical adolescent* **2** *informal* wildly funny ▷ **hysterically** *adv*

hysterics *n* **1** an attack of hysteria **2** *informal* wild uncontrollable bursts of laughter

Hywel Dda *or* **Howel Dda** *n* known as *Hywel the Good*. died 950 AD, Welsh prince. He united S and N Wales and codified Welsh law

Hz hertz

I i

the imaginary number √-1

pron used by a speaker or writer to refer to himself or herself as the subject of a verb [Old English *ic*]

I **1** *chem* iodine **2** the Roman numeral for one

I **1** Independent **2** Institute **3** International **4** Island; Isle

Ia. *or* **IA** Iowa

iamb (eye-am) *or* **iambus** *n, pl* **iambs** *or* **iambuses** *prosody* a metrical foot of two syllables, a short one followed by a long one [Greek *iambos*]

iambic (eye-am-bik) *prosody adj* **1** written in metrical units of one short and one long syllable ▷ *n* **2** an iambic foot, line, or stanza

Iaşi *n* a city in NE Romania: capital of Moldavia (1565–1859); university (1860). Pop: 280 000 (2005 est). German name: **Jassy**

IBA (in Britain) Independent Broadcasting Authority

Ibadan *n* a city in SW Nigeria, capital of Oyo state: university (1948). Pop: 2 375 000 (2005 est)

Ibagué *n* a city in W central Colombia. Pop: 440 000 (2005 est)

Iberia *n* **1** the Iberian Peninsula **2** an ancient region in central Asia, south of the Caucasus corresponding approximately to present-day Georgia

Iberian *adj* **1** of or relating to Iberia or its inhabitants ▷ *n* **2** a native or inhabitant of Iberia

Iberian Peninsula *n* a peninsula of SW Europe, occupied by Spain and Portugal

Ibero- *combining form* indicating Iberia or Iberian: *Ibero-Caucasian*

Ibert *n* Jacques (François Antoine). 1890–1962, French composer; his works include the humorous orchestral *Divertissement* (1930)

Iberville *n* Pierre le Moyne, Sieur d'. 1661–1706, French-Canadian explorer, who founded (1700) the first French colony in Louisiana

ibex (ibe-eks) *n, pl* **ibexes** *or* **ibex** a wild mountain goat with large backward-curving horns [Latin: chamois]

ibid. in the same place: used to refer to a book, page, or passage previously cited [Latin *ibidem*]

ibis (ibe-iss) *n, pl* **ibises** *or* **ibis** a large wading bird with a long thin curved bill [Egyptian *hby*]

Ibiza, Iviza *or* **Eivissa** *n* **1** a Spanish island in the W Mediterranean, one of the Balearic Islands: hilly, with a rugged coast; tourism. Pop: 40 175 (2003 est). Area: 541 sq km (209 sq miles) **2** the capital of Ibiza, a port on the south of the island. Pop: 16 000 (latest est)

ibn-al-Arabi *n* Muhyi-l-din. 1165–1240, Muslim mystic and poet, born in Spain, noted for his influence on Sufism

ibn-Batuta *n* 1304–?68, Arab traveller, who wrote the *Rihlah*, an account of his travels (1325–54) in Africa and Asia

ibn-Ezra *n* Abraham Ben Meir. 1093–1167, Jewish poet, scholar, and traveller, born in Spain

ibn-Gabirol *n* Solomon. ?1021–?58, Jewish philosopher and poet, born in Spain. His work *The Fountain of Life* influenced Western medieval philosophers

ibn-Khaldun *n* 1332–1406, Arab historian and philosopher. His *Kitab al-'ibar* (*Book of Examples*) is a history of Islam

ibn-Saud *n* Abdul-Aziz. 1880–1953, first king of Saudi Arabia (1932–53)

Ibo (ee-boh) *n* **1** (*pl* **Ibos** *or* **Ibo**) a member of an African people of S Nigeria **2** their language

Ibrahim Pasha *n* 1789–1848, Albanian general; son of Mehemet Ali, whom he succeeded as viceroy of Egypt (1848)

Ibsen *n* Henrik. 1828–1906, Norwegian dramatist and poet. After his early verse plays *Brand* (1866) and *Peer Gynt* (1867), he began the series of social dramas in prose, including *A Doll's House* (1879), *Ghosts* (1881), and *The Wild Duck* (1886), which have had a profound influence on modern drama. His later plays, such as *Hedda Gabler* (1890) and *The Master Builder* (1892), are more symbolic

Içá *n* the Brazilian part of the river **Putumayo**

Icaria *n* a Greek island in the Aegean Sea, in the Southern Sporades group. Area: 256 sq km (99 sq miles). Modern Greek name: **Ikaría**. Also called: **Nikaria**

Icarian *adj* **1** of or relating to Icaria or its inhabitants ▷ *n* **2** an inhabitant of Icaria

Icarian Sea *n* the part of the Aegean Sea between the islands of Patmos and Leros and the coast of Asia Minor, where, according to legend, Icarus fell into the sea

Icarus *n Greek myth* the son of Daedalus, with whom he escaped from Crete, flying with wings made of wax and feathers. Heedless of his father's warning he flew too near the sun, causing the wax to melt, and fell into the Aegean and drowned

ICBM intercontinental ballistic missile

ice *n* **1** water that has frozen and become solid **2** *chiefly Brit* a portion of ice cream **3 break the ice** to relax the atmosphere, esp. between strangers **4 on ice** in readiness or reserve **5 on thin ice** in a dangerous situation: *he knew he was on thin ice* **6 the Ice** *NZ informal* Antarctica ▷ *vb* **icing, iced 7** (foll. by *up* or *over*) to become covered with ice **8** to cover with icing **9** to cool or chill with ice [Old English *īs*]

Ice. Iceland(ic)

ice age *n* any period of time during which a large part of the earth's surface was covered with ice, caused by the advance of glaciers

ice beer *n* a beer that is chilled after brewing so that any water is turned to ice and then removed

iceberg *n* **1** a large mass of ice floating in the sea **2 tip of the iceberg** the small visible part of a problem that is much larger [probably Middle Dutch *ijsberg* ice mountain]

iceberg lettuce *n* a type of lettuce with very crisp pale leaves tightly enfolded

iceboat *n* another name for **icebreaker**

icebox *n* **1** *US and Canad* a refrigerator **2** a compartment in a refrigerator for making or storing ice **3** a container packed with ice for keeping food and drink cold

icebreaker *n* a ship designed to break a channel through ice

icecap *n* a thick mass of glacial ice that permanently covers an area

ice cream *n* a sweet frozen food, made from cream, milk, or a custard base, flavoured in various ways

iced *adj* **1** served very cold **2** covered with icing

ice field *n* a large expanse of floating sea ice

ice floe *n* a sheet of ice floating in the sea

ice hockey *n* a game like hockey played on ice by two teams wearing skates

İçel *n* another name for **Mersin**

Iceland *n* an island republic in the N Atlantic, regarded as part of Europe: settled by Norsemen, who established a legislative assembly in 930; under Danish rule (1380–1918); gained independence in 1918 and became a republic in 1944; contains large areas of glaciers, snowfields, and lava beds with many volcanoes and hot springs (the chief source of domestic heat); inhabited chiefly along the SW coast. The economy is based largely on fishing and tourism. Official language: Icelandic. Official religion: Evangelical Lutheran. Currency: króna. Capital: Reykjavik. Pop: 315 281 (2013 est). Area: 102 828 sq km (39 702 sq miles)

Icelander *n* a native or inhabitant of Iceland

Icelandic *adj* **1** of or relating to Iceland or its inhabitants ▷ *n* **2** the official language of Iceland

ice lolly *n* Brit informal a water ice or an ice cream on a stick

ice pack *n* **1** a bag or folded cloth containing crushed ice, applied to a part of the body to reduce swelling **2** same as **pack ice**

ice skate *n* **1** a boot with a steel blade fitted to the sole which enables the wearer to glide over ice ▷ *vb* **ice-skate** (-skating, -skated) **2** to glide over ice on ice skates ❯ **ice-skater** *n*

icewine *n* Canad a dessert wine made from grapes that have frozen before being harvested

Ichang or **I-ch'ang** *n* a variant transliteration of the Chinese name of **Yichang**

I Ching *n* an ancient Chinese book of divination and a source of Confucian and Taoist philosophy

ichneumon (ik-new-mon) *n* a greyish-brown mongoose

ichthyology (ik-thi-ol-a-jee) *n* the study of fishes [Greek *ikhthus* fish + -LOGY] ❯ **ichthyological** *adj* ❯ **ichthyologist** *n*

icicle *n* a tapering spike of ice hanging where water has dripped [from ICE + Old English *gicel* icicle]

icing *n* **1** Also (esp. US and Canad.): **frosting** a mixture of sugar and water or egg whites used to cover and decorate cakes **2** the formation of ice on a ship or aircraft **3 icing on the cake** any unexpected extra or bonus

icing sugar *n* a very finely ground sugar used for making icing or sweets

icon or **ikon** *n* **1** a picture of Christ, the Virgin Mary, or a saint, venerated in the Orthodox Church **2** a picture on a computer screen representing a computer function that can be activated by moving the cursor over it **3** a person or thing regarded as a symbol of a belief or cultural movement: *a feminist icon* [Greek *eikōn* image]

Iconium *n* the ancient name for **Konya**

iconoclast *n* **1** a person who attacks established or traditional ideas or principles **2** a destroyer of religious images or objects [Late Greek *eikōn* icon + *klastēs* breaker] ❯ **iconoclasm** *n* ❯ **iconoclastic** *adj*

icosahedron (ike-oh-sa-heed-ron) *n, pl* **-drons** or **-dra** (-dra) a solid figure with 20 faces [Greek *eikosi* twenty + -*edron* -sided]

Ictinus *n* 5th century BC, Greek architect, who designed the Parthenon with Callicrates

icy *adj* **icier, iciest 1** freezing or very cold **2** covered with ice: *an icy runway* **3** cold or reserved in manner ❯ **icily** *adv* ❯ **iciness** *n*

id *n psychoanalysis* the primitive instincts and energies in the unconscious mind that underlie all psychological impulses [Latin: it]

ID 1 Idaho **2** identification

Id. Idaho

I'd I had *or* I would

Ida *n* **Mount Ida 1** a mountain in central Crete: the highest on the island; in ancient times associated with the worship of Zeus. Height: 2456 m (8057 ft). Modern Greek name: **Idhi 2** a mountain in NW Turkey, southeast of the site of ancient Troy. Height: 1767 m (5797 ft). Turkish name: **Kaz Daği**

Ida. Idaho

Idaho *n* a state of the northwestern US: consists chiefly of ranges of the Rocky Mountains, with the Snake River basin in the south; important for agriculture (**Idaho potatoes**), livestock, and silver-mining. Capital: Boise. Pop: 1 366 332 (2003 est). Area: 216 413 sq km (83 557 sq miles) Abbreviation: **Id., Ida.,** (with zip code) **ID**

Idahoan *n* **1** a native or inhabitant of Idaho ▷ *adj* **2** of or relating to Idaho or its inhabitants

idea *n* **1** any product of mental activity; thought **2** a scheme, intention, or plan **3** the thought of something: *the idea excites me* **4** a belief or opinion **5** a vague notion; inkling: *they had no idea of the severity of my injuries* **6** a person's conception of something: *his idea of integrity is not the same as mine* **7** aim or purpose: *the idea is to economize on transport* **8** *philosophy* (in Plato) a universal model of which all things in the same class are only imperfect imitations [Greek: model, outward appearance]

> **USAGE** It is usually considered correct to say that someone has *the idea of doing* something, rather than *the idea to do* it: *he had the idea of taking* (not *the idea to take*) *a short holiday.*

ideal *n* **1** (*often pl*) a principle or model of ethical behaviour **2** a conception of something that is perfect **3** a person or thing considered to represent perfection **4** something existing only as an idea ▷ *adj* **5** most suitable: *they seem to have adopted an ideal man as their candidate* **6** of, involving, or existing only as an idea; imaginary: *an ideal world* ❯ **ideally** *adv*

idealism *n* **1** belief in or striving towards ideals **2** the tendency to represent things in their ideal forms, rather than as they are **3** *philosophy* the doctrine that material objects and the external world do not exist in reality, but are creations of the mind ❯ **idealist** *n* ❯ **idealistic** *adj*

idealize or **-lise** *vb* **-lizing, -lized** or **-lising, -lised** to consider or represent (something) as ideal or more nearly perfect than is true ❯ **idealization** or **-lisation** *n*

idée fixe (ee-day feeks) *n, pl* **idées fixes** (ee-day feeks) an idea with which a person is obsessed [French]

idem *pron, adj* the same: used to refer to an article, chapter, or book already quoted [Latin]

identical *adj* **1** that is the same: *they got the identical motel room as last year* **2** exactly alike or equal **3** (of twins) developed from a single fertilized ovum that has split into two, and thus of the same sex and very much alike [Latin *idem* the same] ❯ **identically** *adv*

identification parade *n* a group of people, including one suspected of a crime, assembled to discover whether a witness can identify the suspect

identify *vb* **-fies, -fying, -fied 1** to prove or recognize as being a certain person or thing; determine the identity of **2** (*often foll. by* with) to understand and sympathize with a person or group because one regards oneself as being similar or similarly situated **3** to consider or treat as the same **4** to connect or associate closely: *he was closely identified with the community charge* ❯ **identifiable** *adj* ❯ **identification** *n*

Identikit *n* **1** trademark a composite picture, assembled from descriptions given, of a person wanted by the police ▷ *adj* **identikit 2** artificially created; formulaic: *an identikit pop group* **3** stereotypical: *the identikit Scots midfield mauler*

dentity *n, pl* **-ties 1** the state of being a specified person or thing: *the identity of his murderers was not immediately established* **2** the individual characteristics by which a person or thing is recognized **3** the state of being the same **4** *maths* Also called: **identity element** a member of a set that when combined with any other member of the set, leaves it unchanged: *the identity for multiplication of numbers is 1* [Latin *idem* the same]

dentity theft *n* the fraudulent use of another person's name and personal details to open a bank account, obtain credit, etc.

deo- *combining form* of or indicating ideas: *ideology* [from French *idéo-*, from Greek *idea* idea]

deogram *or* **ideograph** *n* a character or symbol that directly represents a concept or thing, rather than the sounds that form its name [Greek *idea* idea + *gramma* a drawing]

deology *n, pl* **-gies** the body of ideas and beliefs of a person, group, or nation [from IDEO- + -LOGY] ❭ **ideological** *adj* ❭ **ideologically** *adv* ❭ **ideologist** *n*

des *n* (in the ancient Roman calendar) the 15th day in March, May, July, and October and the 13th of the other months [Latin *idus*]

dhi *n* a transliteration of the Modern Greek name for (Mount) **Ida** (1)

diocy *n, pl* **-cies 1** utter stupidity **2** a foolish act or remark

diom *n* **1** a group of words which, when used together, have a different meaning from the one suggested by the individual words, for example *it was raining cats and dogs* **2** linguistic usage that is grammatical and natural to native speakers **3** the characteristic vocabulary or usage of a person or group **4** the characteristic artistic style of an individual or school [Greek *idios* private, separate] ❭ **idiomatic** *adj*

diosyncrasy *n, pl* **-sies** a personal peculiarity of mind, habit, or behaviour; quirk [Greek *idios* private, separate + *sunkrasis* mixture] ❭ **idiosyncratic** *adj*

diot *n* **1** a foolish or senseless person **2** *no longer in technical use* a person with severe mental retardation [Greek *idiōtēs* private person, ignoramus] ❭ **idiotic** *adj* ❭ **idiotically** *adv*

dle *adj* **1** not doing anything **2** not operating or being used **3** not wanting to work; lazy **4** ineffective or useless: *it would be idle to look for a solution at this stage* **5** frivolous or trivial: *idle pleasures* **6** without basis; unfounded: *idle rumours* ▷ *vb* **idling, idled 7** (often foll. by *away*) to waste or pass (time) in idleness **8** (of an engine) to run at low speed without transmitting any power [Old English *īdel*] ❭ **idleness** *n* ❭ **idler** *n* ❭ **idly** *adv*

dol (**eye**-dl) *n* **1** an object of excessive devotion or admiration **2** an image of a god used as an object of worship [Greek *eidōlon* image]

dolatry (ide-ol-a-tree) *n* **1** the worship of idols **2** excessive devotion or reverence ❭ **idolater** *n* ❭ **idolatrous** *adj*

dolize *or* **-lise** *vb* **-lizing, -lized** *or* **-lising, -lised 1** to love or admire excessively **2** to worship as an idol ❭ **idolization** *or* **-lisation** *n*

dyll *or US sometimes* **idyl** (id-ill) *n* **1** a scene or time of peace and happiness **2** a poem or prose work describing a charming rural scene or episode [Greek *eidullion*] ❭ **idyllic** *adj*

i.e. that is to say [Latin *id est*]

IED improvised explosive device

Ieper *n* the Flemish name for **Ypres**

if *conj* **1** in the event that, or on condition that: *if you work hard you'll succeed* **2** used to introduce an indirect question to which the answer is either *yes* or *no*; whether: *it doesn't matter if the play is any good or not* **3** even though: *a splendid if slightly decaying house* **4** used to introduce an unfulfilled

wish, with *only*: *if only you had told her* ▷ *n* **5** a condition or stipulation: *there are no hidden ifs or buts* [Old English *gif*]

Ife *n* a town in W central Nigeria: one of the largest and oldest Yoruba towns; university (1961); centre of the cocoa trade. Pop: 229 000 (2005 est)

iffy *adj* **iffier, iffiest** *informal* full of uncertainty

Ifni *n* a former Spanish province in S Morocco, on the Atlantic: returned to Morocco in 1969

IFS Irish Free State (now called Republic of Ireland)

igloo *n, pl* **-loos** a dome-shaped Inuit house, built of blocks of solid snow [Inuktitut *iglu*]

Ignatiev *n* Count **Nikolai Pavlovich**. 1832–1908, Russian diplomat and politician. As ambassador to Turkey (1864–77), he negotiated the Treaty of San Stefano (1878) ending the Russo-Turkish War

Ignatius *n* Saint, surnamed *Theophorus*. died ?110 AD, bishop of Antioch. His seven letters, written on his way to his martyrdom in Rome, give valuable insight into the early Christian Church. Feast day: Oct 17 or Dec 17 or 20

Ignatius Loyola *n* Saint. 1491–1556, Spanish ecclesiastic. He founded the Society of Jesus (1534) and was its first general (1541–56). His *Spiritual Exercises* (1548) remains the basic manual for the training of Jesuits. Feast day: July 31

igneous (ig-nee-uss) *adj* **1** (of rocks) formed as molten rock cools and hardens **2** of or like fire [Latin *ignis* fire]

ignis fatuus (ig-niss fat-yew-uss) *n, pl* **ignes fatui** (ig-neez fat-yew-eye) same as **will-o'-the-wisp** [Medieval Latin, literally: foolish fire]

ignite *vb* **-niting, -nited 1** to catch fire **2** to set fire to [Latin *ignis* fire] ❭ **ignitable** *adj*

ignition *n* **1** the system used to ignite the fuel in an internal-combustion engine **2** an igniting or the process of igniting

ignoble *adj* **1** dishonourable **2** of low birth or origins [Latin *in-* not + *nobilis* noble] ❭ **ignobly** *adv*

ignominy (ig-nom-in-ee) *n, pl* **-minies** disgrace or public shame: *the ignominy of being replaced* [Latin *ignominia* disgrace] ❭ **ignominious** *adj*

ignoramus *n, pl* **-muses** an ignorant person [Latin, literally: we have no knowledge of]

ignorance *n* lack of knowledge or education

ignorant *adj* **1** lacking in knowledge or education **2** rude through lack of knowledge of good manners: *an ignorant remark* **3 ignorant of** lacking in awareness or knowledge of: *ignorant of Asian culture*

ignore *vb* **-noring, -nored** to refuse to notice; disregard deliberately [Latin *ignorare* not to know]

Iguaçú *or* **Iguassú** *n* a river in SE South America, rising in S Brazil and flowing west to join the Paraná River, forming part of the border between Brazil and Argentina. Length: 1200 km (745 miles)

Iguaçú Falls *n* a waterfall on the border between Brazil and Argentina, on the Iguaçú River: divided into hundreds of separate falls by forested rocky islands. Width: about 4 km (2.5 miles). Height: 82 m (269 ft)

iguana *n* a large tropical tree lizard of the W Indies and S America with a spiny back [S American Indian *iwana*]

Ihimaera *n* **Witi**, full name *Witi Tame Ihimaera-Smiler*. born 1944, New Zealand Māori novelist and short-story writer; his novels include *The Whale Rider* (1987) and *The Uncle's Story* (2002)

IJssel *or* **Yssel** *n* a river in the central Netherlands: a distributary of the Rhine, flowing north to the IJsselmeer. Length: 116 km (72 miles)

IJsselmeer *or* **Ysselmeer** *n* a shallow lake in the NW Netherlands; formed from the S part of the Zuider Zee by the construction of the **IJsselmeer Dam** in 1932; salt water gradually replaced by fresh water from the IJssel River; fisheries (formerly marine fish, now esp. eels). Area: (before reclamation) 3690 sq km (1425 sq miles). Estimated final area: 1200 sq km (465 sq miles). English name: **IJssel Lake**

i

Ikaría n a transliteration of the Modern Greek name for Icaria

ikebana (eek-a-bah-na) n the Japanese art of flower arrangement [Japanese]

Ikeja n a town in SW Nigeria, capital of Lagos state: residential and industrial suburb of Lagos. Pop (local government area): 313 196 (2006)

ikon n same as **icon**

IL Illinois

il- prefix same as in-¹, in-²

Île-de-France n **1** a region of N France, in the Paris Basin: part of the duchy of France in the 10th century **2** a former name (1715–1810) for **Mauritius**

Île du Diable n the French name for **Devil's Island**

Îles Comores pl n the French name for the **Comoros**

Îles du Salut pl n the French name for the **Safety Islands**

Ilesha n a town in W Nigeria. Pop: 500 000 (2005 est)

Îles Mascareignes pl n the French name for the **Mascarene Islands**

Îles sous le Vent pl n the French name for the **Leeward Islands** (3)

ileum n the third and lowest part of the small intestine [Latin: flank, groin]

ilex n **1** a genus of trees or shrubs that includes holly **2** same as **holm oak** [Latin]

Ilía n a transliteration of the Modern Greek name for **Elia**

Iliamna n **1** a lake in SW Alaska: the largest lake in Alaska. Length: about 130 km (80 miles). Width: 40 km (25 miles) **2** a volcano in SW Alaska, northwest of Iliamna Lake. Height: 3076 m (10 092 ft)

Iligan n a city in the Philippines, a port on the N coast of Mindanao. Pop: 306 000 (2005 est)

Ilion n a transliteration of the Greek name for ancient **Troy**

ilium n, pl **-ia** the uppermost and widest of the three sections of the hipbone

Ilium n the Latin name for ancient **Troy**

ilk n **1** a type or class: three or four others of the same ilk **2** of that ilk Scot of the place of the same name: used to indicate that the person named is proprietor or laird of the place named: Moncrieff of that ilk [Old English ilca the same family]

> **USAGE** Although the use of ilk to mean a type or class is sometimes condemned as being the result of a misunderstanding of a Scottish expression of that ilk, it is nevertheless well established and generally acceptable.

Ilkeston n a town in N central England, in SE Derbyshire. Pop: 37 270 (2001)

Ilkley n a town in N England, in Bradford unitary authority, West Yorkshire: nearby is **Ilkley Moor** (to the south). Pop: 13 472 (2001)

ill adj **worse, worst 1** not in good health **2** bad, harmful, or hostile: ill effects **3** promising an unfavourable outcome: ill omen **4** at ease unable to relax ▷ n **5** evil or harm ▷ adv **6** badly, wrongly: the title ill befits him **7** with difficulty; hardly: we can ill afford another scandal [Old Norse illr bad]

ill. **1** illustrated **2** illustration

Ill. Illinois

I'll I will or I shall

ill-advised adj **1** (of a plan or action) badly thought out **2** (of a person) acting without reasonable care or thought

Illampu n one of the two peaks of Mount Sorata

Illawarra n **1** a coastal district of E Australia, in S New South Wales. Pop: 404 626 (2002 est) **2** an Australian breed of shorthorn dairy cattle noted for its high milk yield and ability to survive on poor pastures

ill-bred adj lacking good manners > **ill-breeding** n

ill-disposed adj unfriendly or unsympathetic

Ille-et-Vilaine n a department of NW France, in E

Brittany. Capital: Rennes. Pop: 894 625 (2003 est). Area: 6992 sq km (2727 sq miles)

illegal adj against the law > **illegality** n > **illegally** adv

illegible adj unable to be read or deciphered > **illegibility** n

illegitimate adj **1** born of parents who were not married to each other at the time **2** illegal; unlawful > **illegitimacy** n

ill-fated adj doomed or unlucky

ill-favoured adj ugly or unattractive

ill-founded adj not based on proper proof or evidence

ill-gotten adj obtained dishonestly or illegally: ill-gotten gains

ill-health n the condition of being unwell

illiberal adj **1** narrow-minded or intolerant **2** not generous; mean **3** lacking in culture or refinement > **illiberality** n

Illich n Ivan. 1926–2002. US teacher and writer, born in Austria. His books include Deschooling Society (1971), Medical Nemesis (1975), and In the Mirror of the Past (1991)

illicit adj **1** same as **illegal 2** forbidden or disapproved of by society: an illicit kiss

Illimani n a mountain in W Bolivia, in the Andes near La Paz. Height: 6882 m (22 580 ft)

Illinois n **1** a state of the N central US, in the Midwest: consists of level prairie crossed by the Illinois and Kaskaskia Rivers; mainly agricultural. Capital: Springfield. Pop: 12 653 544 (2003 est). Area: 144 858 sq km (55 930 sq miles). Abbreviation: **Ill.**, (with zip code) **IL 2** a river in Illinois, flowing SW to the Mississippi. Length: 439 km (273 miles)

Illinoisan, Illinoian or **Illinoisian** n **1** a native or inhabitant of Illinois ▷ adj **2** of or relating to Illinois or its inhabitants

illiterate adj **1** unable to read and write **2** uneducated or ignorant: linguistically illiterate ▷ n **3** an illiterate person > **illiteracy** n

ill-mannered adj having bad manners

illness n **1** a disease or indisposition **2** a state of ill health

illogical adj **1** senseless or unreasonable **2** not following logical principles > **illogicality** n > **illogically** adv

ill-starred adj very unlucky or unfortunate

ill-tempered adj having a bad temper

ill-timed adj done or happening at an unsuitable time

ill-treat vb to treat cruelly or harshly > **ill-treatment** n

illuminant n **1** something that gives off light ▷ adj **2** giving off light

illuminate vb **-nating, -nated 1** to light up **2** to make easily understood; explain: the report obscures rather than illuminates the most relevant facts **3** to decorate with lights **4** to decorate (an initial letter or manuscript) with designs of gold, silver, or bright colours [Latin illuminare to light up] > **illuminating** adj > **illuminative** adj

illumination n **1** an illuminating or being illuminated **2** a source of light **3** illuminations chiefly Brit lights used as decorations in streets or towns **4** the decoration in colours, gold, or silver used on some manuscripts

illumine vb **-mining, -mined** literary same as **illuminate**

illusion n **1** a false appearance or deceptive impression of reality: her upswept hair gave the illusion of above average height **2** a false or misleading idea or belief: we may suffer from the illusion that we are special [Latin illusio deceit]

illusionist n a conjuror

illusory or **illusive** adj seeming to be true, but actually false: the economic benefits of such reforms were largely illusory

> **USAGE** Illusive is sometimes wrongly used where elusive is meant: they fought hard, but victory remained elusive (not illusive).

illustrate vb **-trating, -trated 1** to clarify or explain by use of examples or comparisons **2** to provide (a book or text) with pictures **3** to be an example of [Latin illustrare to make light, explain] > **illustrative** adj > **illustrator** n

lustration *n* **1** a picture or diagram used to explain or decorate a text **2** an example: *an illustration of the brutality of the regime* **3** the art of illustrating

lustrious *adj* famous and distinguished [Latin *illustris* bright, famous]

ll will *n* unkind feeling; hostility

llyria *n* an ancient region of uncertain boundaries on the E shore of the Adriatic Sea, including parts of present-day Croatia, Montenegro, and Albania

llyrian *n* **1** a member of the group of related Indo-European peoples who occupied Illyria from the late third millennium to the early first millennium BC **2** the extinct and almost unrecorded language of these peoples: of uncertain relationship within the Indo-European family, but thought by some to be the ancestor of modern Albanian ▷ *adj* **3** of, characteristic of, or relating to Illyria, its people, or their language

llyricum *n* a Roman province founded after 168 BC, based on the coastal area of Illyria

lmen *n* Lake Ilmen a lake in NW Russia, in the Novgorod Region: drains through the Volkhov River into Lake Ladoga. Area: between 780 sq km (300 sq miles) and 2200 sq km (850 sq miles), according to the season

loilo *n* a port in the W central Philippines, on SE Panay Island. Pop: 408 000 (2005 est)

lorin *n* a city in W Nigeria, capital of Kwara state: agricultural trade centre. Pop: 714 000 (2005 est)

lves *n* Toomas Hendrik. born 1953, Estonian politician, president of Estonia from 2006

lyushin *n* Sergei Vladimirovich. 1894–1977, Soviet aircraft designer. He designed the dive bomber Il-2 Stormovik and the jet airliner Il-62

IM instant messaging

im- *prefix* same as in-¹, in-²

'm I am

image *n* **1** a mental picture of someone or something produced by the imagination or memory **2** the appearance or impression given to the public by a person or organization **3** a simile or metaphor **4** a representation of a person or thing in a work of art or literature **5** an optical reproduction of an object, formed by the lens of an eye or camera, or by a mirror **6** a person or thing that resembles another closely **7** a personification of a specified quality; epitome: *the image of good breeding* ▷ *vb* **imaging, imaged 8** to picture in the mind **9** to mirror or reflect an image of **10** to portray or describe [Latin *imago*]

imagery *n, pl* **-ries 1** figurative or descriptive language in a literary work **2** mental images **3** images collectively, esp. statues or carvings

imaginary *adj* **1** existing only in the imagination **2** *maths* relating to the square root of a negative number

imagination *n* **1** the faculty or action of producing mental images of what is not present or in one's experience **2** creative mental ability

imaginative *adj* **1** produced by or showing a creative imagination **2** having a vivid imagination

imagine *vb* **-ining, -ined 1** to form a mental image of **2** to think, believe, or guess: *I would imagine they'll be here soon* [Latin *imaginari*] ▷ **imaginable** *adj*

imaginings *pl n* speculative thoughts about what might be the case or what might happen; fantasies: *lurid imaginings*

imago (im-**may**-go) *n, pl* **imagoes** or **imagines** (im-**maj**-in-eez) a sexually mature adult insect [Latin: likeness]

imam *n Islam* **1** a leader of congregational prayer in a mosque **2** the title of some Muslim leaders [Arabic]

IMAX (**eye**-max) *n* a film projection process that produces an image ten times larger than standard

imbalance *n* a lack of balance, for instance in emphasis or proportion: *a chemical imbalance in the brain*

imbecile (im-**biss**-eel) *n* **1** *informal* an extremely stupid person **2** *old-fashioned* a person of abnormally low intelligence ▷ *adj* **3** stupid or senseless: *imbecile fanaticism*

[Latin *imbecillus* feeble] ▷ **imbecility** *n*

imbed *vb* **-bedding, -bedded** same as **embed**

imbibe *vb* **-bibing, -bibed** *formal* **1** to drink (alcoholic drinks) **2** to take in or assimilate (ideas): *values she had imbibed as a child* [Latin *imbibere*]

imbroglio (imb-**role**-ee-oh) *n, pl* **-glios** a confusing and complicated situation [Italian]

Imbros *n* a Turkish island in the NE Aegean Sea, west of the Gallipoli Peninsula: occupied by Greece (1912–14) and Britain (1914–23). Area: 280 sq km (108 sq miles). Turkish name: **Imroz**

imbue *vb* **-buing, -bued** to fill or inspire (with ideals or principles) [Latin *imbuere* to stain]

IMF International Monetary Fund

Imhotep *n* c. 2600 BC, Egyptian physician and architect. After his death he was worshipped as a god; the Greeks identified him with Asclepius

imitate *vb* **-tating, -tated 1** to copy the manner or style of, or take as a model: *he remains rock's most imitated guitarist* **2** to mimic or impersonate, esp. for amusement **3** to make a copy of; reproduce or duplicate [Latin *imitari*] ▷ **imitable** *adj* ▷ **imitator** *n*

imitation *n* **1** a copy of an original or genuine article **2** an instance of imitating someone: *her Coward imitations were not the best thing she did* **3** behaviour modelled on the behaviour of someone else: *to learn by imitation* ▷ *adj* **4** made to resemble something which is usually superior or more expensive: *imitation leather*

imitative *adj* **1** imitating or tending to copy **2** copying or reproducing an original, esp. in an inferior manner: *imitative painting* **3** onomatopoeic

Imittós *n* a transliteration of the Modern Greek name for Hymettus

immaculate *adj* **1** completely clean or tidy: *an immaculate pinstripe suit* **2** completely flawless: *his equestrian pedigree is immaculate* [Latin *in-* not + *macula* blemish] ▷ **immaculately** *adv*

immanent *adj* **1** present within and throughout something **2** (of God) present throughout the universe [Latin *immanere* to remain in] ▷ **immanence** *n*

immaterial *adj* **1** of no real importance or relevance **2** not formed of matter

immature *adj* **1** not fully grown or developed **2** lacking wisdom, insight, or stability because of youth ▷ **immaturity** *n*

immeasurable *adj* too great to be measured ▷ **immeasurably** *adv*

immediate *adj* **1** taking place without delay: *an immediate cut in interest rates* **2** next or nearest in space, time, or relationship: *our immediate neighbour* **3** present; current: *they have no immediate plans to close it* [Latin *in-* not + *mediare* to be in the middle] ▷ **immediacy** *n* ▷ **immediately** *adv*

immemorial *adj* having existed or happened for longer than anyone can remember: *this has been the custom since time immemorial*

immense *adj* **1** huge or vast **2** *informal* very great [Latin *immensus* unmeasured] ▷ **immensely** *adv* ▷ **immensity** *n*

immerse *vb* **-mersing, -mersed 1** to plunge or dip into liquid **2** to involve deeply: *he immersed himself in the history of Rome* **3** to baptize by dipping the whole body into water [Latin *immergere*] ▷ **immersion** *n*

immersion heater *n* an electrical device in a domestic hot-water tank for heating water

immigrant *n* a person who comes to a foreign country in order to settle there

immigration *n* the act of coming to a foreign country in order to settle there [Latin *immigrare* to go into] ▷ **immigrate** *vb*

imminent *adj* likely to happen soon [Latin *imminere* to project over] ▷ **imminence** *n*

Immingham *n* a port in NE England, in North East Lincolnshire unitary authority, Lincolnshire: docks opened in 1912, principally for the exporting of coal; now handles chiefly bulk materials, esp. imported iron ore. Pop: 11 090 (2001)

immiscible *adj* (of liquids) incapable of being mixed: *oil and water are immiscible* > **immiscibility** *n*

immobile *adj* 1 not moving 2 not able to move or be moved > **immobility** *n*

immobilize *or* **-lise** *vb* **-lizing, -lized** *or* **-lising, -lised** to make unable to move or work: *a device for immobilizing steering wheels* > **immobilization** *or* **-lisation** *n*

immoderate *adj* excessive or unreasonable: *immoderate consumption of alcohol* > **immoderately** *adv*

immodest *adj* 1 behaving in an indecent or improper manner 2 behaving in a boastful or conceited manner > **immodesty** *n*

immolate *vb* **-lating, -lated** *literary* to kill or offer as a sacrifice, esp. by fire [Latin *immolare*] > **immolation** *n*

immoral *adj* 1 morally wrong; corrupt 2 sexually depraved or promiscuous > **immorality** *n*

immortal *adj* 1 not subject to death or decay 2 famous for all time 3 everlasting ▷ *n* 4 a person whose fame will last for all time 5 an immortal being > **immortality** *n*

immortalize *or* **-ise** *vb* **-izing, -ized** *or* **-ising, -ised** 1 to give everlasting fame to: *a name immortalized by countless writers* 2 to give immortality to

immovable *or* **immoveable** *adj* 1 unable to be moved 2 unwilling to change one's opinions or beliefs 3 not affected by feeling; emotionless 4 unchanging 5 *law* (of property) consisting of land or houses > **immovability** *or* **immoveability** *n* > **immovably** *or* **immoveably** *adv*

immune *adj* 1 protected against a specific disease by inoculation or as the result of natural resistance 2 exempt from obligation or penalty 3 **immune to** secure against: *football is not immune to economic recession* [Latin *immunis* exempt from a public service]

immune system *n* the mechanism by which a body reacts to foreign materials, involving the production of antibodies

immunity *n, pl* **-ties** 1 the ability of an organism to resist disease 2 freedom from prosecution, tax, etc.

immunize *or* **-nise** *vb* **-nizing, -nized** *or* **-nising, -nised** to make (someone) immune to a disease, esp. by inoculation > **immunization** *or* **-nisation** *n*

immunodeficiency *n* a deficiency in or breakdown of a person's ability to fight diseases

immunology *n* the branch of medicine concerned with the study of immunity > **immunological** *adj* > **immunologist** *n*

immure *vb* **-muring, -mured** 1 *archaic or literary* to imprison 2 to shut (oneself) away from society [Latin *im-* in + *murus* wall]

immutable (im-**mute**-a-bl) *adj* unchangeable or unchanging: *the immutable sequence of night and day* > **immutability** *n*

Imo *n* a state of SE Nigeria. Capital: Owerri. Pop: 3 934 899 (2006). Area: 5100 sq km (1969 sq miles)

imp *n* 1 a small demon 2 a mischievous child [Old English *impa* bud, hence offspring, child]

imp. 1 imperative 2 imperfect

impact *n* 1 the effect or impression made by something 2 the act of one object striking another; collision 3 the force of a collision ▷ *vb* 4 to press firmly against or into 5 **impact on** to have an effect on [Latin *impactus* pushed against] > **impaction** *n*

impacted *adj* (of a tooth) unable to grow out because of being wedged against another tooth below the gum

impair *vb* to damage or weaken in strength or quality [Old French *empeirer* to make worse] > **impairment** *n*

impala (imp-**ah**-la) *n, pl* **-las** *or* **-la** an African antelope with lyre-shaped horns [Zulu]

impale *vb* **-paling, -paled** to pierce through or fix with a sharp object: *they impaled his severed head on a spear* [Latin *im-* on + *palus* pole] > **impalement** *n*

impalpable *adj formal* 1 not able to be felt by touching:

impalpable shadows 2 difficult to understand > **impalpability** *n*

impart *vb* 1 to communicate (information or knowledge) 2 to give (a specified quality): *flavouring to impart a sweet taste* [Latin *im-* in + *partire* to share]

impartial *adj* not favouring one side or the other > **impartiality** *n* > **impartially** *adv*

impassable *adj* (of terrain or roads) not able to be travelled through or over > **impassability** *n*

impasse (am-**pass**) *n* a situation in which progress or escape is impossible [French]

impassible *adj* 1 *rare* not susceptible to pain or injury 2 impassive; unmoved > **impassibility** *or* **impassibleness** *n*

impassioned *adj* full of emotion: *an impassioned plea to the United Nations*

impassive *adj* not showing or feeling emotion > **impassively** *adv* > **impassivity** *n*

impasto *n* the technique of applying paint thickly, so that brush marks are evident [Italian]

impatient *adj* 1 irritable at any delay or difficulty 2 restless to have or do something > **impatience** *n* > **impatiently** *adv*

impeach *vb* 1 *chiefly US* to charge (a public official) with an offence committed in office 2 *Brit and Austral criminal law* to accuse of treason or serious crime 3 to challenge or question (a person's honesty or honour) [Late Latin *impedicare* to entangle] > **impeachable** *adj* > **impeachment** *n*

impeccable *adj* without flaw or error: *impeccable manners* [Latin *in-* not + *peccare* to sin] > **impeccably** *adv*

impecunious *adj formal* without money; penniless [Latin *in-* not + *pecuniosus* wealthy]

impedance (imp-**eed**-anss) *n electronics* the total effectiv resistance in an electric circuit to the flow of an alternating current

impede *vb* **-peding, -peded** to block or make progress or action difficult [Latin *impedire*]

impediment *n* 1 a hindrance or obstruction 2 a physica disability that makes speech or walking difficult

impedimenta *pl n* any objects that impede progress, esp. the baggage and equipment carried by an army

impel *vb* **-pelling, -pelled** 1 to urge or force (a person) to do something 2 to push, drive, or force into motion [Latin *impellere* to drive forward]

impending *adj* (esp. of something bad) about to happen [Latin *impendere* to overhang]

impenetrable *adj* 1 impossible to get through: *an impenetrable barrier* 2 impossible to understand 3 not receptive to ideas or influence: *impenetrable ignorance* > **impenetrability** *n* > **impenetrably** *adv*

impenitent *adj* not sorry or penitent > **impenitence** *n*

imperative *adj* 1 extremely urgent; essential 2 commanding or authoritative: *an imperative tone of voice* 3 *grammar* denoting a mood of verbs used in commands ▷ *n* 4 *grammar* the imperative mood [Latin *imperare* to command]

imperceptible *adj* too slight, subtle, or gradual to be noticed > **imperceptibly** *adv*

imperfect *adj* 1 having faults or errors 2 not complete 3 *grammar* denoting a tense of verbs describing continuous, incomplete, or repeated past actions ▷ *n* 4 *grammar* the imperfect tense > **imperfectly** *adv*

imperfection *n* 1 the state of being imperfect 2 a fault or defect

imperial *adj* 1 of an empire, emperor, or empress 2 majestic; commanding 3 exercising supreme authority; imperious 4 (of weights or measures) conforming to the standards of a system formerly official in Great Britain ▷ *n* 5 a wine bottle holding the equivalent of eight normal bottles [Latin *imperium* authority]

imperialism *n* 1 the policy or practice of extending a country's influence over other territories by conquest, colonization, or economic domination **2** an imperial system, authority, or government **> imperialist** *adj*, *n* **> imperialistic** *adj*

imperil *vb* **-rilling, -rilled** or US **-riling, -riled** *formal* to put in danger

imperious *adj* used to being obeyed; domineering [Latin *imperium* power] **> imperiously** *adv*

imperishable *adj* unable to disappear or be destroyed

impermanent *adj* not permanent; fleeting **> impermanence** *n*

impermeable *adj* (of a substance) not allowing fluid to pass through: *an impermeable layer* **> impermeability** *n*

impermissible *adj* not allowed

impersonal *adj* **1** without reference to any individual person; objective: *Buddhism began as a very impersonal doctrine* **2** without human warmth or sympathy: *an impersonal manner* **3** *grammar* **a** (of a verb) having no subject, as in *it is raining* **b** (of a pronoun) not referring to a person **> impersonality** *n* **> impersonally** *adv*

impersonate *vb* **-ating, -ated 1** to pretend to be (another person) **2** to imitate the character or mannerisms of (another person) for entertainment **> impersonation** *n* **> impersonator** *n*

impertinent *adj* disrespectful or rude [Latin *impertinens* not belonging] **> impertinence** *n*

imperturbable *adj* not easily upset; calm **> imperturbability** *n* **> imperturbably** *adv*

impervious *adj* **1** not letting water etc. through **2** not influenced by a feeling, argument, etc.

impetigo (imp-it-**tie**-go) *n* a contagious skin disease causing spots or pimples [Latin: scabby eruption]

impetuous *adj* **1** acting without consideration **2** done rashly or hastily [Late Latin *impetuosus* violent] **> impetuosity** *n*

impetus (imp-it-**uss**) *n*, *pl* **-tuses 1** an incentive or impulse **2** *physics* the force that starts a body moving or that tends to resist changes in its speed or direction once it is moving [Latin: attack]

Imphal *n* a city in NE India, capital of Manipur Territory, on the Manipur River: formerly the seat of the Manipur kings: site of a major Anglo-Indian victory over the Japanese (1944), which was a turning point in the British recovery of Burma (now officially called Myanmar). Pop: 217 275 (2001)

impi *n*, *pl* **-pi** or **-pies** a group of Zulu warriors [Nguni (language group of southern Africa) *impi* regiment, army]

impiety *n* lack of respect or religious reverence

impinge *vb* **-pinging, -pinged** (often foll. by on) to encroach (on), affect or restrict: *international economic forces impinging on the local economy* [Latin *impingere* to dash against] **> impingement** *n*

impious (imp-e-**uss**) *adj* showing a lack of respect or religious reverence

impish *adj* mischievous **> impishness** *n*

implacable *adj* **1** incapable of being appeased or pacified **2** unyielding **> implacability** *n* **> implacably** *adv*

implant *vb* **1** to fix firmly in the mind: *to implant sound moral principles* **2** to plant or embed **3** *surgery* to graft or insert (a tissue or hormone) into the body ▷ *n* **4** anything implanted in the body, such as a tissue graft **> implantation** *n*

implausible *adj* not easy to believe **> implausibility** *n*

implement *vb* **1** to carry out (instructions etc.): *she refused to implement the agreed plan* ▷ *n* **2** a tool or other piece of equipment [Late Latin *implementum*, literally: a filling up] **> implementation** *n*

implicate *vb* **-cating, -cated 1** to show (someone) to be involved, esp. in a crime **2** to imply [Latin *implicare* to involve]

implication *n* **1** something that is suggested or implied **2** an act or instance of suggesting, implying, or being implied **3** a probable consequence (of something)

implicit *adj* **1** expressed indirectly: *an implicit agreement* **2** absolute and unquestioning: *implicit trust* **3** contained

in, although not stated openly: *this view of the mind was implicit in all his work* [Latin *implicitus*] **> implicitly** *adv*

implied *adj* hinted at or suggested: *an implied criticism*

implode *vb* **-ploding, -ploded** to collapse inwards [*im-* in + *(ex)plode*]

implore *vb* **1** to bring in (goods) from another country beg desperately [Latin *implorare*]

imply *vb* **-plies, -plying, -plied 1** to express or indicate by a hint; suggest **2** to suggest or involve as a necessary consequence: *a spending commitment implies a corresponding tax imposition* [Old French *emplier*]

USAGE See at **infer**.

---

impolite *adj* discourteous; rude **> impoliteness** *n*

impolitic *adj* ill-advised; unwise

imponderable *adj* **1** unable to be weighed or assessed ▷ *n* **2** something difficult or impossible to assess

import *vb* **1** to bring in (goods) from another country **2** *formal* to signify; mean: *to import doom* ▷ *n* **3** something imported **4** *formal* importance: *his new work is of great import* **5** meaning **6** *Canad slang* a sportsman who is not native to the area where he plays [Latin *importare* to carry in] **> importer** *n* **> importation** *n*

important *adj* **1** of great significance, value, or consequence **2** of social significance: *an important man in the company hierarchy* **3** of great concern: *it was important to me to know* [Medieval Latin *importare* to signify, from Latin: to carry in] **> importance** *n* **> importantly** *adv*

USAGE The use of *more importantly* as in *more importantly, the local council is opposed to this proposal* has become very common, but many people still prefer to use *more important*.

---

importunate *adj* *formal* persistent or demanding

importune *vb* **-tuning, -tuned** *formal* to harass with persistent requests [Latin *importunus* tiresome] **> importunity** *n*

impose *vb* **-posing, -posed 1** to establish (a rule, condition, etc.) as something to be obeyed or complied with **2** to force (oneself) on others **3** *printing* to arrange (pages) in the correct order for printing **4** to pass off (something) deceptively on someone **5** *impose on* to take advantage of (a person or quality): *she imposed on his kindness* [Latin *imponere* to place upon]

imposing *adj* grand or impressive: *an imposing building*

imposition *n* **1** the act of imposing **2** something imposed, esp. unfairly on someone **3** the arrangement of pages for printing **4** *old-fashioned* a task set as a school punishment

impossibility *n*, *pl* **-ties 1** the state or quality of being impossible **2** something that is impossible

impossible *adj* **1** not able to be done or to happen **2** absurd or unreasonable **3** *informal* intolerable or outrageous: *those children are impossible* **> impossibly** *adv*

impostor or **imposter** *n* a person who cheats or swindles by pretending to be someone else [Late Latin *impostor* deceiver]

imposture *n* *formal* deception, esp. by pretending to be someone else

impotent (imp-a-**tent**) *adj* **1** not having the power to influence people or events **2** (of a man) incapable of sexual intercourse **> impotence** *n*

impound *vb* **1** to take legal possession of; confiscate **2** to confine (an animal) in a pound

impoverish *vb* **1** to make (someone) poor **2** weaken the quality of something [Old French *empovrir*] **> impoverished** *adj* **> impoverishment** *n*

impracticable *adj* **1** not able to be put into practice **2** unsuitable for a desired use **> impracticability** *n*

impractical *adj* **1** not sensible or workable: *the use of force was viewed as impractical* **2** not having practical skills **> impracticality** *n*

imprecation *n formal* a curse [Latin *imprecari* to invoke]
> **imprecate** *vb*

imprecise *adj* inexact or inaccurate > **imprecision** *n*

impregnable *adj* **1** unable to be broken into or taken by force: *an impregnable fortress* **2** unable to be affected or overcome: *a confident, impregnable person* [Old French *imprenable*] > **impregnability** *n*

impregnate *vb* **-nating, -nated** **1** to saturate, soak, or fill throughout **2** to make pregnant **3** to imbue or permeate: *the party has been impregnated with an enthusiasm for reform* [Latin *in-* in + *praegnans* pregnant] > **impregnation** *n*

impresario *n, pl* **-sarios** a person who runs theatre performances, concerts, etc. [Italian]

impress *vb* **1** to make a strong, lasting, or favourable impression on: *he was impressed by the standard of play* **2** to stress or emphasize **3** to imprint or stamp by pressure: *a pattern impressed in paint on the rock* ▷ *n* **4** an impressing **5** a mark produced by impressing [Latin *imprimere* to press into] > **impressible** *adj*

impression *n* **1** an effect produced in the mind by a person or thing: *she was keen to create a relaxed impression* **2** a vague idea or belief: *he only had a vague impression of how it worked* **3** a strong, favourable, or remarkable effect **4** an impersonation for entertainment **5** an imprint or mark produced by pressing **6** *printing* the number of copies of a publication printed at one time

impressionable *adj* easily impressed or influenced: *the promotion of smoking to the impressionable young* > **impressionability** *n*

Impressionism *n* a style of painting developed in 19th-century France, with the aim of reproducing the immediate impression or mood of things, esp. the effects of light and atmosphere, rather than form or structure

impressionist *n* **1** **Impressionist** an artist who painted in the style of Impressionism **2** a person who imitates the character or mannerisms of another person for entertainment

impressionistic *adj* **1** **Impressionistic** of or about Impressionism **2** based on subjective observations or impressions rather than systematic study or facts: *Mitchell was making impressionistic documentaries*

impressive *adj* capable of impressing, esp. by size, magnificence, or importance > **impressively** *adv*

imprimatur (imp-rim-ah-ter) *n* official approval for something to be printed, usually given by the Roman Catholic Church [New Latin: let it be printed]

imprint *n* **1** a mark or impression produced by pressing, printing, or stamping **2** the publisher's name and address, often with the date of publication, printed on the title page of a book ▷ *vb* **3** to produce (a mark) by pressing, printing, or stamping: *T-shirts imprinted with slogans* **4** to establish firmly; impress: *he couldn't dislodge the images imprinted on his brain*

imprison *vb* to confine in or as if in prison
> **imprisonment** *n*

improbable *adj* not likely or probable > **improbability** *n*
> **improbably** *adv*

improbity *n, pl* **-ties** *formal* dishonesty or wickedness

impromptu *adj* **1** without planning or preparation; improvised ▷ *adv* **2** in a spontaneous or improvised way: *he spoke impromptu* ▷ *n* **3** a short piece of instrumental music resembling improvisation **4** something that is impromptu [Latin *in promptu* in readiness]

improper *adj* **1** indecent **2** irregular or incorrect
> **improperly** *adv*

improper fraction *n* a fraction in which the numerator is greater than the denominator, as 7/6

impropriety (imp-roe-pry-a-tee) *n, pl* **-ties** *formal* unsuitable or slightly improper behaviour

improve *vb* **-proving, -proved** **1** to make or become better in quality **2** **improve on** to achieve a better standard or quality in comparison with: *both had improved on their previous performance* [Anglo-French *emprouer* to turn to profit] > **improvable** *adj*

improvement *n* **1** the act of improving or the state of being improved **2** a change that makes something better or adds to its value: *home improvements* **3** *Austral and NZ* a building on a piece of land, adding to its value

improvident *adj* **1** not providing for the future **2** incautious or rash > **improvidence** *n*

improvise *vb* **-vising, -vised** **1** to do or make quickly from whatever is available, without previous planning **2** to make up (a piece of music, speech, etc.) as one goes along [Latin *improvisus* unforeseen] > **improvisation** *n*

imprudent *adj* not carefully thought out; rash
> **imprudence** *n*

impudent *adj* impertinent or insolent [Latin *impudens* shameless] > **impudence** *n* > **impudently** *adv*

impugn (imp-yoon) *vb formal* to challenge or attack as false [Latin *impugnare* to fight against] > **impugnment** *n*

impulse *n* **1** a sudden desire or whim **2** an instinctive drive; urge: *the mothering impulse* **3** *physics* **a** the product of a force acting on a body and the time for which it acts **b** the change in the momentum of a body as a result of a force acting upon it **4** *physiol* a stimulus transmitted in a nerve or muscle [Latin *impulsus* incitement]

impulsive *adj* **1** tending to act without thinking first: *an impulsive man* **2** done without thinking first **3** forceful or impelling

impunity (imp-yoon-it-ee) *n* with impunity without punishment or unpleasant consequences [Latin *impunis* unpunished]

impure *adj* **1** having unwanted substances mixed in **2** immoral or obscene: *impure thoughts* **3** dirty or unclean

impurity *n, pl* **-ties** **1** an impure element or thing: *impurities in the water* **2** the quality of being impure

impute *vb* **-puting, -puted** **1** to attribute (blame or a crime) to a person **2** to attribute to a source or cause: *I impute your success to nepotism* [Latin *in-* in + *putare* to think]
> **imputation** *n*

Imran Khan *n* full name *Imran Ahmad Khan Niazi*. born 1952, Pakistani cricketer and politician: an all-rounder, he played in 88 test matches and captained Pakistan to victory in the 1992 World Cup

Imroz *n* the Turkish name for **Imbros**

in *prep* **1** inside; within: *in the room* **2** at a place where there is: *in the shade* **3** indicating a state, situation, or condition: *in silence* **4** when (a period of time) has elapsed: *come back in one year* **5** using: *written in code* **6** wearing: *the man in the blue suit* **7** with regard to (a specified activity or occupation): *in journalism* **8** while performing the action of: *in crossing the street he was run over* **9** having as purpose: *in honour of the president* **10** (of certain animals) pregnant with: *in calf* **11** into: *he fell in the water* **12** **have it in one** to have the ability (to do something) **13** **in that** *or* **in so far as** because or to the extent that: *it was of great help in that it gave me more confidence* ▷ *adv* **14** in or into a particular place; indoors: *come in* **15** at one's home or place of work: *he's not in at the moment* **16** in office or power: *the Conservatives got in at the last election* **17** so as to enclose: *block in* **18** (in certain games) so as to take one's turn of the play: *you have to get the other side out before you go in* **19** *Brit* (of a fire) alight **20** (*in combination*) indicating an activity or gathering, esp. one organized to protest against something: *teach-in*; *work-in* **21** **have got it in for** *informal* to wish or intend harm towards **22** **in for** about to experience (something, esp. something unpleasant): *they're in for a shock* **23** **in on** acquainted with or sharing in: *I was in on all his plans* **24** **in with** friendly with ▷ *adj* **25** fashionable; modish: *the in thing to do* ▷ *n* **26** **ins and outs** the detailed points or facts (of a situation) [Old English]

In *chem* indium

IN Indiana

in. inch(es)

in-¹, il-, im- *or* **ir-** *prefix* **a** not; non: *incredible*; *illegal*; *imperfect*; *irregular* **b** lack of: *inexperience* [Latin]

in-², **il-**, **im-** *or* **ir-** *prefix* in; into; towards; within; on: *infiltrate* [from *in*]

inability *n* the fact of not being able to do something

in absentia *adv* in the absence of (someone indicated) [Latin]

inaccessible *adj* 1 impossible or very difficult to reach 2 unable to be used or seen: *his works are inaccessible to English-speaking readers* 3 difficult to understand or appreciate: *Webern's music is still considered inaccessible* > **inaccessibility** *n*

inaccuracy *n, pl* **-cies** 1 lack of accuracy; imprecision 2 an error or mistake > **inaccurate** *adj*

inaction *n* lack of action; inertia

inactive *adj* 1 idle; not active 2 *chem* (of a substance) having little or no reactivity > **inactivity** *n*

inadequacy *n, pl* **-cies** 1 lack or shortage 2 the state of being or feeling inferior 3 a weakness or failing: *their own failures or inadequacies*

inadequate *adj* 1 not enough; insufficient 2 not good enough > **inadequately** *adv*

inadmissible *adj* not allowable or acceptable

inadvertent *adj* done unintentionally > **inadvertence** *n* > **inadvertently** *adv*

inadvisable *adj* unwise; not sensible

inalienable *adj* not able to be taken away or transferred to another: *the inalienable rights of the citizen*

inamorata *or masc* **inamorato** *n, pl* **-tas** *or masc* **-tos** *literary* a sweetheart or lover [Italian *innamorata, innamorato*]

inane *adj* senseless or silly: *inane remarks* [Latin *inanis* empty] > **inanity** *n*

inanimate *adj* lacking the qualities of living beings: *inanimate objects*

inanition *n formal* exhaustion or weakness, as from lack of food [Latin *inanis* empty]

inapplicable *adj* not suitable or relevant

inapposite *adj* not suitable or appropriate > **inappositeness** *n*

inappropriate *adj* not suitable or proper > **inappropriately** *adv*

inapt *adj* 1 not apt or fitting 2 lacking skill > **inaptitude** *n*

inarticulate *adj* unable to express oneself clearly or well

inasmuch as *conj* 1 since; because 2 in so far as

inattentive *adj* not paying attention > **inattention** *n*

inaudible *adj* not loud enough to be heard > **inaudibly** *adv*

inaugural *adj* 1 of or for an inauguration ▷ *n* 2 US a speech made at an inauguration

inaugurate *vb* **-rating, -rated** 1 to open or celebrate the first public use of ceremonially: *the newest electrified line was inaugurated today* 2 to formally establish (a new leader) in office 3 to begin officially or formally [Latin *inaugurare* to take omens, hence to install in office after taking auguries] > **inauguration** *n* > **inaugurator** *n*

inauspicious *adj* unlucky; suggesting an unfavourable outcome

inboard *adj* 1 (of a boat's motor or engine) situated within the hull 2 situated close to the fuselage of an aircraft ▷ *adv* 3 within the sides of, or towards the centre of, a vessel or aircraft

inborn *adj* existing from birth: *an inborn sense of optimism*

inbox *n* a folder in a computer mailbox in which incoming messages are stored

inbred *adj* 1 produced as a result of inbreeding 2 inborn or ingrained: *inbred good manners*

inbreed *vb* **-breeding, -bred** to breed from closely related individuals

inbreeding *n* breeding from closely related individuals

inbuilt *adj* (of a quality or feeling) present from the beginning: *an inbuilt prejudice*

Inc. *US and Austral* (of a company) incorporated

Inca *n* 1 (*pl* **Inca** *or* **Incas**) a member of a S American indigenous people whose empire, centred on Peru, lasted until the early 1530s 2 the language of this people

incalculable *adj* impossible to estimate or predict > **incalculability** *n*

in camera *adv* in private session: *the proceedings were held in camera* [Latin]

incandescent *adj* 1 glowing with heat 2 (of artificial light) produced by a glowing filament [Latin *incandescere* to glow] > **incandescence** *n*

incandescent lamp *n* a lamp that contains a filament which is electrically heated to incandescence

incantation *n* 1 ritual chanting of magic words or sounds 2 a magic spell [Latin *incantare* to repeat magic formulas] > **incantatory** *adj*

incapable *adj* 1 helpless: *drunk and incapable* 2 **incapable of** lacking the ability to

incapacitate *vb* **-tating, -tated** to deprive (a person) of strength, power, or ability; disable

incapacity *n, pl* **-ties** 1 lack of power, strength, or ability 2 *law* legal disqualification or ineligibility

incarcerate *vb* **-rating, -rated** *formal* to confine or imprison [Latin *in-* in + *carcer* prison] > **incarceration** *n*

incarnate *adj* 1 possessing human form: *a devil incarnate* 2 personified or typified: *stupidity incarnate* ▷ *vb* **-nating, -nated** 3 to give a bodily or concrete form to 4 to be representative or typical of [Late Latin *incarnare* to make flesh]

incarnation *n* 1 the act of embodying or state of being embodied in human form 2 a person or thing that typifies some quality or idea

Incarnation *n Christian theol* God's coming to earth in human form as Jesus Christ

incautious *adj* (of a person or action) careless or rash

incendiary (in-send-ya-ree) *adj* 1 (of bombs etc.) designed to cause fires 2 tending to create strife or violence 3 relating to the illegal burning of property or goods ▷ *n, pl* **-aries** 4 a bomb that is designed to start fires 5 a person who illegally sets fire to property or goods [Latin *incendere* to kindle] > **incendiarism** *n*

incense¹ *n* 1 an aromatic substance burnt for its fragrant odour, esp. in religious ceremonies 2 the odour or smoke so produced ▷ *vb* **-censing, -censed** 3 to burn incense to (a deity) 4 to perfume or fumigate with incense [Church Latin *incensum*]

incense² *vb* **-censing, -censed** to make very angry [Latin *incensus* set on fire] > **incensed** *adj*

incentive *n* 1 something that encourages effort or action 2 an additional payment made to employees to increase production ▷ *adj* 3 encouraging greater effort: *an incentive scheme for workers* [Latin *incentivus* setting the tune]

inception *n* the beginning of a project [Latin *incipere* to begin]

incessant *adj* never stopping [Latin *in-* not + *cessare* to cease] > **incessantly** *adv*

incest *n* sexual intercourse between two people who are too closely related to marry [Latin *in-* not + *castus* chaste] > **incestuous** *adj*

inch *n* 1 a unit of length equal to one twelfth of a foot (2.54cm) 2 *meteorol* the amount of rain or snow that would cover a surface to a depth of one inch 3 a very small distance, degree, or amount: *neither side was prepared to give an inch* 4 **every inch** in every way: *she arrived looking every inch a star* 5 **inch by inch** gradually 6 **within an inch of** one's life almost to death ▷ *vb* 7 to move very slowly or gradually: *I inched my way to the bar* [Old English *ynce*]

inchoate (in-koe-ate) *adj formal* just begun and not yet properly developed [Latin *incohare* to make a beginning]

Inchon *or* **Incheon** *n* a port in W South Korea, on the Yellow Sea: the chief port for Seoul; site of a major strategic amphibious assault by UN troops, liberating Seoul (Sept 15, 1950). Pop: 2 642 000 (2005 est.). Former name: **Chemulpo**

incidence *n* 1 extent or frequency of occurrence: *the rising incidence of car fires* 2 *physics* the arrival of a beam of light or particles at a surface **3** *geometry* the partial overlapping of two figures or a figure and a line

incident *n* **1** an occurrence or event, esp. a minor one **2** a relatively insignificant event that might have serious consequences **3** a public disturbance ▷ *adj* **4** *physics* (of a beam of light or particles) arriving at or striking a surface **5 incident to** *formal* likely to occur in connection with: *the dangers are incident to a policeman's job* [Latin *incidere* to happen]

incidental *adj* **1** happening in connection with or resulting from something more important **2** secondary or minor: *incidental expenses* ▷ **incidentally** *adv*

incidental music *n* background music for a film or play

incidentals *pl n* minor expenses, events, or action

incinerate *vb* **-ating, -ated** to burn up completely [Latin *in-* to + *cinis* ashes] ▷ **incineration** *n*

incinerator *n* a furnace for burning rubbish

incipient *adj formal* just starting to be or happen [Latin *incipere* to begin]

incise *vb* **-cising, -cised** to cut into with a sharp tool [Latin *incidere* to cut into]

incision *n* a cut, esp. one made during a surgical operation

incisive *adj* direct and forceful: *witty and incisive comments*

incisor *n* a sharp cutting tooth at the front of the mouth

incite *vb* **-citing, -cited** to stir up or provoke to action [Latin *in-* in, on + *citare* to excite] ▷ **incitement** *n*

incivility *n, pl* **-ties 1** rudeness **2** an impolite act or remark

incl. 1 including **2** inclusive

inclement *adj formal* (of weather) stormy or severe ▷ **inclemency** *n*

inclination *n* **1** a liking, tendency, or preference: *he showed no inclination to change his routine* **2** the degree of slope from a horizontal or vertical plane **3** a slope or slant **4** *surveying* the angular distance of the horizon below the plane of observation

incline *vb* **-clining, -clined 1** to veer from a vertical or horizontal plane; slope or slant **2** to have or cause to have a certain tendency or disposition: *that does not incline me to think that you are right* **3** to bend or lower (part of the body, esp. the head) **4 incline one's ear** to listen favourably ▷ *n* **5** an inclined surface or slope [Latin *inclinare* to cause to lean] ▷ **inclined** *adj*

inclined plane *n* a sloping plane used to enable a load to be raised or lowered by pushing or sliding, which requires less force than lifting

include *vb* **-cluding, -cluded 1** to have as part of the whole **2** to put in as part of a set, group, or category [Latin *in-* in + *claudere* to close]

inclusion *n* **1** an including or being included **2** something included

inclusive *adj* **1** including everything: *capital inclusive of profit* **2** including the limits specified: *Monday to Friday inclusive* **3** comprehensive

incognito (in-kog-nee-toe) *adv, adj* **1** under an assumed name or appearance ▷ *n, pl* **-tos 2** a false identity **3** a person who is incognito [Latin *incognitus* unknown]

incognizant *adj* **incognizant of** unaware of ▷ **incognizance** *n*

incoherent *adj* **1** unable to express oneself clearly **2** not logically connected or ordered: *an incoherent argument* ▷ **incoherence** *n*

income *n* the total amount of money earned from work or obtained from other sources over a given period of time

income support *n* (in Britain) an allowance paid by the government to people with a very low income

income tax *n* a personal tax levied on annual income

incoming *adj* **1** about to arrive **2** about to come into office

incommensurable *adj* **1** not able to be judged, measured, or compared **2** *maths* not having a common divisor other than 1, such as 2 and √-5

▷ **incommensurability** *n*

incommensurate *adj* **1** inadequate or disproportionate: *gains incommensurate with the risk involved* **2** incommensurable

incommode *vb* **-moding, -moded** *formal* to bother, disturb, or inconvenience [Latin *incommodus* inconvenient]

incommodious *adj formal* inconveniently small; cramped

incommunicado *adv, adj* not allowed to communicate with other people, for instance while in solitary confinement [Spanish *incomunicado*]

incomparable *adj* so excellent as to be beyond or above comparison ▷ **incomparably** *adv*

incompatible *adj* not able to exist together in harmony; conflicting or inconsistent ▷ **incompatibility** *n*

incompetent *adj* **1** not having the necessary ability or skill to do something **2** *law* not legally qualified: *an incompetent witness* ▷ *n* **3** an incompetent person ▷ **incompetence** *n*

incomplete *adj* not finished or whole

incomprehension *n* inability to understand ▷ **incomprehensible** *adj*

inconceivable *adj* so unlikely to be true as to be unthinkable ▷ **inconceivability** *n*

inconclusive *adj* not giving a final decision or result

incongruous *adj* out of place; inappropriate: *an incongruous figure among the tourists* ▷ **incongruity** *n* ▷ **incongruously** *adv*

inconnu (in-kon-new) *n Canad* a whitefish of Arctic waters [French, literally: unknown]

inconsequential *or* **inconsequent** *adj* **1** unimportant or insignificant **2** not following logically as a consequence ▷ **inconsequentially** *adv*

inconsiderable *adj* **1** not worth considering; insignificant **2 not inconsiderable** fairly large: *he gets not inconsiderable royalties from his musicals* ▷ **inconsiderably** *adv*

inconsiderate *adj* lacking in care or thought for others; thoughtless ▷ **inconsiderateness** *n*

inconsistent *adj* **1** unstable or changeable in behaviour or mood **2** containing contradictory elements: *an inconsistent argument* **3** not in accordance: *actions inconsistent with high office* ▷ **inconsistency** *n*

inconsolable *adj* very distressed ▷ **inconsolably** *adv*

inconspicuous *adj* not easily noticed or seen

inconstant *adj* **1** liable to change one's loyalties or opinions **2** variable: *their household income is inconstant* ▷ **inconstancy** *n*

incontestable *adj* impossible to deny or argue with

incontinent *adj* **1** unable to control the bladder and bowels **2** lacking self-restraint, esp. sexually [Latin *in-* not + *continere* to restrain] ▷ **incontinence** *n*

incontrovertible *adj* absolutely certain; undeniable ▷ **incontrovertibly** *adv*

inconvenience *n* **1** a state or instance of trouble or difficulty ▷ *vb* **-iencing, -ienced 2** to cause trouble or difficulty to (someone) ▷ **inconvenient** *adj*

incorporate *vb* **-rating, -rated 1** to include or be included as part of a larger unit **2** to form a united whole or mass **3** to form into a corporation ▷ *adj* **4** incorporated [Latin *in-* in + *corpus* body] ▷ **incorporated** *adj* ▷ **incorporation** *n*

incorporeal *adj* without material form, substance, or existence

incorrect *adj* **1** wrong: *an incorrect answer* **2** not proper: *incorrect behaviour* ▷ **incorrectly** *adv*

incorrigible *adj* (of a person or behaviour) beyond correction or reform; incurably bad ▷ **incorrigibility** *n* ▷ **incorrigibly** *adv*

incorruptible *adj* **1** too honest to be bribed or corrupted **2** not prone to decay or disintegration ▷ **incorruptibility** *n*

increase *vb* **-creasing, -creased 1** to make or become greater in size, degree, or frequency ▷ *n* **2** a rise in size, degree, or frequency **3** the amount by which something increases **4 on the increase** becoming more common [Latin *in-* in + *crescere* to grow] **〉increasingly** *adv*

incredible *adj* **1** unbelievable **2** *informal* marvellous; amazing **〉incredibility** *n* **〉incredibly** *adv*

incredulity *n* unwillingness to believe

incredulous *adj* not prepared or willing to believe something

increment *n* **1** the amount by which something increases **2** a regular salary increase **3** *maths* a small positive or negative change in a variable or function [Latin *incrementum* increase] **〉incremental** *adj*

incriminate *vb* **-nating, -nated 1** to make (someone) seem guilty of a crime **2** to charge (someone) with a crime [Late Latin *incriminare* to accuse] **〉incrimination** *n* **〉incriminatory** *adj*

incrust *vb* same as **encrust**

incubate (in-cube-ate) *vb* **-bating, -bated 1** (of birds) to hatch (eggs) by sitting on them **2** to cause (bacteria) to develop, esp. in an incubator or culture medium **3** (of disease germs) to remain inactive in an animal or human before causing disease **4** to develop gradually [Latin *incubare*] **〉incubation** *n*

incubator *n* **1** *med* a heated enclosed apparatus for rearing premature babies **2** an apparatus for hatching birds' eggs or growing bacterial cultures

incubus (in-cube-uss) *n, pl* **-bi** or **-buses 1** a demon believed in folklore to have sexual intercourse with sleeping women **2** a nightmarish burden or worry [Latin *incubare* to lie upon]

inculcate *vb* **-cating, -cated** to fix in someone's mind by constant repetition [Latin *inculcare* to tread upon] **〉inculcation** *n*

inculpate *vb* **-pating, -pated** *formal* to incriminate [Latin *in-* on + *culpare* to blame]

incumbency *n, pl* **-cies** the office, duty, or tenure of an incumbent

incumbent *formal n* **1** a person who holds a particular office or position ▷ *adj* **2** morally binding as a duty: *it is incumbent on cricketers to respect the umpire's impartiality* [Latin *incumbere* to lie upon]

incur *vb* **-curring, -curred** to bring (something undesirable) upon oneself [Latin *incurrere* to run into]

incurable *adj* **1** not able to be cured: *an incurable tumour* **2** not able to be changed: *he is an incurable romantic* ▷ *n* **3** a person with an incurable disease **〉incurability** *n* **〉incurably** *adv*

incurious *adj* showing no curiosity or interest **〉incuriously** *adv*

incursion *n* **1** a sudden or brief invasion **2** an inroad or encroachment: *a successful incursion into the American book-shop market* [Latin *incursio* attack] **〉incursive** *adj*

Ind *n* **1** a poetic name for **India 2** an obsolete name for the **Indies**

ind. 1 independent **2** index **3** indicative **4** indirect **5** industrial

Ind. 1 Independent **2** India **3** Indian **4** Indiana **5** Indies

indaba (in-dah-ba) *n* **1** (among native peoples of southern Africa) a meeting to discuss a serious topic **2** *S African informal* a matter of concern or for discussion [Zulu]

indebted *adj* **1** owing gratitude for help or favours **2** owing money **〉indebtedness** *n*

indecent *adj* **1** morally or sexually offensive **2** unseemly or improper: *indecent haste* **〉indecency** *n* **〉indecently** *adv*

indecent assault *n* a sexual attack which does not include rape

indecent exposure *n* the showing of one's genitals in public

indecipherable *adj* impossible to read

indecisive *adj* **1** unable to make decisions **2** not decisive or conclusive: *an indecisive argument* **〉indecision** or **indecisiveness** *n*

indeed *adv* **1** certainly; actually: *indeed, the sea featured heavily in his poems* **2** truly, very: *it has become a dangerous place indeed* **3** in fact; what is more: *it is necessary, indeed indispensable* ▷ *interj* **4** an expression of doubt or surprise

indefatigable *adj* never getting tired or giving up: *Mitterrand was an indefatigable organizer* [Latin *in-* not + *defatigare*, from *fatigare* to tire] **〉indefatigably** *adv*

indefensible *adj* **1** (of behaviour or statements) unable to be justified or supported **2** (of places or buildings) impossible to defend against attack **〉indefensibility** *n*

indefinable *adj* difficult to describe or explain completely

indefinite *adj* **1** without exact limits: *an indefinite number* **2** vague or unclear **〉indefinitely** *adv*

indefinite article *n grammar* either of the words 'a' or 'an'

indelible *adj* **1** impossible to erase or remove **2** making indelible marks: *indelible ink* [Latin *in-* not + *delere* to destroy] **〉indelibly** *adv*

indelicate *adj* **1** offensive, embarrassing, or tasteless **2** coarse, crude, or rough **〉indelicacy** *n*

indemnify *vb* **-fies, -fying, -fied 1** to secure against loss, damage, or liability **2** to compensate for loss or damage **〉indemnification** *n*

indemnity *n, pl* **-ties 1** insurance against loss or damage **2** compensation for loss or damage **3** legal exemption from penalties incurred [Latin *in-* not + *damnum* damage]

indent *vb* **1** to start (a line of writing) further from the margin than the other lines **2** to order (goods) using a special order form **3** to notch (an edge or border) **4** to write out (a document) in duplicate **5** to bind (an apprentice) by indenture ▷ *n* **6** *chiefly Brit* an official order for goods, esp. foreign merchandise [Latin *in-* in + *dens* tooth]

indentation *n* **1** a hollow, notch, or cut, as on an edge or on a coastline **2** an indenting or being indented **3** Also: **indention** the leaving of space or the amount of space left between a margin and the start of an indented line

indenture *n* **1** a contract, esp. one binding an apprentice to his or her employer ▷ *vb* **-turing, -tured 2** to bind (an apprentice) by indenture **3** to enter into an agreement by indenture

Independence *n* a city in W Missouri, near Kansas City: starting point for the Santa Fe, Oregon, and California Trails (1831–44). Pop: 112 079 (2003 est)

independent *adj* **1** free from the influence or control of others **2** not dependent on anything else for function or validity **3** not relying on the support, esp. financial support, of others **4** capable of acting for oneself or on one's own **5** of or having a private income large enough to enable one to live without working: *independent means* **6** *maths* (of a variable) not dependent on another variable ▷ *n* **7** an independent person or thing **8** a politician who does not represent any political party **〉independence** *n* **〉independently** *adv*

independent school *n* a school that is neither financed nor controlled by the government or local authorities

in-depth *adj* detailed or thorough: *an in-depth analysis*

indescribable *adj* too intense or extreme for words **〉indescribably** *adv*

indestructible *adj* not able to be destroyed

indeterminate *adj* **1** uncertain in extent, amount, or nature **2** left doubtful; inconclusive: *an indeterminate reply* **3** *maths* **a** having no numerical meaning, as the fraction $\frac{0}{0}$ **b** (of an equation) having more than one variable and an unlimited number of solutions **〉indeterminable** *adj* **〉indeterminacy** *n*

index (in-dex) *n, pl* **-dexes** or **-dices 1** an alphabetical list of names or subjects dealt with in a book, indicating where they are referred to **2** a file or catalogue in a library which enables a book or reference to be found **3** a number indicating the level of wages or prices as compared with some standard value **4** an indication or sign: *national birth rate was once an index of military power* **5** *maths* **a** same as **exponent b** a superscript number placed to the left of a radical sign indicating the root to be extracted: *the index of* $^3\sqrt{8}$ *is 3* **6** a number or ratio indicating a specific characteristic or property: *refractive index* ▷ *vb* **7** to put an index in (a book) **8** to enter (a word or item) in an index **9** to make index-linked [Latin: pointer]

indexation *or* **index-linking** *n* the act of making wages, pensions, or interest rates index-linked

index finger *n* the finger next to the thumb. Also called: forefinger

index-linked *adj* (of pensions, wages, or interest rates) rising and falling in line with the cost of living

India *n* **1** a republic in S Asia: history dates from the Indus Valley civilization (3rd millennium BC); came under British supremacy in 1763 and passed to the British Crown in 1858; nationalist movement arose under Gandhi (1869–1948); Indian subcontinent divided into Pakistan (Muslim) and India (Hindu) in 1947; became a republic within the Commonwealth in 1950. It consists chiefly of the Himalayas, rising over 7500 m (25 000 ft) in the extreme north, the Ganges plain in the north, the Thar Desert in the northwest, the Chota Nagpur plateau in the northeast, and the Deccan Plateau in the south. Official and administrative languages: Hindi and English; each state has its own language. Parts of the SE coast suffered badly in the Indian Ocean tsunami of December 2004. Religion: Hindu majority, Muslim minority. Currency: rupee. Capital: New Delhi. Pop: 1 220 800 359 (2013 est). Area: 3 268 100 sq km (1 261 813 sq miles). Hindi name: **Bharat 2** *communications* a code word for the letter *i*

Indiaman *n, pl* **-men** (formerly) a merchant ship engaged in trade with India

Indian *adj* **1** of or relating to India or its inhabitants **2** *old-fashioned, taboo* of the original inhabitants of the American continent ▷ *n* **3** a native or inhabitant of India **4** *old-fashioned, taboo* a person descended from the original inhabitants of the American continent

Indiana *n* a state of the N central US, in the Midwest: consists of an undulating plain, with sand dunes and lakes in the north and limestone caves in the south. Capital: Indianapolis. Pop: 6 195 643 (2003 est). Area: 93 491 sq km (36 097 sq miles). Abbreviation: **Ind.**, (with zip code) **IN**

Indianapolis *n* a city in central Indiana: the state capital. Pop: 783 438 (2003 est)

Indian club *n* a heavy bottle-shaped club, usually swung in pairs for exercise

Indian corn *n* same as **maize**

Indian Desert *n* another name for the **Thar Desert**

Indian Empire *n* British India and the Indian states under indirect British control, which gained independence as India and Pakistan in 1947

Indian file *n* same as **single file**

Indian hemp *n* same as **hemp**

Indianian *n* **1** a native or inhabitant of Indiana ▷ *adj* **2** of or relating to Indiana or its inhabitants

Indian ink *or especially US and Canad* **India ink** *n* a black ink made from a fine black soot

Indian Ocean *n* an ocean bordered by Africa in the west, Asia in the north, and Australia in the east and merging with the Antarctic Ocean in the south. Average depth: 3900 m (13 000 ft). Greatest depth (off the Sunda Islands): 7450 m (24 442 ft). In December 2004 a major undersea earthquake off Sumatra triggered a tsunami which affected large areas of the ocean as far away as east Africa, and killed an estimated 226 435 people. Area: about 73 556 000 sq km (28 400 000 sq miles)

Indian summer *n* **1** a period of warm sunny weather in autumn **2** a period of tranquillity or of renewed productivity towards the end of a person's life or career

India paper *n* a thin soft opaque printing paper

originally made in the Orient

Indic *adj* **1** of a branch of Indo-European consisting of many of the languages of India, including Sanskrit, Hindi, and Urdu ▷ *n* **2** this group of languages

indicate *vb* **-cating, -cated 1** to be or give a sign or symptom of: *to concede 18 goals in 7 games indicates a serious malaise* **2** to point out or show **3** to state briefly **4** to switch on the indicators in a motor vehicle to show that one is changing direction **5** (of measuring instruments) to show a reading of **6** (*usually passive*) to recommend or require: *surgery seems to be indicated for this patient* [Latin *indicare*] ❯ **indication** *n*

indicative (in-dik-a-tiv) *adj* **1** indicative of suggesting: *the symptoms aren't indicative of anything serious* **2** *grammar* denoting a mood of verbs used to make a statement ▷ *n* **3** *grammar* the indicative mood

indicator *n* **1** something that acts as a sign or indication: *an indicator of the moral decline of our society* **2** a device for indicating that a motor vehicle is about to turn left or right, esp. two pairs of lights that flash **3** an instrument, such as a gauge, that registers or measures something **4** *chem* a substance used to indicate the completion of a chemical reaction, usually by a change of colour

indices (in-diss-seez) *n* a plural of **index**

indict (in-dite) *vb* to charge (a person) formally with a crime, esp. in writing [Latin *in-* against + *dictare* to declare] ❯ **indictable** *adj*

indictment *n* **1** *criminal law* a formal charge of crime, esp. in writing: *the indictment contained three similar charges against each of the defendants* **2** a serious criticism: *a scathing indictment of faith healing*

indie *n informal* an independent record company

Indies *n* the Indies **1** the territories of S and SE Asia included in the East Indies, India, and Indochina **2** See **East Indies 3** See **West Indies**

indifference *n* **1** lack of concern or interest: *elite indifference to mass opinion* **2** lack of importance: *a matter of indifference to me*

indifferent *adj* **1** showing no concern or interest: *he was indifferent to politics* **2** of only average standard or quality **3** not at all good: *she had starred in several very indifferent movies* **4** unimportant **5** showing or having no preferences [Latin *indifferens* making no distinction]

indigenous (in-dij-in-uss) *adj* originating or occurring naturally in a country or area: *the indigenous population is under threat* [Latin *indigenus*]

indigent *adj formal* so poor as to lack even necessities: *the indigent widow of a fellow writer* [Latin *indigere* to need] ❯ **indigence** *n*

indigestible *adj* difficult or impossible to digest ❯ **indigestibility** *n*

indigestion *n* difficulty in digesting food, accompanied by stomach pain, heartburn, and belching

indignant *adj* feeling or showing indignation [Latin *indignari* to be displeased with] ❯ **indignantly** *adv*

indignation *n* anger aroused by something felt to be unfair or wrong

indignity *n, pl* **-ties** embarrassing or humiliating treatment

indigo *adj* **1** deep violet-blue ▷ *n, pl* **-gos** *or* **-goes 2** a dye of this colour originally obtained from plants [Spanish *indico*, from Greek *Indikos* of India]

indirect *adj* **1** done or caused by someone or something else: *indirect benefits* **2** not going in a direct course or line: *he took the indirect route home* **3** not coming straight to the point: *an indirect question* ❯ **indirectly** *adv*

indirect object *n grammar* the person or thing indirectly affected by the action of a verb and its direct object, as *John* in the sentence *I bought John a newspaper*

indirect speech *n* same as **reported speech**

indirect tax *n* a tax levied on goods or services which is paid indirectly by being added to the price

indiscernible *adj* not able or scarcely able to be seen

indiscipline *n* lack of discipline

indiscreet *adj* incautious or tactless in revealing secrets

indiscretion *n* **1** lack of discretion **2** an indiscreet act or remark

indiscriminate *adj* lacking discrimination or careful choice: *an indiscriminate bombing campaign* 〉**indiscriminately** *adv* 〉**indiscrimination** *n*

indispensable *adj* absolutely necessary: *an indispensable guide for any traveller* 〉**indispensability** *n*

indisposed *adj* **1** sick or ill **2** unwilling [Latin *indispositus* disordered] 〉**indisposition** *n*

indisputable *adj* beyond doubt

indissoluble *adj* permanent: *joining a political party is not an indissoluble marriage*

indistinct *adj* unable to be seen or heard clearly 〉**indistinctly** *adv*

indistinguishable *adj* so similar as to be difficult to tell apart

indium *n chem* a rare soft silvery metallic element. Symbol: In [Latin *indicum* indigo]

individual *adj* **1** of, relating to, or meant for a single person or thing: *small sums from individual donors* **2** separate or distinct from others of its kind: *please mark the individual pages* **3** characterized by unusual and striking qualities ▷ *n* **4** a single person, esp. when regarded as distinct from others: *respect for the individual* **5** *informal* a person: *a most annoying individual* **6** *biology* a single animal or plant, esp. as distinct from a species [Latin *individuus* indivisible] 〉**individually** *adv*

individualism *n* **1** the principle of leading one's life in one's own way **2** same as **laissez faire** **3** egotism 〉**individualist** *n* 〉**individualistic** *adj*

individuality *n*, *pl* **-ties 1** distinctive or unique character or personality: *a house of great individuality* **2** the qualities that distinguish one person or thing from another **3** a separate existence

individualize *or* **-ise** *vb* **-izing, -ized** *or* **-ising, -ised** to make individual or distinctive in character

indivisible *adj* **1** unable to be divided **2** *maths* leaving a remainder when divided by a given number

Indo- *combining form* denoting India or Indian: *Indo-European*

Indochina *or* **Indo-China** *n* **1** Also called: **Farther India** a peninsula in SE Asia, between India and China: consists of Myanmar, Thailand, Laos, Cambodia, Vietnam, and Malaysia **2** the former French colonial possessions of Cochin China, Annam, Tonkin, Laos, and Cambodia

Indochinese *or* **Indo-Chinese** *adj* **1** of or relating to Indochina or its inhabitants ▷ *n*, *pl* **-nese 2** a native or inhabitant of Indochina

indoctrinate *vb* **-nating, -nated** to teach (someone) systematically to accept a doctrine or opinion uncritically 〉**indoctrination** *n*

Indo-European *adj* **1** of a family of languages spoken in most of Europe and much of Asia, including English, Russian, and Hindi ▷ *n* **2** the Indo-European family of languages

indolent *adj* lazy; idle [Latin *indolens* not feeling pain] 〉**indolence** *n*

indomitable *adj* too strong to be defeated or discouraged: *an indomitable work ethic* [Latin *indomitus* untamable]

Indonesia *n* a republic in SE Asia, in the Malay Archipelago, consisting of the main islands of Sumatra, Java and Madura, Bali, Sulawesi (Celebes), Lombok, Sumbawa, Flores, the Moluccas, part of Timor, part of Borneo (Kalimantan), Papua (formerly Irian Jaya), and over 3000 small islands in the Indian and Pacific Oceans: became the Dutch East Indies in 1798; declared independence in 1945; became a republic in 1950; East Timor (illegally annexed in 1975) became independent in 2002. Parts of Sumatra suffered badly in the Indian Ocean tsunami of December 2004. Official language: Bahasa Indonesia. Religion: Muslim majority. Currency: rupiah. Capital: Jakarta. Pop: 251 160 124 (2013 est). Area: 1 919 317 sq km (741 052 sq miles). Former names (1798–1945): **Dutch East Indies, Netherlands East Indies**

Indonesian *adj* **1** of or relating to Indonesia or its inhabitants ▷ *n* **2** a native or inhabitant of Indonesia

indoor *adj* situated, happening, or used inside a building: *an indoor pool*

indoors *adv*, *adj* inside or into a building

Indore *n* **1** a city in central India, in W Madhya Pradesh. Pop: 1 597 441 (2001) **2** a former state of central India: became part of Madhya Bharat in 1948, which in turn became part of Madhya Pradesh in 1956

indrawn *adj* drawn or pulled in: *he heard her indrawn breath*

Indre *n* a department of central France in the Centre region. Capital: Châteauroux. Pop: 230 954 (2003 est). Area: 6906 sq km (2693 sq miles)

Indre-et-Loire *n* a department of W central France in the Centre region: contains many famous châteaux along the Loire. Capital: Tours. Pop: 563 062 (2003 est). Area: 6158 sq km (2402 sq miles)

indubitable (in-dew-bit-a-bl) *adj* beyond doubt; definite [Latin *in-* not + *dubitare* to doubt] 〉**indubitably** *adv*

induce *vb* **-ducing, -duced 1** to persuade or use influence on **2** to cause or bring about **3** *med* to cause (labour) to begin by the use of drugs or other means **4** *logic obsolete* to draw (a general conclusion) from particular instances **5** to produce (an electromotive force or electrical current) by induction **6** to transmit (magnetism) by induction [Latin *inducere* to lead in] 〉**inducible** *adj*

inducement *n* **1** something that encourages someone to do something **2** the act of inducing

induct *vb* **1** to bring in formally or install in a job, rank, or position **2** to initiate in knowledge of (a group or profession): *boys are inducted into the world of men* [Latin *inductus* led in]

inductance *n* the property of an electric circuit as a result of which an electromotive force is created by a change of current in the same or in a neighbouring circuit

induction *n* **1** *logic* a process of reasoning by which a general conclusion is drawn from particular instances **2** *med* the process of inducing labour **3** the process by which electrical or magnetic properties are transferred, without physical contact, from one circuit or body to another **4** a formal introduction or entry into an office or position **5** (in an internal-combustion engine) the drawing in of mixed air and fuel from the carburettor to the cylinder 〉**inductional** *adj*

induction coil *n* a transformer for producing a high voltage from a low voltage. It consists of a soft-iron core, a primary coil of few turns, and a concentric secondary coil of many turns

induction course *n* a training course to help familiarize someone with a new job

inductive *adj* **1** *logic* of or using induction: *inductive reasoning* **2** of or operated by electrical or magnetic induction

inductor *n* a device designed to create inductance in an electrical circuit

indulge *vb* **-dulging, -dulged 1** (often foll. by *in*) to yield to or gratify (a whim or desire for): *to indulge in new clothes* **2** to allow (someone) to have or do everything he or she wants: *he had given her too much, indulged her in everything* **3** to allow (oneself) the pleasure of something: *he indulged himself* **4** *informal* to take alcoholic drink [Latin *indulgere* to concede]

indulgence *n* **1** something that is allowed because it gives pleasure; extravagance **2** the act of indulging oneself or someone else **3** liberal or tolerant treatment **4** something granted as a favour or privilege **5** *RC Church* a remission of the temporal punishment for sin after its guilt has been forgiven

indulgent *adj* kind or lenient, often to excess 〉**indulgently** *adv*

Indus n a river in S Asia, rising in SW Tibet in the Kailas Range of the Himalayas and flowing northwest through Kashmir, then southwest across Pakistan to the Arabian Sea: important throughout history, esp. for the Indus Civilization (about 3000 to 1500 BC), and for irrigation. Length: about 2900 km (1800 miles)

industrial adj **1** of, used in, or employed in industry **2** with an economy relying heavily on industry: *northern industrial cities*

industrial action n action, such as a strike or work-to-rule, by which workers complain about their conditions

industrial estate n Brit, Austral, NZ and S African an area of land set aside for factories and warehouses

industrialism n an organization of society characterized by large-scale manufacturing industry rather than trade or farming

industrialist n a person who owns or controls large amounts of money or property in industry

industrialize or **-lise** vb **-lizing, -lized** or **-lising, -lised** to develop industry on a large scale in (a country or region) **>** **industrialization** or **-lisation** n

industrial relations pl n the relations between management and workers

Industrial Revolution n the Industrial Revolution the transformation in the 18th and 19th centuries of Britain and other countries into industrial nations

industrious adj hard-working

industry n, pl **-tries 1** the work and process involved in manufacture: *Japanese industry increased output considerably last year* **2** a branch of commercial enterprise concerned with the manufacture of a specified product: *the steel industry* **3** the quality of working hard [Latin *industrius* active]

Indy Car racing n a form of motor racing around banked oval tracks [after the *Indianapolis 500* motor race]

Ine n died after 726, king of Wessex (688–726)

inebriate n **1** a person who is habitually drunk ▷ adj **2** drunk, esp. habitually [Latin *ebrius* drunk] **>** **inebriation** n

inebriated adj drunk

inedible adj not fit to be eaten

ineducable (in-ed-yuke-a-bl) adj incapable of being educated, esp. on account of mental retardation

ineffable adj too great or intense to be expressed in words [Latin *in*- not + *effabilis* utterable] **>** **ineffably** adv

ineffective adj having no effect or an inadequate effect

ineffectual adj having no effect or an inadequate effect: *the raids were costly and ineffectual*

inefficient adj not performing a task or function to the best advantage **>** **inefficiency** n

inelegant adj lacking elegance or refinement

ineligible adj not qualified for or entitled to something

ineluctable adj formal impossible to avoid: *the ineluctable collapse of the coalition* [Latin *in*- not + *eluctari* to escape]

inept adj **1** awkward, clumsy, or incompetent **2** not suitable or fitting; out of place [Latin *in*- not + *aptus* fitting] **>** **ineptitude** n

inequable adj **1** unfair **2** not uniform

inequality n, pl **-ties 1** the state or quality of being unequal **2** an instance of this **3** lack of smoothness or regularity of a surface **4** maths a statement indicating that the value of one quantity or expression is not equal to another

inequitable adj unjust or unfair

inequity n, pl **-ties 1** injustice or unfairness **2** something which is unjust or unfair

ineradicable adj impossible to remove or root out: *an ineradicable distrust of foreigners*

inert adj **1** without the power to move or to resist motion **2** inactive or lifeless **3** having only a limited ability to react chemically [Latin *iners* unskilled]

inertia n **1** a feeling of unwillingness to do anything **2** physics the tendency of a body to remain still or continue moving unless a force is applied to it **>** **inertial** adj

inertia selling n Brit the illegal practice of sending unrequested goods to householders, followed by a bill for the goods if they do not return them

inescapable adj not able to be avoided

inessential adj **1** not necessary ▷ n **2** an unnecessary thing

inestimable adj too great to be calculated

inevitable adj **1** unavoidable; sure to happen **2** informal so regular as to be predictable: *the inevitable guitar solo* ▷ n **3** (often preceded by *the*) something that is unavoidable [Latin *in*- not + *evitare* to avoid] **>** **inevitability** n **>** **inevitably** adv

inexact adj not exact or accurate

inexcusable adj too bad to be justified or tolerated

inexhaustible adj incapable of being used up; endless

inexorable adj unable to be prevented from continuing or progressing: *an inexorable trend* [Latin *in*- not + *exorare* to prevail upon] **>** **inexorably** adv

inexpensive adj not costing a lot of money

inexperienced adj having no knowledge or experience of a particular situation, activity, etc. **>** **inexperience** n

inexpert adj lacking skill

inexpiable adj (of sin) incapable of being atoned for; unpardonable

inexplicable adj impossible to explain

inexpressible adj (of a feeling) too strong to be expressed in words

in extremis adv **1** in dire straits **2** at the point of death

inextricable adj **1** impossible to escape from: *an inextricable dilemma* **2** impossible to disentangle or separate: *an inextricable mass of twisted metal* **>** **inextricably** adv

inf. 1 infantry **2** infinitive **3** informal **4** information

infallible adj **1** incapable of error **2** always successful: *an infallible cure* **3** (of the Pope) incapable of error in setting forth matters of doctrine on faith and morals **>** **infallibility** n **>** **infallibly** adv

infamous (in-fam-uss) adj well-known for something bad

infamy n, pl **-mies 1** the state of being infamous **2** an infamous act or event [Latin *infamis* of evil repute]

infancy n, pl **-cies 1** the state or period of being an infant **2** an early stage of growth or development: *virtual reality is in its infancy* **3** law the state or period of being a minor

infant n **1** a very young child; baby **2** law same as **minor** (4) **3** Brit a young school child ▷ adj **4** of, relating to, or designed for young children: *infant school* **5** in an early stage of development: *an infant democracy* [Latin *infans*, literally: speechless]

infanta n **1** (formerly) a daughter of a king of Spain or Portugal **2** the wife of an infante [Spanish and Portuguese]

infante n (formerly) any son of a king of Spain or Portugal, except the heir to the throne [Spanish and Portuguese]

infanticide n **1** the act of killing an infant **2** a person who kills an infant [INFANT + Latin *caedere* to kill]

infantile adj **1** childishly immature **2** of infants or infancy

infantile paralysis n same as **poliomyelitis**

infantry n, pl **-tries** soldiers who fight on foot [Italian *infanteria*]

infant school n (in England and Wales) a school for children aged between 5 and 7

infatuate vb **-ating, -ated** to inspire or fill with an intense and unreasoning passion [Latin *infatuare*] **>** **infatuation** n

infatuated adj (often foll. by *with*) carried away by an intense and unreasoning passion for someone

infect vb **1** to contaminate (a person or thing) with a germ or virus or its consequent disease **2** to taint or contaminate **3** to affect with an opinion or feeling as if by contagion: *even she was infected by the excitement* [Latin *inficere* to stain]

infection *n* **1** an infectious disease **2** contamination of a person or thing by a germ or virus or its consequent disease

infectious *adj* **1** (of a disease) capable of being transmitted without actual contact **2** causing or transmitting infection **3** spreading from one person to another: *infectious laughter*

infectious mononucleosis *n* same as **glandular fever**

infelicity *n, pl* **-ties** *formal* **1** something, esp. a remark or expression, that is inapt **2** the state or quality of being unhappy or unfortunate **>** **infelicitous** *adj*

infer *vb* **-ferring, -ferred** **1** to conclude by reasoning from evidence; deduce **2** *not standard* to imply or suggest [Latin *inferre* to bring into]

> **USAGE** The use of *infer* to mean *imply* is common in both speech and writing, but is regarded by many people as incorrect.

inference *n* **1** the act or process of reaching a conclusion by reasoning from evidence **2** an inferred conclusion or deduction

inferential *adj* of or based on inference

inferior *adj* **1** lower in quality, quantity, or usefulness **2** lower in rank, position, or status **3** of poor quality **4** lower in position **5** *printing* (of a character) printed at the foot of an ordinary character **▷** *n* **6** a person inferior to another, esp. in rank [Latin: lower] **>** **inferiority** *n*

inferiority complex *n psychiatry* a disorder arising from a feeling of inferiority to others, characterized by aggressiveness or extreme shyness

infernal *adj* **1** of or relating to hell **2** *informal* irritating: *stop that infernal noise* [Latin *infernus* lower]

inferno *n, pl* **-nos** **1** an intense raging fire **2** a place or situation resembling hell, because it is crowded and noisy **3 the inferno** hell [Late Latin *infernus* hell]

infertile *adj* **1** not capable of producing offspring **2** (of soil) not productive; barren **>** **infertility** *n*

infest *vb* to inhabit or overrun (a place, plant, etc.) in unpleasantly large numbers: *the area was infested with moles* [Latin *infestare* to molest] **>** **infestation** *n*

infidel *n* **1** a person who has no religious belief **2** a person who rejects a specific religion, esp. Christianity or Islam **▷** *adj* **3** of unbelievers or unbelief [Latin *infidelis* unfaithful]

infidelity *n, pl* **-ties** **1** sexual unfaithfulness to one's husband, wife, or lover **2** an act or instance of unfaithfulness

infield *n* **1** *cricket* the area of the field near the pitch **2** *baseball* the area of the playing field enclosed by the base lines **>** **infielder** *n*

infighting *n* **1** rivalry or quarrelling between members of the same group or organization **2** *boxing* combat at close quarters

infiltrate *vb* **-trating, -trated** **1** to enter (an organization, area, etc.) gradually and in secret, so as to gain influence or control: *they infiltrated the party structure* **2** to pass (a liquid or gas) through (a substance) by filtering or (of a liquid or gas) to pass through (a substance) by filtering **>** **infiltration** *n* **>** **infiltrator** *n*

infinite (in-fin-it) *adj* **1** having no limits or boundaries in time, space, extent, or size **2** extremely or immeasurably great or numerous: *infinite wealth* **3** *maths* having an unlimited or uncountable number of digits, factors, or terms **>** **infinitely** *adv*

infinitesimal *adj* **1** extremely small: *an infinitesimal risk* **2** *maths* of or involving a small change in the value of a variable that approaches zero as a limit **▷** *n* **3** *maths* an infinitesimal quantity

infinitive (in-fin-it-iv) *n grammar* a form of the verb which in most languages is not inflected for tense or person and is used without a particular subject: in

English, the infinitive usually consists of the word *to* followed by the verb

infinitude *n literary* **1** the state or quality of being infinite **2** an infinite extent or quantity

infinity *n, pl* **-ties** **1** an infinitely great number or amount **2** endless time, space, or quantity **3** *maths* the concept of a value greater than any finite numerical value

infirm *adj* physically or mentally weak, esp. from old age

infirmary *n, pl* **-ries** a place for the treatment of sick or injured people; hospital

infirmity *n, pl* **-ties** **1** the state of being infirm **2** physical weakness or frailty

infix *vb* **1** to fix firmly in **2** to instil or impress on the mind by repetition **>** **infixation** *or* **infixion** *n*

in flagrante delicto (in flag-grant-ee dee-lick-toe) *adv chiefly law* while committing the offence [Latin]

inflame *vb* **-flaming, -flamed** **1** to make angry or excited **2** to increase or intensify; aggravate **3** to produce inflammation in or become inflamed **4** to set or be set on fire

inflammable *adj* **1** liable to catch fire **2** easily aroused to anger or passion **>** **inflammability** *n*

> **USAGE** See at **flammable**.

inflammation *n* **1** the reaction of living tissue to injury or infection, characterized by heat, redness, swelling, and pain **2** an inflaming or being inflamed

inflammatory *adj* **1** likely to provoke anger **2** characterized by or caused by inflammation

inflatable *adj* **1** capable of being inflated **▷** *n* **2** a plastic or rubber object which can be inflated

inflate *vb* **-flating, -flated** **1** to expand or cause to expand by filling with gas or air **2** to give an impression of greater importance than is justified: *something to inflate their self-esteem* **3** to cause or undergo economic inflation [Latin *inflare* to blow into]

inflation *n* **1** an inflating or being inflated **2** *econ* a progressive increase in the general level of prices brought about by an increase in the amount of money in circulation or by increases in costs **3** *informal* the rate of increase of prices **>** **inflationary** *adj*

inflect *vb* **1** to change (the voice) in tone or pitch **2** *grammar* to change (the form of a word) by inflection **3** to bend or curve [Latin *inflectere* to curve, alter] **>** **inflective** *adj*

inflection *or* **inflexion** *n* **1** change in the pitch of the voice **2** *grammar* a change in the form of a word, signalling change in such grammatical functions as tense or number **3** an angle or bend **4** an inflecting or being inflected **5** *maths* a change in curvature from concave to convex or vice versa **>** **inflectional** *or* **inflexional** *adj*

inflexible *adj* **1** unwilling to be persuaded; obstinate **2** (of a rule etc.) firmly fixed: *inflexible schedules* **3** incapable of being bent: *inflexible joints* **>** **inflexibility** *n*

inflict *vb* **1** to impose (something unpleasant) on **2** to deliver (a blow or wound) [Latin *infligere* to strike (something) against] **>** **infliction** *n* **>** **inflictor** *n*

in-flight *adj* happening or provided during flight in an aircraft: *in-flight meals*

inflorescence *n botany* **1** the part of a plant that consists of the flower-bearing stalks **2** the arrangement of the flowers on the stalks **3** the process of flowering; blossoming [Latin *in-* into + *florescere* to bloom]

inflow *n* **1** something, such as a liquid or gas, that flows in **2** the act of flowing in; influx

influence *n* **1** an effect of one person or thing on another **2** the power of a person or thing to have such an effect **3** power resulting from ability, wealth, or position **4** a person or thing with influence **5 under the influence** *informal* drunk **▷** *vb* **-encing, -enced** **6** to have an effect upon (actions or events) **7** to persuade or induce [Latin *influere* to flow into]

influential *adj* having or exerting influence

influenza *n* a highly contagious viral disease characterized by fever, muscular pains, and catarrh [Italian: influence, hence incursion, epidemic]

influx *n* **1** the arrival or entry of many people or things **2** the act of flowing in [Latin *influere* to flow into]

info *n informal* short for **information**

inform *vb* **1** to give information to; tell: *he informed me that he would be free after lunch* **2** to make knowledgeable (about) or familiar (with): *he'll be informed of his rights* **3** to give incriminating information to the police **4** to impart some essential or formative characteristic to **5** to animate or inspire [Latin *informare* to describe] **>** **informed** *adj*

informal *adj* **1** relaxed and friendly: *an informal interview* **2** appropriate to everyday life or use rather than formal occasions: *informal clothes* **3** (of speech or writing) appropriate to ordinary conversation rather than to formal written language **>** **informality** *n* **>** **informally** *adv*

informant *n* a person who gives information

information *n* **1** knowledge acquired in any manner; facts **2** *computers* **a** the meaning given to data by the way it is interpreted **b** same as **data** (2)

information superhighway *n* the concept of a worldwide network of computers transferring information at high speed

information technology *n* the production, storage, and communication of information using computers and electronic technology

information theory *n* the study of the processes of communication and the transmission of information

informative *adj* giving useful information

informer *n* a person who informs to the police

infra dig *adj informal* beneath one's dignity [Latin *infra dignitatem*]

infrared *adj* **1** of or using rays with a wavelength just beyond the red end of the visible spectrum ▷ *n* **2** the infrared part of the spectrum [Latin *infra* beneath]

infrasonic *adj* having a frequency below the range audible to the human ear [Latin *infra* beneath]

infrasound *n* infrasonic waves

infrastructure *n* **1** the basic structure of an organization or system **2** the stock of facilities, services, and equipment in a country, including factories, roads, and schools, that are needed for it to function properly [Latin *infra* beneath]

infrequent *adj* not happening often **>** **infrequently** *adv*

infringe *vb* -**fringing,** -**fringed 1** to violate or break (a law or agreement) **2 infringe on** *or* **upon** to encroach or trespass on: *the press infringed on their privacy* [Latin *infringere* to break off] **>** **infringement** *n*

infuriate *vb* -**ating,** -**ated** to make very angry [Medieval Latin *infuriare*] **>** **infuriating** *adj* **>** **infuriatingly** *adv*

infuse *vb* -**fusing,** -**fused 1** to fill with (an emotion or quality) **2** to soak or be soaked in order to extract flavour [Latin *infundere* to pour into]

infusible *adj* unable to be fused or melted **>** **infusibility** *n*

infusion *n* **1** the act of infusing **2** a liquid obtained by infusing

Inge *n* William Ralph, known as *the Gloomy Dean.* 1860–1954, English theologian, noted for his pessimism; dean of St Paul's Cathedral (1911–34)

Ingenhousz *n* Jan. 1730–99, Dutch plant physiologist and physician, who discovered photosynthesis

ingenious (in-jean-ee-uss) *adj* showing cleverness and originality: *a truly ingenious invention* [Latin *ingenium* natural ability]

ingenue (an-jay-new) *n* an innocent or inexperienced young woman, esp. as a role played by an actress [French]

ingenuity (in-jen-new-it-ee) *n* cleverness at inventing things [Latin *ingenuitas* a freeborn condition; meaning influenced by INGENIOUS]

ingenuous (in-jen-new-uss) *adj* **1** unsophisticated and trusting **2** frank and straightforward [Latin *ingenuus* freeborn, virtuous]

Ingerland *or* **Ingerlund** *n informal* a jocular spelling of England, as pronounced in the chants of sports, esp. football, supporters

ingest *vb* to take (food or liquid) into the body [Latin *ingerere* to put into] **>** **ingestion** *n*

ingle *n archaic or dialect* a fire in a room or a fireplace [probably Scottish Gaelic *aingeal* fire]

Ingleborough *n* a mountain in N England, in North Yorkshire: potholes. Height: 723 m (2373 ft)

inglenook *n Brit* a corner by a fireplace

inglorious *adj* dishonourable or shameful

ingoing *adj* going in; entering

Ingolstadt *n* a city in S central Germany, in Bavaria on the River Danube: oil-refining. Pop: 119 528 (2003 est)

ingot *n* a piece of metal cast in a form suitable for storage, usually a bar [origin unknown]

ingrained *or* **engrained** *adj* **1** (of a habit, feeling, or belief) deeply impressed or instilled **2** (of dirt) worked into or through the fibre or pores [*dyed in grain* dyed with kermes through the fibre]

ingratiate *vb* -**ating,** -**ated** to act in order to bring (oneself) into favour (with someone) [Latin *in-* in + *gratia* favour] **>** **ingratiating** *adj*

ingratitude *n* lack of gratitude or thanks

ingredient *n* a component of a mixture or compound, esp. in cooking [Latin *ingrediens* going into]

Ingres *n* Jean Auguste Dominique. 1780–1867, French classical painter, noted for his draughtsmanship

ingress *n formal* **1** the act of going or coming in **2** the right or permission to enter [Latin *ingressus*]

ingrowing *adj* (esp. of a toenail) growing abnormally into the flesh **>** **ingrown** *adj*

Ingush Republic *n* a constituent republic of S Russia: part of the Checheno-Ingush Autonomous Republic from 1936 until 1992. Capital: Magas (formerly at Nazran). Pop: 468 900 (2002). Area: 3600 sq km (1390 sq miles). Also called: **Ingushetia**

inhabit *vb* to live or dwell in [Latin *inhabitare*] **>** **inhabitable** *adj*

inhabitant *n* a person or animal that is a permanent resident of a particular place or region

inhalant (in-hale-ant) *n* a medicinal preparation inhaled to help breathing problems

inhale *vb* -**haling,** -**haled** to breathe in (air, smoke, or vapour) [Latin *in-* in + *halare* to breathe] **>** **inhalation** *n*

inhaler *n* a container used to administer an inhalant

Inhambane *n* a port in SE Mozambique on an inlet of the Mozambique Channel (**Inhambane Bay**). Pop: about 70 000 (latest est)

inharmonious *adj* lacking harmony; discordant; disagreeing

inhere *vb* -**hering,** -**hered** inhere in to be an inseparable part (of) [Latin *inhaerere* to stick in]

inherent *adj* existing as an inseparable part **>** **inherently** *adv*

inherit *vb* **1** to receive money, property, or a title from someone who has died **2** to receive (a characteristic) from an earlier generation by heredity **3** to receive (a position or situation) from a predecessor: *he inherited a mess* [Old French *enheriter*] **>** **inheritor** *n*

inheritable *adj* **1** capable of being transmitted by heredity from one generation to a later one **2** capable of being inherited

inheritance *n* **1** *law* **a** hereditary succession to an estate or title **b** the right of an heir to succeed on the death of an ancestor **2** something inherited or to be inherited **3** the act of inheriting **4** the fact of receiving characteristics from an earlier generation by heredity

inheritance tax *n* (in Britain) a tax consisting of a percentage levied on the part of an inheritance that exceeds a specified allowance

inhibit *vb* **1** to restrain or hinder (an impulse or desire) **2** to prohibit or prevent: *an attempt to inhibit nuclear proliferation* **3** *chem* to stop, prevent, or decrease the rate of (a chemical reaction) [Latin *inhibere*] **> inhibited** *adj* **> inhibitor** *n*

inhibition *n* **1** *psychol* a feeling of fear or embarrassment that stops one from behaving naturally **2** an inhibiting or being inhibited **3** the process of stopping or retarding a chemical reaction

inhospitable *adj* **1** not welcoming; unfriendly **2** (of a place or climate) not easy to live in; harsh

inhuman *adj* **1** cruel or brutal **2** not human

inhumane *adj* extremely cruel or brutal

inhumanity *n, pl* **-ties 1** lack of kindness or compassion **2** an inhumane act

inimical *adj* **1** adverse or unfavourable: *inimical to change* **2** unfriendly or hostile [Latin *in-* not + *amicus* friendly]

inimitable *adj* impossible to imitate **> inimitably** *adv*

iniquity *n, pl* **-ties 1** injustice or wickedness **2** a wicked act [Latin *iniquus* unfair] **> iniquitous** *adj*

initial *adj* **1** of or at the beginning ▷ *n* **2** the first letter of a word, esp. a person's name **3** *printing* a large letter set at the beginning of a chapter or work ▷ *vb* **-tialling, -tialled** *or US* **-tialing, -tialed 4** to sign with one's initials, esp. to indicate approval [Latin *initium* beginning] **> initially** *adv*

initiate *vb* **-ating, -ated 1** to begin or set going: *more women initiate divorce today* **2** to accept (new members) into a group, often through secret ceremonies **3** to teach the fundamentals of a skill or knowledge to (someone) ▷ *n* **4** a person who has been initiated, esp. recently **5** a beginner [Latin *initiare*] **> initiation** *n* **> initiator** *n*

initiative *n* **1** a first step; a commencing move: *a peace initiative* **2** the right or power to initiate something: *it forced local people to take the initiative* **3** enterprise: *the drive and initiative to create new products* **4 on one's own initiative** without being prompted

inject *vb* **1** *med* to put (a fluid) into the body with a syringe **2** to introduce (a new element): *to inject a dose of realism into the assessment* [Latin *injicere* to throw in] **> injection** *n*

injudicious *adj* showing poor judgment; unwise

injunction *n* **1** *law* a court order not to do something **2** an authoritative command [Latin *injungere* to enjoin] **> injunctive** *adj*

injure *vb* **-juring, -jured 1** to hurt physically or mentally **2** to do wrong to (a person), esp. by an injustice: *the injured party* **3** to damage: *an opportunity to injure your reputation* **> injured** *adj*

injurious *adj* **1** causing harm **2** abusive, slanderous, or libellous

injury *n, pl* **-ries 1** physical hurt **2** a specific instance of this: *a leg injury* **3** harm done to the feelings **4** damage: *inflict no injury on the wealth of the nation* [Latin *injuria* injustice]

injury time *n sport* playing time added at the end of a match to compensate for time spent treating injured players. Also called: **stoppage time**

injustice *n* **1** unfairness **2** an unfair action

ink *n* **1** a black or coloured liquid used for printing, writing, and drawing **2** a dark brown fluid squirted for self-concealment by an octopus or cuttlefish ▷ *vb* **3** to mark or cover with ink **4 ink in** to arrange or confirm definitely [Old French *enque*]

Inkerman *n* a village in S Crimea, east of Sevastopol: scene of a battle during the Crimean War in which British and French forces defeated the Russians (1854)

inkhosi (in-koh-see) *n, pl* **amakhosi** *S African* a tribal chief [Zulu]

inkling *n* a vague idea or suspicion [Middle English *inclen* to hint at]

inkstand *n* a stand or tray for holding writing tools and containers for ink

inkwell *n* a small container for ink, often fitted into the surface of a desk

inky *adj* **inkier, inkiest 1** dark or black, like ink **2** stained with ink **> inkiness** *n*

inlaid *adj* **1** set in another material so that the surface is smooth, such as a design in wood **2** made in this way: *an inlaid table-top*

inland *adj* **1** of or in the interior of a country or region, away from a sea or border **2** *chiefly Brit* operating within a country or region; domestic: *inland trade* ▷ *n* **3** the interior of a country or region ▷ *adv* **4** towards or into the interior of a country or region

Inland Revenue *n* (in New Zealand and formerly in Britain) a government department that collects major direct taxes, such as income tax

Inland Sea *n* a sea in SW Japan, between the islands of Honshu, Shikoku, and Kyushu. Japanese name: **Seto Naikai**

in-law *n* **1** a relative by marriage ▷ *adj* **2** (*in combination*) related by marriage: *his brother-in-law*

inlay *vb* **-laying, -laid 1** to decorate (an article, esp. of furniture) by inserting pieces of wood, ivory, or metal so that the surfaces are smooth and flat ▷ *n* **2** decoration made by inlaying **3** an inlaid article **4** *dentistry* a filling shaped to fit a cavity

inlet *n* **1** a narrow strip of water extending from the sea into the land **2** a passage or valve through which a liquid or gas enters a machine

in-line skate *n* another name for **Rollerblade**

in loco parentis (par-rent-iss) in place of a parent: said of a person acting for a parent [Latin]

inmate *n* a person who is confined to an institution such as a prison or hospital

inmost *adj* same as **innermost**

inn *n* a pub or small hotel providing food and accommodation [Old English]

Inn *n* a river in central Europe, rising in Switzerland in Graubünden and flowing northeast through Austria and Bavaria to join the River Danube at Passau: forms part of the border between Austria and Germany. Length: 514 km (319 miles)

innards *pl n informal* **1** the internal organs of the body, esp. the entrails **2** the working parts of a machine [variant of *inwards*]

innate *adj* existing from birth, rather than acquired; inborn: *his innate decency* [Latin *innasci* to be born in] **> innately** *adv*

inner *adj* **1** happening or located inside or further inside: *the door to the inner office* **2** of the mind or spirit: *her inner self* **3** exclusive or private: *the inner sanctum of the party secretariat* **4** more profound; less apparent: *the inner meaning* ▷ *n* **5** *archery* **a** the red innermost ring on a target **b** a shot which hits this ring

inner child *n psychol* the part of the psyche that retains the feelings as they were experienced in childhood

inner city *n* the parts of a city in or near its centre, where there are often social and economic problems

Inner Hebrides *pl n* See **Hebrides**

inner man *or fem* **inner woman** *n* **1** the mind or soul **2** *humorous* the stomach

Inner Mongolia *n* an autonomous region of NE China: consists chiefly of the Mongolian plateau, with the Gobi Desert in the north and the Great Wall of China in the south. Capital: Hohhot. Pop: 23 800 000 (2003 est). Area: 1 177 500 sq km (459 225 sq miles)

innermost *adj* **1** most intimate or private: *innermost secrets* **2** furthest within

inner tube *n* an inflatable rubber tube inside a pneumatic tyre casing

inning *n baseball* a division of the game consisting of a turn at batting and a turn in the field for each side [Old English *innung* a going in]

innings *n* **1** *cricket* **a** the batting turn of a player or team **b** the runs scored during such a turn **2** a period of opportunity or action

Inniskilling *n* the former name of **Enniskillen**

innkeeper n an owner or manager of an inn

innocence n the quality or state of being innocent [Latin *innocentia* harmlessness]

innocent adj **1** not guilty of a particular crime **2** without experience of evil **3** harmless or innocuous **4 innocent of** without or lacking: *innocent of prejudice* ▷ n **5** an innocent person, esp. a young child or a naive adult > **innocently** adv

Innocent II n original name *Gregorio Papareschi*. died 1143, pope (1130–43). He condemned Abelard's teachings

Innocent III n original name *Giovanni Lotario de' Conti*. ?1161–1216, pope (1198–1216), under whom the temporal power of the papacy reached its height. He instituted the Fourth Crusade (1202) and a crusade against the Albigenses (1208), and called the fourth Lateran Council (1215)

Innocent IV n original name *Sinibaldo de' Fieschi*. died 1254, pope (1243–54); an unrelenting enemy of Emperor Frederick II and his heirs

innocuous adj having no adverse or harmful effect [Latin *innocuus*]

innovate vb **-vating, -vated** to introduce new ideas or methods [Latin *innovare* to renew] > **innovative** or **innovatory** adj > **innovator** n

innovation n **1** something newly introduced, such as a new method or device **2** the act of innovating

Innsbruck n a city in W Austria, on the River Inn at the foot of the Brenner Pass: tourist centre. Pop: 113 392 (2001)

Innu n **1** a member of an Algonquian people living in Labrador and northern Quebec **2** the Algonquian language of this people

innuendo n, pl **-dos** or **-does** an indirect or subtle reference to something rude or unpleasant [Latin: by hinting]

Innuit (in-new-it) n same as **Inuit**

innumerable adj too many to be counted > **innumerably** adv

innumerate adj having no understanding of mathematics or science > **innumeracy** n

inoculate vb **-lating, -lated 1** to protect against disease by injecting with a vaccine **2** to introduce (microorganisms, esp. bacteria) into (a culture medium) [Latin *inoculare* to implant] > **inoculation** n

inoffensive adj causing no harm or annoyance

İnönü n Ismet. 1884–1973, Turkish statesman; president of Turkey (1938–50) and prime minister (1923–37; 1961–65)

inoperable adj surgery unable to be safely operated on: *an inoperable tumour*

inoperative adj not working or functioning: *continued shelling has rendered the ceasefire inoperative*

inopportune adj badly timed or inappropriate

inordinate adj **1** excessive: *an inordinate amount of time spent arguing* **2** unrestrained, as in behaviour or emotion: *inordinate anger* [Latin *inordinatus* disordered] > **inordinately** adv

inorganic adj **1** not having the structure or characteristics of living organisms **2** chem of or denoting chemical compounds that do not contain carbon **3** not resulting from or produced by growth; artificial: *inorganic fertilizers*

inorganic chemistry n the branch of chemistry concerned with the elements and compounds which do not contain carbon

inpatient n a patient who stays in a hospital for treatment

input n **1** resources, such as money, labour, or power, put into a project **2** computers the data fed into a computer ▷ vb **-putting, -put 3** to enter (data) in a computer

inquest n **1** an official inquiry into an unexplained, sudden, or violent death, held by a coroner **2** informal an investigation or discussion [Latin *in-* into + *quaesitus* investigation]

inquietude n formal restlessness or anxiety

inquire or **enquire** vb **-quiring, -quired 1** to seek information (about) **2 inquire after** to ask about the health or progress of (a person) **3 inquire into** to make an investigation **4 inquire of** to ask (a person) for information: *I'll inquire of my aunt when she is coming* [Latin *inquirere*] > **inquirer** or **enquirer** n

inquiry or **enquiry** n, pl **-ries 1** a question **2** an investigation

inquisition n **1** a thorough investigation **2** an official inquiry, esp. one held by a jury before an officer of the Crown > **inquisitional** adj

Inquisition n history an organization within the Catholic Church (1232–1820) for suppressing heresy

inquisitive adj **1** excessively curious about other people's business **2** eager to learn > **inquisitively** adv > **inquisitiveness** n

inquisitor n **1** a person who inquires, esp. deeply or ruthlessly **2 Inquisitor** an officer of the Inquisition

inquisitorial adj **1** of or like an inquisition or an inquisitor **2** offensively curious > **inquisitorially** adv

inquorate adj without enough people present to make a quorum

in re (in ray) prep in the matter of; concerning [Latin]

INRI Jesus of Nazareth, king of the Jews (the inscription placed over Christ's head during the Crucifixion) [Latin *Iesus Nazarenus Rex Iudaeorum*]

inroads pl n **make inroads into** to start affecting or reducing: *my gambling has made great inroads into my savings*

inrush n a sudden and overwhelming inward flow

ins. 1 inches **2** insurance

insane adj **1** mentally ill **2** stupidly irresponsible: *acting on an insane impulse* > **insanely** adv

insanitary adj dirty or unhealthy

insanity n, pl **-ties 1** the state of being insane **2** stupidity

insatiable (in-saysh-a-bl) adj impossible to satisfy > **insatiability** n > **insatiably** adv

inscribe vb **-scribing, -scribed 1** to mark or engrave with (words, symbols, or letters) **2** to write one's name, and sometimes a brief dedication, on (a book) before giving to someone **3** to enter (a name) on a list **4** geometry to draw (a geometric construction) inside another construction so that the two are in contact at as many points as possible but do not intersect [Latin *inscribere*]

inscription n **1** something inscribed, esp. words carved or engraved on a coin, tomb, or ring **2** a signature or brief dedication in a book or on a work of art

inscrutable adj mysterious or enigmatic [Latin *in-* not + *scrutari* to examine] > **inscrutability** n

insect n **1** a small animal that has six legs and usually has wings, such as an ant, fly, or butterfly **2** (loosely) any similar invertebrate, such as a spider, tick, or centipede [Latin *insectum* (animal that has been) cut into]

insecticide n a substance used to destroy insects [*insect* + Latin *caedere* to kill]

insectivore n **1** a small mammal, such as a hedgehog or a shrew, that eats invertebrates **2** a plant or animal that eats insects [*insect* + Latin *vorare* to swallow] > **insectivorous** adj

insecure adj **1** anxious or uncertain **2** not adequately protected: *low-paid or insecure employment* **3** unstable or shaky > **insecurity** n

inseminate vb **-nating, -nated** to impregnate (a female) with semen [Latin *in-* in + *semen* seed] > **insemination** n

insensate adj **1** lacking sensation or consciousness **2** insensitive or unfeeling **3** foolish

insensible adj **1** unconscious **2** without feeling **3** imperceptible **4 insensible of** or **to** unaware of or indifferent to: *insensible to suffering* > **insensibility** n

insensitive adj unaware of or ignoring other people's feelings > **insensitivity** n

inseparable adj **1** constantly together because of mutual liking: *they became inseparable companions* **2** too closely connected to be separated > **inseparably** adv

insert vb **1** to place or fit (something) inside something else **2** to introduce (a clause or comment) into text or a speech ▷ *n* **3** something inserted, esp. an advertisement in between the pages of a magazine [Latin *inserere* to plant in]

insertion *n* **1** the act of inserting **2** something inserted, such as an advertisement in a newspaper

in-service *adj* denoting training that is given to employees during the course of employment: *an in-service course*

inset *vb* **-setting, -set 1** to place in or within; insert ▷ *n* **2** something inserted **3** *printing* a small map or diagram set within the borders of a larger one ▷ *adj* **4** decorated with something inserted

inshore *adj* **1** in or on the water, but close to the shore: *inshore fishermen* ▷ *adv, adj* **2** towards the shore from the water: *the boat was forced inshore; a strong wind blowing inshore*

inside *prep* **1** in or to the interior of: *a bomb had gone off inside the parliament building* **2** in a period of time less than: *they took the lead inside seven minutes* ▷ *adj* **3** on or of the inside: *an article on the paper's inside pages* **4** by or from someone within an organization, esp. illicitly: *inside information* **5** of or being the lane in a road which is nearer the side than other lanes going in the same direction: *all the lorries were in the inside lane* ▷ *adv* **6** in, on, or to the inside; indoors: *when the rain started we took our drinks inside* **7** *Brit, Austral and NZ slang* in or into prison ▷ *n* **8** the inner side, surface, or part of something **9 inside out** with the inside facing outwards **10 know inside out** to know thoroughly ▶ See also **insides**

USAGE See at **outside.**

---

inside job *n informal* a crime committed with the assistance of someone employed by or trusted by the victim

insider *n* a member of a group or organization who therefore has exclusive information about it

insider dealing *n* the illegal practice of a person on the stock exchange or in the civil service taking advantage of early confidential information in order to deal in shares for personal profit

insides *pl n informal* the stomach and bowels

insidious *adj* working in a subtle or apparently harmless way, but nevertheless dangerous or deadly: *an insidious virus* [Latin *insidiae* an ambush] **> insidiously** *adv* **> insidiousness** *n*

insight *n* **1** a penetrating understanding, as of a complex situation or problem **2** the ability to perceive clearly or deeply the inner nature of things

insignia (in-**sig**-nee-a) *n, pl* **-nias** *or* **-nia** a badge or emblem of membership, office, or honour [Latin: badges]

insignificant *adj* having little or no importance **> insignificance** *n*

insincere *adj* pretending what one does not feel **> insincerely** *adv* **> insincerity** *n*

insinuate *vb* **-ating, -ated 1** to suggest indirectly by allusion, hints, or innuendo **2** to get (someone, esp. oneself) into a position by gradual manoeuvres: *she insinuated herself into the conversation* [Latin *insinuare* to wind one's way into]

insinuation *n* **1** an indirect or devious hint or suggestion **2** an act or the practice of insinuating

insipid *adj* **1** dull and boring **2** lacking flavour [Latin *in-* not + *sapidus* full of flavour] **> insipidity** *n*

insist *vb* (often foll. by *on* or *upon*) **1** to make a determined demand (for): *he insisted on his rights* **2** to express a convinced belief (in) or assertion (of): *she insisted that she had been given permission* [Latin *insistere* to stand upon, urge]

insistent *adj* **1** making continual and persistent demands **2** demanding attention: *the chirruping of an insistent bird* **> insistence** *n* **> insistently** *adv*

in situ *adv, adj* in the original position [Latin]

in so far as *or* **insofar as** *prep* to the degree or extent that

insole *n* **1** the inner sole of a shoe or boot **2** a loose inner sole used to give extra warmth or to make a shoe fit

insolent *adj* rude and disrespectful [Latin *in-* not + *solere* to be accustomed] **> insolence** *n* **> insolently** *adv*

insoluble *adj* **1** impossible to solve **2** not able to be dissolved **> insolubility** *n*

insolvent *adj* **1** unable to pay one's debts ▷ *n* **2** a person who is insolvent **> insolvency** *n*

insomnia *n* inability to sleep [Latin *in-* not + *somnus* sleep] **> insomniac** *n, adj*

insomuch *adv* **1** (foll. by *as* or *that*) to such an extent or degree **2** (foll. by *as*) because of the fact (that)

insouciant *adj* carefree or unconcerned [French] **> insouciance** *n*

inspan *vb* **-spanning, -spanned** *chiefly S African* **1** to harness (animals) to (a vehicle); yoke **2** to press (people) into service [Middle Dutch *inspannen*]

inspect *vb* **1** to examine closely, esp. for faults or errors **2** to examine officially [Latin *inspicere*] **> inspection** *n*

inspector *n* **1** an official who checks that things or places meet certain regulations and standards **2** a police officer ranking below a superintendent and above a sergeant

inspectorate *n* **1** a group of inspectors **2** the position or duties of an inspector

inspiration *n* **1** stimulation of the mind or feelings to activity or creativity **2** a person or thing that causes this state **3** an inspired idea or action **> inspirational** *adj*

inspire *vb* **-spiring, -spired 1** to stimulate (a person) to activity or creativity **2** to arouse (an emotion or a reaction): *he inspires confidence* [Latin *in-* into + *spirare* to breathe]

inspired *adj* **1** brilliantly creative: *his most inspired compositions* **2** very clever and accurate: *an inspired guess*

inst. *old-fashioned* instant (this month)

instability *n* lack of steadiness or reliability

install *vb* **1** to put in and prepare (equipment) for use **2** to place (a person) formally in a position or rank **3** to settle (a person, esp. oneself) in a position or state: *Tony installed himself in an armchair* [Medieval Latin *installare*]

installation *n* **1** installing **2** equipment that has been installed **3** a place containing equipment for a particular purpose: *radar installation*

installment plan *n* Also (Canad): **instalment plan** US same as **hire-purchase**

instalment *or* US **installment** *n* **1** one of the portions into which a debt is divided for payment at regular intervals **2** a portion of something that is issued, broadcast, or published in parts [probably from Old French *estal* something fixed]

instance *n* **1** a case or particular example **2** urgent request or order: *at the instance of* **3 for instance** as an example **4 in the first instance** in the first place; initially ▷ *vb* **-stancing, -stanced 5** to mention as an example [Latin *instantia* a being close upon]

instant *n* **1** a very brief time; moment **2** a particular moment: *at the same instant* ▷ *adj* **3** immediate **4** (of foods) able to be prepared very quickly and easily: *instant coffee* **5** urgent or pressing **6** of the present month: *a letter of the 7th instant* [Latin *instans* present, pressing closely]

instantaneous *adj* happening at once: *the applause was instantaneous* **> instantaneously** *adv*

instantly *adv* immediately

instant message *n* **1** an electronic message sent in real time over a computer network ▷ *vb* **instant-message 2** to communicate with (another person) using such messages **> instant messaging** *n*

instead *adv* **1** as a replacement or substitute for the person or thing mentioned **2 instead of** in place of or as an alternative to [*in stead* in place]

instep *n* **1** the middle part of the foot forming the arch between the ankle and toes **2** the part of a shoe or stocking covering this

instigate *vb* **-gating, -gated 1** to cause to happen: *to* *instigate rebellion* **2** to urge on to some action [Latin *instigare*] **> instigation** *n* **> instigator** *n*

instil *or US* **instill** *vb* **-stilling, -stilled 1** to introduce (an idea or feeling) gradually in someone's mind **2** *rare* to pour in or inject drop by drop [Latin *instillare* to pour in a drop at a time] **> instillation** *n* **> instiller** *n*

instinct *n* **1** the inborn tendency to behave in a particular way without the need for thought: *maternal instinct* **2** natural reaction: *my first instinct was to get out of the car* **3** intuition: *Mr Barr's mother said she knew by instinct that her son was safe* [Latin *instinctus* roused]

instinctive *or* **instinctual** *adj* done or happening without any logical thought: *an instinctive understanding of people* **> instinctively** *or* **instinctually** *adv*

institute *n* **1** an organization set up for a specific purpose, esp. research or teaching **2** the building where such an organization is situated **3** a rule, custom, or precedent ▷ *vb* **-tuting, -tuted 4** to start or establish **5** to install in a position or office [Latin *instituere*, from *statuere* to place]

institution *n* **1** a large important organization such as a university or bank **2** a hospital etc. for people with special needs **3** an established custom, law, or principle: *the institution of marriage* **4** *informal* a well-established person or feature: *the programme has became an institution* **5** an instituting or being instituted

institutional *adj* **1** of or relating to an institution: *institutional care* **2** dull, routine, and uniform: *institutional meals* **> institutionalism** *n*

institutionalize *or* **-lise** *vb* **-lizing, -lized** *or* **-lising, -lised 1** (*often passive*) to subject (a person) to institutional life, often causing apathy and dependence on routine **2** to make or become an institution: *institutionalized religion* **3** to place in an institution

instruct *vb* **1** to order to do something **2** to teach (someone) how to do something **3** to brief (a solicitor or barrister) [Latin *instruere*]

instruction *n* **1** a direction or order **2** the process or act of teaching **> instructional** *adj*

instructions *pl n* information on how to do or use something: *the plane had ignored instructions from air traffic controllers*

instructive *adj* informative or helpful

instructor *n* **1** a person who teaches something **2** *US and Canad* a college teacher ranking below assistant professor

instrument *n* **1** a tool or implement, esp. one used for precision work **2** *music* any of various devices that can be played to produce musical sounds **3** a measuring device to show height, speed, etc.: *the pilot's eyes never left his instruments* **4** *informal* a person used by another to gain an end **5** an important factor in something: *her evidence was an instrument in his arrest* **6** a formal legal document [Latin *instrumentum*]

instrumental *adj* **1** helping to cause **2** played by or composed for musical instruments **3** of or done with an instrument: *instrumental error*

instrumentalist *n* a person who plays a musical instrument

instrumentation *n* **1** a set of instruments in a car etc. **2** the arrangement of music for instruments **3** the list of instruments needed for a piece of music

instrument panel *n* a panel holding the instruments in a vehicle or on a machine

insubordinate *adj* not submissive to authority **> insubordination** *n*

insubstantial *adj* **1** flimsy, fine, or slight **2** imaginary or unreal

insufferable *adj* unbearable **> insufferably** *adv*

insufficient *adj* not enough for a particular purpose **> insufficiency** *n* **> insufficiently** *adv*

insular *adj* **1** not open to change or new ideas: *theatre tradition become rather insular* **2** of or like an island [Latin *insula* island] **> insularity** *n*

insulate *vb* **-lating, -lated 1** to prevent or reduce the transfer of electricity, heat, or sound by surrounding or lining with a nonconducting material **2** to isolate or set apart [Late Latin *insulatus* made into an island] **> insulator** *n*

insulation *n* **1** material used to insulate something **2** the act of insulating

insulin (in-syoo-lin) *n* a hormone produced in the pancreas which controls the amount of sugar in the blood [Latin *insula* islet (of tissue in the pancreas)]

insult *vb* **1** to treat or speak to rudely: *they insulted us and even threatened to kill us* ▷ *n* **2** an offensive remark or action **3** a person or thing producing the effect of an insult: *their explanation is an insult to our intelligence* [Latin *insultare* to jump upon]

insuperable *adj* impossible to overcome; insurmountable **> insuperability** *n*

insupportable *adj* **1** impossible to tolerate **2** incapable of being upheld or justified: *an insupportable accusation*

insurance *n* **1** the agreement by which one makes regular payments to a company who pay an agreed sum if damage, loss, or death occurs **2** the money paid for insurance or by an insurance company **3** a means of protection: *sensible insurance against heart attacks*

insurance policy *n* a contract of insurance

insure *vb* **-suring, -sured 1** to guarantee or protect (against risk or loss) **2** (often foll. by *against*) to issue (a person) with an insurance policy or take out an insurance policy (on): *the players were insured against accidents* **3** *chiefly US* same as **ensure** **> insurability** *n* **> insurable** *adj*

insured *n* **the insured** the person covered by an insurance policy

insurer *n* a person or company that sells insurance

insurgent *adj* **1** rebellious or in revolt against an established authority ▷ *n* **2** a person who takes part in a rebellion [Latin *insurgens* rising] **> insurgency** *n*

insurmountable *adj* impossible to overcome: *insurmountable problems*

insurrection *n* the act of rebelling against an established authority [Latin *insurgere* to rise up] **> insurrectionist** *n, adj*

int. 1 internal **2** Also: **Int** international

intact *adj* not changed or damaged in any way [Latin *intactus*]

intaglio (in-tah-lee-oh) *n, pl* **-lios** *or* **-li 1** a seal or gem decorated with an engraved design **2** an engraved design [Italian] **> intagliated** *adj*

intake *n* **1** a thing or a quantity taken in: *an intake of students* **2** the act of taking in **3** the opening through which fluid or gas enters a pipe or engine

intangible *adj* **1** difficult for the mind to grasp: *intangible ideas* **2** incapable of being felt by touch **> intangibility** *n*

integer *n* any positive or negative whole number or zero, as opposed to a number with fractions or decimals [Latin: untouched]

integral *adj* **1** being an essential part of a whole **2** whole or complete **3** *maths* **a** of or involving an integral **b** involving or being an integer ▷ *n* **4** *maths* the sum of a large number of minute quantities, summed either between stated limits (**definite integral**) or in the absence of limits (**indefinite integral**)

integral calculus *n* *maths* the branch of calculus concerned with the determination of integrals and their use in solving differential equations

integrand *n* *maths* a mathematical function to be integrated

integrate *vb* **-grating, -grated 1** to make or be made into a whole **2** to amalgamate (a racial or religious group) with an existing community **3** to designate (an institution) for use by all races or groups **4** *maths* to determine the integral of a function or variable [Latin *integrare*] **> integration** *n*

integrated circuit *n* a tiny electronic circuit

integrity n **1** honesty **2** the quality of being whole or united: *respect for a state's territorial integrity* **3** the quality of being unharmed or sound: *the integrity of the cell membrane* [Latin *integritas*]

integument n any natural protective covering, such as a skin, rind, or shell [Latin *integumentum*]

intellect n **1** the ability to understand, think, and reason **2** a particular person's mind or intelligence, esp. a brilliant one: *his intellect is wasted on that job* **3** *informal* a person who has a brilliant mind [Latin *intellectus* comprehension]

intellectual adj **1** of, involving, or appealing to the intellect: *intellectual literature* **2** clever or intelligent ▷ n **3** a person who has a highly developed intellect ⟩ **intellectuality** n ⟩ **intellectually** adv

intelligence n **1** the ability to understand, learn, and think things out quickly **2** the collection of secret information, esp. for military purposes **3** a group or department collecting military information **4** *old-fashioned* news or information [Latin *intellegere* to understand, literally: to choose between]

intelligence quotient n a measure of the intelligence of a person calculated by dividing the person's mental age by his or her actual age and multiplying the result by 100. Abbreviation: **IQ**

intelligent adj **1** having or showing intelligence: *an intelligent child*; *an intelligent guess* **2** (of a computerized device) able to initiate or modify action in the light of ongoing events ⟩ **intelligently** adv

intelligent design n a theory that rejects the theory of natural selection, arguing for an intelligent cause in the form of a creator

intelligentsia n the intelligentsia the educated or intellectual people in a society [Russian *intelligentsiya*]

intelligible adj able to be understood ⟩ **intelligibility** n

intemperate adj **1** unrestrained or uncontrolled: *intemperate remarks* **2** drinking alcohol too much or too often **3** extreme or severe: *an intemperate climate* ⟩ **intemperance** n

intend vb **1** to propose or plan (something or to do something) **2** to have as one's purpose **3** to mean to express or indicate: *no criticism was intended* **4** (often foll. by *for*) to design or destine (for a certain purpose or person): *the plane was never intended for combat* [Latin *intendere* to stretch forth]

intended adj **1** planned or future ▷ n **2** *informal* a person whom one is to marry

intense adj **1** of very great force, strength, degree, or amount: *intense heat* **2** characterized by deep or forceful feelings: *an intense person* [Latin *intensus* stretched] ⟩ **intensely** adv ⟩ **intenseness** n

USAGE *Intense* is sometimes wrongly used where *intensive* is meant: *the land is under intensive* (not *intense*) *cultivation. Intensely* is sometimes wrongly used where *intently* is meant: *he listened intently* (not *intensely*).

intensifier n a word, esp. an adjective or adverb, that intensifies the meaning of the word or phrase that it modifies, for example, *very* or *extremely*

intensify vb **-fies, -fying, -fied** to make or become intense or more intense ⟩ **intensification** n

intensity n, pl **-ties** **1** the state or quality of being intense **2** extreme force, degree, or amount **3** *physics* the amount or degree of strength of electricity, heat, light, or sound per unit area of volume

intensive adj **1** of or needing concentrated effort or resources: *intensive training* **2** using one specified factor more than others: *labour-intensive* **3** *agriculture* designed to increase production from a particular area: *intensive farming* **4** *grammar* (of a word) giving emphasis, for example, *very* in *the very same* ⟩ **intensively** adv ⟩ **intensiveness** n

USAGE See at **intense**.

intensive care n thorough, continuously supervised treatment of an acutely ill patient in a hospital

intent n **1** something that is intended **2** *law* the will or purpose to commit a crime: *loitering with intent* **3** to all intents and purposes in almost every respect; virtually ▷ adj **4** having one's attention firmly fixed: *an intent look* **5** intent on or upon strongly resolved on: *intent on winning the election* [Late Latin *intentus* aim] ⟩ **intently** adv ⟩ **intentness** n

USAGE See at **intense**.

intention n something intended; a plan, idea, or purpose: *he had no intention of resigning*

intentional adj done on purpose ⟩ **intentionally** adv

inter (in-ter) vb **-terring, -terred** to bury (a corpse) [Latin *in-* into + *terra* earth]

inter- prefix **1** between or among: *international* **2** together, mutually, or reciprocally: *interdependent* [Latin]

interact vb to act on or in close relation with each other ⟩ **interaction** n ⟩ **interactive** adj

inter alia (in-ter ale-ya) adv among other things [Latin]

interbreed vb **-breeding, -bred** **1** to breed within a related group so as to produce particular characteristics in the offspring **2** same as **crossbreed** (1)

intercede vb **-ceding, -ceded** **1** to plead in favour of **2** to act as a mediator in order to end a disagreement: *a policeman was watching the beatings without interceding* [Latin *inter-* between + *cedere* to move]

intercept vb **1** to stop or seize on the way from one place to another **2** *maths* to mark off or include (part of a line, curve, plane, or surface) between two points or lines ▷ n **3** *maths* **a** a point at which two figures intersect **b** the distance from the origin to the point at which a line, curve, or surface cuts a coordinate axis [Latin *intercipere* to seize before arrival] ⟩ **interception** n ⟩ **interceptor** n

intercession n **1** the act of interceding **2** a prayer offered to God on behalf of others ⟩ **intercessor** n

interchange vb **-changing, -changed** **1** to change places or cause to change places ▷ n **2** the act of interchanging **3** a motorway junction of interconnecting roads and bridges designed to prevent streams of traffic crossing one another ⟩ **interchangeable** adj ⟩ **interchangeably** adv

Intercity adj trademark (in Britain) denoting a fast train (service) travelling between cities

intercom n an internal communication system with loudspeakers [short for *intercommunication*]

intercommunicate vb **-cating, -cated** **1** to communicate mutually **2** (of two rooms) to interconnect ⟩ **intercommunication** n

intercommunion n association between Churches, involving mutual reception of Holy Communion

interconnect vb to connect with one another ⟩ **interconnected** adj ⟩ **interconnection** n

intercontinental adj travelling between or linking continents

intercourse n **1** the act of having sex **2** communication or dealings between individuals or groups [Latin *intercurrere* to run between]

interdenominational adj among or involving more than one denomination of the Christian Church

interdepartmental adj of or between different departments

interdependent adj dependent on one another ⟩ **interdependence** n

interdict n **1** *law* an official prohibition or restraint **2** *RC Church* the exclusion of a person or place from certain sacraments, although not from communion ▷ vb **3** to prohibit or forbid [Latin *interdicere* to forbid] ⟩ **interdiction** n ⟩ **interdictory** adj

interdisciplinary adj involving more than one branch of learning

interest n **1** curiosity or concern about something or someone **2** the power of causing this: *to have great interest* **3** something in which one is interested; a hobby or pursuit **4** (*often pl*) advantage: *in one's own interests* **5** money paid for the use of credit or borrowed money: *she borrowed money at 25 per cent interest* **6** (*often pl*) a right, share, or claim, esp. in a business or property **7** (*often pl*) a group of people with common aims: *foreign interests* ▷ vb **8** to arouse the curiosity or concern of **9** to cause to become interested or involved in something [Latin: it concerns]

interested adj **1** showing or having interest **2** involved in or affected by: *a consultation paper sent to interested parties*

interest group n a group of persons who attempt to influence legislators on behalf of a particular interest

interesting adj causing interest ⟩ **interestingly** adv

interface n **1** an area where two things interact or link: *the interface between Islamic culture and Western modernity* **2** an electrical circuit linking one device, esp. a computer, with another **3** *physics, chem* a surface that forms the boundary between two liquids or chemical phases that cannot be mixed ▷ vb **-facing, -faced** to connect or be connected with by interface ⟩ **interfacial** adj

interfacing n **1** a piece of fabric sewn beneath the facing of a garment to give shape and firmness **2** same as interlining

interfaith adj relating to, between, or involving different religions

interfere vb **-fering, -fered 1** to try to influence other people's affairs where one is not involved or wanted **2** *physics* to produce or cause to produce interference **3** interfere with **a** to clash with or hinder: *child-bearing may interfere with your career* **b** *Brit, Austral and NZ euphemistic* to abuse sexually [Old French *s'entreferir* to collide] ⟩ **interfering** adj

interference n **1** the act of interfering **2** any undesired signal that interferes with the reception of radio waves **3** *physics* the meeting of two waves which reinforce or neutralize each other depending on whether they are in or out of phase

interferon n *biochem* a protein made by cells that stops the development of an invading virus

interfuse vb **-fusing, -fused 1** to mix or become mixed **2** to blend or fuse together ⟩ **interfusion** n

intergalactic adj occurring or located between different galaxies

interim adj **1** temporary or provisional: *an interim government* ▷ n **2** in the interim during the intervening time [Latin: meanwhile]

interior n **1** a part or region that is on the inside: *the interior of the earth* **2** the inside of a building or room, with respect to design and decoration **3** the central area of a country or continent, furthest from the sea **4** a picture of the inside of a room or building ▷ adj **5** of, situated on, or suitable for the inside **6** mental or spiritual: *interior development* **7** coming or acting from within **8** of a nation's domestic affairs [Latin]

interior angle n an angle of a polygon contained between two adjacent sides

interior decoration n **1** the decoration and furnishings of the interior of a room or house **2** Also called: **interior design** the art or business of planning this ⟩ **interior decorator** n

interj. interjection

interject vb to make (a remark) suddenly or as an interruption [Latin *interjicere* to place between]

interjection n a word or phrase which is used on its own and which expresses sudden emotion

interlace vb **-lacing, -laced** to join by lacing or weaving together: *interlaced fingers*

Interlaken n a town and resort in central Switzerland, situated between Lakes Brienz and Thun on the River Aar. Pop: 5119 (2000)

interlard vb to insert in or occur throughout: *to interlard one's writing with foreign phrases*

interlay vb **-laying, -laid** to insert (layers) between: *to interlay gold among the silver*

interleaf n, pl **-leaves** an extra leaf which is inserted

interleave vb **-leaving, -leaved** to insert, as blank leaves in a book, between other leaves

interleukin (in-ter-loo-kin) n *biochem* a substance obtained from white blood cells that stimulates their activity against infection and may be used to fight some forms of cancer

interline[1] vb **-lining, -lined** to write or print (matter) between the lines of (a text or book)

interline[2] vb **-lining, -lined** to provide (a part of a garment) with a second lining

interlining n the material used to interline parts of garments

interlink vb to connect together

interlock vb **1** to join or be joined firmly together ▷ n **2** a device used to prevent a mechanism from operating independently or unsafely

interlocutor (in-ter-lock-yew-ter) n *formal* a person who takes part in a conversation [Latin *inter-* between + *loqui* to talk]

interlocutory (in-ter-lock-yew-tree) adj **1** *law* pronounced during the course of legal proceedings; provisional: *an interlocutory injunction* **2** *formal* of dialogue; conversational

interloper (in-ter-lope-er) n a person in a place or situation where he or she has no right to be

interlude n **1** a period of time or different activity between longer periods or events **2 a** a pause between the acts of a play **b** a brief piece of music or other entertainment performed during this pause [Latin *inter-* between + *ludus* play]

intermarry vb **-ries, -rying, -ried 1** (of different races, religions, or social groups) to become connected by marriage **2** to marry within one's own family or tribe ⟩ **intermarriage** n

intermediary n, pl **-aries 1** a person who tries to bring about agreement between others **2** a messenger ▷ adj **3** acting as an intermediary **4** intermediate

intermediate adj **1** occurring between two points or extremes **2** (of a class, course, etc.) suitable for learners with some level of skill or competence ▷ n **3** something intermediate **4** *chem* a substance formed between the first and final stages of a chemical process [Latin *inter-* between + *medius* middle] ⟩ **intermediation** n

interment n a burial

intermezzo (in-ter-met-so) n, pl **-zos** or **-zi 1** a short piece of instrumental music performed between the acts of a play or opera **2 a** a short composition between two longer movements in an extended musical work **b** a similar composition intended for independent performance [Italian]

interminable adj seemingly endless because boring: *an interminable rambling anecdote* ⟩ **interminably** adv

intermingle vb **-gling, -gled** to mix together

intermission n an interval between parts of a play, film, etc. [Latin *intermittere* to leave off, cease]

intermittent adj occurring at intervals ⟩ **intermittently** adv

intern vb **1** to imprison, esp. during wartime ▷ n **2 a** student or recent graduate receiving practical training in a working environment **3** *chiefly US* a trainee doctor in a hospital [Latin *internus* internal] ⟩ **internment** n

internal adj **1** of, situated on, or suitable for the inside **2** *anatomy* affecting or relating to the inside of the body: *internal bleeding* **3** of a nation's domestic affairs: *internal politics* **4** coming or acting from within an organization: *an internal reorganization* **5** spiritual or mental: *internal conflict* [Latin *internus*] ⟩ **internally** adv

internal-combustion engine n an engine in which power is produced by the explosion of a fuel-and-air mixture within the cylinders

international *adj* **1** of or involving two or more nations **2** controlling or legislating for several nations: *an international court* **3** available for use by all nations: *international waters* ▷ *n* **4** *sport* **a** a game or match between the national teams of different countries **b** a member of a national team **›internationally** *adv*

International *n* any of several international socialist organizations

International Date Line *n* the line approximately following the 180° meridian from Greenwich on the east side of which the date is one day earlier than on the west

internationalism *n* the ideal or practice of cooperation and understanding for the good of all nations **›internationalist** *n*

International Phonetic Alphabet *n* a series of signs and letters for the representation of human speech sounds. Abbreviation: **IPA**

International Style or **Modernism** *n* a 20th-century architectural style characterized by undecorated straight forms and the use of glass, steel, and reinforced concrete

internecine *adj formal* destructive to both sides: *internecine war* [Latin *internecare* to destroy]

internee *n* a person who is interned

internet *n* (*sometimes cap*) a large public access computer network linked to others worldwide

internet service provider *n* a business providing its customers with connection to the internet and other related services. Abbreviation: **ISP**

internist *n* a physician who specializes in internal medicine

interpenetrate *vb* **-trating, -trated 1** to penetrate (something) thoroughly **2** to penetrate each other or one another mutually **›interpenetration** *n*

interpersonal *adj* of or relating to relationships between people: *interpersonal conflict at work*

interplanetary *adj* of or linking planets

interplay *n* the action and reaction of things upon each other

Interpol International Criminal Police Organization: an association of over 100 national police forces, devoted chiefly to fighting international crime

interpolate (in-ter-pole-ate) *vb* **-lating, -lated 1** to insert (a comment or passage) into (a conversation or text) **2** *maths* to estimate (a value of a function) between the values already known [Latin *interpolare* to give a new appearance to] **›interpolation** *n*

interpose *vb* **-posing, -posed 1** to place (something) between or among other things **2** to interrupt (with comments or questions) **3** to put forward so as to interrupt: *he ended the discussion by interposing a veto* [Latin *inter-* between + *ponere* to put] **›interposition** *n*

interpret *vb* **1** to explain the meaning of **2** to work out the significance of: *his remarks were widely interpreted as a promise not to raise taxes* **3** to convey the meaning of (a poem, song, etc.) in performance **4** to act as an interpreter [Latin *interpretari*] **›interpretive** *adj*

interpretation *n* **1** the act or result of interpreting or explaining **2** the particular way in which a performer expresses his or her view of a composition: *an interpretation of Mahler's fourth symphony* **3** explanation, as of a historical site, provided by the use of original objects, visual display material, etc.

interpreter *n* **1** a person who translates orally from one language into another **2** *computers* a program that translates a statement in a source program to machine language and executes it before translating and executing the next statement

interpretive centre *n* a building situated at a place of interest, such as a country park or historical site, that provides information about the site by showing videos, exhibiting objects, etc.

interracial *adj* between or among people of different races

interregnum *n, pl* **-nums** or **-na** a period between the end of one ruler's reign and the beginning of the next [Latin *inter-* between + *regnum* reign] **›interregnal** *adj*

interrelate *vb* **-lating, -lated** to connect (two or more things) or (of two or more things) to become connected to each other **›interrelation** *n* **›interrelationship** *n*

interrogate *vb* **-gating, -gated** to question (someone) closely [Latin *interrogare*] **›interrogation** *n* **›interrogator** *n*

interrogative (in-ter-rog-a-tiv) *adj* **1** used in asking a question: *an interrogative pronoun* **2** of or like a question: *an interrogative look* ▷ *n* **3** an interrogative word, phrase, sentence, or construction

interrogatory (in-ter-rog-a-tree) *adj* **1** expressing or involving a question ▷ *n, pl* **-tories 2** a question or interrogation

interrupt *vb* **1** to break into (a conversation or discussion) by questions or comment **2** to stop (a process or activity) temporarily [Latin *inter-* between + *rumpere* to break] **›interrupted** *adj* **›interruptive** *adj*

interrupter or **interruptor** *n* a device for opening and closing an electric circuit

interruption *n* **1** something that interrupts, such as a comment or question **2** an interval or intermission **3** the act of interrupting or the state of being interrupted

interscholastic *adj* occurring between two or more schools: *an interscholastic competition*

intersect *vb* **1** (of roads or lines) to cross (each other) **2** to divide or mark off (a place, area, or surface) by passing through or across [Latin *intersecare* to divide]

intersection *n* **1** a point at which things intersect, esp. a road junction **2** the act of intersecting or the state of being intersected **3** *maths* **a** a point or set of points common to two or more geometric figures **b** the set of elements that are common to two sets **›intersectional** *adj*

intersex *n* **1** the condition of having characteristics in between those of a male and a female **2** an individual exhibiting such characteristics

intersperse *vb* **-spersing, -spersed 1** to scatter among, between, or on **2** to mix (something) with other things scattered here and there [Latin *inter-* between + *spargere* to sprinkle] **›interspersion** *n*

interstellar *adj* between or among stars

interstice (in-ter-stiss) *n* (*usually pl*) **1** a small gap or crack between things **2** *physics* the space between adjacent atoms in a crystal lattice [Latin *interstitium* interval]

intertwine *vb* **-twining, -twined** to twist together

interval *n* **1** the period of time between two events **2** *Brit and Austral* a short period between parts of a play, concert, etc. **3** *music* the difference of pitch between two notes **4 at intervals a** now and then: *turn the chicken at intervals* **b** with a certain amount of space between: *the poles were placed at intervals of twenty metres* [Latin *intervallum*, literally: space between two palisades]

intervene *vb* **-vening, -vened 1** (often foll. by *in*) to involve oneself in a situation, esp. to prevent conflict **2** to interrupt a conversation **3** to happen so as to stop something: *he hoped to play but a serious injury intervened* **4** to come or be among or between: *ten years had intervened since he had seen Joe* [Latin *intervenire* to come between]

intervention *n* the act of intervening, esp. to influence or alter a situation in some way **›interventionist** *n, adj*

interview *n* **1** a formal discussion, esp. one in which an employer assesses a job applicant **2** a conversation in which a well-known person is asked about his or her views, career, etc., by a reporter ▷ *vb* **3** to question (someone) [Old French *entrevue*] **›interviewee** *n* **›interviewer** *n*

interwar *adj* of or happening in the period between World War I and World War II

interweave *vb* **-weaving, -wove** or **-weaved, -woven** or **-weaved** to weave together

intestate *adj* **1** (of a person) not having made a will ▷ *n*

2 a person who dies without having made a will [Latin *intestatus*] > **intestacy** *n*

intestine *n* the part of the alimentary canal between the stomach and the anus. See **large intestine, small intestine** [Latin *intestinus* internal] > **intestinal** *adj*

intifada (in-tiff-ah-da) *n* the Palestinian uprising against Israel in the West Bank and Gaza Strip [Arabic]

intimacy *n, pl* **-cies 1** close or warm friendship **2** (*often pl*) intimate words or acts within a close relationship

intimate¹ *adj* **1** characterized by a close or warm personal relationship: *an intimate friend* **2** deeply personal, private, or secret **3** (of knowledge) extensive and detailed **4** *euphemistic* having sexual relations **5** having a friendly quiet atmosphere: *an intimate nightclub* ▷ *n* **6** a close friend [Latin *intimus* innermost] > **intimately** *adv*

intimate² *vb* **-mating, -mated** *formal* **1** to make (something) known in an indirect way: *he has intimated his intention to retire* **2** to announce [Late Latin *intimare* to proclaim] > **intimation** *n*

intimidate *vb* **-dating, -dated** to subdue or influence (someone) through fear [Latin *in-* in + *timidus* fearful] > **intimidating** *adj* > **intimidation** *n*

into *prep* **1** to the inner part of: *they went into the house* **2** to the middle of so as to be surrounded by: *into the bushes* **3** against; up against: *he drove into a wall* **4** used to indicate the result of a change: *they turned the theatre into a garage* **5** *maths* used to indicate division: *three into six is two* **6** *informal* interested in: *I'm really into healthy food*

intolerable *adj* more than can be endured > **intolerably** *adv*

intolerant *adj* refusing to accept practices and beliefs that differ from one's own > **intolerance** *n*

intonation *n* **1** the sound pattern produced by variations in the voice **2** the act of intoning **3** *music* the ability to play or sing in tune > **intonational** *adj*

intone *vb* **-toning, -toned 1** to speak or recite in a monotonous tone **2** to speak with a particular tone [Medieval Latin *intonare*]

in toto *adv* totally or entirely [Latin]

intoxicant *n* **1** something, such as an alcoholic drink, that causes intoxication ▷ *adj* **2** causing intoxication

intoxicate *vb* **-cating, -cated 1** (of an alcoholic drink) to make (a person) drunk **2** to stimulate or excite to a point beyond self-control [Latin *in-* in + *toxicum* poison] > **intoxicated** *adj* > **intoxicating** *adj*

intoxication *n* **1** the state of being drunk **2** great excitement and exhilaration

Intracoastal Waterway *n* short for **Atlantic Intracoastal Waterway**

intractable *adj* **1** (of a person) difficult to influence or direct **2** (of a problem or illness) difficult to solve or cure > **intractability** *n* > **intractably** *adv*

intramural *adj chiefly US and Canad* operating within or involving those within a school or college: *intramural sports* [Latin *intra-* inside + *murus* wall]

intranet *n computers* an internal network that makes use of internet technology [*intra-* + INTERNET]

intransigent *adj* **1** refusing to change one's attitude ▷ *n* **2** an intransigent person, esp. in politics [Latin *in-* not + *transigere* to settle] > **intransigence** *n*

intransitive *adj* (of a verb) not taking a direct object: *'to faint' is an intransitive verb* > **intransitively** *adv*

intrapreneur *n Brit and US* a person who while remaining within a larger organization uses entrepreneurial skills to develop new services or systems as a subsidiary of the organization [*intra-* inside + *(entre)preneur*]

intrauterine *adj* situated within the womb [Latin *intra-* inside + *uterus* womb]

intrauterine device *n* a contraceptive device in the shape of a coil, inserted into the womb

intravenous (in-tra-vee-nuss) *adj anatomy* into a vein: *intravenous drug users* [Latin *intra-* inside + *vena* vein] > **intravenously** *adv*

in-tray *n* a tray used in offices for incoming letters or documents requiring attention

intrepid *adj* fearless or bold [Latin *in-* not + *trepidus* fearful] > **intrepidity** *n* > **intrepidly** *adv*

intricate *adj* **1** difficult to sort out: *an intricate problem* **2** full of complicated detail: *intricate Arab mosaics* [Latin *intricare* to entangle] > **intricacy** *n* > **intricately** *adv*

intrigue *vb* **-triguing, -trigued 1** to make interested or curious: *a question which has intrigued him for years* **2** to plot secretly or dishonestly ▷ *n* **3** secret plotting **4** a secret love affair [French *intriguer*] > **intriguing** *adj* > **intriguingly** *adv*

intrinsic *adj* **1** essential to the real nature of a thing: *hedgerows are an intrinsic part of the countryside* **2** *anatomy* situated within or peculiar to a part: *intrinsic muscles* [Latin *intrinsecus* inwardly] > **intrinsically** *adv*

intro *n, pl* **-tros** *informal* short for **introduction**

introduce *vb* **-ducing, -duced 1** to present (someone) by name (to another person) **2** to present (a radio or television programme) **3** to present for consideration or approval: *he introduced the bill to Parliament in 1967* **4** to bring into use: *Latvia has introduced its own currency into circulation* **5** to insert **6 introduce to** to cause to experience for the first time: *his father introduced him to golf* **7 introduce with** to start: *he introduced his talk with some music* [Latin *introducere* to bring inside] > **introducible** *adj*

introduction *n* **1** the act of introducing something or someone **2** a preliminary part, as of a book or musical composition **3** a book that explains the basic facts about a particular subject to a beginner **4** a presentation of one person to another or others

introductory *adj* serving as an introduction

introit *n* **1** RC *Church* a short prayer said or sung as the celebrant is entering the sanctuary to celebrate Mass **2** *Church of England* a hymn or psalm sung at the beginning of a service [Latin *introitus* entrance]

introspection *n* the examining of one's own thoughts, impressions, and feelings [Latin *introspicere* to look within] > **introspective** *adj*

introversion *n psychol* the directing of interest inwards towards one's own thoughts and feelings rather than towards the external world or making social contacts

introvert *adj* **1** shy and quiet **2** *psychol* concerned more with inner feelings than with external reality ▷ *n* **3** such a person [Latin *intro-* inward + *vertere* to turn] > **introverted** *adj*

intrude *vb* **-truding, -truded** to come in or join in without being invited [Latin *intrudere* to thrust in]

intruder *n* a person who enters a place without permission

intrusion *n* **1** the act of intruding; an unwelcome visit, etc.: *an intrusion into her private life* **2** *geology* **a** the forcing of molten rock into spaces in the overlying strata **b** molten rock formed in this way > **intrusive** *adj*

intrust *vb* same as **entrust**

intuition *n* instinctive knowledge of or belief about something without conscious reasoning: *intuition told her something was wrong* [Latin *intueri* to gaze upon] > **intuitional** *adj*

intuitive *adj* of, possessing, or resulting from intuition: *an intuitive understanding* > **intuitively** *adv*

Inuit *n, pl* **-it** *or* **-its** an indigenous inhabitant of North America or Greenland [Inuktitut, plural of *inuk* person]

Inuk *n* a member of the Inuit people

Inuktitut *n* the language of the Inuit

inundate *vb* **-dating, -dated 1** to cover completely with water **2** to overwhelm, as if with a flood: *the police were inundated with calls* [Latin *inundare*] > **inundation** *n*

inured *adj* able to tolerate something unpleasant because one has become accustomed to it: *he became inured to the casual brutality of his captors* [Middle English *enuren* to accustom] > **inurement** *n*

invade *vb* **-vading, -vaded 1** to enter (a country or territory) by military force **2** to enter in large numbers:

the town was invaded by rugby supporters **3** to disturb (privacy, etc.) [Latin *invadere*] **> invader** *n*

invalid[1] *n* **1** a person who is disabled or chronically ill ▷ *adj* **2** sick or disabled ▷ *vb* **3** *chiefly Brit* to dismiss (a soldier etc.) from active service because of illness [Latin *in-* not + *validus* strong] **> invalidism** *n*

invalid[2] *adj* **1** having no legal force: *an invalid cheque* **2** (of an argument, result, etc.) not valid because it has been based on a mistake **> invalidity** *n* **> invalidly** *adv*

invalidate *vb* **-dating, -dated** **1** to make or show (an argument) to be invalid **2** to take away the legal force of (a contract) **> invalidation** *n*

invaluable *adj* having great value that is impossible to calculate

invariable *adj* unchanging **> invariably** *adv*

invasion *n* **1** the act of invading with armed forces **2** any intrusion: *an invasion of privacy* **> invasive** *adj*

invective *n* abusive speech or writing [Late Latin *invectivus* scolding]

inveigh (in-vay) *vb* **inveigh against** *formal* to make harsh criticisms against [Latin *invehi*, literally: to be carried in, hence assail]

inveigle *vb* **-gling, -gled** to coax or manipulate (someone) into an action or situation [Old French *avogler* to blind, deceive] **> inveiglement** *n*

invent *vb* **1** to think up or create (something new) **2** to make up (a story, excuse, etc.) [Latin *invenire* to find] **> inventor** *n*

invention *n* **1** something that is invented **2** the act of inventing **3** creative power; inventive skill **4** *euphemistic* a lie: *his story is a malicious invention*

inventive *adj* creative and resourceful: *her inventive use of colour*

inventory (in-ven-tree) *n, pl* **-tories** **1** a detailed list of the objects in a particular place ▷ *vb* **-tories, -torying, -toried** **2** to make a list of [Medieval Latin *inventorium*]

Inveraray *n* a town in W Scotland, in Argyll and Bute: Inveraray Castle is the seat of the Dukes of Argyll. Pop: about 700 (2001)

Invercargill *n* a city in New Zealand, on South Island: regional trading centre for sheep and agricultural products. Pop: 51 700 (2004 est)

Inverclyde *n* a council area of W central Scotland: created in 1996 from part of Strathclyde region. Administrative centre: Greenock. Pop: 83 050 (2003 est). Area: 162 sq km (63 sq miles)

Inverness *n* **1** a city in N Scotland, administrative centre of Highland: tourism and specialized engineering. Pop: 40 949 (2001) **2** (*sometimes not cap*) an overcoat with a removable cape

Inverness-shire *n* (until 1975) a county of NW Scotland, now part of Highland

inverse *adj* **1** opposite in effect, sequence, direction, etc. **2** *maths* linking two variables in such a way that one increases as the other decreases ▷ *n* **3** the exact opposite: *the inverse of this image* **4** *maths* an inverse element

inversion *n* **1** the act of inverting or state of being inverted **2** something inverted, esp. a reversal of order, functions, etc.: *an inversion of their previous relationship* **> inversive** *adj*

invert *vb* **1** to turn upside down or inside out **2** to reverse in effect, sequence, or direction ▷ *n* **3** a homosexual [Latin *in-* in + *vertere* to turn] **> invertible** *adj*

invertebrate *n* **1** any animal without a backbone, such as an insect, worm, or octopus ▷ *adj* **2** of or designating invertebrates

inverted commas *pl n* same as **quotation marks**

invest *vb* **1** (often foll. by *in*) to put (money) into an enterprise with the expectation of profit **2** (often foll. by *in*) to devote (time or effort to a project) **3** to give power or authority to: *invested with the powers of government* **4** (often foll. by *in*) to install someone (in an official position) **5** (foll. by *with* or *in*) to credit or provide (a person with qualities): *he was invested with great common sense* **6 invest in**

to buy: *she invested in some barbecue equipment* **7 invest with** usually poetic to cover, as if with a coat: *when spring invests the trees with leaves* [Medieval Latin *investire* to clothe] **> investor** *n*

investigate *vb* **-gating, -gated** to inquire into (a situation or problem) thoroughly in order to discover the truth: *the police are currently investigating the case* [Latin *investigare* to search after] **> investigative** *adj* **> investigator** *n*

investigation *n* a careful search or examination in order to discover facts

investiture *n* the formal installation of a person in an office or rank

investment *n* **1** the act of investing **2** money invested **3** something in which money is invested

investment trust *n* a financial enterprise that invests its subscribed capital in a wide range of securities for its investors' benefit

inveterate *adj* **1** deep-rooted or ingrained: *an inveterate enemy of Marxism* **2** confirmed in a habit or practice: *an inveterate gambler* [Latin *inveteratus* of long standing] **> inveteracy** *n*

invidious *adj* likely to cause resentment or unpopularity [Latin *invidia* envy]

invigilate (in-vij-il-late) *vb* **-lating, -lated** *Brit* to supervise people who are sitting an examination [Latin *invigilare* to watch over] **> invigilation** *n* **> invigilator** *n*

invigorate *vb* **-rating, -rated** to give energy to or refresh [Latin *in-* in + *vigor* vigour] **> invigorating** *adj*

invincible *adj* incapable of being defeated: *an army of invincible strength* [Latin *in-* not + *vincere* to conquer] **> invincibility** *n* **> invincibly** *adv*

inviolable *adj* that must not be broken or violated: *an inviolable oath* **> inviolability** *n*

inviolate *adj* free from harm or injury **> inviolacy** *n*

invisible *adj* **1** not able to be seen by the eye: *invisible radiation* **2** concealed from sight **3** *econ* relating to services, such as insurance and freight, rather than goods: *invisible earnings* **> invisibility** *n* **> invisibly** *adv*

invitation *n* **1** a request to attend a dance, meal, etc. **2** the card or paper on which an invitation is written

invite *vb* **-viting, -vited** **1** to ask (a person) in a friendly or polite way (to do something, attend an event, etc.) **2** to make a request for, esp. publicly or formally: *we invite applications for six scholarships* **3** to bring on or provoke: *his theory invites disaster* **4** to tempt ▷ *n* **5** *informal* an invitation [Latin *invitare*]

inviting *adj* tempting or attractive

in vitro *adv, adj* (of biological processes or reactions) happening outside the body of the organism in an artificial environment [New Latin, literally: in glass]

invocation *n* **1** the act of invoking **2** a prayer to God or another deity asking for help, forgiveness, etc. **> invocatory** *adj*

invoice *n* **1** a bill for goods and services supplied ▷ *vb* **-voicing, -voiced** **2** to present (a customer) with an invoice [Old French *envois*, plural of *envoi* message]

invoke *vb* **-voking, -voked** **1** to put (a law or penalty) into use: *chapter 8 of the UN charter was invoked* **2** to bring about: *the hills invoked a feeling of serenity* **3** to call on (God or another deity) for help, inspiration, etc. **4** to summon (a spirit) by uttering magic words [Latin *invocare* to appeal to]

USAGE *Invoke* is sometimes wrongly used where *evoke* is meant: *this proposal evoked* (not *invoked*) *a strong reaction.*

---

involuntary *adj* **1** carried out without one's conscious wishes; unintentional **2** *physiol* (esp. of a movement or muscle) performed or acting without conscious control **> involuntarily** *adv*

involute *adj* also: **involuted** **1** complex, intricate, or involved **2** rolled inwards or curled in a spiral ▷ *n*

3 *geometry* the curve described by the free end of a thread as it is wound around another curve on the same plane [Latin *involutus*]

involve *vb* **-volving, -volved 1** to include as a necessary part **2** to have an effect on: *around fifty riders were involved and some were hurt* **3** to implicate: *several people were involved in the crime* **4** to make complicated: *the situation was further involved by her disappearance* [Latin *in-* in + *volvere* to roll] **> involvement** *n*

involved *adj* **1** complicated **2 involved in** concerned in

invulnerable *adj* not able to be wounded or damaged **> invulnerability** *n*

inward *adj* **1** directed towards the middle of something **2** situated within **3** of the mind or spirit: *inward meditation* **4** of one's own country or a specific country: *inward investment* ▷ *adv* **5** same as **inwards**

inwardly *adv* **1** within the private thoughts or feelings: *inwardly troubled, he kept smiling* **2** not aloud: *to laugh inwardly* **3** in or on the inside

inwards *or* **inward** *adv* towards the inside or middle of something

inwrought *adj* worked or woven into material, esp. decoratively

in-your-face *adj slang* aggressive and confrontational: *in-your-face advertising*

Io *chem* ionium

Ioánnina *or* **Yanina** *n* a city in NW Greece: belonged to the Serbs (1349–1430) and then the Turks (until 1913); seat of Ali Pasha, the "Lion of Janina", from 1788 to 1822. Pop: 78 000 (2005 est.). Serbian name: **Janina**

iodide *n chem* a compound containing an iodine atom, such as methyl iodide

iodine *n chem* a bluish-black element found in seaweed and used in medicine, photography, and dyeing. Symbol: **I** [Greek *iōdēs* rust-coloured, but mistakenly derived from *ion* violet]

iodize *or* **-dise** *vb* **-dizing, -dized** *or* **-dising, -dised** to treat with iodine **> iodization** *or* **-disation** *n*

IOM Isle of Man

ion *n* an electrically charged atom or group of atoms formed by the loss or gain of one or more electrons [Greek, literally: going]

Iona *n* an island off the W coast of Scotland, in the Inner Hebrides: site of St Columba's monastery (founded in 563) and an important early centre of Christianity. Area: 854 ha (2112 acres)

Ionesco *n* Eugène. 1912–94, French dramatist, born in Romania; a leading exponent of the theatre of the absurd. His plays include *The Bald Prima Donna* (1950) and *Rhinoceros* (1960)

ion exchange *n* the process in which ions are exchanged between a solution and an insoluble solid. It is used to soften water

Ionia *n* an ancient region of W central Asia Minor, including adjacent Aegean islands: colonized by Greeks in about 1100 BC

Ionian *n* **1** a member of a Hellenic people who settled in Attica in about 1100 BC and later colonized the islands and E coast of the Aegean Sea ▷ *adj* **2** of or relating to this people or their dialect of Ancient Greek **3** of or relating to Ionia

Ionian Islands *pl n* a group of Greek islands in the Ionian Sea, consisting of Corfu, Cephalonia, Zante, Levkas, Ithaca, Cythera, and Paxos: ceded to Greece in 1864. Pop: 212 984 (2001). Area: 2307 sq km (891 sq miles)

Ionian Sea *n* the part of the Mediterranean Sea between SE Italy, E Sicily, and Greece

ionic *adj* of or in the form of ions

Ionic *adj* of a style of classical architecture characterized by fluted columns with scroll-like ornaments on the capital

ionize *or* **-ise** *vb* **-izing, -ized** *or* **-ising, -ised** to change or become changed into ions **> ionization** *or* **-isation** *n*

ionosphere *n* a region of ionized layers of air in the earth's upper atmosphere, which reflects radio waves **> ionospheric** *adj*

iota (eye-oh-ta) *n* **1** the ninth letter in the Greek alphabet (I, ι) **2** a very small amount: *I don't feel one iota of guilt*

Iō-tō *n* the official Japanese name for **Iwo Jima**

IOU *n* a written promise or reminder to pay a debt [representing *I owe you*]

IOW Isle of Wight

Iowa *n* a state of the N central US, in the Midwest: consists of rolling plains crossed by many rivers, with the Missouri forming the western border and the Mississippi the eastern. Capital: Des Moines. Pop: 2 944 062 (2003 est.). Area: 144 887 sq km (55 941 sq miles). Abbreviation: **Ia.**, (with zip code) **IA**

Iowan *n* **1** a native or inhabitant of Iowa ▷ *adj* **2** of or relating to Iowa or its inhabitants

IP *computers* internet protocol: a code used to label packets of data sent across the internet, identifying both the sending and the receiving computers

IPA International Phonetic Alphabet

iPad *n trademark* a small portable computer activated by touching the screen

IP address *computers* internet protocol address: a unique code that identifies each computer connected to the internet

Ipatieff *n* Vladimir Nikolaievich. 1867–1952, US physicist, born in Russia. He discovered the structure of isoprene (1897) and later developed high-octane fuels

ipecacuanha (ip-pee-kak-yew-ann-a) *or* **ipecac** (ip-pee-kak) *n* a drug made from the dried roots of a S American plant, used to cause vomiting [S American Indian *ipekaaguéne*]

I-pin *n* a variant transliteration of the Chinese name for Yibin

iPod *n trademark* a small portable digital audio player capable of storing thousands of tracks in a variety of formats including MP3

Ipoh *n* a city in Malaysia, capital of Perak state: tin-mining centre. Pop: 643 000 (2005 est)

Ipsambul *n* another name for **Abu Simbel**

ipso facto *adv* by that very fact or act [Latin]

Ipsus *n* an ancient town in Asia Minor, in S Phrygia: site of a decisive battle (301 BC) in the Wars of the Diadochi in which Lysimachus and Seleucus defeated Antigonus and Demetrius

Ipswich *n* a town in E England, administrative centre of Suffolk, a port at the head of the Orwell estuary: financial services, telecommunications. Pop: 138 718 (2001)

IQ intelligence quotient

Iqaluit *n* a town in N Canada, capital of Nunavut. Pop: 6699 (2011). Former name: **Frobisher Bay**

Iqbal *n* Sir Muhammad. 1875–1938, Indian Muslim poet, philosopher, and political leader, who advocated the establishment of separate nations for Indian Hindus and Muslims and is generally regarded as the originator of Pakistan

Iquique *n* a port in N Chile: oil refineries. Pop: 243 000 (2005 est)

Iquitos *n* an inland port in NE Peru, on the Amazon 3703 km (2300 miles) from the Atlantic: head of navigation for large steamers. Pop: 389 000 (2005 est)

Ir *chem* iridium

Ir. **1** Ireland **2** Irish

IRA Irish Republican Army

Iráklion *n* a port in Greece, in N Crete: former capital of Crete (until 1841); ruled by Venetians (13th–17th centuries). Pop: 150 000 (2005 est). Italian name: **Candia**. Also called: **Heraklion, Herakleion**

Iran *n* a republic in SW Asia, between the Caspian Sea and the Persian Gulf: a monarchy until an Islamic revolution in 1979 headed by the Ayatollah Khomeini when the Shah was obliged to leave the country. Consists chiefly of a high central desert plateau almost completely surrounded by mountains, a semitropical fertile region along the Caspian coast, and a hot and dry area beside the Persian Gulf. Oil is the most important export. Official language: Persian (Iranian or Farsi). Official religion: Muslim majority. Currency: rial. Capital: Tehran. Pop: 79 853 900 (2013 est). Area: 1 647 050 sq km (635 932 sq miles). Former name (until 1935): **Persia**. Official name: **Islamic Republic of Iran**

Iranian *adj* **1** of or relating to Iran or its inhabitants ▷ *n* **2** a native or inhabitant of Iran **3** a branch of the Indo-European family of languages, including Persian

Iraq *n* a republic in SW Asia, on the Persian Gulf: coextensive with ancient Mesopotamia; became a British mandate in 1920, independent in 1932, and a republic in 1958. The Iraqi invasion of Kuwait (1990) led to their defeat in the first Gulf War (1991) by US-led UN forces. The second Gulf War (2003) took place when Iraq was invaded by a coalition of US, UK, and other forces; government elected in 2005, although there is continuing violence and resistance to the coalition presence; the last coalition troops left the country in 2011. Iraq consists chiefly of the mountains of Kurdistan in the northeast, part of the Syrian Desert, and the lower basin of the Rivers Tigris and Euphrates. Oil is the major export. Official language: Arabic; Kurdish is official in the Kurdish Autonomous Region only. Official religion: Muslim. Currency: dinar. Capital: Baghdad. Pop: 31 858 481 (2013 est). Area: 438 446 sq km (169 284 sq miles)

Iraqi *adj* **1** of or relating to Iraq or its inhabitants ▷ *n* **2** a native or inhabitant of Iraq

irascible *adj* easily angered [Latin *ira* anger] **> irascibility** *n* **> irascibly** *adv*

irate *adj* very angry [Latin *iratus* enraged]

Irbid *n* a town in NW Jordan. Pop: 280 000 (2005 est)

Irbil *n* a variant of Erbil

ire *n literary* anger [Latin *ira*]

Ire. Ireland

Ireland¹ *n* **1** an island off NW Europe: part of the British Isles, separated from Britain by the North Channel, the Irish Sea, and St George's Channel; contains large areas of peat bog, with mountains that rise over 900 m (3000 ft) in the southwest and several large lakes. It was conquered by England in the 16th and early 17th centuries and ruled as a dependency until 1801, when it was united with Great Britain until its division in 1921 into the Irish Free State and Northern Ireland. Latin name: **Hibernia** **2** Republic of Ireland, Irish Republic *or* Southern Ireland a republic in NW Europe occupying most of Ireland: established as the Irish Free State (a British dominion) in 1921 and declared a republic in 1949; joined the European Community (now the European Union) in 1973. Official languages: Irish (Gaelic) and English. Currency: euro. Capital: Dublin. Pop: 4 775 982 (2013 est). Area: 70 285 sq km (27 137 sq miles) ▶ Gaelic name: **Eire**. See also **Northern Ireland**

Ireland² *n* John (Nicholson). 1879–1962, English composer, esp. of songs

Irene *n* **1** ?752–803 AD, Byzantine ruler (780–90, 792–97, joint ruler with her son Constantine VI; 797–802). She is venerated as a saint in the Greek Orthodox Church **2** *Greek myth* the goddess of peace

Ireton *n* Henry. 1611–51, English Parliamentarian general in the Civil War; son-in-law of Oliver Cromwell. His plan for a constitutional monarchy was rejected by Charles I (1647), whose death warrant he signed; lord deputy of Ireland (1650–51)

Irian Barat *n* a former Indonesian name for Papua (2)

Irian Jaya *n* a former Indonesian name (1973–2001) for Papua (2)

iridaceous (ir-rid-**day**-shuss) *adj* of or belonging to the iris family

iridescent *adj* having shimmering changing colours like a rainbow [Latin *irid-* iris] **> iridescence** *n*

iridium *n chem* a hard yellowish-white chemical element that occurs in platinum ores and is used as an alloy with platinum. Symbol: Ir [Latin *irid-* iris]

iris *n* **1** the coloured muscular membrane in the eye that surrounds and controls the size of the pupil **2** a tall plant with long pointed leaves and large flowers [Greek: rainbow]

Irish *adj* **1** of or relating to Ireland or its inhabitants ▷ *n* **2** same as **Irish Gaelic 3** the dialect of English spoken in Ireland ▷ *pl n* **4 the Irish** the people of Ireland

Irish coffee *n* hot coffee mixed with Irish whiskey and topped with double cream

Irish Free State *n* a former name (1921–37) for (the Republic of) Ireland

Irish Gaelic *n* the Celtic language of Ireland

Irishman *or fem* **Irishwoman** *n, pl* **-men** *or fem* **-women** a native or inhabitant of Ireland

Irish moss *n* same as carrageen

Irish Republic *n* See Ireland (2)

Irish Sea *n* an arm of the North Atlantic Ocean between Great Britain and Ireland

irk *vb* to irritate or vex [Middle English *irken* to grow weary]

irksome *adj* annoying or tiresome

Irkutsk *n* a city in S Russia; situated on the Trans-Siberian railway; university (1918); one of the largest industrial centres in Siberia, esp. for heavy engineering. Pop: 587 000 (2005 est)

iron *n* **1** a strong silvery-white metallic element, widely used for structural and engineering purposes. Symbol: Fe **2** a tool made of iron **3** a small electrically heated device with a weighted flat bottom for pressing clothes **4** *golf* a club with an angled metal head **5** a splintlike support for a malformed leg **6** great strength or resolve: *a will of iron* **7 strike while the iron is hot** to act at a suitable moment ▷ *adj* **8** made of iron **9** very hard or merciless: *iron determination* **10** very strong: *an iron constitution* ▷ *vb* **11** to smooth (clothes or fabric) by removing (creases) with an iron ▶ See also **iron out, irons** [Old English *irēn*]

Iron Age *n* a phase of human culture that began in the Middle East about 1100 BC, during which iron tools and weapons were used

ironbark *n* an Australian eucalyptus with hard rough bark

Ironbridge Gorge *n* a gorge formed by the river Severn in Shropshire; named after the Iron Bridge (1779), the first iron bridge of its kind in the world, now a monument to the Industrial Revolution

ironclad *adj* **1** covered or protected with iron: *an ironclad warship* **2** unable to be contradicted: *ironclad proof* ▷ *n* **3** *history* a large wooden 19th-century warship with armoured plating

Iron Curtain *n* (formerly) the guarded border between the countries of the Soviet bloc and the rest of Europe

Iron Gate *or* **Iron Gates** *n* a gorge of the River Danube on the border between Romania and Serbia. Length: 3 km (2 miles). Romanian name: **Porţile de Fier**

ironic *or* **ironical** *adj* of, characterized by, or using irony **> ironically** *adv*

ironing *n* clothes to be ironed

ironing board *n* a narrow cloth-covered board, usually with folding legs, on which to iron clothes

iron lung *n* an airtight metal cylinder enclosing the entire body up to the neck and providing artificial respiration

iron maiden *n* a medieval instrument of torture, consisting of a hinged case (often shaped in the form of a woman) lined with iron spikes

ironmaster *n Brit history* a manufacturer of iron

ironmonger *n Brit* a shopkeeper or shop dealing in hardware **> ironmongery** *n*

iron out *vb* to settle (a problem or difficulty) through negotiation or discussion

iron pyrites *n* same as pyrite

iron rations *pl n* emergency food supplies, esp. for military personnel in action

irons *pl n* **1** fetters or chains **2 have several irons in the fire** to have several projects or plans at once

Irons *n* Jeremy. born 1948, British film and stage actor. His films include *The French Lieutenant's Woman* (1981), *The Mission* (1986), *Reversal of Fortune* (1990), and *Lolita* (1997)

ironstone *n* **1** any rock consisting mainly of iron ore **2** a tough durable earthenware

ironwood *n* **1** any of various trees, such as hornbeam, with exceptionally hard wood **2** the wood of any of these trees

ironwork *n* work done in iron, esp. decorative work

ironworks *n* a building in which iron is smelted, cast, or wrought

irony *n, pl* **-nies** **1** the mildly sarcastic use of words to imply the opposite of what they normally mean **2** a situation or result that is the direct opposite of what was expected or intended [Greek *eirōneia*]

irradiate *vb* **-ating, -ated** **1** *physics* to subject to or treat with light or other electromagnetic radiation **2** to make clear or bright intellectually or spiritually **3** to light up; illuminate ▷ **irradiation** *n*

irrational *adj* **1** not based on logical reasoning **2** incapable of reasoning **3** *maths* (of an equation or expression) involving radicals or fractional exponents ▷ **irrationality** *n* ▷ **irrationally** *adv*

irrational number *n maths* any real number that cannot be expressed as the ratio of two integers, such as π

Irrawaddy *n* the main river in Myanmar, rising in the north in two headstreams and flowing south through the whole length of Myanmar, to enter the Andaman Sea by nine main mouths. Length: 2100 km (1300 miles)

irreconcilable *adj* not able to be resolved or settled: *irreconcilable differences* ▷ **irreconcilability** *n*

irrecoverable *adj* not able to be recovered

irredeemable *adj* **1** not able to be reformed, improved, or corrected **2** (of bonds or shares) not able to be bought back directly or paid off **3** (of paper money) not able to be converted into coin ▷ **irredeemably** *adv*

irredentist *n* a person in favour of seizing territory that was once part of his or her country [Italian *irredenta*, from the phrase *Italia irredenta* Italy unredeemed] ▷ **irredentism** *n*

irreducible *adj* impossible to put in a reduced or simpler form ▷ **irreducibility** *n*

irrefutable *adj* impossible to deny or disprove

irregular *adj* **1** uneven in shape, position, arrangement, etc. **2** not conforming to accepted practice or routine **3** (of a word) not following the usual pattern of formation in a language **4** not occurring at expected or equal intervals: *an irregular pulse* **5** (of troops) not belonging to regular forces ▷ *n* **6** a soldier not in a regular army ▷ **irregularity** *n* ▷ **irregularly** *adv*

irrelevant *adj* not connected with the matter in hand ▷ **irrelevance** or **irrelevancy** *n*

irreligious *adj* **1** lacking religious faith **2** indifferent or opposed to religion

irremediable *adj* not able to be improved or cured

irremovable *adj* not able to be removed ▷ **irremovably** *adv*

irreparable *adj* not able to be repaired or put right: *irreparable damage to his reputation* ▷ **irreparably** *adv*

irreplaceable *adj* impossible to replace: *acres of irreplaceable moorland were devastated*

irrepressible *adj* not capable of being repressed, controlled, or restrained ▷ **irrepressibility** *n* ▷ **irrepressibly** *adv*

irreproachable *adj* blameless or faultless ▷ **irreproachability** *n*

irresistible *adj* **1** not able to be resisted or refused: *irresistible pressure from the financial markets* **2** extremely attractive: *an irresistible woman* ▷ **irresistibility** *n* ▷ **irresistibly** *adv*

irresolute *adj* unable to make decisions ▷ **irresolution** *n*

irrespective *adj* **irrespective of** without taking account of

irresponsible *adj* **1** not showing or done with due care for the consequences of one's actions or attitudes; reckless **2** not capable of accepting responsibility ▷ **irresponsibility** *n* ▷ **irresponsibly** *adv*

irretrievable *adj* impossible to put right or make good ▷ **irretrievability** *n* ▷ **irretrievably** *adv*

irreverence *n* **1** lack of due respect **2** a disrespectful remark or act ▷ **irreverent** *adj*

irreversible *adj* not able to be reversed or put right again: *irreversible loss of memory* ▷ **irreversibly** *adv*

irrevocable *adj* not possible to change or undo ▷ **irrevocably** *adv*

irrigate *vb* **-gating, -gated** **1** to supply (land) with water through ditches or pipes in order to encourage the growth of crops **2** *med* to bathe (a wound or part of the body) [Latin *irrigare*] ▷ **irrigation** *n* ▷ **irrigator** *n*

irritable *adj* **1** easily annoyed or angered **2** *pathol* abnormally sensitive **3** *biology* (of all living organisms) capable of responding to such stimuli as heat, light, and touch ▷ **irritability** *n*

irritant *n* **1** something that annoys or irritates **2** a substance that causes a part of the body to become tender or inflamed ▷ *adj* **3** causing irritation

irritate *vb* **-tating, -tated** **1** to annoy or anger (someone) **2** *pathol* to cause (an organ or part of the body) to become inflamed or tender **3** *biology* to stimulate (an organ) to respond in a characteristic manner [Latin *irritare* to provoke] ▷ **irritation** *n*

irrupt *vb* to enter forcibly or suddenly [Latin *irrumpere*] ▷ **irruption** *n* ▷ **iruptive** *adj*

Irtysh *or* **Irtish** *n* a river in central Asia, rising in China in the Altai Mountains and flowing west through Kazakhstan, then northwest into Russia to join the Ob River as its chief tributary. Length: 4444 km (2760 miles)

Irvine¹ *n* a town on the W coast of Scotland, the administrative centre of North Ayrshire: designated a new town in 1966. Pop: 33 090 (2001)

Irvine² *n* Alexander Andrew Mackay, Baron, known as *Derry*. born 1940, British lawyer and Labour politician; Lord Chancellor (1997–2003)

Irving *n* **1** Sir Henry. real name *John Henry Brodribb*. 1838–1905, English actor and manager of the Lyceum Theatre in London (1878–1902) **2** Washington. 1783–1859, US essayist and short-story writer, noted for *The Sketch Book of Geoffrey Crayon* (1820), which contains the stories *Rip Van Winkle* and *The Legend of Sleepy Hollow*

Irwin *n* Steve, full name *Stephen Robert Irwin*, known as 'The Crocodile Hunter'. 1962–2006, Australian zoologist, environmentalist, and maker of television wildlife documentaries; died following wounding by a stingray

is *vb* third person singular of the present tense of **be** [Old English]

ISA (eye-sa) *n* (in Britain) individual savings account

Isabella *n* original name *Elizabeth Farnese*. 1692–1766, second wife (1714–46) of Philip V of Spain and mother of Charles III of Spain

Isabella I *n* known as *Isabella the Catholic*. 1451–1504, queen of Castile (1474–1504) and, with her husband, Ferdinand V, joint ruler of Castile and Aragon (1479–1504)

Isabella II *n* 1830–1904, queen of Spain (1833–68), whose accession precipitated the first Carlist war (1833–39). She was deposed in a revolution

Isabella of France *n* 1292–1358, wife (1308–27) of Edward II of England, whom, aided by her lover, Roger de Mortimer, she deposed; mother of Edward III

isallobar (ice-sal-oh-bar) *n* a line on a map connecting places with equal pressure changes [Greek *isos* equal + *allos* other + *baros* weight]

Isar *n* a river in central Europe, rising in W Austria and flowing generally northeast through S Germany into the Danube. Length: over 260 km (160 miles)

sauria *n* an ancient district of S central Asia Minor, chiefly on the N slopes of the W Taurus Mountains

saurian *adj* **1** of or relating to Isauria or its inhabitants ▷ *n* **2** a native or inhabitant of Isauria

SBN International Standard Book Number

schia *n* a volcanic island in the Tyrrhenian Sea, at the N end of the Bay of Naples. Area: 47 sq km (18 sq miles)

sère *n* **1** a department of SE France, in Rhône-Alpes region. Capital: Grenoble. Pop: 1 128 755 (2003 est). Area: 7904 sq km (3083 sq miles) **2** a river in SE France, rising in the Graian Alps and flowing west and southwest to join the River Rhône near Valence. Length: 290 km (180 miles)

sfahan *or* **Eşfahān** *n* a city in central Iran: the second largest city in the country; capital of Persia in the 11th century and from 1598 to 1722. Pop: 1 547 000 (2005 est). Ancient name: **Aspadana**

sherwood *n* **Christopher,** full name *Christopher William Bradshaw-Isherwood.* 1904–86, US novelist and dramatist, born in England. His works include the novel *Goodbye to Berlin* (1939) and three verse plays written in collaboration with W.H. Auden

shiguro *n* **Kazuo.** born 1954, British novelist, born in Japan. His novels include *An Artist of the Floating World* (1986), the Booker-prizewinning *The Remains of the Day* (1989), and *Never Let Me Go* (2005)

sidore of Seville *n* **Saint,** Latin name *Isidorus Hispalensis.* ?560–636 AD, Spanish archbishop and scholar, noted for his *Etymologies,* an encyclopedia. Feast day: April 4

singlass (ize-ing-glass) *n* **1** a gelatine made from the air bladders of freshwater fish **2** same as **mica** [Middle Dutch *huysenblase* sturgeon bladder]

sis¹ *n* an Egyptian fertility goddess

sis² *n* the local name for the River Thames at Oxford

SIS Islamic State of Iraq and Syria, an Islamist terrorist organization formed in the early 21st century

skenderun *n* a port in S Turkey, on the **Gulf of Iskenderun.** Pop: 161 000 (2005 est). Former name: **Alexandretta**

sl. 1 Island **2** Isle

slam *n* **1** the Muslim religion teaching that there is only one God and that Mohammed is his prophet **2** Muslim countries and civilization [Arabic: surrender (to God)] ❯ **Islamic** *adj* ❯ **Islamist** *adj, n*

slamabad *n* the capital of Pakistan, in the north on the Potwar Plateau: site chosen in 1959; surrounded by the Capital Territory of Islamabad for 909 sq km (351 sq miles). Pop: 770 000 (2005 est)

sland *n* **1** a piece of land that is completely surrounded by water **2** something isolated, detached, or surrounded **3** See **traffic island.** Related adjective: **insular** [Old English *īgland*]

slander *n* **1** a person who lives on an island **2** Islander NZ a Pacific Islander

slands *pl n* **the Islands** NZ the islands of the South Pacific

slay *n* an island off the W coast of Scotland: the southernmost of the Inner Hebrides; separated from the island of Jura by the **Sound of Islay.** Pop: 3457 (2001). Area: 606 sq km (234 sq miles)

sle *n* (except when part of a place name) a poetic name for an island

sle of Dogs *n* See (Isle of) **Dogs**

sle of Man *n* See (Isle of) **Man**

sle of Pines *n* the former name of (Isle of) **Youth**

sle of Sheppey *n* See (Isle of) **Sheppey**

sle of Wight *n* See (Isle of) **Wight**

sle of Youth *n* See (Isle of) **Youth**

Isle Royale *n* an island in the northeast US, in NW Lake Superior: forms, with over 100 surrounding islands, **Isle Royale National Park.** Area: 541 sq km (209 sq miles)

slet *n* a small island

slington *n* a borough of N Greater London. Pop: 180 100 (2003 est). Area: 16 sq km (6 sq miles)

ism *n* *informal, often used to show contempt* a doctrine, system, or practice, esp. one whose name ends in *-ism,* such as *communism* or *fascism*

-ism *suffix* **1** indicating a political or religious belief: *socialism; Judaism* **2** indicating a characteristic quality: *heroism* **3** indicating an action: *exorcism* **4** indicating prejudice on the basis specified: *sexism*

Ismailia *n* a city in NE Egypt, on the Suez Canal: founded in 1863 by the former Suez Canal Company; devastated by Israeli troops in the October War (1973). Pop: 299 000 (2005 est)

Ismail Pasha *n* 1830–95, viceroy (1863–66) and khedive (1867–79) of Egypt, who brought his country close to bankruptcy. He was forced to submit to Anglo-French financial control (1876) and to abdicate (1879)

Ismoil Somoni *n* a mountain in SE Tajikistan in the Pamirs: the highest mountain in the former Soviet Union. Height: 7495 m (24 590 ft). Former names: **Stalin Peak, Communism Peak**

isn't is not

iso- *or before a vowel* **is-** *combining form* equal or identical: *isomagnetic* [Greek *isos* equal]

isobar (ice-oh-bar) *n* **1** a line on a map connecting places of equal atmospheric pressure **2** *physics* any of two or more atoms that have the same mass number but different atomic numbers [Greek *isobarēs* of equal weight] ❯ **isobaric** *adj* ❯ **isobarism** *n*

isochronal *or* **isochronous** *adj* **1** equal in length of time **2** occurring at equal time intervals [Greek *isos* equal + *khronos* time] ❯ **isochronism** *n*

Isocrates *n* 436–338 BC, Athenian rhetorician and teacher

isohel *n* a line on a map connecting places with an equal period of sunshine [Greek *isos* equal + *hēlios* sun]

isohyet (ice-oh-hie-it) *n* a line on a map connecting places having equal rainfall [Greek *isos* equal + *huetos* rain]

isolate *vb* **-lating, -lated 1** to place apart or alone **2** *chem* to obtain (a substance) in an uncombined form **3** *med* to quarantine (a person or animal) with a contagious disease [Latin *insulatus,* literally: made into an island] ❯ **isolation** *n*

isomer (ice-oh-mer) *n chem* a substance whose molecules contain the same atoms as another but in a different arrangement ❯ **isomeric** *adj*

isometric *adj* **1** having equal dimensions or measurements **2** *physiol* relating to muscular contraction that does not produce shortening of the muscle **3** (of a three-dimensional drawing) having the three axes equally inclined and all lines drawn to scale [Greek *isometria* equal measurement] ❯ **isometrically** *adv*

isometrics *n* a system of isometric exercises

isomorphism *n* **1** *biology* similarity of form, as in different generations of the same life cycle **2** *chem* the existence of two or more substances of different composition in a similar crystalline form **3** *maths* a one-to-one correspondence between the elements of two or more sets ❯ **isomorph** *n* ❯ **isomorphic** *or* **isomorphous** *adj*

isosceles triangle (ice-soss-ill-eez) *n* a triangle with two sides of equal length [Greek *isos* equal + *skelos* leg]

isotherm (ice-oh-therm) *n* a line on a map linking places of equal temperature [Greek *isos* equal + *thermē* heat]

isotonic *adj* **1** *physiol* (of two or more muscles) having equal tension **2** (of a drink) designed to replace the fluid and salts lost from the body during exercise

isotope (ice-oh-tope) *n* one of two or more atoms with the same number of protons in the nucleus but a different number of neutrons [Greek *isos* equal + *topos* place] ❯ **isotopic** *adj* ❯ **isotopy** *n*

isotropic *or* **isotropous** *adj* having uniform physical properties, such as elasticity or conduction in all directions ❯ **isotropy** *n*

ISP internet service provider: a business providing its

customers with connection to the internet

Israel n 1 a republic in SW Asia, on the Mediterranean Sea: established in 1948, in the former British mandate of Palestine, as a primarily Jewish state; 8 disputes with Arab neighbours (who did not recognize the state of Israel), erupted into full-scale wars in 1948, 1956, 1967 (the Six Day War), and 1973 (the Yom Kippur War). In 1993 Israel agreed to grant autonomous status to the Gaza Strip and the West Bank, according to the terms of a peace agreement with the PLO. Official languages: Hebrew and Arabic. Religion: Jewish majority, Muslim and Christian minorities. Currency: shekel. Capital: Jerusalem (international recognition withheld as East Jerusalem was annexed (1967) by Israel: UN recognized capital: Tel Aviv). Pop: 7 707 042 (2013 est). Area (including Golan Heights and East Jerusalem): 21 946 sq km (8473 sq miles) 2 a the ancient kingdom of the 12 Hebrew tribes at the SE end of the Mediterranean b the kingdom in the N part of this region formed by the ten northern tribes of Israel in the 10th century BC and destroyed by the Assyrians in 721 BC 3 informal the Jewish community throughout the world

Israeli adj 1 of or relating to Israel or its inhabitants ▷ n, pl **-lis** or **-li** 2 a native or inhabitant of Israel

Israelite n Bible a member of the ethnic group claiming descent from Jacob; a Hebrew

Isserlis n Steven (John). born 1958, British cellist

Issigonis n Sir Alec (Arnold Constantine). 1906–88, British car designer born in Smyrna. He is noted for his designs for the Morris Minor (1948) and the Mini (1959)

issue n 1 a topic of interest or discussion 2 an important subject requiring a decision 3 a particular edition of a magazine or newspaper 4 a consequence or result 5 law the descendants of a person 6 the act of sending or giving out something 7 the act of emerging; outflow 8 something flowing out, such as a river 9 at issue a under discussion b in disagreement 10 force the issue to compel decision on some matter 11 join issue to join in controversy 12 take issue to disagree ▷ vb **-suing, -sued** 13 to make (a statement etc.) publicly 14 to supply officially (with) 15 to send out or distribute 16 to publish 17 to come forth or emerge [Old French eissue way out] ▷ **issuable** adj

Issus n an ancient town in S Asia Minor, in Cilicia north of present-day Iskenderun: scene of a battle (333 BC) in which Alexander the Great defeated the Persians

Issyk-Kul n a lake in NE Kyrgyzstan in the Tian Shan mountains, at an altitude of 1609 m (5280 ft): one of the largest mountain lakes in the world. Area: 6200 sq km (2390 sq miles)

Istanbul n a port in NW Turkey, on the western (European) shore of the Bosporus: the largest city in Turkey; founded in about 660 BC by Greeks; refounded by Constantine the Great in 330 AD as the capital of the Eastern Roman Empire; taken by the Turks in 1453 and remained capital of the Ottoman Empire until 1922; industrial centre for shipbuilding, textiles, etc. Pop: 9 760 000 (2005 est). Ancient name: **Byzantium**. Former name (330–1926): **Constantinople**

Isthmian adj relating to or situated in the Isthmus of Corinth or the Isthmus of Panama

isthmus (iss-muss) n a narrow strip of land connecting two relatively large land areas [Greek isthmos]

Istria n a peninsula in the N Adriatic Sea: passed from Italy to Yugoslavia (except for Trieste) in 1947 and to Croatia in 1991

Istrian adj 1 of or relating to Istria or its inhabitants ▷ n 2 a native or inhabitant of Istria

it pron 1 refers to a nonhuman, animal, plant, or inanimate thing, or sometimes to a small baby 2 refers to something unspecified or implied or to a previous or understood clause, phrase, or word: I knew it 3 used to represent human life or experience in respect of the present situation: how's it going? 4 used as the subject of

impersonal verbs: it is snowing; it's Friday 5 informal the crucial or ultimate point: the steering failed and I thought that was it ▷ n 6 informal a sexual intercourse b sex appeal 7 a desirable quality or ability [Old English hit]

IT information technology

It. 1 Italian 2 Italy

ITA initial teaching alphabet: a partly phonetic alphabet used to teach reading

Ital. 1 Italian 2 Italy

Italia n the Italian name for **Italy**

Italian adj 1 of or relating to Italy or its inhabitants ▷ n 2 a native or inhabitant of Italy 3 the official language of Italy and one of the official languages of Switzerland

Italianate adj Italian in style or character

Italian East Africa n a former Italian territory in E Africa, formed in 1936 from the possessions of Eritrea, Italian Somaliland, and Ethiopia: taken by British forces in 1941

Italian Somaliland n a former Italian colony in E Africa, united with British Somaliland in 1960 to form the independent republic of Somalia

italic adj 1 of a style of printing type in which the characters slant to the right ▷ n 2 italics italic type or print, used for emphasis [Latin Italicus of Italy (where it was first used)]

italicize or **-cise** vb **-cizing, -cized** or **-cising, -cised** to print (text) in italic type ▷ **italicization** or **-cisation** n

Italo- combining form indicating Italy or Italian: Italophobia; Italo-German

Italy n a republic in S Europe, occupying a peninsula in the Mediterranean between the Tyrrhenian and the Adriatic Seas, with the islands of Sardinia and Sicily to the west: first united under the Romans but became fragmented into numerous political units in the Middle Ages; united kingdom proclaimed in 1861; under the dictatorship of Mussolini (1922–43); became a republic in 1946; a member of the European Union. It is generally mountainous, with the Alps in the north and the Apennines running the length of the peninsula. Official language: Italian. Religion: Roman Catholic majority. Currency: euro. Capital: Rome. Pop: 61 482 297 (2013 est) Area: 301 247 sq km (116 312 sq miles). Italian name: **Italia**

itch n 1 a skin irritation causing a desire to scratch 2 a restless desire 3 any skin disorder, such as scabies, characterized by intense itching ▷ vb 4 to feel an irritating or tickling sensation 5 to have a restless desire (to do something): they were itching to join the fight [Old English giccean to itch]

itchy adj **itchier, itchiest** 1 having an itch 2 have itchy feet to have a desire to travel ▷ **itchiness** n

it'd it would or it had

item n 1 a single thing in a list or collection 2 a piece of information: a news item 3 accounting an entry in an account 4 informal a couple [Latin: in like manner]

itemize or **-ise** vb **-izing, -ized** or **-ising, -ised** to put on a list or make a list of ▷ **itemization** or **-isation** n

Iténez n the Spanish name for the **Guaporé**

iterate vb **-ating, -ated** to say or do again [Latin iterum again] ▷ **iteration** n ▷ **iterative** adj

Ithaca n a Greek island in the Ionian Sea, the smallest of the Ionian Islands: regarded as the home of Homer's Odysseus. Area: 93 sq km (36 sq miles). Modern Greek name: **Itháki**

Ithacan adj 1 of or relating to Ithaca or its inhabitants ▷ n 2 a native or inhabitant of Ithaca

itinerant adj 1 working for a short time in various places ▷ n 2 an itinerant worker or other person [Latin iter a journey]

itinerary n, pl **-aries** 1 a detailed plan of a journey 2 a record of a journey 3 a guidebook for travellers

-itis suffix forming nouns indicating inflammation of a specified part: tonsillitis [Greek -itēs belonging to]

it'll it will or it shall

Ito n Prince **Hirobumi**. 1841–1909, Japanese statesman; premier (1884–88; 1892–96; 1898; 1900–01). He led the movement to modernize Japan and helped to draft the Meiji constitution (1889); assassinated

its adj **1** of or belonging to it: *its left rear wheel*; *I can see its logical consequence* ▷ pron **2** something belonging to it: *its is over there*

it's it is or it has

itself pron **1 a** the reflexive form of it: *the cat scratched itself* **b** used for emphasis: *even the money itself won't convince me* **2** its normal or usual self: *my parrot doesn't seem itself these days*

Itúrbide n **Agustín de**. 1783–1824, Mexican nationalist and emperor (1822–23). He was forced to abdicate and later executed

ITV (in Britain) Independent Television

IUD intrauterine device: a coil-shaped contraceptive fitted into the womb

Ivan III n known as *Ivan the Great*. 1440–1505, grand duke of Muscovy (1462–1505). He expanded Muscovy, defeated the Tatars (1480), and assumed the title of Ruler of all Russia (1472)

Ivan IV n known as *Ivan the Terrible*. 1530–84, grand duke of Muscovy (1533–47) and first tsar of Russia (1547–84). He conquered Kazan (1552), Astrakhan (1556), and Siberia (1581), but was defeated by Poland in the Livonian War (1558–82) after which his rule became increasingly oppressive

Ivanovo n a city in W central Russia, on the Uvod River: textile centre. Pop: 423 000 (2005 est.). Former name (1871–1932): **Ivanovo-Voznesensk**

I've I have

Ives n **1 Charles (Edward)**. 1874–1954, US composer, noted for his innovative use of polytonality, polyrhythms, and quarter tones. His works include *Second Piano Sonata: Concord* (1915), five symphonies, chamber music, and songs **2 Frederick Eugene**. 1856–1937, US inventor of halftone photography

IVF in vitro fertilization

Iviza n a variant spelling of **Ibiza**

Ivorian n **1** a native or inhabitant of the Côte d'Ivoire ▷ adj **2** of or relating to the Côte d'Ivoire or its inhabitants

ivories pl n slang **1** the keys of a piano **2** the teeth **3** dice

ivory n, pl **-ries 1** a hard smooth creamy white type of bone that makes up a major part of the tusks of elephants ▷ adj **2** yellowish-white [Latin *ebur*] ▷ **ivory-like** adj

Ivory n **James**. born 1928, US film director. With the producer Ismael Merchant, his films include *Shakespeare Wallah* (1964), *Heat and Dust* (1983), *A Room With a View* (1986), and *The Golden Bowl* (2000)

Ivory Coast n the **Ivory Coast** the former name (until 1986) of **Côte d'Ivoire**

ivory tower n remoteness from the realities of everyday life ▷ **ivory-towered** adj

IVR International Vehicle Registration

ivy n, pl **ivies 1** a woody climbing or trailing plant with evergreen leaves and black berry-like fruits **2** any of various other climbing or creeping plants, such as the poison ivy [Old English *īfig*]

iwi (ee-wee) n NZ a Māori tribe [Māori]

Iwo n a city in SW Nigeria. Pop: 479 000 (2005 est)

Iwo Jima n an island in the W Pacific, about 1100 km (700 miles) south of Japan: one of the Volcano Islands; scene of prolonged fighting between US and Japanese forces until taken by the US in 1945; returned to Japan in 1968. Area: 20 sq km (8 sq miles). Official Japanese name: Iō-tō

ixia n a southern African plant of the iris family with showy ornamental funnel-shaped flowers [Greek *ixos* mistletoe]

Ixtaccihuatl or **Iztaccihuatl** n a dormant volcano in central Mexico, southeast of Mexico City. Height: (central peak) 5286 m (17 342 ft)

Iyeyasu or **Ieyasu** n **Tokugawa**. 1542–1616, Japanese general and statesman; founder of the Tokugawa shogunate (1603–1867)

Izetbegović n **Alija**. 1925–2003, Bosnia and Herzegovinian politician: president (1992–2000), he led the country to independence and during the subsequent civil war

Izhevsk n an industrial city in central Russia, capital of the Udmurt Republic. Pop: 632 000 (2005 est)

Izmir n a port in W Turkey, on the Gulf of Izmir: the third largest city in the country; university (1955). Pop: 2 500 000 (2005 est). Former name: **Smyrna**

Izmit n a town in NW Turkey, on the Gulf of Izmit. Pop: 306 000 (2005 est)

Iznik n the modern Turkish name of **Nicaea**

Iztaccihuatl n a variant spelling of **Ixtaccihuatl**

i

Jj

J joule(s)

ja *interj S African* yes

jab *vb* **jabbing, jabbed** **1** to poke sharply ▷ *n* **2** a quick short punch **3** *informal* an injection: *a flu jab* **4** a sharp poke [variant of *job*]

Jabalpur *or* **Jubbulpore** *n* a city in central India, in central Madhya Pradesh. Pop: 951 469 (2001)

jabber *vb* **1** to speak very quickly and excitedly; chatter ▷ *n* **2** quick excited chatter [imitative]

Jabir ibn Hayyan *n* ?721–?815. Arab alchemist, whose many works enjoyed enormous esteem among later alchemists, such as Geber

jabiru *n* a large white-and-black Australian stork

jacaranda *n* a tropical American tree with sweet-smelling wood and pale purple flowers [from a Native American langauge]

jack *n* **1** a mechanical device used to raise a motor vehicle or other heavy object **2** a playing card with a picture of a pageboy on it **3** *bowls* a small white bowl at which the players aim their bowls **4** *electrical engineering* a socket into which a plug can be inserted **5** a flag flown at the bow of a ship, showing nationality **6** one of the pieces used in the game of jacks **7 every man jack** everyone without exception ▶ See also **jack in, jacks, jack up** [from short form of *John*]

jackal *n* a doglike wild animal of Africa and Asia, which feeds on the decaying flesh of dead animals [Persian *shagāl*]

jackanapes *n Brit* a mischievous child [literally: Jack of the ape, nickname of first Duke of Suffolk, whose badge showed an ape's ball and chain]

jackaroo *or* **jackeroo** *n, pl* **-roos** *Austral* a trainee on a sheep station [from *jack* man + (*kang*)*aroo*]

jackass *n* **1** a fool **2** a male donkey **3 laughing jackass** same as **kookaburra** [*jack* (male) + *ass*]

jackboot *n* **1** a leather military boot reaching up to the knee **2** brutal and authoritarian rule

jackdaw *n* a large black-and-grey crowlike bird of Europe and Asia [*jack* + *daw*, obsolete name for jackdaw]

jacket *n* **1** a short coat with a front opening and long sleeves **2** the skin of a potato **3** same as **dust jacket** [Old French *jaquet*]

jacket potato *n* a potato baked in its skin

Jack Frost *n* frost represented as a person

jack in *vb Brit slang* to abandon (an attempt or enterprise)

jack-in-the-box *n* a toy consisting of a box containing a figure on a compressed spring, which jumps out when the lid is opened

jackknife *vb* **-knifing, -knifed** **1** (of an articulated lorry) to go out of control in such a way that the trailer swings round at a sharp angle to the cab ▷ *n, pl* **-knives** **2** a knife with a blade that can be folded into the handle **3** a dive in which the diver bends at the waist in midair

Jacklin *n* **Tony,** full name *Anthony Jacklin.* born 1944, English golfer: won the British Open Championship (1969) and the US Open Championship (1970)

jack of all trades *n, pl* **jacks of all trades** a person who can do many different kinds of work; handyman

jackpot *n* **1** the most valuable prize that can be won in a gambling game **2 hit the jackpot** *informal* to be very fortunate or very successful [probably from *jack* (playing card)]

jack rabbit *n* a hare of W North America with very long hind legs and large ears [*jackass-rabbit*, referring to its long ears]

jacks *n* a game in which metal, bone, or plastic pieces are thrown and then picked up between throws of a small ball [*jackstones*, variant of *checkstones* pebbles]

Jackson¹ *n* a city in and state capital of Mississippi, on the Pearl River. Pop: 179 599 (2003 est)

Jackson² *n* **1 Andrew.** 1767–1845, US statesman, general, and lawyer; seventh president of the US (1829–37). He became a national hero after successfully defending New Orleans from the British (1815). During his administration the spoils system was introduced and the national debt was fully paid off **2 Colin** (**Ray**). born 1967, Welsh athlete: gold medallist in the 110m hurdles at the world championships (1993, 1999), European Championships (1990, 1994, 1998, 2002), and Commonwealth Games (1990, 1994) **3 Glenda.** born 1936, British stage, film, and television actress, and Labour politician. Her films include *Women in Love* (1969) for which she won an Oscar, *The Music Lovers* (1970), *Sunday Bloody Sunday* (1971), and *Turtle Diary* (1985); member of parliament (1992–2015) **4 Jesse** (**Louis**). born 1941, US Democrat politician and clergyman; Black campaigner for minority rights **5 Michael** (**Joe**). 1958–2009, US pop singer, lead vocalist with the Jacksons (originally the Jackson 5) (1969–86). His solo albums include *Thriller* (1982), *Bad* (1987), and *Invincible* (2001) **6 Peter.** born 1961, New Zealand film director, screenwriter, and producer; his films include *Heavenly Creatures* (1994), *The Lord of the Rings* trilogy (2001–03), *King Kong* (2005), and *The Hobbit: An Unexpected Journey* (2012) **7 Thomas Jonathan,** known as *Stonewall Jackson.* 1824–63, Confederate general in the American Civil War, noted particularly for his command at the first Battle of Bull Run (1861)

Jacksonville *n* a port in NE Florida: the leading commercial centre of the southeast. Pop: 773 781 (2003 est)

Jack Tar *n chiefly literary* a sailor

Jack the Ripper *n* an unidentified murderer who killed at least seven prostitutes in London's East End between August and November 1888

jack up *vb* **1** to raise (a motor vehicle) with a jack **2** to increase (prices or salaries) **3** *NZ informal* to organize something through unorthodox channels ▷ *n* **jack-up** **4** *NZ informal* something achieved dishonestly

Jacobean (jak-a-bee-an) *adj* of or in the reign of James I of England and Ireland (1603–25) [Latin *Jacobus* James]

Jacobi *n* **1 Sir Derek** (**George**). born 1938, British actor **2 Karl Gustav Jacob.** 1804–51, German mathematician.

Independently of N. H. Abel, he discovered elliptic functions (1829). He also made important contributions to the study of determinants and differential equations

acobite *n history* a supporter of James II and his descendants [Latin *Jacobus* James]

acobsen *n* Arne. 1902–71, Danish architect and designer. His buildings include the Town Hall at Rodovre (1955)

acopo della Quercia *n* ?1374–1438, Italian Renaissance sculptor: best known for his marble reliefs of scenes from Genesis around the portal of San Petronio, Bologna (1425–35)

acquard (jak-ard) *n* a fabric with an intricate design incorporated into the weave [after J. M. *Jacquard*, its inventor]

acuzzi (jak-oo-zee) *n trademark* a large circular bath with a mechanism that swirls the water

ade *n* **1** an ornamental semiprecious stone, usually green in colour ▷ *adj* **2** bluish-green [obsolete Spanish *piedra de ijada* colic stone, because it was believed to cure colic]

aded *adj* tired or bored from overindulgence or overwork

adotville *n* the former name of **Likasi**

aén *n* a city in S Spain. Pop: 115 638 (2003 est)

affa *n* **1** a port in W Israel, on the Mediterranean: incorporated into Tel Aviv in 1950; an old Canaanite city. Biblical name: **Joppa**. Hebrew name: **Yafo 2** a large variety of orange, having a thick skin

affna *n* a port in N Sri Lanka: for many centuries the capital of a Tamil kingdom. Pop: 149 000 (2005 est)

ag¹ *n Scot informal* same as **jab** (3) [origin unknown]

ag² *n slang* a period of uncontrolled indulgence in an activity: *all-night crying jags* [origin unknown]

agged (jag-gid) *adj* having an uneven edge with sharp points [from *jag* a sharp point]

agger *n* Sir **Mick**, full name *Michael Philip Jagger*. born 1943, English rock singer and songwriter: lead vocalist with the Rolling Stones

aguar *n* a large wild cat of south and central America, with a spotted coat [from S American Indian]

ail *or* **gaol** *n* **1** a prison ▷ *vb* **2** to confine in prison [Old French *jaiole* cage]

ailbird *n informal* a person who is or has often been in jail

ailer *or* **gaoler** *n* a person in charge of a jail

aipur *n* a city of great beauty in N India, capital of Rajasthan state: University of Rajasthan (1947). Pop: 2 324 319 (2001)

akarta *n* the capital of Indonesia, in N West Java: founded in 1619 and ruled by the Dutch until 1945; the chief trading centre of the East in the 17th century; University of Indonesia (1947). Pop: 8 347 083 (2000). Former name (until 1949): **Batavia**. Former spelling: **Djakarta**

ake *adj* she's jake *Austral and NZ slang* it is all right [probably from the name *Jake*]

akobson *n* Roman (Osipovič). 1896–1982, US linguist, born in Russia. His publications include *Children's Speech* (1941) and *Fundamentals of Language* (1956)

alalabad *n* a city in NE Afghanistan, capital of Nangarhar province; a trading, military, and tourist centre on the main route between Kabul and the Khyber Pass. Pop: 96 000 (2004 est)

alandhar *n* a city in NW India, in central Punjab. Pop: 701 223 (2001)

alapa *n* a city in E central Mexico, capital of Veracruz State, at an altitude of 1427 m (4681 ft): resort. Pop: 525 000 (2005 est)

alisco *n* a state of W Mexico, on the Pacific: crossed by the Sierra Madre; valuable mineral resources. Capital: Guadalajara. Pop: 6 321 278 (2000). Area: 80 137 sq km (30 934 sq miles)

alopy (jal-lop-ee) *n, pl* **-lopies** *informal* a dilapidated old car [origin unknown]

am¹ *vb* **jamming, jammed 1** to wedge (an object) into a

tight space or against another object: *the table was jammed against the wall* **2** to fill (a place) with people or vehicles: *the surrounding roads were jammed for miles* **3** to make or become stuck or locked: *the window was jammed open* **4** *radio* to prevent the clear reception of (radio communications) by transmitting other signals on the same wavelength **5** *slang* to play in a jam session **6** **jam on the brakes** to apply the brakes of a vehicle very suddenly ▷ *n* **7** a situation where a large number of people or vehicles are crowded into a place: *a traffic jam* **8** *informal* a difficult situation: *you are in a bit of a jam* **9** same as **jam session** [probably imitative]

jam² *n* a food made from fruit boiled with sugar until the mixture sets, used for spreading on bread [perhaps from JAM¹ (the act of squeezing)]

Jam. **1** Jamaica **2** *Bible* James

Jamaica *n* an island and state in the Caribbean: colonized by the Spanish from 1494 onwards; large numbers of Black slaves being imported; captured by the British in 1655 and established as a colony in 1866; gained full independence in 1962; a member of the Commonwealth. Exports: chiefly bauxite and alumina, sugar, and bananas. Official language: English. Religion: Protestant majority. Currency: Jamaican dollar. Capital: Kingston. Pop: 2 909 714 (2013 est). Area: 10 992 sq km (4244 sq miles)

Jamaican *adj* **1** of or relating to Jamaica or its inhabitants ▷ *n* **2** a native or inhabitant of Jamaica

jamb *n* a side post of a doorframe or window frame [Old French *jambe* leg, jamb]

Jambi *n* a port in W Indonesia, in SE Sumatra on the Hari River. Pop: 417 507 (2000). Former spelling: **Djambi**. Also called: **Telanaipura**

jamboree *n* a large gathering or celebration [origin unknown]

James *n* **1 Clive**. born 1939, Australian journalist, critic and broadcaster. His books include the memoirs *Unreliable Memoirs* (1980) and *North Face of Soho* (2006) and the novel *Brilliant Creatures* (1983) **2 Henry** 1843–1916, British novelist, short-story writer, and critic, born in the US. Among his novels are *Washington Square* (1880), *The Portrait of a Lady* (1881), *The Bostonians* (1886), *The Wings of the Dove* (1902), *The Ambassadors* (1903), and *The Golden Bowl* (1904) **3 Jesse**(Woodson). 1847–82, US outlaw **4 P**(**hyllis**) **D**(**orothy**), Baroness James of Holland Park. 1920–2014, British detective novelist. Her books include *Death of an Expert Witness* (1977), *Original Sin* (1994), and *Death in Holy Orders* (2001) **5 William**, brother of Henry James. 1842–1910, US philosopher and psychologist, whose theory of pragmatism is expounded in *Essays in Radical Empiricism* (1912). His other works include *The Will to Believe* (1897), *The Principles of Psychology* (1890), and *The Varieties of Religious Experience* (1902) **6** *New Testament* **a** known as *James the Great*. one of the twelve apostles, a son of Zebedee and brother to John the apostle (Matthew 4:21). Feast day: July 25 or April 30 **b** known as *James the Less*. one of the twelve apostles, son of Alphaeus (Matthew 10:3). Feast day: May 3 or Oct 9 **c** known as *James the brother of the Lord*. a brother or close relative of Jesus (Mark 6:3; Galatians 1:19). Feast day: Oct 23 **d** the book ascribed to his authorship (in full **The Epistle of James**)

James I *n* **1** called *the Conqueror*. 1208–76, king of Aragon (1216–76). He captured the Balearic Islands and Valencia from the Muslims, thus beginning Aragonese expansion in the Mediterranean **2** 1394–1437, king of Scotland (1406–37), second son of Robert III **3** 1566–1625, king of England and Ireland (1603–25) and, as James VI, king of Scotland (1567–1625), in succession to Elizabeth I of England and his mother, Mary Queen of Scots, respectively. He alienated Parliament by his assertion of the divine right of kings, his favourites, esp. the Duke of Buckingham, and his subservience to Spain

James II *n* **1** 1430–60, king of Scotland (1437–60), son of James I **2** 1633–1701, king of England, Ireland, and, as

j

James VII, of Scotland (1685–88); son of Charles I. His pro-Catholic sympathies and arbitrary rule caused the Whigs and Tories to unite in inviting his eldest surviving daughter, Mary, and her husband, William of Orange, to take the throne as joint monarchs. James was defeated at the Boyne (1690) when he attempted to regain the throne

James III *n* 1451–88, king of Scotland (1460–88), son of James II

James IV *n* 1473–1513, king of Scotland (1488–1513); he invaded England (1496) in support of Perkin Warbeck; he was killed at Flodden

James V *n* 1512–42, king of Scotland (1513–42), son of James IV

James Bay *n* the S arm of Hudson Bay, in central Canada. Area: 108 780 sq km (42 000 sq miles)

Jameson *n* Sir Leander Starr. 1853–1917, British administrator in South Africa, who led the Jameson Raid; prime minister of Cape Colony (1904–08)

Jamestown *n* a ruined village in E Virginia, on Jamestown Island (a peninsula in the James River): the first permanent settlement by the English in America (1607); capital of Virginia (1607–98); abandoned in 1699

Jammu *n* a city in N India, winter capital of the state of Jammu and Kashmir. Pop: 378 431 (2001)

Jammu and Kashmir *n* the official name for the part of Kashmir under Indian control

jammy *adj* **-mier, -miest 1** covered with or tasting like jam **2** *Brit slang* lucky: *jammy so-and-sos!*

Jamnagar *n* a city in India, in Gujarat: noted for its palaces and temples: cement, pottery, textiles. Pop: 447 734 (2001)

jam-packed *adj* filled to capacity

jam session *n slang* an improvised performance by jazz or rock musicians [probably from JAM¹]

Jamshedpur *n* a city in NE India, in Jharkhand: large iron and steel works (1907–11); a major industrial centre. Pop: 570 349 (2001)

Jan. January

Janáček *n* Leoš. 1854–1928, Czech composer. His music is influenced by Czech folksong and speech rhythms and is remarkable for its integration of melody and language. His works include the operas *Jenufa* (1904) and *The Cunning Little Vixen* (1924), the *Glagolitic Mass* (1927), as well as orchestral and chamber music and songs

jandal *n* NZ a rubber-soled sandal attached to the foot by a thong between the big toe and the next toe

Janet *n* Pierre Marie Félix. 1859–1947, French psychologist and neurologist, noted particularly for his work on the origins of hysteria

jangle *vb* **-gling, -gled 1** to make a harsh unpleasant ringing noise **2** to produce an irritating or unpleasant effect on: *the caffeine in coffee can jangle the nerves* [Old French *jangler*]

Janiculum *n* a hill in Rome across the River Tiber from the Seven Hills

Janina *n* the Serbian name for **Ioánnina**

janitor *n chiefly Scot, US and Canad* the caretaker of a school or other building [Latin: doorkeeper]

janjaweed *or* **janjawid** (jan-juh-weed) *n* an armed tribal militia group in the Darfur region of Sudan [Arabic]

Jan Mayen *n* an island in the Arctic Ocean, between Greenland and N Norway: volcanic, with large glaciers; former site of Dutch whaling stations; annexed to Norway in 1929. Area: 373 sq km (144 sq miles)

Jansen *n* Cornelis. Latin name *Cornelius Jansenius*. 1585–1638, Dutch Roman Catholic theologian. In *Augustinus* (1640) he defended the teachings of St Augustine, esp. on free will, grace, and predestination

Jansky *n* Karl Guthe 1905–50, US electrical engineer. He discovered a source of radio waves outside the solar system (1932) and pioneered radio astronomy

January *n* the first month of the year [Latin *Januarius*]

japan *n* **1** a glossy black lacquer, originally from the Orient, which is used on wood or metal ▷ *vb* **-panning, -panned 2** to varnish with japan

Japan *n* **1** an archipelago and empire in E Asia, extending for 3200 km (2000 miles) between the Sea of Japan and the Pacific and consisting of the main islands of Hokkaido, Honshu, Shikoku, and Kyushu and over 3000 smaller islands: feudalism abolished in 1871, followed by industrialization and expansion of territories, esp. during World Wars I and II, when most of SE Asia came under Japanese control; dogma of the emperor's divinity abolished in 1946 under a new democratic constitution; by the 1980s, rapid economic growth made Japan the most industrialized nation in the Far East. Official language: Japanese. Religion: Shintoist majority, large Buddhist minority. Currency: yen. Capital: Tokyo. Pop: 127 253 075 (2013 est). Area: 369 660 sq km (142 726 sq miles). Japanese names: Nippon, Nihon **2** Sea of Japan the sea between mainland Asia and Japan. Korean name **East Sea**

Japan Current *n* a warm ocean current flowing northeastwards off the E coast of Japan towards the North Pacific. Also called: **Kuroshio**

Japanese *adj* **1** of or relating to Japan or its inhabitants ▷ *n* **2** (*pl* **-nese**) a native or inhabitant of Japan **3** the language of Japan

jape *n old-fashioned* a joke or prank [origin unknown]

japonica *n* **1** a Japanese shrub with red flowers and yellowish fruit **2** same as **camellia** [New Latin *Japonia* Japan]

Japurá *n* a river in NW South America, rising in SW Colombia and flowing southeast across Colombia and Brazil to join the Amazon near Tefé: known as the Caquetá in Colombia. Length: about 2800 km (1750 miles). Spanish name: **Yapurá**

Jaques-Dalcroze *n* Émile. 1865–1950, Swiss composer and teacher: invented eurythmics

jar¹ *n* **1** a wide-mouthed cylindrical glass container, used for storing food **2** *Brit informal* a glass of beer [Arabic *jarrah* large earthen vessel]

jar² *vb* **jarring, jarred 1** to have an irritating or unpleasant effect: *sometimes a light remark jarred on her father* **2** to be in disagreement or conflict: *their very different temperaments jarred* **3** to jolt or bump ▷ *n* **4** a jolt or shock [probably imitative] ▷ **jarring** *adj*

jardiniere *n* an ornamental pot or stand for plants [French]

jargon *n* **1** specialized language relating to a particular subject, profession, or group **2** pretentious or unintelligible language [Old French]

Jarman *n* Derek. 1942–94, British film director and writer; his films include *Jubilee* (1977), *Caravaggio* (1986), and *Wittgenstein* (1993)

jarrah *n* an Australian eucalypt yielding valuable timber

Jarrett *n* Keith born 1945, US jazz pianist and composer

Jarrow *n* a port in NE England, in South Tyneside unitary authority, Tyne and Wear: ruined monastery where the Venerable Bede lived and died; its unemployed marched on London in the 1930s; shipyards, oil installations, iron and steel works. Pop: 27 526 (2001)

Jarry *n* Alfred. 1873–1907, French dramatist and poet, who anticipated the theatre of the absurd with his play *Ubu Roi* (1896)

Jaruzelski *n* Wojciech. 1923–2014, Polish statesman and soldier; prime minister (1981–85); head of state 1985–90 (as president from 1989)

Jas. James

jasmine *n* a shrub or climbing plant with sweet-smelling flowers [Persian *yāsmin*]

jasper *n* a kind of quartz, usually red in colour, which is used as a gemstone and for ornamental decoration [Greek *iaspis*]

Jasper National Park *n* a national park in SW Canada, in W Alberta in the Rockies: wildlife sanctuary. Area: 10 900 sq km (4200 sq miles)

Jaspers *n* Karl. 1883–1969, German existentialist philosopher

Jassy *n* the German name for Iaşi

jaundice *n* yellowing of the skin and the whites of the eyes, caused by an excess of bile pigments in the blood [French *jaune* yellow]

jaundiced *adj* **1** bitter or cynical: *the financial markets are taking a jaundiced view of the Government's motives* **2** having jaundice

jaunt *n* **1** a pleasure trip or outing ▷ *vb* **2** to go on a jaunt [origin unknown]

jaunty *adj* **-tier, -tiest** **1** cheerful and energetic: *he was worried beneath the jaunty air* **2** smart and attractive: *a jaunty little hat* [French *gentil* noble] ▷ **jauntily** *adv*

Jaurès *n* Jean Léon. 1859–1914, French politician and writer, who founded the socialist paper *l'Humanité* (1904), and united the French socialist movement into a single party (1905); assassinated

Java¹ *n* an island of Indonesia, south of Borneo, from which it is separated by the Java Sea: politically the most important island of Indonesia; it consists chiefly of active volcanic mountains and is densely forested. It came under Dutch control in 1596 and became part of Indonesia in 1949. It is one of the most densely populated areas in the world. Capital: Jakarta. Pop (with Madura): 121 352 608 (2000 est). Area: 132 174 sq km (51 032 sq miles). Former spelling: **Djawa**

Java² *n trademark* a computer programming language that is widely used on the internet [after *Java* coffee from the Indonesian island, allegedly drunk by its creators]

Javan *adj* **1** of or relating to Java or its inhabitants ▷ *n* **2** a native or inhabitant of Java

Javanese *adj* **1** of or relating to the island of Java or its inhabitants ▷ *n* **2** (*pl* **-nese**) a native or inhabitant of Java **3** the language of Java

Javari *or* **Javary** *n* a river in South America, flowing northeast as part of the border between Peru and Brazil to join the Amazon. Length: about 1050 km (650 miles). Spanish name: **Yavarí**

javelin *n* a light spear thrown in a sports competition [Old French *javeline*]

jaw *n* **1** either of the bones that hold the teeth and frame the mouth **2** the lower part of the face below the mouth **3** *slang* a long chat ▷ *vb* **4** *slang* to have a long chat [probably Old French *joue* cheek]

Jawara *n* Sir Dawda. born 1924, Gambian statesman; president of The Gambia (1970–94); overthrown in a military coup

jawbone *n* the bone in the lower jaw of a person or animal

ja well no fine *interj S African* used to indicate reluctant acceptance

jaws *pl n* **1** the mouth of a person or animal **2** the parts of a machine or tool that grip an object **3** the narrow opening of a gorge or valley **4** a dangerous or threatening position: *to snatch victory from the jaws of defeat*

Jaxartes *n* the ancient name for Syr Darya

jay *n* a bird of Europe and Asia with a pinkish-brown body and blue-and-black wings [Old French *jai*]

Jay *n* John 1745–1829, American statesman, jurist, and diplomat; first chief justice of the Supreme Court (1789–95). He negotiated the Jay's Treaty

Jaya *n* Mount Jaya a mountain in E Indonesia, in Papua (formerly Irian Jaya) in the Sudirman Range: the highest mountain in New Guinea. Height: 5039 m (16 532 ft). Former spelling: **Djaya**. Former names: **Mount Carstensz, Sukarno Peak**

Jayapura *n* a port in NE Indonesia, capital of Papua (formerly Irian Jaya), on the N coast. Pop: 155 548 (2000). Former spelling: **Djajapura**. Former names: **Sukarnapura, Kotabaru, Hollandia**

Jayawardene *n* Junius Richard. 1906–96, Sri Lankan statesman; prime minister (1977–78) and first president of Sri Lanka (1978–89)

jaywalking *n* crossing the road in a dangerous or careless manner [*jay* (in sense: a foolish person)] ▷ **jaywalker** *n*

jazz *n* **1** a kind of popular music of African-American origin that has an exciting rhythm and often involves improvisation **2 and all that jazz** *slang* and other related things [origin unknown]

jazz up *vb informal* **1** to play (a piece of music) in a jazzy style **2** to make (something) appear more interesting or lively: *never seek to jazz up a plain story*

jazzy *adj* **-zier, -ziest** **1** colourful and modern: *jazzy shop fronts* **2** of or like jazz

JCB *n trademark Brit* a large machine used in building, that has a shovel on the front and a digger arm on the back [initials of Joseph Cyril Bamford, its manufacturer]

jealous *adj* **1** suspicious or fearful of being displaced by a rival **2** envious: *I was jealous of the girls who had boyfriends* **3** resulting from jealousy: *my jealous tears* [Late Latin *zelus* emulation] ▷ **jealously** *adv*

jealousy *n, pl* **-ousies** the state of or an instance of feeling jealous

Jean *n* **1** born 1921, full name *Jean Benoît Guillaume Robert Antoine Louis Marie Adolphe Marc d'Aviano*, grand duke of Luxembourg (1964–2000) **2 Michaelle**. born 1957, in Haiti. Canadian stateswoman and broadcaster; governor-general from 2005

Jean de Meung *n* real name *Jean Clopinel*. ?1250–?1305, French poet, who continued Guillaume de Lorris' *Roman de la Rose*. His portion of the poem consists of some 18 000 lines and contains satirical attacks on women and the Church

Jean Paul *n* real name *Johann Paul Friedrich Richter*. 1763–1825, German novelist

jeans *pl n* casual denim trousers [from *jean* fustian fabric from Genoa]

Jeans *n* Sir James Hopwood. 1877–1946, English astronomer, physicist, and mathematician, best known for his popular books on astronomy. He made important contributions to the kinetic theory of gases and the theory of stellar evolution

Jebel Musa *n* a mountain in NW Morocco, near the Strait of Gibraltar: one of the Pillars of Hercules. Height: 850 m (2790 ft)

Jedda *n* another name for Jiddah

Jeep *n trademark* a small road vehicle with four-wheel drive [perhaps *general-purpose (vehicle)*, influenced by Eugene the *Jeep*, creature in a comic strip]

Jeeps *n* Dickie. born 1931, English Rugby Union footballer: halfback for England (1956–62) and the British Lions (1959–62)

jeer *vb* **1** to be derisive towards (someone) ▷ *n* **2** a cry of derision [origin unknown] ▷ **jeering** *adj, n*

Jefferies *n* Richard. 1848–87, British writer and naturalist, noted for his observation of English country life: his books include *Bevis* (1882) and collections of essays such as *The Open Air* (1885)

Jefferson *n* Thomas. 1743–1826, US statesman: secretary of state (1790–93); third president (1801–09). He was the chief drafter of the Declaration of Independence (1776), the chief opponent of the centralizing policies of the Federalists under Hamilton, and effected the Louisiana Purchase (1803) ▷ **Jeffersonian** *adj, n*

Jefferson City *n* a city in central Missouri, the state capital, on the Missouri River. Pop: 37 550 (2003 est)

Jeffrey *n* Francis, Lord. 1773–1850, Scottish judge and literary critic. As editor of the *Edinburgh Review* (1803–29), he was noted for the severity of his criticism of the romantic poets, esp. Wordsworth

Jeffreys *n* George, 1st Baron Jeffreys of Wem. ?1645–89, English judge, notorious for his brutality at the "Bloody Assizes" (1685), where those involved in Monmouth's rebellion were tried

jeggings *pl n* women's leggings designed to look like tight denim jeans [blend of *jeans* + *leggings*]

Jehol n 1 a former province of NE China, north of the Great Wall: divided among Hebei, Liaoning, and Inner Mongolia in 1956. Area: 192 380 sq km (74 278 sq miles) 2 a region of NE China, in Hebei and Liaoning provinces: mountainous

Jehovah n God [Hebrew *Yahweh*]

Jehovah's Witness n a member of a Christian Church whose followers believe that the end of the world is near

jejune adj 1 simple and unsophisticated 2 dull and uninteresting [Latin *jejunus* empty]

jejunum (jij-**june**-um) n anatomy the part of the small intestine between the duodenum and the ileum [Latin] > **jejunal** adj

Jekyll n Gertrude. 1843–1932, British landscape gardener: noted for her simplicity of design and use of indigenous plants

Jekyll and Hyde n a person with two distinct personalities, one good and the other evil [after the character in a novel by R. L. Stevenson]

jell vb 1 to take on a definite form: *the changes have had little time to jell* 2 same as **gel** (2) [from *jelly*]

jellaba n a loose robe with a hood, worn by some Arab men [Arabic *jallabah*]

Jellicoe n John Rushworth, 1st Earl Jellicoe. 1859–1935, British admiral, who commanded the Grand Fleet at the Battle of Jutland (1916), which incapacitated the German fleet for the rest of World War I

jellied adj prepared in a jelly: *jellied eels*

jellies pl n slang gelatine capsules of temazepam, dissolved and injected as a recreational drug [from GELATINE]

jelly n, pl **-lies** 1 a fruit-flavoured dessert set with gelatine 2 a food made from fruit juice boiled with sugar until the mixture sets, used for spreading on bread 3 a savoury food preparation set with gelatine ▶ See also **jellies** [Latin *gelare* to freeze] > **jelly-like** adj

jellyfish n, pl **-fish** a small sea creature with a jelly-like umbrella-shaped body and trailing tentacles

Jemappes n a town in SW Belgium, in Hainaut province west of Mons: scene of a battle (1792) during the French Revolutionary Wars, in which the French defeated the Austrians

jemmy or US **jimmy** n, pl **-mies** a short steel crowbar, used by burglars to prise open doors and windows [from short form of *James*]

Jena n a city in E central Germany, in Thuringia: university (1558), at which Hegel and Schiller taught; site of the battle (1806) in which Napoleon Bonaparte defeated the Prussians; optical and precision instrument industry. Pop: 102 634 (2003 est)

Jenkins n Roy (Harris), Baron Jenkins of Hillhead. 1920–2003, British politician and author; Labour home secretary (1965–67, 1974–76) and chancellor of the exchequer (1967–70); president of the European Commission (1977–80); cofounder of the Social Democratic Party (1981); leader of party (1982–83); Chancellor of Oxford University (1987–2003)

Jenner n 1 Edward 1749–1823, English physician, who discovered vaccination by showing that injections of cowpox virus produce immunity against smallpox (1796) 2 Sir William. 1815–98, English physician and pathologist, who differentiated between typhus and typhoid fevers (1849)

jenny n, pl **-nies** a female donkey, ass, or wren [from the name *Jenny*]

Jensen n Johannes Vilhelm. 1873–1950, Danish novelist, poet, and essayist: best known for his novel sequence about the origins of mankind *The Long Journey* (1908–22). Nobel prize for literature 1944

jeopardize or **-dise** vb **-dizing, -dized** or **-dising, -dised** to put (something) at risk: *the escalating violence that is jeopardizing current peace moves*

jeopardy n danger of harm, loss, or death: *the survival of public hospitals is in jeopardy* [Old French *jeu parti*, literally:

Jerba n a variant spelling of **Djerba**

jerboa n a small rodent of Asia and N Africa with long hind legs used for jumping [Arabic *yarbū'*]

jeremiad n a long mournful complaint [French *jérémiade* referring to the Lamentations of Jeremiah in the Bible]

jerepigo (jer-ree-**pee**-go) n S African a sweet fortified wine similar to port [Portuguese *jeropiga*]

Jerez n a town in SW Spain: famous for the making of sherry. Pop: 191 002 (2003 est). Official name: **Jerez de la Frontera**. Former name: **Xeres**

Jericho n a town in the West Bank near the N end of the Dead Sea, 251 m (825 ft) below sea level: on the site of an ancient city, the first place to be taken by the Israelites under Joshua after entering the Promised Land in the 14th century BC (Joshua 6)

jerk vb 1 to move with an irregular or spasmodic motion 2 to pull or push (something) abruptly or spasmodically ▷ n 3 an abrupt or spasmodic movement 4 an irregular jolting motion: *the irritating jerk that heralded a gear change* 5 slang, chiefly US and Canad a stupid or ignorant person [probably variant of *yerk* to pull stitches tight]

jerkin n a short jacket [origin unknown]

jerky adj jerkier, jerkiest having an irregular jolting motion: *avoid any sudden or jerky movements* > **jerkily** adv > **jerkiness** n

Jerome n 1 Latin name *Eusebius Hieronymus*. ?347–?420 AD, Christian monk and scholar, whose outstanding work was the production of the Vulgate. Feast day: Sept 30 2 Jerome K(lapka). 1859–1927, English humorous writer; author of *Three Men in a Boat* (1889)

Jerry n old-fashioned, Brit slang (pl **-ries**) a German, esp. a German soldier 2 Germans collectively

jerry-built adj (of houses) built badly with cheap materials

jerry can n a flat-sided can used for carrying petrol or water [from *Jerry* German soldier]

jersey n 1 a knitted garment covering the upper part of the body 2 a soft, slightly stretchy, machine-knitted fabric [originally referring to a type of woollen fabric made in JERSEY]

Jersey n 1 an island in the English Channel, the largest of the Channel Islands: forms, with two other islands, the bailiwick of Jersey; colonized from Normandy in the 11th century and still officially French-speaking; noted for finance, market gardening, dairy farming, and tourism. Capital: St Helier. Pop: 95 732 (2013 est). Area: 116 sq km (45 sq miles) 2 a breed of dairy cattle producing milk with a high butterfat content, originating from the island of Jersey

Jersey City n an industrial city in NE New Jersey, opposite Manhattan on a peninsula between the Hudson and Hackensack Rivers: part of the Port of New York; site of one of the greatest railway terminals in the world. Pop: 239 097 (2003 est)

Jerusalem n 1 the de facto capital of Israel (recognition of this has been withheld by the United Nations), situated in the Judaean hills: became capital of the Hebrew kingdom after its capture by David around 1000 BC; destroyed by Nebuchadnezzar of Babylon in 586 BC; taken by the Romans in 63 BC; devastated in 70 AD and 135 AD during the Jewish rebellions against Rome; fell to the Arabs in 637 and to the Seljuk Turks in 1071; ruled by Crusaders from 1099 to 1187 and by the Egyptians and Turks until conquered by the British (1917); centre of the British mandate of Palestine from 1920 to 1948, when the Arabs took the old city and the Jews held the new city; unified after the Six Day War (1967) under the Israelis; the holy city of Jews, Christians, and Muslims. Pop: 693 200 (2003 est) 2 a the New Jerusalem Christianity Heaven b any ideal city

Jerusalem artichoke n a small yellowish-white vegetable that grows underground [altered from Italian *girasole* sunflower]

Jervis Bay *n* an inlet of the Pacific in SE Australia, in Jervis Bay Territory on the coast of S New South Wales: regarded for some purposes as part of the Australian Capital Territory: site of the Royal Australian Naval College

Jespersen *n* (Jens) **Otto** (Harry). 1860–1943, Danish philologist: author of *Modern English Grammar* (1909–31)

Jesselton *n* the former name of **Kota Kinabalu**

jest *n* **1** something done or said to amuse people **2 in jest** as a joke: *many a true word is spoken in jest* ▷ *vb* **3** to do or say something to amuse people [variant of *gest* exploit]

jester *n* a professional clown employed by a king or nobleman during the Middle Ages

Jesuit (jezz-yew-it) *n* a member of the Society of Jesus, a Roman Catholic religious order [New Latin *Jesuita*]
▷ **Jesuitical** *adj*

Jesus *n* **1** Also called: **Jesus Christ, Jesus of Nazareth** ?4 BC–?29 AD, founder of Christianity, born in Bethlehem and brought up in Nazareth as a Jew. He is believed by Christians to be the Son of God and to have been miraculously conceived by the Virgin Mary, wife of Joseph. With 12 disciples, he undertook two missionary journeys through Galilee, performing miracles, teaching, and proclaiming the coming of the Kingdom of God. His revolutionary Sermon on the Mount (Matthew 5–8), which preaches love, humility, and charity, the essence of his teaching, aroused the hostility of the Pharisees. After the Last Supper with his disciples, he was betrayed by Judas and crucified. He is believed by Christians to have risen from his tomb after three days, appeared to his disciples several times, and ascended to Heaven after 40 days **2** *Son of Sirach*. 3rd century BC, author of the Apocryphal book of Ecclesiasticus ▷ *interj also* **Jesus wept** **3** *taboo, slang* used to express intense surprise, dismay, etc. [via Latin from Greek *Iēsous*, from Hebrew *Yeshūa'*, shortened from *Yehōshūa'* God is help, JOSHUA]

jet¹ *n* **1** an aircraft driven by jet propulsion **2** a thin stream of liquid or gas forced out of a small hole **3** an outlet or nozzle through which a stream of liquid or gas is forced ▷ *vb* **jetting, jetted 4** to travel by jet aircraft [Old French *jeter* to throw]

jet² *n* a hard black mineral that is polished and used in jewellery [Old French *jaiet*]

jet-black *adj* deep black

jetboat *n* a motorboat propelled by a jet of water

jet engine *n* an aircraft engine that uses jet propulsion for forward motion

jet lag *n* a feeling of fatigue and disorientation often experienced by air passengers who have crossed several time zones in a short space of time

jet-propelled *adj* driven by jet propulsion

jet propulsion *n* a method of propulsion by which an aircraft is moved forward by the force of the exhaust gases ejected from the rear

jetsam *n* **1** goods thrown overboard to lighten a ship during a storm **2 flotsam and jetsam** See **flotsam** (2) [from *jettison*]

jet set *n* rich and fashionable people who travel widely for pleasure ▷ **jet-setter** *n* ▷ **jet-setting** *adj*

jet ski *n* a small self-propelled vehicle resembling a scooter, which skims across water on a flat keel ▷ **jet skiing** *n*

jettison *vb* **1** to abandon or give up: *jettisoning democracy in favour of fascism* **2** to throw overboard [Latin *jactatio* a tossing about]

jetty *n, pl* **-ties 1** a landing pier or dock **2** a structure built from a shore out into the water to protect a harbour [Old French *jetee* projecting part]

Jevons *n* **William Stanley**. 1835–82, English economist and logician: introduced the concept of final or marginal utility in *The Theory of Political Economy* (1871)

Jew *n* **1** a person whose religion is Judaism **2** a descendant of the ancient Hebrews [Hebrew *yehūdāh* Judah]

jewel *n* **1** a precious or semiprecious stone **2** a person or thing regarded as precious or special: *a fantastic little car, a real little jewel* **3** a gemstone used as part of the machinery of a watch [Old French *jouel*]

jewelled *or US* **jeweled** *adj* decorated with jewels

jeweller *or US* **jeweler** *n* a person who buys, sells, and repairs jewellery

jewellery *or US* **jewelry** *n* objects such as rings, necklaces, and bracelets, worn for decoration

Jewess *n often offensive* a woman whose religion is Judaism

jewfish *n Austral* a freshwater catfish

Jewish *adj* of Jews or Judaism

Jewish Autonomous Region *n* an administrative division of SE Russia, in E Siberia: colonized by Jews in 1928; largely agricultural. Capital: Birobidzhan. Pop: 190 900 (2002). Area: 36 000 sq km (13 895 sq miles). Also called: **Birobidzhan, Birobijan**

Jewry *n* Jews collectively

jew's-harp *n* a small musical instrument held between the teeth and played by plucking a metal strip with the finger

Jezebel *n* a wicked or shameless woman [after the wife of Ahab, in the Bible]

Jezreel *n* **Plain of Jezreel** another name for **Esdraelon**

Jezreelite *n* a native or inhabitant of Jezreel

Jhabvala *n* **Ruth Prawer**, original name *Ruth Prawer*. 1927–2013, British writer living in India and the US, born in Germany to Polish parents: author of the Booker-prizewinning novel *Heat and Dust* (1975) and scripts for films by James Ivory

Jhansi *n* a city in central India, in SW Uttar Pradesh: scene of a mutiny against the British in 1857. Pop: 383 248 (2001)

Jharkhand *n* a state of NE India, created in 2000 from the S part of Bihar: consists of part of the Chota Nagpur plateau; mineral extraction, including coal and mica. Capital: Ranchi. Pop: 26 909 428 (2001). Area: 74 677 sq km (28 833 sq miles)

Jhelum *n* a river in Pakistan and Kashmir, rising in W central Kashmir and flowing northwest through the Vale of Kashmir, then southwest into NW Punjab to join the Chenab River: important for irrigation, having the Mangla Dam (Pakistan), completed in 1967. Length: about 720 km (450 miles)

Jiang Qing *or* **Chiang Ch'ing** *n* 1913–91, Chinese Communist actress and politician; widow of Mao Tse-tung. She was a leading member of the Gang of Four

Jiangsu *or* **Kiangsu** *n* a province of E China, on the Yellow Sea: consists mostly of the marshy delta of the Yangtze River, with some of China's largest cities and most densely populated areas. Capital: Nanjing. Pop: 74 060 000 (2003 est). Area: 102 200 sq km (39 860 sq miles)

Jiangxi *or* **Kiangsi** *n* a province of SE central China, in the basins of the Kan River and Poyang Lake: mineral resources include coal and tungsten. Capital: Nanchang. Pop: 42 220 000 (2003 est). Area: 164 800 sq km (64 300 sq miles)

Jiang Zemin *n* born 1926, Chinese Communist politician: president (1993–2003)

Jiaozhou *or* **Kiaochow** *n* a territory of NE China, in SE Shandong province, surrounding **Jiaozhou Bay** (an inlet of the Yellow Sea): leased to Germany from 1898 to 1914. Area: about 520 sq km (200 sq miles)

jib¹ *n* **1** *nautical* a triangular sail set in front of the foremast **2 the cut of someone's jib** a person's manner or style [origin unknown]

jib² *vb* **jibbing, jibbed** *chiefly Brit* **1** (of an animal) to stop short and refuse to go forwards: *my animal jibbed three times* **2 jib at** to object to: *he jibs at any suggestion that his side are the underdogs* [origin unknown]

jib³ *n* the projecting arm of a crane [probably from *gibbet*]

jibe¹ *n* **1** an insulting or taunting remark ▷ *vb* **jibing,**

jibed 2 to make insulting or taunting remarks

jibe² vb **jibing, jibed** informal to be in accord or be consistent: *their apparent devotion hardly jibed with what he had heard about them*

jibe³ vb **jibing, jibed**, n nautical same as **gybe**

Jibouti or **Jibuti** n variant spellings of Djibouti

Jiddah or **Jedda** n a port in W Saudi Arabia, on the Red Sea: the diplomatic capital of the country; the port of entry for Mecca, 80 km (50 miles) east. Pop: 3 807 000 (2005 est)

jiffy n, pl **jiffies** informal a very short time: *won't be a jiffy!* [origin unknown]

Jiffy bag n trademark a large padded envelope

jig n 1 a lively folk dance 2 music for this dance 3 a mechanical device that holds and locates a part during machining ▷ vb **jigging, jigged** 4 to dance a jig 5 to move with quick jerky movements [origin unknown]

Jigawa n a state of N Nigeria. Capital: Dutse. Pop: 4 348 649 (2006). Area: 23 154 sq km (8940 sq miles)

jigger n a small whisky glass

jiggered adj old-fashioned, informal damned or blowed: *well, I'm jiggered, so that's where it went!* [probably euphemism for **buggered**]

jiggery-pokery n informal, chiefly Brit dishonest behaviour; cheating [Scots dialect *joukery-pawkery*]

jiggle vb **-gling, -gled** to move with quick jerky movements [frequentative of *jig*]

jigsaw n 1 Also called: **jigsaw puzzle** a puzzle in which the player has to put together a picture that has been cut into irregularly shaped interlocking pieces 2 a mechanical saw with a fine steel blade for cutting along curved or irregular lines in sheets of material [*jig* (to jerk up and down) + SAW¹]

jihad n Islamic holy war against unbelievers

Jilin or **Kirin** n 1 a province of NE China, in central Manchuria. Capital: Changchun. Pop: 27 040 000 (2003 est). Area: 187 000 sq km (72 930 sq miles) 2 Also called: **Chi-lin** a river port in NE China, in N central Jilin province on the Songhua River. Pop: 1 496 000 (2005 est)

Jilolo n a variant spelling of Djailolo. See **Halmahera**

Jilong n the Pinyin transliteration of the Chinese name for Chilung

jilt vb to leave or reject (a lover) abruptly or callously [dialect *jillet* flighty girl]

Jim Crow n US 1 the policy or practice of segregating Black people 2 offensive a Black person [from name of song]

Jiménez n Juan Ramón. 1881–1958, Spanish lyric poet. His most famous work is *Platero y yo* (1917), a prose poem: Nobel prize for literature 1956

Jiménez de Cisneros n Francisco. 1436–1517, Spanish cardinal and statesman; regent of Castile (1506–07) and Spain (1516–17) and grand inquisitor for Castile and León (1507–17). Also: **Ximenes de Cisneros**

Jinan, Chinan or **Tsinan** n an industrial city in NE China, capital of Shandong province; probably over 3000 years old. Pop: 2 654 000 (2005 est)

Jingdezhen, Fowliang or **Fou-liang** n a city in SE China, in NE Jiangxi province east of Poyang Lake: famous for its porcelain industry, established in the sixth century. Pop: 416 000 (2005 est)

jingle n 1 a short catchy song used to advertise a product on radio or television 2 a light ringing sound ▷ vb **-gling, -gled** 3 to make a light ringing sound [probably imitative]

jingoism n excessive and aggressive patriotism [after the use of *by Jingo!* in a 19th-century song] ▷ **jingoistic** or **jingoist** adj

Jinja n a town in Uganda, on the N shore of Lake Victoria. Pop: 86 520 (2002 est)

Jinjiang n a former spelling of Zhenjiang

jink vb to move quickly or jerkily in order to dodge someone: *he jinked free and won a race to the line to level the scores* [Scots]

jinks pl n **high jinks** boisterous or mischievous behaviour [origin unknown]

Jinnah n Mohammed Ali 1876–1948, Indian Muslim statesman. He campaigned for the partition of India into separate Hindu and Muslim states, becoming first governor general of Pakistan (1947–48)

jinni or **djinni** n, pl **jinn** or **djinn** a being or spirit in Muslim belief that could take on human or animal form [Arabic]

jinx n 1 someone or something believed to bring bad luck ▷ vb 2 to bring bad luck to [perhaps from Greek *iunx* wryneck, a bird used in magic]

Jinzhou, Chin-Chou or **Chin-chow** n a city in NE China, in SW Liaoning province. Pop: 888 000 (2005 est) Former name (1913–47): **Chin-hsien**

jitterbug n 1 a fast jerky American dance that was popular in the 1940s ▷ vb **-bugging, -bugged** 2 to dance the jitterbug

jitters pl n **the jitters** informal a feeling of extreme nervousness experienced before an important event: *I had a case of the jitters before my first two speeches* [origin unknown]

jittery adj nervous

jive n 1 a lively jerky dance that was popular in the 1940s and 1950s ▷ vb **jiving, jived** 2 to dance the jive [origin unknown] ▷ **jiver** n

Jnr Junior

Joachim n 1 Joseph. 1831–1907, Hungarian violinist and composer 2 Saint. 1st century BC, traditionally the father of the Virgin Mary; feast day: July 25 or Sept 9

Joachim of Fiore n ?1132–1202 AD, Italian mystic and philosopher, best known for teaching that history can be divided into three ages, those of the Father, Son, and Holy Ghost

Joan n 1 known as *the Fair Maid of Kent*. 1328–85, wife of Edward the Black Prince; mother of Richard II 2 Pope legendary female pope, first mentioned in the 13th century: said to have been elected while disguised as a man and to have died in childbirth

Joan of Arc n Saint known as *the Maid of Orléans*; French name *Jeanne d'Arc*. ?1412–31, French national heroine, who led the army that relieved Orléans in the Hundred Years' War, enabling Charles VII to be crowned at Reims (1429) After being captured (1430), she was burnt at the stake as a heretic. She was canonized in 1920. Feast day: May 30

João Pessoa n a port in NE Brazil, capital of Paraíba state. Pop: 931 000 (2005 est)

job n 1 a person's occupation or paid employment 2 a piece of work; task 3 the performance of a task: *he made a good job of the repair* 4 informal a difficult task: *they are having a job to fill his shoes* 5 Brit, Austral and NZ informal a crime, esp a robbery 6 **just the job** informal exactly what is required 7 **make the best of a bad job** to cope as well as possible in unsatisfactory circumstances [origin unknown]

jobbing adj doing individual jobs for payment: *a jobbing gardener*

Jobcentre or **job centre** n (in Britain) a government office where advertisements of available jobs are displayed

Jobclub or **job club** n (in Britain) a group of unemployed people which meets every weekday and is given advice on and help with job seeking

jobless adj 1 unemployed ▷ pl n 2 people who are unemployed: *the young jobless*

job lot n a miscellaneous collection of articles sold together

Jobs n Steve, full name *Steven Paul Jobs*. 1955–2011, US computer scientist and executive: co-founder (with Steve Wozniak, 1976) of the Apple computer company

Job's comforter n a person who adds to someone else's distress while pretending to be sympathetic [after *Job* in the Bible]

jobseeker's allowance n (in Britain) a social-security payment for unemployed people

485 | job sharing - John o'Groats

job sharing *n* an arrangement by which a job is shared by two part-time workers

Jochum *n* Eugen. 1902–87, German orchestral conductor

jockey *n* **1 a** a person who rides horses in races as a profession ▷ *vb* **2 jockey for position** to try to obtain an advantage by skilful manoeuvring [from the name *Jock*]

jockstrap *n* an elasticated belt with a pouch to support the genitals, worn by male athletes. Also called: **athletic support** [slang *jock* penis]

jocose (joke-**kohss**) *adj old-fashioned* playful or humorous [Latin *jocus* joke] **> jocosely** *adv*

jocular *adj* **1** (of a person) often joking; good-humoured **2** (of a remark) meant lightly or humorously [Latin *joculus* little joke] **> jocularity** *n* **> jocularly** *adv*

jocund (jok-kund) *adj literary* cheerful or merry [Latin *jucundus* pleasant]

Jodhpur *n* **1** a former state of NW India, one of the W Rajputana states: now part of Rajasthan **2** a walled city in NW India, in W Rajasthan: university (1962). Pop: 846 408 (2001)

Jodhpuri *adj* of or relating to Jodhpur or its inhabitants

jodhpurs *pl n* trousers worn for riding, which are loose-fitting around the thighs and tight-fitting below the knees [from JODHPUR (1)]

Jodl *n* Alfred. 1890–1946, German general, largely responsible for German strategy during World War II: executed as a war criminal

Jodrell Bank *n* an astronomical observatory in NW England, in Cheshire: radio telescope with a steerable parabolic dish, 75 m (250 ft) in diameter

joey *n Austral* a young kangaroo

Joffre *n* Joseph Jacques Césaire. 1852–1931, French marshal. He commanded the French army (1914–16) and was largely responsible for the Allies' victory at the Marne (1914), which halted the German advance on Paris

jog *vb* **jogging, jogged 1** to run at a gentle pace for exercise **2** to nudge slightly **3 jog along** to continue in a plodding way: *many people jog along in second gear for the whole of their lives* **4 jog** someone's memory to remind someone of something ▷ *n* **5** a slow run as a form of exercise [probably variant of *shog* to shake] **> jogger** *n* **> jogging** *n*

joggle *vb* **-gling, -gled** to shake or move with a slightly jolting motion [frequentative of *jog*]

Jogjakarta *n* a former spelling of Yogyakarta

jog trot *n* an easy bouncy pace, midway between a walk and a trot

Johannesburg *n* a city in N South Africa; the capital of Gauteng province: South Africa's largest city and chief industrial centre; grew with the establishment in 1886 of the gold-mining industry; University of Witwatersrand (1922). Pop: 957 441 (2011)

john *n slang, chiefly US and Canad* a toilet [special use of the name]

John *n* **1** *New Testament* **a** the apostle John, the son of Zebedee, identified with the author of the fourth Gospel, three epistles, and the book of Revelation. Feast day: Dec 27 or Sept 26 **b** the fourth Gospel **c** any of three epistles (in full **The First, Second,** and **Third Epistles of John**) **2** See **John the Baptist 3** known as *John Lackland*. 1167–1216, king of England (1199–1216); son of Henry II. He succeeded to the throne on the death of his brother Richard I, having previously tried to usurp the throne. War with France led to the loss of most of his French possessions. After his refusal to recognize Stephen Langton as archbishop of Canterbury an interdict was imposed on England (1208–14). In 1215 he was compelled by the barons to grant the Magna Carta **4** called *the Fearless*. 1371–1419, duke of Burgundy (1404–19). His attempt to control the mad king Charles VI and his murder of the king's brother led to civil war: assassinated **5 Augustus (Edwin).** 1878–1961, British painter, esp. of portraits **6 Barry** born 1945, Welsh Rugby Union footballer: halfback for Wales (1966–72) and the

British Lions (1968–71) **7** Sir **Elton (Hercules).** original name *Reginald Dwight*. born 1947, British rock pianist, composer, and singer; his hits include "Goodbye Yellow Brick Road" (1973) and "Candle in the Wind 1997" (1997), a tribute to Diana, Princess of Wales **8 Gwen,** sister of Augustus John. 1876–1939, British painter, working in France: noted esp. for her portraits of women

John I *n* **1** surnamed *Tzimisces*. 925–976 AD, Byzantine emperor (969–976): extended Byzantine power into Bulgaria and Syria **2** called *the Great*. 1357–1433, king of Portugal (1385–1433). He secured independence for Portugal by his victory over Castile (1385) and initiated Portuguese overseas expansion

John II *n* **1** called *the Good*. 1319–64, king of France (1350–64): captured by the English at Poitiers (1356) and forced to sign treaties (1360) surrendering SW France to England **2** called *the Perfect*. 1455–95, king of Portugal (1481–95): sponsored Portuguese expansion in the New World and reduced the power of the aristocracy **3** surnamed *Casimir Vasa*. 1609–72, king of Poland (1648–68), who lost much territory to neighbouring countries: abdicated

John III *n* **1** 1507–57, king of Portugal (1521–57): his reign saw the expansion of the Portuguese empire overseas but the start of economic decline at home **2** surnamed *Sobieski*. 1624–96, king of Poland (1674–96). He raised the Turkish siege of Vienna (1683)

John IV *n* called *the Fortunate*. 1604–56, king of Portugal (1640–56). As duke of Braganza he led a revolt against Spanish rule and became king: lost most of Portugal's Asian possessions to the Dutch

John VI *n* ?1769–1826, king of Portugal (1816–26): recognized the independence of Brazil (1825)

John XXII *n* original name *Jacques Duèse*. ?1244–1334, pope (1316–34), residing at Avignon; involved in a long conflict with the Holy Roman Emperor Louis IV and opposed the Franciscan Spirituals

John XXIII *n* Saint. original name *Angelo Giuseppe Roncalli*. 1881–1963, pope (1958–63). He promoted ecumenism and world peace and summoned the second Vatican Council (1962–65); canonized in 2014. Feast day: Oct 11 or June 4

John Bull *n* England represented as a man

John Chrysostom *n* Saint. ?345–407 AD, Greek bishop and theologian; one of the Fathers of the Greek Church, noted for his eloquence. Feast day: Sept 13

johnny *n, pl* **-nies** *Brit old-fashioned, informal* a chap: *you legal johnnies*

Johnny Canuck (kan-**nuk**) *n Canad informal* Canada personified as a man

John of Austria *n* called *Don John*. 1547–78, Spanish general: defeated the Turks at Lepanto (1571)

John of Damascus *n* Saint. ?675–749 AD, Syrian theologian, who defended the veneration of icons and images against the iconoclasts. Feast day: Dec 4

John of Gaunt *n* Duke of Lancaster. 1340–99, son of Edward III: virtual ruler of England during the last years of his father's reign and during Richard II's minority [*Gaunt*, variant of GHENT, where he was born]

John of Leyden *n* original name *Jan Bockelson*. ?1509–36, Dutch Anabaptist leader. He established a theocracy in Münster (1534) but was tortured to death after the city was recaptured (1535) by its prince bishop

John of Salisbury *n* died 1180, English ecclesiastic and scholar; bishop of Chartres (1176–80). He supported Thomas à Becket against Henry II

John of the Cross *n* Saint. original name *Juan de Yepis y Alvarez*. 1542–91, Spanish Carmelite monk, poet, and mystic. He founded the Discalced Carmelites with Saint Teresa (1568). Feast day: Dec 14

John o'Groats *n* a village at the northeasternmost tip of the Scottish mainland: considered to be the northernmost point of the mainland of Great Britain although Dunnet Head, slightly to the west, lies further north. See also **Land's End**

John Paul I n original name *Albino Luciani*. 1912–78, pope (1978) whose brief 33-day reign was characterized by a simpler papal style and anticipated an emphasis on pastoral rather than administrative priorities

John Paul II n Saint. original name *Karol Wojtyla*. 1920–2005, pope (1978–2005), born in Poland: the first non-Italian to be elected since 1522; canonized in 2014. Feast day: Oct 22

Johns n 1 Andrew (Gary). born 1974, Australian Rugby League footballer: halfback for Australia (1995–2006) 2 Jasper. born 1930, US artist, noted for his collages and constructions

Johnson n 1 Amy 1903–41, British aviator, who made several record flights, including those to Australia (1930) and to Cape Town and back (1936) 2 Andrew 1808–75, US Democrat statesman who was elected vice president under the Republican Abraham Lincoln; 17th president of the US (1865–69), became president after Lincoln's assassination. His lenience towards the South after the American Civil War led to strong opposition from radical Republicans, who tried to impeach him 3 (Alexander) Boris (de Pfeffel). born 1964, British Conservative politician; mayor of London from 2008 4 Earvin, known as *Magic*. born 1959, US basketball player 5 Eyvind. 1900–76, Swedish novelist and writer, whose novels include the *Krilon* trilogy (1941–43): joint winner of the Nobel prize for literature 1974 6 Jack 1878–1946, US boxer; world heavyweight champion (1908–15) 7 Lionel (Pigot) 1867–1902, British poet and critic, best known for his poems "Dark Angel" and "By the Statue of King Charles at Charing Cross" 8 Lyndon Baines known as *LBJ*. 1908–73, US Democrat statesman; 36th president of the US (1963–69). His administration carried the Civil Rights Acts of 1964 and 1965, but he lost popularity by increasing US involvement in the Vietnam war 9 Martin. born 1970, English Rugby Union footballer; captain of the England team that won the World Cup in 2003. 10 Michael (Duane) born 1967, US athlete: world (1995) and Olympic (1996) 200- and 400-metre gold medallist 11 Philip (Cortelyou). 1906–2005, US architect and writer; his buildings include the New York State Theater (1964) and the American Telephone and Telegraph building (1978–83), both in New York 12 Robert ?1898–1937, US blues singer and guitarist 13 Samuel known as *Dr. Johnson*. 1709–84, British lexicographer, critic, and conversationalist, whose greatest works are his *Dictionary* (1755), his edition of Shakespeare (1765), and his *Lives of the Most Eminent English Poets* (1779–81). His fame, however, rests as much on Boswell's biography of him as on his literary output

John the Baptist n New Testament Saint. the son of Zacharias and Elizabeth and the cousin and forerunner of Jesus, whom he baptized. He was beheaded by Herod (Matthew 14:1–2). Feast day: June 24

Johore or **Johor** n a state of Malaysia, on the S Malay Peninsula: mostly forested, with large swamps; bauxite- and iron-mining. Capital: Johore Bahru. Pop: 2 740 625 (2000). Area: 18 986 sq km (7331 sq miles)

Johore Bahru or **Johor Bahru** n a city in S Malaysia, capital of Johore state: important trading centre, situated at the sole crossing point of Johore Strait (between Malaya and Singapore Island). Pop: 719 000 (2005 est)

joie de vivre (zhwah de veev-ra) n enjoyment of life [French, literally: joy of living]

join vb 1 to become a member of (a club or organization) 2 to become part of (a queue or list) 3 to meet (someone) as a companion: *join me for a beer* 4 to take part in (an activity): *join the war effort* 5 (of two roads or rivers) to meet and come together 6 to bring into contact: *join hands* 7 **join forces** to combine efforts with someone ▷ n 8 a place where two things are joined together ▶ See also **join in, join up** [Latin *jungere* to yoke]

joined-up adj integrated by an overall strategy: *joined-up government*

joiner n a person whose job is making finished woodwork, such as window frames and stairs

joinery n the skill or work of a joiner

join in vb to take part in (an activity)

joint adj 1 shared by or belonging to two or more parties: *the two countries have issued a joint statement* ▷ n 2 anatomy the junction between two or more bones: *a hip joint* 3 a junction of two or more parts or objects: *a mortar joint* 4 a piece of meat suitable for roasting 5 slang a building or place of entertainment: *strip joints* 6 slang a cannabis cigarette 7 **out of joint a** informal out of order or out of keeping: *they find their routine lives out of joint with their training* **b** (of a bone) knocked out of its normal position 8 **put someone's nose out of joint** See nose (10) ▷ vb 9 to provide a joint or joints 10 to cut or divide (meat) into joints ﹥ **jointed** adj ﹥ **jointly** adv

joint-stock company n a business firm whose capital is owned jointly by shareholders

join up vb to become a member of a military organization

Joinville n Jean de. ?1224–1317, French chronicler, noted for his *Histoire de Saint Louis* (1309)

joist n a beam made of timber, steel, or concrete, used as a support in the construction of floors and roofs [Old French *giste*]

jojoba (hoe-**hoe**-ba) n a shrub whose seeds contain an oil used in cosmetics [Mexican Spanish]

joke n 1 something that is said or done to amuse people 2 someone or something that is ridiculous: *the country's inexperienced leaders are regarded as something of a joke* 3 **no joke** informal a serious or difficult matter: *getting over mountain passes at ten thousand feet is no joke* ▷ vb **joking, joked** 4 to say or do something to amuse people [Latin *jocus*] ﹥ **jokey** adj ﹥ **jokingly** adv

joker n 1 a person who jokes a lot 2 slang a person regarded without respect: *waiting for the next jokers to sign up* 3 an extra playing card in a pack, which can replace any other card in some games 4 Austral and NZ informal a chap

Jokjakarta n a former spelling of Yogyakarta

jol (joll) S African slang n 1 a party ▷ vb **jolling, jolled** 2 to have a good time [Dutch]

Jolie n Angelina. born 1975, US actor and campaigner for humanitarian causes: her films include *Girl Interrupted* (1999), *Lara Croft, Tomb Raider* (2001), *A Mighty Heart* (2007), *Changeling* (2008), and *Salt* (2010). She was awarded an honorary damehood in 2014

Joliot-Curie n Jean-Frédéric, 1900–58, and his wife, Irène, 1897–1956, French physicists: shared the Nobel prize for chemistry in 1935 for discovering artificial radioactivity

Jolliet n Louis. 1645–1700, French-Canadian explorer, with Jaques Marquette, of the Mississippi river

jollification n a merry festivity

jollity n the condition of being jolly

jolly adj **-lier, -liest** 1 full of good humour 2 involving a lot of fun: *big jolly birthday parties* ▷ adv 3 Brit informal very: *I'm going to have a jolly good try* ▷ vb **-lies, -lying, -lied** 4 **jolly along** informal to try to keep (someone) cheerful by flattery or cheerful chat [Old French *jolif*]

Jolly Roger n the traditional pirate flag, depicting a white skull and crossbones on a black background

Jolo n an island in the SW Philippines: the main island of the Sulu Archipelago. Pop: 87 998 (2000). Area: 893 sq km (345 sq miles)

Jolson n Al, real name *Asa Yoelson*. 1886–1950, US singer and film actor, born in Russia; star of the first talking picture *The Jazz Singer* (1927)

jolt n 1 a severe shock 2 a sudden violent movement ▷ vb 3 to surprise or shock: *he was momentarily jolted by the news* 4 to bump against (someone or something) with a sudden violent movement 5 to move in a jerking manner [origin unknown]

Jonah n a person believed to bring bad luck to those around him or her [after Jonah in the Bible]

Jones n 1 **Carwyn** (**Howell**). born 1967, Welsh Labour politician; first minister of Wales from 2009 2 **Daniel**. 1881–1967, British phonetician 3 **Daniel**. 1912–93, Welsh composer. He wrote nine symphonies and much chamber music 4 **David**. 1895–1974, British artist and writer: his literary works, which combine poetry and prose, include In Parenthesis (1937), an account of World War I, and The Anathemata (1952) 5 **Digby** (**Marritt**). Baron. born 1956, British businessman and politician; director-general of the Confederation of British Industry (2000–06); Minister of State for Trade and Investment (2007–08) 6 **Inigo**. 1573–1652, English architect and theatrical designer, who introduced Palladianism to England. His buildings include the Banqueting Hall of Whitehall. He also designed the settings for court masques, being the first to use the proscenium arch and movable scenery in England 7 **John Paul**, original name John Paul. 1747–92, US naval commander, born in Scotland: noted for his part in the War of American Independence 8 (**Everett**) **Le Roi**, Muslim name Imanu Amìri Baraka. born 1934, US Black poet, dramatist, and political figure 9 **Quincy**. born 1933, US composer, arranger, conductor, record producer, and trumpeter, noted esp. for his film scores and his collaborations in the recording studio with Michael Jackson 10 **Robert Tyre**, known as Bobby Jones. 1902–71, US golfer: won a unique 'grand slam' in 1930 of US Open, US Amateur, British Open, and British Amateur championships

Jongkind n Johann Barthold. 1819–91, Dutch landscape painter and etcher, working in Paris: best known for his atmospheric seascapes

Jönköping n a city in S Sweden, on the S shore of Lake Vättern: scene of the conclusion of peace between Sweden and Denmark in 1809. Pop: 119 971 (2004 est)

jonquil n a narcissus with sweet-smelling yellow or white flowers [French jonquille]

Jonson n Ben. 1572–1637, English dramatist and poet, who developed the "comedy of humours", in which each character is used to satirize one particular humour or temperament. His plays include Volpone (1606), The Alchemist (1610), and Bartholomew Fair (1614), and he also wrote court masques

Joplin n 1 Janis 1943–70, US rock singer, noted for her hoarse and passionate style. Her albums include Cheap Thrills (1968) and Pearl (1971) 2 **Scott** 1868–1917, US pianist and composer: creator of ragtime

Joppa n the biblical name of Jaffa, the port from which Jonah embarked (Jonah 1:3)

Jordaens n Jacob. 1593–1678, Flemish painter, noted for his naturalistic depiction of peasant scenes

Jordan¹ n 1 a kingdom in SW Asia: coextensive with the biblical Moab, Gilead, and Edom; made a League of Nations mandate and emirate under British control in 1922 and became an independent kingdom in 1946; territories west of the River Jordan and the Jordanian part of Jerusalem (intended to be part of an autonomous Palestine) were occupied by Israel after the war of 1967. It contains part of the Great Rift Valley and consists mostly of desert. Official language: Arabic. Official religion: (Sunni) Muslim. Currency: dinar. Capital: Amman. Pop: 6 482 081 (2013 est). Area: 89 185 sq km (34 434 sq miles). Official name: **Hashemite Kingdom of Jordan**. Former name (1922–49): **Trans-Jordan** 2 the chief and only perennial river of Israel and Jordan, rising in several headstreams in Syria and Lebanon, and flowing south through the Sea of Galilee to the Dead Sea: occupies the N end of the Great Rift Valley system and lies mostly below sea level. Length: over 320 km (200 miles)

Jordan² n 1 **Michael** (**Jeffrey**). born 1963, US basketball player 2 **Neil**. born 1950, Irish film director and writer;

his films include The Company of Wolves (1984), Mona Lisa (1986), The Crying Game (1992), Michael Collins (1996), The End of the Affair (2000), and The Brave One (2007)

Jordanian adj 1 of or relating to Jordan or its inhabitants ▷ n 2 a native or inhabitant of Jordan

Jos n a city in central Nigeria, capital of Plateau state on the **Jos Plateau**: major centre of the tin-mining industry. Pop: 685 000 (2005 est)

Joseph II n 1741–90, Holy Roman emperor (1765–90); son of Francis I. He ruled Austria jointly with his mother, Maria Theresa, until her death (1780). He reorganized taxation, abolished serfdom, curtailed the feudal power of the nobles, and asserted his independence from the pope

Joseph Bonaparte Gulf n an inlet of the Timor Sea in N Australia. Width: 360 km (225 miles)

Josephine n Empress, previous name Joséphine de Beauharnais; real name Marie Joséphine Tascher de la Pagerie. 1763–1814, empress of France as wife of Napoleon Bonaparte (1796–1809)

Josephus n Flavius. real name Joseph ben Matthias. ?37–?100 AD, Jewish historian and general; author of History of the Jewish War and Antiquities of the Jews

josh vb slang to joke or tease [origin unknown]

Jospin n Lionel (**Robert**) born 1937, French politician; prime minister (1997–2002)

joss stick n a stick of incense, giving off a sweet smell when burnt [joss (a Chinese idol) from Portuguese deos god]

jostle vb **-tling, -tled** 1 to bump or push roughly: television crews filming the scene were jostled by police 2 to compete with someone: jostling for power [Old French jouster to joust]

jot vb **jotting, jotted** 1 **jot down** to write a brief note of: quickly jot down the answers to these questions ▷ n 2 the least bit: it makes not one jot of difference [Greek iōta iota, smallest letter]

jotter n a small notebook

jottings pl n notes jotted down

joual (**zhwahl**) n a nonstandard variety of Canadian French [French]

joule (**jool**) n physics the SI unit of work or energy [after J. P. JOULE]

Joule n James Prescott. 1818–89, English physicist, who evaluated the mechanical equivalent of heat and contributed to the study of heat and electricity

journal n 1 a newspaper or magazine 2 a daily record of events [Latin diurnalis daily]

journalese n a superficial style of writing regarded as typical of newspapers and magazines

journalism n the profession of collecting, writing, and publishing news through newspapers and magazines or by radio and television

journalist n a person who writes or edits news items for a newspaper or magazine or for radio or television ▷ **journalistic** adj

journey n 1 the process of travelling from one place to another 2 the time taken or distance travelled on a journey ▷ vb 3 to make a journey [Old French journee a day, a day's travelling]

journeyman n, pl **-men** a qualified craftsman who works for an employer [journey (in obsolete sense: a day's work)]

joust history n 1 a combat with lances between two mounted knights ▷ vb 2 to take part in such a tournament [Old French jouster]

Jove n 1 Jupiter (the god) 2 **by Jove** old-fashioned an exclamation of surprise or for emphasis

jovial adj happy and cheerful [Latin jovialis of (the planet) Jupiter] ▷ **joviality** n ▷ **jovially** adv

Jovian n full name Flavius Claudius Jovianus. ?331–364 AD, Roman emperor (363–64): he made peace with Persia, relinquishing Roman provinces beyond the Tigris, and restored privileges to the Christians

j

Jowett n Benjamin. 1817–93, British classical scholar and educator: translated the works of Plato

jowl[1] n **1** the lower jaw **2** cheek by jowl See cheek **3** jowls cheeks [Old English *ceafl* jaw] **>** **jowled** adj

jowl[2] n fatty flesh hanging from the lower jaw [Old English *ceole* throat]

joy n **1** deep happiness and contentment **2** something that brings deep happiness: *a thing of beauty is a joy for ever* **3** *informal* success or satisfaction: *we checked ports and airports without any joy* [Latin *gaudium*]

Joyce n **1** James (Augustine Aloysius). 1882–1941, Irish novelist and short-story writer. He profoundly influenced the development of the modern novel by his use of complex narrative techniques, esp. stream of consciousness and parody, and of compound and coined words. His works include the novels *Ulysses* (1922) and *Finnegans Wake* (1939) and the short stories *Dubliners* (1914) **2** William, known as *Lord Haw-Haw*. 1906–46, British broadcaster of Nazi propaganda to Britain, who was executed for treason

joyful adj feeling or bringing great joy: *joyful crowds; a joyful event* **>** **joyfully** adv

joyless adj feeling or bringing no joy

joyous adj extremely happy and enthusiastic **>** **joyously** adv

joyride n a drive in a car one has stolen **>** **joyrider** n **>** **joyriding** n

joystick n the control lever of an aircraft or a computer

JP (in Britain) Justice of the Peace

JPEG (jay-peg) n *computers* **a** a standard compressed file format used for pictures **b** a picture held in this file format

Jr Junior

JSA jobseeker's allowance: in Britain, a payment made to unemployed people

Juan Carlos n born 1938, king of Spain (1975–2014): nominated by Franco as the first king of the restored Spanish monarchy that was to follow his death; abdicated in favour of his son Felipe

Juan de Fuca n Strait of Juan de Fuca a strait between Vancouver Island (Canada) and NW Washington (US). Length: about 129 km (80 miles). Width: about 24 km (15 miles)

Juan Fernández Islands pl n a group of three islands in the S Pacific Ocean, administered by Chile: volcanic and wooded. Area: about 180 sq km (70 sq miles)

Juantorena n Alberto. born 1951, Cuban runner: won the 400 metres and the 800 metres in the 1976 Olympic Games

Juárez[1] n short for Ciudad Juárez

Juárez[2] n Benito Pablo. 1806–72, Mexican statesman. As president (1861–65; 1867–72) he thwarted Napoleon III's attempt to impose an empire under Maximilian and introduced many reforms

Juba n **1** a river in NE Africa, rising in S central Ethiopia and flowing south across Somalia to the Indian Ocean: the chief river of Somalia. Length: about 1660 km (1030 miles) **2** the capital of South Sudan, on the White Nile river. Pop: 250 000 (2006 est)

Jubbulpore n a variant spelling of Jabalpur

jube n *Austral and NZ informal* same as jujube

jubilant adj feeling great joy [Latin *jubilare* to give a joyful cry] **>** **jubilantly** adv

jubilation n a feeling of great joy and celebration

jubilee n a special anniversary, esp. a 25th (**silver jubilee**) or 50th one (**golden jubilee**) [Old French *jubile*, ultimately from Hebrew *yōbhēl* ram's horn, used for proclamation]

Judaea or **Judea** n the S division of ancient Palestine, succeeding the kingdom of Judah: a Roman province during the time of Christ

Judaean or **Judean** adj **1** of or relating to Judaea, or its inhabitants ▷ n **2** a native or inhabitant of Judaea

Judah ha-Levi n ?1075–1141, Jewish poet and philosopher, born in Spain; his major works include the collection in *Diwan* and the prose work *Sefer ha-Kuzari*, which presented his philosophy of Judaism in dialogue form

Judah ha-Nasi n ?135–?220 AD, rabbi and patriarch of the Sanhedrin, who compiled the Mishnah

Judaic adj of Jews or Judaism

Judaism n the religion of the Jews, based on the Old Testament and the Talmud

Judas n a person who betrays a friend [after *Judas* Iscariot the apostle who betrayed Jesus to his enemies in the Bible]

Judas Maccabaeus n Jewish leader, whose revolt (166–161 BC) against the Seleucid kingdom of Antiochus IV (Epiphanes) enabled him to recapture Jerusalem and rededicate the Temple

judder vb *informal, chiefly Brit* to shake or vibrate violently: *the van juddered before it moved away* [probably blend of jar (jolt) + shudder]

judder bar n NZ a raised strip across a road designed to slow down vehicles

Judea n a variant spelling of Judaea

judge n **1** a public official with authority to hear cases and pass sentences in a court of law **2** a person appointed to determine the result of a competition **3** a person whose opinion on a particular subject is usually reliable: *a fine judge of men* ▷ vb **judging, judged 4** to determine the result of (a competition) **5** to appraise critically: *she hopes people judge her on her work rather than her appearance* **6** to decide (something) after inquiry: *we use a means test to judge the most needy cases* **7** to believe or consider: *doctors judged that the benefits of such treatment outweighed the risk* [Latin *judex*]

judgment or **judgement** n **1** a decision formed after careful consideration: *the editorials reserve their judgment about the new political plan* **2** the verdict pronounced by a court of law **3** the ability to make critical distinctions and achieve a balanced viewpoint: *their judgment was unsound on foreign and defence issues* **4** the formal decision of the judge of a competition **5** against one's better judgment contrary to what one thinks is sensible: *again my better judgment, I asked for another bourbon* **6** pass judgment to give one's opinion, usually a critical one, on a matter

judgmental or **judgemental** adj making judgments, esp. critical ones, about other people's conduct

Judgment Day n *Christianity* the occasion of the Last Judgment by God at the end of the world

judicial adj **1** of judges or the administration of justice **2** showing or using good judgment: *judicial self-restraint* [Latin *judicium* judgment] **>** **judicially** adv

judiciary n the branch of the central authority in a country that administers justice

judicious adj having or showing good judgment: *the judicious use of charge cards* **>** **judiciously** adv

judo n a sport derived from jujitsu, in which the two opponents try to throw or force each other on to the ground [Japanese *jū* gentleness + *dō* way]

jug n a container with a handle and a small spout, used for holding and pouring liquids [origin unknown]

jugged hare n hare stewed in an earthenware pot

juggernaut n **1** Brit a very large heavy lorry **2** any terrible force that demands complete self-sacrifice [Hindi *Jagannath* lord of the world]

juggle vb **-gling, -gled 1** to throw and catch several objects continuously so that most are in the air at the same time **2** to keep (several activities) in progress at the same time: *women who are adept at juggling priorities* **3** to manipulate (facts or figures) to suit one's purpose [Old French *jogler* to perform as a jester] **>** **juggler** n

Jugoslav or **Jugoslavian** adj, n same as Yugoslav, Yugoslavian

Jugoslavia n a variant spelling of Yugoslavia

jugular n a large vein in the neck that carries blood to the heart from the head. Also called: **jugular vein** [Latin *iugulum* throat]

Jugurtha *n* died 104 BC, king of Numidia (?112–104), who waged war against the Romans (the **Jugurthine War**, 112–105) and was defeated and executed

juice *n* **1** a drink made from the liquid part of a fruit or vegetable: *grapefruit juice* **2** *informal* **a** petrol **b** electricity **3 juices a** the fluids in a person's or animal's body: *digestive juices* **b** the liquid that comes out of meat when it is cooked [Old French *jus*]

juicy *adj* **juicier, juiciest 1** full of juice **2** *informal* interesting and exciting: *juicy details*

Juiz de Fora *n* a city in SE Brazil, in Minas Gerais state on the Rio de Janeiro–Belo Horizonte railway: textiles. Pop: 502 000 (2005 est)

jujitsu *n* the traditional Japanese system of unarmed self-defence [Japanese *jū* gentleness + *jutsu* art]

juju *n* **1** a magic charm or fetish used by some tribes in W Africa **2** the power associated with a juju [probably from W African *djudju* evil spirit, fetish]

jujube *n* a chewy sweet made of flavoured gelatine [Medieval Latin *jujuba*]

jukebox *n* an automatic coin-operated record player [*juke* (from a Black American language) bawdy]

jukskei *n* S African a game in which a peg is thrown over a fixed distance at a stake fixed into the ground [Afrikaans *juk* yoke + *skei* pin]

Jul. July

julep *n* a sweet alcoholic drink, usually garnished with sprigs of mint

Julian *n* known as *Julian the Apostate*; Latin name *Flavius Claudius Julianus*. 331–363 AD, Roman emperor (361–363), who attempted to revive paganism in the Roman empire while remaining tolerant to Christians and Jews

Juliana *n* full name *Juliana Louise Emma Marie Wilhelmina*. 1909–2004, queen of the Netherlands (1948–80). She abdicated in favour of her eldest daughter Beatrix

Julian Alps *pl n* a mountain range in Slovenia: an E range of the Alps

Julian calendar *n* the calendar introduced by Julius Caesar, in which leap years occur every fourth year and in every centenary year

Julian of Norwich *n* ?1342–?1413, English mystic and anchoress: best known for the *Revelations of Divine Love* describing her visions

julienne *adj* **1** (of vegetables or meat) cut into thin shreds ▷ *n* **2** a clear soup containing thinly shredded vegetables [French]

Julius II *n* original name *Giuliano della Rovere*. 1443–1513, pope (1503–13). He completed the restoration of the Papal States to the Church, began the building of St Peter's, Rome (1506), and patronized Michelangelo, Raphael, and Bramante

Jullundur *n* the former name of **Jalandhar**

July *n*, *pl* **-lies** the seventh month of the year [after *Julius* Caesar]

jumble *n* **1** a disordered mass or state **2** articles donated for a jumble sale ▷ *vb* **-bling, -bled 3** to mix up [origin unknown]

jumble sale *n* a sale, usually of second-hand articles, often in aid of charity

jumbo *adj* **1** *Brit, Austral and NZ informal* very large: *jumbo prawns* ▷ *n*, *pl* **-bos 2** short for **jumbo jet** [after a famous elephant exhibited by P. T. Barnum]

jumbo jet *n* *informal* a very large jet-propelled airliner

jumbuck *n* *Austral old-fashioned, slang* sheep [from a native Australian language]

Jumna *n* a river in N India, rising in Uttarakhand in the Himalayas and flowing south and southeast to join the Ganges just below Allahabad (a confluence held sacred by Hindus). Length: 1385 km (860 miles)

jump *vb* **1** to move suddenly up into the air by using the muscles in the legs and feet **2** to move quickly: *he jumps on a No. 6 bus* **3** to jerk with astonishment or shock: *he

jumped when he heard a loud noise* **4** (of prices) to rise suddenly or abruptly **5** to change quickly from one subject to another: *any other comments before I jump on to the next section?* **6** *informal* to attack without warning: *the officer was jumped by three prisoners who broke his jaw* **7 jump down someone's throat** *informal* to speak sharply to someone **8 jump the gun** See **gun** (3) **9 jump the queue a** to take a place in a queue ahead of people who are already queuing **b** to have an unfair advantage over other people: *squatters should not be able to jump the queue for housing* **10 jump to it** *informal* to begin doing something immediately ▷ *n* **11** the act or an instance of jumping **12** *sport* any of several contests that involve jumping: *the long jump* **13** a sudden rise: *a 78% jump in taxable profits* **14** a sudden change from one subject to another: *stunning jumps from thought to thought* **15** a step or degree: *one jump ahead of the competition* **16 take a running jump** *informal* a contemptuous expression of dismissal ▷ See also **jump at, jump on** [probably imitative]

jump at *vb* to accept eagerly: *I jumped at the chance to return to English county cricket*

jumped-up *adj informal* having suddenly risen in significance and appearing arrogant: *a jumped-up bunch of ex-student-leaders*

jumper¹ *n* **1** *Brit and Austral* a knitted garment covering the upper part of the body **2** *US and Canad* a pinafore dress [obsolete *jump* man's loose jacket]

jumper² *n* a person or animal that jumps

jump jet *n informal* a fixed-wing jet aircraft that can land and take off vertically

jump leads *pl n* two heavy cables used to start a motor vehicle with a flat battery by connecting the flat battery to the battery of another vehicle

jump on *vb informal* to make a sudden physical or verbal attack on: *the press really jumped on him*

jump-start *vb* **1** to start the engine of (a motor vehicle) by pushing or rolling it and then engaging the gears ▷ *n* **2** the act of starting a motor vehicle in this way

jump suit *n* a one-piece garment combining trousers and top

jumpy *adj* **jumpier, jumpiest** nervous or apprehensive

Jun. **1** June **2** Junior

Junagadh *n* a town in India, in Gujarat: noted for its Buddhist caves and temples. Pop: 168 686 (2001)

Juncker *n* Jean-Claude born 1954, Luxembourgish politician; prime minister of Luxembourg (1995–2013); president of the European Commission from 2014

junction *n* a place where roads or railway lines meet, link, or cross each other [Latin *junctio* a joining]

juncture *n* a point in time, esp. a critical one: *trade has been halted at a crucial juncture*

Jundiaí *n* an industrial city in SE Brazil, in São Paulo state. Pop: 332 000 (2005 est)

June *n* the sixth month of the year [probably from Latin *Junius* of the goddess Juno]

Juneau *n* a port in SE Alaska: state capital. Pop: 31 187 (2003 est)

Jung *n* Carl Gustav. 1875–1961, Swiss psychologist. His criticism of Freud's emphasis on the sexual instinct ended their early collaboration. He went on to found analytical psychology, developing the concepts of the collective unconscious and its archetypes and of the extrovert and introvert as the two main psychological types

Jungfrau *n* a mountain in S Switzerland, in the Bernese Alps south of Interlaken. Height: 4158 m (13 642 ft)

Junggar Pendi, Dzungaria *or* **Zungaria** *n* an arid region of W China, in N Xinjiang between the Altai Mountains and the Tian Shan

jungle *n* **1** a forest area in a hot country with luxuriant vegetation **2** a confused or confusing situation: *the administrative jungle* **3** a situation where there is an intense struggle for survival: *the economic jungle* **4** a type of fast electronic dance music [Hindi *jangal*]

j

junior *adj* **1** lower in rank or position: *junior officers* **2** younger: *world junior champion* **3** (in England and Wales) of school children between the ages of 7 and 11 approximately **4** US of the third year of a four-year course at college or high school ▷ *n* **5** a person holding a low rank or position **6** a person who is younger than another person: *the man she is to marry is 20 years her junior* **7** (in England and Wales) a junior school child **8** US a junior student [Latin: younger]

Junior *adj* the younger of two: usually used after a name to distinguish between two people of the same name: *Harry Connick Junior*

junior lightweight *n* a professional boxer weighing up to 130 pounds (59 kg)

juniper *n* an evergreen shrub with purple berries which are used to make gin [Latin *juniperus*]

Junius *n* pen name of the anonymous author of a series of letters (1769–72) attacking the ministries of George III of Great Britain and Ireland now generally believed to have been written by Sir Philip Francis

junk¹ *n* **1** old or unwanted objects **2** informal rubbish: *the sheer junk written about astrology* **3** slang narcotic drugs, esp. heroin [Middle English *jonke* old useless rope]

junk² *n* a Chinese sailing boat with a flat bottom and square sails [Portuguese *junco*, from Javanese *jon*]

junk bond *n* finance a security that offers a high yield but often involves a high risk of default

Junkers *n* Hugo. 1859–1935, German aircraft designer. His military aircraft were used in both World Wars

junket *n* **1** an excursion made by a public official and paid for out of public funds **2** a sweet dessert made of flavoured milk set with rennet **3** a feast [Middle English: rush basket, hence custard served on rushes] ▷ **junketing** *n*

junk food *n* food with a low nutritional value

junkie *n* informal a drug addict

junk mail *n* unsolicited mail advertising goods or services

Juno *n* the queen of the Roman gods

junta *n* a group of military officers holding the power in a country after a revolution [Spanish: council]

Jupiter *n* **1** the king of the Roman gods **2** the largest planet

Jura *n* **1** a department of E France, in Franche-Comté region. Capital: Lons-le-Saunier. Pop: 253 309 (2003 est)). Area: 5055 sq km (1971 sq miles) **2** a canton of Switzerland, bordering the French frontier: formed in 1979 from part of Bern. Capital: Delémont. Pop: 69 200 (2002 est). Area: 838 sq km (323 sq miles) **3** an island off the W coast of Scotland, in the Inner Hebrides, separated from the mainland by the **Sound of Jura**. Pop: 200 (2004 est). Area: 381 sq km (147 sq miles) **4** a mountain range in W central Europe, between the Rivers Rhine and Rhône: mostly in E France, extending into W Switzerland **5** a range of mountains in the NE quadrant of the moon lying on the N border of the Mare Imbrium

Jurassic *adj* geology of the geological period about 180 million years ago, during which dinosaurs flourished [after the Jura (Mountains) in W central Europe]

juridical *adj* of law or the administration of justice [Latin *jus* law + *dicere* to say]

jurisdiction *n* **1** the right or power to administer justice and to apply laws **2** the exercise or extent of such a right or power **3** authority in general: *under the jurisdiction of the referee* [Latin *jurisdictio*]

jurisprudence *n* the science or philosophy of law [Latin *juris prudentia*]

jurist *n* a person who is an expert on law [French *juriste*]

juror *n* a member of a jury [Old French *jurer* to take an oath]

Juruá *n* a river in South America, rising in E central Peru and flowing northeast across NW Brazil to join the Amazon. Length: 1900 km (1200 miles)

jury *n, pl* **-ries 1** a group of, usually, twelve people, sworn to deliver a true verdict according to the evidence upon case presented in a court of law **2** a group of people appointed to judge a competition [Old French *jurer* to swear]

jury box *n* an enclosure where the jury sits in a court of law

jury-rigged *adj* chiefly nautical set up in a makeshift manner [origin unknown]

just *adv* **1** very recently: *the results have just been published* **2** at this very instant or in the very near future: *news is just coming in of a nuclear explosion* **3** no more than; only: *nothing fancy, just solid German fare* **4** exactly: *just the opposite* **5** barely: *the swimmers arrived just in time for the opening ceremony* **6** just about practically or virtually: *just about everyone* **7** just about to very soon going to: *it was just about to explode* **8** just a moment or second or minute an expression requesting someone to wait for a short time **9** just now **a** a short time ago: *as you said just now* **b** at the present time: *he needs all the support he can get just now* **c** S African informal in a little while **10** just so arranged with precision: *a cottage with the gardens and rooms all just so* ▷ *adj* **11** fair and right: *a just war* [Latin *jus* justice] ▷ **justly** *adv* ▷ **justness** *n*

> **USAGE** The use of *just* with *exactly* (*it's just exactly what they want*) is redundant and should be avoided: *it's exactly what they want.*

justice *n* **1** the quality of being just **2** the administratio of law according to prescribed and accepted principles **3** a judge **4** bring to justice to capture, try, and punish (a criminal) **5** do justice to to show to full advantage: *she wore white slacks and a sleeveless blouse that did full justice to her trim figure* [Latin *justitia*]

justice of the peace *n* **1** (in Britain) a magistrate who is authorized to act as a judge in a local court of law **2** (i New Zealand) a person authorized to act in a limited judicial capacity

justifiable *adj* having a good cause or reason: *I reacted with justifiable indignation* ▷ **justifiably** *adv*

justify *vb* **-fies, -fying, -fied 1** to prove (something) to be just or valid: *the idea of the end justifying the means* **2** to defend (an action) as being warranted: *an essay justifying his conversion to Catholicism* **3** to arrange (text) when typin or printing so that both margins are straight [Latin *justificare*] ▷ **justification** *n*

Justinian I *n* called *the Great*; Latin name *Flavius Anicius Justinianus*. 483–565 AD, Byzantine emperor (527–565). He recovered North Africa, SE Spain, and Italy, largely owing to the brilliance of generals such as Belisarius. H sponsored the Justinian Code

Justinian II *n* 669–711 AD, Byzantine emperor (685–95, 705–11). Banished (695) after a revolt against his oppressive rule, he regained the throne with the help o the Bulgars. He was killed in a second revolt

Justin Martyr *n* Saint. ?100–?165 AD, Christian apologis and philosopher. Feast day: June 1

jute *n* a fibre that comes from the bark of an East Indian plant, used in making rope, sacks, and mats [Bengali *jhuto*]

Jutland *n* a peninsula of N Europe: forms the continental portion of Denmark and geographically includes the N part of the German province of Schleswig-Holstein, while politically it includes only the mainland of Denmark and the islands north of Limfjorden; a major but inconclusive naval battle was fought off its NW coast in 1916 between the British and German fleets. Danish name: **Jylland**

Jutlander *n* a native or inhabitant of Jutland

jut out *vb* **jutting, jutted** to stick out [variant of JET¹]

Juvenal *n* Latin name *Decimus Junius Juvenalis*. ?60–?140 AD, Roman satirist. In his 16 verse satires, he denounced th vices of imperial Rome

juvenile *adj* **1** young; not fully adult: *juvenile offenders* **2** of or for young people: *juvenile court* **3** immature in behaviour ▷ *n* **4** a young person [Latin *juvenilis*]

juvenile delinquent *n* a young person who is guilty of a crime **›** **juvenile delinquency** *n*

juvenilia *pl n* works produced in an artist's youth

juxtapose *vb* **-posing, -posed** to place (two objects or ideas) close together or side by side [Latin *juxta* next to + POSITION] **›** **juxtaposition** *n*

Jylland *n* the Danish name for Jutland

Kk

K **1** kelvin(s) **2** *chess* king **3** *chem* potassium **4** one thousand **5** *computers* a unit of 1024 words, bits, or bytes

K2 *n* a mountain in the Karakoram Range on the Kashmir-Xinjiang border: the second highest mountain in the world. Height: 8611 m (28 250 ft). Also called: **Godwin-Austen, Dapsang**

kabaddi *n* a game in which players try to touch opposing players but avoid being captured by them

Kabalega Falls *pl n* rapids on the lower Victoria Nile, about 35 km (22 miles) east of Lake Albert, where the Nile drops 120 m (400 ft). Also: **Murchison Falls**

Kabardino-Balkar Republic *n* a constituent republic of S Russia, on the N side of the Caucasus Mountains. Capital: Nalchik. Pop: 900 500 (2002). Area: 12 500 sq km (4825 sq miles). Also called: **Kabardino-Balkaria**

Kabila *n* Laurent. 1940–2001, Congolese politician and guerrilla leader: he overthrew the Mobutu regime in Zaïre, becoming president of the renamed Democratic Republic of Congo (1997–2001): assassinated

Kabir *n* 1440–1518, Indian religious leader who pioneered a religious movement that combined elements of Islam and Hinduism and is considered the precursor of Sikhism

kabloona *n* a person who is not of Inuit ancestry, esp. a white person

Kabul *or* **Kabol** *n* **1** the capital of Afghanistan, in the northeast of the country at an altitude of 1800 m (5900 ft) on the **Kabul River**: over 3000 years old, with a strategic position commanding passes through the Hindu Kush and main routes to the Khyber Pass; destroyed and rebuilt many times; capital of the Mogul Empire from 1504 until 1738 and of Afghanistan from 1773; university (1932). Pop: 3 288 000 (2005 est) **2** a river in Afghanistan and Pakistan, rising in the Hindu Kush and flowing east into the Indus at Attock, Pakistan. Length: 700 km (435 miles)

Kaczynski *n* Lech. 1949–2010, Polish politician, president of Poland from 2005

Kádár *n* János. 1912–89, Hungarian statesman; Communist prime minister of Hungary (1956–58; 1961–65) and first secretary of the Communist Party (1956–88)

Kaddish *n, pl* **Kaddishim** *Judaism* an ancient Jewish liturgical prayer, recited esp. by mourners [Aramaic *qaddīsh* holy]

Kaduna *n* **1** a state of N Nigeria. Capital: Kaduna. Pop: 6 066 562 (2006). Area: 46 053 sq km (17 781 sq miles). Former name (until 1976): **North-Central State 2** a city in N central Nigeria, capital of Kaduna state on the **Kaduna River** (a principal tributary of the Niger). Pop: 1 329 000 (2005 est)

Kaesŏng *n* a city in SW North Korea: former capital of Korea (938–1392). Pop: 621 000 (2005 est)

Kaffir (kaf-fer) *n S African offensive, obsolete* a Black African [Arabic *kāfir* infidel]

Kaffraria *n* a former region of S central South Africa:

inhabited chiefly by people then known as the Kaffirs; British Kaffraria was a crown colony established in 185 in the southwest of the region and annexed to Cape Colony in 1865

Kaffrarian *adj* **1** of or relating to Kaffraria or its inhabitants ▷ *n* **2** a native or inhabitant of Kaffraria

Kafiristan *n* the former name of **Nuristan**

Kafka *n* Franz. 1883–1924, Czech novelist writing in German. In his two main novels *The Trial* (1925) and *The Castle* (1926), published posthumously against his wishes, he portrays man's fear, isolation, and bewilderment in a nightmarish dehumanized world ▷ **Kafkaesque** *adj*

kaftan *or* **caftan** *n* **1** a long loose garment worn by men in eastern countries **2** a woman's dress resembling this [Turkish *qaftān*]

Kagera *n* a river in E Africa, rising in headstreams on the border between Tanzania and Rwanda and flowing east to Lake Victoria: the most remote headstream of th Nile and largest tributary of Lake Victoria. Length: about 480 km (300 miles)

Kagoshima *n* a port in SW Japan, on S Kyushu. Pop: 544 840 (2002 est)

kahawai *n* a food and game fish of New Zealand [Māori]

Kahn *n* **1** Herman. 1922–83, US mathematician and futurologist; director of the Hudson Institute (1961–83) **2** Louis I(sadore). 1901–74, US architect, noted for his art museums at Yale (1951–53), Fort Worth (1966–72), and New Haven (1969–74)

kai *n NZ informal* food [Māori]

Kaieteur Falls *pl n* a waterfall in Guyana, on the Potaro River. Height: 226 m (741 ft). Width: about 107 m (350 ft)

Kaifeng *n* a city in E China, in N Henan on the Yellow River: one of the oldest cities in China and its capital (a Pien-liang) from 907 to 1126. Pop: 810 000 (2005 est)

kail *n* same as **kale**

Kairouan, Kairwan *or* **Qairwan** *n* a city in NE Tunisia one of the holy cities of Islam; pilgrimage and trading centre. Pop: 124 000 (2005 est)

kaiser (kize-er) *n history* a German or Austro-Hungarian emperor [German, from Latin *Caesar* emperor]

Kaiser *n* Georg. 1878–1945, German expressionist dramatist

Kaiserslautern *n* a city in W Germany, in S Rhineland-Palatinate. Pop: 999 095 (2003 est)

kak (kuck) *n S African taboo* **1** faeces **2** rubbish [Afrikaans]

kaka *n* a parrot of New Zealand [Māori]

kakapo *n, pl* **-pos** a ground-living nocturnal New Zealand parrot that resembles an owl [Māori]

Kalahari *n* the Kalahari an extensive arid plateau of South Africa, Namibia, and Botswana. Area: 260 000 sq km (100 000 sq miles). Also known as: the Kalahari Desert

Kalamazoo *n* a city in SW Michigan, midway between Detroit and Chicago: aircraft, missile parts. Pop: 75 513 (2003 est)

Kalashnikov n a Russian-made automatic rifle [after M. *Kalashnikov*, its designer]

Kalat or **Khelat** n a region of SW Pakistan, in S Baluchistan: formerly a princely state ruled by the Khan of Kalat, which joined Pakistan in 1948

kale n a type of cabbage with crinkled leaves [Old English *cāl*]

kaleidoscope n **1** a tube-shaped toy lined with angled mirrors and containing loose pieces of coloured paper that form intricate patterns when viewed through a hole in the end **2** any complicated or rapidly changing set of colours, circumstances, etc.: *a kaleidoscope of shifting political groups and alliances* [Greek *kalos* beautiful + *eidos* form + *skopein* to look at] **> kaleidoscopic** adj

kalends pl n same as **calends**

kaleyard n Scot a vegetable garden [literally: cabbage garden]

Kalgan n a former name of **Zhangjiakou**

Kalgoorlie n a city in Western Australia, adjoining the town of Boulder: a centre of the Coolgardie gold rushes of the early 1890s; declining gold resources superseded by the discovery of nickel ore in 1966. Pop: 28 281 (including Boulder) (2001)

Kalidasa n ?5th century AD, Indian dramatist and poet, noted for his romantic verse drama *Sakuntala*

Kalimantan n the Indonesian name for Borneo: applied to the Indonesian part of the island only, excluding the Malaysian states of Sabah and Sarawak and the sultanate of Brunei. Pop: 11 341 558 (2000)

Kalinin¹ n the former name (until 1991) of **Tver**

Kalinin² n Mikhail Ivanovich. 1875–1946, Soviet statesman: titular head of state (1919–46); a founder of *Pravda* (1912)

Kaliningrad n a port in W Russia, on the Pregolya River: severely damaged in World War II as the chief German naval base on the Baltic; ceded to the Soviet Union in 1945 and is now Russia's chief Baltic naval base. Pop: 436 000 (2005 est). Former name (until 1946): **Königsberg**

Kalisz n a town in central Poland, on an island in the Prosna River: textile industry. Pop: 110 000 (2005 est). Ancient name: **Calissia**

Kallis n Jacques (Henry), born 1975, South African cricketer; an all-rounder, in 166 tests (1995–2013) he scored 13,289 runs and took 292 wickets

Kalmar n a port in SE Sweden, partly on the mainland and partly on a small island in the **Sound of Kalmar** opposite Öland: scene of the signing of the Union of Kalmar, which united Sweden, Denmark, and Norway into a single monarchy (1397–1523). Pop: 60 734 (2004 est)

Kalmyk Republic or **Kalmuck Republic** n a constituent republic of S Russia, on the Caspian Sea: became subject to Russia in 1646. Capital: Elista. Pop: 292 400 (2002). Area: 76 100 sq km (29 382 sq miles). Also: **Kalmykia**

Kaluga n a city in central Russia, on the Oka River. Pop: 340 000 (2005 est)

Kama n a river in central Russia, rising in the Ural Mountains and flowing to the River Volga, of which it is the largest tributary. Length: 2030 km (1260 miles)

Kamakura n a city in central Japan, on S Honshu: famous for its Great Buddha (Daibutsu), a 13th-century bronze, 15 m (49 ft) high. Pop: 169 714 (2002 est)

Kamasutra (kah-ma-soo-tra) n the **Kamasutra** an ancient Hindu text on sex [Sanskrit *kāma* love + *sūtra* thread, rule]

Kamchatka n a peninsula in E Russia, between the Sea of Okhotsk and the Bering Sea. Length: about 1200 km (750 miles)

Kamchatkan adj **1** of or relating to Kamchatka or its inhabitants **▷** n **2** a native or inhabitant of Kamchatka

Kamensk-Uralski n an industrial city in S Russia. Pop: 183 000 (2005 est)

Kamerlingh-Onnes n Heike. 1853–1926, Dutch physicist: a pioneer of the physics of low-temperature

materials and discoverer (1911) of superconductivity. Nobel prize for physics 1913

Kamerun n the German name for **Cameroon**

Kamet n a mountain on the border of China and India, west of Nepal in the Himalayas. Height: 7756 m (25 447 ft)

kamik n a traditional Inuit boot made of caribou hide or sealskin

kamikaze (kam-mee-**kah**-zee) n **1** (in World War II) a Japanese pilot who performed a suicidal mission **▷** adj **2** (of an action) undertaken in the knowledge that it will result in the death or injury of the person performing it: *a kamikaze attack* [Japanese *kami* divine + *kaze* wind]

Kamloops trout n a bright silvery rainbow trout common in British Columbia, Canada

Kammerer n Paul. 1880–1926, Austrian zoologist: noted for his controversial experiments, esp. with the midwife toad, apparently demonstrating the inheritance of acquired characteristics. Accused of fraud, he committed suicide

Kampala n the capital and largest city of Uganda, in Central region on Lake Victoria: Makerere University (1961). Pop: 1 208 544 (2002 est)

Kampuchea n the name (1976–89) of **Cambodia**

Kampuchean adj **1** of or relating to Kampuchea or its inhabitants **▷** n **2** a native or inhabitant of Kampuchea

Kan. or **Kans.** Kansas

Kananga n a city in the SW Democratic Republic of Congo: a commercial centre on the railway from Lubumbashi to Port Francqui. Pop: 424 000 (2005 est). Former name (until 1966): **Luluabourg**

Kanara or **Canara** n a region of SW India, in Karnataka on the Deccan Plateau and the W Coast. Area: about 155 000 sq km (60 000 sq miles)

Kanazawa n a port in central Japan, on W Honshu: textile and porcelain industries. Pop: 439 892 (2002 est)

Kanchenjunga n a variant spelling of **Kangchenjunga**

Kanchipuram n a city in SE India, in Tamil Nadu: a sacred Hindu town known as "the Benares of the South"; textile industries. Pop: 152 984 (2001)

Kandahar n a city in S Afghanistan: an important trading centre, built by Ahmad Shah Durrani (1724–73) as his capital on the site of several former cities. Pop: 436 000 (2005 est)

Kandinsky n Vasili. 1866–1944, Russian expressionist painter and theorist, regarded as the first to develop an entirely abstract style: a founder of *der Blaue Reiter*

Kandy n a city in central Sri Lanka: capital of the kingdom of Kandy from 1480 until 1815, when occupied by the British; sacred Buddhist temple; University of Sri Lanka. Pop: 112 000 (2005 est)

kangaroo n, pl **-roos** a large Australian marsupial with powerful hind legs used for leaping [probably Aboriginal]

kangaroo court n an unofficial court set up by a group to discipline its members

Kangaroo Island n an island in the Indian Ocean, off South Australia. Area: 4350 sq km (1680 sq miles)

kangaroo paw n an Australian plant with green-and-red flowers

Kangchenjunga, Kanchenjunga or **Kinchinjunga** n a mountain on the border between Nepal and Sikkim, in the Himalayas: the third highest mountain in the world. Height: 8598 m (28 208 ft)

KaNgwane n (formerly) a Bantu homeland in South Africa; abolished in 1994. Capital: Schoemansdal. Former name: **Swazi Territory**

Kano n **1** a state of N Nigeria: consists of wooded savanna in the south and scrub vegetation in the north. Capital: Kano. Pop: 9 383 682 (2006). Area: 20 131 sq km (7773 sq miles) **2** a city in N Nigeria, capital of Kano state: transport and market centre. Pop: 674 100 (1996 est)

Kanpur n an industrial city in NE India, in S Uttar Pradesh on the River Ganges: scene of the massacre by

Nana Sahib of British soldiers and European families and his later defeat by British forces in 1857. Pop: 2 532 138 (2001). Former name: **Cawnpore**

Kansan *n* **1** a native or inhabitant of Kansas ▷ *adj* **2** of or relating to Kansas or its inhabitants

Kansas *n* a state of the central US: consists of undulating prairie, drained chiefly by the Arkansas, Kansas, and Missouri Rivers; mainly agricultural. Capital: Topeka. Pop: 2 723 507 (2003 est). Area: 213 096 sq km (82 277 sq miles). Abbreviation: **Kan.**, **Kans.**, (with zip code) **KS**

Kansas City *n* **1** a city in W Missouri, at the confluence of the Missouri and Kansas Rivers: important centre of livestock and meat-packing industry. Pop: 442 768 (2003 est) **2** a city in NE Kansas, adjacent to Kansas City, Missouri. Pop: 145 757 (2003 est)

Kansu *n* a variant transliteration of the Chinese name for **Gansu**

Kant *n* Immanuel. 1724–1804, German idealist philosopher. He sought to determine the limits of man's knowledge in *Critique of Pure Reason* (1781) and propounded his system of ethics as guided by the categorical imperative in *Critique of Practical Reason* (1788)

Kaohsiung, Kao-hsiung *or* **Gaoxiong** *n* a port in SW Taiwan, on the South China Sea: the chief port of the island. Pop: 1 506 000 (2005 est). Japanese name: **Takao**

Kaolack *n* a port in SW Senegal, on the Saloum River. Pop: 299 000 (2005 est)

kaolin *n* a fine white clay used in making porcelain and in some medicines [*Kaoling*, Chinese mountain where supplies for Europe were first obtained]

kapa haka *n* NZ the traditional Māori performing arts, often performed competitively [Māori]

ka pai *interj* NZ good! well done! [Māori]

Kapfenberg *n* an industrial town in E Austria, in Styria. Pop: 22 234 (2001)

Kapil Dev *n* (Ramlal) Nikhanj. born 1959, Indian cricketer: an all-rounder, he played in 131 test matches and captained India to victory in the 1983 World Cup

Kapitza *n* Piotr Leonidovich. 1894–1984, Russian physicist. He worked in England and the USSR, doing research in several areas, particularly cryogenics; Nobel prize for physics in 1978

kapok *n* a fluffy fibre from a tropical tree, used for stuffing pillows and padding sleeping bags [Malay]

Kapoor *n* Sir Anish. born 1954, British sculptor, born in Bombay; winner of the Turner Prize (1991); noted for the *ArcelorMittal Orbit*, a sculpture and observation tower exhibited at the London Olympic Park from 2012

kaput (kap-**poot**) *adj informal* ruined or broken: *the chronometer, incidentally, is kaput* [German *kaputt*]

Karachai-Cherkess Republic *or* **Karachayevo-Cherkess Republic** *n* a constituent republic of W Russia, on the N side of the Caucasus Mountains. Capital: Cherkessk. Pop: 439 700 (2002). Area: 14 100 sq km (5440 sq miles). Also called: **Karachai-Cherkessia**

Karachi *n* a port in S Pakistan, on the Arabian Sea: capital of Pakistan (1947–60); university (1950); chief port: commercial and industrial centre. Pop: 11 819 000 (2005 est)

Karadžić *n* Radovan. born 1945, Bosnian Serb political leader during the Bosnian war (1992–95); evaded capture until arrested in 2008; tried on charges of genocide and war crimes by an international criminal tribunal at The Hague (2010–2014) and ongoing

Karafuto *n* transliteration of the Japanese name for Sakhalin

Karaganda *n* a city in E central Kazakhstan, founded in 1857: a major coal-mining and industrial centre. Pop: 412 000 (2005 est). Also called: **Qaraghandy**

Karajan *n* Herbert von. 1908–89, Austrian conductor

Kara-Kalpak Autonomous Republic *n* an administrative division in NW Uzbekistan, on the Aral Sea: came under Russian rule by stages from 1873 until

Uzbekistan became independent in 1991. Capital: Nukus. Pop: 1 633 900 (2002 est). Area: 165 600 sq km (63 900 sq miles). Also called: **Kara-Kalpakia, Kara-Kalpakstan**

Karakoram *or* **Karakorum** *n* a mountain system in N Kashmir, extending for about 480 km (300 miles) from northwest to southeast: contains the second highest peak in the world (K2); crossed by several high passes, notably the **Karakoram Pass** 5575 m (18 290 ft)

Karakorum *n* a ruined city in Mongolia: founded in 1220 by Ghenghis Khan; destroyed by Kublai Khan when his brother rebelled against him, after Kublai Khan had moved his capital to Peking (now Beijing)

karakul *n* **1** a sheep of central Asia, the lambs of which have soft curled dark hair **2** the fur prepared from these lambs [Russian]

Kara Kum *n* a desert in Turkmenistan, covering most of the country: extensive areas now irrigated. Area: about 300 000 sq km (120 000 sq miles)

Karamanlis *n* Konstantinos. 1907–98, Greek statesman: prime minister of Greece (1955–58; 1958–61; 1961–63; 1974–80): president of Greece (1980–85; 1990–95)

Karan *n* Donna. born 1948, US fashion designer; creator of the DKNY clothing label

karaoke *n* a form of entertainment in which members of the public sing well-known songs over a prerecorded backing tape [Japanese *kara* empty + *ōkesutora* orchestra]

Kara Sea *n* a shallow arm of the Arctic Ocean off the N coast of Russia: ice-free for about three months of the year

karate *n* a Japanese system of unarmed combat, in which punches, chops, and kicks are made with the hands, feet, elbows, and legs [Japanese: empty hand]

Karbala *or* **Kerbela** *n* a town in central Iraq: the chief holy city of Iraq and centre of Shiah Muslim pilgrimage: burial place of Mohammed's grandson Husain. Pop: 460 000 (2005 est)

Karelia *n* **1** a region of NE Europe comprising areas of both Finland and Russia. Following the Russo-Finnish War (1939–40) a large part of what had been Finnish Karelia was annexed by the former Soviet Union; together with the part of Karelia which already belonged to Russia at that time, it corresponds roughly to the modern Karelian Republic in Russia **2** another name for the **Karelian Republic**

Karelian *adj* **1** of or relating to Karelia, its people, or the language ▷ *n* **2** a native or inhabitant of Karelia **3** the dialect of Finnish spoken in Karelia

Karelian Isthmus *n* a strip of land, now in Russia, between the Gulf of Finland and Lake Ladoga: annexed by the former Soviet Union after the Russo-Finnish War (1939–40)

Karelian Republic *n* a constituent republic of NW Russia between the White Sea and Lakes Onega and Ladoga. Capital: Petrozavodsk. Pop: 716 700 (2002). Area: 172 400 sq km (66 560 sq miles)

Kariba *n* Lake Kariba a lake on the Zambia-Zimbabwe border, created by the building of the **Kariba Dam** across the Zambezi for hydroelectric power. Length: 282 km (175 miles)

Karl-Marx-Stadt *n* the former name (1953–90) of Chemnitz

Karloff *n* Boris, real name *William Pratt*. 1887–1969, English film actor, famous for his roles in horror films, esp. *Frankenstein* (1931)

Karlovy Vary *n* a city in the W Czech Republic, at the confluence of the Tepla and OhĐe Rivers: warm mineral springs. Pop: 50 691 (2007 est). German name: **Karlsbad, Carlsbad**

Karlskrona *n* a port in S Sweden: Sweden's main naval base since 1680. Pop: 61 097 (2004 est)

Karlsruhe *n* a city in SW Germany, in Baden-Württemberg: capital of the former Baden state. Pop: 282 595 (2003 est)

arma n Hinduism, Buddhism a person's actions affecting nis or her fate in the next reincarnation [Sanskrit: action, effect]

arnak n a village in E Egypt, on the Nile: site of the N part of the ruins of ancient Thebes

arnataka n a state of S India, on the Arabian Sea: consists of a narrow coastal plain rising to the South Deccan plateau; mainly agricultural. Capital: Bangalore. Pop: 52 733 958 (2001). Area: 191 791 sq km 74 051 sq miles). Former name (1956–73): **Mysore**

ärnten n the German name for **Carinthia**

aroo or **Karroo** n, pl **-roos** (often not cap) **1** any of several nigh arid plateaus in South Africa, esp. the **Central** Karoo and the **Little Karoo**. The highveld, north of the Central Karoo, is sometimes called the **Northern Karoo 2** a period or rock system in Southern Africa equivalent to the period or system extending from the Upper Carboniferous to the Lower Jurassic: divided into **Lower** and **Upper Karoo** ▷ adj **3** of, denoting, or formed in the Karoo period [C18: from Afrikaans karo, probably from Khoikhoi garo desert]

aross (ka-ross) n S African a blanket made of animal skins sewn together [Khoi (language of southern Africa) karos animal-skin blanket]

arpov n Anatoly. born 1951, Russian chess player and politician: world champion (1975–85); FIDE world champion (1993–99); member of the Russian Civic Chamber from 2005

arri n, pl **-ris 1** an Australian eucalypt **2** its wood, used for building

arsh n Yousuf. 1908–2002, Canadian photographer noted for portraits, esp. of famous subjects

art n same as **go-kart**

arzai n Hamid. born 1957, Afghan military and political leader: acting president (2001–04); president 2004–2014)

asai n a river in southwestern Africa, rising in central Angola and flowing east then north as part of the border between Angola and the Democratic Republic of Congo, continuing northwest through the Democratic Republic of Congo to the River Congo. Length: 2154 km 1338 miles)

asbah n same as **casbah**

ashi or **Kashgar** n an oasis city in W China, in W Xinjiang. Pop: 318 000 (2005 est)

ashmir n a region of SW central Asia: from the 16th century ruled by the Moguls, Afghans, Sikhs, and British successively; since 1947 disputed between India, Pakistan, and China; 84 000 sq km (33 000 sq miles) in the northwest are held by Pakistan and in part known as Azad Kashmir (Free Kashmir), part as the Northern Areas; an area of 42 735 sq km (16 496 sq miles) in the east the Aksai Chin) is held by China; the remainder was in 1956 officially incorporated into India as the state of Jammu and Kashmir; traversed by the Himalaya and Karakoram mountain ranges and the Rivers Jhelum and Indus; a fruit-growing and cattle-grazing region, with a woollen industry. Capitals: (Jammu and Kashmir) Srinagar (summer), Jammu (winter); (Azad Kashmir) Muzaffarabad; (Northern Areas) Gilgit

ashmiri adj **1** of or relating to Kashmir, its people, or their language ▷ n **2** (pl **-miris** or **-miri**) a member of the people of Kashmir **3** the state language of Kashmir, belonging to the Dardic group of the Indo-European family of languages

ashmirian adj **1** of or relating to Kashmir, its people, or their language ▷ n **2** a member of the people of Kashmir

asparov n Garry, real name Garik Weinstein. born 1963, Armenian-Jewish chess player, born in Azerbaijan: world champion (1985–93); PCA world champion 1993–2000); since retiring from chess he has been involved in politics in Russia, forming the United Civil Front in 2005

assa n the Hungarian name for **Košice**

Kassala n a city in the E Sudan: founded as a fort by the Egyptians in 1834. Pop: 430 000 (2005 est)

Kassel or **Cassel** n a city in central Germany, in Hesse; capital of Westphalia (1807–13) and of the Prussian province of Hesse-Nassau (1866–1945). Pop: 194 322 (2003 est)

Kastrop-Rauxel n a variant spelling of **Castrop-Rauxel**

Katanga n a region of SE Democratic Republic of Congo: site of a secessionist movement during the 1960s and again in 1993; important for hydroelectric power and rich mineral resources (copper and tin ore). Pop: estimates vary between 4 000 000 (1998) and 8 000 000 (2006). Area: 496 964 sq km (191 878 sq miles). Former name (1972–97): **Shaba**

Katar n a variant spelling of **Qatar**

Katari adj, n a variant spelling of **Qatari**

Kathiawar n a large peninsula of W India, in Gujarat between the Gulf of Kutch and the Gulf of Cambay. Area: about 60 690 sq km (23 430 sq miles)

katipo n, pl **-pos** a small venomous New Zealand spider, commonly black with a red or orange stripe on the abdomen [Māori]

Katla n an ice-capped volcano in the Mýrdalsjökull glacier in south Iceland. Its last major eruption was in 1918. Height: 1512 m (4961 ft) [named after an Icelandic witch]

Katmai n Mount Katmai a volcano in SW Alaska, in the Aleutian Range: erupted in 1912 forming the Valley of Ten Thousand Smokes, a region with numerous fumaroles; established as **Katmai National Monument**, 10 917 sq km (4215 sq miles), in 1918. Height: 2100 m (7000 ft). Depth of crater: 1130 m (3700 ft). Width of crater: about 4 km (2.5 miles)

Katmandu or **Kathmandu** n the capital of Nepal, in the east at the confluence of the Baghmati and Vishnumati Rivers. Pop: 814 000 (2005 est)

Katowice n an industrial city in S Poland. Pop: 2 914 000 (2005 est). Former name (1953–56): **Stalinogrod**

Katrine n Loch Katrine a lake in central Scotland, east of Loch Lomond: noted for its associations with Sir Walter Scott's Lady of the Lake. Length: about 13 km (8 miles)

Katsina n **1** a state of N Nigeria. Capital: Katsina. Pop: 5 792 578 (2006). Area: 24 192 sq km (9341 sq miles) **2** a city in N Nigeria, in Katsina state: a major intellectual and cultural centre of the Hausa people (16th–18th centuries). Pop: 530 000 (2005 est)

Kattegat n a strait between Denmark and Sweden: linked to the Sound, the Great Belt, and the Little Belt with the Baltic Sea and by the Skagerrak with the North Sea. Former spelling: **Cattegat**

katydid n a large green grasshopper of North America [imitative]

Katz n Sir Bernard. 1911–2003, British neurophysiologist, born in Germany. Shared the Nobel prize for physiology or medicine (1970) with Julius Axelrod and Ulf von Euler

Kauai n a volcanic island in NW Hawaii, northwest of Oahu. Chief town: Lihue. Pop (Kauai county): 60 747 (2003 est). Area (island): 1433 sq km (553 sq miles)

Kauffmann n Angelica. 1741–1807, Swiss painter, who worked chiefly in England

Kaufman n George S(imon). 1889–1961, US dramatist who, with Moss Hart, collaborated on many Broadway comedy hits

Kaunas n a city in central Lithuania at the confluence of the Neman and Viliya Rivers: ceded by Poland to Russia in 1795; became the provisional capital of Lithuania (1920–40); incorporated into the Soviet Union 1944–91; university (1922). Pop: 364 000 (2005 est). Russian name: **Kovno**

Kaunda n Kenneth (David). born 1924, Zambian statesman. He became Zambia's first president (1964–91)

kauri n a large New Zealand conifer grown for its valuable wood and resin [Māori]

Kaválla *n* a port in E Greece, in Macedonia East and Thrace region on the **Bay of Kaválla**, an important Macedonian fortress of the Byzantine empire; ceded to Greece by Turkey after the Balkan War (1912–13). Pop (municipality): 63 572 (2001). Ancient name: **Neapolis**

Kaveri *n* a variant spelling of **Cauvery**

Kavir Desert *n* another name for the **Dasht-i-Kavir**

Kawabata *n* Yasunari. 1899–1972, Japanese novelist, author of *Yukiguni* (*Snow Country*, 1948) and *Yama no oto* (*The Sound of the Mountain*, 1954): Nobel prize for literature 1968

Kawasaki *n* an industrial port in central Japan, on SE Honshu, between Tokyo and Yokohama. Pop: 1 245 780 (2002 est)

kayak *n* **1** an Inuit canoe-like boat consisting of a frame covered with animal skins **2** a fibreglass or canvas-covered canoe of similar design [Inuktitut]

Kayseri *n* a city in central Turkey: trading centre since ancient times as the chief city of Cappadocia. Pop: 605 000 (2005 est). Ancient name: **Caesarea Mazaca**

Kazakhstan *or* **Kazakstan** *n* a republic in central Asia: conquered by Mongols in the 13th century; came under Russian control in the 18th and 19th centuries; was a Soviet republic from 1936 until it gained independence in 1991. It has rich mineral deposits and agriculture is important. Official language: Kazakh. Religion: nonreligious, Muslim, and Christian. Official currency: tenge. Capital: Astana (formerly Akmola, Akmolinsk, or Tselinograd); capital functions moved from Almaty (formerly Alma-Ata) in 1997. Pop: 17 736 896 (2013 est). Area: 2 715 100 sq km (1 048 030 sq miles)

Kazan¹ *n* a city in W Russia, capital of the Tatar Autonomous Republic on the River Volga: capital of an independent khanate in the 15th century; university (1804); a major industrial centre. Pop: 1 108 000 (2005 est)

Kazan² *n* Elia, real name *Elia Kazanjoglous* 1909–2003, US stage and film director and writer, born in Turkey. His films include *Gentleman's Agreement* (1947) and *On the Waterfront* (1954) for both of which he won Oscars, and *East of Eden* (1955)

Kazan Retto *n* transliteration of the Japanese name for the **Volcano Islands**

Kazantzakis *n* Nikos. 1885–1957, Greek novelist, poet, and dramatist, noted esp. for his novels *Zorba the Greek* (1946) and *Christ Recrucified* (1954) and his epic poem *The Odyssey* (1938)

Kazbek *n* Mount Kazbek an extinct volcano in N Georgia in the central Caucasus Mountains. Height: 5047 m (16 558 ft)

Kaz Daği *n* the Turkish name for (Mount) **Ida** (2)

kazoo *n*, *pl* **-zoos** a cigar-shaped metal musical instrument that produces a buzzing sound when the player hums into it [probably imitative]

KBE (in Britain) Knight (Commander of the Order) of the British Empire

kbps *computers* kilobits per second

kbyte *computers* kilobyte

kcal kilocalorie

KCB (in Britain) Knight Commander of the Bath

kea *n* a large brown-green parrot of New Zealand [Māori]

Kéa *n* transliteration of the Modern Greek name for **Keos**

Kean *n* Edmund. ?1789–1833, English actor, noted for his Shakespearean roles

Keating *n* Paul. born 1944, Australian Labor politician; prime minister of Australia (1991–96)

Keaton *n* Buster, real name *Joseph Francis Keaton* 1895–1966, US film comedian who starred in silent films such as *The Navigator* (1924), *The General* (1926), and *Steamboat Bill Junior* (1927)

Keats *n* John. 1795–1821, English poet. His finest poetry is contained in *Lamia and other Poems* (1820), which includes *The Eve of St Agnes*, *Hyperion*, and the odes *On a Grecian Urn*, *To a Nightingale*, *To Autumn*, and *To Psyche*

kebab *n* a dish consisting of small pieces of meat and vegetables, usually threaded onto skewers and grilled [Arabic *kabāb* roast meat]

Kebbi *n* a state of Nigeria, in the NW. Capital: Birnin-Kebbi. Pop: 3 238 628 (2006). Area: 36 800 sq km (14 208 sq miles)

Keble *n* John. 1792–1866, English clergyman. His sermon on national apostasy (1833) is considered to have inspired the Oxford Movement

kecks *or* **keks** *pl n* N English dialect trousers [from dialect *kicks* breeches]

Kecskemét *n* a city in central Hungary: vineyards and fruit farms. Pop: 107 604 (2003 est)

Kedah *n* a state of NW Malaysia: under Thai control until it came under the British in 1909; the chief export are rice, tin, and rubber. Capital: Alor Star. Pop: 1 648 750 (2000). Area: 9426 sq km (3639 sq miles)

kedge *nautical vb* **kedging, kedged 1** to move (a boat) along by hauling in on the cable of a light anchor ▷ *n* **2** a light anchor used for kedging [Middle English *caggen* to fasten]

kedgeree *n chiefly Brit* a dish consisting of rice, fish, and eggs [Hindi *khicarī*]

Kediri *n* a city in Indonesia, in E Java: commercial centr. Pop: 244 519 (2000)

Kedleston Hall *n* a mansion near Derby in Derbyshire, rebuilt (1759–65) for the Curzon family by Matthew Brettingham, James Paine, and Robert Adam

Keegan *n* Kevin. born 1951, English footballer and manager; his clubs included Liverpool, Hamburg, and Newcastle United whom he also managed; played for England (1972–82), scoring 21 goals in 63 games, and managed them (1999–2000); European Footballer of the Year (1978, 1979)

keek *vb*, *n Scot* same as **peep¹** [probably from Middle Dutch *kīken* to look]

keel *n* **1** one of the main lengthways steel or timber pieces along the base of a ship, to which the frames are fastened **2 on an even keel** working or progressing smoothly without any sudden changes [Old Norse *kjǫlr*]

keelhaul *vb* **1** to reprimand (someone) harshly **2** *history* to drag (someone) under the keel of a ship as a punishment

Keeling Islands *pl n* another name for the **Cocos Island**

keel over *vb* **1** (of an object) to turn upside down **2** *informal* (of a person) to collapse suddenly

keelson *or* **kelson** *n* a lengthways beam fastened to the keel of a ship for strength [probably from Low German *kielswin* keel swine]

Keelung *n* another name for **Chilung**

keen¹ *adj* **1** eager or enthusiastic: *a keen gardener* **2** intense or strong: *a keen interest in environmental issues* **3** astute, quick, and perceptive: *a keen sense of humour* **4** (of sight, smell, or hearing) capable of recognizing fine distinctions **5** (of a knife or blade) having a sharp cutting edge **6** very strong and cold: *a keen wind* **7** very competitive: *keen prices* **8 keen on** fond of; devoted to: *he very keen on sport* [Old English *cēne*] ⟩ **keenly** *adv* ⟩ **keenness** *n*

keen² *vb* **1** to lament the dead ▷ *n* **2** a lament for the dead [Irish Gaelic *caoine*]

keep *vb* **keeping, kept 1** to have or retain possession of (something) **2** to have temporary charge of: *he'd kept my broken beads in his pocket for me all evening* **3** to store in a customary place: *I keep it at the back of the drawer with my journal* **4** to remain or cause (someone or something) to remain in a specified state or condition: *keep still* **5** to continue or cause (someone) to continue: *keep going straight on* **6** to stay (in, on, or at a place or position): *keep to the paths* **7** to have as part of normal stock: *they keep a small stock of first-class German wines* **8** to support (someone) financially **9** to detain (someone) **10** to be faithful to (something): *to keep a promise* **11** (of food) to stay in good condition for a certain time: *fish doesn't keep very well* **12** to observe (a religious festival) with rites or ceremonies

3 to maintain by writing regular records in: *he keeps a ature diary in his spare time* **14** to look after or maintain for se, pleasure, or profit: *an old man who kept goats and cows* **5** to associate with: *she has started keeping bad company* **6** how are you keeping? are you well? **17** keep in with to tay friendly with someone as they may be useful to you ▸ *n* **18** the cost of food and other everyday expense: *I have o earn my keep* **19** the main tower within the walls of a nedieval castle or fortress **20** for keeps *informal* ermanently ▸ See also keep at, keep away, etc. [Old nglish *cēpan* to observe]

eep at *vb* **1** to persist in (an activity) **2** to compel (a erson) to continue doing (a task)

eep away *vb* (often foll. by *from*) to prevent (someone) rom going (somewhere)

eep back *vb* to refuse to reveal (something)

eep down *vb* **1** to hold (a group of people) under control to cause (numbers or costs) not to increase **3** to lie low to cause (food) to stay in the stomach; not vomit

eeper *n* **1** a person in charge of animals in a zoo **2** a erson in charge of a museum, collection, or section of a nuseum **3** a person who supervises a person or thing: *he self-appointed keeper of the village conscience* **4** short for amekeeper, goalkeeper, wicketkeeper

eep fit *n* exercises designed to promote physical fitness f performed regularly

eep from *vb* **1** to restrain (oneself or someone else) rom (doing something) **2** to preserve or protect someone) from (something): *this will keep you from falling sleep*

eeping *n* **1** in keeping with suitable or appropriate to or or **2** out of keeping with unsuitable or inappropriate to or for

eep off *vb* **1** to stay or cause (someone) to stay at a listance (from) **2** to avoid or cause to avoid (something): o keep off alcohol; to keep babies off sugar **3** to avoid or cause someone) to avoid (a topic)

eep on *vb* **1** to persist in (doing something): *petrol onsumption keeps on rising* **2** to continue to employ: *a keleton staff of 20 is being kept on* **3** keep on about to persist n talking about **4** keep on at to nag (a person)

eep out *vb* **1** to remain or cause (someone) to remain utside **2** keep out of **a** to cause (someone) to remain nexposed to (an unpleasant situation) **b** to avoid: *to keep out of trouble*

eepsake *n* a gift kept in memory of the giver

eep to *vb* **1** to do exactly what was expected of one: *he ept to his normal schedule* **2** to be confined to: *she kept to her ed until her flu had cleared up* **3** keep oneself to oneself to void the company of others **4** keep to oneself **a** to avoid he company of others **b** to avoid giving away information)

eep up *vb* **1** to maintain at the present level **2** to naintain in good condition **3** keep up with **a** to naintain a pace set by (someone) **b** to remain informed bout: *he liked to think he kept up with current musical trends* **c** to emain in contact with (someone) **4** keep up with the oneses *informal* to compete with one's friends or neighbours in material possessions

eewatin *n* a former administrative district of the Northwest Territories of Canada stretching from the istrict of Mackenzie to Hudson Bay; became part of Nunavut in 1999: mostly tundra

efallonia *n* another name for Cephalonia

eflavík *n* a port in SW Iceland: NATO airbase, fishing. Pop: 7963 (2003 est)

eg *n* a small barrel in which beer is transported and tored [Scandinavian]

eighley *n* a town in N England, in Bradford unitary uthority, West Yorkshire, on the River Aire: textile ndustry. Pop: 49 453 (2001)

eijo *n* transliteration of the Japanese name for Seoul

eitel *n* Wilhelm. 1882–1946, German field marshal; chief f the supreme command of the armed forces (1938–45).

He was convicted at the Nuremberg trials and executed

Kekkonen *n* Urho. (1900–86), Finnish statesman; president (1956–81)

Kekulé von Stradonitz *n* (Friedrich) August. 1829–96, German chemist. His elucidation of the concepts of valence and single, double, and triple bonds enabled him to suggest the structure of many molecules, notably benzene (**Kekulé structure**)

Kelantan *n* a state of NE Malaysia: under Thai control until it came under the British in 1909; produces rice and rubber. Capital: Kota Bharu. Pop: 1 313 014 (2000). Area: 14 920 sq km (5761 sq miles)

Keller *n* **1** Gottfried. 1819–90, Swiss novelist and short-story writer, who wrote in German: noted esp. for the novel *Der Grüne Heinrich* (1855, rewritten 1880) **2** Helen (Adams). 1880–1968, US author and lecturer. Blind and deaf from infancy, she was taught to read, write, and speak and became noted for her work for disabled people

Kells *n* a town in the Republic of Ireland, in Co Meath: *The Book of Kells*, an illuminated manuscript of the Gospels, was produced at the monastery here in the 8th century. Pop: 4421 (2002)

Kelly *n* **1** Gene, full name *Eugene Curran Kelly*. 1912–96, US dancer, choreographer, film actor, and director. His many films include *An American in Paris* (1951) and *Singin' in the Rain* (1952) **2** Grace. 1929–82, US film actress. Her films included *High Noon* (1952) and *High Society* (1956). She married Prince Rainier III of Monaco in 1956 and died following a car crash **3** Ned. 1855–80, Australian horse and cattle thief and bushranger, active in Victoria: captured by the police and hanged

Kelmscott Manor *n* a Tudor house near Lechlade in Oxfordshire: home (1871–96) of William Morris

kelp *n* a large brown seaweed rich in iodine and potash [origin unknown]

kelpie *n* **1** (in Scottish folklore) a water spirit in the form of a horse **2** an Australian sheepdog with a smooth coat and upright ears [origin unknown]

kelson *n* same as **keelson**

kelt *n* a salmon that has recently spawned [origin unknown]

Kelt *n* same as **Celt**

kelvin *n physics* the basic SI unit of thermodynamic temperature [after W. T. *Kelvin*, physicist]

Kelvin *n* William Thomson, 1st Baron Kelvin. 1824–1907, British physicist, noted for his work in thermodynamics, inventing the Kelvin scale, and in electricity, pioneering undersea telegraphy

Kelvin scale *n physics* a thermodynamic temperature scale starting at absolute zero

Kemble *n* **1** Frances Anne, known as *Fanny*. 1809–93, English actress, in the US from 1832 **2** her uncle, John Philip. 1757–1823, English actor and theatrical manager

Kemerovo *n* a city in S Russia: a major coal-mining centre of the Kuznetsk Basin, with important chemical plants. Pop: 479 000 (2005 est). Former name (until 1932): Shcheglovsk

Kempe *n* **1** Margery. ?1373–?1440, English mystic. Her autobiography, *The Book of Margery Kempe*, describes her mystical experiences and pilgrimages in Europe and Palestine **2** Rudolf. 1910–76, German orchestral conductor, noted esp. for his interpretations of Wagner

Kempis *n* Thomas à. ?1380–1471, German Augustinian monk, generally regarded as the author of the devotional work *The Imitation of Christ*

ken *n* **1** beyond one's ken beyond one's range of knowledge ▸ *vb* kenning, kenned or kent **2** *Scot and N English dialect* to know [Old English *cennan*]

Ken. Kentucky

Kendal *n* a town in NW England, in Cumbria: a gateway town to the Lake District, with an ancient woollen industry. Pop: 28 030 (2001)

Kendall *n* Edward Calvin. 1886–1972, US biochemist, who isolated the hormone thyroxine (1916). He shared the

k

Nobel prize for physiology or medicine (1950) with Phillip Hench and Tadeus Reichstein for their work on hormones

kendo *n* the Japanese sport of fencing using wooden staves [Japanese]

Kendrew *n* Sir John Cowdery. 1917–97, British biochemist. Using X-ray diffraction he discovered the structure of myoglobin, for which he shared a Nobel Prize (1962) with Max Perutz

Keneally *n* Thomas (**Michael**). born 1935, Australian writer. His novels include the Booker prizewinner *Schindler's Ark* (1982); other works are *The Playmaker* (1987), *The Great Shame* (1998), and *The Woman and Her Hero* (2007)

Kenilworth *n* a town in central England, in Warwickshire: ruined 12th-century castle, subject of Sir Walter Scott's novel *Kenilworth*. Pop: 22 218 (2001)

Kénitra *n* a port in NW Morocco, on the Sebou River 16 km (10 miles) from the Atlantic. Pop: 598 000 (2003). Also called: **Mina Hassan Tani**. Former name (1932–56): **Port Lyautey**

Kennedy¹ *n* **Cape Kennedy** a former name (1963–73) of (Cape) **Canaveral**

Kennedy² *n* **1** Charles Peter. (1959–2015), British politician, leader of the Liberal Democrats (1999–2006) **2** Edward (**Moore**), known as *Ted*. 1932–2009, US Democrat politician; senator 1962–2009 **3** his brother, John (**Fitzgerald**), known as *JFK*. 1917–63, US Democrat statesman; 35th president of the US (1961–63), the first Roman Catholic and the youngest man ever to be president. He demanded the withdrawal of Soviet missiles from Cuba (1962) and prepared civil rights reforms; assassinated **4** Nigel (**Paul**). born 1956, British violinist, noted for his flamboyant style **5** Robert (**Francis**), known as *Bobby*, brother of John Kennedy. 1925–68, US Democrat statesman; attorney general (1961–64) and senator for New York (1965–68); assassinated

kennel *n* **1** a hutlike shelter for a dog **2** kennels a place where dogs are bred, trained, or boarded ▷ *vb* **-nelling, -nelled** *or US* **-neling, -neled 3** to keep (a dog) in a kennel [Latin *canis* dog]

Kennelly *n* Arthur Edwin. 1861–1939, US electrical engineer: independently of Heaviside, he predicted the existence of an ionized layer in the upper atmosphere, known as the Kennelly-Heaviside layer or E region

Kenneth I *n* surnamed *MacAlpine*. died 858, king of the Scots of Dalriada and of the Picts (?844–858): considered the first Scottish king

Kenny *n* **1** Brett. born 1961, Australian rugby league player; scored 10 tries in 17 games for Australia (1982–87) **2** Yvonne, born 1950, Australian opera singer, noted for her performances in Mozart and Handel operas

Kensington and Chelsea *n* a borough of Greater London, on the River Thames: **Kensington Palace** (17th century) and gardens. Pop: 174 400 (2003 est). Area: 12 sq km (5 sq miles)

Kent¹ *n* a county of SE England, on the English Channel: the first part of Great Britain to be colonized by the Romans; one of the seven kingdoms of Anglo-Saxon England until absorbed by Wessex in the 9th century AD. Apart from the Downs it is mostly low-lying and agricultural, specializing in fruit and hops. The Medway towns of Rochester and Gillingham became an independent unitary authority in 1998. Administrative centre: Maidstone. Pop (excluding Medway): 1 348 800 (2003 est). Area (excluding Medway): 3526 sq km (1361 sq miles)

Kent² *n* William. ?1685–1748, English architect, landscape gardener, and interior designer

Kentuckian *n* **1** a native or inhabitant of Kentucky ▷ *adj* **2** of or relating to Kentucky or its inhabitants

Kentucky *n* **1** a state of the S central US: consists of an undulating plain in the west, the Bluegrass region in the centre, the Tennessee and Ohio River basins in the

southwest, and the Appalachians in the east. Capital: Frankfort. Pop: 4 117 827 (2003 est). Area: 102 693 sq km (39 650 sq miles). Abbreviation: **Ken., Ky.,** (with zip code) **KY 2** a river in central Kentucky, rising in the Cumberland Mountains and flowing northwest to the Ohio River. Length: 417 km (259 miles)

Kenwood House *n* a 17th-century mansion on Hampstead Heath in London: remodelled and decorated by Robert Adam: contains the Iveagh bequest, a noted art collection

Kenya *n* **1** a republic in E Africa, on the Indian Ocean: became a British protectorate in 1895 and a colony in 1920; gained independence in 1963 and is a member of the Commonwealth. Tea and coffee constitute about a third of the total exports. Official languages: Swahili and English. Religions: Christian majority, animist minority. Currency: shilling. Capital: Nairobi. Pop: 44 037 656 (2013 est). Area: 582 647 sq km (224 960 sq miles) **2** Mount Kenya an extinct volcano in central Kenya: the second highest mountain in Africa; girth at 2400 m (8000 ft) is about 150 km (95 miles). The regions above 3200 m (10 500 ft) constitute **Mount Kenya National Park**. Height: 5199 m (17 058 ft). Local name: **Kirinyaga**

Kenyan *adj* **1** of or relating to Kenya or its inhabitants ▷ *n* **2** a native or inhabitant of Kenya

Kenyatta *n* Jomo. ?1891–1978, Kenyan statesman: imprisoned as a suspected leader of the Mau Mau revolt (1953–59); elected president of the Kenya African National Union (1961); prime minister of independent Kenya (1963) and president (1964–78)

Keos *n* an island in the Aegean Sea, in the NW Cyclades. Pop: 2412 (2001). Area: 174 sq km (67 sq miles). Italian name: **Zea**. Modern Greek name: **Kéa**

Kephallinía *n* a transliteration of the Modern Greek name for **Cephalonia**

kepi *n* a French military cap with a flat top and a horizontal peak [French]

Kepler *n* Johannes. 1571–1630, German astronomer. As discoverer of Kepler's laws of planetary motion he is regarded as one of the founders of modern astronomy

kept *vb* **1** the past of **keep 2 kept woman** *or* **man** a person financially supported by someone in return for sexual favours

Kerala *n* a state of SW India, on the Arabian Sea: formed in 1956, it includes the former state of Travancore-Cochin; has the highest population density of any Indian state. Capital: Trivandrum (Thiruvananthapuram). Pop: 31 838 619 (2001). Area: 38 863 sq km (15 005 sq miles)

keratin *n* a fibrous protein found in the hair and nails

kerb *or US and Canad* **curb** *n* a line of stone or concrete forming an edge between a pavement and a roadway [Old French *courbe* bent]

kerb crawling *n* *Brit* the act of driving slowly beside a kerb to pick up a prostitute ❭ **kerb crawler** *n*

Kerbela *n* a variant of Karbala

kerbstone *or US and Canad* **curbstone** *n* one of a series of stones that form a kerb

Kerch *n* a port in S Ukraine on the **Kerch Peninsula** and the **Strait of Kerch** (linking the Black Sea with the Sea of Azov): founded as a Greek colony in the 6th century BC; ceded to Russia in 1774; iron-mining, steel production, and fishing. Pop: 153 000 (2005 est)

kerchief *n* a piece of cloth worn over the head or round the neck [Old French *cuevrechef*]

Kerenski *or* **Kerensky** *n* Aleksandr Fyodorovich. 1881–1970, Russian liberal revolutionary leader; prime minister (July–October 1917): overthrown by the Bolsheviks

kerfuffle *n* *informal* a noisy and disorderly incident [Scot *curfuffle, carfuffle*]

Kerguelen *n* an archipelago in the S Indian Ocean: consists of one large volcanic island (Kerguelen or Desolation Island) and 300 small islands; part of the rench Southern and Antarctic Territories

erkrade *n* a town in the SE Netherlands, in Limburg: ne of the oldest coal-mining centres in Europe. Pop: 0 000 (2003 est)

erkyra *n* transliteration of the Modern Greek name for Corfu

erman *n* a city in SE Iran: carpet-making centre. Pop: 46 000 (2005 est)

ermanshah *n* a city in W Iran, in the valley of the Qareh Su: oil refinery. Pop: 832 000 (2005 est). Former name (1987–1995): **Bakhtaran**

ermes (kur-meez) *n* the dried bodies of female scale nsects, used as a red dyestuff [Arabic *qirmiz*]

ern *n* Jerome (David). 1885–1945, US composer of musical comedies, most notably *Show Boat* (1927)

ernel *n* **1** the edible seed of a nut or fruit within the hell or stone **2** the grain of a cereal, such as wheat, consisting of the seed in a hard husk **3** the central or essential part of something: *there is a kernel of truth in these remarks* [Old English *cyrnel* a little seed]

ernow *n* the Cornish name for **Cornwall**

erosene *n US, Canad, Austral and NZ* same as **paraffin** (1) [Greek *kēros* wax]

erouac *n* Jack, real name *Jean-Louis Lebris de Kérouac*. 922–69, US novelist and poet of the Beat Generation. His works include *On the Road* (1957) and *Big Sur* (1962)

err *n* Sir John Robert. 1914–91, Australian public servant. As governor general of Australia (1974–77), he dismissed the Labor prime minister Gough Whitlam 1975) amid great controversy

erry¹ *n* **1** a county of SW Republic of Ireland, in W Munster province: mostly mountainous (including the highest peaks in Ireland), with a deeply indented coast and many offshore islands. County town: Tralee. Pop: 32 527 (2002). Area: 4701 sq km (1815 sq miles) **2** a small black breed of dairy cattle, originally from Kerry

erry² *n* John Forbes. born 1943, US politician; unsuccessful Democratic Party candidate in the presidential election of 2004; secretary of state from 013

esey *n* Ken. 1935–2001, US novelist, best-known for *One lew Over the Cuckoo's Nest* (1962)

esselring *n* Albert. 1885–1960, German field marshal. He commanded the Luftwaffe attacks on Poland, France, and Britain (1939–40), and was supreme commander in Italy (1943–45) and on the western front 1945)

esteven *n* Parts of Kesteven an area in E England constituting a former administrative division of Lincolnshire

estrel *n* a small falcon that feeds on small animals such as mice [Old French *cresserele*]

eswick *n* a market town in NW England, in Cumbria in the Lake District: tourist centre. Pop: 4984 (2001)

etch *n* a two-masted sailing ship [Middle English *cache*]

etchup *n* a thick cold sauce, usually made of tomatoes [Chinese *kōetsiap* brine of pickled fish]

etone (kee-tone) *n chem* any of a class of compounds with the general formula R´COR, where R and R´ are alkyl or aryl groups [German *Keton*, from *Aketon* acetone]

ettering *n* a town in central England, in Northamptonshire: footwear industry. Pop: 51 063 (2001)

ettle *n* **1** a metal container with a handle and spout, for boiling water **2** any of various metal containers for heating liquid, cooking, etc. **3 a different kettle of fish** a different matter entirely **4 a fine kettle of fish** a difficult or awkward situation ▷ *vb* **-tling, -tled 5** (of police) to force (demonstrators) into an enclosed space [Old Norse *etill*]

ettledrum *n* a large bowl-shaped metal drum that can be tuned to play specific notes

ew *n* part of the Greater London borough of Richmond-upon-Thames, on the River Thames: famous for **Kew Gardens** (the Royal Botanic Gardens), established in 1759 and given to the nation in 1841

key¹ *n* **1** a specially shaped metal instrument for moving the bolt of a lock so as to lock or unlock a door, suitcase, etc. **2** an instrument that is turned to operate a valve, clock winding mechanism, etc. **3** any of a set of levers pressed to operate a typewriter, computer, or musical keyboard instrument **4** a scale of musical notes that starts at one specific note **5** something that is crucial in providing an explanation or interpretation **6** a means of achieving a desired end: *education is the key to success in most walks of life today* **7** a list of explanations of symbols, codes, or abbreviations **8** pitch: *he spoke in a low key* ▷ *adj* **9** of great importance: *key prosecution witnesses have been giving evidence* ▷ *vb* **10** to harmonize with: *training and educational programmes uniquely keyed for local needs* **11** to adjust or fasten (something) with a key or some similar device **12** same as **keyboard**. See also **key in** [Old English *cæg*]

key² *n* same as **cay**

Key *n* John(Phillip). born 1961, New Zealand politician; prime minister from 2008

keyboard *n* **1** a set of keys on a typewriter, computer, or piano **2** a musical instrument played using a keyboard ▷ *vb* **3** to enter (text) in type using a keyboard
> **keyboarder** *n*

keyed up *adj* very excited or nervous

key grip *n* the person in charge of moving and setting up camera tracks and scenery in a film or television studio

keyhole *n* an opening for inserting a key into a lock

keyhole surgery *n* surgery carried out using very small instruments, performed through a narrow hole cut in the body rather than through a major incision

key in *vb* to enter (information or instructions) into a computer by means of a keyboard

key money *n Brit* a sum of money required from a new tenant of a house or flat before he or she moves in

Keynes *n* John Maynard, 1st Baron Keynes. 1883–1946, English economist. In *The General Theory of Employment, Interest and Money* (1936) he argued that unemployment was characteristic of an unregulated market economy and therefore to achieve a high level of employment it was necessary for governments to manipulate the overall level of demand through monetary and fiscal policies (including, when appropriate, deficit financing). He helped to found the International Monetary Fund and the World Bank > **Keynesian** *adj, n*
> **Keynesianism** *n*

keynote *n* **1** a central or dominant idea in a speech or literary work **2** the note on which a scale or key is based ▷ *adj* **3** central or dominating: *his keynote speech to the party conference*

keypad *n* a small panel with a set of buttons for operating a TV remote control, electronic calculator, etc.

keyring *n* a metal ring, often decorative, for keeping keys on

key signature *n music* a group of sharps or flats at the beginning of each stave line to indicate the key

keystone *n* **1** the most important part of a process, organization, etc.: *the keystone of the government's economic policy* **2** the central stone at the top of an arch

keyword *n computers* a word or phrase that a computer will search for in order to locate the information or file that the computer user has requested

key worker *n chiefly Brit* **1** a social worker, mental health worker, or nursery nurse assigned to an individual case, patient, or child **2** (in Britain) a worker in a public sector profession considered by the government to be essential to society

kg kilogram

KG (in Britain) Knight of the Order of the Garter

KGB (formerly) the Soviet secret police [Russian *Komitet Gosudarstvennoi Bezopasnosti* State Security Committee]

Khabarovsk *n* a port in E Russia, on the Amur River: it was the administrative centre of the whole Soviet Far

k

Eastern territory until 1938; a major industrial centre. Pop: 579 000 (2005 est)

Khachaturian n Aram (Ilich). 1903–78, Russian composer. His works, which often incorporate Armenian folk tunes, include a piano concerto and the ballets *Gayaneh* (1942) and *Spartacus* (1954)

Khadijah n 554–619 AD, the first wife of the Prophet Mohammed, regarded as the first convert to Islam

Khafre n Greek name *Chephren*. king of Egypt (*c.* 2550 BC) of the 4th dynasty. He built the second pyramid and is thought to have built the Sphinx at Giza

Khakass Republic n a constituent republic of S central Russia, formerly in Krasnoyarsk Territory: formed in 1930. Capital: Abakan. Pop: 546 100 (2002). Area: 61 900 sq km (23 855 sq miles). Also called: *Russian* **Khakassia**

khaki adj 1 dull yellowish-brown ▷ n 2 a hard-wearing fabric of this colour, used for military uniforms [Urdu, from Persian: dusty]

Khalid ibn Abdul Aziz n 1913–82, king and President of the Council of Ministers of Saudi Arabia (1975–82)

Khalkidíki n a transliteration of the Modern Greek name for **Chalcidice**

Khalkís n a transliteration of the Modern Greek name for **Chalcis**

Khama n Sir Seretse. 1921–80, Botswana statesman; the first president of Botswana (1966–80)

Khamenei n Ayatollah Seyed Ali. born 1940, Iranian political and religious leader: president (1981–89); supreme leader from 1989

khan n a title of respect in Afghanistan and central Asia [Turkish]

Khan n See **Imran Khan**

Khaniá n a transliteration of the Modern Greek name for **Chania**

Khan Tengri n a mountain in central Asia, on the border between Kyrgyzstan and the Xinjiang Uygur Autonomous Region of W China. Height: 6995 m (22 951 ft)

Kharkov n a city in E Ukraine: capital of the Ukrainian Soviet Socialist Republic (1917–34); university (1805). Pop: 1 436 000 (2005 est)

Khartoum or **Khartum** n the capital of Sudan, at the junction of the Blue and the White Nile: with adjoining Khartoum North and Omdurman, the largest conurbation in the country; destroyed by the Mahdists in 1885 when General Gordon was killed; seat of the Anglo-Egyptian government of Sudan until 1954, then capital of the new republic. Pop: 4 495 000 (2005 est)

Khatami n Seyed Mohammad. born 1943, Iranian politician: president of Iran (1997–2005)

Khayyám n See **Omar Khayyám**

Khelat n a variant spelling of **Kalat**

Kherson n a port in S Ukraine on the Dnieper River near the Black Sea: shipyards. Pop: 320 000 (2005 est)

Khingan Mountains pl n a mountain system of NE China, in W Manchuria. Highest peak: 2034 m (6673 ft)

Khíos n a transliteration of the Modern Greek name for **Chios**

Khirbet Qumran n an archaeological site in NW Jordan, near the NW shore of the Dead Sea: includes the caves where the Dead Sea Scrolls were found

Khiva n a former khanate of W Asia, on the Amu Darya River: divided between the former Uzbek and Turkmen Soviet Socialist Republics in 1924

Khmer Republic n the former official name (1970–76) of Cambodia

Khoikhoi n 1 a member of a race of people of Southern Africa, of short stature and a dark yellowish-brown complexion, who formerly occupied the region near the Cape of Good Hope and are now almost extinct 2 any of the languages of this people, belonging to the Khoisan family

Khojent, Khodzhent or **Khujand** n a town in Tajikistan on the Syr Darya River: one of the oldest

towns in central Asia; textile industries. Pop: 146 000 (2005 est). Former name (1936–91): **Leninabad**

Khomeini n Ruholla, known as *Ayatollah Khomeini*. 1900–89, Iranian Shiite Muslim religious and political leader. Following the overthrow of the shah of Iran (1979) he returned from exile and instituted an Islamic republic. His rule saw deteriorating relations with the West and war (1980–88) with Iraq

Khotan n another name for **Hotan**

Khrushchev n Nikita Sergeyevich. 1894–1971, Soviet statesman; premier of the Soviet Union (1958–64). After Stalin's death he became first secretary of the Soviet Communist Party (1953–64) and initiated a policy to remove the influence of Stalin (1956). As premier, he pursued a policy of peaceful coexistence with the West but alienated Communist China

Khujand n a variant spelling of **Khojent**

Khulna n a city in S Bangladesh. Pop: 1 497 000 (2005 est

Khyber Pass n a narrow pass over the Safed Koh Range between Afghanistan and Pakistan, over which came the Persian, Greek, Tatar, Mogul, and Afghan invasion of India; scene of bitter fighting between the British and Afghans (1838–42, 1878–80). Length: about 53 km (33 miles). Highest point: 1072 m (3518 ft)

kHz kilohertz

Kiangsi n a variant transliteration of the Chinese nam for **Jiangxi**

Kiangsu n a variant transliteration of the Chinese nam for **Jiangsu**

Kiaochow n a variant transliteration of the Chinese name for **Jiaozhou**

kia ora interj NZ a Māori greeting [Māori]

kibbutz n, pl **kibbutzim** a farm, factory, or other workplace in Israel, owned and run communally by its members [Modern Hebrew *qibbūs* gathering]

kibosh n put the kibosh on slang to put a stop to [origin unknown]

kick vb 1 to drive, push, or hit with the foot or feet 2 to strike out with the feet, as in swimming 3 to raise a leg high, as in dancing 4 rugby to score (a conversion, drop kick, or penalty) with a kick: *he kicked his third penalty* 5 (o a firearm) to recoil when fired 6 informal to object or resist: *school uniforms give children something to kick against* 7 informal to free oneself of (an addiction): *smokers who want to kick the habit* 8 alive and kicking informal active an in good health 9 kick someone upstairs to promote someone to a higher but effectively powerless position ▷ n 10 a thrust or blow with the foot 11 any of certain rhythmic leg movements used in swimming 12 the recoil of a firearm 13 informal an exciting effect: *we get a kick out of attacking opposing fans and overturning their buses; a few small bets just for kicks* 14 informal the intoxicating effec of an alcoholic drink: *a cocktail with a kick in it* 15 kick in th teeth slang a humiliating rebuff ▶ See also **kick about, kick in,** etc. [Middle English *kiken*]

kick about or **kick around** vb informal 1 to treat (someone) harshly 2 to discuss (ideas) informally 3 to lie neglected or forgotten: *there's a copy of that book kicking about somewhere*

kickback n 1 part of an income paid to a person in retu for an opportunity to make a profit, often by some illegal arrangement 2 a strong reaction

kick in vb to start or become activated

kick off vb 1 to start play in a game of football by kickin the ball from the centre of the field 2 informal to commence (a discussion, event, etc.) ▷ n kick-off 3 a th kick that officially starts a game of football b the time when the first kick is due to take place 4 informal the time when an event is due to begin

kick out vb informal to dismiss (someone) or throw (someone) out forcefully

kickstand n a short metal bar on a motorcycle, which when kicked into a vertical position holds the cycle upright when stationary

ck-start *n* **1** Also: **kick-starter** a pedal on a motorcycle that is kicked downwards to start the engine **2** an action r event that reactivates something ▷ *vb* **3** to start (a notorcycle) with a kick-start **4** to do something bold or rastic in order to begin or improve the performance of omething: *to kick-start the economy*

ck up *vb informal* to cause (trouble)

d¹ *n* **1** *informal* a young person; child **2** a young goat soft smooth leather made from the hide of a kid ▷ *adj* younger: *my kid sister* ▷ *vb* **kidding, kidded** **5** (of a goat) o give birth to (young) [from Old Norse]

d² *vb* **kidding, kidded** *informal* **1** to tease or deceive someone) for fun **2** to fool (oneself) into believing omething: *don't kid yourself that no-one else knows* [probably rom KID¹] **> kidder** *n*

d *n* a variant spelling of (Thomas) **Kyd**

dd *n* William, known as *Captain Kidd.* 1645–1701, Scottish rivateer, pirate, and murderer; hanged

dderminster *n* **1** a town in W central England, in N Worcestershire on the River Stour: carpet industry. Pop: 5 610 (2001) **2** a type of ingrain reversible carpet riginally made at Kidderminster

ddie *n informal* a child

d gloves *pl n* **handle someone with kid gloves** to treat omeone with great tact in order not to upset them

idman *n* Nicole. born 1967, Australian film actress, orn in Hawaii. Her films include *To Die For* (1995), *Eyes Vide Shut* (1999), *The Hours* (2002), *The Golden Compass* 2007), and *The Railway Man* (2014)

dnap *vb* **-napping, -napped** *or US* **-naping, -naped** to apture and hold (a person), usually for ransom [KID¹ - obsolete *nap* to steal] **> kidnapper** *or US* **-naper** *n* • **kidnapping** *or US* **-naping** *n*

dney *n* **1** either of two bean-shaped organs at the back f the abdominal cavity. They filter waste products from he blood, which are excreted as urine **2** the kidneys of ertain animals used as food [origin unknown]

dney bean *n* a reddish-brown kidney-shaped bean, dible when cooked

dney machine *n* a machine carrying out the unctions of damaged human kidneys

dology *n informal* the practice of bluffing or deception n order to gain a psychological advantage over someone

iel *n* a port in N Germany, capital of Schleswig-Holstein tate, on the **Kiel Canal** (connecting the North Sea with he Baltic): joined the Hanseatic League in 1284; became art of Denmark in 1773 and passed to Prussia in 1866; an mportant naval base in World Wars I and II; hipbuilding and engineering industries. Pop: 233 039 2003 est)

ielce *n* an industrial city in S Poland. Pop: 206 796 2007 est)

ierkegaard *n* Søren Aabye. 1813–55, Danish hilosopher and theologian. He rejected organized Christianity and anticipated the existentialists in mphasizing man's moral responsibility and freedom f choice. His works include *Either/Or* (1843), *The Concept of Dread* (1844), and *The Sickness unto Death* (1849) • **Kierkegaardian** *adj, n*

ieślowski *n* Krzysztof. 1941–96, Polish film director, vhose later films were made in France; his work ncludes the television series *Decalogue* (1988–89) and the ilm trilogy *Three Colours* (1993–94)

iev *n* the capital of Ukraine, on the Dnieper River: ormed the first Russian state by the late 9th century; niversity (1834). Pop: 2 623 000 (2005 est)

igali *n* the capital of Rwanda, in the central part. Pop: 82 000 (2005 est)

igoma-Ujiji *n* a city in W Tanzania, on the shore of ake Tanganyika; formed by the merger of the towns of Kigoma and Ujiji in the 1960s

ikládhes *n* a transliteration of the Modern Greek name or **Cyclades**

ilauea *n* a crater on the E side of Mauna Loa volcano, on SE Hawaii island: the world's largest active crater. Height: 1247 m (4090 ft). Width: 3 km (2 miles)

Kildare *n* a county of E Republic of Ireland, in Leinster province: mostly low-lying and fertile. County town: Naas. Pop: 163 944 (2002). Area: 1694 sq km (654 sq miles)

Kilimanjaro *n* a volcanic massif in N Tanzania: the highest peak in Africa; extends from east to west for 80 km (50 miles). Height: 5895 m (19 340 ft)

Kilkenny *n* **1** a county of SE Republic of Ireland, in Leinster province: mostly agricultural. County town: Kilkenny. Pop: 80 339 (2002). Area: 2062 sq km (796 sq miles) **2** a market town in SE Republic of Ireland, county town of Co Kilkenny: capital of the ancient kingdom of Ossory. Pop: 9500 (latest est)

kill *vb* **1** to cause the death of (a person or animal) **2** *informal* to cause (someone) pain or discomfort: *my feet are killing me* **3** to put an end to: *his infidelity had killed his marriage* **4** *informal* to quash or veto: *the main opposition party tried to kill the bill* **5** *informal* to overwhelm (someone) completely with laughter, attraction, or surprise: *her jokes really kill me* **6 kill oneself** *informal* to overexert oneself **7 kill time** to spend time on something unimportant or trivial while waiting for something: *I'm just killing time until I can talk to the other witnesses* **8 kill two birds with one stone** to achieve two results with one action ▷ *n* **9** the act of causing death at the end of a hunt or bullfight **10** the animal or animals killed during a hunt **11 in at the kill** present when something comes to a dramatic end with unpleasant results for someone else [Middle English *cullen*] **> killer** *n*

Killarney *n* a town in SW Republic of Ireland, in Co Kerry: a tourist centre near the **Lakes of Killarney**. Pop: 13 137 (2002)

killer whale *n* a black-and-white toothed whale, most common in cold seas

Killiecrankie *n* a pass in central Scotland, in the Grampians: scene of a battle (1689) in which the Jacobites defeated William III's forces but lost their leader, Viscount Dundee

killing *adj* **1** *informal* very tiring: *a killing pace* **2** *informal* extremely funny **3** causing death; fatal ▷ *n* **4** the act of causing death; slaying **5 make a killing** *informal* to have a sudden financial success

killjoy *n* a person who spoils other people's pleasure

Kilmarnock *n* a town in SW Scotland, the administrative centre of East Ayrshire: associations with Robert Burns; engineering and textile industries; whisky blending. Pop: 43 588 (2001)

kiln *n* a large oven for burning, drying, or processing pottery, bricks, etc. [Latin *culina* kitchen]

kilo *n*, *pl* **kilos** short for **kilogram, kilometre**

kilo- *combining form* **1** denoting one thousand (10^3): *kilometre* **2** (in computers) denoting 2^{10} (1024): *kilobyte*. In computer usage, *kilo-* is restricted to sizes of storage (for example *kilobit*) when it means 1024: in other computer contexts it retains its usual meaning of 1000 [Greek *khilioi* thousand]

kilobit *n computers* 1024 bits

kilobyte *n computers* 1024 bytes

kilocalorie *n* one thousand calories

kilocycle *n* an old word for **kilohertz**

kilogram *or* **kilogramme** *n* **1** one thousand grams **2** the basic SI unit of mass

kilohertz *n*, *pl* **kilohertz** one thousand hertz; one thousand cycles per second

kilojoule *n* one thousand joules

kilolitre *or US* **kiloliter** *n* a measure of volume equivalent to one thousand litres

kilometre *or US* **kilometer** *n* a unit of length equal to one thousand metres

kiloton *n* **1** one thousand tons **2** an explosive power, esp. of a nuclear weapon, equal to the power of 1000 tons of TNT

kilovolt *n* one thousand volts

k

kilowatt *n* one thousand watts

kilowatt-hour *n* a unit of energy equal to the work done by a power of 1000 watts in one hour

kilt *n* **1** a knee-length pleated tartan skirt-like garment, worn by men in Highland dress and by women and girls ▷ *vb* **2** to put pleats in (cloth) [Scandinavian] **› kilted** *adj*

Kilung *n* another name for **Chilung**

Kilvert *n* Francis. 1840–79, British clergyman and diarist. His diary (published 1938–40) gives a vivid account of life in the Welsh Marches in the 1870s

Kimberley *n* **1** a city in central South Africa; the capital of Northern Cape province: besieged (1899–1900) for 126 days during the Boer War; diamond-mining and -marketing centre, with heavy engineering works. Pop: 62 526 (2001) **2** Also called: **the Kimberleys** a plateau region of NW Australia, in N Western Australia: consists of rugged mountains surrounded by grassland. Area: about 360 000 sq km (140 000 sq miles)

Kim Il-sung *n* 1912–94, North Korean statesman and marshal; prime minister (1948–72) and president (1972–94) of North Korea

Kim Jong-il *n* 1942–2011, North Korean politician; supreme leader of North Korea (1994–2011): son of Kim Il-sung

Kim Jong-un *n* born 1984, Korean politician; supreme leader of North Korea from 2011: son of Kim Jong-il

kimono (kim-moan-no) *n, pl* **-nos 1** a loose wide-sleeved Japanese robe, fastened with a sash **2** a European dressing gown resembling this [Japanese: clothing]

kin *n* **1** a person's relatives collectively **2** See next of kin [Old English *cyn*]

Kinabalu *n* a mountain in Malaysia, on N Borneo in central Sabah: the highest peak in Borneo. Height: 4125 m (13 533 ft)

Kincardineshire *n* a former county of E Scotland: became part of Grampian region in 1975 and part of Aberdeenshire in 1996. Also called: **the Mearns**

Kinchinjunga *n* a variant of **Kangchenjunga**

kind¹ *adj* **1** considerate, friendly, and helpful: *a good, kind man; a few kind words* **2** cordial; courteous: *reprinted by kind permission* [Old English *gecynde* natural, native]

kind² *n* **1** a class or group having characteristics in common: *what kind of music do you like?* **2** essential nature or character: *differences of degree rather than of kind* **3** in kind **a** (of payment) in goods or services rather than in money **b** with something of the same sort: *the government threatened to retaliate in kind to any use of nuclear weapons* **4** kind of to a certain extent; loosely: *kind of hard; a kind of socialist* **5** of a kind of a poorer quality or standard than is wanted or expected: *a few farmers wrest subsistence of a kind from the thin topsoil* [Old English *gecynd* nature]

> **USAGE** The mixture of plural and singular constructions, although often used informally with *kind* and *sort*, should be avoided in serious writing: *children enjoy those kinds* (not *those kind*) *of stories; these sorts* (not *these sort*) *of distinctions are becoming blurred.*

kindergarten *n* a class or school for children under six years old [from German, literally: children's garden]

kind-hearted *adj* considerate and sympathetic

kindle *vb* **-dling, -dled 1** to set (a fire) alight or (of a fire) to start to burn **2** to arouse or be aroused: *his passions were kindled as quickly as her own* [Old Norse *kynda*]

kindling *n* material for starting a fire, such as dry wood or straw

kindly *adj* **-lier, -liest 1** having a warm-hearted and caring nature **2** pleasant or agreeable: *a kindly climate* ▷ *adv* **3** in a considerate or humane way **4** please: *will you kindly stop prattling on about it!* **5** not take kindly to to react unfavourably towards **› kindliness** *n*

kindness *n* **1** the quality of being kind **2** a kind or helpful act

kindred *adj* **1** having similar qualities: *cholera, and other kindred diseases* **2** related by blood or marriage **3** kindred spirit a person with whom one has something in common ▷ *n* **4** relationship by blood or marriage **5** similarity in character **6** a person's relatives collectively [Middle English *kinred*]

kindy or **kindie** *n, pl* **-dies** *Austral and NZ informal* a kindergarten

kine *pl n archaic* cows or cattle [Old English *cȳna* of cows]

kinematics (kin-nim-mat-iks) *n physics* the study of the motion of bodies without reference to mass or force [Greek *kinēma* movement] **› kinematic** *adj*

kinetic (kin-net-ik) *adj* relating to or caused by motion [Greek *kinein* to move] **› kinetically** *adv*

kinetic art *n* art, such as sculpture, that moves or has moving parts

kinetic energy *n physics* the energy of motion of a body equal to the work it would do if it were brought to rest

kinetics *n physics* the branch of mechanics concerned with the study of bodies in motion

king *n* **1** a male ruler of a country who has inherited the throne from his parents **2** a ruler or chief: *the king of the fairies* **3** a person, animal, or thing considered as the best or most important of its kind: *the king of rock and roll* **4** a playing card with a picture of a king on it **5** a chessman able to move one square in any direction: the object of the game is to checkmate one's opponent's king **6** *draughts* a piece which has moved entirely across the board and been crowned and which may therefore move backwards as well as forwards [Old English *cyning*] **› kingship** *n*

King *n* **1** B.B., real name *Riley B. King*.1925–2015, US blues singer and guitarist **2** Billie Jean (née *Moffitt*). born 1943, US tennis player: winner of twelve Grand Slam singles titles, including Wimbledon (1966–68, 1972–73, and 1975 and the US Open (1967, 1971–72, and 1974) **3** Martin Luther. 1929–68, US Baptist minister and civil-rights leader. He advocated nonviolence in his campaigns against the segregation of Black people in the South: assassinated: Nobel Peace Prize 1964 **4** Mervyn (Allister) Baron. born 1948, British banker; governor of the Bank of England (2003–13); a cross-bench peer in the House of Lords from 2013 **5** Stephen (Edwin). born 1947, US writer esp of horror novels; his books, many of which have been .filmed, include *Carrie* (1974), *The Shining* (1977), *Mise* (1988), and *Everything's Eventual* (2002) **6** William Lyon Mackenzie. 1874–1950, Canadian Liberal statesman; prime minister (1921–26; 1926–30; 1935–48)

King Country *n* the King Country an area in the centre of North Island, New Zealand: home of the King Movement, a nineteenth-century Māori separatist movement

kingcup *n Brit* a yellow-flowered plant; marsh marigold

kingdom *n* **1** a territory or state ruled by a king or queen **2** any of the three groups into which natural objects may be divided: the animal, plant, and mineral kingdoms **3** a place or area considered to be under the total power and control of a person, organization, or thing: *the kingdom of God*

kingfisher *n* a fish-eating bird with a greenish-blue and orange plumage [originally *king's fisher*]

kingklip *n* an edible eel-like marine fish of S Africa [Afrikaans]

king-of-arms *n, pl* **kings-of-arms** a person holding the highest rank of heraldic office

kingpin *n* **1** the most important person in an organization: *a Mexican narcotics kingpin* **2** a pivot pin that provides a steering joint in a motor vehicle

king post *n building* a vertical post connecting the apex of a triangular roof truss to the tie beam

king prawn *n* a large prawn, fished commercially in Australian waters

Kingsford-Smith *n* Sir Charles (Edward). 1897–1935,

ustralian aviator and pioneer (with Charles Ulm) of
ans-Pacific and trans-Tasman flights

ng-size or **king-sized** adj larger than a standard size

ngsley n **1** Sir Ben. born 1943, British actor. He won an
scar for his performance in the title role of the film
andhi (1982); his later films include Schindler's List (1993)
nd Sexy Beast (2000) **2** Charles. 1819–75, British
lergyman and author. His works include the historical
omances Westward Ho! (1855) and Hereward the Wake (1866)
nd the children's story The Water Babies (1863) **3** his
rother, **Henry**. 1830–76, British novelist, editor, and
ournalist, who spent some time in Australia. His works
nclude Ravenshoe (1861) and the Anglo-Australian novels
he Recollections of Geoffrey Hamlyn (1859) and The Hillyars and
he Burtons (1865)

ng's Lynn n a market town in E England, in Norfolk
n the estuary of the Great Ouse near the Wash: a
eading port in the Middle Ages. Pop: 40 921 (2001). Also
alled: **Lynn, Lynn Regis**

ng-Smith n Ronald Gordon, known as Dick. 1922–2011,
ritish writer for children; his numerous books include
he Sheep Pig (1984) and the Sophie series

ngston n **1** the capital and chief port of Jamaica, on
he SE coast: University of the West Indies. Pop: 574 000
005 est) **2** a port in SE Canada, in SE Ontario: the chief
aval base of Lake Ontario and a large industrial centre;
niversity (1841). Pop: 108 158 (2001) **3** the capital of
lorfolk Island, in the S Pacific Ocean **4** short for
ingston upon Thames

ngston upon Hull n **1** the official name of **Hull** **2** a
nitary authority in NE England, in the East Riding of
orkshire: formerly (1974–96) part of the county of
lumberside. Pop: 247 900 (2003 est). Area: 71 sq km
27 sq miles)

ngston upon Thames n a borough of SW Greater
ondon, on the River Thames: formed in 1965 by the
malgamation of several former boroughs of Surrey;
dministrative centre of Surrey. Pop: 150 400 (2003 est).
rea: 38 sq km (15 sq miles)

ngstown n the capital of St Vincent and the
renadines: a port and resort. p.: 31 000 (2005 est)

nk n **1** a twist or bend in something such as a rope or
air **2** informal a flaw or quirk in someone's personality
vb **3** to form or cause to form a kink [Dutch]

nky adj kinkier, kinkiest **1** slang given to unusual sexual
ractices **2** tightly looped or curled

nnock n Neil (Gordon). Baron. born 1942, British
abour politician, born in Wales; leader of the Labour
arty (1983–92); a European commissioner (1995–2004)
nd vice-president of the European Commission
1999–2004)

nross-shire n a former county of E central Scotland:
ecame part of Tayside region in 1975 and part of Perth
nd Kinross in 1996

nsey n Alfred Charles. 1894–1956, US zoologist, who
irected a survey of human sexual behaviour

nsfolk pl n one's family or relatives

nshasa n the capital of the Democratic Republic of
ongo, on the River Congo opposite Brazzaville: became
apital of the Belgian Congo in 1929 and of Zaïre in 1960;
niversity (1954). Pop: 5 717 000 (2005 est). Former name
until 1966): **Léopoldville**

nship n **1** blood relationship **2** the state of having
ommon characteristics

nsman n, pl -**men** a relation by blood or marriage
kinswoman fem n

osk n **1** a small booth from which cigarettes,
ewspapers, and sweets are sold **2** chiefly Brit a public
elephone box [French kiosque bandstand, from Persian
üshk pavilion]

oto n a variant spelling of **Kyoto**

p Brit slang n **1** sleep: a couple of hours' kip **2** a bed ▷ vb
ipping, kipped 3 to sleep or take a nap **4** kip down to
leep in a makeshift bed [origin unknown]

Kipling n (Joseph) Rudyard. 1865–1936, English poet,
short-story writer, and novelist, born in India. His works
include Barrack-Room Ballads (1892), the two Jungle Books
(1894, 1895), Stalky and Co (1899), Kim (1901), and the Just So
Stories (1902): Nobel prize for literature 1907

kipper n **1** a herring that has been cleaned, salted, and
smoked ▷ vb **2** to cure (a herring) by salting and
smoking it [Old English cypera]

Kirchhoff n Gustav Robert. 1824–87, German physicist.
With Bunsen he developed the method of spectrum
analysis that led to their discovery of caesium (1860) and
rubidium (1861): also worked on electrical networks

Kirchner n Ernst Ludwig. 1880–1938, German
expressionist painter and printmaker; a founder of the
group die Brücke (1905)

Kirghizia or **Kirgizia** n the former Russian name for
Kyrgyzstan

Kirghiz Steppe n a variant spelling of **Kyrgyz Steppe**

Kiribati n an independent republic in the W Pacific:
comprises 33 islands including Banaba (Ocean Island),
the Gilbert and Phoenix Islands, and eight of the Line
Islands; part of the British colony of the Gilbert and
Ellice Islands until 1975; became self-governing in 1977
and gained full independence in 1979 as the Republic of
Kiribati; a member of the Commonwealth. Official
languages: English, I-Kiribati (Gilbertese) is widely
spoken. Religion: Christian majority. Currency:
Australian dollar. Capital: Bairiki islet, in Tarawa atoll.
Pop: 103 248 (2013 est). Area: 684 sq km (264 sq miles)

Kirin n a variant transliteration of the Chinese name for
Jilin

Kirinyaga n the local name of **Mount Kenya**. See
Kenya (2)

Kiritimati n an island in the central Pacific, in Kiribati:
one of the Line Islands; the largest atoll in the world.
Pop: 5115 (2005). Former name: **Christmas Island**

kirk n Scot a church [Old Norse kirkja]

Kirk n Norman. 1923–74, prime minister of New Zealand
(1972–74)

Kirkby[1] n a town in NW England, in Knowsley unitary
authority, Merseyside. Pop: 40 006 (2001)

Kirkby[2] n Dame Emma. born 1949, British soprano,
specializing in performances of early music with period
instruments

Kirkcaldy n a port in E Scotland, in SE Fife on the Firth
of Forth. Pop: 46 912 (2001)

Kirkcudbrightshire n a former county of SW Scotland,
part of Dumfries and Galloway since 1975

Kirklees n a unitary authority in N England, in West
Yorkshire. Pop: 391 400 (2003 est). Area: 410 sq km
(158 sq miles)

Kirkpatrick n Mount Kirkpatrick a mountain in
Antarctica, in S Victoria Land in the Queen Alexandra
Range. Height: 4528 m (14 856 ft)

Kirkuk n a city in NE Iraq: centre of a rich oilfield with
pipelines to the Mediterranean. Pop: 548 000 (2005 est)

Kirkwall n a town on the N coast of Mainland in the
Orkney Islands: administrative centre of the island
authority of Orkney: cathedral built by Norsemen
(begun in 1137). Pop: 6206 (2001)

Kirov[1] n a city in NW Russia, on the Vyatka River: an
early trading centre; engineering industries. Pop:
454 000 (2005 est). Former name (1780–1934): **Vyatka**

Kirov[2] n Sergei Mironovich. 1888–1934, Soviet politician;
one of Stalin's chief aides. His assassination was the
starting point for Stalin's purge of the Communist Party
(1934–38)

Kirovabad n the former name (1936–91) of **Gandzha**

Kirovograd n a city in S central Ukraine on the Ingul
River: manufacturing centre of a rich agricultural area.
Pop: 250 000 (2005 est). Former names: (until 1924)
Yelisavetgrad, (1924–36) **Zinovievsk**

Kirribilli House n the official Sydney residence of the
Australian Prime Minister

k

Kirsch or **Kirschwasser** n a brandy distilled from black cherries [German *Kirschwasser* cherry water]

Kiruna n a town in N Sweden: iron-mining centre. Pop: 23 273 (2004 est)

Kisangani n a city in the N Democratic Republic of Congo, at the head of navigation of the River Congo below Boyoma Falls (Stanley Falls): Université Libre du Congo (1963). Pop: 475 000 (2005 est). Former name (until 1966): **Stanleyville**

Kishinev n the Russian name for **Chişinău**

Kismayu n another name for **Chisimaio**

kismet n fate or destiny [Persian *qismat*]

kiss vb **1** to touch with the lips as an expression of love, greeting, or respect **2** to join lips with another person as an act of love or desire **3** literary to touch lightly: *a long high free kick that kissed the top of the crossbar* ▷ n **4** a caress with the lips **5** a light touch [Old English *cyssan*] ▷ **kissable** adj

kissagram n Brit, Austral and NZ a greetings service in which a person is employed to present greetings by kissing the person celebrating

kiss curl n a circular curl of hair pressed flat against the cheek or forehead

kisser n slang the mouth or face

kissing crust n NZ the soft end of a loaf of bread where two loaves have been separated

Kissinger n Henry (Alfred). born 1923, US academic and diplomat, born in Germany; assistant to President Nixon for national security affairs (1969–75); Secretary of State (1973–77): shared the Nobel peace prize 1973

kiss of life n the kiss of life mouth-to-mouth resuscitation in which a person blows gently into the mouth of an unconscious person

kist n Scot and S African a large wooden chest

Kistna n another name for the (River) **Krishna**

Kisumu n a port in W Kenya, in Nyanza province on the NE shore of Lake Victoria: fishing and trading centre. Pop: 433 000 (2005 est)

kit¹ n **1** a set of tools or supplies for use together or for a purpose: *a first-aid kit* **2** the container for such a set **3** a set of parts sold ready to be assembled: *a model aircraft kit* **4** a large basket **5** clothing and other personal effects, such as those of a soldier: *a complete set of school team kit* ▶ See also **kit out** [Middle Dutch *kitte* tankard]

kit² n NZ a flax basket [Māori *kete*]

Kitaj n R. B. 1932–2007, US painter working in Britain, noted for such large figurative works as *If Not, Not* (1976)

Kitakyushu n a port in Japan, on N Kyushu: formed by the amalgamation of the cities of Wakamatsu, Yawata, Tobata, Kokura, and Moji; one of Japan's largest industrial centres. Pop: 999 806 (2002 est)

kitbag n a canvas or other bag for a serviceman's kit

kitchen n a room equipped for preparing and cooking food [Late Latin *coquina*]

Kitchener¹ n an industrial town in SE Canada, in S Ontario: founded in 1806 as Dutch Sand Hills, it was renamed Berlin in 1830 and Kitchener in 1916. Pop: 190 399 (2001)

Kitchener² n Horatio Herbert, 1st Earl Kitchener of Khartoum. 1850–1916, British field marshal. As head of the Egyptian army (1892–98), he expelled the Mahdi from Sudan (1898), occupying Khartoum; he also commanded British forces (1900–02) in the Boer War and (1902–09) in India. He conducted the mobilization of the British army for World War I as war minister (1914–16); he was drowned on his way to Russia

kitchenette n a small kitchen or part of a room equipped for use as a kitchen

kitchen garden n a garden for growing vegetables, herbs, etc.

kitchen tea n Austral and NZ a party held before a wedding to which guests bring kitchen equipment as presents

kite n **1** a light frame covered with a thin material flown in the wind at the end of a length of string **2** a bird of prey with a long forked tail and large wings **3** a four-sided geometrical shape in which each side is equal in length to one of the sides joining it [Old Engli c̄yta]

Kite mark n Brit the official mark in the form of a kite articles approved by the British Standards Institution

kith n kith and kin old-fashioned one's friends and relatio [Old English *cȳthth*]

Kíthira n a transliteration of the Modern Greek name f Cythera

kit out or **kit up** vb **kitting, kitted** chiefly Brit to provide with clothes or equipment needed for a particular activity

kitsch n tawdry or sentimental art or literature [from German] ▷ **kitschy** adj

kitten n **1** a young cat **2** have kittens informal to react with disapproval or anxiety: *she had kittens when she discovered the price* [Old French *caton*]

kittenish adj lively and flirtatious

kittiwake n a type of seagull with pale grey black-tipp wings and a square-cut tail [imitative]

kitty¹ n, pl **-ties** a diminutive or affectionate name for a kitten, cat

kitty² n, pl **-ties 1** any shared fund of money **2** the pool certain gambling games [probably from KIT¹]

Kitty Hawk n a village in NE North Carolina, near Kill Devil Hill, where the Wright brothers made the world first aeroplane flight (1903)

Kitwe n a city in N Zambia: commercial centre of the Copper Belt. Pop: 545 000 (2005 est)

Kitzbühel n a town in W Austria, in the Tirol: centre fo winter sports. Pop: 8574 (2001)

Kiushu n a variant spelling of **Kyushu**

Kivu n Lake Kivu a lake in central Africa, between the Democratic Republic of Congo and Rwanda at an altitu of 1460 m (4790 ft). Area: 2698 sq km (1042 sq miles). Depth: (maximum) 475 m (1558 ft)

kiwi n, pl **kiwis 1** a flightless bird of New Zealand with a long beak, stout legs, and no tail **2** informal a New Zealander [Māori]

kiwi fruit n an edible fruit with a fuzzy brown skin and green flesh

Kizil Irmak n a river in Turkey, rising in the Kizil Dag and flowing southwest, northwest, and northeast to t Black Sea: the longest river in Asia Minor. Length: abov 1150 km (715 miles). Ancient name: **Halys**

kJ kilojoule(s)

kl kilolitre(s)

Klagenfurt n a city in S Austria, capital of Carinthia province: tourist centre. Pop: 90 141 (2001)

Klaipeda n a port in Lithuania on the Baltic: shipbuilding and fish canning. Pop: 190 000 (2005 est) German name: **Memel**

Klaus n Vaclav. born 1941, Czech politician: prime minister of the Czech Republic (1993–97); president (2003–13)

Klausenburg n the German name for **Cluj**

klaxon n a type of loud horn used on fire engines and ambulances as a warning signal [former trademark]

Kléber n Jean Baptiste. 1753–1800, French general, who succeeded Napoleon as commander in Egypt (1799); assassinated

Klee n Paul. 1879–1940, Swiss painter and etcher. A founder member of *der Blaue Reiter*, he subsequently evolved an intensely personal style of unusual fantasy and wit

Klein n **1** Calvin (Richard). born 1942, US fashion design **2** Melanie. 1882–1960, Austrian psychoanalyst resident in England (from 1926), noted for her work on child behaviour

kleinhuisie (klayn-hay-see) n S African an outside toilet [Afrikaans, literally: little house]

Kleist n (Bernd) Heinrich (Wilhelm) von. 1777–1811, German dramatist, poet, and short-story writer. His plays include *The Broken Pitcher* (1808), *Penthesilea* (1808), and *The Prince of Homburg* (published 1821)

Klemperer *n* Otto. 1885–1973, orchestral conductor, born in Germany. He was best known for his interpretations of Austro-German classics

kleptomania *n psychol* a strong impulse to steal [Greek *kleptein* to steal + *mania* madness] **> kleptomaniac** *n*

Klimt *n* Gustav. 1862–1918, Austrian painter. He founded the Vienna Sezession (1897), a group of painters influenced by Art Nouveau

Kline *n* Franz. 1910–62, US abstract expressionist painter. His works are characterized by heavy black strokes on a white or grey background

Klint *n* Kaara. 1888–1954, Danish furniture designer; founder of the contemporary Scandinavian style

klipspringer *n* a small agile antelope of rocky regions of Africa south of the Sahara [Afrikaans: rock jumper]

Klondike *n* 1 a region of NW Canada, in the Yukon in the basin of the Klondike River: site of rich gold deposits, discovered in 1896 but largely exhausted by 1910. Area: about 2100 sq km (800 sq miles) 2 a river in NW Canada, rising in the Yukon and flowing west to the Yukon River. Length: about 145 km (90 miles) **>** Also spelt: **Klondyke**

kloof *n S African* a mountain pass or gorge [Afrikaans]

Klopstock *n* Friedrich Gottlieb. 1724–1803, German poet, noted for his religious epic *Der Messias* (1748–73) and for his odes

km kilometre(s)

km/h kilometres per hour

knack *n* 1 a skilful way of doing something 2 an ability to do something difficult with apparent ease [probably from Middle English *knak* sharp knock]

knacker *n Brit* a person who buys up old horses for slaughter [origin unknown]

knackered *adj slang* 1 extremely tired: *they'd been marching for three hours and were absolutely knackered* 2 broken or no longer functioning: *a knackered TV set*

knapsack *n* a canvas or leather bag carried strapped on the back or shoulder [Low German *knappen* to eat + *sack* bag]

knapweed *n* a plant with purplish thistle-like flowers [Middle English *knopwed*]

knave *n* 1 *cards* the jack 2 *archaic* a dishonest man [Old English *cnafa*] **> knavish** *adj*

knavery *n*, *pl* **-eries** *old-fashioned* dishonest behaviour

knead *vb* 1 to work and press (a soft substance, such as dough) into a smooth mixture with the hands 2 to squeeze or press with the hands [Old English *cnedan*] **> kneader** *n*

Knebworth House *n* a Tudor mansion in Knebworth in Hertfordshire: home of Sir Edward Bulwer-Lytton; decorated (1843) in the Gothic style

knee *n* 1 the joint of the leg between the thigh and the lower leg 2 the area around this joint 3 the upper surface of a sitting person's thigh: *a little girl being cuddled on her father's knee* 4 the part of a garment that covers the knee 5 **bring someone to his knees** to force someone into submission **>** *vb* **kneeing, kneed** 6 to strike, nudge, or push with the knee [Old English *cnēow*]

kneecap *n* 1 *anatomy* a small flat triangular bone in front of and protecting the knee **>** *vb* **-capping, -capped** 2 (of terrorists) to shoot (a person) in the kneecap

knee-deep *adj* 1 so deep as to reach or cover the knees 2 a sunk to the knees: *knee-deep in mud* b deeply involved: *knee-deep in work*

knee-high *adj* as high as the knee

knee-jerk *n* 1 *physiol* a sudden involuntary kick of the lower leg caused by a sharp tap on the tendon just below the kneecap **>** *adj* **kneejerk** 2 made or occurring as a predictable and automatic response: *a kneejerk reaction*

kneel *vb* **kneeling, knelt** *or* **kneeled** 1 to rest, fall, or support oneself on one's knees **>** *n* 2 the act or position of kneeling [Old English *cnēowlian*]

knees-up *n Brit informal* a party

knell *n* 1 the sound of a bell rung to announce a death or a funeral 2 something that indicates death or destruction **>** *vb* 3 to ring a knell 4 to proclaim by a tolling bell [Old English *cnyll*]

Kneller *n* Sir Godfrey. ?1646–1723, portrait painter at the English court, born in Germany

knelt *vb* the past of **kneel**

knew *vb* the past tense of **know**

knickerbockers *pl n* loose-fitting short trousers gathered at the knee or calf [after Diedrich *Knickerbocker*, fictitious author of Washington Irving's *History of New York*]

knickers *pl n* a woman's or girl's undergarment covering the lower trunk and having separate legs or leg-holes [contraction of *knickerbockers*]

knick-knack *n* a small ornament or trinket [reduplication of obsolete *knack* a toy]

knife *n*, *pl* **knives** 1 a cutting instrument or weapon consisting of a sharp-edged blade of metal fitted into a handle **>** *vb* **knifing, knifed** 2 to stab or kill with a knife [Old English *cnīf*] **> knifelike** *adj*

knife edge *n* 1 the sharp cutting edge of a knife 2 a critical point in the development of a situation: *and at this point the election result is still poised on a knife edge*

knight *n* 1 a man who has been given a knighthood in recognition of his achievements 2 a (in medieval Europe) a person who served his lord as a mounted and heavily armed soldier b (in medieval Europe) a devoted male admirer of a noblewoman, esp. her champion in a jousting tournament 3 a chessman shaped like a horse's head, able to move either two squares horizontally and one square vertically or two squares vertically and one square horizontally **>** *vb* 4 to make (a man) a knight [Old English *cniht* servant]

Knight *n* Dame Laura. 1887–1970, British painter, noted for her paintings of Gypsies, the ballet, and the circus

knight errant *n*, *pl* **knights errant** (esp. in medieval romance) a knight who wanders in search of deeds of courage, chivalry, etc. **> knight errantry** *n*

knighthood *n* an honorary title given to a man by the British sovereign in recognition of his achievements

knightly *adj* of, resembling, or appropriate for a knight **> knightliness** *n*

knit *vb* **knitting, knitted** *or* **knit** 1 to make (a garment) by looping (wool) using long eyeless needles or a knitting machine 2 to join together closely 3 to draw (one's eyebrows) together **>** *n* 4 a fabric made by knitting [Old English *cnyttan* to tie in] **> knitter** *n*

knitting *n* knitted work or the process of producing it

knitwear *n* knitted clothes, such as sweaters

knives *n* the plural of **knife**

knob *n* 1 a rounded projection from a surface, such as a rotating switch on a radio 2 a rounded handle of a door or drawer 3 a small amount of butter or margarine [Middle Low German *knobbe* knot in wood] **> knoblike** *adj*

knobbly *adj* having or covered with small bumps: *a curious knobbly root vegetable*

knobkerrie *n S African* a club or a stick with a rounded end [Khoi (language of southern Africa) *kirri* stick]

knock *vb* 1 to give a blow or push to 2 to rap sharply with the knuckles: *he knocked on the door of the guest room* 3 to make by striking: *he knocked a hole in the wall* 4 to collide (with) 5 to bring into a certain condition by hitting: *he was knocked unconscious in a collision* 6 *informal* to criticize adversely 7 to emit a regular banging sound as a result of a fault: *the engine was knocking badly* 8 **knock on the head** to prevent the further development of (a plan) **>** *n* 9 a a blow, push, or rap: *he gave the table a knock* b the sound so caused 10 the sound of knocking in an engine or bearing 11 *informal* a misfortune, rejection, or setback 12 *informal* criticism **>** See also **knock about, knock back,** etc. [Old English *cnocian*]

knock about *or* **knock around** *vb* 1 to wander or travel about: *I have knocked about the world through three continents*

2 (foll. by *with*) to associate **3** to treat brutally: *she looked knocked about, with bruises and cuts to her head* **4** to consider or discuss informally ▷ *adj* **knockabout 5** (of comedy) lively, boisterous, and physical

knock back *vb informal* **1** to drink quickly: *he fell over after knocking back eight pints of lager* **2** to cost: *lunch for two here will knock you back £50* **3** to reject or refuse: *I don't know any man who'd knock back an offer like that* ▷ *n* **knockback 4** *slang* a refusal or rejection

knock down *vb* **1** to strike to the ground with a blow, such as in boxing **2** (in auctions) to declare an article sold **3** to demolish **4** *informal* to reduce (a price) ▷ *adj* **knockdown 5** powerful: *a knockdown argument* **6** *chiefly Brit* (of a price) very cheap **7** easily dismantled: *knockdown furniture*

knocker *n* **1** a metal object attached to a door by a hinge and used for knocking **2 knockers** *slang* a woman's breasts

knock-knees *pl n* legs that are bent inwards at the knees ❯ **knock-kneed** *adj*

knock off *vb* **1** *informal* to finish work: *around ten, the day shift knocked off* **2** *informal* to make or do hastily or easily: *she knocked off 600 books in all during her long life* **3** *informal* to take (an amount) off the price of (an article): *I'll knock off 10% if you pay cash* **4** *Brit, Austral and NZ informal* to steal **5** *slang* to kill **6** *slang* to stop doing something; used as a command: *knock it off!*

knock-on *rugby n* **1** the foul of playing the ball forward with the hand or arm ▷ *vb* **knock on 2** to play (the ball) forward with the hand or arm

knock-on effect *n* the indirect result of an action or decision

knockout *n* **1** the act of rendering someone unconscious **2** *boxing* a blow that renders an opponent unable to continue after the referee has counted to ten **3** a competition in which competitors are eliminated progressively **4** *informal* a person or thing that is very impressive or attractive: *at my youngest sister's wedding she was a knockout in navy and scarlet* ▷ *vb* **knock out 5** to render (someone) unconscious **6** *boxing* to defeat (an opponent) by a knockout **7** to destroy: *communications in many areas were knocked out by the earthquake* **8** to eliminate from a knockout competition **9** *informal* to amaze: *the fantastic audience reaction knocked me out*

knock up *vb* **1** Also: **knock together** *informal* to make or assemble quickly: *my boyfriend can knock up a wonderful lasagne* **2** *Brit informal* to waken: *to knock someone up early* **3** *slang* to make pregnant **4** to practise before a game of tennis, squash, or badminton ▷ *n* **knock-up 5** a practice session at tennis, squash, or badminton

Knole *n* a mansion in Sevenoaks in Kent: built (1454) for Thomas Bourchier, Archbishop of Canterbury; later granted to the Sackville family, who made major alterations (1603–08)

knoll *n* a small rounded hill [Old English *cnoll*]

Knossos or **Cnossus** *n* a ruined city in N central Crete: remains of the Minoan Bronze Age civilization

knot *n* **1** a fastening formed by looping and tying pieces of rope, cord, or string **2** a tangle, such as in hair **3** a decorative bow, such as of ribbon **4** a small cluster or huddled group: *a knot of passengers gathered on the platform* **5** a bond: *to tie the knot of friendship* **6 a** a hard mass of wood where a branch joins the trunk of a tree **b** a cross section of this, visible in timber **7** a feeling of tightness, caused by tension or nervousness: *a dull knot of anxiety that sat in the pit of her stomach* **8** a unit of speed used by ships and aircraft, equal to one nautical mile per hour **9 at a rate of knots** very fast **10 tie someone in knots** to confuse someone completely ▷ *vb* **knotting, knotted 11** to tie or fasten in a knot **12** to form into a knot **13** to entangle or become entangled [Old English *cnotta*] ❯ **knotless** *adj* ❯ **knotted** *adj*

knothole *n* a hole in a piece of wood where a knot has been

knotty *adj* **-tier, -tiest 1** full of knots **2** extremely difficult or puzzling: *a knotty problem*

know *vb* **knowing, knew, known 1** to be or feel certain of the truth or accuracy of (a fact, answer, or piece of information) **2** to be acquainted with: *I'd known him for many years, since I was seventeen* **3** to have a grasp of or understand (a skill or language) **4** to understand or be aware of (something, or how to do or be something): *she knew how to get on with people* **5** to experience: *you had to have known poverty before you could give money its true value, he claimed* **6** to be intelligent, informed, or sensible enough (to do something): *how did he know to send the letter in the first place?* **7** to be able to distinguish: *I don't know one flower from another* **8** *know what's what* to know how one thing or things in general work **9** *you never know* things are uncertain ▷ *n* **10 in the know** *informal* aware or informed [Old English *gecnāwan*] ❯ **knowable** *adj*

know-all *n informal, disparaging* a person who pretends or appears to know a lot more than other people

know-how *n informal* the ability to do something that is difficult or technical

knowing *adj* **1** suggesting secret knowledge: *Paul saw the knowing look that passed between them* **2** cunning or shrewd **3** deliberate ❯ **knowingly** *adv* ❯ **knowingness** *n*

knowledge *n* **1** the facts or experiences known by a person or group of people **2** the state of knowing **3** specific information about a subject **4 to my knowledge** as I understand it

knowledgeable or **knowledgable** *adj* intelligent or well-informed ❯ **knowledgeably** or **knowledgably** *adv*

Knowles *n* Beyoncé. born 1981, US singer, songwriter, and actress. A member of the girl band Destiny's Child, she later found solo success with the singles "Crazy in Love" (2003) and "Single Ladies (Put a Ring on It)" (2008)

known *vb* **1** the past participle of **know** ▷ *adj* **2** identified *consorting with known criminals*

Knowsley *n* a unitary authority of NW England, in Merseyside. Pop: 150 200 (2003 est). Area: 97 sq km (38 sq miles)

Knox *n* **1** John. ?1514–72, Scottish theologian and historian. After exile in England and on the Continent (1547–59), he returned to Scotland in 1559 and established the Presbyterian Church of Scotland (1560). His chief historical work was the *History of the Reformation in Scotland* (1586) **2 Ronald (Arbuthnott).** 1888–1957, British priest and author. A convert to Roman Catholicism, he is noted for his translation of the Vulgate (1945–49)

Knox-Johnston *n* Sir Robin (William Robert Patrick). born 1939, British yachtsman. He was the first to sail round the world alone nonstop (1968–69)

Knoxville *n* an industrial city in E Tennessee, on the Tennessee River: state capital (1796–1812; 1817–19). Pop: 173 278 (2003 est)

knuckle *n* **1** a joint of a finger **2** the knee joint of a calf or pig **3 near the knuckle** *informal* likely to offend people because of frankness or rudeness ▶ See also **knuckle down, knuckle under** [Middle English]

knuckle down *vb* **-ling, -led** *informal* to apply oneself conscientiously: *he's never been able to knuckle down and study anything for long*

knuckle-duster *n* a metal appliance worn over the knuckles to add force to a blow

knuckle under *vb* **-ling, -led** to give way under pressure or authority

knurl *n* a small ridge, often one of a series [probably from *knur* a knot in wood]

Knussen *n* (Stuart) Oliver. born 1952, British composer and conductor. His works include the opera *Where the Wild Things Are* (1981) and three symphonies

KO or **k.o.** *vb* **KO'ing, KO'd** or **k.o.'ing, k.o.'d 1** to knock out ▷ *n, pl* **KO's** or **k.o.'s 2** a knockout

koala or **koala bear** *n* a tree-dwelling Australian marsupial with dense grey fur [Aboriginal]

Kobarid *n* a village in Slovenia on the Isonzo River: part of Italy until 1947; scene of the defeat of the Italians by Austro-German forces (1917). Italian name: **Caporetto**

Kobe *n* a port in S Japan, on S Honshu on Osaka Bay: formed in 1889 by the amalgamation of Hyogo and Kobe; a major industrial complex, producing ships, steel, and rubber goods. Pop: 1 478 380 (2002 est)

Kobe beef (koh-bi) *n* a grade of beef from cattle raised in Kobe, Japan, which is extremely tender and full-flavoured

København *n* the Danish name for **Copenhagen**

Koblenz *or* **Coblenz** *n* a city in W central Germany, in the Rhineland-Palatinate at the confluence of the Rivers Moselle and Rhine: ruled by the archbishop-electors of Trier from 1018 until occupied by the French in 1794; passed to Prussia in 1815, becoming capital of the Rhine Province (1824–1945) and of the Rhineland-Palatinate (1946–50); wine trade centre. Pop: 107 608 (2003 est). Latin name: **Confluentes**

Koch *n* Robert. 1843–1910, German bacteriologist, who isolated the anthrax bacillus (1876), the tubercle bacillus (1882), and the cholera bacillus (1883): Nobel prize for physiology or medicine 1905

Kochi *n* **1** a port in SW Japan, on central Shikoku on Urado Bay. Pop: 326 490 (2002 est) **2** another name for **Cochin** (2)

Kodály *n* Zoltán. 1882–1967, Hungarian composer. His works were often inspired by native folk songs and include the comic opera *Háry János* (1926) and *Psalmus Hungaricus* (1923) for chorus and orchestra

Kodiak *n* an island in S Alaska, in the Gulf of Alaska: site of the first European settlement in Alaska, made by Russians in 1784. Pop: 13 466 (2004 est). Area: 8974 sq km (3465 sq miles)

Kodok *n* the modern name for **Fashoda**

koeksister (kook-sist-er) *n S African* a plaited doughnut deep-fried and soaked in syrup [Afrikaans]

Koestler *n* Arthur. 1905–83, British writer, born in Hungary. Of his early antitotalitarian novels *Darkness at Noon* (1940) is outstanding. His later works, *The Sleepwalkers* (1959), *The Act of Creation* (1964), and *The Ghost in the Machine* (1967) reflect his interest in science, philosophy, and psychology. He committed suicide

Kofu *n* a city in central Japan, on S Honshu: textiles. Pop: 190 098 (2002 est)

Kogi *n* a state of W Nigeria. Capital: Lokoja. Pop: 3 278 487 (2006). Area: 29 833 sq km (11 519 sq miles)

kohanga reo *or* **kohanga** *n NZ* an infant class where children are taught in Māori [Māori: language nest]

Kohima *n* a city in NE India, capital of Nagaland, near the Burmese border: centre of fierce fighting in World War II, when it was surrounded by the Japanese but not captured (1944). Pop: 78 584 (2001)

kohl *n* a cosmetic powder used to darken the area around the eyes [Arabic]

Kohl *n* Helmut. born 1930, German statesman: chancellor of West Germany (1982–90) and of Germany (1990–98)

Köhler *n* Wolfgang. 1887–1967, German psychologist, a leading exponent of Gestalt psychology

kohlrabi (kole-rah-bee) *n, pl* **-bies** a type of cabbage with an edible stem [Italian *cavolo* cabbage + *rapa* turnip]

Koizumi *n* Junichiro. born 1941, Japanese politician; prime minister (2001–06)

Kokand *n* a city in NE Uzbekistan, in the Fergana valley. Pop: 211 000 (2005 est)

kokanee (coke-can-ee) *n* a freshwater salmon of lakes and rivers in W North America [after *Kokanee* Creek, in British Columbia]

Koko Nor *or* **Kuku Nor** *n* a lake in W China, in Qinghai province in the NE Tibetan Highlands at an altitude of about 3000 m (10 000 ft): the largest lake in China. Area: about 4100 sq km (1600 sq miles). Chinese name: **Qinghai**

Kokoschka *n* Oskar. 1886–1980, Austrian expressionist painter and dramatist, noted for his landscapes and portraits

kola *n* same as **cola**

Kola Peninsula *n* a peninsula in NW Russia, between the Barents and White Seas: forms most of the Murmansk region. Area: about 130 000 sq km (50 000 sq miles)

Kolar Gold Fields *n* a city in S India, in SE Karnataka: a major gold-mining centre since 1881. Pop: 176 000 (2005 est)

Kolding *n* a port in Denmark, in E Jutland at the head of Kolding Fjord (an inlet of the Little Belt). Pop: 54 941 (2004 est)

Kolhapur *n* a city in W India, in S Maharashtra: university (1963). Pop: 485 183 (2001)

Kolkata *n* a port in E India, capital of West Bengal state, on the Hooghly River: former capital of the country (1833–1912); major commercial and industrial centre; many universities. Pop: 4 580 544 (2001). Former official name: **Calcutta**

kolkhoz (kol-hawz) *n* (formerly) a collective farm in the Soviet Union [Russian]

Kollwitz *n* Käthe. 1867–1945, German lithographer and sculptress

Kolmar *n* the German name for **Colmar**

Kolmogorov *n* Andrei Nikolaevich. (1903–87), Soviet mathematician, who made important contributions to the theoretical foundations of probability

Köln *n* the German name for **Cologne**

Kolomna *n* a city in the W central Russia, at the confluence of the Moskva and Oka Rivers: railway engineering centre. Pop: 151 500 (1999 est)

Kolozsvár *n* the Hungarian name for **Cluj**

Kolyma *n* a river in NE Russia, rising in the Kolyma Mountains north of the Sea of Okhotsk and flowing generally north to the East Siberian Sea. Length: 2600 km (1615 miles)

Kolyma Range *n* a mountain range in NE Russia, in NE Siberia, extending about 1100 km (700 miles) between the Kolyma River and the Sea of Okhotsk. Highest peak: 1862 m (6109 ft)

Komati *n* a river in southern Africa, rising in E South Africa and flowing east through Swaziland and Mozambique to the Indian Ocean at Delagoa Bay. Length: about 800 km (500 miles)

komatik (koh-ma-tik) *n Canad* a sledge with wooden runners and crossbars bound with animal hides [Inuktitut]

Komi Republic *n* a constituent republic of NW Russia: annexed by the princes of Moscow in the 14th century. Capital: Syktyvkar. Pop: 1 019 000 (2002). Area: 415 900 sq km (160 540 sq miles)

Kommunarsk *n* the former name (until 1992) of **Alchevsk**

Komsomolsk *n* an industrial city in W Russia, on the Amur River: built by members of the Komsomol (Communist youth league) in 1932. Pop: 275 000 (2005 est)

Konakry *or* **Konakri** *n* variant spellings of **Conakry**

Kongur Shan, Kungur *or* **Qungur** *n* a mountain in China, in W Xinjiang: the highest peak in the Pamirs. Height: 7719 m (25 325 ft)

Königgrätz *n* the German name for **Hradec Králové**

Königsberg *n* the former name (until 1946) of **Kaliningrad**

Königshütte *n* the German name for **Chorzów**

Konstanz *n* the German name for **Constance**

Konya *or* **Konia** *n* a city in SW central Turkey: in ancient times a Phrygian city and capital of Lycaonia. Pop: 883 000 (2005 est). Ancient name: **Iconium**

kook *n US and Canad informal* an eccentric or foolish person [probably from *cuckoo*] > **kooky** *or* **kookie** *adj*

kookaburra *n* a large Australian kingfisher with a cackling cry [Aboriginal]

Koolhaas n Rem. born 1944, Dutch architect and theorist, co-founder of the Office for Metropolitan Architecture (1975); buildings include the Grand Palais and associated developments in Lille, France (1989–96); books include S, M, L, XL (1996)

koori n, pl **-ris** an Australian Aborigine

Kootenay or **Kootenai** n a river in W North America, rising in SE British Columbia and flowing south into NW Montana, then north into Idaho before re-entering British Columbia, broadening into **Kootenay Lake**, then flowing to the Columbia River. Length: 655 km (407 miles)

kopeck n a former Russian monetary unit worth one hundredth of a rouble [Russian kopeika]

Kopeisk or **Kopeysk** n a city in SW central Russia, in Chelyabinsk province: lignite mining. Pop: 24 000 (2005 est). Former name: **Kopi**

kopje or **koppie** (kop-ee) n S African a small isolated hill [Afrikaans]

Koran n the sacred book of Islam, believed by Muslims to be the infallible word of God dictated to Mohammed [Arabic qur'ān reading, book] ⟩ **Koranic** adj

Korbut n Olga. born 1955, Soviet gymnast: noted for her highly individualistic style, which greatly increased the popularity of the sport, esp. following her performance in the 1972 Olympic Games

Korçë n a market town in SE Albania. Pop: 60 000 (2003 est)

Korchnoi n Victor. born 1931, Soviet-born chess player: Soviet champion 1960, 1962, and 1964: defected to the West in 1976

Korda n Sir Alexander, real name Sandor Kellner. 1893–1956, British film producer and director, born in Hungary: his films include The Scarlet Pimpernel (1934), Anna Karenina (1948), and The Third Man (1949)

Kordofan n a region of the central and S Sudan: consists of a plateau with rugged uplands (the Nuba Hills). Area: 380 548 sq km (146 930 sq miles)

Kordofanian n **1** a group of languages spoken in the Kordofan and Nuba Hills of the S Sudan: classed as an independent family, probably distantly related to Niger-Congo ⟩ adj **2** denoting, relating to, or belonging to this group of languages **3** of or relating to Kordofan

Korea n a former country in E Asia, now divided into two separate countries, North Korea and South Korea. Korea occupied the peninsula between the Sea of Japan (East Sea) and the Yellow Sea: an isolated vassal of Manchu China for three centuries until the opening of ports to Japanese trade in 1876; gained independence in 1895; annexed to Japan in 1910 and divided in 1945 into two occupation zones (Russian in the north, American in the south), which became North Korea and South Korea in 1948. Japanese name (1910–45): **Chosen**. See **North Korea, South Korea**

Korean adj **1** of or relating to Korea or its inhabitants ⟩ n **2** a native or inhabitant of Korea **3** the official language of North and South Korea

Korea Strait n a strait between South Korea and SW Japan, linking the Sea of Japan (East Sea) with the East China Sea

Kórinthos n transliteration of the Modern Greek name for Corinth

korma n a type of mild Indian dish consisting of meat or vegetables cooked in water, yoghurt, or cream [from Urdu]

Kortrijk n the Flemish name for Courtrai

Korzybski n Alfred (Habdank Skarbek). 1879–1950, US originator of the theory and study of general semantics, born in Poland

Kos or **Cos** n an island in the SE Aegean Sea, in the Greek Dodecanese Islands: separated from SW Turkey by the **Kos Channel**; settled in ancient times by Dorians and became famous for literature and medicine. Pop: 30 947 (2001). Area: 282 sq km (109 sq miles)

Kosciusko n Thaddeus, Polish name Tadeusz Kościuszko. 1746–1817, Polish general: fought for the colonists in the American War of Independence and led an unsuccessful revolt against the partitioning of Poland (1794)

Kosciuszko n Mount Kosciuszko a mountain in Australia, in SE New South Wales in the Australian Alps the highest peak in Australia. Height: 2230 m (7316 ft)

kosher (koh-sher) adj **1** Judaism **a** conforming to religious law **b** (of food) prepared in accordance with the dietary laws **2** informal legitimate, genuine, or proper ⟩ n **3** kosher food [Yiddish]

Košice n a city in E Slovakia: passed from Hungary to Czechoslovakia in 1920 and to Slovakia in 1993. Pop: 236 093 (2001). Hungarian name: **Kassa**

Kosovar or **Kosovan** adj **1** of or relating to Kosovo or its inhabitants ⟩ n **2** a native or inhabitant of Kosovo

Kosovo or **Kosova** n an autonomous province of Serbia, in the SW: chiefly Albanian in population since the 13th century; Serb suppression of separatists escalated to a policy of ethnic cleansing in 1998, provoking NATO airstrikes against Serbia in 1999 and takeover by UN administration; unilaterally declared independence in 2008. Mainly a plateau. Capital: Priština. Pop: 1 847 708 (2013 est). Area: 10 887 sq km (4203 sq miles). Full Serbian name: **Kosovo-Metohija**

Kossoff n Leon. born 1926, British painter, esp. of London scenes

Kossuth n Lajos. 1802–94, Hungarian statesman. He led the revolution against Austria (1848) and was provisional governor (1849), but he fled when the revolt was suppressed (1849)

Kostroma n a city in W central Russia, on the River Volga: fought over bitterly by Novgorod, Tver, and Moscow, until annexed by Moscow in 1329; textile centre. Pop: 280 000 (2005 est)

Kostunica n Vojislav. born 1944, Serbian politician; president of the Federal Republic of Yugoslavia (2000–03); prime minister of Serbia and Montenegro (2004–06); prime minister of Serbia (2006–08)

Kosygin n Aleksei Nikolayevich. 1904–80, Soviet statesman; premier of the Soviet Union (1964–80)

Kota or **Kotah** n a city in NW India, in Rajasthan on the Chambal River: textile industry. Pop: 695 899 (2001)

Kotabaru n a former name of Jayapura

Kota Bharu or **Bahru** n a port in NE Peninsular Malaysia: capital of Kelantan state on the delta of the Kelantan River. Pop: 263 000 (2005 est)

Kota Kinabalu n a port in Malaysia, capital of Sabah state on the South China Sea: exports timber and rubber. Pop: 439 000 (2005 est). Former name: **Jesselton**

Kourou n a town in N central French Guiana; site of the European Space Agency's launch and research base. Pop: 19 107 (1999)

Kovno n transliteration of the Russian name for Kaunas

Kovrov n a city in W central Russia, on the Klyazma River: textiles and heavy engineering. Pop: 155 000 (2005 est)

Kowait n a variant of Kuwait

Kowaiti adj, n a variant of Kuwaiti

kowhai (koh-wye, koh-fye) n a small tree of New Zealand and Chile with clusters of yellow flowers [Māori]

Kowloon n **1** a peninsula of SE China, opposite Hong Kong Island: part of the former British colony of Hong Kong. Area: 10 sq km (3.75 sq miles) **2** a port in Hong Kong, on Kowloon Peninsula. Pop: 2 019 533 (2006 est)

kowtow vb **1** to be humble and very respectful (towards) the senior editors accused each other of kowtowing to his demands **2** to touch the forehead to the ground in deference ⟩ n **3** the act of kowtowing [Chinese k'o to strike, knock + t'ou head]

Kozhikode n a port in SW India, in W Kerala on the Malabar coast: important European trading post (1511–1765): formerly calico-manufacturing. Pop: 436 527 (2001). Also called: **Calicut**

kph kilometres per hour

Kr *chem* krypton

Kra *n* **Isthmus of Kra** an isthmus of SW Thailand, between the Bay of Bengal and the Gulf of Thailand: the narrowest part of the Malay Peninsula. Width: about 56 km (35 miles)

kraal *n* **1** a Southern African hut village surrounded by a strong fence **2** *S African* an enclosure for livestock [Afrikaans, from Portuguese *curral* enclosure]

Krafft-Ebing *n* Richard, Baron von Krafft-Ebing. 1840–1902, German neurologist and psychiatrist who pioneered the systematic study of sexual behaviour in *Psychopathia Sexualis* (1886)

Kragujevac *n* a town in E central Serbia; capital of Serbia (1818–39); automobile industry. Pop: 145 890 (2002)

Krakatoa *or* **Krakatau** *n* a volcanic island in Indonesia, in the Sunda Strait between Java and Sumatra: partially destroyed by its eruption in 1883, the greatest in recorded history. Further eruptions 44 years later formed a new island, **Anak Krakatau** ("Child of Krakatau"). Also called: **Rakata**

Krakau *n* the German name for **Cracow**

kraken *n* a legendary sea monster [Norwegian]

Kraków *n* the Polish name for **Cracow**

Kramatorsk *n* a city in Ukraine: a major industrial centre of the Donets Basin. Pop: 177 000 (2005 est)

Kranj *n* the Slovene name for **Carniola**

krans (krahnss) *n S African* a sheer rock face [Afrikaans]

Krasnodar *n* an industrial city in SW Russia, on the Kuban River. Pop: 650 000 (2005 est). Former names (until 1920): **Yekaterinodar, Ekaterinodar**

Krasnoyarsk *n* a city in E central Russia, on the Yenisei River: the country's largest hydroelectric power station is nearby. Pop: 912 000 (2005 est)

Krebs *n* Sir Hans Adolf. 1900–81, British biochemist, born in Germany, who shared a Nobel prize for physiology or medicine (1953) for the discovery of the Krebs cycle, a series of biochemical reactions occurring during respiration in animal and plant cells

Krefeld *n* a city in Germany, in W North Rhine-Westphalia: textile industries. Pop: 238 565 (2003 est)

Kreisler *n* Fritz. 1875–1962, US violinist, born in Austria

Kremenchug *n* an industrial city in E central Ukraine on the Dnieper River. Pop: 234 000 (2005 est)

Kremer *n* Gidon. born 1947, Latvian violinist, now based in the US

kremlin *n* the citadel of any Russian city [Russian *kreml*]

Kremlin *n* **1** the 12th-century citadel in Moscow, containing the former Imperial Palace, three Cathedrals, and the offices of the Russian government **2** (formerly) the central government of the Soviet Union

Krems *n* a town in NE Austria, in Lower Austria on the River Danube. Pop: 23 713 (2001)

krill *n, pl* **krill** a small shrimplike crustacean [Norwegian *kril* young fish]

Krishna[1] *n* a Hindu god, the incarnation of Vishnu

Krishna[2] *n* a river in S India, rising in the Western Ghats and flowing generally southeast to the Bay of Bengal. Length: 1300 km (800 miles). Also called: **Kistna**

Krishna Menon *n* See Menon

Kristeva *n* Julia. born 1941, French semiotician, born in Bulgaria. Her works include *La Révolution du langage poétique* (1974), *Histoires d'amour* (1983), and the autobiographical novel *Les Samouraïs* (1990)

Kristiania *n* a former name (1877–1924) of **Oslo**

Kristiansand *or* **Christiansand** *n* a port in S Norway, on the Skagerrak: shipbuilding. Pop: 75 280 (2004 est)

Kristiansen *n* Ingrid. born 1956, Norwegian long-distance runner: world 10 000 metres record holder (1986–93)

Kristianstad *n* a town in S Sweden: founded in 1614 as a Danish fortress, it was finally acquired by Sweden in 1678. Pop: 75 590 (2004 est)

Kríti *n* transliteration of the Modern Greek name for **Crete**

Krivoy Rog *n* a city in SE Ukraine: founded in the 17th century by Cossacks; iron-mining centre; iron- and steelworks. Pop: 658 000 (2005 est)

krona *n, pl* **-nor** the standard monetary unit of Sweden [Swedish, from Latin *corona* crown]

krone (kroh-na) *n, pl* **-ner** (-ner) the standard monetary unit of Norway and Denmark [Danish or Norwegian, from Latin *corona* crown]

Kronstadt *n* **1** a port in NW Russia, on Kotlin island in the Gulf of Finland: naval base. Pop: 42 800 (2006 est) **2** the German name for **Braşov**

Kropotkin *n* Prince Peter, Russian name *Pyotr Alexeyevich*. 1842–1921, Russian anarchist: his books include *Mutual Aid* (1902) and *Modern Science and Anarchism* (1903)

Kruger *n* Paul, full name *Stephanus Johannes Paulus*. 1825–1904, Boer statesman; president of the Transvaal (1883–1900). His opposition to Cecil Rhodes and his denial of civil rights to the Uitlanders led to the Boer War (1899–1902)

Kruger National Park *n* a wildlife sanctuary in NE South Africa, the world's largest game reserve. Area: over 21 700 sq km (8400 sq miles)

krugerrand *n* a one-ounce gold coin minted in South Africa [Paul Kruger + *rand*]

Krugersdorp *n* a city in NE South Africa, in the Witwatersrand, at an altitude of 1720 m (5650 ft): a gold-, manganese-, and uranium-mining centre. Pop: 86 618 (2001)

Krupp *n* a German family of steel and armaments manufacturers, including **Alfred**, 1812–87, his son **Friedrich Alfred**, 1854–1902, and the latter's son-in-law, **Gustav Krupp von Bohlen und Halbach**, 1870–1950

Krušné Hory *n* the Czech name for the **Erzgebirge**

Krym *or* **Krim** *n* transliteration of the Russian name for **Crimea**

krypton *n chem* an inert gaseous element occurring in trace amounts in air and used in fluorescent lights and lasers. Symbol: **Kr** [Greek *kruptos* hidden]

KS Kansas

Kt Knight

KT (in Britain) Knight of the Order of the Thistle

kt. kiloton

Kuala Lumpur *n* a city in Malaysia, in the SW Malay Peninsula: formerly (until 1999) the capital of Malaysia; became capital of the Federated Malay States in 1895, and of Malaysia in 1963; capital of Selangor state from 1880 to 1973, when it was made a federal territory. Pop: 1 392 000 (2005 est)

Kuban *n* a river in SW Russia, rising in the Caucasus Mountains and flowing north and northwest to the Sea of Azov. Length: 906 km (563 miles)

Kubelik *n* Raphael. 1914–96, Czech conductor and composer

Kublai Khan *n* ?1216–94, Mongol emperor of China: grandson of Genghis Khan. He completed his grandfather's conquest of China by overthrowing the Sung dynasty (1279) and founded the Yuan dynasty (1279–1368)

Kubrick *n* Stanley. 1928–99, US film writer, director, and producer. He directed *Lolita* (1962), *Dr Strangelove* (1963), *2001: A Space Odyssey* (1968), *A Clockwork Orange* (1971), *The Shining* (1980), *Full Metal Jacket* (1987), and *Eyes Wide Shut* (1999)

Kuch Bihar *n* a variant spelling of **Cooch Behar**

Kuching *n* a port in E Malaysia, capital of Sarawak state, on the Sarawak River 24 km (15 miles) from its mouth. Pop: 152 310 (2000)

kudos (kew-doss) *n* personal fame or glory [Greek]

kudu *or* **koodoo** *n* a spiral-horned African antelope [Afrikaans, from Khoi (language of southern Africa)]

Kuenlun *n* a variant spelling of **Kunlun**

kugel (koog-el) *n S African* a rich, fashion-conscious, materialistic young Jewish woman [from Yiddish *kugel*, a type of savoury pudding popular in Jewish cookery]

Kuibyshev or **Kuybyshev** n the former name (until 1991) of **Samara**

Ku Klux Klan n a secret organization of White Protestant Americans who use violence against black and Jewish people [probably based on Greek *kuklos* circle + CLAN] **> Ku Klux Klanner** n

kukri n a heavy, curved knife used by Gurkhas [Hindi]

Kuku Nor n a variant of **Koko Nor**

kulak n (formerly) a property-owning Russian peasant [Russian]

Kulun n the Chinese name for **Ulan Bator**

Kum n a variant spelling of **Qom**

Kumamoto n a city in SW Japan, on W central Kyushu: Kumamoto Medical University (1949). Pop: 653 835 (2002 est)

Kumaratunga n Chandrika Bandaranaike. born 1945, Sri Lankan politician: prime minister (1994); president (1994–2005)

Kumasi n a city in S Ghana: seat of Ashanti kings since 1663; university (1961); market town for a cocoa-producing region. Pop: 862 000 (2005 est)

Kumayri n a city in NW Armenia: textile centre. Pop: 144 000 (2005 est). Former names: (1840–1924) **Aleksandropol**, (1924–91) **Leninakan**

kumera or **kumara** n NZ a tropical root vegetable with yellow flesh [Māori]

kümmel n a German liqueur flavoured with aniseed and cumin [from German]

kumquat (kumm-kwott) n a citrus fruit resembling a tiny orange [Cantonese Chinese *kam kwat* golden orange]

Kun n Béla. 1886–?1937, Hungarian Communist leader, president of the short-lived Communist republic in Hungary (1919). He was forced into exile and died in a Stalinist purge

Kundera n Milan. born 1929, Czech novelist living in France. His novels include *The Book of Laughter and Forgetting* (1979), *The Unbearable Lightness of Being* (1984), and *Ignorance* (2002)

Küng n Hans. born 1928, Swiss Roman Catholic theologian, who questioned the doctrine of infallibility: his licence to teach was withdrawn in 1979. His books include *Global Responsibility* (1991)

kung fu n any of various Chinese systems of martial art, esp. unarmed combat in which punches, chops, and kicks are made with the hands and feet; certain styles involve the use of weapons [Chinese: skill; accomplishment]

Kungur n a variant transliteration of the Chinese name for **Kongur Shan**

Kunlun, Kuenlun or **Kwenlun** n a mountain range in China, between the Tibetan plateau and the Tarim Basin, extending over 1600 km (1000 miles) east from the Pamirs: the largest mountain system of Asia. Highest peak: Ulugh Muztagh, 7723 m (25 338 ft)

Kunming or **K'un-ming** n a city in SW China, capital of Yunnan province, near Lake Tien: important during World War II as a Chinese military centre, American air base, and transport terminus for the Burma Road; Yunnan University (1934). Pop: 1 748 000 (2005 est)

Kuopio n a city in S central Finland. Pop: 88 250 (2003 est)

Kura n a river in W Asia, rising in NE Turkey and flowing across Georgia and Azerbaijan to the Caspian Sea. Length: 1515 km (941 miles)

kura kaupapa Māori n NZ a primary school where the teaching is done in Māori

Kurdistan, Kurdestan or **Kordestan** n a large plateau and mountainous region, between the Caspian Sea and the Black Sea, south of the Caucasus. Area: over 29 000 sq km (74 000 sq miles)

Kure n a port in SW Japan, on SW Honshu: a naval base; shipyards. Pop: 202 628 (2002 est)

Kurgan n a city in W Russia, on the Tobol River: industrial centre for an agricultural region. Pop: 344 000 (2005 est)

Kuril Islands or **Kurile Islands** pl n a chain of 56 volcanic islands off the NE coast of Asia, extending for 1200 km (750 miles) from the S tip of the Kamchatka Peninsula to NE Hokkaido. Area: 14 990 sq km (6020 sq miles). Japanese name: **Chishima**

Kurland n a variant spelling of **Courland**

Kurosawa n Akira. 1910–99, Japanese film director. His works include *Rashomon* (1950), *The Seven Samurai* (1954), *The Throne of Blood* (1957), *Kagemusha* (1980), *Ran* (1985), and *Madadayo* (1993)

Kuroshio n another name for **Japan Current**

kurrajong n an Australian tree or shrub with tough fibrous bark [from a native Australian language]

Kursk n a city in W Russia: industrial centre of an agricultural region: scene of a major Soviet victory (1943). Pop: 410 000 (2005 est)

Kurzeme n the Latvian name for **Courland**

Kuskokwim n a river in SW Alaska, rising in the Alaska Range and flowing generally southwest to **Kuskokwim Bay**, an inlet of the Bering Sea. Length: about 970 km (600 miles)

Kutaisi n an industrial city in W Georgia on the Rioni River: one of the oldest towns of the Caucasus. Pop: 175 000 (2005 est)

Kutch or **Cutch** n **1** a former state of W India, on the **Gulf of Kutch** (an inlet of the Arabian Sea): part of Gujarat state since 1960 **2 Rann of Kutch** an extensive salt waste in W central India, and S Pakistan: consists of the Great Rann in the north and the Little Rann in the southeast; seasonal alternation between marsh and desert; some saltworks. In 1968 an international tribunal awarded about 10 per cent of the border area to Pakistan. Area: 23 000 sq km (9000 sq miles)

Kutuzov n Prince Mikhail Ilarionovich. 1745–1813, Russian field marshal, who harried the French army under Napoleon throughout their retreat from Moscow (1812–13)

Kuwait or **Koweit** n **1** a state on the NW coast of the Persian Gulf: came under British protection in 1899 and gained independence in 1961; invaded by Iraq in 1990; liberated by US-led UN forces 1991 in the Gulf War: mainly desert. The economy is dependent on oil. Official language: Arabic. Official religion: Muslim. Currency: dinar. Capital: Kuwait. Pop: 2 695 316 (2013 est). Area: 24 280 sq km (9375 sq miles) **2** the capital of Kuwait: a port on the Persian Gulf. Pop: 1 225 000 (2005 est)

Kuwaiti or **Koweiti** adj **1** of or relating to Kuwait or its inhabitants ▷ n **2** a native or inhabitant of Kuwait

Kuznets n Simon. 1901–85, US economist born in Russia. His books include *National Income and its Composition (1919–1938)* (1941) and *Economic Growth of Nations* (1971). He was awarded the Nobel Prize for economics in 1971

Kuznetsk Basin or **Kuzbass** n a region of S Russia, in the Kemerovo Region of W Siberia: the richest coalfield in the country, with reserves of iron ore. Chief industrial centre: Novokuznetsk. Area: about 69 900 sq km (27 000 sq miles)

kV kilovolt

Kvaløy n two islands in the Arctic Ocean, off the N coast of Norway: **North Kvaløy**, 329 sq km (127 sq miles), and **South Kvaløy**, 735 sq km (284 sq miles)

kvetch vb slang, chiefly US to complain or grumble [Yiddish]

kW kilowatt

Kwajalein n an atoll in the W Pacific, in the W Marshall Islands, in the central part of the Ralik Chain. Length: about 125 km (78 miles)

Kwangchow n a variant transliteration of the Chinese name for **Canton**

Kwangchowan n a territory of SE China, in SW Kwantung province: leased to France as part of

French Indochina from 1898 to 1945. Area: 842 sq km (325 sq miles)

Kwangju *n* a city in SW South Korea: an important military base during the Korean War; cotton textile industry. Pop: 1 448 000 (2005 est)

Kwangsi-Chuang Autonomous Region *n* another spelling of **Guangxi Zhuang Autonomous Region**

Kwangtung *n* a variant transliteration of the Chinese name for **Guangdong**

Kwantung Leased Territory *n* a strategic territory of NE China, at the S tip of the Liaodong Peninsula of Manchuria: leased forcibly by Russia in 1898; taken over by Japan in 1905; occupied by the Soviet Union in 1945 and subsequently returned to China on the condition of shared administration; made part of Liaoning province by China in 1954. Area: about 3400 sq km (1300 sq miles). Also called: **Kuan-tung**

Kwanzaa *n* an African-American festival held from December 26 until January 1 [from Swahili (*matunda ya*) *kwanza* first (fruits)]

Kwara *n* a state of W Nigeria: mainly wooded savanna. Capital: Ilorin. Pop: 2 371 089 (2006). Area: 36 825 sq km (14 218 sq miles)

kwashiorkor *n* severe malnutrition of young children, caused by not eating enough protein [native word in Ghana]

KwaZulu *n* (formerly) a Bantu homeland in South Africa, in Natal: abolished in 1993 and became part of the new province of KwaZulu-Natal in 1994. Capital: Ulundi

KwaZulu-Natal *n* a province of NE South Africa; replaced the former province of Natal in 1994: service industries. Capital: Pietermaritzburg. Pop: 10 267 300 (2011 est). Area: 92 180 sq km (35 591 sq miles)

Kweichow *or* **Kueichou** *n* a variant transliteration of the Chinese name for **Guizhou**

Kweilin *or* **Kuei-lin** *n* a variant transliteration of the Chinese name for **Guilin**

Kweisui *n* the former name of **Hohhot**

Kweiyang *or* **Kuei-yang** *n* a variant transliteration of the Chinese name for **Guiyang**

kwela (kway-luh) *n* a type of South African popular music performed using simple instruments [Zulu: jump up]

kWh kilowatt-hour

KWIC *computers* keyword in context

KWOC *computers* keyword out of context

Ky *n* Nguyen Kao. 1930–2011, Vietnamese military and political leader; premier of South Vietnam (1965–67); vice president (1967–71)

Ky. *or* **KY** Kentucky

Kyd *or* **Kid** *n* Thomas. 1558–94, English dramatist, noted for his revenge play *The Spanish Tragedy* (1586)

kyle *n Scot* a narrow strait or channel: *Kyle of Lochalsh* [Gaelic *caol* narrow]

Kyongsong *n* another name for **Seoul**

Kyoto *or* **Kioto** *n* a city in central Japan, on S Honshu: the capital of Japan from 794 to 1868; cultural centre, with two universities (1875, 1897). Pop: 1 387 264 (2002 est)

Kyrgyzstan, Kirghizstan *or* **Kirgizstan** *n* a republic in central Asia: came under Russian rule in the 19th century, became a Soviet republic in 1936 and gained independence in 1991; it has deposits of minerals, oil, and gas. Official languages: Kyrgyz and Russian. Religion: nonreligious, Muslim. Currency: som. Capital: Bishkek. Pop: 5 548 042 (2013 est). Area: 198 500 sq km (76 460 sq miles)

Kyrgyz Steppe *n* a vast steppe region in central Kazakhstan. Also called: **the Steppes**

Kythera *n* a variant spelling of **Cythera**

Kyushu *or* **Kiushu** *n* an island of SW Japan: the southernmost of Japan's four main islands, with over 300 surrounding small islands; coalfield and chemical industries. Chief cities: Fukuoka, Kitakyushu, and Nagasaki. Pop: 14 786 000 (2002 est). Area: 35 659 sq km (13 768 sq miles)

Kyzyl Kum *n* a desert in Kazakhstan and Uzbekistan

KZN (in South Africa) KwaZulu-Natal

k

Ll

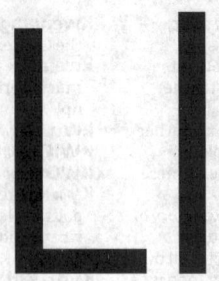

l litre(s)

L 1 large 2 Latin 3 learner driver 4 usually written: £ pound 5 the Roman numeral for 50

L. or **l.** 1 lake 2 left 3 length 4 (pl **LL** or **ll**) line

la n music same as **lah**

La chem lanthanum

LA 1 Los Angeles 2 Louisiana

La. Louisiana

laager n (in Africa) a camp defended by a circular formation of wagons [Afrikaans lager]

Laaland n a variant spelling of **Lolland**

lab n informal short for **laboratory**

Lab politics Labour

Labe n the Czech name for the (River) **Elbe**

label n 1 a piece of card or other material attached to an object to show its contents, ownership, use, or destination 2 a brief descriptive term given to a person, group, or school of thought: we would need a handy label to explain the new company ▷ vb **-belling, -belled** or US **-beling, -beled** 3 to attach a label to 4 to describe or classify in a word or phrase [Old French: ribbon]

labial (lay-bee-al) adj 1 of or near the lips 2 phonetics relating to a speech sound made using the lips ▷ n 3 phonetics a speech sound such as English p or m, that involves the lips [Latin labium lip]

labiate (lay-bee-ate) n 1 any of a family of plants with square stems, aromatic leaves, and a two-lipped flower, such as mint or thyme ▷ adj 2 of this family [Latin labium lip]

Labiche n Eugène Marin. 1815–88, French dramatist, noted for his farces of middle-class life, which include Le Chapeau de paille d'Italie (1851) and Le Voyage de Monsieur Perrichon (1860)

labium (lay-bee-um) n, pl **-bia** (-bee-a) 1 a lip or liplike structure 2 any one of the four lip-shaped folds of the vulva [Latin: lip]

labor n US, Austral and sometimes Canad same as **labour**

laboratory n, pl **-ries** a building or room equipped for conducting scientific research or for teaching practical science [Latin laborare to work]

Labor Day n 1 (in the US and Canada) public holiday in honour of labour, held on the first Monday in September 2 (in Australia) public holiday observed on different days in different states

laborious adj involving great exertion or prolonged effort ▶ **laboriously** adv

Labor Party n the main left-wing political party in Australia

labour or US, Austral and sometimes Canad **labor** n 1 productive work, esp. physical work done for wages 2 the people involved in this, as opposed to management 3 the final stage of pregnancy, leading to childbirth 4 difficult work or a difficult job ▷ vb 5 to do physical work: the girls were labouring madly on it 6 to work hard (for something) 7 to make one's way with difficulty: she was now labouring down the return length 8 to emphasize too

persistently: I have laboured the point 9 (usually foll. by under) to be at a disadvantage because of a mistake or false belief: she laboured under the illusion that I understood her [Latin labor]

Labour Day n 1 a public holiday in honour of work, held in Britain on May 1 2 (in New Zealand) a public holiday commemorating the introduction of the eight-hour day held on the 4th Monday in October

laboured or US, Austral and sometimes Canad **labored** adj undertaken with difficulty: laboured breathing

labourer or US, Austral and sometimes Canad **laborer** n a person engaged in physical work

labour exchange n Brit the former name for a Jobcentre

Labour Party n 1 the main left-wing political party in a number of countries including Britain and New Zealand 2 any similar party in various other countries

labour-saving adj (of a method or piece of equipment) reducing the amount of work or effort needed to carry out a task

Labrador[1] n 1 Also called: **Labrador-Ungava** a large peninsula of NE Canada, on the Atlantic, the Gulf of St Lawrence, Hudson Strait, and Hudson Bay: contains most of Quebec and the mainland part of the province of Newfoundland and Labrador; geologically part of the Canadian Shield. Area: 1 619 000 sq km (625 000 sq miles) 2 Also called: **Coast of Labrador** a region of NE Canada, on the Atlantic and consisting of the mainland part of Newfoundland and Labrador province

Labrador[2] or **Labrador retriever** n a powerfully built dog with short dense black, brown, or golden hair

La Bruyère n Jean de. 1645–96, French moralist, noted for his Caractères (1688), satirical character studies, including portraits of contemporary public figures

Labuan n an island off the NW coast of Borneo, forming a federal territory of Malaysia: part of the Straits Settlements until 1946, when transferred to North Borneo. Chief town: Victoria (or Labuan). Area: 98 sq km (38 sq miles)

laburnum n a small ornamental tree that has clusters of yellow drooping flowers. It is highly poisonous [Latin]

labyrinth (lab-er-inth) n 1 a mazelike network of tunnels or paths, either natural or man-made 2 any complex or confusing system 3 the interconnecting cavities of the internal ear [Greek laburinthos] ▶ **labyrinthine** adj

lac n a resinous substance secreted by certain insects (**lac insects**), used in the manufacture of shellac [Hindi lākh resin]

Lacan n Jacques. 1901–81, French psychoanalyst, who reinterpreted Freud in terms of structural linguistics: an important influence on poststructuralist thought

Laccadive, Minicoy, and Amindivi Islands pl n the former name (until 1973) of the **Lakshadweep Islands**

lace n 1 a delicate decorative fabric made from threads woven in an open web of patterns 2 a cord or string drawn through eyelets to fasten a shoe or garment ▷ vb

lacing, laced 3 to fasten (shoes) with a lace **4** to draw (a cord or thread) through holes as when tying shoes **5** to add a small amount of alcohol, a drug, or poison to (food or drink) **6** to intertwine; interlace [Latin *laqueus* noose]

Lacedaemon *n* another name for **Sparta, Laconia**

Lacedaemonian *adj, n* another word for **Spartan**

lacerate (lass-er-rate) *vb* **-ating, -ated 1** to tear (the flesh) jaggedly **2** to hurt (the feelings): *it would only lacerate an overburdened conscience* [Latin *lacerare* to tear] **> laceration** *n*

lace up *vb* **1** to fasten (clothes or footwear) with laces ▷ *adj* **lace-up 2** (of footwear) to be fastened with laces ▷ *n* **lace-up 3** a shoe or boot which fastens with a lace

Lachlan *n* a river in SE Australia, rising in central New South Wales and flowing northwest then southwest to the Murrumbidgee River. Length: about 1450 km (900 miles) [named after Lachlan Macquarie, governor of New South Wales (1809–21)]

lachrymal *adj* same as **lacrimal**

lachrymose *adj* **1** given to weeping; tearful **2** mournful; sad [Latin *lacrima* a tear]

lacing *n* chiefly Brit informal a severe beating

lack *n* **1** shortage or absence of something required or desired: *a lack of confidence* ▷ *vb* **2** (often foll. by in) to be short (of) or have need (of): *lacking in sparkle* [related to Middle Dutch *laken* to be wanting]

lackadaisical *adj* **1** lacking vitality and purpose **2** lazy and careless in a dreamy way [earlier *lackadaisy*]

lackey *n* **1** a servile follower; hanger-on **2** a liveried male servant or valet [Catalan *lacayo, alacayo*]

lacklustre *or US* **lackluster** *adj* lacking brilliance, force, or vitality

Laclos *n* Pierre Choderlos de. 1741–1803, French soldier and writer, noted for his novel in epistolary form *Les Liaisons dangereuses* (1782)

Laconia *n* an ancient country of S Greece, in the SE Peloponnese, of which Sparta was the capital: corresponds to the present-day department of Lakonia

Laconian *n* **1** a native or inhabitant of Laconia, the ancient Greek country of which Sparta was the capital ▷ *adj* **2** of or relating to Laconia or its inhabitants

laconic *adj* (of a person's speech) using few words [Greek *Lakōnikos* Spartan; referring to the Spartans' terseness of speech] **> laconically** *adv*

La Coruña *n* a port in NW Spain, on the Atlantic: point of departure for the Spanish Armada (1588); site of the defeat of the French by the British under Sir John Moore in the Peninsular War (1809). Pop: 243 902 (2003 est.). Galician name: **A Coruña**. English name: **Corunna**

lacquer *n* **1** a hard glossy coating made by dissolving natural or synthetic resins in a solvent that evaporates quickly **2** a black resin, obtained from certain trees, used to give a hard glossy finish to wooden furniture **3** a clear sticky substance for spraying onto the hair to hold a style in place [Portuguese *laca* lac]

lacquered *adj* coated with lacquer

lacrimal *or* **lachrymal** (lack-rim-al) *adj* of tears or the glands that secrete tears [Latin *lacrima* a tear]

lacrosse *n* a sport in which two teams try to propel a ball into each other's goal using long-handled sticks with a pouched net at the end [Canadian French: the hooked stick]

lactate¹ *vb* **-tating, -tated** (of mammals) to secrete milk

lactate² *n* an ester or salt of lactic acid

lactation *n* **1** the secretion of milk from the mammary glands **2** the period during which milk is secreted

lacteal *adj* **1** of or like milk **2** (of lymphatic vessels) conveying or containing chyle ▷ *n* **3** any of the lymphatic vessels that convey chyle from the small intestine to the blood [Latin *lacteus* of milk]

lactic *adj* relating to or derived from milk [Latin *lac* milk]

lactic acid *n* a colourless syrupy acid found in sour milk and used as a preservative (**E270**) for foodstuffs

lactose *n* a white crystalline sugar occurring in milk

La Cumbre *n* another name for the **Uspallata Pass**

lacuna (lak-kew-na) *n, pl* **-nae** (-nee) a gap or space in a book or manuscript [Latin: pool, cavity]

lacy *adj* **lacier, laciest** of or like lace

lad *n* **1** a boy or young man **2** informal any male **3** the lads informal a group of males [perhaps from Old Norse]

ladder *n* **1** a portable frame consisting of two long parallel supports connected by steps, for climbing up or down **2** any system thought of as having a series of ascending stages: *the career ladder* **3** chiefly Brit a line of connected stitches that have come undone in tights or stockings ▷ *vb* **4** chiefly Brit to have or cause to have a line of undone stitches [Old English *hlǣdder*]

ladder back *n* a chair in which the back is made of horizontal slats between two uprights

laddish *adj* Brit, Austral and NZ informal, often disparaging characteristic of young men, esp. by being rowdy or immature

lade *vb* **lading, laded, laden** *or* **laded 1** to put cargo on board (a ship) or (of a ship) to take on cargo **2** (foll. by with) to burden or load [Old English *hladen* to load]

laden *adj* **1** loaded **2** burdened

la-di-da *or* **lah-di-dah** *adj* informal affected or pretentious in speech or manners [mockingly imitative of affected speech]

ladies *n* informal a women's public toilet

lading *n* a load; cargo; freight

Ladislaus I *or* **Ladislas I** *n* Saint. 1040–95, king of Hungary (1077–95). He extended his country's boundaries and suppressed paganism. Feast day: June 27

ladle *n* **1** a long-handled spoon with a deep bowl for serving soup, stew, etc. ▷ *vb* **-dling, -dled 2** to serve out as with a ladle [Old English *hlædel*]

ladle out *vb* informal to distribute (money, gifts, etc.) generously

lad mag *n* a magazine aimed at or appealing to men, focusing on fashion, gadgets, and often featuring scantily dressed women

Ladoga *n* Lake Ladoga a lake in NW Russia, in the SW Karelian Republic: the largest lake in Europe; drains through the River Neva into the Gulf of Finland. Area: about 18 000 sq km (7000 sq miles). Russian name: Ladozhskoye Ozero

Ladrone Islands *pl n* the former name (1521–1668) of the **Mariana Islands**

lady *n, pl* **-dies 1** a woman regarded as having the characteristics of a good family, such as dignified manners **2** a polite name for a woman ▷ *adj* **3** female: *a lady chef* [Old English *hlǣfdige*]

Lady *n, pl* **-dies 1** (in Britain) a title borne by various classes of women of the peerage **2** Our Lady a title of the Virgin Mary

ladybird *n* a small red beetle with black spots [after Our Lady, the Virgin Mary]

ladyboy *n* informal a transvestite or transsexual, esp. one from the Far East

Lady Day *n* March 25, the feast of the Annunciation of the Virgin Mary: a quarter day in England, Wales, and Ireland

lady-in-waiting *n, pl* **ladies-in-waiting** a lady who attends a queen or princess

lady-killer *n* informal a man who is, or believes he is, irresistible to women

ladylike *adj* refined and fastidious

Ladyship *n* (preceded by Your or Her) a title used to address or refer to any peeress except a duchess

Ladysmith *n* a city in E South Africa: besieged by Boers for four months (1899–1900) during the Boer War. Pop: 41 427 (2001)

lady's-slipper *n* an orchid with reddish or purple flowers

Laënnec *n* René Théophile Hyacinthe. 1781–1826, French physician, who invented the stethoscope

Lafayette *or* **La Fayette** *n* **1** Marie Joseph Paul Yves

Roch Gilbert du Motier, Marquis de Lafayette. 1757–1834, French general and statesman. He fought on the side of the colonists in the War of American Independence and, as commander of the National Guard (1789–91; 1830), he played a leading part in the French Revolution and the revolution of 1830 **2 Marie-Madeleine**, Comtesse de Lafayette. 1634–93, French novelist, noted for her historical romance *La Princesse de Clèves* (1678)

La Fontaine *n* Jean de. 1621–95, French poet, famous for his *Fables* (1668–94)

Laforgue *n* Jules. 1860–87, French symbolist poet. An originator of free verse, he had a considerable influence on modern poetry

lag¹ *vb* **lagging, lagged 1** (often foll. by *behind*) to hang (back) or fall (behind) in movement, progress, or development **2** to fall away in strength or intensity ▷ *n* **3** a slowing down or falling behind **4** the interval of time between two events, esp. between an action and its effect: *the time lag between mobilization and combat* [origin unknown]

lag² *vb* **lagging, lagged 1** to wrap (a pipe, cylinder, or boiler) with insulating material to prevent heat loss ▷ *n* **2** the insulating casing of a steam cylinder or boiler [Scandinavian]

lag³ *n* old lag *Brit, Austral and NZ slang* a convict or ex-convict [origin unknown]

Lagarde *n* Christine (**Madeleine Odette**). born 1956, French politician; managing director of the International Monetary Fund from 2011

lager *n* a light-bodied effervescent beer, fermented in a closed vessel using yeasts that sink to the bottom of the brew [German *Lagerbier* beer for storing]

Lagerfeld *n* Karl (**Otto**). born 1938, German fashion designer working mainly in Paris

Lagerkvist *n* Pär (**Fabian**). 1891–1974, Swedish novelist and dramatist. His works include the novels *The Dwarf* (1944) and *Barabbas* (1950): Nobel prize for literature 1951

Lagerlöf *n* Selma. 1858–1940, Swedish novelist, noted esp. for her children's classic *The Wonderful Adventures of Nils* (1906–07): Nobel prize for literature 1909

laggard *n* a person who lags behind

lagging *n* insulating material wrapped around pipes, boilers, or tanks to prevent loss of heat

lagoon *n* a body of water cut off from the open sea by coral reefs or sand bars [Latin *lacuna* pool]

Lagoon Islands *pl n* a former name of **Tuvalu**

Lagos *n* **1** the former capital and chief port of Nigeria, on the Bight of Benin: first settled in the sixteenth century; a slave market until the nineteenth century; ceded to Britain (1861); university (1962). Pop: 11 135 000 (2005 est) **2** a state of SW Nigeria. Capital: Ikeja. Pop: 9 013 534 (2006). Area: 3345 sq km (1292 sq miles)

Lagrange *n* Comte Joseph Louis. 1736–1813, French mathematician and astronomer, noted particularly for his work on harmonics, mechanics, and the calculus of variations ❭ **Lagrangian** *adj*

La Granja *n* another name for **San Ildefonso**

La Guaira *or* **La Guayra** *n* the chief seaport of Venezuela, on the Caribbean. Pop: 26 669 (1990 est)

La Guardia *n* Fiorello H(**enry**). 1882–1947, US politician. As mayor of New York (1933–45), he organized slum-clearance and labour safeguard schemes and suppressed racketeering

lah *n music* (in tonic sol-fa) the sixth note of any ascending major scale

La Hogue *n* a roadstead off the NW coast of France: scene of the defeat of the French by the Dutch and English fleet (1692)

Lahore *n* **1** a city in NE Pakistan: capital of the former province of West Pakistan (1955–70); University of the Punjab (1882). Pop: 6 373 000 (2005 est) **2** a variety of large domestic fancy pigeon having a black-and-white plumage

Lahti *n* a town in S Finland: site of the main Finnish

radio and television stations; furniture industry. Pop: 98 253 (2003 est)

Laibach *n* the German name for **Ljubljana**

laid *vb* the past of **lay¹**

laid-back *adj* relaxed in style or character

laid paper *n* paper with a regular pattern of lines impressed upon it

lain *vb* the past participle of **lie²**

Laine *n* Dame Cleo, full name *Clementina Dinah Laine*. born 1927, British jazz singer, noted esp. for her recordings with her husband John Dankworth

Laing *n* R(**onald**) D(**avid**). 1927–89, Scottish psychiatrist; his best known books include *The Divided Self* (1960), *The Politics of Experience and the Bird of Paradise* (1967), and *Knots* (1970)

lair *n* **1** the resting place of a wild animal **2** *informal* a place of seclusion or hiding [Old English *leger*]

laird *n* Scot a landowner, esp. of a large estate [Scots variant of *lord*]

laissez faire *or* **laisser faire** (less-ay fair) *n* the policy of nonintervention, esp. by a government in commerce [French, literally: let (them) act]

laity (lay-it-ee) *n* **1** people who are not members of the clergy **2** all the people who do not belong to a specific profession [from LAY³]

lake¹ *n* an expanse of water entirely surrounded by land [Latin *lacus*]

lake² *n* **1** a bright pigment produced by combining organic colouring matter with an inorganic compound **2** a red dye obtained by combining a metallic compound with cochineal [variant of *lac*]

Lake District *n* a region of lakes and mountains in NW England, in Cumbria: includes England's largest lake (Windermere) and highest mountain (Scafell Pike); national park; literary associations (the Lake Poets); tourist region. Also called: **Lakeland**

Lakeland *n* **1** another name for the **Lake District** ▷ *adj* **2** of or relating to the Lake District

Lake of the Woods *n* a lake in N central North America, mostly in W central Ontario, Canada: fed chiefly by the Rainy River; drains into Lake Winnipeg by the Winnipeg River; many islands; tourist region. Area: 3846 sq km (1485 sq miles)

Lake Success *n* a village in SE New York State, on W Long Island: headquarters of the United Nations Security Council from 1946 to 1951. Pop: 2832 (2003 est)

lake trout *n* a yellow-spotted trout of the Great Lakes region of Canada

lakh (lahk) *n* (in India) 100 000, esp. referring to this sum of rupees [Hindi *lākh*]

Lakshadweep Islands *pl n* a group of 26 coral islands and reefs in the Arabian Sea, off the SW coast of India: a union territory of India since 1956. Administrative centre: Kavaratti Island. Pop: 60 595 (2001). Area: 28 sq km (11 sq miles). Former name (until 1973): **Laccadive, Minicoy, and Amindivi Islands**

La-La land *n slang* **1** a nickname for **Los Angeles 2** (*not capitals*) a place that is remote from reality [C20: reduplication of the initials LA]

La Línea *n* a town in SW Spain, on the Bay of Gibraltar. Pop: 61 892 (2003 est). Official name: **La Línea de la Concepción**

Lalique *n* René (**Jules**). 1860–1945, French Art- Nouveau jeweller, glass-maker, and designer: noted esp. for his frosted glassware

Lallans *or* **Lallan** *n* **1** a literary version of the variety of English spoken and written in the Lowlands of Scotland ▷ *adj* **2** of or relating to the Lowlands of Scotland or their dialects [Scottish variant of LOWLANDS]

Lalo *n* (**Victor-Antoine-**)Édouard (edwar). 1823–92, French composer of Spanish descent. His works include the *Symphonie espagnole* (1873) and the ballet *Namouna* (1882)

lam¹ *vb* **lamming, lammed** *slang* to attack vigorously [Scandinavian]

lam² n on the lam US and Canad slang **a** making an escape **b** in hiding [origin unknown]

lama n a Buddhist priest or monk in Mongolia or Tibet [Tibetan blama]

La Mancha n a plateau of central Spain, between the mountains of Toledo and the hills of Cuenca: traditionally associated with episodes in Don Quixote. Average height: 600 m (2000 ft)

La Manche n See Manche (2)

Lamarck n Jean Baptiste Pierre Antoine de Monet, Chevalier de Lamarck. 1744–1829, French naturalist. He outlined his theory of organic evolution (Lamarckism) in Philosophie Zoologique (1809)

Lamartine n Alphonse (Marie Louis de Prat) de. 1790–1869, French romantic poet, historian, and statesman: his works include Méditations poétiques (1820) and Histoire des Girondins (1847)

lamb n **1** the young of a sheep **2** the meat of a young sheep eaten as food **3** someone who is innocent, gentle, and good ▷ vb **4** (of a ewe) to give birth [Old English]

Lamb¹ n the Lamb a title given to Christ

Lamb² n **1** Charles, pen name Elia. 1775–1834, English essayist and critic. He collaborated with his sister Mary on Tales from Shakespeare (1807). His other works include Specimens of English Dramatic Poets (1808) and the largely autobiographical essays collected in Essays of Elia (1823; 1833) **2** William. See (2nd Viscount) Melbourne **3** Willis Eugene. 1913–2008, US physicist. He detected the small difference in energy between two states of the hydrogen atom (Lamb shift). Nobel prize for physics 1955

Lambaréné n a town in W Gabon on the Ogooué River: site of the hospital built by Albert Schweitzer, who died and was buried there (1965). Pop: 9000 (2003 est)

lambast or **lambaste** vb **1** to beat severely **2** to reprimand severely [LAM¹ + BASTE³]

lambent adj **1** (of a flame or light) flickering softly over a surface **2** (of wit or humour) light or brilliant [Latin lambere to lick] ▷ **lambency** n

Lambert n Constant. 1905–51, English composer and conductor. His works include much ballet music and The Rio Grande (1929), a work for chorus, orchestra, and piano, using jazz idioms

Lambeth n **1** a borough of S Greater London, on the Thames: contains Lambeth Palace (the London residence of the Archbishop of Canterbury). Pop: 268 500 (2003 est). Area: 27 sq km (11 sq miles) **2** the Archbishop of Canterbury in his official capacity

lambing n **1** the birth of lambs at the end of winter **2** the shepherd's work of tending the ewes and newborn lambs at this time

lamb's fry n Austral and NZ lamb's liver for cooking

lambskin n the skin of a lamb, usually with the wool still on, used to make coats, slippers, etc.

lame adj **1** disabled or crippled in the legs or feet **2** weak; unconvincing: lame arguments ▷ vb **laming, lamed 3** to make lame [Old English lama] ▷ **lamely** adv ▷ **lameness** n

lamé (lah-may) n a fabric interwoven with gold or silver threads [Old French lame gold or silver thread]

lame duck n a person who is unable to cope without the help of other people

lament vb **1** to feel or express sorrow or regret (for or over) ▷ n **2** an expression of sorrow **3** a poem or song in which a death is lamented [Latin lamentum] ▷ **lamentation** n

lamentable adj very unfortunate or disappointing ▷ **lamentably** adv

lamented adj grieved for: usually said of someone dead

Lamerie n Paul de. 1688–1751, English silversmith of French Huguenot descent, noted for his lavish rococo designs

lamina n, pl **-nae** a thin plate, esp. of bone or mineral [Latin: thin plate] ▷ **laminar** adj

laminate vb **-nating, -nated 1** to make (material in sheet form) by sticking together thin sheets **2** to cover with a thin sheet of material **3** to split or be split into thin sheets ▷ n **4** a material made by sticking sheets together ▷ adj **5** composed of lamina; laminated ▷ **lamination** n

laminated adj **1** composed of many layers stuck together **2** covered with a thin protective layer of plastic

lamington n Austral and NZ a sponge cake covered with a sweet coating

Lammas n August 1, formerly observed in England as a harvest festival: a quarter day in Scotland [Old English hlāfmæsse loaf mass]

lamp n **1** a device that produces light: an electric lamp; a gas lamp; an oil lamp **2** a device that produces radiation, esp. for therapeutic purposes: an ultraviolet lamp [Greek lampein to shine]

lampblack n a fine black soot used as a pigment in paint and ink

Lampedusa¹ n an island in the Mediterranean, between Malta and Tunisia. Area: about 21 sq km (8 sq miles)

Lampedusa² n Giuseppe Tomasi di. 1896–1957, Italian novelist: author of the historical novel The Leopard (1958)

lampoon n **1** a piece of writing ridiculing a person ▷ vb **2** to ridicule and criticize (someone) in a lampoon [French lampon] ▷ **lampooner** or **lampoonist** n

lamppost n a metal or concrete pole supporting a lamp in a street

lamprey n an eel-like fish with a round sucking mouth [Late Latin lampreda]

LAN computers local area network

Lanai n an island in central Hawaii, west of Maui island. Pop: 3193 (2000). Area: 363 sq km. (140 sq miles)

Lanarkshire n a historical county of S Scotland: became part of Strathclyde region in 1975; since 1996 administered by the council areas of North Lanarkshire, South Lanarkshire, and Glasgow

Lancashire n **1** a county of NW England, on the Irish Sea: became a county palatine in 1351 and a duchy attached to the Crown; much reduced in size after the 1974 boundary changes, losing the Furness district to Cumbria and much of the south to Greater Manchester, Merseyside, and Cheshire: Blackburn with Darwen and Blackpool became independent unitary authorities in 1998. It was traditionally a cotton textiles manufacturing region. Administrative centre: Preston. Pop (excluding unitary authorities): 1 147 000 (2003 est). Area (excluding unitary authorities): 2889 sq km (1115 sq miles). Abbreviation: **Lancs 2** a mild whitish-coloured cheese with a crumbly texture

Lancaster n a city in NW England, former county town of Lancashire, on the River Lune: castle (built on the site of a Roman camp); university (1964). Pop: 45 952 (2001)

Lancastrian n **1** a native or inhabitant of Lancashire or Lancaster **2** a supporter of the house of Lancaster in the Wars of the Roses (1455–85) ▷ adj **3** of or relating to Lancashire or Lancaster **4** of the house of Lancaster

lance n **1** a long weapon with a pointed head used by horsemen ▷ vb **lancing, lanced 2** to pierce (an abscess or boil) with a lancet **3** to pierce with or as with a lance [Latin lancea]

lance corporal n a noncommissioned officer of the lowest rank

lanceolate adj narrow and tapering to a point at each end, like some leaves [Latin lanceola small lance]

lancer n (formerly) a cavalryman armed with a lance

lancet n **1** a pointed surgical knife with two sharp edges **2** short for lancet arch, lancet window [Old French lancette small lance]

lancet arch n a narrow acutely pointed arch

lancet window n a narrow window with a lancet arch

lancewood n a New Zealand tree with slender leaves

Lanchow or **Lan-chou** n a variant transliteration of the Chinese name for Lanzhou

Lancs Lancashire

land n **1** the solid part of the surface of the earth as distinct from seas and lakes. Related adjective: **terrestrial 2** ground, esp. with reference to its use or quality: *agricultural land* **3** rural or agricultural areas: *he couldn't leave the land* **4** *law* ground owned as property **5** a country, region, or area: *to bring peace and riches to your land* ▷ *vb* **6** to come down or bring (something) down to earth after a flight or jump **7** to transfer (something) or go from a ship to the shore: *sacks of malt were landed from barges* **8** to come to or touch shore **9** *informal* to obtain: *he landed a handsomely paid job at Lloyd's* **10** *angling* to retrieve (a hooked fish) from the water **11** *informal* to deliver (a blow or punch) ▶ See also **land up** [Old English] ⟩ **landless** *adj*

Land *n* Edwin Herbert. 1909–91, US inventor of the Polaroid Land camera

land agent *n* a person in charge of a landed estate

landau (lan-daw) *n* a four-wheeled horse-drawn carriage with two folding hoods [after *Landau*, a town in Germany, where first made]

Landau *n* Lev Davidovich. 1908–68, Soviet physicist, noted for his researches on quantum theory and his work on the theories of solids and liquids: Nobel prize for physics 1962

landed *adj* **1** owning land: *landed gentry* **2** consisting of land: *landed property*

Landes *n* **1** a department of SW France, in Aquitaine region. Capital: Mont-de-Marsan. Pop: 341 254 (2003 est). Area: 9364 sq km (3652 sq miles) **2** a region of SW France, on the Bay of Biscay: occupies most of the Landes department and parts of Gironde and Lot-et-Garonne; consists chiefly of the most extensive forest in France. Area: 14 000 sq km (5400 sq miles)

landfall *n* the act of sighting or nearing land, esp. from the sea

landfill *n* disposing of rubbish by covering it with earth

land girl *n* a girl or woman who does farm work, esp. in wartime

land-holder *n* a person who owns or occupies land ⟩ **land-holding** *adj*, *n*

landing *n* **1** the floor area at the top of a flight of stairs **2** the act of coming to land, esp. after a flight or sea voyage **3** a place of disembarkation

landing field *n* an area of land on which aircraft land and from which they take off

landing gear *n* the undercarriage of an aircraft

landlady *n*, *pl* **-dies 1** a woman who owns and leases property **2** a woman who owns or runs a lodging house or pub

land line *n* a telecommunications wire or cable laid over land

landlocked *adj* (of a country) completely surrounded by land

landlord *n* **1** a man who owns and leases property **2** a man who owns or runs a lodging house or pub

landlubber *n* *nautical* any person without experience at sea

landmark *n* **1** a prominent object in or feature of a particular landscape **2** an important or unique event or development: *a landmark in scientific progress*

landmass *n* a large continuous area of land

land mine *n* *military* an explosive device placed in the ground, usually detonated when someone steps on it or drives over it

Land of the Midnight Sun *n* **1** any land north of the Arctic Circle, which has continuous daylight throughout the short summer, esp. N parts of Norway, Sweden, and Finland **2** an informal name for **Lapland**

Landor *n* Walter Savage. 1775–1864, English poet, noted also for his prose works, including *Imaginary Conversations* (1824–29)

landowner *n* a person who owns land ⟩ **landowning** *n*, *adj*

Landowska *n* Wanda. 1877–1959, US harpsichordist, born in Poland

landscape *n* **1** an extensive area of land regarded as being visually distinct **2** a painting, drawing, or photograph depicting natural scenery ▷ *vb* **-scaping**, **-scaped 3** to improve the natural features of (an area of land) [Middle Dutch *lantscap* region]

landscape gardening *n* the art of laying out grounds in imitation of natural scenery ⟩ **landscape gardener** *n*

Landseer *n* Sir Edwin Henry. 1802–73, English painter, noted for his studies of animals

Land's End *n* a granite headland in SW England, on the SW coast of Cornwall: the westernmost point of England

Landshut *n* a city in SE Germany, in Bavaria: Trausnitz castle (13th century); manufacturing centre for machinery and chemicals. Pop: 60 282 (2003 est)

landside *n* the part of an airport farthest from the aircraft

landslide *n* **1** Also called: **landslip a** the sliding of a large mass of rocks and soil down the side of a mountain or cliff **b** the material dislodged in this way **2** an overwhelming electoral victory

Landsteiner *n* Karl. 1868–1943, Austrian immunologist, who discovered (1900) human blood groups and introduced the ABO classification system. He also discovered (1940) the Rhesus (Rh) factor in blood and researched into poliomyelitis. Nobel prize for physiology or medicine (1930)

land up *vb* to arrive at a final point or condition

landward *adj* **1** lying, facing, or moving towards land **2** in the direction of the land ▷ *adv* also: **landwards 3** towards land

lane *n* **1** a narrow road, esp. in the country **2** one of the parallel strips into which the carriageway of a major road or motorway is divided **3** any well-defined route or course, such as for ships or aircraft **4** one of the parallel strips into which a running track or swimming bath is divided for races [Old English *lane*, *lanu*]

Lanfranc *n* ?1005–89, Italian ecclesiastic and scholar; archbishop of Canterbury (1070–89) and adviser to William the Conqueror. He instituted many reforms in the English Church

Lang *n* **1** Cosmo Gordon, 1st Baron Lang of Lambeth. 1864–1945, British churchman; archbishop of Canterbury (1928–42) **2** Fritz. 1890–1976, Austrian film director, later in the US, most notable for his silent films, such as *Metropolis* (1926), *M* (1931), and *The Testament of Dr. Mabuse* (1932) **3** Jack (John Thomas). 1876–1975, Labor premier of New South Wales from 1925–27 and from 1930–32, who introduced much social welfare legislation and was dismissed by the governor, Sir Philip Game, in 1932 for acting unconstitutionally

lang. language

Lange *n* David (Russell). 1942–2005, New Zealand statesman: prime minister (1984–89)

Langer *n* Bernhard. born 1957, German professional golfer: won the US Masters (1985, 1993)

Langland *n* William. ?1332–?1400, English poet. The allegorical religious poem in alliterative verse, *The Vision of William concerning Piers the Plowman*, is attributed to him

Langley *n* Samuel Pierpont. 1834–1906, US astronomer and physicist: invented the bolometer (1878) and pioneered the construction of heavier-than-air flying machines

Langmuir *n* Irving. 1881–1957, US chemist. He developed the gas-filled tungsten lamp and the atomic hydrogen welding process: Nobel prize for chemistry 1932

Langres Plateau *n* a calcareous plateau of E France north of Dijon between the Seine and the Saône, reaching over 580 m (1900 ft): forms a watershed between rivers flowing to the Mediterranean and to the English Channel

Langton *n* Stephen. ?1150–1228, English cardinal; archbishop of Canterbury (1213–28). He was consecrated archbishop by Pope Innocent III in 1207 but was kept out of his see by King John until 1213. He was partly responsible for the Magna Carta (1215)

Langtry n Lillie, known as *the Jersey Lily*, real name *Émilie Charlotte le Breton*. 1852–1929, English actress, noted for her beauty and for her friendship with Edward VII

language n **1** a system of spoken sounds or conventional symbols for communicating thought **2** the language of a particular nation or people **3** the ability to use words to communicate **4** any other means of communicating: *body language* **5** the specialized vocabulary used by a particular group: *legal language* **6** a particular style of verbal expression: *rough language* **7** computers See **programming language** [Latin *lingua* tongue]

language laboratory n a room in a school or college equipped with tape recorders etc., for learning foreign languages

Languedoc n **1** a former province of S France, lying between the foothills of the Pyrenees and the River Rhône: formed around the countship of Toulouse in the 13th century; important production of bulk wines **2** a wine from this region

Languedoc-Roussillon n a region of S France, on the Gulf of Lions: consists of the departments of Lozère, Gard, Hérault, Aude, and Pyrénées-Orientales; mainly mountainous with a coastal plain

languid adj lacking energy; dreamy and inactive [Latin *languere* to languish] ➤ **languidly** adv

languish vb literary **1** to suffer deprivation, hardship, or neglect: *she won't languish in jail for it* **2** to lose or diminish in strength or energy: *the design languished into oblivion* **3** (often foll. by *for*) to be listless with desire; pine [Latin *languere*] ➤ **languishing** adj

languor (lang-ger) n literary a pleasant state of dreamy relaxation [Latin *languere* to languish] ➤ **languorous** adj

lank adj **1** (of hair) straight and limp **2** thin or gaunt: *a lank bespectacled boy* [Old English *hlanc* loose]

Lankester n Sir Edwin Ray. 1847–1929, English zoologist, noted particularly for his work in embryology and study of protozoans

lanky adj **lankier, lankiest** ungracefully tall and thin ➤ **lankiness** n

lanolin n a yellowish sticky substance extracted from wool: used in some ointments [Latin *lana* wool + *oleum* oil]

Lansbury n George. 1859–1940, British Labour politician, who led the Labour Party in opposition (1931–35). A committed pacifist, he resigned over the party's reaction to Mussolini's seizure of Ethiopia

Lansing n a city in S Michigan, on the Grand River: the state capital. Pop: 118 379 (2003 est)

lantana (lan-tay-na) n a shrub with orange or yellow flowers, considered a weed in Australia

lantern n **1** a light with a transparent protective case **2** a raised part on top of a dome or roof which lets in light or air **3** the upper part of a lighthouse that houses the light [Greek *lampein* to shine]

lantern jaw n a long hollow jaw that gives the face a drawn appearance ➤ **lantern-jawed** adj

lanthanide series n chem a class of 15 chemically related elements (**lanthanides**) with atomic numbers from 57 (lanthanum) to 71 (lutetium)

lanthanum n chem a silvery-white metallic element of the lanthanide series: used in electronic devices and glass manufacture. Symbol: **La** [Greek *lanthanein* to lie unseen]

Lanús n a city in E Argentina: a S suburb of Buenos Aires. Pop: 212 152 (2001)

lanyard n **1** a cord worn round the neck to hold a whistle or knife **2** nautical a line for extending or tightening rigging [Old French *lasne* strap]

Lanzarote n the most easterly of the Canary Islands; mountainous, with a volcanic landscape; tourism, fishing. Pop: 109 942 (2002 est). Area: 795 sq km (307 sq miles)

Lanzhou, Lanchow or **Lan-chou** n a city in N China, capital of Gansu province, on the Yellow River: situated on the main route between China and the West. Pop: 1 788 000 (2005 est)

Lao adj, n another name for **Laotian**

Laoag n a city in the N Philippines, on NW Luzon: trade centre for an agricultural region. Pop: 94 466 (2000)

Laodicea n the ancient name of several Greek cities in W Asia, notably at Latakia

laodicean (lay-oh-**diss**-see-an) adj indifferent, esp. in religious matters [referring to the early Christians of Laodicea (Revelation 3:14–16)]

Laoighis n a variant spelling of **Laois**

Laois n a county of central Republic of Ireland, in Leinster province: formerly boggy but largely reclaimed for agriculture. County town: Portlaoise. Pop: 58 774 (2002). Area: 1719 sq km (664 sq miles). Also called: **Laoighis, Leix.** Former name: **Queen's County**

Laos n a republic in SE Asia: first united as the kingdom of Lan Xang ("million elephants") in 1353, after being a province of the Khmer Empire for about four centuries; made part of French Indochina in 1893 and gained independence in 1949; became a republic in 1975. It is generally forested and mountainous, with the Mekong River running almost the whole length of the W border. Official language: Laotian. Religion: Buddhist majority, tribal religions. Currency: kip. Capital: Vientiane. Pop: 6 695 166 (2013 est). Area: 236 800 sq km (91 429 sq miles). Official name: **People's Democratic Republic of Laos**

Laotian or **Lao** n **1** (pl **Laotians, Lao** or **Laos**) a member of a Buddhist people of Laos and NE Thailand, related to the Thais **2** the language of this people, closely related to Thai ▷ adj **3** of or relating to this people or their language or to Laos

Lao Zi or **Lao-tzu** n ?604–?531 BC, Chinese philosopher, traditionally regarded as the founder of Taoism and the author of the *Tao-te Ching*

lap[1] n **1** the area formed by the upper surface of the thighs of a seated person **2** a protected place or environment: *in the lap of luxury* **3** the part of a person's clothing that covers the lap **4 drop in someone's lap** to give someone the responsibility of [Old English *læppa* flap]

lap[2] n **1** one circuit of a racecourse or track **2** a stage or part of a journey **3 a** an overlapping part **b** the extent of overlap ▷ vb **lapping, lapped 4** to overtake (an opponent) in a race so as to be one or more circuits ahead **5** to enfold or wrap around **6** to place or lie partly or completely over, or project beyond: *deep-pile carpet that lapped against his ankles* **7** to envelop or surround with comfort, love, or peace: *she was lapped by the luxury of Seymour House* [probably same as LAP[1]]

lap[3] vb **lapping, lapped 1** (of small waves) to wash against (the shore or a boat) with light splashing sounds **2** (often foll. by *up*) (esp. of animals) to scoop (a liquid) into the mouth with the tongue ▷ n **3** the act or sound of lapping ▶ See also **lap up** [Old English *lapian*]

La Palma n an island in the N Atlantic, in the NW Canary Islands: administratively part of Spain. Chief town: Santa Cruz de la Palma. Pop: 85 547 (2002 est). Area: 725 sq km (280 sq miles)

laparoscopy n an investigative surgical procedure in which an optical instrument is inserted through a small incision in the abdomen [Greek *lapara* flank + *skopein* to look at] ➤ **laparoscopic** adj

La Paz n a city in W Bolivia, at an altitude of 3600 m (12 000 ft): seat of government since 1898 (though Sucre is still the official capital); the country's largest city; founded in 1548 by the Spaniards; university (1830). Pop: 1 533 000 (2005 est)

lap dancing n a form of entertainment in which scantily dressed women dance erotically for individual members of the audience

lapdog n a small pet dog

lapel (lap-**pel**) n the part on the front of a jacket or coat that folds back towards the shoulders [from LAP[1]]

lapidary *n, pl* **-daries 1** a person who cuts, polishes, sets, or deals in gemstones ▷ *adj* **2** of or relating to gemstones or the work of a lapidary [Latin *lapidarius,* from *lapis* stone]

lapis lazuli (lap-iss lazz-yew-lie) *n* a brilliant blue mineral used as a gemstone [Latin *lapis* stone + Medieval Latin *lazulum* azure]

lap joint *n* a joint made by fastening together overlapping parts

Laplace *n* Pierre Simon, Marquis de Laplace. 1749–1827, French mathematician, physicist, and astronomer. He formulated the nebular hypothesis (1796). He also developed the theory of probability

Lapland *n* an extensive region of N Europe, mainly within the Arctic Circle: consists of the N parts of Norway, Sweden, Finland, and the Kola Peninsula of the extreme NW of Russia. Also called (informal): **Land of the Midnight Sun**

La Plata *n* **1** a port in E Argentina, near the Río de la Plata estuary: founded in 1882 and modelled on Washington DC; university (1897). Pop: 758 000 (2005 est) **2** See (Río de la) **Plata**

lap of honour *n* a ceremonial circuit of a racing track by the winner of a race

Lapp *n* **1** Also: **Laplander** a member of a nomadic people living chiefly in N Scandinavia **2** the language of this people ▷ *adj* **3** of this people or their language

lappet *n* **1** a small hanging flap or piece of lace **2** *zoology* a flap of flesh or membrane, such as the ear lobe or a bird's wattle [LAP¹ + -*et* (diminutive suffix)]

lapse *n* **1** a temporary drop in standard as a result of forgetfulness or lack of concentration **2** a moment or instance of bad behaviour, esp. by someone who is usually well-behaved **3** a period of time sufficient for a change to take place: *the lapse between phone call and now* **4** a gradual decline to a lower degree, condition, or state: *its lapse from the tradition of Disraeli* **5** *law* the loss of some right by neglecting to exercise or renew it ▷ *vb* **lapsing, lapsed 6** to drop in standard or fail to maintain a standard **7** to decline gradually in status, condition, or degree **8** to allow to end or become no longer valid, esp. through negligence: *a bid that lapsed last July* **9** (usually foll. by *into*) to drift (into a condition): *she appeared to lapse into a brief reverie* **10** (often foll. by *from*) to turn away (from beliefs or standards) **11** (of time) to slip away [Latin *lapsus* error] > **lapsed** *adj*

Laptev Sea *n* a shallow arm of the Arctic Ocean, along the N coast of Russia between the Taimyr Peninsula and the New Siberian Islands. Former name: **Nordenskjöld Sea**

laptop *adj* (of a computer) small and light enough to be held on the user's lap

lap up *vb* **1** to eat or drink **2** to accept (information or attention) eagerly: *the public are lapping up the scandal*

lapwing *n* a bird of the plover family with a crested head. Also called: **peewit** [Old English *hlēapewince* plover]

Lara *n* Brian Charles. born 1969, Trinidadian cricketer: scored 11,953 runs in 131 test matches (1990–2006) for the West Indies; holder of records for highest individual score in first-class cricket (501 not out for Warwickshire, 1994) and for highest test innings (400 not out against England, 2004)

larboard *n nautical* an old word for **port²** (1) [Middle English *laddeborde*]

larceny *n, pl* **-nies** *law* theft [Old French *larcin*] > **larcenist** *n*

larch *n* **1** a coniferous tree with deciduous needle-like leaves and egg-shaped cones **2** the wood of this tree [Latin *larix*]

lard *n* **1** the soft white fat obtained from pigs and prepared for use in cooking ▷ *vb* **2** to prepare (lean meat or poultry) by inserting small strips of bacon or fat before cooking **3** to add unnecessary material to (speech or writing) [Latin *laridum* bacon fat]

larder *n* a room or cupboard used for storing food [Old French *lardier*]

Lardner *n* Ring(old Wilmer). 1885–1933, US short-story writer and journalist, whose best-known works are collected in *How to Write Short Stories* (1924) and *The Love Nest* (1926)

lardy cake *n Brit* a sweet cake made of bread dough, lard, sugar, and dried fruit

Laredo *n* a city in the US, in Texas, on the Mexican border: founded by the Spanish in 1755 on the Rio Grande. Pop: 197 488 (2003 est)

large *adj* **1** having a relatively great size, quantity, or extent; big **2** of wide or broad scope, capacity, or range; comprehensive: *a large effect* ▷ *n* **3 at large a** as a whole; in general: *both the Navy and the country at large* **b** (of a dangerous criminal or wild animal) out of captivity; free **c** in full detail ▷ *vb* **larging, larged 4 large it** *Brit slang* to enjoy oneself or celebrate in an extravagant way [Latin *largus* ample] > **largeness** *n*

large intestine *n* the part of the alimentary canal consisting of the caecum, colon, and rectum

largely *adv* principally; to a great extent

large-scale *adj* **1** wide-ranging or extensive **2** (of maps and models) constructed or drawn to a big scale

largesse *or* **largess** (lar-jess) *n* the generous giving of gifts, favours, or money [Old French]

largish *adj* fairly large

largo *music adv* **1** in a slow and stately manner ▷ *n, pl* **-gos 2** a piece or passage to be performed in a slow and stately manner [Italian]

lariat *n US and Canad* **1** a lasso **2** a rope for tethering animals [Spanish *la reata* the lasso]

Larisa *or* **Larissa** *n* a city in E Greece, in E Thessaly: fortified by Justinian; annexed to Greece in 1881. Pop: 130 000 (2005 est)

lark¹ *n* a small brown songbird, esp. the skylark [Old English *lāwerce, lǣwerce*]

lark² *informal n* **1** a carefree adventure or frolic **2** a harmless piece of mischief **3** an activity or job viewed with disrespect ▷ *vb* **4 lark about** to have a good time frolicking or playing pranks [origin unknown] > **larky** *adj*

Larkin *n* Philip. 1922–85, English poet: his verse collections include *The Less Deceived* (1955) and *The Whitsun Weddings* (1964)

larkspur *n* a plant with blue, pink, or white flowers with slender spikes at the base [LARK¹ + SPUR]

Larne *n* a district of NE Northern Ireland, in Co Antrim. Pop: 30 948 (2003 est). Area: 336 sq km (130 sq miles)

La Rochefoucauld *n* François, Duc de La Rochefoucauld. 1613–80, French writer. His best-known work is *Réflexions ou sentences et maximes morales* (1665), a collection of epigrammatic and cynical observations on human nature

La Rochelle *n* a port in W France, on the Bay of Biscay: a Huguenot stronghold until its submission through famine to Richelieu's forces after a long siege (1627–28). Pop: 80 014 (2006)

Larousse *n* Pierre Athanase. 1817–75, French grammarian, lexicographer, and encyclopedist. He edited and helped to compile the *Grand Dictionnaire universel du XIX siècle* (1866–76)

larrikin *n Austral and NZ old-fashioned, slang* a mischievous or unruly person

larva *n, pl* **-vae** the immature form of many insects before it develops into its adult form [New Latin] > **larval** *adj*

Larwood *n* Harold. 1904–95, English cricketer. An outstanding fast bowler, he played 21 times for England between 1926 and 1933

laryngeal *adj* of or relating to the larynx

laryngitis *n* inflammation of the larynx, causing huskiness or loss of voice

larynx (lar-rinks) *n, pl* **larynges** (lar-rin-jeez) *or* **larynxes**

hollow organ forming part of the air passage to the lungs: it contains the vocal cords [Greek *larunx*]

lasagne *or* **lasagna** (laz-zan-ya) *n* **1** a form of pasta in wide flat sheets **2** a dish made from layers of lasagne, meat, and cheese [Italian, from Latin *lasanum* cooking pot]

La Salle[1] *n* a city in SE Canada, in Quebec: a S suburb of Montreal. Pop (with Émard): 100 327 (2006)

La Salle[2] *n* Sieur **Robert Cavelier de**. 1643–87, French explorer and fur trader in North America; founder of Louisiana (1682)

La Scala *n* the chief opera house in Italy, in Milan (opened 1776)

lascar *n* an East Indian seaman

Lascaux *n* the site of a cave in SW France, in the Dordogne: contains Palaeolithic wall drawings and paintings

lascivious (lass-iv-ee-uss) *adj* showing or producing sexual desire; lustful [Latin *lascivia* wantonness] **> lasciviously** *adv*

Lasdun *n* Sir **Denys**. 1914–2001, British architect. He is best known for the University of East Anglia (1968) and the National Theatre in London (1976)

laser (lay-zer) *n* **1 a** a device that produces a very narrow intense beam of light, which is used for cutting very hard materials and in surgery etc. *▷ vb* **2** to use a laser on (something), esp. as part of medical treatment **3** Also: **laser off** to remove (a tattoo, fat, etc.) with laser treatment [from light amplification by stimulated emission of radiation]

laser printer *n* a computer printer that uses a laser beam to produce characters which are then transferred to paper

lash[1] *n* **1** an eyelash **2** a sharp cutting blow from a whip **3** the flexible end of a whip *▷ vb* **4** to hit (a person or thing) sharply with a whip, esp. formerly as punishment **5** (of rain or waves) to beat forcefully against **6** to attack (someone) with words of ridicule or scolding **7** to flick or wave sharply to and fro: *his tail lashing in irritation* **8** to urge as with a whip: *to lash the audience into a violent mood* **▶** See also **lash out** [perhaps imitative]

lash[2] *vb* to bind or secure with rope, string, or cord [Latin *laqueus* noose]

lashing[1] *n* **1** a flogging **2** a scolding

lashing[2] *n* rope, string, or cord used for binding or securing

lashings *pl n old-fashioned, informal* large amounts; lots: *lashings of cream*

Lashio *n* a town in NE central Myanmar: starting point of the Burma Road to Chongqing, China

Lashkar *n* a former city in N India, in Madhya Pradesh: capital of the former states of Gwalior and Madhya Bharat; now part of the city of Gwalior

Lashkar Gah *n* a city in S Afghanistan, situated between the Arghandab and Helmand rivers: capital of Helmand province. Pop: 201 546 (2006 est)

lash out *vb* **1** to make a sudden verbal or physical attack **2** *informal* to spend extravagantly

Lasker *n* **Emanuel**. 1868–1941, German chess player: world champion (1894–1921)

Laski *n* **Harold (Joseph)**. 1893–1950, English political scientist and socialist leader

Las Palmas *n* a port and resort in the central Canary Islands, on NE Grand Canary: a major fuelling port on the main shipping route between Europe and South America. Capital of the Canary Islands. Pop: 377 600 (2003 est)

La Spezia *n* a port in NW Italy, in Liguria, on the **Gulf of Spezia**: the chief naval base in Italy. Pop: 91 391 (2001)

lass *n* a girl or young woman [origin unknown]

Lassa *n* a variant spelling of **Lhasa**

Lassa fever *n* a serious viral disease of Central West Africa, characterized by high fever and muscular pains

[after *Lassa*, the Nigerian village where it was first identified]

Lassalle *n* **Ferdinand**. 1825–64, German socialist and writer: a founder of the first German workers' political party (1863), which later became the Social Democratic Party

Lassen Peak *n* a volcano in S California, in the S Cascade Range. An area of 416 sq km (161 sq miles) was established as **Lassen Volcanic National Park** in 1916. Height: 3187 m (10 457 ft)

lassie *n Scot and N English informal* a little lass; girl

lassitude *n* physical or mental weariness [Latin *lassus* tired]

lasso (lass-oo) *n, pl* **-sos** *or* **-soes 1** a long rope with a noose at one end used for catching horses and cattle *▷ vb* **-soing, -soed 2** to catch as with a lasso [Spanish, from Latin *laqueus* noose] **> lassoer** *n*

Lassus *n* **Roland de**. Italian name *Orlando di Lasso*. ?1532–94, Flemish composer, noted for his mastery in both sacred and secular music

last[1] *adj* **1** being, happening, or coming at the end or after all others **2** most recent: *last April* **3** only remaining: *that's the last one* **4** most extreme; utmost **5** least suitable or likely: *China was the last place on earth he intended to go ▷ adv* **6** after all others **7** most recently: *we last saw him on Thursday night* **8** as the last or latest item *▷ n* **9 the last a** a person or thing that is last **b** the final moment; end **10** the final appearance, mention, or occurrence: *the last of this season's visitors* **11 at last** in the end; finally **12 at long last** finally, after difficulty or delay [variant of Old English *latest, lætest*]

> **USAGE** Since *last* can mean either *after all others* or *most recent*, it is better to avoid using this word where ambiguity might arise, as in *her last novel*. *Final* or *latest* should be used in such contexts to avoid ambiguity.

last[2] *vb* **1** to continue to exist for a length of time: *the soccer war lasted 100 hours* **2** to be sufficient for the needs of (a person) for a length of time: *I shall make a couple of bottles to last me until next summer* **3** to remain fresh, uninjured, or unaltered for a certain time: *the flowers haven't lasted well* **▶** See also **last out** [Old English *lǣstan*]

last[3] *n* the wooden or metal form on which a shoe or boot is made or repaired [Old English *lāst* footprint]

last-ditch *adj* done as a final resort: *a last-ditch attempt*

lasting *adj* existing or remaining effective for a long time

Last Judgment *n* the Last Judgment *theol* God's verdict on the destinies of all human beings at the end of the world

lastly *adv* **1** at the end or at the last point **2** finally

last-minute *adj* given or done at the latest possible time: *last-minute changes*

last name *n* same as **surname**

last out *vb* **1** to be sufficient for one's needs: *if the energy supply lasts out* **2** to endure or survive: *I might not last out my hours of duty*

last post *n military* **1** a bugle call used to signal the time to retire at night **2** a similar call sounded at military funerals

last rites *pl n Christianity* religious rites for those close to death

last straw *n* a small incident, irritation, or setback that coming after others is too much to cope with

Last Supper *n* the Last Supper the meal eaten by Christ with his disciples on the night before his Crucifixion

Las Vegas *n* a city in SE Nevada: famous for luxury hotels and casinos. Pop: 517 017 (2003 est)

lat. latitude

Lat. Latin

Latakia *or* **Lattakia** *n* the chief port of Syria, in the northwest: tobacco industry. Pop: 486 000 (2005 est). Latin name: **Laodicea ad Mare**

latch *n* **1** a fastening for a gate or door that consists of a bar that may be slid or lowered into a groove, hole, or notch **2** a spring-loaded door lock that can only be opened by a key from outside ▷ *vb* **3** to fasten, fit, or be fitted with a latch [Old English *læccan* to seize]

latchkey child *n Brit, Austral and NZ* a child who has to let himself or herself in at home after school, as both parents are out at work

latch on *vb informal* **1** (often foll. by *to*) to attach oneself (to): *he should latch on to a man with a deal to do* **2** to understand: *it took a while to latch on to what he was trying to say*

late *adj* **1** occurring or arriving after the correct or expected time: *the plane will be late* **2** towards or near the end: *the late afternoon* **3** occurring or being at a relatively advanced time: *a late starter, his first novel was effectively his last* **4** at an advanced time in the evening or at night: *it's late, I have to get back* **5** having died recently: *her late father* **6** recent: *recollect the late defeats which your enemies have experienced* **7** former: *the late manager of the team* **8** **of late** recently ▷ *adv* **9** after the correct or expected time: *Mark Wright arrived late* **10** at a relatively advanced age: *coming late to motherhood* **11** recently: *as late as in 1983, only 9 per cent of that labour force was unionized* **12** **late in the day a** at a late or advanced stage **b** too late [Old English *læt*] ❯ **lateness** *n*

> USAGE Since *late* can mean *deceased*, many people think it is better to avoid using this word to refer to the person who held a post or position before its present holder: *the previous* (not *the late*) *editor of The Times.*

lateen *adj nautical* denoting a rig with a triangular sail bent to a yard hoisted to the head of a low mast [French *voile latine* Latin sail]

Late Greek *n* the Greek language from about the 3rd to the 8th centuries AD

Late Latin *n* the form of written Latin used from the 3rd to the 7th centuries AD

lately *adv* in recent times; of late

latent *adj* lying hidden and not yet developed within a person or thing [Latin *latere* to lie hidden] ❯ **latency** *n*

later *adj, adv* **1** the comparative of **late** ▷ *adv* **2** afterwards

lateral (lat-ter-al) *adj* of or relating to the side or sides [Latin *latus* side] ❯ **laterally** *adv*

lateral thinking *n* a way of solving problems by apparently illogical methods

latest *adj, adv* **1** the superlative of **late** ▷ *adj* **2** most recent, modern, or new: *the latest fashions* ▷ *n* **3** **at the latest** no later than the time specified

latex *n* a milky fluid produced by many plants: latex from the rubber plant is used in the manufacture of rubber [Latin: liquid]

lath *n, pl* **laths** one of several thin narrow strips of wood used as a supporting framework for plaster or tiles [Old English *lætt*]

lathe *n* a machine for shaping metal or wood by turning it against a fixed tool [perhaps from Old Norse]

lather *n* **1** foam formed by soap or detergent in water **2** foamy sweat, as produced by a horse **3** *informal* a state of agitation ▷ *vb* **4** to coat or become coated with lather **5** to form a lather **6** *informal* to beat; flog [Old English *lēathor* soap] ❯ **lathery** *adj*

Latimer *n* Hugh. ?1485–1555, English Protestant bishop: burnt at the stake for refusing to disavow his Protestant beliefs when Mary I assumed the throne

Latin *n* **1** the language of ancient Rome and the Roman Empire **2** a member of any of those peoples whose languages are derived from Latin ▷ *adj* **3** of the Latin language **4** of those peoples whose languages are derived from Latin **5** of the Roman Catholic Church [Latin *Latinus* of Latium]

Latina *n* a city in W central Italy, in Lazio: built as a planned town in 1932 on reclaimed land of the Pontine Marshes. Pop: 107 898 (2001). Former name (until 1947): Littoria

Latin America *n* those areas of America whose official languages are Spanish and Portuguese, derived from Latin: South America, Central America, Mexico, and certain islands in the Caribbean

Latin American *n* **1** a native or inhabitant of Latin America ▷ *adj* **2** of or relating to Latin America or its inhabitants

Latin Quarter *n* an area of Paris, on the S bank of the River Seine: contains the city's main educational establishments; centre for students and artists

latish *adj, adv* rather late

latitude *n* **1 a** an angular distance measured in degrees north or south of the equator **b** (*often pl*) a region considered with regard to its distance from the equator **2** scope for freedom of action and thought [Latin *latus* broad] ❯ **latitudinal** *adj*

latitudinarian *adj* **1** liberal, esp. in religious matters ▷ *n* **2** a person with latitudinarian views

Latium *n* an ancient territory in W central Italy, in modern Lazio, on the Tyrrhenian Sea: inhabited by the Latin people from the 10th century BC until dominated by Rome (4th century BC). Italian name: **Lazio**

Latour *n* Maurice Quentin de 1704–88, French pastelist noted for the vivacity of his portraits

La Tour *n* Georges de. ?1593–1652, French painter, esp. of candlelit religious scenes

latrine *n* a toilet in a barracks or camp [Latin *lavatrina* bath]

latter *n* **1 the latter** the second or second mentioned of two ▷ *adj* **2** near or nearer the end: *the latter half of the season* **3** more advanced in time or sequence; later [Old English *lætra*]

> USAGE *The latter* should only be used to refer to the second of two items: *many people choose to go by hovercraft rather than use the ferry, but I prefer the latter.* The last of three or more items can be referred to as *the last-named.*

latter-day *adj* present-day; modern

latterly *adv* recently; lately

lattice (lat-iss) *n* **1** Also called: **latticework** a framework of strips of wood or metal interlaced in a diagonal pattern **2** a gate, screen, or fence formed of such a framework **3** an array of atoms, ions, or molecules in a crystal, or an array of points indicating their positions in space ▷ *vb* **-ticing, -ticed 4** to make, adorn, or supply with a lattice [Old French *latte* lath] ❯ **latticed** *adj*

Latvia *n* a republic in NE Europe, on the Gulf of Riga and the Baltic Sea: ruled by Poland, Sweden, and Russia since the 13th century, Latvia was independent from 1919 until 1940 and was a Soviet republic (1940–91), gaining its independence after conflict with Soviet forces; it joined the EU in 2004. Latvia is mostly forested. Official language: Latvian. Religion: nonreligious, Christian. Currency: euro. Capital: Riga. Pop: 2 178 443 (2013 est). Area: 63 700 sq km (25 590 sq miles)

Latvian *adj* **1** of or relating to Latvia or its inhabitants ▷ *n* **2** a native or inhabitant of Latvia **3** the language of Latvia

laud *literary vb* **1** to praise or glorify ▷ *n* **2** praise or glorification [Latin *laudare* to praise]

Laud *n* William. 1573–1645, English prelate; archbishop of Canterbury (1633–45). His persecution of Puritans and his High Church policies in England and Scotland were a cause of the Civil War; he was impeached by the Long Parliament (1640) and executed

Lauda *n* Niki. born 1949, Austrian motor-racing driver: Formula One world champion 1975, 1977, 1984

laudable *adj* deserving praise; commendable ❯ **laudability** *n* ❯ **laudably** *adv*

laudanum (lawd-a-num) *n* a sedative extracted from opium [New Latin]

laudatory *adj* (of speech or writing) expressing praise

Lauder *n* Sir Harry. real name *Hugh MacLennan*. 1870–1950, Scottish ballad singer and music-hall comedian

Laue *n* Max Theodor Felix von. 1879–1960, German physicist. He pioneered the technique of measuring the wavelengths of X-rays by their diffraction by crystals and contributed to the theory of relativity: Nobel prize for physics 1914

laugh *vb* 1 to express amusement or happiness by producing a series of inarticulate sounds 2 to utter or express with laughter: *he laughed his derision at the play* 3 to bring or force (oneself) into a certain condition by laughter: *laughing herself silly* 4 **laugh at** to make fun of; jeer at 5 **laugh up one's sleeve** to laugh secretly ▷ *n* 6 the act or an instance of laughing 7 *informal* a person or thing that causes laughter: *he's a laugh, that one* 8 **the last laugh** final success after previous defeat ▶ See also **laugh off** [Old English *læhan, hliehhen*] > **laughingly** *adv*

laughable *adj* ridiculous because so obviously inadequate or unsuccessful

laughing gas *n* nitrous oxide used as an anaesthetic: it may cause laughter and exhilaration when inhaled

laughing stock *n* a person or thing that is treated with ridicule

laugh off *vb* to treat (something serious or difficult) lightly

laughter *n* the action or noise of laughing [Old English *hleahtor*]

Laughton *n* Charles. 1899–1962, US actor, born in England: noted esp. for his films of the 1930s, such as *The Private Life of Henry VIII* (1933), for which he won an Oscar, and *Mutiny on the Bounty* (1935)

Launceston *n* a city in Australia, the chief port of the island state of Tasmania on the Tamar River, 64 km (40 miles) from Bass Strait. Pop: 68 443 (2001)

launch¹ *vb* 1 to move (a vessel) into the water, esp. for the first time 2 a to start off or set in motion: *to launch an appeal* b to put (a new product) on the market 3 to set (a rocket, missile, or spacecraft) into motion 4 to involve (oneself) totally and enthusiastically: *Francis launched himself into the transfer market with gusto* 5 **launch into** to start talking or writing (about) 6 (usually foll. by *out*) to start (out) on a new enterprise ▷ *n* 7 an act or instance of launching [Late Latin *lanceare* to use a lance, hence to set in motion] > **launcher** *n*

launch² *n* an open motorboat [Malay *lancharan* boat, from *lanchar* speed]

launch pad *or* **launching pad** *n* a platform from which a spacecraft, rocket, or missile is launched

launder *vb* 1 to wash and iron (clothes and linen) 2 to make (money illegally obtained) appear to be legally gained by passing it through foreign banks or legitimate enterprises [Latin *lavare* to wash]

Launderette *n* Brit, Austral and NZ trademark an establishment where clothes can be washed and dried, using coin-operated machines. Also called (US, Canad, Austral, NZ): **Laundromat**

laundry *n*, *pl* **-dries** 1 the clothes or linen to be laundered or that have been laundered 2 a place where clothes and linen are washed and ironed

laundry list *n* US and Canad a list of items perceived as being long

Laurasia *n* one of the two ancient supercontinents produced by the first split of the even larger supercontinent Pangaea about 200 million years ago, comprising what are now North America, Greenland, Europe, and Asia (excluding India) [C20: from New Latin *Laur(entia)* (referring to the ancient N American landmass, from *Laurentian* strata of the Canadian Shield) + *(Eur)asia*]

laureate (lor-ee-at) *adj* 1 *literary* crowned with laurel leaves as a sign of honour ▷ *n* 2 short for **poet laureate** [Latin *laurea* laurel] > **laureateship** *n*

laurel *n* 1 a small Mediterranean evergreen tree with glossy leaves 2 **laurels** a wreath of laurel, worn on the head as an emblem of victory or honour in classical times 3 **laurels** honour, distinction, or fame 4 **look to one's laurels** to be on guard against one's rivals 5 **rest on one's laurels** to be satisfied with what one has already achieved and stop striving for further success [Latin *laurus*]

Laurel and Hardy *n* a team of US film comedians, **Stan Laurel**, 1890–1965, born in Britain, the thin one, and his partner, **Oliver Hardy**, 1892–1957, the fat one

Lauren *n* Ralph. born 1939, US fashion designer

Laurence *n* Margaret, full name *Jean Margaret Laurence*, 1926–87, Canadian novelist and short story writer; her novels include *The Stone Angel* (1964)

Laurentian *adj* 1 of, relating to, or situated near the St Lawrence River in SE Canada 2 same as **Lawrentian**

Laurentian Mountains *pl n* a range of low mountains in E Canada, in Quebec between the St Lawrence River and Hudson Bay. Highest point: 1191 m (3905 ft). Also called: **Laurentides**

Laurier *n* Sir Wilfrid. 1841–1919, Canadian Liberal statesman; the first French-Canadian prime minister (1896–1911)

Lausanne *n* a city in W Switzerland, capital of Vaud canton, on Lake Geneva; cultural and commercial centre; university (1537). Pop: 116 300 (2002 est)

lav *n* Brit informal short for **lavatory**

lava *n* 1 molten rock discharged by volcanoes 2 any rock formed by the solidification of lava [Latin *lavare* to wash]

Laval¹ *n* a city in SE Canada, in Quebec: a NW suburb of Montreal. Pop: 343 005 (2001)

Laval² *n* Pierre. 1883–1945, French statesman. He was premier of France (1931–32; 1935–36) and premier of the Vichy government (1942–44). He was executed for collaboration with Germany

lavatorial *adj* characterized by frequent reference to excretion: *lavatorial humour*

lavatory *n*, *pl* **-ries** same as **toilet** [Latin *lavare* to wash]

lavender *n* 1 a plant grown for its bluish-purple flowers and as the source of a sweet-smelling oil 2 its dried flowers, used to perfume clothes ▷ *adj* 3 pale bluish-purple [Medieval Latin *lavendula*]

lavender water *n* a light perfume made from lavender

Laver *n* Rod(ney) (George). born 1938, Australian tennis player: won eleven Grand Slam singles titles (1960–69), including all four in a single year twice (1962, 1969)

Lavigne *n* Avril. born 1984, Canadian rock singer and songwriter; her recordings include *Let Go* (2002), *Under My Skin* (2004) and *The Best Damn Thing* (2007)

lavish *adj* 1 great in quantity or richness: *lavish banquets* 2 very generous in giving 3 extravagant; wasteful: *lavish spending habits* ▷ *vb* 4 to give or spend very generously or in great quantities [Old French *lavasse* torrent] > **lavishly** *adv*

Lavoisier *n* Antoine Laurent. 1743–94, French chemist; one of the founders of modern chemistry. He disproved the phlogiston theory, named oxygen, and discovered its importance in respiration and combustion

law *n* 1 a rule or set of rules regulating what may or may not be done by members of a society or community 2 a rule or body of rules made by the legislature or other authority. Related adjectives: **legal, judicial, juridical** 3 the control enforced by such rules: *scant respect for the rule of law* 4 **the law** a the legal or judicial system b the profession or practice of law c *informal* the police or a policeman 5 **law and order** the policy of strict enforcement of the law, esp. against crime and violence 6 a rule of behaviour: *an unwritten law that Nanny knows best* 7 Also called: **law of nature** a generalization based on a recurring fact or event 8 the science or knowledge of law; jurisprudence 9 a general principle, formula, or rule in mathematics, science, or philosophy: *the law of* *gravity* **10 the Law** the laws contained in the first five books of the Old Testament **11 go to law** to resort to legal proceedings on some matter **12 lay down the law** to speak in an authoritative manner [Old English *lagu*]

Law *n* **1 Andrew Bonar**. 1858–1923, British Conservative statesman, born in Canada; prime minister (1922–23) **2 Denis**. born 1940, Scottish footballer; a striker, he played for Manchester United (1962–73) and Scotland (30 goals in 55 games, 1958–74); European Footballer of the Year (1964) **3 John**. 1671–1729, Scottish financier. He founded the first bank in France (1716) and the Mississippi Scheme for the development of Louisiana (1717), which collapsed due to excessive speculation **4 Jude**. born 1972, British film actor, who starred in *The Talented Mr Ripley* (1999), *Cold Mountain* (2003), and *Sherlock Holmes* (2009) **5 William**. 1686–1761, British Anglican divine, best known for *A Serious Call to a Holy and Devout Life* (1728)

law-abiding *adj* obeying the laws: *a law-abiding citizen*

lawbreaker *n* a person who breaks the law ⊳ **lawbreaking** *n, adj*

Lawes *n* **1 Henry**. 1596–1662, English composer, noted for his music for Milton's masque *Comus* (1634) and for his settings of some of Robert Herrick's poems **2** his brother, **William**. 1602–45, English composer, noted for his harmonically experimental instrumental music

lawful *adj* allowed, recognized, or sanctioned by law; legal ⊳ **lawfully** *adv*

lawgiver *n* **1** the giver of a code of laws **2** Also called: **lawmaker** a maker of laws ⊳ **lawgiving** *n, adj*

lawless *adj* **1** breaking the law, esp. in a wild or violent way: *lawless butchery* **2** not having laws ⊳ **lawlessness** *n*

Law Lords *pl n* (in Britain) members of the House of Lords who sit as the highest court of appeal

lawn¹ *n* an area of cultivated and mown grass [Old French *lande*]

lawn² *n* a fine linen or cotton fabric [probably from *Laon*, town in France where made]

lawn mower *n* a hand-operated or power-operated machine for cutting grass

lawn tennis *n* **1** tennis played on a grass court **2** same as tennis

Lawrence *n* **1 Saint**. died 258 AD, Roman martyr: according to tradition he was roasted to death on a gridiron. Feast day: Aug 10 **2 D**(avid) **H**(erbert). 1885–1930, British novelist, poet, and short-story writer. Many of his works deal with the destructiveness of modern industrial society, contrasted with the beauty of nature and instinct, esp. the sexual impulse. His novels include *Sons and Lovers* (1913), *The Rainbow* (1915), *Women in Love* (1920), and *Lady Chatterley's Lover* (1928) **3 Ernest Orlando**. 1901–58, US physicist, who invented the cyclotron (1931): Nobel prize for physics 1939 **4 Gertrude**. 1898–1952, British actress, noted esp. for her roles in comedies such as Noël Coward's *Private Lives* (1930) **5 Sir Thomas**. 1769–1830, British portrait painter **6 T**(homas) **E**(dward), known as *Lawrence of Arabia*. 1888–1935, British soldier and writer. He took a major part in the Arab revolt against the Turks (1916–18), proving himself an outstanding guerrilla leader. He described his experiences in *The Seven Pillars of Wisdom* (1926)

lawrencium *n chem* an element artificially produced from californium. Symbol: Lr [after E. O. LAWRENCE]

Lawrentian *adj* of or resembling the style of D. H. Lawrence or T. E. Lawrence. Also: **Laurentian**

Lawson *n* **1 Henry Archibald**. 1867–1922, Australian poet and short-story writer, whose work is taken as being most representative of the Australian outback, esp. in *While the Billy Boils* (1896) and *Joe Wilson and his Mates* (1901) **2 Nigel**, Baron. born 1932, British Conservative politician; Chancellor of the Exchquer (1983–89). **3** his daughter, **Nigella**. born 1960, British journalist, broadcaster, and cookery writer

lawsuit *n* a case in a court of law brought by one person or group against another

lawyer *n* a member of the legal profession who can advise clients about the law and represent them in court

lax *adj* lacking firmness; not strict [Latin *laxus* loose] ⊳ **laxity** *n*

laxative *n* **1** a medicine that induces the emptying of the bowels ⊳ *adj* **2** easing the emptying of the bowels [Latin *laxare* to loosen]

Laxness *n* Halldór (Kiljan). 1902–98, Icelandic novelist, noted for his treatment of rural working life in Iceland. His works include *Salka Valka* (1932) and *Independent People* (1935). Nobel prize for literature 1955

lay¹ *vb* **lays, laying, laid** **1** to put in a low or horizontal position; cause to lie: *Mary laid a clean square of white towelling carefully on the grass* **2** to establish as a basis: *ready to lay your new fashion foundations?* **3** to place or be in a particular state or position: *underneath lay a key* **4** to regard as the responsibility of: *ridiculous attempts to lay the loss at the door of the Admiralty* **5** to put forward: *ruses by which we lay claim on one another* **6** to arrange or prepare: *she would lay her plans* **7** to place in position: *he laid a wreath* **8** (of birds, esp. the domestic hen) to produce (eggs) **9** to make (a bet) with (someone): *I'll lay money he's already gone home* **10** to arrange (a table) for a meal **11** to prepare (a fire) by arranging fuel in the grate **12** *taboo, slang* to have sexual intercourse with **13 lay bare** to reveal or explain: *a century of neurophysiology has now laid bare the structures of the brain* **14 lay hold of** to seize or grasp **15 lay oneself open** to make oneself vulnerable (to criticism or attack) **16 lay open** to reveal or disclose **17 lay waste** to destroy completely ⊳ *n* **18** the manner or position in which something lies or is placed **19** *taboo, slang* **a** an act of sexual intercourse **b** a sexual partner ▸ See also **lay aside, lay down**, etc. [Old English *lecgan*]

> **USAGE** In standard English, the verb *lay* can only be used with an object, and *lie* can only be used without one: *the Queen laid a wreath; he was lying on the floor.*

lay² *vb* the past tense of **lie²**

lay³ *adj* **1** of or involving people who are not members of the clergy **2** nonprofessional or nonspecialist [Greek *laos* people]

lay⁴ *n* a short narrative poem intended to be sung [Old French *lai*]

layabout *n* a lazy person

Layamon or **Lawman** *n* 12th-century English poet and priest; author of the *Brut*, a chronicle providing the earliest version of the Arthurian story in English

Layard *n* Sir Austen Henry. 1817–94, English archaeologist, noted for his excavations at Nimrud and Nineveh

lay aside *vb* **1** to abandon or reject **2** to put aside (one thing) in order to take up another **3** to store or reserve for future use

lay-by *n* **1** *Brit* a place where drivers can stop by the side of a main road **2** *Austral and NZ* a system of payment whereby a buyer pays a deposit on an article, which is reserved for him or her until he or she has paid the full price

lay down *vb* **1** to place on the ground or a surface **2** to sacrifice: *willing to lay down their lives for the truth* **3** to formulate (a rule or principle) **4** to record (plans) on paper **5** to store or stock: *the speed with which we lay down extra, unwanted fat*

layer *n* **1** a single thickness of something, such as a cover or a coating on a surface **2** a laying hen **3** *horticulture* a shoot that forms its own root while still attached to the parent plant ⊳ *vb* **4** to form or make a layer or layers [from LAY¹]

layette *n* a complete set of clothing, bedclothes, and other accessories for a newborn baby [Middle Dutch *laege* box]

lay figure *n* **1** an artist's jointed dummy, used esp. for studying effects of drapery **2** a person considered to be subservient or unimportant [Dutch *leeman*, literally: joint-man]

lay in *vb* to accumulate and store: *they've already laid in five hundred bottles of great vintages*

lay into *vb informal* to attack or scold severely

layman *or fem* **laywoman** *n, pl* **-men** *or* **-women 1** a person who is not a member of the clergy **2** a person who does not have specialized knowledge of a subject: *the layman's guide to nuclear power*

lay off *vb* **1** to suspend (staff) during a slack period at work **2** *informal* to leave (a person, thing, or activity) alone: *'Lay off the defence counsel bit!' he snapped* ▷ *n* **lay-off 3** a period of imposed unemployment

lay on *vb* **1** to provide or supply: *they laid on a treat for the entourage* **2 lay it on thick** *slang* to exaggerate, esp. when flattering

lay out *vb* **1** to arrange or spread out **2** to plan or design: *the main streets were laid out on a grid system* **3** to prepare (a corpse) for burial or cremation **4** *informal* to spend (money), esp. lavishly **5** *informal* to knock (someone) unconscious ▷ *n* **layout 6** the arrangement or plan of something, such as a building **7** the arrangement of printed material

lay reader *n* **1** *Church of England* a person licensed to conduct religious services other than the Eucharist **2** *RC Church* a layman chosen to read the epistle at Mass

lay up *vb* **1** *informal* to confine through illness: *laid up with a bad cold* **2** to store for future use

laze *vb* **lazing, lazed 1** to be idle or lazy **2** (often foll. by *away*) to spend (time) in idleness ▷ *n* **3** time spent lazing [from *lazy*]

Lazio *n* **1** a region of W central Italy, on the Tyrrhenian Sea: includes the plain of the lower Tiber, the reclaimed Pontine Marshes, and Campagna. Capital: Rome. Pop: 5 145 805 (2003 est) **2** the Italian name for **Latium**

lazy *adj* **lazier, laziest 1** not inclined to work or exert oneself **2** done in a relaxed manner with little effort **3** moving in a sluggish manner: *the lazy drift of the bubbles* [origin unknown] **> lazily** *adv* **> laziness** *n*

lazybones *n informal* a lazy person

lb 1 pound (weight) **2** *cricket* leg bye

lbw *cricket* leg before wicket

lc 1 loco citato: in the place cited **2** *printing* lower case

LCD 1 liquid crystal display **2** Also: **lcd** lowest common denominator

lcm *or* **LCM** lowest common multiple

lea¹ *n* **1** *poetic* a meadow or field **2** grassland [Old English *lēah*]

LEA (in Britain) Local Education Authority

leach *vb* **1** to remove or be removed from a substance by a liquid passing through it **2** to lose soluble substances by the action of a liquid passing through [perhaps Old English *leccan* to water]

Leach *n* Bernard (**Howell**). 1887–1979, British potter, born in Hong Kong

Leacock *n* Stephen Butler. 1869–1944, Canadian humorist and economist: his comic works include *Literary Lapses* (1910) and *Frenzied Fiction* (1917)

lead¹ *vb* **leading, led 1** to show the way to (an individual or a group) by going with or ahead: *he led her into the house* **2** to guide, control, or direct: *he dismounted and led his horse back* **3** to influence someone to act, think, or behave in a certain way: *researching our family history has led her to correspond with relatives abroad* **4** to have the principal part in (something): *planners led the development of policy* **5** to go at the head of or have the top position in (something): *the pair led the field by almost two minutes* **6** (of a road or way) to be the means of reaching a place: *the footbridge leads on to a fine promenade* **7** to pass or spend: *I've led a happy life* **8** to guide or be guided by physical means: *he took her firmly by the arm and led her home* **9** to direct the course of (water, a rope, or wire) along, or as if along, a channel **10** (foll. by *with*) to have as the most important item: *the Review leads with a critique of A Place of Greater Safety* **11** *Brit music* to play first violin in (an orchestra) **12** to begin a round of cards by putting down the first card ▷ *n* **13** the first or most prominent place **14** example or leadership: *some of his children followed his lead* **15** an advantage over others: *Essex have a lead of 24 points* **16** an indication; clue: *we've got a lead on how the body got into the water* **17** a length of leather, nylon, or chain used to walk or control a dog **18** the principal role in a play, film, or other production, or the person playing such a role **19** the most important news story in a newspaper: *the shooting makes the lead in the Times* **20** the act of playing the first card in a round of cards or the card so played **21** a wire, cable, or other conductor for making an electrical connection ▷ *adj* **22** acting as a leader or lead: *lead singer* ▶ See also **lead off, lead on**, etc. [Old English *lǣdan*]

lead² *n* **1** a heavy toxic bluish-white metallic element: used in alloys, cable sheaths, paints, and as a radiation shield. Symbol: **Pb 2 a** graphite used for drawing **b** a thin stick of this as the core of a pencil **3** a lead weight suspended on a line, used to take soundings of the depth of water **4** lead weights or shot, as used in cartridges or fishing lines **5** a thin strip of lead for holding small panes of glass or pieces of stained glass **6 leads a** thin sheets or strips of lead used as a roof covering **b** a roof covered with such sheets **7** Also called: **leading** *printing* a thin strip of metal, formerly used for spacing between lines of type ▷ *adj* **8** of, relating to, or containing lead ▷ *vb* **9** to surround, cover, or secure with lead or leads [Old English *lēad*]

Leadbelly *n* real name *Huddie Ledbetter*. 1888–1949, US blues singer and guitarist

leaded *adj* (of windows) made from many small panes of glass held together by lead strips

leaden *adj* **1** heavy or sluggish: *my limbs felt leaden* **2** of a dull greyish colour: *leaden November sky* **3** made of lead **4** gloomy, spiritless, or lifeless: *hollow characters and leaden dialogue*

leader *n* **1** a person who rules, guides, or inspires others; head **2** *Brit and Austral* the leading editorial in a newspaper. Also: **leading article 3** *music* the principal first violinist of an orchestra who acts as the conductor's deputy **4** the person or animal who is leading in a race **5** the best or the most successful of its kind: *the company is a world leader in its field* **6** the leading horse or dog in a team **7** a strip of blank film or tape at the beginning of a reel **8** *botany* any of the long slender shoots that grow from the stem or branch of a tree **> leadership** *n*

leaderboard *n* a board displaying the current scores of the leading competitors, esp. in a golf tournament

lead-in *n* an introduction to a subject

leading *adj* **1** principal or primary: *the leading designers* **2** in the first position: *the leading driver*

leading aircraftman *n* the rank above aircraftman in the British air force **> leading aircraftwoman** *fem n*

leading light *n* an important and influential person in an organization or campaign

leading question *n* a question worded to suggest the desired answer, such as *What do you think of the horrible effects of pollution?*

leading rating *n* a rank in the Royal Navy comparable to a corporal in the army

lead off *vb* to begin

lead on *vb* to trick (someone) into believing or doing something wrong

lead pencil *n* a pencil containing a thin stick of a graphite compound

lead poisoning *n* acute or chronic poisoning by lead

lead time *n* *manufacturing* the time between the design of a product and its production

lead up to *vb* **1** to act as a preliminary or introduction to **2** to approach (a topic) gradually or cautiously

leaf *n, pl* **leaves 1** one of the flat usually green blades attached to the stem of a plant **2** the foliage of a tree or plant: *shrubs have been planted for their leaf interest* **3 in leaf** (of shrubs or trees) with all its leaves fully opened **4** a very thin sheet of metal **5** one of the sheets of paper in a book **6** a hinged, sliding, or detachable part, such as an extension to a table **7 take a leaf out of someone's book** to imitate someone in a particular course of action **8 turn over a new leaf** to begin a new and improved course of behaviour ▷ *vb* **9** (usually foll. by *through*) to turn pages casually or hurriedly without reading them **10** (of plants) to produce leaves [Old English *lēaf*] **> leafless** *adj*

leafage *n* the leaves of plants

leaflet *n* **1** a sheet of printed matter distributed, usually free, for advertising or information **2** any small leaf **3** one of the divisions of a compound leaf ▷ *vb* **-leting, -leted 4** to distribute leaflets (to)

leaf mould *n* a rich soil consisting of decayed leaves

leafy *adj* **leafier, leafiest 1** covered with leaves **2** having many trees or shrubs: *a leafy suburb*

league¹ *n* **1** an association of people or nations formed to promote the interests of its members **2** an association of sporting clubs that organizes matches between member teams **3** *informal* a class or level: *the guy is not even in the same league* **4 in league (with)** working or planning together with ▷ *vb* **leaguing, leagued 5** to form or be formed into a league [Latin *ligare* to bind]

league² *n* an obsolete unit of distance of varying length: commonly equal to 3 miles (4.8 km) [Late Latin *leuga, leuca*]

leak *n* **1 a** a crack or hole that allows the accidental escape or entrance of liquid, gas, radiation, etc. **b** such escaping or entering liquid, etc. **2** a disclosure of secret information **3** the loss of current from an electrical conductor because of faulty insulation **4** the act or an instance of leaking **5** *slang* urination ▷ *vb* **6** to enter or escape, or allow to enter or escape, through a crack or hole **7** to make (secret information) public, esp. deliberately [from Old Norse] **> leaky** *adj*

leakage *n* the act, an instance, or the result of leaking: *the leakage of 60 tonnes of oil*

Leakey *n* **1** Louis Seymour Bazett. 1903–72, British anthropologist and archaeologist, settled in Kenya. He discovered fossil remains of manlike apes in E Africa **2** his son **Richard**. born 1944, Kenyan anthropologist, who discovered the remains of primitive man over 2 million years old in E Africa

Leamington Spa *n* a town in central England, in central Warwickshire: saline springs. Pop: 61 595 (2001). Official name: **Royal Leamington Spa**

lean¹ *vb* **leaning, leaned** *or* **leant 1** (foll. by *against* or *on* or *upon*) to rest or put (something) so that it rests against a support **2** to bend or make (something) bend from an upright position **3** (foll. by *to* or *towards*) to have or express a tendency or preference ▷ *n* **4** the condition of bending from an upright position ▶ See also **lean on** [Old English *hleonian, hlinian*]

lean² *adj* **1** (esp. of a person) having a trim body with no surplus flesh **2** (of meat) having little or no fat **3** (of a period) sparse, difficult, or causing hardship: *these are lean days in Baghdad* ▷ *n* **4** the part of meat that contains little or no fat [Old English *hlǣne*] **> leanness** *n*

Lean *n* Sir David. 1908–91, English film director. His films include *In Which We Serve* (1942), *Blithe Spirit* (1945), *Brief Encounter* (1946), *Great Expectations* (1946), *Oliver Twist* (1948), *The Bridge on the River Kwai* (1957), *Lawrence of Arabia* (1962), *Dr Zhivago* (1965), and *A Passage to India* (1984)

leaning *n* a tendency or inclination

lean on *vb* **1** *informal* to try to influence (someone) by using threats **2** to depend on (someone) for help and advice

leant *vb* a past of **lean¹**

lean-to *n, pl* **-tos** a building with a sloping roof attached to another building or a wall

leap *vb* **leaping, leapt** *or* **leaped 1** to jump suddenly from one place to another **2** (often foll. by *at*) to move or react quickly **3** to jump over ▷ *n* **4** the act of jumping **5** an abrupt or important change or increase: *a leap to full European union* **6 a leap in the dark** an action performed without knowledge of the consequences **7 by leaps and bounds** with unexpectedly rapid progress [Old English *hlēapan*]

leapfrog *n* **1** a children's game in which each player in turn leaps over the others' bent backs ▷ *vb* **-frogging, -frogged 2 a** to play leapfrog **b** to leap over (something) **3** to advance by jumps or stages

leap year *n* a calendar year of 366 days, February 29 (**leap day**) being the additional day, that occurs every four years

Lear *n* Edward. 1812–88, English humorist and painter, noted for his illustrated nonsense poems and limericks

learn *vb* **learning, learned** *or* **learnt 1** to gain knowledge (of something) or acquire skill in (some art or practice) **2** to memorize (something) **3** to gain by experience, example, or practice: *I learned everything the hard way* **4** (often foll. by *of* or *about*) to become informed; find out: *Captain Nelson learned of the disaster from his wireless* [Old English *leornian*] **> learnable** *adj* **> learner** *n*

learned (lurn-id) *adj* **1** having great knowledge **2** involving or characterized by scholarship: *your learned paper on the subject*

learning *n* knowledge gained by studying

learning difficulties *pl n* difficulty experienced in reaching the average standard of people of the same age group in intellectual and cognitive skills

lease *n* **1** a contract by which an owner rents buildings or land to another person for a specified period **2 a new lease of life** a prospect of renewed energy, health, or happiness ▷ *vb* **leasing, leased 3** to let or rent (land or buildings) by lease [Old French *laissier* to let go]

leasehold *n* **1** land or property held under a lease **2** the holding of such property under lease **> leaseholder** *n*

leash *n* **1** a dog's lead **2** straining at the leash eagerly impatient to begin something ▷ *vb* **3** to put a leash on [Old French *laissier* to loose (hence to let a dog run on a leash)]

least *adj, adv* **1 the least** the superlative of **little**: *without encountering the least sign of civilization; he is the least well-educated prime minister* ▷ *adj* **2** of very little importance **3** smallest ▷ *adv* **4 at least** if nothing else: *at least I wrote* **5 at the least** at the minimum: *at the very least you should have some self-respect* **6 not in the least** not at all: *you're not detaining me, not in the least* [Old English *lǣst*, superlative of *lǣssa* less]

leastways *or US and Canad* **leastwise** *adv informal* at least; anyway

leather *n* **1** the skin of an animal made smooth and flexible by tanning and removing the hair **2 leathers** leather clothes, esp. as worn by motorcyclists ▷ *adj* **3** made of leather ▷ *vb* **4** to whip as if with a leather strap **5** to dress in leather [Old English *lether-* (in compound words)]

Leatherhead *n* a town in S England, in Surrey. Pop: 42 885 (2001)

leatherjacket *n* **1** any of various tropical fishes having a leathery skin **2** the tough-skinned larva of certain crane flies, which destroy the roots of grasses

leathery *adj* looking or feeling like leather, esp. in toughness

leave¹ *vb* **leaving, left 1** to go away (from a person or place) **2** to cause to remain behind, often by mistake, in a place: *I left the paper under the table* **3** to cause to be or remain in a specified state: *the poll leaves the parties neck-and-neck* **4** to stop attending or belonging to a particular organization or institution: *at seventeen she left the convent* **5** to not eat something or not deal with something: *he left a half-eaten lunch* **6** to result in; cause: I *have been terribly hurt by women, it leaves indelible marks* **7** to allow (someone) to do something without interfering: *the governor left them to it for a further few hours* **8** to be survived by (members of one's family): *he leaves a widow and one daughter* **9** to bequeath: *her adored son left his millions to an unknown half-sister* **10** to have as a remainder: *37 - 14 leaves 23* **11 leave (someone) alone a** to stop annoying (someone) **b** to permit to stay or be alone ▸ See also **leave off, leave out** [Old English *lǣfan*]

leave² *n* **1** permission to be absent, for instance from work: *so I asked for leave* **2** the length of such absence: *weekend leave* **3** permission to do something: *they were refused leave to appeal* **4 on leave** officially excused from work or duty **5 take (one's) leave of** to say farewell to [Old English *lēaf*]

leaven (lev-ven) *n* also: **leavening 1** any substance, such as yeast, that produces fermentation in dough and makes it rise **2** an influence that produces a gradual change ▷ *vb* **3** to cause fermentation in (dough) **4** to spread through, causing a gradual change [Latin *levare* to raise]

Leavenworth *n* a city in NE Kansas, on the Missouri River: the state's oldest city, founded in 1854 by proslavery settlers from Missouri. Pop: 35 211 (2003 est)

leave off *vb* **1** to stop; cease **2** to stop wearing or using

leave out *vb* to omit or exclude: *leave out everything not necessary to living*

leaves *n* the plural of **leaf**

leave-taking *n* a departing; a farewell

leavings *pl n* things left behind unwanted, such as food on a plate

Leavis *n* F(rank) R(aymond). 1895–1978, English literary critic. He edited *Scrutiny* (1932–53) and his books include *The Great Tradition* (1948) and *The Common Pursuit* (1952) ▸ **Leavisite** *adj, n*

Lebanese *adj* **1** of or relating to the Lebanon or its inhabitants ▷ *n, pl* **-nese 2** a native or inhabitant of the Lebanon

Lebanon *n* the Lebanon a republic in W Asia, on the Mediterranean: an important centre of the Phoenician civilization in the third millennium BC; part of the Ottoman Empire from 1516 until 1919; gained independence in 1941 (effective by 1945). Official language: Arabic; French and English are also widely spoken. Religion: Muslim and Christian. Currency: Lebanese pound. Capital: Beirut. Pop: 4 131 583 (2013 est). Area: 10 400 sq km (4015 sq miles)

Lebanon Mountains *pl n* a mountain range in central Lebanon, extending across the whole country parallel with the Mediterranean coast. Highest peak: 3104 m (10 184 ft). Arabic name: **Jebel Liban**

Lebensraum (lay-benz-rowm) *n* territory claimed by a nation or state because it is necessary for survival or growth [German: living space]

Leblanc *n* Nicolas. ?1742–1806, French chemist, who invented a process for the manufacture of soda from common salt

Lebowa *n* a former Bantu homeland in NE South Africa, consisting of three separate territories with several smaller exclaves: abolished in 1993

Lebrun *n* **1** Albert. 1871–1950, French statesman; president (1932–40) **2** Also: *Le Brun* **Charles**. 1619–90, French historical painter. He was court painter to Louis XIV and executed much of the decoration of the palace of Versailles

Le Carré *n* John, real name *David John Cornwell*. born 1931, English novelist, esp. of spy thrillers such as *The Spy who came in from the Cold* (1963), *Tinker, Tailor, Soldier, Spy* (1974), *Smiley's People* (1980), *The Tailor of Panama* (1996), and *The Mission Song* (2006)

Le Cateau *n* a town in NE France: site (August 26, 1914) of the largest British battle since Waterloo, which led to the disruption of the German attack on the Allies. Pop: 6998 (2009)

Lecce *n* a walled city in SE Italy, in Puglia: Greek and Roman remains. Pop: 83 303 (2001)

Lech *n* a river in central Europe, rising in SW Austria and flowing generally north through S Germany to the River Danube. Length: 285 km (177 miles)

lecherous (letch-er-uss) *adj* (of a man) having or showing strong and uncontrolled sexual desire [Old French *lechier* to lick] ▸ **lecher** *n* ▸ **lechery** *n*

lecithin (less-sith-in) *n biochem* a yellow-brown compound found in plant and animal tissues, esp. egg yolk: used in making cosmetics and inks, and as an emulsifier and stabilizer (**E322**) in foods [Greek *lekithos* egg yolk]

Lecky *n* William Edward Hartpole. 1838–1903, Irish historian; author of *The History of England in the 18th Century* (1878–90)

Le Clos *n* Chad. born 1992, South African swimmer; won gold in the 200m butterfly at the 2012 Olympics

Leconte de Lisle *n* Charles Marie René. 1818–94, French Parnassian poet

Le Corbusier *n* real name *Charles Édouard Jeanneret*. 1887–1965, French architect and town planner, born in Switzerland. He is noted for his use of reinforced concrete and for his modular system, which used units of a standard size. His works include Unité d'Habitation at Marseilles (1946–52) and the city of Chandigarh, India (1954)

Le Creusot *n* a town in E central France: metal, machinery, and armaments industries. Pop: 26 283 (1999)

lectern *n* a sloping reading desk, esp. in a church [Latin *legere* to read]

lecture *n* **1** a talk on a particular subject delivered to an audience **2** a lengthy scolding ▷ *vb* **-turing, -tured 3** to deliver a lecture (to an audience or class) **4** to scold (someone) at length [Latin *legere* to read] ▸ **lecturer** *n* ▸ **lectureship** *n*

led *vb* the past of **lead¹**

LED *electronics* light-emitting diode: a semiconductor that gives out light when an electric current is applied to it

Lederberg *n* Joshua. 1925–2008, US geneticist, who discovered the principle of transduction in bacteria. Nobel prize for physiology or medicine 1958 with George Beadle and Edward Tatum

ledge *n* **1** a narrow horizontal surface that projects from a wall or window **2** a narrow shelflike projection on a cliff or mountain [perhaps Middle English *leggen* to lay]

ledger *n accounting* the principal book in which the commercial transactions of a company are recorded [perhaps Middle English *leggen* to lay (because kept in a specific place)]

Ledger *n* Heath(cliffe) Andrew. 1979–2008, Australian film actor. His films include *The Patriot* (2000), *A Knight's Tale* (2001) and *Brokeback Mountain* (2005)

ledger line *n music* a short line above or below the staff used to indicate the pitch of notes higher or lower than the range of the staff

Led Zeppelin *n* British rock group (1968–80); comprised Jimmy Page (born 1944), Robert Plant (born 1948), John Paul Jones (born 1946), and John Bonham (1948–80): recordings include *Led Zeppelin I* (1969), *Led Zeppelin IV* (1971), and *Physical Graffiti* (1975)

lee *n* **1** a sheltered part or side; the side away from the direction from which the wind is blowing ▷ *adj* **2** *nautical* on, at, or towards the side away from the wind: *her lee rail was awash* [Old English *hlēow* shelter]

Lee¹ *n* a river in SW Republic of Ireland, flowing east into Cork Harbour. Length: about 80 km (50 miles)

Lee² *n* **1** Ang. born 1954, Taiwanese film director; his films include *Sense and Sensibility* (1995), *Crouching Tiger, Hidden Dragon* (2000), *Brokeback Mountain* (2005), and *Life of Pi* (2012) **2 Bruce**, original name *Lee Yuen Kam*. 1940–73, US film actor and kung fu expert who starred in such films as *Enter the Dragon* (1973) **3 Gypsy Rose**, original name *Rose Louise Hovick*. 1914–70, US striptease and burlesque artiste, who appeared in the Ziegfeld Follies (1936) and in films **4 Laurie**. 1914–97, British poet and writer, best known for the autobiography *Cider with Rosie* (1959) **5 Richard Henry**. 1732–94, American Revolutionary statesman, who moved the resolution in favour of American independence (1776) **6 Robert E(dward)**. 1807–70, American general; commander-in-chief of the Confederate armies in the Civil War **7 Spike**, real name *Shelton Jackson Lee*. born 1957, US film director: his films include *She's Gotta Have It* (1985), *Malcolm X* (1992), and the documentary *When the Levees Broke: A Requiem in Four Acts* (2008) **8 T(sung)-D(ao)**. born 1926, US physicist, born in China. With Yang he disproved the principle that parity is always conserved and shared the Nobel prize for physics in 1957

leech *n* **1** a worm which has a sucker at each end of the body and feeds on the blood or tissues of other animals **2** a person who lives off another person; parasite [Old English *lǣce*]

Leeds *n* **1** a city in N England, in Leeds unitary authority, West Yorkshire on the River Aire: linked with Liverpool and Goole by canals; a former centre of the clothing industry; two universities (1904, 1992). Pop: 443 247 (2001) **2** a unitary authority in N England, in West Yorkshire. Pop: 715 200 (2003 est). Area: 562 sq km (217 sq miles)

Leeds Castle *n* a castle near Maidstone in Kent: the home of several medieval queens of England

leek *n* a vegetable of the onion family with a slender white bulb and broad flat green overlapping leaves: the national emblem of Wales [Old English *lēac*]

Lee Kuan Yew *n* 1923–2015, Singaporean statesman; prime minister of Singapore 1959–90, during which period his party's authoritarian rule was criticized but the country's economy progressed rapidly

leer *vb* **1** to give a sneering or suggestive look or grin ▷ *n* **2** such a look [Old English *hlēor* cheek]

leery *adj* **leerier, leeriest 1** *slang* (foll. by *of*) suspicious or wary **2** *chiefly dialect* knowing or sly [perhaps obsolete sense (to look askance) of *leer*]

lees *pl n* the sediment from an alcoholic drink [plural of obsolete *lee*, from Old French]

leet *n Scot* a list of candidates for an office [perhaps Anglo-French *litte*, variant of LIST¹]

Leeuwarden *n* a city in the N Netherlands, capital of Friesland province. Pop: 91 000 (2003 est)

Leeuwenhoek *n* Anton van. 1632–1723, Dutch microscopist, whose microscopes enabled him to give the first accurate description of blood corpuscles, spermatozoa, and microbes

leeward 1 *chiefly nautical* ▷ *adj* **2** of, in, or moving in the direction towards which the wind blows ▷ *n* **3** the side towards the lee ▷ *adv* **4** towards the lee

Leeward Islands *pl n* **1** a group of islands in the Caribbean, in the N Lesser Antilles between Puerto Rico and Martinique **2** a former British colony in the E Caribbean (1871–1956), consisting of Antigua, Barbuda, Redonda, Saint Kitts, Nevis, Anguilla, Montserrat, and the British Virgin Islands **3** a group of islands in the S Pacific, in French Polynesia in the W Society Archipelago: Huahiné, Raiatéa, Tahaa, Bora-Bora, and Maupiti. Pop: 30 221 (2002). French name: **Îles sous le Vent**

leeway *n* **1** flexibility of action or expenditure: *he gave me a lot of leeway in the work I did* **2** sideways drift of a boat or aircraft

Le Fanu *n* (Joseph) Sheridan. 1814–73, Irish writer, best known for his stories of mystery and the supernatural, esp. *Uncle Silas* (1864) and the collection *In a Glass Darkly* (1872)

Lefkoşa *n* the Turkish name for **Nicosia**

left¹ *adj* **1** denoting the side of something or someone that faces west when the front is turned towards the north **2** on the left side of the body: *I grabbed it with my left hand* **3** liberal, radical, or socialist ▷ *adv* **4** on or in the direction of the left ▷ *n* **5** a left side, direction, position, area, or part **6 the left** the people in a political party or society who have more socialist or liberal views: *the biggest party of the French Left* **7** *boxing* **a** a blow with the left hand **b** the left hand [Old English: idle, weak]

left² *vb* the past of **leave¹**

Left Bank *n* a district of Paris, on the S bank of the River Seine; frequented by artists, students, etc.

left field *n* **1** *baseball* **a** the area of the outfield to the batter's left **b** the fielder who covers this area **2 out of left field** unexpected or surprising: *Their proposal came out of left field* ▷ *adj* **left-field 3** *US and Canad informal* unconventional or outside the mainstream

left-hand *adj* **1** of, on, or towards the left **2** for the left hand

left-handed *adj* **1** better at using the left hand than the right **2** done with the left hand **3** designed for use by the left hand **4** awkward or clumsy **5** ambiguous or insincere: *a left-handed compliment* **6** turning from right to left; anticlockwise ▷ *adv* **7** with the left hand: *I write left-handed* ▷ **left-hander** *n*

leftist *adj* **1** of or relating to the political left or its principles ▷ *n* **2** a person who supports the political left ▷ **leftism** *n*

left-luggage office *n Brit* a place at a railway station or airport where luggage may be left for a small charge

leftover *n* **1** (*often pl*) an unused portion, esp. of cooked food ▷ *adj* **2** left as an unused portion

leftward *adj, adv* also: **leftwards** on or towards the left

left-wing *adj* **1** socialist or radical: *the party ditched many of its more left-wing policies* **2** belonging to the more radical part of a political party: *a group of left-wing Conservatives* ▷ *n* **left wing 3** (*often caps*) the more radical or progressive section, esp. of a political party: *the Left Wing of the Labour Party* **4** *sport* **a** the left-hand side of the field of play **b** a player positioned in this area in certain games ▷ **left-winger** *n*

lefty *n, pl* **lefties** *informal* **1** *Brit, Austral and NZ* a left-winger **2** *chiefly US and Canad* a left-handed person

leg *n* **1** either of the two lower limbs in humans, or any similar structure in animals, that is used for movement or support **2** the part of a garment that covers the leg **3** a lower limb of an animal, esp. the thigh, used for food: *leg of lamb* **4** something similar to a leg in appearance or function, such as one of the supports of a chair **5** a section of a journey **6** a single stage, lap, or length in a relay race **7** one of a series of games, matches, or parts of games **8** *cricket* the side of the field to the left of a right-handed batsman as he faces the bowler **9 not have a leg to stand on** *informal* to have no reasonable basis for an opinion or argument **10 on one's last legs** worn out or exhausted **11 to pull someone's leg** *informal* to tease or make fun of someone **12 shake a leg** *informal* to hurry up **13 stretch one's legs** to stand up or walk around, esp. after sitting for some time ▷ *vb* **legging, legged 14 leg it** *informal* to walk, run, or hurry [Old Norse *leggr*]

legacy *n, pl* **-cies 1** money or personal property left to someone by a will **2** something handed down to a successor [Medieval Latin *legatia* commission]

legal *adj* **1** established by or permitted by law; lawful **2** of or relating to law **3** relating to or characteristic of lawyers [Latin *legalis*] ▷ **legally** *adv*

legal aid *n* financial assistance available to people who are unable to meet the full cost of legal proceedings

legalese *n* the conventional language in which legal documents are written

legalism *n* strict adherence to the letter of the law ▷ **legalist** *n, adj* ▷ **legalistic** *adj*

legality *n, pl* **-ties** the state or quality of being legal or lawful

legalize *or* **-lise** *vb* **-lizing, -lized** *or* **-lising, -lised** to make lawful or legal › **legalization** or **-lisation** n

legal tender n currency that a creditor must by law accept to pay a debt

Legaspi n a port in the Philippines, on SE Luzon on the Gulf of Albay. Pop: 178 000 (2005 est)

legate n a messenger, esp. one representing the Pope [Latin *legare* to delegate]

legatee n the recipient of a legacy

legation n 1 a diplomatic mission headed by a minister 2 the official residence and office of a diplomatic minister

legato (leg-ah-toe) *music adv* 1 smoothly and evenly ▷ n, pl **-tos** 2 a style of playing with no gaps between notes [Italian]

leg before wicket n *cricket* a dismissal on the grounds that a batsman has been struck on the leg by a bowled ball that otherwise would have hit the wicket. Abbreviation: **lbw**

leg break n *cricket* a bowled ball that spins from leg to off on pitching

leg bye n *cricket* a run scored after the ball has hit the batsman's leg or some other part of his body, except his hand, without touching the bat. Abbreviation: **lb**

legend n 1 a popular story handed down from earlier times which may or may not be true 2 such stories collectively 3 a person whose fame makes him or her seem exceptional: *he is a living legend* 4 modern stories about a famous person which may or may not be true: *no Garland fan could complain about sordid revelations tarnishing the legend* 5 words written on something to explain it: *a pub mirror spelling out the legend 'Saloon Bar'* 6 an explanation on a table, map, or chart, of the symbols used [Medieval Latin *legenda* passages to be read]

legendary adj 1 very famous: *the legendary beauty of the Alps* 2 of or relating to legend 3 described in legend: *the legendary birthplace of Aphrodite*

Legendre n Adrien Marie. 1752–1833, French mathematician, noted for his work on the theory of numbers, the theory of elliptical functions, and the method of least squares

Léger n Fernand. 1881–1955, French cubist painter, influenced by industrial technology

legerdemain (lej-er-de-main) n 1 same as **sleight of hand** 2 cunning deception [Old French: light of hand]

leger line n same as **ledger line**

leggings pl n 1 an extra outer covering for the lower legs 2 close-fitting trousers for women or children

leggy adj 1 having unusually long legs 2 (of a plant) having a long weak stem

leghorn n 1 a type of Italian wheat straw that is woven into hats 2 any hat made from this straw [English name for *Livorno*, in Italy]

Leghorn n 1 the English name for **Livorno** 2 a breed of domestic fowl laying white eggs

legible adj (of handwriting) able to be read [Latin *legere* to read] › **legibility** n › **legibly** adv

legion n 1 any large military force: *the French Foreign Legion* 2 (often pl) any very large number 3 an infantry unit in the ancient Roman army of three to six thousand men 4 an association of veterans [Latin *legio*] › **legionary** adj, n

legionnaire n (often cap) a member of a legion

Legionnaire's disease n a serious bacterial infection, with symptoms similar to pneumonia [after the outbreak at a meeting of the American Legion in Philadelphia in 1976]

legislate vb **-lating, -lated** 1 to make or pass laws 2 to bring into effect by legislation [Latin *lex, legis* law + *latus*, past participle of *ferre* to bring] › **legislator** n

legislation n 1 the act or process of making laws 2 the laws so made

legislative adj 1 of or relating to the process of making laws 2 having the power or function of making laws: *the election to Singapore's new legislative assembly*

legislature n a body of people authorized to make, amend, and repeal laws

legitimate adj 1 authorized by or in accordance with law: *legitimate accounting practices* 2 based on correct or acceptable principles of reasoning: *a legitimate argument* 3 (of a child) born of parents legally married to each other 4 of, relating to, or ruling by hereditary right: *under their legitimate ruling house* 5 of or relating to serious drama as distinct from films, television, or vaudeville ▷ vb **-mating, -mated** 6 to make, pronounce, or show to be legitimate [Medieval Latin *legitimatus* made legal] › **legitimacy** n › **legitimately** adv

legitimize or **-mise** vb **-mizing, -mized** or **-mising, -mised** to make legitimate; legalize › **legitimization** or **-misation** n

legless adj 1 without legs 2 *slang* very drunk

Legnica n an industrial town in SW Poland. Pop: 105 025 (2007 est). German name: **Liegnitz**

Lego n *trademark* a construction toy consisting of plastic bricks and other components that fit together [Danish *leg godt* play well]

leg-pull n *Brit informal* a practical joke

legroom n space to move one's legs comfortably, as in a car

leguaan n a large amphibious S African lizard [Dutch, from French *l'iguane* the iguana]

legume n 1 the pod of a plant of the pea or bean family 2 the seed from such pods, esp. beans or peas [Latin *legere* to pick (a crop)]

leguminous adj of or relating to any family of flowering plants having pods (or legumes) as fruits

Lehár n Franz. 1870–1948, Hungarian composer of operettas, esp. *The Merry Widow* (1905)

Le Havre n a port in N France, on the English Channel at the mouth of the River Seine: transatlantic trade; oil refining. Pop: 185 311 (2006)

Lehmann n 1 Lilli. 1848–1929, German soprano 2 Lotte. 1888–1976, US soprano, born in Germany 3 Rosamond (Nina). 1903–90, British novelist. Her books include *Dusty Answer* (1927), *Invitation to the Waltz* (1932), and *The Echoing Grove* (1953)

Lehmbruck n Wilhelm. 1881–1919, German sculptor and graphic artist

lei n (in Hawaii) a garland of flowers, worn around the neck [Hawaiian]

Leibnitz or **Leibniz** n Baron Gottfried Wilhelm von. 1646–1716, German rationalist philosopher and mathematician. He conceived of the universe as a hierarchy of independent units or monads, synchronized by pre-established harmony. His works include *Théodicée* (1710) and *Monadologia* (1714). He also devised a system of calculus, independently of Newton › **Leib'nitzian** adj

Leibniz Mountains pl n a mountain range on the SW limb of the moon, containing the highest peaks (10 000 metres) on the moon

Leibovitz n Annie. born 1949, US photographer, known for her portraits of celebrities

Leicester[1] n 1 a city in central England, in Leicester unitary authority, on the River Soar: administrative centre of Leicestershire: Roman remains and a ruined Norman castle; two universities (1957, 1992); light engineering, hosiery, and footwear industries. Pop: 283 900 (2003 est) 2 a unitary authority in central England, in Leicestershire. Pop: 330 574 (2001). Area: 73 sq km (28 sq miles) 3 short for **Leicestershire** 4 a breed of sheep with long wool, originally from Leicestershire 5 a fairly mild dark orange whole-milk cheese, similar to Cheddar

Leicester[2] n Earl of. title of *Robert Dudley*. ?1532–88, English courtier; favourite of Elizabeth I. He led an unsuccessful expedition to the Netherlands (1585–87)

Leicestershire n a county of central England: absorbed the small historical county of Rutland in 1974; Rutland

and Leicester city became independent unitary authorities in 1997: largely agricultural. Administrative centre: Leicester. Pop (excluding Leicester city): 619 200 (2003 est). Area (excluding Leicester city): 2084 sq km (804 sq miles). Shortened form: **Leicester**. Abbreviation: **Leics**

Leichhardt *n* Friedrich Wilhelm Ludwig. 1813–48, Australian explorer, born in Prussia. He disappeared during an attempt to cross Australia from East to West

Leics Leicestershire

Leiden *or* **Leyden** *n* a city in the W Netherlands, in South Holland province: residence of the Pilgrim Fathers for 11 years before they sailed for America in 1620; university (1575). Pop: 118 000 (2003 est)

Leigh[1] *n* a town in NW England, in Wigan unitary authority, Greater Manchester: engineering industries. Pop: 43 006 (2001)

Leigh[2] *n* **1** Mike. born 1943, British dramatist and theatre, film, and television director, noted for his use of improvisation. His plays include *Abigail's Party* (1977), and his films include *High Hopes* (1988), *Secrets and Lies* (1996), *Vera Drake* (2004), and *Happy-Go-Lucky* (2008) **2** Vivien, real name Vivian Hartley. 1913–67, English stage and film actress. Her films include *Gone with the Wind* (1939) and *A Streetcar Named Desire* (1951), for both of which she won Oscars

Leighton *n* Frederic, 1st Baron Leighton of Stretton. 1830–96, British painter and sculptor of classical subjects: president of the Royal Academy (1878)

Leinster *n* a province of E and SE Republic of Ireland: it consists of the counties of Carlow, Dublin, Kildare, Kilkenny, Laois, Longford, Louth, Meath, Offaly, Westmeath, Wexford, and Wicklow. Pop: 2 105 579 (2002). Area: 19 632 sq km (7580 sq miles)

Leipzig *n* a city in E central Germany, in Saxony: famous fairs, begun about 1170; publishing and music centre; university (1409); scene of a decisive defeat for Napoleon Bonaparte in 1813. Pop: 497 531 (2003 est)

Leiria *n* a city in central Portugal: site of the first printing press in Portugal (1466). Pop: 119 870 (2001)

leisure *n* **1** time or opportunity for relaxation or hobbies **2 at leisure a** having free time **b** not occupied **3 at one's leisure** when one has free time [Old French *leisir*] ▷ **leisured** *adj*

leisure centre *n* a building providing facilities, such as a swimming pool, gym, and café, for a range of leisure pursuits

leisurely *adj* **1** unhurried; relaxed ▷ *adv* **2** in a relaxed way ▷ **leisureliness** *n*

Leith *n* a port in SE Scotland, on the Firth of Forth: part of Edinburgh since 1920

leitmotif *or* **leitmotiv** (lite-mote-eef) *n* **1** *music* a recurring melodic phrase used to suggest a character, thing, or idea **2** an often repeated image in a literary work [German: leading motif]

Leitrim *n* a county of N Republic of Ireland in Connacht province, on Donegal Bay: agricultural. County town: Carrick-on-Shannon. Pop: 25 799 (2002). Area: 1525 sq km (589 sq miles)

Leix *n* another name for Laois

Leizhou Peninsula *or* **Luichow Peninsula** *n* a peninsula of SE China, in SW Guangdong province, separated from Hainan Island by Hainan Strait

lekgotla (leh-hot-luh) *or* **kgotla** (hot-luh) *n* S African **1** a meeting place for village assemblies, court cases, and meetings of village leaders **2** a conference or business meeting [Sotho, Tswana]

lekker *adj* S African slang pleasing, enjoyable, or tasty [Afrikaans, from Dutch]

Lely *n* Sir Peter. Dutch name *Pieter van der Faes*. 1618–80, Dutch portrait painter in England

Lemaître *n* Abbé Georges (Édouard). 1894–1966, Belgian astronomer and priest, who first proposed the big-bang theory of the universe (1927)

Lemalu *n* Jonathan (Fa'afetai). born 1976, New Zealand singer of Samoan descent; a bass-baritone noted esp. for his lieder recitals

Léman *n* Lac Léman the French name for (Lake) **Geneva**

Le Mans *n* a city in NW France: scene of the first experiments in motoring and flying; annual motor race. Pop: 148 169 (2006)

Lemberg *n* the German name for Lvov

lemming *n* **1** a small rodent of northern and arctic regions, reputed to rush into the sea in large groups and drown **2** a member of any group following an unthinking course towards destruction [Norwegian]

Lemnian *adj* **1** of or relating to Lemnos or its inhabitants ▷ *n* **2** a native or inhabitant of Lemnos

Lemnos *n* a Greek island in the N Aegean Sea: famous for its medicinal earth (**Lemnian seal**). Chief town: Kastron. Pop: 18 104 (2001). Area: 477 sq km (184 sq miles). Modern Greek name: **Límnos**

lemon *n* **1 a** a yellow oval edible fruit with juicy acidic flesh that grows on an evergreen tree in warm and tropical regions **2** *slang* a person or thing considered to be useless or defective ▷ *adj* **3** light yellow [Arabic *laymūn*] ▷ **lemony** *adj*

lemonade *n* a drink made from lemon juice, sugar, and water, or from carbonated water, citric acid, and sweetener

lemon sole *n* an edible European flatfish

Lemper *n* Ute. born 1963, German singer and actress, noted esp. for her performances of songs by Kurt Weill

lemur *n* a nocturnal animal, related to the monkey, with a foxy face and long tail, found on Madagascar [Latin *lemures* ghosts]

Lena *n* a river in Russia, rising in S Siberia and flowing generally north through the Sakha Republic to the Laptev Sea by an extensive delta: the longest river in Russia. Length: 4271 km (2653 miles)

lend *vb* **lending, lent** **1** to permit the temporary use of **2** to provide (money) temporarily, often at interest **3** to contribute (some abstract quality): *a painted trellis lends a classical air to any garden* **4** **lend an ear** to listen **5 lend oneself** *or* **itself** to be appropriate for: *the building lends itself to loft conversion* [Old English *lēnan*] ▷ **lender** *n*

Lendl *n* Ivan. born 1960, Czech tennis player and coach; won eight Grand Slam singles titles (1984–90)

Lenglen *n* Suzanne. 1899–1938, French tennis player: Wimbledon champion (1919-25)

length *n* **1** the extent or measurement of something from end to end **2** a specified distance, esp. between two positions: *the length of a cricket-pitch* **3** a period of time, as between specified limits or moments **4** the quality, state, or fact of being long rather than short **5** a piece of something, usually longer than it is wide: *a length of twine* **6** (usually pl) the amount of trouble taken in doing something: *to go to great lengths* **7** *prosody, phonetics* the duration of a vowel or syllable **8 at length a** after a long interval or period of time **b** in great detail [Old English *lengthu*]

lengthen *vb* to make or become longer

lengthways *or* **lengthwise** *adv, adj* in, according to, or along the direction of length

lengthy *adj* **lengthier, lengthiest** very long or tiresome ▷ **lengthily** *adv* ▷ **lengthiness** *n*

lenient (lee-nee-ent) *adj* tolerant, not strict or severe [Latin *lenis* soft] ▷ **leniency** *n* ▷ **leniently** *adv*

Lenin *n* Vladimir Ilyich, original surname Ulyanov. 1870–1924, Russian statesman and Marxist theoretician; first premier of the Soviet Union. He formed the Bolsheviks (1903) and led them in the October Revolution (1917), which established the Soviet Government. He adopted the New Economic Policy (1921) after the Civil War had led to the virtual collapse of the Russian economy, formed the Comintern (1919), and was the originator of the guiding doctrine of the Soviet Union, Marxism-Leninism. After the Soviet

Union broke up in 1991, many statues of Lenin were demolished

Leninabad *n* the former name (1937–91) of **Khojent**

Leninakan *n* the former name (1925–91) of **Kumayri**

Leningrad *n* the former name (1937–91) of **Saint Petersburg**

Lenin Peak *n* a mountain on the border of Kyrgyzstan and Tajikistan; the highest peak in the Trans Alai Range. Height: 7134 m (23 406 ft)

lenity *n, pl* **-ties** mercy or clemency

Lennon *n* John (Ono), original name *John Winston Lennon*. 1940–80, English rock guitarist, singer, and songwriter: member of the Beatles (1962–70). His subsequent recordings, many in collaboration with his wife Yoko Ono, include "Instant Karma" (1970), *Imagine* (1971), and *Double Fantasy* (1980). He was shot dead in front of his home in New York City

Leno *n* Dan, original name *George Galvin*. 1860–1904, British music-hall entertainer, noted esp. for his pantomime performances: he died insane

Le Nôtre *n* André. 1613–1700, French landscape gardener, who created the gardens at Versailles for Louis XIV

lens *n* **1** a piece of glass or other transparent material with a curved surface or surfaces, used to bring together or spread rays of light passing through it: used in cameras, telescopes, and spectacles **2** *anatomy* a transparent structure in the eye, behind the iris, that focuses images on the retina [Latin: lentil]

Lens *n* an industrial town in N France, in the Pas de Calais department; badly damaged in both World Wars. Pop: 36 257 (2006)

lent *vb* the past of **lend**

Lent *n* *Christianity* the period from Ash Wednesday to Easter Saturday, during which some Christians give up doing something they enjoy [Old English *lencten, lengten* spring, literally: lengthening (of hours of daylight)]
> **Lenten** *adj*

lentil *n* any of the small edible seeds of a leguminous Asian plant [Latin *lens*]

lento *music adv* **1** slowly ▷ *n, pl* **-tos** **2** a movement or passage performed slowly [Italian]

Lenya *n* Lotte, original name *Caroline Blamauer*. 1900–81, Austrian singer and actress, associated esp. with the songs of her husband Kurt Weill

Leo *n* *astrol* the fifth sign of the zodiac; the Lion [Latin]

Leo I *n* Saint, known as *Leo the Great*. ?390–461 AD, pope (440–461). He extended the authority of the papacy in the West and persuaded Attila not to attack Rome (452). Feast day: Nov 10 or Feb 18

Leo III *n* **1** called *the Isaurian*. ?675–741 AD, Byzantine emperor (717–41): he checked Arab expansionism and began the policy of iconoclasm, which divided the empire for the next century **2** Saint. ?750–816 AD, pope (795–816). He crowned Charlemagne emperor of the Romans (800). Feast day: June 12

Leo IX *n* Saint, original name *Bruno of Egisheim*. 1002–54, pope (1049–54): first of the great medieval reforming popes. Conflict with the Eastern Church led to the schism between Rome and Constantinople (1054). Feast day: April 19

Leo X *n* original name *Giovanni de' Medici*. 1475–1521, pope (1513–21): noted for his patronage of Renaissance art and learning; excommunicated Luther (1521)

Leo XIII *n* original name *Gioacchino Pecci*. 1810–1903, pope (1878–1903). His many important encyclicals include *Rerum novarum* (1891) on the need for Roman Catholics to take action on various social problems

Leoben *n* a city in E central Austria, in Styria on the Mur River: lignite mining. Pop: 25 804 (2001)

León *n* **1** a region and former kingdom of NW Spain, which united with Castile in 1230 **2** a city of NW Spain: capital of the kingdom of León (10th century). Pop: 135 634 (2003 est) **3** a city in central Mexico, in W Guanajuato state: commercial centre of a rich

agricultural region. Pop: 1 438 000 (2005 est). Official name: **León de los Aldamas 4** a city in W Nicaragua: one of the oldest towns of Central America, founded in 1524; capital of Nicaragua until 1855; university (1812). Pop: 168 000 (2005 est)

Leonard *n* **1** Sugar Ray, real name *Ray Charles Leonard*. born 1956, US boxer: the first man to have won world titles at five officially recognized weights **2** Elmore. 1925–2013, US novelist and screenwriter, noted for westerns and thrillers. His works include *3:10 to Yuma* (filmed 1957, 2007), *Get Shorty* (1990; filmed 1996), and *Rum Punch* (1992) filmed as *Jackie Brown* (1997) by Quentin Tarantino

Leonardo da Vinci *n* 1452–1519, Italian painter, sculptor, architect, and engineer: the most versatile talent of the Italian Renaissance. His most famous paintings include *The Virgin of the Rocks* (1483–85), the *Mona Lisa* (or *La Gioconda*, 1503), and the *Last Supper* (?1495–97). His numerous drawings, combining scientific precision in observation with intense imaginative power, reflect the breadth of his interests, which ranged over biology, physiology, hydraulics, and aeronautics. He invented the first armoured tank and foresaw the invention of aircraft and submarines
> **Leonardesque** *adj*

Leoncavallo *n* Ruggiero. 1858–1919, Italian composer of operas, notably I *Pagliacci* (1892)

Leonidas *n* died 480 BC, king of Sparta (?490–480), hero of the Battle of Thermopylae, in which he was killed by the Persians under Xerxes

leonine *adj* of or like a lion [Latin *leo* lion]

Leonine *adj* **1** connected with one of the popes called Leo **2** Leonine City a district of Rome on the right bank of the Tiber fortified by Pope Leo IV **3** of or relating to certain prayers in the Mass prescribed by Pope Leo XIII ▷ *n* **4** Also called: **Leonine verse a** a type of medieval hexameter or elegiac verse having internal rhyme **b** a type of English verse with internal rhyme

Leonov *n* Aleksei Arkhipovich. born 1934, Soviet cosmonaut; the first man to walk in space (1965)

leopard *or fem* **leopardess** *n* a large African and Asian mammal of the cat family, which has a tawny yellow coat with black spots. Also called: **panther** [Greek *leōn* lion + *pardos* panther]

Leopardi *n* Count Giacomo. 1798–1837, Italian poet and philosopher, noted esp. for his lyrics, collected in I *Canti* (1831)

Leopold I *n* **1** 1640–1705, Holy Roman Emperor (1658–1705). His reign was marked by wars with Louis XIV of France and with the Turks **2** 1790–1865, first king of the Belgians (1831–65)

Leopold II *n* **1** 1747–92, Holy Roman Emperor (1790–92). He formed an alliance with Prussia against France (1792) after the downfall of his brother-in-law Louis XVI **2** 1835–1909, king of the Belgians (1865–1909); son of Leopold I. He financed Stanley's explorations in Africa, becoming first sovereign of the Congo Free State (1885)

Leopold III *n* 1901–83, king of the Belgians (1934–51); son of Albert I. His surrender to the Nazis (1940) forced his eventual abdication in favour of his son, Baudouin

Léopoldville *n* the former name (until 1966) of **Kinshasa**

leotard *n* a tight-fitting garment covering the body from the shoulders to the thighs and worn by acrobats, ballet dancers, and people doing exercises [after Jules *Léotard*, acrobat]

Lepanto *n* **1** a port in W Greece, between the Gulfs of Corinth and Patras: scene of a naval battle (1571) in which the Turkish fleet was defeated by the fleets of the Holy League. Pop (municipality): 18 259 (2001). Greek name: **Návpaktos 2** Gulf of Lepanto another name for the (Gulf of) **Corinth**

Lepaya *n* a variant spelling of **Liepāja**

Le Pen *n* **1** Jean-Marie. born 1928, French politician; leader of the extreme right-wing Front National

(1972–2011); runner-up in the presidential election of 2002 **2** his daughter **Marine**. born 1968, French politician: leader of the Front National from 2011

leper *n* **1** *offensive* a person who has leprosy **2** a person who is avoided [Greek *lepros* scaly]

> **USAGE** The use of *leper* can be offensive and should be avoided. Instead you should talk about *a person with leprosy*.

lepidopteran *n*, *pl* **-terans** *or* **-tera 1** an insect that has two pairs of fragile wings and develops from a caterpillar; a butterfly or moth ▷ *adj* also: **lepidopterous 2** denoting such an insect [Greek *lepis* scale + *pteron* wing]

lepidopterist *n* a person who studies or collects moths and butterflies

Lepidus *n* Marcus Aemilius. died ?13 BC, Roman statesman: formed the Second Triumvirate with Octavian (later Augustus) and Mark Antony

Lepontine Alps *pl n* a range of the S central Alps, in S Switzerland and N Italy. Highest peak: Monte Leone, 3553 m (11 657 ft)

Leppard *n* Raymond. born 1927, British conductor and musicologist, in the US from 1977: noted esp. for his revivals of early opera

leprechaun *n* (in Irish folklore) a mischievous elf [Irish Gaelic *leipreachān*]

leprosy *n pathol* a chronic infectious disease, characterized by painful inflamed lumps beneath the skin and disfigurement and wasting away of affected parts ▷ **leprous** *adj*

lepton *n physics* any of a group of elementary particles with weak interactions [Greek *leptos* thin]

Lérida *n* a city in NE Spain, in Catalonia: commercial centre of an agricultural region. Pop: 118 035 (2003 est). Catalan name: **Lleida**

Lermontov *n* Mikhail Yurievich. 1814–41, Russian novelist and poet: noted esp. for the novel *A Hero of Our Time* (1840)

Lerner *n* Alan Jay. 1914–86, US songwriter and librettist. With Frederick Loewe he wrote *My Fair Lady* (1956) and *Camelot* (1960) as well as a number of film scripts, including *Gigi* (1958)

Lerwick *n* a town in Shetland, administrative centre of the island authority of Shetland, on the island of Mainland: the most northerly town in the British Isles; knitwear, oil refining. Pop: 6830 (2001)

Le Sage *or* **Lesage** *n* Alain-René. 1668–1747, French novelist and dramatist, author of the picaresque novel *Gil Blas* (1715–35)

lesbian *n* **1** a female homosexual ▷ *adj* **2** of or characteristic of lesbians [from LESBOS] ▷ **lesbianism** *n*

Lesbos *n* an island in the E Aegean, off the NW coast of Turkey: a centre of lyric poetry, led by Alcaeus and Sappho (6th century BC); annexed to Greece in 1913. Chief town: Mytilene. Pop: 90 642 (2001). Area: 1630 sq km (630 sq miles). Modern Greek name: **Lésvos**. Former name: **Mytilene**

Les Cayes *n* a port in SW Haiti, on the S Tiburon Peninsula. Pop: 45 904 (1995). Also called: **Cayes**. Former name: **Aux Cayes**

lese-majesty (lezz-maj-ist-ee) *n* **1** an offence against the sovereign power in a state; treason **2** an act of disrespect towards authority [from Latin *laesa majestas* wounded majesty]

lesion *n* **1** any structural change in an organ or tissue resulting from injury or disease **2** an injury or wound [Late Latin *laesio* injury]

Lesotho *n* a kingdom in southern Africa, forming an enclave in the Republic of South Africa: annexed to British Cape Colony in 1871; made a protectorate in 1884; gained independence in 1966; a member of the Commonwealth. It is generally mountainous, with temperate grasslands throughout. Languages: Sesotho

and English. Religion: Christian majority. Currency: loti and South African rand. Capital: Maseru. Pop: 1 936 181 (2013 est). Area: 30 344 sq km (11 716 sq miles). Former name (1884–1966): **Basutoland**

less *adj* **1** the comparative of **little**: *less fibre* **2** *not standard* fewer ▷ *adv* **3** the comparative of **little**: *eat less* **4** **less of** to a smaller extent or degree: *it would become less of a problem* **5** **no less** *sometimes humorous* used to indicate admiration or surprise: *sculpted by a famous Frenchman, Rodin no less* ▷ *prep* **6** minus: *a two pounds-a-week rise (less tax)* [Old English *lǣssa, lǣs*]

> **USAGE** *Less* should not be confused with *fewer*. *Less* refers strictly only to quantity and not to number: *there is less water than before. Fewer* means smaller in number: *there are fewer people than before.*

lessee *n* a person to whom a lease is granted [Old French *lesser* to lease]

lessen *vb* to make or become less

lesser *adj* not as great in quantity, size, or worth

Lesser Antilles *pl n* the Lesser Antilles a group of islands in the Caribbean, including the Leeward Islands, the Windward Islands, Barbados, and the Netherlands Antilles. Formerly called: **the Caribbees**

Lesser Sunda Islands *pl n* the English name of **Nusa Tenggara**

Lessing *n* **1** Doris (May). 1919–2013, English novelist and short-story writer, brought up in Rhodesia: her novels include the five-novel sequence *Children of Violence* (1952–69), *The Golden Notebook* (1962), a series of science-fiction works (1979–83), *The Good Terrorist* (1985), and *The Sweetest Dream* (2001). Nobel prize for literature 2007 **2** Gotthold Ephraim. 1729–81, German dramatist and critic. His plays include *Miss Sara Sampson* (1755), the first German domestic tragedy, and *Nathan der Weise* (1779). He is noted for his criticism of French classical dramatists, and for his treatise on aesthetics *Laokoon* (1766)

lesson *n* **1 a** a single period of instruction in a subject **b** the content of such a period **2** material assigned for individual study **3** something from which useful knowledge or principles can be learned: *one could still learn an important lesson from these masters* **4** an experience that serves as a warning or example: *the experience will prove a sobering lesson for the military* **5** a passage of Scripture read during a church service [Old French *leçon*]

lessor *n* a person who grants a lease of property

lest *conj* **1** so as to prevent any possibility that: *one grabbed it lest a neighbour got there first* **2** for fear that: *his anxiety lest anything mar the family event* [Old English *thy lǣs the*, literally: whereby less that]

Lésvos *n* transliteration of the Modern Greek name for **Lesbos**

let¹ *vb* **letting, let 1** to allow: *a child lets a friend play with his favourite toy* **2 a** an auxiliary expressing a request, proposal, or command, or conveying a warning or threat: *well, let's try it; just let me catch you here again!* **b** an auxiliary expressing an assumption or hypothesis: *let 'a' equal 'b'* **c** an auxiliary used to convey resigned acceptance of the inevitable: *let the worst happen* **3** to allow someone to rent (property or accommodation) **4** to cause the movement of (something) in a specified direction: *he let air out of the tyre* **5** **let alone** not to mention: *I could hardly think, let alone find words to say* **6** **let alone** *or* **be** stop annoying or interfering with: *let the poor cat alone* **7** **let go** to relax one's hold (on) **8** **let loose a** to allow (a person or animal) to leave or escape **b** *informal* to make (a sound) suddenly: *he let loose a laugh* **c** *informal* to fire (ammunition) from a gun ▷ *n* **9** *Brit and Austral* the act of letting property or accommodation ▶ See also **let down**, **let off**, etc. [Old English *lǣtan* to permit]

let² *n* **1** *tennis, squash* a minor infringement or obstruction of the ball, requiring a point to be replayed **2 without let or hindrance** without obstruction [Old English *lettan* to hinder]

Letchworth *n* a town in SE England, in N Hertfordshire: the first garden city in Great Britain (founded in 1903). Pop: 32 932 (2001)

let down *vb* **1** to fail to satisfy the expectations of (someone); disappoint **2** to lower **3** to lengthen a garment by decreasing the hem **4** to deflate: *to let down a tyre* ▷ *n* **letdown 5** a disappointment

lethal *adj* capable of causing death [Latin *letum* death] > **lethally** *adv*

lethargy *n*, *pl* -**gies 1** sluggishness or dullness **2** an abnormal lack of energy [Greek *lēthargos* drowsy] > **lethargic** *adj* > **lethargically** *adv*

Lethbridge *n* a city in Canada, in S Alberta. Pop: 67 374 (2001)

let off *vb* **1** to excuse from (work or duties): *I'll let you off homework for a week* **2** to spare (someone) the expected punishment: *lots were let off because they couldn't be bothered to prosecute anybody* **3** to explode or fire (a bomb, gun, or firework) **4** to release (liquid, air, or steam)

let on *vb informal* **1** to reveal (a secret) **2** to pretend: *he let on that he was a pilgrim*

let out *vb* **1** to emit: *he let out a scream* **2** to allow to leave; release **3** to make (property) available for people to rent **4** to make (a garment) wider by reducing the seams **5** to reveal (a secret) ▷ *n* **let-out 6** a chance to escape

letter *n* **1** a written or printed message, usually enclosed in an envelope and sent by post **2** any of a set of conventional symbols used in writing or printing a language: character of the alphabet **3** the strict meaning of an agreement or document; exact wording: *the letter of the law* **4 to the letter** precisely: *you have to follow treatment to the letter for it to be effective* ▷ *vb* **5** to write or mark letters on (a sign) [Latin *littera* letter of the alphabet] > **lettering** *n*

letter bomb *n* an explosive device in an envelope or parcel that explodes when the envelope or parcel is opened

letter box *n chiefly Brit* **1** a slot in a door through which letters are delivered **2** Also called: **pillar box, postbox** a public box into which letters and postcards are put for collection

lettered *adj* **1** well educated **2** printed or marked with letters

letterhead *n* a printed heading on stationery giving the name and address of the sender

letter of credit *n* a letter issued by a bank entitling the bearer to draw money from other banks

letterpress *n* a method of printing in which ink is transferred from raised surfaces to paper by pressure

letters *pl n* **1** literary knowledge or ability: *a man of letters* **2** literary culture in general

letters patent *pl n* See **patent** (3)

lettuce *n* a plant cultivated for its large edible leaves, which are used in salads [Latin *lactuca*, from *lac* milk, because of its milky juice]

let up *vb* **1** to diminish or stop **2** (foll. by *on*) *informal* to be less harsh (towards someone) ▷ *n* **let-up 3** *informal* a lessening: *there has been no let-up in the war*

Leucas *n* a variant spelling of **Leukas**

Leucippus *n* 5th century BC Greek philosopher, who originated the atomist theory of matter, developed by his disciple, Democritus

leucocyte (loo-koh-site) *n* any of the various large white cells in the blood of vertebrates [Greek *leukos* white + *kutos* vessel]

Leuctra *n* an ancient town in Greece southwest of Thebes in Boeotia: site of a victory of Thebes over Sparta (371BC), which marked the end of Spartan military supremacy in Greece

leukaemia *or especially US* **leukemia** (loo-kee-mee-a) *n* an acute or chronic disease characterized by extreme overproduction of white blood cells [Greek *leukos* white + *haima* blood]

Leukas *or* **Leucas** *n* another name for **Levkás**

Leuven *n* the Flemish name for **Louvain**

Levant *n* the **Levant** a former name for the area of the E Mediterranean now occupied by Lebanon, Syria, and Israel [C15: from Old French, from the present participle of *lever* to raise (referring to the rising of the sun in the east), from Latin *levāre*]

Levantine *adj* **1** of or relating to the Levant ▷ *n* **2** (esp. formerly) an inhabitant of the Levant

levee[1] *n US* **1** a natural or artificial river embankment **2** a quay [French, from Latin *levare* to raise]

levee[2] *n* a formal reception held by a sovereign just after rising from bed [French, from Latin *levare* to raise]

level *adj* **1** on a horizontal plane **2** having an even surface **3** being of the same height as something else: *the floor of the lean-to was level with the patio* **4** equal to or even with (something or someone else): *Johnson was level with the overnight leader* **5** not exceeding the upper edge of (a spoon etc.) **6** consistent or regular: *a level pulse* **7** one's level best the best one can do ▷ *vb* **-velling, -velled** *or US* **-veling, -veled 8** (sometimes foll. by *off*) to make horizontal or even **9** to make equal in position or status **10** to direct (an accusation or criticism) emphatically at someone **11** to focus (a look) directly at someone **12** to aim (a weapon) horizontally **13** to demolish completely ▷ *n* **14** a horizontal line or plane **15** a device, such as a spirit level, for determining whether a surface is horizontal **16** position or status in a scale of values: *a high-level delegation* **17** stage or degree of progress: *primary school level* **18** a specified vertical position: *floor level* **19** the topmost horizontal line or plane from which the height of something is calculated: *sea level* **20** a flat even surface or area of land **21** a degree or intensity reached on a measurable or notional scale: *noise level* **22 on the level** *informal* sincere or genuine [Latin *libella*, diminutive of *libra* scales]

level crossing *n Brit, Austral and NZ* a point at which a railway line and a road cross

level-headed *adj* calm and sensible

Leven *n* **Loch Leven 1** a lake in E central Scotland: one of the shallowest of Scottish lochs, with seven islands, on one of which Mary, Queen of Scots was imprisoned (1567–8). Length: 6 km (3.7 miles). Width: 4 km (2.5 miles) **2** a sea loch in W Scotland, extending for about 14 km (9 miles) east from Loch Linnhe

lever *n* **1** a handle used to operate machinery **2** a bar used to move a heavy object or to prise something open **3** a rigid bar that turns on a fixed support (fulcrum) to transfer effort and motion, for instance to move a load **4** a means of exerting pressure in order to achieve an aim: *using the hostages as a lever to gain concessions from the west* ▷ *vb* **5** to open or move with a lever [Latin *levare* to raise]

leverage *n* **1** the mechanical advantage gained by using a lever **2** the ability to influence people or events: *information gives leverage*

leveraged buyout *n* a takeover bid in which a small company uses its assets, and those of the target company, to raise the loans required to finance the takeover

leveret (lev-ver-it) *n* a young hare [Latin *lepus* hare]

Leverhulme *n* William Hesketh, 1st Viscount. 1851–1925, English soap manufacturer and philanthropist, who founded (1881) the model industrial town Port Sunlight

Leverkusen *n* a town in NW Germany, in North Rhine-Westphalia on the Rhine: chemical industries. Pop: 161 543 (2003 est)

Leverrier *n* Urbain Jean Joseph. 1811–77, French astronomer: calculated the existence and position of the planet Neptune

Levi *n* **1 Carlo.** 1902–75, Italian physician, painter, and writer. Best known for his novel *Christ Stopped at Eboli* (1947), his other works include *The Watch* (1952) and *Words*

are Stones (1958) **2 Primo.** 1919–87, Italian novelist. His book *If This is a Man* (1947) relates his experiences in Auschwitz. Other books include *The Periodic Table* (1956) and *The Drowned and the Saved* (1988), published after his suicide

leviathan (lev-vie-ath-an) *n* any huge or powerful thing [Hebrew *liwyāthān*, a Biblical sea monster]

Levis *pl n trademark* denim jeans

Lévi-Strauss *n* Claude. (1908–2009) French anthropologist, leading exponent of structuralism. His books include *The Elementary Structures of Kinship* (1969), *Totemism* (1962), *The Savage Mind* (1966), *Mythologies* (1964–71), and *Saudades do Brazil* (Memories of Brazil; 1994)

levitate *vb* **-tating, -tated** to rise or cause to rise, suspended, in the air [Latin *levis* light] ▸ **levitation** *n*

levity *n, pl* **-ties** a frivolous or too light-hearted attitude to serious matters [Latin *levis* light]

Levkás, Leukas *or* **Leucas** *n* a Greek island in the Ionian Sea, in the Ionian Islands. Pop: 20 751 (2001). Area: 295 sq km (114 sq miles). Italian name: **Santa Maura**

Levkosia *or* **Leukosia** *n* the Greek name for **Nicosia**

levy (lev-vee) *vb* **levies, levying, levied 1** to impose and collect (a tax, tariff, or fine) **2** to conscript troops for service ▷ *n, pl* **levies 3 a** the imposition and collection of taxes, tariffs, or fines **b** the money so raised **4** troops conscripted for service [Latin *levare* to raise]

Lévy-Bruhl *n* Lucien. 1857–1939, French anthropologist and philosopher, noted for his study of the psychology of primitive peoples

lewd *adj* indecently vulgar; obscene [Old English *lǣwde* lay, ignorant] ▸ **lewdly** *adv* ▸ **lewdness** *n*

Lewes *n* a market town in S England, administrative centre of East Sussex, on the River Ouse: site of a battle (1264) in which Henry III was defeated by Simon de Montfort. Pop: 15 988 (2001)

Lewis¹ *n* the N part of the island of Lewis with Harris, in the Outer Hebrides. Pop: about 17 000 (2001). Area: 1634 sq km (631 sq miles)

Lewis² *n* **1** Carl. full name *Frederick Carleton Lewis*. born 1961, US athlete; winner of the long jump, 100 metres, 200 metres, and 4 × 100 metres relay at the 1984 Olympic Games; winner of the 100 metres in the 1988 Olympic Games; winner of the long jump in the 1992 and 1996 Olympic Games **2** See **Day-Lewis 3** C(live) S(taples). 1898–1963, English novelist, critic, and Christian apologist, noted for his critical work, *Allegory of Love* (1936), his theological study, *The Screwtape Letters* (1942), and for his children's books chronicling the land of Narnia **4** Lennox. born 1965, Canadian and British boxer; won Olympic gold (1988) for Canada in the superheavyweight division; won various professional heavyweight titles between 1994 and 2004 **5 Matthew Gregory**, known as *Monk Lewis*. 1775–1818, English novelist and dramatist, noted for his Gothic horror story *The Monk* (1796) **6** Meriwether. 1774–1807, American explorer who, with William Clark, led an overland expedition from St Louis to the Pacific Ocean (1804–06) **7** (John) Saunders. 1893–1985, Welsh poet, dramatist, critic, and politician: founder (1926) and president (1926–39) of the Welsh Nationalist Party **8** (Harry) Sinclair. 1885–1951, US novelist. He satirized the complacency and philistinism of American small-town life, esp. in *Main Street* (1920) and *Babbitt* (1922): Nobel prize for literature 1930 **9 Wally.** born 1959, Australian rugby league player; played 33 matches for Australia (1981–91), scoring 11 tries **10** (Percy) Wyndham. 1884–1957, British painter, novelist, and critic, born in the US: a founder of vorticism. His writings include *Time and Western Man* (1927), *The Apes of God* (1930), and the trilogy *The Human Age* (1928–55)

Lewisham *n* a borough of S Greater London, on the River Thames. Pop: 248 300 (2003 est). Area: 35 sq km (13 sq miles)

Lewis with Harris *or* **Lewis and Harris** *n* an island in the Outer Hebrides, separated from the NW coast of Scotland by the Minch: consists of Lewis in the north and Harris in the south; many lakes and peat moors; economy based chiefly on the Harris tweed industry, with some fishing. Chief town: Stornoway. Pop: 19 918 (2001). Area: 2134 sq km (824 sq miles)

lexical *adj* **1** relating to the vocabulary of a language **2** relating to a lexicon ▸ **lexically** *adv*

lexicography *n* the process or profession of compiling dictionaries ▸ **lexicographer** *n*

lexicon *n* **1** a dictionary, esp. one of an ancient language such as Greek **2** the vocabulary of a language or of an individual [Greek *lexis* word]

Lexington *n* **1** a city in NE central Kentucky, in the bluegrass region: major centre for horse-breeding. Pop (including Fayette): 266 798 (2003 est) **2** a city in Massachusetts, northwest of Boston: site of the first action (1775) of the War of American Independence. Pop: 30 631 (2003 est)

ley *n* land temporarily under grass [variant of *lea*]

Leyden *n* a variant spelling of **Leiden**

Leyden jar (lide-en) *n physics* an early type of capacitor consisting of a glass jar with the lower part of the inside and outside coated with tinfoil [from *Leiden*, city in the Netherlands]

Leyte *n* an island in the central Philippines, in the Visayan Islands. Chief town: Tacloban. Pop: 1 592 336 (2000). Area: 7215 sq km (2786 sq miles)

Leyte Gulf *n* an inlet of the Pacific in the E Philippines, east of Leyte and south of Samar: scene of a battle (Oct 23–26, 1944) during World War II, in which the Americans defeated almost the entire Japanese navy, thereby ensuring ultimate Allied victory

LGBT lesbian, gay, bisexual, and transgender

LGBTI lesbian, gay, bisexual, transgender, and intersex

LGV (in Britain) large goods vehicle

Lhasa *or* **Lassa** *n* a city in SW China, capital of Tibet, at an altitude of 3606 m (11 830 ft): for centuries the sacred city of Lamaism and residence of the Dalai Lamas from the 17th century until 1950: known as the Forbidden City because it was closed to Westerners until the beginning of the 20th century; annexed by China in 1951. The Dalai Lama fled after an unsuccessful revolt against Chinese rule in 1959. Pop: 131 000 (2005 est)

Li *chem* lithium

LI 1 Long Island **2** Light Infantry

liability *n, pl* **-ties 1** someone or something that is a problem or embarrassment **2** the state of being legally responsible **3** (*often pl*) sums of money owed by an organization

liable *adj* **1** probable or likely: *weak and liable to give way* **2** commonly suffering a condition: *he's liable to colds in the chest* **3** legally obliged or responsible; answerable [Old French *lier* to bind]

> **USAGE** The use of *liable to* to mean *probable or likely* was formerly considered incorrect, but is now acceptable.

liaise *vb* **-aising, -aised** (usually foll. by *with*) to communicate and maintain contact with

liaison *n* **1** communication and cooperative contact between groups **2** a secretive or adulterous sexual relationship [Old French *lier* to bind]

Liákoura *n* a transliteration of the Modern Greek name for (Mount) **Parnassus**

liana *n* a woody climbing and twining plant of tropical forests [French]

Lianyungang, Sinhailien *or* **Hsin-hai-lien** *n* a city in E China, near the coast of Jiangsu. Pop: 645 000 (2005 est)

Liao *n* a river in NE China, rising in SE Inner Mongolia and flowing northeast then southwest to the Gulf of Liaodong. Length: about 1100 km (700 miles)

Liaodong *or* **Liaotung** *n* **1** Liaodong Peninsula a peninsula of NE China, in S Manchuria extending south into the Yellow Sea: forms the S part of Liaoning province **2** Gulf of Liaodong the N part of the Gulf of Chihli, west of the Liaodong Peninsula

Liaoning *n* a province of NE China, in S Manchuria. Capital: Shenyang. Pop: 42 100 000 (2003 est). Area: 150 000 sq km (58 500 sq miles)

Liaoyang *n* a city in NE China, in S Manchuria, in Liaoning province: a regional capital in the early dynasties. Pop: 752 000 (2005 est)

liar *n* a person who tells lies

Liard *n* a river in W Canada, rising in the SE Yukon and flowing east and then northwest to the Mackenzie River. Length: 885 km (550 miles)

lib *n informal* liberation: used in the name of certain movements: *women's lib; gay lib*

Lib *Brit, Austral and S African politics* Liberal

libation (lie-bay-shun) *n* **a** the pouring out of wine in honour of a deity **b** the wine so poured out [Latin *libare* to pour an offering of drink]

Libau *n* the German name for **Liepāja**

Libava *n* transliteration of the Russian name for **Liepāja**

Libby *n* Willard Frank. 1908–80, US chemist, who devised the technique of radiocarbon dating: Nobel prize for chemistry 1960

libel *n* **1** *law* the publication of something false which damages a person's reputation **2** any damaging or unflattering representation or statement ▷ *vb* **-belling, -belled** *or US* **-beling, -beled 3** *law* to make or publish a false damaging statement or representation about (a person) [Latin *libellus* a little book] **> libellous** *or US* **libelous** *adj*

liberal *adj* **1** having social and political views that favour progress and reform **2** generous in temperament or behaviour **3** tolerant of other people **4** using or existing in large quantities; lavish: *the world's finest gadgetry, in liberal quantities* **5** not rigid; free: *a more liberal interpretation* **6** (of an education) designed to develop general cultural interests and intellectual ability **7** Liberal of or relating to a Liberal Party ▷ *n* **8** a person who has liberal ideas or opinions [Latin *liber* free] **> liberalism** *n* **> liberally** *adv*

Liberal Democrat *n* a member or supporter of the Liberal Democrats, a British centrist political party that advocates proportional representation

liberality *n, pl* **-ties 1** generosity **2** the quality of being broad-minded

liberalize *or* **-lise** *vb* **-lizing, -lized** *or* **-lising, -ised** to make (a law) less strict **> liberalization** *or* **-lisation** *n*

Liberal Party *n* **1** *history* a British non-Socialist political party which advocated progress and reform **2** any similar party in various other countries **3** the main right-wing political party in Australia

liberate *vb* **-rating, -rated 1** to free (someone) from social prejudices or injustices **2** to give liberty to; make free **3** to release (a country) from enemy occupation **> liberation** *n* **> liberator** *n*

liberated *adj* **1** not bound by traditional sexual and social roles: *a liberated woman* **2** given liberty **3** released from enemy occupation

Liberec *n* a city in the N Czech Republic, on the Neisse River: a centre of the German Sudeten movement in 1938. Pop: 97 000 (2005 est). German name: **Reichenberg**

Liberia *n* a republic in W Africa, on the Atlantic: originated in 1822 as a home for freed Afro-American slaves, with land purchased by the American Colonization Society; republic declared in 1847; exports are predominantly rubber and iron ore. Official language: English. Religion: Christian majority, also animist. Currency: dollar. Capital: Monrovia. Pop: 3 989 703 (2013 est). Area: 111 400 sq km (43 000 sq miles)

Liberian *adj* **1** of or relating to Liberia or its inhabitants ▷ *n* **2** a native or inhabitant of Liberia

libertarian *n* **1** a person who believes in freedom of thought and action ▷ *adj* **2** believing in freedom of thought and action

libertine (lib-er-teen) *n* **1** a person who is promiscuous and unscrupulous ▷ *adj* **2** promiscuous and unscrupulous [Latin *libertus* freed]

liberty *n, pl* **-ties 1** the freedom to choose, think, and act for oneself **2** the right of unrestricted movement and access; freedom **3** (*often pl*) a social action regarded as being forward or improper **4** at liberty free or unconfined **5** at liberty to unrestricted or authorized: *I am not at liberty to divulge his name* **6** take liberties (with) to be overfamiliar (towards someone) [Latin *libertas*]

Liberty Island *n* a small island in upper New York Bay: site of the Statue of Liberty. Area: 5 hectares (12 acres). Former name (until 1956): **Bedloe's Island**

Libeskind *n* Daniel. born 1946, US architect, born in Poland. Based in Berlin, he designed the Jewish Museum there (1999), the Imperial War Museum in Manchester (2000), and the "Freedom Tower" that will replace the World Trade Center in New York

Libia *n* the Italian name for **Libya**

libidinous *adj* characterized by excessive sexual desire **> libidinously** *adv*

libido (lib-ee-doe) *n, pl* **-dos 1** *psychoanalysis* psychic energy from the id **2** sexual urge or desire [Latin: desire] **> libidinal** *adj*

Libra *n astrol* the seventh sign of the zodiac; the Scales [Latin]

librarian *n* a person in charge of or assisting in a library **> librarianship** *n*

library *n, pl* **-braries 1** a room or building where books and other literary materials are kept **2** a collection of literary materials, films, tapes, or records, kept for borrowing or reference **3** the building or institution that houses such a collection **4** a set of books published as a series, often in a similar format **5** *computers* a collection of standard programs, usually stored on disk [Latin *liber* book]

libretto *n, pl* **-tos** *or* **-ti** a text written for an opera [Italian: little book] **> librettist** *n*

Libreville *n* the capital of Gabon, in the west on the estuary of the Gabon River: founded as a French trading post in 1843 and expanded with the settlement of freed slaves in 1848. Pop: 649 000 (2005 est)

Libya *n* a republic in N Africa, on the Mediterranean: became an Italian colony in 1912; divided after World War II into Tripolitania and Cyrenaica (under British administration) and Fezzan (under French); gained independence in 1951; monarchy overthrown by a military junta led by Colonel Gaddafi in 1969; Gaddafi's authoritarian regime overthrown in 2011 following a popular uprising. It consists almost wholly of desert and is a major exporter of oil. Official language: Arabic. Official religion: (Sunni) Muslim. Currency: Libyan dinar. Capital: Tripoli. Pop: 6 002 347 (2013 est). Area: 1 760 000 sq km (680 000 sq miles). Official name: Dawlat Libya

Libyan *adj* **1** of or relating to Libya or its inhabitants ▷ *n* **2** a native or inhabitant of Libya

Libyan Desert *n* a desert in N Africa, in E Libya, W Egypt, and the NW Sudan: the NE part of the Sahara

lice *n* the plural of **louse**

licence *or US* **license** *n* **1** a document giving official permission to do, use, or own something **2** formal permission or exemption **3** intentional disregard of conventional rules to achieve a certain effect: *poetic licence* **4** excessive freedom [Latin *licet* it is allowed]

license *vb* **-censing, -censed 1** to grant a licence to or for **2** to give permission to or for **> licensable** *adj*

licensee *n* a person who holds a licence, esp. one to sell alcoholic drink

license plate *n* the US and Canadian term for **numberplate**

licentiate *n* a person who holds a certificate of

competence to practise a certain profession

licentious *adj* sexually unrestrained or promiscuous [Latin *licentia* licence] **> licentiousness** *n*

lichee *n* same as lychee

lichen *n* any of various small mossy plants that grow in patches on tree trunks, bare ground, rocks, and stone walls [Greek *leikhein* to lick]

Lichfield *n* a city in central England, in SE Staffordshire: cathedral with three spires (13th-14th century); birthplace of Samuel Johnson, during whose lifetime the **Lichfield Group** (a literary circle) flourished. Pop: 28 435 (2001)

lich gate *n* same as lych gate

Lichtenstein *n* Roy. 1923–97, US pop artist

licit *adj formal* lawful; permitted [Latin *licere* to be permitted]

lick *vb* **1** to pass the tongue over in order to taste, wet, or clean **2** to flicker over or round (something): *flames licked the gutters* **3** *informal* **a** to defeat **b** to thrash **4 lick into shape** to put into a satisfactory condition **5 lick one's wounds** to retire after a defeat ▷ *n* **6** an instance of passing the tongue over something **7** a small amount: *a lick of paint* **8** *informal* a blow **9** *informal* a fast pace: *a pulsating rhythm taken at a lick* **10 a lick and a promise** something hastily done, esp. a hurried wash [Old English *liccian*]

licorice *n US and Canad* same as liquorice

lid *n* **1** a removable or hinged cover: *a saucepan lid* **2** short for **eyelid 3 put the (tin) lid on** *informal* to put an end to [Old English *hlid*] **> lidded** *adj*

Liddell Hart *n* Sir Basil Henry. 1895–1970, British military strategist and historian: he advocated the development of mechanized warfare before World War II

Lidice *n* a mining village in the Czech Republic: destroyed by the Germans in 1942 in reprisal for the assassination of Reinhard Heydrich; rebuilt as a national memorial

lido (lee-doe) *n, pl* **-dos** *Brit* an open-air swimming pool or a part of a beach used by the public for swimming and sunbathing [*Lido*, island bathing beach near Venice]

lie¹ *vb* **lying, lied 1** to speak untruthfully with the intention of deceiving **2** to convey a false impression: *the camera cannot lie* ▷ *n* **3** an untrue statement deliberately used to mislead **4** something that is deliberately intended to deceive **5 give the lie to a** to disprove **b** to accuse of lying [Old English *lyge, lēogan*]

lie² *vb* **lying, lay, lain 1** (often foll. by *down*) to place oneself or be in a horizontal position **2** to be situated: *I left the money lying on the table; Nepal became the only country lying between China and India* **3** to be and remain (in a particular state or condition): *others of their species lie asleep* **4** to stretch or extend: *an enormous task lies ahead* **5** (usually foll. by *in*) to exist or comprise: *her charm lies in her inner beauty* **6** (foll. by *with*) to rest (with): *the fault lies with them* ▷ *n* **7** the manner, place, or style in which something is situated **8** an animal's lair **9 lie of the land** the way in which a situation is developing ▶ See also lie down, lie in [Old English *licgan*]

USAGE See at lay¹.

Lie *n* Trygve Halvdan. 1896–1968, Norwegian statesman; first secretary-general of the United Nations (1946–52)

Liebfraumilch (leeb-frow-milk) *n* a sweet white wine from the German Rhine [German: from *Liebfrau* the Virgin Mary + *Milch* milk]

Liebig *n* Justus, Baron von Liebig. 1803–73, German chemist, who founded agricultural chemistry. He also contributed to organic chemistry, esp. to the concept of radicals, and discovered chloroform

Liebknecht *n* **1** Karl. 1871–1919, German socialist leader: with Rosa Luxemburg he led an unsuccessful Communist revolt (1919) and was assassinated **2** his

father, **Wilhelm**. 1826–1900, German socialist leader and journalist, a founder (1869) of what was to become (1891) the German Social Democratic Party

Liechtenstein *n* a small mountainous principality in central Europe on the Rhine: formed in 1719 by the uniting of the lordships of Schellenberg and Vaduz, which had been purchased by the Austrian family of Liechtenstein; customs union formed with Switzerland in 1924. Official language: German. Religion: Roman Catholic majority. Currency: Swiss franc. Capital: Vaduz. Pop: 37 009 (2003 est). Area: 160 sq km (62 sq miles)

Liechtensteiner *n* **1** a native or inhabitant of Liechtenstein ▷ *adj* **2** of or relating to Liechtenstein or its inhabitants

lied (leed) *n, pl* **lieder** *music* a musical setting for solo voice and piano of a romantic or lyrical poem [German: song]

lie detector *n informal* a device used to measure any increase in blood pressure, pulse rate, etc., of someone being questioned, which is thought to indicate that the person is lying

lie down *vb* **1** to place oneself or be in a horizontal position in order to rest **2** to yield to: *never take any attack on your candidate lying down* ▷ *n* **lie-down 3** a rest

liege (leej) *adj* **1** (of a lord) owed feudal allegiance: *their liege lord* **2** (of a vassal or subject) owing feudal allegiance: *a liege subject* **3** faithful; loyal ▷ *n* **4** a liege lord **5** a subject [Old French *lige*]

Liège *n* **1** a province of E Belgium: formerly a principality of the Holy Roman Empire, much larger than the present-day province. Pop: 1 029 605 (2004 est). Area: 3877 sq km (1497 sq miles) **2** a city in E Belgium, capital of Liège province: the largest French-speaking city in Belgium; river port and industrial centre. Pop: 185 488 (2004 est) ▶ Flemish name: **Luik**

Liegnitz *n* the German name for Legnica

lie in *vb* **1** to remain in bed late into the morning ▷ *n* **lie-in 2** a long stay in bed in the morning

lien *n law* a right to retain possession of someone else's property until a debt is paid [Latin *ligamen* bond]

Liepāja or **Lepaya** *n* a port in W Latvia on the Baltic Sea; founded by the Teutonic Knights in 1263: a naval and industrial centre, with a fishing fleet. Pop: 86 985 (2002 est). Russian name: **Libava**. German name: **Libau**

Liestal *n* a city in NW Switzerland, capital of Basel-Land demicanton. Pop: 12 930 (2000)

Lietuva *n* the Lithuanian name for Lithuania

lieu (lyew) *n* **in lieu of** instead of [Old French]

Lieut. lieutenant

lieutenant (lef-ten-ant, *US* loo-ten-ant) *n* **1** a junior officer in the army, navy, or the US police force **2** a person who acts as principal assistant [Old French, literally: place-holding] **> lieutenancy** *n*

lieutenant colonel *n* an officer in an army, air force, or marine corps immediately junior to a colonel

lieutenant commander *n* an officer in a navy immediately junior to a commander

lieutenant general *n* a senior officer in an army, air force, or marine corps

lieutenant governor *n* **1** a deputy governor **2** (in Canada) the representative of the Crown in a province

Lifar *n* Serge. 1905–86, Russian ballet dancer and choreographer: ballet master at the Paris Opera Ballet (1932–58). His ballets include *Prométhée* (1929), *Icare* (1935), and *Phèdre* (1950)

life *n, pl* **lives 1** the state or quality that identifies living beings, characterized chiefly by growth, reproduction, and response to stimuli **2** the period between birth and death or between birth and the present time **3** a living person or being: *riots which claimed 22 lives* **4** the remainder or extent of one's life: *with that lady for the rest of her life* **5** the process of living: *rituals gave his life stability* **6** *informal* a sentence of life imprisonment, usually approximating to fifteen years **7** a characteristic state or mode of existence: *country life is best* **8** the length of time that something is active or functioning: *the life of a battery* **9** a present condition or mode of existence: *they are leading a joyous life* **10** a biography **11** the sum or course of human events and activities **12** liveliness or high spirits: *full of life* **13** a source of strength, animation, or vitality: *he was the life of the show* **14** all living things collectively: *there is no life on Mars; marine life* **15** a matter of life and death a matter of extreme urgency **16 as large as life** *informal* real and living **17 not on your life** *informal* certainly not **18 to the life** (of a copy of a painting or drawing) resembling the original exactly **19 true to life** faithful to reality [Old English *līf*]

life assurance *n* insurance that provides for a sum of money to be paid to the insured person at a certain age, or to the spouse or children on the death of the insured. Also called: **life insurance**

life belt *n* an inflatable ring used to keep a person afloat when in danger of drowning

lifeblood *n* **1** the blood vital to life **2** something that is essential for existence, development, or success

lifeboat *n* a boat used for rescuing people at sea

life buoy *n* a buoyant device to keep people afloat in an emergency

life coach *n* a person whose job it is to improve the quality of his or her client's life, by offering advice on professional and personal matters, such as careers, health, personal relationships, etc.

life cycle *n* the series of changes occurring in each generation of an animal or plant

lifeguard *n* a person at a beach or pool whose job is to rescue people in danger of drowning

life jacket *n* an inflatable sleeveless jacket worn to keep a person afloat when in danger of drowning

lifeless *adj* **1** inanimate; dead **2** lacking liveliness or animation **3** unconscious

lifelike *adj* closely resembling or representing life

lifeline *n* **1** a single means of contact or support on which a person or an area relies **2** a rope used for life-saving

lifelong *adj* lasting for a lifetime

life peer *n Brit* a peer whose title ceases at his or her death

life preserver *n* **1** *Brit* a bludgeon kept for self-defence **2** *US and Canad* a life belt or life jacket

lifer *n informal* a prisoner sentenced to life imprisonment

life raft *n* a raft for emergency use at sea

life-saver *n* **1** same as **lifeguard 2** *informal* a person or thing that gives help in time of need **> life-saving** *adj, n*

life science *n* any of the sciences concerned with the structure and behaviour of living organisms, such as biology, botany, or zoology

life-size *or* **life-sized** *adj* representing actual size

lifestyle *n* a set of attitudes, habits, and possessions regarded as typical of a particular group or an individual

life-support *adj* (of equipment or treatment) necessary to sustain life

lifetime *n* **1** the length of time a person is alive **2 of a lifetime** (of an opportunity or experience) the most important or memorable

Liffey *n* a river in E Republic of Ireland, rising in the Wicklow Mountains and flowing west, then northeast through Dublin into Dublin Bay. Length: 80 km (50 miles)

Lifford *n* the county town of Donegal, Republic of Ireland; market town. Pop: 1395 (2002)

lift *vb* **1** to rise or raise upwards to a higher place: *the breakdown truck was lifting the lorry* **2** to move upwards: *he slowly lifted his hand* **3** to raise in status or estimation: *lifted from poverty* **4** to revoke or cancel: *the government lifted its restrictions on imported beef* **5** to remove (plants or underground crops) from the ground for harvesting **6** to disappear or disperse: *the tension lifted* **7** *informal* to plagiarize (music or writing) **> n 8 a** a compartment raised or lowered in a vertical shaft to transport people

or goods to another floor in a building **b** See **chairlift, ski lift 9** a ride in a car or other vehicle as a passenger **10** a rise in morale or feeling of cheerfulness **11** the act of lifting **12** the force that lifts airborne objects [from Old Norse]

liftoff *n* the initial movement of a rocket as it leaves its launch pad

lig *Brit slang n* **1** (esp. in the media) a function with free entertainment and refreshments **> vb ligging, ligged 2** to attend such a function **> ligger** *n* **> ligging** *n*

ligament *n anatomy* a band of tough tissue that connects various bones or cartilage [Latin *ligare* to bind]

ligature *n* **1** a link, bond, or tie **2** *printing* a character of two or more joined letters, such as ff **3** *music* a slur or the group of notes connected by it **> vb -turing, -tured 4** to bind with a ligature [Latin *ligare* to bind]

Ligeti *n* György. 1923–2006, Hungarian composer, resident in Vienna. His works, noted for their experimentalism, include *Atmosphères* (1961) for orchestra, *Volumina* (1962) for organ, and a requiem mass (1965)

light[1] *n* **1** the natural medium, electromagnetic radiation, that makes sight possible **2** anything that illuminates, such as a lamp or candle **3** See **traffic light 4** a particular type of light: *dim yellow light* **5 a** daylight **b** daybreak; dawn **6** anything that lets in light, such as a window **7** an aspect or view: *we have seen the world in a new light* **8** mental understanding or spiritual insight: *suddenly he saw the light* **9** an outstanding person: *a leading light of the movement* **10** brightness of countenance, esp. a sparkle in the eyes **11 a** something that ignites, such as a spark or flame **b** something used for igniting, such as a match **12** See **lighthouse 13 come to light** to become known or visible **14 in (the) light of** taking into account **15 see the light** to understand **16 see the light (of day) a** to come into being **b** to come to public notice **> adj 17** full of light **18** (of a colour) pale: *light blue* **> vb lighting, lighted** *or* **lit 19** to ignite **20** (often foll. by *up*) to illuminate or cause to illuminate **21** to guide by light **▸** See also **light up** [Old English *lēoht*] **> lightish** *adj*

light[2] *adj* **1** not heavy; weighing relatively little **2** relatively low in density, strength, amount, degree, etc.: *light oil; light alloy* **3** lacking sufficient weight **4** not bulky or clumsy: *light bedclothes* **5** not serious or difficult to understand; entertaining: *light music* **6** graceful or agile: *light movements* **7** without strong emphasis or serious meaning: *he gazed about with a light inattentive smile* **8** easily digested: *a light lunch* **9** relatively low in alcohol: *a light wine* **10** without burdens, difficulties, or problems: *a light heart lives longest* **11** dizzy or unclear: *a light head* **12** (of bread or cake) spongy or well risen **13 a** (of transport) designed to carry light loads **b** (of a vessel, aircraft, or other transport) not loaded **c** carrying light arms or equipment: *light infantry* **15** (of an industry) producing small consumer goods using light machinery **16 make light of** to treat as insignificant or unimportant **> adv 17** with little equipment or luggage: *travelling light* **> vb lighting, lighted** *or* **lit 18** (esp. of birds) to settle or land after flight **19** (foll. by *on* or *upon*) to discover by chance **▸** See also **lights** [Old English *lēoht*] **> lightish** *adj* **> lightly** *adv* **> lightness** *n*

light bulb *n* a hollow rounded glass fitting containing a gas and a thin metal filament that gives out light when an electric current is passed through it

lighten[1] *vb* **1** to make less dark **2** to shine; glow **3** (of lightning) to flash

lighten[2] *vb* **1** to make or become less heavy **2** to make or become less burdensome **3** to make or become more cheerful or lively

lighter[1] *n* a small portable device for lighting cigarettes, etc.

lighter[2] *n* a flat-bottomed barge used in loading or unloading a ship [probably from Middle Dutch]

light-fingered *adj* skilful at thieving, esp. by picking pockets

light flyweight *n* a professional boxer weighing up to 108 pounds (49 kg) or an amateur boxer weighing up to 48 kg

Lightfoot *n* Gordon. born 1938, Canadian singer and songwriter; his recordings include 'If You Could Read My Mind' (1970), *Dream Street Rose* (1980) and *Harmony* (2004)

light-footed *adj* having a light tread

light-headed *adj* giddy; feeling faint

light-hearted *adj* cheerful or carefree in mood or disposition ➤ **light-heartedly** *adv*

light heavyweight *n* a professional boxer weighing up to 175 pounds (79.5 kg) or an amateur weighing up to 81 kg

lighthouse *n* a tower with a light to guide ships and warn of obstructions

lighting *n* 1 the apparatus for and design of artificial light effects to a stage, film, or television set 2 the act or quality of illumination

lighting-up time *n* the time when vehicles are required by law to have their lights on

light middleweight *n* a professional boxer weighing up to 154 pounds (70 kg) or an amateur boxer weighing up to 71 kg

lightning *n* 1 a flash of light in the sky caused by a discharge of electricity ▷ *adj* 2 fast and sudden: *a lightning attack* [variant of *lightening*]

lightning conductor *or* **lightning rod** *n* a metal rod attached to the highest part of a building to divert lightning safely to earth

light pen *n* a penlike photoelectric device that in conjunction with a computer can be used to draw lines or identify symbols on a VDU screen

light pollution *n* the glow from the lighting in streets and buildings that obscures the night sky

light rail *n* a transport system using small trains or trams

lights *pl n* the lungs of sheep, bullocks, and pigs, used for feeding pets [because of the light weight of the lungs]

lightship *n* a moored ship equipped as a lighthouse

lights out *n* the time when residents of an institution are expected to retire to bed

light up *vb* 1 to illuminate 2 to make or become cheerful or animated: *their faces lit up and one dug the other in the ribs* 3 to light a cigarette or pipe

lightweight *adj* 1 not serious 2 of relatively light weight ▷ *n* 3 *informal* a person of little importance or influence 4 a person or animal of relatively light weight 5 a professional boxer weighing up to 135 pounds (61 kg) or an amateur weighing up to 60 kg

light welterweight *n* a professional or an amateur boxer weighing up to 140 pounds (63.5 kg)

light year *n* *astronomy* the distance travelled by light in one mean solar year, i.e. 9.4607×10^{15} metres

ligneous *adj* of or like wood [Latin *lignum* wood]

lignite (lig-nite) *n* a brown sedimentary rock with a woody texture: used as a fuel

lignum vitae (lig-num vite-ee) *n* a tropical American tree with heavy resinous wood [Late Latin, literally: wood of life]

Liguria *n* a region of NW Italy, on the **Ligurian Sea** (an arm of the Mediterranean): the third smallest of the regions of Italy. Pop: 1 572 197 (2003 est). Area: 5410 sq km (2089 sq miles)

Ligurian *adj* 1 of or relating to Liguria or its inhabitants ▷ *n* 2 a native or inhabitant of Liguria

Likasi *n* a city in the S Democratic Republic of Congo: a centre of copper and cobalt production. Pop: 345 000 (2005 est). Former name: **Jadotville**

like¹ *adj* 1 resembling ▷ *prep* 2 in the manner of; similar to: *she was like a child; it looks like a traffic cone* 3 such as: *a modern material, like carbon fibre* 4 characteristic of ▷ *adv* 5 in the manner of: *cheering like mad* 6 *dialect* likely ▷ *conj* 7 *not standard* as though; as if: *I don't want to make it seem like*

I had this bad childhood 8 in the same way that: *she doesn't dance like you do* ▷ *n* 9 the equal or counterpart of a person or thing 10 the like similar things: *magic, supernormal powers and the like* 11 the likes *or* like of people or things similar to (someone or something specified): *the theatre was not meant for the likes of him* [Old English *gelīc*]

USAGE The use of *like* to mean *such as* was formerly thought to be undesirable in formal writing, but has now become acceptable. It was also thought that *as* rather than *like* should be used to mean *in the same way that*, but now both *as* and *like* are acceptable: *they hunt and catch fish as/like their ancestors used to.* The use of *look like* and *seem like* before a clause, although very common, is thought by many people to be incorrect or non-standard: *it looks as though he won't come* (not *it looks like he won't come*).

like² *vb* **liking, liked** 1 to find enjoyable 2 to be fond of 3 to prefer or choose: *I'd like to go home* 4 to feel disposed or inclined; choose; wish: *do as you like* ▷ *n* 5 (*usually pl*) a favourable feeling, desire, or preference: *tell me your likes and dislikes* [Old English *līcian*] ➤ **likeable** *or* **likable** *adj*

likelihood *n* chance; probability

likely *adj* 1 tending or inclined: *likely to win* 2 probable: *the likely effects of the tunnel* 3 appropriate for a purpose or activity: *a likely candidate* ▷ *adv* 4 probably or presumably 5 not likely *informal* definitely not [Old Norse *līkligr*]

USAGE *Likely* as an adverb is preceded by another, intensifying adverb, as in *it will very likely rain* or *it will most likely rain*. Its use without an intensifier, as in *it will likely rain*, is regarded as unacceptable by most users of British English, though it is common in colloquial US English.

like-minded *adj* sharing similar opinions

liken *vb* to compare

likeness *n* 1 resemblance 2 portrait 3 an imitative appearance; semblance: *in the likeness of a dragon*

likewise *adv* 1 in addition; also 2 similarly

liking *n* 1 fondness 2 what one likes or prefers: *if it's not to your liking, do let me know*

lilac *n* 1 a small tree with large sprays of purple or white sweet-smelling flowers ▷ *adj* 2 pale purple [Persian *nīlak* bluish]

Lilburn *n* Douglas (Gordon). 1915–2001, New Zealand composer; noted esp. for his pioneering use of electronic music in combination with more traditional orchestration

Lilburne *n* John. ?1614-57, English Puritan pamphleteer and leader of the Levellers, a radical group prominent during the Civil War

Lilienthal *n* Otto. 1848–96, German aeronautical engineer, a pioneer of glider design

Liliuokalani *n* Lydia Kamekeha. 1838–1917, queen and last sovereign of the Hawaiian Islands (1891–95)

Lille *n* an industrial city in N France: the medieval capital of Flanders; forms with Roubaix and Tourcoing one of the largest conurbations in France. Pop: 232 432 (2006)

Lille Bælt *n* the Danish name for the **Little Belt**

Lillee *n* Dennis (Keith). born 1949, Australian cricketer; a fast bowler, he took 355 wickets in 70 test matches (1971–84)

Lilliputian (lil-lip-pew-shun) *n* 1 a tiny person or being ▷ *adj* 2 tiny; very small [from *Lilliput*, an imaginary country of tiny people in Swift's *Gulliver's Travels*]

Lilo *n*, *pl* **-los** *trademark* a type of inflatable plastic mattress

Lilongwe *n* the capital of Malawi, in the central part west of Lake Malawi. Pop: 655 000 (2005 est)

lilt *n* 1 a pleasing musical quality in a speaking voice 2 (in music) a jaunty rhythm 3 a graceful rhythmic motion ▷ *vb* 4 (of a voice, tune, or song) to rise and fall in a pleasant way **5** to move gracefully and rhythmically [origin unknown] **> lilting** *adj*

lily *n, pl* **lilies 1** a perennial plant, such as the tiger lily, with scaly bulbs and showy white or coloured flowers **2** a water lily [Latin *lilium*]

lily-livered *adj old-fashioned* cowardly

lily of the valley *n, pl* **lilies of the valley** a small plant with spikes of sweet-smelling white bell-shaped flowers

Lima *n* **1** the capital of Peru, near the Pacific coast on the Rímac River: the centre of Spanish colonization in South America; university founded in 1551 (the oldest in South America); an industrial centre with a port at nearby Callao. Pop: 8 180 000 (2005 est) **2** *communications* a code word for the letter L

Limassol *n* a port in S Cyprus: trading centre. Pop: 163 000 (2005 est). Ancient name: **Lemessus**

Limavady *n* a district of N Northern Ireland, in Co Londonderry. Pop: 33 571 (2003 est). Area: 586 sq km (226 sq miles)

limb¹ *n* **1** an arm, leg, or wing **2** any of the main branches of a tree **3 out on a limb a** in a precarious or questionable position **b** *Brit and NZ* isolated, esp. because of unpopular opinions [Old English *lim*] **> limbless** *adj*

limb² *n* the apparent outer edge of the sun, a moon, or a planet [Latin *limbus* edge]

limber¹ *adj* **1** pliant; supple **2** able to move or bend the body freely; agile [origin unknown]

limber² *n* **1** part of a gun carriage, consisting of an axle, pole, and two wheels ▷ *vb* **2** to attach the limber (to a gun) [Middle English *lymour* shaft of a gun carriage]

limber up *vb* to loosen stiff muscles by exercise

limbo¹ *n, pl* **-bos 1** (*often cap*) RC Church (formerly) the supposed region intermediate between heaven and hell for the unbaptized **2 in limbo** not knowing the result or next stage of something and powerless to influence it [Medieval Latin *in limbo* on the border (of hell)]

limbo² *n, pl* **-bos** a West Indian dance in which dancers lean backwards and pass under a horizontal bar which is gradually lowered [origin unknown]

Limbourg *n* the French name for **Limburg** (3)

Limburg¹ *n* **1** a medieval duchy of W Europe: divided between the Netherlands and Belgium in 1839 **2** a province of the SE Netherlands: contains a coalfield and industrial centres. Capital: Maastricht. Pop: 1 142 000 (2003 est). Area: 2253 sq km (809 sq miles) **3** a province of NE Belgium: contains the industrial regions of the Kempen coalfield. Capital: Hasselt. Pop: 805 786 (2004 est). Area: 2422 sq km (935 sq miles). French name: **Limbourg**

Limburg² *or* **Limbourg** *n* de. active ?1400–?1416, a Dutch family of manuscript illuminators. The three brothers Pol, Herman, and Jehanequin are best known for illustrating the *Très Riches Heures du Duc de Berry*, one of the finest examples of the International Gothic style

lime¹ *agriculture n* **1** calcium hydroxide spread as a dressing on acidic land ▷ *vb* **liming, limed 2** to spread a calcium compound upon (land) [Old English *līm*]

lime² *n* the green oval fruit of a small Asian citrus tree with acid fleshy pulp rich in vitamin C [Arabic *līmah*]

lime³ *n* a European linden tree planted for ornament [Old English *lind* linden]

lime-green *adj* light yellowish-green

limekiln *n* a kiln in which calcium carbonate is burned to produce quicklime

limelight *n* **1 the limelight** glare of publicity: *this issue will remain in the limelight* **2 a** a type of lamp, formerly used in stage lighting, in which lime is heated to white heat **b** brilliant white light produced in this way

limerick (lim-mer-ik) *n* a form of comic verse consisting of five lines [allegedly from *will you come up to Limerick?* a refrain sung between nonsense verses at a party]

Limerick *n* **1** a county of SW Republic of Ireland, in N Munster province: consists chiefly of an undulating plain with rich pasture and mountains in the south. County town: Limerick. Pop: 175 304 (2002). Area: 2686 sq km (1037 sq miles) **2** a port in SW Republic of Ireland, county town of Limerick, at the head of the Shannon estuary. Pop: 86 998 (2002)

limestone *n* rock consisting mainly of calcium carbonate: used as a building stone and in making cement

limey *n US, Canad and Austral slang* **1** a British person **2** a British sailor or ship [from *lime-juicer*, because British sailors drank lime juice as a protection against scurvy]

limit *n* **1** (*sometimes pl*) the ultimate extent or amount of something: *each soloist was stretched to his or her limit by the demands of the vocal writing* **2** (*often pl*) the boundary of a specific area: *beyond the city limits* **3** the largest quantity or amount allowed **4 the limit** *informal* a person or thing that is intolerably exasperating ▷ *vb* **-iting, -ited 5** to restrict [Latin *limes* boundary] **> limitable** *adj*

limitation *n* **1** a restriction or controlling of quantity, quality, or achievement **2 limitations** the limit or extent of an ability to achieve something: *learn your own limitations*

limited *adj* **1** having a limit; restricted **2** without fullness or scope; narrow **3** (of governing powers or sovereignty) restricted by a constitution, laws, or an assembly: *limited government* **4** *Brit and NZ* (of a business enterprise) owned by shareholders whose liability for the enterprise's debts is restricted

limited edition *n* an edition of something, such as a book, which has been restricted to a particular number of copies

limn *vb old-fashioned* to represent in drawing or painting [Latin *inluminare* to brighten]

Límnos *n* transliteration of the Modern Greek name for **Lemnos**

Limoges *n* a city in S central France, on the Vienne River: a centre of the porcelain industry since the 18th century. Pop: 139 026 (2006)

Limousin *n* a region and former province of W central France, in the W part of the Massif Central

limousine *n* any large luxurious car [French, literally: cloak]

limp¹ *vb* **1** to walk with an uneven step, esp. with a weak or injured leg **2** to advance in a labouring or faltering manner ▷ *n* **3** an uneven walk or progress [Old English *lemphealt* lame] **> limping** *adj, n*

limp² *adj* **1** lacking firmness or stiffness **2** not energetic or vital **3** (of the binding of a book) paperback [probably Scandinavian] **> limply** *adv*

limpet *n* **1** a conical shellfish that clings tightly to rocks with its muscular foot ▷ *adj* **2** denoting certain weapons that are magnetically attached to their targets and resist removal: *limpet mines* [Old English *lempedu*]

limpid *adj* **1** clear or transparent **2** (of speech or writing) clear and easy to understand [Latin *limpidus* clear] **> limpidity** *n*

Limpopo *n* **1** a province of NE South Africa, comprising the N part of the former province of Transvaal: agriculture and service industries. Capital: Polokwane (formerly Pietersburg). Pop: 5 404 868 (2011 est). Area: 123 910 sq km (47 842 sq miles). Former name (1994–2002): **Northern Province 2** a river in SE Africa, rising in E South Africa and flowing northeast, then southeast as the border between South Africa and Zimbabwe and through Mozambique to the Indian Ocean. Length: 1770 km (1100 miles)

limy¹ *adj* **limier, limiest** of, like, or smeared with birdlime

limy² *adj* **limier, limiest** of or tasting of lime (the fruit)

Linacre *n* Thomas. ?1460–1524, English humanist and physician: founded the Royal College of Physicians (1518)

linage *n* **1** the number of lines in written or printed matter **2** payment according to the number of lines

Linares *n* a city in S Spain: site of Scipio Africanus'

defeat of the Carthaginians (208 BC); lead mines. Pop: 58 257 (2003 est)

linchpin or **lynchpin** n 1 a pin inserted through an axle to keep a wheel in position 2 an essential person or thing: *she was the linchpin of the experiment* [Old English *lynis*]

Lincoln¹ n 1 a city in E central England, administrative centre of Lincolnshire: an important ecclesiastical and commercial centre in the Middle Ages; Roman ruins, a castle (founded by William the Conqueror) and a famous cathedral (begun in 1086). Pop: 85 963 (2001). Latin name: **Lindum** 2 a city in SE Nebraska: state capital; University of Nebraska (1869). Pop: 235 594 (2003 est) 3 short for **Lincolnshire** 4 a breed of long-woolled sheep, originally from Lincolnshire

Lincoln² n **Abraham.** 1809–65, US Republican statesman; 16th president of the US. His fame rests on his success in saving the Union in the Civil War (1861–65) and on his emancipation of slaves (1863); assassinated by John Wilkes Booth

Lincoln Center n a centre for the performing arts in New York City, including theatres, a library, and a school. Official name: **Lincoln Center for the Performing Arts**

Lincolnshire n a county of E England, on the North Sea and the Wash: mostly low-lying and fertile, with fenland around the Wash and hills (the **Lincoln Wolds**) in the east; one of the main agricultural counties of Great Britain: the geographical and ceremonial county includes the unitary authorities of North Lincolnshire and North East Lincolnshire (both part of Humberside county from 1974 to 1996). Administrative centre: Lincoln. Pop (excluding unitary authorities): 665 300 (2003 est). Area (excluding unitary authorities): 5880 sq km (2270 sq miles). Abbreviation: **Lincs**

Lincs Lincolnshire

linctus n, pl **-tuses** a soothing syrupy cough mixture [Latin *lingere* to lick]

Lind n 1 **James.** 1716–94, British physician. He demonstrated (1754) that citrus fruits can cure and prevent scurvy, a remedy adopted by the British navy in 1796 2 **Jenny,** original name *Johanna Maria Lind Goldschmidt.* 1820–87, Swedish coloratura soprano

Lindbergh n **Charles Augustus.** 1902–74, US aviator, who made the first solo nonstop flight across the Atlantic (1927)

Lindemann n **Frederick Alexander,** 1st Viscount Cherwell. 1886–1957, British physicist, born in Germany; Churchill's scientific adviser during World War II

linden n a large tree with heart-shaped leaves and fragrant yellowish flowers. See also **lime³** [Old English *linde* lime tree]

Lindesnes n a cape at the S tip of Norway, projecting into the North Sea. Also called: **the Naze**

Lindisfarne n another name for **Holy Island**

Lindsay n 1 See (Sir David) **Lyndsay** 2 **Norman Alfred William.** 1879–1969, Australian artist and writer 3 (**Nicholas**) **Vachel.** 1879–1931, US poet; best known for *General William Booth* (1913) and *The Congo* (1914)

Lindsey n **Parts of Lindsey** an area in E England constituting a former administrative division of Lincolnshire

Lindwall n **Ray**(mond Russell). 1921–96, Australian cricketer. A fast bowler, he played for Australia 61 times between 1946 and 1958

line¹ n 1 a narrow continuous mark, such as one made by a pencil or brush 2 a thin indented mark or wrinkle on skin 3 a continuous length without breadth 4 a boundary: *the United Nations established a provisional demarcation line* 5 *sport* a a white band indicating a division on a field or track b a mark or imaginary mark at which a race begins or ends 6 a boundary or limit: *the invidious dividing line between universities and polytechnics* 7 the edge or contour of a shape: *the shoulder line* 8 a wire or string with a particular function: *a long washing line* 9 a

telephone connection: *it was a very bad line* 10 a conducting wire, cable, or circuit for electric-power transmission or telecommunications 11 a system of travel or transportation: *a shipping line* 12 a route between two points on a railway 13 a railway track 14 a course or direction of movement: *the birds' line of flight* 15 a course of action or behaviour: *to adopt a more aggressive line* 16 a policy or prescribed way of thinking: *city commentators supported the CBI line* 17 a field of interest or activity: *heroin – that was their line* 18 straight or orderly alignment: *stand in line* 19 one kind of product or article: *a line of smart suits* 20 a row of people or things 21 a row of printed or written words 22 a unit of verse consisting of words in a single row 23 one of a number of narrow horizontal bands forming a television picture 24 *music* any of the five horizontal marks that make up the stave 25 the most forward defensive position: *the front line* 26 a formation of ships or soldiers abreast of each other 27 the combatant forces of certain armies and navies 28 *US and Canad* a queue 29 **all along the line** at every stage in a series 30 **draw the line (at)** to object (to) or set a limit (on): *I'm not a killer, I draw the line at that* 31 **drop someone a line** to send someone a short note 32 **get a line on** *informal* to obtain information about 33 **in line for** likely to receive: *high achievers are in line for cash bonuses* 34 **in line with** conforming to 35 **lay** or **put on the line** a to speak frankly and directly b to risk (one's career or reputation) on something ▷ vb **lining, lined** 36 to mark with a line or lines 37 to be or form a border: *the square was lined with stalls selling snacks* 38 to place in or form a row, series, or alignment ▸ See also **lines, line-up** [Old French *ligne* + Old English *līn*] ⟩ **lined** adj

line² vb **lining, lined** 1 to attach an inside layer to 2 to cover the inside of: *the works of Shakespeare lined his walls* 3 **line one's pockets** to make a lot of money, esp. dishonestly [Latin *linum* flax]

lineage (lin-ee-ij) n direct descent from an ancestor

lineal adj 1 being in a direct line of descent from an ancestor 2 of or derived from direct descent 3 linear [Latin *linea* line]

lineament n (often pl) a facial outline or feature [Latin *lineare* to draw a line]

linear (lin-ee-er) adj 1 of or in lines 2 of or relating to length 3 represented by a line or lines ⟩ **linearity** n

linear measure n a unit or system of units for the measurement of length

lineation (lin-ee-ay-shun) n 1 the act of marking with lines 2 an arrangement of lines

line dancing n a form of dancing performed by rows of people to country and western music

line drawing n a drawing formed with lines only

Line Islands pl n a group of coral islands in the central Pacific, including Tabuaeran, Teraina, and Kiritimati: part of Kiribati, with Palmyra and Jarvis administered by the US

Lineker n **Gary** (**Winston**). born 1960, English footballer and TV presenter: a striker, he scored 48 goals in 80 matches for England (1984–92); his clubs included Leicester City, Everton, Barcelona, and Tottenham Hotspur

linen n 1 a hard-wearing fabric woven from the spun fibres of flax 2 articles, such as sheets or tablecloths, made from linen cloth or from cotton [Latin *linum* flax]

line of fire n the flight path of a bullet discharged from a firearm

line printer n an electromechanical device that prints a line of characters at a time: used in printing and in computer systems

liner¹ n 1 a passenger ship or aircraft, esp. one that is part of a commercial fleet 2 Also called: **eyeliner** a cosmetic used to outline the eyes

liner² n something used as a lining: *a plastic bin liner*

lines pl n 1 the words of a theatrical role: *shaky sets, fluffed lines, and wooden plots* 2 *informal, chiefly Brit* a marriage certificate: *marriage lines* **3** a school punishment of writing out the same sentence or phrase a specified number of times **4 read between the lines** to find an implicit meaning in addition to the obvious one

linesman *n, pl* **-men 1** an official who helps the referee or umpire in various sports, by indicating when the ball has gone out of play **2** a person who maintains railway, electricity, or telephone lines

line-up *n* **1** people or things assembled for a particular purpose: *Christmas TV line-up* **2** the members of such an assembly ▷ *vb* **line up 3** to form or organize a line-up

ling[1] *n, pl* **ling** or **lings** a fish with a long slender body [probably Low German]

ling[2] *n* heather [Old Norse *lyng*]

Lingayen Gulf *n* a large inlet of the South China Sea in the Philippines, on the NW coast of Luzon: site of the Japanese landing in the 1941 invasion

linger *vb* **1** to delay or prolong departure **2** to survive in a weakened condition for some time before death **3** to spend a long time doing or considering something [Old English *lengan* prolong] ▷ **lingering** *adj*

lingerie (lan-zher-ee) *n* women's underwear and nightwear [French, from Latin *lineus* linen]

lingo *n, pl* **-goes** *informal* any foreign or unfamiliar language or jargon [perhaps from LINGUA FRANCA]

lingua franca *n, pl* **lingua francas** or **linguae francae 1** a language used for communication among people of different mother tongues **2** any system of communication providing mutual understanding [Italian: Frankish tongue]

lingual *adj* **1** *anatomy* of the tongue **2** articulated with the tongue **3** *rare* of language or languages ▷ **lingually** *adv*

linguist *n* **1** a person who is skilled in foreign languages **2** a person who studies linguistics [Latin *lingua* tongue]

linguistic *adj* **1** of language **2** of linguistics ▷ **linguistically** *adv*

linguistics *n* the scientific study of language

liniment *n* a medicated oily liquid applied to the skin to relieve pain or stiffness [Latin *linere* to smear]

lining *n* **1** material used to line a garment or curtain **2** any interior covering: *the lining of the womb*

link *n* **1** any of the separate rings that form a chain **2** an emotional or logical relationship between people or things; association **3** a connecting part or episode **4** a type of communications connection: *a rail link; radio link* ▷ *vb* **5** (often foll. by *up*) to connect with or as if with links **6** to connect by association [from Old Norse]

linkage *n* **1** the act of linking or the state of being linked **2** a system of links

linkman *n, pl* **-men** a presenter of a television or radio programme consisting of a number of items broadcast from different locations

Linköping *n* a city in S Sweden: a political and ecclesiastical centre in the Middle Ages; engineering industry. Pop: 137 004 (2004 est)

links *pl n* a golf course [Old English *hlincas*, plural of *hlinc* ridge]

link-up *n* a joining together of two systems or groups

Linlithgow *n* **1** a town in SE Scotland, in West Lothian: ruined palace, residence of Scottish kings and birthplace of Mary, Queen of Scots. Pop: 13 370 (2001) **2** the former name of **West Lothian**

Linnaeus *n* **Carolus**, original name *Carl von Linné*. 1707–78, Swedish botanist, who established the binomial system of biological nomenclature that forms the basis of modern classification

linnet *n* a brownish finch: the male has a red breast and forehead [Old French *linotte*, from Latin *līnum* flax (because the bird feeds on flaxseeds)]

Linnhe *n* **Loch Linnhe** a sea loch of W Scotland, at the SW end of the Great Glen. Length: about 32 km (20 miles)

lino *n* short for linoleum

linocut *n* **1** a design cut in relief in linoleum mounted on a block of wood **2** a print made from such a block

linoleum *n* a floor covering made of hessian or jute with a smooth decorative coating of powdered cork [Latin *linum* flax + *oleum* oil]

Linotype *n trademark* a typesetting machine that casts an entire line of text on one piece of metal

Lin Piao or **Lin Biao** *n* 1908–71, Chinese Communist general and statesman. He became minister of defence (1959) and second in rank to Mao Tse-tung (1966). He fell from grace and is reported to have died in an air crash while attempting to flee to the Soviet Union

linseed *n* the seed of the flax plant [Old English *līn* flax + *sǣd* seed]

linseed oil *n* a yellow oil extracted from flax seeds and used in making paints, inks, linoleum, and varnish

lint *n* **1** an absorbent material with raised fibres on one side, used to dress wounds **2** tiny shreds of yarn or cloth; fluff [probably Latin *linteus* made of linen, from *linum* flax]

lintel *n* a horizontal beam over a door or window [probably ultimately from Latin *limes* boundary]

Linz *n* a port in N Austria, capital of Upper Austria, on the River Danube: cultural centre; steelworks. Pop: 183 504 (2001). Latin name: **Lentia**

lion *n* **1** a large animal of the cat family found in Africa and India, with a tawny yellow coat and, in the male, a shaggy mane **2** a courageous and strong person **3** the **lion's share** the largest portion [Latin *leo*] ▷ **lioness** *fem n*

lion-hearted *adj* very brave; courageous

lionize or **-nise** *vb* **-nizing, -nized** or **-nising, -nised** to treat as a celebrity

Lions *n* **Gulf of Lions** a wide bay of the Mediterranean off the S coast of France, between the Spanish border and Toulon. French name: **Golfe du Lion**

lip *n* **1** *anatomy* either of the two fleshy folds surrounding the mouth **2** any structure resembling a lip, such as the rim of a jug **3** *slang* impudent talk or backchat **4 bite one's lip** to avoid showing feelings of anger or distress **5 keep a stiff upper lip** to maintain one's composure during a time of trouble **6 lick** or **smack one's lips** to anticipate or recall something with glee or relish [Old English *lippa*]

Lipari Islands *pl n* a group of volcanic islands under Italian administration off the N coast of Sicily: remains that form a continuous record from Neolithic times. Chief town: Lipari. Pop: 10 554 (2001). Area: 114 sq km (44 sq miles). Also called: **Aeolian Islands**. Italian name: **Isole Eolie**

lipase *n biochem* any of a group of enzymes that digest fat and are produced in the stomach and pancreas and occur in seeds

Lipchitz *n* **Jacques**. 1891–1973, US sculptor, born in Lithuania: he pioneered cubist sculpture

Li Peng *n* born 1928, Chinese Communist politician: premier (1988–98)

Lipetsk *n* a city in central Russia, on the Voronezh River: steelworks. Pop: 518 000 (2005 est)

lipid *n biochem* any of a group of organic compounds including fats, oils, waxes, and sterols [Greek *lipos* fat]

lipo *n informal* short for liposuction

Li Po or **Li T'ai-po** *n* ?700–762 AD, Chinese poet. His lyrics deal mostly with wine, nature, and women and are remarkable for their imagery

lipogram *n* a piece of writing in which all words containing a particular letter have been deliberately omitted

liposuction *n* a cosmetic surgical operation in which fat is removed from the body by suction

Lippe *n* **1** a former state of NW Germany, now part of the German state of North Rhine-Westphalia **2** a river in NW Germany, flowing west to the Rhine. Length: about 240 km (150 miles)

Lippershey or **Lippersheim** *n* **Hans**. died ?1619, Dutch lens grinder, who built the first telescope

Lippi *n* **1 Filippino**. ?1457–1504, Italian painter of the

Florentine school **2** his father, **Fra Filippo**. ?1406–69, Italian painter of the Florentine school, noted particularly for his frescoes at Prato Cathedral (1452–64)

Lippmann *n* Gabriel. 1845–1921, French physicist. He devised the earliest process of colour photography: Nobel prize for physics 1908

lippy *informal adj* **-pier, -piest 1** insolent or cheeky ▷ *n, pl* **-pies 2** lipstick

lip-read *vb* **-reading, -read** to interpret speech by lip-reading

lip-reading *n* a method used by deaf people to understand spoken words by interpreting movements of the speaker's lips **> lip-reader** *n*

lip service *n* pay lip service to to appear to support or obey something publicly while actually disregarding it

lipstick *n* a cosmetic in the form of a stick, for colouring the lips

liquefy *vb* **-fies, -fying, -fied** (esp. of a gas) to make or become liquid [Latin *liquefacere* to make liquid] **> liquefaction** *n*

liqueur (lik-*cure*) *n* a highly flavoured sweetened alcoholic spirit, intended to be drunk after a meal [French]

liquid *n* **1** a substance in a physical state which can change shape but not size ▷ *adj* **2** of or being a liquid: *liquid medicines* **3** shining and clear: *liquid sunlight days* **4** flowing, fluent, or smooth **5** (of assets) in the form of money or easily convertible into money [Latin *liquere* to be fluid]

liquidate *vb* **-dating, -dated 1** to settle or pay off (a debt or claim) **2** to dissolve a company and divide its assets among creditors **3** to convert (assets) into cash **4** to eliminate or kill

liquidation *n* **1 a** the dissolving of a company by selling its assets to pay off its debts **b go into liquidation** (of a business firm) to have its affairs so terminated **2** destruction; elimination

liquidator *n* an official appointed to liquidate a business

liquid-crystal display *n* a display of numbers, characters, or images, esp. on a calculator, using cells containing a liquid with crystalline properties, that change their reflectivity when an electric field is applied to them

liquidity *n* the state of being able to meet financial obligations

liquidize *or* **-dise** *vb* **-dizing, -dized** *or* **-dising, -dised 1** to make or become liquid; liquefy **2** to process (food) in a liquidizer to make it liquid

liquidizer *or* **-diser** *n* a kitchen appliance with blades for liquidizing food

liquid measure *n* a unit or system of units for measuring volumes of liquids or their containers

liquid oxygen *n* oxygen liquefied by cooling: used in rocket fuels

liquid paraffin *n* an oily liquid obtained by petroleum distillation and used as a laxative

liquor *n* **1** spirits or other alcoholic drinks **2** any liquid in which food has been cooked [Latin *liquere* to be liquid]

liquorice *or US and Canad* **licorice** (lik-ker-iss) *n* **1** a chewy black sweet with a strong flavour **2** the dried black root of a Mediterranean plant, used as a laxative and in confectionery [Greek *glukus* sweet + *rhiza* root]

lira *n, pl* **lire** *or* **liras 1** a former monetary unit of Italy **2** the standard monetary unit of Turkey [Italian, from Latin *libra* pound]

Lisbon *n* the capital and chief port of Portugal, in the southwest on the Tagus estuary: became capital in 1256; subject to earthquakes and severely damaged in 1755; university (1911). Pop: 1 892 891 (2001). Portuguese name: Lisboa

Lisburn *n* **1** a city in Northern Ireland in Lisburn district, Co Antrim, noted for its linen industry: headquarters of the British Army in Northern Ireland. Pop: 71 465 (2001)

2 a district of S Northern Ireland, in Co Antrim and Co Down. Pop: 109 565 (2003 est). Area: 446 sq km (172 sq miles)

Lisieux *n* a town in NW France: Roman Catholic pilgrimage centre, for its shrine of St Thérèse, who lived there. Pop: 22 109 (2006)

lisle (rhymes with **mile**) *n* a strong fine cotton thread or fabric, formerly used to make stockings [after *Lisle* (now Lille), in France]

lisp *n* **1** a speech defect in which *s* and *z* are pronounced like the *th* sounds in English *thin* and *then* respectively ▷ *vb* **2** to speak with a lisp [Old English *wlisp* lisping (imitative)]

LISP *n* a high-level computer programming language suitable for work in artificial intelligence [*lis*(t) *p*(*rocessing*)]

lissom *or* **lissome** *adj* slim and graceful and agile in movement [variant of *lithesome*, from *lithe* + *-some* of a specific nature]

list¹ *n* **1** an item-by-item record of names or things, usually written one below the other ▷ *vb* **2** to make a list of **3** to include in a list [Old English *líste*]

list² *vb* **1** (esp. of ships) to lean to one side ▷ *n* **2** a leaning to one side: *developed a list to starboard* [origin unknown]

listed building *n* (in Britain, Australia, and New Zealand) a building protected from demolition or alteration because of its special historical or architectural interest

listen *vb* **1** to concentrate on hearing something **2** to take heed or pay attention: *listen, let me explain* [Old English *hlysnan*] **> listener** *n*

listen in *vb* (often foll. by *on* or *to*) to listen secretly to; eavesdrop

Lister *n* Joseph, 1st Baron Lister. 1827–1912, British surgeon, who introduced the use of antiseptics

listeriosis *n* a serious form of food poisoning, caused by bacteria of the genus *Listeria* [after Joseph LISTER]

listing *n* **1** a list or an entry in a list **2 listings** lists of films, concerts, etc. printed in newspapers and magazines, and showing details such as times and venues

listless *adj* lacking interest or energy [obsolete *list* desire] **> listlessly** *adv*

Liston *n* Sonny, real name *Charles*. 1922–70, US boxer: former world heavyweight champion

list price *n* the selling price of merchandise as quoted in a catalogue or advertisement

lists *pl n* **1** *history* the enclosed field of combat at a tournament **2 enter the lists** to engage in a conflict or controversy [plural of Old English *líste* border]

Liszt *n* Franz. 1811–86, Hungarian composer and pianist. The greatest piano virtuoso of the 19th century, he originated the symphonic poem, pioneered the one-movement sonata form, and developed new harmonic combinations. His works include the symphonies *Faust* (1861) and *Dante* (1867), piano compositions and transcriptions, songs, and church music

lit *vb* a past of light¹, light²

lit. **1** literal(ly) **2** literary **3** literature

litany *n, pl* **-nies 1** *Christianity* a prayer consisting of a series of invocations, each followed by the same response **2** any tedious recital: *a litany of complaints* [Late Greek *litaneia* prayer]

litchi *n* same as lychee

lite *adj* **1** (of food or drink) containing few calories or little alcohol or fat **2** denoting a less extreme version of a person or thing: *reggae lite* [variant spelling of LIGHT²]

liter *n US* same as litre

literacy *n* **1** the ability to read and write **2** the ability to use language effectively

literal *adj* **1** in exact accordance with the explicit meaning of a word or text **2** word for word: *a literal translation* **3** dull or unimaginative: *she's very, very literal and* flat in how she interprets what she sees **4** true; actual ▷ n **5** a misprint or misspelling in a text [Latin *littera* letter] **> literally** *adv*

literalism *n* the tendency to take words and statements in their literal sense **> literalist** *n*

literary *adj* **1** of or characteristic of literature: *literary criticism* **2** knowledgeable about literature **3** (of a word) used chiefly in written work; not colloquial [Latin *litterarius* concerning reading and writing] **> literariness** *n*

literate *adj* **1** able to read and write **2** educated ▷ n **3** a literate person [Latin *litteratus* learned]

literati *pl n* literary or scholarly people [Latin]

literature *n* **1** written material such as poetry, novels, or essays **2** the body of written work of a particular culture, people, or era: *Elizabethan literature* **3** written or printed matter of a particular type or genre: *medical literature* **4** the art or profession of a writer **5** *informal* printed matter on any subject [Latin *litteratura* writing]

Lith. Lithuania(n)

lithe *adj* attractively graceful and supple in movement [Old English *lithe* (in the sense: gentle; later: supple)]

lithium *n chem* a soft silvery element of the alkali metal series: the lightest known metal. Symbol: Li [Greek *lithos* stone]

litho *n, pl* **-thos** short for **lithography, lithograph**

lithograph *n* **1** a print made by lithography ▷ vb **2** to reproduce (pictures or text) by lithography **> lithographic** *adj* **> lithographically** *adv*

lithography (lith-og-ra-fee) *n* a method of printing from a metal or stone surface on which the printing areas are made ink-receptive [Greek *lithos* stone + *graphein* to write] **> lithographer** *n*

Lithuania *n* a republic in NE Europe, on the Baltic Sea: a grand duchy in medieval times; united with Poland in 1569; occupied by Russia in 1795 and by Germany during World War I; independent Lithuania formed in 1918, but occupied by Soviet troops in 1919 and then by Poland; became a Soviet republic in 1940; unilaterally declared independence from the Soviet Union in 1990; recognized as independent in 1991; joined the EU in 2004. Official language: Lithuanian. Religion: Roman Catholic majority. Currency: euro. Capital: Vilnius. Pop: 3 515 858 (2013 est). Area: 65 200 sq km (25 174 sq miles). Also called: **Lithuanian Republic.** Lithuanian name: **Lietuva**

Lithuanian *adj* **1** of or relating to Lithuania or its inhabitants ▷ n **2** a native or inhabitant of Lithuania **3** the language of Lithuania

litigant *n* a person involved in a lawsuit

litigate *vb* **-gating, -gated 1** to bring or contest a lawsuit **2** to engage in legal proceedings [Latin *lis, lit-* lawsuit + *agere* to carry on] **> litigator** *n*

litigation *n* the process of bringing or contesting a lawsuit

litigious (lit-ij-uss) *adj* frequently going to law

litmus *n* a soluble powder obtained from lichens, which is turned red by acids and blue by alkalis. Paper treated with it (**litmus paper**) is used as an indicator in chemistry [perhaps Scandinavian]

litmus test *n* something which is regarded as a simple and accurate test of a particular thing, such as a person's attitude to an issue

litotes *n, pl* **-tes** understatement used for effect, for example 'She was not a little upset' meaning 'She was extremely upset' [Greek *litos* small]

litre *or US* **liter** *n* a measure of volume equivalent to 1 cubic decimetre [Greek *litra* a unit of weight]

litter *n* **1** small items of rubbish carelessly dropped in public places **2** a disordered or untidy collection of objects **3** a group of animals produced at one birth **4** straw or hay used as bedding for animals **5** dry material used to line a receptacle in which a domestic cat can urinate and defecate **6** (esp. formerly) a bed or seat held between parallel poles and used for carrying people ▷ vb **7** to strew with litter **8** to scatter or be scattered in an untidy fashion **9** (of animals) to give birth to offspring **10** to provide (an animal) with straw or hay for bedding [Latin *lectus* bed]

litter lout *Brit or US, Canad, Austral and NZ* **litterbug** *n slang* a person who drops refuse in public places

little *adj* **1** of small or less than average size **2** young: *a little boy* **3** endearingly familiar: *he was a sweet little man* **4** contemptible, mean, or disagreeable: *some of my best friends were little squirts* **5** of small quantity, extent, or duration: *there was little money circulating; I could see little evidence of it* ▷ adv **6** (usually preceded by *a*) to a small extent or degree; not a lot: *to sleep a little* **7** not at all, or hardly: *army life varied little as the years passed* **8** not much or often: *we go there very little now* **9** **little by little** by small degrees ▷ n **10** **make little of** to treat as insignificant: *one episode in their history is made little of in the guide books* **11** **think little of** to have a low opinion of ▶ See also **less, lesser, least** [Old English *lytel*]

Little America *n* originally the chief US base in the Antarctic, on the Ross Ice Shelf: first established by Admiral Richard E. Byrd (1928); used for polar exploration. It closed in the 1960s

Little Belt *n* a strait in Denmark, between Jutland and Funen Island, linking the Kattegat with the Baltic. Length: about 48 km (30 miles). Width: up to 29 km (18 miles). Danish name: **Lille Bælt**

Little Bighorn *n* a river in the W central US, rising in N Wyoming and flowing north to the Bighorn River. Its banks were the scene of the defeat (1876) and killing of General Custer and his command by Indians

Little Diomede *n* the smaller of the two Diomede Islands in the Bering Strait: administered by the US Area: about 10 sq km (4 sq miles)

little people *pl n folklore* small supernatural beings, such as elves

Little Rock *n* a city in central Arkansas, on the Arkansas River: state capital. Pop: 184 053 (2003 est)

Little Russia *n* a region of the former Soviet Union, consisting chiefly of Ukraine

Little St Bernard Pass *n* a pass over the Savoy Alps, between Bourg-Saint-Maurice, France, and La Thuile, Italy: 11th-century hospice. Height: 2187 m (7177 ft)

Littlewood *n* (Maud) **Joan.** 1914–2002, British theatre director, who founded the Theatre Workshop Company (1945) with the aim of bringing theatre to the working classes: noted esp. for her production of *Oh, What a Lovely War!* (1963)

littoral *adj* **1** of or by the shore ▷ n **2** a coastal region [Latin *litus* shore]

Littoria *n* the former name (until 1947) of **Latina**

liturgy *n, pl* **-gies** the forms of public services officially prescribed by a Church [Greek *leitourgia*] **> liturgical** *adj*

Liu Shao Qi *or* **Liu Shao-ch'i** *n* 1898–1974, Chinese Communist statesman; chairman of the People's Republic of China (1959–68); deposed during the Cultural Revolution

livable *or* **liveable** *adj* (foll. by *with*) tolerable or pleasant to live (with)

live¹ *vb* **living, lived 1** to show the characteristics of life; be alive **2** to remain alive or in existence **3** to exist in a specified way: *to live at ease* **4** to have one's home: *he went to live in Switzerland* **5** to continue or last: *his childhood had always lived inside him* **6** (foll. by *on* or *upon* or *by*) to support one's style of life: *forest dwellers who live by extracting rubber* **7** (foll. by *with*) to endure the effects of (a crime or mistake); tolerate **8** to pass or spend (one's life) **9** to enjoy life to the full: *he likes to live every day to the full* **10** to put into practice in one's daily life: *the freedom to live his own life as he chooses* **11** **live and let live** to be tolerant ▶ See also **live down, live in**, etc. [Old English *libban, lifian*]

live² *adj* **1** alive; living **2** *radio, television* transmitted at the time of performance, rather than being prerecorded: *a live broadcast* **3** actual: *I was able to speak to a real live Hurricane* pilot **4** (of a record) recorded during a performance **5** connected to a source of electric power: *a live cable* **6** of current interest; controversial: *the document has become a live political issue* **7** loaded or capable of exploding: *a live firing exercise with a 4.5in gun* **8** (of a coal or ember) glowing or burning ▷ *adv* **9** during, at, or in the form of a live performance [shortened from *on live* alive]

liveblog *vb* **liveblogging, liveblogged** to report (an event) on one's blog as it happens

live down *vb* to withstand people's reactions to a crime or mistake until they forget it

live in *vb* **1** to have one's home at the place where one works ▷ *adj* **live-in 2** resident: *a live-in nanny is a must; her live-in girlfriend*

livelihood *n* one's job or other source of income

livelong (liv-long) *adj chiefly poetic* long or seemingly long: *all the livelong day*

lively *adj* **-lier, -liest 1** full of life or vigour **2** vivacious or animated **3** vivid ▶ **liveliness** *n*

liven *vb* (usually foll. by *up*) to make or become lively; enliven

liver¹ *n* **1** a large glandular organ which secretes bile, balances nutrients, and removes certain poisons from the body **2** the liver of certain animals used as food [Old English *lifer*]

liver² *n* a person who lives in a specified way: *a fast liver*

liveried *adj* wearing livery

liverish *adj* **1** *informal* having a disorder of the liver **2** feeling disagreeable and slightly irritable

Liverpool¹ *n* **1** a city in NW England, in Liverpool unitary authority, Merseyside, on the Mersey estuary: second largest seaport in Great Britain; developed chiefly in the 17th century with the industrialization of S Lancashire; Liverpool University (1881) and John Moores University (1992). Pop: 469 017 (2001) **2** a unitary authority in NW England, in Merseyside. Pop: 441 800 (2003 est). Area: 113 sq km (44 sq miles)

Liverpool² *n* Robert Banks Jenkinson, 2nd Earl of Liverpool. 1770–1828, British Tory statesman; prime minister (1812–27). His government was noted for its repressive policies until about 1822, when more liberal measures were introduced by such men as Peel and Canning

Liverpudlian *adj* **1** of or relating to Liverpool or its inhabitants ▷ *n* **2** a native or inhabitant of Liverpool

liver sausage *n* a sausage containing liver

liverwort *n* a plant growing in wet places and resembling green seaweeds or leafy mosses [late Old English *liferwyrt*]

livery *n, pl* **-eries 1** the identifying uniform of a servant **2** distinctive dress or outward appearance **3** the stabling, keeping, or hiring out of horses for money [Old French *livrée* allocation]

lives *n* the plural of **life**

livestock *n* animals kept on a farm

live together *vb* (of an unmarried couple) to live in the same house; cohabit

live up to *vb* to fulfil (an expectation, obligation, or principle)

live wire *n* **1** *informal* an energetic person **2** a wire carrying an electric current

Livia Drusilla *n* 58 BC–29 AD, Roman noblewoman: wife (from 39 BC) of Emperor Augustus and mother of Emperor Tiberius

livid *adj* **1** *informal* extremely angry **2** of a dark grey or purple colour: *livid bruises* [Latin *livere* to be black and blue]

living *adj* **1** possessing life; not dead or inanimate **2** currently in use or valid: *a living alliance* **3** seeming to be real: *a living doll* **4** (of people or animals) existing in the present age **5** very: *the living image* **6** of or like everyday life: *living costs* **7** of or involving those now alive: *one of our greatest living actors* ▷ *n* **8** the condition of being alive **9** the manner of one's life: *high living* **10** one's financial means **11** *Church of England* a benefice

living room *n* a room in a private house or flat used for relaxation and entertainment

Livingston *n* a town in SE Scotland, the administrative centre of West Lothian: founded as a new town in 1962. Pop: 50 826 (2001)

Livingstone *n* **1** David. 1813–73, Scottish missionary and explorer in Africa. After working as a missionary in Botswana, he led a series of expeditions and was the first European to discover Lake Ngami (1849), the Zambezi River (1851), the Victoria Falls (1855), and Lake Malawi (1859). In 1866 he set out to search for the source of the Nile and was found in dire straits and rescued (1871) by the journalist H. M. Stanley **2** Kenneth Robert, known as *Ken*. born 1945, Labour leader of the Greater London Council (1981–86); Member of Parliament (1987–2001); Mayor of London (2000–08)

living wage *n* a wage adequate for a worker to live on and support a family in reasonable comfort

living will *n* a document that states that a person who becomes terminally ill does not want their life to be prolonged by artificial means

Livonia *n* **1** a former Russian province on the Baltic, north of Lithuania: became Russian in 1721; divided between Estonia and Latvia in 1918 **2** a city in SE Michigan, west of Detroit. Pop: 99 487 (2003 est)

Livonian *adj* **1** of or relating to Livonia, a former Russian Baltic province, or its inhabitants ▷ *n* **2** a native or inhabitant of Livonia

Livorno *n* a port in W central Italy, in Tuscany on the Ligurian Sea: shipyards; oil-refining. Pop: 156 274 (2001). English name: **Leghorn**

Livy *n* Latin name *Titus Livius*. 59 BC–17 AD, Roman historian; of his history of Rome in 142 books, only 35 survive

lizard *n* a reptile with an elongated body, four limbs, and a long tail [Latin *lacerta*]

Lizard *n* the Lizard a promontory in SW England, in SW Cornwall: the southernmost point in Great Britain. Also known as: **Lizard Head, the Lizard Peninsula**

Ljubljana *n* the capital of Slovenia: capital of Illyria (1816–49); part of Yugoslavia (1918–91); university (1595). Pop: 265 881 (2002). German name: **Laibach**

ll. lines (of written matter)

llama *n* a South American mammal of the camel family, that is used as a beast of burden and is valued for its woolly fleece [from a Native American language]

Llandaff *or* **Llandaf** *n* a town in SE Wales, now a suburb of Cardiff; the oldest bishopric in Wales (6th century)

Llandudno *n* a town and resort in NW Wales, in Conwy county borough on the Irish Sea. Pop: 14 872 (2001)

Llanelli *or* **Llanelly** *n* an industrial town in S Wales, in SE Carmarthenshire on an inlet of Carmarthen Bay. Pop: 46 357 (2001)

Llanfairpwllgwyngyll, Llanfairpwll *or* **Llanfair P. G.** *n* a village in NW Wales, in SE Anglesey: reputed to be the longest place name in Great Britain when unabbreviated; means: St Mary's Church in the hollow of the white hazel near the rapid whirlpool of Llandysilio of the red cave. Full name: **Llanfairpwllgwyn gyllgogerychwyrndrobwllllantysiliogogogoch**

Llangollen *n* a town in NE Wales, in Denbighshire on the River Dee: International Musical Eisteddfod held annually since 1946. Pop: 2930 (2001)

Llano Estacado *n* the S part of the Great Plains of the US, extending over W Texas and E New Mexico: oil and natural gas resources. Chief towns: Lubbock and Amarillo. Area: 83 700 sq km (30 000 sq miles). Also called: **Staked Plain**

LLB Bachelor of Laws [Latin *Legum Baccalaureus*]

LLD Doctor of Laws [Latin *Legum Doctor*]

Lleida *n* the Catalan name for **Lérida**

Llewellyn *n* Colonel Harry. 1911–99, Welsh show-jumping rider: on Foxhunter, he was a member of the

British team that won the gold medal at the 1952 Olympic Games

Lleyn Peninsula *n* a peninsula in NW Wales between Cardigan Bay and Caernarfon Bay

LLM Master of Laws [Latin *Legum Magister*]

Lloyd *n* **1 Clive (Hubert)**. born 1944, West Indian (Guyanese) cricketer; played in 110 tests (1966–84), scoring 7,515 runs; captained the West Indies in 74 tests and to two World Cup wins (1975, 1979) **2 Harold (Clayton)**. 1893–1971, US comic film actor **3 Marie**, real name *Matilda Alice Victoria Wood*. 1870–1922, English music-hall entertainer

Lloyd George *n* David, 1st Earl Lloyd George of Dwyfor. 1863–1945, British Liberal statesman: prime minister (1916–22). As chancellor of the exchequer (1908–15) he introduced old age pensions (1908), a radical budget (1909), and an insurance scheme (1911)

Lloyd Webber *n* **1 Andrew**, Baron Lloyd-Webber. born 1948, English composer. His musicals include *Joseph and the Amazing Technicolour Dreamcoat* (1968), *Jesus Christ Superstar* (1970), and *Evita* (1978), all with lyrics by Tim Rice, and *Cats* (1981), *Phantom of the Opera* (1986), *Sunset Boulevard* (1993), and *The Beautiful Game* (2000) **2** his brother, **Julian**. born 1951, British cellist

Llywelyn ap Gruffudd *n* died 1282, prince of Wales (1258–82): the only Welsh ruler to be recognized as such by the English

Llywelyn ap Iorwerth *n* called *Llywelyn the Great*. died 1240, prince of Gwynedd, N Wales (1194–1238), who extended his rule over most of Wales

lo *interj* old-fashioned look! see!: *lo and behold* [Old English *lā*]

loach *n* a freshwater fish with a long narrow body and barbels around the mouth [Old French *loche*]

Loach *n* Ken(neth). born 1936, British television and film director; his works for television include *Cathy Come Home* (1966) and his films include *Kes* (1970), *Riff-Raff* (1991), *Bread and Roses* (2000), *The Wind that Shakes the Barley* (2006), and *The Angels' Share* (2012)

load *n* **1** something to be borne or conveyed; weight **2** the amount borne or conveyed **3** something that weighs down or burdens: *I have enough of a load to carry right now* **4** *electronics* the power delivered by a machine, generator, or circuit **5** an external force applied to a component or mechanism **6** a load of *informal* a quantity of: *a load of half-truths* **7 get a load of** *informal* to pay attention to ▷ *vb* **8** to place cargo or goods upon (a ship or vehicle) **9** to burden or oppress **10** to supply in abundance: *other treats are loaded with fat* **11** to cause to be biased: *the dice are loaded* **12** to put ammunition into (a firearm) **13** *photog* to insert film in (a camera) **14** to weight or bias (a roulette wheel or dice) **15** *computers* to transfer (a program) to a memory ▶ See also **loads** [Old English *lād* course; in meaning, influenced by LADE] **> loader** *n*

loaded *adj* **1** carrying a load **2** charged with ammunition **3** (of a question or statement) containing a hidden trap or implication **4** (of dice or a roulette wheel) weighted or otherwise biased **5** *slang* wealthy **6** *slang, chiefly US and Canad* drunk

loads *pl n informal* (often foll. by *of*) a lot

load shedding *n chiefly S African, Austral and Indian* the act of temporarily cutting or reducing the supply of electricity to an area

loadstar *n* same as **lodestar**

loadstone *n* same as **lodestone**

loaf¹ *n*, *pl* **loaves 1** a shaped mass of baked bread **2** any shaped or moulded mass of food, such as cooked meat **3** *slang* the head; common sense: *use your loaf!* [Old English *hlāf*]

loaf² *vb* to loiter or lounge around in an idle way [perhaps from *loafer*]

loafer *n* **1** a person who avoids work; idler **2** a moccasin-like shoe [perhaps German *Landläufer* vagabond]

loam *n* fertile soil consisting of sand, clay, and decaying organic material [Old English *lām*] **> loamy** *adj*

loan *n* **1** money lent at interest for a fixed period of time **2** the act of lending: *I am grateful to her for the loan of her book* **3** property lent **4 on loan** lent out; borrowed ▷ *vb* **5** to lend (something, esp. money) [Old Norse *lān*]

Loanda *n* a variant spelling of **Luanda**

loan shark *n* a person who lends money at an extremely high interest rate, esp. illegally

loath *or* **loth** (rhymes with *both*) *adj* (usually foll. by *to*) reluctant or unwilling [Old English *lāth* (in the sense: hostile)]

loathe *vb* **loathing, loathed** to feel strong disgust for [Old English *lāthian*]

loathing *n* strong disgust

loathsome *adj* causing loathing

loaves *n* the plural of **loaf¹**

lob *sport n* **1** a ball struck or bowled in a high arc ▷ *vb* **lobbing, lobbed 2** to hit or kick (a ball) in a high arc **3** *informal* to throw [probably Low German]

Lobachevsky *n* Nikolai Ivanovich, 1793–1856, Russian mathematician; a founder of non-Euclidean geometry

lobar (loh-ber) *adj* of or affecting a lobe

lobate *adj* with or like lobes

lobby *n*, *pl* **-bies 1** a room or corridor used as an entrance hall or vestibule **2** a group which attempts to influence legislators on behalf of a particular interest **3** *chiefly Brit* a hall in a legislative building used for meetings between legislators and members of the public **4** *chiefly Brit* one of two corridors in a legislative building in which members vote ▷ *vb* **-bies, -bying, -bied 5** to attempt to influence (legislators) in the formulation of policy [Old High German *lauba* arbor]

lobbyist *n* a person who lobbies on behalf of a particular interest

lobe *n* **1** any rounded projection **2** the fleshy lower part of the external ear **3** any subdivision of a bodily organ [Greek *lobos* lobe of the ear or of the liver]

lobelia *n* a plant with blue, red, white, or yellow five-lobed flowers [Matthias de *Lobel*, botanist]

Lobengula *n* ?1836–94, last Matabele king (1870–93); his kingdom was destroyed by the British

Lobito *n* the chief port in Angola, in the west on **Lobito Bay**: terminus of the railway through Benguela to Mozambique. Pop: 470 000 (2005 est)

lobola *n S African* (in southern Africa) an African custom by which a bridegroom's family makes a payment in cattle or cash to the bride's family shortly before the marriage [Nguni (language group of southern Africa) *ukulobola* to give bride price]

lobotomy *n*, *pl* **-mies** the surgical cutting of nerves in the frontal lobe of the brain to treat severe mental disorders [Greek *lobos* lobe + *tomē* a cutting]

lobscouse *n* a sailor's stew of meat, vegetables, and hardtack [perhaps dialect *lob* to boil + *scouse* broth]

lobster *n*, *pl* **-sters** *or* **-ster 1** a large edible crustacean with large pincers and a long tail, which turns red when boiled **2** *Austral informal* a $20 note [Old English *loppestre*, from *loppe* spider]

lobster pot *n* a round basket made of open slats, used to catch lobsters

local *adj* **1** of or concerning a particular area **2** restricted to a particular place **3** *med* of, affecting, or confined to a limited area or part: *a local anaesthetic* **4** (of a train or bus) stopping at all stations or stops ▷ *n* **5** an inhabitant of a specified locality: *we swim, sunbathe, meet the locals, unwind* **6** *Brit informal* a pub close to one's home [Latin *locus* place] **> locally** *adv*

local anaesthetic *n med* See **anaesthesia**

local authority *n* the governing body of a county, district, or region

locale (loh-kahl) *n* the place where something happens or has happened [French, from Latin *locus* place]

local government *n* the government of the affairs of counties, towns, and districts by locally elected political bodies

localism *n* **1** the policy of devolving power from a central or federal government to local bodies **2** a pronunciation, phrase, etc., peculiar to a particular locality ➤ **localist** *n*

locality *n, pl* **-ties** **1** a neighbourhood or area **2** the site or scene of an event

localize *or* **-lise** *vb* **-lizing, -lized** *or* **-lising, -lised** to restrict (something) to a particular place

Locarno *n* a town in S Switzerland, in Ticino canton at the N end of Lake Maggiore: tourist resort. Pop: 14 561 (2000)

locate *vb* **-cating, -cated** **1** to discover the whereabouts of; find **2** to situate or build: *located around the corner from the church* **3** to become established or settled

location *n* **1** a site or position; situation **2** the act of locating or the state of being located: *make their location and rescue a top priority* **3** a place outside a studio where filming is done: *shot on location* **4** (in South Africa) a Black African or Coloured township [Latin *locare* to place]

loc. cit. (in textual annotation) in the place cited [Latin *loco citato*]

loch *n Scot* **1** a lake **2** a long narrow arm of the sea [Gaelic]

loci (loh-sigh) *n* the plural of **locus**

lock[1] *n* **1** a device for fastening a door, drawer, lid, etc., and preventing unauthorized access **2** a section of a canal or river closed off by gates between which the water level can be altered to aid boats moving from one level to the next **3** *Brit and NZ* the extent to which a vehicle's front wheels will turn: *they adopted more steering lock* **4** the interlocking of parts **5** a mechanism that fires a gun **6** lock, stock, and barrel completely; entirely **7** a wrestling hold **8** Also called: **lock forward** *rugby* a player in the second row of the scrum ▷ *vb* **9** to fasten or become fastened to prevent entry or exit **10** to secure (a building) by locking all doors and windows **11** to fix or become fixed together securely **12** to become or cause to become immovable: *just before your knees lock* **13** to clasp or entangle in a struggle or embrace ➤ See also **lock out, lock up** [Old English *loc*]

lock[2] *n* **1** a strand or curl of hair **2 locks** *chiefly literary* hair [Old English *loc*]

Locke *n* **1** John. 1632–1704, English philosopher, who discussed the concept of empiricism in his *Essay Concerning Human Understanding* (1690). He influenced political thought, esp. in France and America, with his *Two Treatises on Government* (1690), in which he sanctioned the right to revolt **2** Matthew. ?1630–77, English composer, esp. of works for the stage

locker *n* a small compartment with a lock, used for temporarily storing clothes, valuables, or luggage

Lockerbie *n* a town in SW Scotland, in Dumfries and Galloway: scene (1988) of the UK's worst air disaster when a passenger jet (Pan Am flight 103) was brought down by a terrorist bomb, killing 270 people, including eleven residents of the town. Pop: 4009 (2001)

locket *n* a small hinged ornamental pendant that holds a picture or keepsake [French *loquet* latch]

lockjaw *n pathol* a nontechnical name for **trismus, tetanus**

lock out *vb* **1** to prevent from entering by locking a door **2** to prevent (employees) from working during an industrial dispute, by shutting them out of the premises ▷ *n* **lockout** **3** the closing of a place of employment by an employer, in order to force employees to accept terms

locksmith *n* a person who makes or repairs locks

lock up *vb* **1** to imprison **2** to secure a building by locking all the doors and windows ▷ *n* **lockup** **3** a jail **4** *Brit* a garage or store separate from the main premises **5** *Brit* a small shop with no attached quarters for the owner ▷ *adj* **lock-up** **6** *Brit and NZ* (of premises) without living quarters: *a lock-up garage*

Lockyer *n* Sir Joseph Norman. 1836–1920, English astronomer: a pioneer in solar spectroscopy, he was the first to observe helium in the sun's atmosphere (1868)

loco[1] *n informal* a locomotive

loco[2] *adj slang, chiefly US* insane [Spanish: crazy]

locomotion *n* the act or power of moving [Latin *loco* from a place + MOTION]

locomotive *n* **1** a self-propelled engine for pulling trains ▷ *adj* **2** of locomotion

Locrian *or* **Lokrian** *adj* **1** of or relating to Locris or its inhabitants ▷ *n* **2** a native or inhabitant of Locris

Locris *or* **Lokris** *n* an ancient region of central Greece

locum *n* a person who stands in temporarily for a doctor or clergyman [Medieval Latin *locum tenens* (someone) holding the place (of another)]

locus (loh-kuss) *n, pl* **loci** **1** an area or place where something happens **2** *maths* a set of points or lines whose location satisfies, or is determined by, one or more specified conditions: *the locus of points equidistant from a given point is a circle* [Latin]

locust *n* **1** an African insect, related to the grasshopper, which travels in vast swarms, stripping large areas of vegetation **2** a North American leguminous tree with prickly branches; the carob tree [Latin *locusta*]

locution *n* **1** manner or style of speech **2** a word, phrase, or expression [Latin *locutio* an utterance]

Lod *n* a town in central Israel, southeast of Tel Aviv: Israel's chief airport. Pop: 66 800 (2003 est). Also called: **Lydda**

lode *n* a vein of metallic ore [Old English *lād* course]

lodestar *n* **1** a star, esp. the North Star, used in navigation or astronomy as a point of reference **2** something that serves as a guide

lodestone *n* **1 a** magnetic iron ore **b** a piece of this, used as a magnet **2** a person or thing regarded as a focus of attraction

lodge *n* **1** *chiefly Brit* the gatekeeper's house at the entrance to the grounds of a country mansion **2** a house or cabin used occasionally by hunters, skiers, etc.: *a hunting lodge* **3** *chiefly Brit* a room used by porters in a university or college **4** a local branch of certain societies **5** a beaver's home ▷ *vb* **lodging, lodged** **6** to provide or be provided with rented accommodation **7** to live temporarily in rented accommodation **8** to embed or be embedded: *the bullet lodged in his brain* **9** to leave for safety or storage: *he lodged his wages in the bank* **10** to bring (a charge or accusation) against someone: *the Brazilians lodged a complaint* **11** (often foll. by *in* or *with*) to place (authority or power) in the control (of someone) [Old French *loge*]

Lodge[1] *n* **1** David (John). born 1935, British novelist and critic. His books include *Changing Places* (1975), *Small World* (1984), *Nice Work* (1988), *Therapy* (1995), and *Thinks...* (2001) **2** Sir Oliver (Joseph). 1851–1940, British physicist, who made important contributions to electromagnetism, radio reception, and attempted to detect the ether. He also studied allegedly psychic phenomena **3** Thomas. ?1558–1625, English writer. His romance *Rosalynde* (1590) supplied the plot for Shakespeare's *As You Like It*

Lodge[2] *n* the Lodge the official Canberra residence of the Australian Prime Minister

lodger *n* a person who pays rent in return for accommodation in someone else's home

lodging *n* **1** a temporary residence: *where might I find a night's lodging?* **2 lodgings** a rented room or rooms in another person's home

Lodi *n* a town in N Italy, in Lombardy: scene of Napoleon's defeat of the Austrians in 1796. Pop: 40 805 (2001)

Łódź *n* a city in central Poland: the country's second largest city; major centre of the textile industry; university (1945). Pop: 943 000 (2005 est)

Loeb *n* Jacques. 1859–1924, US physiologist, born in Germany, noted esp. for his pioneering work on artificial parthenogenesis

loess (loh-iss) *n* a fine-grained soil, found mainly in river valleys, originally deposited by the wind [Swiss German *lösch* loose]

Loewe¹ n Frederick. 1904–88, US composer of such musical comedies as *Brigadoon* (1947), *My Fair Lady* (1956), and *Camelot* (1960), all with librettos by Alan Jay Lerner

Loewe² or **Löwe** n (Johann) Karl (Gottfried). 1796–1869, German composer, esp. of songs, such as *Der Erlkönig* (1818)

Loewi n Otto. 1873–1961, US pharmacologist, born in Germany. He shared a Nobel prize for physiology or medicine (1936) with Dale for their work on the chemical transmission of nerve impulses

Lofoten and Vesterålen *pl* n a group of islands off the NW coast of Norway, within the Arctic Circle. Largest island: Hinnøy. Pop: 54 589 (2004 est). Area: about 5130 sq km (1980 sq miles)

loft n **1** the space inside a roof **2** a gallery in a church **3** a room over a stable used to store hay **4** a raised house or coop in which pigeons are kept **5** *golf* **a** the angle of the face of the club used to elevate a ball **b** the height reached by a struck ball ▷ *vb* **6** *sport* to strike or kick (a ball) high in the air [Old Norse *lopt* air, ceiling]

lofty *adj* **loftier, loftiest** **1** of majestic or imposing height **2** morally admirable: *lofty ideals* **3** unpleasantly superior: *a lofty contempt* ❯ **loftily** *adv* ❯ **loftiness** n

log¹ n **1 a** a section of a felled tree stripped of branches **2 a** a detailed record of a voyage of a ship or aircraft **b** a record of the hours flown by pilots and aircrews **c** a book in which these records are made; logbook **3** a device consisting of a float with an attached line, formerly used to measure the speed of a ship **4 sleep like a log** to sleep without stirring ▷ *vb* **logging, logged** **5** to saw logs from (trees) **6** to enter (a distance or event) in a logbook or log ▶ See also **log in, log out** [origin unknown]

log² n short for **logarithm**

Logan n Mount Logan a mountain in NW Canada, in SW Yukon in the St Elias Range: the highest peak in Canada and the second highest in North America. Height (after a re-survey in 1993): 5959 m (19 550 ft)

loganberry n, *pl* **-ries** a purplish-red fruit, similar to a raspberry, that grows on a trailing prickly plant [after J. H. *Logan*, who first grew it]

logarithm n the exponent indicating the power to which a fixed number, the base, must be raised to obtain a given number or variable [Greek *logos* ratio + *arithmos* number] ❯ **logarithmic** *adj*

logbook n **1** a book containing the official record of trips made by a ship or aircraft **2** *Brit informal* the registration document of a car

loggerhead n **1** a large-headed turtle occurring in most seas **2 at loggerheads** engaged in dispute or confrontation [probably dialect *logger* wooden block + HEAD]

loggia (loj-ya) n a covered gallery on the side of a building [Italian]

logging n the work of felling, trimming, and transporting timber ❯ **logger** n

logic n **1** the branch of philosophy that analyses the patterns of reasoning **2** a particular system of reasoning **3** reasoned thought or argument, as distinguished from irrationality **4** the interdependence of a series of events or facts **5** *electronics, computers* the principles underlying the units in a computer system that produce results from data [Greek *logikos* concerning speech or reasoning]

logical *adj* **1** relating to or characteristic of logic **2** using or deduced from the principles of logic: *a logical conclusion* **3** capable of or using clear and valid reasoning **4** reasonable because of facts or events: *the logical choice* ❯ **logically** *adv*

logic gate n *electronics* same as **gate** (4)

logician n a person who specializes in or is skilled at logic

log in or **log on** *vb* to gain entrance to a computer system by keying in a special command

logistics n the detailed planning and organization of a large complex operation, such as a military campaign

[French *loger* to lodge] ❯ **logistical** or **logistic** *adj* ❯ **logistically** *adv*

log jam n *chiefly US and Canad* **1** a blockage caused by the crowding together of logs floating in a river **2** a deadlock

logo (loh-go) n, *pl* **-os** a special design that identifies a company or an organization and appears on all its products, printed material, etc. [shortened from *logotype* badge, symbol]

log out *vb* to exit from a computer system by keying in a special command

Logroño n a walled city in N Spain, on the Ebro River: trading centre of an agricultural region noted for its wine. Pop: 139 615 (2003 est)

-logy *combining form* **1** indicating the science or study of: *musicology* **2** indicating writing or discourse: *trilogy*; *phraseology* [Greek *logos* word] ❯ **-logical** or **-logic** *combining form* ❯ **-logist** *combining form*

loin n **1** the part of the body between the pelvis and the ribs **2** a cut of meat from this part of an animal ▶ See also **loins** [Old French *loigne*]

loincloth n a piece of cloth covering only the loins

loins *pl* n **1** the hips and the inner surface of the legs where they join the body **2** *euphemistic* the genitals

Loire n **1** a department of E central France, in Rhône-Alpes region. Capital: St Étienne. Pop: 726 613 (2003 est). Area: 4799 sq km (1872 sq miles) **2** a river in France, rising in the Massif Central and flowing north and west in a wide curve to the Bay of Biscay: the longest river in France. Its valley is famous for its wines and châteaux. Length: 1020 km (634 miles). Ancient name: Liger

Loire-Atlantique n a department of W France, in Pays de la Loire region. Capital: Nantes. Pop: 1 174 120 (2003 est). Area: 6980 sq km (2722 sq miles)

Loiret n a department of central France, in Centre region. Capital: Orléans. Pop: 629 377 (2003 est). Area: 6812 sq km (2657 sq miles)

Loir-et-Cher n a department of N central France, in Centre region. Capital: Blois. Pop: 318 853 (2003 est). Area: 6422 sq km (2505 sq miles)

loiter *vb* to stand or wait aimlessly or idly [perhaps Middle Dutch *löteren* to wobble]

Lolita (low-lee-ta) n a sexually precocious young girl [after the character in Nabokov's novel *Lolita*]

loll *vb* **1** to lounge in a lazy manner **2** to hang loosely: *a wet lolling tongue; his head lolled back and forth* [perhaps imitative]

Lolland or **Laaland** n an island of Denmark in the Baltic Sea, south of Sjælland. Pop: 69 796 (2003 est). Area: 1240 sq km (480 sq miles)

lollipop n **1** a boiled sweet stuck on a small wooden stick **2** *Brit* an ice lolly [perhaps dialect *lolly* the tongue + POP²]

lollipop man or **lollipop lady** n *Brit informal* a person holding a circular sign on a pole who stops traffic to enable children to cross the road safely

lollop *vb* *chiefly Brit* to walk or run with a clumsy or relaxed bouncing movement [probably *loll* + *-op*, as in *gallop*]

lolly n, *pl* **-lies** **1** *informal* a lollipop **2** *Brit* short for **ice lolly** **3** *Brit, Austral and NZ slang* money **4** *Austral and NZ informal* a sweet [shortened from *lollipop*]

Lomax n Alan. 1915–2002, and his father John Avery (1867–1948), US folklorists

Lombard¹ n **1** a native or inhabitant of Lombardy **2** Also called: **Langobard** a member of an ancient Germanic people who settled in N Italy after 568 AD ▷ *adj also* **Lombardic** **3** of or relating to Lombardy or the Lombards

Lombard² n Peter. ?1100–?60, Italian theologian, noted for his *Sententiarum libri quattuor*

Lombardi n Vincent Thomas, known as *Vince*. 1913–70, American football coach, whose team won the first two Superbowls, and after whom the Superbowl trophy is named

Lombardy n a region of N central Italy, bordering on the Alps: dominated by prosperous lordships and city-states during the Middle Ages; later ruled by Spain and then by Austria before becoming part of Italy in 1859; intensively cultivated and in parts highly industrialized. Pop: 9 108 645 (2003 est). Area: 23 804 sq km (9284 sq miles). Italian name: **Lombardia**

Lombok n an island of Indonesia, in the Lesser Sunda Islands (Nusa Tenggara) east of Java: came under Dutch rule in 1894; important biologically as being transitional between Asian and Australian in flora and fauna, the line of demarcation beginning at **Lombok Strait** (a channel between Lombok and Bali, connecting the Flores Sea with the Indian Ocean). Chief town: Mataram. Pop: 2 536 000 (2004 est). Area: 4730 sq km (1826 sq miles)

Lombroso n Cesare. 1836–1909, Italian criminologist: he postulated the existence of a criminal type

Lomé n the capital and chief port of Togo, on the Bight of Benin. Pop: 865 000 (2005 est)

Lomond n 1 **Loch Lomond** a lake in W Scotland, north of Glasgow: the largest Scottish lake; designated a national park in 2002. Length: about 38 km (24 miles). Width: up to 8 km (5 miles) 2 See **Ben Lomond**

Lomu n Jonah. born 1975, New Zealand Rugby Union player; scored 37 tries in 63 games for the All Blacks (1994–2002)

London¹ n 1 the capital of the United Kingdom, a port in S England on the River Thames near its estuary on the North Sea: consists of the **City** (the financial quarter), the **West End** (the entertainment and major shopping centre), the **East End** (the industrial and former dock area), and extensive suburbs. Latin name: **Londinium.** See also **City 2 Greater London** the administrative area of London, consisting of the City of London and 32 boroughs (13 Inner London boroughs and 19 Outer London boroughs): formed in 1965 from the City, parts of Surrey, Kent, Essex, and Hertfordshire, and almost all of Middlesex, and abolished for administrative purposes in 1996: a Mayor of London and a new London Assembly took office in 2000. Pop: 8 308 369 (2012 est). Area: 1579 sq km (610 sq miles) 3 a city in SE Canada, in SE Ontario on the Thames River: University of Western Ontario (1878). Pop: 337 318 (2001) 4 it's London to a brick Austral and NZ slang it is certain

London² n Jack, full name John Griffith London. 1876–1916, US novelist, short-story writer, and adventurer. His works include Call of the Wild (1903), The Sea Wolf (1904), The Iron Heel (1907), and the semiautobiographical John Barleycorn (1913)

Londonderry or **Derry** n 1 a historical county of NW Northern Ireland, on the Atlantic: in 1973 replaced for administrative purposes by the districts of Coleraine, Derry, Limavady, and Magherafelt. Area: 2108 sq km (814 sq miles) 2 a port in N Northern Ireland, second city of Northern Ireland: given to the City of London in 1613 to be colonized by Londoners; besieged by James II's forces (1688–89). Pop: 83 699 (2001) ▶ See also **Derry**

Londoner n a native or inhabitant of London

London Eye n a large ferris wheel located on the south bank of the River Thames in London; erected in 1999. Height: 135 m (443 ft)

Londonistan n an informal name for London, as considered by some people as a base for radical Islamists [C20: from LONDON + Persian -stan place of; modelled on PAKISTAN and AFGHANISTAN]

London pride n a rock plant with a rosette of leaves and pink flowers

Londrina n a city in S Brazil, in Paraná: centre of a coffee-growing area. Pop: 679 000 (2005 est)

lone adj 1 solitary: a lone figure 2 isolated: a lone isle guarded by the great Atlantic swell 3 Brit unmarried or widowed: a lone parent [from the mistaken division of alone into a lone]

lonely adj -lier, -liest 1 unhappy as a result of solitude 2 resulting from the state of being alone: command can be a lonely business 3 isolated and not much visited by people: a lonely beach ▶ **loneliness** n

lonely hearts adj of or for people seeking a congenial companion or marriage partner: lonely hearts ads

loner n informal a person who prefers to be alone

lonesome adj 1 chiefly US and Canad lonely 2 causing feelings of loneliness: it was lonesome up here on the mountain

long¹ adj 1 having relatively great length in space or time 2 having greater than the average or expected range, extent, or duration: a long session of talks 3 seeming to occupy a greater time than is really so: she was quiet a long moment 4 of a specified extent or duration: trimmed to about two cms long 5 consisting of a large number of parts: a long list 6 phonetics, prosody (of a vowel) of relatively considerable duration 7 from end to end; lengthwise 8 finance having large holdings of securities or commodities in anticipation of rising prices 9 **in the long run** ultimately; after or over a period of time 10 **long on** informal plentifully supplied or endowed with: long on show-biz gossip ▷ adv 11 for a certain time or period: how long have we got? 12 for or during an extensive period of time: to talk long into the night 13 a considerable amount of time: long after I met you; long ago 14 **as** or **so long as a** for or during the same length of time that **b** provided that; if ▷ n 15 anything that is long 16 **before long** soon 17 **for long** for a long time 18 **the long and the short of it** the essential points or facts [Old English lang] ▶ **longish** adj

long² vb to have a strong desire for something or to do something: I longed for a baby; the more I think of him the more I long to see him [Old English langian]

Long n Crawford Williamson. 1815–78, US surgeon. He was the first to use ether as an anaesthetic

long. longitude

long- adv (in combination) for or lasting a long time: long-established; long-lasting

Long Beach n a city in SW California, on San Pedro Bay: resort and naval base; oil-refining. Pop: 475 460 (2003 est)

Longbenton n a town in N England, in North Tyneside unitary authority, Tyne and Wear. Pop: 34 878 (2001)

longboat n 1 the largest boat carried aboard a commercial ship 2 same as **longship**

longbow n a large powerful hand-drawn bow

long-distance adj 1 covering relatively long distances: a long-distance race 2 (of a telephone call) connecting points relatively far apart

Long Eaton n a town in N central England, in SE Derbyshire. Pop: 46 490 (2001)

longevity (lon-jev-it-ee) n long life [Latin longus long + aevum age]

long face n a glum expression

Longfellow n Henry Wadsworth. 1807–82, US poet, noted particularly for his long narrative poems Evangeline (1847) and The Song of Hiawatha (1855)

Longford n 1 a county of N Republic of Ireland, in Leinster province. County town: Longford. Pop: 31 068 (2002). Area: 1043 sq km (403 sq miles) 2 a town in N Republic of Ireland, county town of Co Longford. Pop: 7557 (2002)

longhand n ordinary handwriting, as opposed to typing or shorthand

longhorn n a British breed of beef cattle with long curved horns

longing n 1 a strong feeling of wanting something one is unlikely ever to have ▷ adj 2 having or showing desire: longing glances ▶ **longingly** adv

Longinus n Dionysius. ?2nd century AD, supposed author of the famous Greek treatise on literary criticism, On the Sublime ▶ **Longinean** adj

Long Island n an island in SE New York State, separated from the S shore of Connecticut by **Long Island Sound** (an arm of the Atlantic): contains the New York City boroughs of Brooklyn and Queens in the west, many resorts (notably Coney Island), and two large airports (La Guardia and John F. Kennedy). Area: 4462 sq km (1723 sq miles)

longitude n distance in degrees east or west of the prime meridian at 0° [Latin *longitudo* length]

longitudinal adj 1 of longitude or length 2 placed or extended lengthways

long johns pl n informal long underpants

long jump n an athletic contest of jumping the greatest length from a fixed mark

Longleat House n an Elizabethan mansion near Warminster in Wiltshire, built (from 1568) by Robert Smythson for Sir John Thynne; the grounds, landscaped by Capability Brown, now contain a famous safari park

long-life adj (of milk, batteries, etc.) lasting longer than the regular kind

long-lived adj living or lasting for a long time

long-playing adj old-fashioned of or relating to an LP

long-range adj 1 of or extending into the future: *a long-range economic forecast* 2 (of vehicles, aircraft, or weapons) capable of covering great distances

longship n a narrow open boat with oars and a square sail, used by the Vikings

longshore drift n the movement of material along a beach, due to waves approaching the shore at an oblique angle

longshoreman n, pl **-men** US and Canad a docker

long shot n 1 an undertaking, guess, or possibility with little chance of success 2 a bet against heavy odds 3 **not by a long shot** not by any means: *she wasn't beaten, not by a long shot*

long-sighted adj 1 able to see only distant objects in focus 2 far-sighted

Longs Peak n a mountain in N Colorado, in the Front Range of the Rockies: the highest peak in the Rocky Mountain National Park. Height: 4345 m (14 255 ft)

long-standing adj existing for a long time

long-suffering adj enduring trouble or unhappiness without complaint

long-term adj 1 lasting or extending over a long time: *a long-term commitment* ▷ n **long term** 2 **in the long term** over a long period of time: *in the long term the cost of energy will have to go up*

longtime adj of long standing: *his longtime colleague; his longtime relationship with Sue*

Longueuil n a city in SE Canada, in S Quebec: a suburb of Montreal. Pop: 128 016 (2001)

Longus n ?3rd century AD, Greek author of the prose romance *Daphnis and Chloe*

long wave n a radio wave with a wavelength greater than 1000 metres

longways or US and Canad **longwise** adv lengthways

long-winded adj tiresomely long ▸ **long-windedness** n

Longyearbyen n a village on Spitsbergen island, administrative centre of the Svalbard archipelago: coal-mining

Lons-le-Saunier n a town in E France: saline springs; manufactures sparkling wines. Pop: 18 763 (2006)

loo n, pl **loos** Brit and NZ informal a toilet [perhaps from French *lieux d'aisance* water closet]

loofah n a long rough-textured bath sponge made from the dried pod of a gourd [Arabic *lūf*]

look vb 1 (often foll. by at) to direct the eyes (towards): *he turned to look at her* 2 (often foll. by at) to consider: *let's look at the issues involved* 3 to give the impression of being; seem: *Luxembourg's timetable looks a winner* 4 to face in a particular direction: *Morgan's Rock looks south* 5 (foll. by for) to search or seek: *the department looks for reputable firms* 6 (foll. by into) to carry out an investigation 7 to direct a look at (someone) in a specified way: *she looks at Teresina suspiciously* 8 to match in appearance with (something): *looking your best* 9 to expect or hope (to do something): *we would look to derive a procedure that would account for most cases* 10 **look alive** or **lively** or **sharp** or **smart** to hurry up; get busy 11 **look here** an expression used to attract someone's attention or add emphasis to a statement ▷ n 12 an instance of looking: *a look of icy contempt* 13 a view or

sight (of something): *take a look at my view* 14 (often pl) appearance to the eye or mind; aspect: *I'm not happy with the look of things here; better than you by the looks of it* 15 style or fashion: *the look made famous by the great Russian* ▷ conj 16 an expression demanding attention or showing annoyance: *look, I won't be coming back* ▸ See also **look after**, **look back**, etc. [Old English *lōcian*] ▸ **looker** n

---

USAGE See at **like¹**.

---

look after vb to take care of

lookalike n a person or thing that is the double of another, often well-known, person or thing

look back vb 1 to think about the past 2 **never looked back** was extremely successful: *he became the station's first major signing and never looked back*

look down vb (foll. by on or upon) to treat as inferior or unimportant

look forward to vb to anticipate with pleasure

look-in informal n 1 a chance to be chosen or participate: *before anyone else gets a look-in* ▷ vb **look in** 2 to pay a short visit

looking glass n a mirror

look on vb 1 to be a spectator 2 to consider or regard: *I just looked on her as a friend* ▸ **looker-on** n

lookout n 1 the act of watching for danger or for an opportunity: *on the lookout for attack* 2 a person or people keeping such a watch 3 a viewpoint from which a watch is kept 4 informal worry or concern: *that is my lookout rather than theirs* 5 chiefly Brit chances or prospect: *it's a bad lookout for Europe* ▷ vb **look out** 6 to be careful 7 to watch out for: *look out particularly for oils that have been flavoured* 8 to find and take out: *little time to look out clothes that she might need* 9 (foll. by on or over) to face in a particular direction: *looking out over the courtyard*

look over vb 1 to inspect or examine ▷ n **look-over** 2 an inspection

look-see n slang a brief inspection

look up vb 1 to discover or confirm by checking in a reference book 2 to improve: *things were looking up* 3 **look up to** to have respect for: *she looked up to him as a kind of father* 4 to visit (a person): *I'll look you up when I'm in town*

loom¹ n a machine for weaving yarn into cloth [variant of Old English *gelōma* tool]

loom² vb 1 to appear indistinctly, esp. as a tall and threatening shape 2 (of an event) to seem ominously close [perhaps East Frisian *lomen* to move slowly]

loon¹ n US and Canad same as **diver** (3) [Scandinavian]

loon² n informal a simple-minded or stupid person

loonie n Canad slang 1 a Canadian dollar coin with a loon bird on one of its faces 2 the Canadian currency

loony slang adj **loonier**, **looniest** 1 insane 2 foolish or ridiculous ▷ n, pl **loonies** 3 a foolish or insane person [shortened from *lunatic*]

loop n 1 the rounded shape formed by a curved line that crosses itself: *a loop of the highway* 2 any round or oval-shaped thing that is closed or nearly closed 3 *electronics* a closed circuit through which a signal can circulate 4 a flight manoeuvre in which an aircraft flies vertically in a complete circle 5 a continuous strip of film or tape 6 *computers* a series of instructions in a program, performed repeatedly until some specified condition is satisfied ▷ vb 7 to make into a loop 8 to fasten or encircle with a loop 9 Also: **loop the loop** to fly or be flown vertically in a complete circle [origin unknown]

loophole n an ambiguity or omission in the law, which enables one to evade it

loopy adj **loopier**, **loopiest** informal slightly mad or crazy

Loos n Adolf. 1870–1933, Austrian architect: a pioneer of modern architecture, noted for his plain austere style in such buildings as Steiner House, Vienna (1910)

loose adj 1 (of clothing) not close-fitting: *the jacket loose and unbuttoned* 2 free or released from confinement or restraint **3** not tight, fastened, fixed, or tense **4** not bundled, fastened, or put in a container: *loose tobacco* **5** inexact or imprecise: *a loose translation* **6** (of cash) accessible: *a lot of the loose money is floating around the city* **7** *old-fashioned* sexually promiscuous **8** lacking a sense of propriety: *loose talk* **9 at a loose end** bored because one has nothing to do ▷ *n* **10 on the loose** free from confinement or restraint **11 the loose** *rugby* the part of play when the forwards close round the ball in a ruck or loose scrum ▷ *adv* **12** in a loose manner; loosely ▷ *vb* **loosing, loosed 13** to free or release from restraint or obligation: *he loosed the dogs* **14** to unfasten or untie: *the guards loosed his arms* **15** to make or become less strict, tight, firmly attached, or compact **16** to let fly (a bullet, arrow, or other missile) [Old Norse *lauss* free] ⟩ **loosely** *adv* ⟩ **looseness** *n*

loosebox *n* an enclosed stall with a door in which an animal can be kept

loose cannon *n* a person or thing, with the potential to cause considerable damage, that appears to be out of control

loose-jointed *adj* supple and lithe

loose-leaf *adj* (of a binder) allowing the removal and addition of pages

loosen *vb* **1** to make or become less tight: *loosen and relax the ankle* **2** (often foll. by *up*) to make or become less firm, compact, or rigid: *massage is used first to loosen up the muscles* **3** to untie **4** (often foll. by *up*) to make or become less strict: *the churches loosen up on sexual teachings*

loot *n* **1** goods stolen in wartime or during riots; plunder **2** *informal* money ▷ *vb* **3** to plunder (a city) during war or riots **4** to steal (money or goods) during war or riots [Hindi *lūt*] ⟩ **looter** *n*

lop *vb* **lopping, lopped** (usually foll. by *off*) **1** to cut (parts) off a tree or body **2** to cut out or eliminate any unnecessary parts: *some parts of the legislature were lopped off* [Middle English *loppe* branches cut off]

lope *vb* **loping, loped 1** to move or run with a long easy stride ▷ *n* **2** a long steady gait or stride [Old Norse *hlaupa* to leap]

lop-eared *adj* (of animals) having ears that droop

Lope de Vega *n* full name *Lope Felix de Vega Carpio*. 1562–1635, Spanish dramatist, novelist, and poet. He established the classic form of Spanish drama and was a major influence on European, esp. French, literature. Some 500 of his 1800 plays are extant

Lopez *n* Jennifer. born 1970, Puerto Rican singer and film actress, known as *J-Lo*; her films include *Out of Site* (1997) and *The Wedding Planner* (2001) and her records include *On the 6* (1999) and *This is Me…Then* (2002)

lopsided *adj* greater in weight, height, or size on one side

loquacious *adj* talkative [Latin *loqui* to speak] ⟩ **loquacity** *n*

Lorca¹ *n* a town in SE Spain, on the Guadalentín River. Pop: 82 511 (2003 est)

Lorca² *n* Federico García. 1898–1936, Spanish poet and dramatist. His poetry, such as *Romancero gitano* (1928), shows his debt to Andalusian folk poetry. His plays include the trilogy *Bodas de sangre* (1933), *Yerma* (1934), and *La Casa de Bernarda Alba* (1936)

lord *n* **1** a person with power or authority over others, such as a monarch or master **2** a male member of the nobility **3** (in medieval Europe) a feudal superior **4 my lord** a respectful form of address used to a judge, bishop, or nobleman ▷ *vb* **5 lord it over someone** to act in a superior manner towards someone [Old English *hlāford* bread keeper]

Lord *n* **1** *Christianity* a title given to God or Jesus Christ **2** *Brit* a title given to certain male peers **3** *Brit* a title given to certain high officials and judges ▷ *interj* **4** an exclamation of dismay or surprise: *Good Lord!*

Lord Chancellor *n Brit government* the cabinet minster who is head of the judiciary and Speaker of the House of Lords

Lord Chief Justice *n* (in England and Wales) the judge who is second only to the Lord Chancellor and president of one division of the High Court of Justice

Lord Howe Island *n* an island in the Tasman Sea, southeast of Australia: part of New South Wales. Area: 17 sq km (6 sq miles). Pop: 401 (2001)

Lord Lieutenant *n* **1** (in Britain) the representative of the Crown in a county **2** (formerly) the British viceroy in Ireland

lordly *adj* **-lier, -liest 1** haughty or arrogant **2** of or suitable to a lord ⟩ **lordliness** *n*

Lord Mayor *n* the mayor in the City of London, in certain other English boroughs, and in some Australian cities

Lord Privy Seal *n* (in Britain) the senior cabinet minister without official duties

Lords *n* **the Lords** short for **House of Lords**

Lord's *n* a cricket ground in N London; headquarters of the MCC

lordship *n* the position or authority of a lord

Lordship *n* (preceded by *Your* or *His*) *Brit* a title used to address or refer to a bishop, a judge of the high court, or any peer except a duke

Lord's Prayer *n* **the Lord's Prayer** the prayer taught by Jesus Christ to his disciples

Lords Spiritual *pl n* (in Britain) the Anglican archbishops and senior bishops who are members of the House of Lords

Lord's Supper *n* **the Lord's Supper** same as **Holy Communion**

Lords Temporal *pl n* (in Britain) the peers other than bishops in their capacity as members of the House of Lords

lore *n* collective knowledge or wisdom on a particular subject [Old English *lār*]

Loren *n* Sophia, real name *Sophia Scicolone*. born 1934, Italian film actress. Her films include *Two Women* (1961) for which she won an Oscar, *The Millionairess* (1961), *Man of La Mancha* (1972), *The Cassandra Crossing* (1977), and *Prêt à Porter* (1994)

Lorentz *n* Hendrik Antoon. 1853–1928, Dutch physicist: shared the Nobel prize for physics (1902) with Zeeman for their work on electromagnetic theory

Lorenz *n* Konrad Zacharias 1903–89, Austrian zoologist, who founded ethology. His works include *On Aggression* (1966): shared the Nobel prize for physiology or medicine 1973

lorgnette (lor-nyet) *n* a pair of spectacles or opera glasses mounted on a long handle [French, from *lorgner* to squint]

Lorient *n* a port in W France, on the Bay of Biscay. Pop: 60 286 (2006)

lorikeet *n* a small brightly coloured Australian parrot

Lorraine *n* **1** a region and former province of E France; ceded to Germany in 1871 after the Franco-Prussian war and regained by France in 1919; rich iron-ore deposits. German name: **Lothringen 2 Kingdom of Lorraine** an early medieval kingdom on the Meuse, Moselle, and Rhine rivers: later a duchy **3** a former duchy in E France, once the S half of this kingdom

lorry *n*, *pl* **-ries** *Brit and S African* a large motor vehicle for transporting heavy loads [perhaps dialect *lurry* to pull]

Los Alamos *n* a town in the US, in New Mexico: the first atomic bomb was developed here. Pop: 18 343 (2000 est)

Los Angeles *n* a city in SW California, on the Pacific: the second largest city in the US, having absorbed many adjacent townships; industrial centre and port; with several universities. Pop: 3 819 951 (2003 est). Abbreviation: **LA**

lose *vb* **losing, lost 1** to come to be without, through carelessness or by accident or theft **2** to fail to keep or maintain: *to lose control* **3** to suffer the loss of: *he will lose his redundancy money* **4** to get rid of: *I've lost a stone this summer* **5** to fail to get or make use of: *Lysenko never lost a chance to* *show his erudition* **6** to be defeated in a fight or competition **7** to fail to see, hear, or understand: *she lost sight of him* **8** to waste: *so I'd lost a fortune* **9** to go astray from: *psychologists lose the trail* **10** to allow to go astray or out of sight: *he lost, at the Gare de Lyon, a case with most of his early manuscripts* **11** to cause the loss of: *I came in to have the gear attended to, which lost me a lap* **12** to absorb or engross: *lost in thought* **13** to die or cause the death of: *two lost as yacht sinks in storm* **14** to outdistance or escape from: *there's some satisfaction in knowing that they've lost us* **15** (of a timepiece) to run slow (by a specified amount) [Old English *losian* to perish]

lose out *vb informal* **1** to be defeated or unsuccessful **2 lose out on** to fail to secure or make use of: *the yard has already lost out on a number of valuable orders this year*

loser *n* **1** a person or thing that loses **2** *informal* a person or thing that seems destined to fail: *he's a bit of a loser*

Losey *n* Joseph. 1909–84, US film director, in Britain from 1952. His films include *The Servant* (1963), *The Go-Between* (1971), and *Don Giovanni* (1979)

losing *adj* unprofitable or failing: *a losing streak that cost him millions*

loss *n* **1** the act or an instance of losing **2** the person, thing, or amount lost: *the only loss was a sleeping-bag* **3** the disadvantage or deprivation resulting from losing: *a loss of sovereignty* **4 at a loss a** uncertain what to do; bewildered **b** with income less than outlay: *they cannot afford to run branches at a loss* [Old English *lōsian* to be destroyed]

loss leader *n* an article offered at a low price to attract customers

lost *vb* **1** the past of **lose** ▷ *adj* **2** unable to find one's way **3** unable to be found or recovered **4** confused or bewildered: *she seemed a bit lost* **5** (sometimes foll. by *on*) not used, noticed, or understood by: *not that the propaganda value of the game was lost on the authorities* **6** no longer possessed or existing: *lost credit* **7** (foll. by *in*) engrossed (in): *he remained lost in his own thoughts* **8** morally fallen: *a lost woman* **9** damned: *a lost soul*

lost cause *n* something with no chance of success

lot *pron* **1 a lot** a great number or quantity: *not that there was a lot to tell; a lot of people* ▷ *n* **2** a collection of things or people: *your lot have wasted enough time* **3** destiny or fortune: *the refugees did not choose their lot* **4** any object, such as a straw or slip of paper, drawn from others at random to make a selection or choice: *they could only be split by the drawing of lots; the casting by lots* **5** the use of lots in making a choice: *chosen by lot* **6** an item or set of items for sale in an auction **7** *US, Canad, Austral and NZ* an area of land: *to the parking lot* **8 a bad lot** an unpleasant or disreputable person **9 cast** *or* **throw in one's lot with someone** to join with voluntarily and share the fortunes of someone **10 the lot** the entire amount or number ▷ *adv* **11** (preceded by *a*) *informal* to a considerable extent, degree, or amount: *steroids are used a lot in weightlifting* ▶ See also **lots** [Old English *hlot*]

Lot *n* **1** a department of S central France, in Midi-Pyrénées region. Capital: Cahors. Pop: 164 413 (2003 est). Area: 5226 sq km (2038 sq miles) **2** a river in S France, rising in the Cévennes and flowing west into the Garonne River. Length: about 483 km (300 miles)

Lot-et-Garonne *n* a department of SW France, in Aquitaine. Capital: Agen. Pop: 309 993 (2003 est). Area: 5385 sq km (2100 sq miles)

loth (rhymes with **both**) *adj* same as **loath**

Lothair I *n* ?795–855 AD, Frankish ruler and Holy Roman Emperor (823–30, 833–34, 840–55); son of Louis I, whom he twice deposed from the throne

Lothair II *n* called *the Saxon*. ?1070–1137, German king (1125–37) and Holy Roman Emperor (1133–37). He was elected German king over the hereditary Hohenstaufen claimant

Lothario (loh-thah-ree-oh) *n, pl* **-os** a seducer [after a character in a play]

Lothian Region *n* a former local government region in

SE central Scotland, formed in 1975 from East Lothian, most of Midlothian, and West Lothian; replaced in 1996 by the council areas of East Lothian, Midlothian, West Lothian, and Edinburgh

Lothians *pl n* the **Lothians** three historic counties of SE central Scotland (now council areas): East Lothian, West Lothian, and Midlothian (including Edinburgh)

Lothringen *n* the German name for **Lorraine**

lotion *n* a liquid preparation having a soothing, cleansing, or antiseptic action, applied to the skin [Latin *lotio* a washing]

lots *informal pron* **1** (often foll. by *of*) great numbers or quantities: *lots of friends; you can read lots into Nostradamus* ▷ *adv* **2** a great deal

lottery *n, pl* **-teries 1** a method of raising money by selling tickets by which a winner is selected at random **2** a venture whose outcome is a matter of luck: *hospital treatment is a lottery* [Middle Dutch *loterije*]

lotto *n* **1** a game of chance similar to bingo **2 Lotto** (in certain countries) the national lottery [Italian]

lotus *n* **1** (in Greek mythology) a fruit that induces dreamy forgetfulness in those who eat it **2** any of several water lilies of tropical Africa and Asia, regarded as sacred **3** a symbolic representation of such a plant [Greek *lōtos*]

lotus-eater *n* a person who lives in lazy forgetfulness

lotus position *n* a seated cross-legged position with each foot on top of the opposite thigh, used in yoga and meditation

loud *adj* **1** (of sound) relatively great in volume: *loud applause* **2** making or able to make sounds of relatively great volume: *a loud voice* **3** insistent and emphatic: *loud appeals* **4** (of colours or patterns) harsh to look at **5** noisy, vulgar, and offensive ▷ *adv* **6** in a loud manner **7 out loud** audibly [Old English *hlud*] ▶ **loudly** *adv* ▶ **loudness** *n*

loud-hailer *n* a portable loudspeaker with a built-in amplifier and microphone

loudmouth *n* a person who talks too much, esp. in a boastful or indiscreet way ▶ **loudmouthed** *adj*

loudspeaker *n* a device for converting electrical signals into sounds

lough *n Irish* **1** a lake **2** a long narrow arm of the sea [Irish *loch* lake]

Loughborough *n* a town in central England, in N Leicestershire: university (1966). Pop: 55 258 (2001)

Louis *n* Joe, real name *Joseph Louis Barrow*, nicknamed *the Brown Bomber*. 1914–81, US boxer; world heavyweight champion (1937–49)

Louis I *n* known as *Louis the Pious* or *Louis the Debonair*. 778–840 AD, king of France and Holy Roman Emperor (814–23, 830–33, 834–40): he was twice deposed by his sons

Louis II *n* **1** known as *Louis the German*. ?804–876 AD, king of Germany (843–76); son of Louis I **2 de Bourbon.** See (Prince de) **Condé**

Louis IV *n* known as *Louis the Bavarian*. ?1287–1347, king of Germany (1314–47) and Holy Roman Emperor (1328–47)

Louis V *n* known as *Louis le Fainéant*. ?967–987 AD, last Carolingian king of France (986–87)

Louis VII *n* known as *Louis le Jeune. c.* 1120–80, king of France (1137–80). He engaged in frequent hostilities (1152–74) with Henry II of England

Louis VIII *n* known as *Coeur-de-Lion*. 1187–1226, king of France (1223–26). He was offered the English throne by opponents of King John but his invasion failed (1216)

Louis IX *n* known as *Saint Louis*. 1214–70, king of France (1226–70): led the Sixth Crusade (1248–54) and was held to ransom (1250); died at Tunis while on another crusade

Louis XI *n* 1423–83, king of France (1461–83): involved in a struggle with his vassals, esp. the duke of Burgundy, in his attempt to unite France under an absolute monarchy

Louis XII *n* 1462–1515, king of France (1498–1515), who fought a series of unsuccessful wars in Italy

Louis XIII n 1601–43, king of France (1610–43). His mother (Marie de Médicis) was regent until 1617; after 1624 he was influenced by his chief minister Richelieu

Louis XIV n known as *le roi soleil* (the Sun King). 1638–1715, king of France (1643–1715); son of Louis XIII and Anne of Austria. Effective ruler from 1661, he established an absolute monarchy. His attempt to establish French supremacy in Europe, waging almost continual wars from 1667 to 1714, ultimately failed. But his reign is regarded as a golden age of French literature and art

Louis XV n 1710–74, king of France (1715–74); great-grandson of Louis XIV. He engaged France in a series of wars, esp. the disastrous Seven Years' War (1756–63), which undermined the solvency and authority of the crown

Louis XVI n 1754–93, king of France (1774–92); grandson of Louis XV. He married Marie Antoinette in 1770 and they were guillotined during the French Revolution

Louis XVII n 1785–95, titular king of France (1793–95) during the Revolution, after the execution of his father Louis XVI; he died in prison

Louis XVIII n 1755–1824, king of France (1814–24); younger brother of Louis XVI. He became titular king after the death of Louis XVII (1795) and ascended the throne at the Bourbon restoration in 1814. He was forced to flee during the Hundred Days

Louisbourg n a fortress in Canada, in Nova Scotia on SE Cape Breton Island: founded in 1713 by the French and strongly fortified (1720–40); captured by the British (1758) and demolished; reconstructed as a historic site

Louisiana n a state of the southern US, on the Gulf of Mexico: originally a French colony; bought by the US in 1803 as part of the Louisiana Purchase; chiefly low-lying. Capital: Baton Rouge. Pop: 4 496 334 (2003 est). Area: 116 368 sq km (44 930 sq miles). Abbreviation: **La.**, (with zip code) **LA**

Louisiana Purchase n the large region of North America sold by Napoleon I to the US in 1803 for 15 million dollars: consists of the W part of the Mississippi basin. Area: about 2 292 150 sq km (885 000 sq miles)

Louis of Nassau n 1538–74, a leader (1568–74) of the revolt of the Netherlands against Spain: died in battle

Louis Philippe n known as the *Citizen King*. 1773–1850, king of the French (1830–48). His régime became excessively identified with the bourgeoisie and he was forced to abdicate by the revolution of 1848

Louisville n a port in N Kentucky, on the Ohio River: site of the annual Kentucky Derby; university (1837). Pop: 248 762 (2003 est)

lounge n **1** a living room in a private house **2** same as **lounge bar 3** a communal room in a hotel, ship, or airport, used for waiting or relaxing in **4** the act of lounging ▷ vb **lounging, lounged 5** (often foll. by *about* or *around*) to sit or lie in a relaxed manner **6** to pass time lazily or idly [origin unknown]

lounge bar n a more expensive and comfortable bar in a pub or hotel

lounge suit n a man's suit for daytime wear

lour vb same as **lower²**

Lourdes n a town in SW France: a leading place of pilgrimage for Roman Catholics after a peasant girl, Bernadette Soubirous, had visions of the Virgin Mary in 1858. Pop: 15 698 (2006)

Lourenço Marques n the former name (until 1975) of Maputo

lourie (rhymes with **dowry**) or **loerie** n a type of African bird with either crimson or grey plumage [Afrikaans, from Malay]

louse n **1** (pl **lice**) a wingless blood-sucking insect which feeds off man and some animals **2** (pl **louses**) slang an unpleasant or dishonourable person [Old English *lūs*]

louse up vb **lousing, loused** slang to ruin or spoil

lousy adj **lousier, lousiest 1** slang very mean or unpleasant **2** slang inferior or bad **3** slang ill or unwell **4** infested with lice

lout n a crude or oafish person; boor [perhaps Old English *lūtan* to stoop] ▷ **loutish** adj

Louth n a county of NE Republic of Ireland, in Leinster province on the Irish Sea: the smallest of the counties. County town: Dundalk. Pop: 101 821 (2002). Area: 821 sq km (317 sq miles)

Louvain n a town in central Belgium, in Flemish Brabant province: capital of the duchy of Brabant (11th–15th centuries) and centre of the cloth trade; university (1426). Pop: 89 777 (2004 est). Flemish name: **Leuven**

louvre or US **louver** (loo-ver) n **a** any of a set of horizontal slats in a door or window, slanted to admit air but not rain **b** the slats and frame supporting them [Old French *lovier*] ▷ **louvred** or US **louvered** adj

Louvre n the national museum and art gallery of France, in Paris: formerly a royal palace, begun in 1546; used for its present purpose since 1793

lovage n a European herb with greenish-white flowers [Old French *luvesche*, from Latin *ligusticum*, literally: Ligurian (plant)]

love vb **loving, loved 1** to have a great affection for a person or thing **2** to have passionate desire for someone **3** to like (to do something) very much ▷ n **4** an intense emotion of affection towards a person or thing **5** a deep feeling of sexual attraction **6** wholehearted liking for or pleasure in something **7** a beloved person: often used as an endearment **8** *Brit informal* a commonplace term of address, not necessarily restricted to people one knows or has regard for **9** (in tennis, squash, etc.) a score of zero **10** fall in love to become in love **11** for love or money in any circumstances **12** in love feeling a strong emotional and sexual attraction **13** make love to **a** to have sexual intercourse with **b** archaic to court [Old English *lufu*] ▷ **lovable** or **loveable** adj

love affair n a romantic or sexual relationship between two people who are not married to each other

lovebird n any of several small African parrots often kept as cage birds

lovebite n a temporary red mark left on a person's skin by a partner biting or sucking it during lovemaking

love child n euphemistic a child whose parents have not been married to each other

Lovelace n **1 Countess of**, title of *Ada Augusta King*. 1815–52, English mathematician and personal assistant to Charles Babbage: daughter of Lord Byron. She wrote the first computer program **2 Richard.** 1618–58, English Cavalier poet, noted for *To Althea from Prison* (1642) and *Lucasta* (1649)

loveless adj without love: *a loveless marriage*

love-lies-bleeding n a plant with drooping spikes of small red flowers

love life n a person's romantic or sexual relationships

Lovell n Sir Bernard. 1913–2012 English radio astronomer; founder (1951) and director of Jodrell Bank

lovelorn adj miserable because of unreturned love or unhappiness in love

lovely adj **-lier, -liest 1** very attractive or beautiful **2** highly pleasing or enjoyable: *thanks for a lovely evening* ▷ n, pl **-lies 3** slang an attractive woman: *curvaceous lovelies* ▷ **loveliness** n

lovemaking n **1** sexual play and activity between lovers, including sexual intercourse **2** archaic courtship

lover n **1** a person having a sexual relationship with another person outside marriage **2** (often pl) either of the people involved in a love affair **3** someone who loves a specified person or thing: *an animal-lover*

lovesick adj pining or languishing because of love ▷ **lovesickness** n

lovey-dovey adj making a sentimental or showy display of affection

loving adj feeling or showing love and affection ▷ **lovingly** adv

loving cup n a large two-handled cup out of which people drink in turn

low¹ adj **1** having a relatively small distance from base to top: a low wall **2** of less than usual amount, degree, quality, or cost: low score; low inflation **3** situated at a relatively short distance above the ground, sea level, or the horizon: heavy weather with low driving cloud **4** (of numbers) small **5** involving or containing a relatively small amount of something: low-alcohol summer drinks **6** having little value or quality: it sounds as if your self-confidence is low **7** coarse or vulgar: low comedy **8** unworthy or contemptible: Oh, that's low, Justin **9** inferior in culture or status **10** in a weakened physical or mental state **11** with a hushed tone: in a low, scared voice **12** low-necked: a low evening gown **13** music of or having a relatively low pitch **14** (of latitudes) situated not far north or south of the equator **15** having little or no money **16** unfavourable: he has a low opinion of Ford **17** deep: a low bow **18** (of a gear) providing a relatively low speed ▷ adv **19** in a low position, level, or degree: the pilot flew low over the area **20** at a low pitch; deeply: he's singing very low **21** cheaply: the bank is having to buy high and sell low **22** lay low **a** to make (someone) fall by a blow **b** to overcome or destroy **23** lie low to keep or be concealed or quiet ▷ n **24** a low position, level, or degree: shares hit new low **25** an area of low atmospheric pressure; depression [Old Norse lāgr] **> lowness** n

low² n **1** Also: **lowing** the sound uttered by cattle; moo ▷ vb **2** to make a mooing sound [Old English hlōwan]

Low n Sir David. 1891–1963, British political cartoonist, born in New Zealand: created Colonel Blimp

low-alcohol adj (of beer or wine) containing only a small amount of alcohol

Low Archipelago n another name for the **Tuamotu Archipelago**

lowborn adj rare of ignoble or common parentage

lowbrow disparaging n **1** a person with uncultivated or nonintellectual tastes ▷ adj **2** of or for such a person

Low Church n a section of the Church of England which stresses evangelical beliefs and practices **> Low-Church** adj

low comedy n comedy characterized by slapstick and physical action

Low Countries pl n the lowland region of W Europe, on the North Sea: consists of Belgium, Luxembourg, and the Netherlands

low-down informal adj **1** mean, underhand, and dishonest ▷ n **lowdown 2** the **lowdown** information

Lowell n **1** Amy (Lawrence). 1874–1925, US imagist poet and critic **2** James Russell. 1819–91, US poet, essayist, and diplomat, noted for his series of poems in Yankee dialect, Biglow Papers (1848; 1867) **3** Robert (Traill Spence). 1917–77, US poet. His volumes of verse include Lord Weary's Castle (1946), Life Studies (1959), For the Union Dead (1964), and a book of free translations of European poems, Imitations (1961)

lower¹ adj **1** being below one or more other things: the lower branches **2** reduced in amount or value: lower rates **3** Lower geology denoting the early part of a period or formation ▷ vb **4** to cause or allow to move down: she lowered her head **5** to behave in a way that damages one's respect: she'd never lowered herself enough to make a call **6** to lessen or become less: the cholesterol was lowered by medication **7** to make quieter or reduce the pitch of

lower² or **lour** vb (of the sky or weather) to be overcast and menacing [Middle English louren to scowl] **> lowering** or **louring** adj

Lower Austria n a state of NE Austria: the largest Austrian province, containing most of the Vienna basin. Capital: Sankt Pölten. Pop: 1 552 848 (2003 est). Area: 19 170 sq km (7476 sq miles). German name: **Niederösterreich**

Lower California n a mountainous peninsula of NW Mexico, between the Pacific and the Gulf of California: administratively divided into the states of Baja California (or Baja California Norte) and Baja California Sur. Spanish name: **Baja California**

Lower Canada n (from 1791 to 1841) the official name of the S region of the present-day province of Quebec. Compare **Upper Canada**

lower case n (in printing) small letters, as opposed to capital letters **> lower-case** adj

lower class n the class with the lowest position in society **> lower-class** adj

Lower Egypt n one of the two main administrative districts of Egypt: consists of the Nile Delta

lower house n one of the houses of a parliament that has two chambers: usually the larger and more representative

Lower Hutt n an industrial town in New Zealand on the S coast of North Island. Pop: 100 300 (2004 est)

Lower Lakes pl n chiefly Canad Lakes Erie and Ontario

Lower Saxony n a state of N Germany, on the North Sea and including the E Frisian Islands: a leading European producer of petroleum. Capital: Hanover. Pop: 7 993 000 (2003 est). Area: 47 408 sq km (18 489 sq miles). German name: **Niedersachsen**

lowest common denominator n maths the smallest integer or polynomial that is exactly divisible by each denominator of a set of fractions

lowest common multiple n maths the smallest number or quantity that is exactly divisible by each member of a set of numbers or quantities

Lowestoft n a fishing port and resort in E England, in NE Suffolk on the North Sea. Pop: 68 340 (2001)

low frequency n any radio frequency lying between 300 and 30 kilohertz

Low German n a language of N Germany, spoken in rural areas

low-key or **low-keyed** adj **1** restrained or subdued **2** having a low intensity or tone

lowland n **1** relatively low ground **2** (often pl) a low generally flat region ▷ adj **3** of a lowland or lowlands **> lowlander** n

Lowland adj of or relating to the Lowlands of Scotland or the dialect of English spoken there

Lowlands pl n the Lowlands a low generally flat region of central Scotland, around the Forth and Clyde valleys, separating the Southern Uplands from the Highlands **> Lowlander** n

lowlight n **1** an unenjoyable or unpleasant part of an event **2** (usually pl) a streak of darker colour artificially applied to the hair

lowly adj -lier, -liest **1** humble in position or status **2** simple and unpretentious **> lowliness** n

Low Mass n a simplified form of Mass that is spoken rather than sung

low-minded adj having a vulgar or crude mind **> low-mindedness** n

low-pitched adj **1** pitched low in tone **2** (of a roof) with a shallow slope

low profile n a deliberate shunning of publicity: he kept a low profile **> low-profile** adj

Lowry n **1** L(awrence) S(tephen). 1887–1976, English painter, noted for his bleak northern industrial scenes, often containing primitive or stylized figures **2** (Clarence) Malcolm. 1909–57, British novelist and writer, best known for his semiautobiographical novel Under the Volcano (1947)

low-spirited adj depressed or dejected

low-tech adj **1** of or using low technology **2** in the style of interior design that uses items associated with low technology

low technology n unsophisticated technology that is limited to the production of basic necessities

low tide n the tide at its lowest level or the time at which it reaches this

low water n **1** low tide **2** the lowest level which a stretch of water reaches

loyal adj **1** faithful to one's friends, country, or government **2** of or expressing loyalty: *the loyal toast* [Latin *legalis* legal] ➤ **loyally** adv

loyalist n a patriotic supporter of the sovereign or government ➤ **loyalism** n

Loyalist n (in Northern Ireland) a Protestant wishing to retain Ulster's link with Britain

loyalty n, pl **-ties 1** the quality of being loyal **2** a feeling of friendship or duty towards someone or something

loyalty card n a swipe card issued by a supermarket or chain store to a customer, used to record credit points awarded for money spent in the store

Loyang n a variant transliteration of the Chinese name for Luoyang

lozenge n **1** *med* a medicated tablet held in the mouth until it has dissolved **2** *geometry* a rhombus [Old French *losange*]

Lozère n a department of S central France, in Languedoc-Roussillon region. Capital: Mende. Pop: 74 234 (2003 est). Area: 5180 sq km (2020 sq miles)

LP n a gramophone record of 12 inches in diameter, which holds about 20 or 25 minutes of sound on each side [shortened from *long player*]

L-plate n *Brit and Austral* a red 'L' on a white square attached to a motor vehicle to indicate that the driver is a learner

L'pool Liverpool

Lr *chem* lawrencium

LSD n lysergic acid diethylamide, an illegal hallucinogenic drug

L.S.D., £.s.d. or **l.s.d.** pounds, shillings, pence [Latin *librae, solidi, denarii*]

Lt Lieutenant

Ltd *Brit* Limited (Liability)

Lu *chem* lutetium

Lualaba n a river in the SE Democratic Republic of Congo, rising in Katanga province and flowing north as the W headstream of the River Congo. Length: about 1800 km (1100 miles)

Luanda or **Loanda** n the capital of Angola, a port in the west, on the Atlantic: founded in 1576, it became a centre of the slave trade to Brazil in the 17th and 18th centuries; oil refining. Pop: 2 839 000 (2005 est). Official name: **São Paulo de Loanda**

Luang Prabang n a market town in N Laos, on the Mekong River: residence of the monarch of Laos (1946–75). Pop: 26 400 (2003 est)

lubber n **1** a big, awkward, or stupid person **2** short for landlubber [probably from Old Norse] ➤ **lubberly** adj, adv ➤ **lubberliness** n

Lubbock n a city in NW Texas: cotton market. Pop: 206 481 (2003 est)

Lübeck n a port in N Germany, in Schleswig-Holstein on the Baltic: the leading member of the Hanseatic League, and a major European commercial centre until the 15th century. Pop: 212 754 (2003 est)

Lubitsch n Ernst. 1890–1947, US film director, born in Germany; best known for such sophisticated comedies as *Forbidden Paradise* (1924) and *Ninotchka* (1939)

Lublin n an industrial city in E Poland: provisional seat of the government in 1918 and 1944. Pop: 397 000 (2005 est). Russian name: **Lyublin**

lubricant n a lubricating substance, such as oil

lubricate (loo-brik-ate) vb **-cating, -cated 1** to cover with an oily substance to lessen friction **2** to make greasy, slippery, or smooth [Latin *lubricare* to make slippery] ➤ **lubrication** n

lubricious (loo-brish-uss) adj *formal* or *literary* lewd [Latin *lubricus* slippery]

Lubumbashi n a city in the S Democratic Republic of Congo: founded in 1910 as a copper-mining centre; university (1955). Pop: 1 102 000 (2005 est).

Former name (until 1966): **Elisabethville**

Lucan n Latin name *Marcus Annaeus Lucanus*. 39–65 AD, Roman poet. His epic poem *Pharsalia* describes the civil war between Caesar and Pompey

Lucania n the Latin name for Basilicata

Lucas n George. born 1944, US film director, producer, and writer of screenplays. Films include *American Graffiti* (1973) and *Star Wars* (1977) and its prequels *The Phantom Menace* (1999), *Attack of the Clones* (2002), and *Revenge of the Sith* (2005)

Lucas van Leyden n ?1494–1533, Dutch painter and engraver

Lucca n a city in NW Italy, in Tuscany: centre of a rich agricultural region, noted for the production of olive oil. Pop: 81 862 (2001). Ancient name: **Luca**

lucerne n *Brit and Austral* same as alfalfa

Lucerne n **1** a canton in central Switzerland, northwest of Lake Lucerne: joined the Swiss Confederacy in 1332. Pop: 352 300 (2002 est). Area: 1494 sq km (577 sq miles) **2** a city in central Switzerland, capital of Lucerne canton, on Lake Lucerne: tourist centre. Pop: 59 496 (2000) **3 Lake Lucerne** a lake in central Switzerland: fed and drained chiefly by the River Reuss. Area: 115 sq km (44 sq miles). German name: **Vierwaldstättersee** ▸ German name (for senses 1 and 2): **Luzern**

Lucian n 2nd century AD, Greek writer, noted esp. for his satirical *Dialogues of the Gods* and *Dialogues of the Dead*

lucid adj **1** clear and easily understood **2** capable of clear thought, particularly between periods of insanity or delirium **3** shining or glowing [Latin *lucidus* full of light] ➤ **lucidity** n ➤ **lucidly** adv

Lucifer n Satan [Latin: light-bearer, from *lux* light + *ferre* to bear]

Lucilius n Gaius. ?180–102 BC, Roman satirist, regarded as the originator of poetical satire

luck n **1** events that are subject to chance; fortune, good or bad **2** success or good fortune **3 down on one's luck** lacking good fortune to the extent of suffering hardship **4 no such luck** *informal* unfortunately not **5 try one's luck** to attempt something that is uncertain [Middle Dutch *luc*]

luckless adj unfortunate or unlucky

Lucknow n a city in N India, capital of Uttar Pradesh: capital of Oudh (1775–1856); the British residency was besieged (1857) during the Indian Mutiny. Pop: 2 207 340 (2001)

lucky adj **luckier, luckiest 1** having or bringing good fortune **2** happening by chance, esp. as desired ➤ **luckily** adv

lucky dip n *Brit, Austral and NZ* a box filled with sawdust containing small prizes for which children search

lucrative adj profitable

lucre (loo-ker) n *usually facetious* money or wealth: *filthy lucre* [Latin *lucrum* gain]

Lucretius n full name *Titus Lucretius Carus*. ?96–55 BC, Roman poet and philosopher. In his didactic poem *De rerum natura*, he expounds Epicurus' atomist theory of the universe ➤ **Lucretian** adj

Lucullus n Lucius Licinius. ?110–56 BC, Roman general and consul, famous for his luxurious banquets. He fought Mithradates VI (74–66)

Lucy n Saint. died ?303 AD, a virgin martyred by Diocletian in Syracuse. Feast day: Dec 13

Lüda or **Lü-ta** n a joint name sometimes used for the two port cities of Lüshun and Dalian in NE China, in Liaoning province at the S end of the Liaodong peninsula

Luddite *Brit history* n **1** any of the textile workers opposed to mechanization, who organized machine-breaking between 1811 and 1816 **2** any opponent of industrial change or innovation ▷ adj **3** of the Luddites [after Ned Ludd, who destroyed machinery]

Ludendorff n Erich Friedrich Wilhelm von. 1865–1937, German general, Hindenburg's aide in World War I

Lüdenscheid *n* a city in W Germany, in North Rhine-Westphalia: manufacturing centre for aluminium and plastics. Pop: 79 829 (2003 est)

luderick *n* an Australian fish, usually black or dark brown in colour

Lüderitz *n* a port in Namibia: diamond-mining centre. Pop (admin. constituency): 13 276 (2001)

Ludhiana *n* a city in N India, in the central Punjab: Punjab Agricultural University (1962). Pop: 1 395 053 (2001)

ludicrous *adj* absurd or ridiculous [Latin *ludus* game] **> ludicrously** *adv*

Ludlow *n* a market town in W central England, in Shropshire: castle (11th–16th century). Pop: 9548 (2001)

ludo *n Brit and Austral* a simple board game in which players move counters forward by throwing dice [Latin: I play]

Ludwig II *n* 1845–86, king of Bavaria (1864–86): noted for his extravagant castles and his patronage of Wagner. Declared insane (1886), he drowned himself

Ludwigsburg *n* a city in SW Germany, in Baden-Württemberg north of Stuttgart: expanded in the 18th century around the palace of the dukes of Württemberg. Pop: 87 581 (2003 est)

Ludwigshafen *n* a city in SW Germany, in the Rhineland-Palatinate, on the Rhine: chemical industry. Pop: 162 836 (2003 est)

luff *vb* 1 *nautical* to sail (a ship) into the wind 2 to move the jib of a crane in order to shift a load [Old French *lof*]

lug¹ *vb* **lugging, lugged** to carry or drag with great effort [probably from Old Norse]

lug² *n* 1 a projecting piece by which something is connected, supported, or lifted 2 *informal, Scot* an ear [Scots: ear]

Lugano *n* a town in S Switzerland, on Lake Lugano: a financial centre and tourist resort. Pop: 26 560 (2000)

Lugansk *n* an industrial city in E Ukraine, in the Donbass mining region: established in 1795 as an iron-founding centre. Pop: 454 000 (2005 est). Former name (1935–91): **Voroshilovgrad**

luggage *n* suitcases, trunks, and bags [perhaps LUG¹ + *-age*, as in *baggage*]

lugger *n nautical* a small working boat with an oblong sail [origin unknown]

Lugo *n* a city in NW Spain: Roman walls; Romanesque cathedral. Pop: 91 158 (2003 est). Latin name: **Lucus Augusti**

lugubrious (loo-goo-bree-uss) *adj* mournful or gloomy [Latin *lugere* to grieve]

lugworm *n* a large worm which lives in burrows on sandy shores and is often used as bait by fishermen [origin unknown]

Luhrmann *n* Baz (**Mark Anthony**). born 1962, Australian film director and screenwriter; his films include *Strictly Ballroom* (1992), *Romeo and Juliet* (1996), *Moulin Rouge* (2001), *Australia* (2008), and *The Great Gatsby* (2013)

Luichow Peninsula *n* a variant transliteration of the Chinese name for **Leizhou Peninsula**

Luik *n* the Flemish name for **Liège**

Lukács *n* Georg, original name *György*. 1885–1971, Hungarian Marxist philosopher and literary critic, whose works include *History and Class Consciousness* (1923), *Studies in European Realism* (1946), and *The Historical Novel* (1955)

lukewarm *adj* 1 (of a liquid) moderately warm; tepid 2 lacking enthusiasm or conviction [probably from Old English *hlēow* warm]

Lula da Silva *n* Luiz Inácio. born 1945, Brazilian socialist politician; president of Brazil (2003–2011)

Luleå *n* a port in N Sweden, on the Gulf of Bothnia: industrial and shipbuilding centre; icebound in winter. Pop: 72 608 (2004 est)

lull *vb* 1 to soothe (a person or animal) by soft sounds or motions 2 to calm (fears or suspicions) by deception ▷ *n* 3 a short period of calm [perhaps imitative of crooning sounds]

lullaby *n, pl* **-bies** a quiet song to lull a child to sleep [perhaps a blend of *lull* + *goodbye*]

Lully *n* 1 Jean Baptiste, Italian name *Giovanni Battista Lulli*. 1632–87, French composer, born in Italy; founder of French opera. With Philippe Quinault as librettist, he wrote operas such as *Alceste* (1674) and *Armide* (1686); as superintendent of music at the court of Louis XIV, he wrote incidental music to comedies by Molière 2 Also: **Lull Raymond** or **Ramón**. ?1235–1315, Spanish philosopher, mystic, and missionary. His chief works are *Ars generalis sive magna* and the Utopian novel *Blaquerna*

Luluabourg *n* the former name (until 1966) of **Kananga**

lumbago (lum-**bay**-go) *n* pain in the lower back; low backache [Latin *lumbus* loin]

lumbar *adj* relating to the lower back [Latin *lumbus* loin]

lumbar puncture *n med* insertion of a hollow needle into the lower spinal cord to withdraw fluid for diagnosis

lumber¹ *n* 1 *Brit* unwanted disused household articles 2 *chiefly US and Canad* logs; sawn timber ▷ *vb* 3 *informal* to burden with something unpleasant: *somebody gets lumbered with the extra costs* 4 to fill up with useless household articles 5 *chiefly US and Canad* to convert trees into marketable timber [perhaps from LUMBER²]

lumber² *vb* to move awkwardly and heavily [Middle English *lomeren*] **> lumbering** *adj*

lumberjack *n* (esp. in North America) a person who fells trees and prepares the timber for transport

Lumière *n* Auguste Marie Louis Nicolas. 1862–1954, and his brother, **Louis Jean**, 1864–1948, French chemists and cinema pioneers, who invented a cinematograph and a process of colour photography

luminary *n, pl* **-naries** 1 a a famous person b an expert in a particular subject 2 *literary* something, such as the sun or moon, that gives off light

luminescence *n physics* the emission of light at low temperatures by any process other than burning **> luminescent** *adj*

luminous *adj* 1 reflecting or giving off light: *luminous colours* 2 *no longer in technical use* luminescent: *luminous sparklers* 3 enlightening or wise [Latin *lumen* light] **> luminosity** *n*

lump¹ *n* 1 a small solid mass without definite shape 2 *pathol* any small swelling or tumour 3 *informal* an awkward, heavy, or stupid person 4 a lump in one's throat a tight dry feeling in one's throat, usually caused by great emotion 5 the lump *Brit* self-employed workers in the building trade considered collectively ▷ *adj* 6 in the form of a lump or lumps: *lump sugar* ▷ *vb* 7 (often foll. by *together*) to consider as a single group, often without justification 8 to grow into lumps or become lumpy [probably related to Scandinavian dialect: block]

lump² *vb* **lump it** *informal* to accept something irrespective of personal preference: *if you don't like it, you can lump it* [origin unknown]

lumpectomy *n, pl* **-mies** surgical removal of a tumour in a breast [*lump* + Greek *tomē* a cutting]

lumpish *adj* stupid, clumsy, or heavy **> lumpishness** *n*

lump sum *n* a relatively large sum of money, paid at one time

lumpy *adj* **lumpier, lumpiest** full of or having lumps **> lumpiness** *n*

Lumumba *n* Patrice. 1925–61, Congolese statesman; first prime minister of the Democratic Republic of Congo (1960); assassinated

lunacy *n, pl* **-cies** 1 foolishness 2 (formerly) any severe mental illness

lunar *adj* relating to the moon: *lunar eclipse* [Latin *luna* the moon]

lunatic *adj* 1 foolish; eccentric 2 *archaic* insane ▷ *n* 3 a foolish or annoying person 4 *archaic* a person who is insane [Latin *luna* moon]

lunatic asylum *n offensive* a home or hospital for the mentally ill

lunatic fringe *n* the members of a group who adopt views regarded as extreme

lunch *n* **1** a meal eaten during the middle of the day ▷ *vb* **2** to eat lunch [shortened from *luncheon*]

luncheon *n* a lunch, often a formal one [probably variant of *nuncheon*, from Middle English *none* noon + *schench* drink]

luncheon meat *n* a ground mixture of meat (often pork) and cereal, usually tinned

luncheon voucher *n Brit* a voucher for a specified amount issued to employees and accepted by some restaurants as payment for food

lunchroom *n US and Canad* a room where lunch is served or where students or employees may eat lunches they bring

Lund *n* a city in SE Sweden, northeast of Malmö: founded in about 1020 by the Danish King Canute; the archbishopric for all Scandinavia in the Middle Ages; university (1668). Pop: 101 427 (2004 est)

Lundy *n* an island in SW England, in Devon, in the Bristol Channel: now a bird sanctuary. Pop: 28 (2007)

Lundy's Lane *n* the site, near Niagara Falls, of a major battle (1814) in the War of 1812, in which British and Canadian forces defeated the Americans

Lüneburg *n* a city in N Germany, in Lower Saxony: capital of the duchy of Brunswick-Lüneburg from 1235 to 1369; prominent Hanse town; saline springs. Pop: 70 614 (2003 est)

Lunéville *n* a city in NE France: scene of the signing of the **Peace of Lunéville** between France and Austria (1801). Pop: 20 505 (2008)

lung *n* the part of the body that allows an animal or bird to breathe air. Humans have two lungs, contained within the chest cavity [Old English *lungen*]

lunge *n* **1** a sudden forward motion **2** *fencing* a thrust made by advancing the front foot and straightening the back leg ▷ *vb* **lunging, lunged** **3** to move with a lunge **4** *fencing* to make a lunge [French *allonger* to stretch out (one's arm)]

lungfish *n, pl* **-fish** *or* **-fishes** a freshwater fish with an air-breathing lung

Lungki *or* **Lung-chi** *n* a former name of **Zhangzhou**

Luoyang *or* **Loyang** *n* a city in E China, in N Henan province on the Luo River near its confluence with the Yellow River; an important Buddhist centre in the 5th and 6th centuries; a commercial and industrial centre. Pop: 1 594 000 (2005 est)

lupin *n* a garden plant with large spikes of brightly coloured flowers and flattened pods [Latin *lupinus* wolfish; from the belief that it ravenously exhausted the soil]

lupine *adj* of or like a wolf [Latin *lupus* wolf]

lupus *n* an ulcerous skin disease [Latin: wolf; so called because it rapidly eats away the affected part]

> **USAGE** In current usage the word *lupus* alone is generally understood to signify *lupus vulgaris*. *Lupus erythematosus* is normally referred to in full or by the abbreviation LE.

lurch¹ *vb* **1** to lean or tilt suddenly to one side **2** to stagger ▷ *n* **3** a lurching movement [origin unknown]

lurch² *n* **leave someone in the lurch** to abandon someone in trouble [French *lourche*, a game similar to backgammon]

lure *n* **luring, lured** **1** (sometimes foll. by *away* or *into*) to tempt or attract by the promise of reward ▷ *n* **2** a person or thing that lures **3** *angling* a brightly coloured artificial spinning bait **4** *falconry* a feathered decoy to which small pieces of meat can be attached [Old French *loirre* falconer's lure]

Luria *n* **1** Alexander Romanovich. 1902–77, Russian psychologist, a pioneer of modern neuropsychology. His most important work concerns the psychological effects of brain tumours **2** Isaac (ben Solomon). 1534–72, Jewish mystic living in Egypt and Palestine: noted for his interpretation of the Cabbala

lurid *adj* **1** vivid in shocking detail; sensational: *magazines whose lurid covers sickened him* **2** glaring in colour: *a lurid red tartan* **3** horrible in savagery or violence: *reporting lurid crimes* [Latin *luridus* pale yellow] **› luridly** *adv*

Lurie *n* Alison. born 1926, US novelist. Her novels include *Imaginary Friends* (1967), *The War Between the Tates* (1974), *Foreign Affairs* (1985), and *The Last Resort* (1998)

lurk *vb* **1** to move stealthily or be concealed, esp. for evil purposes **2** to be present in an unobtrusive way; be latent [probably frequentative of *lour*]

lurking *adj* lingering but almost unacknowledged: *it confirms a lurking suspicion*

Lusaka *n* the capital of Zambia, in the southeast at an altitude of 1280 m (4200 ft): became capital of Northern Rhodesia in 1932 and of Zambia in 1964; University of Zambia (1966). Pop: 1 450 000 (2005 est)

Lusatia *n* a region of central Europe, lying between the upper reaches of the Elbe and Oder Rivers: now mostly in E Germany, extending into SW Poland; inhabited chiefly by Sorbs

Lusatian *adj* **1** of or relating to Lusatia, its people, or their language ▷ *n* **2** a native or inhabitant of Lusatia; a Sorb **3** the Sorbian language

luscious (lush-uss) *adj* **1** extremely pleasurable to taste or smell **2** very attractive [perhaps short for *delicious*]

lush¹ *adj* **1** (of vegetation) growing thickly and healthily **2** luxurious, elaborate, or opulent **3** *slang* very attractive or pleasing [Latin *laxus* loose]

lush² *n slang* an alcoholic [origin unknown]

Lüshun *n* a port in NE China, in S Liaoning province, at the S end of the Liaodong peninsula; together with the city of Dalian it comprises the port complex of Lüda: jointly held by China and the Soviet Union (1945–55). Former name: **Port Arthur**

Lusitania *n* an ancient region of the W Iberian Peninsula: a Roman province from 27 BC to the late 4th century AD; corresponds to most of present-day Portugal and the Spanish provinces of Salamanca and Cáceres

Lusitanian *adj* **1** *chiefly poetic* of or relating to Lusitania or Portugal **2** *biology* denoting flora or fauna characteristically found only in the warm, moist, west-facing coastal regions of Portugal, Spain, France, and the west and southwest coasts of Great Britain and Ireland

lust *n* **1** a strong sexual desire **2** a strong desire or drive: *a lust for power* ▷ *vb* **3** (often foll. by *after* or *for*) to have a passionate desire (for) [Old English] **› lustful** *adj* **› lustfully** *adv*

lustre *or US* **luster** *n* **1** soft shining light reflected from a surface; sheen **2** great splendour or glory **3** a shiny metallic surface on some pottery and porcelain [Latin *lustrare* to make bright] **› lustrous** *adj*

lusty *adj* **lustier, lustiest** **1** healthy and full of strength and energy **2** strong or invigorating **› lustily** *adv* **› lustiness** *n*

Lü-ta *n* a variant transliteration of the Chinese name for Lüda

lute *n* an ancient plucked stringed instrument with a long fingerboard and a body shaped like a half pear [Arabic *al 'ūd*, literally: the wood]

Lutetia *or* **Lutetia Parisiorum** *n* an ancient name for Paris (1)

lutetium (loo-tee-shee-um) *n chem* a silvery-white metallic element of the lanthanide series. Symbol: Lu [*Lutetia*, ancient name of Paris]

Luther *n* Martin. 1483–1546, German leader of the Protestant Reformation. As professor of biblical theology at Wittenberg University from 1511, he began preaching the crucial doctrine of justification by faith rather than by works, and in 1517 he nailed 95 theses to the church door at Wittenberg, attacking Tetzel's sale of indulgences. He was excommunicated and outlawed by the Diet of Worms (1521) as a result of his refusal to recant, but he was protected in Wartburg Castle by Frederick III of Saxony (1521–22). He translated the Bible into German (1521–34) and approved Melanchthon's Augsburg Confession (1530), defining the basic tenets of Lutheranism ➤ **ˈLutherism** n

Lutheran n **1** a follower of Martin Luther or a member of a Lutheran Church ▷ adj **2** of or relating to Luther, his doctrines, or any of the Churches that follow these doctrines ➤ **Lutheranism** n

Luthuli or **Lutuli** n Chief Albert John. 1899–1967, South African political leader. As president of the African National Congress (1952–60), he campaigned for nonviolent resistance to apartheid: Nobel peace prize 1961

Luton n **1** a town in SE central England, in Luton unitary authority, S Bedfordshire: airport; motor-vehicle industries; university (1993). Pop: 185 543 (2001) **2** a unitary authority in SE central England, in Bedfordshire. Pop: 185 200 (2003 est). Area: 43 sq km (17 sq miles)

Luton Hoo n a mansion near Luton in Bedfordshire: built (1766–67) for the 3rd Earl of Bute by Robert Adam; rebuilt in the 19th century: houses the Wernher Collection of tapestries, porcelain, and paintings

Lutosławski n Witold. 1913–94, Polish composer, whose works frequently juxtapose aleatoric and notated writing

Lutyens n **1** Sir Edwin. 1869–1944, British architect, noted for his neoclassical country houses and his planning of New Delhi, India **2** his daughter, **Elisabeth**. 1906–83, British composer

Lützen n a town near Leipzig in E Germany, in Saxony; site of a battle (1632) in the Thirty Years' War in which the army of the Holy Roman Empire under Wallenstein was defeated by the Swedes under Gustavus Adolphus, who died in the battle

Lützow-Holm Bay n an inlet of the Indian Ocean on the coast of Antarctica, between Enderby Land and Queen Maud Land

luvvie or **luvvy** n, pl **-vies** facetious a person who is involved in acting or the theatre

lux n, pl **lux** the SI unit of illumination [Latin: light]

Lux. Luxembourg

luxe n See de luxe

Luxembourg n **1** a grand duchy in W Europe: it formed the Benelux customs union with the Belgium and the Netherlands in 1948 and was a founder member of the Common Market, now the European Union. Languages: French, German, and Luxemburgish. Religion: Roman Catholic majority. Currency: euro. Capital: Luxembourg. Pop: 514 862 (2013 est). Area: 2586 sq km (999 sq miles) **2** the capital of Luxembourg, on the Alzette River: an industrial centre. Pop: 77 300 (2003 est) **3** a province in SE Belgium, in the Ardennes. Capital: Arlon. Pop: 254 120 (2004 est). Area: 4416 sq km (1705 sq miles)

Luxembourger n a native or inhabitant of Luxembourg

Luxemburg n Rosa. 1871–1919, German socialist leader, led an unsuccessful Communist revolt (1919) with Karl Liebknecht and was assassinated

Luxor n a town in S Egypt, on the River Nile: the southern part of the site of ancient Thebes; many ruins and tombs, notably the temple built by Amenhotep III (about 1411–1375 BC). Pop: 183 000 (2005 est)

luxuriant adj **1** rich and abundant; lush: luxuriant foliage **2** very elaborate or ornate [Latin luxuriare to abound to excess] ➤ **luxuriance** n ➤ **luxuriantly** adv

USAGE See at luxurious.

luxuriate vb **-ating, -ated 1** luxuriate in to take

self-indulgent pleasure in; revel in **2** to flourish profusely

luxurious adj **1** characterized by luxury **2** enjoying or devoted to luxury ➤ **luxuriously** adv

USAGE Luxurious is sometimes wrongly used where luxuriant is meant: he had a luxuriant (not luxurious) moustache; the walls were covered with a luxuriant growth of wisteria.

luxury n, pl **-ries 1** indulgence in rich and sumptuous living **2** something considered an indulgence rather than a necessity ▷ adj **3** relating to, indicating, or supplying luxury: a luxury hotel [Latin luxuria excess]

Luzern n the German name for **Lucerne**

Luzon n the main and largest island of the Philippines, in the N part of the archipelago, separated from the other islands by the Sibuyan Sea: important agriculturally, producing most of the country's rice, with large forests and rich mineral resources; industrial centres at Manila and Batangas. Capital: Quezon City. Pop: 39 500 000 (2000). Area: 108 378 sq km (41 845 sq miles)

LV (in Britain) luncheon voucher

Lviv n the Ukrainian name for **Lvov**

Lvov n an industrial city in W Ukraine: it has belonged to Poland (1340–1772; 1919–39), Austria (1772–1918), Germany (1939–45), and the Soviet Union (1945–91); Ukrainian cultural centre, with a university (1661). Pop: 719 000 (2005 est). Ukrainian name: **Lviv**. Polish name: **Lwów**. German name: **Lemberg**

Lwów n the Polish name for **Lvov**

lx lux

Lyallpur n the former name (until 1979) of **Faisalabad**

Lyautey n Louis Hubert Gonzalve. 1854–1934, French marshal and colonial administrator; resident general in Morocco (1912–25)

Lycaonia n an ancient region of S Asia Minor, north of the Taurus Mountains; corresponds to present-day S central Turkey

lyceum n (now chiefly in the names of buildings) a public building for events such as concerts and lectures [after the LYCEUM]

Lyceum n the Lyceum **1** a school and sports ground of ancient Athens: site of Aristotle's discussions with his pupils **2** the Aristotelian school of philosophy [from Greek Lukeion, named after a temple nearby dedicated to Apollo Lukeios, an epithet of unknown origin]

lychee (lie-chee) n a Chinese fruit with a whitish juicy pulp [Cantonese lai chi]

lych gate or **lich gate** n a roofed gate to a churchyard, formerly used as a temporary shelter for a coffin [Old English līc corpse]

Lycia n an ancient region on the coast of SW Asia Minor: a Persian, Rhodian, and Roman province

Lycian adj **1** of or relating to Lycia, its inhabitants, or their language ▷ n **2** an inhabitant of Lycia **3** the extinct language of the Lycians, belonging to the Anatolian group or family

Lycra n trademark a synthetic elastic fabric used for tight-fitting garments, such as swimsuits

Lycurgus n 9th century BC, Spartan lawgiver. He is traditionally regarded as the founder of the Spartan constitution, military institutions, and educational system

Lydda n another name for **Lod**

Lydgate n John. ?1370–?1450, English poet and monk. His vast output includes devotional works and translations, such as that of a French version of Boccaccio's The Fall of Princes (1430–38)

Lydia n an ancient region on the coast of W Asia Minor: a powerful kingdom in the century and a half before the Persian conquest (546 BC). Chief town: Sardis

Lydian adj **1** of or relating to Lydia, its inhabitants, or their language ▷ *n* **2** an inhabitant of Lydia **3** the extinct language of the Lydians, thought to belong to the Anatolian group or family

lye *n* **1** a caustic solution obtained from wood ash **2** a concentrated solution of sodium hydroxide or potassium hydroxide [Old English *lēag*]

Lyell *n* Sir **Charles**. 1797–1875, Scottish geologist. In *Principles of Geology* (1830–33) he advanced the theory of uniformitarianism, refuting the doctrine of catastrophism

lying *vb* the present participle of **lie¹**, **lie²**

lying-in *n*, *pl* **lyings-in** *old-fashioned* confinement in childbirth

Lyle *n* **Sandy**, full name *Alexander Walter Barr Lyle*. born 1958, Scottish professional golfer: won the British Open Championship (1985) and the US Masters (1988)

Lyly *n* **John**. ?1554–1606, English dramatist and novelist, noted for his two romances, *Euphues, or the Anatomy of Wit* (1578) and *Euphues and his England* (1580), written in an elaborate style

Lyme Regis *n* a resort in S England, in Dorset, on the English Channel: noted for finds of prehistoric fossils. Pop: 4406 (2001)

Lymington *n* a market town in S England, in SW Hampshire, on the Solent: yachting centre and holiday resort. Pop: 14 227 (2001)

lymph *n* the almost colourless body fluid containing chiefly white blood cells [Latin *lympha* water] ▷ **lymphatic** *adj*

lymphatic system *n* a network of fine vessels by which lymph circulates throughout the body

lymph node *n* any of many bean-shaped masses of tissue in the lymphatic system that help to protect against infection

lymphocyte *n* a type of white blood cell [*lymph* + Greek *kutos* vessel]

Lynagh *n* **Michael**. born 1963, Australian Rugby Union player; won 72 caps (1984–95) and scored 911 points (an Australian record)

lynch *vb* (of a mob) to kill (a person) for some supposed offence without a trial [after Captain William *Lynch* of Virginia, US] ▷ **lynching** *n*

Lynch *n* **1** **David**. born 1946, US film director; his work includes the films *Eraserhead* (1977), *Blue Velvet* (1986), *Wild at Heart* (1990), *Mulholland Drive* (2001), and *Inland Empire* (2006), and the television series *Twin Peaks* (1990) **2** **John**, known as *Jack Lynch*. 1917–99, Irish statesman; prime minister of the Republic of Ireland (1966–73; 1977–79)

lynchpin *n* same as **linchpin**

Lyndsay or **Lindsay** *n* Sir **David**. 1486–1554, Scottish poet and courtier, author of *Ane Pleasant Satyre of the Three Estates* (1552)

Lynn¹ *n* another name for **King's Lynn**. Also called: **Lynn Regis**

Lynn² *n* Dame **Vera**, original name *Vera Margaret Lewis*. born 1917, British singer popular during World War II and known as "the forces' sweetheart". Her best-known songs are "We'll Meet Again" and "White Cliffs of Dover"

lynx *n*, *pl* **lynxes** or **lynx** a mammal of the cat family, with grey-brown mottled fur, tufted ears, and a short tail [Greek *lunx*]

lynx-eyed *adj* having keen sight

Lyon *n* a city in SE central France, capital of Rhône department, at the confluence of the Rivers Rhône and Saône: the third largest city in France; a major industrial centre and river port. Pop: 480 778 (2006). English name: **Lyons**. Ancient name: **Lugdunum**

Lyonnais *n* a former province of E central France, on the Rivers Rhône and Saône: occupied by the present-day departments of Rhône and Loire. Chief town: Lyon

Lyons *n* **Joseph Aloysius**. 1879–1939, Australian statesman; prime minister of Australia (1931–39)

lyre *n* an ancient Greek U-shaped stringed instrument, similar to a harp but plucked with a plectrum [Greek *lura*]

lyrebird *n* an Australian bird, the male of which spreads its tail into the shape of a lyre during courtship

lyric *adj* **1 a** (of poetry) expressing the writer's personal feelings **b** (of poetry) having the form and manner of a song **2** of or relating to such poetry **3** (of a singing voice) light and melodic ▷ *n* **4** a short poem of songlike quality **5 lyrics** the words of a popular song: *Cole invests all her lyrics with a touch of drama* [Greek *lura* lyre] ▷ **lyrically** *adv*

lyrical *adj* **1** same as **lyric** (1, 2) **2** enthusiastic or effusive

lyricism *n* **1** the quality or style of lyric poetry **2** emotional outpouring

lyricist *n* a person who writes the words for a song, opera, or musical

Lysander *n* died 395 BC, Spartan naval commander of the Peloponnesian War

Lysenko *n* **Trofim Denisovich**. 1898–1976, Russian biologist and geneticist

Lysias *n* ?450–?380 BC, Athenian orator

Lysimachus *n* ?360–281 BC, Macedonian general under Alexander the Great; king of Thrace (323–281); killed in battle by Seleucus I

Lysippus *n* 4th century BC, Greek sculptor. He introduced a new naturalism into Greek sculpture

Lytham Saint Anne's *n* usually abbreviated to: **Lytham St Anne's** a resort in NW England, in Lancashire on the Irish Sea. Pop: 41 327 (2001).

Lyttelton *n* **Humphrey**. 1921–2008, British jazz trumpeter and band leader who influenced the British revival of New Orleans jazz

Lytton *n* **1st Baron**, title of *Edward George Earle Lytton Bulwer-Lytton*. 1803–73, British novelist, dramatist, and statesman, noted particularly for his historical romances

Lyublin *n* transliteration of the Russian name for **Lublin**

IMPROVE YOUR WRITING:
hints and tips for better communication

1 General skills

The ability to write, speak, and generally communicate effectively is one of the keys to success at school, college, work, and beyond. To be able to adapt the language you use to suit the situation, audience, and purpose is an important life skill.

In this supplement, you will find practical guidance on writing for different purposes and audiences, and advice on how to adapt your tone, style, and content to different forms of communication, from letters and emails to essays and speeches.

Improving your writing style

- The more you read, the better your writing will become. You will find it easier to recognize what works and what does not.

- Use a thesaurus, which will give you alternatives for a large number of everyday words, to expand your vocabulary and look up words you don't know; precise and thoughtful word choices from a wide-ranging vocabulary make for more effective writing and stimulating reading.

- Think about the tone of what you are writing. Avoid using informal and slang terms in a formal piece; by the same token, if you are writing a personal letter or email, a more informal tone may be appropriate.

- Try varying the length of your sentences to make your writing read more interestingly.

- You may find it useful to read your work aloud to check that you have expressed yourself clearly.

- If a sentence does not read well as it is, try rearranging it. Just moving the end of a sentence to the beginning can work wonders.

Planning

Whatever you are writing, plan it before you start. This means:

- thinking through your ideas to make sure you have a clear picture of the task and of how you are going to tackle it

- thinking about the person or group for whom you are writing, what they need to know and how it should be presented

- deciding what you are going to include in the introduction, development, and conclusion

Finding the right reference materials

If you are working on an informative or academic piece, you may want to supplement your material with information from:

- reference books in the library or at home
- the internet
- TV and radio programmes
- people with first-hand experience of your topic

Remember that not all websites are equally reliable; concentrate on academic and other authoritative sites, such as government ones or those of well-known institutions.

Some golden rules

General

- Don't lose sight of the person or group for whom you are writing.
- Don't try to write in an overcomplicated style.
- Avoid irrelevant details.
- Be careful not to endlessly repeat a particular word or expression.
- Make sure that what you write makes sense and that your argument follows logically.
- Always check what you write in terms of spelling and punctuation (including apostrophes).

Paragraphs

- Don't clutter paragraphs with too many ideas. Aim for one unifying idea per paragraph.
- Sketch out what point each paragraph is covering at or near the start of it.
- Try to organize your paragraphs so that they lead on naturally from one another.

Signposting

Use signposting words and phrases to show the progress of an argument.

- To show progress:

    firstly
    I would like to begin by
    now let us turn to
    let us now consider

finally
I would like to conclude by

■ To provide more support for a case:

moreover
in addition
furthermore

■ To introduce a counter-argument:

however
nevertheless
in contrast
let us look at this from the point of view of

■ To round up:

in conclusion
to summarize
all in all
all of this points to the fact that

Sentences

■ Link sentences together logically.

■ Avoid sentences that are longer than three lines. If a sentence looks too long, break it up.

■ Use short sentences for impact and longer sentences to explore an idea.

■ Avoid saying the same thing twice in a sentence. Make every word count.

Written conventions to remember

Abbreviations

There are no set rules about how to write abbreviations, but these guidelines will help:

■ Use a full stop after any abbreviation that does not end with the final letter of the word, e.g. *Co.*; *Jan.*; *misc.*

■ A full stop is unnecessary when the last letter of the abbreviation is the final letter of the word, e.g. *Dr*; *Mr*; *Mrs*; *Revd*

■ Only use abbreviations in formal writing when it would look odd to write the full form of the word.

■ The first time you mention an abbreviation that is uncommon in everyday speech and writing, make sure you always explain what it is by giving the full form too.

Capital letters

Use a capital letter in the following cases:

- for the first word in each line of most poems:

  > *Hence, loathed Melancholy,*
  > *Of Cerberus, and blackest Midnight born...*

- for official, royal, and courtesy titles: *Prime Minister; Prince William*

- to begin all significant words in book and film titles: *Far from the Madding Crowd; Despicable Me*

- for trade names: *Dyson®*

- for the names of countries: *Sri Lanka*

- for the names of peoples and languages: *Spanish; Thai*

- for religions and holy books: *Sikhism; Koran*

- for adjectives derived from proper nouns: *Islamic; Russian*

Use a lower-case letter when referring to points of the compass, the seasons, and for the first word after a semicolon: *It was a long hot summer; we were heading north to escape the heat.*

Numbers

- Generally, write out numbers from one to ten, use numerals from 11 to 99, but use common sense to judge if the number should be written in words, e.g. *two million; five thousand.*

- Hyphenate numbers from 21 to 99 if written out: *twenty-one; thirty-five.* Again, use common sense to decide. If it will look unwieldy, avoid writing it out in words.

- Use commas when giving figures greater than 999:

  1,354
  3,078,000

2 Writing for your audience

Who are you writing for?

It is very important that you keep in mind who you are writing for, that is, your target audience. You might ask yourself:

- What is their age?
- What is their social background?
- What is their educational background?
- How much do they know already about your topic?

With the answers to the above questions in mind, you might ask yourself:

- Do they expect to hear mostly formal language, or might they accept, or even respond better to, informal words and structures?
- Will they be able to follow longer, more complicated sentences, or should you use mainly short sentences?
- Will they expect straightforward vocabulary, or might they understand or expect more 'difficult' vocabulary?
- Will they understand any technical words you want to use, or will you have to explain them?
- If you are creating a text on a computer, which fonts and layouts would they prefer?

Whatever you are trying to achieve, you will have to decide if the language you use is **appropriate** for your audience and the situation.

Formal and informal language

Depending on your audience and context, formal or informal language may be appropriate. These different levels of language are known as **registers**.

Formal language

Most written texts, unless they have been written in a deliberately informal style, are formal in register. In an essay, a letter to a lawyer, or a conversation with an employer, for example, formal language is appropriate. The following are features of formal language:

- impersonal subjects: *This section of the report covers ...*

- passive constructions, where someone 'has something done to them' and the person who did it is not always identified, that help make language less personal: *He was proved to be a liar* rather than *His cousin proved he was a liar*.

- complex sentences containing a number of ideas: *He was proved to be a liar, which surprised and upset me but strengthened my resolve to speak to him*.

- static nouns rather than active verbs: *It strengthened my resolve* rather than *I firmly resolved to ...*

- connecting words and phrases: *therefore; consequently; in conclusion*

- full-out words and phrases: *I am* rather than *I'm*; *because* rather than *coz*

- standard English words and phrases, i.e. English which is considered correct and acceptable by educated native speakers, with no dialect or slang words

Informal language

You are more likely to choose an informal register with people you know well. In a letter to a relative or a conversation with a friend, for example, informal language might be used. The following are features of informal language:

- active sentences, where someone 'does something': *I found out he lied*.

- shorter sentences containing one or two ideas at most: *I found out he lied, and I'm going to talk to him*.

- abbreviations and contracted (shortened) words and phrases: *btw*; *I'm* rather than *I am*

- words and structures from your regional dialect: *wee* rather than *small*; *I ain't* rather than *I am not*

- words and structures from your own social dialect – the language you use in your social group: *I was like, 'What?' and she was like, 'I'm not going'*.

- possibly, slang words and phrases. Note that slang is very informal language that you only use with people you know very well.

3 Writing to achieve a purpose

Why are you writing?

It is important that you keep in mind why you are writing, that is, what you are trying to achieve with your work. This section looks at the possible reasons for a communication and the language features you can use to achieve your purpose.

Informing

If you are writing to inform, it is crucial for your audience's understanding that the information is clearly structured and expressed.

As with any communication, think about the person or group for whom you are writing and what and how much they need to be told to get a picture of what is happening.

- Introduce the subject clearly, giving an outline and the context of what you are talking about.

- Summarize the facts briefly, clearly, and in a logical order using simple language. The language should be straightforward and 'mean what it says' rather than rely on connotation or suggestion. If you use a technical term, explain it if necessary.

- Paragraphs should be neither too long nor too short. Use bullet points or numbered lists if they help to convey the information clearly. Make clear links between your paragraphs.

- Give the facts in an objective and balanced way. You are presenting facts rather than opinions.

- Use information from more than one source to achieve a balanced view.

- Include statistics and examples, but be careful not to include a lot of irrelevant detail.

- If you are working on a computer, try experimenting with different page layouts and type sizes to help divide up the information and draw the reader's attention to the most important facts.

Explaining

As with informing, think about your audience and how much or how little you need to explain so they understand what is happening.

- Break the explanation down into its important parts. Plan your explanation so that it follows a sensible order and is easy to understand.

- Use connecting words between parts:

  firstly
  next
  finally

- Your text should explain 'how' and/or 'why'. Use words and phrases that show how one thing explains another:

  as a consequence
  therefore
  it follows that
  and this will cause
  in view of the fact that

- Give the explanation in an objective way, without your personal opinions. Give specific examples that support your explanation.

- Use clear, formal language to explain. If you use a technical term, explain it if necessary.

- Be careful not to include a lot of irrelevant and confusing detail but give your audience all the key information.

- Aim to make your piece lively in order to engage and maintain your audience's interest. For example, include an anecdote, or an unusual or unexpected detail about the topic.

Persuading

When writing to persuade, you are trying to bring your audience round to your point of view. Think about who you are writing for and how to get them on your side by appealing to their aspirations and interests. If you want to convince your audience to support a worthwhile cause, you might appeal to their sympathy by emphasizing the differences between their circumstances and those of the less fortunate group for whom you are seeking support.

- Have a strong opening to get the attention of your audience.

- You need to sound reasonable. If you rant, this will distance your readers.

- A common technique is to present opinion as fact:

  This is clearly the right thing to do.
  We have no choice but to ...

- Use language that appeals to people's emotions, for example, strong adjectives and adverbs:

  unbelievable
  desperate
  shamefully
  shockingly

- If the people you are addressing might respond to colloquial, familiar terms, use them to emphasize your connection with them.

- Use personal address to involve your audience:

    Think what you would do if you were in this position.
    Can you deny that these people need your help?

- Also use inclusive language, for example the pronouns *we* and *us*, to include your audience in what you are saying and suggest your ideas are shared.

    Let's do something about this.
    We really should …

- Use I when you want to emphasize your personal involvement.

    I was delighted with the progress I saw.

- Imperative structures and short sentences give urgency to your points:

    We must help.
    Act now.

- Use devices such as rhetorical questions (e.g. *Why do we put up with this?*), repetition, lists, and three-part phrases (e.g. *He could, he should, and he will*) to make your point more forcefully.

- Make a closing statement that emphasizes the strength of your point.

Advising

If you are writing to advise, you want to convince your audience that a particular course of action is the right one.

- Address the audience directly using 'you':

    You must see a doctor.

- Use imperative structures:

    Give this up now.

- You could use a 'question and answer' structure:

    What do you do if … ? You should …
    What would I do in this situation? I would …

- Give several suggestions, and give the advantages and disadvantages of any options you propose.

- Come to a clear conclusion so the audience knows exactly what you are advising them to do:

    I would strongly advise …
    It would certainly be best to …
    It makes complete sense to …
    It is entirely in your interest to …

- Give reasons for the course of action you advise. To make your advice sound well thought out, back it up with facts or an anecdote.

    The reasons for this are ...
    This can be justified by the fact that ...
    As a result of ...

Arguing

When presenting an argument, you are supporting a particular point of view and trying to discredit any others. Therefore, you need to look at both sides of the argument, even if you focus more attention on the side you support.

- Make sure your line of argument is reasonable and takes all the necessary facts into account.
- Do justice to the opposing side by convincingly and politely countering their arguments:

    Some politicians argue that computer games make people violent, but the evidence would suggest this is not the case.
    These arguments do not give sufficient grounds for ...
    But is ... really the only explanation for ... ?

- Back up your argument with specific examples, facts, and statistics, or perhaps a quote from an expert.
- Never resort to abusive comments or statements you cannot back up.
- Structure your argument logically. Use connectives such as *however* and *because* and words that reinforce your argument:

    clearly
    obviously
    therefore
    in fact

- Try to sum up the key points and draw conclusions from these. You might use impersonal language to sound objective:

    From this it can be seen that ...
    It is clear from the facts that ...
    The conclusion can be drawn that ...

- Use devices such as rhetorical questions (*Why do we put up with this?*), repetition, lists, balanced sentences (e.g. *He could be right, he could be wrong*), and three-part phrases (e.g. *He could, he should, and he will*) to make your point more forcefully.
- Come to a clear conclusion so the audience is in no doubt about your point of view.

Analysing, reviewing, and commenting

When you analyse, review, or comment, you may be discussing a piece of literature, a film, an event, etc. You should first establish the main facts and then move on to your analysis, review, or comment.

Remember your audience is likely to be familiar with the subject you are writing about. Look at a variety of newspapers and magazines, on paper or online, to see how journalists analyse, review, and comment on current affairs. Note how their approaches and focuses vary to suit their differing readerships.

When you **analyse**, you make an objective exploration of the facts, considering different viewpoints and how valid they are.

- Present your ideas objectively, in the third person rather than using I or me, and without letting your feelings affect your writing.

- You may use quotations or other evidence to illustrate your points.

When you **review**, you give a detached presentation of the facts about a topic followed by impressions and opinions, and give reasons for them.

- You may present your ideas as your own opinions, not necessarily fact:

  in my view
  in my opinion
  My feeling is …
  I can't help thinking that …

- You might compare positive and negative aspects with signposting words and phrases:

  however
  in comparison
  on the other hand
  … does not match …

- You might suggest improvements:

  The director could have …
  The writer ought to …
  The programme makers would be advised to …

- You may use quotations or other evidence to illustrate your points or justify what you have said.

When you **comment**, you give an opinion, either personal or political, on the overall topic.

- You may present your ideas as your own opinions. You might use devices such as rhetorical questions to make your point more forcefully:

  Why would the government choose to do this?
  Why must we tolerate this?
  When did this stop being wrong?

- You may use quotations or other evidence to illustrate your points or justify what you have said.

Describing

When writing to describe, your aim is to show the interesting aspects of something through the use of carefully chosen words and contrasts.

- Remember all your senses. Think about how things look, taste, sound, smell, or feel.

- Bring in your own feelings and personal reactions to the situation you are describing. Were you angry, excited, sad? You might write in the first person: *I was delighted to see …* .

- Use lots of different types of words, even unusual ones. Use adjectives and adverbs to give the appropriate amount of detail that will allow the reader to get a vivid picture of what you are describing.

- Avoid using too many adjectives at once. It is generally better to pick a strong adjective that captures a feeling or impression rather than using three less punchy ones.

- Use words and imagery to create an atmosphere or mood. You can do this through colour, for example: *The steely grey sky seemed to bear down on us.*

- It is often useful to use comparison, metaphor, and simile to make it interesting for your reader: *He prowled the room like a cat.*

- Vary the length of your sentences. Longer sentences can help 'slow down' your text, while shorter sentences seem more dynamic and can be used to describe exciting action.

- Vary the structure of your sentences so your text is not repetitive. For example, change *He opened the door cautiously* to *Cautiously, he opened the door*.

- Open with a strong sentence to get the attention of the reader, and end with a memorable one.

Entertaining

Many of the techniques outlined in **Describing** above also apply to creative writing, the purpose of which is primarily to entertain. However, creative writing involves more imagination.

Before you begin

- If you are writing a story, make an outline of your plot. Decide who the main characters are, what happens to them and what they do, and how any conflict at the centre of your story is resolved. This way, you will keep to a structure and sequence of events and not ramble.

- Decide where and when the action takes place. Use the setting to create a mood or atmosphere. For example, a city on a foggy evening has an eerie aspect; a crowded beach could be either lively or claustrophobic, depending on the point of view of the narrator.

- Decide who is narrating the events. A first person narrator (*I*) has immediacy and can convey a personal response, so you are likely to use one if you are retelling a personal experience. However, a first person narrator cannot convey the thoughts of another person or events outside his or her own perception. A third person narrator (*he/she*) allows you to describe events happening elsewhere and the thoughts of other people, which gives you more options when writing a story.

Once you have started

- Open the text with an arresting or engaging sentence or image: *You've got to love summer, haven't you?*

- If you are writing a story, it is important to develop and describe the characters involved. Think about what they look like, how they dress, how they move.

- Use vivid imagery to create an atmosphere or mood. You might do this through personification, simile, or metaphor, for example: *The shy sun finally revealed itself and spread its warm blanket over us.*

- Remember to describe using as many senses as possible. Create an image for your reader of how something looks, tastes, sounds, smells, or feels.

- Use vivid adjectives and adverbs. If appropriate, use an unexpected or unusual word or phrase that will make the reader take notice. Experiment with language.

- As well as using adjectives and adverbs to describe, use nouns and verbs to reveal something about character and mood. For example, you could say that a character *strides*, rather than *walks*, to suggest an air of purpose or confidence.

- Leave out any details that do not contribute to the overall plot or atmosphere, or the piece will not cohere and the reader will be distracted.

- Any dialogue you include should also be relevant or useful to the story, perhaps to reveal more about a character or create a tense situation.

- Vary your sentence and paragraph lengths to change the pace of your writing. Longer sentences can help 'slow down' your text, while shorter sentences seem more dynamic and can be used to describe exciting action.

- Vary the structure of your sentences to change their emphasis. For example, moving the subject of your sentence to the end can create tension: *Down the alley, onto the street and across the road, he ran for his life.*

4 Types of written communication

This section looks at the features of different written media and supplies some tips for producing them effectively.

Letters

Although people are writing fewer letters than they did in the past, being able to compose a letter, especially a formal one, is still an important skill.

The structure of a letter

- Your address and other contact details
- Date
- Greeting
- Body of letter
- Ending

Formal letters

When you compose a formal letter, you should incorporate the following features:

- a greeting, called a **salutation**. This can address the person by name (e.g. *Dear Ms Brown*) or, if you do not know the name, *Dear Sir*, *Dear Madam*, or *Dear Sir or Madam*.

- an ending, called a **complimentary close**. If you have addressed the person by name, use *Yours sincerely*. If you have used *Dear Sir* or *Dear Madam*, use *Yours faithfully*.

- a clear structure in the main part of the letter. Each paragraph should be short and to the point.

- formal language

- correct punctuation and spelling

55 Torrance Close
Gorton
NSW 2234

25 August 2015

Mr L Dylan
Terrigan Building Ltd
340 Shorter Street
Terrigan
NSW 2234

Dear Mr Dylan

Estimate for extension to living room, 55 Torrance Close

I am writing to thank you for the written estimate which I received this morning. I have queries about a couple of details in your letter which I would like to be resolved before we proceed any further.

First, can you say exactly when you would propose to begin work on the extension? I realize this depends, to some extent, on how quickly you can finish your current project. I need to know which week work would commence in, however, so that I can make arrangements to store the living room furniture.

Second, can you tell me when you propose to fit the additional plumbing, so that I can arrange to stay with friends while there is no running water? Also, are there any other times when you anticipate that I shall be without water or electricity?

Finally, there is no mention of additional costs for materials. Can I assume, therefore, that these are included in the estimate you have provided for the overall cost of the extension?

Assuming I receive satisfactory answers in writing to these queries, I shall be happy to accept your proposal and go ahead with the project as discussed.

Yours sincerely

Jane Brown

Jane Brown

Letters of complaint

Complaining about faulty goods or services is an unpleasant but common experience. Here are some useful phrases you can use in a letter of complaint:

- *I am writing to express my dissatisfaction with the service I received from ...*

- *I wish to draw your attention to an error in ...*

- *At the time of booking it was agreed that ...*

- *However, on our arrival, we discovered that ...*

- *I recently bought ...* (include colour, model, and price) *in your shop in ...*

- *When I tried to use this item, I discovered that ...*

- *I regret to say that ... was unsatisfactory.*

- *I have contacted you by telephone three times and each time you have promised to visit and put the faults right.*

- *To date these problems have not been resolved.*

- *Under the terms of your guarantee, I would like to request a full reimbursement of the amount paid.*

- *I am withholding payment of the above invoice until I have heard your response to the points outlined above.*

15 High Street
Corton
LANCS
LA12 3SH
fheadley@email.com

17 August 2015

Mr D Bryant
High Fi
3 The Parade
Soulton
LANCS
LA23 8GG

Dear Mr Bryant,

I am writing to complain about the Soundalive 411 headphones which I bought from your company, High Fi in Soulton, on 14 August.

When I plugged the headphones into my iPhone and listened to music through them, the sound in the left headphone was distorted at even low levels of volume – it was clear to me that they were faulty.

I returned them to your shop, a thirty mile round trip, but the salesperson who I originally dealt with disputed my claim - stating that the item had been sold in a satisfactory state. He suggested that I take up the complaint with you, as the owner of the shop.

The Sale of Goods Act 1979 makes it clear that goods be as described, fit for purpose and of satisfactory quality. I am therefore rejecting the headphones and request that you refund the £89 I paid, as the condition of the goods I received constitutes a breach of contract. I have enclosed a copy of my receipt.

I also require you to confirm whether you will arrange for the headphones to be collected from me at the above address, or will reimburse me for the cost of returning them by post?

I expect to receive a response detailing your proposals to satisfactorily settle my claim within seven days of this date.

Yours sincerely

F Headley

Mr F Headley

A resignation letter

A lot of letter correspondence within an organization is about HR issues – resignation letters or changes to terms and conditions, for example. These require a signature, are often 'private and confidential' and, like the work contract, may be required for future reference. For these two reasons, formal letters are the appropriate form of writing. Here is an example of a resignation letter.

Anna Wozniaki
Account Manager
Upside Down Records
Flintrock
Sussex
B45 8EP

17 June 2015

Dear Anna

Please accept this as formal notice of my resignation from the position of Account Executive, with effect from today 17th June, 2015.

In accordance with my contract of employment I am happy to continue to work until the end of my notice period which by my calculations is the 15th July.

While I believe that I am moving for good reasons, I am sorry to leave, and I thank you for your support during my time with the company, which I have found enjoyable and fulfilling.

Please let me know the arrangements for returning equipment – my company phone and laptop – and handing over outstanding work and responsibilities.

Yours sincerely

Martin Fry

Martin Fry

- A letter like this is polite, formal, and shows that you want to help to ease the process of your leaving.
- It offers no suggestions about improvements or criticisms of the company – you might be given an opportunity to do that in person at an exit interview.

An invitation

Invitations are frequently made by email or by text, but there are occasions when a written or printed invitation is still the prevalent form of communication.

Boris and Isabel Andrews

request the pleasure of the company of

Phillip and Sally Bairstow

at the wedding of their daughter Florence

to James Chater

on Saturday July 18 2015

at St Bart's Church, Eggleton at 2pm.

R.S.V.P.

Isabel Andrews, The Gildings, Foxton Lane, Biblington, BB13 5TR

Tel: 01286 5543077.

- The most important feature of an invitation is that it must possess all the necessary information to allow the recipient to respond with an acceptance or a refusal. There is no point sending out wedding invitations to 400 guests without the date on them!

- Social invitations can be informal or formal. Formal invitations – to a wedding or a christening, for example – will usually be printed.

Informal letters

If you write an informal letter, perhaps to a friend or relative, it might a similar layout to a formal one, but it will often display the following differences:

- a greeting that addresses a person by their first name: *Dear Raj*; *My dearest Aunt Anne*

- a less formal ending: *Best wishes*; *Kind regards*; or even a very informal one, if it is appropriate for the person you are addressing: *Bye for now*; *With love*

- a looser structure in the main part of the letter. Paragraphs may be longer and more discursive.

- informal language

A thank-you letter

Hi Moz,

I'm just popping this note through your letterbox to thank you so much for dinner on Saturday. Nigel and I had a wonderful evening. It was lovely to meet Sharon and Graham at last – you've talked about them so much over the years – and they were delightful company. I hope Ben has found the champagne cork (sorry about that!)

By the way, please, please send me your recipe for the chocolate mousse – it was exquisite, and Nigel talked of nothing else on Sunday.

You must come to ours for dinner soon.

Love to you both and thanks again,

Lizzie.

Letters of condolence

46 Cork Lane
Lamington
Herts

12 May

Dear Stephen

I am writing to say how sorry I was to hear of your loss, and that I am thinking of you at this difficult time. Although I was aware that Helen was ill, I was nevertheless shocked to hear of her passing.

I know she was never happier than when she had met you, and the two of you made a lovely couple. She seemed to light up the life of everyone who met her.

I shall certainly attend the memorial service next Thursday, but if there is anything I can do in the meantime Stephen, please don't hesitate to call me. I'm sure Jo and Max are a great comfort to you at the moment.

Thinking of you all with love and affection.

Fiona

- In a letter of condolence, you should be acutely sensitive to the addressee's feelings, rather than trying to express your own emotions (as you might in a thank-you letter). The references made to the deceased in this letter are mainly in the context of her relationship with the bereaved partner, rather than the writer.

- A handwritten note can be more appropriate than a phone call in situations of grief and loss like this. Writing a letter also gives you more time to think about what you want to say, and how you want to say it.

- Note that the sample letter, although it is informal in address and tone, still has a discernible structure: the introductory sentence explains the purpose of the letter; the middle paragraph expands on the theme with the writer's memories of the deceased; and the final paragraph acknowledges the future by accepting an invitation and offering support.

A note of apology

If you feel compelled to apologize for your actions and wish to send the person concerned a letter of apology you should start by making it clear that you are saying sorry.

- State plainly what you are apologizing for and explain your actions or the mistake (as the case may be) as far as you can.

- Accept responsibility if you are at fault and try to suggest a means by which you can right the wrong. At the end of the letter, reiterate your apology.

Here are some useful phrases to use in a note of apology:

- *I am writing to apologize for ...*
- *I've just realized that ...*
- *I can't tell you how sorry I am.*
- *I deeply regret ...*
- *I am sorry that ...*
- *Due to ..., I was unable to ...*
- *I know it's no excuse, but ...*
- *Unfortunately ...*
- *I hope you will accept ...*
- *Can you forgive me for ...?*
- *Would you agree to ...?*
- *Again, please accept my apologies (for ...).*
- *In the meantime, many apologies again.*

Emails

Emails are an important form of communication in many people's lives, and the default means of communication for most businesses. As with any writing, your audience is important.

Informal emails

In emails to friends and family you can be relaxed in your style and tone, and it is acceptable to have the following:

- no greetings or closes, or very informal ones: *Hi*; *Thanks*; *Best*
- informal vocabulary and syntax
- a loose structure
- less emphasis on correct spelling, grammar, and punctuation, e.g. the correct use of capitals
- use of abbreviations: *ASAP*; *BTW*
- use of emoticons and emojis to express feelings: ☺

Hiya Jane,

some drawing classes are starting up. there's one on 16th January if you fancy it. There's also one in feb for teaching drawing. BTW Liz who takes the class teaches kids to draw, and thought that may be of interest to you?

Have a look at the attached and let me know if you fancy it, I'll then book it for us.
Cheers!
S
xx

Formal emails

A piece of professional correspondence or a formal email to someone you don't know should have some of the features of a formal letter (see page 16).

- It is usual to use a greeting of some sort when you begin your email. 'Dear' rarely strikes the wrong note. If the contact is long-standing and you are on a familiar footing then 'Hi' or 'Hello' is acceptable.

- If you are emailing someone for the first time without being invited to, it is polite to explain at the very start of the email who you are and why you are writing to them.

- Don't leave the subject line blank. In most formal or professional correspondence you should aim to keep the email to one subject. Think clearly what the email is about and be as precise as you can. Keep the subject as short as possible.

- If the email is going to be long it is polite to indicate this in the opening few sentences of the email.

- Structure your email so that each point is addressed in a separate paragraph. If you wish, it is entirely acceptable to add a heading to each paragraph. Your reader can then see at a glance the points you are covering.

- Avoid using texting abbreviations or emojis and emoticons.

- When you end your email use the same rules as with formal letters, using 'Yours faithfully' or 'Yours sincerely' as appropriate. As your correspondence gets onto a slightly less formal footing then 'Kind regards' or 'Best wishes' is fine.

Dear Jane,

Thank you for your email.

If you cannot remember your password, and passwords do expire after 12 months, you can use the Forgotten Password facility which is accessible from the Login page. This will allow you to reset your own password.

Could I please direct you, Jane, to use the link below to access our website, perhaps keep this in your favourites.

Yours sincerely,

Stella
Customer Services

Job applications

A covering letter and CV are usually the first things any prospective employer will see of you. If you want to get an interview for a job, it is important that these documents present you in the best possible light. These sections deal with how to construct and write your covering letter and CV, and provide tips on how to apply for a job online.

Covering letter

Your covering letter should convey confidence, enthusiasm, and technical knowledge, and demonstrate an understanding of what the job entails. It need not be long and it should not be a rehash of the accompanying CV. A short, clear, well-written covering letter can make all the difference between two candidates.

Your covering letter should alert the employer to the key points of your CV and show the match between your skills and experience and the job being advertised. In general it will consist of three paragraphs or so:

- **First paragraph.** Introduce yourself, say which job you are applying for and where you saw it. You can also include a general statement of why you want to apply for the job and how you feel about the company.

- **Second paragraph.** Provide information about your skills, strengths, qualifications, and experience. Give specific examples of why you are the ideal candidate and don't simply restate your CV.

- **Final paragraph.** Conclude the letter expressing your desire to get the job and requesting an interview. You should also say what the best way to contact you is, and if there are any inconvenient dates. Always thank the employer for considering your application.

Useful phrases

First of all, identify the job you are applying for:

- *I would like to inquire as to whether there are any openings for junior telesales operators in your company.*

- *I am writing to apply for the post of senior marketing manager.*

- *I would like to apply for the position of online learning coordinator, as advertised on your website.*

- *I am writing to apply for the above post, as advertised in the Guardian of 6 August 2015.*

Next, give some examples of personal achievements:

- *I have gained experience in several major aspects of publishing.*

- *I co-ordinated the changeover from one accounting system to another.*

- I developed designs for a new range of knitwear.
- I have supervised a team of telesales operators on several projects.
- I contributed to the development of our new database software.

Then outline your personal qualities:

- I see myself as systematic and meticulous in my approach to work.
- I am a fair and broad-minded person, with an ability to get on well with people from all walks of life.
- I am hardworking and business minded, and I tend to thrive under pressure.

Explain why you want this job:

- I am now keen to find a post with more responsibility.
- I now wish to find a more permanent full-time position.
- I would like to further my career in the field of production.
- I feel that your company's activities most closely match my own values and interests.

Express your willingness to attend an interview.

Avoid just sending a letter or email with 'Please find my CV attached'.

Remember that this application is a two-stage process to try to get an interview. Each step in the process (covering letter and CV) has to make the employer want to take the next step.

Remember the basics:

- Check all spelling and grammar two or three times.
- Make sure you have spelled all names correctly.
- Include all contact details.
- Include any information that the job advertisement has specifically asked you to provide.

An example covering letter is shown on the next page.

Here is an example of a covering letter:

15 Sandybank Drive
Derby
DX27 9LC
joelmanners@email.com
01245 645201

27 July 2015

Mr H Carson
Personnel Manager
Allied Derby Building Society
HR House
Illingworth Way
DERBY
DX3 9DF

Dear Mr Carson

Customer Services Manager

I am responding to the job advertised in the *Derby Express* and on your website on the 22nd July.

I feel the job is just what I have been looking for, and reading the job description, I am sure that I have the right level of experience, aptitude and training. Your company's support and promotion of ethical investment has always impressed and inspired me and I would very much like to contribute to your success. My CV is attached.

For the past three years I have been Senior Customer Services Adviser at Cathedral County Bank, leading a team of seven people. Since I took on the role our positive response rate has risen by 10 per cent and customer satisfaction in the area I look after by 15 per cent. I was voted Employee of the Month three times by my colleagues in the period. While I am very happy in my job, the opportunities for promotion are limited and I do want to take on a more responsible role in my area of expertise.

I would welcome the opportunity to discuss my application further. Email is the best way to contact me and I am available for interview at your convenience. Thank you for taking the time to read my application.

Yours sincerely

Joel Manners

Mr Joel Manners

Your CV

Your CV exists to give a brief description of who you are, what you have done, and what you can do.

- The language should always be 'active'. Avoid passive statements like 'Turnover growth of 25 per cent was achieved in the period,' say instead, 'I increased turnover for the period by 25 per cent.' Active language simplifies your statements and makes them easier to read.

- Use positive adverbs so that your CV will convey a positive impression to your prospective employer:

    efficiently
    successfully
    effectively

CV structure

The most common CV format is called 'reverse chronological', meaning you start with your current job and work backwards. If your earliest jobs have little relevance to your current application, you can simply list the job title, company, and the dates you worked there. Summarize your education after the employment section, and then add any additional skills and interests that may be of use to support your application.

Top ten CV tips

1. Adapt your CV to the job or prospective employer.

2. You have 30-60 seconds to attract your reader's attention as he or she glances through your CV, so lay it out clearly – use a plain font like Arial, Trebuchet, or Times New Roman – and keep it to the point. It should not be longer than 3 sides.

3. Remember the CV is a means of getting an interview, not getting the job.

4. Avoid gimmicks like thumbnail images or pictures – they distract from the words you are writing about yourself.

5. Focus your description of your current and previous experience on achievements and the contribution you made to the organizations.

    If possible, quantify your achievements – 'my actions led to a saving of £xx' or 'as a result profits were up by x per cent'.

6. Give examples of your skills and qualities. Don't just say 'I am a natural leader' – write a brief description of when you showed this attribute.

7. Avoid bullet points when describing your current and previous jobs. It's much better to write short paragraphs because you can give examples.

8. Format the document to make sure that the printed version reflects what you see on screen. Try not to waste paper by leaving just two or three sentences at the top of the last page.

9. Use 'active' verbs such as 'achieve', 'lead', 'manage'.

10. Finally carefully proofread your CV and, if you can, ask someone else to look at it as well.

Helena Shapur

12 Green Lane, Brighton, Sussex BT1 3EY
Email: h.sharpur@email.com
Mobile: 07123 456789

Personal profile

An enthusiastic, self-motivated professional, highly qualified in the field of online team management. My motivation is to use the web to help make the most of all businesses I work for. I have an in-depth understanding of a wide range of web technologies from Java to Ruby.

Career summary

2009 – present Development Team Leader, GoGetting.com

I joined the online travel company GoGetting.com as a development officer before being promoted in August 2012 to my current position. Since becoming team leader the site has had a threefold increase in unique visitors thanks to an extensive linking program I developed. As a result of the increased traffic, the company has given me extra responsibility to drive the marketing of the site with selected web partners. I manage a team of seven development officers and am in charge of a budget of £250,000.

2004 – 2009 Web Developer, Toprank Recruitment

Having learned a lot at my first company and really enjoyed the experience of working in web development, I joined this small recruitment start-up specializing in the catering trade. During the time I helped program the site's search engine and learned ASP, Java and SQL. I was very proud to have seen one key module of the search engine's development through from design to implementation. The module generated five per cent extra revenue for the company while I was there. I learned a lot about effective teamwork in the process.

2002 – 2004 Junior programmer, Oakhampton Systems

This was a perfect job after graduation. I was part of a small graduate intake whose job was to develop and code account and customer databases. I went on site visits to understand what a client needed and understand the way the business works. I taught myself HTML in this period and designed the company's first website.

Education and qualifications

1998 – 2001 University of Windsor, BSC Computer Science (2:1)
1991 – 1998 Greenglades School, Windsor
3 A-levels: Mathematics (A), Physics (A), Chemistry (B)
10 GCSEs

Hobbies and interests

Between leaving school and starting university I worked for six months so that I could spend three months doing charity runs for Famine Relief, whom I continue to work for as a volunteer. I run long-distance competitively, enjoy cinema, computer games and chess.

References available on request.

Online applications

Sometimes you will be asked to complete an application form online. Here are some tips to do this effectively:

- As for written job applications, you should write in a formal style.

- The online system will probably dictate the particular text format (the font and size of type) – you should take this into account when you draft your answers.

- It is useful to prepare a draft of the application and then transfer the information to the online form.

- Copy and save your answers regularly into a normal document in case the system crashes or you have to break off your application and start again.

- Just because the application is automatically filed online, it does not mean you should be any less rigorous in the editing and proofreading you do. If you can print the document out before you submit it, get someone you trust to read it over to look for errors and omissions.

Social media

The development of social media has significantly changed the way we communicate with each other. You are not speaking to a few specific people but with tens, hundreds, or even hundreds of thousands at once. As well as words, you use pictures, clips, and internet links to share information. The best way to describe what you are doing when you use social media, like Facebook, Twitter, or a blog, is that you are projecting a representation of yourself to a wide audience. This makes them very powerful and positive communication tools – for everyone from teenage friends to large corporations. The downside is that you have to be careful about what information you share, and how you share it: how you represent yourself.

As social media like Facebook and Twitter are constantly developing – in terms of their reach and the purposes for which they are being used – the ground rules for successfully using them are changeable. There are, however, definitely some fundamental 'do's and don'ts'. This section focuses on Facebook and Twitter, because they are currently the most popular forms of social media. There are many others – like Instagram and Linkedin – which have different formats and purposes, but most of the advice here will still be applicable.

Social media 'do's'

- **Decide why you're using it.** Is it to keep in touch with friends, be entertained, promote a business or service, or a mixture of all three? Blogging, Twitter, and Facebook are used for all the above reasons, and they have different strengths and weaknesses.

- **Try to be consistent.** If you want to attract more followers on Twitter and other media, this is more likely to happen if people grow to trust and like your opinions or tweets.

- **Be positive.** It's a good principle to keep in mind, even if you don't always follow it. Anger and negativity do not generally translate well into social media, but a positive response to a negative issue can be effective and motivating. Consider whether you might say the same thing, or share the same information, if your audience were in the room with you. If the answer is 'no', then think twice about posting. This is true whether your audience is made up of personal or business contacts, particularly true if it contains both.

- **Be clear.** Nouns and facts work better on Facebook and Twitter than adjectives and adverbs – there is less room for misinterpretation of intention or mood if the message is clear and unambiguous. Of course, if you're casually chatting with friends on Instagram or Twitter, then it's a different matter.

- **Check your privacy settings.** This will help you avoid inadvertently sharing private information on Facebook and other media, or being embarrassed by something posted on your wall to a wider audience than you would like.

- **Reread your message, status update, or tweet before you post it.** It's very easy to make mistakes in spelling or tone, especially if you're posting from a mobile phone with a very small keyboard. Consider using emoticons if you suspect your message is ambiguous.

Social media 'don'ts'

- **'Retweet' (RT) too often.** It can be off-putting to followers. Sharing a link to a video or article you've enjoyed is often welcomed, but be sparing to make a greater impact.

- **Post or tag pictures of friends or acquaintances on Facebook.** Unless you're sure they won't mind, keep intimate details of shared events for private Facebook messaging.

- **Be rude.** It's very tempting to react angrily to tweets or posts that we strongly disagree with – don't. Arguments can escalate very quickly in the online environment and you will almost certainly say things from behind your computer screen that you would not say in real life. A well-reasoned objection, or counter argument, will have more influence than an abusive message, but serious issues are unlikely to be resolved online. If someone you're following, or you've 'friended' on Facebook, is a continual source of annoyance, then unfollow or block them.

- **Get upset if you are 'unfollowed'.** Twitter is a more impersonal medium than Facebook, and people chop and change whom they follow with great frequency.

- **Mix up your work life and personal life.** This applies particularly on Facebook. Your work colleagues may be amused by a picture of you at last night's party but your boss, who may be a Facebook friend of one of them, might find it less amusing – especially if you call in sick the next day.

- **Post sensitive news which might be better relayed by telephone.** It's very easy to say things online that it might be difficult to express over the phone, but this doesn't necessarily make it the better option.

- **Be repetitive in your posts and tweets.** Many people repeat variations on a theme they consider important, hoping to elicit a response, while their audience gets fed up with reading the same information over and over again.

- **Ramble.** On Twitter you're usually restricted to 140 characters, which is good practice for learning how to express yourself succinctly. Try to keep Facebook updates to one or two lines, if possible. If you have a lot to say, you might be better off sending an email or video calling.

- **Forget to punctuate.** The simple fact that messages are short doesn't mean that they will make sense without commas, full stops, and other punctuation marks.

Blogs

With online communications, as with all other forms of writing, you should use language that is appropriate for your audience and purpose.

The characteristics of some blogs you might write, for example for a company or other organization, might differ very little from those of an essay. In such blogs, you must be aware that you are speaking to an audience who is not so much interested in your personal views as in the organization you work for or represent.

- Because they have information to convey to the reader, such posts should be well structured, with clear paragraphs, each dealing with a separate point.

- You should give the blog a title to attract the reader's attention and give an indication of content.

- Use relatively formal or standard language, and conventional spelling and punctuation. However, the tone can still be friendly.

A personal blog might be written with the purpose of convincing the reader of a point of view or conveying a personal experience. These blogs can mimic the more informal features of conversation.

- They can be more loosely structured.

- They give a personal opinion or view, so you can write in the first person.

- You can make references to yourself and your personal experiences in the course of the blog.

- You might want to address the reader directly.
- Informal or conversational words and phrases can be included.

> A certain poet once named April the cruellest month, but I'd wager for most of us, it's January: the holidays are over, but the winter is just getting underway, and those annoying New Year's Resolutions probably only serve to remind us of the ones we failed to keep last year. If only we could just ditch the entire month, eh?

In all cases, you should keep posts short and interesting. People tend to 'scan' blogs for words and images of interest – they may not be paying full attention. For this reason, try to keep sentences short and punchy. Include images and links to other web pages that reinforce your opinions or make the page look attractive. Add headings to break up the text, and keep paragraphs short.

Texts and instant messages

Texts and IMs are short and tend to be written quickly, and your 'audience' is more likely to be someone you know well. This affects the language you might use:

- less emphasis on correct spelling, grammar, and punctuation. Informal spelling might be used deliberately: *luv*; *soz*
- abbreviations: *ASAP*; *BTW*; *LOL*
- if predictive text is not used, words shortened by using single letters or numbers: *THX*; *B4*

Such messages show some characteristics more often associated with spoken language and conversation:

- a loose structure
- informal language and syntax
- use of dialect – words and phrases you use in your social group or the area where you live
- contracted sentences: *Same here; Never!*

In other types of writing, you have plenty of room to express exactly what you want to say. Because of limited space, the language of texts might be imprecise, so texters sometimes worry that what they say is ambiguous and might be misunderstood. Therefore, text messages sometimes have conventions that deliberately emulate how speech conveys feeling, e.g. through volume or tone of voice.

- emojis to express how the speaker is feeling and avoid ambiguity: ☺
- capital letters to suggest shouting: *I am NOT KIDDING*
- asterisks around words to give emphasis: *I am *not* kidding*
- expression of reactions in brackets, mimicking non-verbal elements: *(chortle)*

> Ta 4 text about lunch ☺
> Brill c u then on 15th x

Essays

If you are writing an essay in response to a set question, read the question closely. Look up any unfamiliar words and, if a quotation is included, make sure you know its context.

Pay close attention to the meaning of the verbs used in the question:

Analyse Break up into parts; investigate

Compare Look for similarities and differences between

Contrast Bring out the differences between

Define Give the meaning of

Describe Give a detailed account of

Discuss Investigate, giving reasons for and against

Distinguish Indicate the differences between

Enumerate List in order

Evaluate Give a judgment based on evidence

Examine Look closely into

Explain Give reasons for

Explore Consider from a variety of viewpoints

Illustrate Make clear by using examples

Interpret Show the meaning of

Justify Respond to the most obvious objections concerning

Outline Give only the main features of

Relate Tell in order

Relate to Show how one thing is connected to another

State Present in a clear form

Summarize Give a concise account of, omitting details

Trace Show the development of a topic from a particular point

Language

In general, an essay should not contain informal or slang language. Structure your sentences in a clear, straightforward way, with no ambiguity of meaning.

Planning

Include all the ideas you have under each heading at the planning stage even if you reject some afterwards. Your written plan may consist of just a few key words per heading to help you stay on track, but you might find it works better if it contains quotations, ideas, and sentences. If you write any data that you want to include beside the relevant points in your plan, it will make it less likely that you will forget something vital when you write your essay.

Structure

Introduction

This should typically be a concise paragraph that includes a short, clear statement of the subject you are going to discuss, your definition of any technical terms used in the question, and an indication of how you are going to tackle the question.

Recently, a politician claimed that school uniform should be made compulsory in all schools in the UK, saying it encourages social equality among students. The purpose of this essay is to examine whether this theory has any real foundation and if school uniform does have such positive effects. It will be argued that, despite evidence that uniform does counter some perceived social differences, children and teenagers will still discriminate against some of their peers on the basis of their social background, whether or not uniform is worn.

Development

Keep to your plan, be aware of the question at all times, and keep your writing relevant. A good essay has a clear structure where each main point is dealt with in a separate paragraph.

Conclusion

Like the introduction, this will be fairly short and should summarize the essence of the essay, bringing together all of the major points and referring back to the question to demonstrate that you have answered it. Don't be afraid to make a bold statement on the subject at this point or to include a choice quotation which supports your conclusion; similarly, if there are further questions that have occurred to you in the course of planning or writing the essay, you could include these here, provided they offer an interesting natural progression from what has gone before.

> In conclusion, although there is some evidence that school uniform promotes social equality among students, it does not provide an easy solution to problems of discrimination. Various studies have found that in schools where uniform is compulsory, children have found other reasons to discriminate against their peers. Even having uniform does not guarantee that pupils will not single each other out on the basis of dress: a pupil from a poor household is unlikely to have the smartest or newest uniform. What is more, young people are imaginative enough to adapt the uniform in their own ways, rendering the notion of uniform itself almost redundant.

Conventions for using quotations and references

- Put "…" or '…' around quotations if the words are not your own.

- You can include a brief quotation inside a sentence: *Macbeth says life is "a walking shadow"*.

- If you are quoting a couple of lines of poetry, show where the line breaks with a slash: *Macbeth calls life "a walking shadow, a poor player, / That struts and frets his hour upon the stage"*.

- When quoting a longer piece of poetry, keep the lines and indent the entire section quoted: *As Macbeth says:*

    "Life's but a walking shadow, a poor player,
    That struts and frets his hour upon the stage,
    And then is heard no more".

- Indicate missing words in a quotation with '…' and put square brackets round any words that are not in the actual quotation, but that you have added so that it makes sense: *"My father [the football manager John Johnson] had a great influence on me," he said*.

- If quoting the title of a book or film in a handwritten text, underline it. If working on a computer, use italics.

- Indicate your sources, either by using footnotes or briefly in the text immediately after the quotation. Include the title, author's name, and if quoting from a play, the act, scene, and line number(s).

- If required, supply a bibliography listing all of your sources, including websites, at the end of the essay. For each source significantly referred to or quoted, you should include: author, title, publisher, and place and date of publication. Arrange the sources alphabetically.

Summaries

Summarizing stories, articles, and reports is a skill everyone employs from time to time, whether it is explaining to a friend what happened in the latest episode of a television serial, or whether it is condensing the findings of a long report for the benefit of others.

What are the features of a good summary?

- It is <u>concise</u> and to the point. There is no irrelevant detail.

- It provides an <u>accurate</u> overview of what was discussed in the original.

- It is <u>objective</u> and therefore does not reveal the views of the summarizer.

- It is written in the summarizer's <u>own words</u> and does not plagiarize.

- From the start, it contains phrases which clarify whose views are being presented:

    Murphy argues that ...
    The writer claims that ...

Tips for summary writing

- Read the text once or twice, mentally identifying the main points.

- Next, jot these down from memory.

- Go through the text highlighting or noting any other key points made by the writer and amending your jottings as necessary.

- Now write the summary in your own words as concisely as you can or as required.

- After you have done this, reread the text to check that you have mentioned all the essential points.

- If a word count has been given, count the words you have used and make sure your summary is the right length. If not, you will need to edit it.

- Once the summary is the right length and contains everything it should, reread it to ensure that it follows on logically and that you have not accidentally cut something vital for it to make sense.

Reports

For some school or university subjects, or in some work situations, you may be called upon to write a report presenting the results of a field trip or project.

Language

- In general, an essay should not contain informal or slang language.
- Structure your sentences in a clear, straightforward way, with no ambiguity of meaning.
- Avoid using I or we; adopt an objective tone instead:

    The field trip was conducted in order to ...
    The aim of the project was to ...

- Use passive constructions to help maintain an impersonal tone:

    The information gathered showed that...

Clear presentation

In a report, you can use presentational features that are different from those of an essay or summary.

- Where helpful, use simple graphs and bar and pie charts to represent data. These provide a quick overview of the results and can aid understanding.
- Organize the information into different sections, giving each one a clear heading to help the reader navigate the report.
- If there are a lot of sections, it may be helpful to number them. If one section is composed of several smaller sections, number them as follows:

    1. [Section heading]
    1.1 [Subsection heading]
    1.2 [Subsection heading]

- If you need to include a large amount of data in the report but do not want to interrupt the flow of the text, put it in an appendix.
- Be consistent in your presentation; pay attention to the numbering of sections and appendices.

Structure

To achieve a really professional-looking report, try structuring it as follows:

- **Title page**
  This includes the title, author, and date.
- **Abstract**
  This is a short summary of the report, including aims, methods, and conclusions.

- **Contents**

  This lists the different sections of the report along with the corresponding page numbers.

- **Introduction**

  This explains the purpose of the report and the methods used.

- **Development**

  This contains the information you have collected for the report in a number of clearly headed sections.

- **Conclusion and recommendations**

  This is a brief, easy-to-understand section saying what you have found and what you think needs to be done.

- **Appendices**

  These contain additional information that has been omitted from the main body of the text but which is relevant to the report as a whole.

- **Notes**

  These give details that would be too cumbersome to include in the main text.

- **Bibliography**

  In academic contexts in particular, a bibliography gives an alphabetical list of books, journals, websites, newspapers, etc., to which you have referred during your investigation or in the text itself. Included with the source is the author, title, publisher, and place and date of publication.

5 Types of spoken communication

Presentations

A presentation for work, school, or university is like an essay in some ways. It should have a clear introduction, a main body that develops your ideas, and a strong conclusion. However, a talk will be heard only once, so its language and content must be very straightforward so that each point can be understood immediately.

You must bear in mind your audience and what they will understand and respond to. One of the advantages of a talk is that you can gauge your audience's response right away. A good talk or presentation will involve direct engagement and interaction with your audience.

Preparation

- If you are working in a pair, decide at the outset who will say what and what each person's role is.

- Don't learn your presentation by heart or write it down word for word. Such strategies make for very boring presentations.

- Make notes to refer to during the presentation in case you dry up. If you write these on index cards, you will be able to put each card to the back of the pile once you have used it and will therefore not lose your place.

- Try practising your presentation in front of a supportive friend or family member. Ask him or her to point out any distracting habits you may have and which you should avoid; for example, fiddling with your hair or saying "you know" too often can be very off-putting to your audience.

Structure

As with writing, one of the keys to giving a good spoken presentation is organizing your material. Your talk should be logically thought through and have a clear structure that the audience can recognise and follow.

- Greet your audience and introduce yourself in order to build a rapport.

- Try to start with something exciting but relevant to make your audience sit up and listen.

- Tell your audience what your presentation is about:

    Today I am/we are going to talk to you about ...
    Today I/we will explain ...
    Today I/we want to tell you why ...

- Give an introductory outline of the structure of your presentaton:

  My talk is divided into three areas ...
  In the first part I/we will talk about ...
  Secondly I/we will explain ...
  In the third and final part I/we will demonstrate ...

- In the main body of your talk, make sure you stick to your outline. Avoid introducing a completely new subject later, especially an important one.

- Use linking sentences to lead from one point to the next, as this will keep the structure of the talk clear for both you and your audience:

  I/we would like to begin by ...
  That's all I/we have to say about ...
  Moving on, I/we would like to look at ...
  To bring my/our talk to a conclusion, I/we will ...

- If you are presenting an argument, build from the weakest to the strongest point.

- Your presentation should end with a quick recap of the main points and a strong, and preferably exciting, conclusion.

- Finish by thanking your audience for their attention and inviting their questions and comments.

Language

- Your topic should be clearly stated, and explained interestingly and purposefully enough to hold the attention of your audience.

- Use standard English grammar so everyone in your audience understands what you are saying.

- Use straightforward vocabulary to maintain the comprehension of your audience. Do not use obscure or technical words unless you intend to explain them as part of your talk.

- Use concise sentences. None of your sentences should be long or complicated. In a written piece, a long sentence can be reread, but in a talk, the audience needs to understand immediately.

- Use plenty of connecting words and phrases between sentences so your talk flows:

  firstly
  next
  finally
  as I/we mentioned earlier
  as i/we will explain later

- Use direct address to involve your audience:

  > *As all of you will be aware ...*
  > *No doubt you have all seen ...*

- Especially in spoken language, devices such as rhetorical questions (*Why do we continue to do this?*), repetition, and three-part phrases (e.g. *He could, he should, and he will*) help you make your point more forcefully.

What to include

- Give specific examples – this gives the audience something to discuss in any question-and-answer session after the talk.

- Do not include too many facts and figures – everything in your talk has to make sense immediately, so too many could overwhelm your audience.

- Include a few light jokes or puns to entertain your audience, but remember that they should be appropriate to the overall tone and used *sparingly*.

- Try to bring your own experience and perspective to the presentation material – there may be facts that are known to people in your audience but anything extra you can add will be of interest.

  > *For my part, I ...*
  > *In my experience ...*
  > *I always find that ...*

- Don't be afraid to express your opinions.

  > *What I find most interesting here ...*
  > *What I particularly like about this is ...*

- Consider including some aspect of audience participation, provided it is not intimidating and provided you are not dependent on getting a reaction – audiences do not always cooperate. In general, some degree of interaction makes a presentation more interesting. Ask your audience if they can think of examples or their own reasons for something happening, or for their own opinions on something.

  > *How do you view ... ?*
  > *What is your attitude to ... ?*
  > *I'd be interested to hear what you have to say about ...*

Visual aids

Use visuals to illustrate your presentation, bearing in mind they should be simple, clearly visible, and above all, useful.

If you have access to a computer, you might like to use a presentation program such as PowerPoint®, with slides projected onto a whiteboard. You could use video clips if you feel comfortable doing so.

- If you are going to use a computer or overhead projector in your presentation, make sure you are familiar with how it works beforehand. Fumbling for an on-switch in front of your audience will not increase your confidence!

- Do not overdo the number of visual aids; the last thing you want is to overwhelm your audience with too much visual information and to distract them from your talk. Illustrations should only be used where they really do help to explain or exemplify a point.

- If using PowerPoint® slides, keep the number of slides to a minimum and have a maximum of four bullet points per slide. Keep each one short and to the point.

- If giving your audience hand-outs, make sure you have enough for everyone. Do not rely on being able to print copies at the last minute.

Timing

- Practise giving your presentation in advance, making sure that you tailor it to fit the time you have been given. Failing to complete your talk on time, especially if another speaker is due to come on can be stressful and look unprofessional. Finding yourself left with too much time to fill can have the same effect.

- When you practise your presentation and when you give it, make sure you do not talk too quickly. Take your time. Don't speak at the same rate as you would when chatting to a friend. Slow down and pause for breath between points. This also helps the audience recognize when you are moving on to a different subject.

Your body language

- Stand up straight and keep your chin up as you talk. Posture says a lot about how you feel and a positive, strong stance will both improve your confidence and convince the audience that you have something interesting to say.

- If you are nervous, standing behind a lectern or table may help you feel less vulnerable, as well as give you something to lean on and to put any notes on.

- Use your hands to point to visuals or emphasize important points, but try not to use too many or over-dramatic hand gestures as it can be distracting.

- Smile from time to time. It will relax you and encourage a link with your audience.

- Look members of your audience very briefly in the eye when you can, though avoid looking at any one individual for too long. Look round the faces with a sweeping glance.

Your voice

- Have some water to hand in case your throat becomes dry during your talk.

- If you feel nervous before you begin speaking, practise deep breathing and rehearse your opening sentences to yourself. It is more likely you will sound calm when you start to speak.

- Speak sincerely and with warmth.

- Speak loudly enough so that everyone can hear you, but don't shout. Make sure you speak up when you come to an important point.

- Vary your tone of voice. Slightly exaggerate the rising and falling notes to add interest.

- Vary your pace, but do not talk too fast as you will lose your audience. Speak more slowly to emphasize an essential detail.

- Allow pauses for audience reaction.

- Don't be put off if you make a mistake during the presentation. Apologize quickly and move on.

    I must apologize, what I should have said was ...
    I'm sorry, let me just refer back to ... to make an additional point.

Answering questions

- Try to anticipate the kind of questions that might be asked so you are ready to answer them confidently.

- Use the same techniques you used during your talk while responding to questions – a question-and-answer session can be an important part of the overall presentation and may very well consolidate a positive impression.

- If someone makes a disapproving comment, or asks you a tricky question or one which you cannot answer immediately, thank them for it and answer tactfully:

    That's an interesting comment. However, I maintain ...
    That's a very good question and not one I can answer right now.
    I'm afraid I can't answer that question, but I will try to find out.

Speeches

At some point in your life you're going to have to stand up in front of a group of people and make a speech. It could be at a wedding, at work, or at a friend's significant birthday party or your own. Whatever the occasion, there are some basic language rules you should follow to make your speech successful and memorable.

Preparation

As with all written work, preparation is the key to writing a good speech. There are some basics you should cover before you start to write:

- Make sure you know who you're speaking to. Always keep in mind all of your audience when you start preparing your speech. If the occasion is going to have a mix of people some of whom you know well and others you know less well, then the tone and content will be less intimate than if you are speaking to good friends and family.

- Decide or establish with the hosts how long your speech should be. This could depend on the number of other speakers, the length of time the venue has been hired for, or what other entertainment or activities are planned.

- Start your research early. For example, if you are making a speech for a colleague's retirement, try and speak to old as well as current workmates so that you have a range of stories and views to draw from.

- Think about the venue. Is it likely to be noisy? Are the audience going to be sitting down and comfortable or standing and eager to move? A long, detailed speech in uncomfortable surroundings will quickly lose the audience's attention.

- Decide on your main theme. All good speeches have a central idea that the speaker wants to make – it doesn't matter whether the occasion is a eulogy, wedding, or a speech to the student union.

Structure and content

When you have covered this ground, you can start to write the speech. There are three main parts to it:

The opening

This is perhaps the most important part of the speech. Work hard to make it effective:

- Try to grab your audience's attention from the start. Make a joke, a controversial statement (if the context is appropriate), or do something unexpected and entertaining. The opening sets the tone for the rest of the speech.

- Give a brief outline of what you are going to say. This will help the audience anticipate which parts might be of particular interest to them, and give them a rough idea of how far into the speech you are at any one time.

    I am going to talk to you about ...
    I will then discuss ...
    I will then move on to ...

The body

Having got your audience's attention, you now need to develop your themes:

- The main theme. Use the main theme as a thread working through the body of the speech. If you are going to spend a little time talking about related but not central themes, tell your audience what you are doing and why.

- Use anecdotes. If possible illustrate your themes with anecdotes. If you're saying what a kind person the bride or a colleague is, tell a story that shows this.

- Use stories from other people. Include quotes from friends, famous people, or colleagues to vary the tone of the speech.

- Above all remember that regardless of the precise aim of the speech, your duty is to entertain: you've asked for people's attention; it is your job to reward them.

The finish

Just as with the opening, you need to finish in a way that will make the speech memorable.

- Recapping. Before you end your speech, you should signal to the audience that you are winding up by recapping the points you have made and saying what you hope to have achieved.

- Thanking your audience. You should always thank them for their time and attention and leave them with a memorable phrase, statistic, or story.

Mm

m 1 metre(s) 2 mile(s) 3 milli- 4 million 5 minute(s)
M 1 mach 2 *currency* mark(s) 3 medium 4 mega- 5 (in
Britain) motorway 6 the Roman numeral for 1000
m. 1 male 2 married 3 masculine 4 meridian 5 month
M. 1 Majesty 2 Master 3 (in titles) Member 4 (*pl* **MM.** *or*
MM) Monsieur
ma *n* an informal word for mother
Ma *n* Yo-Yo. born 1955, US cellist, born in France to
Chinese parents
MA 1 Massachusetts 2 Master of Arts
ma'am *n* short for **madam** (1)
Maarianhamina *n* the Finnish name for **Mariehamn**
maas (**mahs**) *n S African* thick soured milk [Nguni
(language group of southern Africa) *amasi* milk]
Maas *n* the Dutch name for the **Meuse**
Maastricht *or* **Maestricht** *n* a city in the SE
Netherlands near the Belgian and German borders:
capital of Limburg province, on the River Maas (Meuse);
a European Community treaty (**Maastricht Treaty**) was
signed here in 1992, setting out the terms for the
creation of the European Union. Pop: 122 000 (2003 est)
Mabuse *n* Jan. original name *Jan Gossaert*. ?1478–?1533,
Flemish painter
mac *or* **mack** *n Brit informal* a mackintosh
Mac *n chiefly US and Canad* an informal term of address to a
man [Gaelic *mac* son of]
macabre (**mak-kahb**-ra) *adj* strange and horrible;
gruesome [French]
macadam *n* a road surface made of compressed layers of
small broken stones, esp. one bound together with tar or
asphalt [after John *McAdam*, engineer]
macadamia (**mak-a-day**-mee-a) *n* an Australian tree
with edible nuts [after John *Macadam*, Australian
chemist]
macadamize *or* -**ise** *vb* -**izing**, -**ized** *or* -**ising**, -**ised** to
pave a road with macadam
McAleese *n* Mary (**Patricia**). born 1951, Irish politician;
president of Ireland (1997–2011)
Macao *n* a special administrative region of China, in the
south of the country, across the estuary of the Zhu Jiang
from Hong Kong: chief centre of European trade with
China in the 18th century; attained partial autonomy in
1976; formerly (until 1999) a Portuguese overseas
province under a long-term lease from China, as with
Hong Kong (a UK territory until 1997); transit trade with
rest of China; tourism and financial services. It retains
its own currency, the pataca. Pop: 583 003 (2013 est).
Area: 16 sq km (6 sq miles). Portuguese name: **Macau**
Macapá *n* a town in NE Brazil, capital of the federal
territory of Amapá, on the Canal do Norte of the Amazon
delta. Pop: 377 000 (2005 est)
macaque (**mak-kahk**) *n* any of various Asian and African
monkeys with cheek pouches and either a short tail or
no tail [W African *makaku*]
macaroni *n*, *pl* -**nis** *or* -**nies** 1 pasta tubes made from
wheat flour 2 (in 18th-century Britain) a man who was

excessively concerned with his clothes and appearance
[Italian (dialect) *maccarone*]
macaroon *n* a sweet biscuit made of ground almonds
[French *macaron*]
Macarthur *n* John. 1767–1834, Australian military
officer, pastoralist, and entrepreneur, born in England.
He established the breeding of merino sheep in
Australia and was influential in founding the
Australian wool industry
MacArthur *n* 1 Douglas. 1880–1964, US general. During
World War II he became commanding general of US
armed forces in the Pacific (1944) and accepted the
surrender of Japan, the Allied occupation of which he
commanded (1945–51). He was commander in chief of
United Nations forces in Korea (1950–51) until dismissed
by President Truman 2 Dame Ellen (**Patricia**). born 1976,
English yachtswoman; in 2005 she set a new world
record for the fastest solo world circumnavigation
Macassar *n* a variant spelling of **Makassar**
Macau *n* the Portuguese name for **Macao**
Macaulay *n* 1 Dame Rose. 1881–1958, British novelist.
Her books include *Dangerous Ages* (1921) and *The Towers of
Trebizond* (1956) 2 Thomas Babington, 1st Baron. 1800–59,
English historian, essayist, and statesman. His *History of
England from the Accession of James the Second* (1848–61) is
regarded as a classic of the Whig interpretation of
history
macaw *n* a large tropical American parrot with a long
tail and brightly coloured feathers [Portuguese *macau*]
Macbeth *n* died 1057, king of Scotland (1040–57):
succeeded Duncan, whom he killed in battle; defeated
and killed by Duncan's son Malcolm III
MacBride *n* Sean. 1904–88, Irish statesman; minister for
external affairs (1948–51); chairman of Amnesty
International (1961–75); Nobel Peace Prize 1974; UN
commissioner for Namibia (1974–76)
McBride *n* Willie John. born 1940, Irish Rugby Union
footballer. A forward, he played for Ireland (1962–75) and
the British Lions (1962–74)
McCahon *n* Colin. 1919–87, influential New Zealand
painter; noted esp. for landscapes and bold abstract
paintings, many featuring lettering and Christian
imagery
McCarthy *n* 1 Cormac. born 1933, US writer; his novels
include *Suttree* (1979), *Blood Meridian* (1985), *All the Pretty
Horses* (1992), *No Country for Old Men* (2005) and *The Road*
(2006) 2 Joseph R(aymond). 1908–57, US Republican
senator, who led (1950–54) the notorious investigations
of alleged Communist infiltration into the US
government 3 Mary (**Therese**). 1912–89, US novelist and
critic; her works include *The Group* (1963)
McCartney *n* 1 Sir Paul. born 1942, English rock
musician and songwriter; member of the Beatles
(1961–70); leader of Wings (1971–81). His recordings
include "Band on the Run" (1973), "Mull of Kintyre"
(1977), "Flowers in the Dirt" (1989), and "Driving Rain"

(2001) **2** his daughter, **Stella**. born 1971, British fashion designer

Macclesfield n a market town in NW England, in Cheshire: former centre of the silk industry; pharmaceuticals, services. Pop: 50 688 (2001)

McConnell n Jack (Wilson), Baron. born 1960, Scottish Labour politician; first minister of the Scottish Parliament (2001–07)

McCormack n John. 1884–1945, Irish tenor: became US citizen 1919

McCormick n Cyrus Hall. 1809–84, US inventor of the reaping machine (1831)

McCoy n Tony, full name *Anthony Peter McCoy*. born 1974, Northern Irish national hunt jockey: champion jockey every season from 1995/96 to 2014/15 during which he rode a record 4,348 winners

McCullers n Carson. 1917–67, US writer, whose novels include *The Heart is a Lonely Hunter* (1940)

MacDiarmid n Hugh, pen name of *Christopher Murray Grieve*. 1892–1978, Scottish poet; a founder of the Scottish National Party. His poems include *A Drunk Man Looks at the Thistle* (1926)

Macdonald n **1** Flora. 1722–90, Scottish heroine, who helped the Young Pretender to escape to Skye after his defeat at the battle of Culloden (1746) **2** Sir John Alexander. 1815–91, Canadian statesman, born in Scotland, who was the first prime minister of the Dominion of Canada (1867–73; 1878–91)

MacDonald n (James) Ramsay. 1866–1937, British statesman, who led the first and second Labour Governments (1924 and 1929–31). He also led a coalition (1931–35), which the majority of the Labour Party refused to support

McDonald n Sir Trevor. born 1939, British television journalist, born in Trinidad; presenter of ITV's *News at Ten* (1990–99)

Macdonnell Ranges pl n a mountain system of central Australia, in S central Northern Territory, extending about 160 km (100 miles) east and west of Alice Springs. Highest peak: Mount Zeil, 1531 m (5024 ft)

mace¹ n **1** a ceremonial staff carried by certain officials **2** a club with a spiked metal head used in the Middle Ages [probably Vulgar Latin *mattea*]

mace² n a spice made from the dried outer casing of the nutmeg [Latin *macir*]

macebearer n a person who carries a mace in processions or ceremonies

Maced. Macedonia(n)

Macedon or **Macedonia** n a region of the S Balkans, now divided among Greece, Bulgaria, and Macedonia (Former Yugoslav Republic of Macedonia). As a kingdom in the ancient world it achieved prominence under Philip II (359–336 BC) and his son Alexander the Great

Macedonia n **1 a** a country in SE Europe, comprising the NW half of ancient Macedon: it became part of the kingdom of Serbs, Croats, and Slovenes (subsequently Yugoslavia) in 1913; it declared independence in 1992, but Greece objected to the use of the historical name Macedonia; in 1993 it was recognized by the UN under its current official name. Official language: Macedonian. Religion: Christian majority, Muslim, nonreligious, and Jewish minorities. Currency: denar. Capital: Skopje. Pop: 2 087 171 (2013 est). Area: 25 713 sq km (10 028 sq miles). Serbian name: **Makedonija**. Official name: **Former Yugoslav Republic of Macedonia, FYROM 2** an area of N Greece, comprising the regions of Macedonia Central, Macedonia West, and part of Macedonia East and Thrace. Modern Greek name: **Makedhonia 3** a district of SW Bulgaria, now occupied by Blagoevgrad province. Area: 6465 sq km (2496 sq miles)

Macedonian adj **1** of or relating to Macedonia, its inhabitants, or any of their languages or dialects ▷ n **2** a native or inhabitant of Macedonia **3** the language of the Former Yugoslav Republic of Macedonia, belonging to the south Slavonic branch of the Indo-European family **4** an extinct language spoken in ancient Macedonia

Maceió n a port in NE Brazil, capital of Alagôas state, on the Atlantic. Pop: 1 137 000 (2005 est)

McEnroe n John (Patrick Jr). born 1959, US tennis player: US singles champion (1979–81; 1984) and doubles champion (1979; 1981;1983;1989): Wimbledon singles champion (1981; 1983; 1984) and doubles champion (1979; 1981; 1983; 1984; 1992)

macerate (mass-er-ate) vb **-ating, -ated** to soften or be softened by soaking [Latin *macerare* to soften]
› macerated adj **› maceration** n

McEwan n Ian (Russell). born 1948, British novelist and short-story writer. His books include *First Love, Last Rites* (1975), *The Child in Time* (1987), *The Innocent* (1990), *Amsterdam* (which won the Booker prize in 1998), *Atonement* (2001), *Saturday* (2005), and *On Chesil Beach* (2007)

McEwen n Sir John. 1900–80, Australian politician: prime minister of Australia (1967–68)

Macgillicuddy's Reeks pl n a range of mountains in SW Republic of Ireland in Kerry: includes Ireland's highest mountain (Carrantuohill)

McGlashan n Don(ald). born 1959, New Zealand musician and songwriter in the bands Blam Blam Blam, the Front Lawn, and the Mutton Birds

McGonagall n William. 1830–?1902, Scottish writer of doggerel, noted for its bathos, repetitive rhymes, poor scansion, and ludicrous effect

McGrath n Glenn (Donald). born 1970, Australian cricketer: played 124 test matches (1993–2007) and took 563 wickets, a record for a fast bowler

MacGregor n Joanna (Clare). born 1959, British concert pianist and broadcaster; recordings include the "crossover" album *Play* (2001)

McGregor n Ewan. born 1971, Scottish actor; his films include *Shallow Grave* (1994), *Trainspotting* (1996), *Moulin Rouge* (2001), *Big Fish* (2004), and *Salmon Fishing in the Yemen* (2011)

McGuinness n (James) Martin (Pacelli). born 1950, Irish Sinn Féin politician; deputy first minister of Northern Ireland from 2007

Mach¹ (mak) n a unit for expressing the speed of an aircraft as a multiple of the speed of sound: *an airliner capable of cruising at Mach 2*. See also **Mach number**

Mach² n Ernst. 1838–1916, Austrian physicist and philosopher. He devised the system of speed measurement using the Mach number. He also founded logical positivism, asserting that the validity of a scientific law is proved only after empirical testing

Machado n Joaquim Maria. 1839–1908, Brazilian author of novels and short stories, whose novels include *Epitaph of a Small Winner* (1881) and *Dom Casmurro* (1899)

Machaut n Guillaume de. c. 1300–77, French composer and poet; a leading exponent of ars nova

Machel n Samora (Moises). 1933–86, Mozambique statesman; president of Mozambique from 1975–86

machete (mash-**ett**-ee) n a broad heavy knife used for cutting or as a weapon [Spanish]

Machiavelli n Niccolò. 1469–1527, Florentine statesman and political philosopher; secretary to the war council of the Florentine republic (1498–1512). His most famous work is *Il Principe* (*The Prince*, 1532)

Machiavellian (mak-ee-a-**vel**-yan) adj cleverly deceitful and unscrupulous [after MACHIAVELLI]
› Machiavellianism n

machinations (mak-in-**nay**-shuns) pl n cunning schemes or plots to gain power or harm an opponent: *the machinations of a power-hungry institution* [Latin *machinari* to plan]

machine n **1** an assembly of components arranged so as to perform a particular task and usually powered by electricity **2** a vehicle, such as a car or aircraft **3** a system within an organization that controls activities and policies: *the party machine* ▷ *vb* **-chining, -chined 4** to shape, cut, or make something using a machine [Latin *machina*] ❭ **machinable** *adj*

machine code *or* **machine language** *n* instructions for a computer in binary or hexadecimal code that require no conversion or translation by the computer

machine gun *n* **1** a rapid-firing automatic gun, using small-arms ammunition ▷ *vb* **machine-gun (-gunning, -gunned) 2** to shoot or fire at with a machine gun

machine-readable *adj* in a form suitable for processing by a computer

machinery *n*, *pl* **-eries 1** machines, machine parts, or machine systems collectively **2** the mechanism of a machine **3** the organization and procedures by which a system functions: *the machinery of international politics*

machine shop *n* a workshop in which machine tools are operated

machine tool *n* a power-driven machine, such as a lathe, for cutting and shaping metal, wood, or plastic

machinist *n* **1** a person who operates machines to cut or process materials **2** a maker or repairer of machines

machismo (mak-**izz**-moh) *n* strong or exaggerated masculinity [from Mexican Spanish *macho* male]

Mach number (mak) *n* the ratio of the speed of a body in a particular medium to the speed of sound in that medium [after Ernst MACH]

macho (match-oh) *adj* **1** strongly or exaggeratedly masculine ▷ *n* **2** strong or exaggerated masculinity [Mexican Spanish *macho* male]

Machu Picchu *n* a ruined Incan city in S Peru

Macías Nguema *n* the former name (until 1979) of Bioko

McIndoe *n* Sir **Archibald Hector**. 1900–60, New Zealand plastic surgeon; noted for his pioneering work with wounded World War II airmen

mack *n Brit informal* same as **mac**

Mackay *n* a port in E Australia, in Queensland: artificial harbour. Pop: 57 649 (2001)

Mackellar *n* **Dorothea**. 1885–1968, Australian poet, who wrote *My Country*, Australia's best known poem

McKellen *n* Sir **Ian (Murray)**. born 1939, British actor, noted esp. for his Shakespearean roles; films include *The Lord of the Rings* trilogy (2001–03)

McKenna *n* **Siobhán**. 1923–86, Irish actress, whose notable roles included Pegeen Mike in Synge's *The Playboy of the Western World* and Shaw's *Saint Joan*

Mackenzie[1] *n* a river in NW Canada, in the Northwest Territories and Nunavut, flowing northwest from Great Slave Lake to the Beaufort Sea: the longest river in Canada; navigable in summer. Length: 1770 km (1100 miles)

Mackenzie[2] *n* **1** Sir **Alexander**. ?1755–1820, Scottish explorer and fur trader in Canada. He explored the Mackenzie River (1789) and was the first European to cross America north of Mexico (1793) **2 Alexander**. 1822–92, Canadian statesman; first Liberal prime minister (1873–78) **3** Sir **Compton**. 1883–1972, English author. His works include *Sinister Street* (1913–14) and the comic novel *Whisky Galore* (1947) **4** Sir **Thomas**. 1854–1930, New Zealand statesman born in Scotland: prime minister of New Zealand (1912) **5 William Lyon**. 1795–1861, Canadian journalist and politician, born in Scotland. He led an unsuccessful rebellion against the oligarchic Family Compact (1837)

McKenzie *n* **Bret**. born 1976, New Zealand comic actor, noted for his partnership with Jemaine Clement as the musical comedy duo Flight of the Conchords

mackerel *n*, *pl* **-rel** *or* **-rels** an edible sea fish [Old French *maquerel*]

Mackerras *n* Sir **Charles**. 1925–2010, Australian conductor, esp. of opera; resident in England

Mackinac *n* a wooded island in N Michigan, in the **Straits of Mackinac** (a channel between the lower and upper peninsulas of Michigan): an ancient Indian

burial ground; state park. Length: 5 km (3 miles)

mackinaw *n chiefly US and Canad* a thick short double-breasted plaid coat [from a variant of *Mackinac*, an island in N Michigan]

Mackinder *n* Sir **Halford John**. 1861–1947, British geographer noted esp. for his work in political geography. His writings include *Democratic Ideas and Reality* (1919)

McKinley[1] *n* **Mount McKinley** *or* **Denali** a mountain in S central Alaska, in the Alaska Range: the highest peak in North America. Height: 6194 m (20 320 ft)

McKinley[2] *n* **William**. 1843–1901, 25th president of the US (1897–1901). His administration was marked by high tariffs and by expansionist policies. He was assassinated

McKinnon *n* Sir **Don(ald) (Charles)**. born 1939, New Zealand politician; secretary-general of the Commonwealth (2000–08); deputy prime minister of New Zealand (1990–96)

mackintosh *or* **macintosh** *n Brit* **1** a raincoat made of rubberized cloth **2** any raincoat [after Charles *Macintosh*, who invented it]

Mackintosh *n* **1** Sir **Cameron (Anthony)**. born 1946, British producer of musicals and theatre owner; his productions include *Cats* (1981), *Les Misérables* (1985), *Miss Saigon* (1987), and *My Fair Lady* (2001) **2 Charles Rennie**. 1868–1928, Scottish architect and artist, exponent of the Art Nouveau style; designer of the Glasgow School of Art (1896)

Maclean *n* **1 Donald**. 1913–83, British civil servant, who spied for the Russians: fled to the former Soviet Union (with Guy Burgess) in 1951 **2 Sorley**. 1911–96, Scottish Gaelic poet. His works include *Dàin do Eimhir agus Dàin Eile* (1943) and *Spring Tide and Neap Tide* (1977)

Macleish *n* **Archibald**. 1892–1982, US poet and public official; his works include *Collected Poems* (1952) and *J.B.* (1958)

Macleod *n* **John James Rickard**. 1876–1935, Scottish physiologist: shared the Nobel prize for physiology or medicine (1923) with Banting for their part in discovering insulin

McLuhan *n* **(Herbert) Marshall**. 1911–80, Canadian author of works analysing the mass media, including *Understanding Media* (1964) and *The Medium is the Message* (1967)

Macmahon *n* **Marie Edme Patrice Maurice**, Comte de Macmahon. 1808–93, French military commander. He commanded the troops that suppressed the Paris Commune (1871) and was elected president of the Third Republic (1873–79)

McMahon *n* Sir **William**. 1908–88, Australian statesman; prime minister of Australia (1971–72)

Macmillan *n* **(Maurice) Harold**, 1st Earl of Stockton. 1894–1986, British statesman; Conservative prime minister (1957–63)

MacMillan *n* **1** Sir **James (Loy)**. born 1959, Scottish composer and conductor; his works include 3 symphonies, the orchestral work *Confession of Isobel Gowdie* (1990), and the operas *Ines de Castro* (1996) and *The Sacrifice* (2007) **2** Sir **Kenneth**. 1929–92, British choreographer, dancer, and ballet director; chief choreographer for the Royal Ballet from 1970

McMillan *n* **Edwin M(attison)**. 1907–91, US physicist; Nobel prize for chemistry 1951 (with Glenn Seaborg) for the discovery of transuranic elements

McMurdo Sound *n* an inlet of the Ross Sea in Antarctica, north of Victoria Land

MacNeice *n* **Louis**. 1907–63, British poet, born in Northern Ireland. His works include *Autumn Journal* (1939) and *Solstices* (1961) and a translation of *Agamemnon* (1936)

Macon *n* a city in the US, in central Georgia, on the Ocmulgee River. Pop: 95 267 (2003 est)

Mâcon *n* **1** a city in E central France, in the Saône valley: a centre of the wine-producing region of lower Burgundy. Pop: 35 393 (2006) **2** a red or white wine from the Mâcon area, heavier than the other burgundies

Maconchy n Dame **Elizabeth**, married name *Elizabeth LeFanu*. 1907–94, British composer of Irish parentage; noted esp. for her chamber music, which includes 13 string quartets and *Romanza* (1980) for viola and ensemble

Macpherson n **James**. 1736–96, Scottish poet and translator. He published supposed translations of the legendary Gaelic poet Ossian, in reality largely his own work

McPherson n **Conor**. born 1971, Irish playwright and theatre director; his plays include *The Weir* (1997) and *Port Authority* (2001)

Macquarie¹ n **1** an Australian island in the Pacific, SE of Tasmania: noted for its species of albatross and penguin. Area: about 168 sq km (65 sq miles) **2** a river in SE Australia, in E central New South Wales, rising in the Blue Mountains and flowing NW to the Darling. Length: about 1200 km (750 miles)

Macquarie² n **Lachlan**. 1762–1824, Australian colonial administrator; Governor of New South Wales (1809–21), noted for his reformist policies towards ex-convicts and for his record in public works such as road-building in the colony

McQueen n **1 Alexander**. 1969–2011, British fashion designer **2 Steve**. 1930–80, US film actor, noted for his portrayal of tough characters **3 Steve** (n **Rodney**). born 1969, British video artist and film-maker; won the Turner Prize (1999); his films include *Hunger* (2008) and *12 Years a Slave* (2013) which won an Academy Award for best picture

macramé (mak-rah-mee) n **1** the art of knotting and weaving coarse thread into patterns **2** ornaments made in this way [Turkish *makrama* towel]

Macready n **William Charles**. 1793–1873, English actor and theatre manager

macro- or before a vowel **macr-** combining form large, long, or great: *macroscopic* [Greek *makros*]

macrobiotics n a dietary system which advocates whole grains and vegetables grown without chemical additives [Greek *makros* long + *biōtikos*, from *bios* life] ❭ **macrobiotic** adj

macrocarpa n a large Californian coniferous tree, used in New Zealand and elsewhere as a windbreak on farms and for rough timber [Greek *makros* large + *karpos* fruit]

macrocosm n a complex structure, such as the universe or society, regarded as a whole [Greek *makros kosmos* great world]

macroeconomics n the branch of economics concerned with the relationships between aggregates, such as consumption and investment, in a large economic system ❭ **macroeconomic** adj

macromolecule n any very large molecule, such as a protein or synthetic polymer

macron n a mark (¯) placed over a letter to represent a long vowel [Greek *makros* long]

macroscopic adj **1** large enough to be visible to the naked eye **2** concerned with large units [Greek *makros* large + *skopein* to look at]

macula (mak-kew-la) n, pl **-ulae** (-yew-lee) anatomy a small spot or area of distinct colour, such as a freckle [Latin]

mad adj **madder, maddest 1** mentally deranged; insane **2** extremely foolish; senseless: *that was a mad thing to do!* **3** informal angry or annoyed: *he's mad at her for the unjust accusation* **4** extremely excited or confused: *a mad rush* **5 a** (of animals) unusually ferocious: *a mad bear* **b** (of animals) afflicted with rabies **6 like mad** informal with great energy, enthusiasm, or haste **7 mad about** or *on* or **over** wildly enthusiastic about or fond of [Old English *gemǣded* made insane] ❭ **madness** n

Madag. Madagascar

Madagascan adj **1** of or relating to Madagascar or its inhabitants ▷ n **2** a native or inhabitant of Madagascar

Madagascar n an island republic in the Indian Ocean, off the E coast of Africa: made a French protectorate in 1895; became autonomous in 1958 and fully independent in 1960; contains unique flora and fauna. Languages: Malagasy and French. Religions: animist and Christian. Currency: franc. Capital: Antananarivo. Pop: 22 599 098 (2013 est). Area: 587 041 sq km (266 657 sq miles). Official name (since 1975): **Democratic Republic of Madagascar**. Former name (1958–75): **Malagasy Republic**

madam n, pl **madams 1** (pl **mesdames**) a polite term of address for a woman **2** a woman who runs a brothel **3** *Brit and Austral* informal a spoilt or pert girl: *she is a thoroughly precocious little madam if ever there was one* [Old French *ma dame* my lady]

madame (mad-dam) n, pl **mesdames** (may-dam) a French form of address equivalent to *Mrs*

madcap adj **1** impulsive, reckless, or unlikely to succeed: *a madcap expansion of council bureaucracy* ▷ n **2** an impulsive or reckless person

mad cow disease n informal same as **BSE**

madden vb to make or become mad or angry ❭ **maddening** adj

madder n **1** a plant with small yellow flowers and a red fleshy root **2** a dark reddish-purple dye formerly obtained from its root **3** an artificial pigment of this colour [Old English *mædere*]

made vb **1** the past of **make** ▷ adj **2** (in combination) produced or shaped as specified: *handmade* **3 get** or **have it made** informal to be assured of success

Madeira n **1** a group of volcanic islands in the N Atlantic, west of Morocco: since 1976 an autonomous region of Portugal; consists of the chief island, Madeira, Porto Santo, and the uninhabited Deserta and Selvagen Islands. Capital: Funchal. Pop: 245 012 (2001). Area: 797 sq km (311 sq miles) **2** a river in W Brazil, flowing northeast to the Amazon below Manaus. Length: 3241 km (2013 miles) **3** a rich strong fortified white wine made on Madeira

Madeira cake n a type of rich sponge cake

mademoiselle (mad-mwah-zel) n, pl **mesdemoiselles** (maid-mwah-zel) **1** a French form of address equivalent to *Miss* **2** a French teacher or governess

made-to-measure adj (of a piece of clothing) made specifically to fit the person who has ordered it

made-up adj **1** invented or fictitious **2** wearing make-up **3** put together: *some made-up carpet shampoo* **4** (of a road) surfaced with tarmac or concrete

madhouse n informal **1** a state of uproar or confusion **2** old-fashioned a mental hospital

Madhya Bharat n a former state of central India: part of Madhya Pradesh since 1956

Madhya Pradesh n a state of central India, situated on the Deccan Plateau: rich in mineral resources, with several industrial cities: formerly the largest Indian state, it lost much of the SE to the new state of Chhattisgarh in 2000. Capital: Bhopal. Pop: 60 385 118 (2001). Area: 308 332 sq km (119 016 sq miles)

Madison¹ n a city in the US, in S central Wisconsin, on an isthmus between Lakes Mendota and Monona: the state capital. Pop: 218 432 (2003 est)

Madison² n **James**. 1751–1836, US statesman; 4th president of the US (1809–17). He helped to draft the US Constitution and Bill of Rights. His presidency was dominated by the War of 1812

Madison Avenue n a street in New York City: a centre of American advertising and public-relations firms and a symbol of their attitudes and methods

madly adv **1** in an insane or foolish manner **2** with great speed and energy **3** informal extremely or excessively: *she was madly in love with him*

madman or fem **madwoman** n, pl **-men** or **-women** a person who is insane

Madoff n **Bernard** (**Lawrence**), known as *Bernie*. born 1938, US financier; chairman of the NASDAQ stock exchange (1990, 1991, 1993); convicted (2009) of running a $65bn (£40bn) Ponzi scheme

Madonna¹ *n* **1** *chiefly RC Church* the Virgin Mary **2** a picture or statue of the Virgin Mary [Italian: my lady]

Madonna² *n* full name *Madonna Louise Veronica Ciccone*. born 1958, US rock singer and film actress. Her records include *Like a Virgin* (1985), *Like a Prayer* (1989), *Ray of Light* (1998), *Music* (2000), and *MDNA* (2012). Her films include *Desperately Seeking Susan* (1985) and *Evita* (1996)

Madonsela *n* Thuli. born 1962, South African advocate; Public Protector from 2009, during which tenure she has exposed political corruption

madras *n* a medium-hot curry: *chicken madras* [after the *Madras* area of India]

Madras *n* **1** the former official name of **Chennai** **2** the former name (until 1968) for the state of **Tamil Nadu**

Madre de Dios *n* a river in NE South America, rising in SE Peru and flowing northeast to the Beni River in N Bolivia. Length: about 965 km (600 miles)

Madrid *n* the capital of Spain, situated centrally in New Castile: the highest European capital, at an altitude of about 700 m (2300 ft); a Moorish fortress in the 10th century, captured by Castile in 1083 and made capital of Spain in 1561; university (1836). Pop: 3 092 759 (2003 est)

madrigal *n* a type of 16th- or 17th-century part song for unaccompanied voices [Medieval Latin *matricale* primitive] **> madrigalist** *n*

Madura *n* an island in Indonesia, off the NE coast of Java: extensive forests and saline springs. Capital: Pamekasan. Area: 5472 sq km (2113 sq miles)

Madurai *n* a city in S India, in S Tamil Nadu: centre of Dravidian culture for over 2000 years; cotton industry. Pop: 922 913 (2001). Former name: **Madura**

Madurese *adj* **1** of or relating to Madura or its inhabitants ▷ *n*, *pl* **-ese** **2** a native or inhabitant of Madura

Maeander *or* **Meander** *n* ancient name of the river Menderes (1)

Maebashi *n* a city in central Japan, on central Honshu: centre of sericulture and silk-spinning; university (1949). Pop: 283 005 (2002 est)

Maecenas *n* **1** Gaius. ?70–8 BC, Roman statesman; adviser to Augustus and patron of Horace and Virgil **2** a wealthy patron of the arts

maelstrom (male-strom) *n* **1** a large powerful whirlpool **2** any confused, violent, and destructive turmoil: *a maelstrom of adulterous passion* [Old Dutch *malen* to whirl round + *stroom* stream]

Maelstrom *n* a strong tidal current in a restricted channel in the Lofoten Islands off the NW coast of Norway

maenad (mean-ad) *n* **1** *classical history* a female disciple of Dionysus, the Greek god of wine **2** a frenzied woman [Greek *mainas* madwoman]

Maestricht *n* an obsolete spelling of **Maastricht**

maestro (my-stroh) *n*, *pl* **-tri** *or* **-tros** **1** a distinguished musician or conductor **2** any master of an art: *Milan's maestro of minimalism* [Italian: master]

Maeterlinck *n* Comte Maurice. 1862–1949, Belgian poet and dramatist, noted particularly for his symbolist plays, such as *Pelléas et Mélisande* (1892), which served as the basis for an opera by Debussy, and *L'Oiseau bleu* (1909). Nobel prize for literature 1911

mae west *n slang* an inflatable life jacket [after *Mae West*, actress renowned for her large bust]

Maewo *n* an almost uninhabited island in Vanuatu. Also called: **Aurora**

Mafeking *n* the former name (until 1980) of **Mafikeng**

Mafia *n* **the Mafia** a secret criminal organization founded in Sicily, and carried to the US by Italian immigrants [Sicilian dialect, literally: hostility to the law]

Mafikeng *n* a town in N South Africa: besieged by the Boers for 217 days (1899–1900) during the second Boer War: administrative headquarters of the British protectorate of Bechuanaland until 1965, although outside its borders. Pop: 23 650 (2001). Former name (until 1980): **Mafeking**

mafioso (maf-fee-oh-so) *n*, *pl* **-sos** *or* **-si** (-see) a member of the Mafia

mag *n* short for **magazine** (1)

Magallanes *n* the former name of **Punta Arenas**

Magaluf *n* a resort town on the SW coast of Majorca

magazine *n* **1** a periodic paperback publication containing written pieces and illustrations **2** a television or radio programme made up of short nonfictional items **3** a metal case holding several cartridges used in some firearms **4** a rack for automatically feeding slides through a projector **5** a place for storing weapons, explosives, or military equipment [Arabic *makhāzin* storehouses]

Magdalena *n* a river in SW Colombia, rising on the E slopes of the Andes and flowing north to the Caribbean near Barranquilla. Length: 1540 km (956 miles)

Magdalena Bay *n* an inlet of the Pacific on the coast of NW Mexico, in Lower California

Magdeburg *n* an industrial city and port in central Germany, on the River Elbe, capital of Saxony-Anhalt: a leading member of the Hanseatic League, whose local laws, the **Magdeburg Laws** were adopted by many European cities. Pop: 227 535 (2003 est)

Magellan¹ *n* **Strait of Magellan** a strait between the mainland of S South America and Tierra del Fuego, linking the S Pacific with the S Atlantic. Length: 600 km (370 miles). Width: up to 32 km (20 miles)

Magellan² *n* **Ferdinand**. Portuguese name *Fernão de Magalhães*. ?1480–1521, Portuguese navigator in the service of Spain. He commanded an expedition of five ships that set out to sail to the East Indies via the West. He discovered the Strait of Magellan (1520), crossed the Pacific, and reached the Philippines (1521), where he was killed by natives. One of his ships reached Spain (1522) and was therefore the first to circumnavigate the world

magenta (maj-jen-ta) *adj* deep purplish-red [after *Magenta*, Italy]

Maggiore *n* **Lake Maggiore** a lake in N Italy and S Switzerland, in the S Lepontine Alps

maggot *n* the limbless larva of various insects, esp. the housefly and blowfly [earlier *mathek*] **> maggoty** *adj*

Magherafelt *n* a district of N Northern Ireland, in Co Londonderry. Pop: 40 837 (2003 est). Area: 572 sq km (221 sq miles)

Maghreb *or* **Maghrib** *n* NW Africa, including Morocco, Algeria, Tunisia, and sometimes Libya [from Arabic, literally: the West]

Maghrebi *or* **Maghribi** *adj* **1** of or relating to the Maghreb or its inhabitants ▷ *n* **2** a native or inhabitant of the Maghreb

magi (maje-eye) *pl n*, *sing* **magus** (may-guss) **1** See **magus** **2** **the three Magi** *Christianity* the wise men from the East who came to worship the infant Jesus (Matthew 2:1–12) [see MAGUS]

magic *n* **1** the supposed power to make things happen by using supernatural means **2** tricks done to entertain; conjuring **3** any mysterious or extraordinary quality or power: *the magic of Placido Domingo* **4** like **magic** very quickly ▷ *adj* also: **magical** **5** of magic **6** possessing or considered to possess mysterious powers **7** unaccountably enchanting **8** *informal* wonderful or marvellous ▷ *vb* **-gicking**, **-gicked** **9** to transform or produce as if by magic: *he had magicked up a gourmet meal at a moment's notice* [Greek *magikē* witchcraft] **> magically** *adv*

magic away *vb* to cause to disappear as if by magic: *to magic away pollution*

magic carpet *n* (in fairy stories) a carpet which can carry people through the air

magician *n* **1** a conjuror **2** a person with magic powers

magic lantern *n* an early type of slide projector

magisterial *adj* **1** commanding and authoritative **2** of a magistrate [Latin *magister* master] **> magisterially** *adv*

magistracy *n, pl* **-cies 1** the office or function of a magistrate **2** magistrates collectively

magistrate *n* **1** a public officer concerned with the administration of law **2** same as **justice of the peace 3** *Austral and NZ* a former name for **district court judge** [Latin *magister* master]

magistrates' court *n* (in England) a court that deals with minor crimes, certain civil actions, and preliminary hearings

magma *n, pl* **-mas** or **-mata** hot molten rock within the earth's crust which sometimes finds its way to the surface where it solidifies to form igneous rock [Greek: salve made by kneading]

Magna Carta *n English history* the charter granted by King John at Runnymede in 1215, recognizing the rights and privileges of the barons, church, and freemen [Medieval Latin: great charter]

Magna Graecia *n* (in the ancient world) S Italy, where numerous colonies were founded by Greek cities [Latin: Great Greece]

magnanimous *adj* generous and forgiving, esp. towards a defeated enemy [Latin *magnanimus* great-souled] **> magnanimity** *n* **> magnanimously** *adv*

magnate *n* an influential or wealthy person, esp. in industry [Late Latin *magnates* great men]

magnesia *n* a white tasteless substance used as an antacid and laxative; magnesium oxide [Greek *Magnēsia* of *Magnēs*, ancient mineral-rich region]

magnesium *n chem* a light silvery-white metallic element that burns with a very bright white flame. Symbol: **Mg** [from MAGNESIA]

magnet *n* **1** a piece of iron, steel, or lodestone that has the property of attracting iron to it **2** a person or thing that exerts a great attraction: *these woods are a magnet for bird watchers* [Greek *magnēs*]

magnetic *adj* **1** of, producing, or operated by means of magnetism **2** of or like a magnet **3** capable of being made into a magnet **4** exerting a powerful attraction: *political leaders of magnetic appeal* **> magnetically** *adv*

magnetic disk *n* a computer storage disk

magnetic field *n* an area around a magnet in which its power of attraction is felt

magnetic mine *n* a mine which detonates when a magnetic field, such as that generated by the metal of a ship's hull, is detected

magnetic needle *n* a slender magnetized rod used in certain instruments, such as the magnetic compass, for indicating the direction of a magnetic field

magnetic north *n* the direction in which a compass needle points, at an angle from the direction of true (geographic) north

magnetic pole *n* either of two variable points on the earth's surface towards which a magnetic needle points

magnetic storm *n* a sudden severe disturbance of the earth's magnetic field, caused by emission of charged particles from the sun

magnetic tape *n* a long plastic strip coated with a magnetic substance, used to record sound or video signals or to store information in computers

magnetism *n* **1** the property of attraction displayed by magnets **2** powerful personal charm **3** the branch of physics concerned with magnetic phenomena

magnetite *n* a black magnetizable mineral that is an important source of iron

magnetize or **-tise** *vb* **-tizing, -tized** or **-tising, -tised 1** to make a substance or object magnetic **2** to attract strongly: *he was magnetized by her smile* **> magnetizable** or **-tisable** *adj* **> magnetization** or **-tisation** *n*

magneto (mag-nee-toe) *n, pl* **-tos** a small electric generator in which the magnetic field is produced by a permanent magnet, esp. one used to provide the spark in an internal-combustion engine [short for *magnetoelectric generator*]

magnetron *n* an electronic valve used with a magnetic field to generate microwave oscillations, used. esp. in radar [*magnet* + *electron*]

Magnificat *n Christianity* the hymn of the Virgin Mary (Luke 1:46–55), used as a canticle [from its opening word]

magnification *n* **1** the act of magnifying or the state of being magnified **2** the degree to which something is magnified **3** a magnified copy of something

magnificent *adj* **1** splendid or impressive in appearance **2** superb or very fine: *a magnificent performance* [Latin *magnificus* great in deeds] **> magnificence** *n* **> magnificently** *adv*

magnify *vb* **-fies, -fying, -fied 1** to make something look bigger than it really is, for instance by using a lens or microscope **2** to make something seem more important than it really is; exaggerate: *you are magnifying the problem out of all proportion* **3** to make something sound louder than it really is: *the stethoscope magnifies internal body sounds* **4** *archaic* to glorify or praise [Latin *magnificare* to praise] **> magnified** *adj*

magnifying glass or **magnifier** *n* a convex lens used to produce an enlarged image of an object

magniloquent *adj* (of speech) excessively grand, literary, and pompous [Latin *magnus* great + *loqui* to speak] **> magniloquence** *n*

Magnitogorsk *n* a city in central Russia, on the Ural River: founded in 1930 to exploit local magnetite ores; site of one of the world's largest metallurgical plants. Pop: 415 000 (2005 est)

magnitude *n* **1** relative importance: *an evil of the first magnitude* **2** relative size or extent **3** *astronomy* the apparent brightness of a celestial body expressed on a numerical scale on which bright stars have a low value [Latin *magnitudo* size]

magnolia *n* an Asian and North American tree or shrub with white, pink, purple, or yellow showy flowers [after Pierre *Magnol*, botanist]

magnox *n* an alloy composed mainly of magnesium, used in fuel elements of some nuclear reactors (**magnox reactors**) [from *mag*(nesium) *n*(o) *ox*(idation)]

magnum *n, pl* **-nums** a wine bottle of twice the normal size, holding 1.5 litres [Latin: a big thing]

magnum opus *n* a great work of art or literature, esp. the greatest single work of an artist [Latin]

magpie *n* **1** a bird of the crow family with black-and-white plumage, a long tail, and a chattering call **2** any of various similar Australian birds, for example the butcherbird **3** *Brit* a person who hoards small objects [from *Mag*, diminutive of *Margaret* + *pie*, obsolete name for the magpie]

Magritte *n* René. 1898–1967, Belgian surrealist painter. By juxtaposing incongruous objects, depicted with meticulous realism, his works create a bizarre and disturbing impression

magus (may-guss) *n, pl* **magi** (maje-eye) **1** a Zoroastrian priest **2** an astrologer or magician of ancient times [Old Persian: magician]

Magyar *n* **1** a member of the main ethnic group of Hungary **2** the Hungarian language ▷ *adj* **3** of the Magyars

Magyarország *n* the Hungarian name for **Hungary**

Mahajanga *n* a port in NW Madagascar, on Bombetoka Bay. Pop: 147 000 (2005 est). Former name: **Majunga**

Mahalla el Kubra *n* a city in N Egypt, on the Nile delta: one of the largest diversified textile centres in Egypt. Pop: 433 000 (2005 est)

Mahanadi *n* a river in E India, rising in Chhattisgarh and flowing north, then south and east to the Bay of Bengal. Length: 885 km (550 miles)

maharaja or **maharajah** *n* the head of one of the royal families which formerly ruled parts of India [Hindi: great raja]

maharani or **maharanee** n the wife of a maharaja [Hindi: great rani]

Maharashtra n a state of W central India, formed in 1960 from the Marathi-speaking S and E parts of former Bombay state: lies mainly on the Deccan plateau; mainly agricultural. Capital: Mumbai (Bombay). Pop: 96 752 247 (2001). Area: 307 690 sq km (118 800 sq miles)

maharishi n Hinduism a teacher of religious and mystical knowledge [Hindi: great sage]

mahatma n a person revered for his holiness or wisdom: often used as a title or form of address: *Mahatma Gandhi* [Sanskrit *mahā* great + *ātman* soul]

Mahavira n the title of **Vardhamana** 599–527 BC, Indian ascetic and religious teacher, regarded as the founder of Jainism

Mahdi n **1** the title assumed by *Mohammed Ahmed*. ?1843–85, Sudanese military leader, who led a revolt against Egypt (1881) and captured Khartoum (1885) **2** *Islam* any of a number of Muslim messiahs expected to convert all mankind to Islam [Arabic *mahdīy* one who is guided, from *madā* to guide aright] **> Mahdism** n **> Mahdist** n, adj

Mahé n an island in the Indian Ocean, the chief island of the Seychelles. Capital: Victoria. Pop: 71 900 (2002 est). Area: 147 sq km (57 sq miles)

Mahfouz or **Mahfuz** n Naguib. 1911–2006, Egyptian novelist and writer, author of the trilogy of novels *Bain al-Kasrain* (1945–57). His novel *Children of Gebelawi* (1959) was banned by the Muslim authorities in Egypt: Nobel prize for literature 1988

mah jong or **mah-jongg** n a game of Chinese origin, played using tiles bearing various designs, in which the players try to obtain a winning combination of tiles [Chinese, literally: sparrows]

Mahler n Gustav. 1860–1911, Austrian composer and conductor, whose music links the romantic tradition of the 19th century with the music of the 20th century. His works include nine complete symphonies for large orchestras, the symphonic song cycle *Das Lied von der Erde* (1908), and the song cycle *Kindertotenlieder* (1902)

mahogany n, pl -nies **1** the hard reddish-brown wood of any of several tropical trees ▷ adj **2** reddish-brown: *wonderful mahogany tones* [origin unknown]

mahout (ma-howt) n (in India and the East Indies) an elephant driver or keeper [Hindi *mahāut*]

Mähren n the German name for **Moravia**

Mahy n Margaret. 1936–2012, New Zealand writer for children. Her books include *A Lion in the Meadow* (1969), *The Changeover* (1984), and *Alchemy* (2002)

maid n **1** a female servant **2** archaic or literary a young unmarried girl; maiden [form of *maiden*]

maiden n **1** archaic or literary a young unmarried girl, esp. a virgin **2** horse racing a horse that has never won a race ▷ adj **3** unmarried: *a maiden aunt* **4** first or earliest: *maiden voyage* [Old English *mægden*] **> maidenhood** n **> maidenly** adj

maidenhair fern n a fern with delicate hairlike fronds of small pale green leaflets

maidenhead n **1** the hymen **2** virginity or maidenhood

Maidenhead n a town in S England, in Windsor and Maidenhead unitary authority, Berkshire, on the River Thames. Pop: 58 848 (2001)

maiden name n a woman's surname before marriage

maiden over n cricket an over in which no runs are scored

maid of honour n **1** an unmarried lady attending a queen or princess **2** US and Canad the principal unmarried attendant of a bride

maidservant n a female servant

Maidstone n a town in SE England, administrative centre of Kent, on the River Medway. Pop: 89 684 (2001)

Maiduguri n a city in NE Nigeria, capital of Bornu State; agricultural trade centre. Pop: 828 000 (2005 est). Also called: **Yerwa-Maiduguri**

Maikop n a city in SW Russia, capital of the Adygei Republic: extensive oilfields to the southwest; mineral springs. Pop: 165 000 (2005 est)

mail¹ n **1** letters and packages transported and delivered by the post office **2** the postal system **3** a single collection or delivery of mail **4** a train, ship, or aircraft that carries mail **5** short for **e-mail** ▷ vb **6** chiefly US and Canad to send by mail **7** to contact or send by e-mail [Old French *male* bag]

mail² n flexible armour made of riveted metal rings or links [Old French *maille* mesh] **> mailed** adj

mailbag n a large bag for transporting or delivering mail

mailbox n **1** US, Canad and Austral a box outside a house into which the postman puts letters for the occupiers of the house **2** (on a computer) the directory in which e-mail messages are stored

mail coach n history a fast stagecoach designed primarily for carrying mail

Mailer n Norman. 1923–2007, US author. His works, which are frequently critical of modern American society, include the war novel *The Naked and the Dead* (1948), *An American Dream* (1965), his account of the 1967 peace march on Washington *The Armies of the Night* (1968), *The Executioner's Song* (1979), and *Barbary Shore* (1998)

mailing list n a register of names and addresses to which information or advertising matter is sent by post or e-mail

Maillol n Aristide. 1861–1944, French sculptor, esp. of monumental female nudes

mailman n, pl -men US and Canad a postman

mail merge n computers a word-processing facility that can produce personalized letters by combining data from two different files

mail order n a system of buying and selling goods by post

mailshot n a posting of circulars, leaflets, or other advertising to a selected large number of people at once

maim vb to injure badly or cruelly, with some permanent damage resulting [Old French *mahaignier* to wound]

Maimonides n also called Rabbi *Moses ben Maimon*. 1135–1204, Jewish philosopher, physician, and jurist, born in Spain. He codified Jewish law in *Mishneh Torah* (1180) **> Maimonidean** adj, n

main adj **1** chief or principal ▷ n **2** a principal pipe or line in a system used to distribute water, electricity, or gas **3** mains the main distribution network for water, gas, or electricity **4** great strength or force: *with might and main* **5** literary the open ocean **6** in the main on the whole [Old English *mægen* strength]

Main n a river in central and W Germany, flowing west through Würzburg and Frankfurt to the Rhine. Length: about 515 km (320 miles)

mainbrace n nautical **1** the rope that controls the movement of the spar of a ship's mainsail **2** splice the mainbrace See **splice**

main clause n grammar a clause that can stand alone as a sentence

Maine n a state of the northeastern US, on the Atlantic: chiefly hilly, with many lakes, rivers, and forests. Capital: Augusta. Pop: 1 305 728 (2003 est). Area: 86 156 sq km (33 265 sq miles). Abbreviation: **Me.**, (with zip code) **ME**

Maine-et-Loire n a department of W France, in Pays de la Loire region. Capital: Angers. Pop: 745 486 (2003 est). Area: 7218 sq km (2815 sq miles)

mainframe n computers a high-speed, general-purpose computer, with a large storage capacity

mainland n the main part of a land mass as opposed to an island

Mainland n **1** an island off N Scotland: the largest of the Shetland Islands. Chief town: Lerwick. Pop: 17 550 (2001). Area: about 583 sq km (225 sq miles) **2** Also called: **Pomona** an island off N Scotland: the largest of the Orkney Islands. Chief town: Kirkwall. Pop: 15 315 (2001).

Area: 492 sq km (190 sq miles) **3 the Mainland** NZ a South Islanders' name for **South Island**

main line *n* **1** *railways* the chief route between two points, usually fed by branch lines ▷ *vb* **mainline 2** *slang* to inject a drug into a vein

mainly *adv* for the most part; principally

mainmast *n nautical* the chief mast of a sailing vessel with two or more masts

mainsail *n nautical* the largest and lowermost sail on the mainmast

mainspring *n* **1** the chief cause or motive of something: *the mainspring of a dynamic economy* **2** the chief spring of a watch or clock

mainstay *n* **1** a chief support **2** *nautical* a rope securing a mainmast

mainstream *n* **1** the people or things representing the most common or generally accepted ideas and styles in a society, art form, etc.: *the mainstream of academic life* **2** the main current of a river ▷ *adj* **3** belonging to the social or cultural mainstream: *mainstream American movies*

mainstream media *n* newspapers, magazines, television, and radio, as opposed to social media

mainstreeting *n Canad* the practice of a politician walking about a town or city to try to gain votes

maintain *vb* **1** to continue or keep in existence: *we must maintain good relations with them* **2** to keep in proper or good condition: *an expensive car to maintain* **3** to sustain or keep up a particular level or speed: *he set off at a high speed, but couldn't maintain it all the way* **4** to enable a person to have the money, food and other things he or she needs to live: *the money maintained us for a month* **5** to assert: *he had always maintained that he never wanted children* **6** to defend against contradiction: *he maintained his innocence* [from Latin *manu tenere* to hold in the hand]

maintenance *n* **1** the act of maintaining or the state of being maintained **2** the process of keeping a car, building, etc. in good condition **3** *law* financial provision ordered to be made by way of periodical payments or a lump sum, usually for a separated or divorced spouse

Maintenon *n* Marquise de, title of *Françoise d'Aubigné*. 1635–1719, the mistress and, from about 1685, second wife of Louis XIV

Mainz *n* a port in W Germany, capital of the Rhineland-Palatinate, at the confluence of the Main and Rhine: an archbishopric from about 780 until 1801; important in the 15th century for the development of printing (by Johann Gutenberg). Pop: 185 532 (2003 est). French name: **Mayence**

maisonette *n Brit and S African* a flat with more than one floor [French, diminutive of *maison* house]

Maistre *n Joseph de*. 1753–1821, French writer and diplomat, noted for his extreme reactionary views, expounded in such works as *Les Soirées de St Petersbourg* (1821)

Maitland¹ *n* a town in SE Australia, in E New South Wales: industrial centre of an agricultural region. Pop: 53 470 (2001)

Maitland² *n* Frederic William. 1850–1906, English legal historian

maitre d'hotel (met-ra dote-tell) *n, pl* **maitres d'hotel** a head waiter [French]

maize *n* a type of corn grown for its large yellow edible grains, which are used for food and as a source of oil. See also **sweet corn** [Spanish *maiz*]

Maj. Major

majestic *adj* beautiful, dignified, and impressive ▷ **majestically** *adv*

majesty *n* **1** great dignity and grandeur **2** supreme power or authority [Latin *majestas*]

Majesty *n, pl* **-ties** (preceded by *Your* or *His* or *Her* or *Their*) a title used to address or refer to a sovereign or the wife or widow of a sovereign

Maj. Gen. Major General

majolica *or* **maiolica** *n* a type of porous pottery glazed with bright metallic oxides. It was extensively made in Renaissance Italy [Italian, from Late Latin *Majorica* Majorca]

major *adj* **1** greater in size, frequency, or importance than others of the same kind: *the major political parties* **2** very serious or significant: *a major investigation* **3** main or principal: *a major road* **4** *music* **a** (of a scale) having notes separated by a whole tone, except for the third and fourth notes, and seventh and eighth notes, which are separated by a semitone **b** of or based on the major scale: *the key of D major* ▷ *n* **5** a middle-ranking military officer **6** *music* a major key, chord, mode, or scale **7** a person who has reached the age of legal majority **8** *US, Canad, S African, Austral and NZ* the principal field of study of a student ▷ *vb* **9** *US, Canad, S African, Austral and NZ* to study as one's principal subject: *he majored in economics* [Latin: greater]

Major *n* Sir John. born 1943, British Conservative politician: Chancellor of the Exchequer (1989–90); prime minister (1990–97)

Majorca *n* an island in the W Mediterranean: the largest of the Balearic Islands; tourism. Capital: Palma. Pop: 730 778 (2002 est). Area: 3639 sq km (1465 sq miles). Spanish name: **Mallorca**

major-domo *n, pl* **-mos** the chief steward or butler of a great household [Medieval Latin *major domus* head of the household]

majorette *n* one of a group of girls who practise formation marching and baton twirling

major general *n* a senior military officer

majority *n, pl* **-ties 1** the greater number or part of something **2** (in an election) the number of votes or seats by which the strongest party or candidate beats the combined opposition or the runner-up **3** the largest party or group that votes together in a meeting, council or parliament **4** the age at which a person legally becomes an adult **5 in the majority** forming or part of the group of people or things made up of more than half of a larger group [Medieval Latin *majoritas*]

> **USAGE** *The majority of* can only refer to a number of things or people. When talking about an amount, *most of* should be used: *most of* (not *the majority of*) *the harvest was saved.*

Majunga *n* the former name of **Mahajanga**

Makalu *n* a massif in NE Nepal, on the border with Tibet in the Himalayas

Makarios III *n* original name *Mikhail Christodoulou Mouskos*. 1913–77, Cypriot archbishop, patriarch, and statesman; first president of the republic of Cyprus (1960–74; 1974–77)

Makassar, Makasar *or* **Macassar** *n* a port in central Indonesia, on SW Sulawesi: an important native port before Portuguese (16th century) and Dutch (17th century) control; capital of the Dutch East Indies (1946–49); a major Indonesian distribution and transshipment port. Pop: 1 100 019 (2000). Former name (1971–99): **Ujung Pandang**

make *vb* **making, made 1** to create, construct, establish, or draw up; bring into being: *houses made of stone; he will have to make a will* **2** to cause to do or be; compel or induce: *please make her go away* **3** to bring about or produce: *don't make a noise* **4** to carry out or perform: *he made his first trip to China in 1987; she made an obscene gesture* **5** to appoint: *they made him caretaker manager* **6** to come into a specified state or condition: *to make merry* **7** to become: *she will make a good diplomat* **8** to cause or ensure the success of: *that news has made my day* **9** to amount to: *5 and 5 make 10* **10** to earn or be paid: *they must be making a fortune* **11** to have the qualities of or be suitable for: *what makes this book such a good read?* **12** to prepare for use: *she forgot to make her bed* **13** to be the essential element in: *confidence makes a good salesman* **14** to use for a specified purpose: *they will make this town their base* **15** to deliver: *he made a very good speech* **16** to consider to be: *what time do you make it?* **17** to cause to seem or represent as being: *her girlish pigtails made her look younger than she was; she made the experience sound most unpleasant* **18** to acquire: *she doesn't make friends easily* **19** to engage in: *they made war on the Turks* **20** to travel a certain distance or to a certain place: *we can make at least three miles before it gets dark* **21** to arrive in time for: *he didn't make the first act of the play* **22** to win or score: *he made a break of 125* **23** *informal* to gain a place or position on or in: *to make the headlines* **24 make a day** or **night of it** to cause an activity to last a day or night **25 make eyes at** *old-fashioned* to flirt with or ogle **26 make it** *informal* **a** to be able to attend: *I'm afraid I can't make it to your party* **b** to be successful **27 make like** *slang, chiefly US and Canad* **a** to imitate **b** to pretend **28 make to** or **as if to** or **as though to** to act with the intention or with a show of doing something: *she made as if to hit him* ▷ *n* **29** manufacturer; brand: *what make of car is that?* **30** the way in which something is made **31 on the make** *slang* out for profit or conquest ▶ See also **make away, make for**, etc. [Old English *macian*] **⟩ maker** *n*

make away *vb* **1** to depart in haste **2 make away with a** to steal **b** to kill or get rid of

Makeba *n* Miriam. 1932–2008, South African singer and political activist; banned from South Africa from 1960 to 1990

make believe *vb* **1** to pretend ▷ *n* **make-believe 2** a fantasy or pretence

Makedhonia *n* a transliteration of the Modern Greek name for Macedonia (2)

make do *vb* to manage with an inferior alternative

make for *vb* **1** to head towards **2** to prepare to attack **3** to help bring about: *this will make for a spectacular race*

make of *vb* to interpret as the meaning of: *what did she make of it all?*

make off *vb* **1** to go or run away in haste **2 make off with** to steal or abduct

make out *vb* **1** to manage to see or hear **2** to understand **3** to write out: *how shall I make out the cheque?* **4** to attempt to establish or prove: *she made me out to be a crook* **5** to pretend: *he made out that he could play the piano* **6** to manage or get on: *how did you make out in the exam?*

make over *vb* **1** to renovate or remodel: *she made over the dress to fit her sister* ▷ *n* **makeover 2** a complete remodelling **3** a series of alterations, including beauty treatments and new clothes, intended to make an improvement to someone's appearance

Maker *n* a title given to God

makeshift *adj* serving as a temporary substitute

make-up *n* **1** cosmetics, such as powder or lipstick **2** the cosmetics used by an actor to adapt his or her appearance **3** the arrangement of the parts of something **4** mental or physical constitution ▷ *vb* **make up 5** to form or constitute: *these arguments make up the case for the defence* **6** to devise or compose, sometimes with the intent to deceive: *she was well known for making up stories about herself* **7** to supply what is lacking in; complete: *I'll make up the difference* **8** Also: **make it up** to settle differences amicably **9 make up for** to compensate for: *one good year can make up for several bad ones* **10** to apply cosmetics to the face **11 make up to** *informal* **a** to make friendly overtures to **b** to flirt with

makeweight *n* an unimportant person or thing added to make up a lack

Makeyevka *n* a city in SE Ukraine: coal-mining centre. Pop: 380 000 (2005 est)

Makhachkala *n* a port in SW Russia, capital of the Dagestan Republic, on the Caspian Sea: fishing fleet; oil refining. Pop: 503 000 (2005 est). Former name (until 1921): Petrovsk

making *n* **1** the act or process of producing something **2 be the making of** to cause the success of **3 in the making** in the process of becoming or being made

makings *pl n* **have the makings of** to have the potentials, qualities, or materials necessary to make or become something: *it had the makings of a classic showdown*

Makkah or **Makah** *n* transliteration of the Arabic name for Mecca

mako *n, pl* **makos** a powerful shark of the Atlantic and Pacific Oceans [Māori]

Makurdi *n* a port in E central Nigeria, capital of Benue State on the Benue River: agricultural trade centre. Pop: 259 000 (2005 est)

mal- *combining form* bad or badly; wrong or wrongly: *maladjusted; malfunction* [Latin *malus* bad, *male* badly]

Malabar Coast or **Malabar** *n* a region along the SW coast of India, extending from Goa to Cape Comorin: includes most of Kerala state

Malabo *n* the capital and chief port of Equatorial Guinea, on the island of Bioko in the Gulf of Guinea. Pop: 105 000 (2005 est). Former name (until 1973): **Santa Isabel**

Malacca or **Melaka** *n* a state of SW Peninsular Malaysia: rubber plantations. Capital: Malacca. Pop: 635 791 (2000). Area: 1683 sq km (650 sq miles)

malachite (mal-a-kite) *n* a green mineral used as a source of copper, and for making ornaments [Greek *molokhitis*]

Malachy *n* Saint. 1094–1148, Irish prelate; he became Archbishop of Armagh (1132) and founded (1142) the first Cistercian abbey in Ireland. Feast day: Nov 3

maladjustment *n psychol* a failure to meet the demands of society, such as coping with problems and social relationships **⟩ maladjusted** *adj*

maladminister *vb* to administer badly, inefficiently, or dishonestly **⟩ maladministration** *n*

maladroit (mal-a-droyt) *adj* clumsy, awkward, or tactless [French *mal* badly + ADROIT] **⟩ maladroitly** *adv* **⟩ maladroitness** *n*

malady (mal-a-dee) *n, pl* **-dies** *old-fashioned* any disease or illness [Vulgar Latin *male habitus* in poor condition]

Málaga *n* **1** a port and resort in S Spain, in Andalusia on the Mediterranean. Pop: 547 105 (2003 est) **2** a sweet fortified dessert wine from Málaga

Malagasy *n* **1** (*pl* **-gasy** or **-gasies**) a native or inhabitant of Madagascar **2** the official language of Madagascar belonging to the Malayo-Polynesian family ▷ *adj* **3** of or relating to Madagascar, its people, or their language

Malagasy Republic *n* the former name (1958–75) of Madagascar

malaise (mal-laze) *n* **1** a vague feeling of unease, illness, or depression **2** a complex of problems affecting a country, economy, etc.: *Belgium's political malaise* [Old French *mal* bad + *aise* ease]

Malamud *n* Bernard. 1914–86, US novelist and short-story writer. His works include *The Fixer* (1966) and *Dubin's Lives* (1979)

Malan *n* Daniel F(rançois). 1874–1959, South African politician; prime minister (1948–54). He passed legislation to introduce apartheid

Malang *n* a city in S Indonesia, on E Java: commercial centre. Pop: 756 982 (2000)

malapropism *n* the comic misuse of a word by confusion with one which sounds similar, for example *under the affluence of alcohol* [after Mrs *Malaprop* in Sheridan's play *The Rivals*]

Mälaren *n* Lake Mälaren a lake in S Sweden, extending 121 km (75 miles) west from Stockholm, where it joins with an inlet of the Baltic Sea (the **Saltsjön**). Area: 1140 sq km (440 sq miles). Also called: **Mälar**

malaria *n* a disease with recurring attacks of fever, caused by the bite of some types of mosquito [Italian *mala aria* bad air] **⟩ malarial** *adj*

malarkey *n slang* nonsense or rubbish [origin unknown]

Malatya *n* a city in E central Turkey: nearby is the ruined Roman and medieval city of Melitene (Old Malatya). Pop: 448 000 (2005 est)

Malawi *n* **1** a republic in E central Africa: established as a British protectorate in 1891; became independent in 1964 and a republic, within the Commonwealth, in 1966; lies along the Great Rift Valley, with Lake Nyasa (Malawi) along the E border, the Nyika Plateau in the northwest, and the Shire (or Shiré) Highlands in the southeast. Official language: Chichewa; English and various other Bantu languages are also widely spoken. Religion: Christian majority, Muslim, and animist minorities. Currency: kwacha. Capital: Lilongwe. Pop: 16 777 547 (2013 est). Area: 118 484 sq km (45 747 sq miles). Former name: **Nyasaland 2 Lake Malawi** the Malawi name for (Lake) **Nyasa**

Malawian *adj* **1** of or relating to Malawi or its inhabitants ▷ *n* **2** a native or inhabitant of Malawi

Malay *n* **1** a member of a people living chiefly in Malaysia and Indonesia **2** the language of this people ▷ *adj* **3** of the Malays or their language

Malaya *n* **1 States of the Federation of Malaya** part of Malaysia, in the S Malay Peninsula, constituting Peninsular Malaysia: consists of the former Federated Malay States, the former Unfederated Malay States, and the former Straits Settlements. Capital: Kuala Lumpur. Pop: 17 144 322 (2000). Area: 131 587 sq km (50 806 sq miles) **2 Federation of Malaya** a federation of the nine Malay States of the Malay Peninsula and two of the Straits Settlements (Malacca and Penang): formed in 1948: became part of the British Commonwealth in 1957 and joined Malaysia in 1963

Malayan *adj* **1** of or relating to Malaya or its inhabitants ▷ *n* **2** a native or inhabitant of Malaya

Malay Archipelago *n* a group of islands in the Indian and Pacific Oceans, between SE Asia and Australia: the largest group of islands in the world; includes over 3000 Indonesian islands, about 7000 islands of the Philippines, and, sometimes, New Guinea

Malay Peninsula *n* a peninsula of SE Asia, extending south from the Isthmus of Kra in Thailand to Cape Tanjong Piai in Malaysia: consists of SW Thailand and the states of Malaya (Peninsular Malaysia). Ancient name: **Chersonesus Aurea**

Malaysia *n* a federation in SE Asia (within the Commonwealth), consisting of **Peninsular Malaysia** on the Malay Peninsula, and **East Malaysia** (Sabah and Sarawak), occupying the N part of the island of Borneo: formed in 1963 as a federation of Malaya, Sarawak, Sabah, and Singapore (the latter seceded in 1965); densely forested and mostly mountainous. Official language: Malay; English and various Chinese and Indian minority languages are also spoken. Official religion: Muslim. Currency: ringgit. Capital: Kuala Lumpur. Federal seat of government: Putrajaya. Pop: 29 628 392 (2013 est). Area: 329 847 sq km (127 355 sq miles)

Malaysian *adj* **1** of or relating to Malaysia or its inhabitants ▷ *n* **2** a native or inhabitant of Malaysia

Malay States *pl n* the former states of the Malay Peninsula that, together with Penang and Malacca, formed the Union of Malaya (1946) and the Federation of Malaya (1948). Perak, Selangor, Negri Sembilan, and Pahang were established as the Federated Malay States by the British in 1895 and Perlis, Kedah, Kelantan, and Trengannu as the Unfederated Malay States in 1909 (joined by Johore in 1914)

Malcolm *n* George. 1917–97, British harpsichordist

Malcolm III *n* died 1093, king of Scotland (1057–93). He became king after Macbeth

Malcolm X *n* original name *Malcolm Little*. 1925–65, US Black civil-rights leader: assassinated

malcontent *n* a person who is discontented with the existing situation [Old French]

Maldives *pl n* **Republic of Maldives** a republic occupying an archipelago of 1087 coral islands in the Indian Ocean, southwest of Sri Lanka: came under British protection in 1887; became independent in 1965 and a republic in

1968; a member of the Commonwealth. The economy and infrastructure were severely damaged in the Indian Ocean tsunami of December 2004. Official language: Divehi. Official religion: (Sunni) Muslim. Currency: rufiyaa. Capital: Malé. Pop: 393 988 (2013 est). Area: 298 sq km (115 sq miles). Also known as: **the Maldive Islands**

Maldivian *or* **Maldivan** *adj* **1** of or relating to the Maldives or their inhabitants ▷ *n* **2** a native or inhabitant of the Maldives

Maldon *n* a market town in SE England, in Essex; scene of a battle (991) between the East Saxons and the victorious Danes, celebrated in *The Battle of Maldon*, an Old English poem; notable for Maldon salt, used in cookery. Pop: 20 731 (2001)

male *adj* **1** of the sex that can fertilize female reproductive cells **2** of or characteristic of a man **3** for or composed of men or boys: *a male choir* **4** (of flowers) bearing stamens but lacking a pistil **5** *electronics, engineering* having a projecting part or parts that fit into a hollow counterpart: *a male plug* ▷ *n* **6** a male person, animal, or plant [Latin *masculus* masculine] ❭ **maleness** *n*

Malé *n* the capital of the Republic of Maldives, on Malé Island in the centre of the island group. Pop: 90 000 (2005 est)

Malebranche *n* Nicolas. 1638–1715, French philosopher. Originally a follower of Descartes, he developed the philosophy of occasionalism, esp. in *De la recherche de la vérité* (1674)

male chauvinism *n* the belief, held by some men, that men are better and more important than women ❭ **male chauvinist** *n, adj*

malediction (mal-lid-**dik**-shun) *n* the utterance of a curse against someone or something [Latin *maledictio* a reviling] ❭ **maledictory** *adj*

malefactor (**mal**-if-act-or) *n* a criminal or wrongdoer [Latin *malefacere* to do evil] ❭ **malefaction** *n*

Malema *n* Julius (Sello). born 1981, South African politician; President of the ANC Youth League from 2008 until he was expelled in 2012; founded the Economic Freedom Fighters (2013)

Malenkov *n* Georgi Maksimilianovich. 1902–88, Soviet politician; prime minister (1953–55). He was removed from the party presidium (1957) for plotting against Khrushchev; expelled from the Communist Party (1961)

Malevich *n* Kasimir. 1878–1935, Russian painter. He founded the abstract art movement known as Suprematism

malevolent (mal-**lev**-a-lent) *adj* wishing evil to others; malicious [Latin *malevolens*] ❭ **malevolence** *n* ❭ **malevolently** *adv*

malfeasance (mal-**fee**-zanss) *n law* wrongful or illegal behaviour, esp. by a public official [Old French *mal faisant* evil-doing]

malformation *n* **1** the condition of being faulty or abnormal in form or shape **2** *pathol* a deformity, esp. when congenital ❭ **malformed** *adj*

malfunction *vb* **1** to fail to function properly or fail to function at all ▷ *n* **2** failure to function properly or failure to function at all

Malherbe *n* François de. 1555–1628, French poet and critic. He advocated the classical ideals of clarity and concision of meaning

Mali *n* a landlocked republic in West Africa: conquered by the French by 1898 and incorporated (as French Sudan) into French West Africa; became independent in 1960; settled chiefly in the basins of the Rivers Senegal and Niger in the south. Official language: French. Religion: Muslim majority, also animist. Currency: franc. Capital: Bamako. Pop: 15 968 882 (2013 est). Area: 1 248 574 sq km (482 077 sq miles). Former name (1898–1959): **French Sudan**

Malian *n* **1** an inhabitant or native of Mali ▷ *adj* **2** of or relating to Mali or its people

malice (mal-iss) *n* the desire to do harm or cause mischief to others [Latin *malus* evil] **> malicious** *adj* **> maliciously** *adv*

malice aforethought *n law* a deliberate intention to do something unlawful

malign (mal-line) *vb* **1** to say unpleasant and untrue things about someone; slander ▷ *adj* **2** evil in influence or effect [Latin *malignus* spiteful]

malignant (mal-lig-nant) *adj* **1** seeking to harm others **2** tending to cause great harm; injurious **3** *pathol* (of a tumour) uncontrollable or resistant to therapy [Late Latin *malignare* to behave spitefully] **> malignancy** *n*

malignity (mal-lig-nit-ee) *n* the condition of being malign or deadly

Malines *n* the French name for **Mechelen**

malinger (mal-ling-ger) *vb* to pretend to be ill, or exaggerate how ill one is, to avoid work [French *malingre* sickly] **> malingerer** *n*

Malinowski *n* Bronislaw Kasper. 1884–1942, Polish anthropologist in England and the US, who researched into the sexual behaviour of primitive people in New Guinea and Melanesia

mall (mawl) *n* **1** *US, Canad, Austral and NZ* short for **shopping mall 2** a shaded avenue, esp. one open to the public [after *the Mall*, an avenue in St James's Park, London]

mallard *n, pl* **-lard** or **-lards** a common N hemisphere duck, the male of which has a dark green head [Old French *mallart*]

Mallarmé *n* Stéphane. 1842–98, French symbolist poet, noted for his free verse, in which he chooses words for their evocative qualities; his works include *L'Après-midi d'un Faune* (1876), *Vers et prose* (1893), and *Divagations* (1897)

Malle *n* Louis. 1932–95, French film director: his films include *Le Feu follet* (1963), *Au revoir les enfants* (1987), and *Vanya on 42nd Street* (1994)

malleable (mal-lee-a-bl) *adj* **1** (esp. of metal) capable of being hammered or pressed into shape without breaking **2** able to be influenced [Medieval Latin *malleabilis*] **> malleability** *n* **> malleably** *adv*

mallee *n* a low-growing eucalypt found in dry regions of Australia

mallet *n* **1** a hammer with a large wooden head **2** a long stick with a head like a hammer used to strike the ball in croquet or polo [Old French *maillet* wooden hammer]

Mallorca *n* the Spanish name for **Majorca**

mallow *n* any of a group of plants, with purple, pink, or white flowers [Latin *malva*]

Malmédy *n* See **Eupen and Malmédy**

Malmö *n* a port in S Sweden, on the Sound: part of Denmark until 1658; industrial centre. Pop: 268 971 (2004 est)

malnourished *adj* physically weak due to lack of healthy food

malnutrition *n* physical weakness resulting from insufficient food or an unbalanced diet

malodorous (mal-lode-or-uss) *adj* having an unpleasant smell: *the malodorous sludge of Boston harbour*

Malory *n* Sir Thomas. 15th-century English author of *Le Morte d'Arthur* (?1470), a prose collection of Arthurian legends, translated from the French

Malouf *n* David. born 1934, Australian novelist, short-story writer, and poet. His novels include *An Imaginary Life* (1978), *Remembering Babylon* (1993), *The Conversations at Curlow Creek* (1996), and *Ransom* (2009)

Malpighi *n* Marcello. 1628–94, Italian physiologist. A pioneer in microscopic anatomy, he identified the capillary system (1661) **> Malpighian** *adj*

malpractice *n* illegal, unethical, or negligent professional conduct

Malraux *n* André. 1901–76, French writer and statesman. His novels include *La Condition humaine* (1933) on the Kuomintang revolution (1927–28) and *L'Espoir* (1937) on the Spanish Civil War, in both of which events he took

part. He also wrote on art, notably in *Les Voix du silence* (1951)

malt *n* **1** grain, such as barley, that is kiln-dried after it has been germinated by soaking in water **2** See **malt whisky** ▷ *vb* **3** to make into or become malt **4** to make from malt or to add malt to [Old English *mealt*] **> malted** *adj* **> malty** *adj*

Malta *n* a republic occupying the islands of Malta, Gozo, and Comino, in the Mediterranean south of Sicily; governed by the Knights Hospitallers from 1530 until Napoleon's conquest in 1798; French driven out, with British help, 1800; became British dependency 1814; suffered severely in World War II; became independent in 1964 and a republic in 1974; joined the EU in 2004; a member of the Commonwealth. Official languages: Maltese and English. Official religion: Roman Catholic. Currency: euro (from January 2008 replacing the Maltese lira). Capital: Valletta. Pop: 411 277 (2013 est). Area: 316 sq km (122 sq miles)

Maltese *adj* **1** of or relating to Malta or its inhabitants ▷ *n* **2** (*pl* **-tese**) a native or inhabitant of Malta **3** the language of Malta

Maltese cross *n* a cross with triangular arms that taper towards the centre, sometimes with the outer sides curving in

Malthus *n* Thomas Robert. 1766–1834, English economist. He propounded his population theory in *An Essay on the Principle of Population* (1798)

Malthusian (malth-yew-zee-an) *adj* of the theory stating that increases in population tend to exceed increases in the food supply and that therefore sexual restraint should be exercised [after T. R. MALTHUS]

maltose *n* a sugar formed by the action of enzymes on starch [*malt* + *-ose* indicating a sugar]

maltreat *vb* to treat badly, cruelly, or violently [French *maltraiter*] **> maltreatment** *n*

malt whisky *n* whisky made from malted barley

Maluku *n* the Indonesian name for the **Moluccas**

Malvern *n* a town and resort in W England, in S Worcestershire on the E slopes of the **Malvern Hills**: annual dramatic festival; mineral springs. Pop: 35 588 (2001)

malversation *n rare* professional or public misconduct [French *malverser* to behave badly]

Malvinas *pl n* **Islas Malvinas** the Argentine name for the **Falkland Islands**

malware *n* a computer program designed specifically to damage or disrupt a system, such as a virus

mam *n informal or dialect* same as **mother**

mama or *especially US* **mamma** (mam-mah) *n old-fashioned, informal* same as **mother** [reduplication of childish syllable *ma*]

mamba *n* a very poisonous tree snake found in tropical and Southern Africa [Zulu *im-amba*]

mambo *n, pl* **-bos** a Latin American dance resembling the rumba [American Spanish]

Mamet *n* David. born 1947, US dramatist and film director. His plays include *Sexual Perversity in Chicago* (1974), *American Buffalo* (1976), *Glengarry Glen Ross* (1983), and *Oleanna* (1992); films include *House of Games* (1987) and *Spartan* (2004)

mammal *n* a warm-blooded animal, such as a human being, dog or whale, the female of which produces milk to feed her babies [Latin *mamma* breast] **> mammalian** *adj, n*

mammary *adj* of the breasts or milk-producing glands [Latin *mamma* breast]

mammary gland *n* any of the milk-producing glands in mammals, such as a woman's breast or a cow's udder

mammon *n* wealth regarded as a source of evil and corruption, personified in the New Testament as a false god (**Mammon**) [New Testament Greek *mammōnas* wealth]

mammoth *n* **1** a large extinct elephant with a hairy coat and long curved tusks ▷ *adj* **2** gigantic [Russian *mamot*]

Mammoth Cave National Park *n* a national park in W central Kentucky: established in 1941 to protect a system of limestone caverns

mammy *n*, *pl* **-mies** *informal or dialect* same as **mother**

Mamoré *n* a river in central Bolivia, flowing north to the Beni River to form the Madeira River. Length: about 1500 km (930 miles)

mampara (mum-puh-ruh) *n* *S African slang* an incompetent fool [Sotho]

man *n*, *pl* **men 1** an adult male human being, as distinguished from a woman **2** a human being of either sex; person: *all men are born equal* **3** human beings collectively; mankind. Related adjective: **anthropoid 4** a human being regarded as representative of a particular period or category: *Neanderthal man* **5** an adult male human being with qualities associated with the male, such as courage or virility: *take it like a man* **6** an employee, servant, or representative **7** a member of the armed forces who is not an officer **8** a member of a group or team **9** a husband, boyfriend, or male lover **10** a movable piece in various games, such as draughts **11** *S African slang* any person: used as a term of address **12 as one man** with unanimous action or response **13** he's your man he's the person needed **14 man and boy** from childhood **15 sort out the men from the boys** to discover who can cope with difficult or dangerous situations and who cannot **16 to a man** without exception ▷ *vb* **manning, manned 17** to provide with sufficient people for operation or defence **18** to take one's place at or near in readiness for action [Old English *mann*] **> manhood** *n*

> **USAGE** The use of words ending in *-man* is avoided as implying a male in job advertisements, where sexual discrimination is illegal, and in many other contexts where a term that is not gender-specific is available, such as *salesperson, barperson, camera operator*.

Man *n* **Isle of Man** an island in the British Isles, in the Irish Sea between Cumbria and Northern Ireland: a UK Crown Dependency (but not part of the United Kingdom), with its own ancient parliament, the Court of Tynwald; a dependency of Norway until 1266, when for a time it came under Scottish rule; its own language, Manx, became extinct in the 19th century but has been revived to some extent. Capital: Douglas. Pop: 86 159 (2013 est). Area: 588 sq km (227 sq miles)

Man. Manitoba

mana *n* NZ authority, influence and prestige

manacle (man-a-kl) *n* **1** a metal ring or chain put round the wrists or ankles, used to restrict the movements of a prisoner or convict ▷ *vb* **-cling, -cled 2** to put manacles on [Latin *manus* hand]

Manado *n* a variant of **Menado**

manage *vb* **-naging, -naged 1** to succeed in doing something: *we finally managed to sell our old house* **2** to be in charge of; administer: *the company is badly managed* **3** to have room or time for: *can you manage lunch tomorrow?* **4** to keep under control: *she disapproved of taking drugs to manage stress* **5** to struggle on despite difficulties, esp. financial ones: *most people cannot manage on a cleaner's salary* [Italian *maneggiare* to train (esp. horses)] **> manageable** *adj*

management *n* **1** the people responsible for running an organization or business **2** managers or employers collectively **3** the technique or practice of managing or controlling

manager *n* **1** a person who manages an organization or business **2** a person in charge of a sports team **3** a person who controls the business affairs of an actor or entertainer **> manageress** *fem n*

managerial *adj* of a manager or management

managing director *n* the senior director of a company, who has overall responsibility for the way it is run

Managua *n* **1** the capital of Nicaragua, on the S shore of Lake Managua: chosen as capital in 1857. Pop: 1 159 000 (2005 est) **2 Lake Managua** a lake in W Nicaragua: drains into Lake Nicaragua by the Tipitapa River. Length: 61 km (38 miles). Width: about 26 km (16 miles)

Manama *n* the capital of Bahrain, at the N end of Bahrain Island: transit port. Pop: 142 000 (2005 est)

mañana (man-yah-na) *n*, *adv* **a** tomorrow **b** some other and later time [Spanish]

Manáos *n* a variant spelling of **Manaus**

Manassas *n* a town in NE Virginia, west of Alexandria: site of the victory of Confederate forces in the Battles of Bull Run, or First and Second Manassas (1861; 1862), during the American Civil War. Pop: 37 166 (2003 est)

man-at-arms *n*, *pl* **men-at-arms** a soldier, esp. a medieval soldier

manatee *n* a large plant-eating mammal occurring in tropical coastal waters of the Atlantic [Carib *Manattouí*]

Manaus *or* **Manáos** *n* a port in N Brazil, capital of Amazonas state, on the Rio Negro 19 km (12 miles) above its confluence with the Amazon: chief commercial centre of the Amazon basin. Pop: 1 673 000 (2005 est)

Manc *n*, *adj* *Brit informal* short for **Mancunian**

Manche *n* **1** a department of NW France, in Basse-Normandie region. Capital: St-Lô. Pop: 484 967 (2003 est). Area: 6412 sq km (2501 sq miles) **2 La Manche** the French name for the **English Channel**

Manchester *n* **1** a city in NW England, in Manchester unitary authority, Greater Manchester: linked to the Mersey estuary by the **Manchester Ship Canal**: commercial, industrial, and cultural centre; formerly the centre of the cotton and textile trades; two universities. Pop: 394 269 (2001). Latin name: **Mancunium 2** a unitary authority in NW England, in Greater Manchester. Pop: 432 500 (2003 est). Area: 116 sq km (45 sq miles)

Manchu *n*, *pl* **-chus** *or* **-chu** a member of a Mongoloid people of Manchuria, a region of NE China, who conquered China in the 17th century, ruling until 1912

Manchukuo *or* **Manchoukuo** *n* a former state of E Asia (1932–45), consisting of the three provinces of old Manchuria and Jehol

Manchuria *n* a region of NE China, historically the home of the Manchus, rulers of China from 1644 to 1912: includes part of Inner Mongolia and the provinces of Heilongjiang, Jilin, and Liaoning. Area: about 1 300 000 sq km (502 000 sq miles)

Manchurian *adj* **1** of or relating to Manchuria or its inhabitants ▷ *n* **2** a native or inhabitant of Manchuria

Mancunian (man-kew-nee-an) *adj* **1** of or relating to Manchester or its inhabitants ▷ *n* **2** a native or inhabitant of Manchester [Medieval Latin *Mancunium* Manchester]

mandala *n* *Buddhist art* a circular design symbolizing the universe [Sanskrit: circle]

Mandalay *n* a city in central Myanmar, on the Irrawaddy River: the second largest city in the country and former capital of Burma and of Upper Burma; Buddhist religious centre. Pop: 927 000 (2005 est)

mandarin *n* **1** (in the Chinese Empire) a member of a senior grade of the bureaucracy **2** a high-ranking official with extensive powers **3** a person of standing and influence, esp. in literary or intellectual circles **4** a small citrus fruit resembling the tangerine [Sanskrit *mantrin* counsellor]

Mandarin Chinese *or* **Mandarin** *n* the official language of China since 1917

mandate *n* **1** an official or authoritative command to carry out a particular task: *the UN force's mandate does not allow it to intervene* **2** *politics* the political authority given to a government or an elected representative through an electoral victory **3** Also: **mandated territory** (formerly) a territory administered by one country on behalf of an international body ▷ *vb* **-dating, -dated 4** to delegate authority to **5** to assign territory to a nation under a mandate [Latin *mandare* to command]

mandatory *adj* **1** obligatory; compulsory **2** having the nature or powers of a mandate ⟩ **mandatorily** *adv*

Mandela *n* **1** Nelson (Rolihlahla). 1918–2013, Black South African statesman: president of South Africa (1994–99). Jailed in 1962 for 5 years and, in 1964, for life, he was released in 1990 after a long international campaign; deputy president of the African National Congress (1990–91) and president (1991–97); elected president of South Africa in 1994; Nobel peace prize jointly with F. W. de Klerk in 1993 **2** (**Numzano**) **Winnie**. born 1934, Black South African political activist: campaigned for the release of her husband Nelson Mandela; they divorced in 1996

Mandelstam *or* **Mandelshtam** *n* **1** Nadezhda (Yakovlevna), born *Nadezhda Khazina*. 1899–1980, Soviet writer, wife of Osip Mandelstam: noted for her memoirs *Hope against Hope* (1971) and *Hope Abandoned* (1973) describing life in Stalin's Russia **2** Osip (Emilyevich). 1891–?1938, Soviet poet and writer, born in Warsaw; he was persecuted by Stalin and died in a labour camp. His works include *Tristia* (1922), *Poems* (1928), and the autobiographical *Journey to Armenia* (1933)

Mandeville *n* **1** Bernard de. ?1670–1733, English author, born in Holland, noted for his satire *The Fable of the Bees* (1723) **2** Sir John. 14th century, English author of *The Travels of Sir John Mandeville*. The book claims to be an account of the author's journeys in the East but is largely a compilation from other works

mandible *n* **1** the lower jawbone of a vertebrate **2** either of the jawlike mouthparts of an insect **3** either part of the bill of a bird, esp. the lower part [Late Latin *mandibula* jaw]

mandolin *n* a musical instrument with four pairs of strings stretched over a small light body, usually played with a plectrum [Italian *mandolino* small lute]

mandrake *n* a plant with a forked root. It was formerly thought to have magic powers and a narcotic was prepared from its root [Latin *mandragoras*]

mandrel *or* **mandril** *n* **1** a spindle on which the object being worked on is supported in a lathe **2** a shaft on which a machining tool is mounted [perhaps from French *mandrin* lathe]

mandrill *n* a monkey of W Africa. The male has red and blue markings on its face and buttocks [*man* + *drill* an Old-World monkey]

mane *n* **1** the long hair that grows from the neck in such mammals as the lion and horse **2** long thick human hair [Old English *manu*] ⟩ **maned** *adj*

manège (man-nayzh) *n* **1** the art of training horses and riders **2** a riding school [from French, Italian *maneggiare* to manage]

Manet *n* Édouard. 1832–83, French painter. His painting *Le Déjeuner sur l'herbe* (1863), which was condemned by the Parisian establishment, was acclaimed by the Impressionists, whom he decisively influenced

maneuver *n, vb* US same as **manoeuvre**

man Friday *n* **1** a loyal male servant or assistant **2** Also: **girl Friday, person Friday** any person who does all the odd jobs that arise, esp. in an office [after a character in *Robinson Crusoe*]

manful *adj* determined and brave ⟩ **manfully** *adv*

Mangalore *n* a port in S India, in Karnataka on the Malabar Coast. Pop: 398 745 (2001)

manganese *n chem* a brittle greyish-white metallic element used in making steel. Symbol: **Mn** [probably altered from Medieval Latin *magnesia*]

mange *n* a skin disease of domestic animals, characterized by itching and loss of hair [Old French *mangeue* itch]

mangelwurzel *n* a variety of beet with a large yellowish root [German *Mangold* beet + *Wurzel* root]

manger *n* a trough in a stable or barn from which horses or cattle feed [Old French *maingeure*]

mangetout (mawnzh-too) *n* a variety of garden pea with an edible pod [French: eat all]

mangle¹ *vb* **-gling, -gled 1** to destroy or damage by crushing and twisting **2** to spoil [Norman French *mangler*] ⟩ **mangled** *adj*

mangle² *n* **1** a machine for pressing or squeezing water out of washed clothes, consisting of two heavy rollers between which the clothes are passed ⟩ *vb* **-gling, -gled 2** to put through a mangle [Dutch *mangel*]

mango *n, pl* **-goes** *or* **-gos** the egg-shaped edible fruit of a tropical Asian tree, with a smooth rind and sweet juicy flesh [Malay *mangā*]

mangrove *n* a tropical evergreen tree or shrub with intertwining aerial roots that forms dense thickets along coasts [older *mangrow* (changed through influence of *grove*), from Portuguese *mangue*]

mangy *adj* **-gier, -giest 1** having mange **2** scruffy or shabby ⟩ **mangily** *adv* ⟩ **manginess** *n*

manhandle *vb* **-handling, -handled 1** to handle or push someone about roughly **2** to move something by manpower rather than by machinery

Manhattan *n* **1** an island at the N end of New York Bay, between the Hudson, East, and Harlem Rivers: administratively (with adjacent islets) a borough of New York City; a major financial, commercial, and cultural centre. Pop: 1 537 195 (2000). Area: 47 sq km (22 sq miles) **2** a mixed drink consisting of four parts whisky, one part vermouth, and a dash of bitters

Manhire *n* Bill. born 1946, New Zealand poet and writer. His poetry collections include *How to Take Off Your Clothes at the Picnic* (1977), *Zoetropes* (1984), *Sunshine* (1996), and *Lifted* (2005)

manhole *n* a hole with a detachable cover, through which a person can enter a sewer or pipe to inspect or repair it

man-hour *n* a unit of work in industry, equal to the work done by one person in one hour

manhunt *n* an organized search, usually by police, for a wanted man or fugitive

Mani *n* ?216–?276 AD, Persian prophet who founded Manichaeism. Also: **Manes, Manichaeus**

mania *n* **1** an obsessional enthusiasm or liking **2** a mental disorder characterized by great or violent excitement [Greek: madness]

-mania *combining form* indicating extreme or abnormal excitement aroused by something: *kleptomania*

maniac *n* **1** a wild disorderly person **2** a person who has a great craving or enthusiasm for something [Late Latin *maniacus* belonging to madness] ⟩ **maniacal** (man-eye-ak-kl) *adj*

manic *adj* **1** extremely excited or energetic; frenzied: *manic, cavorting dancers* **2** of, involving, or affected by mania: *deep depression broken by periods of manic excitement*

manic-depressive *psychiatry adj* **1** denoting a mental disorder characterized by an alternation between extreme euphoria and deep depression ⟩ *n* **2** a person afflicted with this disorder

manicure *n* **1** cosmetic care of the hands and fingernails ⟩ *vb* **-curing, -cured 2** to care for the fingernails and hands [Latin *manus* hand + *cura* care] ⟩ **manicurist** *n*

manifest *adj* **1** easily noticed, obvious ⟩ *vb* **2** to reveal or display: *an additional symptom now manifested itself* **3** to show by the way one behaves: *he manifested great personal bravery* **4** (of a disembodied spirit) to appear in visible form ⟩ *n* **5** a customs document containing particulars of a ship and its cargo **6** a list of the cargo and passengers on an aeroplane [Latin *manifestus* plain] ⟩ **manifestation** *n*

manifesto *n, pl* **-tos** *or* **-toes** a public declaration of intent or policy issued by a group of people, for instance by a political party [Italian]

manifold *adj formal* **1** numerous and varied: *her talents are manifold* ⟩ *n* **2** a pipe with a number of inlets or outlets, esp. one in a car engine [Old English *manigfeald*]

manikin n 1 a little man; dwarf or child 2 a model of the human body [Dutch *manneken*]

manila or **manilla** n a strong usually brown paper used to make envelopes [after MANILA]

Manila n 1 the chief port of the Philippines, on S Luzon on Manila Bay: capital of the republic until 1948 and from 1976; seat of the Far Eastern University and the University of Santo Tomas (1611). Pop: 10 677 000 (2005 est) 2 a type of cigar made in this city

Manila Bay n an almost landlocked inlet of the South China Sea in the Philippines, in W Luzon: mostly forms Manila harbour. Area: 1994 sq km (770 sq miles)

man in the street n the average person

manioc n same as cassava [S American Indian *mandioca*]

manipulate vb -lating, -lated 1 to handle or use skilfully 2 to control something or someone cleverly or deviously [Latin *manipulus* handful] › **manipulation** n › **manipulator** adj › **manipulator** n

Manipur n a state in NE India: largely densely forested mountains. Capital: Imphal. Pop: 2 388 634 (2001). Area: 22 327 sq km (8621 sq miles)

Manisa n a city in W Turkey: the Byzantine seat of government (1204–1313). Pop: 237 000 (2005 est)

Manitoba n 1 a province of W Canada: consists of prairie in the southwest, with extensive forests in the north and tundra near Hudson Bay in the northeast. Capital: Winnipeg. Pop: 1 208 268 (2011). Area: 650 090 sq km (251 000 sq miles). Abbreviation: **MB** 2 **Lake Manitoba** a lake in W Canada, in S Manitoba: fed by the outflow from Lake Winnipegosis; drains into Lake Winnipeg. Area: 4706 sq km (1817 sq miles)

Manitoban n 1 a native or inhabitant of Manitoba ▷ adj 2 of or relating to Manitoba or its inhabitants

Manitoulin Island n an island in N Lake Huron in Ontario: the largest freshwater island in the world. Length: 129 km (80 miles). Width: up to 48 km (30 miles)

Manizales n a city in W Colombia, in the Cordillera Central of the Andes at an altitude of 2100 m (7000 ft): commercial centre of a rich coffee-growing area. Pop: 401 000 (2005 est)

mankind n 1 human beings collectively 2 men collectively

USAGE Some people object to the use of *mankind* to refer to all human beings and prefer the term *humankind*.

Manley n Michael (Norman). 1924–97, Jamaican statesman; prime minister of Jamaica (1972–80; 1989–92)

manly adj -lier, -liest 1 possessing qualities, such as vigour or courage, traditionally regarded as appropriate to a man; masculine 2 characteristic of a man › **manliness** n

man-made adj made by humans; artificial

Mann n 1 Heinrich. 1871–1950, German novelist: works include *Professor Unrat* (1905), which was filmed as *The Blue Angel* (1928), and *Man of Straw* (1918) 2 his brother, Thomas. 1875–1955, German novelist, in the US after 1937. His works deal mainly with the problem of the artist in bourgeois society and include the short story *Death in Venice* (1913) and the novels *Buddenbrooks* (1900), *The Magic Mountain* (1924), and *Doctor Faustus* (1947): Nobel prize for literature 1929

manna n 1 *Bible* the miraculous food which sustained the Israelites in the wilderness (Exodus 16:14–36) 2 a windfall: *manna from heaven* [Hebrew *mān*]

Mannar n **Gulf of Mannar** the part of the Indian Ocean between SE India and the island of Sri Lanka: pearl fishing

manned adj having a human staff or crew: *thirty years of manned space flight*

mannequin n 1 a woman who wears the clothes displayed at a fashion show; model 2 a life-size dummy of the human body used to fit or display clothes [French]

manner n 1 the way a thing happens or is done 2 a person's bearing and behaviour 3 the style or customary way of doing something: *sculpture in the Greek manner* 4 type or kind 5 **in a manner of speaking** in a way; so to speak 6 **to the manner born** naturally fitted to a specified role or activity [Old French *maniere*]

mannered adj 1 (of speech or behaviour) unnaturally formal and put on to impress others 2 having manners as specified: *ill-mannered*

Mannerheim n Baron Carl Gustaf Emil. 1867–1951, Finnish soldier and statesman; president of Finland (1944–46)

mannerism n 1 a distinctive and individual gesture or way of speaking 2 excessive use of a distinctive or affected manner, esp. in art or literature

mannerly adj well-mannered and polite › **mannerliness** n

manners pl n 1 a person's social conduct viewed in the light of whether it is regarded as polite or acceptable or not: *his manners leave something to be desired*; *shockingly bad manners* 2 a socially acceptable way of behaving: *it's not manners to point*

Mannheim[1] n a city in SW Germany, in Baden-Württemberg at the confluence of the Rhine and Neckar: one of Europe's largest inland harbours; a cultural and musical centre. Pop: 308 353 (2003 est)

Mannheim[2] n Karl. 1893–1947, Hungarian sociologist, living in Britain from 1933: author of *Ideology and Utopia* (1929) and *Man and Society in an Age of Reconstruction* (1941)

Manning n 1 Henry Edward. 1808–92, British churchman. Originally an Anglican, he was converted to Roman Catholicism (1851) and made archbishop of Westminster (1865) and cardinal (1875) 2 Olivia. 1908–80, British novelist and short-story writer, best known for her novel sequence *Fortunes of War*, comprising the *Balkan Trilogy* (1960–65) and the *Levant Trilogy* (1977–80)

mannish adj (of a woman) displaying qualities regarded as typical of a man

manoeuvre or US **maneuver** (man-noo-ver) vb -vring, -vred or US -vering, -vered 1 to move or do something with dexterity and skill: *she manoeuvred the car easily into the parking space* 2 to manipulate a situation in order to gain some advantage 3 to perform a manoeuvre or manoeuvres ▷ n 4 a movement or action requiring dexterity and skill 5 a contrived, complicated, and possibly deceptive plan or action 6 **manoeuvres** military or naval exercises, usually on a large scale 7 a change in course of a ship or aircraft, esp. a complicated one 8 room for manoeuvre the possibility of changing one's plans or behaviour if it becomes necessary or desirable [French, from Medieval Latin *manuopera* manual work] › **manoeuvrable** or US **maneuverable** adj › **manoeuvrability** or US **maneuverability** n

manoeuvring or US **maneuvering** n the skilful manipulation of a situation to gain some advantage

man-of-war n, pl **men-of-war** 1 a warship 2 short for Portuguese man-of-war

Manolete n original name *Manuel Rodríguez y Sánchez*. 1917–47, Spanish bullfighter

manor n 1 (in medieval Europe) the lands and property controlled by a lord 2 *Brit* a large country house and its lands 3 *Brit slang* an area of operation, esp. of a local police force [Old French *manoir* dwelling] › **manorial** adj

manor house n chiefly *Brit* a large country house, esp. one that was originally part of a medieval manor

manpower n the number of people needed or available for a job

manqué (mong-kay) adj unfulfilled; would-be: *an actor manqué* [French, literally: having missed]

Manresa n a city in NE Spain: contains a cave used as the spiritual retreat of St Ignatius Loyola. Pop: 67 269 (2003 est)

mansard n a roof with two slopes on both sides and both ends, the lower slopes being steeper than the upper [after François MANSART]

Mansart n **1** François. 1598–1666, French architect, who established the classical style in French architecture **2** his great-nephew, **Jules Hardouin**. 1646–1708, French architect and town planner, who completed the Palace of Versailles

manse n the house provided for a minister of some Christian denominations [Medieval Latin *mansus* dwelling]

Mansell n Nigel (**Ernest James**). born 1953, English motor-racing driver: Formula One world champion (1992)

manservant n, pl **menservants** a male servant, esp. a valet

Mansfield¹ n a town in central England, in W Nottinghamshire: former coal-mining and cotton-textiles industries. Pop: 69 987 (2001)

Mansfield² n Katherine, real name *Kathleen Mansfield Beauchamp*. 1888–1923, British writer, born in New Zealand, noted for her short stories, such as those in *Bliss* (1920) and *The Garden Party* (1922)

Mansholt n Sicco Leendert. 1908–95, Dutch economist and politician; vice president (1958–72) and president (1972–73) of the European Economic Community Commission. He was the author of the Mansholt Plan for the agricultural organization of the European Economic Community

mansion n **1** a large and imposing house **2 Mansions** *Brit* a name given to some blocks of flats as part of their address: *18 Wilton Mansions* [Latin *mansio* a remaining]

Mansion House n the Mansion House **1** the residence of the Lord Mayor of London **2** the residence of the Lord Mayor of Dublin

manslaughter n *law* the unlawful but not deliberately planned killing of one human being by another

Manson n Sir Patrick. 1844–1922, British physician, who established that mosquitoes transmit certain parasites responsible for human diseases

Mansur n Abu Ja'far al-. 712–75 AD, 2nd caliph of the Abbasid dynasty (754–75). He founded Baghdad (762) and made it the Islamic capital

Mansûra n See El Mansûra

Mantegna n Andrea. 1431–1506, Italian painter and engraver, noted esp. for his frescoes, such as those in the Ducal Palace, Mantua

mantel n a wooden, stone, or iron frame around a fireplace [variant of *mantle*]

Mantel n Dame Hilary (**Mary**). born 1952, English writer. Her novels include *Wolf Hall* (2009) and *Bring Up the Bodies* (2012), both of which won the Booker Prize

mantelpiece n a shelf above a fireplace often forming part of the mantel. Also: **mantel shelf, chimneypiece**

manticore n a mythical beast with a lion's body, a scorpion's tail, and a man's head with three rows of teeth [Persian *mardkhora* man-eater]

mantilla n a woman's lace or silk scarf covering the shoulders and head, worn esp. in Spain [Spanish *manta* cloak]

Mantinea or **Mantineia** n (in ancient Greece) a city in E Arcadia; site of several battles

mantis n, pl **-tises** or **-tes** a carnivorous insect resembling a grasshopper, that rests with the first pair of legs raised as if in prayer. Also: **praying mantis** [Greek: prophet]

mantissa n the part of a common logarithm consisting of the decimal point and the figures following it: *the mantissa of 2.4771 is .4771* [Latin: something added]

mantle n **1** old-fashioned a loose wrap or cloak **2** anything that covers completely or envelops: *a mantle of snow covered the ground* **3** the responsibilities and duties which go with a particular job or position: *he refuses to accept the mantle of leader* **4** a small mesh dome used to increase illumination in a gas or oil lamp by becoming incandescent **5** *geology* the part of the earth between the crust and the core ▷ vb **-tling, -tled 6** to spread over or become spread over: *mountains mantled in lush vegetation* [Latin *mantellum* little cloak]

man-to-man adj characterized by frankness and sincerity: *a man-to-man discussion*

Mantova n the Italian name for Mantua

mantra n **1** *Hinduism, Buddhism* any sacred word or syllable used as an object of concentration **2** *Hinduism* a Vedic psalm of praise [Sanskrit: speech, instrument of thought]

Mantua n a city in N Italy, in E Lombardy, surrounded by lakes: birthplace of Virgil. Pop: 47 790 (2001). Italian name: **Mantova**

manual adj **1** of a hand or hands: *manual dexterity* **2** physical as opposed to mental: *manual labour* **3** operated or done by human labour rather than automatic or computer-aided means: *a manual gearbox* ▷ n **4** a book of instructions or information **5** *music* one of the keyboards on an organ [Latin *manus* hand] › **manually** adv

Manuel I n called *the Fortunate*. 1469–1521, king of Portugal (1495–1521); his reign saw the discovery of Brazil and the beginning of Portuguese trade with India and the East

manufacture vb **-turing, -tured 1** to process or make goods on a large scale, esp. using machinery **2** to invent or concoct evidence, an excuse, etc. ▷ n **3** the production of goods, esp. by industrial processes [Latin *manus* hand + *facere* to make] › **manufacturer** n › **manufacturing** n, adj

manuka (mah-nook-a) n a New Zealand tree with strong elastic wood and aromatic leaves [Māori]

manuka honey n honey from the nectar of the manuka tree; its antibacterial agent is used for medicinal purposes. See also **UMF**

Manukau n a city in New Zealand, on **Manukau Harbour** (an inlet of the Tasman Sea) near Auckland on NW North Island. Pop: 326 200 (2004 est)

manumit (man-new-mit) vb **-mitting, -mitted** to free from slavery [Latin *manumittere* to release] › **manumission** n

manure n **1** animal excrement used as a fertilizer ▷ vb **-nuring, -nured 2** to spread manure upon fields or soil [Anglo-French *mainoverer*]

manuscript n **1** a book or other document written by hand **2** the original handwritten or typed version of a book or article submitted by an author for publication [Medieval Latin *manuscriptus* handwritten]

Manx adj **1** of the Isle of Man ▷ n **2** an almost extinct Celtic language of the Isle of Man ▷ pl n **3** the Manx the people of the Isle of Man [Scandinavian]

Manx cat n a short-haired breed of cat without a tail

Manxman or feminine **Manxwoman** n, pl **-men** or **-women** a native or inhabitant of the Isle of Man

many adj **1** a large number of; numerous: *many times*; *many people think the government is incompetent* ▷ pron **2** a number of people or things, esp. a large one: *many are seated already*; *have as many as you want* **3 many a** each of a considerable number of: *many a man* ▷ n **4** the many the majority of mankind, esp. the common people [Old English *manig*]

Manzoni n Alessandro. 1785–1873, Italian romantic novelist and poet, famous for his historical novel *I Promessi sposi* (1825–27)

Maoism n Communism as interpreted in the theories and policies of Mao Tse-tung (1893–1976), Chinese statesman › **Maoist** n, adj

Māori n **1** (pl **-ri** or **-ris**) a member of the Polynesian people living in New Zealand since before the arrival of European settlers **2** the language of this people ▷ adj **3** of this people or their language

Māoriland n an obsolete name for New Zealand

Māorilander n an obsolete name for a New Zealander

Mao Tse-tung or **Mao Ze Dong** n 1893–1976, Chinese Marxist theoretician and statesman. The son of a peasant farmer, he helped to found the Chinese Communist Party (1921) and established a soviet republic in SE China (1931–34). He led the retreat of Communist forces to NW China known as the Long

March (1935–36), emerging as leader of the party. In opposing the Japanese in World War II, he united with the Kuomintang regime, which he then defeated in the ensuing civil war. He founded the People's Republic of China (1949) of which he was chairman until 1959. As party chairman until his death, he instigated the Cultural Revolution in 1966

map *n* **1** a diagrammatic representation of the earth's surface or part of it, showing the geographical distributions or positions of features such as roads, towns, relief, and rainfall **2** a diagrammatic representation of the stars or of the surface of a celestial body **3** *maths* same as **function 4 put on the map** to make (a town or company) well-known: *William Morris put Kelmscott on the map* ▷ *vb* **mapping, mapped 5** to make a map of **6** *maths* to represent or transform (a function, figure, or set) ▶ See also **map out** [Latin *mappa* cloth]

Map or **Mapes** *n* Walter. ?1140–?1209, Welsh ecclesiastic and satirical writer. His chief work is the miscellany *De Nugis curialium*

maple *n* **1** any of various trees or shrubs with five-pointed leaves and winged seeds borne in pairs **2** the hard wood of any of these trees ▶ See also **sugar maple** [Old English *mapeltrēow* maple tree]

maple leaf *n* the leaf of the maple tree, the national emblem of Canada

maple syrup *n* a very sweet syrup made from the sap of the sugar maple

map out *vb* to plan or design

mapping *n* *maths* same as **function**

Maputo *n* the capital and chief port of Mozambique, in the south on Delagoa Bay: became capital in 1907; the nearest port to the Rand gold-mining and industrial region of South Africa. Pop: 1 316 000 (2005 est). Former name (until 1975): **Lourenço Marques**

maquis (mah-kee) *n, pl* **-quis** (-kee) **1** the French underground movement that fought against the German occupying forces in World War II **2** a type of shrubby, mostly evergreen, vegetation found in coastal regions of the Mediterranean area [French]

mar *vb* **marring, marred** to spoil or be the one bad feature of: *Sicily's coastline is marred by high-rise hotels* [Old English *merran*]

Mar. March

marabou *n* **1** a large black-and-white African stork **2** the soft white down of this bird, used to trim hats etc. [Arabic *murābit* holy man]

maraca (mar-rak-a) *n* a shaken percussion instrument, usually one of a pair, consisting of a gourd or plastic shell filled with dried seeds or pebbles [Brazilian Portuguese]

Maracaibo *n* **1** a port in NW Venezuela, on the channel from Lake Maracaibo to the Gulf of Venezuela: the second largest city in the country; University of Zulia (1891); major oil centre. Pop: 2 182 000 (2005 est) **2 Lake Maracaibo** a lake in NW Venezuela, linked with the Gulf of Venezuela by a dredged channel: centre of the Venezuelan and South American oil industry. Area: about 13 000 sq km (500 sq miles)

Maracanda *n* the ancient name for **Samarkand**

Maracay *n* a city in N central Venezuela: developed greatly as the headquarters of Juan Vicente Gómez (1857–1935) during his dictatorship; textile industries. Pop: 1 138 000 (2005 est)

Maradona *n* Diego (Armando). born 1960, Argentinian footballer and manager: his clubs included Argentinos Juniors, Boca Juniors, Barcelona, and Napoli; scored 34 goals in 91 internationals (1977–94); under his captaincy Argentina won the World Cup in 1986

marae (mar-rye) *n* NZ **1** an enclosed space in front of a Māori meeting house **2** a Māori meeting house and its buildings [Māori]

Marajó *n* an island in N Brazil, at the mouth of the Amazon. Area: 38 610 sq km (15 444 sq miles)

Maranhão *n* a state of NE Brazil, on the Atlantic: forested and humid in the northwest, with high plateaus in the east and south. Capital: São Luís. Pop: 5 803 224 (2002). Area: 328 666 sq km (128 179 sq miles)

Marañón *n* a river in NE Peru, rising in the Andes and flowing northwest into the Ucayali River, forming the Amazon. Length: about 1450 km (900 miles)

Maraş *n* a town in S Turkey: noted formerly for the manufacture of weapons but now for carpets and embroidery. Pop: 366 000 (2005 est)

maraschino (mar-rass-kee-no) *n* a liqueur made from a type of sour cherry having a taste like bitter almonds [Italian]

maraschino cherry *n* a cherry preserved in maraschino

Marat *n* Jean Paul. 1743–93, French revolutionary leader and journalist. He founded the radical newspaper *L'Ami du peuple* and was elected to the National Convention (1792). He was instrumental in overthrowing the Girondists (1793); he was stabbed to death in his bath by Charlotte Corday

Marathi or **Mahratti** *adj* **1** of or relating to Maharashtra state in India, its people, or their language ▷ *n* **2** the state language of Maharashtra, belonging to the Indic branch of the Indo-European family

marathon *n* **1** a race on foot of 26 miles 385 yards (42.195 kilometres) **2** any long or arduous task or event ▷ *adj* **3** of or relating to a race on foot of 26 miles 385 yards (42.195 kilometres): *marathon runners* **4** long and arduous: *a marathon nine hour meeting* [referring to the feat of the messenger said to have run 26 miles from Marathon to Athens to bring the news of victory in 490 BC]

Marathon *n* a plain in Attica northeast of Athens: site of a victory of the Athenians and Plataeans over the Persians (490 BC)

maraud *vb* to wander or raid in search of plunder [French *marauder* to prowl] ▷ **marauder** *n* ▷ **marauding** *adj*

Marbella *n* a coastal resort in S Spain, on the Costa del Sol. Pop: 100 000 (2004 est)

marble *n* **1** a hard limestone rock, which usually has a mottled appearance and can be given a high polish **2** a block of marble or work of art made of marble **3** a small round glass ball used in playing marbles ▷ *vb* **-bling, -bled 4** to mottle with variegated streaks in imitation of marble [Greek *marmaros*] ▷ **marbled** *adj*

marbles *n* a game in which marbles are rolled at one another

marbling *n* **1** a mottled effect or pattern resembling marble **2** the streaks of fat in lean meat

Marburg *n* **1** a city in W central Germany, in Hesse: famous for the religious debate between Luther and Zwingli in 1529; Europe's first Protestant university (1527). Pop: 78 511 (2003 est) **2** the German name for **Maribor**

marc *n* **1** the remains of grapes or other fruit that have been pressed for wine-making **2** a brandy distilled from these [French]

Marc *n* Franz. 1880–1916, German expressionist painter; cofounder with Kandinsky of the *Blaue Reiter* group (1911). He is noted for his symbolic compositions of animals

marcasite *n* **1** a pale yellow form of iron pyrites used in jewellery **2** a cut and polished form of steel used for making jewellery [Arabic *marqashīta*]

Marceau *n* Marcel. 1923–2007, French mime artist

Marcel *n* Gabriel (Honoré). 1889–1973, French Christian existentialist philosopher and dramatist, whose philosophical works include *Being and Having* (1949) and *The Mystery of Being* (1951)

Marcellus *n* Marcus Claudius. ?268–208 BC, Roman general and consul, who captured Syracuse (212) in the Second Punic War

march[1] *vb* **1** to walk with very regular steps, like a soldier

2 to walk in a quick and determined manner, esp. when angry: *he marched into the kitchen without knocking* **3** to make a person or group proceed: *he was marched back to his cell* **4** (of an army, procession, etc.) to walk as an organized group: *the demonstrators marched down the main street* **5** to advance or progress steadily: *time marches on* ▷ n **6** a regular stride **7** a long or exhausting walk **8** the steady development or progress of something: *the continuous march of industrial development* **9** a distance covered by marching **10** an organized protest in which a large group of people walk somewhere together: *a march against racial violence* **11** a piece of music suitable for marching to **12 steal a march on** to gain an advantage over, esp. by a trick [Old French *marchier* to tread] ▷ **marcher** n ▷ **marching** adj

march² n **1** a border or boundary **2** the land lying along a border or boundary, often of disputed ownership [Old French *marche*]

March¹ n the third month of the year [Latin *Martius* (month) of Mars]

March² n the German name for the **Morava** (1)

Marche n a former province of central France

Marches n the **Marches 1** the border area between England and Wales or Scotland, both characterized by continual feuding (13th–16th centuries) **2** a region of central Italy. Capital: Ancona. Pop: 1 484 601 (2003 est). Area: 9692 sq km (3780 sq miles). Italian name: **Le Marche 3** any of various other border regions

March hare n a hare during its breeding season in March, noted for its wild and excitable behaviour

marching girl n NZ a girl who does team formation marching as a sport

marching orders pl n **1** *informal* dismissal, esp. from employment **2** military orders, giving instructions about a march

marchioness (marsh-on-ness) n **1** a woman who holds the rank of marquis or marquess **2** the wife or widow of a marquis or marquess [Medieval Latin *marchionissa*]

marchpane n *archaic* marzipan [French]

Marciano n **Rocky**. original name *Rocco Francis Marchegiano* 1923–69, US heavyweight boxer; world heavyweight champion, 1952–56

Marconi n **Guglielmo**. 1874–1937, Italian physicist, who developed radiotelegraphy and succeeded in transmitting signals across the Atlantic (1901): Nobel prize for physics 1909

Marcos n **1 Ferdinand (Edralin)**. 1917–89, Filipino statesman; president of the Philippines from 1965; deposed and exiled in 1986 **2** his wife, **Imelda (Remedios Visitación Trinidad Romuáldez)**. born 1929, Filipino politician; governor of Manila (1976–86); notorious for her profligacy as first lady

Marcus Aurelius Antoninus n original name *Marcus Annius Verus*. 121–180 AD, Roman emperor (161–180) noted particularly for his *Meditations*, propounding his stoic view of life

Marcuse n **Herbert**. 1898–1979, US philosopher, born in Germany. In his later works he analysed the situation of man under monopoly capitalism and the dehumanizing effects of modern technology. His works include *Eros and Civilization* (1958) and *One Dimensional Man* (1964)

Mar del Plata n a city and resort in E Argentina, on the Atlantic: fishing port. Pop: 552 000 (2005 est)

Mardi Gras (mar-dee grah) n the festival of Shrove Tuesday, celebrated in some cities with great revelry [French: fat Tuesday]

mare¹ n the adult female of a horse or zebra [Old English *mere*]

mare² (mar-ray) n, pl **maria** one of many huge dry plains on the surface of the moon or Mars, visible as dark markings [Latin: sea]

Marengo n a village in NW Italy: site of a major battle in which Napoleon decisively defeated the Austrians (1800)

mare nostrum *Latin* n the Latin name for the Mediterranean [literally: our sea]

Marenzio n **Luca**. 1553–99, Italian composer of madrigals

mare's-nest n a discovery imagined to be important but proving to be worthless

Margaret n **1** called the *Maid of Norway*. ?1282–90, queen of Scotland (1286–90); daughter of Eric II of Norway. Her death while sailing to England to marry the future Edward II led Edward I to declare dominion over Scotland **2** 1353–1412, queen of Sweden (1388–1412) and regent of Norway and Denmark (1380–1412), who united the three countries under her rule **3 Princess**. 1930–2002, younger sister of Queen Elizabeth II of Great Britain and Northern Ireland

Margaret of Anjou n 1430–82, queen of England. She married the mentally unstable Henry VI of England in 1445 to confirm the truce with France during the Hundred Years' War. She became a leader of the Lancastrians in the Wars of the Roses and was defeated at Tewkesbury (1471) by Edward IV

Margaret of Navarre n Also: **Margaret of Angoulême** 1492–1549, queen of Navarre (1544–49) by marriage to Henry II of Navarre; sister of Francis I of France. She was a poet, a patron of humanism, and author of the *Heptaméron* (1558)

Margaret of Scotland n **Saint**. 1045–93, queen consort of Malcolm III of Scotland. Her piety and benefactions to the church led to her canonization (1250). Feast days: June 10, Nov 16

Margaret of Valois n 1553–1615, daughter of Henry II of France and Catherine de' Medici; queen of Navarre (1572) by marriage to Henry of Navarre. The marriage was dissolved (1599) after his accession as Henry IV of France: noted for her *Mémoires*

margarine n a butter substitute made from vegetable and animal fats [Greek *margaron* pearl]

Margarita n an island in the Caribbean, off the NE coast of Venezuela: pearl fishing. Capital: La Asunción

Margate n a town and resort in SE England, in E Kent on the Isle of Thanet. Pop: 58 465 (2001)

marge n *Brit and Austral informal* margarine

margin n **1** an edge, rim, or border: *we came to the margin of the wood; people on the margin of society* **2** the blank space surrounding the text on a page **3** an additional amount or one beyond the minimum necessary: *the margin of victory was seven lengths; a small margin of error* **4** *chiefly Austral* a payment made in addition to a basic wage, esp. for special skill or responsibility **5** a limit beyond which something can no longer exist or function: *the margin of physical survival* **6** *econ* the minimum return below which an enterprise becomes unprofitable [Latin *margo* border]

marginal adj **1** of, in, on, or forming a margin **2** not important; insignificant: *he remained a rather marginal political figure* **3** close to a limit, esp. a lower limit: *marginal legal ability* **4** *econ* relating to goods or services produced and sold at the margin of profitability: *marginal cost* **5** *politics* of or designating a constituency in which elections tend to be won by small margins: *a marginal seat* **6** designating agricultural land on the edge of fertile areas ▷ n **7** *politics, chiefly Brit and NZ* a marginal constituency ▷ **marginally** adv

marginalia pl n notes in the margin of a book, manuscript, or letter

margrave n (formerly) a German nobleman ranking above a count [Middle Dutch *markgrave* count of the frontier]

Margrethe II n born 1940, queen of Denmark from 1972

marguerite n a garden plant with flowers resembling large daisies [French: daisy]

Margulies n **Donald**. born 1955, US playwright; plays include *The Loman Family Picnic* (1989) and the Pulitzer Prize-winning *Dinner with Friends* (1999)

Maria de' Medici n French name *Marie de Médicis*. 1573–1642, queen of France (1600–10) by marriage to

Henry IV of France; daughter of Francesco, grand duke of Tuscany. She became regent for her son (later Louis XIII) but continued to wield power after he came of age (1614). She was finally exiled from France in 1631 after plotting to undermine Richelieu's influence at court

Mariana Islands *pl n* a chain of volcanic and coral islands in the W Pacific, east of the Philippines and north of New Guinea: divided politically into Guam (a US unincorporated territory) and the islands north of Guam constituting the Northern Mariana Islands (a US commonwealth territory). Area: 1018 sq km (393 sq miles). Former name (1521–1668): **Ladrone Islands**

Marianao *n* a city in NW Cuba, adjacent to W Havana city: the chief Cuban military base. Pop: 133 016 (1989)

Mariánské Lázně *n* a town in the W Czech Republic: a fashionable spa in the 18th and 19th centuries. Pop: 13 872 (2007 est). German name: **Marienbad**

Maria Theresa *n* 1717–80, archduchess of Austria and queen of Hungary and Bohemia (1740–80); the daughter and heiress of Emperor Charles VI of Austria; the wife of Emperor Francis I; the mother of Emperor Joseph II. In the War of the Austrian Succession (1740–48) she was confirmed in all her possessions except Silesia, which she attempted unsuccessfully to regain in the Seven Years' War (1756–63)

Maribor *n* an industrial city in N Slovenia on the Drava River: a flourishing Hapsburg trading centre in the 13th century; resort. Pop: 110 668 (2002). German name: Marburg

Marie *n* 1875–1938, queen consort of Ferdinand I of Romania. A granddaughter of Queen Victoria, she secured Romania's support for the Allies in World War I

Marie Antoinette *n* 1755–93, queen of France (1774–93) by marriage to Louis XVI of France. Her opposition to reform during the Revolution contributed to the overthrow of the monarchy; guillotined

Marie Byrd Land *n* the former name of **Byrd Land**

Marie de France *n* 12th century AD, French poet, who probably lived in England; noted for her *lais* (verse narratives) based on Celtic tales

Marie Galante *n* an island in the E Caribbean southeast of Guadeloupe, of which it is a dependency. Chief town: Grand Bourg. Pop: 12 488 (1999). Area: 155 sq km (60 sq miles)

Mariehamn *n* a city in SW Finland, chief port of the Åland Islands. Pop: 10 693 (2004 est). Finnish name: Maarianhamina

Marie Louise *n* 1791–1847, empress of France (1811–15) as the second wife of Napoleon I; daughter of Francis I of Austria. On Napoleon's abdication (1815) she became Duchess of Parma

Mari El Republic *n* a constituent republic of W central Russia, in the middle Volga basin. Capital: Yoshkar-Ola. Pop: 728 000 (2002). Area: 23 200 sq km (8955 sq miles)

Marienbad *n* the German name for **Mariánské Lázně**

marigold *n* any of various plants cultivated for their yellow or orange flowers [from *Mary* (the Virgin) + *gold*]

marijuana *or* **marihuana** (mar-ree-wah-na) *n* the dried leaves and flowers of the hemp plant, used as a drug, esp. in cigarettes [Mexican Spanish]

Marikana *n* a town in the North West Province of South Africa; the platinum mine was the scene of a strike and armed conflict in 2012 during which 47 people, mostly mineworkers, died. Pop: 19 522 (2011)

marimba *n* a percussion instrument consisting of a set of hardwood plates placed over tuned metal resonators, played with soft-headed sticks [West African]

Marin *n* John. 1870–1953, US painter, noted esp. for his watercolour landscapes and seascapes

marina *n* a harbour for yachts and other pleasure boats [Latin: marine]

marinade *n* 1 a mixture of oil, wine, vinegar, etc., in which meat or fish is soaked before cooking ▷ *vb* -nading, -naded 2 same as **marinate** [French]

marinate *vb* -nating, -nated to soak in marinade [Italian *marinare* to pickle] ⟩ **marinated** *adj*

Marinduque *n* an island of the central Philippines, east of Mindoro: forms, with offshore islets, a province of the Philippines. Capital: Boac. Pop (Marinduque province): 217 392 (2000). Area: 960 sq km (370 sq miles)

marine *adj* 1 of, found in, or relating to the sea 2 of shipping or navigation 3 used or adapted for use at sea ▷ *n* 4 (esp. in Britain and the US) a soldier trained for land and sea combat 5 a country's shipping or navy collectively: *the merchant marine* [Latin *marinus* of the sea]

mariner (mar-in-er) *n* a sailor

Marinetti *n* Filippo Tommaso. 1876–1944, Italian poet; founder of futurism (1909)

marionette *n* a puppet whose limbs are moved by strings [French, from the name *Marion*]

Maritain *n* Jacques. 1882–1973, French neo-Thomist Roman Catholic philosopher

marital *adj* of or relating to marriage [Latin *maritus* married] ⟩ **maritally** *adv*

maritime *adj* 1 of or relating to shipping 2 of, near, or living near the sea [Latin *maritimus* of the sea]

Maritime Alps *pl n* a range of the W Alps in SE France and NW Italy. Highest peak: Argentera, 3297 m (10 817 ft)

Maritime Provinces *or* **Maritimes** *pl n* the Maritime Provinces another name for the Atlantic Provinces of Canada, but often excluding Newfoundland and Labrador

Maritsa *n* a river in S Europe, rising in S Bulgaria and flowing east into Turkey, then south from Edirne as part of the border between Turkey and Greece to the Aegean. Length: 483 km (300 miles). Turkish name: **Meriç**. Greek name: **Évros**

Mariupol *n* a port in SE Ukraine, on an estuary leading to the Sea of Azov. Pop: 485 000 (2005 est). Former name (1948–91): **Zhdanov**

Marius *n* Gaius. ?155–86 BC, Roman general and consul. He defeated Jugurtha, the Cimbri, and the Teutons (107–101), but his rivalry with Sulla caused civil war (88). He was exiled but returned (87) and took Rome

Marivaux *n* Pierre Carlet de Chamblain de. 1688–1763, French dramatist and novelist, noted particularly for his comedies, such as *Le Jeu de l'amour et du hasard* (1730) and *La Vie de Marianne* (1731–41)

marjoram *n* a plant with sweet-scented leaves, used for seasoning food and in salads [Medieval Latin *marjorana*]

mark¹ *n* 1 a visible impression on a surface, such as a spot or scratch 2 a sign, symbol, or other indication that distinguishes something 3 a written or printed symbol, as used for punctuation 4 a letter, number, or percentage used to grade academic work 5 a thing that indicates position; marker 6 an indication of some quality: *a mark of respect* 7 a target or goal 8 impression or influence: *this book displays the mark of its author's admiration of Kafka* 9 (in trade names) a particular model or type of a vehicle, machine, etc.: *the Ford Escort Mark Two* 10 one of the temperature settings at which a gas oven can work: *bake at gas mark 5 for thirty minutes* 11 make one's mark to achieve recognition 12 on your mark *or* marks a command given to runners in a race to prepare themselves at the starting line 13 up to the mark meeting the desired standard ▷ *vb* 14 to make a visible impression, trace, or stain on 15 to have a tendency to become dirty, scratched, or damaged: *this material marks easily* 16 to characterize or distinguish: *the gritty determination that has marked his career* 17 to designate someone as a particular type of person: *she would now be marked as a troublemaker* 18 to label, esp. to indicate price 19 to celebrate or commemorate an occasion or its anniversary: *a series of concerts to mark the 200th anniversary of Mozart's death* 20 to pay attention to: *mark my words* 21 to observe or notice 22 to grade or evaluate academic work 23 *sport* to stay close to an opponent to hamper his or her play 24 mark off *or* out to set boundaries or limits on

25 mark time a to move the feet alternately as in marching but without advancing **b** to wait for something more interesting to happen ▸ See also markdown, mark-up [Old English *mearc*]

mark² *n* See Deutschmark [Old English *marc* unit of weight of precious metal]

markdown *n* **1** a price reduction ▷ *vb* **mark down 2** to reduce in price **3** to make a written note of: *she marked down the number of the getaway car*

marked *adj* **1** obvious or noticeable: *a marked improvement* **2** singled out, esp. as the target of attack: *a marked man* ❭ **markedly** (mark-id-lee) *adv*

marker *n* **1** an object used to show the position of something **2** Also called: **marker pen** a thick felt-tipped pen used for drawing and colouring

market *n* **1** an occasion at which people meet to buy and sell merchandise **2** a place at which a market is held **3** the buying and selling of goods and services, esp. when unrestrained by political or social considerations: *the market has been brought into health care* **4** the trading opportunities provided by a particular group of people: *the youth market* **5** demand for a particular product **6** short for **stock market 7** be in the market for to wish to buy **8** on the market available for purchase **9** seller's *or* buyer's market a market characterized by excess demand (or supply) and thus favourable to sellers (or buyers) ▷ *adj* **10** of, relating to, or controlled by the buying and selling of goods and services, esp. when unrestrained by political or social considerations: *a market economy* ▷ *vb* **-keting, -keted 11** to offer or produce for sale [Latin *mercari* to trade] ❭ **marketable** *adj*

market forces *pl n* the effect of supply and demand on trading within a free market

market garden *n chiefly Brit and NZ* a place where fruit and vegetables are grown for sale ❭ **market gardener** *n*

marketing *n* the part of a business which controls the way that goods or services are sold

market maker *n Stock Exchange* a dealer in securities on the London Stock Exchange who can also deal with the public as a broker

marketplace *n* **1** a place where a public market is held **2** the commercial world of buying and selling

market price *n* the prevailing price at which goods may be bought or sold

market research *n* the study of customers' wants and purchases, and of the forces influencing them

market-test *vb* to put (a section of a public-sector service) out to tender, often before full privatization

market town *n chiefly Brit* the main town in an agricultural area, usually one where a market is regularly held

Markham *n* Mount Markham a mountain in Antarctica, in Victoria Land. Height: 4350 m (14 272 ft)

Markiewicz *n* Constance, Countess, original name *Constance Gore-Booth*. 1868–1927, Irish nationalist, married to a Polish count. She fought in the Easter Rising (1916) and was sentenced to death but reprieved. The first woman elected to the British parliament (1918), she refused to take her seat

marking *n* **1** the arrangement of colours on an animal or plant **2** the assessment and correction of pupils' or students' written work by teachers

Markova *n* Dame Alicia. real name *Lilian Alicia Marks*. (1910–2004), English ballerina

marksman *n, pl* **-men** a person skilled in shooting ❭ **marksmanship** *n*

mark-up *n* **1** an amount added to the cost of something to provide the seller with a profit ▷ *vb* **mark up 2** to increase the cost of something by an amount or percentage in order to make a profit

marl *n* a fine-grained rock consisting of clay, limestone, and silt used as a fertilizer [Late Latin *margila*] ❭ **marly** *adj*

Marlborough¹ *n* a town in S England, in Wiltshire: besieged and captured by Royalists in the Civil War (1642); site of Marlborough College, a public school founded in 1843. Pop: 7713 (2001)

Marlborough² *n* 1st Duke of. title of *John Churchill*. 1650–1722, English general; commander of British forces in the War of the Spanish Succession (1701–14), in which he won victories at Blenheim (1704), Ramillies (1706), Oudenaarde (1708), and Malplaquet (1709)

Marley *n* Bob, full name *Robert Nesta Marley*. 1945–81, Jamaican reggae singer, guitarist, and songwriter. With his group, the Wailers, his albums included *Burnin'* (1973), *Natty Dread* (1975), *Rastaman Vibration* (1976), and *Exodus* (1977)

marlin *n, pl* **-lin** *or* **-lins** a large fish with a long spear-like upper jaw, found in warm and tropical seas [after MARLINSPIKE (because of its long jaw)]

marlinspike *or* **marlinespike** (mar-lin-spike) *n nautical* a pointed metal tool used in separating strands of rope [Dutch *marlijn* light rope + SPIKE]

Marlowe *n* Christopher. 1564–93, English dramatist and poet, who established blank verse as a creative form of dramatic expression. His plays include *Tamburlaine the Great* (1590), *Edward II* (?1592), and *Dr Faustus* (1604). He was stabbed to death in a tavern brawl

marmalade *n* a jam made from citrus fruits, esp. oranges [Portuguese *marmelo* quince]

Marmara *or* **Marmora** *n* Sea of Marmara a deep inland sea in NW Turkey, linked with the Black Sea by the Bosporus and with the Aegean by the Dardanelles: separates Turkey in Europe from Turkey in Asia. Area: 11 471 sq km (4429 sq miles). Ancient name: Propontis

Marmolada *n* a mountain in NE Italy: highest peak in the Dolomites. Height: 3342 m (10 965 ft)

marmoreal (mar-more-ee-al) *adj* of or like marble [Latin *marmoreus*]

marmoset *n* a small South American monkey with a long bushy tail [Old French *marmouset* grotesque figure]

marmot *n* any of various burrowing rodents of Europe, Asia, and North America. They are heavily built and have coarse fur [French *marmotte*]

Marne *n* **1** a department of NE France, in Champagne-Ardenne region. Capital: Châlons-sur-Marne. Pop: 563 027 (2003 est). Area: 8205 sq km (3200 sq miles) **2** a river in NE France, rising on the plateau of Langres and flowing north, then west to the River Seine, north of Paris: linked by canal with the Rivers Saône, Rhine, and Aisne; scene of two unsuccessful German offensives (1914, 1918) during World War I. Length: 525 km (326 miles)

Maroc *n* the French name for Morocco

maroon¹ *vb* **1** to abandon someone in a deserted area, esp. on an island **2** to isolate in a helpless situation: *we're marooned here until the snow stops* [American Spanish *cimarrón* wild] ❭ **marooned** *adj*

maroon² *adj* **1** dark purplish-red ▷ *n* **2** an exploding firework or flare used as a warning signal [French: chestnut]

Maros *n* the Hungarian name for the Mureș

Marprelate *n* Martin, the pen name of the anonymous author or authors of a series of satirical Puritan tracts (1588–89), attacking the bishops of the Church of England

Marquand *n* J(ohn) P(hillips). 1893–1960, US novelist, noted for his stories featuring the Japanese detective Mr Moto and for his satirical comedies of New England life, such as *The Late George Apley* (1937)

marque (mark) *n* a brand of product, esp. of a car [French]

marquee *n* a large tent used for a party, exhibition, etc. [invented singular form of MARQUISE]

Marquesan *adj* **1** of or relating to the Marquesas Islands or their inhabitants ▷ *n* **2** a native or inhabitant of the Marquesas Islands

Marquesas Islands *pl n* a group of volcanic islands in

the S Pacific, in French Polynesia. Pop: 8712 (2002). Area: 1287 sq km (497 sq miles). French name: Îles Marquises

marquess (mar-kwiss) *n* **1** (in the British Isles) a nobleman ranking between a duke and an earl **2** See **marquis**

marquetry *n, pl* **-quetries** a pattern of inlaid veneers of wood or metal used chiefly as ornamentation in furniture [Old French *marqueter* to inlay]

Marquette *n* Jacques, known as *Père Marquette*. 1637–75, French Jesuit missionary and explorer, with Louis Jolliet, of the Mississippi river

marquis *n, pl* **-quises** *or* **-quis** (in various countries) a nobleman ranking above a count, corresponding to a British marquess [Old French *marchis* count of the frontier]

Marquis *n* Don(ald Robert Perry). 1878–1937, US humorist; author of *archy and mehitabel* (1927)

marquise (mar-keez) *n* **1** (in various countries) a marchioness **2** a gemstone cut in a pointed oval shape [French]

Marrakech *or* **Marrakesh** *n* a city in W central Morocco: several times capital of Morocco; tourist centre. Pop: 672 000 (2003)

marram grass *n* a grass that grows on sandy shores: often planted to stabilize sand dunes [Old Norse *marálmr*]

marriage *n* **1** the state or relationship of being married: *the institution of marriage* **2** the contract made by two people to live together in a partnership. Related adjectives: **connubial, nuptial 3** the ceremony formalizing this union; wedding **4** a close union or relationship: *the marriage of scientific knowledge and industry*

marriageable *adj* suitable for marriage, usually with reference to age

marriage guidance *n* advice given by trained counsellors to couples who have problems in their married life

married *adj* **1** having a husband or wife **2** of marriage or married people: *married life* ▷ *n* **3** marrieds married people: *young marrieds*

Marriner *n* Sir Neville. born 1924, British conductor and violinist; founder (1956) and director of the Academy of St Martin in the Fields, which specializes in baroque music

marrow *n* **1** the fatty tissue that fills the cavities of bones **2** short for **vegetable marrow** [Old English *mærg*]

marrowfat pea *or* **marrow pea** *n* a variety of large pea

marry¹ *vb* **-ries, -rying, -ried 1** to take (someone) as one's partner in marriage **2** to join or give in marriage **3** Also: **marry up** to fit together or unite; join: *their playing marries Irish traditional music and rock* [Latin *maritare*]

marry² *interj archaic* an exclamation of surprise or anger [euphemistic for the Virgin *Mary*]

Marryat *n* Frederick, known as *Captain Marryat*. 1792–1848, English novelist and naval officer; author of novels of sea life, such as *Mr Midshipman Easy* (1836), and children's stories, such as *The Children of the New Forest* (1847)

Mars *n* **1** the Roman god of war **2** the fourth planet from the sun

Marsala *n* **1** a port in W Sicily: landing place of Garibaldi at the start of his Sicilian campaign (1860). Pop: 77 784 (2001) **2** (*sometimes not cap*) a dark sweet dessert wine made in Sicily

Marsalis *n* Wynton. born 1961, US jazz and classical trumpeter

Marseillaise (mar-say-**yaze**) *n* the Marseillaise the French national anthem [French (*chanson*) *marseillaise* (song) of Marseilles (first sung in Paris by the battalion of Marseilles)]

Marseille *n* a port in SE France, on the Gulf of Lions: second largest city in the country and a major port; founded in about 600 BC by Greeks from Phocaea; oil refining. Pop: 860 363 (2007). Ancient name: **Massilia**. English name: **Marseilles**

marsh *n* low poorly drained land that is wet, muddy, and sometimes flooded [Old English *merisc*] ▷ **marshy** *adj*

Marsh *n* **1** Dame (**Edith**) Ngaio. 1899–1981, New Zealand crime writer, living in Britain (from 1928). Her many detective novels include *Final Curtain* (1947) and *Last Ditch* (1977) **2** Rodney (**William**). born 1947, Australian cricketer: a wicketkeeper, he took 355 dismissals in 96 test matches (1970–84)

marshal *n* **1** (in some armies and air forces) an officer of the highest rank: *Field Marshall* **2** an officer who organizes or controls ceremonies or public events **3** US the chief police or fire officer in some states **4** (formerly in England) an officer of the royal family or court ▷ *vb* **-shalling, -shalled** *or* US **-shaling, -shaled 5** to arrange in order: *she marshalled her facts and came to a conclusion* **6** to assemble and organize people or vehicles in readiness for onward movement **7** to guide or lead, esp. in a ceremonious way: *she marshalled them towards the lecture theatre* [Old French *mareschal*] ▷ **marshalcy** *n*

Marshall *n* **1** Alfred. 1842–1924, English economist, author of *Principles of Economics* (1890) **2** Barry (**James**). born 1951, Australian microbiologist who, with Robin Warren, demonstrated that the bacterium *Helicobacter pylori* is the cause of most peptic ulcers, for which they won the Nobel Prize in Physiology or Medicine (2005) **3** George Catlett. 1880–1959, US general and statesman. He was chief of staff of the US army (1939–45) and, as secretary of state (1947–49), he proposed the Marshall Plan (1947): Nobel peace prize 1953 **4** John. 1755–1835, US jurist and statesman. As chief justice of the Supreme Court (1801–35), he established the principles of US constitutional law **5** Sir John Ross. 1912–88, New Zealand politician; prime minister (1972)

marshalling yard *n railways* a place where railway wagons are shunted and made up into trains

Marshall Islands *pl n* a republic, consisting of a group of 34 coral islands in the W central Pacific: formerly part of the Trust Territory of the Pacific Islands (1947–87); status of free association with the US from 1986; consists of two parallel chains, Ralik and Ratak. Official languages: Marshallese and English. Religion: Roman Catholic majority. Currency: US dollar. Capital: Delap-Uliga-Djarrit, on Majuro atoll. Pop: 69 747 (2013 est.) Area: (land) 181 sq km (70 sq miles); (lagoon) 11 655 sq km (4500 sq miles)

Marshal of the Royal Air Force *n* the highest rank in the Royal Air Force

marsh gas *n* a gas largely composed of methane formed when plants decay in the absence of air

marshland *n* land consisting of marshes

marshmallow *n* a spongy pink or white sweet

marsh mallow *n* a plant that grows in salt marshes and has pale pink flowers. It was formerly used to make marshmallows

Marsilius of Padua *n* Italian name *Marsiglio dei Mainardini*. ?1290–?1343, Italian political philosopher, best known as the author of the *Defensor pacis* (1324), which upheld the power of the temporal ruler over that of the church

Marston *n* John. ?1576–1634, English dramatist and satirist. His works include the revenge tragedies *Antonio and Mellida* (1602) and *Antonio's Revenge* (1602) and the satirical comedy *The Malcontent* (1604)

Marston Moor *n* a flat low-lying area in NE England, west of York: scene of a battle (1644) in which the Parliamentarians defeated the Royalists

marsupial (mar-**soop**-ee-al) *n* **1** a mammal, such as a kangaroo or an opossum, the female of which carries her babies in a pouch at the front of her body until they reach a mature state ▷ *adj* **2** of or like a marsupial [Latin *marsupium* purse]

mart *n* a market or trading centre [Middle Dutch: market]

Martaban *n* Gulf of Martaban an inlet of the Bay of Bengal in Myanmar

Martello tower n a round tower used for coastal defence, formerly much used in Europe [after Cape *Mortella* in Corsica]

marten n, pl **-tens** or **-ten 1** any of several agile weasel-like mammals with bushy tails and golden-brown to blackish fur **2** the fur of these animals [Middle Dutch *martren*]

Martha n **Saint Martha** *New Testament* a sister of Mary and Lazarus, who lived at Bethany and ministered to Jesus (Luke 10:38–42). Feast day: July 29 or June 4

martial adj of or characteristic of war, soldiers, or the military life: *martial music* [Latin *martialis* of Mars, god of war]

Martial n Latin name *Marcus Valerius Martialis*. ?40–?104 AD, Latin epigrammatist and poet, born in Spain

martial art n any of various philosophies and techniques of self-defence originating in the Far East, such as judo or karate

martial law n rule of law maintained by military forces in the absence of civil law

Martian (marsh-an) adj **1** of the planet Mars ▷ n **2** an inhabitant of Mars, in science fiction

martin n a bird of the swallow family with a square or slightly forked tail [probably after St *Martin*, because the birds were believed to migrate at Martinmas]

Martin 1 Archer John Porter. 1910–2002, British biochemist; Nobel prize for chemistry 1952 (with Richard Synge; 1914–94) for developing paper chromatography (1944). He subsequently developed gas chromatography (1953) **2 Chris(topher Anthony John)**. born 1977, English rock musician; lead singer of Coldplay **3 Frank**. 1890–1974, Swiss composer. He used a modified form of the twelve-note technique in some of his works, which include *Petite Symphonie Concertante* (1946) and the oratorio *Golgotha* (1949) **4 Sir George (Henry)**. born 1926, British record producer and arranger, noted for his work with the Beatles **5 John**. 1789–1854, British painter, noted for his visionary landscapes and large-scale works with biblical subjects **6 Michael (John)**. Baron. born 1945, Scottish Labour politician; speaker of the House of Commons (2000–09) **7 Paul (Edgar Philippe)**. born 1938, Canadian Liberal politician; prime minister of Canada (2003–06) **8 Saint**. called *Saint Martin of Tours*. ?316–?397 AD, bishop of Tours (?371–?397); a patron saint of France. He furthered monasticism in Gaul. Feast day: Nov 11 or 12 **9 Steve(n)**. born 1945, US film actor and comedian; his films include *The Jerk* (1979), *Roxanne* (1987), and *Bowfinger* (1999)

Martin V n original name *Oddone Colonna*. 1368–1431, pope (1417–31). His election at the Council of Constance brought to an end the Great Schism

Martin du Gard n **Roger**. 1881–1958, French novelist, noted for his series of novels, *Les Thibault* (1922–40): Nobel prize for literature 1937

Martineau n **1 Harriet**. 1802–76, English author of books on political economy and of novels and children's stories **2** her brother, **James**. 1805–1900, English Unitarian theologian and minister

martinet n a person who maintains strict discipline [after General *Martinet*, drillmaster under Louis XIV]

martingale n a strap from the reins to the girth of a horse, preventing it from carrying its head too high [French]

martini n **1** (*often cap*) trademark an Italian vermouth **2** a cocktail of gin and vermouth

Martini n **Simone**. ?1284–1344, Sienese painter

Martinican adj **1** of or relating to Martinique or its inhabitants ▷ n **2** a native or inhabitant of Martinique

Martinique n an island in the E Caribbean, in the Windward Islands of the Lesser Antilles: administratively an overseas region of France. Capital: Fort-de-France. Pop: 403 795 (2007 est). Area: 1090 sq km (420 sq miles)

Martinmas n the feast of St Martin on November 11: a quarter day in Scotland

Martinů n **Bohuslav**. 1890–1959, Czech composer

martyr n **1** a person who chooses to die rather than renounce his or her religious beliefs **2** a person who suffers greatly or dies for a cause or belief **3 a martyr to** suffering constantly from: *a martyr to arthritis* ▷ vb **4** to make a martyr of [Late Greek *martur-* witness] **⟩ martyrdom** n

marvel vb **-velling, -velled** or US **-veling, -veled 1** to be filled with surprise or wonder ▷ n **2** something that causes wonder [Old French *merveille*]

Marvell n **Andrew**. 1621–78, English poet and satirist. He is noted for his lyrical poems and verse and prose satires attacking the government after the Restoration

marvellous or US **marvelous** adj **1** excellent or splendid: *a marvellous idea* **2** causing great wonder or surprise; extraordinary: *electricity is a marvellous thing* **⟩ marvellously** or US **marvelously** adv

Marx n **Karl**. 1818–83, German founder of modern communism, in England from 1849. With Engels, he wrote *The Communist Manifesto* (1848). He developed his theories of the class struggle and the economics of capitalism in *Das Kapital* (1867; 1885; 1895). He was one of the founders of the International Workingmen's Association (First International) (1864)

Marx Brothers n the. a US family of film comedians, esp. **Arthur Marx**, known as *Harpo* (1888–1964), **Herbert Marx**, known as *Zeppo* (1901–79), **Julius Marx**, known as *Groucho* (1890–1977), and **Leonard Marx**, known as *Chico* (1886–1961). Their films include *Animal Crackers* (1930), *Monkey Business* (1931), *Horsefeathers* (1932), *Duck Soup* (1933), and *A Day at the Races* (1937)

Marxism n the economic and political theories of Karl Marx, which argue that class struggle is the basic agency of historical change, and that capitalism will be superseded by communism **⟩ Marxist** n, adj

Mary I n family name *Tudor*, known as *Bloody Mary*. 1516–58, queen of England (1553–58). The daughter of Henry VIII and Catherine of Aragon, she married Philip II of Spain in 1554. She restored Roman Catholicism to England and about 300 Protestants were burnt at the stake as heretics

Mary II n 1662–94, queen of England, Scotland, and Ireland (1689–94), ruling jointly with her husband William III. They were offered the crown by parliament, which objected to the arbitrary rule of her father James II

Maryland n a state of the eastern US, on the Atlantic: divided into two unequal parts by Chesapeake Bay: mostly low-lying, with the Alleghenies in the northwest Capital: Annapolis. Pop: 5 508 909 (2003 est). Area: 31 864 sq km (12 303 sq miles). Abbreviation: **Md.**, (with zip code) **MD**

Mary, Queen of Scots n family name *Stuart*. 1542–87, queen of Scotland (1542–67); daughter of James V of Scotland and Mary of Guise. She was married to Francis II of France (1558–60), her cousin Lord Darnley (1565–67), and the Earl of Bothwell (1567–71), who was commonly regarded as Darnley's murderer. She was forced to abdicate in favour of her son (later James VI of Scotland) and fled to England. Imprisoned by Elizabeth I until 1587, she was beheaded for plotting against the English crown

marzipan n a mixture made from ground almonds, sugar, and egg whites that is put on top of cakes or used to make sweets [Italian *marzapane*]

Masaccio n original name *Tommaso Guidi*. 1401–28, Florentine painter. He was the first to apply to painting the laws of perspective discovered by Brunelleschi. His chief work is the frescoes in the Brancacci chapel in the church of Santa Maria del Carmine, Florence

Masada n an ancient mountaintop fortress in Israel, 400 m (1300 ft) above the W shore of the Dead Sea: the last Jewish stronghold during a revolt in Judaea

m

(66–73 AD). Besieged by the Romans for a year, almost all of the inhabitants killed themselves rather than surrender. The site is an Israeli national monument

masala n Indian cookery a mixture of spices ground into a paste

Masan n a port in SE South Korea, on an inlet of the Korea Strait: first opened to foreign trade in 1899. Pop: 428 000 (2005 est)

Masaryk n 1 Jan. 1886–1948, Czech statesman; foreign minister (1941–48). He died in mysterious circumstances after the Communists took control of the government 2 his father, **Tomáš Garrigue**. 1850–1937, Czech philosopher and statesman; a founder of Czechoslovakia (1918) and its first president (1918–35)

Masbate n 1 an island in the central Philippines, between Negros and SE Luzon: agricultural, with resources of gold, copper, and manganese. Pop (Masbate province): 707 668 (2000). Area: 4045 sq km (1562 sq miles) 2 the capital of this island, a port in the northeast. Pop: 71 441 (2000)

masc. masculine

Mascagni n Pietro. 1863–1945, Italian composer of operas, including Cavalleria rusticana (1890)

mascara n a cosmetic for darkening the eyelashes [Spanish: mask]

Mascarene Islands pl n a group of volcanic islands in the W Indian Ocean, east of Madagascar: consists of the islands of Réunion, Mauritius, and Rodrigues. French name: **Îles Mascareignes**

mascarpone (mass-car-po-nee) n a soft Italian cream cheese [from Italian dialect mascherpa ricotta]

mascot n a person, animal, or thing considered to bring good luck [French mascotte]

masculine adj 1 possessing qualities or characteristics considered typical of or appropriate to a man; manly 2 unwomanly; not feminine 3 grammar denoting a gender of nouns that includes some male animate things 4 prosody denoting a rhyme between pairs of single final stressed syllables [Latin masculinus] > **masculinity** n

Masefield n John. 1878–1967, English poet, novelist, and critic; poet laureate (1930–67)

maser n a device for amplifying microwaves, working on the same principle as a laser [m(icrowave) a(mplification by) s(timulated) e(mission of) r(adiation)]

Maseru n the capital of Lesotho, in the northwest near the W border with South Africa; established as capital of Basutoland in 1869. Pop: 175 000 (2005 est)

mash n 1 a soft pulpy mass 2 agriculture bran, meal, or malt mixed with warm water and used as food for horses, cattle, or poultry 3 Brit informal mashed potatoes ▷ vb 4 to beat or crush into a mash [Old English mēsc-] > **mashed** adj

Masherbrum or **Masharbrum** n a mountain in N India, in N Kashmir in the Karakoram Range of the Himalayas. Height: 7822 m (25 660 ft)

Mashhad or **Meshed** n a city in NE Iran: an important holy city of Shi'ite Muslims; carpet manufacturing. Pop: 2 147 000 (2005 est)

Masinissa or **Massinissa** n ?238–?149 BC, king of Numidia (?210–149), who fought as an ally of Rome against Carthage in the Second Punic War

mask n 1 any covering for the whole or a part of the face worn for amusement, protection, or disguise 2 behaviour that hides one's true feelings: his mask of detachment 3 surgery a sterile gauze covering for the nose and mouth worn to minimize the spread of germs 4 a device placed over the nose and mouth to facilitate or prevent inhalation of a gas 5 a moulded likeness of a face or head, such as a death mask 6 the face or head of an animal such as a fox ▷ vb 7 to cover with or put on a mask 8 to hide or disguise: a high brick wall that masked the front of the building 9 to cover so as to protect [Arabic maskharah clown] > **masked** adj

masking tape n an adhesive tape used to protect surfaces surrounding an area to be painted

masochism (mass-oh-kiz-zum) n 1 psychiatry a condition in which pleasure, esp. sexual pleasure, is obtained from feeling pain or from being humiliated 2 a tendency to take pleasure from one's own suffering [after Leopold von Sacher Masoch, novelist] > **masochist** n, adj > **masochistic** adj

mason n a person skilled in building with stone [Old French masson]

Mason n a Freemason

Masonic adj of Freemasons or Freemasonry

masonry n 1 stonework or brickwork 2 the craft of a mason

Masonry n Freemasonry

Masqat n a transliteration of the Arabic name for Muscat

masque (mask) n a dramatic entertainment of the 16th to 17th centuries, consisting of dancing, dialogue, and song [variant of mask] > **masquer** n

masquerade (mask-er-aid) vb -ading, -aded 1 to pretend to be someone or something else ▷ n 2 an attempt to keep secret the real identity or nature of something: he was unable to keep up his masquerade as the war's victor 3 a party at which the guests wear masks and costumes [Spanish mascara mask]

mass n 1 a large body of something without a definite shape 2 a collection of the component parts of something: a mass of fibres 3 a large amount or number, as of people 4 the main part or majority 5 the size of a body; bulk 6 physics a physical quantity expressing the amount of matter in a body 7 (in painting or drawing) an area of unified colour, shade, or intensity ▷ adj 8 done or occurring on a large scale: mass hysteria 9 consisting of a mass or large number, esp. of people: a mass meeting ▷ vb 10 to join together into a mass ▶ See also **masses** [Latin massa] > **massed** adj

Mass n 1 (in the Roman Catholic Church and certain other Christian churches) a service in which bread and wine are consecrated to represent the body and blood of Christ 2 a musical setting of parts of this service [Church Latin missa]

Mass. Massachusetts

Massa n a town in W Italy, in NW Tuscany. Pop: 66 769 (2001)

Massachusetts n a state of the northeastern US, on the Atlantic: a centre of resistance to English colonial policy during the War of American Independence; consists of a coastal plain rising to mountains in the west. Capital: Boston. Pop: 6 433 422 (2003 est). Area: 20 269 sq km (7826 sq miles). Abbreviation: **Mass.**, (with zip code) **MA**

Massachusetts Bay n an inlet of the Atlantic on the E coast of Massachusetts

massacre (mass-a-ker) n 1 the wanton or savage killing of large numbers of people 2 informal an overwhelming defeat ▷ vb -cring, -cred 3 to kill people indiscriminately in large numbers 4 informal to defeat overwhelmingly [Old French]

massage (mass-ahzh) n 1 the kneading or rubbing of parts of the body to reduce pain or stiffness or help relaxation ▷ vb -saging, -saged 2 to give a massage to 3 to manipulate statistics or evidence to produce a desired result [French masser to rub]

massage parlour n 1 a commercial establishment providing massages 2 euphemistic a place where men pay to have sex with prostitutes

massasauga (mass-a-saw-ga) n a North American venomous snake with a horny rattle at the end of the tail [after the Missisauga River, Ontario, Canada]

Massasoit n died 1661, Wampanoag Indian chief, who negotiated peace with the Pilgrim Fathers (1621)

Massawa or **Massaua** n a port in E central Eritrea, on the Red Sea: capital of Eritrea during Italian occupation, from 1885 until 1900. Pop: 36 700 (2004 est)

Masséna n André, Prince d'Essling. 1758–1817, French marshal under Napoleon I: victories at Saorgio (1794), Loano (1795), Rivoli (1797), Zürich (1799), and Caldiero (1805): defeated by Wellington in the Peninsular War (1810–11)

Massenet n Jules (Émile Frédéric). 1842–1912, French composer of operas, including Manon (1884), Werther (1892), and Thaïs (1894)

masses pl n **1 the masses** ordinary people as a group **2 masses of** informal, chiefly Brit a great number or quantity of: masses of food

masseur (mass-ur) or fem **masseuse** (mass-uhz) n a person who gives massages

Massey n **1** Raymond.1896–1983, Canadian actor and film star. His films include The Scarlet Pimpernel (1934) and East of Eden (1955). He also appeared in the television series Dr Kildare (1961–65) **2** Vincent. 1887–1967, Canadian statesman: first Canadian-born governor general of Canada (1952–59) **3** William Ferguson. 1856–1925, New Zealand statesman, born in Ireland: prime minister of New Zealand (1912–25)

massif (mass-seef) n a series of connected masses of rock forming a mountain range [French]

Massif Central n a mountainous plateau region of S central France, occupying about one sixth of the country: contains several extinct volcanic cones, notably Puy de Dôme, 1465 m (4806 ft). Highest point: Puy de Sancy, 1886 m (6188 ft). Area: about 85 000 sq km (33 000 sq miles)

Massine n Léonide. 1896–1979, US ballet dancer and choreographer, born in Russia

Massinger n Philip. 1583–?1640, English dramatist, noted esp. for his comedy A New Way to pay Old Debts (1633)

massive adj **1** (of objects) large, bulky, heavy, and usually solid **2** impressive or imposing **3** intensive or considerable: a massive overdose [French massif] **> massively** adv

mass-market adj of, for, or appealing to a large number of people; popular: mass-market newspapers

mass media pl n the means of communication that reach large numbers of people, such as television, newspapers, and radio

mass noun n a noun that refers to an extended substance rather than to each of a set of objects, for example water as opposed to lake

mass number n the total number of protons and neutrons in the nucleus of an atom

mass-produce vb **-producing, -produced** to manufacture standardized goods on a large scale by extensive use of machinery **> mass-produced** adj **> mass-production** n

mass spectrometer n an instrument for analysing the composition of a sample of material, in which ions, produced from the sample, are separated by electric or magnetic fields according to their ratios of charge to mass

Massys, Matsys or **Metsys** n Quentin. 1466–1530, Flemish painter, based in Antwerp; noted for his portraits and scenes of everyday life

mast¹ n **1** nautical a vertical pole for supporting sails, radar equipment, etc., above the deck of a ship **2** a tall upright pole used as an aerial for radio or television broadcasting: a television mast **3 before the mast** nautical as an apprentice seaman [Old English mæst]

mast² n the fruit of forest trees, such as beech or oak, used as food for pigs [Old English mæst]

mastaba n a mud-brick superstructure above tombs in ancient Egypt [Arabic: bench]

mastectomy (mass-tek-tom-ee) n, pl **-mies** surgical removal of a breast [Greek mastos breast + ek out + tomē a cutting]

master n **1** the man who has authority over others, such as the head of a household, the employer of servants, or the owner of slaves or animals **2** a person with

exceptional skill at a certain thing: B.B. King is a master of the blues **3** a person who has complete control of a situation: the master of his portfolio **4** an original copy or tape from which duplicates are made **5** a craftsman fully qualified to practise his trade and to train others **6** a player of a game, esp. chess or bridge, who has won a specified number of tournament games **7** a highly regarded teacher or leader **8** a graduate holding a master's degree **9** the chief officer aboard a merchant ship **10** chiefly Brit a male teacher **11** the superior person or side in a contest **12** the heir apparent of a Scottish viscount or baron: the Master of Ballantrae ▷ adj **13** (of a craftsman) fully qualified to practise and to train others **14** overall or controlling: master plan **15** designating a mechanism that controls others: master switch **16** main or principal: master bedroom ▷ vb **17** to become thoroughly proficient in **18** to overcome or defeat [Latin magister teacher]

Master n a title of address for a boy who is not old enough to be called Mr

master aircrew n a rank in the Royal Air Force, equal to warrant officer

masterful adj **1** showing great skill **2** domineering or authoritarian **> masterfully** adv

master key n a key that opens all the locks of a set; passkey

masterly adj showing great skill; expert

mastermind vb **1** to plan and direct a complex task or project ▷ n **2** a person who plans and directs a complex task or project

Master of Arts n a degree, usually postgraduate in a nonscientific subject, or a person holding this degree

master of ceremonies n a person who presides over a public ceremony, formal dinner, or entertainment, introducing the events and performers

Master of Science n a degree, usually postgraduate in a scientific subject, or a person holding this degree

Master of the Rolls n (in England) the senior civil judge in the country and the head of the Public Record Office

masterpiece or **masterwork** n **1** an outstanding work or performance **2** the most outstanding piece of work of an artist or craftsman

Masters n Edgar Lee. 1868–1950, US poet; best known for Spoon River Anthology (1915)

masterstroke n an outstanding piece of strategy, skill, or talent

mastery n, pl **-teries 1** outstanding skill or expertise **2** complete power or control: he had complete mastery over the country

masthead n **1** nautical the highest part of a mast **2** the name of a newspaper or periodical printed at the top of the front page

mastic n **1** an aromatic resin obtained from a Mediterranean tree and used to make varnishes and lacquers **2** any of several putty-like substances used as a filler, adhesive, or seal [Greek mastikhē]

masticate vb **-cating, -cated** to chew food [Greek mastikhan to grind the teeth] **> mastication** n

mastiff n a large powerful short-haired dog, usually fawn or brown with dark streaks [Latin mansuetus tame]

mastitis n inflammation of the breast

mastodon n an extinct elephant-like mammal [New Latin, literally: breast-tooth, referring to the nipple-shaped projections on the teeth]

mastoid adj **1** shaped like a nipple or breast ▷ n **2** a nipple-like projection of bone behind the ear **3** informal mastoiditis [Greek mastos breast]

mastoiditis n inflammation of the mastoid

Mastroianni n Marcello. 1924–96, Italian film actor; his films include Le notti bianche (1957), La dolce vita (1960), Ginger and Fred (1985), and Prêt à Porter (1995)

masturbate vb **-bating, -bated** to fondle one's own genitals, or those of someone else, to cause sexual pleasure [Latin *masturbari*] **>** **masturbation** *n*

Masuria *n* a region of NE Poland: until 1945 part of East Prussia: includes the **Masurian Lakes**, scene of Russian defeats by the Germans (1914, 1915) during World War I

Masurian *adj* **1** of or relating to Masuria or its inhabitants **▷** *n* **2** a native or inhabitant of Masuria

mat¹ *n* **1** a thick flat piece of fabric used as a floor covering, a place to wipe one's shoes, etc. **2** a small pad of material used to protect a surface from heat or scratches from an object placed upon it **3** a large piece of thick padded material put on the floor as a surface for wrestling, gymnastics, etc. **▷** *vb* **matting, matted** **4** to tangle or become tangled into a dense mass [Old English *matte*]

mat² *adj* same as **matt** [French, literally: dead]

Matabeleland *n* a region of W Zimbabwe, between the Rivers Limpopo and Zambezi, comprises three provinces, Matabeleland North, Matabeleland South, and Bulawayo: rich gold deposits. Chief town: Bulawayo. Area: 181 605 sq km (70 118 sq miles)

Matadi *n* the chief port of the Democratic Republic of Congo, in the west at the mouth of the River Congo. Pop: 256 000 (2005 est)

matador *n* the bullfighter armed with a sword, who attempts to kill the bull [Spanish, from *matar* to kill]

Mata Hari *n* real name *Gertrud Margarete Zelle*. 1876–1917, Dutch dancer in France, who was executed as a German spy in World War I

matai *n* a New Zealand tree, the wood of which is used for timber for building [Māori]

Matamoros *n* a port in NE Mexico, on the Río Grande: scene of bitter fighting during the US-Mexican War; centre of a cotton-growing area. Pop: 481 000 (2005 est)

Matanzas *n* a port in W central Cuba: founded in 1693 and developed into the second city of Cuba in the mid-19th century; exports chiefly sugar. Pop: 130 000 (2005 est)

Matapan *n* Cape Matapan a cape in S Greece, at the S central tip of the Peloponnese: the southern point of the mainland of Greece. Modern Greek name: **Taínaron**

match¹ *n* **1** a formal game or sports event in which people or teams compete **2** a person or thing able to provide competition for another: *he has met his match* **3** a person or thing that resembles, harmonizes with, or is equivalent to another: *the colours aren't a perfect match, but they're close enough; white wine is not a good match for steak* **4** a person or thing that is an exact copy or equal of another **5** a partnership between a man and a woman, as in marriage **6** a person regarded as a possible partner in marriage: *for any number of men she would have been a good match* **▷** *vb* **7** to fit parts together **8** to resemble, harmonize with, or equal one another or something else: *our bedroom curtains match the bedspread; she walked at a speed that he could barely match* **9** to find a match for **10** **match with** *or* **against** **a** to compare in order to determine which is the superior **b** to arrange a competition between [Old English *gemæcca* spouse] **>** **matching** *adj*

match² *n* **1** a thin strip of wood or cardboard tipped with a chemical that ignites when scraped against a rough or specially treated surface **2** a fuse used to fire cannons' explosives [Old French *meiche*]

matchbox *n* a small box for holding matches

match-fit *adj sport* in good physical condition for competing in a match

matchless *adj* unequalled

matchmaker *n* a person who introduces people in the hope that they will form a couple **>** **matchmaking** *n, adj*

match play *n golf* scoring according to the number of holes won and lost

match point *n sport* the final point needed to win a match

matchstick *n* **1** the wooden part of a match **▷** *adj* **2** (esp. of drawn figures) thin and straight: *little matchstick men*

matchwood *n* **1** wood suitable for making matches **2** splinters

mate¹ *n* **1** **a** *informal, chiefly Brit, Austral and NZ* a friend: often used as a term of address between males: *I spotted my mate Jimmy McCrae at the other end of the bar; that's all right, mate* **b** (*in combination*) an associate or colleague: *a classmate; the governor's running mate* **2** the sexual partner of an animal **3** a marriage partner **4** *nautical* any officer below the master on a commercial ship **5** (in some trades) an assistant: *a plumber's mate* **6** one of a pair of matching items **▷** *vb* **mating, mated** **7** to pair (a male and female animal) or (of animals) to pair for breeding **8** to marry **9** to join as a pair [Low German]

mate² *n*, *vb* **mating, mated** *chess* same as **checkmate**

mater *n Brit humorous* mother: often used facetiously [Latin]

material *n* **1** the substance of which a thing is made **2** cloth **3** ideas or notes that a finished work may be based on: *the material of the story resembles an incident in his own life* **▷** *adj* **4** concerned with or composed of physical matter or substance; not relating to spiritual or abstract things: *the material universe* **5** of or affecting economic or physical wellbeing: *material prosperity* **6** relevant or pertinent: *material evidence* **▶** See also **materials** [Latin *materia* matter]

materialism *n* **1** excessive interest in and desire for money or possessions **2** the belief that only the material world exists **>** **materialist** *n, adj* **>** **materialistic** *adj*

materialize *or* **-lise** *vb* **-lizing, -lized** *or* **-lising, -lised** **1** to become fact; actually happen: *the promised pay rise never materialized* **2** to appear after being invisible: *trees materialized out of the gloom* **3** to take shape: *after hours of talks, a plan began to materialize* **>** **materialization** *or* **-lisation** *n*

materially *adv* to a significant extent: *we were not materially affected*

materials *pl n* the equipment necessary for a particular activity: *building materials*

materiel (mat-ear-ee-**ell**) *n* the materials and equipment of an organization, esp. of a military force [French]

maternal *adj* **1** of or characteristic of a mother **2** related through the mother's side of the family: *his maternal uncle* [Latin *mater* mother] **>** **maternally** *adv*

maternity *n* **1** motherhood **2** motherliness **▷** *adj* **3** relating to women during pregnancy or childbirth: *maternity leave*

mate's rates *pl n chiefly Austral and NZ informal* reduced charges offered to a friend or colleague

matey *adj Brit informal* friendly or intimate

math *n US and Canad informal* short for **mathematics**

mathematical *adj* **1** using, used in, or relating to mathematics **2** having the precision of mathematics **>** **mathematically** *adv*

mathematician *n* an expert or specialist in mathematics

mathematics *n* **1** a group of related sciences, including algebra, geometry, and calculus, which use a specialized notation to study number, quantity, shape, and space **2** numerical calculations involved in the solution of a problem [Greek *mathēma* a science]

maths *n Brit and Austral informal* short for **mathematics**

Mathura *n* a city in N India, in W Uttar Pradesh on the Jumna River: a place of Hindu pilgrimage, revered as the birthplace of Krishna. Pop: 298 827 (2001). Former name: **Muttra**

Matilda *n* known as *the Empress Maud*. 1102–67, only daughter of Henry I of England and wife of Geoffrey of Anjou. After her father's death (1135) she unsuccessfully waged a civil war with Stephen for the English throne; her son succeeded as Henry II

matinee (mat-in-**nay**) *n* an afternoon performance of a play or film [French]

matins *n* an early morning service in various Christian Churches [Latin *matutinus* of the morning]

Matisse n Henri. 1869–1954, French painter and sculptor; leader of Fauvism

Matlock n a town in England, on the River Derwent, administrative centre of Derbyshire: mineral springs. Pop: 11 265 (2001)

Mato Grosso or **Matto Grosso** n 1 a high plateau of SW Brazil: forms the watershed separating the Amazon and Plata river systems 2 a state of W central Brazil: mostly on the Mato Grosso Plateau, with the Amazon basin to the north; valuable mineral resources. Capital: Cuiabá. Pop: 2 604 742 (2002). Area: 881 001 sq km (340 083 sq miles)

Mato Grosso do Sul n a state of W central Brazil: formed in 1979 from part of Mato Grosso state. Capital: Campo Grande. Pop: 2 140 624 (2002). Area: 350 548 sq km (135 318 sq miles)

Matopo Hills or **Matopos** pl n the granite hills south of Bulawayo, Zimbabwe, where Cecil Rhodes chose to be buried

Matosinhos or **Matozinhos** n a port in N Portugal, on the estuary of the Leça River north of Oporto: fishing industry. Pop: 167 026 (2001)

matriarch (mate-ree-ark) n the female head of a tribe or family [Latin mater mother + Greek arkhein to rule] > **matriarchal** adj

matriarchy n, pl **-chies** a form of social organization in which a female is head of the family or society, and descent and kinship are traced through the female line

matrices (may-triss-seez) n a plural of **matrix**

matricide n 1 the act of killing one's mother 2 a person who kills his or her mother [Latin mater mother + caedere to kill] > **matricidal** adj

matriculate vb **-lating, -lated** to enrol or be enrolled in a college or university [Medieval Latin matriculare to register] > **matriculation** n

matrilineal (mat-rill-in-ee-al) adj relating to descent through the female line

matrimony n the state of being married [Latin matrimonium wedlock] > **matrimonial** adj

matrix (may-trix) n, pl **-trices** or **matrixes** 1 the context or framework in which something is formed or develops: a highly complex matrix of overlapping interests 2 the rock in which fossils or pebbles are embedded 3 a mould, esp. one used in printing 4 maths a rectangular array of elements set out in rows and columns [Latin: womb]

matron n 1 a staid or dignified married woman 2 a woman in charge of the domestic or medical arrangements in an institution 3 Brit (formerly) the administrative head of the nursing staff in a hospital [Latin matrona] > **matronly** adj

matron of honour n, pl **matrons of honour** a married woman attending a bride

Matsu or **Mazu** n an island group in Formosa Strait, off the SE coast of mainland China: belongs to Taiwan. Pop: 9800 (2007 est). Area: 44 sq km (17 sq miles)

Matsuyama n a port in SW Japan, on NW Shikoku: textile and chemical industries; Ehime University (1949). Pop: 473 039 (2002 est)

matt or **matte** adj having a dull surface rather than a shiny one

matted adj tangled into a thick mass

matter n 1 the substance of which something, esp. a physical object, is made; material 2 substance that occupies space and has mass, as distinguished from substance that is mental or spiritual 3 substance of a specified type: vegetable matter 4 an event, situation, or subject: a matter of taste; the break-in is a matter for the police 5 a quantity or amount: a matter of a few pounds 6 the content of written or verbal material as distinct from its style or form 7 written material in general: advertising matter 8 a secretion or discharge, such as pus 9 **for that matter** as regards that 10 **no matter** regardless of; irrespective of: you have to leave, no matter what she thinks 11 **the matter** wrong; the trouble: there's nothing the matter

▷ vb 12 to be of importance ▷ interj **no matter** 13 it is unimportant [Latin materia cause, substance]

Matterhorn n a mountain on the border between Italy and Switzerland, in the Pennine Alps. Height: 4477 m (14 688 ft). French name: **Mont Cervin**. Italian name: Monte Cervino

matter of fact n 1 **as a matter of fact** actually; in fact ▷ adj **matter-of-fact** 2 unimaginative or emotionless: he conducted the executions in a completely matter-of-fact manner

Matthews n Sir Stanley. 1915–2002, English footballer

Matthias n 1 1557–1619, Holy Roman Emperor (1612–19); king of Hungary (1608–18) and Bohemia (1611–17) 2 **Saint Matthias** New Testament the disciple chosen by lot to replace Judas as one of the 12 apostles (Acts 1:15–26). Feast day: May 14 or Aug 9

Matthias I Corvinus n ?1440–90, king of Hungary (1458–90): built up the most powerful kingdom in Central Europe. A patron of Renaissance art, he founded the Corvina library, one of the finest in Europe. Hungarian name: **Mátyás Hollós**

matting n a coarsely woven fabric used as a floor covering

mattock n a type of large pick that has one flat, horizontal end to its blade, used for loosening soil [Old English mattuc]

Matto Grosso n a variant spelling of **Mato Grosso**

mattress n a large flat cushion with a strong cover, filled with cotton, foam rubber, etc., and often including coiled springs, used as a bed [Arabic almatrah place where something is thrown]

maturation n the process of becoming mature

mature adj 1 fully developed physically or mentally; grown-up 2 (of plans or theories) fully considered and thought-out 3 sensible and balanced in personality and emotional behaviour 4 due or payable: a mature insurance policy 5 (of fruit, wine, or cheese) ripe or fully aged ▷ vb **-turing, -tured** 6 to make or become mature 7 (of bills or bonds) to become due for payment or repayment [Latin maturus early, developed] > **maturity** n

matzo n, pl **matzos** a large very thin biscuit of unleavened bread, traditionally eaten by Jews during Passover [Hebrew matsāh]

Maubeuge n an industrial town in N France, near the border with Belgium. Pop: 33 546 (1999)

maudlin adj foolishly or tearfully sentimental, esp. as a result of drinking [Middle English Maudelen Mary Magdalene, often shown weeping]

Maugham n W(illiam) Somerset. 1874–1965, English writer. His works include the novels Of Human Bondage (1915) and Cakes and Ale (1930), short stories, and comedies

Maui n a volcanic island in S central Hawaii: the second largest of the Hawaiian Islands. Pop: 117 644 (2000). Area: 1885 sq km (728 sq miles)

maul vb 1 to tear with the claws: she was badly mauled by a lion 2 to criticize a play, performance, etc., severely: the film was mauled by the critics 3 to handle roughly or clumsily ▷ n 4 rugby a loose scrum [Latin malleus hammer]

Maulmain n a variant spelling of **Moulmein**

Mauna Kea n an extinct volcano in Hawaii, on N central Hawaii island: the highest island mountain in the world. Height: 4206 m (13 799 ft)

Mauna Loa n an active volcano in Hawaii, on S central Hawaii island. Height: 4171 m (13 684 ft)

maunder vb to move, talk, or act aimlessly or idly [origin unknown]

Maundy Thursday n Christianity the Thursday before Easter observed as a commemoration of the Last Supper [Latin mandatum commandment]

Maupassant n (Henri René Albert) Guy de. 1850–93, French writer, noted esp. for his short stories, such as Boule de suif (1880), La Maison Tellier (1881), and Mademoiselle Fifi (1883). His novels include Bel Ami (1885) and Pierre et Jean (1888)

Maupertuis n Pierre Louis Moreau de. 1698–1759, French

mathematician, who originated the principle of least action (or Maupertuis principle)

Mauretania *n* an ancient region of N Africa, corresponding approximately to the N parts of modern Algeria and Morocco

Mauretanian *adj* **1** of or relating to Mauretania or its inhabitants ▷ *n* **2** a native or inhabitant of Mauretania

Mauriac *n* François. 1885–1970, French novelist, noted esp. for his psychological studies of the conflict between religious belief and human desire. His works include *Le Désert de l'amour* (1925), *Thérèse Desqueyroux* (1927), and *Le Nœud de vipères* (1932): Nobel prize for literature 1952

Maurice *n* **1** 1521–53, duke of Saxony (1541–53) and elector of Saxony (1547–53). He was instrumental in gaining recognition of Protestantism in Germany **2** known as *Maurice of Nassau*. 1567–1625, prince of Orange and count of Nassau; the son of William the Silent, after whose death he led the United Provinces of the Netherlands in their struggle for independence from Spain (achieved by 1609) **3** Frederick Denison. 1805–72, English Anglican theologian and pioneer of Christian socialism

Mauritania *n* a republic in NW Africa, on the Atlantic: established as a French protectorate in 1903 and a colony in 1920; gained independence in 1960; lies in the Sahara; contains rich resources of iron ore. Official language: Arabic; Fulani, Soninke, Wolof, and French are also spoken. Official religion: Muslim. Currency: ouguiya. Capital: Nouakchott. Pop: 3 437 610 (2013 est). Area: 1 030 700 sq km (398 000 sq miles). Official name: **Islamic Republic of Mauritania**

Mauritanian *adj* **1** of or relating to Mauritania or its inhabitants ▷ *n* **2** a native or inhabitant of Mauritania

Mauritian *adj* **1** of or relating to Mauritius or its inhabitants ▷ *n* **2** a native or inhabitant of Mauritius

Mauritius *n* an island and state in the Indian Ocean, east of Madagascar: originally uninhabited, it was settled by the Dutch (1638–1710) then abandoned; taken by the French in 1715 and the British in 1810; became an independent member of the Commonwealth in 1968. It is economically dependent on sugar. Official language: English; a French creole is widely spoken. Religion: Hindu majority, large Christian minority. Currency: rupee. Capital: Port Louis. Pop: 1 322 238 (2013 est). Area: 1865 sq km (720 sq miles). Former name (1715–1810): **Île-de-France**

Maurois *n* André, pen name of Émile Herzog. 1885–1967, French writer, best known for his biographies, such as those of Shelley, Byron, and Proust

Maurras *n* Charles. 1868–1952, French writer and political theorist, who founded (1899) the extreme right-wing group L'Action Française: sentenced (1945) to life imprisonment for supporting Pétain during World War II

Maury *n* Matthew Fontaine. 1806–73, US pioneer hydrographer and oceanographer

mausoleum (maw-so-**lee**-um) *n* a large stately tomb [Greek *mausōleion* the tomb of king *Mausōlos*]

mauve *adj* light purple [Latin *malva* mallow]

maverick *n* **1** a person of independent or unorthodox views **2** (in the US and Canada) an unbranded stray calf ▷ *adj* **3** (of a person or his or her views) independent and unorthodox [after Samuel A. *Maverick*, Texas rancher]

maw *n* the mouth, throat, or stomach of an animal [Old English *maga*]

mawkish *adj* foolishly or embarrassingly sentimental [obsolete *mawk* maggot] **> mawkishness** *n*

Mawson *n* Sir Douglas. 1882–1958, Australian Antarctic explorer, born in England

max *n informal* **1** the most significant or greatest thing **2 to the max** to the ultimate extent

max. maximum

maxi *adj* **1** (of a garment) very long **2** large or considerable [from *maximum*]

maxilla *n, pl* **-lae 1** the upper jawbone of a vertebrate

2 any part of the mouth in insects and other arthropods [Latin: jaw] **> maxillary** *adj*

maxim *n* a brief expression of a general truth, principle, or rule of conduct [Latin *maxima*, in the phrase *maxima propositio* basic axiom]

Maxim *n* Sir Hiram Stevens. 1840–1916, British inventor of the first automatic machine gun (1884), born in the US

maximal *adj* of or being a maximum; the greatest possible

Maximilian *n* full name *Ferdinand Maximilian Joseph*. 1832–67, archduke of Austria and emperor of Mexico (1864–67). After the French had partially conquered Mexico, he was offered the throne but was defeated and shot by the Mexicans under Juárez

Maximilian I *n* 1459–1519, king of Germany (1486–1519) and Holy Roman Emperor (1493–1519)

maximize *or* **-mise** *vb* **-mizing, -mized** *or* **-mising, -mised** to make as high or great as possible; increase to a maximum **> maximization** *or* **-misation** *n*

maximum *n, pl* **-mums** *or* **-ma 1** the greatest possible amount or degree: *he gave the police the maximum of cooperation* **2** the greatest amount recorded, allowed, or reached: *keep to a maximum of two drinks a day* ▷ *adj* **3** of, being, or showing a maximum or maximums: *maximum speed* [Latin: greatest]

maxwell *n* the cgs unit of magnetic flux [after J. C. MAXWELL]

Maxwell *n* **1** James Clerk. 1831–79, Scottish physicist. He made major contributions to the electromagnetic theory, developing the equations (**Maxwell equations**) upon which classical theory is based. He also contributed to the kinetic theory of gases, and colour vision **2** (Ian) Robert, original name *Robert Hoch*. 1923–91, British publisher, born in Slovakia: founder (1949) of Pergamon Press; chairman of Mirror Group Newspapers Ltd. (1984–91); theft from his employees' pension funds and other frauds discovered after his death led to the collapse of his business

may¹ *vb, past* **might 1** used as an auxiliary to indicate that permission is requested by or granted to someone: *she may leave* **2** used as an auxiliary to indicate the possibility that something could happen: *problems which may well have tragic consequences* **3** used as an auxiliary to indicate ability or capacity, esp. in questions: *may I help you?* **4** used as an auxiliary to indicate a strong wish: *long may she reign* [Old English *mæg*, from *magan* to be able]

> **USAGE** It was formerly considered correct to use *may* rather than *can* when referring to permission as in: *you may use the laboratory for your experiments*, but this use of *may* is now almost entirely restricted to polite questions such as: *may I open the window?* The use of *may* with *if* in constructions such as *your analysis may have been more credible if...* is generally regarded as incorrect, *might* being preferred: *your analysis might have been more credible if...*

may² *or* **may tree** *n Brit* same as **hawthorn** [from *May*]

May¹ *n* the fifth month of the year [probably from *Maia*, Roman goddess]

May² *n* Robert McCredie, Baron. born 1936, Australian biologist and ecologist

Maya *n* **1** (*pl* **-ya** *or* **-yas**) a member of an indigenous people of Central America, who once had an advanced civilization **2** the language of this people **> Mayan** *n, adj*

Mayagüez *n* a port in W Puerto Rico; needlework industry. Pop: 97 627 (2003 est)

Mayakovski *or* **Mayakovsky** *n* Vladimir Vladimirovich. 1893–1930, Russian Futurist poet and dramatist. His poems include *150 000 000* (1921) and *At the Top of my Voice* (1930); his plays include *Vladimir Mayakovsky — a Tragedy* (1913) and *The Bedbug* (1929)

maybe *adv* perhaps

Mayday n the international radio distress signal [phonetic spelling of French m'aidez help me]

May Day n the first day of May, traditionally a celebration of the coming of spring: in some countries now a holiday in honour of workers

Mayence n the French name for **Mainz**

Mayenne n a department of NW France, in Pays de la Loire region. Capital: Laval. Pop: 290 780 (2003 est). Area: 5212 sq km (2033 sq miles)

Mayer n **1** Julius Robert von. 1814–78, German physicist whose research in thermodynamics (1842) contributed to the discovery of the law of conservation of energy **2** Louis B(urt). 1885–1957, US film producer, born in Russia; founder and first head (1924–48) of the Metro-Goldwyn-Mayer (MGM) film company

Mayfair n a fashionable district of west central London

mayfly n, pl **-flies** a short-lived insect with large transparent wings

mayhem n **1** any violent destruction or confusion: a driver caused motorway mayhem **2** law the maiming of a person [Anglo-French mahem injury]

Mayhew n Henry. 1812–87, British social commentator, journalist, and writer; a founder of Punch (1841): best known for London Labour and the London Poor (1851–62)

mayn't may not

Mayo¹ n a county of NW Republic of Ireland, in NW Connacht province, on the Atlantic: has many offshore islands and several large lakes. County town: Castlebar. Pop: 117 446 (2002). Area: 5397 sq km (2084 sq miles)

Mayo² n a family of US medical practitioners. They pioneered group practice and established (1903) the **Mayo Clinic** in Rochester, Minnesota. Foremost among them were **William Worrall Mayo** (1819–1911), his sons **William James Mayo** (1861–1939) and **Charles Horace Mayo** (1865–1939), and Charles's son, **Charles William Mayo** (1898–1968)

Mayon n a volcano in the Philippines, on SE Luzon: Height: 2421 m (7943 ft)

mayonnaise n a thick creamy sauce made from egg yolks, oil, and vinegar [French]

mayor n the civic head of a municipal council in many countries [Latin maior greater] **> mayoral** adj

mayoralty n, pl **-ties** the office or term of office of a mayor

mayoress n **1** chiefly Brit the wife of a mayor **2** a female mayor

Mayotte n an island in the Indian Ocean, northwest of Madagascar; administered by France. Pop (including Pamanzi): 186 026 (2004 est). Area: 374 sq km (146 sq miles)

maypole n a tall pole around which people dance during May-Day celebrations

May queen n a girl chosen to preside over May-Day celebrations

Mazar-e-Sharif or **Mazar-i-Sharif** n a city in N Afghanistan, reputed burial place of the caliph Ali; trading, agricultural, and military centre. Pop: 254 000 (2005 est)

Mazarin n Jules, original name Giulio Mazarini. 1602–61, French cardinal and statesman, born in Italy. He succeeded Richelieu (1642) as chief minister to Louis XIII and under the regency of Anne of Austria (1643–61). Despite the disturbances of the Fronde (1648–53), he strengthened the power of France in Europe

Mazatlán n a port in W Mexico, in S Sinaloa on the Pacific: situated opposite the tip of the peninsula of Lower California, for which it is the chief link with the mainland. Pop: 406 000 (2005 est)

maze n **1** a complex network of paths or passages designed to puzzle people who try and find their way through or out of it **2** a puzzle in which the player must trace a path through a complex network of lines without touching or crossing any of them **3** any confusing network or system: a maze of regulations [from amaze]

Mazu n the Pinyin transliteration of the Chinese name for **Matsu**

mazurka n **1** a lively Polish dance in triple time **2** music for this dance [Polish]

Mazzini n Giuseppe. 1805–72, Italian nationalist. In 1831, in exile, he established the Young Italy association in Marseille, which sought to unite Italy as a republic. In 1849 he was one of the triumvirate that ruled the short-lived Roman republic

mb millibar

Mb computers megabyte

MB **1** Bachelor of Medicine **2** Manitoba

Mbabane n the capital of Swaziland, in the northwest: administrative and financial centre, with a large iron mine nearby. Pop: 71 000 (2005 est)

MBE (in Britain) Member of the Order of the British Empire

Mbeki n Thabo (Mvuyelwa). born 1942, South African politician: a member of the African National Congress (ANC); deputy president of South Africa (1994–99); president (1999–2008)

Mbujimayi n a city in S Democratic Republic of Congo: diamond mining. Pop: 821 000 (2005 est)

MC **1** Master of Ceremonies **2** (in the US) Member of Congress **3** (in Britain) Military Cross

MCC (in Britain) Marylebone Cricket Club

MCh Master of Surgery [Latin Magister Chirurgiae]

Md chem mendelevium

MD **1** Doctor of Medicine **2** Managing Director **3** Maryland

Md. Maryland

MDF medium density fibreboard: a wood-substitute material used in interior decoration

MDMA methylenedioxymethamphetamine: the chemical name for the drug ecstasy

MDT (in the US and Canada) Mountain Daylight Time

me¹ pron (objective) **1** refers to the speaker or writer: that hurts me ▷ n **2** informal the personality of the speaker or writer or something that expresses it: the real me [Old English mē]

> **USAGE** It was formerly regarded as correct to use I, he, she, etc. rather than me, him, her, after the verb to be, as in: it is I who told him. Since both I and me can sound strange in a sentence like this, it is better to use a different construction: I am the one who told him. The use of a possessive before an -ing form of a verb was formerly thought to be preferable to using me, etc., but now both forms are acceptable: he didn't like my/me having a job of my own.

me² or **mi** n music (in tonic sol-fa) the third note of any ascending major scale

ME **1** Maine **2** Middle English **3** myalgic encephalomyelitis: see **chronic fatigue syndrome**

Me. Maine

mea culpa (may-ah cool-pah) an acknowledgment of guilt [Latin, literally: my fault]

mead¹ n a wine-like alcoholic drink made from honey, often with spices added [Old English meodu]

mead² n archaic or poetic a meadow [Old English mǣd]

Mead¹ n Lake Mead a reservoir in NW Arizona and SE Nevada, formed by the Hoover Dam across the Colorado River: one of the largest man-made lakes in the world. Area: 588 sq km (227 sq miles)

Mead² n Margaret. 1901–78, US anthropologist. Her works include Coming of Age in Samoa (1928) and Male and Female (1949)

Meade n George Gordon. 1815–72, Union general in the American Civil War. He commanded the Army of the Potomac, defeating the Confederates at Gettysburg (1863)

meadow n **1** a grassy field used for hay or for grazing animals **2** a low-lying piece of grassland, often near a river [Old English mǣdwe]

meadowsweet *n* a plant with dense heads of small fragrant cream-coloured flowers

Meads *n* Sir Colin. born 1936, New Zealand Rugby Union footballer. A forward, he played for the All Blacks (1957–71)

meagre *or US* **meager** *adj* 1 not enough in amount or extent: *meagre wages* 2 thin or emaciated [Old French *maigre*]

meal¹ *n* 1 any of the regular occasions, such as breakfast or dinner, when food is served and eaten 2 the food served and eaten 3 **make a meal of** *informal* to perform a task with unnecessarily great effort [Old English *mǣl* measure, set time, meal]

meal² *n* 1 the edible part of a grain or bean pulse (excluding wheat) ground to a coarse powder 2 *Scot* oatmeal 3 *chiefly US* maize flour [Old English *melu*]
> **mealy** *adj*

mealie *or* **mielie** *n* (*often pl*) *S African* same as **maize** [Afrikaans, from Latin *milium* millet]

meals-on-wheels *n* a service taking hot meals to elderly or disabled people in their own homes

meal ticket *n slang* a person or situation providing a source of livelihood or income [from original US sense of ticket entitling holder to a meal]

mealy-mouthed *adj* unwilling or afraid to speak plainly

mean¹ *vb* **meaning, meant** 1 to intend to convey or express: *what do you mean by that?* 2 to denote, represent, or signify: *a red light means 'stop!'*; *'gravid' is a technical term meaning 'pregnant'* 3 to intend: *I meant to phone you earlier, but didn't have time* 4 to say or do in all seriousness: *the boss means what she says* 5 to have the importance specified: *music means everything to him* 6 to destine or design for a certain person or purpose: *those sweets weren't meant for you* 7 to produce, cause, or result in: *major road works will mean long traffic delays* 8 to foretell: *those black clouds mean rain* 9 **mean well** to have good intentions [Old English *mǣnan*]

> **USAGE** In standard English *mean* should not be followed by *for* when expressing intention: *I didn't mean this to happen* (not *I didn't mean for this to happen*).

mean² *adj* 1 not willing to give or use much of something, esp. money: *she was noticeably mean; don't be mean with the butter* 2 unkind or spiteful: *a mean trick* 3 *informal* ashamed: *she felt mean about not letting the children stay out late* 4 *informal, chiefly US, Canad and Austral* bad-tempered or vicious 5 shabby and poor: *a mean little room* 6 *slang* excellent or skilful: *he plays a mean trumpet* 7 **no mean a** of high quality: *no mean player* **b** difficult: *no mean feat* [Old English *gemǣne* common] > **meanly** *adv*
> **meanness** *n*

mean³ *n* 1 the middle point, state, or course between limits or extremes 2 *maths* **a** the mid-point between the highest and lowest number in a set **b** the average ▷ *adj* 3 intermediate in size or quantity 4 occurring halfway between extremes or limits; average [Late Latin *medianus* median]

meander (mee-and-er) *vb* 1 (of a river, road, etc.) to follow a winding course 2 to wander without definite aim or direction ▷ *n* 3 a curve or bend, as in a river 4 a winding course or movement [Greek *Maiandros* the River Maeander]

Meander *n* a variant spelling of **Maeander**

mean deviation *n statistics* the difference between an observed value of a variable and its mean

meanie *or* **meany** *n informal* 1 *chiefly Brit* a miserly person 2 a nasty ill-tempered person

meaning *n* 1 the sense or significance of a word, sentence, or symbol 2 the inner, symbolic, or true interpretation or message: *the meaning of the New Testament*

meaningful *adj* 1 serious and important: *a meaningful relationship* 2 intended to express a feeling or opinion: *a meaningful pause*

meaningless *adj* having no meaning or purpose; futile

means *n* 1 the medium, method, or instrument used to obtain a result or achieve an end: *a means of transport* ▷ *pl n* 2 income: *a man of means* 3 **by all means** without hesitation or doubt; certainly 4 **by means of** with the use or help of 5 **by no** or **not by any means** on no account; in no way

means test *n* the checking of a person's income to determine whether he or she qualifies for financial aid
> **means-tested** *adj*

meant *vb* the past of **mean¹**

meantime *n* 1 the intervening period: *in the meantime* ▷ *adv* 2 same as **meanwhile**

mean time *or* **mean solar time** *n* the times, at a particular place, measured so as to give 24-hour days (mean solar days) throughout a year

meanwhile *adv* 1 during the intervening period 2 at the same time, esp. in another place

meany *n, pl* **meanies** same as **meanie**

Mearns *n* **the Mearns** another name for **Kincardineshire**

measles *n* a highly contagious viral disease common in children, characterized by fever and a rash of small red spots. See also **German measles** [Low German *masele* spot on the skin]

measly *adj* **-slier, -sliest** 1 *informal* too small in quantity or value 2 having or relating to measles

measure *n* 1 the size, quantity, or degree of something, as discovered by measurement or calculation 2 a device for measuring distance, volume, etc., such as a graduated scale or container 3 a system or unit of measurement: *the joule is a measure of energy* 4 an amount of alcoholic drink, esp. that served as standard in a bar 5 degree or extent: *a measure of success* 6 a particular action intended to achieve an effect: *radical measures are needed to cut unemployment* 7 a legislative bill, act, or resolution 8 *music* same as **bar¹** (9) 9 *prosody* poetic rhythm or metre 10 *prosody* a metrical foot 11 *old-fashioned* a dance 12 **for good measure** as an extra precaution or beyond requirements ▷ *vb* **-suring, -sured** 13 to determine the size, amount, etc., of by measurement: *he measured the room for a new carpet* 14 to indicate or record the size, speed, force, etc., of: *this dial measures the pressure in the pipe* 15 to have the size, quantity, etc., specified: *the room measures six feet* 16 to estimate or assess: *you cannot measure intelligence purely by exam results* 17 to function as a measurement of: *the ohm measures electrical resistance* 18 to bring into competition or conflict with: *he measured his strength against that of his opponent* ▷ See also **measure out**, **measures**, **measure up** [Latin *mensura*] > **measurable** *adj*

measured *adj* 1 slow or stately 2 carefully considered; deliberate

measurement *n* 1 the act or process of measuring 2 an amount, extent, or size determined by measuring 3 a system or unit used for measuring: *the kilometre is the standard measurement of distance in most countries* 4 **measurements** the size of a person's waist, chest, hips, etc., used when buying clothes

measure out *vb* to carefully pour or put the required amount of (something) into a container: *she measured out a large whisky*

measures *pl n* rock strata that contain a particular type of deposit: *coal measures*

measure up *vb* 1 to take the measurement of (an area): *we went round and measured up for curtains* 2 **measure up to** to fulfil (expectations or standards)

measuring *adj* used to measure quantities, esp. in cooking: *a measuring jug*

meat *n* 1 the flesh of animals used as food 2 the essence or gist: *get to the meat of your lecture as quickly as possible* [Old English *mete*] > **meatless** *adj*

meatball *n* minced beef, shaped into a ball before cooking

Meath *n* a county of E Republic of Ireland, in Leinster province on the Irish Sea: formerly a kingdom much larger than the present county; livestock farming. County town: Trim. Pop: 134 005 (2002). Area: 2338 sq km (903 sq miles)

meaty *adj* **meatier, meatiest 1** of, like, or full of meat **2** heavily built; fleshy or brawny **3** full of import or interest: *a meaty historical drama*

Mecca *or* **Mekka** *n* **1** a city in W Saudi Arabia, joint capital (with Riyadh) of Saudi Arabia: birthplace of Mohammed; the holiest city of Islam, containing the Kaaba. Pop: 1 529 000 (2005 est). Arabic name: **Makkah 2** (*sometimes not cap*) a place that attracts many visitors: *Athens is a Mecca for tourists*

mech. 1 mechanical **2** mechanics

mechanic *n* a person skilled in maintaining or operating machinery or motors [Greek *mēkhanē* machine]

mechanical *adj* **1** made, performed, or operated by machinery **2** able to understand how machines work and how to repair or maintain them **3 a** (of an action) done without thought or feeling **b** (of a task) not requiring any thought; routine or repetitive **4** of or involving the science of mechanics ⟩ **mechanically** *adv*

mechanical drawing *n* a drawing to scale of a machine or architectural plan from which dimensions can be taken

mechanical engineering *n* the branch of engineering concerned with the design, construction, and operation of machines

mechanics *n* **1** the scientific study of motion and force **2** the science of designing, constructing, and operating machines ⟩ *pl n* **3** the technical aspects of something

mechanism *n* **1** a system of moving parts that performs some function, esp. in a machine **2** any mechanical device or part of such a device **3** a process or technique: *the body's defence mechanisms* ⟩ **mechanistic** *adj*

mechanize *or* **-nise** *vb* **-nizing, -nized** *or* **-nising, -nised 1** to equip a factory or industry with machinery **2** to make mechanical or automatic **3** *military* to equip an army with armoured vehicles ⟩ **mechanization** *or* **-nisation** *n*

Mechelen *n* a city in N Belgium, in Antwerp province: capital of the Netherlands from 1507 to 1530; formerly famous for lace-making; now has an important vegetable market. Pop: 76 981 (2004 est). French name: **Malines**. English name: **Mechlin**

Mechlin *n* the English name for **Mechelen**

Mecklenburg *n* a historic region and former state of NE Germany, along the Baltic coast; now part of Mecklenburg-West Pomerania

Mecklenburg-West Pomerania *n* a state of NE Germany, along the Baltic coast: consists of the former state of Mecklenburg and those parts of W Pomerania not incorporated into Poland after World War II: part of East Germany until 1990. Pop: 1 732 000 (2003 est)

Med *n* **the Med** *informal* the Mediterranean region

MEd Master of Education

med. 1 medical **2** medicine **3** medieval **4** medium

medal *n* a small flat piece of metal bearing an inscription or image, given as an award or in commemoration of some outstanding event [French *médaille*]

medallion *n* **1** a disc-shaped ornament worn on a chain round the neck **2** a large medal **3** a circular decorative device used in architecture [Italian *medaglia* medal]

medallist *or US* **medalist** *n chiefly sport* a winner of a medal or medals

Medan *n* a city in Indonesia, in NE Sumatra: seat of the University of North Sumatra (1952) and the Indonesian Islam University (1952). Pop: 1 904 273 (2000)

Medawar *n* Sir Peter Brian. 1915–87, English zoologist, who shared the Nobel prize for physiology or medicine (1960) with Sir Macfarlane Burnet for work on immunology

meddle *vb* **-dling, -dled** to interfere annoyingly [Old French *medler*] ⟩ **meddler** *n* ⟩ **meddlesome** *adj*

Medellín *n* a city in W Colombia, at an altitude of 1554 m (5100 ft): the second largest city in the country, with three universities; important coffee centre, with large textile mills; dominated by drug cartels in recent years. Pop: 3 236 000 (2005 est)

media *n* **1** a plural of **medium 2** **the media** the mass media collectively ⟩ *adj* **3** of or relating to the mass media: *media hype*

> **USAGE** When *media* refers to the mass media, it is sometimes treated as a singular form, as in: *the media has shown great interest in these events.* Many people think this use is incorrect and that *media* should always be treated as a plural form: *the media have shown great interest in these events.*

Media *n* an ancient country of SW Asia, south of the Caspian Sea: inhabited by the Medes; overthrew the Assyrian Empire in 612 BC in alliance with Babylonia; conquered by Cyrus the Great in 550 BC; corresponds to present-day NW Iran

mediaeval (med-ee-eve-al) *adj* same as **medieval**

media event *n* an event that is staged for or exploited by the mass media

medial (mee-dee-al) *adj* of or situated in the middle [Latin *medius* middle] ⟩ **medially** *adv*

median *n* **1** a middle point, plane, or part **2** *geometry* a straight line joining one corner of a triangle to the midpoint of the opposite side **3** *statistics* the middle value in a frequency distribution, below and above which lie values with equal total frequencies [Latin *medius* middle]

median strip *n* *US, Canad and NZ* the strip that separates the two sides of a motorway or dual carriageway

mediate (mee-dee-ate) *vb* **-ating, -ated 1** to intervene between people or in a dispute in order to bring about agreement **2** to resolve differences by mediation **3** to be changed slightly by (an experience or event): *clients' attitudes to social workers have often been mediated by their past experiences* [Late Latin *mediare* to be in the middle] ⟩ **mediation** *n* ⟩ **mediator** *n*

medic *n* *informal* a doctor, medical orderly, or medical student [from MEDICAL]

medical *adj* **1** of or relating to the science of medicine or to the treatment of patients without surgery ⟩ *n* **2** *informal* a medical examination [Latin *medicus* physician] ⟩ **medically** *adv*

medical certificate *n* **1** a doctor's certificate giving evidence of a person's unfitness for work **2** a document stating the result of a satisfactory medical examination

medicament (mid-dik-a-ment) *n* a medicine

medicate *vb* **-cating, -cated 1** to treat a patient with a medicine **2** to add a medication to a bandage, shampoo, etc. [Latin *medicare* to heal] ⟩ **medicative** *adj*

medication *n* **1** treatment with drugs or remedies **2** a drug or remedy

Medici *n* **1** an Italian family of bankers, merchants, and rulers of Florence and Tuscany, prominent in Italian political and cultural history in the 15th, 16th, and 17th centuries, including **2 Catherine de'**. See **Catherine de' Medici 3 Cosimo I**, known as *Cosimo the Great*. 1519–74, duke of Florence and first grand duke of Tuscany (1569–74) **4 Cosimo de'**, known as *Cosimo the Elder*. 1389–1464, Italian banker, statesman, and patron of arts, who established the political power of the family in Florence (1434) **5 Giovanni de'**. See **Leo X 6 Giulio de'**. See **Clement VII 7 Lorenzo de'**, known as *Lorenzo the Magnificent*. 1449–92, Italian statesman, poet, and scholar; ruler of Florence (1469–92) and first patron of Michelangelo **8 Maria de'**. See **Maria de' Medici** ▶ French name: **Médicis**

medicinal (mid-diss-in-al) *adj* relating to or having therapeutic properties ⟩ **medicinally** *adv*

medicine *n* **1** any substance used in treating or alleviating the symptoms of disease **2** the science of preventing, diagnosing, or curing disease **3** any nonsurgical branch of medical science **4 take one's medicine** to accept a deserved punishment [Latin *medicina (ars)* (art) of healing]

medicine man *n* (among certain peoples) a person believed to have supernatural powers of healing

medico *n, pl* **-cos** *informal* a doctor or medical student

medieval *or* **mediaeval** (med-ee-**eve**-al) *adj* **1** of, relating to, or in the style of the Middle Ages **2** *informal* old-fashioned or primitive [New Latin *medium aevum* the middle age] ➤ **medievalist** *or* **mediaevalist** *n*

Medieval Greek *n* the Greek language from the 7th to 13th century AD

Medieval Latin *n* the Latin language as used throughout Europe in the Middle Ages

Medina *n* a city in W Saudi Arabia: the second most holy city of Islam (after Mecca), with the tomb of Mohammed; university (1960). Pop: 1 044 000 (2005 est). Arabic name: **Al Madinah**. Ancient Arabic name: **Yathrib**

mediocre (mee-dee-**oak**-er) *adj* not very high quality; average or second rate [Latin *mediocris* moderate] ➤ **mediocrity** (mee-dee-**ok**-rit-ee) *n*

meditate *vb* **-tating, -tated 1** to think about something deeply: *he meditated on the problem* **2** to reflect deeply on spiritual matters **3** to plan, consider, or think of doing something [Latin *meditari* to reflect upon] ➤ **meditative** *adj* ➤ **meditator** *n*

meditation *n* **1** the act of meditating; reflection **2** contemplation of spiritual matters, esp. as a religious practice

Mediterranean *n* **1** short for the **Mediterranean Sea 2** a native or inhabitant of a Mediterranean country ▷ *adj* **3** of, relating to, situated or dwelling on or near the Mediterranean Sea **4** denoting a postulated subdivision of the Caucasoid race, characterized by slender build and dark complexion **5** *meteorol* (of a climate) characterized by hot summers and relatively warm winters when most of the annual rainfall occurs **6** (*often not cap*) *obsolete* situated in the middle of a landmass; inland [C16: from Latin *mediterraneus*, from *medius* middle + *-terraneus*, from *terra* land, earth]

Mediterranean Sea *n* a large inland sea between S Europe, N Africa, and SW Asia: linked with the Atlantic by the Strait of Gibraltar, with the Red Sea by the Suez Canal, and with the Black Sea by the Dardanelles, Sea of Marmara, and Bosporus; many ancient civilizations developed around its shores. Greatest depth: 4770 m (15 900 ft). Length: (west to east) over 3700 km (2300 miles). Greatest width: about 1370 km (850 miles). Area: (excluding the Black Sea) 2 512 300 sq km (970 000 sq miles). Ancient name: **Mare Internum**

medium *adj* **1** midway between extremes of size, amount, or degree: *fry over a medium heat; a man of medium height* ▷ *n, pl* **-dia** *or* **-diums 2** a middle state, degree, or condition: *the happy medium* **3** a substance which has a particular effect or can be used for a particular purpose: *linseed oil is used as a thinning medium for oil paint* **4** a means for communicating information or news to the public **5** a person who can supposedly communicate with the dead **6** the substance or surroundings in which an organism naturally lives or grows **7** *art* the category of a work of art, as determined by its materials: *his works in the photographic medium* [Latin *medius* middle]

> **USAGE** See at media.

medium wave *n* a radio wave with a wavelength between 100 and 1000 metres

medlar *n* the apple-like fruit of a small Eurasian tree, which is not edible until it has begun to decay [Old French *medlier*]

medley *n* **1** a mixture of various elements **2** a musical composition consisting of various tunes arranged as a continuous whole **3** *swimming* a race in which a different

stroke is used for each length [Old French, from *medler* to mix, quarrel]

Médoc *n* **1** a district of SW France, on the left bank of the Gironde estuary: famous vineyards **2** a fine red wine from this district

medulla (mid-**dull**-la) *n, pl* **-las** *or* **-lae** (-lee) **1** *anatomy* the innermost part of an organ or structure **2** *anatomy* the lower stalklike section of the brain **3** *botany* the central pith of a plant stem [Latin: marrow] ➤ **medullary** *adj*

medusa (mid-**dew**-za) *n, pl* **-sas** *or* **-sae** (-zee) jellyfish [*Medusa*, in Greek mythology, who had snakes for hair]

Medvedev *n* Dmitry Anatolyevich. born 1965, Russian politician; president of Russia (2008–12); prime minister of Russia from 2012

Medway *n* **1** a river in SE England, flowing through Kent and the **Medway towns** (Rochester, Chatham, and Gillingham) to the Thames estuary. Length: 110 km (70 miles) **2** a unitary authority in SE England, in Kent. Pop: 251 100 (2003 est). Area: 204 sq km (79 sq miles)

meek *adj* quiet, and ready to do what other people say [related to Old Norse *mjūkr* amenable] ➤ **meekly** *adv*

meerkat *n* a South African mongoose [Dutch: sea-cat]

meerschaum (**meer**-shum) *n* **1** a white, heat-resistant, claylike mineral **2** a tobacco pipe with a bowl made of this mineral [German *Meerschaum*, literally: sea foam]

Meerut *n* an industrial city in N India, in W Uttar Pradesh: founded as a military base by the British in 1806 and scene of the first uprising (1857) of the Indian Mutiny. Pop: 1 074 229 (2001)

meet[1] *vb* **meeting, met 1** to be in or come to the same place at the same time as, either by arrangement or by accident: *I met him in town* **2** to come into contact with something or each other: *his head met the ground with a crack; the town where the Rhine and the Moselle meet* **3** to come to or be at the place of arrival of: *he met his train at noon* **4** to make the acquaintance of, or be introduced to, someone or each other **5** (of people) to gather together for a purpose: *the board meets once a week* **6** to compete, play, or fight against **7** to cope with effectively; satisfy: *they were unable to meet his demands* **8** to pay for (something): *it is difficult to meet the cost of medical insurance* **9** Also: **meet with** to experience or suffer: *he met his death at the Somme* **10** there is more to this than meets the eye there is more involved in this than appears ▷ *n* **11** a sports meeting **12** *chiefly Brit* the assembly of hounds and huntsmen prior to a hunt [Old English *mētan*]

meet[2] *adj archaic* proper, fitting, or correct: *meet and proper* [Old English *gemēte*]

meeting *n* **1** an act of coming together: *a meeting was fixed for the following day* **2** an assembly or gathering of people: *the meeting voted in favour* **3** a sporting competition, as of athletes, or of horse racing

meg *n computers informal* short for **megabyte**

mega *adj slang* extremely good, great, or successful

mega- *combining form* **1** denoting 10^6: *megawatt* **2** (in computer technology) denoting 2^{20} (1 048 576): *megabyte* **3** large or great: *megalith* **4** *informal* very great: *megastar* [Greek *megas* huge, powerful]

megabyte *n computers* 2^{20} or 1 048 576 bytes

megadeath *n* the death of a million people, esp. in a nuclear war or attack

megahertz *n, pl* **megahertz** one million hertz; one million cycles per second

megajoule *n* one million joules

megalith *n* a very large stone, esp. one forming part of a prehistoric monument ➤ **megalithic** *adj*

megalomania *n* **1** a mental illness characterized by delusions of power **2** *informal* a craving for power [Greek *megas* great + *mania* madness] ➤ **megalomaniac** *adj, n*

megaphone *n* a funnel-shaped instrument used to make someone's voice sound louder, esp. out of doors

megapixel *n* one million pixels: used to describe the resolution of digital images

megapode *n* any of various ground-living birds of

Australia, New Guinea, and adjacent islands. Their eggs incubate in mounds of sand or rotting vegetation [Greek *megas* great + *-podos* -footed]

Megara *n* a town in E central Greece: an ancient trading city, founding many colonies in the 7th and 8th centuries BC. Pop (municipality): 27 252 (2001)

megaton *n* **1** one million tons **2** an explosive power, esp. of a nuclear weapon, equal to the power of one million tons of TNT

megavolt *n* one million volts

megawatt *n* one million watts

Meghalaya *n* a state of NE India, created in 1969 from part of Assam. Capital: Shillong. Pop: 2 306 069 (2001). Area: 22 429 sq km (7800 sq miles)

Megiddo *n* an ancient town in N Palestine, strategically located on a route linking Egypt to Mesopotamia: site of many battles, including an important Egyptian victory over rebel chieftains in 1469 or 1468 BC

Mehemet Ali *or* **Mohammed Ali** *n* 1769–1849, Albanian commander in the service of Turkey. He was made viceroy of Egypt (1805) and its hereditary ruler (1841), founding a dynasty that ruled until 1952

Mehta *n* Zubin. born 1936, Indian conductor; musical director of the Israel Philharmonic orchestra from 1969

Meiji *n* **1** *Japanese history* the reign of Emperor Mutsuhito (1867–1912), during which Japan began a rapid process of Westernization, industrialization, and expansion in foreign affairs **2** the throne name of Mutsuhito. 1852–1912, emperor of Japan (1867–1912) [Japanese, from Chinese *ming* enlightened + *dji* government]

Meilhac *n* Henri. 1831–97, French dramatist, who collaborated with Halévy on opera libretti, esp. Offenbach's *La Belle Hélène* (1865) and *La Vie parisienne* (1867)

meiosis (my-oh-siss) *n, pl* **-ses** (-seez) a type of cell division in which reproductive cells are produced, each containing half the chromosome number of the parent nucleus [Greek *meiōn* less]

Meir *n* Golda 1898–1978, Israeli stateswoman, born in Russia; prime minister (1969–74)

Meissen *n* a town in E Germany, in Saxony, in Dresden district on the River Elbe: famous for its porcelain (Dresden china), first made here in 1710. Pop: 28 640 (2003 est)

Meitner *n* Lise. 1878–1968, Austrian nuclear physicist. With Hahn, she discovered protactinium (1918), and they demonstrated with F. Strassmann the fission of uranium

meitnerium *n* *chem* an element artificially produced in small quantities by high-energy ion bombardment. Symbol: Mt [after Lise MEITNER]

Méjico *n* the Spanish name for **Mexico**

Mekka *n* a variant spelling of **Mecca**

Meknès *n* a city in N central Morocco, in the Middle Atlas Mountains: noted for the making of carpets. Pop: 234 000 (2003)

Mekong *n* a river in SE Asia, rising in SW China in Qinghai province: flows southeast forming the border between Laos and Myanmar, and part of the border between Laos and Thailand, then continues south across Cambodia and Vietnam to the South China Sea by an extensive delta, one of the greatest rice-growing areas in Asia. Length: about 4025 km (2500 miles)

Melaka *n* a variant spelling of **Malacca**

melaleuca (mel-a-**loo**-ka) *n* an Australian shrub or tree with a white trunk and black branches [Greek *melas* black + *leukos* white]

melamine *n* a colourless crystalline compound used in making synthetic resins [German *Melamin*]

melancholia (mel-an-**kole**-lee-a) *n* an old name for depression (1)

melancholy (**mel**-an-kol-lee) *n, pl* **-cholies 1** a tendency to gloominess or depression **2** a sad thoughtful state of mind ▷ *adj* **3** characterized by, causing, or expressing

sadness [Greek *melas* black + *kholē* bile] ▷ **melancholic** *adj, n*

Melanchthon *n* Philipp. original surname *Schwarzerd*. 1497–1560, German Protestant reformer. His *Loci Communes* (1521) was the first systematic presentation of Protestant theology and in the Augsburg Confession (1530) he stated the faith of the Lutheran churches. He also reformed the German educational system

Melanesia *n* one of the three divisions of islands in the Pacific (the others being Micronesia and Polynesia); the SW division of Oceania: includes Fiji, New Caledonia, Vanuatu, the Bismarck Archipelago, and the Louisiade, Solomon, Santa Cruz, and Loyalty Islands, which all lie northeast of Australia [C19: from Greek *melas* black + *nēsos* island; with reference to the dark skins of the inhabitants; on the model of *Polynesia*]

melange (may-**lahnzh**) *n* a mixture or assortment: *a melange of historical facts and legends* [French *mêler* to mix]

melanin *n* a black pigment present in the hair, skin, and eyes of humans and animals [Greek *melas* black]

melanoma *n, pl* **-mas** *or* **-mata** *pathol* a tumour composed of dark-coloured cells, occurring in some skin cancers [Greek *melas* black + *-oma*, modelled on *carcinoma*]

Melba *n* **1** Dame Nellie, stage name of *Helen Porter Mitchell*. 1861–1931, Australian operatic soprano **2** do a Melba *Austral slang* to make repeated farewell appearances

Melba toast *n* very thin crisp toast [after Dame Nellie MELBA]

Melbourne¹ *n* a port in SE Australia, capital of Victoria, on Port Phillip Bay: the second largest city in the country; settled in 1835 and developed rapidly with the discovery of rich goldfields in 1851; three universities. Pop: 4 246 345 (2012)

Melbourne² *n* William Lamb, 2nd Viscount. 1779–1848; Whig prime minister (1834; 1835–41). He was the chief political adviser to the young Queen Victoria

Melburnian *n* **1** a native or inhabitant of Melbourne ▷ *adj* **2** of or relating to Melbourne or its inhabitants

Melchior *n* **1** (in Christian tradition) one of the Magi, the others being Balthazar and Caspar **2** Lauritz. 1890–1973, US operatic tenor, born in Denmark

meld *vb* to merge or blend [blend of *melt* + *weld*]

melee (**mel**-lay) *n* a noisy riotous fight or crowd [French, from *mêler* to mix]

Méliès *n* Georges. 1861–1938, French pioneer film director

Melilla *n* the chief town of a Spanish enclave in Morocco, on the Mediterranean coast: founded by the Phoenicians; exports iron ore. Pop: 68 463 (2003 est)

Melitopol *n* a city in SE Ukraine. Pop: 157 000 (2005 est)

Melk *n* a town in N Austria, on the River Danube: noted for its baroque Benedictine abbey. Pop: 5222 (2001)

mellifluous (mel-**lif**-flew-uss) *adj* (of sound) smooth and sweet [Latin *mel* honey + *fluere* to flow]

mellow *adj* **1** (esp. of colours, light, or sounds) soft or rich: *the mellow stillness of a sunny Sunday morning* **2** kind-hearted, esp. through maturity or old age **3** genial and relaxed, for instance through the effects of alcohol or good food **4** (esp. of fruits) sweet, ripe, and full-flavoured **5** (esp. of wine or cheese) having developed a full smooth flavour as a result of maturing **6** (of soil) soft and loamy ▷ *vb* **7** to make or become mellow **8** (foll. by *out*) to make or become calm and relaxed [origin unknown]

melodeon *n* **1** a small accordion **2** a keyboard instrument like a harmonium [German *Melodie* melody]

melodic (mel-**lod**-ik) *adj* **1** of or relating to melody **2** tuneful and pleasant to the ear; melodious ▷ **melodically** *adv*

melodious (mel-**lode**-ee-uss) *adj* **1** pleasant to the ear: *he gave a melodious chuckle* **2** tuneful and melodic ▷ **melodiousness** *n*

melodrama *n* **1** a play or film full of extravagant action and emotion **2** overdramatic emotion or behaviour [Greek *melos* song + *drama* drama] ▷ **melodramatic** *adj* ▷ **melodramatics** *pl n*

melody *n, pl* **-dies 1** *music* a succession of notes forming a distinctive sequence; tune **2** sounds that are pleasant because of their tone or arrangement, esp. words of poetry [Greek *melōidia*]

melon *n* any of various large edible fruits which have a hard rind and juicy flesh [Greek *mēlon* apple]

Melos *n* an island in the SW Aegean Sea, in the Cyclades: of volcanic origin, with hot springs; centre of early Aegean civilization, where the Venus de Milo was found. Pop: 4771 (2001). Area: 132 sq km (51 sq miles). Modern Greek name: **Mílos**

Melpomene (mel-pom-in-nee) *n Greek myth* the Muse of tragedy

Melrose Abbey *n* a ruined Cistercian abbey in Melrose in Scottish Borders: founded in 1136 and sacked by the English in 1385 and 1547: repaired in 1822 by Sir Walter Scott

melt *vb* **1** to change from a solid into a liquid as a result of the action of heat **2** to dissolve: *these sweets melt in the mouth* **3** Also: **melt away** to diminish and finally disappear; fade away: *he felt his inner doubts melt away* **4** to blend so that it is impossible to tell where one thing ends and another begins: *they melted into the trees until the gamekeeper had passed* **5** to make or become emotional or sentimental; soften: *she melted into tears* [Old English *meltan* to digest] **> meltingly** *adv*

meltdown *n* **1** (in a nuclear reactor) the melting of the fuel rods, with the possible escape of radioactivity **2** *informal* a sudden disastrous failure **3** *informal* a process of irreversible decline

melting point *n* the temperature at which a solid turns into a liquid

melting pot *n* a place or situation in which many races, ideas, etc., are mixed

Melton Mowbray *n* a town in central England, in Leicestershire: pork pies and Stilton cheese. Pop: 25 554 (2001)

meltwater *n* melted snow or ice

Melville *n* Herman. 1819–91, US novelist and short-story writer. Among his works, *Moby Dick* (1851) and *Billy Budd* (written 1891, published 1924) are outstanding

Melville Island *n* **1** a Canadian island in the Arctic Ocean, north of Victoria Island: in the Northwest Territories and Nunavut. Area: 41 865 sq km (16 164 sq miles) **2** an island in the Arafura Sea, off the N central coast of Australia, separated from the mainland by Clarence Strait. Area: 6216 sq km (2400 sq miles)

Melville Peninsula *n* a peninsula of N Canada, in Nunavut, between the Gulf of Boothia and Foxe Basin

member *n* **1** a person who belongs to a group or organization such as a club or political party **2** any part of a plant or animal, such as a limb or petal **3** a Member of Parliament: *the member for Glasgow Central* ⊳ *adj* **4** (of a country or group) belonging to an organization or alliance: *a summit of the member countries' heads of state is due* [Latin *membrum* limb, part]

Member of Parliament *n* a person who has been elected to the House of Commons or the equivalent assembly in another country

membership *n* **1** the members of an organization collectively **2** the number of members **3** the state of being a member

membrane *n* a thin flexible tissue that covers, lines, or connects plant and animal organs or cells [Latin *membrana* skin covering a part of the body] **> membranous** *adj*

meme (meem) *n* a video, photo, or story that is viewed by many internet users in a short time

Memel *n* **1** the German name for **Klaipeda 2** the lower course of the Neman River

memento *n, pl* **-tos** *or* **-toes** something that reminds one of past events; a souvenir [Latin, imperative of *meminisse* to remember]

memento mori *n, pl* **memento mori** an object intended to remind people of death [Latin: remember you must die]

Memling *or* **Memlinc** *n* Hans. ?1430–94, Flemish painter of religious works and portraits

memo *n, pl* **memos** short for **memorandum**

memoir (mem-wahr) *n* a biography or historical account based on personal knowledge [Latin *memoria* memory]

memoirs *pl n* **1** a collection of reminiscences about a period or series of events, written from personal experience **2** an autobiography

memorabilia *pl n, sing* **-rabile** objects connected with famous people or events

memorable *adj* worth remembering or easily remembered because it is very special or important [Latin *memorare* to remember] **> memorably** *adv*

memorandum *n, pl* **-dums** *or* **-da 1** a note sent by one person or department to another within a business organization **2** a note of things to be remembered **3** *law* a short written summary of the terms of a transaction [Latin: (something) to be remembered]

memorial *n* **1** something, such as a statue, built or displayed to preserve the memory of someone or something: *a war memorial* ⊳ *adj* **2** in memory of someone or something: *a memorial service* [Late Latin *memoriale* a reminder]

memorize *or* **-rise** *vb* **-rizing, -rized** *or* **-rising, -rised** to commit to memory; learn by heart

memory *n, pl* **-ries 1** the ability of the mind to store and recall past sensations, thoughts, and knowledge: *she can do it from memory* **2** the sum of everything retained by the mind **3** a particular recollection of an event or person: *he started awake with a sudden memory* **4** the length of time one can remember: *my memory doesn't go that far back* **5** commemoration: *in memory of our leader* **6** a person's reputation after death: *a conductor of fond memory* **7** a part of a computer in which information is stored [Latin *memoria*]

memory card *n* a small removable data storage device, used in mobile phones, digital cameras, etc.

Memory Stick *n computers* **1** *trademark* a standard format for memory cards **2 memory stick**. same as **USB drive**

Memphian *adj* **1** of or relating to ancient Memphis or its inhabitants ⊳ *n* **2** an inhabitant or native of ancient Memphis

Memphis *n* **1** a port in SW Tennessee, on the Mississippi River: the largest city in the state; a major cotton and timber market; Memphis State University (1909). Pop: 645 978 (2003 est) **2** a ruined city in N Egypt, the ancient centre of Lower Egypt, on the Nile: administrative and artistic centre, sacred to the worship of Ptah

Memphremagog *n* **Lake** a lake on the border between the US and Canada, in N Vermont and S Quebec. Length: about 43 km (27 miles). Width: up to 6 km (4 miles)

memsahib *n* (formerly, in India) a term of respect used for a European married woman [*ma'am* + *sahib*]

men *n* the plural of **man**

menace *vb* **-acing, -aced 1** to threaten with violence or danger ⊳ *n* **2** a threat; a source of danger **3** *informal* an annoying person or thing; nuisance [Latin *minax* threatening] **> menacing** *adj*

Menado *or* **Manado** *n* a port in NE Indonesia, on NE Sulawesi: founded by the Dutch in 1657. Pop: 372 887 (2000)

ménage (may-nahzh) *n* a household [French]

ménage à trois (ah trwah) *n, pl* **ménages à trois** a sexual arrangement involving a married couple and the lover of one of them [French, literally: household of three]

menagerie (min-naj-er-ee) *n* a collection of wild animals kept for exhibition [French]

Menai Strait *n* a channel of the Irish Sea between the island of Anglesey and the mainland of NW Wales: famous suspension bridge (1819–26) designed by Thomas Telford and tubular bridge (1846–50) by Robert

Stephenson. Length: 24 km (15 miles). Width: up to 3 km (2 miles)

Menam *n* another name for the **Chao Phraya**

Menander *n* **1** ?160 BC–?120 BC, Greek king of the Punjab. A Buddhist convert, he reigned over much of NW India **2** ?342–?292 BC, Greek comic dramatist. The *Dyskolos* is his only complete extant comedy but others survive in adaptations by Terence and Plautus

Mencius *n* Chinese name *Mengzi* or *Meng-tze*. ?372–?289 BC, Chinese philosopher, who propounded the ethical system of Confucius

Mencken *n* H(enry) L(ouis). 1880–1956, US journalist and literary critic, noted for *The American Language* (1919): editor of the *Smart Set* and the *American Mercury,* which he founded (1924)

mend *vb* **1** to repair something broken or not working **2** to heal or recover: *a wound like that will take a while to mend* **3** (esp. of behaviour) to improve; make or become better: *if you don't mend your ways you'll be in serious trouble* ▷ *n* **4** a mended area, esp. on a garment **5** on the mend regaining one's health [from *amend*]

mendacity *n* the tendency to be untruthful [Latin *mendax* untruthful] > **mendacious** *adj*

Mendel *n* Gregor Johann. 1822–84, Austrian monk and botanist; founder of the science of genetics. He developed his theory of organic inheritance from his experiments on the hybridization of green peas. His findings were published (1865) but remained unrecognized until 1900 > **Mendelism** *n*

mendelevium *n* chem an artificially produced radioactive element. Symbol: **Md** [after D. I. MENDELEYEV]

Mendeleyev or **Mendeleev** *n* Dmitri Ivanovich. 1834–1907, Russian chemist. He devised the original periodic table of the elements (1869)

Mendel's laws *pl n* the principles of heredity proposed by Gregor Mendel

Mendelssohn *n* **1** Felix, full name *Jacob Ludwig Felix Mendelssohn-Bartholdy*. 1809–47, German romantic composer. His works include the overtures *A Midsummer Night's Dream* (1826) and *Fingal's Cave* (1832), five symphonies, the oratorio *Elijah* (1846), piano pieces, and songs. He was instrumental in the revival of the music of J. S. Bach in the 19th century **2** his grandfather, **Moses**. 1729–86, German Jewish philosopher. His best-known work is *Jerusalem* (1783), in which he defends Judaism and appeals for religious toleration

Menderes *n* **1** a river in SW Turkey flowing southwest, then west to the Aegean. Length: about 386 km (240 miles). Ancient name: **Maeander 2** a river in NW Turkey flowing west and northwest to the Dardanelles. Length: 104 km (65 miles). Ancient name: **Scamander**

Mendes *n* Sam(uel) (Alexander). born 1965, British theatre and film director, who made his name as artistic director of the Donmar Warehouse, London (1992–2002) before directing the films *American Beauty* (1999), *The Road to Perdition* (2002), *Revolutionary Road* (2008), and *Skyfall* (2012)

Mendès-France *n* Pierre. 1907–82, French statesman; prime minister (1954–55). He concluded the war in Indochina and granted independence to Tunisia

mendicant *adj* **1** begging **2** (of a monk, nun, etc.) dependent on charity for food ▷ *n* **3** a mendicant friar **4** a beggar [Latin *mendicus* beggar]

Mendips *pl n* a range of limestone hills in SW England, in N Somerset: includes the Cheddar Gorge and numerous caves. Highest point: 325 m (1068 ft). Also called: **Mendip Hills**

Mendoza[1] *n* a city in W central Argentina, in the foothills of the Sierra de los Paramillos: largely destroyed by an earthquake in 1861; commercial centre of an intensively cultivated irrigated region; University of Cuyo (1939). Pop: 1 072 000 (2005 est)

Mendoza[2] *n* Pedro de. died 1537, Spanish soldier and explorer; founder of Buenos Aires (1536)

Menelik II *n* 1844–1913, emperor of Abyssinia (1889–1910). He defeated the Italians at Aduwa (1896), maintaining the independence of Abyssinia in an era of European expansion in Africa

Menes *n* the first king of the first dynasty of Egypt (?3100 BC). He is said to have united Upper and Lower Egypt and founded Memphis

menfolk *pl n* men collectively, esp. the men of a particular family

Mengelberg *n* (Josef) Willem. 1871–1951, Dutch orchestral conductor, noted for his performances of the music of Mahler

Mengistu Haile Mariam *n* born 1937, Ethiopian soldier and statesman; head of state from 1977 until 1991 when rebels seized power and he fled into exile

menhir (men-hear) *n* a single standing stone, dating from prehistoric times [Breton *men* stone + *hir* long]

menial (mean-nee-al) *adj* **1** involving or doing boring work of low status ▷ *n* **2** a domestic servant [Old French *meinie* household]

Meninga *n* Mal. born 1960, Australian rugby league player: scored 21 tries in 46 internationals (1982–94)

meninges (min-in-jeez) *pl n, sing* **meninx** (mean-inks) the three membranes that surround the brain and spinal cord [Greek, plural of *meninx* membrane]

meningitis (men-in-jite-iss) *n* inflammation of the meninges, caused by infection and causing severe headache, fever, and rigidity of the neck muscles

meniscus *n, pl* **-nisci** or **-niscuses 1** the curved upper surface of a liquid standing in a tube, produced by the surface tension **2** a crescent-shaped lens [Greek *mēniskos* crescent]

Menon *n* Vengalil Krishnan Krishna. 1897–1974, Indian diplomat and politician, who was a close associate of Nehru and played a key role in the Indian nationalist movement

menopause *n* the period during which a woman's menstrual cycle ceases, normally at an age of 45 to 50 [Greek *mēn* month + *pausis* halt] > **menopausal** *adj*

menorah (min-or-a) *n* Judaism a seven-branched candelabrum used as an emblem of Judaism [Hebrew: candlestick]

Menorca *n* the Spanish name for **Minorca** (1)

Menotti *n* Gian Carlo. 1911–2007, Italian composer, in the US from 1928. His works include the operas *The Medium* (1946), *The Consul* (1950), *Amahl and the Night Visitors* (1951), and *Giorno di Nozze* (1988)

menses (men-seez) *n* same as **menstruation** [Latin, plural of *mensis* month]

menstrual *adj* of or relating to menstruation: *the menstrual cycle*

menstruate *vb* **-ating, -ated** to undergo menstruation [Latin *menstruare*, from *mensis* month]

menstruation *n* the approximately monthly discharge of blood from the womb in women of childbearing age who are not pregnant

mensuration *n* **1** the study of the measurement of geometric magnitudes such as length **2** the act or process of measuring [Latin *mensura* measure]

menswear *n* clothing for men

mental *adj* **1** of, done by, or involving the mind: *mental alertness* **2** done in the mind without using speech or writing: *mental arithmetic* **3** affected by mental illness: *a mental patient* **4** concerned with mental illness: *a mental hospital* **5** slang extremely foolish or eccentric [Latin *mens* mind] > **mentally** *adv*

mental age *n* the age which a person is considered to have reached in thinking ability, judged by comparing his or her ability with the average for people of various ages: *a twenty-one-year-old woman with a mental age of only ten*

mental handicap *n* any intellectual disability resulting from injury to or abnormal development of the brain > **mentally handicapped** *adj*

mental illness _n_ any of various disorders in which a person's thoughts, emotions, or behaviour are so abnormal as to cause suffering to himself, herself, or other people

mentality _n, pl_ **-ties** a particular attitude or way of thinking: _the traditional civil service mentality_

menthol _n_ an organic compound found in peppermint oil and used as an antiseptic, decongestant, and painkiller [Latin _mentha_ mint] **> mentholated** _adj_

mention _vb_ **1** to refer to or speak about briefly or incidentally **2** to include in a report, list etc., because of high standards or an outstanding achievement: _the hotel is mentioned in all the guidebooks; he was twice mentioned in dispatches during the war_ **3 not to mention (something)** to say nothing of (something too obvious to mention) **>** _n_ **4** a slight reference or allusion **5** a recognition or acknowledgment of high quality or an outstanding achievement [Latin _mentio_ a calling to mind]

Mentmore _n_ a mansion in Mentmore in Buckinghamshire: built by Sir Joseph Paxton in the 19th century for the Rothschild family; now owned by the Maharishi University of Natural Law

Menton _n_ a town and resort in SE France, on the Mediterranean: belonged to Monaco from the 14th century until 1848, then an independent republic until purchased by France in 1860. Pop: 28 833 (2008)

mentor _n_ an adviser or guide [_Mentor_, adviser of Telemachus in Homer's _Odyssey_]

menu _n_ **1** a list of dishes served at a meal or that can be ordered in a restaurant **2** a list of options displayed on a visual display unit from which the operator can choose [French: small, detailed (list)]

Menuhin _n_ Yehudi, Baron. 1916–99, British classical and jazz violinist, born in the US

Menzies _n_ Sir Robert Gordon. 1894–1978, Australian statesman; prime minister (1939–41; 1949–66)

meow _or_ **miaow** (mee-ow) _n_ **1** the characteristic high-pitched cry of a cat; mew **>** _vb_ **2** to make such a sound

MEP (in Britain) Member of the European Parliament

Mephistopheles (mef-iss-stoff-ill-eez) _n_ a devil in medieval mythology to whom Faust sold his soul **> Mephisphelean** _adj_

Merano _n_ a town and resort in NE Italy, in the foothills of the central Alps: capital of the Tyrol (12th–15th century); under Austrian rule until 1919. Pop: 33 656 (2001). German name: **Meran**

Merca _n_ a port in S Somalia on the Indian Ocean. Pop: 189 000 (2005 est)

mercantile _adj_ of trade or traders; commercial [Italian _mercante_ merchant]

Mercator _n_ Gerardus. Latinized name of _Gerhard Kremer_. 1512–94, Flemish cartographer and mathematician

Mercator projection (mer-kate-er) _n_ a way of drawing maps in which latitude and longitude form a rectangular grid, scale being exaggerated with increasing distance from the equator [after G. MERCATOR]

mercenary _n, pl_ **-naries 1** a soldier who fights for a foreign army for money **>** _adj_ **2** motivated by greed or the desire for gain: _calculating and mercenary businessmen_ **3** of or relating to a mercenary or mercenaries [Latin _merces_ wages]

Mercer _n_ Johnny, full name _John Herndon Mercer_. 1909–76, US popular songwriter and singer. His most popular songs include "Blues in the Night" (1941) and "Moon River" (1961)

mercerized _or_ **-rised** _adj_ (of cotton) treated with an alkali to make it strong and shiny [after John _Mercer_, maker of textiles]

merchandise _n_ **1** goods for buying, selling, or trading with; commodities **>** _vb_ **-dising, -dised 2** to engage in the commercial purchase and sale of goods or services; trade

merchandising _n_ **1** the selection and display of goods in a retail outlet **2** commercial goods, esp. ones issued to exploit the popularity of a pop group, sporting event, etc.

merchant _n_ **1** a person who buys and sells goods in large quantities and usually of one type: _a wine merchant_ **2** _chiefly Scot, US and Canad_ a person engaged in retail trade; shopkeeper **3** _slang_ a person dealing in something undesirable: _a gossip merchant_ **>** _adj_ **4** of ships involved in commercial trade or their crews: _a merchant sailor; the British merchant fleet_ [Latin _mercari_ to trade]

Merchant _n_ Ismail. 1936–2005, Indian film producer, noted for his collaboration with James Ivory on such films as _Shakespeare Wallah_ (1965), _The Europeans_ (1979), _A Room with a View_ (1986), _The Remains of the Day_ (1993), and _The Golden Bowl_ (2000)

merchant bank _n_ a financial institution that deals primarily with foreign trade and business finance **> merchant banker** _n_

merchantman _n, pl_ **-men** a merchant ship

merchant navy _n_ the ships or crew engaged in a nation's commercial shipping

Mercia _n_ a kingdom and earldom of central and S England during the Anglo-Saxon period that reached its height under King Offa (757–96)

merciful _adj_ **1** (of an act or event) giving relief from pain or suffering: _after months of illness, death came as a merciful release_ **2** showing or giving mercy; compassionate **> mercifully** _adv_

merciless _adj_ without mercy; pitiless, cruel, or heartless **> mercilessly** _adv_

Merckx _n_ Eddy. born 1945, Belgian professional cyclist: five times winner of the Tour de France, including four consecutive victories (1969–72)

Mercouri _n_ Melina. 1925–94, Greek actress and politician: her films include _Never on Sunday_ (1960); minister of culture (1981–85 and 1993–94)

mercurial (mer-cure-ee-al) _adj_ **1** lively and unpredictable: _a mercurial and temperamental chess player_ **2** of or containing mercury [Latin _mercurialis_]

mercuric _adj_ of or containing mercury in the divalent state

mercurous _adj_ of or containing mercury in the monovalent state

mercury _n, pl_ **-ries** _chem_ a silvery toxic metal, the only element liquid at normal temperatures, used in thermometers, barometers, lamps, and dental amalgams. Symbol: **Hg** [Latin _Mercurius_, messenger of Jupiter]

Mercury _n_ **1** _Roman myth_ the messenger of the gods **2** the second smallest planet and the one nearest the sun

mercy _n, pl_ **-cies 1** compassionate treatment of, or attitude towards, an offender or enemy who is in one's power **2** the power to show mercy: _they threw themselves on the King's mercy_ **3** a relieving or welcome occurrence or act: _it was a mercy you turned up when you did_ **4 at the mercy of** in the power of **>** _adj_ **5** done or undertaken in an attempt to relieve suffering or bring help: _a mercy mission_ [Latin _merces_ recompense]

mercy killing _n_ same as euthanasia

mere¹ _adj_ nothing more than: _the election in Slovenia seems a mere formality_ [Latin _merus_ pure] **> merely** _adv_

mere² _n Brit dialect or archaic_ a lake [Old English: sea, lake]

Meredith _n_ George. 1828–1909, English novelist and poet. His works, notable for their social satire and analysis of character, include the novels _Beauchamp's Career_ (1876) and _The Egoist_ (1879) and the long tragic poem _Modern Love_ (1862)

meretricious _adj_ superficially or garishly attractive but of no real value [Latin _meretrix_ prostitute]

merganser (mer-gan-ser) _n, pl_ **-sers** _or_ **-ser** a large crested marine diving duck [Latin _mergere_ to plunge + _anser_ goose]

merge _vb_ **merging, merged 1** to combine, esp. so as to become part of a larger whole: *the two airlines merged in 1983* **2** to blend gradually, without any sudden change being apparent: *late afternoon merged imperceptibly into early evening* [Latin *mergere* to plunge]

merger *n* the act of merging, esp. the combination of two or more companies

Mergui Archipelago *n* a group of over 200 islands in the Andaman Sea, off the Tenasserim coast of S Myanmar: mountainous and forested

Meriç *n* the Turkish name for the **Maritsa**

Mérida *n* **1** a city in SE Mexico, capital of Yucatán state: founded in 1542 on the site of the ancient Mayan city of T'ho; centre of the henequen industry; university. Pop: 919 000 (2005 est) **2** a city in W Venezuela: founded in 1558 by Spanish conquistadores; University of Los Andes (1785). Pop: 319 000 (2005 est) **3** a market town in W Spain, in Extremadura, on the Guadiana River: founded in 25 BC; became the capital of Lusitania and one of the chief cities of Iberia. Pop: 52 110 (2003 est). Latin name: **Augusta Emerita**

meridian *n* **1** one of the imaginary lines joining the north and south poles at right angles to the equator, designated by degrees of longitude from 0° at Greenwich to 180° **2** (in acupuncture etc.) any of various channels through which vital energy is believed to circulate round the body [Latin *meridies* midday]

meridional *adj* **1** of or along a meridian **2** of or in the south, esp. the south of Europe

Mérimée *n* Prosper. 1803–70, French novelist, dramatist, and short-story writer, noted particularly for his short novels *Colomba* (1840) and *Carmen* (1845), on which Bizet's opera was based

meringue (mer-**rang**) *n* **1** stiffly beaten egg whites mixed with sugar and baked **2** a small cake made from this mixture [French]

merino *n*, *pl* **-nos 1** a sheep with long fine wool, originally reared in Spain **2** the yarn made from this wool [Spanish]

Merionethshire *n* (until 1974) a county of N Wales, now part of Gwynedd

merit *n* **1** worth or superior quality; excellence: *the film had two sequels, neither of much merit* **2** an admirable or advantageous quality: *the relative merits of film and video as a medium of communication* **3** **have the merit of** to have a positive feature or advantage that the alternatives do not have: *the first version has the merit of being short* **4** **on its merits** on its intrinsic qualities or virtues ▷ *vb* **-riting, -rited 5** to be worthy of; deserve: *the issue merits much fuller discussion* [Latin *meritum* reward]

meritocracy (mer-it-**tok**-rass-ee) *n*, *pl* **-cies** a social system in which power is held by the most talented or intelligent people ❭ **meritocrat** *n* ❭ **meritocratic** *adj*

meritorious *adj* deserving praise for being good or worthwhile [Latin *meritorius* earning money]

Merkel *n* Angela. born 1954, German politician; chair of the Christian Democratic Union from 2000; chancellor of Germany from 2005 (the first woman to hold the office)

Merleau-Ponty *n* Maurice. 1908–61, French phenomenological philosopher

merlin *n* a small falcon with dark plumage [Old French *esmerillon*]

mermaid *n* an imaginary sea creature with a woman's head and upper body and a fish's tail [*mere* sea + *maid*] ❭ **merman** *masc n*

Meroë *n* an ancient city in N Sudan, on the Nile; capital of a kingdom that flourished from about 700 BC to about 350 AD

merry *adj* **-rier, -riest 1** cheerful and jolly **2** *Brit and Austral informal* slightly drunk **3** **make merry** to take part in noisy cheerful celebrations or fun [Old English *merige* agreeable] ❭ **merrily** *adv* ❭ **merriment** *n*

merry-go-round *n* **1** a fairground roundabout **2** a whirl of activity

merrymaking *n* noisy cheerful celebrations or fun ❭ **merrymaker** *n*

Merse *n* **the Merse** a fertile lowland area of SE Scotland, in the Scottish Borders, north of the Tweed

Merseburg *n* a city in E Germany, on the Saale River, in Saxony-Anhalt: residence of the dukes of Saxe-Merseburg (1656–1738); chemical industry. Pop: 35 358 (2003 est)

Mersey *n* a river in W England, rising in N Derbyshire and flowing northwest and west to the Irish Sea through a large estuary on which is situated the port of Liverpool. Length: about 112 km (70 miles)

Merseyside *n* a metropolitan county of NW England, administered since 1986 by the unitary authorities of Sefton, Liverpool, St Helens, Knowsley, and Wirral. Area: 652 sq km (252 sq miles)

Mersin *n* a port in S Turkey, on the Mediterranean: oil refinery. Pop: 603 000 (2005 est). Also called: **Içel**

Merthyr Tydfil *n* **1** a town in SE Wales, in Merthyr Tydfil county borough: formerly an important centre for the mining industry. Pop: 30 483 (2001) **2** a county borough in SE Wales, created from part of N Mid Glamorgan in 1996. Pop: 55 400 (2003 est). Area: 111 sq km (43 sq miles)

Merton¹ *n* a borough in SW Greater London. Pop: 191 400 (2003 est). Area: 38 sq km (15 sq miles)

Merton² *n* Thomas (**Feverel**). 1915–68, US writer, monk, and mystic; noted esp. for his autobiography *The Seven Storey Mountain* (1948)

mesa *n* a flat-topped hill found in arid regions [Spanish: table]

mésalliance (mez-**zal**-ee-anss) *n* a marriage with a person of lower social status [French]

Mesa Verde *n* a high plateau in SW Colorado: remains of numerous prehistoric cliff dwellings, inhabited by the Pueblo Indians

mescal (mess-**kal**) *n* **1** a globe-shaped cactus without spines found in Mexico and the southwestern US **2** a Mexican alcoholic spirit similar to tequila [Mexican Indian *mexcalli*]

mescaline *n* a hallucinogenic drug derived from the button-like top of the mescal cactus

mesdames (may-**dam**) *n* the plural of **madame, madam** (1)

mesdemoiselles (maid-mwah-**zel**) *n* the plural of **mademoiselle**

mesembryanthemum *n* a low-growing plant with fleshy leaves and bright daisy-like flowers [Greek *mesēmbria* noon + *anthemon* flower]

mesh *n* **1** a material resembling a net made from intersecting strands with a space between each strand **2** an open space between the strands of a net or network: *the minimum permitted size of fishing net mesh* **3** (*often pl*) the strands surrounding these spaces **4** anything that ensnares or holds like a net ▷ *adj* **5** made from mesh: *a wire mesh fence* ▷ *vb* **6** to entangle or become entangled **7** (of gear teeth) to engage or interlock **8** to fit together closely or work in harmony: *she schedules her holidays to mesh with theirs* [probably Dutch *maesche*]

Meshed *n* a variant of Mashhad

mesmerize *or* **-ise** *vb* **-izing, -ized** *or* **-ising, -ised 1** to fascinate and hold spellbound: *his voice had the entire audience mesmerized* **2** *archaic* to hypnotize ❭ **mesmerism** *n* ❭ **mesmerizing** *adj*

Mesoamerica *or* **Meso-America** *n* another name for **Central America** ❭ **Mesoamerican** *or* **Meso-American** *adj*

Mesolithic (mess-oh-**lith**-ik) *adj* of the middle period of the Stone Age, in Europe from about 12 000 to 3000 BC [Greek *mesos* middle + *lithos* stone]

Mesolonghi *n* a variant of Missolonghi

Mesolóngion *n* transliteration of the Modern Greek name for Missolonghi

mesomorph *n physiol* a person with a muscular body

build. See also **ectomorph, endomorph** [Greek *mesos* middle + *morphē* shape] ⊳ **mesomorphic** *adj*

meson (mee-zon) *n physics* any of a group of elementary particles that has a mass between those of an electron and a proton [Greek *mesos* middle + *-on*, indicating an elementary particle]

Mesopotamia *n* a region of SW Asia between the lower and middle reaches of the Tigris and Euphrates rivers: site of several ancient civilizations [Latin from Greek *mesopotamia (khōra)* (the land) between rivers]

Mesopotamian *adj* **1** of or relating to Mesopotamia or its inhabitants ⊳ *n* **2** a native or inhabitant of Mesopotamia

mesosphere (mess-oh-sfeer) *n* the atmospheric layer above the stratosphere

Mesozoic (mess-oh-zoh-ik) *adj geology* of the geological era that began 225 million years ago and lasted about 155 million years, during which the dinosaurs emerged, flourished, then became extinct [Greek *mesos* middle + *zōion* animal]

mess *n* **1** a state of untidiness or confusion, esp. a dirty or unpleasant one: *the house was in a mess* **2** a confused and difficult situation; muddle: *the firm is in a terrible financial mess* **3** *informal* a dirty or untidy person or thing: *there was a nasty burnt mess in the saucepan* **4** a building providing catering, and sometimes recreation, facilities for service personnel **5** a group of service personnel who regularly eat together **6** *old-fashioned* a portion of soft or runny food: *a mess of pottage* ⊳ *vb* **7** (of service personnel) to eat in a group ▸ See also **mess about, mess up, mess with** [Old French *mes* dish of food]

mess about *or* **mess around** *vb* **1** to pass the time doing trivial or silly things without any particular purpose or plan: *messing about in boats* **2** to interfere or meddle: *you have no business messing around here* **3** *chiefly US* to engage in adultery

message *n* **1** a communication from one person or group to another **2** an implicit meaning or moral, as in a work of art **3** a religious or political belief that someone attempts to communicate to others: *paintings with a fierce feminist message* **4 get the message** *informal* to understand [Old French, from Latin *mittere* to send]

message board *n* an internet discussion forum

Messager *n* André (**Charles Prosper**). 1853–1929, French composer and conductor

messages *pl n Scot and N English dialect* household shopping

messaging *n* the sending of a message by any form of electronic communication: *text messaging*

Messalina *n* Valeria. died 48 AD, wife of the Roman emperor Claudius, notorious for her debauchery and cruelty

Messene *n* an ancient Greek city in the SW Peloponnese: founded in 369 BC as the capital of Messenia

messenger *n* a person who takes messages from one person or group to another [Old French *messagier*]

Messenia *n* the southwestern area of the Peloponnese in S Greece

Messerschmitt *n* Willy. 1898–1978, German aeronautical engineer. His military planes figured prominently in World War II, including the Me-262, the first jet fighter

Messi *n* Lionel (**Andrés**). born 1987, Argentinian footballer; a prolific goalscorer for both Barcelona (from 2004) and Argentina (from 2005)

Messiaen *n* Olivier. 1908–92, French composer and organist. His music is distinguished by its rhythmic intricacy; he was influenced by Hindu and Greek rhythms and bird song

Messiah *n* **1** *Judaism* the awaited king of the Jews, who will be sent by God to free them **2** *Christianity* Jesus Christ, when regarded in this role **3** a liberator of a country or people [Hebrew *māshīach* anointed]

Messianic *adj* **1** of or relating to a Messiah, or the arrival

on Earth of a Messiah **2 messianic** of or relating to the belief that someone or something will bring about a complete transformation of the existing social order: *a messianic zeal for the free market*

messieurs (may-syuh) *n* the plural of **monsieur**

Messina *n* a port in NE Sicily, on the **Strait of Messina**: colonized by Greeks around 730 BC; under Spanish rule (1282–1676 and 1678–1713); university (1549). Pop: 252 026 (2001)

mess jacket *n* a waist-length jacket, worn by officers in the mess for formal dinners

mess kit *n* a soldier's eating utensils for use in the field

Messrs (mess-erz) *n* the plural of **Mr**

mess up *vb informal* **1** to make untidy or dirty **2** to spoil something, or do something badly: *he messed up his driving test*

mess with *vb informal, chiefly US* to interfere in, or become involved with, a dangerous person, thing, or situation: *he had started messing with drugs*

messy *adj* **messier, messiest 1** untidy **2** dirty **3** unpleasantly confused or complicated: *the messy, uncontrollable world of real life* ⊳ **messily** *adv* ⊳ **messiness** *n*

Meštrović *n* Ivan. 1883–1962, US sculptor, born in Austria: his works include portraits of Sir Thomas Beecham and Pope Pius XI

met *vb* the past of **meet**[1]

Met *adj* **1** Meteorological: *the Met Office* ⊳ *n* **2 the Met** the Metropolitan Police, who operate in London

Meta *n* a river in Colombia, rising in the Andes and flowing northeast and east, forming part of the border between Colombia and Venezuela, to join the Orinoco River. Length: about 1000 km (620 miles)

metabolic syndrome *n* a condition associated with obesity, which increases the risk of cardiovascular disease and diabetes

metabolism (met-tab-ol-liz-zum) *n* the chemical processes that occur in living organisms, resulting in growth, production of energy, and elimination of waste [Greek *metaballein* to change] ⊳ **metabolic** *adj*

metabolize *or* **-lise** *vb* **-lizing, -lized** *or* **-lising, -lised** to produce or be produced by metabolism

metacarpus *n, pl* **-pi** the set of five long bones in the hand between the wrist and the fingers [Greek *meta* after + *karpos* wrist] ⊳ **metacarpal** *adj, n*

metal *n* **1 a** *chem* a chemical element, such as iron or copper, that reflects light and can be shaped, forms positive ions, and is a good conductor of heat and electricity **b** an alloy, such as brass or steel, containing one or more of these elements **2** short for **road metal 3** *informal* short for **heavy metal 4 metals** the rails of a railway ⊳ *adj* **5** made of metal [Greek *metallon* mine]

metalanguage *n* the language or system of symbols used to discuss another language or system

metalled *or* US **metaled** *adj* (of a road) surfaced with crushed rock or small stones: *a metalled driveway*

metallic *adj* **1** of or consisting of metal **2** sounding like two pieces of metal hitting each other: *a metallic click* **3** (of a voice) harsh, unpleasant, and unemotional **4** shining like metal: *metallic paint* **5** (of a taste) unpleasantly harsh and bitter

metalliferous *adj* containing a metallic element [Latin *metallum* metal + *ferre* to bear]

metallography *n* the study of the composition and structure of metals

metalloid *n chem* a nonmetallic element, such as arsenic or silicon, that has some of the properties of a metal

metallurgy *n* the scientific study of the structure, properties, extraction, and refining of metals [*metal* + Greek *-urgia*, from *ergon* work] ⊳ **metallurgical** *adj* ⊳ **metallurgist** *n*

metal road *n* NZ an unsealed road covered in gravel

metalwork *n* **1** the craft of making articles from metal **2** articles made from metal **3** the metal part of something ⊳ **metalworker** *n*

metamorphic *adj* **1** (of rocks) altered considerably from the original structure and composition by pressure and heat **2** of metamorphosis or metamorphism

metamorphism *n* the process by which metamorphic rocks are formed

metamorphose *vb* **-phosing, -phosed** to change from one state or thing into something different: *the media personality metamorphosed into society hostess*

metamorphosis (met-a-mor-foss-is) *n, pl* **-ses** (-seez) **1** a complete change of physical form or substance **2** a complete change of character or appearance **3** *zoology* the change of form that accompanies transformation into an adult in certain animals, for example the butterfly or frog [Greek: transformation, from *meta* after + *morphē* form]

metaphor *n* a figure of speech in which a word or phrase is applied to an object or action that it does not literally apply to in order to imply a resemblance, for example *he is a lion in battle* [Greek *metapherein* to transfer] **> metaphorical** *adj* **> metaphorically** *adv*

metaphysical *adj* **1** of metaphysics **2** abstract, abstruse, or unduly theoretical

Metaphysical *adj* denoting certain 17th-century poets who combined intense feeling with elaborate imagery

metaphysics *n* **1** the philosophical study of the nature of reality **2** abstract or subtle discussion or reasoning [Greek *ta meta ta phusika* the things after the physics, from the arrangement of subjects treated in the works of Aristotle]

Metastasio *n* Pietro, original name *Pietro Antonio Domenico Trapassi*. 1698–1782, Italian poet and librettist; Viennese court poet (from 1730). His works include *La clemenza di Tito* (1732)

metastasis (mit-tass-tiss-iss) *n, pl* **-ses** (-seez) **1** *pathol* the spreading of a disease, esp. cancer, from one part of the body to another **2** the spreading of a problem into new areas [Greek: transition] **> metastasize** *or* **-sise** *vb*

metatarsus *n, pl* **-si** the set of five long bones in the foot between the toes and the ankle [Greek *meta* after + *tarsos* instep] **> metatarsal** *adj, n*

metathesis (mit-tath-iss-iss) *n, pl* **-ses** (-seez) the transposition of two sounds or letters in a word [Greek *metatithenai* to transpose]

metazoan (met-a-zoh-an) *n* **1** any animal having a body composed of many cells: includes all animals except sponges and protozoans **> adj 2** of the metazoans [New Latin *Metazoa*]

Metchnikoff *n* Élie. 1845–1916, Russian bacteriologist in France. He formulated the theory of phagocytosis and shared the Nobel prize for physiology or medicine 1908

meteor *n* **1** a small piece of rock or metal that has entered the earth's atmosphere from space **2** Also: **shooting star** the bright streak of light appearing in the sky due to a piece of rock or metal burning up because of friction as it falls through the atmosphere [Greek *meteōros* lofty]

meteoric (meet-ee-or-rik) *adj* **1** of or relating to meteors **2** brilliant and very rapid: *his meteoric rise to power* **> meteorically** *adv*

meteorite *n* the rocklike remains of a meteoroid that has collided with the earth

meteoroid *n* any of the small celestial bodies that are thought to orbit the sun. When they enter the earth's atmosphere, they become visible as meteors

meteorol. *or* **meteor.** **1** meteorological **2** meteorology

meteorology *n* the study of the earth's atmosphere and weather-forming processes, esp. for weather forecasting **> meteorological** *adj* **> meteorologist** *n*

mete out *vb* **meting, meted** to impose or deal out something, usually something unpleasant: *the sentence meted out to him has proved controversial* [Old English *metan* to measure]

meter¹ *n* **1** any device that measures and records the quantity or number of units of something that was used during a specified period or is being used at that moment: *a gas meter* **2** short for **parking meter 3** short for **taximeter > vb 4** to measure the amount of something used, or a rate of flow, with a meter [Old English *metan* to measure]

meter² *n* US same as **metre¹, metre²**

-meter *combining form* **1** indicating an instrument for measuring: *barometer* **2** *prosody* indicating a verse having a specified number of feet: *pentameter* [Greek *metron* measure]

methadone *n* a drug similar to morphine, sometimes prescribed as a heroin substitute [(di)meth(yl) + a(mino) + d(iphenyl) + -one, indicating a ketone]

methamphetamine *n* a variety of amphetamine used for its stimulant action

methanal *n* same as **formaldehyde**

methane *n* a colourless odourless flammable gas, the main constituent of natural gas [meth(yl) + -ane, indicating an alkane]

methane series *n* a series of saturated hydrocarbons with the general formula C_nH_{2n+2}

methanol *n* a colourless poisonous liquid used as a solvent and fuel. Also: **methyl alcohol** [*methane* + -ol, indicating alcohol]

methicillin *n* a semisynthetic penicillin used to treat various infections

methinks *vb, past* **methought** *archaic* it seems to me that

method *n* **1** a way of doing something, esp. a systematic or regular one **2** orderliness of thought or action **3** the techniques of a particular field or subject [Greek *methodos*, literally: a going after]

Method *n* an acting technique in which the actor bases his or her role on the inner motivation of the character played

methodical *adj* careful, well-organized, and systematic **> methodically** *adv*

Methodist *n* **1** a member of any of the Christian Nonconformist denominations that derive from the beliefs and practices of John Wesley and his followers **> adj 2** of or relating to Methodists or their Church **> Methodism** *n*

Methodius *n* Saint, with his younger brother Saint Cyril called *the Apostles of the Slavs*. 815–885 AD, Greek Christian theologian sent as a missionary to the Moravians. Feast day: Feb 14 or May 11

methodology *n, pl* **-gies 1** the system of methods and principles used in a particular discipline **2** the philosophical study of method **> methodological** *adj*

methought *vb archaic* the past tense of **methinks**

meths *n Brit, Austral and NZ informal* methylated spirits

methyl *adj* of or containing the monovalent saturated hydrocarbon group of atoms CH_3: *methyl mercury* [from *methylene*]

methyl alcohol *n* same as **methanol**

methylate *vb* **-ating, -ated** to mix with methanol

methylated spirits *n* alcohol that has been rendered undrinkable by the addition of methanol and a violet dye, used as a solvent or as a fuel for small lamps or heaters. Also: **methylated spirit**

methylene *adj* of, consisting of, or containing the divalent group of atoms $-CH_2-$: *a methylene group or radical* [Greek *methu* wine + *hulē* wood + -ene, indicating a double bond]

meticulous *adj* very precise about details; careful and thorough [Latin *meticulosus* fearful] **> meticulously** *adv* **> meticulousness** *n*

métier (met-ee-ay) *n* **1** a profession or trade **2** a person's strong point or speciality [French]

Métis (met-teess) *n, pl* **-tis** (-teess, -teez) a person of mixed parentage, esp. the offspring of a Native American and a French Canadian [French] **> Métisse** *fem n*

metonymy (mit-on-im-ee) *n, pl* **-mies** a figure of speech in which one thing is replaced by another associated with it, for instance the use of *Downing Street* to mean *the British government* [Greek *meta-*, indicating change + *onoma* name]

metre¹ *or US* **meter** *n* the basic SI unit of length, equal to 100 centimetres (39.37 inches): *the majority of people are between one and a half and two metres tall* [same as METRE²]

metre² *or US* **meter** *n* **1** *prosody* the rhythmic arrangement of syllables in verse, usually according to the number and kind of feet in a line **2** *music, chiefly US* the rhythmic arrangement of the beat in a piece of music [Greek *metron* measure]

metre-kilogram-second *n* See **mks units**

metric *adj* of or relating to the metre or metric system: *use either all metric or all imperial measurements*

metrical *or* **metric** *adj* **1** of or relating to measurement **2** of or in poetic metre ⟩ **metrically** *adv*

metricate *vb* **-cating, -cated** to convert a measuring system or instrument to metric units ⟩ **metrication** *n*

metric system *n* any decimal system of units based on the metre. For scientific purposes SI units are used

metric ton *n* (not in technical use) a tonne

metro *n, pl* **-ros** an urban, usually underground, railway system in certain cities, such as Paris [French, from *chemin de fer métropolitain* metropolitan railway]

metronome *n* a device which indicates the speed music should be played at by producing a clicking sound from a pendulum with an adjustable period of swing [Greek *metron* measure + *nomos* law]

metropolis (mit-trop-oh-liss) *n* the main city of a country or region [Greek *mētēr* mother + *polis* city]

metropolitan *adj* **1** of or characteristic of a metropolis **2** of or consisting of a city and its suburbs: *the Tokyo metropolitan region* **3** of or belonging to the home territories of a country, as opposed to overseas territories: *metropolitan France* ⊳ *n* **4** *Christianity* the senior clergyman, esp. an archbishop, in charge of an ecclesiastical province **5** an inhabitant of a large city

Metropolitan Museum of Art *n* the principal museum in New York City: founded in 1870 and housed in its present premises in Central Park since 1880

-metry *combining form* indicating the process or science of measuring: *geometry* [Greek *metron* measure] ⟩ **-metric** *combining form*

Metternich *n* Klemens. 1773–1859, Austrian statesman. He became foreign minister (1809) and made a significant contribution to the Congress of Vienna (1815). From 1821 to 1848 he was both foreign minister and chancellor of Austria and is noted for his defence of autocracy in Europe

mettle *n* **1** courage or spirit: *the lack of mettle evident among British politicians* **2** character or abilities: *the mettle saints are made of* **3** on one's mettle roused to making one's best efforts [variant of *metal*]

Metz *n* a city in NE France on the River Moselle: a free imperial city in the 13th century; annexed by France in 1552; part of Germany (1871–1918); centre of the Lorraine iron-mining region. Pop: 126 776 (2006)

Meurthe-et-Moselle *n* a department of NE France, in Lorraine region. Capital: Nancy. Pop: 718 250 (2003 est). Area: 5280 sq km (2059 sq miles)

Meuse *n* **1** a department of N France, in Lorraine region: heavy fighting occurred here in World War I. Capital: Bar-le-Duc. Pop: 191 728 (2003 est). Area: 6241 sq km (2434 sq miles) **2** a river in W Europe, rising in NE France and flowing north across E Belgium and the S Netherlands to join the Waal River before entering the North Sea. Length: 926 km (575 miles). Dutch name: **Maas**

MeV million electronvolts (10⁶ electronvolts)

mew¹ *n* **1** the characteristic high-pitched cry of a cat; meow ⊳ *vb* **2** to make such a sound [imitative]

mew² *n* a seagull [Old English *mǣw*]

Mewar *n* another name for **Udaipur** (1)

mewl *vb* **1** (esp. of a baby) to cry weakly; whimper ⊳ *n* **2** a weak or whimpering cry [imitative]

mews *n chiefly Brit* **1** a yard or street lined by buildings originally used as stables but now often converted into dwellings ⊳ *adj* **2** (of a flat or house) located in a mews: *a mews cottage* [plural of *mew*, originally referring to royal stables built on the site of hawks' mews (cages)]

Mex. **1** Mexican **2** Mexico

Mexicali *n* a city in NW Mexico, capital of Baja California (Norte) state, on the border with the US adjoining Calexico, California: centre of a rich irrigated agricultural region. Pop: 840 000 (2005 est)

Mexican *adj* **1** of or relating to Mexico or its inhabitants ⊳ *n* **2** a native or inhabitant of Mexico

Mexican wave *n* the rippling effect produced when the spectators in successive sections of a sports stadium stand up while raising their arms and then sit down [first seen at the World Cup finals in *Mexico* in 1986]

Mexico *n* **1** a republic in North America, on the Gulf of Mexico and the Pacific: early Mexican history includes the Maya, Toltec, and Aztec civilizations; conquered by the Spanish between 1519 and 1525 and achieved independence in 1821; lost Texas to the US in 1836 and California and New Mexico in 1848. It is generally mountainous with three ranges of the Sierra Madre (east, west, and south) and a large central plateau. Official language: Spanish. Religion: Roman Catholic majority. Currency: peso. Capital: Mexico City. Pop: 116 220 947 (2013 est). Area: 1 967 183 sq km (761 530 sq miles). Official name: **United Mexican States**. Spanish name: **Méjico 2** a state of Mexico, on the central plateau surrounding Mexico City, which is not administratively part of the state. Capital: Toluca. Pop: 13 096 686 (2000). Area: 21 460 sq km (8287 sq miles) **3 Gulf of Mexico** an arm of the Atlantic, bordered by the US, Cuba, and Mexico: linked with the Atlantic by the Straits of Florida and with the Caribbean by the Yucatán Channel. Area: about 1 600 000 sq km (618 000 sq miles)

Mexico City *n* the capital of Mexico, on the central plateau at an altitude of 2240 m (7350 ft): founded as the Aztec capital (Tenochtitlán) in about 1300; conquered and rebuilt by the Spanish in 1521; forms, with its suburbs, the federal district of Mexico; the largest industrial complex in the country. Pop: 19 013 000 (2005 est)

Meyerbeer *n* Giacomo, real name *Jakob Liebmann Beer*. 1791–1864, German composer, esp. of operas, such as *Robert le diable* (1831) and *Les Huguenots* (1836)

Meyerhof *n* Otto (Fritz). 1884–1951, German physiologist, noted for his work on the metabolism of muscles. He shared the Nobel prize for physiology or medicine 1922

Meyerhold *n* Vsevolod Emilievich, original name *Karl Theodor Kasimir*. 1874–*c*. 1940, Russian theatre director, noted for his experimental nonrealistic productions. He was arrested in 1939 and died in custody

Mézières *n* a town in NE France, on the River Meuse opposite Charleville. See **Charleville-Mézières**

mezzanine (mez-zan-een) *n* an intermediate storey, esp. one between the ground and first floor [Italian *mezzano* middle]

mezzo (met-so) *adv* **1** *music* moderately; quite: *mezzo-forte* ⊳ *n, pl* **-zos 2** short for **mezzo-soprano** [Italian: half]

mezzo-soprano *n, pl* **-nos 1** a female voice lower than soprano but higher than contralto **2** a singer with such a voice

mezzotint (met-so-tint) *n* **1** a method of engraving done by scraping and burnishing the roughened surface of a copper plate **2** a print made from a plate so treated [Italian *mezzotinto* half tint]

mg milligram

Mg *chem* magnesium

M. Glam Mid Glamorgan

Mgr **1** manager **2** monseigneur **3** monsignor

MHz megahertz

mi *n music* same as **me²**

MI Michigan

MI5 Military Intelligence, section five; the part of the British security services which combats spying and subversion in Britain

MI6 Military Intelligence, section six; the part of the British security services which spies on other countries. Also called: **SIS**

Miami *n* a city and resort in SE Florida, on Biscayne Bay: developed chiefly after 1896, esp. with the Florida land boom of the 1920s; centre of an extensive tourist area. Pop: 376 815 (2003 est)

Miami Beach *n* a resort in SE Florida, on an island separated from Miami by Biscayne Bay. Pop: 89 312 (2003 est)

Miandad *n Javed*. born 1957, Pakistani cricketer and coach: a batsman, he played in 124 test matches (1976–93), 34 as captain, scoring 8,832 runs (a Pakistan record)

miasma (mee-azz-ma) *n*, *pl* **-mata** *or* **-mas** an unwholesome or foreboding atmosphere [Greek: defilement]

mica (my-ka) *n* any of a group of minerals consisting of flakelike crystals of aluminium or potassium silicates. They have a high resistance to electricity and heat [Latin: crumb]

mice *n* the plural of **mouse**

Mich. Michigan

Michael *n* **1** 1596–1645, tsar of Russia (1613–45); founder of the Romanov dynasty **2** born 1921, king of Romania (1927–30, as part of a three-part regency; 1940–47), who relinquished the throne (1930–40) in favour of his father, Carol II. He led the coup d'état that overthrew (1944) Antonescu but was forced to abdicate (1947) by the Communists **3 Saint Michael** *Bible* one of the archangels. Feast day: Sept 29 or Nov 8

Michael VIII *n* surnamed *Palaeologus*. 1224–82, Byzantine emperor (1259–82); founder of the Palaeologan dynasty. His reign saw the recovery of Constantinople from the Latins (1261) and the reunion (1274) of the Greek and Roman churches

Michaelmas (mik-kl-mass) *n* Sept 29, the feast of St Michael the archangel: one of the four quarter days in England, Ireland, and Wales

Michaelmas daisy *n Brit* a garden plant with small daisy-shaped purple, pink, or white flowers in autumn

Michelangelo *n* full name *Michelangelo Buonarroti*. 1475–1564, Florentine sculptor, painter, architect, and poet; one of the outstanding figures of the Renaissance. Among his creations are the sculptures of *David* (1504) and of *Moses* which was commissioned for the tomb of Julius II, for whom he also painted the ceiling of the Sistine Chapel (1508–12). *The Last Judgment* (1533–41), also in the Sistine, includes a torturous vision of Hell and a disguised self-portrait. His other works include the design of the Laurentian Library (1523–29) and of the dome of St Peter's, Rome

Michelet *n Jules*. 1798–1874, French historian, noted esp. for his *Histoire de France* (17 vols, 1833–67)

Michelin *n André*. 1853–1931, French industrialist; founder, with his brother **Édouard Michelin** (1859–1940), of the Michelin Tyre Company (1888): the first to use demountable pneumatic tyres on motor vehicles

Michelozzo *n* full name *Michelozzo di Bartolommeo*. 1396–1472, Italian architect and sculptor. His most important design was the Palazzo Riccardo for the Medici family in Florence (1444–59)

Michelson *n Albert Abraham*. 1852–1931, US physicist, born in Germany: noted for his part in the Michelson-Morley experiment: Nobel prize for physics 1907

Michelson-Morley experiment *n* an experiment first performed in 1887 by A. A. Michelson and E. W. Morley, in which an interferometer was used to attempt to detect a difference in the velocities of light in directions parallel and perpendicular to the earth's motion. The negative result was explained by the special theory of relativity

Michigan *n* **1** a state of the N central US, occupying two peninsulas between Lakes Superior, Huron, Michigan, and Erie: generally low-lying. Capital: Lansing. Pop: 10 079 985 (2003 est). Area: 147 156 sq km (56 817 sq miles). Abbreviation: **Mich.**, (with zip code) **MI 2 Lake Michigan** a lake in the N central US between Wisconsin and Michigan: the third largest of the five Great Lakes and the only one wholly in the US; linked with Lake Huron by the Straits of Mackinac. Area: 58 000 sq km (22 400 sq miles)

Michigander *n* a native or inhabitant of Michigan

Michiganite *n* **1** a native or inhabitant of Michigan ▷ *adj* **2** of or relating to Michigan or its inhabitants

Michoacán *n* a state of SW Mexico, on the Pacific: rich mineral resources. Capital: Morelia. Pop: 3 979 177 (2000). Area: 59 864 sq km (23 114 sq miles)

Mick *n offensive, slang* an Irishman [nickname for *Michael*]

mickey *n* **take the mickey (out of)** *informal* to tease (someone) [origin unknown]

Mickey Finn *n slang* a drink containing a drug to make the drinker unconscious [origin unknown]

Mickey Mouse *adj slang* trivial, insignificant, or amateurish: *a Mickey Mouse survey* [after the cartoon character created by Walt Disney]

Mickiewicz *n Adam*. 1798–1855, Polish poet, whose epic *Thaddeus* (1834) is regarded as a masterpiece of Polish literature

mickle *or* **muckle** *archaic or Scot and N English dialect adj* **1** large or abundant ▷ *adv* **2** much; greatly ▷ *n* **3** a great amount [Old Norse *mikell*]

micro *n*, *pl* **micros** short for **microcomputer**, **microprocessor**

micro- *or* **micr-** *combining form* **1** small or minute: *microdot* **2** involving the use of a microscope: *microscopy* **3** denoting 10^{-6}: *microsecond* [Greek *mikros* small]

microbe *n* any microscopic organism, esp. a disease-causing bacterium [MICRO- + Greek *bios* life] **> microbial** *or* **microbic** *adj*

microbiology *n* the branch of biology involving the study of microorganisms

microblog *n* a blog in which there is a limitation on the length of individual postings **> microblogger** *n* **> microblogging** *n*

microchemistry *n* chemical experimentation with minute quantities of material

microchip *n* a tiny wafer of semiconductor material, such as silicon, containing an integrated circuit. Often shortened to: **chip**

microcircuit *n* a miniature electronic circuit in which a number of permanently connected components are contained in one small chip of semiconducting material

microcomputer *n* a compact computer in which the central processing unit is contained in one or more silicon chips

microcosm *n* **1** a miniature representation of something: *this area is a microcosm of France as a whole* **2** man regarded as epitomizing the universe **3 in microcosm** on a small scale [Greek *mikros kosmos* little world] **> microcosmic** *adj*

microdot *n* a greatly reduced photographic copy (about the size of a pinhead) of a document

microeconomics *n* the branch of economics concerned with particular commodities, firms, or individuals and the relationships between them

microelectronics *n* the branch of electronics concerned with microcircuits

microfiche (my-kroh-feesh) *n* same as **fiche** [French, from MICRO- + *fiche* small card]

microfilm *n* **1** a strip of film on which books or documents can be recorded in miniaturized form ▷ *vb* **2** to photograph a page or document on microfilm

microlight *or* **microlite** *n* a very small private aircraft with large wings

micrometer (my-krom-it-er) *n* an instrument for the accurate measurement of small distances or angles

microminiaturization *or* **-risation** *n* the production and use of very small electronic components

micron (my-kron) *n* a unit of length equal to one millionth of a metre [Greek *mikros* small]

Micronesia *n* **1** one of the three divisions of islands in the Pacific (the others being Melanesia and Polynesia); the NW division of Oceania: includes the Mariana, Caroline, Marshall, and Kiribati island groups, and Nauru Island **2 Federated States of Micronesia** an island group in the W Pacific, formerly within the United States Trust Territory of the Pacific Islands: comprises the islands of Truk, Yap, Ponape, and Kosrae: formed in 1979 when the islands became self-governing: status of free association with the US from 1982. Languages: English and Micronesian languages. Religion: Christian majority. Currency: US dollar. Capital: Palikir. Pop: 106 104 (2013 est) [C19: from MICRO- + Greek *nēsos* island; so called from the small size of many of the islands; on the model of *Polynesia*]

microorganism *n* any organism of microscopic size, such as a virus or bacterium

microphone *n* a device for converting sound into electrical energy

microprocessor *n computers* a single integrated circuit which acts as the central processing unit in a small computer

microscope *n* **1** an optical instrument that uses a lens or combination of lenses to produce a greatly magnified image of a small close object **2** any instrument, such as the electron microscope, for producing a greatly magnified visual image of a small object

microscopic *adj* **1** too small to be seen except with a microscope **2** very small; minute **3** of or using a microscope **> microscopically** *adv*

microscopy *n* the use of microscopes

microsecond *n* one millionth of a second

microstructure *n* a structure on a microscopic scale, such as that of a metal or a cell

microsurgery *n* intricate surgery performed using a special microscope and miniature precision instruments

microwave *n* **1** an electromagnetic wave with a wavelength of between 0.3 and 0.001 metres: used in radar and cooking **2** short for **microwave oven** *> vb* **-waving, -waved 3** to cook in a microwave oven

microwave detector *n* a device used by police for recording the speed of a motorist

microwave oven *n* a type of cooker which uses microwaves to cook food quickly

micturate *vb* **-rating, -rated** to urinate [Latin *micturire* to desire to urinate] **> micturition** *n*

mid¹ *n archaic* the middle [Old English]

mid² *or* **'mid** *prep poetic* amid

mid- *combining form* indicating a middle part, point, time, or position: *midday; mid-June; mid-Victorian*

midair *n* some point above ground level, in the air

midday *n* **1** twelve o'clock in the day; noon **2** the middle part of the day, from late morning to early afternoon: *the midday sun*

Middelburg *n* a city in the SW Netherlands, capital of Zeeland province, on Walcheren Island: an important trading centre in the Middle Ages and member of the Hanseatic League; 12th-century abbey; market town. Pop: 46 000 (2003 est)

midden *n Brit and Austral* a dunghill or pile of refuse [from Old Norse]

middle *n* **1** an area or point equal in distance from the ends or edges of a place: *a hotel in the middle of town* **2** the time between the first part and last part of an event or period of time: *the middle of June; the film got a bit boring in the* *middle* **3** the part of the body around the stomach; waist **4 in the middle of** busy doing something: *I'm in the middle of washing the dishes* **> adj 5** equally distant from the ends or outer edges of something; central: *the middle finger* **6** having an equal number of elder and younger brothers and sisters: *he was the middle child of three* **7** intermediate in status or situation: *middle management* **8** avoiding extremes; moderate: *we must find a middle course between authoritarianism and anarchy* [Old English *middel*]

middle age *n* the period of life between youth and old age, usually considered to occur between the ages of 40 and 60 **> middle-aged** *adj*

Middle Ages *n European history* **1** (broadly) the period from the fall of the W Roman Empire in 476 AD to the Italian Renaissance **2** (narrowly) the period from about 1000 AD to the 15th century

middle-age spread *or* **middle-aged spread** *n* the fat that appears round many people's waists when they become middle-aged

Middle America *n* **1** the territories between the US and South America: Mexico, Central America, Panama, and the Greater and Lesser Antilles **2** the US middle class, esp. those groups that are politically conservative

Middle American *adj* **1** of or relating to the territories between the US and South America or their inhabitants **2** of or relating to the US middle class, esp. those groups that are politically conservative *> n* **3** a native or inhabitant of Middle America **4** a member of the US middle class

Middle Atlantic States *or* **Middle States** *pl n* the states of New York, Pennsylvania, and New Jersey

middlebrow *disparaging n* **1** a person with conventional tastes and limited cultural appreciation *> adj* **2** of or appealing to middlebrows

middle C *n music* the note written on the first ledger line below the treble staff or the first ledger line above the bass staff. On a piano it is near the middle of the keyboard

middle class *n* **1** the social class between the working and upper classes. It consists of business and professional people *> adj* **middle-class 2** of or characteristic of the middle class

Middle Congo *n* one of the four territories of former French Equatorial Africa, in W central Africa: became an autonomous member of the French Community, as the Republic of Congo, in 1958

middle-distance *adj* **1** *athletics* of or being a race of a length between the sprints and the distance events, esp. the 800 or 1500 metres: *a middle-distance runner* *> n* **middle distance 2** the part of a painting between the foreground and the far distance

middle ear *n* the sound-conducting part of the ear immediately inside the eardrum

Middle East *n* **1** (loosely) the area around the E Mediterranean, esp. Israel and the Arab countries from Turkey to North Africa and eastwards to Iran **2** (formerly) the area extending from the Tigris and Euphrates to Myanmar

Middle Eastern *adj* of or relating to the Middle East or its inhabitants

Middle England *n* a characterization of a predominantly middle-class, middle-income section of British society, living mainly in suburban and rural England

Middle English *n* the English language from about 1100 to about 1450

Middle High German *n* High German from about 1200 to about 1500

Middle Low German *n* Low German from about 1200 to about 1500

middleman *n, pl* **-men 1** a trader who buys from the producer and sells to the consumer **2** an intermediary or go-between

middle name *n* **1** a name between a person's first name and surname **2** a characteristic quality for which a person is known: *danger is my middle name*

middle-of-the-road *adj* **1** not extreme, esp. in political views; moderate **2** of or denoting popular music of wide general appeal

Middlesbrough *n* an industrial town and unitary authority in NE England; on the Tees estuary; university (1992). The unitary authority was formerly (1974–96) part of Cleveland county. Pop: 135 00 (2008 est.) Area: 54 sq km (21 sq miles)

middle school *n* (in England and Wales) a school for children aged between 8 or 9 and 12 or 13

Middlesex *n* a former county of SE England: became mostly part of N and W Greater London in 1965. Abbreviation: **Middx**

Middle States *pl n* another name for the **Middle Atlantic States**

Middleton[1] *n* a town in NW England, in Rochdale Unitary Authority, Greater Manchester. Pop: 45 314 (2001)

Middleton[2] *n* **1** Kate, real name *Catherine Elizabeth*. born 1982, married Prince William in 2011; created Duchess of Cambridge **2** Thomas. ?1570–1627, English dramatist. His plays include the tragedies *Women beware Women* (1621) and, in collaboration with William Rowley (?1585–?1642), *The Changeling* (1622), and the political satire *A Game at Chess* (1624)

middleweight *n* a professional boxer weighing up to 160 pounds (72.5 kg) or an amateur weighing up to 75 kg

Middle West *n* another name for the **Midwest**

Middle Western *adj* another name for **Midwestern**

Middle Westerner *n* another name for **Midwesterner**

middling *adj* **1** neither very good nor very bad **2** moderate in size **3** fair to middling neither good nor bad, esp. in health ▷ *adv* **4** *informal* moderately: *middling well*

Middx Middlesex

Mideast *n chiefly US* another name for **Middle East**

midfield *n soccer* the area between the two opposing defences

midge *n* a small mosquito-like biting insect occurring in dancing swarms, esp. near water [Old English *mycge*]

midget *n offensive, old-fashioned* **1** a dwarf whose skeleton and features are of normal proportions ▷ *adj* **2** much smaller than normal: *a midget submarine* [*midge* + *-et* small]

Mid Glamorgan *n* a former county of S Wales, formed in 1974 from parts of Breconshire, Glamorgan, and Monmouthshire: replaced in 1996 by the county boroughs of Bridgend, Rhondda Cynon Taff, Merthyr Tydfil, and part of Caerphilly

Midi *n* **1** the south of France **2 Canal du Midi** a canal in S France, extending from the River Garonne at Toulouse to the Mediterranean at Sète and providing a link between the Mediterranean and Atlantic coasts: built between 1666 and 1681. Length: 181 km (150 miles)

MIDI *n* a system for transmitting information to electronic musical instruments [*m(usical) i(nstrument) d(igital) i(nterface)*]

midi- *combining form* of medium or middle size or length: *a midi-skirt*

Midi-Pyrénées *n* a region of SW France: consists of N slopes of the Pyrenees in the south, a fertile lowland area in the west crossed by the River Garonne, and the edge of the Massif Central in the north and east

midi system *n* a complete set of compact hi-fi sound equipment designed as a single unit

midland *n* the central or inland part of a country

Midlander *n* a native or inhabitant of the Midlands of England

Midlands *n* the Midlands (*functioning as sing or pl*) the central counties of England, including Warwickshire, Northamptonshire, Leicestershire, Nottinghamshire, Derbyshire, Staffordshire, the former West Midlands metropolitan county, and Worcestershire: characterized by manufacturing industries

Midlothian *n* a council area of SE central Scotland: the historical county of Midlothian (including Edinburgh) became part of Lothian region in 1975; separate unitary authorities were created for Midlothian and City of Edinburgh in 1996; mainly agricultural. Administrative centre: Dalkeith. Pop: 79 710 (2003 est.). Area: 356 sq km (137 sq miles)

midmost *adj, adv* in the middle or midst

midnight *n* **1** the middle of the night; 12 o'clock at night ▷ *adj* **2** happening or apparent at midnight or in the middle of the night: *midnight Mass* **3 burn the midnight oil** to work or study late into the night

midnight sun *n* the sun visible at midnight during the summer inside the Arctic and Antarctic circles

mid-off *n cricket* the fielding position on the off side closest to the bowler

mid-on *n cricket* the fielding position on the on side closest to the bowler

midpoint *n* **1** the point on a line equally distant from either end **2** a point in time halfway between the beginning and end of an event

midriff *n* **1** the middle part of the human body between waist and chest **2** *anatomy* same as **diaphragm** (1) [Old English *midhrif* mid belly]

midshipman *n, pl* **-men** a naval officer of the lowest commissioned rank

midships *adv, adj nautical* See **amidships**

midst *n* **1 in our midst** among us **2 in the midst of a** surrounded by **b** at a point during

midsummer *n* **1** the middle or height of summer **2** same as **summer solstice**

Midsummer's Day *or* **Midsummer Day** *n* June 24, the feast of St John the Baptist: one of the four quarter days in England, Ireland, and Wales

midtown *n US and Canad* the centre of a town

midway *adj* **1** in or at the middle of the distance; halfway: *the midway point* ▷ *adv* **2** to the middle of the distance

Midway Islands *pl n* an atoll in the central Pacific, about 2100 km (1300 miles) northwest of Honolulu: annexed by the US in 1867: scene of a decisive battle (June, 1942), in which the US combined fleets destroyed Japan's carrier fleet. Pop: 40 (2013 est). Area: 5 sq km (2 sq miles)

midweek *n* the middle of the week

Midwest *or* **Middle West** *n* the N central part of the US; the region consisting of the states from Ohio westwards that border on the Great Lakes, often extended to include the upper Mississippi and Missouri valleys

Midwestern *or* **Middle Western** *adj* of or relating to the Midwest of the US or its inhabitants

Midwesterner *or* **Middle Westerner** *n* a native or inhabitant of the Midwest of the US

mid-wicket *n cricket* the fielding position on the on side, roughly the same distance from both wickets, and halfway towards the boundary

midwife *n, pl* **-wives** a person qualified to deliver babies and to care for women before, during, and after childbirth [Old English *mid* with + *wif* woman] ❯ **midwifery** (mid-wiff-fer-ree) *n*

midwinter *n* **1** the middle or depth of winter **2** same as **winter solstice**

mien (mean) *n literary* a person's manner, bearing, or appearance [probably from obsolete *demean* appearance]

Mieres *n* a city in N Spain, south of Oviedo: steel and chemical industries; iron and coal mines. Pop: 47 618 (2003 est)

Mies van der Rohe *n* Ludwig. 1886–1969, US architect, born in Germany. He directed the Bauhaus (1929–33) and developed a functional style, characterized by geometrical design. His works include the Seagram building, New York (1958)

mifepristone (mi-**fep**-riss-tone) *n* a technical name for **abortion pill**

miffed *adj informal* offended or upset [perhaps imitative of bad temper]

might¹ *vb* **1** the past tense or subjunctive mood of **may**¹: *he might have come* **2** (used as an auxiliary) expressing possibility: *he might well have gone already.* See **may**¹ (2) [Old English *mihte*]

> **USAGE** See at **may**¹.

might² *n* **1** great power, strength, or vigour **2 with all one's might** using all one's strength and energy **3 (with) might and main** See **main** [Old English *miht*]

mighty *adj* **mightier, mightiest 1** powerful or strong **2** very great in extent or importance ▷ *adv* **3** *informal, chiefly US, Canad and Austral* very: *mighty hungry* **> mightily** *adv* **> mightiness** *n*

mignonette (min-yon-**net**) *n* a plant with spikes of small fragrant greenish-white flowers [French, diminutive of *mignon* dainty]

migraine (mee-grain) *n* a throbbing headache usually affecting only one side of the head and commonly accompanied by nausea and visual disturbances [French, from Greek *hēmi* half + *kranion* skull]

migrant *n* **1** a person or animal that moves from one place to another ▷ *adj* **2** moving from one place to another: *migrant farm labourers*

migrate *vb* **-grating, -grated 1** to go from one place to settle in another, esp. in a foreign country **2** (of living creatures, esp. birds) to journey between different habitats at specific times of the year [Latin *migrare* to change one's abode] **> migration** *n* **> migratory** *adj*

mikado *n, pl* **-dos** *archaic* the Japanese emperor [Japanese]

mike *n informal* a microphone

Míkonos *n* transliteration of the Modern Greek name for Mykonos

mil *n photog* short for **millimetre**: *35-mil film* [Latin *millesimus* thousandth]

milady *n, pl* **-dies** (formerly) a continental title for an English gentlewoman

Milan *n* a city in N Italy, in central Lombardy: Italy's second largest city and chief financial and industrial centre; a centre of the Renaissance under the Visconti and Sforza families. Pop: 1 256 211 (2001). Italian name: Milano. Latin name: **Mediolanum**

Milazzo *n* a port in NE Sicily: founded in the 8th century BC; scene of a battle (1860), in which Garibaldi defeated the Bourbon forces. Pop: 32 108 (2001). Ancient name: Mylae

milch (miltch) *adj chiefly Brit* (esp. of cattle) kept for milk [Old English *-milce* (in compounds)]

mild *adj* **1** (of a taste or sensation) not strong; bland **2** gentle or temperate in character, climate, or behaviour **3** not extreme; moderate: *mild criticism of senior officers* **4** feeble; unassertive: *a mild protest* ▷ *n* **5** *Brit* a dark beer flavoured with fewer hops than bitter [Old English *milde*]

mildew *n* **1** a disease of plants caused by a parasitic fungus **2** same as **mould**² ▷ *vb* **3** to affect or become affected with mildew [Old English *mildēaw* honey dew] **> mildewy** *adj*

mild steel *n* strong tough steel containing a small quantity of carbon

mile *n* **1** Also: **statute mile** a unit of length used in the UK, the US and certain other countries, equal to 1760 yards. 1 mile is equivalent to 1.60934 kilometres **2** See **nautical mile 3** Also: **miles** *informal* a great distance; great deal: *he missed by miles* **4** a race extending over a mile ▷ *adv* **5 miles** very much: *it's miles better than their first album* [Latin *mille passuum* a thousand paces]

mileage *n* **1** a distance expressed in miles **2** the total number of miles that a motor vehicle has travelled **3** the number of miles a motor vehicle will travel on one gallon of fuel **4** *informal* the usefulness or benefit of something: *the opposition is trying to make political mileage out of the issue*

mileometer *or* **milometer** (mile-**om**-it-er) *n Brit* a device that records the number of miles that a vehicle has travelled

milepost *n chiefly US and Canad* a signpost that shows the distance in miles to or from a place

miler *n* an athlete, horse, etc., that specializes in races of one mile

Miles *n* Bernard, Baron Miles of Blackfriars. 1907–91, British actor and theatre manager. He founded the Mermaid Theatre in London, and was known as a character actor

milestone *n* **1** a stone pillar that shows the distance in miles to or from a place **2** a significant event in a life or history: *a milestone in Turkish-Bulgarian relations*

Miletus *n* an ancient city on the W coast of Asia Minor: a major Ionian centre of trade and learning in the ancient world

milfoil *n* same as **yarrow** [Latin *mille* thousand + *folium* leaf]

Milford Haven *n* a port in SW Wales, in Pembrokeshire on **Milford Haven** (a large inlet of St George's Channel): major oil port. Pop: 12 830 (2001)

Milhaud *n* Darius. 1892–1974, French composer; member of Les Six. A notable exponent of polytonality, his large output includes operas, symphonies, ballets, string quartets, and songs

Miliband *n* **1** David (**Wright**). born 1965, British Labour politician; foreign secretary (2007–10) **2** his brother, **Ed** (ward Samuel), born 1969, British Labour politician; leader of the Labour Party (2010–2015)

milieu (meal-yuh) *n, pl* **milieux** *or* **milieus** (meal-yuhz) the social and cultural environment in which a person or thing exists: *the film takes for its milieu an apparently wholesome small town* [French]

militant *adj* **1** very active or aggressive in the support of a cause **2** *formal* warring; engaged in warfare ▷ *n* **3** a militant person [Latin *militare* to be a soldier] **> militancy** *n* **> militantly** *adv*

militarism *n* the pursuit of policies intended to create and maintain aggressive and influential armed forces **> militarist** *n, adj* **> militaristic** *adj*

militarized *or* **-rised** *adj* occupied by armed forces: *one of the most heavily militarized borders in the world* **> militarization** *or* **-risation** *n*

military *adj* **1** of or relating to the armed forces or war **2** of or characteristic of soldiers ▷ *n* **3 the military** the armed services, esp. the army [Latin *miles* soldier] **> militarily** *adv*

military police *n* a corps within an army that performs police duties

militate *vb* **-tating, -tated** (of facts or events) to have a strong influence or effect: *our position militated against counter-attacks*

> **USAGE** See at **mitigate**.

militia (mill-**ish**-a) *n* a military force of trained civilians enlisted for use in emergency only [Latin: soldiery] **> militiaman** *n*

milk *n* **1 a** a whitish fluid secreted by the mammary glands of mature female mammals and used for feeding their young **b** the milk of cows, goats, etc., used by humans as a food and to make cheese, butter, and yogurt **2** any similar fluid, such as the juice of a coconut ▷ *vb* **3** to draw milk from the udder of a cow or other animal **4** to extract as much money, help, or value as possible from: *he was accused of milking the situation for his own ends* [Old English *milc*] **> milker** *n* **> milkiness** *n* **> milky** *adj*

milk-and-water *adj* weak, feeble, or insipid

milk bar *n* (formerly) a snack bar at which milk drinks and light refreshments are served

milk chocolate *n* chocolate that has been made with milk, having a creamy taste

milk float *n Brit* a small electrically powered vehicle used to deliver milk to houses

milkmaid *n* a girl or woman who milks cows

milkman *n, pl* **-men** *Brit, Austral and NZ* a man who delivers milk to people's houses

milk of magnesia *n* a suspension of magnesium hydroxide in water, used as an antacid and laxative

milk pudding *n* a pudding made by cooking milk with a grain, esp. rice

milk round *n* **1** *Brit and NZ* a route along which a milkman regularly delivers milk **2** *Brit* a regular series of visits made by recruitment officers from industry to colleges

milk shake *n* a cold frothy drink made of milk, flavouring, and sometimes ice cream, whisked or beaten together

milksop *n* a feeble or ineffectual man or youth

milk tooth *n* any of the first set of teeth in young children

Milky Way *n* **1** the diffuse band of light stretching across the night sky that consists of millions of distant stars in our galaxy **2** the galaxy in which the Earth is situated [translation of Latin *via lactea*]

mill *n* **1** a building where grain is crushed and ground to make flour **2** a factory, esp. one which processes raw materials: *a steel mill* **3** any of various processing or manufacturing machines, esp. one that grinds, presses, or rolls **4** a small device for grinding solids: *a pepper mill* **5** **go** *or* **be put through the mill** to have an unpleasant experience or ordeal ▷ *vb* **6** to grind, press, or process in or as if in a mill **7** to groove or flute the edge of a coin **8** to move about in a confused manner: *the corridor was full of people milling about* [Latin *molere* to grind]

Mill *n* **1** James. 1773–1836, Scottish philosopher, historian, and economist. He expounded Bentham's utilitarian philosophy in *Elements of Political Economy* (1821) and *Analysis of the Phenomena of the Human Mind* (1829) and also wrote a *History of British India* (1817–18) **2** his son, John Stuart. 1806–73, English philosopher and economist. He modified Bentham's utilitarian philosophy in *Utilitarianism* (1861) and in his treatise *On Liberty* (1859) he defended the rights and freedom of the individual. Other works include *A System of Logic* (1843) and *Principles of Political Economy* (1848)

Millais *n* Sir John Everett. 1829–96, English painter, who was a founder of the Pre-Raphaelite Brotherhood. His works include *The Order of Release* (1853) and *The Blind Girl* (1856)

Millau Bridge *n* a road bridge, the highest in the world, crossing the River Tarn in the Massif Central in SW France; designed by Sir Norman Foster and opened in 2004

Millay *n* Edna St Vincent. 1892–1950, US poet, noted esp. for her sonnets; her collections include *The Buck in the Snow* (1928) and *Fatal Interview* (1931)

milled *adj* **1** crushed or ground in a mill: *freshly milled black pepper* **2** (of a coin) having a grooved and often raised edge

millennium (mill-en-nee-um) *n, pl* **-nia** (-nee-a) *or* **-niums 1** a period of one thousand years **2** **the Millennium** *Christianity* the period of a thousand years of Christ's awaited reign upon earth **3** a future period of peace and happiness [Latin *mille* thousand + *annus* year] ▷ **millennial** *adj*

Millennium Bridge *n* a steel bridge for pedestrians over the River Thames linking the City of London at St Paul's Cathedral with the Tate Modern Gallery at Bankside: it has a span of 325 m (1056 ft)

millennium bug *n computers* any software problem arising from the change in date at the start of the 21st century

millepede *n* same as **millipede**

miller *n history* a person who owns or operates a mill, esp. a corn mill

Miller *n* **1** Arthur. 1915–2005, US dramatist. His plays include *Death of a Salesman* (1949), *The Crucible* (1953), *A View from the Bridge* (1955), and *Mr Peters' Connections* (1998) **2** (Alton) Glenn. 1904–44, US composer, trombonist, and band leader. His popular compositions include "Moonlight Serenade". During World War II he was leader of the US Air Force band in Europe. He disappeared without trace on a flight between England and France **3** Henry (Valentine). 1891–1980, US novelist, author of *Tropic of Cancer* (1934) and *Tropic of Capricorn* (1938) **4** Hugh 1802–56, Scottish geologist and writer **5** Sir Jonathan (Wolfe). born 1934, British doctor, actor, and theatre director. His productions include Shakespeare, Ibsen, and Chekhov as well as numerous operas. He has also presented many television medical programmes

miller's thumb *n* a small freshwater European fish with a flattened body [from the alleged likeness of the fish's head to a thumb]

millesimal (mill-less-im-al) *adj* **1** denoting or consisting of a thousandth ▷ *n* **2** a thousandth part of something [Latin *millesimus*]

millet *n* a cereal grass cultivated for its edible grain and as animal fodder [Latin *milium*]

Millet *n* Jean François. 1814–75, French painter of the Barbizon school, noted for his studies of peasants at work

Millett *n* Kate. full name *Katherine Murray Millett*. born 1934, US feminist writer and artist; books include *Sexual Politics* (1969) and *The Politics of Cruelty* (1994)

milli- *combining form* denoting 10^{-3}: millimetre [Latin *mille* thousand]

milliard *n Brit* (no longer in technical use) a thousand million [French]

millibar *n* a unit of atmospheric pressure equal to 100 newtons per square metre

Milligan *n* Spike, real name *Terence Alan Milligan*. 1918–2002, Irish radio, stage, and film comedian and author, born in India. He appeared in *The Goon Show* (with Peter Sellers and Harry Secombe; BBC Radio, 1952–60) and his films include *Postman's Knock* (1962), *Adolf Hitler, My Part in his Downfall* (1972), *The Three Musketeers* (1974), *The Last Remake of Beau Geste* (1977), and *Yellowbeard* (1982). He was awarded an honorary knighthood in 2000

milligram *or* **milligramme** *n* one thousandth of a gram [French]

Millikan *n* Robert Andrews. 1868–1953, US physicist. He measured the charge of an electron (1910), verified Einstein's equation for the photoelectric effect (1916), and studied cosmic rays; Nobel prize for physics 1923

millilitre *or US* **milliliter** *n* a measure of volume equivalent to one thousandth of a litre

millimetre *or US* **millimeter** *n* a unit of length equal to one thousandth of a metre

milliner *n* a person who makes or sells women's hats [originally *Milaner* a native of *Milan*, once famous for its fancy goods] ▷ **millinery** *n*

million *n, pl* **-lions** *or* **-lion 1** the number equal to one thousand thousands: 1 000 000 or 10^6 **2** (often *pl*) informal an extremely large but unspecified number: *I've got a million things to do today* [early Italian *millione*] ▷ **millionth** *n, adj*

millionaire *n* a person who has money or property worth at least a million pounds, dollars, etc. ▷ **millionairess** *fem n*

millipede *or* **millepede** *n* a small crawling animal with a cylindrical many-segmented body, each segment of which bears two pairs of legs [Latin *mille* thousand + *pes* foot]

millisecond *n* one thousandth of a second

millpond *n* a pool which provides water to turn a millwheel

millrace *n* the current of water that turns a millwheel

Mills *n* **1** Hayley. born 1946, British actress. Her films include *Pollyanna* (1960) and *The Parent Trap* (1961) **2** her father, Sir **John**. 1908–2005, British actor. His films include *This Happy Breed* (1944), *Great Expectations* (1946), and *Ryan's Daughter* (1971)

millstone *n* **1** one of a pair of heavy flat stones that are rotated one against the other to grind grain **2** a heavy burden of responsibility or obligation: *the debt had become a millstone round his neck*

millstream *n* a stream of water used to turn a millwheel

millwheel *n* a water wheel that drives a mill

Milne *n* A(lan) A(lexander). 1882–1956, English writer, noted for his books and verse for children, including *When We Were Very Young* (1924) and *Winnie the Pooh* (1926)

milometer (mile-om-it-er) *n* same as **mileometer**

milord *n* (formerly) a continental title used for an English gentleman [from *my lord*]

Mílos *n* transliteration of the Modern Greek name for Melos

Milošević *n* Slobodan. 1941–2006, Serbian politician, president of Serbia (1989–97) and of the Federal Republic of Yugoslavia (1997–2000). He supported ethnic cleansing in Bosnia-Herzegovina (1992–95) and Kosovo (1998–99). He was ousted in 2000 and brought to trial (2001) for war crimes; died in prison before the trial was concluded

Miłosz *n* Czeslaw. 1911–2004, US poet and writer, born in Lithuania, writing in Polish; author of *The Captive Mind* (1953). Nobel prize for literature 1980

Milstein *n* Nathan. 1904–92, US violinist, born in Ukraine

milt *n* the male reproductive gland, sperm, or semen of a fish [Old English *milte* spleen]

Miltiades *n* ?540–?489 BC, Athenian general, who defeated the Persians at Marathon (490)

Milton *n* John. 1608–74, English poet. His early works, notably *L'Allegro* and *Il Penseroso* (1632), the masque *Comus* (1634), and the elegy *Lycidas* (1637), show the influence of his Christian humanist education and his love of Italian Renaissance poetry. A staunch Parliamentarian and opponent of episcopacy, he published many pamphlets during the Civil War period, including *Areopagitica* (1644), which advocated freedom of the press. His greatest works were the epic poems *Paradise Lost* (1667; 1674), and *Paradise Regained* (1671) and the verse drama *Samson Agonistes* (1671)

Milton Keynes *n* **1** a new town in central England, in Milton Keynes unitary authority, N Buckinghamshire: founded in 1967: electronics, clothing, machinery; seat of the Open University. Pop: 184 506 (2001 est) **2** a unitary authority in central England, in Buckinghamshire. Pop: 215 700 (2003). Area: 310 sq km (119 sq miles)

Milwaukee *n* a port in SE Wisconsin, on Lake Michigan: the largest city in the state; established as a trading post in the 18th century; an important industrial centre. Pop: 586 941 (2003 est)

Milwaukeean *adj* **1** of or relating to Milwaukee or its inhabitants ▷ *n* **2** a native or inhabitant of Milwaukee

mime *n* **1** a style of acting using only gesture and bodily movement and not words **2** a performer specializing in this **3** a performance in this style ▷ *vb* **miming, mimed** **4** to express or describe something in actions or gestures without using speech **5** (of musicians) to pretend to be singing or playing music that is actually prerecorded [Greek *mimos* imitator] ▷ **mimer** *n*

Mimeograph (mim-ee-oh-grahf) *n* **1** *trademark* an office machine for printing multiple copies from a stencil ▷ *vb* **2** to print copies using this machine

mimetic (mim-met-ik) *adj* **1** imitating or representing something: *most photographs are mimetic representations of the real world* **2** *biology* of or showing mimicry [Greek *mimeisthai* to imitate]

mimic *vb* **-icking, -icked** **1** to imitate a person or a way of acting or speaking, esp. to entertain or make fun of **2** to take on the appearance of: *certain flies mimic wasps* **3** to

copy closely or in a servile manner: *social climbers in the colonies began to mimic their conquerors* ▷ *n* **4** a person or an animal, such as a parrot, that is clever at mimicking [Greek *mimikos*]

mimicry *n, pl* **-ries** **1** the act or art of copying or imitating closely **2** *biology* the resemblance shown by one animal species to another dangerous or inedible one, which protects it from predators

mimosa *n* a tropical shrub with ball-like clusters of yellow flowers and leaves sensitive to touch and light [Latin *mimus* mime, because the plant's sensitivity to touch imitates the similar reaction of animals]

min. **1** minimum **2** minute *or* minutes

Min. **1** Minister **2** Ministry

Mina Hassan Tani *n* another name for **Kénitra**

Minamoto Yoritomo *n* 1147–99, Japanese nobleman; the first shogun (1192–99) of the feudal era

minaret *n* a slender tower of a mosque with one or more balconies [Arabic *manārat* lamp]

Minas Basin *n* a bay in E Canada, in central Nova Scotia the NE arm of the Bay of Fundy, with which it is linked by **Minas Channel**

Minas Gerais *n* an inland state of E Brazil: situated on the high plateau of the Brazilian Highlands; large reserves of iron ore and manganese. Capital: Belo Horizonte. Pop: 18 343 517 (2002). Area: 587 172 sq km (226 707 sq miles)

minatory *adj* threatening or menacing [Latin *minari* to threaten]

mince *vb* **mincing, minced** **1** to chop, grind, or cut into very small pieces **2** to walk or speak in an affected dainty manner **3 not mince one's words** to be direct and to the point rather than making an effort to avoid upsetting people ▷ *n* **4** *chiefly Brit and NZ* minced meat [Old French *mincier*, from Late Latin *minutia* smallness] ▷ **minced** *adj* ▷ **mincer** *n*

mincemeat *n* **1** a mixture of dried fruit and spices used for filling pies **2 make mincemeat of** *informal* to defeat completely

mince pie *n* a small round pastry tart filled with mincemeat

Minch *n* **the Minch** a channel of the Atlantic divided into the **North Minch** between the mainland of Scotland and the Isle of Lewis, and the **Little Minch** between the Isle of Skye and Harris and North Uist

mincing *adj* (of a person or their style of walking or speaking) affectedly elegant

mind *n* **1** the part of a person responsible for thought, feelings, and intention. Related adjective: **mental** **2** intelligence as opposed to feelings or wishes **3** memory or recollection: *his name didn't spring to mind immediately* **4** a person considered as an intellectual being: *one of Europe's greatest minds* **5** the condition or state of a person's feelings or thoughts: *a confused state of mind* **6** an intention or desire: *I have a mind to go* **7** attention or thoughts: *keep your mind on the job* **8** a sound mental state; sanity: *he's out of his mind* **9 change one's mind** to alter one's decision or opinion **10 give someone a piece of one's mind** to scold someone severely **11 in two minds** undecided or wavering **12 make up one's mind** to reach a decision **13 on one's mind** in one's thoughts **14 to my mind** in my opinion ▷ *vb* **15** to take offence at: *do you mind if I open a window?* **16** to pay attention to: *to mind one's own business* **17** to make certain; ensure: *mind you tell him* **18** to take care of: *mind the shop* **19** to be cautious or careful about: *mind how you go* **20** *dialect* to remember ▷ See also **mind out** [Old English *gemynd*]

Mindanao *n* the second largest island of the Philippines, in the S part of the archipelago: mountainous and volcanic. Chief towns: Davao, Zamboanga. Pop: 13 626 338 (2000). Area: (including offshore islands) 94 631 sq km (36 537 sq miles)

mind-boggling *adj* so large, complicated, or surprising that it causes surprise and shock: *mind-boggling wealth*

minded *adj* having a mind or inclination as specified: *commercially minded*

minder *n* **1** *slang* an aide or assistant, esp. one employed as a bodyguard or public relations officer for someone **2** short for **child minder**

mindful *adj* **mindful of** being aware of and taking into account: *the company is ever mindful of the need to find new markets*

mindfulness *n* **1** the state of being mindful **2** the practice of giving complete, non-judgmental attention to one's present experience, used as a method to reduce stress

mindless *adj* **1** stupid or careless **2** requiring little or no intellectual effort **3** heedless: *mindless of the risks involved* **> mindlessly** *adv* **> mindlessness** *n*

Mind Map *n trademark* a method of representing ideas in a diagram, with related concepts arranged around a core concept

Mindoro *n* a mountainous island in the central Philippines, south of Luzon. Pop: 1 062 000 (2000 est.). Area: 9736 sq km (3759 sq miles)

mind out *vb* to be careful or pay attention

mind-reader *n* a person seemingly able to make out the thoughts of another

mind's eye *n* **in one's mind's eye** in one's imagination

Mindszenty *n* Joseph. 1892–1975, Hungarian cardinal. He was sentenced to life imprisonment on a charge of treason (1949) but released during the 1956 Revolution

mine¹ *pron* **1** something or someone belonging to or associated with me: *it's a great favourite of mine* **2** of mine belonging to or associated with me **> adj 3** *archaic* same as **my**: *mine eyes; mine host* [Old English mīn]

mine² *n* **1** a place where minerals, esp. coal, ores, or precious stones, are dug from the ground **2** a type of bomb placed in water or under the ground, and designed to destroy ships, vehicles, or people passing over or near it **3** a profitable source or abundant supply: *a mine of information* **> vb mining, mined 4** to dig minerals from the ground: *lead has been mined here for over three centuries* **5** to dig a hole or tunnel, esp. in order to obtain minerals **6** to place explosive mines in or on: *the retreating troops had mined the bridge* [Old French]

mine dump *n S African* a large mound of waste material from gold-mining operations

minefield *n* **1** an area of ground or water containing explosive mines **2** a subject or situation full of hidden problems

minelayer *n* a warship or aircraft for carrying and laying mines

miner *n* a person who works in a mine, esp. a coal mine

mineral *n* **1** a naturally occurring solid inorganic substance with a characteristic chemical composition and structure **2** any inorganic matter **3** any substance obtained by mining, esp. a metal ore **4** *Brit* a soft drink containing carbonated water and flavourings **> adj 5** of, containing, or resembling minerals [Medieval Latin *minera* mine, ore]

mineralogy (min-er-al-a-jee) *n* the scientific study of minerals **> mineralogical** *adj* **> mineralogist** *n*

mineral water *n* water containing dissolved mineral salts or gases

Minerva *n* the Roman goddess of wisdom

minestrone (min-ness-**strone**-ee) *n* a soup made from a variety of vegetables and pasta [Italian, from *minestrare* to serve]

minesweeper *n* a naval vessel equipped to clear mines

Ming *adj* of or relating to Chinese porcelain from the time of the Ming dynasty, which ruled China from 1368 to 1644

minger *n Brit informal* unattractive person

minging *n Brit informal* unattractive or unpleasant

mingle *vb* **-gling, -gled 1** to mix or blend **2** to associate or mix with a group of people: *the performers mingled with the audience after the show* [Old English *mengan* to mix]

Mingus *n* Charles, known as *Charlie Mingus*. 1922–79, US jazz double bassist, composer, and band leader

mingy *adj* **-gier, -giest** *Brit and NZ informal* mean or miserly [probably a blend of *mean + stingy*]

Minho *n* the Portuguese name for the **Miño**

mini *adj* **1** small; miniature **2** (of a skirt or dress) very short **> n, pl minis 3** something very small of its kind, esp. a miniskirt

mini- *combining form* smaller or shorter than the standard size: *minibus; miniseries* [from *miniature + minimum*]

miniature *n* **1** a model or representation on a very small scale **2** a very small painting, esp. a portrait **3** a very small bottle of whisky or other spirits, which can hold 50 millilitres **4** in miniature on a small scale **> adj 5** much smaller than usual; small-scale [Medieval Latin *miniare* to paint red (in illuminating manuscripts), from *minium* red lead] **> miniaturist** *n*

miniaturize *or* **-rise** *vb* **-rizing, -rized** *or* **-rising, -rised** to make a very small version of something, esp. electronic components **> miniaturization** *or* **-risation** *n*

minibus *n* a small bus

minicab *n Brit* an ordinary car used as a taxi

minicomputer *n* a small digital computer which is more powerful than a microcomputer

minidisc *n* a small recordable compact disc

minim *n* **1** a unit of fluid measure equal to one sixtieth of a drachm **2** *music* a note with the time value of half a semibreve [Latin *minimus* smallest]

minimal *adj* of the least possible quantity or degree

minimalism *n* **1** a type of music based on the repetition of simple elements **2** a design or style using the simplest and fewest elements to create the maximum effect **> minimalist** *adj, n*

minimize *or* **-mise** *vb* **-mizing, -mized** *or* **-mising, -mised 1** to reduce to the lowest possible degree or amount: *these measures should help minimize our costs* **2** to regard or treat as less important than it really is; belittle: *I don't want to minimize the importance of her contribution*

minimum *n, pl* **-mums** *or* **-ma 1** the least possible amount, degree, or quantity: *fry the burgers in the minimum of oil* **2** the least amount recorded, allowed, or reached: *soak the beans for a minimum of eight hours* **> adj 3** of, being, or showing a minimum or minimums: *the minimum age* [Latin *minimus* least]

minimum lending rate *n* (formerly) the minimum rate at which the Bank of England would lend money: replaced in 1981 by the base rate

minimum wage *n* the lowest wage that an employer is permitted to pay by law or union contract

mining *n* **1** the act, process, or industry of extracting coal or ores from the earth **2** *military* the process of laying mines

minion *n* a servile assistant [French *mignon* darling]

miniseries *n, pl* **-series** a television programme in several parts that is shown on consecutive days over a short period

miniskirt *n* a very short skirt

minister *n* **1** (esp. in Presbyterian and some Nonconformist Churches) a member of the clergy **2** a head of a government department **3** a diplomat with a lower rank than an ambassador **> vb 4** minister to to attend to the needs of [Latin: servant] **> ministerial** *adj*

minister of state *n* (in the British Parliament) a minister, usually below cabinet rank, appointed to assist a senior minister

Minister of the Crown *n Brit* any Government minister of cabinet rank

ministrations *pl n* the giving of help or service: *the ministrations of the chaplain* [Latin *ministrare* to wait upon]

ministry *n, pl* **-tries 1** the profession or duties of a minister of religion **2** ministers considered as a group **3 a** a government department headed by a minister **b** the buildings of such a department

mink *n, pl* **mink** *or* **minks 1** a mammal of Europe, Asia,

m

and North America, resembling a large stoat **2** its highly valued fur **3** a garment made of this, esp. a woman's coat or stole [Scandinavian]

Minkowski *n* Hermann, 1864–1909, German mathematician, born in Russia. His concept of a four-dimensional space-time continuum (1907) proved crucial for the general theory of relativity developed by Einstein

Minn. Minnesota

Minna *n* a city in W central Nigeria, capital of Niger state. Pop: 278 000 (2005 est)

Minneapolis *n* a city in SE Minnesota, on the Mississippi River adjacent to St Paul: the largest city in the state; important centre for the grain trade. Pop: 373 188 (2003 est)

Minnelli *n* Liza. born 1946, US actress and singer, daughter of Judy Garland. Her films include *Charlie Bubbles* (1968), *Cabaret* (1972), *Arthur* (1981), and *Stepping Out* (1991)

minneola *n* a juicy citrus fruit that is a cross between a tangerine and a grapefruit

Minnesota *n* **1** a state of the N central US: chief US producer of iron ore. Capital: St Paul. Pop: 5 059 375 (2003 est). Area: 218 600 sq km (84 402 sq miles). Abbreviation: **Minn.**, (with zip code) **MN 2** a river in S Minnesota, flowing southeast and northeast to the Mississippi River near St Paul. Length: 534 km (332 miles)

Minnesotan *n* **1** a native or inhabitant of Minnesota ▷ *adj* **2** of or relating to Minnesota or its inhabitants

minnow *n*, *pl* **-nows** or **-now** a small slender European freshwater fish [Old English *myne*]

Miño *n* a river in SW Europe, rising in NW Spain and flowing southwest (as part of the border between Spain and Portugal) to the Atlantic. Length: 338 km (210 miles). Portuguese name: Minho

Minoan (min-no-an) *adj* of or denoting the Bronze Age culture of Crete from about 3000 BC to about 1100 BC [*Minos*, in Greek mythology, king of Crete]

Minogue *n* Kylie. born 1968, Australian singer and actress: records include "I Should Be So Lucky" (1988), *Kylie Minogue* (1994), "Can't Get You Out of My Head" (2001), *X* (2007), and *Kiss Me Once* (2014)

minor *adj* **1** lesser or secondary in size, frequency, or importance than others of the same kind: *a minor poet* **2** not very serious or significant: *minor injuries* **3** *music* **a** (of a scale) having a semitone between the second and third and fifth and sixth notes (**natural minor**) **b** of or based on the minor scale: *his quintet in C minor; a minor third* ▷ *n* **4** a person below the age of legal majority **5** *US, Canad and Austral education* a subsidiary subject **6** *music* a minor key, chord, mode, or scale ▷ *vb* **7** **minor in** *US and Canad education* to study as a subsidiary subject: *to minor in politics* [Latin: less, smaller]

Minorca *n* **1** an island in the W Mediterranean, northeast of Majorca: the second largest of the Balearic Islands. Chief town: Mahón. Pop: 78 796 (2002 est). Area: 702 sq km (271 sq miles). Spanish name: **Menorca 2** a breed of light domestic fowl with glossy white, black, or blue plumage

Minorcan *adj* **1** of or relating to Minorca or its inhabitants ▷ *n* **2** a native or inhabitant of Minorca

minority *n*, *pl* **-ties 1** the smaller of two parts, factions, or groups **2** a group that is different, esp. racially or politically, from a larger group of which it is a part **3 in the minority** forming or part of the group of people or things made up of less than half of a larger group ▷ *adj* **4** relating to or being a minority: *a minority sport*

Minotaur *n Greek myth* a monster with the head of a bull and the body of a man [Greek *Minōtauros*]

Minsk *n* the capital of Belarus: an industrial city and educational and cultural centre, with a university (1921). Pop: 1 709 000 (2005 est)

minster *n Brit* any of certain cathedrals and large churches, usually originally connected to a monastery

[Church Latin *monasterium* monastery]

minstrel *n* **1** a medieval singer and musician **2** a performer in a minstrel show [Old French *menestral*]

minstrel show *n* a theatrical entertainment consisting of songs and dances performed by actors wearing black face make-up

mint¹ *n* **1** any of various plants with aromatic leaves used for seasoning and flavouring **2** a sweet flavoured with mint [Greek *minthē*] ▷ **minty** *adj*

mint² *n* **1** a factory where the official coins of a country are made **2** a very large amount of money ▷ *adj* **3 in mint condition** in perfect condition; as if new ▷ *vb* **4** to make coins by stamping metal **5** to invent or create: *no-one knows who first minted the term 'yuppie'* [Latin *moneta* money, mint]

minuet (min-new-et) *n* **1** a stately court dance of the 17th and 18th centuries in triple time **2** music for this dance [French *menuet* dainty]

minus *prep* **1** reduced by the subtraction of: *six minus two equals four* **2** *informal* without or lacking: *he returned minus his jacket* ▷ *adj* **3** indicating or involving subtraction: *a minus sign* **4** Also: **negative** less than zero: *it's minus eight degrees in Montreal today* **5** *education* slightly below the standard of a particular grade: *a C minus for maths* ▷ *n* **6** short for **minus sign 7** a negative quantity **8** *informal* something detrimental or negative [Latin, neuter of *minor* less]

minuscule (min-niss-skyool) *adj* very small [Latin (*littera*) *minuscula* very small (letter)]

minus sign *n* the symbol -, indicating subtraction, a negative quantity, or a negative electrical charge

minute¹ *n* **1** 60 seconds; one sixtieth of an hour **2** any very short period of time; moment: *I'll be with you in a minute* **3** the distance that can be travelled in a minute: *it's about ten minutes away* **4** a measure of angle equal to one sixtieth of a degree **5** **up to the minute** the very latest or newest ▷ *vb* **-nuting, -nuted 6** to record in minutes: *the decision was minuted in 1990*. See also **minutes** [Medieval Latin *minuta*, noun use of Latin *minutus* minute (small)]

minute² *adj* **1** very small; tiny **2** precise or detailed: *a minute examination* [Latin *minutus*, past participle of *minuere* to diminish] ▷ **minutely** *adv*

minutes *pl n* an official record of the proceedings of a meeting or conference

minute steak *n* a small piece of steak that can be cooked quickly

minutiae (my-new-shee-eye) *pl n*, *sing* **-tia** trifling or precise details [Late Latin, plural of *minutia* smallness]

minx *n* a bold or flirtatious girl [origin unknown]

Minya *n* See El Minya

Miocene (my-oh-seen) *adj geology* of the epoch of geological time about 25 million years ago [Greek *meiōn* less + *kainos* new]

Miquelon *n* a group of islands in the French territory of Saint Pierre and Miquelon

Mirabeau *n* Comte de, title of *Honoré-Gabriel Riqueti*. 1749–91, French Revolutionary politician

miracle *n* **1** an event contrary to the laws of nature and attributed to a supernatural cause **2** any amazing and fortunate event: *it's a miracle that no-one was killed in the accident* **3** a marvellous example of something: *a miracle of organization* [Latin *mirari* to wonder at]

miracle play *n* a medieval play based on a biblical story or the life of a saint

miraculous *adj* **1** like a miracle **2** surprising or remarkable

Miraflores *n* Lake Miraflores an artificial lake in Panama, in the S Canal Zone of the Panama Canal

mirage (mir-rahzh) *n* **1** an image of a distant object or sheet of water, often inverted or distorted, caused by atmospheric refraction by hot air **2** something illusory: *the mirage of economic recovery* [French, from (*se*) *mirer* to be reflected]

Miranda *n* Francisco de. 1750–1816, Venezuelan revolutionary, who planned to liberate South and Central America from Spain. A leader (1811–12) of the Venezuelan uprising, he surrendered to Spain and died in prison

mire *n* **1** a boggy or marshy area **2** mud, muck, or dirt **3** an unpleasant or difficult situation that is difficult to get out of: *the country sank deeper into the economic mire* ▷ *vb* **miring, mired 4** to sink or be stuck in a mire: *the company has been mired in financial scandal* [Old Norse *mȳrr*]

Miró *n* Joan. 1893–1983, Spanish surrealist painter

Mirren *n* Dame **Helen**, original name *Ilyena Vasilievna Mironov*, born 1945, English actor; her films include *Savage Messiah* (1972), *The Long Good Friday* (1980), *The Cook, The Thief, His Wife and Her Lover* (1989) and *The Queen* (2006), for which she won an Academy Award for Best Actress

mirror *n* **1** a sheet of glass with a metal coating on its back, that reflects an image of an object placed in front of it **2** a thing that reflects or depicts something else ▷ *vb* **3** to reflect or represent faithfully: *the book inevitably mirrors my own interests* [Latin *mirari* to wonder at]

mirror ball *n* a large revolving ball covered with small pieces of mirror glass so that it reflects light in changing patterns: used in discos and ballrooms

mirror image *n* an image or object that has left and right reversed as if seen in a mirror

mirth *n* laughter, gaiety, or merriment [Old English *myrgth*] **> mirthful** *adj* **> mirthless** *adj*

MIRV multiple independently targeted re-entry vehicle: a missile that has several warheads, each one being aimed at a different target

Mirvis *n* **Ephraim**. born 1956, British rabbi, born in South Africa; Commonwealth chief rabbi from 2013

mis- *prefix* **1** wrong or bad; wrongly or badly: *misunderstanding*; *mislead* **2** lack of; not: *mistrust* [Old English *mis(se)-*]

misadventure *n* **1** an unlucky event; misfortune **2** *law* accidental death not due to crime or negligence

misaligned *adj* not properly aligned; out of true **> misalignment** *n*

misalliance *n* an unsuitable alliance or marriage

misanthrope (miz-zan-*thrope*) *or* **misanthropist** (miz-*zan*-throp-ist) *n* a person who dislikes or distrusts people in general [Greek *misos* hatred + *anthrōpos* man] **> misanthropic** (miz-zan-*throp*-ik) *adj* **> misanthropy** (miz-*zan*-throp-ee) *n*

misapply *vb* **-plies, -plying, -plied** to use something for a purpose for which it is not intended or is not suited **> misapplication** *n*

misapprehend *vb* to misunderstand **> misapprehension** *n*

misappropriate *vb* **-ating, -ated** to take and use money dishonestly **> misappropriation** *n*

misbegotten *adj* **1** planned or designed badly or with dishonourable motives or aims **2** *literary or dialect* illegitimate; bastard

misbehave *vb* **-having, -haved** to behave badly **> misbehaviour** *or US* **misbehavior** *n*

miscalculate *vb* **-lating, -lated** to calculate or judge wrongly: *we miscalculated the strength of the opposition* **> miscalculation** *n*

miscall *vb* to call by the wrong name

miscarriage *n* **1** spontaneous premature expulsion of a fetus from the womb, esp. before the 20th week of pregnancy **2** an act of mismanagement or failure: *a miscarriage of justice*

miscarry *vb* **-ries, -rying, -ried 1** to expel a fetus prematurely from the womb **2** to fail

miscast *vb* **-casting, -cast** to cast a role or an actor in a play or film inappropriately: *the role of the avaricious boss was miscast; she was miscast as Cassandra*

miscegenation (miss-ij-in-*nay*-shun) *n* interbreeding of races, esp. where differences of colour are involved [Latin *miscere* to mingle + *genus* race]

miscellaneous (miss-sel-*lane*-ee-uss) *adj* composed of or containing a variety of things; mixed or assorted [Latin *miscere* to mix]

miscellany (miss-*sell*-a-nee) *n, pl* **-nies** a mixed assortment of items

mischance *n* **1** bad luck **2** an unlucky event or accident

mischief *n* **1** annoying but not malicious behaviour that causes trouble or irritation **2** an inclination to tease **3** injury or harm caused by a person or thing [Old French *meschief*, from *mes-* mis- + *chef* end]

mischief-maker *n* someone who deliberately causes trouble **> mischief-making** *n*

mischievous (miss-*chiv*-uss) *adj* **1** full of mischief **2** teasing; slightly malicious **3** intended to cause harm: *a purveyor of mischievous disinformation* **> mischievously** *adv*

miscible (miss-*sib*-bl) *adj* able to be mixed: *miscible with water* [Latin *miscere* to mix] **> miscibility** *n*

misconceived *adj* false, mistaken, or badly thought-out: *a misconceived conception of loyalty*

misconception *n* a false or mistaken view, idea, or belief

misconduct *n* behaviour, such as adultery or professional negligence, that is regarded as immoral or unethical

misconstrue *vb* **-struing, -strued** to interpret mistakenly **> misconstruction** *n*

miscreant (miss-*kree*-ant) *n* a wrongdoer or villain [Old French *mescreant* unbelieving]

misdeal *vb* **-dealing, -dealt 1** to deal out cards incorrectly ▷ *n* **2** a faulty deal

misdeed *n* an evil or illegal action

misdemeanour *or US* **misdemeanor** *n* **1** a minor wrongdoing **2** *criminal law* (formerly) an offence less serious than a felony

misdirect *vb* to give someone wrong directions or instructions **> misdirection** *n*

mise en scène (meez on sane) *n* **1** the stage setting and scenery in a play **2** the environment of an event [French]

Miseno *n* a cape in SW Italy, on the N shore of the Bay of Naples: remains of the town of **Misenum**, a naval base constructed by Agrippa in 31 BC

miser *n* a person who hoards money and hates spending it: *I'm married to a miser* [Latin: wretched] **> miserly** *adj*

miserable *adj* **1** unhappy or depressed; wretched **2** causing misery or discomfort: *a miserable existence* **3** sordid or squalid: *miserable living conditions* **4** mean or ungenerous: *a miserable pension* [Latin *miserabilis*] **> miserableness** *n* **> miserably** *adv*

misericord *n* a ledge projecting from the underside of the hinged seat of a choir stall in a church, which the occupant can rest against while standing [Latin *miserere* to pity + *cor* heart]

misery *n, pl* **-eries 1** intense unhappiness or suffering **2** something which causes such unhappiness **3** squalid or poverty-stricken conditions **4** *Brit informal* a person who is habitually depressed: *he is such a misery* [Latin *miser* wretched]

misfire *vb* **-firing, -fired 1** (of a firearm) to fail to fire as expected **2** (of a motor engine or vehicle) to fail to fire at the appropriate time **3** to fail to have the intended result; go wrong: *he was injured when a practical joke misfired* ▷ *n* **4** the act or an instance of misfiring

misfit *n* a person who is not suited to the role, social group, etc., he or she finds himself or herself in

misfortune *n* **1** bad luck **2** an unfortunate event

misgivings *pl n* feelings of uncertainty, fear, or doubt

misgovern *vb* to govern badly **> misgovernment** *n*

misguided *adj* mistaken or unwise

mishandle *vb* **-dling, -dled** to handle or treat badly or inefficiently

mishap *n* a minor accident

mishear *vb* **-hearing, -heard** to fail to hear what someone says correctly

Mishima *n* Yukio. 1925–70, Japanese novelist and

short-story writer, whose works reflect a preoccupation with homosexuality and death. He committed harakiri in protest at the decline of traditional Japanese values

mishit *sport n* **1** a faulty shot, kick, or stroke ▷ *vb* **-hitting, -hit** **2** to hit or kick a ball with a faulty stroke

mishmash *n* a confused collection or mixture [reduplication of *mash*]

misinform *vb* to give incorrect information to ⟩ **misinformation** *n*

misinterpret *vb* to understand or represent something wrongly: *the press misinterpreted the President's remarks* ⟩ **misinterpretation** *n*

misjudge *vb* **-judging, -judged** to judge wrongly or unfairly ⟩ **misjudgment** *or* **misjudgement** *n*

Miskolc *n* a city in NE Hungary: the second most important industrial centre in Hungary; iron and steel industries. Pop: 180 282 (2003 est)

mislay *vb* **-lays, -laying, -laid** to lose something temporarily, esp. by forgetting where it is

mislead *vb* **-leading, -led** to give false or confusing information to

misleading *adj* giving a false or confusing impression: *misleading use of statistical data*

mismanage *vb* **-naging, -naged** to organize or run something badly ⟩ **mismanagement** *n*

mismatch *vb* **1** to form an unsuitable partner, opponent, or set ▷ *n* **2** an unsuitable match ⟩ **mismatched** *adj*

misnamed *adj* having an inappropriate or misleading name: *the grotesquely misnamed Freedom Party*

misnomer (miss-no-mer) *n* **1** an incorrect or unsuitable name for a person or thing **2** the use of the wrong name [Old French *mesnommer* to misname]

misogyny (miss-oj-in-ee) *n* hatred of women [Greek *misos* hatred + *gunē* woman] ⟩ **misogynist** *n* ⟩ **misogynous** *adj*

misplace *vb* **-placing, -placed** **1** to lose something temporarily by forgetting where it was placed **2** to put something in the wrong place

misplaced *adj* **1** (of an emotion or action) directed towards a person or thing that does not deserve it: *misplaced optimism* **2** put in the wrong place: *a scrappy game dominated by misplaced kicking*

misprint *n* **1** an error in printing ▷ *vb* **2** to print a letter incorrectly

misprision *n law* the concealment of the commission of a felony or an act of treason [Old French *mesprision* error]

mispronounce *vb* **-nouncing, -nounced** to pronounce a word or name wrongly ⟩ **mispronunciation** *n*

misquote *vb* **-quoting, -quoted** to quote inaccurately ⟩ **misquotation** *n*

misread *vb* **-reading, -read** **1** to misinterpret or misunderstand: *he misread her politeness as approval* **2** to read incorrectly

misrepresent *vb* to represent wrongly or inaccurately ⟩ **misrepresentation** *n*

misrule *vb* **-ruling, -ruled** **1** to govern inefficiently or without justice ▷ *n* **2** inefficient or unjust government **3** disorder or lawlessness

miss¹ *vb* **1** to fail to notice, see, or hear: *it's right at the top of the hill, so you can't miss it*; *I missed what he said because I was talking at the time* **2** to fail to hit something aimed at: *he threw a stone at the dog but missed* **3** to fail to achieve or reach: *they narrowly missed promotion last season* **4** to fail to take advantage of: *he never missed a chance to make money* **5** to fail or be unable to be present: *he had missed the last three meetings* **6** to be too late for: *we missed the bus and had to walk* **7** to discover or regret the loss or absence of: *the boys miss their father when he's away on business* **8** to escape or avoid narrowly: *it missed the helicopter's rotors by inches* ▷ *n* **9** a failure to hit, reach, etc.: *an easy miss in the second frame gave his opponent the advantage* **10** **give something a miss** to decide not to do, go to, or take part in something: *I'll give the pub a miss and have a quiet night in* ▶ See also **miss out** [Old English *missan*]

miss² *n informal* an unmarried woman or girl [from *mistress*]

Miss *n* a title of a girl or unmarried woman, usually used before the surname: *Miss Brown to you*

Miss. Mississippi

missal *n RC Church* a book containing the prayers and rites of the Masses for a complete year [Church Latin *missale*, from *missa* Mass]

misshapen *adj* badly shaped; deformed

missile *n* **1** a rocket with an exploding warhead, used as a weapon **2** an object or weapon that is thrown, launched, or fired at a target [Latin *mittere* to send]

missing *adj* **1** not in its proper or usual place and unable to be found **2** not able to be traced and not known to be dead: *seven men were reported missing after the raid* **3** not included in something although it perhaps should have been: *two things are missing from the report*

missing link *n* **1** any missing section or part in a series **2** **the missing link** a hypothetical extinct animal, formerly thought to be intermediate between the apes and man

mission *n* **1** a specific task or duty assigned to a person or group of people **2** a task or duty that a person believes he or she must achieve; vocation: *he felt it was his mission to pass on his knowledge to other people* **3** a group of people representing or working for a particular country or organization in a foreign country: *the UN peacekeeping mission* **4** a group of people sent by a church to a foreign country to do religious and social work **5** the place in which a church or government mission is based **6** the dispatch of aircraft or spacecraft to achieve a particular task **7** a charitable centre that offers shelter or aid to poor or needy people **8** *S African* a long and difficult process [Latin *mittere* to send]

missionary *n, pl* **-naries** **1** a person sent abroad by a church to do religious and social work ▷ *adj* **2** of or relating to missionaries: *missionary work* **3** resulting from a desire to convert people to one's own beliefs: *missionary zeal*

Missionary Ridge *n* a ridge in NW Georgia and SE Tennessee: site of a battle (1863) during the Civil War: Northern victory leading to the campaign in Georgia

mission statement *n* an official statement of the aims and objectives of a business or other organization

Mississauga *n* a town in SE Ontario: a SW suburb of Toronto. Pop: 612 925 (2001)

Mississippi *n* **1** a state of the southeastern US, on the Gulf of Mexico: consists of a largely forested undulating plain, with swampy regions in the northwest and on the coast, the Mississippi River forming the W border; cotton, rice, and oil. Capital: Jackson. Pop: 2 881 281 (2003 est). Area: 122 496 sq km (47 296 sq miles). Abbreviation: **Miss.**, (with zip code) **MS** **2** a river in the central US, rising in NW Minnesota and flowing generally south to the Gulf of Mexico through several mouths, known as the Passes: the second longest river in North America (after its tributary, the Missouri), with the third largest drainage basin in the world (after the Amazon and the Congo). Length: 3780 km (2348 miles)

Mississippian *adj* **1** of or relating to the state of Mississippi or the Mississippi River **2** (in North America) of, denoting, or formed in the lower of two subdivisions of the Carboniferous period, which lasted for 30 million years. See also **Pennsylvanian** (2) ▷ *n* **3** an inhabitant or native of the state of Mississippi **4** the **Mississippian** the Mississippian period or rock system equivalent to the lower Carboniferous of Europe

missive *n* a formal or official letter [Latin *mittere* to send]

Missolonghi *or* **Mesolonghi** *n* a town in W Greece, near the Gulf of Patras: famous for its defence against the Turks in 1822–23 and 1825–26 and for its association with Lord Byron, who died here in 1824. Pop (municipality): 18 354 (2001). Modern Greek name: **Mesolóngion**

Missouri *n* **1** a state of the central US: consists of rolling prairies in the north, the Ozark Mountains in the south, and part of the Mississippi flood plain in the southeast, with the Mississippi forming the E border; chief US producer of lead and barytes. Capital: Jefferson City. Pop: 5 704 484 (2003 est). Area: 178 699 sq km (68 995 sq miles). Abbreviation: **Mo.**, (with zip code) **MO 2** a river in the W and central US, rising in SW Montana: flows north, east, and southeast to join the Mississippi above St Louis; the longest river in North America; chief tributary of the Mississippi. Length: 3970 km (2466 miles)

Missourian *n* **1** a native or inhabitant of Missouri ▷ *adj* **2** of or relating to Missouri or its inhabitants

miss out *vb* **1** to leave out or overlook **2** miss out on to fail to take part in (something enjoyable or beneficial): *she'd missed out on going to university*

misspell *vb* **-spelling, -spelt** *or* **-spelled** to spell a word wrongly ⟩ **misspelling** *n*

misspend *vb* **-spending, -spent** to waste or spend unwisely ⟩ **misspent** *adj*

missus *or* **missis** *n* **1** Brit, Austral and NZ informal one's wife or the wife of the person addressed or referred to: *the missus is a fabulous cook* **2** an informal term of address for a woman [spoken version of *mistress*]

missy *n, pl* **missies** informal an affectionate or disparaging form of address to a girl

mist *n* **1** a thin fog **2** a fine spray of liquid, such as that produced by an aerosol container **3** condensed water vapour on a surface **4** something that causes haziness or lack of clarity, such as a film of tears ▷ *vb* **5** to cover or be covered with mist: *the windscreen has misted up again; his eyes misted over and he shook with rage* [Old English] ⟩ **misty** *adj* ⟩ **mistiness** *n*

mistake *n* **1** an error or blunder **2** a misconception or misunderstanding ▷ *vb* **-taking, -took, -taken 3** to misunderstand or misinterpret: *the chaplain quite mistook her meaning* **4** to confuse a person or thing with another: *they saw the HMS Sheffield and mistook her for the Bismarck* **5** to choose badly or incorrectly: *he mistook his path* [Old Norse *mistaka* to take erroneously]

mistaken *adj* **1** wrong in opinion or judgment **2** arising from error in opinion or judgment: *a mistaken viewpoint*

Mistassini *n* Lake Mistassini a lake in E Canada, in N Quebec: the largest lake in the province; drains through the Rupert River into James Bay. Area: 2175 sq km (840 sq miles). Length: about 160 km (100 miles)

mister *n* an informal form of address for a man [variant of *master*]

Mister *n* the full form of **Mr**

Misti *n* See El Misti

mistime *vb* **-timing, -timed** to do or say at the wrong time

Mistinguett *n* original name *Jeanne-Marie Bourgeois*. 1875–1956, French dancer, chanteuse, and entertainer

mistle thrush *or* **missel thrush** *n* a large European thrush with a brown back and spotted breast [Old English *mistel* mistletoe]

mistletoe *n* a Eurasian evergreen shrub with waxy white berries, which grows as a parasite on various trees [Old English *misteltān*, from *mistel* mistletoe + *tān* twig]

mistook *vb* the past tense of **mistake**

mistral *n* a strong cold dry northerly wind of S France [Provençal, from Latin *magistralis* masterful]

Mistral *n* **1** Frédéric. 1830–1914, French Provençal poet, who led a movement to revive Provençal language and literature: shared the Nobel prize for literature 1904 **2** Gabriela, pen name of *Lucila Godoy de Alcayaga*. 1889–1957, Chilean poet, educationalist, and diplomatist. Her poetry includes the collection *Desolación* (1922): Nobel prize for literature 1945

mistreat *vb* to treat badly ⟩ **mistreatment** *n*

mistress *n* **1** a woman who has a continuing sexual relationship with a man who is usually married to somebody else **2** a woman in a position of authority,

ownership, or control **3** a woman having control over something specified: *she is a mistress of disguise* **4** chiefly Brit a female teacher [Old French *maistresse*]

mistrial *n* law a trial which is invalid because of some error

mistrust *vb* **1** to have doubts or suspicions about ▷ *n* **2** lack of trust ⟩ **mistrustful** *adj* ⟩ **mistrustfully** *adv*

misunderstand *vb* **-standing, -stood** to fail to understand properly

misunderstanding *n* **1** a failure to understand properly **2** a disagreement

misunderstood *adj* not properly or sympathetically understood: *a misunderstood adolescent*

misuse *n* **1** incorrect, improper, or careless use: *misuse of drugs* **2** cruel or inhumane treatment ▷ *vb* **-using, -used 3** to use wrongly **4** to treat badly or harshly

Mitchell *n* **1** Joni, original name *Roberta Joan Anderson*. born 1943, Canadian folk-rock singer and songwriter. Her albums include *Blue* (1971), *Court and Spark* (1974), *Mingus* (1979), *Turbulent Indigo* (1994), and *Shine* (2007) **2** Margaret. 1900–49, US novelist; author of *Gone with the Wind* (1936) **3** Reginald Joseph. 1895–1937, British aeronautical engineer; designer of the Spitfire fighter **4** Sir Thomas Livingstone, known as *Major Mitchell*. 1792–1855, Australian explorer born in Scotland

Mitchum *n* Robert. 1917–97, US film actor. His many films include *Night of the Hunter* (1955) and *Farewell my Lovely* (1975)

mite¹ *n* any of numerous very small creatures of the spider family, some of which live as parasites [Old English *mite*]

mite² *n* **1** a very small creature or thing **2** a very small sum of money **3 a mite** informal somewhat: *the main course was a mite bland* [Middle Dutch *mite*]

Mithridates VI *or* **Mithradates VI** *n* called *the Great*. ?132–63 BC, king of Pontus (?120–63). He waged three wars against Rome (88–84; 83–81; 74–64) and was finally defeated by Pompey: committed suicide

mitigate *vb* **-gating, -gated** to make less severe or harsh [Latin *mitis* mild + *agere* to make] ⟩ **mitigating** *adj* ⟩ **mitigation** *n*

> **USAGE** *Mitigate* is sometimes wrongly used where *militate* is meant: *his behaviour militates* (not *mitigates*) *against his chances of promotion.*

Mitilíni *n* transliteration of the Modern Greek name for Mytilene (1)

mitochondrion *n, pl* **-dria** biology a small spherical or rodlike body found in the cytoplasm of most cells [Greek *mitos* thread + *khondrion* grain]

mitosis *n* a type of cell division in which the nucleus divides into two nuclei each containing the same number of chromosomes as the parent nucleus [Greek *mitos* thread]

mitre *or* US **miter** (my-ter) *n* **1** Christianity the headdress of a bishop or abbot, consisting of a tall pointed cleft cap **2** Also: **mitre joint** a corner joint formed by cutting bevels of equal angles at the ends of each piece of material ▷ *vb* **-tring, -tred** *or* **-tering, -tered 3** to join with a mitre joint [Greek *mitra* turban]

mitt *n* **1** a glovelike hand covering that does not cover the fingers **2** short for **mitten 3** slang a hand **4** a baseball glove [from *mitten*]

Mittelland Canal *n* a canal in Germany, linking the Rivers Rhine and Elbe. Length: 325 km (202 miles)

mitten *n* a glove with one section for the thumb and a single section for the fingers [Old French *mitaine*]

Mitterrand *n* François (Maurice Marie). 1916–96, French statesman; first secretary of the socialist party (1971–95); president (1981–95)

mix *vb* **1** to combine or blend into one mass or substance: *mix the water, yeast, and flour into a smooth dough* **2** to be able to combine into one substance: *oil and water do not mix* **3** to form by combining different substances: *to mix cement* **4** to do at the same time: *to mix business and pleasure* **5** to be outgoing in social situations: *he mixed well* **6** *music* to balance and adjust individual performers' parts to make an overall sound by electronic means ▷ *n* **7** something produced by mixing; mixture **8** a mixture of ingredients, esp. one commercially prepared for making a cake **9** *music* the sound produced by mixing ▶ See also mix-up [Latin *miscere*] ⟩ **mixed** *adj*

mixed bag *n informal* something made up of different elements, characteristics, or people

mixed blessing *n* an event or situation with both advantages and disadvantages

mixed doubles *n tennis, badminton* a doubles game with a man and a woman as partners on each side

mixed economy *n* an economy in which some companies are privately owned and others are owned by the government

mixed farming *n* farming involving both the growing of crops and the keeping of livestock ⟩ **mixed farm** *n*

mixed grill *n* a dish of several kinds of grilled meat, tomatoes, and mushrooms

mixed marriage *n* a marriage between people of different races or religions

mixed metaphor *n* a combination of incongruous metaphors, such as *when the Nazi jackboots sing their swan song*

mixed-up *adj* in a state of mental confusion

mixer *n* **1** a kitchen appliance, usually electrical, used for mixing foods **2** any of various other devices or machines used for mixing things: *a cement mixer* **3** a nonalcoholic drink such as tonic water or ginger ale that is mixed with an alcoholic drink **4** *informal* a person considered in relation to his or her ability to mix socially: *he's not a good mixer*

mixture *n* **1** something produced by blending or combining other things: *top with the cheese and breadcrumb mixture* **2** a combination of different things, such as feelings: *he speaks of her with a mixture of loyalty and regret* **3** *chem* a substance consisting of two or more substances mixed together without any chemical bonding between them

mix-up *n* **1** a confused condition or situation ▷ *vb* **mix up** **2** to make into a mixture **3** to confuse: *he mixes Ryan up with Lee* **4** **mixed up in** involved in (an activity or group, esp. one that is illegal): *she's mixed up in a drugs racket*

Mizoguchi *n* Kenji. 1898–1956, Japanese film director. His films include *A Paper Doll's Whisper of Spring* (1925), *Woman of Osaka* (1940), and *Ugetsu Monogatari* (1952)

Mizoram *n* a state (since 1986) in NE India, created in 1972 from the former Mizo Hills District of Assam. Capital: Aijal. Pop: 891 058 (2001). Area: about 21 081 sq km (8140 sq miles)

mizzenmast *n nautical* (on a vessel with three or more masts) the third mast from the bow [Italian *mezzano* middle + MAST]

MJ megajoule

Mk (in trade names) mark

mks units *pl n* a metric system of units based on the metre, kilogram, and second: it forms the basis of the SI units

ml **1** millilitre(s) **2** mile(s)

ML Medieval Latin

Mladic *n* Ratko. born 1943, Bosnian military figure, commander of the Bosnian Serb forces during the civil war of 1992–95; indicted by the UN for war crimes, including the massacre of 6000 Bosnian Muslims at Srebrenica (1995); his trial at an international criminal tribunal in the Hague began in 2012

MLitt Master of Letters [Latin *Magister Litterarum*]

Mlle *or* **Mlle.** *pl* **Mlles** *or* **Mlles.** the French equivalent of *Miss* [from *Mademoiselle*]

MLR minimum lending rate

mm millimetre(s)

Mmabatho *n* the capital of the former homeland of Bophuthatswana

Mme *pl* **Mmes** the French equivalent of *Mrs* [from *Madame, Mesdames*]

MMORPG (more-peg) massive(ly) multi-player online role-playing game: an internet-based computer game set in a virtual world, where many people can play at the same time and interact with each other

MMR a combined vaccine against measles, mumps, and rubella, given to very young children

MMus Master of Music

Mn *chem* manganese

MN Minnesota

mnemonic (nim-on-ik) *n* **1** something, for instance a verse, intended to help the memory ▷ *adj* **2** aiding or meant to aid one's memory [Greek *mnēmōn* mindful] ⟩ **mnemonically** *adv*

mo *n informal, chiefly Brit* short for **moment** (1)

Mo *chem* molybdenum

MO **1** Medical Officer **2** Missouri

Mo. Missouri

m.o. *or* **MO** **1** mail order **2** money order

moa *n* a recently extinct large flightless bird of New Zealand that resembled the ostrich [Māori]

Moab *n Old Testament* an ancient kingdom east of the Dead Sea, in what is now the SW part of Jordan: flourished mainly from the 9th to the 6th centuries BC

Moabite *Old Testament adj* **1** of or relating to Moab or its inhabitants ▷ *n* **2** a native or inhabitant of Moab

moan *n* **1** a low prolonged cry of pain or suffering **2** any similar sound, esp. that made by the wind **3** *informal* a grumble or complaint ▷ *vb* **4** to make a low cry of, or talk in a way suggesting, pain or suffering: *he moaned in pain* **5** to make a sound like a moan: *the wind moaned through the trees* **6** *informal* to grumble or complain [Old English *mǣnan* to grieve over] ⟩ **moaner** *n*

moat *n* a wide ditch, originally filled with water, surrounding a fortified place such as a castle [Old French *motte* mound]

mob *n* **1** a riotous or disorderly crowd of people **2** *informal* any group of people **3** the masses **4** *slang* a gang of criminals ▷ *vb* **mobbing, mobbed** **5** to attack in a group resembling a mob **6** to surround in a crowd to acclaim or attack: *she was mobbed by her fans when she left the theatre* [shortened from Latin *mobile vulgus* the fickle populace]

mobcap *n* a woman's 18th-century cotton cap with a pouched crown [obsolete *mob* woman, esp. loose-living + CAP]

mobile *adj* **1** able to move or be moved: *mobile toilets* **2** changing quickly in expression: *a mobile face* **3** *sociol* (of individuals or social groups) moving within and between classes, occupations, and localities ▷ *n* **4** a light structure suspended in midair with delicately balanced parts that are set in motion by air currents **5** short for **mobile phone** [Latin *mobilis*] ⟩ **mobility** *n*

Mobile *n* a port in SW Alabama, on **Mobile Bay** (an inlet of the Gulf of Mexico): the state's only port and its first permanent settlement, made by French colonists in 1711. Pop: 193 464 (2003 est)

mobile home *n* a large caravan, usually staying in one place, which people live in permanently

mobile phone *n* a portable telephone powered by batteries

mobilize *or* **-lise** *vb* **-lizing, -lized** *or* **-lising, -lised** **1** to prepare for war or another emergency by organizing resources and the armed services **2** to organize for a purpose: *we must mobilize local residents behind our campaign* ⟩ **mobilization** *or* **-lisation** *n*

mobster *n US* a member of a criminal organization; gangster

Mobutu[1] *n* the former name (until 1997) of **Lake Albert**. See **Albert**

Mobutu[2] *n* Sese Seko, original name *Joseph*. 1930–97, Zaïrese statesman; president of Zaïre (now the

Democratic Republic of Congo) (1970–97); accused of corruption and overthrown by rebels in 1997; died in exile

Moçambique n the Portuguese name for **Mozambique**

moccasin n **1** a type of soft leather shoe traditionally worn by some Native American peoples **2** a soft leather shoe with a raised seam at the front above the toe [American Indian]

mocha (mock-a) n **1** a dark brown coffee originally imported from Mocha **2** a flavouring made from coffee and chocolate

Mocha or **Mokha** n a port in Yemen, on the Red Sea; in the former North Yemen until 1990: formerly important for the export of Arabian coffee. Pop: 14 562 (2005 est)

mock vb **1** to behave with scorn or contempt towards a person or thing: *her husband mocked her attempts to educate herself* **2** to imitate or mimic, esp. in fun **3** to defy or frustrate: *the team mocked the visitors' attempts to score* ▷ n **4 mocks** informal (in England and Wales) school examinations taken as practice before public exams ▷ adj **5** sham or imitation: *mock Georgian windows* **6** serving as an imitation or substitute, esp. for practice purposes: *a mock battle* ▶ See also **mock-up** [Old French *mocquer*] ⟩ **mocking** n, adj

mockers pl n **put the mockers on** Brit, Austral and NZ informal to ruin the chances of success of [perhaps from *mock*]

mockery n, pl **-eries 1** ridicule, contempt, or derision **2** a person, thing, or action that is so worthless that it seems like a parody: *the interview was a mockery from start to finish* **3 make a mockery of something** to make something appear worthless or foolish: *the judge's decision makes a mockery of the law*

mock-heroic adj (of a literary work, esp. a poem) imitating the style of heroic poetry in order to satirize an unheroic subject

mockingbird n an American songbird which can mimic the song of other birds

mock orange n a shrub with white fragrant flowers like those of the orange

mock turtle soup n an imitation turtle soup made from a calf's head

mock-up n a working full-scale model of a machine or apparatus for test or research purposes

mod¹ n Brit a member of a group of teenagers, originally in the mid-1960s, who were very clothes-conscious and rode motor scooters [from *modernist*]

mod² n an annual Highland Gaelic meeting with musical and literary competitions [Gaelic *mòd* assembly]

MOD (in Britain) Ministry of Defence

mod. 1 moderate **2** modern

modal (mode-al) adj **1** of or relating to mode or manner **2** grammar (of a verb form or auxiliary verb) expressing possibility, intention, or necessity rather than actuality: 'can', 'might', and 'will' are examples of modal verbs in English **3** music of or relating to a mode ⟩ **modality** n

mod cons pl n informal modern conveniences, such as hot water and heating

mode n **1** a manner or way of doing, acting, or existing **2** a particular fashion or style **3** music any of the various scales of notes within one octave **4** maths the most frequently occurring of a range of values [Latin *modus* manner]

model n **1** a three-dimensional representation, usually on a smaller scale, of a device or structure: *an architect's model of the proposed new housing estate* **2** an example or pattern that people might want to follow: *her success makes her an excellent role model for other young Black women* **3** an outstanding example of its kind: *the report is a model of clarity* **4** a person who poses for a sculptor, painter, or photographer **5** a person who wears clothes to display them to prospective buyers; mannequin **6** a design or style of a particular product: *the cheapest model of this car has a 1300cc engine* **7** a theoretical description of the way a

system or process works: *a working model of the human immune system* ▷ adj **8** excellent or perfect: *a model husband* **9** being a small-scale representation of: *a model aeroplane* ▷ vb **-elling, -elled** or US **-eling, -eled 10** to make a model of: *he modelled a plane out of balsa wood* **11** to plan or create according to a model or models: *it had a constitution modelled on that of the United States* **12** to display (clothing and accessories) as a mannequin **13** to pose for a sculptor, painter, or photographer [Latin *modulus*, diminutive of *modus* mode]

modem (mode-em) n computers a device for transmitting information between two computers by a telephone line, consisting of a modulator that converts computer signals into audio signals and a corresponding demodulator [from *mo(dulator) dem(odulator)*]

Modena n **1** a city in N Italy, in Emilia-Romagna: ruled by the Este family (18th–19th century); university (1678). Pop: 175 502 (2001). Ancient name: **Mutina 2** (*sometimes not cap*) a popular variety of domestic fancy pigeon originating in Modena

moderate adj **1** not extreme or excessive: *a man of moderate views*; *moderate consumption of alcohol* **2** (of a size, rate, intensity, etc.) towards the middle of the range of possible values: *a moderate-sized garden*; *a moderate breeze* **3** of average quality or extent: *moderate success* ▷ n **4** a person who holds moderate views, esp. in politics ▷ vb **-rating, -rated 5** to make or become less extreme or violent: *he has moderated his opinions since then* **6** to preside over a meeting, discussion, etc. [Latin *moderari* to restrain] ⟩ **moderately** adv

moderation n **1** the quality of being moderate **2** the act of moderating **3 in moderation** within moderate or reasonable limits

moderato (mod-er-ah-toe) adv music **1** at a moderate speed **2** with restraint: *allegro moderato* [Italian]

moderator n **1** Presbyterian Church a minister appointed to preside over a Church court, synod, or general assembly **2** a person who presides over a public or legislative assembly **3** a material, such as heavy water, used for slowing down neutrons in nuclear reactors

modern adj **1** of the present or a recent time; contemporary: *there have been very few outbreaks of the disease in modern times* **2** using the latest techniques, equipment, etc.; up-to-date: *modern and efficient railways* **3** of contemporary styles or schools of art, literature, and music, esp. those of an experimental kind ▷ n **4** a contemporary person [Late Latin *modernus*, from *modus* mode] ⟩ **modernity** n

Modern English n the English language since about 1450

modernism n an early- and mid-twentieth century movement in art, literature, and music that rejected traditional styles and techniques ⟩ **modernist** n, adj

modernize or **-nise** vb **-nizing, -nized** or **-nising, -nised 1** to make modern in style, methods, or equipment: *a commitment to modernizing industry* **2** to adopt modern ways or ideas ⟩ **modernization** or **-nisation** n

modern languages pl n the languages spoken in present-day Europe, with the exception of English

modern pentathlon n an athletic contest consisting of five different events: horse riding with jumps, fencing with electric épée, freestyle swimming, pistol shooting, and cross-country running

modest adj **1** having a humble opinion of oneself or one's accomplishments **2** not extreme or excessive: *a modest increase in inflation* **3** not ostentatious or pretentious: *a modest flat in the suburbs* **4** shy or easily embarrassed **5** old-fashioned (esp. of clothes) not revealing much of the body: *a modest dress* [Latin *modestus* moderate] ⟩ **modestly** adv ⟩ **modesty** n

Modi n Narendra. born 1950, Indian politician; prime minister of India from 2014

modicum n a small amount [Latin: a little way]

modifier n grammar a word or phrase that makes the

sense of another word more specific: for example, the noun *garage* is a modifier of *door* in *garage door*

modify *vb* **-fies, -fying, -fied 1** to change or alter slightly **2** to make less extreme or uncompromising **3** *grammar* (of a word or phrase) to act as a modifier to another word or phrase [Latin *modus* measure + *facere* to make] ⟩ **modification** *n*

Modigliani *n* Amedeo. 1884–1920, Italian painter and sculptor, noted esp. for the elongated forms of his portraits

modish (mode-ish) *adj* in the current fashion or style ⟩ **modishly** *adv*

modiste (mode-east) *n* a fashionable dressmaker or milliner [French]

modulate *vb* **-lating, -lated 1** to change the tone, pitch, or volume of (one's voice) **2** to adjust or regulate the degree of: *the hormone which modulates the development of the sexual organs* **3** *music* to change from one key to another **4** *physics, electronics* to superimpose the amplitude, frequency, or phase of a wave or signal onto another wave or signal [Latin *modulari* to modulate] ⟩ **modulation** *n* ⟩ **modulator** *n*

module *n* **1** a standard self-contained unit, such as an assembly of electronic components or a standardized piece of furniture, that can be used in combination with other units **2** *astronautics* a self-contained separable unit making up a spacecraft **3** *education* a short course of study that together with other such courses counts towards a qualification [Latin *modulus*, diminutive of *modus* mode] ⟩ **modular** *adj*

modulus *n, pl* **-li** *physics* a coefficient expressing a specified property, for instance elasticity, of a specified substance [Latin]

modus operandi (mode-uss op-er-an-die) *n, pl* **modi operandi** (mode-eye) method of operating [Latin]

modus vivendi (mode-uss viv-venn-die) *n, pl* **modi vivendi** (mode-eye) a working arrangement between conflicting interests [Latin: way of living]

Moers *n* a city in W Germany, in North Rhine-Westphalia: coalmining centre. Pop: 107 903 (2003 est)

mofussil *n* (in India) a rural or provincial area

Mogadishu *n* the capital and chief port of Somalia, on the Indian Ocean: founded by Arabs around the 10th century; taken by the Sultan of Zanzibar in 1871 and sold to Italy in 1905. Pop: 1 257 000 (2005 est). Local spelling: Muqdisho. Italian name: **Mogadiscio**

Mogador *n* the former name (until 1956) of **Essaouira**

moggy or **mog** *n, pl* **moggies** or **mogs** *Brit, Austral and NZ slang* a cat [dialect *mog*, originally a pet name for a cow]

Mogilev or **Mohilev** *n* an industrial city in E Belarus on the Dnieper River: passed to Russia in 1772 after Polish rule. Pop: 353 000 (2005 est)

mogul (moh-gl) *n* an important or powerful person

Mogul *adj* of or relating to a Muslim dynasty of Indian emperors established in 1526 [Persian *mughul* Mongolian]

MOH (in Britain) Medical Officer of Health

mohair *n* **1** the long soft silky hair of the Angora goat **2** a fabric made from yarn of this hair and cotton or wool [Arabic *mukhayyar*, literally: choice]

Mohammed *n* same as **Muhammad**

Mohammed II *n* ?1430–81, Ottoman sultan of Turkey (1451–81). He captured Constantinople (1453) and conquered large areas of the Balkans

Mohave Desert *n* another name for **Mojave Desert**

Mohawk[1] *n* a river in E central New York State, flowing south and east to the Hudson River at Cohoes: the largest tributary of the Hudson. Length: 238 km (148 miles)

Mohawk[2] *n* **1** a member of a N American Indian people formerly living along the Mohawk river **2** the language of this people

Mohenjo-Daro *n* an excavated city in SE Pakistan, southwest of Sukkur near the River Indus: flourished

during the third millennium BC

mohican *n* a punk hairstyle in which the head is shaved at the sides and the remaining strip of hair is worn stiffly erect and often brightly coloured [after *Mohican*]

Mohican *n* **1** (*pl* **-cans** or **-can**) a member of a N American Indian people formerly living along the Hudson river **2** the language of this people

Moholy-Nagy *n* Laszlo or Ladislaus. 1895–1946, US painter and teacher, born in Hungary. He worked at the Bauhaus (1923–29)

moiety (moy-it-ee) *n, pl* **-ties** *archaic* **1** a half **2** one of two parts or divisions of something [Old French *moitié*]

moire (mwahr) *n* a fabric, usually silk, with a watered effect [French]

moiré (mwahr-ray) *adj* **1** having a watered or wavelike pattern ▷ *n* **2** such a pattern, impressed on fabrics **3** a fabric, usually silk, with such a pattern **4** Also: **moiré pattern** a pattern seen when two geometrical patterns, such as grids, are visually superimposed [French]

moist *adj* slightly damp or wet [Old French]

moisten *vb* to make or become moist

moisture *n* water diffused as vapour or condensed on or in objects

moisturize or **-rise** *vb* **-rizing, -rized** or **-rising, -rised** to add moisture to the air or the skin ⟩ **moisturizer** or **-riser** *n*

Mojave Desert or **Mohave Desert** *n* a desert in S California, south of the Sierra Nevada: part of the Great Basin. Area: 38 850 sq km (15 000 sq miles)

mojo *n, pl* **mojos** or **mojoes** *chiefly US slang* **1** a charm or magic spell **2** the art of casting magic spells **3** uncanny personal power or influence, esp. the power to attract sexually [from West African]

moke *n* **1** *Brit slang* a donkey **2** *Austral and NZ* a horse of inferior quality [origin unknown]

Mokha *n* a variant of **Mocha**

Mokpo *n* a port in SW South Korea, on the Yellow Sea. Pop: 253 000 (2005 est)

mol *chem* mole

mol. **1** molecular **2** molecule

molar *n* **1** a large back tooth specialized for crushing and chewing food ▷ *adj* **2** of any of these teeth [Latin *mola* millstone]

molasses *n* **1** the thick brown bitter syrup obtained from sugar during refining **2** *US and Canad* same as **treacle** [Portuguese *melaço*]

mold *n, vb* US same as **mould[1]**

Moldau *n* **1** the German name for **Moldavia 2** the German name for the **Vltava**

Moldavia *n* **1** another name for **Moldova 2** a former principality of E Europe, consisting of the basins of the Rivers Prut and Dniester: the E part (Bessarabia) became Moldova; the W part remains a province of Romania

Moldavian *adj, n* **1** another name for **Moldovan** ▷ *adj* **2** of or relating to the former E European principality of Moldavia or its inhabitants ▷ *n* **3** a native or inhabitant of Moldavia

Moldova *n* a republic in SE Europe: comprising the E part of the former principality of Moldavia, the E part of which (Bessarabia) was ceded to the Soviet Union in 1940 and formed the Moldavian Soviet Socialist Republic until it gained independence in 1991; Russian forces have remained in Moldova east of the Nistru river supporting the separatist region of Transdniestria which has a Slavic majority population; Moldova has a chiefly agrarian economy noted for fruit, vegetables, wine, and tobacco. Official language: Romanian. Religion: nonreligious and Christian. Currency: leu. Capital: Chişinău (Kishinev). Pop: 3 619 925 (2013 est). Area: 33 670 sq km (13 000 sq miles). Also called: **Moldavia**

Moldovan or **Moldavian** *adj* **1** of or relating to Moldova or its inhabitants ▷ *n* **2** a native or inhabitant of Moldova

mole¹ n a small dark raised spot on the skin

mole² n 1 a small burrowing mammal with velvety dark fur and forelimbs specialized for digging 2 informal a spy who has infiltrated an organization and become a trusted member of it [Middle Dutch mol]

mole³ n chem the basic SI unit of amount of substance: the amount that contains as many elementary entities as there are atoms in 0.012 kilogram of carbon-12 [German Mol, short for Molekül molecule]

mole⁴ n 1 a breakwater 2 a harbour protected by a breakwater [Latin moles mass]

molecular (mol-lek-yew-lar) adj of or relating to molecules

molecular formula n chem a chemical formula indicating the number and type of atoms in a molecule, but not its structure: NH_3 is the molecular formula of ammonia

molecular weight n chem the sum of all the atomic weights of the atoms in a molecule

molecule (mol-lik-kyool) n 1 the simplest unit of a chemical compound that can exist, consisting of two or more atoms held together by chemical bonds 2 a very small particle [New Latin molecula, diminutive of Latin moles mass]

molehill n 1 the small mound of earth thrown up by a burrowing mole 2 **make a mountain out of a molehill** to exaggerate an unimportant matter out of all proportion

molest vb 1 to accost or attack someone, esp. a woman or child, with the intention of assaulting her or him sexually 2 to disturb or injure, esp. by using or threatening violence: killing, capturing, or molesting the local wildlife was strictly forbidden [Latin molestare to annoy]
> **molestation** n > **molester** n

Molière n real name Jean-Baptiste Poquelin. 1622–73, French dramatist, regarded as the greatest French writer of comedy. His works include Tartuffe (1664), Le Misanthrope (1666), L'Avare (1668), Le Bourgeois gentilhomme (1670), and Le Malade imaginaire (1673)

Molise n a region of S central Italy, the second smallest of the regions: separated from **Abruzzi e Molise** in 1965. Capital: Campobasso. Pop: 321 047 (2003 est). Area: 4438 sq km (1731 sq miles)

moll n slang a gangster's female accomplice or girlfriend [from Moll, familiar form of Mary]

mollify vb -fies, -fying, -fied to make someone less angry or upset; soothe: he sought to mollify his critics [Latin mollis soft + facere to make] > **mollification** n

mollusc or US **mollusk** n an invertebrate with a soft unsegmented body and often a shell, such as a snail, mussel, or octopus [Latin molluscus]

mollycoddle vb -coddling, -coddled to give an excessive amount of care and protection to [from Molly, girl's name + coddle]

Molnár n Ferenc. 1878–1952, Hungarian dramatist and novelist. His plays include Liliom (1909)

Molokai n an island in central Hawaii. Pop: 7404 (2000). Area: 676 sq km (261 sq miles)

Molopo n a seasonal river rising in N South Africa and flowing west and southwest to the Orange river. Length: about 1000 km (600 miles)

Molotov¹ n the former name (1940–62) for **Perm**

Molotov² n Vyacheslav Mikhailovich, original surname Skriabin. 1890–1986, Soviet statesman. As commissar and later minister for foreign affairs (1939–49; 1953–56) he negotiated the nonaggression pact with Nazi Germany and attended the founding conference of the United Nations and the Potsdam conference (1945)

Molotov cocktail n a simple bomb made from a bottle filled with petrol and a cloth wick; petrol bomb [after V. M. Molotov]

molt vb, n US same as **moult**

molten adj so hot that it has melted and formed a liquid: molten metal

Moltke n 1 Count Helmuth Johannes Ludwig von. 1848–1916, German general; chief of the German general staff (1906–14) 2 his uncle Count **Helmuth Karl Bernhard von**. 1800–91, German field marshal; chief of the Prussian general staff (1858–88)

molto adv music very: allegro molto; molto adagio [Italian]

Moluccas or **Molucca Islands** pl n a group of islands in the Malay Archipelago, between Sulawesi (Celebes) and New Guinea. Capital: Amboina. Pop: 1 990 598 (2000). Area: about 74 505 sq km (28 766 sq miles). Indonesian name: **Maluku**. Former name: **Spice Islands**

molybdenum (mol-lib-din-um) n chem a very hard silvery-white metallic element used in alloys, esp. to harden and strengthen steels. Symbol: Mo [Greek molubdos lead]

mom n informal, chiefly US, Canad and S African same as **mother**

Mombasa n a port in S Kenya, on a coral island in a bay of the Indian Ocean: the chief port for Kenya, Uganda, and NE Tanzania; became British in 1887, capital of the East African Protectorate until 1907. Pop: 828 000 (2005 est)

moment n 1 a short period of time 2 a specific instant or point in time: at that moment the phone rang 3 **the moment** the present point of time: for the moment he is out of prison 4 importance, significance, or value: a matter of greatest moment 5 physics a a tendency to produce motion, esp. rotation about a point or axis b the product of a physical quantity, such as force or mass, and its distance from a fixed reference point [Latin momentum movement]

momentary adj lasting for only a moment; temporary
> **momentarily** adv

moment of truth n a moment when a person or thing is put to the test

momentous (moh-men-tuss) adj of great significance
> **momentousness** n

momentum (moh-men-tum) n 1 the impetus to go forward, develop, or get stronger: the campaign steadily gathered support and momentum 2 the impetus of a moving body: the sledge gathered momentum as it slid ever faster down the slope 3 physics the product of a body's mass and its velocity [Latin: movement]

momma n chiefly US an informal or childish word for **mother**

Mommsen n Theodor. 1817–1903, German historian, noted esp. for The History of Rome (1854–56): Nobel prize for literature 1902

Mon. Monday

mon- combining form See **mono-**

Monacan adj 1 of or relating to Monaco or its inhabitants ▷ n 2 a native or inhabitant of Monaco

Monaco n a principality in SW Europe, on the Mediterranean and forming an enclave in SE France: the second smallest sovereign state in the world (after the Vatican); consists of **Monaco-Ville** (the capital) on a rocky headland, **La Condamine** (a business area and port), **Monte Carlo** (the resort centre), and **Fontvieille**, a light industrial area. Language: French. Religion: Roman Catholic. Currency: euro. Pop: 30 500 (2013 est). Area: 189 hectares (476 acres). Related adjective: **Monegasque**

monad n 1 philosophy any fundamental singular metaphysical entity 2 a single-celled organism 3 an atom, ion, or radical with a valency of one [Greek monas unit]

Monaghan n 1 a county of NE Republic of Ireland, in Ulster province: many small lakes. County town: Monaghan. Pop: 52 593 (2002). Area: 1292 sq km (499 sq miles) 2 a town in NE Republic of Ireland, county town of Co Monaghan. Pop: 5717 (2002)

monandrous adj 1 biology having only one stamen in each flower 2 having only one male sexual partner over a period of time [Greek monos sole + anēr man]

Mona Passage n a strait between Puerto Rico and the Dominican Republic, linking the Atlantic with the Caribbean

m

monarch n a sovereign head of state, esp. a king, queen, or emperor, who rules by hereditary right [Greek *monos* sole + *arkhein* to rule] **> monarchical** or **monarchic** adj

monarchism n the belief that a country should have a hereditary ruler, such as a king, rather than an elected one **> monarchist** n, adj

monarchy n, pl **-chies 1** a form of government in which supreme authority is held by a single hereditary ruler, such as a king **2** a country reigned over by a monarch

Monash n Sir John. 1865–1931, Australian military commander. Leader of Australian forces in World War I

monastery n, pl **-teries** the building or group of buildings where a community of monks lives [Greek *monazein* to live alone]

monastic adj **1** of or relating to monasteries, monks, or nuns **2** (of a way of life) simple and austere; ascetic **> monasticism** n

monatomic adj chem **1** (of an element) consisting of single atoms **2** (of a compound or molecule) having only one atom or group that can be replaced in a reaction

Mönchengladbach n a city in W Germany, in W North Rhine-Westphalia: headquarters of NATO forces in N central Europe; textile industry. Pop: 262 391 (2003 est). Former name: München-Gladbach

Monck n George. 1st Duke of Albemarle. 1608–70, English general. In the Civil War he was a Royalist until captured (1644) and persuaded to support the Commonwealth. After Cromwell's death he was instrumental in the restoration of Charles II (1660)

Moncton n a city in E Canada, in SE New Brunswick. Pop: 90 359 (2001)

Mondale n Walter (Frederick). born 1928, US Democratic politician; vice president of the US (1977–81)

Monday n the second day of the week, and the first day of the working week [Old English *mōnandæg* moon's day]

Mondrian n Piet. 1872–1944, Dutch painter, noted esp. as an exponent of the abstract art movement De Stijl

Monegasque n **1** a native or inhabitant of Monaco ▷ adj **2** of or relating to Monaco or its inhabitants [from French, from Provençal *mounegasc*, from *Mounegue* Monaco]

Monet n Claude. 1840–1926, French landscape painter; the leading exponent of impressionism. His interest in the effect of light on colour led him to paint series of pictures of the same subject at different times of day. These include *Haystacks* (1889–93), *Rouen Cathedral* (1892–94), the *Thames* (1899–1904), and *Water Lilies* (1899–1906)

monetarism n **1** the theory that inflation is caused by an excess quantity of money in an economy **2** an economic policy based on this theory and a belief in the efficiency of free market forces **> monetarist** n, adj

monetary adj of money or currency [Latin *moneta* money]

money n **1** a means of payment and measure of value: *some cultures used to use shells as money* **2** the official currency, in the form of banknotes or coins, issued by a government **3** moneys or monies law old-fashioned a financial sum or income **4** an unspecified amount of wealth: *money to lend* **5** informal a rich person or rich people: *he married money* **6** for my money in my opinion **7** one's money's worth full value for the money one has paid for something **8** put money on to place a bet on. Related adjective: pecuniary [Latin *moneta*]

moneybags n informal a very rich person

moneychanger n a person engaged in the business of exchanging currencies or money

moneyed or **monied** adj having a great deal of money; rich

money-grubbing adj informal seeking greedily to obtain money **> money-grubber** n

moneylender n a person who lends money at interest as a living

moneymaker n **1** a person whose chief concern is to make money **2** a person or thing that is or might be profitable **> moneymaking** adj, n

money-spinner n informal an enterprise, idea, or thing that is a source of wealth

-monger combining form **1** indicating a trader or dealer: *ar ironmonger* **2** indicating a promoter of something: *a warmonger* [Old English *mangere*]

mongol n offensive (not in technical use) a person affected by Down's syndrome **> mongoloid** n, adj

Mongol n **1** a native or inhabitant of Mongolia, esp. a nomad **2** the Mongolian language

Mongolia n **1** a republic in E central Asia: made a Chinese province in 1691; became autonomous in 1911 and a republic in 1924; multiparty democracy introduce in 1990. It consists chiefly of a high plateau, with the Gobi Desert in the south, a large lake district in the northwest, and the Altai and Khangai Mountains in the west Official language: Khalkha. Religion: nonreligiou majority. Currency: tugrik. Capital: Ulan Bator. Pop: 3 226 516 (2013 est). Area: 1 565 000 sq km (604 095 sq miles) Former names: (until 1924) Outer Mongolia, (1924–92) Mongolian People's Republic **2** a vast region of central Asia, inhabited chiefly by Mongols: now divided into the republic of Mongolia, Inner Mongolia (the Mongol Autonomous Region of China), and the Tuva Republic o S Russia; at its height during the 13th century under Genghis Khan

Mongolian adj **1** of or relating to Mongolia or its inhabitants ▷ n **2** a native or inhabitant of Mongolia **3** the language of Mongolia

Mongolian People's Republic n the former name of Mongolia (1)

mongolism n offensive a former name (not in technical use) for Down's syndrome [the condition produces facia features similar to those of the Mongoloid peoples]

Mongoloid adj of a major racial group of mankind, characterized by yellowish skin, straight black hair, and slanting eyes: includes most of the people of SE Asia, E Asia, and the Arctic area of N America

mongoose n, pl **-gooses** a small long-tailed predatory mammal of Asia and Africa that kills snakes [from Marathi (a language of India) *mangūs*]

mongrel n **1** a dog of mixed breeding **2** something made up of things from a variety of sources: *despite using components from three other cars, this new model is no mongrel* ▷ adj **3** of mixed breeding or origin: *a mongrel race* [from obsolete *mong* mixture]

monied adj same as **moneyed**

monies n law or old-fashioned a plural of **money**

moniker or **monicker** n slang a person's name or nickname [Shelta *munnik*, altered from Irish Gaelic *ainm* name]

monism n philosophy the doctrine that reality consists of only one basic substance or element, such as mind or matter [Greek *monos* sole] **> monist** n, adj

monition n a warning or caution [Latin *monere* to warn]

monitor n **1** a person or device that warns, checks, controls, or keeps a continuous record of something **2** Brit, Austral and NZ a pupil assisting a teacher with various duties **3** a screen used to display certain kinds o information, for example in airports or television studios **4** a large predatory lizard inhabiting warm regions of Africa, Asia, and Australia ▷ vb **5** to act as a monitor of **6** to observe or record the condition or performance of a person or thing **7** to check a broadcast for acceptable quality or content [Latin *monere* to advise] **> monitorial** adj

monitory adj acting as or giving a warning

monk n a male member of a religious community bound by vows of poverty, chastity, and obedience. Related adjective: monastic [Greek *monos* alone] **> monkish** adj

Monk n **1** Thelonious (Sphere). 1920–82, US jazz pianist and composer **2** a variant spelling of (George) **Monck**

monkey n **1** any long-tailed primate that is not a lemur or tarsier **2** (loosely) any primate that is not a human **3** a naughty or mischievous child **4** *slang* £500 or $500 **5 give a monkey's** *Brit slang* to care about or regard as important: *who gives a monkey's what he thinks?* ▷ *vb* **6 monkey around** *or* **about with** to meddle or tinker with [origin unknown]

monkey business *n informal* mischievous or dishonest behaviour or acts

monkey nut *n Brit* a peanut

monkey puzzle *n* a South American coniferous tree with branches shaped like a candelabrum and stiff sharp leaves

monkey tricks *or US* **monkey shines** *pl n informal* mischievous behaviour or acts

monkey wrench *n chiefly Brit* a wrench with adjustable jaws

monkshood *n* a poisonous plant with hooded blue-purple flowers

Monmouth[1] *n* a market town in E Wales, in Monmouthshire: Norman castle, where Henry V was born in 1387. Pop: 8547 (2001)

Monmouth[2] *n* James Scott, Duke of Monmouth. 1649–85, the illegitimate son of Charles II of England, he led a rebellion against James II in support of his own claim to the Crown; captured and beheaded

Monmouthshire *n* a county of E Wales: administratively part of England for three centuries (until 1830); mainly absorbed into the county of Gwent in 1974; reinstated with reduced boundaries in 1996: chiefly agricultural, with the Black Mountains in the N. Administrative centre: Cwmbran. Pop: 86 200 (2003 est). Area: 851 sq km (329 sq miles)

Monnet *n* Jean. 1888–1979, French economist and public servant, regarded as founding father of the European Economic Community. He was first president (1952–55) of the European Coal and Steel Community

mono *adj* **1** short for **monophonic** ▷ *n* **2** monophonic sound

mono- *or before a vowel* **mon-** *combining form* **1** one; single: *monorail; monolingual* **2** *chem* indicating that a chemical compound contains a single specified atom or group: *monoxide* [Greek *monos* alone]

monobasic *adj chem* (of an acid, such as hydrogen chloride) having only one replaceable hydrogen atom per molecule

monochromatic *adj* (of light or other electromagnetic radiation) having only one wavelength

monochrome *adj* **1** *photog, television* black-and-white ▷ *n* **2** a painting or drawing done in a range of tones of a single colour [Greek *monokhrōmos* of one colour]

monocle (mon-a-kl) *n* (formerly) a lens worn for correcting defective sight in one eye only, held in position by the facial muscles [MONO- + Latin *oculus* eye] ❭ **monocled** *adj*

monocline *n* a fold in stratified rocks in which the strata are inclined in the same direction from the horizontal [MONO- + Greek *klinein* to lean] ❭ **monoclinal** *adj, n*

monoclinic *adj crystallog* of the crystal system characterized by three unequal axes, one pair of which are not at right angles to each other

monoclonal antibody *n* an antibody produced from a single clone of cells grown in a culture

monocoque (mon-a-cock) *n* a vehicle body moulded from a single piece of material with no separate load-bearing parts [French]

monocotyledon (mon-no-kot-ill-**leed**-on) *n* any flowering plant with a single embryonic seed leaf, such as the grasses, lilies, palms, and orchids

monocular *adj* having or intended for the use of only one eye [Late Latin *monoculus* one-eyed]

monoculture *n* the continuous growing of one type of crop

monody *n, pl* **-dies 1** (in Greek tragedy) an ode sung by a

single actor **2** *music* a style of composition consisting of a single vocal part, usually with accompaniment [MONO- + Greek *aeidein* to sing] ❭ **monodist** *n*

monoecious (mon-ee-shuss) *adj* **1** (of some flowering plants) having the male and female reproductive organs in separate flowers on the same plant **2** (of some animals and lower plants) hermaphrodite [MONO- + Greek *oikos* house]

monogamy *n* the state or practice of having only one husband or wife at a time [MONO- + Greek *gamos* marriage] ❭ **monogamous** *adj*

monogram *n* a design of one or more letters, esp. initials, on clothing, stationery, etc. [Greek *monogrammatos* consisting of one letter]

monograph *n* a paper, book, or other work concerned with a single subject or aspect of a subject

monolingual *adj* knowing or expressed in only one language

monolith *n* **1** a large block of stone **2** a statue, obelisk, or column cut from one block of stone **3** something which can be regarded as forming one large, single, whole: *the Christian religion should not be thought of as a monolith* [Greek *monolithos* made from a single stone] ❭ **monolithic** *adj*

monologue *n* **1** a long speech made by one actor in a play or film; soliloquy **2** a dramatic piece for a single performer **3** any long speech by one person, esp. one which prevents other people talking or expressing their views [Greek *monologos* speaking alone]

> **USAGE** See at **soliloquy.**

monomania *n* an obsession with one thing or idea ❭ **monomaniac** *n, adj*

monomer *n chem* a compound whose molecules can join together to form a polymer

monomial *n maths* an expression consisting of a single term, such as *5ax* [MONO- + (BIN)OMIAL]

Monongahela *n* a river in the northeastern US, flowing generally north to the Allegheny River at Pittsburgh, Pennsylvania, forming the Ohio River. Length: 206 km (128 miles)

mononucleosis (mon-oh-new-klee-oh-siss) *n* infectious mononucleosis same as **glandular fever**

monophonic *adj* (of a system of broadcasting, recording, or reproducing sound) using only one channel between source and loudspeaker. Short form: mono

monoplane *n* an aeroplane with only one pair of wings

monopolize *or* **-lise** *vb* **-lizing, -lized** *or* **-lising, -lised 1** to have full control or use of, to the exclusion of others **2** to hold exclusive control of a market or supply

monopoly *n, pl* **-lies 1** exclusive control of the market supply of a product or service **2 a** an enterprise exercising this control **b** the product or service so controlled **3** *law* the exclusive right granted to a person or company by the state to trade in a specified commodity or area **4** exclusive control, possession, or use of something [MONO- + Greek *pōlein* to sell] ❭ **monopolist** *n* ❭ **monopolistic** *adj*

Monopoly *n trademark* a board game for two to six players who deal in 'property' as they move tokens around the board

monorail *n* a single-rail railway

monosaccharide *n* a simple sugar, such as glucose, that cannot be broken down into other sugars

monosodium glutamate *n* a substance which enhances protein flavours: used as a food additive

monosyllable *n* a word of one syllable ❭ **monosyllabic** *adj*

monotheism *n* the belief or doctrine that there is only one God ❭ **monotheist** *n, adj* ❭ **monotheistic** *adj*

monotone *n* **1** a single unvaried pitch level in speech or sound **2** a way of speaking which lacks variety of pitch or expression: *he rambled on in a dull monotone* **3** lack of

variety in style or expression ▷ *adj* **4** unvarying
monotonous *adj* tedious because of lack of variety
> **monotonously** *adv*
monotony *n, pl* **-nies** **1** wearisome routine; dullness
2 lack of variety in pitch or tone
monounsaturated *adj* of a group of vegetable oils,
such as olive oil, that have a neutral effect on cholesterol
in the body
monovalent *adj chem* **1** having a valency of one **2** having
only one valency > **monovalence** *or* **monovalency** *n*
monoxide *n* an oxide that contains one oxygen atom per
molecule
Monroe *n* **1** James. 1758–1831, US statesman; fifth
president of the US (1817–25). He promulgated the
Monroe Doctrine (1823) **2** Marilyn, born *Norma Jeane
Mortenson*, later *Norma Jeane Baker*, sometimes spelled
Norma Jean, 1926–62, US film actress. Her films include
Niagara (1952), *Gentlemen Prefer Blondes* (1953), and *Some Like
It Hot* (1959)
Monrovia *n* the capital and chief port of Liberia, on the
Atlantic: founded in 1822 as a home for freed American
slaves; University of Liberia (1862). Pop: 614 000 (2005 est)
Mons *n* a town in SW Belgium, capital of Hainaut
province: scene of the first battle (1914) of the British
Expeditionary Force during World War I. Pop: 91 185
(2004 est). Flemish name: **Bergen**
Monseigneur (mon-sen-**nyur**) *n, pl* **Messeigneurs**
(may-sen-**nyur**) a title given to French prelates and
princes [French, literally: my lord]
monsieur (muss-**syuh**) *n, pl* **messieurs** (may-**syuh**) a
French form of address equivalent to *sir* or *Mr* [French,
literally: my lord]
Monsignor *n, pl* **Monsignors** *or* **Monsignori** *RC Church* a
title given to certain senior clergymen [Italian]
monsoon *n* **1** a seasonal wind of S Asia which blows
from the southwest in summer and from the northeast
in winter **2** the rainy season when the SW monsoon
blows, from about April to October [Arabic *mawsim*
season]
monsoon bucket *n NZ* a large container for water
carried by helicopter and used to extinguish bush and
scrub fires
mons pubis (monz pew-biss) *n, pl* **montes pubis**
(mon-teez) the fatty flesh in human males over the
junction of the pubic bones [New Latin: hill of the
pubes]
monster *n* **1** an imaginary beast, usually frightening in
appearance **2** a very large person, animal, or thing **3** an
exceptionally cruel or wicked person **4** a person, animal,
or plant with a marked deformity [Latin *monstrum*
portent]
monstrance *n RC Church* a vessel in which the
consecrated Host is exposed for adoration [Latin
monstrare to show]
monstrosity *n, pl* **-ties** **1** an outrageous or ugly person or
thing **2** the state or quality of being monstrous
monstrous *adj* **1** hideous or unnatural in size or
character **2** atrocious, unjust, or shocking: *the President
described the invasion as monstrous* **3** huge **4** of or like a
monster **5** (of plants and animals) abnormal in
structure > **monstrously** *adv*
mons veneris (monz ven-er-iss) *n, pl* **montes veneris**
(mon-teez) the fatty flesh in human females over the
junction of the pubic bones [New Latin: hill of Venus]
Mont. Montana
montage (mon-**tahzh**) *n* **1** a picture made by combining
material from various sources, such as other pictures or
photographs **2** the technique of producing pictures in
this way **3** a method of film editing by juxtaposition or
partial superimposition of several shots to form a single
image **4** a film sequence of this kind [French]
Montagu *n* **1** Charles. See (Earl of) **Halifax** (2) **2** Lady
Mary Wortley. 1689–1762, English writer, noted for her
Letters from the East (1763)

Montaigne *n* Michel (Eyquem) de. 1533–92, French
writer. His life's work, the *Essays* (begun in 1571),
established the essay as a literary genre and record the
evolution of his moral ideas
Montale *n* Eugenio. 1896–1981, Italian poet: Nobel prize
for literature 1975
Montana[1] *n* a state of the western US: consists of the
Great Plains in the east and the Rocky Mountains in the
west. Capital: Helena. Pop: 917 621 (2003 est). Area:
377 070 sq km (145 587 sq miles). Abbreviation: **Mont.**,
(with zip code) **MT**
Montana[2] *n* Joe. born 1958, American football
quarterback
Montanan *n* **1** a native or inhabitant of Montana ▷ *adj*
2 of or relating to Montana or its inhabitants
Montauban *n* a city in SW France: a stronghold in the
16th and 17th centuries, taken by Richelieu in 1629. Pop:
51 855 (1999)
Montbéliard *n* an industrial town in E France: former
capital of the duchy of Burgundy. Pop: 27 570 (1999)
Mont Blanc *n* a massif in SW Europe, mainly between
France and Italy: the highest mountain in the Alps;
beneath it is **Mont Blanc Tunnel**, 12 km (7.5 miles) long.
Highest peak (in France): 4807 m (15 771 ft). Italian name:
Monte Bianco
Montcalm *n* Louis Joseph, Marquis de Montcalm de
Saint-Véran. 1712–59, French general in Canada (1756);
killed in Quebec by British forces under General Wolfe
Mont Cenis *n* See (Mont) **Cenis**
Mont Cervin *n* the French name for the **Matterhorn**
Monte Carlo *n* a town and resort forming part of the
principality of Monaco, on the Riviera: famous casino
and the destination of an annual car rally (the **Monte
Carlo Rally**). Pop: 15 507 (2000)
Monte Cassino *n* a hill above Cassino in central Italy:
site of intense battle during World War II: site of
Benedictine monastery (530 AD), destroyed by Allied
bombing in 1944, later restored
Monte Corno *n* See (Monte) **Corno**
Montefeltro *n* an Italian noble family who ruled
Urbino from the 13th to the 16th century. **Federigo
Montefeltro**, duke of Urbino (1422–82), was a noted
patron of the arts and military leader
Montego Bay *n* a port and resort in NW Jamaica: the
second largest town on the island Pop: 96 488 (2001)
Montenegrin *adj* **1** of or relating to Montenegro or its
people, or their language ▷ *n* **2** the language that is
spoken in Montenegro **3 a** a native or inhabitant of
Montenegro **b** a speaker of Montenegrin
Montenegro *n* a republic in S central Europe,
bordering on the Adriatic; declared a kingdom in 1910
and united with Serbia, Croatia, and other territories
in 1918 to form Yugoslavia; remained united with
Serbia as the Federal Republic of Yugoslavia when the
other Yugoslav constituent republics became
independent in 1991–92; Union of Serbia and
Montenegro formed in 2003 and dissolved 2006. Mainly
mountainous. Language: Serbian (Montenegrin).
Religion: Orthodox Christian majority. Currency: euro.
Capital: Podgorica. Pop: 653 474 (2013 est). Area: 13 812 sq km
(5387 sq miles)
Monterey *n* a city in W California: capital of Spain's
Pacific empire from 1774 to 1825; taken by the US (1846).
Pop: 29 960 (2003 est)
Monterrey *n* a city in NE Mexico, capital of Nuevo Léon
state: the third largest city in Mexico; a major industrial
centre, esp. for metals. Pop: 1 353 000 (2005 est)
Montespan *n* Marquise de, title of *Françoise Athénaïs de
Rochechouart*. 1641–1707, French noblewoman; mistress of
Louis XIV of France
Montesquieu *n* Baron de la Brède et de, title of *Charles
Louis de Secondat*. 1689–1755, French political philosopher.
His chief works are the satirical *Lettres persanes* (1721) and
L'Esprit des lois (1748), a comparative analysis of various

forms of government, which had a profound influence on political thought in Europe and the US

Montessori *n* **Maria**. 1870–1952, Italian educational reformer, who evolved the Montessori method of teaching children

Monteux *n* **Pierre**. 1875–1964, US conductor, born in France

Monteverdi *n* **Claudio**. ?1567–1643, Italian composer, noted esp. for his innovations in opera and for his expressive use of dissonance. His operas include *Orfeo* (1607) and *L'Incoronazione di Poppea* (1642) and he also wrote many motets and madrigals

Montevideo *n* the capital and chief port of Uruguay, in the south on the Río de la Plata estuary: the largest city in the country: University of the Republic (1849); resort. Pop: 1 378 707 (1996)

Montez *n* **Lola**, original name *Marie Gilbert*. 1818–61, Irish dancer; mistress of Louis I of Bavaria (1786–1868; reigned 1825–48)

Montezuma II *n* 1466–1520, Aztec emperor of Mexico (?1502–20). He was overthrown and killed by the Spanish conquistador Cortés

Montfort *n* **Simon de**, Earl of Leicester. ?1208–65, English soldier, born in Normandy. He led the baronial rebellion against Henry III and ruled England from 1264 to 1265; he was killed at Evesham

Montgolfier *n* **Jacques Étienne**, 1745–99, and his brother **Joseph Michel**, 1740–1810, French inventors, who built (1782) and ascended in (1783) the first practical hot-air balloon

Montgomery¹ *n* a city in central Alabama, on the Alabama River: state capital; capital of the Confederacy (1861). Pop: 200 123 (2003 est)

Montgomery² *n* **1 Bernard Law**, 1st Viscount Montgomery of Alamein, nicknamed *Monty*. 1887–1976, British field marshal. As commander of the 8th Army in North Africa, he launched the offensive, beginning with the victory at El Alamein (1942), that drove Rommel's forces back to Tunis. He also commanded the ground forces in the invasion of Normandy (1944) and accepted Germany's surrender at Lüneburg Heath (May 7, 1945) **2 L(ucy) M(aud)**. 1874–1942, Canadian writer; her novels include *Anne of Green Gables* (1908) and its sequels.

Montgomeryshire *n* (until 1974) a county of central Wales, now part of Powys

month *n* **1** one of the twelve divisions (**calendar months**) of the calendar year **2** a period of time extending from one date to a corresponding date in the next calendar month **3** a period of four weeks or of 30 days [Old English *mōnath*]

Montherlant *n* **Henri (Millon) de**. 1896–1972, French novelist and dramatist: his novels include *Les Jeunes Filles* (1935–39) and *Le Chaos et la nuit* (1963)

monthly *adj* **1** happening or payable once every month: *a monthly magazine* **2** lasting or valid for a month: *a monthly travel pass* ▷ *adv* **3** once a month ▷ *n, pl* **-lies 4** a magazine published once a month

Montluçon *n* an industrial city in central France, on the Cher River. Pop: 39 492 (2008)

Montmartre *n* a district of N Paris, on a hill above the Seine: the highest point in the city; famous for its associations with many artists

Montparnasse *n* a district of S Paris, on the left bank of the Seine: noted for its cafés, frequented by artists, writers, and students

Montpelier *n* a city in N central Vermont, on the Winooski River: the state capital. Pop: 7945 (2003 est)

Montpellier *n* a city in S France, the chief town of Languedoc: its university was founded by Pope Nicholas IV in 1289; wine trade. Pop: 254 974 (2006)

Montreal *n* a city and major port in central Canada, in S Quebec on **Montreal Island** at the junction of the Ottawa and St Lawrence Rivers. Pop: 1 039 534 (2001). French name: **Montréal**

Montreuil *n* an E suburb of Paris: formerly famous for peaches, but now industrialized. Pop: 102 889 (2006)

Montreux *n* a town and resort in W Switzerland, in Vaud canton on Lake Geneva; annual television festival. Pop: 22 454 (2000)

Montrose¹ *n* a port and resort in E Scotland, in Angus. Pop: 10 845 (2001)

Montrose² *n* **James Graham**, 1st Marquess and 5th Earl of Montrose. 1612–50, Scottish general, noted for his victories in Scotland for Charles I in the Civil War. He was later captured and hanged

Mont-Saint-Michel *n* a rocky islet off the coast of NW France, accessible at low tide by a causeway, in the **Bay of St Michel** (an inlet of the Gulf of St Malo): Benedictine abbey (966), used as a prison from the Revolution until 1863; reoccupied by Benedictine monks since 1966. Area: 1 hectare (3 acres)

Montserrat *n* **1** a volcanic island in the Caribbean, in the Leeward Islands: a UK Overseas Territory: much of the island rendered uninhabitable by volcanic eruptions in 1997. Capital: Brades (replacing Plymouth, effectively destroyed by the eruption). Pop: 5189 (2013 est). Area: 103 sq km (40 sq miles) **2** a mountain in NE Spain, northwest of Barcelona: famous Benedictine monastery. Height: 1235 m (4054 ft). Ancient name: **Mons Serratus**

monument *n* **1** something, such as a statue or building, erected in commemoration of a person or event **2** an ancient building which is regarded as an important part of a country's history **3** an exceptional example of the results of something: *the whole town is a monument to bad sixties' architecture* [Latin *monumentum*]

Monument *n* **the Monument** a tall columnar building designed (1671) by Sir Christopher Wren to commemorate the Fire of London (1666), which destroyed a large part of the medieval city

monumental *adj* **1** large, impressive, or likely to last or be remembered for a long time: *a monumental three-volume biography* **2** of or being a monument **3** *informal* extreme: *a monumental gamble*

Monza *n* a city in N Italy, northeast of Milan: the ancient capital of Lombardy; scene of the assassination of King Umberto I in 1900; motor-racing circuit. Pop: 120 204 (2001)

moo *n* **1** the characteristic deep long sound made by a cow ▷ *vb* **2** to make this sound; low

mooch *vb slang* **1** to loiter or walk aimlessly **2** to cadge or scrounge [perhaps Old French *muchier* to skulk]

mood¹ *n* **1** a temporary state of mind or temper: *a happy mood* **2** a sullen or gloomy state of mind, esp. when temporary: *she's in a mood* **3** a prevailing atmosphere or feeling: *the current mood of disenchantment with politics* **4 in the mood** inclined to do or have (something) [Old English *mōd* mind, feeling]

mood² *n grammar* a form of a verb indicating whether the verb expresses a fact (indicative mood), a wish or supposition (subjunctive mood), or a command (imperative mood) [same as MOOD¹]

moody *adj* **moodier, moodiest 1** sullen, sulky, or gloomy **2** temperamental or changeable **› moodily** *adv* **› moodiness** *n*

Moody *n* **Dwight Lyman**. 1837–99, US evangelist and hymnodist, noted for his revivalist campaigns in Britain and the US with I. D. Sankey

Moog *n music trademark* a type of synthesizer [after Robert *Moog*, engineer]

mooi *adj S African slang* pleasing or nice [Afrikaans]

moolah (moo-luh) *n slang* money [origin unknown]

mooli *n* a type of large white radish [E African native name]

Moomba *n Austral* **1** a festival held annually in Melbourne since 1954, named in the belief that *moomba* was an Aboriginal word meaning "Let's get together and have fun" **2** a natural gas field in South Australia

[from a native Australian language *moom* buttocks, anus]

moon *n* **1** the natural satellite of the earth. Related adjective: **lunar 2** this satellite as it is seen during its revolution around the earth, esp. at one of its phases: *new moon*; *full moon* **3** any natural satellite of a planet **4** a month **5 over the moon** *informal* extremely happy; ecstatic ▷ *vb* **6 moon about** *or* **around** to be idle in a listless or dreamy way [Old English *mōna*]
> **moonless** *adj*

Moon *n* William. 1818–94, British inventor of the Moon writing system in 1847, who, himself blind, taught blind children in Brighton and printed mainly religious works from stereotyped plates of his own designing

moonbeam *n* a ray of moonlight

moon-faced *adj* having a round face

moonlight *n* **1** light from the sun received on earth after reflection by the moon ▷ *adj* **2** illuminated by the moon: *a moonlight walk* ▷ *vb* **-lighting, -lighted 3** *informal* to work at a secondary job, esp. illegally **> moonlighter** *n*

moonlight flit *n Brit and Austral informal* a hurried departure at night to avoid paying rent

moonlit *adj* illuminated by the moon

moonscape *n* the surface of the moon or a picture or model of it

moonshine *n* **1** *US and Canad* illegally distilled or smuggled whisky **2** foolish or nonsensical talk or thought

moonshot *n* the launching of a spacecraft to the moon

moonstone *n* a white translucent form of feldspar, used as a gem

moonstruck *adj* slightly mad or odd, as if affected by the moon

moony *adj* **moonier, mooniest** *Brit, Austral and NZ informal* dreamy or listless

moor¹ *n Brit* an expanse of open uncultivated ground covered with heather, coarse grass, and bracken [Old English *mōr*]

moor² *vb* to secure a ship or boat with cables, ropes, or anchors so that it remains in one place [Germanic]
> **moorage** *n*

Moor *n* a member of a Muslim people of North Africa who ruled Spain between the 8th and 15th centuries [Greek *Mauros*]

Moore *n* **1** Bobby. full name *Robert Frederick Moore*. 1941–93, English footballer, captain of the England team that won the World Cup in 1966 **2** Dudley (**Stuart John**). 1935–2002, British actor, comedian, and musician noted for his comedy partnership (1960–73) with Peter Cook and such films as *10* (1979) and *Arthur* (1981) **3** George. 1852–1933, Irish novelist. His works include *Esther Waters* (1894) and *The Brook Kerith* (1916) **4** G(eorge) E(dward). 1873–1958, British philosopher, noted esp. for his *Principia Ethica* (1903) **5** Gerald. 1899–1987, British pianist, noted as an accompanist esp. to lieder singers **6** Henry. 1898–1986, British sculptor. His works are characterized by monumental organic forms and include the *Madonna and Child* (1943) at St Matthew's Church, Northampton **7** Sir John. 1761–1809, British general; commander of the British army (1808–09) in the Peninsular War: killed at Corunna **8** Marianne (**Craig**). 1887–1972, US poet: her works include *Observations* (1924) and *Selected Poems* (1935) **9** Thomas. 1779–1852, Irish poet, best known for *Irish Melodies* (1807–34)

moorhen *n* a waterfowl with black plumage and a red bill

mooring *n* a place where a ship or boat can be tied up or anchored

moorings *pl n nautical* the ropes and anchors used in mooring a vessel

Moorish *adj* **1** of or relating to the Moors **2** of a style of architecture used in Spain from the 13th to the 16th century, characterized by the horseshoe arch

moorland *n Brit* an area of moor

moose *n, pl* **moose** a large North American deer with large flattened antlers; the American elk [from a Native American language]

Moose Jaw *n* a city in W Canada, in S Saskatchewan. Pop: 32 631 (2001)

moot *adj* **1** subject or open to debate: *a moot point* ▷ *vb* **2** to suggest or bring up for debate: *a compromise proposal, involving building fewer flats, was mooted* ▷ *n* **3** (in Anglo-Saxon England) a local administrative assembly [Old English *gemōt*]

mop *n* **1** a tool with a head made of twists of cotton or sponge and a long handle used for washing or polishing floors **2** a similar tool, except smaller and without a long handle, used to wash dishes **3** a thick untidy mass of hair ▷ *vb* **mopping, mopped 4** to clean or soak up with or as if with a mop: *she mopped her brow with a handkerchief* ▶ See also **mop up** [Latin *mappa* napkin]

mope *vb* **moping, moped 1** to be gloomy or apathetic **2** to walk around in a gloomy and aimless manner [perhaps from obsolete *mope* fool]

moped *n* a light motorcycle not over 50cc [*motor* + *pedal*]

mopes *pl n* **the mopes** low spirits

mopoke *n* **1** a small spotted owl of Australia and New Zealand **2** *Austral slang* a slow or lugubrious person [imitative of the bird's cry]

moppet *n* same as **poppet** [obsolete *mop* rag doll]

mop up *vb* **1** to clean with a mop **2** *informal* to complete the last remaining stages of a job **3** *military* to clear remaining enemy forces after a battle, by killing them or taking them prisoner

moquette *n* a thick velvety fabric used for carpets and upholstery [French]

Mor. Morocco

Moradabad *n* a city in N India, in N Uttar Pradesh. Pop: 641 240 (2001)

moraine *n* a ridge or mound formed from debris deposited by a glacier [French]

moral *adj* **1** concerned with or relating to the distinction between good and bad or right and wrong behaviour: *moral sense* **2** based on a sense of right and wrong according to conscience: *moral duty* **3** displaying a sense of right and wrong; (of support or a victory) psychological rather than practical ▷ *n* **4** a lesson about right or wrong behaviour that is shown in a fable or event **5 morals** principles of behaviour in accordance with standards of right and wrong [Latin *moralis* relating to morals or customs] **> morally** *adv*

morale (mor-**rahl**) *n* the degree of confidence or optimism of a person or group [French]

moralist *n* **1** a person who has a strong sense of right and wrong **2** someone who criticizes other people for not doing what he or she is morally correct
> **moralistic** *adj*

morality *n, pl* **-ties 1** good moral conduct **2** the degree to which something is morally acceptable: *we discussed the morality of fox-hunting* **3** a system of moral principles

morality play *n* a medieval type of drama concerned with the conflict between personified virtues and vices

moralize *or* **-lise** *vb* **-lizing, -lized** *or* **-lising, -lised 1** to discuss or consider something in the light of one's own moral beliefs, esp. with disapproval **2** to interpret or explain in a moral sense **3** to improve the morals of

moral philosophy *n* the branch of philosophy dealing with ethics

Morar *n* Loch Morar a lake in W Scotland, in the SW Highlands: the deepest in Scotland. Length: 18 km (11 miles). Depth: 296 m (987 ft)

morass *n* **1** a tract of swampy low-lying land **2** a disordered, confusing, or muddled state of affairs [Old French *marais* marsh]

moratorium *n, pl* **-ria** *or* **-riums 1** a legally authorized postponement of the payment of a debt **2** an agreed suspension of activity [Latin *mora* delay]

Morava *n* **1** a river in central Europe, rising in the

...udeten Mountains, in the Czech Republic, and flowing ...outh through Slovakia to the Danube: forms part of the ...order between the Czech Republic, Slovakia, and ...ustria. Length: 370 km (230 miles). German name: ...arch **2** a river in E Serbia, formed by the confluence of ...he Southern Morava and the Western Morava near ...talac: flows north to the Danube. Length: 209 km ...130 miles) **3** the Czech name for **Moravia**

...oravia[1] *n* a region of the Czech Republic around the ...orava River, bounded by the Bohemian-Moravian ...ighlands, the Sudeten Mountains, and the W ...arpathians: became a separate Austrian crownland in ...848; part of Czechoslovakia 1918–92; valuable mineral ...esources. Czech name: **Morava**. German name: **Mähren**

...oravia[2] *n* Alberto, pen name of *Alberto Pincherle*. ...907–90, Italian novelist and short-story writer: his ...orks include *The Time of Indifference* (1929), *The Woman of ...ome* (1949), *The Lie* (1966), and *Erotic Tales* (1985)

...oravian *adj* **1** of or relating to Moravia, its people, or ...heir dialect of Czech **2** of or relating to the Moravian ...hurch ▷ *n* **3** the Moravian dialect **4** a native or ...nhabitant of Moravia **5** a member of the Moravian ...hurch ▷ **Moravianism** *n*

...oravian Gate *n* a low mountain pass linking S Poland ...nd Moravia (the Czech Republic), between the SE ...udeten Mountains and the W Carpathian Mountains

...oray *n* a large marine eel marked with brilliant ...olours [Greek *muraina*]

...oray[1] *n* a council area and historical county of NE ...cotland: part of Grampian region from 1975 to 1996: ...ainly hilly, with the Cairngorm mountains in the ...outh Administrative centre: Elgin. Pop: 87 460 (2003 est). ...rea: 2238 sq km (874 sq miles). Former name: **Elgin**

...oray[2] *or* **Murray** *n* 1st Earl of, title of *James Stuart*. ...1531–70, regent of Scotland (1567–70) following the ...abdication of Mary, Queen of Scots, his half-sister. He ...defeated Mary and Bothwell at Langside (1568): ...assassinated by a follower of Mary

...oray Firth *n* an inlet of the North Sea on the NE coast ...f Scotland. Length: about 56 km (35 miles)

...orbid *adj* **1** having an unusual interest in death or ...npleasant events **2** *med* relating to or characterized by ...disease [Latin *morbus* illness] ▷ **morbidity** *n* ▷ **morbidly** *adv*

...orbihan *n* a department of NW France, in S Brittany. ...apital: Vannes. Pop: 665 540 (2003 est). Area: 7092 sq km ...2766 sq miles)

...ordant *adj* **1** sarcastic or caustic: *mordant wit* ▷ *n* **2** a ...substance used in dyeing to fix colours **3** an acid or other ...corrosive fluid used to etch lines on a printing plate ...Latin *mordere* to bite]

...ordecai *n Old Testament* the cousin of Esther who ...averted a massacre of the Jews (Esther 2–9)

...ordvinian Republic *n* a constituent republic of W ...central Russia, in the middle Volga basin. Capital: ...Saransk. Pop: 888 700 (2002). Area: 26 200 sq km ...10 110 sq miles). Also called: **Mordovian Republic**, ...**Mordovia**

...ore *adj* **1** the comparative of **much, many**: *more joy than ...you know*; *even more are leaving the country* **2** additional or ...further: *no more apples* **3** **more of** to a greater extent or ...degree: *more of a nuisance* ▷ *adv* **4** used to form the ...comparative of some adjectives and adverbs: *more quickly* ...**5** the comparative of **much**: *people listen to the radio more now* ...**6** **more or less a** as an estimate; approximately **b** to an ...unspecified extent or degree: *the film was a disaster, more or ...less* [Old English *māra*]

USAGE See at **most**.

...ore *n* **1** Hannah. 1745–1833, English writer, noted for her ...religious tracts, esp. *The Shepherd of Salisbury Plain* **2** Sir ...Thomas. 1478–1535, English statesman, humanist, and ...Roman Catholic Saint; Lord Chancellor to Henry VIII ...(1529–32). His opposition to the annulment of Henry's

marriage to Catherine of Aragon and his refusal to recognize the Act of Supremacy resulted in his execution on a charge of treason. In *Utopia* (1516) he set forth his concept of the ideal state. Feast day: June 22 or July 6

Morea *n* the medieval name for the **Peloponnese**

Moreau *n* **1** Gustave 1826–98, French symbolist painter **2** Jean Victor. 1763–1813, French general in the Revolutionary and Napoleonic Wars **3** Jeanne. born 1928, French stage and film actress. Her films include *Jules et Jim* (1961), *Diary of a Chambermaid* (1964), and *The Proprietor* (1996)

Morecambe[1] *n* a port and resort in NW England, in NW Lancashire on **Morecambe Bay** (an inlet of the Irish Sea). Pop (with Heysham): 49 569 (2001)

Morecambe[2] *n* Eric, real name *John Eric Bartholomew*. 1926–84, British comedian and actor, noted esp. for his comedy partnership (from 1941) with Ernie Wise (real name Ernest Wiseman, 1925–99)

moreish *or* **morish** *adj informal* (of food) causing a desire for more

morel *n* an edible mushroom with a pitted cap [French *morille*]

Morelia *n* a city in central Mexico, capital of Michoacán state: a cultural centre during colonial times; two universities. Pop: 668 000 (2005 est). Former name (until 1828): **Valladolid**

morello *n, pl* **-los** a variety of small very dark sour cherry [Italian: blackish]

Morelos *n* an inland state of S central Mexico, on the S slope of the great plateau. Capital: Cuernavaca. Pop: 1 552 878 (2000 est). Area: 4988 sq km (1926 sq miles)

moreover *adv* in addition to what has already been said

morepork *n chiefly NZ* same as **mopoke**

mores (more-rayz) *pl n* the customs and conventions embodying the fundamental values of a community [Latin: customs]

Moreton Bay bug *n* an Australian flattish edible shellfish

Morgan *n* **1** Edwin (George). (1920–2010), Scottish poet, noted esp. for his collection *The Second Life* (1968) and his many concrete and visual poems; appointed Scottish national poet 2004 **2** Sir Henry. 1635–88, Welsh buccaneer, who raided Spanish colonies in the West Indies for the English **3** John Pierpont. 1837–1913, US financier, philanthropist, and art collector **4** (Hywel) Rhodri. born 1939, Welsh Labour politician; first minister of Wales (2000–09) **5** Thomas Hunt. 1866–1945, US biologist. He formulated the chromosome theory of heredity. Nobel prize for physiology or medicine 1933

morganatic *adj* of or designating a marriage between a person of high rank and a person of low rank, by which the latter is not elevated to the higher rank and any children have no rights to inherit the higher party's titles or property [Medieval Latin *morganaticum* morning-gift after consummation representing the husband's only liability]

morgue *n* **1** a mortuary **2** *informal* a store of clippings and back numbers used for reference in a newspaper [French]

moribund *adj* **1** near death **2** no longer performing effectively or usefully: *Romania's moribund economy* [Latin *mori* to die]

Mörike *n* Eduard. 1804–75, German poet, noted for his lyrics, such as *On a Winter's Morning before Sunrise* and *At Midnight*

morish *adj* same as **moreish**

Morisot *n* Berthe. 1841–95, French impressionist painter; noted for her studies of women and children

Morley[1] *n* an industrial town in N England, in Leeds unitary authority, West Yorkshire. Pop: 54 051 (2001)

Morley[2] *n* **1** Edward Williams. 1838–1923, US chemist who collaborated with A. A. Michelson in the Michelson-Morley experiment **2** John, Viscount Morley of

m

Blackburn. 1838–1923, British Liberal statesman and writer; secretary of state for India (1905–10) **3 Robert.** 1908–92, British actor. His many films include *Major Barbara* (1940), *Oscar Wilde* (1960), and *The Blue Bird* (1976) **4 Thomas.** ?1557–?1603, English composer and organist, noted for his madrigals and his textbook on music, *A Plaine and Easie Introduction to Practicall Musicke* (1597)

Mormon n **1** a member of the Church of Jesus Christ of Latter-day Saints, founded in 1830 in New York by Joseph Smith ▷ adj **2** of the Mormons, their Church, or their beliefs ⟩ **Mormonism** n

morn n *poetic or Austral* morning [Old English *morgen*]

mornay adj served with a cheese sauce: *haddock mornay* [after Philippe de MORNAY]

Mornay n Philippe de, Seigneur du Plessis-Marly. 1549–1623, French Huguenot leader. Also: **Duplessis-Mornay**

morning n **1** the first part of the day, ending at noon **2** daybreak; dawn **3 the morning after** *informal* the aftereffects of excess, esp. a hangover ▷ adj **4** of or in the morning: *morning coffee* [from *morn*, on the model of *evening*]

morning dress n formal daytime dress for men, consisting of a frock coat with the front cut away (**morning coat**), usually with grey trousers and top hat

morning-glory n, pl **-ries** a tropical climbing plant with trumpet-shaped blue, pink, or white flowers, which close in late afternoon

mornings adv *informal* in the morning, esp. regularly, or during every morning

morning sickness n nausea occurring shortly after rising in early pregnancy

morning star n a planet, usually Venus, seen just before sunrise

Moro n Aldo. 1916–78, Italian Christian Democrat statesman; prime minister of Italy (1963–68; 1974–76) and minister of foreign affairs (1965–66; 1969–72; 1973–74). He negotiated the entry of the Italian Communist Party into coalition government before being kidnapped by the Red Brigades in 1978 and murdered

Moroccan adj **1** of or relating to Morocco or its inhabitants ▷ n **2** a native or inhabitant of Morocco

morocco n a fine soft leather made from goatskins [after MOROCCO, where it was originally made]

Morocco n a kingdom in NW Africa, on the Mediterranean and the Atlantic: conquered by the Arabs in about 683, who introduced Islam; at its height under Berber dynasties (11th–13th centuries); became a French protectorate in 1912 and gained independence in 1956. It is mountainous, with the Atlas Mountains in the centre and the Rif range along the Mediterranean coast, with the Sahara in the south and southeast; an important exporter of phosphates. Official language: Arabic; Berber and French are also widely spoken. Official religion: (Sunni) Muslim. Currency: dirham. Capital: Rabat. Pop: 32 649 130 (2013 est). Area: 458 730 sq km (177 117 sq miles). French name: **Maroc**

moron n **1** *informal, disparaging* a foolish or stupid person **2** *no longer in technical use, offensive* a person having an intelligence quotient of between 50 and 70 [Greek *mōros* foolish] ⟩ **moronic** adj

Moroni n the capital of the Comoros, on the island of Njazidja (Grande Comore). Pop: 59 000 (2005 est)

morose (mor-rohss) adj ill-tempered, sullen, and unwilling to talk very much [Latin *morosus* peevish] ⟩ **morosely** adv

Morpeth n a town in NE England, the administrative centre of Northumberland. Pop: 13 555 (2001)

morpheme n *linguistics* a speech element having a meaning or grammatical function that cannot be subdivided into further such elements

morphine *or* **morphia** n a drug extracted from opium: used in medicine as an anaesthetic and sedative [*Morpheus*, in Greek mythology, the god of sleep and dreams]

morphing n a computer technique used for graphics and in films, in which one image is gradually transformed into another image without individual changes being noticeable in the process [from METAMORPHOSIS]

morphology n the science of forms and structures of organisms or words ⟩ **morphological** adj

Morphy n Paul. 1837–84, US chess player, widely considered to have been the world's greatest player

Morris n William. 1834–96, English poet, designer, craftsman, and socialist writer. He founded the Kelmscott Press (1890)

morris dance n an old English folk dance performed b men (**morris men**) who wear a traditional costume decorated with bells [Middle English *moreys daunce* Moorish dance]

Morrison n **1** Herbert (**Stanley**), Baron Morrison of Lambeth. 1888–1965, British Labour statesman, Home Secretary and Minister for Home Security in Churchill War Cabinet (1942–45) **2** Jim, full name *James Douglas Morrison*. 1943–71, US rock singer and songwriter, lead vocalist with the Doors **3** Toni, full name *Chloe Anthony Morrison*. born 1931, US novelist, whose works include *Su* (1974), *Song of Solomon* (1977), *Beloved* (1987), *Jazz* (1992), anc *Paradise* (1998): awarded the Nobel Prize for literature in 1993 **4** Sir Van, full name *George Ivan Morrison*. born 1945, Northern Irish rock singer and songwriter. His albums include *Astral Weeks* (1968), *Moondance* (1970), *Avalon Sunse* (1989), and *Days Like These* (1995)

morrow n **the morrow** *old-fashioned or poetic* **1** the next da **2** the morning [Old English *morgen* morning]

Morse n Samuel (**Finley Breese**). 1791–1872, US inventor and painter. He invented the first electric telegraph an the Morse code

Morse code n a code formerly used internationally for transmitting messages, in which letters and numbers are represented by groups of dots and dashes, or by shorter and longer sounds [after Samuel MORSE]

morsel n a small piece of something, esp. of food [Old French *mors* a bite]

mortal adj **1** (of living beings, esp. humans) destined to die sometime rather than living forever **2** causing death; fatal: *a mortal wound* **3** deadly or unrelenting: *he is my mortal enemy* **4** of or resulting from the fear of death: *mortal terror* **5** of or involving life or the world: *the hangman's noose ended his mortal existence* **6** great or very intense: *mortal pain* **7** *informal* conceivable or possible: *there was no mortal reason to leave* **8** *slang* long and tedious: *for three mortal hours* ▷ n **9** a human being [Latin *mors* death] ⟩ **mortally** adv

mortality n, pl **-ties** **1** the condition of being mortal **2** great loss of life, as in war or disaster **3** the number of deaths in a given period

mortal sin n *Christianity* a sin that will lead to damnatio unless repented of

mortar n **1** a small cannon that fires shells in high arcs **2** a mixture of cement or lime or both with sand and water, used to hold bricks or stones together **3** a vessel, usually bowl-shaped, in which substances are crushed with a pestle ▷ vb **4** to fire on with mortars **5** to join bricks or stones with mortar [Latin *mortarium* basin in which mortar is mixed]

mortarboard n **1** a black tasselled academic cap with a flat square top **2** a small square board with a handle on the underside for carrying mortar

mortgage n **1** an agreement under which a person borrows money to buy property, esp. a house, and the lender can take possession of the property if the borrower fails to repay the money **2** a loan obtained under such an agreement: *a mortgage of three times one's income* **3** a regular repayment of money borrowed under such an agreement: *the monthly mortgage on the building* ▷ v **-gaging, -gaged 4** to pledge a house or other property a security for the repayment of a loan ▷ adj **5** of or relatin to a mortgage: *a mortgage payment* [Old French, literally: dead pledge]

mortgagee *n* the person or organization who lends money in a mortgage agreement

mortgagor *or* **-ger** *n* the person who borrows money in a mortgage agreement

mortice *or* **mortise** (mor-tiss) *n* **1** a slot or recess cut into a piece of wood or stone to receive a matching projection (tenon) on another piece, or a mortice lock ▷ *vb* **-ticing, -ticed** *or* **-tising, -tised** **2** to cut a slot or recess in a piece of wood or stone **3** to join two pieces of wood or stone by means of a mortice and tenon [Old French *mortoise*]

mortice lock *n* a lock set into the edge of a door so that the mechanism of the lock is enclosed by the door

mortician *n chiefly US* same as **undertaker**

mortify *vb* **-fies, -fying, -fied** **1** to make someone feel ashamed or embarrassed **2** *Christianity* to subdue one's emotions, the body, etc., by self-denial **3** (of flesh) to become gangrenous [Latin *mors* death + *facere* to do] ▷ **mortification** *n* ▷ **mortifying** *adj*

Mortimer *n* **1** Sir John (Clifford). 1923–2009, British barrister, playwright, and novelist, best known for the television series featuring the barrister Horace Rumpole. His novels include *Paradise Postponed* (1985) and *The Sound of Trumpets* (1998) **2** Roger de, 8th Baron of Wigmore and 1st Earl of March. 1287–1330, lover of Isabella, the wife of Edward II of England: they invaded England in 1326 and compelled the king to abdicate in favour of his son, Edward III; executed

Morton *n* **1** 4th Earl of, title of *James Douglas*. 1516–81, regent of Scotland (1572–78) for the young James VI. He was implicated in the murders of Rizzio (1566) and Darnley (1567) and played a leading role in ousting Mary, Queen of Scots; executed **2** Jelly Roll, real name *Ferdinand Joseph La Menthe Morton*. 1885–1941, US jazz pianist, singer, and songwriter; one of the creators of New Orleans jazz

mortuary *n*, *pl* **-aries** a building or room where dead bodies are kept before cremation or burial [Latin *mortuarius* of the dead]

mosaic (moh-**zay**-ik) *n* a design or decoration made up of small pieces of coloured glass or stone [Greek *mouseios* of the Muses]

Mosaic *adj* of or relating to Moses or the laws and traditions ascribed to him

Moscow *n* the capital of Russia and of the Moscow Autonomous Region, on the Moskva River: dates from the 11th century; capital of the grand duchy of Russia from 1547 to 1712; capital of the Soviet Union 1918–91; centres on the medieval Kremlin; chief political, cultural, and industrial centre of Russia, with two universities. Pop: 10 672 000 (2005 est). Russian name: Moskva. Related noun: **Muscovite**

Moseley *n* Henry Gwyn-Jeffreys. 1887–1915, English physicist. He showed that the wavelengths of X-rays emitted from the elements are related to their atomic numbers

Moselle *n* **1** a department of NE France, in Lorraine region. Capital: Metz. Pop: 1 027 854 (2003 est). Area: 6253 sq km (2439 sq miles) **2** a river in W Europe, rising in NE France and flowing northwest, forming part of the border between Luxembourg and Germany, then northeast to the Rhine: many vineyards along its lower course. Length: 547 km (340 miles). German name: Mosel **3** (*sometimes not cap*) a German white wine from the Moselle valley

Moses *n* **1** *Old Testament* the Hebrew prophet who led the Israelites out of Egypt to the Promised Land and gave them divinely revealed laws **2** Ed. born 1956, US hurdler; winner of the 400 m hurdles in the 1976 and 1984 Olympic Games **3** Grandma, real name *Anna Mary Robertson Moses*. 1860–1961, US painter of primitives, who began to paint at the age of 75

mosey *vb* mosey along *or* on *informal* to walk slowly and casually; amble [origin unknown]

Moshesh *or* **Moshoeshoe** *n* died 1870, African chief, who founded the Basotho nation, now Lesotho

Mosi-oa-Tunya *pl n* the local name for **Victoria Falls** [from Lozi: 'the smoke that thunders']

Moskva *n* **1** transliteration of the Russian name for Moscow **2** a river in W central Russia, rising in the Smolensk-Moscow upland, and flowing southeast through Moscow to the Oka River: linked with the River Volga by the Moscow Canal. Length: about 500 km (310 miles)

Moslem *n*, *pl* **-lems** *or* **-lem**, *adj* same as **Muslim**

Mosley *n* Sir Oswald Ernald. 1896–1980, British politician; founder of the British Union of Fascists (1932)

mosque *n* a Muslim place of worship [Arabic *masjid* temple]

mosquito *n*, *pl* **-toes** *or* **-tos** a two-winged insect, the females of which pierce the skin of humans and animals to suck their blood [Spanish, diminutive of *mosca* fly]

mosquito net *n* a fine curtain or net to keep mosquitoes away, esp. hung over a bed

moss *n* **1** a very small flowerless plant typically growing in dense mats on trees, rocks, or moist ground **2** *Scot and N English* a peat bog or marsh [Old English *mos* swamp] ▷ **mossy** *adj*

Moss *n* **1** Kate. born 1974, British supermodel. **2** Sir Stirling. born 1929, English racing driver

mossie *n S African* the common sparrow [Afrikaans]

moss rose *n* a variety of rose that has a mossy stem and fragrant pink flowers

most *n* **1** the greatest number or degree: *the most I can ever remember being paid* **2** the majority: *most of his records are dreadful* **3** at (the) most at the maximum: *she is fifteen at the most* **4** make the most of to use to the best advantage: *they made the most of their chances* ▷ *adj* **5** of or being the majority of a group of things or people or the largest part of something: *most people don't share your views* **6** the most the superlative of **many, much**: *he has the most talent* ▷ *adv* **7** the most used to form the superlative of some adjectives and adverbs: *the most beautiful women in the world* **8** the superlative of **much**: *what do you like most about your job?* **9** very; exceedingly: *a most unfortunate accident* [Old English *māst* or *mǣst*]

> **USAGE** *More* and *most* should be distinguished when used in comparisons. *More* applies to cases involving two people, objects, etc., *most* to cases involving three or more: *John is the more intelligent of the two; he is the most intelligent of the students.*

Mostaganem *n* a port in NW Algeria, on the Mediterranean Sea: exports wine, fruit, and vegetables. Pop: 133 000 (2005 est)

mostly *adv* **1** almost entirely; generally: *the men at the party were mostly young* **2** on many or most occasions; usually: *rattlesnakes mostly hunt at night*

Most Reverend *n* (in Britain) a courtesy title applied to archbishops

Mosul *n* a city in N Iraq, on the River Tigris opposite the ruins of Nineveh: an important commercial centre with nearby Ayn Zalah oilfield; university. Pop: 1 236 000 (2005 est)

mot (moh) *n* short for **bon mot** [French: word]

MOT **1** *Brit* short for **MOT test** **2** *Brit* the certificate showing that a vehicle has passed its MOT test **3** *NZ* Ministry of Transport

mote *n* a tiny speck [Old English *mot*]

motel *n* a roadside hotel for motorists [*mo(tor)* + *(ho)tel*]

motet (moh-**tet**) *n* a religious song for a choir in which several voices, usually unaccompanied, sing contrasting parts simultaneously [Old French, diminutive of *mot* word]

moth *n* any of numerous chiefly nocturnal insects resembling butterflies, that typically have stout bodies and do not have club-shaped antennae [Old English *moththe*]

mothball *n* **1** a small ball of camphor or naphthalene placed in stored clothing to repel clothes moths **2 put in mothballs** to postpone work on ▷ *vb* **3** to take something out of operation but maintain it for future use **4** to postpone work on

moth-eaten *adj* **1** decayed or scruffy **2** eaten away by or as if by moths: *a moth-eaten suit*

mother *n* **1** a female who has given birth to offspring **2** a person's own mother **3** a title given to certain members of female religious orders **4** motherly qualities, such as maternal affection: *it appealed to the mother in her* **5** the mother of a female or thing that creates, founds, or protects something: *the mother of modern feminism; necessity is the mother of invention* **6 the mother of all** *informal* the greatest example of its kind: *the mother of all parties* ▷ *adj* **7** of or relating to a female or thing that creates, founds, or protects something: *our mother company is in New York* **8** native or innate: *mother wit* ▷ *vb* **9** to give birth to or produce **10** to nurture or protect [Old English *mōdor*] ▷ **motherless** *adj* ▷ **motherly** *adj*

Mother Carey's chicken *n* same as **stormy petrel** [origin unknown]

Mother City *n S African* an informal name for **Cape Town**

mother country *n* **1** the original country of colonists or settlers **2** a person's native country

motherhood *n* the state of being a mother

Mothering Sunday *n* **1** (in Britain and S Africa) the fourth Sunday in Lent, when mothers traditionally receive presents from their children **2** (in Australia) the second Sunday in May, when mothers traditionally receive presents from their children ▷ Also called: **Mother's Day**

mother-in-law *n*, *pl* **mothers-in-law** the mother of one's wife or husband

motherland *n* a person's native country

mother-of-pearl *n* a hard iridescent substance that forms the inner layer of the shells of certain molluscs, such as the oyster

Mother's Day *n* **1** See **Mothering Sunday** **2** *US and Canad* the second Sunday in May, observed as a day in honour of mothers

mother superior *n*, *pl* **mother superiors** *or* **mothers superior** the head of a community of nuns

mother tongue *n* the language first learned by a child

Motherwell *n* a town in S central Scotland, the administrative centre of North Lanarkshire on the River Clyde: industrial centre. Pop: 30 311 (2001)

mothproof *adj* **1** (esp. of clothes) chemically treated so as to repel clothes moths ▷ *vb* **2** to make mothproof

motif (moh-**teef**) *n* **1** a distinctive idea, esp. a theme elaborated on in a piece of music or literature **2** a recurring shape in a design **3** a single decoration, such as a symbol or name on a piece of clothing [French]

motile *adj* capable of independent movement [Latin *movere* to move] ▷ **motility** *n*

motion *n* **1** the process of continual change in the position of an object; movement: *the motion of the earth round the sun*. Related adjective: **kinetic 2** a movement or gesture: *he made stabbing motions with the spear* **3** a way or style of moving: *massage the back with steady circular motions* **4** a formal proposal to be discussed and voted on in a debate or meeting **5** *Brit* **a** the evacuation of the bowels **b** excrement **6 go through the motions** to do something mechanically or without sincerity **7 set in motion** to make operational or start functioning ▷ *vb* **8** to signal or direct a person by a movement or gesture: *she motioned to me to sit down* [Latin *movere* to move] ▷ **motionless** *adj*

Motion *n* Sir Andrew. born 1952, British poet and biographer; his collections include *Pleasure Steamers* (1978) and *Public Property* (2002): poet laureate (1999–2009)

motion picture *n US and Canad* a film; movie

motivate *vb* **-vating, -vated 1** to give a reason or

inspiration for a course of action to someone: *he was motivated purely by greed* **2** to inspire and encourage someone to do something: *a good teacher must motivate her pupils* ▷ **motivation** *n*

motive *n* **1** the reason, whether conscious or unconscious, for a certain course of action **2** same as **motif** (2) ▷ *adj* **3** of or causing motion: *a motive force* [Late Latin *motivus* moving]

motive power *n* **1** any source of energy used to produce motion **2** the means of supplying power to an engine or vehicle

mot juste (moh **zhoost**) *n*, *pl* **mots justes** the appropriate word or expression [French]

motley *adj* **1** made up of people or things of different types: *a motley assortment of mules, donkeys, and camels* **2** multicoloured ▷ *n* **3** *history* the costume of a jester [perhaps Old English *mot* speck]

motocross *n* the sport of motorcycle racing across rough ground [*moto*(r) + *cross*(-country)]

motor *n* **1** the engine, esp. an internal-combustion engine, of a vehicle **2** a machine that converts energy, esp. electrical energy, into mechanical energy **3** *chiefly Brit informal* a car ▷ *adj* **4** *chiefly Brit* of or relating to cars and other vehicles powered by petrol or diesel engines: *the motor industry* **5** powered by or relating to a motor: *a new synthetic motor oil* **6** *physiol* producing or causing motion ▷ *vb* **7** to travel by car **8** *informal* to move fast [Latin *movere* to move] ▷ **motorized** *or* **-ised** *adj*

motorbicycle *n* **1** a motorcycle **2** a moped

motorbike *n informal* a motorcycle

motorboat *n* any boat powered by a motor

motorcade *n* a procession of cars carrying an important person or people [*motor* + (*caval*)*cade*]

motorcar *n* a more formal word for **car**

motorcycle *n* a two-wheeled vehicle driven by an engine ▷ **motorcyclist** *n*

motorist *n* a driver of a car

motorman *n*, *pl* **-men** *Brit, Austral and NZ* the driver of an electric train

motor scooter *n* a light motorcycle with small wheels and an enclosed engine

motor vehicle *n* a road vehicle driven by an engine

motorway *n Brit, Austral and NZ* a dual carriageway for fast-moving traffic, with no stopping permitted and no crossroads

Motown *n trademark* music combining rhythm and blues and pop [*Mo*(tor) *Town*, nickname for Detroit]

motte *n history* a mound on which a castle was built [Old French]

MOT test *n* (in Britain) a compulsory annual test of the roadworthiness of motor vehicles over 3 years old

mottled *adj* coloured with streaks or blotches of different shades [from *motley*] ▷ **mottling** *n*

motto *n*, *pl* **-toes** *or* **-tos 1** a short saying expressing the guiding maxim or ideal of a family or organization, esp. when part of a coat of arms **2** a verse or maxim contained in a paper cracker **3** a quotation prefacing a book or chapter of a book [Italian]

mould¹ *or US* **mold** *n* **1** a shaped hollow container into which a liquid material is poured so that it can set in a particular shape: *pour the mixture into a buttered mould, cover, and steam for two hours* **2** a shape, nature, or type: *an orthodox Communist in the Stalinist mould* **3** a framework around which something is constructed or shaped: *the heated glass is shaped round a mould inside a kiln* **4** something, esp. a food, made in or on a mould: *salmon mould* ▷ *vb* **5** to make in a mould **6** to shape or form: *a figure moulded out of clay* **7** to influence or direct: *cultural factors moulding our everyday life* [Latin *modulus* a small measure]

mould² *or US* **mold** *n* a coating or discoloration caused by various fungi that develop in a damp atmosphere on food, fabrics, and walls [Northern English dialect *mowlde* mouldy]

mould³ *or US* **mold** *n* loose soil, esp. when rich in organic matter: *leaf mould* [Old English *molde*]

mouldboard *or US* **moldboard** *n* the curved blade of a plough, which turns over the furrow

moulder *or US* **molder** *vb* to crumble or cause to crumble, as through decay: *John Brown's body lies mouldering in the grave* [from MOULD³]

moulding *or US* **molding** *n* a shaped ornamental edging

mouldy *or US* **moldy** *adj* **-dier, -diest** **1** covered with mould **2** stale or musty, esp. from age or lack of use **3** *slang* dull or boring

Moulin *n* Jean. 1899–1943, French lawyer and Resistance hero; Chairman of the National Council of the Resistance (1943): tortured to death by the Nazis

Moulins *n* a market town in central France, on the Allier River. Pop: 21 892 (1999)

Moulmein *or* **Maulmain** *n* a port in S Myanmar, near the mouth of the Salween River: exports teak and rice. Pop: 390 000 (2005 est)

moult *or US* **molt** *vb* **1** (of birds and animals) to shed feathers, hair, or skin so that they can be replaced by a new growth ▷ *n* **2** the periodic process of moulting [Latin *mutare* to change]

mound *n* **1** a heap of earth, debris, etc. **2** any heap or pile **3** a small natural hill [origin unknown]

mount¹ *vb* **1** to climb or ascend: *he mounted the stairs to his flat* **2** to get up on a horse, a platform, etc. **3** Also: **mount up** to increase or accumulate: *costs do mount up; the tension mounted* **4** to fix onto a backing, setting, or support: *sensors mounted on motorway bridges* **5** to organize and stage a campaign, play, etc.: *the Allies mounted a counter attack on the eastern front* ▷ *n* **6** a backing, setting, or support onto which something is fixed: *a diamond set in a gold mount* **7** a horse for riding: *none of his mounts at yesterday's race meeting finished better than third* [same as MOUNT²]

mount² *n* a mountain or hill: used in literature and (when cap.) in proper names: *Mount Etna* [Latin *mons* mountain]

mountain *n* **1** a very large, high, and steep hill: *the highest mountain in the Alps* **2** a huge heap or mass: *a mountain of papers* **3** a surplus of a commodity, esp. in the European Union: *a butter mountain* ▷ *adj* **4** of, found on, or for use on a mountain or mountains: *a mountain village* [Latin *mons*]

mountain ash *n* a tree with clusters of small white flowers and bright red berries; rowan

mountain bike *n* a type of bicycle with straight handlebars and heavy-duty tyres, originally designed for use over rough hilly ground

mountain cat *n* any of various wild animals of the cat family, such as the bobcat, lynx, or puma

mountaineer *n* **1** a person who climbs mountains ▷ *vb* **2** to climb mountains **>** **mountaineering** *n*

mountain goat *n* a wild goat inhabiting mountainous regions

mountain lion *n* a puma

mountainous *adj* **1** having many mountains: *a mountainous region* **2** like a mountain or mountains, esp. in size: *mountainous waves*

mountain oyster *n* NZ *informal* a sheep's testicle eaten as food

mountain sickness *n* nausea, headache, and shortness of breath caused by climbing to high altitudes

Mountbatten *n* Louis (Francis Albert Victor Nicholas), 1st Earl Mountbatten of Burma 1900–79, British naval commander; great-grandson of Queen Victoria. During World War II he was supreme allied commander in SE Asia (1943–46). He was the last viceroy of India (1947) and governor general (1947–48); killed by an IRA bomb

Mount Desert Island *n* an island off the coast of Maine: lakes and granite peaks. Area: 279 sq km (108 sq miles)

mountebank *n* **1** (formerly) a person who sold quack medicines in public places **2** a charlatan or fake [Italian *montambanco* a climber on a bench]

mounted *adj* riding horses: *mounted police*

Mountie *or* **Mounty** *n, pl* **Mounties** *informal* a member of the Royal Canadian Mounted Police [from *mounted*]

mounting *n* same as **mount¹** (6)

Mount Isa *n* a city in NE Australia in NW Queensland: mining of copper and other minerals. Pop: 20 525 (2001)

Mount McKinley National Park *n* the former name of Denali National Park and Preserve

Mount Rainier National Park *n* a national park in W Washington, in the Cascade Range. Area: 976 sq km (377 sq miles)

mourn *vb* to feel or express sadness for the death or loss of someone or something [Old English *murnan*] **>** **mourner** *n*

Mourne Mountains *pl n* a mountain range in SE Northern Ireland. Highest peak: Slieve Donard, 853 m (2798 ft)

mournful *adj* **1** feeling or expressing grief and sadness: *he stood by, a mournful expression on his face* **2** (of a sound) suggestive or reminiscent of grief or sadness: *the locomotive gave a mournful bellow* **>** **mournfully** *adv*

mourning *n* **1** sorrow or grief, esp. over a death **2** the conventional symbols of grief for a death, such as the wearing of black **3** the period of time during which a death is officially mourned ▷ *adj* **4** of or relating to mourning

mouse *n, pl* **mice** **1** a small long-tailed rodent similar to but smaller than a rat **2** a quiet, timid, or cowardly person **3** *computers* a hand-held device used to control cursor movements and computing functions without keying ▷ *vb* **mousing, moused** **4** *rare* to stalk and catch mice [Old English *mūs*]

mouser *n* a cat or other animal that is used to catch mice

mousetrap *n* **1** a spring-loaded trap for killing mice **2** *Brit informal* cheese of mediocre quality

moussaka *n* a dish originating in the Balkan States, consisting of meat, aubergines, and tomatoes, topped with cheese sauce [Modern Greek]

mousse *n* **1** a light creamy dessert made with eggs, cream, and fruit set with gelatine **2** a similar dish made from fish or meat **3** short for **styling mousse** [French: froth]

moustache *or US* **mustache** *n* unshaved hair growing on the upper lip [French, from Italian *mostaccio*]

mousy *or* **mousey** *adj* **mousier, mousiest** **1** (of hair) dull light brown in colour **2** shy or ineffectual **>** **mousiness** *n*

mouth *n, pl* **mouths** **1** the opening through which many animals take in food and issue sounds **2** the visible part of the mouth; lips **3** a person regarded as a consumer of food: *three mouths to feed* **4** a particular manner of speaking: *a foul mouth* **5** *informal* boastful, rude, or excessive talk: *she is all mouth* **6** the point where a river issues into a sea or lake **7** an opening, such as that of a bottle, tunnel, or gun **8 down in the mouth** in low spirits ▷ *vb* **9** to form words with movements of the lips but without speaking **10** to speak or say something insincerely, esp. in public: *ministers mouthing platitudes* [Old English *mūth*]

mouthful *n, pl* **-fuls** **1** the amount of food or drink put into the mouth at any one time when eating or drinking **2** a long word, phrase, or name that is difficult to say **3** *Brit informal* an abusive response: *I asked him to move and he just gave me a mouthful*

mouth organ *n* same as **harmonica**

mouthpiece *n* **1** the part of a wind instrument into which the player blows **2** the part of a telephone receiver into which a person speaks **3** a person or publication expressing the views of an organization

mouthwash *n* a medicated solution for gargling and cleansing the mouth

mouthwatering *adj* (of food) making one want to eat it, because it looks or smells delicious

movable *or* **moveable** *adj* **1** able to be moved; not fixed **2** (of a festival, esp. Easter) varying in date from year to year ▷ *n* **3 movables** movable articles, esp. furniture

move *vb* **moving, moved 1** to go or take from one place to another; change in position: *I moved your books off the table* **2** to start to live or work in a different place: *I moved to Brighton from Bristol last year* **3** to be or cause to be in motion: *the trees were moving in the wind; the car moved slowly down the road* **4** to act or begin to act: *the government plans to move to reduce crime* **5** to cause or prompt to do something: *public opinion moved the President to act* **6** to change the time when something is scheduled to happen: *can I move the appointment to Friday afternoon, please?* **7** to arouse affection, pity, or compassion in; touch: *her story moved me to tears* **8** to change, progress, or develop in a specified way: *the conversation moved to more personal matters* **9** to suggest a proposal formally, as in a debate: *to move a motion* **10** to spend most of one's time with a specified social group: *they both move in theatrical, arty circles* **11** (in board games) to change the position of a piece **12** (of machines) to work or operate **13 a** (of the bowels) to excrete waste **b** to cause the bowels to excrete waste **14** (of merchandise) to be disposed of by being bought **15** to travel quickly: *this car can really move* **16 move heaven and earth** to do everything possible to achieve a result ▷ *n* **17** the act of moving; movement **18** one of a sequence of actions, usually part of a plan: *the first real move towards disarmament* **19** the act of moving one's home or place of business **20 a** (in a boardgame) a player's turn to move his piece **b** (in a boardgame) a manoeuvre of a piece **21 get a move on** *informal* to hurry up **22 make a move** *informal* **a** to prepare or begin to leave a place to go somewhere else: *we'd better make a move if we want to be home before dark* **b** to do something which will produce a response: *neither of us wanted to make the first move* **23 on the move** travelling from place to place [Latin *movere*]

move in *vb* **1** Also: **move into** to start to live in a different house or flat **2** to start to live in the same house or flat as: *he moved in with his girlfriend* **3** to attack a person or place, or try to gain influence or control over a person or activity: *the police moved in to break up the demonstration*

movement *n* **1** the act, process, or an instance of moving **2** the manner of moving: *their movement is jerky* **3 a** a group of people with a common ideology **b** the organized action and campaigning of such a group: *a successful movement to abolish child labour* **4** a trend or tendency: *a movement towards shorter working hours* **5** finance a change in the price or value of shares, a currency, etc.: *adverse currency movements* **6** music a principal self-contained section of a large-scale work, such as a symphony **7 movements** a person's location and activities during a specific time: *police were trying to piece together the recent movements of the two men* **8 a** the evacuation of the bowels **b** the matter evacuated **9** the mechanism which drives and regulates a watch or clock

move on *vb* **1** to leave one place in order to go elsewhere: *we spent three days in Perth before moving on towards Inverness* **2** to order (someone) to leave and go elsewhere: *we were moved on by the police* **3** to finish one thing and turn one's attention to something else: *can we move on to the next question?*

move over *vb* **1** to change one's position in order to make room for someone else: *if you moved over there'd be room for us both on the couch* **2** to leave one's job so that someone else can have it: *she decided to move over to let someone younger onto the board*

mover *n* **1** a person or animal that moves in a particular way: *a slow mover* **2** the person who first puts forward a proposal **3** *US and Canad* a removal firm or a person who works for one

movie *n* **1** *informal* a cinema film **2 the movies** the cinema: *I want to go to the movies tonight*

moving *adj* **1** arousing or touching the emotions: *a moving account of her son's death* **2** changing or capable of changing position: *a moving target* **> movingly** *adv*

moving staircase *or* **moving stairway** *n* an escalator

mow *vb* **mowing, mowed, mowed** *or* **mown 1** to cut down grass or crops: *a tractor chugged along, mowing hay* **2** to cut the growing vegetation of a field or lawn: *to mow a meadow* [Old English *māwan*] **> mower** *n*

mow down *vb* to kill in large numbers, esp. by gunfire

Mowlam *n* **Mo**, full name *Marjorie Mowlam*. 1949–2005, British Labour politician; secretary of state for Northern Ireland (1997–99) and minister for the cabinet office (1999–2001)

mown *vb* the past participle of **mow**

Moya *n* (**John**) **Hidalgo**. 1920–94, British architect: in partnership with Philip Powell, his designs include Skylon, Festival of Britain (1950), Wolfson College, Oxford (1974), and the Queen Elizabeth Conference Centre, Westminster (1986)

Moyle *n* a district of NE Northern Ireland, in Co Antrim. Pop: 16 302 (2003 est). Area: 494 sq km (191 sq miles)

Mozambican *or* **Mozambiquan** *adj* **1** of or relating to Mozambique or its inhabitants ▷ *n* **2** a native or inhabitant of Mozambique

Mozambique *n* a republic in SE Africa: colonized by the Portuguese from 1505 onwards and a slave-trade centre until 1878; made an overseas province of Portugal in 1951; became an independent republic in 1975; became a member of the Commonwealth in 1995. Official language: Portuguese. Religion: animist majority. Currency: metical. Capital: Maputo. Pop: 24 096 669 (2013 est). Area: 812 379 sq km (313 661 sq miles). Portuguese name: **Moçambique**. Also called (until 1975): **Portuguese East Africa**

Mozambique Channel *n* a strait between Mozambique and Madagascar. Length: about 1600 km (1000 miles). Width: 400 km (250 miles)

Mozart *n* **Wolfgang Amadeus**. 1756–91, Austrian composer. A child prodigy and prolific genius, his works include operas, such as *The Marriage of Figaro* (1786), *Don Giovanni* (1787), and *The Magic Flute* (1791), symphonies, concertos for piano, violin, clarinet, and French horn, string quartets and quintets, sonatas, songs, and Masses, such as the unfinished *Requiem* (1791) **> Mozartean** *or* **Mozartian** *adj*

Mo-Zi *or* **Mo-tzu** *n* ?470–?391 BC, Chinese religious philosopher; his teaching, expounded in the book *Mo-Zi*, emphasizes love, frugality, avoidance of aggressive war, and submission to Heaven

mozzarella (mot-sa-**rel**-la) *n* a moist white curd cheese originally made in Italy from buffalo milk [Italian]

MP 1 Member of Parliament **2** Military Police **3** Mounted Police

MP3 *n computers* an audio or video file created using MPEG-1 Audio Layer-3, trade name of a file compression system

MP3 player *n* a small portable digital audio player capable of storing and playing files downloaded from the internet or transferred from a CD

MPEG (**em**-peg) *n computers* **a** a standard compressed file format used for audio and video files **b** a file in this format [from *Motion Picture Experts Group*]

mpg miles per gallon

mph miles per hour

MPhil Master of Philosophy

Mpumalanga *n* a province of E South Africa; formed in 1994 (originally as Eastern Transvaal) from part of the former province of Transvaal: agriculture and service industries. Capital: Nelspruit. Pop: 4 039 939 (2011 est). Area: 78 370 sq km (30 259 sq miles)

MPV multipurpose vehicle

Mr *n*, *pl* **Messrs** a title used before a man's name or before some office that he holds: *Mr Pickwick; Mr President* [from *mister*]

MRI *med* magnetic resonance imaging: a diagnostic scanning technique which gives detailed images of internal tissue by analysing its response to being bombarded with high-frequency radio waves within a strong magnetic field

Mrs *n*, *pl* **Mrs** *or* **Mesdames** a title used before the name of a married woman [from *mistress*]

ms millisecond(s)

Ms (mizz) *n* a title used before the name of a woman to avoid indicating whether she is married or not

MS **1** Mississippi **2** multiple sclerosis

MS. *or* **ms.** *pl* **MSS.** *or* **mss.** manuscript

MSc Master of Science

MSF Manufacturing, Science, and Finance (Union)

MSG monosodium glutamate

MSM mainstream media

MSP (in Britain) Member of the Scottish Parliament

MST Mountain Standard Time

mt megaton

Mt¹ Mount: *Mt Everest*

Mt² *chem* meitnerium

MT Montana

mt. megaton

MTech (in the US) Master of Technology

Mu'awiyah I *n* ?602–680 AD, first caliph (661–80) of the Omayyad dynasty of Damascus; regarded as having secularized the caliphate

Mubarak *n* (Muhammad) Hosni, born 1928, Egyptian statesman: president of Egypt (1981–2011); ousted from office after mass demonstrations

much *adj* **more**, **most 1** a large amount or degree of: *there isn't much wine left* ▷ *n* **2** a large amount or degree **3** a bit **much** *informal* rather excessive **4 make much of a** to make sense of: *he couldn't make much of her letter* **b** to give importance to: *the press made much of the story* **5 not much of** not to any appreciable degree or extent: *he's not much of a cook* **6 not up to much** *informal* of a low standard: *this beer is not up to much* ▷ *adv* **7** considerably: *I'm much better now* **8** practically or nearly: *it's much the same* **9** often or a great deal: *that doesn't happen much these days* **10 (as) much as** even though; although: *much as I'd like to, I can't come* ▶ See also **more**, **most** [Old English *mycel*]

muchness *n* **much of a muchness** *Brit and NZ* very similar

mucilage (mew-sill-ij) *n* **1** a sticky substance used as an adhesive, such as gum or glue **2** a glutinous substance secreted by certain plants [Late Latin *mucilago* mouldy juice] ▷ **mucilaginous** *adj*

muck *n* **1** dirt or filth **2** farmyard dung or decaying vegetable matter **3** *slang, chiefly Brit and NZ* something of poor quality; rubbish: *I don't want to eat this muck* **4 make a muck of** *slang, chiefly Brit and NZ* to ruin or spoil ▷ *vb* **5** to spread manure upon ▶ See also **muck about**, **muck in**, etc. [probably Old Norse]

muck about *or* **muck around** *vb slang* **1** to waste time by misbehaving or being silly **2 muck about with** to interfere with, annoy, or waste the time of

muck in *vb Brit and NZ slang* to share duties or work with other people

muck out *vb* to clean (a barn, stable, etc.)

muckraking *n* seeking out and exposing scandal relating to well-known people ▷ **muckraker** *n*

mucksweat *n Brit informal* profuse sweat

muck up *vb informal* to ruin, spoil, or do very badly: *I mucked up my driving test*

mucky *adj* **1** dirty or muddy: *don't come in here with your mucky boots on!* **2** sexually explicit; obscene: *a mucky book*

mucosa *n* same as **mucous membrane** [Latin *mucosus* slimy] ▷ **mucosal** *adj*

mucous membrane *n* a mucus-secreting tissue that lines body cavities or passages

mucus (mew-kuss) *n* the slimy protective secretion of the mucous membranes [Latin: nasal secretions] ▷ **mucosity** *n* ▷ **mucous** *adj*

mud *n* **1** soft wet earth, as found on the ground after rain or at the bottom of ponds **2 (someone's) name is mud** *informal* (someone) is disgraced **3 throw mud at** *informal* to slander or vilify ▷ *adj* **4** made from mud or dried mud: *a mud hut* [probably Low German *mudde*]

mud bath *n* **1** a medicinal bath in heated mud **2** a dirty or muddy place, occasion, or state: *heavy rain turned the pitch into a mud bath*

muddle *n* **1** a state of untidiness or confusion: *the files are in a terrible muddle* **2** a state of mental confusion or uncertainty: *the government are in a muddle over the economy* ▷ *vb* **-dling**, **-dled 3** Also: **muddle up** to mix up or confuse (objects or items): *you've got your books all muddled up with mine* **4** to make (someone) confused: *don't muddle her with too many suggestions* [perhaps Middle Dutch *moddelen* to make muddy] ▷ **muddled** *adj*

muddleheaded *adj* mentally confused or vague

muddle through *vb* to succeed in spite of lack of organization

muddy *adj* **-dier**, **-diest 1** covered or filled with mud **2** not clear or bright: *muddy colours* **3** cloudy: *a muddy liquid* **4** (esp. of thoughts) confused or vague ▷ *vb* **-dies**, **-dying**, **-died 5** to make muddy **6** to make a situation or issue less clear: *the allegations of sexual misconduct only serve to muddy the issue* ▷ **muddily** *adv*

mud flat *n* an area of low muddy land that is covered at high tide but not at low tide

mud flow *n* the rapid downhill movement of a mass of mud, typically in the shape of a tongue

mudguard *n* a curved part of a bicycle or other vehicle attached above the wheels to reduce the amount of water or mud thrown up by them

mudpack *n* a cosmetic paste applied to the face to improve the complexion

mudpie *n* a mass of mud moulded into a pielike shape by a child

mudslinging *n* the making of malicious personal attacks on an opponent, esp. in politics ▷ **mudslinger** *n*

muesli (mewz-lee) *n* a mixture of rolled oats, nuts, and dried fruit, usually eaten with milk [Swiss German]

muezzin (moo-ezz-in) *n Islam* the official of a mosque who calls the faithful to prayer from the minaret [Arabic *mu'adhdhin*]

muff¹ *n* a tube of fur or cloth into which the hands are placed for warmth [probably Dutch *mof*]

muff² *vb* **1** to do (something) badly: *I muffed my chance to make a good impression* **2** to bungle (a shot or catch) [origin unknown]

muffin *n* **1** a small cup-shaped sweet bread roll, usually eaten hot with butter **2** a thick round baked yeast roll, usually toasted and served with butter [origin unknown]

muffle *vb* **-fling**, **-fled 1** to deaden (a sound or noise), esp. by wrapping the source of it in something: *the sound was muffled by the double glazing* **2** to wrap up in a scarf or coat for warmth **3** to censor or restrict: *an attempt to muffle criticism* [probably Old French *moufle* mitten] ▷ **muffled** *adj*

muffler *n* **1** *Brit* a thick scarf worn for warmth **2** *US and Canad* a device to deaden sound, esp. one on a car exhaust; silencer

mufti *n* civilian clothes worn by a person who normally wears a military uniform [from *Mufti*, Muslim religious leader]

Mufulira *n* a mining town in the Copper Belt of Zambia. Pop: 220 000 (2005 est)

mug¹ *n* **1** a large drinking cup with a handle **2** the quantity held by a mug or its contents: *a mug of coffee* [probably Scandinavian]

mug² *n* **1** *slang* a person's face or mouth: *keep your ugly mug out of this* **2** *slang* a gullible person, esp. one who is swindled easily **3 a mug's game** a worthless activity [perhaps same as MUG¹]

mug³ *vb* **mugging**, **mugged** to attack someone in order to rob them ▷ **mugger** *n* ▷ **mugging** *n*

Mugabe *n* Robert, born 1925, Zimbabwean politician; leader of one wing of the Patriotic Front against the government of Ian Smith of Rhodesia, and of the Zanu party; prime minister (1980–87); president from 1987

muggins n slang **a** a stupid or gullible person **b** a title used humorously to refer to oneself [probably from surname Muggins]

muggy adj **-gier, -giest** (of weather or air) unpleasantly warm and humid [dialect mug drizzle] **> mugginess** n

mug shot n informal a photograph of a person's face, esp. one resembling a police-file picture

mug up vb Brit slang to study a subject hard, esp. for an exam [origin unknown]

Muhammad n ?570–632 AD, the prophet believed by Muslims to be the channel for the final unfolding of God's revelation to mankind: popularly regarded as the founder of Islam. He began to teach in Mecca in 610 but persecution forced him to flee with his followers to Medina in 622. After several battles, he conquered Mecca (630), establishing the principles of Islam (embodied in the Koran) over all Arabia

Muhammad Ali, Muhammed Ali or **Mohammed Ali** n original name Cassius (Marcellus) Clay. born 1942, US boxer, who was world heavyweight champion three times (1964–67; 1974–78; 1978)

Mühlhausen n the German name for **Mulhouse**

Muir n Edwin. 1887–1959, Scottish poet, novelist, and critic

Muir Glacier n a glacier in SE Alaska, in the St Elias Mountains, flowing southeast from Mount Fairweather. Area: about 900 sq km (350 sq miles)

mujaheddin or **mujahedeen** (moo-ja-hed-**deen**) pl n fundamentalist Muslim guerrillas [Arabic mujāhidīn fighters]

Mukden n a former name of **Shenyang**

mukluk n a soft boot, usually of sealskin, worn in the American Arctic [Yupik (native language of Siberia and Alaska) muklok large seal]

mulatto (mew-lat-toe) n, pl **-tos** or **-toes** old-fashioned, offensive a person with one Black and one White parent [Spanish mulato young mule]

mulberry n, pl **-ries** **1** a tree with edible blackberry-like fruit, the leaves of which are used to feed silkworms **2** the fruit of any of these trees ▷ adj **3** dark purple [Latin morum]

mulch n **1** a mixture of half-rotten vegetable matter and peat used to protect the roots of plants or enrich the soil ▷ vb **2** to cover soil with mulch [obsolete mulch soft]

Muldoon n Sir Robert (David). 1921–92, New Zealand statesman; prime minister of New Zealand (1975–84)

mule[1] n **1** the sterile offspring of a male donkey and a female horse **2** a machine that spins cotton into yarn [Latin mulus]

mule[2] n a backless shoe or slipper [Latin mulleus a magistrate's shoe]

muleteer n a person who drives mules

mulga n **1** an Australian acacia shrub growing in desert regions **2** Austral the outback [Aboriginal]

Mulhacén n a mountain in S Spain, in the Sierra Nevada: the highest peak in Spain. Height: 3478 m (11 410 ft)

Mülheim an der Ruhr or **Mülheim** n an industrial city in W Germany, in North Rhine-Westphalia on the River Ruhr: river port. Pop: 170 745 (2003 est)

Mulhouse n a city in E France, on the Rhône-Rhine canal: under German rule (1871–1918); textiles. Pop: 112 260 (2006). German name: **Mühlhausen**

mulish adj stubborn; obstinate

mull n Scot a promontory or headland: the Mull of Galloway [probably Gaelic maol]

Mull n a mountainous island off the west coast of Scotland, in the Inner Hebrides, separated from the mainland by the **Sound of Mull**. Chief town: Tobermory. Pop: 2667 (2001). Area: 909 sq km (351 sq miles)

mullah n (formerly) a Muslim scholar, teacher, or religious leader [Arabic mawlā master]

mulled adj (of wine or ale) flavoured with sugar and spices and served hot [origin unknown]

Muller n Hermann Joseph. 1890–1967, US geneticist, noted for his work on the transmutation of genes by X-rays: Nobel prize for physiology or medicine 1946

Müller n **1** (Friedrich) Max. 1823–1900, British Sanskrit scholar born in Germany **2** Johann. See **Regiomontanus 3** Johannes Peter. 1801–58, German physiologist, anatomist, and experimental psychologist **4** Paul Hermann. 1899–1965, Swiss chemist. He synthesized DDT (1939) and discovered its use as an insecticide: Nobel prize for physiology or medicine 1948

mullet n, pl **mullets** or **mullet** any of various marine food fishes [Greek mullos]

Mulligan n Gerry, full name Gerald Joseph Mulligan. 1927–96, US jazz saxophonist, who pioneered the cool jazz style of the 1950s

mulligatawny n a curry-flavoured soup of Anglo-Indian origin [Tamil milakutanni pepper water]

Mulliken n Robert Sanderson. 1896–1986, US physicist and chemist, who won the Nobel prize for chemistry (1966) for his work on bonding and the electronic structure of molecules

Mullingar n a town in N central Republic of Ireland, the county town of Co Westmeath; site of cathedral; cattle raised. Pop: 15 621 (2002)

mullion n a slender vertical bar between the casements or panes of a window [Old French moinel] **> mullioned** adj

mull over vb to study or ponder: he mulled over the arrangements [probably from muddle]

mulloway n a large Australian sea fish, valued for sport and food

Mulroney n (Martin) Brian. born 1939, Canadian lawyer, businessman, and statesman; Conservative prime minister (1984–93)

Multan n a city in central Pakistan, near the Chenab River. Pop: 1 459 000 (2005 est)

multi- combining form **1** many or much: multimillion **2** more than one: multistorey [Latin multus much, many]

multicoloured adj having many colours: multicoloured balls of wool

multicultural adj of or for the cultures of several different races

multifarious (mull-tee-**fare**-ee-uss) adj many and varied: multifarious religious movements and political divisions sprang up around this time [Late Latin multifarius manifold]

multiflora rose n a climbing rose with clusters of small fragrant flowers

multiform adj having many shapes or forms

multilateral adj of or involving more than two nations or parties: multilateral trade negotiations

multilingual adj **1** able to speak more than two languages **2** written or expressed in more than two languages: a multilingual leaflet

multimedia pl n **1** the combined use of media such as television and slides ▷ adj **2** computers of or relating to systems that can manipulate data in a variety of forms, such as sound, graphics, or text

multimillionaire n a person who has money or property worth several million pounds, dollars, etc.

multinational adj **1** (of a large business company) operating in several countries **2** involving people from several countries: a multinational peacekeeping force ▷ n **3** a large company operating in several countries

multiparous (mull-**tip**-a-russ) adj producing many offspring at one birth [New Latin multiparus]

multiple adj **1** having or involving more than one part, individual, or element ▷ n **2** a number or polynomial which can be divided by another specified one an exact number of times: 6 is a multiple of 2 [Latin multiplus] **> multiply** adv

multiple-choice adj (of a test or question) giving a number of possible answers out of which the correct one must be chosen

multiple sclerosis n a chronic progressive disease of the central nervous system, resulting in speech and visual disorders, tremor, muscular incoordination, and partial paralysis

multiplex *n, pl* **-plexes 1** a purpose-built complex containing several cinemas and usually restaurants and bars ▷ *adj* **2** having many elements; complex [Latin: having many folds]

multiplicand *n* a number to be multiplied by another number (the **multiplier**)

multiplication *n* **1** a mathematical operation, equivalent to adding a number to itself a specified number of times. For instance, 4 multiplied by 3 equals 12 (i.e. 4+4+4) **2** the act of multiplying or state of being multiplied

multiplication sign *n* the symbol ×, placed between numbers to be multiplied

multiplication table *n* a table giving the results of multiplying two numbers together

multiplicity *n, pl* **-ties 1** a large number or great variety **2** the state of being multiple

multiplier *n* a number by which another number (the **multiplicand**) is multiplied

multiply *vb* **-plies, -plying, -plied 1** to increase or cause to increase in number, quantity, or degree **2** to combine numbers or quantities by multiplication **3** to increase in number by reproduction [Latin *multiplicare*]

multipurpose *adj* having many uses: *a giant multipurpose enterprise*

multipurpose vehicle *n* a large car, similar to a van, designed to carry up to eight passengers

multiracial *adj* consisting of or involving people of many races: *a multiracial society* ﹥ **multiracialism** *n*

multistage *adj* (of a rocket or missile) having several stages, each of which can be jettisoned after it has burnt out

multistorey *adj* (of a building) having many storeys

multitrack *adj* (in sound recording) using tape containing two or more tracks

multitude *n* **1** a large number of people or things: *a multitude of different pressure groups* **2** the multitude the common people [Latin *multitudo*] ﹥ **multitudinous** *adj*

multi-user *adj* (of a computer) capable of being used by several people at once

mum¹ *n chiefly Brit informal* same as **mother** [a child's word]

mum² *adj* **1** keep mum remain silent **2** mum's the word keep quiet (about something) [suggestive of closed lips]

Mumbai *n* a port in W India, capital of Maharashtra state, on the Arabian Sea: ceded by Portugal to England in 1661 and of major importance in British India; commercial and industrial centre, esp. for cotton. Pop: 11 914 398 (2001). Former English name: **Bombay**

mumble *vb* **-bling, -bled 1** to speak or say something indistinctly, with the mouth partly closed: *I could hear him mumbling under his breath* ▷ *n* **2** an indistinct or low utterance or sound [Middle English *momelen*, from MUM²]

mumbo jumbo *n* **1** meaningless language; nonsense or gibberish **2** foolish religious ritual or incantation [probably from West African *mama dyumbo*, name of a tribal god]

Mumford *n* Lewis. 1895–1990, US sociologist, whose works are chiefly concerned with the relationship between humans and their environment. They include *The City in History* (1962) and *Roots of Contemporary Architecture* (1972)

mummer *n* one of a group of masked performers in a folk play or mime [Old French *momer* to mime]

mummery *n, pl* **-meries 1** a performance by mummers **2** hypocritical or ostentatious ceremony

mummified *adj* (of a body) preserved as a mummy ﹥ **mummification** *n*

mummy¹ *n, pl* **-mies** *chiefly Brit* an embalmed body as prepared for burial in ancient Egypt [Persian *mūm* wax]

mummy² *n, pl* **-mies** a child's word for **mother** [variant of MUM¹]

mumps *n* an infectious viral disease in which the glands below the ear become swollen and painful [obsolete *mump* to grimace]

munch *vb* to chew noisily and steadily [imitative]

Munch *n* Edvard. 1863–1944, Norwegian painter and engraver, whose works, often on the theme of death, include *The Scream* (1893); a major influence on the expressionists, esp. on *die Brücke*

München *n* the German name for **Munich**

München-Gladbach *n* the former name of Mönchengladbach

mundane *adj* **1** everyday, ordinary, and therefore not very interesting **2** relating to the world or worldly matters [Latin *mundus* world]

mung bean *n* an E Asian bean plant grown for its edible seeds which are used as a source of bean sprouts [Tamil *mūngu*]

Munich *n* a city in S Germany, capital of the state of Bavaria, on the Isar River: became capital of Bavaria in 1508; headquarters of the Nazi movement in the 1920s; a major financial, commercial, and manufacturing centre. Pop: 1 247 873 (2003 est). German name: **München**

municipal *adj* of or relating to a town or city or its local government [Latin *municipium* a free town]

municipality *n, pl* **-ties 1** a city, town, or district enjoying local self-government **2** the governing body of such a unit

munificent (mew-niff-fiss-sent) *adj* very generous [Latin *munus* gift + *facere* to make] ﹥ **munificence** *n*

muniments (mew-nim-ments) *pl n law* the title deeds and other documentary evidence relating to the title to land [Latin *munire* to defend]

munitions (mew-nish-unz) *pl n* military equipment and stores, esp. ammunition

Munnings *n* Sir Alfred. 1878–1959, British painter, best known for his horse paintings

Munro *n* **1** Alice, original name *Alice Laidlaw*. born 1931, Canadian short-story writer; her books include *Lives of Girls and Women* (1971), *The Moons of Jupiter* (1982), and *The Love of a Good Woman* (1999); winner of the Booker international prize (2009) for a lifetime body of work; awarded the Nobel prize for literature (2013) **2** H(ector) H(ugh), pen name Saki. 1870–1916, Scottish author, born in Burma (now Myanmar), noted for his collections of satirical short stories, such as *Reginald* (1904) and *Beasts and Superbeasts* (1914)

Munster *n* a province of SW Republic of Ireland: the largest of the four provinces and historically a kingdom; consists of the counties of Clare, Cork, Kerry, Limerick, Tipperary, and Waterford. Capital: Cork. Pop: 1 100 614 (2002). Area: 24 125 sq km (9315 sq miles)

Münster *n* a city in NW Germany, in North Rhine-Westphalia on the Dortmund-Ems Canal: one of the treaties comprising the Peace of Westphalia (1648) was signed here; became capital of Prussian Westphalia in 1815. Pop: 269 579 (2003 est)

Münsterberg *n* Hugo. 1863–1916, German psychologist, in the US from 1897, noted for his pioneering work in applied psychology

munted *adj* NZ slang **1** destroyed or ruined **2** abnormal or peculiar

Müntzer *n* Thomas. c. 1490–1525, German radical religious and political reformer; executed for organizing the Peasants' War (1524–25)

muon (mew-on) *n* a positive or negative elementary particle with a mass 207 times that of an electron [short for *mu* meson]

mural (myoor-al) *n* **1** a large painting on a wall ▷ *adj* **2** of or relating to a wall [Latin *murus* wall] ﹥ **muralist** *n*

Muralitharan *n* Muttiah. born 1972, Sri Lankan cricketer: a spin bowler, he played in 133 test matches and took a world-record 800 wickets

Murasaki Shikibu *n* 11th-century Japanese court lady, author of *The Tale of Genji*, perhaps the world's first novel

Murat n Joachim. 1767-1815, French marshal, during the Napoleonic Wars; king of Naples (1808-15)

Murchison n Sir Roderick Impey. 1792-1871, Scottish geologist: played a major role in establishing parts of the geological time scale, esp. the Silurian, Permian, and Devonian periods

Murchison Falls n another name for **Kabalega Falls**

Murcia n **1** a region and ancient kingdom of SE Spain, on the Mediterranean: taken by the Moors in the 8th century; an independent Muslim kingdom in the 11th and 12th centuries **2** a city in SE Spain, capital of Murcia province: trading centre for a rich agricultural region; silk industry; university (1915). Pop: 391 146 (2003 est)

murder n **1** the unlawful intentional killing of one human being by another **2** informal something dangerous, difficult, or unpleasant: *shopping on Christmas Eve is murder* **3** cry blue murder informal to make an outcry **4** get away with murder informal to do as one pleases without ever being punished ▷ vb **5** to kill someone intentionally and unlawfully **6** informal to ruin a piece of music or drama by performing it very badly: *he absolutely murdered that song* **7** informal to beat decisively [Old English morthor] > **murderer** n > **murderess** fem n > **murderous** adj

Murdoch n **1** Dame (Jean) Iris. 1919-99, British writer. Her books include *The Bell* (1958), *A Severed Head* (1961), *The Sea, The Sea* (1978), which won the Booker Prize, *The Philosopher's Pupil* (1983), and *Existentialists and Mystics* (1997) **2** (Keith) Rupert. born 1931, US publisher and media entrepreneur, born in Australia; chairman of News International Ltd (including Times Newspapers Ltd), 20th Century-Fox, and HarperCollins

Mureş n a river in SE central Europe, rising in central Romania in the Carpathian Mountains and flowing west to the Tisza River at Szeged, Hungary. Length: 885 km (550 miles). Hungarian name: **Maros**

Murillo n Bartolomé Esteban. 1618-82, Spanish painter, esp. of religious subjects and beggar children

murk n thick gloomy darkness [Old Norse *myrkr* darkness]

murky adj murkier, murkiest **1** gloomy or dark **2** cloudy or hard to see through: *a murky stagnant pond* **3** obscure and suspicious; shady: *murky goings-on*; *his murky past* > **murkily** adv > **murkiness** n

Murman Coast or **Murmansk Coast** n a coastal region of NW Russia, in the north of the Kola Peninsula within the Arctic Circle, but ice-free

Murmansk n a port in NW Russia, on the Kola Inlet of the Barents Sea: founded in 1915; the world's largest town north of the Arctic Circle, with a large fishing fleet. Pop: 316 000 (2005 est)

murmur vb **1** to speak or say in a quiet indistinct way **2** to complain ▷ n **3** a continuous low indistinct sound, such as that of a distant conversation **4** an indistinct utterance: *a murmur of protest* **5** a complaint or grumble: *he left without a murmur* **6** med any abnormal soft blowing sound heard usually over the chest: *a heart murmur* [Latin *murmurare* to rumble] > **murmuring** n, adj > **murmurous** adj

Murphy n **1** Alex. born 1939, English rugby league player and coach; scored 16 tries in 27 test matches for Great Britain (1958-71) **2** Eddie, full name *Edward Regan Murphy*. born 1951, US film actor and comedian. His films include *48 Hours* (1982), *Beverly Hills Cop* (1984), *Coming to America* (1988), *Dr Dolittle* (1998), and, as a voice artist, the *Shrek* series of animated films (2001-10) **3** William Parry. 1892-1987, US physician: with G. R. Minot, he discovered the liver treatment for anaemia and they shared, with G. H. Whipple, the Nobel prize for physiology or medicine in 1934

Murphy-O'Connor n Cormac. born 1932, British cardinal, Archbishop of Westminster (2000-09)

Murphy's Law n same as **Sod's Law**

murrain (murr-rin) n any plaguelike disease in cattle [Old French *morir* to die]

Murray[1] n a river in SE Australia, rising in New South Wales and flowing northwest into SE South Australia, then south into the sea at Encounter Bay: the main river of Australia, important for irrigation and power. Length: 2590 km (1609 miles)

Murray[2] n **1** 1st Earl of. See (1st Earl of) **Moray 2** Sir (George) Gilbert (Aimé). 1866-1957, British classical scholar, born in Australia: noted for his verse translations of Greek dramatists, esp. Euripides **3** Sir James (Augustus Henry). 1837-1915, Scottish lexicographer; one of the original editors (1879-1915) of what became the *Oxford English Dictionary* **4** Les, full name *Leslie Allan Murray*. born 1938, Australian poet; his collections include *The Weatherboard Cathedral* (1969), *The Daylight Moon* (1987), *Subhuman Redneck Poems* (1996), and *The Biplane Houses* (2007) **5** Murray of Epping Forest, Baron, title of *Lionel Murray*, known as *Len*. 1922-2004, British trades union leader; general secretary of the Trades Union Congress (1973-84)

Murrumbidgee n a river in SE Australia, rising in S New South Wales and flowing north and west to the Murray River: important for irrigation. Length: 1690 km (1050 miles)

mus. **1** museum **2** music **3** musical

MusB or **MusBac** Bachelor of Music

Muscat n the capital of the Sultanate of Oman, a port on the Gulf of Oman: a Portuguese port from the early 16th century; controlled by Persia (1650-1741). Pop: 689 000 (2005 est). Arabic name: **Masqat**

Muscat and Oman n the former name (until 1970) of (the Sultanate of) **Oman**

muscle n **1** a tissue in the body composed of bundles of elongated cells which produce movement in an organ or part by contracting or relaxing **2** an organ composed of muscle tissue: *the heart is essentially just another muscle* **3** strength or force: *we do not have the political muscle to force through these reforms* ▷ vb **-cling, -cled 4** muscle in to force one's way into a situation; intrude: *I don't like the way he's trying to muscle in here* [Medical Latin *musculus* little mouse]

muscle-bound adj having overdeveloped and inelastic muscles

muscleman n, pl **-men 1** a man with highly developed muscles **2** a henchman employed to intimidate or use violence upon victims

Muscovite adj **1** of or relating to Moscow or its inhabitants ▷ n **2** a native or inhabitant of Moscow

Muscovy n **1** a Russian principality (13th to 16th centuries), of which Moscow was the capital **2** an archaic name for **Russia, Moscow**

muscular adj **1** having well-developed muscles; brawny **2** of or consisting of muscle: *great muscular effort is needed* **3** forceful or powerful: *a muscular account of Schumann's Fourth Symphony* > **muscularity** n

muscular dystrophy n a hereditary disease in which the muscles gradually weaken and waste away

musculature n the arrangement of muscles in an organ, part, or organism

musculoskeletal adj of or relating to the skeleton and musculature taken together

MusD or **MusDoc** Doctor of Music

muse[1] vb musing, mused to think deeply and at length about: *she mused unhappily on how right her sister had been* [Old French *muser*]

muse[2] n a force or person, esp. a woman, that inspires a creative artist [Greek *Mousa* a Muse]

Muses pl n Greek myth the nine sister goddesses, each of whom was the protector of a different art or science

museum n a building where objects of historical, artistic, or scientific interest are exhibited and preserved [Greek *Mouseion* home of the Muses]

museum piece n informal a very old or old-fashioned object or building

Museveni n Yoweri. born 1944, Ugandan politician; president of Uganda from 1986

Musgrave *n* Thea. born 1928, Scottish composer, noted esp. for her operas

mush¹ *n* **1** a soft pulpy mass **2** *informal* cloying sentimentality [obsolete *moose* porridge]

mush² *Canad interj* **1** an order to dogs in a sled team to start up or go faster ▷ *vb* **2** to travel by or drive a dogsled [perhaps from imperative of French *marcher* to advance]

Musharraf *n* Pervez. born 1943, Pakistani general and politician; became military leader of Pakistan following a coup in 2001; president (2001–08)

mushroom *n* **1** an edible fungus consisting of a cap at the end of a stem **2** something resembling a mushroom in shape or rapid growth ▷ *vb* **3** to grow rapidly: *consumer debt mushroomed rapidly in 1989* [Late Latin *mussirio*]

mushroom cloud *n* the large mushroom-shaped cloud produced by a nuclear explosion

mushy *adj* **mushier, mushiest** **1** soft and pulpy **2** *informal* excessively sentimental

music *n* **1** an art form consisting of sequences of sounds organized melodically, harmonically, and rhythmically **2** such sounds, esp. when produced by singing or musical instruments **3** any written or printed representation of musical sounds: *I can't read music* **4** any sequence of sounds perceived as pleasing or harmonious **5 face the music** *informal* to confront the consequences of one's actions **6 music to one's ears** something, such as a piece of news, that one is pleased to hear [Greek *mousikē (tekhnē)* (art) in the protection of the Muses]

musical *adj* **1** of or used in music **2** talented in or fond of music **3** pleasant-sounding; harmonious: *musical laughter* **4** involving or set to music: *a musical biography of Judy Garland* ▷ *n* **5** a play or film that has dialogue interspersed with songs and dances **> musicality** *n* **> musically** *adv*

musical box *n* a box containing a mechanical instrument that plays tunes when the box is opened

musical chairs *n* **1** a game in which the players run round a row of chairs while music plays. There is one more player than there are chairs, and when the music stops the player who cannot find a chair to sit on is out **2** any situation involving a number of people in a series of interrelated changes: *the dismissal of the Chancellor started a game of musical chairs in the Cabinet*

music centre *n Brit* a single hi-fi unit containing a turntable, radio, compact disc player, and cassette player

music hall *n chiefly Brit* **1** (formerly) a variety entertainment consisting of songs and comic turns **2** a theatre at which such entertainments were staged

musician *n* a person who plays or composes music, esp. as a profession

musicianship *n* the technical and interpretive skills involved in singing or playing music: *the piano part is simple but performed with great musicianship*

musicology *n* the scholarly study of music **> musicologist** *n*

Musil *n* Robert. 1880–1942, Austrian novelist, whose novel *The Man Without Qualities* (1930–42) is an ironic examination of contemporary ills

musk *n* **1** a strong-smelling glandular secretion of the male musk deer, used in perfumery **2** any similar substance produced by animals or plants, or manufactured synthetically [Persian *mushk*]

musk deer *n* a small central Asian mountain deer

muskeg *n chiefly Canad* an area of undrained boggy land [Native American: grassy swamp]

musket *n* a long-barrelled muzzle-loading gun fired from the shoulder, a forerunner of the rifle [Italian *moschetto* arrow, earlier: sparrow hawk] **> musketeer** *n*

Muskie *n* Edmund (Sixtus). 1914–96, US Democratic politician: Governor of Maine (1955–59): senator for Maine (1959–80): Secretary of State (1980–81)

muskmelon *n* any of several varieties of melon, such as the cantaloupe and honeydew

musk ox *n* a large ox, which has a dark shaggy coat, downward-curving horns, and emits a musky smell

muskrat *n, pl* **-rats** *or* **-rat** **1** a North American beaver-like amphibious rodent **2** the brown fur of this animal

musk rose *n* a Mediterranean rose, cultivated for its white musk-scented flowers

musky *adj* **muskier, muskiest** having a heady sweet smell **> muskiness** *n*

Muslim *or* **Moslem** *n, pl* **-lims** *or* **-lim** **1** a follower of the religion of Islam ▷ *adj* **2** of or relating to Islam [Arabic, literally: one who surrenders]

muslin *n* a very fine plain-weave cotton fabric [French *mousseline*]

musquash *n* muskrat fur [from a Native American language]

muss *vb US and Canad informal* to make untidy; rumple: *watch you don't muss up my hair!* [probably a blend of *mess* + *fuss*]

mussel *n* an edible shellfish, with a dark slightly elongated hinged shell, which lives attached to rocks [Latin *musculus*, diminutive of *mus* mouse]

Musset *n* Alfred de. 1810–57, French romantic poet and dramatist: his works include the play *Lorenzaccio* (1834) and the lyrics *Les Nuits* (1835–37), tracing his love affair with George Sand

Mussolini *n* Benito known as *il Duce.* 1883–1945, Italian Fascist dictator. After the Fascist march on Rome, he was appointed prime minister by King Victor Emmanuel III (1922) and assumed dictatorial powers. He annexed Abyssinia and allied Italy with Germany (1936), entering World War II in 1940. He was forced to resign following the Allied invasion of Sicily (1943) and was eventually shot by Italian partisans

Mussorgsky *or* **Moussorgsky** *n* Modest (Petrovich). 1839–81, Russian composer. He translated inflections of speech into melody in such works as the song cycle *Songs and Dances of Death* (1875–77) and the opera *Boris Godunov* (1874). His other works include *Pictures at an Exhibition* (1874) for piano

must¹ *vb* **1** used as an auxiliary to express or indicate the need or necessity to do something: *I must go to the shops* **2** used as an auxiliary to express or indicate obligation or requirement: *you must not smoke in here* **3** used as an auxiliary to express or indicate the probable correctness of a statement: *he must be finished by now* **4** used as an auxiliary to express or indicate inevitability: *all good things must come to an end* **5** used as an auxiliary to express or indicate determination: *I must try and finish this* **6** used as an auxiliary to express or indicate conviction or certainty on the part of the speaker: *you must be kidding!* ▷ *n* **7** an essential or necessary thing: *strong boots are a must for hill walking* [Old English *mōste*, past tense of *mōtan* to be allowed or obliged]

must² *n* the pressed juice of grapes or other fruit ready for fermentation [Latin *mustum* new wine]

mustache *n US* same as **moustache**

mustachio *n, pl* **-chios** *often humorous* a moustache, esp. a bushy or elaborate one [Italian *mostaccio*] **> mustachioed** *adj*

mustang *n* a small breed of horse, often wild or half wild, found in the southwestern US [Mexican Spanish *mestengo*]

mustard *n* **1** a hot, spicy paste made from the powdered seeds of any of a family of plants **2** any of these plants, which have yellow flowers and slender pods ▷ *adj* **3** brownish-yellow [Old French *moustarde*]

mustard and cress *n* seedlings of white mustard and garden cress, used in salads and as a garnish

mustard gas *n* an oily liquid with poisonous vapour used in chemical warfare, esp. in World War I, which can cause blindness, burns, and sometimes death

mustard plaster *n med* a mixture of powdered black mustard seeds applied to the skin

muster *vb* **1** to summon or gather: *I put as much disbelief in* *my expression as I could muster* **2** to call or be called together for duty or inspection: *the battalion mustered on the bank of the river* ▷ *n* **3** an assembly of military personnel for duty or inspection **4** a collection, assembly, or gathering **5 pass muster** to be acceptable [Latin *monstrare* to show]

musty *adj* **-tier, -tiest** **1** smelling or tasting old, stale, or mouldy **2** old-fashioned, dull, or hackneyed: *musty ideas* [perhaps variant of obsolete *moisty*] ➤ **mustily** *adv* ➤ **mustiness** *n*

mutable (mew-tab-bl) *adj* able to or tending to change [Latin *mutare* to change] ➤ **mutability** *n*

mutagen (mew-ta-jen) *n* any substance that can induce genetic mutation [MUTATION + *-gen* (suffix) producing] ➤ **mutagenic** *adj*

mutagenesis (mew-ta-jen-iss-iss) *n* the origin and development of a genetic mutation [MUTATION + GENESIS]

mutant (mew-tant) *n* **1** an animal, organism, or gene that has undergone mutation ▷ *adj* **2** of or resulting from mutation

Mutare *n* a city in E Zimbabwe, near the Mozambique border: rail and trade centre in a mining and tobacco-growing region. Pop: 160 000 (2005 est). Former name (until 1982): **Umtali**

mutate (mew-tate) *vb* **-tating, -tated** to undergo or cause to undergo mutation [Latin *mutare* to change]

mutation (mew-tay-shun) *n* **1** a change or alteration **2** a change in the chromosomes or genes of a cell which may affect the structure and development of the resultant offspring **3** a physical characteristic in an organism resulting from this type of chromosomal change

mute *adj* **1** not giving out sound or speech; silent **2** old-fashioned, offensive unable to speak **3** unspoken or unexpressed: *she shot him a look of mute entreaty* **4** (of a letter in a word) silent: *the 'k' in 'know' is mute* ▷ *n* **5** old-fashioned, offensive a person who is unable to speak **6** any of various devices used to soften the tone of stringed or brass instruments ▷ *vb* **muting, muted** **7** to reduce the volume or soften the tone of a musical instrument by means of a mute or soft pedal **8** to reduce the volume of a sound: *the double glazing muted the noise* [Latin *mutus* silent] ➤ **mutely** *adv* ➤ **muteness** *n*

muted *adj* **1** (of a sound or colour) softened: *a muted pink shirt* **2** (of an emotion or action) subdued or restrained: *his response was muted* **3** (of a musical instrument) being played while fitted with a mute: *muted trumpet*

mute swan *n* the swan most commonly seen in Britain, which has a pure white plumage and an orange-red bill

muti (moo-tee) *n* S African medicine, esp. herbal [Zulu]

Muti *n* Riccardo. born 1941, Italian conductor: musical director of Philharmonia Orchestra, London (1979–82), Philadelphia Orchestra (1980–92), and La Scala, Milan (1986–2005)

mutilate (mew-till-ate) *vb* **-lating, -lated** **1** to injure by tearing or cutting off a limb or essential part; maim **2** to damage a book or text so as to render it unintelligible **3** to spoil or damage severely [Latin *mutilare* to cut off] ➤ **mutilated** *adj* ➤ **mutilation** *n* ➤ **mutilator** *n*

mutineer *n* a person who mutinies

mutinous *adj* **1** openly rebellious **2** characteristic or indicative of mutiny

mutiny (mew-tin-ee) *n, pl* **-nies** **1** open rebellion against authority, esp. by sailors or soldiers against their officers ▷ *vb* **-nies, -nying, -nied** **2** to engage in mutiny: *soldiers who had mutinied and taken control* [Old French *mutin* rebellious]

mutt *n slang* **1** a foolish or stupid person **2** a mongrel dog [from *muttonhead*]

mutter *vb* **1** to say something or speak in a low and indistinct tone: *he muttered an excuse* **2** to grumble ▷ *n* **3** a muttered sound or complaint [Middle English *moteren*] ➤ **muttering** *n, adj*

Mutter *n* Anne-Sophie. born 1963, German violinist

mutton *n* **1** the flesh of mature sheep, used as food **2 mutton dressed as lamb** an older woman dressed up to look young [Medieval Latin *multo* sheep]

mutton bird *n* **1** Austral a migratory sea bird with dark plumage **2** NZ any of a number of migratory sea birds, the young of which are a Māori delicacy

muttonchops *pl n* side whiskers trimmed in the shape of chops

Muttra *n* the former name of **Mathura**

mutual (mew-chew-al) *adj* **1** experienced or expressed by each of two or more people about the other; reciprocal: *mutual respect* **2** common to or shared by two or more people: *a mutual friend* **3** denoting an organization, such as an insurance company, in which the policyholders or investors share the profits and expenses and there are no shareholders [Latin *mutuus* reciprocal] ➤ **mutuality** *n* ➤ **mutually** *adv*

> **USAGE** The use of *mutual* to mean *common to or shared by two or more people* was formerly considered incorrect, but is now acceptable. Tautologous use of *mutual* should be avoided: *cooperation* (not *mutual cooperation*) *between the two countries.*

mutual fund *n* US and Canad an investment trust that issues units for public sale and invests the money in many different businesses

Muybridge *n* Eadweard, original name *Edward James Muggeridge*. 1830–1904, US photographer, born in England; noted for his high-speed photographic studies of animals and people in motion

Muzak *n* trademark recorded light music played in places such as restaurants and shops

Muzorewa *n* Abel (**Tendekayi**) 1925–2010, Zimabwean Methodist bishop and politician; president of the African National Council (1971–85). He was one of the negotiators of an internal settlement (1978–79); prime minister of Rhodesia (1979)

muzzle *n* **1** the projecting part of an animal's face, usually the jaws and nose **2** a guard, made of plastic or strap of strong material, fitted over an animal's nose and jaws to prevent it biting or eating **3** the front end of a gun barrel ▷ *vb* **-zling, -zled** **4** to prevent from being heard or noticed: *an attempt to muzzle the press* **5** to put a muzzle on an animal [Old French *muse* snout]

muzzy *adj* **-zier, -ziest** **1** confused and groggy: *he felt muzzy and hung over* **2** blurred or hazy: *the picture was muzzy and out of focus* [origin unknown] ➤ **muzzily** *adv* ➤ **muzziness** *n*

MV megavolt

MW **1** megawatt **2** radio medium wave

mwah *interj* a representation of the sound of a kiss

Mweru *n* a lake in central Africa, on the border between Zambia and the Democratic Republic of Congo. Area: 4196 sq km (1620 sq miles)

Mx physics maxwell

my *adj* **1** of, belonging to, or associated with the speaker or writer (me): *my own way of doing things* **2** used in various forms of address: *my lord* ▷ *interj* **3** an exclamation of surprise or awe: *my, how you've grown!* [variant of Old English *mīn*]

> **USAGE** See at **me¹**.

myall *n* an Australian acacia with hard scented wood [Aboriginal]

Myanmar or **Myanma** *n* a republic in SE Asia, on the Bay of Bengal and the Andaman Sea: unified from small states in 1752; annexed by Britain (1823–85) and made a province of India in 1886; became independent in 1948. It is generally mountainous, with the basins of the Chindwin and Irrawaddy Rivers in the central part and the Irrawaddy delta in the south. Official language: Burmese. Religion: Buddhist majority. Currency: kyat. Capital: Yangon. Pop: 55 167 330 (2013 est). Area:

676 577 sq km (261 228 sq miles). Official full name: **the Union of Myanmar**. Former official name (until 1989, though still widely used): **Burma**

mycelium (mice-eel-lee-um) *n, pl* **-lia** (-lee-a) the mass forming the body of a fungus [Greek *mukēs* mushroom + *hēlos* nail]

Mycenae *n* an ancient Greek city in the NE Peloponnesus on the plain of Argos

Mycenaean (mice-in-ee-an) *adj* of or relating to the Aegean civilization of Mycenae (1400–1100 BC)

mycology *n* the study of fungi [Greek *mukēs* mushroom + -LOGY]

myelin (my-ill-in) *n* a white tissue forming an insulating sheath around certain nerve fibres [Greek *muelos* marrow]

myeloma (my-ill-oh-ma) *n, pl* **-mas** *or* **-mata** (-ma-ta) a tumour of the bone marrow [Greek *muelos* marrow + -ōma, modelled on *carcinoma*]

Myers *n* L(eopold) H(amilton). 1881–1944, British novelist, best known for his novel sequence *The Near and the Far* (1929–40)

Mykonos *n* a Greek island in the S Aegean Sea, one of the Cyclades: a popular tourist resort with many churches. Pop: 9306 (2001). Greek name: **Míkonos**

My Lai *n* a village in S Vietnam where in 1968 US troops massacred over 400 civilians

mynah *or* **myna** *n* a tropical Asian starling which can mimic human speech [Hindi *mainā*]

Mynheer (min-near) *n* a Dutch title of address equivalent to *Sir* or *Mr* [Dutch *mijnheer* my lord]

myocardium *n, pl* **-dia** the muscular tissue of the heart [Greek *mus* muscle + *kardia* heart] > **myocardial** *adj*

myopia (my-oh-pee-a) *n* inability to see distant objects clearly because the images are focused in front of the retina; short-sightedness [Greek *muōps* short-sighted] > **myopic** (my-op-ik) *adj*

myriad (mir-ree-ad) *adj* **1** innumerable: *the myriad demands of the modern world* > *n* **2** a large indefinite number: *myriads of tiny yellow flowers* [Greek *murias* ten thousand]

myriapod *n* an invertebrate with a long segmented body and many legs, such as a centipede [Greek *murias* ten thousand + *pous* foot]

myrmidon *n* a follower or henchman [after the followers of Achilles in Greek myth]

Myron *n* 5th century BC, Greek sculptor. He worked mainly in bronze and introduced a greater variety of pose into Greek sculpture, as in his *Discobolus*

myrrh (mur) *n* the aromatic resin of an African or Asian shrub or tree, used in perfume, incense, and medicine [Greek *murrha*]

myrtle (mur-tl) *n* an evergreen shrub with pink or white flowers and aromatic blue-black berries [Greek *murtos*]

myself *pron* **1** the reflexive form of I or *me*: *I really enjoyed myself at the party* **2** I or me in person, as distinct from anyone else: *I myself know of no answer* **3** my usual self: *I'm not myself today*

Mysia *n* an ancient region in the NW corner of Asia Minor

Mysian *adj* **1** of or relating to Mysia or its inhabitants > *n* **2** a native or inhabitant of Mysia

Mysore *n* **1** a city in S India, in S Karnataka state: former capital of the state of Mysore; manufacturing and trading centre; university (1916). Pop: 742 261 (2001) **2** the former name (until 1973) of **Karnataka**

mysterious *adj* **1** of unknown cause or nature: *a mysterious illness* **2** creating a feeling of strangeness, curiosity, or wonder: *a fascinating and mysterious old woman* > **mysteriously** *adv*

mystery *n, pl* **-teries 1** an unexplained or inexplicable event or phenomenon **2** a person or thing that arouses curiosity or suspense because of an unknown, obscure, or enigmatic quality **3** a story or film which arouses suspense and curiosity because of facts concealed **4** a religious rite, such as the Eucharist in Christianity [Greek *mustērion* secret rite]

mystery play *n* (in the Middle Ages) a type of drama based on the life of Christ

mystery tour *n* an excursion to an unspecified destination

mystic *n* **1** a person who achieves mystical experience > *adj* **2** same as **mystical** [Greek *mustēs* one who has been initiated]

mystical *adj* **1** relating to or characteristic of mysticism **2** *Christianity* having a sacred significance that is beyond human understanding **3** having occult or metaphysical significance > **mystically** *adv*

mysticism *n* **1** belief in or experience of a reality beyond normal human understanding or experience **2** the use of prayer and meditation in an attempt to achieve direct intuitive experience of the divine

mystify *vb* **-fies, -fying, -fied 1** to confuse, bewilder, or puzzle: *his success mystifies many in the fashion industry* **2** to make obscure: *it is important for us not to mystify the function of the scientist* > **mystification** *n* > **mystifying** *adj*

mystique (miss-steek) *n* an aura of mystery, power, and awe that surrounds a person or thing

myth *n* **1 a** a story about superhuman beings of an earlier age, usually of how natural phenomena or social customs came into existence **b** same as **mythology** (1, 2) **2 a** an idea or explanation which is widely held but untrue or unproven: *the myth that the USA is a classless society* **b** a person or thing whose existence is fictional or unproven: *the Loch Ness Monster is a myth* [Greek *muthos* fable]

myth. 1 mythological **2** mythology

mythical *or* **mythic** *adj* **1** of or relating to myth **2** imaginary or fictitious > **mythically** *adv*

mythology *n, pl* **-gies 1** myths collectively, esp. those associated with a particular culture or person **2** a body of stories about a person, institution, etc. **3** the study of myths > **mythological** *adj*

Mytilene *n* **1** a port on the Greek island of Lesbos: Roman remains; Byzantine fortress. Pop (municipality): 37 881 (2001). Modern Greek name: **Mitilíni 2** a former name for **Lesbos**

myxoedema *or US* **myxedema** (mix-id-deem-a) *n* a disease caused by an underactive thyroid gland, characterized by puffy eyes, face, and hands, and mental sluggishness [Greek *muxa* mucus + *oidēma* swelling]

myxomatosis (mix-a-mat-oh-siss) *n* an infectious and usually fatal viral disease of rabbits causing swellings and tumours [Greek *muxa* mucus + -ōma denoting tumour + -ōsis denoting disease]

m

Nn

n¹ 1 nano- 2 neutron

n² n 1 maths a number whose value is not stated: two to the power n ▷ adj 2 an indefinite number of: there are n objects in the box ⟩ **nth** adj

N 1 chess knight 2 chem nitrogen 3 physics newton(s) 4 North(ern) 5 nuclear: N plant

n. 1 neuter 2 noun 3 number

N. 1 National(ist) 2 Navy 3 New 4 Norse

Na chem sodium [Latin natrium]

NA North America

n/a not applicable: used to indicate that a question on a form is not relevant to the person filling it in

Naafi n 1 Brit Navy, Army, and Air Force Institutes 2 a canteen or shop run by this organization, esp. for military personnel

naan n same as **nan bread**

naartjie (nahr-chee) n S African a tangerine [Afrikaans]

nab vb **nabbing, nabbed** informal 1 to arrest (someone) 2 to catch (someone) doing something wrong [perhaps Scandinavian]

Nablus n a town in the West Bank: near the site of ancient Shechem. Pop: 136 000 (2005 est)

nabob (nay-bob) n informal a rich or important person [Hindi nawwāb; see NAWAB]

Nabokov n Vladimir (Vladimirovich). 1899–1977, US novelist, born in Russia. His works include Lolita (1955), Pnin (1957), Pale Fire (1962), and Ada (1969) ⟩ **Nabokovian** adj

nacelle (nah-**sell**) n a streamlined enclosure on an aircraft, esp. one housing an engine [French: small boat]

nacho n, pl **nachos** Mexican cookery a snack of a piece of tortilla topped with cheese, peppers, etc.

nacre (nay-ker) n mother-of-pearl [Arabic naqqārah shell, drum] ⟩ **nacreous** adj

Nadal n Rafael.. born 1986, Spanish tennis player: winner of fourteen Grand Slam singles titles (from 2005), including a record nine at the French Open

Nadar n real name Gaspard Félix Tournachon. 1820–1910, French photographer, writer, and caricaturist: noted for his portrait photographs of artists and writers and for taking the first aerial photographs (1858)

Nader n Ralph. born 1934, US lawyer and campaigner for consumer rights and the environment: a candidate for US president in 1996, 2000, 2004, and 2008

nadir n 1 the point in the sky directly below an observer and opposite the zenith 2 the lowest or worst point of anything: I had touched the very nadir of despair [Arabic nazīr as-samt, literally: opposite the zenith]

naevus or US **nevus** (nee-vuss) n, pl -**vi** a birthmark or mole [Latin]

naff adj Brit slang in poor taste: naff frocks and trouser suits [perhaps back slang from fan, short for FANNY] ⟩ **naffness** n

nag¹ vb **nagging, nagged** 1 to scold or find fault constantly 2 **nag at** to be a constant source of discomfort or worry to ▷ n 3 a person who nags [Scandinavian] ⟩ **nagging** adj, n

nag² n 1 often disparaging an old horse 2 a small riding horse [Germanic]

Nagaland n a state of NE India: formed in 1962 from parts of Assam and the North-East Frontier Agency; inhabited chiefly by Naga tribes; consists of almost inaccessible forested hills and mountains (the **Naga Hills**); shifting cultivation predominates. Capital: Kohima. Pop: 1 988 636 (2001). Area: 16 579 sq km (6401 sq miles)

Nagano n a city in central Japan, on central Honshu: Buddhist shrine; two universities. Pop: 359 045 (2002 est)

Nagarjuna n c. 150–c. 250 AD, Indian Buddhist monk, founder of the Madhyamika (Middle Path) school of Mahayana Buddhism: noted for his philosophical writings

Nagasaki n a port in SW Japan, on W Kyushu: almost completely destroyed in 1945 by the second atomic bomb dropped on Japan by the US; shipbuilding industry. Pop: 419 901 (2002 est)

Nagorno-Karabakh Autonomous Region n an administrative division in S Azerbaijan. In 1990–94 Armenian claims to the region led to violent unrest and fighting between national forces. Capital: Stepanakert. Pop: 143 000 (2000 est). Area: 4400 sq km (1700 sq miles)

Nagoya n a city in central Japan, on S Honshu on Ise Bay: a major industrial centre. Pop: 2 109 681 (2002 est)

Nagpur n a city in central India, in NE Maharashtra state: became capital of the kingdom of Nagpur (1743); capital of the Central Provinces (later Madhya Pradesh) from 1861 to 1956. Pop: 2 051 320 (2001)

Nagy n Imre. 1896–1958, Hungarian statesman; prime minister (1953–55; 1956). He was removed from office and later executed when Soviet forces suppressed the revolution of 1956; reburied with honours in 1989

Nagyszeben n the Hungarian name for **Sibiu**

Nagyvárad n the Hungarian name for **Oradea**

Naha n a port in S Japan, on the SW coast of Okinawa Island: chief city of the Ryukyu Islands. Pop: 303 146 (2002 est)

naiad (nye-ad) n, pl **naiads** or **naiades** (nye-ad-deez) Greek myth a water nymph [Greek naias]

nail n 1 a piece of metal with a point at one end and a head at the other, hit with a hammer to join two objects together 2 the hard covering of the upper tips of the fingers and toes 3 **hit the nail on the head** to say something exactly correct or accurate 4 **on the nail** at once: he paid always in cash, always on the nail ▷ vb 5 to attach (something) with nails 6 informal to arrest or catch (someone) 7 informal to execute (an act or performance) to the highest level: you nailed that song! [Old English nægl]

nail down vb 1 to secure or fasten down with nails or as if with nails 2 to force an agreement from 3 to settle in a definite way: a compromise was agreed in principle but has not yet been nailed down

nailfile n a small metal file used to shape and smooth the nails

nail varnish *or* **nail polish** *n* a thick liquid applied to the nails as a cosmetic

Naipaul *n* Sir V(idiadhar) S(urajprasad). born 1932, Trinidadian novelist of Indian descent, living in Britain. His works include *A House for Mr Biswas* (1961), *In a Free State* (1971), which won the Booker Prize, *A Bend in the River* (1979), *The Enigma of Arrival* (1987), and *Beyond Belief* (1998): Nobel prize for literature 2001

Nairnshire *n* (until 1975) a county of NE Scotland, now part of Highland

Nairobi *n* the capital of Kenya, in the southwest, at an altitude of 1650 m (5500 ft): founded in 1899; became capital in 1905; commercial and industrial centre; the Nairobi National Park (a game reserve) is nearby. Pop: 2 818 000 (2005 est)

Naismith *n* James. 1861–1939, Canadian sportsman and coach; inventor of basketball

naive *or* **naïve** (nye-eev) *adj* 1 innocent and gullible 2 simple and lacking sophistication: *naive art* [French, from Latin *nativus* native] > **naively** *adv*

naivety (nye-eev-tee) *or* **naïveté** *n* the state or quality of being naive

Najaf *n* a holy city in central Iraq, near the River Euphrates; burial place of the Caliph Ali and a centre of the Shiite faith. Pop: 639 000 (2005 est)

naked *adj* 1 without clothes 2 not concealed: *naked aggression* 3 without any covering: *it was dimly lit by naked bulbs* 4 the naked eye the eye unassisted by any optical instrument: *difficult to spot with the naked eye* [Old English *nacod*] > **nakedly** *adv* > **nakedness** *n*

Nakhichevan *n* a city in W Azerbaijan, capital of the Nakhichevan Autonomous Republic: an ancient trading town; ceded to Russia in 1828. Pop: 66 800 (1994). Ancient name: **Naxuana**

Nakhichevan Autonomous Republic *n* a region belonging to Azerbaijan, from which it is separated by part of Armenia; annexed by Russia in 1828; unilaterally declared secession from the Soviet Union in 1990. Capital: Nakhichevan. Pop: 363 000 (2000 est). Area: 5500 sq km (2120 sq miles)

Nakuru *n* a town in W Kenya, on Lake Nakuru: commercial centre of an agricultural region. Pop: 264 000 (2005 est)

Nalchik *n* a city in SW Russia, capital of the Kabardino-Balkar Republic, in a valley of the Greater Caucasus: health resort. Pop: 283 000 (2005 est)

Nam *or* **'Nam** *n chiefly US informal* Vietnam

Namangan *n* a city in E Uzbekistan. Pop: 471 000 (2005 est)

Namaqualand *n* a semiarid coastal region of SW Africa, extending from near Windhoek, Namibia, into W South Africa: divided by the Orange River into **Little Namaqualand** in South Africa, and **Great Namaqualand** in Namibia; rich mineral resources. Area: 47 961 sq km (18 518 sq miles). Also called: **Namaland**

namby-pamby *adj Brit, Austral and NZ* excessively sentimental or prim [nickname of Ambrose Phillips, 18th-century pastoral poet]

Nam Co *or* **Nam Tso** *n* a salt lake in SW China, in SE Tibet at an altitude of 4629 m (15 186 ft). Area: about 1800 sq km (700 sq miles). Also called: **Tengri Nor**

name *n* 1 a word or term by which a person or thing is known. Related adjective: **nominal** 2 reputation, esp. a good one: *he was making a name for himself* 3 a famous person: *she's a big name now* 4 call someone names *or* a name to insult someone by using rude words to describe him or her 5 in name only not possessing the powers or status implied by one's title: *a leadership in name only* 6 in the name of a for the sake of: *in the name of decency* b by the authority of: *in the name of the law* 7 name of the game the most significant or important aspect of something: *survival is the name of the game in wartime* 8 to one's name in one's possession: *she hasn't a penny to her name* ▷ *vb* **naming, named** 9 to give a name to 10 to refer to by name: *he*
refused to name his source 11 to fix or specify: *he named a time for the meeting* 12 to appoint: *she was named Journalist of the Year* 13 to ban (an MP) from the House of Commons by mentioning him or her formally by name as being guilty of disorderly conduct 14 name names to cite people in order to blame or accuse them [Old English *nama*]

namecheck *vb* 1 to mention (someone) by name ▷ *n* 2 a mention of someone's name, for example on a radio programme

name day *n RC Church* the feast day of a saint whose name one bears

name-dropping *n informal* the practice of referring to famous people as though they were friends, in order to impress others

nameless *adj* 1 without a name 2 unspecified: *the individual concerned had better remain nameless* 3 too horrible to speak about: *the nameless dread*

namely *adv* that is to say

Namen *n* the Flemish name for **Namur**

nameplate *n* a small sign on or next to a door giving the occupant's name and, sometimes, profession

namesake *n* a person or thing with the same name as another [probably originally *for the name's sake*]

Namhoi *n* another name for **Foshan**

Namibe *n* a port in SW Angola: fishing industry. Pop: 132 900 (2004 est)

Namibia *n* a country in southern Africa bordering on South Africa: annexed by Germany in 1884 and mandated by the League of Nations to South Africa in 1920. The mandate was terminated by the UN in 1966 but this was ignored by South Africa, as was the 1971 ruling by the International Court of Justice that the territory be surrendered. Independence was achieved in 1990 and Namibia became a member of the Commonwealth; Walvis Bay remained a South African enclave until 1994, when it was returned to Namibia. Official language: English; Afrikaans and German also spoken. Religion: mostly animist, with some Christians. Currency: dollar. Capital: Windhoek. Pop: 2 182 852 (2013 est). Area: 823 328 sq km (317 887 sq miles). Also called: **South West Africa**. Former name (1885–1919): **German Southwest Africa**

Namibian *adj* 1 of or relating to Namibia or its inhabitants ▷ *n* 2 a native or inhabitant of Namibia

Namier *n* Sir Lewis Bernstein, original name *Ludwik Bernsztajn vel Niemirowski*. 1888–1960, British historian, born in Poland: noted esp. for his studies of 18th-century British politics

Nam Tso *n* a variant transliteration of the Chinese name for **Nam Co**

Namur *n* 1 a province of S Belgium. Capital: Namur. Pop: 452 856 (2004 est). Area: 3660 sq km (1413 sq miles) 2 a town in S Belgium, capital of Namur province: strategically situated on a promontory between the Sambre and Meuse Rivers, besieged and captured many times. Pop: 106 213 (2004 est) ▶ Flemish name: **Namen**

Nana Sahib *n* real name *Dandhu Panth*. ?1825–?1860, Indian nationalist, who led the uprising at Cawnpore during the Indian Mutiny

nan bread *or* **naan** *n* a slightly leavened Indian bread in a large flat leaf shape [Hindi]

Nanchang *or* **Nan-ch'ang** *n* a walled city in SE China, capital of Jiangxi province, on the Kan River: largest city in the Poyang basin. Pop: 1 742 000 (2005 est)

Nan-ching *n* a variant spelling of **Nanjing**

nancy *n, pl* **-cies** *Brit, Austral and NZ offensive, slang* an effeminate or homosexual boy or man. Also called: **nancy boy** [from the girl's name]

Nancy *n* a city in NE France: became the capital of the dukes of Lorraine in the 12th century, becoming French in 1766; administrative and financial centre. Pop: 107 434 (2006)

Nanda Devi *n* a mountain in N India, in Uttarakhand in

the Himalayas. Height: 7817 m (25 645 ft)

Nanga Parbat n a mountain in N India, in NW Kashmir in the W Himalayas. Height: 8126 m (26 660 ft)

Nanhai n the Chinese name for the **South China Sea**

Nanjing, Nanking or **Nan-ching** n a port in E central China, capital of Jiangsu province, on the Yangtze River: capital of the Chinese empire and a literary centre from the 14th to 17th centuries; capital of Nationalist China (1928–37); site of a massacre of about 300 000 civilians by the invading Japanese army in 1937; university (1928). Pop: 2 806 000 (2005 est)

Nanning or **Nan-ning** n a port in S China, capital of Guanxi, on the Xiang River: rail links with Vietnam. Pop: 1 395 000 (2005 est)

nanny n, pl **-nies** **1** a woman whose job is looking after young children ▷ vb **nannies, nannying, nannied** **2** to nurse or look after someone else's children **3** to be too protective towards children [child's name for a nurse]

nanny goat n a female goat

nano- combining form denoting one thousand millionth (10⁻⁹): nanosecond [Latin nanus dwarf]

nanometre n one thousand-millionth of a metre. Symbol: nm

nanotechnology n a branch of technology dealing with the manufacture of objects with dimensions of less than 100 nanometres and the manipulation of individual molecules and atoms

Nansei-shoto n the official Japanese name for **Ryukyu Islands**

Nansen n Fridtjof. 1861–1930, Norwegian arctic explorer, statesman, and scientist. He crossed Greenland (1888–89) and attempted to reach the North Pole (1893–96), attaining a record 86°14′ N (1895). He was the League of Nations' high commissioner for refugees (1920–22): Nobel peace prize 1922

Nan Shan pl n a mountain range in N central China, mainly in Qinghai province, with peaks over 6000 m (20 000 ft)

Nanterre n a town in N France, on the Seine: an industrial suburb of Paris. Pop: 90 903 (2006)

Nantes n a port in W France, at the head of the Loire estuary: scene of the signing of the Edict of Nantes and of the Noyades (drownings) during the French Revolution; extensive shipyards, and large metallurgical and food processing industries. Pop: 290 871 (2006)

Nantong or **Nantung** n a city in E China, in Jiangsu province on the Yangtze estuary. Pop: 898 000 (2005 est)

Nantucket n an island off SE Massachusetts: formerly a centre of the whaling industry; now a resort. Length: nearly 24 km (15 miles). Width: 5 km (3 miles). Pop (county and town): 10 724 (2003 est)

nap¹ n **1** a short sleep ▷ vb **napping, napped** **2** to have a short sleep **3 catch someone napping** to catch someone unprepared: they don't want to be caught napping when the army moves again [Old English hnappian]

nap² n the raised fibres of velvet or similar cloth [probably Middle Dutch noppe]

nap³ n **1** a card game similar to whist **2** horse racing a tipster's choice for a certain winner ▷ vb **napping, napped** horse racing to name (a horse) as a likely winner [shortened from Napoleon]

napalm n **1** a highly inflammable jellied petrol, used in firebombs and flame-throwers ▷ vb **2** to attack (people or places) with napalm [na(phthene) + palm(itate) salt of palmitic acid]

nape n the back of the neck [origin unknown]

naphtha n chem a liquid mixture distilled from coal tar or petroleum: used as a solvent and in petrol [Greek]

naphthalene n chem a white crystalline substance distilled from coal tar or petroleum, used in mothballs, dyes, and explosives [naphtha + al(cohol) + -ene]

Napier¹ n a port in New Zealand, on E North Island on Hawke Bay: wool trade centre. Pop: 56 100 (2004 est)

Napier² n **1** Sir Charles James. 1782–1853, British general and colonial administrator: conquered Sind (1843): governor of Sind (1843–47) **2** John. 1550–1617, Scottish mathematician: invented logarithms and pioneered the decimal notation used today **3** Robert (**Cornelis**), 1st Baron Napier of Magdala. 1810–90, British field marshal, who commanded in India during the Sikh Wars (1845, 1848–49) and the Indian Mutiny (1857–59). He captured Magdala (1868) while rescuing British diplomats from Ethiopia

napkin n **1** a piece of cloth or paper for wiping the mouth or protecting the clothes while eating **2** same as **sanitary towel** [Latin mappa cloth]

Naples n a port in SW Italy, capital of Campania region, on the Bay of Naples: the third largest city in the country; founded by Greeks in the 6th century BC; incorporated into the Kingdom of the Two Sicilies in 1140 and its capital (1282–1503); university (1224). Pop: 1 004 500 (2001). Ancient name: **Neapolis**. Italian name: **Napoli**. Related adjective: **Neapolitan 2 Bay of Naples** an inlet of the Tyrrhenian Sea in the SW coast of Italy

Napoleon I n full name Napoleon Bonaparte. 1769–1821, Emperor of the French (1804–15). He came to power as the result of a coup in 1799 and established an extensive European empire. A brilliant general, he defeated every European coalition against him until, irreparably weakened by the Peninsular War and the Russian campaign (1812), his armies were defeated at Leipzig (1813). He went into exile but escaped and ruled as emperor during the Hundred Days. He was finally defeated at Waterloo (1815). As an administrator, his achievements were of lasting significance and include the Code Napoléon, which remains the basis of French law

Napoleon II n Duke of Reichstadt. 1811–32, son of Napoleon Bonaparte and Marie Louise. He was known as the King of Rome during the first French empire and was entitled Napoleon II by Bonapartists after Napoleon I's death (1821)

Napoleon III n full name Charles Louis Napoleon Bonaparte, known as Louis-Napoleon. 1808–73, Emperor of the French (1852–70); nephew of Napoleon I. He led two abortive Bonapartist risings (1836; 1840) and was elected president of the Second Republic (1848), establishing the Second Empire in 1852. Originally successful in foreign affairs, he was deposed after the disastrous Franco-Prussian War

Napoli n the Italian name for **Naples**

nappy n, pl **-pies** Brit and NZ a piece of soft absorbent material, usually disposable, wrapped around the waist and between the legs of a baby to absorb its urine and excrement [from napkin]

Nara n a city in central Japan, on S Honshu: the first permanent capital of Japan (710–784). Pop: 364 411 (2002 est)

Narayan n R(asipuram) K(rishnaswamy). 1906–2001, Indian novelist writing in English. His books include Swami and Friends (1938), The Man-Eater of Malgudi (1961), Under the Banyan Tree (1985), and Grandmother's Tale (1993)

Narayanganj n a city in central Bangladesh, on the Ganges delta just southeast of Dhaka. Pop: 241 393 (2001)

Narbada n another name for the **Narmada**

Narbonne n a city in S France: capital of the Roman province of **Gallia Narbonensis**; harbour silted up in the 14th century. Pop: 51 996 (2006)

narcissism n an exceptional interest in or admiration for oneself [after Narcissus, a youth in Greek mythology, who fell in love with his reflection] ❯ **narcissistic** adj

narcissus (nahr-siss-uss) n, pl **-cissi** (-siss-eye) a yellow, orange, or white flower related to the daffodil [Greek narkissos, perhaps from narkē numbness, because of narcotic properties attributed to the plant]

narcosis n unconsciousness caused by a narcotic or general anaesthetic [Greek narkē numbness]

narcotic n **1** a drug, such as opium or morphine, that produces numbness and drowsiness, used medicinally but addictive ▷ *adj* **2** of narcotics or narcosis [Greek *narkē* numbness]

nark *slang vb* **1** to annoy ▷ *n* **2** an informer or spy: *copper's nark* **3** Brit someone who complains in an irritating or whining manner [probably from Romany *nāk* nose]

narky *adj* **narkier, narkiest** *slang* irritable, complaining, or sarcastic

Narmada *or* **Narbada** *n* a river in central India, rising in Madhya Pradesh and flowing generally west to the Gulf of Cambay in a wide estuary: the second most sacred river in India. Length: 1290 km (801 miles)

Narragansett Bay *n* an inlet of the Atlantic in SE Rhode Island: contains several islands, including Rhode Island, Prudence Island, and Conanicut Island

narrate *vb* **-rating, -rated** **1** to tell (a story); relate **2** to speak the words accompanying and telling what is happening in a film or TV programme [Latin *narrare* to recount] **> narrator** *n*

narration *n* **1** a narrating **2** a narrated account or story

narrative *n* **1** an account of events **2** the part of a literary work that relates events ▷ *adj* **3** telling a story: *a narrative account of the main events* **4** of narration: *narrative clarity*

narrow *adj* **1** small in breadth in comparison to length **2** limited in range, extent, or outlook: *a narrow circle of academics* **3** with little margin: *a narrow advantage* ▷ *vb* **4** to make or become narrow **5 narrow down** to restrict or limit: *the search can be narrowed down to a single room* ▸ See also **narrows** [Old English *nearu*] **> narrowly** *adv* **> narrowness** *n*

narrow boat *n* Brit a long bargelike canal boat

narrow gauge *n* **1** a railway track with less than 56½ inches (1.435 metres) between the lines ▷ *adj* **narrow-gauge 2** denoting a railway with a narrow gauge

narrow-minded *adj* bigoted, intolerant, or prejudiced **> narrow-mindedness** *n*

narrows *pl n* a narrow part of a strait, river, or current

Narva *n* a port in Estonia on the Narva River near the Gulf of Finland: developed around a Danish fortress in the 13th century; textile centre. Pop: 66 712 (2007 est)

Narvik *n* a port in N Norway: scene of two naval battles in 1940; exports iron ore from Kiruna and Gällivare (Sweden). Pop: 18 542 (2004 est)

narwhal *n* an arctic whale with a long spiral tusk [Old Norse *nāhvalr*, from *nār* corpse + *hvalr* whale]

NASA (in the US) National Aeronautics and Space Administration

nasal *adj* **1** of the nose **2** (of a sound) pronounced with air passing through the nose **3** (of a voice) characterized by nasal sounds [Latin *nasus* nose] **> nasally** *adv*

Nasarawa *or* **Nassarawa** *n* a state of Nigeria, in the centre east of Abuja. Capital: Lafia. Pop: 1 863 275 (2006). Area: 27 117 sq km (10 470 sq miles)

nascent *adj formal* starting to grow or develop [Latin *nasci* to be born]

NASDAQ US National Association of Securities Dealers Automated Quotations (System)

Naseby *n* a village in Northamptonshire: site of a major Parliamentarian victory (1645) in the Civil War, when Cromwell routed Prince Rupert's force

Nash *n* **1** John. 1752–1835, English town planner and architect. He designed Regent's Park, Regent Street, and the Marble Arch in London **2** Ogden. 1902–71, US humorous poet **3** Paul. 1889–1946, English painter, noted esp. as a war artist in both World Wars and for his landscapes **4** Richard, known as *Beau Nash*. 1674–1762, English dandy **5** See (Thomas) **Sir Walter. 1882–1968**, New Zealand Labour statesman, born in England: prime minister of New Zealand (1957–60)

Nashe *or* **Nash** *n* Thomas. 1567–1601, English pamphleteer, satirist, and novelist, author of the first picaresque novel in English, *The Unfortunate Traveller, or the Life of Jack Wilton* (1594)

Nashville *n* a city in central Tennessee, the state capital, on the Cumberland River: an industrial and commercial centre, noted for its recording industry. Pop (including Davidson): 544 765 (2003 est)

Nasik *n* a city in W India, in Maharashtra: a centre for Hindu pilgrims. Pop: 1 076 967 (2001)

Nasiriyah *n* a city in S Iraq, on the River Euphrates; agricultural and trading centre. Pop: 425 000 (2005 est)

Nasmyth *n* James. 1808–90, British engineer; inventor of the steam hammer (1839)

Nassau *n* **1** a region of W central Germany: formerly a duchy (1816–66), from which a branch of the House of Orange arose (represented by the present rulers of the Netherlands and Luxembourg); annexed to the Prussian province of Hesse-Nassau in 1866; corresponds to present-day W Hesse and NE Rhineland-Palatinate states **2** the capital and chief port of the Bahamas, on the NE coast of New Providence Island: resort. Pop: 229 000 (2005 est)

Nasser *n* Gamal Abdel. 1918–70, Egyptian soldier and statesman; president of Egypt (1956–70). He was one of the leaders of the coup that deposed King Farouk (1952) and became premier (1954). His nationalization of the Suez Canal (1956) led to an international crisis, and during his presidency Egypt was twice defeated by Israel (1956; 1967)

Nastase *n* Ilie. born 1946, Romanian tennis player: winner of the US Open (1972) and the French Open (1973)

nasturtium *n* a plant with yellow, red, or orange trumpet-shaped flowers [Latin: kind of cress]

nasty *adj* **-tier, -tiest** **1** unpleasant: *a nasty odour* **2** dangerous or painful: *a nasty burn* **3** (of a person) spiteful or ill-natured ▷ *n, pl* **-ties 4** something unpleasant: *video nasties* [probably related to Dutch *nestig* dirty] **> nastily** *adv* **> nastiness** *n*

nat. 1 national **2** nationalist

natal (nay-tl) *adj* of or relating to birth [Latin *natalis* of one's birth]

Natal *n* **1** a former province of E South Africa, between the Drakensberg and the Indian Ocean: set up as a republic by the Boers in 1838; became a British colony in 1843; joined South Africa in 1910; replaced by KwaZulu-Natal in 1994. Capital: Pietermaritzburg **2** a port in NE Brazil, capital of Rio Grande do Norte state, near the mouth of the Potengi River. Pop: 1 049 000 (2005 est)

nation *n* a large body of people of one or more cultures or races, organized into a single state: *a major industrialized nation* [Latin *natio* birth, tribe]

national *adj* **1** of or serving a nation as a whole **2** characteristic of a particular nation: *the national character* ▷ *n* **3** a citizen of a particular country: *Belgian nationals* **4** a national newspaper **> nationally** *adv*

national anthem *n* a patriotic song adopted by a nation for use on public occasions

National Curriculum *n* (in England and Wales) the curriculum of subjects taught in state schools since 1989

national debt *n* the total outstanding borrowings of a nation's central government

National Gallery *n* a major art gallery in London, in Trafalgar Square. Founded in 1824, it contains the largest collection of paintings in Britain

national grid *n* Brit and NZ **1** a network of high-voltage power lines linking major electric power stations **2** the arrangement of vertical and horizontal lines on an ordnance survey map

National Health Service *n* (in Britain) the system of national medical services financed mainly by taxation

national hunt *n* Brit (often caps) horse racing over courses with fences

national insurance *n* (in Britain) state insurance based on contributions from employees and employers, providing payments to unemployed, sick, and retired people

nationalism *n* **1** a policy of national independence

n

2 patriotism, sometimes to an excessive degree › **nationalist** n, adj › **nationalistic** adj

Nationalist China n an unofficial name for (the Republic of) **China**

nationality n, pl **-ties 1** the fact of being a citizen of a particular nation **2** a group of people of the same race: *young men of all nationalities*

nationalize or **-lise** vb **-lizing, -lized** or **-lising, -lised** to put (an industry or a company) under state control › **nationalization** or **-lisation** n

national park n an area of countryside protected by a national government for its scenic or environmental importance and visited by the public

National Park n a mountainous volcanic region in New Zealand, in the central North Island: ski resort

National Portrait Gallery n an art gallery in London, established in 1856, displaying portraits and photographs of eminent figures in British history

national service n chiefly Brit compulsory military service

National Socialism n German history the doctrines and practices of the Nazis, involving the supremacy of Hitler, anti-Semitism, state control of the economy, and national expansion › **National Socialist** n, adj

national superannuation n NZ a government pension paid to people of 65 years and over; retirement pension

National Theatre n the former name of the Royal National Theatre

National Trust n (in Britain) an organization concerned with the preservation of historic buildings and areas of natural beauty

nationwide adj covering or available to the whole of a nation

native adj **1** relating to a place where a person was born: *native land* **2** born in a specified place: *a native New Yorker* **3** native to originating in: *a plant native to alpine regions* **4** natural or inborn: *native genius* **5** relating to the original inhabitants of a country: *archaeology may uncover magnificent native artefacts* **6** go native (of a settler) to adopt the lifestyle of the local population ▷ n **7** a person born in a specified place: *a native of Palermo* **8** an indigenous animal or plant: *the saffron crocus is a native of Asia Minor* **9** a member of the original race of a country, as opposed to colonial immigrants [Latin *nativus* innate, natural, from *nasci* to be born]

Native American n same as American Indian

native bear n Austral same as koala

native companion n Austral same as brolga

native dog n Austral same as dingo

nativity n, pl **-ties** birth or origin [Late Latin *nativitas* birth]

Nativity n Christianity **1** the birth of Jesus Christ **2** the feast of Christmas celebrating this

NATO or **Nato** North Atlantic Treaty Organization: an international organization established for purposes of collective security

natter Brit and NZ informal vb **1** to talk idly and at length ▷ n **2** a long idle chat [dialect *gnatter* to grumble, imitative]

natterjack n a greyish-brown toad with reddish warty lumps [origin unknown]

natty adj **-tier, -tiest** informal smart and spruce [dialect *net* neat] › **nattily** adv

natural adj **1** as is normal or to be expected: *the natural consequence* **2** genuine or spontaneous: *talking in a relaxed, natural manner* **3** of, according to, existing in, or produced by nature: *natural disasters* **4** not acquired; inborn: *their natural enthusiasm* **5** not created by human beings **6** not synthetic: *natural fibres such as wool* **7** (of a parent) not adoptive **8** (of a child) illegitimate **9** music not sharp or flat: F natural ▷ n **10** informal a person with an inborn talent or skill: *she's a natural at bridge* **11** music a note that is neither sharp nor flat › **naturalness** n

natural gas n a gaseous mixture, consisting mainly of methane, found below ground; used widely as a fuel

natural history n the study of animals and plants in the wild

naturalism n a movement in art and literature advocating detailed realism › **naturalistic** adj

naturalist n **1** a student of natural history **2** a person who advocates or practises naturalism

naturalize or **-lise** vb **-lizing, -lized** or **-lising, -lised 1** to give citizenship to (a person born in another country) **2** to introduce (a plant or animal) into another region **3** to cause (a foreign word or custom) to be adopted › **naturalization** or **-lisation** n

natural logarithm n a logarithm which has the irrational number e as a base

naturally adv **1** of course; surely **2** in a natural or normal way **3** instinctively

natural number n a positive integer, such as 1, 2, 3, 4 etc.

natural philosophy n old-fashioned physics

natural resources pl n naturally occurring materials such as coal, oil, and minerals

natural science n any of the sciences dealing with the study of the physical world, such as biology, physics, chemistry, and geology

natural selection n a process by which only those creatures and plants well adapted to their environment survive

natural wastage n chiefly Brit a reduction in the number of employees through not replacing those who leave, rather than by dismissing employees or making them redundant

nature n **1** the whole system of the existence, forces, and events of the physical world that are not controlled by human beings **2** fundamental or essential qualities: *the theory and nature of science* **3** kind or sort: *problems of a financial nature* **4** temperament or personality: *an amiable and pleasant nature* **5** by nature essentially: *he was by nature a cautious man* **6** in the nature of essentially; by way of: *it was in the nature of a debate rather than an argument* [Latin *natura*, from *nasci* to be born]

nature reserve n an area of land that is preserved and managed in order to protect its animal and plant life

nature study n the study of animals and plants by direct observation

nature trail n a path through countryside, signposted to draw attention to natural features of interest

naturism n same as nudism › **naturist** n, adj

Naucratis n an ancient Greek city in N Egypt, in the Nile delta: founded in the 7th century BC

naught n **1** archaic or literary nothing **2** chiefly US the figure 0 ▷ adv **3** archaic or literary not at all: *I care naught* [Old English *nāwiht*]

naughty adj **-tier, -tiest 1** (of children) mischievous or disobedient **2** mildly indecent: *naughty lingerie* [(originally: needy, poor) from *naught*] › **naughtily** adv › **naughtiness** n

Nauru n an island republic in the SW Pacific, west of Kiribati: administered jointly by Australia, New Zealand, and Britain as a UN trust territory before becoming independent in 1968; a member of the Commonwealth (formerly a special member not represented at all meetings, until 1999). The economy is based on export of phosphates. Languages: Nauruan (a Malayo-Polynesian language) and English. Religion: Christian. Currency: Australian dollar. Capital: Yaren. Pop: 9 434 (2013 est). Area: 2130 hectares (5263 acres). Former name: Pleasant Island

Nauruan adj **1** of or relating to Nauru, its inhabitants, or their language ▷ n **2** a native or inhabitant of Nauru **3** the Malayo-Polynesian language of Nauru

nausea (naw-zee-a) n **1** the feeling of being about to vomit **2** disgust [Greek: seasickness, from *naus* ship]

nauseate vb **-ating, -ated 1** to cause (someone) to feel

sick **2** to arouse feelings of disgust in (someone)
> **nauseating** adj

nauseous adj **1** as if about to be sick: he felt nauseous **2** sickening

nautical adj of the sea, ships, or navigation [Greek nautikos, from naus ship]

nautical mile n a unit of length, used in navigation, standardized as 6080 feet

nautilus n, pl **-luses** or **-li** a sea creature with a shell and tentacles [Greek nautilos sailor]

naval adj of or relating to a navy or ships [Latin navis ship]

Navarino n **1** the Italian name for **Pylos 2** a sea battle (Oct 20, 1827) in which the defeat of the Turkish-Egyptian fleet by a combined British, French, and Russian fleet decided Greek independence

Navarre n a former kingdom of SW Europe: established in the 9th century by the Basques; the parts south of the Pyrenees joined Spain in 1515 and the N parts passed to France in 1589. Capital: Pamplona. Spanish name: Navarra

nave¹ n the long central part of a church [Latin navis ship, from the similarity in shape]

nave² n the hub of a wheel [Old English nafu, nafa]

navel n the slight hollow in the centre of the abdomen, where the umbilical cord was attached [Old English nafela]

navel orange n a sweet orange that has a navel-like hollow at the top

navigable adj **1** wide, deep, or safe enough to be sailed through: the navigable portion of the Nile **2** able to be steered: the boat has to be watertight and navigable

navigate vb **-gating, -gated 1** to direct or plot the course or position of a ship or aircraft **2** to travel over or through safely: your cousin, who's just navigated the Amazon **3** informal to direct (oneself) carefully or safely: he navigated his unsteady way to the bar **4** (of a passenger in a vehicle) to read the map and give directions to the driver [Latin navis ship + agere to drive] > **navigation** n
> **navigational** adj > **navigator** n

Návpaktos n the Greek name for **Lepanto**

Navratilova n Martina. born 1956, Czech-born US tennis player: winner of 59 Grand Slam titles (1974–2006), comprising eighteen singles titles (including a record nine at Wimbledon), 31 doubles titles (a record) , and ten mixed doubles titles

navvy n, pl **-vies** Brit and Austral informal a labourer on a building site or road [from navigator builder of a navigation (in the sense: canal)]

navy n, pl **-vies 1** the branch of a country's armed services comprising warships with their crews, and all their supporting services **2** the warships of a nation > adj **3** short for **navy-blue** [Latin navis ship]

navy-blue adj very dark blue [from the colour of the British naval uniform]

nawab (na-wahb) n (formerly) a Muslim ruler or powerful landowner in India [Hindi nawwāb, from Arabic nuwwāb, plural of na'ib viceroy]

Naxos n a Greek island in the S Aegean, the largest of the Cyclades: ancient centre of the worship of Dionysius. Pop: 18 188 (2001). Area: 438 sq km (169 sq miles)

nay interj **1** old-fashioned no > n **2** a person who votes against a motion > adv **3** used for emphasis: I want, nay, need to know [Old Norse nei]

Nayarit n a state of W Mexico, on the Pacific: includes the offshore Tres Marías Islands. Capital: Tepic. Pop: 919 739 (2000). Area: 27 621 sq km (10 772 sq miles)

Nay Pyi Taw or **Naypyidaw** n the official capital of Myanmar (Burma), built in the centre of the country near Pyinmana in 2005–2006, and superseding Yangon (Rangoon) for main government functions. Pop: officially approaching 1 000 000 in 2007

Nazarene n **1 the Nazarene** Jesus Christ **2** old-fashioned a Christian **3** a native or inhabitant of Nazareth > adj **4** of or relating to Nazareth

Nazareth n a town in N Israel, in Lower Galilee: the home of Jesus in his youth. Pop: 62 700 (2003 est)

Naze n **the Naze 1** a flat marshy headland in SE England, in Essex on the North Sea coast **2** another name for **Lindesnes**

Nazi n, pl **-zis 1** a member of the fascist National Socialist German Workers' Party, which came to power in Germany in 1933 under Adolf Hitler > adj **2** of or relating to the Nazis [German, phonetic spelling of the first two syllables of Nationalsozialist National Socialist]
> **Nazism** n

nb cricket no-ball

Nb chem niobium

NB New Brunswick **2** note well [sense 2 from Latin nota bene]

NC 1 Also: **N.C.** North Carolina **2** Brit education National Curriculum

NCO noncommissioned officer

Nd chem neodymium

N. Dak. or **ND** North Dakota

Ndjamena or **N'djamena** n the capital of Chad, in the southwest, at the confluence of the Shari and Logone Rivers: trading centre for livestock. Pop: 866 000 (2005 est). Former name (until 1973): **Fort Lamy**

Ndola n a city in N Zambia: copper, cobalt, and sugar refineries. Pop: 478 000 (2005 est)

N'Dour n Youssou. born 1959, Senegalese singer and musician, whose work has popularized African music in the West; recordings include Nelson Mandela (1986), Eyes Open (1992), and Nothing's in Vain (2002)

NDT Newfoundland Daylight Time

Ne chem neon

NE¹ 1 Nebraska **2** northeast(ern)

NE² or **N.E.** New England

ne- combining form same as **neo-**: Nearctic

Neagh n Lough Neagh a lake in Northern Ireland, in SW Co Antrim: the largest lake in the British Isles. Area: 388 sq km (150 sq miles)

Neanderthal (nee-ann-der-tahl) adj **1** of a type of primitive man that lived in Europe before 12 000 BC **2** informal having or characterized by excessively conservative views: his notoriously Neanderthal attitude to women [after Neandertal, a valley in Germany]

neap n short for **neap tide** [Old English, as in nēpflōd neap tide]

Neapolitan adj **1** of or relating to Naples or its inhabitants > n **2** a native or inhabitant of Naples [Greek Neapolis new town]

neap tide n a tide that occurs at the first and last quarter of the moon when there is the smallest rise and fall in tidal level

near prep **1** at or to a place or time not far away from > adv **2** at or to a place or time not far away **3** short for **nearly**: the pain damn near crippled him > adj **4** at or in a place or time not far away: in the near future **5** closely connected or intimate: a near relation **6** almost being the thing specified: a mood of near rebellion > vb **7** to draw close (to): the participants are nearing agreement > n **8** the left side of a horse or vehicle [Old English nēar, comparative of nēah close] > **nearness** n

nearby adj **1** not far away: a nearby village > adv **2** close at hand: I live nearby

Near East n **1** another term for the **Middle East** (1) **2** (formerly) the Balkan States and the area of the Ottoman Empire

nearly adv **1** almost **2 not nearly** nowhere near: it's not nearly as easy as it looks

near miss n **1** any attempt that just fails to succeed **2** an incident in which two aircraft or vehicles narrowly avoid collision **3** a bomb or shot that does not quite hit the target

nearside n **1** chiefly Brit the side of a vehicle that is nearer the kerb **2** the left side of an animal

near-sighted adj same as **short-sighted**

near thing n informal an event whose outcome is nearly a failure or a disaster, or only just a success

neat adj **1** clean and tidy **2** smoothly or competently done: a neat answer **3** (of alcoholic drinks) undiluted **4** slang, chiefly US and Canad admirable; excellent [Latin nitidus clean] > **neatly** adv > **neatness** n

neaten vb to make neat

neath prep archaic short for **beneath**

Neath Port Talbot n a county borough in S Wales, created from part of West Glamorgan in 1996. Administrative centre: Port Talbot. Pop: 135 300 (2003 est). Area: 439 sq km (169 sq miles)

neb n archaic or dialect the beak of a bird or the nose of an animal [Old English nebb]

Nebo n Mount Nebo a mountain in Jordan, northeast of the Dead Sea: the highest point of a ridge known as Pisgah, from which Moses viewed the Promised Land just before his death (Deuteronomy 34:1). Height: 802 m (2631 ft)

Nebr. Nebraska

Nebraska n a state of the western US: consists of an undulating plain. Capital: Lincoln. Pop: 1 739 291 (2003 est). Area: 197 974 sq km (76 483 sq miles). Abbreviation: **Nebr.**, (with zip code) **NE**

Nebraskan adj **1** of or relating to Nebraska or its inhabitants ▷ n **2** a native or inhabitant of Nebraska

nebula (neb-yew-la) n, pl **-lae** (-lee) astronomy a hazy cloud of particles and gases [Latin: mist, cloud] > **nebular** adj

nebulize or **-lise** vb **-lizing, -lized** or **-lising, -lised** to turn (a liquid) into a fine spray

nebulizer or **-liser** n a device which turns a drug from a liquid into a fine spray which can be inhaled

nebulous adj vague and unclear: a nebulous concept

NEC (in Britain) National Executive Committee

necessaries pl n essential items: the necessaries and comforts of life

necessarily adv **1** as a certainty: the factors were not necessarily connected with one another **2** inevitably: tourism is an industry that has a necessarily close connection with governments

necessary adj **1** needed in order to obtain the desired result: the necessary skills **2** certain or unavoidable: the necessary consequences ▷ n **3 do the necessary** informal to do something that is necessary in a particular situation **4 the necessary** informal the money required for a particular purpose ▸ See also **necessaries** [Latin necessarius indispensable]

necessitate vb **-tating, -tated** to compel or require

necessitous adj literary very needy

necessity n, pl **-ties 1** a set of circumstances that inevitably requires a certain result: the necessity to maintain safety standards **2** something needed: the daily necessities **3** great poverty **4 of necessity** inevitably

neck n **1** the part of the body connecting the head with the rest of the body **2** the part of a garment around the neck **3** the long narrow part of a bottle or violin **4** the length of a horse's head and neck taken as the distance by which one horse beats another in a race: to win by a neck **5** informal impudence **6 by a neck** by a very small margin: beaten only by a neck **7 get it in the neck** informal to be reprimanded or punished severely **8 neck and neck** absolutely level in a race or competition **9 neck of the woods** informal a particular area: how did they get to this neck of the woods? **10 stick one's neck out** informal to risk criticism or ridicule by speaking one's mind **11 up to one's neck in** informal to be deeply involved in: he was up to his neck in the scandal ▷ vb **12** informal (of two people) to kiss each other passionately [Old English hnecca]

Neckar n a river in SW Germany, rising in the Black Forest and flowing generally north into the Rhine at Mannheim. Length: 394 km (245 miles)

neckband n a band around the neck of a garment

Necker n Jacques. 1732–1804, French financier and statesman, born in Switzerland; finance minister of

France (1777–81; 1788–90). He attempted to reform the fiscal system and in 1789 he recommended summoning the States General. His subsequent dismissal was one of the causes of the storming of the Bastille (1789)

neckerchief n a piece of cloth worn tied round the neck [neck + kerchief]

necklace n a decorative piece of jewellery worn round the neck

neckline n the shape or position of the upper edge of a dress or top

necktie n US same as **tie** (5)

necromancy (neck-rome-man-see) n **1** communication with the dead **2** sorcery [Greek nekros corpse + mantis prophet] > **necromancer** n

necrophilia n sexual attraction for or sexual intercourse with dead bodies [Greek nekros corpse + philos loving]

necropolis (neck-rop-pol-liss) n a cemetery [Greek nekros dead + polis city]

necrosis n **1** biology, med the death of cells in the body, as from an interruption of the blood supply **2** botany death of plant tissue due to disease or frost [Greek nekros corpse] > **necrotic** adj

nectar n **1** a sugary fluid produced by flowers and collected by bees **2** Classical myth the drink of the gods **3** any delicious drink [Greek nektar]

nectarine n a smooth-skinned variety of peach [apparently from nectar]

ned n Scot slang a hooligan [origin unknown]

NEDC (formerly) National Economic Development Council. Also (informal): **Neddy**

Nederland n the Dutch name for the **Netherlands**

née prep indicating the maiden name of a married woman: Jane Gray (née Blandish) [French, past participle (feminine) of naître to be born]

need vb **1** to require or be in want of: they desperately need success **2** to be obliged: the government may need to impose a statutory levy **3** used to express necessity or obligation and does not add -s when used with singular nouns or pronouns: need he go? ▷ n **4** the condition of lacking something: he has need of a new coat **5** a requirement: the need for closer economic co-operation **6** necessity: there was no need for an explanation **7** poverty or destitution: the money will go to those areas where need is greatest **8** distress: help has been given to those in need ▸ See also **needs** [Old English nēad, nied]

needful adj **1** necessary or required ▷ n **2 the needful** informal what is necessary, usually money

needle n **1** a pointed slender piece of metal with a hole in it through which thread is passed for sewing **2** a long pointed rod used in knitting **3** same as **stylus 4** med the long hollow pointed part of a hypodermic syringe, which is inserted into the body **5** a pointer on the scale of a measuring instrument **6** a long narrow stiff leaf: pine needles **7** Brit informal intense rivalry or ill-feeling in a sports match **8** short for **magnetic needle 9 have** or **get the needle** Brit informal to be or become annoyed ▷ vb **-dling, -dled 10** informal to goad or provoke [Old English nǣdl]

needlecord n a fine-ribbed corduroy fabric

needlepoint n **1** embroidery done on canvas **2** lace made by needles on a paper pattern

needless adj not required; unnecessary > **needlessly** adv

needlewoman n, pl **-women** a woman who does needlework

needlework n sewing and embroidery

needs adv **1** necessarily: they must needs be admired ▷ pl n **2** what is required: he provides them with their needs

needy adj **needier, neediest** in need of financial support

Néel n Louis. 1904–2000, French physicist, noted for his research on magnetism; shared the Nobel prize for physics in 1970

ne'er adv poetic never

ne'er-do-well n **1** an irresponsible or lazy person ▷ adj **2** useless; worthless: his ne'er-do-well brother

nefarious (nif-**fair**-ee-uss) *adj literary* evil; wicked [Latin *ne* not + *fas* divine law]

Nefertiti *or* **Nofretete** *n* 14th century BC, Egyptian queen; wife of Akhenaton

neg. negative

negate *vb* **-gating, -gated** 1 to cause to have no value or effect: *his prejudices largely negate his accomplishments* 2 to deny the existence of [Latin *negare*]

negation *n* 1 the opposite or absence of something 2 a negative thing or condition 3 the act of negating

negative *adj* 1 expressing a refusal or denial: *a negative response* 2 lacking positive qualities, such as enthusiasm or optimism 3 *med* indicating absence of the condition for which a test was made 4 *physics* **a** (of an electric charge) having the same electrical charge as an electron **b** (of a body or system) having a negative electric charge; having an excess of electrons 5 same as **minus** (4) 6 measured in a direction opposite to that regarded as positive 7 short for **electronegative** 8 of a photographic negative ▷ *n* 9 a statement or act of denial or refusal 10 *photog* a piece of photographic film, exposed and developed, bearing an image with a reversal of tones or colours, from which positive prints are made 11 a word or expression with a negative meaning, such as *not* 12 a quantity less than zero 13 **in the negative** indicating denial or refusal ⟩ **negatively** *adv*

negative equity *n* the holding of a property of fallen value which is worth less than the amount of mortgage still unpaid

negativism *n* a tendency to be unconstructively critical ⟩ **negativist** *n, adj*

Negev *or* **Negeb** *n* the S part of Israel, on the Gulf of Aqaba: a triangular-shaped semidesert region, with large areas under irrigation; scene of fighting between Israeli and Egyptian forces in 1948. Chief town: Beersheba. Area: 12 820 sq km (4950 sq miles)

neglect *vb* 1 to fail to give due care or attention to: *she had neglected her child* 2 to fail (to do something) through carelessness: *he neglected to greet his guests* 3 to disregard: *he neglected his duty* ▷ *n* 4 lack of due care or attention: *the city had a look of shabbiness and neglect* 5 the state of being neglected [Latin *neglegere*]

neglectful *adj* not paying enough care or attention: *abusive and neglectful parents*

negligee (neg-lee-**zhay**) *n* a woman's light, usually lace-trimmed dressing gown [French]

negligence *n* neglect or carelessness ⟩ **negligent** *adj* ⟩ **negligently** *adv*

negligible *adj* so small or unimportant as to be not worth considering

negotiable *adj* 1 able to be changed or agreed by discussion: *the prices were negotiable* 2 (of a bill of exchange or promissory note) legally transferable

negotiate *vb* **-ating, -ated** 1 to talk with others in order to reach (an agreement) 2 to succeed in passing round or over (a place or a problem) [Latin *negotium* business, from *nec* not + *otium* leisure] ⟩ **negotiation** *n* ⟩ **negotiator** *n*

Negri Sembilan *n* a state of S Peninsular Malaysia: mostly mountainous, with large areas under paddy and rubber. Capital: Seremban. Pop: 859 924 (2000). Area: 6643 sq km (2565 sq miles)

Negro[1] *old-fashioned, offensive n, pl* **-groes** 1 a member of any of the Black peoples originating in Africa ▷ *adj* 2 of Black people [Latin *niger* black]

Negro[2] *n* **Río Negro** 1 a river in NW South America, rising in E Colombia (as the Guainía) and flowing east, then south as part of the border between Colombia and Venezuela, entering Brazil and continuing southeast to join the Amazon at Manáus. Length: about 2250 km (1400 miles) 2 a river in S central Argentina, formed by the confluence of the Neuquén and Limay Rivers and flowing east and southeast to the Atlantic. Length: about 1014 km (630 miles) 3 a river in central Uruguay,

rising in S Brazil and flowing southwest into the Uruguay River. Length: about 467 km (290 miles)

Negroid *adj old-fashioned or offensive* of or relating to the Black peoples originating in Africa

Negropont *n* 1 the former English name for **Euboea** 2 the medieval English name for **Chalcis**

Negros *n* an island of the central Philippines, one of the Visayan Islands. Capital: Bacolod. Pop: 3 700 000 (2000 est). Area: 12 704 sq km (4904 sq miles)

Nehru *n* 1 Jawaharlal. 1889–1964, Indian statesman and nationalist leader. He spent several periods in prison for his nationalist activities and practised a policy of noncooperation with Britain during World War II. He was the first prime minister of the republic of India (1947–64) 2 his father, **Motilal**, known as *Pandit Nehru*. 1861–1931, Indian nationalist, lawyer, and journalist; first president of the reconstructed Indian National Congress

neigh *n* 1 the high-pitched sound made by a horse ▷ *vb* 2 to make this sound [Old English *hnǣgan*]

neighbour *or US* **neighbor** *n* 1 a person who lives near or next to another 2 a person, thing, or country near or next to another [Old English *nēah* near + *būr, gebūr* dweller]

neighbourhood *or US* **neighborhood** *n* 1 a district where people live 2 the immediate environment; surroundings 3 the people in a district 4 **in the neighbourhood of** approximately ▷ *adj* 5 in and for a district: *our neighbourhood cinema*

neighbouring *or US* **neighboring** *adj* situated nearby: *the neighbouring island*

neighbourly *or US* **neighborly** *adj* kind, friendly, and helpful

Neill *n* 1 **A(lexander) S(utherland)**. 1883–1973, Scottish educationalist and writer, who put his progressive educational theories into practice at Summerhill school (founded 1921) 2 **Sam**, real name *Nigel John Dermot Neill*. born 1947, New Zealand film and television actor, born in Northern Ireland; his work includes the television series *Reilly, Ace of Spies*, (1983) and the films *My Brilliant Career* (1979), *Dead Calm* (1989), *Jurassic Park* (1993), and *The Piano* (1993)

Neisse *n* 1 Also called: **Glatzer Neisse** a river in SW Poland, rising on the northern Czech border, and flowing northeast to join the Oder near Brzeg. Length: about 193 km (120 miles). Polish name: **Nysa** 2 Also called: **Lusatian Neisse** a river in E Europe, rising near Liberec in the Czech Republic and flowing north to join the Oder: forms part of the German–Polish border. Length: 225 km (140 miles)

neither *adj* 1 not one nor the other (of two): *neither enterprise went well* ▷ *pron* 2 not one nor the other (of two): *neither completed the full term* ▷ *conj* 3 **a** used preceding alternatives joined by *nor*; not: *sparing neither strength nor courage* **b** same as **nor** (2) ▷ *adv* 4 *not standard* same as **either** (4) [Old English *nāwther*]

> **USAGE** A verb following a compound subject that uses *neither …(nor)* should be in the singular if both subjects are in the singular: *neither Jack nor John has done the work.*

Nejd *n* a region of central Saudi Arabia: formerly an independent sultanate of Arabia; united with Hejaz to form the kingdom of Saudi Arabia (1932)

Nekrasov *n* **Nikolai Alekseyevich**. 1821–77, Russian poet, who wrote chiefly about the sufferings of the peasantry

nelson *n* a wrestling hold in which a wrestler places his arm or arms under his opponent's arm or arms from behind and exerts pressure with his palms on the back of his opponent's neck [from a proper name]

Nelson[1] *n* 1 a town in NW England, in E Lancashire: textile industry. Pop: 28 998 (2001) 2 a port in New Zealand, on N South Island on Tasman Bay. Pop: 45 300 (2004 est) 3 **River Nelson** a river in central Canada, in N central Manitoba, flowing from Lake Winnipeg northeast to Hudson Bay. Length: about 650 km (400 miles)

Nelson n **1** Horatio, Viscount Nelson. 1758–1805, British naval commander during the Revolutionary and Napoleonic Wars. He became rear admiral in 1797 after the battle of Cape St Vincent and in 1798 almost destroyed the French fleet at the battle of the Nile. He was killed at Trafalgar (1805) after defeating Villeneuve's fleet **2** Willie. born 1933, US country singer and songwriter

Nelspruit n a city in NE South Africa, the capital of Mpumalanga province on the Crocodile River: trading and agricultural centre, esp. for fruit, with a growing tourist trade. Pop: 21 541 (2001)

Neman or **Nyeman** n a river in NE Europe, rising in Belarus and flowing northwest through Lithuania to the Baltic. Length: 937 km (582 miles). Polish name: **Niemen**

nematode n a slender unsegmented cylindrical worm [Greek nēma thread + eidos shape]

Nemea n (in ancient Greece) a valley in N Argolis in the NE Peloponnese; site of the **Nemean Games**, a Panhellenic festival and athletic competition held every other year

Nemean adj of or relating to Nemea or its inhabitants

nemesis (nem-miss-iss) n, pl -**ses** (-seez) a means of retribution or vengeance [Greek nemein to distribute what is due]

neo- combining form new, recent, or a modern form of: neoclassicism; neo-Nazi [Greek neos new]

neoclassicism n a late 18th- and early 19th-century style of art and architecture, based on ancient Roman and Greek models > **neoclassical** adj

neocolonialism n political control wielded by one country over another through control of its economy > **neocolonial** adj

neocon n, adj chiefly US short for **neoconservative**

neoconservative adj **1** favouring a return to a set of established (esp. political) conservative values which have been updated to suit current conditions > n **2** a person subscribing to neoconservative philosophy

neodymium n chem a toxic silvery-white metallic element of the lanthanide series. Symbol: Nd [NEO- + didymium, a compound originally thought to be an element]

Neogaea n a zoogeographical area comprising the Neotropical region. Compare **Arctogaea**, **Notogaea** [C19: New Latin, from NEO- + GAEA, from Greek gaia earth]

Neogaean adj of or relating to Neogaea

neoliberalism n a modern political and economic theory that promotes free trade, privatization, reduced public expenditure, and limited control of business > **neoliberal** n, adj

Neolithic adj of the period that lasted in Europe from about 4000 to 2400 BC, characterized by primitive farming and the use of polished stone and flint tools and weapons [NEO- + Greek lithos stone]

neologism (nee-ol-a-jiz-zum) n a newly coined word, or an established word used in a new sense [NEO- + Greek logos word]

neon n **1** chem a colourless odourless rare gas, used in illuminated signs and lights. Symbol: Ne ▷ adj **2** of or illuminated by neon: a flashing neon sign [Greek: new]

neonatal adj relating to the first few weeks of a baby's life > **neonate** n

neon light n a glass tube containing neon, which gives a pink or red glow when a voltage is applied

neophyte n formal **1** a beginner **2** a person newly converted to a religious faith **3** a novice in a religious order [Greek neos new + phuton a plant]

Nepal n a republic in S Asia: the world's only Hindu kingdom until it abandoned its monarchy in 2008; united in 1768 by the Gurkhas; consists of swampy jungle in the south and great massifs, valleys, and

gorges of the Himalayas over the rest of the country, with many peaks over 8000 m (26 000 ft) (notably Everest and Kangchonjunga). A multiparty democracy was instituted in 1990. Official language: Nepali. Official religion: Hinduism; Mahayana Buddhist minority. Currency: rupee. Capital: Katmandu. Pop: 30 430 267 (2013 est). Area: 147 181 sq km (56 815 sq miles). Official name: **Federal Democratic Republic of Nepal**

Nepalese adj **1** of or relating to Nepal or its inhabitants ▷ n, pl -**ese 2** a native or inhabitant of Nepal

Nepali (nip-paw-lee) or **Nepalese** (nep-pal-leez) adj **1** of or relating to Nepal or its inhabitants ▷ n **2** (pl -**pali**, -**palis** or -**palese**) a native or inhabitant of Nepal **3** the language of Nepal

nephew n a son of one's sister or brother [Latin nepos]

nephritis (nif-frite-tiss) n inflammation of the kidney [Greek nephros kidney]

Nepos n Cornelius. ?100–?25 BC, Roman historian and biographer; author of De viris illustribus

nepotism (nep-a-tiz-zum) n favouritism shown to relatives and friends by those with power [Italian nepote nephew]

Neptune n **1** the Roman god of the sea **2** the eighth planet from the sun

neptunium n chem a silvery metallic element synthesized in the production of plutonium. Symbol: Np [after NEPTUNE, the planet]

nerd or **nurd** n slang **1** a boring or unpopular person, esp. one who is obsessed with a particular subject: a computer nerd **2** a stupid and feeble person [origin unknown] > **nerdish** or **nurdish** adj

Neri n Saint Philip. Italian name Filippo de' Neri. 1515–95, Italian priest; founder of the Congregation of the Oratory (1564). Feast day: May 26

Nernst n Walther Hermann. 1864–1941, German physical chemist who formulated the third law of thermodynamics: Nobel prize for chemistry 1920

Nero n full name Nero Claudius Caesar Drusus Germanicus; original name Lucius Domitius Ahenobarbus. 37–68 AD, Roman emperor (54–68). He became notorious for his despotism and cruelty, and was alleged to have started the fire (64) that destroyed a large part of Rome

Neruda n Pablo, real name Neftali Ricardo Reyes. 1904–73, Chilean poet. His works include Veinte poemas de amor y una canción desesperada (1924) and Canto general (1950), an epic history of the Americas: Nobel prize for literature 1971

Nerva n full name Marcus Cocceius Nerva. ?30–98 AD, Roman emperor (96–98), who introduced some degree of freedom after the repressive reign of Domitian. He adopted Trajan as his son and successor

Nerval n Gérard de, real name Gérard Labrunie. 1808–55, French poet, noted esp. for the sonnets of mysticism, myth, and private passion in Les Chimères (1854)

nervate adj (of leaves) with veins

nerve n **1** a cordlike bundle of fibres that conducts impulses between the brain and other parts of the body **2** bravery and determination **3** informal impudence: you've got a nerve! **4 lose one's nerve** to lose self-confidence and become afraid about what one is doing **5 strain every nerve** to make every effort (to do something) ▷ vb **nerving, nerved 6 nerve oneself** to prepare oneself (to do something difficult or unpleasant) ▶ See also **nerves** [Latin nervus]

nerve cell n same as **neuron**

nerve centre n **1** a place from which a system or organization is controlled: an underground nerve centre of intelligence **2** a group of nerve cells associated with a specific function

nerve gas n a poisonous gas which affects the nervous system

nerveless adj **1** (of fingers or hands) without feeling; numb **2** (of a person) fearless

nerve-racking or **nerve-wracking** adj very distressing or harrowing

nerves *pl n informal* **1** anxiety or tension: *nerves can often be the cause of wedding-day hitches* **2** the ability or inability to remain calm in a difficult situation: *his nerves are in a shocking state* **3 get on someone's nerves** to irritate someone

Nervi *n* Pier Luigi. 1891–1979, Italian engineer and architect; noted for his pioneering use of reinforced concrete as a decorative material. He codesigned the UNESCO building in Paris (1953)

nervous *adj* **1** apprehensive or worried **2** excitable; highly strung **3** of or relating to the nerves: *the nervous system* ➤ **nervously** *adv* ➤ **nervousness** *n*

nervous breakdown *n* a mental illness in which the sufferer ceases to function properly, and experiences symptoms including tiredness, anxiety, and deep depression

nervous system *n* the brain, spinal column, and nerves, which together control thought, feeling, and movement. See **neuron**

nervy *adj* **nervier, nerviest** *Brit and Austral informal* excitable or nervous

Nesbit *n* E(dith). 1858–1924, British writer of children's books, including *The Phoenix and the Carpet* (1904) and *The Railway Children* (1906)

ness *n Brit* a headland or cape [Old English *næs*]

Ness *n* Loch Ness a lake in NW Scotland, in the Great Glen: said to be inhabited by an aquatic monster. Length: 36 km (22.5 miles). Depth: 229 m (754 ft)

-ness *suffix* indicating state, condition, or quality: *greatness; selfishness* [Old English *-nes*]

Nesselrode *n* Count Karl Robert. 1780–1862, Russian diplomat: as foreign minister (1822–56), he negotiated the Treaty of Paris after the Crimean War (1856)

nest *n* **1 a** a place or structure in which birds or other animals lay eggs or give birth to young **2** a cosy or secluded place **3** a set of things of graduated sizes designed to fit together: *a nest of tables* ▷ *vb* **4** to make or inhabit a nest **5** (of a set of objects) to fit one inside another **6** *computers* to position (data) within other data at different ranks or levels [Old English]

nest egg *n* a fund of money kept in reserve

nestle *vb* **-tling, -tled** **1** to snuggle or cuddle closely **2** to be in a sheltered position: *honey-coloured stone villages nestling in wooded valleys* [Old English *nestlian*]

nestling *n* a young bird not yet able to fly

Nestorius *n* died ?451 AD, Syrian churchman; patriarch of Constantinople (428–431); deposed for heresy by the Council of Ephesus

net¹ *n* **1** a very fine fabric made from intersecting strands of material with a space between each strand **2** a piece of net, used to protect or hold things or to trap animals **3** (in certain sports) a strip of net over which the ball or shuttlecock must be hit **4** the goal in soccer or hockey **5** a strategy intended to trap people: *innocent fans were caught in the police net* **6** *informal* short for **internet** ▷ *vb* **netting, netted** **7** to catch (a fish or other animal) in a net [Old English *net(t)*]

net² *or* **nett** *adj* **1** remaining after all deductions, as for taxes and expenses: *net income* **2** (of weight) excluding the weight of wrapping or container **3** final or conclusive: *the net effect* ▷ *vb* **netting, netted** **4** to yield or earn as a clear profit [French: neat]

Netanyahu *n* Benjamin. born 1949, Israeli politician: leader of the Likud party (1993–99 and from 2005); prime minister (1996–99 and from 2009)

netball *n* a team game, usually played by women, in which a ball has to be thrown through a net hanging from a ring at the top of a pole

Neth. Netherlands

nether *adj old-fashioned* lower or under: *nether regions* [Old English *nithera*, literally: further down]

Netherlander *n* a native or inhabitant of the Netherlands

Netherlands *n* the Netherlands (*functioning as sing or pl*)

1 Also called: **Holland** a kingdom in NW Europe, on the North Sea: declared independence from Spain in 1581 as the United Provinces; became a major maritime and commercial power in the 17th century, gaining many overseas possessions; formed the Benelux customs union with Belgium and Luxembourg in 1948 and was a founder member of the Common Market, now the European Union. It is mostly flat and low-lying, with about 40 per cent of the land being below sea level, much of it on polders protected by dykes. Official language: Dutch. Religion: Christian majority, Protestant and Roman Catholic, large nonreligious minority. Currency: euro. Capital: Amsterdam, with the seat of government at The Hague. Pop: 16 805 037 (2013 est). Area: 41 526 sq km (16 033 sq miles). Dutch name: **Nederland** **2** the kingdom of the Netherlands together with the Flemish-speaking part of Belgium, esp. as ruled by Spain and Austria before 1581; the Low Countries

Netherlands Antilles *pl n* the Netherlands Antilles two groups of islands in the Caribbean, in the Lesser Antilles: a former constituent country of the Netherlands (since 2010 each island has had a separate status), consisting of the S group of Curaçao, Aruba, and Bonaire, and the N group of Saint Eustatius, Saba, and the S part of Saint Martin; economy based on refining oil from Venezuela. Pop: 222 000 (2004 est). Area: 996 sq km (390 sq miles). Former names: (until 1949) **Curaçao, the Dutch West Indies, the Netherlands West Indies**

Netherlands East Indies *pl n* the Netherlands East Indies a former name (1798–1945) for **Indonesia**

Netherlands Guiana *n* a former name for **Surinam**

Netherlands West Indies *pl n* the Netherlands West Indies a former name for the **Netherlands Antilles**

nethermost *adj* lowest

nether world *n* **1** the underworld **2** hell ▶ Also called: **nether regions**

net profit *n* gross profit minus all operating expenses such as wages and overheads

Netrebko *n* Anna. born 1971, Russian operatic soprano

nett *adj, vb* same as **net²**

netting *n* a fabric or structure made of net

nettle *n* **1** a plant with stinging hairs on the leaves **2 grasp the nettle** to attempt something unpleasant with boldness and courage [Old English *netele*]

nettled *adj* irritated or annoyed

nettle rash *n* a skin condition, usually caused by an allergy, in which itchy red or white raised patches appear

network *n* **1** a system of intersecting lines, roads, veins, etc. **2** an interconnecting group or system: *a network of sympathizers and safe-houses* **3** *radio, television* a group of broadcasting stations that all transmit the same programme at the same time **4** *electronics, computers* a system of interconnected components or circuits ▷ *vb* **5** *radio, television* to broadcast (a programme) over a network

Neubrandenburg *n* a city in NE Germany, in Mecklenburg-West Pomerania: 14th-century city walls. Pop: 69 157 (2003 est)

Neuchâtel *n* **1** a canton in the Jura Mountains of W Switzerland. Capital: Neuchâtel. Pop: 167 000 (2002 est). Area: 798 sq km (308 sq miles) **2** a town in W Switzerland, capital of Neuchâtel canton, on Lake Neuchâtel: until 1848 the seat of the last hereditary rulers in Switzerland. Pop: 32 914 (2000) **3** Lake Neuchâtel a lake in W Switzerland: the largest lake wholly in Switzerland. Area: 216 sq km (83 sq miles) ▶ German name (for senses 1, 2): **Neuenburg**

Neuilly-sur-Seine *n* a town in N France, on the Seine: a suburb of NW Paris. Pop: 61 754 (2010)

Neumann *n* **1** Johann Balthasar. 1687–1753, German rococo architect. His masterpiece is the church of Vierzehnheiligen in Bavaria **2** See (John) **von Neumann**

Neumünster *n* a town in N Germany, in Schleswig-Holstein: manufacturing of textiles and machinery. Pop: 78 951 (2003 est)

neural *adj* of a nerve or the nervous system

neuralgia *n* severe pain along a nerve ❭ **neuralgic** *adj*

neuritis (nyoor-**rite**-tiss) *n* inflammation of a nerve or nerves, often causing pain and loss of function in the affected part

neurology *n med* the scientific study of the nervous system ❭ **neurological** *adj* ❭ **neurologist** *n*

neuron *or* **neurone** *n* a cell specialized to conduct nerve impulses [Greek]

neurosis (nyoor-**oh**-siss) *n, pl* -**ses** (-seez) a mental disorder producing hysteria, anxiety, depression, or obsessive behaviour

neurosurgery *n med* the branch of surgery concerned with the nervous system ❭ **neurosurgeon** *n* ❭ **neurosurgical** *adj*

neurotic *adj* **1** tending to be emotionally unstable **2** afflicted by neurosis ▷ *n* **3** a person afflicted with a neurosis or tending to be emotionally unstable

neurotransmitter *n biochem* a chemical by which a nerve cell communicates with another nerve cell or with a muscle

Neusatz *n* the German name for **Novi Sad**

Neuss *n* an industrial city in W Germany, in North Rhine-Westphalia west of Düsseldorf: founded as a Roman fortress in the 1st century AD. Pop: 152 050 (2003 est). Latin name: **Novaesium**

Neustria *n* the western part of the kingdom of the Merovingian Franks, formed in 561 AD in what is now N France

Neustrian *adj* of or relating to Neustria or its inhabitants

neuter *adj* **1** *grammar* denoting a gender of nouns which are neither male nor female **2** (of animals and plants) sexually underdeveloped ▷ *n* **3** *grammar* **a** the neuter gender **b** a neuter noun **4** a sexually underdeveloped female insect, such as a worker bee **5** a castrated animal ▷ *vb* **6** to castrate (an animal) [Latin *ne* not + *uter* either (of two)]

neutral *adj* **1** not taking any side in a war or dispute **2** of or belonging to a neutral party or country **3** not displaying any emotions or opinions **4** (of a colour) not definite or striking **5** *chem* neither acidic nor alkaline **6** *physics* having zero charge or potential ▷ *n* **7** a neutral person or nation **8** the position of the controls of a gearbox that leaves the gears unconnected to the engine [Latin *neutralis* of neuter gender] ❭ **neutrality** *n*

neutralize *or* **-lise** *vb* **-lizing, -lized** *or* **-lising, -lised 1** to make electrically or chemically neutral **2** to make ineffective by counteracting **3** to make (a country) neutral by international agreement: *the great powers neutralized Belgium in the 19th century* ❭ **neutralization** *or* **-lisation** *n*

neutrino (new-**tree**-no) *n, pl* -**nos** *physics* an elementary particle with no mass or electrical charge [Italian diminutive of *neutrone* neutron]

neutron *n physics* a neutral elementary particle of about the same mass as a proton [from *neutral*, on the model of *electron*]

neutron bomb *n* a nuclear weapon designed to kill people and animals while leaving buildings virtually undamaged

Nev. Nevada

Neva *n* a river in NW Russia, flowing west to the Gulf of Finland by the delta on which Saint Petersburg stands. Length: 74 km (46 miles)

Nevada *n* a state of the western US: lies almost wholly within the Great Basin, a vast desert plateau; noted for production of gold and copper. Capital: Carson City. Pop: 2 241 154 (2003 est). Area: 284 612 sq km (109 889 sq miles). Abbreviation: **Nev.**, (with zip code) **NV**

Nevadan *n* a native or inhabitant of Nevada

never *adv* **1** at no time; not ever **2** certainly not; not at all **3** Also: **well I never!** surely not! [Old English *nǣfre*]

> **USAGE** In informal speech and writing, *never* can be used instead of *not* with the simple past tenses of certain verbs, for emphasis (*I never said that; I never realized how clever he was*), but this usage should be avoided in serious writing.

never-ending *adj* long and boring

nevermore *adv literary* never again

never-never *n* the **never-never** *informal* hire-purchase: *they are buying it on the never-never*

never-never land *n* an imaginary idyllic place

Nevers *n* a city in central France: capital of the former duchy of Nivernais; engineering industry. Pop: 40 131 (2006)

nevertheless *adv* in spite of that

Nevis *n* **1** an island in the Caribbean, part of St Kitts-Nevis; the volcanic cone of **Nevis Peak**, which rises to 1002 m (3287 ft), lies in the centre of the island. Capital: Charlestown. Pop: 11 181 (2001. Area: 129 sq km (50 sq miles) **2** See **Ben Nevis**

new *adj* **1** recently made, brought into being, or acquired: *a new car* **2** of a kind never before existing; novel: *a new approach to monetary policy* **3** recently discovered: *testing new drugs* **4** recently introduced to or inexperienced in a place or situation: *new to this game* **5** fresh; additional: *you can acquire new skills* **6** unknown: *this is new to me* **7** (of a cycle) beginning again: *a new era* **8** (of crops) harvested early: *new potatoes* **9** changed for the better: *she returned a new woman* ▷ *adv* **10** (*usually in combination*) recently, newly: *new-laid eggs* ▶ See also **news** [Old English *nīowe*] ❭ **newish** *adj* ❭ **newness** *n*

New Age *n* **1** a philosophy, originating in the late 1980s, characterized by a belief in alternative medicine, astrology, and spiritualism ▷ *adj* **2** of the New Age: *New Age therapies* ❭ **New Ager** *n*

New Age Music *n* a type of gentle melodic largely instrumental popular music originating in the USA in the late 1980s

New Amsterdam *n* the Dutch settlement established on Manhattan (1624–26); capital of New Netherland; captured by the English and renamed New York in 1664

Newark *n* **1** a town in N central England, in Nottinghamshire. Pop: 35 454 (2001). Official name: **Newark-on-Trent 2** a port in NE New Jersey, just west of New York City, on Newark Bay and the Passaic River: the largest city in the state; founded in 1666 by Puritans from Connecticut; industrial and commercial centre. Pop: 277 911 (2003 est)

New Australia *n* the colony on socialist principles founded by William Lane in Paraguay in 1893

New Australian *n Austral* an Australian name for a recent immigrant, esp. one from Europe

New Bedford *n* a port and resort in SE Massachusetts, near Buzzards Bay: settled by Plymouth colonists in 1652; a leading whaling port (18th–19th centuries). Pop: 94 112 (2003 est)

newbie *n informal* a person new to a job, club, etc.

newborn *adj* recently or just born

New Britain *n* an island in the S Pacific, northeast of New Guinea: the largest island of the Bismarck Archipelago; part of Papua New Guinea; mountainous, with several active volcanoes. Capital: Rabaul. Pop: 161 737 (2000). Area: 36 519 sq km (14 100 sq miles)

New Brunswick *n* a province of SE Canada on the Gulf of St Lawrence and the Bay of Fundy: extensively forested. Capital: Fredericton. Pop: 751 171 (2011 est). Area: 72 092 sq km (27 835 sq miles). Abbreviation: **NB**

New Brunswicker *n* a native or inhabitant of New Brunswick

Newbury *n* a market town in West Berkshire unitary authority, S England: scene of a Parliamentarian victory

(1643) and a Royalist victory (1644) during the Civil War; telecommunications, racecourse. Pop: 32 675 (2001)

Newby Hall *n* a mansion near Ripon in Yorkshire: built in 1705 and altered (1770–76) by Robert Adam

New Caledonia *n* an island in the SW Pacific, east of Australia: forms, with its dependencies, a French Overseas Country; discovered by Captain Cook in 1774; rich mineral resources. Capital: Nouméa. Pop: 264 022 (2013 est). Area: 19 103 sq km (7374 miles). French name: Nouvelle-Calédonie

New Canadian *n Canad* a recent immigrant to Canada

New Castile *n* a region and former province of central Spain. Chief town: Toledo

Newcastle¹ *n* a port in SE Australia, in E New South Wales near the mouth of the Hunter River: important industrial centre, with extensive steel, metalworking, engineering, shipbuilding, and chemical industries. It suffered Australia's first recorded fatal earthquake, in 1989. Pop: 279 975 (2001)

Newcastle² *n* Duke of, the title of *Thomas Pelham Holles*. 1693–1768, English Whig prime minister (1754–56; 1757–62): brother of Henry Pelham

Newcastle-under-Lyme *n* a town in W central England, in Staffordshire. Pop: 74 427 (2001). Often shortened to: **Newcastle**

Newcastle upon Tyne *n* **1** a port in NE England in Newcastle upon Tyne unitary authority, Tyne and Wear, near the mouth of the River Tyne opposite Gateshead: Roman remains; engineering industries, including ship repairs; two universities (1937, 1992). Pop: 189 863 (2001). Often shortened to: **Newcastle** **2** a unitary authority in NE England, in Tyne and Wear. Pop: 266 600 (2003 est). Area: 112 sq km (43 sq miles)

new chum *n Austral and NZ archaic or informal* a recent British immigrant

Newcomb *n* Simon. 1835–1909, US astronomer, noted for his tables of celestial bodies and astronomical constants

Newcombe *n* John (David). born 1944, Australian tennis player; winner of seven Grand Slam singles titles (1967–75), including three at Wimbledon (1967, 1970, 1971)

Newcomen *n* Thomas. 1663–1729, English engineer who invented a steam engine, which James Watt later modified and developed

newcomer *n* a recent arrival or participant

New Delhi *n* See **Delhi**

newel *n* **1** Also called: **newel post** the post at the top or bottom of a flight of stairs that supports the handrail **2** the central pillar of a winding staircase [Old French *nouel* knob]

New England *n* **1** the NE part of the US, consisting of the states of Maine, New Hampshire, Vermont, Massachusetts, Rhode Island, and Connecticut: settled originally chiefly by Puritans in the mid-17th century **2** a region in SE Australia, in the northern tablelands of New South Wales

New Englander *n* a native or inhabitant of New England

New England Range *n* a mountain range in SE Australia, in NE New South Wales: part of the Great Dividing Range. Highest peak: Ben Lomond, 1520 m (4986 ft)

newfangled *adj* objectionably or unnecessarily modern [Middle English *newefangel* liking new things]

Newfie *n informal* **1** a native or inhabitant of Newfoundland **2** the island of Newfoundland

New Forest *n* a region of woodland and heath in S England, in SW Hampshire: a hunting ground of the West Saxon kings; tourist area, noted for its ponies; made into a national park in 2005. Area: 336 sq km (130 sq miles)

new-found *adj* newly or recently discovered: *new-found confidence*

Newfoundland *n* **1** an island of E Canada, separated from the mainland by the Strait of Belle Isle: with the Coast of Labrador, forms the province of Newfoundland and Labrador; consists of a rugged plateau with the Long Range Mountains in the west. Area: 110 681 sq km (42 734 sq miles) **2** the former name for **Newfoundland and Labrador 3** a very large heavy breed of dog similar to a Saint Bernard with a flat coarse usually black coat

Newfoundland and Labrador *n* a province of E Canada, consisting of the island of Newfoundland and the Coast of Labrador: usually known as Newfoundland until its official long form was adopted as the main name in 2001. Capital: St John's. Pop: 514 536 (2011 est). Area: 404 519 sq km (156 185 sq miles). Abbreviation: **NL**

Newfoundlander *n* a native or inhabitant of Newfoundland

New France *n* the former French colonies and possessions in North America, most of which were lost to England and Spain by 1763: often restricted to the French possessions in Canada

Newgate *n* a famous London prison, in use from the Middle Ages: demolished in 1902

New Georgia *n* **1** a group of islands in the SW Pacific, in the Solomon Islands **2** the largest island in this group. Area: about 1300 sq km (500 sq miles)

New Granada *n* **1** a former Spanish presidency and later viceroyalty in South America. At its greatest extent it consisted of present-day Panama, Colombia, Venezuela, and Ecuador **2** the name of Colombia when it formed, with Panama, part of Great Colombia (1819–30)

New Guinea *n* **1** an island in the W Pacific, north of Australia: divided politically into Papua (formerly Irian Jaya, a province of Indonesia) in the west and Papua New Guinea in the east. There is a central chain of mountains and a lowland area of swamps in the south and along the Sepik River in the north. Area: 775 213 sq km (299 310 sq miles) **2 Trust Territory of New Guinea** (until 1975) an administrative division of the former Territory of Papua and New Guinea, consisting of the NE part of the island of New Guinea together with the Bismarck Archipelago; now part of Papua New Guinea

Newham *n* a borough of E Greater London, on the River Thames: established in 1965. Pop: 250 600 (2003 est). Area: 36 sq km (14 sq miles)

New Hampshire *n* a state of the northeastern US: generally hilly. Capital: Concord. Pop: 1 287 687 (2003 est). Area: 23 379 sq km (9027 sq miles). Abbreviation: **N.H.**, (with zip code) **NH**

New Harmony *n* a village in SW Indiana, on the Wabash River: scene of two experimental cooperative communities, the first founded in 1815 by George Rapp, a German religious leader, and the second by Robert Owen in 1825

Newhaven *n* a ferry port and resort on the S coast of England, in East Sussex. Pop: 12 276 (2001)

New Haven *n* an industrial city and port in S Connecticut, on Long Island Sound: settled in 1638 by English Puritans, who established it as a colony in 1643; seat of Yale University (1701). Pop: 124 512 (2003 est)

New Hebrides *pl n* the former name (until 1980) of Vanuatu

Ne Win *n* U. 1911–2002, Burmese statesman and general; prime minister (1958–60), head of the military government (1962–74), and president (1974–81)

New Ireland *n* an island in the S Pacific, in the Bismarck Archipelago, separated from New Britain by St George's Channel: part of Papua New Guinea. Chief town and port: Kavieng. Pop (province): 118 148 (2000). Area (including adjacent islands): 9850 sq km (3800 sq miles)

New Jersey *n* a state of the eastern US, on the Atlantic and Delaware Bay: mostly low-lying, with a heavy industrial area in the northeast and many coastal resorts. Capital: Trenton. Pop: 8 638 396 (2003 est). Area:

19 479 sq km (7521 sq miles). Abbreviation: **N.J.**, (with zip code) **NJ**

New Jerusalem *n Christianity* heaven

Newlands *n* John Alexander. 1838–98, British chemist: classified the elements in order of their atomic weight, noticing similarities in every eighth and thus discovering his law of octaves

New Latin *n* the form of Latin used since the Renaissance, mainly for scientific names

newly *adv* **1** recently **2** again; anew: *newly interpreted*

newlyweds *pl n* a recently married couple

Newman *n* **1** Barnet. 1905–70, US painter, a founder of Abstract Expressionism: his paintings include the series *Stations of the Cross* (1965–66) **2** John Henry. 1801–90, British theologian and writer. Originally an Anglican minister, he was a prominent figure in the Oxford Movement. He became a Roman Catholic (1845) and a priest (1847) and was made a cardinal (1879). His writings include the spiritual autobiography *Apologia pro vita sua* (1864), a treatise on the nature of belief, *The Grammar of Assent* (1870), and hymns **3** Paul. 1925–2008, US film actor and director, who appeared in such films as *Hud* (1963), *Butch Cassidy and the Sundance Kid* (1969), *The Sting* (1973), *The Verdict* (1982), *The Color of Money* (1986), *Nobody's Fool* (1994), and *Road to Perdition* (2002)

New Man *n chiefly Brit* a modern man who allows the caring side of his nature to show by being supportive and by sharing childcare and housework

Newmarket *n* a town in SE England, in W Suffolk: a famous horse-racing centre since the reign of James I. Pop: 16 947 (2001)

new maths *n Brit* an approach to mathematics in which basic set theory is introduced at an elementary level

New Mexican *adj* **1** of or relating to New Mexico or its inhabitants ▷ *n* **2** a native or inhabitant of New Mexico

New Mexico *n* a state of the southwestern US: high semiarid plateaus and mountains, crossed by the Rio Grande and the Pecos River; large Spanish-American and Indian populations; contains over two-thirds of US uranium reserves. Capital: Santa Fé. Pop: 1 874 614 (2003 est). Area: 314 451 sq km (121 412 sq miles). Abbreviation: **N. Mex.**, (with zip code) **NM**

new moon *n* the moon when it appears as a narrow crescent at the beginning of its cycle

New Netherland *n* a Dutch North American colony of the early 17th century, centred on the Hudson valley. Captured by the English in 1664, it was divided into New York and New Jersey

New Orleans *n* a port in SE Louisiana, on the Mississippi River, about 172 km (107 miles) from the sea: the largest city in the state and the second most important port in the US; founded by the French in 1718; belonged to Spain (1763–1803). It is largely below sea level, built around the Vieux Carré (French quarter); famous for its annual Mardi Gras festival and for its part in the history of jazz; a major commercial, industrial, and transportation centre. Pop: 469 032 (2003 est)

New Plymouth *n* a port in New Zealand, on W North Island: founded in 1841. Pop: 69 200 (2004 est)

Newport *n* **1** a city and port in SE Wales, in Newport county borough on the River Usk: electronics. Pop: 116 143 (2001) **2** a county borough in SE Wales, created from part of Gwent in 1996. Pop: 139 300 (2003 est). Area: 190 sq km (73 sq miles) **3** a port in SE Rhode Island: founded in 1639, it became one of the richest towns of colonial America; centre of a large number of US naval establishments. Pop: 26 136 (2003 est) **4** a town in S England, administrative centre of the Isle of Wight. Pop: 22 957 (2001)

Newport News *n (functioning as sing)* a port in SE Virginia, at the mouth of the James River: an industrial centre, with one of the world's largest shipyards. Pop: 181 647 (2003 est)

New Providence *n* an island in the Atlantic, in the Bahamas. Chief town: Nassau. Pop: 210 832 (2000). Area: 150 sq km (58 sq miles)

New Quebec *n* a region of E Canada, formerly the Ungava district of Northwest Territories (1895–1912), extending from the line of the Eastmain and Hamilton Rivers north between Hudson Bay and Labrador; absorbed by Quebec in 1912; contains extensive iron deposits. Area: about 777 000 sq km (300 000 sq miles)

New Romney *n* a market town in SE England, in Kent on Romney Marsh: of early importance as one of the Cinque Ports, but is now over 1.6 km (1 mile) inland. Pop: 9406 (2001). Former name (until 1563): **Romney**

Newry *n* a city and port in Northern Ireland, in Newry and Mourne district, Co Down. Pop: 27 433 (2001)

Newry and Mourne *n* a district of SE Northern Ireland, in Co Down. Pop: 89 644 (2003 est). Area: 909 sq km (351 sq miles)

news *n* **1** important or interesting new happenings **2** information about such events, reported in the mass media **3 the news** a television or radio programme presenting such information **4** interesting or important new information: *it's news to me* **5** a person or thing widely reported in the mass media: *reggae is suddenly big news again*

news agency *n* an organization that collects news reports and sells them to newspapers, magazines, and TV and radio stations

newsagent *n Brit* a shopkeeper who sells newspapers and magazines

newscast *n* a radio or television broadcast of the news [*news* + (*broad*)*cast*] **> newscaster** *n*

news conference *n* same as **press conference**

newsflash *n* a brief item of important news, which interrupts a radio or television programme

newsgroup *n computers* a forum where subscribers exchange information about a specific subject by e-mail

New Siberian Islands *pl n* an archipelago in the Arctic Ocean, off the N mainland of Russia, in the Sakha Republic. Area: about 37 555 sq km (14 500 sq miles)

newsletter *n* a periodical bulletin issued to members of a group

New South *n Austral informal* See **New South Wales**

New South Wales *n* a state of SE Australia: originally contained over half the continent, but was reduced by the formation of other states (1825–1911); consists of a narrow coastal plain, separated from extensive inland plains by the Great Dividing Range; the most populous state; mineral resources. Capital: Sydney. Pop: 7 272 800 (2012). Area: 801 428 sq km (309 433 sq miles)

newspaper *n* a weekly or daily publication consisting of folded sheets and containing news, features, and advertisements

newspeak *n* the language of politicians and officials regarded as deliberately ambiguous and misleading [from the novel *1984* by George Orwell]

newsprint *n* an inexpensive wood-pulp paper used for newspapers

newsreader *n* a news announcer on radio or television

newsreel *n* a short film with a commentary which presents current events

newsroom *n* a room in a newspaper office or radio or television station where news is received and prepared for publication or broadcasting: *a journalist who was in the newsroom at the time*

newsstand *n* a portable stand from which newspapers are sold

New Style *n* the present method of reckoning dates using the Gregorian calendar

newsworthy *adj* sufficiently interesting to be reported as news

newsy *adj* **newsier, newsiest** (of a letter) full of news

newt *n* a small amphibious creature with a long slender body and tail and short legs [mistaken division of *an ewt*; *ewt* from Old English *efeta*]

New Testament *n* the second part of the Christian Bible, dealing with the life and teachings of Christ and his followers

newton *n* the SI unit of force that gives an acceleration of 1 metre per second per second to a mass of 1 kilogram [after Sir Isaac NEWTON]

Newton *n* Sir **Isaac**. 1642–1727, English mathematician, physicist, astronomer, and philosopher, noted particularly for his law of gravitation, his three laws of motion, his theory that light is composed of corpuscles, and his development of calculus independently of Leibnitz. His works include *Principia Mathematica* (1687) and *Opticks* (1704)

Newtown *n* a new town in central Wales, in Powys. Pop: 10 358 (2001)

new town *n* (in Britain) a town planned as a complete unit and built with government sponsorship

Newtownabbey *n* **1** a town in Northern Ireland, in Newtownabbey district, Co Antrim on Belfast Lough: the third largest town in Northern Ireland, formed in 1958 by the amalgamation of seven villages; light industrial centre, esp. for textiles. Pop: 62 056 (2001) **2** a district of E Northern Ireland, in Co Antrim. Pop: 80 285 (2003 est). Area: 151 sq km (58 sq miles)

Newtown St Boswells *n* a village in SE Scotland, administrative centre of Scottish Borders: agricultural centre. Pop: 1199 (2001)

new wave *n* a movement in politics, the arts, or music that consciously breaks with traditional values

New Windsor *n* the official name of **Windsor** (1)

New World *n* **the New World** the Americas; the western hemisphere

New Year *n* the first day or days of the year in various calendars, usually a holiday

New Year's Day *n* January 1, celebrated as a holiday in many countries

New Year's Eve *n* December 31

New York *n* **1** Also called: **New York City** a city in SE New York State, at the mouth of the Hudson River: the largest city and chief port of the US; settled by the Dutch as New Amsterdam in 1624 and captured by the British in 1664, when it was named New York; consists of five boroughs (Manhattan, the Bronx, Queens, Brooklyn, and Staten Island, which was called Richmond until 1975) and many smaller islands, with its commercial and financial centre in Manhattan; the country's leading commercial and industrial centre. Pop: 8 085 742 (2003 est). Abbreviation: **N.Y.C., NYC 2** a state of the northeastern US: consists chiefly of a plateau with the Finger Lakes in the centre, the Adirondack Mountains in the northeast, the Catskill Mountains in the southeast, and Niagara Falls in the west. Capital: Albany. Pop: 19 190 115 (2003 est). Area: 123 882 sq km (47 831 sq miles). Abbreviation: **N.Y.**, (with zip code) **NY**

New York Bay *n* an inlet of the Atlantic at the mouth of the Hudson River: forms the harbour of the port of New York

New Yorker *n* a native or inhabitant of New York

New York State Barge Canal *n* a system of inland waterways in New York State, connecting the Hudson River with Lakes Erie and Ontario and, via Lake Champlain, with the St Lawrence. Length: 845 km (525 miles)

New Zealand *n* an independent dominion within the Commonwealth, occupying two main islands (the North Island and the South Island), Stewart Island, the Chatham Islands, and a number of minor islands in the SE Pacific: original Māori inhabitants ceded sovereignty to the British government in 1840; became a dominion in 1907; a major world exporter of dairy products, wool, and meat. Official languages: English and Māori. Religion: Christian majority, nonreligious and Māori minorities. Currency: New Zealand dollar. Capital: Wellington. Pop: 4 365 113 (2013 est). Area: 270 534 sq km (104 454 sq miles)

New Zealander *n* a native or inhabitant of New Zealand

Nexø *n* **Martin Andersen**. 1869–1954, Danish novelist. His chief works are the novels *Pelle the Conqueror* (1906–10), which deals with the labour movement, and *Ditte, Daughter of Man* (1917–21)

next *adj* **1** immediately following: *the next generation* **2** immediately adjoining: *in the next room* **3** closest to in degree: *the next-best thing* ▷ *adv* **4** at a time immediately to follow: *the patient to be examined next* **5 next to a** adjacent to: *the house next to ours* **b** following in degree: *next to my wife, I love you most* **c** almost: *the evidence is next to totally useless* [Old English *nēhst*, superlative of *nēah* near]

next door *adj, adv* in, at, or to the adjacent house or flat: *the Cabinet retired next door; the people next door*

next of kin *n* a person's closest relative

nexus *n, pl* **nexus 1** a connection or link **2** a connected group or series [Latin, from *nectere* to bind]

Ney *n* **Michel**, Duc d'Elchingen. 1769–1815, French marshal, who earned the epithet *Bravest of the Brave* at the battle of Borodino (1812) in the Napoleonic Wars. He rallied to Napoleon on his return from Elba and was executed for treason (1815)

NF Newfoundland

Nfld. Newfoundland

NG 1 (in the US) National Guard **2** New Guinea **3** Also: **ng** no good

Ngaliema Mountain *n* the Congolese name for (Mount) **Stanley**

ngati (nah-tee) *n, pl* **ngati** NZ (occurring as part of the tribe name) a tribe or clan [Māori]

NH *or* **N.H.** New Hampshire

Nha Trang *n* a port in SE Vietnam, on the South China Sea: nearby temples of the Cham civilization; fishing industry. Pop: 382 000 (2005 est)

NHS (in Britain) National Health Service

Ni *chem* nickel

NI **1** (in Britain) National Insurance **2** Northern Ireland

niacin *n* a vitamin of the B complex that occurs in milk, liver, and yeast. Also called: **nicotinic acid** [from *ni(cotinic) ac(id)* + *-in* denoting a chemical substance]

Niagara *n* **1** a river in NE North America, on the border between W New York State and Ontario, Canada, flowing from Lake Erie to Lake Ontario. Length: 45 km (28 miles) **2** a torrent

Niagara Falls *n* **1** (*functioning as pl*) the falls of the Niagara River, on the border between the US and Canada between Lake Erie and Lake Ontario: divided by Goat Island into the American Falls, 50 m (167 ft) high and approximately 300 m (985 ft) wide, and the Horseshoe or Canadian Falls, 47 m (158 ft) high and by some estimates well over 800 m (2625 ft) wide **2** (*functioning as sing*) a city in W New York State, situated at the falls of the Niagara River. Pop: 78 815 (2001) **3** (*functioning as sing*) a city in S Canada, in SE Ontario on the Niagara River just below the falls: linked to the city of Niagara Falls in the US by three bridges. Pop: 78 815 (2001)

Niamey *n* the capital of Niger, in the southwest, on the River Niger: became capital in 1926; airport and land route centre. Pop: 997 000 (2005 est)

Niarchos *n* **Stavros** (**Spyros**). 1909–96, Greek shipowner. He pioneered the use of supertankers in the 1950s

nib *n* the writing point of a pen [origin unknown]

nibble *vb* **-bling, -bled 1** to take little bites (of) **2** to bite gently: *she nibbled at her lower lip* ▷ *n* **3** a little bite **4** a light hurried meal [related to Low German *nibbelen*]

nibs *n* **his** *or* **her nibs** *slang* a mock title used of an important or self-important person [origin unknown]

Nicaea *n* an ancient city in NW Asia Minor, in Bithynia: site of the **first council of Nicaea** (325 AD), which composed the Nicene Creed. Modern Turkish name: Iznik

Nicaean *adj* a variant of **Nicene**

NICAM near-instantaneous companding system: a technique for coding audio signals into digital form

Nicaragua n 1 a republic in Central America, on the Caribbean and the Pacific: colonized by the Spanish from the 1520s; gained independence in 1821 and was annexed by Mexico, becoming a republic in 1838. Official language: Spanish. Religion: Roman Catholic majority. Currency: córdoba. Capital: Managua. Pop: 5 788 531 (2013 est). Area: 131 812 sq km (50 893 sq miles) **2 Lake Nicaragua** a lake in SW Nicaragua, separated from the Pacific by an isthmus 19 km (12 miles) wide: the largest lake in Central America. Area: 8264 sq km (3191 sq miles)

Nicaraguan adj 1 of or relating to Nicaragua or its inhabitants ▷ n 2 a native or inhabitant of Nicaragua

nice adj 1 pleasant 2 kind: it's really nice of you to worry about me 3 good or satisfactory: a nice clean operation 4 subtle: a nice distinction [Latin nescius ignorant] **> nicely** adv **> niceness** n

Nice n a city in SE France, on the Mediterranean: a leading resort of the French Riviera; founded by Phocaeans from Marseille in about the 3rd century BC. Pop: 348 721 (2007)

Nicene or **Nicaean** adj of or relating to Nicaea or its inhabitants

nicety n, pl **-ties** 1 a subtle point: the niceties of our arguments 2 a refinement or delicacy: social niceties 3 to a nicety precisely

niche (neesh) n 1 a recess in a wall for a statue or ornament 2 a position exactly suitable for the person occupying it: perhaps I will find my niche in a desk job ▷ adj 3 of or aimed at a specialist group or market: niche retailing ventures [Old French nichier to nest]

Nicholas n Saint. 4th-century AD bishop of Myra, in Asia Minor; patron saint of Russia and of children, sailors, merchants, and pawnbrokers. Feast day: Dec 6. See also **Santa Claus**

Nicholas I n 1 Saint, called the Great. died 867 AD, Italian ecclesiastic; pope (858–867). He championed papal supremacy. Feast day: Nov 13 2 1796–1855, tsar of Russia (1825–55). He gained notoriety for his autocracy and his emphasis on military discipline and bureaucracy

Nicholas II n 1868–1918, tsar of Russia (1894–1917). After the disastrous Russo-Japanese War (1904–05), he was forced to summon a representative assembly, but his continued autocracy and incompetence precipitated the Russian Revolution (1917): he abdicated and was shot

Nicholas V n original name Tommaso Parentucelli. 1397–1455, Italian ecclesiastic; pope (1447–55). He helped to found the Vatican Library

Nicholas of Cusa n 1401–64, German cardinal, philosopher, and mathematician: anticipated Copernicus in asserting that the earth revolves around the sun

Nichols n 1 Peter (Richard). born 1927, British dramatist, whose works include A Day in the Death of Joe Egg (1967), the musical Privates on Parade (1977), and Blue Murder (1995) 2 Vincent (Gerard). born 1945, English clergyman: Archbishop of Westminster from 2009

Nicholson n 1 Ben. 1894–1982, English painter, noted esp. for his abstract geometrical works 2 Jack. born 1937, US film actor. His films include Easy Rider (1969), One Flew Over the Cuckoo's Nest (1974), Chinatown (1974), Terms of Endearment (1983), Batman (1989), As Good As It Gets (1998), About Schmidt (2002), and The Departed (2006) 3 John. 1821–57, British general and administrator, born in Ireland: deputy commissioner in the Punjab (1851–56), where he became the object of hero-worship among the natives and kept the Punjab loyal during the Indian Mutiny: played a major role in the capture of Delhi

Nicias n died 414 BC, Athenian statesman and general. He ended the first part of the Peloponnesian War by making peace with Sparta (421)

nick vb 1 to make a small cut in 2 chiefly Brit slang to steal 3 chiefly Brit slang to arrest ▷ n 4 a small notch or cut

5 slang a prison or police station 6 informal condition: in good nick 7 in the nick of time just in time [perhaps Middle English nocke nock]

nickel n 1 chem a silvery-white metallic element that is often used in alloys. Symbol: Ni 2 a US or Canadian coin worth five cents [German Kupfernickel nickel ore, literally: copper demon; it was mistakenly thought to contain copper]

nickelodeon n US an early type of jukebox [nickel + (mel)odeon]

nickel silver n an alloy containing copper, zinc, and nickel

nicker n, pl **nicker** Brit slang a pound sterling [origin unknown]

Nicklaus n Jack. born 1940, US golfer: winner of a record eighteen major championships (1962–86), comprising a record six in the US Masters, five in the USPGA, four in the US Open, and three in the British Open

nick-nack n same as knick-knack

nickname n 1 a familiar, pet, or derisory name given to a person or place ▷ vb **-naming, -named** 2 to call (a person or place) by a nickname: Gaius Caesar Augustus Germanicus, nicknamed Caligula [mistaken division of an ekename an additional name]

Nicobar Islands pl n a group of 19 islands in the Indian Ocean, south of the Andaman Islands, with which they form a territory of India. Area: 1645 sq km (635 sq miles)

Nicolai n (Carl) Otto (Ehrenfried). 1810–49, German composer: noted for his opera The Merry Wives of Windsor (1849)

Nicolson n Sir Harold (George). 1886–1968, British diplomat, politician, and author: married to Vita Sackville-West

Nicosia n the capital of Cyprus, in the central part on the Pedieos River: capital since the 10th century. Pop (Greek and Turkish): 211 000 (2005 est). Greek name: **Levkosia, Leukosia**. Turkish name: **Lefkoşa**

nicotine n a poisonous alkaloid found in tobacco [after J. Nicot, who introduced tobacco into France] **> nicotinic** adj

Nictheroy n another name for Niterói

nictitating membrane n (in reptiles, birds, and some mammals) a thin fold of skin under the eyelid that can be drawn across the eye

Nidaros n the former name (1930–31) of Trondheim

Niebuhr n 1 Barthold Georg. 1776–1831, German historian, noted for his critical approach to sources, esp. in History of Rome (1811–32) 2 Reinhold. 1892–1971, US Protestant theologian. His works include Moral Man and Immoral Society (1932) and The Nature and Destiny of Man (1941–43)

niece n a daughter of one's sister or brother [Latin neptis granddaughter]

Niederösterreich n the German name for **Lower Austria**

Niedersachsen n the German name for **Lower Saxony**

Nielsen n Carl (August) (karl). 1865–1931, Danish composer. His works include six symphonies and the opera Masquerade (1906)

Niemen n the Polish name for the Neman

Niemeyer n Oscar. 1907–2012, Brazilian architect. His work includes many buildings in Brasília, esp. the president's palace (1959) and the cathedral (1964)

Niemöller n Martin. 1892–1984, German Protestant theologian, who was imprisoned (1938–45) for his opposition to Hitler

Niepce n Joseph-Nicéphore. 1765–1833, French inventor. He produced the first photographic image (1816) and the first permanent camera photograph (1826)

Nietzsche n Friedrich Wilhelm. 1844–1900, German philosopher, poet, and critic, noted esp. for his concept of the superman and his rejection of traditional Christian values. His chief works are The Birth of Tragedy (1872), Thus Spake Zarathustra (1883–91), and Beyond Good and

Evil (1886) ❯ **Nietzschean** n, adj ❯ **Nietzscheism** or **Nietzscheanism** n

Nièvre n a department of central France, in Burgundy region. Capital: Nevers. Pop: 222 298 (2003 est). Area: 6888 sq km (2686 sq miles)

niff Brit slang ▷ vb **1** a stink ▷ vb **2** to stink [perhaps from sniff] ❯ **niffy** adj

nifty adj **-tier, -tiest** informal neat or smart [origin unknown]

Niger n **1** a landlocked republic in West Africa: important since earliest times for its trans-Saharan trade routes; made a French colony in 1922 and became fully independent in 1960; exports peanuts and livestock. Official language: French. Religion: Muslim majority. Currency: franc. Capital: Niamey. Pop: 16 899 327 (2013 est). Area: 1 267 000 sq km (489 000 sq miles) **2** a river in West Africa, rising in S Guinea and flowing in a great northward curve through Mali, then southwest through Niger and Nigeria to the Gulf of Guinea: the third longest river in Africa, with the largest delta, covering an area of 36 260 sq km (14 000 sq miles). Length: 4184 km (2600 miles) **3** a state of W central Nigeria. Capital: Minna. Pop: 3 950 249 (2006). Area: 76 363 sq km (29 476 sq miles)

Nigeria n a republic in West Africa, on the Gulf of Guinea: Lagos annexed by the British in 1861; protectorates of Northern and Southern Nigeria formed in 1900 and united as a colony in 1914; gained independence as a member of the Commonwealth in 1960 (membership suspended from 1995 to 1999 following human rights violations); Eastern Region seceded as the Republic of Biafra for the duration of the severe civil war (1967–70); ruled by military governments from 1966. It consists of a belt of tropical rain forest in the south, with semidesert in the extreme north and highlands in the east; the main export is petroleum. Official language: English; Hausa, Ibo, and Yoruba are the chief regional languages. Religion: animist, Muslim, and Christian. Currency: naira. Capital: Abuja. Pop: 174 507 539 (2013 est). Area: 923 773 sq km (356 669 sq miles)

Nigerian adj **1** of or relating to Nigeria or its inhabitants ▷ n **2** a native or inhabitant of Nigeria

Nigerien adj **1** of or relating to Niger or its inhabitants ▷ n **2** a native or inhabitant of Niger

niggard n a stingy person [perhaps from Old Norse]

niggardly adj not generous: it pays its staff on a niggardly scale ❯ **niggardliness** n

nigger n offensive a Black person [Spanish negro]

niggle vb **-gling, -gled 1** to worry slightly **2** to find fault continually ▷ n **3** a small worry or doubt **4** a trivial objection or complaint [Scandinavian] ❯ **niggling** adj

nigh archaic, poetic adv **1** nearly ▷ adj **2** near ▷ prep **3** close to [Old English nēah, nēh]

night n **1** the period of darkness that occurs each 24 hours, between sunset and sunrise. Related adjective: **nocturnal 2** the period between sunset and bedtime; evening **3** the time between bedtime and morning **4** nightfall or dusk **5** an evening designated for a specific activity: opening night **6 make a night of it** to celebrate the whole evening ▷ adj **7** of, occurring, or working at night: the night sky ▶ See also **nights** [Old English niht]

nightcap n **1** a drink taken just before bedtime **2** a soft cap formerly worn in bed

nightclub n a place of entertainment open until late at night, usually offering drink, a floor show, and dancing

nightdress n a loose dress worn in bed by women or girls

nightfall n the approach of darkness; dusk

nightgown n same as **nightdress**

nightie n informal short for **nightdress**

nightingale n a small bird with a musical song, usually heard at night [Old English nihtegale, literally: night singer]

Nightingale n Florence, known as the Lady with the Lamp. 1820–1910, English nurse, famous for her work during the Crimean War. She helped to raise the status and quality of the nursing profession and founded a training school for nurses in London (1860)

nightjar n a nocturnal bird with a harsh cry [night + JAR² (so called from its discordant cry)]

nightlife n the entertainment and social activities available at night in a town or city: New York nightlife

night-light n a dim light left on overnight

nightlong adj, adv throughout the night

nightly adj **1** happening each night ▷ adv **2** each night

nightmare n **1** a terrifying or deeply distressing dream **2** a terrifying or unpleasant experience **3** a thing that is feared: wheels and loose straps are a baggage handler's nightmare [night + Old English mare, mære evil spirit] ❯ **nightmarish** adj

nights adv informal at night or on most nights: he works nights

night safe n a safe built into the outside wall of a bank, in which customers can deposit money when the bank is closed

night school n an educational institution that holds classes in the evening

nightshade n a plant which produces poisonous berries with bell-shaped flowers [Old English nihtscada]

nightshirt n a long loose shirtlike garment worn in bed

night soil n archaic human excrement collected at night from cesspools or privies

nightspot n informal a nightclub

night-time n the time from sunset to sunrise

night watch n **1** a watch or guard kept at night for security **2** the period of time this watch is kept

night watchman n a person who keeps guard at night on a factory or other building

nihilism (nye-ill-liz-zum) n a total rejection of all established authority and institutions [Latin nihil nothing] ❯ **nihilist** n, adj ❯ **nihilistic** adj

Nihon n transliteration of a Japanese name for Japan

Niigata n a port in central Japan, on NW Honshu at the mouth of the Shinano River: the chief port on the Sea of Japan. Pop: 514 678 (2002 est)

Nijinsky n Waslaw or Vaslaw. 1890–1950, Russian ballet dancer and choreographer, who was associated with Diaghilev. His creations include settings of Stravinsky's Petrushka and The Rite of Spring

Nijmegen n an industrial town in the E Netherlands, in Gelderland province on the Waal River: the oldest town in the country; scene of the signing (1678) of the peace treaty between Louis XIV, the Netherlands, Spain, and the Holy Roman Empire. Pop: 156 000 (2003 est). Latin name: **Noviomagus**. German name: **Nimwegen**

-nik suffix forming nouns indicating a person associated with a particular state or quality: refusenik [Russian]

Nikaria n another name for **Icaria**

Nikko n a town in central Japan, on NE Honshu: a major pilgrimage centre, with a 4th-century Shinto shrine, a Buddhist temple (767), and the shrines and mausoleums of the Tokugawa shoguns. Pop: 17 527 (2002 est)

Nikolainkaupunki n the former name of **Vaasa**

Nikolayev n a city in S Ukraine on the Southern Bug about 64 km (40 miles) from the Black Sea: founded as a naval base in 1788; one of the leading Black Sea ports. Pop: 518 000 (2005 est). Former name: **Vernoleninsk**

nil n nothing: esp. as a score in games [Latin]

Nile n a river in Africa, rising in S central Burundi in its remotest headstream, the **Luvironza**: flows into Lake Victoria and leaves the lake as the **Victoria Nile**, flowing to Lake Albert, which is drained by the **Albert Nile**, becoming the **White Nile** at **Lake No**, then flowing through South Sudan; joined by its chief tributary, the **Blue Nile** (which rises near Lake Tana, Ethiopia) at Khartoum, and flows north to its delta on the Mediterranean; the longest river in the world. Length:

n

(from the source of the Luvironza to the Mediterranean) 6741 km (4187 miles)

Nilgiri Hills or **Nilgiris** pl n a plateau in S India, in Tamil Nadu. Average height: 2000 m (6500 ft), reaching 2635 m (8647 ft) in Doda Betta

Nilotic adj 1 of or relating to the Nile 2 of, relating to, or belonging to a tall pastoral people inhabiting South Sudan, parts of Kenya and Uganda, and neighbouring countries 3 relating to or belonging to the group of languages spoken by the Nilotic peoples ▷ n 4 a group of languages of E Africa, including Luo, Dinka, and Masai, now generally regarded as belonging to the Chari-Nile branch of the Nilo-Saharan family [C17: via Latin from Greek *Neilōtikos*, from *Neilos* the NILE]

Nilsson n Birgit. 1918–2006, Swedish operatic soprano

nimble adj 1 agile and quick in movement 2 mentally alert or acute [Old English *nǣmel* quick to grasp + *numol* quick at seizing] > **nimbly** adv

nimbus n, pl -**bi** or -**buses** 1 a dark grey rain cloud 2 a halo [Latin: cloud]

NIMBY not in my back yard: used of people who are opposed to any building or changes that will affect them directly

Nîmes n a city in S France: Roman remains including an amphitheatre and the Pont du Gard aqueduct. Pop: 147 114 (2006)

Nimitz n Chester William. 1885–1966, US admiral; commander in chief of the US Pacific fleet in World War II (1941–45)

Nimrud n an ancient city in Assyria, near the present-day city of Mosul (Iraq): founded in about 1250 BC and destroyed by the Medes in 612 BC; excavated by Sir Austen Henry Layard

Nimwegen n the German name for **Nijmegen**

Nimzowitsch n Aaron Isayevich 1886–1935, Latvian chess player and theorist; influential in enunciating the principles of the hypermodern school, of which he was the main instigator

nincompoop n informal a stupid person [origin unknown]

nine n 1 the cardinal number that is the sum of one and eight 2 a numeral, 9 or IX, representing this number 3 something representing or consisting of nine units 4 dressed up to the nines informal elaborately dressed 5 **999** (in Britain) the telephone number of the emergency services ▷ adj 6 amounting to nine: *nine men* [Old English *nigon*] > **ninth** adj, n

nine-days wonder n something that arouses great interest, but only for a short period

nine-eleven, 9-11 or **9/11** n the 11th of September 2001, the day on which the twin towers of the World Trade Center in New York were flown into and destroyed by aeroplanes hijacked by Islamic fundamentalists. Also called: **September eleven** [from the US custom of expressing dates in figures, the day of the month following the number of the month]

ninefold adj 1 having nine times as many or as much 2 having nine parts ▷ adv 3 by nine times as much or as many

ninepins n the game of skittles

nineteen n 1 the cardinal number that is the sum of ten and nine 2 a numeral, 19 or XIX, representing this number 3 something representing or consisting of nineteen units 4 talk nineteen to the dozen to talk very fast ▷ adj 5 amounting to nineteen: *nineteen years* > **nineteenth** adj, n

nineteenth hole n golf slang the bar in a golf clubhouse [from its being the next objective after a standard 18-hole round]

ninety n, pl -**ties** 1 the cardinal number that is the product of ten and nine 2 a numeral, 90 or XC, representing this number 3 something representing or consisting of ninety units 4 **nineties** the numbers 90 to 99, esp. when used to refer to the years of someone's life

or of a century ▷ adj 5 amounting to ninety: *ninety degrees* > **ninetieth** adj, n

Nineveh n the ancient capital of Assyria, on the River Tigris opposite the present-day city of Mosul (N Iraq): at its height in the 8th and 7th centuries BC; destroyed in 612 BC by the Medes and Babylonians

Ninevite n a native or inhabitant of Nineveh

Ningbo or **Ningpo** n a port in E China, in NE Zhejiang, on the Yung River, about 20 km (12 miles) from its mouth at Hangzhou Bay: one of the first sites of European settlement in China. Pop: 1 188 000 (2005 est)

Ningsia or **Ninghsia** n 1 a former province of NW China: mostly included in Inner Mongolia in 1956, with the smaller part constituted as the Ningxia Hui AR in 1958 2 the former name of **Yinchuan**

Ningxia Hui Autonomous Region n an administrative division of NW China, south of Inner Mongolia. Capital: Yinchuan. Pop: 5 800 000 (2003 est). Area: 66 400 sq km (25 896 sq miles)

Ninian n Saint. ?360–?432 AD, the first known apostle of Scotland; built a stone church (*candida casa*) at Whithorn on his native Solway; preached to the Picts. Feast day: Sept 16

ninja n, pl -**ja** or -**jas** a person skilled in ninjutsu, a Japanese martial art characterized by stealthy movement and camouflage [Japanese]

ninny n, pl -**nies** a stupid person [perhaps from *an innocent*]

Ninus n a king of Assyria and the legendary founder of Nineveh, husband of Semiramis

niobium n chem a white superconductive metallic element. Symbol: **Nb** [Latin after *Niobe* (daughter of Tantalus); because it occurred in tantalite]

Niort n a market town in W France. Pop: 60 486 (2006)

nip[1] vb nipping, nipped 1 informal to hurry 2 to pinch or squeeze 3 to bite lightly 4 (of the cold) to affect (someone) with a stinging sensation 5 to check the growth of (something): *a trite script nips all hope in the bud* ▷ n 6 a pinch or light bite 7 sharp coldness: *a nip in the air* [perhaps from Old Norse]

nip[2] n a small drink of spirits [from *nipperkin* a vessel holding a half-pint or less]

Nipigon n Lake Nipigon a lake in central Canada, in NW Ontario, draining into Lake Superior via the **Nipigon River**. Area: 4843 sq km (1870 sq miles)

Nipissing n Lake Nipissing a lake in central Canada, in E Ontario between the Ottawa River and Georgian Bay. Area: 855 sq km (330 sq miles)

nipper n Brit, Austral and NZ informal a small child

nipple n 1 the small projection in the centre of each breast, which in females contains the outlet of the milk ducts 2 a small projection through which oil or grease can be put into a machine or component [perhaps from *neb* peak, tip]

Nippon n transliteration of a Japanese name for **Japan**

Nipponese adj, n, pl -**nese** another word for **Japanese**

Nippur n an ancient Sumerian and Babylonian city, the excavated site of which is in SE Iraq: an important religious centre, abandoned in the 12th or 13th century

nippy adj -**pier**, -**piest** 1 (of weather) frosty or chilly 2 informal quick or nimble 3 (of a motor vehicle) small and relatively powerful

niqab n a veil of lightweight opaque fabric, covering all the face except the eyes, worn by some Muslim women [Arabic]

Nirenberg n Marshall Warren. 1927–2010, US biochemist; shared the Nobel prize for physiology or medicine (1968) for his role in deciphering the genetic code

nirvana (near-vah-na) n Buddhism, Hinduism the ultimate state of spiritual enlightenment and bliss attained by extinction of all desires and individual existence [Sanskrit: extinction]

Niš or **Nish** n an industrial town in Serbia, in the SE: situated on routes between central Europe and the

Aegean. Pop: 203 670 (2002)

Nishapur n a town in NE Iran, at an altitude of 1195 m (3920 ft): birthplace and burial place of Omar Khayyám. Pop: 208 000 (2005 est)

Nishinomiya n an industrial city in central Japan, on S Honshu, northwest of Osaka. Pop: 436 877 (2002 est)

nisi (nye-sigh) adj See **decree nisi**

Nissen hut n chiefly Brit a tunnel-shaped military shelter made of corrugated steel [after Lt Col. Peter Nissen, mining engineer]

nit¹ n the egg or larva of a louse [Old English hnitu]

nit² n informal short for **nitwit**

Niterói n a port in SE Brazil, on Guanabara Bay opposite Rio de Janeiro: contains Brazil's chief shipyards. Pop: 458 465 (2000). Also called: **Nictheroy**

nit-picking informal n 1 a concern with insignificant details, usually with the intention of finding fault ▷ adj 2 showing such concern

nitrate chem n 1 a salt or ester of nitric acid 2 a fertilizer containing nitrate salts ▷ vb **-trating, -trated** 3 to treat with nitric acid or a nitrate 4 to convert or be converted into a nitrate ❯ **nitration** n

nitre or US **niter** n chem same as **potassium nitrate** [Latin nitrum]

nitric adj chem of or containing nitrogen

nitric acid n chem a colourless corrosive liquid widely used in industry

nitride n chem a compound of nitrogen with a more electropositive element

nitrify vb **-fies, -fying, -fied** chem 1 to treat (a substance) or cause (a substance) to react with nitrogen 2 to treat (soil) with nitrates 3 to convert (ammonium compounds) into nitrates by oxidation ❯ **nitrification** n

nitrite n chem a salt or ester of nitrous acid

nitro- or before a vowel **nitr-** combining form 1 indicating that a chemical compound contains the univalent group, $-NO_2$: nitrobenzene 2 indicating that a chemical compound is a nitrate ester: nitrocellulose [Greek nitron nitre]

nitrogen (nite-roj-jen) n chem a colourless odourless gas that forms four-fifths of the air and is an essential part of all animal and plant life. Symbol: N ❯ **nitrogenous** adj

nitrogen cycle n the natural cycle by which nitrates in the soil, derived from dead organic matter, are absorbed by plants and reduced to nitrates again when the plants and the animals feeding on them die and decay

nitrogen fixation n the conversion of atmospheric nitrogen into nitrogen compounds by soil bacteria

nitroglycerine or **nitroglycerin** n chem a thick pale yellow explosive liquid made from glycerol and nitric and sulphuric acids

nitrous adj chem derived from or containing nitrogen in a low valency state

nitrous acid n chem a weak acid known only in solution and in the form of nitrite salts

nitrous oxide n chem a colourless gas used as an anaesthetic

nitty-gritty n the nitty-gritty informal the basic facts of a matter or situation [perhaps rhyming compound from grit]

nitwit n informal a stupid person [perhaps NIT¹ + WIT¹]

Niue n an island in the S Pacific, between Tonga and the Cook Islands: annexed by New Zealand (1901); achieved full internal self-government in 1974. Chief town and port: Alofi. Pop: 1269 (2012 est). Area: 260 sq km (100 sq miles). Also called: **Savage Island**

Niuean adj 1 of or relating to Niue or its inhabitants ▷ n 2 a native or inhabitant of Niue

Niu Tireni or **Niu Tirani** n a Māori name for **New Zealand** [Māori: from a corruption of European names for New Zealand]

Niven n David. 1909–83, British film actor and author. His films include The Prisoner of Zenda (1937), Around the World in 80 Days (1956), Casino Royale (1967), and Paper Tiger

(1975). He wrote the autobiographical The Moon's a Balloon (1972) and Bring on the Empty Horses (1975)

Nivernais n a former province of central France, around Nevers

Nixon n Richard (**Milhous**). 1913–94, US Republican politician; 37th president from 1969 until he resigned over the Watergate scandal in 1974 ❯ **Nixonian** adj

Nizam al-Mulk n title of Abu Ali Hasan Ibn Ali. ?1018–92, Persian statesman; vizier of Persia (1063–92) for the Seljuk sultans: assassinated

Nizhni Novgorod n a city and port in central Russia, at the confluence of the Volga and Oka Rivers: situated on the Volga route from the Baltic to central Asia; birthplace of Maxim Gorki. Pop: 1 288 000 (2005 est). Former name (1932–91): **Gorki**

Nizhni Tagil n a city in central Russia, on the E slopes of the Ural Mountains: a major metallurgical centre. Pop: 382 000 (2005 est)

NJ or **N.J.** New Jersey

Nkandla n the private residence of Jacob Zuma, South African President from 2009, south of the town of Nkandla, KwaZulu-Natal. The use of state funds to upgrade the property caused controversy

Nkomo n Joshua. 1917–99, Zimbabwean politician; coleader, with Robert Mugabe, of the Patriotic Front (1976–80) against the government of Ian Smith in Rhodesia; minister (1980–82; 1988–99) and vice-president (1990–96).

nkosi (ing-koss-ee) n S African a term of address to a superior; master; chief [Nguni (language group of southern Africa) inkosi chief, lord]

Nkrumah n Kwame. 1909–72, Ghanaian statesman, prime minister (1957–60) and president (1960–66). He led demands for self-government in the 1950s, achieving Ghanaian independence in 1957. He was overthrown by a military coup (1966)

nm nanometre

N. Mex. or **NM** New Mexico

no¹ interj 1 used to express denial, disagreement, or refusal ▷ n, pl **noes** or **nos** 2 an answer or vote of no 3 a person who answers or votes no [Old English nā]

no² adj 1 not any, not a, or not one: I have no money; no comment 2 not at all: he's no exception 3 not: no taller than a child 4 no way! an expression of emphatic refusal or denial [Old English nān none]

No¹ or **Noh** n, pl **No** or **Noh** the stylized classical drama of Japan, using music and dancing [Japanese nō talent]

No² chem nobelium

No³ n Lake No a lake in South Sudan, where the Bahr el Jebel (White Nile) is joined by the Bahr el Ghazal. Area: about 103 sq km (40 sq miles)

No. or **no.** pl **Nos.** or **nos.** number [French numéro]

n.o. cricket not out

nob n chiefly Brit slang a person of wealth or social distinction [origin unknown]

no-ball n cricket an improperly bowled ball, for which the batting side scores a run. Abbreviation: **nb**

nobble vb **-bling, -bled** chiefly Brit, Austral and NZ slang 1 to bribe or threaten 2 to disable (a racehorse) to stop it from winning 3 to steal [a nobbler, a false division of an hobbler one who hobbles horses]

Nobel n Alfred (**Bernhard**). 1833–96, Swedish chemist and philanthropist, noted for his invention of dynamite (1866) and his bequest founding the Nobel prizes

nobelium n chem a radioactive element produced artificially from curium. Symbol: **No** [after Nobel Institute, Stockholm, where it was discovered]

Nobel prize (no-bell) n a prize for outstanding contributions to chemistry, physics, physiology and medicine, literature, economics, and peace that may be awarded annually [after Alfred Nobel]

Nobile n Umberto. 1885–1978, Italian aeronautical engineer and aviator. He flew his Norge airship over the North Pole (1926) with Amundsen and his Italia airship

n

over the Pole in 1928, crashing on the return

nobility *n* **1** the quality of being noble; dignity **2** the class of people who hold titles and high social rank

noble *adj* **1** having or showing high moral qualities: *a noble cause* **2** belonging to a class of people who hold titles and high social rank **3** impressive and magnificent: *a noble beast* **4** *chem* (of certain metals) resisting oxidation ▷ *n* **5** a person who holds a title and high social rank [Latin *nobilis*, originally capable of being known, hence well-known] **> nobly** *adv*

noble gas *n* any of the unreactive gases helium, neon, argon, krypton, xenon, and radon

nobleman *or fem* **noblewoman** *n, pl* **-men** *or* **-women** a person of noble rank

noblesse oblige (no-bless oh-bleezh) *n often humorous* the supposed obligation of the nobility to be honourable and generous [French, lit: nobility obliges]

nobody *pron* **1** no person; no-one ▷ *n, pl* **-bodies 2** a person of no importance

---

USAGE See at **everyone**.

---

no-brainer *n slang* something that requires little or no mental effort

nock *n* **1** a notch on an arrow that fits on the bowstring **2** a groove at either end of a bow that holds the bowstring [related to Swedish *nock* tip]

no-claims bonus *or* **no-claim bonus** *n* a reduction in the cost of an insurance policy made if no claims have been made in a specified period

nocturnal *adj* **1** of the night **2** (of animals) active at night [Latin *nox* night]

nocturne *n* a short dreamy piece of music

nod *vb* **nodding, nodded 1** to lower and raise (one's head) briefly, to express agreement or greeting **2** to express by nodding: *he nodded his approval* **3** to sway or bend forwards and back **4** to let one's head fall forward with sleep **5 nodding acquaintance** a slight knowledge (of a subject or person) ▷ *n* **6** a quick down-and-up movement of the head, in agreement **7 land of Nod** an imaginary land of sleep [origin unknown]

noddle *n chiefly Brit informal* the head or brains [origin unknown]

noddy *n, pl* **-dies 1** a tropical tern with a dark plumage **2** a fool [perhaps from obsolete *noddy* foolish, drowsy]

node *n* **1** *botany* the point on a plant stem from which the leaves grow **2** *maths* a point at which a curve crosses itself **3** a knot or knob **4** *physics* a point in a vibrating body at which there is practically no vibration **5** *anatomy* any natural bulge or swelling: *lymph node* **6** *astronomy* either of the two points at which the orbit of a body intersects the path of the sun or the orbit of another body [Latin *nodus* knot] **> nodal** *adj*

nod off *vb informal* to fall asleep

nodule *n* **1** a small rounded lump, knot, or node **2** a rounded mineral growth on the root of a plant such as clover [Latin *nodulus*] **> nodular** *adj*

Noel *or* **Noël** *n* same as **Christmas** [French, from Latin *natalis* a birthday]

nog *n* an alcoholic drink containing beaten egg [origin unknown]

noggin *n* **1** *informal* the head **2** a small quantity of spirits [origin unknown]

no-go area *n* a district that is barricaded off so that the police or army can enter only by force

Noguchi *n* Hideyo. 1876–1928, Japanese bacteriologist, active in the US. He made important discoveries in the treatment of syphilis

noise *n* **1** a sound, usually a loud or disturbing one **2** loud shouting; din **3** an undesired electrical disturbance in a signal **4** unwanted or irrelevant elements in a visual image: *removing noise from pictures* **5 noises** conventional utterances conveying a reaction: *he made the appropriate noises* ▷ *vb* **noising, noised 6 be noised abroad** (of news or gossip) to be spread [Latin *nausea* seasickness]

noiseless *adj* making little or no sound **> noiselessly** *adv*

noise pollution *n* annoying or harmful noise in an environment

noisette (nwah-zett) *n* a hazelnut chocolate [French]

noisome *adj formal* **1** (of smells) offensive **2** extremely unpleasant [obsolete *noy*, variant of *annoy*]

noisy *adj* **noisier, noisiest 1** making a lot of noise **2** (of a place) full of noise **> noisily** *adv*

Nolan *n* **1** Michael Patrick, Baron. 1928–2007, British judge; chairman of the Committee on Standards in Public Life (1994–97) **2** Sir **Sidney**. 1917–92, Australian painter, whose works explore themes in Australian folklore

Nolde *n* Emil. 1867–1956, German painter and engraver, noted particularly for his violent use of colour and the primitive masklike quality of his figures

Nollekens *n* Joseph. 1737–1823, British neoclassical sculptor of portrait busts, tombs, and mythological subjects

nomad *n* **1** a member of a tribe who move from place to place to find pasture and food **2** a wanderer [Greek *nomas* wandering for pasture] **> nomadic** *adj*

no-man's-land *n* land between boundaries, esp. an unoccupied zone between opposing forces

nom de plume *n, pl* **noms de plume** same as **pen name** [French]

nomenclature (no-men-klatch-er) *n formal* the system of names used in a particular subject [Latin *nomenclatura* list of names]

nominal *adj* **1** in name only: *nominal independence* **2** very small in comparison with real worth: *a nominal amount of aid* [Latin *nomen* name] **> nominally** *adv*

nominalism *n* the philosophical theory that a general word, such as *dog*, is merely a name and does not denote a real object **> nominalist** *n*

nominal value *n* same as **par value**

nominate *vb* **-nating, -nated 1** to propose (someone) as a candidate **2** to appoint (someone) to an office or position [Latin *nomen* name] **> nomination** *n*

nominative *n grammar* a grammatical case in some languages that identifies the subject of a verb [Latin *nominativus* belonging to naming]

nominee *n* a person who is nominated to an office or as a candidate

non- *prefix* **1** indicating negation: *nonexistent* **2** indicating refusal or failure: *noncooperation* **3** indicating exclusion from a specified class: *nonfiction* **4** indicating lack or absence: *nonevent* [Latin *non* not]

nonaddictive *adj* not causing addiction

nonage *n* **1** *law* the state of being under full legal age for various actions **2** a period of immaturity

nonagenarian *n* a person who is from 90 to 99 years old [Latin *nonaginta* ninety]

nonaggression *n* the policy of not attacking other countries

nonagon *n geometry* a figure with nine sides **> nonagonal** *adj*

nonalcoholic *adj* containing no alcohol

nonaligned *adj* (of a country) not part of a major alliance or power bloc **> nonalignment** *n*

nonbeliever *n* a person who does not follow any religious movement

nonbelligerent *adj* (of a country) not taking part in a war

nonce *n* **for the nonce** for the present [a mistaken division of *for then anes*, for the once]

nonce word *n* a word coined for a single occasion

nonchalant (non-shall-ant) *adj* casually unconcerned or indifferent [French, from *nonchaloir* to lack warmth] **> nonchalance** *n* **> nonchalantly** *adv*

non-com *n* short for **noncommissioned officer**

noncombatant *n* a member of the armed forces whose duties do not include fighting, such as a chaplain or surgeon

noncombustible *adj* not capable of igniting and burning

noncommissioned officer *n* (in the armed forces) a person who is appointed as a subordinate officer, from the lower ranks, rather than by a commission

noncommittal *adj* not committing oneself to any particular opinion

noncompliance *n* failure or refusal to do as requested

non compos mentis *adj* of unsound mind [Latin: not in control of one's mind]

nonconductor *n* a substance that is a poor conductor of heat, electricity, or sound

nonconformist *n* **1** a person who does not conform to generally accepted patterns of behaviour or thought ▷ *adj* **2** (of behaviour or ideas) not conforming to accepted patterns: *men who pride themselves on their nonconformist past* ▷ **nonconformity** *n*

Nonconformist *n* **1** a member of a Protestant group separated from the Church of England ▷ *adj* **2** of or relating to Nonconformists

noncontributory *adj* Brit denoting a pension scheme for employees, the premiums of which are paid entirely by the employer

non-cooperation *n* the refusal to do more than is legally or contractually required of one

noncustodial *adj* not involving imprisonment: *a noncustodial sentence*

nondescript *adj* lacking outstanding features [NON- + Latin *descriptus*, past participle of *describere* to copy]

non-domicile *n* Brit a UK resident who claims another country as his or her permanent home, esp. to escape certain taxes. Also shortened to: **non-dom**

non-domiciled *adj* Brit of or denoting a person who is resident in the UK but who claims another country as his or her permanent home

nondrinker *n* a person who does not drink alcohol

none *pron* **1** not any: *none of the men was represented by a lawyer; none of it meant anything to him* **2** no-one; nobody: *none could deny it* **3** **none the** in no degree: *her parents were none the wiser* [Old English *nān*, literally: not one]

> USAGE None is a singular pronoun and should be used with a singular form of a verb: *none of the students has* (not *have*) *a car.*

nonentity (non-enn-tit-tee) *n*, *pl* **-ties** an insignificant person or thing

non-essential *adj* not absolutely necessary

nonetheless *adv* despite that; however

nonevent *n* a disappointing or insignificant occurrence which was expected to be important

nonexistent *adj* not existing in a particular place ▷ **nonexistence** *n*

nonferrous *adj* **1** denoting a metal other than iron **2** not containing iron

nonfiction *n* writing that deals with facts or real events

nonflammable *adj* not easily set on fire

nonfunctional *adj* having no practical function

nonintervention *n* refusal to intervene in the affairs of others

noniron *adj* not requiring ironing

nonmember *n* a person who is not a member of a particular club or organization

nonmetal *n* chem a chemical element that forms acidic oxides and is a poor conductor of heat and electricity ▷ **nonmetallic** *adj*

nonmoral *adj* not involving morality; neither moral nor immoral

non-native *adj* not originating in a particular place

non-nuclear *adj* not involving or using nuclear power or weapons

Nono *n* Luigi. 1924–90, Italian composer of 12-tone music

no-nonsense *adj* sensible, practical, and straightforward: *a no-nonsense approach to crime*

nonpareil (non-par-rail) *n* a person or thing that is unsurpassed [French, from NON- + *pareil* similar]

non-partisan *adj* not supporting any single political party

non-payment *n* failure to pay money owed

nonplussed *or US* **nonplused** *adj* perplexed [Latin *non plus* no further]

nonprofessional *adj* not earning a living at a specified occupation: *nonprofessional investors*

non-profit-making *adj* not intended to make a profit

nonproliferation *n* limitation of the production or spread of something such as nuclear or chemical weapons

nonrepresentational *adj* art same as abstract

nonresident *n* a person who does not live in a particular country or place

nonsectarian *adj* not confined to any specific subdivision of a religious group

nonsense *n* **1** something that has or makes no sense **2** unintelligible language **3** foolish behaviour: *she'll stand no nonsense* ▷ **nonsensical** *adj*

non sequitur (sek-wit-tur) *n* a statement having little or no relation to what preceded it [Latin: it does not follow]

nonslip *adj* designed to prevent slipping: *a nonslip mat*

nonsmoker *n* **1** a person who does not smoke **2** a train carriage or compartment in which smoking is forbidden

nonsmoking *or* **no-smoking** *adj* denoting an area in which smoking is forbidden

nonstandard *adj* denoting words, expressions, or pronunciations that are not regarded as correct by educated native speakers of a language

nonstarter *n* a person or an idea that has little chance of success

nonstick *adj* (of cooking utensils) coated with a substance that food will not stick to when cooked

nonstop *adj* **1** without a stop: *two weeks of nonstop rain* ▷ *adv* **2** without a stop: *most days his phone rings nonstop*

Nonsuch Palace *n* a former royal palace in Cuddington in London: built in 1538 for Henry VIII; later visited by Elizabeth I, James I, Charles I, and Charles II; demolished (1682–1702)

nontoxic *adj* not poisonous

non-U *adj* Brit informal (of language or behaviour) not characteristic of the upper classes

nonunion *adj* **1** (of a company) not employing trade union members: *a nonunion shop* **2** (of a person) not belonging to a trade union

nonverbal *adj* not involving the use of language

nonviolent *adj* using peaceful methods to bring about change ▷ **nonviolence** *n*

nonvoting *adj* finance (of shares in a company) not entitling the holder to vote at company meetings

non-White *adj* **1** belonging to a race of people not European in origin ▷ *n* **2** a member of one of these races

noodle *n* a simpleton [a blend of *noddle* + *noodles*]

noodles *pl n* ribbon-like strips of pasta [German *Nudeln*]

nook *n* **1** a corner or recess **2** a secluded or sheltered place [origin unknown]

noon *n* the middle of the day; 12 o'clock [Latin *nona (hora)* ninth hour (originally 3 pm, the ninth hour from sunrise)]

noonday *adj* happening or appearing at noon

no-one *or* **no one** *pron* no person; nobody

> USAGE See at everyone.

Noordbrabant *n* the Dutch name for **North Brabant**

Noordholland *n* the Dutch name for **North Holland**

noose *n* a loop in the end of a rope, tied with a slipknot, such as one used to hang people [Latin *nodus* knot]

nope *interj* informal no

nor *conj* **1** used to join alternatives, the first of which is preceded by *neither*; and not: *neither willing nor able* **2** and not ... either: *he had not arrived yet, nor had any of the models* [contraction of Old English *nōther*]

Nord *n* a department of N France, in Nord-Pas-de-Calais region. Capital: Lille. Pop: 2 561 800 (2003 est). Area: 5774 sq km (2252 sq miles)

Nordau *n* **Max Simon**, original name *Max Simon Südfeld*. 1849–1923, German author, born in Hungary; a leader of the Zionist movement

Nordenskjöld *n* Baron **Nils Adolf Erik**. 1832–1901, Swedish Arctic explorer and geologist, born in Finland. He was the first to navigate the Northeast Passage (1878–79)

Nordenskjöld Sea *n* the former name of the **Laptev Sea** [named after Nils Adolf Erik Nordenskjöld]

nordic *adj skiing* of competitions in cross-country racing and ski-jumping

Nordic *adj* of Scandinavia or its typically tall, blond, and blue-eyed people [French *nordique* of the north]

Nordkyn Cape *n* a cape in N Norway: the northernmost point of the European mainland

Nord-Pas-de-Calais *n* a region of N France, on the Straits of Dover (the **Pas de Calais**): coal-mining, textile, and metallurgical industries

Nordrhein-Westfalen *n* the German name for **North Rhine-Westphalia**

Norfolk *n* **1** a county of E England, on the North Sea and the Wash: low-lying, with large areas of fens in the west and the Broads in the east; rich agriculturally. Administrative centre: Norwich. Pop: 810 700 (2003 est). Area: 5368 sq km (2072 sq miles) **2** a port in SE Virginia, on the Elizabeth River and Hampton Roads: headquarters of the US Atlantic fleet; shipbuilding. Pop: 241 727 (2003 est)

Norfolk Island *n* an island in the S Pacific, between New Caledonia and N New Zealand: an Australian external territory; discovered by Captain Cook in 1774; a penal settlement in early years. Capital: Kingston. Pop: 2182 (2012). Area: 36 sq km (14 sq miles)

Norge *n* the Norwegian name for **Norway**

Noricum *n* an Alpine kingdom of the Celts, south of the Danube: comprises present-day central Austria and parts of Bavaria; a Roman province from about 16 BC

norm *n* a standard that is required or regarded as normal [Latin *norma* carpenter's square]

normal *adj* **1** usual, regular, or typical: *the study of normal behaviour* **2** free from mental or physical disorder **3** *geometry* same as **perpendicular** (1) ▷ *n* **4** the usual, regular, or typical state, degree, or form **5** *geometry* a perpendicular line or plane [Latin *normalis* conforming to the carpenter's square] > **normality** *or especially US* **normalcy** *n*

normalize *or* **-lise** *vb* **-lizing, -lized** *or* **-lising, -lised** **1** to make or become normal **2** to bring into conformity with a standard > **normalization** *or* **-lisation** *n*

normally *adv* **1** as a rule; usually **2** in a normal manner

Norman¹ *n* **1** a native or inhabitant of Normandy, esp. one of the people who conquered England in 1066 **2** same as **Norman French** ▷ *adj* **3** of the Normans or their dialect of French **4** of or relating to Normandy **5** of a style of architecture used in Britain from the Norman Conquest until the 12th century, with rounded arches and massive masonry walls

Norman² *n* **1 Greg.** born 1955, Australian golfer: winner of the British Open (1986, 1993) **2 Jessye.** born 1945, US soprano: noted for her interpretations of Wagner and Mahler

Normandy *n* a former province of N France, on the English Channel: settled by Vikings under Rollo in the 10th century; scene of the Allied landings in 1944. Chief town: Rouen. French name: **Normandie**

Norman French *n* the medieval Norman and English dialect of Old French

normative *adj* of or establishing a norm or standard: *a normative model*

Norn *n Norse myth* any of the three virgin goddesses of fate [Old Norse]

Norrington *n* **Sir Roger** (**Arthur Carver**). born 1934, British conductor; noted for period performances of early music

Norrköping *n* a port in SE Sweden, near the Baltic. Pop: 124 378 (2004 est)

Norse *adj* **1** of ancient and medieval Scandinavia **2** of Norway ▷ *n* **3 a** the N group of Germanic languages spoken in Scandinavia **b** any one of these languages, esp. in their ancient or medieval forms

Norseman *n, pl* **-men** same as **Viking**

north *n* **1** one of the four cardinal points of the compass, at 0° or 360° **2** the direction along a meridian towards the North Pole **3** the direction in which a compass needle points; magnetic north **4 the north** any area lying in or towards the north ▷ *adj* **5** in or towards the north **6** (esp. of the wind) from the north ▷ *adv* **7** in, to, or towards the north [Old English]

North¹ *n* **1 the North a** the northern part of England, generally regarded as reaching the southern boundaries of Yorkshire, Derbyshire, and Cheshire **b** (in the US) the states north of the Mason-Dixon Line that were known as the Free States during the Civil War **c** the economically and technically advanced countries of the world ▷ *adj* **2** of or denoting the northern part of a country or area

North² *n* **1 Frederick**, 2nd Earl of Guildford, called *Lord North*. 1732–92, British statesman; prime minister (1770–82), dominated by George III. He was held responsible for the loss of the American colonies **2 Sir Thomas**. ?1535–?1601, English translator of Plutarch's *Lives* (1579), which was the chief source of Shakespeare's Roman plays

North Africa *n* the part of Africa between the Mediterranean and the Sahara: consists chiefly of Morocco, Algeria, Tunisia, Libya, and N Egypt

North African *adj* **1** of or relating to North Africa or its inhabitants ▷ *n* **2** a native or inhabitant of North Africa

Northallerton *n* a market town in N England, administrative centre of North Yorkshire. Pop: 15 517 (2001)

North America *n* the third largest continent, linked with South America by the Isthmus of Panama and bordering on the Arctic Ocean, the N Pacific, the N Atlantic, the Gulf of Mexico, and the Caribbean. It consists generally of a great mountain system (the Western Cordillera) extending along the entire W coast, actively volcanic in the extreme north and south, with the Great Plains to the east and the Appalachians still further east, separated from the Canadian Shield by an arc of large lakes (Great Bear, Great Slave, Winnipeg, Superior, Michigan, Huron, Erie, Ontario); reaches its greatest height of 6194 m (20 320 ft) in Mount McKinley, Alaska, and its lowest point of 85 m (280 ft) below sea level in Death Valley, California, and ranges from snowfields, tundra, and taiga in the north to deserts in the southwest and tropical forests in the extreme south. Pop: 332 156 000 (2005 est). Area: over 24 000 000 sq km (9 500 000 sq miles)

North American *adj* **1** of or relating to North America or its inhabitants ▷ *n* **2** a native or inhabitant of North America

Northampton *n* **1** a town in central England, administrative centre of Northamptonshire, on the River Nene: footwear and engineering industries. Pop: 189 474 (2001) **2** short for **Northamptonshire**

Northamptonshire *n* a county of central England: agriculture, food processing, engineering, and footwear industries. Administrative centre: Northampton. Pop: 642 700 (2003 est). Area: 2367 sq km (914 sq miles). Abbreviation: **Northants**

Northants Northamptonshire

North Ayrshire *n* a council area of W central Scotland,

n

on the Firth of Clyde: comprises the N part of the historical county of Ayrshire, including the Isle of Arran; formerly part of Strathclyde Region (1975–96): chiefly agricultural, with fishing and tourism. Administrative centre: Irvine. Pop: 136 030 (2003 est). Area: 884 sq km (341 sq miles)

North Borneo n the former name (until 1963) of **Sabah**

northbound adj going towards the north

North Brabant n a province of the S Netherlands: formed part of the medieval duchy of Brabant. Capital: 's Hertogenbosch. Pop: 2 400 000 (2003 est). Area: 4965 sq km (1917 sq miles). Dutch name: **Noordbrabant**

North Cape n **1** a cape on N Magerøy Island, in the Arctic Ocean off the N coast of Norway **2** a cape on N North Island, New Zealand

North Carolina n a state of the southeastern US, on the Atlantic: consists of a coastal plain rising to the Piedmont Plateau and the Appalachian Mountains in the west. Capital: Raleigh. Pop: 8 407 248 (2003 est). Area: 126 387 sq km (48 798 sq miles). Abbreviation: **N.C.**, (with zip code) **NC**

North Carolinian adj **1** of or relating to North Carolina or its inhabitants ▷ n **2** a native or inhabitant of North Carolina

North Channel n a strait between NE Ireland and SW Scotland, linking the North Atlantic with the Irish Sea

Northcliffe n Viscount. title of Alfred Charles William Harmsworth. 1865–1922, British newspaper proprietor. With his brother, 1st Viscount Rothermere, he built up a vast chain of newspapers. He founded the Daily Mail (1896), the Daily Mirror (1903), and acquired The Times (1908)

North Country n the North Country same as **North**¹ (1a)

Northd Northumberland

North Dakota n a state of the western US: mostly undulating prairies and plains, rising from the Red River valley in the east to the Missouri plateau in the west, with the infertile Bad Lands in the extreme west. Capital: Bismarck. Pop: 633 837 (2003 est). Area: 183 019 sq km (70 664 sq miles). Abbreviation: **N. Dak.**, **N.D.**, (with zip code) **ND**

North Dakotan adj **1** of or relating to North Dakota or its inhabitants ▷ n **2** a native or inhabitant of North Dakota

North Down n a district of E Northern Ireland, in Co Down. Pop: 77 110 (2003 est). Area: 82 sq km (32 sq miles)

northeast n **1** the direction midway between north and east **2** the northeast any area lying in or towards the northeast ▷ adj also: **northeastern 3** (sometimes cap) of or denoting that part of a country or area which lies in the northeast **4** situated in, moving towards, or facing the northeast **5** (esp. of the wind) from the northeast ▷ adv **6** in, to, or towards the northeast **›** **northeasterly** adj, adv, n

Northeast n the Northeast the northeastern part of England, esp. Northumberland, Durham, and the Tyneside area

northeaster n a strong wind or storm from the northeast

North East Frontier Agency n the former name (until 1972) of **Arunachal Pradesh**

North East Lincolnshire n a unitary authority in E England, in Lincolnshire: formerly (1974–96) part of the county of Humberside. Pop: 157 400 (2003 est). Area: 192 sq km (74 sq miles)

northerly adj **1** of or in the north ▷ adv, adj **2** towards the north **3** from the north: a cold northerly wind

northern adj **1** situated in or towards the north **2** facing or moving towards the north **3** (sometimes cap) of or characteristic of the north or North **›** **northernmost** adj

Northern Cape n the largest but least populated province in South Africa, in the NW part of the country; created in 1994 from part of Cape Province: agriculture, mining (esp. diamonds). Capital: Kimberley. Pop:

1 145 861 (2011 est). Area: 139 703 sq km (361 830 sq miles)

Northern Dvina n See Dvina (1)

Northerner n a person from the north of a country or area, esp. England

northern hemisphere n that half of the globe lying north of the equator

Northern Ireland n that part of the United Kingdom occupying the NE part of Ireland: separated from the rest of Ireland, which became independent in law in 1920; remained part of the United Kingdom, with a separate Parliament (Stormont), inaugurated in 1921, and limited self-government; scene of severe conflict between Catholics and Protestants, including terrorist bombing from 1969; direct administration from Westminster from 1972; assembly and powersharing executive established in 1998–99 following the Good Friday Agreement of 1998, suspended in 2002, and reinstated 2007. Capital: Belfast. Pop: 1 810 863 (2011 est). Area: 14 121 sq km (5452 sq miles)

Northern Isles pl n Orkney and Shetland

northern lights pl n same as **aurora borealis**

Northern Mariana Islands n a US commonwealth territory in the N Pacific, formerly part of the Trust Territory of the Pacific Islands (1947–87). Capital: Saipan island (Capitol Hill). Pop: 51 170 (2013 est). Area: 477 sq km (184 sq miles)

Northern Province n the former name for **Limpopo** (1)

Northern Rhodesia n the former name (until 1964) of **Zambia**

Northern Territories pl n a former British protectorate in W Africa, established in 1897; attached to the Gold Coast in 1901; now constitutes the Northern Region of Ghana (since 1957)

Northern Territory n an administrative division of N central Australia, on the Timor and Arafura Seas: the Arunta Desert lies in the east, the Macdonnell Ranges in the south, and Arnhem Land in the north (containing Australia's largest Aboriginal reservation); the Ashmore and Cartier Islands constitute a separate Australian External Territory. Capital: Darwin. Pop: 233 300 (2012 est). Area: 1 347 525 sq km (520 280 sq miles)

North Holland n a province of the NW Netherlands, on the peninsula between the North Sea and IJsselmeer: includes the West Frisian Island of Texel. Capital: Haarlem. Pop: 2 573 000 (2003 est). Area: 2663 sq km (1029 sq miles). Dutch name: **Noordholland**

northings pl n a series of numbers in a grid reference indicating the distance northwards from a given latitude

North Island n the northernmost of the two main islands of New Zealand. Pop: 3 422 000 (2013 est). Area: 114 729 sq km (44 297 sq miles)

North Korea n a republic in NE Asia, on the Sea of Japan (East Sea) and the Yellow Sea: established in 1948 as a people's republic; mostly rugged and mountainous, with fertile lowlands in the west Language: Korean. Currency: won. Capital: Pyongyang. Pop: 24 720 407 (2013 est). Area: 122 313 sq km (47 225 sq miles). Official name: **Democratic People's Republic of Korea**. Korean name: **Chosŏn**

North Korean adj **1** of or relating to North Korea or its inhabitants ▷ n **2** a native or inhabitant of North Korea

North Lanarkshire n a council area of central Scotland: consists mainly of the NE part of the historical county of Lanarkshire; formerly (1974–96) part of Strathclyde Region: engineering and metalworking industries. Administrative centre: Motherwell. Pop: 321 820 (2003 est). Area: 1771 sq km (684 sq miles)

Northland n **1** the peninsula containing Norway and Sweden **2** (in Canada) the far north

Northlander n **1** a native or inhabitant of the peninsula containing Norway and Sweden **2** (in Canada) a native or inhabitant of the far north

North Lincolnshire n a unitary authority of NE

n

England, in Lincolnshire: formerly (1975–96) part of the county of Humberside. Pop: 155 000 (2003 est). Area: 1497 sq km (578 sq miles)

Northman n, pl **-men** same as **Viking**

north of 60 n Canad the area of Canada lying north of a latitude of 60°N

North Ossetian Republic n a constituent republic of S Russia, on the N slopes of the central Caucasus Mountains. Capital: Vladikavkaz. Pop: 709 900 (2002). Area: about 8000 sq km (3088 sq miles). Also called: **North Ossetia, Alania**

North Pole n the northernmost point on the earth's axis, at a latitude of 90°N, which has very low temperatures

North Rhine-Westphalia n a state of W Germany: formed in 1946 by the amalgamation of the Prussian province of Westphalia with the N part of the Prussian Rhine province and later with the state of Lippe; part of West Germany until 1990: highly industrialized. Capital: Düsseldorf. Pop: 18 080 000 (2003 est). Area: 34 039 sq km (13 142 sq miles). German name: **Nordrhein-Westfalen**

North Riding n (until 1974) an administrative division of Yorkshire, now constituting most of North Yorkshire

North Saskatchewan n a river in W Canada, rising in W Alberta and flowing northeast, east, and southeast to join the South Saskatchewan River and form the Saskatchewan River. Length: 1223 km (760 miles)

North Sea n an arm of the Atlantic between Great Britain and the N European mainland. Area: about 569 800 sq km (220 000 sq miles). Former name: **German Ocean**

North Somerset n a unitary authority of SW England, in Somerset: formerly (1974–96) part of the county of Avon. Pop: 191 400 (2003 est). Area: 375 sq km (145 sq miles)

North Star n the North Star same as **Pole Star**

North Tyneside n a unitary authority of NE England, in Tyne and Wear. Pop: 190 800 (2003 est). Area: 84 sq km (32 sq miles)

Northumb. Northumberland

Northumberland¹ n the northernmost county of England, on the North Sea; became a unitary authority in 2009: hilly in the north (the Cheviots) and west (the Pennines), with many Roman remains, notably Hadrian's Wall; shipbuilding, coal mining. Administrative centre: Morpeth. Pop: 310 600 (2007 est). Area: 5032 sq km (1943 sq miles). Abbreviation: **Northd**

Northumberland² n 1st Duke of, title of John Dudley. 1502–53, English statesman and soldier, who governed England (1549–53) during the minority of Edward VI. His attempt (1553) to gain the throne for his daughter-in-law, Lady Jane Grey, led to his execution

Northumbria n **1** (in Anglo-Saxon Britain) a region that stretched from the Humber to the Firth of Forth: formed in the 7th century AD, it became an important intellectual centre; a separate kingdom until 876 AD **2** an area of NE England roughly corresponding to the Anglo-Saxon region of Northumbria

Northumbrian adj **1** of or relating to Northumberland, its inhabitants, or their dialect of English **2** of or relating to ancient Northumbria, its inhabitants, or their dialect

North Vietnam n a region of N Vietnam, on the Gulf of Tonkin: an independent Communist state from 1954 until 1976. Area: 164 061 sq km (63 344 sq miles)

northward adj, adv also: **northwards** **1** towards the north ▷ n **2** the northward part or direction

northwest n **1** the direction midway between north and west **2** the northwest any area lying in or towards the northwest ▷ adj also: **northwestern** **3** (sometimes cap) of or denoting that part of a country or area which lies in the northwest **4** situated in, moving towards, or facing the northwest **5** (esp. of the wind) from the

northwest ▷ adv **6** in, to, or towards the northwest ▷ **northwesterly** adj, adv, n

Northwest n the Northwest **1** the northwestern part of England, esp. Lancashire and the Lake District **2** the northwestern part of the US, consisting of the states of Washington, Oregon, and sometimes Idaho **3** (in Canada) the region north and west of the Great Lakes

North West n a province in N South Africa, created in 1994 from the NE part of Cape Province and part of Transvaal: agriculture and service industries. Capital: Mafikeng. Pop: 3 509 953 (2011 est). Area: 116 320 sq km (44 911 sq miles)

northwester n a strong wind or storm from the northwest

North-West Frontier Province n a province in N Pakistan between Afghanistan and Jammu and Kashmir: part of British India from 1901 until 1947; of strategic importance, esp. for the Khyber Pass. Capital: Peshawar. Pop: 20 170 000 (2003 est). Area: 74 522 sq km (28 773 sq miles)

Northwest Territories pl n a territory of NW Canada including part of Victoria Island and several other islands of the Arctic; comprised over a third of Canada's total area until Nunavut became a separate territory in 1999: rich mineral resources. Pop: 41 462 (2011 est). Area: 2 082 910 sq km (804 003 sq miles). Abbreviation: **NWT**

Northwest Territory n See Old Northwest

Northwich n a town in NW England, in Cheshire: salt and chemical industries. Pop: 39 568 (2001)

North Yemen n a former republic in SW Arabia, on the Red Sea; now part of Yemen; declared a republic in 1962; united with South Yemen in 1990. Official name: **Yemen Republic**. See also **Yemen, South Yemen**

North Yorkshire n a county in N England, formed in 1974 from most of the North Riding of Yorkshire and parts of the East and West Ridings: the geographical and ceremonial county includes the unitary authorities of Middlesbrough, Redcar and Cleveland, and part of Stockton on Tees (all within Cleveland until 1996), and York (created in 1997). Administrative centre: Northallerton. Pop (excluding unitary authorities): 576 100 (2003 est). Area (excluding unitary authorities): 8037 sq km (3102 sq miles)

Norton n Graham, real name Graham Walker. born 1963, Irish comedian and TV presenter noted for his camp humour

Norw. **1** Norway **2** Norwegian

Norway n a kingdom in NW Europe, occupying the W part of the Scandinavian peninsula: first united in the Viking age (800–1050); under the rule of Denmark (1523–1814) and Sweden (1814–1905); became an independent monarchy in 1905. Its coastline is deeply indented by fjords and fringed with islands, rising inland to plateaus and mountains. Norway has a large fishing fleet and its merchant navy is among the world's largest. Official language: Norwegian. Official religion: Evangelical Lutheran. Currency: krone. Capital: Oslo. Pop: 4 722 701 (2013 est). Area: 323 878 sq km (125 050 sq miles). Norwegian name: **Norge**

Norwegian adj **1** of or relating to Norway or its inhabitants ▷ n **2** a native or inhabitant of Norway **3** the language of Norway

Norwegian Sea n part of the Arctic Ocean between Greenland and Norway

nor'wester n NZ a hot dry wind

Norwich n a city in E England, administrative centre of Norfolk: cathedral (founded 1096); University of East Anglia (1963); traditionally a centre of the footwear industry, now has engineering, financial services. Pop: 174 047 (2001)

Nos. or **nos.** numbers

nose n **1** the organ situated above the mouth, used for smelling and breathing **2** the sense of smell **3** the front part of a vehicle **4** the distinctive smell of a wine or perfume **5** instinctive skill in finding something: *he had a nose for media events* **6 get up someone's nose** *informal* to annoy someone **7 keep one's nose clean** to stay out of trouble **8 look down one's nose at** *informal* to be haughty towards **9 pay through the nose** *informal* to pay a high price **10 put someone's nose out of joint** *informal* to make someone envious by doing what he or she would have liked to do or had expected to do **11 rub someone's nose in it** *informal* to remind someone unkindly of a failing or error **12 turn up one's nose at** *informal* to show contempt for **13 win by a nose** to win by a narrow margin ▷ *vb* **nosing, nosed 14** to move forward slowly and carefully: *a motorboat nosed out of the mist* **15** to pry or snoop **16 nose out** to discover by searching or prying [Old English *nosu*]

nosebag *n* a bag containing feed, fastened around the head of a horse

noseband *n* the part of a horse's bridle that goes around the nose

nosebleed *n* bleeding from the nose

nose cone *n* the cone-shaped front section of a missile or spacecraft

nose dive *n* **1** (of an aircraft) a sudden plunge with the nose pointing downwards **2** *informal* a sudden drop: *when we fail our self-confidence takes a nose dive* ▷ *vb* **nose-dive (-diving, -dived) 3** to take a nose dive

nosegay *n* a small bunch of flowers [*nose + gay* (archaic) toy]

nosey or **nosy** *adj* **nosier, nosiest** *informal* prying or inquisitive ❯ **nosiness** *n*

nosey parker *n* *Brit and S African informal* a prying person [arbitrary use of surname *Parker*]

nosh *Brit, Austral and NZ slang n* **1** food ▷ *vb* **2** to eat [Yiddish]

nosh-up *n* *Brit slang* a large meal

Nossal *n* Sir Gustav (Victor Joseph). born 1931, Australian biologist, born in Austria; knighted (1977) for his work on immunology

nostalgia *n* **1** a sentimental yearning for the past **2** homesickness [Greek *nostos* a return home + *algos* pain] ❯ **nostalgic** *adj* ❯ **nostalgically** *adv*

Nostradamus *n* Latinized name of *Michel de Notredame.* 1503–66, French physician and astrologer; author of a book of prophecies in rhymed quatrains, *Centuries* (1555)

nostril *n* either of the two openings at the end of the nose [Old English *nosu* nose + *thyrel* hole]

nostrum *n* **1** a quack medicine **2** a favourite remedy [Latin: our own (make)]

nosy *adj* **nosier, nosiest** same as **nosey**

not *adv* **1** used to negate the sentence, phrase, or word that it modifies: *I will not stand for it* **2 not that** which is not to say that: *not that I've ever heard him complain* [Old English *nāwiht*, from *nā* no + *wiht* creature, thing]

nota bene (note-a ben-nay) note well; take note [Latin]

notable (note-a-bl) *adj* **1** worthy of being noted; remarkable ▷ *n* **2** a person of distinction [Latin *notare* to note] ❯ **notability** *n* ❯ **notably** *adv*

notary or **notary public** (note-a-ree) *n, pl* **notaries** or **notaries public** a public official, usually a solicitor, who is legally authorized to attest and certify documents [Latin *notarius* one who makes notes, a clerk]

notation (no-tay-shun) *n* **1** representation of numbers or quantities in a system by a series of symbols **2** a set of such symbols [Latin *notare* to note]

notch *n* **1** a V-shaped cut **2** *informal* a step or level: *the economy moved up another notch* ▷ *vb* **3** to cut a notch in **4 notch up** *informal* to score or achieve: *he notched up a hat trick of wins* [mistaken division of *an otch*, from Old French *oche* notch]

note *n* **1** a brief informal letter **2** a brief record in writing for future reference **3** a critical comment or explanation in a book **4** an official written communication, as from a government or from a doctor **5** short for **banknote 6** *Brit and NZ* a musical sound of a particular pitch **7** a written symbol representing the pitch and duration of a

musical sound **8** *chiefly Brit* a key on a piano, organ, or other keyboard instrument **9** a particular feeling or atmosphere: *an optimistic note* **10** a distinctive vocal sound, as of a type of animal **11** a sound used as a signal or warning: *the note to retreat was sounded* **12** short for **promissory note 13** of note **a** distinguished or famous **b** important: *nothing of note* **14 strike the right note** to behave appropriately **15 take note of** to pay attention to ▷ *vb* **noting, noted 16** to notice; pay attention to: *such criticism should be noted* **17** to make a written note of: *he noted it in his diary* **18** to remark upon: *I note that you do not wear shoes* [Latin *nota* sign]

notebook *n* a book for writing in

notebook computer *n* a portable computer approximately the size of a sheet of A4 paper

notecase *n* same as **wallet**

noted *adj* well-known: *a noted scholar*

notelet *n* a folded card with a printed design on the front, for writing informal letters

notepad *n* a number of sheets of paper fastened together along one edge, used for writing notes or letters on

notepaper *n* paper used for writing letters

noteworthy *adj* worth noting; remarkable

nothing *pron* **1** not anything: *I felt nothing* **2** a matter of no importance: *don't worry, it's nothing* **3** absence of meaning, value, or worth: *the industry shrank to almost nothing* **4** the figure 0 **5 have** or **be nothing to do with** to have no connection with **6 nothing but** not something other than; only **7 nothing doing** *informal* an expression of dismissal or refusal **8 nothing less than** downright: *nothing less than complete withdrawal* **9 think nothing of something** to regard something as easy or natural ▷ *adv* **10** not at all: *he looked nothing like his brother* ▷ *n* **11** *informal* a person or thing of no importance or significance [Old English *nāthing, nān thing*]

> **USAGE** *Nothing* normally takes a singular verb, but when *nothing but* is followed by a plural form of a noun, a plural verb is usually used: *it was a large room where nothing but souvenirs were sold.*

nothingness *n* **1** nonexistence **2** total insignificance

notice *n* **1** observation or attention: *to attract notice* **2** a displayed placard or announcement giving information **3** advance notification of something such as intention to end a contract of employment: *she handed in her notice* **4** a theatrical or literary review: *the film reaped ecstatic notices* **5 at short notice** with very little notification **6 take no notice of** to ignore or disregard **7 take notice** to pay attention ▷ *vb* **-ticing, -ticed 8** to become aware (of) **9** to point out or remark upon [Latin *notus* known]

noticeable *adj* easily seen or detected ❯ **noticeably** *adv*

notice board *n* a board on which notices are displayed

notifiable *adj* having to be reported to the authorities: *a notifiable disease*

notification *n* **1** the act of notifying someone of something **2** a formal announcement

notify *vb* **-fies, -fying, -fied** to inform: *notify gas and electricity companies of your moving date* [Latin *notus* known + *facere* to make]

notion *n* **1** an idea or opinion **2** a whim [Latin *notio* a becoming acquainted (with)]

notional *adj* hypothetical, imaginary, or unreal: *a notional dividend payment*

Notogaea *n* a zoogeographical area comprising the Australasian region. Compare **Arctogaea, Neogaea** [C19: from Greek *notos* south wind + *gaia* land]

Notogaean *n* **1** a native or inhabitant of Notogaea ▷ *adj* **2** of or relating to Notogaea or its inhabitants

notorious *adj* well known for some bad reason [Medieval Latin *notorius* well-known] ❯ **notoriety** *n* ❯ **notoriously** *adv*

not proven *adj* a verdict in Scottish courts, given when there is insufficient evidence to convict the accused

Notre Dame *n* the early Gothic cathedral of Paris, on the Île de la Cité: built between 1163 and 1257

no-trump *cards n* **1** a bid or hand without trumps ▷ *adj* **2** (of a hand) suitable for playing without trumps

Nottingham *n* **1** a city in N central England, administrative centre of Nottinghamshire, on the River Trent: scene of the outbreak of the Civil War (1642); famous for its associations with the Robin Hood legend; two universities. Pop: 249 584 (2001) **2** a unitary authority in N central England, in Nottinghamshire. Pop: 273 900 (2003 est). Area: 78 sq km (30 sq miles)

Nottinghamshire *n* an inland county of central England: generally low-lying, with part of the S Pennines and the remnant of Sherwood Forest in the east. Nottingham became an independent unitary authority in 1998. Administrative centre: Nottingham. Pop (excluding Nottingham): 755 400 (2003 est). Area (excluding Nottingham): 2086 sq km (805 sq miles). Abbreviation: **Notts**

Nottm Nottingham

Notts Nottinghamshire

notwithstanding *prep* **1** in spite of ▷ *adv* **2** nevertheless

Nouakchott *n* the capital of Mauritania, near the Atlantic coast: replaced St Louis as capital in 1957; situated on important caravan routes. Pop: 559 000 (2002 est)

nougat *n* a hard chewy pink or white sweet containing chopped nuts [French, from Latin *nux* nut]

nought *n* **1** the figure 0 ▷ *n*, *adv* **2** same as **naught** [Old English *nōwiht*, from *ne* not, no + *ōwiht* something]

noughties *pl n informal* the decade from 2000 to 2009

noughts and crosses *n Brit* a game in which two players, one using a nought, the other a cross, alternately mark squares formed by two pairs of crossed lines, the winner being the first to get three of his or her symbols in a row

Nouméa *n* the capital and chief port of the French Overseas Territory of New Caledonia. Pop: 146 000 (2005 est)

noun *n* a word that refers to a person, place, or thing [Latin *nomen* name]

nourish *vb* **1** to provide with the food necessary for life and growth **2** to encourage or foster (an idea or feeling) [Latin *nutrire* to feed] ❯ **nourishing** *adj*

nourishment *n* the food needed to nourish the body

nous *n old-fashioned, slang* common sense [Greek: mind]

nouveau riche (noo-voh **reesh**) *n, pl* **nouveaux riches** (noo-voh **reesh**) a person who has become wealthy recently and is regarded as vulgar [French: new rich]

Nouvelle-Calédonie *n* the French name for **New Caledonia**

nouvelle cuisine (noo-vell kwee-**zeen**) *n* a style of preparing and presenting food with light sauces and unusual combinations of flavours [French: new cooking]

Nov. November

nova *n, pl* **-vae** *or* **-vas** a star that undergoes an explosion and fast increase of brightness, then gradually decreases to its original brightness [New Latin *nova* (*stella*) new (star)]

Novalis *n* real name *Friedrich von Hardenberg.* 1772–1801, German romantic poet. His works include the mystical *Hymnen an die Nacht* (1797; published 1800) and *Geistliche Lieder* (1799)

Nova Lisboa *n* the former name (1928–73) of **Huambo**

Novara *n* a city in NW Italy, in NE Piedmont: scene of the Austrian defeat of the Piedmontese in 1849. Pop: 100 910 (2001)

Nova Scotia *n* **1** a peninsula in E Canada, between the Gulf of St Lawrence and the Bay of Fundy **2** a province of E Canada, consisting of the Nova Scotia peninsula and Cape Breton Island: first settled by the French as Acadia. Capital: Halifax. Pop: 921 727 (2011 est). Area: 52 841 sq km (20 402 sq miles) ▶ Abbreviation: **NS**

Nova Scotian *n* **1** a native or inhabitant of Nova Scotia ▷ *adj* **2** of or relating to Nova Scotia or its inhabitants

Novaya Zemlya *n* an archipelago in the Arctic Ocean, off the NE coast of Russia: consists of two large islands and many islets. Area: about 81 279 sq km (31 382 sq miles)

novel[1] *n* a long fictional story in book form [Latin *novella* (*narratio*) new (story)]

novel[2] *adj* fresh, new, or original: *a novel approach* [Latin *novus* new]

novelette *n* a short novel, usually one regarded as trivial or sentimental

novelist *n* a writer of novels

novella *n, pl* **-las** a short narrative tale or short novel [Italian]

Novello *n* **Ivor**, real name *Ivor Novello Davies.* 1893–1951, Welsh actor, composer, songwriter, and dramatist

novelty *n, pl* **-ties** **1** the quality of being new and interesting **2** a new or unusual experience or thing **3** a small cheap toy or trinket

November *n* the eleventh month of the year [Latin: ninth month]

novena (no-**vee**-na) *n, pl* **-nas** *or* **-nae** (-nee) *RC Church* a set of prayers or services on nine consecutive days [Latin *novem* nine]

Novgorod *n* a city in NW Russia, on the Volkhov River; became a principality in 862 under Rurik, an event regarded as the founding of the Russian state; a major trading centre in the Middle Ages; destroyed by Ivan the Terrible in 1570. Pop: 215 000 (2005 est)

novice (**nov**-viss) *n* **1** a beginner **2** a person who has entered a religious order but has not yet taken vows [Latin *novus* new]

Novi Sad *n* a port in Serbia, in the NE on the River Danube: founded in 1690 as the seat of the Serbian patriarch; university (1960). Pop: 234 151 (2002). German name: **Neusatz**

novitiate *or* **noviciate** *n* **1** the period of being a novice **2** the part of a monastery or convent where the novices live

Novokuznetsk *n* a city in S central Russia: iron and steel works. Pop: 542 000 (2005 est). Former name (1932–61): **Stalinsk**

Novosibirsk *n* a city in W central Russia, on the River Ob: the largest town in Siberia; developed with the coming of the Trans-Siberian railway in 1893; important industrial centre. Pop: 1 425 000 (2005 est)

now *adv* **1** at or for the present time **2** immediately: *bring it now* **3** in these times; nowadays **4** given the present circumstances: *now do you understand why?* **5 a** used as a hesitation word: *now, I can't really say* **b** used for emphasis: *now listen to this* **c** used at the end of a command: *run along now* **6 just now a** very recently: *he left just now* **b** very soon: *I'm going just now* **7 now and again** *or* **then** occasionally **8 now now!** an exclamation used to tell someone off or to calm someone ▷ *conj* **9** Also: **now that** seeing that: *now you're here, you can help me* ▷ *n* **10** the present time: *now is the time to go* [Old English *nū*]

nowadays *adv* in these times: *nowadays his work is regarded as out-of-date*

Nowell *n* same as **Noel**

nowhere *adv* **1** in, at, or to no place **2 getting nowhere** *informal* making no progress **3 nowhere near** far from: *the stadium is nowhere near completion* ▷ *n* **4 in the middle of nowhere** (of a place) completely isolated

no-win *adj* with no possibility of a favourable outcome: *a no-win situation*

nowt *n N English dialect* nothing [from *naught*]

noxious *adj* **1** poisonous or harmful **2** extremely unpleasant [Latin *noxius* harmful]

Noyon *n* a town in N France: scene of the coronations of Charlemagne (768) and Hugh Capet (987); birthplace of John Calvin. Pop: 14 471 (1999)

nozzle *n* a projecting spout from which fluid is discharged [diminutive of *nose*]

Np *chem* neptunium

nr near

NS 1 New Style (method of reckoning dates) **2** Nova Scotia

NSPCC (in Britain) National Society for the Prevention of Cruelty to Children

NST Newfoundland Standard Time

NSW New South Wales

NT 1 (in Britain) National Trust **2** New Testament **3** Northern Territory **4** Nunavut

-n't not: added to *be* or *have,* or auxiliary verbs: *can't*; *don't*; *isn't*

nth *adj* See n²

Nu *n* U, original name *Thakin Nu.* 1907–95, Burmese statesman and writer; prime minister (1948–56, 1957–58, 1960–62). He attempted to establish parliamentary democracy, but was ousted (1962) by Ne Win

nuance (new-ahnss) *n* a subtle difference, as in colour, meaning, or tone [French]

nub *n* the point or gist: *this is the nub of his theory* [Middle Low German *knubbe* knob]

nubble *n* a small lump [from *nub*] **> nubbly** *adj*

Nubia *n* an ancient region of NE Africa, on the Nile, extending from Aswan to Khartoum

Nubian *n* **1** a native or inhabitant of Nubia **2** the language spoken by the people of Nubia *> adj* **3** of or relating to Nubia or its inhabitants **4** *informal* of or relating to Black culture

Nubian Desert *n* a desert in the NE Sudan, between the Nile valley and the Red Sea: mainly a sandstone plateau

nubile (new-bile) *adj* **1** (of a young woman) sexually attractive **2** (of a young woman) old enough or mature enough for marriage [Latin *nubere* to marry]

nubuck (new-buk) *n* (*sometimes cap*) leather that has been rubbed on the flesh side of the skin to give it a fine, velvet-like finish

nuclear *adj* **1** of nuclear weapons or energy **2** of an atomic nucleus: *nuclear fission*

nuclear bomb *n* a bomb whose force is due to uncontrolled nuclear fusion or fission

nuclear energy *n* energy released during a nuclear reaction as a result of fission or fusion

nuclear family *n sociol, anthropol* a family consisting only of parents and their offspring

nuclear fission *n nuclear physics* the splitting of an atomic nucleus, either spontaneously or by bombardment by a neutron: used in atomic bombs and nuclear power plants

nuclear-free *adj* (of an area) barred, esp. by local authorities, from being supplied with nuclear-generated electricity and from storing nuclear waste or weapons

nuclear fusion *n nuclear physics* the combination of two nuclei to form a heavier nucleus with the release of energy: used in hydrogen bombs

nuclear physics *n* the branch of physics concerned with the structure of the nucleus and the behaviour of its particles

nuclear power *n* power produced by a nuclear reactor

nuclear reaction *n physics* a process in which the structure and energy content of an atomic nucleus is changed by interaction with another nucleus or particle

nuclear reactor *n nuclear physics* a device in which a nuclear reaction is maintained and controlled to produce nuclear energy

nuclear winter *n* a theoretical period of low temperatures and little light that has been suggested would occur after a nuclear war

nucleate *adj* **1** having a nucleus *> vb* **-ating, -ated 2** to form a nucleus

nuclei (new-klee-eye) *n* the plural of nucleus

nucleic acid *n biochem* a complex compound, such as DNA or RNA, found in all living cells

nucleon *n physics* a proton or neutron

nucleonics *n* the branch of physics concerned with the applications of nuclear energy **> nucleonic** *adj*

nucleus *n, pl* **-clei 1** *physics* the positively charged centre of an atom, made of protons and neutrons, about which electrons orbit **2** a central thing around which others are grouped **3** a centre of growth or development: *the nucleus of a new relationship* **4** *biology* the part of a cell that contains the chromosomes and associated molecules that control the characteristics and growth of the cell **5** *chem* a fundamental group of atoms in a molecule serving as the base structure for related compounds [Latin: kernel]

nude *adj* **1** completely undressed *> n* **2** a naked figure in painting, sculpture, or photography **3 in the nude** naked [Latin *nudus*] **> nudity** *n*

nudge *vb* **nudging, nudged 1** to push (someone) gently with the elbow to get attention **2** to push (something or someone) lightly: *the dog nudged the stick with its nose* **3** to persuade (someone) gently *> n* **4** a gentle poke or push [origin unknown]

nudism *n* the practice of not wearing clothes, for reasons of health **> nudist** *n, adj*

Nuevo Laredo *n* a city and port of entry in NE Mexico, in Tamaulipas state on the Rio Grande opposite Laredo, Texas: oil industries. Pop: 353 000 (2005 est)

Nuevo León *n* a state of NE Mexico: the first centre of heavy industry in Latin America. Capital: Monterrey. Pop: 3 826 240 (2000). Area: 64 555 sq km (24 925 sq miles)

Nuffield *n* William Richard Morris, 1st Viscount Nuffield. 1877–1963, English motorcar manufacturer and philanthropist. He endowed Nuffield College at Oxford (1937) and the Nuffield Foundation (1943), a charitable trust for the furtherance of medicine and education

nugatory (new-gat-tree) *adj formal* **1** of little value **2** not valid: *their rejection rendered the treaty nugatory* [Latin *nugae* trifling things]

nugget *n* **1** a small lump of gold in its natural state **2** something small but valuable: *a nugget of useful knowledge > vb* **3** *NZ and S African* to polish footwear [origin unknown]

nuisance *n* **1** a person or thing that causes annoyance or bother *> adj* **2** causing annoyance or bother: *nuisance calls* [Old French *nuire* to injure]

NUJ (in Britain) National Union of Journalists

Nu Jiang *n* the Chinese name for the **Salween**

nuke *slang vb* **nuking, nuked 1** to attack with nuclear weapons *> n* **2** a nuclear bomb

Nuku'alofa *n* the capital of Tonga, a port on the N coast of Tongatapu Island. Pop: 36 000 (2005 est)

Nukus *n* a city in Uzbekistan, capital of the Kara-Kalpak Autonomous Republic, on the Amu Darya River. Pop: 325 000 (2005 est)

null *adj* **1 null and void** not legally valid **2 null set** *maths* a set with no members [Latin *nullus* none] **> nullity** *n*

nulla-nulla *n* a wooden club used by Australian Aborigines

Nullarbor Plain *n* a vast low plateau of S Australia: extends north from the Great Australian Bight to the Great Victoria Desert; has no surface water or trees. Area: 260 000 sq km (100 000 sq miles)

nullify *vb* **-fies, -fying, -fied 1** to make (something) ineffective **2** to make (something) legally void [Latin *nullus* of no account + *facere* to make] **> nullification** *n*

NUM (in Britain & S Africa) National Union of Mineworkers

Numantia *n* an ancient city in N Spain: a centre of Celtic resistance to Rome in N Spain; captured by Scipio the Younger in 133 BC

Numantian *adj* **1** of or relating to Numantia or its inhabitants *> n* **2** a native or inhabitant of Numantia

Numa Pompilius *n* the legendary second king of Rome (?715–?673 BC), said to have instituted religious rites

numb *adj* **1** deprived of feeling through cold, shock, or fear **2** unable to move; paralysed *> vb* **3** to make numb

n

[Middle English *nomen*, literally: taken (with paralysis)]
> **numbly** *adv* > **numbness** *n*

numbat *n* a small Australian marsupial with a long snout and tongue

number *n* **1** a concept of quantity that is or can be derived from a single unit, a sum of units, or zero **2** the word or symbol used to represent a number **3** a numeral or string of numerals used to identify a person or thing: *an account number* **4** the person or thing so identified: *he was seeded number two* **5** sum or quantity: *a very large number of people have telephoned* **6** one of a series, as of a magazine **7** a self-contained piece of pop or jazz music **8** a group of people: *one of their number might be willing* **9** *informal* an admired article: *that little number is by Dior* **10** *grammar* classification of words depending on how many people or things are referred to **11** any number of many **12** beyond *or* without number innumerable **13** have someone's number *informal* to have discovered someone's true character or intentions **14** one's number is up *Brit and Austral informal* one is about to die ▷ *vb* **15** to count **16** to assign a number to: *numbered seats* **17** to add up to: *the illustrations numbered well over fifty* **18** to include in a group: *he numbered several Americans among his friends* **19** one's days are numbered something unpleasant, such as death, is likely to happen to one soon [Latin *numerus*]

number crunching *n* computers the large-scale processing of numerical data

numberless *adj* too many to be counted

number one *n* **1** *informal* oneself: *he looks after number one* **2** *informal* the bestselling pop record in any one week ▷ *adj* **3** first in importance, urgency, or quality: *he's their number one suspect*

numberplate *n* a plate on a motor vehicle showing the registration number

Number Ten *n* 10 Downing Street, the British prime minister's official London residence

numbskull *or* **numskull** *n* a stupid person

numeral *n* a word or symbol used to express a sum or quantity [Latin *numerus* number]

numerate *adj* able to do basic arithmetic > **numeracy** *n*

numeration *n* **1** the act or process of numbering or counting **2** a system of numbering

numerator *n* maths the number above the line in a fraction

numerical *or* **numeric** *adj* measured or expressed in numbers: *record the severity of your symptoms in numerical form* > **numerically** *adv*

numerology *n* the study of numbers and of their supposed influence on human affairs

numerous *adj* **1** many: *they carried out numerous bombings* **2** consisting of a large number of people or things: *the cast is not as numerous as one might suppose*

Numidia *n* an ancient country of N Africa, corresponding roughly to present-day Algeria: flourished until its invasion by Vandals in 429; chief towns were Cirta and Hippo Regius

Numidian *adj* **1** of or relating to Numidia or its inhabitants ▷ *n* **2** a native or inhabitant of Numidia

numinous *adj formal* **1** arousing spiritual or religious emotions **2** mysterious or awe-inspiring [Latin *numen* divine will]

numismatics *n* the study or collection of coins or medals [Greek *nomisma* piece of currency] > **numismatist** *n*

numskull *n* same as **numbskull**

nun *n* a female member of a religious order [Late Latin *nonna*]

Nunavut *n* a territory of NW Canada, formed in 1999 from part of the Northwest Territories as a semi-autonomous region for the Inuit; includes Baffin Island and Ellesmere Island. Capital: Iqaluit. Pop: 31 906 (2011 est). Area: 2 093 190 sq km (808 185 sq miles)

nuncio *n, pl* **-cios** *RC Church* a papal ambassador [Latin *nuntius* messenger]

Nuneaton *n* a town in central England, in Warwickshire. Pop: 70 721 (2001)

Nunn *n* Sir Trevor (**Robert**). born 1940, British theatre director; artistic director (1968–86) and chief executive (1968–86) of the Royal Shakespeare Company; artistic director of the Royal National Theatre (1997–2003). His productions include *Nicholas Nickleby* (1980), *Cats* (1981), and *Les Misérables* (1985)

nunnery *n, pl* **-neries** a convent

nunny bag *n Canad* (in Newfoundland) a small sealskin knapsack [probably from Scots dialect *noony* lunch]

nuptial *adj* relating to marriage: *a nuptial blessing* [Latin *nuptiae* marriage]

nuptials *pl n* a wedding

nurd *n slang* same as **nerd**

Nuremberg *n* a city in S Germany, in N Bavaria: scene of annual Nazi rallies (1933–38), the anti-Semitic Nuremberg decrees (1935), and the trials of Nazi leaders for their war crimes (1945–46); important metalworking and electrical industries. Pop: 493 553 (2003 est). German name: **Nürnberg**

Nureyev *n* Rudolf. 1938–93, Austrian ballet dancer, born in the Soviet Union: he lived in England (1961–83) and France (1983–89). He became an Austrian citizen in 1982

Nurhachi *n* 1559–1626, Manchurian leader, who unified the Manchurian state and began (1618) the Manchurian conquest of China

Nuri as-Said *n* 1888–1958, Iraqi soldier and statesman: prime minister of Iraq 14 times between 1930 and 1958: he died during a military coup

Nuristan *n* a region of E Afghanistan: consists mainly of high mountains (including part of the Hindu Kush), steep narrow valleys, and forests. Area: about 13 000 sq km (5000 sq miles). Former name: **Kafiristan**

Nurmi *n* Paavo, known as *The Flying Finn*. 1897–1973, Finnish runner, winner of the 1500, 5000, and 10 000 metres' races at the 1924 Olympic Games in Paris

Nürnberg *n* the German name for **Nuremberg**

nurse *n* **1** a person trained to look after sick people, usually in a hospital **2** short for nursemaid ▷ *vb* **nursing, nursed** **3** to look after (a sick person) **4** to breast-feed (a baby) **5** (of a baby) to feed at its mother's breast **6** to try to cure (an ailment) **7** to harbour or foster (a feeling) **8** to clasp fondly: *she nursed her drink* [Latin *nutrire* to nourish] > **nursing** *n, adj*

Nurse *n* Sir Paul (**Maxime**). born 1949, English cell biologist and geneticist; winner (2001), with LH Hartwell and RT Hunt, of the Nobel Prize for Physiology or Medicine

nursemaid *or* **nurserymaid** *n* a woman employed to look after children

nursery *n, pl* **-ries** **1** a room in a house where children sleep or play **2** a place where children are taken care of when their parents are at work **3** a place where plants and young trees are grown for sale

nurseryman *n, pl* **-men** a person who raises plants and trees for sale

nursery nurse *n* a person trained to look after children of pre-school age

nursery rhyme *n* a short traditional verse or song for children

nursery school *n* a school for young children from three to five years old

nursery slopes *pl n* gentle slopes used by beginners in skiing

nursery stakes *pl n* a race for two-year-old horses

nursing home *n* a private hospital or home for people who are old or ill

nursing officer *n* (in Britain) the administrative head of the nursing staff of a hospital

nurture *n* **1** the act or process of promoting the development of a child or young plant ▷ *vb* **-turing, -tured 2** to promote or encourage the development of [Latin *nutrire* to nourish]

Nusa Tenggara *n* an island chain east of Java, mostly in Indonesia: the main islands are Bali, Lombok, Sumbawa, Sumba, Flores, Alor, and Timor. Pop: 11 112 702 (2000). Area: 73 144 sq km (28 241 sq miles). English name: **Lesser Sunda Islands**

nut *n* **1** a dry one-seeded fruit that grows inside a hard shell **2** the edible inner part of such a fruit **3** a small piece of metal with a hole in it, that screws on to a bolt **4** *slang* an eccentric or insane person **5** *slang* the head **6** *slang* an enthusiast: *a health nut* **7** *Brit* a small piece of coal **8** a hard *or* tough nut to crack a person or thing that presents difficulties **9** do one's nut *Brit and Austral slang* to be very angry ▷ See also **nuts** [Old English *hnutu*]

NUT (in Britain & S Africa) National Union of Teachers

nutcase *n slang* an insane person

nutcracker *n* a device for cracking the shells of nuts. Also: **nutcrackers**

nuthatch *n* a songbird that feeds on insects, seeds, and nuts [Middle English *notehache* nut hatchet, from its habit of splitting nuts]

nutmeg *n* a spice made from the seed of a tropical tree [Old French *nois muguede* musk-scented nut]

nutraceutical *n* See **functional food**

nutria (new-tree-a) *n* the fur of the coypu [Latin *lutra* otter]

nutrient (new-tree-ent) *n* **1** a substance that provides nourishment: *their only source of nutrient* ▷ *adj* **2** providing nourishment [Latin *nutrire* to nourish]

nutriment (new-tree-ment) *n* the food or nourishment required by all living things to grow and stay healthy [Latin *nutrimentum*]

nutrition (new-trish-un) *n* **1** the process of taking in and absorbing nutrients **2** the process of being nourished **3** the study of nutrition [Latin *nutrire* to nourish] ▷ **nutritional** *adj* ▷ **nutritionist** *n*

nutritious *adj* providing nourishment [Latin *nutrix* nurse]

nutritive *adj* of nutrition; nutritious

nuts *adj slang* **1** insane **2** nuts about very fond of or enthusiastic about

nuts and bolts *pl n informal* the essential or practical details: *the nuts and bolts of photography*

nutshell *n* in a nutshell in essence; briefly

nutter *n Brit and NZ slang* an insane person

nutty *adj* **-tier, -tiest** **1** containing or resembling nuts **2** *slang* insane or eccentric ▷ **nuttiness** *n*

Nuuk *n* the capital of Greenland, in the southwest: the oldest Danish settlement in Greenland, founded in 1721. Pop: 14 350 (2004 est). Danish name (official name until 1979): **Godthaab**

nux vomica *n* the seed of a tree, containing strychnine [Medieval Latin: vomiting nut]

nuzzle *vb* **-zling, -zled** to push or rub gently with the nose or snout [from *nose*]

NV Nevada

nvCJD new-variant Creutzfeldt-Jakob disease

NW northwest(ern)

NWT Northwest Territories (of Canada)

NY *or* **N.Y.** New York

Nyasa *or* **Nyassa** *n* Lake Nyasa a lake in central Africa at the S end of the Great Rift Valley: the third largest lake in Africa, drained by the Shire River into the Zambezi. Area: about 28 500 sq km (11 000 sq miles). Malawi name: **(Lake) Malawi**

Nyasaland *n* the former name (until 1964) of **Malawi**

NYC New York City

Nyeman *n* a variant spelling of **Neman**

Nyerere *n* Julius Kambarage. 1922–99, Tanzanian statesman; president (1964–85). He became prime minister of Tanganyika in 1961 and president in 1962, negotiating the union of Tanganyika and Zanzibar to form Tanzania (1964)

Nyíregyháza *n* a market town in NE Hungary. Pop: 116 899 (2003 est)

Nykøbing *n* a port in Denmark, on the W coast of Falster Island. Pop: 16 784 (2004 est)

nylon *n* a synthetic material used for clothing and many other products [originally a trademark]

nylons *pl n* stockings made of nylon

Nyman *n* Michael. born 1944, British composer; works include the opera *The Man Who Mistook His Wife For a Hat* (1986) and scores for films, including *The Piano* (1992) and several films by Peter Greenaway

nymph *n* **1** *myth* a spirit of nature, represented as a beautiful young woman **2** the larva of certain insects, resembling the adult form **3** *chiefly poetic* a beautiful young woman [Greek *numphē*]

nymphet *n* a girl who is sexually precocious and desirable

nympho *n*, *pl* **-phos** *informal* short for **nymphomaniac**

nymphomaniac *n* a woman with an abnormally intense sexual desire [Greek *numphē* nymph + *mania* madness] ▷ **nymphomania** *n*

Nysa *n* the Polish name for the **Neisse** (1)

NZ *or* **N.Z.** New Zealand

NZE New Zealand English

NZRFU New Zealand Rugby Football Union

NZSE40 Index New Zealand Stock Exchange 40 Index

O¹ 1 *chem* oxygen **2** Old **3** same as **nought**

O² ** *interj* same as **oh

o. *or* **O.** old

o' *prep informal or old-fashioned* of: *a cup o' tea*

OA Order of Australia

oaf *n* a stupid or clumsy person [variant of Old English *ælf* elf] **> oafish** *adj*

Oahu *n* an island in central Hawaii: the third largest of the Hawaiian Islands. Chief town: Honolulu. Pop: 876 151 (2000). Area: 1574 sq km (608 sq miles)

oak *n* **1** a large forest tree with hard wood, acorns as fruits, and leaves with rounded projections **2** the wood of this tree, used as building timber and for making furniture [Old English *āc*] **> oaken** *adj*

oak apple *or* **oak gall** *n* a brownish round lump or ball produced on oak trees by certain wasps

Oakham *n* a market town in E central England, the administrative centre of Rutland. Pop: 9620 (2001)

Oakland *n* a port and industrial centre in W California, on San Francisco Bay; damaged by earthquake in 1989. Pop: 398 844 (2003 est)

Oakley *n* Annie, real name *Phoebe Anne Oakley Mozee*. 1860–1926, US markswoman

Oaks *n* the Oaks an annual horse race for three-year-old fillies, run at Epsom [named after an estate near Epsom]

oakum *n* loose fibre obtained by unravelling old rope, used for filling cracks in wooden ships [Old English *ācumba*, literally: off-combings]

Oakville *n* a city in SE Canada, in SE Ontario on Lake Ontario southwest of Toronto: motor-vehicle industry. Pop: 144 738 (2001)

OAM Medal of the Order of Australia

OAP (in Britain) old age pensioner

oar *n* **1** a long pole with a broad blade, used for rowing a boat **2** put *or* stick one's oar in to interfere or interrupt [Old English *ār*]

oarsman *or fem* **oarswoman** *n, pl* **-men** *or* **-women** a person who rows **> oarsmanship** *n*

oasis *n, pl* **-ses 1** a fertile patch in a desert **2** a place or situation offering relief in the midst of difficulty [Greek]

oast *n chiefly Brit* an oven for drying hops [Old English *āst*]

oast house *n chiefly Brit* a building containing ovens for drying hops

Oastler *n* Richard. 1789–1861, British social reformer; he campaigned against child labour and helped achieve the ten-hour day (1847)

oat *n* **1** a hard cereal grown as food **2** oats the edible grain of this cereal **3** sow one's wild oats to have casual sexual relationships while young [Old English *āte*] **> oaten** *adj*

oatcake *n* a thin unsweetened biscuit made of oatmeal

Oates *n* **1** Captain Lawrence Edward Grace. 1880–1912, English explorer. He died on Scott's second Antarctic expedition **2** Titus.. 1649–1705, English conspirator. He fabricated the Popish Plot (1678), a supposed Catholic conspiracy to kill Charles II, burn London, and massacre Protestants. His perjury caused the execution of many innocent Catholics

oath *n, pl* **oaths 1** a solemn promise, esp. to tell the truth in a court of law **2** an offensive or blasphemous expression; a swearword **3** on *or* under oath having made a solemn promise to tell the truth, esp. in a court of law [Old English *āth*]

oatmeal *n* **1** a coarse flour made by grinding oats ▷ *adj* **2** greyish-yellow

Oaxaca *n* **1** a state of S Mexico, on the Pacific: includes most of the Isthmus of Tehuantepec; inhabited chiefly by Indians. Capital: Oaxaca de Juárez. Pop: 3 432 180 (2000). Area: 95 363 sq km (36 820 sq miles) **2** a city in S Mexico, capital of Oaxaca state: founded in 1486 by the Aztecs and conquered by Spain in 1521. Pop: 483 000 (2005 est). Official name: **Oaxaca de Juárez**

Ob *n* a river in N central Russia, formed at Bisk by the confluence of the Biya and Katun Rivers and flowing generally north to the **Gulf of Ob** (an inlet of the Arctic Ocean): one of the largest rivers in the world, with a drainage basin of about 2 930 000 sq km (1 131 000 sq miles). Length: 3682 km (2287 miles)

ob. (on tombstones) he *or* she died [Latin *obiit*]

Obama *n* Barack (Hussein). born 1961, US Democrat politician: 44th president of the US from 2009

Oban *n* a small port and resort in W Scotland, in Argyll and Bute on the Firth of Lorne. Pop: 8120 (2001)

Obasanjo *n* Olusegun. born 1937, Nigerian politician and general; head of the military government (1976–79); president (1999–2007)

obbligato (ob-lig-**gah**-toe) *music adj* **1** not to be omitted in performance ▷ *n, pl* **-tos 2** an essential part or accompaniment: *an aria with bassoon obbligato* [Italian]

obdurate *adj* not to be persuaded; hardhearted or obstinate [Latin *obdurare* to make hard] **> obduracy** *n*

OBE (in Britain) Officer of the Order of the British Empire

obedient *adj* obeying or willing to obey [Latin *oboediens*] **> obedience** *n* **> obediently** *adv*

obeisance (oh-**bay**-sanss) *n formal* **1** an attitude of respect or humble obedience **2** a bow or curtsy showing this attitude [Old French *obéissant* obeying] **> obeisant** *adj*

obelisk (**ob**-bill-isk) *n* **1** a four-sided stone pillar that tapers to a pyramid at the top **2** *printing* same as **dagger** (2) [Greek *obeliskos* a little spit]

Oberammergau *n* a village in S Germany, in Bavaria in the foothills of the Alps: famous for its Passion Play, performed by the villagers every ten years (except during the World Wars) since 1634, in thanksgiving for the end of the Black Death. Pop: 5363 (2003 est)

Oberhausen *n* an industrial city in W Germany, in North Rhine-Westphalia on the Rhine-Herne Canal: site of the first ironworks in the Ruhr. Pop: 220 033 (2003 est)

Oberland *n* the lower parts of the Bernese Alps in central Switzerland, mostly in S Bern canton

Oberösterreich *n* the German name for **Upper Austria**

obese (oh-beess) *adj* very fat [Latin *obesus*] **> obesity** *n*

obey *vb* **1** to carry out instructions or orders; be obedient **2** to act in accordance with one's feelings, an impulse, etc.: *I had obeyed the impulse to open the gate and had walked up the drive* [Latin *oboedire*]

obfuscate *vb* **-cating, -cated** *formal* to make something unnecessarily difficult to understand [Latin *ob-* (intensive) + *fuscare* to blacken] **> obfuscation** *n* **> obfuscatory** *adj*

obituary *n, pl* **-aries** a published announcement of a death, usually with a short biography of the dead person [Latin *obitus* death] **> obituarist** *n*

obj. **1** objection **2** *grammar* object(ive)

object¹ *n* **1** a thing that can be touched or seen **2** a person or thing seen as a focus for feelings, actions, or thought: *she had become for him an object of compassion* **3** an aim or purpose: *the main object of the exercise* **4** *philosophy* that which can be perceived by the mind, as contrasted with the thinking subject **5** *grammar* a noun, pronoun, or noun phrase that receives the action of a verb or is governed by a preposition, such as *the bottle* in *she threw the bottle* **6** **no object** not a hindrance or obstacle: *money's no object* [Late Latin *objectus* something thrown before (the mind)]

object² *vb* **1** to express disapproval or opposition: *my colleagues objected strongly to further delays* **2** to state as one's reason for opposing: *he objected that his small staff would be unable to handle the added work* [Latin *ob-* against + *jacere* to throw] **> objector** *n*

objection *n* **1** an expression or feeling of opposition or disapproval **2** a reason for opposing something: *the planning officer had raised no objection to the proposals*

objectionable *adj* offensive or unacceptable

objective *n* **1** an aim or purpose: *the objective is to highlight the environmental threat to the planet* **2** *grammar* a grammatical case in some languages that identifies the direct object of a verb or preposition **3** *optics* the lens nearest to the object observed in an optical instrument ▷ *adj* **4** not distorted by personal feelings or bias: *I have tried to be as objective as possible in my presentation* **5** of or relating to actual facts as opposed to thoughts or feelings: *stand back and try to take a more objective view of your life as a whole* **6** existing independently of the mind; real **> objectival** *adj* **> objectively** *adv* **> objectivity** *n*

object lesson *n* a practical demonstration of some principle or ideal

objet d'art (ob-zhay dahr) *n, pl* **objets d'art** (ob-zhay dahr) a small object considered to be of artistic worth [French: object of art]

oblate *adj geometry* (of a sphere) flattened at the poles: *the oblate spheroid of the earth* [New Latin *oblatus* lengthened]

oblation *n* **1** *Christianity* the offering of bread and wine to God at Communion **2** any offering made for religious purposes [Medieval Latin *oblatus* offered] **> oblational** *adj*

obligated *adj* being morally or legally bound to do something: *they are obligated to provide temporary accommodation* **> obligative** *adj*

obligation *n* **1** a moral or legal duty **2** the binding power of such a duty: *I feel under some obligation to help you with your education* **3** a sense of being in debt because of a service or favour: *I don't want him marrying me out of obligation*

obligatory *adj* required or compulsory because of custom or law

oblige *vb* **obliging, obliged 1** to compel someone by legal, moral, or physical means to do something **2** to make (someone) indebted or grateful for a favour: *I am obliged to you for your help* **3** to do a favour to someone: *she obliged the guests with a song* [Latin *ob-* towards + *ligare* to bind]

obliging *adj* willing to be helpful **> obligingly** *adv*

oblique (oh-bleak) *adj* **1** at an angle; slanting **2** *geometry* (of lines or planes) neither perpendicular nor parallel to one another **3** indirect or evasive: *only oblique references have been made to the anti-government unrest* ▷ *n* **4** same as **solidus** [Latin *obliquus*] **> obliquely** *adv* **> obliqueness** *n*

oblique angle *n* an angle that is not a right angle or any multiple of a right angle

obliterate *vb* **-rating, -rated** to destroy every trace of; wipe out completely [Latin *oblitterare* to erase] **> obliteration** *n*

oblivion *n* **1** the condition of being forgotten or disregarded: *the Marxist-Leninist wing of the party looks set to sink into oblivion* **2** the state of being unaware or unconscious: *guests seemed to feel a social obligation to drink themselves into oblivion* [Latin *oblivio* forgetfulness]

oblivious *adj* unaware or unconscious: *oblivious of her soaking clothes; I was oblivious to the beauty* **> obliviousness** *n*

oblong *adj* **1** having an elongated, rectangular shape ▷ *n* **2** a figure or object having this shape [Latin *oblongus*]

obloquy (ob-lock-wee) *n, pl* **-quies** *formal* **1** abusive statements or blame: *the British press was held up to moral obloquy* **2** disgrace brought about by this: *the punishment of lifelong public obloquy and private embarrassment* [Latin *obloquium* contradiction]

obnoxious *adj* extremely unpleasant [Latin *obnoxius*] **> obnoxiousness** *n*

oboe *n* a double-reeded woodwind instrument with a penetrating nasal tone [French *haut bois*, literally: high wood (referring to its pitch)] **> oboist** *n*

Obote *n* (Apollo) Milton. 1924–2005, Ugandan politician; prime minister of Uganda (1962–66) and president (1966–71; 1980–85). He was deposed by Amin in 1971 and remained in exile until 1980; deposed again in 1985 by the Acholi army

O'Brien *n* **1** Conor Cruise. 1917–2008, Irish diplomat and writer. As an Irish Labour MP he served in the coalition government of 1973–77, becoming a senator (1977–79). He edited the *Observer* (1978–81) **2** Edna. born 1936, Irish novelist. Her books include *The Country Girls* (1960), *Johnny I Hardly Knew You* (1977), and *In the Forest* (2002) **3** Flann, real name Brian O'Nolan. 1911–66, Irish novelist and journalist. His novels include *At Swim-Two-Birds* (1939) and the posthumously published *The Third Policeman* (1967). As Myles na Gopaleen he wrote a satirical column for the *Irish Times* **4** Kerry. born 1945. Australian journalist and broadcaster

obs. obsolete

obscene *adj* **1** offensive to accepted standards of decency or modesty **2** *law* tending to deprave or corrupt: *an obscene publication* **3** disgusting: *a great dark obscene pool of blood* [Latin *obscenus* inauspicious] **> obscenity** *n*

obscure *adj* **1** not well-known: *the concerts feature several obscure artists* **2** not easily understood: *the contracts are written in obscure language* **3** unclear or indistinct ▷ *vb* **-scuring, -scured 4** to make unclear or vague; hide: *no amount of bluster could obscure the fact that the prime minister had run out of excuses* **5** to cover or cloud over [Latin *obscurus* dark] **> obscuration** *n* **> obscurity** *n*

obsequies (ob-sick-weez) *pl n, sing* **-quy** *formal* funeral rites [Medieval Latin *obsequiae*]

obsequious (ob-seek-wee-uss) *adj* being overattentive in order to gain favour [Latin *obsequiosus* compliant] **> obsequiousness** *n*

observance *n* **1** the observing of a law or custom **2** a ritual, ceremony, or practice, esp. of a religion

observant *adj* quick to notice details around one; sharp-eyed

observation *n* **1** the act of watching or the state of being watched **2** a comment or remark **3** detailed examination of something before analysis, diagnosis, or interpretation: *you may be admitted to hospital for observation and rest* **4** the facts learned from observing **5** the ability to notice things: *she has good powers of observation* **> observational** *adj*

observatory *n, pl* **-ries** a building specially designed and equipped for studying the weather and the stars

observe *vb* **-serving, -served** **1** to see or notice: *after some hours I observed a change in the animal's behaviour* **2** to watch (something) carefully **3** to make scientific examinations of **4** to remark: *the speaker observed that times had changed* **5** to keep (a law or custom) [Latin *observare*] **> observable** *adj* **> observer** *n*

obsessed *adj* thinking about someone or something all the time: *he had become obsessed with her* [Latin *obsessus* besieged] **> obsessive** *adj, n*

obsession *n* **1** something that preoccupies a person to the exclusion of other things: *his principal obsession was with trying to economize* **2** *psychiatry* a persistent idea or impulse, often associated with anxiety and mental illness **> obsessional** *adj*

obsidian *n* a dark glassy volcanic rock [after *Obsius*, the discoverer of a stone resembling obsidian]

obsolescent *adj* becoming obsolete or out of date **> obsolescence** *n*

obsolete *adj* no longer used; out of date [Latin *obsoletus* worn out]

> **USAGE** The word *obsoleteness* is hardly ever used, *obsolescence* standing as the noun form for both *obsolete* and *obsolescent*.

obstacle *n* **1** a situation or event that prevents something being done: *there are obstacles which could slow the development of a vaccine* **2** a person or thing that hinders movement [Latin *obstaculum*, from *ob-* against + *stare* to stand]

obstetrician *n* a doctor who specializes in obstetrics

obstetrics *n* the branch of medicine concerned with pregnancy and childbirth [Latin *obstetrix* a midwife] **> obstetric** *adj*

obstinate *adj* **1** keeping stubbornly to a particular opinion or course of action **2** difficult to treat or deal with: *obstinate weeds* [Latin *obstinatus*] **> obstinacy** *n* **> obstinately** *adv*

obstreperous *adj* noisy and difficult to control: *her obstreperous teenage son* [Latin *ob-* against + *strepere* to roar]

obstruct *vb* **1** to block a way with an obstacle **2** to make progress or activity difficult: *this government will never obstruct the course of justice* **3** to block a clear view of [Latin *obstructus* built against]

obstruction *n* **1** a person or thing that obstructs **2** the act of obstructing or being obstructed **3** *sport* the act of unfairly impeding an opposing player

obstructionist *n* a person who deliberately obstructs legal or parliamentary business **> obstructionism** *n*

obstructive *adj* deliberately causing difficulties or delays **> obstructively** *adv* **> obstructiveness** *n*

obtain *vb* **1** to gain possession of; get **2** *formal* to be customary or accepted: *silence obtains from eight in the evening* [Latin *obtinere* to take hold of] **> obtainable** *adj*

obtrude *vb* **-truding, -truded** **1** to push oneself or one's opinions on others in an unwelcome way **2** to be or make unpleasantly noticeable [Latin *obtrudere*] **> obtrusion** *n*

obtrusive *adj* unpleasantly noticeable: *the music should fit your mood, it shouldn't be too obtrusive* **> obtrusiveness** *n*

obtuse *adj* **1** mentally slow or emotionally insensitive **2** *maths* (of an angle) between 90° and 180° **3** not sharp or pointed; blunt [Latin *obtusus* dulled] **> obtuseness** *n*

obverse *n* **1** a counterpart or opposite: *his true personality being the obverse of his outer image* **2** the side of a coin that bears the main design **3** the front, top, or main surface of anything [Latin *obversus* turned towards]

obviate *vb* **-ating, -ated** *formal* to avoid or prevent (a need or difficulty): *a mediator will obviate the need for independent legal advice* [Latin *obviare*]

> **USAGE** Only things which have not yet occurred can be *obviated*. For example, one can *obviate* a possible future difficulty, but not one which already exists.

obvious *adj* **1** easy to see or understand ▷ *n* **2** **state the obvious** to say something that is unnecessary or already known: *he is prone to stating the obvious* [Latin *obvius*] **> obviously** *adv* **> obviousness** *n*

ocarina *n* a small egg-shaped wind instrument with a mouthpiece and finger holes [Italian: little goose]

O'Casey *n* Sean. 1880–1964, Irish dramatist. His plays include *Juno and the Paycock* (1924) and *The Plough and the Stars* (1926), which are realistic pictures of Dublin slum life

occasion *n* **1** a particular event or the time at which it happens **2** a need or reason to do or be something: *we barely knew him and never had occasion to speak of him* **3** a suitable time or opportunity to do something **4** a special event, time, or celebration: *a wedding day is a truly special occasion* **5** **on occasion** every so often **6** **rise to the occasion** to meet the special demands of a situation ▷ *vb* **7** *formal* to cause, esp. incidentally [Latin *occasio* a falling down]

occasional *adj* happening from time to time; not frequent or regular **> occasionally** *adv*

occasional table *n* a small table with no regular use

Occident *n* the western hemisphere, esp. Europe and America [Latin *occidere* to fall (with reference to the setting sun)] **> Occidental** *adj*

occiput (ox-sip-putt) *n* *anatomy* the back of the head or skull [Latin *ob-* at the back of + *caput* head] **> occipital** *adj*

occlude *vb* **-cluding, -cluded** *formal* **1** to block or stop up a passage or opening: *the arteries are occluded by deposits of plaque* **2** to shut in or out: *slowly occluding him from Nash's vision* **3** *chem* (of a solid) to absorb and retain a gas or other substance [Latin *occludere*] **> occlusion** *n*

occluded front *n* *meteorol* the front formed when the cold front of a depression overtakes a warm front, raising the warm air from ground level

occult *adj* **1** involving mystical or supernatural phenomena or powers **2** beyond ordinary human understanding **3** secret or mysterious ▷ *n* **4** **the occult** the knowledge and study of occult phenomena and powers [Latin *occultus* hidden, secret]

occupancy *n, pl* **-cies** **1** the act of occupying a property **2** the period of time during which one is an occupant of a property

occupant *n* a person occupying a property, position, or place

occupation *n* **1** a person's job or profession **2** any activity on which someone's time is spent: *a pleasant and rewarding occupation* **3** the control of a country by a foreign military power **4** the act of occupying or the state of being occupied: *the occupation of Kuwait* **> occupational** *adj*

occupational hazard *n* something unpleasant that occurs due to your job: *frequent colds are an occupational hazard in teaching*

occupational therapy *n* treatment of people with physical, emotional, or social problems using purposeful activity to help them overcome or learn to accept their problems

occupier *n* *Brit* the person who lives in a particular house, whether as owner or tenant

occupy *vb* **-pies, -pying, -pied** **1** to live, stay, or work in (a house, flat, or office) **2** to keep (someone or someone's mind) busy **3** to take up (time or space) **4** to move in and take control of (a country or other place): *soldiers have occupied the country's television station* **5** to fill or hold (a position or office) [Latin *occupare* to seize hold of]

occur *vb* **-curring, -curred** **1** to happen **2** to be found or be present; exist **3** **occur to** to come into the mind of [Latin *occurrere* to run up to]

> **USAGE** It is usually regarded as incorrect to talk of pre-arranged events *occurring* or *happening*: *the wedding took place* (not *occurred* or *happened*) *in the afternoon*.

occurrence *n* **1** something that happens **2** the fact of occurring: *the likelihood of its occurrence increases with age*

ocean *n* **1** the vast area of salt water covering about 70 per cent of the earth's surface **2** one of the five principal divisions of this: the Atlantic, Pacific, Indian, Arctic, and Antarctic **3** *informal* a huge quantity or expanse: *oceans of replies* **4** *literary* the sea [from *Oceanus*, Greek god of the stream believed to flow round the earth] **> oceanic** *adj*

ocean-going *adj* (of a ship or boat) suited for travel on the open ocean

Oceania *n* the islands of the central and S Pacific, including Melanesia, Micronesia, and Polynesia: sometimes also including Australasia and the Malay Archipelago

Oceanian *adj* **1** of or relating to Oceania or its inhabitants ▷ *n* **2** a native or inhabitant of Oceania

Oceanic *n* **1 a** branch, group, or subfamily of the Malayo-Polynesian family of languages, comprising Polynesian and Melanesian ▷ *adj* **2** of, relating to, or belonging to this group of languages **3** of or relating to Oceania

oceanography *n* the study of oceans and their environment **> oceanographer** *n* **> oceanographic** *adj*

ocelot (oss-ill-lot) *n* a large cat of Central and South America with a dark-spotted yellow-grey coat [Mexican Indian *ocelotl* jaguar]

och *interj Scot and Irish* an expression of surprise, annoyance, or disagreement

oche (ok-kee) *n darts* a mark on the floor behind which a player must stand when throwing a dart [origin unknown]

ochre *or US* **ocher** (oak-er) *n* **1** a yellow or reddish-brown earth used in paints or dyes ▷ *adj* **2** moderate yellow-orange to orange [Greek *ōkhros* pale yellow]

Ockeghem *or* **Okeghem** *n* Johannes, Jean d', *or* Jan van. ?1430–?95, Flemish composer. Also: **Ockenheim**

Ockham *or* **Occam** *n* William of. died ?1349, English nominalist philosopher, who contested the temporal power of the papacy and ended the conflict between nominalism and realism

o'clock *adv* used after a number between one and twelve to specify an hour: *five o'clock in the morning*

O'Connell *n* Daniel. 1775–1847, Irish nationalist leader and orator, whose election to the British House of Commons (1828) forced the acceptance of Catholic emancipation (1829)

O'Connor *n* **1** Feargus. 1794–1855, Irish politician and journalist, a leader of the Chartist movement **2** (**Mary**) **Flannery.** 1925–64, US novelist and short-story writer, author of *Wise Blood* (1952) and *The Violent Bear it Away* (1960) **3** Frank, real name *Michael O'Donovan.* 1903–66, Irish short-story writer and critic **4** Thomas Power, known as *Tay Pay.* 1848–1929, Irish journalist and nationalist leader

OCR optical character recognition: the ability (through a computer device) for letters and numbers to be optically scanned and input to a storage device

Oct. October

octagon *n* a geometric figure with eight sides [Greek *oktagōnos* having eight angles] **> octagonal** *adj*

octahedron (ok-ta-heed-ron) *n*, *pl* **-drons** *or* **-dra** a solid figure with eight plane faces

octane *n* a liquid hydrocarbon found in petroleum

octane number *or* **octane rating** *n* a number indicating the quality of a petrol

octave *n* **1 a** the musical interval between the first note and the eighth note of a major or minor scale **b** the higher of these two notes **c** the series of notes filling this interval **2** *prosody* a rhythmic group of eight lines of verse [Latin *octo* eight]

Octavia *n* died 11 BC, wife of Mark Antony; sister of Augustus

octavo *n*, *pl* **-vos 1** a book size resulting from folding a sheet of paper of a standard size to form eight leaves **2** a book or sheet of this size [New Latin *in octavo* in an eighth (of a sheet)]

octet *n* **1** a group of eight instrumentalists or singers **2** a piece of music for eight performers [Latin *octo* eight]

October *n* the tenth month of the year [Latin *octo* eight, since it was originally the eighth month in Roman reckoning]

octogenarian *n* **1** a person between 80 and 89 years old ▷ *adj* **2** between 80 and 89 years old [Latin *octogenarius* containing eighty]

octopus *n*, *pl* **-puses** a sea creature with a soft oval body and eight long tentacles with suckers [Greek *oktōpous* having eight feet]

ocular *adj* of or relating to the eyes or sight [Latin *oculus* eye]

oculist *n old-fashioned* an ophthalmologist

OD *informal n* **1** an overdose of a drug ▷ *vb* **OD'ing, OD'd 2** to take an overdose of a drug

odalisque (ode-a-lisk) *n* a female slave in a harem [Turkish *ōdalik*]

Oda Nobunaga *n* 1534–82, Japanese general and feudal leader, who unified much of Japan under his control: assassinated

odd *adj* **1** unusual or peculiar: *his increasingly odd behaviour* **2** occasional or incidental: *the odd letter from a friend abroad* **3** leftover or additional: *we use up odd pieces of fabric to make up jerseys in wild designs* **4** (of a number) not divisible by two **5** being part of a pair or set when the other or others are missing: *the drawer was full of odd socks* **6** somewhat more than the round number specified: *I had known him for the past twenty-odd years* **7 odd man** *or* **one out** a person or thing excluded from others forming a group or unit ► See also **odds** [Old Norse *oddi* angle, point, third or odd number] **> oddly** *adv* **> oddness** *n*

oddball *n informal* a strange or eccentric person

oddity *n*, *pl* **-ties 1** an odd person or thing **2** a peculiar characteristic **3** the quality of being or appearing unusual or strange

odd-man rush *n ice hockey* an attacking move when the defence is outnumbered by the opposing team

oddments *pl n* odd pieces or things; leftovers: *oddments of wool*

odds *pl n* **1** the probability, expressed as a ratio, that something will or will not happen: *the odds against an acquittal had stabilized at six to four* **2** the difference, expressed as a ratio, between the money placed on a bet and the amount that would be received as winning payment: *the current odds are ten to one* **3** the likelihood that a certain state of affairs will be so: *the odds are that you are going to fail* **4** the advantage that one contender is judged to have over another: *the odds are in his favour* **5 at odds a** on bad terms **b** at variance **6 it makes no odds** *Brit and Austral* it does not matter **7 over the odds** more than is expected or necessary

odds and ends *pl n* small, usually unimportant, objects, jobs to be done, etc.: *I have brought a few odds and ends with me*

odds-on *adj* having a better than even chance of winning

ode *n* a lyric poem, usually addressed to a particular subject, with lines of varying lengths and metres [Greek *ōidē* song]

Odense *n* a port in S Denmark, on Funen Island: cathedral founded by King Canute in the 11th century. Pop: 145 554 (2004 est)

Oder *n* a river in central Europe, rising in the NE Czech Republic and flowing north and west, forming part of the border between Germany and Poland, to the Baltic. Length: 913 km (567 miles). Czech and Polish name: **Odra**

Oder-Neisse Line *n* the present-day boundary between Germany and Poland along the Rivers Oder and Neisse. Established in 1945, it originally separated the Soviet Zone of Germany from the regions under Polish administration

o

Odessa *n* a port in S Ukraine on the Black Sea: the chief Russian grain port in the 19th century; university (1865); industrial centre and important naval base. Pop: 1 010 000 (2005 est)

Odets *n* Clifford. 1906–63, US dramatist; founder member of the Group Theatre. His plays include *Waiting for Lefty* (1935) and *Golden Boy* (1937)

Odin *n* the chief god in Norse mythology

odious *adj* offensive or hateful: *I steeled myself for the odious task* [see ODIUM] **> odiousness** *n*

Odisha *n* a state of E India, on the Bay of Bengal: part of the province of Bihar and Orissa (1912–36); enlarged by the addition of 25 native states in 1949. Capital: Bhubaneswar. Pop: 36 706 920 (2001). Area: 155 707 sq km (60 119 sq miles). Former name (until 2011): **Orissa**

odium (oh-dee-um) *n formal* widespread dislike or disapproval of a person or action [Latin]

Odoacer *or* **Odovacar** *n* ?434–493 AD, barbarian ruler of Italy (476–493); assassinated by Theodoric

odometer (odd-om-it-er) *n US and Canad* same as **mileometer** [Greek *hodos* way + -METER]

odoriferous *adj formal* having or giving off a pleasant smell

odour *or US* **odor** *n* a particular and distinctive scent or smell [Latin *odor*] **> odorous** *adj* **> odourless** *adj*

Odra *n* the Czech and Polish name for the **Oder**

odyssey (odd-iss-ee) *n* a long eventful journey

OE *NZ informal* overseas experience: *he's away on his OE*

Oë *n* Kenzaburo, born 1935, Japanese novelist and writer; his books include *The Catch* (1958), *A Personal Matter* (1964), and *Silent Cry* (1989): Nobel prize for literature 1994

OECD Organization for Economic Cooperation and Development

oedema *or US* **edema** (id-deem-a) *n, pl* -**mata** *pathol* an abnormal accumulation of fluid in the tissues of the body, causing swelling [Greek *oidēma* swelling]

Oedipus complex (ee-dip-puss) *n psychoanalysis* the usually unconscious sexual desire of a child, esp. a male child, for the parent of the opposite sex **> oedipal** *adj*

Oehlenschläger *or* **Öhlenschläger** *n* Adam Gottlob. 1779–1850, Danish romantic poet and dramatist

o'er *prep, adv poetic* over

oesophagus (ee-soff-a-guss) *or US* **esophagus** *n, pl* -**gi** (-guy) the tube through which food travels from the throat to the stomach; gullet [Greek *oisophagos*] **> oesophageal** *or US* **esophageal** *adj*

oestrogen (ee-stra-jen) *or US* **estrogen** *n* a female sex hormone that controls the reproductive cycle, and prepares the body for pregnancy [from *oestrus* + -*gen* (suffix) producing]

oestrus (ee-struss) *or US* **estrus** *n* a regularly occurring period of fertility and sexual receptivity in the reproductive cycle of most female mammals, except humans; heat [Greek *oistros* gadfly, hence frenzy]

of *prep* **1** belonging to; situated in or coming from; because of: *the inhabitants of former East Germany*; *I saw five people die of chronic hepatitis* **2** used after words or phrases expressing quantities: *a pint of milk* **3** specifying an amount or value: *we had to release the bombs at a height of 400 metres* **4** made up of, containing, or characterized by: *a length of rope*; *she is a woman of enviable beauty* **5** used to link a verbal noun with a following noun or noun phrase that is either the subject or the object of the verb: *the sudden slipping of the plates of the Earth's crust*; *the bombing of civilian targets* **6** at a given distance or space of time from: *you can still find wood within a mile of the village*; *he had been within hours of leaving for Romania* **7** used to specify or give more information about: *the city of Glasgow*; *a meeting on the subject of regional security* **8** about or concerning: *speaking of boycotts* **9** *US* before the hour of: *about quarter of eight in the evening* [Old English]

USAGE See at **off**.

Ofcom *n* (in Britain) Office of Communications: a government body regulating the telecommunications industries

off *prep* **1** so as to be no longer in contact with: *take the wok off the heat* **2** so as to be no longer attached to or associated with: *making use of benefit disqualification to terrorize unemployed people off the register* **3** away from: *he was driven off the road* **4** situated near to or leading away from: *they were laying out a bombing range off the coast* **5** no longer having a liking for: *she's gone off you lately* **6** no longer using: *he was off heroin for a year* ▷ *adv* **7** so as to deactivate or disengage: *turn off the gas supply* **8 a** so as to get rid of: *he was flying at midnight so he had to sleep off his hangover* **b** as a reduction in price: *she took 20% off* **9** spent away from work or other duties: *it was the assistant manager's day off* **10** away; at a distance: *the men dashed back to their car and sped off* **11** away in the future: *the date was six weeks off* **12** so as to be no longer taking place: *the investigation was hastily called off* **13** removed from contact with something: *he took the jacket off* **14** off and on occasionally; not regularly or continuously: *we lived together off and on* ▷ *adj* **15** not on; no longer operating: *her bedroom light was off* **16** cancelled or postponed: *the deal is off and your deposit will be returned in full* **17** in a specified condition, esp. regarding money or provisions: *a married man with four children is better off on the dole*; *how are you off for money?* **18** not up to the usual standard: *an off year for good wine* **19** no longer on the menu: *haddock is off* **20** (of food or drink) having gone bad or sour: *this milk is off* ▷ *n* **21** *cricket* the side of the field to the right of a right-handed batsman when he is facing the bowler [variant of *of*]

USAGE In standard English, *off* is not followed by *of*: *he stepped off* (not *off of*) *the platform.*

Offa *n* died 796 AD, king of Mercia (757–796), who constructed an earthwork (**Offa's Dyke**) between Wales and Mercia

offal *n* the edible internal parts of an animal, such as the heart or liver [*off* + *fall*, referring to parts cut off]

offal pit *or* **offal hole** *n NZ* a place on a farm for the disposal of animal offal

Offaly *n* an inland county of E central Republic of Ireland, in Leinster province: formerly an ancient kingdom, which also included parts of Tipperary, Leix, and Kildare. County town: Tullamore. Pop: 63 663 (2002). Area: 2000 sq km (770 sq miles)

offbeat *adj* unusual, unconventional, or eccentric

off-break *n cricket* a bowled ball that spins from off to leg on pitching

off colour *adj* **1** slightly ill; unwell **2** slightly indecent: *an off-colour joke*

offcut *n* a piece of paper, wood, or fabric remaining after the main pieces have been cut; remnant

Offenbach¹ *n* a city in central Germany, on the River Main in Hesse opposite Frankfurt am Main: leather-goods industry. Pop: 119 208 (2003 est)

Offenbach² *n* Jacques. 1819–80, German-born French composer of many operettas, including *Orpheus in the Underworld* (1858), and of the opera *The Tales of Hoffmann* (1881)

offence *or US* **offense** *n* **1 a** breaking of a law or rule; crime **2** annoyance or anger **3** a cause of annoyance or anger **4 give offence** to cause to feel upset or angry **5 take offence** to feel hurt or offended

offend *vb* **1** to hurt the feelings of (a person); insult **2** to be disagreeable to; disgust: *she was offended by what she saw* **3** to commit a crime [Latin *offendere*] **> offender** *n* **> offending** *adj*

offensive *adj* **1** unpleasant or disgusting to the senses: *there was an offensive smell of beer* **2** causing annoyance or anger; insulting **3** for the purpose of attack rather than defence ▷ *n* **4** an attitude or position of aggression: *to go on the offensive* **5** an attack or hostile action: *troops had* launched a major offensive against the rebel forces **> offensively** *adv*

offer *vb* **1** to present for acceptance or rejection: *I offered her a lift* **2** to provide: *this department offers a wide range of courses* **3** to present itself: *if an opportunity should offer* **4** to be willing (to do something): *his father offered to pay his tuition* **5** to put forward (a proposal, information, or opinion) for consideration: *may I offer a different view?* **6** to present for sale **7** to propose as payment; bid **8** to present (a prayer or sacrifice) as an act of worship **9** to show readiness for: *to offer resistance* ▷ *n* **10** something that is offered **11** the act of offering [Latin *offerre* to present]

offering *n* **1** something that is offered **2** a contribution to the funds of a religious organization **3** a sacrifice to a god

offertory *n, pl* **-tories** *Christianity* **1** the part of a church service when the bread and wine for communion are offered for consecration **2** the collection of money at this service **3** the prayers said or sung while the worshippers' offerings are being brought to the altar

off-grid *adj* not involving or requiring the use of mainstream sources of energy

offhand *adj* also: **offhanded 1** curt or casual in manner: *I felt calm enough to adopt a casual offhand manner* ▷ *adv* **2** without preparation: *I don't know offhand why that should be so* **> offhandedly** *adv* **> offhandedness** *n*

Offiah *n* Martin. born 1965, English Rugby League football player: scored 26 tries in 33 matches for Great Britain (1988–1994)

office *n* **1** a room, set of rooms, or building in which business, professional duties, or clerical work are carried out **2** a department of an organization dealing with particular business: *cheque books were sent from the printer to the bank's sorting office* **3** the group of people working in an office: *she assured him that the office was running smoothly* **4** a government department or agency: *Office of Fair Trading* **5** a position of trust or authority, as in a government: *he would not seek a second term of office* **6** a place where tickets, information, or some service can be obtained: *why don't you give the ticket office a ring?* **7** *Christianity* a religious ceremony or service **8 good offices** the help given by someone to someone else: *Syria's good offices finally led to the release of two Western hostages* **9** in or **out of office** (of a government) in or out of power [Latin *officium* service, duty]

officer *n* **1** a person in the armed services, or on a non-naval ship, who holds a position of authority **2** a policeman or policewoman **3** a person holding a position of authority in a government or organization

official *adj* **1** of an office or position of authority: *I'm not here in any official capacity* **2** approved by or derived from authority: *there has been no official announcement* **3** formal or ceremonial: *he was speaking at an official dinner in Warsaw* ▷ *n* **4** a person holding a position of authority **> officially** *adv*

officialdom *n* officials or bureaucrats collectively

officialese *n* language typical of official documents, esp. when wordy or pompous

Official Receiver *n Brit* an officer appointed by the government to deal with the affairs of a bankrupt person or company

officiate *vb* **-ating, -ated 1** to perform the duties of an office; act in an official capacity: *the referee will officiate at the match* **2** to conduct a religious or other ceremony: *the priest officiated at the wedding* **> officiation** *n* **> officiator** *n*

officious *adj* offering unwanted advice or services; interfering [Latin *officiosus* kindly] **> officiousness** *n*

offing *n* **1** the part of the sea that can be seen from the shore **2 in the offing** *Brit, Austral and NZ* not far off; likely to occur soon

off key *music adj* **1** out of tune: *an off-key rendition* ▷ *adv* **2** out of tune: *he sings off key*

off-licence *n Brit* a shop or a counter in a shop where alcoholic drink is sold for drinking elsewhere

offline *adj* **1** disconnected from a computer or the

internet ▷ *adv* **2** while not connected to a computer or the internet

off-load *vb* to get rid of (something unpleasant), usually by giving it to someone else: *you take all the credit and off-load all the blame*

off-peak *adj* (of services) used at times other than those of greatest demand

off-putting *adj informal* rather unpleasant or disturbing: *it can be very off-putting when you first visit a social security office*

off-road *adj* (of a motor vehicle) designed for use away from public roads

off-roader *n* a motor vehicle designed for use away from public roads

offset *vb* **-setting, -set 1** to cancel out or compensate for **2** to print (something) using the offset process ▷ *n* **3** a printing method in which the impression is made onto a surface, such as a rubber roller, which transfers it to the paper **4** *botany* a short runner in certain plants that produces roots and shoots at the tip

offshoot *n* **1** a shoot growing from the main stem of a plant **2** something that has developed from something else

offshore *adj, adv* **1** away from or at some distance from the shore ▷ *adj* **2** sited or conducted at sea: *he reversed his position on offshore drilling*

offside *adj, adv* **1** *sport* (of a player) in a position illegally ahead of the ball when it is played ▷ *n* **2** *chiefly Brit* the side of a vehicle nearest the centre of the road

off spin *n cricket* a method of spin bowling delivery in which the ball spins from off to leg after bouncing **> off-spinner** *n*

offspring *n* **1** the immediate descendant or descendants of a person or animal **2** a product, outcome, or result: *the women's liberation movement was the offspring of the 1960s*

off-the-peg *adj* (of clothing) ready to wear; not produced especially for the person buying

Ofgem *n* (in Britain) Office of Gas and Electricity Markets: the body which regulates the power supply industries

Ofili *n* Chris(**topher**). born 1968, British painter, noted esp. for his brightly coloured collages using elephant dung: Turner Prize 1998

O'Flaherty *n* Liam. 1897–1984, Irish novelist and short-story writer. His novels include *The Informer* (1925) and *Famine* (1937)

Oflot *n* (in Britain) Office of the National Lottery: the body which oversees the running of the National Lottery

OFS (Orange) Free State

Ofsted *n* (in Britain) Office for Standards in Education: the body which assesses the educational standards of schools in England and Wales

oft *adv old-fashioned or poetic* short for **often** [Old English]

often *adv* **1** frequently; much of the time **2 as often as** not quite frequently **3 every so often** occasionally **4 more often than not** in more than half the instances [Middle English variant of *oft*]

Ofwat *n* (in Britain) Office of Water Services: the body which regulates the activities of the water companies in England and Wales

Ogaden *n* the Ogaden a region of SE Ethiopia, bordering on Somalia: consists of a desert plateau, inhabited by Somali nomads; a secessionist movement, supported by Somalia, has existed within the region since the early 1960s and led to bitter fighting between Ethiopia and Somalia (1977–78)

Ogasawara Gunto *n* transliteration of the Japanese name for the **Bonin Islands**

Ogbomosho *n* a city in SW Nigeria; trading centre for an agricultural region. Pop: 959 000 (2005 est)

Ogden *n* C(**harles**) K(**ay**). 1889–1957, English linguist, who, with I. A. Richards, devised Basic English

Ogdon *n* John (**Andrew Howard**). 1937–89, British pianist and composer

O

ogee arch (oh-jee) *n* a pointed arch made with an S-shaped curve on each side [probably from Old French]

ogle *vb* **ogling, ogled** to stare at (someone) lustfully [probably from Low German *oegeln*]

Oglethorpe *n* James Edward. 1696–1785, English general and colonial administrator; founder of the colony of Georgia (1733)

Ogooué *or* **Ogowe** *n* a river in W central Africa, rising in SW Congo-Brazzaville and flowing generally northwest and north through Gabon to the Atlantic. Length: about 970 km (683 miles)

O grade *n* (formerly) **1** the basic level of the Scottish Certificate of Education **2** a pass in a particular subject at O grade: *she has eight O grades*

ogre *n* **1** (in folklore) a man-eating giant **2** any monstrous or cruel person [French] ▷ **ogreish** *adj* ▷ **ogress** *fem n*

Ogun *n* a state of SW Nigeria. Capital: Abeokuta. Pop: 3 728 098 (2006). Area: 16 762 sq km (6472 sq miles)

oh *interj* an exclamation of surprise, pain, pleasure, fear, or annoyance

OH Ohio

O. Henry *n* pen name of *William Sidney Porter*. 1862–1910, US short-story writer. His collections of stories, characterized by his use of caricature and surprising endings, include *Cabbages and Kings* (1904) and *The Four Million* (1906)

O'Higgins *n* **1** Ambrosio. ?1720–1801, Irish soldier, who became viceroy of Chile (1789–96) and of Peru (1796–1801) **2** his son, Bernardo. 1778–1842, Chilean revolutionary. He was one of the leaders in the struggle for independence from Spain and was Chile's first president (1817–23)

Ohio *n* **1** a state of the central US, in the Midwest on Lake Erie: consists of prairies in the W and the Allegheny plateau in the E, the Ohio River forming the S and most of the E borders. Capital: Columbus. Pop: 11 435 798 (2003 est). Area: 107 044 sq km (41 330 sq miles). Abbreviation and zip code: **OH 2** a river in the eastern US, formed by the confluence of the Allegheny and Monongahela Rivers at Pittsburgh: flows generally W and SW to join the Mississippi at Cairo, Illinois, as its chief E tributary. Length: 1570 km (975 miles)

ohm *n* the SI unit of electrical resistance [after Georg Simon Ohm]

Ohm *n* Georg Simon. 1787–1854, German physicist, who formulated the law named after him

OHMS (in Britain and the Commonwealth) On Her (*or* His) Majesty's Service

oil *n* **1** any of a number of viscous liquids with a smooth sticky feel, which are usually flammable, insoluble in water, and are obtained from plants, animals, or mineral deposits by synthesis **2** same as **petroleum 3** a substance derived from petroleum and used for lubrication **4** *Brit* paraffin as a domestic fuel **5** oil colour or paint **6** an oil painting ▷ *vb* **7** to lubricate with oil or apply oil to **8 oil the wheels** to make things run smoothly [Latin *oleum* (olive) oil]

oilcloth *n* a cotton fabric treated with oil or a synthetic resin to make it waterproof, formerly used esp. for tablecloths

oilfield *n* an area containing reserves of oil

oilfired *adj* using oil as fuel

oil paint *n* a thick paint made of pigment ground in linseed oil

oil painting *n* **1** a picture painted with oil paints **2** the art of painting with oil paints

oil rig *n* a structure used as a base when drilling an oil well

Oil Rivers *pl n* the delta of the Niger River in S Nigeria

oil-seed rape *n* same as **rape²**

oilskin *n* **1** a thick cotton fabric treated with oil to make it waterproof **2** a protective outer garment made of this fabric

oil slick *n* a mass of floating oil covering an area of water

oil well *n* a well bored into the earth or sea bed to a supply of oil

oily *adj* **oilier, oiliest 1** soaked or covered with oil **2** of, containing, or like oil **3** attempting to gain favour by insincere behaviour and flattery ▷ **oiliness** *n*

oink *n* the grunt of a pig or an imitation of this

ointment *n* a smooth greasy substance applied to the skin to heal or protect, or as a cosmetic: *home-made creams and ointments* [Latin *unguentum* unguent]

Oise *n* **1** a department of N France, in Picardy region. Capital: Beauvais. Pop: 776 999 (2003 est). Area: 5887 sq km (2296 sq miles) **2** a river in N France, rising in Belgium, in the Ardennes, and flowing southwest to join the Seine at Conflans. Length: 302 km (188 miles)

Oistrakh *n* **1** David. 1908–74, Russian violinist **2** his son, Igor. born 1931, Russian violinist

Oita *n* an industrial city in SW Japan, on NE Kyushu: dominated much of Kyushu in the 16th century. Pop: 437 699 (2002 est)

OK Oklahoma

O.K. *informal interj* **1** an expression of approval or agreement ▷ *adj* **2** in good or satisfactory condition ▷ *adv* **3** reasonably well or in a satisfactory manner ▷ *vb* **O.K.ing, O.K.ed 4** to approve or endorse ▷ *n, pl* **O.K.s 5** approval or agreement [perhaps from *o(ll) k(orrect)*, jocular alteration of *all correct*]

Okanagan *n* **1** a river in North America that flows south from Okanagan Lake in Canada into the Columbia River in NE Washington, US Length: about 483 km (300 miles). Also (US): **Okanogan 2** Also: **Okanogan, Okinagan** a member of a North American Indian people living in the Okanagan River valley in British Columbia and Washington **3** Also: **Okanogan, Okinagan** the language of this people, belonging to the Salish family

Okanagan Lake *n* a lake in SW Canada, in S British Columbia: drained by the Okanagan River into the Columbia River. Length: about 111 km (69 miles). Width: from 3.2–6.4 km (2–4 miles)

okapi (oh-kah-pee) *n, pl* **-pis** *or* **-pi** an African mammal related to the giraffe, but with a shorter neck, a reddish coat, and white stripes on the legs [from a Central African word]

Okavango *or* **Okovango** *n* a river in SW central Africa, rising in central Angola and flowing southeast, then east as part of the border between Angola and Namibia, then southeast across the Caprivi Strip into Botswana to form a great marsh known as the **Okavango Basin, Delta** *or* **Swamp**. Length: about 1600 km (1000 miles)

okay *interj, adj, adv, vb, n* same as **O.K.**

Okayama *n* a city in SW Japan, on W Honshu on the Inland Sea. Pop: 621 809 (2002 est)

Okeechobee *n* Lake Okeechobee a lake in S Florida, in the Everglades: second largest freshwater lake wholly within the US. Area: 1813 sq km (700 sq miles)

O'Keeffe *n* Georgia. 1887–1986, US painter, best known for her semiabstract still lifes, esp. of flowers: married the photographer Alfred Stieglitz

Okefenokee Swamp *n* a swamp in the US, in SE Georgia and N Florida: protected flora and fauna. Area: 1554 sq km (600 sq miles)

Okhotsk *n* Sea of Okhotsk part of the NW Pacific, surrounded by the Kamchatka Peninsula, the Kurile Islands, Sakhalin Island, and the E coast of Siberia. Area: 1 589 840 sq km (613 838 sq miles)

Okinawa *n* a coral island of SW Japan, the largest of the Ryukyu Islands in the N Pacific: scene of heavy fighting in World War II; administered by the US (1945–72); agricultural. Chief town: Naha. Pop: 1 318 218 (2000). Area: 1176 sq km (454 sq miles)

Okla. Oklahoma

Oklahoma *n* a state in the S central US: consists of plains in the west, rising to mountains in the southwest and east; important for oil. Capital: Oklahoma City. Pop:

3 511 532 (2003 est). Area: 181 185 sq km (69 956 sq miles). Abbreviation: **Okla.**, (with zip code) **OK**

Oklahoma City *n* a city in central Oklahoma: the state capital and a major agricultural and industrial centre. Pop: 523 303 (2003 est)

Oklahoman *n* **1** a native or inhabitant of Oklahoma ▷ *adj* **2** of or relating to Oklahoma or its inhabitants

Okovango *n* a variant spelling of **Okavango**

okra *n* a tall plant with long green pods that are used as food [West African]

Okri *n* Ben. born 1959, Nigerian writer; his books include the Booker-prizewinning *The Famished Road* (1991), *Dangerous Love* (1996), and *In Arcadia* (2002)

Olaf I *or* **Olav I** *n* known as *Olaf Tryggvesson*. ?965–?1000 AD, king of Norway (995–?1000). He began the conversion of Norway to Christianity

Olaf II *or* **Olav II** *n* Saint. 995–1030 AD, king of Norway (1015–28), who worked to complete the conversion of Norway to Christianity; deposed by Canute; patron saint of Norway. Feast day: July 29

Olaf V *or* **Olav V** *n* 1903–91, king of Norway 1957–91; son of Haakon VII

Öland *n* an island in the Baltic Sea, separated from the mainland of SE Sweden by Kalmar Sound: the second largest Swedish island. Chief town: Borgholm. Pop: 24 628 (2004 est). Area: 1347 sq km (520 sq miles)

old *adj* **1** having lived or existed for a long time: *the old woman; burning witches is one old custom I've no desire to see revived* **2** of or relating to advanced years or a long life: *I twisted my knee as I tried to squat and cursed old age* **3** worn with age or use: *the old bathroom fittings* **4** having lived or existed for a specified period: *he is 60 years old* **5** the earlier or earliest of two or more things with the same name: *the old edition; the Old Testament* **6** designating the form of a language in which the earliest known records are written: *Old English* **7** familiar through long acquaintance or repetition: *an old acquaintance; the legalization argument is an old and familiar one* **8** dear: used as a term of affection or familiarity: *always rely on old Tom to turn out* **9** out of date; unfashionable **10** former or previous: *my old housekeeper lent me some money* **11** of long standing: *he's an old and respected member of staff* **12** good old days: an earlier period of time regarded as better than the present ▷ *n* **13** an earlier or past time: *in days of old* [Old English *eald*] ▷ **oldish** *adj*

old age pension *n* a former name for **retirement pension** ▷ **old age pensioner** *n*

Old Bailey *n* the Central Criminal Court of England

old boy *n* **1** a male ex-pupil of a school **2** *informal, chiefly Brit* **a** a familiar form of address used to refer to a man **b** an old man

Old Castile *n* a region of N Spain, on the Bay of Biscay: formerly a province. Spanish name: **Castilla la Vieja**

Oldcastle *n* Sir John, Baron Cobham. ?1378–1417, Lollard leader. In 1411 he led an English army in France but in 1413 he was condemned as a heretic and later hanged and burnt. He is thought to have been a model for Shakespeare's character Falstaff in *Henry IV*

old country *n* the country of origin of an immigrant or an immigrant's ancestors

Old Delhi *n* See **Delhi**

olde *adj* *facetious* quaint [from the former spelling of old]

olden *adj* *archaic or poetic* old: *in the olden days the girls were married young*

Oldenbarneveldt *n* Johan van. 1547–1619, Dutch statesman, regarded as a founder of Dutch independence; the leading figure (from 1586) in the United Provinces of the Netherlands; executed by Maurice of Nassau

Oldenburg¹ *n* **1** a city in NW Germany, in Lower Saxony: former capital of Oldenburg state. Pop: 158 340 (2003 est) **2** a former state of NW Germany: became part of Lower Saxony in 1946

Oldenburg² *n* Claes. born 1929, US pop sculptor and artist, born in Sweden

Old English *n* the English language of the Anglo-Saxons, spoken from the fifth century AD to about 1100. Also called: **Anglo-Saxon**

Old English sheepdog *n* a large sheepdog with thick shaggy hair

old-fashioned *adj* **1** in the style of a previous period; outdated: *she wore her hair in a strangely old-fashioned tight hairdo* **2** favouring or denoting the styles or ideas of a former time: *old-fashioned values*

Oldfield *n* Bruce. born 1950, British fashion designer

old flame *n* *informal, old-fashioned* a person with whom one once had a romantic relationship

Old French *n* the French language in its earliest forms, from about the 9th century up to about 1400

old girl *n* **1** a female ex-pupil of a school **2** *informal, chiefly Brit* **a** a familiar form of address used to refer to a woman **b** an old woman

old guard *n* a group of people in an organization who have traditional values: *the company's old guard is making way for a new, more youthful team* [after Napoleon's imperial guard]

Oldham *n* **1** a town in NW England, in Oldham unitary authority, Greater Manchester. Pop: 103 544 (2001) **2** a unitary authority in NW England, in Greater Manchester. Pop: 218 100 (2003 est). Area: 141 sq km (54 sq miles)

old hand *n* a skilled or experienced person

old hat *adj* old-fashioned or dull

Old High German *n* a group of West Germanic dialects that developed into modern German; High German up to about 1200

old identity *n* NZ a well-known local person who has lived in an area for a long time

oldie *n* *informal* an old song, film, or person

old lady *n* *informal* one's mother or wife

old maid *n* **1** a woman regarded as unlikely ever to marry; spinster **2** *informal* a prim, fussy, or excessively cautious person

old man *n* **1** *informal* one's father **2** one's husband **3** an affectionate form of address used to a man

old master *n* **1** one of the great European painters of the period 1500 to 1800 **2** a painting by one of these

old moon *n* a phase of the moon between last quarter and new moon, when it appears as a waning crescent

Old Nick *n* *informal* Satan

Old Northwest *n* (in the early US) the land between the Great Lakes, the Mississippi, and the Ohio River. Awarded to the US in 1783, it was organized into the Northwest Territory in 1787 and now forms the states of Ohio, Indiana, Illinois, Wisconsin, Michigan, and part of Minnesota. See also **Northwest Territory**

old school *n* a group of people favouring traditional or conservative ideas or practices

old school tie *n* the system of mutual help supposed to operate among the former pupils of independent schools

Old Style *n* the former method of reckoning dates using the Julian calendar

Old Testament *n* the first part of the Christian Bible, containing the sacred Scriptures of the Hebrews

old-time *adj* of or relating to a former time; old-fashioned: *an old-time waltz*

Olduvai Gorge *n* a gorge in N Tanzania, north of the Ngorongoro Crater: fossil evidence of early man and other closely related species, together with artefacts

old wives' tale *n* a belief, usually superstitious or foolish, passed on by word of mouth as a piece of traditional wisdom

old woman *n* **1** *informal* one's mother or wife **2** a timid, fussy, or cautious person ▷ **old-womanish** *adj*

Old World *n* that part of the world that was known to Europeans before the discovery of the Americas; the eastern hemisphere

old-world *adj* of or characteristic of former times; quaint or traditional

oleaginous (oh-lee-**aj**-in-uss) *adj* like or producing oil; oily [Latin *oleaginus*]

oleander (oh-lee-**ann**-der) *n* an evergreen Mediterranean shrub with fragrant white, pink, or purple flowers [Medieval Latin]

O level *n* **1** (formerly, in Britain) the basic level of the General Certificate of Education **2** a pass in a particular subject at O level: *a very intelligent young woman with ten O levels*

olfactory *adj* of the sense of smell [Latin *olere* to smell + *facere* to make]

oligarchy (ol-lee-gark-ee) *n, pl* -**chies** **1** government by a small group of people **2** a state governed this way **3** a small group of people governing such a state [Greek *oligos* few + *arkhein* to rule] **>** **oligarchic** *or* **oligarchical** *adj*

Oligocene (ol-lig-go-seen) *adj geology* of the epoch of geological time about 35 million years ago [Greek *oligos* little + *kainos* new]

oligopoly *n, pl* -**lies** *econ* a market situation in which control over the supply of a commodity is held by a small number of producers [Greek *oligos* few + *pōlein* to sell]

Ólimbos *n* transliteration of the Modern Greek name for (Mount) **Olympus** (1)

Oliphant *n* Sir Mark Laurence Elwin. 1901–2000, British nuclear physicist, born in Australia

Olivares *n* Conde-Ducque de, title of *Gaspar de Guzmán y Pimental*. 1587–1645, Spanish statesman: court favourite and prime minister (1621–43) of Philip IV. His attempts to establish Hapsburg domination of Europe ended in failure

olive *n* **1** an evergreen Mediterranean tree **2** the small green or black fruit of this tree **▷** *adj* **3** short for **olive-green** [Latin *oliva*]

olive branch *n* a peace offering: *I should offer some kind of olive branch and get in touch with them*

olive-green *adj* deep yellowish-green

olive oil *n* a yellowish-green oil pressed from ripe olives and used in cooking and medicines

Oliver *n* **1** one of Charlemagne's 12 paladins. See also Roland **2** Isaac. ?1556–1617, English portrait miniaturist, born in France: he studied under Hilliard and worked at James I's court **3** Jamie (**Trevor**). born 1975, British chef and presenter of television cookery programmes **4** Joseph, known as *King Oliver*. 1885–1938, US pioneer jazz cornetist

Olives *n* Mount of Olives a hill to the east of Jerusalem: in New Testament times the village Bethany (Mark 11:11) was on its eastern slope and Gethsemane on its western one

Olivier *n* Laurence (**Kerr**), Baron Olivier of Brighton. 1907–89, English stage, film, and television actor and director: director of the National Theatre Company (1961–73): films include the Shakespeare adaptations *Henry V* (1944), *Hamlet* (1948), and *Richard III* (1956)

Olmütz *n* the German name for Olomouc

Olomouc *n* a city in the Czech Republic, in North Moravia on the Morava River: capital of Moravia until 1640; university (1576). Pop: 102 000 (2005 est). German name: **Olmütz**

oloroso (ol-ler-**roh**-so) *n* a golden-coloured sweet sherry [Spanish: fragrant]

Olsztyn *n* a town in NE Poland: founded in 1334 by the Teutonic Knights; communications centre. Pop: 176 000 (2005 est)

Olympia *n* **1** a plain in Greece, in the NW Peloponnese: in ancient times a major sanctuary of Zeus and site of the original Olympic Games **2** a port in W Washington, the state capital, on Puget Sound. Pop: 43 963 (2003 est)

Olympiad *n* **1** a staging of the modern Olympic Games **2** an international contest in chess or other games

Olympian *adj* **1** of Mount Olympus or the classical Greek gods **2** majestic or godlike **▷** *n* **3** a competitor in the Olympic Games **4** a god of Mount Olympus

Olympic *adj* of the Olympic Games

Olympic Games *n* **1** an ancient Greek festival, held every fourth year in honour of Zeus, consisting of games and festivities **2** Also called: **the Olympics** the modern revival of these games, consisting of international athletic and sporting contests held every four years in a selected country

Olympic Mountains *pl n* a mountain range in NW Washington: part of the Coast Range. Highest peak: Mount Olympus, 2427 m (7965 ft)

Olympic Peninsula *n* a large peninsula of W Washington

Olympus *n* **1** Mount Olympus a mountain in NE Greece: the highest mountain in Greece, believed in Greek mythology to be the dwelling place of the greater gods. Height: 2911 m (9550 ft). Modern Greek name: **Ólimbos** **2** Mount Olympus a mountain in NW Washington: highest peak of the Olympic Mountains. Height: 2427 m (7965 ft) **3** a poetic word for **heaven** (1)

Olynthus *n* an ancient city in N Greece: the centre of Chalcidice

OM Order of Merit (a Brit. title)

Omagh *n* **1** a market town in Northern Ireland. Pop: 19 910 (2001) **2** a district of W Northern Ireland, in Co Tyrone. Pop: 49 560 (2003 est). Area: 1130 sq km (436 sq miles)

Omaha *n* a city in E Nebraska, on the Missouri River opposite Council Bluffs, Iowa: the largest city in the state; the country's largest livestock market and meat-packing centre. Pop: 404 267 (2003 est)

Oman *n* a sultanate in SE Arabia, on the Gulf of Oman and the Arabian Sea: the most powerful state in Arabia in the 19th century, ruling Zanzibar, much of the Persian coast, and part of Pakistan. Official language: Arabic. Official religion: Muslim. Currency: rial. Capital: Muscat. Pop: 3 154 134 (2013 est). Area: about 306 000 sq km (118 150 sq miles). Former name (until 1970): **Muscat and Oman**

Omani *n* **1** a native or inhabitant of Oman **▷** *adj* **2** of or relating to Oman or its inhabitants

Omar *or* **Umar** *n* died 644 AD, the second caliph of Islam (634–44). During his reign Islamic armies conquered Syria and Mesopotamia: murdered

Omar Khayyám *n* ?1050–?1123, Persian poet, mathematician, and astronomer, noted for the *Rubáiyát*, a collection of quatrains, popularized in the West by Edward Fitzgerald's version (1859)

ombudsman *n, pl* -**men** an official who investigates citizens' complaints against the government or its servants [Swedish: commissioner]

Omdurman *n* a city in the central Sudan, on the White Nile, opposite Khartoum, with which it forms the country's largest city; scene of the **Battle of Omdurman** (1898), in which the Mahdi's successor was defeated by Lord Kitchener's forces. Pop: recent estimates vary between 1 000 000 and 3 000 000

omega *n* **1** the 24th and last letter of the Greek alphabet (Ω, ω) **2** the ending or last of a series

omega-3 *n* an unsaturated fatty acid that occurs naturally in fish oil, valuable in reducing blood cholesterol

omelette *or especially US* **omelet** *n* a dish of beaten eggs cooked in a flat pan and often folded round a savoury filling [French]

omen *n* **1** a thing or occurrence regarded as a sign of future happiness or disaster **2** prophetic significance: *birds of ill omen* [Latin]

OMG Oh my God!: used esp. in emails, text messages, etc.

ominous *adj* warning of evil [Latin *ominosus*] **>** **ominously** *adv*

omission *n* **1** something that has been left out or passed over **2** an act of missing out or failing to do something: *we regret the omission of these and the names of the other fine artists*

omit *vb* **omitting, omitted 1** to fail to include; leave out **2** to fail (to do something) [Latin *omittere*]

omnibus *n, pl* **-buses 1** a collection of works by one author or several works on a similar topic, reprinted in one volume **2** Also called: **omnibus edition** a television or radio programme consisting of two or more episodes of a serial broadcast earlier in the week **3** *old-fashioned* a bus ▷ *adj* **4** consisting of or dealing with several different things at once: *this year's version of an omnibus crime bill* [Latin, literally: for all]

omnipotent (om-nip-a-tent) *adj* having very great or unlimited power [Latin *omnipotens* all-powerful]
> omnipotence *n*

omnipresent *adj* (esp. of a god) present in all places at the same time [Latin *omnis* all + *praesens* present]
> omnipresence *n*

omniscient (om-niss-ee-ent) *adj formal* knowing or seeming to know everything [Latin *omnis* all + *scire* to know] **> omniscience** *n*

omnivore (om-niv-vore) *n* an animal that eats any type of food

omnivorous (om-niv-or-uss) *adj* **1** eating any type of food **2** taking in everything indiscriminately: *his omnivorous sociability has meant constant hard work for his wife* [Latin *omnivorus* all-devouring]

Omsk *n* a city in W central Russia, at the confluence of the Irtysh and Om Rivers: a major industrial centre, with pipelines from the second Baku oilfield. Pop: 1 132 000 (2005 est)

Omuta *n* a city in SW Japan, on W Kyushu on Ariake Bay: former coal-mining centre; chemical industries and manufacturing. Pop: 139 345 (2002 est)

on *prep* **1** in contact with or at the surface of: *let the cakes stand in the tins on a wire rack; she had dirt on her dress* **2** attached to: *a piece of paper on a clipboard* **3** carried with: *the message found on her* **4** near to or along the side of: *the hotel is on the coast* **5** within the time limits of (a day or date): *they returned to Moscow on 22nd September* **6** being performed upon or relayed through the medium of: *a construction of refined sounds played on special musical instruments; what's on television?* **7** at the occasion of: *she had received numerous letters congratulating her on her election* **8** immediately after or at the same time as: *check with the tourist office on arrival* **9** through the use of: *an extraordinarily vigorous man who thrives on physical activity; the program runs on the Unix operating system* **10** regularly taking (a drug): *she's on the pill* **11** by means of (a mode of transport): *his only way up the hill had to be on foot; they get around on bicycles* **12** in the process or course of: *he is away on a climbing expedition; coal miners have been on strike for six weeks* **13** concerned with or relating to: *ten million viewers watched the recent series on homelessness* **14** (of a statement or action) having as basis or grounds: *I have it on good authority* **15** charged to: *all drinks are on the house for the rest of the evening* **16** staked as a bet: *I'll have a bet on the favourite* ▷ *adv* **17** in operation; functioning: *the lights had been left on all night* **18** attached to, surrounding, or placed in contact with something: *they escaped with nothing on except sleeveless shirts and shorts* **19** taking place: *what do you have on tonight?* **20** continuously or persistently: *the crisis must not be allowed to drag on indefinitely* **21** forwards or further: *they trudged on* **22** **on and off** occasionally; not regularly or continuously **23** **on and on** without ceasing; continually ▷ *adj* **24** *informal* performing: *who's on next?* **25** *informal* definitely taking place: *is the party still on?* **26** *informal* tolerable, practicable, or acceptable: *that's just not on* **27** **on at** *informal* nagging: *he was always on at her to stop smoking* ▷ *n* **28** *cricket* the side of the field to the left of a right-handed batsman when he is facing the bowler [Old English *an, on*]

On *n* the ancient Egyptian and biblical name for **Heliopolis**

ON Ontario

onager *n, pl* **-gri** or **-gers** a wild ass of Persia [Greek *onagros*]

onanism *n* **1** withdrawal in sexual intercourse before ejaculation **2** masturbation [after Onan: see Genesis 38:9]

Onassis *n* Aristotle (Socrates). 1906–75, Argentinian (formerly Greek) shipowner, born in Turkey. In 1968 he married Jacqueline, 1929–94, the widow of US President John F. Kennedy

ONC (in Britain) Ordinary National Certificate

once *adv* **1** one time; on one occasion only **2** at some past time, but no longer: *I was in love once* **3** by one degree (of relationship): *he was Deirdre's cousin once removed* **4** **once and for all** conclusively; for the last time **5** **once in a while** occasionally; now and then **6** **once or twice** a few times **7** **once upon a time** used to begin fairy tales and children's stories ▷ *conj* **8** as soon as: *once you have learned good grammar you can leave it to nature and forget it* ▷ *n* **9** one occasion or case: *once is enough* **10** **all at once a** suddenly **b** simultaneously **11** **at once a** immediately **b** simultaneously **12** **for once** this time, even if at no other time [Middle English *ones, anes*]

once-over *n informal* a quick examination or appraisal

oncogene (ong-koh-jean) *n* a gene present in all cells, that when abnormally activated can cause cancer [Greek *onkos* tumour + *-gen* (suffix) producing]

oncoming *adj* coming nearer in space or time; approaching: *oncoming traffic*

OND (in Britain) Ordinary National Diploma

Ondaatje *n* Michael. born 1943, Sri Lankan-born Canadian writer: his works include the poetry collection *There's a Trick with a Knife I'm Learning to Do* (1979), the Booker-prizewinning novel *The English Patient* (1992, filmed 1997), *Anil's Ghost* (2000), and *Divisadero* (2007)

Ondo *n* a state of SW Nigeria, on the Bight of Benin. Capital: Akure. Pop: 3 441 024 (2004). Area: 15 500 sq km (5985 sq miles)

one *adj, n* **1** single or lone (person or thing); not two or more: *one civilian has died and thirty-three have been injured* **2** only or unique (person or thing): *he is the one to make correct judgments and influence the public; she was unique, inimitable, one of a kind* **3** a specified (person or thing) as distinct from another or others of its kind: *place one hand under the knee and the other under the ankle; which one is correct?* **4** **one or two** a few ▷ *adj* **5** a certain, indefinite, or unspecified (time): *one day he would learn the truth about her* **6** *informal, emphatic* a: *we're on to one hell of a story* ▷ *pron* **7** an indefinite person regarded as typical of every person: *one can always hope that there won't be an accident* **8** any indefinite person: *one can catch fine trout in this stream* **9** I or me: *one only wonders what he has against the dogs* ▷ *n* **10** the smallest natural number and first cardinal number **11** a numeral, 1 or I, representing this number **12** something representing or consisting of one unit **13** *informal* a joke or story: *have you heard the one about the actress and the bishop?* **14** **(all) in one** combined or united **15** **all one** of no consequence: *leave if you want to, it's all one to me* **16** **at one with** in agreement or harmony with **17** **one and all** everyone, without exception **18** **one by one** one at a time; individually [Old English *ān*]

one another *pron* each other: *they seem to genuinely care for one another*

one-armed bandit *n informal* a fruit machine operated by pulling down a lever at one side

one-dimensional *adj* **1** having one dimension **2** completely lacking in depth or complexity: *the production staging is one-dimensional and the direction rigid*

Onega *n* a lake in NW Russia, mostly in the Karelian Republic: the second largest lake in Europe. Area: 9891 sq km (3819 sq miles)

one-horse *adj informal* small or insignificant: *a dusty one-horse town in the foothills of the Karakoram mountain range*

Oneida *n, pl* **-das** or **-da 1 Lake Oneida** a lake in central New York State: part of the New York State Barge Canal system. Length: about 35 km (22 miles). Greatest width: 9 km (6 miles) **2 the Oneida** (*functioning as pl*) a North American Indian people formerly living east of Lake

Ontario; one of the Iroquois peoples **3** a member of this people **4** the language of this people, belonging to the Iroquoian family [from Iroquois *onẽýote'*, literally: standing stone]

O'Neill *n* Eugene (Gladstone). 1888–1953, US dramatist. His works, which are notable for their emotional power and psychological analysis, include *Desire under the Elms* (1924), *Strange Interlude* (1928), *Mourning becomes Elektra* (1931), *Long Day's Journey into Night* (1941), and *The Iceman Cometh* (1946): Nobel prize for literature 1936

one-liner *n informal* a short joke or witty remark

oneness *n* **1** agreement **2** uniqueness **3** sameness

one-night stand *n* **1** *informal* a sexual encounter lasting only one evening or night **2** a performance given only once at any one place

one-off *n* something that happens or is made only once

onerous (own-er-uss) *adj* (of a task) difficult to carry out [Latin *onus* load] **> onerousness** *n*

oneself *pron* **1** the reflexive form of *one* **2** one's normal or usual self: *one doesn't feel oneself after such an experience*

one-sided *adj* **1** considering or favouring only one side of a matter: *a one-sided version of events* **2** having all the advantage on one side: *it was a one-sided match with Brazil missing a succession of chances*

onesie *n* a one-piece garment consisting of a long-sleeved top with trousers, with a zip up the front

one-stop *adj* having or providing a range of services or goods in one place: *one-stop shopping*

One Thousand Guineas *n* the One Thousand Guineas an annual horse race for three-year-old fillies, run at Newmarket

one-time *adj* at some time in the past; former

one-to-one *adj* **1** (of two or more things) corresponding exactly **2** denoting a relationship or encounter in which someone is involved with only one other person: *one-to-one meetings* **3** *maths* involving the pairing of each member of one set with only one member of another set, without remainder

one-track *adj informal* obsessed with one idea or subject: *she's got a one-track mind*

one-up *adj informal* having an advantage or lead over someone else **> one-upmanship** *n*

one-way *adj* **1** moving or allowing travel in one direction only: *the town centre has a baffling one-way system* **2** involving no reciprocal obligation or action: *he does not get anything back out of the one-way relationship*

ongoing *adj* in progress; continuing: *there are still ongoing discussions about the future role of NATO*

onion *n* **1** a vegetable with an edible bulb with a strong smell and taste **2 know one's onions** *Brit and NZ slang* to be fully acquainted with a subject [Latin *unio*] **> oniony** *adj*

Onions *n* Charles Talbut. 1873–1965, English lexicographer; an editor of the *Oxford English Dictionary*

Onitsha *n* a port in S Nigeria, in Anambra State on the Niger River: industrial centre. Pop: 565 000 (2005 est)

online *adj* **1** connected to a computer or the internet ▷ *adv* **2** while connected to a computer or the internet

onlooker *n* a person who observes without taking part **> onlooking** *adj*

only *adj* **1** alone of its or their kind: *I will be talking to the only journalist to have been inside the prison* **2** (of a child) having no brothers or sisters **3** unique by virtue of superiority; best: *first class is the only way to travel* **4 one and only** incomparable: *the one and only Diana Ross* ▷ *adv* **5** without anyone or anything else being included; alone: *only you can decide if you can abide by this compromise* **6** merely or just: *it's only Henry* **7** no more or no greater than: *I was talking to a priest only a minute ago* **8** merely: *they had only to turn up to win the competition* **9** not earlier than; not until: *I've only found out today why you wouldn't come* **10** if only or if ... only used to introduce a wish or hope **11 only too** extremely: *they were only too willing to do anything to help* ▷ *conj* **12** but or however: *those countries are going through the same cycle, only a little later than us* [Old English *ānlīc*]

USAGE In informal English, *only* is often used as a sentence connector: *I would have phoned you, only I didn't know your number.* This use should be avoided in formal writing: *I would have phoned you if I'd known your number.* In formal speech and writing, *only* is placed directly before the word or words that it modifies: *she could interview only three applicants in the morning.* In all but the most formal contexts, however, it is generally regarded as acceptable to put *only* before the verb: *she could only interview three applicants in the morning.* Care must be taken not to create ambiguity, esp. in written English, in which intonation will not, as it does in speech, help to show to which item in the sentence *only* applies. A sentence such as *she only drinks tea in the afternoon* is capable of two interpretations and is therefore better rephrased either as *she drinks only tea in the afternoon* (i.e. no other drink) or *she drinks tea only in the afternoon* (i.e. at no other time).

o.n.o. or near(est) offer

onomatopoeia (on-a-mat-a-pee-a) *n* use of a word which imitates the sound it represents, such as *hiss* [Greek *onoma* name + *poiein* to make] **> onomatopoeic** or **onomatopoetic** *adj*

Onondaga *n* **1** Lake Onondaga a salt lake in central New York State. Area: about 13 sq km (5 sq miles) **2** (*pl* **-gas** or **-ga**) a member of a North American Indian Iroquois people formerly living between Lake Champlain and the St Lawrence River **3** the language of this people, belonging to the Iroquoian family [from Iroquois *onõtáge'*, literally: on the top of the hill (the name of their principal village)]

onrush *n* a forceful forward rush or flow; surge

onset *n* a start; beginning

onshore *adj, adv* **1** towards the land: *a stiff onshore wind* **2** on land; not at sea

onside *adj, adv sport* (of a player) in a legal position, for example, behind the ball or with a required number of opponents between oneself and the opposing team's goal line

onslaught *n* a violent attack [Middle Dutch *aenslag*]

Ont. Ontario

Ontarian or **Ontarioan** *n* **1** a native or inhabitant of Ontario ▷ *adj* **2** of or relating to Ontario or its inhabitants

Ontario *n* **1** a province of central Canada: lies mostly on the Canadian Shield and contains the fertile plain of the lower Great Lakes and the St Lawrence River, one of the world's leading industrial areas; the second largest and the most populous province. Capital: Toronto. Pop: 12 851 821 (2011 est). Area: 891 198 sq km (344 092 sq miles). Abbreviation: **Ont., ON 2** Lake Ontario a lake between the US and Canada, bordering on New York State and Ontario province: the smallest of the Great Lakes; linked with Lake Erie by the Niagara River and Welland Canal; drained by the St Lawrence. Area: 19 684 sq km (7600 sq miles)

onto or **on to** *prep* **1** to a position that is on: *step onto the train* **2** having discovered or become aware of: *the police are onto us* **3** into contact with: *get onto the factory*

USAGE *Onto* is now generally accepted as a word in its own right. *On to* is still used, however, where *on* is considered to be part of the verb: *he moved on to a different town* as contrasted with *he jumped onto the stage.*

ontology *n philosophy* the study of the nature of being [Greek *ōn* being + -LOGY] **> ontological** *adj*

onus (own-uss) *n, pl* **onuses** a responsibility, task, or burden: *the courts put the onus on parents* [Latin: burden]

onward *adj* **1** directed or moving forward ▷ *adv* also: **onwards 2** continuing; progressing

onyx *n* a kind of quartz with alternating coloured layers, used as a gemstone [Greek: fingernail (so called from its veined appearance)]

oodles pl n informal great quantities: *he has shown he can raise oodles of cash* [origin unknown]

oolite (oh-a-lite) n a limestone made up of tiny grains of calcium carbonate [New Latin *oolites*, literally: egg stone] > **oolitic** adj

oom n S African a title of respect used to refer to an elderly man [Afrikaans, literally: uncle]

oomiak or **oomiac** n same as **umiak**

oompah n a representation of the sound made by a deep brass instrument, esp. in brass-band music

oomph n informal enthusiasm, vigour, or energy [origin unknown]

oops interj an exclamation of surprise or of apology when someone has a slight accident or makes a mistake

Oort n Jan Hendrick. 1900–92, Dutch astronomer, who confirmed (1927) and developed the theory of galactic rotation. He was the first to propose (1950) the existence of a mass of comets orbiting the sun far beyond the orbit of Pluto (the **Oort cloud**)

OOS occupational overuse syndrome: pain caused by repeated awkward movements while at work

Oostende n the Flemish name for **Ostend**

ooze¹ vb **oozing, oozed 1** to flow or leak out slowly; seep **2** (of a substance) to discharge moisture **3** to overflow with (a feeling or quality): *he oozes confidence* ▷ n **4** a slow flowing or leaking [Old English *wōs* juice] > **oozy** adj

ooze² n a soft thin mud, such as that found at the bottom of a lake, river, or sea [Old English *wāse* mud]

op. opus

opacity (ohp-ass-it-tee) n, pl **-ties 1** the state or quality of being opaque **2** the quality of being difficult to understand; unintelligibility

opal n a precious stone, usually milky or bluish in colour, with shimmering changing reflections [Greek *opallios*]

opalescent adj having shimmering changing reflections, like opal > **opalescence** n

opaque adj **1** not able to be seen through; not transparent or translucent **2** hard to understand; unintelligible [Latin *opacus* shady]

op. cit. (op sit) (in textual annotations) in the work cited [Latin *opere citato*]

OPEC Organization of Petroleum-Exporting Countries

open adj **1** not closed, fastened, or blocked up: *the doctor's office was open* **2** not enclosed, covered, or wrapped: *the parcel was open* **3** extended, expanded, or unfolded: *an open flower* **4** ready for business: *some of the crafts rooms and photography shops are open all night* **5** (of a job) available: *all the positions on the council should be open to females* **6** unobstructed by buildings or trees: *we lived in a small market town surrounded by open countryside* **7** free to all to join in, enter, or use: *there was an open competition and I was appointed* **8** (of a season or period) not restricted for purposes of hunting game of various kinds **9** not decided or finalized: *the legality of these issues is still an open question* **10** ready to consider new ideas: *I was able to approach their problem with an open mind* **11** honest and frank **12** generous: *she has given me love and the open hand* **13** exposed to view; blatant: *there has never been such sustained and open criticism of the President* **14** unprotected; susceptible: *a change of policy which would leave vulnerable youths open to exploitation* **15** having spaces or gaps: *open ranks*; *an open texture* **16** computers designed to an internationally agreed standard to allow communication between computers irrespective of size or manufacturer **17** music **a** (of a string) not stopped with the finger **b** (of a note) played on such a string **18** sport (of a goal or court) unguarded or relatively unprotected **19** (of a wound) exposed to the air ▷ vb **20** to make or become open: *it was easy to open the back door and to slip noiselessly outside*; *she knelt and tried to open the drawer* **21** to set or be set in action; start: *the US will have to open talks on Palestinian rights*; *I want to open a dress shop* **22** to arrange for

(a bank account), usually by making an initial deposit **23** to declare open ceremonially or officially ▷ n **24** sport a competition which anyone may enter **25 the open** any wide or unobstructed area [Old English] > **opener** n > **openly** adv > **openness** n

open air n the place or space where the air is unenclosed; outdoors

open-and-shut adj easily decided or solved; obvious: *an open-and-shut case*

opencast mining n mining by excavating from the surface [open + archaic *cast* ditch, cutting]

open day n a special occasion on which a school, university, or other institution is open for the public to visit

open-ended adj **1** without definite limits; unrestricted: *the schedule is open-ended* **2** (of an activity) done without the aim of attaining a particular result or decision: *the dangers of open-ended military involvement*

open-eyed adj **1** with the eyes wide open, as in amazement **2** watchful; alert

open-handed adj generous

open-hearted adj **1** kind or generous **2** willing to speak one's mind; candid

open-heart surgery n surgical repair of the heart during which the heart is exposed and the blood circulation is maintained mechanically

open house n a situation in which people allow friends or visitors to come to their house whenever they want to

opening n **1** the beginning or first part of something **2** the first performance of a theatrical production **3** a chance or opportunity: *an opening into show business* **4** a hole or gap

opening time n Brit and Austral the time at which public houses can legally open for business

open letter n a letter, esp. one of protest, addressed to an individual but published in a newspaper or magazine for all to read

open market n a process by which prices are decided by supply and demand and goods are sold anywhere

open-minded adj willing to consider new ideas; unprejudiced

open-mouthed adj gaping in surprise

open-plan adj having no or few dividing walls between areas: *the house includes an open-plan living room and dining area*

open prison n a prison in which the prisoners are not locked up, thus extending the range of work they can do

open secret n something that is supposed to be secret but is widely known

open source n **1** intellectual property, esp. computer source code, made freely available to the public by its creators ▷ adj **open-source 2** relating to this code: *open-source software*

open-standard adj (of computer programs, codes, etc.) freely available to all users

Open University n (in Britain) a university teaching by means of broadcasts, online materials, correspondence courses, and summer schools

open up vb **1** to make or become accessible: *the Berlin Wall came down and opened up new territory for dramatists* **2** to speak freely or without self-restraint **3** to start firing a gun or guns **4** informal to increase the speed of (a vehicle)

open verdict n a finding by a coroner's jury of death, without stating the cause

opera¹ n **1** a dramatic work in which most or all of the text is sung to orchestral accompaniment **2** the branch of music or drama relating to operas **3** a group that produces or performs operas **4** a theatre where opera is performed [Latin: work]

opera² n a plural of **opus**

operable adj **1** capable of being treated by a surgical operation **2** capable of being operated or put into practice > **operability** n

opera glasses pl n small low-powered binoculars used by audiences in theatres

opera house n a theatre specially designed for the performance of operas

operand n maths a quantity, variable, or function upon which an operation is performed

operate vb -ating, -ated 1 to work 2 to control the working of (a machine) 3 to manage, direct, or run (a business or system) 4 to perform a surgical operation (upon a person or animal) 5 to conduct military or naval operations [Latin operari to work]

operatic adj 1 of or relating to opera 2 overdramatic or exaggerated: he was about to go out with his operatic strut

operating system n the software controlling a computer

operating theatre or US **operating room** n a room in which surgical operations are performed

operation n 1 the act or method of operating 2 the condition of being in action: there are 20 teleworking centres in operation around the country 3 an action or series of actions done to produce a particular result: a large-scale police operation has been in place to manage the heavy traffic 4 surgery a surgical procedure carried out to remove, replace, or repair a diseased or damaged part of the body 5 a military or naval manoeuvre 6 maths any procedure, such as addition, in which a number is derived from another number or numbers by applying specific rules

operational adj 1 in working order and ready for use 2 of or relating to an action done to produce a particular result

operations research n the analysis of problems in business and industry. Also called: **operational research**

operative (op-rat-tiv) adj 1 in force, effect, or operation: these pension provisions became operative from 1978 2 (of a word) particularly relevant or significant: 'if' is the operative word 3 of or relating to a surgical operation ▷ n 4 a worker with a special skill

operator n 1 a person who operates a machine or instrument, esp. a telephone switchboard 2 a person who runs a business: your tour operator will arrange a visa for you 3 informal a person who manipulates affairs and other people: she considered him a shrewd operator who only liked to appear to be simple 4 maths any symbol, term, or letter used to indicate or express a specific operation or process

operculum (oh-perk-yew-lum) n, pl -la (-la) or -lums a covering flap or lidlike structure in animals or plants [Latin: lid]

operetta n a type of comic or light-hearted opera

ophthalmia n inflammation of the eyeball or conjunctiva [Greek ophthalmos eye]

ophthalmic adj of or relating to the eye

ophthalmic optician n See optician (1)

ophthalmology n the branch of medicine concerned with the eye and its diseases ▷ **ophthalmologist** n

ophthalmoscope n an instrument for examining the interior of the eye

Ophüls n Max. 1902–57, German film director, whose films include Liebelei (1932), La Signora di tutti (1934), La Ronde (1950), Le Plaisir (1952), and Lola Montes (1955)

opiate (oh-pee-ate) n 1 a narcotic or sedative drug containing opium 2 something that causes mental dullness or inactivity

opine vb opining, opined formal to hold or express an opinion: he opined that the navy would have to start again from the beginning [Latin opinari]

opinion n 1 belief not founded on certainty or proof but on what seems probable 2 evaluation or estimation of a person or thing: they seemed to share my high opinion of her 3 a judgment given by an expert: medical opinion 4 a matter of opinion a point open to question [Latin opinio belief]

opinionated adj holding very strong opinions which one is convinced are right

opinion poll n same as poll (1)

opium (oh-pee-um) n an addictive narcotic drug made from the seed capsules of the opium poppy and used in medicine as a painkiller and sedative [Latin: poppy juice]

Oporto n a port in NW Portugal, near the mouth of the Douro River: the second largest city in Portugal, famous for port wine (begun in 1678). Pop: 263 131 (2001). Portuguese name: **Porto**

opossum n, pl -sums or -sum 1 a thick-furred American marsupial, with a long snout and a hairless prehensile tail 2 Austral and NZ a similar Australian animal, such as a phalanger [Native American aposoum]

Oppenheimer n J(ulius) Robert. 1904–67, US nuclear physicist. He was director of the Los Alamos laboratory (1943–45), which produced the first atomic bomb. He opposed the development of the hydrogen bomb (1949) and in 1953 was alleged to be a security risk. He was later exonerated

opponent n a person who opposes another in a contest, battle, or argument [Latin opponere to oppose]

opportune adj formal 1 happening at a time that is suitable or advantageous: there was an opportune knock at the door 2 (of time) suitable for a particular purpose: I have arrived at a very opportune moment [Latin opportunus, from ob- to + portus harbour (originally: coming to the harbour, obtaining timely protection)]

opportunist n 1 a person who adapts his or her actions to take advantage of opportunities and circumstances without regard for principles ▷ adj 2 taking advantage of opportunities and circumstances in this way ▷ **opportunism** n ▷ **opportunistic** adj

opportunity n, pl -ties 1 a favourable combination of circumstances 2 a good chance or prospect

opportunity shop n Austral and NZ a shop selling second-hand clothes, sometimes for charity. Sometimes shortened to: **op-shop**

opposable adj zoology (of the thumb) capable of touching the tip of all the other fingers

oppose vb -posing, -posed 1 Also: be opposed to to be against (something or someone) in speech or action 2 as opposed to in strong contrast with: I'm a realist as opposed to a theorist [Latin opponere] ▷ **opposing** adj

opposite adj 1 situated on the other or further side 2 facing or going in contrary directions: he saw another small craft heading the opposite way 3 completely different: I have a different, in fact, opposite view on this subject 4 maths (of a side in a triangle) facing a specified angle ▷ n 5 a person or thing that is opposite; antithesis ▷ prep 6 facing; across from ▷ adv 7 in an opposite position: fragments smashed through the windows of the house opposite

opposite number n a person holding an equivalent position in another group or organization: a ritual exchange of insults with an opposite number

opposition n 1 the act of opposing or being opposed 2 hostility, resistance, or disagreement 3 a person or group antagonistic or opposed to another 4 a political party or group opposed to the ruling party or government 5 astrol a diametrically opposite position of two heavenly bodies

oppress vb 1 to put down or control by cruelty or force 2 to make anxious or uncomfortable [Latin ob- against + premere to press] ▷ **oppression** n ▷ **oppressor** n

oppressive adj 1 cruel, harsh, or tyrannical 2 uncomfortable or depressing: a small flat can become rather oppressive 3 (of weather) hot and humid ▷ **oppressiveness** n

opprobrium (op-probe-ree-um) n formal 1 the state of being abused or scornfully criticized 2 a cause of disgrace or shame [Latin ob- against + probrum a shameful act] ▷ **opprobrious** adj

oppugn (op-pewn) vb formal to call into question; dispute [Latin ob- against + pugnare to fight]

op-shop n Austral and NZ short for **opportunity shop**

opt vb to show preference (for) or choose (to do something) [Latin optare to choose]

optic adj of the eye or vision [Greek optos visible]

optical adj 1 of or involving light or optics 2 of the eye or the sense of sight; optic 3 (of a lens) helping vision

optical fibre n a thin flexible glass fibre used in fibre optics to transmit information

optician n 1 Also called: **ophthalmic optician** a person who is qualified to examine the eyes and prescribe and supply spectacles and contact lenses 2 Also called: **dispensing optician** a person who supplies and fits spectacle frames and lenses, but is not qualified to prescribe lenses

optic nerve n a cranial nerve of vertebrates that conducts nerve impulses from the retina of the eye to the brain

optics n the science dealing with light and vision

optimal adj best or most favourable

optimism n 1 the tendency to take the most hopeful view in all matters 2 philosophy the doctrine of the ultimate triumph of good over evil [Latin optimus best] ⟩ **optimist** n ⟩ **optimistic** adj ⟩ **optimistically** adv

optimize or **-mise** vb **-mizing, -mized** or **-mising, -mised** to make the most of

optimum n, pl **-ma** or **-mums** 1 the most favourable conditions or best compromise possible ▷ adj 2 most favourable or advantageous; best: balance is a critical part of an optimum diet [Latin: the best (thing)]

option n 1 the power or liberty to choose: we have no option other than to fully comply 2 something that is or may be chosen: the menu includes a vegetarian option 3 an exclusive right, usually for a limited period, to buy or sell something at a future date: a producer could extend his option on the material for another six months 4 keep or leave one's options open not to commit oneself 5 soft option an easy alternative ▷ vb 6 to obtain or grant an option on: the film rights are optioned by an international film director [Latin optare to choose]

optional adj possible but not compulsory; open to choice

optometrist (op-tom-met-trist) n a person qualified to examine the eyes and prescribe and supply spectacles and contact lenses ⟩ **optometry** n

opt out vb 1 (often foll. by of) to choose not to be involved (in) or part (of), used esp. of schools and hospitals that leave the public sector ▷ n **opt-out** 2 the act of opting out, esp. of a local authority administration

opulent (op-pew-lent) adj 1 having or indicating wealth 2 abundant or plentiful [Latin opulens] ⟩ **opulence** n

opus (oh-puss) n, pl **opuses** or **opera** an artistic creation, esp. a musical work by a particular composer, numbered in order of publication: Beethoven's opus 61 [Latin: a work]

or conj 1 used to join alternatives: do you want to go out or stay at home? 2 used to join rephrasings of the same thing: twelve, or a dozen [Middle English contraction of other]

OR Oregon

oracle n 1 a shrine in ancient Greece or Rome at which gods were consulted through the medium of a priest or priestess for advice or prophecy 2 a prophecy or statement made by an oracle 3 any person believed to indicate future action with infallible authority [Latin oraculum]

oracular adj 1 of or like an oracle 2 wise and prophetic 3 mysterious or ambiguous

Oradea n an industrial city in NW Romania, in Transylvania: ceded by Hungary (1919). Pop: 182 000 (2005 est). German name: **Grosswardein**. Hungarian name: **Nagyvárad**

oral adj 1 spoken or verbal; using spoken words 2 of or for use in the mouth: an oral thermometer 3 (of a drug) to be taken by mouth: an oral contraceptive ▷ n 4 an examination in which the questions and answers are spoken rather than written [Latin os, oris mouth] ⟩ **orally** adv

Oran n a port in NW Algeria: the second largest city in the country; scene of the destruction by the British of most of the French fleet in the harbour in 1940 to prevent its capture by the Germans. Pop: 744 000 (2005 est)

orange n 1 a round reddish-yellow juicy citrus fruit

2 the evergreen tree on which it grows 3 a colour between red and yellow; the colour of an orange ▷ adj 4 of a colour between red and yellow [Arabic nāranj]

Orange n 1 a river in S Africa, rising in NE Lesotho and flowing generally west across the South African plateau to the Atlantic: the longest river in South Africa. Length: 2093 km (1300 miles) 2 a town in SE France: a small principality in the Middle Ages, the descendants of which formed the House of Orange. Pop: 27 989 (1999). Ancient name: **Arausio**

orangeade n Brit a usually fizzy orange-flavoured drink

orange blossom n the flowers of the orange tree, traditionally worn by brides

Orange Free State n a former province of central South Africa, between the Orange and Vaal rivers: settled by Boers in 1836 after the Great Trek; annexed by Britain in 1848; became a province of South Africa in 1910; replaced in 1994 by the new province of Free State; economy based on agriculture and mineral resources (esp. gold and uranium). Capital: Bloemfontein

Orangeman n, pl **-men** a member of a political society founded in Ireland in 1795 to uphold Protestantism [after William, prince of Orange, later William III]

orangery n, pl **-eries** a conservatory or greenhouse in which orange trees are grown in cooler climates

orangey adj slightly orange

orang-utan or **orang-utang** n a large ape of the forests of Sumatra and Borneo, with shaggy reddish-brown hair and long arms [Malay ōrang man + hūtan forest]

oration n a formal or ceremonial public speech [Latin oratio]

orator (or-rat-tor) n a person who gives an oration, esp. one skilled in persuasive public speaking

oratorio (or-rat-tor-ee-oh) n, pl **-rios** a musical composition for soloists, chorus, and orchestra, based on a religious theme [Italian]

oratory¹ (or-rat-tree) n the art or skill of public speaking [Latin (ars) oratoria (the art of) public speaking]

oratory² n, pl **-ries** a small room or building set apart for private prayer [Latin orare to pray]

orb n 1 an ornamental sphere with a cross on top, carried by a king or queen in important ceremonies 2 a sphere; globe 3 poetic the eye 4 obsolete or poetic a heavenly body, such as the sun [Latin orbis circle, disc]

Orbison n Roy (Kelton). 1936–89, US pop singer and songwriter. His records include the singles "Only the Lonely" (1960) and "Oh Pretty Woman" (1964) and the album Mystery Girl (1989)

orbit n 1 the curved path followed by something, such as a heavenly body or spacecraft, in its motion around another body 2 a range or sphere of action or influence 3 anatomy the eye socket ▷ vb **-biting, -bited** 4 to move around (a heavenly body) in an orbit 5 to send (a satellite or spacecraft) into orbit [Latin orbis circle] ⟩ **orbital** adj

Orcadian n 1 a native or inhabitant of Orkney ▷ adj 2 of or relating to Orkney or its inhabitants [Latin Orcades the Orkney Islands]

Orcagna n Andrea, original name Andrea di Cione. ?1308–68, Florentine painter, sculptor, and architect

orchard n an area of land on which fruit trees are grown [Old English orceard]

orchestra n 1 a large group of musicians whose members play a variety of different instruments 2 Also called: **orchestra pit** the space, in front of or under the stage, reserved for musicians in a theatre [Greek: the space in the theatre for the chorus] ⟩ **orchestral** adj

orchestrate vb **-trating, -trated** 1 to score or arrange (a piece of music) for orchestra 2 to arrange (something) in order to produce a particular result: he had orchestrated today's meeting ⟩ **orchestration** n

orchid n a plant having flowers of unusual shapes and beautiful colours, usually with one lip-shaped petal which is larger than the other two [Greek orkhis testicle, because of the shape of its roots]

Orczy *n* Baroness **Emmuska**. 1865–1947, British novelist, born in Hungary; author of *The Scarlet Pimpernel* (1905)

Ord *n* a river in NE Western Australia, rising on the Kimberley Plateau and flowing generally north to the Timor Sea: subject of a major irrigation scheme. Length: about 500 km (300 miles)

ordain *vb* **1** to make (someone) a member of the clergy **2** *formal* to decree or order with authority [Late Latin *ordinare*] ▷ **ordainment** *n*

ordeal *n* **1** a severe or trying experience **2** *history* a method of trial in which the accused person was subjected to physical danger [Old English *ordāl, ordēl* verdict]

order *n* **1** an instruction that must be obeyed; command **2** a state in which everything is arranged logically, comprehensibly, or naturally: *she strove to keep more order in the house* **3** an arrangement of things in succession; sequence: *group them by letter and then put them in numerical order* **4** an established or customary system of society: *there is an opportunity here for a new world order* **5** a peaceful or harmonious condition of society: *riot police were called in to restore order* **6 a** an instruction to supply something in return for payment: *the waitress came to take their order* **b** the thing or things supplied **7** a written instruction to pay money: *post the coupon below with a cheque or postal order* **8** a social class: *the result will be harmful to society as a whole and to the lower orders in particular* **9** *biology* one of the groups into which a class is divided, containing one or more families **10** kind or sort: *the orchestra played superbly and the singing was of the highest order* **11** Also called: **religious order** a religious community of monks or nuns **12** a group of people who have been awarded a particular honour: *the Order of the Garter* **13** the office or rank of a Christian minister: *he studied for the priesthood as a young man, but never took Holy Orders* **14** the procedure and rules followed by an assembly or meeting: *a point of order* **15** one of the five major classical styles of architecture, classified by the type of columns used **16 a tall order** something difficult or demanding **17 in order a** in sequence **b** properly arranged: *everything is in order for your trip* **c** appropriate or fitting **18 in order that** so that **19 in order to** so that it is possible to: *a healthy diet is necessary in order to keep fit* **20 in or of the order of** amounting approximately to: *summer temperatures are usually in the order of 35°* **21 keep order** to ensure that people obey the law or behave in an acceptable manner **22 on order** having been ordered but not yet delivered **23 out of order a** not in sequence **b** not working: *the lift was out of order, so we had to use the stairs* **c** not following the rules or customary procedure: *the chairperson ruled the motion out of order* **24 to order** according to a buyer's specifications ▷ *vb* **25** to command or instruct (to do something): *she ordered her son to wash the dishes; the police ordered her into the house* **26** to request (something) to be supplied in return for payment: *I ordered a new car three weeks ago, but it hasn't been delivered yet* **27** to arrange (things) methodically or in their proper places ▷ *interj* **28** an exclamation demanding that orderly behaviour be restored [Latin *ordo*]

order around *or* **order about** *vb* to repeatedly tell (someone) what to do in a bossy or unsympathetic way: *it was intolerable that those two could order her around*

orderly *adj* **1** tidy or well-organized: *they evacuated the building in an orderly manner* **2** well-behaved; law-abiding ▷ *n, pl* **-lies 3** *med* a male hospital attendant **4** *military* a soldier whose duty is to carry out orders or perform minor tasks for a more senior officer ▷ **orderliness** *n*

Order of Merit *n Brit* an order awarded for outstanding achievement in any field

order paper *n* a list indicating the order of business, esp. in Parliament

ordinal number *n* a number indicating position in a sequence, such as *first, second, third*

ordinance *n* an official rule or order [Latin *ordinare* to set in order]

ordinarily *adv* in ordinary or usual practice; usually; normally

ordinary *adj* **1** usual or normal: *it was an ordinary working day for them* **2** not special or different in any way: *what did ordinary Germans feel about reunification?* **3** dull or unexciting: *the restaurant charged very high prices for very ordinary cooking* ▷ *n, pl* **-naries 4** *RC Church* the parts of the Mass that do not vary from day to day **5 out of the ordinary** unusual [Latin *ordinarius* orderly]

Ordinary level *n* (in Britain) the formal name for **O level**

ordinary rating *n* a rank in the Royal Navy equivalent to that of a private in the army

ordinary seaman *n Brit, Austral and NZ* a seaman of the lowest rank

ordinary shares *pl n Brit and Austral* shares issued by a company entitling their holders to a dividend according to the profits of the company and to a claim on net assets

ordinate *n maths* the vertical coordinate of a point in a two-dimensional system of coordinates [Latin *ordinare* to arrange in order]

ordination *n* the act or ceremony of making someone a member of the clergy

ordnance *n* **1** weapons and other military supplies **2 the ordnance** a government department dealing with military supplies [variant of *ordinance*]

Ordnance Survey *n* the British government organization that produces detailed maps of Britain and Ireland

Ordovician (or-doe-vish-ee-an) *adj geology* of the period of geological time about 500 million years ago [Latin *Ordovices*, ancient Celtic tribe in N Wales]

ordure *n* excrement; dung [Old French *ord* dirty]

Ordzhonikidze *or* **Orjonikidze** *n* the former name (1954–91) of **Vladikavkaz**

ore *n* rock or mineral from which valuable substances such as metals can be extracted [Old English *ār, ōra*]

Örebro *n* a town in S Sweden: one of Sweden's oldest towns; scene of the election of Jean Bernadotte as heir to the throne in 1810. Pop: 126 940 (2004 est)

Oreg. Oregon

oregano (or-rig-gah-no) *n* a sweet-smelling herb used as seasoning [Greek *origanon* an aromatic herb]

Oregon *n* a state of the northwestern US, on the Pacific: consists of the Coast and Cascade Ranges in the west and a plateau in the east; important timber production. Capital: Salem. Pop: 3 559 596 (2003 est). Area: 251 418 sq km (97 073 sq miles). Abbreviation: **Oreg.,** (with zip code) **OR**

Oregon trail *n* an early pioneering route across the central US, from Independence, W Missouri, to the Columbia River country of N Oregon: used chiefly between 1804 and 1860. Length: about 3220 km (2000 miles)

Orel *or* **Oryol** *n* a city in W Russia; founded in 1564 but damaged during World War II. Pop: 333 000 (2005 est)

Ore Mountains *pl n* another name for the **Erzgebirge**

Orenburg *n* a city in W Russia, on the Ural River. Pop: 550 000 (2005 est). Former name (1938–57): **Chkalov**

Orense *n* a city in NW Spain, in Galicia on the Miño River: warm springs. Pop: 109 475 (2003 est). Galician name: **Ourense**

Oresme *n* Nicole d'. ?1320–82, French economist, mathematician, and cleric: bishop of Lisieux (1378–82)

Øresund *n* the Danish name for the **Sound**. Swedish name: **Öresund**

Orff *n* Carl. 1895–1982, German composer. His works include the secular oratorio *Carmina Burana* (1937) and the opera *Antigone* (1949)

organ *n* **1** a part in animals and plants that is adapted to perform a particular function, for example the heart or lungs **2 a** a musical keyboard instrument which produces sound by forcing air through pipes of a variety of lengths **b** Also called: **electric organ** a keyboard instrument which produces similar sounds electronically **3** a means of communication, such as a newspaper issued by a specialist group or party **4** euphemistic a penis [Greek *organon* tool]

organdie *n* a fine, slightly stiff cotton fabric [French *organdi*]

organ-grinder *n* (formerly) an entertainer who played a barrel organ in the streets

organic *adj* **1** of, produced by, or found in plants or animals: *the rocks were carefully searched for organic remains* **2** not using, or grown without, artificial fertilizers or pesticides: *organic vegetables; an organic farm* **3** *chem* of or belonging to the class of chemical compounds that are formed from carbon **4** (of change or development) gradual and natural rather than sudden or forced **5** made up of many different parts which contribute to the way in which the whole society or structure works: *an organic whole* **> organically** *adv*

organic chemistry *n chem* the branch of chemistry dealing with carbon compounds

organism *n* **1** an animal or plant **2** anything resembling a living creature in structure, behaviour, or complexity: *cities are more complicated organisms than farming villages*

organist *n* a person who plays the organ

organization *or* **-nisation** *n* **1** an organized group of people, such as a club, society, union, or business **2** the act of organizing: *setting up the European tour took a lot of organization* **3** the structure and arrangement of the different parts of something: *the report recommended radical changes in the organization of the social services department* **4** the state of being organized: *the material in this essay lacks any sort of organization* **> organizational** *or* **-isational** *adj*

organize *or* **-nise** *vb* **-nizing, -nized** *or* **-nising, -nised** **1** to plan and arrange (something): *we organized a protest meeting in the village hall* **2** to arrange systematically: *the files are organized in alphabetical order and by date* **3** to form, join, or recruit (people) into a trade union: *the seasonal nature of tourism makes it difficult for hotel workers to organize* [Medieval Latin *organizare*] **> organizer** *or* **-niser** *n*

organized *or* **-nised** *adj* **1** planned and controlled on a large scale and involving many people: *organized crime* **2** orderly and efficient: *a highly organized campaign* **3** (of the workers in a factory or office) belonging to a trade union: *socialism is especially popular among organized labour*

organza *n* a thin stiff fabric of silk, cotton, or synthetic fibre [origin unknown]

orgasm *n* the most intense point of pleasure and excitement during sexual activity [Greek *orgasmos*] **> orgasmic** *adj*

orgy *n, pl* **-gies** **1** a wild party involving promiscuous sexual activity and excessive drinking **2** an act of immoderate or frenzied indulgence: *the rioters were engaged in an orgy of destruction* [Greek *orgia* secret rites] **> orgiastic** *adj*

oriel window *or* **oriel** *n* a window built out from the wall of a house at an upper level [Old French *oriol* gallery]

orient *vb* **1 2** to position or set (for example a map or chart) with relation to the points of the compass or other specific directions **3** *orient oneself* to adjust or align oneself or one's ideas according to new surroundings or circumstances: *new employees can take some time to orient themselves to the company's procedures* **4** be oriented to or towards to work or act with a particular aim, idea, or person in mind: *many people feel that Britain is too much oriented to the Americans* **▷** *n* **5** *poetic* the east [Latin *oriens* rising (sun)]

Orient *n* the Orient East Asia

oriental *adj* eastern

Oriental *adj* **1** of or relating to the Orient **▷** *n* **2** *offensive* a native or inhabitant of the Orient

orientate *vb* **-tating, -tated** same as **orient**

-orientated *or* **-oriented** *combining form* interested in or directed towards the thing specified: *career-orientated women*

orientation *n* **1** the activities and aims that a person or organization is interested in: *the course has a practical rather than theoretical orientation* **2** the position of an object with relation to the points of the compass or other specific directions: *the room's southerly orientation means that it receives a lot of light* **▷** *adj* **3** of or providing information or training needed to understand a new situation or environment: *nearly every college has an orientation programme*

orienteering *n* a sport in which contestants race on foot over a cross-country course consisting of checkpoints found with the aid of a map and compass [Swedish *orientering*]

orifice (or-rif-fiss) *n* an opening or hole through which something can pass, esp. one in the body such as the mouth or anus [Latin *os* mouth + *facere* to make]

orig. **1** origin **2** original(ly)

origami (or-rig-gah-mee) *n* the art, originally Japanese, of folding paper intricately into decorative shapes [Japanese *ori* a fold + *kami* paper]

Origen *n* ?185–?254 AD, Christian theologian, born in Alexandria. His writings include *Hexapla*, a synopsis of the Old Testament, *Contra Celsum*, a defence of Christianity, and *De principiis*, a statement of Christian theology

origin *n* **1** the point, source, or event from which something develops: *the origin of the term 'jazz' is obscure; the war had its origin in the clash between rival nationalists* **2** the country, race, or social class of a person's parents or ancestors: *an Australian of Greek origin; he was proud of his working-class origins* **3** *maths* the point at which the horizontal and vertical axes intersect [Latin *origo* beginning]

original *adj* **1** first or earliest: *the dining room also has attractive original beams* **2** fresh and unusual; not copied from or based on something else: *the composer's work has created some original and attractive choreography* **3** able to think of or carry out new ideas or concepts: *he is an excitingly original writer* **4** being the first and genuine form of something, from which a copy or translation is made: *all French recipes were translated from the original abridged versions* **▷** *n* **5** the first and genuine form of something, from which others are copied or translated: *the original is in the British Museum* **6** a person or thing used as a model in art or literature: *she claimed to be the original on whom Lawrence based Lady Chatterley* **> originality** *n* **> originally** *adv*

original sin *n* a state of sin believed by some Christians to be inborn in all human beings as a result of Adam's disobedience

originate *vb* **-nating, -nated** to come or bring (something) into existence: *humans probably originated in East Africa* **> origination** *n* **> originator** *n*

Orinoco *n* a river in N South America, rising in S Venezuela and flowing west, then north as part of the border between Colombia and Venezuela, then east to the Atlantic by a great delta: the third largest river system in South America, draining an area of 945 000 sq km (365 000 sq miles); reaches a width of 22 km (14 miles) during the rainy season. Length: about 2575 km (1600 miles)

oriole *n* a songbird with a long pointed bill and a mostly yellow-and-black plumage [Latin *aureolus* golden]

Orissa *n* the former name (until 2011) of **Odisha**

Orizaba *n* **1** a city and resort in SE Mexico, in Veracruz state. Pop: 327 000 (2005 est) **2** Pico de Orizaba the Spanish name for **Citlaltépetl**

Orjonikidze *n* a variant spelling of **Ordzhonikidze**

Orkney, Orkneys *or* **Orkney Islands** *pl n* a group of over 70 islands off the N coast of Scotland, separated from the mainland by the Pentland Firth: constitutes an island authority of Scotland; low-lying and treeless; many important prehistoric remains. Administrative centre: Kirkwall. Pop: 19 310 (2003 est). Area: 974 sq km (376 sq miles). Related word: **Orcadian**

Orkneyman *n, pl* **-men** a native or inhabitant of Orkney

> **Orkneywoman** *fem n*

Orlando *n* a city in the US, in Florida: site of Walt Disney World. Pop: 199 336 (2003 est)

Orléanais *n* a former province of N central France, centred on Orléans

Orléans¹ *n* a city in N central France, on the River Loire: famous for its deliverance by Joan of Arc from the long English siege in 1429; university (1305); an important rail and road junction. Pop: 116 256 (2006)

Orléans² *n* **1** Charles, Duc d'Orléans. 1394–1465, French poet; noted for the poems written during his imprisonment in England; father of Louis XII **2 Louis Philippe Joseph**, Duc d'Orléans, known as *Philippe Égalité* (after 1792). 1747–93, French nobleman, who supported the French Revolution and voted for the death of his cousin, Louis XVI, but was executed after his son, the future king Louis-Philippe, defected to the Austrians

Orlov *n* Count **Grigori Grigorievich**. 1734–83, Russian soldier and a lover of Catherine II. He led (with his brother, Count **Aleksey Grigorievich Orlov**, 1737–1808) the coup that brought Catherine to power

Orly *n* a suburb of SE Paris, France, with an international airport

Ormandy *n* **Eugene**. 1899–1985, US conductor, born in Hungary

ormolu *n* a gold-coloured alloy of copper, tin, or zinc, used to decorate furniture and other articles [French *or moulu* ground gold]

Ormonde *n* **1st Duke of**, title of *James Butler*. 1610–88, Anglo-Irish general; commander (1641–50) of the royalist forces in Ireland; Lord Lieutenant of Ireland (1661–69; 1677–84)

Ormuz *n* a variant spelling of **Hormuz**

ornament *n* **1** anything that adorns someone or something; decoration: *the room's only ornament was a dim, oily picture of the Holy Family* **2** decorations collectively: *he had no watch, nor ornament of any kind* **3** a small decorative object: *I hit a garden ornament while parking* **4** a person whose character or talent makes them an asset to society or the group to which they belong: *an ornament of the firm* **5** music a note or group of notes which embellishes the melody but is not an integral part of it, for instance a trill ▷ *vb* **6** to decorate or adorn: *the hall had a high ceiling, ornamented with plaster fruits and flowers* [Latin *ornamentum*]
> **ornamental** *adj* > **ornamentation** *n* > **ornamented** *adj*

ornate *adj* **1** heavily or elaborately decorated: *an ornate ceiling painted with allegorical figures* **2** (of style in writing) overelaborate; using many literary expressions [Latin *ornare* to decorate] > **ornately** *adv*

Orne *n* a department of NW France, in Basse-Normandie. Capital: Alençon. Pop: 291 274 (2003 est). Area: 6144 sq km (2396 sq miles).

ornithology *n* the study of birds [Greek *ornis* bird]
> **ornithological** *adj* > **ornithologist** *n*

Orontes *n* a river in SW Asia, rising in Lebanon and flowing north through Syria into Turkey, where it turns west to the Mediterranean. Length: 571 km (355 miles). Arabic name: **'Asi**

orotund *adj* **1** (of the voice) resonant and booming **2** (of speech or writing) pompous; containing many long or formal words [Latin *ore rotundo* with rounded mouth]

Orozco *n* **José Clemente**. 1883–1949, Mexican painter, noted for his monumental humanistic murals

orphan *n* **1** a child whose parents are dead ▷ *vb* **2** to cause (someone) to become an orphan: *she was orphaned at 16 when her parents died in a car crash* [Greek *orphanos*]

orphanage *n* a children's home for orphans and abandoned children

orphaned *adj* having no living parents

Orpington *n* a district of SE London, part of the Greater London borough of Bromley from 1965

Orr *n* **Robert Gordon**, known as *Bobby*. born 1948, Canadian ice-hockey player

orrery *n, pl* **-ries** a mechanical model of the solar system in which the planets can be moved around the sun [originally made for the Earl of *Orrery*]

orris *n* **1** a kind of iris that has fragrant roots **2** Also: **orrisroot** the root of this plant prepared and used as perfume [variant of *iris*]

Orsk *n* a city in W Russia, on the Ural River: a major railway and industrial centre, with an oil refinery linked by pipeline with the Emba field (on the Caspian). Pop: 247 000 (2005 est)

Ortega *n* **Daniel**, full surname *Ortega Saavedra*. born 1945, Nicaraguan politician and former resistance leader; president of Nicaragua (1985–90) and from 2007

Ortegal *n* **Cape Ortegal** a cape in NW Spain, projecting into the Bay of Biscay

Ortega y Gasset *n* **José**. 1883–1955, Spanish essayist and philosopher. His best-known work is *The Revolt of the Masses* (1930)

orthodontics *n* the branch of dentistry concerned with correcting irregularities of the teeth [Greek *orthos* straight + *odōn* tooth] > **orthodontic** *adj* > **orthodontist** *n*

orthodox *adj* conforming to traditional or established standards in religion, behaviour, or attitudes: *orthodox medicine; the concerto has a more orthodox structure than is usual for this composer* [Greek *orthos* correct + *doxa* belief]
> **orthodoxy** *n*

Orthodox *adj* **1** of the Orthodox Church of Eastern Europe **2** of or being the form of Judaism characterized by traditional interpretation of and strict adherence to Mosaic Law: *an Orthodox Jew*

Orthodox Church *n* the Christian Church dominant in Eastern Europe, which has the Greek Patriarch of Constantinople as its head

orthography *n* **1** spelling considered to be correct: *British and American orthography is different in many cases* **2** the study of spelling [Greek *orthos* correct + *graphein* to write]
> **orthographic** *adj*

orthopaedics or US **orthopedics** *n* the branch of surgery concerned with disorders of the bones and joints [Greek *orthos* straight + *pais* child] > **orthopaedic** or US **orthopedic** *adj* > **orthopaedist** or US **orthopedist** *n*

Ortles *pl n* a range of the Alps in N Italy. Highest peak: 3899 m (12 792 ft). Also called: **Ortler**

ortolan *n* a small European songbird eaten as a delicacy [Latin *hortulus* a little garden]

Orton *n* **Joe (Kingsley)**. 1933–67, British dramatist, noted for his black comedies: these include *Entertaining Mr Sloane* (1964), *Loot* (1966), and *What the Butler Saw* (1969)

Orumiyeh *n* **Lake Orumiyeh** another name for Lake Urmia

Oruro *n* a city in W Bolivia: a former silver-mining centre; university (1892); tin, copper, and tungsten. Pop: 206 000 (2005 est)

Orvieto *n* **1** a market town in central Italy, in Umbria: Etruscan remains. Pop: 20 705 (2001). Latin name: **Urbs Vetus 2** a light white wine from this region

Orwell *n* **George**, real name *Eric Arthur Blair*. 1903–50, English novelist and essayist, born in India. He is notable for his social criticism, as in *The Road to Wigan Pier* (1932); his account of his experiences of the Spanish Civil War *Homage to Catalonia* (1938); and his satirical novels *Animal Farm* (1945), an allegory on the Russian Revolution, and *1984* (1949), in which he depicts an authoritarian state of the future > **Orwellian** *adj*

Oryol *n* a variant spelling of **Orel**

oryx *n* any of various large straight-horned African antelopes

Os *chem* osmium

OS 1 (in Britain) Ordnance Survey **2** outsize(d)

Osaka *n* a port in S Japan, on S Honshu on **Osaka Bay** (an inlet of the Pacific): the third largest city in Japan (the chief commercial city during feudal times); university (1931); an industrial and commercial centre. Pop: 2 484 326 (2002 est)

Osborne *n* **1 George**, real name *Gideon Oliver Osborne*. born

1971, British Conservative politician; Chancellor of the Exchequer from 2010 **2 John (James).** 1929–94, British dramatist. His plays include *Look Back in Anger* (1956), containing the prototype of the angry young man, Jimmy Porter, *The Entertainer* (1957), and *Inadmissible Evidence* (1964)

Osborne House *n* a house near Cowes on the Isle of Wight: the favourite residence of Queen Victoria, who died there; now a convalescent home

Oscar *n* an award in the form of a small gold statuette awarded annually in the US for outstanding achievements in various aspects of the film industry: *he won an Oscar for Best Supporting Actor in 1974* [said to have been named after a remark made by an official that it reminded her of her uncle Oscar]

Oscar II *n* 1829–1907, king of Sweden (1872–1907) and of Norway (1872–1905)

oscillate (oss-ill-late) *vb* **-lating, -lated 1** to swing repeatedly back and forth: *its wings oscillate up and down many times a second* **2** to waver between two extremes of opinion, attitude, or behaviour: *the government oscillates between a desire for reform and a desire to keep its powers intact* **3** *physics* (of an electric current) to vary between minimum and maximum values [Latin *oscillare* to swing] **> oscillation** *n* **> oscillator** *n*

oscilloscope (oss-sill-oh-scope) *n* an instrument that produces a visual representation of an oscillating electric current on the screen of a cathode-ray tube

Oshawa *n* a city in central Canada, in SE Ontario on Lake Ontario: motor-vehicle industry. Pop: 139 051 (2001)

Oshogbo *n* a city in SW Nigeria: trade centre. Pop: 629 000 (2005 est)

Oshun *or* **Osun** *n* a state of SW Nigeria. Capital: Oshogbo. Pop: 3 423 535 (2006). Area: 9251 sq km (3570 sq miles)

osier (oh-zee-er) *n* **1** a willow tree whose flexible branches or twigs are used for making baskets and furniture **2** a twig or branch from this tree [Old French]

Osijek *n* a town in NE Croatia on the Drava River: under Turkish rule from 1526 to 1687. Pop: 85 000 (2005 est). Ancient name: **Mursa**

Osiris *n* an Egyptian god of the underworld

Osler *n* Sir William. 1849–1919, Canadian physician, pioneer of residency in medical training

Oslo *n* the capital and chief port of Norway, in the southeast at the head of **Oslo Fjord** (an inlet of the Skagerrak): founded in about 1050; university (1811); a major commercial and industrial centre, producing about a quarter of Norway's total output. Pop: 521 886 (2004 est). Former name: (1624–1877) **Christiania**, (1877–1924) **Kristiania**

Osman I *or* **Othman I** *n* 1259–1326, Turkish sultan; founder of the Ottoman Empire

osmium *n chem* a very hard brittle bluish-white metal, the heaviest known element. Symbol: **Os** [Greek *osmē* smell, from its penetrating odour]

osmoregulation *n zoology* the adjustment of the osmotic pressure of a cell or organism in relation to the surrounding fluid

osmosis *n* **1** the diffusion of liquids through a membrane until they are mixed **2** the process by which people or ideas influence each other gradually and subtly [Greek *ōsmos* push] **> osmotic** *adj*

Osnabrück *n* an industrial city in NW Germany, in Lower Saxony: a member of the Hanseatic League in the Middle Ages; one of the treaties comprising the Peace of Westphalia (1648) was signed here. Pop: 165 517 (2003 est)

osprey *n* a large fish-eating bird of prey, with a dark back and whitish head and underparts [Old French *ospres*, apparently from Latin *ossifraga*, literally: bone-breaker]

Ossa *n* a mountain in NE Greece, in E Thessaly: famous in mythology for the attempt of the twin giants, Otus and Ephialtes, to reach heaven by piling Ossa on Olympus and Pelion on Ossa. Height: 1978 m (6489 ft)

osseous *adj* consisting of or like bone [Latin *os* bone]

Ossetia *n* a region of central Asia, in the Caucasus: consists administratively of the North Ossetian Republic in Russia and South Ossetia (formerly an Autonomous Region) in Georgia

Ossetic *or* **Ossetian** *adj* **1** of or relating to Ossetia, its people, or their language ▷ *n* **2** the language of the Ossets, belonging to the East Iranian branch of the Indo-European family

Ossi *n informal* a native, inhabitant, or citizen of that part of Germany that was formerly East Germany [C20: from German *ostdeutsch* East German]

Ossian *n* a legendary Irish hero and bard of the 3rd century AD. See also **Macpherson**

Ossie *adj, n* a variant spelling of **Aussie**

Ossietzky *n* Carl von. 1889–1938, German pacifist leader. He was imprisoned for revealing Germany's secret rearmament (1931–32) and again under Hitler (1933–36): Nobel peace prize 1935

ossify *vb* **-fies, -fying, -fied 1** to change into bone; harden **2** to become rigid, inflexible, or unprogressive: *ossified traditions* [Latin *os* bone + *facere* to make] **> ossification** *n*

Ostend *n* a port and resort in NW Belgium, in West Flanders on the North Sea. Pop: 68 273 (2004 est). French name: **Ostende**. Flemish name: **Oostende**

ostensible *adj* apparent or seeming; alleged: *our ostensible common interest is boats* [Latin *ostendere* to show] **> ostensibly** *adv*

ostensive *adj* directly showing or pointing out: *he gave ostensive definitions to things* [Latin *ostendere* to show]

ostentation *n* pretentious, showy, or vulgar display: *she felt the gold taps in the bathroom were tasteless ostentation* **> ostentatious** *adj* **> ostentatiously** *adv*

osteoarthritis (ost-ee-oh-arth-rite-iss) *n* chronic inflammation of the joints, causing pain and stiffness [Greek *osteon* bone + ARTHRITIS] **> osteoarthritic** *adj*

osteopathy *n* a system of healing based on the manipulation of bones or muscle [Greek *osteon* bone + *patheia* suffering] **> osteopath** *n*

osteoporosis (ost-ee-oh-pore-oh-siss) *n* brittleness of the bones, caused by lack of calcium [Greek *osteon* bone + *poros* passage]

Österreich *n* the German name for **Austria**

Ostia *n* an ancient town in W central Italy, originally at the mouth of the Tiber but now about 6 km (4 miles) inland: served as the port of ancient Rome; harbours built by Claudius and Trajan; ruins excavated since 1854

ostinato *n, pl* **-tos** *music* a persistently repeated phrase or rhythm [Italian, from Latin *obstinatus* obstinate]

ostler *n* (formerly) a stableman at an inn [variant of *hostler*, from *hostel*]

Ostpreussen *n* the German name for **East Prussia**

ostracize *or* **-cise** *vb* **-cizing, -cized** *or* **-cising, -cised** to exclude or banish (a person) from a particular group or from society: *he was ostracized from his family when his affair became known* [Greek *ostrakizein* to select someone for banishment by voting on potsherds] **> ostracism** *n*

Ostrava *n* an industrial city in the E Czech Republic, on the River Oder: the chief coal-mining area in the Czech Republic, in Upper Silesia. Pop: 316 000 (2005 est)

ostrich *n* **1** a large African bird which runs fast but cannot fly, and has a long neck, long legs, and soft dark feathers **2** a person who refuses to recognize an unpleasant truth: *he accused the Minister of being 'an ostrich with its head stuck in the sand, while all around him unemployment soars'* [Greek *strouthion*]

Ostrovsky *n* Aleksandr Nikolayevich. 1823–86, Russian dramatist, noted for his satirical comedies about the bourgeoisie. His plays include *The Bankrupt* (1849) and *The Storm* (1859), a tragedy

Ostwald *n* Wilhelm. 1853–1932, German chemist, noted for his pioneering work in catalysis. He also invented a process for making nitric acid from ammonia and developed a new theory of colour: Nobel prize for chemistry 1909

Osun n a variant spelling of **Oshun**

Oswald n **1 Lee Harvey.** 1939–63, presumed assassin (1963) of US president John F. Kennedy; murdered by Jack Ruby two days later **2 Saint.** ?605–41 AD, king of Northumbria (634–41); with St Aidan he restored Christianity to the region. He was killed in battle by Penda of Mercia. Feast day: Aug 5

Oświęcim n the Polish name for **Auschwitz**

OT Old Testament

Otago n a council region of New Zealand, formerly a province, founded by Scottish settlers in the south of South Island. The University of Otago (1869) in Dunedin is the oldest university in New Zealand. Chief town: Dunedin. Pop: 195 000 (2004 est)

OTC (in Britain) Officers' Training Corps

OTE chiefly Brit (esp. in job adverts) on target earnings: the minimum amount of money a salesman is expected to make

other adj **1** remaining (one or ones) in a group of which one or some have been specified: *she wasn't getting on with the other children* **2** being a different one or ones from the one or ones already specified or understood: *other people might not be so tolerant of your behaviour; are you sure it's not in your other pocket?* **3** refers to a place or time which is not the one the speaker or writer is in: *results in other countries have been most encouraging* **4** additional; further: *there is one other thing for the government to do* **5 every other** every alternate: *the doctor sees me every other week* **6 other than a** apart from: *he knew little of the country other than it was Muslim* **b** different from: *treatment other than a hearing aid will be possible for those with inner ear deafness* **7 or other** used to add vagueness to the preceding word or phrase: *he could take some evening course or other which could lead to an extra qualification; he was called away from the house on some pretext or other* **8 the other day** a few days ago ▷ n **9** an additional person or thing: *show me one other* **10 others** people apart from the person who is being spoken or written about: *she devoted her entire life to helping others* **11 the others** the people or things remaining in a group of which one or some have been specified: *I can't speak for the others* ▷ adv **12** otherwise; differently: *they couldn't behave other than they do* [Old English ōther] ❯ **otherness** n

> **USAGE** See at **otherwise**.

other ranks pl n Brit and Austral (in the armed forces) all those who do not hold a commissioned rank

otherwise conj **1** or else; if not, then: *I was 50 but said I was 40, otherwise I'd never have got a job* ▷ adv **2** differently: *it was fruitless to pretend or to hope otherwise* **3** in other respects: *shrewd psychological twists perk up an otherwise predictable story line* ▷ adj **4** different: *circumstances beyond our control dictated that it should be otherwise* ▷ pron **5 or otherwise** or not; or the opposite: *he didn't want company, talkative or otherwise*

> **USAGE** The expression *otherwise than* means *in any other way than* and should not be followed by an adjective: *no-one taught by this method can be other than* (not *otherwise than*) *successful; you are not allowed to use the building otherwise than as a private dwelling.*

otherworldly adj **1** concerned with spiritual rather than practical matters: *his otherworldly manner concealed a ruthless business mind* **2** mystical or supernatural: *this part of Italy has an otherworldly beauty*

otiose (oh-tee-oze) adj serving no useful purpose: *such a strike is almost otiose* [Latin *otiosus* leisured]

O'Toole n (Seamus) **Peter.** 1932–2013, British actor, born in Ireland. His films include *Lawrence of Arabia* (1962), *The Lion in Winter* (1968), *High Spirits* (1988), *Fairytale* (1998) and *Venus* (2006); stage appearances include *Jeffrey Bernard is Unwell* (1989)

Otranto n a small port in SE Italy, in Apulia on the **Strait of Otranto**: the most easterly town in Italy; dates back to Greek times and was an important Roman port; its ruined castle was the setting of Horace Walpole's *Castle of Otranto*. Pop: 5282 (2001)

OTT slang over the top

Ottawa n **1** the capital of Canada, in E Ontario on the Ottawa River: name changed from Bytown to Ottawa in 1854. Pop: 883 391 (2011) **2** a river in central Canada, rising in W Quebec and flowing west, then southeast to join the St Lawrence River as its chief tributary at Montreal; forms the border between Quebec and Ontario for most of its length. Length: 1120 km (696 miles)

otter n a small freshwater fish-eating animal with smooth brown fur, a streamlined body, and webbed feet [Old English *otor*]

Otterburn n a village in NE England, in central Northumberland: scene of a battle (1388) in which the Scots, led by the earl of Douglas, defeated the English, led by Hotspur

Otto n **Rudolf.** 1869–1937, German theologian: his best-known work is *The Idea of the Holy* (1923)

Otto I or **Otho I** n called the Great. 912–73 AD, king of Germany (936–73); Holy Roman Emperor (962–73)

Otto IV n ?1175–1218. German king and Holy Roman Emperor (1198–1215): invaded S Italy (1210) but was later (1214) defeated by France and deposed

ottoman n, pl **-mans** a storage chest with a padded lid for use as a seat [French *ottomane*, feminine of *Ottoman*]

Ottoman adj **1** history of the Ottomans or the Ottoman Empire, the Turkish empire which lasted from the late 13th century until the end of World War I, and at its height included the Balkans and much of N Africa ▷ n, pl **-mans 2** a member of a Turkish people who formed the basis of this empire [Arabic *Othmāni*]

Otway n **Thomas.** 1652–85, English dramatist, noted for *The Orphan* (1680) and *Venice Preserv'd* (1682)

ou (oh) n S African slang a man, bloke, or chap [Afrikaans]

OU 1 the Open University **2** Oxford University

Ouachita or **Washita** n a river in the S central US, rising in the Ouachita Mountains and flowing east, south, and southeast into the Red River in E Louisiana. Length: 974 km (605 miles)

Ouagadougou n the capital of Burkina Faso, on the central plateau: terminus of the railway from Abidjan (Côte d'Ivoire). Pop: 870 000 (2005 est)

oubaas (oh-bahss) n S African a man in authority [Afrikaans *ou* man + *baas* boss]

Oubangui n the French name for **Ubangi**

oubliette (oo-blee-ett) n history a dungeon, the only entrance to which is a trap door in the ceiling [French *oublier* to forget]

ouch interj an exclamation of sharp sudden pain

Oudh n **1** a region of N India, in central Uttar Pradesh: annexed by Britain in 1856 and a centre of the Indian Mutiny (1857–58); joined with Agra in 1877, becoming the United Provinces of Agra and Oudh in 1902, which were renamed Uttar Pradesh in 1950 **2** another name for **Ayodhya**

Oudry n **Jean-Baptiste.** 1686–1755, French rococo painter and tapestry designer, noted esp. for animal and hunting scenes

Ouessant n the French name for **Ushant**

ought vb **1** used to express duty or obligation: *she ought to tell this to the police* **2** used to express advisability: *we ought to get the roof repaired before the attics get any damper* **3** used to express probability or expectation: *a good lawyer ought to be able to fix it for you* **4** used to express a desire on the part of the speaker: *you ought to have a good breakfast before you hit the road* [Old English *āhte*, past tense of *āgan* to owe]

> **USAGE** In correct English, *ought* is not used with *did* or *had*. *I ought not to do it*, not *I didn't ought to do it*; *I ought not to have done it*, not *I hadn't ought to have done it*.

oughtn't ought not

Ouida *n* real name *Marie Louise de la Ramée*. 1839–1908, British popular novelist, best known for *Under Two Flags* (1867)

Ouija board *or* **Ouija** (**weej**-a) *n trademark* a board on which are marked the letters of the alphabet. Answers to questions are spelt out by a pointer, which is supposedly guided by spirits [French *oui* yes + German *ja* yes]

Oujda *n* a city in NE Morocco, near the border with Algeria: frontier post. Pop: 454 000 (2003)

Oulu *n* an industrial city and port in W Finland, on the Gulf of Bothnia: university (1959). Pop: 125 928 (2003 est). Swedish name: **Uleåborg**

ouma (oh-mah) *n S African* **1** grandmother, often as a title with a surname **2** *slang* any elderly woman [Afrikaans]

ounce *n* **1** a unit of weight equal to one sixteenth of a pound or 28.4 grams **2** short for **fluid ounce** **3** a small amount: *you haven't got one ounce of control over her* [Latin *uncia* a twelfth]

OUP (in Northern Ireland) Official Unionist Party

oupa (oh-pah) *n S African* **1** grandfather, often as a title with a surname **2** *slang* any elderly man [Afrikaans]

our *adj* **1** of, belonging to, or associated with us: *our daughter* **2** a formal word for *my* used by monarchs [Old English *ūre*]

Our Father *n* same as the **Lord's Prayer**

ours *pron* **1** something belonging to us: *ours are smaller guns than those*; *the money is ours* **2** of ours belonging to or associated with us: *my wife and a friend of ours had both deserted me*

ourself *pron archaic* a formal word for *myself* used by monarchs

ourselves *pron* **1 a** the reflexive form of *we* or *us*: *we humiliated ourselves* **b** used for emphasis: *we ourselves will finish it* **2** our usual selves: *we've not been feeling quite ourselves since the accident* **3** *not standard* used instead of *we* or *us* in compound noun phrases: *other people and ourselves*

Ouse *n* **1** Also called: **Great Ouse** a river in E England, rising in Northamptonshire and flowing northeast to the Wash near King's Lynn; for the last 56 km (35 miles) follows mainly artificial channels. Length: 257 km (160 miles) **2** a river in NE England, in Yorkshire, formed by the confluence of the Swale and Ure Rivers: flows southeast to the Humber. Length: 92 km (57 miles) **3** a river in S England, rising in Sussex and flowing south to the English Channel. Length: 48 km (30 miles)

ousel *n* same as **ouzel**

oust *vb* to force (someone) out of a position; expel: *the coup which ousted the President* [Anglo-Norman *ouster*]

ouster *n* US an act or instance of forcing someone out of a position: *the demonstrators called for the ouster of the police chief*

out *adv, adj* **1** away from the inside of a place: *she took her purse out; inspection of the eggs should be done when the hen is out of the nest* **2** away from one's home or place of work for a short time: *I called earlier but you were out; a search party is out looking for survivors* **3** no longer burning, shining, or functioning: *he switched the light out; the living-room fire went out while we were next door eating* **4** used up; not having any more of: *their supplies ran out after two weeks; we're out of milk* **5** public; revealed: *our dirty little secret is out* **6** available to the public: *her biography will be out in December* **7** (of the sun, stars, or moon) visible **8** in bloom: *the roses are out early this year* **9** not in fashion or current usage: *trying to be trendy is out* **10** excluded from consideration: *cost cutting is out of the question* **11** not allowed: *smoking on duty is out* **12** out for or to wanting or intent on (something or doing something): *the young soldiers were out for revenge; they're out to get me* **13** *sport* (of a player in a sport like cricket or baseball) no longer batting because he or she has been dismissed by being caught, bowled, etc. **14** on strike **15** in or into a state of unconsciousness: *he went outside and passed out in an alley* **16** used to indicate a burst of activity as indicated by

a verb: *war broke out in the Gulf* **17** out of existence: *the mistakes were scored out* **18** to the fullest extent: *spread out* **19** loudly; clearly: *he cried out in shock and pain* **20** to a conclusion; completely: *she'd worked it out for herself* **21** existing: *the friendliest dog out* **22** inaccurate or incorrect: *the estimate was out by £60* **23** not in office or authority: *she was finally voted out as party leader* **24** (of a period of time) completed: *before the year is out* **25** openly homosexual: *I came out as a lesbian when I was still in my teens* **26** *old-fashioned* (of a young woman) in or into upper-class society life: *Lucinda had a large party when she came out* **27** out of **a** at or to a point outside: *the train pulled out of the station* **b** away from; not in: *they're out of touch with reality; out of focus* **c** because of; motivated by: *out of jealousy* **d** from (a material or source): *made out of plastic* **e** no longer in a specified state or condition: *out of work; out of practice* ▷ *adj* **28** *informal* not concealing one's homosexuality ▷ *prep* **29** US or not standard out of; out through: *he ran out the door* ▷ *interj* **30 a** an exclamation of dismissal **b** (in signalling and radio) an expression used to signal that the speaker is signing off: *over and out!* ▷ *vb* **31** *informal* to expose (a public figure) as being homosexual **32** *informal* to reveal something embarrassing or unknown about (a person): *he was outed as a talented goal scorer* [Old English *ūt*]

> **USAGE** The use of *out* as a preposition, though common in American English, is regarded as incorrect in standard British English: *he climbed out of* (not *out*) *a window; he went out through* (not *out*) *the door*.

out- *prefix* **1** excelling or surpassing in a particular action: *outlast; outlive* **2** at or from a point away, outside: *outpost; outpatient* **3** going away, outward: *outcrop; outgrowth*

outage *n* a period of power failure

out and about *adj* regularly going out of the house to work, take part in social activity, etc., esp. after an illness

out-and-out *adj* absolute; thorough: *it's an out-and-out lie*

outback *n* the remote bush country of Australia

outbid *vb* **-bidding, -bidded** *or* **-bid** to offer a higher price than (another person)

outboard motor *n* a portable petrol engine that can be attached externally to the stern of a boat to propel it

outbox *n* a folder in a computer mailbox in which outgoing messages are stored

outbreak *n* a sudden occurrence of disease or war

outbuilding *n* same as **outhouse**

outburst *n* **1** a sudden strong expression of emotion, esp. of anger: *such emotional outbursts do nothing to help calm discussion of the matter* **2** a sudden period of violent activity: *this sudden outburst of violence has come as a shock*

outcast *n* a person who is rejected or excluded from a particular group or from society

outclass *vb* to surpass (someone) in performance or quality

outcome *n* the result or consequence of something

outcrop *n* part of a rock formation that sticks out of the earth

outcry *n, pl* **-cries** a widespread or vehement protest: *there was great popular outcry against the plan for a dual carriageway*

outdated *adj* old-fashioned or obsolete

outdistance *vb* **-tancing, -tanced** **1** to surpass (someone) in a particular activity **2** to leave (other competitors) behind in a race

outdo *vb* **-does, -doing, -did, -done** to be more successful or better than (someone or something) in performance: *this car easily outdoes its rivals when it comes to comfort*

outdoor *adj* **1** taking place, existing, or intended for use in the open air: *have a swim at the beach or outdoor pool; she was just taking off her outdoor clothing* **2** fond of the outdoors: *Paul was a butch outdoor type*

outdoors *adv* **1** in the open air; outside: *he hardly ever went*

outdoors ▷ *n* **2** the world outside or far away from buildings; the open air: *he'd forgotten his fear of the outdoors*

outer *adj* **1** on the outside; external: *the building's outer walls were painted pale pink* **2** further from the middle: *the outer suburbs* ▷ *n* **3** *archery* **a** the white outermost ring on a target **b** a shot that hits this ring

Outer Hebrides *pl n* See Hebrides

Outer Mongolia *n* the former name (until 1924) of the republic of **Mongolia**

outermost *adj* furthest from the centre or middle

outer space *n* space beyond the atmosphere of the earth

outface *vb* **-facing, -faced** to subdue or disconcert (someone) by staring

outfall *n Brit, Austral and NZ* the mouth of a river, drain, or pipe: *the survey measured pollution levels near sewer outfalls*

outfield *n* **1** *cricket* the area of the field far from the pitch **2** *baseball* the area of the playing field beyond the lines connecting first, second, and third bases **> outfielder** *n*

outfit *n* **1** a set of clothes worn together **2** *informal* a group of people working together as a unit **3** a set of equipment for a particular task; kit: *a complete anti-snakebite outfit*

outfitter *n old-fashioned* a shop or person that sells men's clothes

outflank *vb* **1** to go around and beyond the side of (an enemy army) **2** to get the better of (someone)

outflow *n* **1** anything that flows out, such as liquid or money **2** the amount that flows out

outfox *vb* to defeat or foil (someone) by being more cunning; outsmart

outgoing *adj* **1** leaving: *some members of the outgoing government continued to attend the peace talks* **2** friendly and sociable

outgoings *pl n* expenses

outgrow *vb* **-growing, -grew, -grown** **1** to grow too large for (clothes or shoes): *it's amazing how quickly children outgrow their clothes* **2** to lose (a way of behaving or thinking) in the course of becoming more mature: *most teenagers outgrow their moodiness as they near adulthood* **3** to grow larger or faster than (someone or something): *the weeds threatened to outgrow and choke the rice plants*

outgrowth *n* **1** a natural development or consequence: *he argued that religion was an outgrowth of magic* **2** a thing growing out of a main body; offshoot

outhouse *n* a building near to, but separate from, a main building

outing *n* **1** a trip or excursion **2** *informal* the naming of prominent homosexuals, often against their will

outlandish *adj* extremely unconventional; bizarre

outlast *vb* to last longer than

outlaw *n* **1** *history* a criminal who has been deprived of legal protection and rights ▷ *vb* **2** to make (something) illegal: *racial discrimination was formally outlawed* **3** *history* to make (someone) an outlaw **> outlawed** *adj*

outlay *n* the money, effort, or time spent on something

outlet *n* **1** a means of expressing one's feelings: *the shock would give her an outlet for her own grief* **2 a** a market for a product: *there is a huge sales outlet for personal computers* **b** a shop or organization selling the goods of a particular producer or wholesaler or manufacturer: *her own brand is now sold to outlets throughout the world* **3** an opening permitting escape or release: *make sure the exhaust outlet is not blocked*

outline *n* **1** a general explanation or description of something, which does not give all the details: *the course gave a brief outline of twentieth-century music* **2** outlines the important features of something: *the outlines of his theory are correct, we just need to fill in the details* **3** the general shape of something, esp. when only the profile and not the details are visible: *it was still light enough to see the outline of the distant mountains* **4** a drawing showing only the external lines of an object ▷ *vb* **-lining, -lined** **5** to give the main features or general idea of (something): *I*

outlined what we had done and what we had still to do **6** to show the general shape of an object but not its details, as light does coming from behind an object: *we could see the towers of the city outlined against the night sky*

outlive *vb* **-living, -lived** **1** to live longer than (someone): *she only outlived her husband by a few months* **2** to live beyond (a date or period): *the sparrow outlived the winter* **3 outlive its usefulness** to be no longer useful or necessary: *some argued that the organization had outlived its usefulness*

outlook *n* **1** a general attitude to life: *my whole outlook on life had changed* **2** the probable condition or outcome of something: *the economic outlook is not good* **3** the weather forecast for the next few days: *the outlook for the weekend* **4** the view from a place: *a dreary outlook of chimneys and smoke*

outlying *adj* far away from the main area

outmanoeuvre *or US* **outmaneuver** *vb* **-vring, -vred** *or US* **-vering, -vered** to gain an advantage over (someone) by skilful dealing: *the management outmanoeuvred us into accepting redundancies*

outmatch *vb* to surpass or outdo (someone)

outmoded *adj* no longer fashionable or accepted

outnumber *vb* to exceed in number: *they were outnumbered by fifty to one*

out of bounds *adj, adv* **1** (often foll. by *to*) not to be entered (by): *the area has been out of bounds to foreign journalists and closed to tourists* **2** (in a sport such as golf) outside the boundaries of the course or playing area

out-of-date *adj, adv* old-fashioned; outmoded

out of doors *adv* in the open air; outside

out of pocket *adj* having lost or spent money: *I was £10 out of pocket after paying for their drinks*

out-of-the-way *adj* remote and isolated: *an out-of-the-way village in the Bavarian Forest*

out-of-work *adj* unemployed: *an out-of-work engineer*

outpace *vb* **-pacing, -paced** **1** to go faster than (someone) **2** to surpass or outdo (someone or something) in growth, development, etc.: *the increase in the number of households is outpacing the number of houses being built*

outpatient *n* a patient who visits a hospital for treatment but does not stay there overnight

outport *n Canad* an isolated fishing village, esp. in Newfoundland

outpost *n* a small settlement in a distant part of the country or in a foreign country, which is used for military or trading purposes

outpouring *n* **1** a great amount of something that is produced very rapidly: *a prolific outpouring of ideas and energy* **2** a passionate outburst: *the hysterical outpourings of fanatics*

output *n* **1** the amount of something that is made or produced: *our weekly output has increased by 240 tonnes* **2** *electronics* the power, voltage, or current delivered by a circuit or component **3** *computers* the information produced by a computer ▷ *vb* **-putting, -putted** *or* **-put** **4** *computers* to produce (data) at the end of a process

outrage *n* **1** deep indignation, anger, or resentment: *she felt a sense of outrage that he should abandon her like that* **2** an extremely vicious or cruel act; gross violation of decency, morality, or honour: *there have been reports of another bombing outrage in the capital* ▷ *vb* **-raging, -raged** **3** to cause deep indignation, anger, or resentment in (someone): *they were outraged by the news of the assassination* [French *outré* beyond]

outrageous *adj* **1** unusual and shocking: *his sense of humour made him say and do the most outrageous things* **2** shocking and socially or morally unacceptable: *I will fight these outrageous accusations of corruption in the courts if necessary* **> outrageously** *adv*

Outram *n* Sir James. 1803–63, British soldier and administrator in India; he participated in the relief of Lucknow (1857) during the Indian Mutiny

outrank *vb* to be of higher rank than (someone)

outré (oo-tray) *adj* eccentric and rather shocking [French: having gone beyond]

outrider *n* a person who rides a motorcycle or horse in front of or beside an official vehicle as an attendant or guard

outrigger *n* **1** a stabilizing framework projecting from the side of a boat or canoe **2** a boat or canoe equipped with such a framework

outright *adj* **1** complete; total: *he is close to an outright victory* **2** straightforward and direct: *outright hostility* ▷ *adv* **3** completely: *the film was banned outright* **4** instantly: *my driver was killed outright* **5** openly: *ask her outright why she treated you as she did*

outrun *vb* **-running, -ran, -run 1** to run faster or further than (someone) **2** to develop faster than (something): *the population of the city is in danger of outrunning the supply of houses*

outsell *vb* **-selling, -sold** to be sold in greater quantities than: *CDs were outselling cassettes*

outset *n* a start; beginning: *we never really hit it off from the outset*

outshine *vb* **-shining, -shone** to be better than (someone) at something: *by university she had begun to outshine me in sports*

outside *prep* **1** on or to the exterior of: *a crowd gathered outside the court* **2** beyond the limits of: *it was outside my experience and beyond my ability* **3** apart from; other than: *no-one knows outside us* ▷ *adj* **4** on or of the outside: *an outside light is also a good idea* **5** remote; unlikely: *I still had an outside chance of the title* **6** coming from outside a particular group or organization: *the patient had been subjected to outside influences* **7** of or being the lane in a road which is further from the side than other lanes going in the same direction: *he was doing 120 in the outside lane* ▷ *adv* **8** outside a thing or place; out of doors: *we went outside to get some fresh air* **9** *slang* not in prison ▷ *n* **10** the external side or surface of something **11** at the outside *informal* at the very most: *I'll be away four days at the outside*

> **USAGE** In British English, the use of *outside of* and *inside of*, although fairly common, is generally thought to be incorrect or non-standard: *she waits outside* (not *outside of*) *the school.*

outside broadcast *n* radio, television a broadcast not made in a studio

outsider *n* **1** a person excluded from a group **2** a contestant thought unlikely to win

outsize *adj* **1** Also: **outsized** very large or larger than normal ▷ *n* **2** an outsize garment

outskirts *pl n* the parts of a town or city that are furthest from the centre: *an office in the northernmost outskirts of Glasgow*

outsmart *vb* same as **outwit**

outsource *vb* **1** to subcontract (work) to another company **2** to buy (components for a product) rather than manufacture them

outspan *S African n* **1** an area on a farm kept available for travellers to rest and refresh their animals ▷ *vb* **-spanning, -spanned 2** to unharness or unyoke (animals) **3** to relax [Afrikaans *uit* out + *spannen* to stretch]

outspoken *adj* **1** saying exactly what one thinks: *an outspoken critic of human rights abuses* **2** spoken candidly: *she is known for her outspoken views* ▷ **outspokenness** *n*

outspread *adj* spread or stretched out as far as possible: *a gull glided by with outspread wings*

outstanding *adj* **1** very good; excellent: *an outstanding performance* **2** still to be dealt with or paid: *outstanding bills; a few outstanding problems have to be put right* **3** very obvious or important: *there are significant exceptions, of which oil is the outstanding example* ▷ **outstandingly** *adv*

outstation *n* a station or post in a remote region

outstay *vb* same as **overstay**

outstretched *adj* extended or stretched out as far as possible: *he pushed a wad of drachma notes into the young man's outstretched hand*

outstrip *vb* **-stripping, -stripped 1** to surpass (someone) in a particular activity: *his newspapers outstrip all others in vulgarity* **2** to go faster than (someone)

outtake *n* an unreleased take from a recording session, film, or television programme

out there *adj slang* unconventional or eccentric

out-tray *n* a shallow basket in an office for collecting letters and documents that are to be sent out

outvote *vb* **-voting, -voted** to defeat (someone) by getting more votes than him or her

outward *adj* **1** apparent or superficial: *to outward appearances the house is largely unchanged today* **2** of or relating to the outside: *outward shape* **3** (of a journey) away from a place to which one intends to return ▷ *adv* also: **outwards 4** in an outward direction; towards the outside ▷ **outwardly** *adv*

outweigh *vb* **1** to be more important, significant, or influential than: *these niggles are outweighed by the excellent cooking and service* **2** to be heavier than

outwit *vb* **-witting, -witted** to gain an advantage over (someone) by cunning or ingenuity

outworks *pl n* military defences which lie outside the main fortifications of a fort etc.

outworn *adj* (of a belief or custom) old-fashioned and no longer of any use or relevance: *there is no point in pandering to outworn superstition*

ouzel *or* **ousel** (ooze-el) *n* same as **dipper** (2) [Old English ōsle]

ouzo (ooze-oh) *n, pl* **ouzos** a strong aniseed-flavoured alcoholic drink from Greece [Modern Greek *ouzon*]

ova *n* the plural of **ovum**

oval *adj* **1** egg-shaped ▷ *n* **2** anything that is oval in shape, such as a sports ground [Latin *ovum* egg]

Oval *n* the Oval a cricket ground in south London, in the borough of Lambeth

Oval Office *n* the Oval Office **1** the private office of the president of the US, a large oval room in the White House **2** the US presidency

ovary *n, pl* **-ries 1** a reproductive organ in women and female animals in which eggs are produced **2** botany the lower part of a pistil, containing the ovules [Latin *ovum* egg] ▷ **ovarian** *adj*

ovate *adj* shaped like an egg: *the tree has bluish-green, ovate leaves* [Latin *ovatus* egg-shaped]

ovation *n* an enthusiastic round of applause [Latin *ovatio* rejoicing]

oven *n* **1** an enclosed heated compartment or container for baking or roasting food, or for drying or firing ceramics ▷ *vb* **2** to cook in an oven [Old English *ofen*]

over *prep* **1** directly above; across the top or upper surface of: *set the frying pan over a low heat* **2** on or to the other side of: *the pilot flew over the Channel* **3** during or throughout (a period of time): *over the next few months it became clear what was happening* **4** throughout the whole extent of: *the effects are being felt all over the country now* **5** by means of (an instrument of telecommunication): *there was an announcement over the Tannoy system* **6** more than: *she had met him over a year ago* **7** concerning; about: *there has been much argument over these figures* **8** while occupied in: *I'll tell you over dinner tonight* **9** having recovered from the effects of: *he appeared to be over his niggling injury problems* **10** all over someone *informal* extremely affectionate or attentive towards someone **11** over and above added to; in addition to ▷ *adv* **12** in a state, condition, or position over something: *to climb over* **13** onto its side: *the jug toppled over* **14** at or to a point across an intervening space: *she carried him over to the other side of the river* **15** covering the whole area: *there's poverty the world over* **16** from beginning to end: *to read a document over* **17** all over **a** finished **b** over one's entire body **c** typically: *that's him all over* **18** over again once more **19** over and over (again)** repeatedly ▷ *interj* **20** (in signalling and radio) it is now your turn to speak ▷ *adj* **21** finished; no longer in progress: *the second round of voting is over* **22** remaining: *there wasn't any money left over*

23 surplus ▷ *n* **24** *cricket* **a** a series of six balls bowled by a bowler from the same end of the pitch **b** the play during this [Old English *ofer*]

over- *prefix* **1** excessive or excessively: *overcharge*; *overdue* **2** superior in rank: *overlord* **3** indicating location or movement above: *overhang* **4** indicating movement downwards: *overthrow*

overabundance *n* more than is really needed; excess

overact *vb* to act in an exaggerated way

overactive *adj* more active than is normal or desirable: *an overactive thyroid gland*

overall *adj* **1** from one end to the other: *the overall length* **2** including everything; total: *the overall cost* ▷ *adv* **3** in general; on the whole: *overall, I think this is the better car* ▷ *n* **4** *Brit and NZ* a coat-shaped work garment worn over ordinary clothes as a protection against dirt **5 overalls** work trousers with a bib and braces or jacket attached, worn over ordinary clothes as a protection against dirt and wear

overambitious *adj* attempting more than one has the ability to do well: *good plain cookery marred by overambitious sauces*

overarching *adj* overall or all-encompassing: *an overarching concept*

overarm *sport adj* **1** bowled, thrown, or performed with the arm raised above the shoulder ▷ *adv* **2** with the arm raised above the shoulder

overawe *vb* **-awing, -awed** to affect (someone) with an overpowering sense of awe: *he was overawed by the prospect of meeting the Prime Minister*

overbalance *vb* **-lancing, -lanced** to lose one's balance

overbearing *adj* **1** imposing one's views in an unpleasant or forceful manner **2** of particular or overriding importance: *an overbearing need*

overblown *adj* inflated or excessive: *humiliation comes from having overblown expectations for yourself*

overboard *adv* **1** from a boat or ship into the water: *many passengers drowned when they jumped overboard to escape the flames* **2 go overboard** *informal* **a** to be extremely enthusiastic **b** to go to extremes **3 throw overboard** to reject or abandon (an idea or a plan)

overburden *vb* to cause to have more of something than it is possible to cope with: *the city's streets are already overburdened by rush-hour motorists*

overcast *adj* (of the sky or weather) cloudy

overcharge *vb* **-charging, -charged** to charge too high a price

overcoat *n* a warm heavy coat worn in cold weather

overcome *vb* **-coming, -came, -come** **1** to deal successfully with or control (a problem or feeling): *once I'd overcome my initial nerves I discovered hang-gliding was great fun* **2** (of an emotion or a feeling) to affect (someone) strongly or make (someone) powerless: *he was overcome by a sudden surge of jealousy* **3** to defeat (someone) in a conflict

overcompensate *vb* **-sating, -sated** to attempt to make up for or cancel out (something) to an unnecessary degree: *when bookings dropped slightly, the company overcompensated by slashing the price of its holidays by 50%*

overconfident *adj* having more belief in one's abilities than is justified

overcook *vb* to spoil food by cooking it for too long

overcrowded *adj* containing more people or things than is desirable: *overcrowded commuter trains*

overcrowding *n* the cramming of too many people into too small a space: *prison overcrowding and poor conditions*

overdo *vb* **-does, -doing, -did, -done** **1** to do (something) to excess **2** to exaggerate (something) **3** to cook (something) too long **4 overdo it** or **things** to do something to a greater degree than is advisable or healthy

overdose *n* **1 a** larger dose of a drug than is safe: *she tried to kill herself with an overdose of alcohol and drugs* ▷ *vb* **-dosing, -dosed** **2** to take more of a drug than is safe, either accidentally or deliberately: *this drug is rarely prescribed because it is easy to overdose fatally on it*

overdraft *n* **1** the withdrawal of more money from a bank account than there is in it **2** the amount of money withdrawn thus

overdraw *vb* **-drawing, -drew, -drawn** to withdraw more money from a bank account than is in it

overdrawn *adj* **1** having overdrawn one's bank account **2** (of an account) in debit

overdressed *adj* wearing clothes which are too elaborate or formal for the occasion

overdrive *n* **1** a very high gear in a motor vehicle, used at high speeds to reduce wear **2** a state of great activity or excitement: *the government propaganda machine went into overdrive to try to play down the Minister's comments*

overdub *vb* **-dubbing, -dubbed** **1** to add (new sounds) to a tape in such a way that the old and the new sounds can be heard ▷ *n* **2** a sound or series of sounds added by this method

overdue *adj* **1** not having arrived or happened by the time expected or desired: *a reassessment of policy on this issue is long overdue* **2** (of money) not having been paid by the required date: *by this time his rent was three weeks overdue* **3** (of a library book) not having been returned to the library by the required date

overeat *vb* **-eating, -ate, -eaten** to eat more than is necessary or healthy

overemphasize or **-sise** *vb* **-sizing, -sized** or **-sising, -sised** to give (something) more importance than is necessary or appropriate

overestimate *vb* **-mating, -mated** to believe something or someone to be bigger, more important, or better than is the case › **overestimation** *n*

overexcited *adj* excessively enthusiastic or agitated

overexert *vb* to exhaust or injure oneself by doing too much › **overexertion** *n*

overexposed *adj* (of a photograph) too light in colour because the film has been exposed to light for too long

overfeed *vb* **-feeding, -fed** to give (a person, plant, or animal) more food than is necessary or healthy

overfill *vb* to put more into (something) than there is room for

overflow *vb* **-flowing, -flowed** or *formerly* **-flown** **1** to flow over (a brim) **2** to be filled beyond capacity so as to spill over **3 overflow with** to be filled with (an emotion): *a letter overflowing with passion and ardour* ▷ *n* **4** something that overflows, usually a liquid **5** an outlet that enables surplus liquid to be drained off **6** the amount by which a limit or capacity is exceeded ▷ *adj* **7** of or being a subsidiary thing for use when there is no room left in the main one: *an overflow car park*

overgraze *vb* **-grazing, -grazed** to graze (land) too intensively so that it is damaged and no longer provides nourishment

overgrown *adj* covered over with plants or weeds: *they headed up the overgrown and winding trail*

overhang *vb* **-hanging, -hung** **1** to project or hang over beyond (something) ▷ *n* **2** an overhanging part or object

overhaul *vb* **1** to examine (a system or an idea) carefully for faults **2** to make repairs or adjustments to (a vehicle or machine) **3** to overtake (a vehicle or person) ▷ *n* **4** a thorough examination and repair

overhead *adj* **1** situated or operating above head height: *overhead compartments* ▷ *adv* **2** over or above head height: *the missile streaked overhead*

overhead projector *n* a projector that throws an enlarged image of a transparency onto a surface above and behind the person using it

overheads *pl n* the general costs of running a business, such as rent, electricity, and stationery

overhear *vb* **-hearing, -heard** to hear (a speaker or remark) unintentionally or without the knowledge of the speaker

overheat *vb* **1** to make or become too hot **2** to cause (an economy) to tend towards inflation **3** become

overheated (of a person, discussion, etc.) to become angry or agitated: *the Colonel becomes overheated if he sees the term 'Ms' in the newspaper*

Overijssel n a province of the E Netherlands: generally low-lying. Capital: Zwolle. Pop: 1 101 000 (2003 est). Area: 3929 sq km (1517 sq miles)

overindulge vb **-dulging, -dulged** to do too much of something pleasant, such as eating or drinking: *nobody ever wants a hangover, but we all overindulge occasionally* **› overindulgence** n

overjoyed adj extremely pleased

overkill n any treatment that is greater than that required: *the overkill in negative propaganda resulted in this upsurge*

overlap vb **-lapping, -lapped 1** (of two things) to share part of the same space as or lie partly over (each other): *slice the meat and lay it in overlapping slices in a serving dish* **2** to coincide partly in time or subject: *their careers have overlapped for the last ten years* **›** n **3** a part that overlaps **4** the amount or length of something overlapping

overlay vb **-laying, -laid 1** to cover (a surface) with an applied decoration: *a woollen cloth overlaid with gold and silver embroidery* **›** n **2** something that is laid over something else; a covering **3** an applied decoration or layer, for example of gold leaf

overleaf adv on the other side of the page

overlie vb **-lying, -lay, -lain** to lie on or cover (something or someone): *a thin layer of black dust overlay everything*

overload vb **1** to put too large a load on or in (something): *the aircraft was dangerously overloaded* **2** to cause (a transport system) to be unable to function properly because too many people or vehicles are using it: *Heathrow Airport was already overloaded by 1972* **3** to try to put more electricity through a system than the system can cope with **›** n **4** an excessive load

overlook vb **1** to fail to notice (something) **2** to disregard or ignore (misbehaviour or a fault): *I'm prepared to overlook your failure, but don't do it again* **3** to give a view of (something) from above: *a cliff overlooking the Atlantic*

overlord n a supreme lord or master

overly adv too; excessively

overman vb **-manning, -manned** to provide with too many staff **› overmanned** adj **› overmanning** n

overmuch adv, adj too much; very much

overnight adv **1** during the night **2** in or as if in the course of one night; suddenly: *we are not saying that a change like this would happen overnight* **›** adj **3** done in, occurring in, or lasting the night: *the army has ordered an overnight curfew* **4** staying for one night: *overnight guests* **5** for use during a single night: *should I pack an overnight case?* **6** happening very quickly; sudden: *he doesn't expect the programme to be an overnight success*

overpaid adj earning more money than one deserves

overpass n same as **flyover**

overplay vb **1** to overemphasize (something) **2 overplay one's hand** to overestimate the worth or strength of one's position

overpopulated adj (of a town or country) having more people living in it than it can support

overpopulation n the state of being overpopulated

overpower vb **1** to conquer or subdue (someone) by superior force **2** to have such a strong effect on (someone) as to make him or her helpless or ineffective: *I was so appalled, so overpowered by my guilt and my shame that I was unable to speak* **› overpowering** adj

overpriced adj costing more than it is thought to be worth

overprint vb **1** to print (additional matter or another colour) onto (something already printed) **›** n **2** additional matter or another colour printed onto something already printed

overqualified adj having more professional or academic qualifications than are required for a job

overrate vb to have too high an opinion of: *the director's role was seriously overrated*

overreach vb **overreach oneself** to fail by trying to be too clever or achieve too much: *he built up a successful media empire before he overreached himself and lost much of his fortune*

overreact vb to react more strongly or forcefully than is necessary: *allergies happen when the body overreacts to a harmless substance* **› overreaction** n

override vb **-riding, -rode, -ridden 1** to set aside or disregard (a person or a person's decisions) by having superior authority or power: *the managing director can override any decision he doesn't like* **2** to be more important than or replace (something): *unsurprisingly the day-to-day struggle for survival overrode all moral considerations* **› overriding** adj

overripe adj (of a fruit or vegetable) so ripe that it has started to decay or go soft

overrule vb **-ruling, -ruled 1** to reverse the decision of (a person or organization with less power): *the President overruled the hardliners in the party who wanted to use force* **2** to rule or decide against (an argument or decision): *the initial judgment was overruled by the Supreme Court*

overrun vb **-running, -ran, -run 1** to conquer (territory) rapidly by force of numbers **2** to spread over (a place) rapidly: *dirty tenements, overrun by lice, rats, and roaches* **3** to extend or run beyond a set limit: *Tuesday's lunch overran by three-quarters of an hour*

overseas adv **1** across the sea; abroad **›** adj **2** of, to, from, or in a distant country or countries **›** n **3** informal a foreign country or foreign countries collectively

oversee vb **-seeing, -saw, -seen** to watch over and direct (someone or something); supervise **› overseer** n

oversell vb **-selling, -sold** to exaggerate the merits or abilities of

oversew vb **-sewing, -sewed, -sewn** or **-sewed** to sew (two edges) with stitches that pass over them both

oversexed adj more interested in sex than is thought decent

overshadow vb **1** to make (someone or something) seem insignificant or less important by comparison **2** to sadden the atmosphere of: *news of their team-mate's injury overshadowed the victory celebrations*

overshoe n a protective shoe worn over an ordinary shoe

overshoot vb **-shooting, -shot** to go beyond (a mark or target): *the plane overshot the main runway*

overshot adj (of a water wheel) driven by a flow of water that passes over the wheel

oversight n a mistake caused by not noticing something

oversimplify vb **-fies, -fying, -fied** to make something seem simpler than it really is: *the Nationalists' analysis oversimplifies the problems facing the country today*

oversized adj much larger than the usual size

oversleep vb **-sleeping, -slept** to sleep beyond the intended time for getting up

overspend vb **-spending, -spent** to spend more than one can afford

overspill n Brit the rehousing of people from crowded cities in smaller towns

overstate vb **-stating, -stated** to state (something) too strongly; overemphasize **› overstatement** n

overstay vb **overstay one's welcome** to stay as a guest longer than one's host or hostess would like

overstayer n a person who remains in a country after his or her permit has expired

overstep vb **-stepping, -stepped 1** to go beyond the limits of what is thought acceptable: *he had overstepped his authority by acting without consulting his superiors* **2 overstep the mark** to go too far and behave in an unacceptable way

overstretch vb **1** to attempt to do more than there is time or capability for: *for the first time in her career she may have overstretched her talents* **2** to damage (something) by stretching it further than it can safely go: *he overstretched* his Achilles tendon **> overstretched** adj

overstrung adj too highly strung; tense

overt adj done or shown in an open and obvious way: jurors were now looking at the defendant with overt hostility [Old French] **> overtly** adv

overtake vb **-taking, -took, -taken 1** chiefly Brit to move past (another vehicle or person) travelling in the same direction **2** to do better than (someone) after catching up with him or her **3** to come upon (someone) suddenly or unexpectedly: a mortal tiredness overtook him

overtax vb **1** to impose too great a strain on: a singer who had overtaxed her voice **2** to tax (people) too heavily

over-the-top adj slang excessive; beyond the usual or acceptable bounds of behaviour

overthrow vb **-throwing, -threw, -thrown 1** to defeat and replace (a ruler or government) by force **2** to replace (standards or values) ▷ n **3** downfall or destruction: the overthrow of the US-backed dictatorship

overtime n **1** work at a regular job done in addition to regular working hours **2** pay for such work ▷ adv **3** in addition to one's regular working hours: she had been working overtime and she fell asleep at the wheel

overtone n **1** an additional meaning or hint: I don't want to deny that from time to time there are political overtones **2** music, acoustics any of the tones, with the exception of the principal or lowest one, that make up a musical sound

overture n **1** music **a** a piece of orchestral music played at the beginning of an opera, oratorio, ballet, musical comedy, or film, often containing the main musical themes of the work **b** a one-movement orchestral piece, usually having a descriptive or evocative title: the 1812 Overture **2** overtures opening moves towards a new relationship or agreement: the German government made a variety of friendly overtures towards the French [Late Latin apertura opening]

overturn vb **1** to turn over or upside down **2** to overrule or reverse (a legal decision) **3** to overthrow or destroy (a government)

overuse vb **1** to use excessively ▷ n **2** excessive use

overvalue vb **-valuing, -valued** to regard (someone or something) as much more important or valuable than is the case: his approach overvalues hard work and undervalues true skill **> overvalued** adj

overview n a general survey

overweening adj (of opinions or qualities) excessive or immoderate: your modesty is a cover for your overweening conceit [obsolete ween to think]

overweight adj **1** (of a person) weighing more than is healthy **2** weighing more than is usual or permitted

overwhelm vb **1** to overpower the thoughts, emotions, or senses of (someone): we were overwhelmed with grief **2** to overcome (people) with irresistible force: gang violence has overwhelmed an ailing police force **> overwhelming** adj **> overwhelmingly** adv

overwork vb **1** to work too hard or too long **2** to use (something) too much: anti-communism was already being overworked by others ▷ n **3** excessive work

overwrite vb **-writing, -wrote, -written 1** to record on a storage medium, such as a magnetic disk, thus destroying what was originally recorded there **2** to write (something) in an excessively ornate style

overwrought adj tense, nervous, and agitated

Ovett n Steve. born 1955, British middle-distance runner: winner of the 800 metres in the 1980 Olympic Games

Ovid n Latin name Publius Ovidius Naso. 43 BC–?17 AD, Roman poet. His verse includes poems on love, Ars Amatoria, on myths, Metamorphoses, and on his sufferings in exile, Tristia **> Ovidian** adj

oviduct n anatomy the tube through which eggs are conveyed from an ovary [Latin ovum egg + ducere to lead]

Oviedo n a city in NW Spain: capital of Asturias from 810 until 1002; centre of a coal- and iron-mining area. Pop: 207 699 (2003 est)

oviform adj biology shaped like an egg [Latin ovum egg + forma shape]

ovine adj of or like a sheep [Latin ovis sheep]

oviparous (oh-**vip**-par-uss) adj zoology producing eggs that hatch outside the body of the mother [Latin ovum egg + -parus bearing]

ovoid (oh-void) adj egg-shaped

ovulate (ov-yew-late) vb **-lating, -lated** biology to produce or release eggs from an ovary **> ovulation** n

ovule n **1** botany the part of a plant that contains the egg cell and develops into the seed after fertilization **2** zoology an immature ovum [Latin ovum egg]

ovum (oh-vum) n, pl **ova** an unfertilized female egg cell [Latin: egg]

owe vb **owing, owed 1** to be under an obligation to pay an amount of money to (someone): he owes me a lot of money **2** to feel an obligation to do or give: I think I owe you an apology **3 owe something to** to have something as a result of: many serving officers owe their present position to the former president [Old English āgan to have]

Owen n **1** David (Anthony Llewellyn), Baron. born 1938, British politician: Labour foreign secretary (1977–79); cofounder of the Social Democratic Party (1981) and its leader (1983–87): leader (1988–90) of the section of the Social Democratic Party that did not merge with the Liberal Party in 1988; peace envoy to Bosnia-Herzegovina (1992–95) **2** Michael (James). born 1979, English footballer: a striker, he scored 40 goals in 89 games for England (1998–2008); his clubs included Liverpool (1996–2004) and Newcastle United (2005–2009) **3** Sir Richard. 1804–92, English comparative anatomist and palaeontologist **4** Robert. 1771–1858, Welsh industrialist and social reformer. He formed a model industrial community at New Lanark, Scotland, and pioneered cooperative societies. His books include New View of Society (1813) **5** Wilfred. 1893–1918, English poet of World War I, who was killed in action

Owens n Jesse, real name John Cleveland Owens. 1913–80, US Black athlete: won four gold medals at the Berlin Olympics (1936)

Owen Stanley Range n a mountain range in SE New Guinea. Highest peak: Mount Victoria, 4073 m (13 363 ft)

Owerri n a market town in S Nigeria, capital of Imo state. Pop (local government areas): 401 873 (2006)

owing adj **1** not yet paid; due: the bailiffs seized goods worth far more than the amount owing **2 owing to** because of; as a result of: the flight was delayed owing to fog

owl n a bird of prey which has a flat face, large eyes, and a small hooked beak, and which is active at night [Old English ūle] **> owlish** adj

own adj (preceded by a possessive) **1** used to emphasize that something belongs to a particular person: rely on your own instincts ▷ pron (preceded by a possessive) **2** the one or ones belonging to a particular person: I had one of my own **3** the people that someone feels loyalty to, esp. relations: we all look after our own around here **4 come into one's own** to fulfil one's potential **5 hold one's own** to have the necessary ability to deal successfully with a situation: he chose a partner who could hold her own with the best **6 on one's own a** without help: you'll never manage to lift that on your own **b** by oneself; alone: he lives on his own in a flat in town ▷ vb **7** to have (something) as one's possession: he owns homes in four countries **8** Also: **own up to** to confess or admit: I own I could not bear to think of it; I thought she was going to own up to an affair [Old English āgen] **> owner** n **> ownership** n

owner-occupier n someone who owns the house in which he or she lives

ownership flat n NZ a flat owned by the occupier

own goal n **1** a goal scored by a player accidentally playing the ball into his or her own team's net **2** informal any action that results in disadvantage to the person who took it or to his or her associates: the minister's admission was the latest in a series of own goals by the government

ox *n, pl* **oxen** a castrated bull used for pulling heavy loads and for meat [Old English *oxa*]

oxalic acid *n* a colourless poisonous acid found in many plants [Latin *oxalis* garden sorrel]

oxbow lake *n* a crescent-shaped lake on the flood plain of a river and constituting the remnant of a former meander

Oxbridge *n Brit* the British universities of Oxford and Cambridge considered together

oxen *n* the plural of **ox**

Oxenstierna *or* **Oxenstjerna** *n* Count Axel. 1583–1654, Swedish statesman. He was chancellor (1612–54) and successfully directed Swedish foreign policy for most of the Thirty Years' War

Oxfam Oxford Committee for Famine Relief

Oxford *n* **1** a city in S England, administrative centre of Oxfordshire, at the confluence of the Rivers Thames and Cherwell: Royalist headquarters during the Civil War; seat of Oxford University, consisting of 40 separate colleges, the oldest being University College (1249), and Oxford Brookes University (1993); motor-vehicle industry. Pop: 143 016 (2001). Related word: **Oxonian** **2** Also called: **Oxford Down** a breed of sheep with middle-length wool and a dark brown face and legs **3** a type of stout laced shoe with a low heel **4** a lightweight fabric of plain or twill weave used esp. for men's shirts

Oxfordshire *n* an inland county of S central England: situated mostly in the basin of the Upper Thames, with the Cotswolds in the west and the Chilterns in the southeast. Administrative centre: Oxford. Pop: 615 200 (2003 est). Area: 2608 sq km (1007 sq miles). Abbreviation: **Oxon**

oxidation *n* the act or process of oxidizing

oxide *n chem* a compound of oxygen with another element [French]

oxidize *or* **-dise** *vb* **-dizing, -dized** *or* **-dising, -dised** to react chemically with oxygen, as in burning or rusting **> oxidization** *or* **-disation** *n*

Oxon Oxfordshire

Oxon. (in degree titles) of Oxford University [Latin *Oxoniensis*]

Oxonian *adj* **1** of or relating to Oxford or Oxford University **> n 2** a member of Oxford University **3** an inhabitant or native of Oxford

oxtail *n* the tail of an ox, used in soups and stews

Oxus *n* the ancient name for the **Amu Darya**

oxyacetylene *n* a mixture of oxygen and acetylene, used in blowlamps for cutting or welding metals at high temperatures

oxygen *n chem* a colourless, odourless gaseous element essential to life processes and to combustion. Symbol: **O** [Greek *oxus* sharp + *-genēs* producing: from former belief that all acids contained oxygen]

oxygenate *vb* **-nating, -nated** to add oxygen to: *to oxygenate blood*

oxygen mask *n* a small bowl-shaped object which is connected via a pipe to a cylinder of oxygen and can be placed over a person's nose and mouth to help him or her breathe

oxygen tent *n med* a transparent enclosure covering a bedridden patient, into which oxygen is released to aid breathing

oxymoron (ox-see-more-on) *n* a figure of speech that combines two apparently contradictory terms, for example *cruel kindness* [Greek *oxus* sharp + *mōros* stupid]

oyez *or* **oyes** *interj* a cry usually uttered three times by a public crier or court official calling for silence and attention [Old French *oiez!* hear!]

Oyo *n* a state of SW Nigeria. Capital: Ibadan. Pop: 5 591 589 (2006). Area: 28 454 sq km (10 986 sq miles)

oyster *n* **1** an edible shellfish, some types of which produce pearls **2 the world is your oyster** you are in a position where there is every possible chance of personal advancement and satisfaction **▷** *adj* **3** greyish-white [Greek *ostreon*]

oystercatcher *n* a wading bird with black-and-white plumage and a long stout red bill

oz *or* **oz.** ounce [Italian *onza*]

Oz *n slang* Australia

Özal *n* Turgut. 1927–93, Turkish statesman: prime minister of Turkey (1983–89); president (1989–93)

Ozark Mountains *or* **Ozarks** *pl n* an eroded plateau in S Missouri, N Arkansas, and NE Oklahoma. Area: about 130 000 sq km (50 000 sq miles). Also called: **Ozark Plateau**

Ozero Baykal *n* the Russian name for (Lake) **Baikal**

ozone *n* **1** a form of oxygen with a strong odour, formed by an electric discharge in the atmosphere **2** *informal* clean bracing air, as found at the seaside [Greek *ozein* to smell]

ozone layer *n* a layer of ozone in the upper atmosphere that absorbs harmful ultraviolet rays from the sun

Pp

p or **P** *n, pl* **p's, P's** or **Ps** **1** the 16th letter of the English alphabet **2 mind one's p's and q's** to be careful to behave correctly and use polite language

p **1** *Brit, Austral and NZ* penny **2** *Brit* pence

P **1** *chem* phosphorus **2** (on road signs) parking **3** *chess* pawn

p. **1** (*pl* **pp.**) page **2** per

pa[1] *n informal* father

pa[2] *n NZ* (formerly) a fortified Māori settlement

Pa **1** *chem* protactinium **2** *physics* pascal

PA **1** Pennsylvania **2** personal assistant **3** public-address system

Pa. Pennsylvania

p.a. yearly [Latin *per annum*]

Pabst *n* G(eorge) W(ilhelm). 1885–1967, German film director, whose films include *Joyless Street* (1925), *Pandora's Box* (1929), and *The Last Act* (1954)

Pac. Pacific

pace[1] *n* **1 a** a single step in walking **b** the length of a step **2** speed of walking or running **3** speed of doing some other activity: *efforts to accelerate the pace of change are unlikely to succeed* **4** manner of walking **5 keep pace with** to advance at the same speed as **6 put someone through his** or **her paces** to test someone's ability **7 set the pace** to determine the speed at which a group advances ▷ *vb* **pacing, paced** **8** to walk with regular steps, often in anxiety or impatience: *he paced up and down the foyer impatiently* **9** to set the speed for (the competitors) in a race **10 pace out** to measure by paces [Latin *passus* step]

pace[2] *prep* with due respect to: used to express polite disagreement [Latin, from *pax* peace]

pacemaker *n* **1** an electronic device positioned in the body, next to the heart, to regulate the heartbeat **2** a competitor who, by leading a race, causes it to be run at a particular speed

Pachelbel *n* Johann. 1653–1706, German organist and composer, noted esp. for his popular *Canon in D Major*

Pachomius *n* Saint. ?290–346 AD, Egyptian hermit; founder of the first Christian monastery (318). Feast day: May 14 or 15

Pachuca *n* a city in central Mexico, capital of Hidalgo state, in the Sierra Madre Oriental: silver mines; university (1961). Pop: 333 000 (2005 est)

pachyderm (pak-ee-durm) *n* a large thick-skinned mammal, such as an elephant or rhinoceros [Greek *pakhus* thick + *derma* skin]

pacific *adj formal* tending to bring peace; non-aggressive; peaceful [Latin *pax* peace + *facere* to make]

Pacific *n* **1 the Pacific** short for **Pacific Ocean** ▷ *adj* **2** of or relating to the Pacific Ocean or its islands

Pacific Islands *pl n* a former Trust Territory; an island group in the W Pacific Ocean, mandated to Japan after World War I and assigned to the US by the United Nations in 1947: comprised 2141 islands (96 inhabited) of the Caroline, Marshall, and Mariana groups (excluding Guam). In 1978 the Northern Marianas became a commonwealth in union with the US. The three remaining entities consisting of the Marshall Islands, the Republic of Palau (or Belau), and the Federated States of Micronesia became self-governing during the period 1979–80. In 1982 they signed agreements of free association with the US. Land area: about 1800 sq km (700 sq miles), scattered over about 7 500 000 sq km (3 000 000 sq miles) of ocean

Pacific Northwest *n* the region of North America lying north of the Columbia River and west of the Rockies

Pacific Ocean *n* the world's largest and deepest ocean, lying between Asia and Australia and North and South America: almost landlocked in the north, linked with the Arctic Ocean only by the Bering Strait, and extending to Antarctica in the south; has exceptionally deep trenches, and a large number of volcanic and coral islands. Area: about 165 760 000 sq km (64 000 000 sq miles). Average depth: 4215 m (14 050 ft). Greatest depth: Challenger Deep (in the Marianas Trench), 11 033 m (37 073 ft). Greatest width: (between Panama and Mindanao, Philippines) 17 066 km (10 600 miles)

pacifier *n US and Canad* a baby's dummy

pacifist *n* a person who is totally opposed to violence and refuses to take part in war ❯ **pacifism** *n*

pacify *vb* **-fies, -fying, -fied** to soothe or calm [Old French *pacifier*; see PACIFIC] ❯ **pacification** *n*

Pacino *n* Al, full name *Alfredo James Pacino*. born 1940, US film actor; his films include *The Godfather* (1972), *Dog Day Afternoon* (1975), *Scent of a Woman* (1992), for which he won an Oscar, and *Insomnia* (2002)

pack[1] *n* **1** a bundle or load carried on the back **2** *Brit and NZ* a complete set of playing cards **3** a group of animals that hunt together: *a pack of hounds* **4** *rugby* the forwards of a team **5** any collection of people or things: *a pack of lies* **6** *chiefly US and Canad* same as **packet** (1) **7** an organized group of Cub Scouts or Brownie Guides **8** same as **rucksack, backpack 9** Also called: **face pack** a cream treatment that cleanses and tones the skin ▷ *vb* **10** to put (articles) in a case or container for moving **11** to roll (articles) up into a bundle **12** to press tightly together; cram: *thousands of people packed into the city's main square* **13** (foll. by *off*) to send away hastily: *their young son came in to say good night and was packed off to bed* **14** *slang* to be able to deliver a specified amount of unexpected or violent force or power: *the film's unexpected ending packs quite a punch* **15** *US informal* to carry (a gun) habitually **16 send someone packing** *informal* to dismiss someone abruptly ▶ See also **pack in, pack up** [origin unknown]

pack[2] *vb* to fill (a committee, jury, or audience) with one's own supporters [perhaps from *pact*]

package *n* **1** a small parcel **2** Also: **package deal** a deal in which separate items are presented together as a unit **3** *US and Canad* same as **packet** (1) ▷ *vb* **-aging, -aged 4** to put (something) into a package ❯ **packaging** *n*

package holiday *n* a holiday in which everything is arranged by one company for a fixed price

packet n **1** a container, together with its contents: a packet of crisps **2** a small parcel **3** Also: **packet boat** a boat that transports mail, passengers, or goods on a fixed short route **4** slang a large sum of money: she was paid a packet **5** computers a unit into which a larger piece of data is broken down for more efficient transmission [Old French pacquet]

packhorse n a horse used to carry goods

pack ice n a large area of floating ice, consisting of pieces that have become massed together

pack in vb informal to stop doing (something): I'm going to pack it in and resign

packing n material, such as paper or plastic, used to protect packed goods

packsack n the US and Canadian word for **haversack**

packthread n a strong thread for sewing or tying up packages

pack up vb **1** to put (articles) in a bag or case before leaving **2** to stop doing (something) **3** (of a machine) to break down

pact n a formal agreement between two or more parties [Latin pactum]

pad¹ n **1** a thick piece of soft material used for comfort, shape, protection, or absorption **2** a number of sheets of paper fastened together along one edge **3** the fleshy cushioned underpart of an animal's paw **4** a level area or flat-topped structure, from which rockets are launched or helicopters take off **5** the floating leaf of the water lily **6** slang a person's residence ▷ vb **padding, padded 7** to fill (something) out with soft material for comfort, shape, or protection **8** **pad out** to lengthen (a speech or piece of writing) with unnecessary words or pieces of information [origin unknown]

pad² vb **padding, padded 1** to walk with a soft or muffled step **2** to travel (a route) on foot: men padding the streets in cheap sneakers [Middle Dutch pad path]

Padang n a port in W Indonesia, in W Sumatra at the foot of the **Padang Highlands** on the Indian Ocean. Pop: 713 242 (2000)

padded cell n a room with padded walls in a psychiatric hospital, in which patients who are likely to injure themselves are placed

padding n **1** any soft material used to pad something **2** unnecessary information put into a speech or written work to make it longer

paddle¹ n **1** a short light oar with a flat blade at one or both ends **2** a paddle wheel used to move a boat **3** a blade of a water wheel or paddle wheel ▷ vb **-dling, -dled 4** to move (a boat) with a paddle **5** to swim with short rapid strokes, like a dog **6** US and Canad informal to spank [origin unknown]

paddle² vb **-dling, -dled 1** to walk barefoot in shallow water **2** to dabble (one's fingers, hands, or feet) in water ▷ n **3** the act of paddling in water [origin unknown]

paddle steamer n a ship propelled by paddle wheels turned by a steam engine

paddle wheel n a large wheel fitted with paddles, turned by an engine to propel a ship

paddock n **1** a small enclosed field for horses **2** (in horse racing) the enclosure in which horses are paraded and mounted before a race **3** Austral and NZ any area of fenced land [Old English pearruc enclosure]

paddy¹ n, pl -dies **1** Also: **paddy field** a field planted with rice **2** rice as a growing crop or when harvested but not yet milled [Malay pādī]

paddy² n, pl -dies Brit and NZ informal a fit of temper [from Paddy, informal name for an Irishman]

pademelon or **paddymelon** (pad-ee-mel-an) n a small Australian wallaby

Paderborn n a market town in NW Germany, in North Rhine-Westphalia: scene of the meeting between Charlemagne and Pope Leo III (799 AD) that led to the foundation of the Holy Roman Empire. Pop: 141 800 (2003 est)

Paderewski n Ignace Jan. 1860–1941, Polish pianist, composer, and statesman; prime minister (1919)

padkos (pudd-koss) n S African snacks and provisions for a journey [Afrikaans, literally: road food]

padlock n **1** a detachable lock with a hinged hoop fastened through a ring on the object to be secured ▷ vb **2** to fasten (something) with a padlock [origin unknown]

Padova n the Italian name for **Padua**

padre (pah-dray) n informal a chaplain to the armed forces [via Spanish or Italian from Latin pater father]

Padua n a city in NE Italy, in Veneto: important in Roman and Renaissance times; university (1222); botanical garden (1545). Pop: 204 870 (2001). Latin name: Patavium. Italian name: **Padova**

Padus n the Latin name for the **Po**

paean (pee-an) n literary an expression of praise or joy [Greek paian hymn to Apollo]

paediatrician or US **pediatrician** n a doctor who specializes in children's diseases

paediatrics or US **pediatrics** n the branch of medicine concerned with children and their diseases [Greek pais, paid- child + iatros physician] ▷ **paediatric** or US **pediatric** adj

paedophile or US **pedophile** n a person who is sexually attracted to children

paedophilia or US **pedophilia** n the condition of being sexually attracted to children [Greek pais, paid- child + philos loving]

paella (pie-ell-a) n a Spanish dish made from rice, shellfish, chicken, and vegetables [Catalan]

Paestum n an ancient Greek colony on the coast of Lucania in S Italy

Páez n José Antonio. 1790–1873, Venezuelan revolutionary leader; first president (1831–46) of independent Venezuela

pagan adj **1** having, being, or relating to religious beliefs, esp. ancient ones, which are not part of any of the world's major religions: this was the site of a pagan temple to the sun **2** irreligious ▷ n **3** a person who does not belong to any of the world's major religions **4** a person without any religion [Church Latin paganus civilian (hence not a soldier of Christ)] ▷ **paganism** n

Paganini n Niccolò. 1782–1840, Italian violinist and composer

page¹ n **1** one side of one of the leaves of a book, newspaper, or magazine **2** one of the leaves of a book, newspaper, or magazine **3** literary a period or event: a new page in the country's political history **4** a screenful of information from a website or teletext service [Latin pagina]

page² n **1** a small boy who attends a bride at her wedding **2** a youth employed to run errands for the guests in a hotel or club **3** medieval history a boy in training for knighthood ▷ vb **paging, paged 4** to summon (a person), by bleeper or loudspeaker, in order to pass on a message [Greek pais child]

Page n **1** Sir Earle (Christmas Grafton). 1880–1961, Australian statesman; co-leader, with S. M. Bruce, of the federal government of Australia (1923–29) **2** Sir Frederick Handley. 1885–1962, English pioneer in the design and manufacture of aircraft

pageant n **1** an outdoor show portraying scenes from history **2** any magnificent display or procession [perhaps via French from Latin pagina scene of a play]

pageantry n spectacular display or ceremony

pageboy n **1** a hairstyle in which the hair is smooth and the same medium length with the ends curled under **2** same as **page²** (1, 2)

pagination n the numbering in sequence of the pages of a book or manuscript ▷ **paginate** vb

Paglia n Camille. born 1947, US writer and academic, noted for provocative cultural studies such as Sexual Personae (1990) and Vamps and Tramps (1995)

Pagnol *n* Marcel (Paul). 1895–1974, French dramatist, film director, and novelist, noted for his depiction of Provençal life in such films as *Manon des Sources* (1952; remade 1986)

pagoda *n* a pyramid-shaped Asian temple or tower [Portuguese *pagode*]

Pago Pago *n* a port in American Samoa, on SE Tutuila Island. Pop: 4278 (2000). Former name: **Pango Pango**

Pahang *n* a state of Peninsular Malaysia, on the South China Sea: the largest Malayan state; mountainous and heavily forested. Capital: Kuantan. Pop: 1 288 376 (2000). Area: 35 965 sq km (13 886 sq miles)

Pahlavi *n* **1** Mohammed Reza. 1919–80, shah of Iran (1941–79); forced into exile (1979) during civil unrest following which an Islamic republic was established led by the Ayatollah Khomeini **2** his father, **Reza.** 1877–1944, shah of Iran (1925–41). Originally an army officer, he gained power by a coup d'état (1921) and was chosen shah by the National Assembly. He reorganized the army and did much to modernize Iran

Pahsien *n* a former name for **Chongqing**

paid *vb* **1** past of **pay 2 put paid to** to end or destroy: *a knee injury put paid to his promising sporting career*

Paignton *n* a town and resort in SW England, in Devon: administratively part of Torbay since 1968

pail *n* **1** a bucket **2** Also called: **pailful** the amount contained in a pail: *a pail of water* [Old English *pægel*]

pain *n* **1** physical hurt or discomfort caused by injury or illness **2** emotional suffering **3** Also called: **pain in the neck** *informal* a person or thing that is annoying or irritating **4 on pain of** subject to the penalty of: *orders which their soldiers were bound to follow on pain of death* ▷ *vb* **5** to cause (a person) physical or mental suffering **6** *informal* to annoy; irritate ▸ See also **pains** [Latin *poena* punishment] ▷ **painless** *adj*

Paine *n* Thomas. 1737–1809, American political pamphleteer, born in England. His works include the pamphlets *Common Sense* (1776) and *Crisis* (1776–83), supporting the American colonists' fight for independence; *The Rights of Man* (1791–92), a justification of the French Revolution; and *The Age of Reason* (1794–96), a defence of deism

pained *adj* having or suggesting pain or distress: *a pained look*

painful *adj* **1** causing pain or distress: *painful inflammation of the joints; he began the painful task of making funeral arrangements* **2** affected with pain: *the symptoms include fever and painful joints* **3** tedious or difficult: *the hours passed with painful slowness* **4** *informal* extremely bad: *a painful so-called comedy* ▷ **painfully** *adv*

painkiller *n* a drug that relieves pain

pains *pl n* care or trouble: *they are at great pains to appear realistic and responsible*

painstaking *adj* extremely careful and thorough ▷ **painstakingly** *adv*

paint *n* **1** a coloured substance, spread on a surface with a brush or a roller, that forms a hard coating **2** a dry film of paint on a surface **3** *informal* face make-up ▷ *vb* **4** to apply paint to paper or canvas to make a picture of **5** to coat (a surface) with paint **6** to describe vividly in words: *the survey paints a dismal picture of growing hunger and disease* **7** to apply make-up to (the face) **8** to apply (liquid) to (a surface): *paint the varnish on and leave it to dry for at least four hours* **9 paint the town red** *informal* to celebrate in a lively way [Latin *pingere* to paint]

paintbrush *n* a brush used to apply paint

Painted Desert *n* a section of the high plateau country of N central Arizona, along the N side of the Little Colorado River Valley: brilliant-coloured rocks; occupied largely by Navaho and Hopi Indians. Area: about 20 000 sq km (7500 sq miles)

painted lady *n* a butterfly with pale brownish-red mottled wings

painter¹ *n* **1** an artist who paints pictures **2** a person who paints surfaces of buildings as a trade

painter² *n* a rope attached to the bow of a boat for tying it up [probably from Old French *penteur* strong rope]

painting *n* **1** a picture produced by using paint **2** the art of producing pictures by applying paints to paper or canvas **3** the act of applying paint to a surface

paintwork *n* the covering of paint on parts of a vehicle, building, etc.: *someone had damaged the Porsche by scraping a key along its paintwork*

pair *n* **1** two identical or similar things matched for use together: *a pair of shoes* **2** two people, animals, or things used or grouped together: *a pair of tickets* **3** an object consisting of two identical or similar parts joined together: *a pair of jeans* **4** a male and a female animal of the same species kept for breeding purposes **5** parliament two opposed members who both agree not to vote on a specified motion **6** two playing cards of the same denomination **7** one member of a matching pair: *I can't find the pair to this glove* ▷ *vb* **8** to group (people or things) in twos **9 pair off** to separate into groups of two [Latin *par* equal]

> **USAGE** Like other collective nouns, *pair* takes a singular or a plural verb according to whether it is seen as a unit or as a collection of two things: *the pair are said to dislike each other; a pair of good shoes is essential.*

Paisley¹ *n* an industrial town in SW Scotland, the administrative centre of Renfrewshire: one of the world's chief centres for the manufacture of thread, linen, and gauze in the 19th century. Pop: 74 170 (2001)

Paisley² *n* **1** Bob. 1919–96, English footballer and manager: played for Liverpool (1939–54); under his management (1974–83) Liverpool won six English titles and the European Cup three times (1977, 1978, 1981) **2** Ian (Richard Kyle) Baron. (1926–2014), Northern Ireland politician and Presbyterian minister; cofounder (1972) and leader of the Democratic Unionist Party until 2008, First Minister of Northern Ireland from 2007 to 2008

paisley pattern or **paisley** *n* a detailed pattern of small curving shapes, used in fabric [after PAISLEY¹]

pajamas *pl n* US pyjamas

Pak *Indian n* **1** Pakistan ▷ *n, adj* **2** Pakistani

pakeha (pah-kee-hah) *n, pl* **pakeha** or **pakehas** NZ a person of European descent, as distinct from a Māori [Māori]

Paki *Brit slang, offensive n* **1** a Pakistani or person of Pakistani descent ▷ *adj* **2** Pakistani or of Pakistani descent

Pakistan *n* **1** a republic in S Asia, on the Arabian Sea: the Union of Pakistan, formed in 1947, comprised West and East Pakistan; East Pakistan gained independence as Bangladesh in 1971 and West Pakistan became Pakistan; a member of the Commonwealth from 1947, it withdrew from 1972 until 1989; contains the fertile plains of the Indus valley rising to mountains in the north and west Official language: Urdu. Official religion: Muslim. Currency: rupee. Capital: Islamabad. Pop: 193 238 868 (2013 est). Area: 801 508 sq km (309 463 sq miles) **2** a former republic in S Asia consisting of the provinces of West Pakistan and East Pakistan (now Bangladesh), 1500 km (900 miles) apart: formed in 1947 from the predominantly Muslim parts of India

Pakistani *adj* **1** of or relating to Pakistan or its inhabitants ▷ *n* **2** a native or inhabitant of Pakistan

pal *informal n* **1** a close friend ▷ *vb* **palling, palled 2 pal up with** to become friends with [Romany: brother]

Pal. Palestine

palace *n* **1** the official residence of a king, queen, president, or archbishop **2** a large and richly furnished building [Latin *Palatium* Palatine, the site of the palace of the emperors in Rome]

Palacio Valdés *n* Armando. 1853–1938, Spanish novelist and critic

paladin n **1** one of the legendary twelve peers of Charlemagne's court **2** (formerly) a knight who did battle for a king or queen [Italian *paladino*]

palaeo- or US **paleo-** combining form old, ancient, or prehistoric: *palaeobotany*

Palaeocene or US **Paleocene** (pal-ee-oh-seen) adj geology of the epoch of geological time about 65 million years ago [Greek *palaeo-* ancient + *kainos* new]

palaeography or US **paleography** (pal-ee-og-ra-fee) n the study of past handwriting [Greek *palaeo-* ancient + -GRAPHY]

Palaeolithic or US **Paleolithic** (pal-ee-oh-lith-ik) adj of the period from about 2.5 to 3 million years ago until about 12 000 BC, during which primitive man emerged and unpolished chipped stone tools were made [Greek *palaeo-* ancient + *lithos* stone]

palaeontology or US **paleontology** (pal-ee-on-tol-a-jee) n the study of past geological periods and fossils [Greek *palaeo-* ancient + *ōn, ont-* being + -LOGY]
 › palaeontologist or US **paleontologist** n

Palaeozoic or US **Paleozoic** (pal-ee-oh-zoh-ik) adj geology of the geological era that lasted from about 600 million years ago to 230 million years ago [Greek *palaeo-* ancient + *zōion* animal]

Palagi (pa-lang-gee) n, pl **-gis** NZ the Samoan name for a Pakeha

palanquin (pal-an-keen) n (formerly, in the Orient) a covered bed in which someone could be carried on the shoulders of four men [Portuguese *palanquim*]

palatable adj **1** (of food or drink) pleasant to taste **2** (of an experience or idea) acceptable or satisfactory

palate n **1** the roof of the mouth **2** the sense of taste: *a range of dishes to tempt every palate* [Latin *palatum*]

> **USAGE** Avoid confusion with **palette** or **pallet**[1].

palatial adj like a palace; magnificent: *his palatial home*

palatinate n a territory ruled by a palatine prince or noble or a count palatine

palatine adj possessing royal prerogatives: *a count palatine* [Latin *palatium* palace]

Palatine n **1** one of the Seven Hills of Rome: traditionally the site of the first settlement of Rome
 ▷ adj **2** of, relating to, or designating this hill

Palau or **Belau** n **Republic of Palau** a republic comprising a group of islands in the W Pacific, in the W Caroline Islands; administratively part of the UN Trust Territory of the Pacific Islands 1947–87; entered into an agreement of free association with the US (1980); became fully independent in 1994. Chief island: Babelthuap. Capital: Melekeok, on Babelthuap (functions moved from Koror in 2006). Pop: 21 108 (2013 est). Area: 476 sq km (184 sq miles). Former name: **Pelew Islands**

palaver (pal-lah-ver) n time-consuming fuss: *all the palaver involved in obtaining a visa* [Portuguese *palavra* talk]

Palawan n an island of the SW Philippines between the South China Sea and the Sulu Sea: the westernmost island in the country; mountainous and forested. Capital: Puerto Princesa. Pop (Palawan province): 755 412 (2000). Area: 11 785 sq km (4550 sq miles)

palazzo pants pl n women's trousers with very wide legs [Italian *palazzo* palace]

pale[1] adj **1** (of a colour) whitish and not very strong: *pale yellow* **2** (of a complexion) having a whitish appearance, usually because of illness, shock, or fear **3** lacking brightness or colour: *the pale, chill light of an October afternoon* ▷ vb **paling, paled** **4** to become pale or paler: *the girl paled at the news* [Latin *pallidus*] **› paleness** n

pale[2] n **1** a wooden post used in fences **2 a** a fence made of pales **b** a boundary **3 beyond the pale** outside the limits of social convention: *the destruction of forests is beyond the pale* [Latin *palus* stake]

paleface n an offensive term for a White person, said to have been used by Native Americans of N America

Palembang n a port in W Indonesia, in S Sumatra; oil refineries; university (1955). Pop: 1 451 419 (2000)

Palencia n a city in N central Spain: earliest university in Spain (1208); seat of Castilian kings (12th–13th centuries); communications centre. Pop: 81 378 (2003 est)

Palenque n the site of an ancient Mayan city in S Mexico famous for its architectural ruins

Palermo n the capital of Sicily, on the NW coast: founded by the Phoenicians in the 8th century BC Pop: 686 722 (2001)

Palestine n **1** Also called: **the Holy Land, Canaan** the area between the Jordan River and the Mediterranean Sea in which most of the biblical narrative is located **2** the province of the Roman Empire in this region **3** the former British mandatory territory created by the League of Nations in 1922 (but effective from 1920), and including all of the present territories of Israel and Jordan between whom it was partitioned by the UN in 1948

Palestinian adj **1** of or relating to Palestine ▷ n **2 a** native or inhabitant of the former British mandate, or their descendants, esp. such Arabs now living in the Palestinian Administered Territories, Jordan, Lebanon, or Israel, or as refugees from Israeli-occupied territory

Palestrina n Giovanni Pierluigi da. ?1525–94, Italian composer and master of counterpoint. His works, nearly all for unaccompanied choir and religious in nature, include the *Missa Papae Marcelli* (1555)

palette n **1** a flat board used by artists to mix paints **2** the range of colours characteristic of a particular artist or school of painting: *he uses a cool palette with no strong red* **3** the range of colours or patterns that can be displayed on the visual display unit of a computer [French]

> **USAGE** Avoid confusion with **palate** or **pallet**[1].

palette knife n a spatula with a thin flexible blade used in painting or cookery

Paley n William. 1743–1805, English theologian and utilitarian philosopher. His chief works are *The Principles of Moral and Political Philosophy* (1785), *Horae Paulinae* (1790), *A View of the Evidences of Christianity* (1794), and *Natural Theology* (1802)

Palgrave n Francis Turner. 1824–97, British critic and poet, editor of the poetry anthology *The Golden Treasury* (1861)

palindrome n a word or phrase that reads the same backwards or forwards, such as *able was I ere I saw Elba* [Greek *palindromos* running back again]

paling n **1** a fence made of pales **2** pales collectively **3** a single pale

palisade n **1** a fence made of stakes driven into the ground **2** one of the stakes used in such a fence [Latin *palus* stake]

Palissy n Bernard. 1510–89, French Huguenot potter and writer on natural history, noted for his rustic glazed earthenware: died in the Bastille

Palk Strait n a channel between SE India and N Sri Lanka. Width: about 64 km (40 miles)

pall[1] n **1** a cloth spread over a coffin **2** a coffin at a funeral ceremony **3** a dark heavy covering: *a pall of smoke and dust hung in the air* **4** a depressing atmosphere: *a pall hung on them all after his death* [Latin *pallium* cloak]

pall[2] vb to become boring or uninteresting, esp. by continuing for too long: *any pleasure had palled long before the two-hour programme was over* [variant of *appal*]

Palladian adj of a style of architecture characterized by symmetry, and the revival and development of ancient Roman styles [after Andrea PALLADIO]

Palladio n Andrea. 1508–80, Italian architect who revived and developed classical architecture, esp. the ancient Roman ideals of symmetrical planning and harmonic proportions. His treatise *Four Books on Architecture* (1570) and his designs for villas and palaces

P

profoundly influenced 18th-century domestic architecture in England and the US

palladium *n chem* a rare silvery-white element of the platinum metal group, used in jewellery. Symbol: **Pd** [after the asteroid *Pallas*]

pallbearer *n* a person who helps to carry or who escorts the coffin at a funeral

pallet[1] *n* a straw-filled mattress or bed [Latin *palea* straw]

pallet[2] *n* **1** a tool with a flat, sometimes flexible, blade used for shaping pottery **2** a portable platform for storing and moving goods [Latin *pala* spade]

USAGE Avoid confusion with **palate** or **palette**.

---

palliasse *n* a straw-filled mattress; pallet [French *paillasse*]

palliate *vb* **-ating, -ated 1** to lessen the severity of (pain or disease) without curing it **2** to cause (an offence) to seem less serious [Latin *pallium* a cloak]

palliative *adj* **1** relieving without curing ▷ *n* **2** something that palliates, such as a sedative drug **3** something that alleviates or lessens a problem: *equal pay was a palliative for the growing unrest among women*

pallid *adj* **1** lacking colour, brightness, or vigour: *a pallid autumn sun* **2** lacking energy or vitality; insipid: *many militants find the party's socialism too pallid* [Latin *pallidus*]

Pall Mall *n* a street in central London, noted for its many clubs

pallor *n* paleness of complexion, usually because of illness, shock, or fear [Latin: whiteness]

pally *adj* **-lier, -liest** *informal* on friendly terms

palm[1] *n* **1** the inner surface of the hand from the wrist to the base of the fingers **2** the part of a glove that covers the palm **3** in the palm of one's hand at one's mercy or command: *he had the jury in the palm of his hand* ▷ *vb* **4** to hide (something) in the hand: *he palmed the key* ▶ See also **palm off** [Latin *palma*]

palm[2] or **palm tree** *n* a tropical or subtropical tree with a straight unbranched trunk crowned with long pointed leaves [Latin *palma*, from the likeness of its spreading fronds to a hand]

Palma[1] *n* the capital of the Balearic Islands, on the SW coast of Majorca: a tourist centre. Pop: 367 277 (2003 est). Official name: **Palma de Mallorca**

Palma[2] *n* Jacopo, known as *Palma Vecchio*, original name *Jacopo Negretti*. ?1480–1528, Venetian painter, noted esp. for his portraits of women

Palmas *n* a city in N Brazil, capital of Tocantins state. Pop: 391 000 (2005 est)

palmate *adj* shaped like an open hand: *palmate leaves*

Palm Beach *n* a town in SE Florida, on an island between Lake Worth (a lagoon) and the Atlantic: major resort and tourist centre. Pop: 9759 (2003 est)

Palme *n* (Sven) Olof (Joachim). 1927–86, Swedish Social Democratic statesman; prime minister (1969–76, 1982–86); assassinated

Palmer *n* **1** Arnold. born 1929, US professional golfer: winner of seven major championships, including four in the US Masters (1958, 1960, 1962, 1964) and two in the British Open (1961,1962) **2** Samuel. 1805–81, English painter of visionary landscapes, influenced by William Blake

Palmer Archipelago *n* a group of islands between South America and Antarctica: part of the British Antarctic Territory, formerly the British colony of the Falkland Islands and Dependencies. (Claims are suspended under the Antarctic Treaty). Former name: Antarctic Archipelago

Palmer Land *n* the S part of the Antarctic Peninsula

Palmer Peninsula *n* the former name (until 1964) for the Antarctic Peninsula

Palmerston[1] *n* the former name (1869–1911) of Darwin

Palmerston[2] *n* Henry John Temple, 3rd Viscount Palmerston. 1784–1865, British statesman; foreign secretary (1830–34; 1835–41; 1846–51); prime minister (1855–58; 1859–65). His talent was for foreign affairs, in which he earned a reputation as a British nationalist and for high-handedness and gunboat diplomacy

Palmerston North *n* a city in New Zealand, in the S North Island on the Manawatu River. Pop: 78 100 (2004 est)

palmetto *n, pl* **-tos** a small palm tree with fan-shaped leaves [Spanish *palmito* a little palm]

Palmira *n* a city in W Colombia: agricultural trading centre. Pop: 253 000 (2005 est)

Palm Islands *pl n* a group of three man-made island systems under construction just off the shore in Dubai, each in the shape of a palm tree

palmistry *n* fortune-telling by examining the lines and bumps of the hand ❯ **palmist** *n*

palm off *vb* **1** to get rid of (someone or something) by passing it on to another: *the risk has to be shared with subcontractors, not simply palmed off on them* **2** to divert (someone) by a lie or excuse: *Mark was palmed off with a series of excuses*

palm oil *n* an oil obtained from the fruit of certain palm trees, used as an edible fat and in soap

Palm Springs *n* a city in the US, in California: a popular tourist resort. Pop: 45 228 (2003 est)

Palm Sunday *n* the Sunday before Easter

palmtop *adj* (of a computer) small enough to be held in the hand

palmy *adj* **palmier, palmiest 1** successful, prosperous and happy: *the palmy days of youth* **2** covered with palm trees: *palmy beaches*

Palmyra *n* **1** an ancient city in central Syria: said to have been built by Solomon. Biblical name: **Tadmor 2** an island in the central Pacific, in the Line Islands: under US administration

Palo Alto *n* **1** a city in W California, southeast of San Francisco: founded in 1891 as the seat of Stanford University. Pop: 57 233 (2003 est) **2** a battlefield in E Mexico, northwest of Monterrey, where the first battle (1846) of the Mexican War took place, in which the Mexicans under General Mariano Arista were defeated by the Americans under General Zachary Taylor

Palomar *n* Mount Palomar a mountain in S California, northeast of San Diego: site of **Mount Palomar Observatory**, which has a large (200-inch) reflecting telescope. Height: 1871 m (6140 ft)

palomino *n, pl* **-nos** a golden or cream horse with a white mane and tail [Spanish: dovelike]

Palos *n* a village and former port in SW Spain: starting point of Columbus' voyage of discovery to America (1492)

palpable *adj* **1** obvious: *palpable nonsense* **2** (of a feeling or an atmosphere) so intense that it seems capable of being touched: *an air of palpable gloom hung over him* [Latin *palpare* to touch] ❯ **palpably** *adv*

palpate *vb* **-pating, -pated** *med* to examine (an area of the body) by touching [Latin *palpare* to stroke] ❯ **palpation** *n*

palpitate *vb* **-tating, -tated 1** (of the heart) to beat rapidly **2** to flutter or tremble [Latin *palpitare*] ❯ **palpitation** *n*

palsy (pawl-zee) *n pathol* paralysis of a specified type: *cerebral palsy* [Old French *paralisie*] ❯ **palsied** *adj*

Paltrow *n* Gwyneth (Kate). born 1972, US film actress; her films include *Emma* (1996), *Sliding Doors* (1998), *Shakespeare in Love* (1998), and *Sylvia* (2003)

paltry *adj* **-trier, -triest** insignificant [Low Germanic *palter, paltrig* ragged]

Pamirs *pl n* the Pamirs a mountainous area of central Asia, mainly in Tajikistan and partly in Kyrgyzstan, extending into China and Afghanistan: consists of a complex of high ranges, from which the Tian Shan projects to the north, the Kunlun and Karakoram to the east, and the Hindu Kush to the west; Ismoil Somoni (formerly Communism Peak) is situated in the Tajik

Pamirs. Highest peak: Kongur Shan, 7719 m (25 326 ft). Also known as: **the Pamir**

Pamlico Sound *n* an inlet of the Atlantic between the E coast of North Carolina and its chain of offshore islands. Length: 130 km (80 miles)

pampas *n* the extensive grassy plains of South America [Native American *bamba* plain]

pampas grass *n* a South American grass with large feathery silver-coloured flower branches

Pampeluna *n* the former name of **Pamplona**

pamper *vb* to treat (someone) with excessive indulgence or care; spoil [Germanic]

pamphlet *n* a thin paper-covered booklet, often on a subject of current interest [Medieval Latin *Pamphilus*, title of a poem]

pamphleteer *n* a person who writes or issues pamphlets

Pamphylia *n* an area on the S coast of ancient Asia Minor

Pamplona *n* a city in N Spain in the foothills of the Pyrenees: capital of the kingdom of Navarre from the 11th century until 1841. Pop: 190 937 (2003 est). Former name: **Pampeluna**

Pamuk *n* Orhan. born 1952, Turkish novelist and writer; author of *The Black Book* (1990), *My Name is Red* (1998), *Snow* (2002), and *Istanbul: Memories of a City* (2003). Nobel prize for literature 2006

pan¹ *n* **1** a wide long-handled metal container used in cooking **2** any of various similar containers used in industry, etc. **3** either of the two dishes on a set of scales **4** *Brit* the bowl of a lavatory **5** a natural or artificial hollow in the ground: *a saltpan* ▷ *vb* **panning, panned 6** to sift gold from (a river) in a shallow pan **7** *informal* to criticize harshly: *his first film was panned by the critics* ▶ See also **pan out** [Old English *panne*]

pan² *vb* **panning, panned 1** to move (a film camera) or (of a film camera) to be moved to follow a moving object or to take in a whole scene ▷ *n* **2** the act of panning [from *panoramic*]

Pan. Panama

pan- *combining form* including or relating to all parts or members: *Pan-American* [Greek]

panacea (pan-a-**see**-a) *n* a remedy for all diseases or problems [Greek *pan*- all + *akos* remedy]

panache (pan-**ash**) *n* a confident and stylish manner: *the orchestra played with great panache* [Old Italian *pennacchio* feather]

Panaji *n* a variant of **Panjim**

Panama *n* **1** a republic in Central America, occupying the Isthmus of Panama: gained independence from Spain in 1821 and joined Greater Colombia; became independent in 1903, with the immediate area around the canal forming the Canal Zone under US jurisdiction; Panama assumed sovereignty over the Canal Zone in 1979 and full control in 1999. Official language: Spanish; English is also widely spoken. Religion: Roman Catholic majority. Currency: balboa. Capital: Panama City. Pop: 3 559 408 (2013 est). Area: 75 650 sq km (29 201 sq miles) **2 Isthmus of Panama** an isthmus linking North and South America, between the Pacific and the Caribbean. Length: 676 km (420 miles). Width (at its narrowest point): 50 km (31 miles). Former name: **Darien, Isthmus of Darien 3 Gulf of Panama** a wide inlet of the Pacific in Panama

Panama Canal *n* a canal across the Isthmus of Panama, linking the Atlantic and Pacific Oceans: extends from Colón on the Caribbean Sea southeast to Balboa on the Gulf of Panama; built by the US (1904–14), after an unsuccessful previous attempt (1880–89) by the French under de Lesseps. Length: 64 km (40 miles)

Panama Canal Zone *n* See **Canal Zone**

Panama City *n* the capital of Panama, near the Pacific entrance of the Panama Canal: developed rapidly with the building of the Panama Canal; seat of the University of Panama (1935). Pop: 950 000 (2005 est)

panama hat *or* **panama** *n* a straw hat with a rounded crown and a wide brim

Panamanian *adj* **1** of or relating to Panama or its inhabitants ▷ *n* **2** a native or inhabitant of Panama

Pan-American *adj* of North, South, and Central America collectively

panatella *n* a long slender cigar [American Spanish *panetela* long thin biscuit]

Panay *n* an island in the central Philippines, the westernmost of the Visayan Islands. Pop: 3 500 000 (2000). Area: 12 300 sq km (4750 sq miles)

pancake *n* **1** a thin flat circle of fried batter **2** Also called: **pancake landing** an aircraft landing made by levelling out a few feet from the ground and then dropping onto it

Pancake Day *n* Shrove Tuesday, when people traditionally eat pancakes

panchromatic *adj photog* (of an emulsion or film) sensitive to light of all colours

pancreas (**pang**-kree-ass) *n* a large gland behind the stomach, that produces insulin and aids digestion [Greek *pan*- all + *kreas* flesh] ▶ **pancreatic** *adj*

panda *n* **1** Also called: **giant panda** a large black-and-white bearlike animal from the high mountain bamboo forests of China **2** Also called: **lesser panda, red panda** a raccoon-like animal of the mountain forests of S Asia, with a reddish-brown coat and ringed tail [Nepalese]

panda car *n Brit* a police patrol car

pandemic *adj* (of a disease) occurring over a wide geographical area [Greek *pandēmos* general]

pandemonium *n* wild confusion; uproar [Greek *pan*- all + *daimōn* demon]

pander *vb* **1** (foll. by *to*) to indulge (a person or his or her desires): *he pandered to popular fears* ▷ *n* **2** *chiefly archaic* a person who procures a sexual partner for someone [after *Pandarus*, in legend, the procurer of Cressida for Troilus]

pandit *n Hinduism* same as **pundit** (2)

Pandit *n* Vijaya Lakshmi. 1900–90, Indian politician and diplomat; sister of Jawaharlal Nehru

Pandora's box *n* a source of many unforeseen difficulties [a box, in Greek myth, from which all human problems were released]

p & p *Brit* postage and packing

pane *n* a sheet of glass in a window or door [Latin *pannus* rag]

panegyric (pan-ee-**jirr**-rik) *n* a formal speech or piece of writing that praises a person or event [Greek *panēguris* public gathering]

panel *n* **1** a distinct section of a larger surface area, such as that in a door **2** any distinct section of something formed from a sheet of material, such as part of a car body **3** a piece of material inserted in a garment **4** a group of people acting as a team, such as in a quiz or a discussion before an audience **5** *law* **a** a list of jurors **b** the people on a jury **6** short for **instrument panel** ▷ *adj* **7** of a group acting as a panel: *a panel game* ▷ *vb* **-elling, -elled** *or US* **-eling, -eled 8** to cover or decorate with panels [Old French: portion]

panel beater *n* a person who repairs damage to car bodies

panelling *or US* **paneling** *n* panels collectively, such as on a wall or ceiling

panellist *or US* **panelist** *n* a member of a panel, usually on radio or television

panel van *n Austral and NZ* a small van

pang *n* a sudden sharp feeling of pain or sadness [Germanic]

Pangaea *or* **Pangea** *n* the ancient supercontinent, comprising all the present continents joined together, which began to break up about 200 million years ago. See also **Laurasia, Gondwanaland** [C20: from Greek, literally: all-earth]

Pang-fou *n* a variant transliteration of the Chinese name for **Bengbu**

pangolin *n* an animal of tropical countries with a scaly body and a long snout for feeding on ants and termites. Also called: **scaly anteater** [Malay *peng-gōling*]

Pango Pango *n* the former name of **Pago Pago**

Pan Gu *or* **P'an Ku** *n* 32–92 AD, Chinese historian and court official, noted for his history of the Han dynasty: died in prison

panic *n* **1** a sudden overwhelming feeling of terror or anxiety, sometimes affecting a whole group of people ▷ *adj* **2** of or resulting from such terror: *panic measures* ▷ *vb* **-nicking, -nicked 3** to feel or cause to feel panic [Greek *panikos* emanating from *Pan*, god of the fields] **> panicky** *adj*

panicle *n* botany a loose, irregularly branched cluster of flowers, such as in the oat [Latin *panicula* tuft]

panic-stricken *adj* affected by panic

panini *n*, *pl* **-ni** *or* **-nis** a type of Italian bread usually served grilled with a variety of fillings

panjandrum *n* a pompous self-important official [after a character in a nonsense work]

Panjim *or* **Panaji** *n* the capital of the Indian state of Goa (formerly capital of the union territory of Goa, Daman, and Diu until 1987): a port on the Arabian Sea on the coast of Goa. Pop: 58 785 (2001)

Pankhurst *n* **1** Dame **Christabel**. 1880–1958, English suffragette **2** her mother, **Emmeline**. 1858–1928, English suffragette leader, who founded the militant Women's Social and Political Union (1903) **3 Sylvia**, daughter of Emmeline Pankhurst. 1882–1960, English suffragette and pacifist

Panmunjom *n* a village in the demilitarized zone of Korea: site of truce talks leading to the end of the Korean War (1950–53)

pannier *n* **1** one of a pair of bags fixed on either side of the back wheel of a bicycle or motorcycle **2** one of a pair of large baskets slung over a beast of burden [Old French *panier*]

Pannonia *n* a region of the ancient world south and west of the Danube: made a Roman province in 6 AD

panoply (pan-a-plee) *n* a magnificent array: *ambassadors equipped with the full panoply of diplomatic bags, codes and cyphers* [Greek *pan-* all + *hopla* armour]

panorama *n* **1 a** a wide unbroken view in all directions: *the beautiful panorama of the Cornish coast* **2** a wide or comprehensive survey of a subject: *the panorama of American life* **3** a picture of a scene unrolled before spectators a part at a time so as to appear continuous [Greek *pan-* all + *horama* view] **> panoramic** *adj*

pan out *vb* **1** informal to work out; result: *Parker's research did not pan out too well* **2** (of gravel) to yield gold by panning

panpipes *pl n* a musical wind instrument made of tubes of decreasing lengths joined together

pansy *n*, *pl* **-sies 1** a garden plant whose flowers have rounded white, yellow, or purple velvety petals **2** offensive, slang an effeminate or homosexual man or boy [Old French *pensée* thought]

pant *vb* **1** to breathe with noisy gasps after exertion **2** to say (something) while breathing in this way **3** (foll. by *for*) to have a frantic desire for ▷ *n* **4** the act of panting [Greek *phantasioun* to have visions]

pantaloons *pl n* baggy trousers gathered at the ankles [French *pantalon* trousers]

pantechnicon *n* Brit a large van used for furniture removals [Greek *pan-* all + *tekhnē* art; originally a London bazaar later used as a furniture warehouse]

Pantelleria *n* an Italian island in the Mediterranean, between Sicily and Tunisia: of volcanic origin; used by the Romans as a place of banishment. Pop: 7679 (2004 est). Area: 83 sq km (32 sq miles). Ancient name: **Cossyra**

pantheism *n* **1** the belief that God is present in everything **2** readiness to worship all gods **> pantheist** *n* **> pantheistic** *adj*

pantheon *n* **1** (in ancient Greece or Rome) a temple built to honour all the gods **2** all the gods of a particular

creed: *the Celtic pantheon of horse gods* **3** a group of very important people: *he deserves a place in the pantheon of social reformers* [Greek *pan-* all + *theos* god]

Pantheon *n* a circular temple in Rome dedicated to all the gods, built by Agrippa in 27 BC, rebuilt by Hadrian 120–24 AD, and used since 609 AD as a Christian church

panther *n* a leopard, usually a black one [Greek]

panties *pl n* women's or children's underpants

pantihose *pl n* US and Austral women's tights

pantile *n* a roofing tile, with an S-shaped cross section [PAN¹ + *tile*]

panto *n*, *pl* **-tos** Brit informal short for **pantomime** (1)

pantograph *n* **1** an instrument for copying drawings or maps to any scale **2** a device on the roof of an electric train to carry the current from an overhead wire [Greek *pant-* all + *graphein* to write]

pantomime *n* **1** (in Britain) a play based on a fairy tale and performed at Christmas time **2** a theatrical entertainment in which words are replaced by gestures and bodily actions **3** informal, chiefly Brit a confused or farcical situation [Greek *pantomimos*]

pantry *n*, *pl* **-tries** a small room or large cupboard in which food is kept [Latin *panis* bread]

pants *pl n* **1** Brit an undergarment with two leg holes, covering the body from the waist or hips to the thighs **2** US, Canad, Austral and NZ trousers or shorts **3** bore or **scare the pants off someone** informal to bore or scare someone very much [shortened from *pantaloons*]

pantyhose *pl n* Austral and NZ women's tights

Panufnik *n* Sir **Andrzej**. 1914–91, British composer and conductor, born in Poland. His works include nine symphonies, the cantata *Winter Solstice* (1972), Polish folk-song settings, and ballet music

Pão de Açúcar *n* the Portuguese name for the **Sugar Loaf Mountain**

Paolozzi *n* Sir **Eduardo** (**Luigi**). 1924–2005, British sculptor and designer, noted esp. for his semiabstract metal figures

Paoting *or* **Pao-ting** *n* a variant transliteration of the Chinese name for **Baoding**

Paotow *n* a variant transliteration of the Chinese name for **Baotou**

pap¹ *n* **1 a** soft food for babies or invalids **2** worthless or oversimplified entertainment or information **3** S African maize porridge [Latin *pappare* to eat]

pap² *n* old-fashioned, Scot dialect, N English dialect a nipple or teat [from Old Norse]

papa (pap-**pah**) *n* old-fashioned, informal father [French]

papacy (**pay**-pa-see) *n*, *pl* **-cies 1** the office or term of office of a pope **2** the system of government in the Roman Catholic Church that has the pope as its head [Medieval Latin *papa* pope]

Papadopoulos *n* **1 Georgios**. 1919–99, Greek army officer and statesman; prime minister (1967–73) and president (1973) in Greece's military government **2 Tassos Nikolaou**. 1934–2008, Cypriot politician: president of Cyprus from 2003

papal *adj* of the pope or the papacy

Papandreou *n* **Andreas** (**George**). 1919–96, Greek economist and socialist politician; prime minister (1981–89; 1993–96)

paparazzo (pap-a-**rat**-so) *n*, *pl* **-razzi** (-**rat**-see) a freelance photographer who specializes in taking shots of famous people without their knowledge or consent [Italian]

papaya (pap-**pie**-a) *n* a large green fruit with a sweet yellow flesh, that grows in the West Indies [Spanish]

Papeete *n* the capital of French Polynesia, on the NW coast of Tahiti: one of the largest towns in the S Pacific. Pop: 130 000 (2005 est)

Papen *n* **Franz von**. 1879–1969, German statesman; chancellor (1932) and vice chancellor (1933–34) under Hitler, whom he was instrumental in bringing to power

paper *n* **1 a** a flexible material made in sheets from wood pulp or other fibres and used for writing on, decorating walls, or wrapping parcels **2** short for **newspaper, wallpaper 3 papers** documents, such as a passport, which can identify the bearer **4** a set of examination questions **5 papers** the collected diaries or letters of someone's private or public life **6** a lecture or an essay on a specific subject **7 on paper** in theory, as opposed to fact: *countless ideas which look good on paper just don't work in practice* ▷ *adj* **8** made of paper: *paper towels; a paper bag* **9** recorded on paper but not yet existing in practice: *a paper profit of more than $50 million* ▷ *vb* **10** to cover (walls) with wallpaper ▶ See also **paper over** [Latin *papyrus*] **> papery** *adj*

paperback *n* **1** a book with covers made of flexible card ▷ *adj* **2** of a paperback or publication of paperbacks: *a paperback novel*

paperboy *or* **papergirl** *n* a boy or girl employed to deliver newspapers to people's homes

paper chase *n* a former type of cross-country run in which a runner lays a trail of paper for others to follow

paperclip *n* a bent wire clip for holding sheets of paper together

paperhanger *n* a person who hangs wallpaper as an occupation

paperknife *n, pl* **-knives** a knife-shaped object with a blunt blade for opening sealed envelopes

paper money *n* banknotes, rather than coins

paper over *vb* to conceal (something unpleasant or difficult)

paperweight *n* a small heavy object placed on top of loose papers to prevent them from scattering

paperwork *n* clerical work, such as the writing of reports or letters

Paphlagonia *n* an ancient country and Roman province in N Asia Minor, on the Black Sea

Paphos *n* a town in SW Cyprus, near the sites of two ancient cities: famous as the centre of Aphrodite worship and traditionally the place at which she landed after her birth among the waves. Pop: 53 060 (2001)

papier-mâché (pap-yay mash-ay) *n* **1** a hard substance made of layers of paper mixed with paste and moulded when moist ▷ *adj* **2** made of papier-mâché [French, literally: chewed paper]

papilla (pap-pill-a) *n, pl* **-lae** (-lee) *biology* a small projection of tissue at the base of a hair, tooth, or feather [Latin: nipple] **> papillary** *adj*

papist *n, adj usually offensive* same as **Roman Catholic** [Church Latin *papa* pope]

papoose *n* a Native American baby [Native American *papoos*]

Pappus of Alexandria *n* 3rd century BC, Greek mathematician, whose eight-volume *Synagoge* is a valuable source of information about Greek mathematics

paprika *n* a mild powdered seasoning made from red peppers [Hungarian]

Pap test *or* **Pap smear** *n med* same as **cervical smear** [after George *Papanicolaou,* anatomist]

Papua *n* **1 Territory of Papua** a former territory of Australia, consisting of SE New Guinea and adjacent islands: now part of Papua New Guinea. Former name: (1888–1906) **British New Guinea 2** the W part of the island of New Guinea: formerly under Dutch rule, becoming a province of Indonesia in 1963. Capital: Jayapura. Pop: 2 220 934 (2000). Area: 416 990 sq km (161 000 sq miles). Former names (until 1962): **Dutch New Guinea, Netherlands New Guinea.** Former Indonesian names: **Irian Barat** (1962-1973), **Irian Jaya** (1973-2001). Former English name: **West Irian** (translation of Irian Barat) **3 Gulf of Papua** an inlet of the Coral Sea in the SE coast of New Guinea

Papuan *adj* **1** of or relating to Papua or any of the languages spoken there ▷ *n* **2** a native or inhabitant of Papua New Guinea **3** any of several languages of Papua New Guinea that apparently do not belong to the Malayo-Polynesian family

Papua New Guinea *n* a country in the SW Pacific; consists of the E half of New Guinea, the Bismarck Archipelago, the W Solomon Islands, Trobriand Islands, D'Entrecasteaux Islands, Woodlark Island, and the Louisiade Archipelago; administered by Australia from 1949 until 1975, when it became an independent member of the Commonwealth. Official language: English; Tok Pisin (English Creole) and Motu are widely spoken. Religion: Christian majority. Currency: kina. Capital: Port Moresby. Pop: 6 431 902 (2013 est). Area: 461 693 sq km (178 260 sq miles)

papyrus (pap-ire-uss) *n, pl* **-ri** (-rye) *or* **-ruses 1** a tall water plant of Africa **2** a kind of paper made from the stem of this plant, used by the ancient Egyptians, Greeks, and Romans **3** an ancient document written on this paper [Greek *papuros* reed]

par *n* **1** the usual or average condition: *I feel slightly below par most of the time* **2** *golf* a standard score for a hole or course that a good player should make: *four under par with two holes to play* **3** *finance* the established value of the unit of one national currency in terms of the unit of another **4** *commerce* short for **par value 5 on a par with** equal or equivalent to: *an environmental disaster on a par with Chernobyl* **6 par for the course** to be expected: *random acts of violence were par for the course in the capital* [Latin: equal]

par. **1** paragraph **2** parenthesis

Par. Paraguay

para *n informal* **1** a paratrooper **2** a paragraph

Pará *n* **1** a state of N Brazil, on the Atlantic: mostly dense tropical rainforest Capital: Belém. Pop: 6 453 683 (2002). Area: 1 248 042 sq km (474 896 sq miles) **2** another name for **Belém 3** an estuary in N Brazil into which flow the Tocantins River and a branch of the Amazon. Length: about 320 km (200 miles)

para- *or before a vowel* **par-** *prefix* **1** beside or near: *parameter* **2** beyond: *parapsychology* **3** resembling: *paratyphoid fever* [Greek]

parable *n* a short story that uses familiar situations to illustrate a religious or moral point [Greek *parabolē* analogy]

parabola (par-ab-bol-a) *n geometry* an open plane curve formed by the intersection of a cone by a plane parallel to its side [Greek *parabolē* a setting alongside] **> parabolic** *adj*

Paracel Islands *n* a group of uninhabited islets and reefs in the N South China Sea, the subject of territorial claims by China and Vietnam. Compare **Spratly Islands**

Paracelsus *n* Philippus Aureolus, real name *Theophrastus Bombastus von Hohenheim.* 1493–1541, Swiss physician and alchemist, who pioneered the use of specific treatment, based on observation and experience, to remedy particular diseases

paracetamol *n* a mild pain-relieving drug [from *para-acetamidophenol*]

parachute *n* **1** a large fabric canopy connected by a harness, that slows the descent of a person or package from an aircraft ▷ *vb* **-chuting, -chuted 2** to land or to drop (supplies or troops) by parachute from an aircraft [French] **> parachutist** *n*

parade *n* **1** an ordered march or procession **2** a public promenade or street of shops **3** a blatant but sometimes insincere display: *a man who made a parade of liking his own company best* ▷ *vb* **-rading, -raded 4** to exhibit or flaunt: *he neither paraded nor disguised his devout faith* **5** to walk or march, esp. in a procession [French: a making ready]

parade ground *n* a place where soldiers assemble regularly for inspection or display

paradigm (par-a-dime) *n* a model or example: *his experience is a paradigm for the young artist* [Greek *paradeigma* pattern]

paradise *n* **1** heaven; where the good go after death **2** the Garden of Eden **3** any place or condition that fulfils a person's desires [Greek *paradeisos* garden]

P

paradise duck *n* a New Zealand duck with bright feathers

paradox *n* **1** a statement that seems self-contradictory but may be true: *it's a strange paradox that a musician must practise improvising to become a good improviser* **2** a self-contradictory proposition, such as *I always tell lies* **3** a person or thing that is made up of contradictory elements [Greek *paradoxos* opposed to existing notions] **>** **paradoxical** *adj* **>** **paradoxically** *adv*

paraffin *n* **1** Brit a liquid mixture distilled from petroleum or shale and used as a fuel or solvent **2** *chem* the former name for **alkane** [Latin *parum* too little + *affinis* adjacent; so called from its chemical inertia]

paraffin wax *n* a white waxlike substance distilled from petroleum and used to make candles and as a sealing agent

paragon *n* a model of perfection: *a paragon of female integrity and determination* [Old Italian *paragone* comparison]

paragraph *n* **1** a section of a piece of writing, usually devoted to one idea, which begins on a new line and is often indented **2** *printing* the character ¶, used to indicate the beginning of a new paragraph **▷** *vb* **3** to put (a piece of writing) into paragraphs [Greek *paragraphos* line drawing attention to part of a text]

Paraguay *n* **1** an inland republic in South America: colonized by the Spanish from 1537, gaining independence in 1811; lost 142 500 sq km (55 000 sq miles) of territory and over half its population after its defeat in the war against Argentina, Brazil, and Uruguay (1865–70). It is divided by the Paraguay River into a sparsely inhabited semiarid region (Chaco) in the west, and a central region of wooded hills, tropical forests, and rich grasslands, rising to the Paraná plateau in the east. Official languages: Spanish and Guarani. Religion: Roman Catholic majority. Currency: guarani. Capital: Asunción. Pop: 6 623 252 (2013 est). Area: 406 750 sq km (157 047 sq miles) **2** a river in South America flowing south through Brazil and Paraguay to the Paraná River. Length: about 2400 km (1500 miles)

Paraguayan *adj* **1** of or relating to Paraguay or its inhabitants **▷** *n* **2** a native or inhabitant of Paraguay

Paraíba *n* **1** a state of NE Brazil, on the Atlantic: consists of a coastal strip, with hills and plains inland; irrigated agriculture. Capital: João Pessoa. Pop: 3 494 893 (2002). Area: 56 371 sq km (21 765 sq miles) **2** Also called: **Paraíba do Sul** a river in SE Brazil, flowing southwest and then northeast to the Atlantic near Campos. Length: 1060 km (660 miles) **3** Also called: **Paraíba do Norte** a river in NE Brazil, in Paraíba state, flowing northeast and east to the Atlantic. Length: 386 km (240 miles) **4** the former name (until 1930) of **João Pessoa**

parakeet *n* a small colourful parrot with a long tail [Spanish *periquito* parrot]

paralegal *n* a person trained to assist lawyers but not qualified to practise law

parallax *n* an apparent change in an object's position due to a change in the observer's position [Greek *parallaxis* change]

parallel *adj* **1** separated by an equal distance at every point: *parallel lines; a path parallel to the main road* **2** precisely corresponding: *we decide our salaries by comparison with parallel jobs in other charities* **3** *computers* operating on several items of information or instructions at the same time **▷** *n* **4** *maths* one of a set of parallel lines or planes **5** something with similar features to another **6** a comparison; similarity between two things: *she attempted to excuse herself by drawing a parallel between her behaviour and ours* **7** Also called: **parallel of latitude** any of the imaginary lines around the earth parallel to the equator, marking degrees of latitude **8** *printing* the character ∥, used as a reference mark **▷** *vb* **9** to correspond to: *the increase in smoking is paralleled by an increase in lung cancer* [Greek *parallēlos* alongside one another]

parallel bars *pl n* *gymnastics* a pair of wooden bars on upright posts used for various exercises

parallelepiped (par-a-lel-ee-**pipe**-ed) *n* *geometry* a solid shape whose six faces are parallelograms [Greek *parallēlos* parallel + *epipedon* plane surface]

parallelism *n* **1** the state of being parallel **2** a close likeness

parallelogram *n* *geometry* a plane figure whose opposite sides are parallel and equal in length [Greek *parallēlos* parallel + *grammē* line]

paralyse *or US* **-lyze** *vb* **-lysing, -lysed** *or US* **-lyzing, -lyzed** **1** *pathol* to affect with paralysis **2** to make immobile: *he was paralysed by fear* [French *paralyser*]

paralysis *n* **1** *pathol* inability to move all or part of the body due to damage to the nervous system **2** a state of inactivity: *the economic chaos and political paralysis into which the country has sunk* [Greek *paralusis*, from *para-* beyond + *lusis* a loosening]

paralytic *adj* **1** of or relating to paralysis **2** *Brit informal* very drunk **▷** *n* **3** a person who is paralysed

Paramaribo *n* the capital and chief port of Surinam, 27 km (17 miles) from the Atlantic on the Surinam River: the only large town in the country. Pop: 261 000 (2005 est)

paramecium (par-a-**mee**-see-um) *n*, *pl* **-cia** (-see-a) a single-celled animal which lives in ponds, puddles, and sewage filters and swims by means of cilia

paramedic *n* a person, such as a member of an ambulance crew, whose work supplements that of the medical profession **>** **paramedical** *adj*

parameter (par-**am**-it-er) *n* **1** *maths* an arbitrary constant that determines the specific form of a mathematical expression, such as *a* and *b* in $y = ax^2 + b$ **2** *informal* any limiting factor: *exchange rates are allowed to fluctuate only within designated parameters* [Greek *para* beside + *metron* measure]

paramilitary *adj* denoting a group of people organized on military lines

paramount *adj* of the greatest importance [Old French *par* by + *-amont* above]

paramour *n* old-fashioned an adulterous lover [Old French, literally: through love]

Paraná *n* **1** a state of S Brazil, on the Atlantic: consists of a coastal plain and a large rolling plateau with extensive forests. Capital: Curitiba. Pop: 9 798 006 (2002). Area: 199 555 sq km (77 048 sq miles) **2** a city in E Argentina, on the Paraná River opposite Santa Fe: capital of Argentina (1853–1862). Pop: 305 000 (2005 est) **3** a river in central South America, formed in S Brazil by the confluence of the Rio Grande and the Paranaíba River and flowing generally south to the Atlantic through the Río de la Plata estuary. Length: 2900 km (1800 miles)

paranoia *n* **1** a mental disorder which causes delusions of grandeur or of persecution **2** *informal* intense fear or suspicion, usually unfounded [Greek *para-* beyond + *noos* mind] **>** **paranoid** *or* **paranoiac** *adj, n*

paranormal *adj* **1** beyond normal scientific explanation **▷** *n* **2** the paranormal paranormal happenings or matters generally

parapet *n* **1** a low wall or railing along the edge of a balcony or roof **2** *military* a mound of sandbags in front of a trench to conceal and protect troops from fire [Italian *parapetto*]

paraphernalia *n* various articles or bits of equipment [Greek *para-* beyond + *phernē* dowry]

paraphrase *n* **1** an expression of a statement or text in other words **▷** *vb* **-phrasing, -phrased** **2** to put (a statement or text) into other words [Greek *paraphrazein* to recount]

paraplegia (para-**pleej**-ya) *n* *pathol* paralysis of the lower half of the body [Greek: a blow on one side] **>** **paraplegic** *adj, n*

parapsychology *n* the study of mental phenomena such as telepathy

Paraquat *n* *trademark* an extremely poisonous weedkiller

parasite n **1** an animal or plant that lives in or on another from which it obtains nourishment **2** a person who habitually lives at the expense of others; sponger [Greek *para-* beside + *sitos* food] › **parasitic** adj

parasol n an umbrella-like sunshade [French]

paratrooper n a member of the paratroops

paratroops pl n troops trained to be dropped by parachute into a battle area

paratyphoid fever n a disease resembling but less severe than typhoid fever

parboil vb to boil (food) until partially cooked [Late Latin *perbullire* to boil thoroughly; modern meaning due to confusion of *par-* with *part*]

parcel n **1** something wrapped up; a package **2** a group of people or things sharing something in common: *a parcel of fools* **3** a distinct portion of land: *he was the recipient of a substantial parcel of land* ▷ vb **-celling, -celled** or US **-celing, -celed** **4** (often foll. by *up*) to wrap (something) up into a parcel **5** (foll. by *out*) to divide (something) into portions: *the children were parcelled out to relatives* [Old French *parcelle*]

parch vb **1** to deprive (something) of water; dry up: *the summer sun parched the hills* **2** to make (someone) very thirsty: *I'm parched. Have we got any lemonade?* [origin unknown]

parchment n **1** a thick smooth material made from animal skin and used for writing on **2** a manuscript made of this material **3** a stiff yellowish paper resembling parchment [Greek *pergamēnē*, from *Pergamēnos* of Pergamum (where parchment was made)]

pardon vb **1** to forgive or excuse (a person) for (an offence, mistake etc.): *I hope you'll pardon the wait* ▷ n **2** forgiveness **3** official release from punishment for a crime ▷ interj **4** Also: **pardon me, I beg your pardon a** sorry; excuse me **b** what did you say? [Medieval Latin *perdonare* to forgive freely] › **pardonable** adj

Pardubice n a city in the central Czech Republic, on the Elbe River: 13th-century cathedral; oil refinery. Pop: 88 559 (2007 est)

pare vb **paring, pared 1** to peel (the outer layer) from (something): *thinly pare the rind from the grapefruit* **2** to trim or cut the edge of **3** to decrease bit by bit: *the government is prepared to pare down the armed forces* [Latin *parare* to make ready]

Paré n Ambroise. 1510–90, French surgeon. He reintroduced ligature of arteries following amputation instead of cauterization

parent n **1** a father or mother **2** a person acting as a father or mother; guardian **3** a plant or animal that has produced one or more plants or animals [Latin *parens*, from *parere* to bring forth] › **parental** adj › **parenthood** n

parentage n ancestry or family

parent company n a company that owns a number of smaller companies

parenthesis (par-en-thiss-iss) n, pl **-ses** (-seez) **1** a word or phrase inserted into a passage, and marked off by brackets or dashes **2** Also called: **bracket** either of a pair of characters, used to enclose such a phrase [Greek: something placed in besides] › **parenthetical** adj › **parenthetically** adv

parenting n the activity of bringing up children

parent teacher association n an organization consisting of the parents and teachers of school pupils formed to organize activities on behalf of the school

Pareto n **1** Vilfredo. 1848–1923, Italian sociologist and economist. He anticipated Fascist principles of government in his *Mind and Society* (1916) ▷ adj **2** denoting a law, mathematical formula, etc., originally used by Pareto to express the frequency distribution of incomes in a society

par excellence adv beyond comparison: *this book justifies its claim to be a reference work par excellence* [French]

parfait (par-fay) n a dessert consisting of layers of ice cream, fruit, and sauce, topped with whipped cream,

and served in a tall glass: *a blackberry and apricot parfait* [French: perfect]

pariah (par-rye-a) n a social outcast: *the man they regard as a pariah* [Tamil *paraiyan* drummer]

Parian adj **1** denoting or relating to a fine white marble mined in classical times in Paros **2** denoting or relating to a fine biscuit porcelain used mainly for statuary **3** of or relating to Paros ▷ n **4** a native or inhabitant of Paros **5** Parian marble **6** Parian porcelain

Paricutín n a volcano in W central Mexico, in Michoacán state, formed in 1943 after a week of earth tremors; grew to a height of 2500 m (8200 ft) in a year and buried the village of Paricutín

parietal (par-rye-it-al) adj anatomy, biology of or forming the walls of a body cavity: *the parietal bones of the skull* [Latin *paries* wall]

paring n something that has been cut off something

Paris¹ n **1** the capital of France, in the north on the River Seine: constitutes a department; dates from the 3rd century BC, becoming capital of France in 987; centre of the French Revolution; centres around its original site on an island in the Seine, the Île de la Cité, containing Notre Dame; university (1150). Pop: 2 203 817 (2006). Ancient name: **Lutetia 2 Treaty of Paris a** a treaty of 1763 signed by Britain, France, and Spain that ended their involvement in the Seven Years' War **b** a treaty of 1783 between the US, Britain, France, and Spain, ending the War of American Independence **c** a treaty of 1898 between Spain and the US bringing to an end the Spanish-American War [via French and Old French, from Late Latin (*Lutetia Parisiorum*) (marshes) of the *Parisii*, a tribe of Celtic Gaul]

Paris² n **1** Greek myth a prince of Troy, whose abduction of Helen from her husband Menelaus started the Trojan War **2** Matthew. ?1200–59, English chronicler, whose principal work is the *Chronica Majora*

parish n **1** an area that has its own church and a priest or pastor. Related adjective: **parochial 2** the people who live in a parish **3** (in England and, formerly, Wales) the smallest unit of local government [Greek *paroikos* neighbour]

parish clerk n an official who performs various (esp. administrative) duties for a church or civil parish

parish council n (in England and, formerly, Wales) the administrative body of a parish. See **parish** (3)

parishioner n a person who lives in a particular parish

parish register n a book in which the births, baptisms, marriages, and deaths in a parish are recorded

Parisian adj **1** of or relating to Paris or its inhabitants ▷ n **2** a native or inhabitant of Paris

parity n **1** equality, for example of rank or pay **2** close or exact equivalence: *the company maintained parity with the competition* **3** finance equivalence between the units of currency of two countries [Latin *par* equal]

park n **1** a large area of open land for recreational use by the public **2** a piece of open land for public recreation in a town **3** Brit a large area of private land surrounding a country house **4** an area designed to accommodate a number of related enterprises: *a science park* **5** US and Canad a playing field or sports stadium **6** the park Brit informal the pitch in soccer ▷ vb **7** to stop and leave (a vehicle) temporarily: *I parked between the two cars already outside; police vans were parked on every street corner* **8** informal to leave or put (someone or something) somewhere: *she parked herself on the sofa and stayed there all evening* [Germanic] › **parking** n

Park n **1** Mungo. 1771–1806, Scottish explorer. He led two expeditions (1795–97; 1805–06) to trace the course of the Niger in Africa. He was drowned during the second expedition **2** Nick, full name *Nicholas Wulstan Park*. born 1958, British animator and film director; his films include *A Grand Day Out* (1992), which introduced the characters Wallace and Gromit, and the feature-length *Chicken Run* (2000) **3** Chung Hee. 1917–79, South Korean

p

politician; president of the Republic of Korea (1963–79); assassinated

parka *n* a long jacket with a quilted lining and a fur-trimmed hood [from Aleutian (language of Aleutian Islands, off Alaska): skin]

parkade *n Canad* a building used as a car park

park and ride *n* a transportation scheme in which drivers park some distance away from a city centre, tourist attraction, etc. and complete their journey by public transport

Parker *n* **1** Sir Alan (**William**). born 1944, British film director and screenwriter; his films include *Bugsy Malone* (1976), *Midnight Express* (1978), *Mississippi Burning* (1988), *The Commitments* (1991), and *Angela's Ashes* (2000); chairman of the British Film Institute (1998–99) and of the Film Council (1999–2004) **2** Charlie. nickname *Bird* or *Yardbird*. 1920–55, US jazz alto saxophonist and composer; the leading exponent of early bop **3** Dorothy (**Rothschild**). 1893–1967, US writer, noted esp. for the ironical humour of her short stories **4** Matthew. 1504–75, English prelate. As archbishop of Canterbury (1559–75), he supervised Elizabeth I's religious settlement

Parker Bowles *n* Camilla (née *Shand*). born 1947, became the second wife of Prince Charles in 2005; created Duchess of Cornwall and Duchess of Rothesay

Parkes *n* Sir Henry. 1815–96, Australian journalist and politician born in England, five times premier of New South Wales, advocate of free trade and Federation, and a founder of the public education system

parkette *n Canad* a small public car park

parkin *n Brit* a moist spicy ginger cake usually containing oatmeal [origin unknown]

parking lot *n US and Canad* area or building where vehicles may be left for a time

parking meter *n* a coin-operated device beside a parking space that indicates how long a vehicle may be left parked

parking ticket *n* the notice of a fine served on a motorist for a parking offence

Parkinson's disease *or* **Parkinsonism** *n* a progressive disorder of the central nervous system which causes tremor, rigidity, and impaired muscular coordination [after J. *Parkinson*, surgeon]

Parkinson's law *n* the notion that work expands to fill the time available for its completion [after C. N. *Parkinson*, historian and writer]

parkland *n* grassland with scattered trees

parky *adj* **parkier**, **parkiest** *Brit informal* (of the weather) chilly [origin unknown]

parlance *n* the manner of speaking associated with a particular group or subject: *he had, in Marxist parlance, a 'petit bourgeois' mentality* [French *parler* to talk]

parley *old-fashioned n* **1** a discussion between members of opposing sides to decide terms of agreement ▷ *vb* **2** to have a parley [French *parler* to talk]

parliament *n* a law-making assembly of a country [Old French *parlement*, from *parler* to speak]

Parliament *n* **1** the highest law-making authority in Britain, consisting of the House of Commons, the House of Lords, and the sovereign **2** the equivalent law-making authority in another country

parliamentarian *n* an expert in parliamentary procedures

parliamentary *adj* **1** of or from a parliament: *parliamentary elections* **2** conforming to the procedures of a parliament: *parliamentary language*

parlour *or US* **parlor** *n* **1** *old-fashioned* a living room for receiving visitors **2** a room or shop equipped as a place of business: *an ice-cream parlour* [Old French *parler* to speak]

parlous *adj archaic or humorous* dangerously bad; dire: *the parlous state of the economy* [variant of *perilous*]

parma *n Austral informal* a dish of chicken in breadcrumbs, topped with Parmesan cheese and a tomato sauce, and served with ham or bacon

[short for *chicken parmigiana*]

Parma *n* **1** a city in N Italy, in Emilia-Romagna: capital of the duchy of Parma and Piacenza from 1545 until it became part of Italy in 1860; important food industry (esp. Parmesan cheese). Pop: 163 457 (2001) **2** a city in NE Ohio, south of Cleveland. Pop: 83 861 (2003 est)

Parmenides *n* 5th century BC, Greek Eleatic philosopher, born in Italy. He held that the universe is single and unchanging and denied the existence of change and motion. His doctrines are expounded in his poem *On Nature*, of which only fragments are extant

Parmesan *adj* **1** of or relating to Parma or its inhabitants ▷ *n* **2** a native or inhabitant of Parma **3** a hard strong-flavoured cheese used grated on pasta dishes and soups

Parmigianino *n* real name *Girolamo Francesco Maria Mazzola*. 1503–40, Italian painter, one of the originators of mannerism. Also: **Parmigiano**

Parnaíba *or* **Parnahiba** *n* a river in NE Brazil, rising in the Serra das Mangabeiras and flowing generally northeast, to the Atlantic. Length: about 1450 km (900 miles)

Parnassian *adj* of or relating to Mount Parnassus

Parnassus *n* **1** Mount Parnassus a mountain in central Greece, in NW Boeotia: in ancient times sacred to Dionysus, Apollo, and the Muses, with the Castalian Spring and Delphi on its slopes. Height: 2457 m (8061 ft). Modern Greek names: **Parnassós**, **Liákoura** **2** a the world of poetry **b** a centre of poetic or other creative activity **3** a collection of verse or belles-lettres

Parnell *n* Charles Stewart. 1846–91, Irish nationalist, who led the Irish Home Rule movement in Parliament (1880–90) with a calculated policy of obstruction. Although Gladstone was converted to Home Rule (1886), Parnell's career was ruined by the scandal over his adultery with Mrs O'Shea ▷ **Parnellism** *n* ▷ **Parnellite** *n*, *adj*

parochial *adj* **1** narrow in outlook; provincial **2** of or relating to a parish [see PARISH] ▷ **parochialism** *n*

parody *n*, *pl* **-dies** **1** a piece of music or literature that mimics the style of another composer or author in a humorous way **2** something done so badly that it seems like an intentional mockery ▷ *vb* **-dies**, **-dying**, **-died** **3** to make a parody of [Greek *parōidia* satirical poem] ▷ **parodist** *n*

parole *n* **1** the freeing of a prisoner before his or her sentence has run out, on condition that he or she behaves well **2** a promise given by a prisoner to behave well if granted liberty or partial liberty **3** on parole conditionally released from prison ▷ *vb* **-roling**, **-roled** **4** to place (a person) on parole [Old French *parole d'honneur* word of honour]

Paros *n* a Greek island in the S Aegean Sea, in the Cyclades: site of the discovery (1627) of the Parian Chronicle, a marble tablet outlining Greek history from before 1000 BC to about 354 BC (now at Oxford University). Pop: 12 853 (2001). Area: 166 sq km (64 sq miles). Modern Greek name: **Páros**

parotid gland *n anatomy* either of a pair of salivary glands in front of and below the ears [Greek *para-* near + *ous* ear]

paroxysm *n* **1** an uncontrollable outburst of emotion: *a paroxysm of grief* **2** *pathol* **a** a sudden attack or recurrence of a disease **b** a fit or convulsion [Greek *paroxunein* to goad] ▷ **paroxysmal** *adj*

parquet (par-kay) *n* **1** a floor covering made of blocks of wood ▷ *vb* **2** to cover (a floor) with parquetry [Old French: small enclosure]

parquetry (par-kit-tree) *n* pieces of wood arranged in a geometric pattern, used to cover floors

parr *n* a salmon up to two years of age [origin unknown]

Parr *n* Catherine. 1512–48, sixth wife of Henry VIII of England

parricide *n* **1** a person who kills one of his or her parents **2** the act of killing either of one's parents [Latin *parricidium* murder of a parent or relative] **> parricidal** *adj*

parrot *n* **1** a tropical bird with a short hooked beak, bright plumage, and an ability to mimic human speech **2** a person who repeats or imitates someone else's words **3** **sick as a parrot** *usually facetious* extremely disappointed ▷ *vb* **-roting, -roted 4** to repeat or imitate (someone else's words) without understanding them [probably from French *paroquet*]

parrot fever *n* same as psittacosis

parrotfish *n* a brightly coloured sea fish

parry *vb* **-ries, -rying, -ried 1** to ward off (an attack) **2** to avoid answering (questions) in a clever way ▷ *n*, *pl* **-ries 3** an instance of parrying **4** a skilful evasion of a question [French *parer* to ward off]

Parry *n* **1** Sir (Charles) Hubert (Hastings). 1848–1918, English composer, noted esp. for his choral works **2** Sir William Edward. 1790–1855, English arctic explorer, who searched for the Northwest Passage (1819–25) and attempted to reach the North Pole (1827)

parse (parz) *vb* **parsing, parsed** to analyse (a sentence or the words in a sentence) grammatically [Latin *pars (orationis)* part (of speech)]

parsec *n* a unit of astronomical distance equivalent to 3.0857×10^{16} metres or 3.262 light years [*parallax* + *second* (of time)]

parsimony *n formal* extreme caution in spending [Latin *parcimonia*] **> parsimonious** *adj*

parsley *n* a herb with curled pleasant-smelling leaves, used for seasoning and decorating food [Middle English *persely*]

parsnip *n* a long tapering cream-coloured root vegetable [Latin *pastinaca*]

parson *n* **1** a parish priest in the Church of England **2** any clergyman **3** NZ a nonconformist minister [Latin *persona* personage]

parsonage *n* the residence of a parson, provided by the parish

Parsons *n* **1** Sir Charles Algernon. 1854–1931, English engineer, who developed the steam turbine **2** Gram, real name *Cecil Connor*. 1946–73 US country-rock singer and songwriter; founder of the Flying Burrito Brothers (1968–70), he later released the solo albums *G.P.* (1973) and *Grievous Angel* (1974) **3** Talcott. 1902–79, US sociologist, author of *The Structure of Social Action* (1937) and *The Social System* (1951)

parson's nose *n* the rump of a fowl when cooked

part *n* **1** a piece or portion **2** one of several equal divisions: *a salad dressing made with two parts oil to one part vinegar* **3** an actor's role in a play **4** a person's duty: *his ancestors had done their part nobly and well at Bannockburn* **5** an involvement in or contribution to something: *he was jailed for his part in the fraud* **6** a region or area: *he's well known in these parts; the weather in this part of the country is extreme* **7** *anatomy* an area of the body **8** a component that can be replaced in a vehicle or machine **9** US, Canad and Austral same as parting (2) **10** *music* a melodic line assigned to one or more instrumentalists or singers **11** **for my part** as far as I am concerned **12** **for the most part** generally **13** **in part** to some degree; partly **14** **on the part of** on behalf of **15** **part and parcel of** an essential ingredient of **16** **play a part a** to pretend to be what one is not **b** (foll. by *in*) to have something to do with: *examinations play a large part in education and in schools* **17** **take part in** to participate in **18** **take someone's part** to support someone, for example in an argument **19** **take something in good part** to respond to (teasing or criticism) with good humour ▷ *vb* **20** to divide or separate from one another: *her lips parted in laughter; the cord parted with a pop* **21** to go away from one another: *we parted with handshakes all round* **22** to split: *the path parts here* **23** to arrange (the hair) in such a way that a line of scalp is left showing **24** **part from** to cause (someone) to give up: *I was astonished at the way Henry parted his audience from their money* **25** **part with** to give up: *check carefully before you part with your cash* ▷ *adv* **26** to some extent; partly: *this book is part history, part travelogue* ▶ See also **parts** [Latin *pars* a part]

partake *vb* **-taking, -took, -taken 1** **partake in** to take part in **2** **partake of** to take (food or drink) [from earlier *part taker*]

> USAGE *Partake of* is sometimes wrongly used as if it were a synonym of *eat* or *drink*. Correctly, one can only *partake of* food or drink which is available for several people to share.

parterre *n* **1** a formally patterned flower garden **2** the pit of a theatre [French]

Parthenon *n* the temple on the Acropolis in Athens built in the 5th century BC and regarded as the finest example of the Greek Doric order

Parthia *n* a country in ancient Asia, southeast of the Caspian Sea, that expanded into a great empire dominating SW Asia in the 2nd century BC It was destroyed by the Sassanids in the 3rd century AD

Parthian *adj* **1** of or relating to Parthia or its inhabitants ▷ *n* **2** a native or inhabitant of Parthia

Parthian shot *n* a hostile remark or gesture delivered while departing [from the custom of archers from Parthia, who shot their arrows backwards while retreating]

partial *adj* **1** relating to only a part; not complete: *partial deafness* **2** biased: *religious programmes can be as partial as they like* **3** **be partial to** to have a particular liking for [Latin *pars* part] **> partiality** *n* **> partially** *adv*

> USAGE See at **partly**.

participate *vb* **-pating, -pated** **participate in** to become actively involved in [Latin *pars* part + *capere* to take] **> participant** *n* **> participation** *n* **> participatory** *adj*

participle *n grammar* a form of a verb that is used in compound tenses or as an adjective. See also **present participle, past participle** [Latin *pars* part + *capere* to take] **> participial** *adj*

particle *n* **1** an extremely small piece or amount: *clean thoroughly to remove all particles of dirt* **2** *grammar* an uninflected part of speech, such as an interjection or preposition **3** *physics* a minute piece of matter, such as an electron or proton [Latin *pars* part]

parti-coloured *or US* **particolored** *adj* having different colours in different parts [from obsolete *party* of more than one colour]

particular *adj* **1** of, belonging to, or being one person or thing; specific: *the particular type of tuition on offer* **2** exceptional or special: *the report voices particular concern over the state of the country's manufacturing industry* **3** providing specific details or circumstances: *a particular account* **4** difficult to please; fussy ▷ *n* **5** a separate distinct item as opposed to a generalization: *moving from the general to the particular* **6** an item of information; detail: *she refused to go into particulars* **7** **in particular** especially or exactly: *three painters in particular were responsible for these developments* [Latin *particula* a small part] **> particularly** *adv*

particularity *n*, *pl* **-ties 1** great attentiveness to detail **2** the state of being particular as opposed to general; individuality

particularize *or* **-rise** *vb* **-rizing, -rized** *or* **-rising, -rised** to give details about (something) **> particularization** *or* **-risation** *n*

parting *n* **1** a departure or leave-taking **2** *Brit and NZ* the line of scalp showing when sections of hair are combed in opposite directions **3** the act of dividing (something): *the parting of the Red Sea*

parting shot *n* a hostile remark or gesture delivered while departing

partisan *n* **1** a person who supports a particular cause or party **2** a member of an armed resistance group within

P

occupied territory ▷ *adj* **3** prejudiced or one-sided [Old Italian *partigiano*] **❭ partisanship** *n*

partition *n* **1** a large screen or thin wall that divides a room **2** the division of a country into two or more independent countries ▷ *vb* **3** to separate (a room) into sections: *the shower is partitioned off from the rest of the bathroom* **4** to divide (a country) into separate self-governing parts: *the subcontinent was partitioned into India and Pakistan* [Latin *partire* to divide]

partitive *grammar adj* **1** (of a noun) referring to part of something. The phrase *some of the butter* is a partitive construction ▷ *n* **2** a partitive word, such as *some* or *any* [Latin *partire* to divide]

partly *adv* not completely

> **USAGE** Partly and *partially* are to some extent interchangeable, but *partly* should be used when referring to a part or parts of something: *the building is partly* (not *partially*) *of stone*, while *partially* is preferred for the meaning *to some extent: his mother is partially* (not *partly*) *sighted*.

partner *n* **1** either member of a couple in a relationship **2** a member of a business partnership **3** one of a pair of dancers or of players on the same side in a game: *her bridge partner* **4** an ally or companion: *the country's main European trading partner* ▷ *vb* **5** to be the partner of (someone) [Middle English *parcener* joint inheritor]

partnership *n* **1** a relationship in which two or more people or organizations work together in a business venture **2** the condition of being a partner

part of speech *n grammar* a class of words, such as a noun, verb, or adjective, sharing important syntactic or semantic features

Parton *n* Dolly. born 1946, US country and pop singer and songwriter

partook *vb* the past tense of **partake**

partridge *n, pl* **-tridges** or **-tridge** a game bird with an orange-brown head, greyish neck, and a short rust-coloured tail [Latin *perdix*]

Partridge *n* Eric (Honeywood). 1894–1979, British lexicographer, born in New Zealand; author of works on English usage, idiom, slang, and etymology

parts *pl n literary* abilities or talents: *a man of many parts*

Parts of Holland *n* See Holland (3)

Parts of Kesteven *n* See (Parts of) Kesteven

Parts of Lindsey *n* See (Parts of) Lindsey

part song *n* a song composed in harmonized parts

part-time *adj* **1** for less than the normal full working time: *a part-time job* ▷ *adv* **part time** **2** on a part-time basis: *he works part time* **❭ part-timer** *n*

parturient *adj formal* giving birth [Latin *parturire* to be in labour]

parturition *n* the process of giving birth [Latin *parturire* to be in labour]

party *n, pl* **-ties 1** a social gathering for pleasure **2** a group of people involved in the same activity: *a search party* **3** a group of people sharing a common political aim **4** the person or people who take part in or are involved in something, esp. a legal action or dispute: *a judge will decide who the guilty party is* **5** *informal, humorous* a person: *he's an odd old party* ▷ *vb* **-ties, -tying, -tied 6** *informal* to celebrate; have a good time [Old French *partie* part]

party line *n* **1** the policies of a political party **2** a telephone line shared by two or more subscribers

party wall *n property law* a common wall separating two properties

par value *n* the value printed on a share certificate or bond at the time of its issue

Parvanov *n* Georgi. born 1957, Bulgarian politician: president of Bulgaria (2000–2012)

parvenu or *fem* **parvenue** (par-ven-new) *n* a person newly risen to a position of power or wealth who is considered to lack culture or education [French]

Pasadena *n* a city in SW California, east of Los Angeles. Pop: 144 413 (2003 est)

Pasargadae *n* an ancient city in Persia, northeast of Persepolis in present-day Iran: built by Cyrus the Great

Pasay *n* a city in the Philippines, on central Luzon just south of Manila, on Manila Bay. Pop: 364 000 (2005 est). Also called: **Rizal**

pascal *n* the SI unit of pressure; the pressure exerted on an area of 1 square metre by a force of 1 newton [after B. PASCAL]

Pascal[1] *n* a high-level computer programming language developed as a teaching language [after B. PASCAL]

Pascal[2] *n* Blaise. 1623–62, French philosopher, mathematician, and physicist. As a scientist, he made important contributions to hydraulics and the study of atmospheric pressure and, with Fermat, developed the theory of probability. His chief philosophical works are *Lettres provinciales* (1656–57), written in defence of Jansenism and against the Jesuits, and *Pensées* (1670), fragments of a Christian apologia

paschal (pask-l) *adj* **1** of or relating to the Passover **2** of or relating to Easter [Hebrew *pesah* Passover]

Pas-de-Calais *n* a department of N France, in Nord-Pas-de-Calais region, on the Straits of Dover (the **Pas de Calais**): the part of France closest to the British Isles. Capital: Arras. Pop: 1 451 307 (2003 est). Area: 6752 sq km (2633 sq miles)

pas de deux (pah de duh) *n, pl* **pas de deux** *ballet* a dance for two people [French: step for two]

pash *Austral and NZ slang vb* **1** to kiss and cuddle ▷ *n* **2** the act of kissing and cuddling [short for *passion*]

pasha *n* (formerly) a high official of the Ottoman Empire: placed after a name when used as a title [Turkish *paşa*]

pashmina (pash-mee-na) *n* a type of cashmere scarf or shawl made from the underfur of Tibetan goats [Persian *pashm* wool]

Pašić *n* Nicola. 1845–1926, Serbian statesman; prime minister of Serbia (1891–92; 1904–05; 1906–08; 1909–11; 1912–18) and of the Kingdom of Serbs, Croats, and Slovenes (1921–24; 1924–26)

Pasifika *Austral and NZ pl n* **1** the people of the Pacific Islands ▷ *adj* **2** of these people or their culture

Pasionaria *n* La, real name *Dolores Ibarruri*. 1895–1989, Spanish Communist leader, who lived in exile in the Soviet Union (1939–75)

Pasmore *n* Victor. 1908–98, British artist. Originally a figurative painter, he devoted himself to abstract paintings and reliefs after 1947

paso doble (pass-so dobe-lay) *n* **1** a modern ballroom dance in fast duple time **2** music for this dance [Spanish: double step]

Pasolini *n* Pier Paolo. 1922–75, Italian film director. His films include *The Gospel according to St Matthew* (1964), *Oedipus Rex* (1967), *Theorem* (1968), *Pigsty* (1969), and *Decameron* (1970)

pas op (pass op) *interj S African* beware [Afrikaans]

paspalum (pass-pale-um) *n Austral and NZ* a type of grass with wide leaves

pasqueflower *n* a small purple-flowered plant of Europe and Asia [French *passefleur*, changed to *pasqueflower* Easter flower, because it blooms at Easter]

pass *vb* **1** to go by or past (a person or thing) **2** to continue or extend in a particular direction: *the road to Camerino passes through some fine scenery* **3** to go through or cause (something) to go through (an obstacle or barrier): *the bullet passed through his head* **4** to be successful in (a test or examination) **5** to spend (time) or (of time) go by: *the time passed surprisingly quickly* **6** to hand over or be handed over: *she passed me her glass* **7** to be inherited by: *his mother's small estate had passed to him after her death* **8** *sport* to hit, kick, or throw (the ball) to another player **9** (of a law-making body) to agree to (a law or proposal): *the bill was passed by parliament last week* **10** to pronounce (judgment): *the court is* expected to pass sentence later today **11** to move onwards or over: *a flicker of amusement passed over his face* **12** to exceed: *Australia's population has just passed the 17 million mark* **13** to go without comment: *the insult passed unnoticed* **14** to choose not to answer a question or not to make a bid or a play in card games **15** to discharge (urine etc.) from the body **16** to come to an end or disappear: *the madness will soon pass* **17** (foll. by *for* or *as*) to be likely to be mistaken for (someone or something else): *the few sunny days that pass for summer in this country* **18** old-fashioned to take place: *what passed at the meeting?* **19 pass away** or **on** *euphemistic* to die ▷ *n* **20** a successful result in an examination or test **21** *sport* the transfer of a ball from one player to another **22** a route through a range of mountains where there is a gap between peaks **23** a permit or licence **24** *military* a document authorizing leave of absence **25** *bridge etc.* an instance of choosing not to answer a question or not to make a bid or a play in card games **26 a pretty pass** a bad state of affairs **27 make a pass at** *informal* to try to persuade (someone) to have sex: *he made a pass at his secretary* ▸ See also **pass off, pass out**, etc. [Latin *passus* step]

USAGE The past participle of *pass* is sometimes wrongly spelt *past*: *the time for recriminations has passed* (not *past*).

pass. passive
passable *adj* **1** adequate or acceptable: *passable if hardly faultless German* **2** (of a road, path, etc.) capable of being travelled along: *most main roads are passable with care despite the snow* ▸ **passably** *adv*
passage *n* **1** a channel or opening providing a way through **2** a hall or corridor **3** a section of a written work, speech, or piece of music **4** a journey by ship **5** the act of passing from one place or condition to another: *Ireland faced a tough passage to qualify for the World Cup finals* **6** the right or freedom to pass: *the aid convoys were guaranteed safe passage through rebel-held areas* **7** the establishing of a law by a law-making body [Old French *passer* to pass]
passageway *n* corridor or passage
Passamaquoddy Bay *n* an inlet of the Bay of Fundy between New Brunswick (Canada) and Maine (US) at the mouth of the St Croix River
passbook *n* **1** a book issued by a bank or building society for recording deposits and withdrawals **2** *S African* formerly, an official identity document
Passchendaele *n* a village in NW Belgium, in West Flanders province: the scene of heavy fighting during the third battle of Ypres in World War I during which 245 000 British troops were lost
passé (pas-say) *adj* out-of-date: *smoking is a bit passé these days* [French]
passenger *n* **1** a person travelling in a vehicle driven by someone else **2** *Brit and NZ* a member of a team who does not take an equal share of the work: *you'll have to pull your weight – we can't afford passengers* [Old French *passager* passing]
passer-by *n, pl* **passers-by** a person who is walking past someone or something
passerine *adj* **1** belonging to an order of perching birds that includes the larks, finches, and starlings ▷ *n* **2** any bird of this order [Latin *passer* sparrow]
passim *adv* throughout: used to indicate that what is referred to occurs frequently in a particular piece of writing [Latin]
passing *adj* **1** momentary or short-lived: *a passing fad* **2** casual or superficial: *a passing resemblance* ▷ *n* **3** *euphemistic* death **4** the ending of something: *the passing of the old order in Eastern Europe* **5 in passing** briefly and without going into detail; incidentally: *this fact is only noted in passing*
passion *n* **1** intense sexual love **2** any strongly felt

emotion **3** a strong enthusiasm for something: *a passion for football* **4** the object of an intense desire or enthusiasm: *flying is his abiding passion* [Latin *pati* to suffer] ▸ **passionless** *adj*
Passion *n* the sufferings of Christ from the Last Supper to his death on the cross
passionate *adj* **1** showing intense sexual desire **2** capable of or revealing intense emotion: *a passionate speech* ▸ **passionately** *adv*
passionflower *n* a tropical plant with brightly coloured showy flowers [parts of the flowers are said to resemble the instruments of the Crucifixion]
passion fruit *n* the edible egg-shaped fruit of the passionflower
Passion play *n* a play about the Passion of Christ
passive *adj* **1** not taking an active part **2** submissive and receptive to outside forces **3** *grammar* denoting a form of verbs used to indicate that the subject is the recipient of the action, as *was broken* in *The glass was broken by that boy over there* **4** *chem* (of a substance) chemically unreactive ▷ *n* **5** *grammar* the passive form of a verb [Latin *passivus* capable of suffering] ▸ **passively** *adv* ▸ **passivity** *n*
passive resistance *n* resistance to a government or the law by nonviolent acts such as fasting, peaceful demonstrations, or refusing to cooperate
passive smoking *n* the unwilling inhalation of smoke from other people's cigarettes by a nonsmoker
passkey *n* **1** a private key **2** same as **master key, skeleton key**
pass law *n* (formerly in South Africa) a law restricting the movement of Black Africans
pass off *vb* **1** to present (something or oneself) under false pretences: *women who passed themselves off effectively as men* **2** to come to a gradual end: *the effects of the gas passed off relatively peacefully* **3** to take place: *the main demonstration passed off peacefully*
pass out *vb* **1** *informal* to become unconscious; faint **2** *Brit* (of an officer cadet) to qualify for a military commission
Passover *n* an eight-day Jewish festival commemorating the sparing of the Israelites in Egypt [*pass over*, translation of Hebrew *pesah*]
pass over *vb* **1** to take no notice of; disregard: *she claims she had been passed over for promotion because she is a woman* **2** to ignore or not discuss: *this disaster cannot be passed over lightly*
passport *n* **1** an official document issued by a government, which identifies the holder and grants him or her permission to travel abroad **2** an asset that gains a person admission or acceptance: *good qualifications are no automatic passport to a job* [French *passer* to pass + *port* port]
pass up *vb informal* to let (something) go by; disregard: *am I passing up my one chance to be really happy?*
password *n* a secret word or phrase that ensures admission by proving identity or membership
Passy *n* Frédéric. 1822–1912, French politician and economist, who campaigned for international arbitration to prevent war: shared the first Nobel peace prize 1901
past *adj* **1** of the time before the present: *the past history of the world* **2** no longer in existence: *past happiness* **3** immediately previous: *the past year* **4** former: *a past president* **5** *grammar* indicating a tense of verbs used to describe actions that have been begun or completed at the time of speaking ▷ *n* **6 the past** the period of time before the present: *a familiar face from the past* **7** the history of a person or nation **8** an earlier disreputable period of someone's life: *a woman with a bit of a past* **9** *grammar* **a** the past tense **b** a verb in the past tense ▷ *adv* **10** on or onwards: *I called but he just walked past* **11** at a time before the present; ago: *three years past* ▷ *prep* **12** beyond in time: *it's past midnight* **13** beyond in place: *a procession of mourners filed past the coffin* **14** beyond the limit of: *riches past his wildest dreams* **15 not put it past someone** to consider someone capable of (a particular action): *I wouldn't put it*

past him to double-cross us **16 past it** *informal* unable to do the things one could do when younger [from *pass*]

pasta *n* a type of food, such as spaghetti, that is made from a dough of flour and water and formed into different shapes [Italian]

paste *n* **1 a** a soft moist mixture, such as toothpaste **2** an adhesive made from water and flour or starch, for use with paper **3** a smooth creamy preparation of fish, meat, or vegetables for spreading on bread: *sausage paste* **4** *Brit and NZ* dough for making pastry **5** a hard shiny glass used to make imitation gems ▷ *vb* **pasting, pasted 6** to attach by paste: *she bought a scrapbook and carefully pasted in it all her clippings* **7** *slang* to beat or defeat (someone) [Greek *pastē* barley porridge]

pasteboard *n* a stiff board made by pasting layers of paper together

pastel *n* **1 a** a crayon made of ground pigment bound with gum **b** a picture drawn with such crayons **2** a pale delicate colour ▷ *adj* **3** (of a colour) pale and delicate: *pastel pink* [Latin *pasta* paste]

pastern *n* the part of a horse's foot between the fetlock and the hoof [Old French *pasture* a tether]

Pasternak *n* Boris (Leonidovich)). 1890–1960, Russian lyric poet, novelist, and translator, noted particularly for his novel of the Russian Revolution, *Dr. Zhivago* (1957). He was awarded the Nobel prize for literature in 1958, but was forced to decline it

paste-up *n printing* a sheet of paper or board with artwork and proofs pasted on it, which is photographed prior to making a plate

Pasteur *n* Louis. 1822–95, French chemist and bacteriologist. His discovery that the fermentation of milk and alcohol was caused by microorganisms resulted in the process of pasteurization. He also devised methods of immunization against anthrax and rabies and pioneered stereochemistry

pasteurize *or* **-rise** *vb* **-rizing, -rized** *or* **-rising, -rised** to destroy bacteria (in beverages or solid foods) by a special heating process [after Louis **Pasteur**] ▶ **pasteurization** *or* **-risation** *n*

pastiche (past-**eesh**) *n* a work of art that mixes styles or copies the style of another artist [French]

pastille *n* a small fruit-flavoured and sometimes medicated sweet [Latin *pastillus* small loaf]

pastime *n* an activity which makes time pass pleasantly

pasting *n* **1** *slang* a thrashing or heavy defeat **2** *informal* strong criticism

past master *n* a person with a talent for or experience in a particular activity: *a past master at manipulating the media*

Pasto *n* a city in SE Colombia, at an altitude of 2590 m (8500 ft). Pop: 404 000 (2005 est)

pastor *n* a member of the clergy in charge of a congregation [Latin: shepherd]

pastoral *adj* **1** of or depicting country life or scenery **2** (of land) used for pasture **3** of or relating to a member of the clergy or his or her duties **4** of or relating to shepherds or their work ▷ *n* **5** a literary work, picture, or piece of music portraying country life **6** a letter from a bishop to the clergy or people of his diocese [Latin *pastor* shepherd]

pastorale (past-or-**ahl**) *n, pl* **-rales** a musical composition that suggests country life [Italian]

pastoralism *n* a system of agriculture in dry grassland regions based on raising stock such as cattle, sheep, or goats ▶ **pastoralist** *n*

past participle *n grammar* a form of verb used to form compound past tenses and passive forms of the verb and to modify nouns: spoken *is the past participle of* speak

pastrami *n* highly seasoned smoked beef [Yiddish]

pastry *n* **1** a dough of flour, water, and fat **2** (*pl* **-tries**) an individual cake or pie **3** baked foods, such as tarts, made with this dough [from *paste*]

pasturage *n* **1** the business of grazing cattle **2** same as pasture

pasture *n* **1** land covered with grass, suitable for grazing by farm animals **2** the grass growing on this land [Latin *pascere* to feed]

pasty¹ (**pay**-stee) *adj* **pastier, pastiest** (of the complexion) pale and unhealthy-looking

pasty² (**past**-ee) *n, pl* **pasties** a round of pastry folded over a filling of meat and vegetables [Old French *pastée*]

pat¹ *vb* **patting, patted 1** to tap (someone or something) lightly with the hand **2** to shape (something) with a flat instrument or the palm of the hand **3 pat someone on the back** *informal* to congratulate someone ▷ *n* **4** a gentle tap or stroke **5** a small shaped lump of something soft, such as butter **6 pat on the back** *informal* an indication of approval [probably imitative]

pat² *adv* **1** Also: **off pat** thoroughly learned: *he had all his answers off pat* **2 stand pat** *chiefly US and Canad* to stick firmly to a belief or decision ▷ *adj* **3** quick, ready, or glib: *a pat generalization* [perhaps adverbial use ('with a light stroke') of PAT¹]

Patagonia *n* **1** the southernmost region of South America, in Argentina and Chile extending from the Andes to the Atlantic. Area: about 777 000 sq km (300 000 sq miles) **2** an arid tableland in the southernmost part of Argentina, rising towards the Andes in the west

Patagonian *adj* **1** of or relating to Patagonia or its inhabitants ▷ *n* **2** a native or inhabitant of Patagonia

patch *n* **1** a piece of material used to cover a hole in a garment **2** a small contrasting section: *there was a bald patch on the top of his head* **3** a small plot of land **4** *med* a protective covering for an injured eye **5** a scrap or remnant **6** the area under someone's supervision, such as a policeman or social worker **7 a bad patch** a difficult time **8 not a patch on** not nearly as good as ▷ *vb* **9** to mend (a garment) with a patch **10 patch together** to produce (something) by piecing parts together hurriedly or carelessly **11 patch up a** to mend (something) hurriedly or carelessly **b** to make up (a quarrel) [perhaps from French *pieche* piece]

patchwork *n* **1** needlework done by sewing together pieces of different materials **2** something made up of various parts

patchy *adj* **patchier, patchiest 1** of uneven quality or intensity: *since then her career has been patchy* **2** having or forming patches

pate *n* *old-fashioned or humorous* the head or the crown of the head [origin unknown]

pâté (**pat**-ay) *n* a spread of finely minced meat, fish, or vegetables often served as a starter [French]

pâté de foie gras (de fwah **grah**) *n* a smooth rich paste made from the liver of specially fattened geese [French: pâté of fat liver]

patella (pat-**tell**-a) *n, pl* **-lae** (-lee) *anatomy* kneecap [Latin] ▶ **patellar** *adj*

paten (**pat**-in) *n* a plate, usually made of silver or gold, used for the bread at Communion [Latin *patina* pan]

patent *n* **1 a** an official document granting the exclusive right to make, use, and sell an invention for a limited period **b** the right granted by such a document **2** an invention protected by a patent ▷ *adj* **3** open or available for inspection: *letters patent* **4** obvious: *their scorn was patent to everyone* **5** concerning protection of or appointment by a patent **6** (of food, drugs, etc.) made or held under a patent ▷ *vb* **7** to obtain a patent for (an invention) [Latin *patere* to lie open]

USAGE The pronunciation **pat**-tunt is heard in *letters patent* and *Patent Office* and is the usual US pronunciation for all senses. In Britain **pat**-tunt is sometimes heard for senses 1, 2 and 3, but **pay**-tunt is commoner and is regularly used in collocations like *patent leather*.

patent leather *n* leather processed with lacquer to

give a hard glossy surface

patently *adv* clearly and obviously: *an outdated and patently absurd promise*

patent medicine *n* a medicine with a patent, available without a prescription

Patent Office *n* a government department that issues patents

pater *n Brit humorous* father [Latin]

Pater *n* Walter (Horatio). 1839–94, English essayist and critic, noted for his prose style and his advocation of the "love of art for its own sake". His works include the philosophical romance *Marius the Epicurean* (1885), *Studies in the History of the Renaissance* (1873), and *Imaginary Portraits* (1887)

paternal *adj* 1 fatherly: *paternal authority* 2 related through one's father: *his paternal grandmother* [Latin *pater* father] > **paternally** *adv*

paternalism *n* authority exercised in a way that limits individual responsibility [Latin *pater* father] > **paternalistic** *adj*

paternity *n* 1 the fact or state of being a father 2 descent or derivation from a father

paternity suit *n* legal proceedings, usually brought by an unmarried mother, in order to gain legal recognition that a particular man is the father of her child

Paternoster *n RC Church* the Lord's Prayer [Latin *pater noster* our father]

Paterson¹ *n* a city in NE New Jersey: settled by the Dutch in the late 17th century. Pop: 150 782 (2003 est)

Paterson² *n* 1 Andrew Barton, known as *Banjo Paterson*. 1864–1941, Australian poet. His works include "Waltzing Matilda" and "The Man from Snowy River" 2 William. 1658–1719, Scottish merchant and banker: founded the Bank of England (1694)

path *n, pl* **paths** 1 a road or way, often a narrow trodden track 2 a surfaced walk, such as through a garden 3 the course or direction in which something moves: *his car skidded into the path of an oncoming lorry* 4 a course of conduct: *the path of reconciliation and forgiveness* [Old English *pæth*]

pathetic *adj* 1 arousing pity or sympathy 2 distressingly inadequate: *his pathetic attempt to maintain a stiff upper lip failed* [Greek *pathos* suffering] > **pathetically** *adv*

pathetic fallacy *n* (in literature) the presentation of inanimate objects in nature as possessing human feelings

pathname *n computers* the name of a file or directory together with its position in relation to other directories

pathogen *n* any agent, such as a bacterium, that can cause disease [Greek *pathos* suffering + *-gen* (suffix) producing] > **pathogenic** *adj*

pathological *adj* 1 of or relating to pathology 2 *informal* compulsively motivated: *pathological jealousy*

pathology *n* the branch of medicine that studies diseases [Greek *pathos* suffering + -LOGY] > **pathologist** *n*

pathos *n* the power, for example in literature, of arousing feelings of pity or sorrow [Greek: suffering]

pathway *n* a path

Patiala *n* a city in N India, in E Punjab: seat of the Punjabi University (1962). Pop: 302 870 (2001)

patience *n* 1 the capacity for calmly enduring difficult situations: *the endless patience of the nurses* 2 the ability to wait calmly for something to happen without complaining or giving up: *he urged the international community to have patience to allow sanctions to work* 3 *Brit and NZ* a card game for one player only [Latin *pati* to suffer]

patient *adj* 1 enduring difficult situations with an even temper 2 persevering or diligent: *his years of patient work may finally pay off* ▷ *n* 3 a person who is receiving medical care > **patiently** *adv*

patina *n* 1 a film formed on the surface of a metal 2 the sheen on the surface of an old object, caused by age and much handling [Italian: coating]

Patinir *or* **Patenier** *n* Joachim. ?1485–1524, Flemish

painter, noted esp. for the landscapes in his paintings on religious themes

patio *n, pl* **-tios** 1 a paved area adjoining a house: *a barbecue on the patio* 2 an open inner courtyard in a Spanish or Spanish-American house [Spanish: courtyard]

patisserie (pat-**eess**-er-ee) *n* 1 a shop where fancy pastries are sold 2 such pastries [French]

Patmore *n* Coventry (Kersey Dighton). 1823–96, English poet. His works, celebrating both conjugal and divine love, include *The Angel in the House* (1854–62) and *The Unknown Eros* (1877)

Patmos *n* a Greek island in the Aegean, in the NW Dodecanese: St John's place of exile (about 95 AD), where he wrote the Apocalypse. Pop: 2984 (2001). Area: 34 sq km (13 sq miles)

Patna *n* a city in NE India, capital of Bihar state, on the River Ganges: founded in the 5th century BC; university (1917); centre of a rice-growing region. Pop: 1 376 950 (2001)

patois (pat-**wah**) *n, pl* **patois** (pat-**wahz**) 1 a regional dialect of a language 2 the jargon of a particular group [Old French: rustic speech]

Paton *n* Alan (Stewart). 1903–88, South African writer, noted esp. for his novel dealing with racism and apartheid in South Africa, *Cry, the Beloved Country* (1965)

Patras *n* a port in W Greece, in the NW Peloponnese on the Gulf of Patras (an inlet of the Ionian Sea): one of the richest cities in Greece until the 3rd century BC; under Turkish rule from 1458 to 1687 and from 1715 until the War of Greek Independence, which began here in 1821. Pop: 193 000 (2005 est). Modern Greek name: **Pátrai**

patrial *n* (in Britain, formerly) a person with a right by statute to live in the United Kingdom, and so not subject to immigration control [Latin *patria* native land]

patriarch *n* 1 the male head of a tribe or family 2 *Bible* any of the men regarded as the fathers of the human race or of the Hebrew people 3 a *RC Church* the pope b *Eastern Orthodox Church* a highest-ranking bishop 4 an old man who is respected [Church Latin *patriarcha*] > **patriarchal** *adj*

patriarchate *n* the office, jurisdiction, or residence of a patriarch

patriarchy *n* 1 a form of social organization in which males hold most of the power 2 (*pl* **-chies**) a society governed by such a system

patrician *n* 1 a member of the nobility of ancient Rome 2 an aristocrat 3 a person of refined conduct and tastes ▷ *adj* 4 (in ancient Rome) of or relating to patricians 5 aristocratic [Latin *patricius* noble]

patricide *n* 1 the act of killing one's father 2 a person who kills his or her father [Latin *pater* father + *caedere* to kill] > **patricidal** *adj*

Patrick *n* Saint. 5th century AD, Christian missionary in Ireland, probably born in Britain; patron saint of Ireland. Feast day: March 17

patrimony *n, pl* **-nies** an inheritance from one's father or other ancestor [Latin *patrimonium* paternal inheritance]

patriot *n* a person who loves his or her country and passionately supports its interests [Greek *patris* native land] > **patriotic** *adj* > **patriotically** *adv* > **patriotism** *n*

patrol *n* 1 the action of going round an area or building at regular intervals for purposes of security or observation 2 a person or group that carries out such an action 3 a group of soldiers or ships involved in patrolling a particular area 4 a division of a troop of Scouts or Guides ▷ *vb* **-trolling, -trolled** 5 to engage in a patrol of (a place): *peacekeepers patrolled several areas of the city* [French *patrouiller*]

patrol car *n* a police car used for patrolling streets

patron *n* 1 a person who financially supports artists, writers, musicians, or charities 2 a regular customer of a shop, hotel, etc. [Latin *patronus* protector]

P

patronage *n* **1** the support or custom given by a patron **2** (in politics) the ability or power to appoint people to jobs **3** a condescending manner

patronize *or* **-nise** *vb* **-nizing, -nized** *or* **-nising, -nised** **1** to treat (someone) in a condescending way **2** to be a patron of ⟩ **patronizing** *or* **-nising** *adj* ⟩ **patronizingly** *or* **-nisingly** *adv*

patron saint *n* a saint regarded as the particular guardian of a country or a group of people

patronymic *n* a name derived from one's father's or a male ancestor [Greek *patēr* father + *onoma* name]

patter¹ *vb* **1** to make repeated light tapping sounds **2** to walk with quick soft steps ▷ *n* **3** a quick succession of light tapping sounds, such as by feet: *the steady patter of rain against the window* [from PAT¹]

patter² *n* **1** the glib rapid speech of comedians or salesmen **2** chatter **3** the jargon of a particular group ▷ *vb* **4** to speak glibly and rapidly [Latin *pater* in *Pater Noster* Our Father]

pattern *n* **1** an arrangement of repeated parts or decorative designs **2** a regular recognizable way that something is done: *I followed a normal eating pattern* **3** a plan or diagram used as a guide to making something: *a knitting pattern* **4** a model worthy of imitation: *a pattern of kindness* **5** a representative sample ▷ *vb* **6** (foll. by *after* or *on*) to model: *an orchestra patterned after Count Basie's* [Medieval Latin *patronus* example]

patterned *n* having a decorative pattern on it: *a selection of plain and patterned fabrics*

Patti *n* Adelina. 1843–1919, Italian operatic coloratura soprano, born in Spain

Patton *n* George Smith. 1885–1945, US general, who successfully developed tank warfare as an extension of cavalry tactics in World War II: captured Palermo, Sicily (1942) and much of France (1944)

patty *n, pl* **-ties** a small round pie filled with meat or vegetables [French *pâté*]

Pau *n* a city in SW France: residence of the French kings of Navarre; tourist centre for the Pyrenees. Pop: 84 978 (2007)

paua (pah-ooh-uh) *n* an edible shellfish of New Zealand, which has a pearly shell used for jewellery [Māori]

paucity *n formal* **1** scarcity **2** smallness of amount or number [Latin *paucus* few]

Paul *n* **1** Saint. Also called: **Paul the Apostle, Saul of Tarsus.** original name *Saul.* died ?67 AD, one of the first Christian missionaries to the Gentiles, who died a martyr in Rome. Until his revelatory conversion he had assisted in persecuting the Christians. He wrote many of the Epistles in the New Testament. Feast day: June 29. Related adjective: **Pauline** **2** Jean. See **Jean Paul** **3** Les, real name *Lester Polfuss.* 1915–2009, US guitarist: creator of the solid-body electric guitar and pioneer in multitrack recording

Paul I *n* **1** 1754–1801, tsar of Russia (1796–1801); son of Catherine II; assassinated **2** 1901–64, king of the Hellenes (1947–64); son of Constantine I

Paul III *n* original name *Alessandro Farnese.* 1468–1549, Italian ecclesiastic; pope (1534–49). He excommunicated Henry VIII of England (1538) and inaugurated the Counter-Reformation by approving the establishment of the Jesuits (1540), instituting the Inquisition in Italy, and convening the Council of Trent (1545)

Paul VI *n* original name *Giovanni Battista Montini.* 1897–1978, Italian ecclesiastic; pope (1963–1978)

Pauli *n* Wolfgang. 1900–58, US physicist, born in Austria. He formulated the exclusion principle (1924) and postulated the existence of the neutrino (1931), later confirmed by Fermi: Nobel prize for physics 1945

Pauling *n* Linus Carl. 1901–94, US chemist, noted particularly for his work on the nature of the chemical bond and his opposition to nuclear tests: Nobel prize for chemistry 1954; Nobel peace prize 1962

Paulinus *n* Saint. died 644 AD, Roman missionary to England; first bishop of York and archbishop of Rochester. Feast day: Oct 10

Paulinus of Nola *n* Saint. ?353–431 AD, Roman consul and Christian poet; bishop of Nola (409–431). Feast day: June 22

Paumotu Archipelago *n* another name for the **Tuamotu Archipelago**

paunch *n* a protruding belly or abdomen [Latin *pantices* bowels] ⟩ **paunchy** *adj*

pauper *n old-fashioned* **1** a person who is extremely poor **2** (formerly) a person supported by public charity [Latin: poor]

Pausanias *n* 2nd century AD, Greek geographer and historian. His *Description of Greece* gives a valuable account of the topography of ancient Greece

pause *vb* **pausing, paused 1** to stop doing (something) for a short time **2** to hesitate: *she answered him without pausing* ▷ *n* **3** a temporary stop or rest in speech or action **4** *music* a continuation of a note or rest beyond its normal length **5** **give someone pause** to cause someone to hesitate: *it gave him pause for reflection* [Greek *pausis*]

pavane (pav-van) *n* **1** a slow and stately dance of the 16th and 17th centuries **2** music for this dance [Spanish *pavana*]

Pavarotti *n* Luciano 1935–2007, Italian operatic tenor, specializing in works by Verdi and Puccini

pave *vb* **paving, paved 1** to cover (a road or area of ground) with a firm surface to make it suitable for walking or travelling on **2** **pave the way for** to prepare or make easier: *the arrests paved the way for the biggest-ever Mafia trial* [Old French *paver*]

pavement *n* **1** a hard-surfaced path for pedestrians, alongside and a little higher than a road **2** the material used in paving **3** *US* the surface of a road [Latin *pavimentum* hard floor]

Pavese *n* Cesare. 1908–50, Italian writer and translator. His works include collections of poems, such as *Verrà la morte e avrà i tuoi occhi* (1953), short stories, such as the collection *Notte di festa* (1953), and the novel *La luna e i falò* (1950)

Pavia *n* a town in N Italy, in Lombardy: noted for its Roman and medieval remains, including the tomb of St Augustine. Pop: 71 214 (2001). Latin name: **Ticinum**

pavilion *n* **1** a building at a sports ground, esp. a cricket pitch, in which players can wash and change **2** an open building or temporary structure used for exhibitions **3** a summerhouse or other decorative shelter **4** a large ornate tent [Latin *papilio* butterfly, tent]

paving *n* **1** a paved surface **2** material used for a pavement

Pavlodar *n* a port in NE Kazakhstan on the Irtysh River: major industrial centre with an oil refinery. Pop: 303 000 (2005 est)

Pavlov *n* Ivan Petrovich. 1849–1936, Russian physiologist. His study of conditioned reflexes in dogs influenced behaviourism. He also made important contributions to the study of digestion: Nobel prize for physiology or medicine 1904

pavlova *n* a meringue cake topped with whipped cream and fruit [after Anna PAVLOVA]

Pavlova *n* Anna. 1885–1931, Russian ballerina

paw *n* **1** a four-legged mammal's foot with claws and pads **2** *informal* a hand ▷ *vb* **3** to scrape or hit with the paws **4** *informal* to touch or caress (someone) in a rough or overfamiliar manner [Germanic]

pawl *n* a pivoted lever shaped to engage with a ratchet to prevent motion in a particular direction [Dutch *pal*]

pawn¹ *vb* **1** to deposit (an article) as security for money borrowed **2** to stake or risk: *I will pawn my honour on this matter* ▷ *n* **3** an article deposited as security **4** the condition of being so deposited: *in pawn* [Old French *pan* security]

pawn² *n* **1** a chessman of the lowest value, usually able to move only one square forward at a time **2** a person or thing manipulated by someone else: *our city is just a pawn in their power games* [Anglo-Norman *poun*, from Medieval Latin *pedo* infantryman]

pawnbroker *n* a person licensed to lend money on goods deposited ▸ **pawnbroking** *n*

Pawnee *n, pl* **Pawnees** *or* **Pawnee 1** a member of a group of Native American peoples, formerly living in Nebraska and Kansas, now chiefly in Oklahoma **2** the language of these peoples

pawnshop *n* the premises of a pawnbroker

pawpaw (paw-paw) *n* same as **papaya**

pax *n* **1** *chiefly RC Church* the kiss of peace ▷ *interj* **2** *Brit children's slang* a call signalling a desire to end hostilities [Latin: peace]

Paxman *n* Jeremy (**Dickson**). born 1950, British journalist, broadcaster, and author, noted esp. for his political interviews

Paxton *n* Sir Joseph. 1801–65, English architect, who designed Crystal Palace (1851), the first large structure of prefabricated glass and iron parts

pay *vb* **pays, paying, paid 1** to give (money) in return for goods or services: *Willie paid for the drinks; nurses are not very well paid* **2** to settle (a debt or obligation) by giving or doing something: *he has paid his debt to society* **3** to suffer: *she paid dearly for her mistake* **4** to give (a compliment, regards, attention, etc.) **5** to profit or benefit (someone): *it doesn't always pay to be honest* **6** to make (a visit or call) **7** to yield a return of: *the account pays 5% interest* **8** **pay one's way a** to contribute one's share of expenses **b** to remain solvent without outside help ▷ *n* **9** money given in return for work or services; a salary or wage **10 in the pay of** employed by ▸ See also **pay back, pay for**, etc. [Latin *pacare* to appease]

payable *adj* **1** (often foll. by *on*) due to be paid: *the instalments are payable on the third of each month* **2** that is capable of being paid: *pensions are payable to those disabled during the wars*

pay back *vb* **1** to repay (a loan) **2** to make (someone) suffer for a wrong he or she has done you: *I want to pay him back for all the suffering he's caused me*

payday *n* the day on which wages or salaries are paid

payday lender *n* a person or company that offers short-term loans, in advance of payday, at high rates of interest

PAYE (in Britain, Australia and New Zealand) pay as you earn; a system by which income tax is deducted by employers and paid directly to the government

payee *n* the person to whom a cheque or money order is made out

pay for *vb* **1** to make payment for **2** to suffer or be punished for (a mistake)

paying guest *n euphemistic* a lodger

payload *n* **1** the amount of passengers, cargo, or bombs which an aircraft can carry **2** the part of a cargo which earns revenue **3** the explosive power of a warhead or bomb carried by a missile or aircraft

paymaster *n* an official responsible for the payment of wages and salaries

payment *n* **1** the act of paying **2** a sum of money paid **3** something given in return; punishment or reward

pay off *vb* **1** to pay the complete amount of (a debt) **2** to pay (someone) all that is due in wages and dismiss him or her from employment **3** to turn out successfully: *her persistence finally paid off* **4** *informal* to give a bribe to ▷ *n* **payoff 5** *informal* the climax or outcome of events **6** *informal* a bribe **7** the final payment of a debt **8** the final settlement, esp. in retribution: *the payoff came when the gang besieged the squealer's house*

payola *n informal* a bribe to secure special treatment, esp. to promote a commercial product

pay out *vb* **1** to spend (money) on a particular thing **2** to release (a rope) gradually, bit by bit ▷ *n* **payout 3** a sum of money paid out

pay-per-view *n* a television broadcasting system where

a charge is made for receiving a specific programme

payphone *n* a coin-operated telephone

payroll *n* a list of employees, giving the salary or wage of each

Paysandú *n* a port in W Uruguay, on the Uruguay River: the third largest city in the country. Pop: 73 272 (2004)

Pays de la Loire *n* a region of W France, on the Bay of Biscay: generally low-lying, drained by the River Loire and its tributaries; agricultural

payslip *n* a note given to an employee stating his or her salary or wage and detailing the deductions

Payton *n* Walter. 1954–99, American footballer and sports administrator

pay up *vb* to pay (money) promptly or in full

paywall *n* a system preventing a user from accessing certain information on a website unless a fee is paid

Paz *n* Octavio. 1914–98, Mexican poet and essayist. His poems include the cycle *Piedra de sol* (1957) and *Blanco* (1967). Nobel prize for literature 1990

Pb *chem* lead [New Latin *plumbum*]

pc 1 per cent **2** postcard

PC 1 personal computer **2** (in Britain) Police Constable **3** *informal* short for **politically correct 4** (in Britain) Privy Council *or* Counsellor **5** (in Canada) Progressive Conservative

PCOS polycystic ovary syndrome

PCV (in Britain) passenger carrying vehicle

pd paid

Pd *chem* palladium

PDA personal digital assistant

PDF portable document format: a format in which documents may be viewed

PDSA (in Britain) People's Dispensary for Sick Animals

PDT Pacific Daylight Time

PE 1 physical education **2** Prince Edward Island

pea *n* **1** an annual climbing plant with green pods containing green seeds **2** the seed of this plant, eaten as a vegetable [from *pease* (incorrectly assumed to be a plural)]

Peabody *n* George. 1795–1869, US merchant, banker, and philanthropist in the US and England

peace *n* **1** stillness or silence **2** absence of mental anxiety: *peace of mind* **3** absence of war **4** harmony between people or groups **5** a treaty marking the end of a war **6** law and order within a state: *a breach of the peace* **7 at peace a** dead: *the old lady is at peace now* **b** in a state of harmony or serenity **8 hold** *or* **keep one's peace** to keep silent **9 keep the peace** to maintain law and order [Latin *pax*]

peaceable *adj* **1** inclined towards peace **2** tranquil or calm

peace dividend *n* additional money available to a government from cuts in defence expenditure because of the end of a period of hostilities

peaceful *adj* **1** not in a state of war or disagreement **2** calm or tranquil ▸ **peacefully** *adv*

peacemaker *n* a person who brings about peace, esp. between others

peace offering *n* something given or said in order to restore peace: *I bought Mum some flowers as a peace offering*

peace pipe *n* a long decorated pipe smoked by Native Americans, esp. as a token of peace

Peace River *n* a river in W Canada, rising in British Columbia as the Finlay River and flowing northeast into the Slave River. Length: 1715 km (1065 miles)

peacetime *n* a period without war

peach *n* **1 a** a soft juicy fruit with a downy skin, yellowish-orange sweet flesh, and a single stone **2** *informal* a person or thing that is especially pleasing: *a peach of a goal* ▷ *adj* **3** pale pinkish-orange [Latin *Persicum malum* Persian apple]

peach melba *n* a dessert made of halved peaches, vanilla ice cream, and raspberries [after Dame Nellie MELBA]

peachy adj **peachier, peachiest** of or like a peach, esp. in colour or texture

peacock n, pl **-cocks** or **-cock 1** a large male bird of the pheasant family with a crested head and a very large fanlike tail with blue and green eyelike spots **2** a vain strutting person [Latin *pavo* peacock + COCK] **> peahen** *fem n*

Peacock n Thomas Love. 1785–1866, English novelist and poet, noted for his satirical romances, including *Headlong Hall* (1816) and *Nightmare Abbey* (1818)

peafowl n a peacock or peahen

peak n **1** a pointed tip or projection: *the peak of the roof* **2 a** the pointed summit of a mountain **b** a mountain with a pointed summit **3** the point of greatest success or achievement: *the peak of his career* **4** a projecting piece on the front of some caps ▷ *vb* **5** to form or reach a peak ▷ *adj* **6** of or relating to a period of greatest demand: *hotels are generally dearer in peak season* [perhaps from *pike* (the weapon)]

Peak District n a region of N central England, mainly in N Derbyshire at the S end of the Pennines: consists of moors in the north and a central limestone plateau; many caves. Highest point: 727 m (2088 ft)

Peake n Mervyn. 1911–68, English novelist, poet, and illustrator. In his trilogy *Gormenghast* (1946–59), he creates, with vivid imagination, a grotesque Gothic world

peaked adj having a peak

peak load n the maximum load on an electrical power-supply system

peaky adj **peakier, peakiest** pale and sickly [origin unknown]

peal n **1** a long loud echoing sound, such as of bells or thunder ▷ *vb* **2** to sound with a peal or peals [Middle English *pele*]

peanut n a plant with edible nutlike seeds which ripen underground. See also **peanuts**

peanut butter n a brownish oily paste made from peanuts

peanuts n slang a trifling amount of money

pear n **1** a sweet juicy fruit with a narrow top and a rounded base **2 go pear-shaped** informal to go wrong: *the plan started to go pear-shaped* [Latin *pirum*]

pearl n **1** a hard smooth greyish-white rounded object found inside the shell of a clam or oyster and much valued as a gem **2** See **mother-of-pearl 3** a person or thing that is like a pearl in beauty or value ▷ *adj* **4** of, made of, or set with pearl or mother-of-pearl ▷ *vb* **5** to set with or as if with pearls **6** to shape into or assume a pearl-like form or colour **7** to dive for pearls [Latin *perna* sea mussel]

pearl barley n barley ground into small round grains, used in soups and stews

Pearl Harbor n an almost landlocked inlet of the Pacific on the S coast of the island of Oahu, Hawaii: site of a US naval base attacked by the Japanese in 1941, resulting in the US entry into World War II

Pearl River n **1** a river in central Mississippi, flowing southwest and south to the Gulf of Mexico. Length: 789 km (490 miles) **2** the English name for the **Zhu Jiang**

pearly adj **pearlier, pearliest 1** resembling a pearl, esp. in lustre **2** decorated with pearls or mother-of-pearl

Pearly Gates pl n informal the entrance to heaven

pearly king or fem **pearly queen** n the London barrow vendor whose ceremonial clothes display the most lavish collection of pearl buttons

Pears n Sir Peter. 1910–86, British tenor, associated esp. with the works of Benjamin Britten

Pearse n Patrick (Henry). 1879–1916, Irish name *Pádraic*. 1879–1916, Irish nationalist, who planned and led the Easter Rising (1916): executed by the British

Pearson n **1** Karl. 1857–1936, British mathematician, noted for his work in statistics, esp. as applied to biological problems **2** Lester B(owles). 1897–1972,

Canadian Liberal statesman; prime minister (1963–68): Nobel peace prize 1957 for helping to resolve the Suez crisis (1956)

Peary n Robert Edwin. 1856–1920, US arctic explorer, generally regarded as the first man to reach the North Pole (1909)

peasant n **1** a member of a low social class employed in agricultural labour **2** informal an uncouth or uncultured person [Old French *païsant*]

peasantry n peasants as a class

pease n, pl **pease** archaic or dialect same as **pea** [Old English *pise, peose*]

pease pudding n (esp. in Britain) a dish of split peas that have been soaked and boiled

peasouper n informal, chiefly Brit thick dirty yellowish fog

peat n decaying vegetable matter found in uplands and bogs and used as a fuel (when dried) and as a fertilizer [perhaps Celtic]

pebble n **1** a small smooth rounded stone, esp. one worn by the action of water ▷ *vb* **-bling, -bled 2** to cover with pebbles [Old English *papolstān* pebble stone] **> pebbly** adj

pebble dash n Brit and Austral a finish for external walls consisting of small stones set in plaster

pec n informal a pectoral muscle: *a gigolo with flowing blond locks and rippling pecs*

pecan (pee-kan) n a smooth oval nut with a sweet oily kernel that grows on hickory trees in the Southern US [Native American *paccan*]

peccadillo n, pl **-loes** or **-los** a trivial misdeed [Spanish *pecadillo*, from Latin *peccare* to sin]

peccary n, pl **-ries** or **-ry** a piglike animal native to American forests [Carib]

Pechenga n a region of NW Russia, a former territory of N Finland, ceded by Soviet Russia to Finland in 1920 and taken back in 1944. Former name: (1920–1944) **Petsamo**

Pechora n a river in N Russia, rising in the Ural Mountains and flowing north in a great arc to the **Pechora Sea** (the SE part of the Barents Sea). Length: 1814 km (1127 miles)

peck¹ vb **1** to strike or pick up with the beak **2** informal to kiss (a person) quickly and lightly **3 peck at** to eat slowly and reluctantly: *pecking away at your lunch* ▷ *n* **4** a quick light blow from a bird's beak **5** a mark made by such a blow **6** informal a quick light kiss [origin unknown]

peck² n an obsolete unit of liquid measure equal to one quarter of a bushel or 2 gallons (9.1 litres) [Anglo-Norman]

Peck n Gregory. 1916–2003, US film actor; his films include *Keys of the Kingdom* (1944), *The Gunfighter* (1950), *The Big Country* (1958), *To Kill a Mockingbird* (1963), *The Omen* (1976), and *Other People's Money* (1991)

pecker n keep one's pecker up Brit and NZ slang to remain cheerful

pecking order n the order of seniority or power in a group: *she came from a family low in the social pecking order*

Peckinpah n Sam(uel David). 1926–84, US film director, esp. of Westerns, such as *The Wild Bunch* (1969). Among his other films are *Straw Dogs* (1971), *Bring me the Head of Alfredo Garcia* (1974), and *Cross of Iron* (1977)

peckish adj informal feeling slightly hungry

Pecos n a river in the southwestern US, rising in N central New Mexico and flowing southeast to the Rio Grande. Length: about 1180 km (735 miles)

Pécs n an industrial city in SW Hungary: university (1367). Pop: 158 942 (2003 est)

pectin n biochem a water-soluble carbohydrate that occurs in ripe fruit: used in the manufacture of jams because of its ability to gel [Greek *pēktos* congealed]

pectoral adj **1** of or relating to the chest, breast, or thorax: *pectoral fins* **2** worn on the breast or chest: *a pectoral cross* ▷ *n* **3** a pectoral organ or part, esp. a muscle or fin [Latin *pectus* breast]

pectoral fin n a fin, just behind the head in fishes, that helps to control the direction of movement

peculate *vb* **-lating, -lated** *literary* to embezzle (public money) [Latin *peculari*] **> peculation** *n*

peculiar *adj* **1** strange or odd: *a peculiar idea* **2** distinct or special **3** (foll. by *to*) belonging exclusively (to): *a fish peculiar to these waters* [Latin *peculiaris* concerning private property]

peculiarity *n, pl* **-ties 1** a strange or unusual habit; eccentricity **2** a distinguishing trait **3** the state or quality of being peculiar

pecuniary *adj* **1** of or relating to money **2** *law* (of an offence) involving a monetary penalty [Latin *pecunia* money]

pedagogue *or US sometimes* **pedagog** *n* a teacher, esp. a pedantic one [Greek *pais* boy + *agōgos* leader] **> pedagogic** *adj*

pedagogy (ped-a-goj-ee) *n* the principles, practice, or profession of teaching

pedal¹ *n* **1** a foot-operated lever used to control a vehicle or machine, or to modify the tone of a musical instrument ▷ *vb* **-dalling, -dalled** *or US* **-daling, -daled 2** to propel (a bicycle) by operating the pedals **3** to operate the pedals of an organ or piano [Latin *pedalis*, from *pes* foot]

pedal² *adj* of or relating to the foot or the feet [Latin *pedalis*, from *pes* foot]

pedant *n* a person who is concerned chiefly with insignificant detail or who relies too much on academic learning [Italian *pedante* teacher] **> pedantic** *adj* **> pedantically** *adv*

pedantry *n, pl* **-ries** the practice of being a pedant, esp. in the minute observance of petty rules or details

peddle *vb* **-dling, -dled 1** to sell (goods) from place to place **2** to sell illegal drugs **3** to advocate (an idea or information) persistently: *the version of events being peddled by his opponents* [from *pedlar*]

pederast *or* **paederast** *n* a man who has homosexual relations with boys [Greek *pais* boy + *erastēs* lover] **> pederasty** *or* **paederasty** *n*

pedestal *n* **1** a base that supports something, such as a statue **2** **put someone on a pedestal** to admire someone very much [Old Italian *piedestallo*]

pedestrian *n* **1** a person who travels on foot ▷ *adj* **2** dull or commonplace: *a pedestrian performance* [Latin *pes* foot]

pedestrian crossing *n Brit and Austral* a path across a road marked as a crossing for pedestrians

pedestrianize *or* **-nise** *vb* **-nizing, -nized** *or* **-nising, -nised** to convert (a street or shopping area) into an area for pedestrians only

pedestrian precinct *n Brit* an area of a town for pedestrians only, esp. an area of shops

pedicure *n* medical or cosmetic treatment of the feet [Latin *pes* foot + *curare* to care for]

pedigree *n* **1** the line of descent of a purebred animal **2** a document recording this **3** a genealogical table, esp. one indicating pure ancestry [Old French *pie de grue* crane's foot, alluding to the spreading lines used in a genealogical chart]

pediment *n* a triangular part over a door, as used in classical architecture [obsolete *periment*, perhaps workman's corruption of *pyramid*]

pedlar *or especially US* **peddler** *n* a person who peddles [Middle English *ped* basket]

pedometer (pid-dom-it-er) *n* a device that measures the distance walked by recording the number of steps taken [Latin *pes* foot + METER]

Pedro I *n* 1798–1834, first emperor of Brazil (1822–31); son of John VI of Portugal: declared Brazilian independence (1822)

Pedro II *n* 1825–91, last emperor of Brazil (1831–89); son of Pedro I. He was deposed when Brazil became a republic (1889)

peduncle *n* **1** *botany* a plant stalk bearing a flower cluster or solitary flower **2** *anatomy, pathol* any stalklike structure [Latin *pediculus* little foot] **> peduncular** *adj*

pee *informal vb* **peeing, peed 1** to urinate ▷ *n* **2** urine **3** the act of urinating [euphemistic for *piss*]

Peebles *n* a town in SE Scotland, in Scottish Borders. Pop: 8065 (2001)

Peeblesshire *n* (until 1975) a county of SE Scotland, now part of Scottish Borders. Also called: **Tweeddale**

peek *vb* **1** to glance quickly or secretly ▷ *n* **2** such a glance [Middle English *pike*]

peel *vb* **1** to remove the skin or rind of (a fruit or vegetable) **2** to come off in flakes **3** (of a person or part of the body) to shed skin in flakes as a result of sunburn ▷ *n* **4** the skin or rind of a fruit, etc. **▸** See also **peel off** [Latin *pilare* to make bald]

Peel *n* **1** John, real name *John Robert Parker Ravenscroft*. 1939–2004, British broadcaster; presented his influential Radio 1 music programme (1967–2004) and Radio 4's *Home Truths* (1998–2004) **2** Sir **Robert**. 1788–1850, British statesman; Conservative prime minister (1834–35; 1841–46). As Home Secretary (1828–30) he founded the Metropolitan Police and in his second ministry carried through a series of free-trade budgets culminating in the repeal of the Corn Laws (1846), which split the Tory party **> Peelite** *n*

Peele *n* George. ?1556–?96, English dramatist and poet. His works include the pastoral drama *The Arraignment of Paris* (1584) and the comedy *The Old Wives' Tale* (1595)

peelings *pl n* strips of skin or rind that have been peeled off: *potato peelings*

peel off *vb* **1** to remove or be removed by peeling: *this softens the paint, which can then be peeled off* **2** *slang* to take off one's clothes or a piece of clothing **3** to leave a group of moving people, vehicles, etc. by taking a course that curves away to one side: *two aircraft peeled off to attack the enemy bombers*

peen *n* the end of a hammer head opposite the striking face, often rounded or wedge-shaped [origin unknown]

Peenemünde *n* a village in N Germany, in Mecklenburg-West Pomerania on the Baltic coast: site of a German rocket-development centre in World War II

peep¹ *vb* **1** to look slyly or quickly, such as through a small opening or from a hidden place **2** to appear partially or briefly: *the sun peeped through the clouds* ▷ *n* **3** a quick or sly look **4** the first appearance: *the peep of dawn* [variant of *peek*]

peep² *vb* **1** (esp. of young birds) to make small shrill noises ▷ *n* **2** a peeping sound [imitative]

Peeping Tom *n* a man who furtively observes women undressing [after the tailor who, according to legend, peeped at Lady Godiva when she rode naked through Coventry]

peepshow *n* a box containing a series of pictures that can be seen through a small hole

peer¹ *n* **1** a member of a nobility **2** a person who holds any of the five grades of the British nobility: duke, marquess, earl, viscount, and baron **3** a person of equal social standing, rank, age, etc.: *he is greatly respected by his peers in the art world* [Latin *par* equal]

peer² *vb* **1** to look intently or as if with difficulty: *Walter peered anxiously at his father's face* **2** to appear dimly: *the sun peered through the fog* [Flemish *pieren* to look with narrowed eyes]

peerage *Brit n* **1** the whole body of peers; aristocracy **2** the position, rank, or title of a peer

peeress *n* **1** (in Britain) a woman holding the rank of a peer **2** the wife or widow of a peer

peer group *n* a social group composed of people of similar age and status

peerless *adj* having no equals; unsurpassed

peer pressure *n* influence from one's peer group

peeve *informal vb* **peeving, peeved 1** to irritate or annoy: *the way he looked at her peeved her* ▷ *n* **2** something that irritates: *my pet peeve* [from *peevish*] **> peeved** *adj*

peevish *adj* fretful or irritable [origin unknown] **> peevishly** *adv*

p

peewee n a black-and-white Australian bird

peewit or **pewit** n same as **lapwing** [imitative of its call]

peg n **1** a small pin or bolt used to join two parts together, to fasten, or to mark **2** a hook or knob for hanging things on **3** music a pin on a stringed instrument which can be turned to tune the string wound around it **4** Also called: **clothes peg** a split or hinged pin for fastening wet clothes to a line to dry **5** Brit a small drink of spirits **6** an opportunity or pretext for doing something: the play's subject matter provides a perfect peg for a discussion of issues like morality and faith **7** bring or take (someone) down a peg to lower the pride of (someone) **8** off the peg Brit and NZ (of clothes) ready-to-wear, as opposed to tailor-made ▷ vb **pegging, pegged 9** to insert a peg into **10** to secure with pegs: the balloon was pegged down to stop it drifting away **11** to mark (a score) with pegs, as in some card games **12** chiefly Brit to work steadily: he pegged away at his job for years **13** to fix or maintain something, such as prices, at a particular level or value: a fixed-rate mortgage, pegged at 9.6 per cent ▷ See also **peg out** [Low Germanic pegge]

pegboard n **1** a board with a pattern of holes into which small pegs can be fitted, used for playing certain games or keeping a score **2** hardboard with rows of holes from which articles may be hung for display

peggy square n NZ a small hand-knitted square

peg leg n informal **1** an artificial leg **2** a person with an artificial leg

peg out vb **1** informal to collapse or die **2** to mark or secure with pegs: the scientists pegged out a hectare of land in order to study every plant in it

Pegu n a city in S Myanmar: capital of a united Burma (16th century). Pop: 307 000 (2005 est)

Péguy n Charles. 1873–1914, French poet and essayist, whose works include Le Mystère de la charité de Jeanne d'Arc (1910); founder of the journal Cahiers de la quinzaine (1900–14): killed in World War I

Pei n I(eoh) M(ing). born 1917, US architect, born in China. His buildings include the E wing of the National Museum of Art, Washington DC (1978), a glass and steel pyramid at the Louvre, Paris (1989), and the Rock and Roll Hall of Fame, Cleveland, USA (1995)

PEI Prince Edward Island

peignoir (pay-nwahr) n a woman's light dressing gown [French]

Peipus n a lake in W Russia, on the boundary with Estonia: drains into the Gulf of Finland. Area: 3512 sq km (1356 sq miles). Russian name: **Chudskoye Ozero**

Peiraeus n a variant spelling of **Piraeus**

Peirce n Charles Sanders. 1839–1914, US logician, philosopher, and mathematician; pioneer of pragmatism

pejorative (pij-jor-a-tiv) adj **1** (of a word or expression) having an insulting or critical sense ▷ n **2** a pejorative word or expression [Late Latin pejorare to make worse]

peke n informal a Pekingese dog

Peking n the former English name of **Beijing**

Pekingese or **Pekinese** n **1** (pl -ese) a small dog with a long straight coat, curled plumed tail, and short wrinkled muzzle **2** the dialect of Mandarin Chinese spoken in Beijing (formerly Peking) **3** (pl -ese) a native or inhabitant of Beijing (formerly Peking) ▷ adj **4** of or relating to Beijing (formerly Peking) or its inhabitants

Pelagian Islands pl n a group of Italian islands (Lampedusa, Linosa, and Lampione) in the Mediterranean, between Tunisia and Malta. Pop: 6066 (2004 est). Area: about 27 sq km (11 sq miles). Italian name: **Isole Pelagie**

Pelagius n ?360–?420 AD, British monk, who originated the body of doctrines known as Pelagianism and was condemned for heresy (417)

pelargonium n a plant with circular leaves and red, pink, or white flowers: includes many cultivated geraniums [Greek pelargos stork]

Pelé n real name Edson Arantes do Nascimento. born 1940, Brazilian footballer: scored 77 goals in 92 games for Brazil (1957–71) and was in the teams that won the World Cup in 1958, 1962, and 1970; awarded an honorary knighthood in 1997

Pelée n Mount Pelée a volcano in the Caribbean, in N Martinique: erupted in 1902, killing every person but one in the town of Saint-Pierre. Height: 1463 m (4800 ft)

Pelew Islands pl n a former name of (the Republic of) Palau

pelf n disparaging money or wealth [Old French pelfre booty]

Pelham n Henry. 1696–1754, British statesman: prime minister (1743–54); brother of Thomas Pelham Holles, 1st Duke of Newcastle

pelican n a large water bird with a pouch beneath its long bill for holding fish [Greek pelekan]

pelican crossing n (in Britain) a type of road crossing with a pedestrian-operated traffic-light system [from pe(destrian) li(ght) con(trolled) crossing, with -con adapted to -can of pelican]

Pelion n a mountain in NE Greece, in E Thessaly. In Greek mythology it was the home of the centaurs. Height: 1548 m (5079 ft). Modern Greek name: **Pílion**

pelisse (pel-leess) n a cloak or loose coat which is usually fur-trimmed [Old French, from Latin pellis skin]

Pella n an ancient city in N Greece: the capital of Macedonia under Philip II

pellagra n pathol a disease caused by a diet lacking in vitamin B, which results in scaling of the skin, diarrhoea and mental disorder [Italian, from pelle skin + Greek agra paroxysm]

pellet n **1** a small round ball, esp. of compressed matter **2 a** an imitation bullet used in toy guns **b** a piece of small shot **3** a small pill [Latin pila ball]

Pelletier n Pierre Joseph. 1788–1842, French chemist, who isolated quinine, chlorophyll, and other chemical substances

pell-mell adv **1** in a confused headlong rush: the hounds ran pell-mell into the yard **2** in a disorderly manner: the things were piled pell-mell in the room [Old French pesle-mesle]

pellucid adj literary **1** transparent or translucent **2** extremely clear in style and meaning [Latin pellucidus]

pelmet n a board or piece of fabric used to conceal the curtain rail [probably from French palmette palm-leaf decoration on cornice moulding]

Peloponnese n the Peloponnese the S peninsula of Greece, joined to central Greece by the Isthmus of Corinth: chief cities in ancient times were Sparta and Corinth, now Patras. Pop: 503 300 (2001). Area: 21 439 sq km (8361 sq miles). Also known as: **Peloponnesus**. Medieval name: **Morea**. Modern Greek name: **Pelopónnisos**

Peloponnesian adj of or relating to the Peloponnese or its inhabitants

pelota n a game played by two players who use a basket strapped to their wrists or a wooden racket to propel a ball against a specially marked wall [Spanish: ball]

Pelotas n a port in S Brazil, in Rio Grande do Sul on the Canal de São Gonçalo. Pop: 323 000 (2005 est)

pelt[1] vb **1** to throw (missiles) at **2** (foll. by along etc.) to hurry **3** to rain heavily ▷ n **4** a blow **5** at full pelt very quickly: she ran down the street at full pelt [origin unknown]

pelt[2] n the skin or fur of an animal, esp. as material for clothing or rugs: the lucrative international trade in beaver pelts [probably from Latin pellis skin]

pelvis n, pl -vises or -ves **1** the framework of bones at the base of the spine, to which the hips are attached **2** the bones that form this structure [Latin: basin] ▷ **pelvic** adj

Pemba n an island in the Indian Ocean, off the E coast of Africa north of Zanzibar: part of Tanzania; produces most of the world's cloves. Chief town: Chake Chake. Pop: 362 166 (2002). Area: 984 sq km (380 sq miles)

Pembroke n **1** a town in SW Wales, in Pembrokeshire on Milford Haven: 11th-century castle where Henry VII was born. Pop (with Pembroke Dock): 15 890 (2001) **2** the smaller variety of corgi, usually having a short tail

Pembrokeshire *n* a county of SW Wales, on the Irish Sea and the Bristol Channel: formerly (1974–96) part of Dyfed: a hilly peninsula with a deeply indented coast: tourism, agriculture, oil refining. Administrative centre: Haverfordwest Pop: 116 300 (2003 est). Area: 1589 sq km (614 sq miles)

pen¹ *n* **1** an instrument for writing or drawing using ink. See also **ballpoint, fountain pen 2 the pen** writing as an occupation ▷ *vb* **penning, penned 3** to write or compose [Latin *penna* feather]

pen² *n* **1** an enclosure in which domestic animals are kept **2** any place of confinement ▷ *vb* **penning, penned** or **pent 3** to enclose (animals) in a pen **4** penned in being or feeling trapped or confined: *she stood penned in by bodies at the front of the crowd* [Old English *penn*]

pen³ *n US and Canad informal* short for **penitentiary** (1)

pen⁴ *n* a female swan [origin unknown]

Pen. Peninsula

penal (pee-nal) *adj* **1** of or relating to punishment **2** used as a place of punishment: *a penal colony* [Latin *poena* penalty] ▷ **penally** *adv*

penal code *n* the body of laws relating to crime and punishment

penalize or **-ise** *vb* **-izing, -ized** or **-ising, -ised 1** to impose a penalty on (someone) for breaking a law or rule **2** to inflict a disadvantage on: *why should I be penalized just because I'm a woman?* ▷ **penalization** or **-isation** *n*

penalty *n, pl* **-ties 1** a legal punishment for a crime or offence **2** loss or suffering as a result of one's own action: *we are now paying the penalty for neglecting to keep our equipment up to date* **3** *sport, games etc.* a handicap awarded against a player or team for illegal play, such as a free shot at goal by the opposing team [Latin *poena*]

penalty box *n* **1** Also called: **penalty area** *soccer* a rectangular area in front of the goal, within which a penalty is awarded for a serious foul by the defending team **2** *ice hockey* a bench for players serving time penalties

penalty corner *n hockey* a free hit from the goal line taken by the attacking side

penalty shoot-out *n sport* a method of deciding the winner of a drawn match, in which players from each team attempt to score with a penalty shot

penance *n* **1** voluntary self-punishment to make amends for a sin **2** *RC Church* a sacrament in which repentant sinners are forgiven provided they confess their sins to a priest and perform a penance [Latin *paenitentia* repentance]

Penang *n* **1** Also called: **Pulau Pinang** a state of Peninsular Malaysia: consists of the island of Penang and the province Wellesley on the mainland, which first united administratively in 1798 as a British colony. Capital: George Town. Pop: 1 313 449 (2000). Area: 1030 sq km (398 sq miles) **2** a forested island off the NW coast of Malaya, in the Strait of Malacca. Area: 293 sq km (113 sq miles). Former name (until about 1867): **Prince of Wales Island 3** another name for **George Town**

pence *n* a plural of **penny**

penchant (pon-shon) *n* strong inclination or liking: *a stylish woman with a penchant for dark glasses* [French]

Penchi *n* a variant transliteration of the Chinese name for Benxi

pencil *n* **1** a rod of graphite encased in wood which is used for writing or drawing ▷ *vb* **-cilling, -cilled** or *US* **-ciling, -ciled 2** to draw, colour, write, or mark with a pencil **3 pencil in** to note, arrange, or include

provisionally or tentatively [Latin *penicillus* painter's brush]

Penda *n* died 655 AD, king of Mercia (?634–55)

pendant *n* **a** an ornament that hangs from a piece of jewellery **b** a necklace with such an ornament: *a beautiful pearl pendant* [Latin *pendere* to hang down]

pendent *adj literary* **1** dangling **2** jutting [see PENDANT]

Penderecki *n* Krzystof. born 1933, Polish composer, noted for his highly individual orchestration. His works include *Threnody for the Victims of Hiroshima* for strings (1960), *Stabat Mater* (1962), *Polish Requiem* (1983–84), and the opera *Ubu Rex* (1991)

pending *prep* **1** while waiting for ▷ *adj* **2** not yet decided or settled **3** imminent: *these developments have been pending for some time*

Pendleton *n* Victoria (**Louise**). born 1980, English track cyclist: in two Olympic Games (2008, 2012) she won one silver and two gold medals for Britain

pendulous *adj literary* hanging downwards and swinging freely [Latin *pendere* to hang down]

pendulum *n* **1** a weight suspended so it swings freely under the influence of gravity **2** such a device used to regulate a clock mechanism **3** a movement from one attitude or belief towards its opposite: *the pendulum has swung back to more punitive measures*

penetrate *vb* **-trating, -trated 1** to find or force a way into or through **2** to diffuse through; permeate: *the smell of cooking penetrated through to the sitting room* **3** to see through: *the sunlight did not penetrate the thick canopy of leaves* **4** (of a man) to insert the penis into the vagina of (a woman) **5** to grasp the meaning of (a principle, etc.) [Latin *penetrare*] ▷ **penetrable** *adj* ▷ **penetrative** *adj*

penetrating *adj* tending to or able to penetrate: *a penetrating mind; a penetrating voice*

penetration *n* **1** the act or an instance of penetrating **2** the ability or power to penetrate **3** keen insight or perception

Peneus *n* the ancient name for the **Salambria**

Penfield *n* Wilder. 1891–1976, Canadian scientist, neurosurgeon, and writer born in the US; he developed a surgical treatment for epilepsy

pen friend *n* a person with whom one exchanges letters, often a person in another country whom one has not met

Penghu or **P'eng-hu** *n* transliteration of the Chinese name for the **Pescadores**

Pengpu *n* a variant transliteration of the Chinese name for Bengbu

penguin *n* a flightless black-and-white sea bird with webbed feet and wings modified as flippers for swimming [origin unknown]

penicillin *n* an antibiotic used to treat diseases caused by bacteria [Latin *penicillus* tuft of hairs]

peninsula *n* a narrow strip of land projecting from the mainland into a sea or lake [Latin, literally: almost an island] ▷ **peninsular** *adj*

Peninsula *n* **the Peninsula** short for the **Iberian Peninsula**

penis *n, pl* **-nises** or **-nes** the organ of copulation in higher vertebrates, also used for urinating in many mammals [Latin] ▷ **penile** *adj*

penitent *adj* **1** feeling regret for one's sins; repentant ▷ *n* **2** a person who is penitent [Church Latin *paenitens* regretting] ▷ **penitence** *n*

penitential *adj* of, showing, or as a penance

penitentiary *n, pl* **-ries 1** (in the US and Canada) a state or federal prison ▷ *adj* **2** of or for penance **3** used for punishment and reformation: *the penitentiary system* [Latin *paenitens* penitent]

p

Penki *n* a variant transliteration of the Chinese name for Benxi

penknife *n, pl* **-knives** a small knife with one or more blades that fold into the handle

penmanship *n formal* style or technique of writing by hand

Penn *n* **1** Irving. 1917–2009, US photographer, noted for his portraits and his innovations in colour photography **2** William. 1644–1718, English Quaker and founder of Pennsylvania

Penn. *or* **Penna.** Pennsylvania

pen name *n* a name used by a writer instead of his or her real name; nom de plume

pennant *n* **1** a long narrow flag, esp. one used by ships as identification or for signalling **2** *chiefly US, Canad and Austral* a flag indicating the winning of a championship in certain sports [probably a blend of *pendant* + *pennon*]

Penney *n* William George, Baron Penney of East Hendred. 1909–91, British mathematician. He worked on the first atomic bomb and became chairman of the UK Atomic Energy Authority (1964–67)

penniless *adj* very poor

Pennine Alps *pl n* a range of the Alps between Switzerland and Italy. Highest peak: Monte Rosa, 4634 m (15 204 ft)

Pennines *pl n* a system of hills in England, extending from the Cheviot Hills in the north to the River Trent in the south: forms the watershed for the main rivers of N England. Highest peak: Cross Fell, 893 m (2930 ft). Also called: **the Pennine Chain**

Pennine Way *n* a long-distance footpath extending from Edale, Derbyshire, for 402 km (250 miles) to Kirk Yetholm, Scottish Borders

pennon *n* **1** a long flag, often tapering and divided at the end, originally a knight's personal flag **2** a small tapering or triangular flag flown by a ship or boat [Latin *penna* feather]

Pennsylvania *n* a state of the northeastern US: almost wholly in the Appalachians, with the Allegheny Plateau to the west and a plain in the southeast; the second most important US state for manufacturing. Capital: Harrisburg. Pop: 12 365 455 (2003 est). Area: 116 462 sq km (44 956 sq miles). Abbreviation: **Pa., Penn., Penna.,** (with zip code) **PA**

Pennsylvanian *adj* **1** of the state of Pennsylvania **2** (in North America) of, denoting, or formed in the upper of two divisions of the Carboniferous period, which lasted 30 million years, during which coal measures were formed. See also **Mississippian** (2) ▷ *n* **3** an inhabitant or native of the state of Pennsylvania **4** the Pennsylvanian the Pennsylvanian period or rock system, equivalent to the Upper Carboniferous of Europe

penny *n, pl* **pennies** *or* **pence 1** a British bronze coin worth one hundredth of a pound **2** a former British and Australian coin worth one twelfth of a shilling **3** (*pl* **pennies**) US and Canad a cent **4** *informal, chiefly Brit* the least amount of money: *I don't have a penny* **5** a pretty penny *informal* a considerable sum of money **6** spend a penny *Brit and NZ informal* to urinate **7** the penny dropped *informal* the explanation of something was finally understood [Old English *penig, pening*]

Penny Black *n* the first adhesive postage stamp, issued in Britain in 1840

penny-dreadful *n, pl* **-fuls** *Brit informal* a cheap, often lurid book or magazine

penny-farthing *n Brit* an early type of bicycle with a large front wheel and a small rear wheel

penny-pinching *adj* **1** excessively careful with money; miserly ▷ *n* **2** miserliness ▷ **penny-pincher** *n*

pennyroyal *n* a Eurasian plant with hairy leaves and small mauve flowers, which provides an aromatic oil used in medicine [Old French *pouliol* pennyroyal + *real* royal]

penny-wise *adj* penny-wise and pound-foolish careful or thrifty in small matters but wasteful in large ventures

pennywort *n* a Eurasian rock plant with whitish-green tubular flowers and rounded leaves

pennyworth *n* **1** the amount that can be bought for a penny **2** a small or insignificant amount of something: *they'd thrown in their pennyworth of opinion*

penology (pee-nol-a-jee) *n* the study of the punishment of criminals and of prison management [Greek *poinē* punishment]

pen pal *n informal* same as **pen friend**

penpusher *n* a person whose work involves a lot of boring paperwork ▷ **penpushing** *adj, n*

Penrith *n* a market town in NW England, in Cumbria. Pop: 14 471 (2001)

Penrose *n* Sir Roger. born 1931, British mathematician and theoretical physicist, noted for his investigation of black holes

Penshurst Place *n* a 14th-century mansion near Tunbridge Wells in Kent: birthplace of Sir Philip Sidney; gardens laid out from 1560

pension¹ *n* **1** a regular payment made by the state or a former employer to a person who has retired or to a widowed or disabled person ▷ *vb* **2** to grant a pension to ▷ See also **pension off** [Latin *pensio* a payment] ▷ **pensionable** *adj* ▷ **pensioner** *n*

pension² (pon-syon) *n* (in France and some other countries) a relatively cheap boarding house [French: extended meaning of *pension* grant]

pension off *vb* to cause (someone) to retire from a job and pay him or her a pension

pensive *adj* deeply thoughtful, often with a tinge of sadness [Latin *pensare* to consider] ▷ **pensively** *adv*

pent *vb* a past of **pen²**

penta- *combining form* five: *pentagon; pentameter* [Greek *pente*]

pentacle *n* same as **pentagram** [Italian *pentacolo* something having five corners]

pentagon *n geometry* a figure with five sides ▷ **pentagonal** *adj*

Pentagon *n* **1** the five-sided building in Arlington, Virginia, that houses the headquarters of the US Department of Defense. Part of the building was severely damaged in the terrorist attacks of 11 September 2001 **2** the military leadership of the US

pentagram *n* a star-shaped figure with five points

pentameter (pen-**tam**-it-er) *n* a line of poetry consisting of five metrical feet

Pentateuch (pent-a-tyuke) *n* the first five books of the Old Testament [Greek *pente* five + *teukhos* scroll case] ▷ **Pentateuchal** *adj*

pentathlon *n* an athletic contest consisting of five different events. See also **modern pentathlon** [Greek *pente* five + *athlon* contest]

pentatonic scale *n music* a scale consisting of five notes

pentavalent *adj chem* having a valency of five

Pentecost *n* a Christian festival occurring on Whit Sunday celebrating the descent of the Holy Ghost to the apostles [Greek *pentēkostē* fiftieth (day after the Resurrection)]

Pentecostal *adj* relating to any of the Christian groups that have a charismatic and fundamentalist approach to Christianity

Pentelikon *n* a mountain in SE Greece, near Athens: famous for its white marble, worked regularly from the 6th century BC, from which the chief buildings and sculptures in Athens are made. Height: 1109 m (3638 ft). Latin name: **Pentelicus**

penthouse *n* a luxurious flat built on the top floor or roof of a building [Middle English *pentis*, later *penthouse*, from Latin *appendere* to hang from]

Pentland Firth *n* a channel between the mainland of N Scotland and the Orkney Islands: notorious for rough seas. Length: 32 km (20 miles). Width: up to 13 km (8 miles)

pent-up *adj* not released; repressed: *full of pent-up emotional violence*

penultimate *adj* second last

penumbra *n, pl* **-brae** *or* **-bras** **1** the partially shadowed region which surrounds the full shadow in an eclipse **2** *literary* a partial shadow [Latin *paene* almost + *umbra* shadow] **> penumbral** *adj*

penurious *adj formal* **1** niggardly with money **2** lacking money or means

penury *n formal* **1** extreme poverty **2** extreme scarcity [Latin *penuria*]

Penza *n* a city in W Russia: manufacturing centre. Pop: 514 000 (2005 est)

Penzance *n* a town in SW England, in SW Cornwall: the westernmost town in England; resort and fishing port. Pop: 20 255 (2001)

Penzias *n* Arno Allan. born 1933, US astrophysicist, who shared the Nobel prize for physics (1978) with Robert W. Wilson for their discovery of cosmic microwave background radiation

peon *n* a Spanish-American farm labourer or unskilled worker [Spanish]

peony *n, pl* **-nies** a garden plant with showy pink, red, white, or yellow flowers [Greek *paiōnia*]

people *pl n* **1** persons collectively or in general **2** a group of persons considered together: *old people suffer from anaemia more often than younger people do* **3** (*pl* **-ples**) the persons living in a particular country: *the American people* **4** one's family or ancestors: *her people originally came from Skye* **5** the people **a** the mass of ordinary persons without rank or privileges **b** the body of persons in a country who are entitled to vote **>** *vb* **-pling, -pled** **6** to provide with inhabitants: *the centre of the continent is sparsely peopled* [Latin *populus*]

USAGE See at **person**.

---

people carrier *n* same as **multipurpose vehicle**

people mover *n Brit, Austral and NZ* same as **multipurpose vehicle**

Peoria *n* a port in N central Illinois, on the Illinois River. Pop: 112 907 (2003 est)

pep *n* **1** high spirits, energy, or vitality **>** *vb* **pepping, pepped** **2 pep up** to make more lively or interesting: *the company has spent thousands trying to pep up its image* [short for *pepper*]

Pepin the Short *n* died 768 AD, king of the Franks (751–768); son of Charles Martel and father of Charlemagne. He deposed the Merovingian king (751) and founded the Carolingian dynasty

peplum *n, pl* **-lums** *or* **-la** a flared ruffle attached to the waist of a garment [Greek *peplos* shawl]

pepper *n* **1** a sharp hot condiment obtained from the fruit of an East Indian climbing plant **2** Also called: **capsicum** a colourful tropical fruit used as a vegetable and a condiment **>** *vb* **3** to season with pepper **4** to sprinkle liberally: *his speech is heavily peppered with Americanisms* **5** to pelt with small missiles [Greek *peperi*]

pepper-and-salt *adj* **1** (of a fabric) marked with a fine mixture of black and white **2** (of hair) streaked with grey

peppercorn *n* the small dried berry of the pepper plant

peppercorn rent *n Brit* a rent that is very low or nominal

pepper mill *n* a small hand mill used to grind peppercorns

peppermint *n* **1** a mint plant which produces a pungent oil, used as a flavouring **2** a sweet flavoured with peppermint

pepperoni *n* a dry sausage of pork and beef spiced with pepper [Italian *peperoni* peppers]

pepper spray *n* a defence spray agent derived from hot cayenne peppers, which causes temporary blindness and breathing difficulty

peppery *adj* **1** tasting of pepper **2** irritable

pep pill *n informal* a tablet containing a stimulant drug

pepsin *n* an enzyme produced in the stomach, which, when activated by acid, breaks down proteins [Greek *peptein* to digest]

pep talk *n informal* a talk designed to increase confidence and enthusiasm

peptic *adj* **1** of or relating to digestion **2** of or caused by pepsin or the action of the digestive juices [Greek *peptein* to digest]

peptic ulcer *n* an ulcer in the stomach or duodenum

peptide *n chem* a compound consisting of two or more amino acids linked by chemical bonding between the amino group of one and the carboxyl group of another

Pepys *n* Samuel. 1633–1703, English diarist and naval administrator. His diary, which covers the period 1660–69, is a vivid account of London life through such disasters as the Great Plague, the Fire of London, and the intrusion of the Dutch fleet up the Thames

per *prep* **1** for every: *three pence per pound*; *30 pounds per week* **2** by; through **3 as per** according to: *proceed as per the instructions* **4 as per usual** *or* **as per normal** *informal* as usual [Latin: by, for each]

Pera *n* the former name of **Beyoğlu**

peradventure *archaic adv* **1** by chance; perhaps **>** *n* **2** chance or doubt [Old French *par aventure* by chance]

Peraea *or* **Perea** *n* a region of ancient Palestine, east of the River Jordan and the Dead Sea

Perak *n* a state of NW Peninsular Malaysia, on the Strait of Malacca: tin mining. Capital: Ipoh. Pop: 2 051 236 (2000). Area: 21 005 sq km (8110 sq miles)

perambulate *vb* **-lating, -lated** *formal* to walk about (a place) [Latin *per-* through + *ambulare* to walk] **> perambulation** *n*

perambulator *n formal* same as **pram**

per annum *adv* in each year [Latin]

per capita *adj, adv* of or for each person: *the average per capita wage has increased* [Latin, literally: according to heads]

perceive *vb* **-ceiving, -ceived** **1** to become aware of (something) through the senses **2** to understand or grasp [Latin *percipere* to seize entirely] **> perceivable** *adj*

per cent *adv* **1** in each hundred. Symbol: **%** **>** *n* also: **percent 2** a percentage or proportion [Medieval Latin *per centum* out of every hundred]

percentage *n* **1** proportion or rate per hundred parts **2** any proportion in relation to the whole: *a small percentage of the population* **3** *informal* profit or advantage

percentile *n* one of 99 actual or notional values of a variable dividing its distribution into 100 groups with equal frequencies

perceptible *adj* able to be perceived; recognizable **> perceptibly** *adv*

perception *n* **1** the act of perceiving **2** insight or intuition: *his acute perception of other people's emotions* **3** the ability to perceive **4** way of viewing: *advertising affects the customer's perception of a product* [Latin *perceptio* comprehension] **> perceptual** *adj*

perceptive *adj* **1** observant **2** able to perceive **> perceptively** *adv* **> perceptiveness** *n*

Perceval *n* Spencer. 1762–1812, British statesman; prime minister (1809–12); assassinated

perch¹ *n* **1** a branch or other resting place above ground for a bird **2** any raised resting place: *from his perch on the bar stool* **>** *vb* **3** (of birds) to alight or rest on a perch: *it fluttered to the branch and perched there for a moment* **4** to place or position precariously: *he was perched uneasily on the edge of his chair* [Latin *pertica* long staff]

perch² *n, pl* **perch** *or* **perches** **1** a spiny-finned edible freshwater fish of Europe and North America **2** any of various similar or related fishes [Greek *perkē*]

perchance *adv archaic or poetic* **1** perhaps **2** by chance [Anglo-French *par chance*]

percipient *adj formal* quick at perceiving; observant

[Latin *percipiens* observing] **> percipience** *n*

percolate *vb* **-lating, -lated** **1** to pass or filter through very small holes: *the light percolating through the stained-glass windows cast coloured patterns on the floor* **2** to spread gradually: *his theories percolated through the academic community* **3** to make (coffee) or (of coffee) to be made in a percolator [Latin *per-* through + *colare* to strain] **> percolation** *n*

percolator *n* a coffeepot in which boiling water is forced up through a tube and filters down through the coffee grounds into a container

percussion *n* **1** the striking of one thing against another **2** *music* percussion instruments collectively [Latin *percutere* to hit] **> percussive** *adj*

percussion cap *n* a detonator which contains material that explodes when struck

percussion instrument *n* a musical instrument, such as the drums, that produces a sound when struck directly

percussionist *n music* a person who plays percussion instruments

Percy *n* **1** Sir **Henry**, known as **Harry Hotspur**. 1364–1403, English rebel, who was killed leading an army against Henry IV **2** **Thomas**. 1729–1811, English bishop and antiquary. His *Reliques of Ancient English Poetry* (1765) stimulated the interest of Romantic writers in old English and Scottish ballads

Perdido *n* **Monte Perdido** a mountain in NE Spain, in the central Pyrenees. Height: 3352 m (10 997 ft). French name: **Mont Perdu, Perdu**

perdition *n* **1** *Christianity* final and unalterable spiritual ruin; damnation **2** same as **hell** [Late Latin *perditio* ruin]

Perdu *n* **Mont Perdu** the French name for (Monte) **Perdido**

Perea *n* a variant spelling of **Peraea**

peregrinate *vb* **-nating, -nated** *formal* to travel or wander about from place to place [Latin *peregrinari* to travel] **> peregrination** *n*

peregrine falcon *n* a European falcon with dark plumage on the back and wings and lighter underparts [Latin *peregrinus* foreign]

Pereira *n* a town in W central Colombia: cattle trading and coffee processing. Pop: 656 000 (2005 est)

Perelman *n* **S**(idney) **J**(oseph). 1904–79, US humorous writer. After scriptwriting for the Marx Brothers, he published many collections of articles, including *Crazy Like a Fox* (1944) and *Eastward, Hi!* (1977)

peremptory *adj* **1** urgent or commanding: *a peremptory knock on the door* **2** expecting immediate obedience without any discussion: *he gave peremptory instructions to his son* **3** dogmatic [Latin *peremptorius* decisive] **> peremptorily** *adv*

perennial *adj* **1** lasting throughout the year or through many years ▷ *n* **2** a plant that continues its growth for at least three years [Latin *per-* through + *annus* year]

Peres *n* **Shimon**. born 1923, Israeli statesman, born in Poland: prime minister (1984–86; 1995–96); president from 2007; Nobel peace prize 1994 jointly with Yasser Arafat and Yitzhak Rabin

perestroika *n* (in the late 1980s) the policy of restructuring the Soviet economy and political system [Russian: reconstruction]

Pérez de Cuéllar *n* **Javier**. born 1920, Peruvian diplomat and UN secretary-general (1982–91)

Pérez Galdós *n* **Benito**. 1843–1920, Spanish novelist. His works include the *Episodios nacionales* (1873–1912), a series of historical novels, and *Fortunata y Jacinta* (1886–87)

Perez-Reverte *n* **Arturo**. born 1951, Spanish novelist and writer; his books include *The Fencing Master* (1988), *The Dumas Club* (1993), *The Queen of the South* (2002), and the historical 'Captain Alatriste' series, beginning with *Captain Alatriste* (1996)

perfect *adj* **1** having all essential elements **2** faultless: *a perfect circle* **3** correct or precise: *perfect timing* **4** utter or

absolute: *a perfect stranger* **5** excellent in all respects: *a perfect day* **6** *maths* exactly divisible into equal integral or polynomial roots: *36 is a perfect square* **7** *grammar* denoting a tense of verbs used to describe a completed action ▷ *n* **8** *grammar* the perfect tense ▷ *vb* **9** to improve to one's satisfaction: *he is in Paris to perfect his French* **10** to make fully accomplished: *he perfected the system* [Latin *perficere* to complete] **> perfectly** *adv*

> **USAGE** For most of its meanings, the adjective *perfect* describes an absolute state, i.e. one that cannot be qualified; thus something is either *perfect* or *not perfect*, and cannot be *more perfect* or *less perfect*. However, when *perfect* means excellent in all respects, a comparative can be used with it without absurdity: *the next day the weather was even more perfect*.

perfectible *adj* capable of becoming or being made perfect **> perfectibility** *n*

perfection *n* the state or quality of being perfect [Latin *perfectio* a completing]

perfectionism *n* the demand for the highest standard of excellence **> perfectionist** *n, adj*

perfect pitch *n* same as **absolute pitch**

perfect storm *n* a combination of events which produce a disastrous outcome

perfidious *adj literary* treacherous or deceitful [Latin *perfidus*] **> perfidy** *n*

perforate *vb* **-rating, -rated** **1** to make a hole or holes in **2** to punch rows of holes between (stamps) for ease of separation [Latin *per-* through + *forare* to pierce] **> perforable** *adj* **> perforator** *n*

perforation *n* **1** a hole or holes made in something **2** a series of punched holes, such as that between individual stamps

perforce *adv formal* of necessity [Old French *par force*]

perform *vb* **1** to carry out (an action): *the hospital performs more than a hundred such operations each year* **2** to present (a play or concert): *he performed a couple of songs from his new album* **3** to fulfil: *you have performed the first of two conditions* [Old French *parfournir*] **> performable** *adj* **> performer** *n*

performance *n* **1** the act or process of performing **2** an artistic or dramatic production: *the concert includes the first performance of a new trumpet concerto* **3** manner or quality of functioning: *the car's overall performance is excellent* **4** *informal* conduct or behaviour, esp. when distasteful: *what did you mean by that performance at the restaurant?*

perfume *n* **1** a liquid cosmetic worn for its pleasant smell **2** a fragrant smell ▷ *vb* **-fuming, -fumed** **3** to impart a perfume to [French *parfum*, from Latin *per* through + *fumare* to smoke] **> perfumed** *adj*

perfumer *n* a person who makes or sells perfume **> perfumery** *n*

perfunctory *adj formal* done only as a matter of routine: *he gave his wife a perfunctory kiss* [Late Latin *perfunctorius* negligent] **> perfunctorily** *adv* **> perfunctoriness** *n*

perfuse *vb* **-fusing, -fused** **1** to permeate (a liquid, colour, etc.) through or over (something) **2** *surgery* to pass (a fluid) through tissue

Pergamum *n* an ancient city in NW Asia Minor, in Mysia: capital of a major Hellenistic monarchy of the same name that later became a Roman province

pergola *n* an arched trellis or framework that supports climbing plants [Italian]

Pergolesi *n* **Giovanni Battista**. 1710–36, Italian composer: his works include the operetta *La Serva padrona* (1733) and the *Stabat Mater* (1736) for women's voices

perhaps *adv* **1** possibly; maybe **2** approximately; roughly: *it would have taken perhaps three or four minutes* [earlier *perhappes*, from *per* by + *happes* chance]

perianth *n botany* the outer part of a flower [Greek *peri-* around + *anthos* flower]

pericardium *n, pl* **-dia** the membranous sac enclosing the heart [Greek *peri-* around + *kardia* heart] **> pericardial** *adj*

pericarp *n botany* the part of a fruit enclosing the seed that develops from the wall of the ovary [Greek *peri-* around + *karpos* fruit]

Pericles *n* ?495–429 BC, Athenian statesman and leader of the popular party, who contributed greatly to Athens' political and cultural supremacy in Greece. In power from about 460 BC, he was responsible for the construction of the Parthenon. He conducted the Peloponnesian War (431–404 BC) successfully until his death

perigee *n astronomy* the point in its orbit around the earth when the moon or a satellite is nearest the earth [Greek *peri-* near + *gē* earth]

Périgueux *n* a town in SW France, capital of the Dordogne: noted for its Roman remains, medieval cathedral, and pâté de foie gras. Pop: 29 080 (2008)

perihelion *n, pl* -**lia** *astronomy* the point in its orbit around the sun when a planet or comet is nearest the sun [Greek *peri-* near + *hēlios* sun]

peril *n* great danger or jeopardy [Latin *periculum*] **> perilous** *adj*

perimeter (per-rim-it-er) *n* 1 *maths* **a** the curve or line enclosing a plane area **b** the length of this curve or line **2** any boundary around something [Greek *perimetros*]

perinatal *adj* of or occurring in the period from about three months before to one month after birth [Greek *peri-* around + Latin *natus* born]

perineum (per-rin-nee-um) *n, pl* -**nea** (-nee-a) *anatomy* the region of the body between the anus and the genitals [Greek *perinaion*] **> perineal** *adj*

period *n* 1 **a** portion of time: *six inches of rain fell in a 24-hour period* **2** a portion of time specified in some way: *the President's first period of office* **3** an occurrence of menstruation **4** *geology* a unit of geological time during which a system of rocks is formed: *the Jurassic period* **5** a division of time at school, college, or university when a particular subject is taught **6** *physics, maths* the time taken to complete one cycle of a regularly recurring phenomenon **7** *chem* one of the horizontal rows of elements in the periodic table **8** *chiefly US and Canad* same as **full stop** ▷ *adj* **9** dating from or in the style of an earlier time: *a performance on period instruments* [Greek *periodos* circuit]

periodic *adj* recurring at intervals **> periodically** *adv* **> periodicity** *n*

periodical *n* 1 a publication issued at regular intervals, usually monthly or weekly ▷ *adj* **2** of or relating to such publications **3** periodic or occasional

periodic law *n chem* the principle that the chemical properties of the elements are periodic functions of their atomic numbers

periodic table *n chem* a table of the elements, arranged in order of increasing atomic number, based on the periodic law

peripatetic (per-rip-a-tet-ik) *adj* 1 travelling from place to place **2** *Brit* employed in two or more educational establishments and travelling from one to another: *a peripatetic violin teacher* ▷ *n* **3** a peripatetic person [Greek *peripatein* to pace to and fro]

peripheral (per-if-er-al) *adj* 1 not relating to the most important part of something; incidental **2** of or relating to a periphery ▷ *n* **3** *computers* any device, such as a disk or modem, concerned with input/output or storage

periphery (per-if-er-ee) *n, pl* -**eries** 1 the boundary or edge of an area or group: *slums sprouted up on the periphery of the city* **2** fringes of a field of activity: *less developed countries on the periphery of the capitalist system* [Greek *peri-* around + *pherein* to bear]

periphrasis (per-if-ra-siss) *n, pl* -**rases** (-ra-seez) a roundabout way of expressing something; circumlocution [Greek *peri-* around + *phrazein* to declare]

periscope *n* an optical instrument used, esp. in submarines, to give a view of objects on a different level [Greek *periskopein* to look around]

perish *vb* 1 to be destroyed or die **2** to cause to suffer: *we were perished with cold* **3** to rot or cause to rot: *to prevent your swimsuit from perishing, rinse it in clean water before it dries* [Latin *perire* to pass away entirely]

perishable *adj* 1 liable to rot ▷ *n* **2** (*often pl*) a perishable article, esp. food

perishing *adj* 1 *informal* (of weather) extremely cold **2** *slang* confounded or blasted: *get rid of the perishing lot!*

peristalsis (per-riss-tal-siss) *n, pl* -**ses** (-seez) *physiol* the wavelike involuntary muscular contractions of the walls of the digestive tract [Greek *peri-* around + *stalsis* compression] **> peristaltic** *adj*

peritoneum (per-rit-toe-nee-um) *n, pl* -**nea** (-nee-a) or -**neums** a serous sac that lines the walls of the abdominal cavity and covers the abdominal organs [Greek *peritonos* stretched around] **> peritoneal** *adj*

peritonitis (per-rit-tone-ite-iss) *n* inflammation of the peritoneum, causing severe abdominal pain

periwig *n obsolete* a wig formerly worn by men [French *perruque*]

periwinkle¹ *n* same as **winkle** (1) [origin unknown]

periwinkle² *n* a Eurasian evergreen plant with trailing stems and blue flowers [Old English *perwince*]

perjure *vb* -**juring**, -**jured** perjure oneself *criminal law* to deliberately give false evidence while under oath [Latin *perjurare*] **> perjurer** *n*

perjury (per-jer-ee) *n, pl* -**juries** *criminal law* the act of deliberately giving false evidence while under oath [Latin *perjurium* a false oath]

perk¹ *n informal* an incidental benefit gained from a job, such as a company car [short for *perquisite*]

perk² *vb informal* short for **percolate** (3)

perk up *vb* 1 to make or become more cheerful **2** to rise or cause to rise briskly: *the dog's ears perked up suddenly* [origin unknown]

perky *adj* **perkier**, **perkiest** 1 jaunty or lively **2** confident or spirited

Perl *n* a computer programming language that is used for text manipulation, esp. on the World Wide Web [practical extraction and report language]

perlemoen (per-la-moon) *n S African* same as **abalone** [Afrikaans, from Dutch]

Perlis *n* a state of NW Peninsular Malaysia, on the Andaman Sea: a dependency of Thailand until 1909. Capital: Kangar. Pop: 204 450 (2000). Area: 810 sq km (313 sq miles)

Perlman *n* Itzhak. born 1945, Israeli violinist; plays seated because of polio

perm¹ *n* 1 a hairstyle with long-lasting waves or curls produced by treating the hair with chemicals ▷ *vb* **2** to give a perm to (hair)

perm² *n informal* short for **permutation** (4)

Perm *n* a port in W Russia, on the Kama River: oil refinery; university (1916). Pop: 984 000 (2005 est). Former name (1940–62): **Molotov**

permafrost *n* ground that is permanently frozen [*perma*(nent) + *frost*]

permanent *adj* 1 existing or intended to exist forever: *a permanent solution* **2** not expected to change: *a permanent condition* [Latin *permanens* continuing] **> permanence** *n* **> permanently** *adv*

permanent wave *n* same as **perm¹** (1)

permanent way *n chiefly Brit* the track of a railway, including the sleepers and rails

permanganate *n* a salt of an acid containing manganese, used as a disinfectant

permeable *adj* capable of being permeated, esp. by liquids **> permeability** *n*

permeate *vb* -**ating**, -**ated** 1 to penetrate or spread throughout (something): *his mystical philosophy permeates everything he creates* **2** to pass through or cause to pass through by osmosis or diffusion: *the rain permeated her anorak* [Latin *permeare*] **> permeation** *n*

Permian *adj geology* of the period of geological time

about 280 million years ago [after PERM]

permissible *adj* permitted or allowable
> permissibility *n*

permission *n* authorization to do something

permissive *adj* tolerant or lenient, esp. in sexual matters: *the so-called permissive society* **> permissiveness** *n*

permit *vb* **-mitting, -mitted 1** to allow (something) to be done or to happen: *smoking is not permitted in the office* **2** to allow (someone) to do something: *her father does not permit her to eat sweets* **3** to allow the possibility (of): *they saw each other as often as time and circumstances permitted* ▷ *n* **4** an official document granting permission to do something [Latin *permittere*]

permutate *vb* **-tating, -tated** to alter the sequence or arrangement (of): *endlessly permutating three basic designs*

permutation *n* **1** *maths* an ordered arrangement of the numbers or terms of a set into specified groups: *the permutations of a, b, and c, taken two at a time, are ab, ba, ac, ca, bc, cb* **2** a combination of items made by reordering **3** a transformation **4** a fixed combination for selections of results on football pools [Latin *permutare* to change thoroughly]

Pernambuco *n* **1** a state of NE Brazil, on the Atlantic: consists of a humid coastal plain rising to a high inland plateau. Capital: Recife. Pop: 8 084 667 (2002). Area: 98 280 sq km (37 946 sq miles) **2** the former name of **Recife**

pernicious *adj formal* **1** wicked or malicious: *pernicious lies* **2** causing grave harm; deadly [Latin *pernicies* ruin]

pernicious anaemia *n* a severe form of anaemia resulting in a reduction of the red blood cells, weakness, and a sore tongue

pernickety *adj informal* **1** excessively fussy about details **2** (of a task) requiring close attention [origin unknown]

Pernik *n* an industrial town in W Bulgaria, on the Struma River. Pop: 84 000 (2005 est). Former name (1949–62): **Dimitrovo**

Perón *n* **1** Juan Domingo. 1895–1974, Argentine soldier and statesman; dictator (1946–55). He was deposed in 1955, remaining in exile until 1973, when he was elected president (1973–74) **2** his third wife, **María Estella**, known as *Isabel*. born 1931, president of Argentina (1974–76); deposed **3** (**María**) **Eva** (**Duarte de**), known as *Evita*. Second wife of Juan Domingo Perón. 1919–52, Argentine film actress: active in politics and social welfare (1946–52) **> Pe'ronist** *n, adj*

peroration *n formal* the concluding part of a speech which sums up the points made previously [Latin *peroratio*]

peroxide *n* **1** hydrogen peroxide used as a hair bleach **2** any of a class of metallic oxides, such as sodium peroxide, Na_2O_2 ▷ *adj* **3** bleached with or resembling peroxide: *a peroxide blonde* ▷ *vb* **-iding, -ided 4** to bleach (the hair) with peroxide

perp *n US and Canad informal* a person who has committed a crime [short for *perpetrator*]

perpendicular *adj* **1** at right angles to a given line or surface **2** upright; vertical **3** denoting a style of English Gothic architecture characterized by vertical lines ▷ *n* **4** *geometry* a line or plane perpendicular to another [Latin *perpendiculum* a plumb line] **> perpendicularity** *n*

perpetrate *vb* **-trating, -trated** to perform or be responsible for (a deception or crime) [Latin *perpetrare*] **> perpetration** *n* **> perpetrator** *n*

> USAGE *Perpetrate* and *perpetuate* are sometimes confused: *he must answer for the crimes he has perpetrated* (not *perpetuated*); *the book helped to perpetuate* (not *perpetrate*) *some of the myths about his early life.*

perpetual *adj* **1** never ending or never changing: *Mexico's colourful scenery and nearly perpetual sunshine* **2** continually repeated: *his mother's perpetual worries about his health* [Latin *perpetualis*] **> perpetually** *adv*

perpetual motion *n* motion of a hypothetical mechanism that continues indefinitely without any external source of energy

perpetuate *vb* **-ating, -ated** to cause to continue: *images that perpetuate stereotypes of Black people* [Latin *perpetuare* to continue without interruption] **> perpetuation** *n*

> USAGE See at **perpetrate**.

perpetuity *n, pl* **-ties 1** eternity **2** the state of being perpetual **3** something perpetual, such as a pension that is payable indefinitely **4** **in perpetuity** forever [Latin *perpetuitas* continuity]

Perpignan *n* a town in S France: historic capital of Roussillon. Pop: 117 500 (2006)

perplex *vb* **1** to puzzle or bewilder **2** to complicate: *this merely perplexes the issue* [Latin *perplexus* entangled] **> perplexing** *adj*

perplexity *n, pl* **-ties 1** the state of being perplexed **2** something that perplexes

perquisite *n formal* same as **perk**[1] [Latin *perquirere* to seek earnestly for something]

Perrault *n* Charles. 1628–1703, French author, noted for his *Contes de ma mère l'oye* (1697), which contains the fairy tales *Little Red Riding Hood*, *Cinderella*, and *The Sleeping Beauty*

Perrin *n* Jean Baptiste. 1870–1942, French physicist. His researches on the distribution and diffusion of particles in colloids (1911) gave evidence for the physical reality of molecules, confirmed the explanation of Brownian movement in terms of kinetic theory, and determined the magnitude of the Avogadro constant. He also studied cathode rays: Nobel prize for physics 1926

perry *n, pl* **-ries** an alcoholic drink made from fermented pear juice [Old French *peré*]

Perry *n* **1** Fred(erick John). 1909–95, English tennis and table-tennis player; world singles table-tennis champion (1929); as a tennis player he won eight Grand Slam singles titles including the US Open three times (1933–34, 1936) and Wimbledon three times (1934–36) **2** Grayson. born 1960, English potter, embroiderer, and film-maker; won the Turner Prize (2003). **3** Matthew Calbraith. 1794–1858, US naval officer, who led a naval expedition to Japan that obtained a treaty (1854) opening up Japan to western trade **4** his brother, Oliver Hazard. 1785–1819, US naval officer. His defeat of a British squadron on Lake Erie (1813) was the turning point in the War of 1812, leading to the recapture of Detroit

Perse *n* Saint-John, real name *Alexis Saint-Léger*. 1887–1975, French poet, born in Guadeloupe. His works include *Anabase* (1922) and *Chronique* (1960). Nobel prize for literature 1960

per se (per say) *adv* in itself [Latin]

persecute *vb* **-cuting, -cuted 1** to oppress or maltreat (someone), because of race or religion **2** to harass (someone) persistently [Latin *persequi* to take vengeance upon] **> persecution** *n* **> persecutor** *n*

Persepolis *n* the capital of ancient Persia in the Persian Empire and under the Seleucids: founded by Darius; sacked by Alexander the Great in 330 BC

perseverance *n* continued steady belief or efforts; persistence

persevere *vb* **-severing, -severed** (often foll. by *with* or *in*) to continue to make an effort despite difficulties [Latin *perseverus* very strict]

Pershing *n* John Joseph, nickname *Black Jack*. 1860–1948, US general. He was commander in chief of the American Expeditionary Force in Europe (1917–19)

Persia *n* the former name (until 1935) of **Iran**

Persian *adj* **1** of or relating to ancient Persia or modern Iran ▷ *n* **2** a native or inhabitant of Persia (now Iran) **3** the language of Iran or of Persia

Persian carpet *n* a hand-made carpet or rug with flowing or geometric designs in rich colours

Persian cat *n* a long-haired variety of domestic cat

Persian Gulf *n* a shallow arm of the Arabian Sea between SW Iran and Arabia: linked with the Arabian Sea by the Strait of Hormuz and the Gulf of Oman; important for the oilfields on its shores. Area: 233 000 sq km (90 000 sq miles)

Persian lamb *n* **1** a black loosely curled fur from the karakul lamb **2** a karakul lamb

persiflage (per-sif-flahzh) *n literary* light frivolous conversation or writing [French]

persimmon *n* a sweet red tropical fruit [from a Native American language]

persist *vb* **1** to continue without interruption: *if the symptoms persist, see your doctor* **2** (often foll. by in or with) to continue obstinately despite opposition: *she persisted in using these controversial methods* [Latin *persistere*]

persistent *adj* **1** unrelenting: *persistent rain* **2** showing persistence: *she was a persistent woman* **> persistence** *n* **> persistently** *adv*

persistent vegetative state *n med* an irreversible condition, resulting from brain damage, characterized by lack of consciousness, thought, and feeling, although reflex activities continue

person *n, pl* **people** *or* **persons** **1** an individual human being **2** the body of a human being: *he was found to have a knife concealed about his person* **3** *grammar* a category into which pronouns and forms of verbs are subdivided to show whether they refer to the speaker, the person addressed, or some other individual or thing **4** **in person** actually doing something or being somewhere oneself: *I had the chance to hear her speak in person* [Latin *persona* mask]

> **USAGE** *People* is the word usually used to refer to more than one individual: *there were a hundred people at the reception. Persons* is rarely used, except in official English: *several persons were interviewed.*

-person *combining form* sometimes used instead of *-man* and *-woman* or *-lady*: *chairperson*

> **USAGE** See at **man**.

persona (per-soh-na) *n, pl* **-nae** (-nee) the personality that a person adopts and presents to other people [Latin: mask]

personable *adj* pleasant in appearance and personality

personage *n* **1** an important or distinguished person **2** any person

personal *adj* **1** of the private aspects of a person's life: *redundancy can put an enormous strain on personal relationships* **2** of a person's body: *personal hygiene* **3** belonging to, or for the sole use of, a particular individual: *he disappeared, leaving his passport, diary and other personal belongings in his flat* **4** undertaken by an individual: *the sponsorship deal requires him to make a number of personal appearances for publicity purposes* **5** offensive in respect of an individual's personality or intimate affairs: *he has suffered a lifetime of personal remarks about his weight* **6** having the attributes of an individual conscious being: *a personal God* **7** *grammar* of person **8** *law* of movable property, such as money

personal assistant *n* a person who is employed to help someone with his or her work, esp. the secretarial and administrative aspects of it

personal column *n* a newspaper column containing personal messages and advertisements

personal computer *n* a small computer used for word processing or computer games

personality *n, pl* **-ties** **1** *psychol* the distinctive characteristics which make an individual unique **2** the distinctive character of a person which makes him or her socially attractive: *some people find him lacking in personality and a bit colourless* **3** a well-known person in a certain field; celebrity **4** a remarkable person: *she is a personality to be reckoned with* **5** (*often pl*) an offensive personal remark: *the argument never degenerated into personalities*

personalize *or* **-lise** *vb* **-lizing, -lized** *or* **-lising, -lised** **1** to base (an argument or discussion) around people's characters rather than on abstract arguments **2** to mark (stationery or clothing) with a person's initials or name **3** same as **personify**

personally *adv* **1** without the help of others: *she had seen to it personally that permission was granted* **2** in one's own opinion: *personally, I think it's overrated* **3** as if referring to oneself: *yes, he was rather rude but it's not worth taking it personally* **4** as a person: *I don't like him personally, but he's fine to work with*

personal organizer *n* **1** a diary for storing personal records, appointments, etc. **2** a pocket-sized electronic device that performs the same functions

personal pronoun *n* a pronoun such as I, you, he, she, it, we, and they that represents a definite person or thing

personal stereo *n chiefly Brit* a small portable audio cassette player used with lightweight headphones

persona non grata (non grah-ta) *n, pl* **personae non gratae** (grah-tee) an unacceptable person [Latin]

personate *vb* **-ating, -ated** *criminal law* to assume the identity of (another person) with intent to deceive **> personation** *n*

personify *vb* **-fies, -fying, -fied** **1** to give human characteristics to (a thing or abstraction) **2** to represent (an abstract quality) in human or animal form **3** (of a person or thing) to represent (an abstract quality), as in art **4** to be the embodiment of: *she can be charm personified* **> personification** *n*

personnel *n* **1** the people employed in an organization or for a service **2** the department in an organization that appoints or keeps records of employees **3** (in the armed forces) people, as opposed to machinery or equipment [French]

perspective *n* **1** a way of regarding situations or facts and judging their relative importance: *the female perspective on sex and love* **2** objectivity: *Kay's problems helped me put my minor worries into perspective* **3** a method of drawing that gives the effect of solidity and relative distances and sizes **4** the appearance of objects or buildings relative to each other, determined by their distance from the viewer [Latin *perspicere* to inspect carefully]

Perspex *n trademark* a clear acrylic resin used as a substitute for glass

perspicacious *adj formal* acutely perceptive or discerning [Latin *perspicax*] **> perspicacity** *n*

perspicuous *adj literary* (of speech or writing) easily understood; lucid [Latin *perspicuus* transparent] **> perspicuity** *n*

perspiration *n* **1** the salty fluid secreted by the sweat glands of the skin; sweat **2** the act of sweating

perspire *vb* **-spiring, -spired** to sweat [Latin *per-* through + *spirare* to breathe]

persuade *vb* **-suading, -suaded** **1** to make (someone) do something by reason or charm: *we tried to persuade him not to come up the mountain with us* **2** to cause to believe; convince: *persuading people of the need for enforced environmental protection may be difficult* [Latin *persuadere*] **> persuadable** *adj*

persuasion *n* **1** the act of persuading **2** the power to persuade **3** a set of beliefs; creed: *the Roman Catholic persuasion; literary intellectuals of the modernist persuasion*

persuasive *adj* able to persuade: *a persuasive argument* **> persuasively** *adv*

pert *adj* **1** saucy or impudent **2** attractive in a neat way: *pert buttocks* [Latin *apertus* open]

pertain *vb* (often foll. by to) **1** to have reference or relevance: *the notes pertaining to the case* **2** to be appropriate: *the product pertains to real user needs* **3** to belong (to) or be a part (of) [Latin *pertinere*]

Perth *n* **1** a city in central Scotland, in Perth and Kinross on the River Tay: capital of Scotland from the 12th century until the assassination of James I there in 1437.

P

Pop: 44 200 (2009 est) **2** a city in SW Australia, capital of Western Australia, on the Swan River: major industrial centre; University of Western Australia (1911). Pop: 1 897 548 (2012)

Perth and Kinross *n* a council area of N central Scotland, corresponding mainly to the historical counties of Perthshire and Kinross-shire: part of Tayside Region from 1975 until 1996: chiefly mountainous, with agriculture, tourism, and forestry. Administrative centre: Perth. Pop: 135 990 (2003 est). Area: 5321 sq km (2019 sq miles)

Perthshire *n* (until 1975) a county of central Scotland, now part of Perth and Kinross council area

pertinacious *adj* **1** doggedly resolute in purpose or belief **2** stubbornly persistent [Latin *per-* (intensive) + *tenax* clinging] **>** **pertinacity** *n*

pertinent *adj* relating to the matter at hand; relevant [Latin *pertinens*] **>** **pertinence** *n*

perturb *vb* **1** to disturb the composure of **2** to throw into disorder [Latin *perturbare* to confuse]

perturbation *n literary* anxiety or worry

Peru *n* a republic in W South America, on the Pacific: the centre of the great Inca Empire when conquered by the Spanish in 1532; gained independence in 1824 by defeating Spanish forces with armies led by San Martín and Bolívar; consists of a coastal desert, rising to the Andes; an important exporter of minerals and a major fishing nation. Official languages: Spanish, Quechua, and Aymara. Official religion: Roman Catholic. Currency: nuevo sol. Capital: Lima. Pop: 29 849 303 (2013 est). Area: 1 285 215 sq km (496 222 sq miles)

Perugia *n* **1** a city in central Italy, in Umbria: centre of the Umbrian school of painting (15th century); university (1308); Etruscan and Roman remains. Pop: 149 125 (2001). Ancient name: **Perusia 2** Lake Perugia another name for (Lake) **Trasimene**

Perugino *n* Il, real name *Pietro Vannucci*. 1446–1523, Italian painter; master of Raphael. His works include the fresco *Christ giving the Keys to Peter* in the Sistine Chapel, Rome

peruke *n obsolete* a wig for men worn in the 17th and 18th centuries [French *perruque*]

peruse *vb* **-rusing, -rused 1** to read or examine with care **2** to browse or read in a leisurely way [*per-* (intensive) + *use*] **>** **perusal** *n*

Perutz *n* Max Ferdinand. 1914–2002, British biochemist, born in Austria. With J. C. Kendrew, he worked on the structure of haemoglobin and shared the Nobel prize for chemistry 1962

Peruvian *adj* **1** of or relating to Peru or its inhabitants ▷ *n* **2** a native or inhabitant of Peru

Peruzzi *n* Baldassare Tommaso. 1481–1536, Italian architect and painter of the High Renaissance. The design of the Palazzo Massimo, Rome, is attributed to him

pervade *vb* **-vading, -vaded** to spread through or throughout (something) [Latin *per-* through + *vadere* to go] **>** **pervasion** *n* **>** **pervasive** *adj*

perverse *adj* **1** deliberately acting in a way different from what is regarded as normal or proper **2** wayward or contrary; obstinate [Latin *perversus* turned the wrong way] **>** **perversely** *adv* **>** **perversity** *n*

perversion *n* **1** any abnormal means of obtaining sexual satisfaction **2** the act of perverting

pervert *vb* **1** to use wrongly or badly **2** to interpret wrongly or badly; distort **3** to lead (someone) into abnormal behaviour, esp. sexually; corrupt **4** to debase ▷ *n* **5** a person who practises sexual perversion [Latin *pervertere* to turn the wrong way] **>** **perverted** *adj*

pervious *adj* **1** able to be penetrated; permeable: *the thin walls were pervious to the slightest sound* **2** receptive to new ideas; open-minded [Latin *per-* through + *via* a way]

Pesach or **Pesah** (pay-sahk) *n* same as **Passover**

Pesaro *n* a port and resort in E central Italy, in the Marches on the Adriatic. Pop: 91 086 (2001). Ancient name: **Pisaurum**

Pescadores *pl n* a group of 64 islands in Formosa Strait, separated from Taiwan (to which it belongs) by the **Pescadores Channel**. Pop: 91 950 (2007 est). Area: 127 sq km (49 sq miles). Chinese names: **Penghu**, **P'eng-hu**

Pescara *n* a city and resort in E central Italy, on the Adriatic. Pop: 116 286 (2001)

peseta (pess-**say**-ta) *n* a former monetary unit of Spain [Spanish]

Peshawar *n* a city in N Pakistan, at the E end of the Khyber Pass: one of the oldest cities in Pakistan and capital of the ancient kingdom of Gandhara; university (1950). Pop: 1 255 000 (2005 est)

pesky *adj* **peskier, peskiest** *informal, chiefly US and Canad* troublesome [probably changed from *pesty*]

peso (pay-so) *n, pl* **-sos** the standard monetary unit of Chile, Colombia, Cuba, the Dominican Republic, Mexico, the Philippines, and Uruguay [Spanish: weight]

pessary *n, pl* **-ries** *med* **1** a device worn in the vagina, either as a support for the uterus or as a contraceptive **2** a vaginal suppository [Greek *pessos* plug]

pessimism *n* **1** the tendency to expect the worst in all things **2** the doctrine of the ultimate triumph of evil over good [Latin *pessimus* worst] **>** **pessimist** *n* **>** **pessimistic** *adj* **>** **pessimistically** *adv*

Pessoa *n* Fernando. 1888–1935, Portuguese poet, who ascribed much of his work to three imaginary poets, Alvaro de Campos, Alberto Caeiro, and Ricardo Reis

pest *n* **1** an annoying person or thing; nuisance **2** any organism that damages crops, or injures or irritates livestock or man [Latin *pestis* plague]

Pestalozzi *n* Johann Heinrich. 1746–1827, Swiss educational reformer. His emphasis on learning by observation exerted a wide influence on elementary education

pester *vb* to annoy or nag continually [Old French *empestrer* to hobble (a horse)]

pesticide *n* a chemical used to destroy pests, esp. insects [*pest* + Latin *caedere* to kill]

pestilence *n literary* any deadly epidemic disease, such as the plague

pestilent *adj* **1** annoying or irritating **2** highly destructive morally or physically **3** likely to cause infectious disease [Latin *pestis* plague] **>** **pestilential** *adj*

pestle *n* a club-shaped instrument for grinding or pounding substances in a mortar [Old French *pestel*]

pet¹ *n* **1** a tame animal kept for companionship or pleasure **2** a person who is favoured or indulged: *teacher's pet* ▷ *adj* **3** kept as a pet: *a pet hamster* **4** of or for pet animals: *pet food* **5** strongly felt or particularly cherished: *a pet hatred; he would not stand by and let his pet project be abandoned* ▷ *vb* **petting, petted 6** to treat as a pet; pamper **7** to pat or stroke affectionately **8** *informal* (of two people) to caress each other in an erotic manner [origin unknown]

pet² *n* a fit of sulkiness [origin unknown]

Pétain *n* (Henri) Philippe (**Omer**). 1856–1951, French marshal, noted for his victory at Verdun (1916) in World War I and his leadership of the pro-Nazi government of unoccupied France at Vichy (1940–44); imprisoned for treason (1945)

petal *n* any of the brightly coloured leaflike parts which form the head of a flower [Greek *petalon* leaf] **>** **petalled** *adj*

petard *n* **1** (formerly) a device containing explosives used to break through a wall or door **2** hoist with one's own petard being the victim of one's own schemes [French: firework]

Peter *n New Testament* **1** Saint. Also called: **Simon Peter**. died ?67 AD, a fisherman of Bethsaida, who became leader of the apostles and is regarded by Roman Catholics as the first pope; probably martyred at Rome. Feast day: June 29 or Jan 18 **2** either of two epistles traditionally ascribed to Peter (in full **The First Epistle** and **The Second Epistle of Peter**)

Peter I *n* known as *Peter the Great*. 1672–1725, tsar of Russia (1682–1725), who assumed sole power in 1689. He introduced many reforms in government, technology, and the western European ideas. He also acquired new territories for Russia in the Baltic and founded the new capital of St Petersburg (1703)

Peter III *n* 1728–62, grandson of Peter I and tsar of Russia (1762): deposed in a coup d'état led by his wife (later Catherine II); assassinated

Peterborough *n* **1** a city in central England, in Peterborough unitary authority, N Cambridgeshire on the River Nene: industrial centre; under development as a new town since 1968. Pop: 136 292 (2001) **2** a unitary authority in central England, in Cambridgeshire. Pop: 158 800 (2003 est). Area: 402 sq km (155 sq miles) **3** Soke of Peterborough a former administrative unit of E central England, generally considered part of Northamptonshire or Huntingdonshire: absorbed into Cambridgeshire in 1974 **4** a city in SE Canada, in SE Ontario: manufacturing centre. Pop: 73 303 (2001) **5** a traditional type of wooden canoe formerly made in Peterborough, SE Ontario

Peterlee *n* a new town in Co Durham, founded in 1948. Pop: 29 936 (2001)

Petermann Peak *n* a mountain in E Greenland. Height: 2932 m (9645 ft)

peter out *vb* to come gradually to an end: *the road petered out into a rutted track* [origin unknown]

Peter Pan *n* a youthful or immature man [after the main character in *Peter Pan*, a play]

Petersburg *n* a city in SE Virginia, on the Appomattox River: scene of prolonged fighting (1864–65) during the final months of the American Civil War. Pop: 33 091 (2003 est)

Peterson *n* Oscar (**Emmanuel**). 1925–2007, Canadian jazz pianist and singer, who led his own trio from the early 1950s

Peter the Hermit *n* ?1050–1115, French monk and preacher of the First Crusade

pethidine (peth-id-een) *n* a white crystalline water-soluble drug used to relieve pain [perhaps a blend of *piperidine* + *ethyl*]

petiole *n* *botany* the stalk which attaches a leaf to a plant [Latin *petiolus* little foot]

Petipa *n* Marius. 1819–1910, French ballet dancer and choreographer of the Russian imperial ballet: collaborated with Tchaikovsky on *The Sleeping Beauty* (1890)

Petit *n* Roland. 1924–2011, French ballet dancer and choreographer. His innovative ballets include *Carmen* (1949), *Kraanerg* (1969), and *The Blue Angel* (1985); he also choreographed films, such as *Anything Goes* (1956) and *Black Tights* (1960)

petit bourgeois (pet-ee boor-zhwah) *n*, *pl* **petits bourgeois** (pet-ee boor-zhwahz) **1** the lower middle class **2** a member of this class [French]

petite (pit-eat) *adj* (of a woman) small and dainty [French]

petit four (pet-ee four) *n*, *pl* **petits fours** (pet-ee fours) a very small fancy cake or biscuit [French, literally: little oven]

petition *n* **1** a written document signed by a large number of people demanding some form of action from a government or other authority **2** any formal request to a higher authority **3** *law* a formal application in writing made to a court asking for some specific judicial action: *she filed a petition for divorce* ▷ *vb* **4** to address or present a petition to (a government or to someone in authority): *he petitioned the Crown for mercy* **5** (foll. by *for*) to seek by petition: *the firm's creditors petitioned for liquidation* [Latin *petere* to seek] **> petitioner** *n*

petit mal (pet-ee mal) *n* a mild form of epilepsy in which there are periods of loss of consciousness for up to 30 seconds [French: little illness]

petit point (pet-ee point) *n* **1** a small diagonal needlepoint stitch used for fine detail **2** work done with such stitches [French: small point]

pet name *n* an affectionate nickname for a close friend or family member

Petőfi *n* Sándor. 1823–49, Hungarian lyric poet and patriot

Petra *n* an ancient city in the south of present-day Jordan; capital of the Nabataean kingdom

Petrarch *n* Italian name *Francesco Petrarca*. 1304–74, Italian lyric poet and scholar, who greatly influenced the values of the Renaissance. His collection of poems *Canzoniere*, inspired by his ideal love for Laura, was written in the Tuscan dialect. He also wrote much in Latin, esp. the epic poem *Africa* (1341) and the *Secretum* (1342), a spiritual self-analysis **> Petrarchan** *adj*

petrel *n* a sea bird with a hooked bill and tubular nostrils, such as the albatross, storm petrel, or shearwater [variant of earlier *pitteral*]

Petri dish (pet-ree) *n* a shallow dish used in laboratories, esp. for producing cultures of bacteria [after J. R. Petri, bacteriologist]

Petrie *n* Sir (William Matthew) Flinders. 1853–1942, British Egyptologist and archaeologist

Petrified Forest *n* a national park in E Arizona, containing petrified coniferous trees about 170 000 000 years old

petrify *vb* -fies, -fying, -fied **1** to stun or daze with fear: *he was petrified of going to jail* **2** (of organic material) to turn to stone **3** to make or become unable to change or develop: *a society petrified by outmoded conventions* [Greek *petra* stone] **> petrification** *n*

petrochemical *n* a substance, such as acetone, obtained from petroleum **> petrochemistry** *n*

petrodollar *n* money earned by a country by exporting petroleum

Petrograd *n* a former name (1914–24) of Saint Petersburg

petrol *n* a volatile flammable liquid obtained from petroleum and used as a fuel for internal-combustion engines [see PETROLEUM]

petrolatum (pet-rol-**late**-um) *n* a translucent jelly-like substance obtained from petroleum: used as a lubricant and in medicine as an ointment base

petrol bomb *n* a simple grenade consisting of a bottle filled with petrol. A piece of cloth is put in the neck of the bottle and set alight just before the bomb is thrown

petroleum *n* a dark-coloured thick flammable crude oil occurring in sedimentary rocks, consisting mainly of hydrocarbons: the source of petrol and paraffin [Latin *petra* stone + *oleum* oil]

petroleum jelly *n* same as **petrolatum**

petrolhead *n* *informal* a person who is excessively interested in motor vehicles or is devoted to travelling by car

petrol station *n* *Brit* same as **filling station**

Petronius *n* Gaius, known as *Petronius Arbiter*. died 66 AD, Roman satirist, supposed author of the *Satyricon*, a picaresque account of the licentiousness of contemporary society

Petropavlovsk *n* a city in N Kazakhstan on the Ishim River. Pop: 190 000 (2005 est)

Petrópolis *n* a city in SE Brazil, north of Rio de Janeiro: resort. Pop: 280 000 (2005 est)

Petrosian *n* Tigran. 1929–84, Soviet chess player; world champion (1963–69)

Petrovsk *n* the former name (until 1921) of Makhachkala

Petrozavodsk *n* a city in NW Russia, capital of the Karelian Autonomous Republic, on Lake Onega: developed around ironworks established by Peter the Great in 1703; university (1940). Pop: 265 000 (2005 est)

Petsamo *n* the former name (1920–1944) for Pechenga

petticoat *n* a woman's underskirt [from *petty* + *coat*]

pettifogging *adj* excessively concerned with unimportant detail [origin unknown] **> pettifogger** *n*

pettish *adj* peevish or fretful [from PET²] **> pettishness** *n*

petty *adj* **-tier, -tiest** **1** trivial or unimportant: *petty details* **2** small-minded: *petty spite* **3** low in importance: *petty criminals* [French *petit* little] **> pettily** *adv* **> pettiness** *n*

petty cash *n* a small cash fund for minor incidental expenses

petty officer *n* a noncommissioned officer in the navy

petulant *adj* unreasonably irritable or peevish [Latin *petulans* bold] **> petulance** *n* **> petulantly** *adv*

petunia *n* a tropical American plant with pink, white, or purple funnel-shaped flowers [obsolete French *petun* variety of tobacco]

Petworth House *n* a mansion in Petworth in Sussex: rebuilt (1688–96) for Charles Seymour, 6th Duke of Somerset; gardens laid out by Capability Brown; subject of paintings by Turner

Pevsner *n* **1** Antoine. 1886–1962, French constructivist sculptor and painter, born in Russia; brother of Naum Gabo **2** Sir Nikolaus. 1902–83, British architectural historian, born in Germany: his series *Buildings of England* (1951–74) describes every structure of account in the country

pew *n* **1a** (in a church) a long benchlike seat with a back, used by the congregation **b** (in a church) an enclosed compartment reserved for the use of a family or group **2 take a pew** take a seat [Greek *pous* foot]

pewter *n* **1** an alloy containing tin, lead, and sometimes copper and antimony **2** dishes or kitchen utensils made from pewter [Old French *peaultre*]

pfennig (fen-ig) *n* a former German monetary unit worth one hundredth of a mark [German: penny]

Pforzheim *n* a city in SW Germany, in W Baden-Württemberg: centre of the German watch and jewellery industry. Pop: 119 046 (2003 est)

PG indicating a film certified for viewing by anyone, but which contains scenes that may be unsuitable for children, for whom parental guidance is necessary

Pg. **1** Portugal **2** Portuguese

pH *n* potential of hydrogen; a measure of the acidity or alkalinity of a solution

Phaedrus *n* ?15 BC–?50 AD, Roman author of five books of Latin verse fables, based chiefly on Aesop

phaeton (fate-on) *n* a light four-wheeled horse-drawn carriage with or without a top [from French, after *Phaethōn*, character in Greek myth]

phagocyte (fag-go-site) *n* a cell or protozoan that engulfs particles, such as microorganisms [Greek *phagein* to eat + *kutos* vessel]

phalanger *n* an Australian marsupial with dense fur and a long tail [Greek *phalangion* spider's web, referring to its webbed hind toes]

phalanx (fal-lanks) *n*, *pl* **phalanxes** *or* **phalanges** (fal-**lan**-jeez) **1** any closely grouped mass of people: *a solid phalanx of reporters and photographers* **2** a number of people united for a common purpose **3** an ancient Greek battle formation of infantry in close ranks [Greek]

phallic *adj* of or resembling a phallus: *a phallic symbol*

phallus (fal-luss) *n*, *pl* **-luses** *or* **-li** (-lie) **1** same as **penis** **2** an image of the penis as a symbol of reproductive power [Greek *phallos*]

phantasm *n* **1** a phantom **2** an unreal vision; illusion [Greek *phantasma*] **> phantasmal** *adj*

phantasmagoria *n* a shifting medley of dreamlike figures [probably from French *fantasmagorie* production of phantoms] **> phantasmagoric** *adj*

phantasy *n*, *pl* **-sies** archaic same as **fantasy**

phantom *n* **1** an apparition or spectre **2** the visible representation of something abstract, such as in a dream or hallucination: *the phantom of liberty* ▷ *adj* **3** deceptive or unreal: *she regularly took days off for what her bosses considered phantom illnesses* [Greek *phantasma*]

Pharaoh (fare-oh) *n* the title of the ancient Egyptian kings [Egyptian *pr-ʾo* great house]

Pharisee *n* **1** a member of an ancient Jewish sect

teaching strict observance of Jewish traditions **2** (*often not cap*) a self-righteous or hypocritical person [Hebrew *pārūsh* separated] **> Pharisaic** *adj*

pharmaceutical *adj* of or relating to drugs or pharmacy

pharmaceutics *n* same as **pharmacy** (1)

pharmacist *n* a person qualified to prepare and dispense drugs

pharmacology *n* the science or study of drugs **> pharmacological** *adj* **> pharmacologist** *n*

pharmacopoeia (far-ma-koh-**pee**-a) *n* an authoritative book containing a list of medicinal drugs along with their uses, preparation and dosages [Greek *pharmakopoiia* art of preparing drugs]

pharmacy *n* **1** the preparation and dispensing of drugs **2** (*pl* **-cies**) a dispensary [Greek *pharmakon* drug]

Pharsalus *n* an ancient town in Thessaly in N Greece. Several major battles were fought nearby, including Caesar's victory over Pompey (48 BC)

pharyngitis (far-rin-**jite**-iss) *n* inflammation of the pharynx, causing a sore throat

pharynx (far-rinks) *n*, *pl* **pharynges** (far-**rin**-jeez) *or* **pharynxes** the part of the alimentary canal between the mouth and the oesophagus [Greek *pharunx* throat] **> pharyngeal** *adj*

phase *n* **1** any distinct or characteristic stage in a sequence of events: *these two CDs sum up two distinct phases in the singer's career* **2** astronomy one of the recurring shapes of the portion of the moon, Mercury, or Venus illuminated by the sun **3** physics a particular stage in a periodic process or phenomenon **4** physics **in** or **out of phase** (of two waves or signals) reaching or not reaching corresponding phases at the same time ▷ *vb* **phasing, phased 5** to do or introduce gradually: *the redundancies will be phased over two years* ▶ See also **phase in, phase out** [Greek *phasis* aspect]

phase in *vb* to introduce in a gradual or cautious manner: *the scheme was phased in over seven years*

phase out *vb* to discontinue gradually: *rent subsidies are being phased out*

PhD Doctor of Philosophy

pheasant *n* a long-tailed bird with a brightly coloured plumage in the male: native to Asia but introduced elsewhere [Latin *phasianus*]

Pheidippides *or* **Phidippides** *n* 5th century BC. Athenian athlete, who ran to Sparta to seek help against the Persians before the Battle of Marathon (490 BC)

Phelps *n* Michael (Fred). born 1985, US swimmer, who won a record eighteen gold medals at three Olympic Games: six in 2004, eight in 2008, and four in 2012

phenobarbitone *or* **phenobarbital** *n* a sedative used to treat insomnia and epilepsy

phenol *n* a white crystalline derivative of benzene, used as an antiseptic and disinfectant and in the manufacture of resins, explosives, and pharmaceutical substances [Greek *phaino-* shining; because originally prepared from illuminating gas]

phenomena *n* a plural of **phenomenon**

phenomenal *adj* **1** extraordinary or outstanding: *a phenomenal success* **2** of or relating to a phenomenon **> phenomenally** *adv*

phenomenalism *n* philosophy the doctrine that all knowledge comes from sense perception **> phenomenalist** *n*, *adj*

phenomenon *n*, *pl* **-ena** *or* **-enons 1** anything that can be perceived as an occurrence or fact **2** any remarkable occurrence or person [Greek *phainomenon*, from *phainesthai* to appear]

USAGE Although *phenomena* is often treated as if it were singular, correct usage is to employ *phenomenon* with a singular construction and *phenomena* with a plural: *that is an interesting phenomenon* (not *phenomena*); *several new phenomena were recorded in his notes.*

phenotype *n* the physical form of an organism as determined by the interaction of its genetic make-up and its environment

phenyl (fee-nile) *adj* of, containing, or consisting of the monovalent group C_6H_5, derived from benzene: *a phenyl group*

phew *interj* an exclamation of relief, surprise, disbelief, or weariness

phial *n* a small bottle for liquid medicine [Greek *phialē* wide shallow vessel]

Phidias *n* 5th century BC, Greek sculptor, regarded as one of the greatest of sculptors. He executed the sculptures of the Parthenon and the colossal statue of Zeus at Olympia, one of the Seven Wonders of the World: neither survives in the original ⊳ **Phidian** *adj*

phil. **1** philharmonic **2** philosophy

Philadelphia *n* a city and port in SE Pennsylvania, at the confluence of the Delaware and Schuylkill Rivers: the fourth largest city in the US; founded by Quakers in 1682; cultural and financial centre of the American colonies and the federal capital (1790–1800); scene of the Continental Congresses (1774–83) and the signing of the Declaration of Independence (1776). Pop: 1 479 339 (2003 est)

philadelphus *n* a shrub grown for its strongly scented showy flowers [Greek *philadelphon*, literally: loving one's brother]

Philae *n* an island in Upper Egypt, in the Nile north of the Aswan Dam: of religious importance in ancient times; almost submerged since the raising of the level of the dam

philander *vb* (of a man) to flirt or have many casual love affairs with women [Greek *philandros* fond of men, used as a name for a lover in literary works] ⊳ **philanderer** *n* ⊳ **philandering** *adj, n*

philanthropy *n, pl* **-pies** **1** the practice of helping people less well-off than oneself **2** love of mankind in general [Greek *philanthrōpia* love of mankind] ⊳ **philanthropic** *adj* ⊳ **philanthropist** *n*

philately (fill-lat-a-lee) *n* the collection and study of postage stamps [Greek *philos* loving + *ateleia* exemption from tax] ⊳ **philatelist** *n*

Philby *n* **1** Harold Adrian Russell, known as *Kim*. 1912–88, English double agent; defected to the Soviet Union (1963) in his father, H(arry) Saint John (Bridger). 1885–1960, British explorer, civil servant, and Arabist

philharmonic *adj* **1** fond of music ⊳ *n* **2** a specific choir, orchestra, or musical society: *the Vienna Philharmonic* [French *philharmonique*]

Philip *n* **1** *New Testament* **a** one of the twelve apostles of Jesus **b** Also: **Philip the Evangelist** one of the seven deacons appointed by the early Church **c** Also: **Philip the Tetrarch** one of the sons of Herod the Great, who was ruler of part of former Judaea (4 BC–34 AD) (Luke 3:1) **2** King, American Indian name *Metacomet*. died 1676, American Indian chief, the son of Massasoit. He waged King Philip's War against the colonists of New England (1675–76) and was killed in battle **3** Prince. another name for the (Duke of) Edinburgh

Philip I *n* **1** known as *Philip the Handsome*. 1478–1506, king of Castile (1506); father of Emperor Charles V and founder of the Hapsburg dynasty in Spain **2** title of Philip II of Spain as king of Portugal

Philip II *n* **1** 382–336 BC, king of Macedonia (359–336); the father of Alexander the Great **2** known as *Philip Augustus*. 1165–1223, Capetian king of France (1180–1223); set out on the Third Crusade with Richard I of England (1190) **3** 1527–98, king of Spain (1556–98) and, as Philip I, king of Portugal (1580–98); the husband of Mary I of England (1554–58). He championed the Counter-Reformation, sending the Armada against England (1588)

Philip IV *n* known as *Philip the Fair*. 1268–1314, king of France (1285–1314): he challenged the power of the papacy, obtaining the elevation of Clement V as pope

residing at Avignon (the beginning of the Babylonian captivity of the papacy)

Philip V *n* 1683–1746, king of Spain (1700–46) and founder of the Bourbon dynasty in Spain. His accession began the War of Spanish Succession (1701–13)

Philip VI *n* 1293–1350, first Valois king of France (1328–50). Edward III of England claimed his throne, which with other disputes led to the beginning of the Hundred Years' War (1337)

Philippe *n* full name *Philippe Léopold Louis Marie*. born 1960, king of Belgium from 2013

Philippeville *n* the former name of **Skikda**

Philippi *n* an ancient city in NE Macedonia: scene of the victory of Antony and Octavian over Brutus and Cassius (42 BC)

Philippian *adj* **1** of or relating to Philippi ⊳ *n* **2** a native or inhabitant of Philippi

philippic *n* a bitter verbal attack [after the orations of Demosthenes against Philip of Macedon]

Philippine *adj, n* same as **Filipino**

Philippines *n* Republic of the Philippines (*functioning as sing*) a republic in SE Asia, occupying an archipelago of about 7100 islands (including Luzon, Mindanao, Samar, and Negros): became a Spanish colony in 1571 but ceded to the US in 1898 after the Spanish-American War; gained independence in 1946. The islands are generally mountainous and volcanic. Official languages: Filipino, based on Tagalog, and English. Religion: Roman Catholic majority. Currency: peso. Capital: Manila. Pop: 105 720 644 (2013 est). Area: 300 076 sq km (115 860 sq miles). Related word: **Filipino**

Philippine Sea *n* part of the NW Pacific Ocean, east and north of the Philippines

Philippopolis *n* transliteration of the Greek name for Plovdiv

Philip the Bold *n* 1342–1404, duke of Burgundy (1363–1404), noted for his courage at Poitiers (1356) in the Hundred Years' War: regent of France for his nephew Charles VI (1368–88, 1392–1404)

Philip the Good *n* 1396–1467, duke of Burgundy (1419–67), under whose rule Burgundy was one of the most powerful states in Europe

Philip the Magnanimous *n* 1504–67, German prince; landgrave of Hesse (1509–67). He helped to crush (1525) the Peasants' Revolt and formed (1531) the League of Schmalkaden, an alliance of German Protestant rulers

Philistia *n* an ancient region on the coast of SW Palestine

Philistian *adj* of or relating to Philistia or its inhabitants

philistine *n* **1** a person who is hostile towards culture and the arts ⊳ *adj* **2** boorishly uncultured ⊳ **philistinism** *n*

Philistine *n* a member of the non-Semitic people who inhabited ancient Palestine

Phillip *n* Arthur. 1738–1814, English naval commander; captain general of the First Fleet, which carried convicts from Portsmouth to Sydney Cove, Australia, where he founded New South Wales

Phillips *n* Captain Mark. born 1948, English three-day-event horseman; married to Anne, the Princess Royal, divorced 1992

Philo Judaeus *n* ?20 BC–?50 AD, Jewish philosopher, born in Alexandria. He sought to reconcile Judaism with Greek philosophy

philology *n* the science of the structure and development of languages [Greek *philologia* love of language] ⊳ **philological** *adj* ⊳ **philologist** *n*

philosopher *n* **1** a person who studies philosophy **2** a person who remains calm and stoical in the face of difficulties or disappointments

philosopher's stone *n* a substance thought by alchemists to be capable of changing base metals into gold

philosophical *or* **philosophic** *adj* **1** of or relating to philosophy or philosophers **2** calm and stoical in the face of difficulties or disappointments **>** **philosophically** *adv*

philosophize *or* **-phise** *vb* **-phizing, -phized** *or* **-phising, -phised** to discuss in a philosophical manner **>** **philosophizer** *or* **-phiser** *n*

philosophy *n, pl* **-phies** **1** the academic study of knowledge, thought, and the meaning of life **2** the particular doctrines of a specific individual or school relating to these issues: *the philosophy of John Locke* **3** any system of beliefs or values **4** a personal outlook or viewpoint [Greek *philosophia* love of wisdom]

philtre *or US* **philter** *n* a drink supposed to arouse desire [Greek *philtron* love potion]

phishing *n* the practice of using fraudulent e-mails and copies of legitimate websites to extract financial data from computer users for criminal purposes

Phiz *n* real name *Hablot Knight Browne.* 1815–82, English painter, noted for his illustrations for Dickens' novels

phlebitis (fleb-bite-iss) *n* inflammation of a vein, usually in the legs [Greek *phleps* vein] **>** **phlebitic** *adj*

phlegm (flem) *n* **1** the thick yellowish substance secreted by the walls of the respiratory tract **2** apathy or stolidity **3** calmness [Greek *phlegma*] **>** **phlegmy** *adj*

phlegmatic (fleg-mat-ik) *adj* having an unemotional disposition

phloem (flow-em) *n botany* the plant tissue that acts as a path for the distribution of food substances to all parts of the plant [Greek *phloos* bark]

phlox *n, pl* **phlox** *or* **phloxes** a plant with clusters of white, red, or purple flowers [Greek, literally: flame]

Phnom Penh *or* **Pnom Penh** *n* the capital of Cambodia, a port in the south at the confluence of the Mekong and Tonle Sap Rivers: capital of the country since 1865; university (1960). Pop: 1 174 000 (2005 est). Official transliteration: Phnum Pêhn

phobia *n psychiatry* an intense and irrational fear of a given situation or thing [Greek *phobos* fear] **>** **phobic** *adj, n*

Phocaea *n* an ancient port in Asia Minor, the northernmost of Ionian cities on the W coast of Asia Minor: an important maritime state (about 1000–600BC)

Phocis *n* an ancient district of central Greece, on the Gulf of Corinth: site of the Delphic oracle

Phoenicia *n* an ancient maritime country extending from the Mediterranean Sea to the Lebanon Mountains, now occupied by the coastal regions of Lebanon and parts of Syria and Israel: consisted of a group of city-states, at their height between about 1200 and 1000 BC, that were leading traders of the ancient world

Phoenician (fon-nee-shun) *adj* **1** of or relating to Phoenicia or its inhabitants ▷ *n* **2** a native or inhabitant of Phoenicia

phoenix *n* a legendary Arabian bird said to set fire to itself and rise anew from the ashes every 500 years [Greek *phoinix*]

Phoenix *n* a city in central Arizona, capital city of the state, on the Salt River. Pop: 1 388 416 (2003 est)

Phoenix Islands *pl n* a group of eight coral islands in the central Pacific: administratively part of Kiribati. Area: 28 sq km (11 sq miles). The islands and surrounding waters form the Phoenix Islands Protected Area, the world's largest marine protected area. Area: 410 500 sq km (158 500 sq miles)

Phomvihane *n* Kaysone. 1920–92, Laotian Communist statesman; prime minister of Laos (1975–91); president (1991–92)

phone *n, vb* **phoning, phoned** short for **telephone**

phonecard *n* a card used instead of coins to operate certain public telephones

phone-in *n* a radio or television programme in which telephone questions or comments from the public are broadcast live as part of a discussion

phoneme *n linguistics* one of the set of speech sounds in any given language that serve to distinguish one word from another [Greek *phōnēma* sound, speech] **>** **phonemic** *adj*

phonemics *n* the classification and analysis of the phonemes of a language

phonetic *adj* **1** of phonetics **2** denoting any perceptible distinction between one speech sound and another **3** conforming to pronunciation: *phonetic spelling* [Greek *phōnein* to make sounds, speak] **>** **phonetically** *adv*

phonetics *n* the study of speech processes, including the production, perception, and analysis of speech sounds

phoney *or especially US* **phony** *informal adj* **-nier, -niest** **1** not genuine: *a phoney Belgian 50-franc coin* **2** (of a person) insincere or pretentious ▷ *n, pl* **-neys** *or especially US* **-nies** **3** an insincere or pretentious person **4** something that is not genuine [origin unknown]

phonograph *n* **1** an early form of record player capable of recording and reproducing sound on wax cylinders **2** *US and Canad* a record player [Greek *phōnē* sound + *graphein* to write]

phonology *n, pl* **-gies** **1** the study of the sound system in a language **2** such a sound system [Greek *phōnē* sound, voice + -LOGY] **>** **phonological** *adj*

phooey *interj informal* an exclamation of scorn or contempt [probably variant of *phew*]

phosgene (foz-jean) *n* a poisonous gas used in warfare [Greek *phōs* light + -*genēs* born]

phosphate *n* **1** any salt or ester of any phosphoric acid **2** (*often pl*) chemical fertilizer containing phosphorous compounds **>** **phosphatic** *adj*

phosphor *n* a substance capable of emitting light when irradiated with particles of electromagnetic radiation [Greek *phōsphoros* phosphorus]

phosphoresce *vb* **-rescing, -resced** to exhibit phosphorescence

phosphorescence *n* **1** *physics* a fluorescence that persists after the bombarding radiation producing it has stopped **2** the light emitted in phosphorescence **>** **phosphorescent** *adj*

phosphoric *adj* of or containing phosphorus in the pentavalent state

phosphorous *adj* of or containing phosphorus in the trivalent state

phosphorus *n chem* a toxic flammable nonmetallic element which appears luminous in the dark. It exists in two forms, white and red. Symbol: P [Greek *phōsphoros* light-bringing]

photo *n, pl* **-tos** short for **photograph**

photo- *combining form* **1** of or produced by light: *photosynthesis* **2** indicating a photographic process: *photolithography* [Greek *phōs, phōt-* light]

photobomb *vb* to intrude into the background of a photograph without the subject's knowledge

photocell *n* a cell which produces a current or voltage when exposed to light or other electromagnetic radiation

photocopier *n* a machine using light-sensitive photographic materials to reproduce written, printed, or graphic work

photocopy *n, pl* **-copies** **1** a photographic reproduction of written, printed, or graphic work ▷ *vb* **-copies, -copying, -copied** **2** to reproduce on photographic material

photoelectric *adj* of or concerned with electric or electronic effects caused by light or other electromagnetic radiation **>** **photoelectricity** *n*

photoengraving *n* **1** a photomechanical process for producing letterpress printing plates **2** a print made from such a plate **>** **photoengrave** *vb*

photo finish *n* a finish of a race in which contestants are so close that a photograph is needed to decide the result

Photofit n trademark a picture of someone wanted by the police which has been made by combining photographs of different facial features resembling those of the wanted person

photoflash n same as **flashbulb**

photoflood n a highly incandescent electric lamp used for indoor photography and television

photogenic adj **1** (esp. of a person) always looking attractive in photographs **2** biology producing or emitting light

photograph n **1** a picture made by the chemical action of light on sensitive film ▷ vb **2** to take a photograph of

photographic adj **1** of or like photography or a photograph **2** (of a person's memory) able to retain facts or appearances in precise detail **> photographically** adv

photography n **1** the process of recording images on sensitized material by the action of light **2** the practice of taking photographs **> photographer** n

photogravure n a process in which an etched metal plate for printing is produced by photography [PHOTO- + French gravure engraving]

photolithography n a lithographic printing process using photographically made plates **> photolithographer** n

photometer (foe-**tom**-it-er) n an instrument used to measure the intensity of light

photometry (foe-**tom**-it-tree) n the branch of physics concerned with the measurement of the intensity of light **> photometrist** n

photomontage (foe-toe-mon-**tahzh**) n **1** the combination of several photographs to produce one picture **2** a picture produced in this way

photon n physics a quantum of electromagnetic radiation energy, such as light, having both particle and wave behaviour

photosensitive adj sensitive to electromagnetic radiation, esp. light

Photoshop n **1** trademark a software application for managing and editing digital images ▷ vb **2** informal to alter (a digital image) using Photoshop or a similar application

photostat n **1** a type of photocopying machine or process **2** any copy made by such a machine ▷ vb **-statting, -statted** or **-stating, -stated 3** to make a photostat copy (of)

photosynthesis n (in plants) the process by which a green plant uses sunlight to build up carbohydrate reserves **> photosynthesize** or **-sise** vb **> photosynthetic** adj

phototropism (foe-toe-**trope**-iz-zum) n the growth of plants towards a source of light [PHOTO- + Greek tropos turn] **> phototropic** adj

phrasal verb n a phrase that consists of a verb plus an adverb or preposition, esp. one whose meaning cannot be deduced from its parts, such as take in meaning deceive

phrase n **1** a group of words forming a unit of meaning in a sentence **2** an idiomatic or original expression **3** music a small group of notes forming a coherent unit of melody ▷ vb **phrasing, phrased 4** to express orally or in a phrase: I could have phrased that better **5** music to divide (a melodic line or part) into musical phrases, esp. in performance [Greek phrasis speech] **> phrasal** adj

phrase book n a book containing frequently used expressions and their equivalent in a foreign language

phraseology n, pl **-gies** the manner in which words or phrases are used

phrasing n **1** the exact words used to say or write something **2** the way in which someone who is performing a piece of music or reading aloud divides up the work being performed by pausing slightly in appropriate places

phrenology n (formerly) the study of the shape and size of the skull as a means of finding out a person's character and mental ability [Greek phrēn mind + -LOGY]

> phrenological adj **> phrenologist** n

Phrygia n an ancient country of W central Asia Minor

Phryne n real name Muesarete. 4th century BC, Greek courtesan; lover of Praxiteles and model for Apelles' painting Aphrodite Rising from the Waves

Phuket n **1** an island and province of S Thailand, in the Andaman Sea: mainly flat; suffered badly in the Indian Ocean tsunami of December 2004. Area: 534 sq km (206 sq miles) **2** the chief town of the island of Phuket; a popular tourist resort

phut informal n **1** a representation of a muffled explosive sound ▷ adv **2 go phut** to break down or collapse [imitative]

Phyfe or **Fife** n Duncan. ?1768–1854, US cabinet-maker, born in Scotland

phylactery n, pl **-teries** Judaism either of the pair of square cases containing biblical passages, worn by Jewish men on the left arm and head during weekday morning prayers [Greek phulaktērion safeguard]

phylum n, pl **-la** biology one of the major groups into which the animal and plant kingdoms are divided, containing one or more classes [Greek phulon race]

physical adj **1** of the body, as distinguished from the mind or spirit **2** of material things or nature: the physical world **3** of or concerned with matter and energy **4** of or relating to physics **> physically** adv

physical education n training and practice in sports and gymnastics

physical geography n the branch of geography that deals with the natural features of the earth's surface

physical jerks pl n Brit and Austral informal repetitive keep-fit exercises

physical science n any of the sciences concerned with nonliving matter, such as physics, chemistry, astronomy, and geology

physician n **1** a medical doctor **2** archaic a healer [Greek phusis nature]

physicist n a person versed in or studying physics

physics n **1** the branch of science concerned with the properties of matter and energy and the relationships between them **2** physical properties of behaviour: the physics of the electron [translation of Greek ta phusika natural things]

physio n **1** short for **physiotherapy 2** (pl **physios**) short for **physiotherapist**

physiognomy (fiz-ee-on-om-ee) n **1** a person's face considered as an indication of personality **2** the outward appearance of something: the changed physiognomy of the forests [Greek phusis nature + gnōmōn judge]

physiography n same as **physical geography** [Greek phusis nature + -GRAPHY]

physiology n **1** the branch of science concerned with the functioning of organisms **2** the processes and functions of all or part of an organism [Greek phusis nature + -LOGY] **> physiologist** n **> physiological** adj

physiotherapy n the treatment of disease or injury by physical means, such as massage or exercises, rather than by drugs [physio- (prefix) physical + therapy] **> physiotherapist** n

physique n person's bodily build and muscular development [French]

pi n, pl **pis 1** the 16th letter in the Greek alphabet (Π, π) **2** maths a number that is the ratio of the circumference of a circle to its diameter; approximate value: 3.141592.... Symbol: π

PI 1 Philippine Islands **2** private investigator

Piacenza n a town in N Italy, in Emilia-Romagna on the River Po. Pop: 95 594 (2001). Latin name: Placentia

Piaf n Edith, real name Edith Giovanna Gassion, known as the Little Sparrow, 1915–63, French singer

Piaget n Jean. 1896–1980, Swiss psychologist, noted for his work on the development of the cognitive functions in children

pianissimo *adj, adv music* to be performed very quietly [Italian]

pianist *n* a person who plays the piano

piano[1] *n, pl* **-anos** a musical instrument played by depressing keys that cause hammers to strike strings and produce audible vibrations [short for *pianoforte*]

piano[2] *adj, adv music* to be performed softly [Italian]

Piano *n* Renzo. born 1937, Italian architect; buildings include the Pompidou Centre, Paris (1977; with Richard Rogers), the Potsdamer Platz redevelopment, Berlin (1998), and The Shard, London (2012)

piano accordion *n* an accordion in which the right hand plays a piano-like keyboard ▷ **piano accordionist** *n*

pianoforte (pee-ann-oh-**for**-tee) *n* the full name for **piano**[1] [Italian *piano e forte* soft and loud]

Pianola (pee-an-oh-la) *n trademark* a type of mechanical piano, the music for which is encoded in perforations in a paper roll

Piauí *n* a state of NE Brazil, on the Atlantic: rises to a semiarid plateau, with the more humid Paranaíba valley in the west. Capital: Teresina. Pop: 2 898 223 (2002). Area: 250 934 sq km (96 886 sq miles)

Piave *n* a river in NE Italy, rising near the border with Austria and flowing south and southeast to the Adriatic: the main line of Italian defence during World War I. Length: 220 km (137 miles)

piazza *n* **1** a large open square in an Italian town **2** *chiefly Brit* a covered passageway or gallery [Italian: marketplace]

pibroch (pee-brok) *n* a form of music for Scottish bagpipes, consisting of a theme and variations [Gaelic *piobaireachd*]

pic *n, pl* **pics** *or* **pix** *informal* a photograph or illustration

pica (pie-ka) *n* **1** a size of printer's type giving six lines to the inch **2** a size of typewriter type that has ten characters to the inch [Latin *pica* magpie; sense connection obscure]

Picabia *n* Francis. 1879–1953, French painter, designer, and writer, associated with the cubist, Dadaist, and surrealist movements

picador *n bullfighting* a horseman who wounds the bull with a lance to weaken it [Spanish]

Picard *n* Jean. 1620–82, French astronomer. He was the first to make a precise measurement of a longitude line, enabling him to estimate the earth's radius

Picardy *n* a region of N France: mostly low-lying; scene of heavy fighting in World War I. French name: **Picardie**

picaresque *adj* of or relating to a type of fiction in which the hero, a rogue, goes through a series of episodic adventures [Spanish *pícaro* a rogue]

Picasso *n* Pablo. 1881–1973, Spanish painter and sculptor, resident in France: a highly influential figure in 20th-century art and a founder, with Braque, of cubism. A prolific artist, his works include *The Dwarf Dancer* (1901), belonging to his blue period; the first cubist painting *Les Demoiselles d'Avignon* (1907); *Three Dancers* (1925), which appeared in the first surrealist exhibition; and *Guernica* (1937), inspired by an event in the Spanish Civil War

picayune (pick-a-yoon) *US and Canad informal adj* **1** of small value or importance **2** mean or petty ▷ *n* **3** any coin of little value, such as a five-cent piece **4** an unimportant person or thing [French *picaillon* coin from Piedmont]

Piccadilly *n* one of the main streets of London, running from Piccadilly Circus to Hyde Park Corner

piccalilli *n* a pickle of mixed vegetables in a mustard sauce [origin unknown]

piccanin *n S African offensive* a Black African child [variant of *piccaninny*]

piccaninny *or especially US* **pickaninny** *n, pl* **-nies** *offensive* a small Black or Aboriginal child [perhaps from Portuguese *pequenino* tiny one]

Piccard *n* **1** Auguste. 1884–1962, Swiss physicist, whose study of cosmic rays led to his pioneer balloon ascents in the stratosphere (1931–32) **2** his twin brother, **Jean Félix**. 1884–1963, US chemist and aeronautical engineer, born in Switzerland, noted for his balloon ascent into the stratosphere (1934)

piccolo *n, pl* **-los** a woodwind instrument an octave higher than the flute [Italian: small]

pick[1] *vb* **1** to choose or select **2** to gather (fruit, berries, or crops) from (a tree, bush, or field) **3** to remove loose particles from: *she picked some bits of fluff off her sleeve* **4** (foll. by *at*) to nibble (at) without appetite **5** to provoke (an argument or fight) deliberately **6** to separate (strands or fibres), as in weaving **7** to steal from (someone's pocket) **8** to open (a lock) with an instrument other than a key **9** to make (one's way) carefully on foot: *they picked their way through the rubble* **10 pick and choose** to select fastidiously or fussily ▷ *n* **11** choice: *take your pick* **12** the best: *the pick of the country's young cricketers* ▶ See also **pick off**, **pick on**, etc. [Middle English *piken*]

pick[2] *n* **1** a tool with a handle and a long curved steel head, used for loosening soil or breaking rocks **2** any tool used for picking, such as an ice pick or toothpick **3** a plectrum ▷ *vb* **4** to pierce or break up (a hard surface) with a pick [perhaps a variant of PIKE[2]]

pickaback *n, adv, adj* same as **piggyback**

pickaxe *or US* **pickax** *n* a large pick

Pickering *n* **1** Edward Charles. 1846–1919, US astronomer, who invented the meridian photometer **2** his brother, **William Henry**. 1858–1938, US astronomer, who discovered Phoebe, the ninth satellite of Saturn, and predicted (1919) the existence and position of Pluto

picket *n* **1** a person or group standing outside a workplace to dissuade strikebreakers from entering **2** a small unit of troops posted to give early warning of attack **3** a pointed stake that is driven into the ground to support a fence ▷ *vb* **-eting, -eted 4** to act as pickets outside (a workplace) [Old French *piquer* to prick]

picket fence *n* a fence consisting of pickets driven into the ground

picket line *n* a line of people acting as pickets

Pickford *n* Mary, real name *Gladys Mary Smith*. 1893–1979, US actress in silent films, born in Canada

pickings *pl n* money or profits acquired easily

pickle *n* **1** (*often pl*) food, esp. vegetables preserved in vinegar or brine **2** a liquid or marinade, such as spiced vinegar, for preserving vegetables, meat, or fish **3** *informal* an awkward or difficult situation: *to be in a pickle; they are in a pickle over what to do with toxic waste* ▷ *vb* **-ling, -led 4** to preserve or treat in a pickling liquid [probably Middle Dutch *pekel*]

pickled *adj* **1** (of food) preserved in a pickling liquid **2** *informal* drunk

pick-me-up *n informal* a tonic, esp. a special drink taken as a stimulant

pick off *vb* to aim at and shoot (people or things) one by one

pick on *vb* to continually treat someone unfairly

pick out *vb* **1** to select for use or special consideration: *she picked out a wide gold wedding ring* **2** to distinguish (an object from its surroundings), such as in painting: *the wall panels are light brown, with their edges picked out in gold* **3** to recognize (a person or thing): *the culprit was picked out at a police identification parade* **4** to play (a tune) tentatively, as by ear

pickpocket *n* a person who steals from the pockets of others in public places

pick up *vb* **1** to lift or raise: *he picked up his glass* **2** to obtain or purchase: *a couple of pictures she had picked up in a flea market in Paris* **3** to improve in health or condition: *the tourist trade has picked up after the slump caused by the Gulf War* **4** to learn as one goes along: *she had a good ear and picked up languages quickly* **5** to raise (oneself) after a fall or setback: *she picked herself up and got on with her life* **6** to resume; return to **7** to accept the responsibility for paying (a bill) **8** to collect or give a lift to (passengers or goods) **9** *informal* to become acquainted with for a sexual purpose **10** *informal* to arrest **11** to receive (sounds or signals)

pick-up *n* **1** a small truck with an open body used for light deliveries **2** *informal* a casual acquaintance made for a sexual purpose **3** *informal* **a** a stop to collect passengers or goods **b** the people or things collected **4** a device which converts vibrations into electrical signals, such as that to which a record player stylus is attached

picky *adj* **pickier, pickiest** *informal* fussy; finicky

picnic *n* **1** an excursion on which people bring food to be eaten in the open air **2** an informal meal eaten out-of-doors **3 no picnic** *informal* a hard or disagreeable task ▷ *vb* **-nicking, -nicked 4** to eat or take part in a picnic [French *piquenique*] ❭ **picnicker** *n*

pico- *combining form* denoting 10⁻¹²: *picofarad* [Spanish *pico* small quantity]

Pico de Aneto *n* See Aneto

Pico della Mirandola *n* Count Giovanni. 1463–94, Italian Platonist philosopher. His attempt to reconcile the ideas of classical, Christian, and Arabic writers in a collection of 900 theses, prefaced by his *Oration on the Dignity of Man* (1486), was condemned by the pope

Pico de Teide *n* See Teide

picot (peek-oh) *n* any of a pattern of small loops, for example on lace

Pict *n* a member of any of the peoples who lived in N Britain in the first to the fourth centuries AD [Late Latin *Picti* painted men] ❭ **Pictish** *adj*

pictograph *n* **1** a picture or symbol standing for a word or group of words, as in written Chinese **2** Also called: **pictogram** a chart on which symbols are used to represent values [Latin *pingere* to paint] ❭ **pictographic** *adj*

pictorial *adj* **1** relating to or expressed by pictures ▷ *n* **2** a periodical containing many pictures [Latin *pingere* to paint]

picture *n* **1** a visual representation produced on a surface, such as in a photograph or painting **2** a mental image: *neither had any clear picture of whom they were looking for* **3** a description or account of a situation considered as an observable scene: *the reports do not provide an accurate picture of the spread of AIDS* **4** a person or thing resembling another: *he is the picture of a perfect host* **5** a person or scene typifying a particular state: *his face was a picture of dejection* **6** the image on a television screen **7** a cinema film **8 in the picture** informed about a situation **9 the pictures** a cinema or film show ▷ *vb* **-turing, -tured 10** to visualize or imagine **11** to describe or depict vividly: *a documentary that had pictured the police as good-natured dolts* **12** to put in a picture or make a picture of: *the women pictured above are all the same age* [Latin *pingere* to paint]

picture rail *n* the rail near the top of a wall from which pictures are hung

picturesque *adj* **1** visually pleasing, as in being striking or quaint: *a small picturesque harbour* **2** (of language) graphic or vivid [French *pittoresque*]

picture window *n* a large window with a single pane of glass, usually facing a view

piddle *vb* **-dling, -dled** *informal* **1** to urinate **2 piddle about** *or* **around** *or* **away** to spend (one's time) aimlessly: *we have been piddling around for seven months* [origin unknown]

piddling *adj informal* petty or trivial: *piddling amounts of money*

pidgin *n* a language made up of elements of two or more languages and used between the speakers of the languages involved [supposed Chinese pronunciation of *business*]

pidgin English *n* a pidgin in which one of the languages involved is English

pie *n* **1** a sweet or savoury filling baked in pastry **2 pie in the sky** illusory hope or promise of some future good [origin unknown]

piebald *adj* **1** marked in two colours, esp. black and

white ▷ *n* **2** a black-and-white horse [dialect *pie* magpie + BALD]

piece *n* **1** a separate bit or part **2** an instance or occurrence: *a piece of luck* **3** an example or specimen of a style or type: *each piece of furniture is crafted from native red pine by traditional methods* **4** a literary, musical, or artistic composition **5** a coin: *a fifty-pence piece* **6** a firearm or cannon **7** a small object used in playing various games: *a chess piece* **8 go to pieces** (of a person) to lose control of oneself; have a breakdown ▷ *vb* **piecing, pieced 9** (often foll. by *together*) to fit or assemble bit by bit **10** (often foll. by *up*) to patch or make up (a garment) by adding pieces [Middle English *pece*]

pièce de résistance (pyess de ray-zeest-onss) *n* the most outstanding item in a series [French]

piece goods *pl n* goods, esp. fabrics, made in standard widths and lengths

piecemeal *adv* **1** bit by bit; gradually ▷ *adj* **2** fragmentary or unsystematic: *a piecemeal approach* [Middle English *pece* piece + *-mele* a measure]

piece of eight *n, pl* **pieces of eight** a former Spanish coin worth eight reals

piecework *n* work paid for according to the quantity produced

pie chart *n* a circular graph divided into sectors proportional to the sizes of the quantities represented

pied *adj* having markings of two or more colours [dialect *pie* magpie]

pied-à-terre (pyay-da-tair) *n, pl* **pieds-à-terre** (pyay-da-tair) a flat or other lodging for occasional use [French, literally: foot on (the) ground]

Piedmont *n* **1** a region of NW Italy: consists of the upper Po Valley; mainly agricultural. Chief town: Turin. Pop: 4 231 334 (2003 est). Area: 25 399 sq km (9807 sq miles). Italian name: **Piemonte 2** a low plateau of the eastern US, between the coastal plain and the Appalachian Mountains

pie-eyed *adj slang* drunk

Piemonte *n* the Italian name for **Piedmont** (1)

Pienaar *n* (Jacobus) François. born 1967, South African Rugby Union footballer; captain of the South African team that won the Rugby World Cup in 1995

pier *n* **1** a structure with a deck that is built out over water and used as a landing place or promenade **2** a pillar or support that bears heavy loads **3** the part of a wall between two adjacent openings [Middle English *per*]

pierce *vb* **piercing, pierced 1** to make a hole in (something) with a sharp point **2** to force (a way) through (something) **3** (of light) to shine through (darkness) **4** (of sounds or cries) to sound sharply through (the silence) **5** to penetrate: *the cold pierced the air* [Old French *percer*] ❭ **piercing** *adj*

Pierce *n* Franklin. 1804–69, US statesman; 14th president of the US (1853–57)

pier glass *n* a tall narrow mirror, designed to hang on the wall between windows

Pieria *n* a region of ancient Macedonia, west of the Gulf of Salonika

Pierian *adj* **1** of or relating to the Muses or artistic or poetic inspiration **2** of or relating to Pieria

Piero della Francesca *n* ?1420–92, Italian painter, noted particularly for his frescoes of the *Legend of the True Cross* in San Francesco, Arezzo

Piero di Cosimo *n* 1462–1521, Italian painter, noted for his mythological works

Pierre *n* a city in central South Dakota, capital of the state, on the Missouri River. Pop: 13 939 (2003 est)

Pierrot (pier-roe) *n* a male character from French pantomime with a whitened face, white costume, and pointed hat

Pietermaritzburg *n* a city in E South Africa, the capital of KwaZulu-Natal: founded in 1839 by the Boers: gateway to Natal's mountain resorts. Pop: 223 519 (2001)

P

pietism *n* exaggerated piety

Pietro da Cortona *n* real name *Pietro Berrettini*. 1596–1669, Italian baroque painter and architect

piety *n, pl* **-ties** **1** dutiful devotion to God and observance of religious principles **2** the quality of being pious **3** a pious action or saying [Latin *pietas*]

piezoelectric effect (pie-eez-oh-ill-ek-trik) *or* **piezoelectricity** *n physics* **a** the production of electricity by applying a mechanical stress to certain crystals **b** the converse effect in which stress is produced in a crystal as a result of an applied voltage [Greek *piezein* to press]

piffle *n informal* nonsense [origin unknown]

piffling *adj informal* worthless; trivial

pig *n* **1** a mammal with a long head, a snout, and bristle-covered skin, which is kept and killed for pork, ham, and bacon. Related adjective: **porcine** **2** *informal* a dirty, greedy, or bad-mannered person **3** *offensive, slang* a policeman **4** a mass of metal cast into a simple shape **5** *Brit informal* something that is difficult or unpleasant: *the coast is a pig for little boats* **6 a pig in a poke** something bought or received without previous sight or knowledge **7 make a pig of oneself** *informal* to overeat ▷ *vb* **pigging, pigged** **8** (of a sow) to give birth **9** (often foll. by *out*) *slang* to eat greedily or to excess: *she had pigged out on pizza before the show* [Middle English *pigge*]

pigeon¹ *n* **1** a bird which has a heavy body, small head, and short legs, and is usually grey in colour **2** *slang* a victim or dupe [Old French *pijon* young dove]

pigeon² *n informal* concern or responsibility: *this is our pigeon – there's nothing to keep you* [from *pidgin*]

pigeonhole *n* **1** a small compartment, such as in a bureau, for filing papers ▷ *vb* **-holing, -holed** **2** to classify or categorize **3** to put aside

pigeon-toed *adj* with the toes or feet turned inwards

piggery *n, pl* **-geries** a place where pigs are kept

piggish *adj* **1** like a pig in appetite or manners **2** stubborn ▷ **piggishness** *n*

Piggott *n* Lester (**Keith**). born 1935, English flat-racing jockey: won 30 English classic races, including the Derby nine times; champion jockey eleven times, his first in 1960 and his last in 1982

piggy *n, pl* **-gies** **1** a child's word for a pig ▷ *adj* **-gier, -giest** **2** same as **piggish**

piggyback *or* **pickaback** *n* **1** a ride on the back and shoulders of another person ▷ *adv, adj* **2** on the back and shoulders of another person

piggy bank *n* a child's bank shaped like a pig with a slot for coins

pig-headed *adj* stupidly stubborn

pig iron *n* crude iron produced in a blast furnace and poured into moulds

Pig Island *n NZ informal* New Zealand

piglet *n* a young pig

pigment *n* **1** any substance which gives colour to paint or dye **2** a substance which occurs in plant or animal tissue and produces a characteristic colour [Latin *pigmentum*] ▷ **pigmentary** *adj*

pigmentation *n* colouring in plants, animals, or humans, caused by the presence of pigments

Pigmy *n, pl* **-mies** same as **Pygmy**

Pigs *n* See Bay of Pigs

pigskin *n* **1** the skin of the domestic pig **2** leather made of this skin **3** *US and Canad informal* a football

pigsty *or US and Canad* **pigpen** *n, pl* **-sties** **1** a pen for pigs **2** an untidy place

pigswill *n* waste food or other edible matter fed to pigs

pigtail *n* a plait of hair or one of two plaits on either side of the face

pike¹ *n, pl* **pike** *or* **pikes** a large predatory freshwater fish with a broad flat snout, strong teeth, and a long body covered with small scales [Old English *pīc* point, from the shape of its jaw]

pike² *n* a medieval weapon consisting of a metal spearhead on a long pole [Old English *pīc* point] ▷ **pikeman** *n*

pikelet *n Brit, Austral and NZ* a small thick pancake

piker *n Austral and NZ slang* shirker

Pikes Peak *n* a mountain in central Colorado, in the Rockies. Height: 4300 m (14 109 ft)

pikestaff *n* **1** the wooden handle of a pike **2 plain as a pikestaff** very obvious or noticeable

pikey *n Brit slang, disparaging* **1** a gypsy or vagrant **2** a member of the underclass

pilaster *n* a shallow rectangular column attached to the face of a wall [Latin *pila* pillar] ▷ **pilastered** *adj*

Pilate *n* Pontius. Roman procurator of Judaea (?26–?36 AD), who ordered the crucifixion of Jesus, allegedly against his better judgment

Pilatus *n* a mountain in central Switzerland, in Unterwalden canton: derives its name from the legend that the body of Pontius Pilate lay in a former lake on the mountain. Height: 2122 m (6962 ft)

pilau *or* **pilaf** *n* a Middle Eastern dish, consisting of rice flavoured with spices and cooked in stock, to which meat, poultry, or fish may be added [Turkish *pilāw*]

pilchard *n* a small edible sea fish of the herring family, with a rounded body covered with large scales [origin unknown]

Pilcomayo *n* a river in S central South America, rising in W central Bolivia and flowing southeast, forming the border between Argentina and Paraguay, to the Paraguay River at Asunción. Length: about 1600 km (1000 miles)

pile¹ *n* **1** a collection of objects laid on top of one another **2** *informal* a large amount: *boxing has made him a pile of money*; *I've got piles of work to do* **3** same as **pyre** **4** a large building or group of buildings **5** *physics* a nuclear reactor ▷ *vb* **piling, piled** **6** (foll. by *in, into, off, out*, etc.) to move in a group, often in a hurried manner: *the crew piled into the van* **7 pile it on** *informal* to exaggerate ▶ See also **pile up** [Latin *pila* stone pier]

pile² *n* a long heavy beam driven into the ground as a foundation for a structure [Latin *pilum*]

pile³ *n* the fibres in a fabric that stand up or out from the weave, such as in carpeting or velvet [Latin *pilus* hair]

pile-driver *n* a machine that drives piles into the ground

piles *pl n* swollen veins in the rectum; haemorrhoids [Latin *pilae* balls]

pile up *vb* **1** to gather or be gathered in a pile ▷ *n* **pile-up** **2** *informal* a traffic accident involving several vehicles

pilfer *vb* to steal (minor items) in small quantities [Old French *pelfre* booty]

pilgrim *n* **1** a person who journeys to a holy place **2** any wayfarer [Latin *peregrinus* foreign]

pilgrimage *n* **1 a** a journey to a shrine or other holy place **2** a journey or long search made for sentimental reasons: *a sentimental pilgrimage to the poet's birthplace*

Pilgrim Fathers *pl n* the English Puritans who founded Plymouth Colony in SE Massachusetts (1620)

Pílion *n* transliteration of the Modern Greek name for Pelion

pill *n* **1** a small mass of medicine intended to be swallowed whole **2 the pill** *informal* an oral contraceptive taken by a woman **3** something unpleasant that must be endured: *her reinstatement was a bitter pill to swallow*; *the pill was sweetened by a reduction in interest* [Latin *pilula* a little ball]

pillage *vb* **-laging, -laged** **1** to steal property violently, often in war ▷ *n* **2** the act of pillaging **3** something obtained by pillaging; booty [Old French *piller* to despoil]

pillar *n* **1** an upright support of stone, brick, or metal; column **2** something resembling this: *a pillar of smoke* **3** a prominent supporter or member: *a pillar of society* **4 from pillar to post** from one place to another [Latin *pila*]

pillar box *n* (in Britain) a red pillar-shaped public letter box situated in the street

Pillars of Hercules *pl n* the two promontories at the E end of the Strait of Gibraltar: the Rock of Gibraltar on the European side and the Jebel Musa on the African side; according to legend, formed by Hercules

pillbox *n* **1** a box for pills **2** a small enclosed fort of reinforced concrete **3** a small round hat

pillion *n* **1** a seat for a passenger behind the rider of a motorcycle or horse ▷ *adv* **2** on a pillion: *the motorbike on which he was riding pillion* [from Gaelic]

pillock *n Brit slang* a stupid or annoying person [Scandinavian dialect *pillicock* penis]

pillory *n, pl* **-ries 1** (formerly) a wooden frame in which offenders were locked by the neck and wrists and exposed to public abuse and ridicule ▷ *vb* **-ries, -rying, -ried 2** to expose to public ridicule **3** to punish by putting in a pillory [Old French *pilori*]

pillow *n* **1** a cloth bag stuffed with feathers, polyester fibre, or pieces of foam rubber used to support the head in bed ▷ *vb* **2** to rest (one's head) on or as if on a pillow: *he pillowed his head in her lap* [Old English *pylwe*]

pillowcase *or* **pillowslip** *n* a removable washable cover for a pillow

Pílos *n* transliteration of the Modern Greek name for Pylos

pilot *n* **1** a person who is qualified to fly an aircraft or spacecraft **2** a person employed to steer a ship into or out of a port **3** a person who acts as a guide ▷ *adj* **4** serving as a test or trial: *a pilot scheme* **5** serving as a guide: *a pilot beacon* ▷ *vb* **-loting, -loted 6** to act as pilot of **7** to guide or lead (a project or people): *the legislation was piloted through its committee stage* [French *pilote*]

pilot light *n* a small flame that lights the main burner of a gas appliance

pilot officer *n* the most junior commissioned rank in certain air forces

Pilsen *n* the German name for **Plzeň**

Piłsudski *n* Józef. 1867–1935, Polish nationalist leader and statesman; president (1918–21) and premier (1926–28; 1930)

pimento *n, pl* **-tos** same as **allspice**, **pimiento**

pimiento (pim-yen-toe) *n, pl* **-tos** a Spanish pepper with a red fruit used as a vegetable [Spanish *pimiento* pepper plant]

pimp *n* **1** a man who obtains customers for a prostitute, in return for a share of his or her earnings ▷ *vb* **2** to act as a pimp [origin unknown]

pimpernel *n* a plant, such as the scarlet pimpernel, typically having small star-shaped flowers [Old French *pimpernelle*]

pimple *n* a small swollen infected spot on the skin [Middle English] **> pimpled** *adj* **> pimply** *adj*

pimp up *or* **pimp out** *vb informal* to make (someone or something, esp. a car) more extravagantly decorated, as with flashy accessories, etc. **> pimped-up** *or* **pimped-out** *adj*

pin *n* **1** a short stiff straight piece of wire with a pointed end and a rounded head: used mainly for fastening **2** short for **cotter pin, hairpin, rolling pin, safety pin 3** a wooden or metal peg **4** a pin-shaped brooch **5** (in various bowling games) a club-shaped wooden object set up in groups as a target **6** a clip that prevents a hand grenade from exploding until it is removed or released **7** *golf* the flagpole marking the hole on a green **8** *informal* a leg ▷ *vb* **pinning, pinned 9** to fasten with a pin or pins **10** to seize and hold fast: *they pinned his arms behind his back* **11** **pin something on someone** *informal* to place the blame for something on someone: *corruption charges are the easiest to pin on former dictators* **▶** See also **pin down** [Old English *pinn*]

PIN Personal Identity Number: a code number used in conjunction with a bank card to enable an account holder to use certain computerized systems, such as cash dispensers

pinafore *n* **1** *chiefly Brit* an apron with a bib **2** a dress with

a sleeveless bodice or bib top, worn over a jumper or blouse [pin + *afore* in front]

Pinar del Río *n* a city in W Cuba: tobacco industry. Pop: 158 000 (2005 est)

pinball *n* an electrically operated table game in which the player shoots a small ball through several hazards

pince-nez (panss-nay) *n, pl* **pince-nez** glasses that are held in place only by means of a clip over the bridge of the nose [French, literally: pinch-nose]

pincers *pl n* **1** a gripping tool consisting of two hinged arms and curved jaws **2** the jointed grasping arms of crabs and lobsters [Old French *pincier* to pinch]

pinch *vb* **1** to squeeze (something, esp. flesh) between a finger and thumb **2** to squeeze by being too tight: *shoes that pinch* **3** to cause stinging pain to: *the cold pinched his face* **4** to make thin or drawn-looking, such as from grief or cold **5** *informal* to steal **6** *informal* to arrest **7** (usually foll. by *out* or *back*) to remove the tips of (a plant shoot) to correct or encourage growth ▷ *n* **8** a squeeze or sustained nip **9** the quantity that can be taken up between a thumb and finger: *a pinch of ground ginger* **10** extreme stress or need: *most companies are feeling the pinch of recession* **11** **at a pinch** if absolutely necessary **12** **feel the pinch** to be forced to economize [probably from Old French]

pinchbeck *n* **1** an alloy of copper and zinc, used as imitation gold ▷ *adj* **2** sham or cheap [after C. *Pinchbeck*, watchmaker who invented the alloy]

Pinckney *n* **1** Charles. 1757–1824, US statesman, who was a leading member of the convention that framed the US Constitution (1787) **2** his cousin, **Charles Cotesworth**. 1746–1825, US soldier, statesman, and diplomat, who also served at the Constitutional Convention **3** his brother, **Thomas**. 1750–1828, US soldier and politician. He was US minister to Britain (1792–96) and special envoy to Spain (1795–96)

Pincus *n* Gregory Goodwin. 1903–67, US physiologist, whose work on steroid hormones led to the development of the first contraceptive pill

pincushion *n* a small cushion in which pins are stuck ready for use

pindan *n* **1** a desert region of Western Australia **2** the vegetation growing in this region [from a native Australian language]

Pindar *n* ?518–?438 BC, Greek lyric poet, noted for his *Epinikia*, odes commemorating victories in the Greek games

pin down *vb* **1** to force (someone) to make a decision or carry out a promise **2** to define clearly: *the courts have found it difficult to pin down what exactly obscenity is*

Pindus *n* a mountain range in central Greece between Epirus and Thessaly. Highest peak: Mount Smólikas, 2633 m (8639 ft). Modern Greek name: **Píndhos**

pine¹ *n* **1** an evergreen tree with long needle-shaped leaves and brown cones **2** the light-coloured wood of this tree [Latin *pinus*]

pine² *vb* **pining, pined 1** (often foll. by *for*) to feel great longing (for) **2** (often foll. by *away*) to become ill or thin through grief or longing [Old English *pīnian* to torture]

Pine *n* Courtney. born 1964, British jazz saxophonist and clarinettist

pineal gland *or* **pineal body** (pin-ee-al) *n* a small cone-shaped gland at the base of the brain [Latin *pinea* pine cone]

pineapple *n* a large tropical fruit with juicy flesh and a thick hard skin [Middle English *pinappel* pine cone]

pine cone *n* the woody seed case of a pine tree

pine marten *n* a mammal of N European and Asian coniferous woods, with dark brown fur and a creamy-yellow patch on the throat

Pinero *n* Sir Arthur Wing. 1855–1934, English dramatist. His works include the farce *Dandy Dick* (1887) and the problem play *The Second Mrs Tanqueray* (1893)

Pines *n* Isle of Pines the former name of the (Isle of) **Youth**

ping n 1 a short high-pitched sound, such as of a bullet striking metal ▷ vb 2 to make such a noise [imitative]

pinger n a device that makes a pinging sound, esp. a timer

Ping-Pong n trademark same as **table tennis**

pinhead n 1 the head of a pin 2 informal a stupid person > **pinheaded** adj

pinhole n a small hole made with or as if with a pin

pinion¹ n 1 chiefly poetic a bird's wing 2 the outer part of a bird's wing including the flight feathers ▷ vb 3 to immobilize (someone) by holding or tying his or her arms 4 to confine [Latin pinna wing]

pinion² n a cogwheel that engages with a larger wheel or rack [French pignon]

Piniós n transliteration of the Modern Greek name for the **Salambria**

pink¹ n 1 a colour between red and white 2 anything pink, such as pink paint or pink clothing: packaged in pink 3 a garden plant with pink, red, or white fragrant flowers 4 **in the pink** in good health ▷ adj 5 of a colour between red and white 6 informal having mild left-wing sympathies 7 informal relating to homosexuals or homosexuality: the pink vote ▷ vb 8 same as **knock** (7) [origin unknown] > **pinkish** or **pinky** adj

pink² vb to cut with pinking shears [perhaps from Low German]

Pinkerton n Allan. 1819–84, US private detective, born in Scotland. He founded the first detective agency in the US (1850) and organized an intelligence system for the Federal States of America (1861)

Pink Floyd n British rock group, formed in 1966: originally comprised Syd Barrett (1946–2006), Roger Waters (born 1944), Rick Wright (1945–2008), and Nick Mason (born 1945); Barrett was replaced by Dave Gilmour (born 1944) in 1968 and Waters left in 1986. Recordings include The Piper at the Gates of Dawn (1967), Dark Side of the Moon (1973), Wish You Were Here (1975), and The Wall (1979)

pinkie or **pinky** n, pl -ies Scot, US, Canad and NZ the little finger [Dutch pinkje]

pinking shears pl n scissors with a serrated edge that give a wavy edge to material cut and so prevent fraying

pin money n a small amount of extra money earned to buy small luxuries

pinna n anatomy the external part of the ear

pinnace n a ship's boat [French pinace]

pinnacle n 1 the highest point of fame or success 2 a towering peak of a mountain 3 a slender spire [Latin pinna wing]

pinnate adj botany (of compound leaves) having leaflets growing opposite each other in pairs [Latin pinna feather]

pinny n, pl -nies an informal or child's name for **pinafore** (1)

Pinochet or **Pinochet Ugarte** n Augusto. 1915–2006, Chilean general and statesman; president of Chile (1974–90) following his overthrow of Allende (1973): charged (2001) with murder and kidnapping but found unfit to stand trial

pinotage (pin-oh-tazh) n a red wine blended from the Pinot Noir and Hermitage grapes that is unique to South Africa

pinpoint vb 1 to locate or identify exactly: we've pinpointed the fault ▷ adj 2 exact: pinpoint accuracy

pinprick n a small irritation or annoyance

pins and needles n informal a tingling sensation in a part of the body

Pinsent n Sir Matthew (Clive). born 1970, British oarsman; won four gold medals in rowing events at consecutive Olympic Games (1992, 1996, 2000, and 2004)

Pinsk n a city in SW Belarus: capital of a principality (13th–14th centuries). Pop: 134 000 (2005 est)

pinstripe n (in textiles) a very narrow stripe in fabric or the fabric itself

pint n 1 Brit a unit of liquid measure equal to one eighth of an imperial gallon (0.568 litre) 2 US a unit of liquid measure equal to one eighth of a US gallon (0.473 litre) 3 Brit informal a pint of beer [Old French pinte]

pinta n Brit informal a pint of milk [phonetic rendering of pint of]

pintail n, pl -tails or -tail a greyish-brown duck with a pointed tail

Pinter n Harold. 1930–2008, English dramatist. His plays, such as The Caretaker (1959), The Homecoming (1964), No Man's Land (1974), Moonlight (1993), and Celebration (2000), are noted for their equivocal and halting dialogue: Nobel prize for literature 2005 > **Pinteresque** adj

pintle n a pin or bolt forming the pivot of a hinge [Old English pintel penis]

pinto US and Canad adj 1 marked with patches of white; piebald ▷ n, pl -tos 2 a pinto horse [American Spanish]

pint-size or **pint-sized** adj informal very small

pin tuck n a narrow, ornamental fold used on shirt fronts and dress bodices

Pinturicchio or **Pintoricchio** n real name Bernardino di Betto. ?1454–1513, Italian painter of the Umbrian school

pin-up n 1 informal a picture of a sexually attractive person, often partially or totally undressed 2 slang a person who has appeared in such a picture: your favourite pin-up 3 a photograph of a famous personality

pinwheel n same as **Catherine wheel**

Pinyin n a system of spelling used to represent Chinese in Roman letters

Pinzón n 1 Martín Alonzo. ?1440–93, Spanish navigator, who commanded the Pinta on Columbus' first expedition (1492–93), which he abandoned in a vain attempt to be the first to arrive back in Spain 2 his brother, **Vicente Yáñez**. ?1460–?1524, Spanish navigator, who commanded the Niña on Columbus' first expedition (1492–93)

pion or **pi meson** n physics any of three subatomic particles which are classified as mesons

pioneer n 1 an explorer or settler of a new land or region 2 an originator or developer of something new ▷ vb 3 to be a pioneer (in or of) 4 to initiate or develop: the new technique was pioneered in France [Old French paonier infantryman]

pious adj 1 religious or devout 2 insincerely reverent; sanctimonious [Latin pius] > **piousness** n

pip¹ n the seed of a fleshy fruit, such as an apple or pear [short for pippin]

pip² n 1 a short high-pitched sound used as a time signal on radio 2 any of the spots on a playing card, dice, or domino 3 informal the emblem worn on the shoulder by junior officers in the British Army, indicating their rank [imitative]

pip³ n 1 a contagious disease of poultry 2 facetious, slang a minor human ailment 3 **get** or **have the pip** NZ slang to sulk 4 **give someone the pip** Brit, NZ and S African slang to annoy someone: it really gives me the pip [Middle Dutch pippe]

pip⁴ vb **pipping, pipped pip someone at the post** Brit and NZ slang to defeat someone whose success seems certain [probably from PIP²]

pipe n 1 a a long tube for conveying water, oil, or gas 2 a a tube with a small bowl at the end for smoking tobacco b the amount of tobacco that fills the bowl of a pipe 3 zoology, botany any of various hollow organs, such as the respiratory passage of certain animals 4 a a tubular instrument in which air vibrates and produces a musical sound b any of the tubular devices on an organ 5 a boatswain's whistle 6 **put that in your pipe and smoke it** informal accept that fact if you can 7 **the pipes** See **bagpipes** ▷ vb **piping, piped 8** to play (music) on a pipe 9 to summon or lead by a pipe: to pipe in the haggis 10 a to signal orders to (the crew) by a boatswain's pipe b to signal the arrival or departure of: he piped his entire ship's company on deck 11 to utter in a shrill tone 12 to convey (water, oil, or gas) by pipe **13** to force cream or icing through a shaped nozzle to decorate food ▸ See also **pipe down, pipe up** [Old English *pīpe*]

pipeclay *n* a fine white pure clay, used in tobacco pipes and pottery and to whiten leather and similar materials

pipe cleaner *n* a short length of wire covered with tiny tufts of yarn: used to clean the stem of a tobacco pipe

piped music *n* light music played as background music in public places

pipe down *vb informal* to stop talking or making noise

pipe dream *n* a fanciful or impossible plan or hope [alluding to dreams produced by smoking an opium pipe]

pipeline *n* **1** a long pipe for transporting oil, water, or gas **2** a means of communication **3 in the pipeline** in preparation

pipe organ *n* same as **organ** (2a)

piper *n* a person who plays a pipe or bagpipes

Piper *n* John. 1903–92, British artist. An official war artist in World War II, he is known esp. for his watercolours of bombed churches and his stained glass in Coventry Cathedral

pipette *n* a slender glass tube for transferring or measuring out liquids [French: little pipe]

pipe up *vb* to speak up unexpectedly

pipi *n*, *pl* **pipi** *or* **pipis** *Austral and NZ* an edible mollusc of Australia and New Zealand [Māori]

piping *n* **1** a system of pipes **2** a string of icing or cream used to decorate cakes and desserts **3** a thin strip of covered cord or material, used to edge hems or cushions **4** the sound of a pipe or bagpipes **5** a shrill voice or whistling sound: *a dove's cool piping* ▷ *adj* **6** making a shrill sound ▷ *adv* **7 piping hot** extremely hot

pipistrelle *n* a type of small brownish bat found throughout the world [Italian *pipistrello*]

pipit *n* a small songbird with a brownish speckled plumage and a long tail [probably imitative]

pippin *n* a type of eating apple [Old French *pepin*]

pipsqueak *n informal* an insignificant or contemptible person

piquant (pee-kant) *adj* **1** having a spicy taste **2** stimulating to the mind: *love was a forbidden piquant secret* [French, literally: prickling] ▸ **piquancy** *n*

pique (peek) *n* **1** a feeling of resentment or irritation, such as from hurt pride ▷ *vb* **piquing, piqued** **2** to hurt (someone's) pride **3** to excite (curiosity or interest) [French *piquer* to prick]

piqué (pee-kay) *n* a stiff ribbed fabric of cotton, silk, or spun rayon [French: pricked]

piquet (pik-ket) *n* a card game for two people played with a reduced pack [French]

piracy *n*, *pl* **-cies** **1** *Brit and NZ* robbery on the seas **2** a crime, such as hijacking, committed aboard a ship or aircraft **3** the unauthorized use of patented or copyrighted material

Piraeus *or* **Peiraeus** *n* a port in SE Greece, adjoining Athens: the country's chief port; founded in the 5th century BC as the port of Athens. Pop (municipality): 181 933 (2001). Modern Greek name: **Piraiévs**

Pirandello *n* Luigi. 1867–1936, Italian short-story writer, novelist, and dramatist. His plays include *Right you are (If you think so)* (1917), *Six Characters in Search of an Author* (1921), and *Henry IV* (1922): Nobel prize for literature 1934

Piranesi *n* Giambattista. 1720–78, Italian etcher and architect: etchings include *Imaginary Prisons* and *Views of Rome*

piranha *n* a small fierce freshwater fish of tropical America, with strong jaws and sharp teeth [S American Indian: fish with teeth]

pirate *n* **1** a person who commits piracy **2** a vessel used by pirates **3** a person who illegally sells or publishes someone else's literary or artistic work **4** a person or group of people who broadcast illegally ▷ *vb* **-rating, -rated 5** to sell or reproduce (artistic work, ideas, etc.) illegally [Greek *peira* an attack] ▸ **piratical** *adj*

piri-piri *n* a hot sauce, of Portuguese colonial origin, made from red chilli peppers [from a Bantu language: pepper]

pirouette *n* **1** a body spin performed on the toes or the ball of the foot ▷ *vb* **-etting, -etted 2** to perform a pirouette [French]

Pisa *n* a city in Tuscany, NW Italy, near the mouth of the River Arno: flourishing maritime republic (11th–12th centuries), contains a university (1343), a cathedral (1063), and the Leaning Tower (begun in 1174 and about 5 m (17 ft) from perpendicular); tourism. Pop: 89 694 (2001)

Pisanello *n* Antonio. ?1395–?1455, Italian painter and medallist; a major exponent of the International Gothic style. He is best known for his portrait medals and drawings of animals

Pisano *n* **1 Andrea**, real name *Andrea de Pontedera*. ?1290–1348, Italian sculptor and architect, noted for his bronze reliefs on the door of the baptistry in Florence **2 Giovanni**, ?1250–?1320, Italian sculptor, who successfully integrated classical and Gothic elements in his sculptures, esp. in his pulpit in St Andrea, Pistoia **3** his father, **Nicola**, ?1220–?84, Italian sculptor, who pioneered the classical style and is often regarded as a precursor of the Italian Renaissance: noted esp. for his pulpit in the baptistry of Pisa Cathedral

piscatorial *adj formal* of or relating to fish, fishing, or fishermen [Latin *piscatorius*]

Pisces *n astrol* the twelfth sign of the zodiac; the Fishes [Latin]

pisciculture (piss-ee-cult-cher) *n formal* the rearing and breeding of fish under controlled conditions [Latin *piscis* fish]

piscine (piss-sign) *adj* of or resembling a fish [Latin *piscis* fish]

Pishpek *n* a variant transliteration of the Kyrgyz name for **Bishkek**

Pisistratus *n* ?600–527 BC, tyrant of Athens: he established himself in firm control of the city following his defeat of his aristocratic rivals at Pallene (546)

piss *taboo vb* **1** to urinate **2** to discharge as or in one's urine: *to piss blood* ▷ *n* **3** an act of urinating **4** urine **5 take the piss** to make fun of mock someone ▸ See also **piss down, piss off** [probably imitative]

pissant *US disparaging, slang n* **1** an insignificant or contemptible person ▷ *adj* **2** insignificant or contemptible [from PISS + ANT]

Pissarro *n* Camille. 1830–1903, French impressionist painter, esp. of landscapes

piss down *vb taboo, slang* to rain heavily

pissed *adj slang* **1** *Brit, Austral, S African and NZ* drunk **2** *US and Canad* angry

piss off *vb taboo, slang* **1** to annoy or disappoint **2** to go away: often used to dismiss a person

pistachio *n*, *pl* **-chios** a Mediterranean nut with a hard shell and an edible green kernel [Persian *pistah*]

piste (peest) *n* a slope or course for skiing [French]

pistil *n* the seed-bearing part of a flower [Latin *pistillum* pestle]

pistillate *adj botany* (of plants) having pistils

Pistoia *n* a city in N Italy, in N Tuscany: scene of the defeat and death of Catiline in 62 BC Pop: 84 274 (2001)

pistol *n* a short-barrelled handgun [Czech *pišt'ala*]

pistol-whip *vb* **-whipping, -whipped** *US* to beat or strike with a pistol barrel

piston *n* a cylindrical part that slides to and fro in a hollow cylinder: in an engine it is attached by a rod to other parts, thus its movement causes the other parts to move [Old Italian *pistone*]

Pistorius *n* Oscar (**Leonard Carl**), born 1986, South African sprinter in races for below-the-knee amputees; winner of six Paralympic gold medals (2004–2012); found guilty for the manslaughter of his girlfriend Reeva Steenkamp (1983–2013)

pit¹ *n* **1** a large deep opening in the ground **2** a coal mine **3** *anatomy* **a** a small natural depression on the surface of a body or organ **b** the floor of any natural bodily cavity: *the pit of the stomach* **4** *pathol* a pockmark **5** a concealed danger or difficulty **6** an area at the side of a motor-racing track for servicing or refuelling vehicles **7** the area occupied by the orchestra in a theatre **8** an enclosure for fighting animals or birds **9** the back of the ground floor of a theatre **10** same as **pitfall** (2) **11 the pit hell** ▷ *vb* **pitting, pitted 12** (often foll. by *against*) to match in opposition, esp. as antagonists: *sister pitted against sister* **13** to mark with small dents or scars **14** to place or bury in a pit **15 pit one's wits against** to compete against in a test or contest ▸ See also **pits** [Old English *pytt*]

pit² *chiefly US and Canad n* **1** the stone of various fruits ▷ *vb* **pitting, pitted 2** to remove the stone from (a fruit) [Dutch: kernel]

pitapat *adv* **1** with quick light taps ▷ *n* **2** such taps [imitative]

pit bull terrier *n* a strong muscular terrier with a short coat

Pitcairn Island *n* an island in the S Pacific: forms with the islands of Ducie, Henderson and Oeno (all uninhabited) a UK Overseas Territory; Pitcairn itself was uninhabited until the landing in 1790 of the mutineers of H.M.S. *Bounty* and their Tahitian companions. Capital: Adamstown. Pop: 48 (2012 est). Area: 4.6 sq km (1.75 sq miles)

pitch¹ *vb* **1** to hurl or throw **2** to set up (a tent or camp) **3** to slope or fall forwards or downwards: *she pitched forwards like a diver* **4** (of a ship or plane) to dip and raise its back and front alternately **5** to set the level or tone of: *his ambitions were pitched too high* **6** to aim to sell (a product) to a specified market or on a specified basis **7** *music* to sing or play (a note or interval) accurately ▷ *n* **8** *chiefly Brit* (in many sports) the field of play **9** a level of emotion: *children can wind their parents up to a pitch of anger and guilt* **10** the degree or angle of slope **11** the distance between corresponding points or adjacent threads on a screw thread **12** the pitching motion of a ship or plane **13** *music* the highness or lowness of a note in relation to other notes: *low pitch* **14** the act or manner of pitching a ball **15** *chiefly Brit* the place where a street or market trader regularly sells **16** *slang* a persuasive sales talk, esp. one routinely repeated ▸ See also **pitch in, pitch into** [Middle English *picchen*]

pitch² *n* **1** a thick sticky substance formed from coal tar and used for paving or waterproofing **2** any similar substance, such as asphalt, occurring as a natural deposit ▷ *vb* **3** to apply pitch to [Old English *pic*]

pitch-black *adj* extremely dark; unlit: *it was a wild night, pitch-black, with howling gales*

pitchblende *n* a blackish mineral which is the principal source of uranium and radium [German *Pechblende*]

pitch-dark *adj* extremely or completely dark

pitched battle *n* a fierce fight

pitcher¹ *n* a large jug, usually rounded with a narrow neck [Old French *pichier*]

pitcher² *n baseball* the player on the fielding team who throws the ball to the batter

pitcher plant *n* a plant with pitcher-like leaves that attract and trap insects, which are then digested

pitchfork *n* **1** a long-handled fork with two or three long curved prongs for tossing hay ▷ *vb* **2** to use a pitchfork on (something)

pitch in *vb* to cooperate or contribute

pitch into *vb informal* to attack (someone) physically or verbally

Pitch Lake *n* a deposit of natural asphalt in the Caribbean, in SW Trinidad. Area: 46 hectares (114 acres)

pitch pine *n* a pine tree of North America: a source of turpentine and pitch

pitch pipe *n* a small pipe that sounds a note to establish the correct starting note for unaccompanied singing

piteous *adj* arousing or deserving pity: *the piteous mewing of an injured kitten* ❯ **piteousness** *n*

pitfall *n* **1** an unsuspected difficulty or danger **2** a trap in the form of a concealed pit, designed to catch men or wild animals [Old English *pytt* + *fealle* trap]

pith *n* **1** the soft white lining inside the rind of fruits such as the orange **2** the essential part: *policy, though, isn't the pith of what happened yesterday* **3** the soft spongy tissue in the centre of the stem of certain plants [Old English *pitha*]

pithead *n* the top of a mine shaft and the buildings and hoisting gear around it

pith helmet *n* a lightweight hat made of the pith of the sola, an E Indian swamp plant, that is worn for protection from the sun

pithy *adj* **pithier, pithiest 1** terse and full of meaning **2** of, resembling, or full of pith ❯ **pithiness** *n*

pitiable *adj* arousing or deserving pity or contempt ❯ **pitiableness** *n*

pitiful *adj* arousing or deserving great pity or contempt ❯ **pitifully** *adv* ❯ **pitifulness** *n*

pitiless *adj* feeling no pity or mercy ❯ **pitilessly** *adv*

Pitman *n* Sir **Isaac**. 1813–97, English inventor of a system of phonetic shorthand (1837)

piton (**peet**-on) *n mountaineering* a metal spike that may be driven into a crack and used to secure a rope [French]

pits *pl n* **the pits** *slang* the worst possible person, place, or thing [perhaps from *armpits*]

pit stop *n* **1** *motor racing* brief stop made at a pit by a racing car for repairs, refuelling, etc. **2** *informal* any stop made during a car journey for refreshment, rest, or refuelling

Pitt *n* **1** (**William**) **Brad(ley)**, born 1963, US actor; his films include *Thelma and Louise* (1991), *Interview with the Vampire* (1994), *Fight Club* (1999), *Babel* (2006), and *Moneyball* (2011) **2 William**, known as *Pitt the Elder*, 1st Earl of Chatham. 1708–78, British statesman. He was first minister (1756–57; 1757–61; 1766–68) and achieved British victory in the Seven Years' War (1756–63) **3** his son **William**, known as *Pitt the Younger*. 1759–1806, British statesman. As prime minister (1783–1801; 1804–06), he carried through important fiscal and tariff reforms. From 1793, his attention was focused on the wars with revolutionary and Napoleonic France

pitta bread *or* **pitta** *n* a flat rounded slightly leavened bread, originally from the Middle East [Modern Greek *pitta* a cake]

pittance *n* a very small amount of money [Old French *pietance* ration]

pitter-patter *n* **1** the sound of light rapid taps or pats, such as of rain drops ▷ *vb* **2** to make such a sound

Pitt-Rivers *n* **Augustus** (**Henry Lane Fox**). 1827–1900, British archaeologist; first inspector of ancient monuments (1882): assembled a major anthropological collection of tools and weapons (now in the **Pitt-Rivers Museum**, Oxford)

Pittsburgh *n* a port in SW Pennsylvania, at the confluence of the Allegheny and Monongahela Rivers, which form the Ohio River: settled around Fort Pitt in 1758; developed rapidly with the discovery of iron deposits and one of the world's richest coalfields; the largest river port in the US and an important industrial centre, formerly with large steel mills. Pop: 325 337 (2003 est)

pituitary *or* **pituitary gland** *n* the gland at the base of the brain which secretes hormones that affect skeletal growth, development of the sex glands, and other functions of the body [Late Latin *pituitarius* slimy]

pity *n, pl* **pities 1** sorrow felt for the sufferings of others **2** a cause of regret: *it's a great pity he did not live longer* **3 have** or **take pity on** to have sympathy or show mercy for ▷ *vb* **pities, pitying, pitied 4** to feel pity for [Latin *pietas* duty] ❯ **pitying** *adj*

Piura *n* a city in NW Peru: the oldest colonial city in Peru, founded by Pizarro in 1532; commercial centre of an agricultural district. Pop: 357 000 (2005 est)

Pius II *n* pen name *Aeneas Silvius*, original name *Enea Silvio de' Piccolomini*. 1405–64, Italian ecclesiastic, humanist, poet, and historian; pope (1458–64)

Pius IV *n* original name *Giovanni Angelo de' Medici*. 1499–1565, pope (1559–65). He reconvened the Council of Trent (1562), confirming its final decrees

Pius V *n* Saint. original name *Michele Ghislieri*. 1504–72, Italian ecclesiastic; pope (1566–72). He attempted to enforce the reforms decreed by the Council of Trent, excommunicated Elizabeth I of England (1570), and organized the alliance that defeated the Turks at Lepanto (1571). Feast day: 30 April

Pius VI *n* original name *Giovanni Angelico Braschi*. 1717–99, Italian ecclesiastic; pope (1775–99). He opposed French attempts to limit papal authority and denounced (1791) the French Revolution: he died a prisoner of the French in the Revolutionary Wars

Pius VII *n* original name *Luigi Barnaba Chiaramonti*. 1740–1823, Italian ecclesiastic; pope (1800–23). He concluded a concordat with Napoleon (1801) and consecrated him as emperor of France (1804), but resisted his annexation of the Papal States (1809)

Pius IX *n* original name *Giovanni Maria Mastai-Ferretti*. 1792–1878, Italian ecclesiastic; pope (1846–78). He refused to recognize the incorporation of Rome and the Papal States in the kingdom of Italy, confining himself to the Vatican after 1870. He decreed the dogma of the Immaculate Conception (1854) and convened the Vatican Council, which laid down the doctrine of papal infallibility (1870)

Pius X *n* Saint. original name *Giuseppe Sarto*. 1835–1914, Italian ecclesiastic; pope (1903–14). He condemned Modernism (1907) and initiated a new codification of canon law. Feast day: Aug 21

Pius XI *n* original name *Achille Ratti*. 1857–1939, Italian ecclesiastic; pope (1922–39). He signed the Lateran Treaty (1929), by which the Vatican City was recognized as an independent state. His encyclicals condemned Nazism and Communism

Pius XII *n* original name *Eugenio Pacelli*. 1876–1958, Italian ecclesiastic; pope (1939–58): his attitude towards Nazi German anti-Semitism has been a matter of controversy

pivot *n* 1 a central shaft around which something turns 2 the central person or thing necessary for progress or success ▷ *vb* **-oting, -oted** 3 to turn on or provide with a pivot [Old French]

pivotal *adj* 1 of crucial importance 2 of or acting as a pivot

pix *n informal* a plural of **pic**

pixel *n* the smallest constituent unit of an image, as on a visual display unit [from *pix* pictures + *el*(*ement*)]

pixie or **pixy** *n, pl* **pixies** (in folklore) a fairy or elf

Pizarro *n* Francisco. ?1475–1541, Spanish conqueror of Peru. He landed in Peru (1532), murdered the Inca King Atahualpa (1533), and founded Lima as the new capital of Peru (1535). He was murdered by his own followers

pizza *n* a dish of Italian origin consisting of a baked disc of dough covered with a wide variety of savoury toppings [Italian]

pizzazz or **pizazz** *n informal* an attractive combination of energy and style [origin obscure]

pizzicato (pit-see-kah-toe) *adj, adv music* (in music for the violin family) to be plucked with the finger [Italian: pinched]

Pl. (in street names) Place

plaas *n S African* a farm [Afrikaans]

placard *n* 1 a notice that is paraded in public ▷ *vb* 2 to attach placards to [Old French *plaquart*]

placate *vb* **-cating, -cated** to calm (someone) to stop him or her feeling angry or upset [Latin *placare*]
▷ **placatory** *adj*

place *n* 1 a particular part of a space or of a surface 2 a geographical point, such as a town or city 3 a position or rank in a sequence or order 4 an open square lined with houses in a city or town 5 space or room 6 a house or living quarters: *he's buying his own place* 7 any building or area set aside for a specific purpose 8 the point reached in reading or speaking: *her finger was pressed to the page as if marking her place* 9 right or duty: *it's not my place to do their job for them* 10 appointment, position, or job: *she won a place at university* 11 position, condition, or state: *you know what your place in the world is* 12 a space or seat, as at a dining table 13 *maths* the relative position of a digit in a number 14 **all over the place** in disorder or disarray 15 **go places** *informal* to become successful 16 **in** or **out of place** in or out of the proper or customary position 17 **in place of a** instead of: *leeks can be used in place of the broccoli* **b** in exchange for: *he gave her it in place of her ring* 18 **know one's place** to be aware of one's inferior position 19 **put someone in his** or **her place** to humble someone who is arrogant, conceited, etc. 20 **take place** to happen or occur 21 **take the place of** to be a substitute for ▷ *vb* **placing, placed** 22 to put in a particular or appropriate place 23 to find or indicate the place of: *I bet you the media couldn't have placed Neath on the map before the by-election* 24 to identify or classify by linking with an appropriate context: *I felt I should know him, but could not quite place him* 25 to make (an order or bet) 26 to find a home or job for (someone) 27 (often foll. by *with*) to put under the care (of) 28 (of a racehorse, greyhound, athlete, etc.) to arrive in first, second, third, or sometimes fourth place [Latin *platea* courtyard]

Place *n* Francis. 1771–1854, British radical, who campaigned for the repeal (1824) of the Combination Acts, which forbade the forming of trade unions, and for parliamentary reform

placebo (plas-**see**-bo) *n, pl* **-bos** or **-boes** *med* an inactive substance given to a patient usually to compare its effects with those of a real drug but sometimes for the psychological benefit gained by the patient through believing that he or she is receiving treatment [Latin: I shall please]

place kick *n rugby, soccer, American football etc.* a kick in which the ball is placed in position before it is kicked

placement *n* 1 arrangement or position 2 a temporary job which someone is given as part of a training course: *many pupils have been on work placements with local businesses* 3 the act or an instance of finding someone a job or a home: *the main task of the adoption agency is to find the best family placement for each child*

placenta (plass-**ent**-a) *n, pl* **-tas** or **-tae** the organ formed in the womb of most mammals during pregnancy, providing oxygen and nutrients for the fetus [Latin, from Greek *plakous* flat cake] ▷ **placental** *adj*

place setting *n* the cutlery, crockery, and glassware laid for one person at a dining table

placid *adj* having a calm appearance or nature: *placid waters*; *a placid temperament* [Latin *placidus* peaceful]
▷ **placidity** or **placidness** *n* ▷ **placidly** *adv*

placket *n dressmaking* an opening at the waist of a dress or skirt for buttons or zips or for access to a pocket [perhaps from Medieval Dutch *plackaet* breastplate]

plagiarize or **-rise** (play-jer-ize) *vb* **-rizing, -rized** or **-rising, -rised** to steal ideas or passages from (another's work) and present them as one's own [Latin *plagium* kidnapping] ▷ **plagiarism** *n* ▷ **plagiarizer** or **-riser** *n*

plague *n* 1 any widespread and usually highly contagious disease with a high fatality rate 2 an infectious disease of rodents transmitted to man by the bite of the rat flea; bubonic plague 3 something that afflicts or harasses: *a plague of locusts* 4 *informal* a nuisance ▷ *vb* **plaguing, plagued** 5 to afflict or harass: *a playing career plagued by injury* 6 *informal* to annoy or pester [Latin *plaga* a blow]

plaice *n, pl* **plaice** or **plaices** an edible European flatfish with a brown body marked with red or orange spots [Greek *platus* flat]

plaid *n* **1** a long piece of tartan cloth worn over the shoulder as part of Highland costume **2** a crisscross weave or cloth [Scottish Gaelic *plaide*]

Plaid Cymru (plide kumm-ree) *n* the Welsh nationalist party [Welsh]

plain *adj* **1** flat or smooth **2** easily understood: *he made it plain what he wanted from me* **3** honest or blunt: *the plain fact is that my mother has no time for me* **4** without adornment: *a plain brown envelope* **5** not good-looking **6** (of fabric) without pattern or of simple weave **7** lowly, esp. in social rank or education: *the plain people of Ireland* **8** *knitting* of or done in plain stitch ▷ *n* **9** a level stretch of country **10** a simple stitch in knitting made by passing the wool round the front of the needle ▷ *adv* **11** clearly or simply: *that's just plain stupid!* [Latin *planus* level, clear] **> plainly** *adv* **> plainness** *n*

plainchant *n* same as plainsong

plain chocolate *n Brit* chocolate with a slightly bitter flavour and dark colour

plain clothes *pl n* ordinary clothes, as opposed to uniform, worn by a detective on duty

plain flour *n* flour to which no raising agent has been added

plain sailing *n* **1** *informal* smooth or easy progress **2** *nautical* sailing in a body of water that is unobstructed; clear sailing

Plains of Abraham *n* (*functioning as sing*) a field in E Canada between Quebec City and the St Lawrence River: site of an important British victory (1759) in the Seven Years' War, which cost the French their possession of Canada

plainsong *n* the style of unaccompanied choral music used in the medieval Church, esp. in Gregorian chant [translation of Medieval Latin *cantus planus*]

plain speaking *n* saying exactly what one thinks **> plain-spoken** *adj*

plaint *n* **1** *archaic* a complaint or lamentation **2** *law* a statement in writing of grounds of complaint made to a court of law [Old French *plainte*]

plaintiff *n* a person who sues in a court of law [Old French *plaintif* complaining]

plaintive *adj* sad and mournful [Old French *plaintif* grieving] **> plaintively** *adv*

plait (platt) *n* **1** a length of hair that has been plaited ▷ *vb* **2** to intertwine (strands or strips) in a pattern [Latin *plicare* to fold]

plan *n* **1** a method thought out for doing or achieving something **2** a detailed drawing to scale of a horizontal section through a building **3** an outline or sketch ▷ *vb* **planning, planned 4** to form a plan (for) **5** to make a plan of (a building) **6** to intend [Latin *planus* flat]

planchette *n* a device on which messages are written under supposed spirit guidance [French: little board]

Planck *n* Max (**Karl Ernst Ludwig**). 1858–1947, German physicist who first formulated the quantum theory (1900): Nobel prize for physics 1918

plane¹ *n* **1** an aeroplane **2** *maths* a flat surface in which a straight line joining any two of its points lies entirely on that surface **3** a level surface: *an inclined plane* **4** a level of existence or attainment: *her ambition was set on a higher plane than pulling pints in a pub* ▷ *adj* **5** level or flat **6** *maths* lying entirely in one plane ▷ *vb* **planing, planed 7** to glide or skim: *they planed over the ice* [Latin *planum* level surface]

plane² *n* **1** a tool with a steel blade for smoothing timber ▷ *vb* **planing, planed 2** to smooth (timber) using a plane **3** (often foll. by *away* or *off*) to remove using a plane [Latin *planare* to level]

planet *n* any of the eight celestial bodies, Mercury, Venus, Earth, Mars, Jupiter, Saturn, Uranus, or Neptune, that revolve around the sun in oval-shaped orbits [Greek *planain* to wander] **> planetary** *adj*

planetarium *n*, *pl* **-riums** or **-ria 1** an instrument for projecting images of the sun, moon, stars, and planets onto a domed ceiling **2** a building in which such an instrument is housed

planetoid (plan-it-oid) *n* See **asteroid**

plane tree *or* **plane** *n* a tree with rounded heads of fruit and leaves with pointed lobes [Greek *platus* wide (because of its broad leaves)]

plangent (plan-jent) *adj* (of sounds) mournful and resounding

plank *n* **1** a long flat piece of sawn timber **2** one of the policies in a political party's programme **3 walk the plank** to be forced by sailors to walk to one's death off the end of a plank jutting out from the side of a ship [Late Latin *planca* board]

planking *n* a number of planks

plankton *n* the small drifting plants and animals on the surface layer of a sea or lake [Greek *planktos* wandering]

planner *n* **1** a person who makes plans, esp. for the development of a town, building, etc. **2** a chart for recording future appointments, etc.

planning permission *n* formal permission granted by a local authority for the construction, alteration, or change of use of a building

plant *n* **1** a living organism that grows in the ground and lacks the power of movement **2** the land, building, and equipment used in an industry or business **3** a factory or workshop **4** mobile mechanical equipment for construction or road-making **5** *informal* a thing positioned secretly for discovery by someone else, often in order to incriminate an innocent person ▷ *vb* **6** to set (seeds or crops) into the ground to grow: *it's the wrong time of year for planting roses* **7** to place firmly in position: *I planted my chair beside hers* **8** to introduce into someone's mind: *once Wendy had planted the idea in the minds of the owners, they quite fancied selling* **9** *slang* to deliver (a blow or kiss) **10** *informal* to position or hide (someone) in order to deceive or observe **11** *informal* to hide or secrete (something), usually for some illegal purpose or in order to incriminate someone [Old English]

plantain¹ *n* a plant with a rosette of broad leaves and a slender spike of small greenish flowers [Latin *planta* sole of the foot]

plantain² *n* **1** a large tropical fruit like a green-skinned banana **2** the tree on which this fruit grows [Spanish *platano*]

plantation *n* **1** an estate, esp. in tropical countries, where cash crops such as rubber or coffee are grown on a large scale **2** a group of cultivated trees or plants **3** (formerly) a colony of settlers

planter *n* **1** the owner or manager of a plantation **2** a decorative pot for house plants

plantigrade *adj* walking on the entire sole of the foot, as humans and bears do [Latin *planta* sole of the foot + *gradus* a step]

plaque *n* **1** a commemorative inscribed stone or metal plate **2** Also called: **dental plaque** a filmy deposit on teeth consisting of mucus, bacteria, and food, that causes decay [French]

plasma *n* **1** the clear yellowish fluid portion of blood which contains the corpuscles and cells **2** a sterilized preparation of such fluid, taken from the blood, for use in transfusions **3** a former name for **protoplasm 4** *physics* a hot ionized gas containing positive ions and free electrons [Greek: something moulded]

plasma screen *n* a type of flat screen on a television or a visual display unit in which the image is created by electric current passing through many gas-filled cells

Plassey *n* a village in NE India, in W Bengal: scene of Clive's victory (1757) over Siraj-ud-daula, which established British supremacy over India

plaster *n* **1** a mixture of lime, sand, and water that is applied to a wall or ceiling as a soft paste and dries as a hard coating **2** *Brit, Austral and NZ* an adhesive strip of material for dressing a cut or wound **3** short for **mustard plaster, plaster of Paris** ▷ *vb* **4** to coat (a wall or ceiling) with plaster **5** to apply like plaster: *he plastered his face with shaving cream* **6** to cause to lie flat or to adhere: *his hair was plastered to his forehead* [Greek *emplastron* healing dressing] **> plasterer** *n*

plasterboard *n* a thin rigid board, made of plaster compressed between two layers of fibreboard, used to form or cover interior walls

plastered *adj slang* drunk

plaster of Paris *n* a white powder that sets to a hard solid when mixed with water, used for making sculptures and casts for setting broken limbs

plastic *n* **1** any of a large number of synthetic materials that can be moulded when soft and then set **2** *informal* Also called: **plastic money** credit cards etc. as opposed to cash ▷ *adj* **3** made of plastic **4** easily influenced **5** capable of being moulded or formed **6** of moulding or modelling: *the plastic arts* **7** *slang* superficially attractive yet artificial or false: *glamorous models with plastic smiles* [Greek *plastikos* mouldable] **> plasticity** *n*

plastic bullet *n* a solid PVC cylinder fired by the police in riot control

plastic explosive *n* an adhesive jelly-like explosive substance

Plasticine *n trademark* a soft coloured material used, esp. by children, for modelling

plasticize *or* **-cise** *vb* **-cizing, -cized** *or* **-cising, -cised** to make or become plastic

plasticizer *or* **-ciser** *n* a substance added to a plastic material to soften it and improve flexibility

plastic surgery *n* the branch of surgery concerned with the repair or reconstruction of missing, injured, or malformed tissues or parts **> plastic surgeon** *n*

Plata *n* **Río de la Plata** an estuary on the SE coast of South America, between Argentina and Uruguay, formed by the Uruguay and Paraná Rivers. Length: 275 km (171 miles). Width: (at its mouth) 225 km (140 miles). Also known as: **La Plata**. English name: **River Plate**

Plataea *n* an ancient city in S Boeotia, traditionally an ally of Athens: scene of the defeat of a great Persian army by the Greeks in 479 BC

plate *n* **1** a shallow dish made of porcelain, earthenware, glass, etc., on which food is served **2** Also called: **plateful** the contents of a plate **3** a shallow dish for receiving a collection in church **4** flat metal of even thickness obtained by rolling **5** a thin coating of metal usually on another metal **6** dishes or cutlery made of gold or silver **7** a sheet of metal, plastic, or rubber having a printing surface produced by a process such as stereotyping **8** a print taken from such a sheet or from a woodcut **9** a thin flat sheet of a substance, such as glass **10** a small piece of metal or plastic with an inscription, fixed to another surface: *a brass name plate* **11** *photog* a sheet of glass coated with photographic emulsion on which an image can be formed by exposure to light **12** *informal* same as **denture 13** *anatomy* any flat platelike structure **14** a cup awarded to the winner of a sporting contest, esp. a horse race **15** any of the rigid layers of the earth's crust **16 have a lot on one's plate** to have many pressing things to deal with **17 on a plate** without having to make any effort oneself: *he got the job handed to him on a plate* ▷ *vb* **plating, plated 18** to coat (a metal surface) with a thin layer of another metal **19** to cover with metal plates, usually for protection **20** to form (metal) into plate, usually by rolling [Old French: something flat]

Plate *n* **River Plate** the English name for the (Río de la) Plata

plateau (plat-oh) *n, pl* **-teaus** *or* **-teaux** (-ohs) **1** a wide level area of high land **2** a relatively long period of stability: *the body temperature rises to a plateau that it keeps until shortly before bedtime* ▷ *vb* **3** to remain stable for a long period [French]

Plateau *n* a state of central Nigeria, formed in 1976 from part of Benue-Plateau State: tin mining. Capital: Jos. Pop: 3 178 712 (2006). Area: 30 913 sq km (11 936 sq miles)

plated *adj* coated with a layer of metal

plate glass *n* glass produced in thin sheets, used for windows and mirrors

platelayer *n Brit* a workman who lays and maintains railway track

platelet *n* a minute particle occurring in the blood of vertebrates and involved in the clotting of the blood

platen *n* **1** the roller on a typewriter, against which the keys strike **2** a flat plate in a printing press that presses the paper against the type [Old French *platine*]

platform *n* **1** a raised floor **2** a raised area at a railway station where passengers get on or off the trains **3** See **drilling platform 4** the declared aims of a political party **5** the thick raised sole of some shoes **6** a type of computer hardware or operating system [French *plat* flat + *forme* layout]

platform game *n* a type of computer game that is played by moving a figure on the screen through a series of obstacles

platform ticket *n* a ticket for admission to railway platforms but not for travel

Plath *n* **Sylvia**. 1932–63, US poet living in England. She wrote two volumes of verse, *The Colossus* (1960) and *Ariel* (1965), and a novel, *The Bell Jar* (1963): she was married to Ted Hughes

plating *n* **1** a coating of metal **2** a layer or covering of metal plates

Platini *n* **Michel**. born 1955, French footballer, manager, and administrator; scored 41 goals in 72 games for France (1976–87); manager of France (1988–92); president of UEFA from 2007; European Footballer of the Year (1983–85)

platinum *n* a silvery-white metallic element, very resistant to heat and chemicals: used in jewellery, laboratory apparatus, electrical contacts, dentistry, electroplating, and as a catalyst. Symbol: **Pt** [Spanish *platina* silvery element]

platinum blonde *n* a girl or woman with silvery-blonde hair

platitude *n* a trite or unoriginal remark: *it's a platitude, but people need people* [French: flatness] **> platitudinous** *adj*

Plato *n* ?427–?347 BC, Greek philosopher: with his teacher Socrates and his pupil Aristotle, he is regarded as the initiator of western philosophy. His influential theory of ideas, which makes a distinction between objects of sense perception and the universal ideas or forms of which they are an expression, is formulated in such dialogues as *Phaedo*, *Symposium*, and *The Republic*. Other works include *The Apology* and *Laws*

platonic *adj* friendly or affectionate but without physical desire: *platonic love*

Platonic *adj* of the philosopher Plato or his teachings

Platonism (plate-on-iz-zum) *n* the teachings of Plato (?427–?347 BC), Greek philosopher, and his followers **> Platonist** *n*

platoon *n military* a subunit of a company, usually comprising three sections of ten to twelve men [French *peloton* little ball, group of men]

Platte *n* a river system of the central US, formed by the confluence of the **North Platte** and **South Platte** at North Platte, Nebraska: flows generally east to the Missouri River. Length: 499 km (310 miles)

platteland *n* the platteland (in South Africa) the country districts or rural areas [Afrikaans]

platter *n* a large shallow, usually oval, dish [Anglo-Norman *plater*]

platypus *or* **duck-billed platypus** *n, pl* **-puses** an Australian egg-laying amphibious mammal, with dense fur, webbed feet, and a ducklike bill [Greek *platus* flat + *pous* foot]

plaudit *n* (usually pl) an expression of enthusiastic approval [Latin *plaudite* applaud!]

Plauen *n* a city in E central Germany, in Saxony: textile centre. Pop: 70 070 (2003 est)

plausible *adj* **1** apparently reasonable or true: *a plausible excuse* **2** apparently trustworthy or believable: *he is an extraordinarily plausible liar* [Latin *plausibilis* worthy of applause] **> plausibility** *n* **> plausibly** *adv*

Plautus *n* Titus Maccius. ?254–?184 BC, Roman comic dramatist. His 21 extant works, adapted from Greek plays, esp. those by Menander, include *Menaechmi* (the basis of Shakespeare's *The Comedy of Errors*), *Miles Gloriosus*, *Rudens*, and *Captivi*

play *vb* **1** to occupy oneself in (a sport or recreation) **2** to compete against (someone) in a sport or game: *I saw Brazil play Argentina recently* **3** to fulfil (a particular role) in a team game: *he usually plays in midfield* **4** (often foll. by *about* or *around*) to behave carelessly: *he's only playing with your affections, you know* **5** to act the part (of) in a dramatic piece: *he has played Hamlet to packed Broadway houses* **6** to perform (a dramatic piece) **7 a** to perform (music) on an instrument **b** to be able to perform on (a musical instrument): *she plays the bassoon* **8** to send out (water) or cause to send out (water): *they played a hose across the wrecked building* **9** to cause (a radio etc.) to emit sound **10** to move freely or quickly: *the light played across the water* **11** *Stock Exchange* to speculate for gain in (a market) **12** *angling* to tire (a hooked fish) by alternately letting out and reeling in the line **13** to put (a card) into play **14** to gamble **15 play fair** or **false with** to act fairly or unfairly with **16 play for time** to gain time to one's advantage by the use of delaying tactics **17 play into the hands of** to act unwittingly to the advantage of (an opponent) **18 play politics a** to negotiate politically **b** to exploit an important issue merely for political gain **c** to make something into a political issue **> n 19 a** a dramatic piece written for performance by actors **b** the performance of such a piece **20** games or other activity undertaken for pleasure **21** the playing of a game or the time during which a game is in progress: *rain stopped play* **22** conduct: *fair play* **23** gambling **24** activity or operation: *radio allows full play to your imagination* **25** scope for freedom of movement: *there was a lot of play in the rope* **26** free or rapidly shifting motion: *the play of light on the water* **27** fun or jest: *I used to throw cushions at her in play* **28 in** or **out of play** (of a ball in a game) in or not in a position for continuing play according to the rules **29 make a play for** *informal* to make an obvious attempt to gain (something) **▶** See also **play along, playback,** etc. [Old English *plega, plegan*] **> playable** *adj*

play along *vb* to cooperate (with) temporarily: *I'll play along with them for the moment*

playback *n* **1** the playing of a recording on magnetic tape **▷ vb play back 2** to listen to or watch (something recorded)

playbill *n* a poster or bill advertising a play

playboy *n* a rich man who devotes himself to such pleasures as nightclubs and female company

playcentre *n* NZ a centre for preschool children run by parents

play down *vb* to minimize the importance of: *she played down the problems of the company*

player *n* **1** a person who takes part in a game or sport **2** a person who plays a musical instrument **3** *informal* a leading participant in a particular field or activity: *one of the key players in Chinese politics* **4** an actor

Player *n* Gary. born 1935, South African golfer: winner of nine major championships (1959–78), including the British Open (1959, 1968, 1974)

player piano *n* a mechanical piano; Pianola

playful *adj* **1** good-natured and humorous: *a playful remark* **2** full of high spirits and fun: *a playful child* **> playfully** *adv*

playgoer *n* a person who goes often to the theatre

playground *n* **1** an outdoor area for children's play, either with swings and slides, or adjoining a school **2** a place or activity enjoyed by a specified person or group:

they oppose turning the island into a tourist playground

playgroup *n* a regular meeting of infants for supervised creative play

playhouse *n* a theatre

playing field *n* (*sometimes pl*) Brit and NZ a field or open space used for sport

playlist *n* a list of records chosen for playing, such as on a radio station

play-lunch *n* Austral and NZ a child's mid-morning snack at school

playmaker *n sport* a player who creates scoring opportunities for his or her team-mates

playmate *n* a companion in play

play off *vb* **1** to set (two people) against each other for one's own ends: *she delighted in playing one parent off against the other* **2** to take part in a play-off **▷ n play-off 3** *sport* an extra contest to decide the winner when there is a tie **4** *chiefly US and Canad* a contest or series of games to determine a championship

play on *vb* to exploit (the feelings or weakness of another): *he played on my sympathy*

play on words *n* same as **pun**

playpen *n* a small portable enclosure in which a young child can safely be left to play

playschool *n* a nursery group for preschool children

PlayStation *n trademark* a video games console

plaything *n* **1 a** a toy **2** a person regarded or treated as a toy

playtime *n* a time for play or recreation, such as a school break

play up *vb* **1** to highlight: *the temptation is to play up the sensational aspects of the story* **2** Brit and Austral informal to behave in an unruly way **3** to give (one) trouble or not be working properly: *my back's playing me up again; the photocopier's started to play up* **4 play up to** to try to please by flattery

playwright *n* a person who writes plays

plaza *n* **1** an open public square, usually in Spain **2** *chiefly US and Canad* a modern shopping complex [Spanish]

PLC or **plc** (in Britain) Public Limited Company

plea *n* **1** an emotional appeal **2** *law* a statement by or on behalf of a defendant **3** an excuse: *his plea of poverty rings a little hollow* [Anglo-Norman *plai*]

plead *vb* **pleading, pleaded, plead** or especially Scot and US **pled 1** (sometimes foll. by *with*) to ask with deep feeling **2** to give as an excuse: *whenever she invites him to dinner, he pleads a prior engagement* **3** *law* to declare oneself to be (guilty or not guilty) of the charge made against one **4** *law* to present (a case) in a court of law [Latin *placere* to please]

pleadings *pl n law* the formal written statements presented by the plaintiff and defendant in a lawsuit

pleasant *adj* **1** pleasing or enjoyable: *what a pleasant surprise* **2** having pleasing manners or appearance: *he was a pleasant boy* [Old French *plaisant*] **> pleasantly** *adv*

Pleasant Island *n* the former name of Nauru

pleasantry *n, pl* **-ries 1** (*often pl*) a polite or jocular remark: *we exchanged pleasantries about the weather* **2** agreeable jocularity [French *plaisanterie*]

please *vb* **pleasing, pleased 1** to give pleasure or satisfaction to (a person) **2** to regard as suitable or satisfying: *he can get almost anyone he pleases to work with him* **3 if you please** if you wish, sometimes used in ironic exclamation **4 pleased with** happy because of **5 please oneself** to do as one likes **▷ adv 6** used in making polite requests or pleading: *please sit down* **7 yes please** a polite phrase used to accept an offer or invitation [Latin *placere*] **> pleased** *adj*

Pleasence *n* Donald. 1919–95, British actor. His films include *Dr Crippen* (1962) and *Cul de Sac* (1966)

pleasing *adj* giving pleasure

pleasurable *adj* enjoyable or agreeable **> pleasurably** *adv*

pleasure *n* **1** a feeling of happiness and contentment:

the pleasure of hearing good music **2** something that gives enjoyment: *his garden was his only pleasure* **3** the activity of enjoying oneself: *business before pleasure* **4** euphemistic sexual gratification: *he took his pleasure of her* **5** a person's preference [Old French *plaisir*]

pleat *n* **1** a fold formed by doubling back fabric and pressing or stitching into place ▷ *vb* **2** to arrange (material) in pleats [variant of *plait*]

pleb *n Brit informal, often offensive* a common vulgar person

plebeian (pleb-**ee**-an) *adj* **1** of the lower social classes **2** unrefined: *plebeian tastes* ▷ *n* **3** one of the common people, usually of ancient Rome **4** a coarse or unrefined person [Latin *plebs* the common people of ancient Rome]

plebiscite (pleb-**iss**-ite) *n* a direct vote by all the electorate on an issue of national importance [Latin *plebiscitum* decree of the people]

plectrum *n, pl* **-trums** *or* **-tra** an implement for plucking the strings of a guitar or similar instrument [Greek *plēktron*]

pled *vb chiefly US and Scot* a past (esp. in legal usage) of **plead**

pledge *n* **1** a solemn promise **2 a** something valuable given as a guarantee that a promise will be kept or a debt paid **b** the condition of being used as security: *in pledge* **3** a token: *a pledge of good faith* **4** an assurance of support or goodwill, given by drinking a toast: *we drank a pledge to their success* **5** take *or* sign the pledge to vow not to drink alcohol ▷ *vb* **pledging, pledged** **6** to promise solemnly **7** to promise to give (money to charity, etc.) **8** to bind by or as if by a pledge: *I was pledged to secrecy* **9** to give (one's word or property) as a guarantee **10** to drink a toast to (a person or cause) [Old French *plege*]

Pleiocene *adj, n* same as **Pliocene**

Pleistocene (ply-**stow**-seen) *adj geology* of the epoch of geological time from about 1.6 million to 10 000 years ago [Greek *pleistos* most + *kainos* recent]

Plekhanov *n* Georgi Valentinovich. 1857–1918, Russian revolutionary; founder of Russian Marxism and leader of the Russian Social Democratic Workers' Party

plenary *adj* **1** (of an assembly) attended by all the members **2** full or complete: *plenary powers* [Latin *plenus* full]

plenipotentiary *adj* **1** (usually of a diplomat) invested with full authority ▷ *n, pl* **-aries** **2** a diplomat or representative who has full authority to transact business [Latin *plenus* full + *potentia* power]

plenitude *n literary* **1** abundance **2** fullness or completeness [Latin *plenus* full]

plenteous *adj literary* **1** abundant: *a plenteous supply* **2** producing abundantly: *a plenteous harvest*

plentiful *adj* existing in large amounts or numbers ⟩ **plentifully** *adv*

plenty *n, pl* **-ties** **1** (often foll. by *of*) a great number or amount: *plenty of time* **2** abundance: *an age of plenty* ▷ *adj* **3** very many: *there's plenty more fish in the sea* ▷ *adv* **4** informal more than adequately: *that's plenty fast enough for me* [Latin *plenus* full]

Plenty *n* Bay of Plenty a large bay of the Pacific on the NE coast of the North Island, New Zealand

pleonasm *n rhetoric* **1** the use of more words than necessary, such as *a tiny little child* **2** an unnecessary word or phrase [Greek *pleonasmos* excess] ⟩ **pleonastic** *adj*

plethora *n* an excess [Greek *plēthōra* fullness]

pleura (ploor-a) *n, pl* **pleurae** (ploor-ee) *anatomy* the thin transparent membrane enveloping the lungs [Greek: side, rib] ⟩ **pleural** *adj*

pleurisy *n* inflammation of the pleura, making breathing painful ⟩ **pleuritic** *adj, n*

Pleven *or* **Plevna** *n* a town in N Bulgaria: taken by Russia from the Turks in 1877 after a siege of 143 days. Pop: 102 000 (2005 est)

Plevneliev *n* Rosen. born 1964, Bulgarian politician: president of Bulgaria from 2012

plexus *n, pl* **-uses** *or* **-us** a complex network of nerves or

blood vessels [Latin *plectere* to braid]

pliable *adj* **1** easily bent: *pliable branches* **2** easily influenced: *his easy and pliable nature* ⟩ **pliability** *n*

pliant *adj* **1** easily bent; supple: *pliant young willow and hazel twigs* **2** easily influenced: *he was a far more pliant subordinate than his predecessor* [Old French *plier* to fold] ⟩ **pliancy** *n*

pliers *pl n* a gripping tool consisting of two hinged arms usually with serrated jaws [from PLY¹]

plight¹ *n* a dangerous or difficult situation: *the plight of the British hostages* [Old French *pleit* fold, and probably influenced by Old English *pliht* peril]

plight² *vb* plight one's troth *old-fashioned* to make a promise to marry [Old English *pliht* peril]

Plimsoll line *n* a line on the hull of a ship showing the level that the water should reach if the ship is properly loaded [after Samuel *Plimsoll*, who advocated its adoption]

plimsolls *pl n Brit* light rubber-soled canvas sports shoes [from the resemblance of the sole to a Plimsoll line]

plinth *n* **1** a base on which a statue stands **2** the slab that forms the base of a column or pedestal [Greek *plinthos* brick]

Pliny *n* **1** known as *Pliny the Elder*. Latin name *Gaius Plinius Secundus*. 23–79 AD, Roman writer, the author of the encyclopedic *Natural History* (77) **2** his nephew, known as *Pliny the Younger*. Latin name *Gaius Plinius Caecilius Secundus*. ?62–?113 AD, Roman writer and administrator, noted for his letters

Pliocene *or* **Pleiocene** (ply-oh-seen) *adj geology* of the epoch of geological time about 10 million years ago [Greek *pleiōn* more + *kainos* recent]

PLO Palestine Liberation Organization

Płock *n* a town in central Poland, on the River Vistula: several Polish kings are buried in the cathedral: oil refining, petrochemical works. Pop: 130 000 (2005 est)

plod *vb* **plodding, plodded** **1** to walk with heavy slow steps **2** to work slowly and steadily ▷ *n* **3** the act of plodding **4** *Brit slang* a policeman [imitative] ⟩ **plodder** *n*

Ploeşti *n* a city in SE central Romania: centre of the Romanian petroleum industry. Pop: 204 000 (2005 est)

Plomer *n* William (Charles Franklyn). 1903–73, British poet, novelist, and short-story writer, born in South Africa. His novels include *Turbott Wolfe* (1926) and *The Case is Altered* (1932)

plonk¹ *vb* **1** to put down heavily and carelessly: *he plonked himself down on the sofa* ▷ *n* **2** the act or sound of plonking [variant of *plunk*]

plonk² *n informal* cheap inferior wine [origin unknown]

plonker *n Brit slang* a stupid person [origin unknown]

plop *n* **1** the sound made by an object dropping into water without a splash ▷ *vb* **plopping, plopped** **2** to drop with such a sound: *a tear rolled down his cheek and plopped into his soup* **3** to fall or be placed heavily or carelessly: *we plopped down on the bed and went straight to sleep* [imitative]

plosive *phonetics adj* **1** pronounced with a sudden release of breath ▷ *n* **2** a plosive consonant [French *explosif* explosive]

plot¹ *n* **1** a secret plan for an illegal purpose **2** the story of a play, novel, or film ▷ *vb* **plotting, plotted** **3** to plan secretly; conspire **4** to mark (a course) on a map **5** to make a plan or map of **6 a** to locate (points) on a graph by means of coordinates **b** to draw (a curve) through these points **7** to construct the plot of (a play, novel, or film) [from PLOT², influenced by obsolete *complot* conspiracy] ⟩ **plotter** *n*

plot² *n* a small piece of land: *there was a small vegetable plot in the garden* [Old English]

Plotinus *n* ?205–?270 AD, Roman Neo-Platonist philosopher, born in Egypt

plough *or US* **plow** *n* **1** an agricultural tool for cutting or turning over the earth **2** a similar tool used for clearing snow ▷ *vb* **3** to turn over (the soil) with a plough **4** to make (furrows or grooves) in (something) with or as if with a plough **5** (sometimes foll. by *through*) to move (through something) in the manner of a plough: *the ship ploughed through the water* **6** (foll. by *through*) to work at slowly or perseveringly **7** to invest (money): *he ploughed the profits back into the business* **8 plough into** (of a vehicle, plane, etc.) to run uncontrollably into (something): *the aircraft ploughed into a motorway embankment* [Old English *plōg* plough land]

Plough *n* the Plough the group of the seven brightest stars in the constellation Ursa Major

ploughman *or US* **plowman** *n, pl* **-men** a man who ploughs

ploughman's lunch *n* a snack lunch consisting of bread and cheese with pickle

ploughshare *or US* **plowshare** *n* the cutting blade of a plough

Plovdiv *n* a city in S Bulgaria on the Maritsa River: the second largest town in Bulgaria; conquered by Philip II of Macedonia in 341 BC; capital of Roman Thracia; commercial centre of a rich agricultural region. Pop: 339 000 (2005 est). Greek name: **Philippopolis**

plover *n* a shore bird with a round head, straight bill, and long pointed wings [Old French *plovier* rainbird]

plow *n, vb US* same as **plough**

Plowright *n* Dame Joan. born 1929, British actress, married to Laurence Olivier (1961–89)

ploy *n* a manoeuvre designed to gain an advantage in a situation: *a cheap political ploy* [from obsolete noun sense of *employ*, meaning an occupation]

pluck *vb* **1** to pull or pick off **2** to pull out the feathers of (a bird for cooking) **3** (foll. by *off*, *away*, etc.) to pull (something) forcibly or violently (from something or someone) **4** to sound the strings of (a musical instrument) with the fingers or a plectrum **5** *slang* to swindle ▷ *n* **6** courage **7** a pull or tug **8** the heart, liver, and lungs of an animal used for food ▶ See also **pluck up** [Old English *pluccian*]

pluck up *vb* to summon up (courage)

plucky *adj* **pluckier, pluckiest** courageous ⟩ **pluckily** *adv* ⟩ **pluckiness** *n*

plug *n* **1** an object used to block up holes or waste pipes **2** a device with one or more pins which connects an appliance to an electricity supply **3** *informal* a favourable mention of a product etc., for example on television, to encourage people to buy it **4** See **spark plug 5** a piece of tobacco for chewing ▷ *vb* **plugging, plugged 6** to block or seal (a hole or gap) with a plug **7** *informal* to make frequent favourable mentions of (a product etc.), for example on television **8** *slang* to shoot: *he lifted the rifle and plugged the deer* **9** *slang* to punch **10** (foll. by *along*, *away*, etc.) *informal* to work steadily ▶ See also **plug in** [Middle Dutch *plugge*]

plug in *vb* to connect (an electrical appliance) to a power source by pushing a plug into a socket

plum *n* **1** an oval dark red or yellow fruit with a stone in the middle, that grows on a small tree **2** a raisin, as used in a cake or pudding **3** *informal* something of a superior or desirable kind ▷ *adj* **4** made from plums: *plum cake* **5** dark reddish-purple **6** very desirable: *plum targets for attack* [Old English *plūme*]

plumage *n* the feathers of a bird [Old French *plume* feather]

plumb *vb* **1** to understand (something obscure): *to plumb a mystery* **2** to test the alignment of or make vertical with a plumb line **3** (foll. by *in* or *into*) to connect (an appliance or fixture) to a water pipe or drainage system: *the shower should be plumbed in professionally* **4 plumb the depths** (usually foll. by *of*) to experience the worst extremes (of something): *to plumb the depths of despair* ▷ *n* **5** a lead weight hanging on the end of a string and used to test the depth of water or to test whether something is vertical **6 out of plumb** not vertical ▷ *adv* **7** vertical or perpendicular **8** *informal, chiefly US* utterly: *plumb stupid* **9** *informal* exactly: *plumb in the centre* [Latin *plumbum* lead]

plumber *n* a person who fits and repairs pipes and

fixtures for water, drainage, or gas systems [Old French *plommier* worker in lead]

plumbing *n* **1** the pipes and fixtures used in a water, drainage, or gas system **2** the trade or work of a plumber

plumb line *n* a string with a metal weight at one end, used to test the depth of water or to test whether something is vertical

plume *n* **1** a large ornamental feather **2** a group of feathers worn as a badge or ornament on a hat **3** something like a plume: *a plume of smoke* ▷ *vb* **pluming, plumed 4** to adorn with plumes **5** (of a bird) to preen (its feathers) **6 plume oneself** (foll. by *on* or *upon*) to be proud of oneself or one's achievements, esp. unjustifiably: *she was pluming herself on her figure* [Old French]

plummet *vb* **-meting, -meted 1** to drop down; plunge ▷ *n* **2** the weight on a plumb line or fishing line [Old French *plommet* ball of lead]

plummy *adj* **-mier, -miest 1** of, full of, or like plums: *a red wine full of ripe plummy fruit* **2** Brit informal (of a voice) deep, rich, and usually upper-class in accent: *his plummy condescending voice* **3** Brit informal desirable: *they lived plummy lives in the hills of Tuscany*

plump¹ *adj* **1** full or rounded: *until puberty I was really quite plump* ▷ *vb* **2** (often foll. by *up* or *out*) to make (something) fuller or rounded: *she plumped up the cushions on the couch* [Middle Dutch *plomp* blunt] ⟩ **plumpness** *n*

plump² *vb* **1** (often foll. by *down*, *into*, etc.) to drop or sit suddenly and heavily: *he plumped down on the seat* **2 plump for** to choose one from a selection ▷ *n* **3** a heavy abrupt fall or the sound of this ▷ *adv* **4** suddenly or heavily **5** directly: *the plane landed plump in the middle of the field* **6** in a blunt, direct, or decisive manner [probably imitative]

plum pudding *n* a boiled or steamed pudding made with flour, suet, and dried fruit

plumy *adj* **plumier, plumiest 1** like a feather **2** covered or adorned with feathers

plunder *vb* **1** to seize (valuables or goods) from (a place) by force, usually in wartime; loot ▷ *n* **2** anything plundered; booty **3** the act of plundering; pillage [probably from Dutch *plunderen*]

plunge *vb* **plunging, plunged 1** (usually foll. by *into*) to thrust or throw (something or oneself) forcibly or suddenly: *they plunged into the sea; he plunged the knife in to the hilt* **2** to throw or be thrown into a certain condition: *the room was plunged into darkness* **3** (usually foll. by *into*) to involve or become involved deeply (in) **4** to move swiftly or impetuously **5** to descend very suddenly or steeply: *temperatures were plunging* **6** *informal* to gamble recklessly ▷ *n* **7** a leap or dive **8** *informal* a swim **9** a pitching motion **10 take the plunge** *informal* to make a risky decision which cannot be reversed later [Old French *plongier*]

plunger *n* **1** a rubber suction cup used to clear blocked drains **2** a device with a plunging motion; piston

plunk *vb* **1** to pluck the strings of (an instrument) to produce a twanging sound **2** (often foll. by *down*) to drop or be dropped heavily ▷ *n* **3** the act or sound of plunking [imitative]

Plunket *or* **Plunkett** *n* Saint Oliver. 1629–81, Irish Roman Catholic churchman and martyr; wrongly executed as a supposed conspirator in the Popish Plot (1678). Feast day: July 11

Plunket baby *n* NZ a baby brought up according to the principles of the Plunket Society

Plunket nurse *n* NZ a nurse working for the Plunket Society

Plunket Society *n* NZ an organization for the care of mothers and babies

pluperfect *grammar adj* **1** denoting a tense of verbs used to describe an action completed before a past time. In English this is a compound tense formed with *had* plus the past participle ▷ *n* **2** the pluperfect tense [Latin *plus quam perfectum* more than perfect]

plural *adj* **1** of or consisting of more than one **2** *grammar* denoting a word indicating more than one ▷ *n* **3** *grammar*

a the plural number **b** a plural form [Latin *plus* more]

pluralism *n* **1** the existence and toleration in a society of a variety of groups of different ethnic origins, cultures, or religions **2** the holding of more than one office by a person ▷ **pluralist** *n, adj* ▷ **pluralistic** *adj*

plurality *n, pl* **-ties 1** the state of being plural **2** maths a number greater than one **3** a large number **4** a majority

pluralize or **-rise** *vb* **-rizing, -rized** or **-rising, -rised** to make or become plural

plus 1 increased by the addition of: *four plus two* **2** with the addition of: *a good salary, plus a company car* ▷ *adj* **3** indicating addition: *a plus sign* **4** maths same as **positive** (7) **5** on the positive part of a scale **6** indicating the positive side of an electrical circuit **7** involving advantage: *a plus factor* **8** informal having a value above the value stated: *it must be worth a thousand pounds plus* **9** slightly above a specified standard: *he received a B plus for his essay* ▷ *n* **10** a plus sign (+), indicating addition **11** a positive quantity **12** informal something positive or an advantage **13** a gain, surplus, or advantage [Latin: more]

> **USAGE** *Plus, together with,* and *along with* do not create compound subjects in the way that *and* does: the number of the verb depends on that of the subject to which *plus, together with,* or *along with* is added: *this task, plus all the others, was* (not *were*) *undertaken by the government; the doctor, together with the nurses, was* (not *were*) *waiting for the patient.*

plus fours *pl n* men's baggy knickerbockers gathered in at the knee, now only worn for hunting or golf [because made with four inches of material to hang over at the knee]

plush *n* **1** a velvety fabric with a long soft pile, used for furniture coverings ▷ *adj* **2** Also: **plushy** informal luxurious [French *pluche*]

plus-one *n* informal someone who accompanies an invited person to a social function

Plutarch *n* ?46–?120 AD, Greek biographer and philosopher, noted for his *Parallel Lives* of distinguished Greeks and Romans

Pluto *n* **1** Classical myth the god of the underworld **2** a dwarf planet in the solar system, classified as a planet until 2006

plutocracy *n, pl* **-cies 1** government by the wealthy **2** a state ruled by the wealthy **3** a group that exercises power on account of its wealth [Greek *ploutos* wealth + *-kratia* rule] ▷ **plutocratic** *adj*

plutocrat *n* a person who is powerful because of being very rich

plutonic *adj* (of igneous rocks) formed from molten rock that has cooled and solidified below the earth's surface [after PLUTO (1)]

plutonium *n* chem a toxic radioactive metallic element, used in nuclear reactors and weapons. Symbol: **Pu** [after PLUTO (2), because Pluto lies beyond Neptune and plutonium was discovered soon after neptunium]

pluvial *adj* geography, geology of or due to the action of rain [Latin *pluvia* rain]

ply[1] *vb* **plies, plying, plied 1** to work at (a job or trade) **2** to use (a tool) **3** (usually foll. by *with*) to provide (with) or subject (to) persistently: *he plied us with drink; he plied me with questions* **4** to work steadily **5** (of a ship) to travel regularly along (a route): *to ply the trade routes* [Middle English *plye*, short for *aplye* to apply]

ply[2] *n, pl* **plies 1** a layer or thickness, such as of fabric or wood **2** one of the strands twisted together to make rope or yarn [Old French *pli* fold]

Plymouth *n* **1** a port in SW England, in Plymouth unitary authority, SW Devon, on **Plymouth Sound** (an inlet of the English Channel): Britain's chief port in Elizabethan times; the last port visited by the Pilgrim Fathers in the *Mayflower* before sailing to America; naval base; university (1992). Pop: 243 795 (2001) **2** a unitary authority in SW England, in Devon. Pop: 241 500 (2003 est). Area: 76 sq km (30 sq miles) **3** a city in SE Massachusetts, on **Plymouth Bay**: the first permanent European settlement in New England; founded by the Pilgrim Fathers. Pop: 54 109 (2003 est) **4** the former capital of Montserrat, in the Caribbean; largely destroyed by volcanic eruption in 1997

Plymouth Brethren *pl n* a Puritanical religious sect with no organized ministry

Plymouth Rock *n* **1** a heavy American breed of domestic fowl bred for meat and laying **2** a boulder on the coast of Massachusetts: traditionally thought to be the landing place of the Pilgrim Fathers (1620)

plywood *n* a board made of thin layers of wood glued together under pressure, with the grain of one layer at right angles to the grain of the next

Plzeň *n* an industrial city in the Czech Republic. Pop: 163 000 (2005 est). German name: **Pilsen**

Pm chem promethium

PM 1 Prime Minister **2** Postmaster **3** Paymaster **4** project manager

p.m. 1 after noon **2** postmortem (examination)

PMG 1 Postmaster General **2** Paymaster General

PMS premenstrual syndrome

PMT premenstrual tension

pneumatic *adj* **1** operated by compressed air: *pneumatic drill* **2** containing compressed air: *a pneumatic tyre* **3** of or concerned with air, gases, or wind [Greek *pneuma* breath, wind]

pneumatics *n* the branch of physics concerned with the mechanical properties of air and other gases

pneumonia *n* inflammation of one or both lungs [Greek *pneumōn* lung]

Pnom Penh *n* a variant spelling of **Phnom Penh**

po *n, pl* **pos** Brit old-fashioned, informal a chamber pot [from POT[1]]

Po[1] chem polonium

Po[2] *n* a river in N Italy, rising in the Cottian Alps and flowing northeast to Turin, then east to the Adriatic: the longest river in Italy. Length: 652 km (405 miles). Latin name: **Padus**

PO 1 Also: **p.o.** Brit postal order **2** Post Office **3** petty officer **4** Pilot Officer

poach[1] *vb* **1** to catch (game or fish) illegally on someone else's land **2 a** to encroach on (someone's rights or duties) **b** to steal (an idea, employee, or player) [Old French *pocher*] ▷ **poacher** *n*

poach[2] *vb* to simmer (food) very gently in liquid [Old French *pochier* to enclose in a bag]

poblano *n, pl* **-nos 1** a variety of chilli pepper **2** US a native of Puebla, Mexico ▷ *adj* **3** US relating to or coming from Puebla, Mexico

Pocahontas *n* original name *Matoaka*; married name *Rebecca Rolfe*. ?1595–1617, Native American, who allegedly saved the colonist Captain John Smith from being killed

pock *n* **1** a pus-filled blister resulting from smallpox **2** a pockmark [Old English *pocc*]

pocket *n* **1** a small pouch sewn into clothing for carrying small articles **2** any pouchlike container, esp. for catching balls at the edge of a snooker table **3** a small isolated area or group: *a pocket of resistance* **4** a cavity in the earth, such as one containing ore **5 in one's pocket** under one's control **6 out of pocket** having made a loss ▷ *vb* **-eting, -eted 7** to put into one's pocket **8** to take secretly or dishonestly **9** billiards etc. to drive (a ball) into a pocket **10** to conceal or suppress: *he pocketed his pride and asked for help* ▷ *adj* **11** small: *a pocket edition* [Anglo-Norman *poket* a little bag]

pocketbook *n* chiefly US a small case for money and papers

pocket borough *n* (before the Reform Act of 1832) an English borough constituency controlled by one person or family

pocketful *n, pl* **-fuls** as much as a pocket will hold

pocketknife *n, pl* **-knives** a small knife with one or more blades that fold into the handle; penknife

pocket money *n* **1** a small weekly sum of money given to children by parents **2** money for small personal expenses

pockmarked *adj* **1** (of the skin) marked with pitted scars after the healing of smallpox **2** (of a surface) covered in many small hollows: *the building is pockmarked with bullet holes* ⟩ **pockmark** *n*

pod *n* **1 a** a long narrow seedcase containing peas, beans, etc. **b** the seedcase as distinct from the seeds ▷ *vb* **podding, podded 2** to remove the pod from [origin unknown]

podcast *n* **1** an audio file similar to a radio broadcast, which can be downloaded and listened to on a computer, MP3 player, etc. ▷ *vb* **-casts, -casting, -cast** *or* **-casted 2** to create such files and make them available for downloading **3** to make (music, interviews, etc.) available using this format ⟩ **podcaster** *n* ⟩ **podcasting** *n*

Podgorica *or* **Podgoritsa** *n* the capital of Montenegro: under Turkish rule (1474–1878). Pop: 230 000 (2005 est). Former name (1946–92): **Titograd**

podgy *adj* **podgier, podgiest** *Brit informal* short and fat [from *podge* a short plump person] ⟩ **podginess** *n*

podiatry (pod-**eye**-a-tree) *n* another word for **chiropody** ⟩ **podiatrist** *n*

podium *n, pl* **-diums** *or* **-dia 1** a small raised platform used by conductors or speakers **2** a plinth that supports a colonnade or wall [Latin: platform]

Podolsk *n* an industrial city in W Russia, near Moscow. Pop: 177 000 (2005 est)

Poe *n* Edgar Allan. 1809–49, US short-story writer, poet, and critic. Most of his short stories, such as *The Fall of the House of Usher* (1839) and the *Tales of the Grotesque and Arabesque* (1840), are about death, decay, and madness. *The Murders in the Rue Morgue* (1841) is regarded as the first modern detective story

poem *n* **1 a** a literary work, often in verse, usually dealing with emotional or descriptive themes in a rhythmic form **2** a literary work that is not in verse but deals with emotional or descriptive themes in a rhythmic form: *a prose poem* **3** anything like a poem in beauty or effect: *his painting is a poem on creation* [Greek *poiēma* something created]

poep (poop) *n S African taboo* **1** an emission of intestinal gas from the anus **2** a mean or despicable person [Afrikaans]

poesy *n archaic* poetry

poet *n* **1** a writer of poetry **2** a person with great imagination and creativity [Greek *poiētēs* maker, poet]

poetaster *n* a writer of inferior verse

poetic *or* **poetical** *adj* **1** like poetry, by being expressive or imaginative **2** of poetry or poets **3** recounted in verse

poetic justice *n* an appropriate punishment or reward for previous actions

poetic licence *n* freedom from the normal rules of language or truth, as in poetry

poet laureate *n, pl* **poets laureate** *Brit* the poet selected by the British sovereign to write poems on important occasions

poetry *n* **1** poems in general **2** the art or craft of writing poems **3** a poetic quality that prompts an emotional response: *her acting was full of poetry* [Latin *poeta* poet]

po-faced *adj* wearing a disapproving stern expression [perhaps from PO + POKER-FACED]

pogey *or* **pogy** (pohg-ee) *n, pl* **pogeys** *or* **pogies** *Canad slang* **1** financial or other relief given to unemployed people by the government; dole **2** unemployment insurance [from earlier *pogie* workhouse]

pogo stick *n* a pole with steps for the feet and a spring at the bottom, so that the user can bounce up, down, and along on it [origin unknown]

pogrom *n* an organized persecution and massacre [Russian: destruction]

Pohai *n* a variant transliteration of the Chinese name for **Bohai**

poi *n* NZ a ball of woven flax swung rhythmically by Māori women during poi dances [Māori]

poi dance *n* NZ a women's formation dance that involves singing and twirling a poi

poignant *adj* **1** sharply painful to the feelings: *a poignant reminder* **2** cutting: *poignant wit* **3** pertinent in mental appeal: *a poignant subject* [Latin *pungens* pricking] ⟩ **poignancy** *n*

Poincaré *n* **1** Jules Henri. 1854–1912, French mathematician, physicist, and philosopher. He made important contributions to the theory of functions and to astronomy and electromagnetic theory **2** his cousin, **Raymond**. 1860–1934, French statesman; premier of France (1912–13; 1922–24; 1926–29); president (1913–20)

poinsettia *n* a shrub of Mexico and Central America, widely grown for its showy scarlet bracts, which resemble petals [after J. P. *Poinsett*, US Minister to Mexico]

point *n* **1** the essential idea in an argument or discussion: *I agreed with the point he made* **2** a reason or aim: *what is the point of this exercise?* **3** a detail or item **4** a characteristic: *he has his good points* **5** a location or position **6** a dot or tiny mark **7** a dot used as a decimal point or a full stop **8** the sharp tip of anything: *the point of the spear* **9** a headland: *the soaring cliffs at Dwerja Point in the southwest of the island* **10** *maths* a geometric element having a position located by coordinates, but no magnitude **11** a specific condition or degree: *freezing point* **12** a moment: *at that point he left* **13** (*often pl*) any of the extremities, such as the tail, ears, or feet, of a domestic animal **14** (*often pl*) *ballet* the tip of the toes **15** a single unit for measuring something such as value, or of scoring in a game **16** *printing* a unit of measurement equal to one twelfth of a pica **17** *nautical* one of the 32 direction marks on the compass **18** *cricket* a fielding position at right angles to the batsman on the off side **19** either of the two electrical contacts that make or break the circuit in the distributor of a motor vehicle **20** *Brit, Austral and NZ* (*often pl*) a movable section of railway track used to direct a train from one line to another **21** *Brit* short for **power point 22** *boxing* a mark awarded for a scoring blow or knockdown **23** beside the point irrelevant **24** make a point of **a** to make a habit of (something) **b** to do (something) because one thinks it important **25** on *or* at the point of about to; on the verge of: *on the point of leaving* **26** to the point relevant **27** up to a point not completely ▷ *vb* **28** (usually foll. by *at* or *to*) to show the position or direction of something by extending a finger or other pointed object towards it **29** (usually foll. by *at* or *to*) to single out one person or thing from among several: *all the symptoms pointed to epilepsy* **30** to direct or face in a specific direction: *point me in the right direction* **31** to finish or repair the joints in brickwork with mortar or cement **32** (of gun dogs) to show where game is lying by standing rigidly with the muzzle turned towards it ▶ See also **point out** [Latin *pungere* to pierce]

point-blank *adj* **1** fired at a very close target **2** plain or blunt: *a point-blank refusal to discuss the matter* ▷ *adv* **3** directly or bluntly: *the Minister was asked point-blank if he intended to resign* [point + blank (centre spot of an archery target)]

Point de Galle *n* a former name of **Galle**

point duty *n* the control of traffic by a policeman at a road junction

Pointe-à-Pitre *n* the chief port of Guadeloupe, on SW Grande-Terre Island in the Caribbean. Pop: 17 541 (2006)

pointed *adj* **1** having a sharp tip **2** cutting or incisive: *pointed wit* **3** obviously directed at a particular person: *a pointed remark* **4** emphasized or obvious: *pointed ignorance* ⟩ **pointedly** *adv*

Pointe-Noire *n* a port in S Congo-Brazzaville, on the Atlantic: the country's chief port and former capital

(1950–58). Pop: 638 000 (2005 est)

pointer n 1 something that is a helpful indicator of how a situation has arisen or may turn out: *a significant pointer to the likely resumption of talks* 2 an indicator on a measuring instrument 3 a long stick used by teachers, to point out particular features on a map, chart, etc. 4 a large smooth-coated gun dog

pointillism (pwan-till-iz-zum) n a technique used by some impressionist painters, in which dots of colour are placed side by side so that they merge when seen from a distance [French] > **pointillist** n, adj

pointing n the insertion of mortar between the joints in brickwork

pointless adj without meaning or purpose

point of no return n a point at which one is committed to continuing with an action

point of order n, pl **points of order** an objection in a meeting to the departure from the proper procedure

point of view n, pl **points of view** 1 a mental viewpoint or attitude: *she refuses to see the other person's point of view* 2 a way of considering something: *a scientific point of view*

point out vb to draw someone's attention to

point-to-point n Brit a steeplechase organized by a hunt

poise n 1 dignified manner 2 physical balance: *the poise of a natural model* 3 mental balance: *he recovered his poise* ▷ vb **poising, poised** 4 to be balanced or suspended 5 to be held in readiness: *the cats poised to spring on her* [Old French *pois* weight]

poised adj 1 absolutely ready 2 behaving with or showing poise

poison n 1 a substance that causes death or injury when swallowed or absorbed 2 something that destroys or corrupts: *the poison of Nazism* ▷ vb 3 to give poison to someone 4 to add poison to something 5 to have a harmful or evil effect on 6 (foll. by *against*) to turn (a person's mind) against: *he poisoned her mind against me* [Latin *potio* a drink, esp. a poisonous one] > **poisoner** n

poison ivy n a North American climbing plant that causes an itching rash if it touches the skin

poisonous adj 1 of or like a poison 2 malicious

poison-pen letter n a malicious anonymous letter

Poisson n Siméon Denis. 1781–1840, French mathematician, noted for his application of mathematical theory to physics, esp. electricity and magnetism

Poitiers n a city in S central France: capital of the former province of Poitou until 1790; scene of the battle (1356) in which the English under the Black Prince defeated the French; university (1432). Pop: 91 395 (2006)

Poitou n a former province of W central France, on the Atlantic. Chief town: Poitiers

Poitou-Charentes n a region of W central France, on the Bay of Biscay: mainly low-lying

poke¹ vb **poking, poked** 1 to jab or prod with an elbow, finger, etc. 2 to make a hole by poking 3 (sometimes foll. by *at*) to thrust (at): *she poked at the food with her fork* 4 (usually foll. by *in, through*, etc.) to thrust forward or out: *yellow hair poked from beneath his cap* 5 to stir (a fire) by poking 6 (often foll. by *about* or *around*) to search or pry 7 **poke one's nose into** to meddle in ▷ n 8 a jab or prod [Low German & Middle Dutch *poken*]

poke² n 1 dialect a pocket or bag 2 **a pig in a poke** See **pig** [Old French *poque*]

poker¹ n a metal rod with a handle for stirring a fire

poker² n a card game of bluff and skill in which players bet on the hands dealt [origin unknown]

poker face n informal an expressionless face, such as that of a poker player trying to hide the value of his or her cards > **poker-faced** adj

pokerwork n the art of producing pictures or designs on wood by burning it with a heated metal point

poky adj **pokier, pokiest** (of a room) small and cramped > **pokiness** n

pol. 1 political 2 politics

Pol. 1 Poland 2 Polish

Pola n the Italian name for **Pula**

Poland n a republic in central Europe, on the Baltic: first united in the 10th century; dissolved after the third partition effected by Austria, Russia, and Prussia in 1795; re-established independence in 1918; invaded by Germany in 1939; ruled by a Communist government from 1947 to 1989, when a multiparty system was introduced; joined the EU in 2004. It consists chiefly of a low undulating plain in the north, rising to a low plateau in the south, with the Sudeten and Carpathian Mountains along the S border. Official language: Polish. Religion: Roman Catholic majority. Currency: złoty. Capital: Warsaw. Pop: 38 383 809 (2013 est). Area: 311 730 sq km (120 359 sq miles). Polish name: **Polska**

Polanski n Roman. born 1933, Polish film director with a taste for the macabre, as in *Repulsion* (1965) and *Rosemary's Baby* (1968): later films include *Tess* (1980), *Death and the Maiden* (1995), and *The Pianist* (2002)

polar adj 1 of or near either of the earth's poles or the area inside the Arctic or Antarctic Circles 2 of or having a pole or polarity 3 directly opposite in tendency or nature: *polar opposites*

polar bear n a white bear of coastal regions of the North Pole

polar circle n the Arctic or Antarctic Circle

polarity n, pl **-ties** 1 the state of having two directly opposite tendencies or opinions 2 the condition of a body which has opposing physical properties, usually magnetic poles or electric charge 3 the particular state of a part with polarity: *an electrode with positive polarity*

polarization or **-risation** n 1 the condition of having or giving polarity 2 physics the condition in which waves of light or other radiation are restricted to certain directions of vibration

polarize or **-rise** vb **-rizing, -rized** or **-rising, -rised** 1 to cause people to adopt directly opposite opinions: *political opinion had polarized since the restoration of democracy* 2 to have or give polarity or polarization

Polaroid n trademark 1 a type of plastic that polarizes light: used in sunglasses to eliminate glare 2 **Polaroid camera** a camera that produces a finished print by developing and processing it inside the camera within a few seconds 3 **Polaroids** sunglasses with Polaroid plastic lenses

polder n a stretch of land reclaimed from the sea [Middle Dutch *polre*]

pole¹ n 1 a long slender rounded piece of wood, metal, or other material 2 **up the pole** Brit, Austral and NZ informal a slightly mad b in a predicament [Latin *palus* a stake]

pole² n 1 either end of the earth's axis of rotation. See also **North Pole, South Pole** 2 physics a either of the opposite forces of a magnet b either of two points at which there are opposite electric charges 3 either of two directly opposite tendencies or opinions 4 **poles apart** having widely divergent opinions or tastes [Greek *polos* pivot]

Pole¹ n a native or inhabitant of Poland

Pole² n Reginald. 1500–58, English cardinal; last Roman Catholic archbishop of Canterbury (1556–58)

poleaxe or US **poleax** vb **-axing, -axed** 1 to hit or stun with a heavy blow ▷ n 2 an axe formerly used in battle or used by a butcher [Middle English *pollax* battle-axe]

polecat n, pl **-cats** or **-cat** 1 a dark brown mammal like a weasel that gives off a foul smell 2 US a skunk [origin unknown]

pole dancing n a form of entertainment in which a scantily dressed woman dances erotically, turning on and posing against a vertically fixed pole on stage > **pole dancer** n

polemic (pol-em-ik) n 1 a fierce attack on or defence of a particular opinion, belief, etc.: *anti-capitalist polemic* ▷ adj also: **polemical** 2 of or involving dispute or controversy

[Greek *polemos* war] **> polemicist** *n*
polemics *n* the art of dispute
pole position *n* **1** (in motor racing) the starting position on the inside of the front row, generally considered the best one **2** an advantageous starting position
pole star *n* a guiding principle or rule
Pole Star *n* **the Pole Star** the star closest to the northern celestial pole
pole vault *n* **1 the pole vault** a field event in which competitors try to clear a high bar with the aid of a very flexible long pole ▷ *vb* **pole-vault 2** to perform or compete in the pole vault **> pole-vaulter** *n*
Poliakoff *n* Stephen. born 1952, British playwright and film director; work includes the stage plays *Breaking the Silence* (1984) and *Blinded by the Sun* (1996) and the television serials *The Lost Prince* (2003), *Friends and Crocodiles* (2005), and *Dancing on the Edge* (2013)
police *n* **1** (often preceded by *the*) the organized civil force in a state which keeps law and order **2** the men and women who are members of such a force **3** an organized body with a similar function: *security police* ▷ *vb* **-licing, -liced 4** to maintain order or control by means of a police force or similar body [French, from Latin *politia* administration]
police dog *n* a dog trained to help the police
policeman *or fem* **policewoman** *n*, *pl* **-men** *or fem* **-women** a member of a police force
police procedural *n* a novel, film, or television drama that deals with police work
police state *n* a state in which a government controls people's freedom through the police
police station *n* the office of the police force of a district
policy¹ *n*, *pl* **-cies 1** a plan of action adopted by a person, group, or government **2** *archaic* wisdom or prudence [Old French *policie*, from Latin *politia* administration]
policy² *n*, *pl* **-cies** a document containing an insurance contract [Old French *police* certificate] **> policyholder** *n*
Polignac *n* Prince de, title of *Auguste Jules Armand Marie de Polignac*. 1780–1847, French statesman; prime minister (1829–30) to Charles X: his extreme royalist and ultramontane policies provoked the 1830 revolution and cost Charles X the throne
polio *n* short for **poliomyelitis**
poliomyelitis (pole-ee-oh-my-el-**lite**-iss) *n* a viral disease which affects the brain and spinal cord, often causing paralysis [Greek *polios* grey + *muelos* marrow]
polish *vb* **1** to make smooth and shiny by rubbing **2** to perfect or complete: *media experts he had hired to polish his image* **3** to make or become elegant or refined: *not having polished his south London accent didn't help his career* ▷ *n* **4** a substance used for polishing **5** a shine or gloss **6** elegance or refinement ▸ See also **polish off, polish up** [Latin *polire* to polish]
Polish *adj* **1** of or relating to Poland or its inhabitants ▷ *n* **2** the language of Poland
Polish Corridor *n* the strip of land through E Pomerania providing Poland with access to the sea (1919–39), given to her in 1919 in the Treaty of Versailles, and separating East Prussia from the rest of Germany. It is now part of Poland
polished *adj* **1** accomplished: *a polished actor* **2** done or performed well or professionally: *a polished performance*
polish off *vb informal* **1** to finish completely **2** to dispose of or kill
polish up *vb* **1** to make smooth and shiny by polishing **2** to improve (a skill or ability) by working at it: *I'm going to evening classes to polish up my German*
Politburo *n* formerly, the chief decision-making committee of a Communist country [Russian]
polite *adj* **1** having good manners; courteous **2** cultivated or refined: *polite society* **3** socially correct but insincere: *he smiled a polite response and stifled an urge to scream* [Latin *politus* polished] **> politely** *adv* **> politeness** *n*
Politian *n* Italian name *Angelo Polliziano*; original name

Angelo Ambrogini. 1454–94, Florentine humanist and poet
politic *adj* **1** wise or possibly advantageous: *I didn't feel it was politic to mention it* **2** artful or shrewd: *a politic manager* **3** crafty; cunning: *a politic old scoundrel* **4** *archaic* political. See also **body politic** [Old French *politique*, from Greek *polis* city]
political *adj* **1** of the state, government, or public administration **2** relating to or interested in politics: *she was always a very political person* **3** of the parties and the partisan aspects of politics: *the government blames political opponents for fanning the unrest* **> politically** *adv*
politically correct *adj* displaying progressive attitudes, esp. in using vocabulary which is intended to avoid any implied prejudice
political prisoner *n* a person imprisoned for holding particular political beliefs
political science *n* the study of the state, government, and politics **> political scientist** *n*
politician *n* a person actively engaged in politics, esp. a member of parliament
politicize *or* **-cise** *vb* **-cizing, -cized** *or* **-cising, -cised 1** to make political or politically aware **2** to take part in political discussion or activity **> politicization** *or* **-cisation** *n*
politics *n* **1** (*functioning as sing*) the art and science of government **2** (*functioning as pl*) political opinions or sympathies: *his conservative politics* **3** (*functioning as pl*) political activities or affairs: *party politics* **4** (*functioning as sing*) the business or profession of politics **5** (*functioning as sing or pl*) any activity concerned with the acquisition of power: *company politics are often vicious*
polity *n*, *pl* **-ties** *formal* **1** a politically organized state, church, or society **2** a form of government of a state, church, or society [Greek *politeia* citizenship, from *polis* city]
Polk *n* James Knox. 1795–1849, US statesman; 11th president of the US (1845–49). During his administration, Texas and territory now included in New Mexico, Colorado, Utah, Nevada, Arizona, Oregon, and California were added to the Union
polka *n* **1 a** lively 19th-century dance **2** music for this dance ▷ *vb* **-kaing, -kaed 3** to dance a polka [Czech *pulka* half-step]
polka dots *pl n* a regular pattern of small bold spots on a fabric
poll *n* **1** Also called: **opinion poll** the questioning of a random sample of people to find out the general opinion **2** the casting, recording, or counting of votes in an election **3** the result of such a voting: *a marginal poll* **4** the head ▷ *vb* **5** to receive (a certain number of votes) **6** to record the votes of: *he polled the whole town* **7** to question (a person, etc.) as part of an opinion poll **8** to vote in an election **9** to clip or shear **10** to remove or cut short the horns of (cattle) [Middle Low German *polle* hair, head, top of a tree]
pollack *or* **pollock** *n*, *pl* **-lacks, -lack** *or* **-locks, -lock** a food fish related to the cod, found in northern seas [origin unknown]
Pollack *n* Sydney. 1934–2008, US film director. His films include *Tootsie* (1982), *Out of Africa* (1986), and *The Firm* (1993)
Pollaiuolo *n* **1** Antonio, ?1432–98, Florentine painter, sculptor, goldsmith, and engraver: his paintings include the *Martyrdom of St Sebastian* **2** his brother **Piero**. ?1443–96, Florentine painter and sculptor
pollard *n* **1** an animal that has shed its horns or has had them removed **2** a tree with its top cut off to encourage a more bushy growth ▷ *vb* **3** to cut off the top of (a tree) to make it grow bushy [see **POLL**] **> pollarded** *adj*
pollen *n* a fine powder produced by flowers to fertilize other flowers of the same species [Latin: powder]
Pollen *n* Daniel. 1813–96, New Zealand statesman, born in Ireland: prime minister of New Zealand (1876)
pollen count *n* a measure of the amount of pollen in

the air over a 24-hour period, often published as a warning to hay fever sufferers

pollinate *vb* **-nating, -nated** to fertilize by the transfer of pollen **> pollination** *n*

polling booth *n* a compartment in which a voter can mark his or her ballot paper in private during an election

polling station *n* a building where voters go during an election to cast their votes

pollock *n* same as **pollack**

Pollock *n* **1** Sir Frederick. 1845–1937, English legal scholar: with Maitland, he wrote *History of English Law before the Time of Edward I* (1895) **2** Jackson. 1912–56, US abstract expressionist painter; chief exponent of action painting in the US

pollster *n* a person who conducts opinion polls

poll tax *n* any tax levied per head of adult population, esp. the tax which replaced domestic rates (in Scotland from 1989 and England and Wales from 1990, until 1993)

pollutant *n* a substance that pollutes, usually the chemical waste of an industrial process

pollute *vb* **-luting, -luted** **1** to contaminate with poisonous or harmful substances **2** to corrupt morally [Latin *polluere* to defile] **> pollution** *n*

polly *n, pl* **-lies** *informal, chiefly Austral* short for **politician**

polo *n* **1** a game like hockey played on horseback with long-handled mallets and a wooden ball **2** short for **water polo** [Tibetan *pulu* ball]

Polo *n* Marco. 1254–1324, Venetian merchant, famous for his account of his travels in Asia. After travelling overland to China (1271–75), he spent 17 years serving Kublai Khan before returning to Venice by sea (1292–95)

Polokwane *n* a town in NE South Africa, the capital of Limpopo province: commercial and agricultural centre. Pop: 90 398 (2001). Former name: **Pietersburg**

polonaise *n* **1** a stately Polish dance **2** music for this dance [French *danse polonaise* Polish dance]

polo neck *n* a sweater with a high tight turned-over collar

polonium *n chem* a rare radioactive element found in trace amounts in uranium ores. Symbol: **Po** [Medieval Latin *Polonia* Poland; in honour of the nationality of its discoverer, Marie Curie]

polo shirt *n* a cotton short-sleeved shirt with a collar and three-button opening at the neck

Pol Pot *n* original name *Kompong Thom*. 1925–98, Cambodian Communist statesman; prime minister of Kampuchea (1976; 1977–79); his policies led to the deaths of thousands in labour camps before he was overthrown by Vietnamese forces; in 1997 his former supporters in the Khmer Rouge captured him and claimed to have tried and sentenced him to life imprisonment

Polska *n* the Polish name for **Poland**

Poltava *n* a city in E Ukraine: scene of the victory (1709) of the Russians under Peter the Great over the Swedes under Charles XII; centre of an agricultural region. Pop: 319 000 (2005 est)

poltergeist *n* a spirit believed to be responsible for noises and acts of mischief, such as throwing objects about [German *poltern* to be noisy + *Geist* ghost]

poltroon *n obsolete* a complete coward [Old Italian *poltrone* lazy good-for-nothing]

poly *n, pl* **polys** *informal* short for **polytechnic**

poly- *combining form* many or much: *polyhedron*; *polysyllabic* [Greek *polus*]

polyandry *n* the practice of having more than one husband at the same time [Greek *polus* many + *anēr* man] **> polyandrous** *adj*

polyanthus *n, pl* **-thuses** a hybrid garden primrose with brightly coloured flowers [Greek: having many flowers]

Polybius *n* ?205–?123 BC, Greek historian. Under the patronage of Scipio the Younger, he wrote in 40 books a history of Rome from 264 BC to 146 BC

Polycarp *n* Saint. ?69–?155 AD, Christian martyr and bishop of Smyrna, noted for his letter to the church at Philippi. Feast day: Feb 23

polychromatic *adj* **1** having many colours **2** (of radiation) containing more than one wavelength

Polyclitus, Polycleitus *or* **Polycletus** *n* 5th-century BC Greek sculptor, noted particularly for his idealized bronze sculptures of the male nude, such as the *Doryphoros*

Polycrates *n* died ?522 BC, Greek tyrant of Samos, who was crucified by a Persian satrap

polycystic ovary syndrome *n* a hormonal disorder preventing ovulation, leading to reduced fertility, hirsutism, and weight gain. Abbreviation: **PCOS**

polyester *n* a synthetic material used to make plastics and textile fibres

polyethylene *n* same as **polythene**

polygamy (pol-ig-a-mee) *n* the practice of having more than one wife or husband at the same time [Greek *polus* many + *gamos* marriage] **> polygamist** *n* **> polygamous** *adj*

polyglot *adj* **1** able to speak many languages **2** written in or using many languages ▷ *n* **3** a person who can speak many languages [Greek *poluglōttos* many-tongued]

Polygnotus *n* 5th century BC, Greek painter: associated with Cimon in rebuilding Athens

polygon *n* a geometrical figure with three or more sides and angles [Greek *polugōnon* figure with many angles] **> polygonal** *adj*

polygraph *n* an instrument for recording pulse rate and perspiration, often used as a lie detector [Greek *polugraphos* writing copiously]

polygyny *n* the practice of having more than one wife at the same time [Greek *polus* many + *gunē* woman] **> polygynous** *adj*

polyhedron *n, pl* **-drons** *or* **-dra** a solid figure with four or more sides [Greek *polus* many + *hedron* side] **> polyhedral** *adj*

Polyhymnia *n Greek myth* the muse of singing, mime, and sacred dance

polymath *n* a person of great and varied learning [Greek *polumathēs* having much knowledge]

polymer *n* a natural or synthetic compound with large molecules made up of simple molecules of the same kind

polymeric *adj* of or being a polymer: *polymeric materials such as PVC* [Greek *polumerēs* having many parts]

polymerization *or* **-isation** *n* the process of forming a polymer **> polymerize** *or* **-ise** *vb*

polymorphous *or* **polymorphic** *adj* having, or passing through many different forms or stages [Greek *polus* many + *morphē* form]

Polynesia *n* one of the three divisions of islands in the Pacific, the others being Melanesia and Micronesia: includes Samoa, Society, Marquesas, Mangareva, Tuamotu, Cook, and Tubuai Islands, and Tonga [C18: via French from POLY- + Greek *nēsos* island]

Polynesian *adj* **1** of or relating to Polynesia or its inhabitants ▷ *n* **2** a native or inhabitant of Polynesia **3** any of the languages of Polynesia

polynomial *maths adj* **1** consisting of two or more terms ▷ *n* **2** an algebraic expression consisting of the sum of a number of terms

polyp *n* **1** *zoology* a small sea creature that has a hollow cylindrical body with a ring of tentacles around the mouth **2** *pathol* a small growth on the surface of a mucous membrane [Greek *polupous* having many feet]

polyphonic *adj music* consisting of several melodies played together

polyphony (pol-if-on-ee) *n, pl* **-nies** polyphonic style of composition or a piece of music using it [Greek *poluphōnia* diversity of tones]

polysaccharide *n* a carbohydrate which consists of a number of linked sugar molecules, such as starch or cellulose

p

polystyrene *n* a synthetic material used esp. as white rigid foam for insulating and packing

polysyllable *n* a word having more than two syllables **>** **polysyllabic** *adj*

polytechnic *n* **1** *Brit* (in New Zealand and formerly in Britain) college offering courses in many subjects at and below degree level ▷ *adj* **2** of or relating to technical instruction [Greek *polutekhnos* skilled in many arts]

polytheism *n* belief in more than one god **>** **polytheist** *n* **>** **polytheistic** *adj*

polythene *n* a light plastic material made from ethylene, usually made into thin sheets or bags

polyunsaturated *adj* of a group of fats that are less likely to contribute to the build-up of cholesterol in the body

polyurethane *n* a synthetic material used esp. in paints

polyvinyl chloride *n* See PVC

pom *n Austral and NZ slang* a British person. See also pommy

pomace (pumm-iss) *n* apple pulp left after pressing for juice [Latin *pomum* apple]

pomade *n* a perfumed oil put on the hair to make it smooth and shiny, esp. formerly [French *pommade*]

pomander *n* **1** a mixture of sweet-smelling substances in a container, used to perfume drawers or cupboards **2** a container for such a mixture [Medieval Latin *pomum ambrae* apple of amber]

Pombal *n* Marquês de. title of *Sebastião José de Carvalho e Mello*. 1699–1782, Portuguese statesman, who dominated Portuguese government from 1750 to 1777 and instituted many administrative and economic reforms

pomegranate *n* a round tropical fruit with a tough reddish rind containing many seeds in a juicy red pulp [Latin *pomum* apple + *granatus* full of seeds]

pomelo (pom-ill-oh) *n, pl* **-los** the edible yellow fruit, like a grapefruit, of a tropical tree [Dutch *pompelmoes*]

Pomerania *n* a region of N central Europe, extending along the S coast of the Baltic Sea from Stralsund to the Vistula River: now chiefly in Poland, with a small area in NE Germany. German name: **Pommern**. Polish name: **Pomorze**

Pomeranian *adj* **1** of or relating to Pomerania or its inhabitants ▷ *n* **2** a native or inhabitant of Pomerania, esp. a German **3** a toy dog with a long straight silky coat [after POMERANIA]

pomfret (pum-frit) *or* **pomfret-cake** *n* a small black rounded liquorice sweet [from *Pomfret*, earlier form of *Pontefract*, Yorks., where originally made]

pommel *n* **1** the raised part on the front of a saddle **2** a knob at the top of a sword handle ▷ *vb* **-melling, -melled** *or US* **-meling, -meled 3** same as pummel [Old French *pomel* knob]

Pommern *n* the German name for **Pomerania**

pommy *n, pl* **-mies** *(sometimes cap) Austral and NZ slang* a British person. Sometimes shortened to: **pom** [origin unknown]

Pomona *n* (in Orkney) another name for **Mainland**

Pomorze *n* the Polish name for **Pomerania**

pomp *n* **1** stately display or ceremony **2** ostentatious display [Greek *pompē* procession]

Pompadour *n* Marquise de, title of *Jeanne Antoinette Poisson*. 1721–64, mistress of Louis XV of France (1745–64), whom she greatly influenced

Pompeii *n* an ancient city in Italy, southeast of Naples: buried by an eruption of Vesuvius (79 AD); excavation of the site, which is extremely well preserved, began in 1748

Pompeiian *adj* **1** of or relating to Pompeii or its inhabitants ▷ *n* **2** a native or inhabitant of Pompeii

Pompey[1] *n* an informal name for **Portsmouth**

Pompey[2] *n* called *Pompey the Great*; Latin name *Gnaeus Pompeius Magnus*. 106–48 BC, Roman general and statesman; a member with Caesar and Crassus of the first triumvirate (60). He later quarrelled with Caesar, who defeated him at Pharsalus (48). He fled to Egypt and was murdered

Pompidou *n* Georges. 1911–74, French statesman; president of France (1969–74)

pompom *n* **1** a decorative ball of tufted silk or wool **2** the small round flower head of some dahlias and chrysanthemums [French]

pom-pom *n* an automatic rapid-firing gun [imitative]

pompous *adj* **1** foolishly dignified or self-important **2** foolishly grand in style: *a pompous speech* **>** **pomposity** *n* **>** **pompously** *adv*

ponce *offensive, slang, chiefly Brit n* **1** an effeminate man **2** same as pimp ▷ *vb* **poncing, ponced 3** (often foll. by *around* or *about*) *Brit and Austral* to act stupidly or waste time [from Polari, an English slang derived from the lingua franca of the Mediterranean ports]

Ponce *n* a port in S Puerto Rico, on the Caribbean: the second largest town on the island; settled in the 16th century. Pop: 185 930 (2003 est)

Ponce de León *n* Juan. ?1460–1521, Spanish explorer. He settled (1509) and governed (1510–12) Puerto Rico and discovered (1513) Florida

poncho *n, pl* **-chos** a type of cloak made of a piece of cloth with a hole in the middle for the head [American Spanish]

pond *n* a pool of still water [Middle English *ponde* enclosure]

ponder *vb* (sometimes foll. by *on* or *over*) to consider thoroughly or deeply [Latin *ponderare* to weigh, consider] **>** **ponderable** *adj*

ponderous *adj* **1** serious and dull: *much of the film is ponderous and pretentious* **2** heavy or huge **3** (of movement) slow and clumsy [Latin *ponderosus* of great weight]

Pondicherry *n* the former official name (until 2006) for Puducherry

pondok *or* **pondokkie** *n* (in southern Africa) a crudely made house or shack [Malay *pondók* leaf house]

Pondoland *n* an area in SE central South Africa: inhabited chiefly by the Pondo people

pondweed *n* a plant which grows in ponds and slow streams

pong *Brit and Austral informal n* **1** a strong unpleasant smell ▷ *vb* **2** to give off a strong unpleasant smell [origin unknown] **>** **pongy** *adj*

ponga (pong-a) *n* a tall New Zealand tree fern with large leathery leaves [Māori]

poniard (pon-yerd) *n* a small slender dagger [Old French *poignard*]

Ponta Delgada *n* a port in the E Azores, on S São Miguel Island: chief commercial centre of the archipelago. Pop: 65 853 (2001)

Pontchartrain *n* Lake Pontchartrain a shallow lagoon in SE Louisiana, linked with the Gulf of Mexico by a narrow channel, the **Rigolets**: resort and fishing centre. Area: 1620 sq km (625 sq miles)

Pontefract *n* an industrial town in N England, in Wakefield unitary authority, West Yorkshire: castle (1069), in which Richard II was imprisoned and murdered (1400). Pop: 28 250 (2001)

Pontevedra *n* a port in NW Spain: takes its name from a 12-arched Roman bridge, the Pons Vetus. Pop: 77 993 (2003 est)

Pontiac *n* died 1769, chief of the Ottawa Indians, who led a rebellion against the British (1763–66)

Pontianak *n* a port in Indonesia, on W coast of Borneo almost exactly on the equator. Pop: 464 534 (2000)

Pontic *adj* denoting or relating to the Black Sea [from Greek *Pontos* PONTUS]

pontiff *n* the Pope [Latin *pontifex* high priest]

pontifical *adj* **1** of a pontiff **2** pompous or dogmatic in manner

pontificate *vb* **-cating, -cated 1** to speak in a dogmatic manner **2** to officiate as a pontiff ▷ *n* **3** the term of office of a Pope

Pontine Marshes *pl n* an area of W Italy, southeast of Rome: formerly malarial swamps, drained in 1932–34 after numerous attempts since 160 BC had failed. Italian name: **Agro Pontino**

Ponting *n* Ricky (**Thomas**). born 1974, Australian cricketer; a batsman, he played in 168 test matches (1995–2012), 77 as captain; scored 13,378 runs in tests (an Australian record), and captained Australia to two World Cup wins (2003, 2007)

pontoon¹ *n* a floating platform used to support a bridge [Latin *ponto* punt]

pontoon² *n* a card game in which players try to obtain sets of cards worth 21 points [probably an alteration of French *vingt-et-un* twenty-one]

Pontoppidan *n* Henrik. 1857–1943, Danish novelist and short-story writer, author of the novel sequences *The Promised Land* (1891–95), *Lykke-Per* (1898–1904), and *The Empire of Death* (1912–16). Nobel prize for literature 1917

Pontormo *n* Jacopo da. original name *Jacopo Carrucci*. 1494–1556, Italian mannerist painter

Pontus *n* an ancient region of NE Asia Minor, on the Black Sea: became a kingdom in the 4th century BC; at its height under Mithridates VI (about 115–63 BC), when it controlled all Asia Minor; defeated by the Romans in the mid-1st century BC

Pontus Euxinus *n* the Latin name of the **Black Sea**

Pontypool *n* an industrial town in E Wales, in Torfaen county borough: famous for lacquered ironware in the 18th century. Pop: 35 447 (2001)

Pontypridd *n* an industrial town in S Wales, in Rhondda Cynon Taff county borough. Pop: 29 781 (2001)

pony *n, pl* **-nies** a breed of small horse [Scots *powney*, perhaps from Latin *pullus* young animal, foal]

ponytail *n* a hairstyle in which the hair is tied in a bunch at the back of the head and hangs down like a tail

pony trekking *n* the pastime of riding ponies cross-country

poodle *n* a dog with curly hair, which is sometimes clipped [German *Pudel*]

poof *n* Brit, Austral and NZ offensive, slang a male homosexual [French *pouffe* puff] **> poofy** *adj*

pooh *interj* an exclamation of disdain, scorn, or disgust

pooh-pooh *vb* to express disdain or scorn for

pool¹ *n* **1** a small body of still water **2** a small body of spilt liquid: *a pool of blood* **3** See **swimming pool** **4** a deep part of a stream or river [Old English *pōl*]

pool² *n* **1** a shared fund of resources or workers: *a typing pool* **2** a billiard game in which all the balls are potted with the cue ball **3** the combined stakes of those betting in many gambling games **4** *commerce* a group of producers who agree to maintain output levels and high prices ⊳ *vb* **5** to put into a common fund [French *poule*, literally: hen used to signify stakes in a card game]

Poole *n* **1** a port and resort in S England, in Poole unitary authority, Dorset, on **Poole Harbour**; seat of Bournemouth University (1992). Pop: 144 800 (2001) **2** a unitary authority in S England, in Dorset. Pop: 137 500 (2003 est). Area: 37 sq km (14 sq miles)

Pool Malebo *n* the Congolese name for **Stanley Pool**

pools *pl n* **the pools** chiefly Brit a nationwide mainly postal form of gambling which bets on the results of football matches

Poona *or* **Pune** *n* a city in W India, in W Maharashtra: under British rule served as the seasonal capital of the Bombay Presidency. Pop: 2 540 069 (2001)

poop *n nautical* a raised part at the back of a sailing ship [Latin *puppis*]

pooped *adj* US, Canad, Austral and NZ slang exhausted or tired: *if I wasn't so pooped I'd run and have a look at it* [Middle English *poupen* to blow]

Poopó *n* Lake Poopó a lake in SW Bolivia, at an altitude of 3688 m (12 100 ft): fed by the Desaguadero River. Area: 2540 sq km (980 sq miles)

poor *adj* **1** having little money and few possessions **2** less than is necessary or expected: *it was a poor reward for all his effort* **3** (sometimes foll. by *in*) lacking in (something): *a food which is rich in energy but poor in vitamins* **4** inferior: *poor quality* **5** disappointing or disagreeable: *a poor play* **6** pitiable; unlucky: *poor John is ill* **7** poor man's (something): *pewter, sometimes known as poor man's silver* [Latin *pauper*]

poorhouse *n* same as **workhouse**

poor law *n* English history a law providing for support of poor people from parish funds

poorly *adv* **1** badly ⊳ *adj* **2** informal rather ill

poor White *n often offensive* a poverty-stricken White person, usually in the southern US or South Africa

pop¹ *vb* **popping, popped 1** to make or cause to make a small explosive sound **2** (often foll. by *in, out,* etc.) informal to enter or leave briefly or suddenly: *his mother popped out to buy him an ice cream* **3** to place suddenly or unexpectedly: *Benny popped a sweet into his mouth* **4** to burst with a small explosive sound **5** (of the eyes) to protrude **6** informal to pawn **7 pop the question** informal to propose marriage ⊳ *n* **8** a light sharp explosive sound **9** Brit informal a nonalcoholic fizzy drink ⊳ *adv* **10** with a pop ▶ See also **pop off** [imitative]

pop² *n* **1** music of general appeal, esp. to young people, that usually has a strong rhythm and uses electrical amplification ⊳ *adj* **2** relating to pop music: *a pop concert* **3** informal short for **popular**

pop³ *n informal* **1** father **2** an old man

POP 1 point of presence: a device that enables access to the internet **2** post office protocol: a protocol which brings e-mail to and from a mail server

pop. **1** population **2** popular(ly)

pop art *n* a movement in modern art that uses the methods, styles, and themes of popular culture and mass media

popcorn *n* grains of maize heated until they puff up and burst

Pope¹ *n* the bishop of Rome as head of the Roman Catholic Church [Greek *pappas* father]

Pope² *n* Alexander. 1688–1744, English poet, regarded as the most brilliant satirist of the Augustan period, esp. with his *Imitations of Horace* (1733–38). His technical virtuosity is most evident in *The Rape of the Lock* (1712–14). Other works include *The Dunciad* (1728; 1742), the *Moral Essays* (1731–35), and *An Essay on Man* (1733–34)

popery (pope-er-ee) *n offensive* Roman Catholicism

popeyed *adj* **1** staring in astonishment **2** having bulging eyes

popgun *n* a toy gun that fires a pellet or cork by means of compressed air

popinjay *n* a conceited, foppish, or overly talkative person [Arabic *babaghā* parrot]

popish (pope-ish) *adj offensive* relating to Roman Catholicism

poplar *n* a tall slender tree with light soft wood, triangular leaves, and catkins [Latin *populus*]

poplin *n* a strong plain-woven fabric, usually of cotton, with fine ribbing [French *papeline*]

Popocatépetl *n* a volcano in SE central Mexico, southeast of Mexico City. Height: 5452 m (17 887 ft)

pop off *vb informal* **1** to depart suddenly **2** to die suddenly

Popov *n* **1** Alexander Stepanovich. 1859–1906, Russian physicist, the first to use an aerial in experiments with radio waves **2** Oleg (**Konstantinovich**). born 1930, Russian clown, a member of the Moscow Circus

poppadom *or* **poppadum** *n* a thin round crisp fried Indian bread [Hindi]

popper *n* Brit informal a press stud

Popper *n* Sir Karl. 1902–94, British philosopher, born in Vienna. In *The Logic of Scientific Discovery* (1934), he proposes that knowledge cannot be absolutely confirmed, but rather that science progresses by the experimental refutation of the current theory and its consequent replacement by a new theory, equally provisional but covering more of the known data. *The Open Society and its Enemies* (1945) is a critique of dogmatic political philosophies, such as Marxism. Other works are *The Poverty of Historicism* (1957), *Conjectures and Refutations* (1963), and *Objective Knowledge* (1972) **> Popperian** *n, adj*

poppet *n* a term of affection for a small child or sweetheart [variant of *puppet*]

popping crease *n cricket* a line in front of and parallel with the wicket where the batsman stands [from obsolete *pop* to hit]

poppy *n, pl* **-pies 1** a plant with showy red, orange, or white flowers **2** a drug, such as opium, obtained from these plants **3** an artificial red poppy worn to mark Remembrance Sunday and in New Zealand to mark Anzac Day ▷ *adj* **4** reddish-orange [Old English *popæg*]

poppycock *n informal* nonsense [Dutch dialect *pappekak*, literally: soft excrement]

Poppy Day *n informal* Remembrance Sunday

Popsicle *n trademark* the US and Canadian term for **ice lolly**

populace *n* the common people; masses [Latin *populus*]

popular *adj* **1** widely liked or admired **2** (often foll. by *with*) liked by a particular person or group: *the bay is popular with windsurfers and water-skiers* **3** common among the general public: *the groundswell of popular feeling* **4** designed to appeal to a mass audience: *an attack on him in the popular press* [Latin *popularis* of the people] **> popularity** *n* **> popularly** *adv*

popular front *n* a left-wing group or party opposed to fascism

popularize *or* **-rise** *vb* **-rizing, -rized** *or* **-rising, -rised 1** to make popular **2** to make easily understandable **> popularization** *or* **-risation** *n*

populate *vb* **-lating, -lated 1** (*often passive*) to live in: *a mountainous region populated mainly by Armenians* **2** to provide with inhabitants [Latin *populus* people] **> populated** *adj*

population *n* **1** all the inhabitants of a place **2** the number of such inhabitants **3** all the people of a particular class in a place: *the bulk of the rural population lives in poverty* **4** *ecology* a group of individuals of the same species inhabiting a given area: *a population of grey seals*

populism *n* a political strategy based on a calculated appeal to the interests or prejudices of ordinary people: *they preach a heady message of populism and religion* **> populist** *adj, n*

populous *adj* containing many inhabitants

pop-up *adj* **1** (of an appliance) characterized by or having a mechanism that pops up **2** (of a book) having pages that rise when opened, to simulate a three-dimensional form **3** *computers* (of a menu on a computer screen, etc.) suddenly appearing when an option is selected **4** (of a shop, restaurant, etc.) intentionally trading for a short time only: *a pop-up boutique* ▷ *n* **5** *computers* something that appears over or above the open window on a computer screen

porangi (pore-ang-ee) *adj NZ informal* crazy; mad [Māori]

porbeagle *n* a kind of shark

porcelain *n* **1** a delicate type of china **2** an object or objects made of this [French *porcelaine*, from Italian *porcellana* cowrie shell]

porch *n* a covered approach to the entrance of a building [French *porche*]

porcine *adj* of or like a pig [Latin *porcus* a pig]

porcupine *n* a large rodent covered with long pointed quills [Middle English *porc despyne* pig with spines]

pore¹ *vb* **poring, pored** **pore over** to examine or study intently: *a wife who pored over account books and ledgers all day* [Middle English *pouren*]

> **USAGE** See at pour.

pore² *n* **1** a small opening in the skin or surface of an animal or plant **2** any small hole, such as a tiny gap in a rock [Greek *poros* passage, pore]

Pori *n* a port in SW Finland, on the Gulf of Bothnia. Pop: 76 189 (2003 est). Swedish name: **Björneborg**

poriferan (por-riff-er-an) *n biology* a sponge [from New Latin *porifer* bearing pores]

Porirua *n* a city in New Zealand, on the North Island just north of Wellington. Pop: 50 600 (2004 est)

pork *n* the flesh of pigs used as food [Latin *porcus* pig]

porker *n* a pig fattened for food

pork pie *n* a pie with a minced pork filling

porky¹ *adj* **porkier, porkiest 1** of or like pork **2** *informal* fat or obese

porky² *n, pl* **porkies** *slang, chiefly Brit and Austral* a lie [rhyming slang *pork pie*]

porn *or* **porno** *n, adj informal* short for **pornography, pornographic**

pornography *n* writings, pictures, or films designed to be sexually exciting [Greek *pornographos* writing of prostitutes] **> pornographer** *n* **> pornographic** *adj*

porous *adj* **1** allowing air and liquids to be absorbed **2** *biology, geology* having pores [Late Latin *porus* passage, pore] **> porosity** *n*

porphyry (por-fir-ee) *n, pl* **-ries** a reddish-purple rock with large crystals of feldspar in it [Greek *porphuros* purple] **> porphyritic** *adj*

Porphyry *n* original name *Malchus*. 232–305 AD, Greek Neo-Platonist philosopher, born in Syria; disciple and biographer of Plotinus

porpoise *n, pl* **-poises** *or* **-poise** a small mammal of the whale family with a blunt snout [Latin *porcus* pig + *piscis* fish]

porridge *n* **1** a dish made of oatmeal or other cereal, cooked in water or milk **2** *chiefly Brit slang* a term of imprisonment [variant of *pottage*]

porringer *n* a small dish, often with a handle, used esp. formerly for soup or porridge [Middle English *potinger*]

Porson *n* Richard. 1759–1808, English classical scholar, noted for his editions of Aeschylus and Euripides

port¹ *n* a town with a harbour where ships can load and unload [Latin *portus*]

port² *n* **1** the left side of an aircraft or ship when facing the front of it ▷ *vb* **2** to turn or be turned towards the port [origin unknown]

port³ *n* a strong sweet fortified wine, usually dark red [after OPORTO, from where it came originally]

port⁴ *n* **1** *nautical* **a** an opening with a watertight door in the side of a ship, used for loading, etc. **b** See **porthole 2** *electronics* a logical circuit for the input and output of data [Latin *porta* gate]

port⁵ *vb computers* to change (programs) from one system to another [probably from PORT⁴]

Port. **1** Portugal **2** Portuguese

portable *adj* **1** easily carried ▷ *n* **2** an article designed to be easily carried, such as a television or typewriter [Latin *portare* to carry] **> portability** *n*

Port Adelaide *n* the chief port of South Australia, near Adelaide on St Vincent Gulf. Pop: 33 145 (2006)

Portadown *n* a town in S Northern Ireland, in the district of Armagh. Pop: 25 958 (2001)

portage *n* **1** the transporting of boats and supplies overland between navigable waterways **2** the route used for such transport ▷ *vb* **-taging, -taged 3** to transport (boats and supplies) in this way [French]

portal *n* **1** *literary* a large and impressive gateway or doorway **2** *computers* an internet site providing links to other sites [Latin *porta* gate]

Port Arthur *n* **1** a former penal settlement (1833–70) in Australia, on the S coast of the Tasman Peninsula, Tasmania **2** the former name of **Lüshun**

Port-au-Prince *n* the capital and chief port of Haiti, in the south on the Gulf of Gonaïves; founded in 1749 by the French; university (1944). Pop: 2 090 000 (2005 est)

Port Blair *n* the capital of the Indian Union Territory of the Andaman and Nicobar Islands, a port on the SE coast of South Andaman Island: a former penal colony. Pop: 100 186 (2001)

portcullis n an iron grating suspended in a castle gateway, that can be lowered to bar the entrance [Old French *porte coleïce* sliding gate]

Port Elizabeth n a port in S South Africa, on Algoa Bay: motor-vehicle manufacture, fruit canning; resort. Pop: 312 392 (2011)

portend vb to be an omen of: *the 0.5% increase certainly portends higher inflation ahead* [Latin *portendere* to indicate]

portent n **1** a sign of a future event **2** great or ominous significance: *matters of great portent* **3** a marvel [Latin *portentum* sign]

portentous adj **1** of great or ominous significance **2** self-important or pompous: *there was nothing portentous or solemn about him*

porter[1] n **1** a man employed to carry luggage at a railway station or hotel **2** a hospital worker who transfers patients between rooms [Latin *portare* to carry]
 〉**porterage** n

porter[2] n chiefly Brit a doorman or gatekeeper of a building [Latin *porta* door]

porter[3] n Brit a dark sweet ale brewed from black malt [short for *porter's ale*]

Porter n **1** Cole. 1893–1964, US composer and lyricist of musical comedies. His most popular songs include *Night and Day* and *Let's do It* **2 George**, Baron Porter of Luddenham. 1920–2002, British chemist, who shared a Nobel prize for chemistry in 1967 for his work on flash photolysis **3 Katherine Anne**. 1890–1980, US short-story writer and novelist. Her best-known collections of stories are *Flowering Judas* (1930) and *Pale Horse, Pale Rider* (1939) **4 Peter**. 1929–2010, Australian poet, lived in Britain **5 Rodney Robert**. 1917–85, British biochemist: shared the Nobel prize for physiology or medicine 1972 for determining the structure of an antibody **6 William Sidney**. original name of O. Henry

porterhouse n a thick, choice beef steak. Also called: **porterhouse steak** [formerly, a place that served porter, beer, and sometimes meals]

portfolio n, pl **-os 1** a flat case for carrying maps, drawings, or papers **2** selected examples, such as drawings or photographs, that show an artist's recent work **3** the area of responsibility of the head of a government department: *the defence portfolio* **4** a list of investments held by an investor **5 Minister without portfolio** a cabinet minister without responsibility for a government department [Italian *portafoglio*]

Port-Gentil n the chief port of Gabon, in the west near the mouth of the Ogooué River: oil refinery. Pop: 150 000 (2009 est)

Port Harcourt n a port in S Nigeria, capital of Rivers state on the Niger delta: the nation's second largest port; industrial centre. Pop: 942 000 (2005 est)

porthole n a small round window in a ship or aircraft

portico n, pl **-coes** or **-cos** a porch or covered walkway with columns supporting the roof [Italian, from Latin *porticus*]

Porţile de Fier n the Romanian name for the **Iron Gate**

portion n **1** a part of a whole **2** a part belonging to a person or group **3** a helping of food served to one person **4** law a dowry **5** literary someone's fate or destiny: *utter disaster was my portion* ▷ vb **6** to divide (something) into shares. **portion out** [Latin *portio*]

portion out vb to distribute or share (something) among a group of people: *the British portioned out the oil-rich lands to various sheikhs*

Port Jackson n an inlet of the Pacific on the coast of SE Australia, forming a fine natural harbour: site of the city of Sydney, spanned by Sydney Harbour Bridge

Portland[1] n **1 Isle of Portland** a rugged limestone peninsula in SW England, in Dorset, connected to the mainland by a narrow isthmus and by Chesil Bank: the lighthouse of **Portland Bill** lies at the S tip; famous for the quarrying of **Portland stone**, a fine building

material **2** an inland port in NW Oregon, on the Willamette River: the largest city in the state; shipbuilding and chemical industries. Pop: 538 544 (2003 est) **3** a port in SW Maine, on Casco Bay: the largest city in the state; settled by the English in 1632, destroyed successively by French, Indian, and British attacks, and rebuilt; capital of Maine (1820–32). Pop: 63 635 (2003 est)

Portland[2] n **3rd Duke of**. title of *William Henry Cavendish Bentinck*. 1738–1809, British statesman; prime minister (1783; 1807–09); father of Lord William Cavendish Bentinck

Portlaoise n a town in central Republic of Ireland, county town of Laois: site of a top-security prison. Pop: 12 127 (2002)

Port Louis n the capital and chief port of Mauritius, on the NW coast on the Indian Ocean. Pop: 146 876 (2002 est)

portly adj **-lier, -liest** stout or rather fat [from *port* (in the sense: deportment)]

Port Lyautey n the former name (1932–56) of **Kénitra**

portmanteau n, pl **-teaus** or **-teaux** old-fashioned a large suitcase made of stiff leather that opens out into two compartments [French: cloak carrier]

portmanteau word n a word made by joining together the beginning and end of two other words, such as *brunch*. Also called: **blend**

Port Moresby n the capital and chief port of Papua New Guinea, on the SE coast on the Gulf of Papua: important Allied base in World War II. Pop: 290 000 (2005 est)

Port Nicholson n **1** the first British settlement in New Zealand, established on Wellington Harbour in 1840: grew into Wellington **2** the former name for Wellington Harbour [C19: named after Capt John *Nicholson*, Australian naval officer]

Porto n the Portuguese name for **Oporto**

Porto Alegre n a port in S Brazil, capital of the Rio Grande do Sul state: the country's chief inland port; the chief commercial centre of S Brazil, with two universities (1936 and 1948). Pop: 3 795 000 (2005 est)

Portobelo n a small port in Panama, on the Caribbean northeast of Colón: the most important port in South America in colonial times; declined with the opening of the Panama Canal. Pop: 3300 (1997)

Port of Spain n the capital and chief port of Trinidad and Tobago, on the W coast of Trinidad. Pop: 56 000 (2005 est)

Porto Novo n the capital of Benin, in the southwest on a coastal lagoon: formerly a centre of Portuguese settlement and the slave trade. Pop: 253 000 (2005 est)

Porto Rican adj, n a former name for **Puerto Rican**

Porto Rico n the former name (until 1932) of **Puerto Rico**

Porto Velho n a city in W Brazil, capital of the federal territory of Rondônia on the Madeira River. Pop: 301 000 (2005 est)

Port Phillip Bay or **Port Phillip** n a bay in SE Australia, which forms the harbour of Melbourne

portrait n **1** a painting, drawing, or photograph of a person, often only of the face **2** a description [French]
 〉**portraitist** n

portraiture n **1** the art of making portraits **2** a description **3 a** a portrait **b** portraits collectively

portray vb to describe or represent (someone) by artistic means, such as in writing or on film [Old French *portraire* to depict] 〉**portrayal** n

Port Royal n **1** a fortified town in SE Jamaica, at the entrance to Kingston harbour: capital of Jamaica in colonial times **2** the former name (until 1710) of **Annapolis Royal 3** an educational institution about 27 km (17 miles) west of Paris that flourished from 1638 to 1704, when it was suppressed by papal bull as it had become a centre of Jansenism. Its teachers were noted esp. for their work on linguistics: their *Grammaire générale et raisonnée* exercised much influence

Port Said n a port in NE Egypt, at the N end of the Suez

Canal: founded in 1859 when the Suez Canal was begun; became the largest coaling station in the world and later an oil-bunkering port; damaged in the Arab-Israeli wars of 1967 and 1973. Pop: 546 000 (2005 est)

Portsmouth n **1** Informal name: **Pompey** a port in S England, in Portsmouth unitary authority, Hampshire, on the English Channel: Britain's chief naval base; university (1992). Pop: 187 056 (2001) **2** a unitary authority in S England, in Hampshire. Pop: 188 700 (2003 est). Area: 37 sq km (14 sq miles) **3** a port in SE Virginia, on the Elizabeth River: naval base; shipyards. Pop: 99 617 (2003 est)

Port Sudan n the chief port of Sudan, in the NE on the Red Sea. Pop: 499 000 (2005 est)

Port Talbot n a port in SE Wales, in Neath Port Talbot county borough on Swansea Bay: established as a coal port in the mid-19th century; large steelworks; ore terminal. Pop: 35 633 (2001)

Portugal n a republic in SW Europe, on the Atlantic: became an independent monarchy in 1139 and expelled the Moors in 1249 after more than four centuries of Muslim rule; became a republic in 1910; under the dictatorship of Salazar from 1932 until 1968, when he was succeeded by Dr Caetano, who was overthrown by a junta in 1974; constitutional government restored in 1976. Portugal is a member of the European Union. Official language: Portuguese. Religion: Roman Catholic majority. Currency: euro. Capital: Lisbon. Pop: 10 799 270 (2013 est). Area: 91 831 sq km (35 456 sq miles)

Portuguese adj **1** of or relating to Portugal or its inhabitants ▷ n **2** (pl **-guese**) a native or inhabitant of Portugal **3** the language of Portugal and Brazil

Portuguese East Africa n a former name (until 1975) of Mozambique

Portuguese Guinea n the former name (until 1974) of Guinea-Bissau

Portuguese Guinean adj **1** of or relating to Portuguese Guinea or its inhabitants ▷ n **2** a native or inhabitant of Portuguese Guinea

Portuguese India n a former Portuguese overseas province on the W coast of India, consisting of Goa, Daman, and Diu: established between 1505 and 1510; annexed by India in 1961

Portuguese man-of-war n a large sea creature like a jellyfish, with long stinging tentacles

Portuguese Timor n a former name for **East Timor**

Portuguese West Africa n a former name (until 1975) of Angola

pose vb **posing, posed 1** to take up a particular position to be photographed or drawn **2** to behave in an affected way in order to impress others (often foll. by as) to pretend to be (someone one is not) **4** to create or be (a problem, threat, etc.): dressing complicated wounds has always posed a problem for doctors **5** to put forward or ask: the question you posed earlier ▷ n **6** a position taken up for an artist or photographer **7** behaviour adopted for effect [Old French poser to set in place]

Poseidon n Greek myth the god of the sea

Posen n the German name for **Poznań**

poser¹ n **1** Brit, Austral and NZ informal a person who likes to be seen in trendy clothes in fashionable places **2** a person who poses

poser² n a baffling question

poseur n a person who behaves in an affected way in order to impress others [French]

posh adj informal, chiefly Brit **1** smart or elegant **2** upper-class [probably from obsolete slang posh a dandy]

posit (pozz-it) vb **-iting, -ited** to lay down as a basis for argument: the archetypes posited by modern psychology [Latin ponere to place]

position n **1** place or location: the hotel is in an elevated position above the River Wye **2** the proper or usual place **3** the way in which a person or thing is placed or arranged: an upright position **4** point of view; attitude: the Catholic Church's position on contraception **5** social status, esp. high social standing **6** a job; appointment **7** sport a player's allotted role or place in the playing area **8** military a place occupied for tactical reasons **9 in a position to** able to: you were not in a position to repay the money ▷ vb **10** to put into the proper or usual place; locate [Latin ponere to place] ▷ **positional** adj

positive adj **1** expressing certainty: a positive answer **2** definite or certain: are you absolutely positive about the date? **3** tending to emphasize what is good; constructive: positive thinking **4** tending towards progress or improvement: investment that could have a positive impact on the company's fortunes **5** philosophy constructive rather than sceptical **6** informal complete; downright: a positive delight **7** maths having a value greater than zero: a positive number **8** grammar denoting the unmodified form of an adjective as opposed to its comparative or superlative form **9** physics (of an electric charge) having an opposite charge to that of an electron **10** physics short for **electropositive** **11** med (of the result of an examination or test) indicating the presence of a suspected condition or organism ▷ n **12** something positive **13** maths a quantity greater than zero **14** photog a print showing an image whose colours and tones correspond to those of the original subject **15** grammar the positive degree of an adjective or adverb **16** a positive object, such as a terminal in a cell [Late Latin positivus] ▷ **positively** adv ▷ **positiveness** or **positivity** n

positive discrimination n the provision of special opportunities for a disadvantaged group

positive vetting n Brit the thorough checking of all aspects of a person's life to ensure his or her suitability for a position that may involve national security

positivism n a system of philosophy that accepts only things that can be seen or proved ▷ **positivist** n, adj

positron n physics the antiparticle of the electron, having the same mass but an equal and opposite charge [posi(tive) + (elec)tron]

poss. **1** possession **2** possessive **3** possible **4** possibly

posse (poss-ee) n **1** US a selected group of men on whom the sheriff may call for assistance **2** informal a group of friends or associates: a posse of reporters **3** (in W Canada) a troop of horses and riders who perform at rodeos [Latin: to be able]

possess vb **1** to have as one's property; own **2** to have as a quality or attribute: he possessed an innate elegance, authority, and wit on screen **3** to gain control over or dominate: absolute terror possessed her [Latin possidere] ▷ **possessor** n

possessed adj **1** (foll. by of) owning or having: he is possessed of a calm maturity far beyond his years **2** under the influence of a powerful force, such as a spirit or strong emotion: possessed by the devil; she was possessed by a frenzied urge to get out of Moscow

possession n **1** the state of possessing; ownership: how had this compromising picture come into the possession of the press? **2** anything that is possessed **3** possessions wealth or property **4** the state of being controlled by or as if by evil spirits **5** the occupancy of land or property: troops had taken possession of the airport **6** a territory subject to a foreign state **7** the criminal offence of having something illegal on one's person: arrested for drug dealing and possession **8** sport control of the ball by a team or player: City had most of the possession, but couldn't score

possessive adj **1** of possession **2** desiring excessively to possess or dominate: a possessive husband **3** grammar denoting a form of a noun or pronoun used to convey possession, as my or Harry's: a possessive pronoun ▷ n **4** grammar **a** the possessive case **b** a word in the possessive case ▷ **possessiveness** n

possibility n, pl **-ties 1** the state of being possible **2** anything that is possible **3** a competitor or candidate with a chance of success **4** a future prospect or potential: all sorts of possibilities began to open up

possible adj **1** capable of existing, happening, or proving true: *the earliest possible moment* **2** capable of being done: *I am grateful to the library staff for making this work possible* **3** having potential: *a possible buyer* **4** feasible but less than probable: *it's possible that's what he meant, but I doubt it* ▷ *n* **5** same as **possibility** (3) [Latin *possibilis*]

> **USAGE** Although it is very common to talk about something being *very possible* or *more possible*, these uses are generally thought to be incorrect, since *possible* describes an absolute state, and therefore something can only be *possible* or *not possible*: *it is very likely* (not *very possible*) *that he will resign; it has now become easier* (not *more possible*) *to obtain an entry visa*.

possibly *adv* **1** perhaps or maybe **2** by any means; at all: *he can't possibly come*

possum *n* **1** *informal* an opossum **2** *Austral and NZ* a phalanger **3** **play possum** to pretend to be dead, ignorant, or asleep in order to deceive an opponent

post¹ *n* **1** an official system of mail delivery **2** letters or packages that are transported and delivered by the Post Office; mail **3** a single collection or delivery of mail **4** a postbox or post office: *take this to the post* **5** *computers* an item of e-mail made publicly available ▷ *vb* **6** to send by post **7** *computers* to make (e-mail) publicly available **8** *accounting* **a** to enter (an item) in a ledger **b** (often foll. by *up*) to enter all paper items in (a ledger) **9** **keep someone posted** to inform someone regularly of the latest news [Latin *posita* something placed]

post² *n* **1** a length of wood, metal, or concrete fixed upright to support or mark something **2** *horse racing* **a** either of two upright poles marking the beginning and end of a racecourse **b** the finish of a horse race ▷ *vb* **3** (sometimes foll. by *up*) to put up (a notice) in a public place **4** to publish (a name) on a list [Latin *postis*]

post³ *n* **1** a position to which a person is appointed; job **2** a position to which a soldier or guard is assigned for duty **3** a permanent military establishment **4** *Brit* either of two military bugle calls (**first post** and **last post**) giving notice of the time to retire for the night ▷ *vb* **5** *Brit and Austral* to send (someone) to a new place to work **6** to assign to or station at a particular place or position: *guards were posted at the doors* [French *poste*, from Latin *ponere* to place]

post- *prefix* **1** after in time: *postgraduate* **2** behind: *postorbital* [Latin]

postage *n* the charge for sending a piece of mail by post

postage stamp *n* same as **stamp** (1)

postal *adj* of a post office or the mail-delivery service

postal order *n* a written money order sent by post and cashed at a post office by the person who receives it

postbag *n* **1** *chiefly Brit* a mailbag **2** the mail received by a magazine, radio programme, or public figure

postbox *n* same as **letter box** (2)

postcard *n* a card, often with a picture on one side, for sending a message by post without an envelope

post chaise (**shaze**) *n* old-fashioned a four-wheeled horse-drawn coach formerly used as a rapid means of carrying mail and passengers

postcode *n* a system of letters and numbers used to aid the sorting of mail

post-consumer *adj* (of a consumer item) discarded for disposal or recovery having been recycled: *made from 75% post-consumer waste*

postdate *vb* **-dating, -dated 1** to write a future date on (a cheque or document) **2** to occur at a later date than **3** to assign a date to (an event or period) that is later than its previously assigned date

poster *n* **1** a large notice displayed in a public place as an advertisement **2** a large printed picture

poste restante *n* a post-office department where mail is kept until it is called for [French, literally: mail remaining]

posterior *n* **1** *formal or humorous* the buttocks ▷ *adj* **2** at the

back of or behind something: *posterior leg muscles* **3** coming after in a series or time [Latin: latter]

posterity *n* **1** future generations **2** all of one's descendants [Latin *posterus* coming after]

postern *n* a small back door or gate [Old French *posterne*]

post-free *adv, adj* **1** *Brit and Austral* with the postage prepaid **2** free of postal charge

postgraduate *n* **1** a person who is studying for a more advanced qualification after obtaining a degree ▷ *adj* **2** of or for postgraduates

posthaste *adv* with great speed

posthumous (poss-tume-uss) *adj* **1** happening after one's death **2** born after the death of one's father **3** (of a book) published after the author's death [Latin *postumus* the last] **> posthumously** *adv*

postie *n* *Scot, Austral and NZ informal* a postman

postilion *or* **postillion** *n* (esp. formerly) a person who rides one of a pair of horses drawing a coach [French *postillon*]

postimpressionism *n* a movement in painting in France at the end of the 19th century which rejected Impressionism but adapted its use of pure colour to paint with greater subjective emotion **> postimpressionist** *n, adj*

posting *n* **1** a job to which someone is assigned by his or her employer, which involves moving to a particular town or country: *Bonn was his third posting overseas* **2** *computers* an e-mail message that is publicly available

postman *or fem* **postwoman** *n, pl* **-men** *or fem* **-women** a person who collects and delivers mail as a profession

postmark *n* **1** an official mark stamped on mail, showing the place and date of posting ▷ *vb* **2** to put such a mark on (mail)

postmaster *n* **1** Also (fem): **postmistress** an official in charge of a post office **2** the person who manages the e-mail at a site

postmaster general *n, pl* **postmasters general** the executive head of the postal service

postmeridian *adj* occurring after noon [Latin *postmeridianus*]

postmortem *n* **1** In full: **postmortem examination** medical examination of a dead body to discover the cause of death **2** analysis of a recent event: *a postmortem on the party's recent appalling by-election results* ▷ *adj* **3** occurring after death [Latin, literally: after death]

postnatal *adj* occurring after childbirth: *postnatal depression*

post office *n* a building where stamps are sold and postal business is conducted

Post Office *n* a government department responsible for postal services

postoperative *adj* of or occurring in the period after a surgical operation

postpaid *adv, adj* with the postage prepaid

postpone *vb* **-poning, -poned** to put off until a future time [Latin *postponere* to put after] **> postponement** *n*

postpositive *adj grammar* (of an adjective) placed after the word it modifies

postprandial *adj formal* after dinner [Latin *post-* after + *prandium* midday meal]

postscript *n* a message added at the end of a letter, after the signature [Late Latin *postscribere* to write after]

post-traumatic stress disorder *n* a psychological condition, characterized by anxiety, withdrawal, and a proneness to physical illness, that may follow a traumatic experience

postulant *n* an applicant for admission to a religious order [Latin *postulare* to ask]

postulate *formal vb* **-lating, -lated 1** to assume to be true as the basis of an argument or theory **2** to ask, demand, or claim ▷ *n* **3** something postulated [Latin *postulare* to ask for] **> postulation** *n*

posture *n* **1** a position or way in which a person stands, walks, etc.: *good posture* **2** a mental attitude: *a cooperative* *posture* **3** an affected attitude: *an intellectual posture* ▷ *vb* **-turing, -tured 4** to behave in an exaggerated way to attract attention **5** to assume an affected attitude [Latin *positura*] ❭ **postural** *adj*

postviral fatigue syndrome *or* **postviral syndrome** *n* same as **chronic fatigue syndrome**

postwar *adj* occurring or existing after a war

posy *n, pl* **-sies** a small bunch of flowers [variant of *poesy*]

pot¹ *n* **1** a round deep container, often with a handle and lid, used for cooking **2** the amount that a pot will hold **3** short for **flowerpot, teapot 4** a handmade piece of pottery **5** *billiards etc.* a shot by which a ball is pocketed **6** a chamber pot **7** the money in the pool in gambling games **8** (*often pl*) *informal* a large sum of money **9** *informal* a cup or other trophy **10** See **potbelly 11 go to pot** to go to ruin ▷ *vb* **potting, potted 12** to put (a plant) in soil in a flowerpot **13** *billiards etc.* to pocket (a ball) **14** to preserve (food) in a pot **15** to shoot (game) for food rather than for sport **16** to shoot casually or without careful aim **17** *informal* to capture or win [Old English *pott*]

pot² *n slang* cannabis [perhaps from Mexican Indian *potiguaya*]

potable (pote-a-bl) *adj formal* drinkable [Latin *potare* to drink]

potage (po-tahzh) *n* thick soup [French]

potash *n* **1** potassium carbonate, used as fertilizer **2** a compound containing potassium: *permanganate of potash* [from *pot ashes*, because originally obtained by evaporating the lye of wood ashes in pots]

potassium *n chem* a light silvery element of the alkali metal group. Symbol: **K** [New Latin *potassa* potash]

potassium nitrate *n* a crystalline compound used in gunpowders, fertilizers, and as a preservative for foods (E252)

potation *n formal* **1** the act of drinking **2** a drink, usually alcoholic [Latin *potare* to drink]

potato *n, pl* **-toes 1** a starchy vegetable that grows underground **2** the plant from which this vegetable is obtained [Spanish *patata*, from a Native American language]

potato beetle *n* same as **Colorado beetle**

potato chip *n* the US and Canadian term for **crisp** (7)

potato crisp *n* same as **crisp** (7)

potbelly *n, pl* **-lies 1** a bulging belly **2** a person with such a belly

potboiler *n informal* an inferior work of art produced quickly to make money

pot-bound *adj* (of a pot plant) having roots too big for its pot, so that it is unable to grow further

poteen *or* **poitín** *n* (in Ireland) illegally made alcoholic drink [Irish *poitín* little pot]

Potemkin *or* **Potyomkin** *n* **1** Grigori Aleksandrovich. 1739–91, Russian soldier and statesman; lover of Catherine II, whose favourite he remained until his death, and who is reputed to have erected sham villages along the route of the Empress's 1787 tour of the Crimea **2** apparently impressive but actually sham or artificial: *North Korea's Potemkin hospital*

potent *adj* **1** having great power or influence **2** (of arguments) persuasive or forceful **3** highly effective: *a potent poison* **4** (of a male) capable of having sexual intercourse [Latin *potens* able] ❭ **potency** *n*

potentate *n* a ruler or monarch [Latin *potens* powerful]

potential *adj* **1 a** possible but not yet actual: *potential buyers* **b** capable of being or becoming; latent: *potential danger* ▷ *n* **2** ability or talent not yet in full use: *she has great potential as a painter* **3** In full: **electric potential** the work required to transfer a unit positive electric charge from an infinite distance to a given point [Latin *potentia* power] ❭ **potentially** *adv*

potential difference *n* the difference in electric potential between two points in an electric field, measured in volts

potential energy *n* the energy which an object has

stored up because of its position

potentiality *n, pl* **-ties** latent capacity for becoming or developing

pother (rhymes with **bother**) *n literary* a fuss or commotion [origin unknown]

potherb *n* a plant whose leaves, flowers, or stems are used in cooking

pothole *n* **1** a hole in the surface of a road **2** a deep hole in a limestone area

potholing *n* the sport of exploring underground caves ❭ **potholer** *n*

pothook *n* **1** an S-shaped hook for suspending a pot over a fire **2** an S-shaped mark in handwriting

potion *n* a drink of medicine, poison, or some supposedly magic liquid [Latin *potio* a drink, esp. a poisonous one]

pot luck *n* **take pot luck** *informal* to accept whatever happens to be available: *we'll take pot luck at whatever restaurant might still be open*

Potomac *n* a river in the E central US, rising in the Appalachian Mountains of West Virginia: flows northeast, then generally southeast to Chesapeake Bay. Length (from the confluence of headstreams): 462 km (287 miles)

potoroo *n, pl* **-roos** an Australian leaping rodent

Potosí *n* a city in S Bolivia, at an altitude of 4066 m (13 340 ft): one of the highest cities in the world; developed with the discovery of local silver in 1545; tin mining; university (1571). Pop: 144 000 (2005 est)

potpourri (po-poor-ee) *n, pl* **-ris 1** a fragrant mixture of dried flower petals **2** an assortment or medley [French, literally: rotten pot]

pot roast *n* meat cooked slowly in a covered pot with very little liquid

Potsdam *n* a city in Germany, the capital of Brandenburg on the Havel River: residence of Prussian kings and German emperors and scene of the **Potsdam Conference** of 1945, at which the main Allied powers agreed on a plan to occupy Germany at the end of the Second World War. Pop: 144 979 (2003 est)

potsherd *n* a broken piece of pottery [*pot* + *schoord* piece of broken crockery]

pot shot *n* **1** a shot taken without careful aim **2** a shot fired at an animal within easy range

pottage *n* a thick soup or stew [Old French *potage* contents of a pot]

potted *adj* **1** grown in a pot: *potted plant* **2** cooked or preserved in a pot: *potted shrimps* **3** *informal* shortened or abridged: *a potted history*

potter¹ *n* a person who makes pottery

potter² *or especially US and Canad* **putter** *vb* **1** to move with little energy or direction: *I saw him pottering off to see to his canaries* **2 potter about** *or* **around** *or* **away** to be busy in a pleasant but aimless way: *he potters away doing God knows what all day* [Old English *potian* to thrust]

Potter *n* **1** (Helen) Beatrix. 1866–1943, British author and illustrator of children's animal stories, such as *The Tale of Peter Rabbit* (1902) **2** Dennis (Christopher George). 1935–94, British dramatist. His TV plays include *Pennies from Heaven* (1978), *The Singing Detective* (1986), and *Blackeyes* (1989) **3** Paulus. 1625–54, Dutch painter, esp. of animals **4** Stephen. 1900–70, British humorist and critic. Among his best-known works are *Gamesmanship* (1947) and *One-Upmanship* (1952), on the art of achieving superiority over others

Potteries *pl n* **the Potteries** (*sometimes functioning as sing*) a region of W central England, in Staffordshire, in which the china and earthenware industries are concentrated

potter's wheel *n* a flat spinning disc on which clay is shaped by hand

pottery *n, pl* **-teries 1** articles made from baked clay **2** a place where such articles are made **3** the craft of making such articles

potting shed *n* a garden hut in which plants are put in flowerpots and potting materials are stored

potty¹ adj **-tier, -tiest** informal **1** slightly crazy **2** trivial or insignificant **3** (foll. by about) very keen (on) [origin unknown] ⟩ **pottiness** n

potty² n, pl **-ties** a bowl used as a toilet by a small child

pouch n **1** a small bag **2** a baglike pocket in various animals, such as the cheek fold in hamsters ▷ vb **3** to place in or as if in a pouch **4** to make or be made into a pouch [Old French poche bag]

pouf or **pouffe** (poof) n a large solid cushion used as a seat [French]

Poulenc n Francis. 1899–1963, French composer; a member of Les Six. His works include the operas Les Mamelles de Tirésias (1947) and Dialogues des Carmélites (1957), and the ballet Les Biches (1924)

poulterer n Brit a person who sells poultry

poultice (pole-tiss) n med a moist dressing, often heated, applied to painful and swollen parts of the body [Latin puls a thick porridge]

poultry n domestic fowls [Old French pouletrie]

pounce vb **pouncing, pounced 1** (often foll. by on or upon) to spring open suddenly to attack or capture ▷ n **2** the act of pouncing; a spring or swoop [origin unknown]

pound¹ n **1** the standard monetary unit of the United Kingdom and some other countries, made up of 100 pence. Official name: **pound sterling 2** the standard monetary unit of various other countries, such as Cyprus and Malta **3** a unit of weight made up of 16 ounces and equal to 0.454 kilograms [Old English pund]

pound² vb **1** (sometimes foll. by on or at) to hit heavily and repeatedly **2** to crush to pieces or to powder **3** (foll. by out) to produce, by typing heavily **4** (of the heart) to throb heavily **5** to run with heavy steps [Old English pūnian]

pound³ n an enclosure for stray dogs or officially removed vehicles [Old English pund-]

Pound n Ezra (**Loomis**). 1885–1972, US poet, translator, and critic, living in Europe. Indicted for treason by the US government (1945) for pro-Fascist broadcasts during World War II, he was committed to a mental hospital until 1958. He was a founder of imagism and championed the early work of such writers as T. S. Eliot, Joyce, and Hemingway. His life work, the Cantos (1925–70), is an unfinished sequence of poems, which incorporates mythological and historical materials in several languages as well as political, economic, and autobiographical elements

poundage n **1** a charge of so much per pound of weight **2** a charge of so much per pound sterling

-pounder combining form **1** something weighing a specified number of pounds: a 200-pounder **2** something worth a specified number of pounds: a ten-pounder **3** a gun that discharges a shell weighing a specified number of pounds: a two-pounder

pour vb **1** to flow or cause to flow out in a stream **2** to rain heavily **3** to be given or obtained in large amounts: foreign aid is pouring into Iran **4** to move together in large numbers: the fans poured onto the pitch [origin unknown]

> **USAGE** The verbs pour and pore are sometimes confused: she poured cream over her strudel; she pored (not poured) over the manuscript.

pourboire (poor-bwahr) n a tip or gratuity [French, literally: for drinking]

Poussin n Nicolas. 1594–1665, French painter, regarded as a leader of French classical painting. He is best known for the austere historical and biblical paintings and landscapes of his later years

pout vb **1** to thrust out (the lips) sullenly or provocatively **2** to swell out; protrude ▷ n **3** a pouting [origin unknown]

pouter n a breed of domestic pigeon that can puff out its crop

poutine (poo-teen) n Canad a dish of chipped potatoes topped with curd cheese and a tomato-based sauce

poverty n **1** the state of lacking adequate food or money **2** lack or scarcity: a poverty of information **3** inferior quality or inadequacy: the poverty of political debate in this country [Old French poverté]

poverty-stricken adj extremely poor

poverty trap n the situation of being unable to raise one's living standard because any extra income would result in state benefits being reduced or withdrawn

pow interj an exclamation to indicate that a collision or explosion has taken place

POW prisoner of war

powder n **1** a substance in the form of tiny loose particles **2** a medicine or cosmetic in this form ▷ vb **3** to cover or sprinkle with powder [Old French poldre, from Latin pulvis dust] ⟩ **powdery** adj

powdered adj **1** sold in the form of a powder, esp. one which has been formed by grinding or drying the original material: powdered milk **2** covered or made up with a cosmetic in the form of a powder: liveried footmen in powdered wigs

powder keg n **1** a potential source of violence or disaster: a political powder keg **2** a small barrel for holding gunpowder

powder puff n a soft pad used to apply cosmetic powder to the skin

powder room n a ladies' cloakroom or toilet

Powell n **1** Anthony (**Dymoke**). 1905–2000, British novelist, best known for his sequence of novels under the general title A Dance to the Music of Time (1951–75) **2** Cecil Frank. 1903–69, British physicist, who was awarded the Nobel prize for physics in 1950 for his discovery of the pi-meson **3** Colin (**Luther**). born 1937, US politician and general; Republican secretary of state (2001–05) **4** Earl, known as Bud Powell. 1924–1966, US modern-jazz pianist **5** (**John**) Enoch. 1912–98, British politician. An outspoken opponent of Commonwealth immigration into Britain and of British membership of the Common Market (now the European Union), in 1974 he resigned from the Conservative Party, returning to Parliament as a United Ulster Unionist Council member (1974–87) **6** Michael. 1905–90, British film writer, producer, and director, best known for his collaboration (1942–57) with Emeric Pressburger. Films include The Life and Death of Colonel Blimp (1943), A Matter of Life and Death (1946), The Red Shoes (1948), and Peeping Tom (1960)

power n **1** ability to do something **2** (often pl) a specific ability or faculty **3** political, financial, or social force or authority: men's use of power over women in a subordinate position in the workforce; economic power is the bedrock of political power **4** a position of control, esp. over the running of a country: he seized power in a coup in 1966 **5** a state with political, industrial, or military strength **6** a person or group having authority **7** a prerogative or privilege: the power of veto **8** official or legal authority **9** maths the value of a number or quantity raised to some exponent **10** physics, engineering a measure of the rate of doing work expressed as the work done per unit of time **11** the rate at which electrical energy is fed into or taken from a device or system, measured in watts **12** mechanical energy as opposed to manual labour **13** a particular form of energy: nuclear power **14** the magnifying capacity of a lens or optical system **15** informal a great deal: a power of good **16 the powers that be** established authority ▷ vb **17** to supply with power ▷ adj **18** producing or using electrical energy: a large selection of power tools [Anglo-Norman poer]

powerboat n a fast powerful motorboat

power cut n a temporary interruption in the supply of electricity

powerful adj **1** having great power or influence **2** having great physical strength **3** extremely effective: a powerful drug ⟩ **powerfully** adv ⟩ **powerfulness** n

powerhouse n **1** informal a forceful person or thing

2 an electrical generating station

powerless *adj* without power or authority; unable to act › **powerlessly** *adv* › **powerlessness** *n*

power of attorney *n* **1** legal authority to act for another person **2** the document conferring such authority

power play *n* **1** behaviour or tactics intended to magnify a person's influence or power **2** the use of brute strength or force of numbers in order to achieve an objective

power point *n* an electrical socket fitted into a wall for plugging in electrical appliances

power pole *n Austral and NZ* a pole carrying an overhead power line

power-sharing *n* a political arrangement in which opposing groups in a society participate in government

power station *n* an installation for generating and distributing electricity

power steering *n* a type of steering in vehicles in which the turning of the steering wheel is assisted by power from the engine

Powhatan *n* American Indian name *Wahunsonacock.* died 1618, American Indian chief of a confederacy of tribes; father of Pocahontas

powwow *n* **1 a** talk or meeting **2** a meeting of Native Americans of N America ▷ *vb* **3** to hold a powwow [from a Native American language]

Powys¹ *n* a county in E Wales, formed in 1974 from most of Breconshire, Montgomeryshire, and Radnorshire. Administrative centre: Llandrindod Wells. Pop: 129 300 (2003 est). Area: 5077 sq km (1960 sq miles)

Powys² *n* **1** John Cowper. 1872–1963, British novelist, essayist, and poet, who spent much of his life in the US. His novels include *Wolf Solent* (1929), *A Glastonbury Romance* (1932), and *Owen Glendower* (1940) **2** his brother, **Llewelyn.** 1884–1939, British essayist and journalist **3** his brother, **T**(heodore) **F**(rancis). 1875–1953, British novelist and short-story writer, noted for such religious fables as *Mr Weston's Good Wine* (1927) and *Unclay* (1931)

pox *n* **1 a** disease in which pus-filled blisters or pimples form on the skin **2 the pox** *informal* syphilis [changed from *pocks,* plural of *pock*]

Poyang Lake *or* **P'o-yang** *n* a lake in E China, in N Jiangxi province, connected by canal with the Yangtze River: the second largest lake in China. Area (at its greatest): 2780 sq km (1073 sq miles)

Poznań *n* a city in W Poland, on the Warta River: the centre of Polish resistance to German rule (1815–1918, 1939–45). Pop: 661 000 (2005 est). German name: **Posen**

Pozsony *n* the Hungarian name for **Bratislava**

Pozzuoli *n* a port in SW Italy, in Campania on the Gulf of Pozzuoli (an inlet of the Bay of Naples): in a region of great volcanic activity; founded in the 6th century BC by the Greeks. Pop: 78 754 (2001)

pp **1** past participle **2** (in signing documents on behalf of someone else) by delegation to [Latin *per procurationem*]

USAGE In formal correspondence, when Brenda Smith is signing on behalf of Peter Jones, she should write *Peter Jones pp Brenda Smith,* not the other way about.

pp. pages

PPS **1** parliamentary private secretary **2** additional postscript [Latin *post postscriptum*]

PPTA (in New Zealand) Post Primary Teachers Association

PQ **1** Province of Quebec **2** (in Canada) Parti Québécois

PQE *or* **Pqe** post-qualification experience

pr *pl* **prs** pair

Pr *chem* praseodymium

PR **1** proportional representation **2** public relations **3** Puerto Rico

pr. **1** price **2** pronoun

practicable *adj* **1** capable of being done **2** usable [French *praticable*] › **practicability** *n*

USAGE See at **practical.**

practical *adj* **1** involving experience or actual use rather than theory **2** concerned with everyday matters: *the kind of practical and emotional upheaval that divorce can bring* **3** sensible, useful, and effective rather than fashionable or attractive: *it's a marvellous design, because it's comfortable, it's practical, and it actually looks good* **4** involving the simple basics: *practical skills* **5** being very close to (a state); virtual: *it's a practical certainty* ▷ *n* **6** an examination or lesson in which something has to be made or done [Greek *praktikos,* from *prattein* to experience] › **practicality** *n* › **practically** *adv*

USAGE A distinction is usually made between *practical* and *practicable. Practical* refers to a person, idea, project, etc., as being more concerned with or relevant to practice than theory: *he is a very practical person; the idea had no practical application. Practicable* refers to a project or idea as being capable of being done or put into effect: *the plan was expensive, yet practicable.*

practical joke *n* a trick intended to make someone look foolish › **practical joker** *n*

practice *n* **1** something done regularly or repeatedly **2** repetition of an activity in order to gain skill: *regular practice is essential if you want to play an instrument well* **3** the business or surgery of a doctor or lawyer **4** the act of doing something: *I'm not sure how effective these methods will be when put into practice* **5 in practice** *a* what actually happens as distinct from what is supposed to happen: *many ideas which look good on paper just don't work in practice* **b** skilled in something through having had a lot of regular recent experience at it: *I still go shooting, just to keep in practice* **6 out of practice** not having had much regular recent experience at an activity: *although out of practice, I still love playing my violin* [Greek *praktikē* practical work]

practise *or US* **practice** *vb* **-tising, -tised** *or* **-ticing, -ticed** **1** to do repeatedly in order to gain skill **2** to take part in or follow (a religion etc.): *none of them practise Islam* **3** to work at (a profession): *he originally intended to practise medicine* **4** to do regularly: *they practise meditation* [Greek *prattein* to do]

practised *or US* **practiced** *adj* expert or skilled because of long experience in a skill or field: *the doctor answered with a practised smoothness*

practising *or US* **practicing** *adj* taking part in an activity or career on a regular basis: *a practising barrister*

practitioner *n* a person who practises a profession

Prado *n* an art gallery in Madrid housing an important collection of Spanish paintings

praetor (pree-tor) *n* (in ancient Rome) a senior magistrate ranking just below the consuls [Latin] › **praetorian** *adj, n*

Praetorius *n* Michael. 1571–1621, German composer and musicologist, noted esp. for his description of contemporary musical practices and instruments, *Syntagma musicum* (1615–19)

pragmatic *adj* **1** concerned with practical consequences rather than theory **2** *philosophy* of pragmatism [Greek *pragmatikos*] › **pragmatically** *adv*

pragmatism *n* **1** policy dictated by practical consequences rather than by theory **2** *philosophy* the doctrine that the content of a concept consists only in its practical applicability › **pragmatist** *n, adj*

Prague *n* the capital and largest city of the Czech Republic, on the Vltava River: a rich commercial centre during the Middle Ages; site of Charles University (1348) and a technical university (1707); scene of defenestrations (1419 and 1618) that contributed to the outbreak of the Hussite Wars and the Thirty Years' War respectively. Pop: 1 164 000 (2005 est). Czech name: **Praha**

Praha n the Czech name for **Prague**

Praia n the capital of Cape Verde; a port and submarine cable station. Pop: 115 000 (2005 est)

prairie n (often pl) a large treeless area of grassland of North America [French, from Latin pratum meadow]

prairie dog n a rodent that lives in burrows in the N American prairies

Prairie Provinces pl n the Canadian provinces of Manitoba, Saskatchewan, and Alberta, which lie in the N Great Plains region of North America: the chief wheat and petroleum producing area of Canada

praise vb **praising, praised 1** to express admiration or approval for **2** to express thanks and worship to (one's God) ▷ n **3** the expression of admiration or approval **4 sing someone's praises** to praise someone highly [Latin pretium prize]

praiseworthy adj deserving praise; commendable

praline (prah-leen) n a sweet made of nuts with caramelized sugar [French]

pram n a four-wheeled carriage for a baby, pushed by a person on foot [altered from perambulator]

prance vb **prancing, pranced 1** to walk with exaggerated movements **2** (of an animal) to move with high springing steps ▷ n **3** the act of prancing [origin unknown]

Prandtl n Ludwig. 1875–1953, German physicist, who made important contributions to aerodynamics and aeronautics

prang Brit and Austral slang n **1** a crash in an aircraft or car ▷ vb **2** to crash or damage (an aircraft or car) [perhaps imitative]

prank n a mischievous trick [origin unknown] **> prankster** n

Prasad n Rajendra. 1884–1963, Indian statesman and journalist; first president of India (1950–62)

praseodymium (pray-zee-oh-dim-ee-um) n chem a silvery-white element of the lanthanide series of metals. Symbol: Pr [New Latin]

prat n Brit, Austral and NZ slang an incompetent or ineffectual person [probably special use of earlier prat buttocks, origin unknown]

Pratchett n Sir Terence (David John), known as Terry. (1948–2015), British writer, noted for his comic fantasy novels in the Discworld series

prate vb **prating, prated 1** to talk idly and at length ▷ n **2** chatter [Germanic]

Prato n a walled city in central Italy, in Tuscany: woollen industry. Pop: 172 499 (2001). Official name: **Prato in Toscana**

prattle vb **-tling, -tled 1** to chatter in a foolish or childish way ▷ n **2** foolish or childish talk [Middle Low German pratelen to chatter]

prawn n a small edible shellfish [origin unknown]

praxis n **1** practice as opposed to the theory **2** accepted practice or custom [Greek: deed, action]

Praxiteles n 4th-century BC Greek sculptor: his works include statues of Hermes at Olympia, which survives, and of Aphrodite at Cnidus

pray vb **1** to say prayers (to one's God) **2** to ask earnestly; beg ▷ adv **3** archaic I beg you; please: pray, leave us alone [Latin precari to implore]

prayer¹ n **1** a thanksgiving or an appeal spoken to one's God **2** a set form of words used in praying: the Lord's Prayer **3** an earnest request **4** the practice of praying: call the faithful to prayer **5** (often pl) a form of devotion spent mainly praying: morning prayers **6** something prayed for

prayer² n a person who prays

prayer book n a book of prayers used in church or at home

prayer mat or **prayer rug** n the small carpet on which a Muslim performs his or her daily prayers

prayer wheel n Buddhism (in Tibet) a cylinder inscribed with prayers, each turning of which is counted as an uttered prayer

praying mantis n same as **mantis**

PRC People's Republic of China

pre- prefix before in time or position: predate; pre-eminent [Latin prae]

preach vb **1** to talk on a religious theme as part of a church service **2** to speak in support of (something) in a moralizing way [Latin praedicare to proclaim]

preacher n a person who preaches

preamble n an introduction that comes before something spoken or written [Latin prae before + ambulare to walk]

prearranged adj arranged beforehand **> prearrangement** n

prebend n **1** the allowance paid by a cathedral or collegiate church to a canon or member of the chapter **2** the land or tithe from which this is paid [Old French prébende] **> prebendal** adj

prebendary n, pl **-daries** a clergyman who is a member of the chapter of a cathedral

Precambrian or **Pre-Cambrian** adj geology of the earliest geological era, lasting from about 4500 million years ago to 600 million years ago

precancerous adj relating to cells that show signs that they may develop cancer

precarious adj (of a position or situation) dangerous or insecure [Latin precarius obtained by begging] **> precariously** adv

precaution n an action taken in advance to prevent an undesirable event [Latin prae before + cavere to beware] **> precautionary** adj

precede vb **-ceding, -ceded** to go or be before (someone or something) in time, place, or rank [Latin praecedere]

precedence (press-i-denss) n formal order of rank or position

precedent n **1** a previous occurrence used to justify taking the same action in later similar situations **2** law a judicial decision that serves as an authority for deciding a later case ▷ adj **3** preceding

precentor n a person who leads the singing in church services [Latin prae before + canere to sing]

precept n **1** a rule of conduct **2** a rule for morals **3** law a writ or warrant [Latin praeceptum] **> preceptive** adj

preceptor n rare an instructor **> preceptorial** adj

precession n **1** the act of preceding **2** the motion of a spinning body, in which the axis of rotation sweeps out a cone **3 precession of the equinoxes** the slightly earlier occurrence of the equinoxes each year [Latin praecedere to precede]

precinct n **1** Brit, Austral and S African an area in a town closed to traffic: a shopping precinct **2** Brit, Austral and S African an enclosed area around a building **3** US an administrative area of a city [Latin praecingere to surround]

precincts pl n the surrounding region

preciosity (presh-ee-oss-it-ee) n, pl **-ties** affectation

precious adj **1** very costly or valuable: precious jewellery **2** loved and treasured **3** very affected in speech, manners, or behaviour ▷ adv **4** informal very: there's precious little to do in this town [Latin pretiosus valuable]

precious metal n gold, silver, or platinum

precious stone n a rare mineral, such as diamond, ruby, or opal, that is highly valued as a gem

precipice n the very steep face of a cliff [Latin praecipitium steep place]

precipitant adj **1** hasty or rash **2** rushing or falling rapidly ▷ n **3** something which helps bring about an event or condition: stressful events are often the precipitant for a manic attack

precipitate vb **-tating, -tated 1** to cause to happen earlier than expected: the scandal could bring the government down, precipitating a general election **2** to condense or cause to condense and fall as snow or rain **3** chem to cause to be deposited in solid form from a solution **4** to throw from a height: *the encircled soldiers chose to precipitate themselves into the ocean* ▷ *adj* **5** done rashly or hastily **6** rushing ahead ▷ *n* **7** *chem* a precipitated solid [Latin *praecipitare* to throw down headlong]

precipitation *n* **1** the formation of a chemical precipitate **2** *meteorol* **a** rain, hail, snow, or sleet formed by condensation of water vapour in the atmosphere **b** the falling of these **3** rash haste: *they decamped with the utmost precipitation*

precipitous *adj* **1** very steep: *precipitous cliffs* **2** very quick and severe: *a precipitous decline* **3** rapid and unplanned; hasty: *European governments urged the Americans not to make a precipitous decision*

> **USAGE** The use of *precipitous* to mean *hasty* is thought by some people to be incorrect.

précis (pray-see) *n*, *pl* **précis 1** a short summary of a longer text ▷ *vb* **2** to make a précis of [French]

precise *adj* **1** particular or exact: *this precise moment* **2** strictly correct in amount or value: *precise measurements* **3** working with total accuracy: *precise instruments* **4** strict in observing rules or standards [Latin *prae* before + *caedere* to cut] > **precisely** *adv*

precision *n* **1** the quality of being precise ▷ *adj* **2** accurate: *precision engineering*

preclude *vb* **-cluding, -cluded** *formal* to make impossible to happen [Latin *prae* before + *claudere* to close]

precocious *adj* having developed or matured early or too soon [Latin *prae* early + *coquere* to ripen] > **precocity** *n*

precognition *n* *psychol* the alleged ability to foresee future events [Latin *praecognoscere* to foresee]

preconceived *adj* (of ideas etc.) formed without real experience or reliable information > **preconception** *n*

precondition *n* something that is necessary before something else can come about

precursor *n* **1** something that comes before and signals something to follow; a forerunner **2** a predecessor [Latin *praecursor* one who runs in front]

pred. predicate

predacious *adj* (of animals) habitually hunting and killing other animals for food [Latin *praeda* plunder]

predate *vb* **-dating, -dated 1** to occur at an earlier date than **2** to write a date on (a document) that is earlier than the actual date

predator *n* an animal that kills and eats other animals

predatory (pred-a-tree) *adj* **1** (of animals) habitually hunting and killing other animals for food **2** eager to gain at the expense of others [Latin *praedari* to pillage]

predecease *vb* **-ceasing, -ceased** to die before (someone else)

predecessor *n* **1** a person who precedes another in an office or position **2** an ancestor **3** something that precedes something else: *the library will be more extravagant than its predecessors* [Latin *prae* before + *decedere* to go away]

predestination *n* *Christian theol* the belief that future events have already been decided by God

predestined *adj* *Christian theol* determined in advance by God [Latin *praedestinare* to resolve beforehand]

predetermine *vb* **-mining, -mined 1** to determine beforehand **2** to influence or bias > **predetermined** *adj*

predicable *adj* capable of being predicated

predicament *n* an embarrassing or difficult situation [see PREDICATE]

predicant (pred-ik-ant) *adj* **1** of preaching ▷ *n* **2** a member of a religious order founded for preaching, usually a Dominican [Latin *praedicans* preaching]

predicate *n* **1** *grammar* the part of a sentence in which something is said about the subject **2** *logic* something that is asserted about the subject of a proposition ▷ *vb* **-cating, -cated 3** to base or found: *political aims which are predicated upon a feminist view of women's oppression* **4** to declare or assert: *it has been predicated that if we continue with*

our current sexual behaviour every family will have an AIDS victim **5** *logic* to assert (something) about the subject of a proposition [Latin *praedicare* to assert publicly] > **predication** *n* > **predicative** *adj*

predict *vb* to tell about in advance; prophesy [Latin *praedicere*] > **predictable** *adj* > **predictably** *adv* > **predictor** *n*

prediction *n* **1** the act of forecasting in advance **2** something that is forecast in advance

predictive *adj* **1** relating to or able to make predictions **2** (of a word processor) able to complete words after only part of a word has been keyed

predikant (pred-ik-ant) *n* a minister in the Dutch Reformed Church in South Africa [Dutch]

predilection *n* *formal* a preference or liking [French *prédilection*]

predispose *vb* **-posing, -posed** (often foll. by *to*) **1** to influence (someone) in favour of something: *some scientists' social class background predisposes them to view the natural world in a certain way* **2** to make (someone) susceptible to something: *a high-fat diet appears to predispose men towards heart disease* > **predisposition** *n*

predominant *adj* being more important or noticeable than others: *improved living conditions probably played the predominant role in reducing disease in the nineteenth century* > **predominance** *n* > **predominantly** *adv*

predominate *vb* **-nating, -nated 1** to be the most important or controlling aspect or part: *the image of brutal repression that has tended to predominate since the protests were crushed* **2** to form the greatest part or be most common: *women predominate in this gathering* [Latin *prae* before + *dominari* to rule]

pre-eminent *adj* outstanding > **pre-eminence** *n*

pre-empt *vb* to prevent an action by doing something which makes it pointless or impossible: *he pre-empted his expulsion from the party by resigning*

pre-emption *n* *law* the purchase of or right to buy property in advance of others [Medieval Latin *praeemere* to buy beforehand]

pre-emptive *adj* *military* designed to damage or destroy an enemy's attacking strength before it can be used: *a pre-emptive strike*

preen *vb* **1** (of birds) to clean or trim (feathers) with the beak **2** to smarten (oneself) carefully **3 preen oneself** (often foll. by *on*) to be self-satisfied [Middle English *preinen*]

pref. 1 preface **2** prefatory **3** preference **4** preferred **5** prefix

prefab *n* a prefabricated house

prefabricated *adj* (of a building) made in shaped sections for quick assembly

preface (pref-iss) *n* **1** an introduction to a book, usually explaining its intention or content **2** anything introductory ▷ *vb* **-facing, -faced 3** to say or do something before proceeding to the main part **4** to act as a preface to [Latin *praefari* to say in advance]

prefatory *adj* concerning a preface [Latin *praefari* to say in advance]

prefect *n* **1** *Brit, Austral and NZ* a senior pupil in a school with limited power over the behaviour of other pupils **2** (in some countries) the chief administrative officer in a department [Latin *praefectus* one put in charge]

prefecture *n* the office or area of authority of a prefect

prefer *vb* **-ferring, -ferred 1** to like better: *most people prefer television to reading books* **2** *law* to put (charges) before a court for judgment **3** (*often passive*) to promote over another or others [Latin *praeferre* to carry in front, prefer]

> **USAGE** Normally, *to* is used after *prefer* and *preferable*, not *than*: *I prefer Brahms to Tchaikovsky; a small income is preferable to no income at all*, but *than* or *rather than* should be used to link infinitives: *I prefer to walk than/rather than to catch the train.*

preferable *adj* more desirable or suitable **> preferably** *adv*

> **USAGE** Since *preferable* already means *more desirable*, you should not say something is *more preferable* or *most preferable*. See also at **prefer**.

preference *n* 1 a liking for one thing above the rest 2 a person or thing preferred

preference shares *pl n* shares issued by a company which give their holders a priority over ordinary shareholders to payment of dividend

preferential *adj* 1 showing preference: *preferential treatment* 2 indicating a special favourable status in business affairs: *the President is to renew China's preferential trading status* 3 indicating a voting system which allows voters to rank candidates in order of preference: *a multi-option referendum with preferential voting*

preferment *n* promotion to a higher position

prefigure *vb* **-guring, -gured** 1 to represent or suggest in advance 2 to imagine beforehand

prefix *n* 1 *grammar* a letter or group of letters put at the beginning of a word to make a new word, such as *un-* in *unhappy* 2 a title put before a name, such as *Mr* ▷ *vb* 3 *grammar* to add (a letter or group of letters) as a prefix to the beginning of a word 4 to put before

pregnant *adj* 1 carrying a fetus or fetuses within the womb 2 full of meaning or significance: *a pregnant pause* [Latin *praegnans*] **> pregnancy** *n*

prehensile *adj* capable of curling round objects and grasping them: *a prehensile tail* [Latin *prehendere* to grasp]

prehistoric *adj* of man's development before the appearance of the written word **> prehistory** *n*

preindustrial *adj* of a time before the mechanization of industry

prejudge *vb* **-judging, -judged** to judge before knowing all the facts

prejudice *n* 1 an unreasonable or unfair dislike or preference 2 intolerance of or dislike for people because they belong to a specific race, religion, or group: *class prejudice* 3 the act or condition of holding such opinions 4 harm or detriment: *conduct to the prejudice of good order and military discipline* 5 **without prejudice** *law* without harm to an existing right or claim ▷ *vb* **-dicing, -diced** 6 to cause (someone) to have a prejudice 7 to harm: *the incident prejudiced his campaign* [Latin *prae* before + *judicium* sentence]

prejudicial *adj* harmful; damaging

prelacy *n, pl* **-cies** 1 a the office or status of a prelate b prelates collectively 2 *often offensive* government of the Church by prelates

prelate (prel-it) *n* a clergyman of high rank, such as a bishop [Church Latin *praelatus*, from Latin *praeferre* to hold in special esteem]

preliminaries *pl n* same as prelims

preliminary *adj* 1 occurring before or in preparation; introductory ▷ *n, pl* **-naries** 2 an action or event occurring before or in preparation for an activity: *the discussions are a preliminary to the main negotiations* 3 a qualifying contest held before a main competition [Latin *prae* before + *limen* threshold]

prelims *pl n* 1 the pages of a book, such as the title page and contents, which come before the main text 2 the first public examinations in some universities [a contraction of *preliminaries*]

prelude (prel-yewd) *n* 1 a an introductory movement in music b a short piece of music for piano or organ 2 an event introducing or preceding the main event ▷ *vb* **-luding, -luded** 3 to act as a prelude to (something) 4 to introduce by a prelude [Latin *prae* before + *ludere* to play]

premarital *adj* occurring before marriage: *premarital sex*

premature *adj* 1 happening or done before the normal or expected time: *premature ageing* 2 impulsive or hasty: *a premature judgment* 3 (of a baby) born weeks before the

date when it was due to be born [Latin *prae* in advance + *maturus* ripe] **> prematurely** *adv*

premedication *n surgery* any drugs given to prepare a patient for a general anaesthetic

premeditated *adj* planned in advance **> premeditation** *n*

premenstrual *adj* occurring or experienced before a menstrual period

premenstrual syndrome *or* **premenstrual tension** *n* symptoms, such as nervous tension, that may be experienced because of hormonal changes in the days before a menstrual period starts

premier *n* 1 a prime minister 2 a head of government of a Canadian province or Australian state ▷ *adj* 3 first in importance or rank: *Torbay, Devon's premier resort* 4 first in occurrence [Latin *primus* first] **> premiership** *n*

premiere *n* 1 the first public performance of a film, play, or opera ▷ *vb* **-ering, -ered** 2 to give, or (of a film, play, or opera) be, a premiere: *the play was premiered last year in Johannesburg; the movie premieres tomorrow* [French, feminine of *premier* first]

Preminger *n* Otto (Ludwig). 1906–86, US film director, born in Austria. His films include *Carmen Jones* (1954) and *Anatomy of a Murder* (1959)

premise *or* **premiss** *n logic* a statement that is assumed to be true and is used as a basis for an argument [Medieval Latin *praemissa* sent on before]

premises *pl n* 1 a piece of land together with its buildings 2 *law* (in a deed) the matters referred to previously

premium *n* 1 an extra sum of money added to a standard rate, price, or wage: *the superior taste persuades me to pay the premium for bottled water* 2 the (regular) amount paid for an insurance policy 3 the amount above the usual value at which something sells: *some even pay a premium of up to 15% for the privilege* 4 great value or regard: *we do put a very high premium on common sense* 5 **at a premium** a in great demand, usually because of scarcity b at a higher price than usual [Latin *praemium* prize]

Premium Savings Bonds *pl n* (in Britain) savings certificates issued by the government, on which no interest is paid, but there is a monthly draw for cash prizes. Also called: **premium bonds**

premolar *n* a tooth between the canine and first molar in adult humans

premonition *n* a feeling that something unpleasant is going to happen; foreboding [Latin *prae* before + *monere* to warn] **> premonitory** *adj*

prenatal *adj* before birth; during pregnancy

preoccupy *vb* **-pies, -pying, -pied** to fill the thoughts or mind of (someone) to the exclusion of other things [Latin *praeoccupare* to capture in advance] **> preoccupation** *n*

preordained *adj* decreed or determined in advance

preowned *adj euphemistic* already used; second-hand

prep *n Brit informal* short for **preparation** (4)

prep. 1 preparation 2 preparatory 3 preposition

prepacked *adj* (of goods) sold already wrapped

prepaid *adj* paid for in advance

preparation *n* 1 the act of preparing or being prepared 2 (often pl) something done in order to prepare for something else: *to make preparations for a wedding* 3 something that is prepared, such as a medicine 4 *Brit old-fashioned* a homework b the period reserved for this

preparatory (prip-par-a-tree) *adj* 1 preparing for: *a preparatory meeting to organize the negotiations* 2 introductory 3 **preparatory to** before: *Jack cleared his throat preparatory to speaking*

preparatory school *n* 1 *Brit and S African* a private school for children between the ages of 6 and 13, generally preparing pupils for public school 2 (in the US) a private secondary school preparing pupils for college

prepare *vb* **-paring, -pared** 1 to make or get ready: *the army prepared for battle* 2 to put together using parts or ingredients: *he had spent most of the afternoon preparing the meal* **3** to equip or outfit, as for an expedition **4 be prepared to** to be willing and able to: *I'm not prepared to say* [Latin *prae* before + *parare* to make ready]

prepay *vb* **-paying, -paid** to pay for in advance **> prepayment** *n*

preponderant *adj* greater in amount, force, or influence **> preponderance** *n*

preponderate *vb* **-ating, -ated** to be more powerful, important, or numerous (than): *the good preponderate over the bad* [Late Latin *praeponderare* to be of greater weight]

preposition *n* a word used before a noun or pronoun to relate it to the other words, for example *in* in *he is in the car* [Latin *praepositio* a putting before] **> prepositional** *adj*

USAGE The practice of ending a sentence with a preposition (*Venice is a place I should like to go to*) was formerly regarded as incorrect, but is now acceptable and is the preferred form in many contexts.

prepossess *vb* **1** to make a favourable impression in advance **2** to preoccupy or engross mentally **> prepossession** *n*

prepossessing *adj* making a favourable impression; attractive

preposterous *adj* utterly absurd [Latin *praeposterus* reversed]

prep school *n informal* See **preparatory school**

prepuce (pree-pyooss) *n* **1** the retractable fold of skin covering the tip of the penis; foreskin **2** the retractable fold of skin covering the tip of the clitoris [Latin *praeputium*]

Pre-Raphaelite (pree-raff-a-lite) *n* **1** a member of a group of painters in the nineteenth century who revived the style considered typical of Italian painting before Raphael **> adj 2** of or in the manner of Pre-Raphaelite painting and painters

prerecord *vb* to record (music or a programme) in advance so that it can be played or broadcast later **> prerecorded** *adj*

prerequisite *n* **1** something that is required before something else is possible **> adj 2** required before something else is possible

prerogative *n* a special privilege or right [Latin *praerogativa* privilege]

pres. 1 present (time) **2** presidential

Pres. President

presage (press-ij) *vb* **-aging, -aged 1** to be a warning or sign of something about to happen: *the windless air presaged disaster* **> n 2** an omen **3** a misgiving [Latin *praesagire* to perceive beforehand]

presbyopia *n med* a gradual inability of the eye to focus on nearby objects [Greek *presbus* old man + *ōps* eye]

presbyter *n* **1** (in some episcopal Churches) an official with administrative and priestly duties **2** (in the Presbyterian Church) an elder [Greek *presbuteros* an older man] **> presbyterial** *adj*

presbyterian *adj* **1** of or designating Church government by lay elders **> n 2** someone who supports this type of Church government **> presbyterianism** *n*

Presbyterian *adj* **1** of any of the Protestant Churches governed by lay elders **> n 2** a member of a Presbyterian Church **> Presbyterianism** *n*

presbytery *n, pl* **-teries 1** Presbyterian Church a local Church court **2** RC Church the residence of a parish priest **3** elders collectively **4** the part of a church east of the choir; a sanctuary [see PRESBYTER]

preschool *adj* of or for children below the age of five: *a preschool playgroup*

prescience (press-ee-enss) *n formal* knowledge of events before they happen [Latin *praescire* to know beforehand] **> prescient** *adj*

Prescott *n* **1** John (**Leslie**). Baron. born 1938, British

politician: deputy leader of the Labour Party (1994–2007); deputy prime minister (1997–2007) **2** William **Hickling**. 1796–1859, US historian, noted for his work on the history of Spain and her colonies

prescribe *vb* **-scribing, -scribed 1** med to recommend the use of (a medicine or other remedy) **2** to lay down as a rule [Latin *praescribere* to write previously]

prescript *n* something laid down or prescribed

prescription *n* **1 a** written instructions from a doctor for the preparation and use of a medicine **b** the medicine prescribed **2** written instructions from an optician specifying the lenses needed to correct bad eyesight **3** a prescribing [Legal Latin *praescriptio* an order]

prescriptive *adj* **1** laying down rules **2** based on tradition

presence *n* **1** the fact of being in a specified place: *the test detects the presence of sugar in the urine* **2** impressive personal appearance or bearing: *a person of dignified and commanding presence* **3** the company or nearness of a person: *she seemed completely unaware of my presence* **4** military a force stationed in another country: *the American-led military presence in the Gulf* **5** an invisible spirit felt to be nearby: *I felt a presence in the room* [Latin *praesentia* a being before]

presence of mind *n* the ability to stay calm and act sensibly in a crisis

present[1] *adj* **1** being in a specified place: *he had been present at the birth of his son* **2** existing or happening now **3** current: *the present exchange rate* **4** grammar of a verb tense used when the action described is happening now **> n 5** grammar the present tense **6 at present** now **7 for the present** for now; temporarily **8 the present** the time being; now **> See also presents** [Latin *praesens*]

present[2] *n* (prez-int) **1** a gift **> vb** (pri-zent) **2** to introduce (a person) formally to another **3** to introduce to the public: *the Museum of Modern Art is presenting a retrospective of his work* **4** to introduce and compere (a radio or television show) **5** to show or exhibit: *they took advantage of every tax dodge that presented itself* **6** to bring about: *the case presented a large number of legal difficulties* **7** to put forward or submit: *they presented a petition to the Prime Minister* **8** to give or offer formally: *he was presented with a watch to celebrate his twenty-five years with the company* **9** to hand over for action or payment: *to present a bill* **10** to portray in a particular way: *her lawyer presented her as a naive woman who had got into bad company* **11** to aim (a weapon) **12 present arms** to salute with one's weapon [Latin *praesentare* to exhibit]

presentable *adj* **1** fit to be seen by or introduced to other people **2** acceptable: *the team reached a presentable total* **> presentability** *n*

presentation *n* **1** the act of presenting or being presented **2** the manner of presenting **3** a talk or lecture; the manner of presenting **4** a formal ceremony in which an award is made **5** a public performance, such as a play or a ballet

present-day *adj* of the modern day; current: *even by present-day standards these were large aircraft*

presenter *n* a person who introduces a radio or television show and links the items in it

presentiment (priz-zen-tim-ent) *n* a sense that something unpleasant is about to happen; premonition [obsolete French *pressentir* to sense beforehand]

presently *adv* **1** soon: *you will understand presently* **2** chiefly Scot, US and Canad at the moment: *these methods are presently being developed*

present participle *n* grammar a form of verb, ending in -ing, which is used to describe action that is happening at the same time as that of the main verb

present perfect *adj, n* grammar same as **perfect** (7, 8)

presents *pl n* law used in a deed or document to refer to itself: *know all men by these presents*

preservative *n* **1** a chemical added to foods to prevent decay **> adj 2** preventing decay

preserve *vb* **-serving, -served 1** to keep safe from change or extinction; protect: *we are interested in preserving world peace* **2** to protect from decay or damage: *the carefully preserved village of Cregneish* **3** to treat (food) in order to prevent it from decaying **4** to maintain; keep up: *the 1.2% increase in earnings needed to preserve living standards* ▷ *n* **5** an area of interest restricted to a particular person or group: *working-class preserves such as pigeon racing* **6** (*usually pl*) fruit preserved by cooking in sugar **7** an area where game is kept for private hunting or fishing [Latin *prae* before + *servare* to keep safe] **> preservation** *n*

preset *vb* **-setting, -set 1** to set the timer on a piece of equipment so that it starts to work at a specific time ▷ *adj* **2** (of equipment) with the controls set in advance

preshrunk *adj* (of fabric or a garment) having been shrunk during manufacture so that further shrinkage will not occur when washed

preside *vb* **-siding, -sided 1** to chair a meeting **2** to exercise authority: *he presided over the burning of the books* [Latin *praesidere* to superintend]

presidency *n, pl* **-cies** the office or term of a president

president *n* **1** the head of state of a republic, esp. of the US **2** the head of a company, society, or institution **3** a person who presides over a meeting **4** the head of certain establishments of higher education [Late Latin *praesidens* ruler] **> presidential** *adj*

presidium *n* (in Communist countries) a permanent administrative committee [Russian *prezidium*, from Latin *praesidium*, from *praesidere* to superintend]

Presley *n* Elvis (**Aaron** or **Aron**). 1935–77, US rock and roll singer. His recordings include "That's all Right (Mama)" (1954), "Heartbreak Hotel" (1956), "Hound Dog" (1956), numbers from the films *Loving You* and *Jailhouse Rock* (both 1957), and "Suspicious Minds" (1970)

press¹ *vb* **1** to apply weight or force to: *he pressed the button on the camera* **2** to squeeze: *she pressed his hand* **3** to compress to alter in shape **4** to smooth out creases by applying pressure or heat **5** to make (objects) from soft material by pressing with a mould **6** to crush to force out (juice) **7** to urge (someone) insistently: *they pressed for an answer* **8** to force or compel: *I was pressed into playing rugby at school* **9** to plead or put forward strongly: *they intend to press their claim for damages in the courts* **10** to be urgent: *time presses* **11** (sometimes foll. by *on* or *forward*) to continue in a determined way: *they pressed on with their journey* **12** to crowd; push: *shoppers press along the pavements* **13** pressed for short of: *pressed for time* ▷ *n* **14** any machine that exerts pressure to form or cut materials or to extract liquids or compress solids **15** See **printing press 16** the art or process of printing **17** the opinions and reviews in the newspapers: *the government is not receiving a good press at the moment* **18** the act of pressing or state of being pressed: *at the press of a button* **19** a crowd: *a press of people at the exit* **20** *chiefly Scot and Irish* a cupboard for storing clothes or linen **21** go to press to go to be printed: *when is this book going to press?* **22** the press **a** news media collectively, esp. newspapers **b** journalists collectively [Old French *presser*]

press² *vb* **1** to recruit (men) forcibly for military service **2** to use for a purpose other than intended: *press into service* [from *prest* to recruit soldiers]

press agent *n* a person employed to obtain favourable publicity for an individual or organization

press box *n* a room at a sports ground reserved for reporters

Pressburg *n* the German name for **Bratislava**

Pressburger *n* Emeric. 1902–88, Hungarian film writer and producer, living in Britain: best known for his collaboration (1942–57) with Michael Powell. Films include *The Life and Death of Colonel Blimp* (1943), *I Know Where I'm Going* (1945), and *A Matter of Life and Death* (1946)

press conference *n* an interview for reporters given by a famous person

press gallery *n* an area for newspaper reporters, esp. in a parliament

press gang *n* **1** (formerly) a group of men used to

capture men and boys and force them to join the navy ▷ *vb* **press-gang 2** to force (a person) to join the navy by a press gang **3** to persuade (someone) to do something that he or she does not want to do: *he was press-ganged into joining the family business*

pressie or **prezzie** (prez-zee) *n informal* a present

pressing *adj* **1** demanding immediate attention ▷ *n* **2** a large number of gramophone records produced at one time

press release *n* an official announcement or account of a news item circulated to the press

press stud *n* Brit a fastener in which one part with a projecting knob snaps into a hole on another part

press-up *n* an exercise in which the body is raised from and lowered to the floor by straightening and bending the arms

pressure *n* **1** the state of pressing or being pressed **2** the application of force by one body on the surface of another **3** urgent claims or demands: *to work under pressure* **4** a condition that is hard to bear: *the pressure of grief* **5** *physics* the force applied to a unit area of a surface **6** bring pressure to bear on to use influence or authority to persuade ▷ *vb* **-suring, -sured 7** to persuade forcefully: *he was pressured into resignation* [Late Latin *pressura* a pressing, from Latin *premere* to press]

pressure cooker *n* an airtight pot which cooks food quickly by steam under pressure **> pressure-cook** *vb*

pressure group *n* a group that tries to influence policies or public opinion

pressurize or **-rise** *vb* **-rizing, -rized** or **-rising, -rised 1** to increase the pressure in (an aircraft cabin, etc.) in order to maintain approximately atmospheric pressure when the external pressure is low **2** to make insistent demands of (someone): *do not be pressurized into making a decision* **> pressurization** or **-risation** *n*

prestidigitation *n formal* same as **sleight of hand** [French] **> prestidigitator** *n*

prestige *n* **1** high status or respect resulting from success or achievements: *a symbol of French power and prestige* **2** the power to impress: *a humdrum family car with no prestige* [Latin *praestigiae* tricks] **> prestigious** *adj*

presto *music adv, adj* **1** very fast ▷ *n, pl* **-tos 2** a passage to be played very quickly [Italian]

Preston *n* a city in NW England, administrative centre of Lancashire, on the River Ribble: developed as a weaving centre (17th–18th centuries); university (1992). Pop: 184 836 (2001)

Prestonpans *n* a small town and resort in SE Scotland, in East Lothian on the Firth of Forth: scene of the battle (1745) in which the Jacobite army of Prince Charles Edward defeated government forces under Sir John Cope. Pop: 7153 (2001)

Prestwich *n* a town in NW England, in Bury unitary authority, Greater Manchester. Pop: 31 693 (2001)

Prestwick *n* a town in SW Scotland, in South Ayrshire on the Firth of Clyde; international airport, golf course: tourism. Pop: 14 934 (2001)

presumably *adv* one supposes or guesses; probably: *he emerged from what was presumably the kitchen carrying a tray*

presume *vb* **-suming, -sumed 1** to take (something) for granted: *I presume he's dead* **2** to dare (to): *I would not presume to lecture you on medical matters, Dr Jacobs* **3** (foll. by *on* or *upon*) to rely or depend: *don't presume on his agreement* **4** (foll. by *on* or *upon*) to take advantage (of): *I'm afraid I presumed on Aunt Ginny's generosity* [Latin *praesumere* to take in advance] **> presumedly** *adv* **> presuming** *adj*

presumption *n* **1** the act of presuming **2** a basis on which an assumption is made **3** bold insolent behaviour **4** a belief or assumption based on reasonable evidence **> presumptive** *adj*

presumptuous *adj* bold and insolent

presuppose *vb* **-posing, -posed 1** to require as a previous condition in order to be true: *the idea of integration presupposes a disintegrated state* **2** to take for granted **> presupposition** *n*

P

preteen *n* a boy or girl approaching his or her teens

pretence *or US* **pretense** *n* **1** an action or claim that could mislead people into believing something which is not true: *the pretence that many unemployed people are on 'training schemes'* **2** a false display; affectation: *she abandoned all pretence of work and watched me* **3** a claim, esp. a false one, to a right, title, or distinction **4** make-believe **5** a pretext: *they were placed in a ghetto on the pretence that they would be safe there*

pretend *vb* **1** to claim or give the appearance of (something untrue): *he pretended to be asleep* **2** to make believe: *the children pretended to be pop stars* **3** (foll. by *to*) to present a claim, esp. a doubtful one: *to pretend to the throne* [Latin *praetendere* to stretch forth, feign]

pretender *n* a person who makes a false or disputed claim to a throne or title

pretension *n* **1** (*often pl*) a false claim to merit or importance **2** the quality of being pretentious

pretentious *adj* **1** making (unjustified) claims to special merit or importance: *many critics thought her work and ideas pretentious and empty* **2** vulgarly showy; ostentatious: *a family restaurant with no pretentious furnishing*

preterite *or especially US* **preterit** (pret-er-it) *grammar n* **1** a past tense of verbs, such as *jumped, swam* **2** a verb in this tense ▷ *adj* **3** expressing such a past tense [Late Latin *praeteritum (tempus)* past (time)]

preternatural *adj* beyond what is natural; supernatural [Latin *praeter naturam* beyond the scope of nature]

pretext *n* a false reason given to hide the real one: *delivering the book had been a good pretext for seeing her again* [Latin *praetextum* disguise, from *praetexere* to weave in front]

Pretoria *n* a city in N South Africa, the administrative capital of South Africa; formerly capital of Transvaal province: two universities (1873, 1930); large steelworks. Pop: 741 651 (2011). Also called: **Tshwane**

Pretorius *n* **1** Andries Wilhelmus Jacobus. 1799–1853, a Boer leader in the Great Trek (1838) to escape British sovereignty; he also led an expedition to the Transvaal (1848). The town Pretoria was named after him **2** his son, **Marthinus Wessels**. 1819–1901, first president of the South African Republic (1857–71) and of the Orange Free State (1859–63)

prettify *vb* **-fies, -fying, -fied** to make pretty

pretty *adj* **-tier, -tiest** **1** attractive in a delicate or graceful way **2** pleasant to look at **3** *informal, often humorous* excellent or fine: *well, this is a pretty state of affairs to have got into* ▷ *adv* **4** *informal* fairly: *I think he and Nicholas got on pretty well* **5** **sitting pretty** *informal* in a favourable state [Old English *prættig* clever] > **prettily** *adv* > **prettiness** *n*

pretty-pretty *adj informal* excessively pretty

pretzel *n* a brittle salted biscuit in the shape of a knot [from German]

Preussen *n* the German name for **Prussia**

prevail *vb* **1** (*often foll. by* over *or* against) to prove superior; gain mastery: *moderate nationalists have until now prevailed over the radicals* **2** to be the most important feature: *a casual good-natured mood prevailed* **3** to be generally established: *this attitude has prevailed for many years* **4** **prevail on** *or* **upon** to succeed in persuading: *he had easily been prevailed upon to accept a lift* [Latin *praevalere* to be superior in strength]

prevailing *adj* **1** widespread: *the prevailing mood* **2** most usual: *the prevailing wind is from the west*

prevalent *adj* widespread or common > **prevalence** *n*

prevaricate *vb* **-cating, -cated** to avoid giving a direct or truthful answer [Latin *praevaricari* to walk crookedly] > **prevarication** *n* > **prevaricator** *n*

prevent *vb* **1** to keep from happening: *vitamin C prevented scurvy* **2** (*often foll. by* from) to keep (someone from doing something): *circumstances prevented her from coming* [Latin *praevenire*] > **preventable** *adj* > **prevention** *n*

preventive *adj* **1** intended to prevent or hinder **2** *med* tending to prevent disease ▷ *n* **3** something that serves to prevent **4** *med* any drug or agent that tends to prevent disease ▶ Also: **preventative**

Prévert *n* Jacques. 1900–77, Parisian poet, satirist, and writer of film scripts, noted esp. for his song poems. He was a member of the surrealist group from 1925 to 1929

preview *n* **1** an opportunity to see a film, exhibition, or play before it is shown to the public ▷ *vb* **2** to view in advance

Previn *n* André. born 1929, US orchestral conductor, born in Germany; living in Britain; awarded an honorary knighthood (1996)

previous *adj* **1** coming or happening before **2** *informal* happening too soon; premature: *such criticism is a bit previous because no definite decision has yet been taken* **3** **previous to** before [Latin *praevius* leading the way] > **previously** *adv*

Prévost d'Exiles *n* Antoine François, known as *Abbé Prévost*. 1697–1763, French novelist, noted for his romance *Manon Lescaut* (1731), which served as the basis for operas by Puccini and Massenet

prewar *adj* relating to the period before a war, esp. before World War I or II

prey *n* **1** an animal hunted and killed for food by another animal **2** the victim of a hostile person, influence, emotion, or illness: *children are falling prey to the disease* **3** **bird** *or* **beast of prey** a bird *or* animal that kills and eats other birds or animals ▷ *vb* (*often foll. by* on *or* upon) **4** to hunt and kill for food **5** to worry or obsess: *it preyed on his conscience* **6** to make a victim (of others), by profiting at their expense [Old French *preie*]

Pribilof Islands *pl n* a group of islands in the Bering Sea, off SW Alaska, belonging to the US: the breeding ground of the northern fur seal. Area: about 168 sq km (65 sq miles). Also called: **Fur Seal Islands**

price *n* **1** the amount of money for which a thing is bought or sold **2** the cost at which something is obtained: *the price of making the wrong decision* **3** *gambling* odds **4** **at any price** whatever the price or cost **5** **at a price** at a high price **6** **what price (something)?** what are the chances of (something) happening now? ▷ *vb* **pricing, priced** **7** to fix the price of **8** to discover the price of [Latin *pretium*]

price-fixing *n* the setting of prices by agreement among producers and distributors

priceless *adj* **1** extremely valuable **2** *informal* extremely amusing

pricey *adj* **pricier, priciest** *informal* expensive

prick *vb* **1** to pierce lightly with a sharp point **2** to cause a piercing sensation (in): *a needle pricked her finger* **3** to cause a sharp emotional pain (in): *the film pricked our consciences about the plight of the Afghan refugees* **4** **prick up one's ears a** (of a dog) to make the ears stand erect **b** (of a person) to listen attentively ▷ *n* **5** a sudden sharp pain caused by pricking **6** a mark made by a sharp point **7** a sharp emotional pain: *a prick of conscience* **8** *taboo, slang* a penis **9** *offensive, slang* a man who provokes contempt [Old English *prica* point, puncture]

prickle *n* **1** *botany* a thorn or spike on a plant **2** a pricking or stinging sensation ▷ *vb* **-ling, -led** **3** to feel a stinging sensation [Old English *pricel*]

prickly *adj* **-lier, -liest** **1** having prickles **2** tingling or stinging: *he had a prickly feeling down his back* **3** touchy or irritable: *Canadians are notoriously prickly about being taken for Americans*

prickly heat *n* an itchy rash that occurs in very hot moist weather

prickly pear *n* **1** a tropical cactus with edible oval fruit **2** the fruit of this plant

pride *n* **1** satisfaction in one's own or another's success or achievements: *his obvious pride in his son's achievements* **2** an excessively high opinion of oneself **3** a sense of dignity and self-respect: *he must swallow his pride and ally himself with his political enemies* **4** one of the better or most admirable parts of something: *the pride of the main courses is* *the Japanese fish and vegetable tempura* **5** a group of lions **6 pride and joy** the main source of pride: *the car was his pride and joy* **7 pride of place** the most important position ▷ *vb* **priding, prided 8** (foll. by *on* or *upon*) to take pride in (oneself) for [Old English *prýde*]

Pride *n* Thomas. died 1658, English soldier on the Parliamentary side during the Civil War. He expelled members of the Long Parliament hostile to the army (Pride's Purge, 1648) and signed Charles I's death warrant

prie-dieu (pree-**dyuh**) *n* an upright frame with a ledge for kneeling upon, for use when praying [French *prier* to pray + *Dieu* God]

priest *n* **1** (in the Christian Church) a person ordained to administer the sacraments and preach **2** a minister of any religion **3** an official who performs religious ceremonies [Old English *prēost*, apparently from *presbyter*] ❭ **priestess** *fem n* ❭ **priesthood** *n* ❭ **priestly** *adj*

Priestley *n* **1** J(ohn) B(oynton). 1894–1984, English author. His works include the novels *The Good Companions* (1929) and *Angel Pavement* (1930) and the play *An Inspector Calls* (1946) **2** Joseph. 1733–1804, English chemist, political theorist, and clergyman, in the US from 1794. He discovered oxygen (1774) independently of Scheele and isolated and described many other gases

prig *n* a person who is smugly self-righteous and narrow-minded [origin unknown] ❭ **priggish** *adj* ❭ **priggishness** *n*

Prigogine *n* Viscount Ilya. 1917–2003, Belgian chemist, born in Russia: Nobel prize for chemistry 1977 for his work on nonequilibrium thermodynamics

prim *adj* **primmer, primmest** affectedly proper, or formal, and rather prudish [origin unknown] ❭ **primly** *adv*

prima ballerina *n* a leading female ballet dancer [Italian: first ballerina]

primacy *n, pl* **-cies 1** the state of being first in rank, grade, or order **2** *Christianity* the office of an archbishop

prima donna *n, pl* **prima donnas 1** a leading female opera singer **2** *informal* a temperamental person [Italian: first lady]

primaeval *adj* same as **primeval**

prima facie (prime-a **fay**-shee) *adv, adj* as it seems at first [Latin]

primal *adj* **1** of basic causes or origins **2** chief or most important [Latin *primus* first]

primarily *adv* **1** chiefly or mainly **2** originally

primary *adj* **1** first in importance **2** first in position or time, as in a series: *he argued that the country was only in the primary stage of socialism* **3** fundamental or basic: *the new policy will put the emphasis on primary health care rather than hospital care* **4** being the first stage; elementary: *all new recruits participated in the same primary training courses* **5** relating to the education of children up to the age of 11 or 12 **6** (of an industry) involving the obtaining of raw materials **7** (of the flight feathers of a bird's wing) outer and longest **8** being the part of an electric circuit in which a changing current causes a current in a neighbouring circuit: *a primary coil* ▷ *n, pl* **-ries 9** a person or thing that is first in position, time, or importance **10** (in the US) an election in which the voters of a state choose a candidate for office. Full name: **primary election 11** a primary school **12** a primary colour **13** any of the outer and longest flight feathers of a bird's wing **14** a primary part of an electric circuit [Latin *primarius* principal]

primary accent *or* **primary stress** *n linguistics* the strongest accent in a word

primary colour *n* **1** *physics* any of the colours red, green, and blue from which all other colours can be obtained by mixing **2** *art* any of the colours red, yellow, and blue from which all other colours can be obtained by mixing

primary school *n* **1** (in England and Wales) a school for children between the ages of 5 and 11 **2** (in Scotland, Australia and New Zealand) a school for children

between the ages of 5 and 12 **3** (in the US and Canada) a school equivalent to the first three or four grades of elementary school

primate[1] *n* a mammal with flexible hands and feet and a highly developed brain, such as a monkey, an ape, or a human being

primate[2] *n* an archbishop [Latin *primas* principal]

prime *adj* **1** first in importance: *the prime aim* **2** of the highest quality: *prime beef* **3** typical: *a prime example* ▷ *n* **4** the time when a thing is at its best **5** a period of power, vigour, and activity: *he was in the prime of life* **6** *maths* short for **prime number** ▷ *vb* **priming, primed 7** to give (someone) information in advance to prepare him or her **8** to prepare (a surface) for painting **9** to prepare (a gun or mine) before detonating or firing **10** to fill (a pump) with its working fluid, to expel air from it before starting **11** to prepare (something) [Latin *primus* first]

prime meridian *n* the 0° meridian from which the other meridians are worked out, usually taken to pass through Greenwich

Prime Minister *n* the leader of a government

prime mover *n* a person or thing which was important in helping create an idea, situation, etc.: *he was the prime mover behind the coup*

prime number *n* an integer that cannot be divided into other integers but is only divisible by itself or 1, such as 2, 3, 5, 7, and 11

primer[1] *n* **1** a substance applied to a surface as a base coat or sealer **2** a device for detonating the main charge in a gun or mine [see PRIME (verb)]

primer[2] *n* an introductory text, such as a school textbook [Medieval Latin *primarius (liber)* a first (book)]

prime stock *n* NZ livestock in peak condition and ready for killing

primeval (prime-**ee**-val) *adj* of the earliest age of the world [Latin *primus* first + *aevum* age]

primitive *adj* **1** of or belonging to the beginning **2** *biology* of an early stage in development: *primitive amphibians* **3** characteristic of an early simple state, esp. in being crude or basic: *a primitive dwelling* ▷ *n* **4** a primitive person or thing **5** a painter of any era whose work appears childlike or untrained **6** a work by such an artist [Latin *primitivus* earliest of its kind]

Primo de Rivera *n* **1** José Antonio. 1903–36, Spanish politician; founded Falangism **2** his father, Miguel. 1870–1930, Spanish general; dictator of Spain (1923–30)

primogeniture *n* **1** *formal* the state of being the first-born child **2** *law* the right of an eldest son to inherit all the property of his parents [Medieval Latin *primogenitura* birth of a first child]

primordial *adj formal* existing at or from the beginning [Late Latin *primordialis* original]

primp *vb* to tidy (one's hair or clothes) fussily [probably from *prim*]

primrose *n* **1** a wild plant which has pale yellow flowers in spring ▷ *adj* **2** Also: **primrose yellow** pale yellow **3** of primroses [Medieval Latin *prima rosa* first rose]

primrose path *n* (often preceded by *the*) a pleasurable way of life

primula *n* a type of primrose with brightly coloured funnel-shaped flowers [Medieval Latin *primula (veris)* little first one (of the spring)]

Primus *n trademark* a portable paraffin cooking stove, used esp. by campers

prince *n* **1** a male member of a royal family, esp. the son of the king or queen **2** the male ruler of a small country **3** an outstanding member of a specified group: *Dryden, that prince of poets* [Latin *princeps* first man, ruler]

Prince *n* full name *Prince Rogers Nelson*. born 1958, US rock singer, songwriter, record producer, and multi-instrumentalist. His albums include *Dirty Mind* (1981), *Purple Rain* (1984), *Parade* (1986), and *Sign o' the Times* (1987)

prince consort *n* the husband of a queen, who is himself a prince

P

Prince Edward Island *n* an island in the Gulf of St Lawrence that constitutes the smallest Canadian province. Capital: Charlottetown. Pop: 140 204 (2011 est). Area: 5656 sq km (2184 sq miles). Abbreviations: **PE, PEI**

Prince Edward Islander *n* a native or inhabitant of Prince Edward Island

princely *adj* **-lier, -liest 1** of or characteristic of a prince **2** generous or lavish

Prince of Wales[1] *n* the eldest son of the British sovereign

Prince of Wales[2] *n* **Cape Prince of Wales** a cape in W Alaska, on the Bering Strait opposite the coast of the extreme northeast of Russia: the westernmost point of North America

Prince of Wales Island *n* **1** an island in N Canada, in Nunavut. Area: about 36 000 sq km (14 000 sq miles) **2** an island in SE Alaska, the largest island in the Alexander Archipelago. Area: about 4000 sq km (1500 sq miles) **3** an island in NE Australia, in N Queensland in the Torres Strait **4** the former name (until about 1867) of the island of **Penang**

Prince Rupert *n* a port in W Canada, on the coast of British Columbia: one of the W termini of the Canadian National transcontinental railway. Pop: 14 643 (2001)

princess *n* **1** a female member of a royal family, esp. the daughter of the king or queen **2** the wife of a prince

Princess Royal *n* a title sometimes given to the eldest daughter of the British sovereign

Princeton *n* a town in central New Jersey: settled by Quakers in 1696; an important educational centre, seat of Princeton University (founded at Elizabeth in 1747 and moved here in 1756); scene of the battle (1777) during the War of American Independence in which Washington's troops defeated the British on the university campus. Pop: 13 577 (2003 est)

principal *adj* **1** first in importance, rank, or value: *salt is the principal source of sodium in our diets; the Republic's two principal parties* ▷ *n* **2** the head of a school or other educational institution **3** a person who holds one of the most important positions in an organization: *she became a principal in the home finance department* **4** the leading actor in a play **5** *law* **a** a person who engages another to act as his or her agent **b** a person who takes an active part in a crime **c** the person held responsible for fulfilling an obligation **6** *finance* **a** capital or property, as contrasted with income **b** the original amount of a debt on which interest is calculated [Latin *principalis* chief]
▷ **principally** *adv*

> USAGE See at principle.

principal boy *n Brit* the leading male role in a pantomime, traditionally played by a woman

principality *n, pl* **-ties** a territory ruled by a prince

principal parts *pl n grammar* the main verb forms, from which all other verb forms may be deduced

Príncipe *n* an island in the Gulf of Guinea, off the W coast of Africa: part of São Tomé and Príncipe. Area: 150 sq km (58 sq miles)

principle *n* **1** a moral rule guiding personal conduct: *he'd stoop to anything – he has no principles* **2** a set of such moral rules: *a man of principle* **3** a basic or general truth: *the principle of freedom of expression* **4** a basic law or rule underlying a particular theory or philosophy: *the government has been deceitful and has violated basic principles of democracy* **5** a general law in science: *the principle of the conservation of mass* **6** *chem* a constituent of a substance that determines its characteristics **7** in principle in theory though not always in practice **8** on principle because of one's beliefs [Latin *principium* beginning, basic tenet]

> USAGE *Principle* and *principal* are often confused: *the principal* (not *principle*) *reason for his departure; the plan was approved in principle* (not *in principal*).

principled *adj* (of a person or action) guided by moral rules: *principled opposition to the war*

prink *vb* **1** to dress (oneself) finely **2** to preen oneself [probably changed from *prank* to adorn]

print *vb* **1** to reproduce (a newspaper, book, etc.) in large quantities by mechanical or electronic means **2** to reproduce (text or pictures) by applying ink to paper **3** to write in letters that are not joined up **4** to stamp (fabric) with a design **5** to produce (a photograph) from a negative **6** to fix in the mind or memory ▷ *n* **7** printed content, such as newsprint **8** a printed publication, such as a book **9** a picture printed from an engraved plate or wood block **10** printed text, with regard to the typeface: *italic print* **11** a photograph produced from a negative **12** a fabric with a printed design **13** a mark made by pressing something onto a surface **14** See **fingerprint 15 in print a** in printed or published form **b** (of a book) available from a publisher **16 out of print** no longer available from a publisher ▶ See also **print out** [Old French *preindre* to make an impression]

printed circuit *n* an electronic circuit in which the wiring is a metallic coating printed on a thin insulating board

printer *n* **1** a person or business engaged in printing **2** a machine that prints **3** *computers* a machine that prints out results on paper

printing *n* **1** the process of producing printed matter **2** printed text **3** all the copies of a book printed at one time **4** a form of writing in which the letters are not joined together

printing press *n* a machine used for printing

print out *vb* **1** *computers* to produce (printed information) ▷ *n* **print-out, printout 2** printed information from a computer

prior[1] *adj* **1** previous: *prior knowledge* **2** prior to before [Latin: previous]

prior[2] *n* **1** the head monk in a priory **2** the abbot's deputy in a monastery [Late Latin: head] ▷ **prioress** *fem n*

Prior *n* Matthew. 1664–1721, English poet and diplomat, noted for his epigrammatic occasional verse

priority *n, pl* **-ties 1** the most important thing that must be dealt with first **2** the right to be or go before others

priory *n, pl* **-ories** a religious house where certain orders of monks or nuns live

Pripet *n* a river in E Europe, rising in NW Ukraine and flowing northeast into Belarus across the **Pripet Marshes** (the largest swamp in Europe), then east into the Dnieper River. Length: about 800 km (500 miles). Russian name: **Pripyat**

Priscian *n* Latin name *Priscianus Caesariensis*. 6th century AD, Latin grammarian

prise *or* **prize** *vb* **prising, prised** *or* **prizing, prized** to force open or out by levering [Old French *prise* a taking]

prism *n* **1** a transparent block, often with triangular ends and rectangular sides, used to disperse light into a spectrum or refract it in optical instruments **2** *maths* a polyhedron with parallel bases and sides that are parallelograms [Greek *prisma* something shaped by sawing]

prismatic *adj* **1** of or shaped like a prism **2** exhibiting bright spectral colours; rainbow-like: *prismatic light*

prison *n* **1** a public building used to hold convicted criminals and accused people awaiting trial **2** any place of confinement [Old French *prisun*, from Latin *prensio* a capturing]

prisoner *n* **1** a person kept in prison as a punishment for a crime, or while awaiting trial **2** a person confined by any restraints: *he's a prisoner of his own past* **3 take (someone) prisoner** to capture and hold (someone) as a prisoner

prisoner of war *n* a serviceman captured by an enemy in wartime

prissy *adj* **-sier, -siest** prim and prudish [probably from *prim + sissy*] ▷ **prissily** *adv*

Priština *n* the capital of Kosovo: under Turkish control until 1912; severely damaged in the Kosovo conflict of 1999; nearby is the 14th-century Gračanica monastery. Pop: 261 000 (2005 est)

pristine *adj* **1** completely new, clean, and pure: *pristine white plates* **2** of or involving the original, unchanged, and unspoilt period or state: *the viewing of wild game in its pristine natural state* [Latin *pristinus* primitive]

Pritchett *n* Sir V(ictor) S(awdon). 1900–97, British short-story writer, novelist, essayist, and autobiographer; his works include *Mr Beluncle* (1951) and *A Careless Widow* (1989)

privacy *n* **1** the condition of being private **2** secrecy

private *adj* **1** not for general or public use: *a private bathroom* **2** confidential or secret: *a private conversation* **3** involving someone's domestic and personal life rather than his or her work or business: *what I do in my private life is none of your business* **4** owned or paid for by individuals rather than by the government: *private enterprise* **5** not publicly known: *they had private reasons for the decision* **6** having no public office, rank, or position: *the Red Cross received donations from private citizens* **7** (of a place) quiet and secluded: *the garden is completely private* **8** (of a person) quiet and retiring: *she was private – her life was her own* ▷ *n* **9** a soldier of the lowest rank in the army **10 in private** in secret [Latin *privatus* belonging to one individual, withdrawn from public life] **> privately** *adv*

private bill *n* a bill presented to Parliament on behalf of a private individual or corporation

private company *n* a limited company that does not issue shares for public subscription

private detective *n* a person hired by a client to do detective work

privateer *n* **1** a privately owned armed vessel authorized by the government to take part in a war **2** a captain of such a ship

private eye *n informal* a private detective

private income *n* income from sources other than employment, such as investment

private member *n* a Member of Parliament who is not a government minister

private member's bill *n* a law proposed by a Member of Parliament who is not a government minister

private parts *or* **privates** *pl n euphemistic* the genitals

private school *n* a school controlled by a private body, accepting mostly fee-paying pupils

private sector *n* the part of a country's economy that consists of privately owned enterprises

privation *n formal* loss or lack of the necessities of life [Latin *privatio* deprivation]

privative (priv-a-tiv) *adj* **1** causing privation **2** *grammar* expressing lack or absence, for example *-less* and *un-*

privatize *or* **-tise** *vb* **-tizing, -tized** *or* **-tising, -tised** to sell (a state-owned company) to individuals or a private company **> privatization** *or* **-tisation** *n*

privet *n* a bushy evergreen shrub used for hedges [origin unknown]

privilege *n* **1** a benefit or advantage granted only to certain people: *a privilege of rank* **2** the opportunity to do something which gives you great satisfaction and which most people never have the chance to do: *I had the privilege of meeting the Queen when she visited our school* **3** the power and advantages that come with great wealth or high social class: *the use of violence to protect class privilege and thwart popular democracy* [Latin *privilegium* law relevant to rights of an individual]

privileged *adj* enjoying a special right or immunity

privy *adj* **privier, priviest 1** *archaic* secret **2 privy to** sharing in the knowledge of something secret ▷ *n, pl* **privies 3** *obsolete* a toilet, esp. an outside one [Old French *privé* something private]

Privy Council *n* **1** the private council of the British king or queen **2** (in Canada) a formal body of advisers of the governor general **> Privy Counsellor** *n*

privy purse *n* an allowance voted by Parliament for the private expenses of the king or queen

privy seal *n* (in Britain) a seal affixed to certain documents of state

prize¹ *n* **1** something of value, such as a trophy, given to the winner of a contest or game **2** something given to the winner of any game of chance, lottery, etc. **3** something striven for ▷ *adj* **4** winning or likely to win a prize: *a prize bull* [Old French *prise* a capture]

prize² *vb* **prizing, prized** to value highly [Old French *preisier* to praise]

prize³ *vb, n* a variant spelling of **prise**

prizefight *n* a boxing match for a prize or purse **> prizefighter** *n*

pro¹ *adv* **1** in favour of a motion etc. ▷ *prep* **2** in favour of ▷ *n, pl* **pros 3** (usually *pl*) an argument or vote in favour of a proposal or motion. See also **pros and cons** ▶ See also **pros and cons** [Latin: in favour of]

pro² *n, pl* **pros** ▷ *adj informal* **1** short for **professional 2** a prostitute

PRO public relations officer

pro-¹ *prefix* **1** in favour of; supporting: *pro-Chinese* **2** acting as a substitute for: *pronoun* [Latin]

pro-² *prefix* before in time or position: *proboscis* [Greek]

proactive *adj* tending to initiate change rather than reacting to events

probability *n, pl* **-ties 1** the condition of being probable **2** an event or other thing that is likely to happen or be true **3** *statistics* a measure of the likelihood of an event happening

probable *adj* **1** likely to happen or be true **2** most likely: *the probable cause of the accident* ▷ *n* **3** a person who is likely to be chosen for a team, event, etc. [Latin *probabilis* that may be proved]

probably *adv* in all likelihood or probability: *the wedding's probably going to be in late August*

probate *n* **1** the process of officially proving the validity of a will **2** the official certificate stating that a will is genuine [Latin *probare* to inspect]

probation *n* **1** a system of dealing with offenders, esp. juvenile ones, by placing them under supervision **2 on probation a** under the supervision of a probation officer **b** undergoing a test or trial period, such as at the start of a new job [Latin *probare* to test] **> probationary** *adj*

probationer *n* **1** a person on a trial period in a job **2** a person under the supervision of a probation officer

probation officer *n* an officer of a court who supervises offenders placed on probation

probe *vb* **probing, probed 1** to investigate, or look into, closely **2** to poke or examine (something) with or as if with a probe: *he probed carefully with his fingertips* ▷ *n* **3** *surgery* a slender instrument for exploring a wound etc. **4** a thorough inquiry, such as one into corrupt practices **5** See **space probe** [Latin *probare* to test]

probiotic *n* **1** a bacterium that protects the body from harmful bacteria ▷ *adj* **2** of or relating to probiotics: *probiotic yogurts*

probity *n formal* honesty; integrity [Latin *probitas* honesty]

problem *n* **1** something or someone that is difficult to deal with **2** a puzzle or question set for solving **3** *maths* a statement requiring a solution usually by means of several operations ▷ *adj* **4** of a literary work that deals with difficult moral questions: *a problem play* **5** difficult to deal with or creating difficulties for others: *a problem child* [Greek *problēma* something put forward]

problematic *or* **problematical** *adj* difficult to solve or deal with

proboscis (pro-boss-iss) *n* **1** a long flexible trunk or snout, such as an elephant's **2** the elongated mouth part of certain insects [Greek *proboskis* trunk of an elephant]

procedure *n* **1** a way of doing something, esp. an established method **2** the established form of conducting the business of a legislature **> procedural** *adj*

proceed *vb* **1** to advance or carry on, esp. after stopping **2** (often foll. by *with*) to start or continue doing: *he proceeded to pour himself a large whisky* **3** *formal* to walk or go **4** (often foll. by *against*) to start a legal action **5** *formal* to arise (from): *their mutual dislike proceeded from differences of political opinion* [Latin *procedere* to advance]

proceeding *n* **1** an act or course of action **2 proceedings** the events of an occasion: *millions watched the proceedings on television* **3 proceedings** the minutes of the meetings of a society **4 proceedings** legal action

proceeds *pl n* the amount of money obtained from an event or activity

process¹ *n* **1** **a** a series of actions or changes: *a process of genuine national reconciliation* **2** a series of natural developments which result in an overall change: *the ageing process* **3** a method of doing or producing something: *the various production processes use up huge amounts of water* **4 a** a summons to appear in court **b** an action at law **5** a natural outgrowth or projection of a part or organism **6 in the process of** during or in the course of ▷ *vb* **7** to handle or prepare by a special method of manufacture **8** *computers* to perform operations on (data) in order to obtain the required information [Latin *processus* an advancing]

process² *vb* to move in an orderly or ceremonial group: *the cult members processed through the streets to the music of tambourines*

processed *adj* (of food) treated by adding colouring, preservatives, etc., to improve its appearance or the period it will stay edible: *processed cheese*

procession *n* **1** a line of people or vehicles moving forwards in an orderly or ceremonial manner **2** the act of proceeding in a regular formation [Latin *processio* a marching forwards]

processional *adj* **1** of or suitable for a procession: *the processional route* ▷ *n* **2** *Christianity* a hymn sung as the clergy enter church

processor *n* **1** *computers* same as **central processing unit** **2** a person or thing that carries out a process

proclaim *vb* **1** to announce publicly; declare: *Greece was proclaimed an independent kingdom in 1832* **2** to indicate plainly: *the sharp hard glint in the eye proclaimed her determination* [Latin *proclamare* to shout aloud] **> proclamation** *n*

proclivity *n, pl* **-ties** *formal* a tendency or inclination [Latin *proclivitas*]

Proclus *n* ?410–485 AD, Greek Neo-Platonist philosopher

Procopius *n* ?490–?562 AD, Byzantine historian, noted for his account of the wars of Justinian I against the Persians, Vandals, and Ostrogoths

procrastinate *vb* **-nating, -nated** to put off (an action) until later; delay [Latin *procrastinare* to postpone until tomorrow] **> procrastination** *n* **> procrastinator** *n*

procreate *vb* **-ating, -ated** *formal* to produce (offspring) [Latin *procreare*] **> procreative** *adj* **> procreation** *n*

Procrustean *adj* ruthlessly enforcing uniformity [after Procrustes, robber in Greek myth who fitted travellers into his bed by stretching or lopping off their limbs]

proctor *n* a member of the staff of certain universities having duties including the enforcement of discipline [syncopated variant of *procurator*] **> proctorial** *adj*

procurator fiscal *n* (in Scotland) a legal officer who acts as public prosecutor and coroner

procure *vb* **-curing, -cured** **1** to get or provide: *it remained very difficult to procure food and fuel* **2** to obtain (people) to act as prostitutes [Latin *procurare* to look after] **> procurement** *n*

procurer *n* a person who obtains people to act as prostitutes

prod *vb* **prodding, prodded** **1** to poke with a pointed object **2** to rouse (someone) to action ▷ *n* **3** the act of prodding **4** a reminder [origin unknown]

Prodi *n* Romano. born 1939, Italian politician; prime minister (1996–98; 2006–08); president of the European Commission (1999–2004)

prodigal *adj* **1** recklessly wasteful or extravagant **2** prodigal of lavish with: *you are prodigal of both your toil and your talent* ▷ *n* **3** a person who squanders money [Latin *prodigere* to squander] **> prodigality** *n*

prodigious *adj* **1** very large or immense **2** wonderful or amazing [Latin *prodigiosus* marvellous]

prodigy *n, pl* **-gies** **1** a person, esp. a child, with marvellous talent **2** anything that is a cause of wonder [Latin *prodigium* an unnatural happening]

produce *vb* **-ducing, -duced** **1** to bring (something) into existence **2** to present to view: *he produced his passport* **3** to make: *this area produces much of Spain's best wine* **4** to give birth to **5** to present on stage, film, or television: *the girls and boys write and produce their own plays* **6** to act as producer of ▷ *n* **7** food grown for sale: *farm produce* **8** something produced [Latin *producere* to bring forward] **> producible** *adj*

producer *n* **1** a person with the financial and administrative responsibility for a film or television programme **2** a person responsible for the artistic direction of a play **3** a person who supervises the arrangement, performance, and mixing of a recording **4** a person or thing that produces

product *n* **1** something produced **2** a consequence: *their skill was the product of hours of training* **3** *maths* the result achieved by multiplication

production *n* **1** the act of producing **2** anything that is produced **3** the amount produced or the rate at which it is produced **4** *econ* the creation or manufacture of goods and services **5** any work created as a result of literary or artistic effort **6** the presentation of a play, opera, etc. **7** the artistic direction of a play **8** the overall sound of a recording

production line *n* a system in a factory in which an item being manufactured is moved from machine to machine by conveyor belt, and each machine carries out one step in the manufacture of the item

productive *adj* **1** producing or having the power to produce **2** yielding favourable results **3** *econ* producing goods and services that have exchange value: *the country's productive capacity* **4** (foll. by *of*) resulting in: *a period highly productive of books and ideas* **> productivity** *n*

product placement *n* the practice of a company of paying for its product to appear prominently in a film or television programme

proem (pro-em) *n formal* an introduction or preface [Greek *pro-* before + *oimē* song]

Prof. Professor

profane *adj* **1** showing disrespect for religion or something sacred **2** secular **3** coarse or blasphemous: *profane language* ▷ *vb* **-faning, -faned** **4** to treat (something sacred) with irreverence **5** to put to an unworthy use [Latin *profanus* outside the temple] **> profanation** *n*

profanity *n, pl* **-ties** **1** the quality of being profane **2** coarse or blasphemous action or speech

profess *vb* **1** to claim (something as true), often falsely: *he professes not to want the job of prime minister* **2** to acknowledge openly: *he professed great relief at getting some rest* **3** to have as one's belief or religion: *most Indonesians profess the Islamic faith* [Latin *profiteri* to confess openly] **> professed** *adj*

profession *n* **1** a type of work that requires special training, such as in law or medicine **2** the people employed in such an occupation **3** a declaration of a belief or feeling: *a profession of faith* [Latin *professio* public acknowledgment]

professional *adj* **1** of a profession **2** taking part in an activity, such as sport or music, as a means of livelihood **3** displaying a high level of competence or skill: *a professional and polished performance* **4** undertaken or performed by people who are paid: *professional golf* ▷ *n* **5** a professional person > **professionalism** *n* > **professionally** *adv*

professor *n* **1** the highest rank of teacher in a university **2** *chiefly US and Canad* any teacher in a university or college **3** *rare* a person who professes his or her opinions or beliefs [Latin: a public teacher] > **professorial** *adj* > **professorship** *n*

proffer *vb formal* to offer for acceptance [Old French *proffrir*]

proficient *adj* skilled; expert [Latin *proficere* to make progress] > **proficiency** *n*

profile *n* **1** an outline, esp. of the human face, as seen from the side **2** a short biographical sketch [Italian *profilo*]

profiling *n* the practice of categorizing people and predicting their behaviour according to particular characteristics such as race or age

profit *n* **1** (*often pl*) money gained in business or trade **2** a benefit or advantage ▷ *vb* **-iting, -ited 3** to gain a profit or advantage: *we do not want to profit from someone else's problems* [Latin *proficere* to make progress]

profitable *adj* making money or gaining an advantage or benefit > **profitability** *n* > **profitably** *adv*

profit and loss *n accounting* an account showing the year's income and expense items and indicating gross and net profit or loss

profiteer *n* **1** a person who makes excessive profits at the expense of the public ▷ *vb* **2** to make excessive profits > **profiteering** *n*

profit-sharing *n* a system in which a portion of the net profit of a business is shared among its employees

profligate *adj* **1** recklessly extravagant **2** shamelessly immoral ▷ *n* **3** a profligate person [Latin *profligatus* corrupt] > **profligacy** *n*

pro forma *adj* **1** laying down a set form ▷ *adv* **2** performed in a set manner [Latin: for form's sake]

profound *adj* **1** showing or needing great knowledge: *a profound knowledge of Greek literature* **2** strongly felt; intense: *profound relief* **3** extensive: *profound changes* **4** situated at or having a great depth [Latin *profundus* deep] > **profoundly** *adv* > **profundity** *n*

Profumo *n* John (**Dennis**). 1915–2006 British Conservative politician; secretary of state for war (1960–63). He resigned after a scandal that threatened the government of Harold Macmillan

profuse *adj* **1** plentiful or abundant: *he broke out in a profuse sweat* **2** (*often foll. by in*) generous in the giving (of): *he was profuse in his apologies* [Latin *profundere* to pour lavishly] > **profusely** *adv* > **profusion** *n*

progenitor (pro-jen-it-er) *n* **1** a direct ancestor **2** an originator or founder [Latin: ancestor]

progeny (proj-in-ee) *n, pl* **-nies 1** offspring; descendants **2** an outcome [Latin *progenies* lineage]

progesterone *n* a hormone, produced in the ovary, that prepares the womb for pregnancy and prevents further ovulation [PRO-¹ + *ge*(station) + *ster*(ol) + *-one*]

prognathous *adj* having a projecting lower jaw

prognosis *n, pl* **-noses 1** *med* a forecast about the course or outcome of an illness **2** any forecast [Greek: knowledge beforehand]

prognosticate *vb* **-cating, -cated 1** to foretell (future events) **2** to indicate or suggest beforehand [Medieval Latin *prognosticare* to predict] > **prognostication** *n* > **prognosticator** *n*

program *n* **1** a sequence of coded instructions which enables a computer to perform various tasks ▷ *vb* **-gramming, -grammed 2** to arrange (data) so that it can be processed by a computer **3** to feed a program into (a computer) > **programmer** *n*

programmable *or* **programable** *adj* capable of being programmed for computer processing

programme *or US* **program** *n* **1** a planned series of events **2** a broadcast on radio or television **3** a printed list of items or performers in an entertainment ▷ *vb* **-gramming, -grammed** *or US* **-graming, -gramed 4** to schedule (something) as a programme [Greek *programma* written public notice] > **programmatic** *adj*

programming language *n* a language system by which instructions to a computer are coded, that is understood by both user and computer

progress *n* **1** improvement or development **2** movement forward or advance **3** in progress taking place ▷ *vb* **4** to become more advanced or skilful **5** to move forward [Latin *progressus* a going forwards]

progression *n* **1** the act of progressing; advancement **2** the act or an instance of moving from one thing in a sequence to the next **3** *maths* a sequence of numbers in which each term differs from the succeeding term by a fixed ratio

progressive *adj* **1** favouring political or social reform **2** happening gradually: *a progressive illness* **3** (of a dance, card game, etc.) involving a regular change of partners ▷ *n* **4** a person who favours political or social reform > **progressively** *adv*

prohibit *vb* **-biting, -bited 1** to forbid by law or other authority **2** to hinder or prevent: *the paucity of information prohibits us from drawing reliable conclusions* [Latin *prohibere* to prevent] > **prohibitor** *n*

prohibition *n* **1** the act of forbidding **2** a legal ban on the sale or drinking of alcohol **3** an order or decree that forbids > **prohibitionist** *n*

Prohibition *n* the period (1920–33) when making, selling, and transporting alcohol was banned in the US > **Prohibitionist** *n*

prohibitive *adj* **1** (esp. of prices) too high to be affordable **2** prohibiting or tending to prohibit: *a prohibitive distance*

project *n* **1** a proposal or plan **2** a detailed study of a particular subject ▷ *vb* **3** to make a prediction based on known data and observations **4** to cause (an image) to appear on a surface **5** to communicate (an impression): *he wants to project an image of a deep-thinking articulate gentleman* **6** to jut out **7** to cause (one's voice) to be heard clearly at a distance **8** to transport in the imagination: *it's hard to project oneself into his situation* [Latin *proicere* to throw down]

projectile *n* **1** an object thrown as a weapon or fired from a gun ▷ *adj* **2** designed to be thrown forwards **3** projecting forwards [New Latin *projectilis* jutting forwards]

projection *n* **1** a part that juts out **2** a forecast based on known data **3** the process of showing film on a screen **4** the representation on a flat surface of a three-dimensional figure or curved line

projectionist *n* a person who operates a film projector

projector *n* an apparatus for projecting photographic images, film, or slides onto a screen

Prokofiev *n* Sergei (**Sergeyevich**). 1891–1953, Soviet composer. His compositions include the orchestral fairy tale *Peter and the Wolf* (1936), the opera *The Love for Three Oranges* (1921), and seven symphonies

Prokopyevsk *n* a city in S Russia: the chief coal-mining centre of the Kuznetsk Basin. Pop: 216 000 (2005 est)

prolapse *pathol n* **1** Also: **prolapsus** the slipping down of an internal organ of the body from its normal position ▷ *vb* **-lapsing, -lapsed 2** (of an internal organ) to slip from its normal position [Latin *prolabi* to slide along]

prolapsed *adj pathol* (of an internal organ) having slipped from its normal position

prolate *adj geometry* having a polar diameter which is longer than the equatorial diameter [Latin *prolatus* enlarged]

prole *n chiefly Brit offensive, slang* a proletarian

proletarian (pro-lit-**air**-ee-an) *adj* **1** of the proletariat ▷ *n* **2** a member of the proletariat

proletariat (pro-lit-**air**-ee-at) *n* the working class [Latin *proletarius* one whose only contribution to the state was his offspring]

proliferate vb **-rating, -rated 1** to increase rapidly in numbers **2** to grow or reproduce (new parts, such as cells) rapidly [Latin *proles* offspring + *ferre* to bear] > **proliferation** n

prolific adj **1** producing a constant creative output: *a prolific author* **2** producing fruit or offspring in abundance **3** (often foll. by in or of) rich or fruitful [Latin *proles* offspring] > **prolifically** adv

prolix adj (of a speech or piece of writing) overlong and boring [Latin *prolixus* stretched out widely] > **prolixity** n

prologue or US often **prolog** n **1** an introduction to a play or book **2** an event that comes before another: *this success was a happy prologue to their transatlantic tour* [Greek *pro-* before + *logos* discourse]

prolong vb to make (something) last longer [Late Latin *prolongare*] > **prolongation** n

prom n **1** Brit short for **promenade** (1), **promenade concert 2** US and Canad informal a formal dance held at a high school or college

PROM n computers Programmable Read Only Memory

promenade n **1** chiefly Brit a paved walkway along the seafront at a holiday resort **2** old-fashioned a leisurely walk for pleasure or display ▷ vb **-nading, -naded 3** old-fashioned to take a leisurely walk [French]

promenade concert n a concert at which some of the audience stand rather than sit

promethium (pro-**meeth**-ee-um) n chem an artificial radioactive element of the lanthanide series. Symbol: Pm [from *Prometheus*, in Greek mythology, the Titan who gave fire to mankind]

prominent adj **1** standing out from the surroundings; noticeable **2** widely known; famous **3** jutting or projecting outwards: *prominent eyes* [Latin *prominere* to jut out] > **prominence** n > **prominently** adv

promiscuous adj **1** taking part in many casual sexual relationships **2** formal consisting of different elements mingled indiscriminately [Latin *promiscuus* indiscriminate] > **promiscuity** n

promise vb **-mising, -mised 1** to say that one will definitely do or not do something: *I promise I'll have it finished by the end of the week* **2** to undertake to give (something to someone): *he promised me a car for my birthday* **3** to show signs of; seem likely: *she promises to be a fine singer* **4** to assure (someone) of the certainty of something: *everything's fine, I promise you* ▷ n **5** an undertaking to do or not do something **6** indication of future success: *a young player who shows great promise* [Latin *promissum* a promise]

Promised Land n **1** Bible the land of Canaan **2** any longed-for place where one expects to find greater happiness

promising adj likely to succeed or turn out well

promissory note n commerce, chiefly US a written promise to pay a stated sum of money to a particular person on a certain date or on demand

promo n, pl **-mos** informal an item produced to promote a product, esp. a video used to promote a pop record

promontory n, pl **-ries** a point of high land that juts out into the sea [Latin *promunturium* headland]

promote vb **-moting, -moted 1** to encourage the progress or success of: *all attempts to promote a lasting ceasefire have failed* **2** to raise to a higher rank or position **3** to encourage the sale of (a product) by advertising **4** to work for: *he actively promoted reform* [Latin *promovere* to push onwards] > **promotion** n > **promotional** adj

promoter n **1** a person who helps to organize and finance an event, esp. a sports one **2** a person or thing that encourages the progress or success of: *a promoter of terrorism*

prompt vb **1** to cause (an action); bring about: *the killings prompted an anti-Mafia crackdown* **2** to motivate or cause someone to do something: *I still don't know what prompted me to go* **3** to remind (an actor) of lines forgotten during a performance **4** to refresh the memory of ▷ adj **5** done without delay **6** quick to act ▷ adv **7** informal punctually:

at 8 o'clock prompt ▷ n **8** anything that serves to remind [Latin *promptus* evident] > **promptly** adv > **promptness** n

prompter n **a** a person offstage who reminds the actors of forgotten lines **b** a device which performs a similar function for public speakers, TV presenters, etc.

promulgate vb **-gating, -gated 1** to put (a law or decree) into effect by announcing it officially **2** to make widely known [Latin *promulgare*] > **promulgation** n > **promulgator** n

pron. **1** pronoun **2** pronunciation

prone adj **1** having a tendency to be affected by or do something: *I am prone to indigestion* **2** lying face downwards; prostrate [Latin *pronus* bent forward]

prong n a long pointed projection from an instrument or tool such as a fork [Middle English]

pronominal adj grammar relating to or playing the part of a pronoun

pronoun n a word, such as *she* or *it*, that replaces a noun or noun phrase that has already been or is about to be mentioned [Latin *pronomen*]

pronounce vb **-nouncing, -nounced 1** to speak (a sound or sounds), esp. clearly or in a certain way **2** to announce or declare officially: *I now pronounce you man and wife* **3** to declare as one's judgment: *he pronounced the wine drinkable* [Latin *pronuntiare* to announce] > **pronounceable** adj

pronounced adj very noticeable: *he speaks with a pronounced lisp*

pronouncement n a formal announcement

pronto adv informal at once [Spanish: quick]

pronunciation n **1** the recognized way to pronounce sounds in a given language **2** the way in which someone pronounces words

proof n **1** any evidence that confirms that something is true or exists **2** law the total evidence upon which a court bases its verdict **3** maths, logic a sequence of steps or statements that establishes the truth of a proposition **4** the act of testing the truth of something **5** an early copy of printed matter for checking before final production **6** photog a trial print from a negative **7** (esp. formerly) a defined level of alcoholic content used as a standard measure for comparing the alcoholic strength of other liquids: *Moldavian ruby port, 17° proof* ▷ adj **8** (foll. by against) able to withstand: *proof against tears* **9** (esp. formerly) having a level of alcoholic content used as a standard measure for comparing the alcoholic strength of other liquids ▷ vb **10** to take a proof from (type matter) **11** to render (something) proof, esp. to waterproof [Old French *preuve* a test]

proofread vb **-reading, -read** to read and correct (printer's proofs) > **proofreader** n

proof spirit n (in Britain) an alcoholic beverage that contains a standard percentage of alcohol

prop¹ vb **propping, propped** (often foll. by up) **1** to support (something or someone) in an upright position: *she was propped up by pillows* **2** to sustain or support: *the type of measures necessary to prop up the sagging US economy* **3** (often foll. by against) to place or lean ▷ n **4** something that gives rigid support, such as a pole **5** a person or thing giving moral support [perhaps from Middle Dutch *proppe*]

prop² n a movable object used on the set of a film or play

prop³ n informal a propeller

prop. **1** proper(ly) **2** property **3** proposition **4** proprietor

propaganda n **1** the organized promotion of information to assist or damage the cause of a government or movement **2** such information [Italian] > **propagandist** n, adj

propagate vb **-gating, -gated 1** to spread (information or ideas) **2** biology to reproduce or breed **3** horticulture to produce (plants) **4** physics to transmit, esp. in the form of a wave: *the electrical signal is propagated through a specialized group of conducting fibres* [Latin *propagare* to increase (plants) by cuttings] > **propagation** n > **propagator** n

propane n a flammable gas found in petroleum and

used as a fuel [from *propionic (acid)*]

propel *vb* **-pelling, -pelled** to cause to move forwards [Latin *propellere*] **> propellant** *n, adj*

propeller *n* a revolving shaft with blades to drive a ship or aircraft

propene *n* same as **propylene**

propensity *n, pl* **-ties** *formal* a natural tendency: *his problem had always been a propensity to live beyond his means* [Latin *propensus* inclined to]

proper *adj* **1** real or genuine: *a proper home* **2** appropriate or usual: *good wine must have the proper balance of sugar and acid* **3** suited to a particular purpose: *they set out without any proper climbing gear* **4** correct in behaviour: *in many societies it is not considered proper for a woman to show her legs* **5** excessively moral: *she was very strait-laced and proper* **6** being or forming the main or central part of something: *a suburb some miles west of the city proper* **7** *Brit, Austral and NZ informal* complete: *you made him look a proper fool* [Latin *proprius* special] **> properly** *adv*

proper fraction *n* a fraction in which the numerator has a lower absolute value than the denominator, for example $\frac{1}{2}$

proper noun *or* **proper name** *n* the name of a person or place, for example *Iceland* or *Patrick*

Propertius *n* Sextus. ?50–?15 BC, Roman elegiac poet

property *n, pl* **-ties 1** something owned **2** *law* the right to possess, use, and dispose of anything **3** possessions collectively **4** land or buildings owned by someone **5** a quality or attribute: *the oils have healing properties* **6** same as **prop²** [Latin *proprius* one's own]

prophecy *n, pl* **-cies 1** a prediction **2 a** a message revealing God's will **b** the act of uttering such a message **3** the function or activity of a prophet

prophesy *vb* **-sies, -sying, -sied** to foretell

prophet *n* **1** a person supposedly chosen by God to pass on His message **2** a person who predicts the future: *a prophet of doom* **3** a spokesman for, or advocate of, some cause: *a prophet of revolution* [Greek *prophētēs* one who declares the divine will] **> prophetess** *fem n*

Prophet *n* the **the** main name used of Mohammed, the founder of Islam

prophetic *adj* **1** foretelling what will happen **2** of the nature of a prophecy **> prophetically** *adv*

prophylactic *adj* **1** preventing disease ▷ *n* **2** a drug or device that prevents disease **3** *chiefly US* a condom [Greek *prophulassein* to guard by taking advance measures]

propinquity *n formal* nearness in time, place, or relationship [Latin *propinquus* near]

propitiate *vb* **-ating, -ated** to appease (someone, esp. a god or spirit); make well disposed [Latin *propitiare*] **> propitiable** *adj* **> propitiation** *n* **> propitiator** *n* **> propitiatory** *adj*

propitious *adj* **1** favourable or auspicious: *a propitious moment* **2** likely to prove favourable; advantageous: *his origins were not propitious for a literary career* [Latin *propitius* well disposed]

proponent *n* a person who argues in favour of something [Latin *proponere* to propose]

Propontis *n* the ancient name for (the Sea of) **Marmara**

proportion *n* **1** relative size or extent: *a large proportion of our revenue comes from advertisements* **2** correct relationship between parts **3** a part considered with respect to the whole: *the proportion of women in the total workforce* **4 proportions** dimensions or size: *a building of vast proportions* **5** *maths* a relationship between four numbers in which the ratio of the first pair equals the ratio of the second pair **6 in proportion a** comparable in size, rate of increase, etc. **b** without exaggerating ▷ *vb* **7** to adjust in relative amount or size: *the size of the crops are very rarely proportioned to the wants of the inhabitants* **8** to cause to be harmonious in relationship of parts [Latin *pro portione*, literally: for (its, one's) portion]

proportional *adj* **1** being in proportion ▷ *n* **2** *maths* an unknown term in a proportion, for example in *a/b = c/x, x*

is the fourth proportional **> proportionally** *adv*

proportional representation *n* the representation of political parties in parliament in proportion to the votes they win

proportionate *adj* being in proper proportion **> proportionately** *adv*

proposal *n* **1** the act of proposing **2** a suggestion put forward for consideration **3** an offer of marriage

propose *vb* **-posing, -posed 1** to put forward (a plan) for consideration **2** to nominate (someone) for a position **3** to intend (to do something): *I don't propose to waste any more time discussing it* **4** to ask people to drink a toast **5** (often foll. by *to*) to make an offer of marriage [Old French *proposer*, from Latin *proponere* to display]

proposition *n* **1** a proposal or offer **2** *logic* a statement that affirms or denies something and is capable of being true or false **3** *maths* a statement or theorem, usually containing its proof **4** *informal* a person or matter to be dealt with: *even among experienced climbers the mountain is considered a tough proposition* **5** *informal* an invitation to engage in sexual intercourse ▷ *vb* **6** to invite (someone) to engage in sexual intercourse [Latin *propositio* a setting forth]

propound *vb* to put forward for consideration [Latin *proponere* to set forth]

proprietary *adj* **1** denoting a product manufactured and distributed under a trade name **2** possessive: *she watched them with a proprietary eye* **3** privately owned and controlled [Late Latin *proprietarius* an owner]

proprietor *n* an owner of a business establishment **> proprietress** *fem n* **> proprietorial** *adj*

propriety *n, pl* **-ties 1** the quality or state of being appropriate or fitting **2** correct conduct **3 the proprieties** the standards of behaviour considered correct by polite society [Old French *propriété*, from Latin *proprius* one's own]

propulsion *n* **1** a force that moves (something) forward **2** the act of propelling or the state of being propelled [Latin *propellere* to propel] **> propulsive** *adj*

propylene *or* **propene** *n* a gas found in petroleum and used to produce many organic compounds [from *propionic (acid)*]

pro rata *adv, adj* in proportion [Medieval Latin]

prorogue *vb* **-roguing, -rogued** to suspend (Parliament) without dissolving it [Latin *prorogare*, literally: to ask publicly] **> prorogation** *n*

prosaic (pro-**zay**-ik) *adj* **1** lacking imagination; dull **2** having the characteristics of prose **> prosaically** *adv*

pros and cons *pl n* the advantages and disadvantages of a situation [Latin *pro* for + *con(tra)* against]

proscenium *n, pl* **-nia** *or* **-niums** the arch in a theatre separating the stage from the auditorium [Greek *pro* before + *skēnē* stage]

proscribe *vb* **-scribing, -scribed 1** to prohibit (something) **2** to condemn (something); to outlaw or banish [Latin *proscribere* to put up a public notice] **> proscription** *n* **> proscriptive** *adj*

prose *n* **1** ordinary spoken or written language in contrast to poetry **2** a passage set for translation into a foreign language **3** commonplace or dull talk ▷ *vb* **prosing, prosed 4** to speak or write in a tedious style [Latin *prosa oratio* straightforward speech]

Prosecco *n* a sparkling Italian white wine, usually dry

prosecute *vb* **-cuting, -cuted 1** to bring a criminal charge against (someone) **2** to continue to do (something): *the business of prosecuting a cold war through propaganda* **3 a** to seek redress by legal proceedings **b** to institute or conduct a prosecution [Latin *prosequi* to follow] **> prosecutor** *n*

prosecution *n* **1** the act of bringing criminal charges against someone **2** the institution and conduct of legal proceedings against a person **3** the lawyers acting for the Crown to put the case against a person **4** the carrying out of something begun

proselyte (pross-ill-ite) *n* a recent convert [Greek *prosēlutos* recent arrival, convert] **> proselytism** *n*

proselytize *or* **-tise** (pross-ill-it-ize) *vb* **-tizing, -tized** *or* **-tising, -tised** to attempt to convert (someone)

prosody (pross-a-dee) *n* **1** the study of poetic metre and techniques **2** the vocal patterns in a language [Greek *prosōidia* song set to music] **> prosodic** *adj* **> prosodist** *n*

prospect *n* **1** (*pl*) chances or opportunities for future success: *a job with impossible workloads and poor career prospects* **2** expectation, or something anticipated: *she was terrified at the prospect of bringing up two babies on her own* **3** old-fashioned a view or scene: *a prospect of spires, domes, and towers* ▷ *vb* **4** (sometimes foll. by *for*) to search for gold or other valuable minerals [Latin *prospectus* distant view]

prospective *adj* **1** future: *prospective customers* **2** expected or likely: *the prospective loss* **> prospectively** *adv*

prospector *n* a person who searches for gold or other valuable minerals

prospectus *n, pl* **-tuses** a booklet produced by a university, company, etc., giving details about it and its activities

prosper *vb* to be successful [Latin *prosperare* to succeed]

prosperity *n* success and wealth

prosperous *adj* wealthy and successful

Prost *n* Alain. born 1955, French motor-racing driver: Formula One world champion 1985, 1986, 1989, and 1993

prostate *n* a gland in male mammals that surrounds the neck of the bladder. Also called: **prostate gland** [Greek *prostatēs* something standing in front (of the bladder)]

prosthesis (pross-theess-iss) *n, pl* **-ses** (-seez) *surgery* **a** the replacement of a missing body part with an artificial substitute **b** an artificial body part such as a limb, eye, or tooth [Greek: an addition] **> prosthetic** *adj*

prostitute *n* **1** a person who offers sexual intercourse in return for payment ▷ *vb* **-tuting, -tuted** **2** to offer (oneself or another) in sexual intercourse for money **3** to offer (oneself or one's talent) for unworthy purposes [Latin *pro-* in public + *statuere* to cause to stand] **> prostitution** *n*

prostrate *adj* **1** lying face downwards **2** physically or emotionally exhausted ▷ *vb* **-trating, -trated** **3** prostrate oneself to cast (oneself) face downwards, as in submission **4** to exhaust physically or emotionally [Latin *prosternere* to throw to the ground] **> prostration** *n*

prosy *adj* **prosier, prosiest** dull and long-winded **> prosily** *adv*

Prot. **1** Protectorate **2** Protestant

protactinium *n chem* a toxic radioactive metallic element. Symbol: Pa

protagonist *n* **1** a supporter of a cause: *a great protagonist of the ideas and principles of mutuality* **2** the leading character in a play or story [Greek *prōtos* first + *agōnistēs* actor]

Protagoras *n* ?485–?411 BC, Greek philosopher and sophist, famous for his dictum "Man is the measure of all things."

protea (pro-tee-a) *n* an African shrub with showy heads of flowers [after *Proteus*, a sea god who could take many shapes]

protean (pro-tee-an) *adj* capable of constantly changing shape or form: *he is a protean stylist who can move from blues to ballads with consummate ease* [after *Proteus*; see PROTEA]

protect *vb* **1** to defend from trouble, harm, or loss **2** *econ* to assist (domestic industries) by taxing imports [Latin *protegere* to cover before]

protection *n* **1** the act of protecting or the condition of being protected **2** something that keeps (one) safe **3 a** the charging of taxes on imports, to protect domestic industries **b** Also called: **protectionism** the policy of such taxation **4** *informal* Also called: **protection money** money paid to gangsters to avoid attack or damage **> protectionism** *n* **> protectionist** *n, adj*

protective *adj* **1** giving protection: *protective clothing* **2** tending or wishing to protect someone **> protectively** *adv* **> protectiveness** *n*

protector *n* **1** a person or thing that protects **2** *history* a person who acts for the king or queen during his or her childhood, absence, or incapacity **> protectress** *fem n*

protectorate *n* **1** a territory largely controlled by a stronger state **2** the office or term of office of a protector

protégé *or fem* **protégée** (pro-tizh-ay) *n* a person who is protected and helped by another [French *protéger* to protect]

protein *n* any of a large group of nitrogenous compounds that are essential for life [Greek *prōteios* primary]

pro tempore *adv, adj* for the time being. Often shortened to: **pro tem**

protest *n* **1** public, often organized, demonstration of objection **2** a strong objection **3** a formal statement declaring that a debtor has dishonoured a bill **4** the act of protesting ▷ *vb* **5** to take part in a public demonstration to express one's support for or disapproval of an action, proposal, etc.: *the workers marched through the city to protest against the closure of their factory* **6** to disagree or object: *'I'm OK,' she protested* **7** to assert in a formal or solemn manner: *all three repeatedly protested their innocence* **8** US and NZ to object forcefully to: *students and teachers have protested the budget reductions* [Latin *protestari* to make a formal declaration] **> protestant** *adj, n* **> protester** *n*

Protestant *n* **1** a follower of any of the Christian Churches that separated from the Roman Catholic Church in the 16th century ▷ *adj* **2** of or relating to any of these Churches or their followers **> Protestantism** *n*

protestation *n formal* a strong declaration

protium *n* the most common isotope of hydrogen, with a mass number of 1 [from Greek *prōtos* first]

proto- *or sometimes before a vowel* **prot-** *combining form* **1** first: *protomartyr* **2** original: *prototype* [Greek *prōtos* first]

protocol *n* **1** the rules of behaviour for formal occasions **2** a record of an agreement in international negotiations **3** *computers* a standardized format for exchanging data, esp. between different computer systems [Late Greek *prōtokollon* sheet glued to the front of a manuscript]

proton (pro-ton) *n* a positively charged elementary particle, found in the nucleus of an atom [Greek *prōtos* first]

protoplasm *n biology* a complex colourless substance forming the living contents of a cell [Greek *prōtos* first + *plasma* form] **> protoplasmic** *adj*

prototype *n* **1** an early model of a product, which is tested so that the design can be changed if necessary **2** a person or thing that serves as an example of a type

protozoan (pro-toe-zoe-an) *n, pl* **-zoa** a very tiny single-celled invertebrate, such as an amoeba. Also: **protozoon** [Greek *prōtos* first + *zōion* animal]

protract *vb* to lengthen or extend (a situation etc.) [Latin *protrahere* to prolong] **> protracted** *adj* **> protraction** *n*

protractor *n* an instrument for measuring angles, usually a flat semicircular piece of plastic

protrude *vb* **-truding, -truded** to stick out or project [PRO-² + Latin *trudere* to thrust] **> protrusion** *n* **> protrusive** *adj*

protuberant *adj* swelling out; bulging [Late Latin *protuberare* to swell] **> protuberance** *n*

proud *adj* **1** feeling pleasure or satisfaction: *she was proud of her daughter's success* **2** feeling honoured **3** haughty or arrogant **4** causing pride: *the city's proud history* **5** dignified: *too proud to accept charity* **6** (of a surface or edge) projecting or protruding ▷ *adv* **7** do someone proud to entertain someone on a grand scale: *Mum did us all proud last Christmas* [Old French *prud*, *prod* brave] **> proudly** *adv*

proud flesh *n* a mass of tissue formed around a healing wound

Proudhon *n* Pierre Joseph. 1809–65, French socialist, whose pamphlet *What is Property?* (1840) declared that property is theft

Proust n **1** Joseph Louis. 1754–1826, French chemist, who formulated the law of constant proportions **2** Marcel. 1871–1922, French novelist whose long novel À la recherche du temps perdu (1913–27) deals with the relationship of the narrator to themes such as art, time, memory, and society

Prout n **1** Ebenezer. 1835–1909, English musicologist and composer, noted for his editions of works by Handel and J. S. Bach **2** William. 1785–1850, English chemist, noted for his modification of the atomic theory

prov. **1** province **2** provincial **3** provisional

Prov. **1** Bible Proverbs **2** Province **3** Provost

prove vb **proving, proved, proved** or **proven 1** to establish the truth or validity of: such a claim is difficult to prove scientifically **2** law to establish the genuineness of (a will) **3** to show (oneself) to be: he proved equal to the task **4** to be found to be: it proved to be a trap **5** (of dough) to rise in a warm place before baking [Latin probare to test] **>** **provable** adj

proven vb **1** a past participle of **prove 2** See **not proven** ▷ adj **3** known from experience to work: a proven ability to make money

provenance (prov-in-anss) n a place of origin [French]

Provençal (prov-on-sahl) adj **1** of or relating to Provence or its inhabitants ▷ n **2** a language of Provence **3** a native or inhabitant of Provence

Provence n a former province of SE France, on the Mediterranean, and the River Rhône: forms part of the administrative region of Provence-Alpes-Côte d'Azur

provender n old-fashioned fodder for livestock [Old French provendre]

proverb n a short memorable saying that expresses a truth or gives a warning, for example is half a loaf is better than no bread [Latin proverbium]

proverbial adj **1** well-known because commonly or traditionally referred to **2** of a proverb **>** **proverbially** adv

provide vb **-viding, -vided 1** to make available **2** to afford; yield: social activities providing the opportunity to meet new people **3** (often foll. by for or against) to take careful precautions: we provide for the possibility of illness in the examination regulations **4** (foll. by for) to support financially: both parents should be expected to provide for their children **5** formal **provide for** (of a law, treaty, etc.) to make possible: a bill providing for stiffer penalties for racial discrimination [Latin providere to provide for] **>** **provider** n

providence n **1** God or nature seen as a protective force that oversees people's lives **2** the foresight shown by a person in the management of his or her affairs

Providence[1] n Christianity God, esp. as showing foreseeing care of his creatures

Providence[2] n a port in NE Rhode Island, capital of the state, at the head of Narragansett Bay: founded by Roger Williams in 1636. Pop: 176 365 (2003 est)

provident adj **1** thrifty **2** showing foresight [Latin providens foreseeing]

providential adj fortunate, as if through divine involvement

provident society n same as **friendly society**

providing or **provided** conj on condition (that): the deal is on, providing he passes his medical

province n **1** a territory governed as a unit of a country or empire **2** an area of learning, activity, etc. **3** the provinces those parts of a country lying outside the capital [Latin provincia conquered territory]

Provincetown n a village in SE Massachusetts, at the tip of Cape Cod: scene of the first landing place of the Pilgrims (1620) and of the signing of the Mayflower Compact (1620). Pop: 3472 (2003 est)

provincewide Canad adj **1** relating to the whole of a province: a provincewide referendum ▷ adv **2** throughout a province: an advertising campaign to go provincewide

provincial adj **1** of a province **2** unsophisticated or narrow-minded **3** NZ denoting a football team representing a province ▷ n **4** an unsophisticated

person **5** a person from a province or the provinces **>** **provincialism** n

provision n **1** the act of supplying something **2** something supplied **3** provisions food and other necessities **4** a condition incorporated in a document **5** make provision for to make arrangements for beforehand: many restaurants still make no provision for non-smokers ▷ vb **6** to supply with provisions [Latin provisio a providing]

provisional adj temporary or conditional: a provisional diagnosis **>** **provisionally** adv

Provisional n a member of the Provisional IRA or Sinn Féin

proviso (pro-vize-oh) n, pl **-sos** or **-soes** a condition or stipulation [Medieval Latin proviso quod it being provided that] **>** **provisory** adj

provocation n **1** the act of provoking or inciting **2** something that causes indignation or anger

provocative adj provoking or inciting, esp. to anger or sexual desire: a provocative remark **>** **provocatively** adv

provoke vb **-voking, -voked 1** to deliberately act in a way intended to anger someone: waving a red cape, Delgado provoked the animal into charging **2** to incite or stimulate: the army seems to have provoked this latest confrontation **3** (often foll. by into) to cause a person to react in a particular, often angry, way: keeping your true motives hidden may provoke others into being just as two-faced with you **4** to bring about: the case has provoked furious public debate [Latin provocare to call forth] **>** **provoking** adj

provost n **1** the head of certain university colleges or schools **2** the chief councillor of a Scottish town [Old English profost]

provost marshal n the officer in charge of military police in a camp or city

prow n the bow of a vessel [Greek prōra]

prowess n **1** superior skill or ability **2** bravery or fearlessness [Old French proesce]

prowl vb **1** (sometimes foll. by around or about) to move stealthily around (a place) as if in search of prey or plunder ▷ n **2** the act of prowling **3** on the prowl moving around stealthily [origin unknown] **>** **prowler** n

prox. proximo (next month)

proximate adj **1** next or nearest in space or time **2** very near **3** immediately coming before or following in a series **4** approximate [Latin proximus next]

proximity n **1** nearness in space or time **2** nearness or closeness in a series [Latin proximitas closeness]

proxy n, pl **proxies 1** a person authorized to act on behalf of someone else: the firm's creditors can vote either in person or by proxy **2** the authority to act on behalf of someone else [Latin procuratio procuration]

proxy server n computers a computer that acts as an intermediary between a client machine and a server, caching information to save access time

Prozac n trademark an antidepressant drug

prude n a person who is excessively modest or prim, esp. regarding sex [Old French prode femme respectable woman] **>** **prudery** n **>** **prudish** adj

prudent adj **1** sensible and careful **2** discreet or cautious **3** exercising good judgment [Latin prudens far-sighted] **>** **prudence** n **>** **prudently** adv

prudential adj old-fashioned showing prudence: prudential reasons **>** **prudentially** adv

Prudentius n Aurelius Clemens. 348–410 AD, Latin Christian poet, born in Spain. His works include the allegory Psychomachia

Prud'hon n Pierre Paul. 1758–1823, French painter, noted for the romantic and mysterious aura of his portraits

prune[1] n a purplish-black partially dried plum [Latin prunum plum]

prune[2] vb **pruning, pruned 1** to cut off dead or surplus branches of (a tree or shrub) **2** to shorten or reduce [Old French proignier to clip]

prurient adj **1** excessively interested in sexual matters

2 exciting lustfulness [Latin *prurire* to lust after, itch]
> prurience *n*

Prussia *n* a former German state in N and central Germany, extending from France and the Low Countries to the Baltic Sea and Poland: developed as the chief military power of the Continent, leading the North German Confederation from 1867–71, when the German Empire was established; dissolved in 1947 and divided between East and West Germany, Poland, and the former Soviet Union. Area: (in 1939) 294 081 sq km (113 545 sq miles). German name: **Preussen**

Prussian *adj* **1** of or relating to Prussia or its inhabitants ▷ *n* **2** a native or inhabitant of Prussia

prussic acid *n* the extremely poisonous solution of hydrogen cyanide [French *acide prussique* Prussian acid]

Prut *n* a river in E Europe, rising in SW Ukraine and flowing generally southeast, forming part of the border between Romania and Moldova, to join the River Danube. Length: 853 km (530 miles)

pry *vb* **pries, prying, pried** (often foll. by *into*) to make an impertinent or uninvited inquiry (about a private matter) [origin unknown]

Prynne *n* William. 1600–69, English Puritan leader and pamphleteer, whose ears were cut off in punishment for his attacks on Laud

Przemyśl *n* a city in SE Poland, near the border with Ukraine on the San River: a fortress in the early Middle Ages; belonged to Austria (1722–1918). Pop: 66 968 (2007 est)

PS 1 Also: **ps** postscript **2** private secretary

PSA (in New Zealand) Public Service Association

psalm *n* (*often cap*) any of the sacred songs that make up a book (Psalms) of the Old Testament [Greek *psalmos* song accompanied on the harp]

psalmist *n* a writer of psalms

psalmody *n, pl* **-dies** the singing of sacred music

Psalter *n* **1** the Book of Psalms **2** a book containing a version of Psalms [Greek *psaltērion* stringed instrument]

psaltery *n, pl* **-teries** an ancient musical instrument played by plucking strings

PSBR (in Britain) public sector borrowing requirement: the money needed by the public sector of the economy for items not paid for by income

psephology (sef-fol-a-jee) *n* the statistical and sociological study of elections [Greek *psēphos* pebble, vote + -LOGY] **> psephologist** *n*

pseud *n informal* a pretentious person

pseudo *adj informal* not genuine

pseudo- *or sometimes before a vowel* **pseud-** *combining form* false, pretending, or unauthentic: *pseudo-intellectual* [Greek *pseudēs* false]

pseudonym *n* a fictitious name adopted, esp. by an author [Greek *pseudēs* false + *onoma* name]
> pseudonymity *n* **> pseudonymous** *adj*

psittacosis *n* a viral disease of parrots that can be passed on to humans [Greek *psittakos* a parrot]

Pskov *n* **1** a city in NW Russia, on the Velikaya River: one of the oldest Russian cities, at its height in the 13th and 14th centuries. Pop: 203 000 (2005 est) **2** Lake Pskov the S part of Lake Peipus in NW Russia, linked to the main part by a channel 24 km (15 miles) long. Area: about 1000 sq km (400 sq miles)

psoriasis (so-rye-a-siss) *n* a skin disease with reddish spots and patches covered with silvery scales [Greek: itching disease]

psst *interj* a sound made to attract someone's attention, esp. without others noticing

PST Pacific Standard Time

PSV (in Britain, formerly) public service vehicle

psyche *n* the human mind or soul [Greek *psukhē* breath, soul]

psychedelic *adj* **1** denoting a drug that causes hallucinations **2** *informal* having vivid colours and complex patterns similar to those experienced during

hallucinations [Greek *psukhē* mind + *dēlos* visible]

psychiatry *n* the branch of medicine concerned with the study and treatment of mental disorders
> psychiatric *adj* **> psychiatrist** *n*

psychic *adj* **1** relating to or having powers (especially mental powers) which cannot be explained by natural laws **2** relating to the mind ▷ *n* **3** a person who has psychic powers **> psychical** *adj*

psycho *informal n, pl* **-chos 1** same as **psychopath** ▷ *adj* **2** same as **psychopathic**

psycho- *or sometimes before a vowel* **psych-** *combining form* indicating the mind or mental processes: *psychology*; *psychosomatic* [Greek *psukhē* spirit, breath]

psychoactive *adj* capable of affecting mental activity: *a psychoactive drug*

psychoanalyse *or US* **-lyze** *vb* **-lysing, -lysed** *or US* **-lyzing, -lyzed** to examine or treat (a person) by psychoanalysis

psychoanalysis *n* a method of treating mental and emotional disorders by discussion and analysis of the patient's thoughts and feelings **> psychoanalyst** *n* **> psychoanalytical** *or* **psychoanalytic** *adj*

psychogenic *adj psychol* (esp. of disorders or symptoms) of mental, rather than organic, origin

psychological *adj* **1** relating to the mind or mental activity **2** relating to psychology **3** having its origin in the mind: *his backaches are purely psychological*
> psychologically *adv*

psychological moment *n* the best time for achieving the desired response or effect

psychological warfare *n* the military application of psychology, esp. to influence morale in time of war

psychology *n, pl* **-gies 1** the scientific study of all forms of human and animal behaviour **2** *informal* the mental make-up of a person **> psychologist** *n*

psychopath *n* a person afflicted with a personality disorder which causes him or her to commit antisocial and sometimes violent acts **> psychopathic** *adj*

psychopathology *n* the scientific study of mental disorders

psychopathy (sike-op-ath-ee) *n* any mental disorder or disease

psychosis (sike-oh-siss) *n, pl* **-ses** (-seez) a severe mental disorder in which the sufferer's contact with reality becomes highly distorted: *a classic case of psychosis*
> psychotic *adj*

psychosomatic *adj* (of a physical disorder) thought to have psychological causes, such as stress

psychotherapy *n* the treatment of nervous disorders by psychological methods **> psychotherapeutic** *adj* **> psychotherapist** *n*

psych up *vb* to prepare (oneself or another) mentally for a contest or task

pt 1 part **2** past tense **3** point **4** port **5** pro tempore

Pt *chem* platinum

PT *old-fashioned* physical training

pt. pint

PTA Parent Teacher Association

ptarmigan (tar-mig-an) *n* a bird of the grouse family that turns white in winter

Pte. *military* private

pterodactyl (terr-roe-dak-til) *n* an extinct flying reptile with batlike wings [Greek *pteron* wing + *daktulos* finger]

PTO *or* **pto** please turn over

Ptolemaic (tol-lim-may-ik) *adj* relating to Ptolemy, the 2nd-century AD Greek astronomer, or to his belief that the earth was in the centre of the universe

Ptolemy *n* Latin name *Claudius Ptolemaeus*. 2nd century AD, Greek astronomer, mathematician, and geographer. His *Geography* was the standard geographical textbook until the discoveries of the 15th century. His system of astronomy (see **Ptolemaic system**), as expounded in the *Almagest*, remained undisputed until the Copernican system was evolved

Ptolemy I *n* called *Ptolemy Soter*. ?367–283 BC, king of Egypt (323–285 BC), a general of Alexander the Great, who obtained Egypt on Alexander's death and founded the Ptolemaic dynasty: his capital Alexandria became the centre of Greek culture

Ptolemy II *n* called *Philadelphus*. 309–246 BC, the son of Ptolemy I; king of Egypt (285–246). Under his rule the power, prosperity, and culture of Egypt was at its height

ptomaine *or* **ptomain** (toe-main) *n* any of a group of poisonous alkaloids found in decaying matter [Greek *ptōma* corpse]

PTSD post-traumatic stress disorder

Pty *Austral and S African* Proprietary

Pu *chem* plutonium

pub *n* **1** *chiefly Brit* a building with a licensed bar where alcoholic drinks may be bought and drunk **2** *Austral and NZ* a hotel

pub. **1** public **2** publication **3** published **4** publisher **5** publishing

pub-crawl *n* *informal* a drinking tour of a number of pubs

pube *n* *informal* a pubic hair

puberty (pew-ber-tee) *n* the beginning of sexual maturity [Latin *pubertas* maturity] **›** **pubertal** *adj*

pubes *n*, *pl* **pubes** **1** the region above the genitals **2** the plural of **pubis** [Latin]

pubescent *adj* **1** arriving or arrived at puberty **2** covered with down, as some plants and animals [Latin *pubescere* to reach manhood] **›** **pubescence** *n*

pubic (pew-bik) *adj* of or relating to the pubes or pubis: *pubic hair*

pubis *n*, *pl* **-bes** one of the three sections of the hipbone that forms part of the pelvis [New Latin *os pubis* bone of the pubes]

public *adj* **1** relating to the people as a whole **2** provided by the government: *public service* **3** open to all: *public gardens* **4** well-known: *a public figure* **5** performed or made openly: *public proclamation* **6** maintained by and for the community: *a public library* **7** open, acknowledged, or notorious: *a public scandal* **8** go public **a** (of a private company) to offer shares for sale to the public: *few German firms have gone public in recent years* **b** to make information, plans, etc., known: *the group would not have gone public with its suspicions unless it was fully convinced of them* **▷** *n* **9** the community or people in general **10** a particular section of the community: *the racing public* [Latin *publicus*] **›** **publicly** *adv*

public-address system *n* a system of microphones, amplifiers, and loudspeakers for increasing the sound level of speech or music at public gatherings

publican *n* *Brit, Austral and NZ* a person who owns or runs a pub

publication *n* **1** the publishing of a printed work **2** any printed work offered for sale **3** the act of making information known to the public

public bar *n* a bar in a hotel or pub which is cheaper and more basically furnished than the lounge or saloon bar

public company *or* **public limited company** *n* a limited company whose shares may be purchased by the public

public convenience *n* a public toilet

public enemy *n* a notorious person who is considered a danger to the public

public house *n* **1** *Brit* a pub **2** *US and Canad* an inn or small hotel

publicist *n* a person, such as a press agent or journalist, who publicizes something

publicity *n* **1** the process or information used to arouse public attention **2** the public interest so aroused

publicize *or* **-cise** *vb* **-cizing, -cized** *or* **-cising, -cised** to bring to public attention

public lending right *n* the right of authors to receive payment when their books are borrowed from public libraries

public prosecutor *n* *law* an official in charge of prosecuting important cases

Public Protector *n* (in South Africa) an official with powers to investigate irregular government transactions

public relations *n* the practice of gaining the public's goodwill and approval for an organization

public school *n* **1** (in England and Wales) a private independent fee-paying secondary school **2** (in certain Canadian provinces) a public elementary school as distinguished from a separate school **3** (in the US) any school that is part of a free local educational system

public sector *n* the part of a country's economy that consists of state-owned industries and services

public servant *n* **1** an elected or appointed holder of a public office **2** *Austral and NZ* a civil servant

public service *n* *Austral and NZ* the civil service

public-spirited *adj* having or showing an active interest in the good of the community

public utility *n* an organization that supplies water, gas, or electricity to the public

publish *vb* **1** to produce and issue (printed matter) for sale **2** to have one's written work issued for publication **3** to announce formally or in public [Latin *publicare* to make public] **›** **publishing** *n*

publisher *n* **1** a company or person that publishes books, periodicals, music, etc. **2** *US and Canad* the proprietor of a newspaper

Puccini *n* Giacomo. 1858–1924, Italian operatic composer, noted for the dramatic realism of his operas, which include *Manon Lescaut* (1893), *La Bohème* (1896), *Tosca* (1900), and *Madame Butterfly* (1904)

puce *adj* dark brownish-purple: *his face suddenly turned puce with futile rage* [French *couleur puce* flea colour]

puck¹ *n* a small disc of hard rubber used in ice hockey [origin unknown]

puck² *n* a mischievous or evil spirit [Old English *pūca*] **›** **puckish** *adj*

pucker *vb* **1** to gather into wrinkles **▷** *n* **2** a wrinkle or crease [origin unknown]

pudding *n* **1** a dessert, esp. a cooked one served hot **2** a savoury dish with pastry or batter: *steak-and-kidney pudding* **3** a sausage-like mass of meat: *black pudding* [Middle English *poding*]

puddle *n* **1** a small pool of water, esp. of rain **2** a worked mixture of wet clay and sand that is impervious to water **▷** *vb* **-dling, -dled** **3** to make (clay etc.) into puddle **4** to subject (iron) to puddling [Middle English *podel*] **›** **puddly** *adj*

pudenda *pl n* the human genitals, esp. of a female [Latin: the shameful (parts)]

pudgy *adj* **pudgier, pudgiest** *chiefly US* podgy [origin unknown] **›** **pudginess** *n*

Pudovkin *n* Vsevolod. 1893–1953, Russian film director; noted for his silent films, such as *Mother* (1926) and *Storm over Asia* (1928)

Pudsey *n* a town in N England, in Leeds unitary authority, West Yorkshire. Pop: 32 391 (2001)

Puducherry *n* **1** a Union Territory of SE India: transferred from French to Indian administration in 1954 and made a Union Territory in 1962. Capital: Puducherry. Pop: 973 829 (2001 est). Area: 479 sq km (185 sq miles) **2** a port in SE India, capital of the Union Territory of Puducherry (Pondicherry), on the Coromandel Coast. Pop: 220 749 (2001) **▶** Former official name (until 2006): **Pondicherry**

Puebla *n* **1** an inland state of S central Mexico, situated on the Anáhuac Plateau. Capital: Puebla. Pop: 5 070 346 (2000 est). Area: 33 919 sq km (13 096 sq miles) **2** a city in S Mexico, capital of Puebla state: founded in 1532; university (1537). Pop: 1 880 000 (2005 est) **▶** Full name: **Puebla de Zaragoza**

Pueblo *n* a city in Colorado: a centre of the steel industry. Pop: 103 648 (2003 est)

puerile *adj* silly and childish [Latin *puer* a boy] **›** **puerility** *n*

puerperal (pew-er-per-al) *adj* concerning the period following childbirth [Latin *puerperium* childbirth]

puerperal fever *n* a serious, formerly widespread, form of blood poisoning caused by infection during childbirth

puerperium (pure-peer-ee-um) *n* the period after childbirth

Puerto Rican *adj* 1 of or relating to Puerto Rico or its inhabitants ▷ *n* 2 a native or inhabitant of Puerto Rico

Puerto Rico *n* an autonomous commonwealth (in association with the US) occupying the smallest and easternmost of the Greater Antilles in the Caribbean: one of the most densely populated areas in the world; ceded by Spain to the US in 1899. Currency: US dollar. Capital: San Juan. Pop: 3 674 209 (2013 est). Area: 9104 sq km (3515 sq miles). Former name (until 1932): **Porto Rico**. Abbreviation: **PR**

Pufendorf *n* Samuel von. 1632–94, German jurist and philosopher, who lived in Sweden and Denmark. His *De Jure naturae et gentium* (1672) was an important contribution to the philosophy of natural and international law

puff *n* 1 a short quick blast of breath, wind, or smoke 2 the amount of wind or smoke released in a puff 3 the sound made by a puff 4 an act of inhaling and expelling cigarette smoke 5 a light pastry usually filled with cream and jam 6 **out of puff** out of breath: *by the third flight of stairs she was out of puff* ▷ *vb* 7 to blow or breathe in short quick blasts 8 (often foll. by *out*) to cause to be out of breath 9 to take draws at (a cigarette) 10 to move with or by the emission of puffs: *the steam train puffed up the incline* 11 (often foll. by *up* or *out*) to swell [Old English *pyffan*] ▷ **puffy** *adj*

puff adder *n* a large venomous African viper whose body swells when alarmed

puffball *n* a ball-shaped fungus that sends out a cloud of brown spores when mature

puffin *n* a black-and-white sea bird with a brightly coloured beak [origin unknown]

puff pastry *or US* **puff paste** *n* a light flaky pastry

pug *n* a small dog with a smooth coat, lightly curled tail, and a short wrinkled nose [origin unknown]

Pugachov *n* Yemelyan Ivanovich. 1726–75, Russian Cossack rebel, leader of a major revolt against the government of Catherine II: executed

Puget *n* Pierre. 1620–94, French Baroque sculptor, best known for his *Milo of Crotona* (c. 1680)

Puget Sound *n* an inlet of the Pacific in NW Washington. Length: about 130 km (80 miles)

pugilist (pew-jil-ist) *n* a boxer [Latin *pugil* a boxer] ▷ **pugilism** *n* ▷ **pugilistic** *adj*

Pugin *n* Augustus (Welby Northmore). 1812–52, British architect; a leader of the Gothic Revival. He collaborated with Sir Charles Barry on the Palace of Westminster (begun 1836)

Puglia *n* the Italian name for **Apulia**

pugnacious *adj* ready and eager to fight [Latin *pugnax*] ▷ **pugnacity** *n*

pug nose *n* a short stubby upturned nose [from *Pug*] ▷ **pug-nosed** *adj*

puissance *n* a showjumping competition that tests a horse's ability to jump large obstacles [see PUISSANT]

puissant (pew-iss-sant) *adj archaic or poetic* powerful [Old French, from Latin *potens* mighty]

puke *slang vb* **puking, puked** 1 to vomit ▷ *n* 2 the act of vomiting 3 the matter vomited [probably imitative]

pukeko (poo-kek-oh) *n, pl* **-kos** a brightly coloured New Zealand wading bird [Māori]

pukka *adj* 1 properly done, constructed, etc. 2 genuine or real [Hindi *pakkā* firm]

Pula *n* a port in NW Croatia at the S tip of the Istrian Peninsula: made a Roman military base in 178 BC; became the main Austro-Hungarian naval station and passed to Italy in 1919, to Yugoslavia in 1947, and is now in independent Croatia. Pop: 67 000 (2007 est). Latin name: **Pietas Julia**. Italian name: **Pola**

Pulau Pinang *n* another name for **Penang**

pulchritude *n formal or literary* physical beauty [Latin *pulchritudo*] ▷ **pulchritudinous** *adj*

Pulci *n* Luigi. 1432–84, Italian poet. His masterpiece is the comic epic poem *Morgante* (1483)

pule *vb* **puling, puled** *literary* to whine or whimper [imitative]

Pulitzer *n* Joseph. 1847–1911, US newspaper publisher, born in Hungary. He established the Pulitzer prizes

pull *vb* 1 to exert force on (an object) to draw it towards the source of the force 2 to strain or stretch 3 to remove or extract: *he pulled a crumpled tenner from his pocket* 4 *informal* to draw out (a weapon) for use: *he pulled a knife on his attacker* 5 *informal* to attract: *the game is expected to pull a large crowd* 6 to attract a sexual partner 7 (usually foll. by *on* or *at*) to drink or inhale deeply: *he pulled on his pipe* 8 to possess or exercise the power to move: *this car doesn't pull well on hills* 9 to withdraw or remove: *the board pulled their support* 10 *printing* to take (a proof) from type 11 *golf, baseball etc*. to hit (a ball) away from the direction in which the player intended to hit it 12 *cricket* to hit (a ball) to the leg side 13 to row (a boat) or take a stroke of (an oar) in rowing 14 **pull a face** to make a grimace 15 **pull a fast one** *slang* (often foll. by *on*) to play a sly trick 16 **pull apart** *or* **to pieces** to criticize harshly 17 **pull (one's) punches** to limit the force of one's criticisms or blows ▷ *n* 18 the act of pulling 19 the force used in pulling: *the pull of the moon affects the tides* 20 the act of taking in drink or smoke 21 *printing* a proof taken from type 22 something used for pulling, such as a handle 23 *informal* power or influence: *his uncle is chairman of the company, so he has quite a lot of pull* 24 *informal* the power to attract attention or support 25 a single stroke of an oar in rowing 26 the act of pulling the ball in golf, cricket, etc. ▶ See also **pull down, pull in**, etc. [Old English *pullian*]

pull down *vb* to destroy or demolish: *the old houses were pulled down*

pullet *n* a hen less than one year old [Old French *poulet* chicken]

pulley *n* a wheel with a grooved rim in which a belt, chain, or piece of rope runs in order to lift weights by a downward pull [Old French *polie*]

pull in *vb* 1 Also: **pull over** (of a motor vehicle) to draw in to the side of the road 2 (often foll. by *to*) to reach a destination: *the train pulled in to the station* 3 to attract: *his appearance will pull in the crowds* 4 *Brit, Austral and NZ slang* to arrest 5 to earn (money): *he pulls in at least thirty thousand a year*

Pullman[1] *n, pl* **-mans** *chiefly Brit* a luxurious railway coach [after G. M. *Pullman*, its inventor]

Pullman[2] *n* Philip. born 1946, British author. Writing primarily for older children, he is best known for the fantasy trilogy *His Dark Materials* (1997–2000)

pull off *vb informal* to succeed in accomplishing (something difficult): *superheroes who pull off the impossible*

pull out *vb* 1 a (of a motor vehicle) to draw away from the side of the road b (of a motor vehicle) to move out from behind another vehicle to overtake 2 to depart: *the train pulled out of the station* 3 to withdraw: *several companies have pulled out of the student market* 4 to remove by pulling 5 to abandon a situation

pullover *n* a sweater that is pulled on over the head

pull through *vb* to survive or recover, esp. after a serious illness

pull together *vb* 1 to cooperate or work in harmony 2 **pull oneself together** *informal* to regain one's self-control

pull up *vb* 1 (of a motor vehicle) to stop 2 to remove by the roots 3 to rebuke

pulmonary *adj* 1 of or affecting the lungs 2 having lungs or lunglike organs [Latin *pulmo* a lung]

pulp *n* 1 a soft wet substance made from matter which has been crushed or beaten: *mash the strawberries to a pulp*

2 the soft fleshy part of a fruit or vegetable: *halve the tomatoes then scoop the seeds and pulp into a bowl* **3** printed or recorded material with little depth or designed to shock: *pulp fiction; a tape player churned out disco pulp* ▷ *vb* **4** to reduce a material to pulp: *he began to pulp the orange in his fingers* [Latin *pulpa*] **> pulpy** *adj*

pulpit *n* **1** a raised platform in churches used for preaching **2** (usually preceded by *the*) preaching or the clergy [Latin *pulpitum* a platform]

pulpwood *n* pine, spruce, or any other soft wood used to make paper

pulsar *n* a very small star which emits regular pulses of radio waves [from *puls(ating st)ar*]

pulsate *vb* **-sating, -sated 1** to expand and contract rhythmically, like a heartbeat **2** to quiver or vibrate: *the images pulsate with energy and light* **3** *physics* to vary in intensity or magnitude [Latin *pulsare* to push]
> pulsation *n*

pulse¹ *n* **1** *physiol* **a** the regular beating of blood through the arteries at each heartbeat **b** a single such beat **2** *physics, electronics* a sudden change in a quantity, such as a voltage, that is normally constant in a system **3** a regular beat or vibration **4** bustle or excitement: *the lively pulse of a city* **5** the feelings or thoughts of a group as they can be measured: *the political pulse of the capital* ▷ *vb* **pulsing, pulsed 6** to beat, throb, or vibrate [Latin *pulsus* a beating]

pulse² *n* the edible seeds of pod-bearing plants, such as peas, beans, and lentils [Latin *puls* pottage of pulse]

pulverize *or* **-rise** *vb* **-rizing, -rized** *or* **-rising, -rised 1** to reduce to fine particles by crushing or grinding **2** to destroy completely [Latin *pulvis* dust] **> pulverization** *or* **-risation** *n*

puma *n* a large American wild cat with a plain greyish-brown coat and a long tail [S American Indian]

pumice (**pumm-iss**) *n* a light porous stone used for scouring and for removing hard skin. Also called: **pumice stone** [Old French *pomis*]

pummel *vb* **-melling, -melled** *or US* **-meling, -meled** to strike repeatedly with the fists [see POMMEL]

pump¹ *n* **1** a device to force a gas or liquid to move in a particular direction ▷ *vb* **2** (sometimes foll. by *from, out*, etc.) to raise or drive (air, liquid, etc.) with a pump, esp. into or from something **3** (usually foll. by *in* or *into*) to supply in large amounts: *pumping money into the economy* **4** to operate (a handle etc.) in the manner of a pump: *he was warmly applauded, and his hand was pumped by well-wishers* **5** to obtain information from (someone) by persistent questioning **6 pump iron** *slang* to exercise with weights; do body-building exercises [Middle Dutch *pumpe* pipe]

pump² *n* **1** *chiefly Brit* a shoe with a rubber sole, used in games such as tennis; plimsoll **2** *chiefly Brit* a low-cut low-heeled shoe, worn for dancing [origin unknown]

pumpernickel *n* a slightly sour black bread made of coarse rye flour [from German]

pumpkin *n* **1** a large round fruit with a thick orange rind, pulpy flesh, and many seeds **2** the creeping plant that bears this fruit [Greek *pepōn* ripe]

pun *n* **1** the use of words to exploit double meanings for humorous effect, for example *my dog's a champion boxer* ▷ *vb* **2** to make puns [origin unknown]

Punakha *or* **Punaka** *n* a town in W central Bhutan: a former capital of the country

punch¹ *vb* **1** to strike at with a clenched fist ▷ *n* **2** a blow with the fist **3** *informal* point or vigour: *the jokes are mildly amusing but lack any real punch* [probably variant of *pounce* to stamp]

punch² *n* **1** a tool or machine for shaping, piercing, or engraving **2** *computers* a device for making holes in a card or paper tape ▷ *vb* **3** to pierce, cut, stamp, shape, or drive with a punch [Latin *pungere* to prick]

punch³ *n* a mixed drink containing fruit juice and, usually, alcoholic liquor, generally hot and spiced [origin unknown]

Punch *n* the main character in the children's puppet show, Punch and Judy

punchbag *n* a stuffed or inflated bag suspended by a flexible rod, that is punched for exercise, esp. boxing training

punchball *n* a stuffed or inflated ball supported by a flexible rod, that is punched for exercise, esp. boxing training

punchbowl *n* a large bowl for serving punch

punch-drunk *adj* dazed and confused through suffering repeated blows to the head

punched card *or especially US* **punch card** *n computers* a card on which data can be coded in the form of punched holes

Punchinello *n, pl* **-los** *or* **-loes** a clown from Italian puppet shows, the origin of Punch [Italian *Polecenella*]

punch line *n* the last line of a joke or funny story that gives it its point

punch-up *n informal* a fight or brawl

punchy *adj* **punchier, punchiest** *informal* effective or forceful: *learn to compose short concise punchy letters*

punctilious *adj formal* **1** paying careful attention to correct social behaviour **2** attentive to detail [Latin *punctum* a point] **> punctiliously** *adv*

punctual *adj* **1** arriving or taking place at an arranged time **2** (of a person) always keeping exactly to arranged times [Medieval Latin *punctualis* concerning detail]
> punctuality *n* **> punctually** *adv*

punctuate *vb* **-ating, -ated 1** to insert punctuation marks into (a written text) **2** to interrupt at frequent intervals: *the meeting was punctuated by heckling* **3** to emphasize: *he punctuated the question by pressing the muzzle into the pilot's neck* [Latin *pungere* to puncture]

punctuation *n* **1** the use of symbols, such as commas, to indicate speech patterns and meaning not otherwise shown by the written language **2** the symbols used for this purpose

punctuation mark *n* any of the signs used in punctuation, such as a comma

puncture *n* **1** a small hole made by a sharp object **2** a tear and loss of pressure in a tyre **3** the act of puncturing or perforating ▷ *vb* **-turing, -tured 4** to pierce a hole in (something) with a sharp object **5** to cause (a tyre etc.) to lose pressure by piercing [Latin *pungere* to prick]

pundit *n* **1** an expert on a subject who often speaks or writes about it for a non-specialist audience: *Spain's leading sports pundit, who hosts two TV programmes* **2** a Hindu scholar learned in Sanskrit, religion, philosophy, or law [Hindi *pandit*]

Pune *n* another name for **Poona**

pungent *adj* **1** having a strong sharp bitter smell or taste **2** (of speech or writing) biting; critical [Latin *pungens* piercing] **> pungency** *n*

punish *vb* **1** to force (someone) to undergo a penalty for some crime or misbehaviour **2** to inflict punishment for (some crime or misbehaviour) **3** to treat harshly, esp. by overexertion: *he continued to punish himself in the gym* [Latin *punire*] **> punishable** *adj* **> punishing** *adj*

punishment *n* **1** a penalty for a crime or offence **2** the act of punishing or state of being punished **3** *informal* rough physical treatment: *the boxer's face could not withstand further punishment*

punitive (**pew-nit-tiv**) *adj* relating to punishment: *punitive measures*

Punjab *n* **1** (formerly) a province in NW British India: divided between India and Pakistan in 1947 **2** a state of NW India: reorganized in 1966 as a Punjabi-speaking state, a large part forming the new state of Haryana; mainly agricultural. Capital: Chandigarh. Pop: 24 289 296 (2001). Area: 50 255 sq km (19 403 sq miles) **3** a province of W Pakistan: created in 1947. Capital: Lahore. Pop: 82 710 000 (2003 est). Area: 205 344 sq km (127 595 sq miles)

Punjabi *or* **Panjabi** *n* **1** a member of the chief people of the Punjab **2** the state language of the Punjab, belonging to the Indic branch of the Indo-European family ▷ *adj* **3** of or relating to the Punjab, its people, or their language

Punjab States *pl n* (formerly) a group of states in NW India, amalgamated in 1956 with Punjab state

punk *n* **1** a worthless person **2** a youth movement of the late 1970s, characterized by anti-Establishment slogans, short spiky hair, and the wearing of worthless articles such as safety pins for decoration **3** short for **punk rock** **4** a follower of the punk movement or of punk rock ▷ *adj* **5** relating to the punk youth movement of the late 1970s: *a punk band* **6** worthless or insignificant [origin unknown]

punkah or **punka** *n* (in India) a ceiling fan made of a cloth stretched over a rectangular frame [Hindi *paṅkhā*]

punk rock *n* rock music of the punk youth movement of the late 1970s, characterized by energy and aggressive lyrics and performance ❭ **punk rocker** *n*

punnet *n* a small basket for fruit [origin unknown]

punster *n* a person who is fond of making puns

punt¹ *n* **1** an open flat-bottomed boat, propelled by a pole ▷ *vb* **2** to propel (a punt) by pushing with a pole on the bottom of a river [Latin *ponto*]

punt² *n* **1** a kick in certain sports, such as in rugby, in which the ball is dropped and kicked before it hits the ground ▷ *vb* **2** to kick (a ball) using a punt [origin unknown]

punt³ *chiefly Brit vb* **1** to gamble or bet ▷ *n* **2** a gamble or bet, esp. against the bank, such as in roulette **3** **take a punt at** *Austral and NZ* to make an attempt at [French *ponter*]

punt⁴ *n* a former monetary unit of the Republic of Ireland

Punta Arenas *n* a port in S Chile, on the Strait of Magellan: the southernmost city in the world. Pop: 118 000 (2005 est). Former name: **Magallanes**

punter *n* **1** a person who places a bet **2** *Brit, Austral and NZ informal* any member of the public, esp. when a customer: *the punters are flocking into the sales*

puny *adj* **-nier, -niest** small and weakly [Old French *puisné* born later]

pup *n* **1 a** a young dog; puppy **b** the young of various other animals, such as the seal ▷ *vb* **pupping, pupped** **2** (of dogs, seals, etc.) to give birth to pups

pupa (pew-pa) *n, pl* **-pae** (-pee) or **-pas** an insect at the stage of development between larva and adult [Latin: a doll] ❭ **pupal** *adj*

pupil¹ *n* a student who is taught by a teacher [Latin *pupus* a child]

pupil² *n* the dark circular opening at the centre of the iris of the eye [Latin *pupilla*, diminutive of *pupa* doll; from the tiny reflections in the eye]

puppet *n* **1** a small doll or figure moved by strings attached to its limbs or by the hand inserted in its cloth body **2** a person or state that appears independent but is controlled by another: *the former cabinet ministers have denied that they are puppets of a foreign government* [Latin *pupa* doll]

puppeteer *n* a person who operates puppets

puppy *n, pl* **-pies** **1** a young dog **2** *informal, disparaging* a brash or conceited young man [Old French *popée* doll] ❭ **puppyish** *adj*

puppy fat *n* fatty tissue that develops in childhood or adolescence and usually disappears with maturity

purblind *adj* **1** partly or nearly blind **2** lacking in understanding [*pure* (that is, utterly) *blind*]

Purcell *n* **1** Edward Mills. 1912–97, US physicist, noted for his work on the magnetic moments of atomic nuclei: shared the Nobel prize for physics (1952) **2** Henry. ?1659–95, English composer, noted chiefly for his rhythmic and harmonic subtlety in setting words. His works include the opera *Dido and Aeneas* (1689), music for the theatrical pieces *King Arthur* (1691) and *The Fairy Queen* (1692), several choral odes, fantasias, sonatas, and church music

purchase *vb* **-chasing, -chased** **1** to obtain (goods) by payment **2** to obtain by effort or sacrifice: *he had purchased his freedom at the expense of his principles* ▷ *n* **3** something that is bought **4** the act of buying **5** the mechanical advantage achieved by a lever **6** a firm leverage or grip [Old French *porchacier* to strive to obtain] ❭ **purchaser** *n*

purdah *n* the custom in some Muslim and Hindu communities of keeping women in seclusion, with clothing that conceals them completely when they go out [Hindi *parda* veil]

pure *adj* **1** not mixed with any other materials or elements: *pure wool* **2** free from tainting or polluting matter: *pure water* **3** innocent: *pure love* **4** complete: *Pamela's presence on that particular flight was pure chance* **5** (of a subject) studied in its theoretical aspects rather than for its practical applications: *pure mathematics* **6** of unmixed descent [Latin *purus* unstained] ❭ **purely** *adv* ❭ **pureness** *n*

purebred *adj* denoting a pure strain obtained through many generations of controlled breeding

puree (pure-ray) *n* **1** a smooth thick pulp of sieved fruit, vegetables, meat, or fish ▷ *vb* **-reeing, -reed** **2** to make (foods) into a puree [French]

purgative *med n* **1** a medicine for emptying the bowels ▷ *adj* **2** causing emptying of the bowels

purgatory *n* **1** *chiefly RC Church* a place in which the souls of those who have died undergo limited suffering for their sins on earth before they go to heaven **2** a situation of temporary suffering or torment: *it was purgatory living in the same house as him* [Latin *purgare* to purify] ❭ **purgatorial** *adj*

purge *vb* **purging, purged** **1** to rid (something) of undesirable qualities **2** to rid (an organization etc.) of undesirable people: *the party was purged* **3 a** to empty (the bowels) **b** to cause (a person) to empty his or her bowels **4 a** *law* to clear (a person) of a charge **b** to free (oneself) of guilt by showing repentance **5** to be purified ▷ *n* **6** the act or process of purging **7** the removal of undesirables from a state, organization, or political party **8** a medicine that empties the bowels [Latin *purgare* to purify]

Puri *n* a port in E India, in Odisha (formerly Orissa) on the Bay of Bengal: 12th-century temple of Jagannath. Pop: 157 610 (2001)

purify *vb* **-fies, -fying, -fied** **1** to free (something) of harmful or inferior matter **2** to free (a person) from sin or guilt **3** to make clean, for example in a religious ceremony [Latin *purus* pure + *facere* to make] ❭ **purification** *n*

purism *n* strict insistence on the correct usage or style, such as in grammar or art ❭ **purist** *adj, n* ❭ **puristic** *adj*

puritan *n* **1** a person who follows strict moral or religious principles ▷ *adj* **2** of or like a puritan: *he maintained a streak of puritan self-denial* [Late Latin *puritas* purity] ❭ **puritanism** *n*

Puritan *history n* **1** a member of the extreme English Protestants who wished to strip the Church of England of most of its rituals ▷ *adj* **2** of or relating to the Puritans ❭ **Puritanism** *n*

puritanical *adj* **1** *usually disparaging* strict in moral or religious outlook **2** (*sometimes cap*) of or relating to a puritan or the Puritans ❭ **puritanically** *adv*

purity *n* the state or quality of being pure

purl¹ *n* **1** a knitting stitch made by doing a plain stitch backwards **2** a decorative border, such as of lace ▷ *vb* **3** to knit in purl stitch [dialect *pirl* to twist into a cord]

purl² *vb literary* (of a stream) to flow with a gentle movement and a murmuring sound [probably imitative]

purlieu (per-lyoo) *n* **1** *English history* land on the edge of a royal forest **2** (*usually pl*) *literary* a neighbouring area; outskirts **3** (*often pl*) *literary* a place one frequents: *the committee was the purlieu of civil servants* [Anglo-French *puralé* a going through]

purlin or **purline** n a horizontal beam that supports the rafters of a roof [origin unknown]

purloin vb formal to steal [Old French porloigner to put at a distance]

purple n 1 a colour between red and blue 2 cloth of this colour, often used to symbolize royalty or nobility 3 the official robe of a cardinal 4 anything purple, such as purple paint or purple clothing: a large lady, unwisely dressed in purple ▷ adj 5 of a colour between red and blue 6 (of writing) excessively elaborate: purple prose [Greek porphura the purple fish (murex)] > **purplish** adj

purple heart n informal, chiefly Brit a heart-shaped purple tablet consisting mainly of amphetamine

Purple Heart n a decoration awarded to members of the US Armed Forces wounded in action

purport vb 1 to claim to be or do something, esp. falsely: painkillers may actually cause the headaches they purport to cure 2 (of speech or writing) to signify or imply ▷ n 3 meaning or significance [Old French porporter to convey]

purpose n 1 the reason for which anything is done, created, or exists 2 a fixed design or idea that is the object of an action 3 determination: his single-minded determination only lightly conceals a clear sense of purpose 4 practical advantage or use: we debated senseless points of dogma for hours to no fruitful purpose 5 **on purpose** intentionally ▷ vb -**posing, -posed** 6 to intend or determine to do (something) [Old French porposer to plan]

purpose-built adj made to serve a specific purpose

purposeful adj with a fixed and definite purpose; determined > **purposefully** adv

---
USAGE Purposefully is sometimes wrongly used where purposely is meant: he had purposely (not purposefully) left the door unlocked.
---

purposely adv on purpose

USAGE See at **purposeful**.
---

purposive adj formal 1 having or showing a definite intention: the establishment of the camps lacks a purposive trend towards a solution 2 useful

purr vb 1 (esp. of cats) to make a low vibrant sound, usually considered as expressing pleasure 2 to express (pleasure) by this sound or by a sound suggestive of purring ▷ n 3 a purring sound [imitative]

purse n 1 a small pouch for carrying money 2 US, Canad, Austral and NZ a woman's handbag 3 wealth or resources: the public purse appeared bottomless 4 a sum of money that is offered as a prize ▷ vb **pursing, pursed** 5 to pull (the lips) into a small rounded shape [Old English purs]

purser n an officer aboard a ship who keeps the accounts

purse strings pl n **hold the purse strings** to control the spending of a particular family, group, etc.

pursuance n formal the carrying out of an action or plan: the pursuance of duty had taken him abroad

pursue vb -**suing, -sued** 1 to follow (a person, vehicle, or animal) in order to capture or overtake 2 to try hard to achieve (some desire or aim) 3 to follow the guidelines of (a plan or policy) 4 to apply oneself to (studies or interests) 5 to follow persistently or seek to become acquainted with: was his desire to pursue and marry Carol based purely on her looks? 6 to continue to discuss or argue (a point or subject) [Old French poursivre] > **pursuer** n

pursuit n 1 the act of pursuing 2 an occupation or pastime

pursuivant (purse-iv-ant) n the lowest rank of heraldic officer [Old French]

purulent (pure-yew-lent) adj of, relating to, or containing pus [Latin purulentus] > **purulence** n

Purús n a river in NW central South America, rising in SE Peru and flowing northeast to the Amazon. Length: about 3200 km (2000 miles)

purvey vb 1 to sell or provide (foodstuffs) 2 to provide or make available: the foreign ministry used him to purvey sensitive items of diplomatic news [Old French porveeir to provide] > **purveyor** n

purview n 1 scope of operation: each designation falls under the purview of a different ministry 2 breadth or range of outlook: he hopes that the purview of science will be widened [Anglo-Norman purveu]

pus n the yellowish fluid that comes from inflamed or infected tissue [Latin]

Pusan n the former name (until 2000) of **Busan**

Pusey n Edward Bouverie. 1800–82, British ecclesiastic; a leader with Keble and Newman of the Oxford Movement

push vb 1 (sometimes foll. by off, away, etc.) to apply steady force to in order to move 2 to thrust (one's way) through something, such as a crowd 3 (sometimes foll. by for) to be an advocate or promoter (of): there are many groups you can join to push for change 4 to spur or drive (oneself or another person) in order to achieve more effort or better results: you must be careful not to push your children too hard 5 informal to sell (narcotic drugs) illegally ▷ n 6 the act of pushing; thrust 7 informal drive or determination: everything depends on him having the push to obtain the money 8 informal a special effort to achieve something: when this push spent itself it was obvious the bid had failed 9 **the push** Brit and NZ informal dismissal from employment ▸ See also **push about, push off,** etc. [Latin pulsare]

push about or **push around** vb informal to bully: don't let them push you around

push-bike n Brit, Austral and NZ informal a bicycle

push button n 1 an electrical switch operated by pressing a button ▷ adj **push-button** 2 operated by a push button: a push-button radio

pushchair n Brit a small folding chair on wheels in which a small child can be wheeled around: escalators are difficult with pushchairs

pushed adj (often foll. by for) informal short of: pushed for time

pusher n informal a person who sells illegal drugs

pushing prep 1 almost or nearly (a certain age, speed, etc.): pushing fifty ▷ adj 2 aggressively ambitious

Pushkin[1] n a town in NW Russia: site of the imperial summer residence and Catherine the Great's palace. Pop: 84 628 (2002). Former name: (1708–1937) **Tsarskoye Selo**

Pushkin[2] n Aleksander (Sergeyevich). 1799–1837, Russian poet, novelist, and dramatist. His works include the romantic verse tale The Prisoner of the Caucasus (1822), the verse novel Eugene Onegin (1833), the tragedy Boris Godunov (1825), and the novel The Captain's Daughter (1836)

push off vb informal to go away; leave

pushover n informal 1 something that is easily achieved 2 a person, team, etc., that is easily taken advantage of or defeated

push-start vb 1 to start (a motor vehicle) by pushing it, thus turning the engine ▷ n 2 this process

push through vb to force to accept: the President wants to push through his economic package

pushy adj **pushier, pushiest** informal offensively assertive or ambitious

pusillanimous adj formal timid and cowardly: pusillanimous behaviour [Latin pusillus weak + animus courage] > **pusillanimity** n

Puskas n Ferenc. 1927–2006, Hungarian footballer; played for Hungary (1945–56) and Real Madrid (1958–66)

puss n 1 informal a cat 2 slang a girl or woman [probably Low German]

pussy[1] n, pl **pussies** 1 Also called: **pussycat** informal a cat 2 taboo, slang the female genitals [from puss]

pussy[2] adj -**sier, -siest** containing or full of pus

pussyfoot vb informal 1 to move about stealthily 2 to avoid committing oneself: don't let's pussyfoot about naming the hit man

pussy willow *n* a willow tree with silvery silky catkins

pustulate *vb* **-lating, -lated** to form into pustules

pustule *n* a small inflamed raised area of skin containing pus [Latin *pustula* a blister] **> pustular** *adj*

put *vb* **putting, put** **1** to cause to be (in a position or place): *he put the book on the table* **2** to cause to be (in a state or condition): *what can be done to put things right?* **3** to lay (blame, emphasis, etc.) on a person or thing: *don't try to put the blame on someone else!* **4** to set or commit (to an action, task, or duty), esp. by force: *she put him to work weeding the garden* **5** to estimate or judge: *I wouldn't put him in the same class as Verdi as a composer* **6** (foll. by *to*) to utilize: *he put his culinary skills to good use when he opened a restaurant* **7** to express: *he didn't put it quite as crudely as that* **8** to make (an end or limit): *opponents claim the scheme will put an end to much of the sailing and boating in the area* **9** to present for consideration; propose: *he put the question to the committee* **10** to invest (money) in or expend (time or energy) on: *they put a lot of money into the sport* **11** to throw or cast: *put the shot* ▷ *n* **12** a throw, esp. in putting the shot ▸ See also **put about, put across,** etc. [Middle English *puten* to push]

put about *vb* **1** to make widely known: *a rumour was put about that he had been drunk* **2** *nautical* to change course

put across *vb* to communicate successfully: *he's not very good at putting his ideas across*

put aside *vb* **1** to save: *try to put some money aside in case of emergencies* **2** to disregard: *put aside adolescent fantasies of romance*

putative (pew-tat-iv) *adj formal* **1** commonly regarded as being: *the desire of the putative father to establish his possible paternity* **2** considered to exist or have existed; inferred: *a putative earlier form* [Latin *putare* to consider]

put away *vb* **1** to save: *it takes a lot of discipline to put away something for your old age* **2** *informal* to lock up in a prison, mental institution, etc.: *we have enough evidence to put him away for life* **3** *informal* to eat or drink in large amounts: *he put away three beers and three huge shots of brandy*

put back *vb* **1** to return to its former place **2** to move to a later time: *the finals could be put back until Monday*

put down *vb* **1** to make a written record of **2** to repress: *the rising was put down with revolting cruelty* **3** to consider: *I'd put him down as a complete fool* **4** to attribute: *the government's defeat in the election can be put down to a general desire for change* **5** to put (an animal) to death **6** *slang* to belittle or humiliate ▷ *n* **put-down** **7** *informal* a cruelly crushing remark

put forward *vb* **1** to propose or suggest **2** to offer the name of; nominate

Putin *n* Vladimir (**Vladimirovich**). born 1952, Russian statesman; president of Russia (2000–08) and from 2012; prime minister (2008–12)

put in *vb* **1** to devote (time or effort): *the competitors who did best were the ones who had put in some practice* **2** (often foll. by *for*) to apply (for a job) **3** to submit: *they have put in an official complaint* **4** *nautical* to bring a vessel into port

Putnam *n* **1** Israel. 1718–90, American general in the War of Independence **2** his cousin **Rufus**. 1738–1824, American soldier in the War of Independence; surveyor general of the US (1796–1803)

put off *vb* **1** to postpone: *ministers have put off making a decision until next month* **2** to evade (a person) by delay: *they tried to put him off, but he came anyway* **3** to cause dislike in: *he was put off by her appearance* **4** to cause to lose interest in: *the accident put him off sailing* **5** to distract: *a swerving cyclist may have put off the driver*

put on *vb* **1** to dress oneself in **2** to adopt (an attitude or feeling) insincerely: *I don't see why you have to put on that fake American accent* **3** to present (a play or show) **4** to add: *I've put on nearly a stone since September* **5** to cause (an electrical device) to function: *she put on the light* **6** to bet (money) on a horse race or game **7** to impose: *the government has put a tax on gas*

put out *vb* **1 a** to annoy or anger **b** to disturb or confuse **2** to extinguish (a fire, light, etc.) **3** to inconvenience (someone): *I hope I'm not putting you out* **4** to select or lay out for use: *she put out two clean cloths in the kitchen* **5** to publish or broadcast: *she put out a statement denying the rumours* **6** to dislocate: *he put his back out digging the garden*

put over *vb informal* to communicate (facts or information)

Putrajaya *n* officially the capital of Malaysia since 1999, in the SW Malay Peninsula, and forming its own federal territory; a high-tech garden city (including nearby Cyberjaya); construction began in 1995 and is expected to be complete in about 2010, with a planned population of over 300 000; government functions transferred in stages from Kuala Lumpur, starting in 1999

putrefy *vb* **-fies, -fying, -fied** *formal* (of organic matter) to rot and produce an offensive smell [Latin *putrefacere*] **> putrefaction** *n*

putrescent *adj formal* becoming putrid; rotting: *putrescent toadstools* [Latin *putrescere* to become rotten] **> putrescence** *n*

putrid *adj* **1** (of organic matter) rotting: *putrid meat* **2** sickening or foul: *a putrid stench* **3** *informal* deficient in quality or value: *a penchant for putrid puns* **4** morally corrupt [Latin *putrere* to be rotten] **> putridity** *n*

putsch *n* a violent and sudden political revolt: *an attempted putsch against the general* [from German]

putt *golf n* **1** a stroke on the green with a putter to roll the ball into or near the hole ▷ *vb* **2** to strike (the ball) in this way [Scot]

puttee *n* (*usually pl*) (esp. as part of a military uniform) a strip of cloth worn wound around the leg from the ankle to the knee [Hindi *pattī*]

putter *n golf* a club, usually with a short shaft, for putting

put through *vb* **1** to connect by telephone: *I'm sorry, you've been put through to the wrong extension* **2** to carry out to a conclusion

putting green *n* (on a golf course) the area of closely mown grass around the hole

Puttnam *n* David, Baron. born 1941, British film producer. Films include *Chariots of Fire* (1981), *The Killing Fields* (1984), *Memphis Belle* (1990), and *My Life So Far* (1999)

putty *n, pl* **-ties 1** a stiff paste used to fix glass into frames and fill cracks in woodwork ▷ *vb* **-ties, -tying, -tied** **2** to fix or fill with putty [French *potée* a pound]

Putumayo *n* a river in NW South America, rising in S Colombia and flowing southeast as most of the border between Colombia and Peru, entering the Amazon in Brazil: scene of the Putumayo rubber scandal (1910–11) during the rubber boom, in which many Indians were enslaved and killed by rubber exploiters. Length: 1578 km (980 miles). Brazilian name: **Içá**

put up *vb* **1** to build or erect: *I want to put up a fence round the garden* **2** to display (a poster, sign, etc.) **3** to accommodate or be accommodated at: *can you put me up for tonight?* **4** to increase (prices) **5** to submit (a plan, case, etc.) **6** to offer: *the factory is being put up for sale* **7** to give: *they put up a good fight* **8** to provide (money) for: *they put up 35% of the film's budget* **9** to nominate or be nominated as a candidate: *the party have yet to decide whether to put up a candidate* **10** **put up to** to incite to: *I wonder who put them up to it?* **11** **put up with** *informal* to endure or tolerate ▷ *adj* **put-up 12** *informal* dishonestly or craftily prearranged: *a put-up job*

put upon *vb* to take advantage of (someone): *he's always being put upon*

putz *n US slang* a despicable or stupid person [Yiddish *puts* ornament]

Puvis de Chavannes *n* Pierre Cécile. 1824–98, French mural painter

Puy de Dôme *n* **1** a department of central France in Auvergne region. Capital: Clermont-Ferrand. Pop: 609 817 (2003 est.). Area: 8016 sq km (3094 sq miles) **2** a mountain in central France, in the Auvergne Mountains: a volcanic plug. Height: 1485 m (4872 ft)

Puy de Sancy *n* a mountain in S central France: highest peak of the Monts Dore. Height: 1886 m (6188 ft)

Pu-yi *n* Henry. 1906–67, last emperor of China as Xuan-Tong (1908–12); emperor of the Japanese puppet state of Manchukuo as Kang-de (1934–45)

puzzle *vb* **-zling, -zled 1** to baffle or bewilder **2 puzzle out** to solve (a problem) by mental effort **3 puzzle over** to think deeply about in an attempt to understand: *he puzzled over the squiggles and curves on the paper* ▷ *n* **4** a problem that cannot be easily solved **5** a toy, game, or question presenting a problem that requires skill or ingenuity for its solution [origin unknown] ▷ **puzzled** *adj* ▷ **puzzlement** *n* ▷ **puzzler** *n* ▷ **puzzling** *adj*

PVC polyvinyl chloride

PVS persistent vegetative state

PW policewoman

PWR pressurized-water reactor

pyaemia *or* **pyemia** *n med* blood poisoning with pus-forming microorganisms in the blood [Greek *puon* pus + *haima* blood]

Pydna *n* a town in ancient Macedonia: site of a major Roman victory over the Macedonians, resulting in the downfall of their kingdom (168 BC)

pye-dog *or* **pi-dog** *n* a half-wild Asian dog with no owner [Hindi *pāhī* outsider]

pygmy *n, pl* **-mies 1** something that is a very small example of its type **2** an abnormally undersized person **3** a person of little importance or significance ▷ *adj* **4** very small: *the pygmy anteater* [Greek *pugmaios* undersized]

Pygmy *n, pl* **-mies** a member of one of the very short peoples of Equatorial Africa

pyjamas *or US* **pajamas** *pl n* a loose-fitting jacket or top and trousers worn to sleep in [Persian *pai* leg + *jāma* garment]

pylon *n* **1** *chiefly Brit* a large vertical steel tower-like structure supporting high-tension electrical cables **2** *US and Canad* a plastic cone used to demarcate areas, esp. on public roads [Greek *pulōn* a gateway]

Pylos *n* a port in SW Greece, in the SW Peloponnese; scene of a defeat of the Spartans by the Athenians (425 BC) during the Peloponnesian War and of the Battle of Navarino. Italian name: **Navarino**. Modern Greek name: **Pílos**. See **Navarino**

Pym *n* **1** Barbara (**Mary Crampton**). 1913–80, British novelist, noted for such comedies of middle-class English life as *Excellent Women* (1952), *A Glass of Blessings* (1958), and *The Sweet Dove Died* (1978) **2** John. ?1584–1643, leading English parliamentarian during the events leading to the Civil War. He took a prominent part in the impeachment of Buckingham (1626) and of Strafford and Laud (1640)

Pynchon *n* Thomas (**Ruggles**). born 1937, US novelist, author of *V* (1963), *The Crying of Lot 49* (1967), *Gravity's Rainbow* (1973), *Mason and Dixon* (1997), and *Against the Day* (2006)

Pyongyang *or* **P'yŏng-yang** *n* the capital of North Korea, in the southwest on the Taedong River: industrial centre; university (1946). Pop: 3 284 000 (2005 est)

pyorrhoea *or especially US* **pyorrhea** (pire-ree-a) *n med* a discharge of pus, esp. in diseases of the gums or tooth sockets [Greek *puon* pus + *rhein* to flow]

pyramid *n* **1** a huge stone building with a square base and four sloping triangular sides meeting in a point, such as the royal tombs built by the ancient Egyptians **2** *maths* a solid figure with a polygonal base and triangular sides that meet in a common vertex [Greek *puramis*] ▷ **pyramidal** *adj*

pyramid selling *n* the practice of selling distributors batches of goods which they then subdivide and sell to other distributors, this process continuing until the final distributors are left with a stock that is unsaleable except at a loss

pyre *n* a pile of wood for cremating a corpse [Greek *pur* fire]

Pyrenean *adj* of or relating to the Pyrenees or their inhabitants

Pyrenees *pl n* a mountain range between France and Spain, extending from the Bay of Biscay to the Mediterranean. Highest peak: Pico de Aneto, 3404 m (11 168 ft)

Pyrénées-Atlantiques *or* **Pyrénées** *n* a department of SW France in Aquitaine region. Capital: Pau. Pop: 614 174 (2003 est). Area: 7712 sq km (3008 sq miles). Former name: **Basses-Pyrénées**

Pyrénées-Orientales *n* a department of S France, in Languedoc-Roussillon region. Capital: Perpignan. Pop: 411 447 (2003 est). Area: 4144 sq km (1616 sq miles)

pyrethrum (pie-reeth-rum) *n* **1** a Eurasian chrysanthemum with white, pink, red, or purple flowers **2** an insecticide prepared from dried pyrethrum flowers [Greek *purethron*]

pyretic (pie-ret-ik) *adj pathol* of, relating to, or characterized by fever [Greek *puretos* fever]

Pyrex *n trademark* a variety of heat-resistant glassware used in cookery and chemical apparatus

pyrite (pie-rite) *n* a yellow mineral consisting of iron sulphide in cubic crystalline form. Formula: FeS_2 [Latin *pyrites* flint]

pyrites (pie-rite-eez) *n, pl* **-tes 1** same as **pyrite 2** a disulphide of a metal, esp. of copper and tin

pyromania *n psychiatry* the uncontrollable impulse and practice of setting things on fire [Greek *pur* fire + *mania* madness] ▷ **pyromaniac** *n, adj*

pyrotechnics *n* **1** the art of making fireworks **2** a firework display **3** a brilliant display of skill: *all those courtroom pyrotechnics* [Greek *pur* fire + *tekhnē* art] ▷ **pyrotechnic** *adj*

Pyrrhic victory (pir-ik) *n* a victory in which the victor's losses are as great as those of the defeated [after PYRRHUS, who defeated the Romans in 279 BC but suffered heavy losses]

Pyrrho *n* ?365–?275 BC, Greek philosopher; founder of scepticism. He maintained that true wisdom and happiness lie in suspension of judgment, since certain knowledge is impossible to attain ▷ **'Pyrrhonism** *n* ▷ **'Pyrrhonist** *n, adj*

Pyrrhus *n* 319–272 BC, king of Epirus (306–272). He invaded Italy but was ultimately defeated by the Romans (275 BC) ▷ **'Pyrrhic** *adj*

Pythagoras *n* ?580–?500 BC, Greek philosopher and mathematician. He founded a religious brotherhood, which followed a life of strict asceticism and greatly influenced the development of mathematics and its application to music and astronomy

Pythagoras' theorem (pie-thag-or-ass) *n* the theorem that in a right-angled triangle the square of the length of the hypotenuse equals the sum of the squares of the other two sides [after PYTHAGORAS]

Pytheas *n* 4th century BC, Greek navigator. He was the first Greek to visit and describe the coasts of Spain, France, and the British Isles and may have reached Iceland

python *n* a large nonpoisonous snake of Australia, Africa, and S Asia which kills its prey by crushing it with its body [after *Python*, a dragon killed by Apollo]

pyx *n Christianity* any receptacle in which the bread used in Holy Communion is kept [Latin *pyxis* small box]

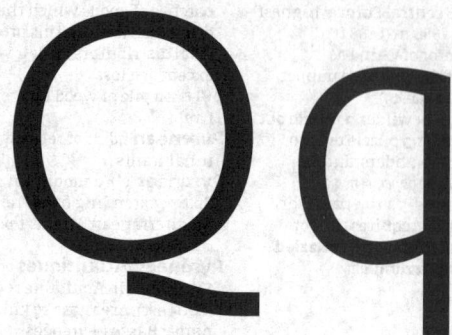

Qq

Q 1 *chess* queen 2 question

q. 1 quart 2 quarter 3 question 4 quire

Q. 1 Queen 2 question

Qabis *n* the Arabic name for **Gabès**

Qaboos bin Said *n* born 1940, Sultan of Oman from 1970

Qairwan *n* a variant of **Kairouan**

Qaraghandy *n* a variant transliteration of the Kazakh name for **Karaganda**

Qatar *or* **Katar** *n* a state in E Arabia, occupying a peninsula in the Persian Gulf: under Persian rule until the 19th century; became a British protectorate in 1916; declared independence in 1971; exports petroleum and natural gas. Official language: Arabic. Official religion: (Sunni) Muslim. Currency: riyal. Capital: Doha. Pop: 2 042 444 (2013 est). Area: about 11 000 sq km (4250 sq miles)

Qatari *or* **Katari** *adj* 1 of or relating to Qatar or its inhabitants ▷ *n* 2 a native or inhabitant of Qatar

Qattara Depression *n* an arid basin in the Sahara, in NW Egypt, impassable to vehicles. Area: about 18 000 sq km (7000 sq miles). Lowest point: 133 m (435 ft) below sea level

QC 1 Queen's Counsel 2 Quebec

QED which was to be shown or proved [Latin *quod erat demonstrandum*]

Qeshm *or* **Qishm** *n* 1 the largest island in the Persian Gulf: part of Iran. Area: 1336 sq km (516 sq miles) 2 the chief town of this island

Qian Long *or* **Ch'ien-lung** *n* original name *Hong-li*. 1711–99, Chinese emperor of the Qing dynasty. He expanded the Chinese empire and was a patron of the arts

Qingdao, Tsingtao *or* **Chingtao** *n* a port in E China, in E Shandong province on Jiazhou Bay, developed as a naval base and fort in 1891. Shandong university (1926). Pop: 2 431 000 (2005 est)

Qinghai, Tsinghai *or* **Chinghai** *n* 1 a province of NW China: consists largely of mountains and high plateaus. Capital: Xining. Pop: 5 340 000 (2003 est). Area: 721 000 sq km (278 400 sq miles) 2 the Pinyin transliteration of the Chinese name for **Koko Nor**

Qiqihar, Chichihaerh, Ch'i-ch'i-haerh *or* **Tsitsihar** *n* a city in NE China, in Heilongjiang province on the Nonni River. Pop: 1 452 000 (2005 est)

Qishm *n* a variant of **Qeshm**

Qld *or* **QLD** Queensland

QM Quartermaster

Qom, Qum *or* **Kum** *n* a city in NW central Iran: a place of pilgrimage for Shiite Muslims. Pop: 1 045 000 (2005 est)

Qomolangma *n* a Chinese name for (Mount) **Everest**

qr. *pl* **qrs** 1 quarter 2 quire

qt *pl* **qt** *or* **qts** quart

q.t. *n* on the q.t. *informal* secretly

qua (kwah) *prep* in the capacity of; by virtue of being [Latin]

quack¹ *vb* 1 (of a duck) to utter a harsh guttural sound 2 to make a noise like a duck ▷ *n* 3 the sound made by a duck [imitative]

quack² *n* 1 an unqualified person who claims medical knowledge 2 *Brit, Austral and NZ informal* a doctor [short for *quacksalver*, from Dutch *quack*, apparently: to hawk + *salf* salve] ▷ **quackery** *n*

quad¹ *n* short for **quadrangle** (1)

quad² *n informal* a quadruplet

quad³ *n* 1 quadraphonics ▷ *adj* 2 quadraphonic

quad bike *or* **quad** *n* a vehicle like a small motorcycle, with four large wheels, designed for agricultural and sporting uses

quadrangle *n* 1 a rectangular courtyard with buildings on all four sides 2 *geometry* a figure consisting of four points connected by four lines [Late Latin *quadrangulum*] ▷ **quadrangular** *adj*

quadrant *n* 1 *geometry* **a** a quarter of the circumference of a circle **b** the area enclosed by two perpendicular radii of a circle 2 a piece of a mechanism in the form of a quarter circle 3 an instrument formerly used in astronomy and navigation for measuring the altitudes of stars [Latin *quadrans* a quarter]

quadraphonic *adj* using four independent channels to reproduce or record sound ▷ **quadraphonics** *n*

quadrate *n* 1 a cube or square, or a square or cubelike object ▷ *vb* **-rating, -rated** 2 to make square or rectangular [Latin *quadrare* to make square]

quadratic *maths n* 1 Also called: **quadratic equation** an equation in which the variable is raised to the power of two, but nowhere raised to a higher power: *solve the quadratic equation $2x^2-3x-6=3$* ▷ *adj* 2 of or relating to the second power

quadrennial *adj* 1 occurring every four years 2 lasting four years

quadri- *or before a vowel* **quadr-** *combining form* four: *quadrilateral* [Latin]

quadriceps *n anatomy* a muscle at the front of the thigh [New Latin]

quadrilateral *adj* 1 having four sides ▷ *n* 2 a polygon with four sides

quadrille *n* 1 a square dance for four couples 2 music for this dance [Spanish *cuadrilla*]

quadrillion *n, pl* **-lions** *or* **-lion** 1 (in Britain, France, and Germany) the number represented as one followed by 24 zeros (10^{24}) 2 (in the US and Canada) the number represented as one followed by 15 zeros (10^{15}) [French *quadrillon*]

quadriplegia *n* paralysis of all four limbs [QUADRI- + Greek *plēssein* to strike] ▷ **quadriplegic** *adj, n*

quadruped (kwod-roo-ped) *n* an animal, esp. a mammal, that has four legs [Latin *quadru-* four + *pes* foot]

quadruple *vb* **-pling, -pled** 1 to multiply by four ▷ *adj* 2 four times as much or as many 3 consisting of four parts 4 *music* having four beats in each bar ▷ *n* 5 a quantity or number four times as great as another

[Latin *quadru-* four + *-plus* -fold]

quadruplet *n* one of four children born at one birth

quadruplicate *adj* **1** fourfold or quadruple ▷ *vb* **-cating, -cated 2** to multiply or be multiplied by four [Latin *quadruplicare* to increase fourfold]

quaff (kwoff) *vb old-fashioned* to drink heartily or in one draught [perhaps imitative]

quagga *n, pl* **-gas** *or* **-ga** a recently extinct zebra, striped only on the head and shoulders [Khoikhoi *qǔagga*]

quagmire (kwog-mire) *n* a soft wet area of land that gives way under the feet; bog [from *quag* bog + *mire*]

Quai d'Orsay *n* the quay along the S bank of the Seine, Paris, where the French foreign office is situated

quail¹ *n, pl* **quails** *or* **quail** a small game bird of the partridge family [Old French *quaille*]

quail² *vb* to shrink back with fear; cower [origin unknown]

quaint *adj* attractively unusual, esp. in an old-fashioned style [Old French *cointe*, from Latin *cognitus* known]

quake *vb* **quaking, quaked 1** to shake or tremble with or as if with fear **2** to shudder because of instability ▷ *n* **3** *informal* an earthquake [Old English *cwacian*]

Quaker *n* a member of a Christian sect, the Religious Society of Friends [originally an offensive nickname] **> Quakerism** *n*

qualification *n* **1** an official record of achievement awarded on the successful completion of a course of training or passing of an examination **2** an ability, quality, or attribute, esp. one that fits a person to perform a particular job or task **3** a condition that modifies or limits; restriction **4** the act of qualifying or being qualified

qualified *adj* **1** having successfully completed a training course or passed the exams necessary in order to be entitled to work in a particular profession: *a qualified lawyer* **2** having the abilities, qualities, or attributes necessary to perform a particular job or task **3** having completed a training or degree course and gained the relevant certificates **4** limited or restricted; not wholehearted: *the mission was only a qualified success*

qualify *vb* **-fies, -fying, -fied 1** to have the abilities or attributes required in order to do or have something, such as a job: *he qualified as a teacher; she did not qualify for a State pension at that time* **2** to moderate or restrict (a statement one has made) **3** to describe or be described as having a particular quality: *it was neither witty nor subtle enough to qualify as a spoof* **4** to be successful in one stage of a competition and as a result progress to the next stage: *Lewis failed to qualify for the 100 metres* **5** *grammar* to modify the sense of (a word) [Latin *qualis* of what kind + *facere* to make] **> qualifier** *n*

qualitative *adj* involving or relating to distinctions based on quality

qualitative analysis *n chem* analysis of a substance to determine its constituents

quality *n, pl* **-ties 1** degree or standard of excellence **2** a distinguishing characteristic or attribute **3** the basic character or nature of something **4** a feature of personality **5** (formerly) high social status ▷ *adj* **6** excellent or superior: *a quality product* [Latin *qualis* of what sort]

quality assurance *n commerce* the process of verifying that a product conforms to required standards, often performed by an independent assessor

quality control *n* checking of the relative quality of a manufactured product, usually by testing samples

qualm (kwahm) *n* **1** a pang of conscience; scruple **2** a sudden sensation of misgiving **3** a sudden feeling of sickness or nausea [Old English *cwealm* death or plague]

quandary *n, pl* **-ries** a situation in which it is difficult to decide what to do; predicament; dilemma [origin unknown]

quandong (kwon-dong) *n* **1** a small Australian tree with edible fruit and nuts used in preserves **2** an Australian tree with pale timber

quango *n, pl* **-gos** a semipublic government-financed administrative body whose members are appointed by the government [*qu(asi-)a(utonomous) n(on)g(overnmental) o(rganization)*]

Quant *n* **Dame Mary.** born 1934, British fashion designer, whose Chelsea Look of miniskirts and geometrically patterned fabrics dominated London fashion in the 1960s

quantify *vb* **-fies, -fying, -fied** to discover or express the quantity of [Latin *quantus* how much + *facere* to make] **> quantifiable** *adj* **> quantification** *n*

quantitative *adj* **1** involving considerations of amount or size **2** capable of being measured

quantitative analysis *n chem* analysis of a substance to determine the proportions of its constituents

quantitative easing *or* **quantitive easing** *n* the practice of increasing the supply of money in order to stimulate economic activity

quantity *n, pl* **-ties 1** a specified or definite amount or number **2** the aspect of anything that can be measured, weighed, or counted **3** a large amount **4** *maths* an entity having a magnitude that may be denoted by a numerical expression [Latin *quantus* how much]

> **USAGE** The use of a plural noun after *quantity of* as in *a large quantity of bananas* was formerly considered incorrect, but is now acceptable.

quantity surveyor *n* a person who estimates the cost of the materials and labour necessary for a construction job

quantum *n, pl* **-ta 1** an amount or quantity, esp. a specific amount **2** *physics* the smallest quantity of some physical property that a system can possess ▷ *adj* **3** of or designating a major breakthrough or sudden advance: *a quantum leap in business computing* [Latin *quantus* how much]

quantum theory *n* a theory concerning the behaviour of physical systems based on the idea that they can only possess certain properties, such as energy and angular momentum, in discrete amounts (quanta)

quarantine *n* **1** a period of isolation, esp. of people or animals arriving from abroad, to prevent the spread of disease ▷ *vb* **-tining, -tined 2** to isolate in or as if in quarantine [Italian *quarantina* period of forty days]

quark *n physics* the hypothetical elementary particle supposed to be a fundamental unit of all baryons and mesons [special use of a word coined by James Joyce in the novel *Finnegans Wake*]

Quarles *n* **Francis.** 1592–1644, English poet

quarrel *n* **1** an angry disagreement; argument **2** a cause of dispute; grievance ▷ *vb* **-relling, -relled** *or US* **-reling, -reled** (often foll. by *with*) **3** to engage in a disagreement or dispute; argue **4** to find fault; complain [Latin *querella* complaint]

quarrelsome *adj* inclined to quarrel or disagree

quarry¹ *n, pl* **-ries 1** a place where stone is dug from the surface of the earth ▷ *vb* **-ries, -rying, -ried 2** to extract (stone) from a quarry [Old French *quarriere*]

quarry² *n, pl* **-ries 1** an animal that is being hunted; prey **2** anything pursued [Middle English *quirre* entrails offered to the hounds]

quarry tile *n* an unglazed floor tile

quart *n* a unit of liquid measure equal to one quarter of a gallon or two pints (1.136 litres) [Latin *quartus* fourth]

quarter *n* **1** one of four equal parts of something such as an object or quantity **2** the fraction equal to one divided by four ($\frac{1}{4}$) **3** a fourth part of a year; three months **4** *Brit informal* a unit of weight equal to four ounces (113.4 grams) **5** a region or district of a town or city: *the French quarter of New Orleans* **6** a region, direction, or point of the compass **7** *US and Canad* a coin worth 25 cents **8** short for **quarter-hour 9** *astronomy* **a** one fourth of the moon's period of revolution around the earth **b** either of two phases of the moon when half of the lighted surface is visible **10** (*sometimes pl*) an unspecified person or group of people: *it met stiff opposition in some quarters* **11** mercy or pity shown to a defeated opponent: *no quarter was asked or given* **12** any of the four limbs of a quadruped ▷ *vb* **13** to divide into four equal parts **14** (*formerly*) to dismember (a human body) **15** to billet or be billeted in lodgings **16** *heraldry* to divide (a shield) into four separate bearings ▷ *adj* **17** being or consisting of one of four equal parts ▶ See also **quarters** [Latin *quartus* fourth]

quarterback *n* a player in American football who directs attacking play

quarter day *n Brit* any of four days in the year when certain payments become due

quarterdeck *n nautical* the rear part of the upper deck of a ship, traditionally for official or ceremonial use

quarterfinal *n* the round before the semifinal in a competition

quarter-hour *n* **1** a period of 15 minutes **2** either of the points of time 15 minutes before or after the hour

quarterlight *n Brit* a small pivoted window in the door of a car for ventilation

quarterly *adj* **1** occurring, done, due, or issued at intervals of three months ▷ *n, pl* **-lies 2** a periodical issued every three months ▷ *adv* **3** once every three months

quartermaster *n* **1** a military officer responsible for accommodation, food, and equipment **2** a naval officer responsible for navigation

quarters *pl n* accommodation, esp. as provided for military personnel

quarter sessions *n* (*formerly*) a court with limited jurisdiction, held four times a year

quarterstaff *n, pl* **-staves** a stout iron-tipped wooden staff about 6ft long, formerly used as a weapon [origin unknown]

quartet *n* **1** a group of four singers or instrumentalists **2** a piece of music for four performers **3** any group of four [Italian *quarto* fourth]

quartier *n* a city district

quartile *n* **1** one of three values of a variable dividing its distribution into four groups with equal frequencies ▷ *adj* **2** of a quartile

quarto *n, pl* **-tos** a book size resulting from folding a sheet of paper into four leaves or eight pages [New Latin *in quarto* in quarter]

quartz *n* a hard glossy mineral consisting of crystalline silicon dioxide [German *Quarz*]

quartz clock *or* **quartz watch** *n* a very accurate clock or watch that is operated by a vibrating quartz crystal

quartz crystal *n* a thin plate or rod cut from a piece of quartz and ground so that it vibrates at a particular frequency

quasar (kway-zar) *n* any of a class of extremely distant starlike objects that are powerful sources of radio waves and other forms of energy [*quas(i-stell)ar (radio source)*]

quash *vb* **1** to officially reject (something, such as a judgment or decision) as invalid **2** to defeat or suppress forcefully and completely [Latin *quassare* to shake]

quasi- (kway-zie) *combining form* **1** almost but not really; seemingly: *a quasi-religious cult* **2** resembling but not actually being; so-called: *a quasi-scholar* [Latin: as if]

Quasimodo *n* **1** a character in Victor Hugo's novel *Notre-Dame de Paris* (1831), a grotesque hunch-backed bellringer of the cathedral of Notre Dame **2 Salvatore**. 1901–68, Italian poet, whose early work expresses symbolist ideas and techniques. His later work is more concerned with political and social issues: Nobel prize for literature 1959 [(sense 1) from the opening words of the Latin introit for that day, *quasimodo geniti infantes* as new-born babies]

quassia (kwosh-a) *n* **1** a tropical American tree with bitter bark and wood **2** the wood of this tree or a bitter compound extracted from it, used in insecticides [after Graman *Quassi*, who discovered its medicinal value]

quaternary *adj* consisting of four parts [Latin *quaterni* by fours]

Quaternary *adj geology* of the most recent period of geological time, which started about one million years ago

Quathlamba *n* the Sotho name for **Drakensberg**

quatrain *n* a stanza or poem of four lines [French, from Latin *quattuor* four]

Quatre Bras *n* a village in Belgium near Brussels; site of a battle in June 1815 where Wellington defeated the French under Marshal Ney, immediately preceding the battle of Waterloo

quatrefoil *n* **1** a leaf composed of four leaflets **2** *archit* a carved ornament of four arcs about a common centre [Old French *quatre* four + *-foil* leaflet]

quattrocento (kwat-roe-**chen**-toe) *n* the 15th century, esp. in reference to Renaissance Italian art [Italian: four hundred (short for fourteen hundred)]

quaver *vb* **1** (esp. of the voice) to quiver or tremble **2** to say or sing (something) with a trembling voice ▷ *n* **3** *music* a note having the time value of an eighth of a semibreve **4** a tremulous sound or note [Germanic] **> quavering** *adj*

quay (kee) *n* a wharf built parallel to the shoreline [Old French *kai*]

Quayle *n* Sir (John) Anthony. 1913–89, British actor and theatrical producer: director (1948–56) of the Shakespeare Memorial Theatre

Que. Quebec

queasy *adj* **-sier, -siest 1** having the feeling that one is about to vomit; nauseous **2** feeling or causing uneasiness [origin unknown] **> queasily** *adv* **> queasiness** *n*

Quebec *n* **1** a province of E Canada: the largest Canadian province; a French colony from 1608 to 1763, when it passed to Britain; lying mostly on the Canadian Shield, it has vast areas of forest and extensive tundra and is populated mostly in the plain around the St Lawrence River. Capital: Quebec. Pop: 7 903 001 (2011). Area: 1 540 680 sq km (594 860 sq miles). Abbreviation: **PQ 2** a port in E Canada, capital of the province of Quebec, situated on the St Lawrence River: founded in 1608 by Champlain; scene of the Plains of Abraham (1759), by which the British won Canada from the French. Pop: 516 622 (2011) **3** *communications* a code word for the letter *q*

queen *n* **1** a female sovereign who is the official ruler or head of state **2** the wife of a king **3** a woman, thing, or place considered the best or most important of her or its kind: *the rose is considered the queen of garden flowers* **4** *slang, offensive* an effeminate male homosexual **5** the only fertile female in a colony of bees, wasps, or ants **6** a playing card with a picture of a queen on it **7** a chessman, able to move in a straight line in any direction ▷ *vb* **8** *chess* to promote (a pawn) to a queen when it reaches the eighth rank **9 queen it** *informal* to behave in an overbearing manner: *she is more beautiful than ever and still queening it over everybody* [Old English *cwēn*] **> queenly** *adj*

Queen *n* Ellery. pseudonym of *Frederic Dannay* (1905–82) and *Manfred B. Lee* (1905–71), US co-authors of detective novels featuring a sleuth also called Ellery Queen

Queen Anne *adj* **1** of or in an 18th-century style of furniture characterized by the use of curves **2** of or in an early 18th-century English architectural style characterized by the use of red bricks and classical ornamentation

Queenborough in Sheppey *n* a town in SE England, in Kent: formed in 1968 by the amalgamation of Queenborough, Sheerness, and Sheppey. Pop: 3471 (2001)

Queen Charlotte Islands *pl n* a group of about 150 islands off the W coast of Canada: part of British Columbia. Pop: about 6000 (latest est). Area: 9596 sq km (3705 sq miles)

queen consort *n* the wife of a reigning king

Queen Elizabeth Islands *pl n* a group of islands off the N coast of Canada: the northernmost islands of the Canadian Arctic archipelago, lying N of latitude 74°N; part of Nunavut. Area: about 390 000 sq km (150 000 sq miles)

Queen Elizabeth Land *n* an area of British Antarctic Territory, situated south of Weddell Sea and between longitudes 20°W and 80°W, stretching from Filchner-Ronne Ice Shelf to the South Pole. Area: 437 000 sq km (169 000 sq miles)

Queen Maud Land *n* the large section of Antarctica between Coats Land and Enderby Land: claimed by Norway in 1939. (Claims are suspended under the Antarctic Treaty of 1959)

Queen Maud Range *n* a mountain range in Antarctica, in S Ross Dependency, extending for about 800 km (500 miles)

queen mother *n* the widow of a former king who is also the mother of the reigning sovereign

queen post *n building* one of a pair of vertical posts that connect the tie beam of a truss to the principal rafters of a roof

Queens *n* a borough of E New York City, on Long Island. Pop: 2 225 486 (2003 est)

Queen's Bench *n* (in Britain) one of the divisions of the High Court of Justice

Queensberry rules *pl n* **1** the code of rules followed in modern boxing **2** *informal* gentlemanly conduct, esp. in a dispute [after the ninth Marquess of *Queensberry*, who originated the rules]

Queen's Counsel *n* **1** (in Britain, Australia and New Zealand) a barrister or advocate appointed Counsel to the Crown **2** (in Canada and New Zealand) an honorary title bestowed on lawyers with long experience

Queen's County *n* the former name of **Laois**

Queen's English *n* correctly spoken and written British English

queen's evidence *n English law* evidence given for the Crown against former associates in crime by an accomplice

Queen's Guide *or* **Queen's Scout** *n* a Guide or Scout who has passed the highest tests of proficiency

queen's highway *n* **1** (in Britain) any public road or right of way **2** (in Canada) a main road maintained by the provincial government

Queen's House *n* **the Queen's House** a Palladian mansion in Greenwich, London: designed (1616–35) by Inigo Jones; now part of the National Maritime Museum; restored 1984–90

Queensland *n* a state of NE Australia: fringed on the Pacific side by the Great Barrier Reef; the Great Dividing Range lies in the east, separating the coastal lowlands from the dry Great Artesian Basin in the south. Capital: Brisbane. Pop: 5 027 889 (2012 est). Area: 1 727 500 sq km (667 000 sq miles)

Queenslander *n* a native or inhabitant of Queensland

Queenstown *n* the former name (1849–1922) of **Cóbh**

queer *adj* **1** not normal or usual; odd or strange **2** dubious; shady **3** *Brit* faint, giddy, or queasy **4** *informal, usually offensive* homosexual **5** *informal* eccentric or slightly mad ▷ *n* **6** *informal, usually offensive* a homosexual ▷ *vb* **7** **queer someone's pitch** *informal* to spoil or thwart someone's chances of something [origin unknown]

> **USAGE** Although the term *queer* meaning homosexual is still considered offensive when used by non-homosexuals, it is now being used by some homosexuals of themselves as a positive term, as in *queer politics, queer cinema.*

queer street *n* **in queer street** *informal* in a difficult financial situation, esp. debt or bankruptcy

quell *vb* **1** to suppress (rebellion or unrest); subdue

2 to overcome or allay [Old English *cwellan* to kill]

Quelpart *n* a former name of **Cheju**

Quemoy *n* an island in Formosa Strait, off the SE coast of China: administratively part of Taiwan. Pop (with associated islets): 80 000 (latest est). Area: 130 sq km (50 sq miles)

quench *vb* **1** to satisfy (one's thirst) **2** to put out; extinguish **3** to suppress or subdue **4** *metallurgy* to cool (hot metal) by plunging it into cold water [Old English *ācwencan* to extinguish]

Queneau *n* Raymond. 1903–76. French writer, influenced in the 1920s by surrealism. His novels include *Zazie dans le métro* (1959)

Querétaro *n* **1** an inland state of central Mexico: economy based on agriculture and mining. Capital: Querétaro. Pop: 1 402 010 (2000). Area: 11 769 sq km (4544 sq miles) **2** a city in central Mexico, capital of Querétaro state: scene of the signing (1848) of the treaty ending the US-Mexican War and of the execution of Emperor Maximilian (1867). Pop: 913 000 (2005 est)

quern *n* a stone hand mill for grinding corn [Old English *cweorn*]

querulous (kwer-yew-luss) *adj* complaining; whining or peevish [Latin *queri* to complain] ▷ **querulously** *adv*

query *n*, *pl* **-ries** **1** a question, esp. one expressing doubt **2** a question mark ▷ *vb* **-ries, -rying, -ried** **3** to express uncertainty, doubt, or an objection concerning (something) **4** to express as a query; ask [Latin *quaere* ask!]

quesadilla *n Mexican cookery* a toasted tortilla filled with cheese and sometimes other ingredients [Spanish, diminutive of *queso* cheese]

Quesnay *n* François. 1694–1774, French political economist, encyclopedist, and physician. He propounded the theory championed by the physiocrats in his *Tableau économique* (1758)

quest *n* **1** a looking for or seeking; search **2** the object of a search; a goal or target ▷ *vb* **3** **quest for** to go in search of **4** (of dogs) to search for game [Old French *queste*]

question *n* **1 a** a form of words addressed to a person in order to obtain an answer; interrogative sentence **2 a** point at issue: *they were silent on the question of social justice* **3** a difficulty or uncertainty **4 a** an act of asking **b** an investigation into some problem **5** a motion presented for debate **6 beyond (all) question** beyond (any) doubt **7 call something into question a** to make something the subject of disagreement **b** to cast doubt upon the validity or truth of something **8 in question** under discussion: *the area in question was not contaminated* **9 out of the question** beyond consideration; impossible ▷ *vb* **10** to put a question or questions to (a person); interrogate **11** to make (something) the subject of dispute **12** to express uncertainty; doubt [Latin *quaestio*]

> **USAGE** *The question whether* should be used rather than *the question of whether* or *the question as to whether*: this leaves open the question whether he acted correctly.

questionable *adj* **1** (esp. of a person's morality or honesty) doubtful **2** of disputable value or authority ▷ **questionably** *adv*

questioner *n* a person who asks a question

questioning *adj* **1** proceeding from or characterized by doubt or uncertainty **2** intellectually inquisitive: *a questioning mind* ▷ *n* **3** interrogation

question mark *n* **1** the punctuation mark (?), used at the end of questions **2** a doubt or uncertainty: *a question mark still hangs over their success*

question master *n Brit* the person chairing a radio or television quiz or panel game

questionnaire *n* a set of questions on a form, used to collect statistical information or opinions from people

question time *n* (in parliamentary bodies of the British type) the time set aside each day for questions to government ministers

q

Quetta *n* a city in W central Pakistan, at an altitude of 1650 m (5500 ft): a summer resort, military station, and trading centre. Pop: 744 000 (2005 est)

queue *n* **1** a line of people or vehicles waiting for something ▷ *vb* **queuing** *or* **queueing, queued 2** (often foll. by *up*) to form or remain in a line while waiting [Latin *cauda* tail]

Quevedo y Villegas *n* Francisco Gómez de. 1580–1645, Spanish poet and writer, noted for his satires and the picaresque novel *La historia de la vida del Buscón* (1626)

Quezon City *n* a city in the Philippines, on central Luzon adjoining Manila: capital of the Philippines from 1948 to 1976; seat of the University of the Philippines (1908). Pop: 2 173 831 (2000)

Quezon y Molina *n* Manuel Luis. 1878–1944, Philippine statesman: first president of the Philippines (from 1935) and head of the government in exile after the Japanese conquest of the islands in World War II

quibble *vb* **-bling, -bled 1** to make trivial objections ▷ *n* **2** a trivial objection or equivocation, esp. one used to avoid an issue **3** *archaic* a pun [origin unknown]

Quiberon *n* a peninsula of NW France, on the S coast of Brittany: a naval battle was fought off its coast in 1759 during the Seven Years' War, in which the British defeated the French

quiche (keesh) *n* a savoury flan with an egg custard filling to which cheese, bacon, or vegetables are added [French]

quick *adj* **1** characterized by rapidity of movement or action; fast **2** lasting or taking a short time **3** immediate or prompt: *her quick action minimized the damage* **4** eager or ready to perform (an action): *quick to condemn* **5** responsive to stimulation; alert; lively: *they were impressed by his quick mind* **6** easily excited or aroused: *he is impulsive and has a quick temper* **7** nimble in one's movements or actions; deft: *she has quick hands* ▷ *n* **8** any area of sensitive flesh, esp. that under a nail **9** cut someone to the quick to hurt someone's feelings deeply **10** the quick *archaic* living people ▷ *adv* **11** in a rapid manner; swiftly [Old English *cwicu* living] **> quickly** *adv* **> quickness** *n*

quick-change artist *n* an actor or entertainer who undertakes several rapid changes of costume during a performance

quicken *vb* **1** to make or become faster; accelerate **2** to impart to or receive vigour or enthusiasm: *science quickens the imagination* **3 a** (of a fetus) to begin to show signs of life **b** (of a pregnant woman) to reach the stage of pregnancy at which movements of the fetus can be felt

quick-freeze *vb* **-freezing, -froze, -frozen** to preserve (food) by subjecting it to rapid refrigeration

quickie *informal n* **1** anything made or done rapidly ▷ *adj* **2** made or done rapidly: *a quickie divorce*

quicklime *n* a white caustic solid, mainly composed of calcium oxide, used in the manufacture of glass and steel

quicksand *n* a deep mass of loose wet sand that submerges anything on top of it

quickset *chiefly Brit adj* **1** (of plants or cuttings) planted so as to form a hedge ▷ *n* **2** a hedge composed of such plants

quicksilver *n* the metal mercury

quickstep *n* **1** a modern ballroom dance in rapid quadruple time **2** music for this dance

quick-tempered *adj* easy to anger

quick-witted *adj* having a keenly alert mind **> quick-wittedness** *n*

quid[1] *n, pl* **quid** *Brit slang* **1** a pound (sterling) **2** be quids in to be in a very favourable or advantageous position [origin unknown]

quid[2] *n* a piece of tobacco for chewing [Old English *cwidu* chewing resin]

quiddity *n, pl* **-ties 1** the essential nature of something **2** a petty or trifling distinction [Latin *quid* what]

quid pro quo *n, pl* **quid pro quos** one thing, esp. an advantage or object, given in exchange for another [Latin: something for something]

quiescent (kwee-ess-ent) *adj formal* quiet, inactive, or dormant [Latin *quiescere* to rest] **> quiescence** *n*

quiet *adj* **1** characterized by an absence of noise **2** calm or tranquil: *the sea is quiet today* **3** untroubled: *a quiet life* **4** not busy: *business is quiet this morning* **5** private or secret: *I had a quiet word with her* **6** free from anger, impatience, or other extreme emotion **7** not showy: *quiet colours; a quiet wedding* **8** modest or reserved: *quiet humour* ▷ *n* **9** the state of being silent, peaceful, or untroubled **10** on the quiet without other people knowing ▷ *vb* **11** to make or become calm or silent [Latin *quies* repose] **> quietly** *adv* **> quietness** *n*

quieten *vb Brit and NZ* **1** (often foll. by *down*) to make or become quiet or silent **2** to allay (fear or doubts)

quietism *n formal* passivity and calmness of mind towards external events **> quietist** *n, adj*

quietude *n formal* quietness, peace, or tranquillity

quietus *n, pl* **-tuses 1** *literary* a release from life; death **2** the discharge or settlement of debts or duties [Latin *quietus est*, literally: he is at rest]

quiff *n Brit* a tuft of hair brushed up above the forehead [origin unknown]

quill *n* **1** Also called: **quill pen** a feather made into a pen **2 a** any of the large stiff feathers of the wing or tail of a bird **b** the hollow stem of a feather **3** any of the stiff hollow spines of a porcupine or hedgehog [origin unknown]

Quiller-Couch *n* Sir Arthur (Thomas), known as Q. 1863–1944, British critic and novelist, who edited the *Oxford Book of English Verse* (1900)

quilling *n* a decorative craftwork in which material such as glass, fabric or paper is formed into small bands or rolls that form the basis of a design

Quilmes *n* a city in E Argentina: a resort and suburb of Buenos Aires. Pop: 518 788 (2001)

quilt *n* **1** a cover for a bed, consisting of a soft filling sewn between two layers of material, usually with crisscross seams **2** a continental quilt; duvet ▷ *vb* **3** to stitch together two layers of (fabric) with padding between them [Old French *coilte* mattress] **> quilted** *adj*

Quimper *n* a city in NW France: capital of Finistère department. Pop: 63 929 (2008)

quin *n* a quintuplet

quince *n* the acid-tasting pear-shaped fruit of an Asian tree, used in preserves [Greek *kudōnion*]

quincunx *n* a group of five objects arranged in the shape of a rectangle with one at each corner and the fifth in the centre [Latin: five twelfths; in ancient Rome, this was a coin marked with five spots]

Quine *n* Willard van Orman. 1908–2000, US philosopher. His works include *Word and Object* (1960), *Philosophy of Logic* (1970), *The Roots of Reference* (1973), and *The Logic of Sequences* (1990)

Qui Nhong *n* a port in SE Vietnam, on the South China Sea. Pop: 163 385 (1992 est)

quinine *n* a bitter drug extracted from cinchona bark, used as a tonic and formerly in malaria therapy [Spanish *quina* cinchona bark]

Quinn *n* Anthony. 1915–2001, US film actor, born in Mexico: noted esp. for his performances in *La Strada* (1954) and *Zorba the Greek* (1964)

quinquennial *adj* occurring once every five years or over a period of five years

quinquereme *n* an ancient Roman galley with five banks of oars [Latin *quinque* five + *remus* oar]

quinsy *n* inflammation of the tonsils and throat, with abscesses [Greek *kuōn* dog + *ankhein* to strangle]

quint *n US and Canad* a quintuplet

quintal *n* **1** a unit of weight equal to (esp. in Britain) 112 pounds (50.85 kg) or (esp. in US) 100 pounds (45.36 kg) **2** a unit of weight equal to 100 kilograms [Arabic *qintār*]

Quintana Roo *n* a state of SE Mexico, on the E Yucatán

Peninsula: hot, humid, forested, and inhabited chiefly by Maya Indians. Capital: Chetumal. Pop: 287 000 (2005 est). Area: 50 350 sq km (19 463 sq miles)

quintessence *n* **1** the perfect representation of a quality or state **2** an extract of a substance containing its central nature in its most concentrated form [Medieval Latin *quinta essentia* the fifth essence] **> quintessential** *adj*

quintet *n* **1** a group of five singers or instrumentalists **2** a piece of music for five performers **3** any group of five [Italian *quintetto*]

Quintilian *n* Latin name *Marcus Fabius Quintilianus*. ?35–?96 AD, Roman rhetorician and teacher

quintillion *n*, *pl* **-lions** *or* **-lion** **1** (in Britain, France, and Germany) the number represented as one followed by 30 zeros (10^{30}) **2** (in the US and Canada) the number represented as one followed by 18 zeros (10^{18}) [Latin *quintus* fifth]

quintuple *vb* **-pling, -pled** **1** to multiply by five **> adj** **2** five times as much or as many **3** consisting of five parts **> n** **4** a quantity or number five times as great as another [Latin *quintus* fifth + -*plus* -fold]

quintuplet *n* one of five children born at one birth

quip *n* **1** a witty saying **> vb** **quipping, quipped** **2** to make a quip [probably from Latin *quippe* indeed, to be sure]

quire *n* a set of 24 or 25 sheets of paper [Old French *quaier*]

Quirinal *n* one of the seven hills on which ancient Rome was built

quirk *n* **1** a peculiarity of character; mannerism or foible **2** an unexpected twist or turn: *a strange quirk of fate* [origin unknown] **> quirky** *adj*

quisling *n* a traitor who aids an occupying enemy force; collaborator [after Vidkun *Quisling*, Norwegian collaborator with the Nazis]

quit *vb* **quitting, quit** **1** to stop (doing something) **2** to resign (from): *the Prime Minister's decision to quit*; *he quit his job as a salesman* **3** to leave (a place) [Old French *quitter*] **> quitter** *n*

quitch *or* **quitch grass** *n* same as **couch grass**

quite *adv* **1** (*not used with a negative*) to a greater than average extent; somewhat: *he found her quite attractive* **2** absolutely: *you're quite right* **3** in actuality; truly **4** quite a *or* an of an exceptional kind: *she is quite a girl* **5** quite something a remarkable thing or person **> interj** **6** an expression used to indicate agreement [adverbial use of *quite* (adjective) quit, free of]

> **USAGE** See at **very**.

Quito *n* the capital of Ecuador, in the north at an altitude of 2850 m (9350 ft), just south of the equator: the oldest capital in South America, existing many centuries before the Incan conquest in 1487; a cultural centre since the beginning of Spanish rule (1534); two universities. Pop: 1 514 000 (2005 est)

quits *adj informal* **1** on an equal footing **2** call it quits to end a dispute or contest, agreeing that honours are even

quittance *n* **1** release from debt or other obligation **2** a document certifying this [Old French *quitter* to release from obligation]

quiver¹ *vb* **1** to shake with a tremulous movement; tremble **> n** **2** a shaking or trembling [obsolete *cwiver* quick, nimble] **> quivering** *adj*

quiver² *n* a case for holding or carrying arrows [Old French *cuivre*]

quixotic (kwik-sot-ik) *adj* unrealistically optimistic or chivalrous [after Don *Quixote* in Cervantes' romance] **> quixotically** *adv*

quiz *n*, *pl* **quizzes** **1** an entertainment in which the knowledge of the players is tested by a series of questions **2** any set of quick questions designed to test knowledge **3** an investigation by close questioning **> vb** **quizzing, quizzed** **4** to investigate by close questioning; interrogate [origin unknown]

quizzical *adj* questioning and mocking or supercilious: *the question elicits a quizzical expression* **> quizzically** *adv*

Qum *n* a variant of Qom

Qumran *n* See Khirbet Qumran

Qungur *n* a variant transliteration of the Chinese name for Kongur Shan

quod *n* Brit slang a jail [origin unknown]

quoin *n* **1** an external corner of a wall **2** the stone forming the outer corner of a wall; a cornerstone **3** a wedge [variant of *coin* (in former sense of corner)]

quoit *n* a large ring used in the game of quoits [origin unknown]

quoits *n* a game in which quoits are tossed at a stake in the ground in attempts to encircle it

quokka *n* a small Australian wallaby

quondam *adj formal* of an earlier time; former: *her quondam employers* [Latin]

quorate *adj* having or being a quorum: *the meeting is now quorate*

Quorn *n* trademark a vegetable protein used as a meat substitute

quorum *n* the minimum number of members required to be present in a meeting or assembly before any business can be transacted [Latin, literally: of whom]

quota *n* **1** the share that is due from, due to, or allocated to a person or group **2** the prescribed number or quantity allowed, required, or admitted [Latin *quotus* of what number]

quotation *n* **1** a written or spoken passage repeated exactly in a later work, speech, or conversation, usually with an acknowledgment of its source **2** the act of quoting **3** an estimate of costs submitted by a contractor to a prospective client

quotation marks *pl n* the punctuation marks used to begin and end a quotation, either '' and '' or ' and '

quote *vb* **quoting, quoted** **1** to repeat (words) exactly from (an earlier work, speech, or conversation), usually with an acknowledgment of their source **2** to state a price for goods or a job of work **3** to put quotation marks round (words) **> n** **4** *informal* a quotation **5** quotes *informal* quotation marks **> interj** **6** an expression used to indicate that the words that follow are a quotation [Medieval Latin *quotare* to assign reference numbers to passages] **> quotable** *adj*

quoth *vb archaic* (foll. by I or *he* or *she*) said [Old English *cwæth*]

quotidian *adj* **1** daily **2** *literary* commonplace **3** (esp. of fever) recurring daily [Latin *quotidianus*]

quotient *n* the result of the division of one number or quantity by another [Latin *quotiens* how often]

Qu Qiu Bai *or* **Ch'ü Ch'iu-pai** *n* 1889–1935, Chinese communist leader who was also an important literary figure: executed by the Nationalist forces in Shanghai

Quran (koo-rahn) *n* same as **Koran**

q.v. (denoting a cross-reference) which (word, item, etc.) see [New Latin *quod vide*]

Qwaqwa *n* (formerly) a Bantu homeland in N South Africa; the only Bantu homeland without exclaves: abolished in 1994. Also called: **Basotho-Qwaqwa**. Former name (until 1972): **Basotho-Ba-Borwa**

qwerty *or* **QWERTY keyboard** *n* the standard English language typewriter or computer keyboard with the characters q, w, e, r, t, and y at the top left of the keyboard

Rr

r 1 radius **2** ratio **3** right **4** *cricket* run(s)

R 1 *chem* radical **2** Regina **3** Registered Trademark **4** *physics, electronics* resistance **5** Rex **6** River **7** *chess* rook

Ra *chem* radium

RA 1 rear admiral **2** (in Britain) Royal Academy **3** (in Britain) Royal Artillery

RAAF Royal Australian Air Force

Rabat *n* the capital of Morocco, in the northwest on the Atlantic coast, served by the port of Salé: became a military centre in the 12th century and a Corsair republic in the 17th century. Pop: 673 000 (2003)

Rabaul *n* a port in Papua New Guinea, on NE New Britain Island, in the Bismarck Archipelago: capital of the Territory of New Guinea until 1941; almost surrounded by volcanoes. Pop: 17 855 (2001 est)

Rabbath Ammon *n Old Testament* the ancient royal city of the Ammonites, on the site of modern Amman

rabbi (rab-bye) *n, pl* **-bis 1** the spiritual leader of a Jewish congregation **2** an expert in or teacher of Jewish Law [Hebrew: my master] **> rabbinical** *adj*

rabbit *n, pl* **-bits** *or* **-bit 1** a common burrowing mammal with long ears and a short fluffy tail *> vb* **-biting, -bited 2** *informal* to talk too much: *he keeps rabbiting on about interrogation* [origin unknown]

rabbit ears *pl n Austral and NZ* an indoor television aerial

rabbit fence *n* a fence to prevent the spread of rabbits

rabbiting *n* go rabbiting to hunt rabbits

rabbit punch *n* a short sharp blow to the back of the neck

rabble *n* **1** a disorderly crowd of noisy people **2 the rabble** *disparaging* the common people [origin unknown]

rabble-rouser *n* a person who stirs up the feelings of the mob **> rabble-rousing** *adj, n*

Rabelais *n* François. ?1494–1553, French writer. His written works, esp. *Gargantua and Pantagruel* (1534), contain a lively mixture of earthy wit, common sense, and satire

Rabelaisian *adj* characterized by broad, often bawdy humour and sharp satire [after the work of François RABELAIS]

Rabi *n* Isidor Isaac. 1898–1988, US physicist, born in Austria, who devised the atomic and molecular beam resonance method of observing atomic spectra. Nobel prize for physics 1944

Rabia *or* **Rabiah** *n* full name *Rabia al-Adawiyyah*. c. 713–801 AD, Islamic saint, mystic, and religious leader; her teachings inspired the Sufi movement

rabid *adj* **1** fanatical: *a rabid separatist* **2** having rabies [Latin *rabidus* frenzied] **> rabidity** *n*

rabies (ray-beez) *n pathol* a fatal infectious viral disease of the nervous system transmitted by dogs and certain other animals [Latin: madness]

Rabin *n* Yitzhak. 1922–95, Israeli statesman; prime minister of Israel (1974–77; 1992–95); assassinated

RAC (in Britain) Royal Automobile Club

raccoon *or* **racoon** *n, pl* **-coons** *or* **-coon** a small American mammal with a long striped tail [from a Native American language]

race¹ *n* **1** a contest of speed **2** any competition or rivalry: *the arms race* **3** a rapid current of water **4** a channel of a stream: *a mill race* **5** *Austral and NZ* a narrow passage through which sheep pass individually, as to a sheep dip *> vb* **racing, raced 6** to take part in a contest of speed with (someone) **7** to enter (an animal or vehicle) in a race: *to race greyhounds* **8** to travel as fast as possible **9** (of an engine) to run faster than normal **10** (of the heart) to beat faster than normal **>** See also **races** [Old Norse *rās* running] **> racer** *n* **> racing** *adj, n*

race² *n* **1** a group of people of common ancestry with distinguishing physical features, such as skin colour or build **2 the human race** human beings collectively **3** a group of animals or plants having common characteristics that distinguish them from other members of the same species [Italian *razza*]

Race *n* Cape Race a cape at the SE extremity of Newfoundland, Canada

race caller *n* a professional horse-racing commentator

racecourse *n* a long broad track on which horses are raced

racehorse *n* a horse specially bred for racing

raceme (rass-eem) *n botany* a cluster of flowers along a central stem, as in the foxglove [Latin *racemus* bunch of grapes]

race meeting *n* a series of horse or greyhound races held at the same place

race relations *pl n* the relations between members of two or more races within a single community

race riot *n* a riot involving violence between people of different races

races *pl n* **the races** a series of contests of speed between horses or greyhounds over a fixed course

racetrack *n* **1** a circuit used for races between cars, bicycles, or runners **2** *US and Canad* a racecourse

Rachel *n* **1** *Old Testament* the second and best-loved wife of Jacob; mother of Joseph and Benjamin (Genesis 29–35) **2** original name *Elisa Félix*. 1820–58, French tragic actress, famous for her roles in the plays of Racine and Corneille

Rachmaninoff *or* **Rachmaninov** *n* Sergei Vassilievich. 1873–1943, Russian piano virtuoso and composer

racial *adj* **1** relating to the division of the human species into races **2** typically associated with any such group **> racially** *adv*

Racine *n* Jean Baptiste. 1639–99, French tragic poet and dramatist. His plays include *Andromaque* (1667), *Bérénice* (1670), and *Phèdre* (1677)

racism *or* **racialism** *n* **1** hostile or oppressive behaviour towards people because they belong to a different race **2** the belief that some races are innately superior to others because of hereditary characteristics **> racist** *or* **racialist** *n, adj*

rack¹ *n* **1** a framework for holding particular articles, such as coats or luggage **2** a straight bar with teeth on ts edge, to work with a cogwheel **3 the rack** *history* an instrument of torture that stretched the body of the victim ▷ *vb* **4** to cause great suffering to: *Germany was racked by food riots* **5 rack one's brains** to try very hard to think of something [probably from Middle Dutch *rec* framework]

> **USAGE** See at **wrack**[1].

rack[2] *n* **go to rack and ruin** to be destroyed through neglect [variant of WRACK[1]]

rack[3] *vb* to clear (wine or beer) by siphoning it off from the dregs

rack[4] *n* the neck or rib part of a joint of meat

rack-and-pinion *n* a device for converting rotary into linear motion and vice versa, in which a gearwheel (the pinion) engages with a flat toothed bar (the rack)

racket[1] *n* **1** a noisy disturbance **2** an illegal activity done to make money **3** *slang* a business or occupation: *I've been in the racket since I was sixteen* ▷ *vb* **-eting, -eted** **4** to make a commotion [probably imitative] **> rackety** *adj*

racket[2] or **racquet** *n* a bat consisting of an oval frame surrounding a mesh of strings, with a handle, used in tennis, badminton, and squash. See also **rackets** [French *raquette*]

racketeer *n* a person who makes money from illegal activities **> racketeering** *n*

rackets *n* a game similar to squash, played by two or four people

Rackham *n* Arthur. 1867–1939, English artist, noted for his book illustrations, esp. of fairy tales

rack-rent *n* an extortionate rent

raclette *n* a Swiss dish of melted cheese, usually served on boiled potatoes [French]

raconteur (rak-on-tur) *n* a person skilled in telling stories [French]

racoon *n*, *pl* **-coons** or **-coon** same as **raccoon**

racquet *n* same as **racket**[2]

racy *adj* **racier, raciest** **1** slightly shocking: *a racy comedy* **2** spirited or lively: *a racy literary style* **> racily** *adv* **> raciness** *n*

rad radian

RADA (in Britain) Royal Academy of Dramatic Art

radar *n* **1** a method of detecting the position and velocity of a distant object by bouncing a narrow beam of extremely high-frequency radio pulses off it **2** the equipment used in this [ra(dio) d(etecting) a(nd) r(anging)]

radar trap *n* a device which uses radar to detect motorists who break the speed limit

Radcliffe *n* **1** Ann. 1764–1823, British novelist, noted for her Gothic romances *The Mysteries of Udolpho* (1794) and *The Italian* (1797) **2** Paula (Jane). born 1973, British athlete, winner of the London Marathon (2002, 2003, 2005), gold medalist in the marathon at the World Championships (2005), and European record holder for the 10,000 m

raddle *vb Austral and NZ* to mark (sheep) for identification

raddled *adj* (of a person) untidy or rundown in appearance [from *rud* red ochre]

Radek *n* Karl (Bernhardovich), original name *Karl Sobelsohn*. 1885–?1939, Soviet politician and journalist who was secretary of Comintern (1920–24). He was accused of treason (1937) and probably died in a labour camp

Radetzky *n* Count Joseph. 1766–1858, Austrian field marshal: served in the war against Sardinia (1848–9), winning brilliant victories at Custozza (1848) and Novara (1849): governor of Lombardy-Venetia in N Italy (1849-57)

radial *adj* **1** spreading out from a common central point **2** of a radius or ray **3** short for **radial-ply** ▷ *n* **4** a radial-ply tyre **> radially** *adv*

radial-ply *adj* (of a tyre) having the fabric cords in the outer casing running radially to enable the sidewalls to be flexible

radian *n* an SI unit of plane angle; the angle between two radii of a circle that cut off on the circumference an arc equal in length to the radius

radiant *adj* **1** characterized by health and happiness: *radiant good looks* **2** shining **3** emitted as radiation: *radiant heat* **4** sending out heat by radiation: *radiant heaters* [Latin *radiare* to shine] **> radiance** *n*

radiant energy *n* energy that is emitted or propagated in the form of particles or electromagnetic radiation

radiate *vb* **-ating, -ated** **1** to spread out from a central point **2** to show (an emotion or quality) to a great degree: *she radiated competence and composure* **3** to emit or be emitted as radiation ▷ *adj* **4** having rays or a radial structure [Latin *radiare* to emit rays]

radiation *n* **1** *physics* **a** the emission of energy as particles, electromagnetic waves or sound **b** the particles or waves emitted **2** the process of radiating

radiation sickness *n* an illness caused by overexposure to radioactive material or X-rays

radiator *n* **1** *Brit* a device for heating a room or building, consisting of a series of pipes containing hot water **2** a device for cooling an internal-combustion engine, consisting of thin-walled tubes containing water **3** *Austral and NZ* an electric fire

radical *adj* **1** favouring fundamental change in political or social conditions: *a radical student movement* **2** of the essential nature of a person or thing; fundamental: *a radical fault* **3** searching or thorough: *a radical interpretation* **4** *maths* of or containing roots of numbers or quantities ▷ *n* **5** a person who favours fundamental change in existing institutions or in political, social, or economic conditions **6** *maths* a root of a number or quantity, such as $^3\sqrt{5}$, $\sqrt{x}$ **7** *chem* an atom or group of atoms that acts as a unit during chemical reactions [Latin *radix* a root] **> radicalism** *n* **> radically** *adv*

radicalize or **-lise** *vb* **-lizing, -lized** or **-lising, -lised** to make (a person, group, or situation) radical or more radical: *the feelings of its own radicalized population*

radical sign *n* the symbol $\sqrt{}$ placed before a number or quantity to indicate the extraction of a root, esp. a square root. The value of a higher root is indicated by a raised digit in front of the symbol, as in $^3\sqrt{}$

radicchio (rad-deek-ee-oh) *n*, *pl* **-chios** an Italian variety of chicory, with purple leaves streaked with white that are eaten raw in salads

radicle *n botany* **1** the part of the embryo of seed-bearing plants that develops into the main root **2** a very small root or rootlike part [Latin *radix* root]

Radiguet *n* Raymond. 1903–23, French novelist; the author of *The Devil in the Flesh* (1923) and *Count d'Orgel* (1924)

radii *n* a plural of **radius**

radio *n*, *pl* **-dios** **1** the use of electromagnetic waves for broadcasting or two-way communication without the use of linking wires **2** an electronic device for converting radio signals into sounds **3** a communications device for sending and receiving messages using radio waves **4** sound broadcasting ▷ *vb* **5** to transmit (a message) by radio ▷ *adj* **6** of, relating to, or using radio broadcasting or radio signals: *a radio interview* **7** using or producing electromagnetic waves in the range used for radio signals: *radio astronomy* [Latin *radius* ray]

radio- *combining form* **1** (denoting) radio **2** (denoting) radioactivity or radiation: *radiocarbon*

radioactive *adj* showing or using radioactivity

radioactivity *n* the spontaneous emission of radiation from atomic nuclei. The radiation can consist of alpha or beta particles, or gamma rays

radio astronomy *n* astronomy using a radio telescope to analyse signals received from radio sources in space

radiocarbon *n* a radioactive isotope of carbon, esp. carbon-14

radiocarbon dating *n* same as **carbon dating**

radiochemistry *n* the chemistry of radioactive substances

r

radio-controlled *adj* controlled by signals sent by radio

radio frequency *n* any electromagnetic frequency that lies in the range 10 kilohertz to 300 000 megahertz and can be used for broadcasting

radiogram *n Brit* an old-fashioned combined radio and record player

radiograph *n* an image produced on a special photographic film or plate by radiation, usually by X-rays

radiography (ray-dee-**og**-ra-fee) *n* the production of radiographs for use in medicine or industry ⟩ **radiographer** *n*

radioisotope *n* a radioactive isotope

radiology (ray-dee-**ol**-a-jee) *n* the use of X-rays and radioactive substances in the diagnosis and treatment of disease ⟩ **radiologist** *n*

radioscopy (ray-dee-**oss**-kop-ee) *n* examination of a person or object by means of a fluorescent screen and an X-ray source

radiosonde *n* an airborne instrument to send meteorological information back to earth by radio [RADIO- + French *sonde* sounding line]

radiotelegraphy *n* telegraphy in which messages are transmitted by radio waves

radiotelephone *n* a telephone which sends and receives messages using radio waves rather than wires ⟩ **radiotelephony** *n*

radio telescope *n* an instrument used in radio astronomy to pick up and analyse radio waves from space

radiotherapy *n* the treatment of disease, esp. cancer, by radiation

radio wave *n* an electromagnetic wave of radio frequency

radish *n* a small hot-flavoured red root vegetable eaten raw in salads [Latin *radix* root]

radium *n chem* a highly radioactive luminescent metallic element, found in pitchblende. Symbol: **Ra** [Latin *radius* ray]

radius (ray-dee-uss) *n, pl* **-dii** (-dee-eye) *or* **-diuses 1** a straight line joining the centre of a circle to any point on the circumference **2** the length of this line **3** *anatomy* the outer, slightly shorter of the two bones of the forearm **4** a circular area of a specified size round a central point: *within a seven-mile radius of the club* [Latin: ray, spoke]

Radnorshire *or* **Radnor** *n* (until 1974) a county of E Wales, now part of Powys

Radom *n* a city in E Poland: under Austria from 1795 to 1815 and Russia from 1815 to 1918. Pop: 232 000 (2005 est)

radon (ray-don) *n chem* a colourless radioactive element of the noble gas group. Symbol: **Rn** [from *radium*]

Raeburn *n* Sir Henry. 1756–1823, Scottish portrait painter

RAF (in Britain) Royal Air Force

Rafferty *or* **Rafferty's rules** *pl n Austral and NZ slang* no rules at all [origin unknown]

raffia *n* a fibre obtained from the leaves of a palm tree, used for weaving [Malagasy]

raffish *adj* unconventional or slightly disreputable [obsolete *raff* rubbish]

raffle *n* **1** a lottery, often to raise money for charity, in which the prizes are goods rather than money ▷ *vb* **-fling, -fled 2** to offer as a prize in a raffle [Old French]

Raffles *n* Sir Thomas Stamford. 1781–1826, British colonial administrator: founded Singapore (1819) as a station for the British East India Company

Rafsanjani *n* Hojatoleslam Hashemi Ali Akbar, born 1934, Iranian politician: president of Iran (1989–97)

raft *n* a floating platform of logs or planks tied together [Old Norse *raptr* rafter]

rafter *n* any of the parallel sloping beams that form the framework of a roof [Old English]

rag¹ *n* **1** a small piece of cloth **2** *Brit, Austral and NZ informal* a newspaper **3** *rags* old tattered clothing **4** **from rags to riches** from being extremely poor to being extremely

wealthy [probably formed from *ragged*, from Old English *raggig*]

rag² *Brit vb* **ragging, ragged 1** to tease **2** to play rough practical jokes on ▷ *n* **3** a boisterous practical joke ▷ *adj* **4** (in British universities and colleges) of various events organized to raise money for charity: *a rag week* [origin unknown]

rag³ *n* a piece of ragtime music

ragamuffin *n* **1** a ragged dirty child **2** same as **ragga** [probably from RAG¹]

rag-and-bone man *n Brit* a man who goes from street to street buying old clothes and furniture

ragbag *n* a confused mixture: *the traditional ragbag of art traders*

rage *n* **1** intense anger or passion **2** a fashion or craze: *the dance was the rage of Europe* **3** aggressive behaviour associated with a specified activity or environment: *road rage; school rage* **4** **all the rage** *informal* very popular **5** *Austral and NZ informal* a dance or party ▷ *vb* **raging, raged 6** to feel or show intense anger **7** to proceed violently and without restraint: *the argument was still raging* [Latin *rabies* madness]

ragga *n* a dance-oriented style of reggae [from RAGAMUFFIN]

ragged (rag-gid) *adj* **1** dressed in shabby or torn clothes **2** (of clothes) tattered and torn **3** having a rough or uneven surface or edge **4** neglected or untidy: *the ragged stone-built village*

ragged robin *n* a plant that has pink or white flowers with ragged petals

raglan *adj* **1** (of a sleeve) joined to the garment by diagonal seams from the collar to the underarm **2** (of a garment) with this style of sleeve [after Lord RAGLAN]

Raglan *n* Fitzroy James Henry Somerset, 1st Baron Raglan. 1788–1855, British field marshal, diplomatist, politician, and protégé of Wellington: commanded British troops (1854–55) in the Crimean War

ragout (rag-**goo**) *n* a richly seasoned stew of meat and vegetables [French]

ragtag *n* **ragtag and bobtail** the common people

ragtime *n* a style of jazz piano music with a syncopated melody [probably *ragged time*]

rag trade *n informal* the clothing business

Ragusa *n* **1** an industrial town in SE Sicily. Pop: 68 956 (2001) **2** the Italian name (until 1918) for **Dubrovnik**

ragwort *n* a plant with ragged leaves and yellow flowers

raid *n* **1** a sudden surprise attack: *a bombing raid* **2** a surprise visit by police searching for people or goods: *a drugs raid* ▷ *vb* **3** to make a raid on **4** to sneak into (a place) in order to steal [Old English *rād* military expedition] ⟩ **raider** *n*

rail¹ *n* **1** a horizontal bar supported by vertical posts, used as a fence or barrier **2** a horizontal bar on which to hang things: *a curtain rail* **3** one of a pair of parallel bars that serve as a running surface for the wheels of a train **4** railway: *by car or by rail* **5** **go off the rails** to start behaving improperly or eccentrically ▷ *vb* **6** to fence (an area) with rails [Old French *raille* rod]

rail² *vb* **rail against** *or* **at** to complain bitterly or loudly about [Old French *railler* to mock]

rail³ *n* a small wading marsh bird [Old French *raale*]

railcard *n Brit* an identity card, which pensioners or young people can buy, entitling them to cheaper rail travel

railhead *n* **1** a terminal of a railway **2** the farthest point reached by completed track on an unfinished railway

railing *n* a fence made of rails supported by posts

raillery *n, pl* **-leries** good-natured teasing [French *railler* to tease]

railroad *n* **1** *US* a railway ▷ *vb* **2** *informal* to force (a person) into an action with haste or by unfair means

railway *n* **1** a track composed of a line of parallel metal rails fixed to sleepers, on which trains run **2** any track on which the wheels of a vehicle may run: *a cable railway*

3 the rolling stock, buildings, and tracks used in such a transport system 4 the organization responsible for operating a railway network

raiment n archaic or poetic clothing [from arrayment]

rain n 1 a water falling from the sky in drops formed by the condensation of water vapour in the atmosphere b a fall of rain. Related adjective: **pluvial** 2 a large quantity of anything falling rapidly: a rain of stones descended on the police 3 (**come**) **rain or shine** regardless of circumstances 4 **right as rain** informal perfectly all right ▷ vb 5 to fall as rain: it's raining back home 6 to fall rapidly and in large quantities: steel rungs and sawdust raining down 7 **rained off** or US and Canad **rained out** cancelled or postponed because of rain ▶ See also **rains** [Old English regn] ▷ **rainy** adj

rainbird n S African a common name for **Burchell's coucal**, a bird whose call is believed to be a sign of impending rain

rainbow n an arched display in the sky of the colours of the spectrum, caused by the refraction and reflection of the sun's rays through rain

Rainbow Bridge n a natural stone bridge over a creek in SE Utah. Height: 94 m (309 ft). Span: 85 m (278 ft)

rainbow nation n S African an epithet, alluding to its multiracial population, of **South Africa** [C20: coined by Nelson MANDELA following the end of apartheid]

rainbow trout n a freshwater trout with black spots and two red stripes

rain check n **take a rain check** informal to request or accept the postponement of an offer

raincoat n a coat made of a waterproof material

rainfall n the amount of rain, hail, or snow in a specified place and time

rainforest n dense forest found in tropical areas of heavy rainfall

Rainier n Mount Rainier a mountain in W Washington State: the highest mountain in the state and in the Cascade Range. Height: 4392 m (14 410 ft)

Rainier III n full name Rainier Louis Henri Maxence Bertrand de Grimaldi. 1923–2005, ruling prince of Monaco from 1949. He married (1956) the US actress Grace Kelly (1929–82)

rains pl n **the rains** the season in the tropics when there is a lot of rain

rainstorm n a storm with heavy rain

rainwater n water from rain

rainy day n a future time of need, esp. financial need

Rais or **Retz** n Gilles de. 1404–40, French nobleman who fought with Joan of Arc: marshal of France (1429–40). He was executed for the torture and murder of more than 140 children

raise vb **raising, raised** 1 to lift to a higher position or level 2 to place in an upright position 3 to increase in amount, quality, or intensity: to raise interest rates 4 to collect or gather together: to raise additional capital; to raise an army 5 to cause to be expressed: to raise a smile 6 to stir up 7 to bring up: to raise a family 8 to grow: to raise a crop 9 to put forward for consideration: they raised controversial issues 10 to arouse from sleep or death 11 to build: to raise a barn 12 to bring to an end: to raise a siege 13 to establish radio communications with: we raised Moscow last night 14 to advance in rank; promote 15 maths to multiply (a number) by itself a specified number of times: 8 is 2 raised to the power 3 16 to cause (dough) to rise, as by the addition of yeast 17 cards to bet more than (the previous player) 18 **raise Cain a** to create a disturbance **b** to protest vehemently ▷ n 19 US, Canad and NZ an increase in pay [Old Norse reisa]

raised adj higher than the surrounding area: a small raised platform

raisin n a dried grape [Old French: grape]

raison d'être (ray-zon det-ra) n, pl **raisons d'être** (ray-zon det-ra) reason or justification for existence [French]

raita (rye-ta) n an Indian dish of chopped cucumber, mint, etc., in yogurt, served with curry [Hindi]

Raj n the Raj the British government in India before 1947 [Hindi]

raja or **rajah** n history an Indian prince or ruler [Hindi]

Rajasthan n a state of NW India, bordering on Pakistan: formed in 1958; contains the Thar Desert in the west; now the largest state in India. Capital: Jaipur. Pop: 56 473 122 (2001). Area: 342 239 sq km (132 111 sq miles)

Rajkot n a city in W India, in S Gujarat. Pop: 966 642 (2001)

Rajputana n a former group of princely states in NW India: now mostly part of Rajasthan

Rakata n another name for **Krakatoa**

rake[1] n 1 a farm or garden tool consisting of a row of teeth set in a headpiece attached to a long shaft and used for gathering leaves or straw, or for smoothing loose earth 2 any of various implements similar in shape or function ▷ vb **raking, raked** 3 to scrape or gather with a rake 4 to smooth (a surface) with a rake 5 Also: **rake out** to clear (ashes) from (a fire) 6 **rake together** or up to gather (items or people) with difficulty, as from a limited supply 7 to search or examine carefully: raking over the past is not always popular 8 to direct (gunfire) along the length of (a target): the machine guns raked up and down their line 9 to scrape or graze: he raked the tip of his shoe across the pavement ▶ See also **rake in, rake-off**, etc. [Old English raca]

rake[2] n an immoral man [short for rakehell]

rake[3] n 1 the degree to which an object slopes ▷ vb **raking, raked** 2 to slope from the vertical, esp. (of a ship's mast) towards the stern 3 to construct with a backward slope [origin unknown]

raked adj (of a surface) sloping so that it is higher at the back than at the front

rake in vb informal to acquire (money) in large amounts

rake-off n slang a share of profits, esp. an illegal one

rake up vb to bring back memories of (a forgotten unpleasant event): she doesn't want to rake up the past

rakish[1] (ray-kish) adj dashing or jaunty: a hat which he wore at a rakish angle [probably from RAKE[3]]

rakish[2] adj immoral: a rakish life of drinking and womanizing [from RAKE[2]] ▷ **rakishly** adv

Raleigh[1] n a city in E central North Carolina, capital of the state. Pop: 316 802 (2003 est)

Raleigh[2] or **Ralegh** n Sir Walter. ?1552–1618, English courtier, explorer, and writer; favourite of Elizabeth I. After unsuccessful attempts to colonize Virginia (1584–89), he led two expeditions to the Orinoco to search for gold (1595; 1616). He introduced tobacco and potatoes into England, and was imprisoned (1603–16) for conspiracy under James I. He was beheaded in 1618

rallentando music adj, adv 1 becoming slower ▷ n 2 a passage in which the music becomes slower [Italian]

rally[1] n, pl **-lies** 1 a large gathering of people for a meeting 2 a marked recovery of strength, as during illness 3 Stock Exchange a sharp increase in price or trading activity after a decline 4 tennis, squash etc. an exchange of several shots before one player wins the point 5 a car-driving competition on public roads ▷ vb **-lies, -lying, -lied** 6 to bring or come together after being dispersed 7 to bring or come together for a common cause 8 to summon up (one's strength or spirits) 9 to recover (sometimes only temporarily) from an illness 10 Stock Exchange to increase sharply after a decline [Old French rallier]

rally[2] vb **-lies, -lying, -lied** to mock or tease (someone) in a good-natured way [Old French railler to tease]

rally round vb to group together to help someone

ram n 1 an uncastrated adult male sheep 2 a hydraulically or pneumatically driven piston 3 the falling weight of a pile driver 4 short for **battering ram** ▷ vb **ramming, rammed** 5 to strike against with force 6 to force or drive: he rammed his sword into the man's belly 7 to stuff or cram 8 **ram something home** to make something clear or obvious: *to ram home the message* **9 ram something down someone's throat** to put forward or emphasize an argument or idea with excessive force [Old English *ramm*]

RAM *computers* random access memory: a temporary storage space which loses its contents when the computer is switched off

Rama *n* a Hindu god, the incarnation of Vishnu

Ramadan *n* **1** the ninth month of the Muslim year, 30 days long, during which strict fasting is observed from sunrise to sunset **2** the fast itself

Ramakrishna *n* Sri. 1834–86, Hindu yogi and religious reformer. He preached the equal value of all religions as different paths to God

Ramallah *n* a town in the West Bank, serving as headquarters of the Palestinian National Authority. Pop: 51 000 (2005 est)

Ramanuja *n* 11th century AD, Indian Hindu philosopher and theologian

Ramaphosa *n* (Matamela) **Cyril**. born 1952, South African statesman and trade unionist; secretary general of the ANC (1991–97); deputy president of South Africa from 2014

Ramat Gan *n* a city in Israel, E of Tel Aviv. Pop: 126 500 (2003 est)

Rambert *n* Dame Marie. 1888–1982, British ballet dancer and teacher, born in Poland: founded the **Ballet Rambert** (1926)

ramble *vb* **-bling, -bled 1** to walk for relaxation, sometimes with no particular direction **2** to speak or write in a confused style **3** to grow or develop in a random fashion ▷ *n* **4** a walk, esp. in the countryside [Middle English *romblen*]

rambler *n* **1** a person who takes country walks **2** a climbing rose

rambling *adj* **1** long and irregularly shaped: *a rambling fourteenth-century church* **2** (of speech or writing) confused and long-winded ▷ *n* **3** the activity of going for long walks in the country

Rambouillet *n* a town in N France, in the Yvelines department: site of the summer residence of French presidents. Pop: 26 454 (2006)

RAMC (in Britain) Royal Army Medical Corps

Rameau *n* Jean Philippe. 1683–1764, French composer. His works include the opera *Castor et Pollux* (1737), chamber music, harpsichord pieces, church music, and cantatas. His *Traité de l'harmonie* (1722) was of fundamental importance in the development of modern harmony

ramekin (ram-ik-in) *n* a small container for baking and serving one portion of food [French *ramequin*]

ramification *n* **1** ramifications the consequences or complications resulting from an action **2** a structure of branching parts

ramify *vb* **-fies, -fying, -fied 1** to become complex **2** to spread in branches; subdivide [French *ramifier*]

Ramillies *n* a village in central Belgium where the Duke of Marlborough defeated the French in 1706

ramjet *n* **a** a type of jet engine in which fuel is burned in a duct using air compressed by the forward speed of the aircraft **b** an aircraft powered by such an engine

ramp *n* **1** a slope that joins two surfaces at different levels **2** a place where the level of a road surface changes because of roadworks **3** a movable stairway by which passengers enter and leave an aircraft **4** *Brit* a small hump on a road to make traffic slow down [Old French *ramper* to crawl, rear]

rampage *vb* **-paging, -paged 1** to rush about violently ▷ *n* **2 on the rampage** behaving violently or destructively [Scots]

rampant *adj* **1** growing or spreading uncontrollably **2** *heraldry* (of a beast) standing on the hind legs, the right foreleg raised above the left: *a lion rampant* [Old French *ramper* to crawl, rear]

rampart *n* a mound of earth or a wall built to protect a fort or city [Old French]

Ramphal *n* Sir Shridath Surendranath, known as *Sunni*. born 1928, Guyanese diplomat and Commonwealth Secretary-General (1975–90)

Ramphele *n* Mamphela. born 1947, Black South African political activist: partner of Steve Biko; a director of the World Bank (2000–04); founded the political party Agang (2013)

rampike *n Canad* a tall tree that has been burned bare of branches

ramp up *vb* **1** to increase or cause to increase **2** to increase the effort involved in a process

Rampur *n* a city in N India, in N Uttar Pradesh. Pop: 281 549 (2001)

ram raid *n informal* a raid on a shop in which a stolen car is driven into the window ▷ **ram raider** *n*

ramrod *n* **1** a long thin rod for cleaning the barrel of a gun or forcing gunpowder into an old-fashioned gun ▷ *adj* **2** (of someone's posture) very straight and upright

Ramsay *n* **1** Allan. ?1686–1758, Scottish poet, editor, and bookseller, noted particularly for his pastoral comedy *The Gentle Shepherd* (1725): first person to introduce the circulating library in Scotland **2** his son, **Allan** 1713–84, Scottish portrait painter **3** James Andrew Broun Ramsay. See Dalhousie (2) **4** Gordon. born 1963, British chef and restaurateur; achieved a third Michelin star (2001) **5** Sir William. 1852–1916, Scottish chemist. He discovered argon (1894) with Rayleigh, isolated helium (1895), and identified neon, krypton, and xenon: Nobel prize for chemistry 1904

Ramses II *or* **Rameses II** *n* died ?1225 BC, king of ancient Egypt (?1292–?25). His reign was marked by war with the Hittites and the construction of many colossal monuments, esp. the rock temple at Abu Simbel

Ramses III *or* **Rameses III** *n* died ?1167 BC, king of ancient Egypt (?1198–?67). His reign was marked by wars in Libya and Syria

Ramsey *n* Sir Alf(red) (Ernest). 1922–99, English footballer and football manager, who played for England 32 times and managed England when they won the World Cup (1966)

Ramsgate *n* a port and resort in SE England, in E Kent on the North Sea coast. Pop: 37 967 (2001)

ramshackle *adj* badly made or cared for: *a curious ramshackle building* [obsolete *ransackle* to ransack]

Ram Singh *n* 1816–85, Indian leader of a puritanical Sikh sect, the Kukas, who tried to remove the British from India through a policy of noncooperation

ran *vb* the past tense of **run**

RAN Royal Australian Navy

Rancagua *n* a city in central Chile. Pop: 217 000 (2005 est)

ranch *n* **1** a large cattle farm in the American West **2** *chiefly US and Canad* a large farm for the rearing of a particular kind of livestock or crop: *he owned a yak ranch in Tibet* ▷ *vb* **3** to run a ranch [Mexican Spanish *rancho* small farm] ▷ **rancher** *n*

Ranchi *n* an industrial city in E India, between the coal and iron belts of the Chota Nagpur Plateau; the capital of Jharkhand from 2000. Pop: 846 454 (2001)

ranchslider *n NZ* a glazed sliding door usually opening onto an outside terrace

rancid *adj* (of fatty foods) stale and having an offensive smell [Latin *rancidus*] ▷ **rancidity** *n*

rancour *or US* **rancor** *n* deep bitter hate [Old French] ▷ **rancorous** *adj*

rand *n* the standard monetary unit of the Republic of South Africa [from *Witwatersrand*, S Transvaal, referring to the gold-mining there]

Rand¹ *n* the Rand short for Witwatersrand

Rand² *n* Ayn, real name *Alisa Zinov'yena Rosenbaum*. 1905–82, US writer born in Russia. Her novels include *The Fountainhead* (1943) and *Atlas Shrugged* (1957);

her philosophical outlook has been an influence among conservatives and libertarians in the US

R & B rhythm and blues

R & D research and development

Randers n a port and industrial centre in Denmark, in E Jutland on **Randers Fjord** (an inlet of the Kattegat). Pop: 55 739 (2004 est)

Randolph n **1** Edmund Jennings, 1753–1813, US politician. He was a member of the convention that framed the US constitution (1787), attorney general (1789–94), and secretary of state (1794–95) **2** John, called *Randolph of Roanoke*. 1773–1833, US politician, noted for his eloquence: in 1820 he opposed the Missouri Compromise that outlawed slavery **3** Sir Thomas; 1st Earl of Moray. Died 1332, Scottish soldier: regent after the death of the Bruce (1329)

random adj **1** lacking any definite plan or prearranged order: *a random sample* ▷ n **2** at random not following any prearranged order [Old French *randir* to gallop] ❭ **randomly** adv ❭ **randomness** n

random access n a method of reading data from a computer file without having to read through the file from the beginning

randy adj **randier, randiest** informal sexually aroused [probably from obsolete *rand* to rant] ❭ **randily** adv ❭ **randiness** n

ranee n same as rani

rang vb the past tense of **ring¹**

> **USAGE** See at ring¹.

rangatira (rung-a-**teer**-a) n NZ a Māori chief of either sex [Māori]

range n **1** the limits within which a person or thing can function effectively: *academic ability range* **2 a** the maximum effective distance of a projectile fired from a weapon **b** the distance between a target and a weapon **3** the total distance which a ship, aircraft, or vehicle can travel without taking on fresh fuel **4** the difference in pitch between the highest and lowest note of a voice or musical instrument **5** a whole set of related things: *a range of treatments was available* **6** the total products of a manufacturer, designer, or stockist: *the latest skin-care range* **7** the limits within which something can lie: *a range of prices* **8** US and Canad an extensive tract of open land on which livestock can graze **9** a chain of mountains **10** an area set aside for shooting practice or rocket testing **11** a large cooking stove with one or more ovens **12** maths the set of values that a function or variable can take ▷ vb **ranging, ranged** **13** to vary between one point and another **14** to cover a specified period or specified things: *attitudes ranged from sympathy to indifference* **15** to roam (over) **16** to establish or be situated in a line or series **17** to put into a specific category: *they ranged themselves with the opposition* [Old French: row]

rangefinder n an instrument for finding how far away an object is

ranger n **1** an official in charge of a park or nature reserve **2** US an armed trooper employed to police a State or district: *a Texas ranger*

Ranger or **Ranger Guide** n Brit and Austral a member of the senior branch of the Guides

Rangoon n the former official name (until 1989, but still widely used) of **Yangon**

rangy (**rain**-jee) adj **rangier, rangiest** having long slender limbs

rani or **ranee** n the wife or widow of a raja [Hindi]

Ranjit Singh n called *the Lion of the Punjab*. 1780–1839; founder of the Sikh kingdom in the Punjab

rank¹ n **1 a** a position within a social organization: *the rank of superintendent* **2** high social or other standing: *accusations were made against people of high rank* **3** a person's social class: *it was too grand for someone of his lowly rank* **4** the position of an item in any ordering or sequence **5** a line

or row of people or things **6** a place where taxis wait to be hired **7** a line of people, esp. soldiers, positioned one beside the other **8** any of the eight horizontal rows of squares on a chessboard **9** **close ranks** to maintain solidarity **10** **pull rank** to get one's own way by virtue of one's superior position **11** **rank and file** the ordinary people or members of a group **12** **the ranks** the common soldiers ▷ vb **13** to give or hold a specific position in an organization or group **14** to arrange in rows or lines **15** to arrange in sequence: *to rank students according to their grades* **16** to have a position on a scale of relative values: *the legendary coronation stone ranks high in the hearts of patriots* [Old French *ranc*]

rank² adj **1** complete or absolute: *rank incompetence* **2** smelling offensively strong **3** growing too quickly: *rank weeds* [Old English *ranc* straight, proud]

Rank n **1** J(oseph) Arthur, 1st Baron. 1888–1972, British industrialist and film executive, whose companies dominated the British film industry in the 1940s and 1950s **2** Otto. 1884–1939, Austrian psychoanalyst, noted for his theory that the trauma of birth may be reflected in certain forms of mental illness

Rankin n Ian. born 1960, Scottish novelist; best known for his series of novels featuring Edinburgh detective Inspector Rebus, beginning with *Knots and Crosses* (1987)

rankle vb **-kling, -kled** to continue to cause resentment or bitterness [Old French *draoncle* ulcer]

ransack vb **1** to search through every part of (a place or thing) **2** to plunder or pillage [Old Norse *rann* house + *saka* to search]

ransom n **1** the money demanded in return for the release of someone who has been kidnapped **2** hold to ransom **a** to keep (a prisoner) in confinement until payment is received **b** to attempt to force (a person) to do something ▷ vb **3** to pay money to obtain the release of (a prisoner) **4** to set free (a prisoner) in return for money [Old French *ransoun*] ❭ **ransomer** n

Ransom n John Crowe. 1888–1974, US poet and critic

Ransome n Arthur. 1884–1967, English writer, best known for his books for children, including *Swallows and Amazons* (1930) and *Great Northern?* (1947)

rant vb **1** to talk in a loud and excited way ▷ n **2** loud excited speech [Dutch *ranten* to rave] ❭ **ranting** adj, n

ranunculus n, pl **-luses** or **-li** a genus of plants including the buttercup [Latin *rana* frog]

RAOC (in Britain) Royal Army Ordnance Corps

rap¹ vb **rapping, rapped** **1** to hit with a sharp quick blow **2** to knock loudly and sharply **3** rap out to utter in sharp rapid speech: *he rapped out his address* **4** to perform a rhythmic monologue with musical backing **5** slang to talk in a relaxed and friendly way **6** to rebuke or criticize sharply **7** rap over the knuckles to reprimand ▷ n **8** a sharp quick blow or the sound produced by it **9** a fast rhythmic monologue over a musical backing **10** a sharp rebuke or criticism **11** slang a legal charge: *a murder rap* **12** take the rap slang to suffer the punishment for a crime, whether guilty or not [probably from Old Norse] ❭ **rapper** n

rap² n not care a rap to not care in the least: *she didn't care a rap for us* [probably from *ropaire*, counterfeit coin formerly current in Ireland]

rapacious adj **1** greedy or grasping **2** (of animals or birds) living by catching prey [Latin *rapax*] ❭ **rapacity** n

Rapacki n Adam. 1909–70, Polish politician: foreign minister (1956–68): proposed (1957) the denuclearization of Poland, Czechoslovakia, East Germany, and West Germany (the **Rapacki Plan**): rejected by the West because of Soviet predominance in conventional weapons

Rapallo n a port and resort in NW Italy, in Liguria on the **Gulf of Rapallo** (an inlet of the Ligurian Sea): scene of the signing of two treaties after World War I. Pop: 29 159 (2001)

Rapa Nui n the Polynesian name for **Easter Island**

r

rape¹ *vb* **raping, raped 1** to force (someone) to submit to sexual intercourse ▷ *n* **2** the act of raping **3** any violation or abuse: *the rape of the country's natural resources* [Latin *rapere* to seize] **> rapist** *n*

rape² *n* a yellow-flowered plant cultivated for its seeds, **rapeseed**, which yield a useful oil, **rape oil**, and as a fodder plant [Latin *rapum* turnip]

Raphael *n* **1** *Bible* one of the archangels; the angel of healing and the guardian of Tobias (Tobit 3:17; 5–12). Feast day: Sept 29 **2** original name *Raffaello Santi* or *Sanzio*. 1483–1520, Italian painter and architect, regarded as one of the greatest artists of the High Renaissance. His many paintings include the *Sistine Madonna* (?1513) and the *Transfiguration* (unfinished, 1520) **> Raphaelesque** *adj*

rapid *adj* **1** (of an action) taking or lasting a short time **2** acting or moving quickly: *a rapid advance* [Latin *rapidus*] **> rapidly** *adv* **> rapidity** *n*

rapid eye movement *n* the movement of the eyeballs while a person is dreaming

rapids *pl n* part of a river where the water is very fast and turbulent

rapier (ray-pyer) *n* a long narrow two-edged sword [Old French *espee rapiere* rasping sword]

rapine (rap-pine) *n* pillage or plundering [Latin *rapina*]

rapport (rap-pore) *n* a sympathetic relationship or understanding [French]

rapprochement (rap-prosh-mong) *n* a re-establishment of friendly relations: *the policy of rapprochement with Eastern Europe* [French]

rapscallion *n* old-fashioned a rascal or rogue [earlier *rascallion*]

rap sheet *n* chiefly US and Canad informal a police record of an individual's criminal history

rapt *adj* **1** totally engrossed: *rapt attention* **2** arising from or showing rapture: *with a rapt look on his face* [Latin *raptus* carried away]

raptor *n* any bird of prey [Latin: robber] **> raptorial** *adj*

rapture *n* **1** extreme happiness or delight **2** raptures ecstatic joy: *they will be in raptures over the rugged scenery* [Latin *raptus* carried away] **> rapturous** *adj*

rare¹ *adj* **1** uncommon or unusual: *a rare plant* **2** not happening or done very often: *a rare appearance in London* **3** of uncommonly high quality: *a rare beauty* **4** (of air at high altitudes) having low density; thin [Latin *rarus* sparse]

rare² *adj* (of meat) very lightly cooked [Old English *hrēr*]

rarebit *n* short for **Welsh rarebit**

rare earth *n chem* **1** any oxide of a lanthanide **2** Also called: **rare-earth element** any element of the lanthanide series

rarefied (rare-if-ide) *adj* **1** highly specialized: *the rarefied world of classical ballet* **2** (of air) thin **3** exalted in character: *the rarefied heights of academic excellence*

rarely *adv* **1** hardly ever **2** to an unusual degree; exceptionally

USAGE Since *rarely* means *hardly ever*, one should not say something *rarely ever* happens.

raring *adj* **raring to do something** keen and willing to do something [*rare*, variant of REAR²]

rarity *n, pl* **-ties 1** something that is valuable because it is unusual **2** the state of being rare

Rarotonga *n* an island in the S Pacific, in the SW Cook Islands: the chief island of the group. Chief settlement: Avarua. Pop: 12 188 (2001). Area: 67 sq km (26 sq miles)

rascal *n* **1** a scoundrel or rogue **2** a mischievous child [Old French *rascaille* rabble] **> rascally** *adj*

rase *vb* **rasing, rased** same as **raze**

rash¹ *adj* acting or done without proper thought or consideration; hasty: *rash actions* [Old High German *rasc* hurried, clever] **> rashly** *adv* **> rashness** *n*

rash² *n* **1** an outbreak of spots or patches on the skin, caused by illness or allergy **2** an outbreak of occurrences:

a rash of censorship trials [Old French *rasche*]

rasher *n* a thin slice of bacon [origin unknown]

Rashid *n* a town in N Egypt, on the Nile delta. Former name: **Rosetta**

Rasht *or* **Resht** *n* a city in NW Iran, near the Caspian Sea: agricultural and commercial centre in a rice-growing area. Pop: 586 000 (2005 est)

Rask *n* **Rasmus Christian**. 1787–1832, Danish philologist. He pioneered comparative philology with his work on Old Norse (1818)

Rasmussen *n* **Knud Johan Victor**. 1879–1933, Danish arctic explorer and ethnologist. He led several expeditions through the Arctic in support of his theory that the North American Indians were originally migrants from Asia

rasp *n* **1** a harsh grating noise **2** a coarse file with rows of raised teeth ▷ *vb* **3** to say or speak in a grating voice **4** to make a harsh grating noise **5** to scrape or rub (something) roughly **6** to irritate (one's nerves) [Old French *raspe*]

raspberry *n, pl* **-ries 1** the red fruit of a prickly shrub of Europe and North America **2** informal a spluttering noise made with the tongue and lips to express contempt: *she blew a loud raspberry* [origin unknown]

Rasputin *n* **Grigori Efimovich**. ?1871–1916, Siberian peasant monk, notorious for his debauchery, who wielded great influence over Tsarina Alexandra. He was assassinated by a group of Russian noblemen

Rastafarian *or* **Rasta** *n* **1** a believer in a religion of Jamaican origin that regards Ras Tafari, the former emperor of Ethiopia, Haile Selassie, as God ▷ *adj* **2** of Rastafarians

raster *n* **1** an image consisting of rows of pixel information, such as a JPEG, GIF etc. **2** a pattern of horizontal scanning lines traced by an electron beam, esp. on a television screen [from German *Raster* screen]

rasterize *vb* to convert (a digitized image) into a form that can be printed or represented on a VDU

rat *n* **1** a long-tailed rodent, similar to but larger than a mouse **2** informal someone who is disloyal or treacherous **3 smell a rat** to detect something suspicious ▷ *vb* **ratting**, **ratted 4 rat on a** to betray (someone): *good friends don't rat on each other* **b** to go back on (an agreement): *his ex-wife claims he ratted on their divorce settlement* **5** to hunt and kill rats [Old English *ræt*]

ratafia (rat-a-fee-a) *n* **1** a liqueur made from fruit **2** an almond-flavoured biscuit [West Indian Creole French]

rat-arsed *adj* Brit and Austral slang drunk

rat-a-tat *or* **rat-a-tat-tat** *n* a repeated knocking or tapping sound

ratatouille (rat-a-twee) *n* a vegetable casserole made of stewed tomatoes, aubergines, etc. [French]

ratbag *n* slang an eccentric, stupid, or unreliable person

ratchet *n* **1** a device in which a toothed rack or wheel is engaged by a pivoted lever which permits motion in one direction only **2** the toothed rack or wheel in such a device **3** to operate using a ratchet **4** (usually foll. by *up* or *down*) to increase or decrease, esp. irreversibly: *Hitchcock ratchets up the tension once again* [French *rochet*]

rate¹ *n* **1** a quantity or amount considered in relation to or measured against another quantity or amount: *he was publishing at the rate of about 10 books a year* **2** a price or charge with reference to a standard or scale: *an exchange rate* **3** the speed of progress or change: *crime is increasing at an alarming rate* **4** a charge made per unit for a commodity or service **5** See **rates 6** relative quality: *a third-rate power* **7 at any rate** in any case ▷ *vb* **rating, rated 8** to assign a position on a scale of relative values: *he is rated as one of the top caterers in the country* **9** to estimate the value of: *we rate your services highly* **10** to consider or regard: *it could hardly be rated a success* **11** to be worthy of: *it barely rates a mention* **12** informal to have a high opinion of: *the cognoscenti have always rated his political skills* [Medieval Latin *rata*]

rate² *vb* **rating, rated** to scold or criticize severely [origin unknown]

rateable *adj* **1** able to be rated or evaluated **2** liable to payment of rates

rateable value *n* (in Britain) a fixed value assigned to a property, used to assess the rates due on it

rate-cap *vb* **-capping, -capped** (formerly in Britain) to put an upper limit on the rates charged by a local council **> rate-capping** *n*

ratepayer *n* a person who pays local rates on a building

rates *pl n* (in some countries) a tax on property levied by a local authority

Rathenau *n* Walther. 1867–1922, German industrialist and statesman: he organized the German war industries during World War I, became minister of reconstruction (1921) and of foreign affairs (1922), and was largely responsible for the treaty of Rapallo with Russia. His assassination by right-wing extremists caused a furore

rather *adv* **1** fairly: *that was a rather narrow escape* **2** to a limited extent: *I rather thought that was the case* **3** more truly or appropriately: *they tend to be cat rather than dog people* **4** more willingly: *I would rather go straight home* ▷ *interj* **5** an expression of strong affirmation: *Is it worth seeing? — Rather!* [Old English hrathor, comparative of hrathe ready, quick]

USAGE Both *would* and *had* are used with *rather* in sentences such as *I would rather* (or *had rather*) *go to the film than to the play. Had rather* is less common and now widely regarded as slightly old-fashioned.

ratify *vb* **-fies, -fying, -fied** to give formal approval to: *they ratified the treaty* [Latin ratus fixed + facere to make] **> ratification** *n*

rating *n* **1** a valuation or assessment **2** a classification according to order or grade **3** a noncommissioned sailor **4 ratings** the size of the audience for a TV or radio programme

ratio *n, pl* **-tios 1** the relationship between two numbers or amounts expressed as a proportion: *a ratio of one instructor to every five pupils* **2** *maths* a quotient of two numbers or quantities [Latin: a reckoning]

ration *n* **1** a fixed allowance of something that is scarce, such as food or petrol in wartime **2 rations** a fixed daily allowance of food, such as that given to a soldier ▷ *vb* **3** to restrict the distribution of (something): *the government has rationed petrol* **4** to distribute a fixed amount of (something) to each person in a group [Latin ratio reckoning] **> rationing** *n*

rational *adj* **1** reasonable or sensible **2** using reason or logic in thinking out a problem **3** capable of reasoning: *man is a rational being* **4** sane: *rational behaviour* **5** *maths* able to be expressed as a ratio of two integers: *a rational number* [Latin rationalis] **> rationality** *n* **> rationally** *adv*

rationale (rash-a-nahl) *n* the reason for an action or belief

rationalism *n* the philosophy that regards reason as the only basis for beliefs or actions **> rationalist** *n* **> rationalistic** *adj*

rationalize *or* **-ise** *vb* **-izing, -ized** *or* **-ising, -ised 1** to find reasons to justify or explain (one's actions) **2** to apply logic or reason to (something) **3** to get rid of unnecessary equipment or staff to make (a business) more efficient **> rationalization** *or* **-isation** *n*

rational number *n* any real number that can be expressed in the form *a/b*, where *a* and *b* are integers and *b* is not zero, as 7 or 7/3

Ratisbon *n* the former English name for **Regensburg**

ratpack *n slang* the members of the press who pursue celebrities and give wide coverage of their private lives: *the royal ratpack*

rat race *n* a continual routine of hectic competitive activity: *get out of the rat race for a while*

rattan *n* a climbing palm with tough stems used for wickerwork and canes [Malay rōtan]

ratter *n* a dog or cat that catches and kills rats

Rattigan *n* Sir Terence Mervyn. 1911–77, English playwright. His plays include *The Winslow Boy* (1946), *Separate Tables* (1954), and *Ross* (1960)

rattle *vb* **-tling, -tled 1** to make a rapid succession of short sharp sounds, such as when loose pellets are shaken in a container **2** to send, move, or drive with such a sound: *rain rattled against the window* **3** to shake briskly causing sharp sounds **4** *informal* to frighten or confuse **5 rattle off** *or* **out** to recite perfunctorily or rapidly **6 rattle on** *or* **away** to talk quickly and at length about something unimportant **7 rattle through** to do (something) very quickly: *she rattled through a translation* ▷ *n* **8** a rapid succession of short sharp sounds **9** a baby's toy filled with small pellets that rattle when shaken [Middle Dutch ratelen] **> rattly** *adj*

Rattle *n* Sir Simon. born 1955, English conductor. Principal conductor (1980–91) and music director (1991–98) of the City of Birmingham Symphony Orchestra; chief conductor of the Berlin Philharmonic Orchestra from 2002

rattlesnake *n* a poisonous snake with loose horny segments on the tail that make a rattling sound

rattletrap *n informal* a broken-down old vehicle

rattling *adv informal, old-fashioned* very: *a rattling good yarn*

ratty *adj* **-tier, -tiest** *informal* **1** cross and irritable **2** (of the hair) straggly and greasy **> rattily** *adv* **> rattiness** *n*

Ratushinskaya *n* Irina. born 1954, Russian poet and writer: imprisoned (1983–86) in a Soviet labour camp on charges of subversion. Her publications include *Poems* (1984), *Grey is the Colour of Hope* (1988), and *The Odessans* (1992)

raucous *adj* loud and harsh [Latin raucus]

raunchy *adj* **-chier, -chiest** *slang* sexy or earthy [origin unknown]

Rauschenberg *n* Robert. 1925–2008, US artist; one of the foremost exponents of pop art

ravage *vb* **-vaging, -vaged 1** to cause extensive damage to ▷ *n* **2 ravages** the damaging effects: *the ravages of weather and pollution* [Old French ravir to snatch away]

rave *vb* **raving, raved 1** to talk in a wild or incoherent manner **2** *informal* to write or speak (about) with great enthusiasm ▷ *n* **3** *informal* an enthusiastically favourable review **4** *slang* a professionally organized large-scale party with electronic dance music **5** a name given to various types of dance music, such as techno, that feature a fast electronic rhythm [probably from Old French resver to wander]

ravel *vb* **-velling, -velled** *or US* **-veling, -veled 1** to tangle or become entangled **2** (of a fabric) to fray out in loose ends; unravel [Middle Dutch ravelen]

Ravel *n* Maurice (Joseph). 1875–1937, French composer, noted for his use of unresolved dissonances and mastery of tone colour. His works include *Gaspard de la Nuit* (1908) and *Le Tombeau de Couperin* (1917) for piano, *Boléro* (1928) for orchestra, and the ballet *Daphnis et Chloé* (1912)

raven *n* **1** a large bird of the crow family with shiny black feathers ▷ *adj* **2** (of hair) shiny black [Old English hræfn]

ravening *adj* (of animals) hungrily searching for prey

Ravenna *n* a city and port in NE Italy, in Emilia-Romagna: capital of the Western Roman Empire from 402 to 476, of the Ostrogoths from 493 to 526, and of the Byzantine exarchate from 584 to 751; famous for its ancient mosaics. Pop: 134 631 (2001)

ravenous *adj* **1** very hungry **2** ravening [Old French ravineux] **> ravenously** *adv*

raver *n slang* **1** *Brit, Austral and S African* a person who leads a wild or uninhibited social life **2** a person who enjoys rave music and goes to raves

ravine (rav-veen) *n* a deep narrow steep-sided valley worn by a stream [Old French: torrent]

raving adj 1 delirious 2 informal great or exceptional: a raving beauty ▷ adv 3 to an excessive degree: raving mad ▷ n 4 ravings frenzied or wildly extravagant talk

ravioli pl n small squares of pasta with a savoury filling, such as meat or cheese [Italian]

ravish vb 1 to enrapture or delight: tourists ravished by our brilliant costumes 2 literary to rape [Latin rapere to seize] > **ravishment** n

ravishing adj lovely or delightful > **ravishingly** adv

raw adj 1 (of food) not cooked 2 in an unfinished or unrefined state: raw sewage 3 not selected or modified: raw data 4 (of the skin or a wound) painful, with the surface scraped away 5 untrained or inexperienced: a raw recruit 6 (of the weather) harshly cold and damp 7 frank or realistic: a raw reality 8 raw deal informal unfair or dishonest treatment ▷ n 9 in the raw a informal naked b in a natural and uncivilized state: to see life in the raw 10 on the raw Brit informal sensitive to upset: my nerves are on the raw today [Old English hrēaw]

Rawalpindi n an ancient city in N Pakistan: interim capital of Pakistan (1959–67) during the building of Islamabad. Pop: 1 794 000 (2005 est)

rawboned adj having a lean bony physique

rawhide n 1 untanned hide 2 a whip or rope made of strips of this

Rawlplug n trademark a short fibre or plastic tube used to provide a fixing in a wall for a screw

Rawsthorne n Alan. 1905–71, English composer, whose works include three symphonies, several concertos, and a set of Symphonic Studies (1939)

ray¹ n 1 a narrow beam of light 2 any of a set of lines spreading from a central point 3 a slight indication: a ray of hope 4 maths a straight line extending from a point 5 a thin beam of electromagnetic radiation or particles 6 any of the spines that support the fin of a fish [Old French rai]

ray² n a sea fish related to the sharks, with a flattened body and a long whiplike tail [Old French raie]

ray³ n music (in tonic sol-fa) the second note of any ascending major scale

Ray¹ n Cape Ray a promontory in SW Newfoundland, Canada

Ray² n 1 John. 1627–1705, English naturalist. He originated natural botanical classification and the division of flowering plants into monocotyledons and dicotyledons 2 Man, real name Emmanuel Rudnitsky. 1890–1976, US surrealist photographer 3 Satyajit. 1921–92, Indian film director, noted for his Apu trilogy (1955–59)

Rayleigh n Lord, title of John William Strutt, 1842–1919, British physicist. He discovered argon (1894) with Ramsay and made important contributions to the theory of sound, the theory of scattering of radiation, etc. Nobel prize for physics 1904

rayon n a textile fibre or fabric made from cellulose [French]

raze or **rase** vb **razing, razed** or **rasing, rased** to destroy (buildings or a town) completely [Old French raser]

razoo n, pl **-zoos** Austral and NZ informal an imaginary coin: we haven't got a brass razoo [origin unknown]

razor n an implement with a sharp blade, used for shaving [Old French raseor]

razorbill n a black-and-white sea bird with a stout sideways flattened bill

razor shell n 1 a burrowing shellfish with a long narrow shell 2 this shell

razor wire n strong wire with pieces of sharp metal set across it at intervals

razzle-dazzle or **razzmatazz** n slang 1 noisy or showy fuss or activity 2 a spree or frolic [rhyming compound from dazzle]

Rb chem rubidium

RC 1 Red Cross 2 Roman Catholic

Rd road

re¹ prep with reference to [Latin res thing]

re² n music same as ray³

Re chem rhenium

RE (in Britain) 1 Religious Education 2 Royal Engineers

re- prefix 1 (used with many main words to mean) repetition of an action: remarry 2 (used with many main words to mean) return to a previous condition: renew [Latin]

reach vb 1 to arrive at or get to (a place) 2 to make a movement (towards), as if to grasp or touch: she reached for her bag 3 to succeed in touching: I can't reach that shelf unless I stand on a chair 4 to make contact or communication with: to reach a wider audience 5 to extend as far as (a point or place): to reach the ceiling 6 to come to (a certain condition or situation): to reach a compromise 7 to arrive at or amount to (an amount or value): temperatures in Greece reached 35° yesterday 8 informal to give (something to a person) with the outstretched hand ▷ n 9 the extent or distance of reaching: within easy reach 10 the range of influence or power: it symbolized America's global reach 11 reaches a section of river, land, or sky: the quieter reaches of the upper Thames [Old English rǣcan] > **reachable** adj

reach-me-down adj Brit informal cheap and ready-made or second-hand: a reach-me-down suit

reacquaint vb reacquaint oneself with or become reacquainted with to get to know (someone or something) again

react vb 1 (of a person or thing) to act in response to another person, a stimulus, or a situation 2 react against to act in an opposing or contrary manner 3 chem to undergo a chemical reaction 4 physics to exert an equal force in the opposite direction to an acting force [Late Latin reagere]

reactance n electronics the resistance to the flow of an alternating current caused by the inductance or capacitance of the circuit

reactant n a substance that participates in a chemical reaction

reaction n 1 a physical or emotional response to a stimulus 2 any action resisting another 3 opposition to change 4 med any effect produced by a drug or by a substance (allergen) to which a person is allergic 5 chem a process that involves changes in the structure and energy content of atoms, molecules, or ions 6 the equal and opposite force that acts on a body whenever it exerts a force on another body 7 reactions someone's ability to act in response to something that happens

USAGE Reaction is used to refer both to an instant response (her reaction was one of amazement) and to a considered response in the form of a statement (the Minister gave his reaction to the court's decision). Some people think this second use is incorrect.

reactionary adj 1 opposed to political or social change ▷ n, pl **-aries** 2 a person opposed to radical change

reactivate vb **-vating, -vated** to make (something) active again > **reactivation** n

reactive adj 1 readily taking part in chemical reactions: ozone is a highly reactive form of oxygen gas 2 of or having a reactance 3 responsive to stimulus > **reactively** adv > **reactivity** n

reactor n short for nuclear reactor

read vb **reading, read** 1 to look at and understand or take in (written or printed matter) 2 to look at and say aloud 3 to have a certain wording: the memorandum read as follows 4 to interpret in a specified way: it can be read as satire 5 to interpret the significance or meaning of: an astrologer who reads Tarot 6 to register or show: the meter reads 100 7 to make out the true nature or mood of: she had read his thoughts 8 to interpret (signs, characters, etc.) other than by visual means: to read Braille 9 to have sufficient knowledge of (a language) to understand the written word 10 to undertake a course of study in (a subject): to *read economics* **11** to gain knowledge by reading: *he read about the war* **12** to hear and understand, esp. when using a two-way radio: *we are reading you loud and clear* **13** *computers* to obtain (data) from a storage device, such as magnetic tape ▷ *n* **14** matter suitable for reading: *this book is a very good read* **15** a spell of reading ▶ See also **read into, read out**, etc. [Old English *rǣdan* to advise, explain]

readable *adj* **1** enjoyable to read **2** (of handwriting or print) legible

Reade *n* Charles. 1814–84, English novelist: author of *The Cloister and the Hearth* (1861), a historical romance

reader *n* **1** a person who reads **2** a person who reads aloud in public **3** a person who reads and judges manuscripts sent to a publisher **4** a book of texts for those learning a foreign language **5** *Brit* a member of staff below a professor but above a senior lecturer at a university **6** a proofreader **7** short for **lay reader**

readership *n* all the readers collectively of a publication or author: *a new format would alienate its readership*

reading *n* **1** the act of reading **2** ability to read: *disputes over methods of teaching reading* **3** material for reading **4** a public recital of a literary work **5** a measurement indicated by a gauge or dial **6** *parliamentary procedure* one of the three stages in the passage of a bill through a legislative assembly **7** the form of a particular word or passage in a given text **8** an interpretation of a situation or something said ▷ *adj* **9** of or for reading: *reading glasses*

Reading *n* **1** a town in S England, in Reading unitary authority, Berkshire, on the River Thames: university (1892). Pop: 232 662 (2001) **2** a unitary authority in S England, in Berkshire. Pop: 144 100 (2003 est). Area: 37 sq km (14 sq miles)

read into *vb* to discover in a statement (meanings not intended by the speaker or writer): *one of the implications we must read into the work*

readjust *vb* to adapt to a new situation ▷ **readjustment** *n*

readmit *vb* **-mitting, -mitted** to let (a person or country) back into a place or organization ▷ **readmission** *n*

read out *vb* **1** to read (something) aloud **2** to retrieve (information) from a computer memory ▷ *n* **read-out** **3** the information retrieved from a computer memory

read up *vb* to read intensively about (a subject) in order to get information: *he had read up on the cases*

read-write head *n computers* an electromagnet that can both read and write information on a magnetic tape or disk

ready *adj* **readier, readiest 1** prepared for use or action **2** prompt or eager: *the ready use of corporal punishment* **3** quick or intelligent: *a ready wit* **4** ready to on the point of or liable to: *ready to pounce* **5** easily available: *his ready tears* ▷ *n* **6** *informal* same as **ready money 7** at the ready poised for use: *with pen at the ready* ▷ *vb* **readies, readying, readied 8** to make ready; prepare [Old English *(ge)rǣde*] ▷ **readily** *adv* ▷ **readiness** *n*

ready-made *adj* **1** for immediate use by any customer **2** extremely convenient or ideally suited: *a ready-made audience*

ready money *n* cash for immediate use. Also: **the ready, the readies**

reaffirm *vb* to state again ▷ **reaffirmation** *n*

reafforest *vb* to plant new trees in (an area that was formerly forested) ▷ **reafforestation** *n*

Reagan *n* Ronald. 1911–2004, US film actor and Republican statesman: Governor of California (1966–74): 40th president of the US (1981–89)

reagent (ree-**age**-ent) *n* a chemical substance that reacts with another, used to detect the presence of the other

real¹ *adj* **1** existing or occurring in the physical world **2** actual: *the real agenda* **3** important or serious: *the real challenge* **4** rightly so called: *a real friend* **5** genuine: *the council has no real authority* **6** (of food or drink) made in a traditional way to ensure the best flavour **7** *maths* involving or containing real numbers alone **8** relating

to immovable property such as land or buildings: *real estate* **9** *econ* (of prices or incomes) considered in terms of purchasing power rather than nominal currency value **10 the real thing** the genuine article, not a substitute or imitation [Latin *res* thing]

real² *n* a former small Spanish or Spanish-American silver coin [Spanish, literally: royal]

real ale *n chiefly Brit* beer that has fermented in the barrel

real estate *n* immovable property, esp. land and houses

realignment (ree-a-**line**-ment) *n* a new arrangement or organization: *there will be a realignment of party allegiances*

realism *n* **1** awareness or acceptance of things as they are, as opposed to the abstract or ideal **2** a style in art or literature that attempts to show the world as it really is **3** *philosophy* the theory that physical objects continue to exist whether they are perceived or not ▷ **realist** *n* ▷ **realistic** *adj* ▷ **realistically** *adv*

reality *n, pl* **-ties 1** the state of things as they are or appear to be, rather than as one might wish them to be **2** something that is real **3** the state of being real **4 in reality** in fact

reality TV *n* television programmes focusing on members of the public living in conditions created especially by the programme makers

realize *or* **-lise** *vb* **-lizing, -lized** *or* **-lising, -lised 1** to be aware of or grasp the significance of **2** to achieve (a plan or ambition) **3** to convert (property or goods) into cash **4** (of goods or property) to sell for (a certain sum): *this table realized a large sum at auction* **5** to produce (a complete work of art) from an idea or draft ▷ **realizable** *or* **-lisable** *adj* ▷ **realization** *or* **-lisation** *n*

really *adv* **1** truly: *really boring* **2** in reality: *it's really quite harmless* ▷ *interj* **3** an exclamation of dismay, doubt, or surprise

---

USAGE See at **very.**

---

realm *n* **1** a kingdom **2** a field of interest or study: *the realm of science* [Old French *reialme*]

real number *n* any rational or irrational number

real tennis *n* an ancient form of tennis played in a four-walled indoor court

real-time *adj* (of a computer system) processing data as it is received

realtor *n US and Canad* an estate agent [from a trademark]

realty *n* same as **real estate**

ream *n* **1** a number of sheets of paper, now equal to 500 or 516 sheets (20 quires) **2** *informal* a large quantity (of written material): *reams of verse* [Arabic *rizmah* bale]

reap *vb* **1** to cut and gather (a harvest) **2** to receive as the result of a previous activity: *reap the benefits of our efforts* [Old English *riopan*]

reaper *n* **1** a person who reaps or a machine for reaping **2 the grim reaper** death

reappear *vb* to come back into view ▷ **reappearance** *n*

reappraise *vb* **-praising, -praised** to consider or review (something) to see if changes are needed ▷ **reappraisal** *n*

rear¹ *n* **1** the back part **2** the area or position that lies at the back **3** *informal* the buttocks **4 bring up the rear** to come last ▷ *adj* **5** of or in the rear: *the rear carriage* [Old French *rer*]

rear² *vb* **1** to care for and educate (children) until maturity **2** to breed (animals) or grow (plants) **3** (of a horse) to lift the front legs in the air and stand nearly upright **4** to place or lift (something) upright [Old English *rǣran*]

rear admiral *n* a high-ranking naval officer

Reardon *n* Ray. born 1932, Welsh snooker player: world champion 1970, 1973–76, 1978

rearguard *n* **1** the troops who protect the rear of a military formation ▷ *adj* **2 rearguard action** an effort to prevent or postpone something that is unavoidable

rear light *or* **rear lamp** *n* a red light, usually one of a pair, attached to the rear of a vehicle. Also called: **tail-light, tail lamp**

rearm *vb* **1** to arm again **2** to equip with better weapons › **rearmament** *n*

rearmost *adj* nearest the back

rearrange *vb* **-ranging, -ranged** to organize differently › **rearrangement** *n*

rear-view mirror *n* a mirror on a motor vehicle enabling the driver to see the traffic behind

rearward *adj* **1** in the rear ▷ *adv* also: **rearwards 2** towards the rear

reason *n* **1** a cause or motive for a belief or action: *he had two reasons for his dark mood* **2** the ability to think or argue rationally **3** an argument in favour of or a justification for something: *there is every reason to encourage people to keep fit* **4** sanity **5 by reason of** because of **6 within reason** within moderate or justifiable bounds **7 it stands to reason** it is logical or obvious ▷ *vb* **8** to think logically in forming conclusions **9** reason with to persuade by logical arguments into doing something **10** reason out to work out (a problem) by reasoning [Latin *reri* to think]

> **USAGE** The expression *the reason is because...* should be avoided. Instead one should say either *this is because...* or *the reason is that...*

reasonable *adj* **1** sensible **2** not making unfair demands **3** logical: *a reasonable explanation* **4** moderate in price **5** average: *a reasonable amount of luck* › **reasonably** *adv* › **reasonableness** *n*

reasoned *adj* well thought out or well presented: *a reasoned explanation*

reasoning *n* **1** the process of drawing conclusions from facts or evidence **2** the conclusions reached in this way

reassemble *vb* **-bling, -bled** to put back together again

reassert *vb* **1** to state or declare again **2** reassert oneself to become significant or noticeable again: *reality had reasserted itself*

reassess *vb* to reconsider the value or importance of › **reassessment** *n*

reassure *vb* **-assuring, -assured** to relieve (someone) of anxieties › **reassurance** *n* › **reassuring** *adj*

rebate¹ *n* a refund or discount [Old French *rabattre* to beat down]

rebate² or **rabbet** *n* **1** a groove cut into a piece of timber into which another piece fits ▷ *vb* **-bating, -bated** or **-beting, -beted 2** to cut a rebate in **3** to join (pieces of timber) with a rebate [Old French *rabattre* to beat down]

rebel *vb* **-belling, -belled 1** to fight against the ruling power **2** to reject accepted conventions of behaviour ▷ *n* **3** a person who rebels **4** a person who rejects accepted conventions of behaviour ▷ *adj* **5** rebelling: *rebel councillors* [Latin *re-* again + *bellum* war]

rebellion *n* **1** organized opposition to a government or other authority involving the use of violence **2** nonviolent opposition to a government or other authority: *a Tory backbenchers' rebellion* **3** rejection of accepted conventions of behaviour [Latin *rebellio*]

rebellious *adj* rebelling or showing a tendency towards rebellion › **rebelliously** *adv*

rebirth *n* a revival or renaissance: *the rebirth of their nation*

reboot *vb* to shut down and then restart (a computer system)

rebore or **reboring** *n* the boring of a cylinder to restore its true shape

reborn *adj* active again after a period of inactivity

rebound *vb* **1** to spring back from a sudden impact **2** (of a plan or action) to misfire so as to hurt the person responsible ▷ *n* **3** the act of rebounding **4 on the rebound** *informal* while recovering from rejection: *she married him on the rebound*

rebrand *vb* to change or update the image of (an organization or product)

rebuff *vb* **1** to snub and reject an offer or suggestion ▷ *n*

2 a blunt refusal; snub [Old French *rebuffer*]

rebuild *vb* **-building, -built 1** to build (a building or town) again, after severe damage **2** to develop (something such as a business or relationship) again after destruction or damage

rebuke *vb* **-buking, -buked 1** to scold sternly ▷ *n* **2** a stern scolding [Old French *rebuker*]

rebus (ree-buss) *n*, *pl* **-buses** a puzzle consisting of pictures and symbols representing syllables and words [Latin: by things]

rebut *vb* **-butting, -butted** to prove that (a claim) is untrue [Old French *reboter*] › **rebuttal** *n*

rec *n* short for **recreation**

recalcitrant *adj* wilfully disobedient [Latin *re-* again + *calcitrare* to kick] › **recalcitrance** *n*

recall *vb* **1** to bring back to mind **2** to order to return **3** to annul or cancel ▷ *n* **4** the ability to remember things **5** an order to return

recant *vb* to take back (a former belief or statement) publicly [Latin *re-* again + *cantare* to sing] › **recantation** *n*

recap *informal vb* **-capping, -capped 1** to recapitulate ▷ *n* **2** a recapitulation

recapitulate *vb* **-lating, -lated** to restate the main points of (an argument or speech) [Late Latin *recapitulare*, literally: to put back under headings]

recapitulation *n* **1** the act of recapitulating **2** *music* the repeating of earlier themes, esp. in the final section of a movement

recapture *vb* **-turing, -tured 1** to relive vividly (a former experience or sensation): *recaptured some of those first feelings* **2** to capture again ▷ *n* **3** the act of recapturing

recast *vb* **-casting, -cast 1** to give a new form or shape to: *he found the organization wholly recast* **2** to change the actors or singers in (a play, musical, or opera) **3** to rework (a piece of writing or music): *she has recast most of my book*

recce *chiefly Brit slang vb* **-ceing, -ced** or **-ceed 1** to reconnoitre ▷ *n* **2** reconnaissance

recede *vb* **-ceding, -ceded 1** to withdraw from a point or limit: *the tide had receded* **2** to become more distant: *the threat of intervention had receded* **3** (of a man's hair) to stop growing at the temples and above the forehead **4** to slope backwards: *a receding chin* [Latin *recedere* to go back]

receipt *n* **1** a written acknowledgment that money or goods have been received **2** the act of receiving **3** receipts money taken in over a particular period by a shop or business [Old French *receite*]

receive *vb* **-ceiving, -ceived 1** to get (something offered or sent to one) **2** to experience: *he received a knife wound* **3** to greet (guests) **4** to have (an honour) bestowed: *he received the Order of the Garter* **5** to admit (a person) to a society or condition: *he was received into the Church* **6** to convert (incoming radio or television signals) into sounds or pictures **7** to be informed of (news) **8** to react to: *the article was well received* **9** to support or sustain (the weight of something) **10** *tennis etc.* to play at the other end from the server **11** *Brit and NZ* to buy and sell stolen goods [Latin *recipere*]

received *adj* generally accepted or believed: *contrary to received wisdom*

Received Pronunciation *n* the accent of standard Southern British English

receiver *n* **1** the detachable part of a telephone that is held to the ear **2** the equipment in a telephone, radio, or television that converts the incoming signals into sound or pictures **3** a person appointed by a court to manage property of a bankrupt **4** a person who receives stolen goods knowing they have been stolen

receivership *n law* the state of being administered by a receiver: *the company went into receivership*

recent *adj* **1** having happened lately **2** new [Latin *recens* fresh] › **recently** *adv*

Recent *adj* same as **Holocene**

receptacle *n* **1** an object used to contain something **2** *botany* the enlarged or modified tip of the flower stalk that bears the flower [Latin *receptaculum* store-place]

reception *n* **1** an area in an office, hotel, etc., where visitors are received or reservations dealt with **2** a formal party for guests, esp. after a wedding **3** the manner in which something is received: *an enthusiastic reception* **4** the act of formally welcoming **5** *radio, television* the quality of a received broadcast: *the reception was poor*

receptionist *n* a person employed to receive guests or clients and deal with reservations and appointments

reception room *n* a room in a private house suitable for entertaining guests

receptive *adj* willing to consider and accept new ideas or suggestions **> receptivity** or **receptiveness** *n*

receptor *n physiol* a sensory nerve ending that changes specific stimuli into nerve impulses

recess *n* **1** a space, such as an alcove, set back in a wall **2** a holiday between sessions of work **3 recesses** secret hidden places: *the recesses of her brain* **4** *US and Canad* a break between classes at a school [Latin *recessus* a retreat]

recessed *adj* hidden or placed in a recess

recession *n* **1** a period of economic difficulty when little is being bought or sold **2** the act of receding

recessional *n* a hymn sung as the clergy and choir withdraw after a church service

recessive *adj* **1** tending to recede **2** *genetics* (in a pair of genes) designating a gene that has a characteristic which will only be passed on if the other gene has the same characteristic

recharge *vb* **-charging, -charged** to cause (a battery) to take in and store electricity again **> rechargeable** *adj*

recherché (rish-air-shay) *adj* **1** studiedly refined or elegant **2** known only to connoisseurs [French: thoroughly sought after]

recidivism *n* habitual relapse into crime [Latin *recidivus* falling back] **> recidivist** *n, adj*

Recife *n* a port at the easternmost point of Brazil on the Atlantic: capital of Pernambuco state; built partly on an island, with many waterways and bridges. Pop: 3 527 000 (2005 est). Former name: **Pernambuco**

recipe *n* **1** a list of ingredients and directions for making a particular dish **2** a method for achieving something: *a recipe for industrial chaos* [Latin, literally: take (it)!]

recipient *n* a person who receives something

reciprocal (ris-sip-pro-kl) *adj* **1** done or felt by each of two people or groups to or about the other: *a reciprocal agreement* **2** given or done in return: *a reciprocal invitation* **3** *grammar* (of a pronoun) indicating that action is given and received by each subject, for example, *each other* in *they started to shout at each other* ▷ *n* **4** Also called: **inverse** *maths* a number or quantity that when multiplied by a given number or quantity gives a product of one: *the reciprocal of 2 is 0.5* [Latin *reciprocus* alternating] **> reciprocally** *adv*

reciprocate *vb* **-cating, -cated 1** to give or feel in return: *not everyone reciprocated his enthusiasm* **2** (of a machine part) to move backwards and forwards **> reciprocation** *n*

reciprocity *n* **1** reciprocal action or relation **2** a mutual exchange of commercial or other privileges

recital (ris-site-al) *n* **1** a musical performance by a soloist or soloists **2** the act of reciting something learned or prepared **3** a narration or description: *she plagued her with the recital of constant ailments and illnesses*

recitation *n* **1** the act of reciting poetry or prose from memory **2** something recited

recitative (ress-it-a-teev) *n* a narrative passage in an opera or oratorio, reflecting the natural rhythms of speech [Italian *recitativo*]

recite *vb* **-citing, -cited 1** to repeat (a poem or passage) aloud from memory before an audience **2** to give a detailed account of [Latin *recitare*]

reckless *adj* having no regard for danger or consequences: *reckless driving* [Old English *recceleās*]

Recklinghausen *n* an industrial city in NW Germany, in North Rhine-Westphalia on the N edge of the Ruhr.

Pop: 123 144 (2003 est)

reckon *vb* **1** *informal* to be of the opinion: *she reckoned she could find them* **2** to consider: *he reckoned himself a failure* **3** to calculate or compute **4** to expect **5 reckon with** to take into account: *there is this ancestral hatred to reckon with* **6 reckon without** to fail to take into account **7 reckon on** or **upon** to rely on or expect: *they can't reckon on your automatic support* [Old English *(ge)recenian* recount]

reckoning *n* **1** counting or calculating: *by his reckoning, he owed him money* **2** retribution for one's actions: *the moment of reckoning came* **3** settlement of an account or bill

reclaim *vb* **1** to get back possession of: *the club is now trying to reclaim the money from the blockaders* **2** to convert (unusable or submerged land) into land suitable for farming or building on **3** to recover (useful substances) from waste products [Latin *reclamare* to cry out] **> reclamation** *n*

recline *vb* **-clining, -clined** to rest in a leaning position [Latin *reclinare*]

reclining *adj* (of a seat) with a back that can be adjusted to slope at various angles

recluse *n* a person who lives alone and avoids people [Late Latin *recludere* to shut away] **> reclusive** *adj*

recognition *n* **1** the act of recognizing **2** acceptance or acknowledgment **3** formal acknowledgment of a government or of the independence of a country **4 in recognition of** as a token of thanks for

recognizance or **recognisance** (rik-og-nizz-anss) *n law* **a** an undertaking made before a court or magistrate to do something specified, such as to appear in court on a stated day **b** a sum of money promised as a guarantee of this undertaking [Old French *reconoissance*]

recognize or **-nise** *vb* **-nizing, -nized** or **-nising, -nised 1** to identify (a person or thing) as someone or something already known **2** to accept or be aware of (a fact or problem): *to recognize change* **3** to acknowledge formally the status or legality of (something or someone): *an organization recognized by the UN* **4** to show approval or appreciation of (something) **5** to make formal acknowledgment of (a claim or duty): *I must ask for her to be recognized as a hostile witness* [Latin *re-* again + *cognoscere* to know] **> recognizable** or **-nisable** *adj*

recoil *vb* **1** to jerk or spring back **2** to draw back in fear or horror **3** (of an action) to go wrong so as to hurt the person responsible ▷ *n* **4** the backward movement of a gun when fired **5** the act of recoiling [Old French *reculer*]

recollect *vb* to remember [Latin *recolligere* to gather again] **> recollection** *n*

recombinant (ree-kom-bin-ant) *adj genetics* produced by the combining of genetic material from more than one origin

recommend *vb* **1** to advise as the best course or choice **2** to praise or commend: *I would wholeheartedly recommend his books* **3** to make attractive or advisable: *she has everything to recommend her* [Latin *re-* again + *commendare* to commend] **> recommendation** *n*

recompense *vb* **-pensing, -pensed 1** to pay or reward for work or help **2** to compensate or make up for loss or injury ▷ *n* **3** compensation for loss or injury **4** reward or repayment [Latin *re-* again + *compensare* to balance]

reconcile *vb* **-ciling, -ciled 1** to make (two apparently conflicting things) compatible or consistent with each other: *in many cases science and religion are reconciled* **2** to re-establish friendly relations with (a person or people) or between (people) **3** to accept or cause to accept an unpleasant situation: *we reconciled ourselves to a change* [Latin *reconciliare*]

reconciliation *n* **1** the state of being reconciled **2** the act of reconciling people or groups **3** *S African* a political term emphasizing the need to acknowledge the wrongs of the past

recondite *adj formal* **1** requiring special knowledge **2** dealing with abstruse or profound subjects [Latin *reconditus* hidden away]

r

recondition *vb* to restore to good condition or working order: *a reconditioned engine* ⟩ **reconditioned** *adj*

reconnaissance (rik-kon-iss-anss) *n* **1** the process of obtaining information about the position and movements of an enemy **2** a preliminary inspection [French]

reconnoitre *or US* **reconnoiter** (rek-a-noy-ter) *vb* to make a reconnaissance of [obsolete French *reconnoître*]

reconsider *vb* to think about again, with a view to changing one's policy or course of action ⟩ **reconsideration** *n*

reconstitute *vb* **-tuting, -tuted 1** to reorganize in a slightly different form **2** to restore (dried food) to its former state by adding water ⟩ **reconstitution** *n*

reconstruct *vb* **1** to build again **2** to reorganize: *three works proved useful in reconstructing the training routine* **3** to form a picture of (a past event, esp. a crime) by piecing together evidence ⟩ **reconstruction** *n*

reconvene *vb* to gather together again after an interval: *we reconvene tomorrow*

record *n* (rek-ord) **1** a document or other thing that preserves information **2 records** information or data on a subject collected over a long period: *dental records* **3** a thin disc of a plastic material upon which sound has been recorded in a continuous spiral groove on each side **4** the best recorded achievement in some field: *her score set a Games record* **5** the known facts about a person's achievements **6** a list of crimes of which an accused person has previously been convicted **7** anything serving as evidence or as a memorial: *the First World War is a record of human folly* **8** *computers* a group of data or piece of information preserved as a unit in machine-readable form **9 for the record** for the sake of strict factual accuracy **10 go on record** to state one's views publicly **11 have a record** to have previous criminal convictions **12 off the record** not for publication **13 on record a** stated in a public document **b** publicly known ▷ *adj* **14** being the highest or lowest, or best or worst ever achieved: *record losses* ▷ *vb* (rik-kord) **15** to put in writing to preserve the true facts: *to record the minutes of a meeting* **16** to preserve (sound, TV programmes, etc.) on plastic disc, magnetic tape, etc., for reproduction on a playback device **17** to show or register [Latin *recordari* to remember]

recorded delivery *n* a postal service by which an official receipt is obtained for the posting and delivery of a letter or parcel

recorder *n* **1** a person or machine that records, esp. a video, cassette, or tape recorder **2** *music* a wind instrument, blown through the end, with finger-holes and a reedlike tone **3** (in England and Wales) a barrister or solicitor appointed to sit as a part-time judge in the crown court

recording *n* **1** something that has been recorded **2** the process of recording sounds or visual signals for later use

record player *n* a device for reproducing the sounds stored on a record

recount *vb* to tell the story or details of [Old French *reconter*]

re-count *vb* **1** to count again ▷ *n* **2** a second or further count, esp. of votes in an election

recoup (rik-koop) *vb* **1** to regain or make good (a loss) **2** to reimburse or compensate (someone) for a loss [Old French *recouper* to cut back] ⟩ **recoupment** *n*

recourse *n* **1 have recourse to** to turn to a source of help or course of action **2** a source of help or course of action that is turned to when in difficulty [Latin *re-* back + *currere* to run]

recover *vb* **1** (of a person) to regain health, spirits, or composure **2** to regain a former and better condition: *real wages have recovered from the recession* **3** to find again or obtain the return of (something lost) **4** to get back or make good (expense or loss) **5** to obtain (useful substances) from waste **6** *law* to gain (something) by the judgment of a court: *it should be possible to recover damages*

[Latin *recuperare*] ⟩ **recoverable** *adj*

recovery *n, pl* **-veries 1** the act of recovering from sickness, a shock, or a setback **2** restoration to a former and better condition **3** the regaining of something lost **4** the extraction of useful substances from waste

recreant *n archaic* a disloyal or cowardly person [Old French *recroire* to surrender]

re-create *vb* **-creating, -created** to make happen or exist again ⟩ **re-creation** *n*

recreation *n* an activity done for pleasure or relaxation [Latin *recreare* to refresh] ⟩ **recreational** *adj*

recreation ground *n* an area of publicly owned land where sports and games may be played

recrimination *n* accusations made by two people or groups about each other: *bitter recrimination* [Latin *re-* back + *criminari* to accuse] ⟩ **recriminatory** *adj*

recrudescence *n literary* an outbreak of trouble or a disease after a period of quiet [Latin *re-* again + *crudus* bloody, raw]

recruit *vb* **1** to enlist (people) for military service **2** to enrol or obtain (members or support) ▷ *n* **3** a newly joined member of a military service **4** a new member or supporter [French *recrute* new growth] ⟩ **recruitment** *n*

rectal *adj* of the rectum

rectangle *n* an oblong shape with four straight sides and four right angles [Latin *rectus* straight + *angulus* angle] ⟩ **rectangular** *adj*

rectify *vb* **-fies, -fying, -fied 1** to put right; correct **2** *chem* to separate (a substance) from a mixture by distillation **3** *electronics* to convert (alternating current) into direct current [Latin *rectus* straight + *facere* to make] ⟩ **rectification** *n* ⟩ **rectifier** *n*

rectilinear (rek-tee-lin-ee-er) *adj formal* **1** in a straight line **2** bounded by or formed of straight lines

rectitude *n* moral or religious correctness: *a model of rectitude* [Latin *rectus* right]

recto *n, pl* **-tos 1** the right-hand page of a book **2** the front of a sheet of printed paper [Latin: on the right]

rector *n* **1** *Church of England* a clergyman in charge of a parish **2** *RC Church* a cleric in charge of a college or congregation **3** *chiefly Brit* the head of certain academic institutions **4** (in Scotland) a high-ranking official in a university, elected by the students [Latin: director] ⟩ **rectorship** *n*

rectory *n, pl* **-ries** the house of a rector

rectum *n, pl* **-tums** *or* **-ta** the lower part of the alimentary canal, ending in the anus [Latin: straight]

recumbent *adj* lying down [Latin *recumbere* to lie back]

recuperate *vb* **-rating, -rated** to recover from illness or exhaustion [Latin *recuperare*] ⟩ **recuperation** *n* ⟩ **recuperative** *adj*

recur *vb* **-curring, -curred 1** to happen or occur again **2** (of a thought or feeling) to come back to the mind [Latin *re-* again + *currere* to run] ⟩ **recurrence** *n* ⟩ **recurrent** *adj* ⟩ **recurring** *adj*

recurring decimal *n* a rational number that contains a pattern of digits repeated indefinitely after the decimal point: *1 divided by 11 gives the recurring decimal 0.09090909...*

recusant (rek-yew-zant) *n* **1** *history* a Roman Catholic who did not attend the services of the Church of England **2** a person who refuses to obey authority [Latin *recusans* refusing] ⟩ **recusancy** *n*

recycle *vb* **-cling, -cled 1** to reprocess (something already used) for further use: *public demand for recycled paper* **2** to pass (a substance) through a system again for further use ⟩ **recyclable** *adj*

red *adj* **redder, reddest 1** of a colour varying from crimson to orange; of the colour of blood **2** reddish in colour or having parts or marks that are reddish: *red deer* **3** flushed in the face from anger or shame **4** (of the eyes) bloodshot **5** (of wine) made from black grapes and coloured by their skins ▷ *n* **6** the colour red; the colour of blood **7** anything red, such as red clothing or red paint: *she had dressed in red* **8 in the red** *informal* in debt **9** see **red**

informal to become very angry [Old English *rēad*]
> redness *n* **> reddish** *adj*

Red *informal* ▷ *n* **1** a Communist or socialist ▷ *adj*
2 Communist or socialist

red admiral *n* a butterfly with black wings with red and white markings

redback spider *n* a small venomous Australian spider with a red stripe on the back of the abdomen

red blood cell *n* same as **erythrocyte**

red-blooded *adj informal* vigorous or virile

redbreast *n* a robin

redbrick *adj* (of a British university) founded in the late 19th or early 20th century

Redbridge *n* a borough of NE Greater London: includes part of Epping Forest Pop: 245 100 (2003 est). Area: 56 sq km (22 sq miles)

Redcar and Cleveland *n* a unitary authority in NE England, in North Yorkshire: formerly (1975–96) part of Cleveland county. Pop: 139 100 (2003 est). Area: 240 sq km (93 sq miles)

red card *soccer* ▷ *n* **1** a piece of red pasteboard raised by a referee to indicate that a player has been sent off ▷ *vb*
red-card 2 to send off (a player)

red carpet *n* very special treatment given to an important guest

Red China *n* an unofficial name for (the People's Republic of) **China**

redcoat *n* **1** *history* a British soldier **2** *Canad informal* a Mountie

Red Crescent *n* the name and symbol used by the Red Cross in Muslim countries

Red Cross *n* an international organization (**Red Cross Society**) which helps victims of war or natural disaster

redcurrant *n* a very small red edible fruit that grows in bunches on a bush

red deer *n* a large deer of Europe and Asia, which has a reddish-brown coat and a short tail

Red Deer *n* **1** a town in S Alberta on the Red Deer River: trade centre for mixed farming, dairying region, and natural gas processing. Pop: 67 707 (2001) **2** a river in W Canada, in SW Alberta, flowing southeast into the South Saskatchewan River. Length: about 620 km (385 miles) **3** a river in W Canada, flowing east through **Red Deer Lake** into Lake Winnipegosis. Length: about 225 km (140 miles)

redden *vb* **1** to make or become red or redder **2** to blush

Redding *n* Otis. 1941–67, US soul singer and songwriter. His recordings include "Respect" (1965), *Dictionary of Soul* (1966), and "(Sittin' on) The Dock of the Bay" (1968)

Redditch *n* a town in W central England, in N Worcestershire: designated a new town in the mid-1960s; metal-working industries. Pop: 74 803 (2001)

redecorate *vb* to paint or wallpaper (a room) again
> redecoration *n*

redeem *vb* **1** to make up for **2** to reinstate (oneself) in someone's good opinion: *he missed a penalty but redeemed himself by setting up the winning goal* **3** *Christianity* (of Christ as Saviour) to free (humanity) from sin by death on the Cross **4** to buy back: *she didn't have the money to redeem it* **5** to pay off (a loan or debt) **6** to convert (bonds or shares) into cash **7** to exchange (coupons) for goods **8** to fulfil (a promise): *I vowed to abide by the bill and have redeemed my pledge* [Latin *re-* back + *emere* to buy] **> redeemable** *adj*
> redeemer *n*

Redeemer *n* the Redeemer *Christianity* Jesus Christ

redeeming *adj* making up for faults or deficiencies: *the soundtrack is the film's only redeeming feature*

redemption *n* **1** the act of redeeming **2** the state of being redeemed **3** *Christianity* deliverance from sin through the incarnation and death of Christ
> redemptive *adj*

redeploy *vb* to assign (people) to new positions or tasks
> redeployment *n*

redevelop *vb* to rebuild or renovate (an area or building)

> redeveloper *n* **> redevelopment** *n*

redfish *n, pl* **-fish** *or* **-fishes** *Canad* same as **kokanee**

red flag *n* **1** a symbol of revolution **2** a warning of danger

Redford *n* Robert. born 1936, US film actor and director. His films include (as actor) *Barefoot in the Park* (1966), *Butch Cassidy and the Sundance Kid* (1969), *The Sting* (1973), *All the President's Men* (1976), *Up Close and Personal* (1996), and (as director) *Ordinary People* (1980), *A River Runs Through It* (1992), and *The Horse Whisperer* (1998)

Redgrave *n* **1** Lynn. 1944–2010, British stage and film actress. Her films include *Georgy Girl* (1966), *The Happy Hooker* (1975), and *Gods and Monsters* (1999) **2** her father, Sir Michael. 1908–85, British stage and film actor. Among his films are *The Lady Vanishes* (1938), *The Dam Busters* (1955), *The Loneliness of the Long Distance Runner* (1963), and *The Go-Between* (1971) **3** Sir Steve. born 1962, British oarsman; won five gold medals in rowing events at consecutive Olympic Games (1984, 1988, 1992, 1996, 2000) **4** Vanessa. Elder daughter of Sir Michael Redgrave. born 1937, British stage and film actress, whose roles include performances in the films *Isadora* (1968), *Julia* (1977), *Howards End* (1992), *The Gathering Storm* (2002), and *Coriolanus* (2011): noted also for her active commitment to left-wing politics

red-handed *adj* catch someone red-handed to catch someone in the act of doing something wrong or illegal

red hat *n* the broad-brimmed crimson hat given to cardinals as the symbol of their rank

redhead *n* a person with reddish hair **> redheaded** *adj*

red herring *n* something which diverts attention from the main issue

red-hot *adj* **1** (of metal) glowing hot **2** extremely hot **3** very keen or excited **4** furious: *one of those red-hot blazes of temper* **5** very recent or topical: *red-hot information*

red-hot poker *n* a garden plant with spikes of red or yellow flowers

Red Indian *n, adj offensive* Native American

redirect *vb* **1** to send in a new direction or course **2** to send (mail) to a different address

redistribute *vb* **-uting, -uted** to share out in a different way: *to redistribute the world's wealth*

redistribution *n* **1** the act of redistributing **2** a revision of the number of seats that each province has in the Canadian House of Commons, made every ten years

red lead *n* a bright-red poisonous insoluble oxide of lead

red-letter day *n* a memorably important or happy occasion [from the red letters in ecclesiastical calendars to indicate saints' days]

red light *n* **1** a traffic signal to stop **2** a danger signal

red-light district *n* an area where many prostitutes work

red meat *n* meat, such as beef or lamb, that is dark brown when cooked

Redmond *n* John Edward. 1856–1918, Irish politician. He led the Parnellites from 1891 and helped to procure the Home Rule bill of 1912, but was considered too moderate by extreme nationalists

redo *vb* **-doing, -did, -done 1** to do over again in order to improve **2** *informal* to redecorate: *we should consider redoing some of the rooms*

redolent *adj* redolent of *or* with **1** reminiscent or suggestive of: *a castle redolent of historical novels* **2** smelling of: *the warm heavy air was redolent of sea and flowers* [Latin *redolens*] **> redolence** *n*

Redon *n* Odilon. 1840–1916, French symbolist painter and etcher. He foreshadowed the surrealists in his paintings of fantastic dream images

redouble *vb* **-bling, -bled 1** to make or become much greater: *the party will have to redouble its efforts* **2** *bridge* to double (an opponent's double)

redoubt *n* **1** a small fort defending a hill top or pass **2** a stronghold [French *redoute*]

redoubtable *adj* to be feared and respected: *the*

redoubtable Mr Brooks [Old French *redouter* to dread]
> redoubtably *adv*

redound *vb* **1 redound to** to have an advantageous or disadvantageous effect on: *individual rights redound to the common good* **2 redound on** *or* **upon** to recoil or rebound on [Latin *redundare* to stream over]

redox *n* a chemical reaction between two substances, in which one is oxidized and the other reduced

red pepper *n* **1** the red ripe fruit of the sweet pepper, eaten as a vegetable **2** same as **cayenne pepper**

redraft *vb* to write a second copy of (a letter, proposal, essay, etc.)

red rag *n* something that infuriates or provokes: *a red rag to businessmen* [so called because red objects supposedly infuriate bulls]

redress *vb* **1** to make amends for **2** to adjust in order to make fair or equal: *to redress the balance* **>** *n* **3** compensation or reparation **4** the setting right of a wrong [Old French *redrecier* to set up again]

Red River *n* **1** Also called: **Red River of the South** a river in the S central US, flowing east from N Texas through Arkansas into the Mississippi in Louisiana. Length: 1639 km (1018 miles) **2** a river in the northern US, flowing north as the border between North Dakota and Minnesota and into Lake Winnipeg, Canada. Length: 515 km (320 miles) **3** a river in SE Asia, rising in SW China in Yunnan province and flowing southeast across N Vietnam to the Gulf of Tongkin: the chief river of N Vietnam, with an extensive delta. Length: 500 km (310 miles). Vietnamese name: **Song Koi**

red salmon *n* a salmon with reddish flesh

Red Sea *n* a long narrow sea between Arabia and NE Africa, linked with the Mediterranean in the north by the Suez Canal and with the Indian Ocean in the south: occasionally reddish in appearance through algae. Area: 438 000 sq km (169 000 sq miles)

redshank *n* a large common European sandpiper with red legs

red shift *n* the appearance of lines in the spectrum of distant stars nearer the red end of the spectrum than on earth: used to calculate the velocity of objects in relation to the earth

redskin *n* informal, offensive a Native American [so called because one now extinct tribe painted themselves with red ochre]

Red Square *n* a large square in central Moscow, Russia, bordered by the Kremlin and Lenin's tomb

red squirrel *n* a reddish-brown squirrel of Europe and Asia

redstart *n* **1** a European songbird of the thrush family, the male of which has an orange-brown tail and breast **2** a North American warbler [Old English *rēad* red + *steort* tail]

red tape *n* time-consuming official rules or procedure [from the red tape used to bind official government documents]

reduce *vb* **-ducing, -duced 1** to bring down or lower: *monitoring could reduce the number of perinatal deaths* **2** to weaken or lessen: *vegetarian diets reduce cancer risk* **3** to bring by force or necessity to some state or action: *it reduced her to helpless laughter* **4** to slim **5** to set out systematically as an aid to understanding: *reducing the problem to three main issues* **6** cookery to thicken (a sauce) by boiling away some of its liquid **7** to impoverish: *to be in reduced circumstances* **8** chem **a** to undergo a chemical reaction with hydrogen **b** to lose oxygen atoms **c** to increase the number of electrons **9** maths to simplify the form of (an expression or equation), esp. by substitution of one term by another [Latin *reducere* to bring back] **> reducible** *adj*

reduction *n* **1** the act of reducing **2** the amount by which something is reduced **3** a reduced form of an original, such as a copy of a document on a smaller scale **> reductive** *adj*

redundant *adj* **1** deprived of one's job because it is no

longer necessary or sufficiently profitable **2** surplus to requirements [Latin *redundans* overflowing]
> redundancy *n*

reduplicate *vb* **-cating, -cated** to make double; repeat

redwood *n* a giant Californian conifer with reddish bark

re-echo *vb* **-oing, -oed** to echo over and over again

reed *n* **1** a tall grass that grows in swamps and shallow water **2** a straight hollow stem of this plant **3** music **a** a thin piece of cane or metal in certain wind instruments, which vibrates producing a musical note when the instrument is blown **b** a wind instrument or organ pipe that sounds by means of a reed [Old English *hrēod*]

Reed *n* **1** Sir **Carol**. 1906–76, English film director. His films include *The Third Man* (1949), *An Outcast of the Islands* (1951), and *Oliver!* (1968), for which he won an Oscar **2** **Lou**. 1942–2013, US rock singer, songwriter, and guitarist: member of the Velvet Underground (1965–70). His albums include *Transformer* (1972), *Berlin* (1973), *Street Hassle* (1978), *New York* (1989), *Set the Twilight Reeling* (1996), and *The Raven* (2003) **3** **Walter**. 1851–1902, US physician, who proved that yellow fever is transmitted by mosquitoes (1900)

reedy *adj* **reedier, reediest 1** harsh or thin in tone: *his reedy, hesitant voice* **2** (of a place) full of reeds **> reedily** *adv* **> reediness** *n*

reef¹ *n* **1** a ridge of rock, sand, or coral, lying just beneath the surface of the sea: *a coral reef* **2** a vein of ore [Middle Dutch *ref*]

reef² *nautical* *n* **1** the part of a sail which can be rolled up to reduce its area **>** *vb* **2** to reduce the area of (sail) by taking in a reef [Middle Dutch *rif*]

Reef *n* the Reef **1** another name for the **Great Barrier Reef** **2** another name for the **Witwatersrand**

reefer *n* **1** Also called: **reefer jacket** a man's short heavy double-breasted woollen jacket **2** old-fashioned, slang a hand-rolled cigarette containing cannabis [from the cigarette's resemblance to the rolled reef of a sail]

reef knot *n* a knot consisting of two overhand knots turned opposite ways

reek *vb* **1** to give off a strong unpleasant smell **2** reek of to give a strong suggestion of: *the scene had reeked of insincerity* **3** dialect to give off smoke or fumes **>** *n* **4** a strong unpleasant smell **5** dialect smoke or steam [Old English *rēocan*]

reel¹ *n* **1** a cylindrical object or frame that turns on an axis and onto which film, tape, wire, or thread is wound **2** a winding device attached to a fishing rod, used for casting and winding in the line **3** a roll of film for projection **>** *vb* **4 reel in** to wind or draw in on a reel [Old English *hrēol*]

reel² *vb* **1** to move unsteadily or spin round, as if about to fall **2** to be in a state of confusion or stress: *my mind was still reeling* [probably from REEL¹]

reel³ *n* **1** a lively Scottish dance **2** music for this dance [from REEL²]

re-elect *vb* to vote for (someone) to retain his or her position, for example as a Member of Parliament **> re-election** *n*

reel off *vb* to recite or write fluently or quickly

re-enact *vb* to act out (a previous event) again **> re-enactment** *n*

re-enter *vb* **1** to come back into (a place, esp. a country) **2** (of a spacecraft) to return into (the earth's atmosphere) **> re-entry** *n*

re-equip *vb* **-equipping, -equipped** to provide with fresh supplies, components, etc.

re-establish *vb* to create or set up (an organization, link, etc.) again **> re-establishment** *n*

reeve *n* **1** English history the local representative of the king in a shire until the early 11th century **2** (in medieval England) a steward who supervised the daily affairs of a manor **3** Canad government (in some provinces) a president of a local council [Old English *gerēfa*]

re-examine *vb* **-examining, -examined** to inspect or investigate again **> re-examination** *n*

ref *n informal* the referee in a sport

refectory *n, pl* **-ries** a dining hall in a religious or academic institution [Latin *refectus* refreshed]

refectory table *n* a long narrow dining table supported by two trestles

refer *vb* **-ferring, -ferred refer to** **1** to mention or allude to **2** to be relevant or relate to: *the word cancer refers to many quite specific different diseases* **3** to seek information from: *he referred to his notes* **4** to direct the attention of (someone) for information: *the reader is referred to the introduction* **5** to direct (a patient or client) to another doctor or agency: *her GP referred her to a specialist* **6** to hand over for consideration or decision: *to refer a complaint to another department* [Latin *re-* back + *ferre* to carry] **> referable** *or* **referrable** *adj* **> referral** *n*

> **USAGE** The common practice of adding *back* to *refer* is tautologous, since this meaning is already contained in the *re-* of *refer*: *this refers to* (not *back to*) *what has already been said.* However, when *refer* is used in the sense of passing a document or question for further consideration to the person from whom it was received, it may be appropriate to say *he referred the matter back.*

referee *n* **1** the umpire in various sports, such as football and boxing **2** a person who is willing to provide a reference for someone for a job **3** a person referred to for a decision or opinion in a dispute **>** *vb* **-reeing, -reed 4** to act as a referee

reference *n* **1** the act of referring **2** a mention: *this book contains several references to the Civil War* **3** direction to a passage elsewhere in a book or to another book **4** a book or passage referred to **5** a written testimonial regarding one's character or capabilities **6** a person referred to for such a testimonial **7** relation or restriction, esp. to or by membership of a specific group: *without reference to sex or age* **8 with reference to** concerning **>** *adj* **9** containing information or facts: *reference books* **> referential** *adj*

referendum *n, pl* **-dums** *or* **-da** a direct vote of the electorate on a question of importance [Latin: something to be carried back]

refill *vb* **1** to fill (something) again **>** *n* **2** a second or subsequent filling: *I held out my glass for a refill* **3** a replacement supply of something in a permanent container **> refillable** *adj*

refine *vb* **-fining, -fined 1** to make free from impurities; purify **2** to improve: *surgical techniques are constantly being refined* **3** to separate (a mixture) into pure constituents: *molasses is a residual syrup obtained during sugar refining*

refined *adj* **1** cultured or polite **2** freed from impurities **3** highly developed and effective: *refined intelligence tests*

refinement *n* **1** an improvement to something, such as a piece of equipment **2** fineness of taste or manners **3** a subtle point or distinction **4** the act of refining

refinery *n, pl* **-neries** a factory for purifying a raw material, such as sugar or oil

refit *vb* **-fitting, -fitted 1** to make (a ship) ready for use again by repairing or re-equipping **>** *n* **2** a repair or re-equipping for further use

reflation *n* an increase in the supply of money and credit designed to encourage economic activity [RE- + -flation, as in *inflation*] **> reflate** *vb* **> reflationary** *adj*

reflect *vb* **1** (of a surface or object) to throw back (light, heat, or sound) **2** (of a mirror) to form an image of (something) by reflection **3** to show: *many of her books reflect her obsession with fine art* **4** to consider carefully **5 reflect on** *or* **upon** to cause to be regarded in a specified way: *the incident reflects very badly on me* **6** to bring as a consequence: *the programme reflected great credit on the technicians* [Latin *re-* back + *flectere* to bend]

reflecting telescope *n* a telescope in which the initial image is formed by a concave mirror

reflection *n* **1** the act of reflecting **2** the return of rays of light, heat, or sound **3** an image of an object given back in a mirror **4** careful or long consideration **5 on reflection** after careful consideration or reconsideration **6** discredit or blame: *it's a sad reflection on modern morality* **7** *maths* a transformation of a shape in which right and left, or top and bottom, are reversed

reflective *adj* **1** characterized by quiet thought or contemplation **2** capable of reflecting: *a reflective coating*

reflector *n* **1** a polished surface for reflecting light **2** a reflecting telescope

reflex *n* **1** an immediate involuntary response to a given stimulus **2** a mechanical response to a particular situation, involving no conscious decision **3** an image produced by reflection **>** *adj* **4** of or caused by a reflex: *a reflex action* **5** reflected **6** *maths* (of an angle) between 180° and 360° [Latin *reflexus* bent back]

reflex camera *n* a camera which uses a mirror to channel light from a lens to the viewfinder, so that the image seen is the same as the image photographed

reflexive *adj* **1** *grammar* denoting a pronoun that refers back to the subject of a sentence or clause. Thus, in *that man thinks a great deal of himself,* the pronoun *himself* is reflexive **2** *grammar* denoting a verb used with a reflexive pronoun as its direct object, as in *to dress oneself* **3** *physiol* of or relating to a reflex **>** *n* **4** a reflexive pronoun or verb

reflexology *n* foot massage as a therapy in alternative medicine **> reflexologist** *n*

reform *n* **1** correction of abuses or malpractices: *a programme of economic reforms* **2** improvement of morals or behaviour **>** *vb* **3** to improve (a law or institution) by correcting abuses **4** to give up or cause to give up a bad habit or way of life [Latin *reformare* to form again] **> reformative** *adj* **> reformer** *n*

reformation (ref-fer-may-shun) *n* **1** a reforming **2 the Reformation** a religious movement in 16th-century Europe that began as an attempt to reform the Roman Catholic Church and resulted in the establishment of the Protestant Churches

reformatory *n, pl* **-ries** (formerly) a place where young offenders were sent to be reformed

Reformed *adj* of a Protestant Church, esp. a Calvinist one

reformist *adj* **1** advocating reform rather than abolition, esp. of a religion or a political movement **>** *n* **2** a person advocating reform

refract *vb* to cause light, heat, or sound to undergo refraction [Latin *re-* back + *frangere* to break] **> refractive** *adj* **> refractor** *n*

refracting telescope *n* a type of telescope in which the image is formed by a set of lenses. Also called: **refractor**

refraction *n physics* **1** the change in direction of a wave, such as light or sound, in passing from one medium to another in which it has a different velocity **2** the amount by which a wave is refracted

refractory *adj* **1** *formal* stubborn or rebellious **2** *med* not responding to treatment **3** (of a material) able to withstand high temperatures without fusion or decomposition

refrain¹ *vb* **refrain from** to keep oneself from doing [Latin *refrenare* to check with a bridle]

refrain² *n* **1** a frequently repeated part of a song **2** a much repeated saying or idea [Latin *refringere* to break into pieces]

refrangible *adj* capable of being refracted

refresh *vb* **1** to revive or reinvigorate, for example through rest, drink, or food **2** to stimulate (the memory) [Old French *refreschir*] **> refresher** *n*

refresher course *n* a course designed to improve or update a person's knowledge of a subject

refreshing *adj* **1** having a reviving effect **2** pleasantly different or new: *refreshing candour*

refreshment *n* **1** the act of refreshing **2** refreshments

r

snacks and drinks served as a light meal

refrigerant *n* **1** a fluid capable of vaporizing at low temperatures, used in refrigerators ▷ *adj* **2** causing cooling or freezing

refrigerate *vb* **-rating, -rated** to chill or freeze in order to preserve [Latin *refrigerare* to make cold] **> refrigeration** *n*

refrigerator *n* the full name for **fridge**

refuel *vb* **-elling, -elled** *or US* **-eling, -eled** to supply or be supplied with fresh fuel

refuge *n* **1** shelter or protection from danger or hardship **2** a place, person, or thing that offers protection or help [Latin *re-* back + *fugere* to escape]

refugee *n* a person who has fled from some danger, such as war or political persecution

refulgent *adj literary* shining brightly [Latin *refulgere* to reflect] **> refulgence** *n*

refund *vb* **1** to give back (money) **2** to pay back (a person) ▷ *n* **3** return of money to a purchaser or the amount returned [Latin *re-* back + *fundere* to pour] **> refundable** *adj*

refurbish *vb* to renovate and brighten up **> refurbishment** *n*

refusal *n* **1** the act of refusing **2** the opportunity to reject or accept: *he was given first refusal on all three scripts*

refuse¹ *vb* **-fusing, -fused** **1** to be determined not (to do something): *he refuses to consider it* **2** to decline to give or allow (something) to (someone): *if the judge refuses bail, he'll appeal* **3** to decline to accept (something offered): *he refused the captaincy* **4** (of a horse) to be unwilling to jump a fence [Latin *refundere* to pour back]

refuse² *n* anything thrown away; rubbish [Old French *refuser* to refuse]

refusenik *n* **1** (formerly) a Jew in the USSR who was refused permission to emigrate **2** a person who refuses to obey a law or cooperate with the government because of strong beliefs

refute *vb* **-futing, -futed** to prove (a statement or theory) to be false or incorrect [Latin *refutare*] **> refutation** *n*

USAGE The use of *refute* to mean *deny* is thought by many people to be incorrect.

regain *vb* **1** to get back or recover **2** to reach again: *to regain the shore*

regal *adj* **1** of or fit for a king or queen **2** splendid and dignified; magnificent: *a luxury cruise liner on her serene and regal way around the better ports* [Latin *regalis*] **> regality** *n* **> regally** *adv*

regale *vb* **-galing, -galed** **1** to give delight or amusement to: *she would regale her friends with stories* **2** to provide with abundant food or drink [French *régaler*]

regalia *n* the ceremonial emblems or robes of royalty or high office [Medieval Latin: royal privileges]

regard *vb* **1** to look upon or think of in a specified way: *angina can therefore be regarded as heart cramp* **2** to look closely or attentively at (something or someone) **3** to take notice of: *he has never regarded the conventions* **4** as regards on the subject of ▷ *n* **5** respect or affection: *you haven't a high regard for her opinion* **6** attention: *he eats what he wants with no regard to health* **7** a gaze or look **8** reference or connection: *with regard to my complaint* **9** regards an expression of goodwill: *give her my regards* [Old French *regarder* to look at, care about]

regardful *adj* regardful of paying attention to

regarding *prep* on the subject of; relating to

regardless *adj* **1** regardless of taking no notice of: *the illness can affect anyone regardless of their social class* ▷ *adv* **2** in spite of everything: *I carried on regardless*

regatta *n* a series of races of boats or yachts [obsolete Italian *rigatta* contest]

regency *n, pl* **-cies** **1** government by a regent **2** the status of a regent **3** a period when a regent is in power [Latin *regere* to rule]

Regency *adj* of the regency (1811–20) of the Prince of Wales (later George IV) or the styles of architecture or furniture produced during it

regenerate *vb* (ri-jen-er-ate) **-rating, -rated** **1** to undergo or cause to undergo physical, economic, or spiritual renewal **2** to come or bring into existence once again **3** to replace (lost or damaged tissues or organs) by new growth ▷ *adj* (ri-jen-er-it) **4** physically, economically, or spiritually renewed **> regeneration** *n* **> regenerative** *adj*

Regensburg *n* a city in SE Germany, in Bavaria on the River Danube: a free Imperial city from 1245 and the leading commercial city of S Germany in the 12th and 13th centuries; the Imperial Diet was held in the town hall from 1663 to 1806. Pop: 128 604 (2003 est). Former English name: **Ratisbon**

regent *n* **1** the ruler of a country during the childhood, absence, or illness of its monarch **2** *US and Canad* a member of the governing board of certain schools and colleges ▷ *adj* **3** acting as a regent: *the Prince Regent* [Latin *regere* to rule]

Regent's Park *n* a park in central London, laid out as Marylebone Park by John Nash; now known for the London Zoo, its open-air theatre, and Nash's curved terraces

Reger *n* Max. 1873–1916, German composer, noted esp. for his organ works

reggae *n* a type of popular music of Jamaican origin with a strong beat [West Indian]

Reggio di Calabria *n* a port in S Italy, in Calabria on the Strait of Messina: founded about 720 BC by Greek colonists. Pop: 180 353 (2001)

Reggio nell'Emilia *n* a city in N central Italy, in Emilia-Romagna: founded in the 2nd century BC by Marcus Aemilius Lepidus; ruled by the Este family in the 15th–18th centuries. Pop: 141 877 (2001)

regicide *n* **1** the killing of a king **2** a person who kills a king [Latin *rex* king + *caedere* to kill]

regifting *n* the practice of giving an unwanted gift to another person

regime (ray-zheem) *n* **1** a system of government **2** a particular administration: *the corrupt regime* **3** *med* a regimen [French]

regimen *n* a prescribed system of diet and exercise [Latin: guidance]

regiment *n* **1** an organized body of troops as a unit in the army **2** a large number or group [Late Latin *regimentum* government] **> regimental** *adj*

regimentals *pl n* **1** the uniform and insignia of a regiment **2** military uniform

regimental sergeant major *n military* the senior warrant officer in a regiment or battalion

regimented *adj* very strictly controlled: *the regimented confines of the school* **> regimentation** *n*

Regina¹ *n* queen: now used chiefly in documents and inscriptions [Latin]

Regina² *n* a city in W Canada, capital and largest city of Saskatchewan: founded in 1882 as Pile O'Bones. Pop: 178 225 (2001)

Regiomontanus *n* original name *Johann Müller*. 1436–76, German mathematician and astronomer, who furthered the development of trigonometry

region *n* **1** an administrative division of a country **2** an area considered as a unit for geographical or social reasons **3** a sphere of activity or interest **4** a part of the body: *the lumbar region* **5** in the region of approximately: *in the region of 100 000 troops* **6** the regions the parts of a country away from the capital: *discord between Moscow and the regions* [Latin *regio*] **> regional** *adj*

regionalism *n* **1** the division of a country or organization into geographical regions each having some autonomy **2** loyalty to one's home region

register *n* **1** an official list recording names, events, or transactions **2** the book in which such a list is written

3 a device that records data, totals sums of money, etc.: *a cash register* **4** a style of speaking or writing, such as slang, used in particular circumstances or social situations **5** *music* **a** the timbre characteristic of a certain manner of voice production **b** any of the stops on an organ in respect of its tonal quality: *the flute register* ▷ *vb* **6** to enter (an event, person's name, ownership, etc.) in a register **7** to show on a scale or other measuring instrument **8** to show in a person's face or bearing: *his face registered surprise* **9** *informal* to have an effect or make an impression: *the news did not register at first* **10** to have (a letter or parcel) insured against loss by the Post Office: *registered mail* [Medieval Latin *registrum*] **>** **registration** *n*

register office *n Brit* a government office where civil marriages are performed and births, marriages, and deaths are recorded

registrar *n* **1** a person who keeps official records **2** an official responsible for student records and enrolment in a college **3** *Brit and NZ* a hospital doctor senior to a houseman but junior to a consultant

registration document *n Brit and Austral* a document giving identification details of a vehicle, including its owner's name

registration number *n Brit* a sequence of letters and numbers given to a motor vehicle when it is registered, displayed on numberplates at the front and rear

registry *n, pl* **-tries 1** a place where official records are kept **2** the registration of a ship's country of origin: *a ship of Liberian registry*

registry office *n Brit and NZ* same as **register office**

Regius professor (reej-yuss) *n Brit* a person appointed by the Crown to a university chair founded by a royal patron [Latin *regius* royal]

regress *vb* **1 a** to return to a former and worse condition ▷ *n* **2** return to a former and worse condition [Latin *regredi* to go back] **>** **regressive** *adj*

regression *n* **1** the act of regressing **2** *psychol* the use by an adult of behaviour more appropriate to a child

regret *vb* **-gretting, -gretted 1** to feel sorry or upset about **2** to express apology or distress about: *we regret any misunderstanding caused* ▷ *n* **3** a feeling of repentance, guilt, or sorrow **4 regrets** a polite expression of refusal: *she had sent her regrets* [Old French *regreter*] **>** **regretful** *adj* **>** **regretfully** *adv* **>** **regrettable** *adj* **>** **regrettably** *adv*

> **USAGE** Regretful and regretfully are sometimes wrongly used where regrettable and regrettably are meant: *he gave a regretful smile; he smiled regretfully; this is a regrettable (not regretful) mistake; regrettably (not regretfully), I shall be unable to attend.*

regroup *vb* **1** to reorganize (military forces) after an attack or a defeat **2** to rearrange into a new grouping

regular *adj* **1** normal, customary, or usual **2** symmetrical or even: *regular features* **3** according to a uniform principle, arrangement, or order **4** occurring at fixed or prearranged intervals: *we run regular advertisements in the press* **5** following a set rule or normal practice **6** *grammar* following the usual pattern of formation in a language: *regular verbs* **7** of or serving in the permanent military services: *the regular armed forces* **8** *maths* (of a polygon) having all its sides and angles the same **9** officially qualified or recognized: *he's not a regular doctor* **10** *informal* not constipated: *eating fresh vegetables helps keep you regular* **11** *US and Canad informal* likeable: *a regular guy* **12** complete or utter: *a regular fool* **13** subject to the rule of an established religious community: *canons regular* ▷ *n* **14** a professional long-term serviceman in a military unit **15** *informal* a frequent customer or visitor [Latin *regula* ruler, model] **>** **regularity** *n* **>** **regularize** or **-rise** *vb* **>** **regularly** *adv*

regulate *vb* **-lating, -lated 1** to control by means of rules: *a code of practice to regulate advertising by schools* **2** to adjust

slightly: *he had to take drugs to regulate his heartbeat* [Late Latin *regulare* to control] **>** **regulatory** *adj*

regulation *n* **1** a rule that governs procedure or behaviour **2** the act of regulating ▷ *adj* **3** in accordance with rules or conventions: *dressed in the orchestra's regulation black tie*

regulator *n* **1** a mechanism that automatically controls pressure, temperature, etc. **2** the mechanism by which the speed of a clock is regulated

Regulus *n* Marcus Atilius. died ?250 BC, Roman general; consul (267; 256). Captured by the Carthaginians in the First Punic War, he was sent to Rome on parole to deliver the enemy's peace terms, advised the Senate to refuse them, and was tortured to death on his return to Carthage

regurgitate *vb* **-tating, -tated 1** to vomit **2** (of some birds and animals) to bring back (partly digested food) to the mouth to feed the young **3** to reproduce (ideas or facts) without understanding them [Medieval Latin *re-* back + *gurgitare* to flood] **>** **regurgitation** *n*

rehabilitate *vb* **-tating, -tated 1** to help (a person) to readapt to society after illness or imprisonment **2** to restore to a former position or rank **3** to restore the good reputation of [Medieval Latin *rehabilitare* to restore] **>** **rehabilitation** *n*

rehash *vb* **1** to use (old or already used ideas) in a slightly different form without real improvement ▷ *n* **2** old ideas presented in a new form [*re-* again + *hash* to chop into pieces]

rehearse *vb* **-hearsing, -hearsed 1** to practise (a play, concert, etc.) for public performance **2** to repeat aloud: *he rehearsed his familiar views on the press* **3** to train (a person) for public performance [Old French *rehercier* to harrow a second time] **>** **rehearsal** *n* **>** **rehearser** *n*

rehouse *vb* **-housing, -housed** to provide with a new and better home

Reich¹ (rike) *n* the former German state, esp. the Nazi dictatorship in Germany from 1933–45 (**Third Reich**) [German: kingdom]

Reich² *n* **1** Steve. born 1936, US composer, whose works are characterized by the repetition and modification of small rhythmic motifs. His works include *Drumming* (1971), *The Desert Music* (1984), and *City Life* (1995) **2** Wilhelm. 1897–1957, Austrian psychologist, lived in the US. An ardent socialist and advocate of sexual freedom, he proclaimed a cosmic unity of all energy and built a machine (the orgone accumulator) to concentrate this energy on human beings. His books include *The Function of the Orgasm* (1927)

Reichenberg *n* the German name for **Liberec**

Reichstag *n* **1** Also called: **diet** (in medieval Germany) the estates or a meeting of the estates **2** the legislative assembly representing the people in the North German Confederation (1867–71) and in the German empire (1871–1919) **3** the sovereign assembly of the Weimar Republic (1919–33) **4** the building in Berlin in which this assembly met and from 1999 in which the German government meets: its destruction by fire on Feb 27, 1933 (probably by agents of the Nazi government) marked the end of Weimar democracy. It was restored in the 1990s following German reunification

Reid *n* **1** Sir George Houston. 1845–1918, Australian statesman, born in Scotland: premier of New South Wales (1894–99); prime minister of Australia (1904–05) **2** Thomas. 1710–96, Scottish philosopher and founder of what came to be known as the philosophy of common sense

Reigate *n* a town in S England, in Surrey at the foot of the North Downs. Pop (including Redhill): 50 436 (2001)

reign *n* **1** the period during which a monarch is the official ruler of a country **2** a period during which a person or thing is dominant: *a reign of terror* ▷ *vb* **3** to rule

r

(a country) **4** to be supreme: *a sense of confusion reigns in the capital* [Old French *reigne*]

> **USAGE** *Reign* is sometimes wrongly written for *rein* in certain phrases: *he gave full rein* (not *reign*) *to his feelings; it will be necessary to rein in* (not *reign in*) *public spending.*

reigning *adj* currently holding a title or championship: *the reigning world champion*

reimburse *vb* **-bursing, -bursed** to repay (someone) for (expenses or losses) [Medieval Latin *imbursare* to put in a moneybag] **> reimbursement** *n*

Reims *or* **Rheims** *n* a city in NE France: scene of the coronation of most French monarchs. Pop: 188 078 (2006)

rein *n* **1 reins a** long narrow straps attached to a bit to control a horse **b** narrow straps attached to a harness to control a young child **c** means of control: *to take up the reins of government* **2 give (a) free rein** to allow a considerable amount of freedom **3 keep a tight rein on** to control carefully: *we have to keep a tight rein on expenditure* ▷ *vb* **4** to restrain or halt with reins **5** to control or limit: *reining her thoughts, she tried to be objective* ▶ See also **rein in** [Old French *resne*]

> **USAGE** See at **reign**.

reincarnate *vb* **-nating, -nated 1** to cause to undergo reincarnation: *souls may be reincarnated in human forms* **2** to be born again in a different body

reincarnation *n* **1** the belief that after death the soul is reborn in another body **2** an instance of rebirth in another body **3** the reappearance in a new form of a principle or idea: *he was the reincarnation of the old Republican Party isolationist*

reindeer *n, pl* **-deer** *or* **-deers** a deer with large branched antlers that lives in the arctic regions [Old Norse *hreindȳri*]

Reindeer Lake *n* a lake in W Canada, in Saskatchewan and Manitoba: drains into the Churchill River via the **Reindeer River**. Area: 6390 sq km (2467 sq miles)

reinforce *vb* **-inforcing, -inforced 1** to give added emphasis to (an idea or feeling): *his tired face reinforced his own weariness* **2** to make physically stronger or harder: *the plastic panels were reinforced with carbon fibre* **3** to give added support to (a military force) by providing more men or equipment: *the army garrison had been reinforced with helicopters* [French *renforcer*] **> reinforcement** *n*

reinforced concrete *n* concrete with steel bars or mesh embedded in it to strengthen it

Reinhardt *n* **1 Django**, real name *Jean Baptiste Reinhardt*. 1910–53, French jazz guitarist, whose work was greatly influenced by Gypsy music. With Stéphane Grappelli, he led the Quintet of the Hot Club of France between 1934 and 1939 **2 Max**, original name *Max Goldmann*. 1873–1943, Austrian theatre producer and director, in the US after 1933

rein in *vb* **1** to stop (a horse) by pulling on the reins **2** to restrict or stop: *either prices or wage packets had to be reined in*

reinstate *vb* **-stating, -stated 1** to restore to a former rank or status **2** to cause to exist or be important again: *reinstate some semblance of order* **> reinstatement** *n*

reinvigorate *vb* to give renewed energy to; refresh

reissue *n* **1** a book, CD, etc., that is published or released again after being unavailable for a time ▷ *vb* **2** to publish or release (a book, CD, etc.) again after a period of unavailability

reiterate *vb* **-rating, -rated** *formal* to repeat again and again [Latin *reiterare*] **> reiteration** *n*

Reith *n* **John (Charles Walsham)**, 1st Baron. 1889–1971, British public servant: first general manager (1922–27) and first director general (1927–38) of the BBC **> Reithian** *or* **Reithean** *adj*

reject *vb* **1** to refuse to accept, use, or believe **2** to deny to (a person) the feelings hoped for: *the boy had been rejected by*

his mother **3** to pass over or throw out as useless **4** (of an organism) to fail to accept (a tissue graft or organ transplant) ▷ *n* **5** a person or thing rejected as not up to standard [Latin *reicere* to throw back] **> rejection** *n*

rejig *vb* **-jigging, -jigged 1** to re-equip (a factory or plant) **2** *informal* to rearrange or manipulate, sometimes in an unscrupulous way: *the promoter hastily rejigged the running order*

rejoice *vb* **-joicing, -joiced** to feel or express great happiness [Old French *resjoir*] **> rejoicing** *n*

rejoin¹ *vb* to come together with (someone or something) again

rejoin² *vb* to reply in a sharp or witty way [Old French *rejoindre*]

rejoinder *n* a sharp or witty reply

rejuvenate *vb* **-nating, -nated** to give back youth or vitality to [Latin *re-* again + *juvenis* young] **> rejuvenation** *n*

rekindle *vb* **-dling, -dled** to arouse (former emotions or interests)

relapse *vb* **-lapsing, -lapsed 1** to fall back into bad habits or illness ▷ *n* **2** the act of relapsing **3** the return of ill health after an apparent or partial recovery [Latin *re-* back + *labi* to slip]

relate *vb* **-lating, -lated 1** to establish a relation between **2** to have reference or relation to **3** to have an understanding (of people or ideas): *the inability to relate to others* **4** to tell (a story) or describe (an event) [Latin *relatus* brought back]

related *adj* **1** linked by kinship or marriage **2** connected or associated: *salts and related compounds*

relation *n* **1** the connection between things or people **2** a person who is connected by blood or marriage **3** connection by blood or marriage **4** an account or narrative **5 in** *or* **with relation to** with reference to: *an inquiry into export controls in relation to Iraq*

relations *pl n* **1** social or political dealings between individuals or groups **2** family or relatives **3** *euphemistic* sexual intercourse

relationship *n* **1** the dealings and feelings that exist between people or groups **2** an emotional or sexual affair **3** the connection between two things: *the relationship between exercise and mental health* **4** association by blood or marriage

relative *adj* **1** true to a certain degree or extent: *a zone of relative affluence* **2** having significance only in relation to something else: *time is relative* **3 relative to** in proportion to: *it will benefit from high growth in earnings relative to prices* **4** respective: *the relative qualities of speed and accuracy* **5** relevant: *the facts relative to the enquiry* **6** *grammar* of a clause (**relative clause**) that modifies a noun or pronoun occurring earlier in the sentence **7** *grammar* of or belonging to a class of words, such as *who, which*, or *that*, which function as conjunctions introducing relative clauses ▷ *n* **8** a person who is related by blood or marriage **> relatively** *adv*

relative atomic mass *n* same as **atomic weight**

relativity *n* **1** either of two theories developed by Albert Einstein, the **special theory of relativity**, which requires that the laws of physics shall be the same as seen by any two different observers in uniform relative motion, and the **general theory of relativity**, which considers observers with relative acceleration and leads to a theory of gravitation **2** the state of being relative

relax *vb* **1** to make or become less tense, looser, or less rigid **2** to ease up from effort or attention **3** to make (rules or discipline) less strict **4** to become more friendly **5** to lessen the intensity of: *he relaxed his vigilance in the lulls between attacks* [Latin *relaxare* to loosen] **> relaxed** *adj*

relaxation *n* **1** rest after work or effort **2** a form of recreation: *his favoured form of relaxation was walking on the local moors* **3** the act of relaxing

relay *n* **1** a fresh set of people or animals relieving others **2** short for **relay race 3** an automatic device that controls a valve or switch, esp. one in which a small change in current or voltage controls the switching on or off of circuits **4** *radio* a combination of a receiver and transmitter designed to receive radio signals and retransmit them ▷ *vb* **5** to pass on (a message) **6** to retransmit (a signal) by means of a relay **7** *Brit* to broadcast (a performance or event) as it happens [Old French *relaier* to leave behind]

relay race *n* a race between teams in which each contestant covers a specified portion of the distance

release *vb* **-leasing, -leased 1** to free (a person or animal) from captivity or imprisonment **2** to free (someone) from obligation or duty **3** to free (something) from (one's grip) **4** to allow (news or information) to be made public or available **5** to allow (something) to move freely: *she released the handbrake* **6** to issue (a CD, film, or book) for sale or public showing: *the CD was originally released six years ago* **7** to give out (heat, energy, radiation, etc.): *the explosion released a cloud of toxic gas* ▷ *n* **8** the act of freeing or state of being freed **9** a statement to the press **10** the act of issuing for sale or publication **11** something issued for sale or public showing [Old French *relesser*]

relegate *vb* **-gating, -gated 1** to put in a less important position **2** to demote (a sports team) to a lower division: *four clubs were relegated from the first division* [Latin *re-* back + *legare* to send] **> relegation** *n*

relent *vb* **1** to change one's mind about some decision **2** to become milder or less severe: *the weather relented* [Latin *re-* back + *lentare* to bend]

relentless *adj* **1** never stopping or reducing in severity: *relentless deterioration in standards* **2** (of a person) determined and pitiless

relevant *adj* to do with the matter in hand [Medieval Latin *relevans*] **> relevance** *n*

reliable *adj* able to be trusted **> reliability** *n* **> reliably** *adv*

reliance *n* the state of relying on or trusting (a person or thing) **> reliant** *adj*

relic *n* **1** an object or custom that has survived from the past **2** something valued for its past associations **3** *relics* remaining parts or traces **4** *RC Church, Eastern Churches* a body part or possession of a saint, venerated as holy [Latin *reliquiae* remains]

relict *n archaic* **1** a relic **2** a widow [Latin *relictus* left behind]

relief *n* **1** a feeling of cheerfulness that follows the removal of anxiety, pain, or distress **2** a temporary pause in anxiety, pain, or distress **3** money, food, or clothing given to people in special need: *disaster relief* **4** the act of freeing a besieged town or fortress: *the relief of Mafeking* **5** a person who replaces another at some task or duty **6** a bus, plane, etc., that carries additional passengers when a scheduled service is full **7** Also called: **relievo** *sculpture, archit* the projection of a carved design from the surface **8** any vivid effect resulting from contrast: *a welcome relief* **9** the difference between the highest and lowest level: *study the map of relief and the rainfall map* **10 on relief** *US and Canad* (of people) in receipt of government aid because of personal need [Old French *relever* to relieve]

relief map *n* a map showing the shape and height of the land surface by contours and shading

relieve *vb* **-lieving, -lieved 1** to lessen (pain, distress, boredom, etc.) **2** to bring assistance to (someone in need): *a plan to relieve those facing hunger* **3** to free (someone) from an obligation: *a further attempt to relieve the taxpayers of their burdens* **4** to take over the duties of (someone): *the night nurse came in to relieve her* **5** to free (a besieged town or fort) **6 relieve oneself** to urinate or defecate **7** to set off by contrast: *painted walls are marginally relieved by some abstract prints* **8** *informal* to take from: *the prince had relieved him of his duties* [Latin *re-* again + *levare* to lighten] **> relieved** *adj*

religion *n* **1** belief in or worship of a supernatural power or powers considered to be divine or to have control of human destiny **2** any formal expression of such belief: *the Christian religion* **3** *chiefly RC Church* the way of life entered upon by monks and nuns: *to enter religion* [Latin *religio*]

religious *adj* **1** of religion **2** pious or devout **3** scrupulous or conscientious: *religious attention to detail* **4** Christianity relating to the way of life of monks and nuns ▷ *n* **5** *Christianity* a monk or nun **> religiously** *adv*

relinquish *vb formal* **1** to give up: *that hope has to be relinquished* **2** to renounce (a claim or right) **3** to release one's hold on [Latin *relinquere*] **> relinquishment** *n*

reliquary (rel-lik-wer-ee) *n, pl* **-quaries** a container for relics of saints

relish *vb* **1** to savour or enjoy (an experience) to the full **2** to anticipate eagerly ▷ *n* **3** liking or enjoyment: *he has an enormous relish for life* **4** pleasurable anticipation: *his early relish for a new challenge* **5** an appetizing or spicy food, such as a pickle, added to a main dish to improve its flavour **6** a zestful quality: *he tells stories with great relish* [earlier *reles* aftertaste]

relive *vb* **-living, -lived** to experience (a sensation or event) again, esp. in the imagination

reload *vb* to put fresh ammunition into (a firearm)

relocate *vb* **-cating, -cated** to move or be moved to a new place of work **> relocation** *n*

reluctance *n* **1** unwillingness to do something **2** *physics* a measure of the resistance of a closed magnetic circuit to a magnetic flux [Latin *reluctari* to resist]

reluctant *adj* unwilling or disinclined **> reluctantly** *adv*

rely *vb* **-lies, -lying, -lied** **rely on** *or* **upon a** to be dependent on: *the organization relies on voluntary contributions* **b** to have trust or confidence in: *you can rely on his judgment* [Old French *relier* to fasten together]

REM rapid eye movement

remain *vb* **1** to continue to be: *the situation remains alarming* **2** to stay behind or in the same place: *to remain at home* **3** to be left after use or the passage of time **4** to be left to be done, said, etc.: *whether this will be a long-term trend remains to be seen* [Latin *remanere*]

remainder *n* **1** a part or portion that is left after use or the passage of time: *we ate some biscuits and the remainder of the jam* **2** *maths* **a** the amount left over when one quantity cannot be exactly divided by another: *for 10 ÷ 3, the remainder is 1* **b** the amount left over when one quantity is subtracted from another **3** a number of copies of a book sold cheaply because it has been impossible to sell them at full price ▷ *vb* **4** to sell (copies of a book) as a remainder

remains *pl n* **1** parts left over from something after use or the passage of time: *the remains of the old Roman fortress* **2** a corpse

remake *vb* **-making, -made 1** to make again in a different way ▷ *n* **2** a new version of an old film

remand *vb* **1** *law* to send (a prisoner or accused person) back into custody or put on bail before trial ▷ *n* **2** the sending of a person back into custody or putting on bail before trial **3 on remand** in custody or on bail awaiting trial [Latin *re-* back + *mandare* to command]

remand centre *n* a place where accused people are detained while awaiting trial

remark *vb* **1** to pass a casual comment (about) **2** to say **3** to observe or notice ▷ *n* **4** a brief casually expressed thought or opinion [Old French *remarquer* to observe]

remarkable *adj* **1** worthy of note or attention: *a remarkable career* **2** striking or extraordinary: *a thing of remarkable beauty* **> remarkably** *adv*

Remarque *n* Erich Maria. 1898–1970, US novelist, born in Germany, noted for his novel of World War I, *All Quiet on the Western Front* (1929)

remarry *vb* **-ries, -rying, -ried** to marry again following a divorce or the death of one's previous spouse **> remarriage** *n*

Rembrandt *n* full name *Rembrandt Harmensz (or Harmenszoon) van Rijn (or van Ryn)*. 1606–69, Dutch painter, noted for his handling of shade and light, esp. in his portraits **> Rembrandtesque** *adj*

REME Royal Electrical and Mechanical Engineers

remedial *adj* **1** providing or intended as a remedy **2** of special teaching for slow learners: *remedial classes* ▷ **remedially** *adv*

remedy *n, pl* **-edies** **1** a drug or treatment for curing pain or disease **2** a way of solving a problem: *every statesman promised a remedy for unemployment* ▷ *vb* **-edies, -edying, -edied** **3** to put right or improve [Latin *remedium* a cure] ▷ **remediable** *adj*

remember *vb* **1** to become aware of (something forgotten) again **2** to keep (an idea, intention, etc.) in one's mind: *remember to write* **3** to give money to (someone), as in a will or in tipping **4** **remember to** to mention (a person's name) to another person, by way of greeting: *remember me to her* **5** to commemorate: *we are here to remember the dead* [Latin *re-* again + *memor* mindful]

remembrance *n* **1** a memory **2** a memento or keepsake **3** the act of honouring some past event or person

Remembrance Day *n* **1** (in Britain) Remembrance Sunday **2** (in Canada and Australia) a statutory holiday observed on November 11 in memory of the dead of both World Wars

Remembrance Sunday *n* (in Britain) the Sunday closest to November 11, on which the dead of both World Wars are commemorated

remind *vb* **1** to cause to remember: *remind her that she was on duty* **2** to put in mind (of someone or something): *you remind me of Alice in Wonderland*

reminder *n* **1** something that recalls the past **2** a note to remind a person of something not done

reminisce *vb* **-niscing, -nisced** to talk or write about old times or past experiences

reminiscence *n* **1** the act of recalling or narrating past experiences **2** something remembered from the past **3** reminiscences stories about a person's life, often presented in a book

reminiscent *adj* **1** reminiscent of reminding or suggestive of **2** characterized by reminiscence [Latin *reminisci* to call to mind]

remiss *adj formal* careless in attention to duty or responsibility [Latin *remissus*]

remission *n* **1** a reduction in the length of a prison term **2** forgiveness for sin **3** easing of intensity of the symptoms of a disease **4** a release from an obligation

remit *vb* (rim-mitt) **-mitting, -mitted** **1** to send (money) for goods or services **2** to cancel (a punishment or debt) **3** *law* to send back (a case) to a lower court for further consideration **4** to slacken or ease off **5** *archaic* to forgive (crime or sins) ▷ *n* (ree-mitt) **6** area of authority: *within the review body's remit* [Latin *re-* back + *mittere* to send]

remittance *n* money sent as payment

remittent *adj* (of a disease) periodically less severe

remix *vb* **1** to change the relative prominence of each performer's part of (a recording) ▷ *n* **2** a remixed version of a recording

remnant *n* **1** a part left over **2** a piece of material from the end of a roll **3** a surviving trace or vestige: *the authorities drafted in the military to crush any remnant of protest* [Old French *remenant* remaining]

remodel *vb* **-delling, -delled** *or US* **-deling, -deled** to give a different shape or form to: *a renaissance of boutiques and remodelled apartments; the country is planning to remodel its armed forces*

remonstrance *n formal* a strong protest about something

remonstrate *vb* **-strating, -strated** *formal* to argue in protest or objection: *the player remonstrated loudly with the official* [Latin *re-* again + *monstrare* to show] ▷ **remonstration** *n*

remorse *n* a sense of deep regret and guilt for something one did [Medieval Latin *remorsus* a gnawing] ▷ **remorseful** *adj*

remorseless *adj* **1** constantly unkind and lacking pity:

remorseless fate **2** continually intense: *the superintendent's remorseless gaze*

remote *adj* **1** far away **2** far from civilization **3** distant in time **4** not relevant: *the issues seem remote from the general population* **5** (of a person's manner) aloof or abstracted **6** slight or faint: *a remote possibility* **7** operated from a distance; remote-controlled: *a remote manipulator arm* [Latin *remotus* far removed] ▷ **remotely** *adv*

remote control *n* control of an apparatus from a distance by radio or electrical signals ▷ **remote-controlled** *adj*

remould *vb* **1** to change completely: *to remould the country* **2** *Brit* to bond a new tread onto the casing of (a worn pneumatic tyre) ▷ *n* **3** *Brit* a tyre made by this process

removable *adj* capable of being removed from a place or released from another object: *a farmer's truck with removable wooden sides*

removal *n* **1** the act of removing or state of being removed **2** the process of moving one's possessions from a previous address to a new one

remove *vb* **-moving, -moved** **1** to take away and place elsewhere **2** to take (clothing) off **3** to get rid of **4** to dismiss (someone) from office **5** *formal* to change the location of one's home or place of business ▷ *n* **6** the degree of difference: *one remove away from complete rebuttal* **7** *Brit* (in certain schools) a class or form designed to prepare pupils for senior classes [Old French *removoir*]

removed *adj* **1** very different or distant: *madness seemed far removed from the sunny order of things* **2** separated by a degree of descent: *the child of a person's first cousin is their first cousin once removed*

Remscheid *n* an industrial city in W Germany, in North Rhine-Westphalia. Pop: 117 717 (2003 est)

remunerate *vb* **-rating, -rated** *formal* to reward or pay for work or service [Latin *remunerari*] ▷ **remuneration** *n* ▷ **remunerative** *adj*

renaissance *n* a renewal of interest or creativity in an area: *a complete renaissance in maze building* [French]

Renaissance *n* **1** the Renaissance the great revival of art, literature, and learning in Europe in the 14th, 15th, and 16th centuries ▷ *adj* **2** of or from the Renaissance

renal (ree-nal) *adj* of the kidneys [Latin *renes* kidneys]

Renan *n* (Joseph) Ernest (ernest). 1823–92, French philosopher, theologian, and historian; best known for his *Life of Jesus* (1863), which discounted the supernatural aspects of the Gospels

renascent *adj literary* becoming active or vigorous again: *renascent nationalism* [Latin *renasci* to be born again] ▷ **renascence** *n*

rend *vb* **rending, rent** *literary* **1** to tear violently **2** (of a sound) to break (the silence) with a shrill or piercing tone [Old English *rendan*]

Rendell *n* Ruth (Barbara), Baroness. 1930–2015, British crime writer: author of detective novels, such as *Wolf to the Slaughter* (1967), and psychological thrillers, such as *The Lake of Darkness* (1980) and (under the name Barbara Vine) *A Fatal Inversion* (1987) and *The Chimney Sweeper's Boy* (1998)

render *vb* **1** to cause to become: *he was rendered unconscious by his wound* **2** to give or provide (aid, a service, etc.) **3** *formal* to present or submit (a bill) **4** to translate **5** to represent in painting, music, or acting **6** to yield or give: *he rendered up his soul to God* **7** to cover with plaster **8** to melt down (fat) [Old French *rendre*] ▷ **rendering** *n*

rendezvous (ron-day-voo) *n, pl* **-vous** (-vooz) **1** an appointment to meet at a specified time and place **2** a place where people meet ▷ *vb* **3** to meet at a specified time or place [French]

rendition *n formal* **1** a performance of a piece of music or a dramatic role **2** a translation

renegade *n* a person who deserts a cause for another [Spanish *renegado*]

renege (rin-nayg) *vb* **-neging, -neged** to go back (on an agreement or promise): *the politicians reneged on every* *promise* [Medieval Latin *renegare* to renounce]

renew *vb* **1** to begin again **2** to take up again after a break: *they wanted to renew diplomatic ties* **3** to make valid again: *we didn't renew the lease* **4** to grow again **5** to restore to a new or fresh condition **6** to replace (an old or worn-out part or piece) **7** to restate or reaffirm (a promise) ⟩ **renewal** *n*

renewable *adj* **1** able to be renewed **2** (of energy or an energy source) inexhaustible or capable of being perpetually replenished ▷ *pl n* **renewables 3** renewable energy sources, such as wind and wave power

Renfrew *n* an industrial town in W central Scotland, in Renfrewshire, W of Glasgow. Pop: 20 251 (2001)

Renfrewshire *n* **1** a council area of W central Scotland, on the River Clyde W of Glasgow: corresponds to part of the historical county of Renfrewshire; part of Strathclyde region from 1975 to 1996: agricultural and residential, with clothing and manufacturing industries in Paisley. Administrative centre: Paisley. Pop: 170 980 (2003 est). Area: 261 sq km (101 sq miles) **2** a former county of W central Scotland, on the Firth of Clyde: became part of Strathclyde region in 1975; now covered by the council areas of Renfrewshire, East Renfrewshire, and Inverclyde

Reni *n* Guido. 1575–1642, Italian baroque painter and engraver

Rennes *n* a city in NW France: the ancient capital of Brittany. Pop: 214 813 (2006)

rennet *n* a substance prepared from the stomachs of calves and used for curdling milk to make cheese [Old English *gerinnan* to curdle]

Rennie *n* John. 1761–1821, British civil engineer who designed bridges, canals, docks, and harbours, including three London bridges and the London and East India docks

Reno *n* a city in W Nevada, at the foot of the Sierra Nevada: noted as a divorce, wedding, and gambling centre by reason of its liberal laws. Pop: 193 882 (2003 est)

Renoir *n* **1** Jean. 1894–1979, French film director: his films include *La grande illusion* (1937), *La règle du jeu* (1939), and *Diary of a Chambermaid* (1945) **2** his father, **Pierre Auguste**. 1841–1919, French painter. One of the initiators of impressionism, he broke away from the movement with his later paintings, esp. his many nude studies, which are more formal compositions

renounce *vb* **-nouncing, -nounced 1** to give up (a belief or habit) voluntarily **2** to give up formally (a claim or right): *he would renounce his rights to the throne* [Latin *renuntiare*]

renovate *vb* **-vating, -vated** to restore to good condition [Latin *re-* again + *novare* to make new] ⟩ **renovation** *n* ⟩ **renovator** *n*

renown *n* widespread good reputation [Old French *renom*]

renowned *adj* famous

rent¹ *vb* **1** to give or have use of (land, a building, a machine, etc.) in return for periodic payments ▷ *n* **2** a payment made periodically for the use of land, a building, a machine, etc. [Old French *rente* revenue]

rent² *n* **1** a slit made by tearing ▷ *vb* **2** the past of **rend**

rental *n* **1** the amount paid or received as rent ▷ *adj* **2** of or relating to rent

rent boy *n* a young male prostitute

rentier (ron-tee-ay) *n* a person who lives off unearned income such as rents or interest

renunciation *n* **1** the act or an instance of renouncing **2** a formal declaration renouncing something

reo *n* NZ a language [Māori]

reopen *vb* to open again after a period of being closed or suspended: *the Supreme Court has agreed to reopen the case*

reorder *vb* to change the order of; organize differently

reorganize *or* **-nise** *vb* **-nizing, -nized** *or* **-nising, -nised** to organize in a new and more efficient way ⟩ **reorganization** *or* **-nisation** *n*

rep¹ *n* theatre short for **repertory company**

rep² *n* **1** a sales representative **2** someone elected to represent a group of people: *the union rep* **3** NZ informal a rugby player selected to represent his district

repair¹ *vb* **1** to restore (something damaged or broken) to good condition or working order **2** to make up for (a mistake or injury) **3** to heal (a breach or division) in (something): *he is attempting to repair his country's relations with America* ▷ *n* **4** the act, task, or process of repairing **5** a part that has been repaired **6** state or condition: *many museums may have to close because they are in such bad repair* [Latin *re-* again + *parare* to make ready] ⟩ **repairable** *adj*

repair² *vb* **repair to** to go to (a place) [Latin *re-* back + *patria* fatherland]

reparable (rep-rab-bl) *adj* able to be repaired or remedied

reparation *n* **1** the act of making up for loss or injury **2** reparations compensation paid by a defeated nation after a war for the damage and injuries it caused [Latin *reparare* to repair]

repartee *n* **1** conversation consisting of witty remarks **2** a sharp witty remark made as a reply [French *repartie*]

repast *n* literary a meal [Old French *repaistre* to feed]

repatriate *vb* **-ating, -ated 1** to send back (a person) to the country of his or her birth or citizenship ▷ *n* **2** a person who has been repatriated: *Algerian repatriates* [Latin *re-* back + *patria* fatherland] ⟩ **repatriation** *n*

repay *vb* **-paying, -paid 1** to refund or reimburse **2** to make a return for (something): *to repay hospitality* ⟩ **repayable** *adj* ⟩ **repayment** *n*

repeal *vb* **1** to cancel (a law) officially ▷ *n* **2** the act of repealing: *the repeal of repressive legislation* [Old French *repeler*] ⟩ **repealable** *adj*

repeat *vb* **1** to say, write, or do again **2** to tell to another person (the secrets told to one by someone else) **3** to recite (a poem, etc.) from memory **4** to occur more than once: *this pattern repeats itself many times* **5** (of food) to be tasted again after eating as the result of belching **6** to say (the words or sounds) uttered by someone else; echo ▷ *n* **7** the act or an instance of repeating **8** a word, action, pattern, etc., that is repeated **9** radio, television a broadcast of a programme which has been broadcast before **10** music a passage that is an exact restatement of the passage preceding it [Latin *repetere* to seek again] ⟩ **repeated** *adj* ⟩ **repeatedly** *adv* ⟩ **repeatable** *adj*

> **USAGE** Since *again* is part of the meaning of *repeat*, one should not say something is *repeated again*.

repeater *n* **1** a gun capable of firing several shots without reloading **2** a clock or watch which strikes the hour or quarter-hour just past, when a spring is pressed

repel *vb* **-pelling, -pelled 1** to cause (someone) to feel disgusted **2** to force or drive back (someone or something) **3** to be effective in keeping away or controlling: *these buzzers are claimed to repel female mosquitoes* **4** to fail to mix with or absorb: *water and oil repel each other* **5** to reject or spurn: *she repelled his advances* [Latin *re-* back + *pellere* to push]

> **USAGE** See at **repulse**.

repellent *adj* **1** disgusting or distasteful **2** resisting water etc. ▷ *n* **3** a chemical used to keep insects or other creatures away

repent *vb* to feel regret for (something bad one has done) [Old French *repentir*] ⟩ **repentance** *n* ⟩ **repentant** *adj*

repercussion *n* **1** repercussions results or consequences of an action or event **2** an echo or reverberation [Latin *repercutere* to strike back]

repertoire *n* **1** all the works that a company or performer can perform **2** the entire stock of skills or techniques that someone or something, such as a computer, is capable of: *a superb repertoire of shots* [French]

repertory *n*, *pl* **-ries 1** same as **repertoire** (2) **2** short for repertory company [Late Latin *repertorium* storehouse]

repertory company *n* a permanent theatre company producing a succession of plays

repetition *n* 1 the act of repeating 2 a thing that is repeated 3 a replica or copy › **repetitious** *adj* › **repetitive** *adj*

rephrase *vb* **-phrasing, -phrased** to express in different words › **rephrasing** *n*

repine *vb* **-pining, -pined** *literary* to be worried or discontented [RE- + PINE²]

replace *vb* **-placing, -placed** 1 to take the place of 2 to substitute a person or thing for (another): *we need to replace that chair* 3 to put (something) back in its rightful place

replacement *n* 1 the act or process of replacing 2 a person or thing that replaces another

replay *n* 1 a showing again of a sequence of action immediately after it happens 2 a second sports match played because an earlier game was drawn ▷ *vb* 3 to play (a recording, match, etc.) again

replenish *vb* to make full or complete again by supplying what has been used up [Old French *replenir*] › **replenishment** *n*

replete *adj* 1 pleasantly full of food and drink 2 well supplied: *a world replete with true horror* [Latin *repletus*] › **repletion** *n*

replica *n* an exact copy [Italian, literally: a reply]

replicate *vb* **-cating, -cated** to make or be an exact copy of; reproduce [Latin *replicatus* bent back] › **replication** *n*

reply *vb* **-plies, -plying, -plied** 1 to make answer (to) in words or writing or by an action 2 to say (something) in answer: *she replied that she did not believe him* ▷ *n, pl* **-plies** 3 an answer or response [Old French *replier* to fold again]

report *vb* 1 to give an account (of) 2 to give an account of the results of an investigation (into): *the commission is to report on global warming* 3 to make a formal report on (a subject) 4 to make a formal complaint about 5 to present (oneself) at an appointed place or for a specific purpose: *report to the manager's office* 6 report to to be responsible to and under the authority of 7 to act as a reporter ▷ *n* 8 an account prepared after investigation and published or broadcast 9 an account of the discussions of a committee or other group of people: *I have the report of the mining union* 10 a story for which there is no absolute proof: *according to report, he is not dead* 11 *Brit and NZ* a statement on the progress of a school child 12 a loud bang made by a gun or explosion 13 comment on a person's character or actions: *he is of good report here* [Latin *re-* back + *portare* to carry] › **reportedly** *adv*

reported speech *n* a report of what someone said that gives the content of the speech without repeating the exact words

reporter *n* a person who gathers news for a newspaper or broadcasting organization

repose¹ *n* 1 a state of quiet restfulness 2 calmness or composure 3 sleep ▷ *vb* **-posing, -posed** 4 to lie or lay down at rest 5 to lie when dead [Old French *reposer*]

repose² *vb* **-posing, -posed** to put (trust) in a person or thing [Latin *reponere* to store up]

reposition *vb* to place in a different position

repository *n, pl* **-ries** 1 a place or container in which things can be stored for safety: *a repository for national treasures* 2 a person to whom a secret is entrusted [Latin *repositorium*]

repossess *vb* (of a lender) to take back (property) from a customer who is behind with payments, for example mortgage repayments › **repossession** *n*

reprehend *vb* to find fault with [Latin *reprehendere*]

reprehensible *adj* deserving criticism: *Willie's reprehensible behaviour*

represent *vb* 1 to act as the authorized delegate for (a person, country, etc.): *she represented her country at the Olympic Games* 2 to act as a substitute (for) 3 to stand as an equivalent of 4 to be a means of expressing: *the lights are relit to represent resurrection* 5 to display the characteristics of: *romanticism in music is represented by Liszt* 6 to describe as having a specified character or quality: *the magical bird was often represented as having two heads* 7 to state or explain 8 to present an image of through a picture or sculpture 9 to bring clearly before the mind [Latin *repraesentare* to exhibit]

representation *n* 1 the state of being represented 2 anything that represents, such as a pictorial portrait 3 representations formal statements made to an official body by a person making a complaint › **representational** *adj*

representative *n* 1 a person chosen to act for or represent a group 2 a person who tries to sell the products or services of a firm 3 a typical example ▷ *adj* 4 typical of a class or kind 5 representing 6 including examples of all the interests or types in a group 7 acting as deputy for another 8 of a political system in which people choose a person to make decisions on their behalf

repress *vb* 1 to keep (feelings) under control 2 to restrict the freedom of: *he continued to repress his people* 3 *psychol* to banish (unpleasant thoughts) from one's conscious mind [Latin *reprimere* to press back] › **repression** *n* › **repressive** *adj*

reprieve *vb* **-prieving, -prieved** 1 to postpone the execution of (a condemned person) 2 to give temporary relief to ▷ *n* 3 a postponement or cancellation of a punishment 4 a warrant granting a postponement or cancellation 5 a temporary relief from pain or harm [Old French *repris* (something) taken back]

reprimand *vb* 1 to blame (someone) officially for a fault ▷ *n* 2 an instance of blaming someone officially [French *réprimande*]

reprint *vb* 1 to print further copies of (a book) ▷ *n* 2 a reprinted copy

reprisal *n* an act of taking revenge: *many residents say they are living in fear of reprisals by the army* [Old French *reprisaille*]

reprise (rip-**preez**) *music* *n* 1 the repeating of an earlier theme ▷ *vb* **-prising, -prised** 2 to repeat an earlier theme

reproach *n* 1 blame or rebuke 2 a scolding 3 beyond reproach beyond criticism ▷ *vb* 4 to express disapproval of (someone's actions) [Old French *reprochier*] › **reproachful** *adj*

reprobate (rep-roh-**bate**) *n* 1 an unprincipled bad person ▷ *adj* 2 morally unprincipled [Late Latin *reprobatus* held in disfavour]

reprobation *n literary* disapproval or blame

reproduce *vb* **-ducing, -duced** 1 to make a copy or representation of 2 *biology* to produce offspring 3 to re-create › **reproducible** *adj*

reproduction *n* 1 *biology* a process by which an animal or plant produces one or more individuals similar to itself 2 a copy of a work of art 3 the quality of sound from an audio system 4 the act or process of reproducing ▷ *adj* 5 made in imitation of an earlier style: *reproduction furniture* › **reproductive** *adj*

reproof *n* a severe blaming of someone for a fault

reprove *vb* **-proving, -proved** to speak severely to (someone) about a fault [Old French *reprover*] › **reprovingly** *adv*

reptile *n* 1 a cold-blooded animal, such as a tortoise, snake, or crocodile, that has an outer covering of horny scales or plates and lays eggs 2 a contemptible grovelling person [Late Latin *reptilis* creeping] › **reptilian** *adj*

Repton *n* Humphry. 1752–1818, English landscape gardener

republic *n* 1 a form of government in which the people or their elected representatives possess the supreme power 2 a country in which the head of state is an elected or nominated president [Latin *respublica*, literally: the public thing]

republican *adj* 1 of or supporting a republic ▷ *n* 2 a

person who supports or advocates a republic
> republicanism n

Republican adj **1** belonging to the Republican Party, the more conservative of the two main political parties in the US **2** belonging to the Irish Republican Army ▷ n **3** a member or supporter of the Republican Party in the US **4** a member or supporter of the Irish Republican Army **> Republicanism** n

Republic of Ireland n See Ireland (2)

repudiate (rip-pew-dee-ate) vb **-ating, -ated 1** to reject the authority or validity of **2** to disown (a person) **3** to refuse to acknowledge or pay (a debt) [Latin *repudium* divorce] **> repudiation** n

repugnant adj offensive or disgusting [Latin *repugnans* resisting] **> repugnance** n

repulse vb **-pulsing, -pulsed 1** to be disgusting to: *this act of feminist rage repulsed as many as it delighted* **2** to drive (an army) back **3** to reject with coldness or discourtesy: *she repulsed his advances* ▷ n **4** a driving back **5** a cold discourteous rejection or refusal [Latin *repellere*]

> **USAGE** Some people think that the use of *repulse* in sentences such as *he was repulsed by what he saw* is incorrect and that the correct word is *repel*.

repulsion n **1** a feeling of disgust or aversion **2** physics a force separating two objects, such as the force between two like electric charges

repulsive adj **1** disgusting or distasteful **2** physics of repulsion **> repulsively** adv

reputable (rep-pew-tab-bl) adj trustworthy or respectable **> reputably** adv

reputation n **1** the opinion generally held of a person or thing **2** a high opinion generally held about a person or thing **3** notoriety or fame, esp. for some specified characteristic [Latin *reputatio*]

repute n good reputation: *a sculptor of international repute* [Latin *reputare* to think over]

reputed adj supposed or rumoured: *the island was reputed to have held a Roman temple; the reputed murderess* **> reputedly** adv

request vb **1** to ask for or politely demand: *we requested a formal meeting with the committee* ▷ n **2** the act or an instance of asking for something: *a polite request* **3** something asked for **4 on request** if asked for: *most companies will send samples on request* [Old French *requeste*]

Requiem (rek-wee-em) n **1** RC Church a Mass celebrated for the dead **2** a musical setting of this Mass [Latin *requies* rest]

require vb **-quiring, -quired 1** to need **2** to impose as a necessary condition: *the decision requires a logical common-sense approach* **3** to insist upon **4** to order or command: *family doctors are required to produce annual reports* [Latin *requirere* to seek to know]

> **USAGE** The use of *require to* as in *I require to see the manager* or *you require to complete a special form* is thought by many people to be incorrect: *I need to see the manager; you are required to complete a special form.*

requirement n **1** something demanded or imposed as an obligation **2** a specific need or want

requisite (rek-wizz-it) adj **1** absolutely essential ▷ n **2** something essential [Latin *requisitus* sought after]

requisition vb **1** to demand and take for use, esp. for military or public use ▷ n **2** a formal request or demand for the use of something **3** the act of taking something over, esp. for military or public use **4** a formal written demand

requite vb **-quiting, -quited** to return to someone (the same treatment or feeling as received): *an Australian who requites her love* [re- back + obsolete *quite* to repay] **> requital** n

reredos (rear-doss) n a screen or wall decoration at the back of an altar [Old French *arere* behind + *dos* back]

reroute vb **-routing, -routed** to send or direct by a different route

rerun n **1** a film or programme that is broadcast again **2** a race that is run again ▷ vb **-running, -ran, -run 3** to put on (a film or programme) again **4** to run (a race) again

resale n the selling again of something purchased

reschedule vb **-duling, -duled 1** to change the time, date, or schedule of: *the show has been rescheduled for August* **2** to arrange a revised schedule for repayment of (a debt)

rescind vb to annul or repeal [Latin *rescindere* to cut off] **> rescission** n

rescue vb **-cuing, -cued 1** to bring (someone or something) out of danger or trouble ▷ n **2** the act or an instance of rescuing [Old French *rescourre*] **> rescuer** n

reseal vb to close or secure tightly again

research n **1** systematic investigation to establish facts or collect information on a subject ▷ vb **2** to carry out investigations into (a subject) [Old French *recercher* to search again] **> researcher** n

resemble vb **-bling, -bled** to be or look like [Old French *resembler*] **> resemblance** n

resent vb to feel bitter or indignant about [French *ressentir*] **> resentful** adj **> resentment** n

reservation n **1** a doubt: *his only reservation was, did he have the stamina?* **2** an exception or limitation that prevents one's wholehearted acceptance: *work I admire without reservation* **3** a seat, room, etc. that has been reserved **4** (esp. in the US) an area of land set aside for American Indian peoples: *the Cherokee reservation* **5** Brit short for central reservation

reserve vb **-serving, -served 1** to keep back or set aside for future use **2** to obtain by arranging beforehand: *I phoned to reserve two tickets* **3** to keep for oneself: *the association reserves the right to charge a fee* **4** to delay announcing (a legal judgment) ▷ n **5** something kept back or set aside for future use **6** the state or condition of being reserved: *we're keeping these two in reserve* **7** sport a substitute **8** an area of publicly owned land used for sport, etc.: *a wildlife reserve* **9** the hiding of one's feelings and personality **10** the part of a nation's armed services not in active service **11 reserves** finance money or assets held by a bank or business to meet future expenses **12** Canad an Indian reservation [Latin *reservare* to keep]

reserved adj **1** not showing one's feelings **2** set aside for use by a particular person

reserve price n the minimum price acceptable to the owner of property being auctioned or sold

reservist n a member of a nation's military reserve

reservoir n **1** a natural or artificial lake for storing water for community use **2** a large supply of something: *a vast reservoir of youthful enthusiasm* [French *réservoir*]

resettle vb **-tling, -tled** to settle to live in a different place **> resettlement** n

Resht n a variant of Rasht

reshuffle n **1** a reorganization of jobs in a government or company ▷ vb **-fling, -fled 2** to reorganize (jobs or duties) in a government or company

reside vb **-siding, -sided** formal **1** to live permanently (in a place): *my daughter resides in Europe* **2** to be present (in): *desire resides in the unconscious* [Latin *residere* to sit back]

residence n **1** a person's home or house **2** a large imposing house **3** the fact of residing in a place **4** a period of residing in a place **5 in residence a** living in a particular place: *the Monarch was not in residence* **b** (of an artist) working for a set period at a college, gallery, etc.: *composer in residence*

resident n **1** a person who lives in a place **2** a bird or animal that does not migrate ▷ adj **3** living in a place **4** living at a place in order to carry out a job: *a resident custodian* **5** employed for one's specialized abilities: *the Museum's resident expert on seventeenth-century Dutch art* **6** (of birds and animals) not in the habit of migrating

r

residential *adj* **1** (of a part of a town) consisting mainly of houses **2** providing living accommodation: *residential clubs for homeless boys*

residential school *n* a government boarding school in N Canada for Indian and Inuit students

residual *adj* **1** of or being a remainder ▷ *n* **2** something left over as a residue

residue *n* **1** what is left over after something has been removed **2** *law* what is left of an estate after the discharge of debts and distribution of specific gifts [Latin *residuus* remaining over]

residuum *n*, *pl* -**ua** same as **residue**

resign *vb* **1** to give up office or a job **2** to accept (an unpleasant fact): *he resigned himself to the inevitable* **3** to give up (a right or claim) [Latin *resignare* to unseal, destroy]

resignation *n* **1** the act of resigning **2** a formal document stating one's intention to resign **3** passive endurance of difficulties: *full of quiet resignation*

resigned *adj* content to endure something unpleasant ▷ **resignedly** *adv*

resilient *adj* **1** (of a person) recovering easily and quickly from misfortune or illness **2** (of an object) capable of regaining its original shape or position after bending or stretching [Latin *resilire* to jump back] ▷ **resilience** *n*

resin (rezz-in) *n* **1** a solid or semisolid substance obtained from certain plants: *cannabis resin* **2** a similar substance produced synthetically [Latin *resina*] ▷ **resinous** *adj*

resist *vb* **1** to stand firm against or oppose: *the party's old guard continue to resist economic reform* **2** to refrain from in spite of temptation: *I couldn't resist a huge portion of almond cake* **3** to refuse to comply with: *to resist arrest* **4** to be proof against: *airport design should be strengthened to help resist explosion* [Latin *resistere*] ▷ **resistible** *adj*

resistance *n* **1** the act of resisting **2** the capacity to withstand something, esp. the body's natural capacity to withstand disease **3** *electronics* the opposition to a flow of electric current through a circuit, component, or substance **4** any force that slows or hampers movement: *wind resistance* **5** line of least resistance the easiest, but not necessarily the best, course of action ▷ **resistant** *adj*, *n*

Resistance *n* the Resistance an illegal organization fighting for national liberty in a country under enemy occupation

Resistencia *n* a city in NE Argentina, on the Paraná River. Pop: 423 000 (2005 est)

resistor *n* an electrical component designed to introduce a known value of resistance into a circuit

resit *Brit vb* -**sitting**, -**sat** **1** to sit (an examination) again ▷ *n* **2** an examination which one must sit again

reskill *vb* to train (workers) to acquire new skills ▷ **reskilling** *n*

Resnais *n* Alain. 1922–2014, French film director, whose films include *Hiroshima mon amour* (1959), *L'Année dernière à Marienbad* (1961), *La Vie est un roman* (1983), and *On Connaît la Chanson* (1998)

resolute *adj* firm in purpose or belief [Latin *resolutus*] ▷ **resolutely** *adv*

resolution *n* **1** firmness or determination **2** a decision to do something **3** a formal expression of opinion by a meeting **4** the act of resolving **5** *music* the process in harmony whereby a dissonant note or chord is followed by a consonant one **6** the ability of a television or digital camera to reproduce fine detail **7** *physics* Also called: **resolving power** the ability of a telescope or microscope to produce separate images of closely placed objects

resolvable *or* **resoluble** *adj* able to be resolved or analysed

resolve *vb* -**solving**, -**solved** **1** to decide or determine firmly **2** to express (an opinion) formally by a vote **3** to separate or cause to separate into (constituent parts) **4** to find the answer or solution to **5** to explain away or dispel: *to resolve the controversy* **6** *music* to follow (a dissonant note or chord) by one producing a consonance **7** *physics* to distinguish between (separate parts) of (an image) as in a microscope, telescope, or other optical instrument ▷ *n* **8** absolute determination: *he spoke of his resolve to deal with the problem of terrorism* [Latin *resolvere* to unfasten, reveal]

resolved *adj* determined

resonance *n* **1** the condition or quality of being resonant **2** sound produced by a body vibrating in sympathy with a neighbouring source of sound [Latin *resonare* to resound]

resonant *adj* **1** resounding or re-echoing **2** producing resonance: *the resonant cavities of the mouth* **3** full of resonance: *his voice is a resonant baritone*

resonate *vb* -**nating**, -**nated** to resound or cause to resound ▷ **resonator** *n*

resort *vb* **1** resort to to have recourse to for help, use, etc.: *some people have resorted to begging for food* **2** to go to, esp. often or habitually: *to resort to the beach* ▷ *n* **3** a place to which many people go for holidays **4** the use of something as a means or aid **5** last resort the last possible course of action open to a person [Old French *resortir* to come out again]

resound (riz-zownd) *vb* **1** to ring or echo with sound **2** (of sounds) to echo or ring **3** to be widely known: *his fame resounded throughout India* [Latin *resonare* to sound again]

resounding *adj* **1** echoing **2** clear and emphatic: *he won a resounding victory* ▷ **resoundingly** *adv*

resource *n* **1** resources sources of economic wealth, esp. of a country or business enterprise: *mineral resources* **2** resources money available for use **3** something resorted to for aid or support: *he saw the university as a resource for the community* **4** the ability to deal with problems: *a man of resource* **5** a means of doing something: *resistance was their only resource* [Old French *resourdre* to spring up again]

resourceful *adj* capable and full of initiative ▷ **resourcefulness** *n*

respect *n* **1** consideration: *respect for my feelings* **2** an attitude of deference or esteem **3** the state of being honoured or esteemed **4** a detail or characteristic: *in virtually all respects boys develop more slowly than girls* **5** in respect of *or* with respect to in reference or relation to **6** respects polite greetings: *he paid his respects to her and left* ▷ *vb* **7** to have an attitude of esteem towards: *she is the person I most respect and wish to emulate* **8** to pay proper attention to or consideration to: *he called on rebel groups to respect a cease-fire* [Latin *respicere* to pay attention to] ▷ **respecter** *n*

respectable *adj* **1** worthy of respect **2** having good social standing or reputation **3** relatively or fairly good: *they obtained respectable results* **4** fit to be seen by other people ▷ **respectability** *n* ▷ **respectably** *adv*

respectful *adj* full of or showing respect ▷ **respectfully** *adv*

respecting *prep* on the subject of

respective *adj* relating separately to each of several people or things: *the culprits will be repatriated to their respective countries*

respectively *adv* (in listing things that refer to another list) separately in the order given: *Diotema and Mantinea were tutors to Pythagoras and Socrates respectively*

Respighi *n* Ottorino. 1879–1936, Italian composer, noted esp. for his suites *The Fountains of Rome* (1917) and *The Pines of Rome* (1924)

respiration (ress-per-ray-shun) *n* **1** breathing **2** the process in living organisms of taking in oxygen and giving out carbon dioxide **3** the breakdown of complex organic substances that takes place in the cells of animals and plants, producing energy and carbon dioxide ▷ **respiratory** *adj*

respirator *n* **1** a device worn over the mouth and nose to prevent the breathing in of poisonous fumes **2** an apparatus for providing artificial respiration

respire *vb* -**spiring**, -**spired** **1** to breathe **2** to undergo respiration [Latin *respirare* to exhale]

respite *n* 1 an interval of rest: *I allowed myself a six month respite to enjoy my family* 2 a temporary delay [Old French *respit*]

resplendent *adj* 1 brilliant or splendid in appearance 2 shining [Latin *re-* again + *splendere* to shine] > **resplendence** *n*

respond *vb* 1 to state or utter (something) in reply 2 to act in reply: *the government must respond accordingly to our recommendations* 3 to react favourably: *most headaches will respond to the use of relaxants* [Old French *respondre*]

respondent *n law* a person against whom a petition is brought

response *n* 1 the act of responding 2 a reply or reaction 3 a reaction to stimulation of the nervous system 4 **responses** *Christianity* the words recited or sung in reply to the priest at a church service

responsibility *n, pl* -**ties** 1 the state of being responsible 2 a person or thing for which one is responsible

responsible *adj* 1 responsible for having control or authority over 2 being the agent or cause (of some action): *only a small number of students were responsible for the disturbances* 3 **responsible to** being accountable for one's actions and decisions to: *management should be made more responsible to shareholders* 4 rational and accountable for one's own actions 5 (of a position or duty) involving decision and accountability [Latin *respondere* to respond] > **responsibly** *adv*

responsive *adj* reacting quickly or favourably to something > **responsiveness** *n*

respray *n* a new coat of paint applied to a vehicle

rest[1] *n* 1 relaxation from exertion or labour 2 a period of inactivity 3 relief or refreshment 4 calm 5 death regarded as repose: *now he has gone to his eternal rest* 6 **at rest** a not moving b calm c dead d asleep 7 a pause or interval 8 a mark in a musical score indicating a pause lasting a specific time 9 a thing or place on which to put something for support or to steady it 10 **lay to rest** to bury (a dead person) > *vb* 11 to become or make refreshed 12 to position (oneself, etc.) for rest or relaxation 13 to place for support or steadying: *he slumped forward to rest his head on his forearms* 14 to depend or rely: *his presidency rested on the outcome of the crisis* 15 to direct (one's eyes) or (of one's eyes) to be directed: *she rested her gaze on the face of the statue* 16 to be at ease 17 to cease or cause to cease from motion or exertion 18 to remain without further attention or action: *she refused to let the matter rest* 19 *law* to finish the introduction of evidence in (a case) 20 to put (pastry) in a cool place to allow the gluten to contract [Old English *ræst, reste*]

rest[2] *n* 1 **the rest** a something left; remainder b the others: *the rest of the world* > *vb* 2 to continue to be (as specified): *your conscience can rest easy* [Old French *rester* to remain]

rest area *n Austral and NZ* a motorist's stopping place off a highway, equipped with tables and seats

restart *vb* to commence (something) or set (something) in motion again

restate *vb* to state or affirm (something) again or in a different way > **restatement** *n*

restaurant *n* a place where meals are prepared and served to customers [French]

restaurant car *n* a railway coach in which meals are served

restaurateur (rest-er-a-**tur**) *n* a person who owns or runs a restaurant

rest-cure *n* a rest taken as part of a course of medical treatment

restful *adj* relaxing or soothing

restitution *n* 1 the act of giving back something that has been lost or stolen 2 *law* compensation for loss or injury [Latin *restituere* to rebuild]

restive *adj* 1 restless or uneasy 2 impatient of control or authority [Old French *restif* balky]

restless *adj* 1 bored or dissatisfied 2 unable to stay still or quiet 3 not restful: *a restless sleep* > **restlessly** *adv* > **restlessness** *n*

restoration *n* 1 the act of restoring to a former or original condition, place, etc. 2 the giving back of something lost or stolen 3 something restored, replaced, or reconstructed 4 a model or representation of a ruin or extinct animal 5 **the Restoration** *Brit* the re-establishment of the monarchy in 1660 or the reign of Charles II (1660–85)

restorative (rist-or-a-tiv) *adj* 1 giving back health or good spirits ▷ *n* 2 a food or medicine that gives back health or good spirits

restore *vb* -**storing**, -**stored** 1 to return (something) to its original or former condition 2 to bring back to health or good spirits 3 to return (something lost or stolen) to its owner 4 to re-enforce or re-establish: *he must restore confidence in himself and his government; they worked to restore the monarchy* 5 to reconstruct (a ruin, extinct animal, etc.) [Latin *restaurare* to rebuild] > **restorer** *n*

restrain *vb* 1 to hold (someone) back from some action 2 to limit or restrict: *restrain any tendency to impulse-buy* 3 to deprive (someone) of liberty [Latin *re-* back + *stringere* to draw]

restrained *adj* not displaying emotion

restraint *n* 1 something that restrains 2 the ability to control one's impulses or passions 3 a restraining or being restrained

restrict *vb* to confine or keep within certain limits [Latin *restrictus* bound up] > **restrictive** *adj*

restriction *n* a rule or situation that limits or controls something or someone: *operating under severe financial restrictions*

restrictive practice *n* 1 a trading agreement against the public interest 2 a practice of a union or other group tending to limit the freedom of other workers or employers

rest room *n US, Canad and Austral* a toilet in a public building

restructure *vb* -**turing**, -**tured** to organize in a different way: *to restructure the world economy*

result *n* 1 the outcome or consequence of an action, policy, etc. 2 the final score of a sporting contest 3 a number or value obtained by solving a mathematical problem 4 a favourable result, esp. a victory or success: *the best chance of a result is at Cheltenham* 5 **results** the marks or grades obtained in an examination ▷ *vb* 6 **result from** to be the outcome or consequence of: *poverty resulting from high unemployment* 7 **result in** to end in (a specified way): *negotiations which resulted in the Treaty of Paris* [Latin *resultare* to spring from]

resultant *adj* 1 arising as a result: *the resultant publicity* ▷ *n* 2 *maths, physics* a single vector that is the vector sum of two or more other vectors, such as a force which results from two other forces acting on a single point

resume *vb* -**suming**, -**sumed** 1 to begin again or go on with (something interrupted) 2 to occupy again or recover: *he will resume his party post today* [Latin *resumere*]

résumé (rezz-yew-may) *n* 1 a short descriptive summary 2 *US, Canad and Austral* a curriculum vitae [French]

resumption *n* the act of resuming or beginning again

resurgence *n* a rising again to vigour: *worldwide religious resurgence* [Latin *resurgere* to rise again] > **resurgent** *adj*

resurrect *vb* 1 to bring or be brought back to life from death 2 to bring back into use or activity

resurrection *n* 1 a return to life by a dead person 2 revival or renewal 3 **the Resurrection** a *Christian theol* the rising again of Christ from the tomb three days after his death b the rising again from the dead of all people at the Last Judgment [Latin *resurgere* to rise again]

resuscitate (ris-suss-it-tate) *vb* -**tating**, -**tated** to restore to consciousness [Latin *re-* again + *suscitare* to raise] > **resuscitation** *n*

retail *n* 1 the sale of goods individually or in small

r

quantities to the public ▷ *adj* **2** of or engaged in such selling: *auctioneers have been successful in cornering the retail market* ▷ *adv* **3** in small amounts or at a retail price ▷ *vb* **4** to sell or be sold in small quantities to the public **5** to relate (gossip or scandal) in detail: *he gleefully retailed the story* [Old French re- again + taillier to cut] **> retailer** *n*

retail therapy *n* the action of shopping for clothes, etc., esp. to cheer oneself up

retain *vb* **1** to keep in one's possession **2** to be able to hold or contain: *with this method the salmon retains its flavour and texture* **3** *law* to engage the services of (a barrister) by payment of a preliminary fee **4** (of a person) to be able to remember (something) without difficulty **5** to hold in position [Latin retinere to hold back]

retainer *n* **1** a fee paid in advance to engage someone's services **2** *Brit, Austral and NZ* a reduced rent paid for a room or flat to reserve it for future use **3** a servant who has been with a family for a long time

retaining wall *n* a wall constructed to hold back earth, loose rock, etc.

retake *vb* **-taking, -took, -taken 1** to recapture: *to retake Jerusalem* **2** to take something, such as an examination or vote, again ▷ *n* **3** *films* a rephotographed scene

retaliate *vb* **-ating, -ated 1** to repay some injury or wrong in kind **2** to cast (accusations) back upon a person [Latin re- back + talis of such kind] **> retaliation** *n* **> retaliatory** *adj*

retard *vb* to delay or slow down the progress or development of (something) [Latin retardare] **> retardant** *n, adj* **> retardation** *n*

retarded *adj old-fashioned, offensive* underdeveloped mentally

retch *vb* **1** to undergo spasms of the stomach as if one is vomiting ▷ *n* **2** an involuntary spasm of the stomach [Old English hræcan]

retention *n* **1** the act of retaining or state of being retained **2** the capacity to remember **3** *pathol* the abnormal holding of something within the body, esp. fluid **> retentive** *adj*

rethink *vb* **-thinking, -thought 1** to think about (something) again with a view to changing one's tactics ▷ *n* **2** the act or an instance of thinking again

Réti *n* Richard. 1889–1929, Hungarian chess player and theorist; influential in enunciating the theories of the hypermodern school

reticent *adj* not willing to say or tell much [Latin reticere to keep silent] **> reticence** *n*

reticulate *adj* in the form of a network or having a network of parts: *a reticulate leaf* [Late Latin reticulatus like a net] **> reticulation** *n*

retina *n, pl* **-nas** *or* **-nae** the light-sensitive inner lining of the back of the eyeball [Medieval Latin] **> retinal** *adj*

retinopathy *n* any of various noninflammatory diseases of the retina, which may have serious effects on vision

retinue *n* a band of attendants accompanying an important person [Old French retenue]

retire *vb* **-tiring, -tired 1** to give up or to cause (a person) to give up work, esp. on reaching pensionable age **2** to go away into seclusion **3** to go to bed **4** to withdraw from a sporting contest, esp. because of injury **5** to pull back (troops) from battle or (of troops) to fall back [French retirer] **> retired** *adj* **> retirement** *n*

retirement pension *n Brit* a regular payment made by the state or a former employee to a retired person over a specified age

retiring *adj* very shy

retort[1] *vb* **1** to reply quickly, wittily, or angrily **2** to use (an argument) against its originator ▷ *n* **3** a sharp, angry, or witty reply **4** an argument used against its originator [Latin re- back + torquere to twist, wrench]

retort[2] *n* **1** a glass vessel with a long tapering neck that is bent down, used for distillation **2** a vessel used for heating ores in the production of metals or heating

coal to produce gas [see RETORT[1]]

retouch *vb* to restore or improve (a painting or photograph) with new touches

retrace *vb* **-tracing, -traced 1** to go back over (one's steps or a route) **2** to go over (a story) from the beginning

retract *vb* **1** to withdraw (a statement, charge, etc.) as invalid or unjustified **2** to go back on (a promise or agreement) **3** to draw in (a part or appendage): *the rear wheels are retracted for tight spaces* [Latin retractare to withdraw] **> retraction** *n*

retractile *adj* capable of being drawn in: *the retractile claws of a cat*

retrain *vb* to train to do a new or different job **> retraining** *n*

retread *vb* **-treading, -treaded 1** to bond a new tread onto (a worn tyre) ▷ *n* **2** a remoulded tyre

retreat *vb* **1** *military* to withdraw or retire in the face of or from action with an enemy **2** to retire or withdraw to seclusion or shelter **3** to alter one's opinion about something ▷ *n* **4** the act of retreating or withdrawing **5** *military* **a** a withdrawal or retirement in the face of the enemy **b** a bugle call signifying withdrawal or retirement **6** a place to which one may retire, esp. for religious contemplation **7** a period of seclusion, esp. for religious contemplation **8** the act of altering one's opinion about something [Old French retret]

retrench *vb* to reduce expenditure [Old French re- off + trenchier to cut] **> retrenchment** *n*

retrial *n* a second trial of a defendant in a court of law

retribution *n* punishment or vengeance for evil deeds [Latin re- back + tribuere to pay] **> retributive** *adj*

retrieve *vb* **-trieving, -trieved 1** to get or fetch back again **2** to bring back to a more satisfactory state: *his attempt to retrieve the situation* **3** to rescue or save **4** to recover (stored information) from a computer system **5** (of dogs) to find and fetch (shot birds and animals) **6** to remember ▷ *n* **7** the chance of being retrieved: *beyond retrieve* [Old French retrover] **> retrievable** *adj* **> retrieval** *n*

retriever *n* a dog trained to retrieve shot birds and animals

retro *adj* associated with or revived from the past: *swap sandals for heeled mules to complete the retro look*

retro- *prefix* **1** back or backwards: *retroactive* **2** located behind: *retrochoir* [Latin]

retroactive *adj* effective from a date in the past: *justice through retroactive legislation is never justice*

retrograde *adj* **1** tending towards an earlier worse condition **2** moving or bending backwards **3** (esp. of order) reverse or inverse ▷ *vb* **-grading, -graded 4** to go backwards or deteriorate [Latin retro- backwards + gradi to walk]

retrogress *vb* to go back to an earlier worse condition [Latin retrogressus having moved backwards] **> retrogression** *n* **> retrogressive** *adj*

retrorocket *n* a small rocket on a larger rocket or a spacecraft, that produces thrust in the opposite direction to the direction of flight in order to slow down

retrospect *n* **in retrospect** when looking back on the past [Latin retrospicere to look back]

retrospective *adj* **1** looking back in time **2** applying from a date in the past: *retrospective legislation* ▷ *n* **3** an exhibition of an artist's life's work

retroussé (rit-troo-say) *adj* (of a nose) turned upwards [French]

retsina *n* a Greek wine flavoured with resin [Modern Greek]

return *vb* **1** to come back to a former place or state **2** to give, put, or send back **3** to repay with something of equivalent value: *she returned the compliment* **4** to hit, throw, or play (a ball) back **5** to recur or reappear: *as he relaxed his appetite returned* **6** to come back or revert in thought or speech: *let's return to what he said* **7** to earn or yield (profit or interest) **8** to answer or reply **9** to vote into office **10** *law* (of a jury) to deliver (a verdict) ▷ *n* **11** the act or an instance of coming back **12** the act of being returned **13** replacement or restoration: *the return of law and order* **14** something that is given or sent back **15** *sport* the act of playing or throwing a ball back **16** a recurrence or reappearance: *the return of tuberculosis* **17** the yield or profit from an investment or venture **18** a statement of one's taxable income (a **tax return**) **19** an answer or reply **20** *Brit, Austral and NZ* short for **return ticket 21 in return** in exchange **22 returns** a statement of the votes counted at an election **23 by return (of post)** *Brit* by the next post back to the sender **24 many happy returns (of the day)** a conventional birthday greeting ▷ *adj* **25** of or being a return: *the team is keen on a return match* [Old French *retorner*] **> returnable** *adj*

returning officer *n* an official in charge of conducting an election in a constituency

return ticket *n Brit, Austral and NZ* a ticket allowing a passenger to travel to a place and back

retweet *vb* to post (another Twitter user's post) for one's own followers

Retz *n* Gilles de Retz See **Rais**

Reuchlin *n* Johann. 1455–1522, German humanist, who promoted the study of Greek and Hebrew

reunify *vb* **-fies, -fying, -fied** to bring together again (something previously divided) **> reunification** *n*

reunion *n* **1** a gathering of people who have been apart **2** the act of coming together again

Réunion *n* an island in the Indian Ocean, in the Mascarene Islands: an overseas region of France, having been in French possession since 1642. A number of far-flung and uninhabited islands, some located on the opposite side of Madagascar, were also politically part of Réunion until 2007, when they were transferred to the French Southern and Antarctic Territories. Capital: Saint-Denis. Pop: 767 000 (2004 est). Area: 2510 sq km (970 sq miles)

reunite *vb* **-niting, -nited** to bring or come together again after a separation

Reus *n* a city in NE Spain, northwest of Tarragona: became commercially important after the establishment of an English colony (about 1750). Pop: 94 407 (2003 est)

reuse *n* **1** the act of using something again ▷ *vb* **-using, -used 2** to use again **> reusable** *adj*

Reuter *n* Baron **Paul Julius von**. original name *Israel Beer Josaphat*. 1816–99, German telegrapher, who founded a news agency in London (1851)

Reutlingen *n* a city in SW Germany, in Baden-Württemberg: founded in the 11th century; an Imperial free city from 1240 until 1802; textile industry. Pop: 112 346 (2003 est)

rev *informal n* **1** revolution per minute (of an engine) ▷ *vb* **revving, revved 2** to increase the speed of revolution of (an engine)

rev. 1 revise(d) **2** revision

Rev. Reverend

Reval *n* the German name for **Tallinn**

revalue *vb* **-valuing, -valued** to adjust the exchange value of (a currency) upwards **> revaluation** *n*

revamp *vb* to patch up or renovate

Revd. Reverend

reveal *vb* **1** to disclose or divulge (a secret) **2** to expose to view or show (something concealed) **3** (of God) to disclose (divine truths) [Latin *revelare* to unveil]

revealing *adj* **1** disclosing information that one did not know: *she made several revealing remarks during the interview* **2** (of clothes) showing more of the body than is usual

reveille (riv-val-ee) *n* a signal given by a bugle or drum to awaken soldiers or sailors in the morning [French *réveillez!* awake!]

revel *vb* **-velling, -velled** *or US* **-veling, -veled 1** **revel in** to take pleasure or wallow in: *he would revel in his victory* **2** to take part in noisy festivities ▷ *n* **3 revels** noisy

merrymaking [Old French *reveler*] **> reveller** *n*

revelation *n* **1** the act of making known a truth which was previously secret **2** a fact newly made known **3** a person or experience that proves to be different from expectations: *New York State could prove a revelation to first-time visitors* **4** *Christianity* God's disclosure of his own nature and his purpose for mankind

Revelation *or* **Revelations** *n informal* the last book of the New Testament, containing visionary descriptions of heaven, and of the end of the world

revelry *n, pl* **-ries** noisy or unrestrained merrymaking

revenge *n* **1** vengeance for wrongs or injury received **2** something done as a means of vengeance ▷ *vb* **-venging, -venged 3** to inflict equivalent injury or damage for (injury received) **4** to take vengeance for (oneself or another) [Old French *revenger*] **> revengeful** *adj*

revenge porn *n* a pornographic image or images posted on the internet without the consent of a participant, for vindictive or malicious reasons

revenue *n* **1** income, esp. that obtained by a government from taxation **2** a government department responsible for collecting taxes [Old French *revenir* to return]

reverberate *vb* **-rating, -rated 1** to resound or re-echo **2** to reflect or be reflected many times [Latin *re-* again + *verberare* to beat] **> reverberation** *n*

revere *vb* **-vering, -vered** to be in awe of and respect deeply [Latin *revereri*]

Revere *n* Paul. 1735–1818, American patriot and silversmith, best known for his night ride on April 18, 1775, to warn the Massachusetts colonists of the coming of the British troops

reverence *n* profound respect **> reverential** *adj*

Reverence *n* Your *or* His Reverence a title sometimes used for a Roman Catholic priest

reverend *adj* **1** worthy of reverence **2** relating to or designating a clergyman ▷ *n* **3** *informal* a clergyman

Reverend *adj* a title of respect for a clergyman

> **USAGE** *Reverend* with a surname alone (*Reverend Smith*), as a term of address ('Yes, *Reverend*'), or in the greeting of a letter (*Dear Rev. Mr Smith*) are all generally considered to be wrong usage. Preferred are (the) *Reverend John Smith* or *Reverend Mr Smith* and *Dear Mr Smith*.

reverent *adj* feeling or expressing reverence

reverie *n* an absent-minded daydream [Old French *resverie* wildness]

revers (riv-veer) *n, pl* **-vers** the turned-back lining of part of a garment, such as the lapel or cuff [French]

reverse *vb* **-versing, -versed 1** to turn or set in an opposite direction, order, or position **2** to change into something different or contrary: *the cabinet intends to reverse the trend of recent polls* **3** to move backwards or in an opposite direction: *as he started to reverse the car, the bomb exploded* **4** to run (machinery) in the opposite direction to normal **5** to turn inside out **6** *law* to revoke or set aside (a judgment or decree) **7 reverse the charges** *Brit* to make a telephone call at the recipient's expense ▷ *n* **8** the opposite or contrary of something **9** the back or rear side of something **10** a change to an opposite position, state, or direction **11** a change for the worse **12** the gear by which a motor vehicle can be made to go backwards **13** the side of a coin bearing a secondary design **14 in reverse** in an opposite or backward direction **15 the reverse of** not at all: *the result was the reverse of his expectations* ▷ *adj* **16** opposite or contrary in direction, position, etc. **17** denoting the gear by which a motor vehicle can be made to go backwards [Latin *reversus* turned back] **> reversal** *n*

reversible *adj* **1** capable of being reversed: *the effect of the operation may not be reversible* **2** (of a garment) made so that either side may be used as the outer side

Reversing Falls n (sometimes not caps) a series of rapids in the Saint John River, New Brunswick, Canada, the flow of which regularly reverses itself owing to the force an incoming tide

reversing lights pl n a pair of lights on the rear of a motor vehicle that go on when the vehicle is moving backwards

reversion n 1 a return to an earlier condition, practice, or belief 2 biology the return of individuals or organs to a more primitive condition or type 3 the rightful passing of property to the owner or designated heir

revert vb 1 to go back to a former state 2 biology (of individuals or organs) to return to a more primitive, earlier, or simpler condition or type 3 to come back to a subject 4 property law (of an estate) to return to its former owner [Latin revertere]

> **USAGE** Since back is part of the meaning of revert, one should not say that someone reverts back to a certain type of behaviour.

review n 1 a critical assessment of a book, film, etc. 2 a publication containing such articles 3 a general survey or report: the new curriculum is to be set up a year after the conclusions of the review are due 4 a formal or official inspection 5 the act or an instance of reviewing 6 a second consideration; re-examination 7 a retrospective survey 8 law a re-examination of a case ▷ vb 9 to hold or write a review of 10 to examine again: the committee will review the ban in the summer 11 to look back upon (a period of time or sequence of events): he reviewed his achievements with pride 12 to inspect formally or officially: when he reviewed the troops they cheered him 13 law to re-examine (a decision) judicially [Latin re- again + videre to see]

reviewer n a person who writes reviews of books, films, etc.

revile vb -viling, -viled to be abusively scornful of: his works were reviled and admired in equal measure [Old French reviler]

revise vb -vising, -vised 1 to change or alter: he grudgingly revised his opinion 2 to prepare a new edition of (a previously printed work) 3 Brit to read (something) several times in order to learn it in preparation for an examination [Latin re- again + visere to inspect]

Revised Version n a revision of the Authorized Version of the Bible published between 1881 and 1885

revision n 1 the act or process of revising 2 a corrected or new version of a book, article, etc.

revisionism n 1 (in Marxist ideology) any dangerous departure from the true interpretation of Marx's teachings 2 the advocacy of revision of some political theory ▷ **revisionist** n, adj

revisory adj of or having the power of revision

revitalize or -lise vb -lizing, -lized or -lising, -lised to make more lively or active

revival n 1 a reviving or being revived 2 a reawakening of religious faith 3 a new production of a play that has not been recently performed 4 a renewed use or interest in: there has been an Art Deco revival

revivalism n a movement that seeks to revive religious faith ▷ **revivalist** n, adj

revive vb -viving, -vived 1 to make or become lively or active again 2 to bring or be brought back to life, consciousness, or strength: revived by a drop of whisky 3 theatre to put on a new production of (an old play) [Latin re- again + vivere to live]

revivify vb -fies, -fying, -fied to give new life to ▷ **revivification** n

revoke vb -voking, -voked 1 to take back or cancel (an agreement, will, etc.) 2 cards to break a rule by failing to follow suit when able to do so ▷ n 3 cards the act of revoking [Latin revocare to call back] ▷ **revocation** n

revolt n 1 a rebellion or uprising against authority 2 in revolt in the state of rebelling ▷ vb 3 to rise up in rebellion against authority 4 to cause to feel disgust [French révolter]

revolting adj horrible and disgusting

revolution n 1 the overthrow of a regime or political system by the governed 2 (in Marxist theory) the transition from one system of production in a society to the next 3 a far-reaching and drastic change 4 a movement in or as if in a circle b one complete turn in a circle: 33 revolutions per minute [Latin revolvere to revolve]

revolutionary adj 1 of or like a revolution 2 advocating or engaged in revolution 3 radically new or different: they have designed revolutionary new materials to build power stations ▷ n, pl -aries 4 a person who advocates or engages in revolution

revolutionize or -**nise** vb -nizing, -nized or -nising, -nised to bring about a radical change in

revolve vb -volving, -volved 1 to move or cause to move around a centre 2 revolve around to be centred or focused upon: the campaign revolves around one man 3 to occur periodically or in cycles 4 to consider or be considered [Latin revolvere] ▷ **revolvable** adj

revolver n a pistol with a revolving cylinder that allows several shots to be fired without reloading

revolving door n a door with four leaves at right angles to each other, revolving about a vertical axis

revue n a theatrical entertainment with topical sketches and songs [French]

revulsion n a violent feeling of disgust [Latin revulsio pulling away]

reward n 1 something given in return for a service 2 a sum of money offered for finding a criminal or missing property 3 something received in return for good or evil: sacrifice provided its own reward ▷ vb 4 to give something to (someone) for a service rendered [Old French rewarder to regard]

rewarding adj giving personal satisfaction: my most professionally rewarding experience

rewarewa (ray-wa-ray-wa) n a tall New Zealand tree with reddish wood [Māori]

rewind vb -winding, -wound to run (a tape or film) back to an earlier point in order to replay

rewire vb -wiring, -wired to provide (a house, engine, etc.) with new wiring

reword vb to alter the wording of

rework vb to improve or bring up to date: they need to rework the system ▷ **reworking** n

rewrite vb -writing, -wrote, -written 1 to write again in a different way ▷ n 2 something rewritten

Rex n king: now used chiefly in documents and inscriptions [Latin]

Reykjavik n the capital and chief port of Iceland, situated in the southwest: its buildings are heated by natural hot water. Pop: 112 490 (2003 est)

Reynaud n Paul. 1878–1966, French statesman: premier during the defeat of France by Germany (1940); later imprisoned by the Germans

Reynolds n 1 Albert. 1932–2014, Irish politician: leader of the Fianna Fáil party and prime minister of the Republic of Ireland (1992–94) 2 Sir Joshua. 1723–92, English portrait painter. He was the first president of the Royal Academy (1768): the annual lectures he gave there, published as Discourses, are important contributions to art theory and criticism

Reynosa n a city in E Mexico, in Tamaulipas state on the Rio Grande. Pop: 847 000 (2005 est)

Rf chem rutherfordium

RFC Rugby Football Club

Rg roentgenium

RGN (in Britain, New Zealand, and Australia) Registered General Nurse

Rh 1 chem rhodium 2 See Rh factor

Rhaetia n an Alpine province of ancient Rome including parts of present-day Tyrol and E Switzerland

Rhaetian n 1 Also called: **Rhaeto-Romanic** a group of

Romance languages or dialects spoken in certain valleys of the Alps, including Romansch, Ladin, and Friulian ▷ *adj* **2** denoting or relating to this group of languages **3** of or relating to Rhaetia

Rhaetian Alps *pl n* a section of the central Alps along E Switzerland's borders with Austria and Italy. Highest peak: Piz Bernina, 4049 m (13 284 ft)

rhapsodize *or* **-dise** *vb* **-dizing, -dized** *or* **-dising, -dised** to speak or write with extravagant enthusiasm

rhapsody *n, pl* **-dies 1** *music* a freely structured and emotional piece of music **2** an expression of ecstatic enthusiasm [Greek *rhaptein* to sew together + *ōidē* song] ❯ **rhapsodic** *adj*

rhea (ree-a) *n* a large fast-running flightless bird of South America, similar to the ostrich [after *Rhea*, mother of Zeus]

Rhee *n* Syngman. 1875–1965, Korean statesman, leader of the campaign for independence from Japan; first president of South Korea (1948–60). Popular unrest forced his resignation

Rheims *n* a variant spelling of **Reims**

Rhein *n* the German name for the **Rhine**

Rheinland *n* the German name for the **Rhineland**

Rheinland-Pfalz *n* the German name for **Rhineland-Palatinate**

Rhemish *adj* of, relating to, or originating in Reims

Rhenish *adj* of or relating to the River Rhine or the lands adjacent to it, esp. the Rhineland-Palatinate

rhenium *n chem* a silvery-white metallic element with a high melting point. Symbol: **Re** [Latin *Rhenus* the Rhine]

rheostat *n* a variable resistor in an electrical circuit, such as one used to dim lights [Greek *rheos* flow + *-statēs* stationary] ❯ **rheostatic** *adj*

rhesus factor (ree-suss) *n* See **Rh factor**

rhesus monkey *n* a small long-tailed monkey of S Asia [Greek *Rhesos*, mythical Thracian king]

rhetoric (ret-a-rik) *n* **1** the art of using speech or writing to persuade or influence **2** artificial or exaggerated language: *there's been no shortage of soaring rhetoric at this summit* [Greek *rhētorikē* (*tekhnē*) (art) of rhetoric] ❯ **rhetorical** (rit-tor-ik-kl) *adj*

rhetorical question *n* a question to which no answer is required, used for dramatic effect, for example *who knows?*

rheum (room) *n* a watery discharge from the eyes or nose [Greek *rheuma* a flow] ❯ **rheumy** *adj*

rheumatic *adj* **1** caused by or affected by rheumatism ▷ *n* **2** a person suffering from rheumatism ❯ **rheumatically** *adv*

rheumatic fever *n* a disease with inflammation and pain in the joints

rheumatics *n informal* rheumatism

rheumatism *n* any painful disorder of joints, muscles, or connective tissue [Greek *rheuma* a flow]

rheumatoid *adj* (of symptoms) resembling rheumatism

rheumatoid arthritis *n* a chronic disease causing painful swelling of the joints

Rh factor *n* an antigen commonly found in human blood: the terms **Rh positive** and **Rh negative** are used to indicate its presence or absence [after the rhesus monkey, in which it was first discovered]

Rhine *n* a river in central and W Europe, rising in SE Switzerland: flows through Lake Constance north through W Germany and west through the Netherlands to the North Sea. Length: about 1320 km (820 miles). Dutch name: **Rijn**. French name: **Rhin**. German name: **Rhein**

Rhineland *n* the region of Germany surrounding the Rhine. German name: **Rheinland**

Rhineland-Palatinate *n* a state of W Germany: formed in 1946 from the S part of the Prussian Rhine province, the Palatinate, and parts of Rhine-Hesse and Hesse-Nassau; part of West Germany until 1990: agriculture (with extensive vineyards) and tourism are important.

Capital: Mainz. Pop: 4 059 000 (2003 est). Area: 19 832 sq km (7657 sq miles). German name: **Rheinland-Pfalz**

rhinestone *n* an imitation diamond made of glass [originally made at Strasbourg, on the Rhine]

rhino *n, pl* **-nos** *or* **-no** a rhinoceros

rhinoceros *n, pl* **-roses** *or* **-ros** a large plant-eating mammal of SE Asia and Africa with one or two horns on the nose and a very thick skin [Greek *rhis* nose + *keras* horn]

rhinovirus *n* any of various viruses that occur in the human respiratory tract and cause diseases, such as the common cold

rhizome *n* a thick horizontal underground stem whose buds develop into new plants [Greek *rhiza* a root]

Rhode Island *n* a state of the northeastern US, bordering on the Atlantic: the smallest state in the US; mainly low-lying and undulating, with an indented coastline in the east and uplands in the northwest. Capital: Providence. Pop: 1 076 164 (2003 est). Area: 2717 sq km (1049 sq miles). Abbreviation: **R.I.**, (with zip code) **RI**

Rhodes¹ *n* **1** a Greek island in the SE Aegean Sea, about 16 km (10 miles) off the Turkish coast: the largest of the Dodecanese and the most easterly island in the Aegean. Capital: Rhodes. Pop (municipality): 55 086 (2001). Area: 1400 sq km (540 sq miles) **2** a port on this island, in the NE: founded in 408 BC; of great commercial and political importance in the 3rd century BC; suffered several earthquakes, notably in 225, when the Colossus was destroyed. Pop: 41 000 (latest est) ▶ Ancient Greek name: Rhodos. Modern Greek name: **Ródhos**

Rhodes² *n* Cecil John. 1853–1902, British colonial financier and statesman in South Africa. He made a fortune in diamond and gold mining and, as prime minister of the Cape Colony (1890–96), he helped to extend British territory. He established the annual Rhodes scholarships to Oxford

Rhodesia *n* a former name (1964–79) for **Zimbabwe**

Rhodesian *adj* **1** of or relating to the former Rhodesia (now Zimbabwe) or its inhabitants ▷ *n* **2** a native or inhabitant of the former Rhodesia

Rhodian *adj* **1** of or relating to the island of Rhodes ▷ *n* **2** a native or inhabitant of Rhodes

rhodium *n chem* a hard silvery-white metallic element, used to harden platinum and palladium. Symbol: **Rh** [Greek *rhodon* rose, from the pink colour of its compounds]

rhododendron *n* an evergreen shrub with clusters of showy flowers [Greek *rhodon* rose + *dendron* tree]

Rhodope Mountains *pl n* a mountain range in SE Europe, in the Balkan Peninsula extending along the border between Bulgaria and Greece. Highest peak: Golyam Perelik (Bulgaria), 2191 m (7188 ft)

Rhodos *n* the Ancient Greek name for **Rhodes**

rhombohedron (rom-boh-heed-ron) *n, pl* **-drons** *or* **-dra** (-dra) a six-sided prism whose sides are parallelograms [RHOMBUS + Greek *-edron* -sided]

rhomboid *n* **1** a parallelogram with adjacent sides of unequal length. It resembles a rectangle but does not have 90° angles ▷ *adj* also: **rhomboidal 2** having such a shape [Greek *rhomboeidēs* shaped like a rhombus]

rhombus (rom-buss) *n, pl* **-buses** *or* **-bi** (-bye) a parallelogram with sides of equal length but no right angles [Greek *rhombos* something that spins] ❯ **rhombic** *adj*

Rhondda *n* an urban area in S Wales, in Rhondda Cynon Taff county borough on two branches of the **Rhondda Valley**: the area developed into a major coal-mining centre after 1807: the last coal mine closed in 1990. Pop (Rhondda ward): 4690 (2001)

Rhondda Cynon Taff *n* a county borough in S Wales, created from part of Mid Glamorgan in 1996. Pop: 231 600 (2003 est). Area: 558 sq km (215 sq miles)

Rhône *n* **1** a river in W Europe, rising in S Switzerland in the **Rhône glacier** and flowing to Lake Geneva, then into

France through gorges between the Alps and Jura and south to its delta on the Gulf of Lion: important esp. for hydroelectricity and for wine production along its valley. Length: 812 km (505 miles) **2** a department of E central France, in the Rhône-Alpes region. Capital: Lyon. Pop: 1 621 718 (2003 est). Area: 3233 sq km (1261 sq miles)

Rhône-Alpes *n* a region of E France: mainly mountainous, rising to the edge of the Massif Central in the west and the French Alps in the east; drained by the Rivers Rhône, Saône, and Isère

rhubarb *n* **1** a large-leaved plant with long green and red stalks which can be cooked and eaten **2** a related plant of central Asia, whose root can be dried and used as a laxative or astringent ▷ *interj, n* **3** the noise made by actors to simulate conversation, esp. by repeating the word *rhubarb* [Old French *reubarbe*]

rhyme *n* **1** sameness of the final sounds in lines of verse or in words **2** a word that is identical to another in its final sound: *'while' is a rhyme for 'mile'* **3** a piece of poetry with corresponding sounds at the ends of the lines **4** rhyme or reason sense or meaning ▷ *vb* **rhyming, rhymed 5** (of a word) to form a rhyme with another word **6** to compose (verse) in a metrical structure [Old French *rime*; spelling influenced by *rhythm*]

rhymester *n* a mediocre poet

rhyming slang *n* slang in which a word is replaced by another word or phrase that rhymes with it, for example *apples and pears* meaning *stairs*

Rhys *n* Jean (Ella Gwendolen Rees Williams). ?1890–1979, Welsh novelist and short-story writer, born in Dominica. Her novels include *Voyage in the Dark* (1934), *Good Morning, Midnight* (1939), and *Wide Sargasso Sea* (1966)

rhythm *n* **1** any regular movement or beat: *the side-effects can cause changes in the rhythm of the heart beat* **2** any regular pattern that occurs over a period of time: *the seasonal rhythm of the agricultural year* **3 a** the arrangement of the durations of and stress on the notes of a piece of music, usually laid out in regular groups (**bars**) of beats **b** any specific arrangement of such groupings: *waltz rhythm* **4** (in poetry) the arrangement of words to form a regular pattern of stresses [Greek *rhuthmos*] ▷ **rhythmic** or **rhythmical** *adj* ▷ **rhythmically** *adv*

rhythm and blues *n* a kind of popular music of Black American origin, derived from and influenced by the blues

rhythm method *n* a method of contraception in which intercourse is avoided at times when conception is most likely

R.I. *or* **RI** Rhode Island

rialto *n, pl* **-tos** a market or exchange [after the RIALTO]

Rialto *n* an island in Venice, Italy, linked with San Marco Island by the **Rialto Bridge** (1590) over the Grand Canal: the business centre of medieval and renaissance Venice

rib¹ *n* **1** one of the curved bones forming the framework of the upper part of the body and attached to the spinal column **2** a cut of meat including one or more ribs **3** a curved supporting part, such as in the hull of a boat **4** one of a series of raised rows in knitted fabric ▷ *vb* **ribbing, ribbed 5** to provide or support with ribs **6** to knit to form a rib pattern [Old English *ribb*] ▷ **ribbed** *adj*

rib² *vb* **ribbing, ribbed** *informal* to tease or ridicule [short for *rib-tickle*] ▷ **ribbing** *n*

RIBA Royal Institute of British Architects

ribald *adj* coarse or obscene in a humorous or mocking way [Old French *ribauld*] ▷ **ribaldry** *n*

riband *or* **ribband** *n* a ribbon awarded for some achievement

Ribbentrop *n* Joachim von. 1893–1946, German Nazi politician: foreign minister under Hitler (1938–45). He was hanged after conviction as a war criminal at Nuremberg

ribbing *n* **1** a pattern of ribs in knitted material

2 a framework or structure of ribs

Ribble *n* a river in NW England, flowing south and west through Lancashire to the Irish Sea. Length: 121 km (75 miles)

ribbon *n* **1** a narrow strip of fine material used for trimming, tying, etc. **2** a long narrow strip of inked cloth or plastic used to produce print in a typewriter **3** a small strip of coloured cloth worn as a badge or as a symbol of an award **4** a long thin strip: *a ribbon of white water* **5** ribbons ragged strips or shreds: *his clothes were torn to ribbons; his credibility was shot to ribbons* [Old French *riban*]

ribbon development *n* the building of houses along a main road

ribbonwood *n* a small evergreen tree of New Zealand

ribcage *n* the bony structure formed by the ribs that encloses the lungs

Ribeirão Prêto *n* a city in SE Brazil, in São Paulo state. Pop: 550 000 (2005 est)

Ribera *n* José de also called *Jusepe de Ribera*, Italian nickname *Lo Spagnoletto* (The Little Spaniard). 1591–1652, Spanish artist, living in Italy. His religious pictures often dwell on horrible suffering, presented in realistic detail

riboflavin (rye-boe-flay-vin) *n* a vitamin of the B complex that occurs in green vegetables, milk, fish, eggs, liver, and kidney: used as a yellow or orange food colouring (**E101**). Also called: **vitamin B₂** [*ribose*, a sugar + Latin *flavus* yellow]

ribonucleic acid *n* the full name of RNA

Ricardo *n* David. 1772–1823, British economist. His main work is *Principles of Political Economy and Taxation* (1817) ▷ **Ricardian** *adj, n*

Ricci *n* Matteo. 1552–1610, Italian Jesuit missionary and scholar, who introduced Christianity to China. He was later censured by the Church for allowing his converts to retain some of their ancient religious customs

rice *n* **1** the edible grain of an erect grass that grows on wet ground in warm climates ▷ *vb* **ricing, riced 2** US and Canad to sieve (potatoes or other vegetables) to a coarse mashed consistency [Greek *orūza*]

Rice *n* Elmer, original name *Elmer Reizenstein*. 1892–1967, US dramatist. His plays include *The Adding Machine* (1923) and *Street Scene* (1929), which was made into a musical by Kurt Weill in 1947

rice paper *n* **1** a thin edible paper made from rice straw **2** a thin Chinese paper made from the rice-paper plant, the pith of which is flattened into sheets

rich *adj* **1** owning a lot of money or property **2** well supplied (with a desirable substance or quality): *a country rich with cultural interest* **3** having an abundance of natural resources, minerals, etc.: *a land rich in unexploited minerals* **4** producing abundantly: *the island is a blend of hilly moorland and rich farmland* **5** luxuriant or prolific: *the meadows rich with corn* **6** (of food) containing much fat or sugar **7** having a full-bodied flavour: *a gloriously rich Cabernet-dominated wine* **8** (of colour) intense or vivid: *her hair had a rich auburn tint* **9** (of sound or a voice) full or resonant **10** very amusing or ridiculous: *a rich joke* **11** (of a fuel-air mixture) containing a relatively high proportion of fuel [Old English *rīce* (originally of people, with sense: great, mighty)] ▷ **richness** *n*

Rich *n* **1** Adrienne. 1929–2012, US poet and feminist writer; her volumes of poetry include *Snapshots of a Daughter-in-Law* (1963) and *Diving Into the Wreck* (1973) **2** Buddy, real name *Bernard Rich*. 1917–87, US jazz drummer and band leader

Richard *n* **1** Sir Cliff, real name *Harry Rodger Webb*. born 1940, British pop singer. Film musicals include *The Young Ones* (1961) and *Summer Holiday* (1962) **2** Maurice, known as *Rocket*. 1921–2000, Canadian ice-hockey player

Richard I *n* nicknamed *Coeur de Lion* or *the Lion-Heart*. 1157–99, king of England (1189–99); a leader of the third crusade (joining it in 1191). On his way home, he was captured in Austria (1192) and held to ransom. After a

r

brief return to England, where he was crowned again (1194), he spent the rest of his life in France

Richard II *n* 1367–1400, king of England (1377–99), whose reign was troubled by popular discontent and baronial opposition. He was forced to abdicate in favour of Henry Bolingbroke, who became Henry IV

Richard III *n* 1452–85, king of England (1483–85), notorious as the suspected murderer of his two young nephews in the Tower of London. He proved an able administrator until his brief reign was ended by his death at the hands of Henry Tudor (later Henry VII) at the battle of Bosworth Field

Richards *n* **1** (vor) A(rmstrong). 1893–1979, British literary critic and linguist, who, with C. K. Ogden, wrote *The Meaning of Meaning* (1923) and devised Basic English **2** Sir **Gordon**. 1904–86, English flat-racing jockey: champion jockey 26 times between 1925 and 1953; won 4870 races, including fourteen English classics **3** Sir **Viv**, full name *Isaac Vivian Alexander Richards*. born 1952, West Indian cricketer, born in Antigua; played in 121 tests, 50 as captain; scored 8,540 test runs

Richardson *n* **1** Dorothy M(iller). 1873–1957, British novelist, a pioneer of stream-of-consciousness writing: author of the novel sequence *Pilgrimage* (14 vols, 1915–67) **2** Henry Handel. pen name of *Ethel Florence Lindesay Richardson*, 1870–1946, Australian novelist; author of the trilogy *The Fortunes of Richard Mahony* (1917–29) **3** Sir **Owen Willans**. 1879–1959, British physicist; a pioneer in the study of atomic physics: Nobel prize for physics 1928 **4** Sir **Ralph** (David). 1902–83, British stage and screen actor **5** Samuel. 1689–1761, British novelist whose psychological insight and use of the epistolary form exerted a great influence on the development of the novel. His chief novels are *Pamela* (1740) and *Clarissa* (1747)

Richelieu *n* Armand Jean du Plessis. 1585–1642, French statesman and cardinal, principal minister to Louis XIII and virtual ruler of France (1624–42). He destroyed the power of the Huguenots and strengthened the crown in France and the role of France in Europe

Richelieu River *n* a river in E Canada, in S Quebec, rising in Lake Champlain and flowing north to the St Lawrence River. Length: 338 km (210 miles)

riches *pl n* valuable possessions or desirable substances: *the unexpected riches of Georgian culture*

Richler *n* Mordecai. 1931–2001, Canadian novelist. His novels include *St Urbain's Horseman* (1971), *Solomon Gursky Was Here* (1990), and *Barney's Version* (1997)

richly *adv* **1** in a rich or elaborate manner: *the rooms are richly decorated with a variety of classical motifs* **2** fully and appropriately: *he left the field to a richly deserved standing ovation*

Richmond *n* **1** a borough of Greater London, on the River Thames: formed in 1965 by the amalgamation of Barnes, Richmond, and Twickenham; site of Hampton Court Palace and the Royal Botanic Gardens at Kew. Pop: 179 200 (2003 est). Area: 55 sq km (21 sq miles). Official name: **Richmond-upon-Thames 2** a town in N England, in North Yorkshire: Norman castle. Pop: 8178 (2001) **3** a port in E Virginia, the state capital, at the falls of the James River: developed after the establishment of a trading post (1637); scene of the Virginia Conventions of 1774 and 1775; Confederate capital in the American Civil War. Pop: 194 729 (2003 est) **4** a county of SW New York City: coextensive with Staten Island borough; consists of Staten Island and several smaller islands

Richter *n* **1** Burton. born 1931, US physicist: shared the 1976 Nobel prize for physics with Samuel Tring for discovering the subatomic particle known as the J/psi particle **2** Johann Friedrich. wrote under the name *Jean Paul*. 1763–1825, German romantic novelist. His works include *Hesperus* (1795) and *Titan* (1800–03) **3** Sviatoslav. 1915–97, Ukrainian concert pianist

Richter scale *n* a scale for expressing the intensity of an earthquake, ranging from 0 to over 8 [after

Charles *Richter*, seismologist]

Richthofen *n* Baron **Manfred von**, nickname *the Red Baron*. 1892–1918, German aviator; commander during World War I of the 11th Chasing Squadron (**Richthofen's Flying Circus**). He was credited with 80 air victories before he was shot down

rick¹ *n* a large stack of hay or straw [Old English *hrēac*]

rick² *vb* **1** to wrench or sprain (a joint) ▷ *n* **2** a wrench or sprain of a joint [variant of *wrick*]

rickets *n* a disease of children, caused by a deficiency of vitamin D and characterized by softening of developing bone, and hence bow legs [origin unknown]

rickety *adj* **1** likely to collapse or break: *a rickety wooden table* **2** resembling or afflicted with rickets
▷ **ricketiness** *n*

rickrack *or* **ricrac** *n* a zigzag braid used for trimming [reduplication of RACK¹]

rickshaw *or* **ricksha** *n* **1** a small two-wheeled passenger vehicle pulled by one or two people, used in parts of Asia **2** a similar vehicle with three wheels, propelled by a person pedalling [Japanese *jinrikisha*]

ricochet (rik-osh-ay) *vb* **-cheting, -cheted** *or* **-chetting, -chetted 1** (of a bullet) to rebound from a surface ▷ *n* **2** the motion or sound of a rebounding bullet [French]

Ricoeur *n* Paul. 1913–2005, French philosopher, noted for his work on theories of interpretation. His books include *Philosophy of the Will* (3 vols, 1950–60), *Freud and Philosophy* (1965), and *The Living Metaphor* (1975)

ricotta *n* a soft white unsalted Italian cheese made from sheep's milk [Italian]

rid *vb* **ridding, rid** *or* **ridded 1** rid of to relieve (oneself) or make a place free of (something undesirable) **2** get rid of to relieve or free oneself of (something undesirable) [Old Norse *rythja*]

riddance *n* good riddance relief at getting rid of someone or something

ridden *vb* **1** the past participle of ride ▷ *adj* **2** afflicted or affected by the thing specified: *the police found three bullet-ridden bodies*

riddle¹ *n* **1** a question, puzzle, or verse phrased so that ingenuity is required to find the answer or meaning **2** a puzzling person or thing ▷ *vb* **-dling, -dled 3** to speak in riddles [Old English *rǣdels(e)*]

riddle² *vb* **-dling, -dled 1** to pierce with many holes **2** to put through a sieve ▷ *n* **3** a coarse sieve [Old English *hriddel* a sieve]

riddled *adj* riddled with full of (something undesirable): *riddled with mistakes*

ride *vb* **riding, rode, ridden 1** to sit on and control the movements of (a horse or other animal) **2** to sit on and propel (a bicycle or motorcycle) **3** to travel on or in a vehicle: *he rides around in a chauffeur-driven Rolls-Royce* **4** to travel over: *they rode the countryside in search of shelter* **5** to travel through or be carried across (sea, sky, etc.): *the moon was riding high* **6** US and Canad to cause to be carried: *to ride someone out of town* **7** (of a vessel) to lie at anchor **8** (usually passive) to tyrannize over or dominate: *ridden by fear* **9** be riding on to be dependent on (something) for success: *a lot is riding on the profits of the film* **10** informal to continue undisturbed: *let it ride* **11** riding high popular and successful ▷ *n* **12** a journey on a bicycle, on horseback, or in a vehicle **13** transport in a vehicle: *most of us have been told not to accept rides from strangers* **14** the type of movement experienced in a vehicle: *a bumpy ride* **15** a path for riding on horseback **16** take for a ride informal to cheat or deceive [Old English *rīdan*]

ride out *vb* to survive (a period of difficulty or danger) successfully

rider *n* **1** a person who rides **2** an extra clause or condition added to a document

ride up *vb* (of a garment) to move up from the proper position

ridge *n* **1** a long narrow raised land formation with sloping sides **2** a long narrow raised strip on a flat surface **3** the top of a roof where the two sloping sides meet **4** *meteorol* an elongated area of high pressure [Old English *hrycg*] **> ridged** *adj* **> ridgy** *adj*

ridgepole *n* **1** a timber along the ridge of a roof, to which the rafters are attached **2** the horizontal pole at the apex of a tent

ridicule *n* **1** language or behaviour intended to humiliate or mock ▷ *vb* **-culing, -culed 2** to make fun of or mock [Latin *ridere* to laugh]

ridiculous *adj* worthy of or causing ridicule

riding¹ *n* the art or practice of horsemanship

riding² *n* **1 Riding** any of the three former administrative divisions of Yorkshire: North Riding, East Riding, and West Riding **2** *Canad* an electoral constituency [Old English *thriding* a third]

riding crop *n* a short whip with a handle at one end for opening gates

Ridley *n* Nicholas. ?1500–55, English bishop, who helped to revise the liturgy under Edward VI. He was burnt at the stake for refusing to disavow his Protestant beliefs when Mary I assumed the throne

Rie *n* Dame Lucie, original name *Lucie Gomperz*. 1902–95, British potter, born in Austria

Riefenstahl *n* Leni. 1902–2003, German photographer and film director, best known for her Nazi propaganda films, such as *Triumph of the Will* (1934)

Riel *n* Louis. 1844–85, Canadian politician; hanged for treason after leading the Métis people in rebellion against the Canadian government

Riemann *n* Georg Friedrich Bernhard. 1826–66, German mathematician whose non-Euclidean geometry was used by Einstein as a basis for his general theory of relativity **> Riemannian** *adj*

Rienzi *or* **Rienzo** *n* Cola di. 1313–54, Italian radical political reformer in Rome

riesling *n* a medium-dry white wine [from German]

Rievaulx Abbey *n* a ruined Cistercian abbey near Helmsley in Yorkshire: built in the 12th century and abandoned at the dissolution of the monasteries; landscaped in the 18th century

Rif, Riff *or* **Rifi** *n* **1** (*pl* **Rifs, Riffs, Rifis** *or* **Rif, Riff, Rifi**) a member of a Berber people, inhabiting the Atlas Mountains in Morocco **2** Also called: **Rifian, Riffian** the dialect of Berber spoken by this people **3** See **Er Rif**

rife *adj* **1** widespread or common **2 rife with** full of: *the media is rife with speculation* [Old English *rífe*]

riff *n* jazz, rock a short series of chords [probably from REFRAIN²]

riffle *vb* **-fling, -fled 1** (often foll. by *through*) to flick through (papers or pages) quickly: *I riffled through the rest of the memos* ▷ *n* **2** *US and Canad* **a** a rapid in a stream **b** a rocky shoal causing a rapid **c** a ripple on water **3** a riffling [probably from *ruffle*]

riffraff *n* worthless or disreputable people [Old French *rif et raf*]

rifle¹ *n* **1** a firearm having a long barrel with a spirally grooved interior, which gives the bullet a spinning motion and thus greater accuracy over a longer range **2 Rifles** a unit of soldiers equipped with rifles: *the Burma Rifles* ▷ *vb* **-fling, -fled 3** to cut spiral grooves inside the barrel of (a gun) [Old French *rifler* to scratch] **> rifled** *adj*

rifle² *vb* **-fling, -fled 1** to search (a house or safe) and steal from it **2** to steal and carry off: *he rifled whatever valuables he could lay his hands on* [Old French *rifler* to plunder, scratch]

rift *n* **1 a** a break in friendly relations between people or groups of people **2** a gap or space made by splitting [Old Norse]

rift valley *n* a long narrow valley resulting from the subsidence of land between two faults

rig *vb* **rigging, rigged 1** to arrange in a dishonest way, for profit or advantage: *he claimed that the poll was rigged* **2** to set up or prepare (something) hastily ready for use **3** *nautical* to equip (a vessel or mast) with (sails or

rigging) ▷ *n* **4** an apparatus for drilling for oil and gas **5** *nautical* the arrangement of the sails and masts of a vessel **6** apparatus or equipment **7** *informal* an outfit of clothes **8** *US, Canad and Austral* an articulated lorry ▸ See also **rig out, rig up** [Scandinavian]

Riga *n* the capital of Latvia, on the **Gulf of Riga** at the mouth of the Western Dvina on the Baltic Sea: a port and major trading centre since Viking times. Pop: 739 232 (2002 est)

-rigged *adj* (of a sailing vessel) having a rig of a certain kind: *a square-rigged ship*

rigging *n* the ropes and cables supporting a ship's masts and sails

right *adj* **1** morally or legally acceptable or correct: *his conduct seemed reasonable, even right* **2** correct or true: *the customer is always right* **3** appropriate, suitable, or proper: *there were problems involved in finding the right candidate* **4** most favourable or convenient: *she waited until the right moment to broach the subject* **5** in a satisfactory condition: *things are right again now* **6** accurate: *is that clock right?* **7** correct in opinion or judgment **8** sound in mind or body **9** of or on the side of something or someone that faces east when the front is turned towards the north **10** conservative or reactionary: *it was alleged he was an agent of the right wing* **11** *geometry* formed by or containing a line or plane perpendicular to another line or plane: *a right angle* **12** of or on the side of cloth worn or facing outwards **13** in one's **right mind** sane **14** she'll be **right** *Austral and NZ informal* that's all right; not to worry **15** the **right side of a** in favour with: *you'd better stay on the right side of him* **b** younger than: *he's still on the right side of fifty* **16** too right *informal* an exclamation of agreement ▷ *adv* **17** correctly: *if we change the structure of local government we must do it right* **18** in the appropriate manner: *do it right next time!* **19** straight or directly: *let's go right to bed* **20** in the direction of the east from the point of view of a person or thing facing north **21** all the way: *he drove right up to the gate* **22** without delay: *I'll be right over* **23** exactly or precisely: *right here* **24** fittingly: *it serves him right* **25** to good or favourable advantage: *it all came out right in the end* ▷ *n* **26** a freedom or power that is morally or legally due to a person: *the defendant had an absolute right to a fair trial* **27** anything that accords with the principles of legal or moral justice **28** in the **right** the state of being in accordance with reason or truth **29** the right side, direction, or part: *the right of the army* **30** the **Right** the supporters or advocates of conservatism or reaction: *the rise of the far Right in France* **31** *boxing* a punch with the right hand **32** rights *finance* the privilege of a company's shareholders to subscribe for new issues of the company's shares on advantageous terms **33** by **right** or **rights** properly: *by rights he should have won* **34** in one's own **right** having a claim or title oneself rather than through marriage or other connection **35** to **rights** consistent with justice or orderly arrangement: *he put the matter to rights* ▷ *vb* **36** to bring or come back to a normal or correct state **37** to bring or come back to a vertical position: *he slipped and righted himself at once* **38** to compensate for or redress: *there is a wrong to be righted* **39** to make (something) accord with truth or facts ▷ *interj* **40** an expression of agreement or compliance [Old English *riht*]

right angle *n* **1** an angle of 90° or π/2 radians **2** at **right angles** perpendicular or perpendicularly **> right-angled** *adj*

right-angled triangle *n* a triangle with one angle which is a right angle

right away *adv* without delay

righteous (rye-chuss) *adj* **1** moral, just, or virtuous: *the lieutenant was a righteous cop* **2** morally justifiable or right: *her eyes were blazing with righteous indignation* [Old English *rihtwís*] **> righteousness** *n*

rightful *adj* **1** in accordance with what is right **2** having a legally or morally just claim: *he is the rightful heir to her fortune* **3** held by virtue of a legal or just claim: *these moves

will restore them to their rightful homes > **rightfully** adv
> **rightfulness** n

right-hand adj **1** of, on, or towards the right: *in the top right-hand corner* **2** for the right hand **3** **right-hand man** a person's most valuable assistant

right-handed adj **1** more adept with the right hand than with the left **2** made for or by the right hand **3** turning from left to right

rightist adj **1** of the political right or its principles ▷ n **2** a supporter of the political right > **rightism** n

rightly adv **1** in accordance with the true facts or justice **2** with good reason: *he was rightly praised for his constancy*

right-minded or **right-thinking** adj holding opinions or principles considered acceptable by the speaker

right of way n, pl **rights of way 1** the right of one vehicle or ship to go before another **2** **a** the legal right of someone to pass over someone else's land **b** the path used by this right

right-on adj informal trendy and socially aware or relevant: *the judges were fed up with right-on comedy*

Right Reverend adj a title of respect for a bishop

rightward adj **1** situated on or directed towards the right ▷ adv also: **rightwards 2** on or towards the right

right whale n a large grey or black whalebone whale with a large head [origin unknown]

right-wing adj **1** conservative or reactionary: *there's a very fast-growing right-wing feeling in our country* **2** belonging to the more conservative part of a political party: *a group of right-wing Labour MPs* ▷ n **right wing 3** (often caps) the more conservative or reactionary section, esp. of a political party: *the Right Wing of the Conservative Party* **4** sport **a** the right-hand side of the field of play **b** a player positioned in this area in certain games > **right-winger** n

Rigi n a mountain in the Alps of N central Switzerland, between Lakes Lucerne, Zug, and Lauerz

rigid adj **1** inflexible or strict: *the talks will be general, without a rigid agenda* **2** physically unyielding or stiff: *use only rigid plastic containers* [Latin rigidus] > **rigidity** n > **rigidly** adv

rigmarole n **1** a long complicated procedure **2** a set of incoherent or pointless statements [earlier ragman roll a list]

rigor mortis n the stiffness of joints and muscles of a dead body [Latin: rigidity of death]

rigorous adj **1** harsh, strict, or severe: *rigorous enforcement of the libel laws* **2** severely accurate: *rigorous scientific testing*

rigour or US **rigor** n **1** a severe or cruel circumstance: *the rigours of forced labour* **2** strictness in judgment or conduct **3** harsh but just treatment [Latin rigor]

rig out vb **1** to dress: *I was rigged out in my usual green shell suit* **2** to equip: *his car is rigged out with gadgets* ▷ n **rigout 3** informal a person's clothing or costume

rig up vb to set up or build temporarily: *they rigged up a loudspeaker system*

Rijeka n a port in Croatia: an ancient town, changing hands many times before passing to Yugoslavia in 1947 until Croatia became independent in 1991. Pop: 135 000 (2005 est). Italian name: **Fiume**

Rijksmuseum n a museum in Amsterdam housing the national art collection of the Netherlands

Rijn n the Dutch name for the **Rhine**

Rijswijk n a town in the SW Netherlands, in South Holland province on the SE outskirts of The Hague: scene of the signing (1697) of the **Treaty of Rijswijk** ending the War of the Grand Alliance. Pop: 48 000 (2003 est). English name: **Ryswick**

rile vb **riling, riled 1** to annoy or anger **2** US and Canad to stir up (a liquid) [variant of roil to agitate]

Riley n **1** Bridget (**Louise**). born 1931, English painter, best known for her black-and-white op art paintings of the 1960s **2** Gina. born 1961, Australian television actress and writer, best known for playing 'Kim' in the comedy series *Kath & Kim* (2002–07)

Rilke n Rainer Maria. 1875–1926, Austro-German poet, born in Prague. Author of intense visionary lyrics,

notably in the *Duino Elegies* (1922) and *Sonnets to Orpheus* (1923)

rill n a small stream [Low German rille]

rim n **1** the raised edge of an object **2** the outer part of a wheel to which the tyre is attached [Old English rima] > **rimless** adj

Rimbaud n Arthur. 1854–91, French poet, whose work, culminating in the prose poetry of *Illuminations* (published 1884), greatly influenced the symbolists. *A Season in Hell* (1873) draws on his tempestuous homosexual affair with Verlaine, after which he abandoned writing (aged about 20) and spent the rest of his life travelling

rime[1] literary n **1** frost formed by the freezing of water droplets in fog onto solid objects ▷ vb **riming, rimed 2** to cover with rime or something resembling it [Old English hrīm] > **rimy** adj

rime[2] n, vb **riming, rimed** archaic same as **rhyme**

Rimini n a port and resort in NE Italy, in Emilia-Romagna on the N Adriatic coast. Pop: 128 656 (2001). Ancient name: **Ariminum**

Rimsky-Korsakov n Nikolai Andreyevich. 1844–1908, Russian composer; noted for such works as the orchestral suite *Scheherazade* (1888) and the opera *Le Coq d'or* (first performed in 1910)

rind n a hard outer layer on fruits, bacon, or cheese [Old English rinde]

ring[1] vb **ringing, rang, rung 1** to give out a clear resonant sound, like that of a bell **2** to cause (a bell) to give out a ringing sound or (of a bell) to give out such a sound **3** chiefly Brit and NZ to call (a person) by telephone **4 ring for** to call by means of a bell: *ring for the maid* **5** (of a building or place) to be filled with sound: *the church rang with singing* **6** (of the ears) to have the sensation of humming or ringing **7** slang to change the identity of (a stolen vehicle) by using the licence plate or serial number of another, usually disused, vehicle **8 ring a bell** to bring something to the mind or memory: *the name doesn't ring a bell* **9 ring down the curtain a** to lower the curtain at the end of a theatrical performance **b ring down the curtain on** to put an end to **10 ring true** or **false** to give the impression of being true or false ▷ n **11** the act of or a sound made by ringing **12** a sound produced by or sounding like a bell **13** informal, chiefly Brit and NZ a telephone call **14** an inherent quality: *it has the ring of possibility to it* ▶ See also **ring in**, **ring off**, etc. [Old English hringan]

USAGE *Rang* and *sang* are the correct forms of the past tenses of *ring* and *sing*, although *rung* and *sung* are still heard informally and dialectally: *he rung (rang) the bell.*

---

ring[2] n **1** a circular band of a precious metal worn on the finger **2** any object or mark that is circular in shape **3** a group of people or things standing or arranged in a circle: *a ring of standing stones* **4** a circular path or course: *crowds of people walking round in a ring* **5** a circular enclosure where circus acts perform or livestock is sold at a market **6** a square raised platform, marked off by ropes, in which contestants box or wrestle **7** a group of people, usually illegal, who control a specified market: *a drugs ring* **8** chem a closed loop of atoms in a molecule **9** one of the systems of circular bands orbiting the planets Saturn, Uranus, and Jupiter **10 the ring** the sport of boxing **11 throw one's hat in the ring** to announce one's intention to be a candidate or contestant **12 run rings around** informal to outclass completely ▷ vb **ringing, ringed 13** to put a ring round **14** to mark (a bird) with a ring or clip for subsequent identification **15** to kill (a tree) by cutting the bark round the trunk **16** to fit a ring in the nose of (a bull, etc.) so that it can be led easily [Old English hring] > **ringed** adj

ring binder n a loose-leaf binder with metal rings that

can be opened to insert perforated paper

ringdove *n* a wood pigeon

ringer *n* **1** Also called: **dead ringer** a person or thing that is almost identical to another **2** *slang* a stolen vehicle the identity of which has been changed by the use of the licence plate or serial number of another, usually disused, vehicle

ring finger *n* the third finger, esp. of the left hand, on which a wedding ring is worn

ring in *vb chiefly Brit and NZ* to report to someone by telephone

ringleader *n* a person who leads others in illegal or mischievous actions

ringlet *n* a lock of hair hanging down in a spiral curl **> ringleted** *adj*

ring main *n* a domestic electrical supply in which outlet sockets are connected to the mains supply through a continuous closed circuit (**ring circuit**)

ringmaster *n* the master of ceremonies in a circus

ring off *vb chiefly Brit and NZ* to end a telephone conversation by replacing the receiver

ring out *vb* to send out a loud resounding noise: *I heard those shots ring out*

ring road *n Brit* a main road that bypasses a town or town centre

ringside *n* **1** the row of seats nearest a boxing or wrestling ring **> adj 2** providing a close uninterrupted view: *a ringside seat for the election*

ringtail *n Austral* a possum with a curling tail used to grip branches while climbing

ringtone *n* a musical tune played by a mobile phone when it receives a call

ring up *vb* **1** *chiefly Brit and NZ* to make a telephone call to **2** to record on a cash register **3 ring up the curtain a** to begin a theatrical performance **b ring up the curtain on** to make a start on

ringworm *n* a fungal infection of the skin producing itchy patches

rink *n* **1 a** a sheet of ice for skating on, usually indoors **2** an area for roller-skating on **3** a building for ice-skating or roller-skating **4 a** a strip of grass or ice on which a game of bowls or curling is played **b** the players on one side in a game of bowls or curling [Old French *renc* row]

rinkhals (rink-hals) *n*, *pl* **-hals** *or* **-halses** a highly venomous snake of Southern Africa capable of spitting its venom accurately at its victim's eyes [Afrikaans]

rink rat *n Canad slang* a youth who helps with odd chores at an ice-hockey rink in return for free admission to games

rinse *vb* **rinsing, rinsed** **1** to remove soap or shampoo from (clothes, dishes, or hair) by washing it out with clean water **2** to wash lightly, esp. without using soap **3** to cleanse (the mouth) by swirling water or mouthwash in it and then spitting the liquid out **4** to give a light tint to (hair) **> n 5** the act or an instance of rinsing **6** *hairdressing* a liquid to tint hair: *a blue rinse* [Old French *rincer*]

Rio Branco *n* **1** a city in W Brazil, capital of Acre state. Pop: 261 000 (2005 est) **2** a river in Brazil, flowing south to the Rio Negro. Length: 644 km (400 miles)

Río Bravo *n* the Mexican name for the **Rio Grande**

Rio de Janeiro *or* **Rio** *n* **1** a port in SE Brazil, on Guanabara Bay: the country's chief port and its capital from 1763 to 1960; backed by mountains, notably Sugar Loaf Mountain; founded by the French in 1555 and taken by the Portuguese in 1567. Pop: 11 469 000 (2005 est). Related noun: **Cariocan 2** a state of E Brazil. Capital: Rio de Janeiro. Pop: 14 724 475 (2002). Area: 42 911 sq km (16 568 sq miles)

Río de la Plata *n* See **Plata**

Río de Oro *n* a former region of W Africa: comprised the S part of the Spanish Sahara (now Western Sahara)

Rio Grande *n* **1** a river in North America, rising in SW Colorado and flowing southeast to the Gulf of Mexico, forming the border between the US and Mexico. Length: about 3030 km (1885 miles). Mexican name: **Río Bravo 2** a port in SE Brazil, in SE Rio Grande do Sul state: serves as the port for Porto Alegre. Pop: 188 000 (2005 est)

Rio Grande do Norte *n* a state of NE Brazil, on the Atlantic: much of it is semiarid plateau. Capital: Natal. Pop: 2 852 784 (2002). Area: 53 014 sq km (20 469 sq miles)

Rio Grande do Sul *n* a state of S Brazil, on the Atlantic. Capital: Porto Alegre. Pop: 10 408 540 (2002). Area: 282 183 sq km (108 951 sq miles)

rioja (ree-oh-ha) *n* a red or white Spanish wine with a vanilla bouquet and flavour [*La Rioja*, area in central N Spain]

Río Negro *n* See **Negro**

riot *n* **1** a disturbance made by an unruly mob **2** *Brit, Austral and NZ* an occasion of lively enjoyment **3** a dazzling display: *the pansies provided the essential riot of colour* **4** *slang* a very amusing person or thing **5 read the riot act to** to reprimand severely **6 run riot a** to behave without restraint **b** (of plants) to grow profusely **> vb 7** to take part in a riot [Old French *riote* dispute] **> rioter** *n* **> rioting** *n*

riotous *adj* **1** unrestrained and excessive: *riotous decadence* **2** unruly or rebellious **3** characterized by unrestrained merriment: *riotous celebration*

riot shield *n* a large shield used by police controlling crowds

rip *vb* **ripping, ripped** **1** to tear or be torn violently or roughly **2** to remove hastily or roughly **3** *informal* to move violently or hurriedly **4 let rip** to act or speak without restraint **> n 5** a tear or split **►** See also **rip off** [origin unknown]

RIP may he, she, *or* they rest in peace [Latin *requiescat or requiescant in pace*]

riparian (rip-pair-ee-an) *adj formal* of or on the bank of a river [Latin *ripa* river bank]

ripcord *n* a cord pulled to open a parachute from its pack

ripe *adj* **1** mature enough to be eaten or used: *a round ripe apple* **2** fully developed in mind or body **3** suitable: *wait until the time is ripe* **4 ripe for** ready or eager to (undertake or undergo an action): *China was ripe for revolution* **5 ripe old age** an elderly but healthy age [Old English *rīpe*]

ripen *vb* **1** to make or become ripe **2** to mature

Ripley *n* George. 1802–80, US social reformer and transcendentalist: founder of the Brook Farm experiment in communal living in Massachusetts (1841)

rip off *slang vb* **1** to cheat by overcharging **2** to steal (something) **> n rip-off 3** a grossly overpriced article **4** the act of stealing or cheating

Ripon *n* a city in N England, in North Yorkshire: cathedral (12th–16th centuries). Pop: 16 468 (2001)

riposte (rip-posst) *n* **1 a** a swift clever reply **2** *fencing* a counterattack made immediately after a successful parry **> vb** **-posting, -posted** **3** to make a riposte [French]

ripple *n* **1 a** a slight wave on the surface of water **2** a slight ruffling of a surface **3** a sound like water flowing gently in ripples: *a ripple of applause* **4** vanilla ice cream with stripes of another ice cream through it: *raspberry ripple* **> vb** **-pling, -pled** **5** to form ripples or flow with a waving motion **6** to make ripples on or in (something) **7** (of sounds) to rise and fall gently [origin unknown] **> rippling** *adj*

rip-roaring *adj informal* boisterous and exciting

ripsaw *n* a handsaw for cutting along the grain of timber

rise *vb* **rising, rose, risen** **1** to get up from a lying, sitting, or kneeling position **2** to get out of bed, esp. to begin one's day: *she rises at 5 am every day to look after her horse* **3** to move from a lower to a higher position or place **4** to appear above the horizon: *as the sun rises higher the mist disappears* **5** to slope upwards: *the road crossed the valley then rose to a low ridge* **6** to increase in height or level: *the tide rose* **7** to swell up: *dough rises* **8** to increase in strength or degree: *frustration is rising amongst sections of the population*

9 to increase in amount or value: *living costs are rising at an annual rate of nine per cent* **10** *informal* to respond (to a challenge or remark) **11** to revolt: *the people rose against their oppressors* **12** (of a court or parliament) to adjourn **13** to be resurrected **14** to become erect or rigid: *the hairs on his neck rose in fear* **15** to originate: *that river rises in the mountains* **16** *angling* (of fish) to come to the surface of the water ▷ *n* **17** the act or an instance of rising **18** a piece of rising ground **19** *Brit* an increase in wages **20** an increase in amount, cost, or quantity **21** an increase in height **22** an increase in status or position **23** an increase in degree or intensity **24** the vertical height of a step or of a flight of stairs **25 get** *or* **take a rise out of** *slang* to provoke an angry reaction from **26 give rise to** to cause the development of [Old English *rīsan*]

riser *n* **1** a person who rises from bed: *an early riser* **2** the vertical part of a step

risible (riz-zib-bl) *adj formal* ridiculous [Latin *ridere* to laugh]

rising *n* **1** a rebellion ▷ *adj* **2** increasing in rank or maturity

rising damp *n* seepage of moisture from the ground into the walls of buildings

risk *n* **1** the possibility of bringing about misfortune or loss **2** a person or thing considered as a potential hazard: *in parts of the world transfusions carry the risk of infection* **3 at risk** in a dangerous situation **4 take** *or* **run a risk** to act without regard to the danger involved ▷ *vb* **5** to act in spite of the possibility of (injury or loss): *if they clamp down they risk a revolution* **6** to expose to danger or loss [French *risque*] ▶ **risky** *adj*

risk assessment *n commerce* an analysis of the level of risk attached to a particular activity

risotto *n, pl* **-tos** a dish of rice cooked in stock with vegetables, meat, etc. [Italian]

risqué (risk-ay) *adj* making slightly rude references to sex: *risqué humour* [French *risquer* to risk]

rissole *n* a mixture of minced cooked meat coated in egg and breadcrumbs and fried [French]

ritardando *adj, adv* same as **rallentando** [Italian]

rite *n* **1** a formal act which forms part of a religious ceremony: *the rite of burial* **2** a custom that is carried out within a particular group: *the barbaric rites of public execution* **3** a particular body of such acts, esp. of a particular Christian Church: *the traditional Anglican rite* [Latin *ritus*]

rite of passage *n* a ceremony or event that marks an important change in a person's life

ritual *n* **1** a religious or other ceremony involving a series of fixed actions performed in a certain order **2** these ceremonies collectively: *people need ritual* **3** regular repeated action or behaviour **4** stereotyped activity or behaviour ▷ *adj* **5** of or like rituals ▶ **ritually** *adv*

ritualism *n* exaggerated emphasis on the importance of rites and ceremonies ▶ **ritualistic** *adj* ▶ **ritualistically** *adv*

ritzy *adj* **ritzier, ritziest** *slang* luxurious or elegant [after the hotels established by César Ritz]

rival *n* **1** a person or group that competes with another for the same object or in the same field **2** a person or thing that is considered the equal of another: *she is without rival in the field of physics* ▷ *adj* **3** in the position of a rival ▷ *vb* **-valling, -valled** *or US* **-valing, -valed** **4** to be the equal or near equal of: *his inarticulateness was rivalled only by that of his brother* **5** to try to equal or surpass [Latin *rivalis*, literally: one who shares the same brook]

rivalry *n, pl* **-ries** active competition between people or groups

riven *adj old-fashioned* **1** split apart: *the party is riven by factions* **2** torn to shreds [Old Norse *rīfa* to tear, rend]

river *n* **1** a large natural stream of fresh water flowing along a definite course into the sea, a lake, or a larger river. Related adjective: **fluvial** **2** an abundant stream or flow: *rivers of blood* [Old French *riviere*]

Rivera *n* Diego. 1886–1957, Mexican painter, noted for his monumental murals in public buildings, which are influenced by Aztec art and depict revolutionary themes

Rivers *n* a state of S Nigeria, in the Niger river delta on the Gulf of Guinea. Capital: Port Harcourt. Pop: 5 185 400 (2006). Area: 11 077 sq km (4277 sq miles)

Riverside *n* a city in SW California. Pop: 281 514 (2003 est)

rivet (riv-vit) *n* **1** a short metal pin for fastening metal plates, with a head at one end, the other end being hammered flat after being put through holes in the plates ▷ *vb* **-veting, -veted** **2** to join by riveting **3** (*often passive*) to cause or be fixed in fascination or horror: *if I'm riveted by something on television I won't answer the phone* [Old French *river* to fasten] ▶ **riveter** *n*

riveting *adj* very interesting or exciting

Riviera *n* the Mediterranean coastal region between Cannes, France, and La Spezia, Italy: contains some of Europe's most popular resorts [C18: from Italian literally: shore, ultimately from Latin *rīpa* bank, shore]

rivulet *n* a small stream [Latin *rivus* stream]

Riyadh *n* the joint capital (with Mecca) of Saudi Arabia, situated in a central oasis: the largest city in the country. Pop: 5 514 000 (2005 est)

Rizal¹ *n* another name for **Pasay**

Rizal² *n* José. 1861–96, Philippine nationalist, executed by the Spanish during the Philippine revolution of 1896

Rizzio *or* **Riccio** *n* David. ?1533–66, Italian musician and courtier who became the secretary and favourite of Mary, Queen of Scots. He was murdered at the instigation of a group of nobles, including Mary's husband, Darnley

RM 1 (in Britain) Royal Mail **2** (in Britain) Royal Marines **3** (in Canada) Rural Municipality **4** (in Canada) Regional Municipality

RMT (in Britain) (National Union of) Rail, Maritime and Transport (Workers)

Rn *chem* radon

RN 1 (in Canada and New Zealand) Registered Nurse **2** (in Britain) Royal Navy

RNA *n biochem* ribonucleic acid: any of a group of nucleic acids, present in all living cells, that play an essential role in the synthesis of proteins

RNLI (in Britain) Royal National Lifeboat Institution

RNZ Radio New Zealand

RNZAF Royal New Zealand Air Force

RNZN Royal New Zealand Navy

roach¹ *n, pl* **roaches** *or* **roach** a European freshwater food fish [Old French *roche*]

roach² *n chiefly US and Canad* a cockroach

Roach *n* Hal, full name *Harald Eugene Roach*. 1892–1992, US film producer, whose company produced numerous comedy films in the 1920s and 1930s, including those featuring Harold Lloyd and Laurel and Hardy

road *n* **1** a route, usually surfaced, used by travellers and vehicles to get from one place to another **2** a street **3** a way or course: *on the road to recovery* **4** *nautical* same as **roadstead** **5 one for the road** *informal* a last alcoholic drink before leaving **6 on the road** travelling about [Old English *rād*]

roadblock *n* a barrier set up across a road by the police or military, in order to stop and check vehicles

road hog *n informal* a selfish or aggressive driver

roadholding *n* the extent to which a vehicle is stable and does not skid on bends or wet roads

roadhouse *n* a pub or restaurant at the side of a road

roadie *n Brit, Austral and NZ informal* a person who transports and sets up equipment for a band

road metal *n* crushed rock or broken stone used in building roads

road rage *n* aggressive behaviour by a motorist in response to the actions of another road user

road show *n* **1** *radio* a live broadcast from a radio van taking a particular programme on a tour of the country **2** a group of entertainers on tour

roadside *n* **1** the edge of a road ▷ *adj* **2** by the edge or side of a road: *a roadside café*

r

roadstead *n nautical* a partly sheltered anchorage

roadster *n* an open car with only two seats

road tax *n* (in Britain) a tax paid on vehicles used on the roads

road test *n* **1** a test of something, such as a vehicle in actual use ▷ *vb* **road-test 2** to test (a vehicle etc.) in actual use

roadway *n* the part of a road that is used by vehicles

roadworks *pl n* repairs to a road or cable under a road, esp. when they block part of the road

roadworthy *adj* (of a motor vehicle) mechanically sound ➤ **roadworthiness** *n*

roam *vb* to walk about with no fixed purpose or direction [origin unknown]

roan *adj* **1** (of a horse) having a brown or black coat sprinkled with white hairs ▷ *n* **2** a horse with such a coat [Spanish *roano*]

Roanoke Island *n* an island off the coast of North Carolina: site of the first attempted English settlement in America. Length: 19 km (12 miles). Average width: 5 km (3 miles)

roar *vb* **1** (of lions and other animals) to make loud growling cries **2** to shout (something) with a loud deep cry: *'Don't do that!' he roared at me* **3** to make a very loud noise: *the engine roared* **4** to laugh in a loud hearty manner **5** (of a fire) to burn fiercely with a roaring sound ▷ *n* **6** a roaring noise: *there was a roar as the train came in* **7** a loud deep cry, uttered by a person or crowd, esp. in anger or triumph: *a roar of approval came from the crowd* [Old English *rārian*]

roaring *adj* **1** a **roaring trade** a brisk and profitable business ▷ *adv* **2** **roaring drunk** noisily or boisterously drunk

roast *vb* **1** to cook (food) by dry heat in an oven or over a fire **2** to brown or dry (coffee or nuts) by exposure to heat **3** to make or be extremely hot **4** *informal* to criticize severely ▷ *n* **5** a roasted joint of meat ▷ *adj* **6** cooked by roasting: *roast beef* [Old French *rostir*] ➤ **roaster** *n*

roasting *informal adj* **1** extremely hot ▷ *n* **2** severe criticism or scolding

rob *vb* **robbing, robbed 1** to take something from (a person or place) illegally **2** to deprive, esp. of something deserved: *I can't forgive him for robbing me of an Olympic gold* [Old French *rober*] ➤ **robber** *n*

Robbe-Grillet *n* Alain.1922–2008, French novelist and screenwriter. Author of *The Voyeur* (1955), *Jealousy* (1957), and *Djinn* (1981): he was one of the leading practitioners of the antinovel

Robben Island *n* a small island in South Africa, 11 km (7 miles) off the Cape Peninsula: formerly used by the South African government to house political prisoners

robbery *n*, *pl* **-beries 1** *criminal law* the stealing of property from a person by using or threatening to use force **2** the act or an instance of robbing

Robbia *n* **1** Andrea della. 1435–1525, Florentine sculptor, best known for his polychrome reliefs and his statues of infants in swaddling clothes **2** his uncle, **Luca della**. ?1400–82, Florentine sculptor, who perfected a technique of enamelling terra cotta for reliefs

Robbins *n* Jerome. 1918–98, US ballet dancer and choreographer. He choreographed the musicals *The King and I* (1951) and *West Side Story* (1957)

robe *n* **1** a long loose flowing garment **2** a dressing gown or bathrobe ▷ *vb* **robing, robed 3** to put a robe on [Old French]

Robert I *n* known as *Robert the Bruce*. 1274–1329, king of Scotland (1306–29): he defeated the English army of Edward II at Bannockburn (1314) and gained recognition of Scotland's independence (1328)

Robert II *n* 1316–90, king of Scotland (1371–90)

Robert III *n* ?1337–1406, king of Scotland (1390–1406), son of Robert II

Roberts *n* **1** Frederick Sleigh, 1st Earl. 1832–1914, British field marshal. He was awarded the Victoria Cross (1858) for his service during the Indian Mutiny and was commander in chief (1899–1900) in the second Boer War **2** Julia. born 1967, US film actress; her films include *Pretty Woman* (1990), *Notting Hill* (1999), *Erin Brockovich* (2000), which earned her an Academy Award, and *Charlie Wilson's War* (2007)

Robertson *n* George (**Islay Macneill**), Baron. born 1946, Scottish Labour politician; secretary-general of NATO (1999–2003)

Robeson *n* Paul. 1898–1976, US bass singer, actor, and leader in the Black civil rights movement

Robespierre *n* Maximilien François Marie Isidore de. 1758–94, French revolutionary and Jacobin leader: established the Reign of Terror as a member of the Committee of Public Safety (1793–94): executed in the coup d'état of Thermidor (1794)

Robey *n* Sir George, original name *George Edward Wade*, known as *the prime minister of mirth*. 1869–1954, British music-hall comedian, who also appeared in films

robin *n* **1** Also called: **robin redbreast** a small Old World songbird with a brown back and an orange-red breast and face **2** a North American thrush similar to but larger than the Old World robin [arbitrary use of name *Robin*]

Robinson *n* **1** Edward G., real name *Emanuel Goldenberg*. 1893–1973, US film actor, born in Romania, famous esp. for gangster roles. His films include *Little Caesar* (1930), *Brother Orchid* (1940), *Double Indemnity* (1944), and *All My Sons* (1948) **2** Edward Arlington. 1869–1935, US poet, author of narrative verse, often based on Arthurian legend. His works include *Collected Poems* (1922), *The Man Who Died Twice* (1924), and *Tristram* (1927) **3** (**William**) Heath. 1872–1944, British cartoonist and book illustrator, best known for his comic drawings of fantastic machines **4** John (**Arthur Thomas**) 1919–83, British bishop and theologian, best known for his controversial *Honest to God* (1963), which popularized radical theological discussion. He was suffragan Bishop of Woolwich (1959–69) **5** Mary. born 1944, Irish barrister and politician: president of Ireland 1990–97; UN high commissioner for human rights (1997–2002) **6** Peter (**David**). born 1948, Northern Irish politician; leader of the Democratic Unionist Party from 2008; first minister of Northern Ireland from 2008 **7** Smokey, real name *William Robinson*. born 1940, US Motown singer, songwriter, and producer. His hits include "The Tears of a Clown" (1970) (with the Miracles) and "Being with You" (1981) **8** "Sugar" Ray, real name *Walker Smith*. 1921–89, US boxer, winner of the world middleweight championship on five separate occasions

robot *n* **1** a machine programmed to perform specific tasks in a human manner, esp. one with a human shape **2** a person of machine-like efficiency **3** *S African* a set of traffic lights [used in *R.U.R.*, a play by a Czech writer, from Czech *robota* work] ➤ **robotic** *adj*

robotics *n* the science of designing, building, and using robots

Rob Roy *n* real name *Robert Macgregor*. 1671–1734, Scottish outlaw

Robson¹ *n* Mount Robson a mountain in SW Canada, in E British Columbia: the highest peak in the Canadian Rockies. Height: 3954 m (12 972 ft)

Robson² *n* **1** Sir Bobby, full name *Robert William*. 1933–2009, English footballer and manager: played in 20 matches for England (1957–62) and managed the team (1982–90); managed Ipswich Town (1969–82) with whom he won the UEFA Cup in 1981; won trophies with clubs in the Netherlands, Portugal, and in Spain where he won the 1997 European Cup Winners' Cup with Barcelona **2** Bryan. born 1957, English footballer and manager: played for Manchester United (1981–94) and was their longest-serving captain: scored 26 goals in 90 games (65 as captain) for England (1980–91) **3** Dame **Flora**. 1902–84, English stage and film actress

robust *adj* **1** very strong and healthy **2** sturdily built: *the new generation of robust lasers* **3** requiring or displaying physical strength: *robust tackles* [Latin *robur* an oak, strength]

roc *n* (in Arabian legend) a bird of enormous size and power [Persian *rukh*]

Roca *n* **Cape Roca** a cape in SW central Portugal, near Lisbon: the westernmost point of continental Europe

Rocard *n* **Michel**. born 1930, French politician: prime minister of France (1988–91)

Rochdale *n* **1 a** a town in NW England, in Rochdale unitary authority, Greater Manchester: former centre of the textile industry. Pop: 95 769 (2001) **2** a unitary authority in NW England, in Greater Manchester. Pop: 206 600 (2003 est). Area: 159 sq km (61 sq miles)

Rochester[1] *n* **1 a** a city in SE England, in Medway unitary authority, Kent, on the River Medway. Pop: 27 123 (2001) **2** a city in NW New York State, on Lake Ontario. Pop: 215 093 (2003 est) **3** a city in the US, in Minnesota: site of the Mayo Clinic. Pop: 92 507 (2003 est)

Rochester[2] *n* **2nd Earl of**, title of *John Wilmot*. 1647–80, English poet, wit, and libertine. His poems include satires, notably *A Satire against Mankind* (1675), love lyrics, and bawdy verse

rock[1] *n* **1** *geology* the mass of mineral matter that makes up part of the earth's crust; stone **2** a large rugged mass of stone **3** *chiefly US, Canad and Austral* a stone **4** a hard peppermint-flavoured sweet, usually in the shape of a long stick **5** a person or thing on which one can always depend: *your loyalty is a rock* **6** *slang* a precious jewel **7 on the rocks a** (of a marriage) about to end **b** (of an alcoholic drink) served with ice [Old French *roche*]

rock[2] *vb* **1** to move from side to side or backwards and forwards **2** to shake or move (something) violently **3** to feel or cause to feel shock: *key events have rocked both countries* **4** to dance to or play rock music **5** *slang* to be very good ▷ *n* **6** Also called: **rock music** a style of pop music with a heavy beat **7** a rocking motion ▷ *adj* **8** of or relating to rock music [Old English *roccian*]

Rock *n* **the Rock 1** an informal name for **Gibraltar 2** a Canadian informal name for **Newfoundland**

rockabilly *n* a fast style of White rock music which originated in the mid-1950s in the US South [*rock and roll* + *hillbilly*]

Rockall *n* an uninhabited British island in the N Atlantic, 354 km (220 miles) W of the Outer Hebrides. Area: 0.07 ha (0.18 acres)

rock and roll *or* **rock'n'roll** *n* a type of pop music originating in the 1950s as a blend of rhythm and blues and country and western

rock bottom *n* the lowest possible level

rock cake *n* a small fruit cake with a rough surface

rock crystal *n* a pure transparent colourless quartz

rock dove *n* a common dove from which domestic and wild pigeons are descended

Rockefeller *n* **1** John D(avison). 1839–1937, US industrialist and philanthropist **2** his son, **John D(avison)**. 1874–1960, US capitalist and philanthropist **3** his son, **Nelson (Aldrich)**. 1908–79, US politician; governor of New York State (1958–74); vice president (1974–76)

rocker *n* **1 a** rocking chair **2** either of two curved supports on which a rocking chair stands **3** a rock music performer or fan **4 off one's rocker** *slang* crazy

rockery *n, pl* **-eries** a garden built of rocks and soil, for growing rock plants

rocket *n* **1** a self-propelling device, usually cylindrical, which produces thrust by expelling through a nozzle the gases produced by burning fuel, such as one used as a firework or distress signal **2** any vehicle propelled by a rocket engine, as a weapon or carrying a spacecraft **3** *informal* a severe reprimand: *my sister gave me a rocket for writing such dangerous nonsense* ▷ *vb* **-eting, -eted 4** to increase rapidly: *within six years their turnover had rocketed*

5 to attack with rockets [Italian *rochetto* little distaff]

rocketry *n* the science and technology of the design and operation of rockets

Rockford *n* a city in N Illinois, on the Rock River. Pop: 151 725 (2003 est)

rock garden *n* a garden featuring rocks or rockeries

Rockhampton *n* a port in Australia, in E Queensland on the Fitzroy River. Pop: 59 475 (2001)

Rockies *pl n* another name for the **Rocky Mountains**

rocking chair *n* a chair set on curving supports so that the sitter may rock backwards and forwards

Rockingham *n* **Marquess of**, title of *Charles Watson-Wentworth*. 1730–82, British statesman and leader of the Whig opposition, whose members were known as the Rockingham Whigs; prime minister (1765–66; 1782). He opposed the war with the American colonists

rocking horse *n* a toy horse mounted on a pair of rocking supports on which a child can rock to and fro

rock melon *n* US, Austral and NZ same as **cantaloupe**

rock pool *n* a small pool between rocks on the seashore

rock salmon *n* Brit a former term for dogfish when used as a food

rock salt *n* common salt as a naturally occurring solid mineral

rock tripe *n* Canad any edible lichen that grows on rocks

Rockwell *n* **Norman**. 1894–1978, US illustrator, noted esp. for magazine covers

rocky[1] *adj* **rockier, rockiest** covered with rocks: *rocky and sandy shores* ❯ **rockiness** *n*

rocky[2] *adj* **rockier, rockiest** shaky or unstable: *a rocky relationship* ❯ **rockiness** *n*

Rocky Mountains *or* **Rockies** *pl n* the chief mountain system of W North America, extending from British Columbia to New Mexico: forms the Continental Divide. Highest peak: Mount Elbert, 4399 m (14 431 ft). Mount McKinley (6194 m (20 320 ft)), in the Alaska Range, is not strictly part of the Rocky Mountains

rococo (rok-**koe**-koe) *adj* **1** relating to an 18th-century style of architecture, decoration, and music characterized by elaborate ornamentation **2** excessively elaborate in style [French]

rod *n* **1** a thin straight pole made of wood or metal **2** a cane used to beat people as a punishment **3** short for **fishing rod 4** a type of cell in the retina, sensitive to dim light [Old English *rodd*] ❯ **rodlike** *adj*

Rodchenko *n* **Alexander (Mikhailovich)**. 1891–1956, Soviet painter, sculptor, designer, and photographer, noted for his abstract geometrical style: a member of the constructivist movement

Roddick *n* **Anita**. 1942–2007, British entrepreneur, founder (1976) of the Body Shop chain, selling natural beauty and health products

rode *vb* the past tense of **ride**

rodent *n* a small mammal with teeth specialized for gnawing, such as a rat, mouse, or squirrel [Latin *rodere* to gnaw] ❯ **rodent-like** *adj*

rodeo *n, pl* **-deos** a display of the skills of cowboys, including bareback riding [Spanish]

Rodgers *n* **Richard**. 1902–79, US composer of musical comedies. He collaborated with the librettist Lorenz Hart on such musicals as *A Connecticut Yankee* (1927), *On Your Toes* (1936), and *Pal Joey* (1940). After Hart's death his librettist was Oscar Hammerstein II. Two of their musicals, *Oklahoma!* (1943) and *South Pacific* (1949), received the Pulitzer Prize

Ródhos *n* transliteration of the Modern Greek name for **Rhodes**

Rodin *n* **Auguste**. 1840–1917, French sculptor, noted for his portrayal of the human form. His works include *The Kiss* (1886), *The Burghers of Calais* (1896), and *The Thinker* (1905)

Rodney *n* **George Brydges**, 1st Baron Rodney. 1719–92, English admiral: captured Martinique (1762): defeated the Spanish at Cape St Vincent (1780) and the French under Admiral de Grasse off Dominica (1782), restoring British superiority in the Caribbean

rodomontade *n literary* boastful words or behaviour [French]

Rodrigo *n* Joaquín. 1902–99, Spanish composer. His works include *Concierto de Aranjuez* (1940) for guitar and orchestra and *Concierto Pastoral* (1978)

roe¹ *n* the ovary and eggs of a female fish, sometimes eaten as food [Middle Dutch *roge*]

roe² *or* **roe deer** *n* a small graceful deer with short antlers [Old English *rā(ha)*]

Roeg *n* Nic(olas). born 1928, British film director and cinematographer. Films include *Walkabout* (1970), *Don't Look Now* (1972), *Insignificance* (1984), and *The Witches* (1990)

roentgen (ront-gan) *n* a unit measuring a radiation dose [after W.K. ROENTGEN]

Roentgen *or* **Röntgen** *n* Wilhelm Konrad. 1845–1923, German physicist, who in 1895 discovered X-rays: Nobel prize for physics 1901

roentgenium *n* a synthetic radioactive element produced in small quantities. Symbol: **Rg** [after W.K. ROENTGEN]

Roeselare *n* the Flemish name for **Roulers**

Roethke *n* Theodore. 1908–63, US poet, whose books include *Words for the Wind* (1957) and *The Far Field* (1964)

roger *interj* **1** (used in signalling) message received **2** an expression of agreement [from the name *Roger*, representing R for *received*]

Roger II *n* 1095–1154, Norman king of Sicily (1130–54). His court was an intellectual centre for Muslim and Christian scholars

Rogers *n* **1** Ginger, real name *Virginia McMath*. 1911–95, US dancer and film actress, who partnered Fred Astaire **2** Richard, Baron Rogers of Riverside. born 1933, British architect. His works include the Pompidou Centre in Paris (1971–77; with Renzo Piano), the Lloyd's building in London (1986), the Millennium Dome in Greenwich (1999), and Heathrow Airport Terminal 5 (2008) **3** William Penn Adair, known as *Will*. 1879–1935, US actor, newspaper columnist, and humorist in the homespun tradition

Roget *n* Peter Mark. 1779–1869, English physician, who on retirement devised a *Thesaurus of English Words and Phrases* (1852), a classified list of synonyms

rogue *n* **1** a dishonest or unprincipled person **2** a mischievous person **3** a crop plant which is inferior, diseased, or of a different variety **4** an inferior or defective specimen ▷ *adj* **5** (of a wild animal) having a savage temper and living apart from the herd: *a rogue elephant* **6** inferior or defective: *rogue heroin* [origin unknown] ▷ **roguish** *adj*

roguery *n, pl* **-gueries** dishonest or immoral behaviour

rogues' gallery *n* a collection of photographs of known criminals kept by the police for identification purposes

Röhm *n* Ernst. 1887–1934, German soldier, who organized (1921–34) Hitler's storm troops: murdered on Hitler's orders

ROI **1** Republic of Ireland **2** *finance* return on investment

roister *vb old-fashioned* to enjoy oneself noisily and boisterously [Old French *rustre* lout] ▷ **roisterer** *n*

Roland *n* the greatest of the legendary 12 peers (paladins, of whom Oliver was another) in attendance on Charlemagne; he died in battle at Roncesvalles (778 AD)

role *n* **1** a task or function: *their role in international relations* **2** an actor's part in a production [French]

role model *n* a person regarded by others, esp. younger people, as a good example to follow

Rolfe *n* Frederick William, also known as *Baron Corvo*. 1860–1913, British novelist. His best-known work is *Hadrian the Seventh* (1904)

roll *vb* **1** to move along by turning over and over **2** to move along on wheels or rollers **3** to curl or make by curling into a ball or tube **4** to move along in an undulating movement **5** to rotate wholly or partially: *he would snort in derision, roll his eyes, and heave a deep sigh* **6** to spread out flat or smooth with a roller or rolling pin: *roll the pastry out thinly* **7** (of a ship or aircraft) to turn from side to side around the longitudinal axis **8** to operate or begin to operate: *the cameras continued to roll as she pulled up to the nightclub* **9** to make a continuous deep reverberating sound: *the thunder rolled* **10** to walk in a swaying manner: *the drunks came rolling home* **11** to appear like a series of waves: *mountain ranges rolling away in every direction* **12** to pass or elapse: *watching the time roll away* **13** (of animals) to turn onto the back and kick **14** to trill or cause to be trilled: *she rolled her r's* **15** to throw (dice) ▷ *n* **16** the act or an instance of rolling **17** anything rolled up into a tube: *a roll of paper towels* **18** a small cake of bread for one person **19** a flat pastry or cake rolled up with a meat, jam, or other filling **20** an official list or register of names: *the electoral roll; the voters' roll* **21** a complete rotation about its longitudinal axis by an aircraft **22** a continuous deep reverberating sound: *the roll of musketry* **23** a swaying or unsteady movement or gait **24** a rounded mass: *rolls of fat* **25** a very rapid beating of the sticks on a drum **26** on a roll *slang* experiencing continued good luck or success **27** strike off the roll to expel from membership of a professional association ▶ See also **roll in**, **roll on**, etc. [Old French *roler*]

Rolland *n* Romain. 1866–1944, French novelist, dramatist, and essayist, known for his novels about a musical genius, *Jean-Christophe*, (1904–12): Nobel prize for literature 1915

roll call *n* the reading aloud of an official list of names, to check who is present

rolled gold *n* a metal, such as brass, coated with a thin layer of gold

roller *n* **1** a rotating cylinder used for smoothing, supporting a thing to be moved, spreading paint, etc. **2** a small tube around which hair may be wound in order to make it curly **3** a long heavy wave of the sea **4** a cylinder fitted on pivots, used to enable heavy objects to be easily moved

Rollerblade *n trademark* a type of roller skate in which the wheels are set in a single straight line under the boot

roller coaster *n* (at a funfair) a narrow railway with open carriages, sharp curves and steep slopes

roller skate *n* **1** a shoe with four small wheels that enable the wearer to glide swiftly over a floor ▷ *vb* **roller-skate** (**-skating, -skated**) **2** to move on roller skates ▶ **roller skater** *n*

roller towel *n* **1** a towel with the two ends sewn together, hung on a roller **2** a towel wound inside a roller enabling a clean section to be pulled out when needed

rollicking *adj* boisterously carefree: *a rollicking read* [origin unknown]

roll in *vb* **1** to arrive in large numbers **2** be rolling in *slang* to have plenty of (money etc.)

rolling *adj* **1** having gentle rising and falling slopes: *rolling hills* **2** (of a walk) slow and swaying **3** subject to regular review and updating: *a 10-year rolling programme* **4** progressing by stages or in succession: *a rolling campaign*

rolling mill *n* **1** a factory where metal ingots are passed between rollers to produce sheets or bars of the required shape **2** a machine with rollers for doing this

rolling pin *n* a cylinder with handles at both ends used for rolling pastry

rolling stock *n* the locomotives and coaches of a railway

rolling stone *n* a restless or wandering person

Rolling Stones *pl n* the. British rock group (formed 1962): comprising Mick Jagger, Keith Richards (born 1943; guitar, vocals), Brian Jones (1942–69; guitar), Charlie Watts (born 1941; drums), Bill Wyman (born 1936; bass guitar; now retired), and subsequently Mick

Taylor (born 1948; guitar; with the group 1969–74) and Ron Wood (born 1947; guitar; with the group from 1975). See also **Jagger**

Rollins *n* Sonny, original name *Theodore Walter Rollins*. born 1930, US jazz tenor saxophonist, noted for his improvisation

rollmop *n* a herring fillet rolled around onion slices and pickled [German *rollen* to roll + *Mops* pug dog]

rollneck *adj* (of a garment) having a high neck that is worn rolled over

Rollo *n* ?860–?930 AD, Norse war leader who received from Charles the Simple a fief that formed the basis of the duchy of Normandy. Also: **Rolf, Rolf the Ganger**

roll of honour *n* a list of those who have died in war for their country

roll on *interj* **1** used to express the wish that an eagerly anticipated event will come quickly: *roll on the next light-hearted romp* ▷ *adj* **roll-on 2** (of a deodorant) applied by means of a revolving ball fitted into the neck of the container

roll-on/roll-off *adj* denoting a ship designed so that vehicles can be driven straight on and straight off

roll over *vb* **1** to overturn **2** to allow (a loan or prize) to continue in force for a further period ▷ *n* **rollover 3** an instance of such a continuance of a loan or prize

roll-top *adj* (of a desk) having a slatted wooden panel that can be pulled down over the writing surface when not in use

roll up *vb* **1** to form into a cylindrical shape: *roll up a length of black material* **2** informal to arrive ▷ *n* **roll-up 3** Brit informal a cigarette made by the smoker from loose tobacco and cigarette papers

roly-poly *adj* **1** plump or chubby ▷ *n, pl* **-lies 2** Brit a strip of suet pastry spread with jam, rolled up, and baked or steamed [probably from *roll*]

ROM *n computers* read only memory: a storage device that holds data permanently and cannot be altered by the programmer

Rom. **1** Roman **2** Romance (languages) **3** Bible Romans **4** Romania(n)

Roma *n* the Italian name for **Rome**

Romagna *n* an area of N Italy: part of the Papal States up to 1860

Romains *n* Jules. pseudonym of *Louis Farigoule*. 1885–1972, French poet, dramatist, and novelist. His works include the novel *Men of Good Will* (1932–46)

roman *adj* **1** in or relating to the vertical style of printing type used for most printed matter ▷ *n* **2** roman type [so called because the style of letters is that used in ancient Roman inscriptions]

Roman *adj* **1** of or relating to Rome or its inhabitants in ancient or modern times **2** of Roman Catholicism or the Roman Catholic Church ▷ *n* **3** a native or inhabitant of ancient or modern Rome

Roman alphabet *n* the alphabet evolved by the ancient Romans for writing Latin, used for writing most of the languages of W Europe, including English

Roman blind *n* a window blind which gathers into horizontal folds from the bottom when drawn up

Roman candle *n* a firework that produces a steady stream of coloured sparks [it originated in Italy]

Roman Catholic *adj* **1** of the Roman Catholic Church ▷ *n* **2** a member of this Church ▷ **Roman Catholicism** *n*

Roman Catholic Church *n* the Christian Church over which the pope presides

romance *n* **1** a love affair: *a failed romance* **2** love, esp. romantic love idealized for its purity or beauty **3** a spirit of or inclination for adventure or mystery **4** a mysterious or sentimental quality **5** a story or film dealing with love, usually in an idealized way **6** a story or film dealing with events and characters remote from ordinary life **7** an extravagant, absurd, or fantastic account **8** a medieval narrative dealing with adventures of chivalrous heroes ▷ *vb* **-mancing, -manced 9** to tell extravagant or improbable lies [Old French *romans*]

Romance *adj* of the languages derived from Latin, such as French, Spanish, and Italian

Romanesque *adj* of or in the style of architecture used in Europe from the 9th to the 12th century, characterized by rounded arches and massive walls

Romania, Rumania *or* **Roumania** *n* a republic in SE Europe, bordering on the Black Sea: united in 1861; became independent in 1878; Communist government set up in 1945; became a socialist republic in 1965; a more democratic regime was installed after a revolution in 1989; joined the EU in 2007. It consists chiefly of a great central arc of the Carpathian Mountains and Transylvanian Alps, with the plains of Walachia, Moldavia, and Dobriya on the south and east and the Pannonian Plain in the west. Official language: Romanian. Religion: Romanian Orthodox (Christian) majority. Currency: leu. Capital: Bucharest. Pop: 21 790 479 (2013 est). Area: 237 500 sq km (91 699 sq miles)

Romanian, Rumanian *or* **Roumanian** *adj* **1** of or relating to Romania or its inhabitants ▷ *n* **2** a native or inhabitant of Romania **3** the language of Romania

Roman nose *n* a nose with a high prominent bridge

Roman numerals *pl n* the letters used as numerals by the Romans, used occasionally today: I (= 1), V (= 5), X (= 10), L (= 50), C (= 100), D (= 500), and M (= 1000). VI = 6 (V + I) but IV = 4 (V - I)

romantic *adj* **1** of or dealing with love **2** idealistic but impractical: *a romantic notion* **3** evoking or given to thoughts and feelings of love: *romantic images* **4** Romantic relating to a movement in European art, music, and literature in the late 18th and early 19th centuries, characterized by an emphasis on feeling and content rather than order and form ▷ *n* **5** a person who is idealistic or amorous **6** a person who likes or produces artistic works in the style of Romanticism ▷ **romantically** *adv*

romanticism *n* **1** idealistic but unrealistic thoughts and feelings **2** Romanticism the spirit and style of the Romantic art, music, and literature of the late 18th and early 19th centuries ▷ **romanticist** *n*

romanticize *or* **-cise** *vb* **-cizing, -cized** *or* **-cising, -cised** to describe or regard (something or someone) in an unrealistic and idealized way: *the Victorian legacy of romanticizing family life*

Romany *n* **1** (*pl* **-nies**) a Gypsy **2** the language of the Gypsies [Romany *romani* (adjective) Gypsy]

Romberg *n* Sigmund. 1887–1951, US composer of operettas, born in Hungary. He wrote *The Student Prince* (1924) and *The Desert Song* (1926)

Rome *n* **1** the capital of Italy, on the River Tiber: includes the independent state of the Vatican City; traditionally founded by Romulus on the Palatine Hill in 753 BC, later spreading to six other hills east of the Tiber; capital of the Roman Empire; a great cultural and artistic centre, esp. during the Renaissance. Pop: 2 546 804 (2001). Italian name: **Roma 2** the Roman Empire **3** the Roman Catholic Church or Roman Catholicism

Romeo *n, pl* **Romeos** an ardent male lover [after the hero of Shakespeare's *Romeo and Juliet*]

Rommel *n* Erwin, nicknamed *the Desert Fox*. 1891–1944, German field marshal, noted for his brilliant generalship in N Africa in World War II. Later a commander in N France, he committed suicide after the officers' plot against Hitler

Romney *n* George. 1734–1802, English painter, who painted more than 50 portraits of Lady Hamilton in various historical roles

Romney Marsh *n* **1** a marshy area of SE England, on the Kent coast between New Romney and Rye: includes Dungeness **2** a type of hardy British sheep from this area, with long wool, bred for mutton

romp *vb* **1** to play or run about wildly or joyfully **2** romp home *or* in to win a race or other competition easily

3 romp through to do (something) quickly and easily ▷ *n* **4** a noisy or boisterous game or prank [probably from Old French *ramper* to crawl, climb]

rompers *pl n* a one-piece baby garment combining trousers and a top. Also called: **romper suit**

Roncesvalles *n* a village in N Spain, in the Pyrenees: a nearby pass was the scene of the defeat of Charlemagne and death of Roland in 778. French name: **Roncevaux**

rondavel *n S African* a small circular building with a cone-shaped roof [origin unknown]

rondeau (ron-doe) *n, pl* **-deaux** (-doe) a poem consisting of 13 or 10 lines with the opening words of the first line used as a refrain [Old French]

rondo *n, pl* **-dos** a piece of music with a leading theme continually returned to: often forms the last movement of a sonata or concerto [Italian]

Rondônia *n* a state of W Brazil: consists chiefly of tropical rainforest; a centre of the Amazon rubber boom until about 1912. Capital: Porto Velho. Pop: 1 431 777 (2002). Area: 243 043 sq km (93 839 sq miles). Former name (until 1956): **Guaporé**

Ronsard *n* Pierre de. 1524–85, French poet, foremost of the *Pléiade*

roo *n, pl* **roos** *Austral informal* a kangaroo

rood *n* **1** *Christianity* the Cross **2** a crucifix [Old English *rōd*]

Roodepoort *n* an industrial city in NE South Africa, in the Witwatersrand. Pop: 172 601 (2001)

rood screen *n* (in a church) a screen separating the nave from the choir

roof *n, pl* **roofs 1** a structure that covers or forms the top of a building **2** the top covering of a vehicle, oven, or other structure **3** the highest part of the mouth or a cave **4 hit** *or* **go through the roof** *informal* to get extremely angry **5 raise the roof** *informal* to be very noisy ▷ *vb* **6** to put a roof on [Old English *hrōf*]

roof garden *n* a garden on a flat roof of a building

roofing *n* material used to build a roof

roof rack *n* a rack for carrying luggage attached to the roof of a car

rooftree *n* same as **ridgepole**

rooibos (roy-boss) *n S African* a kind of tea made from the leaves of a South African wild shrub. Also called: **rooibos tea, bush tea** [Afrikaans *rooi* red + *bos* bush]

rooinek (roy-neck) *n S African* a contemptuous name for an Englishman [Afrikaans *rooi* red + *nek* neck]

rook¹ *n* **1** a large European black bird of the crow family ▷ *vb* **2** *old-fashioned, slang* to cheat or swindle [Old English *hrōc*]

rook² *n* a chessman that may move any number of unoccupied squares in a straight line, horizontally or vertically; castle [Arabic *rukhkh*]

rookery *n, pl* **-eries 1** a group of nesting rooks **2** a colony of penguins or seals

rookie *n informal* a newcomer without much experience [changed from *recruit*]

room *n* **1** an area within a building enclosed by a floor, a ceiling, and walls **2** the people present in a room: *the whole room was laughing* **3** unoccupied or unobstructed space: *there wasn't enough room* **4 room for** opportunity or scope for: *there was no room for acts of heroism* **5** rooms lodgings ▷ *vb* **6** *US* to occupy or share a rented room: *I roomed with him for five years* [Old English *rūm*]

rooming house *n US* a house with self-contained furnished rooms or flats for renting

roommate *n* a person with whom one shares a room or apartment

room service *n* a service in a hotel providing food and drinks in guests' rooms

roomy *adj* **roomier, roomiest** with plenty of space inside: *a roomy entrance hall* ▶ **roominess** *n*

Rooney *n* Wayne. born 1985, English footballer; he played for Everton (2002–2004) and plays for Manchester United (from 2004) and England (from 2003)

Roosevelt *n* **1** (Anna) Eleanor. 1884–1962, US writer,

diplomat, and advocate of liberal causes: delegate to the United Nations (1945–52) **2** her husband, **Franklin Delano**, known as FDR. 1882–1945, 32nd president of the US (1933–45); elected four times. He instituted major reforms (the **New Deal**) to counter the economic crisis of the 1930s and was a forceful leader during World War II **3 Theodore**. 1858–1919, 26th president of the US (1901–09). A proponent of extending military power, he won for the US the right to build the Panama Canal (1903). He won the Nobel peace prize (1906), for mediating in the Russo-Japanese war

roost *n* **1** a place where birds rest or sleep ▷ *vb* **2** to rest or sleep on a roost **3 come home to roost** to have unfavourable repercussions **4 rule the roost** to have authority over people in a particular place [Old English *hrōst*]

rooster *n* the male of the domestic fowl; a cock

root¹ *n* **1** the part of a plant that anchors the rest of the plant in the ground and absorbs water and mineral salts from the soil **2** a plant with an edible root, such as a carrot **3** *anatomy* the part of a tooth, hair, or nail that is below the skin **4 roots** a person's sense of belonging in a place, esp. the one in which he or she was brought up **5** source or origin **6** the essential part or nature of something: *the root of a problem* **7** *linguistics* the form of a word from which other words and forms are derived **8** *maths* a quantity that when multiplied by itself a certain number of times equals a given quantity: *what is the cube root of a thousand?* **9** Also called: **solution** *maths* a number that when substituted for the variable satisfies a given equation **10** *Austral and NZ slang* sexual intercourse **11 root and branch** entirely or utterly. Related adjective: **radical** ▷ *vb* **12** Also: **take root** to establish a root and begin to grow **13** Also: **take root** to become established or embedded **14** *Austral and NZ slang* to have sexual intercourse (with) ▶ See also **root out, roots** [Old English *rōt*]

root² *vb* **1** *Brit* to dig up the earth in search of food, using the snout: *dogs were rooting in the rushes for bones* **2** *informal* to search vigorously but unsystematically: *she was rooting around in her large untidy purse* [Old English *wrōtan*]

root canal *n* the passage in the root of a tooth through which its nerves and blood vessels enter

root crop *n* a crop, such as potato or turnip, cultivated for its roots

root for *vb informal* to give support to (a team or contestant) [origin unknown]

rootle *vb* **-ling, -led** *Brit* same as **root²**

rootless *adj* having no sense of belonging: *a rootless city dweller*

root mean square *n* the square root of the average of the squares of a set of numbers or quantities, for example *the root mean square of 1, 2, and 4 is* $\sqrt{(1^2 + 2^2 + 4^2)/3} = \sqrt{7}$

root out *vb* to get rid of completely: *a major drive to root out corruption*

roots *adj* (of popular music) going back to the origins of a style, esp. in being unpretentious: *roots reggae*

rootstock *n* same as **rhizome**

rope *n* **1** a fairly thick cord made of intertwined fibres or wire **2** a row of objects fastened to form a line: *a twenty-inch rope of pearls* **3 know the ropes** to have a thorough understanding of a particular activity **4 the rope** a rope noose used for hanging someone **b** death by hanging ▷ *vb* **roping, roped 5** to tie with a rope **6 rope off** to enclose or divide with a rope [Old English *rāp*]

rope in *vb* to persuade to take part in some activity

ropey *or* **ropy** *adj* **ropier, ropiest** *Brit informal* **1** poor or unsatisfactory in quality: *a ropey performance* **2** slightly unwell ▶ **ropiness** *n*

Roquefort *n* a strong blue-veined cheese made from ewes' milk [after *Roquefort*, village in S France]

Roraima *n* a state of N Brazil: chiefly rainforest. Capital: Boa Vista. Pop: 346 871 (2002). Area: 230 104 sq km

(89 740 sq miles)

ro-ro *adj* (of a ferry) roll-on/roll-off

rorqual *n* a whalebone whale with a fin on the back [Norwegian *rörhval*]

Rorschach test (ror-shahk) *n psychol* a personality test consisting of a number of unstructured inkblots for interpretation [after H. *Rorschach*, psychiatrist]

rort *Austral informal n* **1 a** dishonest scheme ▷ *vb* **2** to take unfair advantage of something

Rory O'Connor *n* Also called *Roderic*. ?1116–98, king of Connaught and last High King of Ireland

Rosa¹ *n* **Monte Rosa** a mountain between Italy and Switzerland: the highest in the Pennine Alps. Height: 4634 m (15 204 ft)

Rosa² *n* Salvator. 1615–73, Italian artist, noted esp. for his romantic landscapes

rosaceous *adj* of or belonging to a family of plants typically having five-petalled flowers, which includes the rose, strawberry, and many fruit trees

Rosario *n* an inland port in E Argentina, on the Paraná River: the second largest city in the country; industrial centre. Pop: 1 312 000 (2005 est)

rosary *n, pl* **-saries** *RC Church* **1** a series of prayers counted on a string of beads **2** a string of beads used to count these prayers as they are recited [Latin *rosarium* rose garden]

Roscius *n* **1** full name *Quintus Roscius Gallus*. died 62 BC, Roman actor **2** any actor ➤ **Roscian** *adj*

Roscommon *n* **1** an inland county of N central Republic of Ireland, in Connacht: economy based on cattle and sheep farming. County town: Roscommon. Pop: 53 774 (2002). Area: 2463 sq km (951 sq miles) **2** a former name for **Galway** (3)

rose¹ *n* **1 a** a shrub or climbing plant with prickly stems and fragrant flowers **2** the flower of any of these plants **3** a plant similar to this, such as the Christmas rose **4** a perforated cap fitted to a watering can or hose, causing the water to come out in a spray **5 bed of roses** a situation of comfort or ease ▷ *adj* **6** reddish-pink [Latin *rosa*]

rose² *vb* the past tense of **rise**

rosé (roe-zay) *n* a pink wine [French]

roseate (roe-zee-ate) *adj* **1** of the colour rose or pink **2** excessively optimistic

Roseau *n* the capital of Dominica, a port on the SW coast: botanical gardens. Pop: 19 400 (2001 est)

rosebay willowherb *n* a widespread perennial plant that has spikes of deep pink flowers

Rosebery *n* **Earl of**, title of *Archibald Philip Primrose*. 1847–1929, British Liberal statesman; prime minister (1894–95)

rosebud *n* a rose that has not yet fully opened

rose-coloured *adj* **1** reddish-pink **2 see through rose-coloured** *or* **rose-tinted glasses** *or* **spectacles** to view in an unrealistically optimistic light

rosehip *n* the berry-like fruit of a rose plant

rosella *n* a type of Australian parrot

rosemary *n, pl* **-maries** an aromatic European shrub widely cultivated for its grey-green evergreen leaves, which are used in cookery and perfumes [Latin *ros* dew + *marinus* marine]

Rosenberg *n* **1** Alfred. 1893–1946, German Nazi politician and writer, who devised much of the racial ideology of Nazism: hanged for war crimes **2** Isaac. 1890–1918, British poet and painter, best known for his poems about life in the trenches during World War I: died in action **3** Julius. 1918–53, US spy, who, with his wife **Ethel** (1914–53), was executed for passing information about nuclear weapons to the Russians

Rosetta *n* the former name of **Rashid**

rosette *n* a rose-shaped decoration, esp. a circular bunch of ribbons

Rosewall *n* Ken(neth). born 1934, Australian tennis player: won eight Grand Slam singles titles, including the Australian Open four times (1953, 1955, 1971, 1972)

rose-water *n* scented water made by the distillation of rose petals

rose window *n* a circular window with spokes branching out from the centre to form a symmetrical roselike pattern

rosewood *n* a fragrant dark wood used to make furniture

Rosh Hashanah *or* **Rosh Hashana** *n* the festival celebrating the Jewish New Year [Hebrew: beginning of the year]

rosin (rozz-in) *n* **1** a translucent brittle substance produced from turpentine and used for treating the bows of stringed instruments ▷ *vb* **2** to apply rosin to [variant of *resin*]

Roskilde *n* a city in Denmark, on NE Zealand west of Copenhagen: capital of Denmark from the 10th century to 1443; scene of the signing (1658) of the **Peace of Roskilde** between Denmark and Sweden. Pop: 44 205 (2004 est)

ROSPA (in Britain) Royal Society for the Prevention of Accidents

Ross *n* **1** Diana. born 1944, US singer: lead vocalist (1961–69) with Motown group the Supremes, whose hits include "Baby Love" (1964). Her subsequent recordings include *Lady Sings the Blues* (film soundtrack, 1972), and "Chain Reaction" (1986) **2** Sir James Clark. 1800–62, British naval officer; explorer of the Arctic and Antarctic. He located the north magnetic pole (1831) and discovered the Ross Sea during an Antarctic voyage (1839–43) **3** his uncle, Sir John. 1777–1856, Scottish naval officer and Arctic explorer **4** Sir Ronald. 1857–1932, English bacteriologist, who discovered the transmission of malaria by mosquitoes: Nobel prize for physiology or medicine 1902

Ross and Cromarty *n* (until 1975) a county of N Scotland, including the island of Lewis and many islets: now split between the Highland and Western Isles council areas

Ross Dependency *n* a section of Antarctica administered by New Zealand. (Claims are suspended under the Antarctic Treaty of 1959.) Includes the coastal regions of Victoria Land and King Edward VII Land, the Ross Sea and islands, and the Ross Ice Shelf. Area: about 414 400 sq km (160 000 sq miles)

Rossellini *n* Roberto. 1906–77, Italian film director. His films include *Rome, Open City* (1945), *Paisà* (1946), and *L'Amore* (1948)

Rossetti *n* **1** Christina Georgina. 1830–94, British poet **2** her brother, **Dante Gabriel**. 1828–82, British poet and painter: a leader of the Pre-Raphaelites

Ross Ice Shelf *n* the ice shelf forming the S part of the Ross Sea, between Victoria Land and Byrd Land. Also called: **Ross Barrier, Ross Shelf Ice**

Rossini *n* Gioacchino Antonio. 1792–1868, Italian composer, esp. of operas, such as *The Barber of Seville* (1816) and *William Tell* (1829)

Ross Island *n* an island in the W Ross Sea: contains the active volcano Mount Erebus

Rossiya *n* transliteration of the Russian name for **Russia**

Ross Sea *n* a large arm of the S Pacific in Antarctica, incorporating the Ross Ice Shelf and lying between Victoria Land and the Edward VII Peninsula

Rostand *n* Edmond. 1868–1918, French playwright and poet in the romantic tradition; best known for his verse drama *Cyrano de Bergerac* (1897)

roster *n* **1 a** list showing the order in which people are to perform a duty ▷ *vb* **2** to place on a roster [Dutch *rooster* grating or list]

Rostock *n* a port in NE Germany, in Mecklenburg-West Pomerania on the Warnow estuary 13 km (8 miles) from the Baltic and its outport, Warnemünde: the chief port of the former East Germany; university (1419). Pop: 198 303 (2003 est)

r

Rostov or **Rostov-on-Don** n a port in S Russia, on the River Don 48 km (30 miles) from the Sea of Azov: industrial centre. Pop: 1 081 000 (2005 est)

Rostropovich n Mstislav Leopoldovich. 1927–2007, Soviet cellist, composer, and conductor; became a US citizen in 1978 after losing Soviet citizenship (restored in 1990)

rostrum n, pl **-trums** or **-tra** a platform or stage [Latin: beak]

rosy adj **rosier, rosiest 1** of the colour rose or pink: rosy cheeks **2** hopeful or promising: the analysis revealed a far from rosy picture **> rosiness** n

rot vb **rotting, rotted 1** to decay or cause to decay **2** to deteriorate slowly, mentally and physically: I thought he was either dead or rotting in a Chinese jail ▷ n **3** the process of rotting or the state of being rotten **4** something decomposed **5** short for **dry rot 6** a plant or animal disease which causes decay of the tissues **7** nonsense [Old English rotian]

rota n a list of people who take it in turn to do a particular task [Latin: a wheel]

rotary adj **1** revolving **2** operating by rotation ▷ n, pl **-ries 3** US and Canad a traffic roundabout

Rotary Club n a club that is part of **Rotary International**, an international association of professionals and businesspeople who raise money for charity **> Rotarian** n, adj

rotate vb **-tating, -tated 1** to turn around a centre or pivot **2** to follow or cause to follow a set sequence **3** to regularly change (the type of crop) grown on a piece of land in order to preserve the fertility of the soil [Latin rota wheel] **> rotation** n **> rotational** adj

rotator cuff n anatomy the structure around the shoulder joint consisting of the capsule of the joint along with the tendons of the adjacent muscles

Rotavator n trademark a mechanical cultivator with rotary blades

rote adj **1** done by routine repetition: rote learning ▷ n **2** by rote by repetition: we learned by rote [origin unknown]

rotgut n chiefly Brit facetious, slang alcoholic drink of inferior quality

Roth n Philip. born 1933, US novelist. His works include Goodbye, Columbus (1959), Portnoy's Complaint (1969), My Life as a Man (1974), Sabbath's Theater (1995), The Human Stain (2000), and The Plot Against America (2004)

Rotherham n **1** an industrial town in N England, in Rotherham unitary authority, South Yorkshire. Pop: 117 262 (2001) **2** a unitary authority in N England, in South Yorkshire. Pop: 251 500 (2003 est). Area: 283 sq km (109 sq miles)

Rothermere n Viscount. title of Harold Sidney Harmsworth. 1868–1940, British newspaper magnate

Rothesay n a town in SW Scotland, in Argyll and Bute, on the E coast of the Isle of Bute. Pop: 5017 (2001)

Rothko n Mark. 1903–70, US abstract expressionist painter, born in Russia

Rothschild n **1** Lionel Nathan, Baron de Rothschild. 1809–79, British banker and first Jewish member of Parliament **2** his grandfather **Meyer Amschel.** 1743–1812, German financier and founder of the Rothschild banking firm **3** his son, **Nathan Meyer**, Baron de Rothschild. 1777–1836, British banker, born in Germany

rotisserie n a rotating spit on which meat and poultry can be cooked [French]

rotor n **1** the rotating part of a machine or device, such as the revolving arm of the distributor of an internal-combustion engine **2** a rotating device with blades projecting from a hub which produces thrust to lift a helicopter

Rotorua n a city in New Zealand, on N central North Island at the SW end of Lake Rotorua: centre of forestry; noted for volcanic activity. Pop: 67 800 (2004 est)

rotten adj **1** decomposing or decaying: rotten vegetables **2** breaking up through age or hard use: the window frames are rotten **3** informal very bad: what rotten luck! **4** morally corrupt: this country's politics are rotten and out of date **5** informal miserably unwell: I had glandular fever and spent that year feeling rotten **6** informal distressed and embarrassed: I'm feeling rotten as a matter of fact, rotten and guilty ▷ adv **7** informal extremely; very much: men fancy her rotten [Old Norse rotinn]

rotter n chiefly Brit old-fashioned, slang a despicable person

Rotterdam n a port in the SW Netherlands, in South Holland province: the second largest city of the Netherlands and one of the world's largest ports; oil refineries, shipbuilding yards, etc. Pop: 600 000 (2003 est)

Rottweiler (rot-vile-er) n a large sturdy dog with a smooth black-and-tan coat and a docked tail [Rottweil, German city where it was first bred]

rotund (roe-tund) adj **1** round and plump **2** (of speech) pompous or grand [Latin rotundus] **> rotundity** n **> rotundly** adv

rotunda n a circular building or room, esp. with a dome [Italian rotonda]

Rouault n Georges. 1871–1958, French expressionist artist. His work is deeply religious; it includes much stained glass

Roubaix n a city in N France near the Belgian border: forms, with Tourcoing, a large industrial conurbation. Pop: 97 423 (2007)

Roubiliac or **Roubillac** n Louis-François. ?1695–1762, French sculptor: lived chiefly in England: his sculptures include the statue of Handel in Vauxhall Gardens (1737)

rouble or **ruble** (roo-bl) n the standard monetary unit of Russia and Tadzhikistan [Russian rubl]

roué (roo-ay) n a man who leads a sensual and immoral life [French]

Rouen n a city in N France, on the River Seine: the chief river port of France; became capital of the duchy of Normandy in 912; scene of the burning of Joan of Arc (1431); university (1964). Pop: 110 276 (2006)

rouge n **1** a red cosmetic for adding colour to the cheeks ▷ vb **rouging, rouged 2** to apply rouge to [French: red]

Rouget de Lisle n Claude Joseph. 1760–1836, French army officer: composer of the Marseillaise (1792), the French national anthem

rough adj **1** not smooth; uneven or irregular **2** not using enough care or gentleness **3** difficult or unpleasant: tomorrow will be a rough day **4** approximate: a rough guess **5** violent or stormy **6** troubled by violence or crime: he lived in a rough area **7** incomplete or basic: a rough draft **8** lacking refinement: a rough shelter **9** (of ground) covered with scrub or rubble **10** harsh or grating to the ear **11** harsh or sharp: the rough interrogation of my father **12** unfair: rough luck **13** informal ill: Feeling rough? A good stiff drink will soon fix that! **14** shaggy or hairy: the rough wool of her sweater **15** (of work etc.) requiring physical rather than mental effort: wear gloves for any rough work ▷ vb **16** to make rough **17** rough it informal to live without the usual comforts of life ▷ n **18** rough ground **19** a sketch or preliminary piece of artwork **20** informal a violent person **21** in rough in an unfinished or crude state **22** the rough golf the part of the course beside the fairways where the grass is untrimmed **23** the unpleasant side of something: you have to take the rough with the smooth ▷ adv **24** roughly **25** sleep rough to spend the night in the open without shelter ▶ See also **rough out, rough up** [Old English rūh] **> roughly** adv

roughage n the coarse indigestible constituents of food, which help digestion

rough-and-ready adj **1** hastily prepared but adequate for the purpose **2** (of a person) without formality or refinement

rough-and-tumble n **1** a playful fight **2** a disorderly situation

roughcast n **1** a mixture of plaster and small stones for outside walls ▷ vb **-casting, -cast 2** to put roughcast on (a wall)

rough diamond n **1** an unpolished diamond **2** a kind or trustworthy person whose manners are not good

roughen vb to make or become rough

rough-hewn adj roughly shaped or cut without being properly finished

roughhouse n slang rough or noisy behaviour

roughneck n slang **1** a violent person **2** a worker on an oil rig

rough out vb to prepare (a sketch or report) in preliminary form: *he offered to rough out some designs for the sets*

roughshod adv **ride roughshod over** to act with complete disregard for

rough up vb informal to beat up

Rouhani n Hassan. born 1948, Iranian politician; president of Iran from 2013

Roulers n a city in NW Belgium, in West Flanders province. Pop: 55 273 (2004 est). Flemish name: **Roeselare**

roulette n a gambling game in which a ball is dropped onto a revolving wheel with numbered coloured slots [French]

Roumania n a variant of **Romania**

Roumanian n, adj a variant of **Romanian**

round adj **1** having a flat circular shape, like a hoop **2** having the shape of a ball **3** curved; not angular **4** involving or using circular motion **5** complete **6** maths **a** forming or expressed by a whole number, with no fraction **b** expressed to the nearest ten, hundred, or thousand: *in round figures* ▷ adv **7** on all or most sides **8** on or outside the circumference or perimeter: *ponds which are steeply sided all round* **9** in rotation or revolution: *she swung round on me* **10** to all members of a group: *handing cigarettes round* **11** to a specific place: *the boys invited him round* **12** all year round throughout the year ▷ prep **13** surrounding or encircling: *wrap your sash round the wound* **14** on all or most sides of: *the man turned in a circle, looking all round him* **15** on or outside the circumference or perimeter of **16** from place to place in: *a trip round the island in an ancient bus* **17** reached by making a partial circuit about: *just round the corner* **18** revolving about: *if you have two bodies in orbit, they orbit round their common centre of gravity* ▷ vb **19** to move round: *as he rounded the last corner, he raised a fist* ▷ n **20** a round shape or object **21** a session: *a round of talks* **22** a series: *the petty round of domestic matters* **23** a series of calls: *a paper round* **24** the daily round the usual activities of a person's day **25** a playing of all the holes on a golf course **26** a stage of a competition: *the first round of the Portuguese Open* **27** one of a number of periods in a boxing or wrestling match **28** a single turn of play by each player in a card game **29** a number of drinks bought at one time for a group of people **30** a bullet or shell for a gun **31** a single discharge by a gun **32** music a part song in which the voices follow each other at equal intervals **33** circular movement **34 a** a single slice of bread **b** a serving of sandwiches made from two complete slices of bread **35** a general outburst: *a round of applause* **36** in the round **a** in full detail **b** theatre with the audience all round the stage **37** go the rounds (of information or infection) to be passed around from person to person ▶ See also **round down**, **round off**, etc. [Old French *ront*]

USAGE See at **around**.

roundabout n Brit, Austral and NZ **1** a road junction in which traffic moves in one direction around a central island **2** a revolving circular platform, often with seats, on which people ride for amusement ▷ adj **3** not straightforward: *the roundabout sea route; she thought of asking about it in a roundabout way* ▷ adv, prep **round about 4** approximately: *round about 1900*

round dance n **1** a dance in which the dancers form a circle **2** a ballroom dance, such as the waltz, in which couples revolve

round down vb to lower (a number) to the nearest whole number or ten, hundred, or thousand below it

roundel n **1** a circular identifying mark on military aircraft **2** a small circular object [Old French *rondel* little circle]

roundelay n a song in which a line or phrase is repeated as a refrain [Old French *rondelet*]

rounders n Brit and NZ a bat and ball game in which players run between posts after hitting the ball

Roundhead n English history a supporter of Parliament against Charles I during the Civil War [referring to their short-cut hair]

roundhouse n US and Canad a circular building in which railway locomotives are serviced

roundly adv bluntly or thoroughly: *the Church roundly criticized the bill*

round off vb to complete agreeably or successfully: *our afternoon was rounded off with coffee and biscuits*

round on vb to attack or reply to (someone) with sudden irritation or anger

round robin n **1** a petition with the signatures in a circle to disguise the order of signing **2** a tournament in which each player plays against every other player

round-shouldered adj denoting poor posture with drooping shoulders and a slight forward bending of the back

round table n a meeting of people on equal terms for discussion

Round Table n **1** (in Arthurian legend) the table of King Arthur, shaped so that his knights could sit around as equals **2** one of an organization of clubs of young business and professional men who meet in order to further charitable work

round-the-clock adj throughout the day and night

round trip n a journey to a place and back again

round up vb **1** to gather together: *the police had rounded up a circle of drug users* **2** to raise (a number) to the nearest whole number or ten, hundred, or thousand above it ▷ n **roundup 3** a summary or discussion of news and information **4** the act of gathering together livestock or people

roundworm n a worm that is a common intestinal parasite of man

rouse¹ vb **rousing, roused 1** to wake up **2** to provoke or excite: *his temper was roused and he had a gun* **3 rouse oneself** to become energetic [origin unknown]

rouse² (rhymes with **mouse**) vb (foll. by **on**) Austral to scold or rebuke

rouseabout n Austral and NZ a labourer in a shearing shed

rousing adj lively or vigorous: *a rousing speech*

Rousseau n **1** Henri, known as *le Douanier*. 1844–1910, French painter, who created bold dreamlike pictures, often of exotic landscapes in a naive style. Among his works are *Sleeping Gypsy* (1897) and *Jungle with a Lion* (1904–06). He also worked as a customs official **2** Jean Jacques. 1712–78, French philosopher and writer, born in Switzerland, who strongly influenced the theories of the French Revolution and the romantics. Many of his ideas spring from his belief in the natural goodness of man, whom he felt was warped by society. His works include *Du contrat social* (1762), *Émile* (1762), and his *Confessions* (1782) **3** Théodore. 1812–67, French landscape painter: leader of the Barbizon school

Rousseff n Dilma. born 1947, Brazilian socialist politician; president of Brazil from 2011

Roussillon n a former province of S France: united with Aragon in 1172; passed to the French crown in 1659; now forms part of the region of Languedoc-Roussillon

roustabout n **1** an unskilled labourer on an oil rig **2** Austral and NZ another word for **rouseabout**

rout¹ n **1** an overwhelming defeat **2** a disorderly retreat **3** a noisy rabble ▷ vb **4** to defeat and put to flight [Anglo-Norman *rute*]

rout² *vb* **1** to find by searching **2** to drive out: *the dissidents had been routed out* **3** to dig (something) up [variant of ROOT²]

route *n* **1** the choice of roads taken to get to a place **2** a fixed path followed by buses, trains, etc. between two places **3** a chosen way or method: *the route to prosperity* ▷ *vb* **routeing, routed 4** to send by a particular route [Old French *rute*]

> **USAGE** When forming the present participle or verbal noun from the verb *to route* it is preferable to retain the *e* in order to distinguish the word from *routing*, the present participle or verbal noun from *rout¹*, to defeat or *rout²*, to dig, rummage: *the routeing of buses from the city centre to the suburbs*. The spelling *routing* in this sense is, however, sometimes encountered, esp. in American English.

routemarch *n military* a long training march

router *n computers* a device that allows data to be moved efficiently between two points on a network

routine *n* **1** a usual or regular method of procedure **2** the boring repetition of tasks: *mindless routine* **3** a set sequence of dance steps **4** *computers* a program or part of a program performing a specific function: *an input routine* ▷ *adj* **5** relating to or characteristic of routine [Old French *route* a customary way]

roux (roo) *n* a cooked mixture of fat and flour used as a basis for sauces [French: brownish]

rove *vb* **roving, roved 1** to wander about (a place) **2** (of the eyes) to look around [probably from Old Norse] **> rover** *n*

row¹ (rhymes with **know**) *n* **1** an arrangement of people or things in a line: *a row of shops* **2** a line of seats in a cinema or theatre **3** *Brit* a street lined with identical houses **4** *maths* a horizontal line of numbers **5** **in a row** in succession: *five championships in a row* [Old English *rāw*, *rǣw*]

row² (rhymes with **know**) *vb* **1** to propel (a boat) by using oars **2** to carry (people or goods) in a rowing boat **3** to take part in the racing of rowing boats as a sport ▷ *n* **4** an act or spell of rowing **5** an excursion in a rowing boat [Old English *rōwan*] **> rowing** *n*

row³ (rhymes with **cow**) *informal n* **1** a noisy quarrel **2** a controversy or dispute: *the row over Europe* **3** a noisy disturbance: *go to the insurance offices and kick up a row about your money* **4** a reprimand ▷ *vb* **5** to quarrel noisily [origin unknown]

rowan *n* a European tree with white flowers and red berries; mountain ash [Scandinavian]

rowdy *adj* **-dier, -diest 1** rough, noisy, or disorderly ▷ *n, pl* **-dies 2** a person like this [origin unknown] **> rowdily** *adv*

Rowe *n* Nicholas. 1674–1718, English dramatist, who produced the first critical edition of Shakespeare; poet laureate (1715–18). His plays include *Tamerlane* (1702) and *The Fair Penitent* (1703)

rowel (rhymes with **towel**) *n* a small spiked wheel at the end of a spur [Old French *roel* a little wheel]

rowing boat *n* a small pleasure boat propelled by oars. Usual US and Canad word: **rowboat**

Rowlandson *n* Thomas. 1756–1827, English caricaturist, noted for the vigour of his attack on sordid aspects of contemporary society and on statesmen such as Napoleon

Rowley *n* Thomas. ?1586–?1642, English dramatist, who collaborated with John Ford and Thomas Dekker on *The Witch of Edmonton* (1621) and with Thomas Middleton on *The Changeling* (1622)

Rowling *n* J(oanne) K(athleen). born 1965, British novelist; author of the bestselling series of children's books featuring the boy wizard Harry Potter, which began with *Harry Potter and the Philosopher's Stone* (1995)

rowlock (rol-luk) *n* a swivelling device attached to the top of the side of a boat that holds an oar in place

Roxas y Acuña *n* Manuel. 1892–1948, Philippine statesman; first president of the Republic of the Philippines (1946–48)

Roxburghshire *n* (until 1975) a county of SE Scotland, now part of Scottish Borders council area

royal *adj* **1** of or relating to a king or queen or a member of his or her family: *the royal yacht* **2 Royal** supported by or in the service of royalty: *the Royal Society of Medicine* **3** very grand: *royal treatment* ▷ *n* **4** *informal* a king or queen or a member of his or her family [Old French *roial*] **> royally** *adv*

Royal Air Force *n* the air force of the United Kingdom

royal-blue *adj* deep blue

royalist *n* **1** a supporter of a monarch or monarchy ▷ *adj* **2** of or relating to royalists **> royalism** *n*

royal jelly *n* a substance secreted by worker bees and fed to all larvae when very young and to larvae destined to become queens throughout their growth

Royal Leamington Spa *n* the official name of Leamington Spa

Royal Marines *pl n Brit* a corps of soldiers specially trained in amphibious warfare

Royal National Theatre *n* a theatre complex in London, on the S bank of the Thames (opened 1976). The prefix Royal was added in 1988. It houses the Royal National Theatre Company

Royal Navy *n* the navy of the United Kingdom

royalty *n, pl* **-ties 1** royal people **2** the rank or power of a king or queen **3** a percentage of the revenue from the sale of a book, performance of a work, use of a patented invention or of land, paid to the author, inventor, or owner

royal warrant *n* an authorization to a tradesman to supply goods to a royal household

Royce *n* Josiah. 1855–1916, US philosopher of monistic idealism. In his ethical studies he emphasized the need for individual loyalty to the world community

RPI (in Britain) retail price index: a measure of the changes in the average level of retail prices of selected goods

rpm revolutions per minute

RR 1 Right Reverend **2** *US and Canad* rural route

RSA 1 Republic of South Africa **2** (in New Zealand) Returned Services Association **3** Royal Scottish Academy **4** (in Britain) Royal Society of Arts

RSFSR (formerly) Russian Soviet Federative Socialist Republic

RSI repetitive strain injury: pain in the arm caused by repeated awkward movements, such as in typing

RSM (in Britain) regimental sergeant major

RSPCA (in Britain) Royal Society for the Prevention of Cruelty to Animals

RSS Rich Site Summary *or* Really Simple Syndication: a way of allowing web users to receive updated information from selected websites on their browser

RSVP please reply [French *répondez s'il vous plaît*]

RTA *Brit* road traffic accident

Rt Hon. Right Honourable: a title of respect for a Privy Councillor, certain peers, and the Lord Mayor or Lord Provost of certain cities

Ru *chem* ruthenium

RU486 *n* the technical name for **abortion pill**

Ruanda-Urundi *n* a former territory of central Africa: part of German East Africa from 1890; a League of Nations mandate under Belgian administration from 1919; a United Nations trusteeship from 1946; divided into the independent states of Rwanda and Burundi in 1962

rub *vb* **rubbing, rubbed 1** to apply pressure and friction to (something) with a circular or backwards-and-forwards movement **2** to move (something) with pressure along or against (a surface) **3** to clean, polish, or dry by rubbing **4** to spread with pressure, esp. so that it can be absorbed: *rub beeswax into all polishable surfaces* **5** to chafe or fray through rubbing **6** to mix (fat) into flour with the fingertips, as in making pastry **7 rub it in** to emphasize an unpleasant fact **8 rub up the wrong way** to annoy ▷ *n* **9** the act of rubbing **10 the rub** the obstacle or difficulty: *there's the rub* ▷ See also **rub along**, **rub down**, etc. [origin unknown]

Rub' al Khali *n* a desert in S Arabia, mainly in Saudi Arabia, extending southeast from Nejd to Hadramaut and northeast from Yemen to the United Arab Emirates. Area: about 777 000 sq km (300 000 sq miles). English names: **Great Sandy Desert**, **Empty Quarter**. Also called: **Ar Rimal**

rub along *vb* **1** to have a friendly relationship **2** to continue in spite of difficulties

rubato *music n, pl* **-tos 1** flexibility of tempo in performance: *his playing brought much beautifully felt but never sentimental rubato to the music* ▷ *adj, adv* **2** to be played with a flexible tempo [Italian, literally: robbed]

rubber[1] *n* **1** an elastic material obtained from the latex of certain plants, such as the rubber tree **2** a similar substance produced synthetically **3** a piece of rubber used for erasing something written **4** *US slang* a condom **5 rubbers** *US* rubber-coated waterproof overshoes ▷ *adj* **6** made of or producing rubber [the tree was so named because its product was used for rubbing out writing] ▷ **rubbery** *adj*

rubber[2] *n* **1** *bridge, whist* a match of three games **2** a series of matches or games in various sports [origin unknown]

rubber band *n* a continuous loop of thin rubber, used to hold papers together

rubberize *or* **-ise** *vb* **-izing, -ized** *or* **-ising, -ised** to coat or treat with rubber

rubberneck *slang vb* **1** to stare in a naive or foolish manner ▷ *n* **2** a person who stares inquisitively **3** a sightseer or tourist

rubber plant *n* **1** a large house plant with glossy leathery leaves **2** same as **rubber tree**

rubber stamp *n* **1** a device used for imprinting dates or signatures on forms or invoices **2** automatic authorization of something **3** a person or body that gives official approval to decisions taken elsewhere but has no real power ▷ *vb* **rubber-stamp 4** *informal* to approve automatically

rubber tree *n* a tropical tree cultivated for its latex, which is the major source of commercial rubber

rubbing *n* an impression taken of an engraved or raised design by laying paper over it and rubbing with wax or charcoal

rubbish *n* **1** discarded or waste matter **2** anything worthless or of poor quality: *the rubbish on television* **3** foolish words or speech ▷ *vb* **4** *informal* to criticize [origin unknown] ▷ **rubbishy** *adj*

rubble *n* **1** debris from ruined buildings **2** pieces of broken stones or bricks [origin unknown]

Rubbra *n* (Charles) Edmund. 1901–86, English composer of works in a traditional idiom

rub down *vb* **1** to prepare (a surface) for painting by rubbing it with sandpaper **2** to dry or clean (an animal or person) vigorously, esp. after exercise

rubella (roo-bell-a) *n* a mild contagious viral disease characterized by cough, sore throat, and skin rash. Also called: **German measles** [Latin *rubellus* reddish]

Rubens *n* Sir Peter Paul. 1577–1640, Flemish painter, regarded as the greatest exponent of the Baroque: appointed (1609) painter to Archduke Albert of Austria, who gave him many commissions, artistic and diplomatic. He was knighted by Charles I of England in 1629. His prolific output includes the triptych in Antwerp Cathedral, *Descent from the Cross* (1611–14), *The Rape of the Sabines* (1635), and his *Self-Portrait* (?1639)

Rubicon *n* **1** a stream in N Italy: in ancient times the boundary between Italy and Cisalpine Gaul. By leading his army across it and marching on Rome in 49 BC,

Julius Caesar broke the law that a general might not lead an army out of the province to which he was posted and so committed himself to civil war with the senatorial party **2** (*sometimes not cap*) a point of no return **3** a penalty in piquet by which the score of a player who fails to reach 100 points in six hands is added to his opponent's **4 cross the Rubicon** *or* **pass the Rubicon** to commit oneself irrevocably to some course of action

rubicund (roo-bik-kund) *adj old-fashioned* of a reddish colour [Latin *rubicundus*]

rubidium (roo-bid-ee-um) *n chem* a soft highly reactive radioactive metallic element used in electronic valves, photocells, and special glass. Symbol: **Rb** [Latin *rubidus* red]

Rubinstein *n* **1** Anton Grigorevich. 1829–94, Russian composer and pianist **2** Artur. 1886–1982, US pianist, born in Poland

ruble *n* same as **rouble**

Rublyov *or* **Rublev** *n* Andrey. ?1370–1430, Russian icon painter. His masterpiece is *The Old Testament Trinity*

rub off *vb* **1** to remove or be removed by rubbing: *rub the skins off the hazelnuts* **2** to have an effect through close association: *glamour can rub off on you by association*

rub out *vb* **1** to remove or be removed with a rubber **2** *US slang* to murder

rubric (roo-brik) *n* **1** a set of rules of conduct or procedure, esp. one for the conduct of Christian church services **2** a title or heading in a book [Latin *ruber* red]

ruby *n, pl* **-bies 1** a deep red transparent precious gemstone ▷ *adj* **2** deep red **3** denoting a fortieth anniversary: *a ruby wedding* [Latin *ruber* red]

RUC Royal Ulster Constabulary: a former name for the Police Service of Northern Ireland

ruche *n* a strip of pleated or frilled lace or ribbon used to decorate clothes [French, literally: beehive]

ruck[1] *n* **1** the ruck ordinary people, often in a crowd **2** *rugby* a loose scrum that forms around the ball when it is on the ground [probably from Old Norse]

ruck[2] *n* **1** a wrinkle or crease ▷ *vb* **2** to wrinkle or crease: *the toe of his shoe had rucked up one corner of the pale rug* [Scandinavian]

rucksack *n Brit, Austral and S African* a large bag, with two straps, carried on the back [from German]

ruction *n informal* **1** an uproar **2 ructions** an unpleasant row [origin unknown]

Ruda Śląska *n* a town in SW Poland: coalmining. Pop: 144 914 (2007 est)

Rudd *n* **1** Kevin (Michael). born 1957, Australian politician: leader of the Labor Party (2006–10 and 2013); Prime Minister (2007–2010 and 2013) **2** Steele, pen name of Arthur Hoey Davis, 1868–1935, Australian author. His works include *On Our Selection* (1899), *Our New Selection* (1902), *Back at Our Selection* (1906) and *Grandpa's Selection* (1916) which featured the characters Dad and Dave

rudder *n* **1** *nautical* a vertical hinged piece that projects into the water at the stern, used to steer a boat **2** a vertical control surface attached to the rear of the fin used to steer an aircraft [Old English *rōther*] ▷ **rudderless** *adj*

ruddy *adj* **-dier, -diest**. **1** (of the complexion) having a healthy reddish colour **2** red or pink: *a ruddy glow* ▷ *adv, adj* **3** *informal* bloody: *too ruddy slow; I just went through the ruddy ceiling* [Old English *rudig*]

rude *adj* **1** insulting or impolite **2** vulgar or obscene: *rude words* **3** unexpected and unpleasant: *we received a rude awakening* **4** roughly or crudely made: *the rude hovels* **5** robust or sturdy: *the very picture of rude health* **6** lacking refinement [Latin *rudis*] ▷ **rudely** *adv* ▷ **rudeness** *n*

rudiment *n* **1 rudiments a** the simplest and most basic stages of a subject: *the rudiments of painting* **b** a partially developed version of something: *the rudiments of a democratic society* **2** *biology* an organ or part that is incompletely developed or no longer functions [Latin *rudimentum*] ▷ **rudimentary** *adj*

r

Rudolf¹ n Lake Rudolf the former name (until 1979) of (Lake) Turkana

Rudolf² or **Rudolph** n 1858–89, archduke of Austria, son of emperor Franz Joseph: he and his mistress committed suicide at the royal hunting lodge in Mayerling

Rudolf I or **Rudolph I** n 1218–91, king of Germany (1273–91): founder of the Hapsburg dynasty based on the duchies of Styria and Austria

rue¹ vb **ruing, rued** literary to feel regret for [Old English hrēowan]

rue² n an aromatic shrub with bitter evergreen leaves formerly used in medicine [Greek rhutē]

rueful adj feeling or expressing sorrow or regret: a rueful smile ▷ **ruefully** adv

ruff¹ n 1 a circular pleated or fluted cloth collar 2 a natural growth of long or coloured hair or feathers around the necks of certain animals or birds 3 a bird of the sandpiper family [from ruffle]

ruff² n, vb cards same as **trump¹** (1, 2) [Old French roffle]

ruffian n a violent lawless person [Old French rufien]

ruffle vb **-fling, -fled** 1 to disturb the smoothness of: the wind was ruffling Dad's hair 2 to annoy or irritate 3 (of a bird) to erect its feathers in anger or display 4 to flick cards or pages rapidly ▷ n 5 a strip of pleated material used as a trim [Germanic]

rufous adj (of birds or animals) reddish-brown [Latin rufus]

rug n 1 a small carpet 2 a thick woollen blanket 3 slang a wig 4 **pull the rug out from under** to betray or leave defenceless [Scandinavian]

Rugbeian adj 1 of or relating to Rugby School ▷ n 2 a person educated at Rugby School

rugby or **rugby football** n a form of football played with an oval ball in which the handling and carrying of the ball is permitted [after the public school at Rugby, where it was first played]

Rugby n a town in central England, in E Warwickshire: famous public school, founded in 1567. Pop: 61 988 (2001)

rugby league n a form of rugby played between teams of 13 players

rugby union n a form of rugby played between teams of 15 players

rugged (rug-gid) adj 1 rocky or steep: the rugged mountains of Sicily's interior 2 with an uneven or jagged surface 3 (of the face) strong-featured 4 rough, sturdy, or determined in character 5 (of equipment or machines) designed to withstand rough treatment or use in rough conditions [probably from Old Norse]

rugger n chiefly Brit informal rugby

rug rat n informal a young child not yet walking

Ruhr n the chief coalmining and industrial region of Germany: in North Rhine-Westphalia around the valley of the River Ruhr (a tributary of the Rhine 235 km (146 miles) long). German name: **Ruhrgebiet**

ruin vb 1 to destroy or spoil completely: the suit was ruined 2 to cause (someone) to lose money: the first war ruined him ▷ n 3 the state of being destroyed or decayed 4 loss of wealth or position 5 a destroyed or decayed building or town 6 something that is severely damaged: my heart was an aching ruin [Latin ruina a falling down]

ruination n 1 the act of ruining or the state of being ruined 2 something that causes ruin

ruinous adj 1 causing ruin or destruction 2 more expensive than can reasonably be afforded: ruinous rates of exchange ▷ **ruinously** adv

Ruisdael or **Ruysdael** n Jacob van. ?1628–82, Dutch landscape painter

rule n 1 a statement of what is allowed, for example in a game or procedure 2 a customary form or procedure: he has his own rule: be firm, be clear, but never be rude 3 **the rule** the common order of things: humanitarian gestures were more the exception than the rule 4 the exercise of governmental authority or control: the rule of President Marcos 5 the period of time in which a monarch or government has

power: four decades of Communist rule 6 a device with a straight edge for guiding or measuring: a slide rule 7 printing a long thin line or dash 8 Christianity a systematic body of laws and customs followed by members of a religious order 9 law an order by a court or judge 10 **as a rule** usually ▷ vb **ruling, ruled** 11 to govern (people or a political unit) 12 to be pre-eminent or superior 13 to be customary or prevalent: chaos ruled as the scene turned into one of total confusion 14 to decide authoritatively: the judges ruled that men could be prosecuted for rape offences against their wives 15 to mark with straight parallel lines or one straight line 16 to restrain or control [Old French riule]

rule of thumb n a rough and practical approach, based on experience, rather than theory

rule out vb 1 to dismiss from consideration 2 to make impossible

ruler n 1 a person who rules or commands 2 a strip of wood, metal, or plastic, with straight edges, used for measuring and drawing straight lines

ruling adj 1 controlling or exercising authority 2 predominant ▷ n 3 a decision of someone in authority

rum¹ n an alcoholic drink made from sugar cane [origin unknown]

rum² adj **rummer, rummest** Brit slang strange or unusual [origin unknown]

Rumania n a variant of Romania

Rumanian adj, n a variant of Romanian

rumba n 1 a rhythmic and syncopated dance of Cuban origin 2 music for this dance [Spanish]

rumble vb **-bling, -bled** 1 to make or cause to make a deep echoing sound: thunder rumbled overhead 2 to move with such a sound: a slow freight train rumbled past 3 Brit slang to find out about (someone or something): his real identity was rumbled ▷ n 4 a deep resonant sound 5 slang a gang fight [probably from Middle Dutch rummelen] ▷ **rumbling** adj, n

rumbustious adj boisterous or unruly [probably variant of robustious]

Rumford n Count Rumford See **Thompson** (1)

ruminant n 1 a mammal that chews the cud, such as cattle, sheep, deer, goats, and camels ▷ adj 2 of ruminants 3 meditating or contemplating in a slow quiet way

ruminate vb **-nating, -nated** 1 (of ruminants) to chew (the cud) 2 to meditate or ponder [Latin ruminare to chew the cud] ▷ **rumination** n ▷ **ruminative** adj

rummage vb **-maging, -maged** 1 to search untidily ▷ n 2 an untidy search through a collection of things [Old French arrumage to stow cargo]

rummage sale n US and Canad a jumble sale

rummy n a card game based on collecting sets and sequences [origin unknown]

rumour or US **rumor** n 1 information, often a mixture of truth and untruth, told by one person to another 2 gossip or common talk ▷ vb 3 **be rumoured** to be circulated as a rumour: he is rumoured to have at least 53 yachts [Latin rumor]

rump n 1 a person's buttocks 2 the rear part of an animal's or bird's body 3 Also called: **rump steak** a cut of beef from the rump 4 a small core of members within a group who remain loyal to it: the rump of the once-influential communist party [probably from Old Norse]

rumple vb **-pling, -pled** to make or become crumpled or dishevelled [Middle Dutch rompelen]

rumpus n, pl **-puses** a noisy or confused commotion [origin unknown]

rumpy-pumpy n informal sexual intercourse

Rumsfeld n Donald (Henry). born 1932, US Republican politician and businessman: Secretary of Defense (2001–06)

run vb **running, ran, run** 1 to move on foot at a rapid pace 2 to pass over (a distance or route) in running: being a man isn't about running the fastest mile 3 to take part in (a race): I ran a decent race **4** to carry out as if by running: *he is running errands for his big brother* **5** to flee **6** to travel somewhere in a vehicle **7** to give a lift to (someone) in a vehicle: *one wet day I ran her down to the service* **8** to drive or maintain and operate (a vehicle) **9** to travel regularly between places on a route: *trains running through the night* **10** to move or pass quickly: *he ran his hand across his forehead* **11** to function or cause to function: *run the video tape backwards* **12** to manage: *he ran a small hotel* **13** to continue in a particular direction or for a particular time or distance: *a road running alongside the Nile; a performing arts festival running in the city for six weeks* **14** *law* to have legal force or effect: *the club's lease has a year to run* **15** to be subjected to or affected by: *she ran a high risk of losing her hair* **16** to tend or incline: *he was of medium height and running to fat* **17** to recur persistently or be inherent: *the capacity for infidelity ran in the genes* **18** to flow or cause (liquids) to flow: *sweat ran down her face* **19** to dissolve and spread: *the soles of the shoes peeled off and the colours ran* **20** (of stitches) to unravel **21** to spread or circulate: *rumours ran around quickly* **22** to publish or be published in a newspaper or magazine: *our local newspaper ran a story on the appeal* **23** *chiefly US and Canad* to stand as a candidate for political or other office: *he has formally announced his decision to run for the office of President* **24** to get past or through: *the oil tanker was hit as it tried to run the blockade* **25** to smuggle (goods, esp. arms) **26** (of fish) to migrate upstream from the sea, esp. in order to spawn **27** *cricket* to score (a run or number of runs) by hitting the ball and running between the wickets ▷ *n* **28** the act or an instance of running: *he broke into a run* **29** a distance covered by running or a period of running: *it's a short run of about 20 kilometres* **30** a trip in a vehicle, esp. for pleasure: *our only treat is a run in the car to Dartmoor* **31** free and unrestricted access: *he had the run of the house* **32 a** a period of time during which a machine or computer operates **b** the amount of work performed in such a period **33** a continuous or sustained period: *a run of seven defeats* **34** a continuous sequence of performances: *the play had a long run* **35** cards a sequence of winning cards in one suit: *a run of spades* **36** type, class, or category: *he had nothing in common with the usual run of terrorists* **37** a continuous and urgent demand: *a run on the pound* **38** a series of unravelled stitches, esp. in tights **39** a steeply inclined course, esp. a snow-covered one used for skiing **40** an enclosure for domestic fowls or other animals: *the chicken run* **41** (esp. in Australia and New Zealand) a tract of land for grazing livestock **42** the migration of fish upstream in order to spawn **43** *music* a rapid scalelike passage of notes **44** *cricket* a score of one, normally achieved by both batsmen running from one end of the wicket to the other after one of them has hit the ball **45** *baseball* an instance of a batter touching all four bases safely, thereby scoring **46 a run for one's money** *informal* **a** a close competition **b** pleasure or success from an activity **47 in the long run** as an eventual outcome **48 on the run** escaping from arrest **49 the runs** *slang* diarrhoea ▶ See also **runabout, run across**, etc. [Old English *runnen*]

runabout *n* **1** a small car used for short journeys ▷ *vb* **run about 2** to move busily from place to place

run across *vb* to meet unexpectedly by chance

run along *vb* to go away

run away *vb* **1** to go away **2** to escape **3** (of a horse) to gallop away uncontrollably: *the horse ran away with him* **4 run away with a** to abscond or elope with: *I ran away with David* **b** to escape from the control of: *he let his imagination run away with him* **c** to win easily or be certain of victory in (a competition): *the Spaniards at one stage seemed to be running away with the match* ▷ *adj* **runaway 5** a person or animal that runs away ▷ *adj* **runaway 6** no longer under control: *a runaway train* **7** (of a race or victory) easily won

Runcie *n* Robert (Alexander Kennedy), Baron. 1921–2000, Archbishop of Canterbury (1980–91)

Runcorn *n* a town in NW England, in Halton unitary authority, N Cheshire, on the Manchester Ship Canal: port and industrial centre; designated a new town in 1964. Pop: 60 072 (2001)

run down *vb* **1** to be rude about: *he is busy running us down and insulting other Europeans* **2** to reduce in number or size: *it should be possible to run down the existing hospitals almost entirely* **3** (of a device such as a clock or battery) to lose power gradually and cease to function **4** to hit and knock to the ground with a moving vehicle **5** to pursue and find or capture: *while I was there, Moscow ran me down, convinced I was ready to defect* ▷ *adj* **rundown 6** tired or ill **7** shabby or dilapidated ▷ *n* **rundown 8** a reduction in number or size **9** a brief review or summary

Rundstedt *n* Karl Rudolf Gerd von. 1875–1953, German field marshal; directed the conquest of Poland and France in World War II; commander of the Western Front (1942–44); led the Ardennes counteroffensive (Dec 1944)

rune *n* **1** any of the characters of the earliest Germanic alphabet **2** an obscure piece of writing using mysterious symbols [Old Norse *rūn* secret] ⟩ **runic** *adj*

Runeberg *n* Johan Ludvig 1804–77, Finnish poet, who wrote in Swedish. His works include the epic *King Fialar* (1844) and patriotic poems including the Finnish national anthem

rung¹ *n* **1** one of the bars forming the steps of a ladder **2** a crosspiece between the legs of a chair [Old English *hrung*]

rung² *vb* the past participle of **ring¹**

run-holder *n* *Austral and NZ* the owner or manager of a sheep or cattle station

run in *vb* **1** to run (an engine) gently, usually when it is new **2** *informal* to arrest ▷ *n* **run-in 3** *informal* an argument or quarrel **4** an approach to the end of an event: *the run-in for the championship*

run into *vb* **1** to be beset by: *the mission has run into difficulty* **2** to meet unexpectedly **3** to extend to: *businessmen denied losses running into the thousands* **4** to collide with

runnel *n* *literary* a small stream [Old English *rynele*]

runner *n* **1** a competitor in a race **2** a messenger for a firm **3** a person involved in smuggling **4 a** either of the strips of metal or wood on which a sledge runs **b** the blade of an ice skate **5** *botany* a slender horizontal stem of a plant, such as the strawberry, that grows along the surface of the soil and produces new roots and shoots **6** a long strip of cloth used to decorate a table or as a rug **7** a roller or guide for a sliding component **8 do a runner** *slang* to run away to escape trouble or to avoid paying for something

runner bean *n* the edible pod and seeds of a type of climbing bean plant

runner-up *n*, *pl* **runners-up** a person who comes second in a competition

running *adj* **1** maintained continuously: *a running battle* **2** without interruption: *for the third day running* **3** flowing: *rinse them under cold running water* **b** supplied through a tap: *there is no electricity, no running water, and no telephone* **4** operating: *running costs* **5** discharging pus: *a running sore* **6** accomplished at a run: *a running jump* **7** moving or slipping easily, as a rope or a knot ▷ *n* **8** the act of moving or flowing quickly **9** management or organization: *the running of the farm* **10** the operation or maintenance of a machine **11 in** or **out of the running** having or not having a good chance in a competition **12 make the running** to set the pace in a competition or race

running board *n* a board along the side of a vehicle, for help in stepping into it

running head *n* *printing* a heading printed at the top of every page of a book

running mate *n* **1** *US* a candidate for the lesser of two linked positions, esp. a candidate for the vice-presidency **2** a horse that pairs another in a team

running repairs *pl n* repairs that are done without greatly disrupting operations

r

runny *adj* **-nier, -niest 1** tending to flow: *a runny egg* **2** producing moisture: *a runny nose*

Runnymede *n* a meadow on the S bank of the Thames near Windsor, where King John met his rebellious barons in 1215 and acceded to Magna Carta

run off *vb* **1** to leave quickly **2 run off with a** to run away with in order to marry or live with **b** to steal **3** to produce (copies of a document) on a machine **4** to drain (liquid) or (of liquid) to be drained ▷ *n* **run-off 5** an extra race or contest to decide the winner after a tie **6** NZ grazing land for cattle

run-of-the-mill *adj* ordinary or average

run on *vb* to continue without interruption

run out *vb* **1** to use up or (of a supply) to be used up: *we soon ran out of gas* **2** to become invalid: *my passport has run out* **3 run out on** *informal* to desert or abandon **4** *cricket* to dismiss (a running batsman) by breaking the wicket with the ball while he is running between the wickets ▷ *n* **run-out 5** *cricket* dismissal of a batsman by running him out

run over *vb* **1** to knock down (a person) with a moving vehicle **2** to overflow **3** to examine hastily

runt *n* **1** the smallest and weakest young animal in a litter **2** an undersized or inferior person [origin unknown]

run through *vb* **1** to practise or rehearse **2** to pierce with a sword or other weapon ▷ *n* **run-through 3** a practice or rehearsal

run to *vb* **1** to reach an amount or size: *the testimony ran to a million words* **2** to be or have enough money for: *we do not run to these luxuries, I am afraid*

run up *vb* **1** to amass: *running up massive debts* **2** to make by sewing together quickly **3 run up against** to experience (difficulties) ▷ *n* **run-up 4** the time just before an event: *the run-up to the elections*

runway *n* a hard level roadway where aircraft take off and land

Runyon *n* **(Alfred) Damon.** 1884–1946, US short-story writer, best known for his humorous tales about racy Broadway characters. His story collections include *Guys and Dolls* (1932), which became the basis of a musical (1950)

rupee *n* the standard monetary unit of a number of countries including India and Pakistan [Hindi *rupaīyā*]

Rupert *n* **Prince.** 1619–82, German-born nephew of Charles I: Royalist general during the Civil War (until 1646) and commander of the Royalist fleet (1648–50). After the Restoration he was an admiral of the English fleet in wars against the Dutch

Rupert's Land *n* (formerly, in Canada) the territories granted by Charles II to the Hudson's Bay Company in 1670 and ceded to the Canadian Government in 1870, comprising all the land watered by rivers flowing into Hudson Bay

rupture *n* **1** the act of breaking or the state of being broken **2** a breach of peaceful or friendly relations **3** *pathol* a hernia ▷ *vb* **-turing, -tured 4** to break or burst **5** to cause a breach in relations or friendship **6** to affect or be affected with a hernia [Latin *rumpere* to burst forth]

rural *adj* in or of the countryside [Latin *ruralis*]

rural dean *n* *chiefly Brit* a clergyman with authority over a group of parishes

rural route *n* US and Canad a mail service or route in a rural area

Rurik *or* **Ryurik** *n* died 879. Varangian (Scandinavian Viking) leader who founded the Russian monarchy. He gained control over Novgorod (?862) and his dynasty, the Rurikids, ruled until 1598

Ruritania *n* **1** an imaginary kingdom of central Europe: setting of several novels by English novelist Anthony Hope (1863–1933), esp. *The Prisoner of Zenda* (1894) **2** any setting of adventure, romance, and intrigue

Ruritanian *adj* **1** of or relating to Ruritania **2** involving adventure, romance, and intrigue ▷ *n* **3** a native or inhabitant of Ruritania

ruse (rooz) *n* an action or plan intended to mislead someone [Old French]

Ruse *n* a city in NE Bulgaria, on the River Danube: the chief river port and one of the largest industrial centres in Bulgaria. Pop: 172 000 (2005 est)

rush¹ *vb* **1** to move or do very quickly **2** to force (someone) to act hastily **3** to make a sudden attack upon (a person or place): *scores of pubescent girls rushed the stage* **4** to proceed or approach in a reckless manner **5** to come or flow quickly or suddenly: *the water rushed in, and the next instant the boat was swamped* ▷ *n* **6** a sudden quick or violent movement **7** a sudden demand or need **8** a sudden surge towards someone or something: *the gold rush* **9** a sudden surge of sensation **10** a sudden flow of air or liquid **11 rushes** (in film-making) the initial prints of a scene before editing ▷ *adj* **12** done with speed or urgency: *a rush job* [Old French *ruser* to put to flight]

rush² *n* a plant which grows in wet places and has a slender pithy stem [Old English *risce, rysce*] ▷ **rushy** *adj*

Rush *n* **Geoffrey (Roy).** born 1951, Australian film actor. His films include *Shine* (1996), for which he won an Academy Award, *Quills* (2000), and *The King's Speech* (2010)

Rushdie *n* **Sir (Ahmed) Salman.** born 1947, British writer, born in India, whose novels include *Midnight's Children* (1981), which won the Booker prize, *Shame* (1983), *The Ground Beneath Her Feet* (1998), and *Shalimar the Clown* (2005). His novel *The Satanic Verses* (1988) was regarded as blasphemous by many Muslims and he was forced into hiding (1989) when the Ayatollah Khomeini called for his death; knighted in 2007

rush hour *n* a period at the beginning and end of the working day when large numbers of people are travelling to or from work

rush light *n* an old-fashioned candle made of rushes

Rushmore *n* **Mount Rushmore** a mountain in W South Dakota, in the Black Hills: a national memorial, with the faces of Washington, Lincoln, Jefferson, and Roosevelt carved into its side by Gutzon Borglum between 1927 and 1941. Height: 1841 m (6040 ft)

rusk *n* a hard brown crisp biscuit, often used for feeding babies [Spanish or Portuguese *rosca* screw, bread shaped in a twist]

Rusk *n* **(David) Dean.** 1909–94, US statesman: secretary of state (1961–69). He defended US military involvement in Vietnam and opposed recognition of communist China

Ruskin *n* **John.** 1819–1900, English art critic and social reformer. He was a champion of the Gothic Revival and the Pre-Raphaelites and saw a close connection between art and morality. From about 1860 he argued vigorously for social and economic planning. His works include *Modern Painters* (1843–60), *The Stones of Venice* (1851–53), *Unto this Last* (1862), *Time and Tide* (1867), and *Fors Clavigera* (1871–84)

Russ. Russia(n)

Russborough House *n* a mansion near Blessington in Co Wicklow, Republic of Ireland: built by Richard Castle and Francis Bindon for the 1st Earl of Miltown from 1740

Russell *n* **1 Bertrand (Arthur William), 3rd Earl.** 1872–1970, British philosopher and mathematician. His books include *Principles of Mathematics* (1903), *Principia Mathematica* (1910–13) with A. N. Whitehead, *Introduction to Mathematical Philosophy* (1919), *The Problems of Philosophy* (1912), *The Analysis of Mind* (1921), and *An Enquiry into Meaning and Truth* (1940): Nobel prize for literature 1950 **2 George William** pen name **æ.** 1867–1935, Irish poet and journalist **3 Henry Norris.** 1877–1957, US astronomer and astrophysicist, who originated one form of the Hertzsprung–Russell diagram **4 John, 1st Earl.** 1792–1878, British statesman; prime minister (1846–52; 1865–66). He led the campaign to carry the 1832 Reform Act **5 Ken.** 1927–2011, British film director. His films include *Women in Love* (1969), *The Music Lovers* (1970), *The Boy Friend* (1971), *Valentino* (1977), *Gothic* (1986), and *The Rainbow* (1989)

russet *adj* **1** *literary* reddish-brown: *a disarray of russet curls* ▷ *n* **2** an apple with a rough reddish-brown skin [Latin *russus*]

Russia *n* **1** the largest country in the world, covering N Eurasia and bordering on the Pacific and Arctic Oceans and the Baltic, Black, and Caspian Seas: originating from the principality of Muscovy in the 17th century, it expanded to become the Russian Empire; the Tsar was overthrown in 1917 and the Communist Russian Soviet Federative Socialist Republic was created; this merged with neighbouring Soviet Republics in 1922 to form the Soviet Union; on the disintegration of the Soviet Union in 1991 the Russian Federation was established as an independent state; Russia's annexation of the Ukrainian region of Crimea in 2014 has not been internationally recognized. Official language: Russian. Religion: nonreligious and Russian orthodox Christian. Currency: rouble. Capital: Moscow. Pop: 142 500 482 (2013 est). Area: 17 074 984 sq km (6 592 658 sq miles) **2** another name for the former **Soviet Union 3** another name for the former **Russian Soviet Federative Socialist Republic** ▶ Russian name: **Rossiya**

Russian *adj* **1** of or relating to Russia or its inhabitants ▷ *n* **2** a native or inhabitant of Russia **3** the official language of Russia and, formerly, of the Soviet Union

Russian doll *n* any of a set of hollow wooden figures, each of which splits in half to contain the next smallest figure, down to the smallest

Russian Federation *n* See Russia

Russian roulette *n* an act of bravado in which a person spins the cylinder of a revolver loaded with only one cartridge and presses the trigger with the barrel against his or her own head

Russian Soviet Federative Socialist Republic *n* (formerly) the largest administrative division of the Soviet Union. Abbreviation: RSFSR

Russian Turkestan *n* See Turkestan

Russian Zone *n* another name for the **Soviet Zone**

rust *n* **1** a reddish-brown oxide coating formed on iron or steel by the action of oxygen and moisture **2** a fungal disease of plants which produces a reddish-brown discoloration ▷ *adj* **3** reddish-brown ▷ *vb* **4** to become coated with a layer of rust **5** to deteriorate through lack of use: *my brain had rusted up* [Old English *rūst*]

rust belt *n* an area where heavy industry is in decline, esp. in the Midwest of the United States

rustic *adj* **1** of or resembling country people **2** of or living in the country **3** crude, awkward, or uncouth **4** made of untrimmed branches: *rustic furniture* ▷ *n* **5** a person from the country [Latin *rusticus*] ▶ **rusticity** *n*

rusticate *vb* **-cating, -cated 1** *Brit* to send (a student) down from university for a specified time as a punishment **2** to retire to the country **3** to make or become rustic [Latin *rus* the country]

rustle¹ *vb* **-tling, -tled 1** to make a low crisp whispering sound: *the leaves rustled in the breeze* ▷ *n* **2** this sound [Old English *hrūstlian*]

rustle² *vb* **-tling, -tled** *chiefly US and Canad* to steal (livestock) [probably from RUSTLE¹ (in the sense: to move with a quiet sound)] ▶ **rustler** *n*

rustle up *vb informal* to prepare or find at short notice: *Bob rustled up a meal*

rusty *adj* **rustier, rustiest 1** affected by rust: *a rusty old freighter* **2** reddish-brown **3** out of practice in a skill or subject: *your skills may be a little rusty, but your past experience will more than make up for that* ▶ **rustily** *adv* ▶ **rustiness** *n*

rut¹ *n* **1** a groove or furrow in a soft road, caused by wheels **2** dull settled habits or way of living: *his career was in a rut* [probably from French *route* road]

rut² *n* **1** a recurrent period of sexual excitement in certain male ruminants ▷ *vb* **rutting, rutted 2** (of male ruminants) to be in a period of sexual excitement [Old French *rut* noise, roar]

rutabaga *n* the US and Canadian term for **swede**

Ruth *n* **1** *Old Testament* **a** a Moabite woman, who left her own people to remain with her mother-in-law Naomi, and became the wife of Boaz; an ancestress of David **b** the book in which these events are recounted **2 George Herman**, nicknamed *Babe*. 1895–1948, US professional baseball player from 1914 to 1935

Ruthenia *n* a region of E Europe on the south side of the Carpathian Mountains: belonged to Hungary from the 14th century, to Czechoslovakia from 1918 to 1939, and was ceded to the former Soviet Union in 1945; in 1991 it became part of the newly independent Ukraine. Also called: **Carpatho-Ukraine**

Ruthenian *adj* **1** of or relating to Ruthenia, its people, or their dialect of Ukrainian ▷ *n* **2** a dialect of Ukrainian **3** a native or inhabitant of Ruthenia

ruthenium *n chem* a rare hard brittle white metallic element. Symbol: **Ru** [Medieval Latin *Ruthenia* Russia, where it was discovered]

Rutherford *n* **1 Ernest**, 1st Baron. 1871–1937, British physicist, born in New Zealand, who discovered the atomic nucleus (1909). Nobel prize for chemistry 1908 **2 Dame Margaret**. 1892–1972, British stage and screen actress. Her films include *Passport to Pimlico* (1949), *Murder She Said* (1962), and *The VIPs* (1963) **3 Mark**, original name *William Hale White*. 1831–1913, British novelist and writer, whose work deals with his religious uncertainties: best known for *The Autobiography of Mark Rutherford* (1881) and the novel *The Revolution in Tanner's Lane* (1887)

rutherfordium *n chem* an artificially produced radioactive element. Symbol: **Rf** [after E. RUTHERFORD]

ruthless *adj* **1** feeling or showing no mercy **2** thorough and forceful, regardless of effect: *the ruthless pursuit of cost-effectiveness* [*ruth* pity] ▶ **ruthlessly** *adv* ▶ **ruthlessness** *n*

Rutland *n* an inland county of central England: the smallest of the historical English counties, it became part of Leicestershire in 1974 but was reinstated as an independent unitary authority in 1997: mainly agricultural. Administrative centre: Oakham. Pop: 35 700 (2003 est). Area: 394 sq km (152 sq miles)

rutted *adj* (of a road) very uneven because of ruts

Ruwenzori *n* a mountain range in central Africa, on the border between Uganda and the Democratic Republic of Congo between Lakes Edward and Albert: generally thought to be Ptolemy's "Mountains of the Moon". Highest peak: Mount Stanley, 5109 m (16 763 ft)

Ruyter *n* **Michiel Adriaanszoon de**. 1607–76, Dutch admiral, noted for actions in the Anglo-Dutch wars in 1652–53, 1665–67, 1672, and 1673, when he prevented an Anglo-French invasion

RV Revised Version (of the Bible)

Rwanda *n* a republic in central Africa: part of German East Africa from 1899 until 1917, when Belgium took over the administration; became a republic in 1961 after a Hutu revolt against the Tutsi (1959); fighting between the ethnic groups broke out repeatedly after independence, culminating in the genocide of Tutsis by Hutus in 1994; member of the Commonwealth from 2009. Official languages: Kinyarwanda, English, French, and Swahili. Religion: Roman Catholic, African Protestant, Muslim, and animist. Currency: Rwanda franc. Capital: Kigali. Pop: 12 012 589 (2013 est). Area: 26 338 sq km (10 169 sq miles). Former name (until 1962): **Ruanda**

Rwandan *adj* **1** of or relating to Rwanda or its inhabitants ▷ *n* **2** a native or inhabitant of Rwanda

Ryazan *n* a city in W central Russia: capital of a medieval principality; oil refineries and engineering industries. Pop: 523 000 (2005 est)

Rybinsk *n* a city in W central Russia, on the River Volga: an important river port, terminal of the Mariinsk Waterway (between Saint Petersburg and the Volga) at the SE end of the **Rybinsk Reservoir** (area: 4700 sq km

r

(1800 sq miles)). Pop: 218 000 (2005 est). Former names: (from the Revolution until 1957) **Shcherbakov,** (1984–91) **Andropov**

Rydal *n* a village in NW England, in Cumbria on **Rydal Water** (a small lake). **Rydal Mount,** home of Wordsworth from 1813 to 1850, is situated here

Ryder *n* Susan, Baroness Ryder of Warsaw. 1923–2000, British philanthropist; founder of the Sue Ryder Foundation for the Sick and Disabled, which is funded by a chain of charity shops: married to Leonard Cheshire

rye *n* **1** a tall grasslike cereal grown for its light brown grain **2** the grain of this plant **3** Also called: **rye whiskey** whisky distilled from rye **4** US short for **rye bread** [Old English *ryge*]

Rye *n* a resort in SE England, in East Sussex: one of the Cinque Ports. Pop: 4195 (2001)

rye bread *n* bread made entirely or partly from rye flour

rye-grass *n* any of several grasses grown for fodder

Ryle *n* **1** Gilbert. 1900–76, British philosopher. His works include *The Concept of Mind* (1949) **2** Sir **Martin.** 1918–84, British astronomer, noted for his research on radio astronomy: Astronomer Royal 1972–82; shared the Nobel prize for physics in 1974

Ryswick *n* the English name for **Rijswijk**

Ryukyu Islands *pl n* a chain of 55 islands in the W Pacific, extending almost 650 km (400 miles) from S Japan to N Taiwan: an ancient kingdom, under Chinese rule from the late 14th century, invaded by Japan in the early 17th century, under full Japanese sovereignty from 1879 to 1945, and US control from 1945 to 1972; now part of Japan again. They are subject to frequent typhoons. Chief town: Naha (on Okinawa). Pop: 1 318 220 (2000). Area: 2196 sq km (849 sq miles). Japanese name: **Nansei-shoto**

r

Ss

s second (of time)

S 1 South(ern) 2 *chem* sulphur 3 *physics* siemens

S. 1 (*pl* **SS**) Saint 2 school 3 Sea 4 Signor 5 Society [Latin *socius*]

-'s *suffix* 1 forming the possessive singular of nouns and some pronouns: *woman's*; *one's* 2 forming the possessive plural of nouns whose plurals do not end in -s: *children's* 3 forming the plural of numbers, letters, or symbols: *20's* 4 *informal* contraction of *is* or *has*: *it's over* 5 *informal* contraction of *us* with *let*: *let's go*

SA 1 Salvation Army 2 South Africa 3 South America 4 South Australia

SAA South African Airways

Saar *n* 1 a river in W Europe, rising in the Vosges Mountains and flowing north to the Moselle River in Germany. Length: 246 km (153 miles). French name: **Sarre** 2 **the Saar** another name for **Saarland**

Saarbrücken *n* an industrial city in W Germany, capital of Saarland state, on the Saar River. Pop: 181 860 (2003 est)

Saarinen *n* Eero. 1910–61, US architect, born in Finland. His works include the US Embassy, London (1960)

Saarland *n* a state of W Germany: formed in 1919; under League of Nations administration until 1935; occupied by France (1945–57); part of West Germany (1957–90): contains rich coal deposits and is a major industrial region. Capital: Saarbrücken. Pop: 1 060 000 (2003 est). Area: 2567 sq km (991 sq miles)

Saba *n* 1 an island in the NE Caribbean, part of the Netherlands Antilles until their dissolution in 2010, now a special municipality of the Netherlands. Pop: 1491 (2007 est). Area: 13 sq km (5 sq miles) 2 another name for **Sheba** (1)

Sabadell *n* a town in NE Spain, near Barcelona: textile manufacturing. Pop: 191 057 (2003 est)

Sabaean *or* **Sabean** *n* 1 an inhabitant or native of ancient Saba 2 the ancient Semitic language of Saba ▷ *adj* 3 of or relating to ancient Saba, its inhabitants, or their language [C16: from Latin *Sabaeus*, from Greek *Sabaios* belonging to Saba (Sheba)]

Sabah *n* a state of Malaysia, occupying N Borneo and offshore islands in the South China and Sulu Seas: became a British protectorate in 1888; gained independence and joined Malaysia in 1963. Capital: Kota Kinabalu. Pop: 2 603 485 (2000). Area: 73 620 sq km (28 425 sq miles). Former name (until 1963): **North Borneo**

Sabatier *n* Paul. 1854–1941, French chemist, who discovered a process for the hydrogenation of organic compounds: shared the Nobel prize for chemistry (1912)

Sabbath *n* 1 Saturday, observed by Jews as the day of worship and rest 2 Sunday, observed by Christians as the day of worship and rest [Hebrew *shābath* to rest]

sabbatical *adj* 1 denoting a period of leave granted at intervals to university teachers for rest, study, or travel: *a sabbatical year* ▷ *n* 2 a sabbatical period [see SABBATH]

SABC South African Broadcasting Corporation

Sabin *n* Albert Bruce. 1906–93, US microbiologist, born in Poland. He developed the **Sabin vaccine** (1955), taken orally to immunize against poliomyelitis

sable *n*, *pl* **-bles** *or* **-ble** 1 a marten of N Asia, N Europe, and America, with dark brown luxuriant fur 2 the highly valued fur of this animal, used to make coats and hats ▷ *adj* 3 dark brown-to-black [Slavic]

Sable *n* **Cape Sable** 1 a cape at the S tip of Florida: the southernmost point of continental US 2 the southernmost point of Nova Scotia, Canada

sable antelope *n* a large black African antelope with stout backward-curving horns

sabot (**sab**-oh) *n* a heavy wooden or wooden-soled shoe; clog [French]

sabotage *n* 1 the deliberate destruction or damage of equipment, for example by enemy agents or dissatisfied employees 2 deliberate obstruction of or damage to a cause or effort ▷ *vb* **-taging, -taged** 3 to destroy or disrupt by sabotage [French]

saboteur *n* a person who commits sabotage [French]

sabre *or* US **saber** *n* 1 a heavy single-edged cavalry sword with a curved blade 2 a light sword used in fencing, with a narrow V-shaped blade [German (dialect) *Sabel*]

sac *n* a pouch or pouchlike part in an animal or plant [Latin *saccus*]

saccharin *n* an artificial sweetener [Greek *sakkharon* sugar]

saccharine *adj* 1 excessively sweet or sentimental: *saccharine ballads* 2 like or containing sugar or saccharin

Sacco *n* Nicola. 1891–1927, US radical agitator, born in Italy. With Bartolomeo Vanzetti, he was executed for murder (1927) despite suspicions that their political opinions influenced the verdict: the case caused international protests

sacerdotal *adj formal* of priests or the priesthood [Latin *sacerdos* priest]

sachet *n* 1 a small sealed usually plastic envelope containing a small portion of a substance such as shampoo 2 a small soft bag of perfumed powder, placed in drawers to scent clothing [French]

Sachs *n* 1 Hans. 1494–1576, German master shoemaker and Meistersinger, portrayed by Wagner in *Die Meistersinger von Nürnberg* 2 Nelly (**Leonie**). 1891–1970, German Jewish poet and dramatist, who escaped from Nazi Germany and settled in Sweden. Her works include *Eli: A Mystery Play of the Sufferings of Israel* (1951) and *O the Chimneys*, a poem about the Nazi extermination camps. Nobel prize for literature 1966 jointly with Shmuel Yosef Agnon

Sachsen *n* the German name for **Saxony**

sack¹ *n* 1 a large bag made of coarse cloth or thick paper and used for carrying or storing goods 2 the amount contained in a sack 3 **the sack** *informal* dismissal from employment 4 *slang* bed 5 **hit the sack** *slang* to go to bed ▷ *vb* 6 *informal* to dismiss from employment [Greek *sakkos*] ❯ **sacklike** *adj*

sack² *n* **1** the plundering of a captured town or city by an army or mob ▷ *vb* **2** to plunder and partially destroy (a town or city) [French *mettre à sac* to put (loot) in a sack]

sackbut *n* a medieval form of trombone [French *saqueboute*]

sackcloth *n* **1** same as **sacking 2** garments made of such cloth, worn formerly to indicate mourning **3 sackcloth and ashes** an exaggerated attempt to apologize or compensate for a mistake or wrongdoing

sacking *n* coarse cloth woven from flax, hemp, or jute, and used to make sacks

Sacks *n* Jonathan (**Henry**). Baron. born 1948, British rabbi; Commonwealth chief rabbi (1991–2013)

Sackville *n* Thomas, 1st Earl of Dorset. 1536–1608, English poet, dramatist, and statesman. He collaborated with Thomas Norton on the early blank-verse tragedy *Gorboduc* (1561)

Sackville-West *n* Victoria (**Mary**), known as *Vita*. 1892–1962, British writer and gardener, whose works include the novel *The Edwardians* (1930) and the poem *The Land* (1931). She is also noted for the gardens at Sissinghurst Castle, Kent. Married to Harold Nicolson

sacrament *n* **1** a symbolic religious ceremony in the Christian Church, such as baptism or communion **2** Holy Communion **3** something regarded as sacred [Latin *sacrare* to consecrate] ▸ **sacramental** *adj*

Sacramento *n* **1** an inland port in N central California, capital of the state at the confluence of the American and Sacramento Rivers: became a boom town in the gold rush of the 1850s. Pop: 445 335 (2003 est) **2** a river in N California, flowing generally south to San Francisco Bay. Length: 615 km (382 miles)

sacred *adj* **1** exclusively devoted to a god or gods; holy **2** connected with religion or intended for religious use: *sacred music* **3** regarded as too important to be changed or interfered with: *sacred principles of free speech* **4 sacred to** dedicated to: *the site is sacred to Vishnu* [Latin *sacer* holy]

sacred cow *n informal* a person, custom, belief, or institution regarded as being beyond criticism [alluding to the Hindu belief that cattle are sacred]

sacrifice *n* **1** a surrender of something of value in order to gain something more desirable or prevent some evil **2** a ritual killing of a person or animal as an offering to a god **3** a symbolic offering of something to a god **4** the person or animal killed or offered ▷ *vb* **-ficing, -ficed 5** to make a sacrifice (of) **6** *chess* to permit or force one's opponent to capture (a piece) as a tactical move [Latin *sacer* holy + *facere* to make] ▸ **sacrificial** *adj*

sacrilege *n* **1** the misuse of or disrespect shown to something sacred **2** disrespect for a person who is widely admired or a belief that is widely accepted: *it is a sacrilege to offend democracy* [Latin *sacrilegus* temple robber] ▸ **sacrilegious** *adj*

sacristan *n* a person in charge of the contents of a church; sexton [Latin *sacer* holy]

sacristy *n, pl* **-ties** a room attached to a church or chapel where the sacred objects are kept

sacrosanct *adj* regarded as too important to be criticized or changed: *weekend rest days were considered sacrosanct by staff* [Latin *sacer* holy + *sanctus* hallowed] ▸ **sacrosanctity** *n*

sacrum (say-krum) *n, pl* **-cra** *anatomy* the large wedge-shaped bone in the lower part of the back [Latin *os sacrum* holy bone, because it was used in sacrifices]

sad *adj* **sadder, saddest 1** feeling sorrow; unhappy **2** causing, suggesting, or expressing sorrow: *a sad story* **3** deplorably bad: *the garden was in a sad state* **4** regrettable: *it's rather sad he can't be with us* **5** *Brit informal* ridiculously pathetic: *a sad, boring little wimp* ▷ *n* **6 pack a sad** *NZ slang* to strongly express sadness or displeasure [Old English *sæd* weary] ▸ **sadly** *adv* ▸ **sadness** *n*

Sadat *n* (Mohammed) Anwar El. 1918–81, Egyptian statesman: president of Egypt (1970–81); assassinated; Nobel peace prize jointly with Begin 1978

sadden *vb* to make (someone) sad

saddle *n* **1** a seat for a rider, usually made of leather, placed on a horse's back and secured under its belly **2** a similar seat on a bicycle, motorcycle, or tractor **3** a cut of meat, esp. mutton, consisting of both loins **4 in the saddle** in a position of control ▷ *vb* **-dling, -dled 5** to put a saddle on (a horse): *we saddled up at dawn* **6 saddle with** to burden with (a responsibility): *he was also saddled with debt* [Old English *sadol, sadul*]

saddleback *n* **1** an animal with a marking resembling a saddle on its back **2** a hill with a concave outline at the top ▸ **saddle-backed** *adj*

saddlebag *n* a pouch or small bag attached to the saddle of a horse, bicycle, or motorcycle

saddle horse *n* a horse trained for riding only

saddler *n* a person who makes, deals in, or repairs saddles and other leather equipment for horses

saddlery *n, pl* **-dleries 1** saddles and harness for horses collectively **2** the work or place of work of a saddler

saddle soap *n* a soft soap used to preserve and clean leather

saddletree *n* the frame of a saddle

saddo *n Brit informal* a pathetic or socially inadequate person

Sadducee (sad-yew-see) *n Judaism* a member of an ancient Jewish sect that denied the resurrection of the dead and accepted only the traditional written law

Sade *n* Comte **Donatien Alphonse François de**, known as the *Marquis de Sade*. 1740–1814, French soldier and writer, whose exposition of sexual perversion gave rise to the term sadism

sadhu (sah-doo) *n* a Hindu wandering holy man [Sanskrit]

Sadi *or* **Saadi** *n* original name *Sheikh Muslih Addin*. ?1184–1292, Persian poet. His best-known works are *Gulistān* (Flower Garden) and *Būstān* (Tree Garden), long moralistic poems in prose and verse

sadism (say-diz-zum) *n* the gaining of pleasure, esp. sexual pleasure, from infliction of suffering on another person [after the Marquis de SADE] ▸ **sadist** *n* ▸ **sadistic** *adj* ▸ **sadistically** *adv*

Sadler's Wells *n* (*functioning as sing*) a theatre in London. It was renovated in 1931 by Lilian Baylis and became the home of the Sadler's Wells Opera Company and the Sadler's Wells Ballet (now the Royal Ballet) [named after the medicinal *wells* on the site and its owner Thomas *Sadler*, who founded the original theatre on the site]

sadomasochism *n* **1** the combination of sadistic and masochistic elements in one person, characterized by both submissive and aggressive periods in relationships with others **2** a sexual practice in which one partner adopts a masochistic role and the other a sadistic one ▸ **sadomasochist** *n* ▸ **sadomasochistic** *adj*

Sadowa *n* a village in the Czech Republic, in NE Bohemia: scene of the decisive battle of the Austro-Prussian war (1866) in which the Austrians were defeated by the Prussians. Czech name: **Sadová**

s.a.e. *Brit, Austral and NZ* stamped addressed envelope

safari *n, pl* **-ris** an overland expedition for hunting or observing animals, esp. in Africa [Swahili: journey]

safari park *n* an enclosed park in which wild animals are kept uncaged in the open and can be viewed by the public from cars or buses

safe *adj* **1** giving security or protection from harm: *a safe environment* **2** free from danger: *she doesn't feel safe* **3** taking or involving no risks: *a safe bet* **4** not dangerous: *the beef is safe to eat* **5 on the safe side** as a precaution ▷ *n* **6** a strong metal container with a secure lock, for storing money or valuables [Old French *salf*] ▸ **safely** *adv*

safe-conduct *n* **1** a document giving official permission to travel through a dangerous region, esp. in time of war **2** the protection given by such a document

safe-deposit *or* **safety-deposit** *n* a place or building with facilities for the safe storage of money and valuables

safeguard *vb* **1** to protect (something) from being harmed or destroyed ▷ *n* **2** a person or thing that ensures protection against danger or harm: *safeguards to prevent air collisions*

safekeeping *n* protection from theft or damage: *I put my money in a bank for safekeeping*

safe sex *or* **safer sex** *n* nonpenetrative sex, or intercourse using a condom, intended to prevent the spread of HIV

safety *n, pl* **-ties 1** the quality or state of being free from danger **2** shelter: *they swam to safety*

safety belt *n* same as **seat belt**

safety catch *n* a mechanism on a gun that prevents it from being fired accidentally

safety curtain *n* a fireproof curtain that can be lowered to separate the auditorium from the stage in a theatre to prevent the spread of a fire

Safety Islands *pl n* a group of three small French islands in the Atlantic, off the coast of French Guiana. French name: **Îles du Salut**

safety lamp *n* a miner's oil lamp designed to prevent it from igniting combustible gas

safety match *n* a match that will light only when struck against a specially prepared surface

safety net *n* **1** a large net under a trapeze or high wire to catch performers if they fall **2** something that can be relied on for help in the event of difficulties: *the social security safety net*

safety pin *n* a pin bent back on itself so that it forms a spring, with the point shielded by a guard when closed

safety razor *n* a razor with a guard over the blade or blades to protect the skin from deep cuts

safety valve *n* **1** a valve in a boiler or machine that allows fluid or gases to escape at excess pressure **2** an outlet that allows one to express strong feelings without harming or offending other people: *sport acted as a safety valve for his pent-up frustrations*

safflower *n* a thistle-like plant with orange-yellow flowers, which yields a dye and an oil used in paints, medicines, and cooking [Old French *saffleur*]

saffron *n* **1** a type of crocus with purple or white flowers with orange stigmas **2** the dried orange-coloured stigmas of this plant, used for colouring or flavouring ▷ *adj* **3** orange-yellow [Arabic *za'farān*]

Safi *n* a port in W Morocco, 170 km (105 miles) northwest of Marrakech, to which it is the nearest port. Pop: 470 000 (2003)

Safid Rud *n* a river in N Iran, flowing northeast to a delta on the Caspian Sea. Length: about 785 km (490 miles)

S.Afr. South Africa(n)

sag *vb* **sagging, sagged 1** to sink in the middle, under weight or pressure: *the bed sagged nearly to the floor* **2** (of courage or spirits) to weaken or tire **3** (of clothes) to hang loosely or unevenly **4** to fall in value: *the stock market sagged* ▷ *n* **5** the act or state of sagging [from Old Norse] ▷ **saggy** *adj*

saga (sah-ga) *n* **1** a medieval Scandinavian legend telling the adventures of a hero or a family **2** *informal* a long story or series of events: *the long-running saga of the hostage issue* [Old Norse]

sagacious *adj formal* wise or sensible [Latin *sagax*] ▷ **sagaciously** *adv* ▷ **sagacity** *n*

Sagan *n* **1** Carl (Edward) 1934–96, US astronomer and writer on scientific subjects; presenter of the television series *Cosmos* (1980) **2** original name Françoise Quoirez. 1935–2004, French writer, best-known for the novels *Bonjour Tristesse* (1954) and *Aimez-vous Brahms?* (1959)

Sagarmatha *n* the Nepalese name for (Mount) **Everest**

sage¹ *n* **1** a person, esp. an old man, regarded as being very wise ▷ *adj* **2** very wise or knowledgeable, esp. as the result of age or experience [Latin *sapere* to be sensible]

sage² *n* **1** a Mediterranean plant with grey-green leaves which are used in cooking for flavouring **2** short for

sagebrush [Latin *salvus* in good health (from its curative properties)]

sagebrush *n* an aromatic plant of W North America, with silver-green leaves and large clusters of small white flowers

Saghalien *n* a variant of **Sakhalin**

Sagittarius *n astrol* the ninth sign of the zodiac; the Archer [Latin]

sago *n* an edible starch from the powdered pith of the sago palm tree, used for puddings and as a thickening agent [Malay *sāgū*]

Saguenay *n* a river in SE Canada in S Quebec, rising as the Péribonca River on the central plateau and flowing south, then east to the St Lawrence. Length: 764 km (475 miles)

Sagunto *n* an industrial town in E Spain, near Valencia: allied to Rome and made a heroic resistance to the Carthaginian attack led by Hannibal (219–218 BC). Pop: 58 287 (2003 est). Ancient name: **Saguntum**

Sahara *n* a desert in N Africa, extending from the Atlantic to the Red Sea and from the Mediterranean to central Mali, Niger, Chad, and the Sudan: the largest desert in the world, occupying over a quarter of Africa; rises to over 3300 m (11 000 ft) in the central mountain system of the Ahaggar and Tibesti massifs; large reserves of iron ore, oil, and natural gas. Area: 9 100 000 sq km (3 500 000 sq miles). Average annual rainfall: less than 254 mm (10 in.). Highest recorded temperature: 58°C (136.4°F)

Saharan *n* **1** a group of languages spoken in parts of Chad and adjacent countries, now generally regarded as forming a branch of the Nilo-Saharan family ▷ *adj* **2** relating to or belonging to this group of languages **3** of or relating to the Sahara

sahib *n* an Indian term of address equivalent to *sir*, formerly used as a mark of respect to a European man [Urdu]

said *adj* **1** named or mentioned already: *she had heard that the said lady was also a medium* ▷ *vb* **2** the past of **say**

Saida *n* a port in SW Lebanon, on the Mediterranean: on the site of ancient Sidon; terminal of the Trans-Arabian pipeline from Saudi Arabia. Pop: 150 000 (2005 est)

Saigon *n* the former name (until 1976) of **Ho Chi Minh City**

Saigo Takamori *n* 1828–77, Japanese samurai, who led (1868) the coup that restored imperial government. In 1877 he reluctantly led a samurai rebellion, committing suicide when it failed

sail *n* **1** a sheet of canvas or other fabric, spread on rigging to catch the wind and move a ship over water **2** a voyage on such a ship: *a relaxing sail across the lake* **3** a ship or ships with sails: *to travel by sail* **4** one of the revolving arms of a windmill **5 set sail** to begin a voyage by water **6 under sail a** under way **b** with sail hoisted ▷ *vb* **7** to travel in a boat or ship: *to sail around the world* **8** to begin a voyage: *he hoped to sail at eleven* **9** (of a ship) to move over the water **10** to navigate (a ship): *she sailed the schooner up the channel* **11** to sail over: *he had already sailed the Pacific* **12** to move along smoothly **13 sail into** *informal* to make a violent attack on **14 sail through** to progress quickly or effortlessly: *the top seed sailed through to the second round* [Old English *segl*]

sailboard *n* a board with a mast and a single sail, used for windsurfing

sailcloth *n* **1** the fabric used for making sails **2** a canvas-like cloth used for clothing

sailfish *n, pl* **-fish** *or* **-fishes** a large tropical game fish, with a long sail-like fin on its back

sailor *n* **1** any member of a ship's crew, esp. one below the rank of officer **2** a person considered as liable or not liable to seasickness: *a good sailor*

sainfoin (san-foin) *n* a Eurasian plant with pink flowers, widely grown as feed for grazing farm animals [Medieval Latin *sanum faenum* wholesome hay]

S

Sainsbury *n* David John, Baron. born 1940, British businessman and politician, chief executive of the Sainsbury supermarket chain from 1992; science minister (1998–2006)

saint *n* **1** a person who after death is formally recognized by a Christian Church as deserving special honour because of having lived a very holy life **2** an exceptionally good person [Latin *sanctus* holy] ⟩ **sainthood** *n* ⟩ **saintlike** *adj*

Saint Albans *n* usually abbreviated to: **St Albans** a city in SE England, in W Hertfordshire: founded in 948 AD around the Benedictine abbey first built in Saxon times on the site of the martyrdom (about 303 AD) of St Alban; present abbey built in 1077; Roman ruins. Pop: 82 429 (2001). Latin name: **Verulamium**

Saint Andrews *n* usually abbreviated to: **St Andrews** a city in E Scotland, in Fife on the North Sea: the oldest university in Scotland (1411); famous golf links. Pop: 14 209 (2001)

Saint Augustine *n* usually abbreviated to: **St Augustine** a resort in NE Florida, on the Intracoastal Waterway: the oldest town in North America (1565); the northernmost outpost of the Spanish colonial empire for over 200 years. Pop: 11 915 (2003 est)

Saint Austell *n* usually abbreviated to: **St Austell** a town in SW England, in S Cornwall on **St Austell Bay** (an inlet of the English Channel): centre for the now-declining china clay industry; the Eden Project, a rainforest environment in the world's largest greenhouse, is nearby; administratively part of St Austell with Fowey 1968-74. Pop (with Fowey): 22 658 (2001)

Saint-Barthélemy *n* an island in the E Caribbean, in the Leeward Islands, belonging to France (as a dependency of Guadeloupe until 2007, then as a separate French Overseas Collectivity). Capital: Gustavia. Pop: 6852 (1999 census). Area: 21 sq km (8.1 sq miles)

Saint Bernard *n* a very large dog with a dense red-and-white coat, formerly used as a mountain-rescue dog

Saint Bernard Pass *n* usually abbreviated to: **St Bernard Pass** either of two passes over the Alps: the **Great St Bernard Pass** 2472 m (8110 ft) high, east of Mont Blanc between Italy and Switzerland, or the **Little St Bernard Pass** 2157 m (7077 ft) high, south of Mont Blanc between Italy and France

Saint-Brieuc *n* usually abbreviated to: **St-Brieuc** a market town in NW France, near the N coast of Brittany. Pop: 46 087 (1999)

Saint Catharines *n* usually abbreviated to: **St Catharines** an industrial city in S central Canada, in S Ontario on the Welland Canal. Pop: 129 170 (2001)

Saint Christopher *n* usually abbreviated to: **St Christopher** another name for **Saint Kitts**

Saint Christopher-Nevis *n* usually abbreviated to: **St Christopher-Nevis** the official name of **Saint Kitts-Nevis**

Saint Clair *n* **Lake Saint Clair** a lake between SE Michigan and Ontario: linked with Lake Huron by the **St Clair River** and with Lake Erie by the Detroit River. Area: 1191 sq km (460 sq miles).

Saint-Cloud *n* usually abbreviated to: **St-Cloud** a residential suburb of Paris: former royal palace; Sèvres porcelain factory. Pop: 29 981 (2006)

Saint Croix *n* usually abbreviated to: **St Croix** an island in the Caribbean, the largest of the Virgin Islands of the US: purchased from Denmark by the US in 1917. Chief town: Christiansted. Pop: 53 234 (2000). Area: 207 sq km (80 sq miles). Also called: **Santa Cruz**

Saint Croix River *n* usually abbreviated to: **St Croix River** a river on the border between the northeast US and SE Canada, flowing from the Chiputneticook Lakes to Passamaquoddy Bay, forming the border between Maine, US, and New Brunswick, Canada. Length: 121 km (75 miles)

Saint David's *n* usually abbreviated to: **St David's** a town in SW Wales, in Pembrokeshire: its cathedral was a place of pilgrimage in medieval times. Pop: 1627 (2001)

Saint-Denis *n* usually abbreviated to: **St-Denis 1** a town in N France, on the Seine: 12th-century Gothic abbey church, containing the tombs of many French monarchs; an industrial suburb of Paris. Pop: 105 749 (2009) **2** the capital of the French overseas region of Réunion, a port on the N coast. Pop: 143 000 (2007)

Sainte-Beuve *n* Charles Augustin. 1804–69, French critic, best known for his collections of essays *Port Royal* (1840–59) and *Les Causeries du Lundi* (1851–62)

sainted *adj* **1** formally recognized by a Christian Church as a saint **2** having the qualities, such as patience and kindness, of a saint **3** hallowed or holy

Sainte Foy *n* usually abbreviated to: **Ste Foy** a SW suburb of Quebec, on the St Lawrence River. Pop: 72 547 (2001)

Saint Elias Mountains *pl n* usually abbreviated to: **St Elias Mountains** a mountain range between SE Alaska and the SW Yukon, Canada. Highest peak: Mount Logan, 5959 m (19 550 ft)

Saint-Étienne *n* usually abbreviated to: **St-Étienne** a town in E central France: a major producer of textiles and armaments. Pop: 178 530 (2007 est)

Saint-Exupéry *n* Antoine de. 1900–44, French novelist and aviator. His novels of aviation include *Vol de nuit* (1931) and *Terre des hommes* (1939). He also wrote the fairy tale *Le petit prince* (1943)

Saint Gall *n* usually abbreviated to: **St Gall 1** a canton of NE Switzerland. Capital: St Gall. Pop: 455 200 (2002 est). Area: 2012 sq km (777 sq miles) **2** a town in NE Switzerland, capital of St Gall canton: an important educational centre in the Middle Ages. Pop: 72 626 (2000) ▶ German name: **Sankt Gallen**

Saint George's *n* usually abbreviated to: **St George's** the capital of Grenada, a port in the southwest. Pop: 3908 (2001)

Saint George's Channel *n* usually abbreviated to: **St George's Channel** a strait between Wales and Ireland, linking the Irish Sea with the Atlantic. Length: about 160 km (100 miles). Width: up to 145 km (90 miles)

Saint Gotthard *n* usually abbreviated to: **St Gotthard 1** a range of the Lepontine Alps in SE central Switzerland **2** a pass over the St Gotthard mountains, in S Switzerland. Height: 2114 m (6935 ft)

Saint Helena *n* usually abbreviated to: **St Helena** a volcanic island in the SE Atlantic, forming a UK Overseas Territory with its dependencies Tristan da Cunha and Ascension, and the uninhabited Gough, Inaccessible, and Nightingale Islands: discovered by the Portuguese in 1502 and annexed by England in 1651; scene of Napoleon's exile and death. Capital: Jamestown. Pop: 4255 (2013 est). Area: 122 sq km (47 sq miles)

Saint Helens *n* usually abbreviated to: **St Helens 1** a town in NW England, in St Helens unitary authority, Merseyside: glass industry. Pop: 102 629 (2001) **2** a unitary authority in NW England, in Merseyside. Pop: 176 700 (2003 est). Area: 130 sq km (50 sq miles) **3** a volcanic peak in S Washington state; it erupted in 1980 after lying dormant from 1857

Saint Helier *n* usually abbreviated to: **St Helier** a market town and resort in the Channel Islands, the capital of Jersey, on the S coast. Pop: 28 310 (2001)

Saint James's Palace *n* usually abbreviated to: **St James's Palace** a palace in Pall Mall, London: a residence of British monarchs from 1697 to 1837

Saint John *n* in most cases, usually abbreviated to: **St John 1** a port in E Canada, at the mouth of the Saint John River: the largest city in New Brunswick; very often not abbreviated to 'St'. Pop: 90 762 (2001) **2** an island in the Caribbean, in the Virgin Islands of the US. Pop: 4197 (2000). Area: 49 sq km (19 sq miles) **3 Lake Saint John** a lake in Canada, in S Quebec: drained by the Saguenay River. Area: 971 sq km (375 sq miles) **4** a river in E North America, rising in Maine, US, and flowing northeast to New Brunswick, Canada, then generally southeast to the Bay of Fundy. Length: 673 km (418 miles)

Saint John's *n* usually abbreviated to: **St John's 1** a port in Canada, capital of Newfoundland and Labrador, on the E coast of the Avalon Peninsula. Pop: 122 709 (2001) **2** the capital of Antigua and Barbuda: a port on the NW coast of the island of Antigua. Pop: 24 226 (2000 est)

Saint John's wort *n* a plant with yellow flowers

Saint-Just *n* Louis Antoine Léon de. 1767–94, French Revolutionary leader and orator. A member of the Committee of Public Safety (1793–94), he was guillotined with Robespierre

Saint Kilda *n* usually abbreviated to: **St Kilda 1** a group of volcanic islands in the Atlantic, in the Outer Hebrides: uninhabited since 1930; bird sanctuary **2** Also called: **Hirta** the main island of this group

Saint Kitts *n* usually abbreviated to: **St Kitts** an island in the E Caribbean, in the Leeward Islands: part of the state of St Kitts-Nevis. Capital: Basseterre. Pop: 34 703 (2001). Area: 168 sq km (65 sq miles). Also called: **Saint Christopher**

Saint Kitts-Nevis *n* usually abbreviated to: **St Kitts-Nevis** an independent state in the E Caribbean; comprises the two islands of St Kitts and Nevis: with the island of Anguilla formed a colony (1882–1967) and a British associated state (1967–83); Anguilla formally separated from the group in 1983; gained full independence in 1983 as a member of the Commonwealth. Official language: English. Religion: Protestant majority. Currency: E Caribbean dollar. Capital: Basseterre. Pop: 51 134 (2013 est). Area: 262 sq km (101 sq miles)

Saint Laurent *n* usually abbreviated to: **St Laurent** a W suburb of Montreal, Canada. Pop: 77 391 (2001)

Saint-Laurent *n* **1** Yves, full name *Yves-Mathieu*. 1936–2008, French couturier: popularized trousers for women for all occasions **2** Louis. 1882–1973, Canadian politician; prime minister of Canada (1948–57)

Saint Lawrence *n* usually abbreviated to: **St Lawrence 1** a river in SE Canada, flowing northeast from Lake Ontario, forming part of the border between Canada and the US, to the Gulf of St Lawrence: commercially one of the most important rivers in the world as the easternmost link of the St Lawrence Seaway. Length: 1207 km (750 miles). Width at mouth: 145 km (90 miles) **2** Gulf of Saint Lawrence a deep arm of the Atlantic off the E coast of Canada between Newfoundland and the mainland coasts of Quebec, New Brunswick, and Nova Scotia

Saint Lawrence Seaway *n* usually abbreviated to: **St Lawrence Seaway** an inland waterway of North America, passing through the Great Lakes, the St Lawrence River, and connecting canals and locks: one of the most important waterways in the world. Length: 3993 km (2480 miles)

Saint Leger *n* an annual horse race for three-year-old horses, run at Doncaster

Saint Leonard *n* usually abbreviated to: **St Leonard** a N suburb of Montreal, Canada. Pop: 69 604 (2001)

Saint-Lô *n* usually abbreviated to: **St-Lô** a market town in NW France: a Calvinist stronghold in the 16th century. Pop: 20 537 (2007)

Saint Louis *n* usually abbreviated to: **St Louis** a port in E Missouri, on the Mississippi River near its confluence with the Missouri: the largest city in the state; university; major industrial centre. Pop: 332 223 (2003 est)

Saint-Louis *n* usually abbreviated to: **St-Louis** a port in NW Senegal, on an island at the mouth of the Senegal River: the first French settlement in W Africa (1689); capital of Senegal until 1958. Pop: 183 000 (2005 est)

Saint Lucia *n* usually abbreviated to: **St Lucia** an island state in the Caribbean, in the Windward Islands group of the Lesser Antilles: a volcanic island; gained self-government in 1967 as a British Associated State; attained full independence within the Commonwealth in 1979. Official language: English. Religion: Roman Catholic majority. Currency: E Caribbean dollar. Capital: Castries. Pop: 162 781 (2013 est). Area: 616 sq km (238 sq miles)

saintly *adj* behaving in a very good, patient, or holy way **›saintliness** *n*

Saint Martin *n* usually abbreviated to: **St Martin** an island in the E Caribbean, in the Leeward Islands: administratively divided since 1648, the north belonging to France (as a dependency of Guadeloupe until 2007, then as a separate French Overseas Collectivity) and the south belonging to the Netherlands (as part of the Netherlands Antilles until 2010, then as a constituent country of the Kingdom of the Netherlands); salt industry. Capital (French part): Marigot; (Dutch part): Philipsburg. Pop: (French) 36 824 (2009); (Dutch) 37 429 (2010 est). Areas: (French) 52 sq km (20 sq miles); (Dutch) 33 sq km (13 sq miles). Dutch name: **Sint Maarten**

Saint-Maur-des-Fossés *n* usually abbreviated to: **St-Maur-des-Fossés** a town in N France, on the River Marne: a residential suburb of SE Paris. Pop: 76 698 (2006)

Saint-Mihiel *n* usually abbreviated to: **St-Mihiel** a village in NE France, on the River Meuse: site of a battle in World War I, in which the American army launched its first offensive in France

Saint Moritz *n* usually abbreviated to: **St Moritz** a village in E Switzerland, in Graubünden canton in the Upper Engadine, at an altitude of 1856 m (6089 ft): sports and tourist centre. Pop: 5589 (2000)

Saint-Nazaire *n* usually abbreviated to: **St-Nazaire** a port in NW France, at the mouth of the River Loire: German submarine base in World War II; shipbuilding. Pop: 71 373 (2006)

Saint-Ouen *n* usually abbreviated to: **St-Ouen** a town in N France, on the Seine: an industrial suburb of Paris; famous flea market. Pop: 46 510 (2009)

Saint Paul *n* usually abbreviated to: **St Paul** a port in SE Minnesota, capital of the state, at the head of navigation of the Mississippi: now contiguous with Minneapolis (the Twin Cities). Pop: 280 404 (2003 est)

Saint Paul's *n* usually abbreviated to: **St Paul's** a cathedral in central London, built between 1675 and 1710 to replace an earlier cathedral destroyed during the Great Fire (1666): regarded as Wren's masterpiece

Saint Peter Port *n* usually abbreviated to: **St Peter Port** a port and resort in the Channel Islands: the capital of the Bailiwick of Guernsey, on the E coast of the island of Guernsey. Pop: 28 310 (2001)

Saint Peter's *n* usually abbreviated to: **St Peter's** the basilica of the Vatican City, built between 1506 and 1615 to replace an earlier church: the largest church in the world, 188 m (615 ft) long, and chief pilgrimage centre of Europe; designed by many architects, notably Bramante, Raphael, Sangallo, Michelangelo, and Bernini

Saint Petersburg *n* usually abbreviated to: **St Petersburg 1** a city and port in Russia, on the Gulf of Finland at the mouth of the Neva River: founded by Peter the Great in 1703 and built on low-lying marshes subject to frequent flooding; capital of Russia from 1712 to 1918; a cultural and educational centre, with a university (1819); a major industrial centre, with engineering, shipbuilding, chemical, textile, and printing industries. Pop: 5 315 000 (2005 est). Former names: **Petrograd** (1914–24), **Leningrad** (1924–91) **2** a city and resort in W Florida, on Tampa Bay. Pop: 247 610 (2003 est)

S

Saint-Pierre[1] *n* usually abbreviated to: **St-Pierre** a town on the coast of the French island of Martinique, destroyed by the eruption of Mont Pelée in 1902 with the loss of about 30 000 lives; later partly rebuilt

Saint-Pierre[2] *n* Jacques Henri Bernardin de. 1737–1814, French author; his work, which was greatly influenced by the writings of Rousseau, includes *Voyage à l'Île de France* (1773), *Études de la nature* (1784, 1788), and *La chaumière indienne* (1791)

Saint Pierre and Miquelon *n* usually abbreviated to: **St Pierre and Miquelon** an archipelago in the Atlantic, off the S coast of Newfoundland: an overseas department of France, the only remaining French possession in North America; consists of the islands of St Pierre, with most of the population, and Miquelon, about ten times as large; fishing industries. Capital: St Pierre. Pop: 5774 (2013 est). Area: 242 sq km (94 sq miles)

Saint Pölten *n* See Sankt Pölten

Saint-Quentin *n* usually abbreviated to: **St-Quentin** a town in N France, on the River Somme: textile industry. Pop: 56 843 (2008)

Saint-Saëns *n* (Charles) Camille (kamij). 1835–1921, French composer, pianist, and organist. His works include the symphonic poem *Danse Macabre* (1874), the opera *Samson and Delilah* (1877), the humorous orchestral suite *Carnival of the Animals* (1886), five symphonies, and five piano concertos

Saintsbury *n* George Edward Bateman. 1845–1933, British literary critic and historian; author of many works on English and French literature

Saint-Simon *n* **1** Comte de, title of *Claude Henri de Rouvroy*. 1760–1825, French social philosopher, generally regarded as the founder of French socialism. He thought society should be reorganized along industrial lines and that scientists should be the new spiritual leaders. His most important work is *Nouveau Christianisme* (1825) **2** Duc de, title of *Louis de Rouvroy*. 1675–1755, French soldier, statesman, and writer: his *Mémoires* are an outstanding account of the period 1694–1723, during the reigns of Louis XIV and Louis XV

Saint Thomas *n* usually abbreviated to: **St Thomas 1** an island in the E Caribbean, in the Virgin Islands of the US. Capital: Charlotte Amalie. Pop: 51 181 (2000). Area: 83 sq km (28 sq miles) **2** the former name (1921–37) of **Charlotte Amalie**

Saint Vincent *n* usually abbreviated to: **St Vincent 1** Cape Saint Vincent a headland at the SW extremity of Portugal: scene of several important naval battles, notably in 1797, when the British defeated the French and Spanish **2** Gulf Saint Vincent a shallow inlet of SE South Australia, to the east of the Yorke Peninsula: salt industry

Saint Vincent and the Grenadines *n* usually abbreviated to: **St Vincent and the Grenadines** an island state in the Caribbean, in the Windward Islands of the Lesser Antilles: comprises the island of St Vincent and the Northern Grenadines; formerly a British associated state (1969–79); gained full independence in 1979 as a member of the Commonwealth. Official language: English. Religion: Protestant majority. Currency: Caribbean dollar. Capital: Kingstown. Pop: 103 220 (2013 est). Area: 389 sq km (150 sq miles)

Saint Vitus's dance *n* pathol a nontechnical name for chorea

Saipan *n* an island in the W Pacific, administrative centre of the US associated territory of the Northern Mariana Islands (on Capitol Hill); captured by the Americans and used as an air base until the end of World War II. Pop: 62 392 (2000). Area: 180 sq km (70 sq miles)

Saïs *n* (in ancient Egypt) a city in the W Nile delta; the royal capital of the 24th dynasty (about 730–715 BC) and the 26th dynasty (about 664–525 BC)

Saite *n* a native or inhabitant of the ancient Egyptian city of Saïs

saithe *n* Brit a dark-coloured food fish found in northern seas [Old Norse *seithr* coalfish]

Saitic *adj* of or relating to the ancient Egyptian city of Saïs or its inhabitants

Sakai *n* a port in S Japan, on S Honshu on Osaka Bay: an industrial satellite of Osaka. Pop: 787 833 (2002 est)

sake[1] *n* **1** for someone's *or* one's own sake for the benefit or interest of someone *or* oneself **2** for the sake of something for the purpose of obtaining or achieving something **3** for its own sake for the enjoyment obtained by doing something **4** used in various exclamations of annoyance, impatience, or urgency: *for God's sake* [Old English *sacu* lawsuit (hence, a cause)]

sake[2] *or* **saki** (sah-kee) *n* a Japanese alcoholic drink made from fermented rice [Japanese]

Sakhalin *or* **Saghalien** *n* an island in the Sea of Okhotsk, off the SE coast of Russia north of Japan: fishing, forestry, and mineral resources (coal and petroleum). Capital: Yuzhno-Sakhalinsk. Pop: 546 500 (2002). Area: 76 000 sq km (29 300 sq miles). Japanese name (1905–24): **Karafuto**

Sakha Republic *or* **Yakutia** *n* an administrative division in E Russia, in NE Siberia on the Arctic Ocean: the coldest inhabited region of the world; it has rich mineral resources. Capital: Yakutsk. Pop: 948 100 (2002). Area: 3 103 200 sq km (1 197 760 sq miles)

Sakharov *n* Andrei. 1921–89, Soviet physicist and human-rights campaigner: Nobel peace prize 1975

salaam (sal-ahm) *n* **1** a Muslim greeting consisting of a deep bow with the right palm on the forehead **2** a greeting signifying peace ▷ *vb* **3** to make a salaam (to) [Arabic *salām* peace]

salacious *adj* **1** having an excessive interest in sex **2** (of books, films, or jokes) concerned with sex in an unnecessarily detailed way [Latin *salax* fond of leaping] **> salaciousness** *n*

salad *n* a dish of raw vegetables, often served with a dressing, eaten as a separate course or as part of a main course [Old French *salade*]

salad days *pl n* a period of youth and inexperience

salad dressing *n* a sauce for salad, such as oil and vinegar or mayonnaise

Saladin *n* Arabic name *Salah-ed-Din Yusuf ibn-Ayyub*. ?1137–93, sultan of Egypt and Syria and opponent of the Crusaders. He defeated the Christians near Tiberias (1187) and captured Acre, Jerusalem, and Ashkelon. He fought against Richard I of England and Philip II of France during the Third Crusade (1189–92)

Salado *n* **1** a river in N Argentina, rising in the Andes as the Juramento and flowing southeast to the Paraná River. Length: 2012 km (1250 miles) **2** a river in W Argentina, rising near the Chilean border as the Desaguadero and flowing south to the Colorado River. Length: about 1365 km (850 miles)

Salamanca *n* a city in W Spain: a leading cultural centre of Europe until the end of the 16th century; market town. Pop: 157 906 (2003 est)

salamander *n* **1** a tailed amphibian which looks like a lizard **2** a mythical creature supposed to live in fire [Greek *salamandra*]

Salambria *n* a river in N Greece, in Thessaly, rising in the Pindus Mountains and flowing southeast and east to the Gulf of Salonika. Length: about 200 km (125 miles). Ancient name: **Peneus**. Modern Greek name: **Piniós**

salami *n* a highly spiced sausage, usually flavoured with garlic [Italian]

Salamis *n* an island in the Saronic Gulf, Greece: scene of the naval battle in 480 BC, in which the Greeks defeated the Persians. Pop (municipality): 28 423 (2001). Area: 95 sq km (37 sq miles). Modern Greek name: **Salamina**

salaried *adj* earning or providing a salary: *a salaried employee; a salaried position*

salary *n, pl* **-ries** a fixed regular payment made by an employer, usually monthly, for professional or office work [Latin *salarium* the sum given to Roman soldiers to buy salt]

Salazar *n* Antonio de Oliveira. 1889–1970, Portuguese statesman; dictator (1932–68)

Salduba *n* the pre-Roman (Celtiberian) name for Zaragoza

sale *n* **1** the exchange of goods or property for an agreed sum of money **2** the amount sold **3** an event at which goods are sold at reduced prices **4** an auction **5 sales** the department dealing with selling its company's products [Old English *sala*]

Sale *n* **1** a town in NW England, in Trafford unitary authority, Greater Manchester: a residential suburb of Manchester. Pop: 55 234 (2001) **2** a city in SE Australia, in SE Victoria: centre of an agricultural region. Pop: 12 854 (2001)

Salé *n* a port in NW Morocco, on the Atlantic adjoining Rabat. Pop: 880 000 (2003)

saleable *or US* **salable** *adj* fit for selling or capable of being sold ▷ **saleability** *or US* **salability** *n*

Salem *n* **1** a city in S India, in Tamil Nadu: textile industries. Pop: 693 236 (2001) **2** a city in NE Massachusetts, on the Atlantic: scene of the execution of 19 people after the witch hunts of 1692. Pop: 42 067 (2003 est) **3** a city in the NW USA, the state capital of Oregon: food-processing. Pop: 142 914 (2003 est) **4** an Old Testament name for Jerusalem (Genesis 14:18; Psalms 76:2). See Jerusalem

sale of work *n* a sale of articles, often handmade, the proceeds of which go to a charity

Salerno *n* a port in SW Italy, in Campania on the **Gulf of Salerno**: first medical school of medieval Europe. Pop: 138 188 (2001)

saleroom *n chiefly Brit* a room where objects are displayed for sale by auction

salesgirl *n* a young woman who sells goods in a shop

salesman *n, pl* **-men 1** a man who sells goods in a shop **2** short for **travelling salesman**

salesmanship *n* the technique of or skill in selling

salesperson *n, pl* **-people** *or* **-persons** a person who sells goods in a shop

sales pitch *or* **sales talk** *n* persuasive talk used by a salesperson in persuading a customer to buy something

saleswoman *n, pl* **-women** a woman who sells goods in a shop

saleyard *n Austral and NZ* an area with pens for holding animals before auction

Salford *n* **1** a city in NW England in Salford unitary authority, Greater Manchester, on the Manchester Ship Canal: a major centre of the cotton industry in the 19th century; extensive dock area, now redeveloped, includes the Lowry arts centre; university (1967). Pop: 72 750 (2001) **2** a unitary authority in NW England, in Greater Manchester. Pop: 216 500 (2003 est). Area: 97 sq km (37 sq miles)

salicylic acid (sal-liss-**ill**-ik) *n* a white crystalline substance used to make aspirin and as a fungicide [Latin *salix* willow]

salient (**say**-lee-ent) *adj* **1** (of points or facts) most important: *the salient points of his speech* ▷ *n* **2** *military* a projection of the forward line of an army into enemy-held territory [Latin *salire* to leap]

Salieri *n* Antonio. 1750–1825, Italian composer and conductor, who worked in Vienna (from 1766). The suggestion that he poisoned Mozart has no foundation

saline (**say**-line) *adj* **1** of or containing salt: *a saline flavour* **2** *med* of or relating to a saline: *a saline drip* ▷ *n* **3** *med* a solution of sodium chloride and water [Latin *sal* salt] ▷ **salinity** *n*

Salinger *n* J(erome) D(avid) 1919–2010, US writer, noted particularly for his novel of adolescence *The Catcher in the Rye* (1951). His first novel for 34 years, *Hapworth 16, 1924* was published in 1997

salinization *or* **-nisation** *n* the process by which salts accumulate in undrained land, damaging its potential for plant growth

Salisbury[1] *n* **1** the former name (until 1982) of Harare **2** a city in S Australia: an industrial suburb of N Adelaide. Pop: 118 422 (2006) **3** a city in S England, in SE Wiltshire: nearby Old Sarum was the site of an Early Iron Age hill fort; its cathedral (1220–58) has the highest spire in England. Pop: 43 355 (2001). Ancient name: **Sarum**. Official name: **New Sarum**

Salisbury[2] *n* Robert Gascoyne Cecil, 3rd Marquess of Salisbury. 1830–1903, British statesman; Conservative prime minister (1885–86; 1886–92; 1895–1902). His greatest interest was in foreign and imperial affairs

Salisbury Plain *n* an open chalk plateau in S England, in Wiltshire: site of Stonehenge; military training area. Average height: 120 m (400 ft)

saliva (sal-**lie**-va) *n* the watery fluid secreted by glands in the mouth, which aids digestion [Latin] ▷ **salivary** *adj*

salivate *vb* **-vating, -vated** to produce saliva, esp. an excessive amount ▷ **salivation** *n*

Salk *n* Jonas Edward. 1914–95, US virologist: developed an injected vaccine against poliomyelitis (1954)

sallee *n Austral* **1** a SE Australian eucalyptus with a pale grey bark **2** an acacia tree

sallow *adj* (of human skin) of an unhealthy pale or yellowish colour [Old English *salu*] ▷ **sallowness** *n*

Sallust *n* full name *Gaius Sallustius Crispus*. 86–?34 BC, Roman historian and statesman, noted for his histories of the Catiline conspiracy and the Roman war against Jugurtha

sally *n, pl* **-lies 1** a witty remark **2** a sudden brief attack by troops **3** an excursion ▷ *vb* **-lies, -lying, -lied 4 sally forth a** to set out on a journey **b** to set out in an energetic manner [Latin *salire* to leap]

salmon *n, pl* **-mons** *or* **-mon** a large pink-fleshed fish which is highly valued for food and sport: salmon live in the sea but return to fresh water to spawn [Latin *salmo*]

Salmond *n* **1** Alex(ander Elliot Anderson). born 1954, Scottish Nationalist politician; first minister of the Scottish Parliament (2007–2014) **2** Dame **Mary** (**Anne**). born 1945, New Zealand anthropologist, historian, and writer

salmonella (sal-mon-**ell**-a) *n* a kind of bacteria that can cause food poisoning [after Daniel E. *Salmon*, veterinary surgeon]

salmon ladder *n* a series of steps designed to enable salmon to move upstream to their breeding grounds

salon *n* **1** a commercial establishment in which hairdressers or fashion designers carry on their business **2** an elegant room in a large house in which guests are received **3** an informal gathering, esp. in the 18th, 19th, and early 20th centuries, of major literary, artistic, and political figures in a fashionable household **4** an art exhibition [French]

Salonika *or* **Salonica** *n* the English name for Thessaloníki

saloon *n* **1** a two-door or four-door car with a fixed roof **2** a comfortable but more expensive bar in a pub or hotel **3** a large public room on a passenger ship **4** *chiefly US and Canad* a place where alcoholic drink is sold and consumed [from *salon*]

Salop *n* a former name (1974–80) of Shropshire

Salopian *n* **1** a native or inhabitant of Shropshire ▷ *adj* **2** of or relating to Shropshire or its inhabitants [from *Salop*, a former name of Shropshire]

salsa *n* **1** a lively Puerto Rican dance **2** big-band music accompanying this dance [Spanish, literally: sauce]

salsify *n, pl* **-fies** a Mediterranean plant with a long white edible root [Italian *sassefrica*]

salt *n* **1** sodium chloride, a white crystalline substance, used for seasoning and preserving food **2** *chem* a crystalline solid compound formed from an acid by replacing its hydrogen with a metal **3** lively wit: *his humour added salt to the discussion* **4 old salt** an experienced sailor **5 rub salt into someone's wounds** to make an unpleasant situation even worse for someone **6 salt of the earth** a person or people regarded as the finest of their kind **7 take something with a pinch of salt** to refuse to believe something is completely true or accurate **8 worth one's salt** worthy of one's pay; efficient ▷ *vb* **9** to season or preserve with salt **10** to scatter salt over (an iced road or path) to melt the ice ▷ *adj* **11** preserved in or tasting of salt: *salt beef* ▸ See also **salt away, salts** [Old English *sealt*] ▸ **salted** *adj*

SALT Strategic Arms Limitation Talks *or* Treaty

Salta *n* a city in NW Argentina: thermal springs. Pop: 504 000 (2005 est)

salt away *vb* to hoard or save (money) for the future

saltbush *n* a shrub that grows in alkaline desert regions

saltcellar *n* a small container for salt used at the table [changed from *salt saler; saler* from Old French *saliere* container for salt]

Saltillo *n* a city in N Mexico, capital of Coahuila state: resort and commercial centre of a mining region. Pop: 698 000 (2005 est)

saltire *n* **1** *heraldry* a diagonal cross on a shield **2** the national flag of Scotland, a white diagonal cross on a blue background

Salt Lake City *n* a city in N central Utah, near the Great Salt Lake at an altitude of 1330 m (4300 ft): state capital; founded in 1847 by the Mormons as world capital of the Mormon Church; University of Utah (1850). Pop: 179 894 (2003 est)

salt lick *n* **1** a place where wild animals go to lick salt deposits **2** a block of salt given to domestic animals to lick

Salto *n* a port in NW Uruguay, on the Uruguay River. It is Uruguay's second largest city. Pop: 105 000 (2005 est)

saltpetre *or US* **saltpeter** *n* same as **potassium nitrate** [Latin *sal petrae* salt of rock]

salts *pl n* **1** *med* mineral salts used as a medicine **2** like a **dose of salts** *informal* very quickly

saltwater *adj* of or inhabiting salt water, esp. the sea: *saltwater fish*

salty *adj* **saltier, saltiest 1** of, tasting of, or containing salt **2** (esp. of humour) sharp and witty ▸ **saltiness** *n*

salubrious *adj* favourable to health [Latin *salus* health] ▸ **salubrity** *n*

Saluki *n* a tall hound with a smooth coat and long fringes on the ears and tail [from *Saluq*, ancient Arabian city]

salutary *adj* **1** (of an experience) producing a beneficial result despite being unpleasant: *a salutary reminder* **2** promoting health [Latin *salutaris* wholesome]

salutation *n formal* a greeting by words or actions [Latin *salutare* to greet]

salute *vb* **-luting, -luted 1** to greet with friendly words or gestures of respect, such as bowing **2** to acknowledge with praise: *the statement salutes the changes of the past year* **3** *military* to pay formal respect to (someone) by raising the right hand to the forehead ▷ *n* **4** the act of saluting as a formal military gesture of respect **5** the act of firing guns as a military greeting of honour [Latin *salutare* to greet]

Salvador *n* a port in E Brazil, capital of Bahia state: founded in 1549 as capital of the Portuguese colony, which it remained until 1763; a major centre of the African slave trade in colonial times. Pop: 3 331 000 (2005 est). Former name: **Bahia**. Official name: **São Salvador da Bahia de Todos os Santos**

Salvadorian¹, Salvadorean *or* **Salvadoran** *n* **1** a native or inhabitant of El Salvador ▷ *adj* **2** of or relating to El Salvador, or its people, culture, etc.

Salvadorian² *n* **1** a native or inhabitant of Salvador ▷ *adj* **2** of or relating to Salvador or its inhabitants

salvage *n* **1** the rescue of a ship or its cargo from loss at sea **2** the saving of any goods or property from destruction or waste **3** the goods or property so saved **4** compensation paid for the salvage of a ship or its cargo ▷ *vb* **-vaging, -vaged 5** to save (goods or property) from shipwreck, destruction, or waste **6** to gain (something beneficial) from a failure: *it's too late to salvage anything from the whole dismal display* [Latin *salvare* to save] ▸ **salvageable** *adj*

salvation *n* **1** the act of preserving someone or something from harm **2** a person or thing that preserves from harm **3** *Christianity* the fact or state of being saved from the influence or consequences of sin [Latin *salvatus* saved]

Salvation Army *n* a Christian body organized on military lines for working among poor and homeless people and spreading the Christian faith

salve *n* **1** an ointment for wounds **2** anything that heals or soothes ▷ *vb* **salving, salved 3 salve one's conscience** to do something in order to feel less guilty [Old English *sealf*]

salver *n* a tray, usually a silver one, on which something is presented [Spanish *salva* tray from which the king's taster sampled food]

salvia *n* any small plant or shrub of the sage genus [Latin]

salvo *n, pl* **-vos** *or* **-voes 1** a simultaneous discharge of guns in battle or on a ceremonial occasion **2** an outburst of applause or questions [Italian *salva*, from Latin *salve!* greetings!]

sal volatile (**sal** vol-**at**-ill-ee) *n* a solution of ammonium carbonate, used as smelling salts [New Latin: volatile salt]

Salween *n* a river in SW Asia, rising in the Tibetan Plateau and flowing east and south through SW China and Myanmar to the Gulf of Martaban. Length: 2400 km (1500 miles)

Salzburg *n* **1** a city in W Austria, capital of Salzburg province: 7th-century Benedictine abbey; a centre of music since the Middle Ages and birthplace of Mozart; tourist centre. Pop: 142 662 (2001) **2** a state of W Austria. Pop: 521 238 (2003 est). Area: 7154 sq km (2762 sq miles)

Salzgitter *n* an industrial city in central Germany, in SE Lower Saxony. Pop: 109 855 (2003 est)

SAM surface-to-air missile

S.Am. South America(n)

Samar *n* an island in the E central Philippines, separated from S Luzon by the San Bernardino Strait: the third largest island in the republic. Capital: Catbalogan. Pop: 641 124 (2000). Area: 13 080 sq km (5050 sq miles)

Samara *n* a port in SW Russia, on the River Volga: centre of an important industrial complex; oil refining. Pop: 1 140 000 (2005 est). Former name (1935–91): **Kuibyshev, Kuybyshev**

Samarang *n* a variant spelling of **Semarang**

Samaria *n* **1** the region of ancient Palestine that extended from Judaea to Galilee and from the Mediterranean to the River Jordan; the N kingdom of Israel **2** the capital of this kingdom; constructed northwest of Shechem in the 9th century BC

Samaritan *n* **1** short for **Good Samaritan 2** a member of a voluntary organization (**the Samaritans**) which offers counselling to people in despair, esp. by telephone

samarium *n chem* a silvery metallic element of the rare-earth series. Symbol: **Sm** [after Col. von *Samarski*, Russian inspector of mines]

Samarkand *n* a city in E Uzbekistan: under Tamerlane it became the chief economic and cultural centre of central Asia, on trade routes from China and India (the "silk road"). Pop: 289 000 (2005 est). Ancient name: **Maracanda**

samba *n*, *pl* **-bas 1** a lively Brazilian dance **2** music for this dance [Portuguese]

Sambre *n* a river in W Europe, rising in N France and flowing east into Belgium to join the Meuse at Namur. Length: 190 km (118 miles)

same *adj* (usually preceded by *the*) **1** being the very one: *she is wearing the same hat* **2** being the one previously referred to: *it causes problems for the same reason* **3** alike in kind or quantity: *the same age* **4** unchanged in character or nature: *his attitude is the same as ever* **5** all the same *or* just the same nevertheless; even so **6** be all the same to be a matter of indifference: *it was all the same to me* ▷ *adv* **7** in the same way; similarly: *I felt much the same* ▷ *n* **8** the same something that is like something else in kind or quantity: *this is basically much more of the same* [Old Norse *samr*] ▷ **sameness** *n*

> **USAGE** The use of *same* exemplified in *if you send us your order for the materials, we will deliver same tomorrow* is common in business and official English. In general English, however, this use of the word is avoided: *may I borrow your book? I'll return it* (not *same*) *tomorrow*.

Samian *adj* **1** of or relating to Samos or its inhabitants ▷ *n* **2** a native or inhabitant of Samos

samizdat *n* (in the former Soviet Union) a system of secret printing and distribution of banned literature [Russian]

Samnium *n* an ancient country of central Italy inhabited by Oscan-speaking Samnites: corresponds to the present-day regions of Abruzzi, Molise, and part of Campania

Samoa *n* **1** an independent state occupying four inhabited islands and five uninhabited islands in the S Pacific archipelago of the Samoa Islands: established as a League of Nations mandate under New Zealand administration in 1920 and a UN trusteeship in 1946; gained independence as Western Samoa in 1962 as the first fully independent Polynesian state; officially changed its name to Samoa in 1997; a member of the Commonwealth. Languages: Samoan and English. Religion: Christian. Currency: tala. Capital: Apia. Pop: 195 476 (2013 est). Area: 2841 sq km (1097 sq miles) **2** Also called: **Samoa Islands** a group of islands in the S Pacific, northeast of Fiji: an independent kingdom until the mid 19th century, when it was divided administratively into **American Samoa** (in the east) and **German Samoa** (in the west); the latter was mandated to New Zealand in 1919 and gained full independence in 1962 as Western Samoa, now called Samoa (as detailed in sense 1). Area: 3038 sq km (1173 sq miles)

Samoan *adj* **1** of or relating to Samoa, its people, or their language ▷ *n* **2** a member of the people that inhabit Samoa **3** the language of Samoa, belonging to the Polynesian family of languages

Samos *n* a Greek island in the E Aegean Sea, off the SW coast of Turkey: a leading commercial centre of ancient Greece. Pop: 33 809 (2001). Area: 492 sq km (190 sq miles)

samosa *n* (in Indian cookery) a small fried triangular spiced meat or vegetable pasty. Also (in S Africa): **samoosa** [Hindi]

Samothrace *n* a Greek island in the NE Aegean Sea: mountainous. Pop: 2723 (2001)

samovar *n* a Russian metal tea urn in which the water is heated by an inner container [Russian]

Samoyed *n* a dog with a thick white coat and a tightly curled tail [Russian *Samoed*]

sampan *n* a small flat-bottomed boat with oars, used esp. in China [Chinese *san* three + *pan* board]

samphire *n* a plant found on rocks by the seashore [French *herbe de Saint Pierre* Saint Peter's herb]

sample *n* **1** a small part of anything, taken as being representative of a whole ▷ *vb* **-pling, -pled 2** to take a sample or samples of **3** *music* **a** to take a short extract from (one record) and mix it into a different backing track **b** to record (a sound) and feed it into a computerized synthesizer so that it can be reproduced at any pitch [Latin *exemplum*] ▷ **sampling** *n*

sampler *n* **1** a piece of embroidery done to show the embroiderer's skill in using many different stitches **2** *music* a piece of electronic equipment used for sampling

Sampras *n* **Pete**. born 1971, US tennis player: winner of fourteen Grand Slam single titles (1990–2002), including the US Open (1990, 1993, 1995, 1996, 2002) and Wimbledon (1993–95, 1997–2000)

Samson *n* a man of outstanding physical strength [from the biblical character who was renowned for his strength]

Samsun *n* a port in N Turkey, on the Black Sea. Pop: 395 000 (2005 est). Ancient name: **Amisus**

samurai *n*, *pl* **-rai** a member of the aristocratic warrior caste of feudal Japan [Japanese]

San *n* a river in E central Europe, rising in W Ukraine and flowing northwest across SE Poland to the Vistula River. Length: about 450 km (280 miles)

San'a *or* **Sanaa** *n* the administrative capital of Yemen, on the central plateau at an altitude of 2350 m (7700 ft): formerly the capital of North Yemen. Pop: 1 621 000 (2005 est)

San Antonian *adj* **1** of or relating to San Antonio or its inhabitants ▷ *n* **2** a native or inhabitant of San Antonio

San Antonio *n* a city in S Texas: site of the Alamo; the leading town in Texas until about 1930. Pop: 1 214 725 (2003 est)

sanatorium *or US* **sanitarium** *n*, *pl* **-riums** *or* **-ria 1** an institution providing medical treatment and rest for invalids or convalescents **2** *Brit* a room in a boarding school where sick pupils may be treated [Latin *sanare* to heal]

San Bernardino *n* a city in SE California: founded in 1851 by Mormons from Salt Lake City. Pop: 195 357 (2003 est)

San Bernardino Pass *n* a pass over the Lepontine Alps in SE Switzerland. Highest point: 2062 m (6766 ft)

San Blas *n* **1 Isthmus of San Blas** the narrowest part of the Isthmus of Panama. Width: about 50 km (30 miles) **2 Gulf of San Blas** an inlet of the Caribbean on the N coast of Panama

San Cristóbal *n* **1** an island in the Pacific, in the Galápagos Islands. Area: 505 sq km (195 sq miles). Former name: **Chatham Island 2** a city in SW Venezuela: founded in 1561 by Spanish conquistadores. Pop: 395 000 (2005 est)

sanctify *vb* **-fies, -fying, -fied 1** to make holy **2** to free from sin **3** to approve (an action or practice) as religiously binding: *she is trying to make amends for her marriage not being sanctified* [Latin *sanctus* holy + *facere* to make] ▷ **sanctification** *n*

sanctimonious *adj* pretending to be very religious and virtuous [Latin *sanctimonia* sanctity]

sanction *n* **1** permission granted by authority: *official sanction* **2** support or approval: *they could not exist without his sanction* **3** something that gives binding force to a law, such as a penalty for breaking it or a reward for obeying it **4 sanctions** coercive measures, such as boycotts and trade embargoes, taken by one or more states against another guilty of violating international law ▷ *vb* **5** to officially approve of or allow: *they do not want to sanction direct payments* **6** to confirm or ratify [Latin *sancire* to decree]

sanctity *n* the quality of something considered so holy or important that it must be respected totally: *the sanctity of the Sabbath; the sanctity of marriage*

sanctuary *n*, *pl* **-aries 1** a holy place, such as a consecrated building or shrine **2** the part of a church nearest the main altar **3** a place of refuge or protection for someone who is being chased or hunted **4** refuge or safety: *the sanctuary of your own home* **5** a place, protected by law, where animals can live and breed without interference [Latin *sanctus* holy]

sanctum *n, pl* **-tums** *or* **-ta 1** a sacred or holy place **2** a room or place of total privacy [Latin]

sand *n* **1** a powdery substance consisting of very small rock or mineral grains, found on the seashore and in deserts **2 sands** a large sandy area, esp. on the seashore or in a desert ▷ *vb* **3** to smooth or polish the surface of (something) with sandpaper or a sander **4** to fill with sand: *the channel sanded up* [Old English]

Sand *n* George, pen name of *Amandine Aurore Lucie Dupin.* 1804–76, French novelist, best known for such pastoral novels as *La Mare au diable* (1846) and *François le Champi* (1847–48) and for her works for women's rights to independence

Sandage *n* Allan Rex.1926–2010, US astronomer, who discovered the first quasar (1961)

Sandakan *n* a port in Malaysia, on the NE coast of Sabah: capital (until 1947) of North Borneo. Pop: 347 334 (2000)

sandal *n* a light shoe consisting of a sole held on the foot by thongs or straps [Greek *sandalon*] ▷ **sandalled** *or US* **sandaled** *adj*

sandalwood *n* **1** the hard light-coloured wood of a S Asian or Australian tree, which is used for carving and for incense, and which yields an aromatic oil used in perfumes **2** a tree yielding this wood [Sanskrit *candana*]

Sandalwood Island *n* the former name for **Sumba**

sandbag *n* **1** a sack filled with sand used to make a temporary defence against gunfire or flood water ▷ *vb* **-bagging, -bagged 2** to protect or strengthen with sandbags

sandbank *or* **sand bar** *n* a bank of sand in a sea or river, that may be exposed at low tide

sandblast *n* **1** a jet of sand blown from a nozzle under air or steam pressure ▷ *vb* **2** to clean or decorate (a surface) with a sandblast ▷ **sandblaster** *n*

sandboy *n* **happy as a sandboy** very happy

Sandburg *n* Carl. 1878–1967, US writer, noted esp. for his poetry, often written in free verse

sand castle *n* a model of a castle made from sand

sander *n* a power-driven tool for smoothing surfaces, removing layers of paint from walls, etc.

Sanderson *n* Tessa. born 1956, British javelin-thrower: won gold at the 1984 Olympics

Sandhurst *n* a village in S England, in Bracknell unitary authority, Berkshire: seat of the Royal Military Academy for the training of officer cadets in the British Army. Pop: 19 546 (2001)

San Diego *n* a port in S California, on the Pacific: naval base; two universities. Pop: 1 266 753 (2003 est)

S & M *informal* sadomasochism

sandman *n, pl* **-men** (in folklore) a magical person supposed to put children to sleep by sprinkling sand in their eyes

sand martin *n* a small brown European songbird which nests in tunnels bored in sand or river banks

sandpaper *n* **1** a strong paper coated with sand or other abrasive material for smoothing or polishing a surface ▷ *vb* **2** to smooth or polish (a surface) with sandpaper

sandpiper *n* a wading shore bird with a long bill and slender legs

sandpit *n Brit* a shallow pit or container holding sand for children to play in

Sandringham *n* a village in E England, in Norfolk near the E shore of the Wash: site of **Sandringham House**, a residence of the royal family

sandshoes *pl n* light canvas shoes with rubber soles

sandstone *n* a sedimentary rock consisting mainly of sand grains, much used in building

sandstorm *n* a strong wind that whips up clouds of sand, esp. in a desert

Sandwell *n* a unitary authority in central England, in

West Midlands. Pop: 285 000 (2003 est). Area: 86 sq km (33 sq miles)

sandwich *n* **1** two or more slices of bread, usually buttered, with a layer of food between them ▷ *vb* **2** to place between two other things: *shops sandwiched between flats* [after 4th Earl of *Sandwich*, who ate sandwiches rather than leave the gambling table for meals]

sandwich board *n* one of two connected boards that are hung over the shoulders in front of and behind a person to display advertisements

sandwich course *n Brit* an educational course consisting of alternate periods of study and industrial work

Sandwich Islands *pl n* the former name of **Hawaii**

sandy *adj* **sandier, sandiest 1** resembling, containing, or covered with sand **2** (of hair) reddish-yellow ▷ **sandiness** *n*

sane *adj* **1** having a normal healthy mind **2** sensible or well-judged: *sane advice* [Latin *sanus* healthy]

San Fernando *n* **1** a port in Trinidad and Tobago, on Trinidad on the Gulf of Paria: the second-largest town in the country. Pop: 55 149 (2000) **2** an inland port in W Venezuela, on the Apure River. Pop: 84 180 (latest est). Official name: **San Fernando de Apure 3** a port in SW Spain, on the Isla de León SE of Cádiz; site of an arsenal (founded 1790) and of the most southerly observatory in Europe. Pop: 88 490 (2003 est)

San Franciscan *n* **1** a native or inhabitant of San Francisco ▷ *adj* **2** of or relating to San Francisco or its inhabitants

San Francisco *n* a port in W California, situated around the Golden Gate: developed rapidly during the California gold rush; a major commercial centre and one of the world's finest harbours. Pop: 751 682 (2003 est)

San Francisco Bay *n* an inlet of the Pacific in W California, linked with the open sea by the Golden Gate strait. Length: about 80 km (50 miles). Greatest width: 19 km (12 miles)

sang *vb* the past tense of **sing**

> **USAGE** See at **ring[1]**.

sanger *n Austral slang* a sandwich

Sanger *n* **1** Frederick. 1918–2013, English biochemist, who determined the molecular structure of insulin: awarded two Nobel prizes for chemistry (1958; 1980) **2** Margaret (**Higgins**). 1883–1966, US leader of the birth-control movement

sang-froid (sahng-**frwah**) *n* composure and calmness in a difficult situation [French, literally: cold blood]

sangoma (sang-**go**-ma) *n S African* a witch doctor [Nguni (language group of southern Africa) *isangoma* a diviner]

Sangre de Cristo Mountains *pl n* a mountain range in S Colorado and N New Mexico: part of the Rocky Mountains. Highest peak: Blanca Peak, 4364 m (14 317 ft)

sangria *n* a Spanish drink of red wine, sugar, spices, and fruit [Spanish: a bleeding]

sanguinary *adj formal* **1** (of a battle or fight) involving much violence and bloodshed **2** (of a person) eager to see violence and bloodshed **3** of or stained with blood [Latin *sanguinarius*]

sanguine *adj* **1** cheerful and confident **2** (of the complexion) ruddy [Latin *sanguineus* bloody]

Sanhedrin (san-**id**-rin) *n Judaism* the highest court and supreme council of the ancient Jewish nation

San Ildefonso *n* a town in central Spain, near Segovia: site of the 18th-century summer palace of the kings of Spain. Also called: **La Granja**

sanitary *adj* **1** promoting health by getting rid of dirt and germs **2** free from dirt or germs; hygienic [Latin *sanitas* health]

sanitary towel *or especially US* **sanitary napkin** *n* a pad worn externally by women during menstruation to absorb the flow of blood

sanitation *n* **1** the use of sanitary measures to maintain public health **2** the drainage and disposal of sewage

sanitize *or* **-tise** *vb* **-tizing, -tized** *or* **-tising, -tised** to omit unpleasant details to make (news) more acceptable

sanity *n* **1** the state of having a normal healthy mind **2** good sense or soundness of judgment [Latin *sanitas* health]

San Jose *n* a city in W central California: a leading world centre of the fruit drying and canning industry. Pop: 898 349 (2003 est)

San José *n* the capital of Costa Rica, on the central plateau: a major centre of coffee production in the mid-19th century; University of Costa Rica (1843). Pop: 1 145 000 (2005 est)

San Juan *n* **1** the capital and chief port of Puerto Rico, on the NE coast; University of Puerto Rico; manufacturing centre. Pop: 433 733 (2003 est) **2** a city in W Argentina: almost completely destroyed by an earthquake in 1944. Pop: 455 000 (2005 est)

San Juan Bautista *n* the former name of **Villahermosa**

San Juan Islands *pl n* a group of islands between NW Washington, US, and SE Vancouver Island, Canada: administratively part of Washington

San Juan Mountains *pl n* a mountain range in SW Colorado and N New Mexico: part of the Rocky Mountains. Highest peak: Uncompahgre Peak, 4363 m (14 314 ft)

sank *vb* the past tense of **sink**

Sankara *n* 8th century AD, Hindu philosopher, the leading exponent of the Vedantic school: noted for his commentaries on the great Hindu texts

Sankey *n* Ira David. 1840–1908, US evangelist and hymnodist, noted for his revivalist campaigns in Britain and the US with D. L. Moody

Sankt Pölten *n* a city in NE Austria, the capital of Lower Austria state. Pop: 49 121 (2001). Abbreviation: St Pölten

San Luis Potosí *n* **1** a state of central Mexico: mainly high plateau; economy based on mining (esp. silver) and agriculture. Capital: San Luis Potosí. Pop: 927 000 (2005 est). Area: 62 849 sq km (24 266 sq miles) **2** an industrial city in central Mexico, capital of San Luis Potosí state, at an altitude of 1850 m (6000 ft). Pop: 628 134 (2000 est)

San Marinese *or* **Sammarinese** *adj* **1** of or relating to San Marino or its inhabitants ▷ *n* **2** a native or inhabitant of San Marino

San Marino *n* a republic in S central Europe in the Apennines, forming an enclave in Italy: the smallest republic in Europe, according to tradition founded by St Marinus in the 4th century. Official language: Italian. Religion: Roman Catholic majority. Currency: euro. Capital: San Marino. Pop: 32 448 (2013 est). Area: 62 sq km (24 sq miles)

San Martín *n* José de. 1778–1850, South American patriot, who played an important part in gaining independence for Argentina, Chile, and Peru. He was protector of Peru (1821–22)

Sanmicheli *n* Michele. ?1484–1559, Italian mannerist architect

San Pedro Sula *n* a city in NW Honduras: the country's chief industrial centre. Pop: 610 000 (2005 est)

San Remo *n* a port and resort in NW Italy, in Liguria on the slopes of the Maritime Alps; flower market. Pop: 50 608 (2001)

San Salvador *n* the capital of El Salvador, situated in the SW central part: became capital in 1841; ruined by earthquakes in 1854 and 1873; university (1841). Pop: 1 472 000 (2005 est)

San Salvador Island *n* an island in the central Bahamas: the first land in the New World seen by Christopher Columbus (1492). Area: 156 sq km (60 sq miles). Also called: **Watling Island**

sans-culotte (sanz-kew-**lot**) *n* a revolutionary extremist [French, literally: without knee breeches, because

during the French Revolution the revolutionaries wore trousers]

San Sebastián *n* a port and resort in N Spain on the Bay of Biscay: former summer residence of the Spanish court. Pop: 181 811 (2003 est). Official name: Donostia-San Sebastián

Sanskrit *n* the classical literary language of India, used since ancient times for religious purposes [Sanskrit *samskrta* perfected] ▷ **Sanskritic** *adj*

San Stefano *n* a village in NW Turkey, near Istanbul on the Sea of Marmara: scene of the signing (1878) of the treaty ending the Russo-Turkish War. Turkish name: Yeşilköy

Santa Ana *n* **1** a city in NW El Salvador: the second largest city in the country; coffee-processing industry. Pop: 172 000 (2005 est) **2** a city in SW California: commercial and processing centre of a rich agricultural region. Pop: 342 510 (2003 est)

Santa Catalina *n* an island in the Pacific, off the coast of SW California: part of Los Angeles county: resort. Area: 181 sq km (70 sq miles). Also called: **Catalina Island**

Santa Catarina *n* a state of S Brazil, on the Atlantic: consists chiefly of the Great Escarpment. Capital: Florianópolis. Pop: 5 527 707 (2002). Area: 95 985 sq km (37 060 sq miles)

Santa Clara *n* a city in W central Cuba: sugar and tobacco industries. Pop: 216 000 (2005 est)

Santa Claus *n* the legendary patron saint of children, who brings presents to children on Christmas Eve, commonly identified with Saint Nicholas

Santa Cruz¹ *n* **1** a province of S Argentina, on the Atlantic: consists of a large part of Patagonia, with the forested foothills of the Andes in the west. Capital: Río Gallegos. Pop: 206 897 (2000 est). Area: 243 940 sq km (94 186 sq miles) **2** a city in E Bolivia: the second largest town in Bolivia. Pop: 1 352 000 (2005 est) **3** another name for **Saint Croix**

Santa Cruz² *n* Alvaro de Bazán. 1526–88, Spanish naval commander, who proposed, assembled, and prepared the Spanish Armada but died shortly before it sailed for England

Santa Cruz de Tenerife *n* a port and resort in the W Canary Islands, on NE Tenerife: oil refinery. Pop: 220 022 (2003 est)

Santa Fe *n* **1** a city in N central New Mexico, capital of the state: one of the oldest European settlements in North America, founded in 1610 as the capital of the Kingdom of New Mexico; developed trade with the US by the Santa Fe Trail in the early 19th century. Pop: 66 476 (2003 est) **2** an inland port in E Argentina, on the Salado River: University of the Littoral (1920). Pop: 492 000 (2005 est)

Santa Fean *adj* **1** of or relating to Santa Fe or its inhabitants ▷ *n* **2** a native or inhabitant of Santa Fe

Santa Fe Trail *n* an important trade route in the western US from about 1821 to 1880, linking Independence, Missouri to Santa Fe, New Mexico

Santa Isabel *n* the former name (until 1973) of **Malabo**

Santa Maria *n* **1** a city in S Brazil, in Rio Grande do Sul state. Pop: 252 000 (2005 est) **2** an active volcano in SW Guatemala. Height: 3768 m (12 362 ft)

Santa Marta *n* a port in NW Colombia, on the Caribbean: the oldest city in Colombia, founded in 1525; terminus of the Atlantic railway from Bogotá (opened 1961). Pop: 454 000 (2005 est)

Santa Maura *n* the Italian name for **Levkás**

Santander *n* a port and resort in N Spain, on an inlet of the Bay of Biscay: noted for its prehistoric collection from nearby caves; shipyards and an oil refinery. Pop: 184 778 (2003 est)

Santarém *n* a port in N Brazil, in Pará state where the Tapajós River flows into the Amazon. Pop: 190 000 (2005 est)

Santa Rosa de Copán *n* a village in W Honduras:

noted for the ruined Mayan city of Copán, which lies to the west

Santayana n George. 1863–1952, US philosopher, poet, and critic, born in Spain. His works include *The Life of Reason* (1905–06) and *The Realms of Being* (1927–40)

Santee n a river in SE central South Carolina, formed by the union of the Congaree and Wateree Rivers: flows southeast to the Atlantic; part of the **Santee-Wateree-Catawba River System** an inland waterway 866 km (538 miles) long. Length: 230 km (143 miles)

Santer n Jacques. born 1937, Luxembourg politician: prime minister of Luxembourg (1984–95); president of the European Commission (1995–99)

Santiago n **1** the capital of Chile, at the foot of the Andes: commercial and industrial centre; two universities. Pop: 5 623 000 (2005 est). Official name: **Santiago de Chile 2** a city in the N Dominican Republic. Pop: 479 000 (2005 est). Official name: **Santiago de los Caballeros**

Santiago de Compostela n a city in NW Spain: place of pilgrimage since the 9th century and the most visited (after Jerusalem and Rome) in the Middle Ages; cathedral built over the tomb of the apostle St James. Pop: 92 339 (2003 est). Latin name: **Campus Stellae**

Santiago de Cuba n a port in SE Cuba, on **Santiago Bay** (a large inlet of the Caribbean): capital of Cuba until 1589; university (1947); industrial centre. Pop: 456 000 (2005 est)

Santiago del Estero n a city in N Argentina: the oldest continuous settlement in Argentina, founded in 1553 by Spaniards from Peru. Pop: 385 000 (2005 est)

Santo Domingo n **1** the capital and chief port of the Dominican Republic, on the S coast: the oldest continuous European settlement in the Americas, founded in 1496; university (1538). Pop: 1 920 000 (2005 est). Former name (1936–61): **Ciudad Trujillo 2** the former name (until 1844) of the **Dominican Republic 3** another name (esp. in colonial times) for **Hispaniola**

Santos n a port in S Brazil, in São Paulo state: the world's leading coffee port. Pop: 1 634 000 (2005 est)

Santos-Dumont n Alberto. 1873–1932, Brazilian aeronaut, living in France. He constructed dirigibles and aircraft, including a monoplane (1909)

São Francisco n a river in E Brazil, rising in SW Minas Gerais state and flowing northeast, then southeast to the Atlantic northeast of Aracajú. Length: 3200 km (1990 miles)

São Luís or **São Luíz** n a port in NE Brazil, capital of Maranhão state, on the W coast of São Luís Island: founded in 1612 by the French and taken by the Portuguese in 1615. Pop: 982 000 (2005 est)

São Miguel n an island in the E Azores: the largest of the group. Pop: 131 609 (2001). Area: 854 sq km (333 sq miles)

Saône n a river in E France, rising in Lorraine and flowing generally south to join the Rhône at Lyon, as its chief tributary: canalized for 375 km (233 miles) above Lyon; linked by canals with the Rhine, Marne, Seine, and Loire Rivers. Length: 480 km (298 miles)

Saône-et-Loire n a department of central France, in Burgundy region. Capital: Mâcon. Pop: 543 848 (2003 est). Area: 8627 sq km (3365 sq miles)

São Paulo n **1** a state of SE Brazil: consists chiefly of tableland draining west into the Paraná River. Capital: São Paulo. Pop: 38 177 742 (2002). Area: 247 239 sq km (95 459 sq miles) **2** a city in S Brazil, capital of São Paulo state: the largest city and industrial centre in Brazil, with one of the busiest airports in the world; three universities. Pop: 25 000 (1874); 2 017 025 (1950); 18 333 000 (2005 est)

Saorstat Eireann n the Gaelic name for the **Irish Free State**

São Salvador n short for São Salvador da Bahia de Todos os Santos, the official name for Salvador. See **Salvador**

São Tomé and Príncipe or **São Tomé e Príncipe** n a republic in the Gulf of Guinea, off the W coast of Africa, on the Equator: consists of the islands of Príncipe and São Tomé; colonized by the Portuguese in the late 15th century; became independent in 1975. Official language: Portuguese. Religion: Roman Catholic majority. Currency: dobra. Capital: São Tomé. Pop: 186 817 (2013 est). Area: 1001 sq km (386 sq miles)

sap¹ n **1 a** thin liquid that circulates in a plant, carrying food and water **2** slang a gullible person ▷ vb **sapping, sapped 3** to drain of sap [Old English *sæp*]

sap² vb **sapping, sapped 1** to weaken or exhaust the strength or confidence of **2** to undermine (an enemy position) by digging saps ▷ n **3** a deep and narrow trench used to approach or undermine an enemy position [Italian *zappa* spade]

sapient (say-pee-ent) adj often humorous having great wisdom or sound judgment [Latin *sapere* to taste, know]
> sapience n

Sapir n Edward. 1884–1939, US anthropologist and linguist, noted for his study of the ethnology and languages of North American Indians

sapling n a young tree

saponify vb **-fies, -fying, -fied** chem to convert (a fat) into a soap by treatment with alkali [Latin *sapo* soap]
> saponification n

sapper n **1** a soldier who digs trenches **2** (in the British Army) a private of the Royal Engineers

Sapper n real name Herman Cyril McNeile. 1888–1937, British novelist, author of the popular thriller *Bull-dog Drummond* (1920) and its sequels

sapphire n **1** a transparent blue precious stone ▷ adj **2** deep blue [Greek *sappheiros*]

Sappho n 6th century BC, Greek lyric poetess of Lesbos

Sapporo n a city in N Japan, on W Hokkaido: commercial centre; university (1918). Pop: 1 822 992 (2002 est)

sappy adj **-pier, -piest** (of plants) full of sap

saprophyte n biology any plant, such as a fungus, that lives and feeds on dead organic matter [Greek *sapros* rotten + *phuton* plant]

sarabande or **saraband** n **1** a stately slow Spanish dance **2** music for this dance [Spanish *zarabanda*]

Saracen n **1** an Arab or Muslim who opposed the Crusades ▷ adj **2** of the Saracens [Late Greek *Sarakēnos*]

Saragossa n the English name for **Zaragoza**

Sarajevo or **Serajevo** n the capital of Bosnia-Herzegovina: developed as a Turkish town in the 15th century; capital of the Turkish and Austro-Hungarian administrations in 1850 and 1878 respectively; scene of the assassination of Archduke Franz Ferdinand in 1914, precipitating World War I; besieged by Bosnian Serbs (1992–95). Pop: 603 000 (2005 est)

Saramago n José. 1922–2010, Portuguese novelist and writer; his works include the novel *O ano da morte de Ricardo Reis* (1984): Nobel prize for literature 1998

Sarandon n Susan Abigail. born 1946, US film actress: her films include *Thelma and Louise* (1991), *Lorenzo's Oil* (1992), *The Client* (1994), *Dead Man Walking* (1996), and *Moonlight Mile* (2002)

Saransk n a city in W central Russia, capital of the Mordovian Republic: university (1957). Pop: 304 000 (2005 est)

Saratov n an industrial city in W Russia, on the River Volga: university (1919). Pop: 868 000 (2005 est)

Sarawak n a state of Malaysia, on the NW coast of Borneo on the South China Sea: granted to Sir James Brooke by the Sultan of Brunei in 1841 as a reward for helping quell a revolt; mainly agricultural. Capital: Kuching. Pop: 2 071 506 (2000). Area: about 124 449 sq km (48 050 sq miles)

Sarazen n Gene, original name Eugenio Saraceni. 1902–99, US golfer; won seven major tournaments between 1922 and 1935

sarcasm n **1** mocking or ironic language intended to insult someone **2** the use or tone of such language

[Greek *sarkazein* to rend the flesh]

sarcastic *adj* **1** full of or showing sarcasm **2** tending to use sarcasm: *a sarcastic critic* **> sarcastically** *adv*

sarcoma *n pathol* a malignant tumour beginning in connective tissue [Greek *sarkōma* fleshy growth]

sarcophagus (sahr-**koff**-a-guss) *n*, *pl* **-gi** (-guy) *or* **-guses** a stone or marble coffin or tomb, esp. one bearing sculpture or inscriptions [Greek *sarkophagos* flesh-devouring]

Sardegna *n* the Italian name for **Sardinia**

sardine *n*, *pl* **-dines** *or* **-dine 1** a small fish of the herring family, often preserved in tightly packed tins **2 like sardines** very closely crowded together [Latin *sardina*]

Sardinia *n* the second-largest island in the Mediterranean: forms, with offshore islands, an administrative region of Italy; ceded to Savoy by Austria in 1720 in exchange for Sicily and formed the Kingdom of Sardinia with Piedmont; became part of Italy in 1861. Capital: Cagliari. Pop: 1 637 639 (2003 est). Area: 24 089 sq km (9301 sq miles). Italian name: **Sardegna**

Sardis *or* **Sardes** *n* an ancient city of W Asia Minor: capital of Lydia

sardonic *adj* (of behaviour) mocking or scornful [Greek *sardonios*] **> sardonically** *adv*

sardonyx *n* a type of gemstone with alternating reddish-brown and white parallel bands [Greek *sardonux*]

Sardou *n* Victorien. 1831–1908, French dramatist. His plays include *Fédora* (1882) and *La Tosca* (1887), the source of Puccini's opera

Sargasso Sea *n* a calm area of the N Atlantic, between the Caribbean and the Azores, where there is an abundance of floating seaweed of the genus *Sargassum*

sargassum *n* a floating brown seaweed with long stringy fronds containing air sacs [Portuguese *sargaço*]

sarge *n informal* sergeant

Sargent *n* **1** Sir (Harold) Malcolm (Watts). 1895–1967, English conductor **2** John Singer. 1856–1925, US painter, esp. of society portraits; in London from 1885

Sargeson *n* Frank. 1903–82, New Zealand short-story writer and novelist. His work includes the short-story collection *That Summer and Other Stories* (1946) and the novel *I Saw in my Dream* (1949)

Sargodha *n* a city in NE Pakistan: grain market. Pop: 556 000 (2005 est)

Sargon II *n* died 705 BC, king of Assyria (722–705). He developed a policy of transporting conquered peoples to distant parts of his empire

Sargon of Akkad *n* 24th to 23rd century BC, semilegendary Mesopotamian ruler whose empire extended from the Gulf to the Mediterranean

sari *or* **saree** *n*, *pl* **-ris** *or* **-rees** the traditional dress of Hindu women, consisting of a very long piece of cloth swathed around the body with one end over the shoulder [Hindi]

Sark *n* an island in the English Channel in the Channel Islands, consisting of **Great Sark** and **Little Sark**, connected by an isthmus: ruled by a hereditary Seigneur or Dame. Pop: 591 (2000). Area: 5 sq km (2 sq miles). French name: **Sercq**

Sarka *n* a variant spelling of **Zarqa**

sarking *n Scot, N English, Austral and NZ* flat planking supporting the roof cladding of a building [Scots *sark* shirt]

Sarkozy *n* Nicolas. born 1955, French centre-right politician, president of France from 2007 to 2012

sarky *adj* **-kier, -kiest** *informal* sarcastic

Sarmatia *n* the ancient name of a region between the Volga and Vistula Rivers now covering parts of Poland, Belarus, and SW Russia

Sarmatian *n* **1** a native or inhabitant of Sarmatia, an ancient region of E Europe ▷ *adj* **2** of or relating to Sarmatia or its inhabitants

Sarmatic *adj* of or relating to Sarmatia or its inhabitants

sarmie *n S African children's slang* a sandwich

Sarnen *n* a town in central Switzerland, capital of Obwalden demicanton: resort. Pop: 9145 (2000)

Sarnia *n* an inland port in S central Canada, in SW Ontario at the S end of Lake Huron: oil refineries. Pop: 78 577 (2001)

sarnie *n S Brit informal* a sandwich

sarong *n* a garment worn by Malaysian men and women, consisting of a long piece of cloth tucked around the waist or under the armpits [Malay]

Saronic Gulf *n* an inlet of the Aegean on the SE coast of Greece. Length: about 80 km (50 miles). Width: about 48 km (30 miles). Also called: **Aegina, Gulf of Aegina**

Saros *n* **Gulf of Saros** an inlet of the Aegean in NW Turkey, north of the Gallipoli Peninsula. Length: 59 km (37 miles). Width: 35 km (22 miles)

Sarpi *n* Paolo, real name *Pietro Soave Polano*. 1552–1623, Italian scholar, theologian, and patriot, who championed the Venetian republic in its dispute with Pope Paul V, arguing against papal absolutism and for the separation of church and state

Sarraute *n* Nathalie. 1900–99, French novelist, noted as an exponent of the antinovel. Her novels include *Portrait of a Man Unknown* (1948), *Martereau* (1953), and *Ici* (1995)

Sarre *n* the French name for the **Saar**

SARS 1 severe acute respiratory syndrome; a severe and contagious viral infection of the lungs characterized by high fever, a dry cough, and breathing difficulties **2** South African Revenue Service

sarsaparilla *n* a nonalcoholic drink prepared from the roots of a tropical American climbing plant [Spanish *sarzaparrilla*]

Sarthe *n* a department of NW France, in Pays de la Loire region. Capital: Le Mans. Pop: 536 857 (2003 est). Area: 6245 sq km (2436 sq miles)

Sarto *n* Andrea del. 1486–1531, Florentine painter. His works include *The Nativity of the Virgin* (1514) in the church of Sant' Annunziata, Florence

sartorial *adj formal* of men's clothes or tailoring: *sartorial elegance* [Latin *sartor* a tailor]

Sartre *n* Jean-Paul. 1905–80, French philosopher, novelist, and dramatist; chief French exponent of atheistic existentialism. His works include the philosophical essay *Being and Nothingness* (1943), the novels *Nausea* (1938) and *Les Chemins de la liberté* (1945–49), a trilogy, and the plays *Les Mouches* (1943), *Huis clos* (1944), and *Les Mains sales* (1948)

Sarum *n* the ancient name of **Salisbury** (3)

SAS (in Britain) Special Air Service

Sasebo *n* a port in SW Japan, on NW Kyushu on Omura Bay: naval base. Pop: 242 474 (2002 est)

sash¹ *n* a long piece of cloth worn around the waist or over one shoulder, usually as a symbol of rank [Arabic *shāsh* muslin]

sash² *n* **1** a frame that contains the panes of a window or door **2** a complete frame together with panes of glass [French *châssis* a frame]

sashay *vb informal* to move or walk in a casual or a showy manner: *the models sashayed down the catwalk* [French *chassé* a gliding dance step]

sash cord *n* a strong cord connecting a weight to the sliding half of a sash window

sashimi (sah-**shee**-mee) *n* a Japanese dish of thin fillets of raw fish [Japanese *sashi* piercing + *mi* fish]

sash window *n* a window consisting of two sashes placed one above the other so that the window can be opened by sliding one frame over the front of the other

Sask. Saskatchewan

Saskatchewan *n* **1** a province of W Canada: consists of part of the Canadian Shield in the north and open prairie in the south; economy based chiefly on agriculture and mineral resources. Capital: Regina. Pop: 1 033 381 (2011 est). Area: 651 900 sq km (251 700 sq miles). Abbreviation: **Sask, SK 2** a river in W Canada, formed by the confluence of the North and South Saskatchewan

S

Rivers: flows east to Lake Winnipeg. Length: 596 km (370 miles)

Saskatchewanian *n* **1 a** native or inhabitant of Saskatchewan ▷ *adj* **2** of or relating to Saskatchewan or its inhabitants

Saskatoon *n* a city in W Canada, in S Saskatchewan on the South Saskatchewan River: oil refining; university (1907). Pop: 196 816 (2001)

sassafras *n* a tree of North America, with aromatic bark used medicinally and as a flavouring [Spanish *sasafras*]

Sassari *n* a city in NW Sardinia, Italy: the second-largest city on the island; university (1565). Pop: 120 729 (2001)

Sassenach *n Scot and sometimes Irish* an English person [Gaelic *Sassunach*]

Sassoon *n* **1** Siegfried (**Lorraine**). 1886–1967, British poet and novelist, best known for his poems of the horrors of war collected in *Counterattack* (1918) and *Satirical Poems* (1926). He also wrote a semi-fictitious autobiographical trilogy *The Memoirs of George Sherston* (1928–36) **2** Vidal. 1928–2012, British hair stylist: founder and chairman of Vidal Sassoon Inc

sat *vb* the past of **sit**

Sat. Saturday

Satan *n* the Devil [Hebrew: plotter]

satanic *adj* **1** of Satan **2** supremely evil or wicked

Satanism *n* the worship of Satan ﹥ **Satanist** *n, adj*

satchel *n* a small bag, usually with a shoulder strap [Old French *sachel*]

sate *vb* **sating, sated** to satisfy (a desire or appetite) fully [Old English *sadian*]

satellite *n* **1** a man-made device orbiting the earth or another planet, used in communications or to collect scientific information **2** a heavenly body orbiting a planet or star: *the earth is a satellite of the sun* **3** a country controlled by or dependent on a more powerful one ▷ *adj* **4** of, used in, or relating to the transmission of television signals from a satellite to the home: *satellite TV; a satellite dish* [Latin *satelles* an attendant]

satiate (**say-she-ate**) *vb* **-ating, -ated** to provide with more than enough, so as to disgust or weary: *enough cakes to satiate several children* [Latin *satiare*] ﹥ **satiable** *adj* ﹥ **satiation** *n*

Satie *n* Erik (**Alfred Leslie**). 1866–1925, French composer, noted for his eccentricity, experimentalism, and his direct and economical style. His music, including numerous piano pieces and several ballets, exercised a profound influence upon other composers, such as Debussy and Ravel

satiety (**sat-tie-a-tee**) *n formal* the feeling of having had too much

satin *n* **1** a fabric, usually made from silk or rayon, closely woven to give a smooth glossy surface on one side ▷ *adj* **2** like satin in texture: *satin polyurethane varnish* [Arabic *zaitūnī*] ﹥ **satiny** *adj*

satinwood *n* **1** a hard wood with a satiny texture, used in fine furniture **2** the East Indian tree yielding this wood

satire *n* **1** the use of ridicule to expose incompetence, evil, or corruption **2** a play, novel, or poem containing satire [Latin *satira* a mixture] ﹥ **satirical** *adj*

satirist *n* **1** a writer of satire **2** a person who uses satire

satirize *or* **-rise** *vb* **-rizing, -rized** *or* **-rising, -rised** to ridicule (a person or thing) by means of satire ﹥ **satirization** *or* **-risation** *n*

satisfaction *n* **1** the pleasure obtained from the fulfilment of a desire **2** something that brings fulfilment: *craft workers get satisfaction from their work* **3** compensation or an apology for a wrong done: *consumers unable to get satisfaction from their gas provider*

satisfactory *adj* **1** adequate or acceptable **2** giving satisfaction ﹥ **satisfactorily** *adv*

satisfy *vb* **-fies, -fying, -fied** **1** to fulfil the desires or needs of (a person): *his answer didn't satisfy me* **2** to provide sufficiently for (a need or desire): *to satisfy public demand*

3 to convince: *that trip did seem to satisfy her that he was dead* **4** to fulfil the requirements of: *unable to satisfy the conditions set by the commission* [Latin *satis* enough + *facere* to make] ﹥ **satisfiable** *adj* ﹥ **satisfying** *adj*

satnav *n* motoring informal satellite navigation

Sato Eisaku *n* 1901–75, Japanese statesman: prime minister (1964–72). During his term of office Japan became a major economic power. He shared the Nobel peace prize (1974) for opposing the proliferation of nuclear weapons

satrap *n* (in ancient Persia) a provincial governor or subordinate ruler [Old Persian *khshathrapāvan*, literally: protector of the land]

SATs *Brit* standard assessment tasks

satsuma *n* a small loose-skinned variety of orange with easily separable segments [Satsuma]

Satsuma *n* a former province of SW Japan, on S Kyushu: famous for its porcelain

saturate *vb* **-rating, -rated** **1** to soak completely **2** to fill so completely that no more can be added: *saturating the area with their men* **3** *chem* to combine (a substance) or (of a substance) to be combined with the greatest possible amount of another substance [Latin *saturare*]

saturation *n* **1** the process or state that occurs when one substance is filled so full of another substance that no more can be added **2** *military* the use of very heavy force, esp. bombing, against an area

saturation point *n* **1** the point at which the maximum amount of a substance has been absorbed **2** the point at which some capacity is at its fullest; limit: *the market is close to saturation point*

Saturday *n* the seventh day of the week [Latin *Saturni dies* day of Saturn]

Saturn *n* **1** the Roman god of agriculture and vegetation **2** the sixth planet from the sun, second largest in the solar system, around which revolve concentric rings

Saturnalia *n, pl* **-lia** *or* **-lias** **1** the ancient Roman festival of Saturn, renowned for its unrestrained revelry **2** **saturnalia** a wild party or orgy [Latin *Saturnalis* relating to Saturn]

saturnine *adj* having a gloomy temperament or appearance [Latin *Saturnus* Saturn, from the gloomy influence attributed to the planet]

satyr *n* **1** *Greek myth* a woodland god represented as having a man's body with the ears, horns, tail, and legs of a goat **2** a man who has strong sexual desires [Greek *saturos*]

sauce *n* **1** a liquid added to food to enhance its flavour **2** anything that adds interest or zest **3** *chiefly Brit informal* impudent language or behaviour [Latin *salsus* salted]

sauce boat *n* a boat-shaped container for serving sauce

saucepan *n* a metal pan with a long handle and often a lid, used for cooking food

saucer *n* **1** a small round dish on which a cup is set **2** something shaped like a saucer [Old French *saussier* container for sauce] ﹥ **saucerful** *n*

saucy *adj* **saucier, sauciest** **1** cheeky or slightly rude in an amusing and light-hearted way **2** jaunty and boldly smart: *a saucy hat* ﹥ **sauciness** *n*

Saud *n* full name *Saud ibn Abdul-Aziz*. 1902–69, king of Saudi Arabia (1953–64); son of Ibn Saud. He was deposed by his brother Faisal

Saudi *or* **Saudi Arabian** *adj* **1** of or relating to Saudi Arabia or its inhabitants ▷ *n* **2** a native or inhabitant of Saudi Arabia

Saudi Arabia *n* a kingdom in SW Asia, occupying most of the Arabian peninsula between the Persian Gulf and the Red Sea: founded in 1932 by Ibn Saud, who united Hejaz and Nejd; consists mostly of desert plateau; large reserves of petroleum and natural gas. Official language: Arabic. Official religion: (Sunni) Muslim. Currency: riyal. Capital: Riyadh (royal and administrative), Jiddah (diplomatic). Pop: 26 939 583 (2013 est). Area: 2 260 353 sq km (872 722 sq miles)

sauerkraut *n* a German dish of finely shredded pickled cabbage [German *sauer* sour + *Kraut* cabbage]

sault (**soo**) *n Canad* a waterfall or rapids [French *saut* a leap]

Sault Sainte Marie *n* usually abbreviated to: **Sault Ste Marie** **1** an inland port in central Canada, in Ontario on the St Mary's River, which links Lake Superior and Lake Huron, opposite Sault Ste Marie, Michigan: canal bypassing the rapids completed in 1895. Pop: 67 385 (2001) **2** an inland port in NE Michigan, opposite Sault Ste Marie, Ontario: canal around the rapids completed in 1855, enlarged and divided in 1896 and 1919 (popularly called **Soo Canals**). Pop: 14 184 (2003 est)

sauna *n* **1** a Finnish-style hot steam bath, usually followed by a cold plunge **2** the place in which such a bath is taken [Finnish]

Saunders *n* Dame **Cicely**. 1918–2005, British philanthropist: founded St Christopher's Hospice in 1967 for the care of the terminally ill, upon which the modern hospice movement is modelled. Her books include *Living with Dying* (1983)

saunter *vb* **1** to walk in a leisurely manner; stroll ▷ *n* **2** a leisurely pace or stroll [origin unknown]

saurian *adj* of or resembling a lizard [Greek *sauros* lizard]

sausage *n* **1** finely minced meat mixed with fat, cereal, and seasonings, in a tube-shaped casing **2** an object shaped like a sausage **3 not a sausage** *informal* nothing at all [Old French *saussiche*]

sausage dog *n informal* same as **dachshund**

sausage roll *n* a roll of sausage meat in pastry

sausage sizzle *n Austral and NZ* an event at which sausages are barbecued, often to raise money for a school or other organization

Saussure *n* **Ferdinand de**. 1857–1913, Swiss linguist. He pioneered structuralism in linguistics and the separation of scientific language description from historical philological studies ▷ **Saussurean** *adj, n*

sauté (**so-tay**) *vb* **-téing** or **-téeing, -téed** **1** to fry (food) quickly in a little fat ▷ *n* **2** a dish of sautéed food ▷ *adj* **3** sautéed until lightly brown: *sauté potatoes* [French: tossed]

Sauternes (**so-turn**) *n* a sweet white wine produced in the southern Bordeaux district of France

Sava or **Save** *n* a river in SE Europe, rising in NW Slovenia and flowing east and south to the Danube at Belgrade. Length: 940 km (584 miles)

savage *adj* **1** wild and untamed: *savage tigers* **2** fierce and cruel: *savage cries* **3** (of peoples) uncivilized or primitive: *savage tribes* **4** rude, crude, and violent: *savage behaviour on the terraces* **5** (of terrain) wild and uncultivated ▷ *n* **6** a member of an uncivilized or primitive society **7** a fierce or vicious person ▷ *vb* **-vaging, -vaged 8** to attack ferociously and wound: *savaged by a wild dog* **9** to criticize extremely severely: *savaged by the press for incompetence* [Latin *silvaticus* belonging to a wood] ▷ **savagely** *adv*

Savage *n* **Michael Joseph**. 1872-1940, New Zealand statesman; prime minister of New Zealand (1935-40)

Savage Island *n* another name for **Niue**

savagery *n, pl* **-ries** viciousness and cruelty

Savaii *n* the largest island in Samoa: mountainous and volcanic. Pop: 42 400 (2001). Area: 1174 sq km (662 sq miles)

savannah or **savanna** *n* open grasslands, usually with scattered bushes or trees, in Africa [Spanish *zavana*]

Savannah *n* **1** a port in the US, in E Georgia, near the mouth of the Savannah River: port of departure of the *Savannah* for Liverpool (1819), the first steamship to cross the Atlantic. Pop: 127 573 (2003 est) **2** a river in the southeastern US, formed by the confluence of the Tugaloo and Seneca Rivers in NW South Carolina: flows southeast to the Atlantic. Length: 505 km (314 miles)

savant *n* a very wise and knowledgeable man [French] ▷ **savante** *fem n*

save[1] *vb* **saving, saved** **1** to rescue or preserve (a person or thing) from danger or harm **2** to avoid the spending, waste, or loss of (something): *an appeal on television for the public to save energy* **3** to set aside or reserve (money or goods) for future use: *I'm saving for a vintage Mercedes* **4** to treat with care so as to preserve **5** to prevent the necessity for: *a chance saved him from having to make up his mind* **6** *sport* to prevent (a goal) by stopping (a ball or puck) **7** *Christianity* to free (someone) from the influence or consequences of sin ▷ *n* **8** *sport* the act of saving a goal **9** *computers* an instruction to write information from the memory onto a tape or disk [Old French *salver*] ▷ **savable** or **saveable** *adj* ▷ **saver** *n*

save[2] *old-fashioned prep* **1** (often foll. by *for*) with the exception of: *the stage was empty save for a single chair* ▷ *conj* **2** but [Middle English *sauf*]

save as you earn *n* (in Britain) a savings-related share scheme which allows employees to buy shares in the company they work for at a fixed price

saveloy *n Brit, Austral and NZ* a highly seasoned smoked sausage made from salted pork [Italian *cervellato*]

Savery *n* **Thomas**. ?1650–1715, English engineer, who built (1698) the first practical steam engine, used to pump water from mines

Savigny *n* **Friedrich Karl von**. 1779–1861, German legal scholar, who pioneered the historical approach to jurisprudence, emphasizing custom and precedent

Savile Row *n* a street in Mayfair, London, famous for expensive and fashionable clothes shops

saving *n* **1** preservation from destruction or danger **2** a reduction in the amount of time or money used **3 savings** money saved for future use ▷ *adj* **4** tending to rescue or preserve ▷ *prep* **5** with the exception of

saving grace *n* a good quality in a person that prevents him or her from being entirely bad or worthless

saviour or US **savior** *n* a person who rescues another person or a thing from danger or harm [Church Latin *Salvator* the Saviour]

Saviour or US **Savior** *n Christianity* Jesus Christ, regarded as the saviour of people from sin

Savitskaya *n* **Svetlana**. born 1949, Soviet cosmonaut, the first woman to walk in space (1984). She was elected to the former Soviet parliament (1989)

Savoie *n* **1** a department of E France, in Rhône-Alpes region. Capital: Chambéry. Pop: 386 246 (2003 est). Area: 6188 sq km (2413 sq miles) **2** the French name for **Savoy**

savoir-faire (**sav-wahr-fair**) *n* the ability to say and do the right thing in any situation [French]

Savona *n* a port in NW Italy, in Liguria on the Mediterranean: an important centre of the Italian iron and steel industry. Pop: 59 907 (2001)

Savonarola *n* **Girolamo**. 1452–98, Italian religious and political reformer. As a Dominican prior in Florence he preached against contemporary sinfulness and moral corruption. When the Medici were expelled from the city (1494) he instituted a severely puritanical republic but lost the citizens' support after being excommunicated (1497). He was hanged and burned as a heretic

savory *n, pl* **-vories** an aromatic plant whose leaves are used in cooking [Latin *satureia*]

savour or US **savor** *vb* **1** to enjoy and appreciate (food or drink) slowly **2** to enjoy (a pleasure) for as long as possible: *an experience to be savoured* **3 savour of a** to have a suggestion of: *that could savour of ostentation* **b** to possess the taste or smell of: *the vegetables savoured of coriander* ▷ *n* **4** the taste or smell of something **5** a slight but distinctive quality or trace [Latin *sapor* taste]

savoury or US **savory** *adj* **1** salty or spicy: *savoury foods* **2** attractive to the sense of taste or smell **3** pleasant or acceptable: *one of the book's less savoury characters* ▷ *n, pl* **-ries** **4** *chiefly Brit* a savoury dish served before or after a meal ▷ **savouriness** or US **savoriness** *n*

savoy *n* a cabbage with a compact head and wrinkled leaves [after the Savoy region in France]

Savoy *n* an area of SE France, bordering on Italy, mainly in the Savoy Alps: a duchy in the late Middle Ages and part of the Kingdom of Sardinia from 1720 to 1860, when it became part of France. French name: **Savoie**

Savoy Alps *pl n* a range of the Alps in SE France. Highest peak: Mont Blanc, 4807 m (15 772 ft)

Savoyard *n* **1** a native of Savoy **2** the dialect of French spoken in Savoy ▷ *adj* **3** of or relating to Savoy, its inhabitants, or their dialect

savvy *slang vb* **-vies, -vying, -vied 1** to understand ▷ *n* **2** understanding or common sense ▷ *adj* **3** shrewd [corruption of Spanish *sabe (usted)* (you) know]

saw[1] *n* **1** a cutting tool with a toothed metal blade or edge, either operated by hand or powered by electricity ▷ *vb* **sawing, sawed, sawed** *or* **sawn 2** to cut with or as if with a saw **3** to form by sawing **4** to move (an object) from side to side as if moving a saw [Old English *sagu*]

saw[2] *vb* the past tense of **see**[1]

saw[3] *n* old-fashioned a wise saying or proverb [Old English *sagu* a saying]

saw doctor *n NZ* a sawmill specialist who sharpens and services saw blades

sawdust *n* particles of wood formed by sawing

sawfish *n*, *pl* **-fish** *or* **-fishes** a sharklike ray with a long toothed snout resembling a saw

sawhorse *n Austral and NZ* a structure for supporting wood that is being sawn

sawmill *n* a factory where timber is sawn into planks

sawn *vb* a past participle of **saw**[1]

sawn-off *or especially US* **sawed-off** *adj* (of a shotgun) having the barrel cut short to make concealment of the weapon easier

saw-off *n Canad* **1** a deadlock or stalemate **2** a compromise

sawyer *n* a person who saws timber for a living

sax *n informal* short for **saxophone**

Saxe[1] *n* the French name for **Saxony**

Saxe[2] *n* Hermann Maurice, comte de Saxe. 1696–1750, French marshal born in Saxony: he distinguished himself in the War of the Austrian Succession (1740–48)

saxifrage *n* an alpine rock plant with small white, yellow, purple, or pink flowers [Late Latin *saxifraga*, literally: rock breaker]

Saxo Grammaticus *n* ?1150–?1220, Danish chronicler, noted for his *Gesta Danorum*, a history of Denmark down to 1185, written in Latin, which is partly historical and partly mythological, and contains the Hamlet (Amleth) legend

Saxon *n* **1** a member of a West Germanic people who raided and settled parts of Britain in the fifth and sixth centuries AD **2** any of the West Germanic dialects spoken by the ancient Saxons ▷ *adj* **3** of the ancient Saxons or their language [Late Latin *Saxon-*, *Saxo*]

Saxony *n* **1** a state in E Germany, formerly part of East Germany. Pop: 4 321 000 (2003 est) **2** a former duchy and electorate in SE and central Germany, whose territory changed greatly over the centuries **3** (in the early Middle Ages) any territory inhabited or ruled by Saxons ▸ German name: **Sachsen**. French name: **Saxe**. Compare **Saxony-Anhalt, Lower Saxony**

Saxony-Anhalt *n* a state of E Germany: created in 1947 from the state of Anhalt and those parts of Prussia formerly ruled by the duchy of Saxony: part of East Germany until 1990. Pop: 2 523 000 (2003 est)

saxophone *n* a brass wind instrument with keys and a curved metal body [after Adolphe *Sax*, who invented it] ▸ **saxophonist** *n*

say *vb* **saying, said 1** to speak or utter **2** to express (an idea) in words: *I can't say what I feel* **3** to state (an opinion or fact) positively: *I say you are wrong* **4** to indicate or show: *the clock says ten to nine* **5** to recite: *to say grace* **6** to report or allege: *they say we shall have rain today* **7** to suppose as an example or possibility: *let us say that he is lying* **8** to convey by means of artistic expression: *what does the artist have to*

say *in this picture?* **9** to make a case for: *there is much to be said for it* **10** go without saying to be so obvious as to need no explanation **11 to say the least** at the very least ▷ *adv* **12** approximately: *there were, say, 20 people present* **13** for example: *choose a number, say, four* ▷ *n* **14** the right or chance to speak: *the opposition has hardly had a say in these affairs* **15** authority, esp. to influence a decision: *he has a lot of say* [Old English *secgan*]

Sayan Mountains *pl n* a mountain range in S central Russia, in S Siberia. Highest peak: Munku-Sardyk, 3437 m (11 457 ft)

SAYE (in Britain) save as you earn

Sayers *n* Dorothy L(eigh). 1893–1957, English detective-story writer

saying *n* a well-known phrase or sentence expressing a belief or a truth

Sb *chem* antimony [New Latin *stibium*]

Sc *chem* scandium

SC South Carolina

scab *n* **1** the dried crusty surface of a healing skin wound or sore **2** *disparaging* a person who refuses to support a trade union's actions, and continues to work during a strike **3** a contagious disease of sheep, caused by a mite **4** a fungal disease of plants ▷ *vb* **scabbing, scabbed 5** to become covered with a scab **6** *disparaging* to work as a scab [Old English *sceabb*]

scabbard *n* a holder for a sword or dagger [Middle English *scauberc*]

scabby *adj* **-bier, -biest 1** *pathol* covered with scabs **2** *informal* mean or despicable ▸ **scabbiness** *n*

scabies (**skay**-beez) *n* a contagious skin infection caused by a mite, characterized by intense itching [Latin *scabere* to scratch]

scabious (**skay**-bee-uss) *n* a plant with showy blue, red, or whitish dome-shaped flower heads [Medieval Latin *scabiosa herba* the scabies plant]

scabrous (**skay**-bruss) *adj* **1** rough and scaly **2** indecent or crude: *scabrous stand-up comedy* [Latin *scaber* rough]

Scafell Pike *n* a mountain in NW England, in Cumbria in the Lake District: the highest peak in England. Height: 977 m (3206 ft)

scaffold *n* **1** a temporary framework used to support workmen and materials during the construction or repair of a building **2** a raised wooden platform on which criminals are hanged; gallows [Old French *eschaffaut*]

scaffolding *n* **1** a scaffold or scaffolds **2** the building materials used to make scaffolds

Scala *n* See La Scala

scalar *maths n* **1** a quantity, such as time or temperature, that has magnitude but not direction ▷ *adj* **2** having magnitude but not direction [Latin *scala* ladder]

scald *vb* **1** to burn with hot liquid or steam **2** to sterilize with boiling water **3** to heat (a liquid) almost to boiling point ▷ *n* **4** a burn caused by scalding [Late Latin *excaldare* to wash in warm water]

scale[1] *n* **1** one of the thin flat overlapping plates covering the bodies of fishes and reptiles **2** a thin flat piece or flake **3** a coating which sometimes forms in kettles and hot-water pipes in areas where the water is hard **4** tartar formed on the teeth ▷ *vb* **5** to remove the scales or coating from **6** to peel off in flakes or scales **7** to cover or become covered with scales [Old French *escale*] ▸ **scaly** *adj*

scale[2] *n* **1** (*often pl*) a machine or device for weighing **2** one of the pans of a balance **3 tip the scales** to have a decisive influence **4 tip the scales at** to amount in weight to [Old Norse *skāl* bowl]

scale[3] *n* **1** a sequence of marks at regular intervals, used as a reference in making measurements **2** a measuring instrument with such a scale **3** the ratio between the size of something real and that of a representation of it: *the map has a scale of 1:10 000* **4** a series of degrees or graded system of things: *the Western wage scale for the same work* **5** a relative degree or extent: *growing flowers on a very small scale* **6** *music* a sequence of notes taken in ascending or descending order, esp. within one octave **7** *maths* the notation of a given number system: *the decimal scale* ▷ *vb* **scaling, scaled 8** to climb to the top of (an object or height): *the men scaled a wall* **9 scale up** or **down** to increase or reduce proportionately in size: *the design can easily be scaled up; after five days the search was scaled down* [Latin *scala* ladder]

scalene *adj maths* (of a triangle) having all sides of unequal length [Greek *skalēnos*]

Scaliger *n* **1** Joseph Justus. 1540–1609, French scholar, who revolutionized the study of ancient chronology by his work *De Emendatione temporum* (1583) **2** his father, Julius Caesar. 1484–1558, Italian classical scholar, and writer on biology and medicine

scallion *n* a spring onion [Anglo-French *scalun*]

scallop *n* **1** an edible marine mollusc with two fluted fan-shaped shells **2** a single shell of this mollusc **3** one of a series of small curves along an edge [Old French *escalope* shell] **> scalloping** *n*

scalloped *adj* decorated with small curves along the edge

scallywag *n informal* a badly behaved but likeable person; rascal [origin unknown]

scalp *n* **1** *anatomy* the skin and hair covering the top of the head **2** (formerly among Native Americans of N America) a part of this removed as a trophy from a slain enemy ▷ *vb* **3** to cut the scalp from **4** *informal, chiefly US* to buy and resell so as to make a high or quick profit [probably from Old Norse *skálpr* sheath]

scalpel *n* a small surgical knife with a very sharp thin blade [Latin *scalper* a knife]

scam *n slang* a stratagem for gain; a swindle

Scamander *n* the ancient name for the Menderes (2)

scamp *n* a mischievous person, esp. a child [probably from Middle Dutch *schampen* to decamp]

scamper *vb* **1** to run about hurriedly or quickly ▷ *n* **2** the act of scampering [see SCAMP]

scampi *n* large prawns, usually eaten fried in breadcrumbs [Italian]

scan *vb* **scanning, scanned 1** to scrutinize carefully **2** to glance over quickly **3** *prosody* to analyse (verse) by examining its rhythmic structure **4** *prosody* (of a line or verse) to be metrically correct **5** to examine or search (an area) by systematically moving a beam of light or electrons, or a radar or sonar beam over it **6** *med* to obtain an image of (a part of the body) by means of ultrasound or a scanner ▷ *n* **7** an instance of scanning **8** *med* **a** the examination of part of the body by means of a scanner **b** the image produced by a scanner [Latin *scandere* to climb]

scandal *n* **1** a disgraceful action or event: *the chairman resigned after a loans scandal* **2** shame or outrage arising from a disgraceful action or event: *the figures were a national scandal* **3** malicious gossip [Greek *skandalon* a trap] **> scandalous** *adj* **> scandalously** *adv*

scandalize or **-ise** *vb* **-izing, -ized** or **-ising, -ised** (*often passive*) to shock or be shocked by improper behaviour

scandalmonger *n* a person who spreads or enjoys scandal or gossip

Scanderbeg *n* original name *George Castriota*; Turkish name *Iskender Bey*. ?1403–68, Albanian patriot. He was an army commander for the sultan of Turkey until 1443, when he changed sides and drove the Turks from Albania

Scandinavia *n* **1** Also called: **the Scandinavian Peninsula** the peninsula of N Europe occupied by Norway and Sweden **2** the countries of N Europe, esp. considered as a cultural unit and including Norway, Sweden, Denmark, and often Finland, Iceland, and the Faeroes

Scandinavian *adj* **1** of or relating to Scandinavia or its inhabitants ▷ *n* **2** a native or inhabitant of Scandinavia **3** the northern group of Germanic languages, consisting

of Swedish, Danish, Norwegian, Icelandic, and Faeroese

scandium *n chem* a rare silvery-white metallic element. Symbol: **Sc** [Latin *Scandia* Scandinavia, where discovered]

scanner *n* **1** an aerial or similar device designed to transmit or receive signals, esp. radar signals **2** a device used in medical diagnosis to obtain an image of an internal organ or part

scansion *n* the metrical scanning of verse

scant *adj* scarcely sufficient: *some issues will get scant attention* [Old Norse *skamt* short]

scanty *adj* **scantier, scantiest** barely sufficient or not sufficient **> scantily** *adv* **> scantiness** *n*

Scapa Flow *n* an extensive landlocked anchorage off the N coast of Scotland, in the Orkney Islands: major British naval base in both World Wars. Length: about 24 km (15 miles). Width: 13 km (8 miles)

scapegoat *n* **1** a person made to bear the blame for others ▷ *vb* **2** to make a scapegoat of [*escape* + *goat*, coined to translate Biblical Hebrew *azāzēl*, probably goat for Azazel, mistakenly thought to mean 'goat that escapes']

scapula (skap-pew-la) *n*, *pl* **-lae** (-lee) the technical name for **shoulder blade** [Late Latin: shoulder]

scapular *adj* **1** *anatomy* of the scapula ▷ *n* **2** a loose sleeveless garment worn by monks over their habits

scar¹ *n* **1** a mark left on the skin following the healing of a wound **2** a permanent effect on a person's character resulting from emotional distress **3** a mark on a plant where a leaf was formerly attached **4** a mark of damage ▷ *vb* **scarring, scarred 5** to mark or become marked with a scar **6** to permanently effect or be permanently affected by mental trauma: *their divorce will scar those kids for life* [Greek *eskhara* scab]

scar² *n* a bare craggy rock formation [Old Norse *sker* low reef]

scarab *n* **1** the black dung-beetle, regarded by the ancient Egyptians as divine **2** an image or carving of this beetle [Latin *scarabaeus*]

Scarborough *n* a fishing port and resort in NE England, in North Yorkshire on the North Sea: developed as a spa after 1660; ruined 12th-century castle. Pop: 38 364 (2001)

scarce *adj* **1** insufficient to meet the demand: *scarce water resources* **2** not common; rarely found **3 make oneself scarce** *informal* to go away ▷ *adv* **4** *archaic, literary* scarcely [Old French *scars*]

scarcely *adv* **1** hardly at all **2** *often humorous* probably or definitely not: *that is scarcely justification for your actions*

> **USAGE** See at hardly.

scarcity *n*, *pl* **-ties** an inadequate supply

scare *vb* **scaring, scared 1** to frighten or be frightened **2 scare away** or **off** to drive away by frightening ▷ *n* **3** a sudden attack of fear or alarm: *you gave me a scare* **4** a period of general fear or alarm: *the latest AIDS scare* [Old Norse *skirra*]

scarecrow *n* **1** an object, usually in the shape of a man, made out of sticks and old clothes, to scare birds away from crops **2** *informal* a raggedly dressed person

scaremonger *n* a person who starts or spreads rumours of disaster to frighten people **> scaremongering** *n*

scarf¹ *n*, *pl* **scarves** or **scarfs** a piece of material worn around the head, neck, or shoulders [origin unknown]

scarf² *n*, *pl* **scarfs 1** a joint between two pieces of timber made by notching the ends and strapping or gluing the two pieces together ▷ *vb* **2** to join (two pieces of timber) by means of a scarf [probably from Old Norse]

Scarfe *n* Gerald. born 1936, British cartoonist, famous for his scathing caricatures of politicians and celebrities

Scargill *n* Arthur. born 1938, British trades union leader; president of the National Union of Mineworkers (1982–2002). He led the miners in a long and bitter strike (1984–85), but failed to prevent pit closures

scarify *vb* **-fies, -fying, -fied 1** *surgery* to make slight incisions in (the skin) **2** *agriculture* to break up and loosen

S

(topsoil) **3** to criticize without mercy [Latin *scarifare* to scratch open] > **scarification** *n*

> **USAGE** *Scarify* is sometimes wrongly thought to mean the same as *scare: a frightening* (not *scarifying*) film.

scarlatina *n* the technical name for **scarlet fever** [Italian *scarlatto* scarlet]

Scarlatti *n* **1** Alessandro. ?1659–1725, Italian composer; regarded as the founder of modern opera **2** his son, **(Giuseppe) Domenico.** 1685–1757, Italian composer and harpsichordist, in Portugal and Spain from 1720. He wrote over 550 single-movement sonatas for harpsichord, many of them exercises in virtuoso technique

scarlet *adj* bright red [Old French *escarlate* fine cloth]

scarlet fever *n* an acute contagious disease characterized by fever, a sore throat, and a red rash on the body

scarp *n* **1** a steep slope or ridge of rock **2** *fortifications* the side of a ditch cut nearest to a rampart [Italian *scarpa*]

scarper *vb* *chiefly Brit slang* to run away or escape [origin unknown]

Scarron *n* Paul. 1610–60, French comic dramatist and novelist, noted particularly for his picaresque novel *Le Roman comique* (1651–57)

Scart *or* **SCART** *n* *electronics* a plug-and-socket system which carries pictures and sound, used in home entertainment systems

scarves *n* a plural of **scarf¹**

scary *adj* **scarier, scariest** *informal* quite frightening

scat¹ *vb* **scatting, scatted** *informal* to go away in haste [origin unknown]

scat² *n* **1** a type of jazz singing using improvised vocal sounds instead of words ▷ *vb* **scatting, scatted 2** to sing jazz in this way [perhaps imitative]

scathing *adj* harshly critical: *there was a scathing review of the play in the paper* [Old Norse *skathi* harm] > **scathingly** *adv*

scatology *n* preoccupation with obscenity, esp. with references to excrement [Greek *skat-* excrement + *-LOGY*] > **scatological** *adj*

scatter *vb* **1** to throw about in various directions: *scatter some oatmeal on top of the cake* **2** to separate and move in various directions; disperse: *the infantry were scattering* ▷ *n* **3** the act of scattering **4** a number of objects scattered about [probably variant of *shatter*]

scatterbrain *n* a person who is incapable of serious thought or concentration > **scatterbrained** *adj*

scattershot *adj* wide-ranging but indiscriminate: *a scattershot approach to conservation*

scatty *adj* **-tier, -tiest** *informal* rather absent-minded [from *scatterbrained*] > **scattiness** *n*

scavenge *vb* **-enging, -enged** to search for (anything usable) among discarded material

scavenger *n* **1** a person who collects things discarded by others **2** any animal that feeds on discarded or decaying matter [Old French *escauwer* to scrutinize]

SCE (in Scotland) Scottish Certificate of Education

scenario *n, pl* **-narios 1** a summary of the plot and characters of a play or film **2** an imagined sequence of future events: *the likeliest scenario is another general election* [Italian]

scene *n* **1** the place where an action or event, real or imaginary, occurs **2** an incident or situation, real or imaginary, esp. as described or represented **3** a division of an act of a play, in which the setting is fixed and the action is continuous **4** *films* a shot or series of shots that constitutes a unit of the action **5** the backcloths or screens used to represent a location in a play or film set **6** the view of a place or landscape **7** a display of emotion or loss of temper in public: *you do not want to cause a scene* **8** *informal* a particular activity or aspect of life, and all the

things associated with it: *the club scene* **9** behind the scenes **a** backstage **b** in secret or in private [Greek *skēnē* tent, stage]

scenery *n, pl* **-eries 1** the natural features of a landscape **2** *theatre* the painted backcloths or screens used to represent a location in a theatre or studio

scenic *adj* **1** of or having beautiful natural scenery: *untouched scenic areas* **2** of the stage or stage scenery: *scenic artists*

scent *n* **1** a distinctive smell, esp. a pleasant one **2** a smell left in passing, by which a person or animal may be traced **3** a trail or series of clues by which something is followed: *he must have got on to the scent of the story through you* **4** perfume ▷ *vb* **5** to become aware of by smelling **6** to suspect: *he scented the beginnings of irritation in the car* **7** to fill with odour or fragrance [Old French *sentir* to sense] > **scented** *adj*

sceptic *or US* **skeptic** (skep-tik) *n* **1** a person who habitually doubts generally accepted beliefs **2** a person who doubts the truth of a religion [Greek *skeptikos* one who reflects upon] > **sceptical** *or US* **skeptical** *adj* > **sceptically** *or US* **skeptically** *adv* > **scepticism** *or US* **skepticism** *n*

sceptre *or US* **scepter** *n* an ornamental rod symbolizing royal power [Greek *skeptron* staff] > **sceptred** *or US* **sceptered** *adj*

Schadenfreude (shah-den-froy-da) *n* one person's delight in another's misfortune [German *Schaden* harm + *Freude* joy]

Schaerbeek *n* a city in central Belgium: an industrial suburb of Brussels. Pop: 110 253 (2004 est)

Schaffhausen *n* **1** a small canton of N Switzerland. Pop: 73 900 (2002 est). Area: 298 sq km (115 sq miles) **2** a town in N Switzerland, capital of Schaffhausen canton, on the Rhine. Pop: 33 628 (2000) ▶ French name: **Schaffhouse**

Schama *n* Simon (**Michael**). born 1945, British historian, art critic, and broadcaster, based in the US; his work includes *The Embarrassment of Riches* (1987), *Landscape and Memory* (1995), and the BBC television series *A History of Britain* (2000–02)

Schaumburg-Lippe *n* a former state of NW Germany, between Westphalia and Hanover: part of Lower Saxony since 1946

schedule *n* **1** a timed plan of procedure for a project **2** a list of details or items: *the schedule of priorities* **3** a timetable ▷ *vb* **-uling, -uled 4** to plan and arrange (something) to happen at a certain time **5** to make a schedule or include in a schedule [Latin *scheda* sheet of paper]

Scheele *n* Karl Wilhelm. 1742–86, Swedish chemist. He discovered oxygen, independently of Priestley, and many other substances

Scheldt *n* a river in W Europe, rising in NE France and flowing north and northeast through W Belgium to Antwerp, then northwest to the North Sea in the SW Netherlands. Length: 435 km (270 miles). Flemish and Dutch name: **Schelde**. French name: **Escaut**

Schelling *n* Friedrich Wilhelm Joseph von. 1775–1854, German philosopher. He expanded Fichte's idea that there is one reality, the infinite and absolute Ego, by regarding nature as an absolute being working towards self-consciousness. His works include *Ideas towards a Philosophy of Nature* (1797) and *System of Transcendental Idealism* (1800) > **Schellingian** *adj*

schema *n, pl* **-mata** an outline of a plan or theory [Greek: form]

schematic *adj* presented as a diagram or plan > **schematically** *adv*

schematize *or* **-tise** *vb* **-tizing, -tized** *or* **-tising, -tised** to form into or arrange in a systematic arrangement or plan

scheme *n* **1** a systematic plan for a course of action **2** a systematic arrangement of parts or features: *colour scheme* **3** a secret plot **4** a chart, diagram, or outline **5** a plan formally adopted by a government or organization: *a pension scheme* ▷ *vb* **scheming, schemed 6** to plan in an underhand manner [Greek *skhēma* form] ▶ **schemer** *n* ▶ **scheming** *adj, n*

Schepisi *n* Fred, full name *Frederick Alan Schepisi*. born 1939, Australian film director. His films include *The Chant of Jimmie Blacksmith* (1978), *A Cry in the Dark* (1988), *Last Orders* (2001), and *The Eye of the Storm* (2011)

scherzo (skairt-so) *n, pl* **-zos** a quick lively piece of music, often the second or third movement in a sonata or symphony [Italian: joke]

Schiaparelli *n* **1** Elsa. 1896–1973, Italian couturière, noted esp. for the dramatic colours of her designs **2** Giovanni Virginio. 1835–1910, Italian astronomer, who discovered the asteroid Hesperia (1861) and the so-called canals of Mars (1877)

Schiedam *n* a port in the SW Netherlands, in South Holland province west of Rotterdam: gin distilleries. Pop: 76 000 (2003 est)

Schiele *n* Egon. 1890–1918, Austrian painter and draughtsman: a leading exponent of Austrian expressionism

Schiff *n* Sir Andras. born 1953, Hungarian concert pianist; became British citizen in 2001; knighted (2014) for services to music

Schiller *n* Johann Christoph Friedrich von. 1759–1805, German poet, dramatist, historian, and critic. His concern with the ideal freedom of the human spirit to rise above the constraints placed upon it is reflected in his great trilogy *Wallenstein* (1800) and in *Maria Stuart* (1800)

schilling *n* a former monetary unit of Austria [from German: shilling]

schism (skizz-um) *n* the division of a group, esp. a religious group, into opposing factions, due to differences in doctrine [Greek *skhizein* to split] ▶ **schismatic** *adj*

schist (skist) *n* a crystalline rock which splits into thin layers [Greek *skhizein* to split]

schistosomiasis (shiss-ta-so-**my**-a-siss) *n* same as bilharzia

schizo (skit-so) *offensive adj* **1** schizophrenic ▷ *n, pl* **-os 2** a schizophrenic person

schizoid *adj* **1** *psychol* having a personality disorder characterized by extreme shyness and extreme sensitivity **2** *informal* characterized by conflicting or contradictory ideas or attitudes ▷ *n* **3** *offensive* a person who has a schizoid personality

> **USAGE** The use of *schizoid* as a noun can be offensive and should be avoided. Instead you should talk about *a person with a schizoid personality*.

schizophrenia *n* **1** a psychotic disorder characterized by withdrawal from reality, hallucinations, or emotional instability **2** *informal* behaviour that seems to be motivated by contradictory or conflicting principles [Greek *skhizein* to split + *phrēn* mind] ▶ **schizophrenic** *adj, n*

Schlegel *n* **1** August Wilhelm von. 1767–1845, German romantic critic and scholar, noted particularly for his translations of Shakespeare **2** his brother, **Friedrich von**. 1772–1829, German philosopher and critic; a founder of the romantic movement in Germany

Schleiermacher *n* Friedrich Ernst Daniel. 1768–1834, German Protestant theologian and philosopher. His works include *The Christian Faith* (1821–22)

Schlesien *n* the German name for **Silesia**

Schlesinger *n* John (Richard). 1926–2003, British film and theatre director. Films include *Billy Liar* (1963), *Midnight Cowboy* (1969), *Sunday Bloody Sunday* (1971), and *Eye for an Eye* (1995)

Schleswig *n* **1** a fishing port in N Germany, in Schleswig-Holstein state: on an inlet of the Baltic. Pop: 24 288 (2003 est) **2** a former duchy, in the S Jutland Peninsula: annexed by Prussia in 1864; N part returned to Denmark after a plebiscite in 1920; S part forms part of the German state of Schleswig-Holstein. Danish name: **Slesvig**

Schleswig-Holstein *n* a state of N Germany: drained chiefly by the River Elbe; mainly agricultural. Capital: Kiel. Pop: 2 823 000 (2003 est). Area: 15 658 sq km (6045 sq miles)

Schlick *n* Moritz. 1882–1936, German philosopher, working in Austria, who founded (1924) the Vienna Circle to develop the doctrine of logical positivism. His works include the *General Theory of Knowledge* (1918) and *Problems of Ethics* (1930)

Schlieffen *n* Alfred, Count von Schlieffen. 1833–1913, German field marshal, who devised the **Schlieffen Plan** (1905): it was intended to ensure German victory over a Franco-Russian alliance by holding off Russia with minimal strength and swiftly defeating France by a massive flanking movement through the Low Countries. In a modified form, it was unsuccessfully employed in World War I (1914)

Schliemann *n* Heinrich. 1822–90, German archaeologist, who discovered nine superimposed city sites of Troy (1871–90). He also excavated the site of Mycenae (1876)

schmaltz *n* excessive sentimentality, esp. in music [Yiddish: melted fat] ▶ **schmaltzy** *adj*

Schmidt *n* Helmut (Heinrich Waldemar). born 1918, German Social Democrat statesman; chancellor of West Germany (1974–82)

Schnabel *n* Artur. 1882–1951, US pianist and composer, born in Austria

schnapps *n* a strong dry alcoholic drink distilled from potatoes [German *Schnaps*]

Schnittke *n* Alfred. 1934–98, Russian composer: his works include four symphonies, four violin concertos, choral, chamber, and film music

schnitzel *n* a thin slice of meat, esp. veal [German: cutlet]

Schnitzler *n* Arthur. 1862–1931, Austrian dramatist and novelist. His best-known works are *Anatol* (1893) a series of one-act plays, and *Reigen* (1900), both of which reveal his psychological insight and preoccupation with sexuality

Schoenberg *or* **Schönberg** *n* Arnold. 1874–1951, Austrian composer and musical theorist, in the US after 1933. The harmonic idiom of such early works as the string sextet *Verklärte Nacht* (1899) gave way to his development of atonality, as in the song cycle *Pierrot Lunaire* (1912), and later of the twelve-tone technique. He wrote many choral, orchestral, and chamber works and the unfinished opera *Moses and Aaron*

scholar *n* **1** a person who studies an academic subject **2** a student who has a scholarship **3** a pupil [Latin *schola* school] ▶ **scholarly** *adj*

scholarship *n* **1** academic achievement; learning gained by serious study **2** financial aid provided for a scholar because of academic merit

scholastic *adj* **1** of schools, scholars, or education **2** of or relating to scholasticism ▷ *n* **3** a scholarly person **4** a disciple or adherent of scholasticism [Greek *skholastikos* devoted to learning]

scholasticism *n* the system of philosophy, theology, and teaching that dominated medieval Europe and was based on the writings of Aristotle

Schongauer *n* Martin. ?1445–91, German painter and engraver

school¹ *n* **1** a place where children are educated **2** the staff and pupils of a school **3** a regular session of instruction in a school: *we stayed behind after school* **4** a faculty or department specializing in a particular subject: *the dental school* **5** a place or sphere of activity that instructs: *the school of hard knocks* **6** a group of artists, writers, or thinkers, linked by the same style, teachers,

S

or methods **7** *informal* a group assembled for a common purpose, such as gambling: *a card school* ▷ *vb* **8** to educate or train: *she schooled herself to be as ambitious as her sister* [Greek *skholē* leisure spent in the pursuit of knowledge]

school² *n* a group of sea-living animals that swim together, such as fish, whales, or dolphins [Old English *scolu* shoal]

schoolboy *n* a boy attending school

schooled *adj* **schooled in** trained or educated in: *well schooled in history*

schoolgirl *n* a girl attending school

schoolhouse *n* **1** a building used as a school **2** a house attached to a school

schoolie *n Austral informal* a schoolteacher or a high-school student

schoolies week *n Austral informal* a week of post-exam celebrations for students who have just completed their final year of high school

schooling *n* the education a person receives at school

schoolmarm *n informal* **1** a woman schoolteacher **2** a woman who is old-fashioned and easily shocked by bad language or references to sex

schoolmaster *or fem* **schoolmistress** *n* a person who teaches in or runs a school

schoolteacher *n* a person who teaches in a school

school year *n* **1** a twelve-month period, usually of three terms, during which pupils remain in the same class **2** the time during this period when the school is open

schooner *n* **1** a sailing ship with at least two masts, one at the back and one at the front **2** *Brit* a large glass for sherry **3** *US, Canad, Austral and NZ* a large glass for beer [origin unknown]

Schopenhauer *n* Arthur. 1788–1860, German pessimist philosopher. In his chief work, *The World as Will and Idea* (1819), he expounded the view that will is the creative primary factor and idea the secondary receptive factor ▷ **Schopenhauerian** *adj* ▷ **Schopenhauerism** *n*

schottische *n* **1** a 19th-century German dance resembling a slow polka **2** music for this dance [German *der schottische Tanz* the Scottish dance]

Schouten Islands *pl n* a group of islands in the Pacific, off the N coast of Papua New Guinea. Area: 3185 sq km (1230 sq miles)

Schreiner *n* Olive (Emilie Albertina). 1855–1920, South African novelist and feminist writer, whose works include the autobiographical *The Story of an African Farm* (1883) and *Women and Labour* (1911)

Schröder *n* Gerhard. born 1944, German Social Democrat politician; chancellor of Germany from 1998–2005

Schrödinger *n* Erwin. 1887–1961, Austrian physicist, who discovered the wave equation: shared the Nobel prize for physics 1933

Schubert *n* Franz (Peter) (frants). 1797–1828, Austrian composer; the originator and supreme exponent of the modern German lied. His many songs include the cycles *Die Schöne Müllerin* (1823) and *Die Winterreise* (1827). His other works include symphonies and much piano and chamber music including string quartets and the *Trout* piano quintet (1819)

Schumacher *n* **1** Ernst Friedrich. 1911–77, British economist, born in Germany. He is best known for his book *Small is Beautiful* (1973) **2** Michael. born 1969, German motor racing driver: won a record seven Formula One world championships (1994–1995, 2000–2004) and a record 91 Grand Prix

Schuman *n* **1** Robert. 1886–1963, French statesman; prime minister (1947–48). He proposed (1950) pooling the coal and steel resources of W Europe **2** William (Howard). 1910–91, US composer

Schumann *n* **1** Elisabeth. 1885–1952, German soprano, noted esp. for her interpretations of lieder **2** Robert Alexander. 1810–56, German romantic composer, noted esp. for his piano music, such as *Carneval* (1835) and *Kreisleriana* (1838), his songs, and four symphonies

schuss (shooss) *n skiing* a straight high-speed downhill run [from German]

Schuster *n* Leon. born 1951, South African comedian and film maker. His films include *You Must Be Joking* (1986) and *Mr Bones* (2001)

Schwaben *n* the German name for **Swabia**

Schwann *n* Theodor. 1810–82, German physiologist, who founded the theory that all animals consist of cells or cell products

Schütz *n* Heinrich. 1585–1672, German composer, esp. of church music and madrigals

Schwarzkopf *n* **1** Elisabeth. 1915–2006, Austro-British operatic soprano, born in Germany **2** Norman, nicknamed *Stormin' Norman*. 1934–2012, US general. As head of Central Command, the US military district covering the Middle East, he became the victorious commander-in-chief of the US-led forces in the Gulf War (1991)

Schwarzwald *n* the German name for the **Black Forest**

Schweinfurt *n* a city in central Germany, in N Bavaria on the River Main. Pop: 54 601 (2003 est)

Schweitzer *n* Albert. 1875–1965, Franco-German medical missionary, philosopher, theologian, and organist, born in Alsace. He took up medicine in 1905 and devoted most of his life after 1913 to a medical mission at Lambaréné, Gabon: Nobel peace prize 1952

Schweiz *n* the German name for **Switzerland**

Schwerin *n* a city in N Germany, in Mecklenburg-West Pomerania on Lake Schwerin. Pop: 97 694 (2003 est)

Schwitters *n* Kurt. 1887–1948, German dadaist painter and poet, noted for his collages composed of discarded materials

Schwyz *n* **1** a canton of central Switzerland: played an important part in the formation of the Swiss confederation, to which it gave its name. Capital: Schwyz. Pop: 133 300 (2002 est). Area: 908 sq km (351 sq miles) **2** a town in E central Switzerland, capital of Schwyz canton: tourism. Pop: 13 802 (2000)

sciatic *adj* **1** *anatomy* of the hip or the hipbone **2** of or afflicted with sciatica: *a sciatic injury* [Greek *iskhia* hip joint]

sciatica *n* severe pain in the large nerve in the back of the leg

science *n* **1** the study of the nature and behaviour of the physical universe, based on observation, experiment, and measurement **2** the knowledge obtained by these methods **3** any particular branch of this knowledge: *medical science* **4** any body of knowledge organized in a way resembling that of the physical sciences but concerned with other subjects: *political science* [Latin *scientia* knowledge]

science fiction *n* stories and films that make imaginative use of scientific knowledge or theories

Science Museum *n* a museum in London, originating from 1852 and given its present name and site in 1899: contains collections relating to the history of science, technology, and industry

science park *n* an area where scientific research and commercial development are carried on in cooperation

scientific *adj* **1** relating to science or a particular science: *scientific discovery* **2** done in a systematic way, using experiments or tests ▷ **scientifically** *adv*

scientist *n* a person who studies or practises a science

sci-fi *n* short for **science fiction**

Scillonian *adj* **1** of or relating to the Scilly Isles or their inhabitants ▷ *n* **2** a native or inhabitant of the Scilly Isles

Scilly Isles, Scilly Islands *or* **Scillies** *pl n* a group of about 140 small islands (only five inhabited: Bryher, St Agnes, St Martin's, St Mary's, Tresco) off the extreme SW coast of England: tourist centre. Capital: Hugh Town (on St Mary's). Pop: 2100 (2003 est). Area: 16 sq km (6 sq miles)

scimitar n a curved oriental sword [probably from Persian *shimshīr*]

scintilla (sin-till-a) n a very small amount; hint or trace [Latin: a spark]

scintillate vb -lating, -lated to give off (sparks); sparkle [Latin *scintilla* a spark] **> scintillation** n

scintillating adj (of conversation or humour) very lively and amusing

scion (sy-on) n **1** a descendant or young member of a family **2** a shoot of a plant for grafting onto another plant [Old French *cion*]

Scipio n **1** full name *Publius Cornelius Scipio Africanus Major*. 237–183 BC, Roman general. He commanded the Roman invasion of Carthage in the Second Punic War, defeating Hannibal at Zama (202) **2** full name *Publius Cornelius Scipio Aemilianus Africanus Minor*. ?185–129 BC, Roman statesman and general; the grandson by adoption of Scipio Africanus Major. He commanded an army against Carthage in the last Punic War and razed the city to the ground (146). He became the leader (132) of the opposition in Rome to popular reforms

scissors pl n a cutting instrument held in one hand, with two crossed blades pivoted so that they close together on what is to be cut [Old French *cisoires*]

sclera (skleer-a) n biology the tough white substance that forms the outer covering of the eyeball [Greek *sklēros* hard]

sclerosis (skleer-oh-siss) n, pl **-ses** (-seez) pathol an abnormal hardening or thickening of body tissues, esp. of the nervous system or the inner wall of arteries [Greek *sklērōsis* a hardening]

sclerotic (skleer-rot-ik) adj **1** of or relating to the sclera **2** of, relating to, or having sclerosis

scoff[1] vb **1** (often foll. by *at*) to speak in a scornful and mocking way about (something) ▷ n **2** a mocking expression; jeer [probably from Old Norse] **> scoffing** adj, n

scoff[2] vb informal to eat (food) fast and greedily [variant of *scaff* food]

Scofield n (**David**) **Paul**. (1922–2008), English stage and film actor

scold vb **1** to find fault with or rebuke (a person) harshly **2** old-fashioned to use harsh or abusive language ▷ n **3** a person, esp. a woman, who constantly scolds [from Old Norse *skáld*] **> scolding** n

scollop n, vb same as **scallop**

sconce n a bracket fixed to a wall for holding candles or lights [Late Latin *absconsa* dark lantern]

scone n a small plain cake baked in an oven or on a griddle [Scots]

Scone n a parish in Perth and Kinross, E Scotland, consisting of the two villages of New Scone and Old Scone, formerly the site of the Pictish capital and the stone upon which medieval Scottish kings were crowned. The stone was removed to Westminster Abbey by Edward I in 1296; it was returned to Scotland in 1996 and placed in Edinburgh Castle. Scone Palace was rebuilt in the Neo-Gothic style in the 19th century

scoop n **1** a spoonlike tool with a deep bowl, used for handling loose or soft materials such as flour or ice cream **2** the deep shovel of a mechanical digger **3** the amount taken up by a scoop **4** the act of scooping or dredging **5** a news story reported in one newspaper before all the others ▷ vb **6** (often foll. by *up*) to take up and remove (something) with or as if with a scoop **7 scoop out** to hollow out with or as if with a scoop **8** to beat (rival newspapers) in reporting a news item **9** to win (a prize, a large sum of money, etc.) [Germanic]

scoot vb to leave or move quickly [origin unknown]

scooter n **1** a child's small cycle which is ridden by pushing the ground with one foot **2** a light motorcycle with a small engine

Scopas n 395–350 BC, Greek sculptor and architect

scope n **1** opportunity for using abilities: *ample scope for creative work* **2** range of view or grasp: *that is outside my scope* **3** the area covered by an activity or topic: *the scope of his essay was vast* [Greek *skopos* target]

Scopus n **Mount Scopus** a mountain in central Israel, east of Jerusalem: a N extension of the Mount of Olives; site of the Hebrew University (1925). Height: 834 m (2736 ft)

scorbutic (score-byewt-ik) adj of or having scurvy [Medieval Latin *scorbutus*]

scorch vb **1** to burn or become burnt slightly on the surface **2** to parch or shrivel from heat **3** informal to criticize harshly ▷ n **4** a slight burn **5** a mark caused by the application of excessive heat [probably from Old Norse *skorpna* to shrivel up] **> scorching** adj

scorcher n informal a very hot day

score n **1** the total number of points made by a side or individual in a game **2** the act of scoring a point or points: *there was no score and three minutes remained* **3** the **score** informal the actual situation: *what's the score on this business?* **4** old-fashioned a group or set of twenty: *three score years and ten* **5 scores of** lots of: *we received scores of letters* **6** music a written version of a piece of music showing parts for each musician **7 a** the incidental music for a film or play **b** the songs and music for a stage or film musical **8** a mark or scratch **9** a record of money due: *what's the score for the drinks?* **10** an amount recorded as due **11** a reason: *some objections were made on the score of sentiment* **12** a grievance: *a score to settle* **13 over the score** informal excessive or unfair ▷ vb **scoring, scored 14** to gain (a point or points) in a game or contest **15** to make a total score of **16** to keep a record of the score (of) **17** to be worth (a certain number of points) in a game: *red aces score twenty* **18** to make cuts or lines in or on **19** slang to purchase an illegal drug **20** slang to succeed in finding a sexual partner **21** to arrange (a piece of music) for specific instruments or voices **22** to write the music for (a film or play) **23** to achieve (success or an advantage): *your idea scored with the boss* [Old English *scora*]

scoreboard n sport a board for displaying the score of a game or match

scorecard n **1** a card on which scores are recorded in games such as golf **2** a card identifying the players in a sports match, esp. cricket

score off vb to make a clever or insulting reply to what someone has just said: *they spent the evening scoring off each other*

scorer n **1** a player of a sport who scores a goal, run, or point: *Ireland's record goal scorer has announced his retirement* **2** a person who keeps note of the score of a match or competition as it is being played

scoria (score-ee-a) n **1** geology a mass of solidified lava containing many cavities **2** refuse left after ore has been smelted [Latin: dross]

scorn n **1** open contempt for a person or thing ▷ vb **2** to treat with contempt: *she attacked the government for scorning her profession* **3** to refuse to have or do (something) because it is felt to be undesirable or wrong: *youths who scorn traditional morals* [Old French *escharnir*] **> scornful** adj **> scornfully** adv

Scorpio n astrol the eighth sign of the zodiac; the Scorpion [Latin]

scorpion n a small lobster-shaped animal with a sting at the end of a jointed tail [Greek *skorpios*]

Scorsese n **Martin**. born 1942, US film director, whose films include *Taxi Driver* (1976), *Raging Bull* (1980), the controversial *The Last Temptation of Christ* (1988), *Goodfellas* (1990), *Casino* (1995), and *The Departed* (2006), for which he won an Academy Award for Best Director

Scot n a native or inhabitant of Scotland

Scot. **1** Scotland **2** Scottish

scotch vb **1** to put an end to: *she had scotched the idea of bingo in the church* **2** to wound without killing [origin unknown]

S

Scotch¹ *not standard adj* **1** same as **Scottish** ▷ *pl n* **2** the Scotch the Scots

> **USAGE** In the north of England and in Scotland, *Scotch* is not used outside fixed expressions such as *Scotch whisky*. The use of *Scotch* for *Scots* or *Scottish* is otherwise felt to be incorrect, esp. when applied to people.

Scotch² *n* whisky distilled in Scotland from fermented malted barley

Scotch broth *n Brit* a thick soup made from mutton or beef stock, vegetables, and pearl barley

Scotch egg *n* a hard-boiled egg encased in sausage meat and breadcrumbs, and fried

Scotch mist *n* a heavy wet mist or drizzle

scot-free *adv, adj* without harm or punishment: *the real crooks got off scot-free* [obsolete *scot* a tax]

Scotland *n* a country that is part of the United Kingdom, occupying the north of Great Britain; the English and Scottish thrones were united under one monarch in 1603 and the parliaments in 1707; a devolved Scottish parliament was established in 1999; referendum (2014) decided in favour of Scotland staying within the UK. Scotland consists of the Highlands in the north, the central Lowlands, and hilly uplands in the south; has a deeply indented coastline, about 800 offshore islands (mostly in the west), and many lochs. Capital: Edinburgh. Pop: 5 295 403 (2011 est). Area: 78 768 sq km (30 412 sq miles). Related adjectives: **Scots**, **Caledonian**, **Scottish**

Scotland Yard *n* the headquarters of the police force of metropolitan London

Scots *adj* **1** of Scotland ▷ *n* **2** any of the English dialects spoken or written in Scotland

Scotsman *or fem* **Scotswoman** *n, pl* **-men** *or* **-women** a native or inhabitant of Scotland

Scots pine *n* **1** a coniferous tree found in Europe and Asia, with needle-like leaves and brown cones **2** the wood of this tree

Scott *n* **1 Adam** (**Derek**). born 1980, Australian golfer: first Australian to win the US Masters (2013) **2** Sir **George Gilbert**. 1811–78, British architect, prominent in the Gothic revival. He restored many churches and cathedrals and designed the Albert Memorial (1863) and St Pancras Station (1865) **3** his grandson, **Sir Giles Gilbert**. 1880–1960, British architect, whose designs include the Anglican cathedral in Liverpool (1904–78) and the new Waterloo Bridge (1939–45) **4 Paul** (**Mark**). 1920–78, British novelist, who is best known for the series of novels known as the "Raj Quartet": *The Jewel in the Crown* (1966), *The Day of the Scorpion* (1968), *The Towers of Silence* (1972), and *A Division of the Spoils* (1975). *Staying On* (1977) won the Booker Prize **5** Sir **Peter** (**Markham**). 1909–89, British naturalist, wildlife artist, and conservationist, noted esp. for his paintings of birds. He founded (1946) the Slimbridge refuge for waterfowl in Gloucestershire **6** his father, **Robert Falcon**. 1868–1912, British naval officer and explorer of the Antarctic. He commanded two Antarctic expeditions (1901–04; 1910–12) and reached the South Pole on Jan 18, 1912, shortly after Amundsen; he and the rest of his party died on the return journey **7** Sir **Walter**. 1771–1832, Scottish romantic novelist and poet. He is remembered chiefly for the "Waverley" historical novels, including *Waverley* (1814), *Rob Roy* (1817), *The Heart of Midlothian* (1818), inspired by Scottish folklore and history, and *Ivanhoe* (1819), *Kenilworth* (1821), *Quentin Durward* (1823), and *Redgauntlet* (1824). His narrative poems include *The Lay of the Last Minstrel* (1805), *Marmion* (1808), and *The Lady of the Lake* (1810)

Scottish *adj* of or relating to Scotland or its inhabitants

Scottish Borders *n* a council area in SE Scotland, on the English border: created in 1996, it has the same boundaries as the former Borders Region: it is mainly hilly, with agriculture (esp. sheep farming) the chief economic activity. Administrative centre: Newtown St Boswells. Pop: 108 280 (2003 est). Area: 4734 sq km (1827 sq miles)

scoundrel *n old-fashioned* a person who cheats and deceives [origin unknown]

scour¹ *vb* **1** to clean or polish (a surface) by rubbing with something rough **2** to clear (a channel) by the force of water ▷ *n* **3** the act of scouring [Old French *escurer*] **> scourer** *n*

scour² *vb* **1** to search thoroughly and energetically: *he had scoured auction salerooms* **2** to move quickly over (land) in search or pursuit [probably from Old Norse *skūr* shower]

scourge *n* **1** a person who or thing that causes affliction or suffering **2** a whip formerly used for punishing people ▷ *vb* **scourging, scourged 3** to cause severe suffering to **4** to whip [Latin *excoriare* to whip]

Scouse *Brit informal n* **1** Also called: **Scouser** a native or inhabitant of Liverpool **2** the Liverpool dialect ▷ *adj* **3** of or relating to Liverpool, its inhabitants, or their dialect [from *lobscouse* a sailor's stew]

scout *n* **1** *military* a person sent to find out the position of the enemy **2** same as **talent scout 3** the act or an instance of scouting ▷ *vb* **4** to examine or observe (something) in order to obtain information **5 scout about** *or* **around** to go in search of something [Old French *ascouter* to listen to]

Scout *or* **scout** *n* a member of the Scout Association, an organization for young people which aims to develop character and promote outdoor activities **> Scouting** *n*

scow *n* an unpowered barge used for carrying freight [Low German *schalde*]

scowl *vb* **1** to have an angry or bad-tempered facial expression ▷ *n* **2** an angry or bad-tempered facial expression [probably from Old Norse]

scrabble *vb* **-bling, -bled 1** to scrape at or grope for something with hands, feet, or claws: *scrabbling with his feet to find a foothold* **2** to move one's hands about in order to find something one cannot see: *scrabbling in her handbag for a comb* [Middle Dutch *schrabbelen*]

Scrabble *n trademark* a board game in which words are formed by placing letter tiles in a pattern similar to a crossword puzzle

scrag *n* **1** the thin end of a neck of veal or mutton **2** a thin or scrawny person or animal [perhaps variant of *crag*]

scraggy *adj* **-gier, -giest** unpleasantly thin and bony **> scragginess** *n*

scram¹ *vb* **scramming, scrammed** *informal* to leave very quickly [from *scramble*]

scram² *n* **1** an emergency shutdown of a nuclear reactor ▷ *vb* **scramming, scrammed 2** (of a nuclear reactor) to shut down or be shut down in an emergency [perhaps from SCRAM¹]

scramble *vb* **-bling, -bled 1** to climb or crawl hurriedly by using the hands to aid movement **2** to go hurriedly or in a disorderly manner **3** to compete with others in a rough and undignified way: *spectators scrambled for the best seats* **4** to jumble together in a haphazard manner **5** to cook (eggs that have been whisked up with milk) in a pan **6** *military* (of a crew or aircraft) to take off quickly in an emergency **7** to make (transmitted speech) unintelligible by the use of an electronic scrambler ▷ *n* **8** the act of scrambling **9** a climb or trek over difficult ground **10** a rough and undignified struggle to gain possession of something **11** *military* an immediate takeoff of crew or aircraft in an emergency **12** *Brit* a motorcycle race across rough open ground [blend of SCRABBLE + RAMP]

scrambler *n* an electronic device that makes broadcast or telephone messages unintelligible without a special receiver

scramjet *n* **a** a type of ramjet in which the forward motion of the craft forces oxygen to mix with fuel (usually hydrogen) at supersonic speeds within a duct in the engine **b** an aircraft powered by such an engine [from s(*upersonic*) + c(*ombustion*) + RAMJET]

Scranton *n* an industrial city in NE Pennsylvania: university (1888). Pop: 74 320 (2003 est)

scrap¹ *n* **1** a small piece of something larger; fragment **2** waste material or used articles, often collected and reprocessed **3** scraps pieces of leftover food ▷ *vb* **scrapping, scrapped** **4** to discard as useless [Old Norse *skrap*]

scrap² *informal* *n* **1** a fight or quarrel ▷ *vb* **scrapping, scrapped** **2** to quarrel or fight [perhaps from *scrape*]

scrapbook *n* a book of blank pages in which newspaper cuttings or pictures are stuck

scrape *vb* **scraping, scraped** **1** to move (a rough or sharp object) across (a surface) **2** (often foll. by *away* or *off*) to remove (a layer) by rubbing **3** to produce a grating sound by rubbing against (something else) **4** to injure or damage by scraping: *he had scraped his knees* **5 scrimp and scrape** See scrimp (2) ▷ *n* **6** the act or sound of scraping **7** a scraped place: *a scrape on the car door* **8** *informal* an awkward or embarrassing situation **9** *informal* a conflict or struggle [Old English *scrapian*] **> scraper** *n*

scrape through *vb* to succeed in or survive with difficulty: *both teams had scraped through their semifinals*

scrape together *or* **scrape up** *vb* to collect with difficulty: *he scraped together enough money to travel*

scrapheap *n* **on the scrapheap** (of people or things) no longer required: *I was tossed on the scrapheap at a very early age*

scrappy *adj* **-pier, -piest** badly organized or done: *a scrappy draft of a chapter of my thesis*

scratch *vb* **1** to mark or cut (the surface of something) with a rough or sharp instrument **2** (often foll. by *at, out,* etc.) to tear or dig with the nails or claws **3** to scrape (the surface of the skin) with the nails to relieve itching **4** to rub against (the skin) causing a slight cut **5** to make or cause to make a grating sound **6** (sometimes foll. by *out*) to erase or cross out **7** to withdraw from a race or (in the US) an election ▷ *n* **8** the act of scratching **9** a slight cut on a person's or an animal's body **10** a mark made by scratching **11** a slight grating sound **12 from scratch** *informal* from the very beginning **13 not up to scratch** *informal* not up to standard ▷ *adj* **14** put together at short notice: *a scratch team* **15** *sport* with no handicap allowed: *a scratch golfer* [Germanic] **> scratchy** *adj*

scratchcard *n* a ticket that reveals whether or not the holder is eligible for a prize when the surface is removed by scratching

scratchie *n Austral and NZ informal* short for **scratchcard**

scratching *n music* a sound produced when the record groove in contact with the stylus of a record player is moved back and forth by hand

scrawl *vb* **1** to write carelessly or hastily ▷ *n* **2** careless or scribbled writing [perhaps blend of SPRAWL + CRAWL] **> scrawly** *adj*

scrawny *adj* **scrawnier, scrawniest** very thin and bony [dialect *scranny*] **> scrawniness** *n*

scream *vb* **1** to make a sharp piercing cry or sound because of fear or pain **2** (of a machine) to make a high-pitched noise **3** to laugh wildly **4** to utter with a scream: *he screamed abuse up into the sky* **5** to be unpleasantly conspicuous: *bad news screaming out from the headlines* ▷ *n* **6** a sharp piercing cry or sound, esp. of fear or pain **7** *informal* a very funny person or thing [Germanic]

scree *n* a pile of rock fragments at the foot of a cliff or hill, often forming a sloping heap [Old English *scrīthan* to slip]

screech¹ *n* **1** a shrill or high-pitched sound or cry ▷ *vb* **2** to utter a shrill cry [earlier *scritch*, imitative] **> screechy** *adj*

screech² *n Canad* a dark rum [origin unknown]

screech owl *n* **1** *Brit* same as **barn owl 2** a small North American barn owl

screed *n* a long tiresome speech or piece of writing [probably from Old English *scrēade* shred]

screen *n* **1** the blank surface of a television set, VDU, or radar receiver, on which a visible image is formed **2** the white surface on which films or slides are projected **3 the screen** the film industry or films collectively **4** a light movable frame, panel, or partition used to shelter, divide, or conceal **5** anything that shelters, protects, or conceals: *a screen of leaves blocking out the sun* **6** a frame containing a mesh that is used to keep out insects ▷ *vb* **7** (sometimes foll. by *off*) to shelter, protect, or conceal with or as if with a screen **8** to test or check (an individual or group) so as to assess suitability for a task or to detect the presence of a disease or weapons: *women screened for breast cancer* **9** to show (a film) in the cinema or show (a programme) on television [Old French *escren*]

screenplay *n* the script for a film, including instructions for sets and camera work

screen process *n* a method of printing by forcing ink through a fine mesh of silk or nylon, some parts of which have been treated so as not to let the ink pass

screen saver *n computers* software that produces changing images on a monitor when the computer is operating but idle

screenshot *n* an image created by copying part or all of the display on a computer screen at a particular moment

screenwriter *n* a person who writes screenplays

screw *n* **1** a metal pin with a spiral ridge along its length, twisted into materials to fasten them together **2** a threaded cylindrical rod that engages with a similarly threaded cylindrical hole **3** a thread in a cylindrical hole corresponding with the one on the screw with which it is designed to engage **4** anything resembling a screw in shape **5** *slang* a prison guard **6** *taboo, slang* an act of or partner in sexual intercourse **7 have a screw loose** *informal* to be insane **8 put the screws on** *slang* to use force on or threatening behaviour against ▷ *vb* **9** to rotate (a screw or bolt) so as to drive it into or draw it out of a material **10** to twist or turn: *she screwed up the sheet of paper* **11** to attach or fasten with or as if with a screw or screws **12** *informal* to take advantage of, esp. illegally: *screwed by big business* **13** *informal* to distort or contort: *his face was screwed up in pain* **14** (often foll. by *out of*) *informal* to force out of; extort **15** *taboo, slang* to have sexual intercourse (with) **16 have one's head screwed on the right way** *informal* to be sensible ▶ See also **screw up** [French *escroe*]

screwball *slang, chiefly US and Canad* *n* **1** an odd or eccentric person ▷ *adj* **2** crazy or eccentric: *a screwball comedy*

screwdriver *n* **1** a tool used for turning screws, consisting of a long thin metal rod with a flattened tip that fits into a slot in the head of the screw **2** a drink consisting of orange juice and vodka

screw top *n* **1** a bottle top that screws onto the bottle, allowing the bottle to be resealed after use **2** a bottle with such a top

screw up *vb* **1** *informal* to mishandle or spoil (something): *that screws up all my arrangements* **2** to twist out of shape or distort **3 screw up one's courage** to force oneself to be brave **> screwed-up** *adj*

screwy *adj* **screwier, screwiest** *informal* crazy or eccentric

Scriabin *or* **Skryabin** *n* Aleksandr Nikolayevich. 1872–1915, Russian composer, whose works came increasingly to express his theosophic beliefs. He wrote many piano works; his orchestral compositions include *Prometheus* (1911)

scribble *vb* **-bling, -bled** **1** to write or draw quickly and roughly **2** to make meaningless or illegible marks (on) ▷ *n* **3** something written or drawn quickly or roughly **4** meaningless or illegible marks [Latin *scribere* to write] **> scribbler** *n* **> scribbly** *adj*

scribe *n* **1** a person who made handwritten copies of manuscripts or documents before the invention of printing **2** *Bible* a recognized scholar and teacher of the Jewish Law [Latin *scriba* clerk]

Scribe *n* Augustin Eugène. 1791–1861, French author or coauthor of over 350 vaudevilles, comedies, and libretti for light opera

scrimmage *n* **1** a rough or disorderly struggle ▷ *vb* **-maging, -maged 2** to take part in a scrimmage [earlier *scrimish*]

scrimp *vb* **1** to be very sparing in the use of something: *they were scrimping by on the last of the potatoes* **2 scrimp and save** or **scrape** to spend as little money as possible [Scots]

scrip¹ *n finance* a certificate representing a claim to shares or stocks [short for *subscription receipt*]

scrip² or **script** *n informal* a medical prescription [from PRESCRIPTION]

script *n* **1** the text of a play, TV programme, or film for the use of performers **2** an alphabet or system of writing: *Cyrillic script* **3** a candidate's answer paper in an examination **4** handwriting **5** a typeface which looks like handwriting ▷ *vb* **6** to write a script for [Latin *scriptum* something written]

scripture *n* the sacred writings of a religion [Latin *scriptura* written material] ❯ **scriptural** *adj*

Scripture *n Christianity* the Old and New Testaments

scriptwriter *n* a person who writes scripts, esp. for a film or TV programme ❯ **scriptwriting** *n*

scrofula *n no longer in technical use* tuberculosis of the lymphatic glands [Medieval Latin] ❯ **scrofulous** *adj*

scroggin *n NZ* a mixture of nuts and dried fruits

scroll *n* **1** a roll of parchment or paper, usually inscribed with writing **2** an ancient book in the form of a roll of parchment, papyrus, or paper **3** a decorative carving or moulding resembling a scroll ▷ *vb* **4** *computers* to move (text) on a screen in order to view a section that cannot be fitted into a single display [Middle English *scrowle*]

Scrooge *n* a mean or miserly person [after a character in Dickens' story *A Christmas Carol*]

scrotum *n* the pouch of skin containing the testicles in most male mammals [Latin]

scrounge *vb* **scrounging, scrounged** *informal* to get (something) by asking for it rather than buying it or working for it [dialect *scrunge* to steal] ❯ **scrounger** *n*

scrub¹ *vb* **scrubbing, scrubbed 1** to rub (something) hard in order to clean it **2** to remove (dirt) by rubbing with a brush and water **3 scrub up** (of a surgeon) to wash the hands and arms thoroughly before operating **4** *informal* to delete or cancel (an idea or plan) ▷ *n* **5** the act of scrubbing [Middle Low German *schrubben* or Middle Dutch *schrobben*]

scrub² *n* **1** vegetation consisting of stunted trees or bushes growing in a dry area **2** an area of dry land covered with such vegetation ▷ *adj* **3** stunted or inferior: *scrub pines* [variant of *shrub*]

scrubber *n* **1** *Brit and Austral offensive, slang* a woman who has many sexual partners **2** a device that removes pollutants from the gases that are produced when coal is burned industrially

scrubby *adj* **-bier, -biest 1** (of land) rough, dry, and covered with scrub **2** (of plants) stunted **3** *Brit informal* shabby or untidy

scrubs *pl n* the hygienic clothing worn by surgeons and other operating-theatre staff during an operation

scruff¹ *n* the nape of the neck: *the sergeant had him by the scruff of the neck* [perhaps from Old Norse *skoft* hair]

scruff² *n informal* a very untidy person

scruffy *adj* **scruffier, scruffiest** dirty and untidy in appearance

scrum *n* **1** *rugby* a formation in which players from each side form a tight pack and push against each other in an attempt to get the ball, which is thrown on the ground between them **2** *informal* a disorderly struggle ▷ *vb* **scrumming, scrummed 3** (usually foll. by *down*) *rugby* to form a scrum [from *scrummage*]

scrum half *n rugby* a player who puts in the ball at

scrums and tries to regain its possession in order to pass it to his team's backs

scrummage *n, vb* **-maging, -maged 1** *rugby* same as **scrum 2** same as **scrimmage** [variant of *scrimmage*]

scrump *vb Brit dialect* to steal (apples) from an orchard or garden [variant of *scrimp*]

scrumptious *adj informal* delicious or very attractive [probably changed from *sumptuous*]

scrumpy *n Brit* a rough dry cider brewed in the West Country of England [dialect *scrump* withered apples]

scrunch *vb* **1** to press or crush noisily or be pressed or crushed noisily ▷ *n* **2** the act or sound of scrunching: *the scrunch of tyres on gravel* [variant of *crunch*]

scrunchie *n* a loop of elastic covered loosely with fabric, used to hold the hair in a ponytail

scruple *n* **1** a doubt or hesitation as to what is morally right in a certain situation: *he had no scruples about the drug trade* ▷ *vb* **-pling, -pled 2** to have doubts (about), esp. on moral grounds [Latin *scrupulus* a small weight]

scrupulous *adj* **1** taking great care to do what is fair, honest, or morally right **2** very careful or precise: *scrupulous attention to detail* [Latin *scrupulosus*] ❯ **scrupulously** *adv*

scrutinize or **-nise** *vb* **-nizing, -nized** or **-nising, -nised** to examine carefully or in minute detail

scrutiny *n, pl* **-nies 1** very careful study or observation **2** a searching look [Late Latin *scrutari* to search]

scuba (skew-ba) *n* an apparatus used in skin diving, consisting of cylinders containing compressed air attached to a breathing apparatus [*s(elf-)c(ontained) u(nderwater) b(reathing) a(pparatus)*]

scud *vb* **scudding, scudded 1** (esp. of clouds) to move along quickly **2** *nautical* to run before a gale ▷ *n* **3** the act of scudding **4** spray, rain, or clouds driven by the wind [probably Scandinavian]

scuff *vb* **1** to drag (the feet) while walking **2** to scrape (one's shoes) by doing so ▷ *n* **3** a mark caused by scuffing **4** the act or sound of scuffing [probably imitative]

scuffle *vb* **-fling, -fled 1** to fight in a disorderly manner ▷ *n* **2** a short disorganized fight **3** a scuffling sound [Scandinavian]

scull *n* **1** a single oar moved from side to side over the back of a boat **2** one of a pair of small oars, both of which are pulled by one oarsman **3** a racing boat rowed by one oarsman pulling two oars ▷ *vb* **4** to row (a boat) with a scull [origin unknown] ❯ **sculler** *n*

scullery *n, pl* **-leries** *chiefly Brit* a small room where washing-up and other kitchen work is done [Anglo-Norman *squillerie*]

Scullin *n* James Henry. 1876–1953, Australian statesman; prime minister of Australia (1929–31)

scullion *n archaic* a servant employed to do the hard work in a kitchen [Old French *escouillon* cleaning cloth]

sculpt *vb* same as **sculpture**

sculptor or *fem* **sculptress** *n* a person who makes sculptures

sculpture *n* **1** the art of making figures or designs in wood, plaster, stone, or metal **2** works or a work made in this way ▷ *vb* **-turing, -tured 3** to carve (a material) into figures or designs **4** to represent (a person or thing) in sculpture **5** to form or be formed in the manner of sculpture: *limestone sculptured by fast-flowing streams* [Latin *sculptura* a carving] ❯ **sculptural** *adj*

scum *n* **1** a layer of impure or waste matter that forms on the surface of a liquid: *the build-up of soap scum* **2** a person or people regarded as worthless or criminal ▷ *vb* **scumming, scummed 3** to remove scum from **4** *rare* to form a layer of or become covered with scum [Germanic] ❯ **scummy** *adj*

scumbag *n slang* an offensive or despicable person [perhaps from earlier US sense: condom]

scungy (skun-jee) *adj* **scungier, scungiest** *Austral and NZ slang* miserable, sordid, or dirty [origin unknown]

scunner *dialect, chiefly Scot vb* **1** to produce a feeling of dislike in ▷ n **2 take a scunner to** to take a strong dislike to **3** a person or thing that is disliked [Scots *skunner*]

Scunthorpe n a town in E England, in North Lincolnshire unitary authority, Lincolnshire: developed rapidly after the discovery of local iron ore in the late 19th century; iron and steel industries have declined. Pop: 72 660 (2001)

scupper[1] *n nautical* a drain or spout in a ship's side allowing water on the deck to flow overboard [origin unknown]

scupper[2] *vb* **1** *Brit and NZ slang* to defeat or ruin: *a deliberate attempt to scupper the peace talks* **2** to sink (one's ship) deliberately [origin unknown]

scurf *n* **1** same as **dandruff 2** any flaky or scaly matter sticking to or peeling off a surface [Old English] **> scurfy** *adj*

scurrilous *adj* untrue or unfair, insulting, and designed to damage a person's reputation: *scurrilous allegations* [Latin *scurra* buffoon] **> scurrility** *n*

scurry *vb* **-ries, -rying, -ried 1** to run quickly with short steps ▷ *n, pl* **-ries 2** a quick hurrying movement or the sound of this movement **3** a short shower of rain or snow [probably from *hurry-scurry*]

scurvy *n* **1** a disease caused by a lack of vitamin C, resulting in weakness, spongy gums, and bleeding beneath the skin ▷ *adj* **-vier, -viest 2** *old-fashioned* deserving contempt [from *scurf*] **> scurviness** *n*

scut *n* the short tail of animals such as the deer and rabbit [probably from Old Norse]

Scutari *n* **1** the former name of **Üsküdar 2** the Italian name for **Shkodër**

scuttle[1] *n* same as **coal scuttle** [Latin *scutella* bowl]

scuttle[2] *vb* **-tling, -tled 1** to run with short quick steps ▷ *n* **2** a hurried pace or run [probably from *scud*]

scuttle[3] *vb* **-tling, -tled 1** *nautical* to cause (a ship) to sink by making holes in the sides or bottom **2** to ruin (hopes or plans) or have them ruined: *a new policy scuttled by popular resistance* ▷ *n* **3** *nautical* a small hatch in a ship's deck or side [Spanish *escotilla* a small opening]

Scylla (**sill-a**) *n* **1** (in classical mythology) a sea monster believed to drown sailors navigating the Straits of Messina **2 between Scylla and Charybdis** in an awkward situation in which avoidance of either of two dangers means exposure to the other

Scyros *n* a variant spelling of **Skyros**

scythe *n* **1** a long-handled tool for cutting grass or grain, with a curved sharpened blade that is swung parallel to the ground ▷ *vb* **scything, scythed 2** to cut (grass or grain) with a scythe [Old English *sīgthe*]

Scythia *n* an ancient region of SE Europe and Asia, north of the Black Sea: now part of Ukraine

Scythian *adj* **1** of or relating to ancient Scythia, its inhabitants, or their language ▷ *n* **2** a member of an ancient nomadic people of Scythia **3** the extinct language of this people, belonging to the East Iranian branch of the Indo-European family

SD South Dakota

S. Dak. South Dakota

Sderot *n* a city in the W Negev in S Israel, close to the border with Gaza; a target for sustained rocket attack by Hamas since 2001. Population: 19 800 (2006 est)

SDI Strategic Defense Initiative

SDLP (in Northern Ireland) Social Democratic and Labour Party

Se *chem* selenium

SE southeast(ern)

sea *n* **1 the sea** the mass of salt water that covers three-quarters of the earth's surface **2 a** one of the smaller seas that are part of this: *the Irish Sea* **b** a large inland area of water: *the Caspian Sea* **3** the area on or close to the edge of the sea, esp. as a place where holidays are taken: *a day by the sea* **4** strong and uneven swirling movement of waves: *rough seas* **5** anything resembling the sea in size or movement: *a sea of red and yellow flags* **6 at sea a** on the

ocean **b** in a state of confusion or uncertainty **7 go to sea** to become a sailor **8 put out to sea** to start a sea voyage [Old English *sǣ*]

sea anchor *n nautical* a canvas-covered frame, dragged in the water behind a ship to slow it down or reduce drifting

sea anemone *n* a marine animal with a round body and rings of tentacles which trap food from the water

sea bird *n* a bird that lives on or near the sea

seaboard *n* land bordering on the sea

Seaborg *n* Glenn Theodore. 1912–99, US chemist and nuclear physicist. With E.M. McMillan, he discovered several transuranic elements, including plutonium (1940), curium, and americium (1944), and shared a Nobel prize for chemistry 1951

seaborgium *n chem* a synthetic element. Symbol: **Sg** [after Glenn **Seaborg**]

seaborne *adj* **1** carried on or by the sea **2** transported by ship: *seaborne reinforcements*

sea breeze *n* a breeze blowing inland from the sea

sea cow *n* **1** a whalelike mammal such as a dugong or manatee **2** *archaic* a walrus

sea dog *n* an experienced or old sailor

seafarer *n* **1** a traveller who goes by sea **2** a sailor

seafaring *adj* **1** travelling by sea **2** working as a sailor ▷ *n* **3** the act of travelling by sea **4** the work of a sailor

seafood *n* edible saltwater fish or shellfish

seafront *n* a built-up area facing the sea

seagoing *adj* built for travelling on the sea

sea-green *adj* bluish-green

seagull *n* same as **gull**

Seahenge *n* a Bronze Age timber circle discovered off the coast of Norfolk in E England. Dating from 2050 BC, it is thought to have been used as a ceremonial site

sea horse *n* a small marine fish with a horselike head, which swims upright

Sea Islands *pl n* a chain of islands in the Atlantic off the coasts of South Carolina, Georgia, and Florida

sea kale *n* a European coastal plant with broad fleshy leaves and asparagus-like shoots that can be eaten

seal[1] *n* **1** a special design impressed on a piece of wax, lead, or paper, fixed to a letter or document as a mark of authentication **2** a stamp or signet ring engraved with a design to form such an impression **3** a substance placed over an envelope or container, so that it cannot be opened without the seal being broken **4** something that serves as an official confirmation of approval: *seal of approval* **5** any substance or device used to close an opening tightly **6 set the seal on** to confirm: *the experience set the seal on their friendship* ▷ *vb* **7** to close or secure with or as if with a seal: *once the manuscripts were sealed up, they were forgotten about* **8 seal off** to enclose or isolate (a place) completely **9** to close tightly so as to make airtight or watertight **10** to inject a compound around the edges of (something) to make it airtight or watertight **11** to attach a seal to or stamp with a seal **12** to finalize or authorize **13 seal one's fate** to make sure one dies or fails **14 seal one's lips** to promise not to reveal a secret [Latin *signum* a sign] **> sealable** *adj*

seal[2] *n* **1** a fish-eating mammal with four flippers, which lives in the sea but comes ashore to breed **2** sealskin ▷ *vb* **3** to hunt seals [Old English *seolh*]

sealant *n* any substance, such as wax, used for sealing, esp. to make airtight or watertight

sea legs *pl n informal* the ability to maintain one's balance on board ship and to avoid being seasick

sea level *n* the average level of the sea's surface in relation to the land

sealing wax *n* a hard material made of shellac and turpentine, which softens when heated and which is used to make a seal

sea lion *n* a type of large seal found in the Pacific Ocean

Sea Lord *n* (in Britain) a naval officer on the admiralty board of the Ministry of Defence

S

sealskin *n* the skin or prepared fur of a seal, used to make coats

seam *n* **1** the line along which pieces of fabric are joined by stitching **2** a ridge or line made by joining two edges: *the seam between the old and the new buildings* **3** a long narrow layer of coal, marble, or ore formed between layers of other rocks **4** a mark or line like a seam, such as a wrinkle or scar ▷ *adj* **5** *cricket* of a style of bowling in which the bowler uses the stitched seam round the ball in order to make it swing in flight and after touching the ground: *a seam bowler* ▷ *vb* **6** to join together by or as if by a seam **7** to mark with furrows or wrinkles [Old English *sēam*]

seaman *n*, *pl* **-men 1** a man ranking below an officer in a navy **2** a sailor

seamanship *n* skill in navigating and operating a ship

seamer *or* **seam bowler** *n cricket* a fast bowler who makes the ball bounce on its seam so that it will change direction

seamless *adj* **1** (of a garment) without seams **2** continuous or flowing: *a seamless performance* ▷ **seamlessness** *n*

seamstress *n* a woman who sews, esp. professionally

seamy *adj* **seamier**, **seamiest** involving the sordid and unpleasant aspects of life, such as crime, prostitution, poverty, and violence ▷ **seaminess** *n*

seance *or* **séance** (say-onss) *n* a meeting at which a spiritualist attempts to communicate with the spirits of the dead [French]

seaplane *n* an aircraft that is designed to land on and take off from water

seaport *n* a town or city with a harbour for boats and ships

sear *vb* **1** to scorch or burn the surface of **2** to cause to wither [Old English *sēarian* to become withered]

search *vb* **1** to look through (a place) thoroughly in order to find someone or something **2** to examine (a person) for hidden objects **3** to look at or examine (something) closely: *I searched my heart for one good thing she had done* **4 search out** to find by searching **5** to make a search **6 search me** *informal* I don't know ▷ *n* **7** an attempt to find something or someone by looking somewhere [Old French *cerchier*]

search engine *n computers* an internet service enabling users to search for items of interest

Search Engine Optimization *n* the process of improving a website's page ranking in a search engine

searching *adj* keen or thorough: *a searching analysis* ▷ **searchingly** *adv*

searchlight *n* **1** a light with a powerful beam that can be shone in any direction **2** the beam of light produced by this device

search warrant *n* a legal document allowing a policeman to enter and search premises

Searle *n* Ronald (**William Fordham**). 1920–2011, British cartoonist, best known as the creator of the schoolgirls of St Trinian's

seascape *n* a drawing, painting, or photograph of a scene at sea

Sea Scout *n* a member of the branch of the Scouts which gives training in seamanship

seashell *n* the empty shell of a marine mollusc

seashore *n* land bordering on the sea

seasick *adj* suffering from nausea and dizziness caused by the movement of a ship at sea ▷ **seasickness** *n*

seaside *n* an area, esp. a holiday resort, bordering on the sea

season *n* **1** one of the four divisions of the year (spring, summer, autumn, and winter), each of which has characteristic weather conditions **2** a period of the year characterized by particular conditions or activities: *the typhoon season*; *the football season* **3** the period during which any particular species of animal, bird, or fish is legally permitted to be caught or killed: *the deer season* **4** any

definite or indefinite period: *the busy season* **5** any period during which a show or play is performed at one venue: *the show ran for three seasons* **6 in season a** (of game) permitted to be killed **b** (of fresh food) readily available **c** (of animals) ready to mate ▷ *vb* **7** to add herbs, salt, pepper, or spice to (food) in order to enhance the flavour **8** (in the preparation of timber) to dry and harden **9** to make experienced: *old men seasoned by living* [Latin *satio* a sowing] ▷ **seasoned** *adj*

seasonable *adj* **1** suitable for the season: *a seasonable Christmas snow scene* **2** coming or happening just at the right time: *seasonable advice*

seasonal *adj* of or depending on a certain season or seasons of the year: *seasonal employment* ▷ **seasonally** *adv*

seasoning *n* something that is added to food to enhance the flavour

season ticket *n* a ticket for a series of events or number of journeys, usually bought at a reduced rate

seat *n* **1** a piece of furniture designed for sitting on, such as a chair **2** the part of a chair or other piece of furniture on which one sits **3** a place to sit in a theatre, esp. one that requires a ticket: *there were two empty front-row seats at the pageant* **4** the buttocks **5** the part of a garment covering the buttocks **6** the part or surface on which an object rests **7** the place or centre in which something is based: *the seat of government* **8** *Brit* a country mansion **9** a membership or the right to membership of a legislative or administrative body: *a seat on the council* **10** *chiefly Brit* a parliamentary constituency **11** the manner in which a rider sits on a horse ▷ *vb* **12** to bring to or place on a seat **13** to provide seats for: *the dining hall seats 150 people* **14** to set firmly in place [Old English *gesete*]

seat belt *n* a strap attached to a car or aircraft seat, worn across the body to prevent a person being thrown forward in the event of a collision

seating *n* **1** seats which are provided somewhere, esp. in a public place: *the grandstand has seating for 10 000*; *hard plastic seating* ▷ *adj* **2** of or relating to the provision of places to sit: *the delegation leader complained about the seating arrangements*

Seaton Valley *n* a region in NE England, in SE Northumberland: consists of a group of former coal-mining villages

Seattle *n* a port in W Washington, on the isthmus between Lake Washington and Puget Sound: the largest city in the state and chief commercial centre of the Northwest; two universities. Pop: 569 101 (2003 est)

sea urchin *n* a small sea animal with a round body enclosed in a spiny shell

seaward *adv* also: **seawards 1** towards the sea ▷ *adj* **2** directed or moving towards the sea

seawater *n* salt water from the sea

seaweed *n* any plant growing in the sea or on the seashore

seaworthy *adj* (of a ship) in a fit condition for a sea voyage ▷ **seaworthiness** *n*

sebaceous *adj* of, like, or secreting fat [Latin *sebum* tallow]

sebaceous glands *pl n* the small glands in the skin that secrete oil into hair follicles and onto most of the body surface

Sebastian *n* Saint. died ?288 AD, Christian martyr. According to tradition, he was first shot with arrows and then beaten to death. Feast day: Jan 20

Sebastopol *n* the English name for **Sevastopol**

sebum (see-bum) *n* the oily substance secreted by the sebaceous glands [Latin: tallow]

sec¹ *adj* (of wines) dry [French]

sec² *n informal* a second (of time): *hang on a sec*

sec³ *n* secant

sec. 1 second (of time) **2** secondary **3** secretary

secant (seek-ant) *n* **1** (in trigonometry) the ratio of the length of the hypotenuse to the length of the adjacent side in a right-angled triangle; the reciprocal of cosine

2 a straight line that intersects a curve [Latin *secare* to cut]

secateurs *pl n* a small pair of gardening shears for pruning [French]

secede *vb* **-ceding, -ceded** to make a formal withdrawal of membership from a political alliance, federation, or group: *it will secede from the federation within six months* [Latin *se-* apart + *cedere* to go]

secession *n* the act of seceding **> secessionism** *n* **> secessionist** *n, adj*

seclude *vb* **-cluding, -cluded 1** to remove from contact with others **2** to shut off or screen from view [Latin *secludere*]

secluded *adj* **1** kept apart from the company of others: *a secluded private life* **2** private and sheltered: *a secluded cottage*

seclusion *n* the state of being secluded; privacy: *the seclusion of his winter retreat*

second¹ *adj* **1** coming directly after the first in order **2** rated, graded, or ranked between the first and third levels **3** alternate: *every second Saturday* **4** another of the same kind; additional: *a second chance* **5** resembling or comparable to a person or event from the past: *a second Virgin Mary* **6** of lesser importance or position; inferior **7** denoting the second lowest forward gear in a motor vehicle **8** *music* denoting a musical part, voice, or instrument subordinate to or lower in pitch than another (the first): *the second tenors* **9 at second hand** by hearsay **> n 10** a person or thing that is second **11** *Brit education* an honours degree of the second class **12** the second lowest forward gear in a motor vehicle **13** (in boxing or duelling) an attendant who looks after a boxer or duellist **14 seconds a** *informal* a second helping of food or the second course of a meal **b** goods that are sold cheaply because they are slightly faulty **> vb 15** to give aid or backing to **16** (in boxing or duelling) to act as second to (a boxer or duellist) **17** to express formal support for (a motion proposed in a meeting) **> adv 18** Also: **secondly** in the second place [Latin *secundus* next in order]

second² *n* **1** the basic SI unit of time, equal to $\frac{1}{60}$ of a minute **2** $\frac{1}{60}$ of a minute of angle **3** a very short period of time [Latin *pars minuta secunda* the second small part (a minute being the first small part of an hour)]

second³ (sik-**kond**) *vb Brit and NZ* to transfer (a person) temporarily to another job [French *en second* in second rank] **> secondment** *n*

secondary *adj* **1** below the first in rank or importance: *a secondary consideration* **2** coming next after the first: *secondary cancers* **3** derived from or depending on what is primary or first: *a secondary source* **4** of or relating to the education of people between the ages of 11 and 18 or, in New Zealand, between 13 and 18: *secondary education* **5** (of an industry) involving the manufacture of goods from raw materials **> n, pl -aries 6** a person or thing that is secondary

secondary colour *n* a colour formed by mixing two primary colours

secondary picketing *n* the picketing by striking workers of the premises of a firm that supplies or distributes goods to or from their employer

secondary school *n* a school for young people, usually between the ages of 11 and 18

second-best *adj* **1** next to the best **> adv second best 2 come off second best** *informal* to fail to win against someone **> n second best 3** an inferior alternative

second chamber *n* the upper house of a two-chamber system of government

second childhood *n* the time in an old person's life when he or she starts to suffer from memory loss and confusion; senility

second class *n* **1** the class or grade next in value, rank, or quality to the first **> adj second-class 2** of the class or grade next to the best in value, rank, or quality **3** shoddy or inferior **4** denoting the class of accommodation in a

hotel or on a train, aircraft, or ship, lower in quality and price than first class **5** (of mail) sent by a cheaper type of postage and taking slightly longer to arrive than first-class mail **> adv 6** by second-class mail, transport, etc.

Second Coming *n* the prophesied return of Christ to earth at the Last Judgment

second cousin *n* the child of one's parent's first cousin

second-degree burn *n* a burn in which blisters appear on the skin

second fiddle *n informal* a person who has a secondary status

second floor *n* the storey of a building immediately above the first and two floors up from the ground

second hand *n* a pointer on the face of a watch or clock that indicates the seconds

second-hand *adj* **1** previously owned or used **2** not from an original source or one's own experience: *second-hand opinions* **3** dealing in or selling goods that are not new: *second-hand furniture shops* **> adv 4** from a source of previously owned or used goods: *they preferred to buy second-hand* **5** not directly or from one's own experience: *his knowledge had been gleaned second-hand*

second lieutenant *n* an officer holding the lowest commissioned rank in an army or navy

secondly *adv* same as **second¹** (18)

second nature *n* a habit or characteristic practised for so long that it seems to be part of one's character

second person *n* the form of a pronoun or verb used to refer to the person or people being addressed

second-rate *adj* **1** not of the highest quality; mediocre **2** second in importance or rank: *a second-rate citizen*

second sight *n* the supposed ability to foresee the future or see actions taking place elsewhere

second thoughts *pl n* a revised opinion or idea on a matter already considered

second wind *n* **1** the return of comfortable breathing following difficult or strenuous exercise **2** renewed ability to continue in an effort

secrecy *n, pl* **-cies 1** the state of being secret **2** the ability or tendency to keep things secret

secret *adj* **1** kept hidden or separate from the knowledge of all or all but a few others **2** secretive: *she had become a secret drinker* **3** operating without the knowledge of outsiders: *secret organizations* **> n 4** something kept or to be kept hidden **5** something unrevealed; a mystery: *the secrets of nature* **6** an underlying explanation or reason: *the secret of great-looking hair* **7 in secret** without the knowledge of others [Latin *secretus* concealed] **> secretly** *adv*

secret agent *n* a person employed by a government to find out the military and political secrets of other governments

secretaire (sek-rit-**air**) *n* same as **escritoire**

secretariat *n* **1 a** an office responsible for the secretarial, clerical, and administrative affairs of a legislative body or international organization **b** the staff of such an office or department **2** the premises of a secretariat [French]

secretary *n, pl* **-taries 1** a person who handles correspondence, keeps records, and does general clerical work for an individual or organization **2** the official manager of the day-to-day business of a society, club, or committee **3** (in Britain) a senior civil servant who assists a government minister **4** (in the US) the head of a government administrative department [Medieval Latin *secretarius* someone entrusted with secrets] **> secretarial** *adj*

secretary bird *n* a large long-legged African bird of prey

secretary-general *n, pl* **secretaries-general** the chief administrative official of a legislative body or international organization

secretary of state *n* **1** (in Britain) the head of a major government department **2** (in the US) the head of the government department in charge of foreign affairs

secrete¹ *vb* **-creting, -creted** (of a cell, organ, or gland) to produce and release (a substance) ❯ **secretory** (sik-**reet**-or-ee) *adj*

secrete² *vb* **-creting, -creted** to put in a hiding place [variant of obsolete *secret* to hide away]

secretion *n* **1** a substance that is released from a cell, organ, or gland **2** the process involved in producing and releasing such a substance [Latin *secretio* a separation]

secretive *adj* hiding feelings and intentions ❯ **secretively** *adv*

secret police *n* a police force that operates secretly to suppress opposition to the government

secret service *n* a government agency or department that conducts intelligence or counterintelligence operations

sect *n* **1** a subdivision of a larger religious or political group, esp. one regarded as extreme in its beliefs or practices **2** a group of people with a common interest or philosophy [Latin *secta* faction]

sectarian *adj* **1** of or belonging to a sect **2** narrow-minded as a result of supporting a particular sect ▷ *n* **3** a member of a sect ❯ **sectarianism** *n*

section *n* **1** a part cut off or separated from the main body of something: *a non-smoking section* **2** a part or subdivision of a piece of writing or a book: *the business section* **3** a distinct part of a country or community: *the Arabic section* **4** *surgery* the act or process of cutting or separating by cutting **5** *geometry* a plane surface formed by cutting through a solid **6** short for **Caesarean section** **7** NZ a plot of land for building on **8** *Austral and NZ* a fare stage on a bus ▷ *vb* **9** to cut or divide into sections **10** to commit (a mentally disturbed person) to a mental hospital [Latin *secare* to cut]

sectional *adj* **1** concerned with a particular area or group within a country or community, esp. to the exclusion of others: *narrow sectional interests* **2** made of sections **3** of a section

sector *n* **1** a part or subdivision, esp. of a society or an economy: *the public sector* **2** *geometry* either portion of a circle bounded by two radii and the arc cut off by them **3** a portion into which an area is divided for military operations [Latin: a cutter]

secular *adj* **1** relating to worldly as opposed to sacred things **2** not connected with religion or the church **3** (of clerics) not bound by religious vows to a monastic or other order [Late Latin *saecularis*]

secularism *n* the belief that religion should have no place in civil affairs ❯ **secularist** *n*, *adj*

secularize or **-rise** *vb* **-rizing, -rized** or **-rising, -rised** to change (something, such as education) so that it is no longer connected with religion or the Church ❯ **secularization** or **-risation** *n*

Secunderabad *n* a former town in S central India, in N Andra Pradesh: one of the largest British military stations in India: now part of Hyderabad city

secure *adj* **1** free from danger or damage **2** free from fear, doubt, or care **3** tightly locked or well protected **4** fixed or tied firmly in position **5** able to be relied on: *secure profits* ▷ *vb* **-curing, -cured** **6** to obtain: *to secure a change in German policy* **7** to make or become free from danger or fear **8** to make safe from loss, theft, or attack **9** to attach; make fast or firm **10** to guarantee (payment of a loan) by giving something as security [Latin *securus* free from care] ❯ **securely** *adv*

security *n*, *pl* **-ties** **1** precautions taken to ensure against theft, espionage, or other danger **2** the state of being free from danger, damage, or worry **3** assured freedom from poverty: *the security of a weekly pay cheque* **4** a certificate of ownership, such as a share, stock, or bond **5** something given or pledged to guarantee payment of a loan

security risk *n* someone or something thought to be a threat to state security

sedan *n* US, *Canad, Austral and NZ* a saloon car [origin unknown]

Sedan *n* a town in NE France, on the River Meuse: passed to France in 1642; a Protestant stronghold (16th–17th centuries); scene of a French defeat (1870) during the Franco-Prussian War and of a battle (1940) in World War II, which began the German invasion of France. Pop: 19 219 (2008)

sedan chair *n* an enclosed chair for one passenger, carried on poles by two bearers, commonly used in the 17th and 18th centuries

sedate¹ *adj* **1** quiet, calm, and dignified **2** slow or unhurried: *a sedate walk to the beach* [Latin *sedare* to soothe] ❯ **sedately** *adv*

sedate² *vb* **-dating, -dated** to calm down or make sleepy by giving a sedative drug to

sedation *n* **1** a state of calm, esp. when brought about by sedatives **2** the administration of a sedative

sedative *adj* **1** having a soothing or calming effect ▷ *n* **2** *med* a sedative drug or agent that makes people sleep or calm down [Latin *sedatus* assuaged]

Seddon *n* Richard John, known as *King Dick*. 1845–1906, New Zealand statesman, born in England; prime minister of New Zealand (1893–1906)

sedentary (sed-en-tree) *adj* **1** done sitting down and involving very little exercise: *a sedentary job* **2** tending to sit about without taking much exercise [Latin *sedere* to sit]

sedge *n* a coarse grasslike plant growing on wet ground [Old English *secg*] ❯ **sedgy** *adj*

Sedgemoor *n* a low-lying plain in SW England, in central Somerset: scene of the defeat (1685) of the Duke of Monmouth

sedge warbler *n* a European songbird living in marshy areas

Sedgwick *n* Adam. 1785–1873, English geologist; played a major role in establishing parts of the geological time scale, esp. the Cambrian and Devonian periods

sediment *n* **1** matter that settles to the bottom of a liquid **2** material that has been deposited by water, ice, or wind [Latin *sedimentum* a settling] ❯ **sedimentary** *adj*

sedition *n* speech, writing, or behaviour intended to encourage rebellion or resistance against the government [Latin *seditio* discord] ❯ **seditionary** *n*, *adj* ❯ **seditious** *adj*

Sedna *n* a red planet-like object, roughly half the size of the Earth's moon, orbiting the sun but considerably beyond Pluto; discovered in 2003 [C21: after the Inuit goddess of the ocean]

seduce *vb* **-ducing, -duced** **1** to persuade to have sexual intercourse **2** to tempt into wrongdoing [Latin *seducere* to lead apart] ❯ **seduction** *n*

seductive *adj* **1** (of a woman) sexually attractive **2** very attractive or tempting: *a seductive argument* ❯ **seductively** *adv* ❯ **seductiveness** *n*

sedulous *adj* diligent or painstaking: *a sedulous concern with the achievements of western thought* [Latin *sedulus*] ❯ **sedulously** *adv*

sedum *n* a rock plant with thick clusters of white, yellow, or pink flowers [Latin]

see¹ *vb* **seeing, saw, seen** **1** to look at or recognize with the eyes **2** to understand: *I explained the problem but he could not see it* **3** to perceive or be aware of: *she had never seen him so angry* **4** to view, watch, or attend: *we had barely seen a dozen movies in our lives* **5** to foresee: *they could see what their fate was to be* **6** to find out (a fact): *I was ringing to see whether you'd got it* **7** to make sure (of something) or take care (of something): *see that he is never in a position to do these things again; you must see to it* **8** to consider or decide: *see if you can come next week* **9** to have experience of: *he had seen active service in the revolution* **10** to meet or pay a visit to: *I see my specialist every three months* **11** to receive: *the Prime Minister will see the deputation now* **12** to frequent the company of: *we've been seeing each other since then* **13** to accompany: *she saw him* *to the door* **14** to refer to or look up: *see page 35* **15** (in gambling, esp. in poker) to match (another player's bet) or match the bet of (another player) by staking an equal sum **16 see fit** to consider it proper (to do something): *I did not see fit to send them home* **17 see you** or **see you later** or **be seeing you** an expression of farewell ▶ See also **see about, see into**, etc. [Old English *sēon*]

see² *n* the diocese of a bishop or the place within it where his cathedral is situated [Latin *sedes* a seat]

see about *vb* **1** to take care of: *I'll see about some coffee* **2** to investigate: *to see about a new car*

seed *n* **1** *botany* the mature fertilized grain of a plant, containing an embryo ready for germination. Related adjective: **seminal 2** such seeds used for sowing **3** the source, beginning, or origin of anything: *the seeds of dissent* **4** *chiefly Bible* descendants; offspring: *the seed of David* **5** *sport* a player ranked according to his or her ability **6 go** or **run to seed a** (of plants) to produce and shed seeds after flowering **b** to lose strength or usefulness ▷ *vb* **7** to plant (seeds) in (soil) **8** (of plants) to produce or shed seeds **9** to remove the seeds from (fruit or plants) **10** to scatter silver iodide in (clouds) in order to cause rain **11** to arrange (the draw of a tournament) so that outstanding teams or players will not meet in the early rounds [Old English *sǣd*] ▷ **seedless** *adj*

seedbed *n* **1** an area of soil prepared for the growing of seedlings before they are transplanted **2** the place where something develops: *a seedbed of immorality*

seedling *n* a plant produced from a seed, esp. a very young plant

seed pearl *n* a very small pearl

seed pod *n* *botany* a carpel or pistil enclosing the seeds of a plant, esp. a flowering plant

seedy *adj* **seedier, seediest 1** shabby in appearance: *a seedy cinema* **2** *informal* physically unwell **3** (of a plant) at the stage of producing seeds ▷ **seediness** *n*

Seeger *n* Pete. 1919–2014. US folk singer and songwriter, noted for his protest songs, which include "We shall Overcome" (1960), "Where have all the Flowers gone?" (1961), "If I had a Hammer" (1962), and "Little Boxes" (1962)

seeing *n* **1** the sense or faculty of sight ▷ *conj* **2** (often foll. by *that* or *as*) in light of the fact (that)

USAGE The use of *seeing as how* as in *seeing as (how) the bus is always late, I don't see any reason to hurry* is generally thought to be incorrect or non-standard.

see into *vb* to discover the true nature of: *he could see into my intentions*

seek *vb* **seeking, sought 1** to try to find by searching: *to seek employment* **2** to try to obtain: *to seek a diplomatic solution* **3** to try (to do something): *we seek to establish a stable relationship* [Old English *sēcan*]

seek out *vb* to search hard for and find (a specific person or thing): *you should seek out healthy role models*

Seeland *n* the German name for **Zealand**

seem *vb* **1** to appear to the mind or eye; give the impression of: *the car seems to be running well* **2** to appear to be: *there seems no need for all this nonsense* **3** to have the impression: *I seem to remember you were there too* [Old Norse *sōma* to be suitable]

USAGE See at **like¹**.

seeming *adj* apparent but not real: *his seeming willingness to participate* ▷ **seemingly** *adv*

seemly *adj* **-lier, -liest** *formal* proper or fitting

seen *vb* the past participle of **see¹**

see off *vb* **1** to be present at the departure of (a person going on a journey): *your sisters came to see you off* **2** *informal* to cause to leave or depart, esp. by force

seep *vb* to leak through slowly; ooze [Old English *sīpian*] ▷ **seepage** *n*

seer *n* a person who can supposedly see into the future

seersucker *n* a light cotton fabric with a slightly crinkled surface [Hindi *śīrŝakar*]

seesaw *n* **1** a plank balanced in the middle so that two people seated on the ends can ride up and down by pushing on the ground with their feet **2** an up-and-down or back-and-forth movement ▷ *vb* **3** to move up and down and back or back and forth alternately [reduplication of *saw*, alluding to the movement from side to side, as in sawing]

seethe *vb* **seething, seethed 1** to be in a state of extreme anger or indignation without publicly showing these feelings **2** (of a liquid) to boil or foam [Old English *sēothan*] ▷ **seething** *adj*

see through *vb* **1** to perceive the true nature of: *it was difficult to see through people* **2** to remain with until the end or completion: *not all of them saw it through* **3** to help out in a time of need or trouble: *he helped see her through her divorce* ▷ *adj* **see-through 4** (of clothing) made of thin cloth so that the wearer's body or underclothes are visible

Seferis *n* George. pen name of *Georgios Seferiades*. 1900–71, Greek poet and diplomat: Nobel prize for literature 1963

Sefton *n* a unitary authority in NW England, in Merseyside. Pop: 281 600 (2003 est). Area: 150 sq km (58 sq miles)

segment *n* **1** one of several parts or sections into which an object is divided **2** *maths* **a** a part of a circle cut off by an intersecting line **b** a part of a sphere cut off by an intersecting plane or planes ▷ *vb* **3** to cut or divide into segments [Latin *segmentum*] ▷ **segmental** *adj* ▷ **segmentation** *n*

Segovia¹ *n* a town in central Spain: site of a Roman aqueduct, still in use, and the fortified palace of the kings of Castile (the Alcázar). Pop: 55 640 (2003 est)

Segovia² *n* Andrés, Marquis of Salobreña. 1893–1987, Spanish classical guitarist

Segrè *n* Emilio. 1905–89, US physicist, born in Italy, who was the first to produce an artificial element. He shared the Nobel prize for physics (1959) with Owen Chamberlain for their discovery (1955) of the antiproton

segregate *vb* **-gating, -gated 1** to set apart from others or from the main group **2** to impose segregation on (a racial or minority group) [Latin *se-* apart + *grex* a flock]

segregation *n* **1** the practice or policy of creating separate facilities within the same society for the use of a racial or minority group **2** the act of segregating ▷ **segregational** *adj* ▷ **segregationist** *n*

Seifert *n* Jaroslav. 1901–86, Czech poet and journalist, noted esp. for poems dealing with the German occupation of Prague during World War II. Nobel prize for literature 1984

seigneur *n* a feudal lord, esp. in France [Old French] ▷ **seigneurial** *adj*

seine (sane) *n* **1** a large fishing net that hangs vertically in the water by means of floats at the top and weights at the bottom ▷ *vb* **2** to catch (fish) using **seining, seined** this net [Old English *segne*]

Seine *n* a river in N France, rising on the Plateau de Langres and flowing northwest through Paris to the English Channel: the second longest river in France, linked by canal with the Rivers Somme, Scheldt, Meuse, Rhine, Saône, and Loire. Length: 776 km (482 miles)

Seine-et-Marne *n* a department of N central France, in Île-de-France region. Capital: Melun. Pop: 1 232 467 (2003 est). Area: 5931 sq km (2313 sq miles)

Seine-Maritime *n* a department of N France, in Haute-Normandie region. Capital: Rouen. Pop: 1 237 263 (2003 est). Area: 6342 sq km (2473 sq miles)

Seine-Saint-Denis *n* a department of N central France, in Île-de-France region. Capital: Bobigny. Pop: 1 396 122 (2003 est). Area: 236 sq km (92 sq miles)

seismic *adj* relating to or caused by earthquakes [Greek *seismos* earthquake]

seismograph *n* an instrument that records the

intensity and duration of earthquakes [Greek *seismos* earthquake + -GRAPH] **> seismographer** *n*
> seismography *n*

seismology *n* the branch of geology concerned with the study of earthquakes [Greek *seismos* earthquake + -LOGY]
> seismologist *n*

seismometer *n* same as seismograph

seize *vb* **seizing, seized** 1 to take hold of forcibly or quickly; grab 2 to take immediate advantage of: *real journalists would have seized the opportunity* 3 to take legal possession of 4 (sometimes foll. by *on* or *upon*) to understand quickly: *she immediately seized his idea* 5 to affect or fill the mind of suddenly: *a wild frenzy seized her* 6 to take by force or capture: *the rebels seized a tank factory* 7 (often foll. by *up*) (of mechanical parts) to become jammed through overheating [Old French *saisir*]

seizure *n* 1 *pathol* a sudden violent attack of an illness, such as an epileptic convulsion 2 the act of seizing: *a seizure of drug traffickers' assets*

Sekondi *n* a port in SW Ghana, 8 km (5 miles) northeast of Takoradi: linked administratively with Takoradi in 1946. Pop (with Takoradi): 335 000 (2005 est)

Selangor *n* a state of Peninsular Malaysia, on the Strait of Malacca: established as a British protectorate in 1874, became a Federated Malay State in 1896 and part of Malaysia in 1946; tin producer. Capital: Shah Alam. Pop: 4 188 876 (2000). Area: 7955 sq km (3071 sq miles)

Selby *n* an inland port in N England, in North Yorkshire, on the River Ouse: centre for a coalfield since 1983; agricultural products. Pop: 15 807 (2001)

Selden *n* John. 1584–1654, English antiquary and politician. As a Member of Parliament, he was twice imprisoned for opposing the king

seldom *adv* rarely; not often [Old English *seldon*]

select *vb* 1 to choose (someone or something) in preference to another or others ▷ *adj* 2 chosen in preference to others 3 restricted to a particular group; exclusive: *a select audience* [Latin *seligere* to sort]
> selector *n*

select committee *n* a small committee of Members of Parliament, set up to investigate and report on a specified matter

selection *n* 1 a selecting or being selected 2 a thing or number of things that have been selected 3 a range from which something may be selected: *a good selection of reasonably priced wines* 4 *biology* the process by which certain organisms or individuals are reproduced and survive in preference to others

selective *adj* 1 tending to choose carefully or characterized by careful choice: *they were selective in their reading* 2 of or characterized by selection **> selectively** *adv* **> selectivity** *n*

selenium *n chem* a nonmetallic element used in photocells, solar cells, and in xerography. Symbol: Se [Greek *selēnē* moon]

Seles *n* Monica. born 1973, US tennis player, born in Yugoslavia: winner of nine Grand Slam singles titles, including the US Open (1991–93) and the French Open (1990–92); stabbed while on court in an unprovoked attack

Seleucia *n* 1 an ancient city in Mesopotamia, on the River Tigris: founded by Seleucus Nicator in 312 BC; became the chief city of the Seleucid empire; sacked by the Romans around 162 AD 2 an ancient city in SE Asia Minor, on the River Calycadnus (modern Goksu Nehri): captured by the Turks in the 13th century; site of present-day Silifke (Turkey). Official name: **Seleucia Tracheotis, Seleucia Trachea** 3 an ancient port in Syria, on the River Orontes: the port of Antioch, of military importance during the wars between the Ptolemies and Seleucids; largely destroyed by earthquake in 526; site of present-day Samanda? (Turkey). Official name: **Seleucia Pieria**

Seleucus I *n* surname *Nicator.* ?358–280 BC, Macedonian

general under Alexander the Great, who founded the Seleucid kingdom

self *n, pl* **selves** 1 the distinct individuality or identity of a person or thing 2 a person's typical bodily make-up or personal characteristics: *back to my old self after the scare* 3 one's own welfare or interests: *he only thinks of self* 4 an individual's consciousness of his or her own identity or being ▷ *pron* 5 *not standard* myself, yourself, himself, or herself: *setting goals for self and others* [Old English]

self- *combining form* 1 (used with many main words to mean) of oneself or itself: *self-defence* 2 (used with many main words to mean) by, to, in, due to, for, or from the self: *self-employed; self-respect* 3 (used with many main words to mean) automatic or automatically: *self-propelled*

self-abnegation *n* the denial of one's own interests in favour of the interests of others

self-absorption *n* preoccupation with oneself to the exclusion of others **> self-absorbed** *adj*

self-abuse *n old-fashioned* masturbation

self-addressed *adj* addressed for return to the sender

self-aggrandizement *or* **self-aggrandisement** *n* the act of increasing one's own power, wealth, or importance

self-appointed *adj* having assumed authority without the agreement of others: *self-appointed moralists*

self-assertion *n* the act of putting forward one's own opinions or demanding one's rights, esp. in an aggressive or confident manner **> self-assertive** *adj*

self-assurance *n* confidence in oneself, one's abilities, or one's judgment **> self-assured** *adj*

self-catering *adj* (of accommodation) for tenants providing and preparing their own food

self-centred *or US* **self-centered** *adj* totally preoccupied with one's own concerns

self-certification *n* (in Britain) the completion of a form by a worker stating that his or her absence was due to sickness

self-coloured *or US* **self-colored** *adj* 1 having only a single and uniform colour: *a self-coloured tie* 2 (of cloth or wool) having the natural or original colour

self-confessed *adj* according to one's own admission: *a self-confessed addict*

self-confidence *n* confidence in oneself, one's abilities, or one's judgment **> self-confident** *adj*

self-conscious *adj* embarrassed or ill at ease through being unduly aware of oneself as the object of the attention of others **> self-consciously** *adv* **> self-consciousness** *n*

self-contained *adj* 1 containing within itself all parts necessary for completeness 2 (of a flat) having its own kitchen, bathroom, and toilet not shared by others

self-control *n* the ability to control one's feelings, emotions, or reactions **> self-controlled** *adj*

self-deception *or* **self-deceit** *n* the act or an instance of deceiving oneself

self-defence *or US* **self-defense** *n* 1 the act or skill of defending oneself against physical attack 2 the act of defending one's actions, ideas, or rights

self-denial *n* the repression or sacrifice of one's own desires **> self-denying** *adj*

self-determination *n* 1 the ability to make a decision for oneself without influence from outside 2 the right of a nation or people to determine its own form of government **> self-determined** *adj*

self-discipline *n* the act of controlling or power to control one's own feelings, desires, or behaviour **> self-disciplined** *adj*

self-drive *adj* relating to a hired vehicle that is driven by the hirer

self-educated *adj* educated through one's own efforts without formal instruction

self-effacement *n* the act of making oneself or one's actions seem less important than they are because of modesty or timidity **> self-effacing** *adj*

self-employed *adj* earning one's living in one's own business, rather than as the employee of another

self-esteem *n* respect for or a favourable opinion of oneself

self-evident *adj* so obvious that no proof or explanation is needed ❭ **self-evidently** *adv*

self-explanatory *adj* understandable without explanation

self-expression *n* the expression of one's own personality or feelings, esp. in the creative arts ❭ **self-expressive** *adj*

self-government *n* the government of a country, nation, or community by its own people ❭ **self-governing** *adj*

self-help *n* **1** the use of one's own abilities and resources to help oneself without relying on the assistance of others **2** the practice of solving one's problems within a group of people with similar problems

selfie *n informal* a photograph taken by pointing the camera at oneself

selfie stick *n* an extendable rod to which a camera may be attached to take a photograph of oneself

self-image *n* one's own idea of oneself or sense of one's worth

self-important *adj* having an unduly high opinion of one's own importance ❭ **self-importance** *n*

self-improvement *n* the improvement of one's position, skills, or education by one's own efforts

self-indulgent *adj* tending to allow oneself to have or do things that one enjoys ❭ **self-indulgence** *n*

self-interest *n* **1** one's personal interest or advantage **2** the pursuit of one's own interest ❭ **self-interested** *adj*

selfish *adj* **1** caring too much about oneself and not enough about others **2** (of behaviour or attitude) motivated by self-interest ❭ **selfishly** *adv* ❭ **selfishness** *n*

selfless *adj* putting other people's interests before one's own ❭ **selflessly** *adv* ❭ **selflessness** *n*

self-made *adj* having achieved wealth or status by one's own efforts

self-opinionated *adj* clinging stubbornly to one's own opinions

self-pity *n* pity for oneself, esp. when greatly exaggerated ❭ **self-pitying** *adj*

self-pollination *n botany* the transfer of pollen from the anthers to the stigma of the same flower

self-possessed *adj* having control of one's emotions or behaviour, esp. in difficult situations ❭ **self-possession** *n*

self-preservation *n* the instinctive behaviour that protects one from danger or injury

self-propelled *adj* **1** (of a vehicle) driven by its own engine rather than drawn by a locomotive, horse, etc. **2** (of a rocket launcher or artillery piece) mounted on a motor vehicle ❭ **self-propelling** *adj*

self-raising *adj* (of flour) having a raising agent, such as baking powder, already added

self-realization *or* **-isation** *n* the fulfilment of one's own potential or abilities

self-regard *n* **1** concern for one's own interest **2** proper esteem for oneself

self-reliance *n* reliance on oneself or one's own abilities ❭ **self-reliant** *adj*

self-reproach *n* the act of finding fault with or blaming oneself

self-respect *n* a feeling of confidence and pride in one's own abilities and worth ❭ **self-respecting** *adj*

self-restraint *n* control imposed by oneself on one's own feelings, desires, or actions

self-righteous *adj* thinking oneself more virtuous than others ❭ **self-righteousness** *n*

self-sacrifice *n* the giving up of one's own interests for the wellbeing of others ❭ **self-sacrificing** *adj*

selfsame *adj* the very same: *this was the selfsame woman I'd met on the train*

self-satisfied *adj* smug and complacently satisfied with oneself or one's own actions ❭ **self-satisfaction** *n*

self-sealing *adj* **1** (of an envelope) sealable by pressure alone **2** (of a tyre) automatically sealing small punctures

self-seeking *n* **1** the act or an instance of seeking one's own profit or interests ▷ *adj* **2** inclined to promote only one's own profit or interests: *self-seeking politicians* ❭ **self-seeker** *n*

self-service *adj* **1** of or denoting a shop or restaurant where the customers serve themselves and then pay a cashier ▷ *n* **2** the practice of serving oneself and then paying a cashier

self-serving *adj* continually seeking one's own advantage, esp. at the expense of others

self-starter *n* **1** an electric motor used to start an internal-combustion engine **2** a person who is strongly motivated and shows initiative at work

self-styled *adj* using a title or name that one has given oneself, esp. without right or justification; so-called: *the self-styled leader of the rebellion*

self-sufficient *adj* able to provide for or support oneself without the help of others ❭ **self-sufficiency** *n*

self-supporting *adj* **1** able to support or maintain oneself without the help of others **2** able to stand up or hold firm without support, props, or attachments

self-willed *adj* stubbornly determined to have one's own way, esp. at the expense of others

self-winding *adj* (of a wristwatch) having a mechanism which winds itself automatically

Selkirk *n* Alexander. original name *Alexander Selcraig*. 1676–1721, Scottish sailor, who was marooned on one of the islets of Juan Fernández and is regarded as the prototype of Defoe's *Robinson Crusoe*

Selkirk Mountains *pl n* a mountain range in SW Canada, in SE British Columbia. Highest peak: Mount Sir Sandford, 3533 m (11 590 ft)

Selkirkshire *n* (until 1975) a county of SE Scotland, now part of Scottish Borders

sell *vb* **selling, sold 1** to exchange (something) for money **2** to deal in (objects or property): *he sells used cars* **3** to give up or surrender for a price or reward: *to sell one's honour* **4 sell for** to have a specified price: *they sell for 10 pence each* **5** to promote the sale of (objects or property): *sex sells cigarettes* **6** to gain acceptance of: *he'll sell an idea to a producer* **7** to be in demand on the market: *his books did not sell well enough* **8 sell down the river** *informal* to betray **9 sell oneself a** to convince someone else of one's potential or worth **b** to give up one's moral standards for a price or reward **10 sell someone short** *informal* to undervalue someone ▷ *n* **11** the act or an instance of selling: *the hard sell* ▶ See also **sell off, sell out, sell up** [Old English *sellan* to give, deliver] ❭ **seller** *n*

Sella *n* Phillipe. French Rugby Union football player; played 111 internationals for France (1982–95)

Sellafield *n* the site of an atomic power station and nuclear reprocessing plant in NW England, in W Cumbria. Former name: **Windscale**

sell-by date *n* **1** *Brit* the date printed on packaged food specifying the date after which the food should not be sold **2** past one's **sell-by date** beyond one's prime

Sellers *n* Peter. 1925–80, English radio, stage, and film actor and comedian: noted for his gift of precise vocal mimicry, esp. in *The Goon Show* (with Spike Milligan and Harry Secombe; BBC Radio, 1952–60). His films include *I'm All Right, Jack* (1959), *The Millionairess* (1961), *The Pink Panther* (1963), *Dr Strangelove* (1964), and *Being There* (1979)

sell off *vb* to sell (remaining items) at reduced prices

Sellotape *n* **1** *Brit trademark* a type of transparent adhesive tape ▷ *vb* **-taping, -taped 2** to seal or stick using adhesive tape

sell out *vb* **1 a** to dispose of (something) completely by selling **b** (of items for sale) to be bought up completely: *these tickets will sell out in minutes* **2** *informal* to abandon one's

S

principles, standards, etc. **3** *informal* to betray in order to gain an advantage or benefit ▷ *n* **sellout 4** *informal* a performance of a show etc. for which all tickets are sold **5** a commercial success **6** *informal* a betrayal

sell-through *adj* of the sale of prerecorded video cassettes or DVDs, without their first being for hire only

sell up *vb chiefly Brit and Austral* to sell all one's goods or property

selvage *or* **selvedge** *n* a specially woven edge on a length of fabric to prevent it from unravelling [SELF + EDGE] ▷ **selvaged** *adj*

selves *n* the plural of self

Selznick *n* David O(liver). 1902–62, US film producer, who produced such films as *A Star is Born* (1937), *Gone with the Wind* (1939), and *A Farewell to Arms* (1957)

semantic *adj* **1** of or relating to the meanings of words **2** of or relating to semantics [Greek *sēma* a sign]

semantics *n* the branch of linguistics that deals with the study of meaning

semaphore *n* **1** a system of signalling by holding two flags in different positions to represent letters of the alphabet ▷ *vb* **-phoring, -phored 2** to signal (information) by semaphore [Greek *sēma* a signal + *-phoros* carrying]

Semarang *or* **Samarang** *n* a port in S Indonesia, in N Java on the Java Sea. Pop: 1 348 803 (2000)

semblance *n* outward or superficial appearance: *some semblance of order had been established* [Old French *sembler* to seem]

semen *n* the thick whitish fluid containing spermatozoa that is produced by the male reproductive organs and ejaculated from the penis [Latin: seed]

Semenya *n* Caster. born 1991, South African female athlete; won gold in the 800 metres at the 2009 World Championships; subjected to gender testing then returned to competitive athletics in 2010

Semeru *n* a volcano in Indonesia: the highest peak in Java. Height: 3676 m (12 060 ft). Former spelling: Semeroe

semester *n* either of two divisions of the academic year [Latin *semestris* half-yearly]

semi *n Brit, Austral and S African informal* short for semidetached (2)

semi- *prefix* **1** half: *semicircle* **2** partly or almost: *semiprofessional* **3** occurring twice in a specified period: *semiweekly* [Latin]

semiannual *adj* **1** occurring every half-year **2** lasting for half a year

semiarid *adj* denoting land that lies on the edges of a desert but has a slightly higher rainfall (above 300 mm) so that some farming is possible

semiautomatic *adj* **1** (of a firearm) self-loading but firing only one shot at each pull of the trigger ▷ *n* **2** a semiautomatic firearm

semibreve *n Brit music* a note, now the longest in common use, with a time value that may be divided by any power of 2 to give all other notes

semicircle *n* **1** one half of a circle **2** anything having the shape or form of half a circle ▷ **semicircular** *adj*

semicolon *n* the punctuation mark (;) used to separate clauses or items in a list, or to indicate a pause longer than that of a comma and shorter than that of a full stop

semiconductor *n physics* a substance, such as silicon, which has an electrical conductivity that increases with temperature

semiconscious *adj* not fully conscious ▷ **semiconsciousness** *n*

semidetached *adj* **1** (of a house) joined to another house on one side by a common wall ▷ *n* **2** Brit a semidetached house: *the mock Georgian semidetached*

semifinal *n* the round before the final in a competition ▷ **semifinalist** *n*

seminal *adj* **1** highly original and influential: *seminal thinkers* **2** potentially capable of development **3** of

semen: *seminal fluid* **4** biology of seed [Latin *semen* seed]

seminar *n* **1** a small group of students meeting regularly under the guidance of a tutor for study and discussion **2** one such meeting [Latin *seminarium* a nursery garden]

seminary *n, pl* **-naries** a college for the training of priests [Latin *seminarium* a nursery garden] ▷ **seminarian** *n*

semiotics *n* the study of human communication, esp. communication using signs and symbols [Greek *sēmeion* a sign] ▷ **semiotic** *adj*

Semipalatinsk *n* a city in NE Kazakhstan on the Irtysh River; an important communications centre. Pop: 282 000 (2005 est)

semipermeable *adj* (of a cell membrane) allowing small molecules to pass through but not large ones

semiprecious *adj* (of certain stones) having less value than a precious stone

semiprofessional *adj* **1** (of a person) engaged in an activity or sport part time for pay **2** (of an activity or sport) engaged in by semiprofessional people ▷ *n* **3** a semiprofessional person

semiquaver *n music* a note having the time value of one-sixteenth of a semibreve

Semiramis *n* the legendary founder of Babylon and wife of Ninus, king of Assyria, which she ruled with great skill after his death

semirigid *adj* (of an airship) maintaining shape by means of a main supporting keel and internal gas pressure

semiskilled *adj* partly skilled or trained but not sufficiently so as to perform specialized work

Semite *n* a member of the group of peoples who speak a Semitic language, such as the Jews and Arabs [New Latin *semita* descendant of Shem, eldest of Noah's sons]

Semitic *n* **1** a group of languages that includes Arabic, Hebrew, and Aramaic ▷ *adj* **2** of this group of languages **3** of any of the peoples speaking a Semitic language, esp. the Jews or the Arabs **4** same as Jewish

semitone *n* the smallest interval between two notes in Western music represented on a piano by the difference in pitch between any two adjacent keys ▷ **semitonic** *adj*

semitrailer *n chiefly Austral, US and Canad* a large truck in two separate sections joined by a pivoted bar. Also called: semi

semitropical *adj* bordering on the tropics; nearly tropical ▷ **semitropics** *pl n*

semivowel *n phonetics* a vowel-like sound that acts like a consonant, such as the sound *w* in *well*

Semmelweis *n* Ignaz Philipp. 1818–65, Hungarian obstetrician, who discovered the cause of puerperal infection and pioneered the use of antiseptics

semolina *n* the large hard grains of wheat left after flour has been milled, used for making puddings and pasta [Italian *semolino*]

Sempach *n* a village in central Switzerland, in Lucerne canton on Lake Sempach: scene of the victory (1386) of the Swiss over the Hapsburgs

Semtex *n* a pliable plastic explosive

Sen *n* Ivan. born 1972, Australian filmmaker. His films include *Beneath Clouds* (2002), *Dreamland* (2010), and *Toomelah* (2011)

SEN (in Britain) State Enrolled Nurse

Sen. *or* **sen.** **1** senate **2** senator **3** senior

senate *n* the main governing body at some universities [Latin *senatus* council of the elders]

Senate *n* the upper chamber of the legislatures of Australia, the US, Canada, and many other countries

senator *n* a member of a Senate ▷ **senatorial** *adj*

send *vb* **sending, sent 1** to cause (a person or thing) to go or be taken or transmitted to another place: *send a cheque or postal order* **2 send for** to dispatch a request or command for (someone or something): *she had sent for me* **3** to cause to go to a place or point: *the bullet sent him flying into the air* **4** to bring to a state or condition: *his schemes to send her mad*

5 to cause to happen or come: *the thunderstorm sent by the gods* **6** *old-fashioned, slang* to move to excitement or rapture: *this music really sends me* [Old English *sendan*]
> **sender** *n*

Sendai *n* a city in central Japan, on NE Honshu; severely damaged during the 2011 tsunami; university (1907). Pop: 1 001 387 (2007)

Sendak *n* Maurice (**Bernard**). 1928–2012, US artist, writer, and set designer, best known as an illustrator of children's books, including *Where the Wild Things Are* (1963), which he also wrote, *In the Night Kitchen* (1971), and *Nutcracker* (1984)

send down *vb* **1** *Brit* to expel from a university **2** *informal* to send to prison

sendoff *n* **1** *informal* a show of good wishes to a person about to set off on a journey or start a new career ▷ *vb* **send off** **2** to dispatch (something, such as a letter) **3** *sport* (of a referee) to dismiss (a player) from the field of play for some offence

send up *informal* *vb* **1** to make fun of by doing an imitation or parody ▷ *n* **send-up** **2** a parody or imitation

Seneca *n* **1** Lucius Annaeus, called *the Younger*. ?4 BC–65 AD, Roman philosopher, statesman, and dramatist; tutor and adviser to Nero. He was implicated in a plot to murder Nero and committed suicide. His works include Stoical essays on ethical subjects and tragedies that had a considerable influence on Elizabethan drama **2** his father, **Marcus** or **Lucius Annaeus,** called *the Elder* or *the Rhetorician*. ?55 BC–?39 AD, Roman writer on oratory and history

Senefelder *n* (Johan Nepomuk Franz) **Aloys**. 1771–1834, German dramatist and engraver, born in Czechoslovakia, who invented (1796) lithography

Senegal *n* a republic in West Africa, on the Atlantic: made part of French West Africa in 1895; became fully independent in 1960; joined with The Gambia to form the Confederation of Senegambia (1982–89); mostly low-lying, with semidesert in the north and tropical forest in the southwest. Official language: French. Religion: Muslim majority. Currency: franc. Capital: Dakar. Pop: 13 300 410 (2013 est). Area: 197 160 sq km (76 124 sq miles)

Senegalese *adj* **1** of or relating to Senegal or its inhabitants ▷ *n* **2** a native or inhabitant of Senegal

Senegambia *n* a region of W Africa, between the Senegal and Gambia Rivers: now mostly in Senegal

senescent *adj* *formal* growing old [Latin *senescere* to grow old] > **senescence** *n*

seneschal (sen-ish-al) *n history* a steward of the household of a medieval prince or nobleman [Old French]

Senghor *n* Léopold Sédar. 1906–2001, Senegalese statesman and writer; president of Senegal (1960–80)

senile *adj* mentally or physically weak or infirm on account of old age [Latin *senex* an old man] > **senility** *n*

senior *adj* **1** higher in rank or length of service **2** older in years: *senior citizens* **3** education of or designating more advanced or older pupils or students ▷ *n* **4** a senior person [Latin: older]

Senior *adj chiefly US* being older than someone of the same name: *Joe Yule Senior*

senior aircraftman *n* (in Britain) an ordinary rank in the Royal Air Force

senior citizen *n* an old person, esp. a pensioner

seniority *n, pl* **-ties 1** the state of being senior **2** the degree of power or importance in an organization from length of continuous service

senior service *n Brit* the Royal Navy

Senkaku Islands *pl n* a group of uninhabited islets in the East China Sea; claimed by China and Japan. Chinese name: **Diaoyu Islands**

Senlac *n* a hill in Sussex: site of the Battle of Hastings in 1066

senna *n* **1** a tropical plant with yellow flowers and long pods **2** the dried leaves and pods of this plant, used as a laxative [Arabic *sanā*]

Senna *n* Ayrton. 1960–94, Brazilian racing driver: Formula One world champion (1988, 1990, 1991)

Sennacherib *n* died 681 BC, king of Assyria (705–681); son of Sargon II. He invaded Judah twice, defeated Babylon, and rebuilt Nineveh

Sennar *n* **1** a region of the E Sudan, between the White Nile and the Blue Nile: a kingdom from the 16th to 19th centuries **2** a town in this region, on the Blue Nile: the nearby **Sennar Dam** (1925) supplies irrigation water to Gezira. Pop: 135 000 (2005 est)

Sennett *n* Mack, original name *Michael Sinott*. 1884–1960, US film producer and director, born in Canada, who produced many silent comedy films featuring the Keystone Kops, Charlie Chaplin, and Harold Lloyd, for the Keystone Company

señor (sen-**nyor**) *n* a Spanish form of address equivalent to *sir* or *Mr*

señora (sen-**nyor**-a) *n* a Spanish form of address equivalent to *madam* or *Mrs*

señorita (sen-nyor-**ee**-ta) *n* a Spanish form of address equivalent to *madam* or *Miss*

sensation *n* **1** the power of feeling things physically: *I lose all sensation in my hands* **2** a physical feeling: *a burning sensation in the throat* **3** a general feeling or awareness: *a sensation of vague resentment* **4** a state of excitement: *imagine the sensation in Washington!* **5** an exciting person or thing: *you'll be a sensation* [Late Latin *sensatus* endowed with feelings]

sensational *adj* **1** causing intense feelings of shock, anger, or excitement: *sensational allegations* **2** *informal* extremely good: *the views are sensational* **3** of the senses or sensation > **sensationally** *adv*

sensationalism *n* the deliberate use of sensational language or subject matter to arouse feelings of shock, anger, or excitement > **sensationalist** *adj, n*

sense *n* **1** any of the faculties (sight, hearing, touch, taste, and smell) by which the mind receives information about the external world or the state of the body **2** the ability to perceive **3** a feeling perceived through one of the senses: *a sense of warmth* **4** a mental perception or awareness: *a sense of security* **5** ability to make moral judgments: *a sense of honour* **6** (usually pl) sound practical judgment or intelligence: *a man lost his senses and killed his wife* **7** reason or purpose: *no sense in continuing* **8** general meaning: *he couldn't understand every word but he got the sense of what they were saying* **9** specific meaning; definition: *the three senses of the word* **10** **make sense** to be understandable or practical ▷ *vb* **sensing, sensed 11** to perceive without the evidence of the senses: *he sensed that she was impressed* **12** to perceive through the senses [Latin *sentire* to feel]

senseless *adj* **1** having no meaning or purpose: *a senseless act of violence* **2** unconscious > **senselessly** *adv* > **senselessness** *n*

sense organ *n* a part of the body that receives stimuli and transmits them as sensations to the brain

sensibility *n, pl* **-ties 1** (often pl) the ability to experience deep feelings **2** (usually pl) the tendency to be influenced or offended: *its sheer callousness offended her sensibilities* **3** the ability to perceive or feel

sensible *adj* **1** having or showing good sense or judgment **2** (of clothing and footwear) practical and hard-wearing **3** capable of receiving sensation **4** capable of being perceived by the senses **5** perceptible to the mind **6** *literary* aware: *sensible of your kindness* [Latin *sentire* to feel] > **sensibly** *adv*

sensitive *adj* **1** easily hurt; tender **2** responsive to feelings and moods **3** responsive to external stimuli or impressions **4** easily offended or shocked **5** (of a subject or issue) liable to arouse controversy or strong feelings **6** (of an instrument) capable of registering small differences or changes in amounts **7** *photog* responding readily to light: *a sensitive emulsion* **8** *chiefly US* connected with matters affecting national security [Latin *sentire* to feel] ⟩ **sensitively** *adv* ⟩ **sensitivity** *n*

sensitize *or* **-tise** *vb* **-tizing, -tized** *or* **-tising, -tised** to make sensitive ⟩ **sensitization** *or* **-tisation** *n*

sensor *n* a device that detects or measures a physical property, such as radiation

sensory *adj* relating to the physical senses

sensual *adj* **1** giving pleasure to the body and senses rather than the mind: *soft sensual music* **2** having a strong liking for physical, esp. sexual, pleasures **3** of the body and senses rather than the mind or soul [Latin *sensus* feeling] ⟩ **sensualist** *n*

sensuality *n* **1** the quality or state of being sensual **2** enjoyment of physical, esp. sexual, pleasures

sensuous *adj* **1** pleasing to the senses of the mind or body: *the sensuous rhythms of the drums* **2** (of a person) appreciating qualities perceived by the senses ⟩ **sensuously** *adv*

sent *vb* the past of **send**

sentence *n* **1** a sequence of words constituting a statement, question, or a command that begins with a capital letter and ends with a full stop when written down **2 a** the decision of a law court as to what punishment is passed on a convicted person **b** the punishment passed on a convicted person ▷ *vb* **-tencing, -tenced 3** to pronounce sentence on (a convicted person) in a law court [Latin *sententia* a way of thinking] ⟩ **sentential** *adj*

sententious *adj formal* **1** trying to sound wise **2** making pompous remarks about morality [Latin *sententiosus* full of meaning] ⟩ **sententiously** *adv*

sentient (sen-tee-ent, sen-shent) *adj* capable of perception and feeling [Latin *sentiens* feeling] ⟩ **sentience** *n*

sentiment *n* **1** a mental attitude based on a mixture of thoughts and feelings: *anti-American sentiment* **2** (often pl) a thought, opinion, or attitude expressed in words: *his sentiments were echoed by subsequent speakers* **3** feelings such as tenderness, romance, and sadness, esp. when exaggerated: *a man without the softness of sentiment* [Latin *sentire* to feel]

sentimental *adj* **1** feeling or expressing tenderness, romance, or sadness to an exaggerated extent **2** appealing to the emotions, esp. to romantic feelings: *she kept the ring for sentimental reasons* ⟩ **sentimentalism** *n* ⟩ **sentimentalist** *n* ⟩ **sentimentality** *n* ⟩ **sentimentally** *adv*

sentimentalize *or* **-lise** *vb* **-lizing, -lized** *or* **-lising, -lised** to make sentimental or behave sentimentally

sentimental value *n* the value of an article to a particular person because of the emotions it arouses

sentinel *n old-fashioned* a sentry [Old French *sentinelle*]

sentry *n, pl* **-tries** a soldier who keeps watch and guards a camp or building [perhaps from obsolete *centrinel* *sentinel*]

sentry box *n* a small shelter with an open front in which a sentry stands during bad weather

SEO search engine optimization

Seoul *n* the capital of South Korea, in the west on the Han River: capital of Korea from 1392 to 1910, then seat of the Japanese administration until 1945; became capital of South Korea in 1948; cultural and educational centre. Pop: 9 592 000 (2005 est)

sepal *n botany* a leaflike division of the calyx of a flower [New Latin *sepalum*]

separable *adj* able to be separated

separate *vb* **-rating, -rated 1** to act as a barrier between: *the narrow stretch of water which separates Europe from Asia* **2** to part or be parted from a mass or group **3** to distinguish: *it's what separates the women from the boys* **4** to divide or be divided into component parts **5** to sever or be severed **6** (of a couple) to stop living together ▷ *adj* **7** existing or considered independently: *a separate issue* **8** set apart

from the main body or mass **9** distinct or individual [Latin *separare*] ⟩ **separately** *adv* ⟩ **separateness** *n* ⟩ **separator** *n*

separates *pl n Brit, Austral and NZ* clothes, such as skirts, blouses, and trousers, that only cover part of the body and are designed to be worn together or separately

separate school *n* (in certain Canadian provinces) a school for a large religious minority financed by provincial grants in addition to the education tax

separation *n* **1** the act of separating: *the separation of child from mother* **2** *family law* the living apart of a married couple without divorce **3** a mark, line, or object that separates one thing from another

separatist *n* a person who advocates the separation of his or her own group from an organization or country ⟩ **separatism** *n*

sepia *adj* dark reddish-brown, like the colour of very old photographs [Latin: a cuttlefish]

sepoy *n* (formerly) an Indian soldier in the service of the British [Urdu *sipāhī*]

sepsis *n* poisoning caused by the presence of pus-forming bacteria in the body [Greek: a rotting]

sept *n* a clan, esp. in Ireland or Scotland [perhaps variant of *sect*]

Sept. September

September *n* the ninth month of the year [Latin: the seventh (month)]

septennial *adj* **1** occurring every seven years **2** lasting seven years [Latin *septem* seven + *annus* a year]

septet *n* **1** a group of seven performers **2** a piece of music for seven performers **3** a group of seven people or things [Latin *septem* seven]

septic *adj* of or caused by harmful bacteria ⟩ **septicity** *n*

septicaemia *or* **septicemia** (sep-tis-see-mee-a) *n* an infection of the blood which develops in a wound [Greek *sēptos* decayed + *haima* blood]

septic tank *n* a tank in which sewage is decomposed by the action of bacteria

septuagenarian *n* **1** a person who is between 70 and 79 years old ▷ *adj* **2** between 70 and 79 years old [Latin *septuaginta* seventy]

Septuagint (sept-yew-a-jint) *n* the ancient Greek version of the Old Testament, including the Apocrypha [Latin *septuaginta* seventy]

septum *n, pl* **-ta** *biology, anatomy* a dividing partition between two tissues or cavities, such as in the nose [Latin *saeptum* wall]

septuple *vb* **-pling, -pled 1** to multiply by seven ▷ *adj* **2** seven times as much or as many **3** consisting of seven parts ▷ *n* **4** a quantity or number seven times as great as another [Latin *septem* seven]

sepulchral (sip-pulk-ral) *adj* **1** gloomy and solemn, like a tomb or grave **2** of a sepulchre

sepulchre *or US* **sepulcher** (sep-pulk-er) *n* **1** a burial vault, tomb, or grave ▷ *vb* **-chring, -chred** *or US* **-chering, -chered 2** to bury in a sepulchre [Latin *sepulcrum*]

sepulture (sep-pult-cher) *n* the act of placing in a sepulchre

sequel *n* **1** a novel, play, or film that continues the story of an earlier one **2** anything that happens after or as a result of something else: *there was an amusing sequel to this incident* [Latin *sequi* to follow]

sequence *n* **1** an arrangement of two or more things in a successive order **2** the successive order of two or more things: *chronological sequence* **3** an action or event that follows another or others **4** *maths* an ordered set of numbers or other quantities in one-to-one correspondence with the integers 1 to *n* **5** a section of a film forming a single uninterrupted episode ▷ *vb* **6** to arrange in a sequence [Latin *sequi* to follow]

sequential *adj* happening in a fixed order or sequence

sequester *vb* **1** to seclude: *he could sequester himself in his own home* **2** *law* same as **sequestrate** [Late Latin *sequestrare* to surrender for safekeeping]

sequestrate *vb* **-trating, -trated** *law* to confiscate (property) temporarily until creditors are satisfied or a court order is complied with **› sequestration** *n* **› sequestrator** *n*

sequin *n* a small piece of shiny metal foil used to decorate clothes [Italian *zecchino*] **› sequined** *adj*

sequoia *n* a giant Californian coniferous tree [after *Sequoya*, a Native American scholar]

Sequoia National Park *n* a national park in central California, in the Sierra Nevada Mountains: established in 1890 to protect groves of giant sequoias, some of which are about 4000 years old. Area: 1556 sq km (601 sq miles)

seraglio (sir-ah-lee-oh) *n, pl* **-raglios** 1 the part of a Muslim house or palace where the owner's wives live 2 a Turkish sultan's palace [Italian *serraglio* animal cage]

Serajevo *n* a variant of **Sarajevo**

Seram or **Ceram** *n* an island in Indonesia, in the Moluccas, separated from New Guinea by the **Ceram Sea**: mountainous and densely forested. Area: 17 150 sq km (6622 sq miles). Also called: **Serang**

seraph *n, pl* **-raphim** *theol* a member of the highest order of angels [from Hebrew] **› seraphic** *adj*

Serb *adj, n* same as **Serbian**

Serbia *n* a republic in SE Europe: declared a kingdom in 1882; precipitated World War I by the conflict with Austria; became part of the Kingdom of the Serbs, Croats, and Slovenes (later called Yugoslavia) in 1918; with Montenegro formed the Federal Republic of Yugoslavia when the other constituent republics became independent in 1991–92; a Union of Serbia and Montenegro formed in 2003 and dissolved in 2006. The autonomous region of Kosovo (administered by the UN following the conflict of 1999) unilaterally declared its independence from Serbia in 2008. Mountainous in the S, with the Danube plains in the N. Religion: Serbian Orthodox majority, with Roman Catholic and Muslim minorities. Currencies: new dinar and euro (in Kosovo). Capital: Belgrade. Pop: 7 243 007 (2013). Area: 88 361 sq km (34 109 sq miles). Former name: **Servia**. Serbian name: **Srbija**

Serbia and Montenegro *n* a former country in SE Europe, consisting of the republics of Serbia and Montenegro; replaced the Federal Republic of Yugoslavia in 2003, and dissolved in 2006 following Montenegro's decision to secede

Serbian *adj* 1 of or relating to Serbia or its inhabitants ▷ *n* 2 a native or inhabitant of Serbia 3 the dialect of Serbo-Croat spoken in Serbia

Serbo-Croat or **Serbo-Croatian** *n* 1 the chief official language of Serbia and Croatia ▷ *adj* 2 of this language

Sercq *n* the French name for **Sark**

Seremban *n* a town in Peninsular Malaysia, capital of Negri Sembilan state. Pop: 332 000 (2005 est)

serenade *n* 1 a piece of music played or sung to a woman by a lover 2 a piece of music suitable for this 3 an orchestral suite for a small ensemble ▷ *vb* **-nading, -naded** 4 to sing or play a serenade to (someone) [French]

serendipity *n* the gift of making fortunate discoveries by accident [from the fairy tale *The Three Princes of Serendip*, in which the heroes possess this gift]

serene *adj* 1 peaceful or calm 2 (of the sky) clear or bright [Latin *serenus*] **› serenely** *adv* **› serenity** *n*

serf *n* (esp. in medieval Europe) a labourer who could not leave the land on which he worked [Latin *servus* a slave] **› serfdom** *n*

serge *n* a strong fabric made of wool, cotton, silk, or rayon, used for clothing [Old French *sarge*]

sergeant *n* 1 a noncommissioned officer in the armed forces 2 (in Britain, S Africa, Australia, and NZ) a police officer ranking between constable and inspector [Old French *sergent*]

sergeant at arms *n* a parliamentary or court officer responsible for keeping order

sergeant major *n* a noncommissioned officer of the highest rank in the army

Sergipe *n* a state of NE Brazil: the smallest Brazilian state; a centre of resistance to Dutch conquest (17th century). Capital: Aracajú. Pop: 1 846 039 (2002). Area: 13 672 sq km (8492 sq miles)

serial *n* 1 a story published or broadcast in instalments at regular intervals 2 a publication that is regularly issued and consecutively numbered ▷ *adj* 3 of, in, or forming a series: *serial pregnancies* 4 published or presented as a serial [Latin *series* series] **› serially** *adv*

serialize or **-ise** *vb* **-izing, -ized** or **-ising, -ised** to publish or present in the form of a serial **› serialization** or **-isation** *n*

serial killer *n* a person who commits a number of murders

serial monogamy *n* the practice of having a number of long-term romantic or sexual partners in succession

serial number *n* any of the consecutive numbers given to objects in a series for identification

series *n, pl* **-ries** 1 a group or succession of related things 2 a set of radio or television programmes dealing with the same subject, esp. one having the same characters but different stories 3 *maths* the sum of a finite or infinite sequence of numbers or quantities 4 *electronics* an arrangement of two or more components connected in a circuit so that the same current flows in turn through each of them: *a number of resistors in series* 5 *geology* a set of layers that represent the rocks formed during an epoch [Latin: a row]

Seringapatam *n* a small town in S India, in Karnataka on **Seringapatam Island** in the Cauvery River: capital of Mysore from 1610 to 1799, when it was besieged and captured by the British. Pop: 23 448 (2001)

seriocomic (seer-ee-oh-**kom**-ik) *adj* mixing serious and comic elements

serious *adj* 1 giving cause for concern: *the situation is serious* 2 concerned with important matters: *there are some serious questions that need to be answered* 3 not cheerful; grave: *I am a serious person* 4 in earnest; sincere: *he believes we are serious* 5 requiring concentration: *a serious book* 6 *informal* impressive because of its substantial quantity or quality: *serious money* [Latin *serius*] **› seriously** *adv* **› seriousness** *n*

serjeant *n* same as **sergeant**

Serlio *n* Sebastiano 1475–1554, Italian architect and painter, best known for his treatise *Complete Works on Architecture and Perspective* (1537–75), the first to set out the principles of classical architecture and to give rules for their application

sermon *n* 1 a speech on a religious or moral subject given by a clergyman as part of a church service 2 *disparaging* a serious talk on behaviour, morals, or duty, esp. a long and tedious one [Latin *sermo* discourse]

seropositive (seer-oh-**poz**-zit-iv) *adj* (of a person whose blood has been tested for a specific disease, such as AIDS) showing a significant level of serum antibodies, indicating the presence of the disease

serotonin (ser-roe-**tone**-in) *n* *biochem* a compound that occurs in the brain, intestines, and blood platelets and acts as a neurotransmitter

serous (**seer**-uss) *adj* of, containing, or like serum

serpent *n* 1 *literary* a snake 2 a devious person [Latin *serpens* a creeping thing]

serpentine¹ *adj* twisting like a snake

serpentine² *n* a soft green or brownish-red mineral [so named from its snakelike patterns]

serrated *adj* having a notched or sawlike edge [Latin *serratus* saw-shaped] **› serration** *n*

serried *adj* *literary* in close formation: *the serried ranks of fans* [Old French *serré* close-packed]

Sertorius *n* Quintus. ?123–72 BC, Roman soldier who fought with Marius in Gaul (102) and led an insurrection

S

in Spain against Sulla until he was assassinated

serum (seer-um) n 1 the yellowish watery fluid left after blood has clotted 2 this fluid from the blood of immunized animals used for inoculation or vaccination 3 *physiol, zoology* any clear watery animal fluid [Latin: whey]

serval n a slender African wild cat with black-spotted tawny fur

servant n 1 a person employed to do household work for another person 2 a person or thing that is useful or provides a service: *a distinguished servant of this country* [Old French: serving]

serve vb **serving, served** 1 to be of service to (a person, community, or cause); help 2 to perform an official duty or duties: *he served on several university committees* 3 to attend to (customers) in a shop 4 to provide (guests) with food or drink: *he served dinner guests German wine* 5 to provide (food or drink) for customers: *breakfast is served from 7 am* 6 to provide with something needed by the public: *the community served by the school* 7 to work as a servant for (a person) 8 to go through (a period of police or military service, apprenticeship, or imprisonment) 9 to meet the needs of: *they serve a purpose* 10 to perform a function: *the attacks only served to strengthen their resolve* 11 (of a male animal) to mate with (a female animal) 12 *tennis, squash etc.* to put (the ball) into play 13 to deliver (a legal document) to (a person) 14 **serve someone right** *informal* to be what someone deserves, esp. for doing something stupid or wrong ▷ n 15 *tennis, squash etc.* short for **service** (12) [Latin *servus* a slave]

server n 1 *computers* a computer or program that supplies data to other machines on a network 2 a person who serves

Servetus n **Michael**, Spanish name *Miguel Serveto*. 1511–53, Spanish theologian and physician. He was burnt at the stake by order of Calvin for denying the divinity of Christ

Servia n the former name of **Serbia**

Servian adj, n a former word for **Serbian**

service n 1 an act of help or assistance 2 an organization or system that provides something needed by the public: *a consumer information service* 3 a department of public employment and its employees: *the diplomatic service* 4 the installation or maintenance of goods provided by a dealer after a sale 5 availability for use by the public: *the new plane could be in service within fifteen years* 6 a regular check made on a machine or vehicle in which parts are tested, cleaned, or replaced if worn 7 the serving of guests or customers: *service is included on the wine list* 8 one of the branches of the armed forces 9 the serving of food: *silver service* 10 a set of dishes, cups, and plates for use at table 11 a formal religious ceremony 12 *tennis, squash etc.* a the act, manner, or right of serving the ball b the game in which a particular player serves: *she dropped only one point on her service* ▷ adj 13 of or for the use of servants or employees: *a service elevator* 14 serving the public rather than producing goods: *service industries* ▷ vb **-vicing, -viced** 15 to provide service or services to 16 to check and repair (a vehicle or machine) 17 (of a male animal) to mate with (a female animal) ▶ See also **services** [Latin *servitium* condition of a slave]

Service n **Robert** (**William**). 1874–1958, Canadian poet, born in England; noted for his ballad-like poems of gold-rush era Yukon, such as *The Shooting of Dan McGrew*; his books include *Songs of a Sourdough* (1907)

serviceable adj 1 performing effectively: *serviceable boots* 2 able or ready to be used: *five remaining serviceable aircraft* > **serviceability** n

service area n a place on a motorway with a garage, restaurants, and toilets

service charge n a percentage added to a bill in a hotel or restaurant to pay for service

service flat n *Brit* a flat where domestic services are provided by the management

serviceman n, pl **-men** 1 a person in the armed services 2 a man employed to service and maintain equipment > **servicewoman** *fem* n

service road n *Brit and Austral* a narrow road running parallel to a main road that provides access to houses and shops situated along its length

services pl n 1 work performed in a job: *the OBE for her services to the community* 2 **the services** the armed forces 3 a system of providing the public with something it needs, such as gas or water

service station n 1 a place that sells fuel, oil, and spare parts for motor vehicles 2 same as **service area**

serviette n *chiefly Brit and Canad* a table napkin [Old French]

servile adj 1 too eager to obey people; fawning 2 of or suitable for a slave [Latin *servus* slave] > **servility** n

serving n a portion of food

servitor n *archaic* a servant or attendant

servitude n *formal* 1 slavery or bondage 2 the state or condition of being completely dominated [Latin *servus* a slave]

servomechanism n a device which converts a small force into a larger force, used esp. in steering mechanisms

sesame (sess-am-ee) n a plant of the East Indies, grown for its seeds and oil, which are used in cooking [Greek]

sesh n *slang* short for **session** (1)

Sesostris I n 20th century BC, king of Egypt of the 12th dynasty. He conquered Nubia and brought ancient Egypt to the height of its prosperity. The funerary complex at Lisht was built during his reign

Sesshu n original family name *Oda*, also called *Toyo*. 1420–1506, Japanese landscape painter, who introduced the Chinese technique of ink painting on long scrolls to Japan

sessile adj 1 (of flowers or leaves) having no stalk 2 (of animals such as the barnacle) fixed in one position [Latin *sessilis* concerning sitting]

session n 1 any period devoted to a particular activity 2 a meeting of a court, parliament, or council 3 a series or period of such meetings 4 a school or university term or year [Latin *sessio* a sitting] > **sessional** adj

Sessions n **Roger** (**Huntington**). 1896–1985, US composer

sestet n 1 *prosody* the last six lines of a sonnet 2 same as **sextet** (1) [Italian *sesto* sixth]

Sestos n a ruined town in NW Turkey, at the narrowest point of the Dardanelles: N terminus of the bridge of boats built by Xerxes in 481 BC for the crossing of his armies of invasion

set¹ vb **setting, set** 1 to put in a specified position or state: *I set him free* 2 **set to** or **on** to bring (something) into contact with (something else): *three prisoners set fire to their cells* 3 to put into order or make ready: *set the table* 4 to make or become firm or rigid: *before the eggs begin to set* 5 to put (a broken bone) or (of a broken bone) to be put into a normal position for healing 6 to adjust (a clock or other instrument) to a particular position 7 to arrange or establish: *to set a date for diplomatic talks; it set the standards of performance* 8 to prescribe or assign (a task or material for study): *the examiners have set 'Paradise Lost'* 9 to arrange (hair) while wet, so that it dries in position 10 to place a jewel in (a setting): *a ring set with diamonds* 11 to provide music for (a poem or other text to be sung) 12 *printing* a to arrange (type) for printing b to put (text) into type 13 to arrange (a stage or television studio) with scenery and props 14 **set to** or **on** to value (something) at a specified price or worth: *he set a high price on his services* 15 (of the sun or moon) to disappear beneath the horizon 16 (of plants) to produce (fruits or seeds) or (of fruits or seeds) to develop 17 to place (a hen) on (eggs) to incubate them 18 (of a gun dog) to turn in the direction of game birds ▷ n 19 the act of setting 20 a condition of firmness or hardness 21 manner of standing; posture: *the set of his shoulders* 22 the scenery and other props used in a play or film **23** same as sett ▷ adj **24** fixed or established by authority or agreement: *set hours of work* **25** rigid or inflexible: *she is set in her ways* **26** unmoving; fixed: *a set expression on his face* **27** conventional or stereotyped: *she made her apology in set phrases* **28 set in** (of a scene or story) represented as happening at a certain time or place: *a European film set in Africa* **29 set on** or **upon** determined to (do or achieve something): *why are you so set upon avoiding me?* **30** ready: *all set to go* **31** (of material for study) prescribed for students' preparation for an examination ▶ See also **set about, set against,** etc. [Old English *settan*]

set² n **1** a number of objects or people grouped or belonging together: *a set of slides* **2** a group of people who associate with each other or have similar interests: *the tennis set* **3** *maths* a collection of numbers or objects that satisfy a given condition or share a property **4** a television or piece of radio equipment **5** the scenery and other props used in a dramatic production, film, etc. **6** *sport* a group of games or points in a match, of which the winner must win a certain number **7** a series of songs or tunes performed by a musician or group on a given occasion: *the front row spent the rest of the set craning their necks* [Old French *sette*]

set about vb **1** to start or begin **2** to attack

set against vb **1** to balance or compare **2** to cause to be unfriendly to: *the war set brother against brother*

set aside vb **1** to reserve for a special purpose **2** to discard or reject

set back vb **1** to delay or hinder **2** *informal* to cost (a person) a specified amount ▷ n **setback 3** anything that delays progress

set down vb **1** to record in writing **2** *Brit* to allow (passengers) to get off a bus etc.

set forth vb *formal, archaic* **1** to state or present (an argument or facts) **2** to start out on a journey: *he set forth on foot*

set in vb **1** to begin and continue for some time: *decadence has set in* **2** to insert

set off vb **1** to start a journey **2** to cause (a person) to act or do something, such as laugh **3** to cause to explode **4** to act as a contrast to: *blue suits you, sets off the colour of your hair*

Seton n Ernest Thompson. 1860–1946, US author and illustrator of animal books, born in England

set on or **set upon** vb to attack or cause to attack: *they set the dogs on him*

Seto Naikai n transliteration of the Japanese name for the **Inland Sea**

set out vb **1** to present, arrange, or display **2** to give a full account of: *the policy was set out in an interview with the BBC* **3** to begin or embark on an undertaking, esp. a journey

set piece n **1** a work of literature, music, or art, intended to create an impressive effect **2** *football, hockey etc.* an attacking move from a corner or free kick

set square n a thin flat piece of plastic or metal in the shape of a right-angled triangle, used in technical drawing

sett or **set** n **1** a badger's burrow **2** a small rectangular paving block made of stone [variant of SET¹ (noun)]

settee n a seat, for two or more people, with a back and usually with arms; couch [from SETTLE²]

setter n a large long-haired dog originally bred for hunting

set theory n *maths* the branch of mathematics concerned with the properties and interrelationships of sets

setting n **1** the surroundings in which something is set **2** the scenery, properties, or background used to create the location for a stage play or film **3** a piece of music written for the words of a text **4** the decorative metalwork in which a gem is set **5** the plates and cutlery for a single place at a table **6** one of the positions or levels to which the controls of a machine can be adjusted

settle¹ vb **-tling, -tled 1** to put in order: *he settled his affairs before he died* **2** to arrange or be arranged firmly or comfortably: *he settled into his own chair by the fire* **3** to come down to rest: *a bird settled on top of the hedge* **4** to establish or become established as a resident: *they eventually settled in Glasgow* **5** to establish or become established in a way of life or a job **6** to migrate to (a country) and form a community; colonize **7** to make or become quiet, calm, or stable **8** to cause (sediment) to sink to the bottom in a liquid or (of sediment) to sink thus **9** to subside: *the dust settled* **10** (sometimes foll. by *up*) to pay off (a bill or debt) **11** to decide or dispose of: *to settle an argument* **12** (often foll. by *on* or *upon*) to agree or fix: *they settled on an elementary code* **13** (usually foll. by *on* or *upon*) to give (a title or property) to a person by gift or legal deed: *he settled his property on his wife* **14** to decide (a legal dispute) by agreement without court action: *they settled out of court* [Old English *setlan*]

settle² n a long wooden bench with a high back and arms, sometimes having a storage space under the seat [Old English *setl*]

settle down vb **1** to make or become quiet and orderly **2 settle down to** to remove all distractions and concentrate on: *we settled down to a favourite movie* **3** to adopt an orderly and routine way of life, esp. after marriage

settle for vb to accept or agree to in spite of dissatisfaction

settlement n **1** an act of settling **2** a place newly settled; colony **3** subsidence of all or part of a building **4** an official agreement ending a dispute **5** *law* **a** an arrangement by which property is transferred to a person's possession **b** the deed transferring such property

settler n a person who settles in a new country or a colony

set to vb **1** to begin working **2** to start fighting ▷ n **set-to 3** *informal* a brief disagreement or fight

set-top box n a device which converts the signals from a digital television broadcast into a form which can be viewed on a standard television set

Setúbal n a port in SW Portugal, on **Setúbal Bay** south of Lisbon: an earthquake in 1755 destroyed most of the old town. Pop: 113 937 (2001)

set up vb **1** to build or construct: *the soldiers had actually set up a munitions factory* **2** to put into a position of power or wealth **3** to begin or enable (someone) to begin (a new venture): *he set up a small shop* **4** to begin or produce: *to set up a nuclear chain reaction* **5** to establish: *Broad set up a world record* **6** *informal* to cause (a person) to be blamed or accused **7** to restore the health of: *a pub lunch set me up nicely* ▷ n **setup 8** *informal* the way in which anything is organized or arranged **9** *slang* an event the result of which is prearranged

Seurat n Georges. 1859–91, French neoimpressionist painter. He developed the pointillist technique of painting, characterized by brilliant luminosity, as in *Dimanche à la Grande-Jatte* (1886)

Sevan n **Lake Sevan** a lake in Armenia at an altitude of 1914 m (6279 ft). Area: 1417 sq km (547 sq miles)

Sevastopol n a port, resort, and naval base in the Crimea, on the Black Sea: captured and destroyed by British, French, and Turkish forces after a siege of 11 months (1854–55) during the Crimean War; taken by the Germans after a siege of 8 months (1942) during World War II. Pop: 338 000 (2005 est). English name: Sebastopol

seven n **1** the cardinal number that is the sum of one and six **2** a numeral, 7 or VII, representing this number **3** something representing or consisting of seven units ▷ adj **4** amounting to seven: *seven weeks* [Old English *seofon*] **> seventh** adj, n

sevenfold adj **1** having seven times as many or as much **2** composed of seven parts ▷ adv **3** by seven times as many or as much

S

Seven Hills of Rome *pl n* the hills on which the ancient city of Rome was built: the Palatine, Capitoline, Quirinal, Caelian, Aventine, Esquiline, and Viminal

seven seas *pl n old-fashioned* all the oceans of the world

seventeen *n* **1** the cardinal number that is the sum of ten and seven **2** a numeral, 17 or XVII, representing this number **3** something representing or consisting of seventeen units ▷ *adj* **4** amounting to seventeen: *seventeen children* ❭ **seventeenth** *adj, n*

seventh heaven *n* a state of supreme happiness

seventy *n, pl* **-ties** **1** the cardinal number that is the product of ten and seven **2** a numeral, 70 or LXX, representing this number **3** something representing or consisting of seventy units ▷ *adj* **4** amounting to seventy: *seventy countries* ❭ **seventieth** *adj, n*

sever *vb* **1** to cut right through or cut off (something): *it accidentally severed the electrical cable* **2** to break off (a tie or relationship) [Latin *separare* to separate] ❭ **severable** *adj* ❭ **severance** *n*

several *adj* **1** more than a few: *I spoke to several doctors* **2** *formal* various or separate: *the members with their several occupations* **3** *formal* distinct or different: *misfortune visited her three several times* [Medieval Latin *separalis*]

severally *adv formal* individually or separately: *the Western nations severally rather than jointly decided that they would have to act without Russia*

severance pay *n* compensation paid by a firm to an employee who has to leave because the job he or she was appointed to do no longer exists

severe *adj* **1** strict or harsh in the treatment of others: *a severe parent* **2** serious in appearance or manner: *a severe look; a severe hairdo* **3** very intense or unpleasant: *severe chest pains; the punishments are severe* **4** causing discomfort by its harshness: *severe frost* **5** hard to perform or accomplish: *a severe challenge* [Latin *severus*] ❭ **severely** *adv* ❭ **severity** *n*

Severn *n* **1** a river in E Wales and W England, rising in Powys and flowing northeast and east into England, then south to the Bristol Channel. Length: about 354 km (220 miles) **2** a river in SE central Canada, in Ontario, flowing northeast to Hudson Bay. Length: about 676 km (420 miles)

Severnaya Zemlya *n* an archipelago in the Arctic Ocean off the coast of N central Russia

Severus *n* Lucius Septimius. 146–211 AD, Roman soldier and emperor (193–211). He waged war successfully against the Parthians (197–202) and spent his last years in Britain (208–211)

Seveso *n* a town in N Italy, near Milan: the site of a major air pollution incident in 1976 when a poisonous cloud of dioxin gas was released from a factory. Pop: 22 877 (2010)

Sévigné *n* Marquise de, title of *Marie de Rabutin-Chantal*. 1626–96, French letter writer. Her correspondence with her daughter and others provides a vivid account of society during the reign of Louis XIV

Seville *n* a port in SW Spain, on the Guadalquivir River: chief town of S Spain under the Vandals and Visigoths (5th–8th centuries); centre of Spanish colonial trade (16th–17th centuries); tourist centre. Pop: 709 975 (2003 est). Ancient name: **Hispalis**. Spanish name: **Sevilla**

Seville orange *n* a bitter orange used to make marmalade [after SEVILLE]

Sèvres (sev-ra) *n* a kind of fine French porcelain [after Sèvres, near Paris]

sew *vb* **sewing, sewed, sewn** *or* **sewed** **1** to join with thread repeatedly passed through with a needle **2** to attach, fasten, or close by sewing ▶ See also **sew up** [Old English *sēowan*]

sewage *n* waste matter or excrement carried away in sewers or drains

sewage farm *n* a place where sewage is treated so that it can be used as manure or disposed of safely

Seward *n* William Henry. 1801–72, US statesman; secretary of state (1861–69). He was a leading opponent

of slavery and was responsible for the purchase of Alaska (1867)

Seward Peninsula *n* a peninsula of W Alaska, on the Bering Strait. Length: about 290 km (180 miles)

Sewell *n* Henry. 1807–79, New Zealand statesman, born in England: first prime minister of New Zealand (1856)

sewer *n* a drain or pipe, usually underground, used to carry away surface water or sewage [Old French *essever* to drain]

sewerage *n* **1** a system of sewers **2** the removal of surface water or sewage by means of sewers

sewing *n* **1** a piece of fabric or an article, that is sewn or to be sewn **2** the act of fastening together (pieces of fabric, etc.) with needle and thread

sewing machine *n* a machine that sews material with a needle driven by an electric motor

sewn *vb* a past participle of **sew**

sew up *vb* **1** to fasten or mend completely by sewing **2** *informal* to complete or negotiate successfully: *the deal was sewn up just before the deadline*

sex *n* **1** the state of being either male or female **2** either of the two categories, male or female, into which organisms are divided **3** sexual intercourse **4** feelings or behaviour connected with having sex or the desire to have sex **5** sexual matters in general ▷ *adj* **6** of sexual matters: *sex education* **7** based on or resulting from the difference between the sexes: *sex discrimination* ▷ *vb* **8** to find out the sex of (an animal) [Latin *sexus*]

sexagenarian *n* **1** a person who is between 60 and 69 years old ▷ *adj* **2** between 60 and 69 years old [Latin *sexaginta* sixty]

sex appeal *n* sexual attractiveness

sex chromosome *n* either of the chromosomes that determine the sex of an animal

sexism *n* discrimination against the members of one sex, usually women ❭ **sexist** *n, adj*

sexless *adj* **1** neither male nor female **2** having no sexual desires **3** sexually unattractive

sex object *n* someone, esp. a woman, regarded only in terms of physical attractiveness and not as a person

sexology *n* the study of sexual behaviour in human beings ❭ **sexologist** *n*

sextant *n* an instrument used in navigation for measuring angular distance, for example between the sun and the horizon, to calculate the position of a ship or aircraft [Latin *sextans* one sixth of a unit]

sextet *n* **1** a group of six performers **2** a piece of music for six performers **3** a group of six people or things [variant of *sestet*]

sexton *n* a person employed to look after a church and its churchyard [Medieval Latin *sacristanus* sacristan]

sextuple *vb* **-pling, -pled** **1** to multiply by six ▷ *adj* **2** six times as much or as many **3** consisting of six parts ▷ *n* **4** a quantity or number six times as great as another [Latin *sextus* sixth]

sextuplet *n* one of six children born at one birth

sexual *adj* **1** of or characterized by sex **2** (of reproduction) characterized by the union of male and female reproductive cells **3** of or relating to the differences between males and females ❭ **sexuality** *n* ❭ **sexually** *adv*

sexual harassment *n* the unwelcome directing of sexual remarks, looks, or advances, usually at a woman in the workplace

sexual intercourse *n* the sexual act in which the male's erect penis is inserted into the female's vagina, usually followed by the ejaculation of semen

sex up *vb informal* to make (something) more exciting

sexy *adj* **sexier, sexiest** *informal* **1** sexually exciting or attractive: *a sexy voice* **2** interesting, exciting, or trendy: *a sexy project; a sexy new car* ❭ **sexiness** *n*

Seychelles *pl n* a group of volcanic islands in the W Indian Ocean: taken by the British from the French in 1744: became an independent republic within the Commonwealth in 1976, incorporating the British

Indian Ocean Territory islands of Aldabra, Farquhar, and Desroches. Languages: Creole, English, and French. Religion: Roman Catholic majority. Currency: rupee. Capital: Victoria. Pop: 90 846 (2013 est). Area: 455 sq km (176 sq miles)

Seyhan *n* another name for **Adana**

Seymour *n* **Jane**. ?1509–37, third wife of Henry VIII of England; mother of Edward VI

SF *or* **sf** science fiction

SFA Scottish Football Association

Sfax *n* a port in E Tunisia, on the Gulf of Gabès: the second largest town in Tunisia; commercial centre of a phosphate region. Pop: 570 000 (2005 est)

SFO (in Britain) Serious Fraud Office

Sforza *n* **1** Count **Carlo**. 1873–1952, Italian statesman; leader of the anti-Fascist opposition **2** **Francesco**. 1401–66, duke of Milan (1450–66) **3** his father **Giacomuzzo** *or* **Muzio**, original name *Attendolo*. 1369–1424, Italian condottiere and founder of the dynasty that ruled Milan (1450–1535) **4** **Lodovico**, called *the Moor*. 1451–1508, duke of Milan (1494–1500), but effective ruler from 1480; patron of Leonardo da Vinci

Sg *chem* seaborgium

's Gravenhage *n* a Dutch name for (The) **Hague**

Sgt. Sergeant

sh *interj* be quiet!

Shaanxi *or* **Shensi** *n* a province of NW China: one of the earliest centres of Chinese civilization; largely mountainous. Capital: Xi'an. Pop: 36 900 000 (2003 est). Area: 195 800 sq km (75 598 sq miles)

Shaba *n* the former name (1972–97) of **Katanga**

shabby *adj* **-bier, -biest** **1** old and worn in appearance **2** wearing worn and dirty clothes **3** behaving in a mean or unfair way: *shabby manoeuvres* [Old English *sceabb* scab] ▷ **shabbily** *adv* ▷ **shabbiness** *n*

Shache, Soche *or* **So-ch'e** *n* a town in W China, in the W Xinjiang: a centre of the caravan trade between China, India, and Transcaspian areas. Also called: **Yarkand**

shack *n* **1** a roughly built hut ▷ *vb* **2** **shack up with** *slang* to live with (a lover) [perhaps from dialect *shackly* ramshackle]

shackle *n* **1** one of a pair of metal rings joined by a chain for securing someone's wrists or ankles **2** **shackles** anything that confines or restricts freedom: *free from the shackles of its feudal past* **3** a metal loop or link closed by a bolt, used for securing ropes or chains ▷ *vb* **-ling, -led** **4** to fasten with shackles **5** to restrict or hamper: *an economy shackled by central control* [Old English *sceacel*]

Shackleton *n* Sir **Ernest Henry**. 1874–1922, British explorer. He commanded three expeditions to the Antarctic (1907–09; 1914–17; 1921–22), during which the south magnetic pole was located (1909)

shad *n*, *pl* **shad** *or* **shads** a herring-like food fish [Old English *sceadd*]

Shadbolt *n* **Maurice**. 1932–2004, New Zealand novelist

shade *n* **1** relative darkness produced by blocking out sunlight **2** a place sheltered from the sun by trees, buildings, etc. **3** something used to provide a shield or protection from a direct source of light, such as a lamp shade **4** a shaded area in a painting or drawing **5** any of the different hues of a colour: *a much darker shade of grey* **6** a slight amount: *a shade of reluctance* **7** **put someone** or **something in the shade** to be so impressive as to make another person or thing seem unimportant by comparison **8** *literary* a ghost ▷ *vb* **shading, shaded** **9** to screen or protect from heat or light **10** to make darker or dimmer **11** to represent (a darker area) in (a painting or drawing), by graded areas of tone, lines, or dots **12** to change slightly or by degrees [Old English *sceadu*]

shades *pl n* **1** *slang* sunglasses **2** **shades of** a reminder of: *shades of Margaret Thatcher*

shading *n* the graded areas of tone, lines, or dots, indicating light and dark in a painting or drawing

shadow *n* **1** a dark image or shape cast on a surface when something stands between a light and the surface **2** a patch of shade **3** the dark portions of a picture **4** a hint or faint trace: *a shadow of a doubt* **5** a person less powerful or vigorous than his or her former self **6** a threatening influence: *news of the murder cast a shadow over the village* **7** a person who always accompanies another **8** a person who trails another in secret, such as a detective ▷ *adj* **9** *Brit and Austral* designating a member or members of the main opposition party in Parliament who would hold ministerial office if their party were in power: *the shadow chancellor* ▷ *vb* **10** to cast a shade or shadow over **11** to make dark or gloomy **12** to follow or trail secretly [Old English *sceadwe*]

shadow-box *vb* *boxing* to box against an imaginary opponent for practice ▷ **shadow-boxing** *n*

shadowy *adj* **1** (of a place) full of shadows; shady **2** faint or dark like a shadow: *a shadowy figure* **3** mysterious or not well known: *the shadowy world of espionage*

Shadwell *n* **Thomas**. ?1642–92, English dramatist; poet laureate (1688–92). He was satirized by Dryden

shady *adj* **shadier, shadiest** **1** full of shade; shaded **2** giving or casting shade **3** *informal* of doubtful honesty or legality: *shady business dealings* ▷ **shadiness** *n*

Shaffer *n* Sir **Peter**. born 1926, British dramatist. His plays include *The Royal Hunt of the Sun* (1964), *Equus* (1973), *Amadeus* (1979), and *The Gift of the Gorgon* (1992)

shaft *n* **1 a** a spear or arrow **b** its long narrow stem **2** **shaft of wit** *or* **humour** a clever or amusing remark **3** a ray or streak of light **4** the long straight narrow handle of a tool or golf club **5** a revolving rod in a machine that transmits motion or power **6** one of the bars between which an animal is harnessed to a vehicle **7** *archit* the middle part of a column or pier, between the base and the capital **8** a vertical passageway through a building for a lift **9** a vertical passageway into a mine [Old English *sceaft*]

Shaftesbury *n* **1** **1st Earl of**, title of *Anthony Ashley Cooper*. 1621–83, English statesman, a major figure in the Whig opposition to Charles II **2** **7th Earl of**, title of *Anthony Ashley Cooper*. 1801–85, English evangelical churchman and social reformer. He promoted measures to improve conditions in mines (1842), factories (1833; 1847; 1850), and schools

shag¹ *n* **1** coarse shredded tobacco **2** a matted tangle of hair or wool ▷ *adj* **3** (of a carpet) having long thick woollen threads [Old English *sceacga*]

shag² *n* a kind of cormorant [special use of SHAG¹ (with reference to its crest)]

shag³ *vb* **shagging, shagged** *Brit, Austral and NZ slang* **1** *taboo* to have sexual intercourse with (a person) **2** **shagged out** exhausted [origin unknown]

shaggy *adj* **-gier, -giest** **1** having or covered with rough unkempt fur, hair, or wool: *shaggy cattle* **2** rough and untidy ▷ **shagginess** *n*

shagreen *n* **1** the skin of a shark, used as an abrasive **2** a rough grainy leather made from certain animal hides [French *chagrin*]

shah *n* a ruler of certain Middle Eastern countries, esp. (formerly) Iran [Persian: king]

Shah Jahan *n* 1592–1666, Mogul emperor (1628–58). During his reign the finest monuments of Mogul architecture in India were built, including the Taj Mahal and the Pearl Mosque at Agra

Shahjahanpur *n* a city in N India, in central Uttar Pradesh: founded in 1647 in the reign of Shah Jahan. Pop: 297 932 (2001)

Shahn *n* **Ben**. 1898–1969, US artist, born in Lithuania, best known as an exponent of social realism, esp. in the series (1931–32) inspired by the executions of Sacco and Vanzetti

Shaka *or* **Chaka** *n* died 1828, Zulu military leader, who founded the Zulu Empire in southern Africa

shake *vb* **shaking, shook, shaken** **1** to move up and down or back and forth with short quick movements **2** to be or make unsteady **3** (of a voice) to tremble because of anger or nervousness **4** to clasp or grasp (the hand) of (a person) in greeting or agreement: *they shook hands* **5 shake on it** *informal* to shake hands in agreement or reconciliation **6** to wave vigorously and angrily: *he shook his fist* **7** (often foll. by *up*) to frighten or unsettle **8** to shock, disturb, or upset: *he was badly shaken but unharmed* **9** to undermine or weaken: *a team whose morale had been badly shaken* **10** *US and Canad informal* to get rid of **11** *music* to perform a trill on (a note) **12 shake one's head** to indicate disagreement or disapproval by moving the head from side to side ▷ *n* **13** the act or an instance of shaking **14** a tremor or vibration **15 the shakes** *informal* a state of uncontrollable trembling **16** *informal* a very short period of time: *in half a shake* **17** *music* same as **trill** (1) **18** short for **milk shake**. See also **shake down, shake off, shake up** [Old English *sceacan*]

shake down *vb* **1** to go to bed, esp. in a makeshift bed ▷ *n* **shakedown** **2** a makeshift bed

shake off *vb* **1** to remove or get rid of: *I have been trying to shake off the stigma for some time* **2** to escape from; get away from: *they switched to a blue car in a bid to shake off reporters*

shaker *n* **1** a container used for shaking a powdered substance onto something: *a flour shaker* **2** a container in which the ingredients of alcoholic drinks are shaken together

Shakespeare *n* William. 1564–1616, English dramatist and poet. He was born and died at Stratford-upon-Avon but spent most of his life as an actor and playwright in London. His plays with approximate dates of composition are: *Henry VI, Parts I–III* (1590); *Richard III* (1592); *The Comedy of Errors* (1592); *Titus Andronicus* (1593); *The Taming of the Shrew* (1593); *The Two Gentlemen of Verona* (1594); *Love's Labour's Lost* (1594); *Romeo and Juliet* (1594); *Richard II* (1595); *A Midsummer Night's Dream* (1595); *King John* (1596); *The Merchant of Venice* (1596); *Henry IV, Parts I–II* (1597); *Much Ado about Nothing* (1598); *Henry V* (1598); *Julius Caesar* (1599); *As You Like It* (1599); *Twelfth Night* (1599); *Hamlet* (1600); *The Merry Wives of Windsor* (1600); *Troilus and Cressida* (1601); *All's Well that ends Well* (1602); *Measure for Measure* (1604); *Othello* (1604); *King Lear* (1605); *Macbeth* (1605); *Antony and Cleopatra* (1606); *Coriolanus* (1607); *Timon of Athens* (1607); *Pericles* (1608); *Cymbeline* (1609); *The Winter's Tale* (1610); *The Tempest* (1611); and, possibly in collaboration with John Fletcher, *Two Noble Kinsmen* (1612) and *Henry VIII* (1612). His *Sonnets*, variously addressed to a fair young man and a dark lady, were published in 1609

Shakespearean *or* **Shakespearian** *adj* **1** of William Shakespeare, English dramatist and poet, or his works ▷ *n* **2** a student of or specialist in Shakespeare's works

shake up *vb* **1** to mix by shaking **2** to reorganize drastically **3** *informal* to shock mentally or physically: *the thunderstorm really shook me up* ▷ *n* **shake-up 4** *informal* a radical reorganization, such as the reorganization of employees in a company

Shakhty *n* an industrial city in W Russia: the chief town of the E Donets Basin; a major coal-mining centre. Pop: 219 000 (2005 est)

shako (shack-oh) *n, pl* **shakos** a tall cylindrical peaked military hat with a plume [Hungarian *csákó*]

shaky *adj* **shakier, shakiest 1** weak and unsteady, esp. due to illness or shock **2** uncertain or doubtful: *their prospects are shaky* **3** tending to shake or tremble ▷ **shakily** *adv*

shale *n* a flaky sedimentary rock formed by compression of successive layers of clay [Old English *scealu* shell]

shall *vb, past* **should 1** (with 'I' or 'we' as subject) used as an auxiliary to make the future tense: *we shall see you tomorrow* **2** (with 'you', 'he', 'she', 'it', 'they', or a noun as subject) **a** used as an auxiliary to indicate determination on the part of the speaker: *you shall pay for this!* **b** used as an auxiliary to indicate compulsion or obligation, now esp. in official documents **3** (with 'I' or 'we' as subject) used as an auxiliary in questions asking for advice or agreement: *what shall we do now?*; *shall I shut the door?* [Old English *sceal*]

USAGE The usual rule given for the use of *shall* and *will* is that where the meaning is one of simple futurity, *shall* is used for the first person of the verb and *will* for the second and third: *I shall go tomorrow; they will be there now*. Where the meaning involves command, obligation, or determination, the positions are reversed: *it shall be done; I will definitely go*. However, *shall* has come to be largely neglected in favour of *will*, which has become the commonest form of the future in all three persons.

shallot (shal-**lot**) *n* a small, onion-like plant used in cooking for flavouring [Old French *eschaloigne*]

shallow *adj* **1** having little depth **2** not involving sincere feelings or serious thought **3** (of breathing) consisting of short breaths ▷ *n* **4** (*often pl*) a shallow place in a body of water [Middle English *shalow*] ▷ **shallowness** *n*

sham *n* **1** anything that is not genuine or is not what it appears to be **2** a person who pretends to be something other than he or she is ▷ *adj* **3** not real or genuine ▷ *vb* **shamming, shammed 4** to fake or feign (something); pretend: *he made a point of shamming nervousness* [origin unknown]

shaman (**sham**-man) *n* **1** a priest of shamanism **2** a medicine man or witch doctor of a similar religion [Russian]

shamanism (**sham**-man-iz-zum) *n* a religion of northern Asia, based on a belief in good and evil spirits who can be influenced or controlled only by the shamans ▷ **shamanist** *n, adj*

shamble *vb* **-bling, -bled 1** to walk or move along in an awkward shuffling way ▷ *n* **2** an awkward or shuffling walk [perhaps from *shambles*, referring to legs of a meat vendor's table] ▷ **shambling** *adj, n*

shambles *n* **1** a disorderly or badly organized event or place: *the bathroom was a shambles* **2** *chiefly Brit* a butcher's slaughterhouse **3** *old-fashioned* any scene of great slaughter [Middle English *shamble* table used by meat vendors]

shambolic *adj informal* completely disorganized

shame *n* **1** a painful emotion resulting from an awareness of having done something wrong or foolish **2** capacity to feel such an emotion: *have they no shame?* **3** loss of respect; disgrace **4** a person or thing that causes this **5** a cause for regret or disappointment: *it's a shame to rush back* **6 put to shame** to show up as being inferior by comparison: *his essay put mine to shame* ▷ *interj* **7** *S African informal* **a** an expression of sympathy **b** an expression of pleasure or endearment ▷ *vb* **shaming, shamed 8** to cause to feel shame **9** to bring shame on **10** (often foll. by *into*) to force someone to do something by making him or her feel ashamed not to: *he was finally shamed into paying the bill* [Old English *scamu*]

shamefaced *adj* embarrassed or guilty [earlier *shamefast*] ▷ **shamefacedly** *adv*

shameful *adj* causing or deserving shame: *a shameful lack of concern* ▷ **shamefully** *adv*

shameless *adj* **1** having no sense of shame: *a shameless manipulator* **2** without decency or modesty: *a shameless attempt to stifle democracy* ▷ **shamelessly** *adv*

Shamir *n* Yitzhak. 1915–2012, Israeli statesman, born in Poland; prime minister (1983–84; 1986–92): foreign minister (1980–83; 1984–86)

shammy *n, pl* **-mies** *informal* a piece of chamois leather [variant of *chamois*]

Shamo *n* transliteration of the Chinese name for the Gobi

shampoo *n* **1** a soapy liquid used to wash the hair **2** a similar liquid for washing carpets or upholstery **3** the process of shampooing ▷ *vb* **-pooing, -pooed 4** to wash (the hair, carpets, or upholstery) with shampoo [Hindi *chāmpo*]

shamrock *n* a small clover-like plant with three round leaves on each stem: the national emblem of Ireland [Irish Gaelic *seamrōg*]

Shandong *or* **Shantung** *n* a province of NE China, on the Yellow Sea and the Gulf of Chihli: part of the earliest organized state of China (1520–1030 BC); consists chiefly of the fertile plain of the lower Yellow River, with mountains over 1500 m (5000 ft) high in the centre. Capital: Jinan. Pop: 91 250 000 (2003 est). Area: 153 300 sq km (59 189 sq miles)

shandy *n, pl* **-dies** a drink made of beer and lemonade [origin unknown]

shanghai *slang vb* **-haiing, -haied 1** to force or trick (someone) into doing something **2** *history* to kidnap (a man) and force him to serve at sea **3** *Austral and NZ* to shoot with a catapult ▷ *n* **4** *Austral and NZ* a catapult [senses 1 and 2 after the city of *Shanghai*; senses 3 and 4 from Scots dialect *shangie, shangan* cleft stick]

Shanghai *n* a port in E China, capital of Shanghai municipality (traditionally in SE Jiangsu) near the estuary of the Yangtze: the largest city in China and one of the largest ports in the world; a major cultural and industrial centre, with many universities. Pop: 12 665 000 (2005 est)

shank *n* **1** the part of the leg between the knee and the ankle **2** a cut of meat from the top part of an animal's shank **3** the long narrow part of a tool, key, spoon, etc. [Old English *scanca*]

Shankar *n* Ravi. 1920–2012 Indian sitarist

Shankaracharya *or* **Shankara** *n* 9th century AD, Hindu philosopher and teacher; chief exponent of Vedanta philosophy

Shankly *n* Bill. 1913–81, Scottish footballer and manager of Liverpool FC (1959–74)

shanks's pony *or US* **shanks's mare** *n informal* one's own legs as a means of transport [from *shank*, the lower part of the leg]

Shannon[1] *n* a river in the Republic of Ireland, rising in NW Co Cavan and flowing south to the Atlantic by an estuary 113 km (70 miles) long: the longest river in the Republic of Ireland. Length: 260 km (161 miles)

Shannon[2] *n* Claude (**Elwood**). 1916–2000, US mathematician, who first developed information theory

Shansi *n* a variant transliteration of the Chinese name for **Shanxi**

Shan State *n* an administrative division of E Myanmar: formed in 1947 from the joining of the Federation of Shan States with the Wa States; consists of the **Shan plateau** crossed by forested mountain ranges reaching over 2100 m (7000 ft). Pop: 4 416 000 (1994 est). Area: 149 743 sq km (57 816 sq miles)

shan't shall not

Shantou *or* **Shantow** *n* a port in SE China, in E Guangdong near the mouth of the Han River: became a treaty port in 1869. Pop: 1 356 000 (2005 est). Also called: **Swatow**

shantung *n* a heavy Chinese silk with a knobbly surface [after province of NE China]

Shantung *n* a variant transliteration of the Chinese name for **Shandong**

shanty[1] *n, pl* **-ties** a small rough hut; crude dwelling [Canadian French *chantier* cabin built in a lumber camp]

shanty[2] *or* **chanty** *n, pl* **-ties** a rhythmic song originally sung by sailors when working [French *chanter* to sing]

shantytown *n* a town of poor people living in shanties

Shanxi *or* **Shansi** *n* a province of N China: China's richest coal reserves and much heavy industry. Capital: Taiyuan. Pop: 33 140 000 (2003 est). Area: 157 099 sq km (60 656 sq miles)

shape *n* **1** the outward form of an object, produced by its outline **2** the figure or outline of the body of a person **3** organized or definite form: *to preserve the union in its present shape* **4** the specific form that anything takes on: *a gold locket in the shape of a heart* **5** a pattern or mould **6** condition or state of efficiency: *in poor shape* **7** **take shape** to assume a definite form ▷ *vb* **shaping, shaped** **8** (often foll. by *into* or *up*) to receive or cause to receive shape or form: *spinach shaped into a ball* **9** to mould into a particular pattern or form **10** to devise or develop: *to shape a system of free trade* ▶ See also **shape up** [Old English *gesceap*, literally: that which is created]

shapeless *adj* **1** (of a person or object) lacking a pleasing shape: *a shapeless dress* **2** having no definite shape or form: *a shapeless mound* ▷ **shapelessness** *n*

shapely *adj* **-lier, -liest** (esp. of a woman's body or legs) pleasing or attractive in shape ▷ **shapeliness** *n*

shape up *vb informal* **1** to progress or develop satisfactorily **2** to develop a definite or proper form **3** to start working efficiently or behaving properly: *shape up or face the sack*

Shapiro *n* Jonathan. publishing as *Zapiro*. born 1958, South African political cartoonist

Shapley *n* Harlow. 1885–1972, US astronomer, director of the Harvard College Observatory (1922–56): noted for his work on the size and structure of the galaxy

shard *n* a broken piece or fragment of pottery, glass, or metal [Old English *sceard*]

Shard *n* **the Shard** a tall building, resembling a shard of glass, in London, at London Bridge. Designed by Renzo Piano and completed in 2012, it is for mixed commercial, residential, and leisure use and is the tallest habitable building in the UK. Height: 310 m (1,016 ft)

share[1] *n* **1** a part or portion of something that belongs to or is contributed by a person or group **2** (*often pl*) any of the equal parts into which the capital stock of a company is divided ▷ *vb* **sharing, shared 3** (often foll. by *out*) to divide and distribute **4** to receive or contribute a portion of: *we shared a bottle of mineral water* **5** to join with another or others in the use of (something): *a programme about four women sharing a house* **6** to go through (a similar experience) as others: *we have all shared the nightmare of toothache* **7** to tell others about (something) **8** to have the same (beliefs or opinions) as others: *universal values shared by both east and west* [Old English *scearu*]

share[2] *n* short for **ploughshare** [Old English *scear*]

shareholder *n* the owner of one or more shares in a company

share index *n* an index showing the movement of share prices

sharemilker *n NZ* a person who works on a dairy farm belonging to someone else and gets a share of the proceeds from the sale of the milk

Shari *n* a variant spelling of **Chari**

sharia *n* the body of doctrines that regulate the lives of Muslims [Arabic]

shark *n* **1** a large, usually predatory fish with a long body, two dorsal fins, and rows of sharp teeth **2** *disparaging* a person who swindles or extorts money from other people [origin unknown]

Shark Bay *n* a large inlet on the W coast of Western Australia, 800 km (500 miles) north of Perth; the coastline is over 1500 km (930 miles) long and has two large shallow embayments and numerous islands: noted for its large sea-grass beds, stromatolites, and colonies of dugong; a World Heritage site. Area: 2.2 million hectares. Pop: 900 (2014 est)

sharkskin *n* a smooth glossy fabric used for sportswear

Sharon[1] *n* Ariel. 1928–2014, Israeli soldier and politician; Likud prime minister (2001–06)

Sharon[2] *n* **Plain of Sharon** a plain in W Israel, between the Mediterranean and the hills of Samaria, extending from Haifa to Tel Aviv

sharp *adj* **1** having a keen cutting edge **2** tapering to an edge or point **3** involving a sudden change in direction: *a sharp bend on a road; a sharp rise in prices* **4** moving, acting, or reacting quickly: *sharp reflexes* **5** clearly defined: *a sharp contrast* **6** quick to notice or understand things; keen-witted **7** clever in an underhand way: *sharp practices* **8** bitter or harsh: *a sharp response* **9** shrill or penetrating: *a sharp cry of horror* **10** having a bitter or sour taste **11** (of pain or cold) acute or biting: *a sharp gust of wind* **12** *music* **a** (of a note) raised in pitch by one semitone: *F sharp* **b** (of an instrument or voice) out of tune by being too high in pitch **13** *informal* neat and stylish: *a sharp dresser* ▷ *adv* **14** promptly **15** exactly: *at ten o'clock sharp* **16** *music* **a** higher than a standard pitch **b** out of tune by being too high in pitch: *she sings sharp* ▷ *n* **17** *music* **a** an accidental that raises the pitch of a note by one semitone. Symbol: # **b** a note affected by this accidental **18** *informal* a cheat; cardsharp [Old English *scearp*] **>** **sharpish** *adj* **>** **sharply** *adv* **>** **sharpness** *n*

Sharp *n* Cecil (James). 1859–1924, British musician, best known for collecting, editing, and publishing English folk songs

sharpen *vb* to make or become sharp or sharper **>** **sharpener** *n*

sharper *n* a person who cheats or swindles; fraud

Sharpeville *n* a town in E South Africa: scene of riots in 1960 (when 69 demonstrators died), 1984, and 1985 (when 19 died)

sharpshooter *n* a skilled marksman

sharp-tongued *adj* very critical or sarcastic

sharp-witted *adj* very intelligent and perceptive

shat *vb taboo* a past tense and past participle of **shit**

Shatt-al-Arab *n* a river in SE Iraq, formed by the confluence of the Tigris and Euphrates Rivers: flows southeast as part of the border between Iraq and Iran to the Persian Gulf. Length: 193 km (120 miles)

shatter *vb* **1** to break suddenly into many small pieces **2** to damage badly or destroy: *to shatter American confidence* **3** to upset (someone) greatly: *the whole experience shattered me* [origin unknown] **>** **shattering** *adj*

shattered *adj informal* **1** completely exhausted **2** badly upset: *he was shattered by the separation*

shave *vb* **shaving, shaved,** *or* **shaven 1** to remove (the beard or hair) from (the face, head, or body) by using a razor or shaver **2** to remove thin slices from (wood or other material) with a sharp cutting tool **3** to touch (someone or something) lightly in passing ▷ *n* **4** the act or an instance of shaving **5** the removal of hair from a man's face by a razor **6** a tool for cutting off thin slices **7** **close shave** *informal* a narrow escape [Old English *sceafan*]

shaver *n* **1** an electrically powered razor **2** *old-fashioned* a young boy

Shavian (**shave-ee-an**) *adj* **1** of or like George Bernard Shaw, Irish dramatist noted for his sharp wit, or his works ▷ *n* **2** an admirer of Shaw or his works

shaving *n* **1** a thin slice of something such as wood, which has been shaved off ▷ *adj* **2** used when shaving: *shaving foam*

Shaw *n* **1** Artie, original name *Arthur Arshawsky*. 1910–2004, US jazz clarinetist, band leader, and composer **2 George Bernard,** often known as GBS. 1856–1950, Irish dramatist and critic, in England from 1876. He was an active socialist and became a member of the Fabian Society but his major works are effective as satiric attacks rather than political tracts. These include *Arms and the Man* (1894), *Candida* (1894), *Man and Superman* (1903), *Major Barbara* (1905), *Pygmalion* (1913), *Back to Methuselah* (1921), and *St Joan* (1923): Nobel prize for literature 1925 **3 Richard Norman.** 1831–1912, English architect **4 Thomas Edward.** the name assumed by (T. E.) **Lawrence** after 1927

shawl *n* a piece of woollen cloth worn over the head or shoulders by a woman or wrapped around a baby [Persian *shāl*]

Shays *n* Daniel. ?1747–1825, American soldier and revolutionary leader of a rebellion of Massachusetts farmers against the US government (1786–87)

Shcheglovsk *n* the former name (until 1932) of **Kemerovo**

Shcherbakov *n* a former name (from the Revolution until 1957) of **Rybinsk**

she *pron* **1** (refers to) the female person or animal previously mentioned or in question: *she is my sister* **2** (refers to) something regarded as female, such as a car, ship, or nation ▷ *n* **3** (refers to) a female person or animal [Old English *sīe*]

sheaf *n, pl* **sheaves 1** a bundle of papers tied together **2** a bundle of reaped corn tied together ▷ *vb* **3** to bind or tie into a sheaf [Old English *scēaf*]

shear *vb* **shearing, sheared** *or Austral and NZ sometimes* **shore, sheared** *or* **shorn 1** to remove (the fleece) of (a sheep) by cutting or clipping **2** to cut or cut through (something) with shears or a sharp instrument **3** *engineering* to cause (a part) to break or (of a part) to break through strain or twisting ▷ *n* **4** breakage caused through strain or twisting ▶ See also **shears** [Old English *sceran*] **>** **shearer** *n*

Shearer *n* Alan. born 1970, English footballer: a striker, he scored 30 goals in 63 matches for England (1992–2000); played for Blackburn Rovers (1992–96) and Newcastle United (1996–2006) during which he scored an English Premier League record 260 goals in 441 matches

shearing shed *n Austral and NZ* a farm building with equipment for shearing sheep

shears *pl n* **1** large scissors, used for sheep shearing **2** a large scissor-like cutting tool with flat blades, used for cutting hedges

sheath *n, pl* **sheaths 1** a case or covering for the blade of a knife or sword **2** *biology* a structure that encloses or protects **3** *Brit, Austral and NZ* same as **condom 4** a close-fitting dress [Old English *scēath*]

sheathe *vb* **sheathing, sheathed 1** to insert (a knife or sword) into a sheath **2** to cover with a sheath or sheathing

sheathing *n* any material used as an outer layer

sheaves *n* the plural of **sheaf**

Sheba *n* **1** Also called: **Saba** the ancient kingdom of the Sabeans: a rich trading nation dealing in gold, spices, and precious stones (I Kings 10) **2** the region inhabited by this nation, located in the SW corner of the Arabian peninsula: modern Yemen

shebeen *or* **shebean** *n Scot, Irish and S African* a place where alcoholic drink is sold illegally [Irish Gaelic *síbín* beer of poor quality]

Shechem *n* the ancient name of **Nablus**

shed¹ *n* **1** a small, roughly made building used for storing garden tools, etc. **2** a large barnlike building used for various purposes at factories, train stations, etc.: *a locomotive shed* [Old English *sced*]

shed² *vb* **shedding, shed 1** to get rid of: *250 workers shed by the company* **2 shed tears** to cry **3 shed light on** to make (a problem or situation) easier to understand **4** to cast off (skin, hair, or leaves): *the trees were already beginning to shed their leaves* **5** to cause to flow off: *this coat sheds water* **6** to separate or divide (a group of sheep) [Old English *sc(e)ādan*]

sheen *n* a glistening brightness on the surface of something: *grass with a sheen of dew on it* [Old English *sciēne*]

Sheene *n* Barry (Stephen Frank). 1950–2003, British racing motorcyclist: 500 cc world champion (1976, 1977)

sheep *n, pl* **sheep 1** a cud-chewing mammal with a thick woolly coat, kept for its wool or meat. Related adjective: **ovine 2** a timid person **3 like sheep** (of a group of people) allowing a single person to dictate their actions or beliefs **4 separate the sheep from the goats** to pick out the members of a group who are superior in some respects [Old English *scēap*] **>** **sheeplike** *adj*

sheep-dip *n* **1** a liquid disinfectant and insecticide in which sheep are immersed **2** a deep trough containing such a liquid

sheepdog *n* **1** a dog used for herding sheep **2** a breed of dog reared originally for herding sheep

sheepfold *n* a pen or enclosure for sheep

sheepish *adj* embarrassed because of feeling foolish **> sheepishly** *adv*

sheepshank *n* a knot made in a rope to shorten it temporarily

sheepskin *n* the skin of a sheep with the wool still attached, used to make clothing and rugs

sheer¹ *adj* **1** absolute; complete: *sheer amazement* **2** perpendicular; very steep: *the sheer rock face* **3** (of textiles) light, delicate, and see-through ▷ *adv* **4** steeply: *the cliff drops sheer to the sea* [Old English *scīr*]

sheer² *vb* **sheer off** *or* **away (from) a** to change course suddenly **b** to avoid (an unpleasant person, thing, or topic) [origin unknown]

Sheerness *n* a port and resort in SE England, in N Kent at the junction of the Medway estuary and the Thames: administratively part of Queenborough in Sheppey since 1968

sheet¹ *n* **1** a large rectangular piece of cloth used as an inner bed cover **2** a thin piece of material such as paper or glass, usually rectangular **3** a broad continuous surface or layer: *a sheet of ice* **4** a newspaper ▷ *vb* **5** to provide with, cover, or wrap in a sheet **6** (often foll. by *down*) to rain very heavily [Old English *scīete*]

sheet² *n nautical* a line or rope for controlling the position of a sail [Old English *scēata* corner of a sail]

sheet anchor *n* **1** *nautical* a large strong anchor for use in an emergency **2** a person or thing that can always be relied on

sheeting *n* any material from which sheets are made

sheet metal *n* metal formed into a thin sheet by rolling or hammering

sheet music *n* music printed on individual sheets of paper

Sheffield *n* **1** a city in N England, in Sheffield unitary authority, South Yorkshire on the River Don: important centre of steel manufacture and of the cutlery industry; Sheffield university (1905) and Sheffield Hallam University (1992). Pop: 439 866 (2001) **2** a unitary authority in N England, in South Yorkshire. Pop: 512 500 (2003 est). Area: 368 sq km (142 sq miles)

sheikh *or* **sheik** (shake) *n* **1** the head of an Arab tribe, village, or family **2** (in Muslim communities) a religious leader [Arabic *shaykh* old man] **> sheikhdom** *or* **sheikdom** *n*

sheila *n Austral and NZ old-fashioned, informal* a girl or woman [from the girl's name *Sheila*]

shekel *n* **1** the monetary unit of Israel **2 shekels** *informal* money [Hebrew *sheqel*]

Shelburne *n* **2nd Earl of,** title of *William Petty Fitzmaurice,* also called (from 1784) 1st Marquess of Lansdowne. 1737–1805, British statesman; prime minister (1782–83)

shelduck *or masc* **sheldrake** *n, pl* **-ducks, -duck** *or* **-drakes, -drake** a large brightly coloured wild duck of Europe and Asia [probably from dialect *sheld* pied]

shelf *n, pl* **shelves** **1** a board fixed horizontally against a wall or in a cupboard, for holding things **2** a projecting layer of ice or rock on land or in the sea **3 off the shelf** (of products in shops) sold as standard **4 on the shelf** put aside or abandoned; used esp. of unmarried women considered to be past the age of marriage [Old English *scylfe* ship's deck]

shelf life *n* the length of time a packaged product will remain fresh or usable

shell *n* **1** the protective outer layer of an egg, fruit, or nut **2** the hard outer covering of an animal such as a crab or tortoise **3** any hard outer case **4** the external structure of a building, car, or ship, esp. one that is unfinished or gutted by fire **5** an explosive artillery projectile that can be fired from a large gun **6** a small-arms cartridge

7 *rowing* a very light narrow racing boat **8 come** *or* **bring out of one's shell** to become *or* help to become less shy and reserved ▷ *vb* **9** to remove the shell or husk from **10** to attack with artillery shells ▶ See also **shell out** [Old English *sciell*] **> shell-like** *adj*

she'll she will *or* she shall

shellac *n* **1** a yellowish resin used in varnishes and polishes **2** a varnish made by dissolving shellac in alcohol ▷ *vb* **-lacking, -lacked** **3** to coat with shellac [*shell* + *lac*]

Shelley *n* **1 Mary (Wollstonecraft).** 1797–1851, British writer; author of *Frankenstein* (1818); the daughter of William Godwin and Mary Wollstonecraft, she eloped with Percy Bysshe Shelley **2 Percy Bysshe.** 1792–1822, British romantic poet. His works include *Queen Mab* (1813), *Prometheus Unbound* (1820), and *The Triumph of Life* (1824). He wrote an elegy on the death of Keats, *Adonais* (1821), and shorter lyrics, including the odes "To the West Wind" and "To a Skylark" (both 1820). He was drowned in the Ligurian Sea while sailing from Leghorn to La Spezia

shellfish *n, pl* **-fish** *or* **-fishes** a sea-living animal, esp. one that can be eaten, having a shell

shell out *vb informal* to pay out or hand over (money)

shell shock *n* a nervous disorder characterized by anxiety and depression that occurs as a result of lengthy exposure to battle conditions **> shell-shocked** *adj*

shell suit *n Brit* a lightweight tracksuit made of a waterproof nylon layer over a cotton layer

Shelta *n* a secret language based on Gaelic, used by some travelling people in Ireland and Britain [origin unknown]

shelter *n* **1** something that provides cover or protection from weather or danger **2** the protection given by such a cover ▷ *vb* **3** to take cover from bad weather **4** to provide with a place to live or a hiding place: *to shelter refugees* [origin unknown]

sheltered *adj* **1** protected from wind and rain **2** protected from unpleasant or upsetting experiences: *a sheltered childhood* **3** specially designed to provide a safe environment for elderly or disabled people: *sheltered housing*

shelve¹ *vb* **shelving, shelved** **1** to put aside or postpone: *to shelve a project* **2** to place (something, such as a book) on a shelf **3** to provide with shelves: *to shelve a cupboard* **4** to dismiss (someone) from active service [from *shelves,* plural of *shelf*]

shelve² *vb* **shelving, shelved** to slope away gradually [origin unknown]

shelves *n* the plural of shelf

shelving *n* **1** material for shelves **2** shelves collectively

Shenandoah National Park *n* a national park in N Virginia: established in 1935 to protect the Blue Ridge Mountains. Area: 782 sq km (302 sq miles)

shenanigans *pl n informal* **1** mischief or nonsense **2** trickery or deception [origin unknown]

Shensi *n* a variant transliteration of the Chinese name for **Shaanxi**

Shenyang *n* a walled city in NE China in S Manchuria, capital of Liaoning province: capital of the Manchu dynasty from 1644–1912; seized by the Japanese in 1931. Pop: 4 916 000 (2005 est). Former name: **Mukden**

Shepard *n* **1 Alan Bartlett, Jr.** 1923–98, US naval officer; first US astronaut in space (1961) **2 Sam,** original name *Samuel Shepard Rogers.* born 1943, US dramatist, film actor, and director. His plays include *Chicago* (1966), *The Tooth of Crime* (1972), and *Buried Child* (1978); films as actor include *Days of Heaven* (1978) and *The Right Stuff* (1983); films as director include *Far North* (1989) and *Silent Tongue* (1994)

shepherd *n* **1** a person employed to tend sheep **2** *Christianity* a clergyman when considered as the moral and spiritual guide of the people in the parish ▷ *vb* **3** to guide or watch over (people) [SHEEP + HERD] **> shepherdess** *fem n*

S

shepherd's pie *n* a baked dish of minced meat covered with mashed potato

Sheppard *n* Jack. 1702–24, English criminal, whose daring escapes from prison were celebrated in many contemporary ballads and plays

Sheppey *n* Isle of Sheppey an island in SE England, off the N coast of Kent in the Thames estuary: separated from the mainland by **The Swale**, a narrow channel. Chief towns: Sheerness, Minster. Pop: 37 852 (2001 est). Area: 80 sq km (30 sq miles)

Sher *n* Sir Antony. born 1953, British actor and writer, born in South Africa

Sheraton *n* **1** Thomas. 1751–1806, English furniture maker, author of the influential *Cabinet-Maker and Upholsterer's Drawing Book* (1791) ▷ *adj* **2** denoting furniture made by or in the style of Thomas Sheraton

sherbet *n* **1** *Brit, Austral and NZ* a fruit-flavoured slightly fizzy powder, eaten as a sweet or used to make a drink **2** *US, Canad and S African* same as **sorbet** [Turkish *şerbet*]

Sherborne *n* a town in S England in Dorset: noted for its medieval abbey, ruined medieval castle, and Sherborne Castle, a mansion built by Sir Walter Raleigh in 1594. Pop: 9350 (2001)

Sherbrooke *n* a city in E Canada, in S Quebec: university. It is an industrial and commercial centre. Pop: 127 354 (2001)

Sheridan *n* **1** Philip Henry. 1831–88, American Union cavalry commander in the Civil War. He forced Lee's surrender to Grant (1865) **2** Richard Brinsley. 1751–1816, Irish dramatist, politician, and orator, noted for his comedies of manners *The Rivals* (1775), *School for Scandal* (1777), and *The Critic* (1779)

sheriff *n* **1** (in the US) the chief elected law-enforcement officer in a county **2** (in Canada) a municipal officer who enforces court orders and escorts convicted criminals to prison **3** (in England and Wales) the chief executive officer of the Crown in a county, having chiefly ceremonial duties **4** (in Scotland) a judge in a sheriff court **5** (in Australia) an officer of the Supreme Court [Old English *scīrgerēfa*]

sheriff court *n* (in Scotland) a court having powers to try all but the most serious crimes and to deal with most civil actions

Sherman *n* William Tecumseh. 1820–91, American Union commander during the Civil War. He led the victorious march through Georgia (1864), becoming commander of the army in 1869

Sherpa *n, pl* **-pas** *or* **-pa** a member of a Tibetan people living on the southern slopes of the Himalayas

Sherriff *n* R(obert) C(edric). 1896–1975, British dramatist and film writer, best known for his play of World War I *Journey's End* (1928). His film scripts include *Goodbye Mr. Chips* (1936) and *The Dam Busters* (1955)

Sherrington *n* Sir Charles Scott. 1857–1952, English physiologist, noted for his work on reflex action, published in *The Integrative Action of the Nervous System* (1906): shared the Nobel prize for physiology or medicine with Adrian (1932)

sherry *n, pl* **-ries** a pale or dark brown fortified wine, originally from southern Spain [Spanish *Xeres*, now *Jerez*, in Spain]

's Hertogenbosch *n* a city in the S Netherlands, capital of North Brabant province: birthplace of Hieronymus Bosch. Pop: 133 000 (2003 est). Also called: **Den Bosch**. French name: **Bois-le-Duc**

Sherwood *n* Robert Emmet. 1896–1955, US dramatist. His plays include *The Petrified Forest* (1935), *Idiot's Delight* (1936), and *There shall be no Night* (1940)

Sherwood Forest *n* an ancient forest in central England, in Nottinghamshire: formerly a royal hunting ground and much more extensive; famous as the home of Robin Hood

Shetland *n* Also called: **Shetland Islands** a group of about 100 islands (fewer than 20 inhabited), off the N coast of Scotland, which constitute an island authority of Scotland: a Norse dependency from the 8th century until 1472; noted for the breeding of Shetland ponies, knitwear manufacturing, and fishing; oil-related industries. Administrative centre: Lerwick. Pop: 21 870 (2003 est). Area: 1426 sq km (550 sq miles). Official name (until 1974): **Zetland**

Shetland pony *n* a very small sturdy breed of pony with a long shaggy mane and tail

Shevardnadze *n* Eduard (Amvrosiyevich). 1928–2014, Georgian statesman; president of Georgia (1992–2003); Soviet minister of foreign affairs (1985–91), who played an important part in arms negotiations with the US

shibboleth *n* **1 a** a slogan or catch phrase, usually considered outworn, that characterizes a particular party or sect: *the shibboleth of Western strategy* **2** a custom, phrase, or use of language that reliably distinguishes a member of one group or class from another [word used in the Old Testament by the Gileadites as a test word for the Ephraimites, who could not pronounce *sh*]

shickered *adj Austral and NZ old-fashioned, slang* drunk [Yiddish *shicker* liquor]

shied *vb* the past of **shy¹, shy²**

shield *n* **1** a piece of defensive armour carried in the hand or on the arm to protect the body from blows or missiles **2** any person or thing that protects, hides, or defends: *a wind shield* **3** *heraldry* a representation of a shield used for displaying a coat of arms **4** anything that resembles a shield in shape, such as a trophy in a sports competition ▷ *vb* **5** to protect, hide, or defend (someone or something) from danger or harm: *an industry shielded from competition* [Old English *scield*]

Shields *n* Carol (Ann). 1935–2003, Canadian novelist and writer, born in the US; her novels include *Happenstance* (1980), *The Stone Diaries* (1995), and *Unless* (2002)

shift *vb* **1** to move from one place or position to another **2** to pass (blame or responsibility) onto someone else: *he was trying to shift the blame to me* **3** to change (gear) in a motor vehicle **4** to remove or be removed: *no detergent can shift these stains* **5** *US* to change for another or others **6** *slang* to move quickly ▷ *n* **7** the act or an instance of shifting **8 a** a group of workers who work during a specific period **b** the period of time worked by such a group **9** a method or scheme **10** a loose-fitting straight underskirt or dress [Old English *sciftan*]

shiftless *adj* lacking in ambition or initiative

shifty *adj* **shiftier, shiftiest** looking deceitful and not to be trusted ▷ **shiftiness** *n*

shih-tzu *n* a small dog with a long straight dense coat and a tail curling over its back [Chinese, literally: lion]

Shijiazhuang, Shihchiachuang *or* **Shihkiachwang** *n* a city in NE China, capital of Hebei province: textile manufacturing. Pop: 1 733 000 (2005 est)

Shikoku *n* the smallest of the four main islands of Japan, separated from Honshu by the Inland Sea: forested and mountainous. Pop: 4 137 000 (2002 est). Area: 17 759 sq km (6857 sq miles)

shillelagh (shil-**lay**-lee) *n* (in Ireland) a heavy club [Irish Gaelic *sail* cudgel + *éille* thong]

shilling *n* **1** a former British coin worth one twentieth of a pound, replaced by the 5p piece in 1970 **2** a former Australian coin, worth one twentieth of a pound **3** the standard monetary unit in several E African countries [Old English *scilling*]

Shillong *n* a city in NE India, capital of Meghalaya: situated on the Shillong Plateau at an altitude of 1520 m (4987 ft); destroyed by earthquake in 1897 and rebuilt. Pop: 132 876 (2001)

shillyshally *vb* **-shallies, -shallying, -shallied** *informal* to be indecisive [*shill I shall I*, reduplication of *shall I*]

Shiloh *n* a town in central ancient Palestine, in Canaan on the E slope of Mount Ephraim: keeping place of the tabernacle and the ark; destroyed by the Philistines

shim *n* **1** a thin strip of material placed between two close surfaces to fill a gap ▷ vb **shimming, shimmed 2** to fit or fill up with a shim [origin unknown]

shimmer vb **1** to shine with a faint unsteady light ▷ n **2** a faint unsteady light [Old English *scimerian*]
› shimmering or **shimmery** adj

Shimonoseki n a port in SW Japan, on SW Honshu: scene of the peace treaty (1895) ending the Sino-Japanese War; a heavy industrial centre. Pop: 246 924 (2002 est)

shin n **1** the front part of the lower leg **2** a cut of beef including the lower foreleg ▷ vb **shinning, shinned 3 shin up** to climb (something, such as a rope or pole) by gripping with the hands or arms and the legs and hauling oneself up [Old English *scinu*]

shinbone n the nontechnical name for **tibia**

shindig or **shindy** n, pl **-digs** or **-dies** slang **1** a noisy party or dance **2** a quarrel or brawl [variant of *shinty*]

shine vb **shining, shone 1** to give off or reflect light **2** to direct the light of (a lamp or torch): *I shone a torch at the ceiling* **3** (*past, past part* **shined**) to make clean and bright by polishing: *they earned money by shining shoes* **4** to be very good at something: *she shone in most subjects; she shone at school* **5** to appear very bright and clear: *her hair shone like gold* ▷ n **6** brightness or lustre **7 take a shine to someone** informal to take a liking to someone [Old English *scīnan*]

shiner n informal a black eye

shingle¹ n **1** a thin rectangular tile laid with others in overlapping rows to cover a roof or a wall **2** a woman's short-cropped hairstyle ▷ vb **-gling, -gled 3** to cover (a roof or a wall) with shingles **4** to cut (the hair) in a short-cropped style [Latin *scindere* to split]

shingle² n coarse gravel found on beaches [Scandinavian]

shingles n a disease causing a rash of small blisters along a nerve [Medieval Latin *cingulum* girdle]

shingle slide n NZ the loose stones on a steep slope

shinny n Canad an informal game similar to ice hockey [variant of SHINTY]

Shinto n a Japanese religion in which ancestors and nature spirits are worshipped [Japanese: the way of the gods] **› Shintoism** n **› Shintoist** n, adj

shinty n **1** a game (of Scottish origin) like hockey but with taller goals **2** (pl **-ties**) the stick used in this game [perhaps Scottish Gaelic *sinteag* a pace]

shiny adj **shinier, shiniest 1** bright and polished **2** (of clothes or material) worn to a smooth and glossy state by continual wear or rubbing

ship n **1 a** large seagoing vessel with engines or sails **2** short for **airship, spaceship 3 when one's ship comes in** when one has become successful ▷ vb **shipping, shipped 4** to send or transport by any carrier, esp. a ship **5** nautical to take in (water) over the side **6** to bring or go aboard a vessel: *to ship oars* **7** (often foll. by *off*) informal to send away: *they were shipped off to foreign countries* **8** to be hired to serve aboard a ship: *I shipped aboard a Liverpool liner* [Old English *scip*]

shipboard adj taking place or used aboard a ship: *a shipboard romance*

shipbuilder n a person or company that builds ships **› shipbuilding** n

Shipka Pass n a pass over the Balkan Mountains in central Bulgaria: scene of a bloody Turkish defeat in the Russo-Turkish War (1877–78). Height: 1334 m (4376 ft)

Shipley n Dame Jenny, full name *Jennifer (Mary) Shipley*. born 1952, New Zealand National Party politician; prime minister (1997–1999)

shipmate n a sailor who serves on the same ship as another

shipment n **1** goods shipped together as part of the same lot: *a shipment of arms* **2** the act of shipping cargo

shipper n a person or company that ships

shipping n **1** the business of transporting freight, esp. by ship **2** ships collectively: *all shipping should stay clear of the harbour*

shipshape adj **1** neat or orderly ▷ adv **2** in a neat and orderly manner

shipwreck n **1** the destruction of a ship at sea **2** the remains of a wrecked ship **3** ruin or destruction: *the shipwreck of the old science* ▷ vb **4** to wreck or destroy (a ship) **5** to bring to ruin or destruction

shipwright n someone, esp. a carpenter, who builds or repairs ships

shipyard n a place where ships are built and repaired

Shiraz n a city in SW Iran, at an altitude of 1585 m (5200 ft): an important Muslim cultural centre in the 14th century; university (1948); noted for fine carpets. Pop: 1 230 000 (2005 est)

shire n **1** Brit a county **2** Austral a rural area with an elected council **3 the Shires** the Midland counties of England [Old English *scīr* office]

Shire or **Shiré** n a river in E central Africa, flowing from Lake Malawi through Mozambique to the Zambezi. Length: 596 km (370 miles)

Shire Highlands or **Shiré Highlands** pl n an upland area of S Malawi. Average height: 900 m (3000 ft)

shire horse n a large powerful breed of working horse

shirk vb to avoid doing (work or a duty); to be negligent: *no-one shirks when he's around* [probably from German *Schurke* rogue] **› shirker** n

shirt n **1** an item of clothing worn on the upper part of the body, usually with a collar and sleeves and buttoning up the front **2 keep your shirt on** informal keep your temper **3 put one's shirt on something** informal to bet all one has on something [Old English *scyrte*]

shirt-lifter n offensive, slang a homosexual

shirtsleeve n **1** the sleeve of a shirt **2 in one's shirtsleeves** not wearing a jacket

shirt-tail n the part of a shirt that extends below the waist

shirtwaister or US **shirtwaist** n a woman's dress with a tailored bodice resembling a shirt

shirty adj **shirtier, shirtiest** slang bad-tempered or annoyed

shish kebab n a dish of small pieces of meat and vegetables grilled on a skewer [Turkish *şiş kebab*]

shit taboo vb **shitting, shitted, shit** or **shat 1** to defecate ▷ n **2** faeces; excrement **3** slang rubbish; nonsense **4** slang a worthless person ▷ interj **5** slang an exclamation of anger or disgust [Old English *scītan* to defecate] **› shitty** adj

Shittim n Old Testament the site to the east of the Jordan and northeast of the Dead Sea where the Israelites encamped before crossing the Jordan (Numbers 25:1–9)

shiver¹ vb **1** to tremble from cold or fear ▷ n **2** a tremble caused by cold or fear **3 the shivers** a fit of shivering through fear or illness [Middle English *chiveren*] **› shivering** n, adj **› shivery** adj

shiver² n **1** to break into fragments ▷ n **2** a splintered piece [Germanic]

Shizuoka n a city in central Japan, on S Honshu: a centre for green tea; university (1949). Pop: 468 775 (2002 est)

Shkodër n a market town in NW Albania, on Lake Shkodër: an Illyrian capital in the first millennium BC. Pop: about 90 000 (2003 est). Italian name: **Scutari**

shoal¹ n **1** a large group of fish swimming together **2** a large group of people or things [Old English *scolu*]

shoal² n **1** a stretch of shallow water **2** a sandbank or rocky area, esp. one that can be seen at low water ▷ vb **3** to make or become shallow [Old English *sceald* shallow]

shock¹ vb **1** to cause (someone) to experience extreme horror, disgust, or astonishment: *the similarity shocked me* **2** to cause a state of shock in (a person) ▷ n **3** a sudden and violent blow or impact **4 a** a sudden and violent emotional disturbance **b** something causing this **5** pathol a condition in which a person's blood cannot flow properly because of severe injury, burns, or fright **6** pain and muscular spasm caused by an electric current passing through a person's body [Old French *choc*] **› shocker** n

S

shock² *n* **1** a number of grain sheaves set on end in a field to dry ▷ *vb* **2** to set up (sheaves) in shocks [probably Germanic]

shock³ *n* a thick bushy mass of hair [origin unknown]

shock absorber *n* any device designed to absorb mechanical shock, esp. one fitted to a motor vehicle to reduce the effects of travelling over bumpy surfaces

shocking *adj* **1** *informal* very bad or terrible: *a shocking match at Leicester* **2** causing dismay or disgust: *a shocking lack of concern* **3 shocking pink** (of) a very bright shade of pink

Shockley *n* William Bradfield. 1910–89, US physicist, born in Britain, who shared the Nobel prize for physics (1956) with John Bardeen and Walter Brattain for developing the transistor. He also held controversial views on the connection between race and intelligence

shockproof *adj* capable of absorbing shock without damage

shock tactics *pl n* the use of unexpected or unexpectedly forceful methods to carry out a plan

shock therapy *or* **shock treatment** *n* the treatment of certain mental conditions by passing an electric current through the patient's brain

shod *vb* the past of **shoe**

shoddy *adj* **-dier, -diest** **1** made or done badly or carelessly: *shoddy goods* **2** of poor quality; shabby [origin unknown] **> shoddily** *adv* **> shoddiness** *n*

shoe *n* **1** one of a matching pair of coverings shaped to fit the foot, made of leather or other strong material and ending below the ankle **2** anything resembling a shoe in shape, function, or position **3** short for **horseshoe** **4 be in a person's shoes** *informal* to be in another person's situation ▷ *vb* **shoeing, shod** **5** to fit (a horse) with horseshoes [Old English *scōh*]

shoehorn *n* a smooth curved piece of metal or plastic inserted at the heel of a shoe to ease the foot into it

shoelace *n* a cord for fastening shoes

shoemaker *n* a person who makes or repairs shoes or boots **> shoemaking** *n*

shoestring *n* **1** same as **shoelace** **2** *informal* a very small amount of money: *the theatre will be run on a shoestring*

shoetree *n* a long piece of metal, plastic, or wood, put into a shoe or boot to keep its shape

Sholapur *n* a city in SW India, in S Maharashtra: major textile centre. Pop: 873 037 (2001)

Sholes *n* Christopher Latham. 1819–90, US inventor, who invented (1868) the typewriter and sold the patent to the Remington company (1873)

Sholokhov *n* Mikhail Aleksandrovich. 1905–84, Soviet author, noted particularly for *And Quiet flows the Don* (1934) and *The Don flows Home to the Sea* (1940), describing the effect of the Revolution and civil war on the life of the Cossacks: Nobel prize for literature 1965

shone *vb* a past of **shine**

shonky *adj* **-kier, -kiest** *Austral and NZ informal* unreliable or unsound

shoo *interj* **1** go away!: used to drive away unwanted or annoying animals or people ▷ *vb* **shooing, shooed** **2** to drive away by crying 'shoo' [imitative]

shook *vb* the past tense of **shake**

shoot *vb* **shooting, shot** **1** to hit, wound, or kill with a missile fired from a weapon **2** to fire (a missile or missiles) from a weapon **3** to fire (a weapon) **4** to hunt game with a gun for sport **5** to send out or be sent out quickly and aggressively: *he shot questions at her* **6** to move very rapidly: *the car shot forward* **7** to go or pass quickly over or through: *he was trying to shoot the white water* **8** to slide or push into or out of a fastening: *she shot the bolt quickly* **9** (of a plant) to sprout (a new growth) **10** to photograph or film **11** *sport* to hit or kick the ball at goal ▷ *n* **12** the act of shooting **13** a new growth or sprout of a plant **14** *chiefly Brit* a meeting or party organized for hunting game with guns **15** an area where game can be hunted with guns **16** *informal* a photographic assignment: *a fashion shoot in*

New York [Old English *scēotan*]

shooter *n* **1** a person or thing that shoots **2** *slang* a gun

shooting gallery *n* a long narrow room where people practise shooting

shooting star *n* *informal* a meteor

shooting stick *n* a walking stick with a spike at one end and a folding seat at the other

shoot-out *n* **1** a gunfight **2** short for **penalty shoot-out**

shoot up *vb* **1** to grow or increase rapidly: *crime rates have shot up; as my peers started to shoot up, I stopped growing* **2** *slang* to inject oneself with heroin or another strong drug

shop *n* **1** a place for the sale of goods and services **2** a place where a specified type of work is done; workshop: *a repair shop* **3 all over the shop** *informal* scattered everywhere: *his papers were all over the shop* **4 shut up shop** to close business at the end of the day or permanently **5 talk shop** *informal* to discuss one's business or work on a social occasion ▷ *vb* **shopping, shopped** **6** (often foll. by *for*) to visit a shop or shops in order to buy (goods) **7** *Brit, Austral and NZ slang* to inform on (someone), esp. to the police [Old English *sceoppa* stall] **> shopper** *n*

shop around *vb* *informal* **1** to visit a number of shops or stores to compare goods and prices **2** to consider a number of possibilities before making a choice

shop assistant *n* a person who serves in a shop

shop floor *n* **1** the production area of a factory **2** workers, esp. factory workers, as opposed to management

shopkeeper *n* a person who owns or manages a shop **> shopkeeping** *n*

shoplifter *n* a customer who steals goods from a shop **> shoplifting** *n*

shopping *n* **1** the act of going to shops and buying things **2** things that have been bought in shops

shopping centre *n* **1** a complex of stores, restaurants, and sometimes banks, usually under the same roof **2** the area of a town where most of the shops are situated

shopping list *n* **1** a written list of things to be bought when out shopping **2** any list of things desired or demanded: *a long shopping list of amendments to the treaty*

shopping mall *n* a large enclosed shopping centre

shopping plaza *n* a shopping centre, usually a small group of stores built as a strip

shopsoiled *adj* slightly dirty or faded, from being displayed in a shop

shop steward *n* a trade-union official elected by his or her fellow workers to be their representative in dealing with their employer

shoptalk *n* conversation about one's work, carried on outside working hours

shopwalker *n* *Brit* (esp. formerly) a person employed by a department store to assist sales personnel and help customers

shore¹ *n* **1** the land along the edge of a sea, lake, or wide river. Related adjective: **littoral** **2** land, as opposed to water: *150 yards from shore* **3 shores** a country: *foreign shores* [probably from Middle Low German, Middle Dutch *schōre*]

shore² *n* **1** a prop placed under or against something as a support ▷ *vb* **shoring, shored** **2 shore up** **a** to prop up (an unsteady building or wall) with a strong support **b** to strengthen or support (something weak): *lower interest rates to shore up the economy* [Middle Dutch *schōre*]

shoreline *n* the edge of a sea, lake, or wide river

shorn *vb* a past participle of **shear**

short *adj* **1** of little length; not long **2** of little height; not tall **3** not lasting long **4** not enough: *the number of places laid at the table was short by four* **5 short of** or on lacking in: *short of cash; short on detail* **6** concise: *a short book* **7** (of drinks) consisting chiefly of a spirit, such as whisky **8** (of someone's memory) lacking the ability to retain a lot of facts **9** (of a person's manner) abrupt and rather rude: *Kemp was short with her* **10** (of betting odds) almost even **11** *finance* **a** not possessing at the time of sale the stocks or commodities one sells **b** relating to such sales, which depend on falling prices for profit **12** *phonetics* (of a vowel) of relatively brief duration **13** (of pastry) crumbly in texture **14 in short supply** scarce **15 short and sweet** brief and to the point **16 short for** a shortened form of ▷ *adv* **17** abruptly: *to stop short* **18 be caught short** to have a sudden need to go to the toilet **19 go short** not to have enough **20 short of** except: *they want nothing short of his removal from power* ▷ *n* **21** a drink of spirits **22** a short film shown before the main feature in a cinema **23** same as **short circuit 24 for short** *informal* as a shortened form: *cystic fibrosis, CF for short* **25 in short** briefly ▷ *vb* **26** to short-circuit ▶ See also **shorts** [Old English *sceort*] **> shortness** *n*

shortage *n* not enough of something needed

shortbread *n* a rich crumbly biscuit made with butter

shortcake *n* **1** shortbread **2** a dessert made of layers of biscuit or cake filled with fruit and cream

short-change *vb* **-changing, -changed 1** to give (someone) less than the correct change **2** *slang* to treat (someone), unfairly, esp. by giving less than is expected

short circuit *n* **1** a faulty or accidental connection in an electric circuit, which deflects current through a path of low resistance, usually causing the failure of the circuit ▷ *vb* **short-circuit 2** to develop a short circuit **3** to bypass (a procedure): *she wrote to them direct and short-circuited the job agency* **4** to hinder or frustrate (a plan)

shortcoming *n* a fault or weakness

shortcrust pastry *n* a type of pastry with a crisp but crumbly texture

short cut *n* **1** a route that is shorter than the usual one **2** a way of saving time or effort

shorten *vb* to make or become short or shorter

shortening *n* butter or other fat, used in pastry to make it crumbly

shortfall *n* **1** failure to meet a requirement **2** the amount of such a failure; deficit

shorthand *n* a system of rapid writing using simple strokes and other symbols to represent words or phrases

short-handed *adj* (of a company or organization) lacking enough staff to do the required work

shorthand typist *n* a person skilled in the use of shorthand and in typing

shorthorn *n* a member of a breed of cattle with short horns

short list *n* **1** Also called (Scot): **short leet** a list of suitable candidates for a job or prize, from which the successful candidate will be selected ▷ *vb* **short-list 2** to put (someone) on a short list

short-lived *adj* lasting only for a short time: *his authority was short-lived*

shortly *adv* **1** in a short time; soon **2** in a cross and impatient manner

shorts *pl n* **1** trousers reaching the top of the thigh or partway to the knee **2** *chiefly US and Canad* men's underpants

short shrift *n* brief and unsympathetic treatment

short-sighted *adj* **1** unable to see faraway things clearly **2** not taking likely future developments into account: *a short-sighted approach to the problem* **> short-sightedness** *n*

short-tempered *adj* easily angered

short-term *adj* of, for, or lasting a short time

short-termism *n* the tendency to concentrate on short-term gains, often at the expense of long-term success

short wave *n* a radio wave with a wavelength in the range 10–100 metres

short-winded *adj* tending to run out of breath easily

Shostakovich *n* Dmitri Dmitriyevich. 1906–75, Soviet composer, noted esp. for his 15 symphonies and his chamber music

shot¹ *n* **1** the act or an instance of firing a gun or rifle **2** *sport* the act or an instance of hitting, kicking, or

throwing the ball **3** small round lead pellets used in shotguns **4** a person with specified skill in shooting: *my father was quite a good shot* **5** *informal* an attempt: *a second shot at writing a better treaty* **6** *informal* a guess **7 a** a single photograph **b** an uninterrupted sequence of film taken by a single camera **8** *informal* an injection of a vaccine or narcotic drug **9** *informal* a drink of spirits **10** the launching of a rocket or spacecraft to a specified destination: *a moon shot* **11** *sport* a heavy metal ball used in the shot put **12 like a shot** without hesitating **13 shot in the arm** *informal* something that brings back energy or confidence **14 shot in the dark** a wild guess [Old English *scot*]

shot² *vb* **1** the past of **shoot** ▷ *adj* **2** (of textiles) woven to give a changing colour effect **3** streaked with colour: *dark hair shot with streaks of grey*

shotgun *n* a gun for firing a charge of shot at short range

shot put *n* an athletic event in which contestants hurl a heavy metal ball called a shot as far as possible **> shot-putter** *n*

should *vb* the past tense of **shall** used to indicate that an action is considered by the speaker to be obligatory (*you should go*) or to form the subjunctive mood (*I should like to see you; if I should die; should I be late, start without me*) [Old English *sceolde*]

> **USAGE** *Should* has, as its most common meaning in modern English, the sense *ought* as in *I should go to the graduation, but I don't see how I can*. However, the older sense of the subjunctive of *shall* is often used with I or *we* to indicate a more polite form than *would*: *I should like to go, but I can't*. In much speech and writing, *should* has been replaced by *would* in contexts of this kind, but it remains in formal English when a conditional subjunctive is used: *should he choose to remain, he would be granted asylum*.

shoulder *n* **1** the part of the body where the arm, wing, or foreleg joins the trunk **2** a cut of meat including the upper part of the foreleg **3** the part of an item of clothing that covers the shoulder **4** the strip of unpaved land that borders a road **5 a shoulder to cry on** a person one turns to for sympathy with one's troubles **6 put one's shoulder to the wheel** *informal* to work very hard **7 rub shoulders with someone** *informal* to mix with someone socially **8 shoulder to shoulder a** side by side **b** working together ▷ *vb* **9** to accept (blame or responsibility) **10** to push with one's shoulder: *he shouldered his way through the crowd* **11** to lift or carry on one's shoulders **12 shoulder arms** *military* to bring one's rifle vertically close to one's right side [Old English *sculdor*]

shoulder blade *n* either of two large flat triangular bones, one on each side of the back part of the shoulder

shoulder strap *n* a strap worn over the shoulder to hold up an item of clothing or to support a bag

shouldn't should not

shout *n* **1** a loud call or cry **2** *informal* one's turn to buy a round of drinks ▷ *vb* **3** to cry out loudly **4** *Austral and NZ informal* to treat (someone) to (something, such as a drink) [probably from Old Norse *skūta* taunt]

shout down *vb* to silence (someone) by talking loudly

shove *vb* **shoving, shoved 1** to give a violent push to **2** to push (one's way) roughly **3** *informal* to put (something) somewhere quickly and carelessly: *shove it into the boot* ▷ *n* **4** a rough push [Old English *scūfan*]

shovel *n* **1** a tool for lifting or moving loose material, consisting of a broad blade attached to a large handle **2** a machine or part of a machine resembling a shovel in function ▷ *vb* **-velling, -velled** *or US* **-veling, -veled 3** to lift or move (loose material) with a shovel **4** to put away large quantities of (something) quickly: *shovelling food into their mouths* [Old English *scofl*]

shove off *vb informal* to go away; depart

S

show vb **showing, showed, shown** or **showed 1** to make, be, or become visible or noticeable: *to show an interest; excitement showed on everyone's face* **2** to present for inspection: *someone showed me the plans* **3** to demonstrate or prove: *evidence showed that this was the most economical way* **4** to instruct by demonstration: *she showed me how to feed the pullets* **5** to indicate: *the device shows changes in the pressure* **6** to grant or bestow: *to show mercy* **7** to exhibit or display works of art, goods, etc.: *three artists are showing at the gallery* **8** to present (a film or play) or (of a film or play) to be presented **9** to guide or escort: *he offered to show me around* **10** *informal* to arrive ▷ n **11** a theatrical or other entertainment: *a magic show* **12** a display or exhibition: *a show of paintings* **13** something done to create an impression: *a show of indignation* **14** vain and conspicuous display: *it was nothing but mere show* **15** *slang, chiefly Brit* a thing or affair: *jolly good show* ▸ See also **show off, show up** [Old English scēawian]

show business *n* the entertainment industry. Also (informal): **show biz**

showcase *n* **1** a setting in which something is displayed to best advantage: *a showcase for young opera singers* **2** a glass case used to display objects in a museum or shop

showdown *n informal* a major confrontation that settles a dispute

shower *n* **1 a** a kind of bathing in which a person stands upright and is sprayed with water from a nozzle **b** a device, room, or booth for such bathing **2** a brief period of rain, hail, sleet, or snow **3** a sudden fall of many small light objects: *a shower of loose gravel* **4** *Brit slang* a worthless or contemptible group of people **5** *US, Canad, Austral and NZ* a party held to honour and present gifts to a prospective bride or prospective mother ▷ vb **6** to take a shower **7** to sprinkle with or as if with a shower: *the walkers were showered by volcanic ash* **8** to present (someone) with things liberally: *he showered her with presents* [Old English scūr] ▸ **showery** adj

showing *n* **1** a presentation, exhibition, or display **2** manner of presentation

showjumping *n* the sport of riding horses in competitions to demonstrate skill in jumping ▸ **showjumper** *n*

showman *n, pl* -men **1** a person skilled at presenting anything in an effective manner **2** a person who presents or produces a show ▸ **showmanship** *n*

shown vb a past participle of **show**

show off vb **1** to exhibit or display (something) so as to invite admiration: *he was eager to show off his new car* **2** *informal* to flaunt skills, knowledge, or looks in order to attract attention or impress people ▷ n **show-off 3** *informal* a person who flaunts his or her skills, knowledge, or looks in order to attract attention or impress people

showpiece *n* **1** anything displayed or exhibited **2** something admired as a fine example of its type: *an orchestral showpiece*

showplace *n* a place visited for its beauty or interest

showroom *n* a room in which goods for sale, esp. cars or electrical or gas appliances, are on display

show up vb **1** to reveal or be revealed clearly **2** to expose the faults or defects of (someone or something) by comparison **3** *informal* to put (someone) to shame; embarrass **4** *informal* to arrive

showy adj **showier, showiest 1** colourful, bright in appearance, and very noticeable, and perhaps rather vulgar: *showy jewellery* **2** making an imposing display ▸ **showily** adv ▸ **showiness** n

shrank vb a past tense of **shrink**

shrapnel *n* **1** an artillery shell containing a number of small pellets or bullets which it is designed to scatter on explosion **2** fragments from this type of shell [after H. Shrapnel, who invented it]

shred *n* **1** a long narrow piece torn off something **2** a very small amount: *not a shred of truth* ▷ vb **shredding,**

shredded or **shred 3** to tear into shreds [Old English scrēad] ▸ **shredder** *n*

Shreveport *n* a city in NW Louisiana, on the Red River: centre of an oil and natural-gas region. Pop: 198 364 (2003 est)

shrew *n* **1** a small mouselike animal with a long snout **2** a bad-tempered nagging woman [Old English scrēawa] ▸ **shrewish** adj

shrewd adj intelligent and making good judgments [from shrew (obsolete verb) to curse, from SHREW] ▸ **shrewdly** adv ▸ **shrewdness** n

Shrewsbury *n* a town in W central England, administrative centre of Shropshire, on the River Severn: strategically situated near the Welsh border; market town. Pop: 67 126 (2001)

shriek *n* **1** a high-pitched scream ▷ vb **2** to utter (words or sounds) in a high-pitched tone [probably from Old Norse skrǣkja to screech]

shrift *n* See short shrift [Old English scrift penance]

shrike *n* a bird with a heavy hooked bill, which kills small animals by dashing them on thorns [Old English scrīc thrush]

shrill adj **1** (of a sound) sharp and high-pitched ▷ vb **2** to utter (words or sounds) in a shrill tone [origin unknown] ▸ **shrillness** n ▸ **shrilly** adv

shrimp *n* **1** a small edible shellfish with a long tail and a pair of pincers **2** *informal* a small person ▷ vb **3** to fish for shrimps [probably Germanic]

shrine *n* **1** a place of worship associated with a sacred person or object **2** a container for sacred relics **3** the tomb of a saint or other holy person **4** a place that is visited and honoured because of its association with a famous person or event: *he'd come to worship at the shrine of Mozart* [Latin scrinium bookcase]

shrink vb **shrinking, shrank** or **shrunk, shrunk** or **shrunken 1** to become or cause to become smaller, sometimes because of wetness, heat, or cold **2** shrink from **a** to withdraw or move away through fear: *they didn't shrink from danger* **b** to feel great reluctance (to perform a task or duty) ▷ n **3** *slang* a psychiatrist [Old English scrincan]

shrinkage *n* **1** the fact of shrinking **2** the amount by which anything decreases in size, value, or weight

shrink-wrap vb -**wrapping,** -**wrapped** to package (a product) in a flexible plastic wrapping which shrinks about its contours to seal it

shrivel vb -**velling,** -**velled** or *US* -**veling,** -**veled** to become dry and withered [probably Scandinavian]

Shropshire *n* **1** a county of W central England: Telford and Wrekin became an independent unitary authority in 1998, and the remaining county of Shropshire became a unitary authority in 2009; mainly agricultural. Administrative centre: Shrewsbury. Pop (excluding Telford and Wrekin): 286 700 (2003 est). Area (excluding Telford and Wrekin): 3201 sq km (1236 sq miles) **2** a breed of medium-sized sheep having a dense fleece, originating from Shropshire and Staffordshire, England

shroud *n* **1** a piece of cloth used to wrap a dead body **2** anything that hides things: *a shroud of smoke* ▷ vb **3** to hide or obscure (something): *shrouded in uncertainty; shrouded by smog* [Old English scrūd garment]

Shrove Tuesday *n* the day before Ash Wednesday [Old English scrīfan to confess one's sins]

shrub *n* a woody plant, smaller than a tree, with several stems instead of a trunk [Old English scrybb] ▸ **shrubby** adj

shrubbery *n, pl* -beries **1** an area planted with shrubs **2** shrubs collectively

shrug vb **shrugging, shrugged 1** to draw up and drop (the shoulders) as a sign of indifference or doubt ▷ n **2** the action of shrugging [origin unknown]

shrug off vb **1** to treat (a matter) as unimportant **2** to get rid of (someone)

shrunk *vb* a past tense and past participle of **shrink**

shrunken *vb* **1** a past participle of **shrink** ▷ *adj* **2** reduced in size

shudder *vb* **1** to shake or tremble suddenly and violently from horror or fear **2** (of a machine) to shake violently ▷ *n* **3** a shiver of fear or horror [Middle Low German *schōderen*]

shuffle *vb* **-fling, -fled 1** to walk or move (the feet) with a slow dragging motion **2** to mix together in a jumbled mass: *the chairman shuffled his papers* **3** to mix up (playing cards) so as to change their order ▷ *n* **4** an instance of shuffling **5** a rearrangement: *a shuffle of top management* **6** a dance with short dragging movements of the feet [probably from Low German *schüffeln*]

shufti *n slang, chiefly Brit* a look; peep [from Arabic]

Shufu *or* **Sufu** *n* transliteration of the Chinese name for Kashi

shun *vb* **shunning, shunned** to avoid deliberately [Old English *scunian*]

shunt *vb* **1** to move (objects or people) to a different position **2** *railways* to transfer (engines or carriages) from track to track ▷ *n* **3** the act of shunting **4** a railway point **5** *electronics* a conductor connected in parallel across a part of a circuit to divert a known fraction of the current **6** *informal* a collision where one vehicle runs into the back of another [perhaps from Middle English *shunen* to shun]

shush *interj* **1** be quiet! hush! ▷ *vb* **2** to quiet (someone) by saying 'shush' [imitative]

Shushan *n* the Biblical name for **Susa**

shut *vb* **shutting, shut 1** to move (something) so as to cover an opening: *shut the door* **2** to close (something) by bringing together the parts: *Ridley shut the folder* **3** **shut up** to close or lock the doors of: *let's shut up the shop* **4** **shut in** to confine or enclose **5** **shut out** to prevent from entering **6** (of a shop or other establishment) to stop operating for the day: *the late-night rush after the pubs shut* ▷ *adj* **7** closed or fastened ▶ See also **shutdown, shut off**, etc. [Old English *scyttan*]

shutdown *n* **1** the closing of a factory, shop, or other business ▷ *vb* **shut down 2** to discontinue operations permanently

Shute *n* Nevil, real name *Nevil Shute Norway*. 1899–1960, English novelist, in Australia after World War II: noted for his novels set in Australia, esp. *A Town like Alice* (1950) and *On the Beach* (1957)

shuteye *n slang* sleep

shut off *vb* **1** to cut off the flow or supply of **2** to turn off and stop working: *I shut off the car engine* **3** to isolate or separate: *ghettoes shut off from the rest of society*

shut out *vb* **1** to keep out or exclude **2** to conceal from sight: *blinds were drawn to shut out the sun*

shutter *n* **1** a hinged doorlike cover, usually one of a pair, for closing off a window **2** **put up the shutters** to close business at the end of the day or permanently **3** *photog* a device in a camera that opens to allow light through the lens so as to expose the film when a photograph is taken ▷ *vb* **4** to close or equip with a shutter or shutters

shuttle *n* **1** a bus, train, or aircraft that makes frequent journeys between two places which are fairly near to each other **2** a bobbin-like device used in weaving to pass the weft thread between the warp threads **3** a small bobbin-like device used to hold the thread in a sewing machine ▷ *vb* **-tling, -tled 4** to travel back and forth [Old English *scytel* dart, arrow]

shuttlecock *n* a rounded piece of cork or plastic with feathers stuck in one end, struck to and fro in badminton

shut up *vb* **1** *informal* to stop talking or cause (someone) to stop talking: often used in commands **2** to confine or imprison (someone)

shy¹ *adj* **1** not at ease in the company of others **2** easily frightened; timid **3** **shy of** cautious or wary of **4** reluctant or unwilling: *camera-shy*; *workshy* ▷ *vb* **shies,**

shying, shied 5 to move back or aside suddenly from fear: *with a terrified whinny the horse shied* **6 shy away from** to draw back from (doing something), through lack of confidence ▷ *n*, *pl* **shies 7** a sudden movement back or aside from fear [Old English *scēoh*] ▶ **shyly** *adv* ▶ **shyness** *n*

shy² *vb* **shies, shying, shied 1** to throw (something) ▷ *n*, *pl* **shies 2** a quick throw [Germanic]

Shylock *n* an unsympathetic and demanding person to whom one owes money [after the heartless usurer in Shakespeare's *The Merchant of Venice*]

Shymkent *n* a city in S Kazakhstan; a major railway junction. Pop: 469 000 (2005 est). Russian name: **Chimkent**

si *n music* same as te

Si¹ *chem* silicon

Si² *or* **Si Kiang** *n* a variant transliteration of the Chinese name for the **Xi**

SI See SI unit

Sialkot *n* a city in NE Pakistan: shrine of Guru Nanak. Pop: 487 000 (2005 est)

Siam *n* **1** the former name (until 1939 and 1945–49) of Thailand **2 Gulf of Siam** an arm of the South China Sea between the Malay Peninsula and Indochina. the former name of (the Gulf of) **Thailand** (2)

Siamese *n*, *pl* **-mese 1** same as **Siamese cat** ▷ *adj*, *n*, *pl* **-mese 2** (formerly) same as **Thai**

Siamese cat *n* a breed of cat with cream fur, dark ears and face, and blue eyes

Siamese twins *pl n* twins born joined together at some part of the body

Sian *n* a variant transliteration of the Chinese name for **Xi'an**

Siang *n* a variant transliteration of the Chinese name for the **Xiang**

Siangtan *n* a variant transliteration of the Chinese name for **Xiangtan**

Sibelius *n* Jean. 1865–1957, Finnish composer, noted for his seven symphonies, his symphonic poems, such as *Finlandia* (1900) and *Tapiola* (1925), and his violin concerto (1905)

Siberia *n* a vast region of Russia and N Kazakhstan: extends from the Ural Mountains to the Pacific and from the Arctic Ocean to the borders with China and Mongolia; colonized after the building of the Trans-Siberian Railway. Area: 13 807 037 sq km (5 330 896 sq miles)

Siberian *adj* **1** of or relating to Siberia or its inhabitants ▷ *n* **2** a native or inhabitant of Siberia

sibilant *adj* **1** having a hissing sound ▷ *n* **2** *phonetics* a consonant, such as *s* or *z*, that is pronounced with a hissing sound [Latin *sibilare* to hiss]

Sibiu *n* an industrial town in W central Romania: originally a Roman city, refounded by German colonists in the 12th century. Pop: 133 000 (2005 est). German name: **Hermannstadt**. Hungarian name: **Nagyszeben**

sibling *n* a brother or sister [Old English: a relative]

sibyl *n* (in ancient Greece and Rome) a prophetess [Greek *Sibulla*] ▶ **sibylline** *adj*

sic¹ *adv* thus: inserted in brackets in a text to indicate that an odd spelling or reading is in fact what was written, even though it is or appears to be wrong [Latin]

sic² *vb* **sicking, sicked 1** to attack: used only in commands to a dog **2** to urge (a dog) to attack (someone) [dialect variant of *seek*]

Sichuan, Szechuan *or* **Szechwan** *n* a province of SW China: the most populous administrative division in the country, esp. in the central Red Basin, where it is crossed by three main tributaries of the Yangtze. Capital: Chengdu. Pop: 81 000 000 (2003 est). Area: about 569 800 sq km (220 000 sq miles)

Sicilian *adj* **1** of or relating to Sicily or its inhabitants ▷ *n* **2** a native or inhabitant of Sicily

Sicily *n* the largest island in the Mediterranean,

separated from the tip of SW Italy by the Strait of Messina: administratively an autonomous region of Italy; settled by Phoenicians, Greeks, and Carthaginians before the Roman conquest of 241 BC; under Normans (12th–13th centuries); formed the **Kingdom of the Two Sicilies** with Naples in 1815; mountainous and volcanic. Capital: Palermo. Pop: 4 972 124 (2003 est). Area: 25 460 sq km (9830 sq miles). Latin names: **Sicilia, Trinacria**. Italian name: **Sicilia**

sick *adj* **1** vomiting or likely to vomit **2** physically or mentally unwell **3** of or for ill people: *sick pay* **4** deeply affected with mental or spiritual distress: *sick at heart* **5** mentally disturbed **6** *informal* making fun of death, illness, or misfortune: *a sick joke* **7** sick of or sick and tired of *informal* disgusted by or weary of: *I'm sick of this town* ▷ *n*, *vb* **8** *informal* same as **vomit** [Old English *sēoc*]

sickbay *n* a room for the treatment of sick people, for example on a ship

sicken *vb* **1** to make (someone) feel nauseated or disgusted **2** sicken for to show symptoms of (an illness)

sickening *adj* **1** causing horror or disgust: *sickening scenes of violence* **2** *informal* extremely annoying ▷ **sickeningly** *adv*

Sickert *n* Walter Richard. 1860–1942, British impressionist painter, esp. of scenes of London music halls

sickie *n informal* a day of sick leave from work

sickle *n* a tool for cutting grass and grain crops, with a curved blade and a short handle [Old English *sicol*]

sick leave *n* leave of absence from work through illness

sickly *adj* **-lier, -liest** **1** weak and unhealthy **2** (of a person) looking pale and unwell: *sickly pallor* **3** unpleasant to smell, taste, or look at **4** showing excessive emotion in a weak and rather pathetic way: *a sickly tune* ▷ *adv* **5** suggesting sickness: *sickly pale* ▷ **sickliness** *n*

sickness *n* **1** a particular illness or disease: *sleeping sickness* **2** the state of being ill or unhealthy: *absent from work due to sickness* **3** a feeling of queasiness in the stomach followed by vomiting

Sicyon *n* an ancient city in S Greece, in the NE Peloponnese near Corinth: declined after 146 BC

Siddons *n* Sarah. 1755–1831, English tragedienne

side *n* **1** a line or surface that borders anything **2** *geometry* a line forming part of the perimeter of a plane figure: *a square has four sides* **3** either of two parts into which an object, surface, or area can be divided: *the right side and the left side* **4** either of the two surfaces of a flat object: *write on both sides of the page* **5** the sloping part of a hill or bank **6** either the left or the right half of the body, esp. the area around the waist: *he took a nine millimetre bullet in the side* **7** the area immediately next to a person or thing: *at the side of my bed* **8** a place within an area identified by reference to a central point: *the south side of the island* **9** the area at the edge of something, as opposed to the centre: *the far side of the square* **10** aspect or part: *there is a positive side to truancy* **11** one of two or more contesting groups or teams: *the two sides will meet in the final* **12** a position held in opposition to another in a dispute **13** a line of descent through one parent: *a relative on his father's side* **14** *informal* a television channel **15** *Brit slang* conceit or cheek: *to put on side* **16** on one side apart from the rest **17** on the side in addition to a person's main work: *she did a little public speaking on the side* **18** side by side close together **19** side by side with beside or near to **20** take sides to support one party in a dispute against another ▷ *adj* **21** situated at the side: *the side entrance* **22** less important: *a side issue* ▷ *vb* **siding, sided** **23** side with to support (one party in a dispute) [Old English *sīde*]

sidebar *n* (on a website) a short article placed alongside a longer one

sideboard *n* a piece of furniture for a dining room, with drawers, cupboards, and shelves to hold tableware

sideboards *or especially US and Canad* **sideburns** *pl n* a

man's whiskers grown down either side of the face in front of the ears

sidecar *n* a small passenger car attached to the side of a motorcycle

side-effect *n* **1** a usually unwanted effect caused by a drug in addition to its intended one **2** any additional effect, usually an undesirable one: *the unforeseen side-effects of the end of the Cold War*

sidekick *n informal* a close friend or associate

sidelight *n* **1** *Brit* either of two small lights at the front of a motor vehicle **2** either of the two navigational lights used by ships at night

sideline *n* an extra job in addition to one's main job

sidelines *pl n* **1** *sport* **a** the lines that mark the side boundaries of a playing area **b** the area just outside the playing area, where substitute players sit **2** on the sidelines **a** only passively involved: *on the sidelines of the modern world* **b** waiting to join in an activity

sidelong *adj* **1** directed to the side; oblique ▷ *adv* **2** from the side; obliquely

sidereal (side-eer-ee-al) *adj* of or determined with reference to the stars: *the sidereal time* [Latin *sidus* a star]

side-saddle *n* **1** a riding saddle originally designed for women in skirts, allowing the rider to sit with both legs on the same side of the horse ▷ *adv* **2** on a side-saddle

sideshow *n* **1** an event or incident considered less important than another: *a mere sideshow compared to the war on the Russian front* **2** a small show or entertainment offered along with the main show at a circus or fair

side-splitting *adj* causing a great deal of laughter

sidestep *vb* **-stepping, -stepped** **1** to step out of the way of (something) **2** to dodge (an issue) ▷ *n* **side step** **3** a movement to one side, such as in dancing or boxing

sideswipe *n* **1** an unexpected criticism of someone or something while discussing another subject **2** a glancing blow along or from the side ▷ *vb* **-swiping, -swiped** **3** to make a sideswipe

sidetrack *vb* to distract (someone) from a main subject

sidewalk *n* *US and Canad* a raised space alongside a road, for pedestrians

sideways *adv* **1** moving, facing, or inclining towards one side **2** from one side; obliquely **3** with one side forward ▷ *adj* **4** moving or directed to or from one side

side whiskers *pl n* same as **sideboards**

Sidi-bel-Abbès *n* a city in NW Algeria: headquarters of the Foreign Legion until Algerian independence (1962). Pop: 201 000 (2005 est)

siding *n* a short stretch of railway track connected to a main line, used for loading and unloading freight and storing engines and carriages

sidle *vb* **-dling, -dled** to walk slowly and carefully, not wanting to be noticed [obsolete *sideling* sideways]

Sidney *or* **Sydney** *n* **1** Algernon. 1622–83, English Whig politician, beheaded for his supposed part in the Rye House Plot to assassinate Charles II and the future James II: author of *Discourses Concerning Government* (1689) **2** Sir Philip. 1554–86, English poet, courtier, and soldier. His works include the pastoral romance *Arcadia* (1590), the sonnet sequence *Astrophel and Stella* (1591), and *The Defence of Poesie* (1595), one of the earliest works of literary criticism in English

Sidon *n* the chief city of ancient Phoenicia: founded in the third millennium BC; wealthy through trade and the making of glass and purple dyes; now the Lebanese city of Saïda

Sidonian *adj* **1** of or relating to the ancient Phoenician city of Sidon or its inhabitants ▷ *n* **2** a native or inhabitant of Sidon

Sidra *n* Gulf of Sidra a wide inlet of the Mediterranean on the N coast of Libya

SIDS sudden infant death syndrome; cot death

Siegbahn *n* **1** Kai. 1918–2007, Swedish physicist who worked on electron spectroscopy: Nobel prize for physics 1981 **2** his father, **Karl Manne Georg**. 1886–1978, Swedish physicist, who discovered the M series in X-ray spectroscopy: Nobel prize for physics 1924

siege *n* **1** a military operation carried out to capture a place by surrounding and blockading it **2** a similar operation carried out by police, for example to force people out of a place **3 lay siege to** to subject (a place) to a siege [Old French *sege* a seat]

Siegen *n* a city in NW Germany, in North Rhine-Westphalia: manufacturing centre; birthplace of Rubens. Pop: 107 768 (2003 est)

siemens *n*, *pl* **siemens** the SI unit of electrical conductance [after E. W. von SIEMENS]

Siemens *n* **1** Ernst Werner von. 1816–92, German engineer, inventor, and pioneer in telegraphy. Among his inventions are the self-excited dynamo and an electrolytic refining process **2** his brother, Sir **William**, original name *Karl Wilhelm Siemens*. 1823–83, British engineer, born in Germany, who invented the open-hearth process for making steel

Siena *n* a walled city in central Italy, in Tuscany: founded by the Etruscans; important artistic centre (13th–14th centuries); university (13th century). Pop: 52 625 (2001)

Sienkiewicz *n* Henryk. 1846–1916, Polish novelist. His best-known works are *Quo Vadis?* (1896), set in Nero's Rome, and the war trilogy *With Fire and Sword* (1884), *The Deluge* (1886), and *Pan Michael* (1888), set in 17th-century Poland: Nobel prize for literature 1905

sienna *n* **1** a natural earth used as a reddish-brown or yellowish-brown pigment ▷ *adj* **2 burnt sienna** reddish-brown **3 raw sienna** yellowish-brown [after SIENA]

sierra *n* a range of mountains with jagged peaks in Spain or America [Spanish, literally: saw]

Sierra Leone *n* a republic in W Africa, on the Atlantic: became a British colony in 1808 and gained independence (within the Commonwealth) in 1961; declared a republic in 1971; became a one-party state in 1978; multiparty democracy restored in 1991 but military rule was imposed following a coup in 1992 which led to a civil war that lasted until 2002 in which two million people were displaced; consists of coastal swamps rising to a plateau in the east. Official language: English. Religion: Muslim majority and animist. Currency: leone. Capital: Freetown. Pop: 5 612 685 (2013 est). Area: 71 740 sq km (27 699 sq miles)

Sierra Leonean *adj* **1** of or relating to Sierra Leone or its inhabitants ▷ *n* **2** a native or inhabitant of Sierra Leone

Sierra Madre *n* (*functioning as sing*) the main mountain system of Mexico, extending for 2500 km (1500 miles) southeast from the N border: consists of the **Sierra Madre Oriental** in the east, the **Sierra Madre Occidental** in the west, and the **Sierra Madre del Sur** in the south. Highest peak: Citlaltépetl, 5636 m (18 492 ft) (disputed)

Sierra Morena *n* (*functioning as sing*) a mountain range in SW Spain, between the Guadiana and Guadalquivir Rivers. Highest peak: Estrella, 1299 m (4262 ft)

Sierra Nevada *n* (*functioning as sing*) **1** a mountain range in E California, parallel to the Coast Ranges. Highest peak: Mount Whitney, 4418 m (14 495 ft) **2** a mountain range in SE Spain, mostly in Granada and Almería provinces. Highest peak: Cerro de Mulhacén, 3478 m (11 411 ft)

sies (siss) *interj S African informal* same as **sis²**

siesta *n* an afternoon nap, taken in hot countries [Spanish]

sieve (siv) *n* **1** a utensil with a mesh through which a substance is sifted or strained ▷ *vb* **sieving, sieved 2** to sift or strain through a sieve [Old English *sife*]

Sieyès *n* Emmanuel Joseph, called *Abbé Sieyès*. 1748–1836, French statesman, political theorist, and churchman, who became prominent during the Revolution following the publication of his pamphlet *Qu'est-ce que le tiers état?* (1789). He was instrumental in bringing Napoleon I to power (1799)

sift *vb* **1** to sieve (a powdery substance) in order to remove the coarser particles **2** to examine (information or evidence) carefully to select what is important [Old English *siftan*]

sigh *vb* **1** to draw in and audibly let out a deep breath as an expression of sadness, tiredness, longing, or relief **2** to make a sound resembling this **3 sigh for** to long for **4** to say (something) with a sigh ▷ *n* **5** the act or sound of sighing [Old English *sīcan*]

sight *n* **1** the ability to see; vision. Related adjective: **visual 2** an instance of seeing **3** the range of vision: *the cemetery was out of sight* **4** anything that is seen **5** point of view; judgment: *nothing has changed in my sight* **6** *informal* anything unpleasant to see: *she looked a sight in the streetlamps* **7** a device for guiding the eye in aiming a gun or making an observation with an optical instrument **8** an aim or observation made with such a device **9 sights** anything worth seeing: *the great sights of Barcelona* **10 a sight** *informal* a great deal: *it's a sight warmer than in the hall* **11 a sight for sore eyes** a welcome sight **12 catch sight of** to glimpse **13 know someone by sight** to be able to recognize someone without having ever been introduced **14 lose sight of a** to be unable to see (something) any longer **b** to forget: *we lose sight of priorities* **15 on sight** as soon as someone or something is seen **16 set one's sights on** to have (a specified goal) in mind **17 sight unseen** without having seen the object concerned: *he would have taken it sight unseen* ▷ *vb* **18** to see (someone or something) briefly or suddenly: *the two suspicious vessels were sighted* **19** to aim (a firearm) using the sight [Old English *sihth*]

sighted *adj* not blind

sightless *adj* blind

sight-read *vb* **-reading, -read** to sing or play (music in a printed form) without previous preparation ▷ **sight-reading** *n*

sightscreen *n cricket* a large white screen placed near the boundary behind the bowler, which helps the batsman see the ball

sightseeing *n informal* visiting famous or interesting sights in a place ▷ **sightseer** *n*

Sigismund *n* 1368–1437, king of Hungary (1387–1437) and of Bohemia (1419–37); Holy Roman Emperor (1411–37). He helped to end the Great Schism in the Church; implicated in the death of Huss

Sigismund II *n* called *Sigismund Augustus*. 1520–72, king of Poland (1548–72), who united Poland, Lithuania, and their dependencies by the Union of Lublin (1569)

sigma *n* **1** the 18th letter in the Greek alphabet (Σ, σ) **2** *maths* the symbol Σ, indicating summation

sign *n* **1** something that indicates a fact or condition that is not immediately or outwardly observable: *a sign of tension* **2** a gesture, mark, or symbol intended to convey an idea or information **3** a board or placard displayed in public and intended to advertise, inform, or warn **4** a conventional mark or symbol that has a specific meaning, for example £ for pounds **5** *maths* **a** any symbol used to indicate an operation: *a minus sign* **b** a symbol used to indicate whether a number or expression is positive or negative **6** a visible indication: *no sign of the enemy* **7** an omen **8** *med* any evidence of the presence of a disease or disorder **9** *astrol* short for **sign of the zodiac** ▷ *vb* **10** to write (one's name) on (a document or letter) to show its authenticity or one's agreement **11** to communicate using sign language **12** to make a sign to someone so as to convey an idea or information **13** to engage or be engaged by signing a contract: *he signed for another team* ▶ See also **sign away, sign in,** etc. [Latin *signum*]

Signac *n* Paul. 1863–1935, French neoimpressionist painter, influenced by Seurat

signal *n* **1** any sign, gesture, sound, or action used to communicate information **2** anything that causes immediate action: *this is the signal for a detailed examination* *of the risk* **3 a** a variable voltage, current, or electromagnetic wave, by which information is conveyed through an electronic circuit **b** the information so conveyed ▷ *adj* **4** *formal* very important: *a signal triumph for the government* ▷ *vb* **-nalling, -nalled** *or US* **-naling, -naled** **5** to communicate (information) by signal [Latin *signum* sign] **> signally** *adv*

signal box *n* a building from which railway signals are operated

signalman *n, pl* **-men** a railwayman in charge of the signals and points within a section

signatory (sig-na-tree) *n, pl* **-ries** **1** a person, organization, or state that has signed a document such as a treaty ▷ *adj* **2** having signed a document or treaty

signature *n* **1** a person's name written by himself or herself, used in signing something **2** a distinctive characteristic that identifies a person or animal **3** *music* a sign at the beginning of a piece to show key or time **4** *printing* a sheet of paper printed with several pages, which when folded becomes a section of a book [Latin *signare* to sign]

signature tune *n* a piece of music used to introduce a particular television or radio programme

sign away *vb* to give up one's right to (something): *she will sign away all rights to these pictures*

signboard *n* a board carrying a sign or notice, often to advertise a business or product

signet *n* a small seal used to make documents official [Medieval Latin *signetum*]

signet ring *n* a finger ring engraved with an initial or other emblem

significance *n* **1** the effect something is likely to have on other things: *an event of important significance in British history* **2** meaning: *the occult significance of the symbol*

significant *adj* **1** very important **2** having or expressing a meaning **> significantly** *adv*

significant figures *pl n maths* **1** the figures of a number that express a magnitude to a specified degree of accuracy: *3.141 59 to four significant figures is 3.142* **2** the number of such figures: *3.142 has four significant figures*

signify *vb* **-fies, -fying, -fied** **1** to indicate or suggest **2** to stand as a symbol or sign for: *a blue line on the map signified a river* **3** to be important [Latin *signum* a mark + *facere* to make]

sign in *vb* **1** to sign a register on arrival at a place **2** to admit (a nonmember) to a club or institution as a guest by signing a register on his or her behalf

signing *n* a system of communication using hand and arm movements, such as one used by deaf people. Also called: **sign language**

sign off *vb* to announce the end of a radio or television programme

sign of the zodiac *n astrol* any of the 12 areas into which the zodiac is divided

sign on *vb* **1** *Brit and Austral* to register and report regularly at an unemployment-benefit office **2** to commit oneself to a job or activity by signing a form or contract

signor (see-nyor) *n* an Italian form of address equivalent to *sir* or *Mr*

signora (see-nyor-a) *n* an Italian form of address equivalent to *madam* or *Mrs*

Signorelli *n* **Luca.** ?1441–1523, Italian painter, noted for his frescoes

Signoret *n* **Simone**, original name *Simone Kaminker*. 1921–85, French stage and film actress, whose films include *La Ronde* (1950), *Casque d'Or* (1952), *Room at the Top* (1958), and *Ship of Fools* (1965): married the actor and singer Yves Montand (1921–91)

signorina (see-nyor-ee-na) *n* an Italian form of address equivalent to *madam* or *Miss*

sign out *vb* to sign a register to indicate that one is leaving a place

signpost *n* **1** a road sign displaying information, such as

the distance to the next town **2** an indication as to how an event is likely to develop or advice on what course of action should be taken ▷ *vb* **3** to mark (the way) with signposts

sign up *vb* **1** to agree to do a job or course by signing a document **2 sign someone up** to hire someone officially to do a job **3** to enlist for military service

Sihanouk *n* King **Norodom**. 1922–2012, Cambodian statesman; king of Cambodia (1941–55 and 1993–2004); prime minister (1955–60), after which he became head of state. He was deposed in 1970 but reinstated (1975–76) following the victory of the Khmer Rouge in the civil war. He was head of state in exile from 1982; returned in 1991 and became monarch in 1993 under a new constitution; abdicated 2004

sik *adj Austral slang* excellent

Sikang *n* a former province of W China: established in 1928 from part of W Sichuan and E Tibet; dissolved in 1955

Sikh (seek) *n* **1** a member of an Indian religion that teaches that there is only one God ▷ *adj* **2** of the Sikhs or their religious beliefs or customs [Hindi: disciple] **> Sikhism** *n*

Si Kiang *n* See Xi

Siking *n* a former name for Xi'an

Sikkim *n* a state of NE India, formerly an independent state: under British control (1861–1947); became an Indian protectorate in 1950 and an administrative division of India in 1975; lies in the Himalayas, rising to 8600 m (28 216 ft) at Kanchenjunga in the north. Capital: Gangtok. Pop: 540 493 (2001). Area: 7096 sq km (2740 sq miles)

Sikkimese *adj* **1** of or relating to Sikkim or its inhabitants ▷ *n* **2** a native or inhabitant of Sikkim

Sikorski *n* **Władysław**. 1881–1943, Polish general and statesman: prime minister (1922–23) and prime minister of the Polish government in exile during World War II: died in an air crash

Sikorsky *n* **Igor**. 1889–1972, US aeronautical engineer, born in Russia. He designed and flew the first four-engined aircraft (1913) and designed the first successful helicopter (1939)

silage (sile-ij) *n* a fodder crop harvested while green and partially fermented in a silo

silence *n* **1** the state or quality of being silent **2** the absence of sound **3** refusal or failure to speak or communicate when expected: *he's broken his silence on the issue* ▷ *vb* **-lencing, -lenced** **4** to cause (someone or something) to become silent **5** to put a stop to: *a way of silencing criticism*

silencer *n* any device designed to reduce noise, for example one fitted to the exhaust system of a motor vehicle or one fitted to the muzzle of a gun

silent *adj* **1** tending to speak very little **2** failing to speak or communicate when expected: *they remained silent as minutes passed* **3** producing no noise: *the silent room* **4** not spoken: *silent reproach* **5** (of a letter) used in the spelling of a word but not pronounced, such as the *k* in *know* **6** (of a film) having no soundtrack [Latin *silere* to be quiet] **> silently** *adv*

Silesia *n* a region of central Europe around the upper and middle Oder valley: mostly annexed by Prussia in 1742 but became almost wholly Polish in 1945; rich coal and iron-ore deposits. Polish name: **Śląsk**. Czech name: Slezsko. German name: Schlesien

Silesian *adj* **1** of or relating to Silesia or its inhabitants ▷ *n* **2** a native or inhabitant of Silesia

silhouette *n* **1** the outline of a dark shape seen against a light background **2** an outline drawing, often a profile portrait, filled in with black ▷ *vb* **-etting, -etted** **3** to show (something) in silhouette [after E. de *Silhouette*, politician]

silica *n* a hard glossy mineral, silicon dioxide, which occurs naturally as quartz and is used in the manufacture of glass [Latin *silex* hard stone]

silicate *n* *mineralogy* a compound of silicon, oxygen, and a metal

silicon *n* **1** *chem* a brittle non-metallic element: used in transistors, solar cells, and alloys. Symbol: Si ▷ *adj* **2** denoting an area of a country that contains much high-technology industry: *the Silicon Glen* [from *silica*]

silicon chip *n* same as **chip** (3)

silicone *n* *chem* a tough synthetic material made from silicon and used in lubricants, paints, and resins

Silicon Valley *n* **1** an industrial strip in W California, extending S of San Francisco, in which the US information technology industry is concentrated **2** any area in which industries associated with information technology are concentrated

silicosis *n* *pathol* a lung disease caused by breathing in silica dust

silk *n* **1** the fine soft fibre produced by a silkworm **2** thread or fabric made from this fibre **3** silks clothing made of this **4** *Brit* **a** the gown worn by a Queen's (or King's) Counsel **b** *informal* a Queen's (or King's) Counsel **c** take silk to become a Queen's (or King's) Counsel [Old English *sioloc*]

silken *adj* **1** made of silk **2** *literary* smooth and soft: *her silken hair*

silk-screen printing *n* same as **screen process**

silkworm *n* a caterpillar that spins a cocoon of silk

silky *adj* **silkier, silkiest 1** soft, smooth, and shiny **2** (of a voice or manner) smooth and elegant ▷ **silkiness** *n*

sill *n* **1** a shelf at the bottom of a window, either inside or outside a room **2** the lower horizontal part of a window or door frame [Old English *syll*]

Sillanpää *n* Frans Eemil. 1888–1964, Finnish writer, noted for his novels *Meek Heritage* (1919) and *The Maid Silja* (1931): Nobel prize for literature 1939

Sillitoe *n* Alan. 1928–2010, British novelist. His best-known works include *Saturday Night and Sunday Morning* (1958) and *The Loneliness of the Long Distance Runner* (1959)

Sills *n* Beverley, original name *Belle Silverman*. 1929–2007, US soprano: director of the New York City Opera (1979–89)

silly *adj* **-lier, -liest 1** behaving in a foolish or childish way **2** *old-fashioned* unable to think sensibly, as if from a blow **3** *cricket* (of a fielding position) near the batsman's wicket: *silly mid-off* ▷ *n, pl* **-lies 4** *informal* a foolish person [Old English *sælig* (unattested) happy] ▷ **silliness** *n*

silo *n, pl* **-los 1** an airtight pit or tower in which silage or grain is made and stored **2** an underground structure in which missile systems are sited for protection [Spanish]

Silone *n* Ignazio. 1900–78, Italian writer, noted for his humanitarian socialist novels, *Fontamara* (1933) and *Bread and Wine* (1937)

silt *n* **1** a fine sediment of mud or clay deposited by moving water ▷ *vb* **2** silt up to fill or choke up with silt: *the channels have been silted up* [probably Old Norse]

Silurian *n* (sile-yoor-ee-an) *adj* *geology* of the period of geological time about 425 million years ago, during which fishes first appeared [after *Silures*, a Welsh tribe who opposed the Romans]

silvan *adj* same as **sylvan**

silver *n* **1** a precious greyish-white metallic element: used in jewellery, tableware, and coins. Symbol: **Ag 2** a coin or coins made of silver **3** any household articles made of silver **4** short for **silver medal** ▷ *adj* **5** greyish-white: *silver hair* **6** (of anniversaries) the 25th in a series: *Silver Jubilee; silver wedding* ▷ *vb* **7** to coat with silver or a silvery substance: *a company that silvers their own mirrors* **8** to cause (something) to become silvery in colour: *the sun silvered the tarmac* [Old English *siolfor*]

silverbeet *n* *Austral and NZ* a beet of Australia and New Zealand with edible spinach-like leaves

silver birch *n* a tree with silvery-white peeling bark

Silverchair *pl n* Australian rock group (formed 1994): comprising Daniel Johns (born 1979; vocals, guitar), Ben Gillies (born 1979, drums) and Chris Joannou (born 1979, bass guitar); their albums include *Frogstomp* (1995) and *Young Modern* (2007)

silverfish *n, pl* **-fish** or **-fishes 1** a small wingless silver-coloured insect **2** a silver-coloured fish

silver goal *n* *soccer* (in certain competitions) a goal scored in a full half of extra time, counting as the winner if it is the only goal scored in the full half or full period of extra time

silver lining *n* a hopeful side of an otherwise desperate or unhappy situation

silver medal *n* a medal of silver awarded to a competitor who comes second in a contest or race

silver plate *n* **1** a thin layer of silver deposited on a base metal **2** articles, such as tableware, made of silver plate ▷ **silver-plate** *vb*

silver screen *n* *informal* films collectively or the film industry

silverside *n* a cut of beef from below the rump and above the leg

silversmith *n* a craftsman who makes or repairs items made of silver

silver thaw *n* *Canad* **1** a freezing rainstorm **2** same as **glitter** (7)

silverware *n* items, such as tableware, made of or plated with silver

silvery *adj* **1** having the appearance or colour of silver: *her silvery eyes* **2** having a clear ringing sound: *a cascade of silvery notes*

silviculture *n* the cultivation of forest trees [Latin *silva* woodland + CULTURE]

sim *n* a computer game that simulates an activity such as flying or playing a sport

Si-ma Qian or **Ssu-ma Ch'ien** *n* ?145–?85 BC, Chinese historian, author of the *Shih-chi*, a history of China from earliest times to the 2nd century BC, usually the greatest historical work in Chinese

Simbirsk *n* the former name (until 1924) of **Ulyanovsk**

Simenon *n* Georges. 1903–89, Belgian novelist. He wrote over two hundred novels, including the detective series featuring Maigret

Simeon Stylites *n* Saint. ?390–459 AD, Syrian monk, first of the ascetics who lived on pillars. Feast day: Jan 5 or Sept 1

Simferopol *n* a city in on the S Crimean Peninsula: capital of Crimea; a Scythian town in the 1st century BC; seized by the Russians in 1736. Pop: 344 000 (2005 est)

simian *adj* **1** of or resembling a monkey or ape ▷ *n* **2** a monkey or ape [Latin *simia* an ape]

similar *adj* **1** alike but not identical **2** *geometry* (of two or more figures) different in size or position, but with exactly the same shape [Latin *similis*] ▷ **similarity** *n* ▷ **similarly** *adv*

> **USAGE** *As* should not be used after *similar*: *Wilson held a similar position to Jones* (not *a similar position as Jones*); *the system is similar to the one in France* (not *similar as in France*).

simile (sim-ill-ee) *n* a figure of speech that likens one thing to another of a different category, introduced by *as* or *like* [Latin: something similar]

similitude *n* *formal* likeness; similarity

Simla *n* a city in N India, capital of Himachal Pradesh state: summer capital of India (1865–1939); hill resort and health centre. Pop: 142 161 (2001). Official name: Shimla

simmer *vb* **1** to cook (food) gently at just below boiling point **2** (of violence or conflict) to threaten to break out: *revolt simmering among rural MPs* ▷ *n* **3** the state of simmering [perhaps imitative]

simmer down *vb* *informal* to calm down after being angry

simnel cake *n* *Brit* a fruit cake with marzipan,

traditionally eaten during Lent or at Easter [Latin *simila* fine flour]

Simon *n* **1** the original name of (Saint) **Peter** (1) **2** *New Testament* **a** Saint Simon Zelotes one of the 12 apostles, who had probably belonged to the Zealot party before becoming a Christian (Luke 6:15). Owing to a misinterpretation of two similar Aramaic words he is also, but mistakenly, called *the Canaanite* (Matthew 10:4). Feast day: Oct 28 or May 10 **b** Also: **Simon the Tanner** a relative of Jesus, who may have been identical with Simon Zelotes (Matthew 13:55) **c** Also: **Simon the Tanner** a Christian of Joppa with whom Peter stayed (Acts of the Apostles 9:43) **3** John (**Allsebrook**), 1st Viscount Simon. 1873–1954, British statesman and lawyer. He was Liberal home secretary (1915–16) and, as a leader of the National Liberals, foreign secretary (1931–35), home secretary (1935–37), Chancellor of the Exchequer (1937–40), Lord Chancellor (1940–45) **4** (**Marvin**). Neil. born 1927, US dramatist and librettist, whose plays include *Barefoot in the Park* (1963), *California Suite* (1976), *Biloxi Blues* (1985), *Lost in Yonkers* (1990), and *London Suite* (1995): many have been made into films **5** Paul. born 1941, US pop singer and songwriter. His albums include: with Art Garfunkel (born 1941), *The Sounds of Silence* (1966), and *Bridge over Troubled Water* (1970); and, solo, *Graceland* (1986), *The Rhythm of the Saints* (1990), and *You're The One* (2000)

Simonides *n* ?556–?468 BC, Greek lyric poet and epigrammatist, noted for his odes to victory

simony (sime-on-ee) *n* *Christianity* the practice of buying or selling Church benefits such as pardons [after *Simon Magus*, a biblical sorcerer who tried to buy magical powers]

simoom *n* a hot suffocating sand-laden desert wind [Arabic *samūm* poisonous]

simper *vb* **1** to smile in a silly and mannered way **2** to say (something) with a simper ▷ *n* **3** a simpering smile [origin unknown] ⟩ **simpering** *adj*

simple *adj* **1** easy to understand or do: *in simple English*; *simple exercises* **2** plain and not elaborate: *a simple red skirt*; *a simple answer* **3** not combined or complex: *simple diagnostic equipment* **4** leading an uncomplicated life: *I am a simple man myself* **5** sincere or frank: *a simple apology* **6** of humble background: *the simple country girl* **7** *informal* lacking in intelligence **8** straightforward: *a simple matter of choice* **9** *music* denoting a time where the number of beats per bar may be two, three, or four [Latin *simplex* plain] ⟩ **simplicity** *n*

simple fraction *n* *maths* a fraction in which the numerator and denominator are both whole numbers

simple fracture *n* a fracture in which the broken bone does not pierce the skin

simple interest *n* *finance* interest paid only on the original amount of a debt

simple-minded *adj* **1** (of people) naive and unsophisticated **2** (of opinions or explanations) not taking the complexity of an issue or subject into account ⟩ **simple-mindedness** *n*

simple sentence *n* a sentence consisting of a single main clause

simpleton *n* a foolish or stupid person

simplify *vb* **-fies, -fying, -fied** **1** to make (something) less complicated **2** *maths* to reduce (an equation or fraction) to its simplest form [Latin *simplus* simple + *facere* to make] ⟩ **simplification** *n*

simplistic *adj* (of an opinion or interpretation) too simple or naive

USAGE Since *simplistic* already has *too* as part of its meaning, it is tautologous to talk about something being *too simplistic* or *over-simplistic*.

Simplon Pass *n* a pass over the Lepontine Alps in S Switzerland, between Brig (Switzerland) and Iselle (Italy). Height: 2009 m (6590 ft)

simply *adv* **1** in a simple manner: *an interesting book, simply*

written **2** merely; just: *he's simply too slow* **3** absolutely: *a simply enormous success*

Simpson *n* **1** Sir James Young. 1811–70, Scottish obstetrician, who pioneered the use of chloroform as an anaesthetic **2** Wallis (**Warfield**). See **Edward VIII**

Simpson Desert *n* an uninhabited arid region in central Australia, mainly in the Northern Territory. Area: about 145 000 sq km (56 000 sq miles)

simulate *vb* **-lating, -lated** **1** to pretend to feel or perform (an emotion or action); imitate: *I tried to simulate anger* **2** to imitate the conditions of (a situation), as in carrying out an experiment: *we can then simulate global warming* **3** to have the appearance of: *the wood had been painted to simulate stone* [Latin *simulare* to copy] ⟩ **simulated** *adj* ⟩ **simulation** *n*

simulator *n* a device that simulates specific conditions for the purposes of research or training: *a flight simulator*

simultaneous *adj* occurring or existing at the same time [Latin *simul* at the same time] ⟩ **simultaneously** *adv* ⟩ **simultaneity** *n*

simultaneous equations *pl n* *maths* a set of equations that are all satisfied by the same values of the variables, the number of variables being equal to the number of equations

sin[1] *n* **1** the breaking of a religious or moral law **2** any offence against a principle or standard **3** live in sin *old-fashioned, informal* (of an unmarried couple) to live together ▷ *vb* **sinning, sinned** **4** to commit a sin [Old English *synn*] ⟩ **sinner** *n*

sin[2] *maths* sine

SIN (in Canada) Social Insurance Number

Sinai *n* **1 a** a mountainous peninsula of NE Egypt at the N end of the Red Sea, between the Gulf of Suez and the Gulf of Aqaba: occupied by Israel in 1967; fully restored by 1982 **2** Mount Sinai the mountain where Moses received the Law from God (Exodus 19–20): often identified as Jebel Musa, sometimes as Jebel Serbal, both on the S Sinai Peninsula

Sinaitic *or* **Sinaic** *adj* **1** of or relating to the Sinai Peninsula **2** of or relating to Mount Sinai

Sinaloa *n* a state of W Mexico. Capital: Culiacán. Pop: 2 534 835 (2000). Area: 58 092 sq km (22 425 sq miles)

Sinatra *n* Francis Albert, known as *Frank*. 1915–98, US popular singer and film actor. His recordings include "One for My Baby (and One More for the Road)" (1955) and "My Way" (1969)

sin bin *n* *slang* (in ice hockey etc.) the area in which players must sit for a specified period after committing a serious foul

since *prep* **1** during the period of time after: *one of their worst winters since 1945* ▷ *conj* **2** continuously from the time given: *they've been standing in line ever since she arrived* **3** for the reason that; because ▷ *adv* **4** from that time: *I have often been asked since* [Old English *siththan*]

USAGE See at *ago*.

sincere *adj* genuine and honest: *sincere concern* [Latin *sincerus*] ⟩ **sincerely** *adv* ⟩ **sincerity** *n*

Sinclair *n* **1** Sir Clive (**Marles**). born 1940, English electronics engineer, inventor, and entrepreneur, who produced such electronic goods as pocket calculators and some of the first home computers; however, the Sinclair C5 (1985), a small light electric vehicle for one person, proved a commercial failure **2** Upton (**Beall**). 1878–1968, US novelist, whose *The Jungle* (1906) exposed the working and sanitary conditions of the Chicago meat-packing industry and prompted the passage of food inspection laws

Sind *n* a province of SE Pakistan, mainly in the lower Indus valley: formerly a province of British India; became a province of Pakistan in 1947; divided in 1955 between Hyderabad and Khairpur; reunited as a province in 1970. Capital: Karachi. Pop: 34 240 000 (2003 est). Area: 140 914 sq km (54 407 sq miles)

S

sine *n* (in trigonometry) the ratio of the length of the opposite side to that of the hypotenuse in a right-angled triangle [Latin *sinus* a bend]

sinecure (sin-ee-cure) *n* a paid job that involves very little work or responsibility [Latin *sine* without + *cura* care]

sine die (sin-ay dee-ay) *adv* without fixing a day for future action or meeting [Latin, literally: without a day]

sine qua non (sin-ay kwah non) *n* an essential requirement [Latin, literally: without which not]

sinew *n* 1 *anatomy* a tough fibrous cord connecting muscle to bone 2 *literary* physical strength [Old English *sinu, seonu*]

sinewy *adj* lean and muscular

sinful *adj* 1 having committed or tending to commit sin: *I am a sinful man* 2 being a sin; wicked: *sinful acts*

sing *vb* **singing, sang, sung** 1 to produce musical sounds with the voice 2 to perform (a song) 3 (of certain birds and insects) to make musical calls 4 **sing of** to tell a story in song about: *the minstrels sang of courtly love* 5 to make a humming, ringing, or whistling sound: *the arrow sang past his ear* 6 (of one's ears) to be filled with a continuous ringing sound 7 to bring (someone) to a given state by singing: *I sang him to sleep* 8 *slang, chiefly US* to act as an informer ▶ See also **sing out** [Old English *singan*] ❯ **singer** *n* ❯ **singing** *adj, n*

> USAGE See at **ring**[1].

sing. singular

Singapore *n* 1 a republic in SE Asia, occupying one main island and over 50 small islands at the S end of the Malay Peninsula: established as a British trading post in 1819 and became part of the Straits Settlements in 1826; occupied by the Japanese (1942–45); a British colony from 1946, becoming self-governing in 1959; part of the Federation of Malaysia from 1963 to 1965, when it became an independent republic (within the Commonwealth). Official languages: Chinese, Malay, English, and Tamil. Religion: Buddhist, Taoist, traditional beliefs, and Muslim. Currency: Singapore dollar. Capital: Singapore. Pop: 5 460 302 (2013 est). Area: now over 700 sq km (270 sq miles), increased in recent years as a result of land reclamation schemes 2 the capital of the republic of Singapore: a major international port; administratively not treated as a city

Singaporean *adj* 1 of or relating to Singapore or its inhabitants ▷ *n* 2 a native or inhabitant of Singapore

singe *vb* **singeing, singed** 1 to burn slightly without setting alight; scorch: *it singed his sheepskin* ▷ *n* 2 a slight burn [Old English *sengan*]

Singer *n* 1 Isaac Bashevis. 1904–91, US writer of Yiddish novels and short stories; born in Poland. His works include *Satan in Goray* (1935), *The Family Moscat* (1950), the autobiographical *In my Father's Court* (1966), and *The King of the Fields* (1989): Nobel prize for literature 1978 2 Isaac Merrit. 1811–75, US inventor, who originated and developed an improved chain-stitch sewing machine (1852)

Singh *n* Manmohan. born 1932, Indian politician; prime minister of India (2004–2014)

Singhalese *n, pl* **-lese** ▷ *adj* same as **Sinhalese**

singing telegram *n* 1 a service by which a person is employed to present greetings to someone on a special occasion by singing 2 the greetings presented in this way 3 the person who presents the greetings

single *adj* 1 existing alone; solitary: *the cottage's single chimney* 2 distinct from others of the same kind: *every single housing society* 3 designed for one user: *a single room* 4 unmarried 5 even one: *there was not a single bathroom* 6 (of a flower) having only one circle of petals 7 **single combat** a duel or fight involving two individuals ▷ *n* 8 a hotel bedroom for one person 9 a gramophone record, CD, or cassette with a short recording of music on it 10 *cricket* a hit from which one run is scored 11 a *Brit* a pound note or coin b *US and Canad* a dollar bill 12 a ticket valid for a one-way journey only ▷ *vb* **-gling, -gled** 13 **single out** to select from a group of people or things: *the judge had singled him out for praise* ▶ See also **singles** [Old French *sengle*]

single-breasted *adj* (of a jacket or coat) having the fronts overlapping only slightly and with one row of buttons

single cream *n Brit* cream which has a relatively low fat content and does not thicken when beaten

single-decker *n Brit informal* a bus with only one passenger deck

single entry *n* a book-keeping system in which all transactions are entered in one account only

single file *n* a line of people, one behind the other

single-handed *adj* 1 alone; unaided: *a single-handed raid on the enemy camp* ▷ *adv* 2 unaided or working alone: *she had to take on the world single-handed* ❯ **single-handedly** *adv*

single-minded *adj* having one purpose or aim only; dedicated ❯ **single-mindedly** *adv* ❯ **single-mindedness** *n*

single-parent family *n* a family consisting of one parent and his or her child or children living together, the other parent being dead or permanently absent

singles *pl n sport* a match played with one person on each side

singles bar *n* a bar that is a social meeting place for single people

singlet *n Brit and NZ* a man's sleeveless vest

single ticket *n* same as **single** (12)

singleton *n cards* the only card of a particular suit held by a player

singly *adv* one at a time; one by one

sing out *vb* to call out loudly

Sing Sing *n* a prison in New York State, in Ossining [variant of *Ossining*]

sing-song *n* 1 an informal group singing session ▷ *adj* 2 (of a voice) having a repetitive rise and fall in tone

singular *adj* 1 *grammar* (of a word or form) denoting only one person or thing: *a singular noun* 2 remarkable; extraordinary: *one of the singular achievements* 3 unusual; odd: *a lovable but very singular old woman* ▷ *n* 4 *grammar* the singular form of a word [Latin *singularis* single] ❯ **singularity** *n* ❯ **singularly** *adv*

Sinhailien *n* a variant transliteration of the alternative name for **Lianyungang**

Sinhalese *or* **Singhalese** *n* 1 (*pl* **-lese**) a member of a people living mainly in Sri Lanka 2 the language of this people ▷ *adj* 3 of this people ▶ See also **Sri Lankan**

Sining *n* variant transliteration of the Chinese name for **Xining**

sinister *adj* 1 threatening or suggesting evil or harm: *a sinister conspiracy* 2 *heraldry* of, on, or starting from the bearer's left side [Latin: on the left-hand side, considered by Roman augurs to be the unlucky one]

sink *vb* **sinking, sank, sunk** 1 to submerge (in liquid) 2 to cause (a ship) to submerge by attacking it with bombs, torpedoes, etc. 3 to appear to descend towards or below the horizon 4 to make or become lower in amount or value: *sterling sank to a record low against the Deutschmark* 5 to move or fall into a lower position, esp. due to tiredness or weakness: *she sank back in her chair* 6 **sink into** to pass into a lower state or condition, esp. an unpleasant one: *to sink into debt* 7 (of a voice) to become quieter 8 to become weaker in health 9 to dig (something sharp) into a solid object: *she sank her teeth into the steak* 10 *informal* to drink (a number of alcoholic drinks) 11 to dig, drill, or excavate (a hole or shaft) 12 to drive (a stake) into the ground 13 **sink in** *or* **into** to invest (money) in (a venture) 14 *golf, snooker* to hit (the ball) into the hole or pocket: *he finally sank the shot for a bogey* ▷ *n* 15 a fixed basin in a kitchen or bathroom, with a water supply and drainpipe ▷ *adj* 16 *informal* (of a housing estate or school) deprived or having low standards of achievement [Old English *sincan*]

S

sinker n a weight attached to a fishing line or net to cause it to sink in water

Sinkiang-Uighur Autonomous Region n a variant transliteration of the Chinese name for the **Xinjiang Uygur Autonomous Region**

sink in vb (of a fact) to become fully understood: *the euphoria started to wear off as the implications of it all sank in*

sinking fund n a fund set aside to repay a long-term debt

Sinn Féin (shin fane) n an Irish Republican political movement linked to the IRA [Irish Gaelic: we ourselves]

Sino- combining form Chinese: *Sino-European; Sinology* [Late Latin *Sinae* the Chinese]

Sinology (sine-ol-a-jee) n the study of Chinese history, language, and culture **> Sinologist** n

Sint Maarten n the Dutch name for **Saint Martin**

Sintra n a town in central Portugal, near Lisbon, in the Sintra mountains: noted for its castles and palaces and the beauty of its setting: tourism. Former name: **Cintra**

Sinŭiju n a port in North Korea, on the Yalu River opposite Dandong, China: developed by the Japanese during their occupation (1910–45); industrial centre. Pop: 349 000 (2005 est)

sinuous adj literary **1** full of curves **2** having smooth twisting movements: *sinuous dances* [Latin *sinuosus* winding] **> sinuosity** n

sinus (sine-uss) n anatomy a hollow space in bone, such as one in the skull opening into a nasal cavity [Latin: a curve]

sinusitis n inflammation of the membrane lining a sinus, esp. a nasal sinus

Sion n **1** a town in SW Switzerland, capital of Valais canton, on the River Rhône. Pop: 27 171 (2000). Latin name: **Sedunum 2** a variant of **Zion**

Sioux (soo) n **1** (pl **Sioux**) a member of a group of Native American peoples, formerly living over a wide area from Lake Michigan to the Rocky Mountains **2** any of the languages of these peoples

sip vb **sipping, sipped 1** to drink (a liquid) in small mouthfuls **> n 2** an amount sipped **3** an instance of sipping [probably from Low German *sippen*]

siphon or **syphon** n **1** a tube which uses air pressure to draw liquid from a container **2** same as **soda siphon > vb 3 siphon off a** to draw (liquid) off through a siphon **b** to redirect (resources or money), esp. dishonestly, into other projects or bank accounts [Greek]

Siple n **Mount Siple** a mountain in Antarctica, on the coast of Byrd Land. Height: 3100 m (10 171 ft)

Siqueiros n David Alfaro. 1896–1974, Mexican painter, noted for his murals expressing a revolutionary message

sir n a polite term of address for a man [variant of SIRE]

Sir n a title placed before the name of a knight or baronet: *Sir David Attenborough*

Siracusa n the Italian name for **Syracuse**

Siraj-ud-daula n ?1728–57, Indian leader who became the Great Mogul's deputy in Bengal (1756); opponent of English colonization. He captured Calcutta (1756) from the English and many of his prisoners suffocated in a crowded room that became known as the Black Hole of Calcutta. He was defeated (1757) by a group of Indian nobles in alliance with Robert Clive

sire n **1** a male parent of a horse or other domestic animal **2** archaic a respectful form of address used to a king **> vb 3** to father [Old French]

siren n **1** a device that gives out a loud wailing sound as a warning or signal **2 Siren** Greek myth a sea nymph whose singing lured sailors to destruction on the rocks **3** a woman who is attractive but dangerous to men [Greek *seirēn*]

Siret n a river in SE Europe, rising in Ukraine and flowing southeast through E Romania to the Danube. Length: about 450 km (280 miles)

sirloin n a prime cut of beef from the upper part of the loin [Old French *surlonge*]

sirocco n, pl **-cos** a hot stifling wind blowing from N Africa into S Europe [Italian]

sis¹ n informal short for **sister**

sis² or **sies** (siss) interj S African informal an exclamation of disgust [Afrikaans]

sisal (size-al) n a stiff fibre obtained from a Mexican plant and used for making rope [after *Sisal*, a port in Mexico]

siskin n a yellow-and-black finch [Middle Dutch *sīseken*]

Sisley n Alfred. 1839–99, French painter, esp. of landscapes; one of the originators of impressionism

Sismondi n Jean Charles Léonard Simonde de. 1773–1842, Swiss historian and economist. His *Histoire des républiques italiennes du moyen âge* (1807–18) contributed to the movement for Italian unification

Sissinghurst Castle n a restored Elizabethan mansion near Cranbrook in Kent: noted for the gardens laid out in the 1930s by Victoria Sackville-West and Harold Nicolson

sissy or **cissy** n, pl **-sies 1** an effeminate, weak, or cowardly person **> adj 2** effeminate, weak, or cowardly [from SIS¹]

sister n **1** a woman or girl having the same parents as another person **2** a female fellow member of a group, race, or profession **3** a female nurse in charge of a ward **4** chiefly RC Church a nun **> adj 5** of the same class, origin, or design, as another: *its sister paper* [Old English *sweostor*]

sisterhood n **1** the state of being sisters or like sisters **2** a religious group of women **3** a group of women united by a common interest or belief

sister-in-law n, pl **sisters-in-law 1** the sister of one's husband or wife **2** the wife of one's sibling

sisterly adj of or like a sister; affectionate

Sistine Chapel n the chapel of the pope in the Vatican at Rome, built for Sixtus IV and decorated with frescoes by Michelangelo and others [Sistine, from Italian *Sistino* relating to *Sisto* Sixtus (Pope Sixtus IV)]

Siswati n a language of Swaziland

sit vb **sitting, sat 1** to rest one's body upright on the buttocks: *she had to sit on the ground* **2** to cause (someone) to rest in such a position: *they sat their grandfather in the shade* **3** (of an animal) to rest with the rear part of its body lowered to the ground **4** (of a bird) to perch or roost **5 sit on** (of a bird) to cover its eggs so as to hatch them **6** to be located: *the bank sits in the middle of the village* **7** to pose for a painting or photograph **8** to occupy a seat in some official capacity: *no police representatives will sit on the committee* **9** (of a parliament or court) to be in session **10** to remain unused: *his car sat in the garage* **11** (of clothes) to fit or hang in a certain way: *that dress sits well on you* **12** Brit to take (an examination): *he's sitting his finals* **13** (in combination) to look after a specified person or thing for someone else: *is someone going to dog-sit for you?* **14 sit for** chiefly Brit to be a candidate for (a qualification): *he sat for a degree in medicine* **15 sit tight** informal **a** to wait patiently **b** to maintain one's position firmly **▸** See also **sit back, sit down,** etc. [Old English *sittan*]

sitar n an Indian stringed musical instrument with a long neck and a rounded body [Hindi]

sit back vb to relax or be passive when action should be taken: *we can't just sit back and let this dreadful situation continue*

sitcom n informal (on television or radio) a comedy series involving the same characters in various everyday situations: *yet another unfunny sitcom set in Liverpool*

sit down vb **1** to adopt or cause (someone) to adopt a sitting position **2 sit down under** to suffer (insults or humiliations) without resistance **> n sit-down 3** a short rest sitting down **> adj sit-down 4** (of a meal) eaten while sitting down at a table

sit-down strike n a strike in which workers refuse to leave their place of employment until a settlement is reached

site n **1** the piece of ground where something was, is, or is intended to be located: *a building site; a car park is to be built on the site of a Roman fort* **2** same as **website** ▷ *vb* **siting, sited 3** to locate (something) on a specific site [Latin *situs* position]

Sithole *n* Ndabaningi. 1920–2000, Zimbabwean clergyman and politician; leader of the Zimbabwe African National Union (1963–74). He was one of the negotiators of the internal settlement (1978) to pave the way for Black majority rule in Rhodesia (now Zimbabwe)

sit-in *n* **1** a protest in which the demonstrators sit in a public place and refuse to move ▷ *vb* **sit in 2 sit in for** to stand in as a substitute for (someone) **3 sit in on** to be present at (a meeting) as an observer

Sitka *n* a town in SE Alaska, in the Alexander Archipelago on W Baranof Island: capital of Russian America (1804–67) and of Alaska (1867–1906). Pop: 8876 (2003 est)

sitka spruce *n* a tall North American spruce tree, now often grown in Britain [after SITKA]

sit on *vb informal* to delay action on: *they are sitting on their information*

sit out *vb* **1** to endure to the end: *just sit it out, and it will pass eventually* **2** to take no part in (a dance or game)

Sitsang *n* a Chinese name for **Tibet**

sitter *n* **1** a person posing for his or her portrait or photograph **2** same as **baby-sitter 3** (*in combination*) a person who looks after a specified person or thing for someone else: *a house-sitter*

Sitter *n* Willem de. 1872–1934, Dutch astronomer, who calculated the size of the universe and conceived of it as expanding

sitting *n* **1** a continuous period of being seated at some activity: *you may not be able to complete it in one sitting* **2** one of the times when a meal is served, when there is not enough space for everyone to eat at the same time: *the second sitting* **3** a period of posing for a painting or photograph **4** a meeting of an official body to conduct business ▷ *adj* **5** current: *a sitting member of Congress* **6** seated: *a sitting position*

Sitting Bull *n* Indian name *Tatanka Yotanka*. ?1831–90, American Indian chief of the Teton Dakota Sioux. Resisting White encroachment on his people's hunting grounds, he led the Sioux tribes against the US Army in the Sioux War (1876–77) in which Custer was killed. The hunger of the Sioux, whose food came from the diminishing buffalo, forced his surrender (1881). He was killed during renewed strife

sitting duck *n informal* a person or thing in a defenceless or vulnerable position

sitting room *n* a room in a house or flat where people sit and relax

sitting tenant *n* a tenant occupying a house or flat

situate *vb* **-ating, -ated** *formal* to place [Late Latin *situare* to position]

situation *n* **1 a** state of affairs **b** a complex or critical state of affairs **2** location and surroundings **3** social or financial circumstances **4** a position of employment

---

USAGE *Situation* is often used in contexts in which it is redundant or imprecise. Typical examples are: *the company is in a crisis situation* or *people in a job situation*. In the first example, *situation* does not add to the meaning and should be omitted. In the second example, it would be clearer and more concise to substitute a phrase such as *people at work*.

---

situation comedy *n* same as **sitcom**

sit up *vb* **1** to raise oneself from a lying position into a sitting one **2** to remain out of bed until a late hour **3** *informal* to become suddenly interested: *make the world sit up and take notice* ▷ *n* **sit-up 4** a physical exercise in which the body is brought into a sitting position from one of lying on the back

Sitwell *n* **1** Dame Edith. 1887–1964, English poet and critic, noted esp. for her collection *Façade* (1922) **2** her brother, Sir Osbert. 1892–1969, English writer, best known for his five autobiographical books (1944–50) **3** his brother, Sir Sacheverell. 1897–1988, English poet and writer of books on art, architecture, music, and travel

SI unit *n* any of the units (metre, kilogram, second, ampere, kelvin, candela, mole, and those derived from them) adopted for international use under the Système International d'Unités, now employed for all scientific and most technical purposes

Siva *n* a Hindu god, the Destroyer

Sivaji *n* 1627–80, Indian king (1674–80), who led an uprising of Hindus against Muslim rule and founded the Masatha kingdom

Sivas *n* a city in central Turkey, at an altitude of 1347 m (4420 ft): one of the chief cities in Asia Minor in ancient times; scene of the national congress (1919) leading to the revolution that established modern Turkey. Pop: 266 000 (2005 est)

six *n* **1** the cardinal number that is the sum of one and five **2** a numeral, 6 or VI, representing this number **3** something representing or consisting of six units **4** *cricket* a score of six runs, obtained by hitting the ball so that it crosses the boundary without bouncing **5 at sixes and sevens** in a state of confusion **6 knock someone for six** *informal* to upset or overwhelm someone completely **7 six of one and half a dozen of the other** a situation in which there is no real difference between the alternatives ▷ *adj* **8** amounting to six: *six days* [Old English *siex*] ▷ **sixth** *adj, n*

Six Counties *pl n* the historic counties of Northern Ireland, which no longer have a local government function

sixfold *adj* **1** having six times as many or as much **2** composed of six parts ▷ *adv* **3** by six times as many or as much

Six Nations *pl n* (in North America) the Indian confederacy of the Cayugas, Mohawks, Oneidas, Onondagas, Senecas, and Tuscaroras. Also called: **Iroquois**

Six Nations Championship *n rugby union* an annual competition involving national sides representing England, France, Ireland, Italy, Scotland, and Wales

six-pack *n informal* **1** a package containing six units, esp. six cans of beer **2** a highly developed set of abdominal muscles in a man

sixpence *n* (formerly) a small British, Australian and New Zealand coin worth six old pennies, or 2½ pence

six-pointer *n informal* a football match between two teams in similar positions in the league table, which gains the winning team three points and denies the losing team three points

six-shooter *n US informal* a revolver that fires six shots without reloading

sixteen *n* **1** the cardinal number that is the sum of ten and six **2** a numeral, 16 or XVI, representing this number **3** something representing or consisting of sixteen units ▷ *adj* **4** amounting to sixteen: *sixteen years* ▷ **sixteenth** *adj, n*

sixth form *n* (in England and Wales) the most senior form in a secondary school, in which pupils over sixteen may take A levels or retake GCSEs ▷ **sixth-former** *n*

sixth sense *n* the supposed ability of knowing something instinctively without having any evidence for it

Sixtus IV *n* original name *Francesco della Rovere*. 1414–84, Italian ecclesiastic; pope (1471–84). Notorious for his nepotism and political intrigue, he was also a patron of the arts and commissioned the building (1473–81) of the Sistine Chapel

Sixtus V *n* original name *Felice Peretti*. 1520–90, Italian ecclesiastic; pope (1585–90). He is noted for vigorous administrative reforms that contributed to the Counter-Reformation

sixty *n, pl* **-ties 1** the cardinal number that is the product of ten and six **2** a numeral, 60 or LX, representing this number **3** something representing or consisting of sixty units ▷ *adj* **4** amounting to sixty: *sixty seconds* ⟩ **sixtieth** *adj, n*

sizable *or* **sizeable** *adj* quite large

size¹ *n* **1** the dimensions, amount, or extent of something **2** large dimensions, amount, or extent: *I was overwhelmed by the sheer size of the city* **3** one of a series of standard measurements for goods: *he takes size 11 shoes* **4** *informal* state of affairs as summarized: *that's about the size of it* ▷ *vb* **sizing, sized 5** to sort (things) according to size [Old French *sise*]

> **USAGE** The use of *-size* and *-sized* after *large* or *small* is redundant, except when describing something which is made in specific sizes: *a large* (not *large-size*) *organization*. Similarly, *in size* is redundant in the expressions *large in size* and *small in size*.

size² *n* **1** a thin gluey substance that is used as a sealer ▷ *vb* **sizing, sized 2** to treat (a surface) with size [origin unknown]

sized *adj* of a specified size: *average-sized*

> **USAGE** See at **size¹**.

size up *vb informal* to make an assessment of (a person or situation)

sizzle *vb* **-zling, -zled 1** to make a hissing sound like the sound of frying fat **2** *informal* to be very hot: *the city was sizzling in a hot summer spell* **3** *informal* to be very angry ▷ *n* **4** a hissing sound [imitative] ⟩ **sizzling** *adj*

Sjælland *n* the Danish name for **Zealand**

sjambok (sham-bock) *S African n* **1** a whip or riding crop made of hide ▷ *vb* **-bokking, -bokked 2** to beat with a sjambok [Malay *tjambok*]

SK Saskatchewan

Skagen *n* Cape Skagen another name for the **Skaw**

Skagerrak *n* an arm of the North Sea between Denmark and Norway, merging with the Kattegat in the southeast

skanky *adj* **skankier, skankiest** *slang* **1** dirty or unattractive **2** promiscuous

Skara Brae *n* a Neolithic village in NE Scotland, in the Orkney Islands: one of Europe's most perfectly preserved Stone Age villages, buried by a sand dune until uncovered by a storm in 1850

skate¹ *n* **1** same as **ice skate, roller skate 2** get one's skates on *informal* to hurry ▷ *vb* **skating, skated 3** to glide on or as if on skates **4** skate on thin ice to place oneself in a dangerous situation [Old French *éschasse* stilt] ⟩ **skater** *n* ⟩ **skating** *n*

skate² *n, pl* **skate** *or* **skates** a large edible marine fish with a broad flat body [Old Norse *skata*]

skateboard *n* **1** a narrow board mounted on roller-skate wheels, usually ridden while standing up ▷ *vb* **2** to ride on a skateboard ⟩ **skateboarding** *n*

skate round *or* **skate over** *vb* to avoid discussing or dealing with (a matter) fully: *friends and admirers skated round the question*

Skaw *n* the Skaw a cape at the N tip of Denmark. Also known as: **Cape Skagen, Skagen**

skean-dhu (skee-an-doo) *n* a dagger worn in the sock as part of Highland dress [Gaelic *sgian* knife + *dhu* black]

skedaddle *vb* **-dling, -dled** *informal* to run off hastily [origin unknown]

skein *n* **1** a length of yarn or thread wound in a loose coil **2** a flock of geese in flight [Old French *escaigne*]

skeleton *n* **1** the hard framework of bones that supports and protects the organs and muscles of the body **2** the essential framework of any structure: *a metal skeleton*

supporting the roof and floors **3** *informal* an extremely thin person or animal **4** an outline consisting of bare essentials: *the mere skeleton of a script* **5** a small steel-frame sledge for racing down an ice-covered run **6** the sport of racing small steel-frame sledges down an ice-covered run **7** skeleton in the cupboard *or* closet an embarrassing or scandalous fact from the past that is kept secret ▷ *adj* **8** reduced to a minimum: *a skeleton staff* [Greek: something dried up] ⟩ **skeletal** *adj*

skeleton key *n* a key designed so that it can open many different locks

skelm *n S African informal* a villain or crook [Afrikaans]

Skelmersdale *n* a town in NW England, in Lancashire: designated a new town in 1962. Pop: 39 279 (2001)

Skelton *n* John. ?1460–1529, English poet celebrated for his short rhyming lines using the rhythms of colloquial speech ⟩ **Skeltonic** *adj*

skeptic *n US or archaic* same as **sceptic**

skerry *n, pl* **-ries** *Scot* a rocky island or reef [Old Norse *sker*]

sketch *n* **1** a quick rough drawing **2** a brief descriptive piece of writing **3** a short funny piece of acting forming part of a show **4** any brief outline ▷ *vb* **5** to make a quick rough drawing (of) **6** sketch out to make a brief description of: *they sketched out plans for the invasion* [Greek *skhedios* unprepared]

sketchbook *n* a book of blank pages for sketching on

sketchy *adj* **sketchier, sketchiest** giving only a rough or incomplete description ⟩ **sketchily** *adv*

skew *adj* **1** having a slanting position ▷ *n* **2** a slanting position ▷ *vb* **3** to take or cause to take a slanting position: *our boat skewed off course* **4** to distort or misrepresent: *the takeover bid has skewed last month's figures* [Old French *escuer* to shun]

skewbald *adj* **1** marked with patches of white and another colour ▷ *n* **2** a horse with this marking [origin unknown]

skewed *adj* distorted or biased because of prejudice or lack of information: *a skewed conception of religion*

skewer *n* **1** a long pin for holding meat together during cooking ▷ *vb* **2** to fasten or pierce with or as if with a skewer [probably from dialect *skiver*]

skewwhiff *adj informal* crooked or slanting

ski *n, pl* **skis** *or* **ski 1** one of a pair of long runners that are used, fastened to boots, for gliding over snow ▷ *vb* **skiing, skied** *or* **ski'd 2** to travel on skis [Norwegian] ⟩ **skier** *n* ⟩ **skiing** *n*

skid *vb* **skidding, skidded 1** (of a vehicle or person) to slide sideways while in motion ▷ *n* **2** an instance of skidding [origin unknown]

skidoo *n, pl* **-doos** *Canad* same as **snowmobile** [*Ski-Doo*, originally a trademark]

skid row *n slang, chiefly US and Canad* a poor and neglected area of a city, inhabited by down-and-outs

Skien *n* a port in S Norway, on the Skien River: one of the oldest towns in Norway; timber industry. Pop: 50 507 (2004 est)

skiff *n* a small narrow boat for one person [French *esquif*]

ski jump *n* a steep snow-covered slope ending in a horizontal ramp from which skiers compete to make the longest jump

Skikda *n* a port in NE Algeria, on an inlet of the Mediterranean: founded by the French in 1838 on the site of a Roman city. Pop: 170 000 (2005 est). Former name: **Philippeville**

skilful *or US* **skillful** *adj* having or showing skill ⟩ **skilfully** *or US* **skillfully** *adv*

ski lift *n* a series of chairs hanging from a power-driven cable for carrying skiers up a slope

skill *n* **1** special ability or expertise enabling one to perform an activity very well **2** something, such as a trade, requiring special training or expertise [Old Norse *skil* distinction] ⟩ **skilled** *adj*

skillet *n* **1** a small frying pan **2** *chiefly Brit* a long-handled cooking pot [origin unknown]

skim *vb* **skimming, skimmed 1** to remove (floating material) from the surface of (a liquid): *skim any impurities off the surface* **2** to glide smoothly over (a surface) **3** to throw (a flat stone) across a surface, so that it bounces: *two men skimmed stones on the surface of the sea* **4** (often foll. by *through*) to read (a piece of writing) quickly and without taking in the details [Middle English *skimmen*]

skimmed or **skim milk** *n* milk from which the cream has been removed

skimp *vb* **1** to be extremely sparing or supply (someone) sparingly **2** to do (something) carelessly or with inadequate materials [perhaps a combination of SCANT + SCRIMP]

skimpy *adj* **skimpier, skimpiest** inadequate in amount or size; scant

skin *n* **1** the tissue forming the outer covering of the body **2** a person's complexion: *sallow skin* **3** any outer layer or covering: *potato skin* **4** a thin solid layer on the surface of a liquid: *custard with a thick skin on it* **5** the outer covering of a furry animal, removed and prepared for use **6** a container for liquids, made from animal skin **7 by the skin of one's teeth** by a narrow margin **8 get under one's skin** *informal* to annoy one **9 no skin off one's nose** *informal* not a matter that concerns one **10 save one's skin** to save one from death or harm **11 skin and bone** extremely thin **12 thick** or **thin skin** an insensitive or sensitive nature ⊳ *vb* **skinning, skinned 13** to remove the outer covering from (fruit, vegetables, dead animals, etc.) **14** to injure (a part of the body) by scraping some of the skin off: *I had skinned my knuckles* **15** *slang* to swindle [Old English *scinn*]
⟩ **skinless** *adj*

skin-deep *adj* not of real importance; superficial: *beauty is only skin-deep*

skin diving *n* underwater swimming using only light breathing apparatus and without a special diving suit
⟩ **skin-diver** *n*

skin flick *n slang* a pornographic film

skinflint *n* a very mean person [referring to a person so greedy that he or she would skin (swindle) a flint]

skin graft *n* a piece of skin removed from one part of the body and surgically grafted at the site of a severe burn or other injury

skinhead *n* **1** a member of a group of White youths, noted for their closely cropped hair, aggressive behaviour, and overt racism **2** a closely cropped hairstyle

Skinner *n* B(urrhus) F(rederic). 1904–90, US behavioural psychologist. His "laws of learning", derived from experiments with animals, have been widely applied to education and behaviour therapy

skinny *adj* **-nier, -niest** extremely thin

skint *adj slang* without money, esp. only temporarily [variant of *skinned*]

skintight *adj* (of garments) fitting tightly over the body; clinging

skip¹ *vb* **skipping, skipped 1** *Brit* to move lightly by hopping from one foot to the other **2** to jump over a skipping-rope **3** to cause (a stone) to skim over a surface or (of a stone) to move in this way **4** to pass over or miss out; omit: *I skipped a few paragraphs* **5 skip through** *informal* to read or deal with (something) quickly or without great effort or concentration **6 skip it!** *informal* it doesn't matter! **7** *informal* to miss deliberately: *she skipped the class* **8** *informal, chiefly US, Canad and Austral* to leave (a place) in a hurry: *he skipped town three years later* ⊳ *n* **9** a skipping movement or action [probably from Old Norse]

skip² *n* **1** *Brit* a large open container for transporting building materials or rubbish **2** a cage used as a lift in mines [variant of *skep* a beehive]

ski pants *pl n* stretch trousers, worn for skiing or leisure, which are kept taut by straps under the feet

skipper *n* **1** the captain of a ship or aircraft **2** the captain of a sporting team ⊳ *vb* **3** to be the captain of [Middle Low German, Middle Dutch *schipper* shipper]

skipping *n chiefly Brit* the act of jumping over a rope held either by the person jumping or by two other people, as a game or for exercise

skipping-rope *n chiefly Brit* a rope that is held in the hands and swung round and down so that the holder or others can jump over it

Skipton *n* a market town in N England, in North Yorkshire: 11th-century castle. Pop: 14 313 (2001)

skirl *Scot and N English dialect n* **1** the sound of bagpipes ⊳ *vb* **2** (of bagpipes) to give out a shrill sound [probably from Old Norse]

skirmish *n* **1** a brief or minor fight or argument ⊳ *vb* **2** to take part in a skirmish [Old French *eskirmir*]

Skíros *n* transliteration of the Modern Greek name for Skyros

skirt *n* **1** a woman's or girl's garment hanging from the waist **2** the part of a dress or coat below the waist **3** a circular hanging flap, for example round the base of a hovercraft **4** *Brit and NZ* a cut of beef from the flank **5 bit of skirt** *offensive, slang* a girl or woman ⊳ *vb* **6** to lie along or form the edge of (something): *a track skirting the foot of the mountain* **7** to go around the outer edge of (something): *we skirted the township* **8** to avoid dealing with (an issue): *I was skirting around the real issues* [Old Norse *skyrta* shirt]

skirting board *n Brit* a narrow board round the bottom of an interior wall where it joins the floor

ski stick or **ski pole** *n* one of a pair of sharp pointed sticks used by skiers to gain speed and maintain balance

skit *n* a short funny or satirical sketch [probably Scandinavian]

skite *Austral and NZ vb* **1** to boast ⊳ *n* **2** a boast

ski tow *n* a device for pulling skiers uphill, usually a motor-driven rope grasped by the skier while riding on his or her skis

skittish *adj* **1** playful or lively **2** (of a horse) excitable and easily frightened [probably from Old Norse]

skittle *n* **1** a bottle-shaped object used as a target in a game of skittles **2 skittles** a bowling game in which players knock over as many skittles as possible by rolling a wooden ball at them [origin unknown]

skive *vb* **skiving, skived** (often foll. by *off*) *Brit informal* to avoid work or responsibility [origin unknown]
⟩ **skiver** *n*

skivvy *chiefly Brit often disparaging n, pl* **-vies 1** a female servant who does menial work; drudge **2** *Austral and NZ* a garment resembling a sweater with long sleeves and a polo neck ⊳ *vb* **-vies, -vying, -vied 3** to work as a skivvy [origin unknown]

skolly or **skollie** *n, pl* **-lies** *S African* a hooligan, usually one of a gang [origin unknown]

skookum *adj W Canad* strong or brave [Chinook]

Skopje *n* the capital of (the Former Yugoslav Republic of) Macedonia, on the Vardar River: became capital of Serbia in 1346 and of Macedonia in 1945; suffered a severe earthquake in 1963; university (1949). Pop: 449 000 (2005 est.). Serbian name: **Skoplje**. Turkish name (1392–1913): **Üsküb**

skua *n* a large predatory gull living in cold marine regions [Faeroese *skúgvur*]

skulduggery or US **skullduggery** *n informal* underhand dealing to achieve an aim [origin unknown]

skulk *vb* **1** to move stealthily, so as to avoid notice **2** to lie in hiding; lurk [from Old Norse]

skull *n* **1** the bony framework of the head **2** *informal* the head or mind: *that would have penetrated even your thick skull* [probably from Old Norse]

skull and crossbones *n* a picture of the human skull above two crossed bones, formerly on the pirate flag, now used as a warning of danger or death

skullcap *n* a closely fitting brimless cap

skunk *n, pl* **skunks** or **skunk 1** a mammal with a black-and-white coat and bushy tail, which gives out a foul-smelling fluid when attacked **2** *informal* an unpleasant or unfair person [from a Native American language]

sky *n, pl* **skies 1** the upper atmosphere as seen from earth **2 praise to the skies** praise rather excessively ▷ *vb* **skies, skying, skied 3** *informal* to hit (a ball) high in the air: *the blond-haired forward skied the ball high over the bar* [Old Norse *skȳ* cloud]

sky-blue *adj* bright clear blue

skydiving *n* the sport of jumping from an aircraft and falling freely or performing manoeuvres before opening the parachute ▶ **skydiver** *n*

Skye *n* a mountainous island off the NW coast of Scotland, the largest island of the Inner Hebrides: tourist centre. Chief town: Portree. Pop: 9232 (2001). Area: 1735 sq km (670 sq miles)

sky-high *adj, adv* **1** very high: *most firms are no longer willing to pay sky-high prices* **2 blow sky-high** to destroy completely

skyjack *vb* to hijack (an aircraft) [SKY + HIJACK]

skylark *n* **1** a lark that sings while soaring at a great height ▷ *vb* **2** *old-fashioned* to play or frolic

skylight *n* a window placed in a roof or ceiling to let in daylight

skyline *n* **1** the line at which the earth and sky appear to meet **2** the outline of buildings, trees, or hills, seen against the sky

Skype *n* trademark **1** a software application by which users can make voice and video calls over the internet ▷ *vb* **Skyping, Skyped 2** to make a call by Skype or call (someone) by Skype

skyrocket *n* **1** same as **rocket** (1) ▷ *vb* **2** *informal* to rise very quickly

Skyros *or* **Scyros** *n* a Greek island in the Aegean, the largest island in the N Sporades. Pop: 2602 (2001). Area: 199 sq km (77 sq miles). Modern Greek name: **Skíros**

skyscraper *n* a very tall building

skyward *adj* **1** towards the sky ▷ *adv* also: **skywards 2** towards the sky

slab *n* **1** a broad flat thick piece of wood, stone, or other material **2** *informal* a package containing 24 cans of beer [origin unknown]

slack¹ *adj* **1** not tight, tense, or taut: *the slack jaw hung open* **2** careless in one's work **3** (esp. of water) moving slowly **4** (of trade) not busy ▷ *n* **5** a part that is slack or hangs loose: *take up the slack* **6** a period of less busy activity ▷ *vb* **7** to neglect one's duty or work in a lazy manner: *stop slacking, you pair!* **8** (often foll. by *off*) to loosen or slacken ▶ See also **slacks** [Old English *slæc, sleac*] ▶ **slackness** *n*

slack² *n* small pieces of coal with a high ash content [probably Middle Low German *slecke*]

slacken *vb* (often foll. by *off*) **1** to make or become looser **2** to make or become slower or less intense: *to slacken the pace of reform*

slacker *n* a person who evades work or duty; shirker

slacks *pl n* old-fashioned casual trousers

slag *n* **1** the waste material left after metal has been smelted **2** *Brit and NZ disparaging, slang* a sexually immoral woman ▷ *vb* **slagging, slagged 3** *Brit, Austral and NZ slang* (often foll. by *off*) to criticize in an unpleasant way: *I don't think anyone can slag it off* [Middle Low German *slagge*] ▶ **slagging** *n* ▶ **slaggy** *adj*

slag heap *n* a pile of waste matter from metal smelting or coal mining

slain *vb* the past participle of **slay**

slake *vb* **slaking, slaked 1** *literary* to satisfy (thirst or desire) **2** to add water to (lime) to produce calcium hydroxide [Old English *slacian*]

slalom *n* *skiing, rowing* a race over a winding course marked by artificial obstacles [Norwegian]

slam¹ *vb* **slamming, slammed 1** to close violently and noisily **2** to throw (something or someone) down violently **3** *slang* to criticize harshly: *his new proposals were slammed by the opposition* **4** to strike with violent force: *he slammed the ball into the back of the net* ▷ *n* **5** the act or noise of slamming [Scandinavian]

slam² *n* the winning of all (**grand slam**) or all but one (**little slam**) of the 13 tricks at bridge [origin unknown]

slam dunk *n* **1** *basketball* a scoring shot in which the player jumps up and forces the ball down through the basket **2** *informal* a task so easy that success in it is deemed a certainty ▷ *vb* **slam-dunk 3** *basketball* to jump up and force (a ball) through a basket

slammer *n* **the slammer** *slang* prison

slander *n* **1** *law* a false and damaging statement about a person **2** the crime of making such a statement ▷ *vb* **3** to utter slander (about) [Old French *escandle*] ▶ **slanderous** *adj*

slang *n* **1** informal language not used in formal speech or writing and often restricted to a particular social group or profession ▷ *vb* **2** to use insulting language to (someone) [origin unknown] ▶ **slangy** *adj*

slanging match *n* an angry quarrel in which people trade insults

slant *vb* **1** to lean at an angle; slope **2** to write or present (information) in a biased way ▷ *n* **3** a sloping line or position **4** a point of view, esp. a biased one: *a right-wing slant on the story* **5 on a** *or* **the slant** sloping ▷ *adj* **6** oblique; sloping [Scandinavian] ▶ **slanting** *adj* ▶ **slantwise** *adv*

slap *n* **1** a sharp blow or smack with something flat, such as the open hand **2** the sound made by or as if by such a blow **3 slap and tickle** *Brit old-fashioned, informal* sexual play **4** a slap in the face an unexpected rejection or insult **5** a slap on the back congratulations ▷ *vb* **slapping, slapped 6** to strike sharply with something flat, such as the open hand **7** to bring (something) down forcefully: *he slapped down a fiver* (usually foll. by *against*) to strike (something) with a slapping sound **9** *informal* to cover with quickly or carelessly: *she slapped on some make-up* **10 slap on the back** to congratulate ▷ *adv informal* **11** exactly: *slap in the middle* **12 slap into** forcibly or abruptly into: *he ran slap into the guard* [Low German *slapp*]

slap-bang *adv informal* **1** directly or exactly: *he's on holiday in LA and has run slap-bang into a famous face* **2** forcefully and abruptly: *he'd gone and run slap-bang into the watchman*

slapdash *adv* **1** carelessly or hastily ▷ *adj* **2** careless or hasty

slap-happy *adj* **-pier, -piest** *informal* cheerfully careless

slaphead *n* *slang* a bald person [from SLAP + HEAD]

slapstick *n* rough and high-spirited comedy in which the characters behave childishly

slap-up *adj* *Brit informal* (esp. of meals) large and expensive

slash *vb* **1** to cut (a person or thing) with sharp sweeping strokes **2** to make large gashes in: *I slashed the tyres of his van* **3** to reduce drastically: *to slash costs* **4** to criticize harshly ▷ *n* **5** a sharp sweeping stroke **6** a cut made by such a stroke **7** same as **solidus 8** *Brit and Austral slang* the act of urinating [origin unknown]

slasher *n* *Austral and NZ* a tool or tractor-drawn machine used for cutting scrub or undergrowth in the bush

Śląsk *n* the Polish name for **Silesia**

slat *n* a narrow thin strip of wood or metal, such as used in a Venetian blind [Old French *esclat* splinter]

slate¹ *n* **1** a dark grey rock that can be easily split into thin layers and is used as a roofing material **2** a roofing tile of slate **3** (formerly) a writing tablet of slate **4** *chiefly US and Canad* a list of candidates in an election **5 wipe the slate clean** forget about past mistakes or failures and start afresh **6 on the slate** *Brit and Austral informal* on credit ▷ *vb* **slating, slated 7** to cover (a roof) with slates **8** *chiefly US* to plan or schedule: *another exercise is slated for tomorrow* [Old French *esclate* fragment] ▶ **slaty** *adj*

slate² *vb* **slating, slated** *informal, chiefly Brit and Austral* to criticize harshly: *the new series was slated by the critics* [probably from Old French *esclate* fragment] ▶ **slating** *n*

Slatkin *n* Leonard. born 1944, US conductor; musical director of the St Louis Symphony Orchestra (1979–96) and of the National Symphony Orchestra (1996–2008)

slattern *n* old-fashioned a dirty and untidy woman

[probably from dialect *slatter* to slop] **> slatternliness** *n*
> slatternly *adj*

slaughter *n* **1** the indiscriminate or brutal killing of large numbers of people **2** the savage killing of a person **3** the killing of animals for food ▷ *vb* **4** to kill indiscriminately or in large numbers **5** to kill brutally **6** to kill (animals) for food **7** *informal* (in sport) to defeat easily [Old English *sleaht*]

slaughterhouse *n* a place where animals are killed for food

Slav *n* a member of any of the peoples of E Europe or the former Soviet Union who speak a Slavonic language [Medieval Latin *Sclavus* a captive Slav]

slave *n* **1** a person legally owned by another for whom he or she has to work without freedom, pay, or rights **2** a person under the domination of another or of some habit or influence: *a slave to party doctrine* **3** *informal* a badly-paid person doing menial tasks ▷ *vb* **slaving, slaved 4** (often foll. by *away* or *over*) to work very hard for little or no money [Medieval Latin *Sclavus* a Slav (the Slavonic races were frequently conquered in the Middle Ages)]

Slave Coast *n* the coast of W Africa between the Volta River and Mount Cameroon, chiefly along the Bight of Benin: the main source of African slaves (16th–19th centuries)

slave-driver *n* **1** a person who makes people work very hard **2** (esp. formerly) a person forcing slaves to work

slaver¹ (slay-ver) *n* **1** (esp. formerly) a dealer in slaves **2** *history* a ship used in the slave trade

slaver² (slav-ver) *vb* **1** to dribble saliva **2** (often foll. by *over*) to drool (over someone), making flattering remarks ▷ *n* **3** saliva dribbling from the mouth **4** *informal* nonsense [probably from Low German]

Slave River *n* a river in W Canada, in the Northwest Territories and NE Alberta, flowing from Lake Athabaska northwest to Great Slave Lake. Length: about 420 km (260 miles). Also called: **Great Slave River**

slavery *n* **1** the state or condition of being a slave **2** the practice of owning slaves **3** hard work with little reward

slave trade *n* the buying and selling of slaves, esp. the transportation of Black Africans to America and the Caribbean from the 16th to the 19th centuries

slavish *adj* **1** of or like a slave **2** imitating or copying exactly without any originality: *a slavish adherence to the conventions of Italian opera* **> slavishly** *adv*

Slavkov *n* the Czech name for **Austerlitz**

Slavonia *n* a region in Croatia, mainly between the Drava and Sava Rivers

Slavonian *adj* **1** of or relating to Slavonia, a region in Croatia, or its inhabitants ▷ *n* **2** a native or inhabitant of Slavonia

Slavonic *or especially US* **Slavic** *n* **1** a group of languages including Bulgarian, Russian, Polish, and Czech ▷ *adj* **2** of this group of languages **3** of the people who speak these languages

slay *vb* **slaying, slew, slain** *archaic, literary* to kill, esp. violently [Old English *slēan*] **> slayer** *n*

sleaze *n informal* behaviour in public life considered immoral, dishonest, or disreputable: *political sleaze*

sleazy *adj* **-zier, -ziest** dirty, rundown, and not respectable: *a sleazy hotel* [origin unknown] **> sleaziness** *n*

sledge¹ *or especially US and Canad* **sled** *n* **1** a vehicle mounted on runners, drawn by horses or dogs, for transporting people or goods over snow **2** a light wooden frame used, esp. by children, for sliding over snow ▷ *vb* **sledging, sledged 3** to travel by sledge [Middle Dutch *sleedse*]

sledge² *n* short for **sledgehammer**

sledgehammer *n* **1** a large heavy hammer with a long handle, used for breaking rocks and concrete ▷ *adj* **2** crushingly powerful: *the sledgehammer approach* [Old English *slecg* a large hammer]

sleek *adj* **1** smooth, shiny, and glossy: *sleek blond hair* **2** (of a person) elegantly dressed [variant of *slick*]

sleep *n* **1** a state of rest during which the eyes are closed, the muscles and nerves are relaxed, and the mind is unconscious **2** a period spent sleeping **3** the substance sometimes found in the corner of the eyes after sleep **4** a state of inactivity, like sleep **5** *poetic* death ▷ *vb* **sleeping, slept 6** to be in or as in the state of sleep **7** to be inactive or unaware: *their defence slept as we scored another try* **8** to have sleeping accommodation for (a certain number): *the villa sleeps ten* **9** *poetic* to be dead **10 sleep on it** to delay making a decision about (something) until the next day, in order to think about it ▶ See also **sleep around, sleep in**, etc. [Old English *slēpan*]

sleep around *vb informal* to have many sexual partners

sleeper *n* **1** a railway sleeping car or compartment **2** one of the blocks supporting the rails on a railway track **3** a small plain gold ring worn in a pierced ear lobe to prevent the hole from closing up **4** *informal* a person or thing that achieves success after an initial period of obscurity

sleep in *vb* to sleep longer than usual

sleeping bag *n* a large well-padded bag for sleeping in, esp. outdoors

sleeping car *n* a railway carriage with small rooms containing beds for passengers to sleep in

sleeping partner *n* a partner in a business who shares in the financing but does not take part in its management

sleeping pill *n* a pill containing a drug that induces sleep

sleeping policeman *n Brit* a bump built across a road to prevent motorists from driving too fast

sleeping sickness *n* an infectious, usually fatal, African disease transmitted by the bite of the tsetse fly, causing fever and sluggishness

sleepless *adj* **1** (of a night) during which one does not sleep **2** unable to sleep **3** *chiefly poetic* always active **> sleeplessness** *n*

sleep off *vb informal* to get rid of by sleeping: *go home and sleep it off*

sleepout *n NZ* a small building for sleeping in

sleep out *vb* to sleep in the open air

sleepover *n* an occasion when a person stays overnight at a friend's house

sleep together *vb* to have sexual intercourse and, usually, spend the night together

sleepwalk *vb* to walk while asleep **> sleepwalker** *n* **> sleepwalking** *n*

sleep with *vb* to have sexual intercourse and, usually, spend the night with

sleepy *adj* **sleepier, sleepiest 1** tired and ready for sleep **2** (of a place) without activity or excitement: *a sleepy little town* **> sleepily** *adv*

sleet *n* **1** partly melted falling snow or hail or (esp. US) partly frozen rain ▷ *vb* **2** to fall as sleet [Germanic]

sleeve *n* **1** the part of a garment covering the arm **2** a tubelike part which fits over or completely encloses another part **3** a flat cardboard container to protect a gramophone record **4 up one's sleeve** secretly ready: *he has a few more surprises up his sleeve* [Old English *slīefe, slēfe*] **> sleeveless** *adj*

sleigh *n* **1** same as **sledge¹** (1) ▷ *vb* **2** to travel by sleigh [Dutch *slee*]

sleight (slite) *n old-fashioned* skill or cunning [Old Norse *slǣgth*]

sleight of hand *n* **1** the skilful use of the hands when performing magic tricks **2** the performance of such tricks

slender *adj* **1** (esp. of a person's figure) slim and graceful **2** of small width relative to length or height **3** small or inadequate in amount or size: *a slender advantage* [origin unknown]

slept *vb* the past of **sleep**

Slesvig *n* the Danish name for **Schleswig**

sleuth (rhymes with **tooth**) *n informal* a detective [Old Norse *slōth* a trail]

slew¹ *vb* the past tense of **slay**

slew² *or especially US* **slue** *vb* **1** to slide or skid sideways: *the bus slewed across the road* ▷ *n* **2** the act of slewing [origin unknown]

Slezsko *n* the Czech name for **Silesia**

slice *n* **1** a thin flat piece or wedge cut from something: *a slice of tomato* **2** a share or portion: *the biggest slice of their income* **3** a kitchen tool having a broad flat blade: *a fish slice* **4** *sport* a shot that causes the ball to go to one side, rather than straight ahead ▷ *vb* **slicing, sliced** **5** to cut (something) into slices **6** (usually foll. by *through*) to cut through cleanly and effortlessly, with or as if with a knife **7** (usually foll. by *off* or *from* or *away*) to cut or be cut from a larger piece **8** *sport* to play (a ball) with a slice [Old French *esclice* a piece split off]

slick *adj* **1** (esp. of speech) easy and persuasive: *a slick answer* **2** skilfully devised or executed: *a slick marketing effort* **3** *informal, chiefly US and Canad* shrewd; sly **4** *informal* well-made and attractive, but superficial: *a slick publication* **5** *chiefly US and Canad* slippery ▷ *n* **6** a slippery area, esp. a patch of oil floating on water ▷ *vb* **7** to make smooth or shiny: *long hair slicked back with gel* [probably from Old Norse]

slide *vb* **sliding, slid** **1** to move smoothly along a surface in continual contact with it: *doors that slide open* **2** to slip: *he slid on his back* **3** (usually foll. by *into* or *out of* or *away from*) to pass or move smoothly and quietly: *she slid out of her seat* **4** (usually foll. by *into*) to go (into a specified condition) gradually: *the republic will slide into political anarchy* **5** (of a currency) to lose value gradually **6 let slide** to allow to change to a worse state by neglect: *past chairmen have undoubtedly let things slide* ▷ *n* **7** the act or an instance of sliding **8** a small glass plate on which specimens are placed for study under a microscope **9** a photograph on a transparent base, mounted in a frame, that can be viewed by means of a projector **10** a smooth surface, such as ice, for sliding on **11** a structure with a steep smooth slope for sliding down in playgrounds **12** *chiefly Brit* an ornamental clip to hold hair in place **13** the sliding curved tube of a trombone that is moved in and out to allow different notes to be played [Old English *slīdan*]

slide rule *n* a device formerly used to make mathematical calculations consisting of two strips, one sliding along a central groove in the other, each strip graduated in two or more logarithmic scales of numbers

slide show *n* **1** any display in the form of a series of static images, such as photographic transparencies on a slide projector or images on a computer screen ▷ *adj* **slide-show** **2** presented as a series of static images: *slide-show presentation*

sliding scale *n* a variable scale according to which things such as wages or prices alter in response to changes in other factors

Slieve Donard *n* a mountain in SE Northern Ireland, in the Mourne Mountains: highest peak in Northern Ireland. Height: 853 m (2798 ft)

slight *adj* **1** small in quantity or extent: *a slight improvement* **2** not very important or lacking in substance: *her political career was honourable but relatively slight* **3** slim and delicate ▷ *vb* **4** to insult (someone) by behaving rudely; snub ▷ *n* **5** an act of snubbing (someone) [Old Norse *slēttr* smooth] **> slightly** *adv*

Sligo *n* **1** a county of NW Republic of Ireland, on the Atlantic: has a deeply indented low-lying coast; livestock and dairy farming. County town: Sligo. Pop: 58 200 (2002). Area: 1795 sq km (693 sq miles) **2** a port in NW Republic of Ireland, county town of Co Sligo on **Sligo Bay**. Pop: 19 735 (2002)

slim *adj* **slimmer, slimmest** **1** (of a person) attractively thin **2** small in width relative to height or length: *a slim book* **3** poor; meagre: *a slim chance of progress* ▷ *vb* **slimming, slimmed** **4** to make or become slim by diets and exercise **5** to reduce in size: *that would slim the overheads* [Dutch: crafty] **> slimmer** *n* **> slimming** *n*

Slim¹ *n* the E African name for AIDS [from its wasting effects]

Slim² *n* William Joseph, 1st Viscount. 1891–1970, British field marshal, who commanded (1943–45) the 14th Army in the reconquest of Burma (now called Myanmar) from the Japanese; governor general of Australia (1953–60)

slime *n* **1** soft runny mud or any sticky substance, esp. when disgusting or unpleasant **2** a thick sticky substance produced by some fish, slugs, and fungi [Old English *slīm*]

slimy *adj* **slimier, slimiest** **1** of, like, or covered with slime **2** pleasant and friendly in an insincere way

sling¹ *n* **1** *med* a wide piece of cloth suspended from the neck for supporting an injured hand or arm **2** a rope or strap by which something may be lifted **3** a simple weapon consisting of a strap tied to cords, in which a stone is whirled and then released ▷ *vb* **slinging, slung** **4** *informal* to throw **5** to carry or hang loosely from or as if from a sling: *her shoulder bag was slung across her chest* **6** to hurl with or as if with a sling [probably from Old Norse]

sling² *n* a sweetened mixed drink with a spirit base: *gin sling* [origin unknown]

slingback *n* a shoe with a strap instead of a complete covering for the heel

sling off at *vb Austral and NZ informal* to mock and jeer

slink *vb* **slinking, slunk** to move or act in a quiet and secretive way from fear or guilt [Old English *slincan*]

slinky *adj* **slinkier, slinkiest** *informal* **1** (of clothes) figure-hugging **2** moving in an alluring way

slip¹ *vb* **slipping, slipped** **1** to lose balance and slide unexpectedly: *he slipped on some leaves* **2** to let loose or be let loose: *the rope slipped from his fingers* **3** to move smoothly and easily: *small enough to slip into a pocket* **4** to place quickly or stealthily: *he slipped the pistol back into his holster* **5** to put on or take off easily or quickly: *we had slipped off our sandals* **6** to pass out of (the mind or memory) **7** to move or pass quickly and without being noticed: *we slipped out of the ballroom* **8** to make a mistake **9** to decline in health or mental ability **10** to become worse or lower: *sales had slipped below the level for June of last year* **11** to dislocate (a disc in the spine) **12** to pass (a stitch) from one needle to another without knitting it **13 let slip a** to allow to escape **b** to say unintentionally ▷ *n* **14** a slipping **15** a mistake or oversight: *one slip in concentration that cost us the game* **16** a woman's sleeveless undergarment, worn under a dress **17** same as **slipway** **18** *cricket* a fielding position a little behind and to the offside of the wicketkeeper **19 give someone the slip** to escape from someone ▶ See also **slip up** [Middle Low German or Dutch *slippen*]

slip² *n* **1** a small piece of paper: *the registration slip* **2** a cutting taken from a plant **3** a young slim person: *a slip of a girl* [probably Middle Low German, Middle Dutch *slippe* to cut]

slip³ *n* clay mixed with water to a thin paste, used for decorating or patching a ceramic piece [Old English *slyppe* slime]

slipe *n* NZ wool removed from the pelt of a slaughtered sheep by immersion in a chemical bath [Middle English *slype* to skin]

slipknot *n* a nooselike knot tied so that it will slip along the rope round which it is made

slip-on *adj* **1** (of a garment or shoe) without laces or buttons so as to be easily and quickly put on ▷ *n* **2** a slip-on garment or shoe

slipped disc *n pathol* a painful condition in which one of the discs which connects the bones of the spine becomes displaced and presses on a nerve

slipper *n* a light soft shoe for indoor wear **> slippered** *adj*

slippery *adj* **1** liable or tending to cause objects to slip:

the road was slippery **2** liable to slip from one's grasp: *a bar of slippery soap* **3** not to be trusted: *slippery politicians* **> slipperiness** *n*

slippy *adj* **-pier, -piest** *informal, dialect* same as **slippery** (1, 2) **> slippiness** *n*

slip road *n Brit* a short road connecting a motorway to another road

slipshod *adj* **1** (of an action) done in a careless way without attention to detail: *a slipshod piece of research* **2** (of a person's appearance) untidy and slovenly

slip-slop *n S African* same as **flip-flop**

slipstream *n* the stream of air forced backwards by an aircraft or car in motion

slip up *informal vb* **1** to make a mistake ▷ *n* **slip-up** **2** a mistake

slipway *n* a large ramp that slopes down from the shore into the water, on which a ship is built or repaired and from which it is launched

slit *n* **1** a long narrow cut or opening ▷ *vb* **slitting, slit** **2** to make a straight long cut in (something) [Old English *slītan* to slice]

slither *vb* **1** to move or slide unsteadily, such as on a slippery surface **2** to move along the ground in a twisting way: *a snake slithered towards the tree* ▷ *n* **3** a slithering movement [Old English *slid(e)rian*] **> slithery** *adj*

sliver (sliv-ver) *n* **1** a small thin piece that is cut or broken off lengthwise ▷ *vb* **2** to cut into slivers [obsolete *sliven* to split]

Sloan *n* John. 1871–1951, US painter and etcher, a leading member of the group of realistic painters known as the Ash Can School. His pictures of city scenes include *McSorley's Bar* (1912) and *Backyards, Greenwich Village* (1914)

Sloane Ranger *n informal* (in Britain) a young upper-class woman having a home in London and in the country, characterized as wearing expensive informal clothes [from *Sloane* Square, London + *Lone Ranger*, cowboy hero]

slob *n informal* a lazy and untidy person [Irish Gaelic *slab* mud] **> slobbish** *adj*

slobber *vb* **1** to dribble (liquid or saliva) from the mouth **2 slobber over** to behave in an excessively sentimental way towards (someone) ▷ *n* **3** liquid or saliva spilt from the mouth [Middle Low German, Middle Dutch *slubberen*] **> slobbery** *adj*

slob ice *n Canad* sludgy masses of floating sea ice

sloe *n* **1** the small sour blue-black fruit of the blackthorn **2** same as **blackthorn** [Old English *slāh*]

sloe-eyed *adj* having dark almond-shaped eyes

slog *vb* **slogging, slogged** **1** to work hard and steadily **2** to make (one's way) with difficulty: *we slogged our way through the snow* **3** to hit hard ▷ *n* **4** long exhausting work **5** a long and difficult walk: *a slog through heather and bracken* **6** a heavy blow [origin unknown]

slogan *n* a catchword or phrase used in politics or advertising [Gaelic *sluagh-ghairm* war cry]

sloop *n* a small sailing ship with a single mast [Dutch *sloep*]

slop *vb* **slopping, slopped** **1** (often foll. by *about*) to splash or spill (liquid) **2 slop over** *informal, chiefly US and Canad* to be excessively sentimental ▷ *n* **3** a puddle of spilt liquid **4 slops** liquid refuse and waste food used to feed animals, esp. pigs **5** (*often pl*) *informal* liquid food [Old English *-sloppe*]

slope *n* **1** a stretch of ground where one end is higher than the other **2 slopes** hills or foothills **3** any slanting surface **4** the angle of such a slant ▷ *vb* **sloping, sloped** **5** to slant or cause to slant **6** (esp. of natural features) to have one end or part higher than another: *the bank sloped sharply down to the river* **7 slope off** or **away** *informal* to go quietly and quickly in order to avoid something or someone **8 slope arms** *military* (formerly) to hold a rifle in a sloping position against the shoulder [origin unknown]

slop out *vb* (of prisoners) to empty chamber pots and collect water

sloppy *adj* **-pier, -piest** **1** *informal* careless or untidy: *sloppy workmanship* **2** *informal* excessively sentimental and romantic **3** wet; slushy **> sloppily** *adv* **> sloppiness** *n*

slosh *vb* **1** *informal* to throw or pour (liquid) carelessly **2** (often foll. by *about* or *around*) *informal* **a** to shake or stir (something) in a liquid **b** (of a person) to splash (around) in water or mud **3** (usually foll. by *about* or *around*) *informal* to shake (a container of liquid) or (of liquid in a container) to be shaken **4** *Brit slang* to deal a heavy blow to ▷ *n* **5** the sound of splashing liquid **6** slush **7** *Brit slang* a heavy blow [variant of SLUSH] **> sloshy** *adj*

sloshed *adj slang, chiefly Brit and Austral* drunk

slot *n* **1** a narrow opening or groove, such as one in a vending machine for inserting a coin **2** *informal* a place in a series or scheme: *the late-night slot when people stop watching TV* ▷ *vb* **slotting, slotted** **3** to make a slot or slots in **4** (usually foll. by *in* or *into*) to fit or be fitted into a slot: *I slotted my card into the machine* [Old French *esclot* the depression of the breastbone]

sloth (rhymes with **both**) *n* **1** a slow-moving shaggy-coated animal of Central and South America, which hangs upside down in trees by its long arms and feeds on vegetation **2** *formal* laziness, esp. regarding work [Old English *slǣwth*]

slothful *adj* lazy and unwilling to work

slot machine *n* a machine, esp. for vending food and cigarettes or featuring an electronic game on which to gamble, worked by placing a coin in a slot

slouch *vb* **1** to sit, stand, or move with a drooping posture ▷ *n* **2** a drooping posture **3 be no slouch** *informal* be very good or talented: *he was no slouch himself as a negotiator* [origin unknown]

slouch hat *n* a soft hat with a brim that can be pulled down over the ears

slough¹ (rhymes with **now**) *n* **1** a swamp or marshy area **2** (rhymes with **blue**) *US and Canad* a large hole where water collects **3** despair or hopeless depression [Old English *slōh*]

slough² (sluff) *n* **1** any outer covering that is shed, such as the dead outer layer of the skin of a snake ▷ *vb* **slough off** **2** to shed (an outer covering) or (of an outer covering) to be shed: *the dead cells would slough off* **3** to get rid of (something unwanted or unnecessary): *she tried hard to slough off her old personality* [Germanic]

Slough *n* **1** an industrial town in SE central England, in Slough unitary authority, Berkshire; food products, high-tech industries. Pop: 126 276 (2001) **2** a unitary authority in SE central England, in Berkshire. Pop: 118 800 (2003 est). Area: 28 sq km (11 sq miles)

Slovak *adj* **1** of or relating to Slovakia or its inhabitants ▷ *n* **2** a native or inhabitant of Slovakia **3** the language of Slovakia

Slovakia *n* a country in central Europe: part of Hungary from the 11th century until 1918, when it united with Bohemia and Moravia to form Czechoslovakia; it became independent in 1993 and joined the EU in 2004. Official language: Slovak. Religion: Roman Catholic majority. Currency: koruna. Capital: Bratislava. Pop: 5 488 339 (2013 est). Area: 49 036 sq km (18 940 sq miles)

Slovakian *adj* **1** of, relating to, or characteristic of Slovakia, its people, or the Slovak language ▷ *adj* **2** a native or inhabitant of Slovakia

sloven *n* a person who is always untidy or careless in appearance or behaviour [origin unknown]

Slovene *adj* **1** Also: **Slovenian** of or relating to Slovenia or its inhabitants ▷ *n* **2** a native or inhabitant of Slovenia **3** the language of Slovenia

Slovenia *n* a republic in S central Europe: settled by the Slovenes in the 6th century; joined Yugoslavia in 1918 and became an autonomous republic in 1946; became fully independent in 1992 and joined the EU in 2004;

S

rises over 2800 m (9000 ft) in the Julian Alps. Official language: Slovene. Religion: Roman Catholic majority. Currency: euro (replacing the tolar in 2007). Capital: Ljubljana. Pop: 1 992 690 (2013 est). Area: 20 251 sq km (7819 sq miles)

slovenly *adj* **1** always unclean or untidy **2** negligent and careless: *to write in such a slovenly style* ▷ *adv* **3** in a slovenly manner ❯ **slovenliness** *n*

slow *adj* **1** taking a longer time than is usual or expected **2** lacking speed: *slow movements* **3** adapted to or producing slow movement: *the slow lane* **4** (of a clock or watch) showing a time earlier than the correct time **5** not quick to understand: *slow on the uptake* **6** dull or uninteresting: *the play was very slow* **7** not easily aroused: *he is slow to anger* **8** (of business) not busy; slack **9** (of a fire or oven) giving off low heat **10** *photog* requiring a relatively long time of exposure: *a slow film* ▷ *adv* **11** in a slow manner ▷ *vb* **12** (often foll. by *up* or *down*) to decrease or cause to decrease in speed or activity [Old English *slāw* sluggish] ❯ **slowly** *adv*

slowcoach *n informal* a person who moves or works slowly

slow motion *n* **1** *films, television* action that is made to appear slower than normal by filming at a faster rate or by replaying a video recording more slowly ▷ *adj* **slow-motion 2** of or relating to such action **3** moving at considerably less than usual speed

slow virus *n* a type of virus that is present in the body for a long time before it becomes active or infectious

slowworm *n* a legless lizard with a brownish-grey snakelike body

sludge *n* **1** soft mud or snow **2** any muddy or slushy sediment **3** sewage [probably related to SLUSH] ❯ **sludgy** *adj*

slug¹ *n* a mollusc like a snail but without a shell [probably from Old Norse]

slug² *n* **1** a bullet **2** *printing* a line of type produced by a Linotype machine **3** *informal* a mouthful of alcoholic drink, esp. spirits: *he poured out a large slug of Scotch* [probably from SLUG¹ (with allusion to the shape of the animal)]

slug³ *vb* **slugging, slugged 1** *chiefly US and Canad* to hit very hard ▷ *n* **2** *US and Canad* a heavy blow [probably from SLUG² (bullet)]

sluggard *n old-fashioned* a very lazy person [Middle English *slogarde*]

sluggish *adj* **1** lacking energy **2** moving or working at slower than the normal rate: *the sluggish waters of the canal*

sluice *n* **1** a channel that carries a rapid current of water, with a sluicegate to control the flow **2** the water controlled by a sluicegate **3** same as **sluicegate 4** *mining* a sloping trough for washing ore ▷ *vb* **sluicing, sluiced 5** to draw off or drain with a sluice **6** to wash with a stream of water **7** (often foll. by *away* or *out*) (of water) to run or flow from or as if from a sluice [Old French *escluse*]

sluicegate *n* a valve or gate fitted to a sluice to control the rate of flow of water

slum *n* **1** an overcrowded and badly maintained house **2** (often *pl*) a poor rundown overpopulated section of a city ▷ *vb* **slumming, slummed 3** to visit slums, esp. for curiosity **4** slum it to temporarily and deliberately experience poorer places or conditions [origin unknown] ❯ **slummy** *adj*

slumber *literary vb* **1** to sleep ▷ *n* **2** sleep [Old English *slūma*] ❯ **slumbering** *adj*

slump *vb* **1** (of commercial activity or prices) to decline suddenly **2** to sink or fall heavily and suddenly: *she slumped back with exhaustion* ▷ *n* **3** a severe decline in commercial activity or prices; depression **4** a sudden or marked decline in demand or failure: *a slump in demand for oil* [probably Scandinavian]

slung *vb* the past of **sling¹**

slunk *vb* the past of **slink**

slur *vb* **slurring, slurred 1** to pronounce or say (words) unclearly **2** to make insulting remarks about **3** *music* to

sing or play (successive notes) smoothly by moving from one to the other without a break **4** (often foll. by *over*) to treat hastily or carelessly ▷ *n* **5** an insulting remark intended to damage someone's reputation **6** a slurring of words **7** *music* **a** a slurring of successive notes **b** the curved line ⌒ or ⌣ indicating this [probably from Middle Low German]

slurp *informal vb* **1** to eat or drink (something) noisily ▷ *n* **2** a slurping sound [Middle Dutch *slorpen* to sip]

slurry *n, pl* **-ries** a thin watery mixture of something such as cement or mud [Middle English *slory*]

slush *n* **1** any watery muddy substance, esp. melting snow **2** *informal* sloppily sentimental language or writing [origin unknown] ❯ **slushy** *adj*

slush fund *n* a fund for financing political or commercial corruption

slut *n offensive* a promiscuous woman [origin unknown] ❯ **sluttish** *adj*

Sluter *n* Claus. ?1345–1406, Dutch sculptor, working in Burgundy, whose realism influenced many sculptors and painters in 15th-century Europe. He is best known for the portal sculptures and the *Well of Moses* in the Carthusian monastery at Champnol

sly *adj* **slyer, slyest** *or* **slier, sliest 1** (of a person's remarks or gestures) indicating that he or she knows something of which other people may be unaware: *she had the feeling they were poking sly fun at her* **2** secretive and skilled at deception: *a sly trickster* **3** roguish: *sly comedy* ▷ *n* **4** on the sly secretively: *they were smoking on the sly behind the shed* [Old Norse *slōegr* clever] ❯ **slyly** *adv*

Sm *chem* samarium

smack¹ *vb* **1** to slap sharply **2** to strike loudly or to be struck loudly **3** to open and close (the lips) loudly to show pleasure or anticipation ▷ *n* **4** a sharp loud slap, or the sound of such a slap **5** a loud kiss **6** a sharp sound made by the lips in enjoyment **7** smack in the eye *informal* a snub or rejection ▷ *adv informal* **8** directly; squarely: *smack in the middle* **9** sharply and unexpectedly: *he ran smack into one of the men* [probably imitative]

smack² *n* **1** a slight flavour or suggestion (of something): *the smack of loss of self-control* ▷ *vb* **2** smack of **a** to have a slight smell or flavour of (something) **b** to have a suggestion of (something): *it smacks of discrimination* [Old English *smæc*]

smack³ *n* a slang word for **heroin** [perhaps from Yiddish *schmeck*]

smack⁴ *n* a small single-masted fishing vessel [Dutch *smak*]

smacker *n slang* **1** a loud kiss **2** a pound note or dollar bill

small *adj* **1** not large in size or amount **2** of little importance or on a minor scale: *a small detail* **3** mean, ungenerous, or petty: *a small mind* **4** modest or humble: *small beginnings* **5** feel small to be humiliated **6** (of a child or animal) young; not mature **7** unimportant or trivial: *a small matter* **8** (of a letter) written or printed in lower case rather than as a capital ▷ *adv* **9** into small pieces: *cut it small* ▷ *n* **10** the small narrow part of the back **11** smalls *informal, chiefly Brit* underwear [Old English *smæl*] ❯ **smallish** *adj* ❯ **smallness** *n*

small beer *n informal, chiefly Brit* people or things of no importance

small change *n* coins of low value

small fry *pl n* **1** people regarded as unimportant **2** young children

small goods *pl n Austral and NZ* meats bought from a delicatessen, such as sausages

smallholding *n* a piece of agricultural land smaller than a farm ❯ **smallholder** *n*

small hours *pl n* the early hours of the morning, after midnight and before dawn

small intestine *n anatomy* the narrow, longer part of the alimentary canal, in which digestion is completed

small-minded *adj* having narrow selfish attitudes; petty

smallpox *n* a contagious disease causing fever, a rash, and blisters which usually leave permanent scars

small print *n* details in a contract or document printed in small type, esp. when considered as containing important information that people may regret not reading

small-scale *adj* of limited size or scope

small screen *n* the small screen television, esp. in contrast to cinema: *despite his film success, he has achieved little on the small screen*

small talk *n* light conversation for social occasions

small-time *adj informal* operating on a limited scale; minor: *a small-time smuggler*

smarm *vb Brit informal* **1** to bring (oneself) into favour (with) **2** *old-fashioned* (often foll. by *down*) to flatten (the hair) with oil [origin unknown]

smarmy *adj* **smarmier, smarmiest** unpleasantly flattering or polite

Smart *n* Christopher. 1722–71, British poet, author of *A Song to David* (1763) and *Jubilate Agno* (written 1758–63, published 1939). He was confined (1756–63) for religious mania and died in a debtors' prison

smart *adj* **1** clean and neatly dressed **2** intelligent and shrewd **3** quick and witty in speech: *a smart talker* **4** (of places or events) fashionable; chic: *smart restaurants* **5** vigorous or brisk: *a smart pace* **6** causing a sharp stinging pain **7** (of a system or machine) using computer technology **8** (of a weapon) containing an electronic device which enables it to be guided to its target: *a smart bomb* ▷ *vb* **9** to feel or cause a sharp stinging physical or mental pain: *I was still smarting from the insult* ▷ *n* **10** a stinging pain or feeling ▷ *adv* **11** in a smart manner ▶ See also **smarts** [Old English *smeortan* be painful] ❯ **smartly** *adv* ❯ **smartness** *n*

smart alec *n informal* a person who thinks he or she is an expert on every subject; know-all

smart card *n* a plastic card with integrated circuits used for storing and processing computer data

smarten *vb* (usually foll. by *up*) to make or become smart

smartphone *n* a mobile phone which allows the user to access the internet and send and receive e-mails

smarts *pl n slang, chiefly US* know-how, intelligence, or wits: *the street smarts of the old crooks*

smash *vb* **1** to break into pieces violently and noisily **2** (often foll. by *against* or *through* or *into*) to throw or crash (against) violently, causing shattering: *his head smashed against a window* **3** to hit or collide forcefully and suddenly **4** *sport* to hit (the ball) fast and powerfully with an overhead stroke **5** to defeat or destroy: *the police had smashed a major drug ring* ▷ *n* **6** an act or sound of smashing **7** a violent collision of vehicles **8** *sport* a fast and powerful overhead stroke **9** *informal* a show, record or film which is very popular with the public ▷ *adv* **10** with a smash [probably imitative]

smash-and-grab *adj informal* of or relating to a robbery in which a shop window is broken and the contents removed

smasher *n informal, chiefly Brit* a person or thing that is very attractive or outstanding

smashing *adj informal, chiefly Brit* excellent or first-rate

smash-up *informal n* **1** a bad collision or crash involving motor vehicles ▷ *vb* **smash up 2** to damage to the point of complete destruction: *two men smashed up a bar*

smattering *n* a slight or superficial knowledge: *I knew a smattering of Russian*

smear *vb* **1** to spread with a greasy or sticky substance **2** to apply (a greasy or sticky substance) thickly **3** to rub so as to produce a smudge **4** to spread false and damaging rumours (about) ▷ *n* **5** a dirty mark or smudge **6** a false but damaging rumour spread by a rival or enemy **7** *med* a small amount of a substance smeared onto a glass slide for examination under a microscope [Old English *smeoru* a smear] ❯ **smeary** *adj*

smear test *n med* same as **Pap test**

smell *vb* **smelling, smelt** *or* **smelled 1** to perceive the scent of (a substance) with the nose **2** to have a specified kind of smell: *it smells fruity; your supper smells good* **3** (often foll. by *of*) to emit an odour (of): *the place smells of milk and babies* **4** to give off an unpleasant odour **5** (often foll. by *out*) to detect through instinct: *I smell trouble* **6** to use the sense of smell; sniff **7 smell of** to indicate or suggest: *anything that smells of devaluation* ▷ *n* **8** the sense by which scents or odours are perceived. Related adjective: **olfactory 9** an odour or scent **10** the act of smelling [origin unknown]

smelling salts *pl n* a preparation containing crystals of ammonium carbonate, used to revive a person feeling faint

smelly *adj* **smellier, smelliest** having a nasty smell ❯ **smelliness** *n*

smelt¹ *vb* to extract (a metal) from (an ore) by heating [Middle Low German, Middle Dutch *smelten*]

smelt² *n, pl* **smelt** *or* **smelts** a small silvery food fish [Old English *smylt*]

smelt³ *vb* a past tense and past participle of **smell**

smelter *n* an industrial plant in which smelting is carried out

Smetana *n* Bedřich. 1824–84, Czech composer, founder of his country's national school of music. His works include *My Fatherland* (1874–79), a cycle of six symphonic poems, and the opera *The Bartered Bride* (1866)

smile *n* **1** a facial expression in which the corners of the mouth are turned up, showing amusement or friendliness ▷ *vb* **smiling, smiled 2** to give a smile **3 smile at a** to look at with a kindly expression **b** to look with amusement at **4 smile on** *or* **upon** to regard favourably: *fortune smiled on us today* **5** to express by a smile: *he smiled a comrade's greeting* [probably from Old Norse]

Smiles *n* Samuel. 1812–1904, British writer: author of the didactic work *Self-Help* (1859)

smiley *adj* **1** cheerful **2** depicting a smile ▷ *n* **3** an image or group of symbols depicting a smile, or other facial expression, used in electronic communication

smirch *vb* **1** to disgrace **2** to dirty or soil ▷ *n* **3** a disgrace **4** a smear or stain [origin unknown]

smirk *n* **1** a smug smile ▷ *vb* **2** to give such a smile [Old English *smearcian*]

smite *vb* **smiting, smote, smitten** *or* **smit** *archaic* **1** to strike with a heavy blow **2** to affect severely: *hunger smites him again* **3** to burden with an affliction in order to punish: *God smote the enemies of the righteous* **4 smite on** to strike abruptly and with force: *the sun smote down on him* [Old English *smītan*]

smith *n* **1** a person who works in metal: *goldsmith* **2** See **blacksmith** [Old English]

Smith *n* **1** Adam. 1723–90, Scottish economist and philosopher, whose influential book *The Wealth of Nations* (1776) advocated free trade and private enterprise and opposed state interference **2** Alexander McCall. born 1948, Scottish writer and academic, born in Zimbabwe. His novels include *The No. 1 Ladies' Detective Agency* (1998), *The Sunday Philosophy Club* (2004) and *44 Scotland Street* (2005) **3** Bessie, known as *Empress of the Blues.* 1894–1937, US blues singer and songwriter **4** Delia. born 1941, British cookery writer and broadcaster: her publications include *The Complete Cookery Course* (1982) **5** F.E. See (1st Earl of) **Birkenhead 6** Ian (**Douglas**). 1919–2007, Zimbabwean statesman; prime minister of Rhodesia (1964–79). He declared independence from Britain unilaterally (1965) **7** John. ?1580–1631, English explorer and writer, who helped found the North American colony of Jamestown, Virginia. He was reputedly saved by the Indian chief's daughter Pocahontas from execution by her tribe. Among his works is a *Description of New England* (1616) **8** John. 1938–94, British Labour politician; leader of the Labour Party 1992–94 **9** Joseph. 1805–44, US religious leader; founder of the Mormon

S

Church **10** Dame **Maggie**. born 1934, British actress. She has appeared in the films *The Prime of Miss Jean Brodie* (1969), *California Suite* (1978), *The Lonely Passion of Judith Hearne* (1988), *The Secret Garden* (1993), *Gosford Park* (2001), the *Harry Potter* series (2001–11), and in the TV series *Downton Abbey* (from 2010) **11 Stevie**, real name *Florence Margaret Smith*. 1902–71, British poet. Her works include *Novel on Yellow Paper* (1936), and the poems 'A Good Time was had by All' (1937) and 'Not Waving but Drowning' (1957) **12 Sydney**. 1771–1845, British clergyman and writer, noted for *The Letters of Peter Plymley* (1807–08), in which he advocated Catholic emancipation **13 Will(ard Christopher)**. born 1968, US film actor and rap singer; star of the television series *The Fresh Prince of Bel Air* (1990–96), the *Men In Black* series of films (1997–2012), *Ali* (2001), and *I Robot* (2004) **14 Wilbur**. born 1933, British novelist, born in Zambia. His novels include *Where the Lion Feeds* (1964), *Monsoon* (1999) and *The Quest* (2007) **15 William**. 1769–1839, English geologist, who founded the science of stratigraphy by proving that rock strata could be dated by the fossils they contained

smithereens *pl n* shattered fragments [Irish Gaelic *smidirīn*]

Smithson *n* James. original name *James Lewes Macie*. 1765–1829, English chemist and mineralogist, who left a bequest to found the Smithsonian Institution

Smithsonian Institution *n* a national museum and institution in Washington, D.C., founded in 1846 from a bequest by James Smithson, primarily concerned with ethnology, zoology, and astrophysics

smithy *n*, *pl* **smithies** the workshop of a blacksmith; forge

smitten *vb* **1** a past participle of **smite** ▷ *adj* **2** deeply affected by love (for)

smock *n* **1** a loose overall worn to protect the clothes **2** a loose blouselike garment worn by women **3** a loose protective overgarment decorated with smocking, worn formerly by farm workers ▷ *vb* **4** to gather (material) by sewing in a honeycomb pattern [Old English *smocc*]

smocking *n* ornamental needlework used to gather material

smog *n* a mixture of smoke and fog that occurs in some industrial areas [SMOKE + FOG] ▷ **smoggy** *adj*

smoke *n* **1** the cloudy mass that rises from something burning **2** the act of smoking tobacco **3** *informal* a cigarette or cigar **4 go up in smoke a** to come to nothing **b** to burn up vigorously ▷ *vb* **smoking, smoked 5** to give off smoke: *a smoking fireplace* **6 a** to draw the smoke of (burning tobacco) into the mouth and exhale it again **b** to do this habitually **7** to cure (meat, cheese, or fish) by treating with smoke [Old English *smoca*]

Smoke *n* **the Smoke** *informal* short for **Big Smoke**

smokeless *adj* having or producing little or no smoke: *smokeless fuel*

smokeless zone *n* an area where only smokeless fuels may be used

smoke out *vb* **1** to drive (a person or animal) out of a hiding place by filling it with smoke **2** to bring (someone) out of secrecy and into the open: *they smoked out the plotters*

smoker *n* **1** a person who habitually smokes tobacco **2** a train compartment where smoking is permitted

smoke screen *n* **1** something said or done to hide the truth **2** *military* a cloud of smoke used to provide cover for manoeuvres

smokestack *n* a tall chimney that carries smoke away from a factory

smoko *or* **smokeho** (smoke-oh) *n*, *pl* **-kos** *or* **-hos** *Austral and NZ informal* **1** a short break from work for tea or a cigarette **2** refreshment taken during this break

smoky *adj* **smokier, smokiest 1** filled with or giving off smoke, sometimes excessively: *smoky coal or wood fires* **2** having the colour of smoke **3** having the taste or smell of smoke **4** made dirty or hazy by smoke ▷ **smokiness** *n*

Smoky Mountains *pl n* See Great Smoky Mountains

Smolensk *n* a city in W Russia, on the Dnieper River: a major commercial centre in medieval times; scene of severe fighting (1941 and 1943) in World War II. Pop: 323 000 (2005 est)

Smollett *n* **Tobias George**. 1721–71, Scottish novelist, whose picaresque satires include *Roderick Random* (1748), *Peregrine Pickle* (1751), and *Humphry Clinker* (1771)

smolt *n* a young salmon at the stage when it migrates from fresh water to the sea [Scots]

smooch *slang vb* **1** (of two people) to kiss and cuddle **2** *Brit* to dance very slowly with one's arms around another person or (of two people) to dance together in such a way ▷ *n* **3** the act of smooching [dialect *smouch*, imitative]

smoodge *or* **smooge** *vb* **smoodging, smoodged** *or* **smooging, smooged** *Austral and NZ* **1** same as **smooch** (1) **2** to attempt to gain favour through flattery

smooth *adj* **1** having an even surface with no roughness, bumps, or holes **2** without obstructions or difficulties: *smooth progress towards an agreement* **3** without lumps: *a smooth paste* **4** free from jolts and bumps: *a smooth landing* **5** not harsh in taste; mellow: *an excellent smooth wine* **6** charming or persuasive but possibly insincere ▷ *adv* **7** in a smooth manner ▷ *vb* **8** (often foll. by *down*) to make or become even or without roughness **9** (often foll. by *out* or *away*) to remove in order to make smooth: *smoothing out the creases* **10** to make calm; soothe **11** to make easier: *Moscow smoothed the path to democracy* ▷ *n* **12** the smooth part of something **13** the act of smoothing [Old English *smōth*] ▷ **smoothly** *adv*

smoothie *n* **1** *slang* a man who is so confident, well-dressed, and charming that one is suspicious of his motives and doubts his honesty **2** a smooth thick drink made from fresh fruit and yoghurt, ice cream, or milk

smooth over *vb* to ease or gloss over: *their fears are now being smoothed over*

smooth-talking *adj* confident and persuasive but not necessarily honest or sincere

smorgasbord *n* a variety of savoury dishes served as hors d'oeuvres or as a buffet meal [Swedish]

smote *vb* the past tense of **smite**

smother *vb* **1** to extinguish (a fire) by covering so as to cut it off from the air **2** to suffocate **3** to surround or overwhelm (with): *she smothered him with her idea of affection* **4** to suppress or stifle: *he smothered an ironic chuckle* **5** to cover over thickly: *ice cream smothered with sauce* [Old English *smorian* to suffocate]

smoulder *or* US **smolder** *vb* **1** to burn slowly without flames, usually giving off smoke **2** (of emotions) to exist in a suppressed state without being released [origin unknown]

SMS short message system: used for sending data to mobile phones

smudge *vb* **smudging, smudged 1** to make or become smeared or soiled ▷ *n* **2** a smear or dirty mark **3** a blurred form or area: *the dull smudge of a ship* [origin unknown] ▷ **smudgy** *adj*

smug *adj* **smugger, smuggest** very pleased with oneself; self-satisfied [Germanic] ▷ **smugly** *adv* ▷ **smugness** *n*

smuggle *vb* **-gling, -gled 1** to import or export (goods that are prohibited or subject to taxation) secretly **2** (often foll. by *into* or *out of*) to bring or take secretly: *he was smuggled out of the country unnoticed* [Low German *smukkelen*] ▷ **smuggler** *n* ▷ **smuggling** *n*

smut *n* **1** stories, pictures, or jokes relating to sex or nudity **2** a speck of soot or a dark mark left by soot **3** a disease of cereals, in which black sooty masses cover the affected parts [Old English *smitte*] ▷ **smutty** *adj*

Smuts *n* **Jan Christiaan**. 1870–1950, South African statesman; prime minister (1919–24; 1939–48). He fought for the Boers during the Boer War, then worked for Anglo-Boer reconciliation and served the Allies during World Wars I and II

Smyrna *n* an ancient city on the W coast of Asia Minor: a major trading centre in the ancient world; a centre of early Christianity. Modern name: **Izmir**

Smyth n Dame Ethel (Mary). 1858–1944, British composer, best known for her operas, such as *The Wreckers* (1906). She was imprisoned for supporting the suffragette movement

Sn *chem* tin [New Latin *stannum*]

snack n **1** a light quick meal eaten between or in place of main meals ▷ vb **2** to eat a snack [probably from Middle Dutch *snacken*]

snack bar n a place where light meals or snacks are sold

snaffle n **1** a mouthpiece for controlling a horse ▷ vb **-fling, -fled 2** *Brit, Austral and NZ informal* to steal or take **3** to fit or control (a horse) with a snaffle [origin unknown]

snafu (snaf-foo) **1** *chiefly military slang* ▷ n **2** confusion or chaos regarded as the normal state ▷ adj **3** confused or muddled up, as usual [s(ituation) n(ormal): a(ll) f(ucked) u(p)]

snag n **1** a small problem or difficulty: *one possible snag in his plans* **2** a sharp projecting point that may catch on things **3** a small hole in a fabric caused by a sharp object **4** a tree stump in a river bed that is a danger to navigation **5** (*often pl*) *Austral slang* a sausage ▷ vb **snagging, snagged 6** to tear or catch on a snag [Scandinavian]

snail n a slow-moving mollusc with a spiral shell [Old English *snæg(e)l*]

snail mail *informal* n **1** conventional post, as opposed to e-mail **2** the conventional postal system ▷ vb **snail-mail 3** to send by the conventional postal system, rather than by e-mail

snail's pace n a very slow speed

snake n **1** a long scaly limbless reptile **2** Also: **snake in the grass** a person, esp. a colleague or friend, who secretly acts against one ▷ vb **snaking, snaked 3** to glide or move in a winding course, like a snake [Old English *snaca*]

snakebite n **1** the bite of a snake **2** a drink of cider and lager

snake charmer n an entertainer who appears to hypnotize snakes by playing music

Snake River n a river in the northwestern US, rising in NW Wyoming and flowing west through Idaho, turning north as part of the border between Idaho and Oregon, and flowing west to the Columbia River near Pasco, Washington. Length: 1670 km (1038 miles)

snakes and ladders n a board game in which players move counters along a series of squares by means of dice, going up the ladders to squares nearer the finish and down the snakes to squares nearer the start

snaky adj **snakier, snakiest 1** twisting or winding **2** treacherous

snap vb **snapping, snapped 1** to break suddenly, esp. with a sharp sound **2** to make or cause to make a sudden sharp cracking sound: *he snapped his fingers* **3** to move or close with a sudden sharp sound: *I snapped the lid shut* **4** to move in a sudden or abrupt way **5** to give way or collapse suddenly under strain: *one day someone's temper will snap* **6** to panic when a situation becomes too difficult to cope with: *he could snap at any moment* **7** (*often foll. by at or up*) to seize suddenly or quickly **8** (*often foll. by at*) (of animals) to bite at suddenly **9** to speak (words) sharply and angrily **10** to take a photograph of **11 snap one's fingers at** *informal* to defy or dismiss contemptuously **12 snap out of it** *informal* to recover quickly, esp. from depression or anger ▷ n **13** the act of breaking suddenly or the sound of a sudden breakage **14** a sudden sharp sound **15** a clasp or fastener that closes with a snapping sound **16** a sudden grab or bite **17** a thin crisp biscuit: *brandy snaps* **18** *informal* an informal photograph taken with a simple camera **19** See **cold snap 20** *Brit and NZ* a card game in which the word *snap* is called when two similar cards are turned up ▷ adj **21** done on the spur of the moment: *snap judgments* ▷ adv **22** with a snap ▷ interj

23 a *cards* the word called while playing snap **b** a cry used to draw attention to the similarity of two things ▶ See also **snap up** [Middle Dutch *snappen* to seize]

snapdragon n a plant with spikes of colourful flowers that can open and shut like a mouth; antirrhinum

snap fastener n same as **press stud**

snapper n a food fish of Australia and New Zealand with a pinkish body covered with blue spots

snappy adj **-pier, -piest 1** smart and fashionable: *snappy designs* **2** Also: **snappish** (of someone's behaviour) irritable, unfriendly, and cross **3** brisk or lively: *short snappy movements* **4 make it snappy** *slang* hurry up! ▷ **snappiness** n

snapshot n same as **snap** (18)

snap up vb to take advantage of eagerly and quickly: *the tickets have been snapped up*

snare[1] n **1** a trap for birds or small animals, usually a flexible loop that is drawn tight around the prey **2** anything that traps someone or something unawares ▷ vb **snaring, snared 3** to catch in or as if in a snare [Old English *sneare*]

snare[2] n *music* a set of strings fitted against the lower head of a snare drum, which produces a rattling sound when the drum is beaten [Middle Dutch *snaer* or Middle Low German *snare* string]

snare drum n *music* a small drum fitted with a snare

snarl[1] vb **1** (of an animal) to growl fiercely with bared teeth **2** to speak or say (something) fiercely: *he snarled out a command to a subordinate* ▷ n **3** a fierce growl or facial expression **4** the act of snarling [Germanic]

snarl[2] n **1** a complicated or confused state **2** a tangled mass ▷ vb **3 snarl up** to become, be, or make tangled, confused, or complicated: *the line became snarled up on the propeller; the postal service was snarled up at Christmas* [from Old Norse]

snarl-up n *informal* a confused, disorganized situation such as a traffic jam

snatch vb **1** to seize or grasp (something) suddenly: *she snatched the paper* **2** (*usually foll. by at*) to attempt to seize suddenly **3** to take hurriedly: *these players had snatched a few hours sleep* **4** to remove suddenly: *she snatched her hand away* ▷ n **5** an act of snatching **6** a small piece or incomplete part: *snatches of song* **7** a brief spell: *snatches of sleep* **8** *slang, chiefly US* an act of kidnapping **9** *Brit slang* a robbery: *a wages snatch* [Middle English *snacchen*]

snazzy adj **-zier, -ziest** *informal* (esp. of clothes) stylish and flashy [origin unknown]

Snead n Sam(uel Jackson). 1912–2002, US golfer; winner of seven major tournaments between 1949 and 1951

sneak vb **1** to move quietly, trying not to be noticed **2** to behave in a cowardly or underhand manner **3** to bring, take, or put secretly: *we sneaked him over the border* **4** *informal, chiefly Brit and NZ* (esp. in schools) to tell tales ▷ n **5** a person who acts in an underhand or cowardly manner ▷ adj **6** without warning: *a sneak attack* [Old English *snīcan* to creep] ▷ **sneaky** adj

sneakers pl n US, Canad, Austral and NZ canvas shoes with rubber soles

sneaking adj **1** slight but nagging: *a sneaking suspicion* **2** secret: *a sneaking admiration* **3** acting in a cowardly and furtive way

sneak thief n a burglar who sneaks into houses through open doors and windows

sneer n **1** a facial expression showing distaste or contempt, typically with a curled upper lip **2** a remark showing distaste or contempt ▷ vb **3** to make a facial expression of scorn or contempt **4** to say (something) in a scornful manner [origin unknown] ▷ **sneering** adj, n

sneeze vb **sneezing, sneezed 1** to expel air from the nose suddenly and without control, esp. as the result of irritation in the nostrils ▷ n **2** the act or sound of sneezing [Old English *fnēosan* (unattested)]

sneeze at vb *informal* to ignore or dismiss lightly: *the money's not to be sneezed at*

Snell *n* Sir **Peter** (**George**). born 1938, New Zealand athlete; winner of three Olympic gold medals: for the 800 metres in 1960, and again in 1964, when he also won gold for the 1500 metres

snib *n* Scot and NZ the catch of a door or window

snick *n* **1** a small cut in something; notch **2** cricket a glancing blow off the edge of the bat ▷ *vb* **3** to make a small cut or notch in (something) **4** cricket to hit (the ball) with a snick [probably Scandinavian]

snicker *n, vb* chiefly US and Canad same as **snigger** [probably imitative]

snide or **snidey** *adj* (of comments) critical in an unfair and nasty way [origin unknown]

sniff *vb* **1** to inhale through the nose in short audible breaths **2** (often foll. by at) to smell by sniffing ▷ *n* **3** the act or sound of sniffing [imitative] **> sniffer** *n*

sniff at *vb* to express contempt or dislike for

sniffer dog *n* a police dog trained to locate drugs or explosives by smell

sniffle *vb* -**fling**, -**fled** **1** to sniff repeatedly when the nasal passages are blocked up ▷ *n* **2** the act or sound of sniffling

sniffles or **snuffles** *pl n* **the sniffles** informal a cold in the head

sniff out *vb* to discover after some searching: they eventually sniffed out a suitable Parliamentary seat for him

sniffy *adj* -**fier**, -**fiest** informal contemptuous or scornful

snifter *n* **1** informal a small quantity of alcoholic drink **2** a pear-shaped brandy glass [origin unknown]

snig *vb* **snigging**, **snigged** Austral and NZ to drag (a felled log) by a chain or cable [English dialect]

snigger *n* **1** a quiet and disrespectful laugh kept to oneself ▷ *vb* **2** to utter such a laugh [variant of snicker]

snip *vb* **snipping**, **snipped** **1** to cut with small quick strokes with scissors or shears ▷ *n* **2** informal, chiefly Brit a bargain **3** the act or sound of snipping **4** a small piece snipped off **5** a small cut made by snipping [Low German, Dutch snippen]

snipe *n, pl* **snipe** or **snipes** **1** a wading bird with a long straight bill ▷ *vb* **sniping**, **sniped** (often foll. by at) **2** to shoot (someone) from a place of hiding **3** (often foll. by at) to make critical remarks (about) [Old Norse snípa] **> sniper** *n*

snippet *n* a small scrap or fragment: the odd snippet of knowledge

snitch slang *vb* **1** to act as an informer **2** to steal small amounts ▷ *n* **3** an informer [origin unknown]

snitchy *adj* **snitchier**, **snitchiest** NZ informal bad-tempered or irritable

snivel *vb* -**velling**, -**velled** or US -**veling**, -**veled** **1** to cry and sniff in a self-pitying way **2** to say (something) tearfully; whine **3** to have a runny nose ▷ *n* **4** the act of snivelling [Middle English snivelen]

snob *n* **1** a person who tries to associate with those of higher social status and who hates those of a lower social status **2** a person who feels smugly superior with regard to his or her tastes or interests: a cultural snob [origin unknown] **> snobbery** *n* **> snobbish** *adj*

snoek (**snook**) *n* a South African edible marine fish [Afrikaans, from Dutch: pike]

snoep (**snoop**) *adj* S African informal mean or tight-fisted [Afrikaans: greedy]

snog Brit, NZ and S African slang *vb* **snogging**, **snogged** **1** to kiss and cuddle ▷ *n* **2** the act of kissing and cuddling [origin unknown]

snood *n* a pouchlike hat loosely holding a woman's hair at the back [Old English snōd]

snook *n* **cock a snook at** Brit **a** to make a rude gesture at (someone) by putting one thumb to the nose with the fingers of the hand outstretched **b** to show contempt for (someone in authority) without fear of punishment [origin unknown]

snooker *n* **1** a game played on a billiard table with 15 red balls, six balls of other colours, and a white cue ball **2** a shot in which the cue ball is left in a position such that another ball blocks the target ball ▷ *vb* **3** to leave (an opponent) in an unfavourable position by playing a snooker **4** to put someone in a position where he or she can do nothing [origin unknown]

snoop informal *vb* **1** (often foll. by about or around) to pry into the private business of others ▷ *n* **2** the act of snooping **3** a person who snoops [Dutch snoepen to eat furtively] **> snooper** *n* **> snoopy** *adj*

snooty *adj* **snootier**, **snootiest** informal behaving as if superior to other people; snobbish [from snoot nose]

snooze informal *vb* **snoozing**, **snoozed** **1** to take a brief light sleep ▷ *n* **2** a nap [origin unknown]

snore *vb* **snoring**, **snored** **1** to breathe with snorting sounds while asleep ▷ *n* **2** the act or sound of snoring [imitative]

snorkel *n* **1** a tube allowing a swimmer to breathe while face down on the surface of the water **2** a device supplying air to a submarine when under water ▷ *vb* -**kelling**, -**kelled** or US -**keling**, -**keled** **3** to swim with a snorkel [German Schnorchel]

Snorri Sturluson *n* 1179–1241, Icelandic historian and poet; author of Younger or Prose Edda (?1222), containing a collection of Norse myths and a treatise on poetry, and the Heimskringla sagas of the Norwegian kings from their mythological origins to the 12th century

snort *vb* **1** to exhale air noisily through the nostrils **2** to express contempt or annoyance by snorting **3** to say with a snort **4** slang to inhale (a powdered drug) through the nostrils ▷ *n* **5** a loud exhalation of air through the nostrils to express contempt or annoyance: Clare gave a snort of disgust [Middle English snorten]

snot *n* usually considered vulgar **1** mucus from the nose **2** slang an annoying or disgusting person [Old English gesnot]

snotty *adj* -**tier**, -**tiest** considered vulgar **1** dirty with nasal discharge **2** having a proud and superior attitude **3** slang contemptible; nasty **> snottiness** *n*

snout *n* **1** the projecting nose and jaws of an animal **2** anything projecting like a snout: the snout of a gun **3** slang a person's nose [Germanic]

snow *n* **1** frozen vapour falling from the sky in flakes **2** a layer of snow on the ground **3** a falling of snow **4** slang cocaine ▷ *vb* **5** (with 'it' as subject) to be the case that snow is falling: it's snowing today **6** to fall as or like snow **7** be **snowed in**, **up** or **over** to be covered by or confined with a heavy fall of snow **8** be **snowed under** to be overwhelmed, esp. with paperwork [Old English snāw] **> snowy** *adj*

Snow *n* C(harles) P(ercy), Baron. 1905–80, British novelist and physicist. His novels include the series Strangers and Brothers (1949–70)

snowball *n* **1** snow pressed into a ball for throwing ▷ *vb* **2** to increase rapidly in size or importance: production snowballed between 1950 and 1970 **3** to throw snowballs at

snowberry *n, pl* -**ries** a shrub grown for its white berries

snow-blind *adj* blinded for a short time by the intense reflection of sunlight from snow **> snow blindness** *n*

snowboard *n* a shaped board, like a skateboard without wheels, on which a person is able to slide across the snow **> snowboarding** *n*

snowbound *adj* shut in or blocked off by snow

snowcap *n* a cap of snow on top of a mountain **> snowcapped** *adj*

Snowdon[1] *n* a mountain in NW Wales, in Gwynedd: the highest peak in Wales. Height: 1085 m (3560 ft). Welsh name: **Yr Wyddfa**

Snowdon[2] *n* **1st Earl of**, title of Antony Armstrong-Jones, born 1930, British photographer, whose work includes television documentaries, photographic books, and the design of the Snowdon Aviary, London Zoo (1965). His marriage (1960–78) to Princess Margaret ended in divorce

Snowdonia *n* **1** a massif in NW Wales, in Gwynedd, the highest peak being Snowdon **2** a national park in NW Wales, in Gwynedd and Conwy: includes the Snowdonia massif in the north. Area: 2189 sq km (845 sq miles)

snowdrift *n* a bank of deep snow driven together by the wind

snowdrop *n* a plant with small drooping white bell-shaped flowers

snowfall *n* **1** a fall of snow **2** *meteorol* the amount of snow that falls in a specified place and time

snowflake *n* a single crystal of snow

snow goose *n* a North American goose with white feathers and black wing tips

snow line *n* (on a mountain) the altitude above which there is permanent snow

snowman *n*, *pl* **-men** a figure like a person, made of packed snow

snowmobile *n* a motor vehicle for travelling on snow, esp. one with caterpillar tracks and front skis

snowplough *or especially US* **snowplow** *n* a vehicle for clearing away snow

snowshoe *n* a racket-shaped frame with a network of thongs stretched across it, worn on the feet to make walking on snow less difficult

snowstorm *n* a storm with heavy snow

Snowy Mountain *adj* of or relating to the Snowy Mountains of Australia or their inhabitants

Snowy Mountains *pl n* a mountain range in SE Australia, part of the Australian Alps: famous hydroelectric scheme. Also called (Austral informal): **the Snowy, the Snowies**

Snowy River *n* a river in SE Australia, rising in SE New South Wales: waters diverted through a system of dams and tunnels across the watershed into the Murray and Murrumbidgee Rivers for hydroelectric power and to provide water for irrigation. Length: 426 km (265 miles)

SNP Scottish National Party

Snr *or* **snr** senior

snub *vb* **snubbing, snubbed 1** to insult (someone) deliberately ▷ *n* **2** a deliberately insulting act or remark ▷ *adj* **3** (of a nose) short and turned up [Old Norse *snubba* to scold]

snub-nosed *adj* having a short turned-up nose

snuff[1] *vb* **1** to inhale through the nose (esp. of an animal) to examine by sniffing ▷ *n* **3** a sniff [probably Middle Dutch *snuffen* to snuffle]

snuff[2] *n* finely powdered tobacco for sniffing up the nostrils [Dutch *snuf*]

snuff[3] *vb* **1** (often foll. by *out*) to put out (a candle) **2** to cut off the charred part of (a candle wick) **3** (usually foll. by *out*) *informal* to put an end to **4 snuff it** *Brit and Austral informal* to die ▷ *n* **5** the burned portion of the wick of a candle [origin unknown]

snuffbox *n* a small container for holding snuff

snuffle *vb* **-fling, -fled 1** to breathe noisily or with difficulty **2** to say or speak through the nose **3** to cry and sniff in a self-pitying way ▷ *n* **4** an act or the sound of snuffling [Low German or Dutch *snuffelen*] **> snuffly** *adj*

snug *adj* **snugger, snuggest 1** comfortably warm and well protected; cosy: *safe and snug in their homes* **2** small but comfortable: *a snug office* **3** fitting closely and comfortably ▷ *n* **4** (in Britain and Ireland) a small room in a pub [Swedish *snygg* tidy] **> snugly** *adv*

snuggery *n*, *pl* **-geries** a cosy and comfortable place or room

snuggle *vb* **-gling, -gled** to nestle (into a person or thing) for warmth or from affection [from SNUG]

so[1] *adv* **1** to such an extent: *the river is so dirty that it smells* **2** to the same extent as: *she is not so old as you* **3** extremely: *it's so lovely* **4** also: *I can speak Spanish and so can you* **5** thereupon: *and so we ended up in France* **6** in the state or manner expressed or implied: *they're happy and will remain so* **7 and so on** *or* **forth** and continuing similarly **8 or so** approximately: *fifty or so people came to see me* **9 so be it** an expression of agreement or resignation **10 so much a** a

certain degree or amount (of) **b** a lot (of): *it's just so much nonsense* **11 so much for a** no more need be said about **b** used to express contempt for something that has failed: *so much for all our plans* ▷ *conj* (often foll. by *that*) **12** in order (that): *to die so that you might live* **13** with the consequence (that): *he was late home, so that there was trouble* **14 so as** in order (to): *to diet so as to lose weight* **15** *not standard* in consequence: *she wasn't needed, so she left* **16 so what!** *informal* that is unimportant ▷ *pron* **17** used to substitute for a clause or sentence, which may be understood: *you'll stop because I said so* ▷ *adj* **18** true: *it can't be so* ▷ *interj* **19** an exclamation of surprise or triumph [Old English *swā*]

> **USAGE** In formal English, *so* is not used as a conjunction to indicate either purpose (*he left by a back door so he could avoid photographers*) or result (*the project was abandoned so his services were no longer needed*). In the former case *to* or *in order to* should be used instead, and in the latter case *and so* or *and therefore* would be more acceptable. The expression *so therefore* should not be used.

so[2] *n* *music* same as **soh**

soak *vb* **1** to put or lie in a liquid so as to become thoroughly wet **2** (usually foll. by *in* or *into*) (of a liquid) to penetrate or permeate **3** (usually foll. by *in* or *up*) to take in; absorb: *white clay soaks up excess oil* ▷ *n* **4** a soaking or being soaked **5** *slang* a person who drinks very heavily [Old English *sōcian*] **> soaking** *n*, *adj*

so-and-so *n*, *pl* **so-and-sos** *informal* **1** a person whose name is not specified **2** *euphemistic* a person regarded as unpleasant; a name used in place of a swear word: *you're a dirty so-and-so*

Soane *n* Sir John. 1753–1837, British architect. His work includes Dulwich College Art Gallery (1811–14) and his own house in Lincoln's Inn Fields, London (1812–13), which is now the Sir John Soane's Museum

soap *n* **1** a compound of alkali and fat, used with water as a cleaning agent **2** *informal* short for **soap opera** ▷ *vb* **3** to apply soap to [Old English *sāpe*]

soapbox *n* a crate used as a platform for making speeches

soap opera *n* an on-going television or radio serial about the daily lives of a group of people [so called because manufacturers of soap were typical sponsors]

soapstone *n* a soft mineral used for making table tops and ornaments

soapsuds *pl n* foam or lather produced when soap is mixed with water

soapy *adj* **soapier, soapiest 1** containing or covered with soap: *a soapy liquid* **2** like soap in texture, smell, or taste: *the cheese had a soapy taste* **3** *slang* flattering or persuasive **> soapiness** *n*

soar *vb* **1** to rise or fly upwards into the air **2** (of a bird or aircraft) to glide while maintaining altitude **3** to rise or increase suddenly above the usual level: *television ratings soared* [Old French *essorer*]

Soares *n* Mário. born 1924, Portuguese statesman; prime minister of Portugal (1976–77; 1978–80; 1983–86); president of Portugal (1986–96)

sob *vb* **sobbing, sobbed 1** to cry noisily, breathing in short gasps **2** to speak with sobs ▷ *n* **3** the act or sound of sobbing [probably from Low German]

sober *adj* **1** not drunk **2** tending to drink only moderate quantities of alcohol **3** serious and thoughtful: *a sober and serious fellow* **4** (of colours) plain and dull **5** free from exaggeration: *a fairly sober version of what happened* ▷ *vb* **6** (usually foll. by *up*) to make or become less drunk [Latin *sobrius*] **> sobering** *adj*

Sobers *n* Sir Garfield St Auburn, known as **Garry**. born 1936, West Indian (Barbadian) cricketer: an all-rounder, he played in 93 test matches (1954–74), 39 as captain, scoring 8,032 runs and taking 235 wickets; first man (1968) to score six sixes in a single over in first-class cricket

S

sobriety n the state of being sober

sobriquet or **soubriquet** (so-brik-ay) n a nickname [French soubriquet]

sob story n a tale of personal misfortune or bad luck intended to arouse sympathy

Sobukwe n Robert (Mangaliso). 1924–78, South African politician. Founder of the Pan-Africanist Congress

Soc. or **soc.** 1 socialist 2 society

soca (soak-a) n a mixture of soul and calypso music popular in the E Caribbean

so-called adj called (in the speaker's opinion, wrongly) by that name: so-called military experts

soccer n a game in which two teams of eleven players try to kick or head a ball into their opponents' goal, only the goalkeeper on either side being allowed to touch the ball with his hands [Assoc(iation) Football]

Soche or **So-ch'e** n a variant transliteration of the Chinese name for Shache

Sochi n a city and resort in SW Russia, in the Krasnodar Territory on the Black Sea: hot mineral springs. Pop: 328 000 (2005 est)

sociable adj 1 friendly and enjoying other people's company 2 (of an occasion) providing the opportunity for relaxed and friendly companionship ▷ **sociability** n ▷ **sociably** adv

social adj 1 living or preferring to live in a community rather than alone 2 of or relating to human society or organization 3 of the way people live and work together in groups: social organization 4 of or for companionship or communal activities: social clubs 5 of or engaged in social services: a social worker 6 relating to a certain class of society: social misfits 7 (of certain species of insects) living together in organized colonies: social bees ▷ n 8 an informal gathering [Latin socius a comrade] ▷ **socially** adv

Social Charter n a proposed declaration of the rights, minimum wages, etc. of workers in the European Union

social climber n a person who tries to associate with people from a higher social class in the hope that he or she will be thought also to be upper-class

social contract or **social compact** n an agreement among individuals to cooperate for greater security, which results in the loss of some personal liberties

social democrat n 1 a person who is in favour of a market or mixed economy but believes the State must play an active role in ensuring social justice and equality of opportunity 2 (formerly) a person who believed in the gradual transformation of capitalism into democratic socialism ▷ **social democracy** n

social exclusion n sociol the failure of society to provide certain people with those rights normally available to its members, such as employment, health care, education, etc.

social fund n (in Britain) a social security fund from which loans or payments may be made to people in cases of extreme need

social inclusion n sociol the provision of certain rights to all people in society, such as employment, health care, education, etc.

social intelligence n the ability to form rewarding relationships with other people

socialism n a political and economic theory or system in which the means of production, distribution, and exchange are owned by the community collectively, usually through the state ▷ **socialist** n, adj

socialite n a person who goes to many events attended by the rich, famous, and fashionable

socialize or **-lise** vb **-lizing, -lized** or **-lising, -lised** 1 to meet others socially 2 to prepare for life in society 3 chiefly US to organize along socialist principles ▷ **socialization** or **-lisation** n

social media n websites and applications that allow users to interact with each other

social networking site n a website that allows

subscribers to interact, esp. by forming online communities based around shared interests, experiences, etc.

social science n the systematic study of society and of human relationships within society ▷ **social scientist** n

social security n state provision for the welfare of elderly, unemployed, or sick people, through pensions and other financial aid

social services pl n welfare services provided by local authorities or a state agency for people with particular social needs

social studies n the study of how people live and organize themselves in society

social welfare n 1 social services provided by a state for the benefit of its citizens 2 (in New Zealand) a government department concerned with pensions and benefits for elderly people, sick people, etc.

social work n social services that give help and advice to elderly people, disabled people, and families with problems ▷ **social worker** n

society n, pl **-ties** 1 human beings considered as a group 2 a group of people forming a single community with its own distinctive culture and institutions 3 the structure, culture, and institutions of such a group 4 an organized group of people sharing a common aim or interest: a dramatic society 5 the rich and fashionable class of society collectively 6 old-fashioned companionship: I enjoy her society [Latin societas]

Society Islands pl n a group of islands in the S Pacific: administratively part of French Polynesia; consists of the Windward Islands and the Leeward Islands; became a French protectorate in 1843 and a colony in 1880. Pop: 214 445 (2002). Area: 1595 sq km (616 sq miles)

Society of Friends n the Quakers

Society of Jesus n the religious order of the Jesuits

Socinus n Faustus, Italian name Fausto Sozzini, 1539–1604, and his uncle, **Laelius**, Italian name Lelio Sozzini, 1525–62, Italian Protestant theologians and reformers

socioeconomic adj of or involving economic and social factors

sociology n the study of the development, organization, functioning, and classification of human societies ▷ **sociological** adj ▷ **sociologist** n

sociopolitical adj of or involving political and social factors

sock¹ n 1 a cloth covering for the foot, reaching to between the ankle and knee and worn inside a shoe 2 **pull one's socks up** informal to make a determined effort to improve 3 **put a sock in it** slang be quiet! [Greek sukkhos a light shoe]

sock² slang vb 1 to hit hard ▷ n 2 a hard blow [origin unknown]

socket n 1 a device into which an electric plug can be inserted in order to make a connection in a circuit 2 anatomy a bony hollow into which a part or structure fits: the hip socket [Anglo-Norman soket a little ploughshare]

Socotra, Sokotra or **Suqutra** n an island in the Indian Ocean, about 240 km (150 miles) off Cape Guardafui, Somalia: administratively part of Yemen. Capital: Hadiboh (Tamrida). Area: 3100 sq km (1200 sq miles)

Socrates n ?470–399 BC, Athenian philosopher, whose beliefs are known only through the writings of his pupils Plato and Xenophon. He taught that virtue was based on knowledge, which was attained by a dialectical process that took into account many aspects of a stated hypothesis. He was indicted for impiety and corruption of youth (399) and was condemned to death. He refused to flee and died by drinking hemlock

Socratic adj of the Greek philosopher Socrates, or his teachings

Socratic method n philosophy the method of instruction used by Socrates, in which a series of questions and answers lead to a logical conclusion

S

sod[1] *n* **1** a piece of grass-covered surface soil; turf **2** *poetic* the ground [Low German]

sod[2] *slang, chiefly Brit n* **1** an unpleasant person **2** *humorous* a person, esp. an unlucky one: *the poor sod hasn't been out for weeks* **3 sod all** *slang* nothing *⊳ interj* **4 sod it** an exclamation of annoyance [from *sodomite*] **> sodding** *adj*

soda *n* **1** a simple compound of sodium, such as sodium carbonate or sodium bicarbonate **2** same as **soda water** **3** *US and Canad* a sweet fizzy drink [perhaps from Arabic]

soda bread *n* a type of bread raised with sodium bicarbonate

soda fountain *n US and Canad* **1** a counter that serves soft drinks and snacks **2** a device dispensing soda water

soda siphon *n* a sealed bottle containing soda water under pressure, which is forced up a tube when a lever is pressed

soda water *n* a fizzy drink made by charging water with carbon dioxide under pressure

sodden *adj* **1** soaking wet **2** (of someone's senses) dulled, esp. by excessive drinking [*soden*, obsolete past participle of *seethe*]

Soddy *n* Frederick. 1877–1956, English chemist, whose work on radioactive disintegration led to the discovery of isotopes: Nobel prize for chemistry 1921

sodium *n chem* a very reactive soft silvery-white metallic element. Symbol: Na [from SODA]

sodium bicarbonate *n* a white soluble crystalline compound used in fizzy drinks, baking powder, and in medicine as an antacid

sodium carbonate *n* a colourless or white soluble crystalline compound used in the manufacture of glass, ceramics, soap, and paper, and as a cleansing agent

sodium chlorate *n* a colourless crystalline compound used as a bleaching agent, antiseptic, and weedkiller

sodium chloride *n* common table salt; a soluble colourless crystalline compound widely used as a seasoning and preservative for food and in the manufacture of chemicals, glass, and soap

sodium hydroxide *n* a white strongly alkaline solid used in the manufacture of rayon, paper, aluminium, and soap

sodomite *n* a person who practises sodomy

sodomy *n* anal intercourse committed by a man with another man or a woman [after *Sodom*, Biblical city, noted for its depravity]

Sod's Law *n informal* a humorous saying stating that if something can go wrong or turn out inconveniently it will

Soemba *n* the former spelling of **Sumba**

Soembawa *n* the former spelling of **Sumbawa**

Soenda Islands *pl n* the former spelling of **Sunda Islands**

Soenda Strait *n* the former spelling of **Sunda Strait**

Soerabaja *n* the former spelling of **Surabaya**

Soerakarta *n* the former spelling of **Surakarta**

sofa *n* a long comfortable seat with back and arms for two or more people [Arabic *suffah*]

Sofia *n* the capital of Bulgaria, in the west: colonized by the Romans in 29 AD; became capital of Bulgaria in 1879; university (1880). Pop: 1 045 000 (2005 est). Ancient name: **Serdica**. Bulgarian name: **Sofiya**

soft *adj* **1** easy to dent, shape, or cut: *soft material* **2** not hard; giving way easily under pressure: *a soft bed* **3** fine, smooth, or fluffy to the touch: *soft fur* **4** (of music or sounds) quiet and pleasing **5** (of light or colour) not excessively bright or harsh **6** (of a breeze or climate) temperate, mild, or pleasant **7** with smooth curves rather than sharp edges: *soft focus* **8** kind or lenient, often to excess **9** easy to influence or make demands on **10** *informal* feeble or silly; simple: *soft in the head* **11** not strong or able to endure hardship **12** (of a drug) nonaddictive **13** *informal* requiring little effort; easy: *a soft job* **14** *chem* (of water) relatively free of mineral salts and therefore easily able to make soap lather **15** loving and

tender: *soft words* **16** *phonetics* denoting the consonants *c* and *g* when they are pronounced sibilantly, as in *cent* and *germ* **17 soft on a** lenient towards: *he was accused of being soft on criminals* **b** experiencing romantic love for *⊳ adv* **18** in a soft manner: *to speak soft* *⊳ interj* **19** *archaic* quiet! [Old English *sōfte*] **> softly** *adv*

softball *n* a game similar to baseball, played using a larger softer ball

soft-boiled *adj* (of an egg) boiled for a short time so that the yolk is still soft

soft coal *n* same as **bituminous coal**

soft drink *n* a nonalcoholic drink

soften *vb* **1** to make or become soft or softer **2** to make or become more sympathetic and less critical: *the farmers softened their opposition to the legislation* **3** to lessen the severity or difficulty of: *foreign relief softened the hardship of a terrible winter* **> softener** *n*

soft furnishings *pl n* curtains, hangings, rugs, and covers

softhearted *adj* kind and sympathetic

softie *or* **softy** *n, pl* **softies** *informal* a person who is easily hurt or upset

soft option *n* the easiest of a number of choices

soft palate *n* the fleshy part at the back of the roof of the mouth

soft-pedal *vb* **-dalling, -dalled** *or US* **-daling, -daled 1** to deliberately avoid emphasizing (something): *he was soft-pedalling the question of tax increases* *⊳ n* **soft pedal 2** a pedal on a piano that softens the tone

soft sell *n* a method of selling based on subtle suggestion and gentle persuasion

soft-soap *vb informal* to flatter (a person)

soft-spoken *adj* speaking or said with a soft gentle voice

soft touch *n informal* a person who is easily persuaded to perform favours for, or lend money to, other people

software *n computers* the programs used with a computer

softwood *n* the wood of coniferous trees

Sogdian *n* **1** a member of the people who lived in Sogdiana **2** the language of this people, now almost extinct, belonging to the East Iranian branch of the Indo-European family *⊳ adj* **3** of or relating to Sogdiana, its people, or their language

Sogdiana *n* a region of ancient central Asia. Its chief city was Samarkand

soggy *adj* **-gier, -giest 1** soaked with liquid: *a soggy running track* **2** moist and heavy: *a soggy sandwich* [probably from dialect *sog* marsh] **> sogginess** *n*

soh *n music* the fifth note of any ascending major scale

Soho *n* a district of central London, in the City of Westminster: a foreign quarter since the late 17th century, now chiefly known for restaurants, nightclubs, striptease clubs, etc.

soigné *or fem* **soignée** (swah-nyay) *adj* neat, elegant, and well-dressed: *the soignée deputy editor of Vogue* [French]

soil[1] *n* **1** the top layer of the land surface of the earth **2** a specific type of this material: *sandy soil* **3** land, country, or region: *the first US side to lose on home soil* [Latin *solium* a seat, confused with *solum* the ground]

soil[2] *vb* **1** to make or become dirty or stained **2** to bring disgrace upon: *he's soiled our reputation* *⊳ n* **3** a soiled spot **4** refuse, manure, or excrement [Old French *soillier*]

soiree (swah-ray) *n* an evening social gathering [French]

Soissons *n* a city in N France, on the Aisne River: has Roman remains and an 11th-century abbey. Pop: 28 523 (2008)

sojourn (soj-urn) *literary n* **1** a short stay in a place *⊳ vb* **2** to stay temporarily: *he sojourned in Basle during a short illness* [Old French *sojorner*]

Sokoto *n* **1** a state of NW Nigeria. Capital: Sokoto. Pop: 3 696 999 (2006). Area: 25 973 sq km (10 028 sq miles) **2** a town in NW Nigeria, capital of Sokoto state: capital of the Fulah Empire in the 19th century; Muslim place of pilgrimage. Pop: 444 000 (2005 est)

S

Sokotra *n* a variant spelling of **Socotra**

sol[1] *n music* same as **soh**

sol[2] *n chem* a liquid colloidal solution

solace (sol-iss) *n* **1** comfort in misery or disappointment: *it drove him to seek increasing solace in alcohol* **2** something that gives comfort or consolation: *his music was a solace to me during my illness* ▷ *vb* **-lacing, -laced 3** to give comfort or cheer to (a person) in time of sorrow or distress [Old French *solas*]

Solana *or* **Solana Madariaga** *n* Javier, born 1942, Spanish socialist politician; minister for foreign affairs (1992–95), secretary-general of NATO (1995–99), and EU high representative for foreign policy (1999–2009)

solar *adj* **1** of the sun: *a solar eclipse* **2** operating by or using the energy of the sun: *solar cell* [Latin *sol* the sun]

solarium *n, pl* **-lariums** *or* **-laria** a place with beds equipped with ultraviolet lights used for giving people an artificial suntan [Latin: a terrace]

solar plexus *n* **1** *anatomy* a network of nerves behind the stomach **2** *no longer in technical use* the vulnerable part of the stomach beneath the diaphragm

solar system *n* the system containing the sun and the planets, comets, and asteroids that go round it

sold *vb* **1** the past of **sell** ▷ *adj* **2 sold on** *slang* enthusiastic and uncritical about

solder *n* **1** an alloy used for joining two metal surfaces by melting the alloy so that it forms a thin layer between the surfaces ▷ *vb* **2** to join or mend or be joined or mended with solder [Latin *solidare* to strengthen]

soldering iron *n* a hand tool with a copper tip that is heated and used to melt and apply solder

soldier *n* **1 a** a person who serves or has served in an army **b** a person who is not an officer in an army ▷ *vb* **2** to serve as a soldier [Old French *soudier*] ▷ **soldierly** *adj*

soldier of fortune *n* a man who seeks money or adventure as a soldier; mercenary

soldier on *vb* to continue one's efforts despite difficulties or pressure

sole[1] *adj* **1** being the only one; only **2** not shared; exclusive: *sole ownership* [Latin *solus* alone]

sole[2] *n* **1** the underside of the foot **2** the underside of a shoe **3** the lower surface of an object ▷ *vb* **soling, soled 4** to provide (a shoe) with a sole [Latin *solea* sandal]

sole[3] *n, pl* **sole** *or* **soles** an edible marine flatfish [Latin *solea* a sandal (from the fish's shape)]

sole charge school *n* NZ a country school with only one teacher

solecism (sol-iss-iz-zum) *n formal* **1** a minor grammatical mistake in speech or writing **2** an action considered not to be good manners [Greek *soloikos* speaking incorrectly] ▷ **solecistic** *adj*

solely *adv* **1** only; completely: *an action intended solely to line his own pockets* **2** without others

solemn *adj* **1** very serious; deeply sincere: *my solemn promise* **2** marked by ceremony or formality: *a solemn ritual* **3** serious or glum: *a solemn look on her face* [Latin *solemnis* appointed] ▷ **solemnly** *adv*

solemnity *n, pl* **-ties 1** the state or quality of being solemn **2** a solemn ceremony or ritual

solemnize *or* **-nise** *vb* **-nizing, -nized** *or* **-nising, -nised 1** to celebrate or perform (a ceremony, esp. of marriage) **2** to make solemn or serious ▷ **solemnization** *or* **-nisation** *n*

solenoid (sole-in-oid) *n* a coil of wire, usually cylindrical, in which a magnetic field is set up by passing a current through it [French *solénoïde*] ▷ **solenoidal** *adj*

Solent *n* the Solent a strait of the English Channel between the coast of Hampshire, on the English mainland, and the Isle of Wight. Width: up to 6 km (4 miles)

Soleure *n* the French name for **Solothurn**

sol-fa *n* short for **tonic sol-fa**

solicit *vb* **1** *formal* to seek or request, esp. formally: *she was*

brushed aside when soliciting his support for the vote **2** to approach a person with an offer of sex in return for money [Latin *sollicitare* to harass] ▷ **solicitation** *n*

solicitor *n Brit, Austral and NZ* a lawyer who advises clients on matters of law, draws up legal documents, and prepares cases for barristers

Solicitor General *n, pl* **Solicitors General** (in Britain) the law officer of the Crown ranking next to the Attorney General (in Scotland to the Lord Advocate) and acting as his assistant

solicitous *adj formal* **1** anxious about someone's welfare **2** eager [Latin *sollicitus* anxious] ▷ **solicitousness** *n*

solicitude *n formal* anxiety or concern for someone's welfare

solid *adj* **1** (of a substance) in a physical state in which it resists changes in size and shape; not liquid or gaseous **2** consisting of matter all through; not hollow **3** of the same substance all through: *solid gold* **4** firm, strong, or substantial: *the solid door of a farmhouse* **5** proved or provable: *solid evidence* **6** law-abiding and respectable: *solid family men* **7** (of a meal or food) substantial **8** without interruption; continuous or unbroken: *solid bombardment* **9** financially sound: *a solid institution* **10** strongly united or established: *a solid marriage* **11** *geometry* having or relating to three dimensions **12** adequate; sound, but not brilliant: *a solid career* **13** of a single uniform colour or tone ▷ *n* **14** *geometry* a three-dimensional shape **15** a solid substance [Latin *solidus* firm] ▷ **solidity** *n* ▷ **solidly** *adv*

solidarity *n, pl* **-ties** agreement in interests or aims among members of a group; total unity

solid geometry *n* the branch of geometry concerned with three-dimensional figures

solidify *vb* **-fies, -fying, -fied 1** to make or become solid or hard **2** to make or become strong or unlikely to change: *a move that solidified the allegiance of our followers* ▷ **solidification** *n*

solid-state *adj* (of an electronic device) using a semiconductor component, such as a transistor or silicon chip, in which current flow is through solid material, rather than a valve or mechanical part, in which current flow is through a vacuum

solidus *n, pl* **-di** a short oblique stroke used in text to separate items, such as *and/or*

Solihull *n* **1** a town in central England, in Solihull unitary authority in the S West Midlands near Birmingham: mainly residential. Pop: 94 753 (2001) **2** a unitary authority in central England, in the West Midlands. Pop: 200 300 (2003 est). Area: 180 sq km (70 sq miles)

soliloquize *or* **-quise** *vb* **-quizing, -quized** *or* **-quising, -quised** to say a soliloquy

soliloquy *n, pl* **-quies** a speech made by a person while alone, esp. in a play [Latin *solus* sole + *loqui* to speak]

> **USAGE** Soliloquy is sometimes wrongly used where *monologue* is meant. Both words refer to a long speech by one person, but a *monologue* can be addressed to other people, whereas in a *soliloquy* the speaker is always talking to himself or herself.

Solimões *n* the Solimões the Brazilian name for the Amazon from the Peruvian border to the Rio Negro

Solingen *n* a city in W Germany, in North Rhine-Westphalia: a major European centre of the cutlery industry. Pop: 164 543 (2003 est)

solipsism *n philosophy* the doctrine that the self is the only thing known to exist [Latin *solus* alone + *ipse* self] ▷ **solipsist** *n*

solitaire *n* **1** a game played by one person, involving moving and taking pegs in a pegboard with the object of being left with only one **2** a gem, esp. a diamond, set alone in a ring **3** *chiefly US* patience (the card game) [French]

solitary *adj* 1 experienced or performed alone: *a solitary dinner* 2 living a life of solitude: *a solitary child* 3 single; alone: *the solitary cigarette in the ashtray* 4 having few friends; lonely 5 (of a place) without people; empty ▷ *n, pl* **-taries** 6 a person who lives on his or her own; hermit 7 *informal* short for **solitary confinement**: *I can't put him back in solitary* [Latin *solitarius*] **> solitariness** *n*

solitary confinement *n* isolation of a prisoner in a special cell

solitude *n* the state of being alone

solo *n, pl* **-los** 1 a piece of music or section of a piece of music for one performer: *a trumpet solo* 2 any performance by an individual without assistance 3 Also: **solo whist** a card game in which each person plays on his or her own ▷ *adj* 4 performed by an individual without assistance: *a solo dance* ▷ *adv* 5 by oneself; alone: *to fly solo across the Atlantic* [Latin *solus* alone] **> soloist** *n*

Solomon *n* any person considered to be very wise [after 10th-century BC king of Israel]

Solomon Islands *pl n* an independent state in the SW Pacific comprising an archipelago extending for almost 1450 km (900 miles) in a northwest–southeast direction: the northernmost islands of the archipelago (Buka and Bougainville) form part of Papua New Guinea; the main islands are Guadalcanal, Malaita, San Cristobal, New Georgia, Santa Isabel, and Choiseul: a member of the Commonwealth. Official language: English. Religion: Christian majority. Currency: Solomon Islands dollar. Capital: Honiara. Pop: 597 248 (2013 est). Area: 29 785 sq km (11 500 sq miles)

Solomon's seal *n* a plant with greenish flowers and long waxy leaves

Solon *n* 763?–?559 BC, Athenian statesman, who introduced economic, political, and legal reforms **> Solonian** *or* **Solonic** *adj*

so long *interj* 1 *informal* farewell; goodbye ▷ *adv* 2 *S African slang* for the time being; meanwhile

solo parent *n* NZ a parent bringing up a child or children alone

Solothurn *n* 1 a canton of NW Switzerland. Capital: Solothurn. Pop: 246 500 (2002 est). Area: 793 sq km (306 sq miles) 2 a town in NW Switzerland, capital of Solothurn canton, on the Aare River. Pop: 15 489 (2000) ▶ French name: **Soleure**

solstice *n* either the shortest day of the year (**winter solstice**) or the longest day of the year (**summer solstice**) [Latin *solstitium* the standing still of the sun]

Solti *n* Sir Georg. 1912–97, British conductor, born in Hungary: conductor of the Chicago Symphony Orchestra (1969–91)

soluble *adj* 1 (of a substance) capable of being dissolved 2 (of a mystery or problem) capable of being solved **> solubility** *n*

solute *n chem* the substance in a solution that is dissolved [Latin *solutus* free]

solution *n* 1 a specific answer to or way of answering a problem 2 the act or process of solving a problem 3 *chem* a mixture of two or more substances in which the molecules or atoms of the substances are completely dispersed 4 the act or process of forming a solution 5 the state of being dissolved: *the sugar is held in solution* [Latin *solutio* an unloosing]

solve *vb* **solving, solved** to find the explanation for or solution to (a mystery or problem) [Latin *solvere* to loosen] **> solvable** *adj*

solvent *adj* 1 having enough money to pay off one's debts 2 (of a liquid) capable of dissolving other substances ▷ *n* 3 a liquid capable of dissolving other substances [Latin *solvens* releasing] **> solvency** *n*

solvent abuse *n* the deliberate inhaling of intoxicating fumes from certain solvents

Solway Firth *n* an inlet of the Irish Sea between SW Scotland and NW England. Length: about 56 km (35 miles)

Solyom *n* Laszlo. born 1942, Hungarian politician, president of Hungary (2005–10)

Solzhenitsyn *n* Alexander Isayevich. 1918–2008, Russian novelist. His books include *One Day in the Life of Ivan Denisovich* (1962), *The First Circle* (1968), *Cancer Ward* (1968), *August 1914* (1971), *The Gulag Archipelago* (1974), and *October 1916* (1985). His works criticize the Soviet regime and he was imprisoned (1945–53) and exiled to Siberia (1953–56). He was deported to the West from the Soviet Union in 1974; all charges against him were dropped in 1991 and he returned to Russia in 1994. Nobel prize for literature 1970

Som. Somerset

Somali *n* 1 (*pl* **-lis** *or* **-li**) a member of a tall dark-skinned people inhabiting Somalia 2 the language of this people, belonging to the Cushitic subfamily of the Afro-Asiatic family of languages ▷ *adj* 3 of, relating to, or characteristic of Somalia, the Somalis, or their language

Somalia *n* a republic in NE Africa, on the Indian Ocean and the Gulf of Aden: the north became a British protectorate in 1884; the east and south were established as an Italian protectorate in 1889; gained independence and united as Somalia (or the Somali Republic) in 1960. In 1991 the former British Somaliland region in the north unilaterally declared itself independent as the Republic of Somaliland, and Puntland and other areas are also operating effectively as separate states, but this has not been recognized officially. Official languages: Arabic and Somali. Official religion: (Sunni) Muslim. Currency: Somali shilling. Capital: Mogadishu. Pop: 10 251 568 (2013 est). Area: 637 540 sq km (246 154 sq miles)

Somalian *adj* 1 of or relating to Somalia or its inhabitants ▷ *n* 2 a native or inhabitant of Somalia

Somaliland *n* a former region of E Africa, between the equator and the Gulf of Aden: includes Somalia, Djibouti, and SE Ethiopia

somatic *adj* of or relating to the body as distinct from the mind: *somatic symptoms* [Greek *sōma* the body]

sombre *or US* **somber** *adj* 1 serious, sad, or gloomy: *a sombre message* 2 (of a place) dim or gloomy 3 (of colour or clothes) dull or dark [Latin *sub* beneath + *umbra* shade] **> sombrely** *or US* **somberly** *adv*

sombrero *n, pl* **-ros** a wide-brimmed Mexican hat [Spanish]

some *adj* 1 unknown or unspecified: *some man called for you* 2 an unknown or unspecified quantity or number of: *I've got some money* 3 a a considerable number or amount of: *he lived some years afterwards* b a little: *show some respect* 4 *informal* an impressive or remarkable: *that was some game!* ▷ *pron* 5 certain unknown or unspecified people or things: *some can teach and others can't* 6 an unknown or unspecified quantity of something or number of people or things: *he will sell some in his pub* ▷ *adv* 7 approximately: *some thirty pounds* [Old English *sum*]

somebody *pron* 1 some person; someone ▷ *n, pl* **-bodies** 2 a person of great importance: *he was a somebody*

USAGE See at everyone.

someday *adv* at some unspecified time in the future
somehow *adv* 1 in some unspecified way 2 for some unknown reason: *somehow I can't do it*
someone *pron* some person; somebody

USAGE See at everyone.

someplace *adv US and Canad informal* same as **somewhere**
somersault *n* 1 a leap or roll in which the head is placed on the ground and the trunk and legs are turned over it ▷ *vb* 2 to perform a somersault [Old French *soubresault*]
Somerset¹ *n* a county of SW England, on the Bristol Channel: the Mendip Hills lie in the north and Exmoor in the west: the geographical and ceremonial county

S

includes the unitary authorities of North Somerset and Bath and North East Somerset (both part of Avon county from 1975 until 1996): mainly agricultural (esp. dairying and fruit). Administrative centre: Taunton. Pop (excluding unitary authorities): 507 500 (2003 est.). Area (excluding unitary authorities): 3452 sq km (1332 sq miles)

Somerset² *n* 1st Duke of, title of *Edward Seymour*. ?1500–52, English statesman, protector of England (1547–49) during Edward VI's minority. He defeated the Scots (1547) and furthered the Protestant Reformation: executed

Somerset House *n* a building in London, in the Strand, built (1776–86) by Sir William Chambers; formerly housed the General Register Office of births, marriages, and deaths: contains (from 1990) the art collections of the Courtauld Institute

Somerset Levels and Moors *pl n* a sparsely populated wetland and coastal plain area extending across parts of the north and centre of the historic county of Somerset, from Ilchester and Langport in the south to Clevedon in the north and Glastonbury in the east. Area: 650 sq km (251 sq miles)

Somerville *n* Mary, original name *Mary Fairfax*. 1780–1872, British scientific writer, author of *Physical Geography* (1848) and other textbooks. Somerville College, Oxford, was named after her

something *pron* 1 an unspecified or unknown thing; some thing: *there was something wrong* 2 an unspecified or unknown amount: *something less than a hundred* 3 an impressive or important person, thing, or event: *isn't that something?* 4 something else *slang, chiefly US* a remarkable person or thing ▷ *adv* 5 to some degree; somewhat: *he looks something like me*

-something *combining form* a person whose age can be approximately expressed by a specific decade: *twentysomethings* [from the US television series *thirtysomething*]

sometime *adv* 1 at some unspecified point of time ▷ *adj* 2 former: *a sometime actress*

USAGE The form *sometime* should not be used to refer to a fairly long period of time: *he has been away for some time* (not *for sometime*).

---

sometimes *adv* now and then; from time to time
someway *adv* in some unspecified manner
somewhat *adv* rather; a bit: *somewhat surprising*
somewhere *adv* 1 in, to, or at some unknown or unspecified place, point, or amount: *somewhere down south*; *somewhere between 35 and 45 per cent* 2 getting somewhere *informal* making progress

Somme *n* 1 a department of N France, in Picardy region. Capital: Amiens. Pop: 557 061 (2003 est.). Area: 6277 sq km (2448 sq miles) 2 a river in N France, rising in Aisne department and flowing west to Amiens, then northwest to the English Channel: scene of heavy fighting in World War I. Length: 245 km (152 miles)

somnambulism *n formal* the condition of walking in one's sleep [Latin *somnus* sleep + *ambulare* to walk] ▷ **somnambulist** *n*

somnolent *adj formal* drowsy; sleepy [Latin *somnus* sleep] ▷ **somnolence** *n*

son *n* 1 a male offspring 2 a form of address for a man or boy who is younger than the speaker 3 a male who comes from a certain place or one closely connected with a certain thing: *a good son of the church*. Related adjective: **filial** [Old English *sunu*]

Son *n Christianity* the second member of the Trinity, Jesus Christ

sonar *n* a device that locates objects by the reflection of sound waves: used in underwater navigation and target detection [so(und) na(vigation and) r(anging)]

sonata *n* a piece of classical music, usually in three or

more movements, for piano or for another instrument with or without piano [Italian]

Sondheim *n* Stephen (Joshua). born 1930, US songwriter. He wrote the lyrics for *West Side Story* (1957), the score for *Company* (1971), and both for *A Little Night Music* (1973), *Into the Woods* (1987), and *Passion* (1994)

son et lumière (sonn ay loom-yair) *n* an entertainment staged at night at a famous building or historical site, at which its history is described by a speaker accompanied by lighting effects and music [French, literally: sound and light]

song *n* 1 a piece of music with words, composed for the voice 2 the tuneful call made by certain birds or insects 3 the act or process of singing: *he broke into song* 4 for a song at a bargain price 5 make a song and dance *informal* to make an unnecessary fuss [Old English *sang*]

songbird *n* any bird that has a musical call

Songhua *n* a river in NE China, rising in SE Jilin province and flowing north and northeast to the Amur River near Tongjiang: the chief river of Manchuria and largest tributary of the Amur; frozen from November to April. Length: over 1300 km (800 miles). Also called: Sungari

Song Koi *or* **Song Coi** *n* transliteration of the Vietnamese name for the **Red River** (3)

songololo (song-gol-loll-o) *n*, *pl* -los *S African* a kind of millipede [Nguni (language group of southern Africa) *ukusonga* to roll up]

songstress *n* a female singer of popular songs

song thrush *n* a common thrush that repeats each note of its song

sonic *adj* of, involving, or producing sound [Latin *sonus* sound]

sonic barrier *n* same as **sound barrier**

sonic boom *n* a loud explosive sound caused by the shock wave of an aircraft travelling at supersonic speed

son-in-law *n*, *pl* **sons-in-law** the husband of one's son or daughter

sonnet *n prosody* a verse form consisting of 14 lines with a fixed rhyme scheme and rhythm pattern [Old Provençal *sonet* a little poem]

sonny *n* a familiar, often patronizing, term of address to a boy or man

Sonora *n* a state of NW Mexico, on the Gulf of California: consists of a narrow coastal plain rising inland to the Sierra Madre Occidental; an important mining area in colonial times. Capital: Hermosillo. Pop: 2 213 370 (2000). Area: 184 934 sq km (71 403 sq miles)

sonorous *adj* 1 (of a sound) deep or rich 2 (of speech) using language that is unnecessarily complicated and difficult to understand; pompous [Latin *sonor* a noise] ▷ **sonority** *n*

Sontag *n* Susan. 1933–2004, US intellectual and essayist, noted esp. for her writings on modern culture. Her works include *Notes on Camp* (1964), *Against Interpretation* (1968), *On Photography* (1977), *Illness as Metaphor* (1978), and the novel *The Volcano Lover* (1992)

Soo Canals *pl n* the **Soo Canals** the two ship canals linking Lakes Superior and Huron. There is a canal on the Canadian and on the US side of the rapids of the St Mary's River. See also **Sault Sainte Marie**

Soochow *n* a variant transliteration of the Chinese name for **Suzhou**

sook *Austral and NZ informal vb* 1 to complain peevishly ▷ *n* 2 a peevish complaint [variant of SULK] ▷ **sooky** *adj*

soon *adv* 1 in or after a short time; before long 2 as soon as at the very moment that: *as soon as he had closed the door* 3 as soon ... as used to indicate that the first alternative is slightly preferable to the second: *they'd just as soon die for him as live* [Old English *sōna*]

sooner *adv* 1 the comparative of **soon**: *I only wish I'd been back sooner* 2 rather; in preference: *he would sooner leave the party than break with me* 3 no sooner ... than immediately after or when: *no sooner had he spoken than the stench drifted up* **4 sooner or later** eventually

> **USAGE** *When* is sometimes used instead of *than* after *no sooner*, but this use is generally regarded as incorrect: *no sooner had he arrived than* (not *when*) *the telephone rang.*

Soong *or* **Song** *n* an influential Chinese family, notably Soong Ch'ing-ling (1890–1981), who married **Sun Yat-sen** and became a vice-chairman of the People's Republic of China (1959); and **Soong Mei-ling** (1898–2003), who married **Chiang Kai-shek**

soot *n* a black powder formed by the incomplete burning of organic substances such as coal [Old English *sōt*]
> **sooty** *adj*

sooth *n* in **sooth** *archaic, poetic* in truth [Old English *sōth*]

soothe *vb* **soothing, soothed 1** to make (a worried or angry person) calm and relaxed **2** (of an ointment or cream) to relieve (pain) [Old English *sōthian* to prove]
> **soothing** *adj*

soothsayer *n* a person who makes predictions about the future; prophet

sop *n* **1 a** a small bribe or concession given or made to someone to keep them from causing trouble: *a sop to her conscience* **2** *informal* a stupid or weak person **3 sops** food soaked in a liquid before being eaten ▷ *vb* **sopping, sopped 4 sop up** to soak up or absorb (liquid) [Old English *sopp*]

Soper *n* Donald (Oliver), Baron. 1903–98, British Methodist minister and publicist, noted esp. for his pacifist convictions. His books include *All His Grace* (1953) and *Calling for Action* (1984)

Sophia *n* 1630–1714, electress of Hanover (1658–1714), in whom the Act of Settlement (1701) vested the English Crown. She was a granddaughter of James I of England and her son became George I of Great Britain and Ireland

sophism *n* an argument that seems reasonable but is actually false and misleading [Greek *sophisma* ingenious trick]

sophist *n* a person who uses clever but false arguments [Greek *sophistēs* a wise man] > **sophistic** *adj*

sophisticate *vb* **-cating, -cated 1** to make (someone) less natural or innocent, such as by education **2** to make (a machine or method) more complex or refined ▷ *n* **3** a sophisticated person [Latin *sophisticus* sophistic]
> **sophistication** *n*

sophisticated *adj* **1** having or appealing to fashionable and refined tastes and habits: *a sophisticated restaurant* **2** intelligent, knowledgeable, or able to appreciate culture and the arts: *a sophisticated concert audience* **3** (of machines or methods) complex and using advanced technology

sophistry *n* **1** the practice of using arguments which seem clever but are actually false and misleading **2** (*pl* **-ries**) an instance of this

Sophocles *n* ?496–406 BC, Greek dramatist; author of seven extant tragedies: *Ajax, Antigone, Oedipus Rex, Trachiniae, Electra, Philoctetes,* and *Oedipus at Colonus*
> **Sophoclean** *adj*

sophomore *n chiefly US and Canad* a second-year student at a secondary (high) school or college [probably from earlier *sophumer*, variant of *sophism*]

soporific *adj* **1** causing sleep ▷ *n* **2** a drug that causes sleep [Latin *sopor* sleep]

sopping *adj* completely soaked; wet through. Also: **sopping wet**

soppy *adj* **-pier, -piest** *informal* foolishly sentimental: *a soppy love song* > **soppily** *adv*

soprano *n, pl* **-pranos 1** the highest adult female voice **2** the voice of a young boy before puberty **3** a singer with such a voice **4** the highest or second highest instrument in a family of instruments ▷ *adj* **5** denoting a musical instrument that is the highest or second highest pitched in its family: *the soprano saxophone* **6** of or relating to the highest female voice, or the voice of a young boy: *the part is quite possibly the most demanding soprano role Wagner ever wrote* [Italian]

Sopwith *n* Sir Thomas Octave Murdoch. 1888–1989, British aircraft designer, who built the Sopwith Camel biplane used during World War I. He was chairman (1935–63) of the Hawker Siddeley Group, which developed the Hurricane fighter

Sorata *n* Mount Sorata a mountain in W Bolivia, in the Andes: the highest mountain in the Cordillera Real, with two peaks, Ancohuma, 6550 m (21 490 ft), and Illampu, 6485 m (21 276 ft)

sorbet (**saw-bay**) *n* a flavoured water ice [French, from Arabic *sharbah* a drink]

Sorbonne *n* the Sorbonne a part of the University of Paris containing the faculties of science and literature: founded in 1253 by Robert de Sorbon as a theological college; given to the university in 1808

sorcerer *or fem* **sorceress** *n* a person who uses magic powers; a wizard [Old French *sorcier*]

sorcery *n, pl* **-ceries** witchcraft or magic [Old French *sorcerie*]

Sordello *n* born ?1200, Italian troubadour

sordid *adj* **1** dirty, depressing, and squalid: *a sordid backstreet in a slum area* **2** relating to sex in a crude or unpleasant way: *the sordid details of his affair* **3** involving immoral and selfish behaviour: *the sordid history of the slave trade* [Latin *sordidus*]

sore *adj* **1** (of a wound, injury, etc.) painfully sensitive; tender **2** causing annoyance and resentment: *a sore point* **3** upset and angered: *she's still sore about last night* **4** *literary* urgent; pressing: *in sore need of firm government* ▷ *n* **5** a painful or sensitive wound or injury ▷ *adv* **6 sore afraid** *archaic* greatly frightened [Old English *sār*]

Sorel *n* Georges (**Eugène**). 1847–1922, French social philosopher, who advocated revolutionary syndicalism and preached the creative role of violence and myth

sorely *adv* greatly: *sorely disappointed*

Sörenstam *n* Annika. born 1970, Swedish golfer; winner of the US Women's Open (1995, 1996, 2006), the LPGA Championship (2003, 2004, 2005), and the British Women's Open (2003)

sorghum *n* a grass grown for grain and as a source of syrup [Italian *sorgo*]

Sorocaba *n* a city in S Brazil, in São Paulo state: industrial centre. Pop: 671 000 (2005 est)

sorority *n, pl* **-ties** *chiefly US* a society of female students [Latin *soror* sister]

Soros *n* George. real name *Schwartz György*. born 1930, US investor and philanthropist, born in Hungary

sorrel *n* a plant with bitter-tasting leaves which are used in salads and sauces [Old French *surele*]

Sorrento *n* a port in SW Italy, in Campania on a mountainous peninsula between the Bay of Naples and the Gulf of Salerno: a resort since Roman times. Pop: 16 536 (2001)

sorrow *n* **1** deep sadness or regret, associated with death or sympathy for another's misfortune **2** a particular cause of this ▷ *vb* **3** *literary* to feel deep sadness (about death or another's misfortunes); mourn [Old English *sorg*] > **sorrowful** *adj* > **sorrowfully** *adv*

sorry *adj* **-rier, -riest 1** (often foll. by *for* or *about*) feeling or expressing pity, sympathy, grief, or regret: *I'm sorry about this* **2** in bad mental or physical condition: *a sorry state* **3** poor: *a sorry performance* ▷ *interj* **4** an exclamation expressing apology or asking someone to repeat what he or she has said [Old English *sārig*]

sort *n* **1** a class, group, or kind sharing certain characteristics or qualities **2** *informal* a type of character: *she was a good sort* **3** a more or less adequate example: *a sort of dream machine* **4 of sorts** *or* **of a sort** *a* of a poorer quality: *she was wearing a uniform of sorts* **b** of a kind not quite as intended or desired: *it was a reward, of sorts, for my efforts*

S

5 out of sorts not in normal good health or temper
6 sort of as it were; rather: *I sort of quit; sort of insensitive* ▷ *vb* **7** to arrange (things or people) according to class or type **8** to put (something) into working order; fix **9** to arrange (computer information) by machine in an order the user finds convenient [Latin *sors* fate]

> **USAGE** See at **kind²**.

sort code *n* a sequence of numbers printed on a cheque or bank card identifying the branch holding the account
sortie *n* **1** a short or relatively short return trip **2** (of troops) a raid into enemy territory **3** an operational flight made by a military aircraft ▷ *vb* **-tieing, -tied 4** to make a sortie [French]
sort out *vb* **1** to find a solution to (a problem): *did they sort out the mess?* **2** to take or separate (things or people) from a larger group: *to sort out the wheat from the chaff* **3** to organize (things or people) into an orderly and disciplined group **4 sort someone out** to deal with a person, esp. an awkward one **5** *informal* to punish or tell off (someone)
SOS *n* **1** an international code signal of distress in which the letters SOS are repeatedly spelt out in Morse code **2** *informal* any call for help
Sosnowiec *n* an industrial town in S Poland. Pop: 223 284 (2007 est)
so-so *informal adj* **1** neither good nor bad ▷ *adv* **2** in an average or indifferent way
sot *n* a person who is frequently drunk [Old English *sott*] **> sottish** *adj*
sotto voce (**sot**-toe **voe**-chay) *adv* with a soft voice [Italian]
sou *n* **1** a former French coin of low value **2** *old-fashioned* a very small amount of money: *the tax man never saw a sou from this income* [French]
soubrette (soo-**brett**) *n* a minor female role in comedy, often that of a pert maid [French]
soubriquet *n* same as **sobriquet**
Soudan *n* the French name for the **Sudan**
soufflé (soo-**flay**) *n* a light fluffy dish made with beaten egg whites and other ingredients such as cheese or chocolate [French]
Soufrière *n* **1** a volcano in the Caribbean, on N St Vincent: erupted in 1902, killing about 2000 people. Height: 1234 m (4048 ft) **2** a volcano in the Caribbean, on S Montserrat: the highest point on the island; erupted 1997, causing the effective destruction of the capital, Plymouth, and requiring the partial evacuation of the island. Height: 915 m (3002 ft) **3** a volcano in the Caribbean, on Guadeloupe. Height: 1484 m (4869 ft)
sough (rhymes with *now*) *vb literary* (of the wind) to make a sighing sound [Old English *swōgan*]
sought (sawt) *vb* the past of **seek**
souk (sook) *n* an open-air marketplace in Muslim countries [Arabic *sūq*]
soul *n* **1** the spiritual part of a person, regarded as the centre of personality, intellect, will, and emotions: believed by many to survive the body after death **2** the essential part or fundamental nature of anything: *the soul of contemporary America* **3** deep and sincere feelings: *you've got no soul* **4** Also called: **soul music** a type of Black music using blues and elements of jazz, gospel, and pop **5** a person regarded as a good example of some quality: *the soul of prudence* **6** a person: *there was hardly a soul there* **7 the life and soul** *informal* a person who is lively, entertaining, and fun to be with: *the life and soul of the campus* [Old English *sāwol*]
soul-destroying *adj* (of an occupation or situation) very boring and repetitive
soul food *n informal* food, such as chitterlings and yams, which is traditionally eaten by African-Americans
soulful *adj* expressing deep feelings: *a soulful performance of one of Tchaikovsky's songs*

soulless *adj* **1** lacking human qualities; mechanical: *soulless materialism* **2** (of a person) lacking in sensitivity or emotion
soul mate *n* a person with whom one gets along well because of having shared interests and experiences
soul-searching *n* deep examination of one's actions and feelings
Soult *n* Nicolas Jean de Dieu. 1769–1851, French marshal under Napoleon I. Under Louis-Philippe he was minister of war (1830–34; 1840–44)
sound¹ *n* **1** anything that can be heard; noise **2** *physics* mechanical vibrations that travel in waves through the air, water, etc. **3** the sensation produced by such vibrations in the organs of hearing **4** the impression one has of something: *I didn't really like the sound of it* **5 sounds** *slang* music, esp. rock, jazz, or pop ▷ *vb* **6** to make or cause (an instrument, etc.) to make a sound **7** to announce (something) by a sound: *guns sound the end of the two minutes silence* **8** to make a noise with a certain quality: *her voice sounded shrill* **9** to suggest (a particular idea or quality): *his argument sounded false* **10** to pronounce (something) clearly: *to sound one's r's* ▶ See also **sound off** [Latin *sonus*]
sound² *adj* **1** free from damage, injury, or decay; in good condition **2** firm or substantial: *sound documentary evidence* **3** financially safe or stable: *a sound investment* **4** showing good judgment or reasoning; wise: *sound advice* **5** morally correct; honest **6** (of sleep) deep and uninterrupted **7** thorough: *a sound defeat* ▷ *adv* **8 sound asleep** in a deep sleep [Old English *sund*] **> soundly** *adv*
sound³ *vb* **1** to measure the depth of (a well, the sea, etc.) **2** *med* to examine (a part of the body) by tapping or with a stethoscope ▶ See also **sound out** [Old French *sonder*]
sound⁴ *n* a channel between two larger areas of sea or between an island and the mainland [Old English *sund*]
Sound *n* **the Sound** a strait between SW Sweden and Zealand (Denmark), linking the Kattegat with the Baltic: busy shipping lane; spanned by a bridge in 2000. Length of the strait: 113 km (70 miles). Narrowest point: 5 km (3 miles). Danish name: **Øresund**. Swedish name: **Öresund**
soundalike *n* a person or thing that sounds like another, often well-known, person or thing
sound barrier *n* a sudden increase in the force of air against an aircraft flying at or above the speed of sound
sound bite *n* a short pithy sentence or phrase extracted from a longer speech for use on television or radio: *complicated political messages cannot be properly reduced to fifteen-second sound bites*
soundcard *n* a printed circuit board inserted into a computer, enabling the output and manipulation of sound
sound effects *pl n* sounds artificially produced to make a play, esp. a radio play, more realistic
sounding board *n* a person or group used to test a new idea or policy
soundings *pl n* **1** measurements of the depth of a river, lake, or sea **2** questions asked of someone in order to find out his or her opinion: *soundings among colleagues had revealed enthusiasm for the plan*
sound off *vb* to speak angrily or loudly
sound out *vb* to question (someone) in order to discover his or her opinion: *you might try sounding him out about his family*
soundproof *adj* **1** (of a room) built so that no sound can get in or out ▷ *vb* **2** to make (a room) soundproof
soundtrack *n* the recorded sound accompaniment to a film
sound wave *n* a wave that carries sound
Souness *n* Graeme. born 1953, Scottish footballer and manager: played for a number of clubs, most notably Liverpool (1978–84), whom he also managed (1991–94); won 54 caps for Scotland (1974–86)
soup *n* **1** a food made by cooking meat, fish, or vegetables

in a stock **2 in the soup** *slang* in trouble or difficulties [Old French *soupe*] **> soupy** *adj*

soupçon (soop-sonn) *n* a slight amount; dash [French]

souped-up *adj slang* (of a car, motorbike, or engine) adjusted so as to be faster or more powerful than normal

Souphanouvong *n* Prince. 1902–95, Laotian statesman; president of Laos (1975–86)

soup kitchen *n* a place where food and drink are served to needy people

sour *adj* **1** having a sharp biting taste like the taste of lemon juice or vinegar **2** made acid or bad, such as when milk ferments **3** (of a person's mood) bad-tempered and unfriendly **4 go** *or* **turn sour** to become less enjoyable or happy: *the dream has turned sour* **> vb 5** to make or become less enjoyable or friendly: *relations soured shortly after the war* [Old English *sūr*] **> sourly** *adv*

Sour *n* a variant spelling of **Sur**

source *n* **1** the origin or starting point: *the source of discontent among fishermen* **2** any person, book, or organization that provides information for a news report or for research **3** the area or spring where a river or stream begins **> vb 4** to establish a supplier of (a product, etc.) **5** (foll. by *from*) to originate from [Latin *surgere* to rise]

source code *n computers* the original form of a computer program before it is converted into a machine-readable code

sour cream *n* cream soured by bacteria for use in cooking

sour grapes *n* the attitude of pretending to hate something because one cannot have it oneself

sourpuss *n informal* a person who is always gloomy, pessimistic, or bitter

Sousa *n* John Philip. 1854–1932, US bandmaster and composer of military marches, such as *The Stars and Stripes Forever* (1897) and *The Liberty Bell* (1893)

souse *vb* **sousing, soused 1** to plunge (something) into water or other liquid **2** to drench **3** to steep or cook (food) in a marinade **> n 4** the liquid used in pickling **5** the act or process of sousing [Old French *sous*]

soused *adj slang* drunk

Sousse, Susa *or* **Susah** *n* a port in E Tunisia, on the Mediterranean: founded by the Phoenicians in the 9th century BC. Pop: 191 000 (2005 est). Ancient name: **Hadrumetum**

soutane (soo-tan) *n RC Church* a priest's robe [French]

south *n* **1** one of the four cardinal points of the compass, at 180° from north **2** the direction along a line of latitude towards the South Pole **3 the south** any area lying in or towards the south **> adj 4** situated in, moving towards, or facing the south **5** (esp. of the wind) from the south **> adv 6** in, to, or towards the south [Old English *sūth*]

South *n* **1 the South a** the southern part of England **b** (in the US) the Southern states that formed the Confederacy during the Civil War **c** the countries of the world that are not technically and economically advanced **> adj 2** of or denoting the southern part of a country, area, etc.

South Africa *n* Republic of South Africa a republic occupying the southernmost part of the African continent: the Dutch Cape Colony (1652) was acquired by Britain in 1806 and British victory in the Boer War resulted in the formation of the Union of South Africa in 1910, which became a republic in 1961; implementation of the apartheid system began in 1948 and was abolished, following an intense civil rights campaign, in 1993, with multiracial elections held in 1994; a member of the Commonwealth, it withdrew in 1961 but was readmitted in 1994. Mainly plateau with mountains in the south and east. Mineral production includes gold, diamonds, coal, and copper. Official languages: Afrikaans; English; Ndebele; Pedi; South Sotho; Swazi; Tsonga; Tswana; Venda; Xhosa; Zulu. Religion: Christian majority. Currency: rand. Capitals: Cape Town

(legislative), Pretoria (administrative), Bloemfontein (judicial). Pop: 48 601 098 (2013 est). Area: 1 221 044 sq km (471 445 sq miles). Former name (1910–61): **Union of South Africa**

South African *adj* **1** of or relating to the Republic of South Africa or its inhabitants **> n 2** a native or inhabitant of the Republic of South Africa

South America *n* the fourth largest of the continents, bordering on the Caribbean in the north, the Pacific in the west, and the Atlantic in the east and joined to Central America by the Isthmus of Panama. It is dominated by the Andes Mountains, which extend over 7250 km (4500 miles) and include many volcanoes; ranges from dense tropical jungle, desert, and temperate plains to the cold wet windswept region of Tierra del Fuego. Pop (Latin America and the Caribbean): 558 281 000 (2005 est). Area: 17 816 600 sq km (6 879 000 sq miles)

South American *adj* **1** of or relating to the continent of South America or its inhabitants **> n 2** a native or inhabitant of South America

Southampton¹ *n* **1** a port in S England, in Southampton unitary authority, Hampshire on **Southampton Water** (an inlet of the English Channel): chief English passenger port; university (1952); shipyards and oil refinery. Pop: 234 224 (2001) **2** a unitary authority in S England, in Hampshire. Pop: 221 100 (2003 est). Area: 49 sq km (19 sq miles)

Southampton² *n* **3rd Earl of,** title of *Henry Wriothesley.* 1573–1624, English courtier and patron of Shakespeare, who dedicated *Venus and Adonis* (1593) and *The Rape of Lucrece* (1594) to him: sentenced to death (1601) for his part in the Essex rebellion, but reprieved

Southampton Island *n* an island in N Canada, in Nunavut at the entrance to Hudson Bay: inhabited chiefly by Inuit. Area: 49 470 sq km (19 100 sq miles)

South Arabia *n* Federation of South Arabia the former name (1963–67) of South Yemen (excluding Aden). See also **South Yemen**

South Arabian *adj* **1** of or relating to the former South Arabia (now South Yemen) or its inhabitants **> n 2** a native or inhabitant of South Arabia

South Australia *n* a state of S central Australia, on the Great Australian Bight: generally arid, with the Great Victoria Desert in the west central part, the Lake Eyre basin in the northeast, and the Flinders Ranges, Murray River basin, and salt lakes in the southeast. Capital: Adelaide. Pop: 1 650 600 (2013 est). Area: 984 395 sq km 380 070 (sq miles)

South Australian *adj* **1** of or relating to the state of South Australia or its inhabitants **> n 2** a native or inhabitant of South Australia

South Ayrshire *n* a council area of SW Scotland, on the Firth of Clyde: comprises the S part of the historical county of Ayrshire; formerly part of Strathclyde Region (1975–96): chiefly agricultural, with fishing and tourism. Administrative centre: Ayr. Pop: 111 580 (2003 est). Area: 1202 sq km (464 sq miles)

South Bend *n* a city in the US, in N Indiana: university (1842). Pop: 105 540 (2003 est)

southbound *adj* going towards the south

South Carolina *n* a state of the southeastern US, on the Atlantic: the first state to secede from the Union in 1860; consists largely of low-lying coastal plains, rising in the northwest to the Blue Ridge Mountains; the largest US textile producer. Capital: Columbia. Pop: 4 147 152 (2003 est). Area: 78 282 sq km (30 225 sq miles). Abbreviation and zip code: **SC**

South Carolinian *adj* **1** of or relating to South Carolina or its inhabitants **> n 2** a native or inhabitant of South Carolina

South China Sea *n* part of the Pacific surrounded by SE China, Vietnam, the Malay Peninsula, Borneo, and the Philippines

S

Southcott *n* Joanna. 1750–1814, British religious fanatic, who claimed that she would give birth to the second Messiah

South Dakota *n* a state of the western US: lies mostly in the Great Plains; the chief US producer of gold and beryl. Capital: Pierre. Pop: 764 309 (2003 est). Area: 196 723 sq km (75 955 sq miles). Abbreviation: **S. Dak.**, (with zip code) **SD**

South Dakotan *adj* **1** of or relating to South Dakota or its inhabitants ▷ *n* **2** a native or inhabitant of South Dakota

South Downs *pl n* a range of low hills in S England, extending from E Hampshire to East Sussex: declared a national park in 2009

southeast *n* **1** the direction midway between south and east **2** the southeast any area lying in or towards the southeast ▷ *adj* also: **southeastern 3** of or denoting that part of a country or area which lies in the southeast **4** situated in, moving towards, or facing the southeast **5** (esp. of the wind) from the southeast ▷ *adv* **6** in, to, or towards the southeast ▸ **southeasterly** *adj, adv, n*

Southeast *n* the Southeast the southeastern part of Britain, esp. the London area

Southeast Asia *n* a region including Brunei, Cambodia, Indonesia, Laos, Malaysia, Myanmar, the Philippines, Thailand, and Vietnam

Southeast Asian *adj* **1** of or relating to Southeast Asia or its inhabitants ▷ *n* **2** a native or inhabitant of Southeast Asia

southeaster *n* a strong wind or storm from the southeast

Southend-on-Sea *n* **1** a town in SE England, in SE Essex on the Thames estuary: one of England's largest resorts, extending for about 11 km (7 miles) along the coast. Pop: 160 257 (2001) **2** a unitary authority in SE England, in Essex. Pop: 160 300 (2003 est). Area: 42 sq km (16 sq miles)

southerly *adj* **1** of or in the south ▷ *adv, adj* **2** towards the south **3** from the south: *light southerly winds*

southern *adj* **1** situated in or towards the south **2** facing or moving towards the south **3** (*sometimes cap*) of or characteristic of the south or South ▸ **southernmost** *adj*

Southern *adj* of, relating to, or characteristic of the south of a particular region or country

Southern Alps *pl n* a mountain range in New Zealand, on South Island: the highest range in Australasia. Highest peak: Mount Cook (also known as Aoraki or Aorangi), 3754 m (12 316 ft)

Southerner *n* a person from the south of a country or area, esp. England or the US

southern hemisphere *n* that half of the globe lying south of the equator

Southern Ireland *n* See Ireland (2)

southern lights *pl n* same as **aurora australis**

Southern Ocean *n* another name for the **Antarctic Ocean**

Southern Rhodesia *n* the former name (until 1964) of Zimbabwe

Southern Rhodesian *adj* **1** of or relating to the former Southern Rhodesia (now Zimbabwe) or its inhabitants ▷ *n* **2** a native or inhabitant of Southern Rhodesia

Southern Uplands *pl n* a hilly region extending across S Scotland: includes the Lowther, Moorfoot, and Lammermuir hills

Southey *n* Robert. 1774–1843, English poet, a friend of Wordsworth and Coleridge, attacked by Byron; poet laureate (1813–43)

South Georgia *n* an island in the S Atlantic, about 1300 km (800 miles) southeast of the Falkland Islands, part of the UK Overseas Territory of South Georgia and the South Sandwich Islands; no permanent population. Area: 3755 sq km (1450 sq miles)

South Georgian *adj* **1** of or relating to South Georgia or its inhabitants ▷ *n* **2** a native or inhabitant of South Georgia

South Glamorgan *n* a former county of S Wales, formed in 1974 from parts of Glamorgan and Monmouthshire plus the county borough of Cardiff: replaced in 1996 by the county boroughs of Cardiff and Vale of Glamorgan

South Gloucestershire *n* a unitary authority of SW England, in Gloucestershire: formerly (1975–96) part of the county of Avon. Pop: 246 800 (2003 est). Area: 510 sq km (197 sq miles)

South Holland *n* a province of the SW Netherlands, on the North Sea: lying mostly below sea level, it has a coastal strip of dunes and is drained chiefly by distributaries of the Rhine, with large areas of reclaimed land; the most densely populated province in the country, intensively cultivated and industrialized. Capital: The Hague. Pop: 3 440 000 (2003 est). Area: 3196 sq km (1234 sq miles). Dutch name: **Zuidholland**

South Island *n* the South Island the largest island of New Zealand, separated from the North Island by the Cook Strait. Pop: 1 048 200 (2013 est). Area: 153 947 sq km (59 439 sq miles)

South Korea *n* a republic in NE Asia: established as a republic in 1948; invaded by North Korea and Chinese Communists in 1950 but division remained unchanged at the end of the war (1953); includes over 3000 islands; rapid industrialization. Language: Korean. Religions: Buddhist, Confucianist, Shamanist, and Chondokyo. Currency: won. Capital: Seoul. Pop: 48 955 203 (2013 est). Area: 98 477 sq km (38 022 sq miles). Korean name: **Hanguk**

South Korean *adj* **1** of or relating to South Korea or its inhabitants ▷ *n* **2** a native or inhabitant of South Korea

South Lanarkshire *n* a council area of S Scotland, comprising the S part of the historical county of Lanarkshire: included within Strathclyde Region from 1975 to 1996: has uplands in the S and part of the Glasgow conurbation in the N: mainly agricultural. Administrative centre: Hamilton. Pop: 303 010 (2003 est). Area: 1771 sq km (684 sq miles)

South Orkney Islands *pl n* an uninhabited group of islands in the S Atlantic, southeast of Cape Horn: formerly a dependency of the Falkland Islands; part of the British Antarctic Territory since 1962 (claims are suspended under the Antarctic Treaty). Area: 621 sq km (240 sq miles)

South Ossetia *n* a disputed region in Georgia on the S slopes of the Caucasus Mountains; in 1990 it voted to join Russia, leading to armed conflict with Georgian forces; it became an autonomous region in 1997 but later lost this status under a nationwide reorganization of local government; it declared itself an independent republic in 2008 following armed conflict in the region between Russian and Georgian forces. Capital: Tskhinvali. Pop: about 70 000 (2000 est). Area: 3900 sq km (1500 sq miles). Georgian name: **Tskhinvali**. Also called: **South Ossetian Autonomous Region**

southpaw *informal n* **1** any left-handed person, esp. a boxer ▷ *adj* **2** left-handed

South Pole *n* the southernmost point on the earth's axis, at a latitude of 90°S, which has very low temperatures

Southport *n* a town and resort in NW England, in Sefton unitary authority, Merseyside on the Irish Sea. Pop: 91 404 (2001)

Southron *n* **1** *chiefly Scot* a Southerner, esp. an Englishman **2** *Scot* the English language as spoken in England **3** *dialect, chiefly Southern US* an inhabitant of the South, esp. at the time of the Civil War ▷ *adj* **4** *chiefly Scot* of or relating to the South or to England [C15: Scottish variant of SOUTHERN]

South Saskatchewan *n* a river in S central Canada, rising in S Alberta and flowing east and northeast to join the North Saskatchewan River, forming the Saskatchewan River. Length: 1392 km (865 miles)

South Sea Islands *pl n* the islands in the S Pacific that constitute Oceania

South Seas *pl n* the seas south of the equator

South Shetland Islands *pl n* a group of uninhabited islands in the S Atlantic, north of the Antarctic Peninsula: formerly a dependency of the Falkland Islands; part of British Antarctic Territory since 1962. (Claims are suspended under the Antarctic Treaty). Area: 4662 sq km (1800 sq miles)

South Shields *n* a port in NE England, in South Tyneside unitary authority, Tyne and Wear, on the Tyne estuary opposite North Shields. Pop: 82 854 (2001)

South Sudan *n* a landlocked republic in NE Africa, in the Sahel region; formerly part of Sudan: became independent after a referendum in 2011, following a long civil war. Languages: English, Arabic. Religions: Christian, animist. Currency: South Sudanese Pound. Capital: Juba. Pop: 11 090 104 (2013 est). Area: 644 329 sq km (248 777 sq miles)

South Tyneside *n* a unitary authority of NE England, in Tyne and Wear. Pop: 151 700 (2003 est). Area: 64 sq km (25 sq miles)

South Tyrol *or* **South Tirol** *n* a former part of the Austrian state of Tyrol: ceded to Italy in 1919, becoming the Bolzano and Trento provinces of the Trentino-Alto Adige Autonomous Region. Area: 14 037 sq km (5420 sq miles)

South Vietnam *n* a former republic (1955–76) occupying the S of present-day Vietnam on the South China Sea and the Gulf of Thailand

South Vietnamese *adj* **1** of or relating to the former South Vietnam (now part of Vietnam) or its inhabitants ▷ *n* **2** a native or inhabitant of South Vietnam

southward *adj, adv* also: **southwards** **1** towards the south ▷ *n* **2** the southward part or direction

Southwark *n* a borough of S central Greater London, on the River Thames: site of the Globe Theatre, now reconstructed; the former docks and warehouses have been redeveloped. Pop: 253 800 (2003 est). Area: 29 sq km (11 sq miles)

Southwell *n* Saint Robert. ?1561–95, English poet and Roman Catholic martyr, who was imprisoned, tortured, and executed for his Jesuit activities. His best-known poem is "The Burning Babe"

southwest *n* **1** the direction midway between west and south **2** the southwest any area lying in or towards the southwest ▷ *adj* also: **southwestern** **3** of or denoting that part of a country or area which lies in the southwest **4** situated in, moving towards, or facing the southwest **5** (esp. of the wind) from the southwest ▷ *adv* **6** in, to, or towards the southwest ⟩ **southwesterly** *adj, adv, n*

Southwest *n* the Southwest the southwestern part of Britain, esp. Cornwall, Devon, and Somerset

South West Africa *n* another name for **Namibia**

southwester *n* a strong wind or storm from the southwest

South Yemen *n* a former republic in SW Arabia, on the Gulf of Aden; now a part of Yemen: became a republic in 1967; merged with North Yemen in 1990. Official name (1967–90): People's Democratic Republic of Yemen. Name from 1963 to 1967 (excluding Aden): **Federation of South Arabia, South Arabia.** See also **Yemen, North Yemen**

South Yorkshire *n* a metropolitan county of N England, administered since 1986 by the unitary authorities of Barnsley, Doncaster, Sheffield, and Rotherham. Area: 1560 sq km (602 sq miles)

Soutine *n* Chaim. 1893–1943, French expressionist painter, born in Russia; noted for his portraits and still lifes, esp. of animal carcasses

souvenir *n* an object that reminds one of a certain place, occasion, or person; memento [French]

sou'wester *n* **1** a seaman's hat with a broad brim that covers the back of the neck **2** same as **southwester** [a contraction of SOUTHWESTER]

sovereign *n* **1** the Royal ruler of a country **2** a former British gold coin worth one pound sterling ▷ *adj* **3** independent of outside authority; not governed by another country: *a sovereign nation* **4** supreme in rank or authority: *a sovereign queen* **5** old-fashioned excellent or outstanding: *a sovereign remedy for epilepsy* [Old French *soverain*]

sovereignty *n, pl* **-ties** **1** the political power a nation has to govern itself **2** the position or authority of a sovereign

Sovetsk *n* a town in W Russia, in the Kaliningrad Region on the Neman River: scene of the signing of the treaty (1807) between Napoleon I and Tsar Alexander I; passed from East Prussia to the Soviet Union in 1945. Former name (until 1945): **Tilsit**

soviet *n* (in the former Soviet Union) an elected government council at the local, regional, and national levels [Russian *sovyet*]

Soviet *adj* **1** of or relating to the former Soviet Union ▷ *n* **2** a person from the former Soviet Union

Soviet Central Asia *n* the region of the former Soviet Union now occupied by Kazakhstan, Kyrgyzstan, Tajikistan, Turkmenistan, and Uzbekistan. Also called: **Russian Turkestan, West Turkestan**

Soviet Russia *n* (formerly) another name for **Russian Soviet Federative Socialist Republic, Soviet Union**

Soviet Union *n* a former federal republic in E Europe and central and N Asia: the revolution of 1917 achieved the overthrow of the Russian monarchy and the Soviet Union (the USSR) was established in 1922 as a Communist state. It was the largest country in the world, occupying a seventh of the total land surface. The collapse of Communist rule in 1991 was followed by declarations of independence by the constituent republics and the consequent break-up of the Soviet Union. Official name: **Union of Soviet Socialist Republics**. Also called: **Russia, Soviet Russia**. Abbreviation: **USSR**

Soviet Zone *n* that part of Germany occupied by Soviet forces in 1945–49: transformed into the German Democratic Republic in 1949–50. Also called: **Russian Zone**

sow[1] *vb* **sowing, sowed, sown** *or* **sowed** **1** to scatter or plant (seed) in or on (the ground) so that it may grow: *sow sweet peas in pots; farmers sow their fields with fewer varieties* **2** to implant or introduce: *to sow confusion among the other members* [Old English *sāwan*]

sow[2] *n* a female adult pig [Old English *sugu*]

Soweto *n* a contiguous group of Black African townships southwest of Johannesburg, South Africa: the largest purely Black African urban settlement in southern Africa: scene of riots (1976) following protests against the use of Afrikaans in schools for Black African children. Area: 62 sq km (24 sq miles). Pop: 858 649 (2001) [C20: from *so(uth) we(st) to(wnship)*]

soya bean *or US and Canad* **soybean** *n* a plant whose bean is used for food and as a source of oil [Japanese *shōyu*]

Soyinka *n* Wole. born 1934, Nigerian dramatist, novelist, poet, and literary critic. His works include the plays *The Strong Breed* (1963), *The Road* (1965), and *Kongi's Harvest* (1966), the novel *The Interpreters* (1965), and the political essays *The Burden of Memory* and *The Muse of Forgiveness* (1999); forced into exile by the military regime (1993–98). Nobel prize for literature 1986

soy sauce *n* a salty dark brown sauce made from fermented soya beans, used in Chinese cookery

sozzled *adj Brit, Austral and NZ informal* drunk [origin unknown]

Sp. **1** Spain **2** Spaniard **3** Spanish

spa *n* a mineral-water spring or a resort where such a spring is found [after SPA]

Spa *n* a town in E Belgium, in Liège province: a resort with medicinal mineral springs (discovered in the 14th century). Pop: 10 491 (2004 est)

S

Spaak *n* Paul Henri, 1899–1972, Belgian statesman, first socialist premier of Belgium (1937–38); a leading advocate of European unity, he was president of the consultative assembly of the Council of Europe (1949–51) and secretary-general of NATO (1957–61)

space *n* **1** the unlimited three-dimensional expanse in which all objects exist **2** an interval of distance or time between two points, objects, or events **3** a blank portion or area **4** unoccupied area or room: *barely enough space to walk around* **5** the region beyond the earth's atmosphere containing other planets, stars, and galaxies; the universe ▷ *vb* **spacing, spaced 6** (often foll. by *out*) to place or arrange (things) at intervals or with spaces between them [Latin *spatium*]

space age *n* **1** the period in which the exploration of space has become possible ▷ *adj* **space-age 2** very modern, futuristic, or using the latest technology: *a space-age helmet*

space-bar *n* a bar on a keyboard or typewriter that is pressed in order to leave a space between words or letters

space capsule *n* the part of a spacecraft in which the crew live and work

spacecraft *n* a vehicle that can be used for travel in space

spaced-out *adj informal* vague and dreamy, as if influenced by drugs

Space Invaders *n trademark* a video game in which players try to defend themselves against attacking enemy spacecraft

spaceman *or fem* **spacewoman** *n, pl* **-men** *or fem* **-women** a person who travels in space

space probe *n* a small vehicle equipped to gather scientific information, normally transmitted back to earth by radio, about a planet or conditions in space

spaceship *n* (in science fiction) a spacecraft used for travel between planets and galaxies

space shuttle *n* a manned reusable spacecraft designed for making regular flights

space station *n* a large manned artificial satellite used as a base for scientific research in space and for people travelling in space

spacesuit *n* a sealed protective suit worn by astronauts

space-time *or* **space-time continuum** *n physics* the four-dimensional continuum having three space coordinates and one time coordinate that together completely specify the location of an object or an event

Spacey *n* Kevin, original name *Kevin Spacey Fowler*. born 1959, US actor; films include *Glengarry Glen Ross* (1992), *The Usual Suspects* (1995), and *American Beauty* (1999), which earned him an Academy Award; artistic director of Old Vic Theatre Company, London, from 2003. He received an honorary knighthood in 2015

spacious *adj* having or providing a lot of space; roomy ▷ **spaciousness** *n*

spade[1] *n* **1 a** a tool for digging, with a flat steel blade and a long wooden handle **2 call a spade a spade** to speak plainly and frankly [Old English *spadu*]

spade[2] *n* **1 a spades** the suit of playing cards marked with a black leaf-shaped symbol **b** a card with one or more of these symbols on it **2** *offensive* a Black person **3 in spades** *informal* in plenty: *all you need is talent in spades* [Italian *spada* sword, used as an emblem on playing cards]

spadework *n* dull or routine work done as preparation for a project or activity

spadix (spade-ix) *n, pl* **spadices** (spade-ice-eez) *botany* a spike of small flowers on a fleshy stem [Greek: torn-off frond]

spaghetti *n* pasta in the form of long strings [Italian]

spaghetti junction *n* a junction between motorways with a large number of intersecting roads [from the nickname of the Gravelly Hill Interchange, Birmingham]

spaghetti western *n* a cowboy film made in Europe by an Italian director

Spain *n* a kingdom of SW Europe, occupying the Iberian peninsula between the Mediterranean and the Atlantic: a leading European power in the 16th century, with many overseas possessions, esp. in the New World; became a republic in 1931; under the fascist dictatorship of Franco following the Civil War (1936–39) until his death in 1975; a member of the European Union. It consists chiefly of a central plateau (the Meseta), with the Pyrenees and the Cantabrian Mountains in the north and the Sierra Nevada in the south. Official language: Castilian Spanish, with Catalan, Galician, and Basque official regional languages. Religion: Roman Catholic majority. Currency: euro. Capital: Madrid. Pop: 47 370 542 (2013 est). Area: 504 748 sq km (194 883 sq miles). Spanish name: **España**

spake *vb archaic* a past tense of **speak**

Spalato *n* the Italian name for **Split**

Spalding *n* a town in E England, in S Lincolnshire: noted for its bulbfields. Pop: 22 081 (2001)

Spallanzani *n* Lazzaro. 1729–99, Italian physiologist, noted esp. for his experimental studies of microorganisms and his work on animal reproduction and digestion

spam *vb* **spamming, spammed 1** *computers slang* to send unsolicited e-mail simultaneously to a number of e-mail addresses or mobile phones ▷ *n* **2** unsolicited e-mail or text messages sent in this way [from the repeated use of the word *Spam* in a popular sketch from the British television show *Monty Python's Flying Circus*]

Spam *n trademark* a cold meat made from pork and spices

span *n* **1** the interval or distance between two points, such as the ends of a bridge **2** the complete extent: *that span of time* **3** short for **wingspan 4** a unit of length based on the width of a stretched hand, usually taken as nine inches (23 cms) ▷ *vb* **spanning, spanned 5** to stretch or extend across, over, or around: *her career spanned fifty years*; *to span the Danube* [Old English *spann*]

spangle *n* **1** a small piece of shiny material used as a decoration on clothes or hair; sequin ▷ *vb* **-gling, -gled 2** to cover or decorate (something) with spangles [Middle English *spange* clasp]

Spaniard *n* a native or inhabitant of Spain

spaniel *n* a dog with long drooping ears and a silky coat [Old French *espaigneul* Spanish (dog)]

Spanish *adj* **1** of or relating to Spain or its inhabitants ▷ *n* **2** the official language of Spain, Mexico, and most countries of South and Central America ▷ *pl n* **3 the Spanish** the people of Spain

Spanish America *n* the parts of America colonized by Spaniards from the 16th century onwards and now chiefly Spanish-speaking: includes all of South America (except Brazil, Guyana, French Guiana, and Surinam), Central America (except Belize), Mexico, Cuba, Puerto Rico, the Dominican Republic, and a number of small Caribbean islands

Spanish-American *adj* **1** of or relating to any of the Spanish-speaking countries or peoples of the Americas ▷ *n* **2** a native or inhabitant of Spanish America **3** a Spanish-speaking person in the US

Spanish fly *n* a beetle, the dried body of which is used in medicine

Spanish Guinea *n* the former name (until 1964) of **Equatorial Guinea**

Spanish Main *n* **1** the N coast of South America **2** the Caribbean Sea, the S part of which was frequented by pirates

Spanish Moroccan *adj* **1** of or relating to the former Spanish colony of Spanish Morocco (now part of Morocco) or its inhabitants ▷ *n* **2** a native or inhabitant of Spanish Morocco

Spanish Morocco *n* a former Spanish colony on the N coast of Morocco: part of the kingdom of Morocco since 1956

S

Spanish Sahara *n* the former name (until 1975) of Western Sahara

Spanish West Africa *n* a former overseas territory of Spain in NW Africa: divided in 1958 into the overseas provinces of Ifni and Spanish Sahara

Spanish West African *adj* **1** of or relating to the former Spanish overseas territory of Spanish West Africa (now the overseas provinces of Ifni and Spanish Sahara) or its inhabitants ▷ *n* **2** a native or inhabitant of Spanish West Africa

spank *vb* **1** to slap (someone) with the open hand, on the buttocks or legs ▷ *n* **2** such a slap [probably imitative]

spanking[1] *n* a series of spanks, usually as a punishment for children

spanking[2] *adj* **1** *informal* outstandingly fine or smart: *spanking new uniforms* **2** very fast: *a spanking pace*

spanner *n* **1** a tool for gripping and turning a nut or bolt **2 throw a spanner in the works** *informal* to cause a problem that prevents things from running smoothly [German *spannen* to stretch]

spanspek *n S African* a cantaloupe melon [Afrikaans]

spar[1] *n* a pole used as a ship's mast, boom, or yard [Old Norse *sperra* beam]

spar[2] *vb* **sparring, sparred** **1** *boxing, martial arts* to fight using light blows for practice **2** to argue with someone ▷ *n* **3** an argument [Old English]

spar[3] *n* a light-coloured, crystalline, easily split mineral [Middle Low German]

spare *adj* **1** extra to what is needed: *there are some spare chairs at the back* **2** able to be used when needed: *a spare parking space* **3** (of a person) tall and thin **4** (of a style) plain and without unnecessary decoration or details; austere: *a spare but beautiful novel* **5** *Brit slang* frantic with anger or worry: *the boss went spare* ▷ *n* **6** an extra thing kept in case it is needed ▷ *vb* **sparing, spared** **7** to stop from killing, punishing, or injuring (someone) **8** to protect (someone) from (something) unpleasant: *spare me the sermon* **9** to be able to afford or give: *can you spare me a moment to talk?* **10 not spare oneself** to try one's hardest **11 to spare** more than is required: *a few hours to spare* [Old English *sparian*]

spare part *n* a replacement piece of mechanical or electrical equipment kept in case the original component becomes damaged or worn

spareribs *pl n* a cut of pork ribs with most of the meat trimmed off

spare tyre *n* **1** an additional tyre kept in a motor vehicle in case of puncture **2** *slang* a roll of fat just above the waist

sparing *adj* (sometimes foll. by *of*) economical (with): *she was mercifully sparing in her use of jargon* ▷ **sparingly** *adv*

spark *n* **1** a fiery particle thrown out from a fire or caused by friction **2** a short flash of light followed by a sharp crackling noise, produced by a sudden electrical discharge through the air **3** a trace or hint: *a spark of goodwill* **4** liveliness, enthusiasm, or humour: *that spark in her eye* ▷ *vb* **5** to give off sparks **6** to cause to start; trigger: *the incident sparked off an angry exchange* [Old English *spearca*]

Spark *n* Dame Muriel (Sarah). 1918–2006, British novelist and writer; her novels include *Memento Mori* (1959), *The Prime of Miss Jean Brodie* (1961), *The Takeover* (1976), *A Far Cry from Kensington* (1988), *Symposium* (1990), and *The Finishing School* (2004)

sparkie *n Brit, Austral and NZ informal* electrician

sparkle *vb* **-kling, -kled** **1** to glitter with many bright points of light **2** (of wine or mineral water) to be slightly fizzy **3** to be lively, witty, and intelligent ▷ *n* **4** a small bright point of light **5** liveliness and wit [Middle English *sparklen*] ▷ **sparkling** *adj*

sparkler *n* **1** a type of hand-held firework that throws out sparks **2** *informal* a sparkling gem; esp. a diamond

spark plug *n* a device in an internal-combustion engine that ignites the fuel by producing an electric spark

sparring partner *n* **1** a person who practises with a

boxer during training **2** a person with whom one has friendly arguments

sparrow *n* a very common small brown or grey bird which feeds on seeds and insects [Old English *spearwa*]

sparrowhawk *n* a small hawk which preys on smaller birds

sparse *adj* small in amount and spread out widely: *a sparse population* [Latin *sparsus*] ▷ **sparsely** *adv*

Sparta *n* an ancient Greek city in the S Peloponnese, famous for the discipline and military prowess of its citizens and for their austere way of life

Spartacus *n* died 71 BC, Thracian slave, who led an ultimately unsuccessful revolt of gladiators against Rome (73–71 BC)

Spartan *adj* **1** of or relating to Sparta or its citizens **2** (*sometimes not cap*) very strict or austere: *a Spartan upbringing* **3** (*sometimes not cap*) possessing courage and resolve ▷ *n* **4** a citizen of Sparta **5** (*sometimes not cap*) a disciplined or brave person **6** a Canadian variety of eating apple ▷ **Spartanism** *n*

spasm *n* **1** a sudden tightening of the muscles, over which one has no control **2** a sudden burst of activity or feeling: *a spasm of applause*; *sudden spasms of anger* [Greek *spasmos* a cramp]

spasmodic *adj* taking place in sudden short spells: *spasmodic bouts of illness* ▷ **spasmodically** *adv*

Spassky *n* Boris. born 1937, Russian chess player; world champion (1969–72)

spastic *n* **1** *old-fashioned, offensive* a person who has cerebral palsy, and therefore has difficulty controlling his or her muscles ▷ *adj* **2** affected by involuntary muscle contractions: *a spastic colon* **3** *old-fashioned, offensive* suffering from cerebral palsy [Greek *spasmos* a cramp]

spat[1] *n* a slight quarrel [probably imitative]

spat[2] *vb* a past of **spit**[1]

spate *n* **1** a large number of things happening within a period of time: *a spate of bombings* **2** a fast flow or outpouring: *an incomprehensible spate of words* **3 in spate** *chiefly Brit* (of a river) flooded [origin unknown]

spathe *n botany* a large leaf that surrounds the base of a flower cluster [Greek *spathē* a blade]

spatial *adj* of or relating to size, area, or position: *spatial dimensions* ▷ **spatially** *adv*

spats *pl n* cloth or leather coverings formerly worn by men over the ankle and instep [obsolete *spatterdash* a long gaiter]

spatter *vb* **1** to scatter or splash (a substance, esp. a liquid) in scattered drops: *spattering mud in all directions* **2** to sprinkle (an object or a surface) with a liquid ▷ *n* **3** the sound of spattering **4** something spattered, such as a spot or splash [imitative]

spatula *n* a utensil with a broad flat blade, used in cooking and by doctors [Latin: a broad piece]

spawn *n* **1** the jelly-like mass of eggs laid by fish, amphibians, or molluscs ▷ *vb* **2** (of fish, amphibians, or molluscs) to lay eggs **3** to cause (something) to be created: *the depressed economy spawned the riots* [Anglo-Norman *espaundre*]

spay *vb* to remove the ovaries from (a female animal) [Old French *espeer* to cut with the sword]

spaza shop (spah-zuh) *n S African slang* a small informal shop in a township [from South African urban slang *spaza* camouflaged]

speak *vb* **speaking, spoke, spoken** **1** to say words; talk **2** to communicate or express (something) in words **3** to give a speech or lecture **4** to know how to talk in (a specified language): *I don't speak French* **5 on speaking terms** on good terms; friendly **6 so to speak** as it were **7 speak one's mind** to express one's opinions honestly and plainly **8 to speak of** of a significant nature: *no licensing laws to speak of* [Old English *specan*]

speakeasy *n, pl* **-easies** *US* a place where alcoholic drink was sold illegally during Prohibition

speaker *n* **1** a person who speaks, esp. someone making a speech **2** a person who speaks a particular language: *a fluent Tibetan and English speaker* **3** same as **loudspeaker**

Speaker *n* the official chairman of a law-making body

speak for *vb* **1** to speak on behalf of (other people) **2 speak for itself** to be so obvious that no further comment is necessary: *his work on the convention speaks for itself* **3 speak for yourself!** *informal* do not presume that other people agree with you!

speak up or **speak out** *vb* **1** to state one's beliefs bravely and firmly **2** to speak more loudly and clearly

spear¹ *n* **1** a weapon consisting of a long pole with a sharp point ▷ *vb* **2** to pierce (someone or something) with a spear or other pointed object: *she took her fork and speared an oyster from its shell* [Old English *spere*]

spear² *n* **1** a slender shoot, such as of grass **2** a single stalk of broccoli or asparagus [probably variant of *spire*]

spearhead *vb* **1** to lead (an attack or a campaign) ▷ *n* **2** the leading force in an attack or campaign

spearmint *n* a minty flavouring used for sweets and toothpaste, which comes from a purple-flowered plant

Spears *n* Britney. born 1981, US pop singer; records include the single "Baby One More Time" (1998) and the album *Britney* (2001)

spec *n* **on spec** *informal* as a risk or gamble: *I still tend to buy on spec*

special *adj* **1** distinguished from or better than others of its kind: *a special occasion* **2** designed or reserved for a specific purpose: *special equipment* **3** not usual; different from normal: *a special case* **4** particular or primary: *a special interest in gifted children* **5** relating to the education of children with disabilities: *a special school* ▷ *n* **6** a product, TV programme, etc., which is only available or shown at a certain time: *a two-hour Christmas special live from Hollywood* **7** a meal, usually at a low price, in a bar or restaurant **8** short for **special constable** [Latin *specialis*] ▷ **specially** *adv*

USAGE See at **especial**.

Special Branch *n* (in Britain and S Africa) the department of the police force that is concerned with political security

special constable *n* a person recruited for occasional police duties, such as in an emergency

special delivery *n* the delivery of a piece of mail outside the time of a scheduled delivery, for an extra fee

special effects *pl n films* techniques used in the production of scenes that cannot be achieved by normal methods: *the special effects and make-up are totally convincing*

specialist *n* **1** a person who is an expert in a particular activity or subject **2** a doctor who concentrates on treating one particular category of diseases or the diseases of one particular part of the body: *an eye specialist* ▷ *adj* **3** particular to or concentrating on one subject or activity: *a specialist comic shop*

speciality or *especially US and Canad* **specialty** *n, pl* **-ties 1** a special interest or skill **2** a service, product, or type of food specialized in

specialize or **-lise** *vb* **-lizing, -lized** or **-lising, -lised 1** (often foll. by *in*) to concentrate all one's efforts on studying a particular subject, occupation, or activity: *an expert who specializes in transport* **2** to modify (something) for a special use or purpose: *plants have evolved and specialized in every type of habitat* ▷ **specialization** or **-lisation** *n*

special licence *n* Brit a licence allowing a marriage to take place without following all the usual legal procedures

specialty *n, pl* **-ties** *chiefly US and Canad* same as **speciality**

specie *n* coins as distinct from paper money [Latin *in specie* in kind]

species *n, pl* **-cies** *biology* one of the groups into which a genus is divided, the members of which are able to interbreed [Latin: appearance]

specific *adj* **1** particular or definite: *a specific area of economic policy* **2** precise and exact: *try and be more specific* ▷ **3 specifics** particular qualities or aspects of something: *the specifics of the situation* **4** *med* any drug used to treat a particular disease [Latin *species* kind + *facere* to make] ▷ **specifically** *adv* ▷ **specificity** *n*

specification *n* **1** a detailed description of features in the design of something: *engines built to racing specification* **2** a requirement or detail which is clearly stated: *the main specification was that a good degree was required* **3** the specifying of something

specific gravity *n physics* the ratio of the density of a substance to the density of water

specific heat capacity *n physics* the quantity of heat required to raise the temperature of unit mass of a substance by one degree centigrade

specify *vb* **-fies, -fying, -fied 1** to state or describe (something) clearly **2** to state (something) as a condition: *the rules specify the number of prisoners to be kept in each cell* [Medieval Latin *specificare* to describe]

specimen *n* **1** an individual or part regarded as typical of its group or class **2** *med* a sample of tissue, blood, or urine taken for analysis **3** *informal* a person: *I'm quite a healthy specimen* [Latin: mark, proof]

specious (spee-shuss) *adj* apparently correct or true, but actually wrong or false [Latin *species* outward appearance]

speck *n* **1** a very small mark or spot **2** a small or tiny piece of something: *a speck of fluff* [Old English *specca*]

speckle *vb* **-ling, -led 1** to mark (something) with speckles ▷ *n* **2** a small mark or spot, such as on the skin or on an egg [Middle Dutch *spekkel*] ▷ **speckled** *adj*

specs *pl n informal* short for **spectacles**

spectacle *n* **1** a strange, interesting, or ridiculous scene **2** an impressive public show: *the opening ceremony of the Olympics was an impressive spectacle* **3 make a spectacle of oneself** to draw attention to oneself by behaving foolishly [Latin *spectare* to watch]

spectacles *pl n* a pair of glasses for correcting faulty vision

spectacular *adj* **1** impressive, grand, or dramatic ▷ *n* **2** a spectacular show ▷ **spectacularly** *adv*

spectate *vb* **-tating, -tated** to be a spectator; watch

spectator *n* a person viewing anything; onlooker [Latin *spectare* to watch]

spectator ion *n chem* an ion which is present in a mixture but plays no part in a reaction

Spector *n* Phil. born 1940, US record producer and songwriter, noted for the densely orchestrated "Wall of Sound" in his work with groups such as the Ronettes and the Crystals; convicted in 2009 for the second-degree murder (2003) of actress Lana Clarkson

spectre or US **specter** *n* **1** a ghost **2** an unpleasant or menacing vision in one's imagination: *the spectre of famine* [Latin *spectrum*] ▷ **spectral** *adj*

spectrometer (speck-trom-it-er) *n physics* an instrument for producing a spectrum, usually one in which wavelength, energy, or intensity can be measured

spectroscope *n physics* an instrument for forming or recording a spectrum by passing a light ray through a prism or grating

spectrum *n, pl* **-tra 1** *physics* the distribution of colours produced when white light is dispersed by a prism or grating: violet, indigo, blue, green, yellow, orange, and red **2** *physics* the whole range of electromagnetic radiation with respect to its wavelength or frequency **3** a range or scale of anything such as opinions or emotions [Latin: image]

speculate *vb* **-lating, -lated 1** to form opinions about something, esp. its future consequences, based on the information available; conjecture: *it is too early to speculate about Jackie getting married* **2** to buy securities or property in the hope of selling them at a profit [Latin *speculari* to spy out] ▷ **speculation** *n* ▷ **speculative** *adj* ▷ **speculator** *n*

sped vb a past of **speed**

speech n **1** the ability to speak: *the loss of speech* **2** spoken language: *Doran's lack of coherent speech* **3** a talk given to an audience: *a speech to parliament* **4** a person's manner of speaking: *her speech was extremely slow* **5** a national or regional language or dialect: *Canadian speech* [Old English *spēc*]

speech day n (in schools) an annual day on which prizes are presented and speeches are made by guest speakers

speechify vb **-fies, -fying, -fied** to make a dull or pompous speech

speechless adj **1** unable to speak for a short time because of great emotion or shock **2** unable to be expressed in words: *speechless disbelief*

speech therapy n the treatment of people with speech problems

speed n **1** the quality of acting or moving fast; swiftness **2** the rate at which something moves or happens **3** a gear ratio in a motor vehicle or bicycle: *five-speed gearbox* **4** *photog* a measure of the sensitivity to light of a particular type of film **5** *slang* amphetamine **6 at speed** quickly **7 up to speed a** operating at an acceptable level **b** in possession of all the necessary information ▷ vb **speeding, sped** or **speeded 8** to move or go somewhere quickly **9** to drive a motor vehicle faster than the legal limit ▶ See also **speed up** [Old English *spēd* (originally: success)]

speedboat n a high-speed motorboat

speed camera n a camera for photographing vehicles breaking the speed limit

speed limit n the maximum speed at which a vehicle may legally travel on a particular road

speedo n, pl **speedos** informal a speedometer

speedometer n a dial in a vehicle which shows the speed of travel

speed trap n a place on a road where the police check that passing vehicles are not being driven at an illegally high speed

speed up vb to accelerate or cause to accelerate

USAGE The past tense and past participle of *speed up* is *speeded up* not *sped up*.

speedway n **1** the sport of racing on light powerful motorcycles round cinder tracks **2** US, Canad and NZ the track or stadium where such races are held

speedwell n a small blue or pinkish-white flower

speedy adj **speedier, speediest 1** done without delay **2** (of a vehicle) able to travel fast ▷ **speedily** adv

speleology n the scientific study of caves [Latin *spelaeum* cave]

spell¹ vb **spelling, spelt** or **spelled 1** to write or name in correct order the letters that make up (a word): *how do you spell that name?* **2** (of letters) to make up (a word): *c-a-t spells cat* **3** to indicate (a particular result): *share price slump spells disaster* ▶ See also **spell out** [Old French *espeller*]

spell² n **1** a sequence of words used to perform magic **2** the effect of a spell: *the wizard's spell was broken* **3 under someone's spell** fascinated by someone [Old English *spell* speech]

spell³ n **1** a period of time of weather or activity: *the dry spell; a short spell in prison* **2** a period of duty after which one person or group relieves another **3** Scot, Austral and NZ a period of rest [Old English *spelian* to take the place of]

spellbinding adj so fascinating that nothing else can be thought of: *his spellbinding speeches*

spellbound adj completely fascinated; as if in a trance

spellchecker n computers a program that highlights any word in a word-processed document that is not recognized as being correctly spelt

spelling n **1** the way a word is spelt: *the British spelling of 'theatre'* **2** a person's ability to spell: *my spelling used to be excellent*

spell out vb **1** to make (something) as easy to understand as possible: *to spell out the implications* **2** to read with difficulty, working out each word letter by letter

spelt vb a past of **spell¹**

Spence n Sir Basil (Unwin). 1907–76, Scottish architect, born in India; designed Coventry Cathedral (1951)

Spencer n **1** Herbert. 1820–1903, English philosopher, who applied evolutionary theory to the study of society, favouring laissez-faire doctrines **2** Sir **Stanley**. 1891–1959, English painter, noted esp. for his paintings of Christ in a contemporary English setting

Spencer Gulf n an inlet of the Indian Ocean in S Australia, between the Eyre and Yorke Peninsulas. Length: about 320 km (200 miles). Greatest width: about 145 km (90 miles)

spend vb **spending, spent 1** to pay out (money) **2** to pass (time) in a specific way or place: *I spent a year in Budapest* **3** to concentrate (effort) on an activity: *a lot of energy was spent organizing the holiday* **4** to use up completely: *the hurricane spent its force* [Latin *expendere*] ▷ **spending** n

Spender n Sir Stephen. 1909–95, English poet and critic, who played an important part in the left-wing literary movement of the 1930s. His works include *Journals 1939–83* (1985) and *Collected Poems* (1985)

spendthrift n **1** a person who spends money wastefully ▷ adj **2** of or like a spendthrift: *a spendthrift policy*

Spengler n Oswald. 1880–1936, German philosopher of history, noted for *The Decline of the West* (1918–22), which argues that civilizations go through natural cycles of growth and decay

Spenser n Edmund. ?1552–99, English poet celebrated for *The Faerie Queene* (1590; 1596), an allegorical romance. His other verse includes the collection of eclogues *The Shephearde's Calendar* (1579) and the marriage poem *Epithalamion* (1594)

spent vb **1** the past of **spend** ▷ adj **2** used up or exhausted

Speranski n Mikhail Mikhailovich. 1772–1839, Russian statesman, chief adviser (1807–12) to Alexander I. His greatest achievement was the codification of Russian law (begun 1826)

sperm n **1** (pl **sperms** or **sperm**) one of the male reproductive cells released in the semen during ejaculation **2** same as **semen** [Greek *sperma*]

spermaceti (sper-ma-**set**-ee) n a white waxy substance obtained from the sperm whale [Medieval Latin *sperma ceti* whale's sperm]

spermatozoon (sper-ma-toe-**zoe**-on) n, pl **-zoa** same as **sperm** (1) [Greek *sperma* seed + *zōion* animal]

spermicide n a substance, esp. a cream or jelly, that kills sperm, used as a means of contraception [SPERM + Latin *caedere* to kill] ▷ **spermicidal** adj

sperm oil n an oil obtained from the head of the sperm whale, used as a lubricant

sperm whale n a large whale which is hunted for spermaceti and ambergris [short for SPERMACETI WHALE]

Sperrin Mountains pl n a mountain range in NW Northern Ireland

spew vb **1** to vomit **2** to send or be sent out in a stream: *the hydrant spewed a tidal wave of water* [Old English *spīwan*]

Spey n a river in E Scotland, flowing generally northeast through the Grampian Mountains to the Moray Firth: salmon fishing; parts of the surrounding area (**Speyside**) are famous for whisky distilleries. Length: 172 km (107 miles)

Speyer n a port in SW Germany, in Rhineland-Palatinate on the Rhine: the scene of 50 imperial diets. Pop: 50 247 (2003 est). English name: **Spires**

SPF sun protection factor: an indicator of how a sun cream, lotion, etc. protects the skin from the harmful rays of the sun

sphagnum n a moss which is found in bogs and which decays to form peat [Greek *sphagnos*]

sphere n **1** *geometry* a round solid figure in which every point on the surface is equally distant from the centre **2** an object having this shape, such as a planet **3** a particular field of activity **4** people of the same rank or with shared interests: *a humbler social sphere* [Greek *sphaira*]

spherical *adj* shaped like a sphere

spheroid *n geometry* a solid figure that is almost but not exactly a sphere

sphincter *n anatomy* a ring of muscle surrounding the opening of a hollow organ and contracting to close it [Greek *sphingein* to grip tightly]

sphinx *n* **1** one of the huge statues built by the ancient Egyptians, with the body of a lion and the head of a man **2** a mysterious person

Sphinx *n* **1** the huge statue of a sphinx near the pyramids at El Gîza in Egypt **2** *Greek myth* a monster with a woman's head and a lion's body, who set a riddle for travellers, killing them when they failed to answer it. Oedipus answered the riddle and the Sphinx then killed herself [Greek]

spice *n* **1 a** an aromatic substance, such as ginger or cinnamon, used as flavouring **b** such substances collectively **2** something that makes life or an activity more exciting ▷ *vb* **spicing, spiced 3** to flavour (food) with spices **4** (often foll. by *up*) to add excitement or interest to (something): *they spiced their letters with pointed demands* [Old French *espice*]

Spice Islands *pl n* the former name of the **Moluccas**

spick-and-span *adj* very neat and clean [obsolete *spick* spike + *span-new* absolutely new, like a freshly cut spike]

spicy *adj* **spicier, spiciest 1** strongly flavoured with spices **2** *informal* slightly scandalous: *spicy new story lines*

spider *n* a small eight-legged creature, many species of which weave webs in which to trap insects for food [Old English *spīthra*] ▷ **spidery** *adj*

spider monkey *n* a tree-living monkey with very long legs, a long tail, and a small head

spiel *n* a prepared speech made to persuade someone to buy or do something [German *Spiel* play]

Spielberg *n* Steven. born 1947, US film director, noted esp. for the commercial success of such films as *Jaws* (1975), *Close Encounters of the Third Kind* (1977), *Raiders of the Lost Ark* (1981) and its sequels, *E.T.* (1982), and *Jurassic Park* (1993). Other films include *The Color Purple* (1986), *Schindler's List* (1993), *Saving Private Ryan* (1998), *The Terminal* (2004), and *Lincoln* (2012)

spigot *n* **1** a stopper for the vent hole of a cask **2** a wooden tap fitted to a cask [probably from Latin *spica* a point]

spike¹ *n* **1 a** a sharp-pointed metal object: *a high fence with iron spikes* **2** anything long and pointed: *a hedgehog bristling with spikes* **3** a long metal nail **4 spikes** sports shoes with metal spikes on the soles for greater grip ▷ *vb* **spiking, spiked 5** to secure or supply (something) with spikes: *spiked shoes* **6** to drive a spike or spikes into **7** to add alcohol to (a drink) [Middle English *spyk*] ▷ **spiky** *adj*

spike² *n botany* **1** an arrangement of flowers attached at the base to a long stem **2** an ear of grain [Latin *spica* ear of corn]

spikenard *n* **1** a fragrant Indian plant with rose-purple flowers **2** an ointment obtained from this plant [Medieval Latin *spica nardi*]

spill¹ *vb* **spilling, spilt** *or* **spilled 1** to pour from or as from a container by accident **2** (of large numbers of people) to come out of a place: *rival groups spilled out from the station* **3** to shed (blood) **4 spill the beans** *informal* to give away a secret ▷ *n* **5** *informal* a fall from a motorbike, bike, or horse, esp. in a competition **6** an amount of liquid spilt [Old English *spillan* to destroy] ▷ **spillage** *n*

spill² *n* a splinter of wood or strip of paper for lighting pipes or fires [Germanic]

Spillane *n* Mickey, original name *Frank Morrison Spillane*. 1918–2006, US detective-story writer, best known for his books featuring the detective Mike Hammer, for example *I, the Jury* (1947) and *The Twisted Thing* (1966)

spillikin *n* Brit a thin strip of wood, cardboard, or plastic used in spillikins

spillikins *n* Brit a game in which players try to pick each spillikin from a heap without moving the others

spin *vb* **spinning, spun 1** to revolve or cause to revolve quickly **2** to draw out and twist (fibres, such as silk or cotton) into thread **3** (of a spider or silkworm) to form (a web or cocoon) from a silky fibre that comes out of the body **4 spin a yarn** to tell an unlikely story **5** *sport* to throw, hit, or kick (a ball) so that it spins and changes direction or changes speed on bouncing **6** same as **spin-dry 7** to grow dizzy: *her head was spinning* **8** *informal* to present information in a way that creates a favourable impression ▷ *n* **9** a fast rotating motion **10** a flight manoeuvre in which an aircraft flies in a downward spiral **11** *sport* a spinning motion given to a ball **12** *informal* a short car drive taken for pleasure **13** *informal* the presenting of information in a way that creates a favourable impression ▶ See also **spin out** [Old English *spinnan*] ▷ **spinning** *n*

spina bifida *n* a condition in which part of the spinal cord protrudes through a gap in the backbone, sometimes causing paralysis [New Latin: split spine]

spinach *n* a dark green leafy vegetable [Arabic *isfānākh*]

spinal column *n* same as **spine** (1)

spinal cord *n* the thick cord of nerve tissue within the spine, which connects the brain to the nerves of the body

spin bowler *n cricket* same as **spinner** (1a)

spindle *n* **1** a rotating rod that acts as an axle **2** a rod with a notch in the top for drawing out, twisting and winding the thread in spinning [Old English *spinel*]

spindly *adj* **-dlier, -dliest** tall, thin, and frail

spin doctor *n informal* a person who provides a favourable slant to a news item or policy on behalf of a political personality or party [from the spin given to a ball in sport to make it go in the desired direction]

spindrift *n* spray blown up from the sea [Scots variant of *spoondrift*, from *spoon* to scud + DRIFT]

spin-dry *vb* **-dries, -drying, -dried** to dry (clothes) in a spin-dryer

spin-dryer *n* a device that removes water from washed clothes by spinning them in a perforated drum

spine *n* **1** the row of bony segments that surround and protect the spinal cord **2** the back of a book, record sleeve, or video-tape box **3** a sharp point on the body of an animal or on a plant [Latin *spina* thorn] ▷ **spinal** *adj*

spine-chiller *n* a frightening film or story ▷ **spine-chilling** *adj*

spineless *adj* **1** behaving in a cowardly way **2** (of an animal) having no spine

spinet *n* a small harpsichord [Italian *spinetta*]

spinifex *n* a coarse spiny Australian grass

spinnaker *n* a large triangular sail on a racing yacht [probably from *spin*, but traditionally from Sphinx, the yacht that first used this type of sail]

spinner *n* **1** *cricket* **a** a bowler who specializes in spinning the ball with his or her fingers to make it change direction when it bounces or strikes the batsman's bat **b** a ball that is bowled with a spinning motion **2** a small round object used in angling to attract fish to the bait by spinning in the water **3** a person who makes thread by spinning

spinneret *n* an organ through which silk threads come out of the body of a spider or insect

spinney *n chiefly Brit* a small wood: *the hollow tree in the spinney* [Old French *espinei*]

spinning jenny *n* an early type of spinning frame with several spindles

spinning wheel *n* a wheel-like machine for spinning at home, having one hand- or foot-operated spindle

spin-off *n* **1** a product or development that unexpectedly results from activities designed to achieve something else: *new energy sources could occur as a spin-off from the space*

S

effort **2** a television series involving some of the characters from an earlier successful series

spin out *vb* **1** to take longer than necessary to do (something) **2** to make (money) last as long as possible

Spinoza *n* Baruch. 1632–77, Dutch philosopher who constructed a holistic metaphysical system derived from a series of hypotheses that he judged self-evident. His chief work is *Ethics* (1677)

spinster *n* an unmarried woman [Middle English, in the sense a woman who spins] ▷ **spinsterish** *adj*

spiny *adj* **spinier, spiniest** (of animals or plants) covered with spines

spiracle (spire-a-kl) *n zoology* a small blowhole for breathing through, such as that of a whale [Latin *spiraculum* vent]

spiraea *or especially US* **spirea** (spire-ee-a) *n* a plant with small white or pink flowers [Greek *speiraia*]

spiral *n* **1** *geometry* a plane curve formed by a point winding about a fixed point at an ever-increasing distance from it **2** something that follows a winding course or that has a twisting form **3** *econ* a continuous upward or downward movement in economic activity or prices ▷ *adj* **4** having the shape of a spiral: *a spiral staircase* ▷ *vb* **-ralling, -ralled** *or US* **-raling, -raled 5** to follow a spiral course or be in the shape of a spiral **6** to increase or decrease with steady acceleration: *oil prices continue to spiral* [Latin *spira* a coil] ▷ **spirally** *adv*

spire *n* the tall cone-shaped structure on the top of a church [Old English *spīr* blade]

Spires *n* the English name for **Speyer**

spirit¹ *n* **1** the nonphysical aspect of a person concerned with profound thoughts and emotions **2** the nonphysical part of a person believed to live on after death **3** a shared feeling: *a spirit of fun and adventure* **4** mood or attitude: *fighting spirit* **5** a person's character or temperament: *the indomitable spirit of the Polish people* **6** liveliness shown in what a person does: *it has been undertaken with spirit* **7** the feelings that motivate someone to survive in difficult times or live according to his or her beliefs: *someone had broken his spirit* **8 spirits** one's emotional state: *in good spirits* **9** the way in which something, such as a law or an agreement, was intended to be interpreted: *they acted against the spirit of the treaty* **10** a supernatural being, such as a ghost ▷ *vb* **-riting, -rited** **11 spirit away** *or* **off** to carry (someone or something) off mysteriously or secretly [Latin *spiritus* breath, spirit]

spirit² *n* **1** (*usually pl*) distilled alcoholic liquor, such as whisky or gin **2** *chem* **a** a solution of ethanol obtained by distillation **b** the essence of a substance, extracted as a liquid by distillation **3** *pharmacol* a solution of a volatile oil in alcohol [special use of SPIRIT¹]

spirited *adj* **1** showing liveliness or courage: *a spirited rendition of Schubert's ninth symphony; a spirited defence of the government's policy* **2** characterized by the mood as specified: *high-spirited; mean-spirited*

spirit gum *n* a solution of gum in ether, used to stick on false hair

spirit lamp *n* a lamp that burns methylated or other spirits instead of oil

spirit level *n* a device for checking whether a surface is level, consisting of a block of wood or metal containing a tube partially filled with liquid set so that the air bubble in it rests between two marks on the tube when the block is level

spiritual *adj* **1** relating to a person's beliefs as opposed to his or her physical or material needs **2** relating to religious beliefs **3 one's spiritual home** the place where one feels one belongs **4** Also called: **Negro spiritual** a type of religious folk song originally sung by Black slaves in the American South ▷ **spirituality** *n* ▷ **spiritually** *adv*

spiritualism *n* the belief that the spirits of the dead can communicate with the living ▷ **spiritualist** *n*

spirituous *adj* containing alcohol

spirogyra (spire-oh-jire-a) *n* a green freshwater plant that floats on the surface of ponds and ditches [Greek *speira* a coil + *guros* a circle]

spit¹ *vb* **spitting, spat** *or* **spit 1** to force saliva out of one's mouth **2** to force (something) out of one's mouth: *he spat tobacco into an old coffee can* **3** (of a fire or hot fat) to throw out sparks or particles violently and explosively **4** to rain very lightly **5** (often foll. by *out*) to say (words) in a violent angry way **6** to show contempt or hatred by spitting **7 spit it out!** *informal* a command given to someone to say what is on his or her mind ▷ *n* **8** same as **spittle 9** *informal, chiefly Brit* same as **spitting image** [Old English *spittan*]

spit² *n* **1** a pointed rod for skewering and roasting meat over a fire or in an oven **2** a long narrow strip of land jutting out into the sea [Old English *spitu*]

spit and polish *n informal* thorough cleaning and polishing

spite *n* **1** deliberate nastiness **2 in spite of** regardless of: *he loved them in spite of their shortcomings* ▷ *vb* **spiting, spited 3** to annoy (someone) deliberately: *it was to spite his father* [variant of DESPITE] ▷ **spiteful** *adj* ▷ **spitefully** *adv*

spitfire *n* a woman or girl who is easily angered

Spithead *n* an extensive anchorage between the mainland of England and the Isle of Wight, off Portsmouth

Spitsbergen *n* another name for **Svalbard**

spitting image *n informal* a person who looks very like someone else [from *spit* likeness]

spittle *n* the fluid that is produced in the mouth; saliva [Old English *spætl* saliva]

spittoon *n* a bowl for people to spit into

spitz *n* a stockily built dog with a pointed face, erect ears, and a tightly curled tail [from German]

Spitz *n* Mark. born 1950, US swimmer, who won seven gold medals at the 1972 Olympic Games

spiv *n Brit, Austral and NZ slang* a smartly dressed man who makes a living by underhand dealings; black marketeer [dialect *spiving* smart]

splash *vb* **1** to scatter (liquid) on (something) **2** to cause (liquid) to fall on or (of liquid) to be scattered in drops **3** to display (a photograph or story) prominently in a newspaper ▷ *n* **4** a splashing sound **5** an amount splashed **6** a patch (of colour or light) **7 make a splash** *informal* to attract a lot of attention **8** a small amount of liquid added to a drink [alteration of *plash*]

splashdown *n* **1** the landing of a spacecraft on water at the end of a flight ▷ *vb* **splash down 2** (of a spacecraft) to make a splashdown

splash out *vb* to spend a lot of money on a treat or luxury: *she planned to splash out on a good holiday*

splatter *vb* **1** to splash (something or someone) with small blobs ▷ *n* **2** a splash of liquid

splay *vb* to spread out, with ends spreading out in different directions: *her hair splayed over the pillow* [short for DISPLAY]

splayfooted *adj* same as **flat-footed**

spleen *n* **1** a spongy organ near the stomach, which filters bacteria from the blood **2** spitefulness or bad temper: *we vent our spleen on drug barons* [Greek *splēn*]

spleenwort *n* a kind of fern that grows on walls

splendid *adj* **1** very good: *a splendid match* **2** beautiful or impressive: *a splendid palace* [Latin *splendere* to shine] ▷ **splendidly** *adv*

splendiferous *adj facetious, old-fashioned* grand in appearance [Latin *splendor* radiance + *ferre* to bring]

splendour *or US* **splendor** *n* **1** beauty or impressiveness **2 splendours** the impressive or beautiful features of something: *the splendours of the Emperor's Palace*

splenetic *adj literary* irritable or bad-tempered [from SPLEEN]

splice *vb* **splicing, spliced 1** to join up the trimmed ends of (two pieces of wire, film, or tape) with an adhesive material **2** to join (two ropes) by interweaving the ends **3 get spliced** *informal* to get married [probably from Middle Dutch *splissen*]

splint *n* a piece of wood used to support a broken bone [Middle Low German *splinte*]

splinter *n* **1** a small thin sharp piece broken off, esp. from wood ▷ *vb* **2** to break or be broken into small sharp fragments [Middle Dutch]

splinter group *n* a number of members of an organization, who split from the main body and form an independent group of their own

split *vb* **splitting, split 1** to break or cause (something) to break into separate pieces **2** to separate (a piece) or (of a piece) to be separated from (something) **3** (of a group) to separate into smaller groups, through disagreement: *the council is split over rent increases* **4** (often foll. by *up*) to divide (something) among two or more people **5** *slang* to leave a place **6 split on** *slang* to betray; inform on: *he didn't tell tales or split on him* **7 split one's sides** to laugh a great deal ▷ *n* **8** a gap or rift caused by splitting **9** a division in a group or the smaller group resulting from such a division **10** a dessert of sliced fruit and ice cream, covered with whipped cream and nuts: *banana split* ▷ *adj* **11** divided (esp. in opinion, etc.) **12** having a split or splits: *split ends* ▶ See also **splits, split up** [Middle Dutch *splitten*]

Split *n* a port and resort in W Croatia on the Adriatic: remains of the palace of Diocletian (295–305). Pop: 188 000 (2005 est). Italian name: **Spalato**

split infinitive *n* (in English grammar) an infinitive used with another word between *to* and the verb, as in *to really finish it*. This is often thought to be incorrect

USAGE The traditional rule against placing an adverb between *to* and its verb is gradually disappearing. Although it is true that a split infinitive may result in a clumsy sentence (*he decided to firmly and definitively deal with the problem*), this is not enough to justify the absolute condemnation that this practice has attracted. Indeed, very often the most natural position of the adverb is between *to* and the verb (*he decided to really try next time*) and to change it would result in an artificial and awkward construction (*he decided really to try next time*). The current view is therefore that the split infinitive is not a grammatical error. Nevertheless, many writers prefer to avoid splitting infinitives in formal written English, since readers with a more traditional point of view are likely to interpret this type of construction as incorrect.

split-level *adj* (of a house or room) having the floor level of one part about half a storey above that of the other

split pea *n* a pea dried and split and used in soups or as a vegetable

split personality *n* **1** the tendency to change mood very quickly **2** a disorder in which a person's mind appears to have separated into two or more personalities

splits *n* (in gymnastics and dancing) the act of sitting with both legs outstretched, pointing in opposite directions, and at right angles to the body

split second *n* **1** an extremely short period of time; instant ▷ *adj* **split-second 2** made in an extremely short time: *split-second timing*

splitting *adj* (of a headache) extremely painful

split up *vb* **1** to separate (something) into parts; divide **2** (of a couple) to end a relationship or marriage **3** (of a group of people) to go off in different directions ▷ *n* **split-up 4** the act of separating

splodge *or US* **splotch** *n* **1** a large uneven spot or stain ▷ *vb* **splodging, splodged 2** to mark (something) with a splodge or splodges [alteration of earlier *splotch*]

splurge *n* **1** a bout of spending money extravagantly ▷ *vb* **splurging, splurged 2** (foll. by *on*) to spend (money)

extravagantly: *they rushed out to splurge their pocket money on chocolate* [origin unknown]

splutter *vb* **1** to spit out (something) from the mouth when choking or laughing **2** to say (words) with spitting sounds when choking or in a rage **3** to throw out or to be thrown out explosively: *sparks spluttered from the fire* ▷ *n* **4** the act or noise of spluttering [variant of SPUTTER]

Spock *n* Benjamin, known as Dr Spock. 1903–98, US paediatrician, noted for his influential work *The Common Sense Book of Baby and Child Care* (1946), which challenged traditional notions of child care, advocating a more permissive approach

Spode *n* china or porcelain manufactured by the English potter Josiah Spode or his company

spoil *vb* **spoiling, spoilt** *or* **spoiled 1** to make (something) less valuable, beautiful, or useful **2** to weaken the character of (a child) by giving it all it wants **3** (of oneself) to indulge one's desires: *go ahead and spoil yourself* **4** (of food) to become unfit for consumption **5 be spoiling for** to have an aggressive urge for: *he is spoiling for a fight* ▶ See also **spoils** [Latin *spolium* booty]

spoilage *n* an amount of material that has been spoilt: *new ways to reduce spoilage*

spoiler *n* **1** a device fitted to an aircraft wing to increase drag and reduce lift **2** a similar device fitted to a car

spoils *pl n* **1** valuables seized during war **2** the rewards and benefits of having political power

spoilsport *n* *informal* a person who spoils the enjoyment of other people

Spokane *n* a city in E Washington: commercial centre of an agricultural region. Pop: 196 624 (2003 est)

spoke¹ *vb* the past tense of **speak**

spoke² *n* **1** a bar joining the centre of a wheel to the rim **2 put a spoke in someone's wheel** *Brit and NZ* to create a difficulty for someone [Old English *spāca*]

spoken *vb* **1** the past participle of **speak** ▷ *adj* **2** said in speech: *spoken commands* **3** having speech as specified: *quiet-spoken* **4 spoken for** engaged or reserved

spokesman, spokesperson *or* **spokeswoman** *n, pl* **-men, -people** *or* **-women** a person chosen to speak on behalf of another person or group

spoliation *n* the act or an instance of plundering: *the spoliation of the countryside* [Latin *spoliare* to plunder]

spondee *n* *prosody* a metrical foot of two long syllables [Greek *spondē* ritual offering of drink] **> spondaic** *adj*

sponge *n* **1** a sea animal with a porous absorbent elastic skeleton **2** the skeleton of a sponge, or a piece of artificial sponge, used for bathing or cleaning **3** a soft absorbent material like a sponge **4** Also called: **sponge cake** a light cake made of eggs, sugar, and flour **5** Also called: **sponge pudding** *Brit and Austral* a light steamed or baked spongy pudding **6** a rub with a wet sponge ▷ *vb* **sponging, sponged 7** (often foll. by *down*) to clean (something) by rubbing it with a wet sponge **8** to remove (marks) by rubbing them with a wet sponge **9** (usually foll. by *off* or *on*) to get (something) from someone by taking advantage of his or her generosity: *stop sponging off the rest of us!* [Greek *spongia*] **> spongy** *adj*

sponge bag *n* a small waterproof bag for holding toiletries when travelling

sponger *n* *informal, disparaging* a person who lives off other people by continually taking advantage of their generosity

sponsor *n* **1** a person or group that promotes another person or group in an activity or the activity itself, either for profit or for charity **2** *chiefly US and Canad* a person or firm that pays the costs of a radio or television programme in return for advertising time **3** a person who presents and supports a proposal or suggestion **4** a person who makes certain promises on behalf of a person being baptized and takes responsibility for his or her Christian upbringing ▷ *vb* **5** to act as a sponsor for (someone or something) [Latin *spondere* to promise solemnly] **>** **sponsored** adj **> sponsorship** n

spontaneous adj **1** not planned or arranged; impulsive: a spontaneous celebration **2** occurring through natural processes without outside influence: a spontaneous explosion [Latin sponte voluntarily] **> spontaneously** adv **> spontaneity** n

spontaneous combustion n chem the bursting into flame of a substance as a result of internal oxidation processes, without heat from an outside source

spoof informal n **1** an imitation of a film, TV programme, etc., that exaggerates in an amusing way the most memorable features of the original **2** a good-humoured trick or deception **>** vb **3** to fool (a person) with a trick or deception [made-up word]

spook informal n **1** a ghost **2** a strange and frightening person **>** vb **3** to frighten: it was the wind that spooked her [Dutch] **> spooky** adj

spool n a cylinder around which film, thread, or tape can be wound [Germanic]

spoon n **1** a small shallow bowl attached to a handle, used for eating, stirring, or serving food **2** **be born with a silver spoon in one's mouth** to be born into a very rich and respected family **>** vb **3** to scoop up (food or liquid) with a spoon **4** old-fashioned, slang to kiss and cuddle [Old English spōn splinter]

spoonbill n a wading bird with a long flat bill

spoonerism n the accidental changing over of the first sounds of a pair of words, often with an amusing result, such as hush my brat for brush my hat [after W. A. Spooner, clergyman]

spoon-feed vb **-feeding, -fed 1** to feed (someone, usually a baby) using a spoon **2** to give (someone) too much help

spoor n the trail of an animal [Afrikaans]

Sporades pl n two groups of Greek islands in the Aegean: the **Northern Sporades**, lying northeast of Euboea, and the **Southern Sporades**, which include the Dodecanese and lie off the SW coast of Turkey

sporadic adj happening at irregular intervals; intermittent: sporadic bursts of gunfire [Greek sporas scattered] **> sporadically** adv

spore n a reproductive body, produced by nonflowering plants and bacteria, that develops into a new individual [Greek spora a sowing]

sporran n a large pouch worn hanging from a belt in front of the kilt in Scottish Highland dress [Scottish Gaelic sporan purse]

sport n **1** an activity for exercise, pleasure, or competition: your favourite sport **2** such activities collectively: the minister for sport **3** the enjoyment gained from a pastime: just for the sport of it **4** playful or good-humoured joking: I only did it in sport **5** informal a person who accepts defeat or teasing cheerfully **6** **make sport of someone** to make fun of someone **7** an animal or plant that is very different from others of the same species, usually because of a mutation **8** Austral and NZ informal a term of address between males **>** vb **9** informal to wear proudly: sporting a pair of bright yellow shorts **▶** See also **sports** [variant of Middle English disporten to disport]

sporting adj **1** of sport **2** behaving in a fair and decent way **3** **a sporting chance** reasonable likelihood of happening: a sporting chance of winning

sportive adj playful or high-spirited

sports adj **1** of or used in sports: a sports arena **>** n **2** Also called: **sports day** Brit a meeting held at a school or college for competitions in athletic events

sports car n a fast car with a low body and usually seating only two people

sportscast n US a programme of sports news **> sportscaster** n

sports jacket n a man's casual jacket, usually made of tweed. Also called: **sports coat** US, Austral and NZ

sportsman n, pl **-men 1** a man who plays sports **2** a person who plays by the rules, and accepts defeat

with good humour **> sportsman-like** adj **> sportsmanship** n

sportsperson n a person who plays sports

sportswear n clothes worn for sport or outdoor leisure wear

sportswoman n, pl **-women** a woman who plays sports

sporty adj **sportier, sportiest 1** (of a person) interested in sport **2** (of clothes) suitable for sport **3** (of a car) small and fast **> sportily** adv **> sportiness** n

spot n **1** a small mark on a surface, which has a different colour or texture from its surroundings **2** a location: a spot where they could sit **3** a small mark or pimple on the skin **4** a feature of something that has the attribute mentioned: the one bright spot in his whole day; the high spot of our trip **5** informal a small amount: a spot of bother **6** informal an awkward situation: I'm sometimes in a spot **7** a part of a show, TV programme, etc., reserved for a specific performer or type of entertainment **8** short for **spotlight** (1) **9** **in a tight spot** in a difficult situation **10** **knock spots off someone** to be much better than someone **11** **on the spot a** immediately: he decided on the spot to fly down **b** at the place in question: the expert weapons man on the spot **c** in an awkward situation: the British government will be put on the spot **12** **soft spot** a special affection for someone: a soft spot for older men **>** vb **spotting, spotted 13** to see (something or someone) suddenly **14** to put stains or spots on (something) **15** (of some fabrics) to be prone to marking by liquids: silk spots easily **16** to take note of (the numbers of trains or planes observed) **17** (of scouts, agents, etc.) to look out for (talented but unknown actors, sportspersons, etc.) **18** Brit to rain lightly [from German]

spot check n a quick unplanned inspection

spotless adj **1** perfectly clean **2** free from moral flaws: a spotless reputation **> spotlessly** adv

spotlight n **1** a powerful light focused so as to light up a small area **2** **the spotlight** the centre of attention: the spotlight moved to the president **>** vb **-lighting, -lit** or **-lighted 3** to direct a spotlight on (something) **4** to focus attention on (something)

spot-on adj informal absolutely correct; very accurate: they're spot-on in terms of style

spotted adj **1** having a pattern of spots **2** marked with stains

spotted dick n Brit suet pudding containing dried fruit

spotter n a person whose hobby is watching for and noting numbers or types of trains or planes

spotty adj **-tier, -tiest 1** covered with spots or pimples **2** not consistent; irregular in quality: a rather spotty performance **> spottiness** n

spouse n a person's partner in marriage [Latin sponsus, sponsa betrothed man or woman]

spout vb **1** (of a liquid or flames) to pour out in a stream or jet **2** informal to talk about (something) in a boring way or without much thought **>** n **3** a projecting tube or lip for pouring liquids **4** a stream or jet of liquid: a spout of steaming water **5** **up the spout** slang **a** ruined or lost: the motor industry is up the spout **b** pregnant [Middle English spouten]

spouting n NZ **a** a rainwater downpipe on the outside of a building **b** such pipes collectively

sprain vb **1** to injure (a joint) by a sudden twist **>** n **2** this injury, which causes swelling and temporary disability [origin unknown]

sprang vb a past tense of **spring**

sprat n a small edible fish like a herring [Old English sprott]

Spratly Islands pl n a widely-scattered group of uninhabited islets and reefs in the S South China Sea, the subject of territorial claims wholly or in part by six neighbouring nations. Compare **Paracel Islands**

sprawl vb **1** to sit or lie with one's arms and legs spread out **2** to spread out untidily over a large area: the pulp mill sprawled over the narrow flats **>** n **3** the part of a city or town that has not been planned and spreads out untidily over a large area: *the huge Los Angeles sprawl* [Old English *spreawlian*] **> sprawling** *adj*

spray¹ *n* **1** fine drops of a liquid **2 a** a liquid under pressure designed to be discharged in fine drops from an aerosol or atomizer: *hair spray* **b** the aerosol or atomizer itself **3** a number of small objects flying through the air: *a spray of bullets* ▷ *vb* **4** to scatter in fine drops **5** to squirt (a liquid) from an aerosol or atomizer **6** to cover with a spray: *spray the crops* [Middle Dutch *sprāien*] **> sprayer** *n*

spray² *n* **1** a sprig or branch with buds, leaves, flowers, or berries **2** an ornament or design like this [Germanic]

spray gun *n* a device for spraying fine drops of paint, etc.

spread *vb* **spreading, spread** **1** to open out or unfold to the fullest width: *spread the material out* **2** to extend over a larger expanse: *the subsequent unrest spread countrywide* **3** to apply as a coating: *spread the paste evenly over your skin* **4** to be displayed to its fullest extent: *the shining bay spread out below* **5** to send or be sent out in all directions or to many people: *the news spread quickly; the sandflies that spread the disease* **6** to distribute or be distributed evenly: *we were advised to spread the workload over the whole year* **7 spread out** (of people) to increase the distance between one another (to widen the scope of a search, for example) ▷ *n* **8** a spreading; distribution, dispersion, or expansion: *the spread of higher education* **9** *informal* a large meal **10** *informal* the wingspan of an aircraft or bird **11** *informal, chiefly US and Canad* a ranch or other large area of land **12** a soft food which can be spread: *cheese spread* **13** two facing pages in a book or magazine **14** a widening of the hips and waist: *middle-age spread* [Old English *sprēdan*]

spread-eagled *adj* with arms and legs outstretched

spreadsheet *n* a computer program for manipulating figures, used for financial planning

spree *n* a session of overindulgence, usually in drinking or spending money [Scots *spreath* plundered cattle]

sprig *n* **1** a shoot, twig, or sprout **2** an ornamental device like this **3** *NZ* a stud on the sole of a soccer or rugby boot [Germanic] **> sprigged** *adj*

sprightly *adj* **-lier, -liest** lively and active [obsolete *spright*, variant of SPRITE] **> sprightliness** *n*

spring *vb* **springing, sprang** *or* **sprung, sprung** **1** to jump suddenly upwards or forwards **2** to return or be returned into natural shape from a forced position by elasticity: *the coil sprang back* **3** to cause (something) to happen unexpectedly: *the national coach sprang a surprise* **4** (usually foll. by *from*) to originate; be descended: *this motivation springs from their inborn curiosity; Truman sprang from ordinary people* **5** (often foll. by *up*) to come into being or appear suddenly: *new courses will spring up* **6** to provide (something, such as a mattress) with springs **7** *informal* to arrange the escape of (someone) from prison ▷ *n* **8** the season between winter and summer **9** a leap or jump **10** a coil which can be compressed, stretched, or bent and then return to its original shape when released **11** a natural pool forming the source of a stream **12** elasticity [Old English *springan*] **> springlike** *adj*

spring balance *or especially US* **spring scale** *n* a device that indicates the weight of an object by the extension of a spring to which the object is attached

springboard *n* **1** a flexible board used to gain height or momentum in diving or gymnastics **2** anything that makes it possible for an activity to begin: *the meeting acted as a springboard for future negotiations*

springbok *n, pl* **-bok** *or* **-boks** **1** a S African antelope which moves in leaps **2** a person who has represented S Africa in a national sports team [Afrikaans]

spring chicken *n* **1** a young chicken, which is tender for cooking **2** he *or* she is no spring chicken *informal* he or she is no longer young

spring-clean *vb* **1** to clean (a house) thoroughly, traditionally at the end of winter ▷ *n* **2** an instance of this **> spring-cleaning** *n*

Springfield *n* **1** a city in S Massachusetts, on the Connecticut River: the site of the US arsenal and armoury (1794–1968), which developed the Springfield and Garand rifles. Pop: 152 157 (2003 est) **2** a city in SW Missouri. Pop: 150 867 (2003 est) **3** a city in central Illinois, capital of the state: the home and burial place of Abraham Lincoln. Pop: 113 586 (2003 est)

spring onion *n* a small onion with a tiny bulb and long green leaves, eaten in salads

spring roll *n* an Oriental dish consisting of a savoury mixture rolled in a thin pancake and fried

Springs *n* a city in E South Africa: developed around a coal mine established in 1885 and later became a major world gold-mining centre, now with uranium extraction. Pop: 80 776 (2001)

Springsteen *n* Bruce. born 1949, US rock singer, songwriter, and guitarist. His albums include *Born to Run* (1975), *Darkness on the Edge of Town* (1978), *Born in the USA* (1984), *The Ghost of Tom Joad* (1995), *The Rising* (2002), *Magic* (2007), and *Wrecking Ball* (2012)

spring tide *n* either of the two tides at or just after new moon and full moon: the greatest rise and fall in tidal level

springtime *n* the season of spring

springy *adj* **springier, springiest** (of an object) having the quality of returning to its original shape after being pressed or pulled **> springiness** *n*

sprinkle *vb* **-kling, -kled** **1** to scatter (liquid or powder) in tiny drops over (something) **2** to distribute over (something): *a dozen mud huts sprinkled around it* [probably from Middle Dutch *sprenkelen*] **> sprinkler** *n*

sprinkling *n* a small quantity or amount: *a sprinkling of diamonds*

sprint *n* **1** *athletics* **a** a short race run at top speed **b** a fast run at the end of a longer race **2** any quick run ▷ *vb* **3** to run or cycle a short distance at top speed [Scandinavian] **> sprinter** *n*

sprit *n nautical* a light pole set diagonally across a sail to extend it [Old English *sprēot*]

sprite *n* **1** (in folklore) a fairy or elf **2** an icon in a computer game which can be manoeuvred around the screen [Latin *spiritus* spirit]

spritsail *n nautical* a sail mounted on a sprit

spritzer *n* a tall drink of wine and soda water [German *spritzen* to splash]

sprocket *n* **1** Also called: **sprocket wheel** a wheel with teeth on the rim, that drives or is driven by a chain **2** a cylindrical wheel with teeth on one or both rims for pulling film through a camera or projector [origin unknown]

sprout *vb* **1** (of a plant or seed) to produce (new leaves or shoots) **2** (often foll. by *up*) to begin to grow or develop ▷ *n* **3** a new shoot or bud **4** same as **Brussels sprout** [Old English *sprūtan*]

spruce¹ *n* **1** an evergreen pyramid-shaped tree with needle-like leaves **2** the light-coloured wood of this tree [obsolete *Spruce* Prussia]

spruce² *adj* neat and smart [perhaps from *Spruce leather*; see SPRUCE¹]

spruce up *vb* **sprucing, spruced** to make neat and smart

sprung *vb* a past tense and the past participle of **spring**

spry *adj* **spryer, spryest** *or* **sprier, spriest** active and lively; nimble [origin unknown]

spud *n informal* a potato [obsolete *spudde* short knife]

Spud Island *n* a slang name for **Prince Edward Island**

spume *n literary* **1** foam or froth on the sea ▷ *vb* **spuming, spumed 2** (of the sea) to foam or froth [Latin *spuma*]

spun *vb* **1** the past of **spin** ▷ *adj* **2** made by spinning: *spun sugar; spun silk*

spunk *n* **1** *old-fashioned, informal* courage or spirit **2** *chiefly Brit considered vulgar, slang* semen **3** *Austral and NZ informal* a sexually attractive person, esp. a male [Scottish Gaelic *spong* tinder, sponge] **> spunky** *adj*

spur *n* **1** an incentive to get something done **2** a sharp spiked wheel on the heel of a rider's boot used to urge the horse on **3** a sharp horny part sticking out from a cock's leg **4** a ridge sticking out from a mountain side **5 on the spur of the moment** suddenly and without planning; on impulse **6 win one's spurs** to prove one's ability ▷ *vb* **spurring, spurred 7** (often foll. by *on*) to encourage (someone) [Old English *spura*]

spurge *n* a plant with milky sap and small flowers [Latin *expurgare* to cleanse]

spurious *adj* not genuine or real [Latin *spurius* of illegitimate birth]

spurn *vb* to reject (a person or thing) with contempt [Old English *spurnan*]

spurt *vb* **1** to gush or cause (something) to gush out in a sudden powerful stream or jet **2** to make a sudden effort ▷ *n* **3** a short burst of activity, speed, or energy **4** a sudden powerful stream or jet [origin unknown]

sputnik *n* a Russian artificial satellite [Russian, literally: fellow traveller]

sputter *vb, n* same as **splutter** [Dutch *sputteren*, imitative]

sputum *n, pl* **-ta** saliva, usually mixed with mucus [Latin]

spy *n, pl* **spies 1** a person employed to find out secret information about other countries or organizations **2** a person who secretly keeps watch on others ▷ *vb* **spies, spying, spied 3** (foll. by *on*) to keep a secret watch on someone **4** to work as a spy **5** to catch sight of (someone or something); notice [Old French *espier*]

spyglass *n* a small telescope

spy out *vb* to discover (something) secretly

spyware *n computers* software surreptitiously installed in a computer via the internet to gather and transmit information about the user

sq. square

Sq. 1 Squadron **2** (in place names) Square

SQL *n* a computer programming language that is used for database management [structured query language]

Sqn. Ldr. squadron leader

squab *n, pl* **squabs** *or* **squab** a young bird yet to leave the nest [probably Germanic]

squabble *vb* **-bling, -bled 1** to quarrel over a small matter ▷ *n* **2** a petty quarrel [probably Scandinavian]

squad *n* **1** the smallest military formation, usually a dozen soldiers **2** any small group of people working together: *the fraud squad* **3** *sport* a number of players from which a team is to be selected [Old French *esquade*]

squadron *n* the basic unit of an air force [Italian *squadrone* soldiers drawn up in square formation]

squadron leader *n* a fairly senior commissioned officer in the air force; the rank above flight lieutenant

squalid *adj* **1** dirty, untidy, and in bad condition **2** unpleasant, selfish, and often dishonest: *this squalid affair* [Latin *squalidus*]

squall¹ *n* a sudden strong wind or short violent storm [perhaps a special use of SQUALL²]

squall² *vb* **1** to cry noisily; yell ▷ *n* **2** a noisy cry or yell [probably Scandinavian]

squalor *n* **1** dirty, poor, and untidy physical conditions **2** the condition of being squalid [Latin]

squander *vb* to waste (money or resources) [origin unknown]

square *n* **1** a geometric figure with four equal sides and four right angles **2** anything of this shape **3** an open area in a town bordered by buildings or streets **4** *maths* the number produced when a number is multiplied by itself: *9 is the square of 3, written 3²* **5** *informal* a person who is dull or unfashionable **6 go back to square one** to return to the start because of failure or lack of progress ▷ *adj* **7** being a square in shape **8 a** having the same area as that of a square with sides of a specified length: *2,500 square metres of hillside* **b** denoting a square having a specified length on each side: *a cell of only four square metres* **9** straight or level: *I don't think that painting is square* **10** fair and honest: *a square deal* **11** *informal* dull or unfashionable

12 having all debts or accounts settled: *if I give you 50 pence, then we'll be square* **13 all square** on equal terms; even in score **14 square peg in a round hole** *informal* a misfit ▷ *vb* **squaring, squared 15** *maths* to multiply (a number or quantity) by itself **16** to position so as to be straight or level: *bravely he squared his shoulders* **17** to settle (a debt or account) **18** to level the score in (a game) **19** to be or cause to be consistent: *it would not have squared with her image* ▷ *adv* **20** *informal* same as **squarely**. See also **square off, square up** [Old French *esquare*]

square-bashing *n Brit military slang* marching and other drill on a parade ground

square bracket *n* either of a pair of characters <b/>, used to separate a section of writing or printing from the main text

square dance *n* a country dance in which the couples are arranged in squares

square leg *n cricket* a fielding position on the on side, at right angles to the batsman

squarely *adv* **1** directly; straight: *he looked her squarely in the eye* **2** in an honest and frank way: *you should face squarely anything that worries you*

square meal *n* a meal which is large enough to leave the eater feeling full: *we gave him his first square meal in days*

square off *vb* to stand up as if ready to start boxing or fighting

square-rigged *adj nautical* having sails set at right angles to the keel

square root *n* a number that when multiplied by itself gives a given number: *the square roots of 4 are 2 and -2*

square up *vb* **1** to settle bills or debts **2 square up to** to prepare to confront (a problem or a person)

squash¹ *vb* **1** to press or squeeze (something) so as to flatten it **2** to overcome (a difficult situation), often with force **3 squash in** *or* **into** to push or force (oneself or a thing) into a confined space **4** to humiliate (someone) with a sarcastic reply ▷ *n* **5** *Brit and Austral* a drink made from fruit juice or fruit syrup diluted with water **6** a crowd of people in a confined space **7** Also called: **squash rackets** a game for two players played in an enclosed court with a small rubber ball and long-handled rackets [Old French *esquasser*]

squash² *n, pl* **squashes** *or* **squash** *chiefly US and Canad* a marrow-like vegetable [from a Native American language]

squashy *adj* **squashier, squashiest** soft and easily squashed

squat *vb* **squatting, squatted 1** to crouch with the knees bent and the weight on the feet **2** *law* to occupy an unused building to which one has no legal right ▷ *adj* **3** short and thick ▷ *n* **4** a building occupied by squatters [Old French *esquater*]

squatter *n* an illegal occupier of an unused building

squaw *n offensive* a Native American woman of N America [from a Native American language]

squawk *n* **1** a loud harsh cry, esp. one made by a bird **2** *informal* a loud complaint ▷ *vb* **3** to make a squawk [imitative]

squeak *n* **1** a short high-pitched cry or sound **2 a narrow squeak** *informal* a narrow escape or success ▷ *vb* **3** to make a squeak **4 squeak through** *or* **by** to pass (an examination), but only just [probably Scandinavian] ❭ **squeaky** *adj* ❭ **squeakiness** *n*

squeaky clean *adj* **1** (of hair) washed so clean that wet strands squeak when rubbed **2** completely clean **3** *informal, disparaging* (of a person) cultivating a virtuous and wholesome image

squeal *n* **1** a long high-pitched yelp ▷ *vb* **2** to make a squeal **3** *slang* to inform on someone to the police **4** *informal, chiefly Brit* to complain loudly [Middle English *squelen*, imitative] ❭ **squealer** *n*

squeamish *adj* easily shocked or upset by unpleasant sights or events [Anglo-French *escoymous*]

squeegee *n* a tool with a rubber blade used for wiping

S

away excess water from a surface [probably imitative]

squeeze *vb* **squeezing, squeezed 1** to grip or press (something) firmly **2** to crush or press (something) so as to extract (a liquid): *squeeze the tomato and strain the juice; freshly squeezed lemon juice* **3** to push (oneself or a thing) into a confined space **4** to hug (someone) closely **5** to obtain (something) by great effort or force: *to squeeze the last dollar out of every deal* ▷ *n* **6** a squeezing **7** a hug **8** a crush of people in a confined space **9** *chiefly Brit and NZ* a restriction on borrowing made by a government to control price inflation **10** an amount extracted by squeezing: *a squeeze of lime* **11 put the squeeze on someone** *informal* to put pressure on someone in order to obtain something [Old English *cwȳsan*]

squelch *vb* **1** to make a wet sucking noise, such as by walking through mud **2** *informal* to silence (someone) with a sarcastic or wounding reply ▷ *n* **3** a squelching sound [imitative] ❯ **squelchy** *adj*

squib *n* **1** a firework that burns with a hissing noise before exploding **2 damp squib** something expected to be exciting or successful but turning out to be a disappointment [probably imitative of a light explosion]

squid *n, pl* **squid** *or* **squids** a sea creature with ten tentacles and a long soft body [origin unknown]

squiffy *adj* **-fier, -fiest** *Brit informal* slightly drunk: *a bit squiffy* [origin unknown]

squiggle *n* a wavy line [perhaps SQUIRM + WIGGLE] ❯ **squiggly** *adj*

squill *n* a Mediterranean plant of the lily family [Greek *skilla*]

squint *vb* **1** to have eyes which face in different directions **2** to glance sideways ▷ *n* **3** an eye disorder in which one or both eyes turn inwards or outwards from the nose **4** *informal* a quick look; glance: *take a squint at the map* ▷ *adj* **5** *informal* not straight; crooked [short for *asquint*]

squire *n* **1** a country gentleman in England, usually the main landowner in a country community **2** *informal, chiefly Brit* a term of address used by one man to another **3** *history* a knight's young attendant ▷ *vb* **squiring, squired 4** *old-fashioned* (of a man) to escort (a woman) [Old French *esquier*]

squirm *vb* **1** to wriggle **2** to feel embarrassed or guilty ▷ *n* **3** a wriggling movement [imitative]

squirrel *n* a small bushy-tailed animal that lives in trees [Greek *skiouros*, from *skia* shadow + *oura* tail]

squirt *vb* **1** to force (a liquid) or (of a liquid) to be forced out of a narrow opening **2** to cover or spatter (a person or thing) with liquid in this way ▷ *n* **3** a jet of liquid **4** a squirting **5** *informal* a small or insignificant person [imitative]

squish *vb* **1** to crush (something) with a soft squelching sound **2** to make a squelching sound ▷ *n* **3** a soft squelching sound [imitative] ❯ **squishy** *adj*

Sr 1 (after a name) senior **2** Señor **3** *chem* strontium

Srbija *n* a transliteration of the Serbian name for **Serbia**

Sri Lanka *n* a republic in S Asia, occupying the island of Ceylon: settled by the Sinhalese from S India in about 550 BC; became a British colony 1802; gained independence in 1948, becoming a republic within the Commonwealth in 1972. Exports include tea, cocoa, cinnamon, and copra. Official languages: Sinhalese and Tamil; English is also widely spoken. Religion: Hinayana Buddhist majority. Currency: Sri Lanka rupee. Capital: Colombo (administrative), Sri Jayewardenepura Kotte (legislative). Parts of the coast suffered badly in the Indian Ocean tsunami of December 2004. Pop: 21 675 648 (2013 est.). Area: 65 610 sq km (25 332 sq miles). Official name (since 1978): **Democratic Socialist Republic of Sri Lanka.** Former name (until 1972): **Ceylon**

Sri Lankan *adj* **1** of or relating to Sri Lanka or its inhabitants ▷ *n* **2** a native or inhabitant of Sri Lanka

Srinagar *n* a city in N India, the summer capital of the

state of Jammu and Kashmir, at an altitude of 1600 m (5250 ft) on the Jhelum River: seat of the University of Jammu and Kashmir (1948). Pop: 894 940 (2001)

SRN (formerly in Britain) State Registered Nurse

SS 1 an organization in the Nazi party that provided Hitler's bodyguard, security forces, and concentration-camp guards **2** steamship [(sense 1) German *Schutzstaffel* protection squad]

SSL *computers* secure sockets layer: a protocol for encrypting and transmitting sensitive data securely over the internet

St 1 Saint **2** Street

st. stone

SSR (formerly) Soviet Socialist Republic

Sta (in the names of places or churches) Saint (female) [Italian *Santa*]

stab *vb* **stabbing, stabbed 1** to pierce with a sharp pointed instrument **2** (often foll. by *at*) to make a thrust (at); jab **3 stab someone in the back** to do harm to someone by betraying him or her ▷ *n* **4** a stabbing **5** a sudden, usually unpleasant, sensation: *a stab of jealousy* **6** *informal* an attempt: *you've got to have a stab at it* **7 stab in the back** an act of betrayal that harms a person [Middle English *stabbe* stab wound] ❯ **stabbing** *n*

stability *n* the quality of being stable: *the security and stability of married life*

stabilize *or* **-lise** *vb* **-lizing, -lized** *or* **-lising, -lised** to make or become stable or more stable ❯ **stabilization** *or* **-lisation** *n*

stabilizer *or* **-liser** *n* **1** a device for stabilizing a child's bicycle, an aircraft, or a ship **2** a substance added to food to preserve its texture

stable¹ *n* **1** a building where horses are kept **2** an organization that breeds and trains racehorses **3** an organization that manages or trains several entertainers or athletes ▷ *vb* **-bling, -bled 4** to put or keep (a horse) in a stable [Latin *stabulum* shed]

stable² *adj* **1** steady in position or balance; firm **2** lasting and not likely to experience any sudden changes: *a stable environment* **3** having a calm personality; not moody **4** *physics* (of an elementary particle) not subject to decay **5** *chem* (of a chemical compound) not easily decomposed [Latin *stabilis* steady]

Stabroek *n* the former name (until 1812) of **Georgetown**

staccato (stak-ah-toe) *adj* **1** *music* (of notes) short and separate **2** consisting of short abrupt sounds: *the staccato sound of high-heels on the stairs* ▷ *adv* **3** in a staccato manner [Italian]

stack *n* **1** a pile of things, one on top of the other **2** a large neat pile of hay or straw **3 stacks** a large amount: *there's still stacks for us to do* **4** same as **chimney stack, smokestack 5** an area in a computer memory for temporary storage ▷ *vb* **6** to place (things) in a stack **7** to load or fill (something) up with piles of objects: *Henry was watching her stack the dishwasher* **8** to control (a number of aircraft) waiting to land at an airport so that each flies at a different altitude [Old Norse *stakkr* haystack]

stack up *vb* to compare with someone or something else: *how does this stack up against what you have?*

stadium *n, pl* **-diums** *or* **-dia** a large sports arena with tiered rows of seats for spectators [Greek *stadion*]

Staël *n* **Madame de.** full name *Baronne Anne Louise Germaine* (née *Necker*) *de Staël-Holstein*. 1766–1817, French writer, whose works, esp. *De l'Allemagne* (1810), anticipated French romanticism

staff *n, pl for senses 1 and 2* **staffs,** *for senses 3 and 4* **staffs** *or* **staves 1** the people employed in a company, school, or organization **2** *military* the officers appointed to assist a commander **3** a stick with some special use, such as a walking stick or an emblem of authority **4** *music* a set of five horizontal lines on which music is written and which, along with a clef, indicates pitch ▷ *vb* **5** to provide (a company, school, or organization) with a staff [Old English *stæf*]

Staffa *n* an island in W Scotland, in the Inner Hebrides west of Mull: site of Fingal's Cave

staff nurse *n* (in Britain) a qualified nurse ranking just below a sister or charge nurse

Stafford[1] *n* a market town in central England, administrative centre of Staffordshire. Pop: 63 681 (2001)

Stafford[2] *n* Sir Edward William. 1819–1901, New Zealand statesman, born in Scotland: prime minister of New Zealand (1856–61; 1865–69; 1872)

Staffordshire *n* a county of central England: lowlands in the east and south rise to the Pennine uplands in the north; important in the history of industry, coal and iron having been worked at least as early as the 13th century. In 1974 the industrial area in the S passed to the new county of West Midlands; Stoke-on-Trent became an independent unitary authority in 1997. Administrative centre: Stafford. Pop (excluding Stoke-on-Trent): 811 000 (2003 est). Area (excluding Stoke-on-Trent): 2624 sq km (1013 sq miles)

Staffs Staffordshire

staff sergeant *n military* a noncommissioned officer in an army or in the US Air Force or Marine Corps

stag *n* the adult male of a deer [Old English *stagga*]

stag beetle *n* a beetle with large branched jaws

stage *n* **1** a step or period of development, growth, or progress **2** the platform in a theatre where actors perform **3** **the stage** the theatre as a profession **4** the scene of an event or action **5** a part of a journey: *the last stage of his tour around France* **6** short for **stagecoach** **7** *Brit and Austral* a division of a bus route for which there is a fixed fare ▷ *vb* **staging, staged** **8** to present (a dramatic production) on stage: *to stage 'Hamlet'* **9** to organize and carry out (an event) [Old French *estage* position]

stagecoach *n* a large four-wheeled horse-drawn vehicle formerly used to carry passengers and mail on a regular route

stage direction *n* an instruction to an actor, written into the script of a play

stage door *n* a door at a theatre leading backstage

stage fright *n* feelings of fear and nervousness felt by a person about to appear in front of an audience

stagehand *n* a person who sets the stage and moves props in a theatre

stage-manage *vb* **-managing, -managed** to arrange (an event) from behind the scenes

stage manager *n* a person who supervises the stage arrangements of a production at a theatre

stage-struck *adj* having a great desire to act

stage whisper *n* **1** a loud whisper from an actor, intended to be heard by the audience **2** any loud whisper that is intended to be overheard

stagflation *n* inflation combined with stagnant or falling output and employment [STAGNATION + INFLATION]

stagger *vb* **1** to walk unsteadily **2** to amaze or shock (someone): *it staggered her that there was any liaison between them* **3** to arrange (events) so as not to happen at the same time: *staggered elections* ▷ *n* **4** a staggering [dialect *stacker*] **›** **staggering** *adj* **›** **staggeringly** *adv*

staggers *n* a disease of horses and other domestic animals that causes staggering

staging *n* a temporary support used in building

Stagira *n* an ancient city on the coast of Chalcidice in Macedonia: the birthplace of Aristotle

Stagirite *n* **1** an inhabitant or native of Stagira **2** an epithet of Aristotle

stagnant *adj* **1** (of water) stale from not moving **2** unsuccessful or dull from lack of change or development [Latin *stagnans*]

stagnate *vb* **-nating, -nated** to become inactive or unchanging: *people in old age only stagnate when they have no interests* **›** **stagnation** *n*

stag night *or* **stag party** *n* a party for men only, held for a man who is about to get married

stagy *or US* **stagey** *adj* **stagier, stagiest** too theatrical or dramatic

staid *adj* serious, rather dull, and old-fashioned in behaviour or appearance [obsolete past participle of STAY]

stain *vb* **1** to discolour (something) with marks that are not easily removed **2** to dye (something) with a lasting pigment ▷ *n* **3** a mark or discoloration that is not easily removed **4** an incident in someone's life that has damaged his or her reputation: *a stain on his character* **5** a liquid used to penetrate the surface of a material, such as wood, and colour it without covering up the surface or grain [Middle English *steynen*]

stained glass *n* glass that has been coloured for artistic purposes

Stainer *n* Sir John. 1840–1901, British composer and organist, noted for his sacred music, esp. the oratorio *The Crucifixion* (1887)

Staines *n* a town in SE England, in N Surrey on the River Thames. Pop: 50 538 (2001)

stainless steel *n* a type of steel that does not rust, as it contains large amounts of chromium

stair *n* **1** one step in a flight of stairs **2** a series of steps: *he fled down the back stair* ▶ See also **stairs** [Old English *stæger*]

staircase *n* a flight of stairs, usually with a handrail or banisters

stairs *pl n* a flight of steps going from one level to another, usually indoors

stairway *n* a staircase

stairwell *n* a vertical shaft in a building that contains a staircase

stake[1] *n* **1** a stick or metal bar driven into the ground as part of a fence or as a support or marker **2** **be burned at the stake** to be executed by being tied to a stake in the centre of a pile of wood that is then set on fire ▷ *vb* **staking, staked** **3** to lay (a claim) to land or rights **4** to support (something, such as a plant) with a stake [Old English *staca* stake, post]

stake[2] *n* **1** the money that a player must risk in order to take part in a gambling game or make a bet **2** an interest, usually financial, held in something: *a 50% stake in a new consortium* **3** **at stake** at risk **4** **stakes a** the money that a player has available for gambling **b** a prize in a race or contest **c** a horse race in which all owners of competing horses contribute to the prize ▷ *vb* **staking, staked** **5** to risk (something, such as money) on a result **6** to give financial support to (a business) [origin unknown]

Staked Plain *n* another name for the **Llano Estacado**

stakeholder *n* **1** a person or group not owning shares in an enterprise but having an interest in its operations, such as the employees, customers, or local community ▷ *adj* **2** relating to policies intended to allow people to participate in decisions made by enterprises in which they have a stake: *stakeholder economy*

stakeout *n* **1** *slang, chiefly US and Canad* a police surveillance of an area or house ▷ *vb* **stake out 2** *slang, chiefly US and Canad* to keep (an area or house) under surveillance **3** to surround (a piece of land) with stakes

stalactite *n* an icicle-shaped mass of calcium carbonate hanging from the roof of a cave: formed by continually dripping water [Greek *stalaktos* dripping]

stalagmite *n* a large pointed mass of calcium carbonate sticking up from the floor of a cave: formed by continually dripping water from a stalactite [Greek *stalagmos* dripping]

stale *adj* **1** (esp. of food) no longer fresh, having being kept too long **2** (of air) stagnant and having an unpleasant smell **3** lacking in enthusiasm or ideas through overwork or lack of variety **4** uninteresting from having been done or seen too many times: *such achievements now seem stale today* **5** no longer new: *her war had become stale news* [probably from Old French *estale* motionless] **›** **staleness** *n*

stalemate *n* **1** a chess position in which any of a player's moves would place his king in check: in this position the game ends in a draw **2** a situation in which further action by two opposing forces is impossible or will not achieve anything; deadlock [obsolete *stale* standing place + CHECKMATE]

Stalin¹ *n* **1** Also called: **Stalino**. a former name (from after the Revolution until 1961) of **Donetsk 2** the former name (1950–61) of **Braşov 3** the former name (1949–56) of **Varna**

Stalin² *n* Joseph. original name *Iosif Vissarionovich Dzhugashvili*. 1879–1953, Soviet leader; general secretary of the Communist Party of the Soviet Union (1922–53). He succeeded Lenin as head of the party and created a totalitarian state, crushing all opposition, esp. in the great purges of 1934–37. He instigated rapid industrialization and the collectivization of agriculture and established the Soviet Union as a world power

Stalinabad *n* the former name (1929–61) of **Dushanbe**

Stalingrad *n* the former name (1925–61) of **Volgograd**

Stalinism *n* the policies associated with Joseph Stalin, general secretary of the Communist Party of the Soviet Union 1922–53, which resulted in rapid industrialization, state terror as a means of political control, and the abolition of collective leadership > **Stalinist** *n, adj*

Stalinogrod *n* the former name (1953–56) for **Katowice**

Stalin Peak *n* a former name for Ismoil Somoni

Stalinsk *n* the former name (1932–61) of **Novokuznetsk**

stalk¹ *n* **1** the main stem of a plant **2** a stem that joins a leaf or flower to the main stem of a plant [probably from Old English *stalu* upright piece of wood]

stalk² *vb* **1** to follow (an animal or person) quietly and secretly in order to catch or kill them **2** to pursue persistently and, sometimes, attack (a person with whom one is obsessed, often a celebrity) **3** to spread over (a place) in a menacing way: *danger stalked the streets* **4** to walk in an angry, arrogant, or stiff way [Old English *bestealcian*] > **stalker** *n*

stalking-horse *n* something or someone used to hide a true purpose; pretext

stall¹ *n* **1** a small stand for the display and sale of goods **2** a compartment in a stable or shed for a single animal **3** any small room or compartment: *a shower stall* ▷ *vb* **4** to stop (a motor vehicle or its engine) or (of a motor vehicle or its engine) to stop, by incorrect use of the clutch or incorrect adjustment of the fuel mixture [Old English *steall* a place for standing]

stall² *vb* to employ delaying tactics towards (someone); be evasive [Anglo-French *estale* bird used as a decoy]

stallion *n* an uncastrated male horse, usually used for breeding [Old French *estalon*]

stalls *n* **1** the seats on the ground floor of a theatre or cinema **2** (in a church) a row of seats, divided by armrests or a small screen, for the choir or clergy

stalwart (stawl-wart) *adj* **1** strong and sturdy **2** loyal and reliable ▷ *n* **3** a hard-working and loyal supporter: *local party stalwarts* [Old English *stǣlwirthe* serviceable]

Stambul *or* **Stamboul** *n* the old part of Istanbul, Turkey, south of the Golden Horn: the site of ancient Byzantium; sometimes used as a name for the whole city

stamen *n* the part of a flower that produces pollen [Latin: the warp in an upright loom]

Stamford *n* a city in SW Connecticut, on Long Island Sound: major chemical research laboratories. Pop: 120 107 (2003 est)

Stamford Bridge *n* a village in N England, east of York: site of a battle (1066) in which King Harold of England defeated his brother Tostig and King Harald Hardrada of Norway, three weeks before the Battle of Hastings

stamina *n* energy and strength sustained while performing an activity over a long time [Latin: the threads of life spun out by the Fates, hence energy]

stammer *vb* **1** to speak or say (something) with involuntary pauses or repetition, as a result of a speech disorder or through fear or nervousness ▷ *n* **2** a speech disorder characterized by involuntary repetitions and pauses [Old English *stamerian*]

stamp *n* **1** a printed paper label attached to a piece of mail to show that the required postage has been paid **2** a token issued by a shop or business after a purchase that can be saved and exchanged for other goods sold by that shop or business **3** the action or an act of stamping **4** an instrument for stamping a design or words **5** a design, device, or mark that has been stamped **6** a characteristic feature: *the stamp of inevitability* **7** *Brit informal* a national insurance contribution, formerly recorded by a stamp on an official card **8** type or class: *men of his stamp* ▷ *vb* **9** (often foll. by *on*) to bring (one's foot) down heavily **10** to walk with heavy or noisy footsteps **11** to characterize: *a performance that stamped him as a star* **12** stamp on to subdue or restrain: *all of which have stamped on dissent* **13** to impress or mark (a pattern or sign) on **14** to mark (something) with an official seal or device **15** to have a strong effect on: *a picture vividly stamped on memory* **16** to stick a stamp on (an envelope or parcel) [probably from Old English *stampian*]

stampede *n* **1** a sudden rush of frightened animals or of a crowd ▷ *vb* **-peding, -peded 2** to run away in a stampede [Spanish *estampar* to stamp]

stamping ground *n* a favourite meeting place

stamp out *vb* **1** to put an end to (something) by force; suppress: *an attempt to stamp out democracy* **2** to put out by stamping: *I stamped out my cigarette*

stance *n* **1** an attitude towards a particular matter: *a tough stance in the trade talks* **2** the manner and position in which a person stands **3** *sport* the position taken when about to play the ball [Latin *stare* to stand]

stanch (stahnch) *vb* same as **staunch²** [Old French *estanchier*]

stanchion *n* a vertical pole or bar used as a support [Old French *estanchon*]

stand *vb* **standing, stood 1** to be upright **2** to rise to an upright position **3** to place (something) upright **4** to be situated: *the property stands in a prime position* **5** to have a specified height when standing: *the structure stands sixty feet above the river* **6** to be in a specified position: *Turkey stands to gain handsomely* **7** to be in a specified state or condition: *how he stands in comparison to others* **8** to remain unchanged or valid: *the Conservatives were forced to let much of the legislation stand* **9** stand at (of a score or an account) to be in the specified position: *now the total stands at nine* **10** to tolerate or bear: *Christopher can't stand him* **11** to survive: *stand the test of time* **12** (often foll. by *for*) to be a candidate: *to stand for president* **13** *informal* to buy: *to stand someone a drink* **14** stand a chance to have a chance of succeeding **15** stand one's ground to maintain a stance or position in the face of opposition **16** stand trial to be tried in a law court ▷ *n* **17** a stall or counter selling goods: *the hot dog stand* **18** a structure at a sports ground where people can sit or stand **19** the act or an instance of standing **20** a firmly held opinion: *its firm stand on sanctions* **21** *US and Austral* a place in a law court where a witness stands **22** a rack on which coats and hats may be hung **23** a base, support, or piece of furniture in or on which articles may be held or stored: *a guitar stand* **24** an effort to defend oneself or one's beliefs against attack or criticism: *a last stand against superior forces* **25** *cricket* a long period at the wicket by two batsmen ▶ See also **stand by, stand down**, etc. [Old English *standan*]

standard *n* **1** a level of quality: *cuisine of a high standard* **2** an accepted example of something against which others are judged or measured: *the work was good by any standard* **3** a moral principle of behaviour **4** a flag of a nation or cause **5** an upright pole or beam used as a support: *a lamp standard* **6** a song that has remained popular for many years ▷ *adj* **7** of a usual, medium, or accepted kind: *a standard cost* **8** of recognized authority: *a* standard reference book **9** denoting pronunciations or grammar regarded as correct and acceptable by educated native speakers [Old French *estandart* gathering place]

standard assessment tasks *pl n* (in Britain) national standardized tests for assessing school pupils

standard-bearer *n* **1** a leader of a movement or party **2** a person who carries a flag in battle or in a march

Standard English *n linguistics* the style of English that is regarded as correct and acceptable by educated native speakers

standard gauge *n* **1** a railway track with a distance of 56½ inches (1.435 m) between the lines: used on most railways ▷ *adj* **standard-gauge 2** denoting a railway with a standard gauge

Standard Grade *n* **1** (in Scotland) an examination designed to test skills and application of knowledge, replacing the O Grade **2** a pass in an examination at this level

standardize *or* **-dise** *vb* **-dizing, -dized** *or* **-dising, -dised** to make (things) standard: *to standardize the preparation process* ▷ **standardization** *or* **-disation** *n*

standard lamp *n* a tall electric lamp that has a shade and stands on a base

standard of living *n* the level of comfort and wealth of a person, group, or country

standard time *n* the official local time of a region or country determined by the distance from Greenwich of a line of longitude passing through the area

stand by *vb* **1** to be available and ready to act if needed: *stand by for firing* **2** to be present as an onlooker or without taking any action: *the military police stood by watching idly* **3** to be faithful to: *his wife will stand by him* ▷ *n* **stand-by 4** a person or thing that is ready for use or can be relied on in an emergency **5** **on stand-by** ready for action or use ▷ *adj* **stand-by 6** not booked in advance but subject to availability: *stand-by planes*

stand down *vb* to resign or withdraw, often in favour of another

stand for *vb* **1** to represent: *AIDS stands for Acquired Immune Deficiency Syndrome* **2** to support and represent (an idea or a belief): *to stand for liberty and truth* **3** *informal* to tolerate or bear: *I won't stand for this!*

stand in *vb* **1** to act as a substitute: *she stood in for her father* ▷ *n* **stand-in 2** a person who acts as a substitute for another

standing *adj* **1** permanent, fixed, or lasting: *it was a standing joke* **2** used to stand in or on: *standing room only* **3** *athletics* (of a jump or the start of a race) begun from a standing position ▷ *n* **4** social or financial status or reputation: *her international standing* **5** duration: *a friendship of at least ten years' standing*

standing order *n* **1** an instruction to a bank to pay a fixed amount to a person or organization at regular intervals **2** a rule or order governing the procedure of an organization

Standish *n* Myles (or Miles). ?1584–1656, English military leader of the Pilgrim Fathers at Plymouth, New England

standoff *n* **1** *US and Canad* the act or an instance of standing off or apart **2** a deadlock or stalemate ▷ *vb* **stand off 3** to stay at a distance

standoffish *adj* behaving in a formal and unfriendly way

stand out *vb* **1** to be more impressive or important than others of the same kind: *his passing ability stood out in this game* **2** to be noticeable because of looking different: *her long fair hair made her stand out from the rest* **3** to refuse to agree or comply: *a hero who stood out against foreign domination*

standpipe *n chiefly Brit* a temporary vertical pipe installed in a street and supplying water when household water supplies are cut off

standpoint *n* a point of view from which a matter is considered

standstill *n* a complete stoppage or halt: *all traffic came to a standstill*

stand to *vb* **1** *military* to take up positions in order to defend against attack **2** **stand to reason** to be obvious or logical: *it stands to reason you will play better*

stand up *vb* **1** to rise to one's feet **2** *informal* to fail to keep a date with (a boyfriend or girlfriend): *sometimes he would stand me up* **3** to be accepted as satisfactory or true: *the decision would not stand up in court* **4** **stand up for** to support or defend **5** **stand up to a** to confront or resist (someone) bravely **b** to withstand and endure (something, such as criticism) ▷ *adj* **stand-up 6** (of a comedian) telling jokes alone to an audience **7** done while standing: *a stand-up breakfast* **8** (of a fight or row) angry and unrestrained ▷ *n* **stand-up 9** stand-up comedy or a stand-up comedian

Stanford *n* Sir Charles (Villiers). 1852–1924, Anglo-Irish composer and conductor, who as a teacher at the Royal College of Music had much influence on the succeeding generation of composers: noted esp. for his church music, oratorios, and cantatas

Stanhope *n* **1** Charles, 3rd Earl. 1753–1816, British radical politician and scientist. His inventions included two calculating machines, a microscope lens, and a stereotyping machine **2** his grandfather, James, 1st Earl. 1673–1721, British soldier and statesman; George I's chief minister (1717–21). He fought under Marlborough in the War of the Spanish Succession (1701–14) and negotiated the Triple Alliance with France and Holland (1717)

Stanislavsky *or* **Stanislavski** *n* Konstantin. 1863–1938, Russian actor and director, cofounder of the Moscow Art Theatre (1897). He is famous for his theory of acting, known as the Method, which directs the actor to find the truth within himself about the role he is playing

Stanisław *or* **Stanislaus** *n* Saint. 1030–79, the patron saint of Poland. As Bishop of Cracow (1072–79) he excommunicated King Bolesław II, who arranged his murder. Feast day: May 11

Stanisław II *n* surnamed *Poniatowski*. 1732–98, the last king of Poland (1764–95), during whose reign Poland was repeatedly invaded and partitioned (1772, 1791, 1795) by its neighbours: abdicated

stank *vb* a past tense of **stink**

Stanley¹ *n* **1** the capital of the Falkland Islands, in NE East Falkland Island: scene of fighting in the Falklands War of 1982. Pop: 1989 (2001) **2** a town in NE England, in N Durham. Pop: 19 072 (2001) **3** Mount Stanley a mountain in central Africa, between Uganda and the Democratic Republic of Congo: the highest peak of the Ruwenzori range. Height: 5109 m (16 763 ft). Congolese name: Ngaliema Mountain

Stanley² *n* Sir Henry Morton. 1841–1904, British explorer and journalist, who led an expedition to Africa in search of Livingstone, whom he found on Nov 10, 1871. He led three further expeditions in Africa (1874–77; 1879–84; 1887–89) and was instrumental in securing Belgian sovereignty over the Congo Free State

Stanley Falls *pl n* the former name of **Boyoma Falls**

Stanley knife *n trademark* a type of knife with a thick metal handle with a short, very sharp, replaceable blade [after F. T. *Stanley*, businessman]

Stanley Pool *n* a lake between the Democratic Republic of Congo and Congo-Brazzaville, formed by a widening of the River Congo. Area: 829 sq km (320 sq miles). Congolese name: Pool Malebo

Stanleyville *n* the former name (until 1966) of **Kisangani**

Stannaries *n* the Stannaries a tin-mining district of Devon and Cornwall, formerly under the jurisdiction of special courts

Stanovoi Range *or* **Stanovoy Range** *n* a mountain range in SE Russia; forms part of the watershed between rivers flowing to the Arctic and the Pacific. Highest peak: Mount Skalisty, 2482 m (8143 ft)

Stans¹ *n* a town in central Switzerland, capital of

S

Nidwalden demicanton, 11 km (7 miles) southeast of Lucerne: tourist centre. Pop: 6983 (2000)

Stans² *pl n* **the Stans** a region in Central Asia that consists of Kazakhstan, Kyrgyzstan, Uzbekistan, and Tajikistan

stanza *n prosody* a verse of a poem [Italian: halting place]

staphylococcus (staff-ill-oh-**kok**-uss) *n*, *pl* **-cocci** (-**kok**-eye) a bacterium occurring in clusters and including many species that cause disease [Greek *staphulē* bunch of grapes + *kokkos* berry]

staple¹ *n* **1** a short length of wire bent into a square U-shape, used to fasten papers or secure things ▷ *vb* **-pling, -pled 2** to secure (things) with staples [Old English *stapol* prop]

staple² *adj* **1** of prime importance; principal: *the staple diet of a country* ▷ *n* **2** something that forms a main part of the product, consumption, or trade of a region **3** a main constituent of anything: *the personal reflections which make up the staple of the book* [Middle Dutch *stapel* warehouse]

stapler *n* a device used to fasten things together with a staple

star *n* **1** a planet or meteor visible in the clear night sky as a point of light **2** a hot gaseous mass, such as the sun, that radiates energy as heat and light, or in some cases as radio waves and X-rays. Related adjectives: **astral, sidereal, stellar 3 stars** same as **horoscope** (1) **4** an emblem with five or more radiating points, often used as a symbol of rank or an award: *the RAC awarded the hotel three stars* **5** same as **asterisk 6** a famous person from the sports, acting, or music professions **7 see stars** to see flashes of light after a blow on the head ▷ *vb* **starring, starred 8** to feature (an actor or actress) or (of an actor or actress) to be featured as a star: *he's starred in dozens of films* **9** to mark (something) with a star or stars [Old English *steorra*]

Stara Zagora *n* a city in central Bulgaria: ceded to Bulgaria by Turkey in 1877. Pop: 163 000 (2005 est)

starboard *n* **1** the right side of an aeroplane or ship when facing forwards ▷ *adj* **2** of or on the starboard [Old English *stēorbord*, literally: steering side]

starch *n* **1** a carbohydrate forming the main food element in bread, potatoes, and rice: in solution with water it is used to stiffen fabric **2** food containing a large amount of starch ▷ *vb* **3** to stiffen (cloth) with starch [Old English *sterced* stiffened]

starchy *adj* **starchier, starchiest 1** of or containing starch **2** (of a person's behaviour) very formal and humourless

star-crossed *adj* (of lovers) destined to misfortune

stardom *n* the status of a star in the entertainment or sport world

stare *vb* **staring, stared 1** (often foll. by *at*) to look (at) for a long time **2 stare one in the face** to be glaringly obvious ▷ *n* **3** a long fixed look [Old English *starian*]

starfish *n*, *pl* **-fish** or **-fishes** a star-shaped sea creature with a flat body and five limbs

star fruit *n* same as **carambola**

stargazer *n informal* an astrologer ▷ **stargazing** *n*

stark *adj* **1** harsh, unpleasant, and plain: *a stark choice* **2** grim, desolate, and lacking any beautiful features: *the stark landscapes* **3** utter; absolute: *in stark contrast* ▷ *adv* **4** completely: *stark staring bonkers* [Old English *stearc* stiff] ▷ **starkly** *adv* ▷ **starkness** *n*

Stark *n* **1** Dame Freya (**Madeline**). 1893–1993, British traveller and writer, whose many books include *The Southern Gates of Arabia* (1936), *Beyond Euphrates* (1951), and *The Journey's Echo* (1963) **2** Johannes. 1874–1957, German physicist, who discovered the splitting of the lines of a spectrum when the source of light is subjected to a strong electrostatic field (**Stark effect**, 1913): Nobel prize for physics 1919

Starkey *n* David. born 1945, British historian and broadcaster, noted for his books and television series on the Tudor period

stark-naked *adj* completely naked. Also (informal): **starkers** [Middle English *stert naket*, literally: tail naked]

starlet *n* a young actress who has the potential to become a star

starlight *n* the light that comes from the stars

starling *n* a common songbird with shiny blackish feathers and a short tail [Old English *stærlinc*]

Starling *n* Ernest Henry. 1866–1927, British physiologist, who contributed greatly to the understanding of many bodily functions and with William Bayliss (1860–1924) discovered the hormone secretin (1902)

starlit *adj* lit by starlight

Star of David *n* a symbol of Judaism, consisting of a star formed by two interlaced equilateral triangles

Starr *n* **1** (Myra) Belle. 1848–89, US outlaw, a famous rustler of horses and cattle **2** Ringo, original name *Richard Starkey*. born 1940, British rock musician; drummer (1962–70) with the Beatles

starry *adj* **-rier, -riest 1** (of a sky or night) full of or lit by stars **2** of or like a star or stars: *a starry cast*

starry-eyed *adj* full of unrealistic hopes and dreams; naive

Stars and Stripes *n* the national flag of the United States of America

star sign *n astrol* the sign of the zodiac under which a person was born

Star-Spangled Banner *n* **1** the national anthem of the United States of America **2** same as **Stars and Stripes**

star-studded *adj* featuring many well-known performers: *a star-studded premiere*

start *vb* **1** to begin (something or to do something); come or cause to come into being: *to start a war*; *this conflict started years ago* **2** to set or be set in motion: *he started the van* **3** to make a sudden involuntary movement from fright or surprise; jump **4** to establish; set up: *to start a state lottery* **5** to support (someone) in the first part of a career or activity **6** *Brit informal* to begin quarrelling or causing a disturbance: *don't start with me* **7 to start with** in the first place ▷ *n* **8** the first part of something **9** the place or time at which something begins **10** a signal to begin, such as in a race **11** a lead or advantage, either in time or distance, in a competitive activity: *he had an hour's start on me* **12** a slight involuntary movement from fright or surprise: *I awoke with a start* **13** an opportunity to enter a career or begin a project **14 for a start** in the first place ▶ See also **start off, start on**, etc. [Old English *styrtan*]

starter *n* **1** *chiefly Brit* the first course of a meal **2 for starters** *slang* in the first place **3** a device for starting an internal-combustion engine **4** a person who signals the start of a race **5** a competitor in a race or contest **6 under starter's orders** (of competitors in a race) waiting for the signal to start

startle *vb* **-tling, -tled** to slightly surprise or frighten (someone) [Old English *steartlian* to kick, struggle] ▷ **startling** *adj*

start off *vb* **1** to set out on a journey **2** to be or make the first step in (an activity): *beginners should start off with a walking programme* **3** to cause (a person) to do something, such as laugh

start on *vb Brit informal* to pick a quarrel with: *they started on me*

start out *vb* **1** to set out on a journey **2** to take the first steps in a career or on a course of action: *I started out as a beautician*; *it started out as a joke*

start up *vb* **1** to come or cause (something, such as a business) to come into being; found **2** to set (something) in motion: *she started up the car*

starve *vb* **starving, starved 1** to die from lack of food **2** to deliberately prevent (a person or animal) from having any food **3** *informal* to be very hungry: *we're both starving* **4 starve of** to deprive (someone) of something needed: *the heart is starved of oxygen* **5 starve into** to force (someone) into a specified state by starving: *an attempt to starve him into submission* [Old English *steorfan* to die] ▷ **starvation** *n*

Star Wars *n* (in the US) a proposed system of artificial satellites armed with lasers to destroy enemy missiles in space

stash *informal vb* **1** (often foll. by *away*) *informal* to store (money or valuables) in a secret place for safekeeping ▷ *n* **2** a secret store, usually of illegal drugs, or the place where this is hidden [origin unknown]

state *n* **1** the condition or circumstances of a person or thing **2** a sovereign political power or community **3** the territory of such a community **4** the sphere of power in such a community: *matters of state* **5** (often cap) one of a number of areas or communities having their own governments and forming a federation under a sovereign government, such as in the US or Australia **6** (often cap) the government, civil service, and armed forces **7** in a state *informal* in an emotional or very worried condition **8** lie in state (of a body) to be placed on public view before burial **9** state of affairs circumstances or condition: *this wonderful state of affairs* **10** grand and luxurious lifestyle, as enjoyed by royalty, aristocrats, or the wealthy: *living in state* ▷ *adj* **11** controlled or financed by a state: *state ownership* **12** of or concerning the State: *state secrets* **13** involving ceremony: *a state visit* ▷ *vb* **stating, stated 14** to express (something) in words [Latin *stare* to stand]

State Enrolled Nurse *n* (in Britain) a nurse who has completed a two-year training course

statehouse *n* NZ a rented house built by the government

stateless *adj* not belonging to any country: *stateless refugees*

stately *adj* **-lier, -liest** having a dignified, impressive, and graceful appearance or manner: *the Rolls-Royce approached him at a stately speed* ▷ **stateliness** *n*

stately home *n* Brit a large old mansion, usually one open to the public

statement *n* **1** something stated, usually a formal prepared announcement or reply **2** *law* a declaration of matters of fact **3** an account prepared by a bank at regular intervals for a client to show all credits and debits and the balance at the end of the period **4** an account containing a summary of bills or invoices and showing the total amount due **5** the act of stating

Staten Island *n* an island in SE New York State, in New York Harbor: a borough of New York city; heavy industry. Pop: 443 728 (2000). Area: 155 sq km (60 sq miles)

state of the art *n* **1** the current level of knowledge and development achieved in a technology, science, or art ▷ *adj* **state-of-the-art 2** the most recent and therefore considered the best; up-to-the-minute: *state-of-the-art computers*

State Registered Nurse *n* (formerly in Britain) a nurse who has completed an extensive three-year training course

stateroom *n* **1** a private room on a ship **2** chiefly Brit a large room in a palace, etc., used on ceremonial occasions

States *pl n* the States *informal* the United States of America

state school *n* a school funded by the state, in which education is free

statesman *n, pl* **-men** an experienced and respected political leader ▷ **statesmanship** *n*

static *adj* **1** not active, changing, or moving; stationary **2** *physics* (of a weight, force, or pressure) acting but causing no movement **3** *physics* of forces that do not produce movement ▷ *n* **4** hissing or crackling or a speckled picture caused by interference in the reception of radio or television transmissions **5** electric sparks or crackling produced by friction [Greek *statikos* causing to stand]

static electricity *n* same as **static** (5)

statics *n* the branch of mechanics concerned with the forces producing a state of equilibrium

statin *n* med any of several drugs that inhibit the production of cholesterol

station *n* **1** a place along a route or line at which a bus or train stops to pick up passengers or goods **2** the headquarters of an organization such as the police or fire service **3** a building with special equipment for some particular purpose: *power station; a filling station* **4** a television or radio channel **5** *military* a place of duty **6** position in society: *he had ideas above his station* **7** Austral and NZ a large sheep or cattle farm **8** the place or position where a person is assigned to stand: *every man stood at his station* ▷ *vb* **9** to assign (someone) to a station [Latin *statio* a standing still]

stationary *adj* not moving: *a line of stationary traffic* [Latin *stationarius*]

> **USAGE** Avoid confusion with **stationery**.

stationer *n* a person or shop selling stationery [Medieval Latin *stationarius* a person having a regular station, hence a shopkeeper]

stationery *n* writing materials, such as paper, envelopes, and pens

> **USAGE** Avoid confusion with **stationary**.

stationmaster *n* the senior official in charge of a railway station

Stations of the Cross *pl n* RC Church **1** a series of 14 crosses with pictures or carvings, arranged around the walls of a church, to commemorate 14 stages in Christ's journey to Calvary **2** a series of 14 prayers relating to each of these stages

station wagon *n* US, Austral and NZ an estate car

statistic *n* a numerical fact collected and classified systematically ▷ **statistical** *adj* ▷ **statistically** *adv* ▷ **statistician** *n*

statistics *n* **1** the science dealing with the collection, classification, and interpretation of numerical information ▷ *pl n* **2** numerical information which has been collected, classified, and interpreted [originally: science dealing with facts of a state, from New Latin *statisticus* concerning state affairs]

Statius *n* **Publius Papinius.** ?45–96 AD, Roman poet; author of the collection *Silvae* and of two epics, *Thebais* and the unfinished *Achilleis*

statuary *n* statues collectively

statue *n* a sculpture of a human or animal figure, usually life-size or larger [Latin *statuere* to set up]

Statue of Liberty *n* a monumental statue personifying liberty, in New York Harbor, on Liberty Island: a gift from France, erected in 1885. Official name: **Liberty Enlightening the World**

statuesque (stat-yoo-**esk**) *adj* (of a woman) tall and well-proportioned; like a classical statue

statuette *n* a small statue

stature *n* **1** the height and size of a person **2** the reputation of a person or their achievements: *a batsman of international stature* **3** moral or intellectual distinction [Latin *stare* to stand]

status *n* **1** a person's position in society **2** the esteem in which people hold a person: *priests feel they have lost some of their status in society* **3** the legal or official standing or classification of a person or country: *the status of refugees; Ireland's non-aligned status* **4** degree of importance [Latin: posture]

status quo *n* the existing state of affairs [literally: the state in which]

status symbol *n* a possession regarded as a mark of social position or wealth

statute *n* **1** a law made by a government and expressed in a formal document **2** a permanent rule made by a company or other institution [Latin *statuere* to set up, decree]

statute law *n* **1** a law made by a government **2** such laws collectively

statutory *adj* **1** required or authorized by law **2** (of an offence) declared by law to be punishable

Stauffenberg *n* Claus, Graf von. 1907–44, German army officer, who tried to assassinate Hitler (1944). He and his fellow conspirators were executed

staunch¹ *adj* strong and loyal: *a staunch supporter* [Old French *estanche*] **⟩ staunchly** *adv*

staunch² *or* **stanch** *vb* to stop the flow of (blood) from someone's body

Stavanger *n* a port in SW Norway: canning and shipbuilding industries. Pop: 112 405 (2004 est)

stave *n* **1** one of the long strips of wood joined together to form a barrel or bucket **2** a stick carried as a symbol of office **3** a verse of a poem **4** *music* same as **staff** ▷ *vb* **staving, stove 5 stave in** to burst a hole in (something) [from *staves*, plural of STAFF]

stave off *vb* **staving, staved** to delay (something) for a short time: *to stave off political rebellion*

staves *n* a plural of **staff, stave**

Stavropol *n* **1** a city in SW Russia: founded as a fortress in 1777. Pop: 362 000 (2005 est). Former name (1940–44): **Voroshilovsk 2** the former name (until 1964) of **Togliatti**

stay¹ *vb* **1** to continue or remain in a place, position, or condition: *to stay away; to stay inside* **2** to lodge as a guest or visitor temporarily: *we stay with friends* **3** *Scot and S African* to reside permanently; live **4** to endure (something testing or difficult): *you have stayed the course this long* ▷ *n* **5** the period spent in one place **6** the postponement of an order of a court of law: *a stay of execution* [Old French *ester*]

stay² *n* something that supports or steadies something, such as a prop or buttress [Old French *estaye*]

stay³ *n* a rope or chain supporting a ship's mast or funnel [Old English *stæg*]

stay-at-home *adj* **1** (of a person) enjoying a quiet, settled, and unadventurous life ▷ *n* **2** a stay-at-home person

staycation (stay-kay-shun) *n informal* a holiday in which leisure activities are pursued while staying at one's own home [from *stay¹* + (VA)CATION]

staying power *n* endurance to complete something undertaken; stamina

stays *pl n* old-fashioned corsets with bones in them

staysail *n* a sail fastened on a stay

STD 1 sexually transmitted disease **2** *Brit, Austral and S African* subscriber trunk dialling **3** *NZ* subscriber toll dialling

STD code *n Brit* a code preceding a local telephone number, allowing a caller to dial direct without the operator's help [*s(ubscriber) t(runk) d(ialling)*]

stead *n* **1 stand someone in good stead** to be useful to someone in the future **2** *rare* the function or position that should be taken by another: *I cannot let you rule in my stead* [Old English *stede*]

Stead *n* Christina (Ellen). 1902–83, Australian novelist. Her works include *Seven Poor Men of Sydney* (1934), *The Man who Loved Children* (1940), and *Cotters' England* (1966)

steadfast *adj* dedicated and unwavering **⟩ steadfastly** *adv* **⟩ steadfastness** *n*

steady *adj* **steadier, steadiest 1** firm and not shaking **2** without much change or variation: *we're on a steady course* **3** continuous: *a steady decline* **4** not easily excited; sober **5** regular; habitual: *the steady drinking of alcohol* ▷ *vb* **steadies, steadying, steadied 6** to make or become steady ▷ *adv* **7** in a steady manner **8 go steady** *informal* to date one person regularly ▷ *n, pl* **steadies 9** *informal* one's regular boyfriend or girlfriend ▷ *interj* **10** a warning to keep calm or be careful [from *stead*] **⟩ steadily** *adv* **⟩ steadiness** *n*

steady state *n physics* the condition of a system when all or most changes or disturbances have been eliminated from it

steak *n* **1** a lean piece of beef for grilling or frying **2** a cut of beef for braising or stewing **3** a thick slice of pork, veal, or fish [Old Norse *steik* roast]

steakhouse *n* a restaurant that specializes in steaks

steal *vb* **stealing, stole, stolen 1** to take (something) from someone without permission or unlawfully **2** to use (someone else's ideas or work) without acknowledgment **3** to move quietly and carefully, not wanting to be noticed: *my father stole up behind her* **4 steal the show** (of a performer) to draw the audience's attention to oneself and away from the other performers **5** to obtain or do (something) stealthily: *I stole a glance behind* ▷ *n* **6** *US, Canad and NZ informal* something acquired easily or at little cost [Old English *stelan*]

stealth *n* **1** moving carefully and quietly, so as to avoid being seen **2** cunning or underhand behaviour ▷ *adj* **3** (of technology) able to render an aircraft almost invisible to radar **4** disguised or hidden [Old English *stelan* to steal] **⟩ stealthy** *adj* **⟩ stealthily** *adv*

stealth tax *n* an indirect tax, such as a tax on fuel or pension plans, esp. one of which people are unaware or one that is felt to be unfair

steam *n* **1** the vapour into which water changes when boiled **2** the mist formed when such vapour condenses in the atmosphere **3** *informal* power, energy, or speed **4 let off steam** *informal* to release pent-up energy or feelings **5 pick up steam** *informal* to gather momentum ▷ *adj* **6** operated, heated, or powered by steam: *a steam train* ▷ *vb* **7** to give off steam **8** (of a vehicle) to move by steam power **9** *informal* to proceed quickly and often forcefully **10** to cook (food) in steam **11** to treat (something) with steam, such as in cleaning or pressing clothes **12 steam open** *or* **off** to use steam in order to open or remove (something): *let me steam open this letter* ▷ See also **steam up** [Old English *stēam*]

steam engine *n* an engine worked by steam

steamer *n* **1** a boat or ship driven by steam engines **2** a container with holes in the bottom, used to cook food by steam

steam iron *n* an electric iron that uses steam to take creases out of clothes

steamroller *n* **1** a steam-powered vehicle with heavy rollers used for flattening road surfaces during road-making ▷ *vb* **2** to make (someone) do what one wants by overpowering force

steamship *n* a ship powered by steam engines

steam up *vb* **1** to cover (windows or glasses) or (of windows or glasses) to become covered with steam **2 steamed up** *slang* excited or angry

steamy *adj* **steamier, steamiest 1** full of steam **2** *informal* (of books, films, etc.) erotic

steatite (stee-a-tite) *n* same as **soapstone** [Greek *stear* fat]

Stębark *n* the Polish name for **Tannenberg**

steed *n archaic, literary* a horse [Old English *stēda* stallion]

steel *n* **1** an alloy of iron and carbon, often with small quantities of other elements **2** a steel rod used for sharpening knives **3** courage and mental toughness ▷ *vb* **4** to prepare (oneself) for coping with something unpleasant: *he had steeled himself to accept the fact* [Old English *stēli*] **⟩ steely** *adj*

Steel *n* **1** Danielle, full name *Danielle Fernande Schüelein-Steel*. born 1950, US writer of romantic fiction **2** Baron David (Martin Scott). born 1938, British politician; leader of the Liberal Party (1976–88); Presiding Officer of the Scottish Parliament (1999–2003)

steel band *n music* a band of people playing on metal drums, popular in the West Indies

Steele *n* Sir Richard. 1672–1729, British essayist and dramatist, born in Ireland; with Joseph Addison he was the chief contributor to the periodicals *The Tatler* (1709–11) and *The Spectator* (1711–12)

steel-grey *adj* dark bluish-grey

steel wool *n* a mass of fine steel fibres, used for cleaning metal surfaces

steelworks *n* a factory where steel is made **⟩ steelworker** *n*

Steen n Jan. 1626–79, Dutch genre painter

steep¹ adj **1** having a sharp slope **2** informal (of a fee, price, or demand) unreasonably high; excessive [Old English stēap] ▷ **steeply** adv ▷ **steepness** n

steep² vb **1** to soak or be soaked in a liquid in order to soften or cleanse **2** steeped in filled with: an industry steeped in tradition [Old English stēpan]

steepen vb to become or cause (something) to become steep or steeper

steeple n a tall ornamental tower on a church roof [Old English stēpel]

steeplechase n **1** a horse race over a course with fences to be jumped **2** a track race in which the runners have to leap hurdles and a water jump ▷ vb **-chasing, -chased 3** to race in a steeplechase [so called because it originally took place cross-country, with a church tower serving as a landmark for the riders in the race]

steeplejack n a person who repairs steeples and chimneys

steer¹ vb **1** to direct the course of (a vehicle or vessel) with a steering wheel or rudder **2** to direct the movements or course of (a person, conversation, or activity) **3** to follow (a specified course): the Dutch government steered a middle course **4** steer clear of to avoid [Old English stīeran]

steer² n a castrated male ox or bull [Old English stēor]

steerage n **1** the cheapest accommodation on a passenger ship **2** steering

steering committee n a committee set up to prepare and arrange topics to be discussed, and the order of business, for a government, etc.

steering wheel n a wheel turned by the driver of a vehicle in order to change direction

steersman n, pl **-men** the person who steers a vessel

Stefan Dušan n 1308–55, king of Serbia (1331–55), who conquered Albania (1343) and large parts of the Byzantine empire, into which he introduced legal and administrative reforms

Stefansson n Vilhjalmur. 1879–1962, Canadian explorer, noted for his books on the Inuit

Steffens n (Joseph) Lincoln. 1866–1936, US political analyst, known for his exposure of political corruption

Steier n a variant spelling of **Steyr**

Steiermark n the German name for **Styria**

stein (stine) n an earthenware beer mug [German Stein, literally: stone]

Stein n **1** Gertrude. 1874–1946, US writer, resident in Paris (1903–1946). Her works include Three Lives (1908) and The Autobiography of Alice B. Toklas (1933) **2** Heinrich Friedrich Carl, Baron Stein. 1757–1831, Prussian statesman, who contributed greatly to the modernization of Prussia and played a major role in the European coalition against Napoleon (1813–15) **3** Jock, full name John. 1922–85, Scottish footballer and manager: managed Celtic (1965–78) and Scotland (1978–85)

Steinbeck n John (Ernst). 1902–68, US writer, noted for his novels about agricultural workers, esp. The Grapes of Wrath (1939): Nobel prize for literature 1962

Steiner n Rudolf. 1861–1925, Austrian philosopher, founder of anthroposophy. He was particularly influential in education

Steinitz n Wilhelm. 1836–1900, US chess player, born in Prague; world champion (1866–94)

Steinway n Henry (Engelhard), original name Heinrich Engelhardt Steinweg. 1797–1871, US piano maker, born in Germany

stela (steal-a) or **stele** (steal-ee) n, pl **stelae** (steal-ee) or **steles** an upright stone slab or column decorated with figures or inscriptions, common in prehistoric times [Greek stēlē]

stellar adj **1** relating to the stars **2** informal outstanding or immense: stellar profits [Latin stella star]

stem¹ n **1** the long thin central part of a plant **2** a stalk that bears a flower, fruit, or leaf **3** the long slender part of anything, such as a wineglass **4** linguistics the form of a word that remains after removal of all inflectional endings ▷ vb **stemming, stemmed 5** stem from originate from: this tradition stems from pre-Christian times [Old English stemn]

stem² vb **stemming, stemmed** to stop or hinder the spread of (something): to stem the flow of firearms [Old Norse stemma]

stem cell n biology an undifferentiated embryonic cell that gives rise to specialized cells, such as blood, bone, etc.

stemmed adj having a stem: long-stemmed roses

stench n a strong and very unpleasant smell [Old English stenc]

stencil n **1** a thin sheet with a cut-out pattern through which ink or paint passes to form the pattern on the surface below **2** a design or letters made in this way ▷ vb **-cilling, -cilled** or US **-ciling, -ciled 3** to make (a design or letters) with a stencil [Old French estenceler to decorate brightly]

Stendhal n original name Marie Henri Beyle. 1783–1842, French writer, who anticipated later novelists in his psychological analysis of character. His two chief novels are Le Rouge et le noir (1830) and La Chartreuse de Parme (1839)

Sten gun n a light sub-machine-gun [S & T (initials of the inventors) + -en, as in Bren gun]

stenographer n US and Canad a shorthand typist [Greek stenos narrow + graphein to write]

stent n a surgical implant used to keep an artery open

stentorian adj (of the voice) very loud: a stentorian tone [after Stentor, a herald in Greek mythology]

step n **1** the act of moving and setting down one's foot, such as when walking **2** the distance covered by such a movement **3** the sound made by such a movement **4** one of a sequence of foot movements that make up a dance **5** one of a sequence of actions taken in order to achieve a goal **6** a degree or rank in a series or scale **7** a flat surface for placing the foot on when going up or down **8** manner of walking: he moved with a purposeful step **9** steps **a** a flight of stairs, usually out of doors **b** same as **stepladder 10** a short easily travelled distance: Mexico and Brazil were only a step away **11** break step to stop marching in step **12** in step **a** marching or dancing in time or at the same pace as other people **b** informal in agreement: in step with the West on this issue **13** out of step **a** not marching or dancing in time or at the same pace as other people **b** informal not in agreement: out of step with the political mood **14** step by step gradually **15** take steps to do what is necessary (to achieve something) **16** watch one's step **a** informal to behave with caution ▷ vb **stepping, stepped 17** to move by taking a step, such as in walking (often foll. by on) **18** to place or press the foot; tread **19** to walk a short distance: please step this way **20** step into to enter (a situation) apparently without difficulty: she stepped into a life of luxury ▶ See also **step down, step in,** etc. [Old English stepe, stæpe]

Step n **1** a set of aerobic exercises which consists of stepping on and off a special box of adjustable height ▷ adj **2** denoting this type of exercise: Step aerobics

stepbrother n a son of one's stepmother or stepfather

stepchild n, pl **-children** a stepson or stepdaughter

stepdaughter n a daughter of one's husband or wife by an earlier relationship

step down vb informal to resign from a position

stepfather n a man who has married one's mother after the death or divorce of one's father

stephanotis (stef-fan-note-iss) n a tropical climbing shrub with sweet-smelling white flowers [Greek: fit for a crown]

Stephen n **1** ?1097–1154, king of England (1135–54); grandson of William the Conqueror. He seized the throne on the death of Henry I, causing civil war with Henry's daughter Matilda. He eventually recognized her son (later Henry II) as his successor **2** Saint. died ?35 AD,

S

the first Christian martyr. Feast day: Dec 26 or 27 **3 Saint**, Hungarian name Istán. ?975–1038 AD, first king of Hungary as Stephen I (997–1038). Feast day: Aug 16 or 20 **4** Sir **Leslie**. 1832–1904, English biographer, critic, and first editor of the *Dictionary of National Biography*; father of the novelist Virginia Woolf

Stephenson n **1 George**. 1781–1848, British inventor of the first successful steam locomotive (1814); constructed the first railway line to carry passengers, the Stockton and Darlington Railway (opened 1825) **2** his son, **Robert**. 1803–59, British engineer, noted for his construction of railway bridges and viaducts, esp. the tubular bridge over the Menai Strait

step in *vb informal* to intervene (in a quarrel or difficult situation)

stepladder n a small folding portable ladder with a supporting frame

stepmother n a woman who has married one's father after the death or divorce of one's mother

step on *vb* **1** to place or press one's foot on (something): *he stepped on the brakes* **2** *informal* to behave badly towards (a person in a less powerful position) **3 step on it** *informal* to go more quickly; hurry up

step out *vb* **1** to leave a room briefly **2** to walk quickly, taking long strides

step-parent n a stepfather or stepmother

steppes *pl n* wide grassy plains without trees [Old Russian *step* lowland]

Steppes *pl n* the Steppes **1** the huge grasslands of Eurasia, chiefly in Ukraine and Russia **2** another name for Kyrgyz Steppe

stepping stone n **1** one of a series of stones acting as footrests for crossing a stream **2** a stage in a person's progress towards a goal: *it was a big stepping stone in his career*

stepsister n a daughter of one's stepmother or stepfather

stepson n a son of one's husband or wife by an earlier relationship

step up *vb* **1** *informal* to increase (something) by stages; accelerate **2 step up to the plate** *US and Canad* **a** baseball to move into batting position **b** to come forward and take responsibility for something

stereo *adj* **1** (of a sound system) using two or more separate microphones to feed two or more loudspeakers through separate channels ▷ n, pl **stereos 2** a music system in which sound is directed through two speakers **3** sound broadcast or played in stereo

stereophonic *adj* same as **stereo** (1) [Greek *stereos* solid + *phōnē* sound]

stereoscopic *adj* having a three-dimensional effect: *stereoscopic vision*

stereotype n **1** a set of characteristics or a fixed idea considered to represent a particular kind of person **2** an idea or convention that has grown stale through fixed usage ▷ *vb* **-typing, -typed 3** to form a standard image or idea of (a type of person) [Greek *stereos* solid + TYPE]

sterile *adj* **1** free from germs **2** unable to produce offspring **3** (of plants) not producing or bearing seeds **4** lacking inspiration or energy; unproductive [Latin *sterilis*] ▷ **sterility** n

sterilize or **-lise** *vb* **-lizing, -lized** or **-lising, -lised** to make sterile ▷ **sterilization** or **-lisation** n

sterling n **1** British money: *sterling fell by almost a pfennig* ▷ *adj* **2** genuine and reliable: first-class: *he has a reputation for sterling honesty* [probably Old English *steorra* star, referring to a small star on early Norman pennies]

Sterling n Peter. born 1960, Australian rugby league player: played 18 matches for Australia (1982–88)

sterling silver n **1** an alloy containing at least 92.5 per cent of silver **2** articles made of sterling silver

Sterlitamak n an industrial city in W Russia, in the Bashkir Republic. Pop: 268 000 (2005 est)

stern¹ *adj* **1** strict and serious: *he's a very stern taskmaster* **2** difficult and often unpleasant: *the stern demands of the*

day **3** (of a facial expression) severe and disapproving [Old English *styrne*] ▷ **sternly** *adv*

stern² n the rear part of a boat or ship [Old Norse *stjōrn* steering]

Stern n Isaac. 1920–2001, US concert violinist, born in (what is now) Ukraine

Sterne n Laurence. 1713–68, English novelist, born in Ireland, author of *The Life and Opinions of Tristram Shandy, Gentleman* (1759–67) and *A Sentimental Journey through France and Italy* (1768)

sternum n, pl **-na** or **-nums** a long flat bone in the front of the body, to which the collarbone and most of the ribs are attached [Greek *sternon*]

steroid n biochem an organic compound containing a carbon ring system, such as sterols and many hormones

sterol n biochem a natural insoluble alcohol such as cholesterol and ergosterol [shortened from *cholesterol, ergosterol*, etc.]

stertorous *adj* (of breathing) laboured and noisy [Latin *stertere* to snore]

stet *vb* **stetting, stetted 1** used as an instruction to indicate to a printer that certain deleted matter is to be kept **2** to mark (matter) in this way [Latin, literally: let it stand]

stethoscope n med an instrument for listening to the sounds made inside the body, consisting of a hollow disc that transmits the sound through hollow tubes to earpieces [Greek *stēthos* breast + *skopein* to look at]

Stetson n trademark a felt hat with a broad brim and high crown, worn mainly by cowboys [after John *Stetson*, American hat maker]

Stettin n the German name for Szczecin

stevedore n chiefly US a person employed to load or unload ships [Spanish *estibador* a packer]

Stevenage n a town in SE England, in N Hertfordshire on the Great North Road: developed chiefly as the first of the new towns (1946). Pop: 81 482 (2001)

Stevens n **1 Thaddeus**. 1792–1868, US Radical Republican politician. An opponent of slavery, he supported Reconstruction and entered the resolution calling for the impeachment of President Andrew Johnson **2 Wallace**. 1879–1955, US poet, whose books include the collections *Harmonium* (1923), *The Man with the Blue Guitar* (1937), and *Transport to Summer* (1947)

Stevenson n **1 Adlai Ewing**. 1900–68, US statesman: twice defeated as Democratic presidential candidate (1952; 1956); US delegate at the United Nations (1961–65) **2 Robert Louis (Balfour)**. 1850–94, Scottish writer: his novels include *Treasure Island* (1883), *Kidnapped* (1886), and *The Master of Ballantrae* (1889)

stew n **1 a** a dish of meat, fish, or other food, cooked slowly in a closed pot **2 in a stew** *informal* in a troubled or worried state ▷ *vb* **3** to cook by long slow simmering in a closed pot **4** *informal* (of a person) to be too hot **5** to cause (tea) to become bitter or (of tea) to become bitter through infusing for too long **6 stew in one's own juice** to suffer, without help, the results of one's actions [Middle English *stuen* to take a very hot bath]

steward n **1** a person who looks after passengers and serves meals on a ship or aircraft **2** an official who helps to supervise a public event, such as a race **3** a person who administers someone else's property **4** a person who manages the eating arrangements, staff, or service at a club or hotel **5** See shop steward ▷ *vb* **6** to act as a steward (of) [Old English *stigweard* hall keeper]

stewardess n a female steward on an aircraft or ship

Stewart n **1** the usual spelling for the royal house of Stuart before the reign of Mary Queen of Scots (Mary Stuart) **2** Sir **Jackie**, full name *John Young Stewart*. born 1939, Scottish motor-racing driver: Formula One world champion 1969, 1971, and 1973 **3 James (Maitland)**. 1908–97, US film actor, known for his distinctive drawl; appeared in many films including *Destry Rides Again* (1939), *It's a Wonderful Life* (1946), *The Glenn Miller Story* (1953), and *Vertigo* (1958) **4 Rod.** born 1945, British rock singer: vocalist with the Faces (1969–75). His albums include *Gasoline Alley* (1970), *Every Picture Tells a Story* (1971), and *Atlantic Crossing* (1975)

Stewart Island *n* the third largest island of New Zealand, in the SW Pacific off the S tip of South Island. Pop: 387 (2001). Area: 1735 sq km (670 sq miles)

stewed *adj* **1** (of food) cooked by stewing **2** *Brit* (of tea) bitter through having been left to infuse for too long **3** *slang* drunk

Steyn *n* **Dale (Willem)**, born 1983, South African cricketer; a fast bowler and prolific wicket-taker in all forms of international cricket

Steyr *or* **Steier** *n* an industrial city in N central Austria, in Upper Austria. Pop: 39 340 (2001)

Sth South

stick¹ *n* **1** a small thin branch of a tree **2 a** a long thin piece of wood **b** such a piece of wood shaped for a special purpose: *a walking stick; a hockey stick* **3** a piece of something shaped like a stick: *a stick of cinnamon* **4** *slang* verbal abuse, criticism: *they gave me a lot of stick* **5 the sticks** a country area considered backward or unsophisticated: *places out in the sticks* **6 sticks** pieces of furniture: *these few sticks are all I have* **7** *informal* a person: *not a bad old stick* **8 get hold of the wrong end of the stick** to misunderstand a situation or an explanation completely [Old English *sticca*]

stick² *vb* **sticking, stuck 1** to push (a pointed object) or (of a pointed object) to be pushed into another object **2** to fasten (something) in position by pins, nails, or glue: *she just stuck the label on* **3** to extend beyond something else; protrude: *he stuck his head out of the door* **4** *informal* to place (something) in a specified position: *stick it in the oven* **5** to fasten or be fastened by or as if by an adhesive **6** to come or be brought to a standstill: *stuck in a rut; two army lorries stuck behind us* **7** to remain for a long time: *the room that sticks in my mind the most* **8** *slang, chiefly Brit* to tolerate; abide: *you couldn't stick it for more than two days* **9 be stuck** *informal* to be at a loss (for); to be baffled or puzzled: *I'm stuck; stuck for words* ▸ See also **stick around, stick by**, etc. [Old English *stician*]

stick around *vb informal* to remain in a place, often when waiting for something

stick by *vb* to remain faithful to: *she's stuck by me for sixty years*

sticker *n* a small piece of paper with a picture or writing on it that can be stuck to a surface

sticking plaster *n* a piece of adhesive material used for covering slight wounds

stick insect *n* a tropical insect with a long thin body and legs, which looks like a twig

stick-in-the-mud *n informal* a person who is unwilling to try anything new or do anything exciting

stickleback *n* a small fish with sharp spines along its back [Old English *sticel* prick, sting + BACK]

stickler *n* a person who insists on something: *a stickler for punctuality*

stick out *vb* **1** to (cause to) project from something else: *she stuck her tongue out at me* **2** *informal* to endure (something unpleasant): *she would stick it out for a year* **3 stick out a mile** *or* **like a sore thumb** *informal* to be very obvious **4 stick out for** to continue to demand (something), refusing to accept anything less

stick to *vb* **1** to adhere or cause (something) to adhere to: *the soil sticks to the blade* **2** to remain faithful to (a person, promise, or rule) **3** not to move away from: *stick to the agreement*

stick-up *n slang, chiefly US* a robbery at gunpoint; hold-up

stick up for *vb informal* to support or defend (oneself, another person, or a principle)

sticky *adj* **stickier, stickiest 1** covered with a substance that sticks to other things: *sticky little fingers* **2** intended to stick to a surface: *sticky labels* **3** *informal* difficult or painful: *a sticky meeting* **4** (of weather) unpleasantly warm and humid ❭ **stickiness** *n*

sticky wicket *n* **on a sticky wicket** *informal* in a difficult situation

Stieglitz *n* **Alfred.** 1864–1946, US photographer, whose work helped to develop photography as an art: among his best photographs are those of his wife Georgia O'Keeffe. He was also well known as a promoter of modern art

stiff *adj* **1** firm and not easily bent **2** moving with pain or difficulty: *stiff and aching joints* **3** not moving easily: *the door is stiff* **4** difficult or severe: *a stiff challenge; stiff penalties* **5** formal and not relaxed **6** fairly firm in consistency; thick **7** powerful: *a stiff breeze* **8** (of a drink) containing a lot of alcohol ▷ *n* **9** *slang* a corpse ▷ *adv* **10** completely or utterly: *I was bored stiff* [Old English *stif*] ❭ **stiffly** *adv* ❭ **stiffness** *n*

stiffen *vb* to make or become stiff or stiffer

stiff-necked *adj* proud and stubborn

stifle *vb* **-fling, -fled 1** to stop oneself from expressing (a yawn or cry) **2** to stop (something) from continuing: *the new leadership stifled all internal debate* **3** to feel discomfort and difficulty in breathing **4** to kill (someone) by preventing him or her from breathing [probably from Old French *estouffer* to smother]

stifling *adj* uncomfortably hot and stuffy

stigma *n, pl* **stigmas** *or* **stigmata 1** a mark of social disgrace: *a stigma attached to being redundant* **2** *botany* the part of a flower that receives pollen **3 stigmata** *Christianity* marks resembling the wounds of the crucified Christ, believed to appear on the bodies of certain people [Greek: brand]

stigmatize *or* **-tise** *vb* **-tizing, -tized** *or* **-tising, -tised** to regard as being shameful

stile *n* a set of steps in a wall or fence to allow people, but not animals, to pass over [Old English *stigel*]

stiletto *n, pl* **-tos 1** Also called: **spike heel, stiletto heel** a high narrow heel on a woman's shoe or a shoe with such a heel **2** a small dagger with a slender tapered blade [Italian: little dagger]

Stilicho *n* **Flavius.** ?365–408 AD, Roman general and statesman, born a Vandal. As the guardian of Emperor Theodosius' son Honorius, he was effective ruler of the Western Roman Empire (395–408), which he defended against the Visigoths

still¹ *adv* **1** continuing now or in the future as in the past: *she still loved the theatre* **2** up to this or that time; yet **3** even or yet: *still more pressure on the government* **4** even then; nevertheless: *the baby has been fed and still cries* ▷ *adj* **5** motionless; stationary **6** undisturbed; silent and calm **7** (of a soft drink) not fizzy ▷ *n* **8** *poetic* silence or tranquillity: *the still of night* **9** a still photograph from a film ▷ *vb* **10** to make or become quiet or calm **11** to relieve or end: *Fowler stilled his conscience* [Old English *stille*] ❭ **stillness** *n*

still² *n* an apparatus for distilling spirits [Latin *stilla* a drip]

stillborn *adj* **1** (of a baby) dead at birth **2** (of an idea or plan) completely unsuccessful ❭ **stillbirth** *n*

still life *n, pl* **still lifes 1** a painting or drawing of objects such as fruit or flowers **2** this kind of painting or drawing

still room *n Brit* **1** a room in which distilling is carried out **2** a room for storing food in a large house

stilt *n* **1** either of a pair of long poles with footrests for walking raised from the ground **2** a long post or column used with others to support a building above ground level [Middle English *stilte*]

stilted *adj* (of speech, writing, or behaviour) formal or pompous; not flowing continuously or naturally

Stilton *n* trademark a strong-flavoured blue-veined cheese [named after *Stilton*, Cambridgeshire]

Stilwell *n* **Joseph W(arren)**, known as *Vinegar Joe*. 1883–1946, US general, who was (1941–44) Chiang Kai-shek's chief of staff and commander of all US forces in China, Burma (Myanmar), and India

S

stimulant *n* **1** a drug, food, or drink that makes the body work faster, increases heart rate, and makes sleeping difficult **2** any stimulating thing ▷ *adj* **3** stimulating

stimulate *vb* **-lating, -lated** **1** to encourage to start or progress further: *a cut in interest rates should help stimulate economic recovery* **2** to fill (a person) with ideas or enthusiasm: *books satisfy a part of the intellect that needs to be stimulated* **3** *physiol* to excite (a nerve or organ) with a stimulus [Latin *stimulare*] **> stimulation** *n*

stimulating *adj* **1** inspiring new ideas or enthusiasm **2** (of a physical activity) making one feel refreshed and energetic; invigorating

stimulus (stim-myew-luss) *n, pl* **-li** (-lie) **1** something that acts as an incentive to (someone) **2** something, such as a drug or electrical impulse, that is capable of causing a response in a person or an animal [Latin: a cattle goad]

Stine *n* R(obert) L(awrence). born 1943, US writer, noted for his numerous bestselling horror novels for older children, esp. those in the *Goosebumps* and *Fear Street* series

sting *vb* **stinging, stung** **1** (of certain animals and plants) to inflict a wound on (someone) by the injection of poison **2** to cause (someone) to feel a sharp physical pain: *her hand was stinging* **3** to offend or upset (someone) with a critical remark: *I was stung by what he said* **4** to provoke (a response) by angering: *the consulate would be stung into convulsive action* **5** *informal* to cheat (someone) by overcharging ▷ *n* **6** a skin wound caused by stinging **7** pain caused by or as if by a sting **8** a mental pain: *the sting of memory* **9** the sharp pointed organ of certain animals or plants used to inject poison **10** *slang* a deceptive trick **11** *slang* a trap set up by the police to entice a person to commit a crime, thereby producing evidence [Old English *stingan*] **> stinging** *adj*

stinging nettle *n* same as **nettle** (1)

stingray *n* a flat fish with a jagged whiplike tail capable of inflicting painful wounds

stingy *adj* **-gier, -giest** very mean [perhaps from *stinge*, dialect variant of STING] **> stinginess** *n*

stink *n* **1** a strong unpleasant smell **2** **make** *or* **create** *or* **kick up a stink** *slang* to make a fuss ▷ *vb* **stinking, stank** *or* **stunk, stunk** **3** to give off a strong unpleasant smell **4** *slang* to be thoroughly bad or unpleasant: *the script stinks, the casting stinks* [Old English *stincan*] **> stinky** *adj*

stink bomb *n* a small glass globe used by practical jokers: it releases a liquid with a strong unpleasant smell when broken

stinker *n* *slang* a difficult or very unpleasant person or thing

stinking *adj* **1** having a strong unpleasant smell **2** *informal* unpleasant or disgusting ▷ *adv* **3** **stinking rich** *informal* very wealthy

stink out *vb* **1** to drive (people) away by a foul smell **2** *Brit and NZ* to cause (a place) to stink: *I won't have it stinking the car out!*

stint *vb* **1** to be miserly with (something): *don't stint on paper napkins* ▷ *n* **2** a given amount of work [Old English *styntan* to blunt]

stipend (sty-pend) *n* a regular salary or allowance, esp. that paid to a member of the clergy [Latin *stipendium* tax] **> stipendiary** *adj*

stipple *vb* **-pling, -pled** to draw, engrave, or paint (something) using dots or flecks [Dutch *stippelen*]

stipulate *vb* **-lating, -lated** to specify (something) as a condition of an agreement [Latin *stipulari*] **> stipulation** *n*

stir[1] *vb* **stirring, stirred** **1** to mix up (a liquid) by moving a spoon or stick around in it **2** to move slightly **3** **stir from** to depart from (one's usual or preferred place) **4** to get up after sleeping **5** to excite or move (someone) emotionally **6** to move (oneself) quickly or vigorously; exert (oneself) **7** to wake up: *to stir someone from sleep* ▷ *n* **8** a stirring **9** a strong reaction, usually of excitement: *she created a stir wherever she went* ► See also **stir up** [Old English *styrian*]

stir[2] *n* chiefly US slang prison: *in stir* [Romany *stariben* prison]

Stir. Stirlingshire

stir-crazy *adj* *slang* mentally disturbed as a result of being in prison

stir-fry *vb* **-fries, -frying, -fried** **1** to cook (food) quickly by stirring it in a wok or frying pan over a high heat ▷ *n, pl* **-fries** **2** a dish cooked in this way

Stirling[1] *n* **1** a city in central Scotland, in Stirling council area on the River Forth: its castle was a regular residence of many Scottish monarchs between the 12th century and 1603. Pop: 32 673 (2001) **2** a council area of central Scotland, created from part of Central Region in 1996; includes most of the historical county of Stirlingshire: the Forth valley rises to the Grampian Mountains in the N. Administrative centre: Stirling. Pop: 86 370 (2003 est). Area: 2173 sq km (839 sq miles)

Stirling[2] *n* Sir James. 1926–92, British architect; buildings include the Neue Staatsgalerie in Stuttgart (1977–84)

Stirlingshire *n* a former county of central Scotland: mostly became part of Central Region in 1975: now covered by the council areas of Stirling, Falkirk, and East Dunbartonshire

stirrer *n* *informal* a person who deliberately causes trouble

stirring *adj* causing emotion, excitement, and enthusiasm

stirrup *n* a metal loop attached to a saddle for supporting a rider's foot [Old English *stig* step + *rāp* rope]

stirrup cup *n* chiefly Brit a cup containing an alcoholic drink offered to riders before a fox hunt

stirrup pump *n* a hand-operated pump, the base of which is placed in a bucket of water: used in fighting fires

stir up *vb* **1** to cause (leaves or dust) to rise up and swirl around **2** to set (something) in motion: *that fact has stirred up resentment*

stitch *n* **1** a link made by drawing a thread through material with a needle **2** a loop of yarn formed around a needle or hook in knitting or crocheting **3** a particular kind of stitch **4** *informal* a link of thread joining the edges of a wound together **5** a sharp pain in the side caused by running or exercising **6** **in stitches** *informal* laughing uncontrollably **7** **not a stitch** *informal* no clothes at all ▷ *vb* **8** to sew or fasten (something) with stitches [Old English *stice* sting] **> stitching** *n*

stitch up *vb* **1** to join by stitching **2** *slang* to incriminate by manufacturing evidence **3** *slang* to prearrange in a clandestine manner ▷ *n* **stitch-up** **4** *slang* a matter that has been prearranged clandestinely

stoat *n* a small brown N European mammal related to the weasel: in winter it has a white coat and is then known as an ermine [origin unknown]

stock *n* **1** the total amount of goods kept on the premises of a shop or business **2** a supply of something stored for future use **3** *finance* **a** the money raised by a company through selling shares entitling their holders to dividends, partial ownership, and usually voting rights **b** the proportion of this money held by an individual shareholder **c** the shares of a specified company or industry **4** farm animals bred and kept for their meat, skins, etc. **5** the original type from which a particular race, family, or group is descended **6** the handle of a rifle, held by the firer against the shoulder **7** a liquid produced by simmering meat, fish, bones, or vegetables, and used to make soups and sauces **8** a kind of plant grown for its brightly coloured flowers **9** *old-fashioned* the degree of status a person has **10** See **laughing stock** **11** **in stock** stored on the premises or available for sale or use **12** **out of stock** not immediately available for sale or use **13** **take stock** to think carefully about a situation before making a decision ▷ *adj* **14** staple; standard: *stock sizes in clothes* **15** being a cliché; hackneyed: *the stock answer* ▷ *vb* **16** to keep (goods) for sale **17** to obtain a store of (something) for future use or sale: *to stock up on food* **18** to supply (a farm) with animals or (a lake or stream) with fish ▶ See also **stocks** [Old English *stocc* tree trunk]

stockade *n* an enclosure or barrier of large wooden posts [Spanish *estacada*]

stockbreeder *n* a person who breeds or rears farm animals

stockbroker *n* a person who buys and sells stocks and shares for customers and receives a percentage of their profits ❭ **stockbroking** *n*

stock car *n* a car that has been strengthened and modified for a form of racing in which the cars often collide

stock cube *n* a small solid cube made from dried meat or vegetables, used to add flavouring to stew, soup, etc.

stock exchange *n* **1 a** a highly organized market for the purchase and sale of stocks and shares, operated by professional stockbrokers and market makers according to fixed rules **b** a place where stocks and shares are traded **2** the prices or trading activity of a stock exchange: *the stock exchange has been rising*

Stockhausen *n* **Karlheinz**. 1928–2007, German composer, whose avant-garde music exploits advanced serialization, electronic sounds, group improvisation, and vocal and instrumental timbres and techniques. Works include *Gruppen* (1959) for three orchestras, *Stimmung* (1968) for six vocalists, and the operas *Donnerstag* (1980) and *Freitag* (1996)

stockholder *n* an owner of some of a company's stock

Stockholm *n* the capital of Sweden, a port in the E central part at the outflow of Lake Mälaren into the Baltic: situated partly on the mainland and partly on islands; traditionally founded about 1250; university (1877). Pop: 765 582 (2004 est)

stockinette *n* a machine-knitted elastic fabric [perhaps from *stocking-net*]

stocking *n* a long piece of close-fitting nylon or knitted yarn covering the foot and part or all of a woman's leg [dialect *stock* stocking]

stockinged *adj* in one's **stockinged feet** wearing stockings, tights, or socks but no shoes

stocking stitch *n* alternate rows of plain and purl in knitting

stock in trade *n* a person's typical behaviour or usual work: *practicality is the farmer's stock in trade*

stockist *n* Brit commerce a dealer who stocks a particular product

stock market *n* same as **stock exchange**

stockpile *vb* **-piling, -piled 1** to store a large quantity of (something) for future use ▷ *n* **2** a large store gathered for future use

Stockport *n* **1** a town in NW England, in Stockport unitary authority, Greater Manchester: an early textile centre and scene of several labour disturbances in the early 19th century; engineering, electronics. Pop: 136 082 (2001) **2** a unitary authority in NW England, in Greater Manchester. Pop: 282 500 (2003 est). Area: 126 sq km (49 sq miles)

stockpot *n* Brit and NZ a pot in which stock for soup is made

stockroom *n* a room in which a stock of goods is kept in a shop or factory

stock route *n* Austral and NZ a route designated for droving farm animals, so as to avoid traffic

stocks *pl n* history an instrument of punishment consisting of a heavy wooden frame with holes in which the feet, hands, or head of an offender were locked

stock-still *adv* absolutely still; motionlessly

stocktaking *n* **1** the counting and valuing of goods in a shop or business **2** a reassessment of a person's current situation and prospects

Stockton *n* an inland port in central California, on the San Joaquin River: seat of the University of the Pacific (1851). Pop: 271 466 (2003 est)

Stockton-on-Tees *n* **1** a former port and industrial centre in NE England, in Stockton-on-Tees unitary authority, Co Durham, on the River Tees: famous for the Stockton and Darlington Railway (1825), the first passenger-carrying railway in the world; now mainly residential. Pop: 80 060 (2001) **2** a unitary authority in NE England, in Co Durham and North Yorkshire: created in 1996 from part of Cleveland county. Pop: 186 300 (2003 est). Area: 195 sq km (75 sq miles)

Stockwood *n* (Arthur) Mervyn. 1913–95, British Anglican prelate; bishop of Southwark (1959–80)

stocky *adj* **stockier, stockiest** (of a person) short but well-built ❭ **stockily** *adv* ❭ **stockiness** *n*

stockyard *n* a large yard with pens or covered buildings where farm animals are sold

stodge *n* Brit, Austral and NZ informal heavy and filling starchy food [perhaps blend of STUFF + *podge* a short plump person]

stodgy *adj* **stodgier, stodgiest 1** (of food) full of starch and very filling **2** (of a person) dull, serious, or excessively formal [from STODGE] ❭ **stodginess** *n*

stoep (stoop) *n* (in South Africa) a verandah [Afrikaans]

stoic (stow-ik) *n* **1 a** a person who suffers great difficulties without showing his or her emotions ▷ *adj* **2** same as **stoical**

Stoic *n* **1** a member of the ancient Greek school of philosophy which believed that virtue and happiness could be achieved only by calmly accepting Fate ▷ *adj* **2** of or relating to the Stoics [Greek *stoa* porch] ❭ **Stoicism** *n*

stoical *adj* suffering great difficulties without showing one's feelings ❭ **stoically** *adv* ❭ **stoicism** (stow-iss-iz-zum) *n*

stoke *vb* **stoking, stoked 1** to feed and tend (a fire or furnace) **2** to excite or encourage (a strong emotion) in oneself or someone else [from STOKER]

stoked *adj* Austral and NZ informal very pleased: *I'm really stoked to have got the job*

stokehold *n* nautical the hold for a ship's boilers; fire room

Stoke-on-Trent *n* **1** a city in central England, in Stoke-on-Trent unitary authority, Staffordshire on the River Trent: a centre of the pottery industry; university (1992). Pop: 259 252 (2001) **2** a unitary authority in central England, in N Staffordshire. Pop: 238 000 (2003 est). Area: 93 sq km (36 sq miles)

stoker *n* a person employed to tend a furnace on a ship or train powered by steam [Dutch *stoken* to stoke]

Stoker *n* Bram, original name *Abraham Stoker*. 1847–1912, Irish novelist, author of *Dracula* (1897)

Stokesay Castle *n* a fortified manor house near Craven Arms in Shropshire: built in the 12th century, with a 16th-century gatehouse

Stokowski *n* Leopold. 1887–1977, US conductor, born in Britain. He did much to popularize classical music with orchestral transcriptions and film appearances, esp. in *Fantasia* (1940)

stole¹ *vb* the past tense of **steal**

stole² *n* a long scarf or shawl, worn by women [Greek *stolē* clothing]

stolen *vb* the past participle of **steal**

stolid *adj* showing little or no emotion or interest in anything [Latin *stolidus* dull] ❭ **stolidity** *n* ❭ **stolidly** *adv*

Stolypin *n* Petr Arkadievich. 1863–1911, Russian conservative statesman: prime minister (1906–11). He instituted agrarian reforms but was ruthless in suppressing rebellion: assassinated

stoma (stow-ma) *n*, *pl* **stomata** (stow-ma-ta) **1** botany a pore in a plant leaf that controls the passage of gases into and out of the plant **2** zoology a mouth or mouthlike part [Greek: mouth]

stomach *n* **1** an organ inside the body in which food is stored until it has been partially digested **2** the front of the body around the waist **3** desire or appetite: *he still has*

S

the stomach for a fight ▷ vb **4** to put up with: *liberals could not stomach the rest of the package* [Greek *stoma* mouth]

stomachache n pain in the stomach, such as from indigestion. Also called: **stomach upset, upset stomach**

stomacher n *history* a decorative V-shaped panel of stiff material worn over the chest and stomach mainly by women

stomach pump n *med* a pump with a long tube used for removing the contents of a person's stomach, for instance after he or she has swallowed poison

stomp vb to tread or stamp heavily [variant of STAMP]

stompie n *S African slang* **1** a cigarette butt **2** a short man [Afrikaans *stomp* stump]

stone n **1** the hard nonmetallic material of which rocks are made **2** a small lump of rock **3** Also called: **gemstone** a precious or semiprecious stone that has been cut and polished **4** a piece of rock used for some particular purpose: *gravestone*; *millstone* **5** the hard central part of fruits such as the peach or date **6** (pl **stone**) *Brit* a unit of weight equal to 14 pounds or 6.350 kilograms **7** *pathol* a hard deposit formed in the kidney or bladder **8 heart of stone** a hard or unemotional personality **9 leave no stone unturned** to do everything possible to achieve something ▷ adj **10** made of stoneware: *the polished stone planter* ▷ vb **stoning, stoned 11** to throw stones at (someone), for example as a punishment **12** to remove the stones from (a fruit) [Old English *stān*]

Stone n **1** Oliver. born 1946, US film director and screenwriter: his films include *Platoon* (1986), *Born on the Fourth of July* (1989), *JFK* (1991), *Nixon* (1995), *Alexander* (2004), and *World Trade Center* (2006) **2** Sharon. born 1958, US film actress: her films include *Basic Instinct* (1991), *Casino* (1995), and *Cold Creek Manor* (2003)

Stone Age n a phase of human culture identified by the use of tools made of stone

stonechat n a songbird that has black feathers and a reddish-brown breast [from its cry, which sounds like clattering pebbles]

stone-cold adj **1** completely cold ▷ adv **2 stone-cold sober** completely sober

stoned adj *slang* under the influence of drugs or alcohol

stone-deaf adj completely deaf

stone fruit n same as **drupe**

stoneground adj **1** (of flour) made by crushing grain between two large stones **2** made with stoneground flour: *stoneground wholemeal bread*

Stonehenge n a prehistoric ruin in S England, in Wiltshire on Salisbury Plain: constructed over the period of roughly 3000–1600 BC; one of the most important megalithic monuments in Europe; believed to have had religious and astronomical purposes

stonemason n a person who is skilled in preparing stone for building

stone's throw n a short distance

stonewall vb **1** to deliberately prolong a discussion by being long-winded or evasive **2** *cricket* (of a batsman) to play defensively

stoneware n a hard type of pottery, fired at a very high temperature

stonewashed adj (of clothes or fabric) given a worn faded look by being washed with many small pieces of stone

stonework n any structure or part of a building made of stone

stonkered adj *NZ slang* completely exhausted or beaten; whacked [from *stonker* to beat, of unknown origin]

stony or **stoney** adj **stonier, stoniest 1** (of ground) rough and covered with stones: *the stony path* **2** (of a face, voice, or attitude) unfriendly and unsympathetic > **stonily** adv

stony-broke adj *slang* completely without money

stood vb the past of **stand**

stooge n **1** an actor who feeds lines to a comedian or acts as the butt of his jokes **2** *slang* someone who is taken

advantage of by someone in a superior position [origin unknown]

stool n **1** a seat with legs but no back **2** waste matter from the bowels [Old English *stōl*]

stool pigeon n an informer for the police

stoop¹ vb **1** to bend (the body) forward and downward **2** to stand or walk with head and shoulders habitually bent forward **3 stoop to** to lower one's normal standards of behaviour; degrade oneself: *no real journalist would stoop to faking* ▷ n **4** the act, position, or habit of stooping [Old English *stūpian*] > **stooping** adj

stoop² n *US* an open porch or small platform with steps leading up to it at the entrance to a building [Dutch *stoep*]

stop vb **stopping, stopped 1** to cease from doing (something); discontinue **2** to cause (something moving) to halt or (of something moving) to come to a halt **3** to prevent the continuance or completion of (something) **4** (often foll. by *from*) to prevent or restrain: *I stopped her from going on any further* **5** to keep back: *no agreement to stop arms supplies* **6 stop up** to block or plug: *to stop up a pipe* **7** to stay or rest: *we stopped at a camp site for a change* **8** to instruct a bank not to honour (a cheque) **9** to deduct (money) from pay **10** *informal* to receive (a blow or hit) **11** *music* to alter the vibrating length of (a string on a violin, guitar, etc.) by pressing down on it at some point with the finger **12 stop at nothing** to be prepared to do anything; be ruthless ▷ n **13** prevention of movement or progress: *you can put a stop to it quite easily* **14** the act of stopping or the state of being stopped: *the car lurched to a stop* **15** a place where something halts or pauses: *a bus stop* **16** the act or an instance of blocking or obstructing **17** a device that prevents, limits, or ends the motion of a mechanism or moving part **18** *Brit* a full stop **19** *music* a knob on an organ that is operated to allow sets of pipes to sound **20 pull out all the stops** to make a great effort [Old English *stoppian* (unattested)]

stopbank n *NZ* an embankment to prevent flooding

stopcock n a valve used to control or stop the flow of a fluid in a pipe

Stopes n Marie Carmichael. 1880–1958, English pioneer of birth control, who established the first birth-control clinic in Britain (1921)

stopgap n a thing that serves as a substitute for a short time until replaced by something more suitable

stop off vb (often foll. by *at*) to halt and call somewhere on the way to another place

stopover n **1** a break in a journey ▷ vb **stop over 2** to make a stopover

stoppage n **1** the act of stopping something or the state of being stopped: *a heart stoppage* **2** a deduction of money, such as taxation, from pay **3** an organized stopping of work during industrial action

stoppage time n *chiefly Brit* same as **injury time**

Stoppard n Sir **Tom**, original name *Thomas Straussler* born 1937, British playwright, born in Czechoslovakia: his works include *Rosencrantz and Guildenstern are Dead* (1967), *Travesties* (1974), *Hapgood* (1988), *The Invention of Love* (1997), and the trilogy *The Coast of Utopia* (2002)

stopper n a plug for closing a bottle, pipe, etc.

stop press n news items inserted into a newspaper after the printing has been started

stopwatch n a watch which can be stopped instantly for exact timing of a sporting event

storage n **1** the act of storing or the state of being stored **2** space for storing **3** *computers* the process of storing information in a computer

storage device n a piece of computer equipment, such as a magnetic tape or a disk in or on which information can be stored

storage heater n an electric device that accumulates and radiates heat generated by cheap off-peak electricity

store vb **storing, stored 1** to keep, set aside, or gather (things) for future use **2** to place (furniture or other possessions) in a warehouse for safekeeping **3** to supply or stock (certain goods) **4** *computers* to enter or keep (information) in a storage device ▷ *n* **5** a shop (in Britain usually a large one) **6** a large supply or stock kept for future use **7** short for **department store 8** a storage place, such as a warehouse **9** *computers, chiefly Brit* same as **memory** (7) **10** **in store** about to happen; forthcoming: *you've got a treat in store* **11** **set great store by something** to value something as important ▶ See also **stores** [Old French *estor*]

Store Bælt *n* the Danish name for the **Great Belt**

storehouse *n* **1** a building where goods are stored **2** a collection of things or ideas: *a storehouse of memories*

storeroom *n* a room in which things are stored

stores *pl n* a supply or stock of food and other essentials for a journey

storey *or especially US* **story** *n, pl* **-reys** *or* **-ries** a floor or level of a building [Anglo-Latin *historia* picture, probably from the pictures on medieval windows]

Storey *n* David (**Malcolm**). born 1933, British novelist and dramatist. His best-known works include the novels *This Sporting Life* (1960) and *A Serious Man* (1998) and the plays *In Celebration* (1969), *Home* (1970), and *Stages* (1992)

stork *n* a large wading bird with very long legs, a long bill, and white-and-black feathers [Old English *storc*]

storm *n* **1** a violent weather condition of strong winds, rain, hail, thunder, lightning, etc. **2** a violent disturbance or quarrel: *a storm of protest from the opposition* **3** (usually foll. by *of*) a heavy discharge of bullets or missiles **4** **take a place by storm a** to capture or overrun a place by a violent attack **b** to surprise people, but receive their praise, by being extremely successful at something ▷ *vb* **5** to attack or capture (a place) suddenly and violently **6** to shout angrily **7** to move or rush violently or angrily: *she stormed into the study* [Old English]

storm centre *n* **1** the centre of a storm, where pressure is lowest **2** the centre of any disturbance or trouble

storm door *n* an additional door outside an ordinary door, providing extra protection against wind, cold, and rain

Stormont *n* a suburb of Belfast: site of Parliament House (1928–30), formerly the seat of the parliament of Northern Ireland (1922–72) and since 1998 of the Northern Ireland assembly, and Stormont Castle, formerly the residence of the prime minister of Northern Ireland and since 1998 the office of the province's first minister

storm trooper *n* a member of the paramilitary wing of the Nazi Party

stormy *adj* **stormier, stormiest 1** (of weather) violent with dark skies, heavy rain or snow, and strong winds **2** involving violent emotions: *a stormy affair*

stormy petrel *or* **storm petrel** *n* **1** a small sea bird with dark feathers and paler underparts **2** a person who brings trouble

Stornoway *n* a port in NW Scotland, on the E coast of Lewis in the Outer Hebrides, administrative centre of the Western Isles. Pop: 5602 (2001)

story¹ *n, pl* **-ries 1** a description of a chain of events told or written in prose or verse **2** Also called: **short story** a piece of fiction, shorter and usually less detailed than a novel **3** Also called: **story line** the plot of a book or film **4** a news report **5** the event or material for such a report **6** *informal* a lie [Latin *historia*]

story² *n, pl* **-ries** *chiefly US* same as **storey**

storybook *n* **1** a book containing stories for children ▷ *adj* **2** better or happier than in real life: *a storybook romance*

Stoss *n* Viet. ?1445–1533, German Gothic sculptor and woodcarver. His masterpiece is the high altar in the Church of St Mary, Cracow (1477–89)

stoup *or* **stoop** (stoop) *n* a small basin in a church for holy water [from Old Norse]

Stour *n* **1** Also called: **Great Stour** a river in S England, in Kent, rising in the Weald and flowing N to the North Sea: separates the Isle of Thanet from the mainland **2** any of several smaller rivers in England

Stourbridge *n* an industrial town in W central England, in Dudley unitary authority, West Midlands. Pop: 55 480 (2001)

Stourhead *n* a Palladian mansion near Mere in Wiltshire: built (1722) for Henry Hoare; famous for its landscaped gardens laid out (1741) by Flitcroft

stoush *Austral and NZ slang vb* **1** to hit or punch (someone) ▷ *n* **2** fighting or violence [origin unknown]

stout *adj* **1** solidly built or fat **2** strong and sturdy: *stout footwear* **3** brave or determined: *we met unexpectedly stout resistance* ▷ *n* **4** strong dark beer [Old French *estout* bold] **> stoutly** *adv*

Stout *n* Sir **Robert.** 1844–1930, New Zealand statesman, born in Scotland: prime minister of New Zealand (1884–87)

stouthearted *adj old-fashioned* determined or brave

stove¹ *n* **1** same as **cooker** (1) **2** any apparatus for heating, such as a kiln [Old English *stofa* bathroom]

stove² *vb* a past tense and past participle of **stave**

stovepipe *n* a pipe that takes fumes and smoke away from a stove

stow *vb* (often foll. by *away*) to pack or store (something) [Old English *stōwian* to keep]

Stow *n* John. 1525–1605, English antiquary, noted for his *Survey of London and Westminster* (1598; 1603)

stowage *n* **1** space, room, or a charge for stowing goods **2** the act of stowing

stowaway *n* **1** a person who hides aboard a ship or aircraft in order to travel free ▷ *vb* **stow away 2** to travel in such a way: *he stowed away on a ferry*

Stowe¹ *n* a mansion near Buckingham in N Buckinghamshire: built and decorated in the 17th and 18th centuries by Vanbrugh, Robert Adam, Grinling Gibbons, and William Kent; formerly the seat of the Dukes of Buckingham; fine landscaped gardens: now occupied by a public school

Stowe² *n* Harriet Elizabeth Beecher. 1811–96, US writer, whose bestselling novel *Uncle Tom's Cabin* (1852) contributed to the antislavery cause

Strabane *n* a district of W Northern Ireland, in Co Tyrone. Pop: 38 565 (2003 est). Area: 862 sq km (333 sq miles)

strabismus *n pathol* same as **squint** (3) [Greek *strabismos*]

Strabo *n* ?63 BC–?23 AD, Greek geographer and historian, noted for his *Geographica*

Strachey *n* (Giles) **Lytton**. 1880–1932, English biographer and critic, best known for *Eminent Victorians* (1918) and *Queen Victoria* (1921)

straddle *vb* **-dling, -dled 1** to have one leg or part on each side of (something) **2** *US and Canad informal* to be in favour of both sides of (an issue or argument) [from *stride*]

Stradivari *n* Antonio. ?1644–1737, Italian violin, viola, and cello maker

Stradivarius *n* a violin manufactured in Italy by Antonio Stradivari (?1644–1737) or his family

strafe *vb* **strafing, strafed** to machine-gun (an enemy) from the air [German *strafen* to punish]

Strafford *n* Thomas Wentworth, Earl of. 1593–1641, English statesman. As lord deputy of Ireland (1632–39) and a chief adviser to Charles I, he was a leading proponent of the king's absolutist rule. He was impeached by Parliament and executed

straggle *vb* **-gling, -gled 1** to spread out in an untidy and rambling way: *the town straggled off to the east* **2** to linger behind or wander from a main line or part [origin unknown] **> straggler** *n* **> straggly** *adj*

straight *adj* **1** continuing in the same direction without bending; not curved or crooked **2** even, level, or upright **3** in keeping with the facts; accurate **4** outright or candid: *a straight rejection* **5** in continuous succession

6 (of an alcoholic drink) undiluted **7** not wavy or curly: *straight hair* **8** in good order **9** (of a play or acting style) straightforward or serious **10** honest, respectable, or reliable **11** slang heterosexual **12** slang conventional in views, customs, or appearance **13** informal no longer owing or being owed something: *if you buy the next round we'll be straight* ▷ adv **14** in a straight line or direct course **15** immediately; at once: *get straight back here* **16** in a level or upright position: *he sat up straight* **17** continuously; uninterruptedly: *we waited for three hours straight* **18** (often foll. by *out*) frankly; candidly: *she asked me straight out* **19** go straight informal to reform after having been a criminal **20** straight away *or* straightaway at once ▷ n **21** a straight line, form, part, or position **22** Brit a straight part of a racetrack **23** slang a heterosexual person [Old English *streccan* to stretch]

straighten vb (sometimes foll. by *up* or *out*) **1** to make or become straight **2** to make (something) neat or tidy

straighten out vb to make (something) less complicated or confused

straight face n a serious facial expression which hides a desire to laugh ❯ **straight-faced** adj

straight fight n a contest between two candidates only

straightforward adj **1** (of a person) honest, frank, and open **2** (of a task) easy to do

straight man n an actor who acts as the butt of a comedian's jokes

strain¹ n **1** tension or tiredness resulting from overwork or worry **2** tension between people or organizations: *there are signs of strain between the economic superpowers* **3** an intense physical or mental effort **4** the damage resulting from excessive physical exertion **5** a great demand on the emotions, strength, or resources **6** a way of speaking: *he would have gone on in this strain for some time* **7** physics the change in dimension of a body caused by outside forces **8** strains music a theme, melody, or tune ▷ vb **9** to subject (someone) to mental tension or stress **10** to make an intense effort: *the rest were straining to follow the conversation* **11** to use (resources) to, or beyond, their limits **12** to injure or damage (oneself or a part of one's body) by overexertion: *he appeared to have strained a muscle* **13** to pour (a substance) through a sieve or filter **14** strain at to push, pull, or work with violent effort on (something) **15** to draw (something) taut or be drawn taut [Latin *stringere* to bind tightly]

strain² n **1** a group of animals or plants within a species or variety, distinguished by one or more minor characteristics **2** a trace or streak: *a strain of ruthlessness in their play* [Old English *strēon*]

strained adj **1** (of an action, expression, etc.) not natural or spontaneous **2** (of an atmosphere, relationship, etc.) not relaxed; tense

strainer n a sieve used for straining sauces, vegetables, or tea

strait n **1** (often pl) a narrow channel of the sea linking two larger areas of sea **2** straits a position of extreme difficulty: *in desperate straits* [Old French *estreit* narrow]

straitened adj in straitened circumstances not having much money

straitjacket n **1** a strong canvas jacket with long sleeves used to bind the arms of a violent person **2** anything which holds back or restricts development or freedom: *exporters are wrapped in a straitjacket of regulations*

strait-laced *or* **straight-laced** adj having a strict code of moral standards; puritanical

Straits Settlements pl n (formerly) a British crown colony of SE Asia that included Singapore, Penang, Malacca, Labuan, and some smaller islands

Stralsund n a port in NE Germany, in Mecklenburg-West Pomerania on a strait of the Baltic: one of the leading towns of the Hanseatic League. Pop: 59 140 (2003 est)

strand¹ vb **1** to leave or drive (ships or fish) ashore **2** to leave (someone) helpless, for example without transport

or money ▷ n **3** chiefly poetic a shore or beach [Old English]

strand² n **1** one of the individual fibres of string or wire that form a rope, cord, or cable **2** a single length of string, hair, wool, or wire **3** a string of pearls or beads **4** a part of something; element: *the many disparate strands of the Anglican Church* [origin unknown]

Strand n the Strand a street in W central London, parallel to the Thames: famous for its hotels and theatres

stranded adj stuck somewhere and unable to leave

strange adj **1** odd or unexpected **2** not known, seen, or experienced before; unfamiliar **3** strange to inexperienced in or unaccustomed to: *they are in some degree strange to it* [Latin *extraneus* foreign] ❯ **strangely** adv ❯ **strangeness** n

stranger n **1** any person whom one does not know **2** a person who is new to a particular place **3** stranger to something a person who is unfamiliar with or new to something: *Paul is no stranger to lavish spending*

strangle vb **-gling, -gled 1** to kill (someone) by pressing his or her windpipe; throttle **2** to prevent the growth or development of: *another attempt at strangling national identity* **3** to stifle (a voice, cry, or laugh) by swallowing suddenly: *the words were strangled by sobs* [Greek *strangalē* a halter] ❯ **strangler** n

stranglehold n **1** a wrestling hold in which a wrestler's arms are pressed against his opponent's windpipe **2** complete power or control over a person or situation

strangulate vb **-lating, -lated 1** pathol to constrict (a hollow organ or vessel) so as to stop the flow of air or blood through it: *a badly strangulated hernia* **2** same as strangle ❯ **strangulation** n

Stranraer n a market town in SW Scotland, in W Dumfries and Galloway: fishing port with a ferry service to Northern Ireland. Pop: 10 851 (2001)

strap n **1** a strip of strong flexible material used for carrying, lifting, fastening, or holding things in place **2** a loop of leather or rubber, hanging from the roof in a bus or train for standing passengers to hold on to **3** short for shoulder strap **4** the strap a beating with a strap as a punishment ▷ vb **strapping, strapped 5** to tie or bind (something) with a strap [variant of STROP]

straphanger n informal a passenger in a bus or train who has to travel standing and holding on to a strap

strapless adj (of women's clothes) without straps over the shoulders

strapped adj strapped for slang badly in need of: *strapped for cash*

strapping adj tall, strong, and healthy-looking: *a strapping young lad* [from strap (in the archaic sense: to work vigorously)]

Strasbourg n a city in NE France, on the Rhine: the chief French inland port; under German rule (1870–1918); university (1567); seat of the Council of Europe and of the European Parliament. Pop: 276 867 (2006). German name: Strassburg

strata n the plural of stratum

> **USAGE** Strata is sometimes wrongly used as a singular noun: *this stratum (not strata) of society is often disregarded*.

stratagem n a clever plan to deceive an enemy [Greek *stratēgos* a general]

strategic (strat-ee-jik) adj **1** planned to achieve an advantage; tactical **2** (of weapons, esp. missiles) directed against an enemy's homeland rather than used on a battlefield ❯ **strategically** adv

strategy n, pl **-gies 1** a long-term plan for success, such as in politics or business **2** the art of the planning and conduct of a war [Greek *stratēgia* function of a general] ❯ **strategist** n

Stratford-on-Avon *or* **Stratford-upon-Avon** n a market town in central England, in SW Warwickshire on the River Avon: the birthplace and burial place of William Shakespeare and home of the Royal Shakespeare Company; tourist centre. Pop: 22 187 (2001)

strath *n Scot* a flat river valley [Scottish & Irish Gaelic *srath*]

Strathclyde Region *n* a former local government region in W Scotland: formed in 1975 from Glasgow, Renfrewshire, Lanarkshire, Buteshire, Dunbartonshire, and parts of Argyllshire, Ayrshire, and Stirlingshire; replaced in 1996 by the council areas of Glasgow, Renfrewshire, East Renfrewshire, Inverclyde, North Lanarkshire, South Lanarkshire, Argyll and Bute, East Dunbartonshire, West Dunbartonshire, North Ayrshire, South Ayrshire, and East Ayrshire

strathspey *n* **1** a Scottish dance with gliding steps, slower than a reel **2** music for this dance [after *Strathspey*, valley of the River Spey]

stratified *adj* **1** (of rocks) formed in horizontal layers of different materials **2** *sociol* (of a society) divided into different classes or groups [New Latin *stratificare* to form in layers] **> stratification** *n*

stratocumulus (strat-oh-**kew**-myew-luss) *n, pl* **-li** (-lie) *meteorol* an unbroken stretch of dark grey cloud

stratosphere *n* the atmospheric layer between about 15 and 50 km above the earth

stratum (strah-tum) *n, pl* **-ta** (-ta) **1** any of the distinct layers into which certain rocks are divided **2** a layer of ocean or atmosphere marked off naturally or decided arbitrarily by man **3** a social class [Latin: something strewn]

stratus (stray-tuss) *n, pl* **-ti** (-tie) a grey layer cloud [Latin: strewn]

Straus *n* Oscar. 1870–1954, French composer, born in Austria, noted for such operettas as *Waltz Dream* (1907) and *The Chocolate Soldier* (1908)

Strauss *n* **1** David Friedrich. 1808–74, German Protestant theologian: in his *Life of Jesus* (1835–36) he treated the supernatural elements of the story as myth **2** Johann. 1804–49, Austrian composer, noted for his waltzes **3** his son, Johann, called the *Waltz King*. 1825–99, Austrian composer, whose works include *The Blue Danube Waltz* (1867) and the operetta *Die Fledermaus* (1874) **4** Richard. 1864–1949, German composer, noted esp. for his symphonic poems, including *Don Juan* (1889) and *Till Eulenspiegel* (1895), his operas, such as *Elektra* (1909) and *Der Rosenkavalier* (1911), and his *Four Last Songs* (1948)

Stravinsky *n* Igor Fyodorovich. 1882–1971, US composer, born in Russia. He created ballet scores, such as *The Firebird* (1910), *Petrushka* (1911), and *The Rite of Spring* (1913), for Diaghilev. These were followed by neoclassical works, including *Oedipus Rex* (1927) and the *Symphony of Psalms* (1930). The 1950s saw him reconciled to serial techniques, which he employed in such works as the *Canticum Sacrum* (1955), the ballet *Agon* (1957), and *Requiem Canticles* (1966)

straw *n* **1** dried stalks of threshed grain, such as wheat or barley **2** a single stalk of straw **3** a long thin hollow paper or plastic tube, used for sucking up liquids into the mouth **4 clutch at straws** to turn in desperation to something with little chance of success **5 draw the short straw** to be the person chosen to perform an unpleasant task **> adj 6** made of straw: *straw baskets* [Old English *strēaw*]

Straw *n* Jack, full name *John Whitaker Straw*. born 1946, British Labour politician; Home Secretary (1997–2001); Foreign Secretary (2001–06); Lord Chancellor (2007–10)

strawberry *n, pl* **-ries** a sweet fleshy red fruit with small seeds on the outside [Old English *strēawberige*]

strawberry blonde *adj* **1** (of hair) reddish-blonde **> n 2** a woman with such hair

strawberry mark *n* a red birthmark

straw-coloured *adj* pale yellow: *straw-coloured hair*

straw poll *or* **straw vote** *n* an unofficial poll or vote taken to find out the opinion of a group or the public on some issue

Strawson *n* Sir Peter (Frederick). 1919–2006, British philosopher. His early work deals with the relationship between language and logic, his later work with metaphysics. His books include *The Bounds of Sense* (1966) and *Freedom and Resentment* (1974)

strawweight *n* a professional boxer weighing under 105 pounds (47 kg). Also called: **mini-flyweight**

stray *vb* **1** to wander away from the correct path or from a given area **2** to move away from the point or lose concentration **3** to fail to live up to certain moral standards: *her man had strayed* **> n 4** a domestic animal that has wandered away from its home **5** old-fashioned a lost or homeless child **> adj 6** (of a domestic animal) having wandered away from its home **7** random or separated from the main group of things of their kind: *stray bombs and rockets* [Old French *estraier*]

Strayhorn *n* Billy, full name *William Strayhorn*. 1915–67, US jazz composer and pianist, noted esp. for his association (1939–67) with Duke Ellington

streak *n* **1** a long thin stripe or trace of some contrasting colour **2** (of lightning) a sudden flash **3** a quality or characteristic: *a nasty streak* **4** a short stretch of good or bad luck: *a losing streak* **5** *informal* an instance of running naked through a public place **> vb 6** to mark (something) with a streak or streaks: *sweat streaking the grime of his face* **7** to move quickly in a straight line **8** *informal* to run naked through a public place [Old English *strica*] **> streaked** *or* **streaky** *adj* **> streaker** *n*

stream *n* **1** a small river **2** any steady flow of water or other liquid **3** something that resembles a stream in moving continuously in a line or particular direction: *the stream of traffic* **4** a fast and continuous flow of speech: *the constant stream of jargon* **5** *Brit, Austral and NZ* a class of school children grouped together because of similar ability **> vb 6** to pour in a continuous flow: *rain streamed down her cheeks* **7** (of a crowd of people or traffic or a herd of animals) to move in unbroken succession **8** *computers* to send video or audio material over the internet so that the receiving system can play it almost simultaneously **9** to float freely or with a waving motion: *a flimsy pink dress that streamed out behind her* **10** *Brit and NZ* to group (school children) in streams [Old English *strēam*] **> streaming** *n* **> streamlet** *n*

streamer *n* **1** a long coiled ribbon of coloured paper that unrolls when tossed **2** a long narrow flag

streaming *n computers* a method of sending video or audio material over the internet so that the receiving system can process and play it almost simultaneously

streamline *vb* **-lining, -lined 1** to improve (something) by removing the parts that are least useful or profitable **2** to make (an aircraft, boat, or vehicle) less resistant to flowing air or water by improving its shape **> streamlined** *adj*

Streep *n* Meryl, original name *Mary Louise Streep*. born 1949, US actress. Her films include *The Deer Hunter* (1978), *Kramer vs Kramer* (1979), *The French Lieutenant's Woman* (1981), *Sophie's Choice* (1982), *Out of Africa* (1986), *The Hours* (2002), *Mamma Mia!* (2008), and *The Iron Lady* (2011)

street *n* **1** a public road that is usually lined with buildings, esp. in a town: *Sauchiehall Street* **2** the part of the road between the pavements, used by vehicles **3** the people living in a particular street **4 on the streets** homeless **5 right up one's street** *informal* just what one knows or likes best **6 streets ahead of** *informal* superior to or more advanced than [Old English *strǣt*]

streetcar *n US and Canad* a tram

street cred *or* **street credibility** *n* a command of the styles, knowledge, etc., associated with urban youngsters who are respected by their contemporaries: *having children was the quickest way to lose your street cred*

street value *n* the price that would be paid for goods, esp. illegal ones such as drugs, by the final user: *cocaine with a street value of £2m was seized at Heathrow airport*

streetwalker *n* a prostitute who tries to find customers in the streets

streetwise *adj* knowing how to survive or succeed in poor and often criminal sections of big cities

Streicher *n* Julius. 1885–1946, German Nazi journalist and politician, who spread anti-Semitic propaganda as editor of *Der Stürmer* (1923–45). He was hanged as a war criminal

Streisand *n* Barbra. born 1942, US singer, actress, and film director: the films she has acted in include *Funny Girl* (1968) and *A Star is Born* (1976); her films as actress and director include *Yentl* (1983), *Prince of Tides* (1990), and *The Mirror has Two Faces* (1996)

strength *n* **1** the state or quality of being physically or mentally strong **2** the ability to withstand great force, stress, or pressure **3** something regarded as valuable or a source of power: *his chief strength is rocketry* **4** potency or effectiveness, such as of a drink or drug **5** power to convince: *the strength of this argument* **6** degree of intensity or concentration of colour, light, sound, or flavour: *a medium-strength cheese* **7** the total number of people in a group: *at full strength; 50 000 men below strength* **8 go from strength to strength** to have ever-increasing success **9 on the strength of** on the basis of or relying upon [Old English *strengthu*]

strengthen *vb* to become stronger or make (something) stronger

strenuous *adj* requiring or involving the use of great energy or effort [Latin *strenuus* brisk] ▷ **strenuously** *adv*

streptococcus (strep-toe-kok-uss) *n, pl* **-cocci** (-kok-eye) a bacterium occurring in chains and including many species that cause disease [Greek *streptos* crooked + *kokkos* berry]

streptomycin *n med* an antibiotic used in the treatment of tuberculosis and other bacterial infections [Greek *streptos* crooked + *mukēs* fungus]

Stresemann *n* Gustav. 1878–1929, German statesman; chancellor (1923) and foreign minister (1923–29) of the Weimar Republic. He gained (1926) Germany's admission to the League of Nations and shared the Nobel peace prize (1926) with Aristide Briand

stress *n* **1** mental, emotional, or physical strain or tension **2** special emphasis or significance **3** emphasis placed upon a syllable by pronouncing it more loudly than those that surround it **4** *physics* force producing a change in shape or volume ▷ *vb* **5** to give emphasis to (a point or subject): *she stressed how difficult it had been* **6** to pronounce (a word or syllable) more loudly than those surrounding it [shortened from *distress*] ▷ **stressful** *adj*

stressed-out *adj informal* suffering from anxiety or tension

stretch *vb* **1 stretch over** *or* **for** to extend or spread over (a specified distance): *the flood barrier stretches for several miles* **2** to draw out or extend (something) or to be drawn out or extended in length or area **3** to distort or lengthen (something) or to be distorted or lengthened permanently **4** to extend (the limbs or body), for example when one has just woken up **5** (often foll. by *out, forward,* etc.) to reach or hold out (a part of one's body) **6** to reach or suspend (a rope, etc.) from one place to another **7** to draw (something) tight; tighten **8** (usually foll. by *over*) to extend in time: *a dinner which stretched over three consecutive evenings* **9** to put a great strain upon (one's money or resources) **10** to make do with (limited resources): *the Walkers decided to stretch their budget* **11** to extend (someone) to the limit of his or her abilities **12** to extend (someone) to the limit of his or her tolerance **13 stretch a point** to make an exception not usually made ▷ *n* **14** the act of stretching **15** a large or continuous expanse or distance: *this stretch of desert* **16** extent in time **17** a term of imprisonment **18 at a stretch** *chiefly Brit and NZ* **a** with some difficulty; by making a special effort **b** at one time: *for hours at a stretch they had no conversation* ▷ *adj* **19** (of clothes) able to be stretched without

permanently losing shape: *a stretch suit* [Old English *streccan*] ▷ **stretchy** *adj*

stretcher *n* a frame covered with canvas, on which an ill or injured person is carried

stretcher-bearer *n* a person who helps to carry a stretcher

Stretford *n* an industrial town in NW England, in Trafford unitary authority, Greater Manchester. Pop: 42 103 (2001)

strew *vb* **strewing, strewed, strewn** to scatter (things) over a surface [Old English *streowian*]

strewth *interj informal* an expression of surprise or alarm [alteration of *God's truth*]

stria (strye-a) *n, pl* **striae** (strye-ee) *geology* a scratch or groove on the surface of a rock crystal [Latin: a groove]

striation *n* **1** an arrangement or pattern of striae **2** same as stria ▷ **striated** *adj*

stricken *adj* badly affected by disease, pain, grief, etc.: *flood-stricken areas* [past participle of STRIKE]

strict *adj* **1** severely correct in attention to behaviour or morality: *a strict disciplinarian* **2** following carefully and exactly a set of rules: *she is a strict vegetarian* **3** (of a rule or law) very precise and requiring total obedience: *a strict code of practice* **4** (of a meaning) exact: *this is not, in the strictest sense, a biography* **5** (of a punishment, etc.) harsh or severe **6** complete; absolute: *strict obedience* [Latin *strictus* drawn tight] ▷ **strictly** *adv* ▷ **strictness** *n*

stricture *n formal* a severe criticism [Latin *strictura* contraction]

stride *n* **1** a long step or pace **2** the length of such a step **3** a striding walk **4** progress or development: *he has made great strides in regaining his confidence* **5** a regular pace or rate of progress: *it put me off my stride* **6 take something in one's stride** to do something without difficulty or effort ▷ *vb* **striding, strode, stridden** **7** to walk with long steps or paces **8 stride over** *or* **across** to cross (over a space or an obstacle) with a stride [Old English *strīdan*]

strident *adj* **1** (of a voice or sound) loud and harsh **2** loud, persistent, and forceful: *a strident critic of the establishment* [Latin *stridens*] ▷ **stridency** *n*

strife *n* angry or violent struggle; conflict [Old French *estrif*]

Strijdom *n* Johannes Gerhardus. 1893–1958, South African statesman; prime minister (1954–58)

strike *vb* **striking, struck 1** (of employees) to stop work collectively as a protest against working conditions, low pay, etc. **2** to hit (someone) **3** to cause (something) to come into sudden or violent contact with something **4 strike at** to attack (someone or something) **5** to cause (a match) to light by friction **6** to sound (a specific note) on a musical instrument **7** (of a clock) to indicate (a time) by the sound of a bell **8** to affect (someone) deeply in a particular way: *he never struck me as the supportive type* **9** to enter the mind of: *a brilliant thought struck me* **10** (of a poisonous snake) to injure by biting **11** (past part **struck** or **stricken**) to change into (a different state): *struck blind* **12** to be noticed by; catch: *the heavy smell of incense struck my nostrils* **13** to arrive at (something) suddenly or unexpectedly: *to strike on a solution* **14** to afflict (someone) with a disease: *she has been struck down by breast cancer* **15** to discover a source of (gold, oil, etc.) **16** to reach (something) by agreement: *to strike a deal* **17** to take up (a posture or an attitude) **18** to take apart or pack up: *to strike camp* **19** to make (a coin) by stamping it **20 strike home** to achieve the desired effect **21 strike it rich** *informal* to have an unexpected financial success ▷ *n* **22** a stopping of work, as a protest against working conditions, low pay, etc.: *a one-day strike* **23** an act or instance of striking **24** a military attack, esp. an air attack on a target on land or at sea: *a pre-emptive strike* **25** *baseball* a pitched ball swung at and missed by the batter **26** *tenpin bowling* the knocking down of all the pins with one bowl **27** the discovery of a source of gold, oil, etc. ▶ See also **strike off, strike out, strike up** [Old English *strīcan*]

strikebreaker *n* a person who tries to make a strike fail by working or by taking the place of those on strike

strike off *vb* to remove the name of (a doctor or lawyer who has done something wrong) from an official register, preventing him or her from practising again

strike out *vb* **1** to score out (something written) **2** to start out or begin: *I'm going to strike out for town*

strike pay *n* money paid to strikers by a trade union

striker *n* **1** a person who is on strike **2** *soccer* an attacking player

strike up *vb* **1** to begin (a conversation or friendship) **2** (of a band or an orchestra) to begin to play (a tune)

striking *adj* **1** attracting attention; impressive: *her striking appearance* **2** very noticeable: *a striking difference* ⊳ **strikingly** *adv*

strimmer *n* trademark an electrical tool for trimming the edges of lawns

strimon *n* a transliteration of the Greek name for the Struma

Strindberg *n* August. 1849–1912, Swedish dramatist and novelist, whose plays include *The Father* (1887), *Miss Julie* (1888), and *The Ghost Sonata* (1907)

Strine *n* a humorous transliteration of Australian pronunciation, as in *Gloria Soame* for *glorious home* [a jocular rendering of the Australian pronunciation of *Australian*]

string *n* **1** thin cord or twine used for tying, hanging, or binding things **2** a group of objects threaded on a single strand: *a string of pearls* **3** a series of things or events: *a string of wins* **4** a tightly stretched wire or cord on a musical instrument, such as the guitar, violin, or piano, that produces sound when vibrated **5** **the strings** *music* **a** violins, violas, cellos, and double basses collectively **b** the section of an orchestra consisting of such instruments **6** a group of characters that can be treated as a unit by a computer program **7** **with no strings attached** (of an offer) without complications or conditions **8** **pull strings** *informal* to use one's power or influence, esp. secretly or unofficially ⊳ *adj* **9** composed of stringlike strands woven in a large mesh: *a string bag* ⊳ *vb* **stringing, strung 10** to hang or stretch (something) from one point to another **11** to provide (something) with a string or strings **12** to thread (beads) on a string **13** to extend in a line or series: *towns strung out along the valley* [Old English *streng*] ⊳ **stringlike** *adj*

string along *vb informal* **1 string along with** to accompany: *I'll string along with you* **2** to deceive (someone) over a period of time: *she had only been stringing him along*

string bean *n* same as **runner bean**

string course *n archit* an ornamental projecting band along a wall

stringed *adj* (of musical instruments) having strings

stringent (strin-jent) *adj* requiring strict attention to rules or detail: *all have particularly stringent environmental laws* [Latin *stringere* to bind] ⊳ **stringency** *n*

stringer *n* **1** *archit* a long horizontal timber beam that connects upright posts **2** a journalist employed by a newspaper on a part-time basis to cover a particular town or area

string quartet *n music* **1** a group of musicians consisting of two violins, one viola, and one cello **2** a piece of music composed for such a group

string up *vb informal* to kill (a person) by hanging

stringy *adj* **stringier, stringiest 1** thin and rough: *stringy hair* **2** (of meat or other food) tough and fibrous

stringy-bark *n* an Australian eucalyptus with a fibrous bark

strip¹ *vb* **stripping, stripped 1** to take (the covering or clothes) off (oneself, another person, or thing) **2 a** to undress completely **b** to perform a striptease **3** to empty (a building) of all furniture **4** to take something away from (someone): *they were stripped of their possessions* **5** to remove (paint) from (a surface or furniture): *she stripped the plaster from the kitchen walls* **6** (often foll. by *down*) to

dismantle (an engine or a mechanism) into individual parts ⊳ *n* **7** the act or an instance of undressing or of performing a striptease [Old English *bestriepan* to plunder]

strip² *n* **1** a long narrow piece of something **2** short for **airstrip 3** *Brit, Austral and NZ* the clothes a sports team plays in [Middle Dutch *strīpe* stripe]

strip cartoon *n* a sequence of drawings in a newspaper or magazine, telling an amusing story or an adventure

strip club *n* a club in which striptease performances take place

stripe¹ *n* **1 a** long band of colour that differs from the surrounding material **2** a chevron or band worn on a uniform to indicate rank ⊳ *vb* **striping, striped 3** to mark (something) with stripes [probably from Middle Dutch *strīpe*] ⊳ **striped, stripy** *or* **stripey** *adj*

stripe² *n* a stroke from a whip, rod, or cane [from Middle Low German *strippe*]

strip lighting *n* a method of electric lighting that uses fluorescent lamps in long glass tubes

stripling *n* a teenage boy or young man

stripper *n* **1 a** person who performs a striptease **2** a tool or liquid for removing paint or varnish

strip-search *vb* **1** (of police, customs officials, etc.) to strip (a prisoner or suspect) naked to search him or her for drugs or smuggled goods ⊳ *n* **2** a search that involves stripping a person naked

striptease *n* an entertainment in which a person gradually undresses to music

strive *vb* **striving, strove, striven** to make a great effort: *to strive for a peaceful settlement* [Old French *estriver*]

strobe *n* short for **strobe lighting, stroboscope**

strobe lighting *n* a flashing beam of very bright light produced by a perforated disc rotating in front of a light source

stroboscope *n* an instrument producing a very bright flashing light which makes moving people appear stationary [Greek *strobos* a whirling + *skopein* to look at]

strode *vb* the past tense of **stride**

Stroessner *n* Alfredo. 1912–2006, Paraguayan soldier and politician; president (1954–89): deposed in a military coup

stroganoff *n* a dish of sliced beef cooked with onions and mushrooms, served in a sour-cream sauce. Also called: **beef stroganoff** [after Count *Stroganoff*, Russian diplomat]

stroke *vb* **stroking, stroked 1** to touch or brush lightly or gently ⊳ *n* **2** a light touch or caress with the fingers **3** *pathol* rupture of a blood vessel in the brain resulting in loss of consciousness, often followed by paralysis and damage to speech **4** a blow, knock, or hit **5** an action or occurrence of the kind specified: *a fantastic stroke of luck*; *a stroke of intuition* **6 a** the striking of a clock **b** the hour registered by this: *at the stroke of twelve* **7** a mark made by a pen or paintbrush **8** same as **solidus** used esp. when dictating or reading aloud **9** the hitting of the ball in sports such as golf or cricket **10** any one of the repeated movements used by a swimmer **11** a particular style of swimming, such as the crawl **12** a single pull on the oars in rowing **13 at a stroke** with one action **14 not a stroke** (of work) no work at all [Old English *strācian*]

stroll *vb* **1** to walk about in a leisurely manner ⊳ *n* **2** a leisurely walk [probably from dialect German *strollen*]

stroller *n US and Canad* a chair-shaped carriage for a baby

Stromboli *n* an island in the Tyrrhenian Sea, in the Lipari Islands off the N coast of Sicily: famous for its active volcano, 927 m (3040 ft) high

strong *adj* **stronger, strongest 1** having physical power **2** not easily broken or injured; solid or robust **3** great in degree or intensity; not faint or feeble: *a strong voice*; *a strong smell of explosive* **4** (of arguments) supported by evidence; convincing **5** concentrated; not weak or diluted **6** having a powerful taste or smell: *strong perfume* **7** (of language) using swear words **8** (of a person)

S

self-confident: *a strong personality* **9** committed or fervent: *a strong believer in free trade* **10** important or having a lot of power or influence: *a strong left-wing tendency within the university* **11** very competent at a particular activity: *they sent a very strong team to the Olympics* **12** containing or having a specified number: *the 700-strong workforce* **13** (of an accent) distinct and indicating where the speaker comes from **14** (of a relationship) stable and likely to last **15** having an extreme or drastic effect: *strong discipline* **16** (of a colour) very bright and intense **17** (of a wind, current, or earthquake) moving fast or intensely **18** (of an economy, an industry, a currency, etc.) growing, successful, or increasing in value ▷ *adv* **19 come on strong** *informal* **a** to show blatantly that one is sexually attracted to someone **b** to make a forceful or exaggerated impression **20 going strong** *informal* working or performing well; thriving [Old English *strang*] ❯ **strongly** *adv*

strong-arm *adj informal* involving physical force or violence: *strong-arm tactics*

strongbox *n* a box in which valuables are locked for safety

strong drink *n* alcoholic drink

stronghold *n* **1** an area in which a particular belief is shared by many people: *a Labour stronghold* **2** a place that is well defended; fortress

strong-minded *adj* not easily persuaded to change beliefs or opinions

strong point *n* something at which one is very good: *diplomacy wasn't his strong point*

strongroom *n* a specially designed room in which valuables are locked for safety

strontium *n chem* a soft silvery-white metallic element: the radioactive isotope **strontium-90** is used in nuclear power sources and is a hazardous nuclear fallout product. Symbol: Sr [after *Strontian*, in Scotland, where discovered]

strop *n* a leather strap for sharpening razors [Greek *strophos* cord]

stroppy *adj* **-pier, -piest** *informal* bad-tempered or deliberately awkward [from *obstreperous*]

strove *vb* the past tense of **strive**

struck *vb* a past of **strike**

structural *adj* **1** of or having structure or a structure **2** of or forming part of the structure of a building **3** *chem* of or involving the arrangement of atoms in molecules: *a structural formula* ❯ **structurally** *adv*

structuralism *n* an approach to social sciences and to literature which sees changes in the subject as caused and organized by a hidden set of universal rules ❯ **structuralist** *n, adj*

structure *n* **1** something that has been built or organized **2** the way the individual parts of something are made, built, or organized into a whole **3** the pattern of interrelationships within an organization, society, etc. **4** an organized method of working, thinking, or behaving **5** *chem* the arrangement of atoms in a molecule of a chemical compound **6** *geology* the way in which a rock is made up of its component parts ▷ *vb* **-turing, -tured 7** to arrange (something) into an organized system or pattern: *a structured school curriculum* [Latin *structura*]

strudel *n* a thin sheet of filled dough rolled up and baked: *apple strudel* [from German]

struggle *vb* **-gling, -gled 1** to work or strive: *the old regime struggled for power; he struggled to keep the conversation flowing* **2** to move about violently in an attempt to escape from something restricting **3** to fight with someone, often for possession of something **4** to go or progress with difficulty **5 struggle on** to manage to do something with difficulty ▷ *n* **6** something requiring a lot of exertion or effort to achieve **7** a fight or battle **8 the struggle** *S African* the concerted opposition to apartheid [origin unknown] ❯ **struggling** *adj*

strum *vb* **strumming, strummed 1** to play (a stringed instrument) by sweeping the thumb or a plectrum across the strings **2** to play (a tune) in this way [probably imitative]

Struma *n* a river in S Europe, rising in SW Bulgaria near Sofia and flowing generally southeast through Greece to the Aegean. Length: 362 km (225 miles). Greek names: **Strimon, Strymon**

strumpet *n archaic* a prostitute or promiscuous woman [origin unknown]

strung *vb* the past of **string**

strung up *adj informal* tense or nervous: *you sound a bit strung up*

strut *vb* **strutting, strutted 1** to walk in a stiff proud way with head high and shoulders back; swagger ▷ *n* **2** a piece of wood or metal that forms part of the framework of a structure [Old English *strūtian* to stand stiffly]

Struve *n* Otto. 1897–1963, US astronomer, born in Russia; noted for his work in stellar spectroscopy and his discovery (1937) of interstellar hydrogen

strychnine (strik-neen) *n* a very poisonous drug formerly used in small quantities as a stimulant [Greek *strukhnos* nightshade]

Strymon *n* transliteration of the Greek name for the **Struma**

Stuart *n* **1** the royal house that ruled in Scotland from 1371 to 1714 and in England from 1603 to 1714. See also **Stewart** (2) **2 Charles Edward**, called the *Young Pretender* or *Bonnie Prince Charlie.* 1720–88, pretender to the British throne. He led the Jacobite Rebellion (1745–46) in an attempt to re-establish the Stuart succession **3** his father, **James Francis Edward**, called the *Old Pretender.* 1688–1766, pretender to the British throne; son of James II (James VII of Scotland) and his second wife, Mary of Modena. He made two unsuccessful attempts to realize his claim to the throne (1708; 1715) **4** Mary. See **Mary, Queen of Scots**

stub *n* **1** a short piece remaining after something has been used: *a cigarette stub* **2** the section of a ticket or cheque which the purchaser keeps as a receipt ▷ *vb* **stubbing, stubbed 3** to strike (one's toe or foot) painfully against a hard surface **4 stub out** to put out (a cigarette or cigar) by pressing the end against a surface [Old English *stubb*]

stubble *n* **1** the short stalks left in a field where a crop has been harvested **2** the short bristly hair on the chin of a man who has not shaved for a while [Old French *estuble*] ❯ **stubbly** *adj*

stubble-jumper *n Canad slang* a prairie grain farmer

stubborn *adj* **1** refusing to agree or give in **2** persistent and determined **3** difficult to handle, treat, or overcome: *the most stubborn dandruff* [origin unknown] ❯ **stubbornly** *adv* ❯ **stubbornness** *n*

Stubbs *n* George. 1724–1806, English painter, noted esp. for his pictures of horses

stubby *adj* **-bier, -biest** short and broad

STUC Scottish Trades Union Congress

stucco *n* **1** plaster used for coating or decorating outside walls ▷ *vb* **-coing, -coed 2** to apply stucco to (a building) [Italian]

stuck *vb* **1** the past of **stick²** ▷ *adj* **2** *informal* baffled by a problem or unable to find an answer to a question **3 be stuck on** *slang* to feel a strong attraction to; be infatuated with **4 get stuck in** *informal* to perform a task with determination

stuck-up *adj informal* proud or snobbish

stud¹ *n* **1** a small piece of metal attached to a surface for decoration **2** a fastener consisting of two discs at either end of a short bar, usually used with clothes **3** *Brit* one of several small round objects attached to the sole of a football boot to give better grip ▷ *vb* **studding, studded 4** to decorate or cover (something) with or as if with studs: *apartment houses studded with satellite dishes* [Old English *studu*]

stud² *n* **1** a male animal, esp. a stallion kept for breeding **2** Also: **stud farm** a place where animals are bred **3** the state of being kept for breeding purposes **4** *slang* a virile or sexually active man [Old English *stōd*]

student *n* **1** a person following a course of study in a school, college, or university **2** a person who makes a thorough study of a subject: *a keen student of opinion polls* [Latin *studens* diligent]

studied *adj* carefully practised or planned: *studied calm*

studio *n, pl* **-dios 1** a room in which an artist, photographer, or musician works **2** a room used to record television or radio programmes or to make films or records **3 studios** the premises of a radio, television, record, or film company [Italian]

studio couch *n* a backless couch that can be converted into a double bed

studio flat *n Brit* a flat with one main room and, usually, a small kitchen and bathroom. Also called: **studio apartment**

studious (styoo-dee-uss) *adj* **1** serious, thoughtful, and hard-working **2** precise, careful, or deliberate [Latin *studiosus* devoted to] > **studiously** *adv*

study *vb* **studies, studying, studied 1** to be engaged in the learning or understanding of (a subject) **2** to investigate or examine (something) by observation and research **3** to look at (something or someone) closely; scrutinize ⊳ *n, pl* **studies 4** the act or process of studying **5** a room used for studying, reading, or writing **6** (*often pl*) work relating to a particular area of learning: *environmental studies* **7** an investigation and analysis of a particular subject **8** a paper or book produced as a result of study **9** a work of art, such as a drawing, done for practice or in preparation for another work **10** a musical composition designed to develop playing technique [Latin *studium* zeal]

stuff *n* **1** substance or material **2** any collection of unnamed things **3** the raw material of something **4** subject matter, skill, etc.: *this journalist knew his stuff* **5** woollen fabric **6 do one's stuff** *informal* to do what is expected of one ⊳ *vb* **7** to pack or fill (something) completely; cram **8** to force, shove, or squeeze (something somewhere): *I stuffed it in my briefcase* **9** to fill (food such as poultry or tomatoes) with a seasoned mixture **10** to fill (a dead animal's skin) with material so as to restore the shape of the live animal **11** *slang* to frustrate or defeat **12 get stuffed!** *Brit, Austral and NZ slang* an exclamation of anger or annoyance with someone **13 stuff oneself** *or* **one's face** to eat a large amount of food [Old French *estoffe*]

stuffed shirt *n informal* a pompous or old-fashioned person

stuffed-up *adj* having the passages of one's nose blocked with mucus

stuffing *n* **1** a mixture of ingredients with which poultry or meat is stuffed before cooking **2** the material used to fill and give shape to soft toys, pillows, furniture, etc.; padding

stuffy *adj* **-ier, -iest 1** lacking fresh air **2** old-fashioned and very formal: *an image of stuffy tradition* > **stuffiness** *n*

stultify *vb* **-fies, -fying, -fied** to dull (the mind) by boring routine [Latin *stultus* stupid + *facere* to make] > **stultifying** *adj*

stumble *vb* **-bling, -bled 1** to trip and almost fall while walking or running **2** to walk in an unsteady or unsure way **3** to make mistakes or hesitate in speech **4 stumble across** *or* **on** *or* **upon** to encounter or discover (someone or something) by accident ⊳ *n* **5** an act of stumbling [Middle English *stomble*]

stumbling block *n* any obstacle that prevents something from taking place or progressing

stump *n* **1** the base of a tree trunk left standing after the tree has been cut down or has been removed **2** the part of something, such as a tooth or limb, that remains after a larger part has been removed **3** *cricket* any of three

upright wooden sticks that, with two bails laid across them, form a wicket ⊳ *vb* **4** to baffle or confuse (someone) **5** *cricket* to dismiss (a batsman) by breaking his wicket with the ball **6** *chiefly US and Canad* to campaign or canvass (an area), by political speech-making **7** to walk with heavy steps; trudge [Middle Low German]

stump up *vb Brit informal* to give (the money required)

stumpy *adj* **stumpier, stumpiest** short and thick like a stump; stubby

stun *vb* **stunning, stunned 1** to shock or astonish (someone) so that he or she is unable to speak or act **2** (of a heavy blow or fall) to make (a person or an animal) unconscious [Old French *estoner* to daze]

stung *vb* the past of **sting**

stunk *vb* a past of **stink**

stunner *n Brit, Austral and NZ informal* a person or thing of great beauty

stunning *adj informal* very attractive or impressive > **stunningly** *adv*

stunt¹ *vb* to prevent or slow down (the growth or development of a plant, animal, or person) [Old English: foolish] > **stunted** *adj*

stunt² *n* **1** an acrobatic or dangerous piece of action in a film or television programme **2** anything spectacular or unusual done to gain publicity ⊳ *adj* **3** of or relating to acrobatic or dangerous pieces of action in films or television programmes: *a stunt man* [origin unknown]

stupefaction *n* the state of being unable to think clearly because of tiredness or boredom

stupefy *vb* **-pefies, -pefying, -pefied 1** to make (someone) feel so bored and tired that he or she is unable to think clearly **2** to confuse or astound (someone) [Old French *stupefier*] > **stupefying** *adj*

stupendous *adj* very large or impressive [Latin *stupere* to be amazed] > **stupendously** *adv*

stupid *adj* **1** lacking in common sense or intelligence **2** trivial, silly, or childish: *we got into a stupid quarrel* **3** unable to think clearly; dazed: *stupid with tiredness* [Latin *stupidus*] > **stupidity** *n* > **stupidly** *adv*

stupor *n* a state of near unconsciousness in which a person is unable to behave normally or think clearly [Latin]

sturdy *adj* **-dier, -diest 1** (of a person) healthy, strong, and unlikely to tire or become injured **2** (of a piece of furniture, shoes, etc.) strongly built or made [Old French *estordi* dazed] > **sturdily** *adv*

sturgeon *n* a bony fish from which caviar is obtained [Old French *estourgeon*]

Sturgeon *n* Nicola (Ferguson), born 1970, Scottish Nationalist politician; first minister of the Scottish Parliament from 2014

Sturt *n* Charles. 1795–1869, English explorer, who led three expeditions (1828–29; 1829; 1844–45) into the Australian interior, discovering the Darling River (1828)

stutter *vb* **1** to speak (a word or phrase) with involuntary repetition of initial consonants ⊳ *n* **2** the tendency to involuntarily repeat initial consonants while speaking [Middle English *stutten*] > **stuttering** *n*

Stuttgart *n* an industrial city in W Germany, capital of Baden-Württemberg state, on the River Neckar: developed around a stud farm (*Stuotgarten*) of the Counts of Württemberg. Pop: 589 161 (2003 est)

Stuyvesant *n* Peter. ?1610–72, Dutch colonial administrator of New Netherland (later New York) (1646–64)

sty *n, pl* **sties** a pen in which pigs are kept [Old English *stīg*]

stye *or* **sty** *n, pl* **styes** *or* **sties** inflammation of a gland at the base of an eyelash [Old English *stīgend* swelling + *ye* eye]

Stygian (stij-jee-an) *adj chiefly literary* dark or gloomy [after the *Styx*, a river in Hades]

style *n* **1** a form of appearance, design, or production:

I like that style of dress **2** the way in which something is done: *a new style of command* **3** elegance or refinement of manners and dress: *he has bags of style* **4** a distinctive manner of expression in words, music, painting, etc.: *a painting in the Expressionist style* **5** popular fashion in dress and looks: *the old ones had gone out of style* **6** a fashionable or showy way of life: *the newly rich could dine in style* **7** the particular kind of spelling, punctuation, and design followed in a book, journal, or publishing house **8** *botany* the stemlike part of a flower that bears the stigma ▷ *vb* **styling, styled 9** to design, shape, or tailor: *neatly styled hair* **10** to name or call: *Walsh, who styled himself the Memory Man* [Latin *stilus* writing implement]

styling mousse *n* a light foam applied to the hair before styling in order to hold the style

stylish *adj* smart, fashionable, and attracting attention ❯ **stylishly** *adv*

stylist *n* **1** a hairdresser who styles hair **2** a person who performs, writes, or acts with great attention to the particular style he or she employs

stylistic *adj* of the techniques used in creating or performing a work of art: *there are many stylistic problems facing the performers of Baroque music* ❯ **stylistically** *adv*

stylized or **-lised** *adj* conforming to an established stylistic form

stylus *n* a needle-like device in the pick-up arm of a record player that rests in the groove in the record and picks up the sound signals [Latin *stilus* writing implement]

stymie *vb* **-mieing, -mied 1** to hinder or foil (someone): *the President was stymied by a reluctant Congress* ▷ *n*, *pl* **-mies 2** *golf* (formerly) a situation in which an opponent's ball is blocking the line between the hole and the ball about to be played [origin unknown]

styptic *adj* **1** used to stop bleeding: *a styptic pencil* ▷ *n* **2** a styptic drug [Greek *stuphein* to contract]

Styria *n* a mountainous state of SE Austria: rich mineral resources. Capital: Graz. Pop: 1 190 574 (2003 est). Area: 16 384 sq km (6326 sq miles). German name: Steiermark

Suakin *n* a port in the NE Sudan, on the Red Sea: formerly the chief port of the African Red Sea; now obstructed by a coral reef. Pop: reliable recent estimates are not available

Suárez *n* Francisco de. 1548–1617, Spanish theologian, considered the leading scholastic philosopher after Aquinas and the principal Jesuit theologian. His works include *Disputationes Metaphysicae* (1597) and *De Legibus* (1612)

suave (swahv) *adj* (esp. of a man) smooth, confident, and sophisticated [Latin *suavis* sweet] ❯ **suavely** *adv*

sub *n* **1** short for **subeditor, submarine, subscription, substitute 2** *Brit informal* an advance payment of wages or salary. Formal term: **subsistence allowance** ▷ *vb* **subbing, subbed 3** to act as a substitute

sub- or before *r* **sur-** *prefix* **1** situated under or beneath: *subterranean* **2** secondary in rank; subordinate: *sublieutenant* **3** falling short of; less than or imperfectly: *subarctic; subhuman* **4** forming a subdivision or less important part: *subcommittee* [Latin]

subaltern *n* a British army officer below the rank of captain [Latin *sub-* under + *alter* another]

subaqua *adj* of or relating to underwater sport: *subaqua swimming*

subatomic *adj* *physics* of, relating to, or being one of the particles making up an atom

subcommittee *n* a small committee consisting of members of a larger committee and which is set up to look into a particular matter

subconscious *adj* **1** happening or existing without one's awareness ▷ *n* **2** *psychol* the part of the mind that contains memories and motives of which one is not aware but which can influence one's behaviour ❯ **subconsciously** *adv*

subcontinent *n* a large land mass that is a distinct part

of a continent, such as India is of Asia

subcontract *n* **1** a secondary contract by which the main contractor for a job puts work out to another company ▷ *vb* **2** to let out (work) on a subcontract ❯ **subcontractor** *n*

subculture *n* a group of people within a society or class with a distinct pattern of behaviour, beliefs, and attitudes

subcutaneous (sub-cute-**ayn**-ee-uss) *adj med* beneath the skin

subdivide *vb* **-viding, -vided** to divide (a part of something) into smaller parts ❯ **subdivision** *n*

subdue *vb* **-duing, -dued 1** to overcome and bring (a person or people) under control by persuasion or force **2** to make (feelings, colour, or lighting) less intense [Latin *subducere* to remove]

subeditor *n* a person who checks and edits text for a newspaper or other publication

subgroup *n* a small group that is part of a larger group

subheading *n* the heading of a subdivision of a piece of writing

subhuman *adj* lacking the intelligence or decency expected of a human being

subject *n* **1** the person, thing, or topic being dealt with or discussed **2** any branch of learning considered as a course of study **3** a person, object, idea, or scene portrayed in a work of art **4** *grammar* a word or phrase that represents the person or thing performing the action of the verb in a sentence; for example, *the cat* in the sentence *the cat catches mice* **5** a person or thing that undergoes an experiment or treatment **6** a person under the rule of a monarch or government: *Zambian subjects* ▷ *adj* **7** being under the rule of a monarch or government: *a subject race* **8 subject to a** showing a tendency towards: *they are expensive and subject to over-runs in cost and time* **b** exposed or vulnerable to: *subject to ridicule* **c** conditional upon: *pay is subject to negotiation* ▷ *adv* **9 subject to** under the condition that something takes place: *my visit was agreed subject to certain conditions* ▷ *vb* (sub-**ject**) **10 subject to a** to cause (someone) to experience (something unpleasant): *they were subjected to beatings* **b** to bring under the control or authority of: *to subject a soldier to discipline* [Latin *subjectus* brought under] ❯ **subjection** *n*

subjective *adj* **1** of or based on a person's emotions or prejudices ▷ *n* **2** *grammar* the grammatical case in certain languages that identifies the subject of a verb ❯ **subjectively** *adv*

sub judice (sub joo-**diss**-ee) *adj* before a court of law: *he declined to comment on the case saying it was sub judice* [Latin]

subjugate *vb* **-gating, -gated** to bring (a group of people) under one's control [Latin *sub-* under + *jugum* yoke] ❯ **subjugation** *n*

subjunctive *grammar adj* **1** denoting a mood of verbs used when the content of the clause is being doubted, supposed, or feared true, for example *were* in the sentence *I'd be careful if I were you* ▷ *n* **2** the subjunctive mood [Latin *subjungere* to add to]

sublet *vb* **-letting, -let** to rent out (property which one is renting from someone else)

sublieutenant *n* a junior officer in a navy

sublimate *vb* **-mating, -mated** *psychol* to direct the energy of (a strong desire, esp. a sexual one) into activities that are socially more acceptable [Latin *sublimare* to elevate] ❯ **sublimation** *n*

sublime *adj* **1** causing deep emotions and feelings of wonder or joy **2** without equal; supreme **3** of great moral, artistic, or spiritual value ▷ *n* **4 the sublime** something that is sublime ▷ *vb* **-liming, -limed 5** *chem, physics* to change directly from a solid to a vapour without first melting [Latin *sublimis* lofty] ❯ **sublimely** *adv*

subliminal *adj* resulting from or relating to mental processes of which the individual is not aware: *the* *subliminal message* [Latin *sub* below + *limen* threshold]

sub-machine-gun *n* a portable automatic or semiautomatic gun with a short barrel

submarine *n* **1** a vessel which can operate below the surface of the sea ▷ *adj* **2** existing or located below the surface of the sea: *submarine cables* ▶ **submariner** *n*

submerge *vb* **-merging, -merged 1** to put or go below the surface of water or another liquid **2** to involve totally: *she submerged herself in her work* [Latin *submergere*] ▶ **submersion** *n*

submersible *adj* **1** capable of operating under water ▷ *n* **2** a small vessel designed to operate under water

submission *n* **1** an act or instance of capitulation **2** the act of submitting (something) **3** something submitted, such as a proposal **4** the state in which someone has to accept the control of another person

submissive *adj* showing quiet obedience ▶ **submissively** *adv* ▶ **submissiveness** *n*

submit *vb* **1** **-mitting, -mitted 1** to accept the will of another person or a superior force **2** to send (an application or proposal) to someone for judgment or consideration **3** to be voluntarily subjected (to medical or psychiatric treatment) [Latin *submittere* to place under]

subnormal *adj* **1** less than the normal: *subnormal white blood cells* **2** *no longer in technical use* having a lower than average intelligence ▷ *n* **3** *no longer in technical use* a subnormal person

subordinate *adj* **1** of lesser rank or importance ▷ *n* **2** a person or thing that is of lesser rank or importance ▷ *vb* **-nating, -nated 3** (usually foll. by *to*) to regard (something) as less important than another: *the army's interests were subordinated to those of the air force* [Latin *sub-* lower + *ordo* rank] ▶ **subordination** *n*

subordinate clause *n grammar* a clause that functions as an adjective, an adverb, or a noun rather than one that functions as a sentence in its own right

suborn *vb formal* to bribe or incite (a person) to commit a wrongful act [Latin *subornare*]

Subotica *n* a town in Serbia, in the NE near the border with Hungary: agricultural and industrial centre. Pop: 107 139 (2002). Hungarian name: **Szabadka**

subplot *n* a secondary plot in a novel, play, or film

subpoena (sub-pee-na) *n* **1** a legal document requiring a person to appear before a court of law at a specified time ▷ *vb* **-naing, -naed 2** to summon (someone) with a subpoena [Latin: under penalty]

sub-post office *n* (in Britain) a post office which is run by a self-employed agent for the Post Office

subprime *adj* **1** (of a loan) made to a borrower with a poor credit rating: *subprime mortgage* ▷ *n* **2** such a loan

sub rosa (sub rose-a) *adv literary* in secret [Latin, literally: under the rose; in ancient times a rose was hung over a table as a mark of secrecy]

subroutine *n* a section of a computer program that is stored only once but can be used at several different points in the program

sub-Saharan *adj* in, of, or relating to Africa south of the Sahara desert

subscribe *vb* **-scribing, -scribed 1** (usually foll. by *to*) to pay (money) as a contribution (to a charity, for a magazine, etc.) at regular intervals **2 subscribe to** to give support or approval to: *I do not subscribe to this view* [Latin *subscribere* to write underneath] ▶ **subscriber** *n*

subscript *printing adj* **1** (of a character) written or printed below the line ▷ *n* **2** a subscript character

subscription *n* **1** a payment for issues of a publication over a specified period of time **2** money paid or promised, such as to a charity, or the fund raised in this way **3** *Brit, Austral and NZ* the membership fees paid to a society **4** an advance order for a new product

subsection *n* any of the smaller parts into which a section may be divided

subsequent *adj* occurring after; succeeding [Latin *subsequens*] ▶ **subsequently** *adv*

subservient *adj* **1** overeager to carry out someone else's wishes **2** of less importance or rank: *the subservient role of women in society* [Latin *subserviens*] ▶ **subservience** *n*

subset *n* a mathematical set contained within a larger set

subside *vb* **-siding, -sided 1** to become less loud, excited, or violent **2** to sink to a lower level **3** (of the surface of the earth) to cave in; collapse [Latin *subsidere* to settle down] ▶ **subsidence** *n*

subsidiarity *n* the principle of taking political decisions at the lowest practical level

subsidiary *n, pl* **-aries 1** Also called: **subsidiary company** a company which is at least half owned by another company **2** a person or thing that is of lesser importance ▷ *adj* **3** of lesser importance; subordinate [Latin *subsidiarius* supporting]

subsidize *or* **-dise** *vb* **-dizing, -dized** *or* **-dising, -dised** to aid or support (an industry, a person, a public service, or a venture) with money

subsidy *n, pl* **-dies 1** financial aid supplied by a government, for example to industry, or for public welfare **2** any financial aid, grant, or contribution [Latin *subsidium* assistance]

subsist *vb* subsist on to manage to live on: *to subsist on a diet of sausage rolls* [Latin *subsistere* to stand firm] ▶ **subsistence** *n*

subsistence farming *n* a type of farming in which most of the produce is consumed by the farmer and his family

subsoil *n* the layer of soil beneath the surface soil

subsonic *adj* being or moving at a speed below that of sound

substance *n* **1** the basic matter of which a thing consists **2** a specific type of matter with definite or fairly definite chemical composition: *a fatty substance* **3** the essential meaning of a speech, thought, or written article **4** important or meaningful quality: *the only evidence of substance against him* **5** material possessions or wealth: *a woman of substance* **6** **in substance** with regard to the most important points [Latin *substantia*]

substandard *adj* below an established or required standard

substantial *adj* **1** of a considerable size or value: *a substantial amount of money* **2** (of food or a meal) large and filling **3** solid or strong: *substantial brick pillars* **4** *formal* available to the senses; real: *substantial evidence* **5** of or relating to the basic material substance of a thing ▶ **substantially** *adv*

substantiate *vb* **-ating, -ated** to establish (a story) as genuine ▶ **substantiation** *n*

substantive *n* **1** *grammar* a noun or pronoun used in place of a noun ▷ *adj* **2** having importance or significance: *substantive negotiations between management and staff* **3** of or being the essential element of a thing [Latin *substare* to stand beneath]

substitute *vb* **-tuting, -tuted 1** (often foll. by *for*) to take the place of or put in place of another person or thing **2** *chem* to replace (an atom or group in a molecule) with (another atom or group) ▷ *n* **3** a person or thing that takes the place of another, such as a player who takes the place of a team-mate [Latin *substituere*] ▶ **substitution** *n*

> **USAGE** *Substitute* is sometimes wrongly used where *replace* is meant: *he replaced* (not *substituted*) *the worn tyre with a new one.*

substitution reaction *n chem* the replacing of an atom or group in a molecule by another atom or group

substrate *n biology* the substance upon which an enzyme acts [Latin *substratus* strewn beneath]

substructure *n* **1** a structure that forms a part of anything **2** a structure that forms a foundation or framework for a building

S

subsume *vb* **-suming, -sumed** *formal* to include (something) under a larger classification or group: *an attempt to subsume fascism and communism under a general concept of totalitarianism* [Latin *sub-* under + *sumere* to take]

subtenant *n* a person who rents property from a tenant **> subtenancy** *n*

subtend *vb geometry* to be opposite (an angle or side) [Latin *subtendere* to extend beneath]

subterfuge *n* a trick or deception used to achieve an objective [Latin *subterfugere* to escape by stealth]

subterranean *adj* **1** found or operating below the surface of the earth **2** existing or working in a concealed or mysterious way: *the resistance movement worked largely by subterranean methods* [Latin *sub* beneath + *terra* earth]

subtext *n* **1** an underlying theme in a piece of writing **2** a message which is not stated directly but can be inferred

subtitle *n* **1 subtitles** *films* a written translation at the bottom of the picture in a film with foreign dialogue **2** a secondary title given to a book or play ▷ *vb* **-tling, -tled** **3** to provide subtitles for (a film) or a subtitle for (a book or play)

subtle *adj* **1** not immediately obvious: *a subtle change in his views* **2** (of a colour, taste, or smell) delicate or faint: *the subtle aroma* **3** using shrewd and indirect methods to achieve an objective **4** having or requiring the ability to make fine distinctions: *a subtle argument* [Latin *subtilis* finely woven] **> subtly** *adv*

subtlety *n* **1** (*pl* **-ties**) a fine distinction **2** the state or quality of being subtle

subtract *vb* **1** *maths* to take (one number or quantity) away from another **2** to remove (a part of something) from the whole [Latin *subtrahere* to draw away from beneath] **> subtraction** *n*

subtropical *adj* of the region lying between the tropics and temperate lands

suburb *n* a residential district on the outskirts of a city or town [Latin *sub-* close to + *urbs* a city]

suburban *adj* **1** of, in, or inhabiting a suburb **2** *disparaging* conventional and unexciting

suburbanite *n* a person who lives in a suburb

suburbia *n* suburbs or the people living in them considered as a distinct community or class in society

subvention *n* *formal* a grant or subsidy, for example one from a government [Late Latin *subventio* assistance]

subversion *n* the act or an instance of attempting to weaken or overthrow a government or an institution

subversive *adj* **1** intended or intending to weaken or overthrow a government or an institution ▷ *n* **2** a person engaged in subversive activities

subvert *vb* to bring about the downfall of (something existing by a system of law, such as a government) [Latin *subvertere* to overturn]

subway *n* **1** *Brit and Austral* an underground passage for pedestrians to cross a road or railway **2** an underground railway

subzero *adj* lower than zero: *subzero temperatures*

succeed *vb* **1** to achieve an aim **2** to turn out satisfactorily: *Grandfather's plan succeeded* **3** to do well in a specified field: *how to succeed in show biz* **4** to come next in order after (someone or something): *the first shock had been succeeded by a different kind of gloom* **5** to take over (a position) from (someone): *Henry VIII succeeded to the throne in 1509; he will be succeeded as president by his deputy* [Latin *succedere* to follow after] **> succeeding** *adj*

success *n* **1** the achievement of something attempted **2** the attainment of wealth, fame, or position **3** a person or thing that is successful [Latin *successus* an outcome]

successful *adj* **1** having a favourable outcome **2** having attained fame, wealth, or position **> successfully** *adv*

succession *n* **1 a** a number of people or things following one another in order **2** the act or right by which one person succeeds another in a position **3 in succession** one after another: *the third time in succession*

successive *adj* following another or others without interruption: *eleven successive victories* **> successively** *adv*

successor *n* a person or thing that follows another, esp. a person who takes over another's job or position

succinct *adj* brief and clear: *a succinct answer to this question* [Latin *succinctus*] **> succinctly** *adv*

succour *or US* **succor** *n* **1** help in time of difficulty ▷ *vb* **2** to give aid to (someone in time of difficulty) [Latin *succurrere* to hurry to help]

succubus *n, pl* **-bi** a female demon fabled to have sex with sleeping men [Latin *succubare* to lie beneath]

succulent *adj* **1** (of food) juicy and delicious **2** (of plants) having thick fleshy leaves or stems ▷ *n* **3** a plant that can exist in very dry conditions by using water stored in its fleshy tissues [Latin *sucus* juice] **> succulence** *n*

succumb *vb* **succumb to a** to give way to the force of or desire for (something) **b** to die of (a disease) [Latin *succumbere*]

such *adj* **1** of the sort specified or understood: *such places* **2** so great or so much: *such a mess* ▷ *adv* **3** extremely: *such a powerful friend* ▷ *pron* **4** a person or thing of the sort specified or understood: *such is the law of the land; fruitcakes and puddings and such* **5** as such in itself or themselves: *the Nordic countries are not lifting sanctions as such* **6** such as for example: *other socialist groups, such as the Fabians* [Old English *swilc*]

such and such *adj* **1** specific, but not known or named: *such and such a percentage* ▷ *n* **2** a specific, but not known or named, person or thing: *you have not taken such and such into account*

suchlike *n* **1** such or similar things: *shampoos, talcs, and suchlike* ▷ *adj* **2** of such a kind; similar: *astrology and suchlike nonsense*

Su-chou *n* a variant transliteration of the Chinese name for Suzhou

Süchow *n* a variant transliteration of the Chinese name for Xuzhou

suck *vb* **1** to draw (a liquid) into the mouth through pursed lips **2** to take (something) into the mouth and moisten, dissolve, or roll it around with the tongue: *suck a mint* **3** to extract liquid from (a solid food): *he sat sucking orange segments* **4** to draw in (fluid) as if by sucking: *the mussel sucks in water* **5** to drink milk from (a mother's breast); suckle **6** (often foll. by *down, in,* etc.) to draw (a thing or person somewhere) with a powerful force **7** *slang* to be contemptible or disgusting ▷ *n* **8** a sucking [Old English *sūcan*]

sucker *n* **1** *slang* a person who is easily deceived or swindled **2** *slang* a person who cannot resist something: *he's a sucker for fast cars* **3** *zoology* a part of the body of certain animals that is used for sucking or sticking to a surface **4** a rubber cup-shaped device attached to objects allowing them to stick to a surface by suction **5** *botany* a strong shoot coming from a mature plant's root or the base of its main stem

suck into *vb* to draw (someone) into (a situation) by using a powerful pressure or inducement: *to be sucked into a guerrilla war*

suckle *vb* **-ling, -led** to give (a baby or young animal) milk from the breast or udder or (of a baby or young animal) to suck milk from its mother's breast or udder

suckling *n* a baby or young animal that is still sucking milk from its mother's breast or udder

Suckling *n* Sir John. 1609–42, English Cavalier poet and dramatist

suck up to *vb informal* to flatter (a person in authority) in order to get something, such as praise or promotion

Sucre¹ *n* the legal capital of Bolivia, in the south central part of the country in the E Andes: university (1624). Pop: 231 000 (2005 est.). Former name (until 1839): **Chuquisaca**

Sucre² *n* Antonio José de. 1795–1830, South American liberator, born in Venezuela, who assisted Bolívar in the colonial revolt against Spain; first president of Bolivia (1826–28)

sucrose (soo-kroze) *n chem* sugar [French *sucre* sugar]

suction *n* **1** the act or process of sucking **2** the force produced by drawing air out of a space to make a vacuum that will suck in a substance from another space [Latin *sugere* to suck]

Sudan *n* **1** a republic in NE Africa, on the Red Sea: conquered by Mehemet Ali of Egypt (1820–22) and made an Anglo-Egyptian condominium in 1899 after joint forces defeated the Mahdist revolt; became a republic in 1956; a lengthy civil war between separatists in the mainly Christian south and the government resulted in independence for South Sudan following a referendum in 2011. It consists mainly of a plateau, with the Nubian Desert in the north. Official language: Arabic. Official religion: Muslim; there are Christian and animist minorities. Currency: Sudanese pound or Sudani (replacing the Sudanese dinar in 2007). Capital: Khartoum. Pop: 34 847 910 (2013 est). Area: 1 861 484 sq km (718 723 sq miles). Former name (1899–1956): **Anglo-Egyptian Sudan**. French name: **Soudan** **2 the Sudan** a region stretching across Africa south of the Sahara and north of the tropical zone

Sudanese *adj* **1** of or relating to the Sudan or its inhabitants ▷ *n*, *pl* **-nese 2** a native or inhabitant of the Sudan

Sudanic *n* **1** a group of languages spoken in scattered areas of the Sudan, most of which are now generally assigned to the Chari-Nile branch of the Nilo-Saharan family ▷ *adj* **2** relating to or belonging to this group of languages **3** of or relating to the Sudan

Sudbury *n* a city in central Canada, in Ontario: a major nickel-mining centre. Pop: 103 879 (2001)

sudden *adj* **1** occurring or performed quickly and without warning ▷ *n* **2 all of a sudden** without warning; unexpectedly [Latin *subitus* unexpected] ▷ **suddenly** *adv* ▷ **suddenness** *n*

sudden death *n sport* an extra period of play to decide the winner of a tied competition: the first player or team to go into the lead is the winner

sudden infant death syndrome *n* same as **cot death**

Sudetenland *n* a mountainous region of the N Czech Republic: part of Czechoslovakia (1919–38; 1945–93); occupied by Germany (1938–45). Also called: **the Sudeten**

Sudetes or **Sudeten Mountains** *pl n* a mountain range in E central Europe, along the N border of the Czech Republic, extending into Germany and Poland: rich in minerals, esp. coal. Highest peak: Schneekoppe, 1603 m (5259 ft)

sudoku (soo-doh-koo) *n* a logic puzzle involving the insertion of numbers so that none is repeated in the same row, column, or internal square of a larger square [from Japanese]

sudorific (syoo-dor-if-ik) *adj* **1** causing sweating ▷ *n* **2** a drug that causes sweating [Latin *sudor* sweat + *facere* to make]

suds *pl n* the bubbles on the surface of water in which soap or detergent has been dissolved; lather [probably from Middle Dutch *sudse* marsh]

sue *vb* **suing**, **sued** to start legal proceedings (against): *we want to sue the council*; *he sued for custody of the three children* [Latin *sequi* to follow]

Sue *n* Eugène. original name *Marie-Joseph Sue*. 1804–57, French novelist, whose works, notably *Les mystères de Paris* (1842–43) and *Le juif errant* (1844–45), were among the first to reflect the impact of the industrial revolution on France

suede *n* a leather with a fine velvet-like surface on one side [French *gants de Suède*, literally: gloves from Sweden]

suet *n* a hard fat obtained from sheep and cattle and used for making pastry and puddings [Old French *seu*]

Suetonius *n* full name *Gaius Suetonius Tranquillus*. 75–150 AD, Roman biographer and historian, whose chief works were *Concerning Illustrious Men* and *The Lives of the Caesars* (from Julius Caesar to Domitian)

Suez *n* **1** a port in NE Egypt, at the head of the Gulf of Suez at the S end of the Suez Canal: an ancient trading site and a major naval station under the Ottoman Empire; port of departure for pilgrims to Mecca; oil-refining centre. It suffered severely in the Arab-Israeli conflicts of 1967 and 1973. Pop: 513 000 (2005 est) **2 Isthmus of Suez** a strip of land in NE Egypt, between the Mediterranean and the Red Sea: links Africa and Asia and is crossed by the Suez Canal **3 Gulf of Suez** the NW arm of the Red Sea: linked with the Mediterranean by the Suez Canal

Suez Canal *n* a sea-level canal in NE Egypt, crossing the Isthmus of Suez and linking the Mediterranean with the Red Sea: built (1854–69) by de Lesseps with French and Egyptian capital; nationalized in 1956 by the Egyptians. Length: 163 km (101 miles)

Suff. **1** Suffolk **2** Suffragan

suffer *vb* **1** to undergo or be subjected to (physical pain or mental distress) **2 suffer from** to be badly affected by (an illness): *he was suffering from depression* **3** to become worse in quality; deteriorate: *his work suffered during their divorce* **4** to tolerate: *he suffers no fools* **5** to be set at a disadvantage: *the strongest of them suffers by comparison* [Latin *sufferre*] ▷ **sufferer** *n* ▷ **suffering** *n*

sufferance *n* **on sufferance** tolerated with reluctance: *I was there on sufferance and all knew it*

suffice (suf-**fice**) *vb* **-ficing**, **-ficed 1** to be enough or satisfactory for a purpose **2 suffice it to say…** it is enough to say…: *suffice it to say that AIDS is on the increase* [Latin *sufficere*]

sufficiency *n*, *pl* **-cies** an adequate amount

sufficient *adj* enough to meet a need or purpose; adequate [Latin *sufficiens*] ▷ **sufficiently** *adv*

suffix *grammar n* **1** a letter or letters added to the end of a word to form another word, such as *-s* and *-ness* in *dogs* and *softness* ▷ *vb* **2** to add (a letter or letters) to the end of a word to form another word [Latin *suffixus* fastened below]

suffocate *vb* **-cating**, **-cated 1** to kill or die through lack of oxygen, such as by blockage of the air passage **2** to feel uncomfortable from heat and lack of air [Latin *suffocare*] ▷ **suffocating** *adj* ▷ **suffocation** *n*

Suffolk *n* a county of SE England, on the North Sea: its coast is flat and marshy, indented by broad tidal estuaries. Administrative centre: Ipswich. Pop: 678 100 (2003 est). Area: 3800 sq km (1467 sq miles)

suffragan *n* a bishop appointed to assist an archbishop [Medieval Latin *suffragium* assistance]

suffrage *n* the right to vote in public elections [Latin *suffragium*]

suffragette *n* (in Britain at the beginning of the 20th century) a woman who campaigned militantly for women to be given the right to vote in public elections

suffragist *n* (in Britain at the beginning of the 20th century) a person who campaigned for women to be given the right to vote in public elections

suffuse *vb* **-fusing**, **-fused** to spread through or over (something): *the dawn suffused the sky with a cold grey wash* [Latin *suffusus* overspread with] ▷ **suffusion** *n*

Sufu *n* a variant spelling of **Shufu**

sugar *n* **1** a sweet carbohydrate, usually in the form of white or brown crystals, which is found in many plants and is used to sweeten food and drinks **2** *informal, chiefly US and Canad* a term of affection ▷ *vb* **3** to add sugar to (food or drink) to make it sweet **4** to cover with sugar: *sugared almonds* **5 sugar the pill** to make something unpleasant more tolerable by adding something pleasant [Old French *çucre*, from Sanskrit *śarkarā*] ▷ **sugared** *adj*

Sugar *n* Alan (**Michael**). Baron. born 1947, British electronics entrepreneur; chairman of Amstrad (1968–2008); noted for his BBC series *The Apprentice* (from 2005)

sugar beet *n* a beet grown for the sugar obtained from its roots

sugar cane *n* a tropical grass grown for the sugar obtained from its tall stout canes

sugar daddy *n* an elderly man who gives a young woman money and gifts in return for her company

sugar glider *n* a common phalanger that glides from tree to tree feeding on insects and nectar

sugaring off *n Canad* the boiling down of maple sap to produce sugar, traditionally a social event in early spring

sugar loaf *n* a large cone-shaped mass of hard refined sugar

Sugar Loaf Mountain *n* a mountain in SE Brazil, in Rio de Janeiro on Guanabara Bay. Height: 390 m (1280 ft). Portuguese name: **Pão de Açúcar**

sugar maple *n* a North American maple tree, grown as a source of sugar, which is extracted from the sap

sugary *adj* 1 of, like, or containing sugar: *sugary snacks* 2 (of behaviour or language) very pleasant but probably not sincere: *sugary sentiment* ❭ **sugariness** *n*

Suger *n* 1081–1151, French ecclesiastic and statesman, who acted as adviser to Louis VI and regent (1147–49) to Louis VII. As abbot of Saint-Denis (1122–51) he influenced the development of Gothic architecture

suggest *vb* 1 to put forward (a plan or an idea) for consideration: *he didn't suggest a meeting* 2 to bring (a person or thing) to the mind by the association of ideas: *a man whose very name suggests blandness* 3 to give a hint of: *her grey eyes suggesting a livelier mood than usual* [Latin *suggerere* to bring up]

suggestible *adj* easily influenced by other people's ideas

suggestion *n* 1 something that is suggested 2 a hint or indication: *the entire castle gave no suggestion of period* 3 *psychol* the process whereby the presentation of an idea to a receptive individual leads to the acceptance of that idea

suggestive *adj* 1 (of remarks or gestures) causing people to think of sex 2 **suggestive of** communicating a hint of

Suharto *n* T. N. J. 1921–2008, Indonesian general and statesman; president (1968–98)

suicidal *adj* 1 wanting to commit suicide 2 likely to lead to danger or death: *a suicidal attempt to rescue her son* 3 likely to destroy one's own career or future: *it would be suicidal for them to ignore public opinion*

suicide *n* 1 the act of killing oneself deliberately: *he tried to commit suicide* 2 a person who kills himself or herself intentionally 3 the self-inflicted ruin of one's own career or future: *such a cut would be political suicide* [Latin *sui* of oneself + *caedere* to kill]

suicide bomber *n* a terrorist who carries out a bomb attack, knowing that he or she will be killed in the explosion

Suisse *n* the French name for **Switzerland**

suit *n* 1 a set of clothes of the same material designed to be worn together, usually a jacket with matching trousers or skirt 2 an outfit worn for a specific purpose: *a diving suit* 3 a legal action taken against someone; lawsuit 4 any of the four types of card in a pack of playing cards: spades, hearts, diamonds, or clubs 5 *slang* a business executive or white-collar worker 6 **follow suit** to act in the same way as someone else 7 **strong suit** or **strongest suit** something one excels in ❭ *vb* 8 to be fit or appropriate for: *that colour suits you* 9 to be acceptable to (someone) 10 **suit oneself** to do what one wants without considering other people [Old French *sieute* set of things] ❭ **suited** *adj*

suitable *adj* appropriate for a particular function or occasion; proper ❭ **suitability** *n* ❭ **suitably** *adv*

suitcase *n* a large portable travelling case for clothing

suite *n* 1 a set of connected rooms in a hotel 2 a matching set of furniture, for example two armchairs and a settee 3 *music* a composition of several movements in the same key [French]

suitor *n* 1 *old-fashioned* a man who wants to marry a woman 2 *law* a person who starts legal proceedings against someone; plaintiff [Latin *secutor* follower]

Suiyüan *n* a former province in N China: now part of the Inner Mongolian Autonomous Region

Sukarnapura *n* a former name of **Jayapura**

Sukarno or **Soekarno** *n* Achmed. 1901–70, Indonesian statesman; first president of the Republic of Indonesia (1945–67)

Sukarno Peak *n* a former name of (Mount) **Jaya**

Sukarnoputri *n* Megawati, born 1947, Indonesian politician; president of Indonesia (2001–04): daughter of Achmed Sukarno

Sukhumi *n* a port and resort in W Georgia, on the Black Sea: site of an ancient Greek colony. Pop: 134 000 (2005 est)

Sukkoth (**sook**-oat) *n* an eight-day Jewish harvest festival, commemorating the period when the Israelites lived in the wilderness

Sulawesi *n* an island in E Indonesia: mountainous and forested, with volcanoes and hot springs. Pop: 14 946 488 (2000). Area (including adjacent islands): 229 108 sq km (88 440 sq miles). Also called: **Celebes**

Suleiman I, Soliman or **Solyman** *n* called the *Magnificent.* ?1495–1566, sultan of the Ottoman Empire (1520–66), whose reign was noted for its military power and cultural achievements

sulk *vb* 1 to be silent and moody as a way of showing anger or resentment: *I went home and sulked for two days* ❭ *n* 2 a mood in which one shows anger or resentment by being silent and moody: *he was just in a sulk*

sulky *adj* **sulkier, sulkiest** moody or silent because of anger or resentment [perhaps from obsolete *sulke* sluggish] ❭ **sulkily** *adv* ❭ **sulkiness** *n*

Sulla *n* full name *Lucius Cornelius Sulla Felix.* 138–78 BC, Roman general and dictator (82–79). He introduced reforms to strengthen the power of the Senate

sullen *adj* unwilling to talk or be sociable; sulky [Latin *solus* alone] ❭ **sullenly** *adv* ❭ **sullenness** *n*

Sullivan *n* 1 Sir Arthur (**Seymour**). 1842–1900, English composer who wrote operettas, such as *H.M.S. Pinafore* (1878) and *The Mikado* (1885), with W. S. Gilbert as librettist 2 Louis (**Henri**). 1856–1924, US pioneer of modern architecture: he coined the slogan "form follows function"

Sullom Voe *n* a deep coastal inlet in the Shetland Islands, on the N coast of Mainland. It is used for the storage and transshipment of oil

sully *vb* **-lies, -lying, -lied** 1 to ruin (someone's reputation) 2 to spoil or make dirty: *the stream had been sullied by the smelter's pollution* [probably from French *souiller* to soil]

Sully *n* Maximilien de Béthune, Duc de Sully. 1559–1641, French statesman; minister of Henry IV. He helped restore the finances of France after the Wars of Religion

Sully-Prudhomme *n* René François Armand. 1839–1907, French poet: Nobel prize for literature 1901

sulpha drug or US **sulfa drug** *n pharmacol* any of a group of sulphonamides that prevent the growth of bacteria: used to treat bacterial infections

sulphate or US **sulfate** *n chem* a salt or ester of sulphuric acid

sulphide or US **sulfide** *n chem* a compound of sulphur with another element

sulphite or US **sulfite** *n chem* any salt or ester of sulphurous acid

sulphonamide or US **sulfonamide** (sulf-**on**-a-mide) *n pharmacol* any of a class of organic compounds that prevent the growth of bacteria

sulphur or US **sulfur** *n chem* a light yellow, highly inflammable, nonmetallic element used in the production of sulphuric acid, in the vulcanization of rubber, and in medicine. Symbol: S [Latin *sulfur*] ❭ **sulphuric** or US **sulfuric** *adj*

sulphur dioxide *n chem* a strong-smelling colourless soluble gas, used in the manufacture of sulphuric acid and in the preservation of foodstuffs

S

sulphureous *or US* **sulfureous** (sulf-**yoor**-ee-uss) *adj* same as **sulphurous** (1)

sulphuric acid *n chem* a colourless dense oily corrosive liquid used in the manufacture of fertilizers and explosives

sulphurize, -rise *or US* **sulfurize** (sulf-**yoor**-rise) *vb* **-rizing, -rized** *or* **-rising, -rised** *chem* to combine with or treat (something) with sulphur or a sulphur compound

sulphurous *or US* **sulfurous** *adj chem* **1** of or resembling sulphur **2** containing sulphur, esp. with a valence of four

sultan *n* the sovereign of a Muslim country [Arabic: rule]

sultana *n* **1** the dried fruit of a small white seedless grape **2** a sultan's wife, mother, daughter, or concubine [Italian]

sultanate *n* **1** the territory ruled by a sultan **2** the office or rank of a sultan

sultry *adj* **-trier, -triest** **1** (of weather or climate) very hot and humid **2** suggesting hidden passion: *a sultry brunette* [obsolete *sulter* to swelter]

Sulu Archipelago *n* a chain of over 500 islands in the SW Philippines, separating the Sulu Sea from the Celebes Sea: formerly a sultanate, ceded to the Philippines in 1940. Capital: Jolo. Pop: 619 668 (2000). Area: 2686 sq km (1037 sq miles)

Sulu Sea *n* part of the W Pacific between Borneo and the central Philippines

sum *n* **1** the result of the addition of numbers or quantities **2** one or more columns or rows of numbers to be added, subtracted, multiplied, or divided **3** a quantity of money: *they can win enormous sums* **4 in sum** as a summary; in short: *in sum, it's been a bad week for the government* ▷ *adj* **5** complete or final: *the sum total* ▷ *vb* **summing, summed** **6** See **sum up** [Latin *summa* the top, sum]

Sumatra *n* a mountainous island in W Indonesia, in the Greater Sunda Islands, separated from the Malay Peninsula by the Strait of Malacca: Dutch control began in the 16th century; joined Indonesia in 1945. Northern coastal areas, esp. Aceh province, suffered devastation as a result of the Indian Ocean tsunami of December 2004. Pop: 42 409 510 (2000). Area: 473 606 sq km (182 821 sq miles). Indonesian spelling: **Sumatera**

Sumatran *adj* **1** of or relating to Sumatra or its inhabitants ▷ *n* **2** a native or inhabitant of Sumatra

Sumba *n* an island in Indonesia, in the Lesser Sunda Islands, separated from Flores by the **Sumba Strait:** formerly important for sandalwood exports. Pop: 355 073 (1990). Area: 11 153 sq km (4306 sq miles). Former spelling: **Soemba**. Former name: **Sandalwood Island**

Sumbawa *n* a mountainous island in Indonesia, in the Lesser Sunda Islands, between Lombok and Flores islands. Pop: 1 540 000 (2000). Area: 14 750 sq km (5695 sq miles). Former spelling: **Soembawa**

Sumer *n* the S region of Babylonia; seat of a civilization of city-states that reached its height in the 3rd millennium BC

Sumerian *n* **1** a member of a people who established a civilization in Sumer during the 4th millennium BC **2** the extinct language of this people, of no known relationship to any other language ▷ *adj* **3** of or relating to ancient Sumer, its inhabitants, or their language or civilization

summarize *or* **-rise** *vb* **-rizing, -rized** *or* **-rising, -rised** to give a short account of (something)

summary *n, pl* **-maries** **1** a brief account giving the main points of something ▷ *adj* **2** performed quickly, without formality or attention to details: *a summary judgment* [Latin *summarium*] ▷ **summarily** *adv*

summation *n* **1** a summary of what has just been done or said **2** the process of working out a sum; addition **3** the result of such a process

summer *n* **1** the warmest season of the year, between spring and autumn **2** *literary* a time of youth, success, or

happiness [Old English *sumor*] ▷ **summery** *adj*

summerhouse *n* a small building in a garden, used for shade in the summer

summer school *n* an academic course held during the summer

summer solstice *n* the time at which the sun is at its northernmost point in the sky (southernmost point in the S hemisphere), appearing at noon at its highest altitude above the horizon. It occurs about June 21 (December 22 in the S hemisphere)

summertime *n* the period or season of summer

summing-up *n* **1** a summary of the main points of an argument, speech, or piece of writing **2** concluding statements made by a judge to the jury before they retire to consider their verdict

summit *n* **1** the highest point or part of a mountain or hill **2** the highest possible degree or state; peak or climax: *the summit of success* **3** a meeting of heads of governments or other high officials [Old French *somet*]

summon *vb* **1** to order (someone) to come **2** to send for (someone) to appear in court **3** to call upon (someone) to do something: *the authorities had summoned the relatives to be available* **4** to convene (a meeting) **5** (often foll. by *up*) to call into action (one's strength, courage, etc.); muster [Latin *summonere* to give a discreet reminder]

summons *n, pl* **-monses** **1** a call or an order to attend a specified place at a specified time **2** an official order requiring a person to attend court, either to answer a charge or to give evidence ▷ *vb* **3** to order (someone) to appear in court: *three others had been summonsed for questioning*

sumo *n* the national style of wrestling of Japan, in which two contestants of great height and weight attempt to force each other out of the ring [Japanese]

sump *n* **1** a container in an internal-combustion engine into which oil can drain **2** same as **cesspool** **3** *mining* a hollow at the bottom of a shaft where water collects [Middle Dutch *somp* marsh]

sumptuary *adj* controlling expenditure or extravagant use of resources [Latin *sumptuarius* concerning expense]

sumptuous *adj* magnificent and very expensive; splendid: *sumptuous decoration* [Latin *sumptuosus* costly]

Sumter *n* See **Fort Sumter**

sum up *vb* **1** to give a short account of (the main points of an argument, speech, or piece of writing) **2** to form a quick opinion of: *how well you have summed me up!*

Sumy *n* a city in Ukraine, on the River Pysol: site of early Slav settlements. Pop: 294 000 (2005 est)

sun *n* **1** the star that is the source of heat and light for the planets in the solar system. Related adjective: **solar** **2** any star around which a system of planets revolves **3** the heat and light received from the sun; sunshine **4 catch the sun** to become slightly suntanned **5 under the sun** on earth; at all: *there are no free lunches under the sun* ▷ *vb* **sunning, sunned** **6** to lie, sit, or walk in the sunshine on a warm day [Old English *sunne*] ▷ **sunless** *adj*

Sun. Sunday

sunbathe *vb* **-bathing, -bathed** to lie or sit in the sunshine, in order to get a suntan ▷ **sunbather** *n* ▷ **sunbathing** *n*

sunbeam *n* a ray of sunlight

Sunbelt *n* the southern states of the USA

sun block *n* a chemical applied to exposed skin to block out all or almost all of the ultraviolet rays of the sun

sunburn *n* painful reddening of the skin caused by overexposure to the sun ▷ **sunburnt** *or* **sunburned** *adj*

Sunbury-on-Thames *n* a town in SE England, in N Surrey. Pop: 27 415 (2001)

sun cream *n* a cream applied to exposed skin to reduce the effect of the ultraviolet rays of the sun

sundae *n* ice cream topped with a sweet sauce, nuts, whipped cream, and fruit [origin unknown]

Sunda Islands *pl n* a chain of islands in the Malay

Archipelago, consisting of the **Greater Sunda Islands** (chiefly Sumatra, Java, Borneo, and Sulawesi) and **Nusa Tenggara** (the Lesser Sunda Islands). Former spelling: Soenda Islands

Sunda Strait *n* a strait between Sumatra and Java, linking the Java Sea with the Indian Ocean. Narrowest point: about 26 km (16 miles). Former spelling: **Soenda Strait**

Sunday *n* the first day of the week and the Christian day of worship [Old English *sunnandæg* day of the sun]

Sunday best *n* a person's best clothes, sometimes regarded as those most suitable for wearing at church

Sunday school *n* a school for teaching children about Christianity, usually held in a church hall on Sunday

Sunderland *n* **1** a city and port in NE England, in Sunderland unitary authority, Tyne and Wear, at the mouth of the River Wear: formerly known for shipbuilding, now has car manufacturing, chemicals; university (1992). Pop: 177 739 (2001) **2** a unitary authority in NE England, in Tyne and Wear. Pop: 283 100 (2003 est). Area: 138 sq km (53 sq miles)

sundial *n* a device used for telling the time during the hours of sunlight, consisting of a pointer that casts a shadow onto a surface marked in hours

sundown *n US* sunset

sundries *pl n* several things of various sorts

sundry *adj* **1** several or various; miscellaneous ▷ *pron* **2** all and sundry everybody [Old English *syndrig* separate]

Sundsvall *n* a port in E Sweden, on the Gulf of Bothnia: icebound in winter; cellulose industries. Pop: 93 623 (2004 est)

sunfish *n, pl* -**fish** *or* -**fishes** a large sea fish with a rounded body

sunflower *n* **1** a very tall plant with large yellow flowers **2** sunflower seed oil the oil extracted from sunflower seeds, used as a salad oil and in margarine

sung *vb* the past participle of **sing**

USAGE See at **ring¹**.

Sungari *n* another name for the **Songhua**

Sungkiang *n* a former province of NE China: now part of the Inner Mongolian Autonomous Region

sunglasses *pl n* glasses with darkened lenses that protect the eyes from bright sunlight

sun-god *n* the sun considered as a god

sunk *vb* a past participle of **sink**

sunken *vb* **1** a past participle of **sink** ▷ *adj* **2** (of a person's cheeks, eyes, or chest) curving inward due to old age or bad health **3** situated at a lower level than the surrounding or usual one: *the sunken garden* **4** situated under water; submerged: *sunken ships*

sun lamp *n* a lamp that gives off ultraviolet rays, used for muscular therapy or for giving people an artificial suntan

sunlight *n* the light that comes from the sun ▷ **sunlit** *adj*

sun lounge *or US* **sun parlor** *n* a room with large windows designed to receive as much sunlight as possible

sunnies *pl n informal* short for **sunglasses**

sunny *adj* -**nier**, -**niest** **1** full of or lit up by sunshine **2** cheerful and happy

sunrise *n* **1** the daily appearance of the sun above the horizon **2** the time at which the sun rises

sunrise industry *n* any of the fast-developing high-technology industries, such as electronics

sunroof *n* a panel in the roof of a car that may be opened to let in air or sunshine

sunset *n* **1** the daily disappearance of the sun below the horizon **2** the time at which the sun sets

sunshade *n* anything used to shade people from the sun, such as a parasol or awning

sunshine *n* **1** the light and warmth from the sun **2** *Brit a* light-hearted term of address

sunspot *n* **1** *informal* a sunny holiday resort **2** a dark cool patch on the surface of the sun **3** *Austral* a small area of skin damage caused by exposure to the sun

sunstroke *n* a condition caused by spending too much time exposed to intensely hot sunlight and producing high fever and sometimes loss of consciousness

suntan *n* a brownish colouring of the skin caused by exposure to the sun or a sun lamp ▷ **suntanned** *adj*

sun-up *n US and Austral* sunrise

Sun Yat-sen *n* 1866–1925, Chinese statesman, who was instrumental in the overthrow of the Manchu dynasty and was the first president of the Republic of China (1911). He reorganized the Kuomintang

Suomi *n* the Finnish name for **Finland**

sup¹ *vb* **supping**, **supped 1** to take (liquid) by swallowing a little at a time ▷ *n* **2** a sip [Old English *sūpan*]

sup² *vb* **supping**, **supped** *archaic* to have supper [Old French *soper*]

super *informal adj* **1** very good or very nice: *they had a super holiday* ▷ *n Austral and NZ* **2** superannuation **3** superphosphate [Latin: above]

super- *prefix* **1** above or over: *superscript* **2** outstanding: *superstar* **3** of greater size, extent, or quality: *supermarket* [Latin]

superabundant *adj* existing in very large numbers or amount ▷ **superabundance** *n*

superannuated *adj* **1** discharged with a pension, owing to age or illness **2** too old to be useful; obsolete [Medieval Latin *superannuatus* aged more than one year]

superannuation *n* **a** a regular payment made by an employee into a pension fund **b** the pension finally paid

superb *adj* extremely good or impressive [Latin *superbus* distinguished] ▷ **superbly** *adv*

Super Bowl *n American football* the championship game held annually between the best team of the American Football Conference and that of the National Football Conference

superbug *n informal* a bacterium resistant to antibiotics

supercharge *vb* -**charging**, -**charged 1** to increase the power of (an internal-combustion engine) with a supercharger **2** to charge (the atmosphere, a remark, etc.) with an excess amount of (tension, emotion, etc.) **3** to apply pressure to (a fluid); pressurize

supercharger *n* a device that increases the power of an internal-combustion engine by forcing extra air into it

supercilious *adj* behaving in a superior and arrogant manner [Latin *supercilium* eyebrow] ▷ **superciliously** *adv* ▷ **superciliousness** *n*

superconductivity *n physics* the ability of certain substances to conduct electric current with almost no resistance at very low temperatures ▷ **superconducting** *adj* ▷ **superconductor** *n*

supercontinent *n* a huge landmass thought to have existed in the geological past and to have split into smaller landmasses and formed the present continents

superego *n, pl* -**egos** *psychoanalysis* that part of the unconscious mind that governs a person's ideas concerning what is right and wrong

supererogation *n* the act of doing more work than is required [Latin *supererogare* to spend over and above]

superficial *adj* **1** not careful or thorough: *a superficial analysis* **2** only outwardly apparent rather than genuine or actual: *those are merely superficial differences* **3** (of a person) lacking deep emotions or serious interests; shallow **4** of, near, or forming the surface: *the gash was superficial* [Late Latin *superficialis*] ▷ **superficiality** *n* ▷ **superficially** *adv*

superfluous (soo-per-flew-uss) *adj* more than is sufficient or required [Latin *superfluus* overflowing] ▷ **superfluity** *n*

superfood *n* any highly nutritious foodstuff

superglue *n* an extremely strong and quick-drying glue

supergrass *n Brit, Austral and NZ* an informer who names a large number of people as terrorists or criminals, esp.

one who gives this information in order to avoid being put on trial

super heavyweight *n* an amateur boxer weighing over 201 pounds (91 kg)

superhuman *adj* beyond normal human ability or experience: *a superhuman effort*

superimpose *vb* **-posing, -posed** to set or place (something) on or over something else

superintend *vb* to supervise (a person or an activity) [Latin *super-* above + *intendere* to give attention to]

superintendent *n* **1** a senior police officer **2** a person who directs and manages an organization or office

superior *adj* **1** greater in quality, quantity, or usefulness **2** higher in rank, position, or status: *he was reprimanded by a superior officer* **3** believing oneself to be better than others **4** of very high quality or respectability: *superior merchandise* **5** *formal* placed higher up: *damage to the superior surface of the wing* **6** *printing* (of a character) written or printed above the line ▷ *n* **7** a person of greater rank or status **8** See **mother superior** [Latin *superus* placed above] ▷ **superiority** *n*

> **USAGE** *Superior* should not be used with *than*: *he is a better* (not *a superior*) *poet than his brother; his poetry is superior to* (not *superior than*) *his brother's.*

Superior *n* **Lake Superior** a lake in the N central US and S Canada: one of the largest freshwater lakes in the world and westernmost of the Great Lakes. Area: 82 362 sq km (31 800 sq miles)

superlative (soo-**per**-lat-iv) *adj* **1** of outstanding quality; supreme **2** *grammar* denoting the form of an adjective or adverb that expresses the highest degree of quality ▷ *n* **3** the highest quality **4** *grammar* the superlative form of an adjective or adverb [Old French *superlatif*]

superman *n, pl* **-men** any man with great physical or mental powers

supermarket *n* a large self-service shop selling food and household goods

supermodel *n* a famous and highly-paid fashion model

supernatural *adj* **1** of or relating to things that cannot be explained by science, such as clairvoyance, ghosts, etc. ▷ *n* **2** **the supernatural** forces, occurrences, and beings that cannot be explained by science

supernova *n, pl* **-vae** *or* **-vas** a star that explodes and, for a few days, becomes one hundred million times brighter than the sun

supernumerary *adj* **1** exceeding the required or regular number; extra **2** employed as a substitute or assistant ▷ *n, pl* **-aries 3** a person or thing that exceeds the required or regular number **4** a substitute or assistant **5** an actor who has no lines to say [Latin *super-* above + *numerus* number]

superphosphate *n* a chemical fertilizer, esp. one made by treating rock phosphate with sulphuric acid

superpower *n* a country of very great military and economic power, such as the US

superscript *printing adj* **1** (of a character) written or printed above the line ▷ *n* **2** a superscript character

supersede *vb* **-seding, -seded 1** to take the place of (something old-fashioned or less appropriate): *cavalry was superseded by armoured vehicles* **2** to replace (someone) in function or office [Latin *supersedere* to sit above]

supersize *adj* also: **supersized 1** larger than standard size ▷ *vb* **-sizes, -sizing, -sized 2** to increase the size of (something, such as a temporary portion of food)

supersonic *adj* being, having, or capable of a speed greater than the speed of sound

superstar *n* an extremely popular and famous entertainer or sportsperson ▷ **superstardom** *n*

superstate *n* a large state, esp. one created from a federation of states

superstition *n* **1** irrational belief in magic and the powers that supposedly bring good luck or bad luck **2** a

belief or practice based on this [Latin *superstitio*] ▷ **superstitious** *adj*

superstore *n* a large supermarket

superstructure *n* **1** any structure or concept built on something else **2** *nautical* any structure above the main deck of a ship

supertanker *n* a very large fast tanker

supertax *n* an extra tax on incomes above a certain level

Super Twelve *n* an annual international southern hemisphere Rugby Union tournament between professional club sides from South Africa, Australia, and New Zealand

supervene *vb* **-vening, -vened** to happen as an unexpected development [Latin *supervenire* to come upon] ▷ **supervention** *n*

supervise *vb* **-vising, -vised 1** to direct the performance or operation of (an activity or a process) **2** to watch over (people) so as to ensure appropriate behaviour [Latin *super-* over + *videre* to see] ▷ **supervision** *n* ▷ **supervisor** *n* ▷ **supervisory** *adj*

supine (soo-**pine**) *adj formal* lying on one's back [Latin *supinus*]

supper *n* **1** an evening meal **2** a late evening snack [Old French *soper*]

Suppiluliumas I *n* king of the Hittites (?1375–?1335 BC); founder of the Hittite empire

supplant *vb* to take the place of (someone or something) [Latin *supplantare* to trip up]

supple *adj* **1** (of a person) moving and bending easily and gracefully **2** (of a material or object) soft and bending easily without breaking [Latin *supplex* bowed] ▷ **suppleness** *n*

supplement *n* **1** an addition designed to make something more adequate **2** a magazine distributed free with a newspaper **3** a section added to a publication to supply further information or correct errors **4** (of money) an additional payment to obtain special services ▷ *vb* **5** to provide an addition to (something), esp. in order to make up for an inadequacy: *a Saturday job to supplement her grant* [Latin *supplementum*] ▷ **supplementary** *adj*

supplicant *n formal* a person who makes a humble request [Latin *supplicans* beseeching]

supplication *n formal* a humble request for help [Latin *supplicare* to beg on one's knees]

supply *vb* **-plies, -plying, -plied 1** to provide with something required: *Nigeria may supply them with oil* ▷ *n, pl* **-plies 2** the act of providing something **3** an amount available for use; stock: *electricity supply* **4** **supplies** food and equipment needed for a trip or military campaign **5** *econ* the amount of a commodity that producers are willing and able to offer for sale at a specified price: *supply and demand* **6** a person who acts as a temporary substitute ▷ *adj* **7** acting as a temporary substitute: *supply teachers* [Latin *supplere* to complete] ▷ **supplier** *n*

support *vb* **1** to carry the weight of (a thing or person) **2** to provide the necessities of life for (a family or person) **3** to give practical or emotional help to (someone) **4** to give approval to (a cause, idea, or political party) **5** to take an active interest in and be loyal to (a particular football or other sports team) **6** to establish the truthfulness or accuracy of (a theory or statement) by providing new facts **7** to speak in a debate in favour of (a motion) **8** (in a concert) to perform earlier than (the main attraction) **9** *films, theatre* to play a less important role to (the leading actor or actress) ▷ *n* **10** the act of supporting or the condition of being supported **11** a thing that bears the weight of an object from below **12** a person who gives someone practical or emotional help **13** the means of providing the necessities of life for a family or person **14** a band or entertainer not topping the bill [Latin *supportare* to bring] ▷ **supportive** *adj*

supporter *n* a person who supports a sports team, politician, etc.

suppose *vb* **-posing, -posed 1** to presume (something) to be true without certain knowledge: *I suppose it will be in the papers* **2** to consider (something) as a possible suggestion for the sake of discussion: *suppose you're arrested on a misdemeanour* **3** (of a theory) to depend on the truth or existence of: *this scenario supposes that he would do so* [Latin *supponere* to substitute]

supposed *adj* **1** supposed to expected to: *spies aren't supposed to be nice* **2** presumed to be true without certain knowledge; doubtful: *the supposed wonders of drug therapy* **> supposedly** *adv*

supposition *n* **1** an idea or a statement believed or assumed to be true **2** the act of supposing: *much of it is based on supposition*

suppositional *adj* deduced from an idea or statement believed or assumed to be true; hypothetical

suppository *n*, *pl* **-ries** *med* a medicine in solid form that is inserted into the vagina or rectum and left to dissolve [Latin *suppositus* placed beneath]

suppress *vb* **1** to put an end to (something) by physical or legal force **2** to prevent the circulation or publication of (information or books) **3** to hold (an emotion or a response) in check; restrain: *he could barely suppress a groan* **4** *electronics* to reduce or eliminate (interference) in a circuit [Latin *suppressus* held down] **> suppression** *n*

suppressant *n* a drug that suppresses an action: *a cough suppressant*

suppurate *vb* **-rating, -rated** *pathol* (of a wound or sore) to produce or leak pus [Latin *suppurare*]

supremacy *n* **1** supreme power; dominance **2** the state or quality of being superior

supreme *adj* **1** of highest status or power: *the Supreme Council* **2** of highest quality or importance: *a supreme player* **3** greatest in degree; extreme: *supreme happiness* [Latin *supremus* highest] **> supremely** *adv*

supremo *n*, *pl* **-mos** *informal* a person in overall authority

Suqutra *n* a variant spelling of Socotra

Sur or **Sour** *n* transliteration of the Arabic name for Tyre

sur-¹ *prefix* over; above; beyond: *surcharge*; *surrealism* [Old French]

sur-² *prefix* See sub-

Surabaya or **Surabaja** *n* a port in Indonesia, on E Java on the **Surabaya Strait**: the country's second port and chief naval base; university (1954); fishing and ship-building industries; oil refinery. Pop: 2 599 796 (2000). Former spelling: **Soerabaja**

Surakarta *n* a town in Indonesia, on central Java: textile manufacturing. Pop: 516 500 (1995 est). Former spelling: **Soerakarta**

Surat *n* a port in W India, in W Gujarat: a major port in the 17th century; textile manufacturing. Pop: 2 433 787 (2001)

surcharge *n* **1** a charge in addition to the usual payment or tax **2** an excessive sum charged, often unlawfully ▷ *vb* **-charging, -charged 3** to charge (someone) an additional sum or tax **4** to overcharge (someone) for something

surd *maths* *n* **1** an irrational number ▷ *adj* **2** of or relating to a surd [Latin *surdus* muffled]

sure *adj* **1** free from doubt or uncertainty (in regard to a belief): *she was sure that she was still at home; I am sure he didn't mean it* **2 sure of** having no doubt, such as of the occurrence of a future state or event: *sure of winning the point* **3** reliable or accurate: *a sure sign of dry rot* **4** bound inevitably (to be or do something); certain: *his aggressive style is sure to please the American fans* **5 sure of** or **about** happy to put one's trust in (someone): *I'm still not quite sure about her* **6 sure of oneself** confident in one's own abilities and opinions **7** not open to doubt: *sure proof* **8** bound to be or occur; inevitable: *victory is sure* **9** physically secure: *a sure footing* **10 be sure** (usually foll. by *to* or *and*) be careful or certain (to do something): *be sure to label each jar* **11 for sure** without a doubt **12 make sure** to make certain: *make sure there is no-one in the car*

13 sure enough *informal* in fact: *sure enough, this is happening* **14 to be sure** it has to be acknowledged; admittedly ▷ *adv* **15** *informal, chiefly US and Canad* without question; certainly: *it sure is bad news* ▷ *interj* **16** *informal* willingly; yes [Old French *seur*] **> sureness** *n*

sure-fire *adj* *informal* certain to succeed: *a sure-fire cure*

sure-footed *adj* **1** unlikely to fall, slip, or stumble **2** unlikely to make a mistake

surely *adv* **1** am I not right in thinking that?; I am sure that: *surely you can see that?* **2** without doubt: *without support they will surely fail* **3** slowly but surely gradually but noticeably ▷ *interj* **4** *chiefly US and Canad* willingly; yes

surety *n*, *pl* **-ties 1** a person who takes legal responsibility for the fulfilment of another's debt or obligation **2** security given as a guarantee that an obligation will be met [Latin *securitas* security]

surf *n* **1** foam caused by waves breaking on the shore or on a reef ▷ *vb* **2** to take part in surfing **3** to move rapidly through a particular medium: *surfing the internet* **4** *informal* to be carried on top of something: *that guy's surfing the audience* [probably variant of *sough*] **> surfer** *n*

surface *n* **1** the outside or top of an object **2** the size of such an area **3** material covering the surface of an object **4** the outward appearance as opposed to the real or hidden nature of something: *on the surface the idea seems attractive* **5** *geometry* **a** the complete boundary of a solid figure **b** something that has length and breadth but no thickness **6** the uppermost level of the land or sea **7 come to the surface** to become apparent after being hidden ▷ *vb* **-facing, -faced 8** to become apparent or widely known **9** to rise to the surface of water **10** to give (an area) a particular kind of surface **11** *informal* to get up out of bed [French]

surface tension *n* *physics* a property of liquids, caused by molecular forces, that leads to the apparent presence of a surface film and to rising and falling in contact with solids

surfboard *n* a long narrow board used in surfing

surfeit *n* *formal* **1** an excessive amount **2** excessive eating or drinking **3** an uncomfortably full or sickened feeling caused by eating or drinking too much [French *sourfait*]

surfie *n* *Austral and NZ informal* a young person whose main interest is surfing

surfing *n* the sport of riding towards shore on the crest of a wave by standing or lying on a surfboard

surge *n* **1** a sudden powerful increase: *a surge in spending* **2** a strong rolling movement of the sea **3** a heavy rolling motion or sound: *a great surge of people* ▷ *vb* **surging, surged 4** to move forward strongly and suddenly **5** to increase quickly and strongly **6** (of the sea) to rise or roll with a heavy swelling motion [Latin *surgere* to rise]

surgeon *n* a medical doctor who specializes in surgery

surgery *n*, *pl* **-geries 1** medical treatment in which a person's body is cut open by a surgeon in order to treat or remove the problem part **2** *Brit* a place where, or time when, a doctor or dentist can be consulted **3** *Brit* a time when an MP or councillor can be consulted [Greek *kheir* hand + *ergon* work]

surgical *adj* **1** involving or used in surgery **2** (of an action) performed with extreme precision: *a surgical air attack* **> surgically** *adv*

surgical spirit *n* methylated spirit used medically for cleaning wounds and sterilizing equipment

Suribachi *n* **Mount Suribachi** a volcanic hill in the Volcano Islands, on Iwo Jima: site of a US victory (1945) over the Japanese in World War II

Surinam or **Suriname** *n* a republic in NE South America, on the Atlantic: became a self-governing part of the Netherlands in 1954 and fully independent in 1975. Official languages: Dutch; English is also widely spoken. Religion: Hindu, Christian, and Muslim. Currency: guilder. Capital: Paramaribo. Pop: 566 846 (2013 est). Area: 163 820 sq km (63 251 sq miles). Former names: **Dutch Guiana, Netherlands Guiana**

surly *adj* **-lier, -liest** bad-tempered and rude [from obsolete *sirly* haughty]

surmise *vb* **-mising, -mised** **1** to guess (something) from incomplete or uncertain evidence ▷ *n* **2** a conclusion based on incomplete or uncertain evidence [Old French *surmettre* to accuse]

surmount *vb* **1** to overcome (a problem) **2** to be situated on top of (something): *the island is surmounted by a huge black castle* [Old French *surmonter*] **> surmountable** *adj*

surname *n* a family name as opposed to a first or Christian name [Old French *sur-* over + *nom* name]

surpass *vb* **1** to be greater in extent than or superior in achievement to (something or someone) **2 surpass oneself** *or* **expectations** to go beyond the limit of what was expected [French *surpasser*]

surplice *n* a loose knee-length garment with wide sleeves, worn by clergymen and choristers [Old French *sourpelis*]

surplus *n* **1 a** a quantity or amount left over in excess of what is required **2** *accounting* an excess of income over spending ▷ *adj* **3** being in excess; extra: *surplus to requirements* [Old French]

surprise *n* **1** the act of taking someone unawares: *the element of surprise* **2** a sudden or unexpected event, gift, etc.: *this is a nice surprise* **3** the feeling of being surprised; astonishment: *to our great surprise* **4 take someone by surprise** to capture someone unexpectedly or catch someone unprepared ▷ *adj* **5** causing surprise: *a surprise attack* ▷ *vb* **-prising, -prised** **6** to cause (someone) to feel amazement or wonder **7** to come upon or discover (someone) unexpectedly or suddenly **8** to capture or attack (someone) suddenly and without warning **9 surprise into** to provoke (someone) to unintended action by a trick or deception [Old French *surprendre* to overtake] **> surprised** *adj* **> surprising** *adj* **> surprisingly** *adv*

surreal *adj* very strange or dreamlike; bizarre

surrealism *n* a movement in art and literature in the 1920s, involving the combination of images that would not normally be found together, as if in a dream [French *surréalisme*] **> surrealist** *n, adj* **> surrealistic** *adj*

surrender *vb* **1** to give oneself up physically to an enemy after defeat **2** to give (something) up to another, under pressure or on demand: *the rebels surrendered their arms* **3** to give (something) up voluntarily to another: *he was surrendering his own chance for the championship* **4** to give in to a temptation or an influence ▷ *n* **5** the act or instance of surrendering [Old French *surrendre*]

surreptitious *adj* done in secret or without permission: *surreptitious moments of bliss* [Latin *surrepticius* furtive] **> surreptitiously** *adv*

Surrey¹ *n* a county of SE England, on the River Thames: urban in the northeast; crossed from east to west by the North Downs and drained by tributaries of the Thames. Administrative centre: Kingston upon Thames. Pop: 1 064 600 (2003 est.). Area: 1679 sq km (648 sq miles)

Surrey² *n* Earl of, title of *Henry Howard*. ?1517–47, English courtier and poet; one of the first in England to write sonnets. He was beheaded for high treason

surrogate *n* **1** a person or thing acting as a substitute ▷ *adj* **2** acting as a substitute: *a surrogate father* [Latin *surrogare* to substitute]

surrogate mother *n* a woman who gives birth to a child on behalf of a couple who cannot have a baby themselves, usually by artificial insemination **> surrogate motherhood** *or* **surrogacy** *n*

surround *vb* **1** to encircle or enclose (something or someone) **2** to exist around (someone or something): *the family members who surround him* ▷ *n* **3** *chiefly Brit* a border, such as the area of uncovered floor between the walls of a room and the carpet [Old French *suronder*] **> surrounding** *adj*

surroundings *pl n* the area and environment around a person, place, or thing

surround sound *n* a system of sound recording and reproduction that uses three or more independent recording channels and loudspeakers in order to give the impression that the listener is surrounded by the sound sources

surtax *n* an extra tax on incomes above a certain level

Surtees *n* **1** John. born 1934, British racing motorcyclist and motor-racing driver. He was motorcycling world champion (1956, 1958–60) and Formula One world champion (1964), the only man to have been world champion in both sports **2** Robert Smith. 1803–64, British journalist and novelist, who satirized the sporting life of the English gentry in such works as *Jorrocks's Jaunts and Jollities* (1838)

surveillance *n* close observation of a person suspected of being a spy or a criminal [French]

survey *vb* **1** to view or consider (something) as a whole: *she surveyed her purchases anxiously* **2** to make a detailed map of (an area of land) by measuring or calculating distances and height **3** *Brit* to inspect (a building) to assess its condition and value **4** to make a detailed investigation of the behaviour, opinions, etc., of (a group of people) ▷ *n* **5** a detailed investigation of the behaviour, opinions, etc., of a group of people **6** the act of making a detailed map of an area of land by measuring or calculating distance and height **7** *Brit* an inspection of a building to assess its condition and value [French *surveoir*] **> surveying** *n* **> surveyor** *n*

survival *n* **1** the condition of having survived something **2** a person or thing that continues to exist in the present despite being from an earlier time, such as a custom ▷ *adj* **3** of, relating to, or assisting the act of surviving: *survival suits*

survive *vb* **-viving, -vived** **1 a** to continue to live or exist **b** to continue to live or exist after (a passage of time or a difficult or dangerous experience) **2** to live after the death of (another) [Old French *sourvivre*] **> survivor** *n*

Susa *n* an ancient city north of the Persian Gulf: capital of Elam and of the Persian Empire; flourished as a Greek polis under the Seleucids and Parthians. Biblical name: Shushan

Susah *or* **Susa** *n* other names for **Sousse**

susceptibility *n, pl* **-ties** **1** the quality or condition of being easily affected or influenced by something **2 susceptibilities** emotional feelings

susceptible *adj* **1 susceptible to a** giving in easily to: *susceptible to political pressure* **b** vulnerable to (a disease or injury): *susceptible to pneumonia* **2** easily affected emotionally; impressionable [Late Latin *susceptibilis*]

sushi (soo-shee) *n* a Japanese dish consisting of small cakes of cold rice with a topping of raw fish [Japanese]

suspect *vb* **1** to believe (someone) to be guilty without having any proof **2** to think (something) to be false or doubtful: *he suspected her intent* **3** to believe (something) to be the case; think probable: *I suspect he had another reason* ▷ *n* **4** a person who is believed guilty of a specified offence ▷ *adj* **5** not to be trusted or relied upon: *her commitment to the cause has always been suspect* [Latin *suspicere* to mistrust]

suspend *vb* **1** to hang (something) from a high place **2** to cause (something) to remain floating or hanging: *a huge orange sun suspended above the horizon* **3** to cause (something) to stop temporarily: *the discussions have been suspended* **4** to remove (someone) temporarily from a job or position, usually as a punishment [Latin *suspendere*]

suspended animation *n* a state in which the body's functions are slowed down to a minimum for a period of time, such as by freezing or hibernation

suspended sentence *n* a sentence of imprisonment that is not served by an offender unless he or she commits a further offence during a specified time

suspender belt *n* a belt with suspenders hanging from it for holding up women's stockings

suspenders *pl n* **1 a** elastic straps attached to a belt or corset, with fasteners for holding up women's stockings **b** similar fasteners attached to garters for holding up men's socks **2** *US and Canad* also called (*Brit*): **braces** a pair of straps worn over the shoulders for holding up the trousers

suspense *n* **1** a state of anxiety or uncertainty: *Sue and I stared at each other in suspense* **2** excitement felt at the approach of the climax of a book, film, or play: *action and suspense abound in this thriller* [Medieval Latin *suspensum* delay] ⟩ **suspenseful** *adj*

suspension *n* **1** the delaying or stopping temporarily of something: *the suspension of the talks* **2** temporary removal from a job or position, usually as a punishment **3** the act of suspending or the state of being suspended **4** a system of springs and shock absorbers that supports the body of a vehicle **5** a device, usually a wire or spring, that suspends or supports something, such as the pendulum of a clock **6** *chem* a mixture in which fine solid or liquid particles are suspended in a fluid

suspension bridge *n* a bridge suspended from cables that hang between two towers and are secured at both ends

suspicion *n* **1** the act or an instance of suspecting; belief without sure proof that something is wrong **2** a feeling of mistrust **3** a slight trace: *the merest suspicion of a threat* **4 above suspicion** not possibly guilty of anything, through having a good reputation **5 under suspicion** suspected of doing something wrong [Latin *suspicio* distrust]

suspicious *adj* **1** causing one to suspect something is wrong: *suspicious activities* **2** unwilling to trust: *I'm suspicious of his motives* ⟩ **suspiciously** *adv*

Susquehanna *n* a river in the eastern US, rising in Otsego Lake and flowing generally south to Chesapeake Bay at Havre de Grace: the longest river in the eastern US. Length: 714 km (444 miles)

Sussex *n* **1** (until 1974) a county of SE England, now divided into the separate counties of East Sussex and West Sussex **2** (in Anglo-Saxon England) the kingdom of the South Saxons, which became a shire of the kingdom of Wessex in the early 9th century AD **3** a breed of red beef cattle originally from Sussex **4** a heavy and long-established breed of domestic fowl used principally as a table bird

suss out *vb Brit, Austral and NZ slang* to work out (a situation or a person's character), using one's intuition [from *suspect*]

sustain *vb* **1** to maintain or continue for a period of time: *I managed to sustain a conversation* **2** to keep up the strength or energy of (someone): *one mouthful of water to sustain him; the merest drop of comfort to sustain me* **3** to suffer (an injury or loss): *he sustained a spinal injury* **4** to support (something) from below **5** to support or agree with (a decision or statement): *objection sustained* [Latin *sustinere* to hold up] ⟩ **sustained** *adj*

sustainable *adj* **1** capable of being sustained **2** (of economic development or energy sources) capable of being maintained at a steady level without exhausting natural resources or causing ecological damage: *sustainable development*

sustained-release *adj* (of a pill or tablet) coated with a chemical substance that controls the dosage released into a patient's system

sustenance *n* means of maintaining health or life; food and drink

Sutcliffe *n* Herbert. 1894–1978, English cricketer, who played for Yorkshire; scorer of 149 centuries and 1000 runs in a season 24 times

Suth. Sutherland

Sutherland¹ *n* (until 1975) a county of N Scotland, now part of Highland

Sutherland² *n* **1** Graham. 1903–80, English artist, noted for his work as an official war artist (1941–44), for his tapestry *Christ in Majesty* (1962) in Coventry Cathedral, and for his portraits **2** Dame **Joan**, 1926–2010 known as *La Stupenda*. Australian operatic soprano

Sutherland Falls *n* a waterfall in New Zealand, on SW South Island. Height: 580 m (1904 ft)

Sutlej *n* a river in S Asia, rising in SW Tibet and flowing west through the Himalayas: crosses Himachal Pradesh and the Punjab (India), enters Pakistan, and joins the Chenab west of Bahawalpur: the longest of the five rivers of the Punjab. Length: 1368 km (850 miles)

Sutton *n* a borough of S Greater London. Pop: 178 500 (2003 est). Area: 43 sq km (17 sq miles)

Sutton Coldfield *n* a town in central England, in Birmingham unitary authority, West Midlands; a residential suburb of Birmingham. Pop: 105 452 (2001)

Sutton Hoo *n* an archaeological site in Suffolk where a Saxon longboat containing rich grave goods, probably for a 7th-century East Anglian king, was found in 1939

Sutton-in-Ashfield *n* a market town in N central England, in W Nottinghamshire. Pop: 41 951 (2001)

suture (soo-tcher) *n surgery* a stitch made with catgut or silk thread, to join the edges of a wound together [Latin *suere* to sew]

SUV sport (*or* sports) utility vehicle: a high-powered car with four-wheel drive, originally designed for off-road use

Suva *n* the capital and chief port of Fiji, on the SE coast of Viti Levu; popular tourist resort; University of the South Pacific (1968). Pop: 219 000 (2005 est)

Suvorov *n* Aleksandr Vasilyevich. 1729–1800, Russian field marshal, who fought successfully against the Turks (1787–91), the Poles (1794), and the French in Italy (1798–99)

Suwannee *or* **Swanee** *n* a river in the southeastern US, rising in SE Georgia and flowing across Florida to the Gulf of Mexico at **Suwannee Sound**. Length: about 400 km (250 miles)

suzerain *n* **1** a state or sovereign that has some degree of control over a dependent state **2** (formerly) a person who had power over many people [French] ⟩ **suzerainty** *n*

Suzhou, Su-chou *or* **Soochow** *n* a city in E China, in S Jiangsu on the Grand Canal: noted for its gardens; produces chiefly silk. Pop: 1 201 000 (2005 est). Also called: **Wuhsien**

Svalbard *n* a Norwegian archipelago in the Arctic Ocean, about 650 km (400 miles) north of Norway: consists of the main group (Spitsbergen, North East Land, Edge Island, Barents Island, and Prince Charles Foreland) and a number of outlying islands; sovereignty long disputed but granted to Norway in 1920; coal mining. Administrative centre: Longyearbyen. Pop: 1970 (2013 est). Area: 62 050 sq km (23 958 sq miles). Also called: **Spitsbergen**

svelte *adj* attractively or gracefully slim; slender [French]

Sverdlovsk *n* the former name (1924–91) of Yekaterinburg

Sverige *n* the Swedish name for Sweden

Svevo *n* Italo, original name *Ettore Schnitz*. 1861–1928, Italian novelist and short-story writer, best known for the novel *Confessions of Zeno* (1923)

Svizzera *n* the Italian name for Switzerland

SW 1 southwest(ern) **2** short wave

Sw. 1 Sweden **2** Swedish

swab *n* **1** *med* a small piece of cotton wool used for applying medication or cleansing a wound ▷ *vb* **swabbing, swabbed 2** to clean or apply medication to (a wound) with a swab **3** to clean (the deck of a ship) with a mop [probably from Middle Dutch *swabbe* mop]

Swabia *n* a region and former duchy (from the 10th century to 1313) of S Germany, now part of Baden-Württemberg and Bavaria: part of West Germany until 1990. German name: **Schwaben**

Swabian *adj* **1** of or relating to the German region of

Swabia or its inhabitants ▷ *n* **2** a native or inhabitant of Swabia

swaddle *vb* **-dling, -dled** to wrap (a baby) in swaddling clothes [Old English *swæthel* swaddling clothes]

swaddling clothes *pl n* long strips of cloth formerly wrapped round a newborn baby

swag *n* **1** *slang* stolen property **2** *Austral and NZ informal* (formerly) a swagman's pack containing personal belongings [probably Scandinavian]

swagger *vb* **1** to walk or behave in an arrogant manner ▷ *n* **2** an arrogant walk or manner [probably from *swag*]

swagger stick *n* a short cane carried by army officers

swagman *n, pl* **-men** *Austral and NZ informal* a labourer who carries his personal possessions in a pack while looking for work

Swahili (swah-**heel**-ee) *n* a language of E Africa that is an official language of Kenya and Tanzania [Arabic *sawāhil* coasts]

swain *n archaic or poetic* **1** a male lover or admirer **2** a young man from the countryside [Old English *swān* swineherd]

swallow¹ *vb* **1** to pass (food, drink, etc.) through the mouth and gullet to the stomach **2** *informal* to believe (something) trustingly: *I was supposed to swallow the lie* **3** not to show: *I believe they should swallow their pride* **4** to make a gulping movement in the throat, such as when nervous **5** to put up with (an insult) without answering back **6 be swallowed up** to be taken into and made a part of something: *the old centre was being swallowed up by new estates* ▷ *n* **7** the act of swallowing **8** the amount swallowed at any single time; mouthful [Old English *swelgan*]

swallow² *n* a small migratory bird with long pointed wings and a forked tail [Old English *swealwe*]

swallow dive *n* a dive in which the legs are kept straight and the arms outstretched while in the air, with entry into the water made headfirst

swallowtail *n* **1** a butterfly with a long tail-like part on each hind wing **2** the forked tail of a swallow or similar bird

swam *vb* the past tense of **swim**

swami (swah-mee) *n* a Hindu religious teacher [Hindi *svāmī*]

swamp *n* **1** an area of permanently waterlogged land; bog ▷ *vb* **2** *nautical* to cause (a boat) to sink or fill with water **3** to overwhelm (a person or place) with more than can be dealt with or accommodated [probably from Middle Dutch *somp*] ❯ **swampy** *adj*

swan *n* **1** a large, usually white, water bird with a long neck ▷ *vb* **2 swan around** *or* **about** *informal* to wander about without purpose, but with an air of superiority [Old English]

Swan¹ *n* a river in SW Western Australia, rising as the Avon northeast of Narrogin and flowing northwest and west to the Indian Ocean below Perth. Length: about 240 km (150 miles)

Swan² *n* Sir Joseph Wilson. 1828–1914, English physicist and chemist, who developed the incandescent electric light (1880) independently of Edison

Swanee *n* a variant spelling of **Suwannee**

swank *informal vb* **1** to show off or boast ▷ *n* **2** showing off or boasting [origin unknown] ❯ **swanky** *adj*

swanndri (swan-dry) *n trademark* NZ a weatherproof woollen shirt or jacket. Also called: **swannie**

Swansea *n* **1** a port in S Wales, in Swansea county on an inlet of the Bristol Channel (**Swansea Bay**); a metallurgical and oil-refining centre; university (1920). Pop: 169 880 (2001) **2** a county of S Wales on the Bristol Channel, created in 1996 from part of West Glamorgan: includes the Swansea conurbation and the Gower peninsula. Administrative centre: Swansea. Pop: 224 600 (2003 est). Area: 378 sq km (146 sq miles)

swan song *n* the last public act of a person before retirement or death

swap *or* **swop** *vb* **swapping, swapped** *or* **swopping, swopped** **1** to exchange (something) for something else ▷ *n* **2** an exchange [originally, to shake hands on a bargain, strike: probably imitative]

SWAPO *or* **Swapo** South-West Africa People's Organization

sward *n* a stretch of turf or grass [Old English *sweard* skin]

swarm¹ *n* **1** a group of bees, led by a queen, that has left the hive to make a new home **2** a large mass of insects or other small animals **3** a moving mass of people ▷ *vb* **4** to move quickly and in large numbers **5** to be overrun: *the place is swarming with cops* [Old English *swearm*]

swarm² *vb* **swarm up** to climb (a ladder or rope) by gripping it with the hands and feet: *the boys swarmed up the rigging* [origin unknown]

swarthy *adj* **swarthier, swarthiest** having a dark complexion [obsolete *swarty*]

swash (swosh) *n* the rush of water up a beach following each break of the waves [probably imitative]

swashbuckling *adj* having the exciting manner or behaviour of pirates, esp. those depicted in films [obsolete *swash* to make the noise of a sword striking a shield + *buckler* shield] ❯ **swashbuckler** *n*

swastika *n* **1** a primitive religious symbol in the shape of a Greek cross with the ends of the arms bent at right angles **2** this symbol with clockwise arms as the emblem of Nazi Germany [Sanskrit *svastika*]

swat *vb* **swatting, swatted** **1** to hit sharply: *swatting the ball with confidence* ▷ *n* **2** a sharp blow [dialect variant of *squat*]

Swat *n* **1** a former princely state of NW India: passed to Pakistan in 1947 **2** a river in Pakistan, rising in the north and flowing south to the Kabul River north of Peshawar. Length: about 640 km (400 miles)

swatch *n* **1** a sample of cloth **2** a collection of such samples [origin unknown]

swath (swawth) *n* same as **swathe** [Old English *swæth*]

swathe *vb* **swathing, swathed** **1** to wrap a bandage, garment, or piece of cloth around (a person or part of the body) ▷ *n* **2** a long strip of cloth wrapped around something **3** the width of one sweep of a scythe or of the blade of a mowing machine **4** the strip cut in one sweep **5** the quantity of cut crops left in one sweep **6** a long narrow strip of land [Old English *swathian*]

Swatow *n* a variant transliteration of the Chinese name for **Shantou**

sway *vb* **1** to swing to and fro: *red poppies swayed in the faint breeze* **2** to lean to one side and then the other: *entire rows swayed in time* **3** to be unable to decide between two or more opinions **4** to influence (someone) in his or her opinion or judgment ▷ *n* **5** power or influence **6** a swinging or leaning movement **7 hold sway** to have power or influence [probably from Old Norse *sveigja* to bend]

Swaziland *n* a kingdom in southern Africa: made a protectorate of the Transvaal by Britain in 1894; gained independence in 1968; a member of the Commonwealth. Official languages: Swazi and English. Religion: Christian majority, traditional beliefs. Currency: lilangeni (plural emalangeni) and South African rand. Capital: Mbabane (administrative), Lobamba (legislative). Pop: 1 403 362 (2013 est). Area: 17 363 sq km (6704 sq miles)

Swazi Territory *n* the former name of **KaNgwane**

swear *vb* **swearing, swore, sworn** **1** to use words considered obscene or blasphemous **2** to promise solemnly on oath; vow: *Sally and Peter swore to love and cherish each other* **3 swear by** to have complete confidence in (something) **4** to state (something) earnestly: *I swear he was all right* **5** to give evidence on oath in a law court [Old English *swerian*]

swear in *vb* to make (someone) take an oath when taking up an official position or entering the witness

S

box to give evidence in court: *a new federal president was sworn in*

swear off *vb* to promise to give up: *I lived with memories of the gooey sundaes I've sworn off*

swearword *n* a word considered rude or blasphemous

sweat *n* 1 the salty liquid that comes out of the skin's pores during strenuous activity in excessive heat or when afraid 2 the state or condition of sweating: *he worked up a sweat* 3 *slang* hard work or effort: *climbing to the crest of Ward Hill was a sweat* 4 **in a sweat** *informal* in a state of worry 5 **no sweat** *slang* no problem ▷ *vb* **sweating, sweat** *or* **sweated** 6 to have sweat come through the skin's pores, as a result of strenuous activity, excessive heat, nervousness, or fear 7 *informal* to suffer anxiety or distress 8 **sweat blood** *informal* **a** to work very hard **b** to be filled with anxiety ▶ See also **sweats** [Old English *swǣtan*] ⟩ **sweaty** *adj*

sweatband *n* a piece of cloth tied around the forehead or around the wrist to absorb sweat during strenuous physical activity

sweater *n* a warm knitted piece of clothing covering the upper part of the body

sweat lodge *n* (among native N American peoples) a structure in which water is poured onto hot stones to make the occupants sweat for religious or medicinal purposes

sweat off *vb informal* to get rid of (weight) by doing exercises

sweat out *vb* **sweat it out** *informal* to endure an unpleasant situation for a time, hoping for an improvement

sweats *pl n* sweatshirts and sweat suit trousers collectively

sweatshirt *n* a long-sleeved casual top made of knitted cotton or cotton mixture

sweatshop *n* a workshop where employees work long hours in poor conditions for low pay

sweat suit *n* a suit worn by athletes for training, consisting of a sweatshirt and trousers made of the same material

swede *n* a round root vegetable with a purplish-brown skin and yellow flesh [introduced from Sweden in the 18th century]

Swede *n* a native or inhabitant of Sweden

Sweden *n* a kingdom in NW Europe, occupying the E part of the Scandinavian Peninsula, on the Gulf of Bothnia and the Baltic: first united during the Viking period (8th–11th centuries); a member of the European Union. About 50 per cent of the total area is forest and 9 per cent lakes. Exports include timber, pulp, paper, iron ore, and steel. Official language: Swedish. Official religion: Church of Sweden (Lutheran). Currency: krona. Capital: Stockholm. Pop: 9 119 423 (2013 est.). Area: 449 793 sq km (173 665 sq miles). Swedish name: **Sverige**

Swedenborg *n* Emanuel. original surname *Svedberg*. 1688–1772, Swedish scientist and theologian, whose mystical ideas became the basis of a religious movement

Swedish *adj* 1 of or relating to Sweden or its inhabitants ▷ *n* 2 the language of Sweden

Sweelinck *n* Jan Pieterszoon. 1562–1621, Dutch composer and organist, whose organ works are important for being the first to incorporate independent parts for the pedals

sweep *vb* **sweeping, swept** 1 to clean (a floor or chimney) with a brush 2 (often foll. by *up*) to remove or collect (dirt or rubbish) with a brush 3 to move smoothly and quickly: *the car swept into the drive* 4 to spread rapidly across or through (a place): *the wave of democracy that had swept through Eastern Europe* 5 to move in a proud and majestic fashion: *the boss himself swept into the hall* 6 to direct (one's eyes, line of fire, etc.) over (a place or target) 7 **sweep away** *or* **off** to overwhelm (someone) emotionally: *I've been swept away by my fears* 8 to brush or lightly touch (a surface): *the dress swept along the ground* 9 to clear away or get rid of (something) suddenly or forcefully: *these doubts were quickly swept aside; bridges have been swept away by the floods* 10 to stretch out gracefully or majestically, esp. in a wide circle: *the hills swept down into the green valley* 11 to win overwhelmingly, esp. in an election: *the umbrella party which swept these elections* 12 **sweep the board** to win every event or prize in a contest ▷ *n* 13 the act or an instance of sweeping 14 a swift or steady movement: *the wide sweep of the shoulders* 15 a wide expanse: *the whole sweep of the bay* 16 any curving line or contour, such as a driveway 17 short for **sweepstake** 18 *chiefly Brit* same as **chimney sweep** 19 **make a clean sweep** to win an overwhelming victory [Middle English *swepen*]

sweeper *n* 1 a device used to sweep carpets, consisting of a long handle attached to a revolving brush 2 *soccer* a defensive player usually positioned in front of the goalkeeper

sweeping *adj* 1 affecting many people to a great extent: *sweeping financial reforms* 2 (of a statement) making general assumptions about an issue without considering the details 3 decisive or overwhelming: *to suffer sweeping losses* 4 taking in a wide area: *a sweeping view of the area*

sweepstake *or especially US* **sweepstakes** *n* 1 a lottery in which the stakes of the participants make up the prize 2 a horse race involving such a lottery [originally referring to someone who *sweeps* or takes all the stakes in a game]

sweet *adj* 1 tasting of or like sugar 2 kind and charming: *that was really sweet of you* 3 attractive and delightful: *a sweet child* 4 (of a sound) pleasant and tuneful: *sweet music* 5 (of wine) having a high sugar content; not dry 6 fresh, clear, and clean: *sweet water; sweet air* 7 **sweet on someone** fond of or infatuated with someone ▷ *n Brit, Austral and NZ* 8 a shaped piece of confectionery consisting mainly of sugar 9 a dessert [Old English *swēte*] ⟩ **sweetly** *adv* ⟩ **sweetness** *n*

Sweet *n* Henry. 1845–1912, English philologist; a pioneer of modern phonetics. His books include *A History of English Sounds* (1874)

sweet-and-sour *adj* (of food) cooked in a sauce made from sugar and vinegar and other ingredients

sweetbread *n* the meat obtained from the pancreas of a calf or lamb

sweetbrier *n* a wild rose with sweet-smelling leaves and pink flowers

sweet corn *n* 1 a kind of maize with sweet yellow kernels, eaten as a vegetable when young 2 the sweet kernels removed from the maize cob, cooked as a vegetable

sweeten *vb* 1 to make (food or drink) sweet or sweeter 2 to be nice to (someone) in order to ensure cooperation 3 to make (an offer or a proposal) more acceptable

sweetener *n* 1 a sweetening agent that does not contain sugar 2 *Brit, Austral and NZ slang* an inducement offered to someone in order to persuade them to accept an offer or business deal

sweetheart *n* 1 an affectionate name to call someone 2 *old-fashioned* one's boyfriend or girlfriend 3 *informal* a lovable or generous person

sweetie *n informal* 1 an affectionate name to call someone 2 *Brit and NZ* same as **sweet** (8) 3 *chiefly Brit* a lovable or generous person

sweetmeat *n old-fashioned* a small delicacy preserved in sugar

sweet pea *n* a climbing plant with sweet-smelling pastel-coloured flowers

sweet pepper *n* the large bell-shaped fruit of the pepper plant, which is eaten unripe (**green pepper**) or ripe (**red pepper**) as a vegetable

sweet potato *n* a root vegetable, grown in the tropics, with pinkish-brown skin and yellow flesh

sweet spot *n sport* the centre area of a racquet, club, etc., from which the cleanest shots are made

sweet-talk *informal vb* **1** to persuade (someone) by flattery: *I thought I could sweet-talk you into teaching me* ▷ *n* **sweet talk** **2** insincere flattery intended to persuade

sweet tooth *n* a strong liking for sweet foods

sweet william *n* a garden plant with clusters of white, pink, red, or purple flowers

swell *vb* **swelling, swelled, swollen** *or* **swelled** **1** (of a part of the body) to grow in size as a result of injury or infection: *his face swelled and became pale* **2** to increase in size as a result of being filled with air or liquid: *a balloon swells if you force in more air* **3** to grow or cause (something) to grow in size, numbers, amount, or degree: *Israel's population is swelling* **4** (of an emotion) to become more intense: *his anger swelled within him* **5** (of the seas) to rise in waves **6** (of a sound) to become gradually louder and then die away ▷ *n* **7** the waving movement of the surface of the open sea **8** an increase in size, numbers, amount, or degree **9** a bulge **10** *old-fashioned, informal* a person who is wealthy, upper class, and fashionably dressed **11** *music* an increase in sound followed by an immediate dying away ▷ *adj* **12** *slang, chiefly US* excellent or fine [Old English *swellan*]

swelling *n* an enlargement of a part of the body as the result of injury or infection

swelter *vb* **1** to feel uncomfortable under extreme heat ▷ *n* **2** a hot and uncomfortable condition: *they left the city swelter for the beach* [Old English *sweltan* to die]

sweltering *adj* uncomfortably hot: *a sweltering summer*

swept *vb* the past of **sweep**

swerve *vb* **swerving, swerved** **1** to turn aside from a course sharply or suddenly ▷ *n* **2** the act of swerving [Old English *sweorfan* to scour]

Sweyn *n* known as *Sweyn Forkbeard*. died 1014, king of Denmark (?986–1014). He conquered England, forcing Ethelred II to flee (1013); father of Canute

swift *adj* **1** moving or able to move quickly; fast **2** happening or performed quickly or suddenly: *a swift glance this way* **3 swift to** prompt to (do something): *swift to retaliate* ▷ *n* **4** a small fast-flying insect-eating bird with long wings [Old English] ▷ **swiftly** *adv* ▷ **swiftness** *n*

Swift *n* **1** Graham Colin. born 1949, English writer: his novels include *Waterland* (1983), *Last Orders* (1996), which won the Booker prize, and *The Light of Day* (2002) **2** Jonathan. 1667–1745, Anglo-Irish satirist and churchman, who became dean of St Patrick's, Dublin, in 1713. His works include *A Tale of a Tub* (1704) and *Gulliver's Travels* (1726) ▷ **Swiftian** *adj*

swig *informal n* **1** a large swallow or deep drink, esp. from a bottle ▷ *vb* **swigging, swigged** **2** to drink (some liquid) in large swallows, esp. from a bottle [origin unknown]

swill *vb* **1** to drink large quantities of (an alcoholic drink) **2** (often foll. by *out*) *chiefly Brit and NZ* to rinse (something) in large amounts of water ▷ *n* **3** a liquid mixture containing waste food, fed to pigs **4** a deep drink, esp. of beer [Old English *swilian* to wash out]

swim *vb* **swimming, swam, swum** **1** to move along in water by movements of the arms and legs, or (in the case of fish) tail and fins **2** to cover (a stretch of water) in this way: *the first person to swim the Atlantic* **3** to float on a liquid: *flies swimming on the milk* **4** to be affected by dizziness: *his head was swimming* **5** (of the objects in someone's vision) to appear to spin or move around: *the faces of the nurses swam around her* **6** (often foll. by *in* or *with*) to be covered or flooded with liquid: *a steak swimming in gravy* ▷ *n* **7** the act, an instance, or a period of swimming **8 in the swim** *informal* fashionable or active in social or political activities [Old English *swimman*] ▷ **swimmer** *n* ▷ **swimming** *n*

swimming bath *n* an indoor swimming pool

swimming costume *or* **bathing costume** *n chiefly Brit, Austral and NZ* same as **swimsuit**

swimmingly *adv* successfully, effortlessly, or well: *everything went swimmingly*

swimming pool *n* a large hole in the ground, tiled and filled with water for swimming in

swimsuit *n* a woman's swimming garment that leaves the arms and legs bare

Swinburne *n* Algernon Charles. 1837–1909, English lyric poet and critic

swindle *vb* **-dling, -dled** **1** to cheat (someone) out of money **2** to obtain (money) from someone by fraud ▷ *n* **3** an instance of cheating someone out of money [German *schwindeln*] ▷ **swindler** *n*

Swindon *n* **1** a town in S England, in NE Wiltshire: railway workshops, high technology. Pop: 155 432 (2001) **2** a unitary authority in S England, in Wiltshire. Pop: 181 200 (2003 est). Area: 230 sq km (89 sq miles)

swine *n* **1** a mean or unpleasant person **2** (*pl* **swine**) same as **pig** [Old English *swīn*] ▷ **swinish** *adj*

swine flu *n* a form of influenza occurring in swine caused by a virus capable of spreading to humans

swing *vb* **swinging, swung** **1** to move backwards and forwards; sway **2** to pivot or cause (something) to pivot from a fixed point such as a hinge: *the door swung open* **3** to wave (a weapon, etc.) in a sweeping motion **4** to move in a sweeping curve: *the headlights swung along the street* **5** to alter one's opinion or mood suddenly **6** to hang so as to be able to turn freely **7** *old-fashioned, slang* to be hanged: *you'll swing for this!* **8** *informal* to manipulate or influence successfully: *it may help to swing the election* **9** (often foll. by *at*) to hit out with a sweeping motion **10** *old-fashioned* to play (music) in the style of swing **11** *old-fashioned, slang* to be lively and modern ▷ *n* **12** the act of swinging **13** a sweeping stroke or punch **14** a seat hanging from two chains or ropes on which a person may swing back and forth **15** popular dance music played by big bands in the 1930s and 1940s **16** *informal* the normal pace at which an activity, such as work, happens: *I'm into the swing of things now* **17** a sudden or extreme change, for example in some business activity or voting pattern **18 go with a swing** to go well; be successful **19 in full swing** at the height of activity [Old English *swingan*]

swing bridge *n* a bridge that can be swung open to let ships pass through

swing by *vb informal* to go somewhere to pay a visit

swingeing (swin-jing) *adj chiefly Brit* severe or causing hardship: *swingeing spending cuts*

Swinney *n* John (Ramsay). born 1964, Scottish politician; leader of the Scottish National Party (2000–04); Scottish government finance minister from 2007

swipe *vb* **swiping, swiped** **1** *informal* to try to hit (someone or something) with a sweeping blow: *he swiped at a boy who ran forward* **2** *slang* to steal (something) **3** to pass (a credit or debit card) through a machine which electronically interprets the information stored in the card **4** to activate by moving one's finger across (an item on a screen) ▷ *n* **5** *informal* a hard blow [origin unknown]

swirl *vb* **1** to turn round and round with a twisting motion ▷ *n* **2** a twisting or spinning motion **3** a twisting shape [probably from Dutch *zwirrelen*] ▷ **swirling** *adj*

swish *vb* **1** to move with or cause (something) to make a whistling or hissing sound ▷ *n* **2** a hissing or rustling sound or movement: *she turned with a swish of her skirt* ▷ *adj* **3** *informal, chiefly Brit, Austral and NZ* smart and fashionable [imitative]

Swiss *adj* **1** of or relating to Switzerland or its inhabitants ▷ *n, pl* **Swiss** **2** a native or inhabitant of Switzerland

Swiss ball *n* a very large inflatable ball made of strong elastic rubber, used for physical exercise and physiotherapy

Swiss Re Tower *n* a bluish cigar-shaped office block, London's first environmental skyscraper. Standing 180 m (585 ft) high, the building was completed in 2004

swiss roll *n* a sponge cake spread with jam or cream and rolled up

S

switch *n* **1** a device for opening or closing an electric circuit **2** a sudden quick change **3** an exchange or swap **4** a flexible rod or twig, used for punishment **5** *US and Canad* a pair of movable rails for diverting moving trains from one track to another ▷ *vb* **6** to change quickly and suddenly **7** to exchange (places) or swap (something for something else) **8** *chiefly US and Canad* to transfer (rolling stock) from one railway track to another ▶ See also **switch off, switch on** [probably from Middle Dutch *swijch* twig]

switchback *n* a steep mountain road, railway, or track which rises and falls sharply many times

switchboard *n* the place in a telephone exchange or office building where telephone calls are connected

switch off *vb* **1** to cause (a device) to stop operating by moving a switch or lever: *she switched off the television* **2** *informal* to become bored and stop paying attention: *when the conversation turned to house prices I switched off*

switch on *vb* **1** to cause (a device) to operate by moving a switch or lever **2** *informal* to produce (a certain type of behaviour or emotion) suddenly or automatically: *she was good at switching on the charm*

swither *Scot vb* **1** to hesitate or be indecisive ▷ *n* **2** a state of hesitation or uncertainty [origin unknown]

Swithin *or* **Swithun** *n* Saint. died 862 AD, English ecclesiastic: bishop of Winchester (?852–862). Feast day: July 15

Switz. *or* **Swit.** Switzerland

Switzerland *n* a federal republic in W central Europe: the cantons of Schwyz, Uri, and Unterwalden formed a defensive league against the Hapsburgs in 1291, later joined by other cantons; gained independence in 1499; adopted a policy of permanent neutrality from 1516; a leading centre of the Reformation in the 16th century. It lies in the Jura Mountains and the Alps, with a plateau between the two ranges. Official languages: German, French, and Italian; Romansch minority. Religion: mostly Protestant and Roman Catholic. Currency: Swiss franc. Capital: Bern. Pop: 7 996 026 (2013 est). Area: 41 288 sq km (15 941 sq miles). German name: **Schweiz**. French name: **Suisse**. Italian name: **Svizzera**. Latin name: **Helvetia**

swivel *vb* **-elling, -elled** *or US* **-eling, -eled** **1** to turn on or swing round on a central point ▷ *n* **2** a coupling device which allows an attached object to turn freely [Old English *swīfan* to turn]

swivel chair *n* a chair, whose seat is joined to the legs by a swivel, enabling it to be spun round

swizz *n Brit, NZ and S African informal* a swindle or disappointment [origin unknown]

swizzle stick *n* a small stick used to stir cocktails

swollen *vb* **1** a past participle of **swell** ▷ *adj* **2** enlarged by swelling

swoon *vb* **1** *literary* to faint because of shock or strong emotion **2** to be deeply affected by passion (for someone): *you've swooned over a string of rotten men* ▷ *n* **3** *literary* a faint [Old English *geswōgen* insensible] **❯ swooning** *adj*

swoop *vb* **1** (usually foll. by *down*) to move quickly through the air in a downward curve: *an owl swooped down from its perch* **2** (usually foll. by *on*) to move suddenly and quickly (towards a place) in order to attack, arrest, or question the people inside: *nine police cars and vans swooped on the premises* ▷ *n* **3** the act of swooping [Old English *swāpan* to sweep]

swoosh *vb* **1** to make a swirling or rustling sound when moving or pouring out ▷ *n* **2** a swirling or rustling sound or movement [imitative]

swop *vb* **swopping, swopped** ▷ *n* same as **swap**

sword *n* **1** a weapon with a long sharp blade and a short handle **2 the sword a** military power **b** death; destruction: *we will put them to the sword* **3 cross swords** to have a disagreement with someone [Old English *sweord*]

sword dance *n* a dance in which the performer dances over swords on the ground

swordfish *n, pl* **-fish** *or* **-fishes** a large fish with a very long upper jaw that resembles a sword

Sword of Damocles (**dam-a-kleez**) *n* a disaster that is about to take place [after a flattering courtier forced by Dionysius, tyrant of ancient Syracuse, to sit under a sword suspended by a hair]

swordplay *n* the action or art of fighting with a sword

swordsman *n, pl* **-men** a person who is skilled in the use of a sword **❯ swordsmanship** *n*

swordstick *n* a hollow walking stick that contains a short sword

swore *vb* the past tense of **swear**

sworn *vb* **1** the past participle of **swear** ▷ *adj* **2** bound by or as if by an oath: *a sworn enemy*

swot¹ *informal vb* **swotting, swotted** **1** (often foll. by *up*) to study (a subject) very hard, esp. for an exam; cram ▷ *n* **2** a person who works or studies hard [variant of *sweat*]

swot² *vb* **swotting, swotted** ▷ *n* same as **swat**

swum *vb* the past participle of **swim**

swung *vb* the past of **swing**

Syal *n* Meera. born 1961, British actress and writer of Punjabi origin, who appeared in the TV comedy series *Goodness Gracious Me* (1998–2001) and *The Kumars at No. 42* (2001–06); her screenplays include *Bhaji on the Beach* (1993)

Sybaris *n* a Greek colony in S Italy, on the Gulf of Taranto: notorious for its luxurious living, founded about 720 BC and sacked in 510

sybarite (**sib-bar-ite**) *n* **1** a lover of luxury and pleasure ▷ *adj* **2** luxurious or sensuous [after SYBARIS] **❯ sybaritic** *adj*

Sybarite *n* a native or inhabitant of Sybaris

Sybaritic *adj* of or relating to Sybaris or its inhabitants

sycamore *n* **1** a tree with five-pointed leaves and two-winged fruits **2** *US and Canad* an American plane tree [Latin *sycomorus*]

sycophant *n* a person who uses flattery to win favour from people with power or influence [Greek *sukophantēs*] **❯ sycophancy** *n* **❯ sycophantic** *adj*

Sydney *n* **1** a port in SE Australia, capital of New South Wales, on an inlet of the S Pacific: the largest city in Australia and the first British settlement, established as a penal colony in 1788; developed rapidly after 1820 with the discovery of gold in its hinterland; large wool market; three universities. Pop: 4 627 345 (2011) **2** a port in SE Canada, in Nova Scotia on NE Cape Breton Island: capital of Cape Breton Island until 1820, when the island united administratively with Nova Scotia. Pop: 32 286 (2006)

Syene *n* transliteration of the Ancient Greek name for Aswan

Syktyvkar *n* a city in NW Russia, capital of the Komi Republic: timber industry. Pop: 230 000 (2005 est)

syllabic *adj* of or relating to syllables

syllabify *vb* **-fies, -fying, -fied** to divide (a word) into syllables **❯ syllabification** *n*

syllable *n* **1** a part of a word which is pronounced as a unit, which contains a single vowel sound, and which may or may not contain consonants: for example, 'paper' has two syllables **2** the least mention: *without a syllable about what went on* **3 in words of one syllable** simply and plainly [Greek *sullabē*]

syllabub *n Brit and Austral* a dessert made from milk or cream beaten with sugar, wine, and lemon juice [origin unknown]

syllabus (**sill-lab-buss**) *n, pl* **-buses** *or* **-bi** (**-bye**) **a** the subjects studied for a particular course **b** a list of these subjects [Late Latin]

syllogism *n* a form of reasoning consisting of two premises and a conclusion, for example *some temples are in ruins; all ruins are fascinating; so some temples are fascinating* [Greek *sullogismos*] **❯ syllogistic** *adj*

sylph *n* **1** a slender graceful girl or young woman **2** an imaginary creature believed to live in the air [New Latin *sylphus*] **❯ sylphlike** *adj*

sylvan or **silvan** adj chiefly poetic of or consisting of woods or forests [Latin silva forest]

Sylvester II n original name Gerbert of Aurillac. c. 940–1003 AD, French ecclesiastic and scholar; pope (999–1003): noted for his achievements in mathematics and astronomy

symbiosis n 1 biology a close association of two different animal or plant species living together to their mutual benefit 2 a similar relationship between different individuals or groups: the symbiosis of the coal and railway industries [Greek: a living together] > **symbiotic** adj

symbol n 1 something that represents or stands for something else, usually an object used to represent something abstract 2 a letter, figure, or sign used in mathematics, music, etc., to represent a quantity, operation, function, etc. [Greek sumbolon sign]

symbolic adj 1 of or relating to a symbol or symbols 2 being a symbol of something > **symbolically** adv

symbolism n 1 the representation of something by the use of symbols 2 an art movement involving the use of symbols to express mystical or abstract ideas > **symbolist** adj, n

symbolize or **-lise** vb **-lizing, -lized** or **-lising, -lised** 1 to be a symbol of (something) 2 to represent with a symbol > **symbolization** or **-lisation** n

symmetry n, pl **-tries** 1 the state of having two halves that are mirror images of each other 2 beauty resulting from a balanced arrangement of parts [Greek summetria proportion] > **symmetrical** adj > **symmetrically** adv

Symonds n John Addington. 1840–93, English writer, noted for his Renaissance in Italy (1875–86) and for studies of homosexuality

Symons n Arthur. 1865–1945, English poet and critic, who helped to introduce the French symbolists to England

sympathetic adj 1 feeling or showing kindness and understanding 2 (of a person) likeable and appealing: the film's only sympathetic character 3 sympathetic to showing agreement with or willing to lend support to: sympathetic to the movement > **sympathetically** adv

sympathize or **-thise** vb **-thizing, -thized** or **-thising, -thised** sympathize with a to feel or express sympathy for: I sympathized with this fear b to agree with or support: Pitt sympathized with these objectives > **sympathizer** or **-thiser** n

sympathy n, pl **-thies** 1 (often foll. by for) understanding of other people's problems; compassion 2 sympathy with agreement with someone's feelings or interests: we have every sympathy with how she felt 3 (often pl) feelings of loyalty or support for an idea or a cause: was this where her sympathies lay? 4 mutual affection or understanding between two people or a person and an animal [Greek sympatheia]

symphony n, pl **-nies** 1 a large-scale orchestral composition with several movements 2 an orchestral movement in a vocal work such as an oratorio 3 short for **symphony orchestra** 4 anything that has a pleasing arrangement of colours or shapes: the garden was a symphony of coloured bunting [Greek sun- together + phōnē sound] > **symphonic** adj

symphony orchestra n music a large orchestra that performs symphonies

symposium n, pl **-sia** or **-siums** 1 a conference at which experts or academics discuss a particular subject 2 a collection of essays on a particular subject [Greek sumposion a drinking party]

symptom n 1 med a sign indicating the presence of an illness or disease 2 anything that is taken as an indication that something is wrong: a growing symptom of grave social injustice [Greek sumptōma chance] > **symptomatic** adj

synagogue n a building for Jewish religious services and religious instruction [Greek sunagōgē a gathering]

synapse n anatomy a gap where nerve impulses pass between two nerve cells [Greek sunapsis junction]

sync or **synch** 1 films, television, computers informal ▷ vb 2 to synchronize ▷ n 3 synchronization: the film and sound are in sync

synchromesh adj 1 (of a gearbox) having a system of clutches that synchronizes the speeds of the gearwheels before they engage ▷ n 2 a gear system having these features [synchronized mesh]

synchronism n the quality or condition of occurrence at the same time or rate

synchronize or **-nise** vb **-nizing, -nized** or **-nising, -nised** 1 (of two or more people) to perform (an action) at the same time: a synchronized withdrawal of Allied forces 2 to cause (two or more clocks or watches) to show the same time 3 films to match (the soundtrack and the action of a film) precisely > **synchronization** or **-nisation** n

synchronous adj occurring at the same time and rate [Greek sun- together + khronos time] > **synchrony** n

syncline n geology a downward slope of stratified rock in which the layers dip towards each other from either side

syncopate vb **-pating, -pated** music to stress the weak beats in (a rhythm or a piece of music) instead of the strong beats [Medieval Latin syncopare to omit a letter or syllable] > **syncopation** n

syncope (sing-kop-ee) n 1 med a faint 2 linguistics the omission of sounds or letters from the middle of a word, as in ne'er for never [Greek sunkopē a cutting off]

syndic n Brit a business or legal agent of some universities or other institutions [Greek sundikos defendant's advocate]

syndicalism n a movement advocating seizure of economic and political power by the industrial working class by means of industrial action, esp. general strikes > **syndicalist** n

syndicate n 1 a group of people or firms organized to undertake a joint project 2 an association of individuals who control organized crime 3 a news agency that sells articles and photographs to a number of newspapers for simultaneous publication ▷ vb **-cating, -cated** 4 to sell (articles and photographs) to several newspapers for simultaneous publication 5 to form a syndicate of (people) [Old French syndicat] > **syndication** n

syndrome n 1 med a combination of signs and symptoms that indicate a particular disease 2 a set of characteristics indicating the existence of a particular condition or problem [Greek sundromē, literally: a running together]

synecdoche (sin-neck-dock-ee) n a figure of speech in which a part is substituted for a whole or a whole for a part, as in 50 head of cattle for 50 cows [Greek sunekdokhē]

synergy n the potential ability for individuals or groups to be more successful working together than on their own [Greek sunergos]

Synge n John Millington. 1871–1909, Irish playwright. His plays, marked by vivid colloquial Irish speech, include Riders to the Sea (1904) and The Playboy of the Western World, produced amidst uproar at the Abbey Theatre, Dublin, in 1907

synod n a special church council which meets regularly to discuss church affairs [Greek sunodos]

synonym n a word that means the same as another word, such as bucket and pail [Greek sun- together + onoma name]

synonymous adj 1 (often foll. by with) having the same meaning (as) 2 (foll. by with) closely associated (with): a family whose name had been synonymous with fine jewellery

synopsis (sin-op-siss) n, pl **-ses** (-seez) a brief review or outline of a subject; summary: they have sent me a monthly synopsis of the plot [Greek sunopsis]

synoptic adj 1 of or relating to a synopsis 2 Bible of or relating to the Gospels of Matthew, Mark, and Luke > **synoptically** adv

synovia (sine-oh-vee-a) n med a clear thick fluid that

lubricates the body joints [New Latin] **> synovial** adj

syntax n the grammatical rules of a language and the way in which words are arranged to form phrases and sentences [Greek *suntassein* to put in order] **> syntactic** or **syntactical** adj

synthesis (sinth-iss-siss) n, pl **-ses** (-seez) **1** the process of combining objects or ideas into a complex whole **2** the combination produced by such a process **3** chem the process of producing a compound by one or more chemical reactions, usually from simpler starting materials [Greek *sunthesis*]

synthesize or **-sise** vb **-sizing, -sized** or **-sising, -sised 1** to combine (objects or ideas) into a complex whole **2** to produce (a compound) by synthesis

synthesizer n a keyboard instrument in which speech, music, or other sounds are produced electronically

synthetic adj **1** (of a substance or material) made artificially by chemical reaction **2** not sincere or genuine: *synthetic compassion* ▷ n **3** a synthetic substance or material [Greek *sunthetikos* expert in putting together] **> synthetically** adv

Syon House n a mansion near Brentford in London: originally a monastery, rebuilt in the 16th century, altered by Inigo Jones in the 17th century, and by Robert Adam in the 18th century; seat of the Dukes of Northumberland; gardens laid out by Capability Brown

syphilis n a sexually transmitted disease that causes sores on the genitals and eventually on other parts of the body [*Syphillis*, hero of a 16th-century Latin poem] **> syphilitic** adj

syphon n, vb same as siphon

Syr. **1** Syria **2** Syrian

Syracuse n **1** a port in SW Italy, in SE Sicily on the Ionian Sea: founded in 734 BC by Greeks from Corinth and taken by the Romans in 212 BC, after a siege of three years. Pop: 123 657 (2001). Italian name: **Siracusa 2** a city in central New York State, on Lake Onondaga: site of the capital of the Iroquois Indian federation. Pop: 144 001 (2003 est)

Syr Darya n a river in central Asia, formed from two headstreams rising in the Tian Shan: flows generally west to the Aral Sea: the longest river in central Asia. Length: (from the source of the Naryn) 2900 km (1800 miles). Ancient name: **Jaxartes**

Syria n **1** a republic in W Asia, on the Mediterranean: ruled by the Ottoman Turks (1516–1918); made a French mandate in 1920; became independent in 1944; joined Egypt in the United Arab Republic (1958–61). Hafez al-Assad elected president in 1971 following a coup; after his death in 2000 Assad's son Bashar took over the presidency; his rule was challenged (from 2012) by an uprising that led to civil war. Official language: Arabic. Religion: Muslim majority. Currency: Syrian pound. Capital: Damascus. Pop: 22 457 336 (2013 est). Area: 185 180 sq km (71 498 sq miles) **2** (formerly) the region between the Mediterranean, the Euphrates, the Taurus, and the Arabian Desert

Syrian adj **1** of or relating to Syria or its inhabitants ▷ n **2** a native or inhabitant of Syria

syringa n same as mock orange, lilac [Greek *surinx* tube (its hollow stems were used for pipes)]

syringe n **1** med a device used for withdrawing or injecting fluids, consisting of a hollow cylinder of glass or plastic, a tightly fitting piston, and a hollow needle ▷ vb **-ringing, -ringed 2** to wash out, inject, or spray with a syringe: *a harmless blue dye is syringed into the uterus* [Greek *surinx* tube]

Syro- combining form indicating Syrian: *Syro-Lebanese* [from Greek *Suro-*, from *Suros* a Syrian]

syrup n **1** a solution of sugar dissolved in water and often flavoured with fruit juice: used for sweetening fruit, etc. **2** a thick sweet liquid food made from sugar or molasses: *maple syrup* **3** a liquid medicine containing a sugar solution: *cough syrup* [Arabic *sharāb* a drink]

syrupy adj **1** (of a liquid) thick or sweet **2** excessively sentimental: *a soundtrack of syrupy violins*

system n **1** a method or set of methods for doing or organizing something: *a new system of production or distribution* **2** orderliness or routine; an ordered manner: *there is no system in his work* **3** the manner in which an institution or aspect of society has been arranged: *the Scottish legal system* **4** the system the government and state regarded as exploiting, restricting, and repressing individuals **5** the manner in which the parts of something fit or function together; structure: *disruption of the earth's weather system* **6** any scheme or set of rules used to classify, explain, or calculate: *the Newtonian system of physics* **7** a network of communications, transportation, or distribution **8** biology an animal considered as a whole **9** biology a set of organs or structures that together perform some function: *the immune system* **10** one's physical or mental constitution: *the intrusion of the ME virus into my system*; *to get the hate out of my system* **11** an assembly of electronic or mechanical parts forming a self-contained unit: *an alarm system* [Greek *sustēma*]

systematic adj following a fixed plan and done in an efficient and methodical way: *a systematic approach to teaching* **> systematically** adv

systematize or **-tise** vb **-tizing, -tized** or **-tising, -tised** to arrange (information) in a system **> systematization** or **-tisation** n

systemic adj biology (of a poison, disease, etc.) affecting the entire animal or body **> systemically** adv

systems analysis n the analysis of the requirements of a task and the expression of these in a form that enables a computer to perform the task **> systems analyst** n

systole (siss-tol-ee) n physiol contraction of the heart, during which blood is pumped into the arteries [Greek *sustolē*] **> systolic** adj

Syzran n a port in W central Russia, on the Volga River: oil refining. Pop: 191 000 (2005 est)

Szabadka n the Hungarian name for Subotica

Szczecin n a port in NW Poland, on the River Oder: the busiest Polish port and leading coal exporter; shipbuilding. Pop: 435 000 (2005 est). German name: **Stettin**

Szechuan or **Szechwan** n a variant transliteration of the Chinese name for Sichuan

Szeged n an industrial city in S Hungary, on the Tisza River. Pop: 162 860 (2003 est)

Szell n George. 1897–1970, US conductor, born in Hungary

Szent-Györgyi n Albert (**von Nagyrapolt**). 1893–1986, US biochemist, born in Hungary, who isolated ascorbic acid and identified it as vitamin C. Nobel prize for physiology or medicine 1937

Szilard n Leo. 1898–1964, US physicist, born in Hungary, who originated the idea of a self-sustaining nuclear chain reaction (1934). He worked on the atomic bomb during World War II but later pressed for the international control of nuclear weapons

Szombathely n a city in W Hungary: site of the Roman capital of Pannonia. Pop: 81 113 (2003 est)

Szymanowski n Karol. 1882–1937, Polish composer, whose works include the opera *King Roger* (1926), two violin concertos, symphonies, piano music, and songs

Szymborska n Wisława. 1923–2012, Polish poet and writer: Nobel prize for literature 1996

S

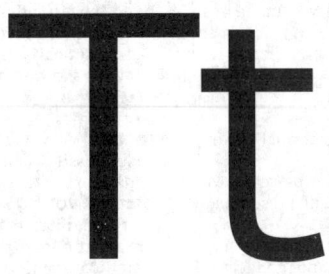

Tt

t or **T** _n, pl_ **t's, T's** or **Ts 1** the 20th letter of the English alphabet **2 to a T a** in every detail: _that's her to a T_ **b** perfectly: _that dress suits you to a T_

t tonne(s)

T 1 _chem_ tritium **2** tera-

t. 1 temperature **2** ton(s)

ta _interj Brit, Austral and NZ informal_ thank you [imitative of baby talk]

Ta _chem_ tantalum

TA (in Britain) Territorial Army

Taal _n_ an active volcano in the Philippines, on S Luzon on an island in the centre of **Lake Taal**. Height: 300 m (984 ft). Area of lake: 243 sq km (94 sq miles)

tab¹ _n_ **1** a small flap of material, esp. one on a garment for decoration or for fastening to a button **2** any similar flap, such as a piece of paper attached to a file for identification **3** _chiefly US and Canad_ a bill, esp. for a meal or drinks **4 keep tabs on** _informal_ to keep a watchful eye on [origin unknown]

tab² _n_ short for **tabulator**

TAB (in New Zealand) Totalisator Agency Board

tabard _n_ **1** a sleeveless jacket, esp. one worn by a medieval knight over his armour **2** a short coat bearing the coat of arms of the sovereign, worn by a herald [Old French _tabart_]

Tabari _n_ Muhammad ibn Jarir al-. 838–923 AD, Arab scholar, whose works include a history of the world from the Creation to 915 AD and a commentary on the Koran

Tabasco¹ _n trademark_ a very hot red sauce made from peppers

Tabasco² _n_ a state in SE Mexico, on the Gulf of Campeche: mostly flat and marshy with extensive jungles; hot and humid climate. Capital: Villahermosa. Pop: 1 889 367 (2000). Area: 24 661 sq km (9520 sq miles)

tabby _n, pl_ **-bies 1** a cat whose fur has dark stripes or wavy markings on a lighter background ▷ _adj_ **2** having dark stripes or wavy markings on a lighter background [from the girl's name _Tabitha_, influenced by _tabby_, old kind of striped silk]

tabernacle _n_ **1 the Tabernacle** _Bible_ the portable sanctuary in which the ancient Israelites carried the Ark of the Covenant **2** any place of Christian worship that is not called a church **3** _RC Church_ a receptacle in which the Blessed Sacrament is kept [Latin _tabernaculum_ a tent]

tabla _n, pl_ **-bla** or **-blas** one of a pair of Indian drums played with the hands [Hindi, from Arabic: drum]

table _n_ **1** a piece of furniture consisting of a flat top supported by legs: _a coffee table_ **2** a set of facts or figures arranged in rows and columns: _a league table_ **3** a group of people sitting round a table for a meal, game, etc.: _the whole table laughed_ **4** _formal_ the food provided at a meal or in a particular house: _he keeps a good table_ **5 turn the tables** to cause a complete reversal of circumstances ▷ _vb_ **-bling, -bled 6** _Brit and Austral_ to submit (a motion) for

discussion by a meeting **7** _US_ to suspend discussion of (a proposal) indefinitely [Latin _tabula_ a writing tablet]

tableau (**tab**-loh) _n, pl_ **-leaux** (-loh) a silent motionless group of people arranged to represent a scene from history, legend, or literature [French]

Table Bay _n_ the large bay on which Cape Town is situated, on the SW coast of South Africa

tablecloth _n_ a cloth for covering the top of a table, esp. during meals

table d'hôte (**tah**-bla **dote**) _adj_ **1** (of a meal) consisting of a set number of courses with a limited choice of dishes offered at a fixed price ▷ _n, pl_ **tables d'hôte** (**tah**-bla **dote**) **2** a table d'hôte meal or menu [French: the host's table]

table football _n Brit_ a game based on soccer, played on a table with sets of miniature human figures mounted on rods allowing them to be tilted or spun to strike the ball. US & Canad name: **foosball**

tableland _n_ a flat area of high ground; plateau

table licence _n Brit_ a licence permitting the sale of alcohol with meals only

Table Mountain _n_ a mountain in SW South Africa, overlooking Cape Town and Table Bay: flat-topped and steep-sided. Height: 1087 m (3567 ft)

tablespoon _n_ **1** a spoon, larger than a dessertspoon, used for serving food **2** Also called: **tablespoonful** the amount contained in such a spoon **3** a unit of capacity used in cooking, equal to half a fluid ounce

tablet _n_ **1** a pill consisting of a compressed medicinal substance **2** a flattish cake of some substance, such as soap **3** a slab of stone, wood, etc., used for writing on before the invention of paper **4** an inscribed piece of stone, wood, etc., that is fixed to a wall as a memorial: _a tablet in memory of those who died_ **5** a handheld personal computer that is operated by touching a screen [Latin _tabula_ a board]

table tennis _n_ a game resembling a miniature form of tennis played on a table with bats and a small light ball

table wine _n_ **1** fairly cheap wine for everyday drinking with meals **2** ordinary wine, as opposed to fortified wine such as sherry or port

tabloid _n_ a newspaper with fairly small pages, usually with many photographs and a concise and often sensational style [from _Tabloid_, originally a trademark for a medicine in tablet form]

taboo or **tabu** _n, pl_ **-boos** or **-bus 1** a restriction or prohibition resulting from social or other conventions **2** a ritual prohibition, esp. of something that is considered holy or unclean ▷ _adj_ **3** forbidden or disapproved of: _a taboo subject_ [Tongan _tapu_]

tabor _n_ a small drum used esp. in the Middle Ages, struck with one hand while the other held a pipe [Old French _tabour_]

Tabor _n_ **Mount Tabor** a mountain in N Israel, near Nazareth: traditionally regarded as the mountain where the Transfiguration took place. Height: 588 m (1929 ft)

Tabriz *n* a city in NW Iran: an ancient city, situated in a volcanic region of hot springs; university (1947); carpet manufacturing. Pop: 1 396 000 (2005 est). Ancient name: **Tauris**

tabular *adj* arranged in parallel columns so as to form a table [Latin *tabula* a board]

tabulate *vb* **-lating, -lated** to arrange (information) in rows and columns ➤ **tabulation** *n*

tabulator *n* a key on a typewriter or word processor that sets stops so that data can be arranged and presented in columns

tachograph *n* a device that measures the speed of a vehicle and the distance that it covers, and produces a record (**tachogram**) of its readings [Greek *takhos* speed + -GRAPH]

tachometer *n* a device for measuring speed, esp. that of a revolving shaft [Greek *takhos* speed + -METER]

tacit (tass-it) *adj* understood or implied without actually being stated: *tacit support* [Latin *tacitus* silent]

taciturn (tass-it-turn) *adj* habitually silent, reserved, or uncommunicative [Latin *tacere* to be silent] ➤ **taciturnity** *n*

Tacitus *n* Publius Cornelius. ?55–?120 AD, Roman historian and orator, famous as a prose stylist. His works include the *Histories*, dealing with the period 68–96, and the *Annals*, dealing with the period 14–68

tack¹ *n* **1** a short sharp-pointed nail with a large flat head **2** *Brit and NZ* a long loose temporary stitch used in dressmaking ▷ *vb* **3** to fasten (something) with a tack or tacks: *the carpet needs to be tacked down* **4** *Brit and NZ* to sew (something) with long loose temporary stitches ▶ See also **tack on** [Middle English *tak* fastening, nail]

tack² *n* **1** *nautical* the course of a boat sailing obliquely into the wind, expressed in terms of the side of the boat against which the wind is blowing: *on the port tack* **2** a course of action or a policy: *telling her to get off my back hadn't worked, so I took a different tack* ▷ *vb* **3** *nautical* to steer (a boat) on a zigzag course, so as to make progress against the wind [from *tack* rope used to secure a sail]

tack³ *n* riding harness for horses, including saddles and bridles [from *tackle*]

tackies or **takkies** *pl n, sing* **tacky** *S African informal* tennis shoes or plimsolls [origin unknown]

tackle *vb* **-ling, -led 1** to deal with (a problem or task) in a determined way **2** to confront (someone) about something: *I intend to tackle both management and union on this issue* **3** to attack and fight (a person or animal) **4** *sport* to attempt to get the ball away from (an opposing player) ▷ *n* **5** *sport* an attempt to get the ball away from an opposing player **6** the equipment required for a particular sport or occupation: *fishing tackle* **7** a set of ropes and pulleys for lifting heavy weights **8** *nautical* the ropes and other rigging aboard a ship [Middle English]

tack on *vb* to attach or add (something) to something that is already complete: *an elegant mansion with a modern extension tacked on at the back*

tack room *n* a room in a stable building in which bridles, saddles, etc. are kept

tacky¹ *adj* **tackier, tackiest** slightly sticky [earlier *tack* stickiness] ➤ **tackiness** *n*

tacky² *adj* **tackier, tackiest** *informal* **1** vulgar and tasteless: *tacky commercialism* **2** shabby or shoddy: *tacky streets* [origin unknown] ➤ **tackiness** *n*

Tacna-Arica *n* a coastal desert region of W South America, long disputed by Chile and Peru: divided in 1929 into the Peruvian department of Tacna and the Chilean department of Arica

taco (tah-koh) *n, pl* **tacos** *Mexican cookery* a tortilla folded into a roll with a filling and usually fried [from Mexican Spanish, from Spanish: literally, a bite to eat]

Tacoma *n* a port in W Washington, on Puget Sound: industrial centre. Pop: 196 790 (2003 est)

tact *n* **1** a sense of the best and most considerate way to deal with people so as not to upset them **2** skill in handling difficult situations [Latin *tactus* a touching] ➤ **tactful** *adj* ➤ **tactfully** *adv* ➤ **tactless** *adj* ➤ **tactlessly** *adv* ➤ **tactlessness** *n*

tactic *n* a move or method used to achieve an aim or task: *he has perfected dissent as a tactic to further his career*. See also **tactics**

tactical *adj* **1** of or employing tactics: *a tactical advantage* **2** (of missiles, bombing, etc.) for use in limited military operations ➤ **tactically** *adv*

tactical voting *n* (in an election) the practice of voting for a candidate or party one would not normally support in an attempt to prevent an even less acceptable candidate or party being elected

tactics *n* **1** *military* the science of the detailed direction of forces in battle to achieve an aim or task ▷ *pl n* **2** the plans and methods used to achieve a particular short-term aim [Greek *tassein* to arrange] ➤ **tactician** *n*

tactile *adj* of or having a sense of touch: *the tactile sense* [Latin *tactilis*]

Tadmor *n* the biblical name for **Palmyra**

tadpole *n* the aquatic larva of a frog or toad, which develops from a limbless tailed form with external gills into a form with internal gills, limbs, and a reduced tail [Middle English *tadde* toad + *pol* head]

Tadzhikistan or **Tadjikistan** *n* variant spellings of **Tajikistan**

Taegu *n* a city in SE South Korea: textile and agricultural trading centre. Pop: 2 510 000 (2005 est)

Taejon *n* a city in W South Korea: market centre of an agricultural region. Pop: 1 464 000 (2005 est)

TAFE (in Australia) Technical and Further Education

taffeta *n* a thin shiny silk or rayon fabric used esp. for women's clothes [Persian *tāftah* spun]

taffrail *n* *nautical* a rail at the back of a ship or boat [Dutch *taffereel* panel]

Tafilelt or **Tafilalet** *n* an oasis in SE Morocco, the largest in the Sahara. Area: about 1300 sq km (500 sq miles)

Taft *n* William Howard. 1857–1930, US statesman; 27th president of the US (1909–13)

tag¹ *n* **1** a piece of paper, leather, etc., for attaching to something as a mark or label: *the price tag* **2** a point of metal or plastic at the end of a cord or lace **3** a brief trite quotation **4** an electronic device worn by a prisoner under house arrest so that his or her movements can be monitored **5** *slang* a graffito consisting of a nickname or personal symbol ▷ *vb* **tagging, tagged 6** to mark with a tag ▶ See also **tag along, tag on** [origin unknown]

tag² *n* **1** a children's game in which one player chases the others in an attempt to touch one of them, who will then become the chaser ▷ *vb* **tagging, tagged 2** to catch and touch (another child) in the game of tag ▶ Also: **tig** [origin unknown]

Tagalog (tag-gah-log) *n* a language spoken in the Philippines

tag along *vb* to accompany someone, esp. when uninvited: *I tagged along behind the gang*

Taganrog *n* a port in SW Russia, on the **Gulf of Taganrog** (an inlet of the Sea of Azov): founded in 1698 as a naval base and fortress by Peter the Great: industrial centre. Pop: 281 000 (2005 est)

tag end *n* the last part of something: *at the tag end of the Ice Age*

tagetes (taj-**eat**-eez) *n, pl* **-tes** any of a genus of plants with yellow or orange flowers, including the French and African marigolds [Latin *Tages*, a god of ancient Etruria]

tagliatelle (tal-yat-**tell**-ee) *n* a form of pasta made in narrow strips [Italian]

Taglioni *n* Marie. 1804–84, Italian ballet dancer, whose romantic style greatly influenced ballet in the 19th century

tag on *vb* to add at the end of something: *a throwaway remark, tagged on at the end of a casual conversation*

Tagore *n* Rabindranath. 1861–1941, Indian poet and philosopher. His verse collections, written in Bengali and English, include *Gitanjali* (1910; 1912): Nobel prize for literature 1913

Tagus *n* a river in SW Europe, rising in E central Spain and flowing west to the border with Portugal, then southwest to the Atlantic at Lisbon: the longest river of the Iberian Peninsula. Length: 1007 km (626 miles). Portuguese name: **Tejo**. Spanish name: **Tajo**

tahini (tah-hee-nee) *n* a paste made from ground sesame seeds, used esp. in Middle Eastern cookery [from Arabic]

Tahiti *n* an island in the S Pacific, in the Windward group of the Society Islands: the largest and most important island in French Polynesia; became a French protectorate in 1842 and a colony in 1880. Capital: Papeete. Pop: 169 674 (2002). Area: 1005 sq km (388 sq miles)

Tahitian *adj* **1** of or relating to Tahiti or its inhabitants ▷ *n* **2** a native or inhabitant of Tahiti

Tahoe *n* Lake Tahoe a lake between E California and W Nevada, in the Sierra Nevada Mountains at an altitude of 1899 m (6229 ft). Area: about 520 sq km (200 sq miles)

Tahrir Square *n* a large square in central Cairo, in Egypt. The name, meaning 'liberation', was used informally after the 1919 revolution and then officially after the 1952 revolution. Scene of mass demonstrations in 2011 against the government of president Hosni Mubarak

t'ai chi (tie chee) *n* a Chinese system of exercises and self-defence characterized by slow rhythmic movements [Chinese *t'ai chi ch'uan* great art of boxing]

Taichung *or* **T'ai-chung** *n* a city in W Taiwan: commercial centre of an agricultural region. Pop: 1 066 000 (2005 est)

taiga (tie-ga) *n* the belt of coniferous forest extending across much of subarctic North America, Europe, and Asia

taikonaut *n* an astronaut from the People's Republic of China [from Cantonese *taikon(g)* cosmos]

tail¹ *n* **1** the rear part of an animal's body, usually forming a long thin flexible part attached to the trunk. Related adjective: **caudal** **2** any long thin part projecting or hanging from the back or end of something: *the waiter produced menus from beneath the tail of his coat* **3** the last part: *the tail of the procession* **4** the rear part of an aircraft **5** *astronomy* the luminous stream of gas and dust particles driven from the head of a comet when it is close to the sun **6** *informal* a person employed to follow and spy upon another **7** **turn tail** to run away **8** **with one's tail between one's legs** completely defeated and demoralized ▷ *adj* **9** at the back: *tail feathers* ▷ *vb* **10** *informal* to follow (someone) stealthily ► See also **tail off, tails** [Old English *tægel*] **> tailless** *adj*

tail² *n law* the limitation of an estate or interest to a person and his or her descendants [Old French *taille* a division]

tailback *n* Brit a queue of traffic stretching back from an obstruction

tailboard *n* a removable or hinged rear board on a lorry or trailer

tail coat *n* a man's black coat which stops at the hips at the front and has a long back split into two below the waist

tailgate *n* **1** same as **tailboard** **2** a door at the rear of a hatchback vehicle ▷ *vb* **3** to drive very close behind (a vehicle) **> tailgater** *n*

tail-light *or* **tail lamp** *n* same as **rear light**

tail off *or* **tail away** *vb* **1** to decrease gradually: *orders tailed off* **2** (of someone's voice) to become gradually quieter and then silent

tailor *n* **1** a person who makes, repairs, or alters outer garments, esp. menswear. Related adjective: **sartorial** ▷ *vb* **2** to cut or style (a garment) to satisfy specific requirements **3** to adapt (something) so as to make it suitable: *activities are tailored to participants' capabilities* [Old French *taillier* to cut] **> tailored** *adj*

tailorbird *n* a tropical Asian warbler that builds a nest by sewing together large leaves using plant fibres

tailor-made *adj* **1** (of clothing) made by a tailor to fit exactly **2** perfect for a particular purpose: *I'm tailor-made for the role*

tailpiece *n* **1** a piece added at the end of something, for example a report **2** a decorative design at the end of a chapter **3** a piece of wood to which the strings of a stringed musical instrument are attached at its lower end

tailpipe *n* a pipe from which exhaust gases are discharged, esp. in a motor vehicle

tailplane *n* a small horizontal wing at the tail of an aircraft to help keep it stable

tails *pl n* **1** *informal* same as **tail coat** ▷ *interj, adv* **2** with the side of a coin uppermost that does not have a portrait of a head on it

tailspin *n* **1** *aeronautics* same as **spin** (10) **2** *informal* a state of confusion or panic

tailwind *n* a wind blowing from behind an aircraft or vehicle

Taimyr Peninsula *n* a large peninsula of N central Russia, between the Kara Sea and the Laptev Sea. Also called: **Taymyr Peninsula**

Tainan *or* **T'ai-nan** *n* a city in the SW Taiwan: an early centre of Chinese emigration from the mainland; formerly the largest city and capital of the island (1638–1885); Chengkung University. Pop: 754 000 (2005 est)

Taínaron *n* a transliteration of the Modern Greek name for (Cape) **Matapan**

Taine *n* Hippolyte Adolphe. 1828–93, French literary critic and historian. He applied determinist criteria to the study of literature, art, history, and psychology, regarding them as products of environment and race. His works include *Histoire de la littérature anglaise* (1863–64) and *Les Origines de la France contemporaine* (1875–93)

taint *vb* **1** to spoil or contaminate by an undesirable quality: *tainted by corruption* ▷ *n* **2** a defect or flaw **3** a trace of contamination or infection [Old French *teindre* to dye] **> tainted** *adj*

taipan *n* a large poisonous Australian snake [Aboriginal]

Taipei *or* **T'ai-pei** *n* the capital of Taiwan (the Republic of China), at the N tip of the island: became capital in 1885; industrial centre; two universities. Pop: 2 473 000 (2005 est)

Taiwan *n* an island in SE Asia between the East China Sea and the South China Sea, off the SE coast of the People's Republic of China: the principal territory of the Republic of China; claimed by the People's Republic of China since its political separation from mainland China in the late 1940s. Pop: 23 299 716 (2013 est). Former name: **Formosa**

Taiwanese *adj* **1** of or relating to Taiwan or its inhabitants ▷ *n* **2** a native or inhabitant of Taiwan

Taiwan Strait *n* another name for **Formosa Strait**

Taiyuan *or* **T'ai-yüan** *n* a city in N China, capital of Shanxi: founded before 450 AD; an industrial centre, surrounded by China's largest reserves of high-grade bituminous coal. Pop: 2 516 000 (2005 est)

Ta'izz *n* a town in SW Yemen, in the former North Yemen until 1990: agricultural trading centre. Pop: 541 000 (2005 est)

Tajikistan, Tadzhikistan *or* **Tadjikistan** *n* a republic in central Asia: under Uzbek rule from the 15th century until taken over by Russia in the 1860s, it became an autonomous Soviet republic in 1929 and gained full independence from the Soviet Union in 1991; it is mainly mountainous. Official language: Tajik or Tajiki. Religion: believers are mainly Muslim. Currency: somoni. Capital: Dushanbe. Pop: 7 910 041 (2013 est). Area: 143 100 sq km (55 240 sq miles)

Taj Mahal *n* a white marble mausoleum in central India, in Agra on the Jumna River: built (1632–43) by the emperor Shah Jahan in memory of his beloved wife, Mumtaz Mahal; regarded as the finest example of Mogul architecture [Urdu, literally: crown of buildings]

Tajo *n* the Spanish name for the **Tagus**

Takamatsu *n* a port in SW Japan, on NE Shikoku on the Inland Sea. Pop: 333 387 (2002 est)

Takao *n* the Japanese name for **Kaohsiung**

take *vb* **taking, took, taken 1** to remove from a place, usually by grasping with the hand: *he took a fifty-dollar note from his wallet* **2** to accompany or escort: *he took me home* **3** to use as a means of transport: *we took a taxi* **4** to conduct or lead: *that road takes you to Preston* **5** to obtain possession of (something), often dishonestly: *they had taken everything most precious to us* **6** to seize or capture: *her husband had been taken by the rebels* **7** (in games such as chess or cards) to win or capture (a piece, trick, etc.) **8** to choose or select (something to use or buy): *I'll take the green one, please* **9** to put an end to: *he took his own life* **10** to require (time, resources, or ability): *this would have taken years to set up* **11** to use as a particular case: *take a friend of mine for example* **12** to find and make use of (a seat, flat, etc.) **13** to accept the duties of: *the legitimate government will take office* **14** to receive in a specified way: *my mother took it calmly* **15** to receive and make use of: *she took the opportunity to splash her heated face* **16** to eat or drink: *all food substances are toxic if taken in excess* **17** to perform (an action, esp. a beneficial one): *she took a deep breath* **18** to accept (something that is offered or given): *she took a job as a waitress* **19** to put into effect: *taking military action simply* **20** to make (a photograph) **21** to write down or copy: *taking notes* **22** to work at or study: *taking painting lessons* **23** to do or sit (a test, exam, etc.) **24** to begin to experience or feel: *he took an interest in psychoanalysis* **25** to accept (responsibility, blame, or credit) **26** to accept as valid: *I take your point* **27** to stand up to or endure: *I can't take this harassment any more* **28** to wear a particular size of shoes or clothes: *what size of shoes do you take?* **29** to have a capacity of or room for: *the Concert Hall can take about 2500 people* **30** to ascertain by measuring: *she comes after breakfast to take her pulse and temperature* **31** to subtract or deduct: *take seven from eleven* **32** to aim or direct: *he took a few steps towards the door* **33** (of a shop, club, etc.) to make (a specified amount of money) from sales, tickets, etc.: *films that take no money at the box office* **34** to have or produce the intended effect: *the dye hasn't taken on your shoes* **35** (of seedlings) to start growing successfully **36 take account of** *or* **take into account** See **account** (9) **37 take advantage of** See **advantage** (4) **38 take care** See **care** (10) **39 take care of** See **care** (11) **40 take it** to assume or believe: *I take it that means they don't want to leave* **41 take part in** See **part** (17) **42 take place** See **place** (20) **43 take upon oneself** to assume the right or duty (to do something) **44 take your time** use as much time as you need ▷ *n* **45** *films, music* one of a series of recordings from which the best will be selected **46** *informal, chiefly US* a version or interpretation: *Minnelli's bleak take on the story* ▶ See also **take after, take against**, etc. [Old English *tacan*]

take after *vb* to resemble in appearance or character: *he takes after his grandfather*

take against *vb informal* to start to dislike, esp. for no good reason: *I took against her right from the start*

take apart *vb* **1** to separate (something) into its component parts: *once I'd taken the clock apart I couldn't fit the bits together again* **2** *informal* to criticize severely

take away *vb* **1** to remove or subtract: *the lymph glands are taken away and examined under a microscope* **2** to detract from or lessen the value of (something): *the fact that he beat his wife doesn't take away from his merits as a writer* ▷ *prep* **3** minus: *six take away two is four* ▷ *adj* **takeaway 4** *Brit, Austral and NZ* sold for consumption away from the premises: *takeaway food* ▷ *n* **takeaway** *Brit, Austral and NZ* **5** a shop or restaurant that sells such food **6** a meal sold for consumption away from the premises

take back *vb* **1** to retract or withdraw (something said or promised): *I take back what I said about him* **2** to regain possession of **3** to return for exchange or a refund: *shopkeepers are often reluctant to take back unsatisfactory goods* **4** to accept (someone) back into one's home, affections, etc.: *I'll only take you back if you promise to behave* **5** to remind (one) of the past: *this takes me back to my childhood*

take down *vb* **1** to record in writing **2** to dismantle or remove **3** to reduce (someone) in power or arrogance: *I do think he needed taking down a peg or two*

take for *vb informal* to consider or suppose to be, esp. mistakenly: *what kind of mug do you take me for?*

take-home pay *n* the remainder of one's pay after income tax and other compulsory deductions have been made

take in *vb* **1** to understand: *I was too tired to take in all of what was being said* **2** *informal* to cheat or deceive: *don't be taken in by his charming manner* **3** to include: *this tour takes in the romance and history of Salzburg, Vienna, and Munich* **4** to receive into one's house: *his widowed mother lived by taking in boarders* **5** to make (clothing) smaller by altering the seams **6** to go to: *taking in a movie*

taken *vb* **1** the past participle of **take** ▷ *adj* **2 taken with** enthusiastically impressed by

take off *vb* **1** to remove (a garment) **2** (of an aircraft) to become airborne **3** *informal* to set out on a journey: *taking off for the Highlands* **4** *informal* to become successful or popular: *the record took off after being used in a film* **5** to deduct (an amount) from a price or total **6** to withdraw or put an end to: *the bus service has been taken off because of lack of demand* **7** *informal* to mimic (someone) ▷ *n* **takeoff 8** the act or process of making an aircraft airborne **9** *informal* an act of mimicry

take on *vb* **1** to employ or hire **2** to assume or acquire: *his eyes took on a strange intensity* **3** to agree to do: *he took on the job of treasurer* **4** to compete against: *we must take on our foreign competitors*

take out *vb* **1** to remove (something) from a place: *she took a comb out of her bag* **2** to obtain: *she took out American citizenship in 1937* **3** to escort or go out with (someone) on a social trip: *can I take you out for a meal some time?* **4** *informal* to kill, destroy, or maim: *most of the enemy's air defences have been taken out* **5 take it** *or* **a lot out of** *informal* to sap the energy or vitality of **6 take it out on** *informal* to vent one's anger on ▷ *adj, n* **takeout 7** *chiefly US and Canad* same as **take away** (4, 5, 6)

take over *vb* **1** to gain control or management of **2** to become responsible for (a job) after another person has stopped doing it: *I'll take over the driving if you want a break* **3 take over from** to become more successful or important than (something), and eventually replace it: *CDs have more or less taken over from records* ▷ *n* **takeover 4** the act of gaining control of a company by buying its shares **5** the act of seizing and taking control of something: *the rebel takeover in Ethiopia*

taker *n* a person who agrees to take something that is offered: *there's only one sweet left – any takers?*

take to *vb* **1** to form a liking for **2** to start using or doing (something) as a habit: *I took to studying the published records of his life*

take up *vb* **1** to occupy or fill (space or time): *looking after the baby takes up most of my time* **2** to adopt the study, practice, or activity of: *I took up architecture* **3** to shorten (a garment) **4** to accept (an offer): *I'd like to take up your offer of help* **5 take up on a** to accept what is offered by (someone): *I might just take you up on that offer* **b** to discuss (something) further with (someone): *I'd like to take you up on that last point* **6 take up with a** to discuss (an issue) with (someone): *take up the matter with the District Council more seriously* **b** to begin to be friendly and spend time with (someone): *he'd already taken up with the woman he would marry*

taking *adj* charming, fascinating, or intriguing

takings *pl n* receipts; earnings

Takoradi *n* the chief port of Ghana, in the southwest on the Gulf of Guinea: modern harbour opened in 1928. Pop (with Sekondi): 335 000 (2005 est)

Talabani n Jalal, born 1933, Iraqi politician, a Kurd, president of Iraq (2005–2014)

talaq or **talak** n a form of divorce under Islamic law in which the husband repudiates the marriage by saying 'talaq' three times [Arabic]

Talavera de la Reina n a walled town in central Spain, on the Tagus River: scene of the defeat of the French by British and Spanish forces (1809) during the Peninsular War; agricultural processing centre. Pop: 79 916 (2003 est)

Talbot n (William Henry) Fox. 1800–77, British scientist, a pioneer of photography, who developed the calotype process

talc or **talcum** n 1 same as **talcum powder** 2 a soft mineral, consisting of magnesium silicate, used in the manufacture of ceramics, paints, and talcum powder [Persian talk]

Talca n a city in central Chile: scene of the declaration of Chilean independence (1818). Pop: 206 000 (2005 est)

Talcahuano n a port in S central Chile, near Concepción on an inlet of the Pacific: oil refinery. Pop: 251 000 (2005 est)

talcum powder n a powder made of purified talc, usually scented, used to dry or perfume the body

tale n 1 a report, account, or story: everyone had their own tale to tell about the flood 2 a malicious piece of gossip 3 **tell tales a** to tell fanciful lies **b** to report malicious stories or trivial complaints, esp. to someone in authority 4 **tell a tale** to reveal something important 5 **tell its own tale** to be self-evident [Old English talu]

talent n 1 a natural ability to do something well: the boy has a real talent for writing 2 a person or people with such ability: he is the major talent in Italian fashion 3 informal attractive members of the opposite sex collectively: there's always lots of talent in that pub 4 any of various ancient units of weight and money [Greek talanton unit of money] > **talented** adj

talent scout n a person whose occupation is the search for talented people, such as sportsmen or performers, for work as professionals

Taliesin n 6th century AD, Welsh bard; supposed author of 12 heroic poems in the Book of Taliesin

talisman n, pl **-mans** a stone or other small object, usually inscribed or carved, believed to protect the wearer from evil influences [Medieval Greek telesma ritual] > **talismanic** adj

talk vb 1 to express one's thoughts or feelings by means of spoken words 2 to exchange ideas or opinions about something: they were talking about where they would go on holiday 3 to give voice to; utter: he was talking rubbish 4 to discuss: the political leaders were talking peace 5 to reveal information: she was ready to talk 6 to be able to speak (a language or style) in conversation: the ferry was full of people talking French 7 to spread rumours or gossip 8 to be effective or persuasive: money talks 9 to get into a particular condition or state of mind by talking: I had talked myself hoarse 10 **now you're talking** informal at last you're saying something agreeable 11 **you can** or **can't talk** informal you are in no position to comment or criticize ▷ n 12 a speech or lecture: a talk on local government reform 13 an exchange of ideas or thoughts: we had a talk about our holiday plans 14 idle chatter, gossip, or rumour 15 (often pl) a conference, discussion, or negotiation ▶ See also **talk back**, **talk down**, etc. [Middle English talkien] > **talker** n

talkative adj given to talking a great deal

talkback n NZ a broadcast in which telephone comments or questions from the public are transmitted live

talk back vb to answer (someone) rudely or cheekily

talk down vb 1 **talk down to** to speak to (someone) in a patronizing manner 2 to give instructions to (an aircraft) by radio to enable it to land

talkie n informal an early film with a soundtrack

Talking Book n trademark a recording of a book, designed to be used by blind people

talking head n (on television) a person, shown only from the shoulders up, who speaks without illustrative material

talking point n something that causes discussion or argument: his appointment as manager was a major talking point in football circles

talking-to n informal a scolding or telling-off

talk into vb to persuade (someone) to do something by talking to him or her: don't let anyone talk you into buying things you don't want

talk out vb 1 to resolve (a problem) by talking: we won't reach a compromise unless we can talk out our differences 2 Brit to block (a bill) in parliament by discussing it for so long that there is no time to vote on it 3 **talk out of** to dissuade (someone) from doing something by talking to him or her

talk round vb 1 to persuade (someone) to agree with one's opinion or suggestion: he didn't want to go, but I talked him round 2 to discuss (a subject) without coming to a conclusion

tall adj 1 of greater than average height 2 having a specified height: five feet tall [Middle English]

Tallahassee n a city in N Florida, capital of the state: two universities. Pop: 153 938 (2003 est)

tallboy n Brit a high chest of drawers made in two sections placed one on top of the other

Talleyrand-Périgord n Charles Maurice. 1754–1838, French statesman; foreign minister (1797–1807; 1814–15). He secretly negotiated with the Allies against Napoleon I from 1808 and was France's representative at the Congress of Vienna (1815)

Tallinn or **Tallin** n the capital of Estonia, on the Gulf of Finland: founded by the Danes in 1219; a port and naval base. Pop: 384 000 (2005 est). German name: **Reval**

Tallis n Thomas. ?1505–85, English composer and organist; noted for his music for the Anglican liturgy

tall order n informal a difficult or unreasonable request

tallow n a hard fatty animal fat used in making soap and candles

tall poppy syndrome n Austral and NZ informal a tendency to disparage any person who is conspicuously successful

tall ship n a large square-rigged sailing ship

tall story n informal an unlikely and probably untrue tale

tally vb **-lies**, **-lying**, **-lied** 1 to agree with or be consistent with something else: this description didn't seem to me to tally with what we saw 2 to keep score ▷ n, pl **-lies** 3 any record of debit, credit, the score in a game, etc. 4 an identifying label or mark 5 a stick used (esp. formerly) as a record of the amount of a debt according to the notches cut in it [Latin talea a stick]

tally-ho interj the cry of a participant at a hunt when the quarry is sighted

Talmud n Judaism the primary source of Jewish religious law [Hebrew talmūdh instruction] > **Talmudic** adj > **Talmudist** n

talon n a sharply hooked claw, such as that of a bird of prey [Latin talus ankle]

tamarillo n, pl **-los** a shrub with a red oval edible fruit

tamarind n a tropical evergreen tree with fruit whose acid pulp is used as a food and to make beverages and medicines [Arabic tamr hindī Indian date]

tamarisk n a tree or shrub of the Mediterranean region and S Asia, with scalelike leaves, slender branches, and feathery flower clusters [Latin tamarix]

Tamatave n the former name (until 1979) of **Toamasina**

Tamaulipas n a state of NE Mexico, on the Gulf of Mexico. Capital: Ciudad Victoria. Pop: 2 747 114 (2000). Area: 79 829 sq km (30 822 sq miles)

Tambo n Oliver. 1917–93, South African politician;

t

president (1977–91) of the African National Congress. He was arrested (1956) with Nelson Mandela but released (1957)

Tambora *n* a volcano in Indonesia, on N Sumbawa: violent eruption of 1815 reduced its height from about 4000 m (13 000 ft) to 2850 m (9400 ft)

tambour *n* an embroidery frame, consisting of two hoops over which the fabric is stretched while being worked [French]

tambourine *n music* a percussion instrument consisting of a single drum skin stretched over a circular wooden frame with pairs of metal discs that jingle when it is struck or shaken [from Old French]

Tambov *n* an industrial city in W Russia: founded in 1636 as a Muscovite fort; a major engineering centre. Pop: 293 000 (2005 est)

tame *adj* **1 a** (of an animal) changed by humans from a wild state into a domesticated state **b** (of an animal) not afraid of or aggressive towards humans **2** (of a person) tending to do what one is told without questioning or criticizing it **3** mild and unexciting: *the love scenes are fairly tame by modern standards* ▷ *vb* **taming, tamed 4** to make (an animal) tame; domesticate **5** to bring under control; make less extreme or dangerous: *many previously deadly diseases have been tamed by antibiotics* [Old English *tam*]

Tamerlane *or* **Tamburlaine** *n* Turkic name *Timur*. ?1336–1405, Mongol conqueror of the area from Mongolia to the Mediterranean; ruler of Samarkand (1369–1405). He defeated the Turks at Angora (1402) and died while invading China

Tameside *n* a unitary authority of NW England, in Greater Manchester. Pop: 213 400 (2003 est). Area: 103 sq km (40 sq miles)

Tamil *n* **1** (*pl* **-ils** *or* **-il**) a member of a people of S India and Sri Lanka **2** the language of the Tamils ▷ *adj* **3** of the Tamils

Tamil Eelam *n* the separate Tamil state that the Tamil Tigers have sought to establish in northern Sri Lanka [from Tamil *eelam* homeland]

Tamil Nadu *n* a state of SE India, on the Coromandel Coast: reorganized in 1956 and 1960 and made smaller; consists of a coastal plain backed by hills, including the Nilgiri Hills in the west Capital: Chennai (formerly called Madras). Pop: 62 110 839 (2001). Area: 130 058 sq km (50 216 sq miles). Former name (until 1968): **Madras**

Tammerfors *n* the Swedish name for **Tampere**

tam-o'-shanter *n* a Scottish brimless woollen cap with a bobble in the centre [after the hero of Burns's poem *Tam o' Shanter*]

tamp *vb* to force or pack (something) down by tapping it several times: *he tamped the bowl of his pipe* [probably from obsolete *tampin* plug for gun's muzzle]

Tampa *n* a port and resort in W Florida, on **Tampa Bay** (an arm of the Gulf of Mexico): two universities. Pop: 317 647 (2003 est)

tamper *vb* (foll. by *with*) **1** to interfere or meddle with without permission: *someone has been tampering with the locks* **2** to attempt to influence someone, esp. by bribery: *an attempt to tamper with the jury* [alteration of *temper* (verb)]

Tampere *n* a city in SW Finland: the second largest town in Finland; textile manufacturing. Pop: 200 966 (2003 est). Swedish name: **Tammerfors**

Tampico *n* a port and resort in E Mexico, in Tamaulipas on the Pánuco River: oil refining. Pop: 702 000 (2005 est)

tampon *n* an absorbent plug of cotton wool inserted into the vagina during menstruation [French]

Tamworth *n* **1** a market town in W central England, in SE Staffordshire. Pop: 71 650 (2001) **2** a city in SE Australia, in E central New South Wales: industrial centre of an agricultural region. Pop: 32 543 (2001)

tan¹ *n* **1** a brown coloration of the skin caused by exposure to ultraviolet rays, esp. those of the sun ▷ *vb* **tanning, tanned 2** (of a person or his or her skin) to go brown after exposure to ultraviolet rays **3** to convert (a skin or hide) into leather by treating it with a tanning

agent **4** *slang* to beat or flog ▷ *adj* **5** yellowish-brown [Medieval Latin *tannare*]

tan² *maths* tangent

Tana *n* **1** Lake Tana *or* Lake Tsana a lake in NW Ethiopia, on a plateau 1800 m (6000 ft) high: the largest lake of Ethiopia; source of the Blue Nile. Area: 3673 sq km (1418 sq miles) **2** a river in E Kenya, rising in the Aberdare Range and flowing in a wide curve east to the Indian Ocean: the longest river in Kenya. Length: 708 km (440 miles) **3** a river in NE Norway, flowing generally northeast as part of the border between Norway and Finland to the Arctic Ocean by Tana Fjord. Length: about 320 km (200 miles). Finnish name: **Teno**

Tanagra *n* a town in ancient Boeotia, famous for terracotta figurines of the same name, first discovered in its necropolis

Tanana *n* a river in central Alaska, rising in the Wrangell Mountains and flowing northwest to the Yukon River. Length: about 765 km (475 miles)

Tananarive *n* the former name of **Antananarivo**

Tancred *n* died 1112, Norman hero of the First Crusade who played a prominent part in the capture of Jerusalem (1099)

tandem *n* **1 a** a bicycle with two sets of pedals and two saddles, arranged one behind the other for two riders **2 in tandem** together or in conjunction: *the two drugs work in tandem to combat the disease* ▷ *adv* **3** one behind the other: *Jim and Ruth arrived, riding tandem* [Latin *tandem* at length]

Tandjungpriok *n* the former spelling of **Tanjungpriok**

tandoor *n* a type of Indian clay oven [Urdu]

tandoori *adj* cooked in a tandoor: *tandoori chicken*

tang *n* **1** a strong sharp taste or smell: *we could already smell the tang of the distant sea* **2** a trace or hint of something: *there was a tang of cloves in the apple pie* **3** the pointed end of a tool, such as a knife or chisel, which fits into the handle [Old Norse *tangi* point] ▷ **tangy** *adj*

Tanga *n* a port in N Tanzania, on the Indian Ocean: Tanzania's second port. Pop: 190 000 (2005 est)

Tanganyika *n* **1** a former state in E Africa: became part of German East Africa in 1884; ceded to Britain as a League of Nations mandate in 1919 and as a UN trust territory in 1946; gained independence in 1961 and united with Zanzibar in 1964 as the United Republic of Tanzania **2 Lake Tanganyika** a lake in central Africa between Tanzania and the Democratic Republic of Congo, bordering also on Burundi and Zambia, in the Great Rift Valley: the longest freshwater lake in the world. Area: 32 893 sq km (12 700 sq miles). Length: 676 km (420 miles)

Tanganyikan *adj* **1** of or relating to the former state of Tanganyika (now part of Tanzania) or its inhabitants ▷ *n* **2** a native of inhabitant of Tanganyika

tangata whenua (**tang-ah-tah fen-noo-ah**) *pl n* NZ **1** the original Polynesian settlers in New Zealand **2** descendants of the original Polynesian settlers [Māori: people of the land]

Tange *n* Kenzo. 1913–2005, Japanese architect. His buildings include the Kurashiki city hall (1960) and St Mary's Cathedral in Tokyo (1962–64)

tangent *n* **1 a** line, curve, or plane that touches another curve or surface at one point but does not cross it **2** (in trigonometry) the ratio of the length of the opposite side to that of the adjacent side of a right-angled triangle **3 go off at a tangent** suddenly take a completely different line of thought or action ▷ *adj* **4** of or involving a tangent **5** touching at a single point [Latin *linea tangens* the touching line]

tangential *adj* **1** only having an indirect or superficial relevance: *Hitler's vegetarianism only has a tangential link with the policies of the Nazis* **2** of or being a tangent: *a street tangential to the market square* ▷ **tangentially** *adv*

tangerine *n* **1** the small orange-like fruit, with a sweet juicy flesh, of an Asian tree ▷ *adj* **2** reddish-orange [from TANGIER]

Tangerine n **1** a native of inhabitant of Tangier ▷ adj **2** of or relating to Tangier or its inhabitants

tangi (tang-ee) n NZ **1** a Māori funeral ceremony **2** informal a lamentation

tangible adj **1** able to be touched; material or physical **2** real or substantial: tangible results [Latin tangere to touch] **> tangibility** **> tangibly** adv

Tangier n a port in N Morocco, on the Strait of Gibraltar: a Phoenician trading post in the 15th century BC; a neutral international zone (1923–56); made the summer capital of Morocco and a free port in 1962; commercial and financial centre. Pop: 526 000 (2003)

tangle n **1** a confused or complicated mass of things, such as hair or fibres, knotted or coiled together: a tangle of wires **2** a complicated problem or situation ▷ vb **-gling, -gled 3** to twist (things, such as hair or fibres) together in a confused mass **4** to come into conflict: the last thing she wanted was to tangle with the police **5** to catch or trap in a net, ropes, etc.: the string of the kite had got tangled in the branches [Middle English tangilen] **> tangled** adj

tango n, pl **-gos 1** a Latin-American dance characterized by long gliding steps and sudden pauses **2** music for this dance ▷ vb **-going, -goed 3** to perform this dance [American Spanish]

Tangshan n an industrial city in NE China, in Hebei province: the 1976 earthquake, which killed an estimated 255 000 people, was the most lethal of the 20th century. Pop: 1 773 000 (2005 est)

Tanguy n Yves. 1900–55, US surrealist painter, born in France

Tanis n an ancient city located in the E part of the Nile delta: abandoned after the 6th century AD; at one time the capital of Egypt. Biblical name: **Zoan**

taniwha (tun-ee-fah) n NZ a mythical Māori monster that lives in rivers and lakes [Māori]

Tanizaki Jun-ichiro n 1886–1965, Japanese novelist, whose works, such as Some Prefer Nettles (1929) and The Makioka Sisters (1943–48), reflect the tension between Western values and Japanese traditions

Tanjore n the former name of **Thanjavur**

Tanjungkarang n a city in Indonesia, in S Sumatra on the Sunda Strait; merged with Telukbetung to form the city of Bandar Lampung

Tanjungpriok n a port in Indonesia, on the NW coast of Java adjoining the capital, Jakarta: a major shipping and distributing centre for the whole archipelago. Former spelling: **Tandjungpriok**

tank n **1** a large container for storing liquids or gases **2** an armoured combat vehicle moving on tracks and armed with guns **3** Also called: **tankful** the quantity contained in a tank [Gujarati (language of W India) tānkh artificial lake]

tankard n a large one-handled beer-mug, sometimes fitted with a hinged lid [Middle English]

tanked up adj slang, chiefly Brit very drunk

tanker n a ship or lorry for carrying liquid in bulk: an oil tanker

tank farming n same as hydroponics **> tank farmer** n

Tannenberg n a village in N Poland, formerly in East Prussia: site of a decisive defeat of the Teutonic Knights by the Poles in 1410 and of a decisive German victory over the Russians in 1914. Polish name: **Stębark**

tannery n, pl **-neries** a place or building where skins and hides are tanned

Tannhäuser n 13th-century German poet, commonly identified with a legendary knight who sought papal absolution after years spent in revelry with Venus. The legend forms the basis of an opera by Wagner

tannic adj of, containing, or produced from tannin or tannic acid

tannie (tun-nee) n S African a title of respect used to refer to an elderly woman [Afrikaans, literally: aunt]

tannin n a yellowish compound found in many plants, such as tea and grapes, and used in tanning and dyeing. Also called: **tannic acid**

Tannoy n trademark Brit a type of public-address system

tansy n, pl **-sies** a plant with yellow flowers in flat-topped clusters [Greek athanasia immortality]

Tanta n a city in N Egypt, on the Nile delta: noted for its Muslim festivals. Pop: 413 000 (2005 est)

tantalize or **-lise** vb **-lizing, -lized** or **-lising, -lised** to tease or make frustrated, for example by tormenting (someone) with the sight of something that he or she wants but cannot have [after Tantalus, a mythological king condemned to stand in water that receded when he tried to drink it and under fruit that moved away when he reached for it] **> tantalizing** or **-lising** adj **> tantalizingly** or **-lisingly** adv

tantalum n chem a hard greyish-white metallic element that resists corrosion. Symbol: **Ta** [after Tantalus (see TANTALIZE), from the metal's incapacity to absorb acids]

tantalus n Brit a case in which bottles of wine and spirits may be locked with their contents tantalizingly visible

tantamount adj tantamount to equivalent in effect to: the raid was tantamount to a declaration of war [Anglo-French tant amunter to amount to as much]

tantrum n a childish outburst of bad temper [origin unknown]

Tan-tung n the former spelling of Dandong

Tanzania n a republic in E Africa, on the Indian Ocean: formed by the union of the independent states of Tanganyika and Zanzibar in 1964; a member of the Commonwealth. Exports include coffee, tea, sisal, and cotton. Official languages: Swahili and English. Religions: Christian, Muslim, and animist. Currency: Tanzanian shilling. Capital: officially Dodoma (though some functions remain in Dar es Salaam). Pop: 48 261 000 (2013 est). Area: 945 203 sq km (364 943 sq miles)

Tanzanian adj **1** of or relating to Tanzania or its inhabitants ▷ n **2** a native or inhabitant of Tanzania

Taoiseach (tee-shack) n the Prime Minister of the Irish Republic

Taoism (rhymes with **Maoism**) n a Chinese system of religion and philosophy advocating a simple honest life and noninterference with the course of natural events **> Taoist** n, adj

tap¹ vb **tapping, tapped 1** to knock lightly and usually repeatedly: she tapped gently on the door **2** to make a rhythmic sound with the hands or feet by lightly and repeatedly hitting a surface with them: he was tapping one foot to the music ▷ n **3** a light blow or knock, or the sound made by it **4** the metal piece attached to the toe or heel of a shoe used for tap-dancing **5** same as **tap-dancing** [Middle English tappen]

tap² n **1** Brit, Austral and NZ a valve by which the flow of a liquid or gas from a pipe can be controlled. Usual US word: **faucet 2** a stopper to plug a cask or barrel **3** a concealed listening or recording device connected to a telephone **4** med the withdrawal of fluid from a bodily cavity: a spinal tap **5 on tap a** informal ready for use **b** (of drinks) on draught rather than in bottles ▷ vb **tapping, tapped 6** to listen in on (a telephone conversation) secretly by making an illegal connection **7** to obtain something useful or desirable from (something): a new way of tapping the sun's energy **8** to withdraw liquid from (something) as if through a tap: to tap a cask of wine **9** to cut into (a tree) and draw off sap from it **10** Brit, Austral and NZ informal to obtain (money or information) from (someone) **11** informal to make an illicit attempt to recruit (a player or employee bound by an existing contract) [Old English tæppa]

Tapajós n a river in N Brazil, rising in N central Mato Grosso and flowing northeast to the Amazon. Length: about 800 km (500 miles)

tapas (tap-ass) pl n (in Spanish cookery) light snacks or appetizers, usually eaten with drinks [Spanish *tapa* cover, lid]

tap-dancing *n* a style of dancing in which the performer wears shoes with metal plates at the heels and toes that make a rhythmic sound on the stage as he or she dances **> tap-dancer** *n* **> tap dance** *n*

tape *n* **1 a** long thin strip of cotton or linen used for tying or fastening: *a parcel tied with pink tape* **2 a** short for **magnetic tape b** a spool or cassette containing magnetic tape, and used for recording or playing sound or video signals: *he put a tape into his stereo* **c** the music, speech, or pictures which have been recorded on a particular cassette or spool of magnetic tape **3** a narrow strip of plastic which has one side coated with an adhesive substance and is used to stick paper, etc., together: *sticky tape* **4** a string stretched across the track at the end of a race course **5** short for **tape measure** ▷ *vb* **taping, taped 6** Also: **tape-record** to record (speech, music, etc.) on magnetic tape **7** to bind or fasten with tape **8 have a person** *or* **situation taped** *Brit and Austral informal* to have full understanding and control of a person or situation [Old English *tæppe*]

tape deck *n* **1** the part of a tape recorder which supports the spools or cassettes, and contains the motor and the playback, recording, and erasing heads **2** the unit in a hi-fi system which fulfils the same function

tape drive *n* a machine for storing or transferring information from a computer onto tape

tape measure *n* a tape or length of metal marked off in centimetres or inches, used for measuring

taper *vb* **1** to become narrower towards one end **2 taper off** to become gradually less: *treatment should be tapered off gradually* ▷ *n* **3** a long thin fast-burning candle **4** a narrowing [Old English *tapor*]

tape recorder *n* an electrical device used for recording and reproducing sounds on magnetic tape

tape recording *n* **1** the act of recording sounds on magnetic tape **2** the magnetic tape used for this: *a tape recording of the interview* **3** the sounds so recorded

tapestry *n, pl* **-tries 1** a heavy woven fabric, often in the form of a picture, used for wall hangings or furnishings **2** same as **needlepoint** (1) **3** a colourful and complicated situation that is made up of many different kinds of things: *the rich tapestry of Hindustani music* [Old French *tapisserie* carpeting]

tapeworm *n* a long flat parasitic worm that inhabits the intestines of vertebrates, including man

tapioca *n* a beadlike starch made from cassava root, used in puddings [S American Indian *tipioca* pressed-out juice]

tapir (tape-er) *n* a piglike mammal of South and Central America and SE Asia, with a long snout, three-toed hind legs, and four-toed forelegs [S American Indian *tapiira*]

tappet *n* a short steel rod in an engine which moves up and down transferring movement from one part of the machine to another [from TAP¹]

taproom *n* old-fashioned the public bar in a hotel or pub

taproot *n* the main root of plants such as the dandelion, which grows straight down and bears smaller lateral roots

tar¹ *n* **1 a** dark sticky substance obtained by distilling organic matter such as coal, wood, or peat **2** same as **coal tar** ▷ *vb* **tarring, tarred 3** to coat with tar **4 tar and feather** to cover (someone) with tar and feathers as a punishment **5 tarred with the same brush** having, or regarded as having, the same faults [Old English *teoru*] **> tarry** *adj*

tar² *n* informal a seaman [short for *tarpaulin*]

Tara *n* a village in Co Meath near Dublin, by the **Hill of Tara**, the historic seat of the ancient Irish kings

Taraba *n* a state of Nigeria, in the E. Capital: Jalingo. Pop: 2 300 736 (2006). Area: 54 473 sq km (21 032 sq miles)

Tarabulus el Gharb *n* transliteration of the Arabic name for Tripoli (1)

Tarabulus esh Sham *n* transliteration of the Arabic name for **Tripoli** (2)

tarakihi (tarr-a-kee-hee) *or* **terakihi** (terr-a-kee-hee) *n* a common edible sea fish of New Zealand waters [Māori]

taramasalata *n* a creamy pale pink pâté, made from the eggs of fish, esp. smoked cod's roe, and served as an hors d'oeuvre [Modern Greek]

Taranaki *n* Mount Taranaki another name for (Mount) **Egmont**

tarantella *n* **1** a peasant dance from S Italy **2** music for this dance [Italian]

Tarantino *n* Quentin. born 1963, US film director and screenwriter, noted for violent quirky dramas including *Reservoir Dogs* (1993), *Pulp Fiction* (1994), *Jackie Brown* (1998), the two parts of *Kill Bill* (2003, 2004), *Inglourious Basterds* (2009), and *Django Unchained* (2012) **> Tarantinoesque** *adj*

Taranto *n* a port in SE Italy, in Apulia on the **Gulf of Taranto** (an inlet of the Ionian Sea): the chief city of Magna Graecia; taken by the Romans in 272 BC. Pop: 202 033 (2001). Latin name: **Tarentum**

tarantula *n* **1** a large hairy spider of tropical America with a poisonous bite **2** a large hairy spider of S Europe [Medieval Latin]

Tarawa *n* an atoll in Kiribati, occupying a chain of islets surrounding a lagoon in the W central Pacific: the capital of Kiribati, Bairiki, is on this atoll. Pop: 45 989 (2005)

Taraz *n* a city in S Kazakhstan: chemical manufacturing. Pop: 339 000 (2005 est). Former names: (1938–91) **Dzhambul**, (1991–97) **Auliye-Ata**

Tarbes *n* a town in SW France: noted for the breeding of Anglo-Arab horses. Pop: 48 166 (2011)

tarboosh *n* a felt or cloth brimless cap, usually red and often with a silk tassel, formerly worn by Muslim men [Arabic *tarbūsh*]

tardy *adj* **-dier, -diest 1** occurring later than it is expected to or than it should: *he spent the weekend writing tardy thank-you letters* **2** slow in progress, growth, etc.: *we made tardy progress across the ice* [Latin *tardus* slow] **> tardily** *adv* **> tardiness** *n*

tare¹ *n* **1** the weight of the wrapping or container in which goods are packed **2** the weight of a vehicle without its cargo or passengers [Arabic *tarhah* something discarded]

tare² *n* **1** any of various vetch plants of Eurasia and N Africa **2** *Bible* a weed, thought to be the darnel [origin unknown]

Tarentum *n* the Latin name of **Taranto**

target *n* **1** the object or person that a weapon, ball, etc., is aimed at: *the station was an easy target for an air attack* **2** an object at which an archer or marksman aims, usually a round flat surface marked with circles **3** a fixed goal or objective: *our sales figures are well below target* **4** a person or thing at which criticism or ridicule is directed: *the Chancellor has been the target of much of the criticism* ▷ *vb* **-geting, -geted 5** to direct: *an advertising campaign targeted at gay men* **6** to aim (a missile) [Old French *targette* a little shield]

Târgu Mureş *n* another spelling of **Tîrgu Mureş**

tariff *n* **1 a** a tax levied by a government on imports or occasionally exports **b** a list of such taxes **2** a list of fixed prices, for example in a hotel **3** *chiefly Brit* a method of charging for services such as gas and electricity by setting a price per unit [Arabic *ta'rīfa* to inform]

Tarim *n* a river in NW China, in Xinjiang: flows east along the N edge of the Taklimakan Shama desert, dividing repeatedly and forming lakes among the dunes, finally disappearing in the Lop Nor depression; the chief river of Xinjiang; drains the great **Tarim Basin** between the Tian Shan and Kunlun mountain systems of central Asia, an area of about 906 500 sq km (350 000 sq miles). Length: 2190 km (1360 miles)

Tarkington *n* (Newton) Booth. 1869–1946, US novelist. His works include the historical romance *Monsieur*

Beaucaire (1900), tales of the Middle West, such as *The Magnificent Ambersons* (1918) and *Alice Adams* (1921), and the series featuring the character Penrod

Tarkovsky *n* Andrei. 1932–86, Soviet film director, whose films include *Andrei Rublev* (1966), *Solaris* (1971), *Nostalgia* (1983), and *The Sacrifice* (1986)

Tarmac *n* **1** *trademark* a paving material made of crushed stone bound with a mixture of tar and bitumen, used for a road or airport runway **2 the tarmac** the area of an airport where planes wait and take off or land: *we had to wait for an hour on the tarmac* ▷ *vb* **tarmac** (**-macking, -macked**) **3** to apply Tarmac to (a surface) [TAR + MAC(ADAM)]

tarn *n chiefly Brit* a small mountain lake [from Old Norse]

Tarn *n* **1** a department of S France, in Midi-Pyrénées region. Capital: Albi. Pop: 350 477 (2003 est). Area: 5780 sq km (2254 sq miles) **2** a river in SW France, rising in the Massif Central and flowing generally west to the Garonne River. Length: 375 km (233 miles)

Tarn-et-Garonne *n* a department of SW France, in Midi-Pyrénées region. Capital: Montauban. Pop: 214 488 (2003 est). Area: 3731 sq km (1455 sq miles)

tarnish *vb* **1** (of a metal) to become stained or less bright, esp. by exposure to air or moisture **2** to damage or taint: *the affair could tarnish the reputation of the prime minister* ▷ *n* **3** a tarnished condition, surface, or film on a surface [Old French *ternir* to make dull] ▷ **tarnished** *adj*

Tarnopol *n* the Polish name for Ternopol

Tarnów *n* an industrial city in SE Poland. Pop: 119 000 (2005 est)

taro *n*, *pl* **-ros** a plant with a large edible rootstock [Tahitian & Polynesian]

tarot (tarr-oh) *n* **1** a special pack of cards, now used mainly for fortune-telling **2** a card in a tarot pack with a distinctive symbolic design [French]

tarpaulin *n* **1** a heavy waterproof canvas coated with tar, wax, or paint **2** a sheet of this canvas, used as a waterproof covering [probably from TAR¹ + PALL¹]

tarragon *n* a European herb with narrow leaves, which are used as seasoning in cooking [Old French *targon*]

Tarragona *n* a port in NE Spain, on the Mediterranean: one of the richest seaports of the Roman Empire; destroyed by the Moors (714). Pop: 121 076 (2003 est). Latin name: **Tarraco**

Tarrasa *n* a city in NE Spain: textile centre. Pop: 184 829 (2003 est). Also called: **Terrassa**

tarry *vb* **-ries, -rying, -ried** *old-fashioned* **1** to delay or linger: *I have no plans to tarry longer than necessary* **2** to stay briefly: *most people tarried only a few hours before moving on* [origin unknown]

tarsal *anatomy adj* **1** of the tarsus or tarsi ▷ *n* **2** a tarsal bone

tarseal *n NZ* **1** the bitumen surface of a road **2 the tarseal** the main highway

tarsier *n* a small nocturnal primate of the E Indies, which has very large eyes

tarsus *n*, *pl* **-si 1** the bones of the ankle and heel collectively **2** the corresponding part in other mammals and in amphibians and reptiles [Greek *tarsos* flat surface, instep]

Tarsus *n* **1** a city in SE Turkey, on the Tarsus River: site of ruins of ancient Tarsus, capital of Cilicia, and birthplace of St Paul. Pop: 231 000 (2005 est) **2** a river in SE Turkey, in Cilicia, rising in the Taurus Mountains and flowing south past Tarsus to the Mediterranean. Length: 153 km (95 miles). Ancient name: **Cydnus**

tart¹ *n* **1** a pastry case, often having no top crust, with a sweet filling, such as jam or custard **2** *chiefly US* a small open pie with a fruit filling [Old French *tarte*]

tart² *adj* **1** (of a flavour) sour or bitter **2** sharp and hurtful: *he made a rather tart comment* [Old English *teart* rough] ▷ **tartly** *adv* ▷ **tartness** *n*

tart³ *n informal* a sexually provocative or promiscuous woman: *you look like a tart.* See also **tart up** [from *sweetheart*]

tartan *n* **1** a design of straight lines, crossing at right angles to give a chequered appearance, esp. one associated with a Scottish clan **2** a fabric with this design [origin unknown]

tartar¹ *n* **1** a hard deposit on the teeth **2** a brownish-red substance deposited in a cask during the fermentation of wine [Medieval Greek *tartaron*]

tartar² *n* a fearsome or formidable person [from TARTAR]

Tartar *or* **Tatar** *n* **1** a member of a Mongoloid people who established a powerful state in central Asia in the 13th century, now scattered throughout Russia and central Asia ▷ *adj* **2** of the Tartars [Persian *Tātār*]

tartaric *adj* of or derived from tartar or tartaric acid

tartaric acid *n* a colourless crystalline acid which is found in many fruits

tartar sauce *n* a mayonnaise sauce mixed with chopped herbs and capers, served with seafood

Tartary *n* a variant spelling of **Tatary**

tartine *n* an open sandwich, esp. one with a rich or elaborate topping [French]

tartrazine (tar-traz-zeen) *n* an artificial yellow dye used as a food additive

Tartu *n* a city in SE Estonia: successively under Polish, Swedish, and Russian rule; university (1632). Pop: 95 000 (2005 est). Former name (11th century until 1918): **Yurev**. German name: **Dorpat**

tart up *vb Brit informal* **1** to decorate in a cheap and flashy way: *the shops were tarted up for Christmas* **2** to try to make (oneself) look smart and attractive

Tarzan *n informal, often humorous* a man with great physical strength, agility, and virility [after the hero of stories by E. R. Burroughs]

Tashkent *n* the capital of Uzbekistan: one of the oldest and largest cities in central Asia; cotton textile manufacturing. Pop: 2 160 000 (2005 est). Uzbek name: **Toshkent**

task *n* **1** a specific piece of work required to be done **2** an unpleasant or difficult job or duty **3 take to task** to criticize or rebuke [Old French *tasche*]

taskbar *n* a row of selectable buttons and icons typically running along the bottom of a computer screen, displaying information such as the names of running programs

task force *n* **1** a temporary grouping of military units formed to undertake a specific mission **2** any organization set up to carry out a continuing task

taskmaster *n* a person who enforces hard or continuous work

Tasman *n* Abel Janszoon. 1603–59, Dutch navigator, who discovered Tasmania, New Zealand, and the Tonga and Fiji Islands (1642–43)

Tasmania *n* an island in the S Pacific, south of mainland Australia: forms, with offshore islands, the smallest state of Australia; discovered by the Dutch explorer Tasman in 1642; used as a penal colony by the British (1803–53); mostly forested and mountainous. Capital: Hobart. Pop: 512 000 (2012 est). Area: 68 332 sq km (26 383 sq miles). Former name (1642–1855): **Van Diemen's Land**

Tasmanian *adj* **1** of or relating to Tasmania or its inhabitants ▷ *n* **2** a native or inhabitant of Tasmania

Tasmanian devil *n* a small flesh-eating marsupial of Tasmania

Tasman Sea *n* the part of the Pacific between SE Australia and NW New Zealand

Tass *n* (formerly) the principal news agency of the Soviet Union

tassel *n* a tuft of loose threads secured by a knot or knob, used to decorate a cushion, piece of clothing, etc. [Old French]

Tassie *or* **Tassy** *n*, *pl* **-sies** *Austral informal* **1** Tasmania **2** a native or inhabitant of Tasmania

Tasso *n* Torquato. 1544–95, Italian poet, noted for his pastoral idyll *Aminta* (1573) and for *Jerusalem Delivered*

t

(1581), dealing with the First Crusade

taste *n* **1** the sense by which the flavour of a substance is distinguished by the taste buds **2** the sensation experienced by means of the taste buds **3** a small amount eaten, sipped, or tried on the tongue **4** a brief experience of something: *a taste of the planter's life* **5** a liking for something: *a taste for puns* **6** the ability to appreciate what is beautiful and excellent: *she's got very good taste in clothes* **7** a person's typical preferences as displayed by what they choose to buy, enjoy, etc.: *the film was good but a bit violent for my taste* **8** the quality of not being offensive or bad-mannered: *that remark was in rather poor taste* ▷ *vb* **tasting, tasted** **9** to distinguish the taste of (a substance) by means of the taste buds: *I've got a stinking cold and can't taste anything* **10** to take a small amount of (a food or liquid) into the mouth, esp. in order to test the flavour **11** to have a flavour or taste as specified: *the pizza tastes delicious* **12** to have a brief experience of (something): *they have tasted democracy and they won't let go* [Old French *taster*]

taste bud *n* any of the cells on the surface of the tongue, by means of which the sensation of taste is experienced

tasteful *adj* having or showing good social or aesthetic taste: *tasteful decor* › **tastefully** *adv*

tasteless *adj* **1** lacking in flavour: *the canteen serves cold, tasteless pizzas* **2** lacking social or aesthetic taste: *a room full of tasteless ornaments; a tasteless remark* › **tastelessly** *adv* › **tastelessness** *n*

taster *n* **1** a person employed to test the quality of food or drink by tasting it **2** a sample of something intended to indicate what the entire thing is like: *the entrance hall was filled with flowers, giving a taster of the splendours in the main exhibition*

tasty *adj* **tastier, tastiest** having a pleasant flavour

tat *n Brit* tatty or tasteless articles

ta-ta *interj chiefly Brit informal* goodbye [origin unknown]

Tatar *n, adj* same as **Tartar**

Tatar Republic *n* a constituent republic of W Russia, around the confluence of the Volga and Kama Rivers. Capital: Kazan. Pop: 3 779 800 (2002). Area: 68 000 sq km (26 250 sq miles)

Tatar Strait *n* an arm of the Pacific between the mainland of SE Russia and Sakhalin Island, linking the Sea of Japan with the Sea of Okhotsk. Length: about 560 km (350 miles). Also called: **Gulf of Tatary**

Tatary *or* **Tartary** *n* **1** a historical region (with indefinite boundaries) in E Europe and Asia, inhabited by Bulgars until overrun by the Tatars in the mid-13th century: extended as far east as the Pacific under Genghis Khan **2 Gulf of Tatary** another name for the **Tatar Strait**

Tate *n* **1** (John Orley) **Allen.** 1899–1979, US poet and critic **2** Sir **Henry.** 1819–99, British sugar refiner and philanthropist; founder of the Tate Gallery **3 Nahum.** 1652–1715, British poet, dramatist, and hymn-writer, born in Ireland: poet laureate (1692–1715). He is best known for writing a version of *King Lear* with a happy ending

Tate Galleries *pl n* two art galleries in London, the original Tate Gallery (1897), now **Tate Britain**, and **Tate Modern**, created in the former Bankside power station in 2000

tater *n Brit dialect* a potato

Tati *n* Jacques, real name *Jacques Tatischeff*. 1908–82, French film director, pantomimist, and comic actor, creator of the character Monsieur Hulot

Tatra Mountains *pl n* a mountain range along the border between Slovakia and Poland, extending for about 64 km (40 miles): the highest range of the central Carpathians. Highest peak: Gerlachovka, 2663 m (8737 ft). Also called: **High Tatra**

tattered *adj* **1** ragged or torn: *a tattered old book* **2** wearing ragged or torn clothing: *the tattered refugees*

tatters *pl n* **1** torn ragged clothing **2 in tatters a** (of

clothing) torn in several places **b** (of an argument, plan, etc.) completely destroyed

Tattersall's *n* **1** a large horse market in London founded in the eighteenth century **2** *Austral* Also (informal): **Tatt's** a large-scale lottery based in Melbourne **3** a name used for sportsmen's clubs in Australia [named after Richard *Tattersall* (died 1795), English horseman, who founded the market]

tatting *n* **1** an intricate type of lace made by looping a thread of cotton or linen with a hand shuttle **2** the work of producing this [origin unknown]

tattle *vb* **-tling, -tled 1** to gossip or chatter ▷ *n* **2** gossip or chatter [Middle Dutch *tatelen*] › **tattler** *n*

tattletale *n chiefly US and Canad* a scandalmonger or gossip

tattoo¹ *n, pl* **-toos 1** a picture or design made on someone's body by pricking small holes in the skin and filling them with indelible dye ▷ *vb* **-tooing, -tooed 2** to make pictures or designs on (a person's skin) by pricking and staining it with indelible colours [Tahitian *tatau*] › **tattooed** *adj* › **tattooist** *n*

tattoo² *n, pl* **-toos 1** (formerly) a signal by drum or bugle ordering soldiers to return to their quarters **2** a military display or pageant **3** any drumming or tapping [Dutch *taptoe*]

tatty *adj* **-tier, -tiest** worn out, shabby, or unkempt [Scots]

Tatum *n* **1** Art, full name *Arthur Tatum*. 1910–56, US jazz pianist **2** Edward Lawrie. 1909–75, US biochemist, who showed how genes regulate biochemical processes in an organism and demonstrated that bacteria reproduce sexually; Nobel prize for physiology or medicine (1958) with Beadle and Lederberg

taught *vb* the past of **teach**

taunt *vb* **1** to tease or provoke (someone) with jeering remarks ▷ *n* **2** a jeering remark [French *tant pour tant* like for like] › **taunting** *adj*

Taunton *n* a market town in SW England, administrative centre of Somerset: scene of Judge Jeffreys' "Bloody Assize" (1685) after the Battle of Sedgemoor. Pop: 58 241 (2001)

Taupo *n* **Lake Taupo** a lake in New Zealand, on central North Island: the largest lake of New Zealand. Area: 616 sq km (238 sq miles)

Tauranga *n* a port in New Zealand, on NE North Island on the Bay of Plenty: exports dairy produce, meat, and timber. Pop: 101 300 (2004 est)

Taurus *n astrol* the second sign of the zodiac; the Bull [Latin]

Taurus Mountains *pl n* a mountain range in S Turkey, parallel to the Mediterranean coast: crossed by the Cilician Gates; continued in the northeast by the Anti-Taurus range. Highest peak: Kaldi Dağ, 3734 m (12 251 ft)

taut *adj* **1** stretched tight: *the cable must be taut* **2** showing nervous strain: *he was looking taut and anxious* **3** (of a film or piece of writing) having no unnecessary or irrelevant details: *a taut thriller* [Middle English *tought*]

tauten *vb* to make or become taut

tautology *n, pl* **-gies** the use of words which merely repeat something already stated, as in *reverse back* [Greek *tautologia*] › **tautological** *or* **tautologous** *adj*

Tavener *n* Sir John (Kenneth). 1944–2013, English composer, whose works include the cantata *The Whale* (1966), the opera *Thérèse* (1979), and the choral work *The Last Discourse* (1998); many of his later works are inspired by the liturgy of the Russian Orthodox Church

tavern *n* **1** old-fashioned a pub **2** *US, Canad, Austral and NZ* a place licensed for the sale and consumption of alcoholic drink [Latin *taberna* hut]

Taverner *n* John. ?1495–1545, English composer, esp. of church music; best known for the mass *Western Wynde*, based on a secular song

tawdry *adj* **-drier, -driest** cheap, showy, and of poor quality: *tawdry Christmas decorations* [Middle English *seynt Audries lace,* finery sold at the fair of St *Audrey*]

Tawney *n* R(ichard) H(enry). 1880–1962, British economic historian, born in India. His chief works are *The Acquisitive Society* (1920), *Religion and the Rise of Capitalism* (1926), and *Equality* (1931)

tawny *adj* brown to brownish-orange [Old French *tané*]

tawny owl *n* a European owl having a reddish-brown plumage and a round head

tawse *n Scot* a leather strap with one end cut into thongs, formerly used by schoolteachers to hit children who had misbehaved [probably plural of obsolete *taw* strip of leather]

tax *n* 1 a compulsory payment to a government to raise revenue, levied on income, property, or goods and services ▷ *vb* 2 to levy a tax on (people, companies, etc.) 3 to make heavy demands on: *the task taxed his ingenuity and patience* 4 **tax someone with** to accuse someone of: *he was taxed with parochialism and meanness* [Latin *taxare* to appraise] › **taxable** *adj* › **taxing** *adj*

taxation *n* the levying of taxes or the condition of being taxed

tax avoidance *n* reduction of tax liability by lawful methods

tax-deductible *adj* legally deductible from income or wealth before tax assessment

tax disc *n* (in Britain) a small disc of paper which must be displayed on a vehicle to show that the tax due on it for that year has been paid

tax evasion *n* reduction of tax liability by illegal methods

tax-free *adj* not needing to have tax paid on it: *a tax-free lump sum*

tax haven *n* a country or state having a lower rate of taxation than elsewhere

taxi *n, pl* **taxis** 1 Also called: **cab, taxicab** a car that may be hired, along with its driver, to carry passengers to any specified destination ▷ *vb* **taxiing, taxied** 2 (of an aircraft) to move along the ground, esp. before takeoff and after landing [*taximeter cab*]

taxidermy *n* the art of preparing, stuffing, and mounting animal skins so that they have a lifelike appearance [Greek *taxis* arrangement + *derma* skin] › **taxidermist** *n*

taximeter *n* a meter fitted to a taxi to register the fare, based on the length of the journey

taxi rank *n* a place where taxis wait to be hired

taxman *n, pl* **-men** 1 a collector of taxes 2 *informal* a tax-collecting body personified: *he was convicted of conspiring to cheat the taxman*

taxonomy *n* 1 the branch of biology concerned with the classification of plants and animals into groups based on their similarities and differences 2 the science or practice of classification [Greek *taxis* order + *nomia* law] › **taxonomic** *adj* › **taxonomist** *n*

taxpayer *n* a person or organization that pays taxes

tax relief *n* a reduction in the amount of tax a person or company has to pay

tax return *n* a declaration of personal income used as a basis for assessing an individual's liability for taxation

tax year *n* a period of twelve months used by a government as a basis for calculating taxes

Tay *n* 1 **Firth of Tay** the estuary of the River Tay on the North Sea coast of Scotland. Length: 40 km (25 miles) 2 a river in central Scotland, flowing northeast through Loch Tay, then southeast to the Firth of Tay: the longest river in Scotland; noted for salmon fishing. Length: 193 km (120 miles) 3 **Loch Tay** a lake in central Scotland, in Stirling council area. Length: 23 km (14 miles)

Taylor *n* 1 A(lan) J(ohn) P(ercivale). 1906–90, British historian whose many works include *The Origins of the Second World War* (1961) 2 **Brook**. 1685–1731, English mathematician, who laid the foundations of differential calculus 3 Dame **Elizabeth**. 1932–2011, US

film actress, born in England: films include *National Velvet* (1944), *Cat on a Hot Tin Roof* (1958), *Suddenly Last Summer* (1959), and *Butterfield 8* (1960) and *Who's Afraid of Virginia Woolf?* (1966), for both of which she won Oscars 4 **Frederick Winslow**. 1856–1915, US engineer, who pioneered the use of time and motion studies to increase efficiency in industry 5 **Jeremy**. 1613–67, English cleric, best known for his devotional manuals *Holy Living* (1650) and *Holy Dying* (1651) 6 **Zachary**. 1784–1850, 12th president of the US (1849–50); hero of the Mexican War

Taymyr Peninsula *n* a variant spelling of **Taimyr Peninsula**

Tayside Region *n* a former local government region in E Scotland: formed in 1975 from Angus, Kinross-shire, and most of Perthshire; replaced in 1996 by the council areas of Angus, City of Dundee, and Perth and Kinross

Tb *chem* terbium

TB tuberculosis

tba *or* **TBA** to be arranged

tbc *or* **TBC** to be confirmed

Tbilisi *n* the capital of Georgia, on the Kura River: founded in 458; taken by the Russians in 1801; university (1918); a major industrial centre. Pop: 1 042 000 (2005 est). Russian name: **Tiflis**

T-bone steak *n* a large choice steak cut from the sirloin of beef, containing a T-shaped bone

tbs. *or* **tbsp.** tablespoon(ful)

Tc *chem* technetium

Tchad *n* the French name for **Chad**

Tchaikovsky *n* Pyotr Ilyich. 1840–93, Russian composer. His works, which are noted for their expressive melodies, include the *Sixth Symphony* (the *Pathétique*; 1893), ballets, esp. *Swan Lake* (1876) and *The Sleeping Beauty* (1889), and operas, including *Eugene Onegin* (1879) and *The Queen of Spades* (1890), both based on works by Pushkin

te *n music* (in tonic sol-fa) the seventh note of any ascending major scale

Te *chem* tellurium

tea *n* 1 a a drink made by infusing the dried chopped leaves of an Asian shrub in boiling water: *would you like a cup of tea?* b the dried chopped leaves of an Asian shrub used to make this drink: *could you get some tea at the grocer's?* c the Asian shrub on which these leaves grow 2 *Brit, Austral and NZ* the main evening meal 3 *chiefly Brit* a light meal eaten in mid-afternoon, usually consisting of tea and cakes, sometimes with sandwiches 4 a drink like tea made from other plants: *mint tea* [Ancient Chinese *d'a*]

tea bag *n* a small bag containing tea leaves, infused in boiling water to make tea

teacake *n chiefly Brit* a flat bun, usually eaten toasted and buttered

teach *vb* **teaching, taught** 1 to tell or show (someone) how to do something 2 to give instruction or lessons in (a subject) to (students) 3 to cause to learn or understand: *life has taught me to seize the day* 4 **teach someone a lesson** to warn or punish someone: *a bully has to be taught a lesson* [Old English *tǣcan*] › **teachable** *adj*

Teach *n* Edward, known as *Blackbeard*. died 1718, English pirate, active in the West Indies and on the Atlantic coast of North America

teacher *n* a person whose job is to teach others, esp. children

tea chest *n* a large light wooden box used for exporting tea or storing things in

teaching *n* 1 the art or profession of a teacher 2 **teachings** the ideas and principles taught by a person, school of thought, etc.: *the teachings of the Catholic Church*

teaching hospital *n* a hospital attached to a medical school, in which students are taught and given supervised practical experience

tea cloth *n* same as **tea towel**

tea cosy *n* a covering for a teapot to keep the contents hot

teacup n **1** a cup out of which tea may be drunk **2** Also called: **teacupful** the amount a teacup will hold

teahouse n a restaurant, esp. in Japan or China, where tea and light refreshments are served

teak n the hard yellowish-brown wood of an East Indian tree, used for furniture making [Malayalam (a language of S India) tēkka]

teal n, pl **teals** or **teal** a small freshwater duck related to the mallard [Middle English tele]

tea leaves pl n, sing **tea leaf** the dried and shredded leaves of the tea shrub, esp. those left behind in a cup or teapot after tea has been made and drunk

team n **1** a group of players forming one of the sides in a sporting contest **2** a group of people organized to work together: a team of scientists **3** two or more animals working together: a sledge pulled by a team of dogs ▷ vb **4 team up with** to join with (someone) in order to work together **5 team with** to match (something) with something else: navy skirts teamed with various coloured blouses [Old English tēam offspring]

team-mate n a fellow member of a team

team spirit n willingness to cooperate as part of a team

teamster n **1** US and Canad a truck driver **2** (formerly) a driver of a team of horses

teamwork n the cooperative work done by a team

teapot n a container with a lid, spout, and handle, in which tea is made and from which it is served

tear¹ n **1** Also called: **teardrop** a drop of salty fluid appearing in and falling from the eye. Related adjectives: **lacrimal, lachrymal, lacrymal 2 in tears** weeping [Old English tēar]

tear² vb **tearing, tore, torn 1** to rip a hole in (something): I tore my jumper on a nail **2** to pull apart or to pieces: eagles have powerful beaks for tearing flesh **3** to hurry or rush **4** to remove or take by force: the sacred things torn from the temples of Inca worshippers **5 tear at someone's heartstrings** to cause someone distress or anguish **6** to injure (a muscle or ligament) by moving or twisting it violently ▷ n **7** a hole or split ▶ See also **tear away, tear down, tear into** [Old English teran]

tear away vb **1** to persuade (oneself or someone else) to leave: she stood and watched, unable to tear herself away from the room ▷ n **tearaway 2** Brit a wild or unruly person

tear down vb to destroy or demolish: it will be cheaper to tear down the old house and build a new one than to repair it

tear duct n a short tube in the inner corner of the eyelid, through which tears drain into the nose

tearful adj weeping or about to weep ▶ **tearfully** adv

tear gas n a gas that stings the eyes and causes temporary blindness, used in warfare and to control riots

tearing adj very urgent: I had been in a tearing hurry to leave the camp

tear into vb informal to attack vigorously and damagingly

tear-jerker n informal an excessively sentimental film or book

tearoom n **1** chiefly Brit a restaurant where tea and light refreshments are served **2** NZ a room in a school or university where hot drinks are served

tease vb **teasing, teased 1** to make fun of (someone) in a provocative and often playful manner **2** to arouse sexual desire in (someone) with no intention of satisfying it **3** to raise the nap of (a fabric) with a teasel ▷ n **4** a person who teases **5** a piece of teasing behaviour [Old English tǣsan] ▶ **teasing** adj

teasel, teazel or **teazle** n **1** a plant of Eurasia and N Africa, with prickly heads of yellow or purple flowers **2** the dried flower head of a teasel, used, esp. formerly, for raising the nap of cloth [Old English tǣsel]

tease out vb **1** to comb (hair, flax, or wool) so as to remove any tangles **2** to extract information with difficulty: it's not easy to tease out the differences between anxiety and depression

teaser n **1** a difficult question **2** a preliminary

advertisement in a campaign that makes people curious to know what product is being advertised

teaspoon n **1** a small spoon used for stirring tea or coffee **2** Also called: **teaspoonful** the amount contained in such a spoon **3** a unit of capacity used in cooking etc., equal to 5 ml

teat n **1** the nipple of a breast or udder **2** something resembling a teat such as the rubber mouthpiece of a feeding bottle [Old French tete]

tea towel or **tea cloth** n a towel for drying dishes

tea tree n a tree of Australia and New Zealand that yields an oil used as an antiseptic

tech n informal a technical college

tech. 1 technical **2** technology

techie or **techy** informal n **1** a person who is skilled in the use of technological devices, such as computers ▷ adj **2** of, relating to, or skilled in the use of such devices

technetium (tek-neesh-ee-um) n chem a silvery-grey metallic element, produced artificially, esp. by the fission of uranium. Symbol: **Tc** [Greek teknētos man-made]

technical adj **1** of or specializing in industrial, practical, or mechanical arts and applied sciences: a technical school **2** skilled in practical activities rather than abstract thinking **3** relating to a particular field of activity: technical jargon **4** according to the letter of the law: a last-minute penalty awarded to the Irish for a technical offence **5** showing technique: technical perfection ▶ **technically** adv

technical college n Brit and Austral an institution for further education that provides courses in art and technical subjects

technical drawing n drawing done by a draughtsman with compasses, T-squares, etc.

technicality n, pl **-ties 1** a petty formal point arising from a strict interpretation of the law or a set of rules: the case was dismissed on a legal technicality **2** a detail of the method used to do something: the technicalities of making a recording

technical knockout n boxing a judgment of a knockout given when a boxer is, in the referee's opinion, too badly beaten to continue without risk of serious injury

technician n a person skilled in a particular technical field: oil technicians

Technicolor n trademark a process of producing colour film for the cinema by superimposing synchronized films of the same scene, each having a different colour filter

technikon n S African a technical college

technique n **1** a method or skill used for a particular task: modern management techniques **2** proficiency in a practical or mechanical skill: he lacks the technique to be a good player [Greek teknē skill]

techno n a type of very fast disco music, using electronic sounds and having a strong technological influence

techno- combining form of or relatinguluk to technology: technophile [Greek teknē skill]

technocracy n, pl **-cies** government by scientists, engineers, and other experts [Greek teknē skill + kratos power] ▶ **technocrat** n ▶ **technocratic** adj

technology n, pl **-gies 1** the application of practical or mechanical sciences to industry or commerce **2** the scientific methods or devices used in a particular field: the latest aircraft technology [Greek teknologia systematic treatment] ▶ **technological** adj ▶ **technologist** n

technophile n **1** a person who is enthusiastic about technology ▷ adj **2** enthusiastic about technology

technophobia n fear of using technological devices, such as computers ▶ **technophobe** n ▶ **technophobic** adj

tectonics n geology the study of the earth's crust and the forces that produce changes in it [Greek tektōn a builder]

Tecumseh n ?1768–1813, American Indian chief of the Shawnee tribe. He attempted to unite western Indian tribes against the White people, but was defeated at Tippecanoe (1811). He was killed while fighting for the British in the War of 1812

ted¹ *vb* **tedding, tedded** to shake out (hay), so as to dry it [Old Norse *tethja*]

ted² *n Brit informal* short for **teddy boy**

Tedder *n* Arthur William, 1st Baron Tedder of Glenguin. 1890–1967, British marshal of the Royal Air Force; deputy commander under Eisenhower of the Allied Expeditionary Force (1944–45)

teddy¹ *n, pl* **-dies** short for **teddy bear**

teddy² *n, pl* **-dies** a woman's one-piece undergarment incorporating a camisole top and French knickers [origin unknown]

teddy bear *n* a stuffed toy bear [after *Teddy* (Theodore) Roosevelt, US president]

teddy boy *n* (in Britain, esp. in the mid-1950s) a youth who wore mock Edwardian fashions [*Teddy*, from *Edward*]

Te Deum (tee **dee**-um) *n Christianity* an ancient Latin hymn beginning Te Deum Laudamus (we praise thee, O God)

tedious *adj* boring and uninteresting › **tediously** *adv* › **tediousness** *n*

tedium *n* the state of being bored or the quality of being boring: *the tedium of a nine-to-five white-collar job* [Latin *taedium*]

tee *n* **1** a support for a golf ball, usually a small wooden or plastic peg, used when teeing off **2** an area on a golf course from which the first stroke of a hole is made **3** a mark used as a target in certain games such as curling and quoits ▸ See also **tee off** [origin unknown]

tee-hee *or* **te-hee** *interj* an exclamation of mocking laughter [imitative]

teem¹ *vb* **teem with** to have a great number of: *the woods were teeming with snakes and bears* [Old English *tēman* to produce offspring]

teem² *vb* (of rain) to pour down in torrents [Old Norse *tœma*]

teen *adj informal* same as **teenage**

teenage *adj* **1** (of a person) aged between 13 and 19 **2** typical of or designed for people aged between 13 and 19: *teenage fashions*

teenager *n* a person between the ages of 13 and 19

teens *pl n* **1** the years of a person's life between the ages of 13 and 19 **2** all the numbers that end in *-teen*

teeny *adj* **-nier, -niest** *informal* extremely small [variant of *tiny*]

teenybopper *n old-fashioned, slang* a young teenager, usually a girl, who is a keen follower of fashion and pop music [*teeny* teenage + *-bopper* someone who bops]

tee off *vb* **teeing, teed** *golf* to hit (the ball) from a tee at the start of a hole

teepee *n* same as **tepee**

Tees *n* a river in N England, rising in the N Pennines and flowing southeast and east to the North Sea at Middlesbrough. Length: 113 km (70 miles)

Teesside *n* the industrial region around the lower Tees valley and estuary: a county borough, containing Middlesbrough, from 1968 to 1974

teeter *vb* to wobble or move unsteadily [Middle English *titeren*]

teeth *n* **1** the plural of **tooth 2** the power to produce a desired effect: *resolution 672 had no teeth* **3** armed to the teeth very heavily armed **4** get one's teeth into to become engrossed in **5** in the teeth of in spite of: *trying to run a business in the teeth of the recession*

teethe *vb* **teething, teethed** (of a baby) to grow his or her first teeth

teething ring *n* a hard ring on which babies may bite while teething

teething troubles *pl n* problems arising during the early stages of a project

teetotal *adj* never drinking alcohol [reduplication of *t* + *total*] › **teetotaller** *n*

TEFL Teaching of English as a Foreign Language

Teflon *n trademark* a substance used for nonstick coatings on saucepans etc.

Tegucigalpa *n* the capital of Honduras, in the south on the Choluteca River: founded about 1579; university (1847). Pop: 1 061 000 (2005 est)

te-hee *interj* same as **tee-hee**

Tehran *or* **Teheran** *n* the capital of Iran, at the foot of the Elburz Mountains: built on the site of the ancient capital Ray, destroyed by Mongols in 1220; became capital in the 1790s; three universities. Pop: 7 352 000 (2005 est)

Tehuantepec *n* Isthmus of Tehuantepec the narrowest part of S Mexico, with the Bay of Campeche on the north coast and the Gulf of Tehuantepec (an inlet of the Pacific) on the south coast

Teide *or* **Teyde** *n* Pico de Teide a volcanic mountain in the Canary Islands, on Tenerife. Height: 3718 m (12 198 ft)

Teilhard de Chardin *n* Pierre. 1881–1955, French Jesuit priest, palaeontologist, and philosopher. *The Phenomenon of Man* (1938–40), uses scientific evolution to prove the existence of God

Tejo *n* the Portuguese name for the **Tagus**

Te Kanawa *n* Dame Kiri. born 1944, New Zealand operatic soprano

tel. telephone

Telanaipura *n* another name for **Jambi**

Tel Aviv *n* a city in W Israel, on the Mediterranean: the largest city and chief financial centre of Israel; incorporated the city of Jaffa in 1950; university (1953): regarded by the international community as the capital of Israel, though most functions of the capital operate from Jerusalem. Pop: 363 400 (2003 est). Official name: Tel Aviv-Jaffa

tele- *combining form* **1** at or over a distance: *telecommunications* **2** television: *telegenic* **3** via telephone or television: *teleconference* [Greek *tele* far]

telecast *vb* **-casting, -cast** *or* **-casted 1** to broadcast by television ▷ *n* **2** a television broadcast › **telecaster** *n*

telecommunications *n* communications using electronic equipment, such as telephones, radio, and television

telecommuting *n* same as **teleworking**

telegram *n* (formerly) a message transmitted by telegraph

telegraph *n* **1** (formerly) a system by which information could be transmitted over a distance, using electrical signals sent along a cable ▷ *vb* **2** (formerly) to send (a message) by telegraph **3** to give advance notice of (something), esp. unintentionally: *the twist in the plot was telegraphed long in advance* **4** *Canad informal* to cast (a vote) illegally by impersonating a registered voter › **telegraphist** *n* › **telegraphic** *adj*

telegraphy *n* (formerly) the science or use of a telegraph

telekinesis *n* movement of a body by thought or willpower, without the application of a physical force › **telekinetic** *adj*

Telemann *n* Georg Philipp. 1681–1767, German composer, noted for his prolific output

telemetry *n* the use of electronic devices to record or measure a distant event and transmit the data to a receiver › **telemetric** *adj*

teleology *n* **1** *philosophy* the doctrine that there is evidence of purpose or design in the universe **2** *biology* the belief that natural phenomena have a predetermined purpose and are not determined by mechanical laws [Greek *telos* end + -LOGY] › **teleological** *adj* › **teleologist** *n*

telepathy *n* the direct communication of thoughts and feelings between minds without the need to use normal means such as speech, writing, or touch [Greek *tele* far + *pathos* suffering] › **telepathic** *adj* › **telepathically** *adv*

telephone *n* **1** a piece of equipment for transmitting speech, consisting of a microphone and receiver mounted on a handset: *the telephone was ringing* **2** the worldwide system of communications using telephones: *reports came in by telephone* ▷ *vb* **-phoning,**

t

-phoned 3 to call or talk to (a person) by telephone ▷ *adj* **4** of or using a telephone: *a telephone call* [Greek *tele* far + *phōnē* voice] **> telephonic** *adj*

telephone box *n* an enclosure from which a paid telephone call can be made

telephone directory *n* a book listing the names, addresses, and telephone numbers of subscribers in a particular area

telephonist *n* a person who operates a telephone switchboard

telephony *n* a system of telecommunications for the transmission of speech or other sounds

telephoto lens *n* a lens fitted to a camera to produce a magnified image of a distant object

teleprinter *n* **1** an apparatus consisting of a keyboard transmitter, which converts a typed message into coded pulses for transmission along a wire or cable, and a printing receiver, which converts incoming signals and prints out the message. US name: **teletypewriter 2** a similar device used for direct input/output of data into a computer at a distant location

Teleprompter *n trademark* a device for displaying a script under a television camera, so that a speaker can read it while appearing to look at the camera

telesales *n* the selling of a commodity or service by telephone

telescope *n* **1** an optical instrument for making distant objects appear closer by use of a combination of lenses **2** See **radio telescope** ▷ *vb* **-scoping, -scoped 3** to shorten (something) while still keeping the important parts: *a hundred years of change has been telescoped into five years* [New Latin *telescopium* far-seeing instrument] **> telescopic** *adj*

telescopic sight *n* a sight on a rifle, etc., consisting of a telescope, used for aiming at distant objects

televangelist *n* US an evangelical preacher who appears regularly on television, preaching the gospel and appealing for donations from viewers [*tele(vision)* + *(e)vangelist*]

televise *vb* **-vising, -vised** to show (a programme or event) on television

television *n* **1** the system or process of producing a moving image with accompanying sound on a distant screen **2** Also called: **television set** a device for receiving broadcast signals and converting them into sound and pictures **3** the content of television programmes: *some people think that television is too violent nowadays* ▷ *adj* **4** of or relating to television: *a television interview* **> televisual** *adj*

teleworking *n* the use of home computers, telephones, etc., to enable a person to work from home while maintaining contact with colleagues or customers **> teleworker** *n*

telex *n* **1** an international communication service which sends messages by teleprinter **2** a teleprinter used in such a service **3** a message sent by telex ▷ *vb* **4** to transmit (a message) by telex [*tel(eprinter) ex(change)*]

Telford¹ *n* a town in W central England, in Telford and Wrekin unitary authority, Shropshire: designated a new town in 1963. Pop: 138 241 (2001)

Telford² *n* Thomas. 1757–1834, Scottish civil engineer, known esp. for his roads and such bridges as the Menai suspension bridge (1825)

Telford and Wrekin *n* a unitary authority in W Central England, in Shropshire. Pop: 160 300 (2003 est). Area: 289 sq km (112 sq miles)

tell *vb* **telling, told 1** to make known in words; notify: *I told her what had happened* **2** to order or instruct (someone to do something): *he had been told to wait in the lobby* **3** to give an account (of an event or situation): *the President had been told of the developments* **4** to communicate by words: *he was woken at 5 am to be told the news* **5** to discover, distinguish, or discern: *she could tell that he was not sorry* **6** to have or produce an impact or effect: *the pressure had begun to tell on him* **7** *informal* to reveal secrets or gossip **8 tell the time** to read the time from a clock **9 you're**

telling me *slang* I know that very well [Old English *tellan*]

Tell *n* William, German name *Wilhelm Tell*. a legendary Swiss patriot, who, traditionally, lived in the early 14th century and was compelled by an Austrian governor to shoot an apple from his son's head with one shot of his crossbow. He did so without mishap

tell apart *vb* to distinguish between: *they're different colours, otherwise how would you tell them apart?*

Tell el Amarna *n* a group of ruins and rock tombs in Upper Egypt, on the Nile below Asyut: site of the capital of Amenhotep IV, built about 1375 BC; excavated from 1891 onwards

teller *n* **1** a narrator **2** a bank cashier **3** a person appointed to count votes

Teller *n* Edward. 1908–2003, US nuclear physicist, born in Hungary: a major contributor to the development of the hydrogen bomb (1952)

telling *adj* having a marked effect or impact: *to inflict telling damage on the enemy*

tell off *vb informal* to reprimand or scold (someone) **> telling-off** *n*

telltale *n* **1** a person who tells tales about others ▷ *adj* **2** giving away information: *examining the hands for telltale signs of age*

tellurian *adj* of the earth [Latin *tellus* the earth]

tellurium *n chem* a brittle silvery-white nonmetallic element. Symbol: **Te** [Latin *tellus* the earth]

telly *n, pl* **-lies** *informal* short for **television**

Teloekbetoeng *n* the former spelling of **Telukbetung**

telomere *n genetics* either of the ends of a chromosome [Greek *telos* end + *meros* part]

Telukbetung *n* a city in Indonesia, in S Sumatra on the Sunda Strait; merged with Tanjungkarang to form the city of Bandar Lampung. Former spelling: **Teloekbetoeng**

Tema *n* a port in SE Ghana on the Atlantic: oil-refining. Pop: 160 000 (2005 est)

temazepam (ti-**maz**-i-pam) *n* (*sometimes cap*) a sedative in the form of a gel-like capsule, which is taken orally or melted and injected by drug users

Témbi *n* a transliteration of the Modern Greek name for Tempe

temerity (tim-**merr**-it-tee) *n* boldness or audacity [Latin *temere* at random]

Temesvár *n* the Hungarian name for **Timişoara**

temp *Brit informal n* **1** a person, esp. a secretary, employed on a temporary basis ▷ *vb* **2** to work as a temp

temp. 1 temperature **2** temporary

Tempe *n* Vale of Tempe a wooded valley in E Greece, in Thessaly between the mountains Olympus and Ossa. Modern Greek name: **Témbi**

temper *n* **1** a sudden outburst of anger: *she stormed out in a temper* **2** a tendency to have sudden outbursts of anger: *you've got a temper all right* **3** a mental condition of moderation and calm: *he lost his temper* **4** a person's frame of mind: *he was in a bad temper* ▷ *vb* **5** to modify so as to make less extreme or more acceptable: *past militancy has been tempered with compassion and caring* **6** to reduce the brittleness of (a hardened metal) by reheating it and allowing it to cool **7** *music* to adjust the frequency differences between the notes of a scale on (a keyboard instrument) [Latin *temperare* to mix]

tempera *n* a painting medium for powdered pigments, consisting usually of egg yolk and water [Italian *temperare* to mingle]

temperament *n* a person's character or disposition [Latin *temperamentum* a mixing]

temperamental *adj* **1** (of a person) tending to be moody and have sudden outbursts of anger **2** *informal* working erratically and inconsistently; unreliable: *the temperamental microphone* **3** of or relating to a person's temperament: *we discussed temperamental and developmental differences* **> temperamentally** *adv*

temperance *n* **1** restraint or moderation, esp. in

yielding to one's appetites or desires **2** abstinence from alcoholic drink [Latin *temperare* to regulate]

temperate *adj* **1** of a climate which is never extremely hot or extremely cold **2** mild or moderate in quality or character: *try to be more temperate in your statements* [Latin *temperatus*]

Temperate Zone *n* those parts of the earth's surface lying between the Arctic Circle and the tropic of Cancer and between the Antarctic Circle and the tropic of Capricorn

temperature *n* **1** the hotness or coldness of something, as measured on a scale that has one or more fixed reference points **2** *informal* an abnormally high body temperature **3** the strength of feeling among a group of people: *his remarks are likely to raise the political temperature considerably* [Latin *temperatura* proportion]

tempest *n literary* a violent wind or storm [Latin *tempestas*]

tempestuous *adj* **1** violent or stormy **2** extremely emotional or passionate: *a tempestuous relationship* ▷ **tempestuously** *adv*

template *n* a wood or metal pattern, used to help cut out shapes accurately [from *temple* a part in a loom that keeps the cloth stretched]

temple¹ *n* a building or place used for the worship of a god or gods [Latin *templum*]

temple² *n* the region on each side of the head in front of the ear and above the cheek bone [Latin *tempus*]

Temple *n* **1** Shirley, married name *Shirley Temple Black*. 1928–2014, US film actress and politician. Her films as a child star include *Little Miss Marker* (1934), *Wee Willie Winkie* (1937), and *Heidi* (1937). She was US ambassador to Ghana (1974–76) and to Czechoslovakia (1989–92) **2** Sir **William**. 1628–99, English diplomat and essayist. He negotiated the Triple Alliance (1668) and the marriage of William of Orange to Mary II **3** William. 1881–1944, English prelate and advocate of social reform; archbishop of Canterbury (1942–44)

Temple of Artemis *n* the large temple at Ephesus, on the W coast of Asia Minor: one of the Seven Wonders of the World

tempo (tem-po) *n, pl* **-pi** (-pee) *or* **-pos** **1** rate or pace: *the slow tempo of change in an overwhelmingly rural country* **2** the speed at which a piece of music is played or meant to be played [Italian]

temporal¹ *adj* **1** of or relating to time **2** of secular as opposed to spiritual or religious affairs: *in the Middle Ages the Pope had temporal as well as spiritual power* **3** not permanent or eternal: *a temporal view of drugs as the No. 1 social problem* [Latin *tempus* time]

temporal² *adj anatomy* of or near the temple or temples

temporal bone *n* either of two compound bones forming the sides of the skull

temporary *adj* lasting only for a short time; not permanent: *temporary accommodation* [Latin *temporarius*] ▷ **temporarily** *adv*

temporize *or* **-rise** *vb* **-rizing, -rized** *or* **-rising, -rised** to delay, act evasively, or protract a negotiation in order to gain time or avoid making a decision: *'Well, I temporized, 'I'll have to ask your mother'* **2** to adapt oneself to circumstances, as by temporary or apparent agreement [Latin *tempus* time]

tempt *vb* **1** to entice (someone) to do something, esp. something morally wrong or unwise: *can I tempt you to have another whisky?* **2** to allure or attract: *she was tempted by the glamour of a modelling career* **3** be tempted to want to do something while knowing it would be wrong or inappropriate to do so: *many youngsters are tempted to experiment with drugs* **4** tempt fate *or* providence to take foolish or unnecessary risks [Latin *temptare* to test] ▷ **tempter** *n* ▷ **temptress** *fem n*

temptation *n* **1** the act of tempting or the state of being tempted **2** a person or thing that tempts

tempting *adj* attractive or inviting: *it's tempting to say I told you so* ▷ **temptingly** *adv*

Temuco *n* a city in S Chile: agricultural trading centre. Pop: 287 000 (2005 est)

ten *n* **1** the cardinal number that is the sum of one and nine **2** a numeral, 10 or X, representing this number **3** something representing or consisting of ten units ▷ *adj* **4** amounting to ten: *ten years* [Old English *tēn*] ▷ **tenth** *adj, n*

tenable *adj* **1** able to be upheld or maintained: *a tenable strategy* **2** (of a job) intended to be held by a person for a particular length of time: *the post will be tenable for three years in the first instance* [Latin *tenere* to hold] ▷ **tenability** *n* ▷ **tenably** *adv*

tenacious *adj* **1** holding firmly: *a tenacious grasp* **2** stubborn or persistent: *tenacious support* [Latin *tenere* to hold] ▷ **tenaciously** *adv* ▷ **tenacity** *n*

tenancy *n, pl* **-cies** **1** the temporary possession or use of lands or property owned by somebody else, in return for payment **2** the period of holding or occupying such property

tenant *n* **1** a person who pays rent for the use of land or property **2** any holder or occupant [Old French: one who is holding]

tenant farmer *n* a person who farms land rented from somebody else

tenantry *n old-fashioned* tenants collectively

tench *n* a European freshwater game fish of the carp family [Old French *tenche*]

Ten Commandments *pl n Bible* the commandments given by God to Moses on Mount Sinai, summarizing the basic obligations of people towards God and their fellow humans

tend¹ *vb* to be inclined (to take a particular kind of action or to be in a particular condition) as a rule: *she tends to be rather absent-minded* [Latin *tendere* to stretch]

tend² *vb* **1** to take care of: *it is she who tends his wounds* **2** tend to to attend to: *excuse me, I have to tend to the other guests* [variant of *attend*]

tendency *n, pl* **-cies** **1** an inclination to act in a particular way **2** the general course or drift of something **3** a faction, esp. within a political party [Latin *tendere* to stretch]

tendentious *adj* expressing a particular viewpoint or opinion, esp. a controversial one, in very strong terms: *a somewhat tendentious reading of French history* ▷ **tendentiously** *adv*

tender¹ *adj* **1** (of cooked food) having softened and become easy to chew or cut **2** gentle and kind: *tender loving care* **3** vulnerable or sensitive: *at the tender age of 9* **4** painful when touched: *his wrist was swollen and tender* [Old French *tendre*] ▷ **tenderly** *adv* ▷ **tenderness** *n*

tender² *vb* **1** to present or offer: *he tendered his resignation* **2** to make a formal offer or estimate for a job or contract: *contractors tendering for government work* ▷ *n* **3** a formal offer to supply specified goods or services at a stated cost or rate: *the government invited tenders to run television and radio services* [Latin *tendere* to extend] ▷ **tenderer** *n* ▷ **tendering** *n*

tender³ *n* **1** a small boat that brings supplies to larger vessels in a port **2** a wagon attached to the rear of a steam locomotive that carries the fuel and water [variant of *attender*]

tenderfoot *n, pl* **-foots** *or* **-feet** a newcomer to a particular activity

tenderize *or* **-rise** *vb* **-rizing, -rized** *or* **-rising, -rised** to make (meat) tender, by pounding it or adding a substance to break down the fibres ▷ **tenderizer** *or* **-riser** *n*

tenderloin *n* a tender cut of pork from between the sirloin and ribs

tendon *n* a band of tough tissue that attaches a muscle to a bone [Medieval Latin *tendo*]

tendril *n* a threadlike leaf or stem by which a climbing plant attaches itself to a support [probably from Old French *tendron*]

Tendulkar n Sachin (Ramesh), born 1973, Indian cricketer: he played in 200 test matches (1989–2013) and was the first batsman to score 15,000 runs in tests (2011) and first to score 100 international centuries (2012)

Tenedos n an island in the NE Aegean, near the entrance to the Dardanelles: in Greek legend the base of the Greek fleet during the siege of Troy. Modern Turkish name: **Bozcaada**

tenement n a large building divided into several different flats [Latin *tenere* to hold]

Tenerife n a Spanish island in the Atlantic, off the NW coast of Africa: the largest of the Canary Islands; volcanic and mountainous; tourism and agriculture. Capital: Santa Cruz. Pop: 778 071 (2002 est). Area: 2058 sq km (795 sq miles)

tenet (ten-nit) n a principle on which a belief or doctrine is based [Latin, literally: he (it) holds]

tenfold adj **1** having ten times as many or as much **2** composed of ten parts ▷ adv **3** by ten times as many or as much

ten-gallon hat n (in the US) a cowboy's broad-brimmed felt hat with a very high crown

Tengri Nor n another name for **Nam Co**

Teniers n David, called the Elder, 1582–1649, and his son David, called the Younger, 1610–90, Flemish painters

Tenn. Tennessee

tenner n Brit, Austral and NZ informal **1** a ten-pound or ten-dollar note **2** the sum of ten pounds or ten dollars: it's worth a tenner at least

Tennessean n **1** a native or inhabitant of Tennessee ▷ adj **2** of or relating to Tennessee or its inhabitants

Tennessee n **1** a state of the E central US: consists of a plain in the west, rising to the Appalachians and the Cumberland Plateau in the east. Capital: Nashville. Pop: 5 841 748 (2003 est). Area: 109 412 sq km (42 244 sq miles). Abbreviation: **Tenn.**, (with zip code) **TN 2** a river in the E central US, flowing southwest from E Tennessee into N Alabama, then west and north to the Ohio River at Paducah: the longest tributary of the Ohio; includes a series of dams and reservoirs under the Tennessee Valley Authority. Length: 1049 km (652 miles)

Tenniel n Sir John, 1820–1914, English caricaturist, noted for his illustrations to Lewis Carroll's *Alice* books and for his political cartoons in *Punch* (1851–1901)

tennis n a game played between two players or pairs of players who use a racket to hit a ball to and fro over a net on a rectangular court. See also **lawn tennis**, **real tennis**, **table tennis** [probably from Anglo-French *tenetz* hold!]

tennis elbow n inflammation of the elbow, typically caused by exertion in playing tennis

Tennyson n Alfred, Lord Tennyson, 1809–92, English poet; poet laureate (1850–92). His poems include *The Lady of Shalott* (1832), *Morte d'Arthur* (1842), the collection *In Memoriam* (1850), *Maud* (1855), and *Idylls of the King* (1859) **›** Tennysonian adj, n

Teno n the Finnish name for **Tana** (3)

Tenochtitlán n an ancient city and capital of the Aztec empire on the present site of Mexico City; razed by Cortés in 1521

tenon n a projecting end of a piece of wood, formed to fit into a corresponding slot in another piece [Old French]

tenor n **1 a** the second highest male voice, between alto and baritone **b** a singer with such a voice **c** a saxophone, horn, or other musical instrument between the alto and baritone or bass **2** a general meaning or character: it was clear from the tenor of the meeting that the chairman's actions are very unpopular ▷ adj **3** denoting a musical instrument between alto and baritone: a tenor saxophone **4** of or relating to the second highest male voice: his voice lacks the range needed for the tenor role [Old French *tenour*]

tenpin bowling n a game in which players try to knock over ten skittles by rolling a ball at them

tense[1] adj **1** having, showing, or causing mental or emotional strain: the tense atmosphere **2** stretched tight: tense muscles ▷ vb **tensing, tensed 3** Also: tense up to make or become tense [Latin *tensus* taut] **›** tensely adv **›** tenseness n

tense[2] n grammar the form of a verb that indicates whether the action referred to in the sentence is located in the past, the present, or the future: 'ate' is the past tense of 'to eat' [Old French *tens* time]

tensile adj of or relating to tension or being stretched: The posts were linked by high tensile wire.

tensile strength n a measure of the ability of a material to withstand lengthwise stress, expressed as the greatest stress that the material can stand without breaking: the addition of linseed oil improved the tensile strength of the cricket bat

tension n **1** a situation or condition of hostility, suspense, or uneasiness: a renewed state of tension between old enemies **2** mental or emotional strain: nervous tension **3** a force that stretches or the state or degree of being stretched tight: keep tension on the line until the fish comes within range of the net **4** physics a force that tends to produce an elongation of a body or structure **5** physics voltage, electromotive force, or potential difference [Latin *tensio*]

tent n **1** a portable shelter made of canvas or other fabric supported on poles, stretched out, and fastened to the ground by pegs and ropes **2** See **oxygen tent** [Old French *tente*]

tentacle n **1** a flexible organ that grows near the mouth in many invertebrates and is used for feeding, grasping, etc. **2** tentacles the unseen methods by which an organization or idea, esp. a sinister one, influences people and events: the tentacles of the secret police [Latin *tentare* to feel] **›** tentacled adj

tentative adj **1** provisional or unconfirmed: a tentative agreement **2** hesitant, uncertain, or cautious: their rather tentative approach [Latin *tentare* to test] **›** tentatively adv **›** tentativeness n

tenterhooks pl n on tenterhooks in a state of tension or suspense [Latin *tentus* stretched + HOOK]

tenth adj, n See ten

tenuous adj insignificant or flimsy: there is only the most tenuous evidence for it [Latin *tenuis*] **›** tenuously adv

tenure n **1** the holding of an office or position **2** the length of time an office or position lasts **3** the holding of a teaching position at a university on a permanent basis **4** the legal right to live in a place or to use land or buildings for a period of time [Latin *tenere* to hold]

Tenzing Norgay n 1914–86, Nepalese mountaineer. With Sir Edmund Hillary, he was the first to reach the summit of Mount Everest (1953)

tepee or **teepee** (tee-pee) n a cone-shaped tent of animal skins, formerly used by American Indians [Sioux *tīpī*]

Tepic n a city in W central Mexico, capital of Nayarit state: agricultural, trading and processing centre. Pop: 341 000 (2005 est)

tepid adj **1** slightly warm **2** lacking enthusiasm: tepid applause [Latin *tepidus*] **›** tepidity n **›** tepidly adv

tequila n a Mexican alcoholic spirit distilled from the agave plant [after *Tequila*, district in Mexico]

tera- combining form denoting one million million (10^{12}): terameter [Greek *teras* monster]

terai n **1** (in India) a belt of marshy land at the foot of mountains, esp. at the foot of the Himalayas in N India **2** a felt hat with a wide brim worn in subtropical regions

teratology (terr-a-tol-a-jee) n the branch of medicine concerned with the development of physical abnormalities during the fetal or early embryonic stage [Greek *teras* monster + -LOGY]

Te Rauparaha n ?1768–1849, Māori warrior chief, head of the Ngāti Toa tribe and signatory to the **Treaty of Waitangi**; noted for his cunning and his prowess in battle, he is also credited with composing "Ka Mate", the All Blacks' usual pre-match haka

terbium n chem a soft silvery-grey element of the

lanthanide series of metals. Symbol: **Tb** [after *Ytterby*, Sweden, where discovered]

Ter Borch *or* **Terborch** *n* Gerard. 1617–81, Dutch genre and portrait painter

Terbrugghen *n* Hendrik. 1588–1629, Dutch painter of the Utrecht school, who specialized in religious subjects, for example the *Incredulity of St Thomas* and the *Calling of St Matthew*

Terceira *n* an island in the N Atlantic, in the Azores: NATO military air base. Pop: 55 833 (2001). Area: 397 sq km (153 sq miles)

tercentenary *or* **tercentennial** *adj* **1** marking a 300th anniversary ▷ *n, pl* **-tenaries** *or* **-tennials** **2** a 300th anniversary [Latin *ter* three times + CENTENARY]

teredo (ter-ree-doh) *n, pl* **-dos** *or* **-dines** (-din-eez) a marine mollusc that bores into and destroys submerged timber [Greek *terēdōn* wood-boring worm]

Terence *n* Latin name *Publius Terentius Afer*. ?190–159 BC, Roman comic dramatist. His six comedies, *Andria*, *Hecyra*, *Heauton Timoroumenos*, *Eunuchus*, *Phormio*, and *Adelphoe*, are based on Greek originals by Menander

Terengganu *n* a variant spelling of **Trengganu**

Teresa *or* **Theresa** *n* **1** Saint, known as *Teresa of Avila*. 1515–82, Spanish nun and mystic. She reformed the Carmelite order and founded 17 convents. Her writings include a spiritual autobiography and *The Way to Perfection*. Feast day: Oct 15 **2** Mother, original name *Agnes Gonxha Bojaxhiu*. 1910–97, Indian Roman Catholic missionary, born in Skopje, now in the Former Yugoslav Republic of Macedonia, of Albanian parents: noted for her work among the starving in Calcutta; Nobel peace prize 1979

Tereshkova *n* Valentina Vladimirovna. born 1937, Soviet cosmonaut; first woman in space (1963)

Teresina *n* an inland port in NE Brazil, capital of Piauí state, on the Parnaíba River: chief commercial centre of the Parnaíba valley. Pop: 895 000 (2005 est). Former name: **Therezina**

Terfel *n* Bryn, real name *Bryn Terfel Jones*. born 1965, Welsh bass baritone, noted for his performances in operas by Mozart and Wagner

tergiversate (tur-jiv-verse-ate) *vb* **-sating, -sated** *formal* **1** to be evasive or ambiguous **2** to change sides or loyalties [Latin *tergiversari* to turn one's back]
▷ **tergiversation** *n* ▷ **tergiversator** *n*

term *n* **1** a word or expression, esp. one used in a specialized field of knowledge: *he coined the term 'inferiority complex'* **2** a period of time: *a four-year prison term* **3** one of the periods of the year when a school, university, or college is open or a lawcourt holds sessions **4** the period of pregnancy when childbirth is imminent **5** *maths* any distinct quantity making up a fraction or proportion, or contained in a sequence, series, etc. **6** *logic* any of the three subjects or predicates occurring in a syllogism **7** full term the end of a specific period of time: *the agony of carrying the child to full term* ▷ *vb* **8** to name, call, or describe as being: *social workers tend to be termed lefties* ► See also **terms** [Latin *terminus* end]

termagant *n literary* an unpleasant, aggressive, and overbearing woman [earlier *Tervagaunt*, after an arrogant character in medieval mystery plays]

terminable *adj* capable of being terminated: *his terminable interest in the property* ▷ **terminability** *n*

terminal *adj* **1** (of an illness) ending in death **2** situated at an end, terminus, or boundary: *the terminal joints of the fingers* **3** *informal* extreme or severe: *terminal boredom* ▷ *n* **4** a place where vehicles, passengers, or goods begin or end a journey: *the ferry terminal* **5** a point at which current enters or leaves an electrical device **6** *computers* a device, usually a keyboard and a visual display unit, having input/output links with a computer [Latin *terminus* end]
▷ **terminally** *adv*

terminal velocity *n physics* the maximum velocity reached by a body falling under gravity through a

liquid or gas, esp. the atmosphere

terminate *vb* **-nating, -nated** **1** to bring or come to an end: *his flying career was terminated by this crash* **2** to put an end to (a pregnancy) by inducing an abortion **3** (of the route of a train, bus, etc.) to stop at a particular place and not go any further: *this train terminates at Leicester* [Latin *terminare* to set boundaries] ▷ **termination** *n*

terminology *n, pl* **-gies** the specialized words and expressions relating to a particular subject
▷ **terminological** *adj* ▷ **terminologist** *n*

terminus (term-in-nuss) *n, pl* **-ni** (-nye) *or* **-nuses** the station or town at one end of a railway line or bus route: *Vienna's Westbahnhof is the terminus for trains to France* [Latin: end]

termite *n* a whitish antlike insect of warm and tropical regions that destroys timber [New Latin *termites* white ants]

terms *pl n* **1** the actual language or mode of presentation used: *the test is carried out in plain non-engineering terms* **2** the conditions of an agreement **3** mutual relationship or standing of a specified nature: *he is on first-name terms with many of the directors* **4** come to terms with to learn to accept (an unpleasant or difficult situation) **5** in terms of as expressed by; with regard to: *he is the best cricketer we have got in fact in terms of pure ability*

tern *n* a gull-like sea bird with a forked tail and long narrow wings [Old Norse *therna*]

ternary *adj* **1** consisting of three items or groups of three items **2** *maths* (of a number system) to the base three [Latin *ternarius*]

Terni *n* an industrial city in central Italy, in Umbria: site of waterfalls created in Roman times. Pop: 105 018 (2001)

Ternopol *n* a town in W Ukraine, on the River Siret: formerly under Polish rule. Pop: 235 000 (2005 est). Polish name: **Tarnopol**

Terpsichore (turp-sick-or-ee) *n* Greek myth the Muse of dance

Terpsichorean (turp-sick-or-ee-an) *adj often facetious* of or relating to dancing [from TERPSICHORE]

Terr. **1** terrace **2** territory

terrace *n* **1** a row of houses, usually identical and joined together by common dividing walls, or the street onto which they face **2** a paved area alongside a building **3** a horizontal flat area of ground, often one of a series in a slope **4** the terraces *or* terracing *Brit and NZ* a tiered area in a stadium where spectators stand ▷ *vb* **-racing, -raced** **5** to make into terraces [Latin *terra* earth]

terraced house *n Brit* a house that is part of a terrace

terracotta *n* **1** a hard unglazed brownish-red earthenware used for pottery ▷ *adj* **2** made of terracotta **3** brownish-orange [Italian, literally: baked earth]

terra firma *n* the ground, as opposed to the sea [Latin]

terraforming *n* planetary engineering designed to enhance the capacity of an extraterrestrial planetary environment to sustain life [Latin *terra* earth]

terrain *n* an area of ground, esp. with reference to its physical character: *mountainous terrain* [Latin *terra* earth]

terra incognita (terr-a in-kog-nit-a) *n* an unexplored region [Latin]

terrapin *n* a small turtle-like reptile of N America that lives in fresh water and on land [from a Native American language]

terrarium *n* **1** an enclosed area or container where small land animals are kept **2** a glass container in which plants are grown [Latin *terra* earth]

terrazzo *n, pl* **-zos** a floor made by setting marble chips into a layer of mortar and polishing the surface [Italian: terrace]

Terre Adélie *n* the French name for **Adélie Land**

terrestrial *adj* **1** of the planet earth **2** of the land as opposed to the sea or air **3** (of animals and plants) living or growing on the land **4** *television* denoting or using a signal sent over land from a transmitter on land, rather than by satellite [Latin *terra* earth]

t

terrible *adj* **1** very serious or extreme: *war is a terrible thing* **2** *informal* very bad, unpleasant, or unsatisfactory: *terrible books* **3** causing fear [Latin *terribilis*] **> terribly** *adv*

terrier *n* any of several small active breeds of dog, originally trained to hunt animals living underground [Old French *chien terrier* earth dog]

terrific *adj* **1** very great or intense: *a terrific blow on the head* **2** *informal* very good; excellent: *a terrific book* [Latin *terrere* to frighten] **> terrifically** *adv*

terrify *vb* **-fies, -fying, -fied** to frighten greatly [Latin *terrificare*] **> terrified** *adj* **> terrifying** *adj* **> terrifyingly** *adv*

terrine (terr-**reen**) *n* **1** an oval earthenware cooking dish with a tightly fitting lid **2** the food cooked or served in such a dish, esp. pâté [French]

territorial *adj* **1** of or relating to a territory or territories **2** of or concerned with the ownership and control of an area of land or water: *a territorial dispute* **3** (of an animal or bird) establishing and defending an area which it will not let other animals or birds into: *the baboon is a territorial species* **4** of or relating to a territorial army **> territorially** *adv* **> territoriality** *n*

Territorial *n* a member of a Territorial Army

Territorial Army *n* (in Britain) a reserve army whose members are not full-time soldiers but undergo military training in their spare time so that they can be called upon in an emergency

territorial waters *pl n* the part of the sea near to a country's coast, which is under the control of the government of that country

territory *n, pl* **-ries 1** any tract of land; district: *mountainous territory* **2** the geographical area under the control of a particular government: *the islands are Japanese territory* **3** an area inhabited and defended by a particular animal or pair of animals **4** an area of knowledge or experience: *all this is familiar territory to readers of her recent novels* **5** a country or region under the control of a foreign country: *a French Overseas Territory* **6** a region of a country, esp. of a federal state, that enjoys less autonomy and a lower status than most constituent parts of the state [Latin *territorium* land surrounding a town]

Territory *n* the Territory *Austral* See **Northern Territory**

terror *n* **1** very great fear, panic, or dread **2** a person or thing that inspires great dread **3** *Brit, Austral and NZ informal* a troublesome person, esp. a child [Latin]

terrorism *n* the systematic use of violence and intimidation to achieve political ends **> terrorist** *n, adj*

terrorize *or* **-rise** *vb* **-rizing, -rized** *or* **-rising, -rised 1** to control or force (someone) to do something by violence, fear, threats, etc.: *he was terrorized into withdrawing his accusations* **2** to make (someone) very frightened **> terrorization** *or* **-risation** *n* **> terrorizer** *or* **-riser** *n*

terry *n* a fabric covered on both sides with small uncut loops, used for towelling and nappies [origin unknown]

Terry *n* **1** Dame **Ellen**. 1847–1928, British actress, noted for her Shakespearean roles opposite Sir Henry Irving and for her correspondence with George Bernard Shaw **2** (**John**) **Quinlan**. born 1937, British architect, noted for his works in neoclassical style, such as the Richmond riverside project (1984)

terse *adj* **1** neatly brief and concise **2** curt or abrupt [Latin *tersus* precise] **> tersely** *adv* **> terseness** *n*

tertiary (**tur**-shar-ee) *adj* **1** third in degree, order, etc. **2** (of education) at university or college level **3** (of an industry) involving services, such as transport and financial services, as opposed to manufacture [Latin *tertius*]

Tertiary *adj geology* of the period of geological time lasting from about 65 million years ago to 600 000 years ago

Tertullian *n* Latin name *Quintus Septimius Florens Tertullianus*. ?160–?220 AD, Carthaginian Christian theologian, who wrote in Latin rather than Greek and originated much of Christian terminology

Teruel *n* a city in E central Spain: 15th-century cathedral; scene of fierce fighting during the Spanish Civil War. Pop: 32 304 (2003 est)

Terylene *n trademark* a synthetic polyester fibre or fabric

TESL Teaching of English as a Second Language

Tesla *n* **Nikola**. 1857–1943, US electrical engineer and inventor, born in Smiljan, now in Croatia. His inventions include a transformer, generators, and dynamos

tessellated *adj* paved or inlaid with a mosaic of small tiles [Latin *tessellatus* checked]

tessera *n, pl* **-serae** a small square tile used in mosaics [Latin]

Tessin *n* the German name for **Ticino**

test[1] *vb* **1** to try (something) out to ascertain its worth, safety, or endurance: *the company has never tested its products on animals* **2** to carry out an examination on (a substance, material, or system) in order to discover whether a particular substance, component, or feature is present: *baby foods are regularly tested for pesticides* **3** to put under severe strain: *the long delay tested my patience* **4** to achieve a result in a test which indicates the presence or absence of something: *he tested positive for cocaine* ▷ *n* **5** a method, practice, or examination designed to test a person or thing **6** a series of questions or problems designed to test a specific skill or knowledge: *a spelling test* **7** a chemical reaction or physical procedure for testing the composition or other qualities of a substance **8** *sport* short for **Test match 9 put to the test** to use (something) in order to gauge its usefulness or effectiveness [Latin *testum* earthen vessel] **> testable** *adj* **> testing** *adj*

test[2] *n* the hard outer covering of certain invertebrates [Latin *testa* shell]

testa (**tess**-ta) *n, pl* **-tae** (-tee) the hard outer layer of a seed [Latin: shell]

testaceous (test-**ay**-shuss) *adj biology* of or having a hard continuous shell [Latin *testacens*, from TESTA]

testament *n* **1** something which provides proof of a fact about someone or something: *the size of the audience was an immediate testament to his appeal* **2** *law* a formal statement of how a person wants his or her property to be disposed of after his or her death: *last will and testament* [Latin *testis* a witness] **> testamentary** *adj*

Testament *n* either of the two main parts of the Bible, the Old Testament or the New Testament

testate *law adj* **1** having left a legally valid will at death ▷ *n* **2** a person who dies and leaves a legally valid will [Latin *testari* to make a will] **> testacy** *n*

testator (test-**tay**-tor) *or fem* **testatrix** (test-**tay**-triks) *n law* a person who has made a will, esp. one who has died testate

test card *n* a complex pattern used to test the characteristics of a television transmission system

test case *n* a legal action that serves as a precedent in deciding similar succeeding cases

testicle *n* either of the two male reproductive glands, in most mammals enclosed within the scrotum, that produce spermatozoa [Latin *testis* a witness (to masculinity)]

testify *vb* **-fies, -fying, -fied 1** *law* to declare or give evidence under oath, esp. in court **2 testify to** to be evidence of: *a piece of paper testifying to their educational qualifications* [Latin *testis* witness]

testimonial *n* **1** a recommendation of the character or worth of a person or thing **2** a tribute given for services or achievements ▷ *adj* **3** of a testimony or testimonial: *a testimonial match*

> **USAGE** *Testimonial* is sometimes wrongly used where *testimony* is meant: *his re-election is a testimony* (not *a testimonial*) *to his popularity with his constituents.*

testimony *n, pl* **-nies 1** a declaration of truth or fact **2** *law* evidence given by a witness, esp. in court under oath **3** evidence proving or supporting something: *that* *they are still talking is a testimony to their 20-year friendship* [Latin *testimonium*]

testis *n*, *pl* **-tes** same as **testicle**

Test match *n* (in various sports, esp. cricket) an international match, esp. one of a series

testosterone *n* a steroid male sex hormone secreted by the testes

test paper *n* **1** the question sheet of a test **2** *chem* paper impregnated with an indicator for use in chemical tests

test pilot *n* a pilot who flies aircraft of new design to test their performance in the air

test tube *n* a cylindrical round-bottomed glass tube open at one end, which is used in scientific experiments

test-tube baby *n* **1** a fetus that has developed from an ovum fertilized in an artificial womb **2** a baby conceived by artificial insemination

testy *adj* **-tier, -tiest** irritable or touchy [Anglo-Norman *testif* headstrong] **> testily** *adv* **> testiness** *n*

tetanus *n* an acute infectious disease in which toxins released from a bacterium cause muscular spasms and convulsions [Greek *tetanos*]

tetchy *adj* **tetchier, tetchiest** cross, irritable, or touchy [probably from obsolete *tetch* defect] **> tetchily** *adv* **> tetchiness** *n*

tête-à-tête *n*, *pl* **-têtes** or **-tête 1** a private conversation between two people **> adv 2** together in private: *they dined tête-à-tête* [French, literally: head to head]

tether *n* **1** a rope or chain for tying an animal to a fence, post, etc., so that it cannot move away from a particular place **2 at the end of one's tether** at the limit of one's patience or endurance **> vb 3** to tie with a tether [Old Norse *tjóthr*]

Tethys *n* the sea that lay between Laurasia and Gondwanaland, the two supercontinents formed by the first split of the larger supercontinent Pangaea. The Tethys Sea can be regarded as the predecessor of today's smaller Mediterranean

Teton Range *n* a mountain range in the N central US, mainly in NW Wyoming. Highest peak: Grand Teton, 4196 m (13 766 ft)

tetra- *combining form* four: *tetrapod*

tetrad *n* a group or series of four [Greek *tetras*]

tetraethyl lead *n* a colourless oily insoluble liquid used in petrol to prevent knocking

tetragon *n* a shape with four angles and four sides [Greek *tetragōnon*] **> tetragonal** *adj*

tetrahedron (tet-ra-heed-ron) *n*, *pl* **-drons** or **-dra** a solid figure with four triangular plane faces [Late Greek *tetraedron*] **> tetrahedral** *adj*

tetralogy *n*, *pl* **-gies** a series of four related books, dramas, operas, etc. [Greek *tetralogia*]

tetrameter (tet-tram-it-er) *n* **1** *prosody* a line of verse consisting of four metrical feet **2** a verse consisting of such lines [Greek *tetra-* four + METER]

Tetrazzini *n* Luisa. 1871–1940, Italian coloratura soprano

Tetuán *n* a city in N Morocco: capital of Spanish Morocco (1912–56). Pop: 499 000 (2003)

Tetzel *or* **Tezel** *n* Johann. ?1465–1519, German Dominican monk. His preaching on papal indulgences provoked Luther's 95 theses at Wittenberg (1517)

Teutoburger Wald *n* a low wooded mountain range in N Germany: possible site of the annihilation of three Roman legions by Germans under Arminius in 9 AD

Teuton (tew-tun) *n* **1** a member of an ancient Germanic people of N Europe **2** a member of any people speaking a Germanic language, esp. a German **> adj 3** Teutonic [Latin *Teutoni* the Teutons]

Teutonic (tew-tonn-ik) *adj* **1** characteristic of or relating to the Germans **2** of the ancient Teutons

Tevere *n* the Italian name for the Tiber

Tevez *n* Carlos (**Alberto**). born 1984, Argentinian footballer; played for Manchester United (2007–09, Manchester City (2009–2013), and Juventus from 2013

Te Waipounamu *n* a Māori name for New Zealand's South Island [Māori, literally: water and greenstone, from the presence of this stone on the South Island]

Tewkesbury *n* a town in W England, in N Gloucestershire at the confluence of the Rivers Severn and Avon: scene of a decisive battle (1471) of the Wars of the Roses in which the Yorkists defeated the Lancastrians; 12th-century abbey. Pop: 9978 (2001)

Tex. 1 Texan **2** Texas

Texan *n* **1 a** native or inhabitant of Texas **> adj 2** of or relating to Texas or its inhabitants

Texas *n* a state of the southwestern US, on the Gulf of Mexico: the second largest state; part of Mexico from 1821 to 1836, when it was declared an independent republic; joined the US in 1845; consists chiefly of a plain, with a wide flat coastal belt rising up to the semiarid Sacramento and Davis Mountains of the southwest; a major producer of cotton, rice, and livestock; the chief US producer of oil and gas; a leading world supplier of sulphur. Capital: Austin. Pop: 22 118 509 (2003 est). Area: 678 927 sq km (262 134 sq miles). Abbreviation: **Tex.**, (with zip code) **TX**

Tex-Mex *adj* **1** combining elements of Texan and Mexican culture **> n 2** Tex-Mex music or cooking

text *n* **1** the main body of a printed or written work as distinct from items such as notes or illustrations **2** any written material, such as words displayed on a visual display unit **3** the written version of the words of a speech, broadcast, or recording: *an advance text of the remarks the president will deliver tonight* **4** a short passage of the Bible used as a starting point for a sermon **5** a book required as part of a course of study: *shelves full of sociology texts* **> vb 6** to send (a text message) by mobile phone **7** to contact (a person) by means of a text message [Latin *texere* to compose]

textbook *n* **1** a book of facts about a subject used by someone who is studying that subject **> adj 2** perfect or exemplary: *a textbook example of an emergency descent*

textile *n* **1** any fabric or cloth, esp. a woven one **> adj 2** of or relating to fabrics or their production: *the world textile market* [Latin *textilis* woven]

text message *n* **1** a message sent in text form, esp. by means of a mobile phone **2** a message appearing on a computer screen **> text messaging** *n*

textual *adj* of, based on, or relating to, a text or texts **> textually** *adv*

texture *n* **1** the structure, appearance, and feel of a substance: *curtains of many textures and colours* **2** the overall sound of a piece of music, resulting from the way the different instrumental parts in it are combined: *a big orchestra weaving rich textures* **> vb -turing, -tured 3** to give a distinctive texture to (something) [Latin *texere* to weave] **> textural** *adj*

Teyde *n* a variant spelling of **Teide**

TGV *n* (in France) a high-speed passenger train [French *train à grande vitesse*]

TGWU (in Britain) Transport and General Workers Union

Th *chem* thorium

Thabana-Ntlenyana *n* a mountain in Lesotho: the highest peak of the Drakensberg Mountains. Height: 3482 m (11 425 ft). Also called: **Thadentsonyane**, **Thabantshonyana**

Thackeray *n* William Makepeace. 1811–63, English novelist, born in India. His novels, originally serialized, include *Vanity Fair* (1848), *Pendennis* (1850), *Henry Esmond* (1852), and *The Newcomes* (1855)

Thadentsonyane *n* another name for **Thabana-Ntlenyana**

Thai *adj* **1** of or relating to Thailand or its inhabitants **> n 2** (*pl* **Thais** *or* **Thai**) a native or inhabitant of Thailand **3** the main language of Thailand

Thailand *n* **1 a** kingdom in SE Asia, on the Andaman Sea and the Gulf of Thailand: united as a kingdom in 1350 and became a major SE Asian power; consists chiefly of a central plain around the Chao Phraya river system, mountains rising over 2400 m (8000 ft) in the northwest, and rainforest the length of the S peninsula. Parts of the SW coast suffered badly in the Indian Ocean tsunami of December 2004. Official language: Thai. Official religion: (Hinayana) Buddhist. Currency: baht. Capital: Bangkok. Pop: 67 448 120 (2013 est). Area: 513 998 sq km (198 455 sq miles). Former name (until 1939 and 1945–49): **Siam** **2 Gulf of Thailand** an arm of the South China Sea between the Malay Peninsula and Indochina. Former name: **Gulf of Siam**

Thaïs *n* 4th-century BC Athenian courtesan; mistress of Alexander the Great

Thales *n* ?624–?546 BC, Greek philosopher, mathematician, and astronomer, born in Miletus. He held that water was the origin of all things and he predicted the solar eclipse of May 28, 585 BC

Thalia *n Greek myth* the Muse of comedy

thalidomide (thal-lid-oh-mide) *n* a drug formerly used as a sedative and hypnotic but withdrawn from use when found to cause abnormalities in developing fetuses [thali(mi)do(glutari)mide]

thallium *n chem* a soft highly toxic white metallic element. Symbol: Tl [Greek *thallos* a green shoot; from the green line in its spectrum]

Thames *n* **1** a river in S England, rising in the Cotswolds in several headstreams and flowing generally east through London to the North Sea by a large estuary. Length: 346 km (215 miles). Ancient name: **Tamesis** **2** a river in SE Canada, in Ontario, flowing south to London, then southwest to Lake St Clair. Length: 217 km (135 miles)

than *conj, prep* **1** used to introduce the second element of a comparison, the first element of which expresses difference: *men are less observant than women and children* **2** used to state a number, quantity, or value in approximate terms by contrasting it with another number, quantity, or value: *temperatures lower than 25 degrees* **3** used after the adverbs *rather* and *sooner* to introduce a rejected alternative: *fruit is examined by hand, rather than by machine* [Old English *thanne*]

> **USAGE** In formal English, *than* is usually regarded as a conjunction governing an unexpressed verb: *he does it far better than I (do)*. The case of any pronoun therefore depends on whether it is the subject or object of the unexpressed verb: *she likes him more than I (like him); she likes him more than (she likes) me*. However in ordinary speech and writing *than* is usually treated as a preposition and is followed by the object form of a pronoun: *my brother is younger than me*.

thane *n* **1** (in Anglo-Saxon England) a nobleman who held land from the king or from a superior nobleman in return for certain services **2** (in medieval Scotland) a person of rank holding land from the king [Old English *thegn*]

Thanet *n* **Isle of Thanet** an island in SE England, in NE Kent, separated from the mainland by two branches of the River Stour: scene of many Norse invasions. Area: 109 sq km (42 sq miles)

Thanjavur *n* a city in SE India, in E Tamil Nadu: headquarters of the earliest Protestant missions in India. Pop: 215 725 (2001). Former name: **Tanjore**

thank *vb* **1** to convey feelings of gratitude to: *he thanked the nursing staff for saving his life* **2** to hold responsible: *he has his father to thank for his familiarity with the film world* **3 thank you** a polite response or expression of gratitude **4 thank goodness, thank heavens** or **thank God** an exclamation of relief [Old English *thancian*]

thankful *adj* grateful and appreciative ⟩ **thankfully** *adv*

thankless *adj* unrewarding or unappreciated: *she took on the thankless task of organizing the office Xmas lunch* ⟩ **thanklessly** *adv* ⟩ **thanklessness** *n*

thanks *pl n* **1** an expression of appreciation or gratitude **2 thanks to** because of: *the birth went very smoothly, thanks to the help of the GHQ medical officer* ▷ *interj* **3** *informal* an exclamation expressing gratitude

thanksgiving *n* a formal public expression of thanks to God

Thanksgiving Day *n* (in North America) an annual holiday celebrated on the fourth Thursday of November in the United States and on the second Monday of October in Canada

Thant *n* U. 1909–74, Burmese diplomat; secretary-general of the United Nations (1962–71)

Thapsus *n* an ancient town near Carthage in North Africa: site of Caesar's victory over Pompey in 46 BC

Thar Desert *n* a desert in NW India, mainly in NW Rajasthan state and extending into Pakistan. Area: over 260 000 sq km (100 000 sq miles). Also called: **Indian Desert, Great Indian Desert**

Tharp *n* Twyla. born 1941, US choreographer, whose work fuses classical ballet with modern dance

Thásos *n* a Greek island in the N Aegean: colonized by Greeks from Paros in the 7th century BC as a gold-mining centre; under Turkish rule (1455–1912). Pop: 13 761 (2001). Area: 379 sq km (146 sq miles)

that *adj* **1** used preceding a noun that has been mentioned or is already familiar: *he'd have to give up on that idea* **2** used preceding a noun that denotes something more remote: *that book on the top shelf* ▷ *pron* **3** used to denote something already mentioned or understood: *that's right* **4** used to denote a more remote person or thing: *is that him over there?* **5** used to introduce a restrictive relative clause: *a problem that has to be overcome* **6 and all that** or **and that** *informal* and similar or related things: *import cutting and all that* **7 that is a** to be precise **b** in other words **8 that's that** there is no more to be said or done ▷ *conj* **9** used to introduce a noun clause: *he denied that the country was suffering from famine* **10** used, usually after *so*, to introduce a clause of purpose: *he turns his face away from her so that she shall not see his tears* **11** used to introduce a clause of result: *a scene so sickening and horrible that it is impossible to describe it* ▷ *adv* **12** Also: **all that** *informal* very or particularly: *the fines imposed have not been that large* [Old English *thæt*]

> **USAGE** Precise writers maintain a distinction between *that* and *which*: *that* is used as a relative pronoun in restrictive clauses and *which* in nonrestrictive clauses. In *the book that is on the table is mine*, the clause *that is on the table* is used to distinguish one particular book (the one on the table) from another or others (which may be anywhere, but not on the table). In *the book, which is on the table, is mine*, the *which* clause is merely descriptive or incidental. The more formal the level of language, the more important it is to preserve the distinction between the two relative pronouns; but in informal or colloquial usage, the words are often used interchangeably.

thatch *n* **1** Also called: **thatching** a roofing material that consists of straw or reeds **2** a roof made of such a material **3** a mass of thick untidy hair on someone's head ▷ *vb* **4** to cover with thatch [Old English *theccan* to cover] ⟩ **thatched** *adj* ⟩ **thatcher** *n*

Thatcher *n* Margaret (Hilda), Baroness (née *Roberts*). 1925–2013, British stateswoman; leader of the Conservative Party (1975–90); prime minister (1979–90)

thaw *vb* **1** to melt or cause to melt: *snow thawing in the gutter* **2** (of frozen food) to become or cause to become unfrozen; defrost **3** (of weather) to be warm enough to cause ice or snow to melt: *it's not freezing, it's thawing again* **4** to become more relaxed or friendly: *only with Llewelyn did he thaw, let his defences down* ▷ *n* **5** the act or process of thawing **6** a spell of relatively warm weather, causing snow or ice to melt [Old English *thawian*]

THC tetrahydrocannabidinol: the active ingredient in cannabis which gives it its narcotic effect

the¹ *adj (definite article)* **1** used preceding a noun that has been previously specified or is a matter of common knowledge: *those involved in the search* **2** used to indicate a particular person or object: *the man called Frank turned to look at it* **3** used preceding certain nouns associated with one's culture, society, or community: *to comply with the law* **4** used preceding an adjective that is functioning as a collective noun: *the unemployed* **5** used preceding titles and certain proper nouns: *the Middle East* **6** used preceding an adjective or noun in certain names or titles: *Alexander the Great* **7** used preceding a noun to make it refer to its class as a whole: *cultivation of the coca plant* **8** used instead of *my, your, her,* etc., with parts of the body: *swelling of tissues in the brain* **9** the best or most remarkable: *it's THE place in town for good Mexican food* [Old English *thē*]

the² *adv* used in front of each of two things which are being compared to show how they increase or decrease in relation to each other: *the smaller the baby, the lower its chances of survival* [Old English *thē, thŷ*]

theatre *or US* **theater** *n* **1** a building designed for the performance of plays, operas, etc. **2** a large room or hall with tiered seats for an audience: *a lecture theatre* **3** a room in a hospital equipped for surgical operations **4** the theatre drama and acting in general **5** a region in which a war or conflict takes place: *a potential theatre of war close to Russian borders* **6** *US, Austral and NZ* same as **cinema** (1) [Greek *theatron*]

theatrical *adj* **1** of or relating to the theatre or dramatic performances **2** exaggerated and affected in manner or behaviour **>** **theatricality** *n* **>** **theatrically** *adv*

theatricals *pl n* dramatic performances, esp. as given by amateurs

Thebaic *adj* **1** of or relating to the ancient Greek city of Thebes or its inhabitants **2** of or relating to the ancient Egyptian city of Thebes or its inhabitants

Thebaid *n* the territory around ancient Thebes in Egypt, or sometimes around Thebes in Greece

Theban *adj* **1** of or relating to the ancient Greek city of Thebes or its inhabitants **2** of or relating to the ancient Egyptian city of Thebes or its inhabitants **▷** *n* **3** a native or inhabitant of Thebes

Thebes *n* **1** (in ancient Greece) the chief city of Boeotia, destroyed by Alexander the Great (336 BC) **2** (in ancient Egypt) a city on the Nile: at various times capital of Upper Egypt or of the entire country

thee *pron old-fashioned* the objective form of **thou¹**

theft *n* **1** the act or an instance of stealing: *he reported the theft of his passport* **2** the crime of stealing: *he had a number of convictions for theft* [Old English *thēofth*]

Theiler *n* Max. 1899–1972, US virologist, born in South Africa, who developed a vaccine against yellow fever. Nobel prize for physiology or medicine 1951

their *adj* of or associated with them: *owning their own land; two girls on their way to school* [Old Norse *theira*]

> **USAGE** See at they.

theirs *pron* **1** something or someone belonging to or associated with them: *it was his fault, not theirs* **2** of theirs belonging to them

theism (thee-iz-zum) *n* **1** belief in one God as the creator of everything in the universe **2** belief in the existence of a God or gods [Greek *theos* god] **>** **theist** *n, adj* **>** **theistic** *adj*

them *pron (objective)* refers to things or people other than the speaker or people addressed: *I want you to give this to them* [Old English *thāem*]

> **USAGE** See at me, they.

theme *n* **1** the main idea or topic in a discussion or

lecture **2** (in literature, music, or art) an idea, image, or motif, repeated or developed throughout a work or throughout an artist's career **3** *music* a group of notes forming a recognizable melodic unit, used as the basis of part or all of a composition **4** a short essay, esp. one set as an exercise for a student [Greek *thema*] **>** **thematic** *adj* **>** **thematically** *adv*

theme park *n* an area planned as a leisure attraction in which all the displays and activities are based on a particular theme, story, or idea: *a Wild West theme park*

theme tune *or* **theme song** *n* a tune or song used to introduce or identify a television or radio programme or performer

Themistocles *n* ?527–?460 BC, Athenian statesman, who was responsible for the Athenian victory against the Persians at Salamis (480). He was ostracized in 470

themselves *pron* **1 a** the reflexive form of *they* or *them*: *two men barricaded themselves into a cell* **b** used for emphasis: *among the targets were police officers themselves* **2** their normal or usual selves: *they don't seem themselves these days*

then *adv* **1** at that time: *he was then at the height of his sporting career* **2** after that: *let's eat first and then we can explore the town* **3** in that case: *then why did he work for you?* **▷** *pron* **4** that time: *since then the list of grievances has steadily grown* **▷** *adj* **5** existing or functioning at that time: *the then Defence Minister* [Old English *thænne, thanne*]

thence *adv formal* **1** from that place: *the train went south into Switzerland, and thence on to Italy* **2** for that reason; therefore [Middle English *thannes*]

thenceforth *or* **thenceforward** *adv formal* from that time on

theocracy *n, pl* **-cies** **1** government by a god or by priests **2** a community under such government [Greek *theos* god + *kratos* power] **>** **theocrat** *n* **>** **theocratic** *adj* **>** **theocratically** *adv*

Theocritus *n* ?310–?250 BC, Greek poet, born in Syracuse. He wrote the first pastoral poems in Greek literature and was closely imitated by Virgil **>** **Theocritan** *or* **Theocritean** *adj, n*

theodolite (thee-odd-oh-lite) *n* an instrument used in surveying for measuring horizontal and vertical angles [origin unknown]

Theodora *n* ?500–548 AD, Byzantine empress; wife and counsellor of Justinian I

Theodorakis *n* Mikis. born 1925, Greek composer, who wrote the music for the films *Zorba the Greek* (1965) and *Serpico* (1973): imprisoned (1967–70) for his opposition to the Greek military government

Theodore I *n* called *Lascaris*. ?1175–1222, Byzantine ruler, who founded a Byzantine state in exile at Nicaea after Constantinople fell to the Crusaders (1204)

Theodoric *or* **Theoderic** *n* called *the Great*. ?454–526 AD, king of the Ostrogoths and founder of the Ostrogothic kingdom in Italy after his murder of Odoacer (493)

Theodosius I *n* called *the Great*. ?346–395 AD, Roman emperor of the Eastern Roman Empire (379–95) and of the Western Roman Empire (392–95)

theologian *n* a person versed in the study of theology

theology *n, pl* **-gies** **1** the systematic study of religions and religious beliefs **2** a specific system, form, or branch of this study: *Muslim theology* [Greek *theos* god + -LOGY] **>** **theological** *adj* **>** **theologically** *adv*

Theophilus *n* died 842 AD, Byzantine emperor (829–42); a patron of learning and supporter of iconoclasm

Theophrastus *n* ?372–?287 BC, Greek Peripatetic philosopher, noted esp. for his *Characters*, a collection of sketches of moral types

theorem *n* a proposition, esp. in maths, that can be proved by reasoning from the basic principles of a subject [Greek *theōrein* to view]

theoretical *or* **theoretic** *adj* **1** based on or concerned with the ideas and abstract principles relating to a particular subject rather than its practical uses: *theoretical physics* **2** existing in theory but perhaps not in reality: *the secret service is under the theoretical control of the government* **>** **theoretically** *adv*

theoretician *n* a person who develops or studies the theory of a subject rather than its practical aspects

theorize *or* **-rise** *vb* **-rizing, -rized** *or* **-rising, -rised** to produce or use theories; speculate **>** **theorist** *n*

theory *n, pl* **-ries 1** a set of ideas, based on evidence and careful reasoning, which offers an explanation of how something works or why something happens, but has not been completely proved: *the theory of cosmology* **2** the ideas and abstract knowledge relating to something: *political theory* **3** an idea or opinion: *it's only a theory, admittedly, but I think it's worth pursuing* **4** **in theory** in an ideal or abstract situation: *in theory, the tax is supposed to limit inflation* [Greek *theōria* a sight]

theosophy *n* a religious or philosophical system claiming to be based on an intuitive insight into the divine nature [Greek *theos* god + *sophia* wisdom] **>** **theosophical** *adj* **>** **theosophist** *n*

Thera *n* a Greek island in the Aegean Sea, in the Cyclades: site of a Minoan settlement and of the volcano that ended Minoan civilization on Crete. Pop: 13 402 (2001). Also called: **Santoríni**. Modern Greek name: **Thíra**

therapeutic (ther-rap-pew-tik) *adj* of or relating to the treatment and cure of disease [Greek *therapeuein* to minister to] **>** **therapeutically** *adv*

therapeutics *n* the branch of medicine concerned with the treatment of disease

therapy *n, pl* **-pies** the treatment of physical, mental, or social disorders or disease [Greek *therapeia* attendance] **>** **therapist** *n*

there *adv* **1** in, at, or to that place or position: *he won't be there* **2** in that respect: *you're right there* **3** **there and then** immediately and without delay: *he walked out there and then* ▷ *adj* **4** **not all there** *informal* mentally defective or silly ▷ *pron* **5** that place: *to return from there* **6** used as a grammatical subject when the true subject follows the verb, esp. the verb 'to be': *there are no children in the house* **7** **so there!** an exclamation, used esp. by children, that usually follows a declaration of refusal or defiance: *you can't come, so there!* **8** **there you are** *or* **go a** an expression used when handing a person something **b** an exclamation of satisfaction or vindication ▷ *interj* **9** an expression of sympathy, for example when consoling a child: *there, there, pet!* [Old English *thǣr*]

> USAGE In correct usage, the verb should agree with the number of the subject in such constructions as *there is a man waiting* and *there are several people waiting*. However, where the subject is compound, it is common in speech to use the singular as in *there's a police car and an ambulance outside*.

thereabouts *or* US **thereabout** *adv* near that place, time, amount, etc.: *meet me at three o'clock or thereabouts*; *Methuselah lived 900 years or thereabouts*

thereafter *adv formal* from that time onwards

thereby *adv formal* by that means or consequently

therefore *adv* for that reason: *the training is long, and therefore expensive*

therein *adv formal* in or into that place or thing

thereof *adv formal* of or concerning that or it

Thérèse de Lisieux *n* Saint, known as *the Little Flower of Jesus*. 1873–97, French Carmelite nun, noted for her autobiography, *The Story of a Soul* (1897). Feast day: Oct 3

thereto *adv formal* **1** to that or it **2** Also: **thereunto** in addition to that

thereupon *adv formal* immediately after that; at that point

Therezina *n* the former name of **Teresina**

therm *n* Brit a unit of heat equal to $1.055\ 056 \times 10^8$ joules [Greek *thermē* heat]

thermal *adj* **1** of, caused by, or generating heat **2** hot or warm: *thermal springs* **3** (of garments) specially made so as

to have exceptional heat-retaining qualities: *thermal underwear* ▷ *n* **4** a column of rising air caused by uneven heating of the land surface, and used by gliders and birds to gain height

thermionic valve *or especially US and Canad* **thermionic tube** *n* an electronic valve in which electrons are emitted from a heated rather than a cold cathode

thermistor (therm-**mist**-or) *n physics* a metal-oxide rod whose resistance falls as temperature rises, used in electronic circuits and as a thermometer

thermocouple *n* a device for measuring temperature, consisting of a pair of wires of different metals joined at both ends

thermodynamics *n* the branch of physical science concerned with the relationship between heat and other forms of energy

thermoelectric *or* **thermoelectrical** *adj* of or relating to the conversion of heat energy to electrical energy

thermometer *n* an instrument used to measure temperature, esp. one in which a thin column of liquid, such as mercury, expands and contracts within a sealed tube marked with a temperature scale

thermonuclear *adj* **1** (of a nuclear reaction) involving a nuclear fusion reaction of a type which occurs at very high temperatures **2** (of a weapon) giving off energy as the result of a thermonuclear reaction **3** involving thermonuclear weapons

thermoplastic *adj* **1** (of a material, esp. a synthetic plastic) becoming soft when heated and rehardening on cooling ▷ *n* **2** a synthetic plastic or resin, such as polystyrene

Thermopylae *n* (in ancient Greece) a narrow pass between the mountains and the sea linking Locris and Thessaly: a defensible position on a traditional invasion route from N Greece; scene of a famous battle (480 BC) in which a greatly outnumbered Greek army under Leonidas fought to the death to delay the advance of the Persians during their attempted conquest of Greece

Thermos *or* **Thermos flask** *n trademark* a type of stoppered vacuum flask used to preserve the temperature of its contents

thermosetting *adj* (of a material, esp. a synthetic plastic) hardening permanently after one application of heat and pressure

thermostat *n* a device which automatically regulates the temperature of central heating, an oven, etc., by switching it off or on when it reaches or drops below a particular temperature **>** **thermostatic** *adj* **>** **thermostatically** *adv*

Theron *n* Charlize born 1975, South African film actress; her films include *The Cider House Rules* (1999) and *Monster* (2003), which earned her an Academy Award

Theroux *n* Paul (Edward). born 1941, US novelist and travel writer. His novels include *Picture Palace* (1978), *The Mosquito Coast* (1981), and *My Other Life* (1996); travel writings include *The Great Railway Bazaar* (1975)

thesaurus (thiss-**sore**-uss) *n, pl* **-ruses** *or* **-ri** a book containing lists of synonyms and related words [Greek *thēsauros* a treasury]

these *adj, pron* the plural of **this**

Thesiger *n* Wilfred (Patrick). 1910–2003, British writer, who explored the Empty Quarter of Arabia (1945–50) and lived with the Iraqi marsh Arabs (1950–58). His books include *Arabian Sands* (1958), *The Marsh Arabs* (1964), and *My Kenya Days* (1994)

thesis (**theess**-siss) *n, pl* **-ses** (-seez) **1** a written work resulting from original research, esp. one submitted for a higher degree in a university **2** an opinion supported by reasoned argument: *it is the author's thesis that Britain has yet to come to terms with the loss of its Empire* **3** *logic* an unproved statement put forward as a premise in an argument [Greek: a placing]

Thespian *n* **1** *often facetious* an actor or actress ▷ *adj* **2** of or relating to drama and the theatre [after THESPIS]

Thespis n 6th century BC, Greek poet, regarded as the founder of tragic drama

Thessalian adj **1** of or relating to the Greek region of Thessaly or its inhabitants ▷ n **2** a native or inhabitant of Thessaly

Thessalonian adj **1** of or relating to ancient Thessalonica (modern Salonika) ▷ n **2** an inhabitant of ancient Thessalonica

Thessaloníki n a port in NE Greece, in central Macedonia at the head of the **Gulf of Salonika** (an inlet of the Aegean): capital of the Roman province of Macedonia; university (1926). Pop: 824 000 (2005 est). Latin name: **Thessalonica**. English name: **Salonika, Salonica**

Thessaly n a region of E Central Greece, on the Aegean: an extensive fertile plain, edged with mountains. Pop: 609 100 (2001). Area: 14 037 sq km (5418 sq miles). Modern Greek name: **Thessalía**

Thetford Mines n a city in SE Canada, in S Quebec: asbestos industry. Pop: 21 651 (2001)

they pron (subjective) **1** refers to people or things other than the speaker or people addressed: they both giggled **2** refers to people in general: they say he beats his wife **3** informal refers to an individual person, whose sex is either not known or not regarded as important: someone could have a nasty accident if they tripped over that [Old Norse their]

> **USAGE** It was formerly considered correct to use he, him, or his after pronouns such as everyone, no-one, anyone, or someone as in everyone did his best, but it is now more common to use they, them, or their, and this use has become acceptable in all but the most formal contexts: everyone did their best.

thiamine or **thiamin** n vitamin B₁, a vitamin found in the outer coat of rice and other grains, a deficiency of which leads to nervous disorders and to beriberi [Greek theion sulphur + VITAMIN]

thick adj **1** having a relatively great distance between opposite surfaces: thick slices **2** having a specified distance between opposite surfaces: fifty metres thick **3** having a dense consistency: thick fog **4** consisting of a lot of things grouped closely together: thick forest **5** (of clothes) made of heavy cloth or wool: a thick jumper **6** informal stupid, slow, or insensitive **7** (of an accent) very noticeable: each word was pronounced in a thick Dutch accent **8** Also: **thick as thieves** informal very friendly **9 a bit thick** Brit informal unfair or unreasonable: £2 an hour, that's a bit thick! **10 thick with a** covered with a lot of: glass panels thick with dust **b** (of a voice) throaty and hard to make out: his voice was thick with emotion ▷ adv **11** in order to produce something thick: the machine sliced the potatoes too thick **12 lay it on thick** informal **a** to exaggerate a story **b** to flatter someone excessively **13 thick and fast** quickly and in large numbers: theories were flying thick and fast ▷ n **14 the thick** the most intense or active part: in the thick of the fighting **15 through thick and thin** in good times and bad [Old English thicce] **> thickly** adv

thicken vb **1** to make or become thick or thicker **2** to become more complicated: the plot thickens **> thickener** n

thickening n **1** something added to a liquid to thicken it **2** a thickened part or piece

thicket n a dense growth of small trees or shrubs [Old English thiccet]

thickhead n slang a stupid or ignorant person **> thickheaded** adj

thickie n slang same as **thicko**

thickness n **1** the state or quality of being thick **2** the dimension through an object, as opposed to length or width **3** a layer: several thicknesses of brown paper

thicko n, pl **thickos** or **thickoes** Brit slang a slow-witted unintelligent person

thickset adj **1** stocky in build **2** planted or placed close together

thick-skinned adj insensitive to criticism or hints; not easily upset

thief n, pl **thieves** a person who steals something from another [Old English thēof] **> thievish** adj

Thiers n Louis Adolphe. 1797–1877, French statesman and historian. After the Franco-Prussian war, he suppressed the Paris Commune and became first president of the Third Republic (1871–73). His policies made possible the paying off of the war indemnity exacted by Germany

thieve vb **thieving, thieved** to steal other people's possessions [Old English thēofian] **> thieving** adj

thigh n the part of the human leg between the hip and the knee [Old English thēh]

thighbone n same as **femur**

thimble n a small metal or plastic cap used to protect the end of the finger from the needle when sewing [Old English thȳmel thumbstall]

Thimbu or **Thimphu** n the capital of Bhutan, in the west in the foothills of the E Himalayas: became the official capital in 1962. Pop: 40 000 (2005 est)

thin adj **thinner, thinnest 1** having a relatively small distance between opposite surfaces: a thin mattress **2** much narrower than it is long: push a thin stick up the pipe in order to clear it **3** (of a person or animal) having no excess body fat **4** made up of only a few, widely separated, people or things: thin hair **5** not dense: a thin film of dust **6** unconvincing because badly thought out or badly presented: the evidence against him was extremely thin **7** (of a voice) high-pitched and not very loud: a thin squeaky voice ▷ adv **8** in order to produce something thin: roll the dough very thin ▷ vb **thinning, thinned 9** to make or become thin or sparse [Old English thynne] **> thinly** adv **> thinness** n

thin client n computers a computer on a network where most functions are carried out on a central server

thine old-fashioned adj **1** (preceding a vowel) of or associated with you (thou): if thine eye offend thee, pluck it out! ▷ pron **2** something belonging to you (thou): the victory shall be thine [Old English thīn]

thing n **1** any physical object that is not alive: there are very few jobs left where people actually make things **2** an object, fact, circumstance, or concept considered as being a separate entity: that would be a terrible thing to do **3** an object or entity that cannot or need not be precisely named: squares and circles and things **4** informal a person or animal: pretty little thing, isn't she? **5** a possession, article of clothing, etc.: have you brought your swimming things? **6** informal a preoccupation or obsession: they have this thing about policemen **7 do one's own thing** to engage in an activity or mode of behaviour satisfying to one's personality **8 make a thing of** to exaggerate the importance of **9 the thing** the latest fashion [Old English: assembly]

thingumabob or **thingamabob** n informal a person or thing the name of which is unknown, temporarily forgotten, or deliberately overlooked. Also: **thingumajig, thingamajig, thingummy**

think vb **thinking, thought 1** to consider, judge, or believe: I think that it is scandalous **2** to make use of the mind, for example in order to make a decision: I'll need to think about what I'm going to do **3** to engage in conscious thought: that made me think **4** to be considerate enough or remember (to do something): no other company had thought to bring high tech down to the user **5 think much** or **a lot of** to have a favourable opinion of: I don't think much of the new design **6 think of a** to remember or recollect: I couldn't think of your surname **b** to conceive of or formulate: for a long time he couldn't think of a response **7 think twice** to consider something carefully before making a decision ▷ n **8** informal a careful open-minded assessment: she had a long hard think [Old English thencan] **> thinker** n

thinking n **1** opinion or judgment: contrary to all fashionable thinking **2** the process of thought ▷ adj **3** using intelligent thought: the thinking man's sport

think over vb to ponder or consider

t

think-tank *n informal* a group of experts employed to study specific problems

think up *vb* to invent or devise

thinner *n* a solvent, such as turpentine, added to paint or varnish to dilute it

thin-skinned *adj* sensitive to criticism or hints; easily upset

third *adj* **1** of or being number three in a series **2** rated, graded, or ranked below the second level **3** denoting the third from lowest forward gear in a motor vehicle ▷ *n* **4** one of three equal parts of something **5** the fraction equal to one divided by three (⅓) **6** the third from lowest forward gear in a motor vehicle **7** *Brit* an honours degree of the third and usually the lowest class **8** *music* the interval between one note and the note four semitones (**major third**) or three semitones (**minor third**) higher or lower than it ▷ *adv* **9** Also: **thirdly** in the third place [Old English *thirda*]

third class *n* **1** the class or grade next in value, rank, or quality to the second ▷ *adj* **third-class 2** of the class or grade next in value, rank, or quality to the second

third degree *n informal* torture or bullying, esp. as used to extort confessions or information

third-degree burn *n* a burn in which both the surface and the underlying layers of the skin are destroyed

third man *n cricket* a fielding position on the off side, near the boundary behind the batsman's wicket

third party *n* **1 a** a person who is involved in an event, legal proceeding, agreement, or other transaction only by chance or indirectly ▷ *adj* **third-party 2** *insurance* providing protection against liability caused by accidental injury or death of other people: *third-party cover*

third person *n* the form of a pronoun or verb used to refer to something or someone other than the speaker or the person or people being addressed

third-rate *adj* mediocre or inferior

Third Reich *n* See Reich¹

Third World *n* the developing countries of Africa, Asia, and Latin America collectively

Thirlmere *n* a lake in NW England, in Cumbria in the Lake District: provides part of Manchester's water supply. Length: 6 km (4 miles)

thirst *n* **1 a** a desire to drink, accompanied by a feeling of dryness in the mouth and throat **2** a craving or yearning: *a thirst for knowledge* ▷ *vb* **3** to feel a thirst [Old English *thurst*]

thirsty *adj* **thirstier, thirstiest 1** feeling a desire to drink **2** causing thirst: *morris dancing is thirsty work* **3** thirsty for feeling an eager desire for: *thirsty for information* ▷ **thirstily** *adv*

thirteen *n* **1** the cardinal number that is the sum of ten and three **2** a numeral, 13 or XIII, representing this number **3** something representing or consisting of thirteen units ▷ *adj* **4** amounting to thirteen: *thirteen people* ▷ **thirteenth** *adj, n*

thirty *n, pl* **-ties 1** the cardinal number that is the product of ten and three **2** a numeral, 30 or XXX, representing this number **3** something representing or consisting of thirty units ▷ *adj* **4** amounting to thirty: *thirty miles* ▷ **thirtieth** *adj, n*

Thirty-nine Articles *pl n* a set of formulas defining the doctrinal position of the Church of England

Thiruvananthapuram *n* the local official name of Trivandrum

this *adj* **1** used preceding a noun referring to something or someone that is closer: *on this side of the Channel* **2** used preceding a noun that has just been mentioned or is understood: *this text has two chief goals* **3** used to refer to something about to be mentioned: *NPR's Anne Garrels has this report* **4** used to refer to the present time or occasion: *this week's edition of the newspaper* **5** *informal* used instead of *a* or *the* in telling a story: *see, it's about this bird who fancies you* ▷ *pron* **6** used to denote a person or thing that is relatively close: *black coral like this* **7** used to denote

something already mentioned or understood: *this didn't seem fair to me* **8** used to denote something about to be mentioned: *just say this: collect Standish from the top of the fire escape* **9** the present time or occasion: *after this it was impossible to talk to him about his feelings* **10** this and that various unspecified and trivial events or facts [Old English *thes, thēos, this* (masculine, feminine, and neuter singular)]

thistle *n* a plant with prickly-edged leaves, dense flower heads, and feathery hairs on the seeds [Old English *thīstel*] ▷ **thistly** *adj*

thistledown *n* the mass of feathery plumed seeds produced by a thistle

thither *adv formal* to or towards that place [Old English *thider*]

tho' *or* **tho** *conj, adv US or poetic* same as *though*

thole¹ *or* **tholepin** *n* one of a pair of wooden pins set upright in the gunwale on either side of a rowing boat to serve as a fulcrum in rowing [Old English *tholl*]

thole² *vb* **tholing, tholed** *Scot and N English* to bear or put up with

Thomas *n* **1** Saint. Also called: **doubting Thomas**. one of the twelve apostles, who refused to believe in Christ's resurrection until he had seen his wounds (John 20:24–29). Feast day: July 3 or Dec 21 or Oct 6 **2** Ambroise. 1811–96, French composer of light operas, including *Mignon* (1866) **3** Dylan (Marlais). 1914–53, Welsh poet and essayist. His works include the prose *Portrait of the Artist as a Young Dog* (1940), the verse collection *Deaths and Entrances* (1946), and his play for voices *Under Milk Wood* (1954) **4** (Philip) Edward, pen name *Edward Eastaway*. 1878–1917, British poet and critic: killed in World War I **5** R(onald) S(tuart). 1913–2000, Welsh poet and clergyman. His collections include *Song at the Year's Turning* (1955), *Not that He Brought Flowers* (1968), and *Laboratories of the Spirit* (1975)

Thomas of Erceldoune *n* called *Thomas the Rhymer*. ?1220–?97, Scottish seer and poet; reputed author of a poem on the Tristan legend

Thomas of Woodstock *n* 1355–97, youngest son of Edward III, who led opposition to his nephew Richard II (1386–89); arrested in 1397, he died in prison

Thompson *n* **1** Benjamin, Count Rumford. 1753–1814, Anglo-American physicist, noted for his work on the nature of heat **2** Daley. born 1958, British athlete: Olympic decathlon champion (1980, 1984) **3** Emma. born 1959, British actress: her films include *Howards End* (1991), *Sense and Sensibility* (1996; also wrote screenplay), *Primary Colors* (1998), and *Love Actually* (2003) **4** Flora (Jane). 1876–1947, British writer, author of the autobiographical *Lark Rise to Candleford* (1945) **5** Francis. 1859–1907, British poet, best known for the mystical poem *The Hound of Heaven* (1893)

Thomson *n* **1** Sir George Paget, son of Joseph John Thomson. 1892–1975, British physicist, who discovered (1927) the diffraction of electrons by crystals: shared the Nobel prize for physics 1937 **2** James. 1700–48, Scottish poet. He anticipated the romantics' feeling for nature in *The Seasons* (1726–30) **3** James, pen name *B.V.* 1834–82, British poet, born in Scotland, noted esp. for *The City of Dreadful Night* (1874), reflecting man's isolation and despair **4** Sir Joseph John. 1856–1940, British physicist. He discovered the electron (1897) and his work on the nature of positive rays led to the discovery of isotopes: Nobel prize for physics 1906 **5** Roy, 1st Baron Thomson of Fleet. 1894–1976, British newspaper proprietor, born in Canada **6** Virgil. 1896–1989, US composer, music critic, and conductor, whose works include two operas, *Four Saints in Three Acts* (1928) and *The Mother of Us All* (1947), piano sonatas, a cello concerto, songs, and film music **7** Sir William. See (1st Baron) Kelvin

Thonburi *n* a city in central Thailand, part of Bangkok Metropolis on the Chao Phraya River; the national capital (1767–82)

thong *n* **1** a thin strip of leather or other material **2** *US*,

Canad and Austral same as **flip-flop 3** a skimpy article of beachwear consisting of thin strips of leather or cloth attached to a piece of material that covers the genitals while leaving the buttocks bare [Old English *thwang*]

Thor *n Norse myth* the god of thunder

thorax (**thaw**-racks) *n*, *pl* **thoraxes** or **thoraces** (thaw-rass-seez) **1** the part of the human body enclosed by the ribs **2** the part of an insect's body between the head and abdomen [Greek: breastplate, chest] **> thoracic** *adj*

Thoreau *n* Henry David. 1817–62, US writer, noted esp. for *Walden, or Life in the Woods* (1854), an account of his experiment in living in solitude. A powerful social critic, his essay *Civil Disobedience* (1849) influenced such dissenters as Gandhi

thorium *n chem* a silvery-white radioactive metallic element. It is used in electronic equipment and as a nuclear power source. Symbol: **Th** [after THOR]

thorn *n* **1** a sharp pointed woody projection from a stem or leaf **2** any of various trees or shrubs having thorns, esp. the hawthorn **3 a thorn in one's side** or **flesh** a source of irritation: *he was sufficiently bright at school to become a thorn in the side of his maths teacher* [Old English] **> thornless** *adj*

Thorn *n* the German name for **Toruń**

Thorndike *n* **1** Edward Lee. 1874–1949, US psychologist, who worked on animals and proposed that all learnt behaviour is regulated by rewards and punishments (**Thorndike's law** or **law of effect**) **2** Dame (**Agnes**) **Sybil**. 1882–1976, British actress

Thornhill *n* Sir James. 1675–1734, English baroque painter. He is best known for decorating the Painted Hall, Greenwich Hospital (1708–27) and the interior of the dome of St Paul's Cathedral (1715–17)

thorny *adj* **thornier, thorniest 1** covered with thorns **2** difficult or unpleasant: *a thorny issue*

thorough *adj* **1** carried out completely and carefully: *he needs a thorough checkup by the doctor* **2** (of a person) painstakingly careful: *he is very thorough if rather unimaginative* **3** great in extent or degree; utter: *a thorough disgrace* [Old English *thurh* through] **> thoroughly** *adv* **> thoroughness** *n*

thoroughbred *adj* **1** obtained through successive generations of selective breeding: *thoroughbred horses* ▷ *n* **2** a pedigree animal, esp. a horse

thoroughfare *n* a way through from one place to another: *the great thoroughfare from the Castle to the Palace of Holyrood*

thoroughgoing *adj* **1** extremely thorough **2** absolute or complete: *a thoroughgoing hatred*

Thorpe *n* **1** Ian. born 1982, Australian swimmer; won three gold medals at the 2000 Olympic Games, six gold medals at the 2002 Commonwealth Games, and two gold medals at the 2004 Olympic Games. **2** James Francis. 1888–1953, American football player and athlete: Olympic pentathlon and decathlon champion (1912) **3** Jeremy. (1929–2014), British politician; leader of the Liberal party (1967–76)

Thorshavn or **Tórshavn** *n* the capital of the Faeroes, a port on the northernmost island. Pop: 17 549 (2004 est)

Thorvaldsen *n* Bertel. 1770–1844, Danish neoclassical sculptor

those *adj, pron* the plural of **that** [Old English *thās*, plural of *this*]

thou¹ *pron old-fashioned* same as **you** used when talking to one person [Old English *thū*]

thou² *n, pl* **thou** *informal* **1** one thousandth of an inch **2** a thousand

though *conj* **1** despite the fact that: *he was smiling with relief and happiness though the tears still flowed down his cheeks* ▷ *adv* **2** nevertheless or however: *he can't dance – he sings well, though* [Old English *thēah*]

thought *vb* **1** the past of **think** ▷ *n* **2** the act or process of thinking **3** a concept or idea **4** ideas typical of a particular time or place: *the development of Western*

intellectual thought **5** detailed consideration: *he appeared to give some sort of thought to the question* **6** an intention, hope, or reason for doing something: *his first thought was to call the guard and have the man arrested* [Old English *thōht*]

thoughtful *adj* **1** considerate in the treatment of other people **2** showing careful thought: *a thoughtful and scholarly book* **3** quiet, serious, and deep in thought **> thoughtfully** *adv* **> thoughtfulness** *n*

thoughtless *adj* not considerate of the feelings of other people **> thoughtlessly** *adv* **> thoughtlessness** *n*

thousand *n, pl* **-sands** or **-sand 1** the cardinal number that is the product of ten and one hundred **2** a numeral, 1000 or 10^3, representing this number **3** a very large but unspecified number: *thousands of bees swarmed out of the hive* **4** something representing or consisting of 1000 units ▷ *adj* **5** amounting to a thousand: *a thousand members* [Old English *thūsend*] **> thousandth** *adj, n*

Thousand Island *adj* of or relating to the Thousand Islands or their inhabitants

Thousand Islands *pl n* a group of about 1500 islands between the US and Canada, in the upper St Lawrence River: administratively divided between the two countries

Thrace *n* **1** an ancient country in the E Balkan Peninsula: successively under the Persians, Macedonians, and Romans **2** a region of SE Europe, corresponding to the S part of the ancient country: divided by the Maritsa River into **Western Thrace** (Greece) and **Eastern Thrace** (Turkey)

Thrale *n* Hester Lynch, known as *Mrs Thrale* or (later) *Mrs Piozzi* (née *Salusbury*). 1741–1821, English writer of memoirs, noted for her friendship with Dr Johnson. Her works include *Anecdotes of the late Samuel Johnson* (1786) and *Letters to and from the late Samuel Johnson* (1788)

thrall *n* the state of being completely in the power of, or spellbound by, a person or thing: *he was held in thrall by her almost supernatural beauty* [Old English *thrǣl* slave]

thrash *vb* **1** to beat (someone), esp. with a stick or whip **2** to defeat totally: *the All Blacks thrashed England 24-3* **3** to move about in a wild manner: *his legs stuck and he fell sideways, thrashing about wildly* **4** same as **thresh** ▷ *n* **5** *informal* a party ▶ See also **thrash out** [Old English *therscan*]

thrashing *n* a severe beating

thrash out *vb* to discuss (a problem or difficulty) fully in order to come to an agreement or decision about it: *we must arrange a meeting to thrash out the details of the scheme*

thread *n* **1** a fine strand or fibre of some material **2** a fine cord of twisted yarns, esp. of cotton, used in sewing or weaving **3** something acting as the continuous link or theme of a whole: *the thread of the story* **4** the spiral ridge on a screw, bolt, or nut **5** a very small amount (of something): *there was a thread of nervousness in his voice* **6** a very thin seam of coal or vein of ore ▷ *pl n* **threads 7** *chiefly US slang* clothes ▷ *vb* **8** to pass thread through the eye of (a needle) before sewing with it **9** to string together: *plastic beads threaded on lengths of nylon line* **10** to make (one's way) through a crowd of people or group of objects: *she threaded and pushed her way through the crowds* [Old English *thrǣd*] **> threadlike** *adj*

threadbare *adj* **1** (of cloth, clothing, or a carpet) having the nap worn off so that the threads are exposed **2** having been used or expressed so often as to be no longer interesting: *threadbare ideas* **3** wearing shabby worn-out clothes

Threadneedle Street *n* a street in the City of London famous for its banks, including the Bank of England, known as **The Old Lady of Threadneedle Street**

threadworm *n* a small threadlike worm that is a parasite of humans

threat *n* **1** a declaration of an intention to inflict harm: *they carried out their threat to kill the hostages* **2** a strong possibility of something dangerous or unpleasant happening: *the wet weather will bring a threat of flooding*

3 a person or thing that is regarded as dangerous and likely to inflict harm: *unemployment is a serious threat to the social order* [Old English *thrēat*]

threaten *vb* **1** to express a threat to (someone): *he threatened John with the sack* **2** to be a threat to: *he was worried about anything that might threaten the health of his child* **3** to be a menacing indication of (something): *the early summer threatened drought* ▷ **threatening** *adj* ▷ **threateningly** *adv*

three *n* **1** the cardinal number that is the sum of one and two **2** a numeral, 3 or III, representing this number **3** something representing or consisting of three units ▷ *adj* **4** amounting to three: *three days* [Old English *thrēo*]

three-dimensional *or* **3-D** *adj* **1** having three dimensions **2** lifelike or realistic: *all the characters are three-dimensional*

three-decker *n* **1** a warship with guns on three decks **2** anything that has three levels, layers, or tiers

threefold *adj* **1** having three times as many or as much **2** composed of three parts ▷ *adv* **3** by three times as many or as much

three-legged race *n* a race in which pairs of competitors run with their adjacent legs tied together

three-ply *adj* made of three thicknesses, layers, or strands

three-point turn *n* a complete turn of a motor vehicle using forward and reverse gears alternately, and completed after only three movements

three-quarter *adj* **1** amounting to three out of four equal parts of something **2** being three quarters of the normal length: *a three-quarter-length coat* ▷ *n* **3** rugby any of the four players between the fullback and the halfbacks

Three Rivers *n* the English name for **Trois-Rivières**

three Rs *pl n* reading, writing, and arithmetic regarded as the three fundamental skills to be taught in primary schools [humorous spelling of *reading, 'riting, and 'rithmetic*]

threescore *adj archaic* sixty

threesome *n* a group of three people

threnody *n, pl* **threnodies** *formal* a lament for the dead [Greek *thrēnōidia*] ▷ **threnodic** *adj* ▷ **threnodist** *n*

thresh *vb* **1** to beat (stalks of ripe corn, rice, etc.), either with a hand tool or by machine to separate the grain from the husks and straw **2** **thresh about** to toss and turn [Old English *therscan*]

thresher *n* any of a genus of large sharks occurring in tropical and temperate seas. They have a very long whiplike tail

threshold *n* **1** the lower horizontal part of an entrance or doorway, esp. one made of stone or hardwood **2** any doorway or entrance: *he had never been over the threshold of a pub before* **3** the starting point of an experience, event, or venture: *she was on the threshold of a glorious career* **4** the point at which something begins to take effect or be noticeable: *the threshold for basic rate tax; he has a low boredom threshold* [Old English *therscold*]

threw *vb* the past tense of **throw**

thrice *adv literary* **1** three times: *twice or thrice in a lifetime* **2** three times as big, much, etc.: *his vegetables are thrice the size of mine* [Old English *thrīwa, thrīga*]

thrift *n* **1** wisdom and caution with money **2** a low-growing plant of Europe, W Asia, and North America, with narrow leaves and round heads of pink or white flowers [Old Norse: success] ▷ **thriftless** *adj*

thrifty *adj* **thriftier, thriftiest** not wasteful with money ▷ **thriftily** *adv* ▷ **thriftiness** *n*

thrill *n* **1** a sudden sensation of excitement and pleasure: *he felt a thrill of excitement* **2** a situation producing such a sensation: *all the thrills of rafting the meandering Dordogne* **3** a sudden trembling sensation caused by fear or emotional shock ▷ *vb* **4** to feel or cause to feel a thrill **5** to vibrate or quiver [Old English *thȳrlian* to pierce] ▷ **thrilling** *adj*

thriller *n* a book, film, or play depicting crime, mystery, or espionage in an atmosphere of excitement and suspense

thrips *n, pl* **thrips** a small slender-bodied insect with piercing mouthparts that feeds on plant sap [Greek: woodworm]

thrive *vb* **thriving, thrived** *or* **throve, thrived** *or* **thriven** **1** to do well; be successful: *Munich has thrived as a centre of European commerce* **2** to grow strongly and vigorously: *the vine can thrive in the most unlikely soils* [Old Norse *thrīfask* to grasp for oneself]

thro' *or* **thro** *prep, adv informal* same as **through**

throat *n* **1** the passage from the mouth and nose to the stomach and lungs **2** the front part of the neck **3** **at each other's throats** quarrelling or fighting with each other **4** **cut one's own throat** to bring about one's own ruin **5** **cut someone's throat** to kill someone **6** **ram** *or* **force something down someone's throat** to insist that someone listen to or accept something **7** **stick in one's throat** to be hard to accept: *his arrogance really sticks in my throat* [Old English *throtu*]

throaty *adj* **throatier, throatiest** **1** hoarse and suggestive of a sore throat: *a throaty 40 fags-a-day bark* **2** deep, husky, or guttural: *she gives a deliciously throaty laugh*

throb *vb* **throbbing, throbbed** **1** to pulsate or beat repeatedly, esp. with abnormally strong force: *her eardrums were throbbing with pain* **2** (of engines, drums, etc.) to have a strong rhythmic vibration or beat ▷ *n* **3** the act or sensation of throbbing: *he felt a throb of fear; the throb of the engines* [imitative] ▷ **throbbing** *adj, n*

Throckmorton *or* **Throgmorton** *n* Francis. 1554–84, English conspirator, who with French and Spanish support plotted (1583) to depose Elizabeth I in favour of Mary, Queen of Scots: executed

throes *pl n* **1** violent pangs, pain, or convulsions: *an animal in its death throes* **2** **in the throes of** struggling to cope with (something difficult or disruptive): *in the throes of a civil war* [Old English *thrāwu* threat]

thrombosis (throm-boh-siss) *n, pl* **-ses** (-seez) coagulation of the blood in the heart or in a blood vessel, forming a blood clot [Greek: curdling] ▷ **thrombotic** (throm-bot-ik) *adj*

throne *n* **1** the ceremonial seat occupied by a monarch or bishop on occasions of state **2** the rank or power of a monarch: *she came to the throne after her father was murdered* [Greek *thronos*]

throng *n* **1** a great number of people or things crowded together ▷ *vb* **2** to gather in or fill (a place) in large numbers: *streets thronged with shoppers* [Old English *gethrang*]

throstle *n poetic* a song thrush [Old English]

throttle *n* **1** a device that controls the fuel-and-air mixture entering an engine ▷ *vb* **-tling, -tled** **2** to kill or injure (someone) by squeezing his or her throat **3** to suppress or censor: *the government is trying to throttle dissent* [Middle English *throtel* throat]

throttle back *vb* to reduce the speed of a vehicle or aircraft by reducing the quantity of fuel entering the engine: *throttling back the engine failed to bring the plane under control*

through *prep* **1** going in at one side and coming out at the other side of: *he drove through the West of the city* **2** occupying or visiting several points scattered around in (an area): *a journey through the Scottish Highlands* **3** as a result of: *diminished responsibility through temporary insanity* **4** during: *driving for five hours through the night* **5** for all of (a period): *it rained all through that summer* **6** *chiefly US* up to and including: *from Monday through Saturday* ▷ *adj* **7** finished: *I'm through with history* **8** having completed a specified amount of an activity: *he tried to stop the investigation halfway through* **9** (on a telephone line) connected **10** no longer able to function successfully in some specified capacity: *they are through, they haven't got a chance* **11** (of a train, plane flight, etc.) going directly to a place, so that passengers do not have to change: *the first ever through train between Singapore and Bangkok* ▷ *adv* **12** through a thing, place, or period of time: *the script gives up around halfway through* **13** extremely or absolutely: *I'm* *soaked through* **14 through and through** to the greatest possible extent: *the boards are rotten through and through* [Old English *thurh*]

throughout *prep* **1** through the whole of (a place or a period of time): *radio stations throughout the UK* ▷ *adv* **2** through the whole of a place or a period of time: *I led both races throughout*

throughput *n* the amount of material processed in a given period, esp. by a computer

throve *vb* a past tense of **thrive**

throw *vb* **throwing, threw, thrown 1** to hurl (something) through the air, esp. with a rapid motion of the arm **2** to put or move suddenly, carelessly, or violently: *she threw her arms round his neck* **3** to bring into a specified state or condition, esp. suddenly: *the invasion threw the region into turmoil* **4** to move (a switch or lever) so as to engage or disengage a mechanism **5** to cause (someone) to fall: *I'm riding the horse that threw me* **6 a** to tip (dice) onto a flat surface **b** to obtain (a specified number) in this way: *one throws a 3 and the other throws a 5* **7** to shape (clay) on a potter's wheel **8** to give (a party) **9** *informal* to confuse or disconcert: *the question threw me* **10** to direct or cast (a look, light, etc.): *the lamp threw a shadow on the ceiling* **11** to project (the voice) so as to make it appear to come from somewhere else **12** *informal* to lose (a contest) deliberately **13 throw a punch** to strike, or attempt to strike, someone with one's fist **14 throw oneself at** to behave in a way which makes it clear that one is trying to win the affection of (someone) **15 throw oneself into** to involve oneself enthusiastically in **16 throw oneself on** to rely entirely upon (someone's goodwill, etc.): *the president threw himself on the mercy of the American people* ▷ *n* **17** the act or an instance of throwing **18** the distance thrown: *a throw of 90 metres* **19** (in sports such as wrestling or judo) a move which causes one's opponent to fall to the floor **20** a decorative blanket or cover **21 a throw** each: *we drank our way through a couple of bottles of claret at £12.50 a throw* ▶ See also **throwaway, throwback,** etc. [Old English *thrāwan* to turn, torment]

throwaway *adj* **1** said or done incidentally: *a throwaway line* **2** designed to be discarded after use: *throwaway cups* ▷ *vb* **throw away 3** to get rid of or discard: *try to recycle glass bottles instead of simply throwing them away* **4** to fail to make good use of: *she threw away the chance of a brilliant career when she got married*

throwback *n* **1** a person or thing that is like something that existed or was common long ago: *his ideas were a throwback to old colonial attitudes* ▷ *vb* **throw back 2** to remind someone of (something he or she said or did previously) in order to upset him or her: *he threw back at me everything I'd said the week before*

throw in *vb* **1** to add at no additional cost: *he'd got good at bargaining them down, making them throw in variations for free* **2** to contribute (a remark) in a discussion **3 throw in the towel** *informal* to give in; accept defeat ▷ *n* **throw-in 4** *soccer etc.* the act of putting the ball back into play when it has gone over one of the sidelines, by throwing it over one's head with both hands

throw off *vb* **1** to take off (clothing) hurriedly **2** *literary* to free oneself of: *Vietnamese farmers threw off their dependency on European seed potatoes*

throw out *vb* **1** to discard or reject: *the court threw out the case* **2** to expel or dismiss, esp. forcibly: *her parents threw her out when they discovered she was pregnant*

throw over *vb old-fashioned* to leave or reject (a lover)

throw together *vb* **1** to assemble (something) hurriedly **2** (of a set of circumstances) to cause (people) to meet and get to know each other

throw up *vb* **1** *informal* to vomit **2** to give up or abandon: *he would threaten to throw up his job* **3** to construct (a building or structure) hastily **4** to produce: *these links are throwing up fresh opportunities*

thru *prep, adv, adj chiefly US* same as **through**

thrum *vb* **thrumming, thrummed 1** to strum

rhythmically but without expression on (a musical instrument) **2** to make a low beating or humming sound: *the air conditioner thrummed* ▷ *n* **3** a repetitive strumming [imitative]

thrush¹ *n* any of a large group of songbirds, esp. one having a brown plumage with a spotted breast, such as the mistle thrush and song thrush [Old English *thrȳsce*]

thrush² *n* **1** a fungal disease, esp. of infants, in which whitish spots form on the mouth, throat, and lips **2** a genital infection caused by the same fungus [origin unknown]

thrust *vb* **thrusting, thrust 1** to push (someone or something) with force: *he took him by the arm and thrust him towards the door* **2** to force (someone) into some condition or situation: *unemployed people have been thrust into the front line of politics* **3** to force (one's way) through a crowd, forest, etc.: *Edward thrust his way towards them* **4** to stick out or up: *she thrust out her lower lip* ▷ *n* **5** a forceful drive, push, stab, or lunge: *the thrust of his spear* **6** a force, esp. one that produces motion **7** the propulsive force produced by the pressure of air and gas forced out of a jet engine or rocket engine **8** the essential or most forceful part: *the main thrust of the report* **9** *physics* a continuous pressure exerted by one part of an object against another **10** *informal* intellectual or emotional drive; forcefulness: *thanks to the ingenuity and enterprising thrust of this company* [Old Norse *thrȳsta*]

thrusting *adj* ambitious and having great drive: *a thrusting young executive*

Thucydides *n* ?460–?395 BC, Greek historian and politician, distinguished for his *History of the Peloponnesian War* ❭ **Thucydidean** *adj*

thud *n* **1** a dull heavy sound **2** a blow or fall that causes such a sound ▷ *vb* **thudding, thudded 3** to make or cause to make such a sound [Old English *thyddan* to strike]

thug *n* a tough and violent man, esp. a criminal [Hindi *thag* thief] ❭ **thuggery** *n* ❭ **thuggish** *adj*

Thule *n* **1** Also called: **ultima Thule** a region believed by ancient geographers to be the northernmost land in the inhabited world: sometimes thought to have been Iceland, Norway, or one of the Shetland Islands **2** an Inuit settlement in NW Greenland: a Danish trading post, founded in 1910, and US air force base

thulium *n chem* a silvery-grey element of the lanthanide series. Symbol: Tm [after THULE]

thumb *n* **1** the short thick finger of the hand set apart from the others **2** the part of a glove shaped to fit the thumb **3 all thumbs** very clumsy **4 thumbs down** an indication of refusal or disapproval **5 thumbs up** an indication of encouragement or approval **6 under someone's thumb** completely under someone else's control ▷ *vb* **7** to touch, mark, or move with the thumb: *he thumbed the volume switch to maximum* **8** to attempt to obtain (a lift in a motor vehicle) by signalling with the thumb: *he thumbed a lift to the station* **9 thumb one's nose at** to behave in a way that shows one's contempt or disregard for: *her mother had always thumbed her nose at convention* **10 thumb through** to flip the pages of (a book or magazine) in order to glance at the contents [Old English *thūma*]

thumb index *n* a series of notches cut into the fore-edge of a book to facilitate quick reference

thumbnail *n* **1** the nail of the thumb ▷ *adj* **2** concise and brief: *a thumbnail sketch*

thumbscrew *n* (formerly) an instrument of torture that pinches or crushes the thumbs

thumbtack *n* the US and Canadian term for **drawing pin**

thump *n* **1** the sound of something heavy hitting a comparatively soft surface **2** a heavy blow with the hand ▷ *vb* **3** to place (something) on or bang against (something) with a loud dull sound: *thumping the table is aggressive* **4** to hit or punch (someone): *stop that at once or I'll thump you!* **5** to throb or beat violently: *he could feel his heart thumping* [imitative]

t

thumping *adj slang* huge or excessive: *a thumping majority*

Thun *n* **1** a town in central Switzerland, in Bern canton on Lake Thun. Pop: 40 377 (2000) **2** a lake in central Switzerland, formed by a widening of the Aar River. Length: about 17 km (11 miles). Width: 3 km (2 miles). German name: **Thuner See**

thunder *n* **1** a loud cracking or deep rumbling noise caused by the rapid expansion of atmospheric gases that are suddenly heated by lightning **2** any loud booming sound: *the thunder of heavy gunfire* **3 steal someone's thunder** to lessen the effect of someone's idea or action by anticipating it ▷ *vb* **4** to make a loud noise like thunder: *an explosion thundered through the shaft* **5** to speak in a loud, angry manner: *'Get out of here this instant!' he thundered* **6** to move fast, heavily, and noisily: *a lorry thundered by* [Old English *thunor*] **> thundery** *adj*

Thunder Bay *n* a port in central Canada, in Ontario on Lake Superior: formed in 1970 by the amalgamation of Fort William and Port Arthur; the head of the St Lawrence Seaway for Canada. Pop: 103 215 (2001)

thunderbolt *n* **1** a flash of lightning accompanying thunder **2** something sudden and unexpected: *his career has been no thunderbolt* **3** myth a weapon thrown to earth by certain gods **4** *sport* a very fast-moving shot or serve

thunderclap *n* **1** a loud outburst of thunder **2** something as violent or unexpected as a clap of thunder

thundercloud *n* a large dark electrically charged cloud associated with thunderstorms

thundering *old-fashioned, slang* *adj* **1** extreme: *a thundering disgrace* ▷ *adv* **2** extremely: *thundering good music*

thunderous *adj* **1** resembling thunder in loudness: *thunderous applause* **2** threatening or angry: *a thunderous scowl*

thunderstorm *n* a storm with thunder and lightning and usually heavy rain or hail

thunderstruck *adj* amazed or shocked

Thurber *n* James (Grover). 1894–1961, US humorist and illustrator. He contributed drawings and stories to the *New Yorker* and his books include *Is Sex Necessary?* (1929), written with E. B. White

Thurgau *n* a canton of NE Switzerland, on Lake Constance: annexed by the confederated Swiss states in 1460. Capital: Frauenfeld. Pop: 229 800 (2002 est). Area: 1007 sq km (389 sq miles). French name: **Thurgovie**

thurible (thyoor-rib-bl) *n* same as **censer** [Latin *turibulum*]

Thuringia *n* a state of central Germany. Pop: 2 373 000 (2003 est). German name: **Thüringen**

Thuringian *adj* **1** of or relating to the German state of Thuringia or its inhabitants ▷ *n* **2** a native or inhabitant of Thuringia

Thuringian Forest *n* a forested mountainous region in E central Germany, rising over 900 m (3000 ft). German name: **Thüringer Wald**

Thurrock *n* a unitary authority in SE England, in Essex. Pop: 145 300 (2003 est). Area: 163 sq km (63 sq miles)

Thurs. Thursday

Thursday *n* the fifth day of the week [Old English *Thursdæg* Thor's day]

Thursday Island *n* an island in Torres Strait, between NE Australia and New Guinea: administratively part of Queensland, Australia. Area: 4 sq km (1.5 sq miles)

thus *adv* **1** as a result or consequence: *the platforms provided a new floor and thus improved and enlarged the premises* **2** in this manner: *I sat thus for nearly half an hour* **3** to such a degree: *the competition has been almost bereft of surprise thus far* [Old English]

Thutmose I *n* died *c.* 1500 BC, king of Egypt of the 18th dynasty, who extended his territory in Nubia and Syria and enlarged the Temple of Amon at Karnak

Thutmose III *n* died *c.* 1450 BC, king of Egypt of the 18th dynasty, who completed the conquest of Syria and dominated the Middle East. He was also a patron of the arts and a famous athlete

thwack *vb* **1** to beat with something flat ▷ *n* **2 a** a blow with something flat **b** the sound made by it [imitative]

thwart *vb* **1** to prevent or foil: *they inflicted such severe losses that they thwarted the invasion* ▷ *n* **2** the seat across a boat where the rower sits [Old Norse *thvert* across]

thy *adj* old-fashioned belonging to or associated in some way with you (thou): *love thy neighbour* [variant of *thine*]

thyme (time) *n* a small shrub with white, pink, or red flowers and scented leaves used for seasoning food [Greek *thumon*]

thymol *n* a white crystalline substance obtained from thyme, used as a fungicide and an antiseptic

thymus (thigh-muss) *n, pl* **-muses** or **-mi** (-my) anatomy a small gland situated near the base of the neck [Greek *thumos* sweetbread]

thyroid anatomy *adj* **1** of or relating to the thyroid gland **2** of or relating to the largest cartilage of the larynx, which forms the Adam's apple in men ▷ *n* **3** the thyroid gland [Greek *thureos* oblong shield]

thyroid gland *n* anatomy an endocrine gland that secretes hormones that control metabolism and body growth

thyself *pron* old-fashioned the reflexive form of **thou**[1]

ti *n* music same as **te**

Ti *chem* titanium

Tia Juana *n* a variant spelling of **Tijuana**

Tianjin, Tientsin *or* **T'ien-ching** *n* an industrial city in NE China, capital of Tianjin municipality (traditionally in Hebei province), on the Grand Canal, 51 km (32 miles) from the Yellow Sea: the third largest city in China; seat of Nankai University (1919). Pop: 9 346 000 (2005 est)

Tian Shan *or* **Tien Shan** *n* a great mountain system of central Asia, in Kyrgyzstan and the Xinjiang Uygur Autonomous Region of W China, extending for about 2500 km (1500 miles). Highest peak: Jengish Chokusu or Tomur Feng (formerly Pobeda Peak), 7439 m (24 406 ft). Russian name: **Tyan-Shan**

tiara *n* **1** a semicircular jewelled headdress worn by some women on formal occasions **2** the triple-tiered crown sometimes worn by the pope [Greek]

Tiber *n* a river in central Italy, rising in the Tuscan Apennines and flowing south through Rome to the Tyrrhenian Sea. Length: 405 km (252 miles). Ancient name: Tiberis. Italian name: Tevere

Tiberias *n* **1** a resort in N Israel, on the Sea of Galilee: an important Jewish centre after the destruction of Jerusalem by the Romans. Pop: 40 100 (2003 est) **2 Lake Tiberias** another name for the (Sea of) **Galilee**

Tiberius *n* full name *Tiberius Claudius Nero Caesar Augustus.* 42 BC–37 AD, Roman emperor (14–37 AD). He succeeded his father-in-law Augustus after a brilliant military career. He became increasingly tyrannical

Tibesti *or* **Tibesti Massif** *n* a mountain range of volcanic origin in NW Chad, in the central Sahara extending for about 480 km (300 miles). Highest peak: Emi Koussi, 3415 m (11 204 ft)

Tibet *n* an autonomous region of SW China; formerly a theocracy and the centre of Lamaism: Europeans strictly excluded in the 19th century; invaded by China in 1950; rebellion (1959) against Chinese rule suppressed and the Dalai Lama fled to India; military rule imposed (1989–90) after continued demands for independence; consists largely of a vast high plateau between the Himalayas and Kunlun Mountains. Capital: Lhasa. Pop: 2 700 000 (2003 est). Area: 1 221 601 sq km (471 660 sq miles). Chinese names: **Xizang Autonomous Region, Sitsang**

tibia (tib-ee-a) *n, pl* **tibiae** (tib-ee-ee) *or* **tibias** the inner and thicker of the two bones of the human leg below the knee; shinbone [Latin: leg; pipe] **> tibial** *adj*

Tibullus *n* Albius. ?54–?19 BC, Roman elegiac poet

Tibur *n* the ancient name for **Tivoli**

tic *n* a spasmodic muscular twitch [French]

Ticino *n* **1** a canton in S Switzerland: predominantly

Italian-speaking and Roman Catholic; mountainous. Capital: Bellinzona. Pop: 314 600 (2002 est). Area: 2810 sq km (1085 sq miles). German name: **Tessin** **2** a river in S central Europe, rising in S central Switzerland and flowing southeast and west to Lake Maggiore, then southeast to the River Po. Length: 248 km (154 miles)

tick¹ *n* **1** a mark (✓) used to check off or indicate the correctness of something **2** a recurrent metallic tapping or clicking sound, such as that made by a clock **3** *informal* a moment or instant: *won't be a tick* ▷ *vb* **4** to mark or check with a tick **5** to produce a recurrent tapping sound or indicate by such a sound: *the clock ticked away* **6 what makes someone tick** *informal* the basic motivation of a person ▸ See also **tick off, tick over** [Low German *tikk* touch]

tick² *n* a small parasitic creature typically living on the skin of warm-blooded animals and feeding on the blood and tissues of their hosts: *a sheep tick* [Old English *ticca*]

tick³ *n* Brit and NZ *informal* account or credit: *a spending spree that was financed on tick* [from *ticket*]

ticker *n slang* the heart

ticker tape *n* (formerly) a continuous paper tape on which current stock quotations were printed by machine

ticket *n* **1** a printed piece of paper or cardboard showing that the holder is entitled to certain rights, such as travel on a train or bus or entry to a place of public entertainment **2** a label or tag attached to an article showing information such as its price and size **3** an official notification of a parking or traffic offence **4** the declared policy of a political party **5 that's (just) the ticket** *informal* that's the right or appropriate thing ▷ *vb* **-eting, -eted 6** to issue or attach a ticket or tickets to [Old French *etiquet*]

tickets *pl n* S African *informal* death or ruin; the end

ticking *n* a strong cotton fabric, often striped, used esp. for mattress and pillow covers [probably from Middle Dutch *tīke*]

tickle *vb* **-ling, -led 1** to touch or stroke (someone), so as to produce laughter or a twitching sensation **2** to itch or tingle **3** to amuse or please **4 tickled pink** *or* **to death** *informal* greatly pleased **5 tickle someone's fancy** to appeal to or amuse someone ▷ *n* **6** a sensation of light stroking or itching: *a tickle in the throat* **7** the act of tickling **8** *Canad* (in the Atlantic Provinces) a narrow strait [Middle English *titelen*]

ticklish *adj* **1** sensitive to being tickled **2** delicate or difficult: *a ticklish problem*

tick off *vb* **1** to mark with a tick, esp. to show that an item on a list has been dealt with **2** *informal* to reprimand or scold (someone) ▸ **ticking-off** *n*

tick over *vb* **1** (of an engine) to run at low speed with the transmission disengaged **2** to run smoothly without any major changes: *the business is just ticking over*

ticktack *n* Brit and Austral a system of sign language, mainly using the hands, by which bookmakers transmit their odds to each other at race courses

ticktock *n* a ticking sound made by a clock

Ticonderoga *n* a village in NE New York State, on Lake George: site of Fort Ticonderoga, scene of battles between the British and French (1758–59) and a strategic point in the War of American Independence

tidal *adj* **1** (of a river, lake, or sea) having tides **2** of or relating to tides: *a tidal surge*

tidal wave *n* **1** *no longer in technical use* same as **tsunami 2** an unusually large incoming wave, often caused by high winds and spring tides **3** a forceful and widespread movement in public opinion, action, etc.: *a tidal wave of scandals and embezzlement*

tiddler *n informal* **1** a very small fish, esp. a stickleback **2** a small child [perhaps from TIDDLY¹]

tiddly¹ *adj* **-dlier, -dliest** Brit very small [childish variant of *little*]

tiddly² *adj* **-dlier, -dliest** *informal, chiefly Brit* slightly drunk [origin unknown]

tiddlywinks *n* a game in which players try to flick discs of plastic into a cup [origin unknown]

tide *n* **1** the alternate rise and fall of sea level caused by the gravitational pull of the sun and moon **2** the current caused by these changes in level: *I got caught by the tide and almost drowned* **3** a widespread tendency or movement: *the rising tide of nationalism* **4** *literary or old-fashioned* a season or time: *Yuletide* [Old English *tīd* time]

tideline *n* the mark or line left by the tide when it retreats from its highest point

tidemark *n* **1** a mark left by the highest or lowest point of a tide **2** *chiefly Brit and NZ* a line of dirt left round a bath after the water has been drained away **3** *informal, chiefly Brit* a dirty mark on the skin, indicating the extent to which someone has washed

tide over *vb* **tiding, tided** to help (someone) to get through a period of difficulty or distress: *they need some form of Social Security to tide them over*

tidings *pl n* information or news [Old English *tīdung*]

tidy *adj* **-dier, -diest 1** neat and orderly **2** Brit, Austral and NZ *informal* quite large: *a tidy sum of money* ▷ *vb* **-dies, -dying, -died 3** to put (things) in their proper place; make neat: *I've tidied up the toys under the bed* ▷ *n, pl* **-dies 4** a small container for odds and ends [(originally: timely, excellent) from *tide*] ▸ **tidily** *adv* ▸ **tidiness** *n*

tie *vb* **tying, tied 1** to fasten or be fastened with string, rope, etc.: *a parcel tied with string* **2** to make a knot or bow in (something): *hang on while I tie my laces* **3** to restrict or limit: *they had children and were consequently tied to the school holidays* **4** to equal the score of a competitor or fellow candidate: *three players tied for second place* ▷ *n* **5** a long narrow piece of material worn, esp. by men, under the collar of a shirt, tied in a knot close to the throat with the ends hanging down the front **6** a bond or link: *he still has close ties to the town where he grew up* **7** a string, wire, etc., with which something is tied **8** *Brit sport* a match in a knockout competition: *whoever wins the tie will play Australia in the semifinals* **9 a** a result in a match or competition in which the scores or times of some of the competitors are the same: *a tie for second place* **b** the match or competition in which the scores or results are equal **10** a regular commitment that limits a person's freedom: *it's a bit of a tie having to visit him every day* **11** something which supports or links parts of a structure **12** US and Canad a sleeper on a railway track **13** *music* a curved line connecting two notes of the same pitch indicating that the sound is to be prolonged for their joint time value ▸ See also **tie in, tie up** [Old English *tīgan*]

tie-break *or* **tie-breaker** *n* an extra game or question that decides the result of a contest that has ended in a draw

Tieck *n* Ludwig. 1773–1853, German romantic writer, noted esp. for his fairy tales

tied *adj* Brit **1** (of a public house) allowed to sell beer from only one particular brewery **2** (of a house) rented out to the tenant for as long as he or she is employed by the owner

tie-dye, tie-dyed *or* **tie and dye** *adj* (of a garment or fabric) dyed in a pattern by tying sections of the cloth together so that they will not absorb the dye: *a tie-dye T-shirt*

tie in *vb* **1** to have or cause to have a close link or connection: *there's no evidence to tie this killing in with the murder of Mrs McGowan* ▷ *n* **tie-in 2** a link or connection **3** a book or other product that is linked with a film or TV programme

Tien Shan *n* a variant transliteration of the Chinese name for the **Tian Shan**

Tientsin *n* a variant transliteration of the Chinese name for **Tianjin**

tiepin *n* an ornamental pin used to pin the two ends of a tie to a shirt

Tiepolo *n* Giovanni Battista. 1696–1770, Italian rococo painter, esp. of frescoes as in the Residenz at Würzburg

tier *n* one of a set of rows placed one above and behind the other, such as theatre seats [Old French *tire*]

Tierra del Fuego *n* an archipelago at the S extremity of South America, separated from the mainland by the Strait of Magellan: the west and south belong to Chile, the east to Argentina. Area: 73 643 sq km (28 434 sq miles)

tie up *vb* **1** to bind (someone or something) securely with string or rope **2** to moor (a vessel) **3** to commit (money etc.) so that it is unavailable for other uses: *people don't want to tie up their savings for a long period* ▷ *n* **tie-up 4** a link or connection

tiff *n* a minor quarrel [origin unknown]

Tiffany *n* Louis Comfort. 1848–1933, US glass-maker and Art-Nouveau craftsman, best known for creating the Favrile style of stained glass

tiffin *n* (in India) a light meal, esp. at midday [probably from obsolete *tiff* to sip]

Tiflis *n* transliteration of the Russian name for **Tbilisi**

tiger *n* **1 a** a large Asian mammal of the cat family which has a tawny yellow coat with black stripes **2** a dynamic, forceful, or cruel person **3** a country, esp. in E Asia, that is achieving rapid economic growth [Greek *tigris*]

tiger lily *n* a lily of China and Japan with black-spotted orange flowers

tiger moth *n* a moth with conspicuously striped and spotted wings

tiger snake *n* a highly venomous brown-and-yellow Australian snake

tight *adj* **1** stretched or drawn taut: *loosening-up of tight muscles* **2** closely fitting: *wearing a jacket that was too tight for him* **3** made, fixed, or closed firmly and securely: *a tight band* **4** constructed so as to prevent the passage of water, air, etc.: *watertight; airtight* **5** cramped and allowing very little room for movement: *they squeezed him into the tight space* **6** unyielding or stringent: *tight security* **7** (of a situation) difficult or dangerous **8** allowing only the minimum time or money for doing something: *we have been working to a tight schedule* **9** Brit, Austral and NZ informal mean or miserly **10** (of a match or game) very close or even **11** informal drunk **12** (of a corner or turn) turning through a large angle in a short distance: *the boat skidded round in a tight turn* ▷ *adv* **13** in a close, firm, or secure way: *they held each other tight* [Old Norse *thēttr* of close texture] **> tightly** *adv* **> tightness** *n*

tighten *vb* to make or become tight or tighter

tight-fisted *adj* unwilling to spend money; mean

tightknit *adj* closely integrated: *a tightknit community*

tight-lipped *adj* **1** unwilling to give any information; secretive: *the Minister remained tight-lipped when it came to answering the press's questions* **2** with the lips pressed tightly together, as through anger: *tight-lipped determination*

tightrope *n* a rope stretched taut on which acrobats perform

tights *pl n* a one-piece clinging garment covering the body from the waist to the feet, worn by women and also by acrobats, dancers, etc.

Tiglath-pileser I *n* king of Assyria (?1116–?1093 BC), who extended his kingdom to the upper Euphrates and defeated the king of Babylonia

Tiglath-pileser III *n* known as *Pulu*. died ?727 BC, king of Assyria (745–727), who greatly extended his empire, subjugating Syria and Palestine

Tigre *or* **Tigray** *n* **1** an autonomous region of N Ethiopia, bordering on Eritrea: formerly a separate kingdom. Capital: Mekele. Pop: 4 334 996 (2005 est) **2** a language of NE Ethiopia, belonging to the SE Semitic subfamily of the Afro-Asiatic family

tigress *n* **1** a female tiger **2** a fierce, cruel, or passionate woman

Tigris *n* a river in SW Asia, rising in E Turkey and flowing southeast through Baghdad to the Euphrates in SE Iraq, forming the delta of the Shatt-al-Arab, which flows into the Persian Gulf: part of a canal and irrigation system as early as 2400 BC, with many ancient cities (including

Nineveh) on its banks. Length: 1900 km (1180 miles)

Tihwa *or* **Tihua** *n* a former name for **Urumchi**

Tijuana *or* **Tia Juana** *n* a city in NW Mexico, in Baja California (Norte). Pop: 1 570 000 (2005 est)

tik *n* S African slang the crystal form of the drug methamphetamine

tike *n* same as **tyke**

tiki (tee-kee) *n* a Māori greenstone neck ornament in the form of a fetus [Māori]

tikka *adj* Indian cookery (of meat) marinated in spices and then dry-roasted: *chicken tikka*

Tikrit *n* a town in N central Iraq on the River Tigris; birthplace of Saladin and Saddam Hussein. Pop: 28 900 (2002 est)

Tilak *or* **Bal Gangadhar**, also called *Lokamanya*. 1856–1920, Indian nationalist leader, educationalist, and scholar, who founded (1914) the Indian Home Rule League

Tilburg *n* a city in the S Netherlands, in North Brabant: textile industries. Pop: 198 000 (2003 est)

Tilbury *n* an area in Essex, on the River Thames: extensive docks; principal container port of the Port of London

tilde *n* a mark (˜) used in some languages to indicate that the letter over which it is placed is pronounced in a certain way, as in Spanish *señor* [Spanish]

Tilden *n* Bill, full name *William Tatem Tilden*, known as *Big Bill*. 1893–1953, US tennis player: won the US singles championship (1920–25, 1929) and the British singles championship (1920–21, 1930)

tile *n* **1 a** a thin piece of ceramic, plastic, etc., used with others to cover a surface, such as a floor or wall **2** a rectangular block used as a playing piece in mah jong and other games **3 on the tiles** informal out having a good time and drinking a lot ▷ *vb* **tiling, tiled 4** to cover (a surface) with tiles [Latin *tegula*] **> tiled** *adj* **> tiler** *n*

tiling *n* **1** tiles collectively **2** something made of or surfaced with tiles

till¹ *conj, prep* same as **until** [Old English *til*]

> **USAGE** Till is a variant of *until* that is acceptable at all levels of language. Until is, however, often preferred at the beginning of a sentence in formal writing: *until his behaviour improves, he cannot become a member.*

till² *vb* to cultivate (land) for the raising of crops: *a constant round of sowing, tilling, and harvesting* [Old English *tilian* to try, obtain] **> tillable** *adj* **> tiller** *n*

till³ *n* a box or drawer into which money taken from customers is put, now usually part of a cash register [origin unknown]

tillage *n* **1** the act, process, or art of tilling **2** tilled land

tiller *n* nautical a handle used to turn the rudder when steering a boat [Anglo-French *teiler* beam of a loom]

Tilley *n* Vesta, original name *Matilda Alice Powles*. 1864–1952, British music-hall entertainer, best known as a male impersonator

Tillich *n* Paul Johannes. 1886–1965, US Protestant theologian and philosopher, born in Germany. His works include *The Courage to Be* (1952) and *Systematic Theology* (1951–63)

Tilly *n* Count Johan Tserclaes von. 1559–1632, Flemish soldier, who commanded the army of The Catholic League (1618–32) and the imperial forces (1630–32) in the Thirty Years' War

Tilsit *n* the former name (until 1945) of **Sovetsk**

tilt *vb* **1** to move into a sloping position with one end or side higher than the other: *Dave tilted his chair back on two legs* **2** to move (part of the body) slightly upwards or to the side: *Marie tilted her head back* **3** to become more influenced by a particular idea or group: *the party is tilting more and more to the right* **4** to compete against someone in a jousting contest ▷ *n* **5** a slope or angle: *a tilt to one side* **6** the act of tilting **7 a** a jousting contest, esp. in medieval Europe **b** a thrust with a lance delivered during a medieval tournament **8** an attempt to win a contest: *a tilt at the world title* **9 at full tilt** at full speed or force [Old English *tealtian*]

tilth *n* **1** the tilling of land **2** the condition of land that has been tilled

Timaru *n* a port and resort in S New Zealand, on E South Island. Pop: 43 100 (2004 est)

timber *n* **1** wood as a building material **2** trees collectively **3** a wooden beam in the frame of a house, boat, etc. ▷ *adj* **4** made out of timber: *timber houses* **5** of or involved in the production or sale of wood as a building material: *a timber merchant* [Old English] **› timbered** *adj* **› timbering** *n*

Timberlake *n* Justin. born 1981, US pop singer; a member of the boy band NSYNC, he later found success with the bestselling solo album *Justified* (2002)

timber limit *n Canad* **1** the area to which rights of cutting timber, granted by a government licence, are limited **2** same as **timber line**

timber line *n* the geographical limit beyond which trees will not grow

timbre (tam-bra) *n* the distinctive quality of sound produced by a particular voice or musical instrument [French]

timbrel *n chiefly Bible* a tambourine [Old French]

Timbuktu *n* **1** a town in central Mali, on the River Niger: terminus of a trans-Saharan caravan route; a great Muslim centre (14th–16th centuries). Pop: 35 600 (2009 est). French name: **Tombouctou** **2** any distant or outlandish place: *from here to Timbuktu*

time *n* **1** the past, present, and future regarded as a continuous whole. Related adjective: **temporal** **2** *physics* a quantity measuring duration, measured with reference to the rotation of the earth or from the vibrations of certain atoms **3** a specific point in time expressed in hours and minutes: *what time are you going?* **4** a system of reckoning for expressing time: *the deadline is 5:00 Eastern Time today* **5** an unspecified interval; a while: *some recover for a time and then relapse* **6** an instance or occasion: *when was the last time you saw it?* **7** a sufficient interval or period: *I need time to think* **8** an occasion or period of specified quality: *they'd had a lovely time* **9** a suitable moment: *the time has come to make peace* **10** a period or point marked by specific attributes or events: *in Victorian times* **11** *Brit* the time at which licensed premises are required by law to stop selling alcoholic drinks **12** the rate of pay for work done in normal working hours: *you get double time for working on a Sunday* **13 a** the system of combining beats in music into successive groupings by which the rhythm of the music is established **b** a specific system having a specific number of beats in each grouping or bar: *duple time* **14 against time** in an effort to complete something in a limited period **15 ahead of time** before the deadline **16 at one time a** once or formerly **b** simultaneously **17 at the same time a** simultaneously **b** nevertheless or however **18 at times** sometimes **19 beat time** to indicate the tempo of a piece of music by waving a baton, hand, etc. **20 do time** *informal* to serve a term in jail **21 for the time being** for the moment; temporarily **22 from time to time** at intervals; occasionally **23 have no time for** to have no patience with **24 in no time** very quickly **25 in one's own time a** outside paid working hours **b** at the speed of one's choice **26 in time a** early or at the appointed time: *he made it to the hospital in time for the baby's arrival* **b** eventually; *in time, the children of intelligent parents will come to dominate* **c** *music* at a correct metrical or rhythmic pulse **27 make time** to find an opportunity **28 on time** at the expected or scheduled time **29 pass the time** to occupy oneself when there is nothing else to do: *they pass the time watching game shows on television* **30 pass the time of day** to have a short casual conversation (with someone) **31 time and again** frequently **32 time of one's life** a memorably enjoyable time **33 time out of mind** from long before

anyone can remember ▷ *vb* **timing, timed** **34** to measure the speed or duration of: *my Porsche was timed at 128 mph* **35** to set a time for: *the attack was timed for 6 am* **36** to do (something) at a suitable time: *her entry could not have been better timed* ▷ *adj* **37** operating automatically at or for a set time: *an electrical time switch* ▷ *interj* **38** the word called out by a publican signalling that it is closing time ▶ See also **times** [Old English *tīma*]

time and a half *n* a rate of pay one and a half times the normal rate, often offered for overtime work

time-and-motion study *n* the analysis of work procedures to work out the most efficient methods of operation

time bomb *n* **1** a bomb containing a timing mechanism that is set so that the bomb will explode at a specified time **2** something that will have a large, often damaging, effect at a later date: *the decline of the manufacturing industry is a political time bomb*

time capsule *n* a container holding articles representative of the current age, buried for discovery in the future

time clock *n* a clock with a device for recording the time of arrival or departure of an employee

time-consuming *adj* taking up a great deal of time

time exposure *n* a photograph produced by exposing film for a relatively long period, usually a few seconds

time-honoured *adj* having been used or done for a long time and established by custom

timekeeper *n* **1** a person or thing that keeps or records time, for instance at a sporting event **2** an employee with a record of punctuality as specified: *a poor timekeeper* **› timekeeping** *n*

time lag *n* a gap or delay between one event and a related event that happens after it: *the time lag between the development and the marketing of new products*

timeless *adj* **1** unaffected by time or by changes in fashion, society, etc.: *the timeless appeal of tailored wool jackets* **2** eternal and everlasting: *the timeless universal reality behind all religions* **› timelessness** *n*

timely *adj, adv* **-lier, -liest** at the right or an appropriate time

time-out *n* **1** *sport, chiefly US, Canad and Austral* an interruption in play during which players rest, discuss tactics, etc. **2 take time out** to take a break from a job or activity

timepiece *n* a device, such as a clock or watch, which measures and indicates time

timer *n* a device for measuring time, esp. a switch or regulator that causes a mechanism to operate at a specific time

times *prep* multiplied by: *ten times four is forty*

timescale *n* the period of time within which events occur or are due to occur

time-served *adj* having successfully completed an apprenticeship or period of training: *a time-served electrician*

timeserver *n* a person who changes his or her views in order to gain support or favour

time sharing *n* **1** a system of part ownership of a property for use as a holiday home whereby each participant owns the property for a particular period every year **2** a system by which users at different terminals of a computer can communicate with it at the same time

time signature *n music* a sign, usually consisting of two figures placed after the key signature, that indicates the number and length of beats in the bar

Times Square *n* a square formed by the intersection of Broadway and Seventh Avenue in New York City, extending from 42nd to 45th Street

timetable *n* **1** a plan of the times when a job or activity should be done: *the timetable for the Royal Visit* **2** a list of departure and arrival times of trains or buses: *a timetable hung on the wall beside the ticket office* **3** a plan of the times when different subjects or classes are taught in a school or college: *a heavy timetable of lectures and practical classes* ▷ *vb* **-tabling, -tabled 4** to set a time when a particular thing should be done: *the meeting is timetabled for 3 o'clock*

time value *n music* the duration of a note relative to other notes in a composition and considered in relation to the basic tempo

time warp *n* an imagined distortion of the progress of time, so that, for instance, events from the past seem to be happening in the present

timeworn *adj* **1** showing the adverse effects of overlong use or of old age: *a timeworn café* **2** having been used so often as to be no longer interesting: *a timeworn cliché*

time zone *n* a region throughout which the same standard time is used

timid *adj* **1** lacking courage or self-confidence: *a timid youth* **2** indicating shyness or fear: *a timid and embarrassed smile* [Latin *timere* to fear] ❯ **timidity** *n* ❯ **timidly** *adv*

timing *n* the ability to judge when to do or say something so as to make the best effect, for instance in the theatre, in playing an instrument, or in hitting a ball in sport

Timişoara *n* a city in W Romania: formerly under Turkish and then Hapsburg rule, being allotted to Romania in 1920; unrest led to the revolution of 1989. Pop: 296 000 (2005 est). Hungarian name: **Temesvár**

Timor *n* an island in the Malay Archipelago, the largest and easternmost of the Lesser Sunda Islands: the west was a Dutch possession (part of the Dutch East Indies) until 1949, when it became part of Indonesia: the east was held by Portugal until 1975, when it declared independence but was immediately invaded by Indonesia; East Timor finally became an independent state in 2002. Area: 30 775 sq km (11 883 sq miles)

Timorese *adj* **1** of or relating to Timor or its inhabitants ▷ *n* **2** a native or inhabitant of Timor

Timor-Leste *n* the official name of **East Timor**

timorous (tim-mor-uss) *adj literary* lacking courage or self-confidence: *a reclusive timorous creature* [Latin *timor* fear] ❯ **timorously** *adv*

Timor Sea *n* an arm of the Indian Ocean between Australia and Timor. Width: about 480 km (300 miles)

Timoshenko *n* Semyon Konstantinovich. 1895–1970, Soviet general in World War II

Timothy *n New Testament* **1** Saint. a disciple of Paul, who became leader of the Christian community at Ephesus. Feast day: Jan 26 or 22 **2** either of the two books addressed to him (in full **The First and Second Epistles of Paul the Apostle to Timothy**), containing advice on pastoral matters

timpani *or* **tympani** (tim-pan-ee) *pl n* a set of kettledrums [Italian] ❯ **timpanist** *or* **tympanist** *n*

tin *n* **1** a soft silvery-white metallic element. Symbol: **Sn 2** a sealed airtight metal container used for preserving and storing food or drink: *a cupboard full of packets and tins* **3** any metal container: *a tin of paint* **4** the contents of a tin **5** *Brit, Austral and NZ* galvanized iron, used to make roofs ▷ *vb* **tinning, tinned 6** to put (food) into tins [Old English]

Tinbergen *n* **1** Jan. 1903–94, Dutch economist, noted for his work on econometrics. He shared (1969) the first Nobel prize for economics with Ragnar Frisch **2** his brother, **Nikolaas.** 1907–88, British zoologist, born in the Netherlands; studied animal behaviour, esp. instincts, and was one of the founders of ethology; Nobel prize for physiology or medicine 1973

tin can *n* a metal food container

tincture *n* a medicine consisting of a small amount of a drug dissolved in alcohol [Latin *tinctura* a dyeing]

tinder *n* dry wood or other easily-burning material used to start a fire [Old English *tynder*] ❯ **tindery** *adj*

tinderbox *n* (formerly) a small box for tinder, esp. one fitted with a flint and steel which could be used to make a spark

tine *n* a slender prong of a fork or a deer's antler [Old English *tind*] ❯ **tined** *adj*

tinfoil *n* a paper-thin sheet of metal, used for wrapping foodstuffs

ting *n* a high metallic sound such as that made by a small bell [imitative]

Ting *n* Samuel Chao Chung. born 1936, US physicist, who discovered the J/psi particle independently of Burton Richter, with whom he shared (1976) the Nobel prize for physics

ting-a-ling *n* the sound of a small bell

tinge *n* **1** a slight tint or colouring: *his skin had an unhealthy greyish tinge* **2** a very small amount: *both goals had a tinge of fortune* ▷ *vb* **tingeing** *or* **tinging, tinged 3** to colour or tint faintly: *the sunset tinged the lake with pink* **4** tinged with having a small amount of a particular quality: *the victory was tinged with sadness* [Latin *tingere* to colour]

tingle *vb* **-gling, -gled 1** to feel a mild prickling or stinging sensation, as from cold or excitement ▷ *n* **2** a mild prickling or stinging feeling [probably a variant of *tinkle*] ❯ **tingling** *adj* ❯ **tingly** *adj*

tin god *n* a self-important person

tinker *n* **1** (esp. formerly) a travelling mender of pots and pans **2** *Scot and Irish* usually disparaging a Gypsy **3** a mischievous child ▷ *vb* **4** tinker with to try to repair or improve (something) by making lots of minor adjustments [origin unknown]

tinker's damn *or* **tinker's cuss** *n* not give a tinker's damn *or* cuss *slang* not to care at all

tinkle *vb* **-kling, -kled 1** to ring with a high tinny sound like a small bell ▷ *n* **2** a high clear ringing sound **3** *Brit informal* a telephone call [imitative] ❯ **tinkly** *adj*

tinned *adj* (of food) preserved by being sealed in a tin

tinny[1] *adj* **-nier, -niest 1** (of a sound) high, thin, and metallic: *the tinny sound of a transistor radio* **2** cheap or shoddy: *a tinny East European car*

tinny[2] *adj* **-nier, -niest** *Austral and NZ slang* lucky

tin-opener *n* a small tool for opening tins

Tin Pan Alley *n* the popular music industry, esp. the more commercial aspects of it

tin plate *n* thin steel sheet coated with a layer of tin to protect it from corrosion

tinpot *adj informal* worthless or unimportant: *a tinpot dictator*

tinsel *n* **1** a decoration consisting of a piece of metallic thread with thin strips of metal foil attached along its length **2** anything cheap, showy, and gaudy: *all their tinsel and show counts for nothing* ▷ *adj* **3** made of or decorated with tinsel **4** cheap, showy, and gaudy [Latin *scintilla* a spark] ❯ **tinselly** *adj*

Tinseltown *n* an informal name for **Hollywood** [C20: from the insubstantial glitter of the film world]

tinsmith *n* a person who works with tin or tin plate

tint *n* **1** a shade of a colour, esp. a pale one: *his eyes had a yellow tint* **2** a colour that is softened by the addition of white: *a room decorated in pastel tints* **3** a dye for the hair ▷ *vb* **4** to give a tint to (something, such as hair) [Latin *tingere* to colour]

Tintagel Head *n* a promontory in SW England, on the W coast of Cornwall: ruins of **Tintagel Castle**, legendary birthplace of King Arthur

tintinnabulation *n* the ringing or pealing of bells [Latin *tintinnare* to tinkle]

Tintoretto *n* Il. original name *Jacopo Robusti*. 1518–94, Italian painter of the Venetian school. His works include *Susanna bathing* (?1550) and the fresco cycle in the Scuola di San Rocco, Venice (from 1564)

tiny *adj* **tinier, tiniest** very small [origin unknown]

tip[1] *n* **1** a narrow or pointed end of something: *the northern tip of Japan* **2** a small piece attached to the end or bottom of something: *boot tips keep boots from getting scuffed* ▷ *vb* **tipping, tipped 3** to make or form a tip on: *the long strips that hang down are tipped with silver cones* [Old Norse *typpi*] ❯ **tipped** *adj*

tip² *n* **1** an amount of money given to someone, such as a waiter, in return for service **2** a helpful hint or warning: *here are some sensible tips to help you avoid sunburn* **3** a piece of inside information, esp. in betting or investing ▷ *vb* **tipping, tipped 4** to give a tip to [origin unknown]

tip³ *vb* **tipping, tipped 1** to tilt: *he tipped back his chair* **2 tip over** to tilt so as to overturn or fall: *the box tipped over and the clothes in it spilled out* **3** *Brit* to dump (rubbish) **4** to pour out (the contents of a container): *he tipped the water from the basin down the sink* ▷ *n* **5** a rubbish dump [origin unknown]

tip-off *n* **1** a warning or hint, esp. one given confidentially and based on inside information ▷ *vb* **tip off 2** to give a hint or warning to: *the police had been tipped off about the robbery*

Tipperary *n* a county of S Republic of Ireland, in Munster province; divided into the North Riding and South Riding: mountainous. County town: Clonmel; Nenagh serves as administrative capital of the North Riding. Pop: 140 131 (2002). Area: 4255 sq km (1643 sq miles)

tippet *n* a scarflike piece of fur, often made from a whole animal skin, worn, esp. formerly, round a woman's shoulders [probably from TIP¹]

Tippett *n* Sir Michael. 1905–98, English composer, whose works include the oratorio *A Child of Our Time* (1941) and the operas *The Midsummer Marriage* (1952), *King Priam* (1961), *The Knot Garden* (1970), *The Ice Break* (1976), and *New Year* (1989)

tipple *vb* **-pling, -pled 1** to drink alcohol regularly, esp. in small quantities ▷ *n* **2** an alcoholic drink [origin unknown] **> tippler** *n*

tipstaff *n* **1** a court official **2** a metal-tipped staff formerly used as a symbol of office

tipster *n* a person who sells tips to people betting on horse races or speculating on the stock market

tipsy *adj* **-sier, -siest** slightly drunk [from TIP³] **> tipsiness** *n*

tiptoe *vb* **-toeing, -toed 1** to walk quietly with the heels off the ground ▷ *n* **2 on tiptoe** on the tips of the toes or on the ball of a foot and the toes: *I stood on tiptoe*

tiptop *adj, adv* of the highest quality or condition

tip-up *adj* able to be turned upwards around a hinge or pivot: *tip-up seats*

Tipu Sahib *or* **Tippoo Sahib** *n* ?1750–99, sultan of Mysore (1782–99): killed fighting the British

TIR International Road Transport [French *Transports Internationaux Routiers*]

tirade *n* a long angry speech or denunciation [French]

Tiran *n* Strait of Tiran a strait between the Gulf of Aqaba and the Red Sea. Length: 16 km (10 miles). Width: 8 km (5 miles)

Tirana *or* **Tiranë** *n* the capital of Albania, in the central part 32 km (20 miles) from the Adriatic: founded in the early 17th century by Turks; became capital in 1920; the country's largest city and industrial centre. Pop: 390 000 (2005 est)

tire¹ *vb* **tiring, tired 1** to reduce the energy of, as by exertion: *she could still do things that would tire women half her age* **2** to become wearied or bored: *he simply stopped talking when she tired of my questions* [Old English *tēorian*] **> tiring** *adj*

tire² *n US* same as **tyre**

tired *adj* **1** weary or exhausted: *they were tired after their long journey* **2** bored with or no longer interested in something: *I'm tired of staying in watching TV every night* **3** having been used so often as to be no longer interesting: *you haven't fallen for that tired old line, have you?* **> tiredness** *n*

Tiree *n* an island off the W coast of Scotland, in the Inner Hebrides. Pop: 770 (2001). Area: 78 sq km (30 sq miles)

tireless *adj* energetic and determined: *a tireless worker for charity* **> tirelessly** *adv*

tiresome *adj* boring and irritating

Tîrgu Mureş *or* **Târgu Mureş** *n* a city in central Romania: manufacturing and cultural centre. Pop: 127 000 (2005 est)

Tirich Mir *n* a mountain in N Pakistan: highest peak of the Hindu Kush. Height: 7690 m (25 230 ft)

Tirol *n* a variant spelling of **Tyrol**

Tirolean *adj, n* a variant spelling of **Tyrolean**

Tirolese *adj, n* a variant spelling of **Tyrolese**

Tirpitz *n* Alfred von. 1849–1930, German admiral: as secretary of state for the Imperial Navy (1897–1916), he created the modern German navy, which challenged British supremacy at sea

Tiruchirapalli *or* **Trichinopoly** *n* an industrial city in S India, in central Tamil Nadu on the Cauvery River: dominated by a rock fortress 83 m (273 ft) high. Pop: 746 062 (2001)

Tirunelveli *n* a city in S India, in Tamil Nadu: site of St Francis Xavier's first preaching in India; textile manufacturing. Pop: 411 298 (2001)

'tis *poetic or dialect* it is

Tisa *n* the Slavonic and Romanian name for **Tisza**

Tissot *n* James Joseph Jacques. 1836–1902, French painter and etcher, best known for scenes of fashionable Victorian life painted in England

tissue *n* **1** a group of cells in an animal or plant with a similar structure and function: *muscular tissue forms 42% of the body tissue* **2** a thin piece of soft absorbent paper used as a disposable handkerchief, towel, etc. **3** short for **tissue paper 4** an interwoven series: *a tissue of lies* [Old French *tissu* woven cloth]

tissue paper *n* very thin soft delicate paper used esp. to wrap breakable goods

Tisza *n* a river in S central Europe, rising in W Ukraine and flowing west, forming part of the border between Ukraine and Romania, then southwest across Hungary into Serbia to join the Danube north of Belgrade. Slavonic and Romanian name: **Tisa**

tit¹ *n* any of various small European songbirds, such as the bluetit, that feed on insects and seeds [Middle English *tite* little]

tit² *n* **1** *slang* a female breast **2** a teat or nipple [Old English *titt*]

titan *n* a person of great strength, importance, or size: *one of the titans of the computer industry* [after the *Titans*, a family of gods in Greek mythology]

titanic *adj* having or requiring colossal strength: *a titanic struggle*

titanium *n chem* a strong white metallic element used in the manufacture of strong lightweight alloys, esp. aircraft parts. Symbol: **Ti** [from TITAN]

titbit *or especially US* **tidbit** *n* **1** a tasty small piece of food **2** a pleasing scrap of scandal: *an interesting titbit of gossip* [origin unknown]

titfer *n old-fashioned, Brit slang* a hat [rhyming slang *tit for tat*]

tit-for-tat *adj* done in return or retaliation for a similar act: *a spate of tit-for-tat killings* [earlier *tip for tap*]

tithe *n* **1** one tenth of one's income or produce paid to the church as a tax **2** a tenth or very small part of anything: *he had accomplished only a tithe of his great dream* ▷ *vb* **tithing, tithed 3** to demand a tithe from **4** to pay a tithe or tithes [Old English *teogotha*] **> tithable** *adj*

tithe barn *n* a large barn where, formerly, the agricultural tithe of a parish was stored

Titian *n* **1** original name *Tiziano Vecellio*. ?1490–1576, Italian painter of the Venetian school, noted for his religious and mythological works, such as *Bacchus and Ariadne* (1523), and his portraits **2** (*sometimes not cap*) reddish-gold, like the hair colour used in many of the works of Titian **> Titianesque** *adj*

Titicaca *n* Lake Titicaca a lake between S Peru and W Bolivia, in the Andes: the highest large lake in the world; drained by the Desaguadero River flowing into Lake Poopó. Area: 8135 sq km (3141 sq miles). Altitude: 3809 m (12 497 ft). Depth: 370 m (1214 ft)

titillate *vb* **-lating, -lated** to arouse or excite pleasurably, esp. in a sexual way [Latin *titillare*] **> titillating** *adj* **> titillation** *n*

titivate *vb* **-vating, -vated** to make smarter or neater [perhaps from *tidy* + *cultivate*] ▷ **titivation** *n*

title *n* **1** the distinctive name of a book, film, record, etc.: *his first album bore the title 'Safe as Milk'* **2** a descriptive name or heading of a section of a book, speech, etc. **3** a book or periodical: *publishers were averaging a total of 500 new titles annually* **4** a name or epithet signifying rank, office, or function: *the job bears the title Assistant Divisional Administrator* **5** a formal designation, such as *Mrs* or *Dr* **6** *sport* a championship: *the Italians have won the title* **7** *law* the legal right to possession of property [Latin *titulus*]

titled *adj* having a title such as 'Lady' or 'Sir' which indicates a high social rank

title deed *n* a document containing evidence of a person's legal right or title to property, esp. a house or land

titleholder *n* a person who holds a title, esp. a sporting championship

title page *n* the page in a book that gives the title, author, publisher, etc.

title role *n* the role of the character after whom a play or film is named

titmouse *n, pl* **-mice** same as **tit¹** [Middle English *tite* little + MOUSE]

Tito *n* Marshal. original name *Josip Broz*. 1892–1980, Yugoslav statesman, who led the communist guerrilla resistance to German occupation during World War II; prime minister of Yugoslavia (1945–53) and president (1953–80)

Titograd *n* the former name (1946–92) of **Podgorica**

titrate (**tite**-rate) *vb* **-trating, -trated** *chem* to measure the volume or concentration of (a solution) by titration [French *titrer*]

titration *n chem* an operation in which a measured amount of one solution is added to a known quantity of another solution until the reaction between the two is complete. If the concentration of one solution is known, that of the other can be calculated

titter *vb* **1** to snigger, esp. derisively or in a suppressed way ▷ *n* **2** a suppressed laugh or snigger [imitative]

tittle *n* a very small amount: *it doesn't matter one jot or tittle what you think* [Latin *titulus* title]

tittle-tattle *n* **1** idle chat or gossip ▷ *vb* **-tattling, -tattled** **2** to chatter or gossip

tittup *vb* **-tupping, -tupped** or US **-tuping, -tuped** **1** to prance or frolic ▷ *n* **2** a caper [probably imitative]

titular *adj* **1** in name only: *titular head of state* **2** of or having a title

Titus *n* **1** *New Testament* **a** Saint. a Greek disciple and helper of Saint Paul. Feast day: Jan 26 or Aug 25 **b** the book written to him (in full **The Epistle of Paul the Apostle to Titus**), containing advice on pastoral matters **2** full name *Titus Flavius Sabinus Vespasianus*. ?40–81 AD, Roman emperor (78–81 AD)

Tivoli *n* a town in central Italy, east of Rome: a summer resort in Roman times; contains the Renaissance Villa d'Este and the remains of Hadrian's Villa. Pop: 49 342 (2001). Ancient name: **Tibur**

Tizard *n* Sir Henry (**Thomas**). 1885–1959, British chemist and scientific administrator, who specialized in the military application of science and backed the development of radar

tizzy *n, pl* **-zies** *informal* a state of confusion or excitement [origin unknown]

Tjirebon *n* a former spelling of **Cirebon**

T-junction *n* a junction where one road joins another at right angles but does not cross it

Tl *chem* thallium

Tlaxcala *n* **1** a state of S central Mexico: the smallest Mexican state; formerly an Indian principality, the chief Indian ally of Cortés in the conquest of Mexico. Capital: Tlaxcala. Pop: 961 912 (2000 est). Area: 3914 sq km (1511 sq miles) **2** a city in E central Mexico, on the central plateau, capital of Tlaxcala state: the church of San Francisco (founded 1521 by Cortés) is the oldest in the Americas. Pop: 15 777 (2005). Official name: **Tlaxcala de Xicohténcatl**

Tlemcen *n* a city in NW Algeria: capital of an Arab kingdom from the 12th to the late 14th century. Pop: 177 000 (2005 est)

Tm *chem* thulium

TN Tennessee

TNT *n* 2,4,6-trinitrotoluene: a type of powerful explosive

to *prep* **1** used to indicate the destination of the subject or object of an action: *he went to the theatre* **2** used to introduce the indirect object of a verb: *talk to him* **3** used to introduce the infinitive of a verb: *I'm going to lie down* **4** as far as or until: *from September 11 to October 25* **5** used to indicate that two things have an equivalent value: *there are 16 ounces to the pound* **6** against or onto: *I put my ear to the door* **7** before the hour of: *17 minutes to midnight* **8** accompanied by: *dancing to a live band* **9** as compared with: *four goals to nil* **10** used to indicate a resulting condition: *burnt to death* **11** working for or employed by: *Chaplain to the Nigerian Chaplaincy in Britain* **12** in commemoration of: *a memorial to the victims of the disaster* ▷ *adv* **13** towards a closed position: *push the door to* [Old English *tō*]

toad *n* **1** an amphibian which resembles a frog, but has a warty skin and spends more time on dry land **2** a loathsome person [Old English *tādige*]

toadflax *n* a plant with narrow leaves and yellow-orange flowers

toad-in-the-hole *n* a traditional British dish made of sausages baked in a batter

toadstool *n* any of various poisonous funguses consisting of a caplike top on a stem

toady *n, pl* **toadies** **1** a person who flatters and ingratiates himself or herself in a fawning way: *a spineless political toady* ▷ *vb* **toadies, toadying, toadied** **2** to fawn on and flatter (someone) [shortened from *toadeater*, originally a quack's assistant who pretended to eat toads, hence a flatterer] ▷ **toadyism** *n*

Toamasina *n* a port in E Madagascar, on the Indian Ocean: the country's chief commercial centre. Pop: 198 000 (2005 est). Former name (until 1979): **Tamatave**

to and fro *adv, adj* also: **to-and-fro** **1** back and forth: *he moved his head to and fro as if dodging blows* **2** from one place to another then back again: *the ferry sailed to and fro across the river* ▷ **toing and froing** *n*

toast¹ *n* **1** sliced bread browned by exposure to heat ▷ *vb* **2** to brown (bread) under a grill or over a fire **3** to warm or be warmed: *toasting his feet at the fire* [Latin *tostus* parched]

toast² *n* **1** a proposal of health or success given to a person or thing and marked by people raising glasses and drinking together **2** a person or thing that is honoured: *his success made him the toast of the British film industry* ▷ *vb* **3** to propose or drink a toast to (a person or thing) [from the spiced toast formerly put in wine]

toaster *n* an electrical device for toasting bread

toastmaster *n* a person who introduces speakers and proposes toasts at public dinners

tobacco *n, pl* **-cos** or **-coes** an American plant with large leaves which are dried for smoking, or chewing, or made into snuff [Spanish *tabaco*]

tobacconist *n* Brit and Austral a person or shop that sells tobacco, cigarettes, pipes, etc.

Tobago *n* an island in the SE Caribbean, northeast of Trinidad: ceded to Britain in 1814; joined with Trinidad in 1888 as a British colony; part of the independent republic of Trinidad and Tobago. Pop: 54 084 (2000)

Tobagonian *adj* **1** of or relating to Tobago or its inhabitants ▷ *n* **2** a native or inhabitant of Tobago

-to-be *adj* about to be; future: *the bride-to-be*

Tobey *n* Mark. 1890–1976, US painter. Influenced by Chinese calligraphy, he devised a style of improvisatory abstract painting called "white writing"

toboggan *n* **1** a long narrow sledge used for sliding over snow and ice ▷ *vb* **2** to ride on a toboggan [from a Native American language]

Tobol *n* a river in central Asia, rising in N Kazakhstan and flowing northeast into Russia to join the Irtysh River. Length: about 1300 km (800 miles)

Tobolsk *n* a town in central Russia, at the confluence of the Irtysh and Tobol Rivers: the chief centre for the early Russian colonization of Siberia. Pop: 100 000 (2000 est)

Tobruk *n* a small port in NE Libya, in E Cyrenaica on the Mediterranean coast road: scene of severe fighting in World War II: taken from the Italians by the British in Jan 1941, from the British by the Germans in June 1942, and finally taken by the British in Nov 1942

toby *n, pl* **-bies** NZ a water stopcock at the boundary of a street and house section [origin unknown]

toby jug *n chiefly Brit* a beer mug or jug in the form of a stout seated man wearing a three-cornered hat and smoking a pipe [from the name *Tobias*]

Tocantins *n* **1** a state of N Brazil, created from the northern part of Goiás state in 1988. Capital: Palmas. Pop: 1 207 014 (2002). Area: 278 421 sq km (107 499 sq miles) **2** a river in E Brazil, rising in S central Goiás state and flowing generally north to the Pará River. Length: about 2700 km (1700 miles)

toccata (tok-**kah**-ta) *n* a piece of fast music for the organ, harpsichord, or piano, usually in a rhythmically free style [Italian]

Toc H *n* a society formed after World War I to encourage Christian comradeship [from initials of *Talbot House*, Poperinge, Belgium, its original headquarters]

Tocqueville *n* **Alexis Charles Henri Maurice Clérel de.** 1805–59, French politician and political writer. His chief works are *De la Démocratie en Amérique* (1835–40) and *L'Ancien régime et la révolution* (1856)

tocsin *n* **1** a warning signal **2** an alarm bell [French]

tod *n* **on one's tod** *Brit slang* by oneself; alone [rhyming slang *Tod Sloan/alone*]

today *n* **1** this day, as distinct from yesterday or tomorrow **2** the present age: *in today's world* ▷ *adv* **3** during or on this day: *I hope you're feeling better today* **4** nowadays: *this is one of the most reliable cars available today* [Old English *tō dæge*, literally: on this day]

Todd *n* **Baron Alexander Robertus.** 1907–97, Scottish chemist, noted for his research into the structure of nucleic acids: Nobel prize for chemistry 1957

toddle *vb* **-dling, -dled** **1** to walk with short unsteady steps, like a young child **2 toddle off** *humorous* to depart: *he toddled off to bed* ▷ *n* **3** the act or an instance of walking with short unsteady steps [origin unknown]

toddler *n* a young child who has only just learned how to walk

toddy *n, pl* **-dies** a drink made from spirits, esp. whisky, hot water, sugar, and usually lemon juice [Hindi *tārī* juice of the palmyra palm]

to-do *n, pl* **-dos** *Brit, Austral and NZ* a commotion, fuss, or quarrel

toe *n* **1** any one of the digits of the foot **2** the part of a shoe or sock covering the toes **3 on one's toes** alert **4 tread on someone's toes** to offend a person, esp. by trespassing on his or her field of responsibility ▷ *vb* **toeing, toed 5** to touch or kick with the toe **6 toe the line** to conform to expected attitudes or standards [Old English *tā*]

toecap *n* a reinforced covering for the toe of a boot or shoe

toehold *n* **1** a small space on a rock, mountain, etc., which can be used to support the toe of the foot in climbing **2** any means of gaining access or advantage: *the French car industry has lost its last toehold in America*

toenail *n* a thin hard clear plate covering part of the upper surface of the end of each toe

toerag *n Brit slang* a contemptible or despicable person

toff *n Brit slang* a well-dressed or upper-class person

[perhaps from *tuft*, nickname for a titled student at Oxford University wearing a cap with a gold tassel]

toffee *n* **1** a sticky chewy sweet made by boiling sugar with water and butter **2 can't (do something) for toffee** *informal* is not competent or talented at (doing something): *she couldn't dance for toffee* [earlier *taffy*]

toffee-apple *n* an apple fixed on a stick and coated with a thin layer of toffee

toffee-nosed *adj slang* snobbish or conceited

tofu *n* a food with a soft cheeselike consistency made from unfermented soya-bean curd [Japanese]

tog *n* unit for measuring the insulating power of duvets

toga (**toe**-ga) *n* a garment worn by citizens of ancient Rome, consisting of a piece of cloth draped around the body [Latin] ▷ **togaed** *adj*

together *adv* **1** with cooperation between people or organizations: *we started a company together* **2** in or into contact with each other: *he clasped his hands together* **3** in or into one place: *the family gets together to talk* **4** at the same time: *'disgusting,' said Julie and Alice together* **5** considered collectively: *the properties together were worth more as a unit* **6** *old-fashioned* continuously: *working for eight hours together* **7 together with** in addition to ▷ *adj* **8** *slang* self-possessed, competent, and well-organized [Old English *tōgædere*]

> **USAGE** See at plus.

togetherness *n* a feeling of closeness to and affection for other people

togged up *adj informal* dressed up in smart clothes. Also: **togged out**

toggle *n* **1** a bar-shaped button inserted through a loop for fastening coats etc. **2** *computers* a key on a keyboard which, when pressed, will turn a function or feature on if it is currently off, and turn it off if it is currently on **3** short for **toggle switch** (1) [origin unknown]

toggle switch *n* **1** an electric switch with a projecting lever that is moved in a particular way to open or close a circuit **2** same as **toggle** (2)

Toghril Beg *n* ?990–1063 AD, Sultan of Turkey (1055–63), who founded the Seljuq dynasty and conquered Baghdad (1055)

Togliatti¹ *n* a city in W central Russia, on the Volga River: automobile industry: renamed in honour of Palmiro Togliatti, an Italian communist. Pop: 718 000 (2005 est). Former name (until 1964): **Stavropol**. Russian name: **Tolyatti**

Togliatti² *n* **Palmiro**. 1893–1964, Italian politician; leader of the Italian Communist Party (1926–64). After Mussolini's fall he became a minister (1944) and vice premier (1945)

Togo¹ *n* a republic in West Africa, on the Gulf of Guinea: became French Togoland (a League of Nations mandate) after the division of German Togoland in 1922; independent since 1960. Official language: French. Religion: animist majority. Currency: franc. Capital: Lomé. Pop: 7 154 237 (2013 est). Area: 56 700 sq km (20 900 sq miles)

Togo² *n* **Marquis Heihachiro**. 1847–1934, Japanese admiral, who commanded the Japanese fleet in the war with Russia (1904–05)

Togoland *n* a former German protectorate in West Africa on the Gulf of Guinea: divided in 1922 into the League of Nations mandates of British Togoland (west) and French Togoland (east); the former joined Ghana in 1957; the latter became independent as Togo in 1960

Togolander *n* a native or inhabitant of the former British Togoland (now part of Ghana) or French Togoland (now Togo)

Togolese *adj* **1** of or relating to Togo or its inhabitants ▷ *n, pl* **-lese** **2** a native or inhabitant of Togo

togs *pl n* **1** *Brit, Austral and NZ informal* clothes **2** *Austral, NZ and Irish* a swimming costume [probably from *toga*]

toheroa (toe-a-roe-a) *n* a large edible mollusc of New Zealand with a distinctive flavour [Māori]

tohunga (toe-hung-a) *n* NZ a Māori priest [Māori]

toil *n* **1** hard or exhausting work: *hours of toil beneath the Catalan sun* ▷ *vb* **2** to work hard: *workers toiling in the fields to produce tea for westerners to drink* **3** to move slowly and with difficulty, for instance because of exhaustion or the steepness of a slope: *Joanna toiled up the steps to the church* [Anglo-French *toiler* to struggle]

toilet *n* **1 a** a bowl fitted with a water-flushing device and connected to a drain, for receiving and disposing of urine and faeces **b** a room with such a fitment **2** *old-fashioned* the act of dressing and preparing oneself [French *toilette* dress]

toilet paper *n* thin absorbent paper used for cleaning oneself after defecation or urination

toilet roll *n* a long strip of toilet paper wound around a cardboard tube

toiletry *n, pl* **-ries** an object or cosmetic used in making up, dressing, etc.

toilette (twah-let) *n* same as **toilet** (2) [French]

toilet water *n* liquid perfume lighter than cologne

toilsome *adj literary* requiring hard work: *a most toilsome job*

Tojo *n* Hideki. 1885–1948, Japanese soldier and statesman; minister of war (1940–41) and premier (1941–44); hanged as a war criminal

Tokelau *or* **Tokelau Islands** *pl n* an island group in the South Pacific composed of three atolls, Nukunono, Atafu, and Fakaofo; dependent territory of New Zealand. Pop: 1368 (2012 est). Area: about 11 sq km (4 sq miles)

token *n* **1** a symbol, sign, or indication of something: *as a token of respect* **2** a gift voucher that can be used as payment for goods of a specified value **3** a metal or plastic disc, such as a substitute for currency for use in a slot machine **4 by the same token** in the same way as something mentioned previously ▷ *adj* **5** intended to create an impression but having no real importance: *as a token gesture of goodwill* [Old English *tācen*]

tokenism *n* the practice of making only a token effort or doing no more than the minimum, esp. in order to comply with a law **> tokenist** *adj*

token strike *n* a brief stoppage of work intended to convey strength of feeling on a disputed issue

Tokyo *n* the capital of Japan, a port on SE Honshu on **Tokyo Bay** (an inlet of the Pacific): part of the largest conurbation in the world (the Tokyo-Yokohama metropolitan area) of over 35 million people; major industrial centre and the chief cultural centre of Japan. Pop (city proper): 8 025 538 (2002 est)

told *vb* the past of **tell**

Toledo *n* **1** a city in central Spain, on the River Tagus: capital of Visigothic Spain, and of Castile from 1087 to 1560; famous for steel and swords since the first century. Pop: 72 549 (2003 est). Ancient name: **Toletum 2** an inland port in NW Ohio, on Lake Erie: one of the largest coal-shipping ports in the world; transportation and industrial centre; university (1872). Pop: 308 973 (2003 est) **3** a fine-tapered sword or sword blade

tolerable *adj* **1** able to be put up with; bearable **2** *informal* fairly good **> tolerably** *adv*

tolerance *n* **1** the quality of accepting other people's rights to their own opinions, beliefs, or actions **2** capacity to endure something, esp. pain or hardship **3** the ability of a substance to withstand heat, stress, etc., without damage **4** *med* the capacity to withstand the effects of a continued or increasing dose of a drug, poison, etc. **5** an acceptable degree of variation in a measurement or value: *the bodywork of the car is precision-engineered with a tolerance of 0.01 millimetres*

tolerant *adj* **1** accepting of the beliefs, actions, etc., of other people **2 tolerant of** able to withstand (heat, stress, etc.) without damage

tolerate *vb* **-ating, -ated 1** to allow something to exist or happen, even although one does not approve of it: *you must learn to tolerate opinions other than your own* **2** to put up with (someone or something): *he found the pain hard to tolerate* [Latin *tolerare* to sustain] **> toleration** *n*

Tolima *n* a volcano in W Colombia, in the Andes. Height: 5215 m (17 110 ft)

Tolkien *n* J(ohn) R(onald) R(euel). 1892–1973, British philologist and writer, born in South Africa. He is best known for *The Hobbit* (1937), the trilogy *The Lord of the Rings* (1954–55), and the posthumously published *The Silmarillion* (1977) **> Tolkienesque** *adj*

toll¹ *vb* **1** to ring (a bell) slowly and regularly **2** to announce by tolling: *the bells tolled the Queen's death* ▷ *n* **3** the slow regular ringing of a bell [origin unknown]

toll² *n* **1** a charge for the use of certain roads and bridges: *the Skye bridge toll* **2** loss or damage from a disaster: *the annual death toll on the roads is about 4500* **3 take a** *or* **its toll** to have a severe and damaging effect: *the continued stress had taken a toll on her health* [Old English *toln*]

Toller *n* Ernst. 1893–1939, German dramatist and revolutionary, noted particularly for his expressionist plays, esp. *Masse Mensch* (1921)

tollgate *n* a gate across a toll road or bridge at which travellers must pay

Tolstoy *n* Leo, Russian name *Count Lev Nikolayevich Tolstoy.* 1828–1910, Russian novelist, short-story writer, and philosopher; author of the two monumental novels *War and Peace* (1865–69) and *Anna Karenina* (1875–77). Following a spiritual crisis in 1879, he adopted a form of Christianity based on a doctrine of nonresistance to evil

tolu (tol-loo) *n* a sweet-smelling balsam obtained from a South American tree, used in medicine and perfume [after *Santiago de Tolu*, Colombia]

Toluca *n* **1** a city in S central Mexico, capital of Mexico state, at an altitude of 2640 m (8660 ft). Pop: 1 987 000 (2005 est). Official name: **Toluca de Lerdo 2 Nevado de Toluca** a volcano in central Mexico, in Mexico state near Toluca: crater partly filled by a lake. Height: 4577 m (15 017 ft)

toluene *n* a flammable liquid obtained from petroleum and coal tar and used as a solvent and in the manufacture of dyes, explosives, etc. [previously obtained from tolu]

tom *n* **1** a male cat ▷ *adj* **2** (of an animal) male: *a tom turkey* [from *Thomas*]

tomahawk *n* a fighting axe used by the Native Americans of N America [from a Native American language]

tomato *n, pl* **-toes 1** a red fleshy juicy fruit with many edible seeds, eaten in salads, as a vegetable, etc. **2** the plant, originally from South America, on which this fruit grows [S American Indian *tomatl*]

tomb *n* **1** a place for the burial of a corpse **2** a monument over a grave **3 the tomb** *poetic* death [Greek *tumbos*]

Tombaugh *n* Clyde William. 1906–97, US astronomer, who discovered (1930) the dwarf planet Pluto

tombola *n Brit* a type of lottery, in which tickets are drawn from a revolving drum [Italian]

Tombouctou *n* the French name for **Timbuktu**

tomboy *n* a girl who behaves or dresses like a boy

tombstone *n* a gravestone

Tombstone *n* a town in the US, in Arizona: scene of the gunfight at the OK Corral in 1881. Pop: 1547 (2003 est)

tome *n* a large heavy book [Greek *tomos* a slice]

tomfoolery *n* foolish behaviour

Tommy *n, pl* **-mies** *Brit old-fashioned, informal* a private in the British Army [originally *Thomas Atkins*, name used in specimen copies of official forms]

Tommy gun *n* a type of light sub-machine-gun [in full *Thompson sub-machine-gun*, from the name of the manufacturer]

tommyrot *n old-fashioned, informal* utter nonsense

tomorrow *n* **1** the day after today: *tomorrow's meeting has been cancelled* **2** the future: *the struggle to build a better*

tomorrow ▷ *adv* **3** on the day after today: *the festival starts tomorrow* **4** at some time in the future: *they live today as millions more will live tomorrow* [Old English *tō morgenne*]

Tomsk *n* a city in central Russia: formerly an important gold-mining town and administrative centre for a large area of Siberia; university (1888); engineering industries. Pop: 486 000 (2005 est)

Tom Thumb *n* **1** General, stage name of *Charles Stratton*. 1838–83, US midget, exhibited in P. T. Barnum's circus **2** a dwarf; midget [after *Tom Thumb*, the tiny hero of several English folk tales]

tomtit *n* Brit a small European bird that eats insects and seeds

tom-tom *n* a long narrow drum beaten with the hands [Hindi *tamtam*]

ton¹ *n* **1** Brit a unit of weight equal to 2240 pounds or 1016.046 kilograms **2** US and Canad a unit of weight equal to 2000 pounds or 907.184 kilograms **3** See **metric ton** **4** **come down on someone like a ton of bricks** to scold someone very severely ▷ *adv* **5** **tons** a lot: *I've got tons of things to do before going on holiday* [variant of TUN]

ton² *n* slang, chiefly Brit a hundred miles per hour [special use of TON¹]

tonal *adj* **1** music written in a key **2** of or relating to tone or tonality

tonality *n, pl* **-ties 1** music the presence of a musical key in a composition **2** the overall scheme of colours and tones in a painting

Tonbridge *n* a market town in SE England, in SW Kent on the River Medway. Pop: 35 833 (2001)

tone *n* **1** sound with reference to its pitch, timbre, or volume **2** US and Canad same as **note** (6) **3** music an interval of two semitones, such as that between doh and ray in tonic sol-fa **4** the quality or character of a sound: *her tone was angry* **5** general aspect, quality, or style: *the tone of the conversation made him queasy* **6** high quality or style: *my car with its patches of rust lowered the tone of the neighbourhood* **7** the quality of a given colour, as modified by mixture with white or black; shade or tint **8** physiol the natural firmness of the tissues and normal functioning of bodily organs in health ▷ *vb* **toning**, **toned 9** to be of a matching or similar tone **10** to give a tone to or correct the tone of [Greek *tonos*] ❯ **toneless** *adj* ❯ **tonelessly** *adv*

Tone *n* (Theobald) Wolfe. 1763–98, Irish nationalist, who founded (1791) the Society of United Irishmen and led (1798) French military forces to Ireland. He was captured and sentenced to death but committed suicide

tone-deaf *adj* unable to distinguish subtle differences in musical pitch

tone down *vb* to moderate in tone: *I sensed some reserve in his manner, so I toned down my enthusiasm*

tone poem *n* music an extended orchestral composition based on nonmusical material, such as a work of literature or a fairy tale

toner *n* **1** a cosmetic applied to the skin to reduce oiliness **2** a powdered chemical that forms the image produced by a photocopier

tone up *vb* to make or become more vigorous, healthy, etc.: *muscle tissue can be toned up*

tong *n* (formerly) a secret society of Chinese Americans [Chinese (Cantonese) *t'ong* meeting place]

Tonga *n* a kingdom occupying an archipelago of more than 150 volcanic and coral islands in the SW Pacific, east of Fiji: inhabited by Polynesians; became a British protectorate in 1900 and gained independence in 1970; a member of the Commonwealth. Official languages: Tongan and English. Religion: Christian majority. Currency: pa'anga. Capital: Nuku'alofa. Pop: 106 322 (2013 est). Area: 750 sq km (290 sq miles). Also called: **Friendly Islands**

tongs *pl n* a tool for grasping or lifting, consisting of two long metal or wooden arms, joined with a hinge or flexible metal strip at one end [Old English *tange*]

tongue *n* **1** a movable mass of muscular tissue attached to the floor of the mouth, used for tasting, eating, and speaking **2** a language, dialect, or idiom: *the Scots tongue* **3** the ability to speak: *taken aback, she could not find her tongue* **4** a manner of speaking: *a sharp tongue* **5** the tongue of certain animals used as food **6** a narrow strip of something that extends outwards: *a narrow tongue of flame* **7** a flap of leather on a shoe **8** the clapper of a bell **9** a projecting strip along an edge of a board that is made to fit a groove in another board **10** **hold one's tongue** to keep quiet **11** **on the tip of one's tongue** about to come to mind **12** **with (one's) tongue in one's cheek** with insincere or ironical intent [Old English *tunge*]

tongue-tie *n* a congenital condition in which movement of the tongue is limited as the result of the fold of skin under the tongue extending too close to the front of the tongue

tongue-tied *adj* speechless, esp. with embarrassment or shyness

tongue twister *n* a sentence or phrase that is difficult to say clearly and quickly, such as the *sixth sick sheikh's sixth sheep's sick*

tonguing *n* a technique of playing a wind instrument by obstructing and uncovering the air passage through the lips with the tongue

tonic *n* **1** a medicine that improves the functioning of the body or increases the feeling of wellbeing **2** anything that enlivens or strengthens: *his dry humour was a stimulating tonic* **3** Also called: **tonic water** a carbonated beverage containing quinine and often mixed with alcoholic drinks: *gin and tonic* **4** music the first note of a major or minor scale and the tonal centre of a piece composed in a particular key ▷ *adj* **5** having an invigorating or refreshing effect: *a tonic bath* **6** music of the first note of a major or minor scale [Greek *tonikos* concerning tone]

tonic sol-fa *n* a method of teaching music, by which syllables are used as names for the notes of the major scale in any key

tonight *n* **1** the night or evening of this present day: *tonight's programme examines the rise of poverty in the 1990s* ▷ *adv* **2** in or during the night or evening of this day: *I want to go out dancing tonight* [Old English *tōniht*]

toning table *n* an exercise table, parts of which move mechanically to exercise specific parts of the body of the person lying on it

Tonkin or **Tongking** *n* **1** a former state of N French Indochina (1883–1946), on the Gulf of Tonkin: forms the largest part of N Vietnam **2** **Gulf of Tonkin** an arm of the South China Sea, bordered by N Vietnam, the Leizhou Peninsula of SW China, and Hainan Island. Length: about 500 km (300 miles)

Tonle Sap *n* a lake in W central Cambodia, linked with the Mekong River by the **Tonle Sap River**. Area: (dry season) about 2600 sq km (1000 sq miles); (rainy season) about 10 000 sq km (3860 sq miles)

tonnage *n* **1** the capacity of a merchant ship expressed in tons **2** the weight of the cargo of a merchant ship **3** the total amount of shipping of a port or nation

tonne (tunn) *n* a unit of mass equal to 1000 kg or 2204.6 pounds [French]

tonsil *n* either of two small oval lumps of spongy tissue situated one on each side of the back of the mouth [Latin *tonsillae* tonsils] ❯ **tonsillar** *adj*

tonsillectomy *n, pl* **-mies** surgical removal of the tonsils [TONSIL + Greek *tomē* a cutting]

tonsillitis *n* inflammation of the tonsils, causing a sore throat and fever

tonsorial *adj* often facetious of a barber or his trade [Latin *tondere* to shave]

tonsure *n* **1 a** (in certain religions and monastic orders) the shaving of the head or the crown of the head only **b** the part of the head left bare by such shaving ▷ *vb* **-suring, -sured 2** to shave the head of [Latin *tonsura* a clipping] ❯ **tonsured** *adj*

too *adv* **1** as well or also: *I'll miss you, too* **2** in or to an excessive degree: *it's too noisy in here* **3** extremely: *you're too kind* **4** *US, Canad and Austral informal* used to emphasize contradiction of a negative statement: *You didn't! — I did too!* [Old English tō]

USAGE See at **very.**

---

took *vb* the past tense of **take**

Tooke *n* John Horne, original name *John Horne*. 1736–1812, British radical, who founded (1771) the Constitutional Society to press for parliamentary reform: acquitted (1794) of high treason. He also wrote the philological treatise *The Diversions of Purley* (1786)

tool *n* **1 a** an implement, such as a hammer, saw, or spade, that is used by hand to help do a particular type of work **b** a power-driven instrument: *machine tool* **2** the cutting part of such an instrument **3** a person used to perform dishonourable or unpleasant tasks for another: *the government is acting as a tool of big business* **4** any object, skill, etc., used for a particular task or in a particular job: *a skilled therapist can use photographs as tools* ▷ *vb* **5** to work, cut, or form (something) with a tool [Old English tōl]

toolbar *n* a row or column of buttons displayed on a computer screen, allowing the user to select a variety of functions

tool-maker *n* a person who specializes in the production or reconditioning of machine tools
› **tool-making** *n*

tool-pusher *n* a person who supervises drilling operations on an oil rig

toonie *or* **twonie** *n* Canad informal a Canadian two-dollar coin

toot *n* **1** a short hooting sound ▷ *vb* **2** to give or cause to give a short blast, hoot, or whistle: *motorists tooted their car horns* [imitative]

tooth *n, pl* **teeth 1** one of the bonelike projections in the jaws of most vertebrates that are used for biting, tearing, or chewing **2** one of the sharp projections on the edge of a comb, saw, zip, etc. **3 long in the tooth** old or ageing **4 a sweet tooth** a liking for sweet food **5 tooth and nail** with great vigour and determination: *the union would oppose compulsory redundancies tooth and nail* ▶ See also **teeth** [Old English tōth]

toothache *n* a pain in or near a tooth

toothbrush *n* a small brush with a long handle, for cleaning the teeth

toothless *adj* **1** having no teeth **2** having no real power: *the proposed Commission will not be as toothless as scoffers suggest*

toothpaste *n* a paste used for cleaning the teeth, applied with a toothbrush

toothpick *n* a small wooden or plastic stick used for extracting pieces of food from between the teeth

tooth powder *n* a powder used for cleaning the teeth, applied with a toothbrush

toothsome *adj* delicious or appetizing in appearance, flavour, or smell

toothy *adj* **toothier, toothiest** having or showing numerous, large, or prominent teeth: *a toothy grin*

tootle *vb* **-tling, -tled 1** to hoot softly or repeatedly ▷ *n* **2** a soft hoot or series of hoots

Toowoomba *n* a city in E Australia, in SE Queensland: agricultural and industrial centre. Pop: 89 338 (2001)

top¹ *n* **1** the highest point or part of anything: *the top of the stairs* **2** the most important or successful position: *at the top of the agenda* **3** a lid or cap that fits on to one end of something, esp. to close it: *he unscrewed the top from a quart of ale* **4** the highest degree or point: *the two people at the top of the Party* **5** the most important person or people in an organization: *the top of the military establishment* **6** the loudest or highest pitch: *she cheered and sang at the top of her voice* **7** a garment, esp. for a woman, that extends from the shoulders to the waist or hips **8** the part of a plant that is above ground: *nettle tops* **9** same as **top gear 10** off

the top of one's head without previous preparation or careful thought **11 on top of a** in addition to: *the average member of staff will get 25% on top of salary* **b** informal in complete control of: *we're on top of our costs and expenses and looking for other opportunities* **12 over the top a** lacking restraint or a sense of proportion: *you went over the top when you called her a religious maniac* **b** military over the edge of a trench ▷ *adj* **13** at, of, or being the top: *men still hold most of the top jobs in industry* ▷ *vb* **topping, topped 14** to put on top of (something): *top your salad with a mild dressing* **15** to reach or pass the top of **16** to be at the top of: *her biggest hit topped the charts for six weeks* **17** to exceed or surpass: *his estimated fortune tops £2 billion* **18 top and tail a** to trim off the ends of (fruit or vegetables) before cooking **b** to wash only a baby's face and bottom ▶ See also **top off, top out, tops,** etc. [Old English topp]

top² *n* **1 a** a toy that is spun on its pointed base **2 sleep like a top** to sleep very soundly [Old English]

topaz (toe-pazz) *n* a hard glassy yellow, pink, or colourless mineral used in making jewellery [Greek *topazos*]

top brass *pl n* the most important or high-ranking officials or leaders

topcoat *n* **1** an overcoat **2** a final coat of paint applied to a surface

top dog *n* informal the leader or chief of a group

top drawer *n* old-fashioned, informal people of the highest social standing

top dressing *n* a layer of fertilizer or manure spread on the surface of land › **top-dress** *vb*

tope¹ *vb* **toping, toped** to drink (alcohol), usually in large quantities [perhaps from French *toper* to take a bet]
› **toper** *n*

tope² *n* a small grey shark of European coastal waters [origin unknown]

topee *or* **topi** (toe-pee) *n* same as **pith helmet** [Hindi *topī* hat]

Topeka *n* a city in E central Kansas, capital of the state, on the Kansas River: university (1865). Pop: 122 008 (2003 est)

Top End *n* the Top End Austral the northern part of the Northern Territory

top-flight *adj* of very high quality

topgallant *n* **1** a mast or sail above a topmast ▷ *adj* **2** of or relating to a topgallant

top gear *n* the highest forward ratio of a gearbox in a motor vehicle

top hat *n* a man's hat with a tall cylindrical crown and narrow brim, now only worn for some formal occasions

top-heavy *adj* unstable through being overloaded at the top

topiary (tope-yar-ee) *n* **1** the art of trimming trees or bushes into artificial decorative shapes **2** trees or bushes trimmed into decorative shapes ▷ *adj* **3** of or relating to topiary [Latin *topia* decorative garden work]
› **topiarist** *n*

topic *n* a subject of a speech, book, conversation, etc. [Greek *topos* place]

topical *adj* of or relating to current affairs › **topicality** *n*
› **topically** *adv*

topknot *n* a crest, tuft, decorative bow, etc., on the top of the head

topless *adj* of or relating to women wearing costumes that do not cover the breasts: *topless bars*

top-level *adj* of, involving, or by those with the highest level of influence or ability: *a top-level meeting*

topmast *n* the mast next above a lower mast on a sailing vessel

topmost *adj* at or nearest the top

top-notch *adj* informal excellent or superb: *top-notch entertainment*

top off *vb* to finish or complete, esp. with some decisive action

topography *n, pl* **-phies 1** the surface features of a region, such as its hills, valleys, or rivers: *the islands are fragile, with a topography constantly changed by wind and wave* **2** the study or description of such surface features **3** the representation of these features on a map [Greek *topos* a place + -GRAPHY] **›** **topographer** *n* **›** **topographical** *adj*

topology *n* a branch of geometry describing the properties of a figure that are unaffected by continuous distortion [Greek *topos* a place + -LOGY] **›** **topological** *adj*

Topolski *n* Feliks. 1907–89, British painter, born in Poland; best known for his sketches and murals, esp. for *Memoir of the Century* (1975–89) painted on viaduct arches on London's South Bank

top out *vb* to place the highest stone on (a building)

topper *n informal* a top hat

topping *n* a sauce or garnish for food

topple *vb* **-pling, -pled** **1** to fall over or cause (something) to fall over, esp. from a height: *he staggered back against the railing and toppled over into the river* **2** to overthrow or oust: *few believe the scandal will topple the government* [from TOP¹ (verb)]

tops *slang n* **1** **the tops** a person or thing of top quality **▷** *adj* **2** excellent: *Pacino's no-holds-barred performance is tops*

topsail *n* a square sail carried on a yard set on a topmast

top-secret *adj* (of military or government information) classified as needing the highest level of secrecy and security

topside *n* a lean cut of beef from the thigh containing no bone

topsoil *n* the surface layer of soil

topsy-turvy *adj* **1** upside down **2** in a state of confusion **▷** *adv* **3** in a topsy-turvy manner [probably *top* + obsolete *tervy* to turn upside down]

top up *vb* **1** to refill (a container), usually to the brim: *I topped up his glass* **2** to add to (an amount) in order to make it sufficient: *the grant can be topped up by a student loan* **▷** *n* **top-up** another serving of a drink in the glass that was used for the first one: *anyone want a top-up?* **▷** *adj* **top-up** **4** serving to top something up: *a top-up loan*

toque (toke) *n* **1** a woman's small round brimless hat **2** *Canad* same as **tuque** (2) [French]

tor *n chiefly Brit* a high hill, esp. a bare rocky one [Old English *torr*]

Torah *n* the whole body of traditional Jewish teaching, including the Oral Law [Hebrew: precept]

Torbay *n* **1** a unitary authority in SW England, in Devon, consisting of Torquay and two neighbouring coastal resorts. Pop: 131 300 (2003 est). Area: 63 sq km (24 sq miles) **2** Also: **Tor Bay** an inlet of the English Channel on the coast of SW England, near Torquay

torch *n* **1** a small portable electric lamp powered by batteries **2** a wooden shaft dipped in wax or tallow and set alight **3** anything regarded as a source of enlightenment, guidance, etc.: *a torch of hope* **4** **carry a torch for** to be in love with (someone), esp. unrequitedly **▷** *vb* **5** *informal* to deliberately set (a building) on fire [Old French *torche* handful of twisted straw]

tore *vb* the past tense of **tear²**

toreador (torr-ee-a-dor) *n* a bullfighter, esp. one on horseback [Spanish]

torero (tor-air-oh) *n, pl* **-ros** a bullfighter, esp. one on foot [Spanish]

Torfaen *n* a county borough of SE Wales, created in 1996 from part of Gwent. Administrative centre: Pontypool. Pop: 90 700 (2003 est). Area: 290 sq km (112 sq miles)

Torino *n* the Italian name for **Turin**

torment *vb* **1** to cause (someone) great pain or suffering **2** to tease or pester (a person or animal) in an annoying or cruel way **▷** *n* **3** physical or mental pain **4** a source of pain or suffering [Latin *tormentum*] **›** **tormentor** *n*

tormentil *n* a creeping plant with yellow four-petalled flowers [Old French *tormentille*]

torn *vb* **1** the past participle of **tear²** **▷** *adj* **2** split or cut **3** divided or undecided, as in preference: *torn between two lovers*

tornado *n, pl* **-dos** *or* **-does** a rapidly whirling column of air, usually characterized by a dark funnel-shaped cloud causing damage along its path [Spanish *tronada* thunderstorm]

Toronto *n* a city in S central Canada, capital of Ontario, on Lake Ontario: the major industrial centre of Canada; two universities. Pop: 2 615 060 (2011)

Torontonian *adj* **1** of or relating to Toronto or its inhabitants **▷** *n* **2** a native or inhabitant of Toronto

torpedo *n, pl* **-does** **1** a cylindrical self-propelled weapon carrying explosives that is launched from aircraft, ships, or submarines and follows an underwater path to hit its target **▷** *vb* **-doing, -doed** **2** to attack or hit (a ship) with one or a number of torpedoes **3** to destroy or wreck: *the Prime Minister warned his party against torpedoing the bill* [Latin: crampfish (whose electric discharges can cause numbness)]

torpedo boat *n* (formerly) a small high-speed warship for torpedo attacks

torpid *adj* **1** sluggish or dull: *he has a rather torpid intellect* **2** (of a hibernating animal) dormant [Latin *torpere* to be numb]

torpor *n* drowsiness and apathy

Torquay *n* a town and resort in SW England, in Torbay unitary authority, S Devon. Pop: 62 968 (2001)

torque (tork) *n* **1** a force that causes rotation around a central point such as an axle **2** an ancient Celtic necklace or armband made of twisted metal [Latin *torques* necklace + *torquere* to twist]

Torquemada *n* Tomás de. 1420–98, Spanish Dominican monk. As first Inquisitor-General of Spain (1483–98), he was responsible for the burning of some 2000 heretics

torr *n, pl* **torr** a unit of pressure equal to one millimetre of mercury (133.3 newtons per square metre) [after E. TORRICELLI]

Torrance *n* a city in SW California, southwest of Los Angeles: developed rapidly with the discovery of oil. Pop: 142 621 (2003 est)

Torre del Greco *n* a city in SW Italy, in Campania near Vesuvius on the Bay of Naples: damaged several times by eruptions. Pop: 90 607 (2001)

Torrens *n* Lake Torrens a shallow salt lake in E central South Australia, about 8 m (25 ft) below sea level. Area: 5776 sq km (2230 sq miles)

torrent *n* **1** a fast or violent stream, esp. of water **2** a rapid flow of questions, abuse, etc. [Latin *torrens*]

torrential *adj* (of rain) very heavy

Torreón *n* an industrial city in N Mexico, in Coahuila state. Pop: 1 057 000 (2005 est)

Torres Strait *n* a strait between NE Australia and S New Guinea, linking the Arafura Sea with the Coral Sea. Width: about 145 km (90 miles)

Torricelli *n* Evangelista. 1608–47, Italian physicist and mathematician, who discovered the principle of the barometer

torrid *adj* **1** (of weather) so hot and dry as to parch or scorch **2** (of land) arid or parched **3** highly charged emotionally: *a torrid affair* [Latin *torrere* to scorch]

Tórshavn *n* the Faeroese name for **Thorshavn**

torsion *n* the twisting of a part by equal forces being applied at both ends but in opposite directions [Latin *torquere* to twist] **›** **torsional** *adj*

torso *n, pl* **-sos** **1** the trunk of the human body **2** a statue of a nude human trunk, esp. without the head or limbs [Italian: stalk, stump]

tort *n law* a civil wrong or injury, for which an action for damages may be brought [Latin *torquere* to twist]

Tortelier *n* Paul. 1914–90, French cellist and composer

tortilla *n Mexican cookery* a kind of thin pancake made from corn meal [Spanish: little cake]

tortoise *n* a land reptile with a heavy dome-shaped shell into which it can withdraw its head and legs [Medieval Latin *tortuca*]

tortoiseshell *n* **1** the horny yellow-and-brown mottled shell of a sea turtle, used for making ornaments and jewellery **2** a domestic cat with black, cream, and brownish markings **3** a butterfly which has orange-brown wings with black markings ▷ *adj* **4** made of tortoiseshell

Tortola *n* an island in the NE Caribbean, in the Leeward Islands group: chief island of the British Virgin Islands. Pop: 23 900 (latest est). Area: 62 sq km (24 sq miles)

Tortuga *n* an island in the Caribbean, off the NW coast of Haiti: haunt of pirates in the 17th century. Area: 180 sq km (70 sq miles). French name: **La Tortue**

tortuous *adj* **1** twisted or winding: *a tortuous route* **2** devious or cunning: *months of tortuous negotiations*

USAGE See at **torture**.

---

torture *vb* **-turing, -tured** **1** to cause (someone) extreme physical pain, esp. to extract information, etc.: *suspects were regularly tortured and murdered by the secret police* **2** to cause (someone) mental anguish ▷ *n* **3** physical or mental anguish **4** the practice of torturing a person **5** something which causes great mental distress: *she was going through the torture of a collapsing marriage* [Latin *torquere* to twist] ❯ **tortured** *adj* ❯ **torturer** *n* ❯ **torturous** *adj*

USAGE The adjective *torturous* is sometimes confused with *tortuous*. One speaks of a *torturous* experience, i.e. one that involves pain or suffering, but of a *tortuous* road, i.e. one that winds or twists.

Toruń *n* an industrial city in N Poland, on the River Vistula: developed around a castle that was founded by the Teutonic Knights in 1230; under Prussian rule (1793–1919). Pop: 214 000 (2005 est). German name: Thorn

Torvill and Dean *n* two British ice dancers, **Jayne Torvill**, born 1957, and **Christopher Dean**, born 1958. They won the world championships in 1981–84, the European championships in 1981–82, 1984, and 1994, and the gold medal in the 1984 Olympic Games

Tory *n*, *pl* **-ries** **1** a member or supporter of the Conservative Party in Great Britain or Canada **2** *history* a member of the English political party that supported the Church and Crown and traditional political structures and opposed the Whigs ▷ *adj* **3** of or relating to a Tory or Tories [Irish *tóraidhe* outlaw] ❯ **Toryism** *n*

tosa (toe-za) *n* a large reddish dog, originally bred for fighting [after a province on the Japanese island of Shikoku]

Toscana *n* the Italian name for **Tuscany**

Toscanini *n* Arturo. 1867–1957, Italian conductor; musical director of La Scala, Milan, and of the NBC symphony orchestra (1937–57) in New York

toss *vb* **1** to throw (something) lightly **2** to fling or be flung about, esp. in a violent way: *the salty sea breeze tossing the branches of the palms* **3** to coat (food) with a dressing by gentle stirring or mixing: *her technique for tossing Caesar salad* **4** (of a horse) to throw (its rider) **5** to move (one's head) suddenly backwards, as in impatience **6** to throw up (a coin) to decide between alternatives by guessing which side will land uppermost **7** **toss and turn** to be restless when trying to sleep ▷ *n* **8** the act or an instance of tossing **9** the act of deciding between alternatives by throwing up a coin and guessing which side will land uppermost: *Essex won the toss and decided to bat first* **10** **argue the toss** to waste time and energy arguing about an unimportant point **11** **not give a toss** *informal* not to care at all [Scandinavian]

toss off *vb* **1** to do or produce (something) quickly and easily: *the tales my sister tossed off so lightly over the dusting* **2** to finish (a drink) in one swallow

toss up *vb* **1** to spin (a coin) in the air in order to decide between alternatives by guessing which side will land uppermost ▷ *n* **toss-up 2** an instance of tossing up a coin

3 *informal* an even chance or risk: *if it's a toss-up for a top position, he gives it to the woman*

Tostig *n* died 1066, earl of Northumbria (1055–65), brother of King Harold II. He joined the Norwegian forces that invaded England in 1066 and died at Stamford Bridge

tot *n* **1** a very young child **2** a small drink of spirits [origin unknown]

total *n* **1** the whole, esp. regarded as the sum of a number of parts **2** **in total** overall: *the company employs over 700 people in total* ▷ *adj* **3** complete: *a total ban on alcohol* **4** being or related to a total: *the total number of deaths* ▷ *vb* **-talling, -talled** *or US* **-taling, -taled 5** to amount to: *the firm's losses totalled more than $2 billion* **6** to add up: *purchases are totalled with a pencil and a notepad* [Latin *totus* all] ❯ **totally** *adv*

totalitarian *adj* **1** of a political system in which there is only one party, which allows no opposition and attempts to control everything: *a totalitarian state* ▷ *n* **2** a person who is in favour of totalitarian policies ❯ **totalitarianism** *n*

totality *n*, *pl* **-ties** **1** the whole amount **2** the state of being total

totalizator, totalizer, totalisator *or* **totaliser** *n* a machine to operate a system of betting on a racecourse in which money is paid out to the winners in proportion to their stakes

tote¹ *vb* **toting, toted** *informal* **1** to carry or wear (a gun) **2** to haul or carry [origin unknown]

tote² *n* the tote *trademark* short for **totalizator**

tote bag *n* a large handbag or shopping bag

totem *n* **1** (esp. among Native Americans) an object or animal symbolizing a clan or family **2** a representation of such an object [from a Native American language] ❯ **totemic** *adj* ❯ **totemism** *n*

totem pole *n* a pole carved or painted with totemic figures set up by certain North American Indians as a tribal symbol

totter *vb* **1** to move in an unsteady manner **2** to sway or shake as if about to fall **3** to be failing, unstable, or precarious: *the world was tottering on the edge of war* [origin unknown]

tot up *vb* **totting, totted** to add (numbers) together: *I'll just tot up what you owe me* [from *total*]

toucan *n* a tropical American fruit-eating bird with a large brightly coloured bill [Portuguese *tucano*]

touch *vb* **1** to cause or permit a part of the body to come into contact with (someone or something): *the baking tin is too hot to touch* **2** to tap, feel, or strike (someone or something): *he touched me on the shoulder* **3** to come or bring (something) into contact with (something else): *the plane's wheels touched the runway* **4** to move or disturb by handling: *we shouldn't touch anything before the police arrive* **5** to have an effect on: *millions of people's lives had been touched by the music of the Beatles* **6** to produce an emotional response in: *the painful truth of it touched her* **7** to eat or drink: *she hardly ever touched alcohol* **8** to compare to in quality or attainment; equal or match: *nothing can touch them for scope and detail* **9** *Brit, Austral and NZ slang* to ask (someone) for a loan or gift of money **10** to fondle in a sexual manner: *I wouldn't let him touch me unless I was in the mood* **11** to strike, harm, or molest: *I never touched him!* **12** **touch on** *or* **upon** to allude to briefly or in passing: *these two issues may be touched upon during the talks* ▷ *n* **13** the sense by which the texture and other qualities of objects can be experienced when they come in contact with a part of the body surface, esp. the tips of the fingers. Related adjective: **tactile 14** the feel or texture of an object as perceived by this sense: *she enjoyed the touch of the damp grass on her feet* **15** the act or an instance of something coming into contact with the body: *he remembered the touch of her hand* **16** a gentle push, tap, or caress: *the switch takes only the merest touch to operate* **17** a small amount; trace: *a touch of luxury* **18** a particular manner or style of doing something: *his songs always reveal his keen melodic touch* **19** a detail of some work: *final touches were now being put to the plans* **20** a slight attack: *a touch of dysentery* **21** (in sports such as football or rugby) the area outside the lines marking the side of the pitch: *he kicked the ball into touch* **22** the technique of fingering a keyboard instrument **23 a touch** slightly or marginally: *it's nice, but a touch expensive* **24 in touch a** regularly speaking to, writing to, or visiting someone **b** having up-to-date knowledge or understanding of a situation or trend **25 lose touch a** to gradually stop speaking to, writing to, or visiting someone **b** to stop having up-to-date knowledge or understanding of a situation or trend **26 out of touch a** no longer speaking to, writing to, or visiting someone **b** no longer having up-to-date knowledge or understanding of a situation or trend ▷ See also **touchdown, touch off, touch up** [Old French *tochier*]

touch and go *adj* risky or critical: *it was touch and go whether the mission would succeed*

touchdown *n* **1** the moment at which a landing aircraft or spacecraft comes into contact with the landing surface **2** *American football* a scoring move in which an attacking player takes the ball into the area behind his opponents' goal ▷ *vb* **touch down 3** (of an aircraft or spacecraft) to land

touché (too-**shay**) *interj* **1** an acknowledgment that a remark or witty reply has been effective **2** an acknowledgment of a scoring hit in fencing [French, literally: touched]

touched *adj* **1** moved to sympathy or emotion: *I was touched by her understanding* **2** slightly mad: *she's a bit touched*

touching *adj* **1** arousing tender feelings ▷ *prep* **2** relating to or concerning: *she might talk about matters touching both of them*

touch judge *n* one of the two linesmen in rugby

touchless *adj* (of a device) able to be controlled without touching a keypad or screen

touchline *n* either of the lines marking the side of the playing area in certain games, such as rugby

touch off *vb* to cause (a disturbance, violence, etc.) to begin: *the death of a teenager in police custody touched off a night of riots*

touchpaper *n* a fuse of dark blue paper on a firework

touch rugby *n* a version of rugby in which players seek to evade being touched (rather than tackled) while in possession of the ball

touchstone *n* a standard by which judgment is made: *this restaurant is the touchstone for genuine Italian cookery in Leeds*

touch-type *vb* **-typing, -typed** to type without looking at the keyboard ▷ **touch-typist** *n*

touch up *vb* to enhance, renovate, or falsify (a picture) by adding extra touches to it

touchwood *n* something, esp. dry wood, used as tinder [*touch* (in the sense: to kindle)]

touchy *adj* **touchier, touchiest 1** easily upset or irritated: *he is a touchy and quick-tempered man* **2** requiring careful and tactful handling: *a touchy subject* ▷ **touchiness** *n*

touchy-feely *adj informal, sometimes offensive* sensitive and caring

tough *adj* **1** strong and difficult to break, cut, or tear: *this fabric is tough and water-resistant* **2** (of meat or other food) difficult to cut and chew; not tender **3** physically or mentally strong and able to cope with hardship: *a tough uncompromising woman, unwilling to take no for an answer* **4** rough or violent: *a tough and ruthless mercenary* **5** strict and firm: *the country's tough drugs laws* **6** difficult or troublesome to do or deal with: *a tough task* **7 tough luck!** *informal* an expression of lack of sympathy for someone else's problems ▷ *n* **8** a rough, vicious, or violent person ▷ *vb* **9 tough it out** *informal* to endure a difficult situation until it improves: *criticism of his performance has reinforced his desire to tough it out* [Old English *tōh*] ▷ **toughness** *n*

toughen *vb* to make or become tough or tougher

Toul *n* a town in NE France: a leading episcopal see in the Middle Ages. Pop: 16 945 (1999)

Toulon *n* a fortified port and naval base in SE France, on the Mediterranean: naval arsenal developed by Henry IV and Richelieu, later fortified by Vauban. Pop: 170 041 (2006)

Toulouse *n* a city in S France, on the Garonne River: scene of severe religious strife in the early 13th and mid-16th centuries; university (1229). Pop: 444 392 (2006). Ancient name: **Tolosa**

Toulouse-Lautrec *n* Henri (Marie Raymond) de. 1864–1901, French painter and lithographer, noted for his paintings and posters of the life of Montmartre, Paris

toupee (**too**-pay) *n* a hairpiece worn by men to cover a bald place [French *toupet* forelock]

tour *n* **1** an extended journey visiting places of interest along the route **2** a trip, by a band, theatre company, etc., to perform in several places **3** an overseas trip made by a cricket team, rugby team, etc., to play in several places **4** *military* a period of service, esp. in one place: *the regiment has served several tours in Northern Ireland* ▷ *vb* **5** to make a tour of (a place) [Old French: a turn]

Touraine *n* a former province of NW central France: at its height in the 16th century as an area of royal residences, esp. along the Loire. Chief town: Tours

Tourane *n* the former name of **Da Nang**

Tourcoing *n* a town in NE France: textile manufacturing. Pop: 93 540 (1999)

tour de force *n, pl* **tours de force** a masterly or brilliant stroke or achievement [French, literally: feat of skill or strength]

Touré *n* (Ahmed) Sékou. 1922–84, president of the Republic of Guinea (1958–84)

tourism *n* tourist travel, esp. when regarded as an industry

tourist *n* **1** a person who travels for pleasure, usually sightseeing and staying in hotels **2** a member of a sports team which is visiting a country to play a series of matches: *the tourists were bowled out for 135* **3** the lowest class of accommodation on a passenger ship ▷ *adj* **4** of or relating to tourists or tourism: *a popular tourist attraction* **5** of the lowest class of accommodation on a passenger ship or aircraft

touristy *adj informal, often disparaging* full of tourists or tourist attractions

tourmaline *n* a hard crystalline mineral used in jewellery and electrical equipment [German *Turmalin*]

Tournai *n* a city in W Belgium, in Hainaut province on the River Scheldt: under several European rulers until 1814. Pop: 67 341 (2004 est). Flemish name: **Doornik**

tournament *n* **1** a sporting competition in which contestants play a series of games to determine an overall winner **2** Also: **tourney** *medieval history* a contest in which mounted knights fought for a prize [Old French *torneiement*]

tournedos (tour-ned-doh) *n, pl* **-dos** (-doze) a thick round steak of beef [French]

Tourneur *n* Cyril. ?1575–1626, English dramatist; author of *The Atheist's Tragedy* (1611) and, reputedly, of *The Revenger's Tragedy* (1607)

tourniquet (**tour**-nick-kay) *n med* a strip of cloth tied tightly round an arm or leg to stop bleeding from an artery [French]

Tours *n* a town in W central France, on the River Loire: nearby is the scene of the defeat of the Arabs in 732, which ended the advance of Islam in W Europe. Pop: 140 252 (2006)

tourtière (tour-tee-**air**) *n Canad* a type of meat pie

tousle (rhymes with **arousal**) *vb* **-sling, -sled** to make (hair or clothes) ruffled and untidy [Low German *tūsen* to shake] ▷ **tousled** *adj*

Toussaint L'Ouverture *n* Pierre Dominique. ?1743–1803, Haitian revolutionary leader. He was made governor of the island by the French Revolutionary

t

government (1794) and expelled the Spanish and British but when Napoleon I proclaimed the re-establishment of slavery he was arrested. He died in prison in France

tout (rhymes with **shout**) vb **1** to seek (business, customers, etc.) or try to sell (goods), esp. in a persistent or direct manner: *he went from door to door touting for business* **2** to put forward or recommend (a person or thing) as a good or suitable example or candidate: *the plant was once touted as a showcase factory* ▷ n **3** a person who sells tickets for a heavily booked event at inflated prices [Old English *tȳtan* to peep]

tow¹ vb **1** to pull or drag (a vehicle), esp. by means of a rope or cable ▷ n **2** the act or an instance of towing **3 in tow** *informal* in one's company or one's charge or under one's influence: *she had an older man in tow* **4 on tow** (of a vehicle) being towed [Old English *togian*]

tow² n fibres of hemp, flax, jute, etc., prepared for spinning [Old English *tōw*]

towards *or US* **toward** *prep* **1** in the direction of: *towards the lake* **2** with regard to: *hostility towards the President* **3** as a contribution to: *the profits will go towards three projects* **4** just before: *towards evening*

towbar n a rigid metal bar attached to the back of a vehicle, from which a trailer or caravan can be towed

towel n **1** a piece of absorbent cloth or paper used for drying things **2 throw in the towel** See **throw in** (3) ▷ vb **-elling, -elled** *or US* **-eling, -eled** **3** to dry or wipe with a towel [Old French *toaille*]

towelling *or US* **toweling** n a soft, fairly thick fabric used to make towels and dressing gowns

tower n **1** a tall, usually square or circular structure, sometimes part of a larger building and usually built for a specific purpose **2 tower of strength** a person who supports or comforts someone else at a time of difficulty ▷ vb **3 tower over** to be much taller than: *sheer walls of limestone towered over us* [Latin *turris*]

tower block n *Brit* a very tall building divided into flats or offices

Tower Hamlets n a borough of E Greater London, on the River Thames: contains the main part of the East End. Pop: 206 600 (2003 est). Area: 20 sq km (8 sq miles)

towering *adj* **1** very tall **2** very impressive or important: *his towering presence on stage* **3** very intense: *in a towering rage*

Tower of London n a fortress in the City of London, on the River Thames: begun 1078; later extended and used as a palace, the main state prison, and now as a museum containing the crown jewels

towheaded *adj* having blonde or yellowish hair [tow²]

town n **1** a large group of houses, shops, factories, etc., smaller than a city and larger than a village. Related adjective: **urban 2** the nearest town or the chief town of an area: *people from town rarely went out to the farm* **3** the central area of a town where most of the shops and offices are: *we're going to a pub in town tonight* **4** the people of a town: *the town is split over the plans for a bypass* **5** built-up areas in general, as opposed to the countryside: *migration from the country to the town* **6 go to town** to make a supreme or unrestricted effort **7 on the town** visiting nightclubs, restaurants, etc.: *we'd a night on the town to celebrate her promotion* [Old English *tūn* village]

town clerk n (currently in Australia and in Britain until 1974) the chief administrative officer of a town

town crier n (formerly) a person employed to make public announcements in the streets

Townes n Charles Hard. 1915–2015, US physicist, noted for his research in quantum electronics leading to the invention of the maser and the laser; shared the Nobel prize for physics in 1964

town hall n a large building in a town often containing the council offices and a hall for public meetings

town house n **1** a terraced house in an urban area, esp. an up-market one **2** a person's town residence as distinct from his or her country residence

townie *or* **townee** n chiefly *Brit informal, often disparaging* a

resident in a town, esp. as distinct from country dwellers

town planning n the comprehensive planning of the physical and social development of a town

Townshend n **1** Charles, 2nd Viscount, nicknamed *Turnip Townshend*. 1674–1738, English politician and agriculturist **2** Pete born 1945, British rock guitarist, singer, and songwriter: member of the Who from 1964 and composer of much of their material

township n **1** a small town **2** (in South Africa) a planned urban settlement of black people or people of mixed racial descent **3** (in the US and Canada) a small unit of local government, often consisting of a town and the area surrounding it **4** (in Canada) a land-survey area, usually 36 square miles (93 square kilometres)

townsman n, pl **-men** an inhabitant of a town ▷ **townswoman** *fem* n

townspeople *or* **townsfolk** pl n the people who live in a town

Townsville n a port in E Australia, in NE Queensland on the Coral Sea: centre of a vast agricultural and mining hinterland. Pop: 119 504 (2001)

towpath n a path beside a canal or river, formerly used by horses pulling barges

towrope n a rope or cable used for towing a vehicle or vessel

toxaemia *or US* **toxemia** (tox-seem-ya) n **1** a form of blood poisoning caused by toxins released by bacteria at a wound or other site of infection **2** a condition in pregnant women characterized by high blood pressure [Latin *toxicum* poison + *haima* blood] ▷ **toxaemic** *or US* **toxemic** *adj*

toxic *adj* **1** poisonous: *toxic fumes* **2** caused by poison: *toxic effects* [Greek *toxikon* (*pharmakon*) (poison) used on arrows] ▷ **toxicity** n

toxicology n the branch of science concerned with poisons and their effects ▷ **toxicological** *adj* ▷ **toxicologist** n

toxin n **1** any of various poisonous substances produced by microorganisms and causing certain diseases **2** any other poisonous substance of plant or animal origin

toy n **1** an object designed for children to play with, such as a doll or model car **2** an object that adults use for entertainment rather than for a serious purpose: *I do use my computer: it's not just a toy* ▷ *adj* **3** being an imitation or model of something for children to play with: *a toy aeroplane* **4** (of a dog) of a variety much smaller than is normal for that breed: *a toy poodle* [origin unknown]

Toyama n a city in central Japan, on W Honshu on **Toyama Bay** (an inlet of the Sea of Japan): chemical and textile centre. Pop: 321 049 (2002 est)

toy boy n the much younger male lover of an older woman

Toynbee n **1** Arnold 1852–83, British economist and social reformer, after whom **Toynbee Hall**, a residential settlement in East London, is named **2** his nephew, Arnold Joseph. 1889–1975, British historian. In his chief work, *A Study of History* (1934–61), he attempted to analyse the principles determining the rise and fall of civilizations

toy-toy *or* **toyi-toyi** *S African* n **1** a dance expressing defiance and protest ▷ vb **2** to dance in this way [origin uncertain]

toy with vb **1** to consider an idea without being serious about it or being able to decide about it: *I've been toying with the idea of setting up my own firm* **2** to keep moving (an object) about with one's fingers, esp. when thinking about something else: *Jessica sat toying with her glass*

Trabzon *or* **Trebizond** n a port in NE Turkey, on the Black Sea: founded as a Greek colony in the 8th century BC at the terminus of an important trade route from central Europe to Asia. Pop: 246 000 (2005 est)

trace vb **tracing, traced 1** to locate or work out (the cause or source of something): *he traced the trouble to a faulty connection* **2** to find (something or someone that was missing): *the police were unable to trace her missing husband* **3** to discover or describe the progress or development of (something): *throughout the 19th century we can trace the development of more complex machinery* **4** to copy (a design, map, etc.) by putting a piece of transparent paper over it and following the lines which show through the paper with a pencil **5** to make the outline of (a shape or pattern): *his index finger was tracing circles on the arm of the chair* ▷ *n* **6** a mark, footprint, or other sign that shows that a person, animal, or thing has been in a particular place: *the police could find no trace of the missing van* **7** an amount of something so small that it is barely noticeable: *I detected a trace of jealousy in her voice* **8** a remnant of something: *traces of an Iron-Age fort remain visible* **9** a pattern made on a screen or a piece of paper by a device that is measuring or detecting something: *a baffling radar trace* [French *tracier*] **>** **traceable** *adj*

trace element *n* a chemical element that occurs in very small amounts in soil, water, etc. and is essential for healthy growth

tracer *n* **1** a projectile that can be observed when in flight by the burning of chemical substances in its base **2** *med* an element or other substance introduced into the body to study metabolic processes

tracer bullet *n* a round of small-arms ammunition containing a tracer

tracery *n*, *pl* **-eries** **1** a pattern of interlacing lines, esp. one in a stained glass window **2** any fine lacy pattern resembling this

traces *pl n* **1** the two side straps that connect a horse's harness to the vehicle being pulled **2 kick over the traces** to escape or defy control [Old French *trait*]

trachea (track-kee-a) *n*, *pl* **-cheae** (-kee-ee) *anatomy, zoology* the tube that carries inhaled air from the throat to the lungs [Greek]

tracheotomy (track-ee-ot-a-mee) *n*, *pl* **-mies** surgical incision into the trachea, as performed when the air passage has been blocked [TRACHEA + Greek *tomē* a cutting]

trachoma (track-oh-ma) *n* a chronic contagious disease of the eye characterized by inflammation of the inner surface of the lids and the formation of scar tissue [Greek *trakhōma* roughness]

tracing *n* **1** a copy of something, such as a map, made by tracing **2** a line traced by a recording instrument

track *n* **1** a rough road or path: *a farm track* **2** the mark or trail left by something that has passed by: *the fox didn't leave any tracks* **3** a rail or pair of parallel rails on which a vehicle, such as a train, runs **4** a course for running or racing on: *a running track* **5** a separate song or piece of music on a record, tape, or CD: *Dolphy switches back to bass clarinet for the final track* **6** a course of action, thought, etc.: *I don't think you're on the right track at all* **7** an endless band on the wheels of a tank, bulldozer, etc. to enable it to move across rough ground **8 keep** or **lose track of** to follow or fail to follow the course or progress of **9 off the beaten track** in an isolated location: *the village where she lives is a bit off the beaten track* ▷ *vb* **10** to follow the trail of (a person or animal) **11** to follow the flight path of (a satellite etc.) by picking up signals transmitted or reflected by it **12** *films* to follow (a moving object) while filming **▶** See also **tracks** [Old French *trac*] **>** **tracker** *n*

track down *vb* to find (someone or something) by tracking or pursuing

tracker dog *n* a dog specially trained to search for missing people

track event *n* a competition in athletics, such as sprinting, that takes place on a running track

track record *n informal* the past record of the accomplishments and failures of a person or organization

tracks *pl n* **1** marks, such as footprints, left by someone or something that has passed **2 in one's tracks** on the very spot where one is standing: *those words stopped her in*

her tracks **3 make tracks** to leave or depart: *it was time to start making tracks*

track shoe *n* a light running shoe fitted with steel spikes for better grip

tracksuit *n* a warm loose-fitting suit worn by athletes etc., esp. during training

tract¹ *n* **1** a large area, esp. of land: *an extensive tract of moorland* **2** *anatomy* a system of organs or glands that has a particular function: *the urinary tract* [Latin *tractus* a stretching out]

tract² *n* a pamphlet, esp. a religious one [Latin *tractatus*]

tractable *adj formal* easy to control, manage, or deal with: *he could easily manage his tractable and worshipping younger brother* [Latin *tractare* to manage] **>** **tractability** *n*

traction *n* **1** pulling, esp. by engine power: *the increased use of electric traction* **2** *med* the application of a steady pull on an injured limb using a system of weights and pulleys or splints: *he was in traction for weeks following the accident* **3** the grip that the wheels of a vehicle have on the ground: *four-wheel drive gives much better traction in wet or icy conditions* [Latin *tractus* dragged]

traction engine *n* a heavy steam-powered vehicle used, esp. formerly, for drawing heavy loads along roads or over rough ground

tractor *n* a motor vehicle with large rear wheels, used to pull heavy loads, esp. farm machinery [Late Latin: one who pulls]

Tracy *n* Spencer. 1900–67, US film actor. His films include *The Power and the Glory* (1933), *Captains Courageous* (1937) and *Boys' Town* (1938), for both of which he won Oscars, *Adam's Rib* (1949), and *Bad Day at Black Rock* (1955)

trade *n* **1** the buying and selling of goods and services **2** a person's job, esp. a craft requiring skill: *he's a plumber by trade* **3** the people and practices of an industry, craft, or business **4** amount of custom or commercial dealings: *a brisk trade in second-hand weapons* **5** a specified market or business: *the wool trade* **6 trades** the trade winds ▷ *vb* **trading, traded** **7** to buy and sell (goods) **8** to exchange: *he traded a job in New York for a life as a cowboy* **9** to engage in trade **10** to deal or do business (with) [Low German: track, hence a regular business] **>** **tradable** or **tradeable** *adj* **>** **trader** *n* **>** **trading** *n*

trade-in *n* **1** a used article given in part payment for the purchase of a new article ▷ *vb* **trade in** **2** to give (a used article) as part payment for a new article

trademark *n* **1 a** the name or other symbol used by a manufacturer to distinguish his or her products from those of competitors **b Registered Trademark** one that is officially registered and legally protected **2** any distinctive sign or mark of a person or thing: *the designer bars which have become the trademark of the city*

trade name *n* **1** the name used by a trade to refer to a product or range of products **2** the name under which a commercial enterprise operates in business

trade-off *n* an exchange, esp. as a compromise: *there is often a trade-off between manpower costs and computer costs*

trade on *vb* to exploit or take advantage of: *a demanding woman who traded on her poor health to get her own way*

Tradescant *n* **1** John. 1570–1638, English botanist and gardener to Charles I. He introduced many plants from overseas into Britain **2** his son, John. 1608–62, English naturalist and gardener, who continued his father's work

tradescantia (trad-dess-kan-shee-a) *n* a widely cultivated plant with striped leaves [after John TRADESCANT]

trade secret *n* a secret formula, technique, or process known and used to advantage by only one manufacturer

tradesman *n*, *pl* **-men** **1** a skilled worker, such as an electrician or painter **2** a shopkeeper **>** **tradeswoman** *fem n*

Trades Union Congress *n* (in Britain and South Africa) the major association of trade unions, which includes all the larger unions

trade union or **trades union** n a society of workers formed to protect and improve their working conditions, pay, etc. ⟩ **trade unionism** or **trades unionism** n ⟩ **trade unionist** or **trades unionist** n

trade wind n a wind blowing steadily towards the equator either from the northeast in the N hemisphere or the southeast in the S hemisphere

trading estate n chiefly Brit a large area in which a number of commercial or industrial firms are situated

tradition n **1** the handing down from generation to generation of customs, beliefs, etc. **2** the unwritten body of beliefs, customs, etc. handed down from generation to generation **3** a custom or practice of long standing **4 in the tradition of** having many features similar to those of a person or thing in the past: a thriller writer in the tradition of Chandler [Latin traditio a handing down]

traditional adj of, relating to, or being a tradition ⟩ **traditionally** adv

traditionalist n a person who supports established customs or beliefs ⟩ **traditionalism** n

traduce vb **-ducing, -duced** formal to speak badly of (someone) [Latin traducere to lead over, disgrace] ⟩ **traducement** n ⟩ **traducer** n

Trafalgar n Cape Trafalgar a cape on the SW coast of Spain, south of Cádiz: scene of the decisive naval battle (1805) in which the French and Spanish fleets were defeated by the British under Nelson, who was mortally wounded

traffic n **1** the vehicles travelling on roads **2** the movement of vehicles or people in a particular place or for a particular purpose: air traffic **3** trade, esp. of an illicit kind: drug traffic **4** the exchange of ideas between people or organizations: a lively traffic in ideas ▷ vb **-ficking, -ficked 5** to carry on trade or business, esp. of an illicit kind: he confessed to trafficking in gold and ivory [Old French trafique] ⟩ **trafficker** n

traffic island n a raised area in the middle of a road designed as a guide for traffic flow and to provide a stopping place for pedestrians crossing

traffic jam n a number of vehicles so obstructed that they can scarcely move

traffic light n one of a set of coloured lights placed at a junction to control the flow of traffic

traffic warden n Brit a person employed to supervise road traffic and report traffic offences

Trafford n a unitary authority in NW England, in Greater Manchester. Pop: 211 800 (2003 est). Area: 106 sq km (41 sq miles)

tragedian (traj-jee-dee-an) or fem **tragedienne** (traj-jee-dee-**enn**) n **1** an actor who specializes in tragic roles **2** a writer of tragedy

tragedy n, pl **-dies 1** a shocking or sad event **2** a serious play, film, or opera in which the main character is destroyed by a combination of a personal failing and adverse circumstances [Greek tragōidia]

tragic adj **1** sad and distressing because it involves death or suffering: she was blinded in a tragic accident **2** of or like a tragedy: a tragic hero **3** sad or mournful: a tragic melody ⟩ **tragically** adv

tragicomedy n, pl **-dies** a play or written work having both comic and tragic elements ⟩ **tragicomic** adj

Traherne n Thomas. 1637–74, English mystical prose writer and poet. His prose works include Centuries of Meditations, which was discovered in manuscript in 1896 and published in 1908

trail n **1** a rough path across open country or through a forest **2** a route along a series of roads or paths that has been specially planned to let people see or do particular things: a nature trail through the woods **3** a print, mark, or scent left by a person, animal, or object: a trail of blood was found down three flights of stairs **4** something that trails behind: a vapour trail **5** a sequence of results from an event: a trail of mishaps ▷ vb **6** to drag or stream along the

ground or through the air behind someone or something: part of her sari trailed behind her on the floor **7** to lag behind (a person or thing): Max had arrived as well, trailing behind the others **8** to follow or hunt (an animal or person), usually secretly, by following the marks or tracks he, she, or it has made: the police had trailed him the length and breadth of the country **9** to be falling behind in a race, match, or competition: they trailed 2-1 at half-time **10** to move wearily or slowly: we spent the afternoon trailing round the shops [Old French trailler to tow]

trail away or **trail off** vb to become fainter, quieter, or weaker: his voice trailed away

trailblazer n a pioneer in a particular field ⟩ **trailblazing** adj, n

trailer n **1** a road vehicle, usually two-wheeled, towed by a motor vehicle and used for carrying goods, transporting boats, etc.: ahead of us was a tractor, drawing a trailer laden with dung **2** the rear section of an articulated lorry **3** an extract or series of extracts from a film, TV, or radio programme, used to advertise it **4** US and Canad same as **caravan** (1)

trailer trash n disparaging poor people living in trailer parks in the US

trailing adj (of a plant) having a long stem which spreads over the ground or hangs loosely: trailing ivy

train vb **1** to instruct (someone) in a skill: soldiers are trained to obey orders unquestioningly **2** to learn the skills needed to do a particular job or activity: she was training to be a computer programmer **3** to do exercises and prepare for a specific purpose: he was training for a marathon **4** to focus on or aim at (something): the warship kept its guns trained on the trawler **5** to discipline (an animal) to obey commands or perform tricks **6** to tie or prune (a plant) so that it grows in a particular way: he had trained the roses to grow up the wall ▷ n **7** a line of railway coaches or wagons coupled together and drawn by a engine **8** a sequence or series: following an earlier train of thought **9** the long back section of a dress that trails along the floor **10 in its train** as a consequence: economic mismanagement brought unemployment and inflation in its train **11 in train** actually happening or being done: the programme of reforms set in train by the new government ▷ adj **12** of or by a train: the long train journey North [Old French trahiner]

trainbearer n an attendant who holds up the train of a dignitary's robe or bride's gown

trainee n **1** a person undergoing training ▷ adj **2** (of a person) undergoing training: a trainee journalist

trainer n **1** a person who coaches a person or team in a sport **2** a person who trains racehorses **3** an aircraft used for training pilots **4** Brit a flat-soled sports shoe of the style used by athletes when training

training n the process of bringing a person to an agreed standard of proficiency by practice and instruction

training shoe n same as **trainer** (4)

train spotter n Brit **1** a person who collects the numbers of railway locomotives **2** informal a person who is obsessed with trivial details, esp. of a subject generally considered uninteresting

traipse informal vb **traipsing, traipsed 1** to walk heavily or tiredly ▷ n **2** a long or tiring walk [origin unknown]

trait n a characteristic feature or quality of a person or thing [French]

traitor n a person who betrays friends, country, a cause, etc. [Latin tradere to hand over] ⟩ **traitorous** adj ⟩ **traitress** fem n

Trajan n Latin name Marcus Ulpius Traianus. ?53–117 AD, Roman emperor (98–117). He extended the empire to the east and built many roads, bridges, canals, and towns

trajectory n, pl **-ries** the path described by an object moving in air or space, esp. the curved path of a projectile [Latin trajectus cast over]

Trakl n Georg. 1887–1914, Austrian poet, noted for his expressionist style: died of a drug overdose while serving as a medical officer in World War I

Tralee n a market town in SW Republic of Ireland, county town of Kerry, near **Tralee Bay** (an inlet of the Atlantic). Pop: 21 987 (2002)

tram n an electrically driven public transport vehicle that runs on rails laid into the road and takes its power from an overhead cable [probably from Low German *traam* beam]

tramlines pl n **1** the tracks on which a tram runs **2** the outer markings along the sides of a tennis or badminton court

trammel vb **-melling, -melled** or US **-meling, -meled 1** to hinder or restrict: *trammelled by family responsibilities* ▷ n **2 trammels** things that hinder or restrict someone: *the trammels of social respectability* [Old French *tramail* three-mesh net]

tramp vb **1** to walk long and far; hike **2** to walk heavily or firmly across or through (a place): *she tramped slowly up the beach* ▷ n **3** a homeless person who travels about on foot, living by begging or doing casual work **4** a long hard walk; hike: *we went for a long tramp over the downs* **5** the sound of heavy regular footsteps: *we could hear the tramp of the marching soldiers* **6** a small cargo ship that does not run on a regular schedule **7** US, Canad, Austral and NZ slang a promiscuous woman [probably from Middle Low German *trampen*]

tramping n NZ the leisure activity of walking in the bush ▷ **tramper** n

trample vb **-pling, -pled 1** Also: **trample on** to tread on and crush: *three children were trampled to death when the crowd panicked and ran* **2 trample on** to treat (a person or his or her rights or feelings) with disregard or contempt [from *tramp*]

trampoline n **1** a tough canvas sheet suspended by springs or cords from a frame, which acrobats, gymnasts, etc., bounce on ▷ vb **-lining, -lined 2** to exercise on a trampoline [Italian *trampolino*]

trance n **1** a hypnotic state resembling sleep in which a person is unable to move or act of his or her own will **2** a dazed or stunned state [Latin *transire* to go over]

tranche (trahnsh) n an instalment or portion, esp. of a loan or share issue: *the new shares will be offered in four tranches around the world*

trannie or **tranny** n, pl **-nies** informal, chiefly Brit a transistor radio

tranquil adj calm, peaceful, or quiet [Latin *tranquillus*] ▷ **tranquilly** adv

tranquillity or US sometimes **tranquility** n a state of calmness or peace

tranquillize, -lise or US **tranquilize** vb **-lizing, -lized** or **-lising, -lised 1** to make or become calm or calmer **2** to give (someone) a drug to make them calm or calmer ▷ **tranquillization, -lisation** or US **tranquilization** n ▷ **tranquillizing, -lising** or US **tranquilizing** adj

tranquillizer, -liser or US **tranquilizer** n a drug that calms someone suffering from anxiety, tension, etc.

trans. 1 transitive **2** translated

trans- prefix **1** across, beyond, crossing, or on the other side of: *transnational* **2** changing thoroughly: *transliterate* [Latin]

transact vb to do, conduct, or negotiate (a business deal) [Latin *transigere* to drive through]

transaction n **1** something that is transacted, esp. a business deal **2 transactions** the records of the proceedings of a society etc.: *an article on land use in the Niagara area taken from the 'Transactions of the Royal Canadian Institute'*

transalpine adj beyond the Alps, esp. as viewed from Italy

Transalpine Gaul n (in the ancient world) that part of Gaul northwest of the Alps

transatlantic adj **1** on or from the other side of the Atlantic **2** crossing the Atlantic

Transcaucasia n a region in central Asia, south of the Caucasus Mountains between the Black and Caspian Seas in Georgia, Armenia, and Azerbaijan: a constituent republic of the Soviet Union from 1918 until 1936

Transcaucasian adj **1** of or relating to the central Asian region of Transcaucasia or its inhabitants ▷ n **2** a native or inhabitant of Transcaucasia

transceiver n a device which transmits and receives radio or electronic signals [*trans(mitter)* + *(re)ceiver*]

transcend vb **1** to go above or beyond what is expected or normal: *a vital party issue that transcends traditional party loyalties* **2** to overcome or be superior to: *to transcend all difficulties* [Latin *transcendere* to climb over]

transcendent adj **1** above or beyond what is expected or normal **2** theol (of God) having existence outside the created world ▷ **transcendence** n

transcendental adj **1** above or beyond what is expected or normal **2** philosophy based on intuition or innate belief rather than experience **3** supernatural or mystical ▷ **transcendentally** adv

transcendentalism n any system of philosophy that seeks to discover the nature of reality by examining the processes of thought rather than the things thought about, or that emphasizes intuition as a means to knowledge ▷ **transcendentalist** n, adj

Transcendental Meditation n a technique (trademarked in the US), based on Hindu traditions, for relaxing and refreshing the mind and body through the silent repetition of a special formula of words

transcribe vb **-scribing, -scribed 1** to write, type, or print out (a text) fully from a speech or notes **2** to make an electrical recording of (a programme or speech) for a later broadcast **3** music to rewrite (a piece of music) for an instrument other than that originally intended [Latin *transcribere*] ▷ **transcriber** n

transcript n **1** a written, typed, or printed copy made by transcribing **2** chiefly US and Canad an official record of a student's school progress

transcription n **1** the act of transcribing **2** something transcribed

Transdniestria n a region of E Moldova: unilaterally declared itself independent in 1990 and was the scene of fighting between government troops and separatists in 1992; to a large extent it functions as a separate republic, but without international recognition

transducer n any device, such as a microphone or electric motor, that converts one form of energy into another [Latin *transducere* to lead across]

transect n biology a sample strip of land used to monitor plant distribution and animal populations within a given area

transept n either of the two shorter wings of a cross-shaped church [Latin *trans-* across + *saeptum* enclosure]

transfer vb **-ferring, -ferred 1** to change or move from one thing, person, place, etc., to another: *he was transferred from prison to hospital* **2** to move (money or property) from the control of one person or organization to that of another: *the money has been transferred into your account* **3** (of a football club) to sell or release (a player) to another club: *he was transferred to Juventus for a world record fee* **4** to move (a drawing or design) from one surface to another ▷ n **5** the act, process, or system of transferring, or the state of being transferred **6** a person or thing that transfers or is transferred **7** a design or drawing that is transferred from one surface to another **8** the moving of (money or property) from the control of one person or organization to that of another [Latin *trans* across + *ferre* to carry] ▷ **transferable** or **transferrable** adj ▷ **transference** n

transfer station n NZ a depot where rubbish is sorted for recycling

transfiguration n a transfiguring or being transfigured

Transfiguration n **1** New Testament the change in the appearance of Christ on the mountain **2** the Church festival held in commemoration of this on August 6

t

transfigure *vb* **-guring, -gured** **1** to change or cause to change in appearance **2** to become or cause to become more exalted [Latin *trans-* beyond + *figura* appearance]

transfix *vb* **-fixing, -fixed** *or* **-fixt** **1** to make (someone) motionless, esp. with horror or shock: *they stood transfixed and revolted by what they saw* **2** to pierce (a person or animal) through with a pointed object: *the Pharaoh is shown transfixing enemies with arrows from a moving chariot* [Latin *transfigere* to pierce through]

transform *vb* **1** to change completely in form or function: *the last forty years have seen the country transformed from a peasant economy to a major industrial power* **2** to change so as to make better or more attractive: *most religions claim to be able to transform people's lives* **3** to convert (one form of energy) to another **4** maths to change the form of (an equation, expression, etc.) without changing its value **5** to change (an alternating current or voltage) using a transformer [Latin *transformare*]

transformation *n* **1** a change or alteration, esp. a radical one **2** the act of transforming or the state of being transformed **3** *S African* a political slogan for demographic change in the power struggle

transformer *n* a device that transfers an alternating current from one circuit to one or more other circuits, usually with a change of voltage

transfuse *vb* **-fusing, -fused** **1** to inject (blood or other fluid) into a blood vessel **2** *literary* to transmit or instil [Latin *transfundere* to pour out]

transfusion *n* **1** the injection of blood, blood plasma, etc., into the blood vessels of a patient **2** the act of transferring something: *a transfusion of new funds*

transgenic *adj* (of an animal or plant) containing genetic material artificially transferred from another species

transgress *vb* *formal* **1** to break (a law or rule) **2** to overstep (a limit): *he had never before been known to transgress the very slowest of walks* [Latin *trans* beyond + *gradi* to step] ❭ **transgression** *n* ❭ **transgressor** *n*

transient *adj* **1** lasting for a short time only: *she had a number of transient relationships with fellow students* **2** (of a person) not remaining in a place for a long time: *the transient population of the inner city* ▷ *n* **3** a transient person or thing [Latin *transiens* going over] ❭ **transience** *n*

transistor *n* **1** a semiconductor device used to amplify and control electric currents **2** *informal* a small portable radio containing transistors [*transfer* + *resistor*]

transistorized *or* **-ised** *adj* (of an electronic device) using transistors

transit *n* **1** the moving or carrying of goods or people from one place to another **2** a route or means of transport: *transit by road* **3** *astronomy* the apparent passage of a celestial body across the meridian **4** *in transit* while travelling or being taken from one place to another: *in transit the fruit can be damaged* ▷ *adj* **5** indicating a place or building where people wait or goods are kept between different stages of a journey: *a transit lounge for passengers who are changing planes* [Latin *transitus* a going over]

transit camp *n* a camp in which refugees, soldiers, etc., live temporarily

transition *n* **1** the process of changing from one state or stage to another: *the transition from dictatorship to democracy* **2** *music* a movement from one key to another [Latin *transitio* a going over] ❭ **transitional** *adj*

transition element *or* **transition metal** *n chem* any element belonging to one of three series of elements with atomic numbers between 21 and 30, 39 and 48, and 57 and 80 (**transition series**). They tend to have more than one valency and to form complexes

transitive *adj grammar* denoting a verb that requires a direct object: *'to find' is a transitive verb*

transitory *adj* lasting only for a short time

Trans-Jordan *n* the former name (1922–49) of Jordan

Trans-Jordanian *adj* **1** of or relating to the former Trans-Jordan (now Jordan) or its inhabitants ▷ *n* **2** a native or inhabitant of Trans-Jordan

Transkei *n* (formerly) the largest of the Bantu homelands in South Africa; declared an independent state in 1976 but this was not recognized outside South Africa; abolished in 1993. Capital: Umtata

Transkeian *adj* **1** of or relating to the former Bantu homeland of Transkei (now part of South Africa) or its inhabitants ▷ *n* **2** a native or inhabitant of Transkei

translate *vb* **-lating, -lated** **1 a** to change (something spoken or written in one language) into another **b** to be capable of being changed from one language into another: *puns do not translate well* **2** to express (something) in a different way, for instance by using a different measurement system or less technical language: *the temperature is 30° Celsius, or if we translate into Fahrenheit, 86°* **3** to transform or convert, for instance by putting an idea into practice: *cheap crops translate into lower feed prices* **4** to interpret the significance of (a gesture, action, etc.): *I gave him what I hoped would be translated as a thoughtful look* **5** to act as a translator: *I had to translate for a party of visiting Greeks* [Latin *translatus* carried over] ❭ **translatable** *adj* ❭ **translator** *n*

translation *n* **1** a piece of writing or speech that has been translated into another language **2** the act of translating something **3** the expression of something in a different way or form: *the book's plot was radically altered during its translation to film* **4** maths a transformation in which the origin of a coordinate system is moved to another position so that each axis retains the same direction ❭ **translational** *adj*

transliterate *vb* **-rating, -rated** to write or spell (a word etc.) into corresponding letters of another alphabet [Latin *trans-* across + *littera* letter] ❭ **transliteration** *n*

translucent *adj* allowing light to pass through, but not transparent [Latin *translucere* to shine through] ❭ **translucency** *or* **translucence** *n*

transmigrate *vb* **-grating, -grated** (of a soul) to pass from one body into another at death ❭ **transmigration** *n*

transmission *n* **1** the sending or passing of something, such as a message or disease from one place or person to another **2** something that is transmitted, esp. a radio or television broadcast **3** a system of shafts and gears that transmits power from the engine to the driving wheels of a motor vehicle

transmit *vb* **-mitting, -mitted** **1** to pass (something, such as a message or disease) from one place or person to another **2 a** to send out (signals) by means of radio waves **b** to broadcast (a radio or television programme) **3** to allow the passage of (particles, energy, etc.): *water transmits sound better than air* **4** to transfer (a force, motion, etc.) from one part of a mechanical system to another: *the chain of the bike transmits the motion of the pedals to the rear wheel* [Latin *transmittere* to send across] ❭ **transmittable** *adj*

transmitter *n* **1** a piece of equipment used for broadcasting radio or television programmes **2** a person or thing that transmits something

transmogrify *vb* **-fies, -fying, -fied** *humorous* to change or transform (someone or something) into a different shape or appearance, esp. a grotesque or bizarre one [origin unknown] ❭ **transmogrification** *n*

transmute *vb* **-muting, -muted** to change the form or nature of: *self-contempt is transmuted into hatred of others* [Latin *transmutare* to shift] ❭ **transmutation** *n*

transom *n* **1** a horizontal bar across a window **2** a horizontal bar that separates a door from a window over it [Old French *traversin*]

transparency *n, pl* **-cies** **1** the state of being transparent **2** a positive photograph on transparent film, usually mounted in a frame or between glass plates, which can be viewed with the use of a slide projector

transparent *adj* **1** able to be seen through; clear **2** easy to understand or recognize; obvious: *transparent honesty* [Latin *trans-* through + *parere* to appear] ❭ **transparently** *adv*

transpire vb **-spiring, -spired 1** to come to light; become known **2** not standard to happen or occur **3** physiol to give off (water or vapour) through the pores of the skin, etc. **4** (of plants) to lose (water vapour) through the stomata [Latin trans- through + spirare to breathe]
> **transpiration** n

> USAGE It is often maintained that transpire should not be used to mean happen or occur, as in the event transpired late in the evening, and that the word is properly used to mean become known, as in it transpired later that the thief had been caught. The word is, however, widely used in the former sense, esp. in spoken English.

transplant vb **1** surgery to transfer (an organ or tissue) from one part of the body or from one person to another **2** to remove or transfer (esp. a plant) from one place to another ▷ n **3** surgery **a** the procedure involved in transferring an organ or tissue **b** the organ or tissue transplanted > **transplantation** n

transponder n a type of radio or radar transmitter-receiver that transmits signals automatically when it receives predetermined signals [trans(mitter) + (res)ponder]

transport vb **1** to carry or move (people or goods) from one place to another, esp. over some distance **2** history to exile (a criminal) to a penal colony **3** to have a strong emotional effect on: transported by joy ▷ n **4** the business or system of transporting goods or people: public transport **5** Brit freight vehicles generally **6** a vehicle used to transport troops **7** a transporting or being transported **8** ecstasy or rapture: transports of delight [Latin trans- across + portare to carry] > **transportable** adj

transportation n **1** a means or system of transporting **2** the act of transporting or the state of being transported **3** history deportation to a penal colony

transport café n Brit an inexpensive eating place on a main road, used mainly by long-distance lorry drivers

transporter n a large vehicle used for carrying cars from the factory to garages for sale

transpose vb **-posing, -posed 1** to change the order of (letters, words, or sentences) **2** music to play (notes, music, etc.) in a different key **3** maths to move (a term) from one side of an equation to the other with a corresponding reversal in sign: transposing 3 in x - 3 = 6 gives x = 6 + 3 [Old French transposer] > **transposition** n

transsexual or **transexual** n **1** a person who believes that his or her true identity is of the opposite sex **2** a person who has had medical treatment to alter his or her sexual characteristics to those of the opposite sex

transship vb **-shipping, -shipped** to transfer or be transferred from one ship or vehicle to another
> **transshipment** n

Trans-Siberian Railway n a railway in S Russia, extending from Moscow to Vladivostok on the Pacific: constructed between 1891 and 1916, making possible the settlement and industrialization of sparsely inhabited regions. Length: 9335 km (5800 miles)

transubstantiation n Christianity the doctrine that the bread and wine consecrated in Communion changes into the substance of Christ's body and blood [Latin trans- over + substantia substance]

transuranic (tranz-yoor-**ran**-ik) adj chem (of an element) having an atomic number greater than that of uranium

Transvaal n former province of NE South Africa: colonized by the Boers after the Great Trek (1836); became a British colony in 1902; joined South Africa in 1910; replaced in 1994 for administrative purposes by a new system of provinces (Eastern Transvaal (later Mpumalanga), Northern Transvaal (later Limpopo), Gauteng, and North West province). Capital: Pretoria

Transvaaler n a native or inhabitant of the former South African province of Transvaal

Transvaalian adj of or relating to the former South African province of Transvaal or its inhabitants

transverse adj crossing from side to side: the transverse arches in the main hall of the college [Latin transvertere to turn across]

transvestite n a person, esp. a man, who seeks sexual pleasure from wearing clothes of the opposite sex [Latin trans- across + vestitus clothed] > **transvestism** n

Transylvania n a region of central and NW Romania: belonged to Hungary from the 11th century until 1918; restored to Romania in 1947

Transylvanian Alps pl n a mountain range in S Romania; a SW extension of the Carpathian Mountains. Highest peak: Mount Negoiu, 2548 m (8360 ft)

trap n **1 a** device or hole in which something, esp. an animal, is caught: a fox trap **2** a plan for tricking a person into being caught unawares **3** a situation from which it is difficult to escape: caught in the poverty trap **4** a bend in a pipe that contains standing water to prevent the passage of gases **5** a boxlike stall in which greyhounds are enclosed before the start of a race **6** a device that hurls clay pigeons into the air to be fired at **7** See **trap door 8** a light two-wheeled carriage: a pony and trap **9** Brit, Austral and NZ slang the mouth: shut your trap! ▷ vb **trapping, trapped 10** to catch (an animal) in a trap **11** to catch (someone) by a trick: the police trapped the drug dealers by posing as potential customers **12** to hold or confine in an unpleasant situation from which it is difficult to escape: trapped in the rubble of collapsed buildings ▶ See also **trap out** [Old English træppe]

Trapani n a port in S Italy, in NW Sicily: Carthaginian naval base, ceded to the Romans after the First Punic War. Pop: 68 346 (2001)

trap door n a hinged door in a ceiling, floor, or stage

trap-door spider n a spider that builds a silk-lined hole in the ground closed by a hinged door of earth and silk

trapeze n a horizontal bar suspended from two ropes, used by circus acrobats [French]

trapezium n, pl **-ziums** or **-zia 1** a quadrilateral having two parallel sides of unequal length **2** chiefly US and Canad a quadrilateral having neither pair of sides parallel [Greek trapeza table] > **trapezial** adj

trapezoid (**trap**-piz-zoid) n **1** a quadrilateral having neither pair of sides parallel **2** US and Canad same as **trapezium** (1) [Greek trapeza table]

trap out vb **trapping, trapped** to dress or adorn [Old French drap cloth]

trapper n a person who traps animals, esp. for their furs or skins

trappings pl n **1** the accessories that symbolize a condition, office, etc.: the trappings of power **2** ceremonial harness for a horse or other animal [probably from Old French drap cloth]

Trappist n a member of an order of Christian monks who follow a rule of strict silence

trash n **1** foolish ideas or talk; nonsense **2** US, Canad, NZ and S African unwanted objects; rubbish **3** chiefly US, Canad and NZ a worthless person or group of people ▷ vb **4** slang to attack or destroy maliciously: we've never trashed a hotel room [origin unknown] > **trashy** adj

Trasimene n **Lake Trasimene** a lake in central Italy, in Umbria: the largest lake in central Italy; scene of Hannibal's victory over the Romans in 217 BC. Area: 128 sq km (49 sq miles). Also known as: **Lake Perugia.** Italian name: **Lago Trasimeno**

trattoria (trat-or-**ee**-a) n an Italian restaurant [Italian]

trauma (**traw**-ma) n **1** psychol an emotional shock that may have long-lasting effects **2** pathol any bodily injury or wound [Greek: a wound] > **traumatic** adj
> **traumatically** adv > **traumatize** or **-ise** vb

travail n literary painful or exceptionally hard work [Old French travaillier]

Travancore n a former princely state of S India which joined with Cochin in 1949 to form **Travancore-Cochin**: part of Kerala state since 1956

travel *vb* **-elling, -elled** *or US* **-eling, -eled 1** to go or move from one place to another **2** to go or journey through or across (an area, region, etc.) *Margaret travelled widely when she was in New Zealand* **3** to go at a specified speed or for a specified distance: *the car was travelling at 30 mph* **4** to go from place to place as a salesman **5** (of perishable goods) to withstand a journey: *not all wines travel well* **6** (of light or sound) to be transmitted or carried from one place to another: *sound travels a long distance in these conditions* **7** (of a machine or part) to move in a fixed path **8** *informal* (of a vehicle) to move rapidly ▷ *n* **9** the act or a means of travelling: *air travel has changed the way people live* **10** a tour or journey: *his travels took him to Dublin* **11** the distance moved by a mechanical part, such as the stroke of a piston [Old French *travaillier* to travail]

travel agency *n* an agency that arranges flights, hotel accommodation, etc., for tourists ❯ **travel agent** *n*

traveller *or US* **traveler** *n* **1** a person who travels, esp. habitually **2** a travelling salesman **3** a Gypsy

traveller's cheque *n* a cheque sold by a bank, travel agency, etc., which the buyer signs on purchase and can cash abroad by re-signing it

travelling salesman *n* a salesman who travels within an assigned area in order to sell goods or get orders for the company he or she represents

travelogue *or US* **travelog** *n* a film or lecture on travels and travelling

travel sickness *n* nausea or vomiting caused by riding in a car or other moving vehicle ❯ **travel-sick** *adj*

Traven *n* B(en), original name *Albert Otto Max Feige*. ?1882–1969, US novelist, born in Germany and living in Mexico from 1920, who kept his identity secret. His novels, originally written in German, include *The Treasure of Sierra Madre* (1934)

Travers *n* Ben(jamin). 1886–1980, British dramatist, best known for such farces as *Rookery Nook* (1926), *Thark* (1927), and *Plunder* (1928)

traverse *vb* **-versing, -versed 1** to move over or back and forth over; cross: *he once traversed San Francisco harbour in a balloon* **2** to reach across **3** to walk, climb, or ski diagonally up or down a slope ▷ *n* **4** something being or lying across, such as a crossbar **5** the act or an instance of traversing or crossing **6** a path or road across ▷ *adj* **7** being or lying across [Latin *transversus* turned across] ❯ **traversal** *n*

travesty *n, pl* **-ties 1** a grotesque imitation or mockery: *a travesty of justice* ▷ *vb* **-ties, -tying, -tied 2** to make or be a travesty of [French *travesti* disguised]

travois (trav-**voy**) *n, pl* **-vois** (-**voyz**) *Canad* a sled used for dragging logs [Canadian French]

trawl *n* **1** a large net, usually in the shape of a sock or bag, dragged at deep levels behind a fishing boat ▷ *vb* **2** to fish using such a net [Middle Dutch *traghelen* to drag]

trawler *n* a ship used for trawling

tray *n* **1** a flat board of wood, plastic, or metal, usually with a rim, on which things can be carried **2** an open receptacle for office correspondence [Old English *trieg*]

TRC *n* (in South Africa) Truth and Reconciliation Commission: a commission which encourages people who committed human rights abuses or acts of terror during the apartheid era to reveal the truth about their crimes in return for immunity from prosecution

treacherous *adj* **1** disloyal and untrustworthy: *he was cruel, treacherous, and unscrupulous* **2** unreliable or dangerous, esp. because of sudden changes: *the tides here can be very treacherous* ❯ **treacherously** *adv*

treachery *n, pl* **-eries** the act or an instance of wilful betrayal [Old French *trecherie*]

treacle *n* a thick dark syrup obtained during the refining of sugar [Latin *theriaca* antidote to poison] ❯ **treacly** *adj*

tread *vb* **treading, trod, trodden** *or* **trod 1** to set one's foot down on or in something: *he trod on some dog's dirt* **2** to crush or squash by treading (on): *treading on a biscuit* **3** to

walk along (a path or road) **4 tread carefully** *or* **warily** to proceed in a delicate or tactful manner **5 tread water** to stay afloat in an upright position by moving the legs in a walking motion ▷ *n* **6** a way of walking or the sound of walking: *he walked, with a heavy tread, up the stairs* **7** the top surface of a step in a staircase **8** the pattern of grooves in the outer surface of a tyre that helps it grip the road **9** the part of a shoe that is generally in contact with the ground [Old English *tredan*]

treadle (tred-dl) *n* a lever operated by the foot to turn a wheel [Old English *tredan* to tread]

treadmill *n* **1** (formerly) an apparatus turned by the weight of men or animals climbing steps on a revolving cylinder or wheel **2** a dreary routine: *they are chained to the treadmill of a job* **3** an exercise machine that consists of a continuous moving belt on which to walk or jog

treason *n* **1** betrayal of one's sovereign or country, esp. by attempting to overthrow the government **2** any treachery or betrayal [Latin *traditio* a handing over] ❯ **treasonable** *adj* ❯ **treasonous** *adj*

treasure *n* **1** a collection of wealth, esp. in the form of money, precious metals, or gems **2** a valuable painting, ornament, or other object: *the museum has many art treasures* **3** *informal* a person who is highly valued: *she can turn her hand to anything, she's a perfect treasure* ▷ *vb* **-suring, -sured 4** to cherish (someone or something) [Greek *thēsauros*]

treasure hunt *n* a game in which players act upon successive clues to find a hidden prize

treasurer *n* a person appointed to look after the funds of a society or other organization

treasure-trove *n law* any articles, such as coins or valuable objects found hidden and without any evidence of ownership [Anglo-French *tresor trové* treasure found]

treasury *n, pl* **-uries 1** a storage place for treasure **2** the revenues or funds of a government or organization

Treasury *n* (in various countries) the government department in charge of finance

treat *vb* **1** to deal with or regard in a certain manner: *her love for a man who treats her abominably* **2** to attempt to cure or lessen the symptoms of (an illness or injury or a person suffering from it): *the drug is prescribed to treat asthma* **3** to subject to a chemical or industrial process: *the wood should be treated with a preservative* **4** to provide (someone) with something as a treat: *I'll treat you to an ice cream* **5 treat of** to deal with (something) in writing or speaking: *this book treats of a most abstruse subject* ▷ *n* **6** a celebration, entertainment, gift, or meal given for or to someone and paid for by someone else **7** any delightful surprise or specially pleasant occasion [Old French *tretier*] ❯ **treatable** *adj*

treatise (treat-izz) *n* a formal piece of writing that deals systematically with a particular subject [Anglo-French *tretiz*]

treatment *n* **1** the medical or surgical care given to a patient **2** a way of handling a person or thing: *the party has had unfair treatment in the press*

treaty *n, pl* **-ties 1** a formal written agreement between two or more states, such as an alliance or trade arrangement: *the Treaty of Rome established the Common Market* **2** an agreement between two parties concerning the purchase of property [Old French *traité*]

Trebizond *n* a variant of Trabzon

treble *adj* **1** three times as much or as many **2** of or denoting a soprano voice or part or a high-pitched instrument **3** of the highest range of musical notes: *these loudspeakers give excellent treble reproduction* ▷ *n* **4** a soprano voice or part or a high-pitched instrument ▷ *vb* **-bling, -bled 5** to make or become three times as much or as many: *sales have trebled in three years* [Latin *triplus* threefold] ❯ **trebly** *adv*

treble chance *n Brit* a method of betting in football pools in which the chances of winning are related to the number of draws and the number of home and away wins forecast by the competitor

treble clef *n music* the clef that establishes G a fifth above middle C as being on the second line of the staff

Treblinka *n* a Nazi concentration camp in central Poland, on the Bug River northeast of Warsaw: chiefly remembered as the place where the Jews of the Warsaw ghetto were put to death

tree *n* **1** any large woody perennial plant with a distinct trunk and usually having leaves and branches. Related adjective: **arboreal 2** See **family tree, shoetree, saddletree 3 at the top of the tree** in the highest position of a profession [Old English *trēow*] **› treeless** *adj*

Tree *n* Sir Herbert Beerbohm. 1853–1917, English actor and theatre manager; half-brother of Sir Max Beerbohm. He was noted for his lavish productions of Shakespeare

tree creeper *n* a small songbird of the N hemisphere that creeps up trees to feed on insects

tree diagram *n maths* a branching diagram showing the probability of various events

tree fern *n* any of numerous large tropical ferns with a trunklike stem

tree kangaroo *n* a tree-living kangaroo of New Guinea and N Australia

tree line *n* same as **timber line**

tree-lined *adj* (of a road) having trees on either side of it: *a pleasant tree-lined avenue in Bristol*

tree surgery *n* the treatment of damaged trees by filling cavities, applying braces, etc. **› tree surgeon** *n*

tree tomato *n* same as **tamarillo**

treetop *n* the highest part of a tree, where the leaves and branches are: *monkeys swung through the treetops*

trefoil (tref-foil) *n* **1** a plant, such as clover, with leaves divided into three smaller leaves **2** *archit* a carved ornament with a shape like such leaves [Latin *trifolium* three-leaved herb] **› trefoiled** *adj*

Treitschke *n* Heinrich von. 1834–96, German historian, noted for his highly nationalistic views

trek *n* **1** a long and often difficult journey, esp. on foot **2** *S African* a journey or stage of a journey, esp. a migration by ox wagon **›** *vb* **trekking, trekked 3** to make a trek [Afrikaans]

trellis *n* a frame made of vertical and horizontal strips of wood, esp. one used to support climbing plants [Old French *treliz* fabric of open texture] **› trelliswork** *n*

tremble *vb* **-bling, -bled 1** to shake with short slight movements: *her hands trembled uncontrollably; he felt the ground trembling beneath him* **2** to experience fear or anxiety: *his parents trembled with apprehension about his future* **3** (of the voice) to sound uncertain or unsteady, for instance through pain or emotion **›** *n* **4** the act or an instance of trembling [Latin *tremere*] **› trembling** *adj*

tremendous *adj* **1** very large or impressive: *a tremendous amount of money* **2** very exciting or unusual: *a tremendous feeling of elation* **3** very good or pleasing: *my wife has given me tremendous support* [Latin *tremendus* terrible] **› tremendously** *adv*

tremolo *n, pl* **-los** *music* **1** (in playing the violin or other stringed instrument) the rapid repetition of a note or notes to produce a trembling effect **2** (in singing) a fluctuation in pitch [Italian: quavering]

tremor *n* **1** an involuntary shudder or vibration: *the slight tremor of excitement* **2** a minor earthquake [Latin]

tremulous *adj literary* trembling, as from fear or excitement: *I managed a tremulous smile* [Latin *tremere* to shake] **› tremulously** *adv*

trench *n* **1** a long narrow ditch in the ground, such as one for laying a pipe in **2** a long deep ditch used by soldiers for protection in a war: *my grandfather fought in the trenches in the First World War* **›** *adj* **3** of or involving military trenches: *trench warfare* [Old French *trenche* something cut]

trenchant *adj* **1** keen or incisive: *a trenchant screenplay* **2** vigorous and effective: *the prime minister's trenchant*

adoption of this issue [Old French: cutting] **› trenchancy** *n*

Trenchard *n* Hugh Montague, 1st Viscount. 1873–1956, British air marshal, who as chief of air staff (1918, 1919–27) and marshal of the RAF (1927–29) established the RAF as a fully independent service. As commissioner of the Metropolitan Police (1931–35) he founded the police college at Hendon

trench coat *n* a belted raincoat similar in style to a military officer's coat

trencher *n history* a wooden board on which food was served or cut [Old French *trencheoir*]

trencherman *n, pl* **-men** a person who enjoys food; hearty eater

trench warfare *n* a type of warfare in which opposing armies face each other in entrenched positions

trend *n* **1** general tendency or direction: *an accelerating trend towards the use of mobile phones* **2** fashionable style: *she set a trend for wearing lingerie as outer garments* **›** *vb* **3** to take a certain trend **4** to be widely discussed on a social media site [Old English *trendan* to turn]

trendsetter *n* a person or thing that creates, or may create, a new fashion **› trendsetting** *adj*

trendy *informal adj* **trendier, trendiest 1** consciously fashionable: *a flat in Glasgow's trendy West End* **›** *n, pl* **trendies 2** a trendy person: *a media trendy* **› trendily** *adv* **› trendiness** *n*

Trengganu *or* **Terengganu** *n* a state of E Peninsular Malaysia, on the South China Sea: under Thai suzerainty until becoming a British protectorate in 1909; joined the Federation of Malaya in 1948; an isolated forested region; mainly agricultural. Capital: Kuala Trengganu. Pop: 898 825 (2000). Area: 12 995 sq km (5002 sq miles)

Trent *n* **1** a river in central England, rising in Staffordshire and flowing generally northeast into the Humber: the chief river of the Midlands. Length: 270 km (170 miles) **2** Also: **Trient**. the German name for **Trento**

Trentino-Alto Adige *n* a region of N Italy: consists of the part of the Tyrol south of the Brenner Pass, ceded by Austria after World War I. Pop: 950 495 (2003 est). Area: 13 613 sq km (5256 sq miles). Former name (until 1947): **Venezia Tridentina**

Trento *n* a city in N Italy, in Trentino-Alto Adige region on the Adige River: Roman military base; seat of the Council of Trent (1545–1563). Pop: 104 946 (2001). Latin name: **Tridentum**. German name: **Trent**

Trenton *n* a city in W New Jersey, capital of the state, on the Delaware River: settled by English Quakers in 1679; scene of the defeat of the British by Washington (1776) during the War of American Independence. Pop: 85 314 (2003 est)

trepidation *n formal* a state of fear or anxiety [Latin *trepidatio*]

trespass *vb* **1** to go onto somebody else's property without permission **›** *n* **2** the act or an instance of trespassing **3** *old-fashioned* a sin or wrongdoing [Old French *trespas* a passage] **› trespasser** *n*

trespass on *or* **trespass upon** *vb formal* to take unfair advantage of (someone's friendship, patience, etc.): *I won't trespass upon your hospitality any longer*

tresses *pl n* a woman's long flowing hair [Old French *trece*]

trestle *n* **1** a support for one end of a table or beam, consisting of two rectangular frameworks or sets of legs which are joined at the top but not the bottom **2** Also called: **trestle table** a table consisting of a board supported by a trestle at each end [Old French *trestel*]

Tretchikoff *n* Vladimir. 1913–2006, South African painter, born in Russia, known for his kitsch appeal, esp. his much-reproduced *Chinese Girl* (1950; also known as *The Green Lady*)

trevally (trih-val-lee) *n, pl* **-lies** *Austral and NZ* any of various food and game fishes [probably alteration of *cavalla*, species of tropical fish]

t

Trevelyan *n* **1** George Macaulay. 1876–1962, British historian, noted for his *English Social History* (1944) **2** his father, Sir George Otto. 1838–1928, British historian and biographer. His works include a biography of his uncle Lord Macaulay (1876)

Trèves *n* the French name for **Trier**

Trevino *n* Lee. born 1939, US professional golfer: winner of the US Open Championship (1968; 1971) and the British Open Championship (1971; 1972)

Treviso *n* a city in N Italy, in Veneto region: agricultural market centre. Pop: 80 144 (2001)

Trevithick *n* Richard. 1771–1833, British engineer, who built the first steam-driven passenger carriage (1801) and the first locomotive to run on smooth wheels on smooth rails (1804)

Trevor *n* William, real name *William Trevor Cox*. born 1928, Irish novelist and short-story writer. His novels include *The Old Boys* (1964), *The Children of Dynmouth* (1977), *Felicia's Journey* (1994), and *The Story of Lucy Gault* (2002)

trews *pl n chiefly Brit* close-fitting trousers of tartan cloth [Scottish Gaelic *triubhas*]

tri- *combining form* **1** three or thrice: *trilingual* **2** occurring every three: *triweekly* [Latin *tres*]

triad *n* **1** a group of three **2** *music* a three-note chord consisting of a note and the third and fifth above it [Greek *trias*] **> triadic** *adj*

Triad *n* a Chinese secret society involved in criminal activities, such as drug trafficking

trial *n* **1** *law* an investigation of a case in front of a judge to decide whether a person is innocent or guilty of a crime by questioning him or her and considering the evidence **2** the act or an instance of trying or proving; test or experiment: *the new drug is undergoing clinical trials* **3** an annoying or frustrating person or thing: *young children can be a great trial at times* **4** a motorcycling competition in which the skills of the riders are tested over rough ground **5** trials a sporting competition for individual people or animals: *horse trials* **6** on trial **a** undergoing trial, esp. before a court of law **b** being tested, for example before a commitment to purchase: *I only have the car out on trial* ▷ *adj* **7** on a temporary basis while being tried out or tested: *a trial run* ▷ *vb* **trialling, trialled** **8** to test or make experimental use of: *the idea has been trialled in several schools* [Anglo-French *trier* to try]

trial and error *n* a method of discovery based on practical experiment and experience rather than on theory: *raising her children has been a matter of trial and error*

trial balance *n accounting* a statement of all the debit and credit balances in the double-entry ledger

triallist *or* **trialist** *n* **1** a person who takes part in a competition **2** *sport* a person who takes part in a preliminary match or heat held to determine selection for a team or event

triangle *n* **1** a geometric figure with three sides and three angles **2** any object shaped like a triangle: *a triangle of streets running up from the river* **3** *music* a percussion instrument that consists of a metal bar bent into a triangular shape, played by striking it with a metal stick **4** any situation involving three people or points of view: *a torrid sex triangle* [TRI- + Latin *angulus* corner] **> triangular** *adj*

triangulate *vb* **-lating, -lated** to survey (an area) by dividing it into triangles

triangulation *n* a method of surveying in which an area is divided into triangles, one side (the base line) and all angles of which are measured and the lengths of the other lines calculated by trigonometry

Triassic *adj geology* of the period of geological time about 230 million years ago [Latin *trias* triad]

triathlon *n* an athletic contest in which each athlete competes in three different events: swimming, cycling, and running [TRI- + Greek *athlon* contest] **> triathlete** *n*

tribalism *n* loyalty to a tribe, esp. as opposed to a modern political entity such as a state

tribe *n* **1** a group of families or clans believed to have a common ancestor **2** *informal* a group of people who do the same type of thing: *a tribe of German yachtsmen* [Latin *tribus*] **> tribal** *adj*

tribesman *n, pl* **-men** a member of a tribe

tribulation *n* great distress: *the tribulations of a deserted wife* [Latin *tribulare* to afflict]

tribunal *n* **1** a special court or committee that is appointed to deal with a particular problem: *an industrial tribunal investigating allegations of unfair dismissal* **2** a court of justice [Latin *tribunus* tribune]

tribune *n* **1** a person who upholds public rights **2** (in ancient Rome) an officer elected by the plebs to protect their interests [Latin *tribunus*]

tributary *n, pl* **-taries** **1** a stream or river that flows into a larger one: *Frankfurt lies on the River Main, a tributary of the Rhine* **2** a person, nation, or people that pays tribute ▷ *adj* **3** (of a stream or river) flowing into a larger stream **4** paying tribute: *Egypt was formerly a tributary province of the Turkish Empire*

tribute *n* **1** something given, done, or said as a mark of respect or admiration **2** a payment by one ruler or state to another, usually as an acknowledgment of submission **3** something that shows the merits of a particular quality of a person or thing: *the car's low fuel consumption is a tribute to the quality of its engine* [Latin *tributum*]

trice *n* **in a trice** in a moment: *she was back in a trice* [originally, at one tug, from *trice* to haul up]

triceps *n* the muscle at the back of the upper arm [Latin]

Trichinopoly *n* another name for **Tiruchirapalli**

trichology (trick-ol-a-jee) *n* the branch of medicine concerned with the hair and its diseases [Greek *thrix* hair] **> trichologist** *n*

trichromatic *or* **trichromic** *adj* **1** having or involving three colours **2** of or having normal colour vision **> trichromatism** *n*

trick *n* **1** a deceitful or cunning action or plan: *she was willing to use any dirty trick to get what she wanted* **2** a joke or prank: *he loves playing tricks on his sister* **3** a clever way of doing something, learned from experience: *an old campers' trick is to use three thin blankets rather than one thick one* **4** an illusory or magical feat or device **5** a simple feat learned by an animal or person **6** a deceptive illusion: *a trick of the light* **7** a habit or mannerism: *she had a trick of saying 'oh dear'* **8** *cards* a batch of cards played in turn and won by the person playing the highest card **9** do the trick *informal* to produce the desired result **10** how's tricks? *slang* how are you? ▷ *vb* **11** to defraud, deceive, or cheat (someone) [Old French *trique*] **> trickery** *n*

trickle *vb* **-ling, -led** **1** to flow or cause to flow in a thin stream or drops: *tears trickled down her cheeks* **2** to move slowly or in small groups: *voters trickled to the polls* ▷ *n* **3** a thin, irregular, or slow flow of something: *a trickle of blood* [probably imitative]

trickle-down *adj* of the theory that granting concessions like tax cuts to the rich will benefit all levels of society by stimulating the economy

trick out *vb* to dress up: *tricked out in chauffeur's rig*

trickster *n* a person who deceives or plays tricks

tricky *adj* **trickier, trickiest** **1** involving snags or difficulties: *a tricky task* **2** needing careful handling: *a tricky situation* **3** sly or wily: *a tricky customer* **> trickily** *adv* **> trickiness** *n*

tricolour *or US* **tricolor** (trick-kol-lor) *n* a flag with three equal stripes in different colours, esp. the French or Irish national flags

tricycle *n* a three-wheeled cycle **> tricyclist** *n*

trident *n* a three-pronged spear [Latin *tridens* three-pronged]

Tridentum *n* the Latin name for **Trento**

tried *vb* the past of **try**

triennial *adj* occurring every three years [TRI- + Latin *annus* year] **> triennially** *adv*

Trient *n* the German name for **Trento**. Also: **Trent**

trier *n* a person or thing that tries

Trier *n* a city in W Germany, in the Rhineland-Palatinate on the Moselle River: one of the oldest towns of central Europe, ancient capital of a Celto-Germanic tribe (the **Treveri**); an early centre of Christianity, ruled by powerful archbishops until the 18th century; wine trade; important Roman remains. Pop: 100 180 (2003 est). Latin name: **Augusta Treverorum**. French name: **Trèves**

Trieste *n* **1** a port in NE Italy, capital of Friuli-Venezia Giulia region, on the **Gulf of Trieste** at the head of the Adriatic Sea: under Austrian rule (1382–1918); capital of the Free Territory of Trieste (1947–54); important transit port for central Europe. Pop: 211 184 (2001). Slovene and Croatian name: **Trst 2 Free Territory of Trieste** a former territory on the N Adriatic: established by the UN in 1947; most of the N part passed to Italy and the remainder to Yugoslavia in 1954

trifle¹ *n* **1** a thing of little or no value or significance **2** *Brit, Austral and NZ* a cold dessert made of sponge cake spread with jam or fruit, soaked in sherry, covered with custard and cream **3 a trifle** to a small extent or degree; slightly: *he is a trifle eccentric* [Old French *trufle* mockery]

trifle² *vb* **trifling, trifled trifle with** to treat (a person or his or her feelings) with disdain or disregard

trifling *adj* insignificant, petty, or frivolous: *a trifling misunderstanding*

trig. trigonometry

trigger *n* **1** a small lever that releases a catch on a gun or machine **2** any event that sets a course of action in motion: *his murder was the trigger for a night of rioting* ▷ *vb* **3** Also: **trigger off** to set (an action or process) in motion: *various factors can trigger off a migraine* [Dutch *trekker*]

trigger-happy *adj informal* too ready or willing to use guns or violence: *trigger-happy border guards*

trigonometry *n* the branch of mathematics concerned with the relations of sides and angles of triangles, which is used in surveying, navigation, etc. [Greek *trigōnon* triangle]

trig point *n* a point on a hilltop etc., used for triangulation by a surveyor

trike *n informal* a tricycle

trilateral *adj* having three sides

trilby *n, pl* **-bies** a man's soft felt hat with an indented crown [after *Trilby*, the heroine of a novel by George Du Maurier]

trill *n* **1** *music* a rapid alternation between a note and the note above it **2** a shrill warbling sound made by some birds: *the canary's high trills* ▷ *vb* **3** (of a bird) to make a shrill warbling sound **4** (of a person) to talk or laugh in a high-pitched musical voice [Italian *trillo*]

Trilling *n* Lionel. 1905–75, US literary critic, whose works include *The Liberal Imagination* (1950) and *Sincerity and Authenticity* (1974)

trillion *n* **-lions** *or* **-lion 1** the number represented as one followed by twelve zeros (10^{12}); a million million **2** (in Britain, originally) the number represented as one followed by eighteen zeros (10^{18}); a million million million ▷ *adj* **3** amounting to a trillion: *a trillion dollars* [French] **> trillionth** *n, adj*

trillium *n* a plant of Asia and North America that has three leaves at the top of the stem with a single white, pink, or purple three-petalled flower [New Latin]

trilobite (**trile-oh-bite**) *n* a small prehistoric marine arthropod, found as a fossil [Greek *trilobos* having three lobes]

trilogy (**trill-a-jee**) *n, pl* **-gies** a series of three books, plays, etc., which form a related group but are each complete works in themselves [Greek *trilogia*]

trim *adj* **trimmer, trimmest 1** neat and spruce in appearance: *trim lace curtains* **2** attractively slim: *his body was trim and athletic* ▷ *vb* **trimming, trimmed 3** to make (something) neater by cutting it slightly without

changing its basic shape: *his white beard was neatly trimmed* **4** to adorn or decorate (something, such as a garment) with lace, ribbons, etc.: *a cotton camisole neatly trimmed with lace* **5 a** to adjust the balance of (a ship or aircraft) by shifting cargo etc. **b** to adjust (a ship's sails) to take advantage of the wind **6** to reduce or lower the size of: *the company has trimmed its pretax profits forecast by $2.3 million* **7** to alter (a plan or policy) by removing parts which seem unnecessary or unpopular: *the government would rather trim its policies than lose the election* **8 trim off** *or* **away** to cut so as to remove: *trim off most of the fat before cooking the meat* ▷ *n* **9** a decoration or adornment: *a black suit with scarlet trim* **10** the upholstery and decorative facings of a car's interior **11** good physical condition: *he had always kept himself in trim* **12** a haircut that neatens but does not alter the existing hairstyle [Old English *trymman* to strengthen]

Trim *n* the county town of Meath, Republic of Ireland; 12th-century castle, medieval cathedral; textiles and machinery. Pop: 5894 (2002)

trimaran (**trime-a-ran**) *n* a boat with one smaller hull on each side of the main hull [TRI- + (CATA)MARAN]

Trimble *n* (**William**) **David**. Baron. born 1944, Northern Irish politician; leader of the Ulster Unionist party (1995–2005); First Minister of Northern Ireland (1998–2002); Nobel peace prize jointly with John Hume in 1998

trimming *n* **1** an extra piece added to a garment for decoration: *a pink nightie with lace trimming* **2 trimmings** usual or traditional accompaniments: *bacon and eggs with all the trimmings*

Trinacria *n* the Latin name for **Sicily**

Trinacrian *adj* of or relating to Trinacria (the Latin name for Sicily) or its inhabitants

Trincomalee *n* a port in NE Sri Lanka, on the **Bay of Trincomalee** (an inlet of the Bay of Bengal); British naval base until 1957: a centre of conflict in the insurgency by the Tamil Tigers (LTTE). Pop: 44 313 (1981 census); more recent official figures are not available

Trinidad *n* an island in the West Indies, off the NE coast of Venezuela: colonized by the Spanish in the 17th century and ceded to Britain in 1802; joined with Tobago in 1888 as a British colony; now part of the independent republic of Trinidad and Tobago. Pop: 1 208 282 (2000)

Trinidad and Tobago *n* an independent republic in the Caribbean, occupying the two southernmost islands of the Lesser Antilles: became a British colony in 1888 and gained independence in 1962; became a republic in 1976; a member of the Commonwealth. Official language: English. Religion: Christian majority, with a large Hindu minority. Currency: Trinidad and Tobago dollar. Capital: Port of Spain. Pop: 1 225 225 (2013 est). Area: 5128 sq km (1980 sq miles)

Trinidadian *adj* **1** of or relating to Trinidad or its inhabitants ▷ *n* **2** a native or inhabitant of Trinidad

Trinitarian *n* **1** a person who believes in the doctrine of the Trinity ▷ *adj* **2** of or relating to the Trinity **> Trinitarianism** *n*

trinitrotoluene *n* the full name for **TNT**

trinity *n, pl* **-ties** a group of three people or things [Latin *trinus* triple]

Trinity *n Christianity* the union of three persons, the Father, Son, and Holy Spirit, in one God

trinket *n* a small or worthless ornament or piece of jewellery [origin unknown]

trio *n, pl* **trios 1** a group of three people or things **2** a group of three instrumentalists or singers **3** a piece of music for three performers [Italian]

trip *n* **1** a journey to a place and back, esp. for pleasure: *they took a coach trip round the island* **2** a false step; stumble **3** the act of causing someone to stumble or fall by catching his or her foot with one's own **4** *informal* a hallucinogenic drug experience **5** a catch on a mechanism that acts as a switch ▷ *vb* **tripping, tripped**

6 Also: **trip up** to stumble or cause (someone) to stumble **7** Also: **trip up** to trap or catch (someone) in a mistake **8** to walk lightly and quickly, with a dancelike motion: *I could see Amelia tripping along beside him* **9** *informal* to experience the effects of a hallucinogenic drug [Old French *triper* to tread]

tripartite *adj* involving or composed of three people or parts **>** **tripartism** *n*

tripe *n* **1** the stomach lining of a cow or pig used as a food **2** *Brit, Austral and NZ informal* nonsense or rubbish [Old French]

Tripitaka (trip-it-tah-ka) *n* the three collections of books making up the Buddhist scriptures [Pali (an ancient language of India) *tri* three + *pitaka* basket]

triple *adj* **1** made up of three parts or things: *a triple murder* **2** (of musical time or rhythm) having three beats in each bar **3** three times as great or as much: *a triple brandy* ▷ *vb* **-pling, -pled** **4** to make or become three times as much or as many: *the company has tripled its sales over the past five years* ▷ *n* **5** something that is, or contains, three times as much as normal **6** a group of three [Latin *triplus*] **>** **triply** *adv*

triple jump *n* an athletic event in which the competitor has to perform a hop, a step, and a jump in a continuous movement

triple point *n chem* the temperature and pressure at which a substance can exist as a solid, liquid, and gas

triplet *n* **1** one of three children born at one birth **2** a group of three musical notes played in the time that two would normally take **3** a group or set of three similar things

triplicate *adj* **1** triple ▷ *vb* **-cating, -cated** **2** to multiply or be multiplied by three ▷ *n* **3** **in triplicate** written out three times: *my request to interview the commander had to be made in triplicate* [Latin *triplicare* to triple] **>** **triplication** *n*

tripod (tripe-pod) *n* **1** a three-legged stand to which a camera can be attached to hold it steady **2** a three-legged stool, table, etc. [TRI- + Greek *pous* a foot]

Tripoli *n* **1** the capital and chief port of Libya, in the northwest on the Mediterranean: founded by Phoenicians in about the 7th century BC; the only city that has survived of the three (Oea, Leptis Magna, and Sabratha) that formed the African Tripolis ("three cities"); fishing and manufacturing centre. Pop: 1 223 300 (2002 est). Ancient name: **Oea**. Arabic name: **Tarabulus el Gharb** **2** a port in N Lebanon, on the Mediterranean: the second largest town in Lebanon; taken by the Crusaders in 1109 after a siege of five years; oil-refining and manufacturing centre. Pop: 212 000 (2005 est). Ancient name: **Tripolis**. Arabic name: **Tarabulus esh Sham**

Tripolitania *n* the NW part of Libya: established as a Phoenician colony in the 7th century BC; taken by the Turks in 1551 and became one of the Barbary states; under Italian rule from 1912 until World War II

Tripolitanian *adj* **1** of or relating to Tripolitania (now part of Libya) or its inhabitants ▷ *n* **2** a native or inhabitant of Tripolitania

tripos (tripe-poss) *n Brit* the final honours degree examinations at Cambridge University [Latin *tripus* tripod]

tripper *n chiefly Brit* a tourist

triptych (trip-tick) *n* a set of three pictures or panels, usually hinged together and often used as an altarpiece [TRI- + Greek *ptux* plate]

Tripura *n* a state of NE India: formerly a princely state, ruled by the Maharajahs for over 1300 years; became a union territory in 1956 and a state in 1972; extensive jungles. Capital: Agartala. Pop: 3 191 168 (2001). Area: 10 486 sq km (4051 sq miles)

trireme (try-reem) *n* an ancient Greek warship with three rows of oars on each side [TRI- + Latin *remus* oar]

trismus *n pathol* the state of being unable to open the mouth because of sustained contractions of the jaw muscles, caused by tetanus. Nontechnical name: **lockjaw** [Greek *trismos* a grinding]

Tristan da Cunha *n* a group of four small volcanic islands in the S Atlantic, about halfway between South Africa and South America: comprises the main island of Tristan and the uninhabited islands of Gough, Inaccessible, and Nightingale; discovered in 1506 by the Portuguese admiral Tristão da Cunha; annexed to Britain in 1816; whole population of Tristan evacuated for two years after the volcanic eruption of 1961. Pop: 264 (2010 est). Area: about 100 sq km (40 sq miles)

triste (treest) *adj old-fashioned* sad [French]

trite *adj* (of a remark or idea) commonplace and unoriginal [Latin *tritus* worn down]

tritium *n* a radioactive isotope of hydrogen. Symbol: **T** or ^{3}**H** [Greek *tritos* third]

triumph *n* **1** the feeling of great happiness resulting from a victory or major achievement **2** an outstanding success, achievement, or victory: *the concert was a musical triumph* **3** (in ancient Rome) a procession held in honour of a victorious general ▷ *vb* **4** to gain control or success: *triumphing over adversity* **5** to rejoice over a victory [Latin *triumphus*] **>** **triumphal** *adj*

triumphant *adj* **1** feeling or displaying triumph: *her smile was triumphant* **2** celebrating a victory or success: *the general's triumphant tour round the city* **>** **triumphantly** *adv*

triumvir (try-umm-vir) *n* (esp. in ancient Rome) a member of a triumvirate [Latin]

triumvirate (try-umm-vir-rit) *n* **1** a group of three people in joint control of something: *the triumvirate of great orchestras which dominates classical music in Europe* **2** (in ancient Rome) a board of three officials jointly responsible for some task

trivalent *adj chem* **1** having a valency of three **2** having three valencies **>** **trivalency** *n*

Trivandrum *n* a city in S India, capital of Kerala, on the Malabar Coast: made capital of the kingdom of Travancore in 1745; University of Kerala (1937). Pop: 744 739 (2001). Local official name: **Thiruvananthapuram**

trivet (triv-vit) *n* **1** a three-legged stand for holding a pot, kettle, etc., over a fire **2** a short metal stand on which hot dishes are placed on a table [Old English *trefet*]

trivia *n* petty and unimportant things or details

trivial *adj* of little importance: *a trivial matter* [Latin *trivialis* common] **>** **triviality** *n* **>** **trivially** *adv*

trivialize *or* **-lise** *vb* **-lizing, -lized** *or* **-lising, -lised** to make (something) seem less important or complex than it is

Troas *n* the region of NW Asia Minor surrounding the ancient city of Troy. Also called: **the Troad**

Trobriand Islands *pl n* a group of coral islands in the Solomon Sea, north of the E part of New Guinea: part of Papua New Guinea. Area: about 440 sq km (170 sq miles)

trochee (troke-ee) *n prosody* a metrical foot of one long and one short syllable [Greek *trekhein* to run] **>** **trochaic** *adj*

trod *vb* the past tense and a past participle of **tread**

trodden *vb* a past participle of **tread**

troglodyte *n* a person who lives in a cave [Greek *trōglodutēs* one who enters caves]

troika *n* **1** a Russian coach or sleigh drawn by three horses abreast **2** a group of three people in authority: *a troika of European foreign ministers* [Russian]

Trois-Rivières *n* a port in E Canada, in Quebec on the St Lawrence River: one of the world's largest centres of newsprint production. Pop: 46 264 (2001). English name: **Three Rivers**

Trojan *adj* **1** of or relating to ancient Troy or its people ▷ *n* **2** a native or inhabitant of ancient Troy **3** a hard-working person **4** a destructive computer program

Trojan Horse *n* **1** *Greek myth* the huge wooden hollow figure of a horse used by the Greeks to enter Troy **2** a trap or trick intended to undermine an enemy

troll¹ *n* (in Scandinavian folklore) a supernatural dwarf or giant that dwells in a cave or mountain [Old Norse: demon]

troll² vb **1** angling to fish by dragging a lure through the water **2** to post deliberately provocative messages on an internet discussion board ▷ n **3** a person who posts deliberately provocative messages on an internet discussion board [Old French troller to run about]

trolley n **1** a small table on casters used for carrying food or drink **2** a wheeled cart or stand used for moving heavy items, such as shopping in a supermarket or luggage at a railway station **3** Brit See **trolley bus 4** US and Canad See **trolley car 5** a device, such as a wheel, that collects the current from an overhead wire, to drive the motor of an electric vehicle **6** Brit and Austral a low truck running on rails, used in factories, mines, etc. [probably from TROLL²]

trolley bus n a bus powered by electricity from two overhead wires but not running on rails

trolley car n US and Canad same as **tram**

trollop n disparaging a promiscuous or slovenly woman [origin unknown]

Trollope n **1** Anthony. 1815–82, English novelist. His most successful novels, such as The Warden (1855), Barchester Towers (1857), and Dr Thorne (1858), are those in the Barsetshire series of studies of English provincial life. The Palliser series of political novels includes Phineas Redux (1874) and The Prime Minister (1876) **2** Joanna. born 1943, British novelist: her works include The Choir (1988), A Village Affair (1989), The Rector's Wife (1991), The Best of Friends (1995), and The Girl From the South (2002)

trombone n a brass musical instrument with a sliding tube which is moved in or out to alter the note played [Italian] > **trombonist** n

Tromp n **1** Cornelius (Martenszoon). 1629–91, Dutch admiral, who fought during the 2nd and 3rd Anglo-Dutch Wars **2** his father, Maarten (Harpertszoon). 1598–1653, Dutch admiral, who fought in the 1st Anglo-Dutch War: killed in action

trompe l'oeil (tromp luh-ee) n, pl **trompe l'oeils** (tromp luh-ee) **1** a painting etc. giving a convincing illusion that the objects represented are real **2** an effect of this kind [French, literally: deception of the eye]

Tromsø n a port in N Norway, on a small island between Kvaløy and the mainland: fishing and sealing centre. Pop: 61 897 (2004 est)

Trondheim n a port in central Norway, on **Trondheim Fjord** (an inlet of the Norwegian Sea): national capital until 1380; seat of the Technical University of Norway. Pop: 154 351 (2004 est). Former name (until the 16th century and from 1930 to 1931): **Nidaros**

troop n **1** a large group: a troop of dogs **2 troops** soldiers: troops have been maintaining an unusually high profile **3** a subdivision of a cavalry or armoured regiment **4** a large group of Scouts made up of several patrols ▷ vb **5** to move in a crowd: we trooped into the room after her **6** military, chiefly Brit and Austral to parade (a flag or banner) ceremonially: trooping the colour [French troupe]

trooper n **1** a soldier in a cavalry regiment **2** US and Austral a mounted policeman **3** US a state policeman **4** a cavalry horse **5** informal, chiefly Brit a troopship

troopship n a ship used to transport military personnel

trope n a word or expression used in a figurative sense [Greek tropos style, turn]

trophy n, pl **-phies 1** a cup, shield, etc., given as a prize **2** a memento of success, esp. one taken in war or hunting: stuffed animal heads and other hunting trophies ▷ adj **3** informal regarded as a highly desirable symbol of wealth or success: a trophy wife [Greek tropaion]

tropic n **1** either of the lines of latitude at about 23½°N (**tropic of Cancer**) and 23½°S (**tropic of Capricorn**) of the equator **2 the tropics** that part of the earth's surface between the tropics of Cancer and Capricorn: the intense heat and humidity of the tropics [Greek tropos a turn; from the belief that the sun turned back at the solstices]

tropical adj belonging to, typical of, or located in, the tropics: tropical rainforests > **tropically** adv

tropism n the tendency of a plant or animal to turn or curve in response to an external stimulus [Greek tropos a turn]

troposphere n the lowest layer of the earth's atmosphere, about 18 kilometres (11 miles) thick at the equator to about 6 km (4 miles) at the Poles [Greek tropos a turn + SPHERE]

Trossachs n the Trossachs (functioning as sing or pl) **1** a narrow wooded valley in central Scotland, between Loch Achray and Loch Katrine: made famous by Sir Walter Scott's descriptions **2** (popularly) the area extending northwards from Loch Ard and Aberfoyle to Lochs Katrine, Achray, and Venachar

trot vb **trotting, trotted 1** (of a horse) to move in a manner faster than a walk but slower than a gallop, in which diagonally opposite legs come down together **2** (of a person) to move fairly quickly, with small quick steps ▷ n **3** a medium-paced gait of a horse, in which diagonally opposite legs come down together **4** a steady brisk pace **5 on the trot** informal one after the other: ten years on the trot **6 the trots** slang diarrhoea [Old French]

Trot n chiefly Brit informal a follower of Trotsky

troth (rhymes with **growth**) n archaic **1** a pledge of fidelity, esp. a betrothal **2 in troth** truly [Old English trēowth]

trot out vb informal to repeat (old information or ideas) without fresh thought: the government trots out the same excuse every time

Trotsky or **Trotski** n Leon, original name Lev Davidovich Bronstein. 1879–1940, Russian revolutionary and Communist theorist. He was a leader of the November Revolution (1917) and, as commissar of foreign affairs and war (1917–24), largely created the Red Army. He was ousted by Stalin after Lenin's death and deported from Russia (1929); assassinated by a Stalinist agent

Trotskyist or **Trotskyite** adj **1** of the theories of Leon Trotsky (1879–1940), Russian Communist, which call for a worldwide revolution by the proletariat ▷ n **2** a supporter of Trotsky or his theories > **Trotskyism** n

trotter n **1** the foot of a pig **2** a horse that is specially trained to trot fast

troubadour (troo-bad-oor) n a travelling poet and singer in S France or N Italy from the 11th to the 13th century who wrote chiefly on courtly love [French]

trouble n **1** difficulties or problems: I'd trouble finding somewhere to park **2** a cause of distress, disturbance, or pain: we must be sensitive to the troubles of other people **3** disease or a problem with one's health: ear trouble **4** a state of disorder, ill-feeling, or unrest: the police had orders to intervene at the first sign of trouble **5** effort or exertion to do something: they didn't even take the trouble to see the film before banning it **6** a personal weakness or cause of annoyance: his trouble is that he's constitutionally jealous **7 in trouble a** likely to be punished for something one has done: in trouble with the public prosecutor **b** pregnant when not married **8 more trouble than it's worth** involving a lot of time or effort for very little reward: making your own pasta is more trouble than it's worth ▷ vb **-bling, -bled 9** to cause trouble to **10** to make an effort or exert oneself: he dismissed the letters as forgeries without troubling to examine them **11** to cause inconvenience or discomfort to: sorry to trouble you! [Old French troubler] > **troubled** adj

troublemaker n a person who causes trouble, esp. between people > **troublemaking** adj, n

troubleshooter n a person employed to locate and deal with faults or problems > **troubleshooting** n, adj

troublesome adj causing trouble

trouble spot n a place where there is frequent fighting or violence: the Balkans have long been one of the major European trouble spots

troublous adj literary unsettled or agitated

trough (troff) n **1** a long open container, esp. one for animals' food or water **2** a narrow channel between two waves or ridges **3** a low point in a pattern that has

t

regular high and low points: *the trough of the slump in pupil numbers was in 1985* **4** *meteorol* a long narrow area of low pressure **5** a narrow channel or gutter [Old English *trōh*]

trounce *vb* **trouncing, trounced** to defeat (someone) utterly [origin unknown]

troupe (troop) *n* a company of actors or other performers [French]

trouper *n* **1** a member of a troupe **2** an experienced person: *Bette plays a showbiz trouper*

trouser *adj* **1** of or relating to trousers: *trouser legs* ▷ *vb* **2** *Brit slang* to take (something, esp. money), often surreptitiously or unlawfully

trousers *pl n* a garment that covers the body from the waist to the ankles or knees with a separate tube-shaped section for each leg [Scottish Gaelic *triubhas* trews]

trousseau (troo-so) *n*, *pl* **-seaux** (-so) the clothes, linen, and other possessions collected by a bride for her marriage [Old French]

trout *n*, *pl* **trout** *or* **trouts** any of various game fishes related to the salmon and found chiefly in fresh water in northern regions [Old English *trūht*]

trove *n* See **treasure-trove**

Trowbridge *n* a market town in SW England, administrative centre of Wiltshire: woollen manufacturing. Pop: 34 401 (2001)

trowel *n* **1** a hand tool resembling a small spade with a curved blade, used by gardeners for lifting plants, etc. **2** a similar tool with a flat metal blade, used for spreading cement or plaster on a surface [Latin *trulla* a scoop]

Troy *n* any of nine ancient cities in NW Asia Minor, each of which was built on the ruins of its predecessor. The seventh was the site of the Trojan War (mid-13th century BC). Also called: **Ilion, Ilium.** Related adjective: **Trojan**

Troyes *n* an industrial city in NE France: became prosperous through its great fairs in the early Middle Ages. Pop: 63 044 (2006)

troy weight *or* **troy** *n* a system of weights used for precious metals and gemstones in which one pound equals twelve ounces [after the city of TROYES, where first used]

Trst *n* the Slovene and Croatian name for **Trieste**

truant *n* **1** a pupil who stays away from school without permission **2 play truant** to stay away from school without permission ▷ *adj* **3** being or relating to a truant: *a truant schoolkid* [Old French: vagabond] **> truancy** *n*

truce *n* a temporary agreement to stop fighting or quarrelling [plural of Old English *trēow* pledge]

Trucial States *pl n* a former name (until 1971) of the **United Arab Emirates.** Also called: **Trucial Sheikhdoms, Trucial Oman, Trucial Coast**

truck¹ *n* **1** *Brit* a railway wagon for carrying freight **2** a large motor vehicle for transporting heavy loads **3** any wheeled vehicle used to move goods ▷ *vb* **4** *chiefly US* to transport goods in a truck [perhaps from *truckle* a small wheel]

truck² *n* **1** *history* the payment of wages in goods rather than in money **2 have no truck with** to refuse to be involved with: *the opposition will have no truck with the planned cut in pensions* [Old French *troquer* (unattested) to barter]

trucker *n* a long-distance lorry driver

truckie *n* *Austral and NZ informal* a truck driver

truckle *vb* **-ling, -led** to yield weakly or give in: *he accused the government of truckling to the right-wing press* [from obsolete *truckle* to sleep in a truckle bed]

truckle bed *n* *chiefly Brit* a low bed on wheels, stored under a larger bed

truculent (truck-yew-lent) *adj* defiantly aggressive or bad-tempered [Latin *trux* fierce] **> truculence** *n* **> truculently** *adv*

Trudeau *n* Pierre Elliott. 1919–2000, Canadian statesman; Liberal prime minister (1968–79; 1980–84)

trudge *vb* **trudging, trudged** **1** to walk or plod heavily or wearily ▷ *n* **2** a long tiring walk [origin unknown]

true *adj* **truer, truest** **1** in accordance with the truth or facts; factual: *not all of the stories about her are true* **2** real or genuine: *he didn't want to reveal his true feelings* **3** faithful and loyal: *a true friend* **4** accurate or precise: *he looked through the telescopic sight until he was convinced his aim was true* **5** (of a compass bearing) according to the earth's geographical rather than magnetic poles: *true north* **6 come true** to actually happen: *fortunately his gloomy prediction didn't come true* ▷ *n* **7 in** *or* **out of true** in or not in correct alignment ▷ *adv* **8** truthfully or rightly: *I'd like to move to Edinburgh, true, but I'd need to get a job there first* [Old English *trīewe*]

true-blue *adj* **1** staunchly loyal, conservative, or patriotic ▷ *n* **true blue 2** *chiefly Brit and Austral* a staunch Conservative or patriot

true-life *adj* taken directly from reality: *true-life TV horror stories*

truelove *n* the person that one loves

Trueman *n* Freddy, full name *Frederick Sewards Trueman.* 1931–2006, English cricketer; a fast bowler, he played for Yorkshire (1949–68) and England (1952–65); first bowler to take 300 test match wickets

true north *n* the direction from any point along a meridian towards the North Pole

Truffaut *n* François. 1932–84, French film director of the New Wave. His films include *Les Quatre cents coups* (1959), *Jules et Jim* (1961), *Baisers volés* (1968), and *Le Dernier Métro* (1980)

truffle *n* **1** a round fungus which grows underground and is regarded as a delicacy **2** Also called: **rum truffle** a sweet flavoured with chocolate or rum [French *truffe*]

trug *n* *Brit* a long shallow basket for carrying garden tools, flowers, etc. [perhaps variant of *trough*]

truism *n* a statement that is clearly true and well known

Trujillo¹ *n* a city in NW Peru: founded 1535; university (1824); centre of a district producing rice and sugar cane. Pop: 686 000 (2005 est)

Trujillo² *n* Rafael (**Léonidas**), original name *Rafael Léonidas Trujillo Molina.* 1891–1961, Dominican dictator, who governed the Dominican Republic (1930–61) with the help of a powerful police force: assassinated

Truk Islands *pl n* a group of islands in the W Pacific, in the E Caroline Islands: administratively part of the US Trust Territory of the Pacific Islands from 1947; became self-governing in 1979 as part of the Federated States of Micronesia; consists of 11 chief islands; a major Japanese naval base during World War II. Pop: 53 381 (2006). Area: 130 sq km (50 sq miles)

truly *adv* **1** in a true, just, or faithful manner **2** really: *a truly awful poem*

Truman *n* Harry S. 1884–1972, US Democratic statesman; 33rd president of the US (1945–53). He approved the dropping of the two atomic bombs on Japan (1945), advocated the postwar loan to Britain, and involved the US in the Korean War

trump¹ *n* **1** same as **trump card** ▷ *vb* **2** *cards* to beat a card by playing a card which belongs to a suit which outranks it **3** to outdo or surpass: *she trumped his news by announcing that she had been picked for the Olympic team* ▶ See also **trumps** [variant of *triumph*]

trump² *n* *archaic, literary* **1** a trumpet or the sound produced by one **2 the last trump** the final trumpet call on the Day of Judgment [Old French *trompe*]

trump card *n* **1** any card from the suit that ranks higher than any other suit in one particular game **2** an advantage, weapon, etc., that is kept in reserve until needed: *the President hoped to use his experience of foreign affairs as a trump card in the election* ▶ Also called: **trump**

trumped up *adj* (of charges, excuses, etc.) made up in order to deceive

trumpery *n*, *pl* **-eries 1** something useless or worthless ▷ *adj* **2** useless or worthless [Old French *tromperie* deceit]

trumpet n 1 a valved brass musical instrument consisting of a narrow tube ending in a flare 2 a loud sound such as that of a trumpet: *the elephant gave a loud trumpet* 3 **blow one's own trumpet** to boast about one's own skills or good qualities ▷ vb **-peting, -peted** 4 to proclaim or state forcefully: *almost every one of the party's loudly trumpeted election claims is untrue* 5 (of an elephant) to make a loud cry [Old French *trompette*] > **trumpeter** n

trumps pl n 1 cards any one of the four suits that outranks all the other suits for the duration of a deal or game 2 **turn up trumps** (of a person) to bring about a happy or successful conclusion, esp. unexpectedly

truncate vb **-cating, -cated** to shorten by cutting [Latin *truncare*] > **truncated** adj > **truncation** n

truncheon n chiefly Brit a small club, esp. one carried by a policeman [Old French *tronchon* stump]

trundle vb **-dling, -dled** to move heavily on or as if on wheels: *a bus trundled along the drive* [Old English *tryndel* circular or spherical object]

trundle bed n US, Canad and NZ a low bed on wheels, stored under a larger bed

trundler n 1 NZ a golf or shopping trolley 2 a child's pushchair

trunk n 1 the main stem of a tree 2 a large strong case or box used to contain clothes when travelling and for storage 3 a person's body excluding the head, neck, and limbs; torso 4 the long nose of an elephant 5 US the boot of a car ▶ See also **trunks** [Latin *truncus*]

trunk call n chiefly Brit and Austral a long-distance telephone call

trunk line n 1 a direct link between two distant telephone exchanges or switchboards 2 the main route or routes on a railway

trunk road n Brit a main road, esp. one maintained by the central government

trunks pl n shorts worn by a man for swimming

Truro n a market town in SW England, administrative centre of Cornwall. Pop: 20 920 (2001)

truss vb 1 to tie or bind (someone) up 2 to bind the wings and legs of (a fowl) before cooking ▷ n 3 med a device for holding a hernia in place 4 a framework of wood or metal used to support a roof, bridge, etc. 5 a cluster of flowers or fruit growing at the end of a single stalk [Old French *trousse*]

trust vb 1 to believe that (someone) is honest and means no harm: *my father warned me never to trust strangers* 2 to feel that (something) is safe and reliable: *I don't trust those new gadgets* 3 to entrust (someone) with important information or valuables: *she's not somebody I would trust with this sort of secret* 4 to believe that (someone) is likely to do something safely and reliably: *I wouldn't trust anyone else to look after my child properly* 5 to believe (a story, account, etc.) 6 to expect, hope, or suppose: *I trust you've made your brother welcome here* ▷ n 7 confidence in the truth, worth, reliability, etc., of a person or thing; faith: *he knew that his father had great trust in him* 8 the obligation of someone in a responsible position: *he was in a position of trust as her substitute father* 9 a a legal arrangement whereby one person looks after property, money, etc., on another's behalf b property that is the subject of such an arrangement 10 (in Britain) a self-governing hospital, group of hospitals, or other body that operates as an independent commercial unit within the National Health Service 11 chiefly US and Canad a group of companies joined together to control the market for any commodity ▷ adj 12 of or relating to a trust or trusts: *trust status* [Old Norse *traust* help, support, confidence]

trustee n 1 a person who administers property on someone else's behalf 2 a member of a board that manages the affairs of an institution or organization

trustful or **trusting** adj characterized by a readiness to trust others > **trustfully** or **trustingly** adv

trust fund n money, securities, etc., held in trust

trustworthy adj (of a person) honest, reliable, or dependable

trusty adj **trustier, trustiest** 1 faithful or reliable: *his trusty steed* ▷ n, pl **trusties** 2 a trustworthy convict to whom special privileges are granted

truth n 1 the quality of being true, genuine, or factual: *there is no truth in the allegations* 2 something that is true: *he finally learned the truth about his parents' marriage* 3 a proven or verified fact, principle, etc.: *some profound truths about biology have come to light* [Old English *trīewth*]

truthful adj 1 telling the truth; honest 2 true; based on facts: *a truthful answer* > **truthfully** adv > **truthfulness** n

try vb **tries, trying, tried** 1 to make an effort or attempt: *you must try to understand* 2 to sample or test (something) to see how enjoyable, good, or useful it is: *I tried smoking once but didn't like it* 3 to put strain or stress on (someone's patience) 4 to give pain, affliction, or vexation to: *sometimes when I've been sorely tried, my temper gets a little out of hand* 5 a to investigate (a case) in a court of law b to hear evidence in order to determine the guilt or innocence of (a person) ▷ n, pl **tries** 6 an attempt or effort 7 rugby a score made by placing the ball down behind the opposing team's goal line [Old French *trier* to sort]

> **USAGE** The use of *and* instead of *to* after *try* is very common, but should be avoided in formal writing: *we must try to prevent* (not *try and prevent*) *this happening.*

trying adj upsetting, difficult, or annoying

try on vb 1 to put on (a garment) to find out whether it fits 2 **try it on** informal to attempt to deceive or fool someone ▷ n **try-on** 3 Brit informal something done to test out a person's tolerance etc.

try out vb 1 to test (something), esp. to find out how good it is ▷ n **tryout** 2 chiefly US and Canad a trial or test, for example of an athlete or actor

trysail n a small fore-and-aft sail set on a sailing vessel to help keep her head to the wind in a storm

tryst n archaic or literary 1 an arrangement to meet, esp. secretly 2 a meeting, esp. a secret one with a lover, or the place where such a meeting takes place [Old French *triste* lookout post]

Tsana n Lake Tsana another name for (Lake) **Tana**

tsar or **czar** (zahr) n (until 1917) the emperor of Russia. Also: **tzar** [Russian, ultimately from CAESAR] > **tsarist** or **czarist** n

tsarevitch or **czarevitch** (zahr-rev-itch) n the eldest son of a Russian tsar

tsarina or **czarina** (zahr-een-a) n the wife of a Russian tsar

Tsaritsyn n a former name (until 1925) of **Volgograd**

Tselinograd n a former name (1961–94) for **Astana**

tsetse fly or **tzetze fly** (tset-see) n a bloodsucking African fly whose bite transmits disease, esp. sleeping sickness [Tswana (language of southern Africa) *tse tse*]

T-shirt or **tee-shirt** n a short-sleeved casual shirt or top [T-shape formed when laid flat]

Tshombe n Moise. 1919–69, Congolese statesman. He led the secession of Katanga (1960) from the newly independent Congo; forced into exile (1963) but returned (1964–65) as premier of the Congo; died in exile

Tshwane n another name for **Pretoria**

Tsinan n a variant transliteration of the Chinese name for **Jinan**

Tsinghai n 1 a variant transliteration of the Chinese name for **Qinghai** 2 a variant transliteration of the Chinese name for **Koko Nor**

Tsingtao n a variant transliteration of the Chinese name for **Qingdao**

Tsingyuan or **Ch'ing-yüan** n the former name of **Baoding**

Tsiolkovski n Konstantin Eduardovich. 1857–1935, Russian aeronautical engineer, a pioneer of rocket and space research. His work on liquid-fuelled rockets anticipated the ideas of Robert Goddard

Tsitsihar *n* a variant transliteration of the Chinese name for Qiqihar

Tskhinvali *n* the Georgian name for **South Ossetia**

tsotsi (tsot-see) *n S African* a Black street thug or gang member [perhaps from Nguni (language group of southern Africa) *tsotsa* to dress flashily]

tsp. teaspoon

T-square *n* a T-shaped ruler used for drawing horizontal lines and to support set squares when drawing vertical and inclined lines

Tsugaru Strait *n* a channel between N Honshu and S Hokkaido islands, Japan. Width: about 30 km (20 miles)

tsunami *n* a large, often destructive, sea wave, usually caused by an earthquake under the sea [Japanese]

Tsushima *n* a group of five rocky islands between Japan and South Korea, in the Korea Strait: administratively part of Japan; scene of a naval defeat for the Russians (1905) during the Russo-Japanese war. Pop: 41 230 (2000). Area: 698 sq km (269 sq miles)

Tsvangirai *n* Morgan. born 1952, Zimbabwean trade unionist and politician; leader of the Movement for Democratic Change, the main opposition party to President Mugabe's Zanu-PF since 1999; prime minister (2009–2013)

Tsvetaeva *n* Marina (Ivanovna). 1892–1941, Russian poet. Opposed to the Revolution, she left Russia (1922) and lived in Paris: when she returned (1939) her husband was shot and she committed suicide

TT 1 teetotal **2** teetotaller **3** tuberculin-tested

Tuamotu Archipelago *n* a group of about 80 coral islands in the S Pacific, in French Polynesia. Pop: 15 973 (2002; including the Gambier Islands). Area: 860 sq km (332 sq miles). Also called: **Low Archipelago, Paumotu Archipelago**

tuatara (too-ah-**tah**-rah) *n* a large lizard-like New Zealand reptile [Māori *tua* back + *tara* spine]

tub *n* **1** a low wide, usually round container **2** a small plastic or cardboard container for ice cream etc. **3** *chiefly US* same as **bath** (1) **4** Also called: **tubful** the amount a tub will hold **5** a slow and uncomfortable boat or ship [Middle Dutch *tubbe*]

tuba (**tube**-a) *n* a low-pitched brass musical instrument with valves [Latin]

tubby *adj* **-bier, -biest** (of a person) fat and short
> **tubbiness** *n*

tube *n* **1** a long hollow cylindrical object, used for the passage of fluids or as a container **2** a flexible cylinder of soft metal or plastic closed with a cap, used to hold substances such as toothpaste **3** *anatomy* any hollow cylindrical structure: *the Fallopian tubes* **4** the tube *Brit* the underground railway system in London **5** *electronics* See **cathode-ray tube 6** *slang, chiefly US* a television set [Latin *tubus*] > **tubeless** *adj*

tuber (**tube**-er) *n* a fleshy underground root of a plant such as a potato [Latin: hump]

tubercle (**tube**-er-kl) *n* **1** a small rounded swelling **2** any abnormal hard swelling, esp. one characteristic of tuberculosis [Latin *tuberculum* a little swelling]

tubercular (tube-**berk**-yew-lar) *or* **tuberculous** *adj* **1** of or symptomatic of tuberculosis **2** of or relating to a tubercle

tuberculin (tube-**berk**-yew-lin) *n* a sterile liquid prepared from cultures of the tubercle bacillus and used in the diagnosis of tuberculosis

tuberculin-tested *adj* (of milk) produced by cows that have been certified as free of tuberculosis

tuberculosis (tube-berk-yew-**lohss**-iss) *n* an infectious disease characterized by the formation of tubercles, esp. in the lungs

tuberous (**tube**-er-uss) *adj* (of plants) forming, bearing, or resembling a tuber or tubers

tubing (**tube**-ing) *n* **1** a length of tube **2** a system of tubes

Tübingen *n* a town in SW Germany, in Baden-

Württemberg: university (1477). Pop: 83 137 (2003 est)

Tubman *n* William Vacanarat Shadrach. 1895–1971, Liberian statesman; president of Liberia (1944–71)

tub-thumper *n* a noisy or ranting public speaker
> **tub-thumping** *adj, n*

Tubuai Islands *pl n* a chain of small islands extending about 1400 km (850 miles) in the S Pacific, in French Polynesia; discovered by Captain Cook in 1777; annexed by France in 1880. Pop: 1979 (2002). Area: 173 sq km (67 sq miles). Also called: **Austral Islands**

tubular (tube-yew-lar) *adj* **1** having the shape of a tube or tubes **2** of or relating to a tube or tubing

tubule (tube-yewl) *n* any small tubular structure, esp. in an animal or plant

TUC (in Britain and South Africa) Trades Union Congress

tuck *vb* **1** to push or fold into a small space or between two surfaces: *she tucked the letter into her handbag* **2** to thrust the loose ends or sides of (something) into a confining space, so as to make it neat and secure: *he tucked his shirt back into his trousers* **3** to make a tuck or tucks in (a garment) ▷ *n* **4** a pleat or fold in a part of a garment, usually stitched down **5** *Brit informal* food, esp. cakes and sweets [Old English *tūcian* to torment]

tuck away *vb informal* **1** to eat (a large amount of food) **2** to store (something) in a safe place: *we knew he had some money tucked away somewhere* **3** to have a quiet, rarely disturbed or visited location: *the chapel is tucked away in a side street*

tucker *n* **1** a detachable yoke of lace, linen, etc., formerly worn over the breast of a low-cut dress **2** *Austral and NZ informal* food **3** one's best bib and tucker *informal* one's best clothes

tuckered *adj* **tuckered out** *informal, chiefly US and Canad* exhausted

tuck in *vb* **1** to put (someone) to bed and make him or her snug **2** to thrust the loose ends or sides of (something) into a confining space: *tuck in the bedclothes* **3** *informal* to eat, esp. heartily

tuck shop *n chiefly Brit* a shop in or near a school, where cakes and sweets are sold

Tucson *n* a city in SE Arizona, at an altitude of 700m (2400 ft): resort and seat of the University of Arizona (1891). Pop: 507 658 (2003 est)

Tucumán *n* a city in NW Argentina: scene of the declaration (1816) of Argentinian independence from Spain; university (1914). Pop: 837 000 (2005 est). Full name: **San Miguel de Tucumán**

Tudor *adj* **1** of or in the reign of the English royal house ruling from 1485 to 1603 **2** denoting a style of architecture characterized by half-timbered houses: *a Tudor cottage*

Tues. Tuesday

Tuesday *n* the third day of the week [Old English *tīwesdæg* day of Tyr, Norse god]

tufa (**tew**-fa) *n* a porous rock formed of calcium carbonate deposited from springs [Italian *tufo*]

tuff *n geology* a porous rock formed from volcanic dust or ash [Old French *tuf*]

tuffet *n* a small mound or low seat [from *tuft*]

tuft *n* a bunch of feathers, grass, hair, threads, etc., held together at the base [probably from Old French *tufe*]
> **tufted** *adj* > **tufty** *adj*

tug *vb* **tugging, tugged 1** to pull or drag with a sharp or powerful movement: *she tugged at my arm* **2** to tow (a ship or boat) by means of a tug ▷ *n* **3** a strong pull or jerk **4** Also called: **tugboat** a boat with a powerful engine, used for towing barges, ships, etc. [Middle English *tuggen*]

Tugela *n* a river in E South Africa, rising in the Drakensberg where it forms the **Tugela Falls**, 856 m (2810 ft) high (highest waterfall in Africa), before flowing east to the Indian Ocean: scene of battles during the Zulu War (1879) and the Boer War (1899–1902). Length: about 500 km (312 miles)

tug-of-love *n* a conflict over the custody of a child between divorced parents or between the child's natural parents and its foster or adoptive parents

tug-of-war *n* **1** a contest in which two people or teams pull opposite ends of a rope in an attempt to drag the opposition over a central line **2** any hard struggle between two people or two groups

Tuileries *n* a former royal residence in Paris: begun in 1564 by Catherine de' Medici and burned in 1871 by the Commune; site of the **Tuileries Gardens** (a park near the Louvre)

tuition *n* **1** instruction, esp. that received individually or in a small group **2** the payment for instruction, esp. in colleges or universities [Latin *tueri* to watch over]

tuktu *n Canad* another name for **caribou**

tuk-tuk *n* (in Thailand) a three-wheeled motor vehicle used as a taxi

Tula *n* an industrial city in W central Russia. Pop: 460 000 (2005 est)

tulip *n* **1** a plant which produces bright cup-shaped flowers in spring **2** the flower or bulb [Turkish *tülbend* turban]

tulip tree *n* a North American tree with tulip-shaped greenish-yellow flowers and long conelike fruits

Tull *n* Jethro. 1674–1741, English agriculturalist, who invented the seed drill

Tullamore *n* the county town of Offaly, Republic of Ireland; food processing and brewing. Pop: 11 098 (2002)

tulle (tewl) *n* a fine net fabric of silk, rayon, etc., used to make evening dresses [French]

Tulsa *n* a city in NE Oklahoma, on the Arkansas River: a major oil centre; two universities. Pop: 387 807 (2003 est)

tumble *vb* **-bling, -bled** **1** to fall or cause to fall, esp. awkwardly or violently: *chairs tumbled over* **2** to roll or twist, esp. in playing: *they rolled and tumbled as wild beasts* **3** to decrease in value suddenly: *interest rates tumbled* **4** to move in a quick and uncontrolled manner: *the crowd tumbled down the stairs* **5** to disturb, rumple, or toss around: *she was all tumbled by the fall* **6** to perform leaps or somersaults ▷ *n* **7** a fall, esp. an awkward or violent one: *he took a tumble down the stairs* **8** a somersault [Old English *tumbian* dance, jump] **> tumbled** *adj*

tumbledown *adj* (of a building) falling to pieces; dilapidated

tumble dryer *or* **tumble drier** *n* an electrically-operated machine that dries wet laundry by rotating it in warmed air inside a metal drum

tumbler *n* **1 a** a flat-bottomed drinking glass with no handle or stem **b** the amount a tumbler will hold **2** a person who performs somersaults and other acrobatic feats **3** a part of the mechanism of a lock

tumble to *vb* to understand or become aware of: *how did he tumble to this?*

tumbril *n* a farm cart that tilts backwards to empty its load, which was used to take condemned prisoners to the guillotine during the French Revolution [Old French *tumberel*]

tumescent (tew-mess-ent) *adj* swollen or becoming swollen

tumid (tew-mid) *adj rare* **1** (of an organ or part of the body) enlarged or swollen **2** pompous or fulsome in style: *a tumid tome* [Latin *tumere* to swell] **> tumidity** *n*

tummy *n, pl* **-mies** an informal or childish word for **stomach**

tumour *or US* **tumor** (tew-mer) *n pathol* **a** any abnormal swelling **b** a mass of tissue formed by a new growth of cells [Latin *tumere* to swell] **> tumorous** *adj*

tumult (tew-mult) *n* **1** a loud confused noise, such as one produced by a crowd **2** a state of confusion and excitement: *a tumult of emotions* [Latin *tumultus*]

tumultuous (tew-mull-tew-uss) *adj* **1** exciting, confused, or turbulent: *this week's tumultuous events* **2** unruly, noisy, or excited: *a tumultuous welcome*

tumulus (tew-myew-luss) *n, pl* **-li** (-lie) *archaeol* no longer in technical use a burial mound [Latin: a hillock]

tun *n* a large beer cask [Old English *tunne*]

tuna (tune-a) *n, pl* **-na** *or* **-nas** **1** a large marine spiny-finned fish **2** the flesh of this fish, often tinned for food [American Spanish]

Tunbridge Wells *n* a town and resort in SE England, in SW Kent: chalybeate spring discovered in 1606; an important social centre in the 17th and 18th centuries. Pop: 60 095 (2001). Official name: **Royal Tunbridge Wells**

tundra *n* a vast treeless Arctic region with permanently frozen subsoil [Russian]

tune *n* **1** a melody, esp. one for which harmony is not essential **2** the correct musical pitch: *many of the notes are out of tune* **3 call the tune** to be in control of the proceedings **4 change one's tune** to alter one's attitude or tone of speech **5 in** *or* **out of tune with** in *or* not in agreement or sympathy with: *in tune with public opinion* **6 to the tune of** *informal* to the amount or extent of ▷ *vb* **tuning, tuned** **7** to adjust (a musical instrument) so each string, key, etc., produces the right note **8** to make small adjustments to (an engine, machine, etc.) to obtain the proper or desired performance **9** to adjust (a radio or television) to receive a particular station or programme: *the radio was tuned to the local station* [variant of *tone*] **> tuner** *n*

tuneful *adj* having a pleasant tune **> tunefully** *adv*

tune in *vb* **1** to adjust (a radio or television) to receive (a station or programme) **2 tuned in to** *slang* aware of or knowledgeable about: *tuned in to European cinema*

tuneless *adj* having no melody or tune

tune up *vb* **1** to adjust (a musical instrument) to a particular pitch **2** to adjust the engine of a car, etc., to improve its performance

tungsten *n chem* a hard greyish-white metallic element. Symbol: W [Swedish *tung* heavy + *sten* stone]

Tungting *or* **Tung-t'ing** *n* a variant transliteration of the Chinese name for the **Dongting**

Tunguska *n* any of three rivers in Russia, in central Siberia, all tributaries of the Yenisei: the **Lower** (Nizhnyaya) **Tunguska** 2690 km (1670 miles) long; the **Stony** (Podkamennaya) **Tunguska** 1550 km (960 miles) long; the **Upper** (Verkhnyaya) **Tunguska** which is the lower course of the Angara. The area was the scene in 1908 of a massive explosion believed to have been the result of the disintegration in the atmosphere of a small comet or meteorite

tunic *n* **1** a close-fitting jacket forming part of some uniforms **2** a loose-fitting knee-length garment [Latin *tunica*]

tuning fork *n* a two-pronged metal fork that when struck produces a pure note of constant specified pitch

Tunis *n* the capital and chief port of Tunisia, in the northeast on the **Gulf of Tunis** (an inlet of the Mediterranean): dates from Carthaginian times, the ruins of ancient Carthage lying to the northeast; university (1960). Pop: 2 063 000 (2005 est)

Tunisia *n* a republic in N Africa, on the Mediterranean: settled by the Phoenicians in the 12th century BC; made a French protectorate in 1881 and gained independence in 1955. It consists chiefly of the Sahara in the south, a central plateau, and the Atlas Mountains in the north. Exports include textiles, petroleum, and phosphates. Official language: Arabic; French is also widely spoken. Official religion: Muslim. Currency: dinar. Capital: Tunis. Pop: 10 835 873 (2013 est). Area: 164 150 sq km (63 380 sq miles)

Tunisian *adj* **1** of or relating to Tunisia or its inhabitants ▷ *n* **2** a native or inhabitant of Tunisia

tunnel *n* **1** an underground passageway, esp. one for trains or cars **2** any passage or channel through or under something: *the carpal tunnel* ▷ *vb* **-nelling, -nelled** *or US* **-neling, -neled** **3** to make one's way through or under (something) by digging a tunnel: *ten men succeeded in tunnelling out of the prisoner-of-war camp* **4** to dig a tunnel (through or under something): *the idea of tunnelling under the English Channel has been around for a long time* [Old French *tonel* cask]

tunnel vision *n* **1** a condition in which a person is unable to see things that are not straight in front **2** narrowness of viewpoint resulting from concentration on only one aspect of a subject or situation

Tunney *n* Gene, original name *James Joseph Tunney.* 1897–1978, US boxer; world heavyweight champion (1926–28)

tunny *n, pl* **-nies** *or* **-ny** same as **tuna** [Latin *thunnus*]

tup *n chiefly Brit* a male sheep [origin unknown]

tupik (**too**-pick) *n* a tent of seal or caribou skin used for shelter by the Inuit in summer [Inuktitut *tupiq*]

Tupolev *n* Andrei Nikolaievich. 1888–1972, Soviet aircraft designer, who designed the first supersonic passenger aircraft, the TU-144 (tested 1969). He also designed supersonic bombers and the TU-104, one of the first passenger jet aircraft (1955)

tuppence *n Brit* same as **twopence** › **tuppenny** *adj*

Tupungato *n* a mountain on the border between Argentina and Chile, in the Andes. Height: 6550 m (21 484 ft)

tuque (rhymes with **fluke**) *n Canad* **1** a knitted cap with a long tapering end **2** a close-fitting knitted hat often with a tassel or pompom [Canadian French]

turban *n* **1** a head-covering worn by a Muslim, Hindu, or Sikh man, consisting of a long piece of cloth wound round the head **2** any head-covering resembling this [Turkish *tülbend*] › **turbaned** *adj*

turbid *adj literary* (of water or air) full of mud or dirt, and frequently swirling around: *the turbid stream of the Loire* [Latin *turbare* to agitate] › **turbidity** *n*

turbine *n* a machine in which power is produced by a stream of water, air, etc., that pushes the blades of a wheel and causes it to rotate [Latin *turbo* whirlwind]

turbocharger *n* a device that increases the power of an internal-combustion engine by using the exhaust gases to drive a turbine › **turbocharged** *adj*

turbofan *n* a type of engine in which a large fan driven by a turbine forces air rearwards to increase the propulsive thrust

turbojet *n* **1** a gas turbine in which the exhaust gases provide the propulsive thrust to drive an aircraft **2** an aircraft powered by turbojet engines

turboprop *n* an aircraft propulsion unit where the propeller is driven by a gas turbine

turbot *n, pl* **-bot** *or* **-bots** a European flatfish, highly valued as a food fish [Old French *tourbot*]

turbulence *n* **1** a state or condition of confusion, movement, or agitation **2** *meteorol* instability in the atmosphere causing gusty air currents

turbulent *adj* **1** involving a lot of sudden changes and conflicting elements: *the city has had a turbulent history* **2** (of people) wild and unruly: *a harsh mountain land inhabited by a score of turbulent tribes* **3** (of water or air) full of violent unpredictable currents: *the turbulent ocean* [Latin *turba* confusion]

turd *n taboo* **1** a piece of excrement **2** *slang* a contemptible person [Old English *tord*]

tureen *n* a large deep dish with a lid, used for serving soups [from TERRINE]

Turenne *n* Vicomte de, title of *Henri de la Tour d'Auvergne.* 1611–75, French marshal. He commanded armies during the Thirty Years' War and the wars of the Fronde

turf *n, pl* **turfs** *or* **turves 1** a layer of thick even grass with roots and soil attached: *a short turf rich in wild flowers* **2** a piece cut from this layer: *we spent the afternoon digging turves* **3** *informal* **a** the area where a person lives and feels at home: *my boyhood turf of east Cork* **b** a person's area of knowledge or influence: *when Kate is at work, she's on her own turf* **4 the turf a** a track where horse races are run **b** horse racing as a sport or industry **5** same as **peat** ▷ *vb* **6** to cover (an area of ground) with pieces of turf [Old English]

turf accountant *n Brit* same as **bookmaker**

turf out *vb informal* to throw (someone or something) out: *the residents fear a new landlord might push up rents and turf them out of their homes*

Turgenev *n* Ivan Sergeyevich. 1818–83, Russian novelist and dramatist. In *A Sportsman's Sketches* (1852) he pleaded for the abolition of serfdom. His novels, such as *Rudin* (1856) and *Fathers and Sons* (1862), are noted for their portrayal of country life and of the Russian intelligentsia. His plays include *A Month in the Country* (1850)

turgid (**tur**-jid) *adj* **1** (of language) pompous, boring, and hard to understand **2** (of water or mud) unpleasantly thick and brown [Latin *turgere* to swell] › **turgidity** *n*

Turgot *n* Anne Robert Jacques. 1727–81, French economist and statesman. As controller general of finances (1774–76), he attempted to abolish feudal privileges, incurring the hostility of the aristocracy and his final dismissal

Turin *n* a city in NW Italy, capital of Piedmont region, on the River Po: became capital of the Kingdom of Sardinia in 1720; first capital (1861–65) of united Italy; university (1405); a major industrial centre, producing most of Italy's cars. Pop: 865 263 (2001). Italian name: **Torino**

Turing *n* Alan Mathison. 1912–54, English mathematician, who was responsible for formal description of abstract automata, and speculation on computer imitation of humans: a leader of the Allied codebreakers at Bletchley Park during World War II; he committed suicide after being prosecuted for homosexuality but was posthumously pardoned in 2013

Turishcheva *n* Ludmilla. born 1952, Soviet gymnast: world champion 1970, 1972 (at the Olympic Games), and 1974

Turk *n* a native or inhabitant of Turkey

Turk. **1** Turkey **2** Turkish

Turkana *n* Lake Turkana a long narrow lake in E Africa, in the Great Rift Valley. Area: 7104 sq km (2743 sq miles). Former name: **Lake Rudolf**

Turkestan *or* **Turkistan** *n* an extensive region of central Asia between Siberia in the north and Tibet, India, Afghanistan, and Iran in the south: formerly divided into **West** (**Russian**) **Turkestan** (also called Soviet Central Asia), comprising present-day Turkmenistan, Uzbekistan, Tajikistan, and Kyrgyzstan and the S part of Kazakhstan, and **East** (**Chinese**) **Turkestan**, approximating to the Xinjiang Uygur Autonomous Region of China

Turkestani *adj* **1** of or relating to the central Asian region of Turkestan or its inhabitants ▷ *n* **2** a native or inhabitant of Turkestan

turkey *n, pl* **-keys** *or* **-key 1** a large bird of North America bred for its meat **2** *informal, chiefly US and Canad* something, esp. a theatrical production, that fails **3 cold turkey** *slang* a method of curing drug addiction by abrupt withdrawal of all doses **4 talk turkey** *informal, chiefly US and Canad* to discuss, esp. business, frankly and practically [used at first of the African guinea fowl (because it was brought through Turkish territory), later applied by mistake to the American bird]

Turkey *n* a republic in W Asia and SE Europe, between the Black Sea, the Mediterranean, and the Aegean: the centre of the Ottoman Empire; became a republic in 1923. The major Asian part, consisting mainly of an arid plateau, is separated from European Turkey by the Bosporus, Sea of Marmara, and Dardanelles. Languages: Turkish (official), Kurdish, and Arabic minority languages. Religion: Muslim majority. Currency: lira. Capital: Ankara. Pop: 80 694 485 (2013 est). Area: 780 576 sq km (301 380 sq miles)

Turkic *n* a family of Asian languages including Turkish and Azerbaijani

Turkish *adj* **1** of or relating to Turkey or its inhabitants ▷ *n* **2** the language of Turkey

Turkish bath *n* **1** a type of bath in which the bather sweats freely in hot dry air, is then washed, often massaged, and has a cold plunge or shower **2 Turkish baths** an establishment for such baths

Turkish coffee *n* very strong black coffee

Turkish delight *n* a jelly-like sweet flavoured with flower essences, usually cut into cubes and covered in icing sugar

Turkmenistan *n* a republic in central Asia: the area has been occupied by a succession of empires; a Turkmen state was established in the 15th century but suffered almost continual civil strife and was gradually conquered by Russia; in 1918 it became a Soviet republic and gained independence from the Soviet Union in 1991: deserts including the Kara Kum cover most of the region; agricultural communities are concentrated around oases; there are rich mineral deposits. Official language: Turkmen. Religion: believers are mainly Muslim. Currency: manat. Capital: Ashkhabad. Pop: 5 113 040 (2013 est). Area: 488 100 sq km (186 400 sq miles)

Turks and Caicos Islands *pl n* a UK Overseas Territory in the Caribbean, southeast of the Bahamas: consists of the eight **Turks Islands**, separated by the Turks Island Passage from the Caicos group, which has six main islands. Capital: Grand Turk. Pop: 47 754 (2013 est). Area: 430 sq km (166 sq miles)

Turku *n* a city and port in SW Finland, on the Gulf of Bothnia: capital of Finland until 1812. Pop: 175 059 (2003 est). Swedish name: **Åbo**

turmeric *n* **1** a tropical Asian plant with yellow flowers and an aromatic underground stem **2** a yellow spice obtained from the root of this plant [Old French *terre merite* meritorious earth]

turmoil *n* disorder, agitation, or confusion: *a period of political turmoil and uncertainty* [origin unknown]

turn *vb* **1** to move to face in another direction **2** to rotate or move round **3** to operate (a switch, key, etc.) by twisting it **4** to aim or point (something) in a particular direction: *they turned their guns on the crowd* **5** to change in course or direction: *the van turned right into Victoria Road* **6** (of a road, river, etc.) to have a bend or curve in it **7** to perform or do (something) with a rotating movement: *a small boy was turning somersaults* **8** to change so as to become: *he turned pale* **9** to reach, pass, or progress beyond in age, time, etc.: *she had just turned fourteen* **10** to find (a particular page) in a book: *turn to page 78* **11** to look at the other side of: *turning the pages of a book* **12** to shape (wood, metal, etc.) on a lathe **13** (of leaves) to change colour in autumn **14** to make or become sour: *the milk is starting to turn* **15** to affect or be affected with nausea or giddiness: *that would turn the strongest stomach* **16** (of the tide) to start coming in or going out **17 turn against** to stop liking (something or someone one previously liked): *people turned against her because she became so dictatorial* **18 turn into** to become or change into: *my mother turned our house into four apartments* **19 turn loose** to set (an animal or a person) free **20 turn someone's head** to affect someone mentally or emotionally **21 turn to a** to direct or apply (one's attention or thoughts) to **b** to stop doing or using one thing and start doing or using (another): *I turned to photography from writing* **c** to appeal or apply to (someone) for help, advice, etc. ▷ *n* **22** the act of turning **23** a movement of complete or partial rotation: *a turn of the dial* **24** a change of direction or position **25** same as **turning** (1) **26** the right or opportunity to do something in an agreed order or succession: *it was her turn to play next* **27** a change in something that is happening or being done: *events took an unhappy turn* **28** a period of action, work, etc. **29** a short walk, ride, or excursion **30** natural inclination: *a liberal turn of mind* **31** distinctive form or style: *she'd a nice turn of phrase* **32** a deed that helps or hinders someone: *I'm trying to do you a good turn* **33** a twist, bend, or distortion in shape **34** a slight attack of an illness: *she's just having one of her turns* **35** *music* a melodic

ornament that alternates the main note with the notes above and below it, beginning with the note above, in a variety of sequences **36** a short theatrical act: *tonight's star turn* **37** *informal* a shock or surprise: *you gave me rather a turn* **38 done to a turn** *informal* cooked perfectly **39 turn and turn about** one after another; alternately ▶ See also **turn down, turn in**, etc. [Old English *tyrnan*] ➤ **turner** *n*

turnaround *or* **turnabout** *n* a complete change or reversal: *a prompt economic turnaround*

turncoat *n* a person who deserts one cause or party to join an opposing one

turn down *vb* **1** to reduce (the volume, brightness, or temperature of something): *turn the heat down* **2** to reject or refuse: *the invitation was turned down* **3** to fold down (sheets, etc.)

Turner *n* **1 Jane.** born 1961, Australian television actress and writer, best known for playing 'Kath' in the comedy series *Kath & Kim* (2002–2007) **2 J(oseph) M(allord) W(illiam).** 1775–1851, British landscape painter; a master of water colours. He sought to convey atmosphere by means of an innovative use of colour and gradations of light **3 Nat.** 1800–31, US rebel slave, who led (1831) Turner's Insurrection, the only major slave revolt in US history: executed **4 Robert Edward III**, known as *Ted.* born 1938, US broadcasting executive and yachtsman; chairman of Turner Broadcasting (1970–96), founder of Cable News Network (1980), and vice-chairman of Time Warner (1996–2003) **5 Tina**, real name *Annie Mae Bullock.* born 1940, US rock singer who performed (1958–75) with her then husband Ike Turner (1931–2007) and later as a solo act. Her recordings include "River Deep, Mountain High" (1966) and "Simply the Best" (1991)

turn in *vb informal* **1** to go to bed for the night **2** to hand in: *turning in my essay* **3** to hand (a suspect or criminal) over to the police: *his own brother turned him in*

turning *n* **1** a road, river, or path that turns off the main way **2** the point where such a way turns off **3** the process of turning objects on a lathe

turning circle *n* the smallest circle in which a vehicle can turn

turning point *n* a moment when a decisive change occurs

turnip *n* a vegetable with a large yellow or white edible root [Latin *napus*]

turnkey *n* old-fashioned a jailer

turn off *vb* **1** to leave (a road or path): *turning off the main road* **2** (of a road or path) to lead away from (another road or path): *a main street with alleys twisting and turning off it* **3** to cause (something) to stop operating by turning a knob, pushing a button, etc. **4** *informal* to cause disgust or disinterest in (someone): *keeping kids from getting turned off by mathematics* ▷ *n* **turn-off 5** a road or other way branching off from the main thoroughfare **6** *informal* a person or thing that causes dislike

turn on *vb* **1** to cause (something) to operate by turning a knob, pushing a button, etc.: *turn on the radio, please* **2** to attack (someone), esp. without warning: *the Labrador turned on me* **3** *informal* to produce suddenly or automatically: *turning on that bland smile* **4** *slang* to arouse emotionally or sexually **5** to depend or hinge on: *the match turned on three double faults by Sampras* ▷ *n* **turn-on 6** *slang* a person or thing that causes emotional or sexual arousal

turn out *vb* **1** to cause (something, esp. a light) to stop operating by moving a switch **2** to produce or create: *turning out two hits a year* **3** to force (someone) out of a place or position: *turned out of office* **4** to empty the contents of (something): *the police ordered him to turn out his pockets* **5** to be discovered or found (to be or do something): *he turned out to be a Finn* **6** to end up or result: *how interesting to see how it all turned out!* **7** to dress and groom: *she is always very well turned out* **8** to assemble or gather: *crowds turned out to see him* **9 turn out for** *informal* to make an appearance, esp. in a sporting competition: *he was asked to turn out for Liverpool*

▷ *n* **turnout 10** a number of people attending an event: *there has been a high turnout of voters in elections in Bulgaria* **11** the quantity or amount produced

turn over *vb* **1** to change position, esp. so as to reverse top and bottom **2** to shift position, for instance by rolling onto one's side: *he turned over and went straight to sleep* **3** to consider carefully: *as I walked, I turned her story over* **4** to give (something) to someone who has a right to it or to the authorities: *the police ordered him to turn over the files to them* **5** (of an engine) to start or function correctly: *when he pressed the starter button, the engine turned over at once* **6** *slang* to rob: *the house had been turned over while they were out* ▷ *n* **turnover 7 a** the amount of business done by a company during a specified period **b** the rate at which stock in trade is sold and replenished **8** a small pastry case filled with fruit or jam: *an apple turnover* **9** the number of workers employed by a firm in a given period to replace those who have left

turnpike *n* **1** *history* a barrier across a road to prevent vehicles or pedestrians passing until a charge (toll) had been paid **2** US a motorway for use of which a toll is charged [*turn* + *pike* a spike]

turnstile *n* a mechanical barrier with arms that are turned to admit one person at a time

turntable *n* **1** the circular platform in a record player that rotates the record while it is being played **2** a circular platform used for turning locomotives and cars

turn up *vb* **1** to arrive or appear: *few people turned up* **2** to find or discover or be found or discovered: *a medical checkup has only turned up a sinus infection* **3** to increase the flow, volume, etc., of: *he turned up the radio* ▷ *n* **turn-up 4** Brit the turned-up fold at the bottom of some trouser legs **5 a turn-up for the books** *informal* an unexpected happening

turpentine *n* **1** a strong-smelling colourless oil distilled from the resin of some coniferous trees, and used for thinning paint, for cleaning, and in medicine **2** a semisolid mixture of resin and oil obtained from various conifers, which is the main source of commercial turpentine **3** *no longer in technical use* any one of a number of thinners for paints and varnishes, consisting of fractions of petroleum [Latin *terebinthina*]

Turpin *n* Dick. 1706–39, English highwayman

turpitude *n* *formal* depravity or wickedness: *newspapers owned by proprietors whose moral turpitude far exceeded anything chronicled in their pages* [Latin *turpitudo* ugliness]

turps *n* short for **turpentine** (1, 3)

turquoise *adj* **1** greenish-blue ▷ *n* **2** a greenish-blue precious stone [Old French *turqueise* Turkish (stone)]

turret *n* **1** a small tower that projects from the wall of a building, esp. a castle **2** (on a tank or warship) a rotating structure on which guns are mounted **3** (on a machine tool) a turret-like steel structure with tools projecting from it that can be rotated to bring each tool to bear on the work [Latin *turris* tower] > **turreted** *adj*

turtle *n* **1** an aquatic reptile with a flattened shell enclosing the body and flipper-like limbs adapted for swimming **2 turn turtle** (of a boat) to capsize [French *tortue* tortoise]

turtledove *n* an Old World dove noted for its soft cooing and devotion to its mate [Old English *turtla*]

turtleneck *n* a round high close-fitting neck on a sweater or a sweater with such a neck

Tuscan *adj* of a style of classical architecture characterized by unfluted columns [from *Tuscany*, a region in central Italy]

Tuscany *n* a region of central Italy, on the Ligurian and Tyrrhenian Seas: corresponds roughly to ancient Etruria; a region of numerous small states in medieval times; united in the 15th and 16th centuries under Florence; united with the rest of Italy in 1861. Capital: Florence. Pop: 3 516 296 (2003 est). Area: 22 990 sq km (8876 sq miles). Italian name: **Toscana**

Tusculan *adj* of or relating to the ancient Italian city

of Tusculum or its inhabitants

Tusculum *n* an ancient city in Latium near Rome

tusk *n* a long pointed tooth in the elephant, walrus, and certain other mammals [Old English *tūsc*] > **tusked** *adj*

Tusk *n* Donald. born 1957, Polish politician; prime minister of Poland (2007–14); president of the European Council from 2014

Tussaud *n* Marie. 1760–1850, Swiss modeller in wax, who founded a permanent exhibition in London of historical and contemporary figures

tussle *n* **1** an energetic fight, struggle, or argument: *she resigned following a protracted boardroom tussle* ▷ *vb* **-sling, -sled 2** to fight or struggle energetically [Middle English *tusen* to pull]

tussock *n* a dense tuft of grass or other vegetation [origin unknown] > **tussocky** *adj*

tut *interj, n, vb* **tutting, tutted** short for **tut-tut**

Tutankhamen or **Tutankhamun** *n* king (1361–1352 BC) of the 18th dynasty of Egypt. His tomb near Luxor, discovered in 1922, contained many material objects

tutelage (tew-till-lij) *n* *formal* **1** instruction or guidance, esp. by a tutor **2** the state of being supervised by a guardian or tutor [Latin *tueri* to watch over]

tutelary (tew-till-lar-ee) *adj* *literary* **1** having the role of guardian or protector **2** of a guardian

tutor *n* **1** a teacher, usually one instructing individual pupils **2** (at a college or university) a member of staff responsible for the teaching and supervision of a certain number of students ▷ *vb* **3** to act as a tutor to (someone) [Latin: a watcher] > **tutorship** *n*

tutorial *n* **1** a period of intensive tuition given by a tutor to an individual student or to a small group of students ▷ *adj* **2** of or relating to a tutor

tutti *adj, adv* *music* to be performed by the whole orchestra, choir, etc. [Italian]

tutti-frutti *n, pl* **-fruttis** an ice cream or other sweet food containing small pieces of candied or fresh fruits [Italian, literally: all the fruits]

tut-tut *interj* **1** an exclamation of mild reprimand, disapproval, or surprise ▷ *vb* **-tutting, -tutted 2** to express disapproval by the exclamation of 'tut-tut' ▷ *n* **3** the act of tut-tutting: *his bright red tennis shorts provoked a few tut-tuts from the traditionalists*

tutu *n* a skirt worn by ballerinas, made of projecting layers of stiffened material [French]

Tutu *n* Desmond. born 1931, South African clergyman, noted for his opposition to apartheid: Anglican Bishop of Johannesburg (1984–86) and Archbishop of Cape Town (1986–96); in 1995 he became leader of the Truth and Reconciliation Commission, established to investigate human rights violations during the apartheid era. Nobel peace prize 1984

Tutuila *n* the largest island of American Samoa, in the SW Pacific. Chief town and port: Pago Pago. Pop: 55 876 (2000). Area: 135 sq km (52 sq miles)

Tutuola *n* Amos. 1920–97, Nigerian writer: his books include *The Palm-Wine Drinkard* (1952) and *Pauper, Brawler and Slanderer* (1987)

Tuvalu *n* a country in the SW Pacific, comprising a group of nine coral islands: established as a British protectorate in 1892. From 1915 until 1975 the islands formed part of the British colony of the Gilbert and Ellice Islands; achieved full independence in 1978; a member of the Commonwealth (formerly a special member not represented at all meetings, until 2000). Languages: English and Tuvaluan. Religion: Christian majority. Currency: Australian dollar; Tuvalu dollars are also used. Capital: Funafuti. Pop: 10 698 (2013 est). Area: 26 sq km (10 sq miles). Former names: **Lagoon Islands, Ellice Islands**

Tuvaluan *adj* **1** relating to, denoting, or characteristic of Tuvalu, its inhabitants, or their language ▷ *n* **2** a native or inhabitant of Tuvalu **3** the Austronesian language of Tuvalu

Tuva Republic *or* **Tyva** *n* a constituent republic of S Russia: mountainous. Capital: Kizyl. Pop: 305 500 (2002). Area: 170 500 sq km (65 800 sq miles). Former name: **Tuvinian Autonomous Republic**

tuxedo *n*, *pl* **-dos** a dinner jacket [after a country club in *Tuxedo Park*, New York]

Tuxtla Gutiérrez *n* a city in SE Mexico, capital of Chiapas state: agricultural centre. Pop: 723 000 (2005 est)

TV television

TVEI *Brit* technical and vocational educational initiative: a national educational scheme in which pupils gain practical experience in technology and industry, often through work placement

Tver *n* a city in central Russia, at the confluence of the Volga and Tversta Rivers: chief port of the upper Volga, linked by canal with Moscow. Pop: 402 000 (2005 est). Former name (1932–91): **Kalinin**

twaddle *n* **1** silly, trivial, or pretentious talk or writing ▷ *vb* **-dling, -dled 2** to talk or write in a silly or pretentious way [earlier *twattle*]

twain *adj*, *n archaic* two [Old English *twēgen*]

Twain *n* **1** Mark, pen name of *Samuel Langhorne Clemens*. 1835–1910, US novelist and humorist, famous for his classics *The Adventures of Tom Sawyer* (1876) and *The Adventures of Huckleberry Finn* (1885) **2** Shania, real name *Eileen Regina Edwards*. born 1965, Canadian country-rock singer; her bestselling recordings include *The Woman In Me* (1995), *Come On Over* (1997), and *UP!* (2002)

twang *n* **1** a sharp ringing sound produced by or as if by the plucking of a taut string **2** a strongly nasal quality in a person's speech: *a high-pitched Texas twang* ▷ *vb* **3** to make or cause to make a twang: *a bunch of angels twanging harps* [imitative] ▷ **twangy** *adj*

twat *n Brit, Austral and NZ taboo, slang* **1** the female genitals **2** a foolish person [origin unknown]

tweak *vb* **1** to twist or pinch with a sharp or sudden movement: *she tweaked his ear* **2** *informal* to make a minor alteration ▷ *n* **3** the act of tweaking **4** *informal* a minor alteration [Old English *twiccian*]

twee *adj informal* excessively sentimental, sweet, or pretty [from *tweet*, affected pronunciation of *sweet*]

tweed *n* **1** a thick woollen cloth produced originally in Scotland **2** tweeds a suit made of tweed [probably from *tweel*, Scots variant of TWILL]

Tweed *n* a river in SE Scotland and NE England, flowing east and forming part of the border between Scotland and England, then crossing into England to enter the North Sea at Berwick. Length: 156 km (97 miles)

Tweeddale *n* another name for **Peeblesshire**

Tweedsmuir *n* Baron Tweedsmuir the title of Scottish novelist John Buchan. See **Buchan**

tweedy *adj* **tweedier, tweediest 1** of, made of, or resembling tweed **2** showing a fondness for a hearty outdoor life, often associated with wearers of tweeds

tweet *n* **1** an imitation of the thin chirping sound made by small birds **2** a short message posted on the Twitter website ▷ *vb* **3** to make this sound **4** to post a short message on the Twitter website [imitative]

tweeter *n* a loudspeaker used in high-fidelity systems for the reproduction of high audio frequencies

tweezers *pl n* a small pincer-like tool used for tasks such as handling small objects or plucking out hairs [obsolete *tweeze* case of instruments]

twelfth *adj* **1** of or being number twelve in a series ▷ *n* **2** number twelve in a series **3** one of twelve equal parts of something

Twelfth Day *n* January 6, the twelfth day after Christmas and the feast of the Epiphany

twelfth man *n* a reserve player in a cricket team

Twelfth Night *n* **a** the evening of January 5, the eve of Twelfth Day **b** the evening of Twelfth Day itself

twelve *n* **1** the cardinal number that is the sum of ten and two **2** a numeral, 12 or XII, representing this

number **3** something representing or consisting of twelve units ▷ *adj* **4** amounting to twelve: *twelve months* [Old English *twelf*]

twelvemonth *n archaic, chiefly Brit* a year

twelve-tone *adj* of or denoting the type of serial music which uses as its musical material a sequence of notes containing all 12 semitones of the chromatic scale

twenty *n*, *pl* **-ties 1** the cardinal number that is the product of ten and two **2** a numeral, 20 or XX, representing this number **3** something representing or consisting of twenty units ▷ *adj* **4** amounting to twenty: *twenty minutes* ▷ **twentieth** *adj*, *n*

Twenty20 *n* form of one-day cricket in which each side bats for twenty overs

twenty-four-seven *or* **24/7** *adv informal* constantly or all the time: *consultants would no longer be available 24/7* [from twenty-four hours a day, seven days a week]

twenty-six counties *pl n* the counties of the Republic of Ireland

twerking *n* a provocative dance performed by moving the hips rapidly back and forth, while pushing the buttocks out

twerp *or* **twirp** *n informal* a silly, stupid, or contemptible person [origin unknown]

twice *adv* **1** two times; on two occasions or in two cases: *I've met her only twice* **2** double in degree or quantity: *twice as big* [Old English *twiwa*]

Twickenham *n* a former town in SE England, on the River Thames: part of the Greater London borough of Richmond-upon-Thames since 1965; contains the English Rugby Football Union ground

twiddle *vb* **-dling, -dled 1** to twirl or fiddle, often in an idle way: *twiddling the knobs of a radio* **2** twiddle one's thumbs **a** to rotate one's thumbs around one another, when bored or impatient **b** to be bored, with nothing to do ▷ *n* **3** an unnecessary decoration, esp. a curly one [probably *twirl* + *fiddle*]

twig¹ *n* a small branch or shoot of a tree [Old English *twigge*] ▷ **twiggy** *adj*

twig² *vb* **twigging, twigged** *informal* to realize or understand: *I should have twigged it earlier* [origin unknown]

twilight *n* **1** the soft dim light that occurs when the sun is just below the horizon after sunset **2** the period in which this light occurs: *soon after twilight we started marching again* **3** a period in which strength, importance, etc., is gradually declining: *the twilight of his political career* ▷ *adj* **4** of or relating to the period towards the end of the day: *the twilight shift* **5** of being a period of decline: *he spent most of his twilight years working on a history of France* **6** denoting irregularity and obscurity: *a twilight existence* [Old English twi- half + LIGHT] ▷ **twilit** *adj*

twilight zone *n* any indefinite or intermediate condition or area: *the twilight zone between sleep and wakefulness*

twill *n* a fabric woven to produce an effect of parallel diagonal lines or ribs in the cloth [Old English *twilic* having a double thread]

twin *n* **1** one of a pair of people or animals conceived at the same time **2** one of a pair of people or things that are identical or very similar ▷ *vb* **twinning, twinned 3** to pair or be paired together [Old English *twinn*]

twin bed *n* one of a pair of matching single beds

twin-bedded *adj* (of a room in a hotel etc.) containing two single beds

twine *n* **1** string or cord made by twisting fibres together ▷ *vb* **twining, twined 2** to twist or wind together: *she twined the flowers into a garland* **3** twine round *or* around to twist or wind around: *she twined her arms around her neck* [Old English *twīn*]

twin-engined *adj* (of an aeroplane) having two engines

twinge *n* **1** a sudden brief darting or stabbing pain **2** a sharp emotional pang: *a twinge of conscience* [Old English *twengan* to pinch]

t

twinkle *vb* **-kling, -kled 1** to shine brightly and intermittently; sparkle **2** (of the eyes) to sparkle, esp. with amusement or delight ▷ *n* **3** a flickering brightness; sparkle [Old English *twinclian*]

twinkling *n* **in the twinkling of an eye** in a very short time

twinset *n* a matching jumper and cardigan

twin town *n* a town that has cultural and social links with a foreign town: *Nuremberg is one of Glasgow's twin towns*

twirl *vb* **1** to move around rapidly and repeatedly in a circle **2** to twist, wind, or twiddle, often idly: *twirling the glass in her hand* ▷ *n* **3** a whirl or twist **4** a written flourish [origin unknown]

twist *vb* **1** to turn one end or part while the other end or parts remain still or turn in the opposite direction: *never twist or wring woollen garments* **2** to distort or be distorted **3** to wind or twine: *the wire had been twisted twice* **4** to force or be forced out of the natural form or position: *I twisted my knee* **5** to change the meaning of; distort: *he'd twisted the truth to make himself look good* **6** to revolve or rotate: *he twisted the switch to turn the radio off* **7** to wrench with a turning action: *he twisted the wheel sharply* **8** to follow a winding course: *the road twisted as it climbed* **9** to dance the twist **10 twist someone's arm** to persuade or coerce someone ▷ *n* **11** the act of twisting: *she gave a dainty little twist to her parasol* **12** something formed by or as if by twisting: *there's a twist in the cable* **13** a decisive change of direction, aim, meaning, or character: *the latest revelations give a new twist to the company's boardroom wranglings* **14** an unexpected development in a story, play, or film **15** a bend: *a twist of the mountain road* **16** a distortion of the original shape or form **17** a jerky pull, wrench, or turn **18** the twist a dance popular in the 1960s, in which dancers vigorously twist the hips **19 round the twist** *slang* mad or eccentric [Old English] ▷ **twisty** *adj*

twisted *adj* (of a person) cruel or perverted

twister *n Brit* a swindling or dishonest person

twit¹ *vb* **twitting, twitted** *Brit* to poke fun at (someone) [Old English *ætwītan*]

twit² *n informal* a foolish or stupid person [from TWIT¹]

twitch *vb* **1** (of a person or part of a person's body) to move in a jerky spasmodic way: *his left eyelid twitched involuntarily* **2** to pull (something) with a quick jerky movement: *she twitched the curtains shut* ▷ *n* **3** a sharp jerking movement, esp. one caused by a nervous condition [Old English *twiccian* to pluck]

twitcher *n Brit informal* a bird-watcher who tries to spot as many rare varieties as possible

twitchy *adj* **twitchier, twitchiest** nervous, worried, and ill-at-ease: *he was twitchy with anticipation*

twitter *vb* **1** (esp. of a bird) to utter a succession of chirping sounds **2** to talk rapidly and nervously in a high-pitched voice: *novelists who twittered about how much they admired him* **3** to post a short message on the Twitter website ▷ *n* **4** the act or sound of twittering **5 in a twitter** in a state of nervous excitement [imitative] ▷ **twitterer** *n* ▷ **twittering** *n* ▷ **twittery** *adj*

Twitter *n trademark* a website where people can post short messages, up to 140 characters in length, about their current activities

two *n* **1** the cardinal number that is the sum of one and one **2** a numeral, 2 or II, representing this number **3** something representing or consisting of two units **4 in two** in or into two parts: *cut the cake in two and take a bit each* **5 put two and two together** to reach an obvious conclusion by considering the evidence available **6 that makes two of us** the same applies to me ▷ *adj* **7** amounting to two: *two years* [Old English *twā*]

twoccing *or* **twocking** *n Brit slang* the act of breaking into a motor vehicle and driving it away [from *T(aking) W(ithout) O(wner's) C(onsent)*, the legal offence] ▷ **twoccer** *or* **twocker** *n*

two-dimensional *adj* **1** having two dimensions **2** somewhat lacking in depth or complexity: *a modern audience is unable to tolerate two-dimensional characters*

two-edged *adj* **1** (of a remark) having both a favourable and an unfavourable interpretation, such as *she looks nice when she smiles* **2** (of a knife, saw, etc.) having two cutting edges

two-faced *adj* deceitful or hypocritical: *he's a two-faced liar and opportunist*

twofold *adj* **1** having twice as many or as much **2** composed of two parts ▷ *adv* **3** by twice as many or as much

two-four *n Canad informal* a box containing 24 bottles of beer

two-handed *adj* **1** requiring the use of both hands **2** requiring the participation of two people: *a two-handed transatlantic yacht race*

twopence *or* **tuppence** (tup-pence) *n Brit* **1** the sum of two pennies **2** the slightest amount: *I don't care twopence who your father is*

twopenny *or* **tuppenny** (tup-pen-ee) *adj chiefly Brit* **1** cheap or tawdry **2** worth or costing two pence **3 not care a twopenny damn** to not care at all

two-piece *adj* **1** consisting of two separate parts, usually matching, such as a woman's suit or swimsuit ▷ *n* **2** such an outfit

two-ply *adj* made of two thicknesses, layers, or strands

Two Sicilies *pl n* **the Two Sicilies** a former kingdom of S Italy, consisting of the kingdoms of Sicily and Naples (1061–1860)

two-sided *adj* **1** having two sides: *two-sided paper* **2** having two aspects or interpretations: *an ambivalent two-sided event*

twosome *n* a group of two people

two-step *n* **1** an old-time dance in duple time: *the next dance was the Military Two-Step* **2** music for this dance

two-stroke *adj* of an internal-combustion engine whose piston makes two strokes for every explosion

Two Thousand Guineas *n* **the Two Thousand Guineas** an annual horse race for three-year-olds, run at Newmarket

two-time *vb* **-timing, -timed** *informal* to deceive (a lover) by having an affair with someone else ▷ **two-timer** *n*

two-way *adj* **1** moving in, or allowing movement in, two opposite directions: *two-way traffic* **2** involving mutual involvement or cooperation: *two-way communication* **3** (of a radio or transmitter) capable of both transmission and reception of messages

TX Texas

Tyan-Shan *n* transliteration of the Russian name for the Tian Shan

Tyburn *n* (formerly) a place of execution in London, on the River Tyburn (a tributary of the Thames, now entirely below ground)

tycoon *n* a businessman of great wealth and power [Japanese *taikun* great ruler]

tyke *or* **tike** *n* **1** *Brit, Austral and NZ informal* a small or cheeky child **2** *Brit dialect* a rough ill-mannered person [Old Norse *tík* bitch]

Tyler *n* **1** John. 1790–1862, US statesman; tenth president of the US (1841–45) **2** Wat. died 1381, English leader of the Peasants' Revolt (1381)

Tylor *n* Sir Edward Burnett. 1832–1917, British anthropologist; first professor of anthropology at Oxford (1896). His *Primitive Culture* (1871) became a standard work

tympani *pl n* same as **timpani**

tympanic membrane *n anatomy* the thin membrane separating the external ear from the middle ear; eardrum

tympanum *n, pl* **-nums** *or* **-na 1** *anatomy* **a** the cavity of the middle ear **b** same as **tympanic membrane 2** *archit* the recessed space between the arch and the lintel above a door [Greek *tumpanon* drum] ▷ **tympanic** *adj*

Tyndale, Tindal *or* **Tindale** *n* William. ?1492–1536, English Protestant and humanist, who translated the

New Testament (1525), the Pentateuch (1530), and the Book of Jonah (1531) into English. He was burnt at the stake as a heretic

Tyndall *n* John. 1820–93, Irish physicist, noted for his work on the radiation of heat by gases, the transmission of sound through the atmosphere, and the scattering of light

Tyne *n* a river in N England, flowing east to the North Sea. Length: 48 km (30 miles)

Tyne and Wear *n* a metropolitan county of NE England, administered since 1986 by the unitary authorities of Newcastle upon Tyne, North Tyneside, Gateshead, South Tyneside, and Sunderland. Area: 540 sq km (208 sq miles)

Tynemouth *n* a port in NE England, in North Tyneside unitary authority, Tyne and Wear, at the mouth of the River Tyne: includes the port and industrial centre of North Shields; fishing, ship-repairing, and marine engineering. Pop: 17 056 (2001)

Tyneside *n* the conurbation on the banks of the Tyne from Newcastle to the coast. Related word: **Geordie**

Tynwald (tin-wold) *n* the Parliament of the Isle of Man [Old Norse *thing* assembly + *vollr* field]

type *n* **1** a kind, class, or category of things, all of which have something in common **2** a subdivision of a particular class; sort: *it is more alcoholic than most wines of this type* **3** the general characteristics distinguishing a particular group: *the old-fashioned type of nanny* **4** *informal* a person, esp. of a specified kind: *a seagoing type* **5** a block with a raised character on it used for printing **6** text printed from type; print ▷ *vb* **typing, typed 7** to write using a typewriter or word processor **8** to be a symbol of or typify **9** to decide the type of; classify [Greek *tupos* image]

typecast *vb* **-casting, -cast** to cast (an actor or actress) in the same kind of role continually

typeface *n* the size and style of printing used in a book, magazine, etc.

typescript *n* any typewritten document

typeset *vb* **-setting, -set** *printing* to set (text for printing) in type

typesetter *n* a person who sets type; compositor

typewriter *n* a machine which prints a letter or other character when the appropriate key is pressed

typewritten *adj* typed on a typewriter or word processor

typhoid *pathol n* **1** short for **typhoid fever** ▷ *adj* **2** of or relating to typhoid fever: *typhoid vaccines*

typhoid fever *n* an acute infectious disease characterized by high fever, spots, abdominal pain, etc. It is spread by contaminated food or water

typhoon *n* a violent tropical storm, esp. one in the China Seas or W Pacific [Chinese *tai fung* great wind]

typhus *n* an acute infectious disease transmitted by lice or mites and characterized by high fever, skin rash, and severe headache [Greek *tuphos* fever]

typical *adj* **1** being or serving as a representative example of a particular type; characteristic: *a typical working day* **2** considered to be an example of some undesirable trait: *it was typical that he should start talking almost before he was inside the room* [Greek *tupos* image] **> typically** *adv*

typify *vb* **-fies, -fying, -fied 1** to be typical of or characterize: *the beers made here typify all that is best about the independent brewing sector* **2** to symbolize or represent: *a number of dissident intellectuals, typified by Andrei Sakharov*

typing *n* **1** the work or activity of using a typewriter or word processor **2** the skill of using a typewriter quickly and accurately

typist *n* a person who types letters, reports, etc., esp. for a living

typo *n, pl* **-pos** *informal* a typographical error

typography *n* **1** the art or craft of printing **2** the style or quality of printing and layout in a book, magazine, etc. **> typographical** *adj* **> typographically** *adv*

tyrannical *adj* of or like a tyrant; unjust and oppressive

tyrannize *or* **-ise** *vb* **-nizing, -nized** *or* **-nising, -nised** to rule or exercise power (over) in a cruel or oppressive manner: *he dominated and tyrannized his younger brother*

tyrannosaurus (tirr-ran-oh-**sore**-uss) *or* **tyrannosaur** *n* a large two-footed flesh-eating dinosaur common in North America in Cretaceous times [Greek *turannos* tyrant + *sauros* lizard]

tyranny *n, pl* **-nies 1 a** a government by a tyrant **b** oppressive and unjust government by more than one person **2** the condition or state of being dominated or controlled by something that makes unpleasant or harsh demands: *the tyranny of fashion drives many women to diet although they are not overweight* **> tyrannous** *adj*

tyrant *n* **1** a person who governs oppressively, unjustly, and arbitrarily **2** any person who exercises authority in a tyrannical manner: *a domestic tyrant* [Greek *turannos*]

tyre *or US* **tire** *n* a ring of rubber, usually filled with air but sometimes solid, fitted round the rim of a wheel of a road vehicle to grip the road [earlier *tire*, probably archaic variant of *attire*]

Tyre *or* **Tyr** *n* a port in S Lebanon, on the Mediterranean: founded about the 15th century BC; for centuries a major Phoenician seaport, famous for silks and its Tyrian-purple dye; now a small market town. Pop: 141 000 (2005 est). Arabic name: **Sur**

tyro *n, pl* **-ros** a novice or beginner [Latin *tiro* recruit]

Tyrol *or* **Tirol** *n* a mountainous state of W Austria: passed to the Hapsburgs in 1363; S part transferred to Italy in 1919. Capital: Innsbruck. Pop: 683 317 (2003 est). Area: 12 648 sq km (4883 sq miles)

Tyrolese *or* **Tyrolean** *adj* **1** of or relating to the Austrian state of Tyrol or its inhabitants ▷ *n* **2** a native or inhabitant of Tyrol

Tyrone *n* a historical county of W Northern Ireland, occupying almost a quarter of the total area of Northern Ireland; in 1973 its administrative functions were devolved to several district councils

Tyrrhenian Sea *n* an arm of the Mediterranean between Italy and the islands of Corsica, Sardinia, and Sicily

Tyson *n* Mike. born 1966, US boxer. World heavyweight champion (1986–90, and 1996): jailed for rape (1992–95) and assault (1999); banned from professional boxing (1997–98) after biting off part of his opponent's ear

Tyumen *n* a port in S central Russia, on the Tura River: one of the oldest Russian towns in Siberia; industrial centre with nearby oil and natural gas reserves. Pop: 518 000 (2005 est)

Tyva *n* another name for **Tuva Republic**

tzar *n* same as **tsar**

Tzara *n* Tristan, original name *Samuel Rosenstock*. 1896–1963, French poet and essayist, born in Romania, best known as the founder of Dada: author of *The Approximate Man* (1931).

tzatziki (tsat-**see**-kee) *n* a Greek dip made from yogurt, chopped cucumber, and mint [Modern Greek]

Tzekung *or* **Tzu-kung** *n* a variant transliteration of the Chinese name for **Zigong**

tzetze fly *n* same as **tsetse fly**

Tzu-po *or* **Tzepo** *n* a variant transliteration of the Chinese name for **Zibo**

Uu

U 1 (in Britain) universal (used to describe a film certified as suitable for viewing by anyone) **2** *chem* uranium ▷ *adj* **3** *Brit informal* (of language or behaviour) characteristic of the upper class

UAE United Arab Emirates

UAR United Arab Republic

UB40 *n* **1** (in Britain) a registration card issued to an unemployed person **2** *informal* (in Britain) a person registered as unemployed

Ubangi *n* a river in central Africa, flowing west and south, forming the border between the Democratic Republic of Congo and the Central African Republic and Congo-Brazzaville, into the River Congo. Length (with the Uele): 2250 km (1400 miles). French name: **Oubangui**

Ubangi-Shari *n* a former name (until 1958) of the **Central African Republic**

ubiquitous (yew-**bik**-wit-uss) *adj* being or seeming to be everywhere at once [Latin *ubique* everywhere] **> ubiquity** *n*

U-boat *n* a German submarine [German *Unterseeboot* undersea boat]

Ubuntu *n S African* humanity or fellow feeling; kindness [Nguni (language group of southern Africa)]

uc *printing* upper case

UCAS (in Britain) Universities and Colleges Admissions Service

Ucayali *n* a river in E Peru, flowing north into the Marañón above Iquitos. Length: 1600 km (1000 miles)

UCCA (formerly, in Britain) Universities Central Council on Admissions

Uccello *n* Paolo. 1397–1475, Florentine painter noted esp. for three paintings of *The Battle of San Romano, 1432* (1456–60)

UCW (in Britain) Union of Communications Workers

Udaipur *n* **1** Also called: **Mewar** a former state of NW India: became part of Rajasthan in 1947 **2** a city in NW India, in S Rajasthan. Pop: 389 317 (2001)

Udall *or* **Uvedale** *n* Nicholas. ?1505–56, English dramatist, whose comedy *Ralph Roister Doister* (?1553), modelled on Terence and Plautus, is the earliest known English comedy

udder *n* the large baglike milk-producing gland of cows, sheep, or goats, with two or more teats [Old English *ūder*]

UDI Unilateral Declaration of Independence

Udine *n* a city in NE Italy, in Friuli-Venezia Giulia region: partially damaged in an earthquake in 1976. Pop: 95 030 (2001)

Udmurt Republic *n* a constituent republic of W central Russia, in the basin of the middle Kama. Capital: Izhevsk. Pop: 1 570 500 (2002). Area: 42 100 sq km (16 250 sq miles)

UEFA Union of European Football Associations

Uele *n* a river in central Africa, rising near the border between the Democratic Republic of Congo and Uganda and flowing west to join the Bomu River and form the Ubangi River. Length: about 1100 km (700 miles)

Ufa *n* a city in W central Russia, capital of the Bashkir Republic: university (1957). Pop: 1 035 000 (2005 est)

Uffizi *n* an art gallery in Florence; built by Giorgio Vasari in the 16th century and opened as a museum in 1765: contains chiefly Italian Renaissance paintings

UFO unidentified flying object

Uganda *n* a republic in E Africa: British protectorate established in 1894–96; gained independence in 1962 and became a republic in 1963; a member of the Commonwealth. It consists mostly of a savanna plateau with part of Lake Victoria in the southeast and mountains in the southwest, reaching 5109 m (16 763 ft) in the Ruwenzori Range. Official language: English; Swahili, Luganda, and Luo are also widely spoken. Religion: Christian majority. Currency: Ugandan shilling. Capital: Kampala. Pop: 34 758 809 (2013 est). Area: 235 886 sq km (91 076 sq miles)

Ugandan *adj* **1** of or relating to Uganda or its inhabitants ▷ *n* **2** a native or inhabitant of Uganda

ugh (uhh) *interj* an exclamation of disgust, annoyance, or dislike

UGLI *n, pl* **-LIS** *or* **-LIES** *trademark* a yellow citrus fruit: a cross between a tangerine, grapefruit, and orange [probably an alteration of *ugly*, from its wrinkled skin]

ugly *adj* **uglier, ugliest** **1** so unattractive as to be unpleasant to look at **2** very unpleasant and involving violence or aggression: *an ugly incident in which one man was stabbed* **3** repulsive or displeasing: *ugly rumours* **4** bad-tempered or sullen: *an ugly mood* [Old Norse *uggligr* dreadful] **> ugliness** *n*

ugly duckling *n* a person or thing, initially ugly or unpromising, that becomes beautiful or admirable [from *The Ugly Duckling* by Hans Christian Andersen]

UHF *radio* ultrahigh frequency

Uhland *n* Johann Ludwig. 1787–1862, German romantic poet, esp. of lyrics and ballads

UHT ultra-heat-treated (milk or cream)

Uinta Mountains *pl n* a mountain range in NE Utah: part of the Rocky Mountains. Highest peak: Kings Peak, 4123 m (13 528 ft)

Ujiji *n* a town in W Tanzania, on Lake Tanganyika: a former slave and ivory centre; the place where Stanley found Livingstone in 1871. It merged with the neighbouring town of Kigoma to form Kigoma-Ujiji in the 1960s

Ujjain *n* a city in W central India, in Madhya Pradesh: one of the seven sacred cities of the Hindus; a major agricultural trade centre. Pop: 429 933 (2001)

Ujung Pandang *n* the former name (1971–1999) for **Makassar**

UK United Kingdom

ukase (yew-**kaze**) *n* (in imperial Russia) a decree from the tsar [Russian *ukaz*]

Ukr. Ukraine

Ukraine *n* a republic in SE Europe, on the Black Sea and the Sea of Azov: ruled by the Khazars (7th–9th centuries), by Ruik princes with the Mongol conquest in the 13th century, then by Lithuania, by Poland, and by Russia; one of the four original republics that formed the Soviet Union in 1922; unilaterally declared independence in 1990, which was recognized in 1991; annexation of Crimea by Russia in 2014 not recognized internationally, despite the mainly Russian population voting in favour of it in a disputed referendum. Consists chiefly of lowlands; economy based on rich agriculture and mineral resources and on the major heavy industries of the Donets Basin. Official language: Ukrainian; Russian is also widely spoken. Religion: believers are mainly Christian. Currency: hryvna. Capital: Kiev. Pop: 44 573 205 (2013 est). Area: 603 700 sq km (231 990 sq miles)

Ukrainian adj **1** of or relating to Ukraine or its inhabitants ▷ n **2** a native or inhabitant of Ukraine **3** the language of Ukraine

ukulele or **ukelele** (yew-kal-**lay**-lee) n a small four-stringed guitar [Hawaiian, literally: jumping flea]

Ulan Bator or **Ulaanbaatar** n the capital of Mongolia, in the N central part: developed in the mid-17th century around the Da Khure monastery, residence until 1924 of successive "living Buddhas" (third in rank of Buddhist-Lamaist leaders), and main junction of caravan routes across Mongolia; university (1942); industrial and commercial centre. Pop: 842 000 (2005 est). Former name (until 1924): **Urga**. Chinese name: **Kulun**

Ulanova n Galina (Sergeyevna) 1910–98, Russian ballet dancer, who performed with the Leningrad Kirov ballet (1928–44) and the Moscow Bolshoi Ballet (1944–62)

Ulan-Ude n an industrial city in SE Russia, capital of the Buryat Republic: an important rail junction. Pop: 361 000 (2005 est). Former name (until 1934): **Verkhne-Udinsk**

Ulbricht n Walter. 1893-1973, East German statesman; largely responsible for the establishment and development of East German communism

ulcer n an open sore on the surface of the skin or a mucous membrane [Latin ulcus]

ulcerated adj made or becoming ulcerous ➤ **ulceration** n

ulcerous adj of, like, or characterized by ulcers

Uleåborg n the Swedish name for **Oulu**

Ulfilas, Ulfila or **Wulfila** n ?311–?382 AD, Christian bishop of the Goths who translated the Bible from Greek into Gothic

Ullswater n a lake in NW England, in Cumbria in the Lake District. Length: 12 km (7.5 miles)

Ulm n an industrial city in S Germany, in Baden-Württemberg on the Danube: a free imperial city (1155–1802). Pop: 119 807 (2003 est)

ulna n, pl **-nae** or **-nas** the inner and longer of the two bones of the human forearm or of the forelimb in other vertebrates [Latin: elbow] ➤ **ulnar** adj

Ulpian n Latin name Domitius Ulpianus. died ?228 AD, Roman jurist, born in Phoenicia

ulster n a man's heavy double-breasted overcoat [ULSTER]

Ulster n **1** a province and former kingdom of N Ireland: passed to the English Crown in 1461; confiscated land given to English and Scottish Protestant settlers in the 17th century, giving rise to serious long-term conflict; partitioned in 1921, six counties forming Northern Ireland and three counties joining the Republic of Ireland. Pop (three Ulster counties of the Republic of Ireland): 46 714 (2002); (six Ulster counties of Northern Ireland): 1 702 628 (2003 est). Area (Republic of Ireland): 8013 sq km (3094 sq miles); (Northern Ireland): 14 121 sq km (5452 sq miles) **2** an informal name for **Northern Ireland**

Ulsterman or fem **Ulsterwoman** n, pl **-men** or **-women** a native or inhabitant of Ulster

ult. ultimo

ulterior (ult-**ear**-ee-or) adj (of an aim, reason, etc.) concealed or hidden: an ulterior motive [Latin: further]

ultimate adj **1** final in a series or process: predictions about the ultimate destination of modern art **2** highest, supreme, or unchallengeable: he has the ultimate power to dismiss the Prime Minister **3** fundamental or essential: a believer in the ultimate goodness of man **4** most extreme: genocide is the ultimate abuse of human rights **5** final or total: she should be able to estimate the ultimate cost ▷ n **6 the ultimate in** the best example of: the ultimate in luxury holidays [Latin ultimus last, distant] ➤ **ultimately** adv

ultima Thule n **1** another name for **Thule 2** any distant or unknown region **3** a remote goal or aim [Latin: the most distant Thule]

ultimatum (ult-im-**may**-tum) n a final warning to someone that they must agree to certain conditions or requirements, or else action will be taken against them: Britain declared war after the Nazis rejected the ultimatum to withdraw from Poland

ultimo adv in or during the previous month. It is rare except when abbreviated to ult. in formal correspondence: your communication of the 1st ultimo [Latin: on the last]

ultra n a person who has extreme or immoderate beliefs or opinions [Latin: beyond]

ultra- prefix **1** beyond a specified extent, range, or limit: ultrasonic **2** extremely: ultraleftist [Latin]

ultraconservative adj **1** highly reactionary ▷ n **2** a reactionary person

ultrahigh frequency n a radio frequency between 3000 and 300 megahertz

ultramarine n **1** a blue pigment originally made from lapis lazuli ▷ adj **2** vivid blue [Latin ultra beyond + mare sea; because the lapis lazuli from which the pigment was made was imported from Asia]

ultramodern adj extremely modern

ultramontane adj **1** on the other side of the mountains, usually the Alps, from the speaker or writer **2** of a movement in the Roman Catholic Church which favours supreme papal authority ▷ n **3** a person from beyond the Alps **4** a member of the ultramontane party of the Roman Catholic Church

ultrasonic adj of or producing sound waves with higher frequencies than humans can hear ➤ **ultrasonically** adv

ultrasonics n the branch of physics concerned with ultrasonic waves

ultrasound n ultrasonic waves, used in echo sounding, medical diagnosis, and therapy

ultrasound scan n an examination of an internal bodily structure by the use of ultrasonic waves, esp. for diagnosing abnormality in a fetus

ultraviolet n **1** the part of the electromagnetic spectrum with wavelengths shorter than light but longer than X-rays ▷ adj **2** of or consisting of radiation lying in the ultraviolet: ultraviolet light

ultra vires (ult-ra **vire**-eez) adv, adj beyond the legal power of a person or organization [Latin, literally: beyond strength]

ululate (yewl-yew-late) vb **-lating, -lated** literary to howl or wail [Latin ululare] ➤ **ululation** n

Ulundi n a town in South Africa: the traditional Zulu capital of KwaZulu-Natal

Uluru n a large isolated desert rock, sometimes described as the world's largest monolith, in the Northern Territory of Australia: sacred to local Aboriginal people. Height: 330m (1100 ft). Base circumference: 9 km (5.6 miles). Also called: **Ayers Rock**

Ulyanovsk n a city in W central Russia on the River Volga: birthplace of Lenin (V. I. Ulyanov), after whom it was renamed in 1924. Pop: 639 000 (2005 est). Former name: **Simbirsk**

Umar Tal n ?1797–1864, African religious and military leader, who created a Muslim empire in W Africa

umbel n a type of compound flower in which the flowers arise from the same point in the main stem and have

stalks of the same length, to give a cluster with the youngest flowers at the centre [Latin *umbella* a sunshade]
> **umbellate** *adj*

umbelliferous *adj* of or denoting a plant with flowers in umbels, such as fennel, parsley, carrot, or parsnip [Latin *umbella* a sunshade + *ferre* to bear]

umber *n* **1** a type of dark brown earth containing ferric oxide (rust) ▷ *adj* **2** dark brown to reddish-brown [French (*terre d'*)*ombre* or Italian (*terra di*) *ombra* shadow (earth)]

Umberto I *n* 1844–1900, king of Italy (1878–1900); son of Victor Emmanuel II: assassinated at Monza

Umberto II *n* 1904–83, the last king of Italy (1946), following the abdication of his father Victor Emmanuel III: abdicated when a referendum supported the abolition of the monarchy

umbilical (um-**bill**-ik-kl) *adj* of or like the navel or the umbilical cord

umbilical cord *n* the long flexible cordlike structure that connects a fetus to the placenta

umbilicus (um-**bill**-ik-kuss) *n anatomy* the navel [Latin: navel, centre]

umbra *n*, *pl* **-brae** or **-bras** a shadow, usually the shadow cast by the moon onto the earth during a solar eclipse [Latin: shade]

umbrage *n* **take umbrage** to take offence [Latin *umbra* shade]

umbrella *n* **1** a portable device used for protection against rain, consisting of a light canopy supported on a collapsible metal frame mounted on a central rod **2** a single organization, idea, etc., that contains or covers many different organizations or ideas **3** anything that has the effect of a protective screen or general cover: *under the umbrella of the Helsinki security conference* ▷ *adj* **4** containing or covering many different organizations, ideas, etc.: *an umbrella group of nationalists and anti-communists* [Italian *ombrella*, from *ombra* shade]
> **umbrella-like** *adj*

Umbria *n* a mountainous region of central Italy, in the valley of the Tiber. Pop: 834 210 (2003 est). Area: 8456 sq km (3265 sq miles)

Umbrian *adj* **1** of or relating to Umbria, its inhabitants, their dialect of Italian, or the ancient language once spoken there **2** of or relating to a Renaissance school of painting that included Raphael ▷ *n* **3** a native or inhabitant of Umbria

UMF *n trademark* a standard for the level of antibacterial agent possessed by manuka honey

umiak, oomiak or **oomiac** (**oo**-mee-ak) *n* a large open boat made of stretched skins, used by Inuit [Inuktitut]

umlaut (**oom**-lout) *n* **1** the mark (¨) placed over a vowel, esp. in German, indicating change in its sound **2** (esp. in Germanic languages) the change of a vowel brought about by the influence of a vowel in the next syllable [German, from *um* around + *Laut* sound]

umlungu (oom-**loong**-goo) *n S African* a White man: used esp. as a term of address [Nguni (language group of southern Africa)]

umpire *n* **1** an official who ensures that the people taking part in a game follow the rules; referee ▷ *vb* **-piring, -pired** **2** to act as umpire in a game [Old French *nomper* not one of a pair]

umpteen *adj informal* very many: *the centre of umpteen scandals* [*umpty* a great deal + *-teen* ten] > **umpteenth** *n*, *adj*

Umtali *n* the former name (until 1982) of **Mutare**

Umtata *n* a city in South Africa, in Eastern Cape province; the capital of the former Transkei Bantu homeland. Pop: 94 778 (2001)

UN United Nations

un-¹ *prefix* (*freely used with adjectives, participles, and their derivative adverbs and nouns; less frequently used with certain other nouns*) not; contrary to; opposite of: *uncertain*; *untidiness*; *unbelief*; *untruth* [Old English *on-*, *un-*]

un-² *prefix* **1** denoting reversal of an action or state: *uncover*; *untie* **2** denoting removal from, release, or deprivation: *unharness* [Old English *un-*, *on-*]

unabashed *adj* not ashamed or embarrassed

unabated *adv* without any reduction in force: *the storm continued unabated*

unable *adj* **unable to** not having the power, ability, or authority to; not able to

unabridged *adj* (of a book or text) complete and not shortened or condensed

unacceptable *adj* too bad to be accepted; intolerable

unaccompanied *adj* **1** not having anyone with one: *unaccompanied female travellers should take care* **2** (of singing or a musical instrument) not being accompanied by musical instruments

unaccountable *adj* **1** without any sensible explanation: *for some unaccountable reason I got on the wrong bus* **2** not having to justify or answer for one's actions to other people: *the secret service remains unaccountable to the public*
> **unaccountably** *adv*

unaccounted *adj* **unaccounted for** unable to be found or traced: *four people were killed in the floods, and eleven remain unaccounted for*

unaccustomed *adj* **1** **unaccustomed to** not used to: *unaccustomed to such behaviour* **2** not familiar: *moments of unaccustomed freedom*

unacknowledged *adj* **1** ignored or not accepted as true or existing **2** not officially recognized as being important

unacquainted *adj* **unacquainted with** not knowing about; unfamiliar with

unadopted *adj Brit* (of a road) not maintained by a local authority

unadorned *adj* not decorated; plain

unadulterated *adj* **1** completely pure, with nothing added: *fresh unadulterated spring water* **2** (of an emotion) not mixed with anything else: *a look of unadulterated terror*

unadventurous *adj* not taking chances or trying anything new

unaffected¹ *adj* unpretentious, natural, or sincere

unaffected² *adj* not influenced or changed

unafraid *adj* not frightened or nervous

unaided *adv* without any help or assistance; independently: *he could not walk unaided for months after the accident*

Unalaska Island *n* a large volcanic island in SW Alaska, in the Aleutian Islands. Length: 120 km (75 miles). Greatest width: about 40 km (25 miles)

unalienable *adj law* same as **inalienable**

unalike *adj* not similar; different

unalloyed *adj literary* not spoiled by being mixed with anything else

unalterable *adj* not able to be changed

unambiguous *adj* having a clear meaning which can only be interpreted in one way

un-American *adj* **1** not in accordance with the aims, ideals, or customs of the US **2** against the interests of the US > **un-Americanism** *n*

Unamuno *n* Miguel de. 1864–1936, Spanish philosopher and writer

unanimous (yew-**nan**-im-uss) *adj* **1** in complete agreement **2** characterized by complete agreement: *unanimous approval* [Latin *unus* one + *animus* mind]
> **unanimity** *n* > **unanimously** *adv*

unannounced *adv* without warning: *she turned up unannounced*

unanswerable *adj* **1** having no possible answer **2** so obviously correct that disagreement is impossible

unappealing *adj* unpleasant or off-putting

unappetizing *adj* tasting, looking, or smelling unpleasant to eat

unappreciated *adj* not given the respect or recognition that is deserved

unapproachable *adj* discouraging friendliness; aloof

unarguable *adj* so obviously correct that disagreement is impossible

unarmed *adj* **1** not carrying any weapons: *they were shooting unarmed peasants* **2** not using any weapons: *unarmed combat*

unashamed *adj* not embarrassed, esp. when doing something some people might find offensive: *unashamed greed* > **unashamedly** *adv*

unasked *adv* **1** without being asked to do something: *he opened the door unasked* ▷ *adj* **2** (of a question) not asked, although sometimes implied

unassailable *adj* not able to be destroyed or overcome: *an unassailable lead*

unassisted *adj* without help from anyone else

unassuming *adj* modest or unpretentious

unattached *adj* **1** not connected with any specific body or group **2** not engaged or married

unattainable *adj* not able to be achieved; impossible

unattended *adj* not being watched or looked after: *unattended baggage*

unattractive *adj* not attractive or appealing

unauthorized *or* **-ised** *adj* done or made without official permission

unavailable *adj* not able to be met, obtained, or contacted

unavailing *adj* useless or futile

unavoidable *adj* unable to be avoided or prevented > **unavoidably** *adv*

unaware *adj* **1** not aware or conscious: *unaware of my surroundings* ▷ *adj* **2** *not standard* same as **unawares**

unawares *adv* **1** by surprise: *death had taken him unawares* **2** without knowing: *had he passed her, all unawares?*

unbalanced *adj* **1** lacking balance **2** mentally deranged **3** biased; one-sided: *his unbalanced summing-up*

unbearable *adj* not able to be endured > **unbearably** *adv*

unbeatable *adj* not able to be bettered

unbecoming *adj* **1** unattractive or unsuitable: *unbecoming garments* **2** not proper or appropriate to a person or position: *acts unbecoming of university students*

unbeknown *adv* (foll. by *to*) without the knowledge of (a person): *unbeknown to her family she had acquired modern ways.* Also (esp. Brit): **unbeknownst** [archaic *beknown* known]

unbelievable *adj* **1** too unlikely to be believed **2** extremely impressive; marvellous **3** *informal* terrible or shocking > **unbelievably** *adv*

unbeliever *n* a person who does not believe in a religion

unbend *vb* **-bending, -bent** to become less strict or more informal in one's attitudes or behaviour

unbending *adj* rigid or inflexible: *an unbending routine*

unbiased *adj* not having or showing prejudice or favouritism; impartial

unbidden *adj literary* not ordered or asked; voluntary or spontaneous: *unbidden thoughts came into Catherine's mind*

unbind *vb* **-binding, -bound** **1** to set free from bonds or chains **2** to unfasten or untie

unblemished *adj* not spoiled or tarnished: *smooth unblemished skins*

unblinking *adj* looking at something without blinking

unblock *vb* to remove a blockage from; clear or free

unblushing *adj* immodest or shameless

unbolt *vb* to unfasten a bolt of a door

unborn *adj* not yet born

unbosom *vb* to relieve oneself of secrets or feelings by telling someone [UN-² + *bosom* (in the sense: centre of the emotions)]

unbounded *adj* having no boundaries or limits

unbowed *adj* not giving in or submitting: *the battered but as yet unbowed general secretary*

unbreakable *adj* not able to be broken; indestructible

unbridled *adj* (of feelings or behaviour) not restrained or controlled in any way: *unbridled passion*

unbroken *adj* **1** complete or whole **2** continuous: *I slept for eight unbroken hours* **3** not disturbed or upset: *an unbroken night* **4** (of a record) not improved upon **5** (of animals, esp. horses) not tamed

unburden *vb* to relieve one's mind or oneself of a worry or trouble by telling someone about it

uncalled-for *adj* unnecessary or unwarranted: *uncalled-for comments*

uncanny *adj* **1** weird or mysterious: *an uncanny silence* **2** beyond what is normal: *an uncanny eye for detail* > **uncannily** *adv* > **uncanniness** *n*

uncared-for *adj* not cared for; neglected

uncaring *adj* showing no concern for other people's suffering and hardship

unceasing *adj* continuing without a break; never stopping

unceremonious *adj* **1** relaxed and informal: *she greeted him with unceremonious friendliness* **2** abrupt or rude: *the answer was an unceremonious 'no'* > **unceremoniously** *adv*

uncertain *adj* **1** not able to be accurately known or predicted: *an uncertain future* **2** not definitely decided: *they are uncertain about the date* **3** not to be depended upon: *an uncertain career* **4** changeable: *an uncertain sky* > **uncertainty** *n*

unchallenged *adj, adv* done or accepted without being challenged: *seventy years of unchallenged rule; her decisions went unchallenged*

unchangeable *adj* not able to be altered

unchanged *adj* remaining the same

uncharacteristic *adj* not typical > **uncharacteristically** *adv*

uncharitable *adj* unkind or harsh > **uncharitably** *adv*

uncharted *adj* **1** (of an area of sea or land) not having had a map made of it, esp. because it is unexplored **2** unknown or unfamiliar: *a whole uncharted universe of emotions*

unchecked *adj* **1** not prevented from continuing or growing: *unchecked population growth* **2** not examined or inspected ▷ *adv* **3** without being stopped or hindered: *the virus could spread unchecked* **4** without being examined or inspected: *the drugs passed unchecked through airport security*

unchristian *or* **un-Christian** *adj* not in accordance with Christian principles

uncial (un-see-al) *adj* **1** of or written in letters that resemble modern capitals, as used in Greek and Latin manuscripts of the third to ninth centuries ▷ *n* **2** an uncial letter or manuscript [Late Latin *unciales litterae* letters an inch long]

uncivil *adj* impolite, rude, or bad-mannered > **uncivilly** *adv*

uncivilized *or* **-lised** *adj* **1** (of a tribe or people) not yet civilized **2** lacking culture or sophistication

unclassified *adj* **1** not arranged in any specific order or grouping **2** (of official information) not secret

uncle *n* **1** a brother of one's father or mother **2** the husband of one's aunt **3** a child's term of address for a male friend of its parents **4** *slang* a pawnbroker [Latin *avunculus*]

unclean *adj* lacking moral, spiritual, or physical cleanliness

unclear *adj* confusing or hard to understand

Uncle Sam *n* a personification of the government of the United States [apparently a humorous interpretation of the letters stamped on army supply boxes during the War of 1812: US]

Uncle Tom *n informal, offensive* a Black person whose behaviour towards White people is regarded as servile [from *Uncle Tom's Cabin* by H. B. Stowe]

unclothed *adj* not wearing any clothes; naked

uncluttered *adj* not containing anything unnecessary; austere and simple

uncoil *vb* to unwind or untwist

uncomfortable *adj* **1** not physically relaxed: *he was forced to sit in an uncomfortable cross-legged position* **2** not comfortable to be in or use: *an uncomfortable chair* **3** causing discomfort or unease: *the uncomfortable truth* > **uncomfortably** *adv*

uncommitted *adj* not bound to a specific opinion, course of action, or cause

uncommon *adj* **1** not happening or encountered often **2** in excess of what is normal: *an uncommon amount of powder*

uncommonly *adv* **1** in an unusual manner or degree **2** extremely: *an uncommonly good humour*

uncommunicative *adj* disinclined to talk or give information

uncomplaining *adj* doing or tolerating something unpleasant or difficult without complaint: *uncomplaining devotion*

uncomplicated *adj* simple and straightforward

uncomplimentary *adj* not expressing respect or praise; insulting

uncomprehending *adj* not understanding what is happening or what has been said

uncompromising *adj* not prepared to compromise; inflexible › **uncompromisingly** *adv*

unconcealed *adj* not hidden or disguised: *a look of unconcealed hatred*

unconcern *n* apathy or indifference

unconcerned *adj* **1** not interested in something and not wanting to become involved **2** not worried or troubled › **unconcernedly** (un-kon-**sern**-id-lee) *adv*

unconditional *adj* without conditions or limitations: *an unconditional ceasefire* › **unconditionally** *adv*

unconfirmed *adj* not yet proved to be true: *unconfirmed reports of a major accident*

uncongenial *adj* (of a place or condition) unpleasant and unfriendly

unconnected *adj* not linked to each other: *a series of unconnected incidents*

unconscionable *adj* **1** unscrupulous or unprincipled: *an unconscionable charmer* **2** excessive in amount or degree: *unconscionable number of social obligations*

unconscious *adj* **1** unable to notice or respond to things which one would normally be aware of through the senses; insensible or comatose **2** not aware of one's actions or behaviour: *unconscious of his failure* **3** not realized or intended: *unconscious duplicity* **4** coming from or produced by the unconscious: *unconscious mental processes* ▷ *n* **5** psychoanalysis the part of the mind containing instincts, impulses, and ideas that are not available for direct examination › **unconsciously** *adv* › **unconsciousness** *n*

unconstitutional *adj* forbidden by the rules or laws which state how an organization or country must function

uncontrollable *adj* **1** unable to be restrained or prevented: *a fit of uncontrollable giggles* **2** (of a person) wild and unmanageable in behaviour: *he became violent and uncontrollable* › **uncontrollably** *adv*

unconventional *adj* not conforming to accepted rules or standards

unconvinced *adj* not certain that something is true or right: *I remained unconvinced by his arguments*

unconvincing *adj* (of a reason, argument, etc.) not good enough to convince people that something is true or right

uncooked *adj* raw

uncooperative *adj* not willing to help other people with what they are trying to do

uncoordinated *adj* **1** not joining or functioning together properly to form a whole **2** (of a person) not able to control his or her movements properly; clumsy

uncork *vb* to remove the cork from a bottle

uncorroborated *adj* not supported by other evidence or proof

uncountable *adj* existing in such large numbers that it is impossible to say how many there are: *uncountable millions*

uncouple *vb* -**pling**, -**pled** to disconnect or become disconnected

uncouth *adj* lacking in good manners, refinement, or grace [Old English *un-* not + *cūth* familiar]

uncover *vb* **1** to remove the cover or top from **2** to reveal or disclose: *they have uncovered a plot to overthrow the government* › **uncovered** *adj*

uncritical *adj* not making a judgment about the merits or morality of something

uncrowned *adj* **1** having the powers, but not the title, of royalty **2** (of a king or queen) not yet crowned

unction *n* **1** chiefly RC Church, Eastern Churches the act of anointing with oil in sacramental ceremonies **2** oily charm **3** an ointment **4** anything soothing [Latin *unguere* to anoint]

unctuous *adj* pretending to be kind and concerned but obviously not sincere [Latin *unctum* ointment]

uncultured *adj* not knowing much about art, literature, etc.

uncut *adj* **1** not shortened or censored **2** not cut **3** (of precious stones) not having shaped and polished surfaces

undamaged *adj* not spoilt or damaged; intact

undaunted *adj* not put off, discouraged, or beaten

undeceive *vb* -**ceiving**, -**ceived** to reveal the truth to someone previously misled or deceived

undecided *adj* **1** not having made up one's mind **2** (of an issue or problem) not agreed or decided upon

undeclared *adj* not acknowledged for tax purposes

undemanding *adj* not difficult to do or deal with: *an undemanding task*

undemonstrative *adj* not showing emotions openly or easily

undeniable *adj* **1** unquestionably true **2** of unquestionable excellence: *of undeniable character* › **undeniably** *adv*

under *prep* **1** directly below; on, to, or beneath the underside or base of: *under the bed* **2** less than: *in just under an hour* **3** lower in rank than: *under a general* **4** subject to the supervision, control, or influence of: *under communism for 45 years* **5** in or subject to certain circumstances or conditions: *the bridge is still under construction; under battle conditions* **6** in (a specified category): *he had filed Kafka's 'The Trial' under crime stories* **7** known by: *under their own names* **8** planted with: *a field under corn* **9** powered by: *under sail* ▷ *adv* **10** below; to a position underneath [Old English]

under- *prefix* **1** below or beneath: *underarm; underground* **2** insufficient or insufficiently: *underemployed* **3** of lesser importance or lower rank: *undersecretary* **4** indicating secrecy or deception: *underhand*

underachieve *vb* -**achieving**, -**achieved** to fail to achieve a performance appropriate to one's age or talents › **underachiever** *n*

underactive *adj* less active than is normal or desirable: *an underactive thyroid gland*

underage *adj* below the required or standard age, usually below the legal age for voting or drinking: *underage sex*

underarm *adj* **1** sport denoting a style of throwing, bowling, or serving in which the hand is swung below shoulder level **2** below the arm ▷ *adv* **3** in an underarm style

underbelly *n*, *pl* -**lies 1** the part of an animal's belly nearest the ground **2** a vulnerable or unprotected part, aspect, or region

underbrush *n* US, Canad and Austral same as **undergrowth**

undercarriage *n* **1** the wheels, shock absorbers, and struts that support an aircraft on the ground and enable it to take off and land **2** the framework supporting the body of a vehicle

undercharge *vb* -**charging**, -**charged** to charge too little for something

underclass *n* a class beneath the usual social scale consisting of the most disadvantaged people, such as the long-term unemployed

underclothes *pl n* also called: **underclothing**. same as **underwear**

undercoat *n* **1** a coat of paint applied before the top coat

2 *zoology* a layer of soft fur beneath the outer fur of animals such as the otter ▷ *vb* **3** to apply an undercoat to a surface

undercook *vb* to cook for too short a time or at too low a temperature

undercover *adj* done or acting in secret: *an undercover investigation*

undercurrent *n* **1** a current that is not apparent at the surface **2** an underlying opinion or emotion

undercut *vb* **-cutting, -cut** **1** to charge less than a competitor in order to obtain trade **2** to undermine or render less effective: *the latest fighting undercuts diplomatic attempts to find a peaceful solution* **3** to cut away the under part of something

underdeveloped *adj* **1** immature or undersized **2** (of a country or its economy) lacking the finance, industries, and organization necessary to advance

underdog *n* a person or team in a weak or underprivileged position

underdone *adj* insufficiently or lightly cooked

underemployed *adj* not fully or adequately employed

underestimate *vb* **-mating, -mated** **1** to make too low an estimate of: *the trust had underestimated the cost of work* **2** to not be aware or take account of the full abilities or potential of: *the police had underestimated him* ▷ *n* **3** too low an estimate › **underestimation** *n*

> **USAGE** *Underestimate* is sometimes wrongly used where *overestimate* is meant: *the importance of his work cannot be overestimated* (not *cannot be underestimated*).

underexpose *vb* **-posing, -posed** *photog* to expose (a film, plate, or paper) for too short a time or with insufficient light › **underexposure** *n*

underfed *adj* not getting enough food to be healthy

underfelt *n* thick felt laid under a carpet to increase insulation

underfoot *adv* **1** underneath the feet; on the ground **2** trample *or* crush underfoot **a** to damage or destroy by stepping on **b** to treat with contempt

undergarment *n* a garment worn under clothes

undergo *vb* **-going, -went, -gone** to experience, endure, or sustain: *he underwent a three-hour operation* [Old English *undergān*]

undergraduate *n* a person studying in a university for a first degree

underground *adv* **1** below ground level: *moles digging underground* **2** secretly: *several political parties had to operate underground for many years* ▷ *adj* **3** beneath the ground: *an underground bunker* **4** secret; clandestine: *an underground organization* **5** (of art, film, music, etc.) avant-garde, experimental, or subversive ▷ *n* **6** a movement dedicated to overthrowing a government or occupation forces **7** (often preceded by *the*) an electric passenger railway operated in underground tunnels

undergrowth *n* small trees and bushes growing beneath taller trees in a wood or forest

underhand *adj* also: **underhanded** **1** sly, deceitful, and secretive **2** *sport* same as **underarm** ▷ *adv* **3** in an underhand manner or style

underinsured *adj* not insured for enough money to cover the replacement value of the goods covered

underlay *n* felt or rubber laid under a carpet to increase insulation and resilience

underlie *vb* **-lying, -lay, -lain** **1** to lie or be placed under **2** to be the foundation, cause, or basis of: *the basic unity which underlies all religion*

underline *vb* **-lining, -lined** **1** to put a line under **2** to emphasize

underling *n disparaging* a subordinate

underlying *adj* **1** not obvious but detectable: *the deeper and underlying aim of her travels* **2** fundamental; basic: *an underlying belief* **3** lying under: *the underlying layers of the skin*

undermanned *adj* not having enough staff to function properly

undermentioned *adj* mentioned below or later

undermine *vb* **-mining, -mined** **1** to weaken gradually or insidiously: *morphia had undermined his grasp of reality* **2** (of the sea or wind) to wear away the base of cliffs

underneath *prep* **1** under or beneath: *a table underneath an olive tree* ▷ *adv* **2** under or beneath: *the chest of drawers was scratched underneath* ▷ *adj* **3** lower ▷ *n* **4** a lower part or surface [Old English *underneothan*]

undernourished *adj* lacking the food needed for health and growth › **undernourishment** *n*

underpaid *adj* not paid as much as the job deserves

underpants *pl n* a man's undergarment covering the body from the waist or hips to the thighs

underpass *n* **1** a section of a road that passes under another road or a railway line **2** a subway for pedestrians

underpay *vb* **-paying, -paid** to pay someone insufficiently › **underpayment** *n*

underpin *vb* **-pinning, -pinned** **1** to give strength or support to: *the principles that underpin his political convictions* **2** to support from beneath with a prop: *to underpin a wall* › **underpinning** *n*

underplay *vb* to achieve (an effect) by deliberate lack of emphasis

underprivileged *adj* **1** lacking the rights and advantages of other members of society; deprived ▷ *n* **2** the underprivileged underprivileged people regarded as a group

underrate *vb* **-rating, -rated** to not be aware or take account of the full abilities or potential of › **underrated** *adj*

underscore *vb* **-scoring, -scored** same as **underline**

undersea *adj, adv* below the surface of the sea

underseal *n* **1** a special coating applied to the underside of a motor vehicle to prevent corrosion ▷ *vb* **2** to apply such a coating to a motor vehicle

undersecretary *n, pl* **-taries** a senior civil servant or junior minister in a government department

undersell *vb* **-selling, -sold** to sell at a price lower than that of another seller

undersexed *adj* having weaker sexual urges than is considered normal

undershirt *n US and Canad* an undergarment covering the body from the shoulders to the hips

undershoot *vb* **-shooting, -shot** *aviation* to land an aircraft short of a runway

underside *n* the bottom or lower surface

undersigned *n* the undersigned the person or people who have signed at the foot of a document, statement, or letter

undersized *adj* smaller than normal

underskirt *n* a skirtlike garment worn under a skirt or dress; petticoat

understaffed *adj* not having enough staff to function properly

understand *vb* **-standing, -stood** **1** to know and comprehend the nature or meaning of: *I understand what you are saying* **2** to know what is happening or why it is happening: *in order to understand the problems that can occur* **3** to assume, infer, or believe: *I understand he is based in this town* **4** to know how to translate or read: *don't you understand Russian?* **5** to be sympathetic to or compatible with: *she needed him to understand her completely* [Old English *understandan*] › **understandable** *adj* › **understandably** *adv*

understanding *n* **1** the ability to learn, judge, or make decisions **2** personal opinion or interpretation of a subject: *my understanding of what he said* **3** a mutual agreement, usually an informal or private one ▷ *adj* **4** kind, sympathetic, or tolerant towards people

understate *vb* **-stating, -stated** **1** to describe or portray something in restrained terms, often to obtain an ironic effect **2** to state that something, such as a number, is less than it is > **understatement** n

understood vb **1** the past of **understand** ▷ adj **2** implied or inferred **3** taken for granted

understudy n, pl **-studies 1** an actor who studies a part so as to be able to replace the usual actor if necessary **2** anyone who is trained to take the place of another if necessary ▷ vb **-studies, -studying, -studied 3** to act as an understudy to

undertake vb **-taking, -took, -taken 1** to agree to or commit oneself to something or to do something: I undertook the worst job in gardening **2** to promise to do something

undertaker n a person whose job is to look after the bodies of people who have died and to organize funerals

undertaking n **1** a task or enterprise **2** an agreement to do something **3** informal the practice of overtaking on an inner lane a vehicle which is travelling in an outer lane

undertone n **1** a quiet tone of voice **2** something which suggests an underlying quality or feeling: an undertone of anger

undertow n a strong undercurrent flowing in a different direction from the surface current, such as in the sea

undervalue vb **-valuing, -valued** to value a person or thing at less than the true worth or importance

underwater adj **1** situated, occurring, or for use under the surface of the sea, a lake, or a river ▷ adv **2** beneath the surface of the sea, a lake, or a river

under way adj **1** in progress; taking place: this test is already under way **2** nautical in motion in the direction headed

underwear n clothing worn under other garments, usually next to the skin

underweight adj weighing less than is average, expected, or healthy

underwent vb the past tense of **undergo**

Underwood n Rory. born 1963, English Rugby Union player: played 85 internationals (1984–96) and scored 49 tries (an England record)

underworld n **1** criminals and their associates **2** Classical myth the regions below the earth's surface regarded as the abode of the dead

underwrite vb **-writing, -wrote, -written 1** to accept financial responsibility for a commercial project or enterprise **2** to sign and issue an insurance policy, thus accepting liability **3** to support > **underwriter** n

undeserved adj not earned or deserved

undesirable adj **1** not desirable or pleasant; objectionable ▷ n **2** a person considered undesirable

undetected adj not having been discovered: an undetected cancer

undeterred adj not put off or dissuaded

undeveloped adj **1** not yet mature or adult **2** (of land) not built on or used for commercial or agricultural purposes

undies pl n Brit, Austral and NZ informal women's underwear

undignified adj foolish or embarrassing

undiluted adj **1** (of a liquid) not having any water added to it; concentrated **2** not mixed with any other feeling or quality: undiluted hatred

undiminished adj not lessened or decreased: his admiration for her remained undiminished

undine (un-dean) n a female water spirit [Latin unda a wave]

undisciplined adj behaving badly, with a lack of self-control

undisguised adj shown openly; not concealed: undisguised curiosity

undismayed adj not upset about something; undaunted

undisputed adj unquestionably true or accurately described: Mao became undisputed leader of China

undistinguished adj not particularly good or bad; mediocre

undisturbed adj **1** quiet and peaceful: an undisturbed village **2** uninterrupted: three hours' undisturbed work **3** not touched, moved, or used by anyone: the wreck has lain undisturbed for centuries

undivided adj **1** total and whole-hearted: her undivided attention **2** not separated into different parts or groups

undo vb **-doing, -did, -done 1** to open, unwrap or untie **2** to reverse the effects of: all the work of the congress would be undone **3** to cause the downfall of

undoing n **1** ruin; downfall **2** the cause of someone's downfall: his confidence was his undoing

undone[1] adj not done or completed; unfinished

undone[2] adj **1** ruined; destroyed **2** unfastened; untied

undoubted adj beyond doubt; certain or indisputable > **undoubtedly** adv

undreamed or **undreamt** adj (often foll. by of) not thought of or imagined

undress vb **1** to take off the clothes of oneself or another ▷ n **2** in a state of undress naked or nearly naked **3** informal or ordinary working clothes or uniform > **undressed** adj

Undset n Sigrid. 1882–1949, Norwegian novelist, best known for her trilogy Kristin Lavransdatter (1920–22): Nobel prize for literature 1928

undue adj greater than is reasonable; excessive: undue attention

USAGE The use of undue in sentences such as there is no cause for undue alarm is redundant and should be avoided.

undulate vb **-lating, -lated 1** to move gently and slowly from side to side or up and down **2** to have a wavy shape or appearance [Latin unda a wave] > **undulation** n

unduly adv excessively

undying adj never ending; eternal

unearned adj **1** not deserved **2** not yet earned

unearned income n income from property or investments rather than work

unearth vb **1** to discover by searching **2** to dig up out of the earth

unearthly adj **1** strange, unnatural, or eerie: unearthly beauty **2** ridiculous or unreasonable: the unearthly hour of seven in the morning > **unearthliness** n

unease n **1** anxiety or nervousness: my unease grew when she was not back by midnight **2** dissatisfaction or tension: unease about the government's handling of the affair

uneasy adj **1** (of a person) anxious or apprehensive **2** (of a condition) precarious or insecure: an uneasy peace **3** (of a thought or feeling) disquieting > **uneasily** adv > **uneasiness** n

uneatable adj (of food) so rotten or unattractive as to be unfit to eat

uneconomic adj not producing enough profit

uneconomical adj not economical; wasteful

uneducated adj not educated well or at all

unemotional adj (of a person) not displaying any emotion

unemployable adj unable or unfit to keep a job

unemployed adj **1** without paid employment; out of work **2** not being used; idle ▷ pl n **3** people who are out of work: the long-term unemployed

unemployment n **1** the condition of being unemployed **2** the number of unemployed workers: unemployment rose again last month

unemployment benefit n (formerly, in the British National Insurance scheme, and currently, in New Zealand) a regular payment to an unemployed person

unencumbered adj not hindered or held back: unencumbered by the responsibilities of childcare

unending adj not showing any signs of ever stopping

unendurable adj too unpleasant to bear

unenthusiastic *adj* not keen about or interested in (something) › **unenthusiastically** *adv*

unenviable *adj* (of a task) so difficult, dangerous, or unpleasant that one is glad not to have to do it oneself: *the unenviable task of phoning the parents of the dead child*

unequal *adj* 1 not equal in quantity, size, rank, or value 2 unequal to inadequate for: *he felt unequal to the job* 3 not offering all people or groups the same opportunities and privileges: *the unequal distribution of wealth* 4 (of a contest) having competitors of different ability › **unequally** *adv*

unequalled *or US* **unequaled** *adj* greater, better, or more extreme than anything else of the same kind

unequivocal *adj* completely clear in meaning; unambiguous › **unequivocally** *adv*

unerring *adj* never mistaken; consistently accurate

UNESCO United Nations Educational, Scientific, and Cultural Organization

unethical *adj* morally wrong

uneven *adj* 1 (of a surface) not level or flat 2 not consistent in quality: *an uneven performance* 3 not parallel, straight, or horizontal 4 not fairly matched: *the uneven battle*

uneventful *adj* ordinary, routine, or quiet › **uneventfully** *adv*

unexampled *adj* without precedent

unexceptionable *adj* not likely to be criticized or objected to

unexceptional *adj* usual, ordinary, or normal

unexciting *adj* slightly dull and boring

unexpected *adj* surprising or unforeseen › **unexpectedly** *adv*

unexplained *adj* strange or unclear because the reason for it is not known

unexpurgated *adj* (of a piece of writing) not censored by having allegedly offensive passages removed

unfailing *adj* continuous or reliable: *his unfailing enthusiasm* › **unfailingly** *adv*

unfair *adj* 1 unequal or unjust 2 dishonest or unethical › **unfairly** *adv* › **unfairness** *n*

unfaithful *adj* 1 having sex with someone other than one's regular partner 2 not true to a promise or vow › **unfaithfulness** *n*

unfamiliar *adj* 1 not known; strange: *an unfamiliar American accent* 2 unfamiliar with not acquainted with: *anyone who is unfamiliar with the language* › **unfamiliarity** *n*

unfashionable *adj* not popular or in vogue

unfasten *vb* to undo, untie, or open or become undone, untied, or opened

unfathomable *adj* too strange or complicated to be understood: *pugs exert a powerful, unfathomable hold over their owners*

unfavourable *or US* **unfavorable** *adj* 1 making a successful or positive outcome unlikely: *unfavourable weather conditions* 2 disapproving: *an unfavourable opinion* › **unfavourably** *or US* **unfavorably** *adv*

Unfederated Malay States *pl n* a former group of native states in the Malay Peninsula that became British protectorates between 1885 and 1909. All except Brunei joined the Malayan Union (later Federation of Malaya) in 1946. Brunei joined the Federation of Malaysia in 1963 but later became an independent nation

unfeeling *adj* without sympathy; callous

unfettered *adj* not limited or controlled: *unfettered competition*

unfinished *adj* 1 incomplete or imperfect 2 (of paint) without an applied finish

unfit *adj* 1 unqualified for or incapable of a particular role or task: *an unfit mother; he was unfit to drive* 2 unsuitable: *this meat is unfit for human consumption* 3 in poor physical condition

unfitted *adj* unsuitable: *unused to and unfitted for any form of manual labour*

unflappable *adj informal* (of a person) not easily upset › **unflappability** *n*

unfledged *adj* 1 (of a young bird) not having developed adult feathers 2 immature and inexperienced

unflinching *adj* not shrinking from danger or difficulty

unfold *vb* 1 to open or spread out from a folded state 2 to reveal or be revealed: *a terrible truth unfolds* 3 to develop or be developed: *the novel unfolds through their recollections*

unfollow *vb* to stop following (a person) on a social networking site

unforeseen *adj* surprising because not expected

unforgettable *adj* making such a strong impression that it is impossible to forget › **unforgettably** *adv*

unforgivable *adj* too bad or cruel to be excused

unforgiving *adj* 1 unwilling to forgive other people's mistakes or wrongdoings 2 (of a machine) allowing little or no opportunity for mistakes to be corrected 3 harsh: *an unforgiving and desolate landscape*

unformed *adj* in an early stage of development; not fully developed or thought out

unforthcoming *adj* not inclined to speak, explain, or communicate

unfortunate *adj* 1 caused or accompanied by bad luck: *an unfortunate coincidence* 2 having bad luck: *my unfortunate daughter* 3 regrettable or unsuitable: *an unfortunate choice of phrase* ▷ *n* 4 an unlucky person › **unfortunately** *adv*

unfounded *adj* (of ideas, fears, or allegations) not based on facts or evidence

unfreeze *vb* **-freezing, -froze, -frozen** 1 to thaw or cause to thaw 2 to relax restrictions or controls on (trade, the transfer of money, etc.): *Congress is considering unfreezing US aid to Jordan*

unfriend *vb* to remove (a person) as a friend on a social networking site

unfriendly *adj* **-lier, -liest** not friendly; hostile

unfrock *vb* to deprive (a person in holy orders) of the status of a priest

unfulfilled *adj* not satisfied

unfurl *vb* to unroll or spread out (an umbrella, flag, or sail) or (of an umbrella, flag, or sail) to be unrolled or spread out

unfurnished *adj* not containing any furniture

ungainly *adj* **-lier, -liest** lacking grace when moving [dialect *gainly* graceful] › **ungainliness** *n*

Ungaretti *n* Giuseppe. 1888–1970, Italian poet, best known for his collection of war poems *Allegria di naufragi* (1919)

Ungava *n* a sparsely inhabited region of NE Canada, in N Quebec east of Hudson Bay, part of the Labrador peninsula: rich mineral resources. Area: 911 110 sq km (351 780 sq miles)

ungenerous *adj* 1 mean or overly thrifty 2 (of a remark or thought) unfair or harsh

ungodly *adj* **-lier, -liest** 1 wicked or sinful 2 *informal* unreasonable or outrageous: *at this ungodly hour* › **ungodliness** *n*

ungovernable *adj* 1 (of an emotion) not able to be controlled or restrained: *an ungovernable rage* 2 (of a country or area) not able to be effectively governed, esp. because of unrest or violence: *years of religious conflict had made much of the island ungovernable*

ungracious *adj* not polite or friendly, esp. when being offered praise or thanks

ungrammatical *adj* not following the rules of grammar

ungrateful *adj* not showing or offering thanks for a favour or compliment

unguarded *adj* 1 unprotected 2 open or frank: *one unguarded briefing* 3 incautious or careless: *an unguarded moment*

unguent (ung-gwent) *n literary* an ointment [Latin *unguere* to anoint]

u

ungulate (ung-gyew-lit) *n* a hoofed mammal [Latin *ungula* hoof]

unhallowed *adj* **1** not consecrated or holy: *unhallowed ground* **2** sinful or wicked

unhand *vb old-fashioned or literary* to release from one's grasp

unhappy *adj* **-pier, -piest 1** sad or depressed **2** unfortunate or wretched **> unhappily** *adv* **> unhappiness** *n*

unharmed *adj* not hurt or damaged in any way

unhealthy *adj* **-healthier, -healthiest 1** likely to cause illness or poor health: *unhealthy foods such as hamburger and chips* **2** not very fit or well **3** caused by or looking as if caused by poor health: *a thin unhealthy look about him* **4** morbid or unwholesome: *an unhealthy interest in computer fraud* **> unhealthiness** *n*

unheard *adj* not listened to; unheeded: *all my warnings went unheard*

unheard-of *adj* **1** without precedent: *an unheard-of phenomenon* **2** highly offensive: *unheard-of behaviour*

unheeded *adj* noticed but ignored: *their protests went unheeded*

unhelpful *adj* doing nothing to improve a situation

unheralded *adj* not announced beforehand

unhindered *adj* **1** not prevented or obstructed: *unhindered access* ▷ *adv* **2** without being prevented or obstructed: *he was able to go about his work unhindered*

unhinge *vb* **combining -hinging, -hinged** to make a person mentally deranged or unbalanced **> unhinged** *adj*

unholy *adj* **-lier, -liest 1** immoral or wicked **2** *informal* outrageous or unnatural: *this unholy mess* **> unholiness** *n*

unhook *vb* **1** to unfasten the hooks of a garment **2** to remove something from a hook

unhurried *adj* done at a leisurely pace, without any rush or anxiety

unhurt *adj* not injured in an accident, attack, etc.

unhygienic *adj* dirty and likely to cause disease or infection

uni *n Brit, Austral and NZ informal* short for **university**

uni- *combining form* of, consisting of, or having only one: *unilateral* [Latin *unus* one]

unicameral *adj* of or having a single legislative chamber: *Denmark's unicameral parliament, known as the Folketing*

UNICEF United Nations Children's Fund

unicellular *adj* (of organisms) consisting of a single cell

Unicode *n computers* a character set for all languages

unicorn *n* a legendary creature resembling a white horse with one horn growing from its forehead [Latin *unus* one + *cornu* a horn]

unicycle *n* a one-wheeled vehicle driven by pedals, used in a circus **> unicyclist** *n*

unidentified *adj* **1** not able to be recognized; unknown: *unidentified gunmen* **2** anonymous or unnamed: *the house of an unidentified Scottish businessman* **> unidentifiable** *adj*

uniform *n* **1 a** a special identifying set of clothes for the members of an organization, such as soldiers ▷ *adj* **2** regular and even throughout: *the mixture must be beaten to a uniform consistency* **3** alike or like: *uniform green metal filing cabinets* [Latin *unus* one + *forma* shape] **> uniformity** *n* **> uniformly** *adv*

unify *vb* **-fies, -fying, -fied** to make or become one; unite [Latin *unus* one + *facere* to make] **> unification** *n*

unilateral *adj* made or done by only one person or group: *unilateral action* **> unilateralism** *n*

unilingual *adj* **1** of or relating to only one language **2** *chiefly Canad* knowing only one language ▷ *n* **3** *chiefly Canad* a person who knows only one language

unimaginable *adj* so unusual, great, or extreme that it is difficult to imagine or understand: *the unimaginable vastness of space*

unimaginative *adj* not having or showing much imagination

Unimak Island *n* an island in SW Alaska, in the Aleutian Islands. Length: 113 km (70 miles)

unimpeachable *adj* completely honest and reliable

unimpeded *adj* not stopped or disrupted by anything

unimportant *adj* trivial or insignificant

uninhabitable *adj* not able to support human life: *an uninhabitable wasteland*

uninhabited *adj* having no people living in or on it: *an uninhabited island*

uninhibited *adj* behaving freely and naturally, without worrying what other people will think

uninitiated *pl n* the uninitiated people who have no special knowledge or experience: *no easy way for the uninitiated to find out what the internet can do*

uninspired *adj* not particularly good or exciting

uninspiring *adj* not likely to make people interested or excited

unintelligible *adj* impossible to make out or understand; incomprehensible: *an unintelligible London accent*

unintended *adj* (of an action or its consequences) not planned or intended: *sometimes drugs have unintended side-effects*

unintentional *adj* (of an action) not done deliberately; accidental: *unintentional discrimination* **> unintentionally** *adv*

uninterested *adj* having or showing no interest in someone or something

> **USAGE** See at **disinterested**.

uninteresting *adj* boring or dull

uninterrupted *adj* continuous, with no breaks or interruptions: *uninterrupted applause*

uninvited *adj* **1** not having been asked: *uninvited guests* ▷ *adv* **2** without having been asked: *he sat down uninvited on the side of the bed*

union *n* **1** the act of merging two or more things to become one, or the state of being merged in such a way **2** short for **trade union** **3** an association of individuals or groups for a common purpose: *the Scripture Union* **4 a** an association or society: *the Students' union* **b** the buildings of such an organization **5** marriage or sexual intercourse **6** *maths* a set containing all the members of two given sets **7** (in 19th-century England) a workhouse maintained by a number of parishes ▷ *adj* **8** of a trade union [Latin *unus* one]

Union *n* the Union **1** *Brit* **a** the union of England and Wales from 1543 **b** the union of the English and Scottish crowns (1603–1707) **c** the union of England and Scotland from 1707 **d** the political union of Great Britain and Ireland (1801–1920) **e** the union of Great Britain and Northern Ireland from 1920 **2** *US* **a** the United States of America **b** the northern states of the US during the Civil War **3** short for the **Union of South Africa**

unionism *n* **1** the principles of trade unions **2** adherence to the principles of trade unions **> unionist** *n, adj*

Unionist *n* a supporter of union between Britain and Northern Ireland

unionize *or* **-ise** *vb* **-izing, -ized** *or* **-ising, -ised** to organize workers into a trade union **> unionization** *or* **-isation** *n*

Union Jack *or* **Union flag** *n* the national flag of the United Kingdom, combining the crosses of Saint George, Saint Andrew, and Saint Patrick

Union of South Africa *n* the former name (1910–61) of (the Republic of) South Africa

Union of Soviet Socialist Republics *n* the official name of the former Soviet Union

union territory *n* one of the 6 administrative territories that, with 28 states, make up the Republic of India

unique (yew-neek) *adj* **1** being the only one of a particular type **2 unique to** concerning or belonging to a particular person, thing, or group: *certain dishes are unique to this restaurant* **3** without equal or like **4** *informal* remarkable [Latin *unicus* unparalleled] **> uniquely** *adv*

> **USAGE** *Unique* is normally taken to describe an absolute state, i.e. one that cannot be qualified; thus something is either *unique* or *not unique*; it cannot be *rather unique* or *very unique*. However *unique* is sometimes used informally to mean remarkable or unusual, and this makes it possible to use comparatives or intensifiers with it, although many people object to this use.

unisex *adj* (of clothing, a hairstyle, or hairdressers) designed for both sexes

unisexual *adj* **1** of one sex only **2** (of an organism) having either male or female reproductive organs but not both

unison *n* **1 in unison** at the same time as another person or other people: *smiling and nodding in unison* **2** (usually preceded by *in*) complete agreement: *to act in unison* **3** *music* a style, technique, or passage in which all the performers sing or play the same notes at the same time [Latin *unus* one + *sonus* sound]

UNISON *n* a British trade union consisting mainly of council and hospital workers

unit *n* **1** a single undivided entity or whole **2** a group or individual regarded as a basic element of a larger whole: *the clan was the basic unit of Highland society* **3** a mechanical part or small device that does a particular job: *a waste disposal unit* **4** a team of people that performs a specific function, and often also their buildings and equipment: *a combat unit* **5** a standard amount of a physical quantity, such as length or energy, used to express magnitudes of that quantity: *the year as a unit of time* **6** *maths* the digit or position immediately to the left of the decimal point **7** a piece of furniture designed to be fitted with other similar pieces: *bedroom units* **8** NZ a self-propelled railcar **9** *Austral and NZ* short for **home unit** [from *unity*]

Unitarian *n* **1** a person who believes that God is one being and rejects the Trinity ▷ *adj* **2** of Unitarians or Unitarianism **> Unitarianism** *n*

unitary *adj* **1** consisting of a single undivided whole: *a unitary state* **2** of a unit or units

unit cost *n* the actual cost of producing one article

unite *vb* **uniting, united** **1** to make or become an integrated whole: *conception occurs when a sperm unites with the egg* **2** to form an association or alliance: *the opposition parties united to fight against privatization* **3** to possess (a combination of qualities) at the same time: *he manages to unite charm and ruthlessness* [Latin *unus* one]

united *adj* **1** produced by two or more people or things in combination: *a united effort* **2** in agreement: *we are united in our opposition to these proposals* **3** in association or alliance

United Arab Emirates *pl n* a group of seven emirates in SW Asia, on the Persian Gulf: consists of Abu Dhabi, Dubai, Sharjah, Ajman, Umm al Qaiwain, Ras el Khaimah, and Fujairah; a former British protectorate; became fully independent in 1971; consists mostly of flat desert, with mountains in the east; rich petroleum resources. Official language: Arabic. Official religion: Muslim. Currency: dirham. Capital: Abu Dhabi. Pop: 5 473 972 (2013 est). Area: 83 600 sq km (32 300 sq miles). Former name (until 1971): **Trucial States**. Abbreviation: **UAE**

United Arab Republic *n* the official name (1958–71) of Egypt

United Arab States *pl n* a federation (1958–61) between the United Arab Republic and Yemen

United Kingdom *n* a kingdom of NW Europe, consisting chiefly of the island of Great Britain together with Northern Ireland: became the world's leading colonial power in the 18th century; the first country to undergo the Industrial Revolution. It became the **United Kingdom of Great Britain and Northern Ireland** in 1921, after the rest of Ireland became autonomous as the Irish Free State. Primarily it is a trading nation, the chief exports being manufactured goods; joined the Common Market (now the European Union) in January 1973. Official language: English; Gaelic, Welsh, and other minority languages. Religion: Christian majority. Currency: pound sterling. Capital: London. Pop: 63 395 574 (2013 est). Area: 244 110 sq km (94 251 sq miles). Abbreviation: **UK**. See also **Great Britain**

United Nations *n* an international organization of independent states, formed to promote peace and international security

United Provinces *pl n* **1** a Dutch republic (1581–1795) formed by the union of the seven northern provinces of the Netherlands, which were in revolt against their suzerain, Philip II of Spain **2** the United Provinces of Agra and Oudh. See **Uttar Pradesh**

United States of America *n* (*functioning as sing or pl*) a federal republic mainly in North America consisting of 50 states and the District of Columbia: colonized principally by the English and French in the 17th century, the native Indians being gradually defeated and displaced; 13 colonies under British rule made the Declaration of Independence in 1776 and became the United States after the War of American Independence. The northern states defeated the South in the Civil War (1861–65). It is the world's most productive industrial nation and also exports agricultural products. It consists generally of the Rocky Mountains in the west, the Great Plains in the centre, the Appalachians in the east, deserts in the southwest, and coastal lowlands and swamps in the southeast. Language: predominantly English; Spanish is also widely spoken. Religion: Christian majority. Currency: dollar. Capital: Washington, DC. Pop: 316 668 567 (2013 est). Area: 9 518 323 sq km (3 675 031 sq miles). Often shortened to: **United States**. Abbreviation: **US, USA**

unit price *n* the price charged per unit

unit trust *n Brit and Austral* an investment trust that issues units for public sale and invests the money in many different businesses

unity *n, pl* **-ties** **1** the state of being one **2** mutual agreement: *unity of intention* **3** the state of being a single thing that is composed of separate parts, organizations, etc.: *moves towards church unity* **4** *maths* the number or numeral one [Latin *unus* one]

Univ. University

univalent *adj chem* same as **monovalent**

universal *adj* **1** of or relating to everyone in the world or everyone in a particular place or society: *the introduction of universal primary education* **2** of, relating to, or affecting the entire world or universe: *the universal laws of physics* **3** true and relevant at all times and in all situations: *there may be no single universal solution* ▷ *n* **4** something which exists or is true in all places and all situations: *universals such as beauty and justice* **> universality** *n* **> universally** *adv*

> **USAGE** The use of *more universal* as in *his writings have long been admired by fellow scientists, but his latest book should have more universal appeal* is acceptable in modern English usage.

universal joint *or* **universal coupling** *n* a form of coupling between two rotating shafts allowing freedom of movement in all directions

universe *n* **1** the whole of all existing matter, energy, and space **2** the world [Latin *universum* the whole world]

university *n, pl* **-ties** **1** an institution of higher education with authority to award degrees **2** the buildings, members, staff, or campus of a university [Medieval Latin *universitas* group of scholars]

Unix (**yew**-nicks) *n trademark* an operating system found on many types of computer

unjust *adj* not fair or just

unjustifiable *adj* inexcusably wrong or unfair

unjustified *adj* not necessary or reasonable

unkempt *adj* **1** (of the hair) uncombed or dishevelled **2** untidy or slovenly: *an unkempt appearance* [Old English *uncembed*, from *cemban* to comb]

unkind *adj* unsympathetic or cruel › **unkindly** *adv* › **unkindness** *n*

unknowing *adj* unaware or ignorant: *unknowing victims of fraud*

unknown *adj* **1** not known, understood, or recognized **2** not famous: *a young and then unknown actor* **3** unknown quantity a person or thing whose action or effect is unknown or unpredictable ▷ *n* **4** an unknown person, quantity, or thing ▷ *adv* **5** unknown to someone without someone being aware: *unknown to him, the starboard engine had dropped off*

unlawful *adj* not permitted by law; illegal

unleaded *adj* (of petrol) containing less tetraethyl lead, in order to reduce environmental pollution

unlearn *vb* **-learning, -learned** *or* **-learnt** to try to forget something learnt or to discard accumulated knowledge

unlearned (un-lurn-id) *adj* ignorant or uneducated

unlearnt *or* **unlearned** *adj* **1** denoting knowledge or skills innately present rather than learnt **2** not learnt or taken notice of: *unlearnt lessons*

unleash *vb* to set loose or cause (something bad): *to unleash war*

unleavened (un-lev-vend) *adj* (of bread) made without yeast or leavening

unless *conj* except under the circumstances that; except on the condition that: *you can't get in unless you can prove you're over eighteen*

unlettered *adj* uneducated or illiterate

unlike *adj* **1** not similar; different ▷ *prep* **2** not like or typical of: *unlike his brother, he could not control his weight* › **unlikeness** *n*

unlikely *adj* not likely; improbable › **unlikeliness** *n*

unlimited *adj* **1** apparently endless: *there was unlimited coffee* **2** not restricted or limited: *unlimited access to the rest of the palace*

unlisted *adj* **1** not entered on a list **2** (of securities) not quoted on a stock exchange **3** *Austral, US and Canad* not listed in a telephone directory by request

unlit *adj* **1** (of a fire, cigarette, etc.) not lit and therefore not burning **2** (of a road) not having any streetlights switched on

unload *vb* **1** to remove cargo from a ship, lorry, or plane **2** to express worries or problems by telling someone about them **3** to remove the ammunition from a gun

unlock *vb* **1** to unfasten a lock or door **2** to release or let loose: *the revelation unlocked a flood of tears*

unlooked-for *adj* unexpected or unforeseen

unloose *or* **unloosen** *vb* **-loosing, -loosed** *or* **-loosening, -loosened** to set free or release

unlovable *adj* too unpleasant or unattractive to be loved

unloved *adj* not loved by anyone

unlovely *adj* unpleasant in appearance or character

unlucky *adj* **1** having bad luck or misfortune: *an unlucky man* **2** caused by bad luck or misfortune: *an unlucky coincidence* **3** regarded as likely to bring about bad luck: *an unlucky number* › **unluckily** *adv*

unmade *adj* **1** (of a bed) with the bedclothes not smoothed and tidied **2** (of a road) not surfaced with tarmac **3** not yet made

unmake *vb* **-making, -made** to undo or destroy

unman *vb* **-manning, -manned** **1** to cause to lose courage or nerve **2** to make effeminate

unmanageable *adj* difficult to use, deal with, or control, esp. because it is too big

unmanly *adj* **1** not masculine or virile **2** cowardly or dishonourable

unmanned *adj* **1** having no personnel or crew: *the border posts were unmanned* **2** (of an aircraft or spacecraft) operated by automatic or remote control

unmannerly *adj* lacking manners; discourteous › **unmannerliness** *n*

unmarked *adj* **1** having no signs of damage or injury **2** not having any identifying signs or markings: *an unmarked police car*

unmarried *adj* not married

unmask *vb* **1** to remove the mask or disguise from **2** to expose or reveal the true nature or character of

unmatched *adj* **1** not equalled or surpassed: *his pace is unmatched by any other modern player* **2** not coordinated or forming a set with anything else: *three unmatched chairs*

unmentionable *adj* unsuitable as a topic of conversation

unmercifully *adv* excessively and relentlessly: *the young boy is hounded unmercifully*

unmistakable *or* **unmistakeable** *adj* clear or unambiguous › **unmistakably** *or* **unmistakeably** *adv*

unmitigated *adj* **1** not reduced or lessened in severity or intensity **2** total and complete: *unmitigated boredom*

unmolested *adv* without disturbance or interference: *the enemy aircraft passed overhead unmolested*

unmoved *adj* not affected by emotion; indifferent

unmoving *adj* still and motionless

unmusical *adj* **1** (of a person) unable to appreciate or play music **2** (of a sound) harsh and unpleasant

unnamed *adj* **1** not mentioned by name; anonymous: *an unnamed government spokesman* **2** not known or described clearly enough to be named: *unnamed fears*

unnatural *adj* **1** strange and slightly frightening because it is not usual; abnormal: *an unnatural silence* **2** not in accordance with accepted standards of behaviour: *an unnatural relationship* **3** affected or forced: *a determined smile which seemed unnatural* **4** inhuman or monstrous: *unnatural evils* › **unnaturally** *adv*

unnecessary *adj* not essential, or more than is essential › **unnecessarily** *adv*

unnerve *vb* **-nerving, -nerved** to cause to lose courage, confidence, or self-control: *he unnerves me* › **unnerving** *adj*

unnoticed *adj* without being seen or noticed

unnumbered *adj* **1** countless; too many to count **2** not counted or given a number

UNO United Nations Organization

unobtainable *adj* impossible to get

unobtrusive *adj* not drawing attention to oneself or itself; inconspicuous

unoccupied *adj* **1** (of a building) without occupants **2** unemployed or idle **3** (of an area or country) not overrun by foreign troops

unofficial *adj* **1** not authorized or approved by the relevant organization or person: *an unofficial strike* **2** not confirmed officially: *unofficial reports of the minister's resignation*

unorganized *or* **-nised** *adj* **1** not arranged into an organized system or structure **2** (of workers) not unionized

unorthodox *adj* **1** (of ideas, methods, etc.) unconventional and not generally accepted **2** (of a person) not conventional in beliefs, behaviour, etc.

unpack *vb* **1** to remove the packed contents of a case **2** to take something out of a packed container

unpaid *adj* **1** without a salary or wage: *unpaid overtime* **2** still to be paid: *unpaid bills*

unpalatable *adj* **1** (of food) unpleasant to taste **2** (of a fact, idea, etc.) unpleasant and hard to accept

unparalleled *adj* not equalled; supreme

unpardonable *adj* unforgivably wrong or rude

unparliamentary *adj* not consistent with parliamentary procedure or practice

unperson *n* a person whose existence is officially denied or ignored

unpick *vb* to undo the stitches of a piece of sewing

unpin *vb* **-pinning, -pinned** **1** to remove a pin or pins from **2** to unfasten by removing pins

unplanned *adj* not intentional or deliberate

unplayable adj sport **1** (of a ball) thrown too fast or too skilfully to be hit **2** (of a pitch or course) too badly affected by rain or frost to be used

unpleasant adj not pleasant or agreeable › **unpleasantly** adv › **unpleasantness** n

unplug vb **-plugging, -plugged** to disconnect a piece of electrical equipment by taking the plug out of the socket

unplugged adj using acoustic rather than electric instruments: an unplugged version of the song

unplumbed adj **1** not measured **2** not understood in depth

unpolished adj **1** not polished **2** not elegant or refined

unpopular adj generally disliked or disapproved of › **unpopularity** n

unpractised or US **unpracticed** adj not experienced or skilled: an unpractised surgical technique

unprecedented adj never having happened before: an unprecedented decision

unpredictable adj not easy to predict or foresee

unprejudiced adj free from bias; impartial

unprepared adj surprised or put at a disadvantage by something because you are not ready to deal with it

unprepossessing adj not very attractive or appealing

unpretentious adj modest, unassuming, and down-to-earth

unprincipled adj lacking moral principles; unscrupulous

unprintable adj unsuitable for printing for reasons of obscenity, libel, or indecency

unproductive adj not producing any worthwhile results: unproductive talks

unprofessional adj not behaving according to the standards expected of a member of a particular profession

unprofitable adj **1** not making a profit **2** not producing any worthwhile results: an unprofitable line of thinking

unpromising adj not likely to turn out well

unprompted adj doing without being urged by anyone else; spontaneous

unpronounceable adj (of a name or word) too difficult to say

unprotected adj not defended or protected from harm

unprovoked adj carried out without any cause or reason: an unprovoked attack

unpunished adj without suffering or resulting in a penalty: the guilty must not go unpunished; such crimes should not remain unpunished

unputdownable adj (of a book, usually a novel) so gripping that one wants to read it at one sitting

unqualified adj **1** lacking the necessary qualifications **2** having no conditions or limitations: an unqualified denial **3** total or complete: unqualified admiration

unquestionable adj not to be doubted; indisputable › **unquestionably** adv

unquestioned adj accepted by everyone without doubt or disagreement: an engineer of unquestioned genius

unquestioning adj accepting a belief or order without thinking about or doubting it in any way: unquestioning obedience › **unquestioningly** adv

unquiet adj chiefly literary anxious or uneasy

unquote interj an expression used to indicate the end of a quotation that was introduced with the word 'quote'

unravel vb **-elling, -elled** or US **-eling, -eled 1** to separate something knitted or woven into individual strands **2** to become separated into individual strands **3** to explain or solve: we unravelled the secrets

unreactive adj (of a substance) not readily partaking in chemical reactions

unread adj **1** (of a book or article) not yet read **2** (of a person) having read little

unreadable adj **1** unable to be read or deciphered; illegible **2** too difficult or dull to read

unreal adj **1** existing only in the imagination or giving the impression of doing so: an unreal quality **2** insincere or artificial › **unreality** n

unrealistic adj **1** not accepting the facts of a situation and not dealing with them in a practical way: he had unrealistic expectations of his son **2** not true to life: an unrealistic portrayal of Scottish life › **unrealistically** adv

unreasonable adj **1** unfair and excessive: an unreasonable request **2** refusing to listen to reason › **unreasonably** adv

unreasoning adj not controlled by reason; irrational

unrecognizable or **-nisable** adj changed or damaged so much that it is hard to recognize

unrecognized or **-nised** adj not properly identified or acknowledged: her talents went unrecognized during her lifetime

unregenerate adj unrepentant or unreformed

unrelated adj not connected with each other: a series of unrelated mishaps

unrelenting adj **1** refusing to relent or take pity **2** not diminishing in determination, effort, or force

unreliable adj not able to be trusted or relied on

unremitting adj never slackening or stopping

unrepentant adj not ashamed of one's beliefs or actions

unrequited adj (of love) not returned

unreserved adj **1** complete and without holding back any doubts: unreserved support **2** open and forthcoming in manner **3** not booked or not able to be booked: all the seats are unreserved › **unreservedly** (un-riz-**zerv**-id-lee) adv

unresolved adj not satisfactorily solved or concluded: the mystery of her death remains unresolved

unresponsive adj not reacting or responding

unrest n **1** a rebellious state of discontent **2** an uneasy or troubled state

unrestrained adj not controlled or limited: the unrestrained use of state power

unrestricted adj not limited by any laws or rules

unrewarding adj not giving any satisfaction

unrighteous adj sinful or wicked

unripe adj not fully matured

unrivalled or US **unrivaled** adj having no equal; matchless

unroll vb **1** to open out or unwind: I unrolled the map **2** (of a series of events or period of time) to happen or be revealed or remembered one after the other

unruffled adj **1** calm and unperturbed **2** smooth and still: unruffled ponds

unruly adj **-lier, -liest** difficult to control or organize; disobedient or undisciplined › **unruliness** n

unsaddle vb **-dling, -dled 1** to remove the saddle from a horse **2** to cause to fall or dismount from a horse

unsafe adj **1** dangerous **2** (of a criminal conviction) based on inadequate or false evidence

unsaid adj not said or expressed

unsaleable adj unable to be sold

unsatisfactory adj not good enough

unsaturated adj **1** chem (of an organic compound) containing a double or triple bond and therefore capable of combining with other substances **2** (of a fat, esp. a vegetable fat) containing a high proportion of fatty acids with double bonds

unsavoury or US **unsavory** adj objectionable or distasteful: an unsavoury divorce

unscathed adj not harmed or injured

unscheduled adj not planned or intended

unscramble vb **-bling, -bled 1** to sort out something confused or disorderly **2** to restore a scrambled message to an intelligible form › **unscrambler** n

unscrew vb **1** to loosen a screw or lid by turning it **2** to unfasten something by removing the screws which fasten it: the mirror had been unscrewed and removed

unscripted adj spoken without a previously prepared text

unscrupulous adj prepared to act in a dishonest or immoral manner

unseasonable adj **1** (of the weather) inappropriate for the season **2** inappropriate or unusual for the time of year: *an unseasonable dip in the sea*

unseat *vb* **1** to throw or displace from a seat or saddle **2** to depose from office or position

unseeded *adj* (of a player in a sport) not given a top player's position in the opening rounds of a tournament

unseeing *adj* not noticing or looking at anything: *staring with unseeing eyes*

unseemly *adj* not according to expected standards of behaviour ⟩ **unseemliness** *n*

unseen *adj* **1** hidden or invisible: *an unseen organist was practising* **2** mysterious or supernatural: *unseen powers* ▷ *adv* **3** without being seen; unnoticed: *the thief entered unseen* ▷ *n* **4** a passage which is given to students for translation without them having seen it in advance

unselfish *adj* concerned about other people's wishes and needs rather than one's own ⟩ **unselfishly** *adv* ⟩ **unselfishness** *n*

unsettle *vb* **-tling, -tled 1** to change or become changed from a fixed or settled condition **2** to confuse or agitate a person or the mind

unsettled *adj* **1** lacking order or stability: *an unsettled time* **2** disturbed and restless: *your child will feel unsettled and insecure* **3** constantly changing or moving from place to place: *his wandering unsettled life* **4** (of an argument or dispute) not resolved **5** (of a debt or bill) not yet paid

unshakable *or* **unshakeable** *adj* (of beliefs) utterly firm and unwavering

unshaken *adj* (of faith or feelings) not having been weakened

unshaven *adj* (of a man who does not have a beard) having stubble on his chin because he has not shaved recently

unsheathe *vb* **-sheathing, -sheathed** to pull a weapon from a sheath

unshockable *adj* not likely to be upset by anything seen, heard, or read

unsightly *adj* unpleasant to look at; ugly ⟩ **unsightliness** *n*

unsigned *adj* (of a letter etc.) anonymous

unskilled *adj* not having or requiring any special skill or training

unsociable *adj* (of a person) not fond of the company of other people

unsocial *adj* **1** not fond of the company of other people **2** (of the hours of work of a job) falling outside the normal working day

unsolicited *adj* given or sent without being asked for: *unsolicited advice; unsolicited junk mail*

unsophisticated *adj* **1** (of a person) lacking experience or worldly wisdom **2** lacking refinement or complexity: *unsophisticated fighter aircraft*

unsound *adj* **1** unhealthy or unstable: *of unsound mind* **2** based on faulty ideas: *unsound judgment* **3** not firm: *unsound foundations* **4** not financially reliable: *his business plan was unsound*

unsparing *adj* **1** very generous; lavish **2** harsh or severe ⟩ **unsparingly** *adv*

unspeakable *adj* **1** incapable of expression in words: *unspeakable gratitude* **2** indescribably bad or evil: *unspeakable atrocities* ⟩ **unspeakably** *adv*

unspoiled *adj* **1** not damaged or harmed **2** (of a place) attractive and not having changed for a long time

unspoken *adj* not openly expressed: *unspoken fears; an unspoken agreement*

unsporting *adj* not following the principles of fair play

unstable *adj* **1** not firmly fixed and likely to wobble or fall: *an unstable pile of books* **2** likely to change suddenly and create difficulties or danger: *the unstable political climate* **3** (of a person) having abrupt changes of mood or behaviour **4** *chem, physics* readily decomposing

unsteady *adj* **1** not securely fixed: *unsteady metal posts* **2** (of a manner of walking, standing, or holding) shaky or staggering ⟩ **unsteadily** *adv* ⟩ **unsteadiness** *n*

unstinting *adj* generous and gladly given: *unstinting praise*

unstoppable *adj* impossible to prevent from continuing or developing

unstrap *vb* **-strapping, -strapped** to undo the straps fastening (something) in position

unstructured *adj* without formal or systematic organization

unstuck *adj* **1** freed from being stuck, glued, or fastened **2** **come unstuck** to suffer failure or disaster

unstudied *adj* natural or spontaneous: *her unstudied elegance and grace*

unsubstantial *adj* **1** lacking weight or firmness **2** having no material existence

unsubstantiated *adj* not yet confirmed or proved to be true: *unsubstantiated rumours*

unsuccessful *adj* not achieving success

unsuitable *adj* not right or appropriate for a particular purpose

unsuited *adj* **1** not appropriate for a particular task or situation: *a likeable man unsuited to a military career* **2** (of a couple) having different personalities or tastes and unlikely to form a lasting relationship: *they are totally unsuited to each other*

unsung *adj* not appreciated or honoured: *an unsung hero*

unsure *adj* **1** lacking assurance or self-confidence **2** uncertain or undecided: *he was unsure who was really in charge*

unsurpassed *adj* better or greater than anything else of its kind

unsuspected *adj* **1** not known to exist: *an unsuspected talent* **2** not under suspicion

unsuspecting *adj* having no idea of what is happening or about to happen

unsweetened *adj* having no sugar or other sweetener added

unswerving *adj* not turning aside; constant

unsympathetic *adj* **1** not feeling or showing sympathy **2** unpleasant and unlikeable **3** (foll. by *to*) opposed or hostile to

untamed *adj* not brought under human control; wild: *an untamed wilderness*

untangle *vb* **-gling, -gled** to free from tangles or confusion

untapped *adj* not yet used or exploited: *untapped mineral reserves*

untaught *adj* **1** without training or education **2** acquired without instruction

untenable *adj* (of a theory, idea, etc.) impossible to defend in an argument

Unter den Linden *n* the main street of Berlin, extending to the Brandenburg Gate

Unterwalden *n* a canton of central Switzerland, on Lake Lucerne: consists of the demicantons of **Nidwalden** (east) and **Obwalden** (west). Capitals: (Nidwalden) Stans; (Obwalden) Sarnen. Pop: (Nidwalden) 38 900 (2002 est); (Obwalden) 33 000 (2002 est). Areas: (Nidwalden) 274 sq km (107 sq miles); (Obwalden) 492 sq km (192 sq miles)

unthinkable *adj* **1** so shocking or unpleasant that one cannot believe it to be true **2** unimaginable or inconceivable

unthinking *adj* **1** thoughtless and inconsiderate **2** done or happening without careful consideration: *an unthinking reflex* ⟩ **unthinkingly** *adv*

untidy *adj* **-dier, -diest** not neat; messy and disordered ⟩ **untidily** *adv* ⟩ **untidiness** *n*

untie *vb* **-tying, -tied** to unfasten or free something that is tied

until *conj* **1** up to a time that: *he lifted the wire until it was taut* **2** before (a time or event): *until the present crisis, they weren't allowed into the country* ▷ *prep* **3** (often preceded by *up*) in or throughout the period before: *up until then I'd never thought about having kids* **4** before: *Baker does not get to Israel until Sunday* [earlier *untill*]

untimely *adj* **1** occurring before the expected or normal time: *his untimely death* **2** inappropriate to the occasion or time: *an untimely idea to raise at the United Nations* **> untimeliness** *n*

unto *prep archaic* to [from Old Norse]

untold *adj* **1** incapable of description: *untold misery* **2** incalculably great in number or quantity: *untold millions* **3** not told

untouchable *adj* **1** above criticism, suspicion or punishment **2** unable to be touched ▷ *n offensive* **3** a member of the lowest class in India, whose touch was formerly regarded as defiling to the four main castes

untouched *adj* **1** not changed, moved, or affected: *a sleepy backwater untouched by mass tourism* **2** not injured or harmed: *the Cathedral survived the war untouched* **3** (of food or drink) not eaten or consumed **4** emotionally unaffected: *he was untouched by the news of his uncle's death*

untoward *adj* **1** causing misfortune or annoyance **2** unfavourable: *untoward reactions* **3** out of the ordinary; out of the way: *nothing untoward had happened*

untrained *adj* without formal or adequate training or education

untrammelled *or US* **untrammeled** *adj* able to act freely and without restrictions

untried *adj* **1** not yet used, done, or tested **2** (of a prisoner) not yet put on trial

untroubled *adj* calm and unworried

untrue *adj* **1** incorrect or false **2** disloyal or unfaithful

untrustworthy *adj* unreliable and not able to be trusted

untruth *n* a statement that is not true; lie

untruthful *adj* **1** (of a person) given to lying **2** (of a statement) not true **> untruthfully** *adv*

untutored *adj* **1** without formal education **2** lacking sophistication or refinement

unusable *adj* not in good enough condition to be used

unused *adj* **1** not being or never having been used **2** (foll. by *to*) not accustomed to

unusual *adj* uncommon or extraordinary **> unusually** *adv*

unutterable *adj* incapable of being expressed in words **> unutterably** *adv*

unvarnished *adj* not elaborated upon; plain: *an unvarnished account of literary life*

unvarying *adj* always staying the same; unchanging

unveil *vb* **1** to ceremonially remove the cover from a new picture, statue, plaque, etc. **2** to make public a secret **3** to remove the veil from one's own or another person's face

unveiling *n* **1** a ceremony involving the removal of a veil covering a statue **2** the presentation of something for the first time

unvoiced *adj* **1** not expressed or spoken **2** *phonetics* voiceless

unwaged *adj* (of a person) not having a paid job

unwanted *adj* not wanted or welcome

unwarranted *adj* not justified or necessary

unwary *adj* not careful or cautious and therefore likely to be harmed **> unwarily** *adv* **> unwariness** *n*

unwavering *adj* (of a feeling or attitude) remaining firm and never weakening

unwelcome *adj* unpleasant and unwanted

unwell *adj* not healthy; ill

unwept *adj* not wept for or lamented

unwholesome *adj* **1** harmful to the body or mind: *unwholesome food* **2** morally harmful: *unwholesome dreams* **3** unhealthy-looking **4** (of food) of inferior quality

unwieldy *adj* too heavy, large, or awkward to be easily handled

unwilling *adj* **1** reluctant **2** done or said with reluctance **> unwillingly** *adv* **> unwillingness** *n*

unwind *vb* **-winding, -wound** **1** to slacken, undo, or unravel: *Paul started to unwind the bandage* **2** to relax after a busy or tense time: *we go out to unwind after work*

unwise *adj* foolish; not sensible **> unwisely** *adv*

unwitting *adj* **1** not intentional **2** not knowing or conscious [Old English *unwitende*] **> unwittingly** *adv*

unwonted *adj* out of the ordinary; unusual

unworkable *adj* impractical and certain to fail: *unworkable proposals for reform*

unworldly *adj* **1** not concerned with material values or pursuits **2** lacking sophistication; naive

unworn *adj* **1** not having deteriorated through use or age **2** (of a garment) never having been worn

unworried *adj* not bothered or perturbed

unworthy *adj* **1** not deserving or meriting: *a person deemed unworthy of membership* **2** (often foll. by *of*) beneath the level considered befitting (to): *unworthy of a prime minister* **3** lacking merit or value **> unworthiness** *n*

unwrap *vb* **-wrapping, -wrapped** to remove the wrapping from something or (of something wrapped) to have the covering removed

unwritten *adj* **1** not printed or in writing **2** operating only through custom: *an unwritten code of conduct*

unyielding *adj* remaining firm and determined

unzip *vb* **-zipping, -zipped** to unfasten the zip of a garment or (of a zip or a garment with a zip) to become unfastened

up *prep* **1** indicating movement to a higher position: *go up the stairs* **2** at a higher or further level or position in or on: *a shop up the road* ▷ *adv* **3** to an upward, higher, or erect position: *the men straightened up from their digging* **4** indicating readiness for an activity: *up and about* **5** indicating intensity or completion of an action: *he tore up the cheque* **6** to the place referred to or where the speaker is: *a man came up to me* **7 a** to a more important place: *up to the city* **b** to a more northerly place: *pensioners who were going up to Norway* **c** to or at university **8** above the horizon: *the sun came up* **9** appearing for trial: *up before the judge* **10** having gained: *ten pounds up on the deal* **11** higher in price: *beer has gone up again* **12** all up with someone *informal* over for or hopeless for someone **13** something's up *informal* something strange is happening **14** up against having to cope with: *look what we're up against now* **15** up for being a candidate or applicant for: *he's up for the job* **16** up to **a** occupied with; scheming: *she's up to no good* **b** dependent upon: *the decision is up to you* **c** equal to or capable of: *are you up to playing in the final?* **d** as far as: *up to his neck in mud* **e** as many as: *up to two years' credit* **f** comparable with: *not up to my usual standard* **17** what's up? *informal* **a** what is the matter? **b** what is happening? ▷ *adj* **18** of a high or higher position **19** out of bed: *aren't you up yet?* **20** (of a period of time) over or completed: *the examiner announced that their time was up* **21** of or relating to a train going to a more important place: *the up platform* ▷ *vb* **upping, upped** **22** to increase or raise **23** up and *informal* to do something suddenly: *he upped and left her* ▷ *n* **24** a high point: *when the ups come along you have to enjoy them* **25** on the up and up **a** Brit trustworthy or honest **b** Brit, Austral and NZ on an upward trend: *our firm's on the up and up* [Old English *upp*]

up-and-coming *adj* likely to be successful in the future; promising

upbeat *adj* **1** *informal* cheerful and optimistic: *the upbeat atmosphere of a thriving metropolis* ▷ *n* **2** *music* **a** an unaccented beat **b** the upward gesture of a conductor's baton indicating this

upbraid *vb* to scold or reproach [Old English *upbrēdan*]

upbringing *n* the education of a person during his or her formative years

upcoming adj coming soon: the upcoming election
upcountry adj 1 of or from the interior of a country ▷ adv 2 towards or in the interior of a country
upcycle vb **-cycling, -cycled** to recycle a disposable or unwanted object into something of greater value or use
update vb **-dating, -dated** 1 to bring up to date 2 inform; relay the most recent information to
Updike n John (Hoyer). 1932–2009, US writer. His novels include Rabbit, Run (1960), Couples (1968), The Coup (1979), Brazil (1993), Seek My Face (2003), and Rabbit is Rich (1982) and Rabbit at Rest (1990), both of which won Pulitzer prizes
upend vb to turn or set or become turned or set on end
upfront adj 1 open and frank 2 (of money) paid at the beginning of a business arrangement ▷ adv **up front** 3 at the front; (in sport) in attack: Liverpool's strikers dominated up front 4 at the beginning of a business arrangement; in advance: we charge up front
upgrade vb **-grading, -graded** 1 to promote a person or job to a higher rank 2 to raise in value, importance, or esteem
Upham n Charles (Hazlitt). 1908–94, New Zealand soldier; hero of World War II and one of only three people to have been awarded the Victoria Cross twice
upheaval n a strong, sudden, or violent disturbance
uphill adj 1 sloping or leading upwards 2 requiring a great deal of effort: an uphill struggle ▷ adv 3 up a slope ▷ n 4 S African a difficulty
uphold vb **-holding, -held** 1 to maintain or defend against opposition 2 to give moral support to › **upholder** n
upholster vb to fit chairs or sofas with padding, springs, and covering › **upholstered** adj › **upholsterer** n
upholstery n the padding, springs, and covering of a chair or sofa
upkeep n 1 the act or process of keeping something in good repair 2 the cost of maintenance
upland adj of or in an area of high or relatively high ground: an upland wilderness
uplands pl n an area of high or relatively high ground: the uplands of Nepal
uplift vb 1 to raise or lift up 2 to raise morally or spiritually 3 Scot to collect or pick up ▷ n 4 the act or process of bettering moral, social, or cultural conditions ▷ adv 5 (of a bra) designed to lift and support the breasts › **uplifting** adj
upload vb 1 to transfer (data or a program) from one computer's memory into that of another ▷ n 2 a file transferred in such a way
upmarket adj expensive and of superior quality
Upolu n an island in the SW central Pacific, in Samoa. Chief town: Apia. Pop: 134 400 (2001). Area: 1114 sq km (430 sq miles)
upon prep 1 on 2 up and on: they climbed upon his lap for comfort [up + on]
upper adj 1 higher or highest in physical position, wealth, rank, or status 2 **Upper** geology denoting the late part of a period or formation: Upper Cretaceous ▷ n 3 the part of a shoe above the sole 4 **on one's uppers** Brit, Austral and NZ very poor; penniless
Upper Austria n a state of N Austria: first divided from Lower Austria in 1251. Capital: Linz. Pop: 1 387 086 (2003 est). Area: 11 978 sq km (4625 sq miles). German name: **Oberösterreich**
Upper Canada n 1 history (1791–1841) the official name of the region of Canada lying southwest of the Ottawa River and north of the lower Great Lakes. Compare **Lower Canada** 2 (esp. in E Canada) another name for **Ontario**
upper-case adj denoting capital letters as used in printed or typed matter
upper class n 1 the highest social class; aristocracy ▷ adj **upper-class** 2 of the upper class
upper crust n Brit, Austral and NZ informal the upper class

uppercut n a short swinging upward punch delivered to the chin
Upper Egypt n one of the four main traditional administrative districts of Egypt: extends south from Cairo to the Sudan
upper hand n the position of control: the hardliners have gained the upper hand
Upper House n the smaller and less representative chamber of a two-chamber parliament, for example the House of Lords or a Senate
uppermost adj 1 highest in position, power, or importance ▷ adv 2 in or into the highest place or position
Upper Peninsula n a peninsula in the northern US between Lakes Superior and Michigan, constituting the N part of the state of Michigan
Upper Silesia n a region of SW Poland, formerly ruled by Germany: coal mining and other heavy industry
Upper Tunguska n See Tunguska
Upper Volta n the former name (until 1984) of **Burkina Faso**
uppish adj Brit informal uppity
uppity adj informal snobbish, arrogant, or presumptuous [up + fanciful ending]
Uppsala or **Upsala** n a city in E central Sweden: the royal headquarters in the 13th century; Gothic cathedral (the largest in Sweden) and Sweden's oldest university (1477). Pop: 182 124 (2004 est)
upright adj 1 vertical or erect 2 honest or just ▷ adv 3 vertically or in an erect position ▷ n 4 a vertical support, such as a post 5 short for **upright piano** 6 the state of being vertical › **uprightness** n
upright piano n a piano which has a rectangular vertical case
uprising n a revolt or rebellion
up-river adj, adv nearer the source of a river: we sailed slowly up-river; the village of Juffure, four days up-river
uproar n 1 a commotion or disturbance characterized by loud noise and confusion 2 angry public criticism or debates: the decision to close the railway led to an uproar
uproarious adj 1 very funny 2 (of laughter) loud and boisterous
uproot vb 1 to pull up by or as if by the roots 2 to displace (a person or people) from their native or usual surroundings 3 to remove or destroy utterly: we must uproot all remnants of feudalism
Upsala n a variant spelling of **Uppsala**
ups and downs pl n alternating periods of good and bad luck or high and low spirits
upscale informal adj (up-skale) 1 of or for the upper end of an economic or social scale; upmarket ▷ vb (up-skale) **-scaling, -scaled** 2 to increase the scale of
upset adj 1 emotionally or physically disturbed or distressed ▷ vb **-setting, -set** 2 to turn or tip over 3 to disrupt the normal state or progress of: bad weather upset their plans 4 to disturb mentally or emotionally ▷ 5 to make physically ill: it still seems to upset my stomach ▷ n 6 an unexpected defeat or reversal, as in a contest or plans 7 a disturbance or disorder of the emotions, mind, or body › **upsetting** adj
upset price n chiefly Scot, US and Canad the lowest price acceptable for something that is for sale by auction, usually a house
upshot n the final result or conclusion; outcome [up + shot]
upside down adj 1 with the bottom where the top would normally be; inverted 2 informal confused or jumbled ▷ adv 3 in an inverted fashion 4 in a chaotic manner or into a chaotic state: recent events have turned many people's lives upside down [by folk etymology, from upsodown]
upsides adv informal, chiefly Brit (foll. by with) equal or level with, as through revenge
upstage adv 1 on, at, or to the rear of the stage ▷ adj 2 at

the back half of the stage ▷ *vb* **-staging, -staged** **3** to move upstage of another actor, forcing him or her to turn away from the audience **4** *informal* to draw attention to oneself and away from someone else

upstairs *adv* **1** to or on an upper floor of a building **2** *informal* to or into a higher rank or office ▷ *n* **3** an upper floor ▷ *adj* **4** situated on an upper floor: *an upstairs bedroom*

upstanding *adj* **1** of good character **2** upright and vigorous in build

upstart *n* a person who has risen suddenly to a position of power and behaves arrogantly

upstream *adv, adj* in or towards the higher part of a stream; against the current

upsurge *n* a rapid rise or swell

upswing *n* **1** *econ* a recovery period in the trade cycle **2** any increase or improvement

upsy-daisy *or* **upsadaisy** *interj* an expression of reassurance, usually used to a child, for example when it stumbles or is being lifted up [originally *up-a-daisy*]

uptake *n* **1** *quick or* **slow on the uptake** *informal* quick or slow to understand or learn **2** the use or consumption of something by a machine or part of the body: *the uptake of oxygen into the blood*

upthrust *n* **1** an upward push **2** *geology* a violent upheaval of the earth's surface

uptight *adj informal* **1** nervously tense, irritable, or angry **2** unable to express one's feelings

up-to-date *adj* modern or fashionable: *an up-to-date kitchen*

up-to-the-minute *adj* the latest or most modern possible: *up-to-the-minute news about what's on in town*

uptown *US and Canad adj, adv* **1** towards, in, or relating to some part of a town that is away from the centre ▷ *n* **2** such a part of town, esp. a residential part

upturn *n* **1** an upward trend or improvement ▷ *vb* **2** to turn or cause to turn over or upside down

UPVC unplasticized polyvinyl chloride

upward *adj* **1** directed or moving towards a higher place or level ▷ *adv* also: **upwards 2** from a lower to a higher place, level, or condition **3** **upward** *or* **upwards of** more than (the stated figure): *a crowd estimated at upward of one hundred thousand people*

upward mobility *n* movement from a lower to a higher economic and social status

upwind *adv* **1** into or against the wind **2** towards or on the side where the wind is blowing ▷ *adj* **3** going against the wind **4** on the windward side

Ur *n* an ancient city of Sumer located on a former channel of the Euphrates

Ural *n* a river in central Russia, rising in the S Ural Mountains and flowing south to the Caspian Sea. Length: 2534 km (1575 miles)

Ural Mountains *or* **Urals** *pl n* a mountain system in W central Russia, extending over 2000 km (1250 miles) from the Arctic Ocean towards the Aral Sea: forms part of the geographical boundary between Europe and Asia; one of the richest mineral areas in the world, with many associated major industrial centres. Highest peak: Mount Narodnaya, 1894 m (6214 ft)

Urania *n Greek myth* the Muse of astronomy

uranium (yew-**rain**-ee-um) *n chem* a radioactive silvery-white metallic element of the actinide series. It is used chiefly as a source of nuclear energy by fission of the radioisotope **uranium 235**. Symbol: U [from URANUS, from the fact that the element was discovered soon after the planet]

Uranus *n* **1** *Greek myth* a god; the personification of the sky **2** the seventh planet from the sun [Greek *Ouranos* heaven]

urban *adj* **1** of or living in a city or town **2** relating to modern pop music of African-American origin, such as hip-hop [Latin *urbs* city]

Urban II *n* original name *Odo or Udo*. ?1042–99, French ecclesiastic; pope (1088–99). He inaugurated the First

Crusade at the Council of Clermont (1095)

Urban VI *n* original name *Bartolomeo Prignano*. ?1318–89, Italian ecclesiastic; pope (1378–89). His policies led to the election of an antipope by the French cardinals, thus beginning the Great Schism in the West

Urban VIII *n* original name *Maffeo Barberini*. 1568–1644, Italian ecclesiastic; pope (1623–44) during the Thirty Years' War, in which he supported Richelieu against the Hapsburgs

urbane *adj* polite, elegant, and sophisticated in manner [Latin *urbanus* of the town]

urbanity *n* the quality of being urbane

urbanize *or* **-nise** *vb* **-nizing, -nized** *or* **-nising, -nised** to make a rural area more industrialized and urban ⟩ **urbanization** *or* **-nisation** *n*

urchin *n* **1** a mischievous child **2** See **sea urchin** [Latin *ericius* hedgehog]

Urdu (oor-doo) *n* an Indic language of the Indo-European family which is an official language of Pakistan and is also spoken in India [Hindustani (*zabāni*) *urdū* (language of the) camp]

urea (**yew**-ree-a) *n* a white soluble crystalline compound found in urine [Greek *ouron* urine]

ureter (yew-**reet**-er) *n* the tube that carries urine from the kidney to the bladder [Greek *ourein* to urinate]

urethra (yew-**reeth**-ra) *n* the tube that in most mammals carries urine from the bladder out of the body [Greek *ourein* to urinate]

urethritis (yew-rith-**rite**-iss) *n* inflammation of the urethra causing a discharge and painful urination ⟩ **urethritic** *adj*

Urey *n* Harold Clayton. 1893–1981, US chemist, who discovered the heavy isotope of hydrogen, deuterium (1932), and worked on methods of separating uranium isotopes: Nobel prize for chemistry 1934

Urfa *n* a city in SE Turkey: market centre. Pop: 451 000 (2005 est). Ancient name: **Edessa**

Urfé *n* Honoré d'. 1568–1625, French writer, whose pastoral *L'Astrée* (1607–27) is considered the first French novel

Urga *n* the former name (until 1924) of **Ulan Bator**

urge *n* **1** a strong impulse, inner drive, or yearning ▷ *vb* **urging, urged 2** to plead with or press someone to do something: *he urged his readers to do the same* **3** to advocate earnestly and persistently: *I have long urged this change* **4** (often foll. by *on*) to force or hasten onwards: *something very powerful urged him on* [Latin *urgere*]

urgent *adj* **1** requiring speedy action or attention: *an urgent inquiry* **2** earnest and forceful: *she heard loud urgent voices in the corridor* [Latin *urgere* to urge] ⟩ **urgency** *n* ⟩ **urgently** *adv*

Uri *n* one of the original three cantons of Switzerland, in the centre of the country: mainly German-speaking and Roman Catholic. Capital: Altdorf. Pop: 35 200 (2002 est). Area: 1075 sq km (415 sq miles)

uric (**yew**-rik) *adj* of or derived from urine

uric acid *n* a white odourless crystalline acid present in the blood and urine

urinal *n* **1** a sanitary fitting, used by men for urination **2** a room containing urinals

urinary *adj anatomy* of urine or the organs that secrete and pass urine

urinary bladder *n* a membranous sac that can expand in which urine excreted from the kidneys is stored

urinate *vb* **-nating, -nated** to excrete urine ⟩ **urination** *n*

urine *n* the pale yellow fluid excreted by the kidneys, containing waste products from the blood. It is stored in the bladder and discharged through the urethra [Latin *urina*]

urinogenital (yew-rin-oh-**jen**-it-al) *adj* same as **urogenital**

URL uniform resource locator: a standardized address of a location on the internet

Urmia *or* **Orumiyeh** *n* **Lake Urmia** a shallow lake in NW

u

Iran, at an altitude of 1300 m (4250 ft): the largest lake in Iran, varying in area from 4000–6000 sq km (1500–2300 sq miles) between autumn and spring

Urmston *n* a town in NW England, in Trafford unitary authority, Greater Manchester. Pop: 40 964 (2001)

urn *n* **1** a vaselike container, usually with a foot and a rounded body **2** a vase used as a container for the ashes of the dead **3** a large metal container, with a tap, used for making and holding tea or coffee [Latin *urna*]

urogenital (yew-roh-jen-it-al) *or* **urinogenital** *adj* of the urinary and genital organs and their functions. Also: **genitourinary**

urology (yew-rol-a-jee) *n* the branch of medicine concerned with the urinary system and its diseases

Urquhart *n* Sir **Thomas**. 1611–60, Scottish author and translator of Rabelais' *Gargantua* and *Pantagruel* (1653; 1693)

Urquhart Castle *n* a castle near Drumnadrochit in Highland, Scotland: situated on Loch Ness

ursine *adj* of or like a bear [Latin *ursus* a bear]

Ursula *n* Saint. a legendary British princess of the fourth or fifth century AD, said to have been martyred together with 11 000 virgins by the Huns at Cologne. Feast day: Oct 21

Uru. Uruguay

Uruapan *n* a city in SW Mexico, in Michoacán state: agricultural trading centre. Pop: 282 000 (2005 est)

Uruguay *n* a republic in South America, on the Atlantic: Spanish colonization began in 1624, followed by Portuguese settlement in 1680; revolted against Spanish rule in 1820 but was annexed by the Portuguese to Brazil; gained independence in 1825. It consists mainly of rolling grassy plains, low hills, and plateaus. Official language: Spanish. Religion: Roman Catholic majority. Currency: peso. Capital: Montevideo. Pop: 3 324 460 (2013 est). Area: 176 215 sq km (68 037 sq miles)

Uruguayan *adj* **1** of or relating to Uruguay or its inhabitants ▷ *n* **2** a native or inhabitant of Uruguay

Urumchi, Ürümqi *or* **Wu-lu-mu-ch'i** *n* a city in NW China, capital of Xinjiang Uygur Autonomous Region: trading centre on a N route between China and central Asia. Pop: 1 562 000 (2005 est). Former name: **Tihwa**

Urundi *n* the former name (until 1962) of **Burundi**

us *pron* (*objective*) **1** refers to the speaker or writer and another person or other people: *the bond between us* **2** refers to all people or people in general: *this table shows us the tides* **3** *informal* me: *give us a kiss!* **4** *formal* same as **me¹** used by monarchs [Old English *ūs*]

USAGE See at me¹.

US *or* **U.S.** United States
USA *or* **U.S.A.** United States of America
usable *adj* able to be used ▷ **usability** *n*
usage *n* **1** regular or constant use: *a move to reduce pesticide usage* **2** the way in which a word is actually used in a language **3** a particular meaning or use that a word can have [Latin *usus* a use]
USB Universal Serial Bus: a standard for connection sockets on computers and other electronic equipment
USB drive *n computers* a small portable data storage device with a USB connection
use *vb* **using, used** **1** to put into service or action; employ for a given purpose: *use a garden fork to mix them together* **2** to choose or employ regularly: *what sort of toothpaste do you use?* **3** to take advantage of; exploit: *I used Jason and he used me* **4** to consume or expend: *a manufacturing plant uses 1000 tonnes of steel a month* ▷ *n* **5** the act or fact of using or being used: *large-scale use of pesticides* **6** the ability or permission to use **7** need or opportunity to use: *the Colombian government had no use for them* **8** usefulness or advantage: *there is no use in complaining* **9** the purpose for which something is used **10** have no use for **a** to have no need of **b** to have a contemptuous dislike for **11** make use of

a to employ; use **b** to exploit (a person) ▶ See also **use up** [Latin *usus* having used] ▷ **user** *n*

use-by date *n* the date on packaged food after which it should not be sold

used *adj* second-hand: *it was a used car*

used to *adj* **1** accustomed to: *I am used to being a medical guinea pig* ▷ *vb* **2** used as an auxiliary to express habitual or accustomed actions or states taking place in the past but not continuing to be the case in the present: *he used to vanish into his studio for days*

USAGE The most common negative form of *used to* is *didn't used to* (or *didn't use to*), but in formal contexts *used not to* is preferred.

useful *adj* **1** able to be used advantageously or for several purposes **2** *informal* commendable or capable: *a useful hurdler* ▷ **usefully** *adv* ▷ **usefulness** *n*

useless *adj* **1** having no practical use **2** *informal* ineffectual, weak, or stupid: *I'm useless at most things* ▷ **uselessly** *adv* ▷ **uselessness** *n*

Usenet *n computers* a vast collection of newsgroups that follow agreed naming, maintaining, and distribution practices

user-friendly *adj* easy to familiarize oneself with, understand, and use

username *n computers* a name that someone uses for identification purposes when logging onto a computer or certain computer applications

use up *vb* to finish a supply of something completely

Ushant *n* an island off the NW coast of France, at the tip of Brittany: scene of naval battles in 1778 and 1794 between France and Britain. Area: about 16 sq km (6 sq miles). French name: **Ouessant**

U-shaped valley *n* a steep-sided valley caused by glacial erosion

usher *n* **1** an official who shows people to their seats, as in a church **2** a person who acts as doorkeeper in a court of law ▷ *vb* **3** to conduct or escort **4** (foll. by *in*) to happen immediately before something or cause it to happen; herald: *the French Revolution ushered in a new age* [Old French *huissier* doorkeeper]

usherette *n* a woman assistant in a cinema, who shows people to their seats

Usk *n* a river in SE Wales, flowing southeast and south to the Bristol Channel. Length: 113 km (70 miles)

Üsküb *n* the Turkish name (1392–1913) for **Skopje**

Üsküdar *n* a town in NW Turkey, across the Bosporus from Istanbul: formerly a terminus of caravan routes from Syria and Asia; base of the British army in the Crimean War. Pop: 495 118 (2000). Former name: **Scutari**

Usman dan Fodio *n* 1754–1817, African mystic and revolutionary leader, who created a Muslim state in Nigeria

USP *econ* unique selling proposition (*or* point)

Uspallata Pass *n* a pass over the Andes in S South America, between Mendoza (Argentina) and Santiago (Chile). Height: 3840 m (12 600 ft). Also called: **La Cumbre**

Ussher *or* **Usher** *n* James. 1581–1656, Irish prelate and scholar. His system of biblical chronology, which dated the creation at 4004 BC, was for long accepted

USSR Union of Soviet Socialist Republics

Ussuri *n* a river in E central Asia, flowing north, forming part of the Chinese border with Russia, to the Amur River. Length: about 800 km (500 miles)

Ústí nad Labem *n* a port in the Czech Republic, on the Elbe River: textile and chemical industries. Pop: 95 000 (2005 est)

Ustinov *n* Sir Peter (Alexander). 1921–2004, British stage and film actor, director, dramatist, and raconteur

Ust-Kamenogorsk *n* a city in E Kazakhstan: centre of a zinc-, lead-, and copper-mining area. Pop: 307 000 (2005 est)

Ustyurt *or* **Ust Urt** *n* an arid plateau in central Asia, between the Caspian and Aral seas in Kazakhstan and Uzbekistan. Area: about 238 000 sq km (92 000 sq miles)

usual *adj* **1** of the most normal, frequent, or regular type: *the usual assortment of stories* ▷ *n* **2** ordinary or commonplace events: *the dirt was nothing out of the usual* **3 as usual** as happens normally **4 the usual** *informal* the habitual or usual drink [Latin *usus* use] **> usually** *adv*

Usumbura *n* the former name of **Bujumbura**

usurp (yewz-**zurp**) *vb* to seize a position or power without authority [Latin *usurpare* to take into use] **> usurpation** *n* **> usurper** *n*

usury (**yewz**-yoor-ree) *n, pl* **-ries** *old-fashioned* **1** the practice of loaning money at an exorbitant rate of interest **2** an unlawfully high rate of interest [Latin *usura* usage] **> usurer** *n*

Ut. *or* **UT** Utah

Utagawa Kuniyoshi *n* original name *Igusa Magosabwo*. 1797–1861, Japanese painter and printmaker of the ukiyo-e school, best known for his prints of warriors and landscapes

Utah *n* a state of the western US: settled by Mormons in 1847; situated in the Great Basin and the Rockies, with the Great Salt Lake in the northwest; mainly arid and mountainous. Capital: Salt Lake City. Pop: 2 351 467 (2003 est). Area: 212 628 sq km (82 096 sq miles). Abbreviation: **Ut.**, (with zip code) **UT**

Utahan *adj* **1** of or relating to Utah or its inhabitants ▷ *n* **2** a native or inhabitant of Utah

Utamaro *n* Kitagawa, original name *Kitagawa Nebsuyoshi*. 1753–1806, Japanese master of wood-block prints, of the ukiyo-e school; noted esp. for his portraits of women

ute *n* Austral and NZ informal a utility truck

utensil *n* a tool or container for practical use: *cooking utensils* [Latin *utensilia* necessaries]

uterine *adj* of or affecting the womb

uterus (**yew**-ter-russ) *n, pl* **uteri** (**yew**-ter-rye) *anatomy* a hollow muscular organ in the pelvic cavity of female mammals, which houses the developing fetus; womb [Latin]

Uthman *n* died 656 AD, third caliph of Islam, who established an authoritative version of the Koran

Utica *n* an ancient city on the N coast of Africa, northwest of Carthage

utilidor (yew-**till**-lid-or) *n Canad* above-ground insulated casing for pipes carrying water, sewerage, and electricity in permafrost regions [UTILITY + -*dor*, from Greek *dōron* gift]

utilitarian *adj* **1** useful rather than beautiful **2** of utilitarianism ▷ *n* **3** an advocate of utilitarianism

utilitarianism *n ethics* the doctrine that the right thing to do is that which brings about the greatest good for the greatest number

utility *n, pl* **-ties 1** usefulness **2** something useful **3** a public service, such as water or electricity ▷ *adj* **4** designed for use rather than beauty: *utility fabrics* [Latin *utilitas* usefulness, from *uti* to use]

utility room *n* a room with equipment for domestic work like washing and ironing

utility truck *n Austral and NZ* a small truck with an open body and low sides

utilize *or* **-lise** *vb* **-lizing, -lized** *or* **-lising, -lised** to make practical or worthwhile use of **> utilization** *or* **-lisation** *n*

utmost *adj* **1** of the greatest possible degree or amount: *the utmost seriousness* **2** at the furthest limit: *the utmost point* ▷ *n* **3** the greatest possible degree or amount: *I was doing my utmost to comply* [Old English *ūtemest*]

Utopia (yew-**tope**-ee-a) *n* any real or imaginary society,

place, or state considered to be perfect or ideal [coined by Sir Thomas More in 1516 as the title of his book that described an imaginary island representing the perfect society, literally: no place, from Greek *ou* not + *topos* a place] **> Utopian** *adj*

Utrecht *n* **1** a province of the W central Netherlands. Capital: Utrecht. Pop: 1 152 000 (2003 est). Area: 1362 sq km (526 sq miles) **2** a city in the central Netherlands, capital of Utrecht province: scene of the signing (1579) of the **Union of Utrecht** (the foundation of the later kingdom of the Netherlands) and of the **Treaty of Utrecht** (1713), ending the War of the Spanish Succession. Pop: 265 000 (2003 est)

Utrillo *n* Maurice. 1883–1955, French painter, noted for his Parisian street scenes

Uttarakhand *n* a state of N India, created in 2000 from the N part of Uttar Pradesh: in the Himalayas, rising to over 7500 m (25 000 ft); rice, tea, and timber. Capital: Dehra Dun. Pop: 8 479 562 (2001). Area: 51 125 sq km (19 739 sq miles). Former name: **Uttaranchal**

Uttar Pradesh *n* a state of N India: the most populous state; originated in 1877 with the merging of Agra and Oudh as the United Provinces; augmented by the states of Rampur, Benares, and Tehri-Garhwal in 1949; the N Himalayan region passed to the new state of Uttaranchal (now Uttarakhand) in 2000; now consists mostly of the Upper Ganges plain; agricultural. Capital: Lucknow. Pop: 166 052 859 (2001). Area: 243 350 sq km (93 933 sq miles)

utter¹ *vb* **1** to express something in sounds or words: *she hadn't uttered a single word* **2** *criminal law* to put counterfeit money or forged cheques into circulation [Middle Dutch *ūteren* to make known]

utter² *adj* total or absolute: *utter amazement* [Old English *ūtera* outer] **> utterly** *adv*

utterance *n* **1** something expressed in speech or writing **2** the expression in words of ideas, thoughts, or feelings

uttermost *adj, n* same as **utmost**

U-turn *n* **1** a turn, made by a vehicle, in the shape of a U, resulting in a reversal of direction **2** a complete change in policy

Utzon *n* Jørn. 1918–2008, Danish architect known primarily for his unique design for the Sydney Opera House (1966)

UV ultraviolet

UV-A *or* **UVA** *n* ultraviolet radiation with a range of 320-380 nanometres

UV-B *or* **UVB** *n* ultraviolet radiation with a range of 280-320 nanometres

uvula (**yew**-view-la) *n* the small fleshy part of the soft palate that hangs in the back of the throat [Medieval Latin, literally: a little grape] **> uvular** *adj*

Uxbridge *n* a town in SE England, part of the Greater London borough of Hillingdon since 1965; chiefly residential; seat of Brunel University (1966)

Uxmal *n* an ancient ruined city in SE Mexico, in Yucatán: capital of the later Maya empire

uxorious (ux-or-ee-uss) *adj* excessively fond of or dependent on one's wife [Latin *uxor* wife]

Uys *n* Pieter-Dirk. born 1945, South African comedian and satirist, noted for creating the female character Evita Bezuidenhout

Uzbekistan *n* a republic in central Asia: annexed by Russia in the 19th century; it became a separate Soviet Socialist republic in 1924 and gained independence in 1991. Official language: Uzbek. Religion: believers are mainly Muslim. Currency: sum. Capital: Tashkent. Pop: 28 661 637 (2013 est). Area: 449 600 sq km (173 546 sq miles)

u

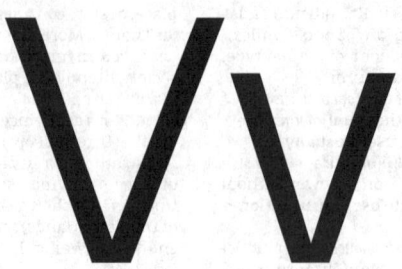

V **1** *chem* vanadium **2** volt **3** the Roman numeral for five

v. **1** verb **2** verse **3** versus **4** volume

VA *or* **Va.** Virginia

Vaal *n* a river in South Africa, rising in the Drakensberg and flowing west to join the Orange River. Length: 1160 km (720 miles)

Vaasa *n* a port in W Finland, on the Gulf of Bothnia: the provisional capital of Finland (1918); textile industries. Pop: 56 953 (2003 est). Former name: **Nikolainkaupunki**

vac *n Brit informal* short for **vacation**

vacancy *n*, *pl* **-cies** **1** an unoccupied job or position: *he had heard of a vacancy for a librarian* **2** an unoccupied room in a hotel or guesthouse: *the last hotel we tried had a vacancy* **3** the state of being unoccupied

vacant *adj* **1** (of a toilet, room, etc.) unoccupied or not being used: *I sat down in a vacant chair* **2** (of a job or position) unfilled at the present time **3** having or suggesting a lack of interest or understanding: *he sat there staring at me with a vacant look* **4** (of a period of time) not set aside for any particular activity: *two slots in his programme have been left vacant* [Latin *vacare* to be empty] **›vacantly** *adv*

vacate *vb* **-cating, -cated** **1** to cause (something) to be empty by leaving: *do you wish us to vacate the room?* **2** to give up (a job or position)

vacation *n* **1** *Brit and S African* a time of the year when the universities or law courts are closed **2** *US, Canad and Austral* same as **holiday** (2) [Latin *vacatio* freedom]

vaccinate *vb* **-nating, -nated** to inject (someone) with a vaccine in order to protect them against a disease: *children vaccinated against meningitis* **›vaccination** *n*

vaccine *n* **1** *med* a substance made from the germs that cause a disease which is given to people to prevent them getting the disease **2** *computers* a piece of software that detects and removes computer viruses from a system [Latin *variolae vaccinae* cowpox (source of the first smallpox vaccine), from *vacca* a cow]

vacillate (vass-ill-late) *vb* **-lating, -lated** to keep changing one's mind or opinions about something: *he vacillated between republican and monarchist sentiments* [Latin *vacillare* to sway] **›vacillation** *n*

vacuity *n* an absence of intelligent thought or ideas: *I suggested to one of his advisers that his vacuity was a handicap in these debates*

vacuous *adj* **1** lacking in intelligent ideas **2** showing no sign of intelligence or understanding: *her smile was vacuous but without malice* [Latin *vacuus* empty]

vacuum *n*, *pl* **vacuums** *or* **vacua** **1** a space which contains no air or other gas **2** a vacant place or position that needs to be filled by someone or something else: *the army moved in to fill the power vacuum* **3** short for **vacuum cleaner** ▷ *vb* **4** to clean (something) with a vacuum cleaner [Latin *vacuus* empty]

vacuum cleaner *n* an electric machine which sucks up dust and dirt from carpets and upholstery **›vacuum cleaning** *n*

vacuum flask *n* a double-walled flask with a vacuum between the walls that keeps drinks hot or cold

vacuum-packed *adj* (of food) packed in an airtight container in order to preserve freshness

vacuum tube *or* **vacuum valve** *n* same as **valve** (3)

vade mecum (vah-dee make-um) *n* a handbook carried for immediate use when needed [Latin, literally: go with me]

Vadodara *n* a city in W India, in SE Gujarat: textile manufacturing. Pop: 1 306 035 (2001). Former name (until 1976): **Baroda**

Vaduz *n* the capital of Liechtenstein, in the Rhine valley: an old market town, dominated by a medieval castle, residence of the prince of Liechtenstein. Pop: 5005 (2003 est)

vagabond *n* a person who travels from place to place and has no fixed home or job [Latin *vagari* to roam]

vagary (vaig-a-ree) *n*, *pl* **-garies** an unpredictable change in a situation or in someone's behaviour: *I was unused to the vagaries of the retailer's world* [probably from Latin *vagari* to roam]

vagina (vaj-jine-a) *n* the passage in most female mammals that extends from the neck of the womb to the external genitals [Latin: sheath] **›vaginal** *adj*

vagrant (vaig-rant) *n* **1** a person who moves from place to place and has no regular home or job ▷ *adj* **2** wandering about [probably from Old French *waucrant*] **›vagrancy** *n*

vague *adj* **1** not expressed or explained clearly: *he thought of his instructions, so vague and imprecise* **2** deliberately withholding information: *he was rather vague about the whole deal* **3** (of a sound or shape) unable to be heard or seen clearly: *he heard some vague sound from downstairs* **4** (of a person) not concentrating or thinking clearly: *she was mumbling to herself in a vague way* **5** not clearly established or known: *it was a vague rumour which would fade away and be forgotten* [Latin *vagus* wandering] **›vaguely** *adv* **›vagueness** *n*

vain *adj* **1** excessively proud of one's appearance or achievements **2** senseless or unsuccessful: *he made a vain attempt to lighten the atmosphere* ▷ *n* **3 in vain** without achieving the desired effects or results: *the old man searched in vain for his son* [Latin *vanus*] **›vainly** *adv*

vainglorious *adj* boastful or proud: *his vainglorious posturing had earned him numerous powerful enemies*

Vajpayee *n* A(tal) B(ihari). born 1924, Indian politician; prime minister of India (1996, 1998–2004)

Valais *n* a canton of S Switzerland: includes the entire valley of the upper Rhône and the highest peaks in Switzerland; produces a quarter of Switzerland's hydroelectricity. Capital: Sion. Pop: 281 000 (2002 est). Area: 5231 sq km (2020 sq miles). German name: **Wallis**

valance (val-lenss) *n* a short piece of decorative material hung round the edge of a bed or above a window [perhaps after VALENCE]

Valdai Hills *pl n* a region of hills and plateaus in

NW Russia, between Moscow and St Petersburg. Greatest height: 346 m (1135 ft)

Val-de-Marne *n* a department of N France, in Île-de-France region. Capital: Créteil. Pop: 1 239 352 (2003 est). Area: 244 sq km (95 sq miles)

Valdivia¹ *n* a port in S Chile, on the **Valdivia River** about 19 km (12 miles) from the Pacific: developed chiefly by German settlers in the 1850s; university (1954). Pop: 136 000 (2005 est)

Valdivia² *n* Pedro de. ?1500–54, Spanish soldier; conqueror of Chile

Val-d'Oise *n* a department of N France, in Île-de-France region. Capital: Pontoise. Pop: 1 121 614 (2003 est). Area: 1249 sq km (487 sq miles)

vale *n literary* a valley [Latin *vallis* valley]

valediction (val-lid-**dik**-shun) *n* a farewell speech [Latin *vale* farewell + *dicere* to say] ❯ **valedictory** *adj*

valence (**vale**-enss) *n chem* the ability of atoms and chemical groups to form compounds

Valence *n* a town in SE France, on the River Rhône. Pop: 64 260 (1999)

Valencia *n* **1** a port in E Spain, capital of Valencia province, on the Mediterranean: the third largest city in Spain; capital of the Moorish kingdom of Valencia (1021–1238); university (1501). Pop: 780 653 (2003 est). Latin name: **Valentia** **2** a region and former kingdom of E Spain, on the Mediterranean **3** a city in N Venezuela: one of the two main industrial centres in Venezuela. Pop: 2 330 000 (2005 est)

Valenciennes *n* a town in N France, on the River Escaut: a coal-mining and heavy industrial centre. Pop: 41 278 (1999)

valency *or especially US and Canad* **valence** *n*, *pl* **-cies** *or* **-ces** *chem* the number of atoms of hydrogen that an atom or chemical group is able to combine with in forming compounds [Latin *valere* to be strong]

Valens *n* ?328–378 AD, emperor of the Eastern Roman Empire (364–378); appointed by his elder brother Valentinian I, emperor of the Western Empire

valentine *n* **1** a card sent, often anonymously, as an expression of love on Saint Valentine's Day, February 14 **2** the person to whom one sends such a card

Valentine *n* Saint. 3rd century AD, Christian martyr, associated by historical accident with the custom of sending valentines; bishop of Terni. Feast day: Feb 14

Valentinian I *or* **Valentinianus I** *n* 321–375 AD, emperor of the Western Roman Empire (364–375); appointed his brother Valens to rule the Eastern Empire

Valentinian II *or* **Valentinianus II** *n* 371–392 AD, emperor of the Western Roman Empire (375–392), reigning jointly with his half brother Gratian until 383

Valentinian III *or* **Valentinianus III** *n* ?419–455 AD, emperor of the Western Roman Empire (425–455). His government lost Africa to the Vandals. With Pope Leo I he issued (444) an edict giving the bishop of Rome supremacy over the provincial churches

Valentino *n* Rudolph, original name *Rodolpho Guglielmi di Valentina d'Antonguolla*. 1895–1926, US silent-film actor, born in Italy. He is famous for his romantic roles in such films as *The Sheik* (1921)

Vale of Glamorgan *n* a county borough of S Wales, created in 1996 from parts of South Glamorgan and Mid Glamorgan. Administrative centre: Barry. Pop: 121 200 (2003 est). Area: 295 sq km (114 sq miles)

valerian *n* a plant with small white or pinkish flowers and a medicinal root [Medieval Latin *valeriana (herba)* (herb) of Valerius]

Valerian *n* Latin name *Publius Licinius Valerianus*. died 260 AD, Roman emperor (253–260): renewed persecution of the Christians; defeated by the Persians

Valéry *n* Paul. 1871–1945, French poet and essayist, influenced by the symbolists, esp. Mallarmé. He wrote lyric poetry, rich in imagery, as in *La Jeune Parque* (1917) and *Album de vers anciens 1890–1900* (1920)

valet *n* **1** a male servant employed to look after another man ▷ *vb* **-eting, -eted** **2** to act as a valet (for) **3** to clean the bodywork and interior of (a car) as a professional service [Old French *vaslet* page]

valeta *or* **veleta** (vel-**lee**-ta) *n* an old-time dance in triple time [Spanish *veleta* weather vane]

Valetta *n* a variant spelling of Valletta

valetudinarian (val-lit-yew-din-**air**-ee-an) *n* **1** a person who is chronically sick **2** a person who continually worries about his or her health [Latin *valetudo* state of health] ❯ **valetudinarianism** *n*

Valhalla *n Norse myth* the great hall of Odin where warriors who die as heroes in battle dwell eternally [Old Norse *valr* slain warriors + *höll* hall]

valiant *adj* very brave: *it was a valiant attempt to rescue the struggling victim* [Latin *valere* to be strong] ❯ **valiantly** *adv*

valid *adj* **1** based on sound reasoning: *I think that's a very valid question* **2** legally acceptable: *she must produce a valid driving licence* **3** important or serious enough to say or do: *religious broadcasting has a valid purpose* [Latin *validus* robust] ❯ **validity** *n*

validate *vb* **-dating, -dated** **1** to prove (a claim or statement) to be true or correct **2** to give legal force or official confirmation to ❯ **validation** *n*

valise (val-**leez**) *n old-fashioned* a small suitcase [Italian *valigia*]

Valium *n trademark* a drug used as a tranquillizer

Valkyrie (val-**keer**-ee) *n Norse myth* any of the beautiful maidens who take the dead heroes to Valhalla [Old Norse *valr* slain warriors + *kyrja* chooser]

Valla *n* Lorenzo. 1405–57, Italian humanist scholar. His writings include *De voluptate* (1431), a philosophical dialogue on pleasure

Valladolid *n* **1** a city in NW Spain: residence of the Spanish court in the 16th century; university (1346). Pop: 321 143 (2003 est) **2** the former name (until 1828) of Morelia

Valle d'Aosta *n* an autonomous region of NW Italy: under many different rulers until passing to the house of Savoy in the 11th century; established as an autonomous region in 1944. Capital: Aosta. Pop: 120 909 (2003 est). Area: 3263 sq km (1260 sq miles)

Valle-Inclán *n* Rámon María del. 1866–1936, Spanish novelist and dramatist. His works include the novel *Tirano Banderas* (1926) and the satirical play *Don Friolera's Horns* (1925)

Vallejo *n* César (Abraham). 1892–1938, Peruvian poet, living in France and Spain from 1923: noted for his experimental style in such works as *Trilce* (1922)

Valletta *or* **Valetta** *n* the capital of Malta, on the NE coast: founded by the Knights Hospitallers, after the victory over the Turks in 1565; became a major naval base after Malta's annexation by Britain (1814). Pop: 84 000 (2005 est)

valley *n* a long stretch of land between hills, often with a river flowing through it [Latin *vallis*]

Valley Forge *n* an area in SE Pennsylvania, northwest of Philadelphia: winter camp (1777–78) of Washington and the American Revolutionary Army

Valley of Ten Thousand Smokes *n* a volcanic region of SW Alaska, formed by the massive eruption of Mount Katmai in 1912; jets of steam issue from vents up to 45 m (150 ft) across

Vallombrosa *n* a village and resort in central Italy, in Tuscany region: 11th-century Benedictine monastery

Valois *n* a historic region and former duchy of N France

Valona *n* another name for Vlorë

valour *or US* **valor** *n literary* great bravery, esp. in battle [Latin *valere* to be strong] ❯ **valorous** *adj*

Valparaíso *n* a port in central Chile, on a wide bay of the Pacific: the third largest city and chief port of Chile; two universities. Pop: 275 000 (2005 est)

valuable *adj* **1** worth a large amount of money: *his house was furnished with valuable antique furniture* **2** of great use or

V

importance: *the investigations will provide valuable information* ▷ *n* **3 valuables** valuable articles of personal property, such as jewellery

valuation *n* **1 a** a formal assessment of how much something is worth: *they will arrange a valuation on your house* **2** the price arrived at by the process of valuing

value *n* **1** the desirability of something, often in terms of its usefulness or exchangeability **2** an amount of money considered to be a fair exchange for something: *50 kilos of cocaine with a high street value* **3** something worth the money it cost: *the set meal was value for money* **4 values** the moral principles and beliefs of a person or group **5** *maths* a particular number or quantity represented by a figure or symbol **6** *music* short for **time value** ▷ *vb* **-uing, -ued 7** to assess the worth or desirability of (something) **8** to hold (someone or something) in high regard [Latin *valere* to be worth] ▷ **valued** *adj* ▷ **valueless** *adj* ▷ **valuer** *n*

value-added tax *n* Brit and S African See **VAT**

value judgment *n* a personal opinion about something based on an individual's beliefs and not on facts which can be checked or proved

valve *n* **1** a part attached to a pipe or tube which controls the flow of gas or liquid **2** *anatomy* a small flap in a hollow organ, such as the heart, that controls the flow and direction of blood **3** a closed tube through which electrons move in a vacuum **4** *zoology* one of the hinged shells of an oyster or clam **5** *music* a device on some brass instruments by which the effective length of the tube may be varied [Latin *valva* a folding door]

valvular *adj* of or relating to valves: *valvular heart disease*

vamoose *vb* **-moosing, -moosed** *slang, chiefly US* to leave a place hurriedly [Spanish *vamos* let's go]

vamp¹ *informal n* **1 a** sexually attractive woman who seduces men ▷ *vb* **2** (of a woman) to seduce (a man) [short for *vampire*]

vamp² *vb* **vamp up** to make (a story, piece of music, etc.) seem new by inventing additional parts [Old French *avantpié* the front part of a shoe]

vampire *n* (in European folklore) a corpse that rises nightly from its grave to drink the blood of living people [from Magyar]

vampire bat *n* a bat of Central and South America that feeds on the blood of birds and mammals

van¹ *n* **1** a road vehicle with a roof and no side windows used to transport goods **2** *Brit* a closed railway wagon used to transport luggage, goods, or mail [shortened from *caravan*]

van² *n* short for **vanguard**

Van *n* **1** a city in E Turkey, on Lake Van. Pop: 377 000 (2005 est) **2 Lake Van** a salt lake in E Turkey, at an altitude of 1650 m (5400 ft): fed by melting snow and glaciers. Area: 3737 sq km (1433 sq miles)

vanadium *n chem* a silvery-white metallic element used to toughen steel. Symbol: **V** [Old Norse *Vanadís*, epithet of the goddess Freya]

Van Allen *n* James Alfred. 1914–2006, US physicist, noted for his use of satellites to investigate cosmic radiation in the upper atmosphere

Van Allen belt *n* either of two belts of charged particles which surround the Earth [after J. A. VAN ALLEN]

Vanbrugh *n* Sir John. 1664–1726, English dramatist and baroque architect. His best-known plays are the Restoration comedies *The Relapse* (1697) and *The Provok'd Wife* (1697). As an architect, he is noted esp. for Blenheim Palace

Van Buren *n* Martin. 1782–1862, US Democratic statesman; 8th president of the US (1837–41)

Vancouver¹ *n* **1** Vancouver Island an island of SW Canada, off the SW coast of British Columbia: separated from the Canadian mainland by the Strait of Georgia and Queen Charlotte Sound, and from the US mainland by Juan de Fuca Strait; the largest island off the W coast of North America. Chief town: Victoria. Pop: 706 243 (2001). Area: 32 137 sq km (12 408 sq miles) **2** a city in SW

Canada, in SW British Columbia: Canada's chief Pacific port, named after Captain George Vancouver: university (1908). Pop: 545 671 (2001) **3 Mount Vancouver** a mountain on the border between Canada and Alaska, in the St Elias Mountains. Height: 4785 m (15 700 ft)

Vancouver² *n* Captain George. 1757–98, English navigator, noted for his exploration of the Pacific coast of North America (1792–94)

V and A (in Britain) Victoria and Albert Museum

vandal *n* someone who deliberately causes damage to personal or public property [from the name of a Germanic tribe of the 3rd and 4th centuries AD] ▷ **vandalism** *n*

vandalize *or* **-lise** *vb* **-lizing, -lized** *or* **-lising, -lised** to cause damage to (personal or public property) deliberately

Vandemonian *n* **1** a native or inhabitant of the former Van Diemen's Land (now Tasmania) ▷ *adj* **2** of or relating to Van Diemen's Land or its inhabitants

Vanderbilt *n* Cornelius, known as *Commodore Vanderbilt*. 1794–1877, US steamship and railway magnate and philanthropist

Van der Hum *n* S African a liqueur made from tangerines [origin uncertain but possibly derived from the humorous uncertainty of the name, equivalent of *whatshisname*]

Van der Post *n* Sir Laurens (Jan). 1906–96, South African writer and traveller. His works include the travel books *Venture to the Interior* (1952), *The Lost World of the Kalahari* (1958), and *Testament to the Bushmen* (1984) and the novels *The Hunter and the Whale* (1967) and *The Admiral's Baby* (1996)

van der Waals *n* Johannes Diderik. 1837–1923, Dutch physicist, noted for his research on the equations of state of gases and liquids: Nobel prize for physics in 1910

van der Weyden *n* Rogier. ?1400–64, Flemish painter, esp. of religious works and portraits

van de Velde *n* **1** Adriaen. 1636–72, Dutch painter of landscapes with animals and figures **2** his uncle, **Esaias**. ?1591–1630, Dutch landscape and genre painter, noted for such works as *The Winter Scene* (1623) **3 Henry**. 1863–1957, Belgian architect and designer, who introduced the British Arts and Crafts movement to the Continent and helped to develop the Art Nouveau style **4 Willem**, known as *the Elder*: father of Adriaen van de Velde. 1611–93, Dutch marine painter, working in England as court painter to Charles II **5** his son, **Willem**, known as *the Younger*. 1633–1707, Dutch marine painter, working in England as court painter to Charles II

Van Diemen Gulf *n* an inlet of the Timor Sea in N Australia, in the Northern Territory

Van Diemen's Land *n* the former name (1642–1855) of Tasmania

Van Dyck *or* **Vandyke** *n* Sir Anthony. 1599–1641, Flemish painter; court painter to Charles I of England (1632–41). He is best known for his portraits of the aristocracy

Vandyke beard *n* a short pointed beard [after Sir Anthony VAN DYCK]

vane *n* **1** one of the blades forming part of the wheel of a windmill, a screw propeller, etc. **2** short for **weather vane** [Old English *fana*]

Vane *n* Sir Henry, known as *Sir Harry Vane*. 1613–62, English Puritan statesman and colonial administrator; governor of Massachusetts (1636–37). He was executed for high treason after the Restoration

Vänern *n* Lake Vänern a lake in SW Sweden: the largest lake in Sweden and W Europe; drains into the Kattegat. Area: 5585 sq km (2156 sq miles)

van Eyck *n* Jan. died 1441, Flemish painter; founder of the Flemish school of painting. His most famous work is the altarpiece *The Adoration of the Lamb*, in Ghent, in which he may have been assisted by his brother **Hubert**, died ?1426

Van Gogh *n* Vincent. 1853–90, Dutch postimpressionist painter, noted for his landscapes and portraits, in which colour is used essentially for its expressive and emotive value

vanguard n **1** the leading division or units of an army **2** the most advanced group or position in scientific research, a movement, etc.: *a distinguished architect in the vanguard of his profession* [Old French *avant-garde* advance guard]

Van Horne n Sir William (**Cornelius**). 1843–1915, Canadian railway executive, born in the US; oversaw the completion of the line from Port Moody to Montreal on the Canadian Pacific Railway

vanilla n **1** a flavouring for food such as ice cream, which comes from the pods of a tropical plant **2** a flavouring extract prepared from the beans of this plant and used in cooking ▷ *adj* **3** flavoured with vanilla: *vanilla essence* **4** *slang* ordinary or conventional: *a vanilla kind of guy* [Spanish *vainilla* pod]

vanish vb **1** to disappear suddenly: *the choppers vanished from radar screens at dawn yesterday* **2** to cease to exist: *the old landmarks had vanished* [Latin *evanescere* to evaporate]

vanishing cream n old-fashioned a cosmetic cream that is colourless once applied

vanishing point n the point in the distance where parallel lines appear to meet

vanity n **1** a feeling of pride about one's appearance or ability **2** (pl **-ties**) something about which one is vain: *it's one of my vanities that I can guess scents* [Latin *vanitas* emptiness]

vanity case n a small bag for holding cosmetics

vanity unit n a hand basin built into a surface, usually with a cupboard below it

vanquish vb literary to defeat (someone) in a battle, contest, or argument [Latin *vincere*]

van Riebeeck n Jan, full name *Johan Anthoniszoon van Riebeeck*. 1619–77, Dutch colonial administrator. Founder of the colony of the Cape of Good Hope (1652)

Van Rompuy n Herman. born 1947, Belgian politician; prime minister of Belgium (2008–09); president of the European Council (2009–14)

Vansittart n Robert Gilbert, 1st Baron Vansittart of Denham. 1881–1957, British diplomat and writer; a fierce opponent of Nazi Germany and of Communism

vantage n a state, position, or opportunity offering advantage [Old French *avantage* advantage]

vantage point n a position that gives one an overall view of a scene or situation

van't Hoff n Jacobus Hendricus. 1852–1911, Dutch physical chemist: founded stereochemistry with his theory of the asymmetric carbon atom; the first to apply thermodynamics to chemical reactions: Nobel prize for chemistry 1901

Vanua Levu n the second largest island of Fiji: mountainous. Area: 5535 sq km (2137 sq miles)

Vanuatu n a republic comprising a group of islands in the W Pacific, W of Fiji: a condominium under Anglo-French joint rule from 1906; attained partial autonomy in 1978 and full independence in 1980 as a member of the Commonwealth. Its economy is based chiefly on copra. Official languages: Bislama; French; English. Religion: Christian majority. Currency: vatu. Capital: Vila (on Efate). Pop: 261 565 (2013 est). Area: about 14 760 sq km (5700 sq miles). Official name: **Republic of Vanuatu**. Former name (until 1980): **New Hebrides**

Vanzetti n Bartolomeo. 1888–1927, US radical agitator, born in Italy: executed with Sacco in a case that had worldwide political repercussions

vape vb vaping, vaped informal to inhale vapour from an e-cigarette

vapid adj dull and uninteresting: *their publications were vapid and amateurish* [Latin *vapidus*] **> vapidity** n

vapor n US same as vapour

vaporize or **-rise** vb **-rizing, -rized** or **-rising, -rised** (of a liquid or solid) to change into vapour **> vaporization** or **-risation** n

vaporous adj resembling or full of vapour

vapour or US **vapor** n **1** a mass of tiny drops of water or other liquids in the air, which appear as a mist **2** the gaseous form of a substance that is usually a liquid or a solid **3 the vapours** old-fashioned a feeling of faintness, dizziness, and depression [Latin *vapor*]

Var n **1** a department of SE France, in Provence-Alpes-Côte-d'Azur region. Capital: Toulon. Pop: 946 305 (2003 est). Area: 6023 sq km (2349 sq miles) **2** a river in SE France, flowing southeast and south to the Mediterranean near Nice. Length: about 130 km (80 miles)

Varah n (**Edward**) **Chad**. 1911–2007, British Anglican clergyman, who founded (1953) the Samaritans counselling service

Varanasi n a city in NE India, in SE Uttar Pradesh on the River Ganges: probably dates from the 13th century BC; an early centre of Aryan philosophy and religion; a major place of pilgrimage for Hindus, Jains, Sikhs, and Buddhists, with many ghats along the Ganges; seat of the Banaras Hindu University (1916), India's leading university, and the Sanskrit University (1957). Pop: 1 100 748 (2001). Former names: **Benares**, **Banaras**

Vardar n a river in S Europe, rising in W Macedonia and flowing northeast, then past Skopje into Greece, where it is called the Axios and enters the Aegean at Thessaloníki. Length: about 320 km (200 miles)

Vardon n Harry. 1870–1937, British golfer

Varese n a historic city in N Italy, in Lombardy near Lake Varese: manufacturing centre, esp. for leather goods. Pop: 80 511 (2001)

Varèse n Edgar(d). 1883–1965, US composer, born in France. His works, which combine extreme dissonance with complex rhythms and the use of electronic techniques, include *Ionisation* (1931) and *Poème électronique* (1958)

Vargas n Getúlio Dornelles. 1883–1954, Brazilian statesman; president (1930–45; 1951–54)

Vargas Llosa n (**Jorge**) **Mario** (**Pedro**) born 1936, Peruvian novelist, writer, and political figure. His novels include *The City and the Dogs* (1963), *Conversation in the Cathedral* (1969), *The Storyteller* (1990), and *The Notebook of Don Rigoberto* (1998). In 1990 he stood unsuccessfully for the presidency of Peru. He won the Nobel Prize in literature 2010

variable adj **1** likely to change at any time: *variable weather* **2** *maths* having a range of possible values ▷ *n* **3** something that is subject to variation **4** *maths* an expression that can be assigned any of a set of values [Latin *variare* to diversify] **> variability** n **> variably** adv

variance n **at variance** not in agreement: *the real record is at variance with the public record*

variant adj **1** differing from a standard or type: *variant spellings* ▷ *n* **2** something that differs from a standard or type

variation n **1** something presented in a slightly different form: *his books are all variations on a main theme* **2** a change in level, amount, or quantity: *there was a variation in the figures* **3** *music* the repetition of a simple tune with the addition of new harmonies or a change in rhythm: *Variations on a Hussar's Song*

varicoloured or US **varicolored** adj having many colours

varicose adj of or resulting from varicose veins: *a varicose ulcer* [Latin *varix* a swollen vein]

varicose veins pl n veins, usually in the legs, which have become knotted, swollen, and sometimes painful

varied adj of different types, sizes, or quantities: *these young men and women would be of varied backgrounds*

variegated adj having patches or streaks of different colours: *variegated holly* **> variegation** n

variety n, pl **-ties 1** the state of being diverse or various **2** different things of the same kind: *I'm cooking the mince with a variety of vegetables* **3** a particular type of something

V

in the same general category: *this variety of pear is extremely juicy* **4** *taxonomy* a race whose distinct characters do not justify classification as a separate species **5** a type of entertainment consisting of short unrelated acts, such as singing, dancing, and comedy [Latin *varietas*]

varifocal *adj* of a lens that is gradated to permit any length of vision between near and distant

varifocals *pl n* a pair of spectacles with varifocal lenses

various *adj* **1** several different: *there are various possible answers to this question* **2** of different kinds: *the causes of high blood pressure are various and complicated* [Latin *varius* changing] **> variously** *adv*

> **USAGE** The use of *different* after *various* should be avoided: *the disease exists in various forms* (not *in various different forms*).

varlet *n old-fashioned* **1** a menial servant **2** a rascal [Old French *vaslet*]

varmint *n informal* an irritating or obnoxious person or animal [dialect variant of *varmin* vermin]

Varna *n* a port in NE Bulgaria, on the Black Sea: founded by Greeks in the 6th century BC; under the Ottoman Turks (1391–1878). Pop: 340 000 (2005 est). Former name (1949–56): **Stalin**

varnish *n* **1** a liquid painted onto a surface to give it a hard glossy finish **2** a smooth surface, coated with or as if with varnish **3** an artificial, superficial, or deceptively pleasing manner or appearance: *those who aspired to become civil servants acquired a varnish of university education* **4** *chiefly Brit* short for **nail varnish** ▷ *vb* **5** to apply varnish to **6** to try to make (something unpleasant) appear more attractive: *when did we start equivocating, camouflaging, varnishing the truth?* [Old French *vernis*]

Varro *n* **Marcus Terentius.** 116–27 BC, Roman scholar and satirist

varsity *n, pl* **-ties** *old-fashioned or informal* short for **university**

vary *vb* **varies, varying, varied 1** to change in appearance, character, or form **2** to be different or cause to be different: *the age of appearance of underarm and body hair varies greatly from person to person* **3** to give variety to: *you can vary the type of exercise you do* **4** to change in accordance with another variable: *an individual's calorie requirement varies with age, sex, and physical activity* [Latin *varius* changing] **> varying** *adj*

vas *n, pl* **vasa** *anatomy, zoology* a vessel or tube that carries a fluid [Latin: vessel]

Vasarely *n* **Victor.** 1908–97, French painter, born in Hungary; a leading exponent of op art

Vasari *n* **Giorgio.** 1511–74, Italian architect, painter, and art historian, noted for his *Lives of the Most Excellent Italian Architects, Painters, and Sculptors* (1550; 1568), a principal source for the history of Italian Renaissance art

vascular *adj biology, anatomy* of or relating to the vessels that conduct and circulate body fluids such as blood or sap [Latin *vas* vessel]

vas deferens *n, pl* **vasa deferentia** *anatomy* either of the two ducts that convey sperm from the testicles to the penis [Latin *vas* vessel + *deferens* carrying away]

vase *n* a glass or pottery jar used as an ornament or for holding cut flowers [Latin *vas* vessel]

vasectomy *n, pl* **-mies** surgical removal of all or part of the vas deferens as a method of contraception [VAS + Greek *tomē* a cutting]

Vaseline *n trademark* petroleum jelly, used as an ointment or a lubricant

vassal *n* **1** (in feudal society) a man who gave military service to a lord in return for protection and often land **2** a person, nation, or state dominated by another [Medieval Latin *vassus* servant] **> vassalage** *n*

vast *adj* unusually large in size, degree, or number [Latin *vastus* deserted] **> vastly** *adv* **> vastness** *n*

Västerås *n* a city in central Sweden, on Lake Mälaren:

Sweden's largest inland port; site of several national parliaments in the 16th century. Pop: 130 960 (2004 est)

vat *n* a large container for holding or storing liquids [Old English *fæt*]

VAT (in Britain and S Africa) value-added tax: a tax levied on the difference between the cost of materials and the selling price of a commodity or service

Vat. Vatican

Vatican *n* **1** the Pope's palace, in Rome **2** the authority of the Pope [Latin *Vaticanus (mons)* Vatican (hill)]

Vatican City *n* an independent state forming an enclave in Rome, with extraterritoriality over 12 churches and palaces in Rome: the only remaining Papal State; independence recognized by the Italian government in 1929; contains St Peter's Basilica and Square and the Vatican; the spiritual and administrative centre of the Roman Catholic Church. Languages: Italian and Latin. Currency: euro. Pop: 836 (2013 est). Area: 44 hectares (109 acres). Italian name: **Città del Vaticano.** Also called: **the Holy See**

Vatnajökull National Park *n* a national park in Iceland, the largest in Europe; contains the Vatnajökull glacier, Europe's largest by volume, and incorporates two existing national parks. Area: 13 000 sq km (5020 sq miles)

Vättern *n* **Lake Vättern** a lake in S central Sweden: the second largest lake in Sweden; linked to Lake Vänern by the Göta Canal; drains into the Baltic. Area: 1912 sq km (738 sq miles)

Vauban *n* **Sébastien Le Prestre de.** 1633–1707, French military engineer and marshal, who greatly developed the science of fortification and devised novel siege tactics using a series of parallel trenches

Vaucluse *n* a department of SE France, in Provence-Alpes-Côte-d'Azur region. Capital: Avignon. Pop: 517 810 (2003 est). Area: 3578 sq km (1395 sq miles)

Vaud *n* a canton of SW Switzerland: mountainous in the southeast; chief Swiss producer of wine. Capital: Lausanne. Pop: 632 000 (2002 est). Area: 3209 sq km (1240 sq miles). German name: **Waadt**

vaudeville *n* variety entertainment consisting of short acts such as song-and-dance routines and comic turns [French]

Vaughan *n* **1 Henry.** 1622–95, Welsh mystic poet, best known for his *Silex Scintillans* (1650; 1655) **2 Dame Janet (Maria).** 1899–1993, British physician and university official: helped set up Britain's first National Blood Transfusion Service (1939): after World War II, became Britain's expert on the effects of radiation on humans; Principal of Somerville College, Oxford (1945–67) **3 Sarah (Lois).** 1924–90, US jazz vocalist and pianist, noted esp. for her skill in vocal improvisation

Vaughan Williams *n* **Ralph.** 1872–1958, English composer, inspired by British folk songs and music of the Tudor period. He wrote operas, symphonies, hymns, and choral music

vault¹ *n* **1** a secure room where money and other valuables are stored safely **2** an underground burial chamber **3** an arched structure that forms a roof or ceiling **4** a cellar for storing wine [Old French *voute, voulte*]

vault² *vb* **1** to jump over (something) by resting one's hands on it or by using a long pole ▷ *n* **2** the act of vaulting [Italian *voltare* to turn] **> vaulter** *n*

vaulted *adj* being or having an arched roof: *an atmospheric vaulted dining room*

vaulting¹ *n* the arrangement of ceiling vaults in a building

vaulting² *adj* excessively confident: *a vaulting ambition for the highest political office*

vaunt *vb* **1** to describe or display (one's success or possessions) boastfully ▷ *n* **2** a boast [Latin *vanus* vain] **> vaunted** *adj*

Vauxhall *n* **1** a district in London, on the south bank of the Thames **2** Also called: **Vauxhall Gardens** a public garden at Vauxhall, laid out in 1661; a fashionable meeting place and site of lavish entertainments. Closed in 1859

Vavilov *n* Nikolai Ivanovich. 1887–?1943, Soviet plant geneticist, noted for his research into the origins of cultivated plants. His findings were regarded as contrary to official ideology and he was arrested (1940), dying in a labour camp

vb verb

VC 1 Vice Chancellor **2** Victoria Cross **3** *history* Vietcong: the Communist-led guerrilla force of South Vietnam

V-chip *n* a device within a television set that allows the set to be programmed not to receive transmissions that have been classified as containing sex, violence, or obscene language

vCJD variant Creutzfeldt-Jakob disease

VCR video cassette recorder

VD venereal disease

VDU visual display unit

veal *n* the meat from a calf, used as food [Latin *vitulus* calf]

Veblen *n* Thorstein. 1857–1929, US economist and social scientist, noted for his analysis of social and economic institutions. His works include *The Theory of the Leisure Class* (1899) and *The Theory of Business Enterprise* (1904)

vector *n* **1** *maths* a variable quantity, such as force, that has magnitude and direction **2** *pathol* an animal, usually an insect, that carries a disease-producing microorganism from person to person [Latin: carrier]

Veda (vay-da) *n* any or all of the most ancient sacred writings of Hinduism [Sanskrit: knowledge] **> Vedic** *adj*

veer *vb* **1** to change direction suddenly: *the plane veered off the runway and careered through the perimeter fence* **2** to change from one position or opinion to another: *her feelings veered from tenderness to sudden spurts of genuine love* ▷ *n* **3** a change of course or direction [Old French *virer*]

veg *n* *informal* a vegetable or vegetables

vegan (**vee**-gan) *n* a person who does not eat meat, fish, or any animal products such as cheese, butter, etc.

vegeburger *or* **veggieburger** *n* a flat cake of chopped vegetables or pulses that is grilled or fried and served in a roll

vegetable *n* **1** a plant, such as potato or cauliflower, with parts that are used as food **2** *offensive* someone who is unable to move or think, as a result of brain damage ▷ *adj* **3** of or like plants or vegetables [Late Latin *vegetabilis* animating]

vegetable marrow *n* a long green vegetable which can be cooked and eaten

vegetable oil *n* any of a group of oils that are obtained from plants

vegetal *adj* of or relating to plant life

vegetarian *n* **1** a person who does not eat meat or fish ▷ *adj* **2** excluding meat and fish: *a vegetarian diet* **> vegetarianism** *n*

vegetate *vb* **-tating, -tated** to live in a dull and boring way with no mental stimulation

vegetation *n* plant life as a whole

vegetative *adj* **1** of or relating to plant life or plant growth **2** (of reproduction) characterized by asexual processes

veggie *informal n* **1** a vegetable **2** a vegetarian ▷ *adj* **3** vegetarian: *a veggie cookbook*

veggieburger *n* same as **vegeburger**

veg out *vb* **vegging, vegged** *slang* to relax in a passive way: *vegging out in front of the television*

vehement *adj* **1** expressing strong feelings or opinions **2** (of actions or gestures) performed with great force or energy [Latin *vehemens* ardent] **> vehemence** *n* **> vehemently** *adv*

vehicle *n* **1** a machine such as a bus or car for transporting people or goods **2** something used to achieve a particular purpose or as a means of expression: *the newspaper was a vehicle for explaining government policies*

3 *pharmacol* an inactive substance mixed with the active ingredient in a medicine **4** a liquid, such as oil, in which a pigment is mixed before it is applied to a surface [Latin *vehere* to carry] **> vehicular** *adj*

Veii *n* an ancient Etruscan city, northwest of Rome: destroyed by the Romans in 396 BC

veil *n* **1** a piece of thin cloth, usually as part of a hat or headdress, used to cover a woman's face **2** something that conceals the truth: *a veil of secrecy* **3 take the veil** to become a nun ▷ *vb* **4** to cover or conceal with or as if with a veil [Latin *velum* a covering]

Veil *n* Simone (**Annie**). born 1927, French stateswoman; president of the European Parliament (1979–82): a survivor of Nazi concentration camps

veiled *adj* (of a comment or remark) presented in a disguised form: *it was a thinly veiled criticism*

vein *n* **1** any of the tubes that carry blood to the heart **2** a thin line in a leaf or in an insect's wing **3** a clearly defined layer of ore or mineral in rock **4** an irregular streak of colour in marble, wood, or cheese **5** a distinctive trait or quality in speech or writing: *critics have exposed a strong vein of moralism in the poem* **6** a temporary mood: *we're in a very humorous vein tonight* [Latin *vena*] **> veined** *adj*

Velázquez *or* **Velásquez** *n* Diego Rodríguez de Silva y. 1599–1660, Spanish painter, remarkable for the realism of his portraits, esp. those of Philip IV of Spain and the royal household

Velcro *n* *trademark* a type of fastening consisting of one piece of fabric with tiny hooked threads and another with a coarse surface that sticks to it

veld *or* **veldt** *n* the open country of South Africa including landscapes which are grassy, bushy, or thinly forested [Afrikaans: field]

veldskoen *or* **velskoen** (felt-skoon) *n* *S African* a sturdy ankle boot [Afrikaans]

veleta *n* same as **valeta**

Vellore *n* a town in SE India, in NE Tamil Nadu: medical centre. Pop: 177 413 (2001)

vellum *n* **1** a fine calf, kid, or lamb parchment **2** a strong good-quality paper that resembles vellum [Old French *velin* of a calf]

velocipede (vel-loss-sip-peed) *n* an early form of bicycle [Latin *velox* swift + *pes* foot]

velocity (vel-loss-it-ee) *n, pl* **-ties** the speed at which something is moving in a particular direction [Latin *velox* swift]

velour *or* **velours** (vel-loor) *n* a silk or cotton cloth similar to velvet [Latin *villus* shaggy hair]

velouté (vuh-loo-tay) *n* a rich white sauce made from stock, eggs, and cream [French, literally: velvety]

Velsen *n* a port in the W Netherlands, in North Holland at the mouth of the canal connecting Amsterdam with the North Sea: fishing and heavy industrial centre. Pop: 68 000 (2003 est)

velskoen *n* same as **veldskoen**

velvet *n* **1** a fabric with a thick close soft pile on one side **2** the furry covering of the newly formed antlers of a deer ▷ *adj* **3** made of velvet **4** soft or smooth like velvet **5 an iron fist** *or* **hand in a velvet glove** determination concealed by a gentle manner [Old French, from Latin *villus* shaggy hair] **> velvety** *adj*

velveteen *n* a cotton fabric that resembles velvet

venal (**vee**-nal) *adj* **1** willing to accept bribes in return for acting dishonestly: *venal politicians* **2** associated with corruption or bribery: *venal greed* [Latin *venum* sale] **> venality** *n*

vend *vb* to sell (goods) [Latin *vendere* to sell]

Venda[1] *n* **1** (*pl* **-da** *or* **-das**) a member of a people of southern Africa, living chiefly in NE South Africa **2** the language of this people

Venda[2] *n* a former Bantu homeland in South Africa, near the Zimbabwe border; abolished in 1993. Capital: Thohoyandou

V

Vendée n a department of W France, in Pays-de-la-Loire region: scene of the Wars of the Vendée, a series of peasant-royalist insurrections (1793–95) against the Revolutionary government. Capital: La Roche-sur-Yon. Pop: 565 230 (2003 est). Area: 7016 sq km (2709 sq miles)

vendetta n 1 a long-lasting quarrel between people or organizations in which they attempt to harm each other: *it's an inexplicable vendetta against the firm and its directors* 2 a private feud between families in which members of one family kill members of the other family in revenge for earlier murders [Italian]

vending machine n a machine that automatically dispenses food, drinks, or cigarettes when money is inserted

Vendôme n Louis Joseph de. 1654–1712, French marshal, noted for his command during the War of the Spanish Succession (1701–14)

vendor n 1 a person who sells goods such as newspapers or hamburgers from a stall or cart 2 *chiefly law* a person who sells property

veneer n 1 a thin layer of wood or plastic used to cover the surface of something made of cheaper material 2 a deceptive but convincing appearance: *nobody penetrated his veneer of modest charm* [Old French *fournir* to furnish]

venerable adj 1 (of a person) entitled to respect because of great age or wisdom 2 (of an object) impressive because it is old or important historically 3 *RC Church* a title given to a dead person who is going to be declared a saint 4 *Church of England* a title given to an archdeacon [Latin *venerari* to venerate]

venerate vb -ating, -ated to hold (someone) in deep respect [Latin *venerari*] ▷ **venerator** n

veneration n a feeling of awe or great respect: *George Gershwin is worthy of the veneration accorded his classical counterparts*

venereal (vin-ear-ee-al) adj 1 transmitted by sexual intercourse: *venereal infections* 2 of the genitals: *venereal warts* [Latin *venus* sexual love]

venereal disease n a disease, such as syphilis, transmitted by sexual intercourse

Venetia n 1 the area of ancient Italy between the lower Po valley and the Alps: later a Roman province 2 the territorial possessions of the medieval Venetian republic that were at the head of the Adriatic and correspond to the present-day region of Veneto and a large part of Friuli-Venezia Giulia

Venetian adj 1 of or relating to Venice or its inhabitants ▷ n 2 a native or inhabitant of Venice

Venetian blind n a window blind made of thin horizontal slats

Veneto n a region of NE Italy, on the Adriatic: mountainous in the north with a fertile plain in the south, crossed by the Rivers Po, Adige, and Piave. Capital: Venice. Pop: 4 577 408 (2003 est). Area: 18 377 sq km (7095 sq miles). Also called: **Venezia-Euganea**

Venez. Venezuela

Venezia n the Italian name for Venice

Venezia Giulia n a former region of NE Italy at the N end of the Adriatic: divided between Yugoslavia and Italy after World War II; now divided between Italy and Slovenia

Venezia Tridentina n the former name (until 1947) of Trentino-Alto Adige

Venezuela n 1 a republic in South America, on the Caribbean: colonized by the Spanish in the 16th century; independence from Spain declared in 1811 and won in 1819 after a war led by Simón Bolívar. It contains Lake Maracaibo and the northernmost chains of the Andes in the northwest, the Orinoco basin in the central part, and the Guiana Highlands in the south. Exports: petroleum, iron ore, and coffee. Official language: Spanish. Religion: Roman Catholic majority. Currency: bolívar. Capital: Caracas. Pop: 28 459 085 (2013 est). Area: 912 050 sq km (352 142 sq miles). Official name:

Bolivarian Republic of Venezuela 2 Gulf of Venezuela an inlet of the Caribbean in NW Venezuela: continues south as Lake Maracaibo

Venezuelan adj 1 of or relating to Venezuela or its inhabitants ▷ n 2 a native or inhabitant of Venezuela

vengeance n 1 the act of killing, injuring, or harming someone for revenge 2 **with a vengeance** to a much greater extent or with much greater force than expected: *my career was beginning to take off with a vengeance* [Old French, from Latin *vindicare* to punish]

vengeful adj wanting revenge

venial (veen-ee-al) adj easily excused or forgiven: *venial sins* [Latin *venia* forgiveness]

Venice n a port in NE Italy, capital of Veneto region, built on over 100 islands and mud flats in the Lagoon of Venice (an inlet of the Gulf of Venice at the head of the Adriatic): united under the first doge in 697 AD; became an independent republic and a great commercial and maritime power, defeating Genoa, the greatest rival, in 1380; contains the Grand Canal and about 170 smaller canals, providing waterways for city transport. Pop: 271 073 (2001). Italian name: **Venezia**. Related adjective: **Venetian**

venison n the flesh of a deer, used as food [Old French *venaison*]

Venizélos n Eleuthérios. 1864–1936, Greek statesman, who greatly extended Greek territory: prime minister (1910–15; 1917–20; 1924; 1928–32; 1933)

Venlo or **Venloo** n a city in the SE Netherlands, in Limburg on the Maas River. Pop: 92 000 (2003 est)

Venn diagram n *maths* a drawing which uses circles to show the relationships between different sets [after John Venn, logician]

venom n 1 a feeling of great bitterness or anger towards someone 2 the poison that certain snakes and scorpions inject when they bite or sting [Latin *venenum* poison, love potion] ▷ **venomous** adj ▷ **venomously** adv

venous (vee-nuss) adj of or relating to veins [Latin *vena* vein]

vent¹ n 1 a small opening in something through which fresh air can enter and fumes can be released 2 the shaft of a volcano through which lava and gases erupt 3 the anal opening of a bird or other small animal 4 **give vent to** to release (an emotion) in an outburst: *she gave vent to her misery and loneliness* ▷ vb 5 to release or express freely: *consumers vented their anger on the group by boycotting its products* 6 to make vents in [Old French *eventer* to blow out]

vent² n a vertical slit in the lower hem of a jacket [Latin *findere* to cleave]

Venter n (John) Craig. born 1946, US biologist: founder of the Institute for Genomic Research (1992) whose work contributed greatly to the mapping of the human genome

ventilate vb -lating, -lated 1 to let fresh air into (a room or building) 2 to discuss (ideas or feelings) openly: *ultra-rightists ventilated anti-Semitic sentiments* [Latin *ventilare* to fan] ▷ **ventilation** n

ventilator n an opening or device, such as a fan, used to let fresh air into a room or building

ventral adj relating to the front part of the body [Latin *venter* abdomen] ▷ **ventrally** adv

ventricle n *anatomy* 1 a chamber of the heart that pumps blood to the arteries 2 any one of the four main cavities of the brain [Latin *ventriculus*] ▷ **ventricular** adj

ventriloquism n the ability to speak without moving the lips so that the words appear to come from another person or from another part of the room [Latin *venter* belly + *loqui* to speak] ▷ **ventriloquist** n

Ventris n Michael George Francis. 1922–56, English architect and scholar, who deciphered the Linear B script, identifying it as an early form of Mycenaean Greek

venture n 1 a project or activity that is risky or of uncertain outcome 2 a business operation in which there is the risk of loss as well as the opportunity for profit ▷ vb **-turing, -tured 3** to do something that involves risk or danger: *I thought it wise to venture into foreign trade* **4** to dare to express (an opinion) **5** to go to an unknown or dangerous place **6** to dare (to do something): *you have asked me so often to come to your place that I ventured to drop in* [variant of *adventure*] ❯ **venturer** *n*

venture capital *n* money provided for investment in new commercial enterprises ❯ **venture capitalist** *n*

Venture Scout *or* **Venturer** *n* a member of the senior branch of the Scouts

venturesome *adj* willing to take risks

Venturi *n* Robert. born 1925, US architect, a pioneer of the postmodernist style. His writings include *Complexity and Contradiction in Architecture* (1966)

venue *n* a place where an organized gathering, such as a concert or a sporting event, is held [Latin *venire* to come]

Venus *n* **1** the Roman goddess of love **2** the planet second nearest to the sun

Venusberg *n* a mountain in central Germany: contains caverns that, according to medieval legend, housed the palace of the goddess Venus

Venus's flytrap *or* **Venus flytrap** *n* a plant that traps and digests insects between hinged leaves

veracious *adj* habitually truthful [Latin *verus* true]

veracity *n* **1** habitual truthfulness **2** accuracy

Veracruz *n* **1** a state of E Mexico, on the Gulf of Mexico: consists of a hot humid coastal strip with lagoons, rising rapidly inland to the central plateau and Sierra Madre Oriental. Capital: Jalapa. Pop: 630 000 (2005 est). Area: 72 815 sq km (28 114 sq miles) **2** the chief port of Mexico, in Veracruz state on the Gulf of Mexico. Pop: 410 000 (2000 est)

verandah *or* **veranda** *n* **1** an open porch attached to a house **2** NZ a continuous overhead canopy outside shops that gives shelter to pedestrians [Portuguese *varanda* railing]

verb *n* a word that is used to indicate the occurrence or performance of an action or the existence of a state, for example *run, make,* or *do* [Latin *verbum* word]

verbal *adj* **1** of or relating to words: *verbal skills* **2** spoken rather than written: *a verbal agreement* **3** grammar of or relating to a verb ❯ **verbally** *adv*

verbalism *n* an exaggerated emphasis on the importance of words

verbalize *or* **-lise** *vb* **-lizing, -lized** *or* **-lising, -lised** to express (an idea or feeling) in words

verbal noun *n* grammar a noun derived from a verb, for example *smoking* in the sentence *smoking is bad for you*

verbatim (verb-**bait**-im) *adv* **1** using exactly the same words: *I'll repeat it verbatim* ▷ *adj* **2** using exactly the same words: *a verbatim account* [Medieval Latin: word by word]

verbena *n* a plant with red, white, or purple sweet-smelling flowers [Latin: sacred bough used by the priest in religious acts]

verbiage *n* the excessive use of words [Latin *verbum* word]

verbose (verb-**bohss**) *adj* using more words than is necessary ❯ **verbosity** *n*

Vercelli *n* a city in NW Italy, in Piedmont: an ancient Ligurian and later Roman city; has an outstanding library of manuscripts (notably the *Codex Vercellensis*, dating from the 10th century). Pop: 45 132 (2001)

Vercingetorix *n* died ?45 BC, Gallic chieftain and hero, executed for leading a revolt against the Romans under Julius Caesar (52 BC)

verdant *adj* literary covered with green vegetation [from Latin *viridis* green]

Verde *n* **Cape Verde** a cape in Senegal, near Dakar: the westernmost point of Africa. See also **Cape Verde**

Verdi *n* Giuseppe. 1813–1901, Italian composer of operas, esp. *Rigoletto* (1851), *Il Trovatore* (1853), *La Traviata* (1853), and *Aïda* (1871)

verdict *n* **1** the decision made by a jury about the guilt or innocence of a defendant **2** an opinion formed after examining the facts [Latin *vere dictum* truly spoken]

verdigris (ver-dig-reess) *n* a green or bluish coating which forms on copper, brass, or bronze that has been exposed to damp [Old French *vert de Grice* green of Greece]

Verdun *n* **1** a fortified town in NE France, on the Meuse: scene of the longest and most severe battle (1916) of World War I, in which the French repelled a powerful German offensive. Pop: 19 624 (1999). Ancient name: Verodunum **2 Treaty of Verdun** an agreement reached in 843 AD by three grandsons of Charlemagne, dividing his empire into an E kingdom (later Germany), a W kingdom (later France), and a middle kingdom (containing what became the Low Countries, Lorraine, Burgundy, and N Italy)

verdure *n* literary flourishing green vegetation [from Latin *viridis* green]

Vereeniging *n* a city in E South Africa: scene of the signing (1902) of the treaty ending the Boer War. Pop: 79 630 (2001)

verge¹ *n* **1** a grass border along a road **2 on the verge of** having almost reached (a point or condition) **3** an edge or rim ▷ *vb* **verging, verged 4 verge on** to be near to: *she was verging on hysteria* [Latin *virga* rod]

verge² *vb* **verging, verged** to move in a specified direction: *verging towards the Irish Sea* [Latin *vergere*]

verger *n* chiefly Church of England **1** a church official who acts as caretaker **2** an official who carries the rod of office before a bishop or dean in ceremonies and processions [Latin *virga* rod, twig]

Verhaeren *n* Émile. 1855–1916, Belgian poet, writing in French. His works include the collections *Les Flamandes* (1883), *Les Soirs* (1887), and *Les Visages de la Vie* (1899)

verify *vb* **-fies, -fying, -fied 1** to check the truth of (something) by investigation **2** to prove (something) to be true [Latin *verus* true + *facere* to make] ❯ **verifiable** *adj* ❯ **verification** *n*

verily *adv* literary truly: *for verily, this was their destiny* [from *very*]

verisimilitude *n* the appearance of truth or reality [Latin *verus* true + *similitudo* similitude]

veritable *adj* rightly called; real: *a veritable mine of information* ❯ **veritably** *adv*

verity *n, pl* **-ties** a true statement or principle [Latin *verus* true]

Verkhne-Udinsk *n* the former name (until 1934) of Ulan-Ude

Verlaine *n* Paul. 1844–96, French poet. His verse includes *Poèmes saturniens* (1866), *Fêtes galantes* (1869), and *Romances sans paroles* (1874). He was closely associated with Rimbaud and was a precursor of the symbolists

Vermeer *n* Jan. full name *Jan van der Meer van Delft* 1632–75, Dutch genre painter, noted esp. for his masterly treatment of light

vermicelli (ver-me-**chell**-ee) *n* **1** very fine strands of pasta, used in soups **2** tiny chocolate strands used as a topping for cakes or ice cream [Italian: little worms]

vermiform *adj* shaped like a worm

vermiform appendix *n* anatomy same as **appendix**

vermilion *adj* **1** orange-red ▷ *n* **2** mercuric sulphide, used as an orange-red pigment; cinnabar [Late Latin *vermiculus* insect from which red dye was prepared]

vermin *pl n* **1** small animals collectively, such as insects and rodents, that spread disease and damage crops **2** unpleasant people [Latin *vermis* worm] ❯ **verminous** *adj*

Vermont *n* a state in the northeastern US: crossed from north to south by the Green Mountains; bounded on the east by the Connecticut River and by Lake Champlain in the northwest. Capital: Montpelier. Pop: 619 107 (2003 est). Area: 24 887 sq km (9609 sq miles). Abbreviation: **Vt.**, (with zip code) **VT**

Vermonter *n* a native or inhabitant of Vermont

vermouth (ver-muth) *n* a wine flavoured with herbs [German *Wermut* wormwood]

vernacular (ver-nak-yew-lar) *n* **1** the commonly spoken language or dialect of a particular people or place ▷ *adj* **2** in or using the vernacular [Latin *vernaculus* belonging to a household slave]

vernal *adj* of or occurring in spring [Latin *ver* spring] **> vernally** *adv*

Verne *n* Jules. 1828–1905, French writer, esp. of science fiction, such as *Twenty Thousand Leagues under the Sea* (1870) and *Around the World in Eighty Days* (1873)

vernier (ver-nee-er) *n* a small movable scale in certain measuring instruments such as theodolites, used to obtain a fractional reading of one of the divisions on the main scale [after Paul *Vernier*, mathematician]

Vernoleninsk *n* the former name of **Nikolayev**

Verny *n* a former name (until 1927) of **Almaty**

Verona *n* a city in N Italy, in Veneto on the Adige River: strategically situated at the junction of major routes between Italy and N Europe; became a Roman colony (89 BC); under Austrian rule (1797–1866); many Roman remains. Pop: 253 208 (2001) **> Veronese** *adj, n*

Veronese *n* Paolo, original name *Paolo Cagliari* or *Caliari*. 1528–88, Italian painter of the Venetian school. His works include *The Marriage at Cana* (1563) and *The Feast of the Levi* (1573)

veronica *n* a plant with small blue, pink, or white flowers [perhaps from the name *Veronica*]

Verrazano or **Verrazzano** *n* Giovanni da. ?1485–?1528, Florentine navigator, the first European to sight what was to become New York (1524)

Verrocchio *n* Andrea del. 1435–88, Italian sculptor, painter, and goldsmith of the Florentine school: noted esp. for the equestrian statue of Bartolommeo Colleoni in Venice

verruca (ver-roo-ka) *n pathol* a wart, usually on the sole of the foot [Latin: wart]

Versace *n* **1** Donatella. born 1955, Italian fashion designer and businesswoman; creative director of the Versace group from 1997 **2** her brother, **Gianni**. 1946–97, Italian fashion designer

Versailles *n* **1** a city in N central France, near Paris: site of an elaborate royal residence built for Louis XIV; seat of the French kings (1682–1789). Pop: 86 477 (2009) **2** Treaty of Versailles **a** the treaty of 1919 imposed upon Germany by the Allies (except for the US and the Soviet Union): the most important of the five peace treaties that concluded World War I **b** another name for (the Treaty of) **Paris** of 1783. See **Paris** (2)

versatile *adj* having many different skills or uses [Latin *versare* to turn] **> versatility** *n*

verse *n* **1** a division of a poem or song **2** poetry as distinct from prose **3** one of the short sections into which chapters of the books of the Bible are divided **4** a poem [Latin *versus* furrow, literally: a turning (of the plough)]

versed *adj* versed in knowledgeable about or skilled in

versify *vb* **-fies, -fying, -fied 1** to put (something) into verse **2** to write in verse [Latin *versus* verse + *facere* to make] **> versification** *n* **> versifier** *n*

version *n* **1** a form of something, such as a piece of writing, with some differences from other forms **2** an account of something from a certain point of view: *so far there's been no official version of the incident* **3** an adaptation, for example of a book or play into a film [Latin *vertere* to turn]

verso *n, pl* **-sos 1** the left-hand page of a book **2** the back of a sheet of printed paper [New Latin *verso (folio)* (the leaf) having been turned]

versus *prep* **1** (in a sporting competition or lawsuit) against **2** in opposition to or in contrast with: *man versus machine* [Latin: turned (in the direction of), opposite]

vertebra (ver-tib-bra) *n, pl* **-brae** (-bree) one of the bony segments of the spinal column [Latin] **> vertebral** *adj*

vertebrate *n* **1** an animal with a backbone, such as a fish, amphibian, reptile, bird, or mammal ▷ *adj* **2** having a backbone

vertex (ver-tex) *n, pl* **-tices** (-tiss-seez) **1** the highest point **2** *maths* **a** the point on a geometric figure where the sides form an angle **b** the highest point of a triangle [Latin: top]

vertical *adj* **1** at right angles to the horizon: *the vertical cliff* **2** straight up and down: *a vertical cut* **3** *econ* of or relating to associated or consecutive, though not identical, stages of industrial activity: *the purchase of a chain of travel agents by a leading tour operator will increase vertical integration in the holiday industry* ▷ *n* **4** a vertical line or direction [from Latin *vertex* top, pole of the sky] **> vertically** *adv*

vertiginous *adj* producing dizziness

vertigo *n pathol* a sensation of dizziness felt because one's balance is disturbed, sometimes experienced when looking down from a high place [Latin: a whirling round]

Verulamium *n* the Latin name of **Saint Albans**

vervain *n* a plant with long slender spikes of purple, blue, or white flowers [Latin *verbena* sacred bough; see VERBENA]

verve *n* great enthusiasm or liveliness [Latin *verba* words, chatter]

Verwoerd *n* Hendrik Frensch. 1901–66, South African politician, born in the Netherlands: prime minister of South Africa (1958–66) and the principal architect of the apartheid system: assassinated

very *adv* **1** used to add emphasis to adjectives and adverbs that are able to be graded: *I'm very happy; he'll be home very soon* ▷ *adj* **2** used with nouns to give emphasis or exaggerated intensity: *the very end of his visit; the very thing I need* [Old French *verai* true]

> **USAGE** In strict usage adverbs of degree such as *very, too, quite, really*, and *extremely* are used only to qualify adjectives: *he is very happy; she is too sad.* By this rule, these words should not be used to qualify past participles that follow the verb *to be*, since they would then be technically qualifying verbs. With the exception of certain participles, such as *tired* or *disappointed*, that have come to be regarded as adjectives, all other past participles are qualified by adverbs such as *much, greatly, seriously*, or *excessively*: *he has been much* (not *very*) *inconvenienced; she has been excessively* (not *too*) *criticized.*

very high frequency *n* a radio-frequency band lying between 30 and 300 megahertz

Very light *n* a coloured flare for signalling at night [after Edward W. *Very*, naval ordnance officer]

Vesalius *n* Andreas. 1514–64, Flemish anatomist, whose *De Humani Corporis fabrica* (1543) formed the basis of modern anatomical research and medicine

vesicle *n biology* **1** a small sac or cavity, esp. one filled with fluid **2** a blister [Latin *vesica* bladder, sac]

Vespasian *n* Latin name *Titus Flavius Sabinus Vespasianus*. 9–79 AD, Roman emperor (69–79), who consolidated Roman rule, esp. in Britain and Germany. He began the building of the Colosseum

vespers *n* an evening service in some Christian churches [Latin *vesper* the evening star]

Vespucci *n* Amerigo, Latin name *Americus Vespucius*. ?1454–1512, Florentine navigator in the New World (1499–1500; 1501–02), after whom the continent of America was named

vessel *n* **1** a ship or large boat **2** an object used as a container for liquid **3** *biology* a tubular structure in animals and plants that carries body fluids, such as blood and sap [Latin *vas*]

vest *n* **1** Brit an undergarment covering the top half of the body **2** US, Canad and Austral a waistcoat ▷ *vb* **3** vest in to settle (power or property) on: *by the power vested in me, I pronounce you man and wife* **4** vest with to bestow on: *the sponsorship has vested these matches with a new interest* [Latin *vestis* clothing]

vestal *adj* **1** chaste or pure ▷ *n* **2** a chaste woman [Latin *Vestalis* virgin priestess of the goddess Vesta]

vestal virgin *n* (in ancient Rome) one of the virgin priestesses dedicated to the goddess Vesta and to maintaining the sacred fire in her temple

vested *adj property law* having an existing right to the immediate or future possession of property

vested interest *n* **1** a strong personal interest someone has in a matter because he or she might benefit from it **2** *property law* an existing right to the immediate or future possession of property

vestibule *n* a small entrance hall [Latin *vestibulum*]

vestige (vest-ij) *n* **1** a small amount or trace **2** *biology* an organ or part that is a small nonfunctional remnant of a functional organ in an ancestor [Latin *vestigium* track]

vestigial (vest-ij-ee-al) *adj* remaining after a larger or more important thing has gone: *a strong seam of vestigial belief*

Vestmannaeyjar *n* a group of islands off the S coast of Iceland: they include the island of Surtsey (emerged 1963) and the volcano Helgafell (erupted 1974). Pop: 4027 (2007). English names: **Westmann Islands, Vestmann Islands**

vestments *pl n* **1** ceremonial clothes worn by the clergy at religious services **2** robes that show authority or rank [Latin *vestire* to clothe]

vestry *n, pl* **-tries** a room in a church used as an office by the priest or minister [probably Old French *vestiarie* wardrobe]

Vesuvius *n* a volcano in SW Italy, on the Bay of Naples: first recorded eruption in 79 AD, which destroyed Pompeii, Herculaneum, and Stabiae; numerous eruptions since then. Average height: 1220 m (4003 ft). Italian name: **Vesuvio**

vet¹ *n* **1** short for **veterinary surgeon** ▷ *vb* **vetting, vetted 2** to make a careful check of (a person or document) for suitability: *guests have to be vetted and vouched for*

vet² *n US, Canad, Austral and NZ* short for **veteran**

vetch *n* **1** a climbing plant with blue or purple flowers **2** the beanlike fruit of the vetch, used as fodder [Latin *vicia*]

veteran *n* **1** a person who has given long service in some capacity **2** a soldier who has seen a lot of active service **3** a person who has served in the military forces ▷ *adj* **4** long-serving: *the veteran American politician* [Latin *vetus* old]

veteran car *n Brit and Austral* a car built before 1919, esp. before 1905

veterinarian *n US, Canad and Austral* a veterinary surgeon

veterinary *adj* relating to veterinary science [Latin *veterinae* draught animals]

veterinary medicine *or* **veterinary science** *n* the branch of medicine concerned with the treatment of animals

veterinary surgeon *n Brit* a person qualified to practise veterinary medicine

veto (vee-toe) *n, pl* **-toes 1** the power to prevent legislation or action proposed by others: *no single state has a veto* **2** the exercise of this power ▷ *vb* **-toing, -toed 3** to refuse consent to (a proposal, such as a government bill) **4** to prohibit or forbid: *the Sports Minister vetoed the appointments* [Latin: I forbid]

Vettel *n* Sebastian, born 1987, German motor racing driver: won four consecutive Formula One world championships (2010–2013)

vex *vb* to cause (someone) to feel annoyance or irritation [Latin *vexare* to jolt (in carrying)] **> vexing** *adj* **> vexation** *n*

vexatious *adj* vexing

vexed *adj* **1** annoyed and puzzled **2** much debated: *the vexed question of pay*

VHF *or* **vhf** *radio* very high frequency

VHS Video Home System: a video cassette recorder system using half-inch magnetic tape

VI 1 Vancouver Island **2** Virgin Islands

via *prep* **1** by way of; through: *he fled to London via Crete* **2** by means of: *working from home and keeping in touch with office life via a video link-up* [Latin]

viable *adj* **1** able to be put into practice: *the party has failed to propose a viable alternative* **2** (of seeds or eggs) capable of growth **3** (of a fetus) sufficiently developed to survive outside the uterus [Latin *vita* life] **> viability** *n*

viaduct *n* a bridge for carrying a road or railway across a valley [Latin *via* way + *ducere* to bring]

Viagra *n trademark* a drug that allows increased blood flow into the penis, used to treat impotence in men

vial *n* same as **phial** [Greek *phialē* a bowl]

viands *pl n old-fashioned* food [Latin *vivenda* things to be lived on]

Viangchan *n* another spelling of **Vientiane**

Viareggio *n* a town and resort in W Italy, in Tuscany on the Ligurian Sea. Pop: 61 103 (2001)

viaticum *n, pl* **-ca** *or* **-cums** *Christianity* Holy Communion given to a person dying or in danger of death [Latin *viaticus* belonging to a journey]

vibes *pl n informal* **1** the emotional reactions between people **2** the atmosphere of a place **3** short for **vibraphone**

Viborg *n* **1** the Swedish name for **Vyborg 2** a town in N central Denmark, in Jutland: formerly a royal town and capital of Jutland. Pop: 33 192 (2004 est)

vibrant (vibe-rant) *adj* **1** full of energy and enthusiasm **2** (of a voice) rich and full of emotion **3** (of a colour) strong and bright [Latin *vibrare* to agitate] **> vibrancy** *n*

vibraphone *n* a musical instrument with metal bars that resonate electronically when hit

vibrate *vb* **-brating, -brated 1** to move backwards and forwards rapidly **2** to have or produce a quivering or echoing sound **3** *physics* to undergo or cause to undergo vibration [Latin *vibrare*] **> vibratory** *adj*

vibration *n* **1** a vibrating **2** *physics* **a** a periodic motion about an equilibrium position, such as in the production of sound **b** a single cycle of such a motion

vibrato *n, pl* **-tos** *music* a slight rapid fluctuation in the pitch of a note

vibrator *n* a device for producing a vibratory motion, used for massage or as a sex aid

viburnum (vie-burn-um) *n* a subtropical shrub with white flowers and berry-like fruits [Latin]

Vic. Victoria (Australian state)

vicar *n* **1** *Church of England* a priest who is in charge of a parish **2** *RC Church* a church officer acting as deputy to a bishop [Latin *vicarius* a deputy] **> vicarial** *adj*

vicarage *n* the house where a vicar lives

vicar apostolic *n RC Church* a clergyman with authority in missionary countries

vicar general *n, pl* **vicars general** an official appointed to assist the bishop in his administrative duties

vicarious (vik-air-ee-uss) *adj* **1** felt indirectly by imagining what another person experiences: *vicarious satisfaction* **2** undergone or done as the substitute for another: *vicarious adventures* **3** delegated: *vicarious power* [Latin *vicarius* substituted] **> vicariously** *adv*

Vicar of Bray *n* **1** a vicar (Simon Aleyn) appointed to the parish of Bray in Berkshire during Henry VIII's reign who changed his faith to Catholic when Mary I was on the throne and back to Protestant when Elizabeth I succeeded and so retained his living **2** Also called: **In Good King Charles's Golden Days** a ballad in which the vicar's changes of faith are transposed to the Stuart period **3** a person who changes his or her views or allegiances in accordance with what is suitable at the time

Vicar of Christ *n RC Church* the Pope as Christ's representative on earth

vice¹ *n* **1** an immoral or evil habit or action: *greed is only one of their vices* **2** a habit regarded as a weakness in someone's character: *one of his few vices is cigars* **3** criminal activities involving sex, drugs, or gambling [Latin *vitium* a defect]

vice² *or US* **vise** *n* a tool with a pair of jaws for holding an object while work is done on it [Latin *vitis* vine, plant with spiralling tendrils]

vice³ *adj* serving in the place of; being next in importance to: *the vice chairman* [Latin *vicis* interchange]

vice admiral *n* a senior commissioned officer in certain navies

vice chancellor *n* the chief executive or administrator at a number of universities

vicegerent *n* a person appointed to exercise all or some of the authority of another [VICE³ + Latin *gerere* to manage]

Vicente *n* Gil. ?1465–?1536, Portuguese dramatist, noted for his court entertainments, religious dramas, and comedies

Vicenza *n* a city in NE Italy, in Veneto: home of the 16th-century architect Andrea Palladio and site of some of his finest works. Pop: 107 223 (2001)

vice president *n* an officer ranking immediately below a president and serving as his or her deputy ⟩ **vice-presidency** *n*

viceregal *adj* 1 of a viceroy 2 *chiefly Austral and NZ* of a governor or governor general

viceroy *n* a governor of a colony or country who represents the monarch [VICE³ + French *roi* king]

vice squad *n* a police division responsible for the enforcement of gaming and prostitution laws

vice versa *adv* the other way round: *there were attacks on northerners by southerners and vice versa* [Latin: relations being reversed]

Vichy *n* a town and spa in central France, on the River Allier: seat of the collaborationist government under Marshal Pétain (1940–44); mineral waters bottled for export. Pop: 26 555 (2006). Latin name: **Vicus Calidus**

Vichy water (vee-shee) *n* a natural mineral water from Vichy in France which is supposed to be good for the health

vicinity (viss-in-it-ee) *n* the area immediately surrounding a place [Latin *vicinus* neighbouring]

vicious *adj* 1 cruel or violent: *vicious attacks* 2 forceful or ferocious: *she gave the chair a vicious jerk* 3 intended to cause hurt or distress: *vicious letters* 4 (of an animal) fierce or hostile [Latin *vitiosus* full of faults] ⟩ **viciously** *adv* ⟩ **viciousness** *n*

vicious circle *n* a situation in which an attempt to resolve one problem creates new problems that recreate the original one

vicissitudes (viss-iss-it-yewds) *pl n* changes in circumstance or fortune [Latin *vicis* change]

Vicksburg *n* a city in W Mississippi, on the Mississippi River: site of one of the most decisive campaigns (1863) of the American Civil War, in which the Confederates were besieged for nearly seven weeks before capitulating. Pop: 26 005 (2003 est)

Vicky *n* professional name of *Victor Weisz*. 1913–66, British left-wing political cartoonist, born in Germany

Vico *n* Giovanni Battista. 1668–1744, Italian philosopher. In *Scienza Nuova* (1721) he postulated that civilizations rise and fall in evolutionary cycles, making use of myths, poetry, and linguistics as historical evidence

victim *n* 1 a person or thing that suffers harm or death 2 a person who is tricked or swindled 3 a living person or animal sacrificed in a religious rite [Latin *victima*]

victimize *or* **-mise** *vb* **-mizing, -mized** *or* **-mising, -mised** to punish or discriminate against (someone) selectively or unfairly ⟩ **victimization** *or* **-misation** *n*

victor *n* 1 a person or nation that has defeated an enemy in war 2 the winner of a contest or struggle [Latin, from *vincere* to conquer]

Victor Emmanuel II *n* 1820–78, king of Sardinia-Piedmont (1849–78) and first king of Italy from 1861

Victor Emmanuel III *n* 1869–1947, last king of Italy

(1900–46): dominated after 1922 by Mussolini, whom he appointed as premier; abdicated

victoria *n* 1 a large sweet red-and-yellow plum 2 a light four-wheeled horse-drawn carriage with a folding hood [after Queen VICTORIA]

Victoria¹ *n* 1 a state of SE Australia: part of New South Wales colony until 1851; semiarid in the northwest, with the Great Dividing Range in the centre and east and the Murray River along the N border. Capital: Melbourne. Pop: 5 713 000 (2013 est). Area: 227 620 sq km (87 884 sq miles) 2 **Lake Victoria** *or* **Victoria Nyanza** a lake in East Africa, in Tanzania, Uganda, and Kenya, at an altitude of 1134 m (3720 ft): the largest lake in Africa and second largest in the world; drained by the Victoria Nile. Area: 69 485 sq km (26 828 sq miles) 3 a port in SW Canada, capital of British Columbia, on Vancouver Island: founded in 1843 by the Hudson's Bay Company; made capital of British Columbia in 1868; university (1963). Pop: 80 032 (2011) 4 the capital of the Seychelles, a port on NE Mahé. Pop: 25 500 (2004 est) 5 an urban area in S China, part of Hong Kong, on N Hong Kong Island: financial and administrative district; university (1911); the name tends not to be used officially since reunification of Hong Kong with China in 1997 6 **Mount Victoria** a mountain in SE Papua New Guinea: the highest peak of the Owen Stanley Range. Height: 4073 m (13 363 ft)

Victoria² *n* 1 1819–1901, queen of the United Kingdom (1837–1901) and empress of India (1876–1901). She married Prince Albert of Saxe-Coburg-Gotha (1840). Her sense of vocation did much to restore the prestige of the British monarchy 2 Tomás Luis de. ?1548–1611, Spanish composer of motets and masses in the polyphonic style

Victoria and Albert Museum *n* a museum of the fine and applied arts in London, originating from 1856 and given its present name and site in 1899. Abbreviation: **V and A**

Victoria Cross *n* the highest decoration for bravery in battle awarded to the British and Commonwealth armed forces

Victoria Day *n* (in Canada) an annual holiday celebrated on the Monday before May 24

Victoria Desert *n* See Great Victoria Desert

Victoria Falls *pl n* a major waterfall on the border between Zimbabwe and Zambia, on the Zambezi River. Height: about 108 m (355 ft). Width: about 1400 m (4500 ft). Local name: **Mosi-oa-Tunya**

Victoria Island *n* a large island in the Canadian Arctic, in Nunavut and the Northwest Territories. Area: about 212 000 sq km (82 000 sq miles)

Victoria Land *n* a section of Antarctica, largely in the Ross Dependency on the Ross Sea

Victorian *adj* 1 of or in the reign of Queen Victoria of Great Britain and Ireland (1837–1901) 2 characterized by prudery or hypocrisy 3 of or relating to Victoria (the state or any of the cities) ▷ *n* 4 a person who lived during the reign of Queen Victoria 5 an inhabitant of Victoria (the state or any of the cities)

Victoriana *pl n* objects of the Victorian period

Victoria Nile *n* See Nile

victorious *adj* 1 having defeated an enemy or opponent: *the victorious allies* 2 of or characterized by victory: *a victorious smile*

victory *n, pl* **-ries** 1 the winning of a war or battle 2 success attained in a contest or struggle [Latin *victoria*]

victual *vb* **-tualling, -tualled** *or US* **-tualing, -tualed** *old-fashioned* to supply with or obtain victuals [Latin *victus* sustenance] ⟩ **victualler** *or US* **-tualer** *n*

victuals (vit-tals) *pl n* old-fashioned food and drink

vicuna (vik-kew-na) *n* 1 a S American mammal like the llama 2 the fine cloth made from its wool [Spanish]

Vidal *n* Gore. 1925–2012 US novelist and essayist. His novels include *Julian* (1964), *Myra Breckinridge* (1968), *Burr* (1974), *Lincoln* (1984), and *The Season of Conflict* (1996)

vide (vie-dee) *see*: used to direct a reader to a specified place in a text or in another book [Latin]

videlicet (vid-**deal**-ee-set) *adv namely*: used to specify items [Latin]

video *n, pl* **-os 1** the recording and showing of films and events using a television set, video tapes, and a video recorder **2** short for **video cassette 3** short for **video cassette recorder** ▷ *vb* **videoing, videoed 4** to record (a television programme or an event) on video ▷ *adj* **5** relating to or used in producing televised images [Latin *videre* to see]

video cassette *n* a cassette containing video tape

video cassette recorder *n* a device for recording and playing back television programmes and films

video game *n* a game that can be played by using an electronic control to move symbols on the screen of a visual display unit

video nasty *n* a film, usually specially made for video, that is explicitly horrific and pornographic

videophone *n* a communications device by which people can both see and speak to each other

video recorder *n* short for **video cassette recorder**

video tape *n* **1** magnetic tape used mainly for recording the video-frequency signals of a television programme or film ▷ *vb* **video-tape** (**-taping, -taped**) **2** to record (a film or programme) on video tape

vie *vb* **vying, vied** to compete (with someone): *the sisters vied with each other to care for her* [probably Old French *envier* to challenge]

Vienna *n* the capital and the smallest state of Austria, in the northeast on the River Danube: seat of the Hapsburgs (1278-1918); residence of the Holy Roman Emperor (1558-1806); withstood sieges by Turks in 1529 and 1683; political and cultural centre in the 18th and 19th centuries, having associations with many composers; university (1365). Pop: 1 590 242 (2003 est). Area: 1075 sq km (415 sq miles). German name: **Wien**. Latin name: **Vindobona**

Vienne *n* **1 a** a department of W central France, in Poitou-Charentes region. Capital: Poitiers. Pop: 402 555 (2003 est). Area: 7044 sq km (2747 sq miles). **b** a town in SE France, on the River Rhône: extensive Roman remains. Ancient name: **Vienna 3** a river in SW central France, flowing west and north to the Loire below Chinon. Length: over 350 km (200 miles)

Viennese *adj* **1** of, relating to, or characteristic of Vienna ▷ *n, pl* **-nese 2** a native or inhabitant of Vienna

Vientiane *or* **Viangchan** *n* the administrative capital of Laos, in the south near the border with Thailand: capital of the kingdom of Vientiane from 1707 until taken by the Thais in 1827. Pop: 776 000 (2005 est)

Vierwaldstättersee *n* the German name for (Lake) Lucerne

Vietnam *or* **Viet Nam** *n* a republic in SE Asia: an ancient empire, conquered by France in the 19th century; occupied by Japan (1940–45) when the Communist-led Vietminh began resistance operations that were continued against restored French rule after 1945. In 1954 the country was divided along the 17th parallel, establishing North Vietnam (under the Vietminh) and South Vietnam (under French control), the latter becoming the independent **Republic of Vietnam** in 1955. From 1959 the country was dominated by war between the Communist Vietcong, supported by North Vietnam, and the South Vietnamese government; increasing numbers of US forces were brought to the aid of the South Vietnamese army until a peace agreement (1973) led to the withdrawal of US troops; further fighting led to the eventual defeat of the South Vietnamese government in March 1975 and in 1976 an elected National Assembly proclaimed the reunification of the country. Official language: Vietnamese. Religion: Buddhist majority. Currency: dong. Capital: Hanoi. Pop: 92 477 857 (2013 est). Area: 331 041 sq km (127 816 sq miles).

Official name: **Socialist Republic of Vietnam**

Vietnamese *adj* **1** of or relating to Vietnam or its inhabitants ▷ *n* **2** (*pl* **-ese**) a native or inhabitant of Vietnam **3** the language of Vietnam

view *n* **1** opinion, judgment, or belief: *in my view that doesn't really work* **2** an understanding of or outlook on something: *a specific view of human history* **3** everything that can be seen from a particular place or in a particular direction: *there was a beautiful view from the window* **4** vision or sight, esp. range of vision: *as they turned into the drive, the house came into view* **5** a picture of a scene **6** the act of seeing or observing **7** **in view of** taking into consideration **8** **on view** exhibited to the public **9** **take a dim** *or* **poor view of** to regard (something) unfavourably **10** **with a view to** with the intention of ▷ *vb* **11** to consider in a specified manner: *they viewed the visit with hardly disguised apprehension* **12** to examine or inspect (a house or flat) carefully with a view to buying it **13** to look at **14** to watch (television) [Latin *videre* to see]

viewer *n* **1** a person who views something, esp. television **2** a hand-held device for looking at photographic slides

viewfinder *n* a device on a camera that lets the user see what will be included in the photograph

viewpoint *n* **1** a person's attitude towards something **2** a place from which one gets a good view

Vigée-Lebrun *n* (**Marie Louise**) **Élisabeth**. 1755–1842, French painter, noted for her portraits of women

vigil (vij-ill) *n* **1** a night-time period of staying awake to look after a sick person, pray, etc. **2** *RC Church, Church of England* the eve of certain major festivals [Latin: alert]

vigilance *n* careful attention

vigilance committee *n* (in the US) a self-appointed body of citizens organized to maintain order

vigilant *adj* on the watch for trouble or danger [Latin *vigilare* to be watchful]

vigilante (vij-ill-**ant**-ee) *n* a person who takes it upon himself or herself to enforce the law [Spanish, from Latin *vigilare* to keep watch]

vignette (vin-**yet**) *n* **1** a short description of the typical features of something **2** a small decorative illustration in a book **3** a photograph or drawing with edges that are shaded off [French, literally: little vine (frequently used to embellish a text)]

Vignola *n* Giacomo Barozzi da. 1507–73, Italian architect, whose cruciform design for Il Gesù, Rome, greatly influenced later Church architecture

Vigny *n* Alfred Victor de. 1797–1863, French romantic poet, novelist, and dramatist, noted for his pessimistic lyric verse *Poèmes antiques et modernes* (1826) and *Les Destinées* (1864), the novel *Cinq-Mars* (1826), and the play *Chatterton* (1835)

Vigo *n* a port in NW Spain, in Galicia on **Vigo Bay** (an inlet of the Atlantic): site of a British and Dutch naval victory (1702) over the French and Spanish. Pop: 292 566 (2003 est)

vigorous *adj* **1** having physical or mental energy **2** displaying or performed with vigour: *vigorous exercise* ▷ **vigorously** *adv*

vigour *or US* **vigor** *n* **1** physical or mental energy: *the vigour of his invective astonished MPs* **2** strong healthy growth [Latin *vigor*]

Viipuri *n* the Finnish name for **Vyborg**

Vijayawada *n* a town in SE India, in E central Andra Pradesh on the Krishna River: Hindu pilgrimage centre. Pop: 825 436 (2001). Former name: **Bezwada**

Viking *n* any of the Scandinavians who raided by sea most of N and W Europe from the 8th to the 11th centuries [Old Norse *víkingr*]

vile *adj* **1** morally wicked: *a vile regime* **2** disgusting: *the vile smell of the man* **3** unpleasant or bad: *I had a vile day at work* [Latin *vilis* cheap] ▷ **vilely** *adv* ▷ **vileness** *n*

vilify (vill-if-fie) *vb* **-fies, -fying, -fied** to speak very badly

V

of (someone) [Latin *vilis* worthless + *facere* to make]
> **vilification** *n*

villa *n* **1** a large house with gardens **2** *Brit* a house rented to holiday-makers [Latin: a farmhouse]

Villa *n* Francisco, called *Pancho Villa*, original name *Doroteo Arango*. ?1877–1923, Mexican revolutionary leader

Villach *n* a city in S central Austria, on the Drava River: nearby hot mineral springs. Pop: 57 497 (2002)

village *n* **1** a small group of houses in a country area **2** the inhabitants of such a community [Latin *villa* a farmhouse] > **villager** *n*

Villahermosa *n* a town in E Mexico, capital of Tabasco state: university (1959). Pop: 583 000 (2005 est). Former name: San Juan Bautista

villain *n* **1** a wicked or evil person **2** the main wicked character in a novel or play [Late Latin *villanus* worker on a country estate]

villainous *adj* of or like a villain

villainy *n*, *pl* **-lainies** evil or vicious behaviour

Villa-Lobos *n* Heitor. 1887–1959, Brazilian composer, much of whose work is based on Brazilian folk tunes

Villars *n* Claude Louis Hector de. 1653–1734, French marshal, distinguished for his command in the War of the Spanish Succession (1701–14)

villein (vill-an) *n* (in medieval Europe) a peasant who was directly subject to his lord, to whom he paid dues and services in return for his land [see VILLAIN]
> **villeinage** *n*

Villeneuve *n* Pierre Charles Jean Baptiste Silvestre de. 1763–1806, French admiral, defeated by Nelson at the Battle of Trafalgar (1805)

Villeurbanne *n* a town in E France: an industrial suburb of E Lyon. Pop: 139 596 (2006)

Villiers de l'Isle Adam *n* August, Comte de. 1838–89, French poet and dramatist; pioneer of the symbolist movement. His works include *Contes cruels* (1883) and the play *Axel* (1885)

Villon *n* **1** François. born 1431, French poet. His poems, such as those in *Le Petit testament* (?1456) and *Le Grand testament* (1461), are mostly ballades and rondeaux, verse forms that he revitalized. He was banished in 1463, after which nothing more was heard of him **2** Jacques, real name *Gaston Duchamp*. 1875–1963, French cubist painter and engraver

villus *n*, *pl* **villi 1** *zoology, anatomy* **2** any of the numerous finger-like projections of the mucous membrane lining the small intestine of many vertebrates **3** any of the finger-like projections formed in the placenta of mammals [from Latin: shaggy hair]

Vilnius *or* **Vilnyus** *n* the capital of Lithuania: passed to Russia in 1795; under Polish rule (1920–39); university (1578); an industrial and commercial centre. Pop: 544 000 (2005 est). Russian name: Vilna. Polish name: Wilno

vim *n* *informal* vigour and energy [Latin *vis* force]

Viminal *n* one of the seven hills on which ancient Rome was built [from Latin *Vīminālis Collis* the Viminal Hill, from *vīminālis* of osiers, from *vīmen* an osier, referring to the willow grove on the hill]

Viña del Mar *n* a city and resort in central Chile, just north of Valparaíso on the Pacific: the second largest city of Chile. Pop: 323 000 (2005 est)

vinaigrette *n* salad dressing made from oil and vinegar with seasonings [French]

Vincennes *n* a suburb of E Paris: 14th-century castle. Pop: 47 845 (2006)

Vincent de Paul *n* Saint. ?1581–1660, French Roman Catholic priest, who founded two charitable orders, the Lazarists (1625) and the Sisters of Charity (1634). Feast day: Sept 27

vindaloo *n*, *pl* **-loos** a type of very hot Indian curry [perhaps from Portuguese *vin d'alho* wine and garlic sauce]

Vindhya Pradesh *n* a former state of central India: merged with the reorganized Madhya Pradesh in 1956

Vindhya Range *or* **Vindhya Mountains** *n* a mountain range in central India: separates the Ganges basin from the Deccan, marking the limits of northern and peninsular India. Greatest height: 1113 m (3651 ft)

vindicate *vb* **-cating, -cated 1** to clear (someone) of guilt or suspicion **2** to provide justification for: *the arrests may vindicate the strong-arm tactics* [Latin *vindex* claimant]
> **vindication** *n*

vindictive *adj* **1** maliciously seeking revenge **2** characterized by spite or ill will [Latin *vindicare* to avenge] > **vindictively** *adv* > **vindictiveness** *n*

vine *n* **1** a plant, such as the grapevine, with long flexible stems that climb by clinging to a support **2** the stem of such a plant [Latin *vinea* vineyard] > **viny** *adj*

vinegar *n* **1** a sour-tasting liquid made by fermentation of beer, wine, or cider, used for salad dressing or for pickling **2** bad temper or spitefulness: *the vinegar in her pen is often a welcome seasoning to duller news* [French *vin* wine + *aigre* sour] > **vinegary** *adj*

Vineland *n* a variant spelling of Vinland

vineyard (vinn-yard) *n* an area of land where grapes are grown [Old English *wīngeard*]

vingt-et-un (van-tay-uhn) *n* same as **pontoon²** [French, literally: twenty-one]

viniculture *n* the process or business of growing grapes and making wine [Latin *vinum* wine + CULTURE]
> **viniculturist** *n*

Vinland *or* **Vineland** *n* the stretch of the E coast of North America visited by Leif Ericson and other Vikings from about 1000 AD

Vinnitsa *n* a city in central Ukraine: passed from Polish to Russian rule in 1793. Pop: 353 000 (2005 est)

vino (vee-noh) *n*, *pl* **-nos** *informal* wine [Spanish or Italian: wine]

vinous (vine-uss) *adj* of or characteristic of wine [Latin *vinum* wine]

vintage *n* **1** the wine obtained from a particular harvest of grapes **2** the harvest from which such a wine is obtained **3** a time of origin: *an open-necked shirt of uncertain vintage* ▷ *adj* **4** (of wine) of an outstandingly good year **5** representing the best and most typical: *a vintage Saint Laurent dress* [Latin *vindemia*]

vintage car *n* a car built between 1919 and 1930

vintner *n* a wine merchant [Latin *vinetum* vineyard]

vinyl (vine-ill) *n* **1** any of various strong plastics made by the polymerization of vinyl compounds, such as PVC **2** conventional records made of vinyl as opposed to compact discs ▷ *adj* **3** *chem* of or containing the monovalent group of atoms CH_2CH-: *vinyl chloride* **4** of or made of vinyl: *vinyl tiles* [Latin *vinum* wine]

viol (vie-oll) *n* a stringed musical instrument that preceded the violin [Old Provençal *viola*]

viola¹ (vee-oh-la) *n* a bowed stringed instrument of the violin family, slightly larger and lower in pitch than the violin [Italian]

viola² (vie-ol-la) *n* a variety of pansy [Latin: violet]

viola da gamba (vee-oh-la da gam-ba) *n* the second largest and lowest member of the viol family [Italian, literally: viol for the leg]

violate *vb* **-lating, -lated 1** to break (a law or agreement): *he violated export laws* **2** to disturb rudely or improperly: *these men who were violating her privacy* **3** to treat (a sacred place) disrespectfully **4** to rape [Latin *violare* to do violence to] > **violation** *n* > **violator** *n*

violence *n* **1** the use of physical force, usually intended to cause injury or destruction **2** great force or strength in action, feeling, or expression [Latin *violentus* violent]

violent *adj* **1** using or involving physical force with the intention of causing injury or destruction: *violent clashes with government supporters* **2** very intense: *I took a violent dislike to him* **3** sudden and forceful: *a violent explosion*
> **violently** *adv*

violet *n* **1** a plant with bluish-purple flowers ▷ *adj* **2** bluish-purple [Latin *viola*]

violin n a musical instrument, the highest member of the violin family, with four strings played with a bow [Italian violino a little viola]

violinist n a person who plays the violin

violist (vee-oh-list) n a person who plays the viola

Viollet-le-Duc n Eugène Emmanuel. 1814–79, French architect and leader of the Gothic Revival in France, noted for his dictionary of French architecture (1854–68) and for his restoration of medieval buildings

violoncello (vie-oll-on-**chell**-oh) n, pl **-los** same as **cello** [Italian]

VIP very important person

viper n a type of poisonous snake [Latin vipera]

virago (vir-rah-go) n, pl **-goes** or **-gos** an aggressive woman [Latin: a manlike maiden]

viral (vie-ral) adj 1 of or caused by a virus ▷ adv 2 **go viral** (of an image, video, story, etc.) to spread quickly and widely among internet users ▷ n 3 an image, video, story, etc. that is spread quickly and widely via the internet

Virchow n Rudolf Ludwig Karl. 1821–1902, German pathologist, who is considered the founder of modern (cellular) pathology

Viren n Lasse. born 1949, Finnish distance runner: winner of the 5000 metres and the 10 000 metres in the 1972 and 1976 Olympic Games

Virgil or **Vergil** n Latin name Publius Vergilius Maro. 70–19 BC, Roman poet, patronized by Maecenas. The Eclogues (42–37), ten pastoral poems, and the Georgics (37–30), four books on the art of farming, established Virgil as the foremost poet of his age. His masterpiece is the Aeneid (30–19) ▷ **Virgilian** or **Vergilian** adj

virgin n 1 a person, esp. a woman, who has never had sexual intercourse 2 a person who is inexperienced in a specified field: a ski virgin ▷ adj 3 not having had sexual intercourse 4 fresh and unused: he found a scrap of virgin paper in a sea of memoranda 5 not yet cultivated, explored, or exploited by people: virgin territory [Latin virgo]

Virgin n 1 **the Virgin** same as **Virgin Mary** 2 a statue or picture of the Virgin Mary

virginal¹ adj 1 like a virgin 2 extremely pure or fresh

virginal² n an early keyboard instrument like a small harpsichord [probably Latin virginalis virginal, perhaps because it was played largely by young ladies]

Virgin Birth n Christianity the doctrine that Jesus Christ was conceived solely by the direct intervention of the Holy Spirit so that Mary remained a virgin

Virginia n a state of the eastern US, on the Atlantic: site of the first permanent English settlement in North America; consists of a low-lying deeply indented coast rising inland to the Piedmont plateau and the Blue Ridge Mountains. Capital: Richmond. Pop: 7 386 330 (2003 est). Area: 103 030 sq km (39 780 sq miles). Abbreviation: **Va.**, (with zip code) **VA**

Virginia Beach n a city and resort in SE Virginia, on the Atlantic. Pop: 439 467 (2003 est)

Virginia creeper n a climbing plant with leaves that turn red in autumn

Virginian adj 1 of or relating to Virginia or its inhabitants ▷ n 2 a native or inhabitant of Virginia

Virgin Islands pl n a group of about 100 small islands (14 inhabited) in the Caribbean, east of Puerto Rico: discovered by Columbus (1493); consists of the British Virgin Islands in the east and the Virgin Islands of the United States in the west and south. Pop: 136 649 (2013 est). Area: 497 sq km (192 sq miles)

Virgin Islands of the United States pl n a territory of the US in the Caribbean, consisting of islands west and south of the British Virgin Islands: purchased from Denmark in 1917 for their strategic importance. Capital: Charlotte Amalie. Pop: 104 737 (2013 est). Area: 344 sq km (133 sq miles). Former name: **Danish West Indies**

virginity n the condition or fact of being a virgin

Virgin Mary n **the Virgin Mary** Christianity Mary, the mother of Christ

Virgin Queen n **the Virgin Queen** another name for Queen Elizabeth I of England. See **Elizabeth I**

Virgo n astrol the sixth sign of the zodiac; the Virgin [Latin]

virile adj 1 having the traditional male characteristics of physical strength and a high sex drive 2 forceful and energetic: a virile Highland fling [Latin virilis manly] ▷ **virility** n

virology n the branch of medicine concerned with the study of viruses ▷ **virological** adj

virtual adj 1 having the effect but not the appearance or form of: the investigation has now come to a virtual standstill 2 computers designed so as to extend the potential of a finite system beyond its immediate limits: virtual memory 3 of or relating to virtual reality [Latin virtus virtue]

virtually adv almost or nearly: he is virtually a prisoner in his own palace

virtual reality n a computer-generated environment that seems real to the user

virtue n 1 moral goodness 2 a positive moral quality: the virtue of humility 3 an advantage or benefit: the added virtue of being harmless 4 chastity, esp. in women 5 **by virtue of** by reason of; because of: they escaped execution by virtue of their high rank [Latin virtus manliness, courage]

virtuoso n, pl **-si** or **-sos** 1 a person with exceptional musical skill 2 a person with exceptional skill in any area ▷ adj 3 showing exceptional skill or brilliance: a virtuoso performance [Italian: skilled] ▷ **virtuosity** n

virtuous adj 1 morally good 2 (of a woman) chaste ▷ **virtuously** adv

virulent (vir-yew-lent) adj 1 extremely bitter or hostile 2 a (of a microorganism) very infectious b (of a disease) having a violent effect 3 extremely poisonous or harmful: the most virulent poison known to man [Latin virulentus full of poison] ▷ **virulence** n

virus n 1 a microorganism that is smaller than a bacterium and can cause disease in humans, animals, or plants 2 informal a disease caused by a virus 3 computers an unsanctioned and self-replicating program which, when activated, corrupts a computer's data and disables its operating system [Latin: slime, poisonous liquid]

visa n an official stamp in a passport permitting its holder to travel into or through the country of the government issuing it [Latin: things seen]

visage (viz-zij) n chiefly literary 1 face 2 appearance [Latin visus appearance]

Visakhapatnam n a variant spelling of **Vishakhapatnam**

vis-à-vis (veez-ah-vee) prep in relation to [French: face-to-face]

Visayan Islands pl n a group of seven large and several hundred small islands in the central Philippines. Chief islands: Negros and Panay. Pop: 15 528 346 (2000). Area: about 61 000 sq km (23 535 sq miles). Spanish name: **Bisayas**

Visby n a port in SE Sweden, on NW Gotland Island in the Baltic: an early member of the Hanseatic League and major N European commercial centre in the Middle Ages. Pop: 22 017 (2000 est)

viscera (viss-er-a) pl n anatomy the large internal organs of the body collectively [Latin: entrails]

visceral adj 1 of or affecting the viscera 2 instinctive rather than rational: visceral hatred of the neighbours

viscid (viss-id) adj sticky [Latin viscum mistletoe, birdlime]

Visconti n 1 the ruling family of Milan from 1277 to 1447 2 Luchino, real name Luchino Visconti de Modrone. 1906–76, Italian stage and film director, whose neorealist films include Ossessione (1942). His other films include The Leopard (1963), Death in Venice (1970), and The Innocents (1976)

viscose n 1 a sticky solution obtained by dissolving cellulose 2 rayon made from this material [Latin viscum birdlime]

V

viscosity *n, pl* **-ties** **1** the state of being viscous **2** *physics* the extent to which a fluid resists a tendency to flow

viscount (vie-count) *n* (in the British Isles) a nobleman ranking below an earl and above a baron [Old French *visconte*] > **viscountcy** *n*

viscountess (vie-count-iss) *n* **1** a woman holding the rank of viscount **2** the wife or widow of a viscount

viscous *adj* (of liquids) thick and sticky

vise *n US* same as **vice²**

Viseu *n* a city in N central Portugal: 12th-century cathedral. Pop: 93 502 (2001)

Vishakhapatnam, Visakhapatnam *or* **Vizagapatam** *n* a port in E India, in NE Andhra Pradesh on the Bay of Bengal: shipbuilding and oil-refining industries. Pop: 969 608 (2001)

Vishnu *n* a Hindu god, the Preserver

visibility *n* **1** the range or clarity of vision: *visibility was good, despite rain* **2** the condition of being visible

visible *adj* **1** able to be seen **2** able to be perceived by the mind: *a visible and flagrant act of aggression* [Latin *visibilis*] > **visibly** *adv*

vision *n* **1** the ability to see **2** a vivid mental image produced by the imagination: *I kept having visions of him being tortured* **3** a hallucination caused by divine inspiration, madness, or drugs: *visions of God* **4** great perception of future developments: *what he had instead of charisma was vision* **5** the image on a television screen **6** a person or thing of extraordinary beauty [Latin *visio* sight, from *videre* to see]

visionary *adj* **1** showing foresight: *a visionary statesman* **2** idealistic but impractical **3** given to having visions **4** of or like visions > *n, pl* **-naries** **5** a visionary person

visit *vb* **-siting, -sited** **1** to go or come to see (a person or place) **2** to stay with (someone) as a guest **3** *old-fashioned* (of a disease or disaster) to afflict **4 visit on** *or* **upon** to inflict (punishment) on **5 visit with** *US informal* to chat with (someone) > *n* **6** the act or an instance of visiting **7** a professional or official call **8** a stay as a guest [Latin *visitare* to go to see]

visitant *n* **1** a ghost or apparition **2** a migratory bird temporarily resting in a particular region

visitation *n* **1** an official visit or inspection **2** a punishment or reward from heaven **3** an appearance of a supernatural being

Visitation *n* **a** the visit made by the Virgin Mary to her cousin Elizabeth (Luke 1: 39–56) **b** the Church festival commemorating this, held on July 2

visiting hours *pl n* the times when visitors are allowed to see someone in a hospital or other institution: *many prisoners' wives complain about the short visiting hours*

visitor *n* a person who visits a person or place

visitor's passport *n* a British passport, valid for one year, that grants access to some countries, usually for a restricted period

Vislinsky Zaliv *n* a transliteration of the Russian name for Vistula (2)

visor (vize-or) *n* **1** a transparent flap on a helmet that can be pulled down to protect the face **2** a small movable screen attached above the windscreen in a vehicle, used as protection against the glare of the sun **3** a peak on a cap [Old French *vis* face]

vista *n* **1** an extensive view **2** a wide range of possibilities or future events: *the vista of opportunity* [Italian]

Vistula *n* **1** a river in central and N Poland, rising in the Carpathian Mountains and flowing generally north and northwest past Warsaw and Torun, then northeast to enter the Baltic via an extensive delta region. Length: 1090 km (677 miles). Polish name: **Wisla**. German name: **Weichsel** **2 Vistula Lagoon** a shallow lagoon on the SW coast of the Baltic Sea, between Danzig and Kaliningrad, crossed by the border between Poland and Russia. German name: **Frisches Haff**. Polish name: **Wislany Zalew**. Russian name: **Vislinsky Zaliv**

visual *adj* **1** done by or used in seeing **2** capable of being

seen [Latin *visus* sight] > **visually** *adv*

visual aids *pl n* objects to be looked at that help the viewer to understand or remember something

visual display unit *n computers* a device with a screen for displaying data held in a computer

visualize *or* **-lise** *vb* **-lizing, -lized** *or* **-lising, -lised** to form a mental image of (something not at that moment visible) > **visualization** *or* **-lisation** *n*

vital *adj* **1** essential or highly important: *marriage isn't such a vital part of his life* **2** energetic or lively: *the epitome of vital youthful manhood* **3** necessary to maintain life: *the vital organs* > *n* **4 vitals** the bodily organs, such as the brain and heart, that are necessary to maintain life [Latin *vita* life] > **vitally** *adv*

vitality *n* physical or mental energy

vitalize *or* **-lise** *vb* **-lizing, -lized** *or* **-lising, -lised** to fill with life or vitality > **vitalization** *or* **-lisation** *n*

vital statistics *pl n* **1** population statistics, such as the numbers of births, marriages, and deaths **2** *informal* the measurements of a woman's bust, waist, and hips

vitamin *n* one of a group of substances that occur naturally in certain foods and are essential for normal health and growth [from Latin *vita* life + AMINE]

Vitebsk *n* a city in E Belarus, a port on the Dvina river: taken by Russia in 1772. Pop: 344 000 (2005 est)

vitiate (vish-ee-ate) *vb* **-ating, -ated** **1** to spoil or weaken the effectiveness of (something) **2** to destroy the legal effect of (a contract) [Latin *vitiare* to injure] > **vitiation** *n*

viticulture *n* the cultivation of grapevines [Latin *vitis* vine]

Viti Levu *n* the largest island of Fiji: mountainous. Chief town (and capital of the state): Suva. Pop: 580 000 (latest est). Area: 10 386 sq km (4010 sq miles)

Vitoria¹ *n* a city in NE Spain: scene of Wellington's decisive victory (1813) over Napoleon's forces in the Peninsular War. Pop: 223 257 (2003 est). Official name (including the Basque name): **Vitoria-Gasteiz**

Vitoria² *n* Francisco de. ?1486–1546, Spanish theologian, sometimes considered the father of international law. He criticized Spanish colonial policy in the New World and argued that war was only defensible in certain strictly defined circumstances

Vitória *n* a port in E Brazil, capital of Espírito Santo state, on an island in the Bay of Espírito Santo. Pop: 1 602 000 (2005 est)

vitreous *adj* **1** of or like glass **2** of or relating to the vitreous humour [Latin *vitrum* glass]

vitreous humour *or* **vitreous body** *n* a transparent gelatinous substance that fills the eyeball between the lens and the retina

vitrify *vb* **-fies, -fying, -fied** to change into glass or a glassy substance > **vitrification** *n*

vitriol *n* **1** language expressing bitterness and hatred **2** sulphuric acid [Latin *vitrum* glass, referring to the glossy appearance of the sulphates]

vitriolic *adj* (of language) severely bitter or harsh

Vitruvius Pollio *n* Marcus. 1st century BC, Roman architect, noted for his treatise *De architectura*, the only surviving Roman work on architectural theory and a major influence on Renaissance architects > **Vitruvian** *adj*

vituperative (vite-tyew-pra-tiv) *adj* bitterly abusive [Latin *vituperare* to blame] > **vituperation** *n*

viva¹ *interj* long live (a specified person or thing) [Italian, literally: may (he) live!]

viva² *Brit* *n* **1** an examination in the form of an interview > *vb* **vivaing, vivaed** **2** to examine (a candidate) in a spoken interview [from VIVA VOCE]

vivace (viv-vah-chee) *adj music* to be performed in a lively manner [Italian]

vivacious *adj* full of energy and enthusiasm [Latin *vivax* lively]

vivacity *n* the quality of being vivacious

Vivaldi *n* Antonio. ?1675–1741, Italian composer and violinist, noted esp. for his development of the solo

V

concerto. His best-known work is *The Four Seasons* (1725)

vivarium *n, pl* **-riums** *or* **-ria** a place where live animals are kept under natural conditions [Latin *vivus* alive]

viva voce (vive-a voh-chee) *adv, adj* **1** by word of mouth ▷ *n* **2** same as **viva²** (1) [Medieval Latin, literally: with living voice]

Vivekananda *n* original name *Narendranath Datta*. 1862–1902, Indian Hindu religious teacher. A disciple of Ramakrishna, he introduced Vedantism to the West

vivid *adj* **1** very bright: *a vivid blue sky* **2** very clear and detailed: *vivid memories* **3** easily forming lifelike images: *a vivid imagination* [Latin *vividus* animated] **> vividly** *adv* **> vividness** *n*

vivify *vb* **-fies, -fying, -fied 1** to bring to life **2** to make more vivid or striking [Latin *vivus* alive + *facere* to make]

viviparous (viv-vip-a-russ) *adj* giving birth to living offspring, as most mammals do [Latin *vivus* alive + *parere* to bring forth]

vivisection *n* the performing of experiments on living animals, involving cutting into or dissecting the body [Latin *vivus* living + *sectio* a cutting] **> vivisectionist** *n*

vixen *n* **1** a female fox **2** *Brit, Austral and NZ informal* a spiteful woman [related to Old English *fyxe*, feminine of *fox*]

viz *adv* namely: used to specify items: *I had only one object, viz, to beat the Germans* [abbreviated from Latin *videlicet* namely]

Vizagapatam *n* a variant spelling of **Vishakhapatnam**

vizier (viz-zeer) *n* a high official in certain Muslim countries [Turkish *vezīr*]

vizor *n* same as **visor**

Vlaardingen *n* a port in the W Netherlands, in South Holland west of Rotterdam: the third largest port in the Netherlands. Pop: 74 000 (2003 est)

Vladikavkaz *n* a city in S Russia, capital of the North Ossetian Republic on the N slopes of the Caucasus. Pop: 318 000 (2005 est). Former names: (1944–54) **Dzaudzhikau**, (1954–91) **Ordzhonikidze**

Vladimir¹ *n* a city in W central Russia: capital of the principality of Vladimir until the court transferred to Moscow in 1328. Pop: 310 000 (2005 est)

Vladimir² *n* Saint, called *the Great*. ?956–1015, grand prince of Kiev (980–1015); first Christian ruler of Russia. Feast day: July 15

Vladivostok *n* a port in SE Russia, on the Sea of Japan: terminus of the Trans-Siberian Railway; the main Russian Pacific naval base since 1872 and chief commercial and civilian Russian port in the Far East; university (1956). Pop: 584 000 (2005 est)

Vlaminck *n* Maurice de. 1876–1958, French painter of the Fauve school

VLF *or* **vlf** *radio* very low frequency

Vlissingen *n* the Dutch name for **Flushing**

vlog *n* **1** a video journal uploaded to the internet ▷ *vb* **vlogging, vlogged 2** to create and upload vlogs **> vlogger** *n* **> vlogging** *n*

Vlorë *or* **Vlonë** *n* a port in SW Albania, on the **Bay of Vlorë**: under Turkish rule from 1462 until Albanian independence was declared here in 1912. Pop: 124 000 (2006 est). Ancient name: **Avlona**. Also called: **Valona**

Vltava *n* a river in the Czech Republic, rising in the Bohemian Forest and flowing generally southeast and then north to the River Elbe near Melnik. Length: 434 km (270 miles). German name: **Moldau**

V neck *n* **a** a neck on a garment that comes down to a point, like the letter V **b** a sweater with a neck like this **> V-neck** *or* **V-necked** *adj*

vocab *n* short for **vocabulary**

vocable *n* *linguistics* a word regarded simply as a sequence of letters or spoken sounds [Latin *vocare* to call]

vocabulary *n, pl* **-laries 1** all the words that a person knows **2** all the words contained in a language **3** the specialist terms used in a given subject **4** a list of words in another language with their translations **5** a range of

symbols or techniques as used in any of the arts or crafts: *the building's vocabulary of materials, textures, and tones* [Latin *vocabulum* vocable]

vocal *adj* **1** of or relating to the voice: *vocal pitch* **2** expressing one's opinions clearly and openly: *a vocal minority with racist views* ▷ *n* **3 vocals** the singing part of a piece of jazz or pop music [Latin *vox* voice] **> vocally** *adv*

vocal cords *pl n* either of two pairs of membranous folds in the larynx, of which the lower pair can be made to vibrate and produce sound by forcing air from the lungs over them

vocalist *n* a singer with a pop group

vocalize *or* **-lise** *vb* **-lizing, -lized** *or* **-lising, -lised 1** to express with or use the voice **2** to make vocal or articulate: *vocalize your discontent* **3** *phonetics* to articulate (a speech sound) with voice **> vocalization** *or* **-lisation** *n*

vocation *n* **1 a** a specified profession or trade **2 a** a special urge to a particular calling or career, esp. a religious one **b** such a calling or career [Latin *vocare* to call]

vocational *adj* directed towards a particular profession or trade: *vocational training*

vocative *n* *grammar* a grammatical case used in some languages when addressing a person or thing [Latin *vocare* to call]

vociferate *vb* **-rating, -rated** to exclaim or cry out about (something) noisily [Latin *vox* voice + *ferre* to bear] **> vociferation** *n*

vociferous *adj* loud and forceful: *a vociferous minority* **> vociferously** *adv*

VOD video on demand: an interactive TV system that allows the viewer to select content and view it at a time of his or her own choosing

vodka *n* a clear alcoholic spirit originating in Russia, made from potatoes or grain [Russian]

voetsak *or* **voetsek** (foot-sak) *interj S African offensive, informal* an expression of dismissal or rejection [Afrikaans, from Dutch *voort se ek* forward, I say, commonly applied to animals]

Vogel *n* Sir Julius. 1835–99, New Zealand statesman; prime minister of New Zealand (1873–75; 1876)

Vogts *n* Hans-Hubert, known as *Berti*. born 1946, German footballer and coach; played in 96 matches for West Germany (1967–79); coach of Germany (1990–98), with whom he won the 1996 European Championships, and Scotland (2002–04)

vogue *n* **1** the popular style at a given time **2 in vogue** fashionable ▷ *adj* **3** fashionable: *a vogue word* [French] **> voguish** *adj*

voice *n* **1** the sound made by the vibration of the vocal cords, esp. when modified by the tongue and mouth **2** a distinctive tone of the speech sounds characteristic of a particular person: *he can recognize her voice* **3** the ability to speak or sing: *he had at last found his voice* **4** the condition or quality of a person's voice: *her voice was kind* **5** the musical sound of a singing voice: *what I have is a good voice and a great love of lyrics* **6** the expression of feeling or opinion: *there was a chorus of dissenting voices* **7** a right to express an opinion: *the party should now move towards a system which will give every member an equal voice* **8** *grammar* a category of the verb that expresses whether it is active or passive **9** *phonetics* the sound characterizing the articulation of several speech sounds, that is produced when the vocal cords are vibrated by the breath **10 with one voice** unanimously ▷ *vb* **voicing, voiced 11** to express verbally: *anyone with an objection has a chance to voice it* **12** to articulate (a speech sound) with voice [Latin *vox*]

voiced *adj* *phonetics* articulated with accompanying vibration of the vocal cords, for example 'b' in English

voiceless *adj* **1** without a voice **2** *phonetics* articulated without accompanying vibration of the vocal cords, for example 'p' in English

voice mail *n* an electronic system for the transfer and storage of telephone messages, which can then be dealt with by the user at his or her convenience

voice-over *n* the voice of an unseen commentator heard during a film

void *n* **1** a feeling or condition of loneliness or deprivation **2** an empty space or area ▷ *adj* **3** having no official value or authority, because the terms have been broken or have not been fulfilled: *the race was declared void and rerun* **4** old-fashioned or literary empty: *behold, the tomb is void!* **5 void of** devoid of or without: *the fact of being punished becomes void of all moral significance* ▷ *vb* **6** to make ineffective or invalid **7** to empty **8** to discharge the contents of (the bowels or bladder) [Latin *vacare* to be empty]

voile (voyl) *n* a light semitransparent dress fabric [French: veil]

Voiotia *n* a department of E central Greece: corresponds to ancient Boeotia and part of ancient Phocis. Pop: 123 913 (2001). Area: 3173 sq km (1225 sq miles)

voip *n informal* voice-over internet protocol: a system for converting analogue signals to digital so that telephone calls may be made over the internet

Vojvodina *or* **Voivodina** *n* an autonomous region of Serbia, in the N. Capital: Novi Sad. Pop: 2 024 487 (2002). Area: 22 489 sq km (8683 sq miles)

vol. volume

volatile (voll-a-tile) *adj* **1** (of circumstances) liable to sudden change **2** (of people) liable to sudden changes of mood and behaviour **3** (of a substance) changing quickly from a solid or liquid form to a vapour [Latin *volare* to fly] ⟩ **volatility** *n*

volatilize *or* **-lise** *vb* **-lizing, -lized** *or* **-lising, -lised** to change from a solid or liquid to a vapour ⟩ **volatilization** *or* **-lisation** *n*

vol-au-vent (voll-oh-von) *n* a very light puff pastry case with a savoury filling [French, literally: flight in the wind]

volcanic *adj* **1** of or relating to volcanoes: *volcanic ash* **2** displaying sudden violence or anger: *their boisterous and often volcanic behaviour*

volcano *n, pl* **-noes** *or* **-nos** **1** an opening in the earth's crust from which molten lava, ashes, dust, and gases are ejected from below the earth's surface **2** a mountain formed from volcanic material ejected from a vent [Italian, from Latin *Volcanus* Vulcan, Roman god of fire]

Volcano Islands *pl n* a group of three volcanic islands in the W Pacific, about 1100 km (700 miles) south of Japan: the largest is Iwo Jima, taken by US forces in 1945 and returned to Japan in 1968. Area: about 28 sq km (11 sq miles). Japanese name: **Kazan Retto**

vole *n* a small rodent with a stocky body and a short tail [short for *volemouse*, from Old Norse *vollr* field + *mus* mouse]

Volga *n* a river in W Russia, rising in the Valdai Range and flowing through a chain of small lakes to the Rybinsk Reservoir and south to the Caspian Sea through Volgograd: the longest river in Europe. Length: 3690 km (2293 miles)

Volgograd *n* a port in SW Russia, on the River Volga: scene of a major engagement (1918) during the civil war and again in World War II (1942–43), in which the German forces were defeated; major industrial centre. Pop: 1 016 000 (2005 est). Former names: (until 1925) **Tsaritsyn,** (1925–61) **Stalingrad**

volition *n* **1** the ability to decide things for oneself **2 of one's own volition** through one's own choice [Latin *volo* I will] ⟩ **volitional** *adj*

volley *n* **1** the simultaneous firing of several weapons **2** the bullets fired **3** a burst of questions or critical comments **4** *sport* a stroke or kick at a moving ball before it hits the ground ▷ *vb* **5** to fire (weapons) in a volley **6** *sport* to hit or kick (a moving ball) before it hits the ground [French *volée* a flight]

volleyball *n* a game in which two teams hit a large ball backwards and forwards over a high net with their hands

Vologda *n* an industrial city in W central Russia. Pop: 295 000 (2005 est)

Vólos *n* a port in E Greece, in Thessaly on the **Gulf of Volos** (an inlet of the Aegean): the third largest port in Greece. Pop: 129 000 (2005 est)

volt *n* the SI unit of electric potential; the potential difference between two points on a conductor carrying a current of 1 ampere, when the power dissipated between these points is 1 watt [after Count Alessandro **Volta**]

Volta[1] *n* **1** a river in W Africa, formed by the confluence of the **Black Volta** and the **White Volta** in N central Ghana: flows south to the Bight of Benin: the chief river of Ghana. Length: 480 km (300 miles); (including the Black Volta) 1600 km (1000 miles) **2 Lake Volta** an artificial lake in Ghana, extending 408 km (250 miles) upstream from the **Volta River Dam** on the Volta River: completed in 1966. Area: 8482 sq km (3275 sq miles)

Volta[2] *n* Count **Alessandro**. 1745–1827, Italian physicist after whom the volt is named. He made important contributions to the theory of current electricity and invented the voltaic pile (1800), the electrophorus (1775), and an electroscope

voltage *n* an electromotive force or potential difference expressed in volts

voltaic *adj* same as **galvanic** (1)

Voltaire *n* pseudonym of *François Marie Arouet*. 1694–1778, French writer, whose outspoken belief in religious, political, and social liberty made him the embodiment of the 18th-century Enlightenment. His major works include *Lettres philosophiques* (1734) and the satire *Candide* (1759). He also wrote plays, such as *Zaïre* (1732), poems, and scientific studies. He suffered several periods of banishment for his radical views ⟩ **Voltairean** *or* **Voltairian** *adj, n*

Volta Redonda *n* a city in SE Brazil, in Rio de Janeiro state on the Paraíba River: founded in 1941; site of South America's largest steelworks. Pop: 419 000 (2005 est)

volte-face (volt-fass) *n, pl* **volte-face** a reversal of opinion [Italian *volta* turn + *faccia* face]

voltmeter *n* an instrument for measuring voltage

Volturno *n* a river in S central Italy, flowing southeast and southwest to the Tyrrhenian Sea: scene of a battle (1860) during the wars for Italian unity, in which Garibaldi defeated the Neapolitans; German line of defence during World War II. Length: 175 km (109 miles)

voluble *adj* talking easily and at length [Latin *volubilis* turning readily] ⟩ **volubility** *n* ⟩ **volubly** *adv*

volume *n* **1** the magnitude of the three-dimensional space enclosed within or occupied by something **2** an amount or total: *the volume of trade between the two countries; the volume of military traffic* **3** loudness of sound **4** the control on a radio etc., for adjusting the loudness of sound **5** a book: *a slim volume* **6** one of several books that make up a series **7** a set of issues of a magazine over a specified period [Latin *volumen* a roll]

volumetric *adj* of or using measurement by volume: *a simple volumetric measurement*

voluminous *adj* **1** (of clothes) large and roomy **2** (of writings) extensive and detailed

voluntary *adj* **1** done or undertaken by free choice: *voluntary repatriation* **2** done or maintained without payment: *voluntary work* **3** (of muscles) having their action controlled by the will ▷ *n, pl* **-taries 4** *music* a composition, usually for organ, played at the beginning or end of a church service [Latin *voluntarius*] ⟩ **voluntarily** *adv*

volunteer *n* **1** a person who offers voluntarily to do something **2** a person who freely undertakes military service ▷ *vb* **3** to offer (oneself or one's services) by choice and without being forced **4** to enlist voluntarily for military service **5** to give (information) willingly **6** to offer the services of (another person)

voluptuary *n, pl* **-aries** a person devoted to luxury and sensual pleasures [Latin *voluptas* pleasure]

voluptuous *adj* **1** (of a woman) sexually alluring because of the fullness of her figure **2** pleasing to the senses: *voluptuous yellow peaches* **> voluptuously** *adv* **> voluptuousness** *n*

volute *n* a spiral or twisting shape or object, such as a carved spiral scroll on an Ionic capital [Latin *volvere* to roll up]

vomit *vb* **-iting, -ited 1** to eject (the contents of the stomach) through the mouth **2** to eject or be ejected forcefully ▷ *n* **3** the partly digested food and drink ejected in vomiting [Latin *vomitare* to vomit repeatedly]

von Braun *n* Wernher. 1912–77, US rocket engineer, born in Germany, where he designed the V-2 missile used in World War II. In the US he worked on the Apollo project

Vondel *n* Joost van den. 1587–1679, Dutch poet and dramatist, author of the Biblical plays *Lucifer* (1654), *Adam in Exile* (1664), and *Noah* (1667)

Vonnegut *n* Kurt. 1922–2007, US novelist. His works include *Cat's Cradle* (1963), *Slaughterhouse Five* (1969), *Galapagos* (1985), *Hocus Pocus* (1990), and *Timequake* (1997)

von Neumann *n* John. 1903–57, US mathematician, born in Hungary. He formulated game theory and contributed to the development of the atomic bomb and to the development of the stored-program computer (**von Neumann machine**)

von Sternberg *n* Joseph, real name *Jonas Sternberg*. 1894–1969, US film director, born in Austria, whose films include *The Blue Angel* (1930), *Blonde Venus* (1932), *The Scarlet Empress* (1934), and the unfinished *I, Claudius* (1937)

von Stroheim *n* Erich, real name *Hans Erich Maria Stroheim von Nordenwall*. 1885–1957, US film director and actor, born in Austria, whose films include *Foolish Wives* (1921) and *Greed* (1923)

voodoo *n* **1** a religion involving ancestor worship and witchcraft, practised by Black people in the West Indies, esp. in Haiti ▷ *adj* **2** of or relating to voodoo: *a voodoo curse* [from West African]

voorkamer (foor-kahm-er) *n* S African the front room of a house [Afrikaans]

voracious *adj* **1** eating or craving great quantities of food **2** very eager or insatiable in some activity: *a voracious collector* [Latin *vorare* to devour] **> voraciously** *adv* **> voracity** *n*

Vorarlberg *n* a mountainous state of W Austria. Capital: Bregenz. Pop: 356 590 (2003 est). Area: 2601 sq km (1004 sq miles)

Voronezh *n* a city in W Russia: engineering, chemical, and food-processing industries; university (1918). Pop: 842 000 (2005 est)

Voroshilov *n* Kliment Yefremovich. 1881–1969, Soviet military leader; president of the Soviet Union (1953–60)

Voroshilovgrad *n* the former name (1935–91) of Lugansk

Voroshilovsk *n* the former name (1940–44) of **Stavropol**

Vorster *n* Balthazar Johannes, known as *John*. 1915–83, South African politician; Nationalist prime minister (1966–78); president (1978)

vortex (vor-tex) *n*, *pl* **-tices** (-tiss-seez) **1** a whirling mass or motion, such as a whirlpool or whirlwind **2** a situation which draws people into it against their will: *the vortex of other people's problems* [Latin: a whirlpool] **> vortical** *adj*

Vosges *n* **1** a mountain range in E France, west of the Rhine valley. Highest peak: 1423 m (4672 ft) **2** a department of NE France, in Lorraine region. Capital: Épinal. Pop: 381 277 (2003 est). Area: 5903 sq km (2302 sq miles)

votary *n*, *pl* **-ries 1** RC Church, Eastern Churches a person who has dedicated himself or herself to religion by taking vows **2** a person devoted to a cause [Latin *votum* a vow] **> votaress** *fem n*

vote *n* **1** a choice made by a participant in a shared decision, esp. in electing a candidate **2** the right to vote **3** the total number of votes cast **4** the opinion of a group of people as determined by voting: *the draft should be put to the vote at a meeting of the Council* **5** a body of votes or voters collectively: *the youth vote* ▷ *vb* **voting, voted 6** to make a choice by vote **7** to authorize or allow by voting: *the organizing committee voted itself controversial new powers* **8** to declare oneself as being (something or in favour of something) by voting: *I've always voted Labour* **9** *informal* to declare by common opinion: *he was voted hotelier of the year for the third time* [Latin *votum* a solemn promise]

vote down *vb* to decide against or defeat in a vote: *a proposed British resolution was voted down*

voter *n* a person who can or does vote

votive *adj* done or given to fulfil a vow [Latin *votivus* promised by a vow]

vouch *vb* **vouch for a** to give personal assurance about: *I can vouch for the man, he's a relative by marriage* **b** to give supporting evidence for or be proof of: *his presence alone vouches for the political nature of the trip* [Latin *vocare* to call]

voucher *n* **1** a ticket or card used instead of money to buy specified goods: *a gift voucher* **2** a document recording a financial transaction [Old French *vo(u)cher* to summon]

vouchsafe *vb* **-safing, -safed 1** *old-fashioned* to give or grant: *she has powers vouchsafed to few* **2** to offer assurances about; guarantee: *he absolutely vouchsafed your integrity* [*vouch + safe*]

vow *n* **1** a solemn and binding promise **2** **take vows** to enter a religious order and commit oneself to its rule of life by the vows of poverty, chastity, and obedience ▷ *vb* **3** to promise or decide solemnly: *she vowed to fight on; I solemnly vowed that some day I would return to live in Europe* [Latin *votum*]

vowel *n* **a** a voiced speech sound made with the mouth open and the stream of breath unobstructed by the tongue, teeth, or lips, for example *a* or *e* **b** a letter representing this [Latin *vocalis (littera)*, from *vox* voice]

vox pop *n* Brit interviews with members of the public on a radio or television programme

vox populi *n* public opinion [Latin: the voice of the people]

voyage *n* **1** a long journey by sea or in space ▷ *vb* **-aging, -aged 2** to go on a voyage: *in this story he voyages to Ireland* [Latin *viaticum* provision for travelling] **> voyager** *n*

voyageur (voy-ahzh-**ur**) *n* **1** formerly a French or Métis canoeman who transported furs from trading posts in the North American interior **2** (in Canada) a woodsman, guide, trapper, boatman, or explorer, esp. in the North [French: voyager]

voyeur *n* a person who obtains sexual pleasure from watching people undressing or having sexual intercourse [French, literally: one who sees] **> voyeurism** *n* **> voyeuristic** *adj*

Voysey *n* Charles (Francis Annesley). 1857–1941, British architect and designer of furniture, fittings, and decor

Voznesensky *n* Andrei (Andreievich).1933–2010, Russian poet, noted for his experimental style

VPL *humorous* visible panty line

VPN virtual private network: a network that uses the internet to transfer information using secure methods

VR virtual reality

vrou (froh) *n* S African an Afrikaner woman, esp. a married woman [Afrikaans]

vs versus

VSA (in New Zealand) Voluntary Service Abroad

V-sign *n* **1** (in Britain and Australia) an offensive gesture made by sticking up the index and middle fingers with the palm of the hand inwards **2** a similar gesture with the palm outwards meaning victory or peace

VSO (in Britain) Voluntary Service Overseas

VSOP very special (or superior) old pale: used of brandy or port

Vt. *or* **VT** Vermont

VTOL vertical takeoff and landing

VTR video tape recorder

Vuelta Abajo *n* a region of W Cuba: famous for its tobacco

V

Vuillard *n* Jean Édouard. 1868–1940, French painter and lithographer

Vulcan *n* the Roman god of fire

vulcanite *n* a hard black rubber produced by vulcanizing natural rubber with sulphur

vulcanize *or* **-nise** *vb* **-nizing, -nized** *or* **-nising, -nised** to treat (rubber) with sulphur under heat and pressure to improve elasticity and strength [after VULCAN]
⟩ **vulcanization** *or* **-nisation** *n*

vulgar *adj* **1** showing lack of good taste, decency, or refinement: *vulgar tabloid sensationalism* **2** denoting a form of a language spoken by the ordinary people, rather than the literary form [Latin *vulgus* the common people]
⟩ **vulgarly** *adv*

vulgar fraction *n* same as **simple fraction**

vulgarian *n* a vulgar person, usually one who is rich

vulgarism *n* a coarse or obscene word or phrase

vulgarity *n, pl* **-ties** **1** the condition of being vulgar **2** a vulgar action or phrase

vulgarize *or* **-rise** *vb* **-rizing, -rized** *or* **-rising, -rised** **1** to make vulgar **2** to make (something little known or difficult to understand) popular ⟩ **vulgarization** *or* **-risation** *n*

Vulgar Latin *n* any of the dialects of Latin spoken in the Roman Empire other than classical Latin

Vulgate *n* the fourth-century Latin version of the Bible

vulnerable *adj* **1** able to be physically or emotionally hurt **2** easily influenced or tempted **3** *military* exposed to attack **4** financially weak and likely to fail: *this company could be vulnerable in a prolonged economic slump* **5** *bridge* (of a side that has won one game towards rubber) subject to increased bonuses or penalties [Latin *vulnus* a wound]
⟩ **vulnerability** *n*

vulpine *adj* **1** of or like a fox **2** clever and cunning [Latin *vulpes* fox]

vulture *n* **1** a very large bird of prey that feeds on flesh of dead animals **2** a person who profits from the misfortune and weakness of others [Latin *vultur*]

vulva *n* the external genitals of human females [Latin: covering, womb, matrix]

vuvuzela *n S African* an elongated plastic instrument that football fans blow to make a loud trumpeting noise [from Zulu]

Vyatka *n* the former name (1780–1934) of **Kirov**

Vyborg *n* a port in NW Russia, at the head of **Vyborg Bay** (an inlet of the Gulf of Finland): belonged to Finland (1918–40). Pop: 79 224 (2002). Finnish name: **Viipuri**. Swedish name: **Viborg**

vying *vb* the present participle of **vie**

Vyshinsky *or* **Vishinsky** *n* Andrei Yanuaryevich. 1883–1954, Soviet jurist, statesman, and diplomat; foreign minister (1949–53). He was public prosecutor (1935–38) at the trials held to purge Stalin's rivals and was the Soviet representative at the United Nations (1945–49; 1953–54)

V

Ww

w *cricket* **1** wicket **2** wide

W **1** *chem* tungsten **2** watt **3** West(ern)

W. **1** Wales **2** Welsh

WA **1** Washington (state) **2** Western Australia

Waadt *n* the German name for **Vaud**

Waal *n* a river in the central Netherlands: the S branch of the Lower Rhine. Length: 84 km (52 miles)

Wabash *n* a river in the E central US, rising in W Ohio and flowing west and southwest to join the Ohio River in Indiana. Length: 764 km (475 miles)

WACA *n* **1** Western Australian Cricket Association **2** the WACA this Association's cricket ground in Perth

Wace *n* Robert. born ?1100, Anglo-Norman poet; author of the *Roman de Brut* and *Roman de Rou*

wacko *chiefly US and Canad informal adj* **1** mad or eccentric ▷ *n, pl* **wackos** **2** a mad or eccentric person [from WACKY]

wacky *adj* **wackier, wackiest** *slang* odd, eccentric, or crazy: *a wacky idea* [dialect: a fool] **>** **wackiness** *n*

wad *n* **1** a small mass of soft material, such as cotton wool, used for packing or stuffing **2** a roll or bundle of banknotes or papers [Late Latin *wadda*]

Wadai *n* a former independent sultanate of NE central Africa: now the E part of Chad

Waddenzee *n* the part of the North Sea between the Dutch mainland and the West Frisian Islands

Waddesdon Manor *n* a mansion near Aylesbury in Buckinghamshire: built (1880–89) in the French style for the Rothschild family: noted for its furnishings and collections of porcelain and paintings

wadding *n* a soft material used for padding or stuffing

Waddington *n* C(onrad) H(all). 1905–75, British embryologist and geneticist: author of *Principles of Embryology* (1956) and *The Ethical Animal* (1960)

waddle *vb* **-dling, -dled** **1** to walk with short steps, rocking slightly from side to side ▷ *n* **2** a swaying walk [from *wade*]

waddy *n, pl* **-dies** a heavy wooden club used by Australian Aborigines

wade *vb* **wading, waded** **1** to walk slowly and with difficulty through water or mud **2 wade in** *or* **into** to begin doing (something) in an energetic way: *wading into the fray* **3 wade through** to proceed with difficulty through: *a stack of literature to wade through* [Old English *wadan*]

Wade *n* born 1945, English tennis player; won three Grand Slam singles titles: US Open (1968), Australian Open (1972), and Wimbledon (1977)

wader *n* a long-legged bird, such as the heron or stork, that lives near water and feeds on fish. Also called: **wading bird**

waders *pl n* long waterproof boots which completely cover the legs, worn by anglers for standing in water

wadi (wod-dee) *n, pl* **-dies** a river in N Africa or Arabia, which is dry except in the rainy season [Arabic]

Wadi Halfa *n* a town in the N Sudan that was partly submerged by Lake Nasser: an important archaeological site

Wad Medani *n* a town in the E Sudan, on the Blue Nile: headquarters of the Gezira irrigation scheme; agricultural research centre. Pop: 332 000 (2005 est)

wafer *n* **1** a thin crisp sweetened biscuit, often served with ice cream **2** *Christianity* a round thin piece of unleavened bread used at Communion **3** *electronics* a small thin slice of germanium or silicon that is separated into numerous individual components or circuits [Old French *waufre*]

wafer-thin *adj* very thin: *wafer-thin meat*

waffle¹ *n* a square crisp pancake with a gridlike pattern [Dutch *wafel*]

waffle² *informal, chiefly Brit, Austral and NZ vb* **-fling, -fled** **1** to speak or write in a vague and wordy manner ▷ *n* **2** vague and wordy speech or writing [origin unknown]

waft *vb* **1** to move gently through the air as if being carried by the wind: *the scent of summer flowers gently wafting through my window* ▷ *n* **2** a scent carried on the air [Middle Dutch *wachter* guard]

wag¹ *vb* **wagging, wagged** **1** to move rapidly and repeatedly from side to side or up and down: *Franklin wagged his tail* **2** *Brit, Austral and NZ slang* to play truant from (school) ▷ *n* **3** an instance of wagging [Old English *wagian*]

wag² *n old-fashioned* a humorous or witty person [origin unknown] **>** **waggish** *adj*

Wag *n informal* the wife or girlfriend of a famous sportsperson

wage *n* **1** Also: **wages** the money paid in return for a person's work, esp. when paid weekly or daily rather than monthly: *a campaign for higher wages* ▷ *vb* **waging, waged** **2** to engage in (a campaign or war) [Old French *wagier* to pledge]

wager *n* **1** a bet on the outcome of an event or activity ▷ *vb* **2** to bet (something, esp. money) on the outcome of an event or activity [Old French *wagier* to pledge]

Wagga Wagga *n* a city in SE Australia, in New South Wales on the Murrumbidgee River: agricultural trading centre. Pop: 44 451 (2001)

waggle *vb* **-gling, -gled** to move with a rapid shaking or wobbling motion [from WAG¹]

Wagner *n* **1** Otto. 1841–1918, Austrian architect, whose emphasis on function and structure in such buildings as the Post Office Savings Bank, Vienna (1904–06), influenced the development of modern architecture **2** (Wilhelm) Richard. 1813–83, German romantic composer noted chiefly for his invention of the music drama. His cycle of four such dramas *The Ring of the Nibelung* was produced at his own theatre in Bayreuth in 1876. His other operas include *Tannhäuser* (1845; revised 1861), *Tristan and Isolde* (1865), and *Parsifal* (1882)

Wagner-Jauregg *n* Julius. 1857–1940, Austrian psychiatrist and neurologist; a pioneer of the use of fever therapy in the treatment of mental disorders. Nobel prize for physiology or medicine 1927

wagon *or* **waggon** *n* **1** a four-wheeled vehicle used for carrying heavy loads, sometimes pulled by a horse or tractor **2** an open railway freight truck **3** a lorry **4 on the wagon** informal abstaining from alcoholic drink [Dutch *wagen*] **> wagoner** or **waggoner** n

Wagram n a village in NE Austria: scene of the defeat of the Austrians by Napoleon in 1809

wagtail n a small songbird of Eurasia and Africa with a very long tail that wags up and down when it walks

Wagyu (**wag**-yoo) n **1** any of several Japanese breeds of beef cattle, raised to produce Kobe beef **2** another name for **Kobe beef**

wahine (wah-**hee**-nay) n NZ a Māori woman, esp. a wife [Māori]

wahoo n a large food and game fish of tropical seas

waif n a person, esp. a child, who is, or who looks as if he or she might be, homeless or neglected [Anglo-Norman]

Waikaremoana n Lake Waikaremoana a lake in the North Island of New Zealand in a dense bush setting. Area: about 55 sq km (21 sq miles)

Waikato n the longest river in New Zealand, flowing northwest across North Island to the Tasman Sea. Length: 350 km (220 miles)

Waikiki n a resort area in Hawaii, on SE Oahu: a suburb of Honolulu

wail vb **1** to utter a prolonged high-pitched cry of pain or sorrow ▷ n **2** a prolonged high-pitched cry of pain or sorrow [from Old Norse] **> wailing** n, adj

Wailing Wall n another name for **Western Wall**

wain n poetic a farm cart [Old English *wægn*]

Wain n John (**Barrington**). 1925–94, British novelist, poet, and critic. His novels include *Hurry on Down* (1953), *Strike the Father Dead* (1962), and *Young Shoulders* (1982)

wainscot n a wooden covering on the lower half of the walls of a room. Also: **wainscoting** [Middle Low German *wagenschot*]

Wainwright n **1** Loudon. born 1946, US rock singer and songwriter. His albums include *Loudon Wainwright III* (1970), *Fame and Wealth* (1983), *Grown Man* (1995) and *Strange Weirdos* (2007) **2** his daughter, **Martha**. born 1976, US rock singer and songwriter. Her recordings include the album *Martha Wainwright* (2005) **3** his son, **Rufus**. born 1973, US rock singer and songwriter. His albums include *Want One* (2003), *Want Two* (2004) and *Release the Stars* (2007)

waist n **1** anatomy the narrow part of the body between the ribs and the hips **2** the part of a garment covering the waist [origin unknown]

waistband n a band of material sewn on to the waist of a garment to strengthen it

waistcoat n a sleeveless upper garment which buttons up the front and is usually worn by men over a shirt and under a jacket

waistline n **1** an imaginary line around the body at the narrowest part of the waist **2** the place where the upper and lower part of a garment are joined together

wait vb **1** to stay in one place or remain inactive in expectation of something: *the delegates have to wait for a reply* **2** to be temporarily delayed: *the celebrations can wait* **3** (of a thing) to be ready or be in store: *waiting for her on the library table was the latest Jilly Cooper novel* ▷ n **4** the act or a period of waiting **5 lie in wait for a** to prepare an ambush for **b** to be ready or be in store for ▶ See also **wait on, wait up** [Old French *waitier*]

Waitangi Day n February 6, the national day of New Zealand commemorating the Treaty Of Waitangi in 1840

Waite n Terry, full name *Terence Hardy Waite*. born 1939, British special envoy to the Archbishop of Canterbury, who negotiated the release of Western hostages held in the Middle East before being taken hostage himself (1987–91) in Lebanon

waiter n a man who serves people with food and drink in a restaurant

waiting game n **play a waiting game** to postpone taking action or making a decision in order to gain an advantage

waiting list n a list of people waiting for something that is not immediately available: *a long waiting list for heart surgery*

waiting room n a room in which people can wait, for example at a railway station or doctor's surgery

wait on vb also **wait upon 1** to serve (people) with food and drink in a restaurant **2** to look after the needs of: *they were waited on by a manservant* ▷ interj **3** NZ stop! hold on!

waitress n **1** a woman who serves people with food and drink in a restaurant ▷ vb **2** to work as a waitress

wait up vb to delay going to bed in order to wait for someone or something: *when he's late, she waits up for him*

Waitz n Grete. 1953–2011, Norwegian long-distance runner and marathon world champion

waive vb **waiving, waived** to refrain from enforcing or claiming (a rule or right) [Old French *weyver*]

waiver n the act or an instance of voluntary giving up a claim or right

Wajda n Andrei or Andrzej. born 1926, Polish film director. His films include *Ashes and Diamonds* (1958), *The Wedding* (1972), *Man of Iron* (1980), *Danton* (1982), *Miss Nobody* (1997), and *Katyń* (2007)

waka n NZ a Māori canoe

Wakayama n an industrial city in S Japan, on S Honshu. Pop: 391 008 (2002 est)

wake[1] vb **waking, woke, woken 1** Also: **wake up** to become conscious again or bring (someone) to consciousness again after a sleep **2 wake up** to make (someone) more alert after a period of inactivity **3 wake up to** to become aware of: *the world did not wake up to this tragedy until many people had died* **4 waking hours** the time when a person is awake: *he often used his waking hours to write music* ▷ n **5** a watch or vigil held over the body of a dead person during the night before burial [Old English *wacian*]

> **USAGE** Where there is an object and the sense is the literal one *wake (up)* and *waken* are the commonest forms: *I wakened him; I woke him (up)*. Both verbs are also commonly used without an object: *I woke up. Awake* and *awaken* are preferred to other forms of *wake* where the sense is a figurative one: *he awoke to the danger*.

wake[2] n **1** the track left by a ship moving through water **2 in the wake of** following soon after: *the arrests come in the wake of the assassination* [Scandinavian]

Wakefield n **1** a city in N England, in Wakefield unitary authority, West Yorkshire: important since medieval times as an agricultural and textile centre. Pop: 76 886 (2001) **2** a unitary authority in N England, in West Yorkshire. Pop: 318 300 (2003 est). Area: 333 sq km (129 sq miles)

wakeful adj **1** unable to sleep **2** without sleep: *wakeful nights* **3** alert: *wakeful readiness* **> wakefulness** n

Wake Island n an atoll in the W central Pacific: claimed by the US in 1899; developed as a civil and naval air station in the late 1930s. Area: 8 sq km (3 sq miles)

waken vb to become conscious again or bring (someone) to consciousness again after a sleep

> **USAGE** See at **wake**[1].

Waksman n Selman Abraham. 1888–1973, US microbiologist, born in Russia. He discovered streptomycin: Nobel prize for physiology or medicine 1952

Walachia or **Wallachia** n a former principality of SE Europe: a vassal state of the Ottoman Empire from the 15th century until its union with Moldavia in 1859, subsequently forming present-day Romania

Walachian or **Wallachian** adj **1** of or relating to the former SE European principality of Walachia (now part of Romania) or its inhabitants ▷ *n* **2** a native or inhabitant of Walachia

Wałbrzych *n* an industrial city in SW Poland. Pop: 176 000 (2005 est). German name: **Waldenburg**

Walcheren *n* an island in the SW Netherlands, in the Scheldt estuary: administratively part of Zeeland province; suffered severely in World War II, when the dykes were breached, and again in the floods of 1953. Area: 212 sq km (82 sq miles)

Walcott *n* **1 Derek (Alton)**. born 1930, St Lucian poet and playwright, whose works include the poetry collections *In a Green Night* (1962) and *The Bounty* (1997), the play *The Dream on Monkey Mountain* (1967), and the long poem *Omeros* (1990): Nobel prize for literature 1992 **2 Jersey Joe**, real name *Arnold Raymond Cream*. 1914–94, US boxer: world heavyweight champion 1951–52

Waldemar I *or* **Valdemar I** *n* known as *Waldemar the Great*. 1131–82, king of Denmark (1157–82). He conquered the Wends (1169), increased the territory of Denmark, and established the hereditary rule of his line

Waldemar II *or* **Valdemar II** *n* known as *Waldemar the Victorious*. 1170–1241, king of Denmark (1202–41); son of Waldemar I. He extended the Danish empire, conquering much of Estonia (1219)

Waldemar IV *or* **Valdemar IV** *n* surnamed *Atterdag*. ?1320–75, king of Denmark (1340–75), who reunited the Danish territories but was defeated (1368) by a coalition of his Baltic neighbours

Waldenburg *n* the German name for **Wałbrzych**

Waldheim *n* **Kurt**. 1918–2007, Austrian diplomat; secretary-general of the United Nations (1972–81); president of Austria (1986–92)

Wales¹ *n* a principality that is part of the United Kingdom, in the west of Great Britain; conquered by the English in 1282; parliamentary union with England took place in 1536: a separate Welsh Assembly with limited powers was established in 1999. Wales consists mainly of moorlands and mountains and has an economy that is chiefly agricultural, with an industrial and former coal-mining area in the south. Capital: Cardiff. Pop: 3 063 456 (2011 est). Area: 20 768 sq km (8017 sq miles). Welsh name: **Cymru**. Medieval Latin name: **Cambria**

Wales² *n* **Jimmy (Donal)**. born 1966, US internet entrepreneur and educator; co-founder (2001) of the open-source online encyclopedia Wikipedia

Wałęsa *n* **Lech**. born 1943, Polish statesman: president of Poland (1990–95); leader of the independent trade union Solidarity 1980–90; Nobel peace prize 1983

Waley *n* **Arthur**. real name *Arthur Schloss*. 1889–1966, English orientalist, best known for his translations of Chinese poetry

Walfish Bay *n* a variant spelling of **Walvis Bay**

walk *vb* **1** to move on foot at a moderate rate with at least one foot always on the ground **2** to pass through, on, or over on foot: *to walk a short distance* **3** to walk somewhere with (a person or a dog) **4 walking on air** very happy and excited **5 walk the streets** to wander about, esp. when looking for work or when homeless ▷ *n* **6** a short journey on foot, usually for pleasure **7** the action of walking rather than running **8** a manner of walking: *a proud slow walk* **9** a place or route for walking **10 walk of life** social position or profession: *people from all walks of life were drawn to her* ▸ See also **walk into**, **walk out**, etc. [Old English *wealcan*] ▷ **walker** *n*

walkabout *n* **1** an occasion when royalty, politicians, or other celebrities walk among and meet the public **2 go walkabout** *Austral* **a** to wander through the bush as a nomad **b** *informal* to be lost or misplaced **c** *informal* to lose one's concentration

Walker *n* **1 Alice (Malsenior)**. born 1944, US writer: her works include *In Love and Trouble: Stories of Black Women* (1973) and the novels *Meridian* (1976), *The Color Purple* (1982), and *Possessing the Secret of Joy* (1992) **2 Sir John**. born 1952, New Zealand middle-distance runner, the first athlete

to run one hundred sub-four-minute miles; won gold in the 1500 metres at the 1976 Olympics

walkie-talkie *n* a small combined radio transmitter and receiver that can be carried around by one person

walking stick *n* a stick or cane carried in the hand to assist walking

walk into *vb* to encounter unexpectedly: *the troop reinforcements had walked into a trap*

Walkman *n trademark* a small portable cassette player with headphones

walk-on *adj* (of a part in a film or play) small and not involving speaking

walk out *vb* **1** to leave suddenly and without explanation, usually in anger **2** (of workers) to go on strike **3 walk out on** *informal* to abandon or desert ▷ *n* **walkout** **4** a strike by workers

walkover *n* **1** *informal* an easy victory ▷ *vb* **walk over 2** to mistreat or bully; take advantage of: *if you don't make your mark early, people will walk all over you*

walkway *n* **1** a path designed for use by pedestrians **2** a passage or pathway between two buildings

wall *n* **1** a vertical structure made of stone, brick, or wood, with a length and height much greater than its thickness, used to enclose, divide, or support. Related adjective: **mural 2** anything that suggests a wall in function or effect: *a wall of elm trees; a wall of suspicion* **3** *anatomy* any lining or membrane that encloses a bodily cavity or structure: *cell walls* **4 drive someone up the wall** *slang* to make someone angry or irritated **5 go to the wall** *informal* to be financially ruined **6 have one's back to the wall** *informal* to be in a very difficult situation, with no obvious way out of it ▷ *vb* **7** to surround or enclose (an area) with a wall **8 wall in** *or* **up** to enclose (someone or something) completely in a room or place [Old English *weall*] ▷ **walled** *adj*

wallaby *n, pl* **-bies** a marsupial of Australia and New Guinea that resembles a small kangaroo [Aboriginal *wolabā*]

Wallace *n* **1 Alfred Russel**. 1823–1913, British naturalist, whose work on the theory of natural selection influenced Charles Darwin **2 Edgar**. 1875–1932, English crime novelist **3 Sir Richard**. 1818–90, English art collector and philanthropist. His bequest to the nation forms the Wallace Collection, London **4 Sir William**. ?1272–1305, Scottish patriot, who defeated the army of Edward I of England at Stirling (1297) but was routed at Falkirk (1298) and later executed

Wallachia *n* a variant spelling of **Walachia**

Wallachian *adj, n* a variant spelling of **Walachian**

wallah (woll-a) *n informal* a person involved with or in charge of a specified thing: *rickshaw wallahs* [Hindi *-wālā*]

wallaroo *n* a large stocky Australian kangaroo of rocky regions

Wallasey *n* a town in NW England, in Wirral unitary authority, Merseyside; near the mouth of the River Mersey, opposite Liverpool. Pop: 58 710 (2001)

wall bars *pl n* a series of horizontal bars attached to a wall and used in gymnastics

Wallenberg *n* **Raoul**. 1912–?, Swedish diplomat, who helped (1944–45) thousands of Hungarian Jews to escape from the Nazis. After his arrest (1945) by the Soviets nothing is certainly known of him; despite claims that he is still alive he is presumed to have died in prison

Wallenstein *or* **Waldstein** *n* **Albrecht Wenzel Eusebius von**, duke of Friedland and Mecklenburg, prince of Sagan. 1583–1634, German general and statesman, born in Bohemia. As leader of the Hapsburg forces in the Thirty Years' War he won many successes until his defeat at Lützen (1632) by Gustavus Adolphus

Waller *n* **1 Edmund**. 1606–87, English poet and politician, famous for his poem "Go, Lovely Rose" **2 Fats**, real name *Thomas Waller*. 1904–43, US jazz pianist and singer

wallet *n* a small folding case, usually of leather, for holding paper money and credit cards [Germanic]

walleye *n* a fish with large staring eyes

walleyed *adj* having eyes with an abnormal amount of white showing because of a squint [Old Norse *vagleygr*]

wallflower *n* **1** a plant grown for its clusters of yellow, orange, red, or purple fragrant flowers **2** *informal* a woman who does not join in the dancing at a party or dance because she has no partner

Wallis¹ *n* the German name for **Valais**

Wallis² *n* Sir **Barnes** (**Neville**). 1887–1979, English aeronautical engineer. He designed the airship R100, the Wellesley and Wellington bombers, and the bouncing bomb (1943), which was used to destroy the Ruhr dams during World War II

Wallis and Futuna Islands *pl n* a French overseas territory in the SW Pacific, west of Samoa. Capital: Mata-Utu. Pop: 15 507 (2013 est). Area: 367 sq km (143 sq miles)

Walloon (wol-**loon**) *n* **1** a French-speaking person from S Belgium or the neighbouring part of France **2** the French dialect of Belgium ▷ *adj* **3** of the Walloons [Germanic]

Walloon Brabant *n* a province of central Belgium, formed in 1995 from the S part of Brabant province: densely populated and intensively farmed, with large industrial centres. Pop: 360 717 (2004 est). Area: 1091 sq km (421 sq miles)

wallop *informal vb* **1** to hit hard ▷ *n* **2** a hard blow [Old French *waloper* to gallop]

walloping *informal n* **1** a severe physical beating ▷ *adj* **2** large or great: *a walloping amount of sodium*

wallow *vb* **1** to indulge oneself in some emotion: *they wallow in self-pity* **2** to lie or roll about in mud or water for pleasure ▷ *n* **3** the act or an instance of wallowing **4** a muddy place where animals wallow [Old English *wealwian* to roll (in mud)]

wallpaper *n* **1** a printed or embossed paper for covering the walls of a room ▷ *vb* **2** to cover (walls) with wallpaper

Wallsend *n* a town in NE England, in North Tyneside unitary authority, Tyne and Wear: situated on the River Tyne at the E end of Hadrian's Wall. Pop: 42 842 (2001)

Wall Street *n* a street in lower Manhattan, New York, where the Stock Exchange and major banks are situated, regarded as the embodiment of American finance

wall-to-wall *adj* (of carpeting) completely covering a floor

wally *n, pl* -**lies** *Brit slang* a stupid or foolish person [from the name *Walter*]

walnut *n* **1** an edible nut with a hard, wrinkled, light brown shell **2** a tree on which walnuts grow **3** the light brown wood of a walnut tree, used for making furniture [Old English *walh-hnutu* foreign nut]

Walpole *n* **1** **Horace**, 4th Earl of Orford. 1717–97, British writer, noted for his letters and for his delight in the Gothic, as seen in his house Strawberry Hill and his novel *The Castle of Otranto* (1764) **2** Sir **Hugh** (**Seymour**). 1884–1941, British novelist, born in New Zealand: best known for *The Herries Chronicle* (1930–33), a sequence of historical novels set in the Lake District **3** Sir **Robert**, 1st Earl of Orford. 1676–1745, English Whig statesman. As first lord of the Treasury and Chancellor of the Exchequer (1721–42) he was effectively Britain's first prime minister

walrus *n, pl* -**ruses** *or* -**rus** a mammal of cold northern seas, with two tusks that hang down from the upper jaw, tough thick skin, and coarse whiskers [Dutch: whale horse]

Walsall *n* **1** an industrial town in central England, in Walsall unitary authority, West Midlands: engineering, electronics. Pop: 170 994 (2001) **2** a unitary authority in central England, in the West Midlands. Pop: 252 400 (2003 est). Area: 106 sq km (41 sq miles)

Walsh *n* **Courtney** (**Andrew**). born 1962, West Indian

cricketer, born in Jamaica: a fast bowler, he took 519 wickets in 132 test matches (1984–2001)

Walsingham¹ *n* a village in E England, in Norfolk: remains of a medieval priory; site of the shrine of Our Lady of Walsingham

Walsingham² *n* Sir **Francis**. ?1530–90, English statesman. As secretary of state (1573–90) to Elizabeth I he developed a system of domestic and foreign espionage and uncovered several plots against the Queen

Walter *n* **1** **Bruno**, real name *Bruno Walter Schlesinger*. 1876–1962, US conductor, born in Germany: famous for his performances of Haydn, Mozart, and Mahler **2** **John**. 1739–1812, English publisher; founded *The Daily Universal Register* (1785), which in 1788 became *The Times*

Waltham Forest *n* a borough of NE Greater London. Pop: 221 600 (2003 est). Area: 40 sq km (15 sq miles)

Walther von der Vogelweide *n* ?1170–?1230, German poet, noted for his lyric verse on political and moral themes

Walton *n* **1** **Ernest Thomas Sinton**. 1903–95, Irish physicist. He succeeded in producing the first artificial transmutation of an atomic nucleus (1932), with whom he shared the Nobel prize for physics 1951 **2** **Izaak**. 1593–1683, English writer, best known for *The Compleat Angler* (1653; enlarged 1676) **3** Sir **William** (**Turner**). 1902–83, English composer. His works include *Façade* (1923), a setting of satirical verses by Edith Sitwell, the *Viola Concerto* (1929), and the oratorio *Belshazzar's Feast* (1931)

waltz *n* **1** a ballroom dance in triple time in which couples spin round as they progress round the room **2** music for this dance ▷ *vb* **3** to dance a waltz **4** *informal* to move in a relaxed and confident way: *he waltzed over to her table to say hello* [German *Walzer*]

Walvis Bay *or* **Walfish Bay** *n* a port in Namibia, on the Atlantic: formed an exclave of South Africa, covering an area of 1124 sq km (434 sq miles) with its hinterland, but has been administered by Namibia since 1992; formally returned to Namibia in 1994; chief port of Namibia and rich fishing centre. Pop: 40 849 (2001)

wampum (wom-**pum**) *n* (formerly) money used by Native Americans of N America, made of shells strung or woven together [Native American *wampompeag*]

wan (rhymes with **swan**) *adj* **wanner**, **wannest** very pale, as a result of illness or unhappiness [Old English *wann* dark] ▷ **wanly** *adv*

WAN *computers* wide area network

Wanchüan *or* **Wan-ch'uan** *n* a former name of Zhangjiakou

wand *n* **1** a rod used by a magician when performing a trick or by a fairy when casting a spell **2** a hand-held electronic device which is pointed at or passed over an item to read the data stored there [Old Norse *vöndr*]

wander *vb* **1** to walk about in a place without any definite purpose or destination **2** (often foll. by *off*) to leave a place where one is supposed to stay: *kids wander off* **3** (of the mind) to lose concentration ▷ *n* **4** the act or an instance of wandering [Old English *wandrian*] ▷ **wanderer** *n* ▷ **wandering** *adj, n*

wanderlust *n* a great desire to travel

Wandsworth *n* a borough of S Greater London, on the River Thames. Pop: 274 100 (2003 est). Area: 35 sq km (13 sq miles)

wane *vb* **waning**, **waned 1** to decrease gradually in size, strength, or power: *the influence of the extremists is waning* **2** (of the moon) to show a gradually decreasing area of brightness from full moon until new moon ▷ *n* **3** on the wane decreasing in size, strength, or power: *his fame was on the wane* [Old English *wanian*] ▷ **waning** *adj*

Wang An Shi *or* **Wang An-shih** *n* 1021–86, Chinese statesman and writer: remembered for his economic reforms, known as the New Policies (1069–76)

Wanganui *n* a port in New Zealand, on SW North Island:

centre for a dairy-farming and sheep-rearing district. Pop: 43 600 (2004 est)

Wang Jing Wei or **Wang Ching-wei** n 1883–1944, Chinese politician. A leading revolutionary, he struggled (1927–32) with Chiang Kai-shek for control of the Kuomintang. During World War II he was head of a Japanese puppet government in Nanjing

wangle vb **-gling, -gled** informal to get (something) by cunning or devious methods: I've wangled you both an invitation [origin unknown]

Wanhsien or **Wan-Hsien** n a variant transliteration of the Chinese name for **Wanxian**

wanigan (wonn-ig-an) n Canad **1** a watertight box or chest used by canoeists or lumberjacks to hold provisions **2** a sled or boat for carrying camping supplies [from a Native American language]

wank taboo, slang vb **1** (of a man) to masturbate ▷ n **2** an instance of masturbating [origin unknown]

wanker n taboo, slang a worthless or stupid person

Wankie n the former name (until 1982) of **Hwange**

wannabe or **wannabee** adj **1** wanting to be, or be like, a particular person or thing: a wannabe actress ▷ n **2** a person who wants to be, or be like, a particular person or thing

Wanne-Eickel n an industrial town in W Germany, in North Rhine-Westphalia on the Rhine-Herne Canal: formed in 1926 by the merging of two townships

want vb **1** to feel a need or longing for: I want a job **2** to wish or desire (to do something): we did not want to get involved **3** Brit, Austral and NZ to have need of or require (doing or being something): what will you do when it wants cleaning? **4** should or ought (to do something): the last person you want to hire is someone who is desperate for a job **5 want for** to be lacking or deficient in: they were convinced I was wealthy and wanted for nothing ▷ n **6** something that is needed, desired, or lacked: attempts to satisfy a number of wants **7** a lack, shortage, or absence: for want of opportunity **8 in want of** needing or lacking: the Chinese peasant farmer may be in want of a roof, a job, a doctor nearby [Old Norse vanta to be deficient]

wanted adj being searched for by the police in connection with a crime that has been committed

wanting adj **1** lacking: I would be wanting in charity if I did not explain the terms **2** not meeting requirements or expectations: she compares herself to her sister and finds herself wanting

wanton adj **1** without motive, provocation, or justification: sheer wanton destruction **2** (of a person) maliciously and unnecessarily cruel **3** old-fashioned (of a woman) sexually unrestrained or immodest ▷ n **4** old-fashioned a sexually unrestrained or immodest woman [Middle English wantowen unruly]

Wanxian, Wanhsien or **Wan-Hsien** n an inland port in central China, in E Sichuan province, on the Yangtze River. Pop: 1 963 000 (2005 est)

WAP n Wireless Application Protocol: a system that allows mobile phone users to access the internet and other information services

wapiti (wop-pit-tee) n, pl **-tis** a large North American deer, now also found in New Zealand [from a Native American language]

war n **1** open armed conflict between two or more countries or groups: this international situation led to war **2** a particular armed conflict: the American war in Vietnam **3** any conflict or contest: a trade war **4 have been in the wars** informal to look as if one has been in a fight ▷ adj **5** relating to war or a war: the war effort; a war correspondent ▷ vb **warring, warred 6** to conduct a war [Old Northern French werre] ▷ **warring** adj

War. Warwickshire

Warangal n a city in S central India, in N Andhra Pradesh: capital of a 12th-century Hindu kingdom. Pop: 528 570 (2001)

waratah n an Australian shrub with crimson flowers

Warbeck n Perkin. ?1474–99, Flemish impostor, pretender to the English throne. Professing to be Richard, Duke of York, he led an unsuccessful rising against Henry VII (1497) and was later executed

warble vb **-bling, -bled** to sing in a high-pitched trilling voice [Old French werbler]

warbler n any of various small songbirds

Warburg n Otto (Heinrich). 1883–1970, German biochemist and physiologist: Nobel prize for physiology or medicine (1931) for his work on respiratory enzymes

war crime n a crime committed in wartime in violation of the accepted customs, such as ill-treatment of prisoners ▷ **war criminal** n

war cry n **1** a rallying cry used by combatants in battle **2** a slogan used to rally support for a cause

ward n **1** a room in a hospital for patients requiring similar kinds of care: the maternity ward **2** one of the districts into which a town, parish, or other area is divided for administration or elections **3** Also called: **ward of court** law a person, esp. a child whose parents are dead, who is placed under the control or protection of a guardian or of a court ▶ See also **ward off** [Old English weard protector] ▷ **wardship** n

Ward n **1** Dame Barbara (Mary), Baroness Jackson. 1914–81, British economist, environmentalist, and writer. Her books include Spaceship Earth (1966) **2** Mrs Humphry, married name of Mary Augusta Arnold. 1851–1920, English novelist. Her novels include Robert Elsmere (1888) and The Case of Richard Meynell (1911) **3** Sir Joseph George. 1856–1930, New Zealand statesman; prime minister of New Zealand (1906–12; 1928–30)

-ward suffix **1** (forming adjectives) indicating direction towards: a backward step **2** (forming adverbs) chiefly US and Canad same as **-wards** [Old English -weard]

warden n **1** a person who is in charge of a building, such as a youth hostel, and its occupants **2** a public official who is responsible for the enforcement of certain regulations: a game warden **3** the chief officer in charge of a prison [Old French wardein]

warder or fem **wardress** n chiefly Brit a prison officer [Old French warder to guard]

ward off vb to prevent (something unpleasant) from happening or from causing harm: to ward off the pangs of hunger; to ward off cancer cells

Wardour Street n **1** a street in Soho where many film companies have their London offices: formerly noted for shops selling antiques and mock antiques **2 Wardour Street English** affectedly archaic speech or writing

wardrobe n **1** a tall cupboard, with a rail or hooks on which to hang clothes **2** the total collection of articles of clothing belonging to one person: your autumn wardrobe **3** the collection of costumes belonging to a theatre or theatrical company [Old French warder to guard + robe robe]

wardrobe mistress n the woman in charge of the costumes in a theatre or theatrical company ▷ **wardrobe master** masc n

wardroom n the quarters assigned to the officers of a warship, apart from the captain

-wards or **-ward** suffix forming adverbs indicating direction towards: a step backwards [Old English -weardes]

ware n articles of the same kind or material: crystal ware. See also **wares** [Old English waru]

warehouse n a place where goods are stored prior to their sale or distribution

wares pl n goods for sale

warfare n **1** the act of conducting a war **2** a violent or intense conflict of any kind: class warfare

war game n **1** a tactical exercise for training military commanders, in which no military units are actually deployed **2** a game in which model soldiers are used to create battles in order to study tactics

warhead n the front section of a missile or projectile that contains explosives

W

Warhol n Andy, real name *Andrew Warhola*. ?1926–87, US artist and film maker; one of the foremost exponents of pop art

warhorse n 1 (formerly) a horse used in battle 2 *informal* a veteran soldier or politician

Warks Warwickshire

Warley n an industrial town in W central England, in Sandwell unitary authority, West Midlands: formed in 1966 by the amalgamation of Smethwick, Oldbury, and Rowley Regis. Pop: 189 854 (2001)

warlike adj 1 of or relating to war: *warlike stores and equipment* 2 hostile and eager to have a war: *a warlike nation*

warlock n a man who practises black magic [Old English *wǣrloga* oath breaker]

Warlock n Peter, real name *Philip Arnold Heseltine*. 1894–1930, British composer and scholar of early English music. His works include song cycles, such as *The Curlew* (1920–22), and the *Capriol Suite* (1926) for strings

warlord n a military leader of a nation or part of a nation

warm adj 1 feeling or having a moderate degree of heat 2 giving heat: *warm clothing* 3 (of colours) predominantly red or yellow in tone 4 kindly or affectionate: *warm embraces* 5 *informal* near to finding a hidden object or guessing facts, for example in a children's game ▷ vb 6 to make warm 7 **warm to a** to become fonder of: *I warmed to him when he defended me* **b** to become more excited or enthusiastic about: *he had warmed to his theme* ▶ See also **warm up** [Old English *wearm*] ﹥ **warmly** adv ﹥ **warmness** n

warm-blooded adj 1 (of an animal, such as a mammal or a bird) having a constant body temperature, usually higher than the surrounding temperature 2 having a passionate nature ﹥ **warm-bloodedness** n

warm-down n light exercises performed to aid recovery from strenuous physical activity

war memorial n a monument to people who have died in a war, esp. local people

warm front n *meteorol* the boundary between a warm air mass and the cold air it is replacing

warm-hearted adj kind, affectionate, or sympathetic

warming pan n a long-handled pan filled with hot coals, formerly pulled over the sheets to warm a bed

warmonger n a person who encourages warlike ideas or advocates war ﹥ **warmongering** n

warmth n 1 the state of being warm 2 affection or cordiality: *the warmth of their friendship*

warm up vb 1 to make or become warm or warmer 2 to prepare for a race, sporting contest, or exercise routine by doing gentle exercises immediately beforehand 3 (of an engine or machine) to be started and left running until the working temperature is reached 4 to become more lively: *wait until things warm up* 5 to reheat (food that has already been cooked) ▷ n **warm-up** 6 a preparatory exercise routine

warn vb 1 to make (someone) aware of a possible danger or problem 2 to inform (someone) in advance: *you'd better warn your girlfriend that you'll be working at the weekend* 3 **warn off** to advise (someone) to go away or not to do something [Old English *wearnian*]

Warne n Shane (Keith). born 1969, Australian cricketer: a leg spinner, he took 708 wickets in 145 test matches (1992–2007)

warning n 1 a hint, threat, or advance notice of a possible danger or problem 2 advice not to do something ▷ adj 3 giving or serving as a warning: *warning signs* ﹥ **warningly** adv

warp vb 1 (esp. of wooden objects) to be twisted out of shape, for example by heat or damp 2 to distort or influence in a negative way: *love warps judgment* ▷ n 3 a fault or an irregularity in the shape or surface of an object 4 a fault or deviation in someone's character 5 See **time warp** 6 the yarns arranged lengthways on a loom through which the weft yarns are woven [Old English *wearp* a throw] ﹥ **warped** adj

war paint n 1 paint applied to the face and body by certain North American Indians before battle 2 *informal* cosmetics

warpath n **on the warpath a** preparing to engage in battle **b** *informal* angry and looking for a fight or conflict

warrant n 1 an official authorization for some action or decision: *Scotland Yard today issued a warrant for the arrest of this man* 2 a document that certifies or guarantees something, such as a receipt or licence ▷ vb 3 to make necessary: *we've no hard evidence to warrant a murder investigation* [Old French *guarant*]

warrant officer n an officer in certain armed services with a rank between those of commissioned and noncommissioned officers

Warrant of Fitness n NZ a six-monthly certificate required for a motor vehicle certifying that it is mechanically sound

warrantor n a person or company that provides a warranty

warranty n, pl -ties a guarantee or assurance that goods meet a specified standard or that the facts in a legal document are as stated [Anglo-French *warantie*]

warren n 1 a series of interconnected underground tunnels in which rabbits live 2 an overcrowded building or area of a city with many narrow passages or streets: *a mountainous concrete warren of apartments* [Anglo-French *warenne*]

Warren[1] n a city in the US, in SE Michigan, northeast of Detroit. Pop: 136 016 (2003 est)

Warren[2] n 1 Earl. 1891–1974, US lawyer; chief justice of the US (1953–69). He chaired the commission that investigated the murder of President Kennedy 2 **(John) Robin**. born 1937, Australian pathologist who, with Barry Marshall, demonstrated that the bacterium *Helicobacter pylori* is the cause of most peptic ulcers, for which they won the Nobel Prize in Physiology or Medicine (2005)

warrigal *Austral* n 1 a dingo ▷ adj 2 wild

Warrington n 1 an industrial town in NW England, in Warrington unitary authority, Cheshire on the River Mersey: dates from Roman times. Pop: 80 661 (2001) 2 a unitary authority in NW England, in N Cheshire. Pop: 193 200 (2003 est). Area: 176 sq km (68 sq miles)

warrior n a person who is engaged in or experienced in war [Old French *werreieor*]

Warsaw n the capital of Poland, in the E central part on the River Vistula: became capital at the end of the 16th century; almost completely destroyed in World War II as the main centre of the Polish resistance movement; rebuilt within about six years; university (1818); situated at the junction of important trans-European routes. Pop: 2 204 000 (2005 est). Polish name: **Warszawa**

warship n a ship designed for naval warfare

wart n 1 a firm abnormal growth on the skin caused by a virus 2 **warts and all** including faults: *she loves him warts and all* [Old English *weart(e)*] ﹥ **warty** adj

Warta n a river in Poland, flowing generally north and west across the whole W Polish Plain to the River Oder. Length: 808 km (502 miles)

Wartburg n a medieval castle in central Germany, in Thuringia southwest of Eisenach: residence of Luther (1521–22) when he began his German translation of the New Testament

warthog n a wild African pig with heavy tusks, wartlike lumps on the face, and a mane of coarse hair

wartime n 1 a time of war ▷ adj 2 of or in a time of war: *the wartime coalition*

Warton n 1 Joseph. 1722–1800, British poet and critic, noted for his poem *The Enthusiast* (1744) and his *Essay on the Writings and Genius of Pope* (1756) 2 his brother **Thomas**. 1728–90, poet laureate (1785–90); author of the poem *The Pleasures of Melancholy* (1747) and the first *History of English Poetry* (1774–81)

Warwick¹ *n* a town in central England, administrative centre of Warwickshire, on the River Avon: 14th-century castle, with collections of armour and waxworks: the university of Warwick (1965) is in Coventry. Pop: 23 350 (2001)

Warwick² *n* **Earl of**, title of *Richard Neville*, known as *the Kingmaker*. 1428–71, English statesman. During the Wars of the Roses, he fought first for the Yorkists, securing the throne (1461) for Edward IV, and then for the Lancastrians, restoring Henry VI (1470). He was killed at Barnet by Edward IV

Warwickshire *n* a county of central England: until 1974, when the West Midlands metropolitan county was created, it contained one of the most highly industrialized regions in the world, centred on Birmingham. Administrative centre: Warwick. Pop: 519 300 (2003 est). Area: 1981 sq km (765 sq miles)

wary (ware-ree) *adj* **warier, wariest** cautious or on one's guard: *be wary of hitchhikers* [Old English *wær* aware, careful] ➤ **warily** *adv* ➤ **wariness** *n*

was *vb* (with 'I', 'he', 'she', 'it', or a sing noun as subject) the past tense of **be** [Old English *wæs*]

Wasatch Range *n* a mountain range in the W central US, in N Utah and SE Idaho. Highest peak: Mount Timpanogos, 3581 m (11 750 ft)

wash *vb* **1** to clean (oneself, part of one's body, or a thing) with soap or detergent and water **2** (of a garment or fabric) to be capable of being washed without damage or loss of colour **3** to move or be moved in a particular direction by water: *houses may be washed away in floods* **4** (of waves) to flow or sweep against or over (a surface or object), often with a lapping sound **5** *informal* to be acceptable or believable: *the masculine pride argument won't wash now when so many women go out to work* ➤ *n* **6** the act or process of washing **7** all the clothes etc. to be washed together on one occasion **8** a thin layer of paint or ink: *a pale wash of blue* **9** the disturbance in the air or water produced at the rear of an aircraft, boat, or other moving object: *we were hit by the wash of a large vessel* **10 come out in the wash** *informal* to become known or apparent in the course of time ▸ See also **wash down, wash out, wash up** [Old English *wæscan, waxan*] ➤ **washable** *adj*

Wash *n* **the Wash** a shallow inlet of the North Sea on the E coast of England, between Lincolnshire and Norfolk

Wash. Washington (state)

washbasin *n* a small sink in a bathroom, used for washing the face and hands. Also: **wash-hand basin**

wash down *vb* **1** to have a drink with or after (food or medicine): *a large steak, washed down with coffee* **2** to wash from top to bottom: *she washed down the staircase*

washed out *adj* **1** exhausted and lacking in energy **2** faded or colourless

washed up *adj informal* no longer as successful or important as previously: *she stands discredited, her career probably washed up*

washer *n* **1** a flat ring of rubber, felt, or metal used to provide a seal under a nut or bolt or in a tap or valve **2** *informal* a washing machine **3** a person who washes things, esp. as a job: *chief cook and bottle washer* **4** *Austral* a small piece of towelling cloth used to wash the face

washerwoman *n, pl* **-women** a woman who washes clothes as a job

washing *n* all the clothes etc. to be washed together on one occasion

washing machine *n* a machine for washing clothes and bed linen in

washing soda *n* crystalline sodium carbonate, used as a cleansing agent

Washington¹ *n* **1** a state of the northwestern US, on the Pacific: consists of the Coast Range and the Olympic Mountains in the west and the Columbia Plateau in the east. Capital: Olympia. Pop: 6 131 445 (2003 est). Area: 172 416 sq km (66 570 sq miles). Abbreviation: **Wash.**, (with zip code) **WA 2** Also called: **Washington, DC** the capital of the US, coextensive with the District of Columbia and situated near the E coast on the Potomac River: site chosen by President Washington in 1790; contains the White House and the Capitol; a major educational and administrative centre. Pop: 563 384 (2003 est) **3** a town in Tyne and Wear: designated a new town in 1964. Pop: 53 388 (2001) **4 Mount Washington** a mountain in N New Hampshire, in the White Mountains: the highest peak in the northeast US; noted for extreme weather conditions. Height: 1917 m (6288 ft) **5 Lake Washington** a lake in W Washington, forming the E boundary of the city of Seattle: linked by canal with Puget Sound. Length: about 32 km (20 miles). Width: 6 km (4 miles)

Washington² *n* **1 Booker T**(aliaferro). 1856–1915, US Black educationalist and writer **2 Denzil**. US film actor; his films include *Glory* (1990), *Malcolm X* (1992), *The Hurricane* (1999), and *John Q.* (2002) **3 George**. 1732–99, US general and statesman; first president of the US (1789–97). He was appointed commander in chief of the Continental Army (1775) at the outbreak of the War of American Independence, which ended with his defeat of Cornwallis at Yorktown (1781). He presided over the convention at Philadelphia (1787) that formulated the constitution of the US and elected him president

Washingtonian *adj* **1** of or relating to the city or state of Washington or their inhabitants ▷ *n* **2** a native or inhabitant of the city or state of Washington

washing-up *n* the act of washing used dishes and cutlery after a meal

wash out *vb* **1** Also: **wash off** to remove or be removed by washing: *the rain washes the red dye out of the cap* **2** to wash the inside of (a container) ▷ *n* **washout 3** a total failure or disaster **4** NZ a part of a road or railway washed away by floodwaters

washroom *n US and Canad* a toilet

washstand *n* a piece of furniture designed to hold a basin for washing the face and hands in

wash up *vb* **1** to wash used dishes and cutlery after a meal **2** *US and Canad* to wash one's face and hands

washy *adj* **washier, washiest 1** overdiluted or weak **2** lacking intensity of colour: *a washy blend of pale brown and pale grey*

Wasim Akram *n* Chaudhry. born 1966, Pakistani cricketer: a fast bowler, he played in 104 test matches (1984–2002), 25 as captain, and took 414 wickets

wasn't was not

wasp *n* a common stinging insect with a slender black-and-yellow striped body [Old English *wæsp*]

Wasp *or* **WASP** (in the US and Canada) White Anglo-Saxon Protestant: a person descended from N European, usually Protestant stock, forming a group often considered to be the most dominant and privileged in N American society

waspish *adj* bad-tempered or spiteful: *waspish comments*

wasp waist *n* a very narrow waist ➤ **wasp-waisted** *adj*

wassail *n* **1** (formerly) a toast drunk to a person during festivities **2** a festivity involving a lot of drinking **3** hot spiced beer or mulled wine drunk at such a festivity ▷ *vb* **4 go wassailing** to go from house to house singing carols at Christmas [Old Norse *ves heill* be in good health]

wastage *n* **1** the act of wasting something or the state of being wasted: *wastage of raw materials* **2** reduction in the size of a workforce by retirement, redundancy, etc.

> **USAGE** Waste and *wastage* are to some extent interchangeable, but many people think that *wastage* should not be used to refer to loss resulting from human carelessness, inefficiency, etc.: *a waste* (not *a wastage*) *of time, money, effort*, etc.

waste *vb* **wasting, wasted 1** to use up thoughtlessly, carelessly, or unsuccessfully **2** to fail to take advantage of: *let's not waste an opportunity to see the children* **3 be wasted**

W

on to be too good for; not be appreciated by: *fine brandy is wasted on you* **4 waste away** to lose one's strength or health: *wasting away from unrequited love* ▷ *n* **5** the act of wasting something or the state of being wasted: *a waste of time* **6** something that is left over because it is in excess of requirements **7** rubbish: *toxic waste* **8** physiol matter discharged from the body as faeces or urine **9 wastes** a region that is wild or uncultivated ▷ *adj* **10** rejected as being useless, unwanted, or worthless: *waste products* **11** not cultivated or productive: *waste ground* **12** physiol discharged from the body as faeces or urine: *waste matter* **13 lay waste** or **lay waste to** to devastate or destroy: *the Bikini atoll, laid waste by nuclear tests* [Latin *vastare* to lay waste]

wasted *adj* **1** unnecessary or unfruitful: *wasted effort* **2** pale, thin, and unhealthy: *the hunched shoulders and the wasted appearance of his body*

wasteful *adj* causing waste: *wasteful expenditure* ❯ **wastefully** *adv*

wasteland *n* **1** a barren or desolate area of land **2** something that is considered spiritually, intellectually, or aesthetically barren: *the TV wasteland*

wastepaper basket *n* a container for paper discarded after use

waster *n informal* a lazy or worthless person

wasting *adj* reducing the vitality and strength of the body: *a pernicious wasting illness*

wastrel *n literary* a lazy or worthless person

Wast Water or **Wastwater** *n* a lake in NW England, in Cumbria in the Lake District. Length: 5 km (3 miles)

watap (wat-**tahp**) *n* a stringy thread made by Native Americans from the roots of conifers [from a Native American language]

watch *vb* **1** to look at or observe closely and attentively **2** to look after (a child or a pet) **3** to maintain a careful interest in or control over: *it reminds me to watch my diet* **4 watch for** to be keenly alert to or cautious about: *the vigilant night watchman hired to watch for thieves* **5 watch it!** be careful! ▷ *n* **6** a small portable timepiece worn strapped to the wrist or in a waistcoat pocket **7** the act or an instance of watching **8** *nautical* any of the periods, usually of four hours, during which part of a ship's crew are on duty **9 keep a close watch on** to maintain a careful interest in or control over: *he keeps a close watch on party opinion* **10 keep watch** to be keenly alert to danger; keep guard **11 on the watch** on the lookout ▶ See also **watch out, watch over** [Old English *wæccan*] ❯ **watcher** *n*

watchable *adj* interesting, enjoyable, or entertaining: *watchable films*

watchdog *n* **1** a dog kept to guard property **2** a person or group that acts as a guard against inefficiency or illegality

watchful *adj* **1** carefully observing everything that happens **2 under the watchful eye of** being closely observed by ❯ **watchfully** *adv* ❯ **watchfulness** *n*

watchmaker *n* a person who makes or mends watches and clocks

watchman *n, pl* **-men** a man employed to guard buildings or property

watch-night service *n* **a** (in Protestant churches) a service held on the night of December 24, to mark the arrival of Christmas Day **b** (in Protestant churches) a service held on the night of December 31, to mark the passing of the old year

watch out *vb* to be careful or on one's guard

watch over *vb* to look after or supervise: *her main ambition is still to watch over the family*

watchstrap *n* a strap attached to a watch for fastening it round the wrist. Also called (US and Canad): watchband

watchtower *n* a tower on which a sentry keeps watch

watchword *n* a slogan or motto: *quality, not quantity, is the watchword*

water *n* **1** a clear colourless tasteless liquid that is

essential for plant and animal life, that falls as rain, and forms seas, rivers, and lakes. Related adjectives: **aquatic, aqueous 2** any area of this liquid, such as a sea, river, or lake **3** the surface of such an area of water: *four-fifths of an iceberg's mass lie below water* **4** the level of the tide: *at high water* **5** physiol **a** any fluid discharged from the body, such as sweat, urine, or tears **b** the fluid surrounding a fetus in the womb **6 hold water** (of an argument or idea) to be believable or reasonable **7 of the first water** of the highest quality or the most extreme degree: *he's a scoundrel of the first water* **8 pass water** to urinate **9 water under the bridge** events that are past and done with ▷ *vb* **10** to moisten or soak with water: *keep greenhouse plants well watered* **11** to give (an animal) water to drink **12** (of the eyes) to fill with tears: *our eyes were watering from the fumes* **13** (of the mouth) to fill with saliva in anticipation of food ▶ See also **water down** [Old English *wæter*] ❯ **waterless** *adj*

water bed *n* a waterproof mattress filled with water

water biscuit *n* a thin crisp unsweetened biscuit, usually eaten with butter or cheese

water buffalo *n* a large black oxlike draught animal of S Asia, with long backward-curving horns

water cannon *n* a machine that pumps a jet of water through a nozzle at high pressure, used to disperse crowds

water chestnut *n* the edible tuber of a Chinese plant, used in Oriental cookery

water closet *n old-fashioned* a toilet. Abbreviation: **WC**

watercolour or US **watercolor** *n* **1** a kind of paint that is applied with water rather than oil **2** a painting done in watercolours

water-cooled *adj* (of an engine) kept from overheating by a flow of water circulating in a casing

watercourse *n* the channel or bed of a river or stream

watercress *n* a plant that grows in ponds and streams, with strong-tasting leaves that are used in salads and as a garnish

water cycle *n geology* the circulation of the earth's water, in which water from the sea evaporates, forms clouds, falls as rain or snow, and returns to the sea by rivers

water diviner *n* a person who can locate the presence of water underground with a divining rod

water down *vb* **1** to weaken (a drink or food) with water **2** to make (a story, plan, or proposal) weaker and less controversial ❯ **watered-down** *adj*

waterfall *n* a cascade of falling water where there is a vertical or almost vertical step in a river

Waterford *n* **1** a county of S Republic of Ireland, in Munster province on the Atlantic: mountainous in the centre and in the northwest County town: Waterford. Pop: 101 546 (2002). Area: 1838 sq km (710 sq miles) **2** a port in S Republic of Ireland, county town of Co Waterford: famous glass industry; fishing. Pop: 44 594 (2002)

waterfowl *n, pl* **-fowl** a bird that swims on water, such as a duck or swan

waterfront *n* the area of a town or city next to an area of water, such as a harbour or dockyard

waterhole *n* a pond or pool in a desert or other dry area, used by animals as a drinking place

Waterhouse *n* **1 Alfred.** 1830–1905, British architect; a leader of the Gothic Revival. His buildings include Manchester Town Hall (1868) and the Natural History Museum, London (1881) **2 George Marsden.** 1824–1906, New Zealand statesman, born in England: prime minister of New Zealand (1872–73) **3 Keith (Spencer).** 1929–2009, British novelist, dramatist, and journalist: best known for the novel *Billy Liar* (1959) and his collaborations with the dramatist Willis Hall (1929–2005)

water ice *n* ice cream made from frozen fruit-flavoured syrup

watering can n a container with a handle and a spout with a perforated nozzle, used to sprinkle water over plants

watering hole n *facetious, slang* a pub

watering place n **1** a place where people or animals can find drinking water **2** *Brit* a spa or seaside resort

water jump n a ditch or brook over which athletes or horses must jump in a steeplechase

water level n **1** the level reached by the surface of an area of water **2** same as **water line**

water lily n a plant with large leaves and showy flowers that float on the surface of an area of water

water line n the level to which a ship's hull will be immersed when afloat

waterlogged adj **1** saturated with water: *waterlogged meadows* **2** (of a boat) having taken in so much water as to be likely to sink

Waterloo n **1** a small town in central Belgium, in Walloon Brabant province south of Brussels: battle (1815) fought nearby in which British and Prussian forces under the Duke of Wellington and Blücher routed the French under Napoleon. Pop: 29 003 (2004 est) **2** a total or crushing defeat (esp. in **meet one's Waterloo**)

water main n a principal supply pipe in an arrangement of pipes for distributing water to houses and other buildings

watermark n **1** a mark impressed on paper during manufacture, visible when the paper is held up to the light **2** a line marking the level reached by an area of water

water meadow n a meadow that remains fertile by being periodically flooded by a stream

watermelon n a large round melon with a hard green rind and sweet watery reddish flesh

water pistol n a toy pistol that squirts a stream of water

water polo n a game played in water by two teams of seven swimmers in which each side tries to throw a ball into the opponents' goal

water power n the power of flowing or falling water to drive machinery or generate electricity

waterproof adj **1** not allowing water to pass through: *waterproof trousers* ▷ n **2** chiefly *Brit* a waterproof garment, such as a raincoat ▷ vb **3** to make waterproof: *the bridge is having its deck waterproofed*

water rat n same as **water vole**

water rate n a charge made for the public supply of water

water-resistant adj (of a fabric or garment) having a finish that resists the absorption of water

Waters n Muddy, real name *McKinley Morganfield*. 1915–83, US blues guitarist, singer, and songwriter. His songs include "Rollin' Stone" (1948) and "Got my Mojo Working" (1954)

watershed n **1** the dividing line between two adjacent river systems, such as a ridge **2** an important period or factor that serves as a dividing line: *a watershed in history*

waterside n the area of land beside a river or lake

watersider n *NZ* a person employed to load and unload ships

water-ski n **1** a type of ski used for gliding over water ▷ vb **-skiing, -skied** or **-ski'd** **2** to ride over water on water-skis while holding a rope towed by a speedboat ▷ **water-skier** n ▷ **water-skiing** n

water softener n a device or substance that removes the minerals that make water hard

waterspout n a tornado occurring over water, which forms a column of water and mist

water table n the level below which the ground is saturated with water

watertight adj **1** not letting water through: *watertight compartments* **2** without loopholes or weak points: *a watertight system*

water tower n a storage tank mounted on a tower so that water can be distributed at a steady pressure

water vapour n water in a gaseous state, esp. when due to evaporation at a temperature below the boiling point

water vole n a small ratlike animal that can swim and lives on the banks of streams and ponds

waterway n a river, canal, or other navigable channel used as a means of travel or transport

water wheel n a large wheel with vanes set across its rim, which is turned by flowing water to drive machinery

water wings pl n an inflatable rubber device shaped like a pair of wings, which is placed under the arms of a person learning to swim

waterworks n **1** an establishment for storing, purifying, and distributing water for community supply ▷ pl n **2** *informal, chiefly Brit euphemistic* the urinary system **3 turn on the waterworks** *informal* to begin to cry deliberately, in order to attract attention or gain sympathy

watery adj **1** of, like, or containing water: *a watery discharge* **2** (of eyes) filled with tears **3** insipid, thin, or weak: *a watery sun had appeared*

Watford n a town in SE England, in SW Hertfordshire: light industries, services. Pop: 120 960 (2001)

Watling Island n another name for **San Salvador Island**

Watson n **1** James Dewey. born 1928, US biologist, whose contribution to the discovery of the helical structure of DNA won him a Nobel prize for Physiology or Medicine shared with Francis Crick and Maurice Wilkins in 1962 **2** John B(roadus). 1878–1958, US psychologist; a leading exponent of behaviourism **3** John Christian. 1867–1941, Australian statesman, born in Chile: prime minister of Australia (1904) **4** Russell. born 1973, English tenor: his albums include *The Voice* (2001) and *Encore* (2002) **5** Tom, full name *Thomas Sturges Watson*. born 1949, US golfer, won eight major titles: the US Masters (1977, 1981), the US Open (1982), and the British Open (1975, 1977, 1980, 1982, 1983)

Watson-Watt n Sir Robert Alexander. 1892–1973, Scottish physicist, who played a leading role in the development of radar

watt (wott) n the SI unit of power, equal to the power dissipated by a current of 1 ampere flowing across a potential difference of 1 volt [after J. WATT]

Watt n James. 1736–1819, Scottish engineer and inventor. His fundamental improvements to the steam engine led to the widespread use of steam power in industry

wattage n the amount of electrical power, expressed in watts, that an appliance uses or generates

Watteau n Jean-Antoine. 1684–1721, French painter, esp. of *fêtes champêtres*, which depicted figures in pastoral settings

Wattenscheid n an industrial town in NW Germany, in North Rhine-Westphalia east of Essen

wattle (wott-tl) n **1** a frame of rods or stakes interwoven with twigs or branches used to make fences **2** a loose fold of brightly coloured skin hanging from the throat of certain birds and lizards **3** an Australian acacia tree with dense golden, yellow, or cream flowers ▷ adj **4** made of, formed by, or covered with wattle: *a wattle fence* [Old English *watol*]

wattle and daub n a building material consisting of interwoven twigs plastered with a mixture of clay and water

Watts n **1** George Frederick. 1817–1904, English painter and sculptor, noted esp. for his painting *Hope* (1886) and his sculpture *Physical Energy* (1904) in Kensington Gardens, London **2** Isaac. 1674–1748, English hymn-writer

Waugh n **1** Evelyn (Arthur St John). 1903–66, English novelist. His early satirical novels include *Decline and Fall* (1928), *Vile Bodies* (1930), *A Handful of Dust* (1934), and *Scoop* (1938). His later novels include the more sombre *Brideshead Revisited* (1945) and the trilogy of World War II *Men at Arms* (1952), *Officers and Gentlemen* (1955), and

W

Unconditional Surrender (1961) **2 Mark (Edward)**, born 1965, Australian cricketer: a batsman, he scored 8029 runs in 128 test matches (1991–2002) **3** his twin brother **Steve**, full name *Stephen Roger Waugh*, born 1965, Australian cricketer: a batsman, he scored 10,927 runs in 168 test matches and captained Australia to victory in the 1999 World Cup

wave *vb* **waving, waved 1** to move (one's hand) to and fro as a greeting **2** to direct (someone) to move in a particular direction by waving: *I waved him on* **3** to hold (something) up and move it from side to side in order to attract attention **4** to move freely to and fro: *flowers waving in the wind* ▷ *n* **5** one of a sequence of ridges or undulations that moves across the surface of the sea or a lake **6** a curve in the hair **7** a sudden rise in the frequency or intensity of something: *a wave of sympathy* **8** a widespread movement that advances in a body: *a new wave of refugees* **9** a prolonged spell of some particular type of weather: *a heat wave* **10** the act or an instance of waving **11** *physics* an energy-carrying disturbance travelling through a medium or space by a series of vibrations without any overall movement of matter **12 make waves** to cause trouble [Old English *wafian*]

waveband *n* a range of wavelengths or frequencies used for a particular type of radio transmission

wave down *vb* to signal to (the driver of a vehicle) to stop

wavelength *n* **1** *physics* the distance between two points of the same phase in consecutive cycles of a wave **2** the wavelength of the carrier wave used by a particular broadcasting station **3 on the same wavelength** *informal* having similar views, feelings, or thoughts

Wavell *n* Archibald (Percival), 1st Earl. 1883–1950, British field marshal. During World War II he was commander in chief in the Middle East (1939–41), defeating the Italians in N Africa. He was commander in chief in India (1941–43) and viceroy of India (1943–47)

waver *vb* **1** to hesitate between possibilities; be indecisive **2** to swing from one thing to another: *she wavered between annoyance and civility* **3** (of a voice or stare) to become unsteady **4** to move back and forth or one way and another: *the barrel of the gun began to waver* [Old Norse *vafra* to flicker] **> wavering** *adj*

wavey *n* Canad a snow goose or other wild goose [from a Native American language]

wavy *adj* **wavier, waviest** having curves: *wavy hair; a wavy line*

wax¹ *n* **1** a solid fatty or oily substance used for making candles and polish, which softens and melts when heated **2** short for **beeswax, sealing wax 3** *physiol* a brownish-yellow waxy substance secreted by glands in the ear ▷ *vb* **4** to coat or polish with wax [Old English *weax*] **> waxed** *adj* **> waxy** *adj*

wax² *vb* **1** to increase gradually in size, strength, or power: *trading has waxed and waned with the economic cycle* **2** (of the moon) to show a gradually increasing area of brightness from new moon until full moon **3** to become: *he waxed eloquent on the disadvantages of marriage* [Old English *weaxan*]

waxed paper *or* **wax paper** *n* paper treated or coated with wax or paraffin to make it waterproof

waxen *adj* **1** resembling wax in colour or texture: *his face is waxen and pale* **2** made of, treated with, or covered with wax: *a waxen image*

waxeye *n* a small New Zealand bird with a white circle round its eye

waxwork *n* a life-size lifelike wax figure of a famous person

waxworks *n* a museum or exhibition of wax figures

way *n* **1** a manner, method, or means: *a new way of life; a tactful way of finding out* **2** a characteristic style or manner: *we are all special in our own way* **3 ways** habits or customs: *he had a liking for British ways* **4** an aspect or detail of something: *the tourist industry is in many ways a success story* **5** a choice or option, for example in a vote: *he thought it* could go either way **6** a route or direction: *the shortest way home* **7** a journey: *you could buy a magazine to read on the way* **8** distance: *they are a long way from Paris* **9** space or room for movement or activity: *you won't be in his way* **10 by the way** incidentally: *by the way, I've decided to leave* **11 by way of a** serving as: *by way of explanation* **b** by the route of: *I went by way of my family home* **12 get one's own way** to have things exactly as one wants them to be **13 give way a** to collapse or break **b** to yield or concede: *I tried to make him understand but he did not give way an inch* **14 give way to a** to be replaced by: *my first feelings of dismay have given way to comparative complacency* **b** to show (an emotion) unrestrainedly **c** to slow down or stop when driving to let (another driver) pass **15 go out of one's way** to take considerable trouble: *he had gone out of his way to reassure me* **16 have it both ways** to enjoy two things that would normally be mutually exclusive **17 in a bad way** *informal* in a poor state of health or a poor financial state **18 in a way** in some respects **19 in no way** not at all **20 make one's way** to proceed or go: *he decided to make his way back in the dark* **21 on the way out** *informal* becoming unfashionable **22 out of the way a** removed or dealt with so as to be no longer a hindrance **b** remote **23 under way** having started moving or making progress ▷ *adv* **24** *informal* far or by far: *that is way out of line* [Old English *weg*]

waybill *n* a document stating the nature, origin, and destination of goods being transported

wayfarer *n* old-fashioned a traveller

waylay *vb* **-laying, -laid 1** to lie in wait for and attack **2** intercept (someone) unexpectedly

Wayne *n* John, real name *Marion Michael Morrison*, 1907–79, US film actor, noted esp. for his many Westerns, which include *Stagecoach* (1939), *The Alamo* (1960), and *True Grit* (1969), for which he won an Oscar

way-out *adj* old-fashioned, informal extremely unconventional

waypoint *n* the co-ordinates of a specific location as defined by a GPS

ways and means *pl n* **1** the methods and resources for accomplishing something **2** the money and the methods of raising the money needed for the functioning of a political unit

wayside *adj* **1** old-fashioned situated by the side of a road: *wayside shrines* ▷ *n* **2 fall by the wayside** to be unsuccessful or stop being successful: *thousands of new diets are dreamed up yearly – many fall by the wayside*

wayward *adj* erratic, selfish, or stubborn [AWAY + -WARD] **> waywardness** *n*

Waziristan *n* a mountainous region of N Pakistan, on the border with Afghanistan

Wb *physics* weber

WC *or* **wc** *n* a toilet

we *pron* (used as the subject of a verb) **1** the speaker or writer and another person or other people: *we arrived in Calais* **2** all people or people in general: *it's an unfair world we live in* **3** *formal* same as **I¹** used by monarchs and editors [Old English *wē*]

weak *adj* **1** lacking in physical or mental strength **2** (of a part of the body) not functioning as well as is normal: *a weak heart* **3** liable to collapse or break: *weak bridges* **4** lacking in importance, influence, or strength: *a weak government* **5** (of a currency or shares) falling in price or characterized by falling prices **6** lacking in moral strength; easily influenced **7** not convincing: *weak arguments* **8** lacking strength or power: *his voice was weak* **9** not having a strong flavour: *weak coffee* [Old English *wāc* soft] **> weakly** *adv*

weaken *vb* to become or make weak or weaker

weak-kneed *adj* informal lacking strength, courage, or resolution

weakling *n* a person who is lacking in physical or mental strength

weak-minded *adj* **1** lacking willpower **2** of low intelligence; foolish

weakness *n* **1** the state of being weak **2** a failing in a person's character: *his weakness is his impetuosity* **3** a self-indulgent liking: *a weakness for gin*

weal¹ *n* a raised mark on the skin produced by a blow [from Old English *walu* ridge]

weal² *n old-fashioned* prosperity or wellbeing: *the public weal* [Old English *wela*]

Weald *n* the Weald a region of SE England, in Kent, Surrey, and East and West Sussex between the North Downs and the South Downs: formerly forested

wealth *n* **1** the state of being rich **2** a large amount of money and valuable material possessions: *redistribution of wealth* **3** a great amount or number: *a wealth of detail* [Middle English *welthe*]

wealthy *adj* **wealthier, wealthiest 1** having a large amount of money and valuable material possessions **2** wealthy in having a great amount or number of: *a continent exceptionally wealthy in minerals*

wean *vb* **1** to start giving (a baby or young mammal) food other than its mother's milk **2** to cause (oneself or someone else) to give up a former habit: *they are unable to wean themselves from the tobacco habit* [Old English *wenian* to accustom] ▷ **weaning** *n*

weapon *n* **1** an object used in fighting, such as a knife or gun **2** anything used to get the better of an opponent: *having a sense of humour is a weapon of self-defence* [Old English *wǣpen*]

weaponry *n* weapons regarded collectively

wear *vb* **wearing, wore, worn 1** to carry or have (a garment or jewellery) on one's body as clothing or ornament **2** to have (a particular facial expression): *she wore a scowl of frank antagonism* **3** to style (the hair) in a particular way: *she wears her hair in a braid* **4** to deteriorate or cause to deteriorate by constant use or action **5** *informal* to accept: *he won't be given a top job – the Party wouldn't wear it* **6** wear thin to lessen or become weaker: *his patience began to wear thin* **7** wear well to remain in good condition for a long time ▷ *n* **8** clothes that are suitable for a particular time or purpose: *evening wear; beach wear* **9** deterioration from constant or normal use **10** the quality of resisting the effects of constant use ▶ See also wear down, wear off, wear out [Old English *werian*] ▷ **wearable** *adj* ▷ **wearer** *n*

Wear *n* a river in NE England, rising in NW Durham and flowing southeast then northeast to the North Sea at Sunderland. Length: 105 km (65 miles)

wear and tear *n* damage or loss resulting from ordinary use

wear down *vb* **1** to make shorter by long or constant wearing or rubbing: *the back of his heels were worn down* **2** to overcome gradually by persistent effort: *to wear down the enemy*

wearing *adj* causing exhaustion and sometimes irritation

wearisome *adj* causing fatigue and irritation

wear off *vb* to have a gradual decrease in effect or intensity: *the cocaine injection was beginning to wear off*

wear out *vb* **1** to make or become unfit for use through wear: *my red trousers are worn out* **2** *informal* to exhaust: *the afternoon's races and games had worn him out*

weary *adj* **-rier, -riest 1** very tired; lacking energy **2** caused by or suggestive of weariness: *he managed a weary smile* **3** causing exhaustion: *a long weary struggle* **4** weary of discontented or bored with: *he was weary of the war* ▷ *vb* **-ries, -rying, -ried 5** to make weary **6** weary of to become discontented or bored with: *he seems to have wearied of her possessiveness* [Old English *wērig*] ▷ **wearily** *adv* ▷ **weariness** *n* ▷ **wearying** *adj*

weasel *n, pl* **-sels** or **-sel** a small meat-eating mammal with reddish-brown fur, a long body and neck, and short legs [Old English *wesle*]

weather *n* **1** the day-to-day atmospheric conditions, such as temperature, cloudiness, and rainfall, affecting a specific place **2** make heavy weather of *informal* to carry out (a task) with great difficulty or needless effort **3** under the weather *informal* feeling slightly ill ▷ *vb* **4** to undergo or cause to undergo changes, such as discoloration, due to the action of the weather **5** to come safely through (a storm, problem, or difficulty) [Old English *weder*]

weather-beaten *adj* **1** tanned by exposure to the weather: *a crumpled weather-beaten face* **2** worn or damaged as a result of exposure to the weather

weatherboard *n* a timber board that is fixed with others in overlapping horizontal rows to form an exterior cladding on a wall or roof ▷ **weatherboarded** *adj*

weathercock *n* a weather vane in the shape of a cock

weather eye *n* keep a weather eye on to keep a careful watch on: *keep a weather eye on your symptoms*

weathering *n* the breakdown of rocks by the action of the weather

weatherman *n, pl* **-men** a man who forecasts the weather on radio or television ▷ **weather girl** *fem n*

weatherproof *adj* able to withstand exposure to weather without deterioration: *a weatherproof roof*

weather vane *n* a metal object on a roof that indicates the direction in which the wind is blowing

weave *vb* **weaving, wove** or **weaved, woven** or **weaved 1** to form (a fabric) by interlacing yarn on a loom **2** to make (a garment or a blanket) by this process **3** to construct (a basket or fence) by interlacing cane or twigs **4** to compose (a story or plan) by combining separate elements into a whole **5** to move from side to side while going forward: *to weave in and out of lanes* **6** get weaving *informal* to hurry ▷ *n* **7** the structure or pattern of a woven fabric: *the rough weave of the cloth* [Old English *wefan*] ▷ **weaver** *n* ▷ **weaving** *n*

web *n* **1** a mesh of fine tough threads built by a spider to trap insects **2** anything that is intricately formed or complex: *a web of relationships* **3** a membrane connecting the toes of some water birds and water-dwelling animals such as frogs **4** the web (often cap) short for World Wide Web ▷ *adj* **5** of or situated on the World Wide Web: *a web server; web pages* [Old English *webb*] ▷ **webbed** *adj*

Web 2.0 *n* the internet viewed as a medium in which interactive experience plays a more important role than simply accessing information

web address *n* another name for URL

Webb *n* **1** Sir Aston. 1849–1930, British architect. His work includes the Victoria and Albert Museum (1909), the Victoria Memorial (1911), and Admiralty Arch (1911) **2** Mary (Gladys). 1881–1927, British novelist, remembered for her novels of rustic life, notably *Precious Bane* (1924) **3** Sidney (James), Baron Passfield. 1859–1947, British economist, social historian, and Fabian socialist. He and his wife (Martha) Beatrice (née Potter), 1858–1943, British writer on social and economic problems, collaborated in *The History of Trade Unionism* (1894) and *English Local Government* (1906–29), helped found the London School of Economics (1895), and started the *New Statesman* (1913)

webbing *n* a strong fabric that is woven in strips and used under springs in upholstery or for straps

webcam *n* a camera that transmits still or moving images over the internet

webcast *n* a broadcast of an event over the internet

weber (vay-ber) *n* the SI unit of magnetic flux (the strength of a magnetic field over a given area) [after W. E. WEBER]

Weber *n* **1** Baron Carl Maria Friedrich Ernst von. 1786–1826, German composer and conductor. His three romantic operas are *Der Freischütz* (1821), *Euryanthe* (1823), and *Oberon* (1826) **2** Ernst Heinrich. 1795–1878, German physiologist and anatomist. He introduced the psychological concept of the just noticeable difference between stimuli **3** Max. 1864–1920, German economist and sociologist, best known for *The Protestant Ethic and the*

Spirit of Capitalism (1904–05) **4** Wilhelm Eduard. 1804–91, German physicist, who conducted research into electricity and magnetism

Webern *n* Anton von. 1883–1945, Austrian composer; pupil of Schoenberg, whose twelve-tone technique he adopted. His works include those for chamber ensemble, such as *Five Pieces for Orchestra* (1911–13)

web-footed *or* **web-toed** *adj* (of certain animals or birds) having webbed feet that aid swimming

weblog *n* a person's online journal

webmail *n* an e-mail system that allows account holders to access mail via an internet site rather than by downloading it onto a computer

website *n* a group of connected pages on the World Wide Web containing information on a particular subject

Webster *n* **1** Daniel. 1782–1852, US politician and orator **2** John. ?1580–?1625, English dramatist, noted for his revenge tragedies *The White Devil* (?1612) and *The Duchess of Malfi* (?1613) **3** Noah. 1758–1843, US lexicographer, famous for his *American Dictionary of the English Language* (1828)

wed *vb* **wedding, wedded** *or* **wed 1** *old-fashioned* to take (a person) as a husband or wife; marry **2** to unite closely: *to wed folklore and magic* [Old English *weddian*]

Wed. Wednesday

wedded *adj* **1** of marriage: *wedded bliss* **2** firmly in support of an idea or institution: *wedded to the virtues of capitalism*

Weddell Sea *n* an arm of the S Atlantic in Antarctica

wedding *n* **1** a marriage ceremony **2** a special wedding anniversary, esp. the 25th (**silver wedding**) or 50th (**golden wedding**)

wedding breakfast *n* the meal usually served after a wedding ceremony or just before the bride and bridegroom leave for their honeymoon

wedding cake *n* a rich iced fruit cake, with one, two, or more tiers, which is served at a wedding reception

wedding ring *n* a plain ring, usually made of a precious metal, worn to indicate that one is married

Wedekind *n* Frank. 1864–1918, German dramatist, whose plays, such as *The Awakening of Spring* (1891) and *Pandora's Box* (1904), bitterly satirize the sexual repressiveness of society

wedge *n* **1** a block of solid material, esp. wood or metal, that is shaped like a narrow V in cross section and can be pushed or driven between two objects or parts of an object in order to split or secure them **2** a slice shaped like a wedge: *a wedge of quiche* **3** *golf* a club with a wedge-shaped face, used for bunker or pitch shots **4** drive a wedge between to cause a split between (people or groups) **5** the thin end of the wedge anything unimportant in itself that implies the start of something much larger ▷ *vb* **wedging, wedged 6** to secure (something) with a wedge **7** to squeeze into a narrow space: *a book wedged between the bed and the table* [Old English *wecg*]

wedge-tailed eagle *n* a large brown Australian eagle with a wedge-shaped tail

Wedgwood *n* **1** Josiah. 1730–95, British potter and industrialist, who founded several pottery works near Stoke-on-Trent in Staffordshire **2** *trademark* pottery produced at the Wedgwood factories, esp. of a type with applied decoration in white on a coloured background

wedlock *n* **1** the state of being married **2** born out of wedlock born when one's parents are not legally married [Old English *wedlāc*]

Wednesday *n* the fourth day of the week [Old English *Wōdnes dæg* Woden's day]

wee¹ *adj* Brit, Austral and NZ small or short [Old English *wǣg* weight]

wee² *informal n* **1** an instance of urinating ▷ *vb* **weeing, weed 2** to urinate ▶ Also: **wee-wee** [origin unknown]

weed *n* **1** any plant that grows wild and profusely, esp. among cultivated plants **2** *slang* **a** marijuana **b** the weed *or* the evil weed tobacco **3** *informal* a thin weak person ▷ *vb* **4** to remove weeds from (a garden) [Old English *wēod*]

weedkiller *n* a chemical or hormonal substance used to kill weeds

weed out *vb* to separate out, remove, or eliminate (an unwanted element): *to weed out the thugs*

weedy *adj* **weedier, weediest 1** *informal* thin or weak: *sick and weedy children* **2** full of weeds: *weedy patches of garden*

week *n* **1** a period of seven consecutive days, esp. one beginning with Sunday **2** a period of seven consecutive days from a specified day: *a week from today* **3** the period of time within a week that is spent at work [Old English *wice, wicu*]

weekday *n* any day of the week other than Saturday or Sunday

weekend *n* Saturday and Sunday

weekly *adj* **1** happening once a week or every week: *a weekly column* **2** determined or calculated by the week: *weekly earnings* ▷ *adv* **3** once a week or every week: *report to the police weekly* ▷ *n*, *pl* **-lies 4** a newspaper or magazine issued every week

Weelkes *n* Thomas. ?1575–1623, English composer of madrigals

weeny *adj* **-nier, -niest** *informal* very small; tiny [from WEE¹]

weep *vb* **weeping, wept 1** to shed tears; cry **2** to ooze liquid: *the skin cracked and wept; the label is weeping black ink in the rain* ▷ *n* **3** a spell of weeping: *together we had a good weep* [Old English *wēpan*]

weeping willow *n* a willow tree with graceful drooping branches

weepy *informal adj* **weepier, weepiest 1** liable or tending to weep ▷ *n*, *pl* **weepies 2** a sentimental film or book

weevil *n* a beetle with a long snout that feeds on plants [Old English *wifel*]

wee-wee *n*, *vb* **-weeing, -weed** *informal, chiefly Brit* same as wee²

weft *n* the yarns woven across the width of the fabric through the lengthways warp yarns [Old English]

Wegener *n* Alfred. 1880–1930, German meteorologist: regarded as the originator of the theory of continental drift

Weichsel *n* the German name for the Vistula (1)

weigh *vb* **1** to have weight as specified: *the tree weighs nearly three tons* **2** to measure the weight of **3** to consider carefully: *the President now has to weigh his options* **4** to be influential: *the authorities did not enter my mind or weigh with me* **5** weigh anchor to raise a ship's anchor **6** weigh out to measure out by weight ▶ See also **weigh down, weigh in**, etc. [Old English *wegan*]

weighbridge *n* a machine for weighing vehicles by means of a metal plate set into a road

weigh down *vb* **1** (of a heavy load) to impede the movements of **2** (of a problem or difficulty) to worry (someone) a great deal

weigh in *vb* **1** (of a boxer or jockey) to be weighed to check that one is of the correct weight for the contest **2** *informal* to contribute to a discussion or conversation: *he weighed in with a few sharp comments* ▷ *n* **weigh-in 3** *sport* the occasion of checking the competitors' weight before a boxing match or a horse race

weigh on *vb* to be oppressive or burdensome to: *the expectations that weigh so heavily on diplomats' wives*

weight *n* **1** the heaviness of an object, substance, or person **2** *physics* the vertical force experienced by a mass as a result of gravitation **3 a** a system of units used to express weight: *metric weight* **b** a unit used to measure weight: *the kilogram is the weight used in the metric system* **4 a** an object of known heaviness used for weighing objects, substances, or people **b** an object of known heaviness used in weight training or weightlifting to strengthen the muscles **5** any heavy load: *with a weight of fish on their backs* **6** force, importance, or influence: *they want their words to carry weight* **7** an oppressive force: *the weight of expectation* **8** pull one's weight *informal* to do one's full share of a task **9** throw one's weight about *informal* to act in an aggressive authoritarian manner ▷ *vb* **10** to add weight to; make heavier **11** to slant (a system) so that it favours one side rather than another [Old English *wiht*]

weighting *n* Brit an allowance paid to compensate for higher living costs: *salary includes Inner London weighting*

weightless *adj* **1** seeming to have very little weight or no weight at all **2** seeming not to be affected by gravity, as in the case of astronauts in an orbiting spacecraft ▷ **weightlessness** *n*

weightlifting *n* the sport of lifting barbells of specified weights in a prescribed manner ▷ **weightlifter** *n*

weight training *n* physical exercise using light or heavy weights in order to strengthen the muscles

weighty *adj* **weightier, weightiest** **1** important or serious: *weighty matters* **2** very heavy

weigh up *vb* to make an assessment of (a person or situation)

Weihai *or* **Wei-hai** *n* a port in NE China, in NE Shandong on the Yellow Sea: leased to Britain as a naval base (1898–1930). Pop: 966 000 (2005 est). Also called: **Weihaiwei**

Weil *n* Simone. 1909–43, French philosopher and mystic, whose works include *Waiting for God* (1951), *The Need for Roots* (1952), and *Notebooks* (1956)

Weill *n* Kurt. 1900–50, German composer, in the US from 1935. He wrote the music for Brecht's *The Rise and Fall of the City of Mahagonny* (1927) and *The Threepenny Opera* (1928)

Weimar *n* a city in E central Germany, in Thuringia: a cultural centre in the 18th and early 19th century; scene of the adoption (1919) of the constitution of the Weimar Republic. Pop: 64 409 (2003 est)

Weinberg *n* Steven. born 1933, US physicist, who shared the Nobel prize for physics (1979) with Sheldon Glashow and Abdus Salam for his role in formulating the electroweak theory

weir *n* **1** a low dam that is built across a river to divert the water or control its flow **2** a fencelike trap built across a stream for catching fish in [Old English *wer*]

Weir *n* **1** David (Russell). born 1979, English wheelchair athlete; won ten medals for Britain, including six golds, over three Olympic Games (2004–2012); won the London Marathon six times **2** Judith. born 1954, Scottish composer: her operas include *A Night at the Chinese Opera* (1987), and *Armida* (2005); Master of the Queen's Music from 2014 **3** Peter. born 1944, Australian film director; his films include *Dead Poets Society* (1989), *The Truman Show* (1998), and *Master and Commander* (2003)

weird *adj* **1** strange or bizarre **2** suggestive of the supernatural; uncanny [Old English *(ge)wyrd* destiny] ▷ **weirdly** *adv* ▷ **weirdness** *n*

weirdo *n, pl* **-dos** *informal* a person who behaves in a bizarre or eccentric manner

Weisshorn *n* a mountain in S Switzerland, in the Pennine Alps. Height: 4505 m (14 781 ft)

Weissmuller *n* John Peter, known as *Johnny*. 1904–84, US swimmer and film actor, who won Olympic gold medals in 1924 and 1928 and played the title role in the early Tarzan films

Weizmann *n* Chaim. 1874–1952, Israeli statesman, born in Russia. As a leading Zionist, he was largely responsible for securing the Balfour Declaration (1917); first president of Israel (1949–52)

Welby *n* Justin (Portal). born 1956, English clergyman; Archbishop of Canterbury from 2013

welch *vb* same as welsh

welcome *vb* **-coming, -comed** **1** to greet the arrival of (a guest) cordially **2** to receive or accept (something) gladly: *I would welcome a chance to speak to him* ▷ *n* **3** the act of greeting or receiving someone or something in a specified manner: *the President was given a warm welcome* ▷ *adj* **4** gladly received or admitted: *I wouldn't want to stay where I'm not welcome* **5** encouraged or invited: *you are welcome to join us at one of our social events* **6** bringing

pleasure: *a welcome change* **7** you're welcome an expression used to acknowledge someone's thanks [Old English *wilcuma*] ▷ **welcoming** *adj*

weld *vb* **1** to join (two pieces of metal or plastic) by softening with heat and hammering or by fusion **2** to unite closely: *the diverse ethnic groups had been welded together by the anti-Fascist cause* ▷ *n* **3** a joint formed by welding [obsolete *well* to melt, weld] ▷ **welder** *n*

Weld *n* Sir Frederick Aloysius. 1823–91, New Zealand statesman, born in England: prime minister of New Zealand (1864–65)

Weldon *n* Fay. born 1931, British novelist and writer. Her novels include *Praxis* (1978), *Life and Loves of a She-Devil* (1984), *Big Women* (1998), and *Rhode Island Blues* (2003)

welfare *n* **1** health, happiness, prosperity, and general wellbeing **2** financial and other assistance given, usually by the government, to people in need [WEL(L)[1] + FARE]

welfare state *n* a system in which the government undertakes responsibility for the wellbeing of its population, through unemployment insurance, old age pensions, and other social-security measures

Welkom *n* a town in central South Africa; developed rapidly following the discovery of gold. Pop: 34 157 (2001)

well[1] *adv* **better, best** **1** satisfactorily or pleasingly: *well proportioned* **2** skilfully: *I played well for the last six holes* **3** thoroughly: *make sure the chicken is well cooked* **4** comfortably or prosperously: *he has lived well from his various nautical exploits* **5** suitably or fittingly: *you can't very well refuse* **6** intimately: *darling Robert, I know him so well* **7** favourably: *it will go down very well with all the people who support him* **8** by a considerable margin: *well over half; she left well before tea* **9** very likely: *the claim may well be true* **10** *informal* extremely: *well cool* **11** all very well used ironically to express discontent or annoyance: *that's all very well, but I'm left to pick up the pieces* **12** as well **a** in addition **b** with equal effect: used to express indifference or reluctance: *I might as well go out* **13** as well as in addition to **14** just as well fortunate or appropriate: *it's just as well I didn't spend all my money* ▷ *adj* **15** in good health: *I'm not feeling well* **16** satisfactory or acceptable: *all was well in the aircraft* ▷ *interj* **17 a** an expression of surprise, indignation, or reproof: *well, what a cheek!* **b** an expression of anticipation in waiting for an answer or remark: *well, what do you think?* [Old English *wel*]

well[2] *n* **1 a** a hole or shaft bored into the earth to tap a supply of water, oil, or gas **2** an open shaft through the floors of a building, used for a staircase ▷ *vb* **3** to flow upwards or outwards: *tears welled up into my eyes* [Old English *wella*]

we'll we will *or* we shall

well-advised *adj* prudent or sensible: *you would be well-advised to cooperate with me*

Welland Canal *n* a canal in S Canada, in Ontario, linking Lake Erie to Lake Ontario: part of the St Lawrence Seaway, with eight locks. Length: 44 km (28 miles). Also called: **Welland Ship Canal**

well-appointed *adj* (of a room or building) equipped or furnished to a high standard

well-balanced *adj* sensible and emotionally stable

well-behaved *adj* having good manners; not causing trouble or mischief

well-being *n* the state of being contented and healthy: *a sense of well-being*

well-born *adj* belonging to a noble or upper-class family

well-bred *adj* having good manners; polite

well-built *adj* strong and well-proportioned

well-connected *adj* having influential or important relatives or friends

well-disposed *adj* inclined to be sympathetic, kindly, or friendly towards a person or idea

well-done *adj* **1** made or accomplished satisfactorily **2** (of food, esp. meat) cooked very thoroughly

Welles *n* (George) Orson. 1915–85, US film director, actor,

W

producer, and screenwriter. His *Citizen Kane* (1941) and *The Magnificent Ambersons* (1942) are regarded as film classics

Wellesley *n* **1** Arthur. See (1st Duke of) **Wellington 2** his brother, **Richard Colley**, Marquis Wellesley. 1760–1842, British administrator. As governor general of Bengal (1797–1805) he consolidated British power in India

Wellesz *n* Egon. 1885–1974, British composer, born in Austria

well-founded *adj* having a sound basis in fact: *a well-founded fear of persecution*

well-groomed *adj* having a smart tidy appearance

well-grounded *adj* having a sound basis in fact: *well-grounded suspicions*

wellhead *n* **1** the source of a well or stream **2** a source, fountainhead, or origin

well-heeled *adj informal* wealthy

wellies *pl n Brit, NZ and Austral informal* Wellington boots

well-informed *adj* knowing a lot about a great variety of subjects or about one particular subject

Wellingborough *n* a town in central England, in Northamptonshire. Pop: 46 959 (2001)

Wellington[1] *n* **1** an administrative district, formerly a province, of New Zealand, on SW North Island: major livestock producer in New Zealand. Capital: Wellington. Pop: 492 500 (2013 est). Area: 28 153 sq km (10 870 sq miles) **2** the capital city of New Zealand. Its port, historically Port Nicholson, on **Wellington Harbour** has a car and rail ferry link between the North and South Islands; university (1899). Pop: 204 000 (2013 est)

Wellington[2] *n* **1st Duke of**, title of *Arthur Wellesley*. 1769–1852, British soldier and statesman; prime minister (1828–30). He was given command of the British forces against the French in the Peninsular War (1808–14) and routed Napoleon at Waterloo (1815)

Wellington boots *or* **wellingtons** *pl n* long rubber boots, worn in wet or muddy conditions [after the 1st Duke of WELLINGTON]

well-intentioned *adj* having good or kindly intentions, usually with unfortunate results

well-known *adj* widely known; famous

well-meaning *adj* having or indicating good intentions, usually with unfortunate results

well-nigh *adv* almost: *a well-nigh impossible task*

well-off *adj* **1** moderately wealthy **2** in a fortunate position: *some people don't know when they are well-off*

well-preserved *adj* not showing signs of ageing: *amazingly well-preserved for a man of 70*

well-read *adj* having read and learned a lot

well-rounded *adj* **1** desirably varied: *his well-rounded team* **2** rounded in shape or well developed: *a voluptuous well-rounded lady*

Wells[1] *n* a city in SW England, in Somerset: 12th-century cathedral. Pop: 10 406 (2001)

Wells[2] *n* **1** Henry. 1805–78, US businessman, who founded (1852) with William Fargo the express mail service Wells, Fargo and Company **2** H(erbert) G(eorge). 1866–1946, British writer. His science-fiction stories include *The Time Machine* (1895), *War of the Worlds* (1898), and *The Shape of Things to Come* (1933). His novels on contemporary social questions, such as *Kipps* (1905), *Tono-Bungay* (1909), and *Ann Veronica* (1909), affected the opinions of his day. His nonfiction works include *The Outline of History* (1920)

well-spoken *adj* having a clear, articulate, and socially acceptable accent and way of speaking

wellspring *n* a source of abundant supply: *the wellspring of truth*

well-thought-of *adj* liked and respected

well-to-do *adj* moderately wealthy

well-versed *adj* knowing a lot about a particular subject

well-wisher *n* a person who shows benevolence or sympathy towards a person or cause

well-worn *adj* **1** (of a word or phrase) having lost its meaning or force through being overused **2** having been

used so much as to show signs of wear: *well-worn leather*

welly *n* **1** *informal* a Wellington boot **2** *Brit slang* energy or commitment: *give it some welly!*

Wels *n* an industrial city in N central Austria, in Upper Austria. Pop: 56 478 (2002)

welsh *or* **welch** *vb* **welsh on** to fail to pay (a debt) or fulfil (an obligation) [origin unknown]

Welsh *adj* **1** of or relating to Wales or its inhabitants ▷ *n* **2** a Celtic language spoken in some parts of Wales ▷ *pl n* **3 the Welsh** the people of Wales [Old English *Wēlisc, Wǣlisc*]

Welshman *or fem* **Welshwoman** *n, pl* **-men** *or* **-women** a native or inhabitant of Wales

Welsh rarebit *n* melted cheese, sometimes mixed with milk or seasonings, served on hot toast. Also called: **Welsh rabbit**

welt *n* **1** a raised mark on the skin produced by a blow **2** a raised or strengthened seam in a garment [origin unknown]

welter *n* a confused mass or jumble: *a welter of facts* [Middle Low German, Middle Dutch *weltern*]

welterweight *n* a professional boxer weighing up to 147 pounds (66.5 kg) or an amateur boxer weighing up to 67 kg

Welty *n* Eudora. 1909–2001, US novelist and short-story writer, noted for her depiction of life in the Mississippi delta. Her novels include *Delta Wedding* (1946) and *The Optimist's Daughter* (1972)

Welwyn Garden City *n* a town in SE England, in Hertfordshire: established (1920) as a planned industrial and residential community. Pop: 43 512 (2001)

Wembley *n* part of the Greater London borough of Brent: site of the English national soccer stadium, replaced by the larger multi-purpose Wembley Stadium in 2007

wen *n pathol* a cyst on the scalp [Old English *wenn*]

Wenceslaus *or* **Wenceslas** *n* **1** 1361–1419, Holy Roman Emperor (1378–1400) and, as **Wenceslaus IV**, king of Bohemia (1378–1419) **2 Saint**, known as *Good King Wenceslaus*. ?907–929, duke of Bohemia (?925–29); patron saint of Bohemia. Feast day: Sept 28

wench *n old-fashioned* **1** *facetious* a girl or young woman **2** a prostitute or female servant [Old English *wencel* child]

wend *vb* to make (one's way) in a particular direction: *it's time to wend our way back home* [Old English *wendan*]

Wendy house *n* a small toy house for a child to play in [after Wendy, the girl in J. M. Barrie's play *Peter Pan*]

wensleydale *n* a white cheese with a flaky texture [after Wensleydale, North Yorkshire]

went *vb* the past tense of **go**

Wentworth *n* **1** Thomas. See (Earl of) **Strafford 2** William Charles. 1790–1872, Australian explorer and statesman who was a member of the exploring party that first crossed the Blue Mountains in 1813 and was later a leader in the movement for self-government in New South Wales

Wenzhou, Wen-chou *or* **Wenchow** *n* a port in SE China, in Zhejiang province: noted for its historic buildings. Pop: 1 475 000 (2005 est)

wept *vb* the past of **weep**

were *vb* the form of the past tense of **be** used after *we, you, they,* or a plural noun, or as a subjunctive in conditional sentences [Old English *wēron, wæron*]

> **USAGE** Were, as a remnant of the past subjunctive in English, is used in formal contexts in clauses expressing hypotheses (*if he were to die, she would inherit everything*), suppositions contrary to fact (*if I were you, I would be careful*), and desire (*I wish he were there now*). In informal speech, however, *was* is often used instead.

we're we are

weren't were not

werewolf *n, pl* **-wolves** (in folklore) a person who can turn into a wolf [Old English *wer* man + *wulf* wolf]

Werfel n Franz. 1890–1945, Austro-Hungarian poet, novelist, and dramatist of the German expressionist movement. His novels include *The Forty Days of Musa Dagh* (1933) and *The Song of Bernadette* (1941)

Wergeland n Henrik Arnold. 1808–45, Norwegian poet and nationalist, remembered for his lyric and narrative verse

Werner n **1** Abraham Gottlieb. 1749–1817, German geologist. He emphasized the importance of field and laboratory observation for understanding the earth **2** Alfred. 1866–1919, Swiss chemist, born in Germany. He developed a coordination theory of the valency of inorganic complexes: Nobel prize for chemistry 1913

Weser n a river in NW Germany: flows northwest to the North Sea at Bremerhaven and is linked by the Mittelland Canal to the Ems, Rhine, and Elbe waterways. Length: 477 km (196 miles)

Wesermünde n the former name (until 1947) of Bremerhaven

Wesker n Sir Arnold. born 1932, British dramatist, whose plays include *Roots* (1959), *Chips With Everything* (1962), *The Merchant* (1976), *Caritas* (1981), and *Break My Heart* (1997)

Wesley n **1** John. 1703–91, English preacher who founded Methodism **2** Mary, pseudonym of *Mary Aline Siepmann*. 1912–2003, British writer: her novels include *The Camomile Lawn* (1984) and *An Imaginative Experience* (1994)

Wessex¹ n **1** an Anglo-Saxon kingdom in S and SW England that became the most powerful English kingdom by the 10th century AD **2** (in Thomas Hardy's works) the southwestern counties of England, esp. Dorset

Wessex² n Earl of Wessex See **Edward** (2)

west n **1** one of the four cardinal points of the compass, at 270° clockwise from north; the direction along a line of latitude towards the sunset **2** the west any area lying in or towards the west ▷ *adj* **3** situated in, moving towards, or facing the west **4** (esp. of the wind) from the west ▷ *adv* **5** in, to, or towards the west [Old English]

West¹ n **1** the West **a** the western part of the world contrasted historically and culturally with the East **b** (esp. formerly) the non-Communist countries of Europe and America contrasted with the Communist states of the East ▷ *adj* **2** of or denoting the western part of a country or region

West² n **1** Benjamin. 1738–1820, US painter, in England from 1763 **2** Kanye, born 1977, US rap singer and producer; his albums include *The College Dropout* (2004) and *Graduation* (2007) **3** Mae. 1892–1980, US film actress **4** Nathanael, real name *Nathan Weinstein*. 1903–40, US novelist: author of *Miss Lonely-Hearts* (1933) and *The Day of the Locust* (1939) **5** Dame Rebecca, real name *Cicily Isabel Andrews* (née *Fairfield*). 1892–1983, British journalist, novelist, and critic

West Atlantic n **1** the W part of the Atlantic Ocean, esp. the N Atlantic around North America **2** a branch of the Niger-Congo family of African languages, spoken in Senegal and in scattered areas eastwards, including Fulani and Wolof ▷ *adj* **3** relating to or belonging to this group of languages

West Bank n the West Bank a semi-autonomous Palestinian region in the Middle East on the W bank of the River Jordan, comprising the hills of Judaea and Samaria and part of Jerusalem: formerly part of Palestine (the entity created by the League of Nations in 1922 and operating until 1948): became part of Jordan after the ceasefire of 1949: occupied by Israel since the 1967 Arab-Israeli War. In 1993 a peace treaty between Israel and the Palestine Liberation Organization provided for the West Bank to become a self-governing Palestinian area; a new Palestinian National Authority assumed control of parts of the territory in 1994–95, but subsequent talks broke down and Israel reoccupied much of this in 2001–02 and continues to maintain most existing Israeli settlements. Pop: 2 676 740 (2013 est). Area: 5879 sq km (2270 sq miles)

West Bengal n a state of E India, on the Bay of Bengal: formed in 1947 from the Hindu area of Bengal; additional territories added in 1950 (Cooch Behar), 1954 (Chandernagor), and 1956 (part of Bihar); mostly low-lying and crossed by the Hooghly River. Capital: Kolkata (Calcutta). Pop: 80 221 171 (2001). Area: 88 752 sq km (34 260 sq miles)

West Berkshire n a unitary authority in S England, in Berkshire. Pop: 144 200 (2003 est). Area: 705 sq km (272 sq miles)

West Berlin n (formerly) the part of Berlin under US, British, and French control

West Berliner n a native or inhabitant of the part of Berlin formerly under US, British, and French control

westbound adj going towards the west

West Bromwich n a town in central England, in Sandwell unitary authority, West Midlands: industrial centre. Pop: 136 940 (2001)

West Country n the West Country the southwest of England, esp. Cornwall, Devon, and Somerset

West Dunbartonshire n a council area of W central Scotland, on Loch Lomond and the Clyde estuary: corresponds to part of the historical county of Dunbartonshire; part of Strathclyde Region from 1975 to 1996: engineering industries. Administrative centre: Dumbarton. Pop: 92 320 (2003 est). Area: 162 sq km (63 sq miles)

West End n the West End a part of W central London containing the main shopping and entertainment areas

Westenra n Hayley (Dee). born 1987, New Zealand singer, known for the purity of her voice in many musical genres

westerly adj **1** of or in the west ▷ *adv, adj* **2** towards the west **3** from the west: *a westerly wind*

western adj **1** situated in or towards the west **2** facing or moving towards the west **3** (*sometimes cap*) of or characteristic of the west or West ▷ n **4** a film or book about cowboys in the western states of the US in the 19th century ⟩ **westernmost** adj

Western adj (esp. formerly) of or characteristic of the Americas and the parts of Europe not under Communist rule

Western Australia n a state of W Australia: mostly an arid undulating plateau, with the Great Sandy Desert, Gibson Desert, and Great Victoria Desert in the interior; settlement concentrated in the southwest; rich mineral resources. Capital: Perth. Pop: 2 517 200 (2013 est). Area: 2 527 636 sq km (975 920 sq miles)

Western Cape n a province of W South Africa, created in 1994 from the SW part of Cape Province: agriculture (esp. fruit), wine making, fishing, various industries in Cape Town. Capital: Cape Town. Pop: 5 822 734 (2011 est). Area: 129 370 sq km (49 950 sq miles). Also called: **Western Province**

Westerner n a person from the west of a country or region

Western Ghats pl n a mountain range in W peninsular India, parallel to the Malabar coast of the Arabian Sea. Highest peak: Anai Mudi, 2695 m (8841 ft)

western hemisphere n the half of the globe that contains the Americas

Western Isles n (*functioning as sing or pl*) **1** an island authority in W Scotland, consisting of the Outer Hebrides; created in 1975. Administrative centre: Stornoway. Pop: 26 100 (2003 est). Area: 2900 sq km (1120 sq miles). Gaelic name: **Eilean Siar 2** Also called: **Western Islands**. another name for **Hebrides**

westernize or **-nise** vb **-nizing, -nized** or **-nising, -nised** to influence or make familiar with the customs or practices of the West ⟩ **westernization** or **-nisation** n

Western Ocean n (formerly) another name for **Atlantic Ocean**

W

Western Province *n* another name for **Western Cape**

Western Sahara *n* a disputed region of NW Africa, on the Atlantic: mainly desert; rich phosphate deposits; a Spanish overseas province from 1958 to 1975; partitioned in 1976 between Morocco and Mauritania who faced growing resistance from the Polisario Front, an organization aiming for the independence of the region as the Democratic Saharan Arab Republic. Mauritania renounced its claim in 1979 and it was taken over by Morocco. Polisario agreed to a UN-brokered ceasefire in 1991 but attempts to settle the status of the region have failed. Pop: 538 811 (2013 est). Area: 266 000 sq km (102 680 sq miles). Former name (until 1975): **Spanish Sahara**

Western Samoa *n* See **Samoa** (1)

Western Wall *n Judaism* a wall in Jerusalem, the last extant part of the Temple of Herod, held sacred by Jews as a place of prayer and pilgrimage. Also called: **Wailing Wall**

Westfalen *n* the German name for **Westphalia**

West Flanders *n* a province of W Belgium: the country's chief agricultural province. Capital: Bruges. Pop: 1 135 802 (2004 est). Area: 3132 sq km (1209 sq miles)

West German *adj* **1** of or relating to the former republic of West Germany (now part of Germany) or its inhabitants ▷ *n* **2** a native or inhabitant of the former West Germany

West Germany *n* a former republic in N central Europe, on the North Sea: established in 1949 from the zones of Germany occupied by the British, Americans, and French after the defeat of Nazi Germany; a member of the European Community; reunited with East Germany in 1990. Official name: **Federal Republic of Germany**. See also **Germany**

West Glamorgan *n* a former county in S Wales, formed in 1974 from part of Glamorgan and the county borough of Swansea: replaced in 1996 by the county of Swansea and the county borough of Neath Port Talbot

West Indian *adj* **1** of or relating to the West Indies ▷ *n* **2** a native or inhabitant of the West Indies

West Indies *n (functioning as sing or pl)* an archipelago off Central America, extending over 2400 km (1500 miles) in an arc from the peninsula of Florida to Venezuela, separating the Caribbean Sea from the Atlantic Ocean: consists of the Greater Antilles, the Lesser Antilles, and the Bahamas; largest island is Cuba. Area: over 235 000 sq km (91 000 sq miles). Also called: **the Caribbean**

West Irian *n* a former English name for **Papua** (2)

West Lothian *n* a council area and historical county of central Scotland, on the Firth of Forth: became part of Lothian region in 1975: reinstated as an independent authority (with revised boundaries) in 1996: agriculture, oil-refining. Administrative centre: Livingston. Pop: 161 020 (2003 est). Area: 425 sq km (164 sq miles)

Westm. Westminster

Westmeath *n* a county of N central Republic of Ireland, in Leinster province: mostly low-lying, with many lakes and bogs. County town: Mullingar. Pop: 71 858 (2002). Area: 1764 sq km (681 sq miles)

West Midlands *n (functioning as sing or pl)* a metropolitan county of central England, administered since 1986 by the unitary authorities of Wolverhampton, Walsall, Dudley, Sandwell, Birmingham, Solihull, and Coventry. Area: 899 sq km (347 sq miles)

Westminster *n* **1** Also called: **City of Westminster** a borough of Greater London, on the River Thames: contains the Houses of Parliament, Westminster Abbey, and Buckingham Palace. Pop: 222 000 (2003 est). Area: 22 sq km (8 sq miles) **2** the Houses of Parliament at Westminster

Westminster Abbey *n* a Gothic church in London: site of a Benedictine monastery (1050–65); scene of the coronations of almost all English monarchs since William I

Westmorland *n* (until 1974) a county of NW England, now part of Cumbria

Weston-super-Mare *n* a town and resort in SW England, in North Somerset unitary authority, Somerset, on the Bristol Channel. Pop: 78 044 (2001)

West Pakistan *n* the former name (until the end of 1971) of Pakistan

Westphalia *n* a historic region of NW Germany, now mostly in the state of North Rhine-Westphalia. German name: **Westfalen**

Westphalian *adj* **1** of or relating to the historic German region of Westphalia or its inhabitants ▷ *n* **2** a native or inhabitant of Westphalia

West Prussia *n* a former province of NE Prussia, on the Baltic: assigned to Poland in 1945. German name: **Westpreussen**

West Riding *n* (until 1974) an administrative division of Yorkshire, now part of West Yorkshire, North Yorkshire, Cumbria, and Lancashire

West Sussex *n* a county of SE England, comprising part of the former county of Sussex: mainly low-lying, with the South Downs in the S. Administrative centre: Chichester. Pop: 758 600 (2003 est). Area: 1989 sq km (768 sq miles)

West Virginia *n* a state of the eastern US: part of Virginia until the outbreak of the American Civil War (1861); consists chiefly of the Allegheny Plateau; bounded on the west by the Ohio River; coal-mining. Capital: Charleston. Pop: 1 810 354 (2003 est). Area: 62 341 sq km (24 070 sq miles). Abbreviation: **W.Va.**, (with zip code) **WV**

West Virginian *adj* **1** of or relating to the state of West Virginia or its inhabitants ▷ *n* **2** a native or inhabitant of West Virginia

westward *adj, adv* also: **westwards** **1** towards the west ▷ *n* **2** the westward part or direction

Westwood *n* Dame Vivienne (Isabel). born 1941, British fashion designer: noted for her punk designs of the late 1970s

West Yorkshire *n* a metropolitan county of N England, administered since 1986 by the unitary authorities of Bradford, Leeds, Calderdale, Kirklees, and Wakefield. Area: 2039 sq km (787 sq miles)

wet *adj* **wetter, wettest** **1** moistened, covered, or soaked with water or some other liquid **2** not yet dry or solid: *wet paint* **3** rainy: *the weather was cold and wet* **4** *Brit and NZ informal* feeble or foolish **5 wet behind the ears** *informal* immature or inexperienced ▷ *n* **6** rainy weather **7** *Brit informal* a feeble or foolish person **8** *Brit informal* a Conservative politician who supports moderate policies ▷ *vb* **wetting, wet** or **wetted** **9** to make wet: *wet the brush before applying the paint* **10** to urinate in (one's clothes or bed) **11 wet oneself** to urinate in one's clothes [Old English *wēt*] **> wetly** *adv* **> wetness** *n*

wet blanket *n informal* a person whose low spirits or lack of enthusiasm have a depressing effect on others

wet dream *n* an erotic dream accompanied by an emission of semen

wether *n* a male sheep, esp. a castrated one [Old English]

wetland *n* an area of marshy land

wet nurse *n* (esp. formerly) a woman hired to breast-feed another woman's baby

wet room *n* a type of waterproofed room with a drain in the floor often serving as an open-plan shower

wet suit *n* a close-fitting rubber suit used by skin-divers and yachtsmen to retain body heat

Wetterhorn *n* a mountain in S Switzerland, in the Bernese Alps. Height: 3701 m (12 143 ft)

Wexford *n* **1** a county of SE Republic of Ireland, in Leinster province on the Irish Sea: the first Irish county to be colonized from England; mostly low-lying and fertile. County town: Wexford. Pop: 116 596 (2002). Area: 2352 sq km (908 sq miles) **2** a port in SE Republic of Ireland, county town of Co Wexford: sacked by Oliver

Cromwell in 1649. Pop: 17 235 (2002)

Weygand n Maxime. 1867–1965, French general; as commander in chief of the Allied armies in France (1940) he advised the French Government to surrender to Germany

Weyl n Hermann. 1885–1955, US mathematician, born in Germany; noted for his work on group theory and the mathematics of relativity

Weymouth n a port and resort in S England, in Dorset on the English Channel: formerly part of the borough of **Weymouth and Melcombe** Regis. Pop (with Melcombe Regis): 48 279 (2001)

whack vb **1** to hit hard: that lad whacked him over the head with a bottle **2** (usually foll. by in or on) informal to put something onto or into (something else) with force or abandon: whack on some sunscreen ▷ n **3** a hard blow or the sound of one: a whack with a blunt instrument **4** informal a share: he took his whack of that money **5 have a whack** to make an attempt **6 out of whack** informal out of order or out of condition: my body is just a little out of whack [imitative]

whacked adj informal completely exhausted

whacking n **1** old-fashioned a severe beating ▷ adv **2** Brit, Austral and NZ informal extremely: a whacking great elm

whale n **1** a very large fishlike sea mammal that breathes through a blowhole on the top of its head **2 have a whale of a time** informal to enjoy oneself very much [Old English hwæl]

whalebone n a thin strip of a horny material that hangs from the upper jaw of some whales, formerly used for stiffening corsets

whalebone whale n any whale with a double blowhole and strips of whalebone between the jaws instead of teeth, including the right whale and the blue whale

whaler n **1** a ship used for hunting whales **2** a person whose job is to hunt whales

whaling n the activity of hunting and killing whales for food or oil

wham interj informal an expression indicating suddenness or forcefulness: suddenly, wham! you are caught up right in the middle of it [imitative]

whammy n, pl -mies informal a devastating setback: the double whammy of drugs and divorce

Whangarei n a port in New Zealand, the northernmost city of North Island: oil refinery. Pop: 72 200 (2004 est)

wharepuni (for-rep-poon-ee) n NZ (in a Māori community) a tall carved building used as a guesthouse [Māori]

wharf n, pl **wharves** or **wharfs** a platform along the side of a waterfront for docking, loading, and unloading ships [Old English hwearf]

wharfie n Austral and NZ a dock labourer

Wharton n Edith (Newbold). 1862–1937, US novelist; author of The House of Mirth (1905) and Ethan Frome (1911)

what pron **1** used in requesting further information about the identity or categorization of something: what was he wearing?; I knew what would happen **2** the person, thing, people, or things that: all was not what it seemed **3** used in exclamations to add emphasis: what a creep! **4 what for?** for what reason? **5 what have you** other similar or related things: qualifications, interests, profession, what have you ▷ adj **6** used with a noun in requesting further information about the identity or categorization of something: what difference can it make now? **7** to any degree or in any amount: they provided what financial support they could [Old English hwæt]

USAGE The use of are in sentences such as what we need are more doctors is common, although many people think is should be used: what we need is more doctors.

whatever pron **1** everything or anything that: I can handle whatever comes up **2** no matter what: whatever you do, keep

your temper **3** informal other similar or related things: a block of wood, rock, or whatever **4** an intensive form of what, used in questions: whatever gave you that impression? ▷ adj **5** an intensive form of what: I can take whatever actions I deem necessary **6** at all: there is no foundation whatever for such opinions

whatnot n informal other similar or related things: groceries, wines, and whatnot

whatsoever adj at all: used for emphasis after a noun phrase that uses words such as none or any: there is nothing whatsoever wrong with your heart; it can be used at any time and under any circumstances whatsoever

wheat n **1** a kind of grain used in making flour and pasta **2** the plant from which this grain is obtained [Old English hwǣte]

wheatear n a small northern songbird with a white rump [probably from white + arse]

wheaten adj made from the grain or flour of wheat: wheaten bread

wheat germ n the vitamin-rich middle part of a grain of wheat

wheatmeal n a brown flour intermediate between white flour and wholemeal flour

wheedle vb -dling, -dled **1** to try to persuade (someone) by coaxing or flattery: wheedling you into giving them their way **2** to obtain (something) in this way: she wheedled money out of him [origin unknown] ▷ **wheedling** adj, n

wheel n **1** a circular object mounted on a shaft around which it can turn, fixed under vehicles to enable them to move **2** anything like a wheel in shape or function: the steering wheel; a spinning wheel **3** something that is repeated in cycles: the wheel of fashion would turn, and the clothes would be back in style **4 at** or **behind the wheel** driving a vehicle ▷ vb **5** to push (a bicycle, wheelchair, or pram) along **6** to turn in a circle **7 wheel and deal** to operate shrewdly and sometimes unscrupulously in order to advance one's own interests **8 wheel round** to change direction or turn round suddenly ▶ See also **wheels** [Old English hwēol, hweowol]

wheelbarrow n a shallow open box for carrying small loads, with a wheel at the front and two handles

wheelbase n the distance between the front and back axles of a motor vehicle

wheelchair n a special chair on large wheels, for use by people who cannot walk properly

wheel clamp n a device fixed onto one wheel of an illegally parked car to prevent the car being driven off

Wheeler n **1** John Archibald. 1911–2008, US physicist, noted for his work on nuclear fission and the development (1949–51) of the hydrogen bomb, also for his work on unified field theory **2** Sir (**Robert Eric**) Mortimer. 1890–1976, Scottish archaeologist, who did much to increase public interest in archaeology. He is noted esp. for his excavations at Mohenjo-Daro and Harappa in the Indus Valley and at Maiden Castle in Dorset

wheelhouse n an enclosed structure on the bridge of a ship from which it is steered

wheelie n a manoeuvre on a cycle or skateboard in which the front wheel or wheels are raised off the ground

wheelie bin n Brit, Austral and NZ a large container for household rubbish, mounted on wheels so that it can be moved more easily

wheeling and dealing n shrewd and sometimes unscrupulous moves made in order to advance one's own interests ▷ **wheeler-dealer** n

wheels pl n **1** informal a car **2** the main force and mechanism of an organization or system: the wheels of the economy **3 wheels within wheels** a series of intricately connected events or plots

wheelwright n a person whose job is to make and mend wheels

wheeze vb wheezing, wheezed **1** to breathe with a

W

rasping or whistling sound ▷ n **2** a wheezing breath or sound **3** Brit old-fashioned, slang a trick or plan: a glorious tax wheeze [probably from Old Norse hvǣsa to hiss] **> wheezy** adj

whelk n an edible sea creature with a strong snail-like shell [Old English weoloc]

whelp n **1** a young wolf or dog **2** offensive a youth ▷ vb **3** (of an animal) to give birth [Old English hwelp]

when adv **1** at what time?: when are they leaving? ▷ conj **2** at the time at which: he was twenty when the war started **3** although: he drives when he could walk **4** considering the fact that: how did you pass the exam when you hadn't studied for it? ▷ pron **5** at which time: she's at the age when girls get interested in boys [Old English hwanne, hwænne]

> **USAGE** When should not be used loosely as a substitute for in which after a noun which does not refer to a period of time: paralysis is a condition in which (not when) parts of the body cannot be moved.

whence conj old-fashioned or poetic from what place, cause, or origin: he would then ask them whence they came [Middle English whannes]

> **USAGE** The expression from whence should be avoided, since whence already means from which place: the tradition whence (not from whence) such ideas flowed.

whenever conj **1** at every or any time that: the filly was trained to stop whenever a jockey used a whip ▷ adv **2** no matter when: I am eager to come whenever you suggest **3** informal at an unknown or unspecified time: the 16th, 17th, or whenever **4** an intensive form of when, used in questions: if we can't exercise restraint now, whenever can we?

where adv **1** in, at, or to what place, point, or position?: where are we going?; I know where he found it ▷ pron **2** in, at, or to which place: he found a sandwich bar where he could get a snack ▷ conj **3** in the place at which: he should have stayed where he was doing well [Old English hwǣr]

whereabouts pl n **1** the place, esp. the approximate place, where a person or thing is: the whereabouts of the president are unknown ▷ adv **2** approximately where: whereabouts will you go?

whereas conj but by contrast: she was crazy about him, whereas for him it was just another affair

whereby pron by or because of which: the process whereby pests become resistant to pesticides

wherefore n **1 the whys and wherefores** the reasons or explanation: the whys and wherefores of the war ▷ conj **2** old-fashioned, formal for which reason

wherein old-fashioned or formal adv **1** in what place or respect?: wherein lies the truth? ▷ pron **2** in which place or thing: the mirror wherein he had been gazing

whereof old-fashioned or formal adv **1** of what or which person or thing? ▷ pron **2** of which person or thing: I know whereof I speak

whereupon conj at which point: they sentenced him to death, whereupon he fainted

wherever pron **1** at, in, or to every place or point which: I got a wonderful reception wherever I went ▷ conj **2** in, to, or at whatever place: wherever they went, the conditions were harsh ▷ adv **3** no matter where: we're going to find him, wherever he is **4** informal at, in, or to an unknown or unspecified place: the jungles of Borneo or wherever **5** an intensive form of where, used in questions: wherever have you been?

wherewithal n **the wherewithal** the necessary funds, resources, or equipment: the wherewithal for making chemical weapons

whet vb **whetting, whetted 1 whet someone's appetite** to increase someone's desire for or interest in something: she gave him just enough information to whet his appetite **2** old-fashioned to sharpen (a knife or other tool) [Old English hwettan]

whether conj **1** used to introduce an indirect question: he asked him whether he had seen the hunter **2** used to introduce a clause expressing doubt or choice: you are entitled to the assistance of a lawyer, whether or not you can afford one; we learn from experience, whether good or bad [Old English hwæther]

whetstone n a stone used for sharpening knives or other tools

whew interj an exclamation of relief, surprise, disbelief, or weariness

whey (way) n the watery liquid that separates from the curd when milk is clotted, for example in making cheese [Old English hwǣg]

which adj **1** used with a noun in requesting that the particular thing being referred to is further identified or distinguished: which way had he gone?; a questionnaire to find out which shops local consumers use **2** any out of several: you have to choose which goods and services you want ▷ pron **3** used in requesting that the particular thing being referred to is further identified or distinguished: which of these occupations would be suitable for you? **4** used in relative clauses referring to a thing rather than a person: a discovery which could have lasting effects **5** and that: her books were all over the dining table, which meant we had to eat in the kitchen [Old English hwelc]

> **USAGE** See at that.

whichever adj **1** any out of several: choose whichever line you feel more comfortable with **2** no matter which: whichever bridge you take, pause mid-stream for a look up and down the river ▷ pron **3** any one or ones out of several: delete whichever is inapplicable **4** no matter which one or ones: whichever you choose, you must be consistent throughout

whiff n **1** a passing odour: I got a whiff of her perfume **2** a trace or hint: the first whiff of jealousy [imitative]

Whig n **1** a member of a British political party of the 18th–19th centuries that sought limited political and social reform and provided the core of the Liberal Party ▷ adj **2** of or relating to Whigs [probably from whiggamore, one of a group of 17th-century Scottish rebels] **> Whiggism** n

while conj **1** at the same time that: anti-inflammatory remedies may be used to alleviate the condition while background factors are investigated **2** at some point during the time that: her father had died while she was gone **3** although or whereas: while she tossed and turned, he fell into a dreamless sleep ▷ n **4** a period of time: I'd like to stay a while [Old English hwīl]

> **USAGE** It was formerly considered incorrect to use while to mean although or whereas, but these uses have now become acceptable.

while away vb **whiling, whiled** to pass (time) idly but pleasantly

whilst conj chiefly Brit same as while

whim n a sudden, passing, and often fanciful idea [origin unknown]

whimper vb **1** to cry, complain, or say (something) in a whining plaintive way ▷ n **2** a soft plaintive whine [imitative]

whimsical adj unusual, playful, and fanciful: a whimsical story **> whimsically** adv

whimsy n **1** (pl **-sies**) a fanciful or playful idea: they thought sparing the rod a foolish whimsy **2** capricious or playful behaviour: sudden flights of whimsy [from whim]

whin n chiefly Brit same as gorse [from Old Norse]

whine n **1** a long high-pitched plaintive cry or moan **2** a peevish complaint ▷ vb **whining, whined 3** to whinge or complain **4** to issue a long high-pitched moan [Old English hwīnan] **> whiner** n **> whining** adj, n

whinge Brit, Austral and NZ informal vb **whingeing, whinged 1** to complain in a moaning manner ▷ n **2** a complaint [Old English hwinsian to whine] **> whinger** n

whinny vb -nies, -nying, -nied 1 (of a horse) to neigh softly or gently ▷ n, pl -nies 2 a gentle or low-pitched neigh [imitative]

whip n 1 a a piece of leather or rope attached at one end to a stiff handle, used for hitting people or animals 2 a a member of a political party who is responsible for urging members to attend Parliament to vote on an important issue b a notice sent to members of a political party by the whip, urging them to attend Parliament to vote in a particular way on an important issue 3 a dessert made from egg whites or cream beaten stiff: raspberry whip ▷ vb **whipping, whipped** 4 to hit with a whip 5 to hit sharply: strands of hair whipped across her cheeks 6 informal to move or go quickly and suddenly: machine-gun bullets whipped past him 7 to beat (cream or eggs) with a whisk or fork until frothy or stiff 8 to rouse (someone) into a particular condition: politicians and businessmen have whipped themselves into a panic about never-ending recession 9 informal to steal (something) ▶ See also whip out, whip-round, whip up [perhaps from Middle Dutch wippen to swing] ⟩ **whipping** n

whip bird n Austral a bird with a whistle ending in a whipcrack note

whip hand n the whip hand an advantage or dominating position: buyers have the whip hand over estate agents

whiplash n 1 a quick lash of a whip 2 short for **whiplash injury**

whiplash injury n an injury to the neck resulting from the head being suddenly thrust forward and then snapped back, for example in a car crash

whip out or **whip off** vb to take (something) out or off quickly and suddenly: she whipped off her glasses

whipper-in n, pl **whippers-in** a huntsman's assistant who manages the hounds

whippersnapper n old-fashioned a young impertinent overconfident person

whippet n a small slender dog similar to a greyhound [perhaps based on whip it! move quickly!]

whipping boy n a person who is expected to take the blame for other people's mistakes or incompetence

whip-round n informal an impromptu collection of money

whipstock n the handle of a whip

whip up vb 1 to excite or arouse: to get people all whipped up about something; to whip up enthusiasm 2 informal to prepare quickly: she had whipped up a rich sauce

whir n, vb whirring, whirred same as whirr

whirl vb 1 to spin or turn round very fast 2 to seem to spin from dizziness or confusion: my mind whirled with half-formed thoughts ▷ n 3 the act or an instance of whirling: he grasps her by the waist and gives her a whirl 4 a round of intense activity: the social whirl of Paris 5 a confused state: my thoughts are in a whirl 6 give something a whirl informal to try something new [Old Norse hvirfla to turn about]

whirligig n 1 a spinning toy, such as a top 2 same as merry-go-round 3 anything that whirls

whirlpool n a powerful circular current of water, into which objects floating nearby are drawn

whirlwind n 1 a column of air whirling violently upwards in a spiral ▷ adj 2 done or happening much more quickly than usual: a whirlwind tour of France

whirr or **whir** n 1 a prolonged soft whizz or buzz: the whirr of the fax machine ▷ vb **whirring, whirred** 2 to produce a prolonged soft whizz or buzz [probably from Old Norse] ⟩ **whirring** n, adj

whisk vb 1 to move or take somewhere swiftly: I was whisked away in a police car 2 to brush away lightly: the waiter whisked the crumbs away with a napkin 3 to beat (cream or eggs) with a whisk or fork until frothy or stiff ▷ n 4 the act or an instance of whisking: a whisk of a scaly tail 5 a utensil for beating cream or eggs until frothy or stiff [Old Norse visk wisp]

whisker n 1 any of the long stiff hairs that grow out from the sides of the mouth of a cat or other mammal 2 any of the hairs growing on a man's face, esp. on the cheeks or chin 3 by a whisker by a very small distance or amount: we missed him by a whisker [Old Norse visk wisp] ⟩ **whiskered** or **whiskery** adj

whiskey n Irish or American whisky

whisky n, pl -kies a strong alcoholic drink made by distilling fermented cereals, esp. in Scotland [Scottish Gaelic uisge beatha water of life]

whisky-jack n Canad same as **Canada jay**

whisper vb 1 to speak or say (something) very softly, using the breath instead of the vocal cords 2 to make a low soft rustling sound: the leaves whispered ▷ n 3 a low soft voice: her voice sank to a whisper 4 informal a rumour: I just picked up a whisper on this killing 5 a low soft rustling sound: a whisper of breeze in the shrubbery [Old English hwisprian] ⟩ **whispered** adj

whist n a card game for two pairs of players [perhaps from whisk, referring to the whisking up of the tricks]

whist drive n a social gathering where whist is played

whistle vb -tling, -tled 1 to produce a shrill sound by forcing breath between pursed lips 2 to produce (a tune) by making a series of such sounds 3 to signal (to) by whistling or blowing a whistle: the doorman whistled a cruising cab 4 to move with a whistling sound: a shell whistled through the upper air 5 (of a kettle or train) to produce a shrill sound caused by steam being forced through a small opening 6 (of a bird) to give a shrill cry 7 whistle in the dark to try to keep up one's confidence in spite of being afraid ▷ n 8 the act or sound of whistling: he gave a whistle of astonishment 9 a metal instrument that is blown down its end to produce a tune, signal, or alarm: he played the tin whistle; the referee's whistle 10 a device in a kettle or a train that makes a shrill sound by means of steam under pressure 11 blow the whistle on informal to reveal and put a stop to (wrongdoing or a wrongdoer): to blow the whistle on corrupt top-level officials 12 wet one's whistle informal to have a drink [Old English hwistlian]

whistle-blower n informal a person who informs on someone or puts a stop to something

whistle for vb informal to expect in vain: he could whistle for his vote in the future

Whistler n James Abbott McNeill. 1834–1903, US painter and etcher, living in Europe. He is best known for his sequence of nocturnes and his portraits

whistle-stop adj denoting a tour, esp. a campaign tour by a political candidate, in which short stops are made at many different places

whit n not a whit not at all: it does not matter a whit [probably variant of obsolete wight a person]

Whit n 1 short for **Whitsuntide** ▷ adj 2 of Whitsuntide: Whit Monday

Whitaker n 1 Sir Frederick. 1812–91, New Zealand statesman, born in England: prime minister of New Zealand (1863–64; 1882–83) 2 Forrest (Steven). born 1961, US actor and film director; his films include (as actor) Ghost Dog (1999) and The Last King of Scotland (2006); (as director) Waiting to Exhale (1995)

Whitbread n Fatima. born 1961, British javelin thrower: won gold at the World Championships (1987)

Whitby n a fishing port and resort in NE England, in E North Yorkshire at the mouth of the River Esk: an important ecclesiastical centre in Anglo-Saxon times; site of an abbey founded in 656. Pop: 13 594 (2001)

white adj 1 having no hue, owing to the reflection of all or almost all light; of the colour of snow 2 pale, because of illness, fear, shock, or another emotion: white with rage 3 (of hair) having lost its colour, usually from age 4 (of coffee or tea) with milk or cream 5 (of wine) made from pale grapes or from black grapes separated from their skins 6 denoting flour, or bread made from flour, that has had part of the grain removed ▷ n 7 the lightest colour; the colour of snow 8 the clear fluid that

W

surrounds the yolk of an egg **9** *anatomy* the white part of the eyeball **10** anything white, such as white paint or white clothing: *a room decorated all in white* ▶ See also **whites** [Old English *hwit*] ❭ **whiteness** *n* ❭ **whitish** *adj*

White¹ *n* **1** a member of a light-skinned race ▷ *adj* **2** of or relating to a White or Whites

White² *n* **1** Gilbert. 1720–93, English clergyman and naturalist, noted for his *Natural History and Antiquities of Selborne* (1789) **2** Jimmy. born 1962, English snooker player **3** Marco Pierre. born 1961, British chef and restaurateur **4** Patrick (Victor Martindale). 1912–90, Australian novelist: his works include *Voss* (1957), *The Eye of the Storm* (1973), and *A Fringe of Leaves* (1976): Nobel prize for literature 1973 **5** T(erence) H(anbury). 1906–64, British novelist: author of the Arthurian sequence *The Once and Future King* (1939–58) **6** Willard (Wentworth). born 1946, British operatic bass, born in Jamaica

whitebait *n* **1** the young of herrings, sprats, or pilchards, cooked and eaten whole **2** any of various small silvery fishes of Australia and New Zealand and of North American coastal regions of the Pacific

white blood cell *n* same as **leucocyte**

whitecaps *pl n* waves with white broken crests

white-collar *adj* denoting workers employed in professional and clerical occupations

white dwarf *n* a small, faint, very dense star

white elephant *n* a possession that is unwanted by its owner

white feather *n* a symbol of cowardice

Whitefield *n* George. 1714–70, English Methodist preacher, who separated from the Wesleys (?1741) because of his Calvinistic views

white fish *n* a sea fish with white flesh that is used for food, such as cod or haddock

white flag *n* a signal of surrender or to request a truce

whitefly *n*, *pl* **-flies** a tiny whitish insect that is harmful to greenhouse plants

White Friar *n* a Carmelite friar

white gold *n* a white lustrous hard-wearing alloy containing gold together with platinum or other metals, used in jewellery

white goods *pl n* large household appliances, such as refrigerators and cookers

Whitehall *n* **1** a street in London stretching from Trafalgar Square to the Houses of Parliament: site of the main government offices **2** the British Government or its central administration

Whitehead *n* Alfred North. 1861–1947, English mathematician and philosopher, who collaborated with Bertrand Russell in writing *Principia Mathematica* (1910–13), and developed a holistic philosophy of science, chiefly in *Process and Reality* (1929)

white heat *n* **1** intense heat that produces a white light **2** *informal* a state of intense emotion: *the white heat of hate*

white hope *n informal* a person who is expected to accomplish a great deal: *the great white hope of Polish cinema*

Whitehorse *n* a town in NW Canada: capital of the Yukon Territory. Pop: 27 889 (2013)

white horses *pl n* same as **whitecaps**

white-hot *adj* **1** at such a high temperature that white light is produced **2** *informal* in a state of intense emotion: *white-hot agony*

White House *n* the US president and the executive branch of the US government: *the White House reviewed the report* [after the official home of the US president in Washington DC]

Whitelaw *n* William (Stephen Ian), 1st Viscount Whitelaw of Penrith. 1918–99, British Conservative politician; Home Secretary (1979–83); leader of the House of Lords (1983–88)

Whiteley *n* Brett. 1939–1992, Australian artist, who travelled widely in Europe and Asia; his works include landscapes, nudes, and portraits

white lie *n* a small lie, usually told to avoid hurting someone's feelings

white light *n* light that contains all the wavelengths of the visible spectrum, as in sunlight

white matter *n* the whitish tissue of the brain and spinal cord, consisting mainly of nerve fibres

white meat *n* meat, such as chicken or pork, that is light in colour when cooked

White Mountains *pl n* **1** a mountain range in the US, chiefly in N New Hampshire: part of the Appalachians. Highest peak: Mount Washington, 1917 m (6288 ft) **2** a mountain range in the US, in E California and SW Nevada. Highest peak: White Mountain, 4342 m (14 246 ft)

whiten *vb* to make or become white or whiter ❭ **whitener** *n* ❭ **whitening** *n*

White Nile *n* See **Nile**

white noise *n* noise that has a wide range of frequencies of uniform intensity

whiteout *n* an atmospheric condition in which blizzards or low clouds make it very difficult to see

white paper *n* an official government report which sets out the government's policy on a specific matter

white pepper *n* a hot seasoning made from the seeds of the pepper plant with the husks removed

White Russia *n* another name for **Belarus**

White Russian *adj* **1** (formerly) of or relating to Byelorussia ▷ *n* **2** (formerly) a native or inhabitant of Byelorussia **3** (formerly) the language of Byelorussia

whites *pl n* white clothes, as worn for playing cricket

white sauce *n* a thick sauce made from flour, butter, seasonings, and milk or stock

White Sea *n* an almost landlocked inlet of the Barents Sea on the coast of NW Russia. Area: 90 000 sq km (34 700 sq miles)

white slave *n* a girl or woman forced or sold into prostitution ❭ **white slavery** *n*

white spirit *n* a colourless liquid obtained from petroleum and used as a substitute for turpentine

White supremacy *n* the theory or belief that White people are superior to people of other races ❭ **White supremacist** *n*, *adj*

white tie *n* **1** a white bow tie worn as part of a man's formal evening dress ▷ *adj* **white-tie 2** denoting an occasion when formal evening dress should be worn: *tickets for the white-tie Shelley Ball*

white trash *n disparaging* poor White people living in the United States, esp. in the South

White Volta *n* a river in W Africa, rising in N Burkina Faso flowing southwest and south to join the Black Volta in central Ghana and form the Volta River. Length: about 885 km (550 miles)

whitewash *n* **1** a mixture of lime or chalk in water, for whitening walls and other surfaces **2** an attempt to conceal the unpleasant truth: *the report was a whitewash* ▷ *vb* **3** to cover with whitewash **4** to conceal the unpleasant truth about ❭ **whitewashed** *adj*

whitewood *n* a light-coloured wood often prepared for staining

Whitgift *n* John. ?1530–1604, English churchman; as archbishop of Canterbury (1583–1604) he tried to curb the influence of Puritanism

whither *conj old-fashioned or poetic* to what place or for what purpose: *they knew not whither they went* [Old English *hwider, hwæder*]

whiting (white-ing) *n* **1** a white-fleshed food fish of European seas **2** *Austral* any of several marine food fishes

Whitlam *n* (Edward) Gough. 1916–2014, Australian Labor statesman: prime minister (1972–75)

Whitley Bay *n* a resort in NE England, in North Tyneside unitary authority, Tyne and Wear, on the North Sea. Pop: 36 544 (2001)

whitlow *n* an inflamed sore on the end of a finger or toe [originally *white* + *flaw*]

W

Whitman n Walt(er). 1819–92, US poet, whose life's work is collected in *Leaves of Grass* (1855 and subsequent enlarged editions). His poems celebrate existence and the multiple elements that make up a democratic society

Whitney[1] n Mount Whitney a mountain in E California: the highest peak in the Sierra Nevada Mountains and in continental US (excluding Alaska). Height: 4418 m (14 495 ft)

Whitney[2] n 1 Eli. 1765–1825, US inventor of a mechanical cotton gin (1793) and pioneer manufacturer of interchangeable parts 2 William Dwight. 1827–94, US philologist, noted esp. for his *Sanskrit Grammar* (1879)

Whitsun n 1 short for **Whitsuntide** ▷ *adj* 2 of Whit Sunday or Whitsuntide

Whit Sunday n the seventh Sunday after Easter [Old English hwīta sunnandæg white Sunday]

Whitsuntide n the week that begins with Whit Sunday

Whittier n John Greenleaf. 1807–92, US poet and humanitarian: a leading campaigner in the antislavery movement. His poems include *Snow-Bound* (1866)

Whittington n Richard, known as *Dick*. died 1423, English merchant, three times mayor of London. According to legend, he walked to London at the age of 13 with his cat and was prevented from leaving again only by the call of the church bells

whittle vb -tling, -tled 1 to make (an object) by cutting or shaving pieces from (a piece of wood) with a small knife 2 whittle down or away to reduce in size or effectiveness gradually: *my self-confidence had been whittled away to almost nothing* [Old English thwītan to cut]

Whittle n Sir Frank. 1907–96, English engineer, who invented the jet engine for aircraft; flew first British jet aircraft (1941)

whizz or **whiz** vb **whizzing, whizzed** 1 to move with a loud humming or buzzing sound: *the bullets whizzed overhead* 2 informal to move or go quickly: *the wind surfers fairly whizzed along the water* ▷ n, pl **whizzes** 3 a loud humming or buzzing sound 4 informal a person who is extremely good at something: *he's a whizz on finance* 5 slang amphetamine [imitative]

whizz kid or **whiz kid** n informal a person who is outstandingly able and successful for his or her age

who pron 1 which person: *who are you?; he didn't know who had started it* 2 used at the beginning of a relative clause referring to a person or people already mentioned: *he is a man who can effect change* [Old English hwā]

USAGE See at **whom**.

WHO World Health Organization

whoa interj a command used to stop horses or to slow down someone who is moving or talking too fast

whodunnit or **whodunit** (hoo-dun-nit) n informal a novel, play, or film about the solving of a murder mystery

whoever pron 1 the person or people who: *whoever bought it for you has to make the claim* 2 no matter who: *I pity him, whoever he is* 3 informal other similar or related people or person: *your best friend, your neighbours, or whoever* 4 an intensive form of *who*, used in questions: *whoever thought of such a thing?*

whole adj 1 constituting or referring to all of something: *I'd spent my whole allowance by Saturday afternoon* 2 unbroken or undamaged ▷ adv 3 in an undivided or unbroken piece: *truffles are cooked whole* 4 informal completely or entirely: *a whole new theory of treatment* ▷ n 5 all there is of a thing: *the whole of my salary* 6 a collection of parts viewed together as a unit: *taking Great Britain as a whole* 7 on the whole a taking all things into consideration: *on the whole he has worked about one year out of twelve* b in general: *on the whole they were not successful* [Old English hāl]
▷ **wholeness** n

wholefood n 1 food that has been refined or processed

as little as possible ▷ *adj* 2 of or relating to wholefood: *a wholefood diet*

wholehearted adj done or given with total sincerity or enthusiasm: *wholehearted support* ➤ **wholeheartedly** adv

wholemeal adj Brit and Austral 1 (of flour) made from the entire wheat kernel 2 made from wholemeal flour: *wholemeal bread*

whole number n maths a number that does not contain a fraction, such as 0, 1, or 2

wholesale n 1 the business of selling goods in large quantities and at lower prices to retailers for resale 2 relating to such business: *wholesale prices* 3 extensive or indiscriminate: *the wholesale destruction of forests* ▷ *adv* 4 by or through the wholesale business: *we buy beef wholesale* 5 extensively or indiscriminately: *buffalo were slaughtered wholesale* ➤ **wholesaler** n

wholesome adj 1 physically beneficial: *wholesome food* 2 morally beneficial: *a wholesome attitude of the mind* [from *whole* healthy]

whole-wheat adj US and Canad same as **wholemeal**

wholly adv completely or totally

whom pron the objective form of *who*: *whom will you tell?; he was devoted to his wife, whom he married in 1960* [Old English hwām]

> **USAGE** It was formerly considered correct to use *whom* whenever the objective form of *who* was required. This is no longer thought to be necessary and the objective form *who* is now commonly used, even in formal writing: *there were several people there who he had met before*. Who cannot be used directly after a preposition – the preposition is usually displaced, as in *the man (who) he sold his car to*. In formal writing *whom* is preferred in sentences like these: *the man to whom he sold his car*. There are some types of sentence in which *who* cannot be used: *the refugees, many of whom were old and ill, were allowed across the border*.

whomever pron the objective form of *whoever*: *this law limits an employer's right to employ whomever he wants*

whoop vb 1 to cry out in excitement or joy 2 whoop it up informal to indulge in a noisy celebration ▷ n 3 a loud cry of excitement or joy [imitative]

whoopee old-fashioned, informal interj 1 an exclamation of joy or excitement ▷ n 2 make whoopee a to indulge in a noisy celebration b to make love

whooping cough n an acute infectious disease mainly affecting children, that causes coughing spasms ending with a shrill crowing sound on breathing in

whoops interj an exclamation of mild surprise or of apology

whopper n informal 1 an unusually large or impressive example of something: *Deauville's beach is a whopper* 2 a big lie

whopping informal adj 1 unusually large: *a whopping 40 per cent* ▷ adv 2 extremely: *it's a whopping great gamble*

whore (hore) n a prostitute or promiscuous woman: often a term of abuse [Old English hōre]

whorehouse n informal a brothel

Whorf n Benjamin Lee. 1897–1943, US linguist, who argued that human language determines perception

whorl n 1 botany a circular arrangement of leaves or flowers round the stem of a plant 2 zoology a single turn in a spiral shell 3 anything shaped like a coil [probably variant of *whirl*]

who's who is or who has

whose pron 1 of whom? belonging to whom?: used in direct and indirect questions: *whose idea was it?; I wondered whose it was* 2 of whom or of which: used as a relative pronoun: *Gran had sympathy for anybody whose life had gone wrong* [Old English hwæs, genitive of hwā who + hwæt what]

whosoever pron old-fashioned or formal same as **whoever**

why adv 1 for what reason?: *why did he marry her?; she avoided*

W

asking him why he was there ▷ *pron* **2** for or because of which: *you can think of all kinds of reasons why you should not believe it* ▷ *n, pl* **whys 3 the whys and wherefores** See **wherefore** (1) ▷ *interj* **4** an exclamation of surprise, indignation, or impatience: *why, I listen to you on the radio twice a week* [Old English *hwȳ, hwī*]

Whyalla *n* a port in S South Australia, on Spencer Gulf: iron and steel and shipbuilding industries. Pop: 21 271 (2001)

WI 1 Wisconsin **2** West Indies **3** *Brit and NZ* Women's Institute

Wichita *n* a city in S Kansas, on the Arkansas River: the largest city in the state; two universities. Pop: 354 617 (2003 est)

wick *n* **1** a cord through the middle of a candle, through which the fuel reaches the flame **2 get on someone's wick** *Brit and Austral slang* to annoy someone [Old English *wēoce*]

Wick *n* a town in N Scotland, in Highland, at the head of **Wick Bay** (an inlet of the North Sea). Pop: 7333 (2001)

wicked *adj* **1** morally bad: *the wicked queen in 'Snow White'* **2** playfully mischievous or roguish: *let's be wicked and go skinny-dipping* **3** dangerous or unpleasant: *there was a wicked cut over his eye* **4** *slang* very good [Old English *wicca* sorcerer, *wicce* witch] ⟩ **wickedly** *adv* ⟩ **wickedness** *n*

wicker *adj* made of wickerwork: *a wicker chair* [from Old Norse]

wickerwork *n* a material consisting of slender flexible twigs woven together

wicket *n cricket* **1** either of two sets of three stumps stuck in the ground with two wooden bails resting on top, at which the batsman stands **2** the playing space between these **3** the act or instance of a batsman being got out [Old French *wiket*]

wicketkeeper *n cricket* the fielder positioned directly behind the wicket

wicking *adj* acting to move moisture by capillary action from the inside to the surface: *wicking fabric*

Wicklow *n* **1** a county of E Republic of Ireland, in Leinster province on the Irish Sea: consists of a coastal strip rising inland to the **Wicklow Mountains**; mainly agricultural, with several resorts. County town: Wicklow. Pop: 114 676 (2002). Area: 2025 sq km (782 sq miles) **2** a port in E Republic of Ireland, county town of Co Wicklow. Pop: 9355 (2002)

wide *adj* **1** having a great extent from side to side: *the wide main street* **2** having a specified extent from side to side: *three metres wide* **3** covering or including many different things: *a wide range of services* **4** covering a large distance or extent: *the proposal was voted down by a wide margin* **5** (of eyes) opened fully ▷ *adv* **6** to a large or full extent: *he swung the door wide* **7 far and wide** See **far** (7) ▷ *n* **8** *cricket* a ball bowled outside the batsman's reach, which scores a run for the batting side [Old English *wīd*] ⟩ **widely** *adv*

wide-angle lens *n* a lens on a camera which can cover a wider angle of view than an ordinary lens

wide-awake *adj* fully awake

wide-eyed *adj* **1** innocent or naive **2** surprised or frightened: *wide-eyed astonishment* ▷ *adv* **3** in a frightened, surprised, or excited manner: *they looked at me wide-eyed*

widen *vb* to make or become wide or wider

wide open *adj* **1** open to the full extent: *the main door was wide open* **2** exposed or vulnerable: *he was leaving himself wide open to problems*

wide-ranging *adj* covering or including many different things or subjects: *a wide-ranging review*

widespread *adj* affecting an extensive area or a large number of people: *widespread damage; widespread public support*

widgeon *n* same as **wigeon**

widget *n* **1** *informal* any small device, the name of which is unknown or forgotten **2** a small device in a beer can which, when the can is opened, releases nitrogen gas into the beer, giving it a head **3** a small computer

program that can be installed on and executed from the desktop of a personal computer [changed from GADGET]

Widnes *n* a town in NW England, in Halton unitary authority, N Cheshire, on the River Mersey: chemical industry. Pop: 55 686 (2001)

widow *n* a woman whose spouse has died and who has not remarried [Old English *widewe*] ⟩ **widowhood** *n*

widowed *adj* denoting a person whose spouse has died and who has not remarried

widower *n* a man whose spouse has died and who has not remarried

widow's weeds *pl n old-fashioned* the black mourning clothes traditionally worn by a widow [from Old English *wǣd* a band worn in mourning]

width *n* **1** the extent or measurement of something from side to side **2** the distance across a rectangular swimming bath, as opposed to its length

Wieland *n* **Christoph Martin.** 1733–1813, German writer, noted esp. for his verse epic *Oberon* (1780)

wield *vb* **1** to handle or use (a weapon or tool) **2** to exert or maintain (power or influence) [Old English *wieldan, wealdan*]

Wien¹ *n* the German name for **Vienna**

Wien² *n* **Wilhelm.** 1864–1928, German physicist, who studied black-body radiation: Nobel prize for physics 1911

Wiener *n* **Norbert.** 1894–1964, US mathematician, who developed the concept of cybernetics

Wiener Neustadt *n* a city in E Austria, in Lower Austria. Pop: 37 627 (2002)

Wiesbaden *n* a city in W Germany, capital of Hesse state: a spa resort since Roman times. Pop: 271 995 (2003 est). Latin name: **Aquae Mattiacorum**

Wiesel *n* **Elie.** born 1928, US human rights campaigner: noted esp. for his documentaries of wartime atrocities against the Jews; Nobel peace prize (1986); honorary knighthood (2006)

Wiesenthal *n* **Simon.** 1908–2005, Austrian investigator of Nazi war crimes. A survivor of the concentration camps, he was active from 1945 in documenting Nazi crimes against the Jews, tracking down their perpetrators, and assisting surviving victims

wife *n, pl* **wives** the woman to whom a person is married [Old English *wīf*] ⟩ **wifely** *adj*

Wi-Fi *n computers* a system of wireless access to the internet

wig *n* an artificial head of hair [from *periwig*]

Wig. Wigtownshire

Wigan *n* **1** an industrial town in NW England, in Wigan unitary authority, Greater Manchester: former coal-mining centre. Pop: 81 203 (2001) **2** a unitary authority in NW England, in Greater Manchester. Pop: 303 800 (2003 est). Area: 199 sq km (77 sq miles)

wigeon *or* **widgeon** *n* a wild marshland duck [origin unknown]

wigging *n Brit old-fashioned, slang* a reprimand [origin unknown]

Wiggins *n* **Sir Bradley (Marc).** born 1980, English racing cyclist; winner of seven Olympic medals, including four golds, for Britain; first British cyclist (2012) to win the Tour de France

wiggle *vb* **-gling, -gled 1** to move with jerky movements from side to side or up and down: *she wiggled her toes in the cool water* ▷ *n* **2** a wiggling movement or walk [Middle Low German, Middle Dutch *wiggelen*]

Wight *n* **Isle of Wight** an island and county of S England in the English Channel. Administrative centre: Newport. Pop: 136 300 (2003 est). Area: 380 sq km (147 sq miles)

Wigner *n* **Eugene Paul.** 1902–95, US physicist, born in Hungary. He is noted for his contributions to nuclear physics: shared the Nobel prize for physics 1963

Wigtownshire *n* (until 1975) a county of SW Scotland, now part of Dumfries and Galloway

W

wigwam n a Native American's tent, made of animal skins [Native American *wĭkwām*]

wiki computers n **1** a website, or page within one, whose content can be edited freely by anyone with access to a web browser ▷ adj **2** of or relating to the software which facilitates such open editing: wiki technology [from Hawaiian wiki-wiki quick]

Wilberforce n **1** Samuel. 1805–73, British Anglican churchman; bishop of Oxford (1845–69) and Winchester (1869–73) **2** his father, William. 1759–1833, British politician and philanthropist, whose efforts secured the abolition of the slave trade (1807) and of slavery (1833) in the British Empire

wilco interj an expression in signalling and telecommunications, indicating that a message just received will be complied with [abbreviation for I will comply]

wild adj **1** (of animals or birds) living in natural surroundings; not domesticated or tame **2** (of plants) growing in a natural state; not cultivated **3** uninhabited and desolate: wild country **4** living in a savage or uncivilized way: a wild mountain man **5** lacking restraint or control: a wild party **6** stormy or violent: a wild windy October morning **7** in a state of extreme emotional intensity: wild with excitement **8** without reason or substance: wild accusations **9** wild about informal very enthusiastic about: his colleagues aren't all that wild about him ▷ adv **10** run wild to behave without restraint: she was allowed to run completely wild ▷ n **11** the wild a free natural state of living: creatures of the wild **12** the wilds a desolate or uninhabited region: the wilds of Africa [Old English wilde] ▷ **wildly** adv ▷ **wildness** n

Wild n Jonathan. ?1682–1725, British criminal, who organized a network of thieves, highwaymen, etc., while also working as an informer: said to have sent over a hundred men to the gallows before being hanged himself

wild card n **1** sport a player or team that is allowed to take part in a competition despite not having met the normal qualifying requirements **2** computers a character that can be substituted for any other in a file

wildcat n, pl **-cats** or **-cat 1** a wild European cat that looks like a domesticated cat but is larger and has a bushy tail **2** informal a quick-tempered person ▷ adj **3** chiefly US risky and financially unsound: a wildcat operation

wildcat strike n a strike begun by workers spontaneously or without union approval

Wilde n Oscar (Fingal O'Flahertie Wills). 1854–1900, Irish writer and screenwriter, famous for such plays as Lady Windermere's Fan (1892) and The Importance of being Earnest (1895). The Picture of Dorian Gray (1891) is a macabre novel about a hedonist and The Ballad of Reading Gaol (1898) relates to his experiences in prison while serving a two-year sentence for homosexuality

wildebeest n, pl **-beests** or **-beest** same as gnu [Afrikaans]

Wilder n **1** Billy, real name Samuel Wilder. 1906–2002, US film director and screenwriter, born in Austria. His films include Double Indemnity (1944), The Lost Weekend (1945), Sunset Boulevard (1950), The Seven Year Itch (1955), Some Like it Hot (1959), The Apartment (1960), and Buddy Buddy (1981) **2** Thornton. 1897–1975 US novelist and dramatist. His works include the novel The Bridge of San Luis Rey (1927) and the play The Skin of Our Teeth (1942)

wilderness n **1** a wild uninhabited uncultivated region **2** a confused mass or tangle: a wilderness of long grass and wild flowers **3** a state of being no longer in a prominent position: a long spell in the political wilderness [Old English wildēornes, from wildēor wild beast]

Wilderness n the Wilderness the barren regions to the south and east of Palestine, esp. those in which the Israelites wandered before entering the Promised Land and in which Christ fasted for 40 days and nights

wildfire n spread like wildfire to spread very quickly or uncontrollably

wild flower n any flowering plant that grows in an uncultivated state

wildfowl pl n wild birds, such as grouse and pheasants, that are hunted for sport or food

wild-goose chase n a search that has little or no chance of success

Wilding n (Frederick) Anthony. 1883–1915, New Zealand tennis player; Wimbledon singles champion (1910–1913) and doubles champion (1907–08, 1910, 1913)

wildlife n wild animals and plants collectively

wild rice n the dark-coloured edible grain of a North American grass that grows on wet ground

Wild West n the western US during its settlement, esp. with reference to its lawlessness

wiles pl n artful or seductive tricks or ploys [from Old Norse vēl craft]

Wilfrid n Saint. 634–709 AD, English churchman; bishop of York (?663–?703). At the Synod of Whitby (664) he argued successfully that Celtic practices should be replaced by Roman ones in the English Church. Feast day: Oct 12

wilful or US **willful** adj **1** determined to do things in one's own way: a wilful and insubordinate child **2** deliberate and intentional: wilful misconduct ▷ **wilfully** adv

Wilhelmina I n 1880–1962, queen of the Netherlands from 1890 until her abdication (1948) in favour of her daughter Juliana

Wilhelmshaven n a port and resort in NW Germany, in Lower Saxony: founded in 1853; was the chief German North Sea naval base until 1945; a major oil port. Pop: 84 586 (2003 est)

Wilhelmstrasse n **1** a street in the centre of Berlin, where the German foreign office and other government buildings were situated until 1945 **2** Germany's ministry of foreign affairs until 1945

Wilkes n **1** Charles. 1798–1877, US explorer of Antarctica **2** John. 1727–97, English politician, who was expelled from the House of Commons and outlawed for writing scurrilous articles about the government. He became a champion of parliamentary reform

Wilkes Land n a region in Antarctica south of Australia, on the Indian Ocean

Wilkins n **1** Sir George Hubert. 1888–1958, Australian polar explorer and aviator **2** Maurice Hugh Frederick. 1916–2004, British biochemist, born in New Zealand. With Crick and Watson, he shared the Nobel prize 1962 for his work on the structure of DNA

Wilkinson n Jonny. born 1979, English Rugby Union player: scored 1,179 points (an England record) in 92 internationals (1998–2011); scored the last-minute drop goal that secured England victory in the final of the 2003 World Cup

will¹ vb, past **would 1** used as an auxiliary to make the future tense: he will go on trial on October 7 **2** to express resolution: they will not consider giving up territories **3** to express a polite request: will you please calm Mummy and Daddy down **4** to express ability: many essential oils will protect clothing from moths **5** to express probability or expectation: his followers will be relieved to hear that **6** to express customary practice: boys will be boys! **7** to express desire: go in very small steps, if you will [Old English willan]

> **USAGE** See at shall.

will² n **1** a strong determination: a fierce will to survive **2** desire or wish: a referendum to determine the will of the people **3** a document setting out a person's wishes regarding the disposal of his or her property after death **4** at will when and as one chooses: customers can withdraw money at will ▷ vb **willing, willed 5** to try to make (something) happen by wishing very hard for it: she willed herself not to cry **6** to wish or desire: if he wills it, we will meet again **7** to leave (property) in one's will: the farm had been willed to her [Old English willa]

W

Willem-Alexander *n* full name *Willem-Alexander Claus George Ferdinand*. born 1967, king of the Netherlands from 2013

Willemstad *n* a port on the SW coast of Curaçao, and that island's capital; formerly the capital of the Netherlands Antilles until their dissolution in 2010: important for refining Venezuelan oil. Pop: 137 000 (2005 est)

William *n* **1** known as *William the Lion*. ?1143–1214, king of Scotland (1165–1214) **2 Prince**. born 1982, Duke of Cambridge, first son of Prince Charles and Diana, Princess of Wales. In 2011 he married Kate Middleton (born 1982); their son, Prince George, was born in 2013; their daughter, Princess Charlotte, was born in 2015

William I *n* **1** known as *William the Conqueror*. ?1027–1087, duke of Normandy (1035–87) and king of England (1066–87). He claimed to have been promised the English crown by Edward the Confessor, after whose death he disputed the succession of Harold II, invading England in 1066 and defeating Harold at Hastings. The conquest of England resulted in the introduction to England of many Norman customs, esp. feudalism. In 1085 he ordered the Domesday Book to be compiled **2** known as *William the Bad*. 1120–66, Norman king of Sicily (1154–66) **3** known as *William the Silent*. 1533–84, prince of Orange and count of Nassau: led the revolt of the Netherlands against Spain (1568–76) and became first stadholder of the United Provinces of the Netherlands (1579–84); assassinated **4** 1772–1843, king of the Netherlands (1815–40): abdicated in favour of his son William II **5** German name *Wilhelm I*. 1797–1888, king of Prussia (1861–88) and first emperor of Germany (1871–88)

William II *n* **1** known as *William Rufus*. ?1056–1100, king of England (1087–1100); the son of William the Conqueror. He was killed by an arrow while hunting in the New Forest **2** known as *William the Good*. 1154–89, last Norman king of Sicily (1166–89) **3** 1792–1849, king of the Netherlands (1840–49); son of William I **4** German name *Kaiser Wilhelm*. 1859–1941, German emperor and king of Prussia (1888–1918): asserted Germany's claim to world leadership; forced to abdicate at the end of World War I

William III *n* known as *William of Orange*. 1650–1702, stadholder of the Netherlands (1672–1702) and king of Great Britain and Ireland (1689–1702). He was invited by opponents of James II to accept the British throne (1688) and ruled jointly with his wife Mary II (James' daughter) until her death in 1694

William IV *n* known as the *Sailor King*. 1765–1837, king of the United Kingdom and of Hanover (1830–37); succeeding his brother George IV; the third son of George III

William of Malmesbury *n* ?1090–?1143, English monk and chronicler, whose *Gesta regum Anglorum* and *Historia novella* are valuable sources for English history to 1142

Williams *n* **1 Hank**, real name *Hiram Williams*. 1923–53, US country singer and songwriter. His songs (all 1948–52) include "Jambalaya", "Your Cheatin' Heart", and "Why Don't you Love me (like you Used to Do?)" **2 John**. born 1941, Australian classical guitarist, living in Britain **3 John (Towner)**. born 1932, US composer of film music; his scores include those for *Jaws* (1975), *Star Wars* (1977), *E.T.* (1982), *Schindler's List* (1993), *Harry Potter and the Philosopher's Stone* (2001), and *Memoirs of a Geisha* (2005) **4 Ralph Vaughan**. See (Ralph) **Vaughan Williams 5 Raymond (Henry)**. 1921–88, British literary critic and novelist, noted esp. for such works as *Culture and Society* (1958) and *The Long Revolution* (1961), which offer a socialist analysis of the relationship between society and culture **6 Robbie**, full name *Robert Peter Williams*. born 1974, British pop singer and songwriter. A member of Take That (1990–95; 2010–12), he found solo success with "Angels" (1997) and the albums *Life Thru a Lens* (1997), *Swing When You're Winning* (2001), and *Escapology* (2002) **7 Robin (McLaurin)**. 1951–2014, US film actor and

comedian; films include *Good Morning, Vietnam* (1987), *Dead Poets' Society* (1989), *Mrs Doubtfire* (1993), and *Insomnia* (2002) **8 Rowan (Douglas)**. Baron. born 1950, Archbishop of Canterbury (2002–2012); Archbishop of Wales (2000–02) **9 Serena**. born 1981, US tennis player, sister of Venus Williams: since 1999 she has won numerous Grand Slam singles titles, including the Australian Open six times, Wimbledon six times, and the US Open six times **10 Tennessee**, real name *Thomas Lanier Williams*. 1911–83, US dramatist. His plays include *The Glass Menagerie* (1944), *A Streetcar Named Desire* (1947), *Cat on a Hot Tin Roof* (1955), and *Night of the Iguana* (1961) **11 Venus**. born 1980, US tennis player: winner of seven Grand Slam singles titles, including Wimbledon five times (2000–01, 2005, 2007–08); with her sister Serena she has won thirteen Grand Slam doubles titles **12 William Carlos**. 1883–1963, US poet, who formulated the poetic concept "no ideas but in things". His works include *Paterson* (1946–58), which explores the daily life of a man living in a modern city, and the prose work *In the American Grain* (1925)

Williamsburg *n* a city in SE Virginia: the capital of Virginia (1693–1779); the restoration of large sections of the colonial city was begun in 1926. Pop: 11 605 (2003 est)

Williamson *n* **1 David**. born 1942, Australian dramatist. His plays include *Don's Party* (1971), *Emerald City* (1987) and *Brilliant Lies* (1993) **2 Henry**. 1895–1977, British novelist, best known for *Tarka the Otter* (1927) and other animal stories **3 Malcolm**. 1931–2003, Australian composer, living in Britain: Master of the Queen's Music (1975–2003). His works include operas and music for children

willies *pl n* give someone the willies *slang* to make someone nervous or frightened [origin unknown]

willing *adj* **1** favourably disposed or inclined: *I'm willing to hear what you have to say* **2** keen and obliging: *willing volunteers* ⟩ **willingly** *adv* ⟩ **willingness** *n*

Willis *n* **1 Norman (David)**. 1933–2014, British trade union leader; general secretary of the Trades Union Congress (1984–93) **2 Ted**. Baron Willis of Chislehurst. 1918–92, British author. His works include the play *Hot Summer Night* (1959) and the novel *Death May Surprise Us* (1974)

will-o'-the-wisp *n* **1** someone or something that is elusive or deceptively alluring: *their freedom was just a will-o'-the-wisp* **2** a pale light that is sometimes seen over marshy ground at night [*Will*, short for *William* + *wisp* twist of hay burning as a torch]

willow *n* a tree that grows near water, with thin flexible branches used in weaving baskets and wood used for making cricket bats [Old English *welig*]

Willow *n* a small town in S Alaska, about 113 km (70 miles) northwest of Anchorage: chosen as the site of the projected new state capital in 1976, a plan which never came to fruition. Pop: 1658 (2000)

willowherb *n* a plant with narrow leaves and purplish flowers

willow pattern *n* a pattern in blue on white china, depicting a Chinese landscape with a willow tree, river, bridge, and figures

willowy *adj* slender and graceful

willpower *n* strong self-disciplined determination to do something

Wills *n* **1 Helen Newington**, married name *Helen Wills Moody Roark*. 1905–98, US tennis player. She was Wimbledon singles champion eight times between 1927 and 1938. She also won the US title seven times and the French title four times **2 William John**. 1834–61, English explorer: Robert Burke's deputy in an expedition on which both men died after crossing Australia from north to south for the first time

willy *n*, *pl* **-lies** *Brit, Austral and NZ informal* a childish or jocular word for **penis**

willy-nilly *adv* **1** in a haphazard fashion; indiscriminately: *spending taxpayers' money willy-nilly*

2 whether desired or not [Old English *wile hē, nyle hē* will he or will he not]

willy wagtail *n Austral* black-and-white flycatcher

willy-willy *n Austral* a small tropical dust storm [from a native Australian language]

Wilmington *n* a port in N Delaware, on the Delaware River: industrial centre. Pop: 72 051 (2003 est)

Wilno *n* the Polish name for Vilnius

Wilson *n* **1** Alexander. 1766–1813, Scottish ornithologist in the US **2** Sir Angus (Frank Johnstone). 1913–91, British writer, whose works include the collection of short stories *The Wrong Set* (1949) and the novels *Anglo-Saxon Attitudes* (1956) and *No Laughing Matter* (1967) **3** Charles Thomson Rees. 1869–1959, Scottish physicist, who invented the cloud chamber: shared the Nobel prize for physics 1927 **4** Edmund. 1895–1972, US critic, noted esp. for *Axel's Castle* (1931), a study of the symbolist movement **5** (James) Harold, Baron Wilson of Rievaulx. 1916–95, British Labour statesman; prime minister (1964–70; 1974–76) **6** Jacqueline. born 1945, British writer for older girls; her best-selling books include *The Story of Tracey Beaker* (1991), *The Illustrated Mum* (1998), and *Girls in Tears* (2002). **7** Richard. 1714–82, Welsh landscape painter **8** (Thomas) Woodrow. 1856–1924, US Democratic statesman; 28th president of the US (1913–21). He led the US into World War I in 1917 and proposed the Fourteen Points (1918) as a basis for peace. Although he secured the formation of the League of Nations, the US Senate refused to support it: Nobel peace prize 1919 ▸ **Wilsonian** *adj*

wilt *vb* **1** (of a flower or plant) to become limp or drooping **2** (of a person) to lose strength or confidence [perhaps from obsolete *wilk* to wither]

Wilton House *n* a mansion in Wilton in Wiltshire: built for the 1st Earl of Pembroke in the 16th century; rebuilt after a fire in 1647 by Inigo Jones and John Webb; altered in the 19th century by James Wyatt; landscaped grounds include a famous Palladian bridge

Wilts Wiltshire

Wiltshire *n* a county of S England, consisting mainly of chalk uplands, with Salisbury Plain in the south and the Marlborough Downs in the north; prehistoric remains (at Stonehenge and Avebury); became a unitary authority in 2009: the geographical and ceremonial county includes Swindon unitary authority (established in 1997). Administrative centre: Trowbridge. Pop (excluding Swindon): 440 800 (2003 est). Area (excluding Swindon): 3481 sq km (1344 sq miles)

wily *adj* **wilier, wiliest** sly or crafty

Wimbledon *n* part of the Greater London borough of Merton: headquarters of the All England Lawn Tennis Club since 1877 and the site of the annual international tennis championships

wimp *informal* *n* **1** a feeble ineffective person ▷ *vb* **2** wimp out of to fail to do (something) through lack of courage [origin unknown] ▸ **wimpish** or **wimpy** *adj*

WIMP *computers* windows, icons, menus (or mice), pointers: denoting a type of user-friendly screen display used on small computers

wimple *n* a piece of cloth draped round the head to frame the face, worn by women in the Middle Ages and now by some nuns [Old English *wimpel*]

win *vb* **winning, won** **1** to achieve first place in (a competition or race) **2** to gain (a prize or first place) in a competition or race **3** to gain victory in (a battle, argument, or struggle) **4** to gain (sympathy, approval, or support) ▷ *n* **5** *informal* a success, victory, or triumph: *three consecutive wins* ▸ See also **win over** [Old English *winnan*] ▸ **winnable** *adj*

wince *vb* **wincing, winced** **1** to draw back slightly, as if in sudden pain ▷ *n* **2** the act of wincing [Old French *wencier*, *guenchir* to avoid]

winch *n* **1** a lifting or hauling device consisting of a rope

or chain wound round a barrel or drum ▷ *vb* **2** to haul or lift using a winch: *two men were winched to safety by a helicopter* [Old English *wince* pulley]

Winchester *n* a city in S England, administrative centre of Hampshire: a Romano-British town; Saxon capital of Wessex; 11th-century cathedral; site of **Winchester College** (1382), English public school. Pop: 41 420 (2001)

Winckelmann *n* Johann Joachim. 1717–68, German archaeologist and art historian; one of the founders of neoclassicism

wind¹ *n* **1** a current of air moving across the earth's surface **2** a trend or force: *the chill wind of change* **3** the power to breathe normally, esp. during or after physical exercise: *if you feel tired during the exercise, persevere – you'll soon get a second wind* **4** gas in the stomach or intestines **5** *informal* foolish or empty talk: *political language is designed to give an appearance of solidity to pure wind* **6 break wind** to release intestinal gas through the anus **7 get wind of** *informal* to find out about: *the media finally got wind of her disappearance* ▷ *adj* **8** *music* of or relating to wind instruments: *the wind section* ▷ *vb* **winding, winded** **9** to cause (someone) to be short of breath: *he fell with a thud that left him winded* **10** to cause (a baby) to bring up wind after feeding [Old English] ▸ **windless** *adj*

wind² *vb* **winding, wound** **1** to twist (something flexible) round some object: *a sweatband was wound round his head* **2** to tighten the spring of (a clock or watch) by turning a key or knob **3** to follow a twisting course: *a narrow path wound through the shrubbery* ▸ See also **wind down, wind up** [Old English *windan*] ▸ **winding** *adj, n*

windbag *n slang* a person who talks a lot but says little of interest

windblown *adj* blown about by the wind: *windblown hair*

windbreak *n* a fence or a line of trees that gives protection from the wind by breaking its force

windcheater *n chiefly Brit* a warm jacket with a close-fitting knitted neck, cuffs, and waistband

wind chill *n* the serious chilling effect of wind and low temperature

wind down *vb* **1** to move downwards by turning a handle: *he wound down the rear window* **2** (of a clock or watch) to slow down before stopping completely **3** to relax after a stressful or tiring time: *I have not had a chance to wind down from a busy day* **4** to diminish gradually: *trading wound down for the day*

winded *adj* temporarily out of breath after physical exercise or a blow to the stomach

Windermere *n* a lake in NW England, in Cumbria in the SE part of the Lake District: the largest lake in England. Length: 17 km (10.5 miles). Sometimes (less correctly) called: **Lake Windermere**

windfall *n* **1** a piece of unexpected good fortune, esp. financial gain **2** a fruit blown off a tree by the wind

windfall tax *n* a tax levied on profits made from the privatization of public utilities

wind farm *n* a large group of wind-driven generators for electricity supply

wind gauge *n* same as **anemometer**

Windhoek *n* the capital of Namibia, in the centre, at an altitude of 1654 m (5428 ft): formerly the capital of German South West Africa. Pop: 252 000 (2005 est)

winding sheet *n* a sheet in which a dead person is wrapped before being buried

wind instrument *n* a musical instrument, such as a flute, that is played by having air blown into it

windjammer *n history* a large merchant sailing ship

windlass *n* a machine for lifting heavy objects by winding a rope or chain round a barrel or drum driven by a motor [Old Norse *vindāss*]

windmill *n* **1** a building containing machinery for grinding corn or for pumping, driven by sails that are turned by the wind **2** *Brit* a toy consisting of a stick with plastic vanes attached, which revolve in the wind

window *n* **1** an opening in a building or a vehicle

W

containing glass within a framework, which lets in light and enables people to see in or out **2** the display area behind a glass window in a shop **3** a transparent area in an envelope which reveals the address on the letter inside **4** an area on a computer screen that can be manipulated separately from the rest of the display area, for example so that two or more files can be displayed at the same time **5** a period of unbooked time in a diary or schedule [Old Norse *vindauga* wind eye]

window box *n* a long narrow box, placed on a windowsill, in which plants are grown

window-dressing *n* **1** the art of arranging goods in shop windows in such a way as to attract customers **2** an attempt to make something seem better than it is by stressing only its attractive features: *do you think that the president's calling for an investigation is window-dressing, or do you think he actually means to do something?* ➤ **window-dresser** *n*

windowpane *n* a sheet of glass in a window

window seat *n* **1** a seat below a window **2** a seat beside a window in a bus, train, or aircraft

window-shopping *n* looking at goods in shop windows without intending to buy anything

windowsill *n* a shelf at the bottom of a window, either inside or outside a room

windpipe *n* a nontechnical name for **trachea**

Wind River Range *n* a mountain range in W Wyoming: one of the highest ranges of the central Rockies. Highest peak: Gannet Peak, 4202 m (13 785 ft)

Windscale *n* the former name of **Sellafield**

windscreen *n Brit, Austral and NZ* the sheet of glass that forms the front window of a motor vehicle

windscreen wiper *n Brit, Austral and NZ* an electrically operated blade with a rubber edge that wipes a windscreen clear of rain

windshield *n US and Canad* the sheet of glass that forms the front window of a motor vehicle

windshield wiper *n US and Canad* an electrically operated blade with a rubber edge that wipes a windshield clear of rain

windsock *n* a cloth cone mounted on a mast, used esp. at airports to indicate the direction of the wind

Windsor¹ *n* **1** a town in S England, in Windsor and Maidenhead unitary authority, Berkshire, on the River Thames, linked by bridge with Eton: site of **Windsor Castle**, residence of English monarchs since its founding by William the Conqueror; **Old Windsor**, royal residence in the time of Edward the Confessor, is 3 km (2 miles) southeast. Pop: 26 747 (2001 est). Official name: **New Windsor 2** a city in SE Canada, in S Ontario on the Detroit River opposite Detroit: motor-vehicle manufacturing; university (1963). Pop: 208 402 (2001)

Windsor² *n* **1** the official name of the British royal family from 1917 **2 Duke of Windsor** the title, from 1937, of **Edward VIII**

Windsor and Maidenhead *n* a unitary authority in S England, in Berkshire. Pop: 135 300 (2003 est). Area: 197 sq km (76 sq miles)

windsurfing *n* the sport of riding on water using a surfboard steered and propelled by an attached sail ➤ **windsurfer** *n*

windswept *adj* **1** exposed to the wind: *the vast windswept plains* **2** blown about by the wind: *his hair was looking a bit windswept*

wind tunnel *n* a chamber through which a stream of air is forced, in order to test the effects of wind on aircraft

wind up *vb* **1** to bring to a conclusion: *we want to wind this conflict up as quickly as possible* **2** *informal* to dissolve (a company) and divide its assets among creditors **3** to tighten the spring of (a clockwork mechanism) by turning a key or knob **4** to move (a car window) upwards by turning a handle **5** *informal* to end up: *to wind up in the hospital* **6** *informal* to make nervous or tense: *as crisis after crisis broke, I became increasingly wound up* **7** *Brit, Austral and NZ*

slang to tease or annoy: *that really used to wind my old man up something rotten* ➤ *adj* **wind-up 8** operated by clockwork: *a wind-up toy* ➤ *n* **wind-up 9** a light-hearted hoax **10** the finish

windward 1 *chiefly nautical* ➤ *adj* **2** of or in the direction from which the wind blows ➤ *n* **3** the windward direction ➤ *adv* **4** towards the wind

Windward Islands *pl n* **1** a group of islands in the SE Caribbean, in the Lesser Antilles: consists of the French Overseas Department of Martinique and the independent states of Grenada, St Lucia, and St Vincent and the Grenadines **2** a group of islands in the S Pacific, in French Polynesia in the W Society Archipelago: Moorea, Maio (Tubuai Manu), and Mehetia and Tetiaroa. Pop: 184 222 (2002). French name: **Îles du Vent**

Windward Passage *n* a strait in the Caribbean, between E Cuba and NW Haiti. Width: 80 km (50 miles)

windy *adj* **windier, windiest 1** denoting a time or conditions in which there is a strong wind: *a windy day* **2** exposed to the wind: *the windy graveyard* **3** long-winded or pompous: *his speeches are long and windy* **4** old-fashioned, slang* frightened

Windy City *n* **the Windy City** *informal* Chicago, Illinois

wine *n* **1 a** an alcoholic drink produced by the fermenting of grapes with water and sugar **b** an alcoholic drink produced in this way from other fruits or flowers: *dandelion wine* ➤ *adj* **2** dark purplish-red ➤ *vb* **wining, wined 3 wine and dine** to entertain (someone) with wine and fine food [Latin *vinum*]

wine bar *n* a bar that specializes in serving wine and usually food

wine box *n* a cubic carton containing wine, with a tap for dispensing

wine cellar *n* **1** a cellar where wine is stored **2** the stock of wines stored there

wineglass *n* a glass for wine, usually with a small bowl on a stem with a flared base

Winehouse *n* **Amy (Jade)**. 1983–2011, English rock singer and songwriter; her albums include *Frank* (2003) and *Back to Black* (2006)

wing *n* **1** one of the limbs or organs of a bird, bat, or insect that are used for flying **2** one of the two winglike supporting parts of an aircraft **3** a projecting part of a building: *converting the unused east wing into a suitable habitation* **4** a faction or group within a political party or other organization: *the youth wing of the African National Congress* **5** *Brit* the part of a car body surrounding the wheels **6** *sport* **a** either of the two sides of the pitch near the touchline **b** same as **winger 7 wings** *theatre* the space offstage to the right or left of the acting area **8 in the wings** ready to step in when needed **9 on the wing** flying **10 spread one's wings** to make fuller use of one's abilities by trying new experiences: *he increasingly spread his wings abroad* **11 take someone under one's wing** to look after someone **12 take wing** to fly away ➤ *vb* **13** to fly: *a lone bird winging its way from the island* **14** to move through the air: *sending a shower of loose gravel winging towards the house* **15** to shoot or wound in the wing or arm **16** to provide with wings [Old Norse *vængr*] ➤ **winged** *adj* ➤ **wingless** *adj*

Wingate *n* **Orde (Charles)**. 1903–44, British soldier. During World War II he organized the Chindits in Burma (Myanmar) to disrupt Japanese communications. He died in an air crash

wing chair *n* an easy chair with side pieces extending forward from a high back

wing commander *n* a middle-ranking commissioned officer in an air force

winger *n sport* a player positioned on a wing

wing nut *n* **1** a threaded nut with two flat projections which allow it to be turned by the thumb and forefinger **2** a foolish or insane person

wingspan *n* the distance between the wing tips of a bird, insect, bat, or aircraft

wink *vb* **1** to close and open one eye quickly as a signal **2** (of a light) to shine brightly and intermittently; twinkle ▷ *n* **3** the act or an instance of winking, esp. as a signal **4** a twinkling of light **5** *informal* the smallest amount of sleep: *I didn't sleep a wink last night* **6 tip someone the wink** *Brit, Austral and NZ informal* to give someone a hint or warning [Old English *wincian*]

Winkelried *n* Arnold von. died ?1386, Swiss hero of the battle of Sempach (1386) against the Austrians

winkle *n* **1** an edible shellfish with a spirally coiled shell ▷ *vb* **-kling, -kled 2 winkle out** *informal, chiefly Brit* **a** to obtain (information) from someone who is not willing to provide it: *try to winkle the real problem out of them* **b** to coax or force out: *he somehow managed to winkle him out of his room*

winkle-pickers *pl n old-fashioned* shoes with very pointed narrow toes

Winnebago *n* **1 Lake Winnebago** a lake in E Wisconsin, fed and drained by the Fox river: the largest lake in the state. Area: 557 sq km (215 sq miles) **2** (*pl* **-gos** or **-go**) a member of a North American Indian people living in Wisconsin and Nebraska **3** the language of this people, belonging to the Siouan family

winner *n* **1** a person or thing that wins **2** *informal* a person or thing that seems sure to be successful

winning *adj* **1** gaining victory: *the winning side* **2** charming or attractive: *her winning smiles*

winnings *pl n* the money won in a competition or in gambling

Winnipeg *n* **1** a city in S Canada, capital of Manitoba at the confluence of the Assiniboine and Red Rivers: University of Manitoba (1877) and University of Winnipeg (1871). Pop: 663 617 (2011) **2 Lake Winnipeg** a lake in S Canada, in Manitoba: drains through the Nelson River into Hudson Bay. Area: 23 553 sq km (9094 sq miles)

Winnipegger *n* a native or inhabitant of Winnipeg

Winnipegosis *n* **Lake Winnipegosis** a lake in S Canada, in W Manitoba. Area: 5400 sq km (2086 sq miles)

winnow *vb* **1** to separate (grain) from (chaff) by a current of air **2** (often foll. by *out*) to separate out (an unwanted element): *the committee will need to winnow out the nonsense* [Old English *windwian*]

wino (wine-oh) *n, pl* **winos** *informal* a destitute person who habitually drinks cheap wine

win over *vb* to gain the support or consent of: *his robust performance won over his critics*

Winslet *n* Kate. born 1975, English film actress; her films include *Sense and Sensibility* (1995), *Titanic* (1997), *Iris* (2001), *Little Children* (2006), and *Revolutionary Road* (2008)

winsome *adj literary* charming or attractive: *a winsome smile* [Old English *wynsum*]

Winstanley *n* Gerrard. ?1609–60, English radical; leader of the Diggers (1649–50) and author of the pamphlet *The Law of Freedom in a Platform* (1652)

Winston *n* Robert (Maurice Lipson), Baron. born 1940, British obstetrician and gynaecologist, noted for his work on human infertility treatment; as a broadcaster, his TV series include *The Human Body* (1998) and *How Science Changed the World* (2010)

Winston-Salem *n* a city in N central North Carolina: formed in 1913 by the uniting of Salem and Winston; a major tobacco manufacturing centre. Pop: 190 299 (2003 est)

winter *n* **1** the coldest season of the year, between autumn and spring ▷ *vb* **2** to spend the winter in a specified place: *wintering in Rome* [Old English]

wintergreen *n* an evergreen shrub from which is obtained a pleasant-smelling oil that is used medicinally and for flavouring

winter solstice *n* the time, about December 22, at which the sun is at its southernmost point in the sky

winter sports *pl n* sports held on snow or ice, such as skiing and skating

Winterthur *n* an industrial town in NE central Switzerland, in Zürich canton: has the largest technical college in the country. Pop: 90 483 (2000)

wintertime *n* the period or season of winter

Winthrop *n* **1** John. 1588–1649, English lawyer and colonist, first governor of the Massachusetts Bay colony: the leading figure among the Puritan settlers of New England **2** his son, John. 1606–76, English lawyer and colonist; a founder of Agawan (now Ipswich), Massachusetts; governor of Connecticut

Winton *n* Tim, full name *Timothy John Winton*. born 1960, Australian writer. His novels include *Cloudstreet* (1992), *The Riders* (1995), and *Dirt Music* (2002)

wintry *adj* **-trier, -triest 1** of or characteristic of winter: *a cold wintry day* **2** cold or unfriendly: *a wintry smile*

win-win *adj* guaranteeing a favourable outcome for everyone involved: *a win-win situation for NATO*

wipe *vb* **wiping, wiped 1** to rub (a surface or object) lightly with a cloth or the hand, in order to remove dirt or liquid from it **2** to remove by wiping: *she made a futile attempt to wipe away her tears* **3** to erase a recording from (a video or audio tape) ▷ *n* **4** the act or an instance of wiping: *a quick wipe* [Old English *wīpian*]

wipe out *vb* to destroy or get rid of completely: *a hail storm wipes out a wheat crop in five minutes*

wiper *n* short for **windscreen wiper**

wire *n* **1** a slender flexible strand of metal **2** a length of this used to carry electric current in a circuit **3** a long continuous piece of wire or cable connecting points in a telephone or telegraph system **4** *old-fashioned, informal* a telegram ▷ *vb* **wiring, wired 5** to fasten with wire **6** to equip (an electrical system, circuit, or component) with wires **7** *informal* to send a telegram to **8** to send by telegraph: *they wired the money for a train ticket* [Old English *wīr*]

wired *adj* **1** *slang* excitable or edgy, usually from stimulant intake: *I don't want coffee, I'm wired enough as it is* **2** using computers to send and receive information, esp. via the internet

wire-haired *adj* (of a dog) having a rough wiry coat

wireless *n* **1** *old-fashioned* same as **radio** ▷ *adj* **2** *computers* communicating without connecting wires: *wireless application protocol*

wire netting *n* a net made of wire, used for fencing

wiretapping *n* the practice of making a connection to a telegraph or telephone wire in order to obtain information secretly

wireworm *n* a destructive wormlike beetle larva

wiring *n* the network of wires used in an electrical system, device, or circuit

Wirral *n* **1 the Wirral** a peninsula in NW England between the estuaries of the Rivers Mersey and Dee **2** a unitary authority in NW England, in Merseyside. Pop: 313 800 (2003 est). Area: 158 sq km (61 sq miles)

wiry *adj* **wirier, wiriest 1** (of a person) slim but strong **2** coarse and stiff: *wiry grass*

Wis. Wisconsin

Wisbech *n* a town in E England, in N Cambridgeshire: market-gardening. Pop: 26 536 (2001)

Wisconsin *n* **1** a state of the N central US, on Lake Superior and Lake Michigan: consists of an undulating plain, with uplands in the north and west; over 168 m (550 ft) above sea level along the shore of Lake Michigan. Capital: Madison. Pop: 5 472 299 (2003 est). Area: 141 061 sq km (54 464 sq miles). Abbreviation: **Wis.**, (with zip code) **WI 2** a river in central and SW Wisconsin, flowing south and west to the Mississippi. Length: 692 km (430 miles)

Wisconsinite *n* a native or inhabitant of Wisconsin

Wisden *n* John. 1826–84, English cricketer; publisher of *Wisden Cricketers' Almanack*, which first appeared in 1864

wisdom *n* **1** the ability to use one's experience and knowledge to make sensible decisions or judgments **2** accumulated knowledge or learning: *the wisdom of Asia and of Africa* [Old English *wīsdōm*]

W

wisdom tooth *n* any of the four molar teeth, one at the back of each side of the jaw, that are the last of the permanent teeth to come through

wise¹ *adj* **1** possessing or showing wisdom: *a wise move* **2 none the wiser** knowing no more than before: *I left the conference none the wiser* **3 wise to** *informal* aware of or informed about: *they'll get wise to our system; he put him wise to the rumour* [Old English *wīs*] ⟩ **wisely** *adv*

wise² *n* old-fashioned way, manner, or respect: *in no wise* [Old English *wīse* manner]

-wise *suffix* forming adverbs **1** indicating direction or manner: *crabwise* **2** with reference to: *moneywise* [Old English *-wisan*]

wiseacre *n* a person who wishes to seem wise [Middle Dutch *wijsseggher* soothsayer]

wisecrack *informal n* **1** a clever, amusing, sometimes unkind, remark ▷ *vb* **2** to make such remarks ⟩ **wisecracking** *adj*

wise guy *n informal* a person who likes to give the impression of knowing more than other people

Wiseman *n* Nicholas Patrick Stephen. 1802–65, British cardinal; first Roman Catholic archbishop of Westminster (1850–65)

wise up *vb* **wising, wised** *slang* (often foll. by *to*) to become aware (of) or informed (about)

wish *vb* **1** to want or desire (something impossible or improbable): *he wished he'd kept quiet* **2** to desire or prefer to be or do something: *the next person who wished to speak* **3** to feel or express a hope concerning the welfare, health, or success of: *we wished him well* **4** to greet as specified: *I wished her a Merry Christmas* ▷ *n* **5** a desire, often for something impossible or improbable: *a desperate wish to succeed as a professional artist* **6** something desired or wished for: *your wishes will come true* **7** the expression of a hope for someone's welfare, health, or success: *give him our best wishes* [Old English *wȳscan*]

wishbone *n* the V-shaped bone above the breastbone of a chicken or turkey

wishful *adj* desirous or longing: *she seemed wishful of prolonging the discussion*

wishful thinking *n* an interpretation of the facts as one would like them to be, rather than as they are: *was it wishful thinking, or had the enemy lost heart?*

wish list *n* a list of things desired by a person or organization: *the government's wish list*

wish on *vb* to want (something unpleasant) to be experienced by: *I wouldn't wish that wretched childhood on anyone*

wishy-washy *adj informal* lacking in character, force, or colour

Wisła *n* the Polish name for **Vistula** (1)

Wislany Zalew *n* the Polish name for the **Vistula** (2)

Wismar *n* a port in NE Germany, on an inlet of the Baltic, in Mecklenburg-West Pomerania: shipbuilding industries. Pop: 45 714 (2003 est)

wisp *n* **1** a thin, delicate, or filmy piece or streak: *little wisps of cloud* **2** a small untidy bundle, tuft, or strand: *a wisp of hair* **3** a slight trace: *a wisp of a smile* [origin unknown]

wispy *adj* **wispier, wispiest** thin, fine, or delicate: *grey wispy hair*

wisteria *n* a climbing plant with large drooping clusters of blue, purple, or white flowers [after Caspar *Wistar*, anatomist]

wistful *adj* sadly wishing for something lost or unobtainable ⟩ **wistfully** *adv* ⟩ **wistfulness** *n*

wit¹ *n* **1** the ability to use words or ideas in a clever, amusing, and imaginative way **2** a person possessing this ability **3** practical intelligence: *do credit me with some wit* ▶ See also **wits** [Old English *witt*]

wit² *vb* **to wit** (used to introduce a statement or explanation) that is to say; namely [Old English *witan*]

witblits (vit-blits) *n S African* an illegally distilled strong alcoholic drink [Afrikaans *wit* white + *blits* lightning]

witch *n* **1** (in former times) a woman believed to possess evil magic powers **2** a person who practises magic or sorcery, esp. black magic **3** an ugly or wicked old woman [Old English *wicce*]

witchcraft *n* the use of magic, esp. for evil purposes

witch doctor *n* a man in certain tribal societies who is believed to possess magical powers, which can be used to cure sickness or to harm people

witchetty grub *n* a wood-boring edible Australian caterpillar

witch hazel *n* a medicinal solution made from the bark and leaves of a N American shrub, which is put on the skin to treat bruises and inflammation

witch-hunt *n* a rigorous campaign to expose and discredit people considered to hold unorthodox views on the pretext of safeguarding the public welfare

with *prep* **1** accompanying; in the company of: *the captain called to the sergeant to come with him* **2** using; by means of: *unlocking the padlock with a key* **3** possessing or having: *a woman with black hair; the patient with angina* **4** concerning or regarding: *be gentle with me* **5** in a manner characterized by: *I know you will handle it with discretion* **6** as a result of: *his voice was hoarse with nervousness* **7** following the line of thought of: *are you with me so far?* **8** having the same opinions as; supporting: *are you with us or against us?* [Old English]

withdraw *vb* **-drawing, -drew, -drawn** **1** to take out or remove: *he withdrew an envelope from his pocket* **2** to remove (money) from a bank account or savings account **3** to leave one place to go to another, usually quieter, place: *he withdrew into his bedroom* **4** (of troops) to leave or be pulled back from the battleground **5** to take back (a statement) formally **6 withdraw from** to give up: *they withdrew from the competition* [*with*, in the sense: away from]

withdrawal *n* **1** the act or an instance of withdrawing **2** the period that a drug addict goes through after stopping using drugs, during which he or she may experience symptoms such as tremors, sweating, and vomiting ▷ *adj* **3** of or relating to withdrawal from an addictive drug: *withdrawal symptoms*

withdrawn *vb* **1** the past participle of **withdraw** ▷ *adj* **2** extremely reserved or shy

wither *vb* **1** to make or become dried up or shrivelled: *the leaves had withered but not fallen* **2** to fade or waste: *deprived of the nerve supply the muscles wither* **3** to humiliate (someone) with a scornful look or remark [probably variant of WEATHER (verb)] ⟩ **withered** *adj*

withering *adj* (of a look or remark) extremely scornful

withers *pl n* the highest part of the back of a horse, between the shoulders [earlier *widersones*]

withhold *vb* **-holding, -held** to keep back (information or money)

within *prep* **1** in or inside: *within the hospital grounds* **2** before (a period of time) has passed: *within a month* **3** not beyond: *within the confines of a low budget; he positioned a low table within her reach* ▷ *adv* **4** *formal* inside or internally: *a glimpse of what was hidden within*

without *prep* **1** not accompanied by: *I can't imagine going through life without him* **2** not using: *our Jeep drove without lights* **3** not possessing or having: *four months without a job; a lot of them came across the border without shoes* **4** in a manner showing a lack of: *without reverence* **5** while not or after not: *she sat without speaking for some while* ▷ *adv* **6** *formal* outside: *seated on the graveyard without*

withstand *vb* **-standing, -stood** to resist or endure successfully: *our ability to withstand stress*

witless *adj* **1** *formal* lacking intelligence or sense **2 scared witless** extremely frightened

witness *n* **1** a person who has seen or can give first-hand evidence of some event: *the only witness to a killing* **2** a person who gives evidence in a court of law: *a witness for the defence* **3** a person who confirms the genuineness of a document or signature by adding his or her own signature **4** evidence proving or supporting something:

W

the Church of England, that historic witness to the power of the Christian faith **5 bear witness to** to be evidence or proof of: the high turn-out bore witness to the popularity of the contest ▷ vb **6** to see, be present at, or know at first hand: I have witnessed many motor-racing accidents **7** to be the scene or setting of: the 1970s witnessed an enormous increase in international lending **8** to confirm the genuineness of (a document or signature) by adding one's own signature **9 witness to** formal to confirm: our aim is to witness to the fact of the empty tomb [Old English witnes]

witness box or especially US **witness stand** n the place in a court of law where witnesses stand to give evidence

wits pl n **1** the ability to think and act quickly: when he was sober his wits were razor-sharp **2 at one's wits' end** at a loss to know what to do **3 have one's wits about one** to be able to think and act quickly **4 live by** or **on one's wits** to gain a livelihood by craftiness rather than by hard work **5 scared out of one's wits** extremely frightened

Witte n Sergei Yulievich. 1849–1915, Russian statesman; prime minister (1905–06). As minister of finance (1892–1903) he tried to modernize the Russian economy

Wittenberg n a city in E Germany, on the River Elbe, in Brandenburg: Martin Luther, as a philosophy teacher at Wittenberg university, began the Reformation here in 1517 by nailing his 95 theses to the doors of a church. Pop: 46 295 (2003 est)

witter vb chiefly Brit informal to chatter or babble pointlessly or at unnecessary length [origin unknown]

Wittgenstein n Ludwig Josef Johann. 1889–1951, British philosopher, born in Austria. After studying with Bertrand Russell, he wrote the Tractatus Logico-Philosophicus (1921), which explores the relationship of language to the world. He was a major influence on logical positivism but later repudiated this, and in Philosophical Investigations (1953) he argues that philosophical problems arise from insufficient attention to the variety of natural language use

witticism n a witty remark

wittingly adv intentionally and knowingly

witty adj **-tier, -tiest** clever and amusing > **wittily** adv

Witwatersrand n a rocky ridge in NE South Africa: contains the richest gold deposits in the world, also coal and manganese; chief industrial centre is Johannesburg. Height: 1500–1800 m (5000–6000 ft). Also called: **the Rand, the Reef**

wives n the plural of **wife**

wizard n **1** a man in fairy tales who has magic powers **2** a person who is outstandingly gifted in some specified field: a financial wizard [from wise]

wizardry n **1** magic or sorcery **2** outstanding skill or accomplishment in some specified field: technological wizardry

wizened (wiz-zend) adj shrivelled, wrinkled, or dried up with age

Władysław II n original name Jogaila. ?1351–1434, grand duke of Lithuania (1377–1401) and king of Poland (1386–1434). He united Lithuania and Poland and founded the Jagiellon dynasty

Władysław IV n 1595–1648, king of Poland (1632–48)

WMD n weapon(s) of mass destruction

woad n a blue dye obtained from a European plant, used by the ancient Britons as a body dye [Old English wād]

wobbegong n an Australian shark with brown-and-white skin

wobble vb **-bling, -bled 1** to move or sway unsteadily **2** to shake: she was having difficulty in controlling her voice, which wobbled about ▷ n **3** a wobbling movement or sound [Low German wabbeln]

wobbly adj **-blier, -bliest 1** unsteady **2** trembling ▷ n **3 throw a wobbly** slang to become suddenly angry or upset

Woburn Abbey n a mansion in Woburn in Bedfordshire: originally an abbey; rebuilt in the 17th century for the Dukes of Bedford, altered by Henry

Holland in the 18th century; deer park landscaped by Humphrey Repton

Wodehouse n Sir P(elham) G(renville). 1881–1975, US author, born in England. His humorous novels of upper-class life in England include the Psmith and Jeeves series > **Wodehousian** adj

wodge n informal a thick lump or chunk: my wodge of Kleenex was a sodden ball [from wedge]

woe n **1** literary intense grief **2 woes** misfortunes or problems: economic woes **3 woe betide someone** someone will or would experience misfortune: woe betide anyone who got in his way [Old English wā, wē]

woebegone adj sad in appearance [woe + obsolete bego to surround]

woeful adj **1** extremely sad **2** pitiful or deplorable: a woeful lack of understanding > **woefully** adv

Woffington n Peg, full name Margaret Woffington. ?1714–60, Irish actress

Wöhler n Friedrich. 1800–82, German chemist, who proved that organic compounds could be synthesized from inorganic compounds

wok n a large bowl-shaped metal Chinese cooking pot, used for stir-frying [Chinese (Cantonese)]

woke vb the past tense of **wake¹**

woken vb the past participle of **wake¹**

Woking n a town in SE England, in central Surrey: mainly residential. Pop: 101 127 (2001)

Wokingham n a unitary authority in SE England, in Berkshire. Pop: 151 200 (2003 est). Area: 179 sq km (69 sq miles)

wold n a large area of high open rolling country [Old English weald wood]

Wolds pl n **the Wolds** a range of chalk hills in NE England: consists of the **Yorkshire Wolds** to the north, separated from the **Lincolnshire Wolds** by the Humber estuary

wolf n, pl **wolves 1** a predatory doglike wild animal which hunts in packs **2** old-fashioned, informal a man who habitually tries to seduce women **3 cry wolf** to give false alarms repeatedly: if you cry wolf too often, people will take no notice ▷ vb **4 wolf down** to eat quickly or greedily: they will wolf down kidneys but refuse tongue [Old English wulf]

Wolf n **1 Friedrich August.** 1759–1824, German classical scholar, who suggested that the Homeric poems, esp. the Iliad, are products of an oral tradition **2 Hugo.** 1860–1903, Austrian composer, esp. of songs, including the Italienisches Liederbuch and the Spanisches Liederbuch **3 Howlin'.** See Howlin' Wolf

Wolfe n **1 James.** 1727–59, English soldier, who commanded the British capture of Quebec, in which he was killed **2 Thomas (Clayton).** 1900–38, US novelist, noted for his autobiographical fiction, esp. Look Homeward, Angel (1929) **3 Tom,** full name Thomas Kennerly Wolfe. born 1931, US author and journalist; his books include The Right Stuff (1979) and the novels Bonfire of the Vanities (1987), and A Man in Full (1998)

Wolfensohn n James D., known as Jim. born 1933, US businessman and international official, born in Australia; president of the International Bank for Reconstruction and Development (the World Bank) (1995–2005); honorary knighthood (1995)

Wolf-Ferrari n Ermanno. 1876–1948, Italian composer born of a German father, in Germany from 1909. His works, mainly in a lyrical style, include operas, such as The Jewels of the Madonna (1911) and Susanna's Secret (1909)

wolfhound n a very large dog, formerly used to hunt wolves

Wolfit n Sir Donald. 1902–68, English stage actor and manager

Wolfram von Eschenbach n died ?1220, German poet: author of the epic Parzival, incorporating the story of the Grail

Wolfsburg n a city in N central Germany, in Lower Saxony: founded in 1938; motor-vehicle industry. Pop: 122 724 (2003 est)

W

wolf whistle *n* **1** a whistle produced by a man to express admiration of a woman's appearance ▷ *vb* **wolf-whistle** (**-whistling, -whistled**) **2** to produce such a whistle

Wollongong *n* a city in E Australia, in E New South Wales on the Pacific: an early centre of dairy farming; now a coal-mining and heavy industrial centre. Pop: 228 846 (2001)

Wollstonecraft *n* **Mary.** 1759–97, British feminist and writer, author of *A Vindication of the Rights of Women* (1792); wife of William Godwin and mother of Mary Shelley

Wolseley *n* **Garnet Joseph, 1st Viscount.** 1833–1913, British field marshal, noted for his army reforms

Wolsey *n* **Thomas.** ?1475–1530, English cardinal and statesman; archbishop of York (1514–30); lord chancellor (1515–29). He dominated Henry VIII's foreign and domestic policies but his failure to obtain papal consent for the annulment of the king's marriage to Catherine of Aragon led to his arrest for high treason (1530); he died on the journey to face trial

Wolverhampton *n* **1** a city in W central England, in Wolverhampton unitary authority, West Midlands: iron and steel foundries; university (1992). Pop: 251 462 (2001) **2** a unitary authority in W central England, in the West Midlands. Pop: 238 900 (2003 est). Area: 69 sq km (27 sq miles)

wolverine *n* a large meat-eating mammal of Eurasia and North America with very thick dark fur [earlier *wolvering*, from *wolf*]

wolves *n* the plural of **wolf**

woman *n, pl* **women 1** an adult female human being **2** adult female human beings collectively: *the very image of woman pared of the trappings of 'femininity'* **3** an adult female human being with qualities associated with the female, such as tenderness or maternalism: *she's more woman than you know* **4** a female servant or domestic help **5** *informal* a wife or girlfriend ▷ *adj* **6** female: *a woman doctor* [Old English *wīfmann*]

womanhood *n* **1** the state of being a woman: *young girls approaching womanhood* **2** women collectively: *Asian womanhood*

womanish *adj* (of a man) looking or behaving like a woman

womanizer *or* **-niser** *n* a man who has casual affairs with many women

womanizing *or* **-nising** *n* (of a man) the practice of indulging in casual affairs with women

womankind *n* all women considered as a group

womanly *adj* possessing qualities generally regarded as typical of, or appropriate to, a woman

womb *n* the nontechnical name for **uterus** [Old English *wamb*]

wombat *n* a furry heavily-built plant-eating Australian marsupial [Aboriginal]

women *n* the plural of **woman**

womenfolk *pl n* **1** women collectively **2** a group of women, esp. the female members of one's family

Women's Liberation *n* a movement promoting the removal of inequalities based upon the assumption that men are superior to women. Also called: **women's lib**

won *vb* the past of **win**

wonder *vb* **1** to think about something with curiosity or doubt: *I wonder why she did that* **2** to be amazed: *I did wonder at her leaving valuable china on the shelves* ▷ *n* **3** something that causes surprise or awe: *it's a wonder she isn't speechless with fright* **4** the feeling of surprise or awe caused by something strange: *the wonder of travel* **5** **do** *or* **work wonders** to achieve spectacularly good results **6** **no** *or* **small wonder** it is not surprising: *no wonder you're going broke* ▷ *adj* **7** causing surprise or awe because of spectacular results achieved: *a new wonder drug for treating migraine* [Old English *wundor*] ▷ **wonderingly** *adv* ▷ **wonderment** *n*

Wonder *n* **Stevie.** real name *Steveland Judkins Morris.* born 1950, US Motown singer, songwriter, and multi-

instrumentalist. His recordings include *Up-Tight* (1966), "Superstition" (1972), *Innervisions* (1973), *Songs in the Key of Life* (1976), and "I Just Called to Say I Love You" (1985)

wonderful *adj* **1** extremely fine; excellent: *I've been offered a wonderful job* **2** causing surprise, amazement, or awe: *a strange and wonderful phenomenon* ▷ **wonderfully** *adv*

wonderland *n* **1** an imaginary land of marvels or wonders **2** an actual place of great or strange beauty: *the apartment was a wonderland of design and colour*

wondrous *adj* old-fashioned or literary causing surprise or awe; marvellous

wonky *adj* **-kier, -kiest** *Brit, Austral and NZ slang* **1** shaky or unsteady: *wonky wheelbarrows; wonky knees* **2** insecure or unreliable: *his marriage is looking a bit wonky* [dialect *wanky*]

Wŏnsan *n* a port in SE North Korea, on the Sea of Japan (East Sea): oil refineries. Pop: 319 000 (2005 est)

wont (rhymes with **don't**) old-fashioned *adj* **1** accustomed: *most murderers, his police friends were wont to say, were male* ▷ *n* **2** a usual practice: *she waded straight in, as was her wont* [Old English *gewunod*]

won't will not

woo *vb* **wooing, wooed 1** to coax or urge: *it will woo people back into the kitchen* **2** old-fashioned to attempt to gain the love of (a woman) [Old English *wōgian*] ▷ **wooing** *n*

wood *n* **1** the hard fibrous substance beneath the bark in trees and shrubs, which is used in building and carpentry and as fuel. Related adjective: **ligneous 2** an area of trees growing together that is smaller than a forest: *a track leading into a wood*. Related adjective: **sylvan 3** *golf* a long-shafted club with a wooden head ▷ *adj* **4** made of, using, or for use with wood: *wood fires* ▶ See also **woods** [Old English *wudu, wudu*]

Wood *n* **1** Mrs **Henry,** married name of *Ellen Price.* 1814–87, British novelist, noted esp. for the melodramatic novel *East Lynne* (1861) **2** Sir **Henry (Joseph).** 1869–1944, English conductor, who founded the Promenade Concerts in London **3** **John,** known as *the Elder.* 1707–54, British architect and town planner, working mainly in Bath, where he designed the North and South Parades (1728) and the Circus (1754) **4** his son, **John,** known as *the Younger.* 1727–82, British architect: designed the Royal Crescent (1767–71) and the Assembly Rooms (1769–71), Bath **5** **Ralph.** 1715–72, British potter, working in Staffordshire, who made the first toby jug (1762)

wood alcohol *n* same as **methanol**

woodbine *n* a wild honeysuckle with sweet-smelling yellow flowers

woodcarving *n* **1** a work of art produced by carving wood **2** the act or craft of carving wood

woodcock *n* a large game bird with a long straight bill

woodcut *n* a print made from a block of wood with a design cut into it

woodcutter *n* a person who cuts down trees or chops wood

wooded *adj* covered with woods or trees

wooden *adj* **1** made of wood **2** lacking spirit or animation: *the man's expression became wooden* ▷ **woodenly** *adv*

wooden spoon *n* a booby prize, esp. in sporting contests

woodland *n* **1** land that is mostly covered with woods or trees ▷ *adj* **2** living in woods: *woodland birds*

woodlouse *n, pl* **-lice** a very small grey creature with many legs that lives in damp places

woodpecker *n* a bird with a strong beak with which it bores into trees for insects

wood pulp *n* pulp made from wood fibre, used to make paper

woodruff *n* a plant with small sweet-smelling white flowers and sweet-smelling leaves [Old English *wudurofe*]

woods *pl n* closely packed trees forming a forest or wood

Woods¹ *n* See **Lake of the Woods**

Woods² *n* **Tiger,** real name *Eldrick Woods.* born 1975, US golfer: youngest US Masters champion and first Black golfer to win a major championship; winner of the US Masters (1997, 2001–02, 2005), US Open (2000, 2002, 2008), British Open Championship (2000, 2005–06), and the PGA Championship (1999, 2000, 2006–07); in 2001 he became the only player to hold all four major titles at once

woodsman *n, pl* **-men** a person who lives in a wood or who is skilled at woodwork or carving

Woodstock *n* a town in New York State, the site of a large rock festival in August 1969. Pop: 6253 (2003 est)

Woodville *n* Elizabeth. ?1437–92, wife of Edward IV of England and mother of Edward V

Woodward *n* **1** Sir Clive. born 1956, English Rugby Union player and subsequently (1997–2004) coach of the England team that won the Rugby World Cup in 2003. **2** R(obert) B(urns). 1917–79, US chemist. For his work on the synthesis of quinine, strychnine, cholesterol, and other organic compounds he won the Nobel prize for chemistry 1965 **3** Sir **Sandy**, full name *John Forster Woodward*. (1932–2013), British admiral; commanded the Royal Navy's task force during the Falklands War (1982)

woodwind *music adj* **1** of or denoting a type of wind instrument, such as the oboe ▷ *n* **2** the woodwind instruments of an orchestra

woodwork *n* **1** the parts of a room or house that are made of wood, such as the doors and window frames: *stark white walls and blue woodwork* **2** the art or craft of making objects from wood **3** crawl out of the woodwork to appear suddenly and in large numbers: *intellectuals and environmentalists crawled out of the woodwork*

woodworm *n* **1** a beetle larva that bores into wooden furniture or beams **2** the damage caused to wood by these larvae

woody *adj* **woodier, woodiest 1** (of a plant) having a very hard stem **2** (of an area) covered with woods or trees

woof[1] *n* same as **weft** [Old English ōwef]

woof[2] *n* an imitation of the bark of a dog

woofer *n* a loudspeaker used in high-fidelity systems for the reproduction of low audio frequencies

Wookey Hole *n* a village in SW England, in Somerset, near Wells: noted for the nearby limestone cave in which prehistoric remains have been found

wool *n* **1** the soft curly hair of sheep and some other animals **2** yarn spun from this, used in weaving and knitting **3** cloth made from this yarn **4** pull the wool over someone's eyes to deceive someone [Old English wull]

Woolf *n* **1** Leonard Sidney. 1880–1969, English publisher and political writer **2** his wife, **Virginia**. 1882–1941, English novelist and critic. Her novels, which include *Mrs Dalloway* (1925), *To the Lighthouse* (1927), *The Waves* (1931), and *Between the Acts* (1941), employ such techniques as the interior monologue and stream of consciousness

woolgathering *n* idle or absent-minded daydreaming

Woollcott *n* Alexander. 1887–1943, US writer and critic. His collected essays include *Shouts and Murmurs* (1922)

woollen *or US* **woolen** *adj* **1** made of wool or of a mixture of wool and another material **2** relating to wool: *woollen mills* ▷ *n* **3** woollens woollen clothes, esp. knitted ones

Woolley *n* Sir (**Charles**) **Leonard**. 1880–1960, British archaeologist, noted for his excavations at Ur in Mesopotamia (1922–34)

woolly *or US* **wooly** *adj* **-lier, -liest 1** made of or like wool **2** confused or indistinct: *woolly ideas* ▷ *n, pl* **-lies 3** a woollen garment, such as a sweater

woolshed *n Austral and NZ* a large building in which sheep shearing takes place

Woolworth *n* Frank Winfield. 1852–1919, US merchant; founder of an international chain of department stores selling inexpensive goods

woomera *n* a notched stick used by Australian Aborigines to aid the propulsion of a spear

Woomera *n* a town in South Australia: site of the Long Range Weapons Establishment. Pop: 602 (2001)

Wootton *n* Barbara (**Frances**), Baroness of Abinger. 1897–1988, English economist, educationalist, social scientist, and criminologist

woozy *adj* **woozier, wooziest** *informal* feeling slightly dizzy [origin unknown]

wop-wops *pl n NZ informal* remote rural areas

Worcester *n* **1** a cathedral city in W central England, the administrative centre of Worcestershire on the River Severn: scene of the battle (1651) in which Charles II was defeated by Cromwell. Pop: 94 029 (2001) **2** an industrial city in the US, in central Massachusetts: Clark University (1887). Pop: 175 706 (2003 est) **3** a town in S South Africa; centre of a fruit-growing region. Pop: 66 349 (2001)

Worcester sauce (wooss-ter) *or* **Worcestershire sauce** *n* a sharp-tasting sauce, made from soy sauce, vinegar, and spices

Worcestershire *n* a county of W central England, formerly (1974–98) part of Hereford and Worcester. Administrative centre: Worcester. Pop: 549 300 (2003 est). Area: 1742 sq km (674 sq miles)

Worcs Worcestershire

word *n* **1** the smallest single meaningful unit of speech or writing. Related adjective: **lexical 2** a brief conversation: *I would like a word with you* **3** a brief statement: *a word of warning* **4** news or information: *let me know if you get word of my wife* **5** a solemn promise: *he had given his word as a rabbi* **6** a command or order: *he had only to say the word and they'd hang him* **7** computers a set of bits used to store, transmit, or operate upon an item of information in a computer **8** by word of mouth by spoken rather than by written means: *their reputation spreads by word of mouth* **9** in a word briefly or in short: *in a word, we've won* **10** my word! Also: **upon my word!** *old-fashioned* an exclamation of surprise or amazement **11** take someone at his *or* her word to accept that someone really means what he or she says: *they're willing to take him at his word when he says he'll change* **12** take someone's word for it to believe what someone says **13** the last word the closing remark of a conversation or argument, often regarded as settling an issue **14** the last word in the finest example of: *the last word in comfort* **15** word for word using exactly the same words: *he repeated almost word for word what had been said* **16** word of honour a solemn promise ▷ *vb* **17** to state in words: *the questions have to be carefully worded* ▶ See also **words** [Old English]

Word *n* the Word the message and teachings contained in the Bible

-word *combining form* (preceded by 'the' and an initial letter) a euphemistic way of referring to a word by its first letter because it is considered to be unmentionable by the user: *the c-word, meaning cancer*

word game *n* any game involving the discovery, formation, or alteration of a word or words

wording *n* the way in which words are used to express something: *the exact wording of the regulation has still not been worked out*

word-perfect *adj* able to repeat from memory the exact words of a text one has learned

word processing *n* the storage and organization of text by electronic means, esp. for business purposes

word processor *n* an electronic machine for word processing, consisting of a keyboard, a VDU incorporating a microprocessor, and a printer

words *pl n* **1** the text of a song, as opposed to the music **2** the text of an actor's part **3** have words to have an argument or disagreement **4** in other words expressing the same idea in a different, more understandable, way **5** put into words to express in speech or writing: *she was reluctant to put her thoughts into words*

Wordsworth *n* **1** Dorothy. 1771–1855, English writer, whose *Journals* are noted esp. for their descriptions of nature **2** her brother, **William**. 1770–1850, English poet, whose work, celebrating nature, was greatly inspired by the Lake District, in which he spent most of his life. *Lyrical Ballads* (1798), to which Coleridge contributed, is often taken as the first example of English romantic poetry and includes his *Lines Written above Tintern Abbey*. Among his other works are *The Prelude* (completed in 1805; revised thereafter and published posthumously) and *Poems in Two Volumes* (1807), which includes *The Solitary Reaper* and *Intimations of Immortality* ▷ **Wordsworthian** *adj, n*

wordy *adj* **wordier, wordiest** using too many words, esp. long words: *wordy explanations*

wore *vb* the past tense of **wear**

work *n* **1** physical or mental effort directed to doing or making something **2** paid employment at a job, trade, or profession **3** duties or tasks: *I had to delegate as much work as I could* **4** something done or made as a result of effort: *a work by a major artist* **5** the place where a person is employed: *accidents at work* **6** *physics old-fashioned* the transfer of energy occurring when a force is applied to move a body **7 at work** working or in action: *the social forces at work in society* ▷ *adj* **8** of or for work: *work experience* ▷ *vb* **9** to do work; labour: *no-one worked harder than Arnold* **10** to be employed: *she worked as a waitress* **11** to make (a person or animal) labour **12** to operate (a machine or a piece of equipment) **13** (of a machine or a piece of equipment) to function, esp. effectively: *he doesn't have to know how things work* **14** (of a plan or system) to be successful **15** to cultivate (land) **16** to move gradually into a specific condition or position: *he picked up the shovel, worked it under the ice, and levered* **17** to make (one's way) with effort: *he worked his way to the top* **18** *informal* to manipulate to one's own advantage: *they could see an angle and they'd know how to work it* ▶ See also **work off, works,** etc. [Old English *weorc*]

workable *adj* **1** able to operate efficiently: *a workable solution* **2** able to be used: *a workable mine*

workaday *adj* commonplace or ordinary: *workaday surroundings*

workaholic *n* a person who is obsessed with work

workbench *n* a heavy table at which a craftsman or mechanic works

worker *n* **1** a person who works in a specified way: *a hard worker* **2** a person who works at a specific job: *a government worker* **3** an employee, as opposed to an employer **4** a sterile female bee, ant, or wasp, that works for the colony

work ethic *n* a belief in the moral value of work

workforce *n* **1** the total number of workers employed by a company **2** the total number of people available for work: *the local workforce*

workhorse *n* a person or thing that does a lot of work, esp. dull or routine work: *this plane is the workhorse of most short-haul airlines*

workhouse *n* (formerly, in England) a public institution where very poor people did work in return for food and accommodation

working *adj* **1** having a job: *the working mother* **2** concerned with, used in, or suitable for work: *working conditions* **3** capable of being operated or used: *a working mechanism* ▷ *n* **4** a part of a mine or quarry that is or has been used **5 workings** the way that something works: *the workings of the human brain*

working capital *n* the amount of capital that a business has available to meet the day-to-day cash requirements of its operations

working class *n* **1** the social group that consists of people who earn wages, esp. as manual workers ▷ *adj* **working-class 2** of or relating to the working class: *a working-class neighbourhood*

working day or *especially US and Canad* **workday** *n* **1** a day when people normally go to work: *the last working day of the week* **2** the part of the day allocated to work: *the long working day of twelve to fourteen hours*

Working for Families Tax Credits *n* (in New Zealand) a tax credit given to families on the basis of their income and family size

working party *n* a committee established to investigate a problem

workload *n* the amount of work to be done, esp. in a specified period: *a heavy workload*

workman *n, pl* **-men** a man who is employed to do manual work

workmanlike *adj* skilfully done: *a neat workmanlike job*

workmanship *n* the degree of skill with which an object is made: *shoddy workmanship*

workmate *n informal* a person who works with another person; fellow worker

work of art *n* **1** a piece of fine art, such as a painting or sculpture **2** an object or a piece of work that has been exceptionally skilfully made or produced: *the doll was truly a work of art*

work off *vb* to get rid of, usually by effort: *he went along to the tennis club and worked off his pique there*

work on *vb* to try to persuade or influence (someone)

work out *vb* **1** to solve, find out, or plan by reasoning or calculation: *working out a new budget* **2** to happen in a particular way: *he decided to wait and see how things worked out* **3** to be successful or satisfactory: *the dates never worked out* **4** to take part in physical exercise **5 work out at** to be calculated at (a certain amount): *the return on capital works out at 15 per cent* ▷ *n* **workout 6** a session of physical exercise for training or to keep fit

work over *vb slang* to give (someone) a severe beating: *whoever worked her over did a thorough job*

works *n* **1** a place where something is manufactured: *a chemical works* ▷ *pl n* **2** the sum total of a writer's or artist's achievements considered together: *the works of Goethe* **3 the works** *slang* everything associated with a particular subject or thing: *traditional Indian music, sitars, the works*

worksheet *n* a sheet of paper containing exercises to be completed by a student

workshop *n* **1** a room or building where manufacturing or other manual work is carried on **2** a group of people engaged in intensive study or work in a creative or practical field: *a writers' workshop*

workshy *adj* not inclined to work; lazy

Worksop *n* a town in N central England, in N Nottinghamshire. Pop: 39 072 (2001)

work station *n* **1** an area in an office where one person works **2** *computers* a component of an electronic office system consisting of a VDU and keyboard

worktable *n* a table at which writing, sewing, or other work may be done

worktop *n* a surface in a kitchen, usually the top of a fitted kitchen unit, which is used for food preparation. Also: **work surface**

work-to-rule *n* a form of industrial action in which employees keep strictly to their employers' rules, with the result of reducing the work rate

work up *vb* **1** to make angry, excited, or upset: *he worked himself up into a rage* **2** to build up or develop: *I'd worked up a thirst* **3** to work on (something) in order to improve it: *there was enough material to be worked up into something publishable* **4 work one's way up** to make progress: *he worked his way up in the catering trade* **5 work up to** to develop gradually towards: *the fete worked up to a climax around lunch time*

world *n* **1** the earth as a planet **2** the human race; people generally: *providing food for the world* **3** any planet or moon, esp. one that might be inhabited **4** a particular group of countries or period of history, or its inhabitants: *the Arab world; the post-Cold War world* **5** an area, sphere, or realm considered as a complete environment: *the art world; the world of nature* **6** the total circumstances and experience of a person that make up his or her life: *there may not ever be a place for us in your world* **7 bring into the world** to deliver or give birth to (a baby) **8 come into the world** to be born **9 for all the world** exactly or very much: *they looked for all the world like a pair of newly-weds* **10 in the world** used to emphasize a statement: *she didn't have a worry in the world* **11 man** or **woman of the world** a man or woman who is experienced in social or public life **12 worlds apart** very different from each other: *this man and I are worlds apart* ▷ *adj* **13** of or concerning the entire world: *the world championship* [Old English w(e)orold]

World *n* **The World** a man-made archipelago of 300 reclaimed islands built off the coast of Dubai in the shape of a map of the world. Area: 63 sq km (24 sq miles)

world-class *adj* being as good as anyone else in the world in a particular field: *he has the makings of a world-class batsman*

World Cup *n* an international competition held between national teams in various sports, most notably association football

worldly *adj* **-lier, -liest 1** not spiritual; earthly or temporal: *as a simple monk he had no interest in politics and other worldly affairs* **2** of or relating to material things: *all his worldly goods* **3** wise in the ways of the world; sophisticated: *a suave, worldly, charming Frenchman* **> worldliness** *n*

worldly-wise *adj* wise in the ways of the world; sophisticated

world music *n* popular music of a variety of ethnic origins and styles

world-shaking *adj* of enormous significance; momentous: *world-shaking events*

World Trade Center *n* a name licensed by World Trade Centers Association to its members to identify any of a number of iconic buildings worldwide to promote world trade and international business relationships; one such former building complex, at 417m (1368 ft), the tallest in the US, stood in Manhattan, New York, from 1974 until its destruction on September 11, 2001, in which 2,750 people died; reconstruction of the complex began in 2002. Abbreviation: (trademark) **WTC**

World War I *n* the war (1914–18) between the Allies (principally France, Russia, Britain, Italy, Australia, Canada, and the US) and the Central Powers (principally Germany, Austria-Hungary, and Turkey). Also: **First World War**

World War II *n* the war (1939–45) between the Allies (Britain, France, Australia, the US, and the Soviet Union) and the Axis (Germany, Italy, and Japan). Also: **Second World War**

world-weary *adj* no longer finding pleasure in life

worldwide *adj* applying or extending throughout the world

World Wide Web *n computers* a vast network of hypertext files, stored on computers throughout the world, that can provide a computer user with information on a huge variety of subjects

worm *n* **1** a small invertebrate animal with a long thin body and no limbs **2** an insect larva that looks like a worm **3** a despicable or weak person **4** a slight trace: *a worm of doubt* **5** a shaft on which a spiral thread has been cut, for example in a gear arrangement in which such a shaft drives a toothed wheel **6** *computers* a type of virus ▷ *vb* **7** to rid (an animal) of worms in its intestines **8 worm one's way a** to go or move slowly and with difficulty: *I had to worm my way out sideways from the bench* **b** to get oneself into a certain situation or position gradually: *worming your way into my good books* **9 worm out of** to obtain (information) from someone who is not willing to provide it: *it took me weeks to worm the facts out of him* ▶ See also **worms** [Old English wyrm]

WORM *n computers* write once read many (times): an optical disk which enables users to store their own data

wormcast *n* a coil of earth or sand that has been excreted by a burrowing worm

worm-eaten *adj* eaten into by worms: *worm-eaten beams*

wormhole *n* a hole made by a worm in timber, plants, or fruit

worms *n* a disease caused by parasitic worms living in the intestines

Worms *n* a city in SW Germany, in Rhineland-Palatinate on the Rhine: famous as the seat of imperial diets, notably that of 1521, before which Luther defended his doctrines in the presence of Charles V; river port and manufacturing centre with a large wine trade. Pop: 81 100 (2003 est)

wormwood *n* a plant from which a bitter oil formerly used in making absinthe is obtained [Old English wormōd, wermōd]

wormy *adj* **wormier, wormiest** infested with or eaten by worms

worn *vb* **1** the past participle of **wear** ▷ *adj* **2** showing signs of long use or wear: *the worn soles of his boots* **3** looking tired and ill: *that worn pain-creased face*

worn-out *adj* **1** worn or used until threadbare, valueless, or useless **2** completely exhausted: *worn-out by their exertions*

worried *adj* concerned and anxious about things that may happen **> worriedly** *adv*

worrisome *adj old-fashioned* causing worry

worry *vb* **-ries, -rying, -ried 1** to be or cause to be anxious or uneasy **2** to annoy or bother: *don't worry yourself with the details* **3** (of a dog) to frighten (sheep or other animals) by chasing and trying to bite them **4 worry away at** to struggle with or work on (a problem) ▷ *n, pl* **-ries 5** a state or feeling of anxiety: *he was beside himself with worry* **6** a cause for anxiety: *having a premature baby is much less of a worry these days* [Old English wyrgan] **> worrier** *n*

worry beads *pl n* a string of beads that supposedly relieves nervous tension when fingered or played with

worrying *adj* causing concern and anxiety

worse *adj* **1** the comparative of **bad 2 none the worse for** not harmed by (adverse events or circumstances) **3 the worse for wear** *informal* in a poor condition; not at one's best: *returning the worse for wear from the pub* ▷ *n* **4 for the worse** into a worse condition: *taking a turn for the worse* ▷ *adv* **5** the comparative of **badly 6 worse off** in a worse condition, esp. financially [Old English wiersa]

worsen *vb* to make or become worse **> worsening** *adj, n*

worship *vb* **-shipping, -shipped** or *US* **-shiped 1** to show profound religious devotion to (one's god), for example by praying **2** to have intense love and admiration for (a person) ▷ *n* **3** religious adoration or devotion **4** formal expression of religious adoration, for example by praying **5** intense love or devotion to a person [Old English weorthscipe] **> worshipper** *n*

Worship *n* **Your** or **His** or **Her Worship** *chiefly Brit* a title for a mayor or magistrate

worshipful *adj* feeling or showing reverence or adoration

worst *adj, adv* **1** the superlative of **bad, badly** ▷ *n* **2** the least good or the most terrible person, thing, or part: *the worst is yet to come* **3 at one's worst** in the worst condition or aspect of a thing or person: *the British male is at his worst in July and August* **4 at worst** in the least favourable interpretation or conditions: *all the questions should ideally be answered 'no', or at worst 'sometimes'* ▷ *vb* **5** *old-fashioned* to defeat or beat [Old English wierrest]

worsted (wooss-tid) *n* a close-textured woollen fabric used to make jackets and trousers [after Worstead, a district in Norfolk]

worth *prep* **1** having a value of: *the fire destroyed property worth $200 million* **2** worthy of; meriting or justifying: *if a job is worth doing, it's worth doing well* **3 worth one's weight in gold** extremely useful or helpful; very highly valued **4 worth one's while** worthy of spending one's time or effort on something: *they needed a wage of at least £140 a week to make it worth their while returning to work* ▷ *n* **5** monetary value: *the corporation's net worth* **6** high quality; value: *the submarine proved its military worth during the Second World War*

W

7 the amount of something that can be bought for a specified price: *$10 billion worth of property* [Old English *weorth*]

Worth *n* Charles Frederick. 1825–95, English couturier, who founded Parisian *haute couture*

Worthing *n* a resort in S England, in West Sussex on the English Channel. Pop: 96 964 (2001)

worthless *adj* **1** without value or usefulness: *worthless junk bonds* **2** without merit: *he sees himself as a worthless creature* **> worthlessness** *n*

worthwhile *adj* sufficiently important, rewarding, or valuable to justify spending time or effort on it

worthy *adj* **-thier, -thiest 1** deserving of admiration or respect: *motives which were less than worthy* **2 worthy of** deserving of: *he would practise extra hard to be worthy of such an honour* **>** *n, pl* **-thies 3** *often facetious* an important person **> worthily** *adv* **> worthiness** *n*

Wotton *n* Sir Henry. 1568–1639, English poet and diplomat

would *vb* **1** used as an auxiliary to form the past tense or subjunctive mood of *will*[1]: *he asked if she would marry him; that would be delightful* **2** to express a polite offer or request: *would you like some lunch?* **3** to describe a habitual past action: *sometimes at lunch time I would choose a painting to go and see*

> **USAGE** See at **should**.

would-be *adj* wanting or pretending to be: *would-be brides*
wouldn't would not

wound[1] *n* **1** an injury to the body such as a cut or a gunshot injury **2** an injury to one's feelings or reputation **>** *vb* **3** to cause an injury to the body or feelings of [Old English *wund*] **> wounding** *adj*

wound[2] *vb* the past of **wind**[2]

wove *vb* a past tense of **weave**

woven *vb* a past participle of **weave**

wow *interj* **1** an exclamation of admiration or amazement **>** *n* **2** *slang* a person or thing that is amazingly successful: *he would be an absolute wow on the chat shows* **>** *vb* **3** *slang* to be a great success with: *the new Disney film wowed festival audiences* [Scots]

wowser *n Austral and NZ slang* **1** a fanatically puritanical person **2** a teetotaller [dialect *wow* to complain]

Wozniak *n* Steve, full name *Stephan Gary Wozniak*. born 1950, US computer scientist and executive: co-founder (with Steve Jobs, 1976) of Apple Inc

wp word processor

WP 1 weather permitting **2** word processing **3** word processor **4** (in South Africa) Western (Cape) Province

WPC (in Britain) woman police constable

wpm words per minute

WR Western Region

WRAC (in Britain) Women's Royal Army Corps

wrack[1] *n* same as **rack**[2] [Old English *wræc* persecution]

> **USAGE** The use of the spelling *wrack* rather than *rack* in sentences such as *she was wracked by grief* or *the country was wracked by civil war* is very common but is thought by many people to be incorrect.

wrack[2] *n* seaweed that is floating in the sea or has been washed ashore [probably from Middle Dutch *wrak* wreckage]

WRAF (in Britain) Women's Royal Air Force

wraith *n literary* a ghost [Scots] **> wraithlike** *adj*

Wrangel Island *n* an island in the Arctic Ocean, off the coast of the extreme NE of Russia: administratively part of Russia; mountainous and mostly tundra. Area: about 7300 sq km (2800 sq miles)

Wrangell *n* Mount Wrangell a mountain in S Alaska, in the W Wrangell Mountains. Height: 4269 m (14 005 ft)

Wrangell Mountains *pl n* a mountain range in SE Alaska, extending into the Yukon, Canada. Highest peak: Mount Blackburn, 5037 m (16 523 ft)

wrangle *vb* **-gling, -gled 1** to argue noisily or angrily **>** *n* **2** a noisy or angry argument [Low German *wrangeln*]

wrap *vb* **wrapping, wrapped 1** to fold a covering round (something) and fasten it securely: *a small package wrapped in brown paper* **2** to fold or wind (something) round a person or thing: *she wrapped a handkerchief around her bleeding palm* **3** to fold, wind, or coil: *she wrapped her arms around her mother* **4** to complete the filming of (a motion picture or television programme) **>** *n* **5** *old-fashioned* a garment worn wrapped round the shoulders **6** (in the filming of a motion picture or television programme) the end of a day's filming or the completion of filming **7** a type of sandwich consisting of filling rolled up in a flour tortilla **8** *Brit slang* a small packet of an illegal drug in powder form: *a wrap of heroin* **9 keep something under wraps** to keep something secret [origin unknown]

wraparound *adj* **1** (of a skirt) designed to be worn wrapped round the body **2** extending in a curve from the front round to the sides: *wraparound shades*

wrap party *n* a party held by cast and crew to celebrate the completion of filming of a motion picture or television programme

wrapper *n* a paper, foil, or plastic cover in which a product is wrapped: *a single sweet wrapper*

wrapping *n* a piece of paper, foil, or other material used to wrap something in

wrap up *vb* **1** to fold paper, cloth, or other material round (something) **2** to put warm clothes on: *remember to wrap up warmly on cold or windy days* **3** *informal* to finish or settle: *he will need 60 to 90 days to wrap up his current business dealings* **4** *slang* to stop talking **5 wrapped up in** giving all one's attention to: *wrapped up in her new baby*

wrasse *n* a brightly coloured sea fish [Cornish *wrach*]

wrath (roth) *n old-fashioned or literary* intense anger [Old English *wræththu*] **> wrathful** *adj*

Wrath *n* Cape Wrath a promontory at the NW extremity of the Scottish mainland

wreak *vb* **1 wreak havoc** to cause chaos or damage: *this Australian sun will wreak havoc with your complexions* **2 wreak vengeance on** to take revenge on [Old English *wrecan*]

> **USAGE** See at **wrought**.

wreath *n, pl* **wreaths 1** a ring of flowers or leaves, placed on a grave as a memorial or worn on the head as a garland or a mark of honour **2** anything circular or spiral: *a wreath of smoke* [Old English *writha*]

wreathe *vb* **wreathing, wreathed** *literary* **1 wreathed in a** surrounded by: *wreathed in pipe smoke* **b** surrounded by a ring of: *wreathed in geraniums* **2 wreathed in smiles** smiling broadly

wreck *vb* **1** to break, spoil, or destroy completely **2** to cause the accidental sinking or destruction of (a ship) at sea **>** *n* **3** something that has been destroyed or badly damaged, such as a crashed car or aircraft **4** a ship that has been sunk or destroyed at sea **5** a person in a poor mental or physical state [from Old Norse]

wreckage *n* the remains of something that has been destroyed or badly damaged, such as a crashed car or aircraft

wrecker *n* **1** a person who destroys or badly damages something: *a marriage wrecker* **2** (formerly) a person who lured ships on to the rocks in order to plunder them **3** *chiefly US, Canad and NZ* a person whose job is to demolish buildings or dismantle cars **4** *US and Canad* a breakdown van

wreckers *pl n NZ* a business which sells material from demolished cars or buildings

Wrekin *n* **1 the Wrekin** an isolated hill in the English Midlands in Telford and Wrekin unitary authority, Shropshire. Height: 400 m (1335 ft) **2 round the Wrekin** or **all round the Wrekin** *Midland English dialect* the long way round: *he went all round the Wrekin instead of explaining clearly*

wren *n* a very small brown songbird [Old English *wrenna*]

Wren[1] *n informal* (formerly, in Britain and certain other nations) a member of the former Women's Royal Naval Service [from abbreviation WRNS]

Wren[2] *n* Sir Christopher. 1632–1723, English architect. He designed St Paul's Cathedral and over 50 other London churches after the Great Fire as well as many secular buildings

wrench *vb* **1** to twist or pull (something) violently, for example to remove it from something to which it is attached: *he grabbed the cable and wrenched it out of the wall socket* **2** to move or twist away with a sudden violent effort: *she wrenched free of his embrace* **3** to injure (a limb or joint) by a sudden twist ▷ *n* **4** a violent twist or pull **5** an injury to a limb or joint, caused by twisting it **6** a feeling of sadness experienced on leaving a person or place: *it would be a wrench to leave Essex after all these years* **7** a spanner with adjustable jaws [Old English *wrencan*]

wrest *vb* **1** to take (something) away from someone with a violent pull or twist **2** to seize forcibly by violent or unlawful means: *she must begin to wrest control of the army and the police* [Old English *wræstan*]

wrestle *vb* **-tling, -tled 1** to fight (someone) by grappling and trying to throw or pin him or her to the ground, often as a sport **2** wrestle with to struggle hard with (a person, problem, or thing): *I wrestled with my conscience* [Old English *wræstlian*] **> wrestler** *n*

wrestling *n* a sport in which each contestant tries to overcome the other either by throwing or pinning him or her to the ground or by forcing a submission

wretch *n old-fashioned* **1** a despicable person **2** a person pitied for his or her misfortune [Old English *wrecca*]

wretched (retch-id) *adj* **1** in poor or pitiful circumstances: *a vast wretched slum* **2** feeling very unhappy **3** of poor quality: *the wretched state of the cabbages* **4** *informal* undesirable or displeasing: *what a wretched muddle* **> wretchedly** *adv* **> wretchedness** *n*

Wrexham *n* **1** a town in N Wales, in Wrexham county borough: seat of the Roman Catholic bishopric of Wales (except the former Glamorganshire); formerly noted for coal-mining. Pop: 42 576 (2001) **2** a county borough in NE Wales, created in 1996 from part of Clwyd. Pop: 129 700 (2003 est). Area: 500 sq km (193 sq miles)

wriggle *vb* **-gling, -gled 1** to twist and turn with quick movements: *he wriggled on the hard seat* **2** to move along by twisting and turning **3** wriggle out of to avoid (doing something that one does not want to do): *he wriggled out of donating blood* ▷ *n* **4** a wriggling movement or action [Middle Low German *wriggeln*]

Wright *n* **1** Frank Lloyd. 1869–1959, US architect, whose designs include the Imperial Hotel, Tokyo (1916), the Guggenheim Museum, New York (1943), and many private houses. His "organic architecture" sought a close relationship between buildings and their natural surroundings **2** Joseph, known as *Wright of Derby*. 1734–97, British painter, noted for his paintings of industrial and scientific subjects, esp. *The Orrery* (?1765) and *The Air Pump* (1768) **3** Joseph. 1855–1930, British philologist; editor of *The English Dialect Dictionary* (1898–1905) **4** Judith (**Arundel**). 1915–2000, Australian poet, critic, and conservationist. Her collections of poetry include *The Moving Image* (1946), *Woman to Man* (1949), and *A Human Pattern* (1990) **5** Richard. 1908–60, US Black novelist and short-story writer, best known for the novel *Native Son* (1940) **6** Wilbur (1867–1912) and his brother, **Orville** (1871–1948), US aviation pioneers, who designed and flew the first powered aircraft (1903) **7** William, known as *Billy*. 1924–94, English footballer: winner of 105 caps

wring *vb* **wringing, wrung 1** Also: **wring out** to squeeze water from (a cloth or clothing) by twisting it tightly **2** to twist (a neck) violently **3** to clasp and twist (one's hands) in anguish **4** to grip (someone's hand) vigorously in greeting **5** to obtain by forceful means: *to wring concessions from the army* **6** wring someone's heart to make someone feel sorrow or pity [Old English *wringan*]

wringer *n* same as **mangle**[1] (2)

wringing *adv* wringing wet extremely wet

wrinkle *n* **1** a slight ridge in the smoothness of a surface, such as a crease in the skin as a result of age ▷ *vb* **-kling, -kled 2** to develop or cause to develop wrinkles [Old English *wrinclian* to wind around] **> wrinkled** *or* **wrinkly** *adj*

wrist *n* **1** the joint between the forearm and the hand **2** the part of a sleeve that covers the wrist [Old English]

wristwatch *n* a watch worn strapped round the wrist

writ *n* a formal legal document ordering a person to do or not to do something [Old English]

write *vb* **writing, wrote, written 1** to draw or mark (words, letters, or numbers) on paper or a blackboard with a pen, pencil, or chalk **2** to describe or record (something) in writing: *he began to write his memoirs* **3** to be an author: *he still taught writing, but he didn't write* **4** to write a letter to or correspond regularly with someone: *don't forget to write!* **5** *informal, chiefly US and Canad* to write a letter to (someone): *I wrote him several times* **6** to say or communicate in a letter or a book: *in a recent letter a friend wrote that everything costs more in Russia now* **7** to fill in the details for (a cheque or document) **8** *computers* to record (data) in a storage device **9** write down to record in writing: *write it down if you find it too embarrassing to talk about* [Old English *wrītan*]

write off *vb* **1** *accounting* to cancel (a bad debt) from the accounts **2** to dismiss from consideration: *he wrote her off as a tense woman* **3** to send a written request (for something): *he wrote off for leaflets on the subject* **4** *informal* to damage (a vehicle) beyond repair ▷ *n* **write-off 5** *informal* a vehicle that is damaged beyond repair

write out *vb* **1** to put into writing or reproduce in full form in writing **2** to remove (a character) from a television or radio series: *another actress is to be written out of the BBC soap*

writer *n* **1** a person whose job is writing; author **2** the person who has written something specified: *the writer of this letter is pretty dangerous*

write up *vb* **1** to describe fully, complete, or bring up to date in writing: *she would write up her diary in bed* ▷ *n* **write-up 2** a published account of something, such as a review in a newspaper or magazine: *I see the Herald didn't give you a very good write-up*

writhe *vb* **writhing, writhed** to twist or squirm in pain: *writhing in agony* [Old English *wrīthan*]

writing *n* **1** something that has been written: *the writing on the outer flap was faint* **2** written form: *permission in writing* **3** short for **handwriting 4** a kind or style of writing: *creative writing* **5** the work of a writer: *Wilde never mentioned chess in his writing*

written *vb* **1** the past participle of **write** ▷ *adj* **2** recorded in writing: *written permission*

WRNS (in Britain, formerly) Women's Royal Naval Service

Wrocław *n* an industrial city in SW Poland, on the River Oder: passed to Austria (1527) and to Prussia (1741); returned to Poland in 1945. Pop: 647 000 (2005 est). German name: **Breslau**

wrong *adj* **1** not correct or accurate: *the wrong answers* **2** acting or judging in error; mistaken: *do correct me if I'm wrong* **3** not in accordance with correct or conventional rules or standards; immoral: *this group argues that even gently slapping a child is wrong* **4** not intended or appropriate: *I ordered the wrong things; you've picked the wrong time to ask such questions* **5** being a problem or trouble: *come on, I know when something's wrong* **6** not functioning properly: *there's something wrong with the temperature sensor* **7** denoting the side of cloth that is worn facing inwards ▷ *adv* **8** in a wrong manner: *I guessed wrong* **9** get someone wrong to misunderstand someone: *don't get me wrong, I'm not making threats* **10** get something wrong to make a mistake about something: *he had got his body language wrong*

W

11 go wrong a to turn out badly or not as intended **b** to make a mistake **c** (of a machine) to stop functioning properly: *pilots must be able to react instantly if the automatic equipment suddenly goes wrong* ▷ *n* **12** something bad, immoral, or unjust: *how can such a wrong be redressed?* **13 in the wrong** mistaken or guilty ▷ *vb* **14** to treat (someone) unjustly **15** to think or speak unfairly of (someone) [Old English *wrang* injustice] **› wrongly** *adv*

wrongdoing *n* immoral or illegal behaviour
› wrongdoer *n*

wrong-foot *vb* **1** *sport* to play a shot in such a way as to catch (an opponent) off-balance: *he constantly wrong-footed his opponent with fine passing* **2** to gain an advantage over (someone) by doing something unexpected: *China wrong-footed Vietnam by supporting the peace plan*

wrongful *adj* unjust or illegal: *wrongful imprisonment*
› wrongfully *adv*

wrong-headed *adj* constantly and stubbornly wrong in judgment

wrote *vb* the past tense of **write**

wroth *adj old-fashioned or literary* angry [Old English *wrāth*]

wrought (rawt) *vb* **1** *old-fashioned* a past of **work** ▷ *adj* **2** *metallurgy* shaped by hammering or beating: *wrought copper and brass*

> **USAGE** *Wrought* is sometimes used as if it were the past tense and past participle of *wreak*, as in *the hurricane wrought havoc in coastal areas*. Many people think this use is incorrect.

wrought iron *n* a pure form of iron with a low carbon content, often used for decorative work

wrung *vb* the past of **wring**

WRVS (in Britain) Women's Royal Voluntary Service

wry *adj* **wrier, wriest** *or* **wryer, wryest 1** drily humorous; sardonic: *wry amusement* **2** (of a facial expression) produced by twisting one's features to denote amusement or displeasure: *a small wry smile twisted the corner of his mouth* [Old English *wrīgian* to turn]
› wryly *adv*

wrybill *n* a New Zealand plover whose bill is bent to one side enabling it to search for food beneath stones

wryneck *n* a woodpecker that has a habit of twisting its neck round

wt. weight

WTC World Trade Center

WTO World Trade Organization

Wu *n* **Harry,** real name *Wu Hongda.* born 1937, Chinese dissident and human-rights campaigner, a US citizen from 1994; held in labour camps (1960–79); exiled to the US in 1985 but returned secretly to document forced labour in Chinese prisons

Wuchang *or* **Wu-ch'ang** *n* a former city of E central China: now a part of Wuhan

Wu Di *or* **Wu Ti** *n* 156 BC–86 BC, Chinese emperor (140–86) of the Han dynasty, who greatly extended the Chinese empire and made Confucianism the state religion

Wuhan *n* a city in SE China, in Hubei province, at the confluence of the Han and Yangtze Rivers: formed in 1950 by the union of the cities of Hanyang, Hankou, and Wuchang (the Han Cities); river port and industrial centre; university (1913). Pop: 6 003 000 (2005 est)

Wu Hou *n* 625–705 AD Chinese empress (655–705) of the Tang dynasty

Wuhsien *n* another name for **Suzhou**

Wuhu *n* a port in E China, in E Anhui province on the Yangtze River. Pop: 701 000 (2005 est)

Wu-lu-mu-ch'i *n* a variant of **Urumchi**

Wundt *n* **Wilhelm Max.** 1832–1920, German experimental psychologist

Wuppertal *n* a city in W Germany, in North Rhine-Westphalia state on the **Wupper River** (a Rhine tributary): formed in 1929 from the amalgamation of the towns of Barmen and Elberfeld and other smaller towns; textile centre. Pop: 362 137 (2003 est)

Württemberg *n* a historic region and former state of S Germany; since 1952 part of the state of Baden-Württemberg

Würzburg *n* a city in S central Germany, in NW Bavaria on the River Main: university (1582). Pop: 132 687 (2003 est)

wuss (woos) *or* **wussy** *n, pl* **wusses** *or* **wussies** *slang, chiefly US* a feeble or effeminate person [perhaps from PUSSY[1]]

Wutsin *n* a former name (until 1949) of **Changzhou**

Wuxi, Wusih *or* **Wu-hsi** *n* a city in E China, in S Jiangsu province on the Grand Canal: textile industry. Pop: 1 192 000 (2005 est)

WV, WVa, *or* **W.Va.** West Virginia

WWI World War One

WWII World War Two

WWW World Wide Web

WY *or* **Wy.** Wyoming

Wyatt *n* **1 James.** 1746–1813, British architect; a pioneer of the Gothic Revival **2 Sir Thomas.** ?1503–42, English poet at the court of Henry VIII

wych-elm *or* **witch-elm** *n* a Eurasian elm with long pointed leaves [Old English *wice*]

Wycherley *n* **William.** ?1640–1716, English dramatist. His Restoration comedies include *The Country Wife* (1675) and *The Plain Dealer* (1676)

Wycliffe *or* **Wyclif** *n* **John.** ?1330–84, English religious reformer. A precursor of the Reformation, whose writings were condemned as heretical, he attacked the doctrines and abuses of the Church. He instigated the first complete translation of the Bible into English. His followers were called Lollards. Also: **Wiclif, Wickliffe**
› Wycliffism *or* **Wyclifism** *n*

Wye *n* a river in E Wales and W England, rising in Powys and flowing southeast into Herefordshire, then south to the Severn estuary. Length: 210 km (130 miles)

Wykeham *n* **William of.** 1324–1404, English prelate and statesman, who founded New College, Oxford, and Winchester College: chancellor of England (1367–71; 1389–91); bishop of Winchester (1367–1404)

Wyndham *n* **John,** pseudonym of *John Wyndham Parkes Lucas Beynon Harris.* 1903–69, British writer of science fiction novels and stories. His works include *The Day of the Triffids* (1951), *The Kraken Wakes* (1953), and *The Midwich Cuckoos* (1957)

Wynette *n* **Tammy,** original name *Virginia Wynette Pugh.* 1942–98, US country singer; her bestselling records include "Your Good Girl's Gonna Go Bad" (1967) and "Stand By Your Man" (1969)

Wyn Jones *n* **Ieuan.** born 1949, Welsh politician; leader of Plaid Cymru (2000–2012)

Wyo. Wyoming

Wyoming *n* a state of the western US: consists largely of ranges of the Rockies in the west and north, with part of the Great Plains in the east and several regions of hot springs. Capital: Cheyenne. Pop: 501 242 (2003 est). Area: 253 597 sq km (97 914 sq miles). Abbreviation: **Wyo., Wy.,** (with zip code) **WY**

Wyomingite *n* a native or inhabitant of Wyoming

WYSIWYG *n, adj computers* what you see is what you get: referring to what is displayed on the screen being the same as what will be printed out

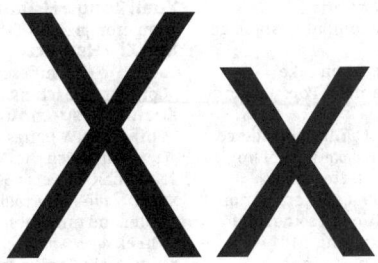

X *maths* **1** (along with y and z) an unknown quantity **2** the multiplication symbol

X 1 indicating an error, a choice, or a kiss **2** indicating an unknown, unspecified, or variable factor, person, or thing: *Miss X* **3** the Roman numeral for ten **4** (formerly) indicating a film that may not be publicly shown to anyone under 18: since 1982 replaced by symbol 18

Xanthian *adj* of or relating to the ancient Lycian city of Xanthus or its inhabitants

Xanthippe *or* **Xantippe** *n* **1** the wife of Socrates, proverbial as a scolding and quarrelsome woman **2** any nagging, peevish, or irritable woman

Xanthus *n* the chief city of ancient Lycia in SW Asia Minor: source of some important antiquities

Xavier *n* Saint Francis, known as the *Apostle of the Indies*. 1506–52, Spanish missionary, who was a founding member of the Jesuit society (1534) and later preached in Goa, Ceylon (Sri Lanka), the East Indies, and Japan. Feast day: Dec 3

X-chromosome *n* the sex chromosome that occurs in pairs in the females of many animals, including humans, and as one of a pair with the Y-chromosome in males

Xe *chem* xenon

Xenakis *n* Iannis. 1922–2001, Greek composer and musical theorist, born in Romania: later a French citizen. He was noted for his use of computers in composition: his works include *ST/10-1, 080262* (1962) and *Dox-orkh* (1991)

Xenocrates *n* ?396–314 BC, Greek Platonic philosopher **>** **Xenocratic** *adj*

xenon *n chem* a colourless odourless gas found in minute quantities in the air. Symbol: **Xe** [Greek: something strange]

Xenophanes *n* ?570–?480 BC, Greek philosopher and poet, noted for his monotheism and regarded as a founder of the Eleatic school

xenophobia (zen-oh-**fobe**-ee-a) *n* hatred or fear of foreigners or strangers [Greek *xenos* foreign + *phobos* fear] **>** **xenophobic** *adj*

Xenophon *n* 431–?355 BC, Greek general and historian; a disciple of Socrates. He accompanied Cyrus the Younger against Artaxerxes II and, after Cyrus' death at Cunaxa (401), he led his army of 10 000 Greek soldiers to the Black Sea, an expedition described in his *Anabasis*. His other works include *Hellenica*, a history of Greece, and the *Memorabilia, Apology*, and *Symposium*, which contain recollections of Socrates

Xeres *n* the former name of **Jerez**

xerography (zeer-**og**-ra-fee) *n* a photocopying process in which an image of the written or printed material is electrically charged on a surface and attracts oppositely charged dry ink particles which are then fixed by heating [Greek *xēros* dry + -GRAPHY] **>** **xerographic** *adj*

Xerox (**zeer**-ox) *n trademark* **1** a machine for copying printed material **2** a copy made by a Xerox machine ▷ *vb*

3 to produce a copy of (a document) using such a machine

Xerxes I *n* ?519–465 BC, king of Persia (485–465), who led a vast army against Greece. His forces were victorious at Thermopylae but his fleet was defeated at Salamis (480) and his army at Plataea (479)

Xhosa (**kawss**-a) *n* **1** (*pl* **-sa** *or* **-sas**) a member of a Black people living in the Republic of South Africa **2** the language of this people **>** **Xhosan** *adj*

Xi, Hsi *or* **Si** *n* a river in S China, rising in Yunnan province and flowing east to the Canton delta on the South China Sea: the main river system of S China. Length: about 1900 km (1200 miles)

Xia Gui *or* **Hsia Kuei** *n* ?1180–1230, Chinese landscape painter of the Sung dynasty; noted for his misty mountain landscapes in ink monochrome

Xiamen *n* a variant transliteration of the Chinese name for **Amoy**

Xi'an, Hsian *or* **Sian** *n* an industrial city in central China, capital of Shaanxi province: capital of China for 970 years at various times between the 3rd century BC and the 10th century AD; seat of the Northwestern University (1937); famous for Qin dynasty emperor Qinshihuang's tomb (207 BC) with 8000-strong terracotta army. Pop: 3 256 000 (2005 est). Former names: **Changan, Siking**

Xiang, Hsiang *or* **Siang** *n* **1** a river in SE central China, rising in NE Guangxi and flowing northeast and north to Dongting Lake. Length: about 1150 km (715 miles) **2** a river in S China, rising in SE Yunnan and flowing generally east to the Hongxiu (the upper course of the Xi River). Length: about 800 km (500 miles)

Xiangtan *or* **Siangtan** *n* a city in S central China, in NE Hunan on the Xiang River: centre of a region noted for tea production. Pop: 592 000 (2005 est)

Xi Jinping *n* born 1953, Chinese Communist statesman; president of China from 2013

Xingú *n* a river in central Brazil, rising on the Mato Grosso plateau and flowing north to the Amazon delta, with over 650 km (400 miles) of rapids in its middle course. Length: 1932 km (1200 miles)

Xining, Hsining *or* **Sining** *n* a city in W China, capital of Qinghai province, at an altitude of 2300 m (7500 ft). Pop: 689 000 (2005 est)

Xinjiang Uygur Autonomous Region *or* **Sinkiang-Uighur Autonomous Region** *n* an administrative division of NW China: established in 1955 for the Uygur ethnic minority, with autonomous subdivisions for other small minorities; produces over half China's wool and contains valuable mineral resources. Capital: Ürümqi. Pop: 19 340 000 (2003 est). Area: 1 646 799 sq km (635 829 sq miles)

Xixón *n* the Asturian name for **Gijón**

Xizang Autonomous Region *n* the Pinyin transliteration of the Chinese name for **Tibet**

Xmas (**eks**-mass) *n informal* short for **Christmas** [from the

Greek letter *chi* (X), first letter of *Khristos* Christ]

XML extensible markup language: a computer language used in text formatting

Xochimilco *n* a town in central Mexico, on Lake Xochimilco: noted for its floating gardens. Pop: 364 647 (2000)

X-rated *adj* **1** (formerly, in Britain) (of a film) considered suitable for viewing by adults only **2** *informal* involving bad language, violence, or sex: *an X-rated conversation*

X-ray *or* **x-ray** *n* **1** a stream of electromagnetic radiation of short wavelength that can pass through some solid materials **2** a picture produced by exposing photographic film to X-rays: used in medicine as a diagnostic aid, since parts of the body, such as bones, absorb X-rays and so appear as opaque areas on the picture ▷ *vb* **3** to photograph, treat, or examine using X-rays

X-ray diffraction *n physics* the scattering of X-rays on contact with matter, resulting in changes in radiation intensity, which is used for studying atomic structure

Xuan Zang *or* **Hsüan-tsang** *n* 602–664 AD, Chinese Buddhist monk, who travelled to India to study the Buddhist scriptures, many of which he translated into Chinese: noted also for his account of his travels

Xuan Zong *or* **Hsüan-tsung** *n* 685–762 AD, Chinese emperor (712–56) of the Tang dynasty

Xun Zi *or* **Hsün-tzu** *n* original name *Hsun Kuang*. c. 300 BC–c. 230 BC, Chinese philosopher, who systematized Confucian teaching

Xuzhou, Hsü-chou *or* **Süchow** *n* a city in N central China, in NW Jiangsu province: scene of a decisive battle (1949) in which the Communists defeated the Nationalists. Pop: 1 662 000 (2005 est)

xylem (zile-em) *n botany* a plant tissue that conducts water and mineral salts from the roots to all other parts [Greek *xulon* wood]

xylene (zile-lean) *n chem* a hydrocarbon existing in three isomeric forms, all three being colourless flammable volatile liquids used as solvents and in the manufacture of synthetic resins, dyes, and insecticides [Greek *xulon* wood]

xylitol *n chem* an artificial sweetener produced from xylose and used esp. in chewing gum

xylophone (zile-oh-fone) *n music* a percussion instrument consisting of a set of wooden bars played with hammers [Greek *xulon* wood] **> xylophonist** *n*

xylose *n* a white crystalline sugar derived from wood and straw

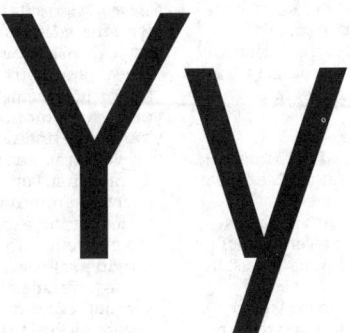

y *maths* (along with *x* and *z*) an unknown quantity

Y 1 an unknown, unspecified, or variable factor, number, person, or thing **2** *chem* yttrium

Y2K *n informal* name for the year 2000 AD (esp. referring to the millennium bug)

ya *interj S African* yes

yabby *n, pl* **-bies** *Austral* **1** a small freshwater crayfish **2** a marine prawn used as bait [from a native Australian language]

Yablonovy Mountains *pl n* a mountain range in Siberia. Highest peak: 1680 m (5512 ft). Also called: **Yablonoi Mountains**

yacht (yott) *n* **1** a large boat with sails or an engine, used for racing or pleasure cruising ▷ *vb* **2** to sail or cruise in a yacht [obsolete Dutch *jaghte*] ▷ **yachting** *n, adj*

yachtsman *or fem* **yachtswoman** *n, pl* **-men** *or* **-women** a person who sails a yacht

yack *n, vb* same as **yak²**

Yafo *n* transliteration of the Hebrew name for **Jaffa** (1)

yah *interj* **1** *informal* same as **yes 2** an exclamation of derision or disgust

yahoo *n, pl* **-hoos** a crude, brutish, or obscenely coarse person [after the brutish creatures in *Gulliver's Travels*]

yahweh *or* **yahveh** *n Bible* a personal name of god [Hebrew YHVH, with conjectural vowels]

yak¹ *n* a Tibetan ox with long shaggy hair [Tibetan *gyag*]

yak² *slang* **1** noisy, continuous, and trivial talk ▷ *vb* **yakking, yakked 2** to talk continuously about unimportant matters [imitative]

yakka *n Austral and NZ informal* work [from a native Australian language]

Yakutsk *n* a port in E Russia, capital of the Sakha Republic (Yakutia), on the Lena River. Pop: 214 000 (2005 est)

Yale lock *n trademark* a type of cylinder lock using a flat serrated key [after L. *Yale*, inventor]

Yalta *n* a port and resort in the Crimea on the Black Sea: scene of a conference (1945) between Churchill, Roosevelt, and Stalin, who met to plan the final defeat and occupation of Nazi Germany. Pop: 80 552 (2005 est)

Yalu *n* a river in E Asia, rising in N North Korea and flowing southwest to Korea Bay, forming a large part of the border between North Korea and NE China. Length: 806 km (501 miles)

yam *n* **1** a twining plant of tropical and subtropical regions, cultivated for its starchy roots which are eaten as a vegetable **2** the sweet potato [Portuguese *inhame*]

Yamagata *n* Prince Aritomo. 1838–1922, Japanese soldier and politician. As war minister (1873) and chief of staff (1878), he modernized Japan's military system. He was premier of Japan (1889–93; 1898)

Yamani *n* Sheikh Ahmed Zaki. born 1930, Saudi Arabian politician; minister of petroleum and mineral resources (1962–86)

Yamasaki *n* Minoru. 1912–86, US architect. His buildings include St Louis Airport, Missouri (1953–55) and the World Trade Center, New York (1970–77)

Yamashita *n* Tomoyuki. 1885–1946, Japanese general. He commanded Japanese forces in the Malayan campaign in World War II and took Singapore (1942); captured (1945) and hanged

yammer *informal vb* **1** to whine in a complaining manner ▷ *n* **2** a yammering sound **3** nonsense or jabber [Old English *geōmrian* to grumble]

Yamoussoukro *n* the capital of Côte d'Ivoire, situated in the S centre of the country. It replaced Abidjan as capital in 1983. Pop: 468 000 (2005 est)

Yanan *or* **Yenan** *n* a city in NE China, in N Shaanxi province: political and military capital of the Chinese Communists (1935–49). Pop: 343 000 (2005 est). Also called: **Fushih**

Yang¹ *n* See Yin and Yang

Yang² *n* Chen Ning. born 1922, US physicist, born in China: with Tsung-Dao Lee, he disproved the physical principle known as the conservation of parity and shared the Nobel prize for physics (1957)

Yangon *n* the largest city and chief port of Myanmar (Burma): officially superseded as capital in 2006 by Nay Pyi Taw (Naypyidaw), though still retaining some of the functions of government; an industrial city and transport centre; dominated by the gold-covered Shwe Dagon pagoda, 112 m (368 ft) high. Pop: 4 082 000 (2005 est). Former name (official until 1989, still widely used in English): **Rangoon**

Yangtze *n* the longest river in China, rising in SE Qinghai province and flowing east to the East China Sea near Shanghai: a major commercial waterway in one of the most densely populated areas of the world. The **Three Gorges dam** near Yichang, the world's biggest hydroelectric and flood-control project, was begun in 1994 and the dam was completed in 2003, with filling taking several years thereafter. Length: 5528 km (3434 miles). Also: **Yangtze Kiang, Chang Jiang, Chang**

Yanina *n* a variant spelling of **Ioánnina**

yank *vb* **1** to pull (someone or something) with a sharp movement: *I yanked myself out of the water* ▷ *n* **2** a sudden pull or jerk [origin unknown]

Yank *n slang* a person from the United States

Yankee *n* **1** *slang* same as **Yank 2** a person from the Northern United States ▷ *adj* **3** of or characteristic of Yankees [perhaps from Dutch *Jan Kees* John Cheese, nickname for English colonists]

Yantai, Yentai *or* **Yen-t'ai** *n* a port in E China, in NE Shandong. Pop: 1 707 000 (2005 est). Also called: **Chefoo**

Yaoundé *or* **Yaunde** *n* the capital of Cameroon, in the southwest: University of Cameroon (1962). Pop: 1 727 000 (2005 est)

yap *vb* **yapping, yapped 1** to bark with a high-pitched sound **2** *informal* to talk at length in an annoying or stupid way ▷ *n* **3** a high-pitched bark **4** *slang* annoying or stupid speech [imitative] ▷ **yappy** *adj*

Yap *n* a group of four main islands in the W Pacific, in the W Caroline Islands: administratively a district of the US Trust Territory of the Pacific Islands from 1947; became self-governing in 1979 as part of the Federated States of Micronesia; important Japanese naval base in World War II. Pop: 11 647 (2006 est). Area: 101 sq km (39 sq miles)

Yapurá *n* the Spanish name for **Japurá**

Yaqui *n* a river in NW Mexico, rising near the border with the US and flowing south to the Gulf of California. Length: about 676 km (420 miles)

yarborough *n bridge, whist* a hand in which no card is higher than nine [supposedly after the second earl of *Yarborough*, said to have bet a thousand to one against its occurrence]

yard¹ *n* **1** a unit of length equal to 3 feet (0.9144 metre) **2** *nautical* a spar slung across a ship's mast to extend the sail [Old English *gierd* rod, twig]

yard² *n* **1** a piece of enclosed ground, often adjoining or surrounded by a building or buildings **2** an enclosed or open area where a particular type of work is done: *a shipbuilding yard* **3** *US, Canad and Austral* the garden of a house **4** *US and Canad* the winter pasture of deer, moose, and similar animals [Old English *geard*]

Yard *n* the Yard *Brit informal* short for **Scotland Yard**

yardarm *n nautical* the outer end of a ship's yard

yardstick *n* **1** a measure or standard used for comparison: *there's no yardstick for judging a problem of this sort* **2** a graduated measuring stick one yard long

Yarkand *n* another name for **Shache**

Yarmouth *n* short for **Great Yarmouth**

yarmulke (yar-mull-ka) *n* a skullcap worn by Jewish men [Yiddish]

yarn *n* **1** a continuous twisted strand of natural or synthetic fibres, used for knitting or making cloth **2** *informal* a long involved story **3 spin a yarn** *informal* to tell such a story [Old English *gearn*]

Yaroslavl *n* a city in W Russia, on the River Volga: a major trading centre since early times and one of the first industrial centres in Russia; textile industries were established in the 18th century. Pop: 609 000 (2005 est)

Yarra River *n* a river in SE Australia, rising in the Great Dividing Range and flowing west and southwest through Melbourne to Port Phillip Bay. Length: 250 km (155 miles)

yarrow *n* a wild plant with flat clusters of white flowers [Old English *gearwe*]

yashmak *n* a veil worn by a Muslim woman to cover her face in public [Arabic]

Yathrib *n* the ancient Arabic name for **Medina**

Yaunde *n* a variant spelling of **Yaoundé**

Yavarí *n* the Spanish name for **Javari**

yaw *vb* **1** (of an aircraft or ship) to turn to one side or from side to side while moving ▷ *n* **2** the act or movement of yawing [origin unknown]

yawl *n* **1** a two-masted sailing boat **2** a ship's small boat [Dutch *jol* or Middle Low German *jolle*]

yawn *vb* **1** to open one's mouth wide and take in air deeply, often when sleepy or bored **2** to be open wide as if threatening to engulf someone or something: *the doorway yawned blackly open at the end of the hall* ▷ *n* **3** the act or an instance of yawning [Old English *geonian*] ▷ **yawning** *adj*

yaws *n* an infectious disease of tropical climates characterized by red skin eruptions [Carib]

Yazd *or* **Yezd** *n* a city in central Iran: a major centre of silk weaving. Pop: 436 000 (2005 est)

Yb *chem* ytterbium

Y-chromosome *n* the sex chromosome that occurs as one of a pair with the X-chromosome in the males of many animals, including humans

yd yard (measure)

YDT Yukon Daylight Time

ye¹ (yee) *pron old-fashioned or dialect* you [Old English *gē*]

ye² *adj* (*definite article*) *old-fashioned or humorous* the: *ye olde*

Rose and Crown pub [a misinterpretation of *the*, written with the old letter thorn (þ), representing *th*]

yea *interj* **1** *old-fashioned* yes ▷ *adv* **2** *old-fashioned or literary* indeed or truly: *they wandered about the church, yea, even unto the altar* [Old English *gēa*]

yeah *interj informal* same as **yes**

year *n* **1** the time taken for the earth to make one revolution around the sun, about 365 days **2** the twelve months from January 1 to December 31 **3** a period of twelve months from any specified date **4** a specific period of time, usually occupying a definite part or parts of a twelve-month period, used for some particular activity: *the financial year* **5** a group of people who have started an academic course at the same time **6 year in, year out** regularly or monotonously, over a long period **7 years a** a long time: *the legal case could take years to resolve* **b** age, usually old age: *a man of his years* [Old English *gēar*]

> **USAGE** In writing spans of years, it is important to choose a style that avoids ambiguity. The practice adopted in this dictionary is, in four-figure dates, to specify the last two digits of the second date if it falls within the same century as the first: *1801–08; 1850–51; 1899–1901*. In writing three-figure BC dates, it is advisable to give both dates in full: *159–156BC*, not *159–56BC* unless of course the span referred to consists of 103 years rather than three years. It is also advisable to specify BC or AD in years under 1000 unless the context makes this self-evident.

yearbook *n* a reference book published once a year containing details of events of the previous year

yearling *n* an animal that is between one and two years old

yearly *adj* **1** occurring, done, or appearing once a year or every year **2** lasting or valid for a year: *the yearly cycle* ▷ *adv* **3** once a year

yearn *vb* **1** to have an intense desire or longing: *he often yearned for life in a country town* **2** to feel tenderness or affection: *I yearn for you* [Old English *giernan*] ▷ **yearning** *n, adj*

yeast *n* a yellowish fungus used in fermenting alcoholic drinks and in raising dough for bread [Old English *giest*] ▷ **yeasty** *adj*

Yeats *n* **1** Jack Butler. 1871–1957, Irish painter **2** his brother W(illiam) B(utler). 1865–1939, Irish poet and dramatist. His collections of verse include *Responsibilities* (1914), *The Tower* (1928), and *The Winding Stair* (1929). Among his plays are *The Countess Cathleen* (1892) and *Cathleen ni Houlihan* (1902); he was a founder of the Irish National Theatre Company at the Abbey Theatre in Dublin. He was awarded the Nobel prize for literature in 1923

yebo *interj S African informal* yes [Zulu *yebo* yes, I agree]

Yeisk, Yeysk *or* **Eisk** *n* a port and resort in SW Russia, on the Sea of Azov. Pop: 86 349 (2002)

Yekaterinburg *or* **Ekaterinburg** *n* a city in NW Russia, in the Ural Mountains: scene of the execution (1918) of Nicholas II and his family; university (1920); one of the largest centres of heavy engineering in Russia. Pop: 1 281 000 (2005 est). Former name (1924–91): **Sverdlovsk**

Yekaterinodar *or* **Ekaterinodar** *n* the former name (until 1920) of **Krasnodar**

Yekaterinoslav *or* **Ekaterinoslav** *n* the former name (1787–96, 1802–1926) of **Dnepropetrovsk**

Yelisavetgrad *or* **Elisavetgrad** *n* the former name (until 1924) of **Kirovograd**

Yelisavetpol *or* **Elisavetpol** *n* the former name (until 1920) of **Gandzha**

yell *vb* **1** to shout, scream, or cheer in a loud or piercing way ▷ *n* **2** a loud piercing cry of pain, anger, or fear [Old English *giellan*]

yellow *n* **1** the colour of a lemon or an egg yolk **2** anything yellow, such as yellow clothing or yellow paint: *painted in yellow* ▷ *adj* **3** of the colour yellow; of the

y

colour of a lemon or an egg yolk **4** *informal* cowardly or afraid **5** having a yellowish complexion ▷ *vb* **6** to make or become yellow or yellower [Old English *geolu*] ❭ **yellowish** *or* **yellowy** *adj*

yellow-belly *n, pl* **-bellies** *slang* a coward ❭ **yellow-bellied** *adj*

yellow card *n soccer* a piece of yellow pasteboard raised by a referee to indicate that a player has been booked for a serious violation of the rules

yellow fever *n* an acute infectious tropical disease causing fever and jaundice, caused by certain mosquitoes

yellowfin tuna *n* a large marine food fish of tropical and subtropical waters

yellowhammer *n* a European songbird with a yellowish head and body [origin unknown]

Yellowknife *n* a city in N Canada, capital of the Northwest Territories on Great Slave Lake. Pop: 19 234 (2011)

Yellow Pages *pl n trademark* a telephone directory that lists businesses under the headings of the type of business or service they provide

Yellow River *n* the second longest river in China, rising in SE Qinghai and flowing east, south, and east again to the Gulf of Bohai south of Tianjin; it has changed its course several times in recorded history. Length: about 4350 km (2700 miles). Chinese name: **Hwang Ho**

Yellow Sea *n* a shallow arm of the Pacific between Korea and NE China. Area: about 466 200 sq km (180 000 sq miles). Chinese name: **Hwang Hai**

Yellowstone *n* a river rising in N Wyoming and flowing north through Yellowstone National Park, then east to the Missouri. Length: 1080 km (671 miles)

Yellowstone Falls *pl n* a waterfall in NW Wyoming, in Yellowstone National Park on the Yellowstone River

Yellowstone National Park *n* a national park in the NW central US, mostly in NW Wyoming: the oldest and largest national park in the US, containing unusual geological formations and geysers. Area: 8956 sq km (3458 sq miles)

yellow streak *n informal* a cowardly or weak trait

yelp *vb* **1** to utter a sharp or high-pitched cry of pain ▷ *n* **2** a sharp or high-pitched cry of pain [Old English *gielpan* to boast]

Yeltsin *n* Boris (**Nicolayevich**). 1931–2007, Russian politician: president of the Russian Soviet Federative Socialist Republic (1990–91); president of Russia (1991–99)

Yemen *n* a republic in SW Arabia, on the Red Sea and the Gulf of Aden: formed in 1990 from the union of North Yemen and South Yemen: consists of arid coastal lowlands, rising to fertile upland valleys and mountains in the west and to the Hadhramaut plateau in the SE: the north and east contains part of the Great Sandy Desert. Official language: Arabic. Official religion: Muslim. Currency: riyal. Capital: San'a. Pop: 25 408 288 (2005 est). Area (including territory claimed by Yemen along the undemarcated eastern border with Saudi Arabia): 472 099 sq km (182 278 sq miles). Official name: **Yemen Republic**. See also **North Yemen, South Yemen**

Yemeni *adj* **1** of or relating to Yemen or its inhabitants ▷ *n* **2** a native or inhabitant of Yemen

yen[1] *n, pl* **yen** the standard monetary unit of Japan [Japanese *en*]

yen[2] *informal n* **1** a longing or desire ▷ *vb* **yenning, yenned 2** to have a longing [perhaps from Chinese *yän* a craving]

Yenan *n* a variant transliteration of the Chinese name for **Yanan**

Yenisei *or* **Yenisey** *n* a river in central Russia, in central Siberia, formed by the confluence of two headstreams in the Tuva Republic: flows west and north to the Arctic Ocean; the largest river in volume in Russia. Length: 4129 km (2566 miles)

Yentai *or* **Yen-t'ai** *n* a variant transliteration of the Chinese name for **Yantai**

yeoman (yo-man) *n, pl* **-men** *history* a farmer owning and farming his own land [perhaps from *yongman* young man]

yeoman of the guard *n* a member of the ceremonial bodyguard (**Yeomen of the Guard**) of the British monarch

yeomanry *n* **1** yeomen collectively **2** (in Britain) a former volunteer cavalry force

yep *interj informal* same as **yes**

Yerevan *n* the capital of Armenia: founded in the 8th century BC; an industrial city and a main focus of trade routes since ancient times; university. Pop: 1 066 000 (2005 est). Also called: **Erevan, Erivan**

Yerwa-Maiduguri *n* another name for **Maiduguri**

yes *interj* **1** used to express consent, agreement, or approval, or to answer when one is addressed **2** used to signal someone to speak or keep speaking, enter a room, or do something ▷ *n* **3** an answer or vote of *yes* **4** a person who answers or votes *yes* [Old English *gēse*]

Yeşil Irmak *n* a river in N Turkey, flowing northwest to the Black Sea. Length: 418 km (260 miles). Ancient name: **Iris**

Yeşilköy *n* the Turkish name for **San Stefano**

yes man *n* a person who always agrees with his or her superior in order to gain favour

yesterday *n* **1** the day before today **2** the recent past ▷ *adv* **3** on or during the day before today **4** in the recent past

yesteryear *formal or literary n* **1** last year or the past in general ▷ *adv* **2** during last year or the past in general

yet *conj* **1** nevertheless or still: *I'm too tired to work, yet I have to go on* ▷ *adv* **2** up until then or now: *this may be her most rewarding book yet* **3** still: *yet more work to do* **4** now (as contrasted with later): *not ready for that yet* **5** eventually in spite of everything: *I'll break your spirit yet!* **6 as yet** up until then or now [Old English *gīeta*]

yeti *n* same as **abominable snowman** [Tibetan]

Yevtushenko *n* Yevgeny Aleksandrovich. born 1933, Russian poet. His often outspoken poetry includes *Babi Yar* (1962), *Bratsk Station* (1966), and *Farewell to Red Banner* (1992)

yew *n* an evergreen tree with needle-like leaves, red berries, and fine-grained elastic wood [Old English *īw*]

Yeysk *n* a variant spelling of **Yeisk**

Yezd *n* a variant of **Yazd**

Y-fronts *pl n trademark* men's or boys' underpants that have a front opening within an inverted Y shape

YHA (in Britain) Youth Hostels Association

Yibin *or* **I-pin** *n* a port in S central China, in Sichuan province: a commercial centre. Pop: 784 000 (2005 est)

Yichang, Ichang *or* **I-ch'ang** *n* a port in S central China, in Hubei province on the Yangtze River 1600 km (1000 miles) from the East China Sea: the Three Gorges dam, the world's biggest hydroelectric and flood-control project, is nearby. Pop: 724 000 (2005 est)

yid *n slang, offensive* a Jew [probably from *Yiddish*]

Yiddish *n* **1** a language derived from High German, spoken by Jews in Europe and elsewhere by Jewish emigrants, and usually written in the Hebrew alphabet ▷ *adj* **2** of this language [German *jüdisch* Jewish]

yield *vb* **1** to produce or bear **2** to give as a return: *some of his policies have yielded large savings* **3** to give up control of; surrender **4** to give way, submit, or surrender, through force or persuasion: *the players finally yielded to the weather* **5** to agree (to): *governments too weak to say no repeatedly yielded to petitions for charters* **6** to grant or allow: *to yield right of way* ▷ *n* **7** the amount produced [Old English *gieldan*]

yielding *adj* **1** compliant or submissive **2** soft or flexible: *he landed on a yielding surface rather than rock or board*

Yin and Yang *n* two complementary principles of Chinese philosophy: Yin is negative, dark, and feminine, Yang is positive, bright, and masculine [Chinese *yin* dark + *yang* bright]

Yinchuan, Yin-ch'uan *or* **Yinchwan** *n* a city in N central China, capital of Ningxia, on the Yellow River. Pop: 642 000 (2005 est)

y

Yingkou or **Yingkow** n a port in NE China, in SW Liaoning province: a major shipping centre for Manchuria. Pop: 723 000 (2005 est)

yippee interj an exclamation of joy, pleasure, or anticipation

YMCA Young Men's Christian Association

yo interj an expression used as a greeting or to attract someone's attention [origin unknown]

yob or **yobbo** n, pl **yobs** or **yobbos** Brit, Austral and NZ slang a bad-mannered aggressive youth [perhaps back slang for boy] › **yobbish** adj

Yobe n a state of Nigeria, in the NE. Capital: Damaturu. Pop: 2 321 591 (2006). Area: 45 502 sq km (17 568 sq miles)

yodel vb **-delling, -delled** or US **-deling, -deled** 1 to sing with abrupt changes back and forth between the normal voice and falsetto, as in folk songs of the Swiss Alps ▷ n 2 the act or sound of yodelling [German jodeln (imitative)] › **yodeller** or US **yodeler** n

yoga n 1 a Hindu system of philosophy aiming at spiritual, mental, and physical wellbeing by means of deep meditation, prescribed postures, and controlled breathing 2 a system of exercising involving such meditation, postures, and breathing [Sanskrit: a yoking]

yogi n a person who practises or is a master of yoga

yogurt or **yoghurt** n a slightly sour custard-like food made from milk curdled by bacteria, often sweetened and flavoured with fruit [Turkish]

Yogyakarta n a city in S Indonesia, in central Java: seat of government of Indonesia (1946–49); university (1949). Pop: 396 711 (2000). Former spellings: **Jogjakarta, Jokjakarta**

yoke n, pl **yokes** or **yoke** 1 a wooden frame with a bar put across the necks of two animals to hold them together so that they can be worked as a team 2 a pair of animals joined by a yoke 3 a frame fitting over a person's shoulders for carrying buckets 4 an oppressive force or burden: people are still suffering under the yoke of slavery 5 a fitted part of a garment to which a fuller part is attached ▷ vb **yoking, yoked** 6 to put a yoke on 7 to unite or link [Old English geoc]

yokel n disparaging a person who lives in the country, esp. one who appears simple and old-fashioned [perhaps from dialect yokel green woodpecker]

Yokohama n a port in central Japan, on SE Honshu on Tokyo Bay: a major port and the country's second largest city situated in the largest and most populous industrial region of Japan. Pop: 3 433 612 (2002 est)

Yokosuka n a port in Japan, in SE Honshu: a major naval base with shipbuilding industries. Pop: 434 613 (2002 est)

yolk n the yellow part in the middle of an egg that provides food for the developing embryo [Old English geoloca]

Yom Kippur n an annual Jewish holiday celebrated as a day of fasting, with prayers of penitence [Hebrew yōm day + kippūr atonement]

yon adj 1 chiefly Scot and N English dialect that: yon dog ▷ adv 2 yonder: he flicked glances hither and yon ▷ pron 3 that person or thing: yon was a pretty sight [Old English geon]

yonder adv 1 over there ▷ adj 2 situated over there: a tree at yonder waterfall [Old English geond]

Yonge n Charlotte M(ary). 1823–1901, British novelist, whose works reflect the religious ideals of the Oxford Movement. Her best-known book is The Heir of Redclyffe (1853)

Yong Lo or **Yung-Lo** n also called Ch'eng Tsu. 1360–1424, Chinese emperor (1404–24) of the Ming dynasty. He moved the capital from Nanjing to Peking (now Beijing), which he rebuilt

Yonkers n a city in SE New York State, near New York City on the Hudson River. Pop: 197 388 (2003 est)

yonks pl n informal a very long time: he must have been planning this for yonks [origin unknown]

Yonne n 1 a department of N central France, in Burgundy region. Capital: Auxerre. Pop: 335 917 (2003 est). Area: 7461 sq km (2910 sq miles) 2 a river in N France, flowing generally northwest to the Seine at Montereau. Length: 290 km (180 miles)

yoo-hoo interj a call to attract a person's attention

yore n of yore a long time ago: in days of yore [Old English geāra]

York[1] n 1 a historic city in NE England, in York unitary authority, North Yorkshire, on the River Ouse: the military capital of Roman Britain; capital of the N archiepiscopal province of Britain since 625, with a cathedral (the Minster) begun in 1154; noted for its cycle of medieval mystery plays; unusually intact medieval walls; university (1963). Pop: 137 505 (2001). Latin name: **Eboracum** 2 a unitary authority in NE England, in North Yorkshire. Pop: 183 100 (2003 est). Area: 272 sq km (105 sq miles) 3 **Cape York** a cape in NE Australia, in Queensland at the N tip of the Cape York Peninsula, extending into the Torres Strait: the northernmost point of Australia

York[2] n 1 the English royal house that reigned from 1461 to 1485 and was descended from Richard Plantagenet, **Duke of York** (1411–60), whose claim to the throne precipitated the Wars of the Roses. His sons reigned as Edward IV and Richard III 2 Alvin C(ullum). 1887–1964, US soldier and hero of World War I 3 **Duke of**, full name Prince Frederick Augustus, Duke of York and Albany. 1763–1827, second son of George III of Great Britain and Ireland. An undistinguished commander-in-chief of the British army (1798–1809), he is the "grand old Duke of York" of the nursery rhyme 4 **Prince Andrew, Duke of**. born 1960, second son of Elizabeth II of Great Britain and Northern Ireland. He married (1986) Miss Sarah Ferguson; they divorced in 1996; their first daughter, Princess Beatrice of York, was born in 1988 and their second, Princess Eugenie of York, in 1990

Yorke Peninsula n a peninsula in South Australia, between Spencer Gulf and St Vincent Gulf: mainly agricultural with several coastal resorts

yorker n cricket a ball bowled so as to pitch just under or just beyond the bat [probably after the Yorkshire County Cricket Club]

Yorkist English history n 1 a supporter of the royal House of York, esp. during the Wars of the Roses ▷ adj 2 of or relating to the supporters or members of the House of York

Yorks. Yorkshire

Yorkshire n a historic county of N England: the largest English county, formerly divided administratively into East, West, and North Ridings. In 1974 it was much reduced in size and divided into the new counties of North, West, and South Yorkshire: in 1996 the East Riding of Yorkshire was reinstated as a unitary authority and parts of the NE were returned to North Yorkshire for geographical and ceremonial purposes

Yorkshire Dales pl n the valleys of the rivers flowing from the Pennines in W Yorkshire: chiefly Ribblesdale, Swaledale, Nidderdale, Wharfedale, and Wensleydale; tourist area. Also called: **the Dales**

Yorkshire pudding n a baked pudding made from a batter of flour, eggs, and milk, often served with roast beef [from YORKSHIRE]

Yorktown n a village in SE Virginia: scene of the surrender (1781) of the British under Cornwallis to the Americans under Washington at the end of the War of American Independence

Yosemite Falls pl n a series of waterfalls in central California, in the Yosemite National Park, with a total drop of 770 m (2525 ft): includes the **Upper Yosemite Falls**, 436 m (1430 ft) high, and the **Lower Yosemite Falls**, 98 m (320 ft) high

Yosemite National Park n a national park in central California, in the Sierra Nevada Mountains: contains the **Yosemite Valley**, at an altitude of about 1200 m

y

(4000 ft), with sheer walls rising about another 1200 m (4000 ft). Area: 3061 sq km (1182 sq miles)

Yoshkar-Ola *n* a city in Russia, capital of the Mari El Republic. Pop: 260 000 (2005 est)

you *pron* **1** (refers to) the person or people addressed: *can I get you a drink?* **2** (refers to) an unspecified person or people in general: *stick to British goods and you can't go wrong* ▷ *n* **3** *informal* the personality of the person being addressed: *that hat isn't really you* [Old English *ēow*]

> USAGE See at me¹.

you'd you had *or* you would
you'll you will *or* you shall
young *adj* **1** having lived or existed for a relatively short time **2** having qualities associated with youth: *their innovative approach and young attitude appealed to him* **3** of or relating to youth: *he'd been a terrorist himself in France in his young days* **4** of a group representing the younger members of a larger organization: *Young Conservatives* ▷ *n* **5** young people in general: *that never seems very important to the young* **6** offspring, esp. young animals: *a deer suckling her young* [Old English *geong*] > **youngish** *adj*

Young *n* **1 Brigham**. 1801–77, US Mormon leader, who led the Mormon migration to Utah and founded Salt Lake City (1847) **2 Edward**. 1683–1765, English poet and dramatist, noted for his *Night Thoughts on Life, Death, and Immortality* (1742–45) **3 Lester**. 1909–59, US saxophonist and clarinettist. He was a leading early exponent of the tenor saxophone in jazz **4 Neil (Percival)**. born 1945, Canadian rock guitarist, singer, and songwriter. His albums include *Harvest* (1972), *Rust Never Sleeps* (1979), *Ragged Glory* (1990), and *Prairie Wind* (2005) **5 Thomas**. 1773–1829, English physicist, physician, and Egyptologist. He helped to establish the wave theory of light by his experiments on optical interference and assisted in the decipherment of the Rosetta Stone

Younghusband *n* **Sir Francis Edward**. 1863–1942, British explorer, mainly of N India and Tibet. He used military force to compel the Dalai Lama to sign (1904) a trade agreement with Britain

youngster *n* a young person
Youngstown *n* a city in NE Ohio: a major centre of steel production: university (1908). Pop: 79 271 (2003 est)

your *adj* **1** of, belonging to, or associated with you: *ask your doctor to make the necessary calls* **2** of, belonging to, or associated with an unspecified person or people in general: *it is not right to take another baby to replace your own* **3** *informal* used to indicate all things or people of a certain type: *these characters are not your average housebreakers* [Old English *ēower*]

Yourcenar *n* **Marguerite**, original name *Marguerite de Crayencour*. 1903–87, French novelist and writer, in the US from 1939; noted for her historical novels, esp. *Mémoires d'Hadrien* (1952)

you're you are
yours *pron* **1** something belonging to you: *my reputation is better than yours* **2** your family: *a blessed Christmas to you and yours* **3** used in closing phrases at the end of a letter: *yours sincerely; yours faithfully* **4 of yours** belonging to you: *that husband of yours*

yourself *pron*, *pl* **-selves 1 a** the reflexive form of *you* **b** used for emphasis: *you've stated publicly that you yourself use drugs* **2** your normal self: *you're not yourself today*

yours truly *pron informal* I or me [from the closing phrase of letters]

Yousafzai *n* **Malala** born 1997, Pakistani women's rights campaigner; survived an attack by a Taliban gunman (2012); Nobel Peace Prize (2014)

youth *n* **1** the period between childhood and maturity **2** the quality or condition of being young, immature, or inexperienced: *his youth told against him in the contest* **3** a young man or boy **4** young people collectively: *there is still hope for today's youth* **5** the freshness, vigour, or vitality

associated with being young [Old English *geogoth*]

Youth *n* **Isle of Youth** an island in the NW Caribbean, south of Cuba: administratively part of Cuba from 1925. Chief town: Nueva Gerona. Pop: 80 600 (2002 est). Area: 3061 sq km (1182 sq miles). Former name: **Isle of Pines**. Spanish name: **Isla de la Juventud**

youth club *n* a club that provides leisure activities for young people

youthful *adj* **1** vigorous or active: *the intermediate section was won by a youthful grandmother* **2** of, relating to, possessing, or associated with youth: *youthful good looks* > **youthfully** *adv* > **youthfulness** *n*

youth hostel *n* an inexpensive lodging place for young people travelling cheaply

YouTube *n* a website on which subscribers can post video files

you've you have
yowl *vb* **1** to produce a loud mournful wail or cry ▷ *n* **2** a wail or howl [Old Norse *gaula*]

yo-yo *n*, *pl* **-yos 1** a toy consisting of a spool attached to a string, the end of which is held while it is repeatedly spun out and reeled in ▷ *vb* **yo-yoing, yo-yoed 2** to change repeatedly from one position to another [originally a trademark for this type of toy]

Ypres *n* a town in W Belgium, in W Flanders province near the border with France: scene of many sieges and battles, esp. in World War I, when it was completely destroyed. Pop: 35 021 (2004 est). Flemish name: **Ieper**

Ypsilanti, Hypsilantis *or* **Hypsilantes** *n* **1 Alexander**. 1792–1828, Greek patriot, who led an unsuccessful revolt against the Turks (1821) **2** his brother, **Demetrios**. 1793–1832, Greek revolutionary leader; commander in chief of Greek forces (1828–30) during the war of independence

yrs 1 years **2** yours
Yser *n* a river in NW central Europe, rising in N France and flowing through SW Belgium to the North Sea: scene of battles in World War I. Length: 77 km (48 miles)

Yssel *n* a variant spelling of **IJssel**
YST Yukon Standard Time
YT Yukon Territory
YTS (in Britain) Youth Training Scheme
ytterbium (it-terb-ee-um) *n chem* a soft silvery element that is used to improve the mechanical properties of steel. Symbol: **Yb** [after *Ytterby*, Swedish quarry where discovered]

yttrium (it-ree-um) *n chem* a silvery metallic element used in various alloys and in lasers. Symbol: **Y** [see YTTERBIUM]

yuan *n*, *pl* **-an** the standard monetary unit of the People's Republic of China [Chinese *yüan* round object]

Yüan *or* **Yüen** *n* a river in SE central China, rising in central Guizhou province and flowing northeast to Lake Tungting. Length: about 800 km (500 miles)

Yuan Shi Kai *n* 1859–1916, Chinese general and statesman: first president (1912–16) of the Chinese republic

Yucatán *n* **1** a state of SE Mexico, occupying the N part of the Yucatán peninsula. Capital: Mérida. Pop: 1 655 707 (2000). Area: 39 340 sq km (15 186 sq miles) **2** a peninsula of Central America between the Gulf of Mexico and the Caribbean, including the Mexican states of Campeche, Yucatán, and Quintana Roo, and part of Belize: a centre of Mayan civilization from about 100 BC to the 18th century. Area: about 181 300 sq km (70 000 sq miles)

Yucatán Channel *n* a channel between W Cuba and the Yucatán peninsula

yucca *n* a tropical plant with spiky leaves and white flowers [from a Native American language]

yucky *or* **yukky** *adj* **yuckier, yuckiest** *or* **yukkier, yukkiest** *slang* disgusting or nasty [from *yuck*, exclamation of disgust]

Yugo. (the former) Yugoslavia
Yugoslav *adj* **1** of or relating to the former Yugoslavia

y

▷ *n* **2** a person from the former Yugoslavia

Yugoslavia *or* **Jugoslavia** *n* **1** Federal Republic of Yugoslavia a former country in SE Europe, comprising Serbia and Montenegro, that was formed in 1991 but not widely internationally recognized until 2000; it was replaced by the Union of Serbia and Montenegro in 2003 (dissolved 2006) **2** a former country in SE Europe, on the Adriatic: established in 1918 from the independent states of Serbia and Montenegro, and regions that until World War I had belonged to Austria-Hungary (Croatia, Slovenia, and Bosnia-Herzegovina); the name was changed from Kingdom of Serbs, Croats, and Slovenes to Yugoslavia in 1929; German invasion of 1941–44 was resisted chiefly by a Communist group led by Tito, who declared a people's republic in 1945; it became the Socialist Federal Republic of Yugoslavia in 1963; in 1991 Slovenia, Croatia, and Bosnia-Herzegovina declared independence, followed by Macedonia in 1992; Serbia and Montenegro formed the Federal Republic of Yugoslavia, subsequently (2003) replaced by the Union of Serbia and Montenegro (dissolved 2006)

Yugoslavian *or* **Jugoslavian** *adj, n* same as Yugoslav

Yukawa *n* Hideki. 1907–81, Japanese nuclear physicist, who predicted (1935) the existence of mesons: Nobel prize for physics 1949

Yukon *n* the Yukon a territory of NW Canada, on the Beaufort Sea, between the Northwest Territories and Alaska: arctic and mountainous, reaching 5959 m (19 550 ft) at Mount Logan, Canada's highest peak; mineral resources. Capital: Whitehorse. Pop: 33 897 (2011). Area: 536 327 sq km (207 076 sq miles). Abbreviation: **YT**

Yukoner *n* a native or inhabitant of the Yukon

Yukon River *n* a river in NW North America, rising in NW Canada on the border between the Yukon Territory and British Columbia: flows northwest into Alaska, US, and then southwest to the Bering Sea; navigable for about 2850 km (1775 miles) to Whitehorse. Length: 3185 km (1979 miles)

Yule *n literary or old-fashioned* Christmas or the Christmas season: *Yuletide* [Old English *geōla*, originally a pagan feast lasting 12 days]

yummy *slang adj* **-mier, -miest 1** delicious or attractive: *yummy sauces* ▷ *interj* **2** Also: **yum-yum** an exclamation indicating pleasure or delight, as in anticipation of delicious food [*yum-yum* (imitative)]

Yunnan *or* **Yünnan** *n* a province of SW China: consists mainly of a plateau broken in the southeast by the Red and Black Rivers, with mountains in the west, rising over 5500 m (18 000 ft); large deposits of tin, lead, zinc, and coal. Capital: Kunming. Pop: 43 760 000 (2003 est). Area: 436 200 sq km (168 400 sq miles)

Yunus *n* Muhammad. born 1940. Bangladeshi economist and social entrepreneur; pioneer of micro-credit; Nobel Peace Prize (2006)

yuppie *n* **1** a young highly-paid professional person, esp. one who has a fashionable way of life ▷ *adj* **2** typical of or reflecting the values of yuppies: *a yuppie accessory* [*y(oung) u(rban)* or *u(pwardly mobile) p(rofessional)*]

yuppify *vb* **-fies, -fying, -fied** to make yuppie in nature: *Mount Pleasant was being yuppified* ❯ **yuppification** *n*

Yurev *n* the former name (11th century until 1918) of Tartu

Yuzovka *n* a former name (1872 until after the Revolution) of Donetsk

Yvelines *n* a department of N France, in Île de France region. Capital: Versailles. Pop: 1 370 443 (2003 est). Area: 2271 sq km (886 sq miles)

YWCA Young Women's Christian Association

y

Zz

z or **Z** *n, pl* **z's, Z's** or **Zs 1** the 26th and last letter of the English alphabet **2** from **A** to **Z** See **a** (3)

z *maths* (along with *x* and *y*) an unknown quantity

Z *chem* atomic number

Zaandam *n* a former town in the W Netherlands, in North Holland: an important shipbuilding centre in the 17th century. It became part of Zaanstad in 1974

Zaanstad *n* a port in the W Netherlands, in North Holland: formed (1974) from Zaandam, Koog a/d Zaan, Zaandijk, Wormerveer, Krommenie, Westzaan, and Assendelft; food and machinery industries. Pop: 139 000 (2003 est)

zabaglione (zab-al-lyoh-nee) *n* a dessert made of egg yolks, sugar, and wine, whipped together [Italian]

Zabrze *n* a city in SW Poland: a Prussian and German town from 1742 until 1945, when it passed to Poland; industrial centre in a coal-mining region. Pop: 189 656 (2007 est). German name: **Hindenburg**

Zacatecas *n* **1** a state of N central Mexico, on the central plateau: rich mineral resources. Capital: Zacatecas. Pop: 1 351 207 (2000). Area: 75 040 sq km (28 973 sq miles) **2** a city in N central Mexico, capital of Zacatecas state: silver mines. Pop: 241 000 (2005 est)

Zacynthus *n* the Latin name for **Zante**

Zagazig or **Zaqaziq** *n* a city in NE Egypt, in the Nile Delta: major cotton market. Pop: 291 000 (2005 est)

Zaghlul *n* Saad. 1857–1927, Egyptian nationalist politician; prime minister (1924)

Zagreb *n* the capital of Croatia, on the River Sava; gothic cathedral; university (1874); industrial centre. Pop: 685 000 (2005 est). German name: **Agram**

Zagros Mountains *pl n* a mountain range in S Iran: has Iran's main oilfields in its W central foothills. Highest peak: Zard Kuh, 4548 m (14 920 ft)

Zaïre *n* **1** the former name (1971–97) of the **Democratic Republic of Congo 2** (formerly) the Zaïrian name (1971–97) for the (River) **Congo** (3)

Zaïrian or **Zaïrean** *adj* **1** of or relating to the former Zaïre (now the Democratic Republic of Congo) or its inhabitants ▷ *n* **2** a native or inhabitant of Zaïre

Zákinthos *n* a transliteration of the Modern Greek name for **Zante**

Zama *n* the name of several ancient cities in N Africa, including the one near the site of Scipio's decisive defeat of Hannibal (202 BC)

Zambezi or **Zambese** *n* a river in S central and E Africa, rising in NW Zambia and flowing across E Angola back into Zambia, continuing south to the Caprivi Strip of Namibia, then east forming the Zambia–Zimbabwe border, and finally crossing Mozambique to the Indian Ocean: the fourth longest river in Africa. Length: 2740 km (1700 miles)

Zambezian *adj* of or relating to the Zambezi River

Zambia *n* a republic in southern Africa: an early site of human settlement; controlled by the British South Africa Company by 1900 and unified as Northern Rhodesia in 1911; made a British protectorate in 1924; part of the Federation of Rhodesia and Nyasaland (1953–63), gaining independence as a member of the Commonwealth in 1964; important mineral exports, esp. copper. Official language: English. Religion: Christian majority, animist minority. Currency: kwacha. Capital: Lusaka. Pop: 14 222 233 (2013 est). Area: 752 617 sq km (290 587 sq miles). Former name (until 1964): **Northern Rhodesia**

Zambian *adj* **1** of or relating to Zambia or its inhabitants ▷ *n* **2** a native or inhabitant of Zambia

Zamboanga *n* a port in the Philippines, on SW Mindanao on Basilan Strait: founded by the Spanish in 1635; tourist centre, with fisheries. Pop: 716 000 (2005 est)

Zamenhof *n* Lazarus Ludwig. 1859–1917, Polish oculist; invented Esperanto

Zamfara *n* a state of Nigeria, in the NW. Capital: Gusau. Pop: 3 259 846 (2006). Area: 39 762 sq km (15 352 sq miles)

Zamora *n* a city in NW central Spain, on the Douro River. Pop: 65 639 (2003 est)

Zamyatin *n* Yevgenii Ivanovich. 1884–1937, Russian novelist and writer, in Paris from 1931, whose works include satirical studies of provincial life in Russia and England, where he worked during World War I, and the dystopian novel *We* (1924)

Zante *n* an island in the Ionian Sea, off the W coast of Greece: southernmost of the Ionian Islands; traditionally belonged to Ulysses, king of Ithaca. Pop: 38 957 (2001). Area: 402 sq km (155 sq miles). Latin name: Zacynthus. Ancient Greek name: **Zakynthos**. Modern Greek name: **Zákinthos**

zany (zane-ee) *adj* **zanier, zaniest** comical in an endearing way [Italian dialect *Zanni*, nickname for *Giovanni* John; traditional name for a clown]

Zanzibar *n* an island in the Indian Ocean, off the E coast of Africa: settled by Persians and Arabs from the 7th century onwards; became a flourishing trading centre for slaves, ivory, and cloves; made a British protectorate in 1890, becoming independent within the Commonwealth in 1963 and a republic in 1964; joined with Tanganyika in 1964 to form the United Republic of Tanzania. Pop: 622 459 (2002)

Zanzibari *adj* **1** of or relating to Zanzibar or its inhabitants ▷ *n* **2** a native or inhabitant of Zanzibar

zap *vb* **zapping, zapped** *slang* **1** to kill, esp. by shooting **2** to change television channels rapidly by remote control **3** to move quickly [imitative]

Zapata *n* Emiliano. ?1877–1919, Mexican guerrilla leader

Zaporozhye *n* a city in E Ukraine on the Dnieper River: developed as a major industrial centre after the construction (1932) of the Dnieper hydroelectric station. Pop: 798 000 (2005 est). Former name (until 1921): **Aleksandrovsk**

Zappa *n* Frank. 1940–93, US rock musician, songwriter, and experimental composer: founder and only permanent member of the Mothers of Invention. His recordings include *Freak Out* (1966), *Hot Rats* (1969), and *Sheik Yerbouti* (1979)

Zaqaziq *n* a variant of **Zagazig**

Zaragoza *n* a city in NE Spain, on the River Ebro: Roman colony established 25 BC; under Moorish rule (714–1118); capital of Aragon (12th–15th centuries); twice besieged by the French during the Peninsular War and captured (1809); university (1474). Pop: 626 081 (2003 est). Pre-Roman name: **Salduba**. Latin name: **Caesaraugusta**. English name: **Saragossa**

Zardari *n* Asif Ali. born 1955, Pakistani politician; president of Pakistan from 2008; widower of Benazir Bhutto

Zaria *n* a city in N central Nigeria: former capital of a Hausa state; agricultural trading centre; university (1962). Pop: 822 000 (2005 est)

Zarqa *n* the second largest town in Jordan, northeast of Amman. Pop: 494 000 (2005 est)

Zatlers *n* Valdis. born 1955, Latvian politician, president of Latvia (2007–2011)

Zátopek *n* Emil. 1922–2000, Czech runner; winner of the 5000 and 10 000 metres and the marathon at the 1952 Olympic Games in Helsinki

Zea *n* the Italian name for **Keos**

zeal *n* great enthusiasm or eagerness, esp. for a religious movement [Greek *zēlos*]

Zealand *n* the largest island of Denmark, separated from the island of Funen by the Great Belt and from S Sweden by the Sound (both now spanned by road bridges). Chief town: Copenhagen. Pop: 2 096 449 (2003 est). Area: 7016 sq km (2709 sq miles). Danish name: **Sjælland**. German name: **Seeland**

zealot (zel-lot) *n* a fanatic or an extreme enthusiast ⟩ **zealotry** *n*

zealous (zel-luss) *adj* extremely eager or enthusiastic ⟩ **zealously** *adv*

Zeami or **Seami** *n* Motokiyo. 1363–1443, Japanese dramatist, regarded as the greatest figure in the history of No drama

zebra *n*, *pl* **-ras** or **-ra** a black-and-white striped African animal of the horse family [Old Spanish: wild ass]

zebra crossing *n* Brit a pedestrian crossing marked by broad black and white stripes: once on the crossing the pedestrian has right of way

zebu (zee-boo) *n* a domesticated ox of Africa and Asia, with a humped back and long horns [French]

zed *n* the British and New Zealand spoken form of the letter z

zee *n* the US spoken form of the letter z

Zeebrugge *n* a port in NW Belgium, in W Flanders on the North Sea: linked by canal with Bruges; German submarine base in World War I

Zeeland *n* a province of the SW Netherlands: consists of a small area on the mainland together with a number of islands in the Scheldt estuary; mostly below sea level. Capital: Middelburg. Pop: 378 000 (2003 est). Area: 1787 sq km (690 sq miles)

Zeelander *n* a native or inhabitant of the Dutch province of Zeeland

Zeffirelli *n* Franco. born 1923, Italian stage and film director and designer, noted esp. for his work in opera; awarded an honorary knighthood (2004)

Zeist *n* a city in the central Netherlands, near Utrecht. Pop: 60 000 (2003 est)

Zeitgeist (tsite-guyst) *n* the spirit or general outlook of a specific time or period [German, literally: time spirit]

Zellweger *n* Renée (Kathleen). born 1969, US film actress: her films include *Nurse Betty* (2000), *Bridget Jones's Diary* (2001) and its sequel *Bridget Jones and the Edge of Reason* (2004), and *Chicago* (2002)

Zemlinsky *n* Alexander. 1871–1942, Austrian composer, living in the US from 1938. His works include the operas

Es war einmal (1900) and *Eine florentische Tragödie* (1917) and the *Lyric Symphony* (1923)

Zen *n* a Japanese form of Buddhism that concentrates on learning through meditation and intuition

Zend-Avesta *n* the Zoroastrian scriptures (the **Avesta**), together with the traditional interpretive commentary known as the **Zend**

zenith *n* **1** the point in the sky directly above an observer **2** the highest or most successful point of anything: *he was at the zenith of his military career* [Arabic *samt arrās* path over one's head] ⟩ **zenithal** *adj*

Zenobia *n* 3rd century AD, queen of Palmyra (?267–272), who was captured by the Roman emperor Aurelian

Zeno of Citium *n* ?336–?264 BC, Greek philosopher, who founded the Stoic school in Athens

Zeno of Elea *n* ?490–?430 BC, Greek Eleatic philosopher; disciple of Parmenides. He defended the belief that motion and change are illusions in a series of paradoxical arguments, of which the best known is that of Achilles and the tortoise

Zephaniah *n* **1** *Old Testament* **a** a Hebrew prophet of the late 7th century BC **b** the book containing his oracles, which are chiefly concerned with the approaching judgment by God upon the sinners of Judah. Douay spelling: **Sophonias 2** Benjamin. born 1958, British poet, writer, and activist, born in Jamaica. His poetry collections include *The Dread Affair* (1985) and *Too Black, Too Strong* (2001)

zephyr (zef-fer) *n* a soft gentle breeze [Greek *zephuros* the west wind]

Zeppelin *n* Count Ferdinand von. 1838–1917, German aeronautical pioneer who designed and manufactured large cylindrical rigid airships (zeppelins)

Zermatt *n* a village and resort in S Switzerland, in Valais canton at the foot of the Matterhorn: cars are not allowed in the area. Pop: 5988 (2000)

zero *n*, *pl* **-ros** or **-roes 1** the cardinal number between +1 and -1 **2** the symbol, 0, representing this number **3** the line or point on a scale of measurement from which the graduations commence **4** the lowest point or degree: *my credibility is down to zero* **5** nothing or nil **6** the temperature, pressure, etc., that registers a reading of zero on a scale ▷ *adj* **7** amounting to zero: *zero inflation* **8** *meteorol* (of visibility) limited to a very short distance ▷ *vb* **-roing, -roed 9** to adjust (an instrument or scale) so as to read zero [Arabic *sifr* empty]

zero gravity *n* the state of weightlessness

zero hour *n* **1** *military* the time set for the start of an operation **2** *informal* a critical time, usually at the beginning of an action

zero in on *vb* **1** to aim a weapon at (a target) **2** to concentrate one's attention on

zero-rated *adj* denoting goods on which the buyer pays no value-added tax

zest *n* **1** invigorating or keen excitement or enjoyment: *he has a zest for life and a quick intellect* **2** added interest, flavour, or charm: *he said that she would provide a new zest for his government* **3** the peel of an orange or lemon, used as flavouring [French *zeste*] ⟩ **zestful** *adj*

Zeta-Jones *n* Catherine, original name *Catherine Jones*. born 1969, Welsh actress, who made her name in the TV series *The Darling Buds of May* (1991–93) before starring in the films *Traffic* (2000), *Chicago* (2002), and *Smoke and Mirrors* (2004)

Zetland *n* the official name (until 1974) of **Shetland**

Zeus *n* Greek myth the ruler of the gods

Zeuxis *n* late 5th century BC, Greek painter, noted for the verisimilitude of his works

Zhangjiakou, Changchiakow or **Changchiak'ou** *n* a city in NE China, in NW Hebei province: a military centre, controlling the route to Mongolia, under the Ming and Manchu dynasties. Pop: 973 000 (2005 est). Former names: **Wanchüan, Kalgan**

Zhangzhou, Changchow or **Ch'ang-chou** *n* a city in

SE China, in S Fujian province on the Saikoe River. Pop 410 000 (2005 est). Former name: **Lungki**

Zhdanov n the former name (1948–91) of **Mariupol**

Zhejiang or **Chekiang** n a province of E China: mountainous and densely populated; a cultural centre since the 12th century. Capital: Hangzhou. Pop: 46 800 000 (2003 est). Area: 102 000 sq km (39 780 sq miles)

Zhengzhou, Chengchow or **Cheng-chou** n a city in E central China, capital of Henan province; an administrative centre. Pop: 2 250 000 (2005 est)

Zhenjiang n a port in E China, in S Jiangsu at the confluence of the Yangtze River and the Grand Canal. Pop: 620 000 (2005 est)

Zhitomir n a city in central Ukraine; centre of an agricultural region. Pop: 282 000 (2005 est)

Zhivkov n Todor. 1911–98, Bulgarian statesman and party leader; prime minister (1962–71); president (1971–89)

Zhuangzi or **Chuang-tzu** n ?369–286 BC, Chinese philosopher, who greatly influenced Chinese religion through the book of Taoist philosophy that bears his name

Zhu Jiang, Chu Chiang or **Chu Kiang** n a river in SE China, in S Guangdong province, flowing southeast from Canton to the South China Sea. Length: about 177 km (110 miles). Also called: **Canton River, Pearl River**

Zhukov n Georgi Konstantinovich. 1896–1974, Soviet marshal. In World War II, he led the offensives that broke the sieges of Stalingrad and Leningrad (1942–43) and later captured Warsaw and Berlin; minister of defence (1955–57)

Zia ul Haq n Mohammed. 1924–88, Pakistani general: president of Pakistan (1978–88), following the overthrow (1977) of Z. A. Bhutto by a military coup. He was killed in an air crash, possibly through sabotage

Zibo, Tzu-po or **Tzepo** n a city in NE China, in Shandong province. Pop: 2 775 000 (2005 est)

Zidane n Zinedine. born 1972, French footballer, known as Zizou; scored 31 goals in 108 games for France (1994–2006), including two in the 1998 World Cup final; sent off in the 2006 World Cup final; his club sides included Juventus and Real Madrid

Ziegfeld n Florenz. 1869–1932, US theatrical producer, noted for his series of extravagant revues (1907–31), known as the Ziegfeld Follies

ziggurat n (in ancient Mesopotamia) a temple in the shape of a pyramid [Assyrian *ziqqurati* summit]

Zigong, Tzekung or **Tzu-kung** n an industrial city in W central China, in Sichuan. Pop: 1 123 000 (2005 est)

zigzag n 1 a line or course having sharp turns in alternating directions ▷ adj 2 formed in or proceeding in a zigzag ▷ adv 3 in a zigzag manner ▷ vb **-zagging, -zagged** 4 to move in a zigzag [German *zickzack*]

zilch n informal nothing [origin unknown]

Zille n Helen. born 1951, South African politician and journalist; mayor of Cape Town (2006–09); leader of the Democratic Alliance party from 2007; premier of Western Cape from 2009

zillion n, pl **-lions** or **-lion** (often pl) informal an extremely large but unspecified number: there are zillions of beautiful spots to visit [after million]

Zimbabwe n 1 a country in SE Africa, formerly a self-governing British colony founded in 1890 by the British South Africa Company, which administered the country until a self-governing colony was established in 1923; joined with Northern Rhodesia (now Zambia) and Nyasaland (now Malawi) as the Federation of Rhodesia and Nyasaland from 1953 to 1963; made a unilateral declaration of independence (UDI) under the leadership of Ian Smith in 1965 on the basis of White minority rule; proclaimed a republic in 1970; in 1976 the principle of Black majority rule was accepted and in 1978 a transitional government was set up; gained independence under Robert Mugabe in 1980; effectively a one-party state since 1987; a member of the Commonwealth until 2003, when it withdrew as a result of conflict with other members. Official language: English. Religion: Christian majority. Currency: Zimbabwe dollar. Capital: Harare. Pop: 13 182 908 (2013 est). Area: 390 624 sq km (150 820 sq miles). Former names: (until 1964) **Southern Rhodesia**, (1964–79) **Rhodesia** 2 Also: **Great Zimbabwe** a ruined fortified settlement in Zimbabwe, which at its height, in the 15th century, was probably the capital of an empire covering SE Africa

Zimbabwean adj 1 of or relating to Zimbabwe or its inhabitants ▷ n 2 a native or inhabitant of Zimbabwe

Zimmer n trademark a tubular frame with rubber feet, used as a support to help disabled or infirm people walk

zinc n chem a brittle bluish-white metallic element that is used in alloys such as brass, to form a protective coating on metals, and in battery electrodes. Symbol: Zn [German *Zink*]

zinc ointment n a medicinal ointment consisting of zinc oxide, petroleum jelly, and paraffin

zinc oxide n chem, pharmacol a white insoluble powder used as a pigment and in making zinc ointment

zing n 1 informal the quality in something that makes it lively or interesting 2 a short high-pitched buzzing sound, like the sound of a bullet or vibrating string [imitative]

zinnia n a plant of tropical and subtropical America, with solitary heads of brightly coloured flowers [after J. G. Zinn, botanist]

Zinoviev n Grigori Yevseevich, original name Ovsel Gershon Aronov Radomylsky. 1883–1936, Soviet politician; chairman of the Comintern (1919–26) executed for supposed complicity in the murder of Kirov. He was the supposed author of the forged 'Zinoviev letter' urging British Communists to revolt, publication of which helped to defeat (1924) the first Labour Government

Zinovievsk n a former name (1924–36) for **Kirovograd**

Zinzendorf n Count Nikolaus Ludwig von. 1700–60, German religious reformer, who organized the Moravian Church

Zion n 1 the hill on which the city of Jerusalem stands 2 a the modern Jewish nation b Israel as the national home of the Jewish people 3 Christianity heaven

Zionism n a political movement for the establishment and support of a national homeland for Jews in what is now Israel ▷ **Zionist** n, adj

zip n 1 Also called: **zip fastener** a fastener with two parallel rows of metal or plastic teeth, one on either side of a closure, which are interlocked by a sliding tab 2 informal energy or vigour 3 a short sharp whizzing sound, like the sound of a passing bullet ▷ vb **zipping, zipped** 4 (often foll. by up) to fasten with a zip 5 to move with a sharp whizzing sound: bullets zipped and ricocheted all around us 6 to hurry or rush [imitative]

zip code n the US equivalent of **postcode** [z(one) i(mprovement) p(lan)]

zipper n US and Canad same as **zip** (1)

zippy adj **-pier, -piest** informal full of energy

zircon n mineralogy a hard mineral consisting of zirconium silicate, used as a gemstone and in industry [German *Zirkon*]

zirconium n chem a greyish-white metallic element, occurring chiefly in zircon, that is exceptionally corrosion-resistant. Symbol: Zr

Ziska or **Žižka** n Jan. ?1370–1424, Bohemian soldier, who successfully led the Hussite rebellion (1420–24) against emperor Sigismund

zit n slang a spot or pimple

zither n a musical instrument consisting of numerous strings stretched over a flat box and plucked to produce notes [Greek *kithara*] ▷ **zitherist** n

Zi Xi or **Tz'u-hsi** n 1835–1908, Chinese empress dowager, who as regent for her son Tong Zhi and her nephew Guang Xu dominated Chinese politics from 1861 to 1908. Her reactionary policies were instrumental in the fall of imperial China

Zlatoust *n* a town in W Russia, on the Ay river: one of the chief metallurgical centres of the Urals since the 18th century. Pop: 192 000 (2005 est)

zloty *n, pl* **-tys** *or* **-ty** the standard monetary unit of Poland [Polish: golden]

Zn *chem* zinc

Zoan *n* the Biblical name for **Tanis**

zodiac *n* **1** an imaginary belt in the sky within which the sun, moon, and planets appear to move, and which is divided into 12 equal areas called **signs of the zodiac**, each named after the constellation which once lay in it **2** *astrol* a diagram, usually circular, representing this belt [Greek *zōidion* animal sign, from *zōion* animal] **›** **zodiacal** *adj*

Zoffany *n* John *or* Johann ?1733–1810, British painter, esp. of portraits; born in Germany

Zog I *n* 1895–1961, king of Albania (1928–39), formerly prime minister (1922–24) and president (1925–28). He allowed Albania to become dominated by Fascist Italy and fled into exile when Mussolini invaded (1939)

Zola *n* Émile. 1840–1902, French novelist and critic; chief exponent of naturalism. In *Les Rougon-Macquart* (1871–93), a cycle of 20 novels, he explains the behaviour of his characters in terms of their heredity: it includes *L'Assommoir* (1877), *Nana* (1880), *Germinal* (1885), and *La Terre* (1887). He is also noted for his defence of Dreyfus in his pamphlet *J'accuse* (1898)

Zomba *n* a city in S Malawi: the capital of Malawi until 1971. Pop: 101 423 (2005)

zombie *or* **zombi** *n, pl* **-bies** *or* **-bis 1** a person who appears to be lifeless, apathetic, or totally lacking in independent judgment **2** a corpse brought to life by witchcraft [W African *zumbi* good-luck fetish]

zone *n* **1** a region, area, or section characterized by some distinctive feature or quality: *a demilitarized zone* **2** *geography* one of the divisions of the earth's surface according to temperature **3** a section on a transport route **4** *maths* a portion of a sphere between two parallel lines intersecting the sphere **5** NZ a catchment area for a specific school *▷ vb* **zoning, zoned 6** to divide (a place) into zones for different uses or activities [Greek *zōnē* girdle] **›** **zonal** *adj* **›** **zoning** *n*

zonked *adj Brit, Austral and NZ slang* **1** highly intoxicated with drugs or alcohol **2** exhausted [imitative]

zoo *n, pl* **zoos** a place where live animals are kept, studied, bred, and exhibited to the public [from *zoological garden*]

zooid (zoh-oid) *n* **1** any independent animal body, such as an individual of a coral colony **2** a cell or body, produced by an organism and capable of independent motion, such as a gamete [Greek *zōion* animal]

zool. 1 zoological **2** zoology

zoological garden *n* the formal term for **zoo**

zoology *n* the study of animals, including their classification, structure, physiology, and history [Greek *zōion* animal + -LOGY] **›** **zoological** *adj* **›** **zoologist** *n*

zoom *vb* **1** to move very rapidly: *the first rocket zoomed into the sky* **2** to increase or rise rapidly: *stocks zoomed on the American exchange* **3** to move with or make a continuous buzzing or humming sound *▷ n* **4** the sound or act of zooming **5** a zoom lens [imitative]

zoom in *or* **zoom out** *vb photog, films, television* to increase or decrease rapidly the magnification of the image of a distant object by means of a zoom lens

zoom lens *n* a lens system that can make the details of a picture larger or smaller while keeping the picture in focus

zoophyte (zoh-a-fite) *n* any animal resembling a plant, such as a sea anemone [Greek *zōion* animal + *phuton* plant]

Zorn *n* Anders Leonhard. 1860–1920, Swedish painter and etcher, esp. of impressionist portraits and landscapes

Zoroaster *n* ?628–?551 BC, Persian prophet; founder of Zoroastrianism. Avestan name: **Zarathustra**

Zoroastrianism (zorr-oh-**ass**-tree-an-iz-zum) *or* **Zoroastrism** *n* the religion founded by the ancient Persian prophet Zoroaster, based on the concept of a continuous struggle between good and evil **›** **Zoroastrian** *adj*

Zorrilla y Moral *n* José. 1817–93, Spanish poet and dramatist, noted for his romantic plays based on national legends, esp. *Don Juan Tenorio* (1844)

Zoug *n* the French name for **Zug**

zounds *interj old-fashioned* a mild oath indicating surprise or indignation [euphemistic shortening of *God's wounds*]

Zr *chem* zirconium

Zsigmondy *n* Richard Adolf. 1865–1929, German chemist, born in Austria, noted for his work on colloidal particles and, with H. Siedentopf, his introduction (1903) of the ultramicroscope: Nobel prize for chemistry 1925

zucchetto (tsoo-ket-toe) *n, pl* **-tos** *RC Church* a small round skullcap worn by clergymen and varying in colour according to the rank of the wearer [Italian]

zucchini (zoo-keen-ee) *n, pl* **-ni** *or* **-nis** *chiefly US, Canad and Austral* a courgette [Italian]

Zuckerberg *n* Mark (Elliot). born 1984, US internet entrepreneur; co-founder (2004) of social networking website Facebook

Zuckerman *n* Solly, Baron. 1904–93, British zoologist, born in South Africa; chief scientific adviser (1964–71) to the British Government. His books include *The Social Life of Monkeys* (1932) and the autobiography *From Apes to Warlords* (1978)

Zug *n* **1** a canton of N central Switzerland: the smallest Swiss canton; mainly German-speaking and Roman Catholic; joined the Swiss Confederation in 1352. Capital: Zug. Pop: 102 200 (2002 est). Area: 239 sq km (92 sq miles) **2** a town in N central Switzerland, the capital of Zug canton, on Lake Zug. Pop: 22 973 (2000) **3** **Lake Zug** a lake in N central Switzerland, in Zug and Schwyz cantons. Area: 39 sq km (15 sq miles) ▶ French name: **Zoug**

Zugspitze *n* a mountain peak in S Germany in the Bavarian Alps, on the Austrian border: the highest peak in Germany. Height: 2963 m (9721 ft)

Zuider Zee *or* **Zuyder Zee** *n* a former inlet of the North Sea in the N coast of the Netherlands sealed off from the sea by a dam in 1932, dividing it into the Waddenzee and the freshwater IJsselmeer, with several large reclaimed areas

Zuidholland *n* the Dutch name for **South Holland**

Zukerman *n* Pinchas. born 1948, Israeli violinist

Zulu *n* **1** (*pl* **-lus** *or* **-lu**) a member of a tall Black people of Southern Africa **2** the language of this people

Zululand *n* a region of E South Africa, on the Indian Ocean; partly corresponds to KwaZulu-Natal. Chief town: Eshowe

Zuma *n* Jacob (Gidleyihlekisa). born 1942, South African politician: Deputy President of South Africa (1999–2005); President of the African National Congress from 2007; President of South Africa from 2009

Zumba *n trademark* a system of dance-like exercises performed to Latin American music

Zungaria *n* another name for **Junggar Pendi**

Zurbarán *n* Francisco de. 1598–1664, Spanish Baroque painter, esp. of religious subjects

Zürich *n* **1** a canton of NE Switzerland: mainly Protestant and German-speaking. Capital: Zürich. Pop: 342 500 (2002 est). Area: 1729 sq km (668 sq miles) **2** a city in NE Switzerland, the capital of Zürich canton, on Lake Zürich: the largest city and industrial centre in Switzerland; centre of the Swiss Reformation; financial centre. Pop: 358 540 (2007) **3** **Lake Zürich** a lake in N Switzerland, mostly in Zürich canton. Area: 89 sq km (34 sq miles)

z

Zuyder Zee *n* a variant spelling of **Zuider Zee**

Zweig *n* **1** Arnold. 1887–1968, German novelist, famous for his realistic war novel *The Case of Sergeant Grischa* (1927) **2** Stefan. 1881–1942, Austrian novelist, dramatist, essayist, and poet

Zwickau *n* a city in E Germany, in Saxony: Anabaptist movement founded here (1521); coal-mining and industrial centre. Pop: 99 846 (2003 est)

Zwicky *n* Fritz. 1898–1974, Swiss astronomer and physicist, working in the US from 1925; noted for his study of supernovae

Zwingli *n* Ulrich or Huldreich. 1484–1531, Swiss leader of the Reformation, based in Zurich. He denied the Eucharistic presence, holding that the Communion was merely a commemoration of Christ's death

Zwolle *n* a town in the central Netherlands, capital of Overijssel province. Pop: 116 365 (2008)

Zworykin *n* Vladimir Kosma. 1889–1982, US physicist and television pioneer, born in Russia. He developed the first practical television camera

zygote *n* the cell resulting from the union of an ovum and a spermatozoon [Greek *zugōtos* yoked]

Z